December 2010.

॥▌▌█▌▌▌▌█▌█▌█▌▌█▌▌█▌▌█▌
♡ **W9-BYE-869**

til love
Christine

Believer's
BIBLE
COMMENTARY

WILLIAM MACDONALD

Edited by Art Farstad

THOMAS NELSON
Since 1798

NASHVILLE   DALLAS   MEXICO CITY   RIO DE JANEIRO   BEIJING

Library of Congress Cataloging-in-Publication Data

MacDonald, William, 1917–
   Believer's Bible commentary : Old and New Testaments / William
MacDonald ; edited with introductions by Arthur Farstad.
     p. cm.
   Originally published in two separate volumes.
   Includes bibliographical references.
   ISBN 0-8407-1972-8
   1. Bible—Commentaries I. Farstad, Arthur L. II. Title.
BS491.2.M33 1995
220.7—dc20
                                                     94-24086
                                                    CIP

CONTENTS

Author's Preface

The purpose of the *Believer's Bible Commentary (BBC)* is to give the average Christian reader a basic knowledge of what the Holy Bible is all about.

The *BBC* is also intended to stimulate such a love and taste for the Bible that the believer will want to delve more deeply into their inexhaustible treasures. While scholars will hopefully find food for their souls, they will be considerate in understanding that the book was not designed primarily for them.

All books have been supplied with introductions, notes, and bibliographies.

With the exception of Psalms, Proverbs, and Ecclesiastes, the exposition of the Old Testament is generally presented in paragraph-by-paragraph rather than in verse-by-verse form. The comments on the text are augmented by practical applications of spiritual truths and by a study of typology, where appropriate.

Passages that point forward to the coming Redeemer are highlighted and handled in greater detail.

The Books of Psalms, Proverbs, and Ecclesiastes are handled verse by verse, either because they do not lend themselves to condensation, or because most believers desire to study them in greater depth. All New Testament books are handled with verse-by-verse comments.

We have tried to face problem texts and to give alternative explanations where possible. Many passages are the despair of commentators, and we must confess that on these we still "see in a mirror, dimly."

More important than any commentary is *the Word of God itself,* as illuminated by the Holy Spirit of God. Without it there is no life, growth, holiness, or acceptable service. We should read it, study it, memorize it, meditate on it, and above all obey it. As someone has said, "Obedience is the organ of spiritual knowledge."

Editor's Introduction

"Don't despise the commentaries." This was the advice of a Bible teacher to his class at Emmaus Bible School (now College) in the late 1950's. At least one student remembered those words through three decades. The teacher was William MacDonald, the author of *Believer's Bible Commentary*. The student was the editor, Arthur Farstad, at that time a callow freshman. He had only read one commentary in his life—*In the Heavenlies* (Ephesians) by Harry A. Ironside. Reading the commentary every night one summer as a teenager, Art Farstad found out what a commentary is.

What a Commentary Is

Exactly what is a commentary and why should we not despise one? Recently a prominent Christian publisher listed *fifteen* types of Bible-related books. If some people don't know exactly how a commentary differs from a study Bible, e.g., or even from a concordance, an atlas, an interlinear, a Bible dictionary—to name five—it should be no surprise.

A commentary comments, or makes (hopefully) helpful remarks on the text, either verse by verse or paragraph by paragraph. Some Christians sneer at commentaries and say, "I only want to hear the spoken word and read the Bible itself!" Sounds pious, but it is not. A commentary merely puts in print the best (and hardest!) type of Bible exposition—the verse by verse teaching and preaching of the Word of God. Some commentaries (such as Ironside's) are quite literally sermons put into print. What's more, the greatest Bible expositions of all ages and tongues are available in

English. Unfortunately many are so long, so dated, and so difficult that the ordinary Christian gets discouraged, not to say overwhelmed. Hence, *Believer's Bible Commentary (BBC)*.

Kinds of Commentaries

Theoretically, anyone interested in the Bible could write a commentary. For this reason they range from extremely liberal to very conservative—with every shade of thought in between. The *BBC* is a very conservative one, accepting the Bible as the inspired and flawless Word of God, totally sufficient for faith and practice.

A commentary can range all the way from highly technical (minute details of Greek and Hebrew syntax, e.g.) to a very breezy sketch. The *BBC* is somewhere in between. What technicalities are needed are largely relegated to the endnotes, but a serious interaction with the details of the text is given with no dodging of difficult passages or convicting applications. Mr. MacDonald's writing is rich in exposition. Its aim is to help produce, not merely garden-variety, lowest-common-denominator Christians, but "disciples."

Commentaries also differ as to theological camp—conservative or liberal, Protestant or Roman Catholic, premillennial or amillennial. The *BBC* is conservative, Protestant, and premillennial.

How to Use This Book

There are several approaches to the *BBC*. We suggest the following, pretty much in this order:

Browsing—If you like or love the Bible you will enjoy leafing through this book, reading bits and pieces here and there to get the flavor of the whole work.

Specific Passage—You may have a question on a verse or paragraph that you need help on. Look it up in the appropriate place in context and you will surely find good material.

A Doctrine—If you are studying creation, the Sabbath, the covenants, the dispensations, or salvation, look up the passages that deal with those subjects. The Table of Contents lists essays[1] on a number of these topics. Use a concordance to help locate key words to guide to central passages for topics other than the ones listed.

Bible Book—Perhaps your Sunday school class or congregation is going through a book of the Bible. You will greatly enrich yourself (and have something to contribute, if there is a discussion) if you read ahead each week the passage to be covered. (Of course, if the leader is also using the

BBC as a main study help, you may want to have two different commentaries!)

The Whole Book—Eventually every Christian should read through the entire Bible. There are hard texts scattered throughout, and a careful, conservative book like the BBC will greatly enhance your study.

Bible study may start out in the "shredded wheat" stage—"nutritious but dry," but as you progress it will become "chocolate pie"!

Mr. MacDonald's advice to me over thirty years ago was, "Don't despise the commentaries." Having studied his Commentaries on the Old and New Testament books with great care while editing them for the New King James text, I can go a step further. My advice: "Enjoy!"

ENDNOTES

[1] Technically a discussion in a commentary that expands on some subject touched upon in the text is called an *excursus*.

Illustrations and Tables

Figures

Tables

Maps

Abbreviations

Abbreviations of Books of the Bible

Old Testament Books

Gen.	Genesis	2 Chron.	2 Chronicles	Dan.	Daniel
Ex.	Exodus	Ezra	Ezra	Hos.	Hosea
Lev.	Leviticus	Neh.	Nehemiah	Joel	Joel
Num.	Numbers	Est.	Esther	Amos	Amos
Deut.	Deuteronomy	Job	Job	Obad.	Obadiah
Josh.	Joshua	Ps.(Pss.)	Psalm(s)	Jon.	Jonah
Judg.	Judges	Prov.	Proverbs	Mic.	Micah
Ruth	Ruth	Eccl.	Ecclesiastes	Nah.	Nahum
1 Sam.	1 Samuel	Song	Song of Solomon	Hab.	Habakkuk
2 Sam.	2 Samuel	Isa.	Isaiah	Zeph.	Zephaniah
1 Kgs.	1 Kings	Jer.	Jeremiah	Hag.	Haggai
2 Kgs.	2 Kings	Lam.	Lamentations	Zech.	Zechariah
1 Chron.	1 Chronicles	Ezek.	Ezekiel	Mal.	Malachi

New Testament Books

Matt.	Matthew	Eph.	Ephesians	Heb.	Hebrews
Mark	Mark	Phil.	Philippians	Jas.	James
Luke	Luke	Col.	Colossians	1 Pet.	1 Peter
John	John	1 Thess.	1 Thessalonians	2 Pet.	2 Peter
Acts	Acts	2 Thess.	2 Thessalonians	1 Jn.	1 John
Rom.	Romans	1 Tim.	1 Timothy	2 Jn.	2 John
1 Cor.	1 Corinthians	2 Tim.	2 Timothy	3 Jn.	3 John
2 Cor.	2 Corinthians	Tit.	Titus	Jude	Jude
Gal.	Galatians	Phmn.	Philemon	Rev.	Revelation

Abbreviations of Bible Versions, Translations, and Paraphrases

ASV	American Standard Version	NEB	New English Bible
FWG	F. W. Grant's *Numerical Bible*	NIV	New International Version
JND	John Nelson Darby's New Translation	NKJV	New King James Version
		NRSV	New Revised Standard Version
KJV	King James Version	RSV	Revised Standard Version
—	Knox Version	RV	Revised Version (England)
LB	Living Bible	—	*The Holy Scriptures* (Jewish
—	Moffatt Translation		Publication Society)
NASB	New American Standard Bible	TEV	Today's English Version

Other Abbreviations

A.D.	*Anno Domini,* in the year of our Lord marginal reading	LXX	Septuagint (ancient Gk. version of the OT)
Aram.	Aramaic	marg.	margin, marginal reading
BBC	*Believer's Bible Commentary*	masc.	masculine
B.C.	Before Christ	ms., mss.	manuscript(s)
c.	*circa,* about	M	Majority Text
cf.	*confer,* compare	MT	Masoretic text
chap.	chapter	n.d.	no date
chaps.	chapters	*NIC*	*New International Commentary*
DSS	Dead Sea Scrolls		
ed.	edited, edition, editor	n.p.	no publisher, no place of publication
eds.	editors		
e.g.	*exempli gratia,* for example	NT	New Testament
et al.	*et alii,* and others	NU	Nestle-Aland/United
fem.	feminine		Bible Societies Greek NT
Gk.	Greek	OT	Old Testament
Heb.	Hebrew	p., pp.	page(s)
ICC	*International Critical Commentary*	trans.	translation, translator, translated
ibid.	*ibidem,* in the same place	vol(s).	volume(s)
i.e.	*id est,* that is	v., vv.	verse(s)
lit.	literal, literally	vs.	versus

Transliteration of Hebrew Words

The Believer's Bible Commentary, being tailor-made for the ordinary Christian who has studied no Hebrew, uses only a handful of Hebrew words in the text, and a few more in the endnotes.

The Hebrew Alphabet

Form	Final Form	Transliterated by	Name	Pronunciation
א		'	'Aleph	(silent)
ב (ב)		b (v)	Bêth	B in boy (v in very)
ג (ג)		g	Gîmel	G in go
ד (ד)		d	Dāleth	D in day (th in them)[1]
ה		h	Hê	H in hat
ו		w	Wāw	W in way[2]
ז		z	Zayin	Z in zeal
ח		ḥ	Hêth	CH in Scottish "loch"
ט		t	Têth	T in toy
י		y	Yôd	Y in yet
כ (כ)	ך	k (kh)	Kaph	K in kick
ל		l	Lāmed	L in let
מ	ם	m	Mêm	M in met
נ	ן	n	Nûn	N in net
ס		s	Sāmekh	S in set
ע		'	'Ayin	(silent)[3]
פ (פ)	ף	p (ph)	Pê	P in pet (ph in phone)
צ	ץ	ts	TSādhê	TS in hits
ק		q	Qôph	Q in Iraq (=k)
ר		r	Rêsh	R in run
שׂ		s	Sîn	S in so
שׁ		sh	SHîn	SH in she
ת (ת)		t (th)	Tāw	T in tin (th in thin)[4]

The Consonants

OT Hebrew has twenty-two letters, all consonants; the early biblical scrolls did not contain vowels. These vowel "points," as they are called, were invented and inserted during the seventh century A.D. Hebrew words are written from right to left, just the opposite from English writing.

We have used a somewhat simplified system of transliteration (similar to what is used in popular transliterations from Israel).

For example, when a *bêth* is pronounced "v" we put a v in the transliteration, not a *b* with a line under it (*nevî'îm*, not *nebî'îm*). Because the difference in sound between *hê* (=h) and *hêth* (=guttural h) is strong, we have put a dot under the *h* when it represents *hêth* (=ḥ).[5]

We have not, however, put marks on English *s's* or *t's* to differentiate minor differences that are too subtle for popular usage.

Names that have become anglicized by frequent usage, such as *Elohim*, are not usually marked with diacritical marks over the English vowels.

The Vowels

Here are a few pointers on how to pronounce the vowels:

The *unmarked* vowels are short: a, e, i, o, u, are pronounced as in c*a*t, p*e*t, k*i*d, d*o*ll, p*u*t.

The vowels marked with either a long mark (ˉ) or a circumflex accent (ˆ) are pronounced as follows:

ā or â as in f*a*ther (e.g.: *Tōrāh*)
ē or ê as in th*ey* (e.g.: *'āmēn*)
 î as in pol*i*ce (e.g.: *'Elōhîm*)
ō or ô as in g*o*ld (e.g.: *shālôm*)
ū or û as in tr*u*th (e.g.: *hallēlû Yah*)

ENDNOTES

[1]In modern (Israeli) Hebrew the letter is always pronounced as a "d."

[2]In modern Hebrew this letter is called *vav* and pronounced as "v."

[3]In biblical times *'ayin* had a guttural sound. For example the Hebrew original of the name *Gaza* began with this letter; apparently it was close enough to a hard "g" sound to make the Hellenists transliterate it here with a *gamma*.

[4]In modern Hebrew this letter is called *tav* and always pronounced as a "t."

[5]This is usually done in scholarly journals and other more technical works.

Transliteration of Greek Words

Greek Name	Greek Letter	English Equivalent	Greek Name	Greek Letter	English Equivalent
alpha	α	a	nu	ν	n
beta	β	b	xi	ξ	x
gamma	γ	g, ng	omicron	o	o (short)
delta	δ	d	pi	π	p
epsilon	ε	e (short)	rho	ρ	r
zeta	ζ	z	sigma	σ (ς)	s
eta	η	e (long)	tau	τ	t
theta	θ	th	upsilon	υ	u, y
iota	ι	i	phi	φ	ph
kappa	κ	k	chi	χ	ch (hard)
lambda	λ	l	psi	ψ	ps
mu	μ	m	omega	ω	o (long)

INTRODUCTION TO
THE OLD TESTAMENT

"For us the supreme sanction of the Old Testament is that which it derived from Christ Himself.... What was indispensable to the Redeemer must always be indispensable to the redeemed."

—Professor G. A. Smith

I. The Name "Old Testament"

Before launching out into the deep seas of OT studies, or even the comparatively small area of studying a particular book, it will prove helpful to outline briefly some general facts about the Sacred Book we call "The Old Testament."

Our word "covenant" translates the Hebrew word *berîth*.[1] In the NT *covenant* and *testament* both translate the same Greek word (*diathēkē*). In the title of the Scriptures the *meaning* "covenant" seems definitely preferable because the Book constitutes a pact, alliance, or *covenant* between God and His people.

It is called the *Old* Testament (or Covenant) to contrast it with the "New" one, although "Older Covenant" might be a better title, since *Old* to some people suggests that it is not worth learning. This would be a deadly error from a spiritual, historical, or cultural viewpoint. Both Testaments are inspired by God and therefore profitable for all Christians. While the believer in Christ frequently turns to that part of the Bible that specifically tells of our Lord, His church, and how He wishes His disciples to live, the importance of the OT for a fully-furnished believer cannot be overstressed.

The relationship between the OT and the NT was nicely expressed by Augustine:

The New is in the Old concealed;
The Old is in the New revealed.[2]

II. The OT Canon

The word *canon* (Gk. *kanōn*) refers to a "rule" by which something is measured or evaluated. The OT Canon is that collection of divinely inspired, and hence authoritative, books recognized by the spiritual leaders of Israel in ancient times. How do we know that these are the *only* books that should be in the canon or that *all* of these thirty-nine writings should be there? Since there were other religious writings (including heretical ones) from early days, how can we be sure that these are the right ones?

It is often said that a Jewish council drew up the canonical list in the late first century of our era. Actually, the books were *canonical* as soon as they were written. Godly and discerning Jews recognized inspired Scriptures from the start. However, there was a dispute for a time over some of the books (Esther, Ecclesiastes, Song of Songs, e.g.) in some quarters.

The Jews divide the OT into three parts: The Torah, the Prophets (Former and Latter), and the Writings.[3]

15

There are several theories as to why, for example, the Book of Daniel, a prophecy, should be among the Writings, and not among the Prophets. A common liberal view is that Daniel was written too late to get into the second section, which they see as already "closed" when Daniel wrote (See Introduction to Daniel.) A conservative view sees Daniel in the third section because he was not a prophet by *office*, but a statesman used by God to write a prophecy. Dr. Merrill F. Unger taught that the three-fold division is determined by the position of the writers[4]:

> This is the conservative and (we believe) the correct view. The Old Testament books were written with the definite purpose of being held sacred and divinely authoritative. Therefore, they possessed the stamp of canonicity from the moment of their appearance. The three-fold division is due to the official position and status of the writers and not to degrees of inspiration, differences of content or chronology.[5]

The council that officially recognized our canon was actually *confirming* what had been generally accepted for centuries. The council drew up not an *inspired list* of books, but a list of *inspired books*.

Even more important for Christians is the fact that our Lord Himself quoted frequently and treated as authoritative books from the three sections of the Hebrew OT. See, for example, Luke 24:27 and 44; endnote 4. Furthermore, Christ never quoted from the so-called apocryphal books.

III. The Apocrypha

Eastern Orthodox, Roman Catholic, and Protestant Bible students all agree on the twenty-seven-book NT Canon, generally[6] in the same order, with the exact same 260 chapters. The situation with the OT is a little more complex.

Protestants and Jews agree on the content of the OT, but the Eastern Orthodox and Roman Catholics[7] accept several Jewish books of history and poetry which they call "deuterocanonical" (Gk. for secondary canon) and Protestants and Jews call "apocryphal" (Gk. for "hidden"[8]).

The thirty-nine books of the *current* King James,[9] New King James, and other truly Protestant versions constitute the exact same materials as the twenty-four books of the Hebrew Bible. The difference in number is because of several combinations in the Jewish editions. For example, the six books of Samuel, Kings, and Chronicles are considered to be just three books, and the Minor Prophets, called "The Book of the Twelve," are seen as just one book.

The Jews wrote many other religious books, often not even in Hebrew, that they did not consider inspired and authoritative. Some, such as 1 and 2 Maccabees, are valuable for inter-testamental history. Others, such as "Bel and the Dragon," need only to be read by the discerning to reveal their non-canonical status.

The least valuable of these Jewish books are called *Pseudepigrapha* (Gk. for "false writings") and the better ones are called *Apocrypha*.

Some ancient Jews and Christians, but especially the Gnostics of Egypt, accepted a larger canon, including some of these books.

When scholarly St. Jerome was asked to translate the apocryphal books into Latin by Damasus, the Bishop of Rome, he did so only *under protest*. This was because he knew his *Hebrew* text well and also that they were not authentic parts of the Jewish Canon. Hence, although Jerome could discern their (at best) secondary status, he did translate these books for the Latin Vulgate. Today they also appear in Roman Catholic versions such as the New American Bible and the Jerusalem Bible, and usually in such ecumenical versions as the New English Bible, the Revised English Bible, and the New Revised Standard Version.

Even the Roman Catholic Church did not *officially* recognize the Apocrypha as canonical until the Counter-Reformation Period (1500's).[10] One reason that the Vatican did this was that a few of her teachings, such as praying for the dead, are found in the Apocrypha. Actually, the Apocrypha is largely *Jewish* literature and history, and not directly relevant to Christian doctrine. While not inspired, some of these books are worth reading from a cultural and historical viewpoint, after one has a firm grip on the inspired books of the Hebrew Canon.

IV. Authorship

The Divine Author of the OT is the Holy Spirit. He moved Moses, Ezra, Isaiah, and the anonymous authors to write under His guidance. The best and correct understanding of this question of how the OT books were produced is called *dual authorship*. The OT is not partly human and partly divine, but totally human and totally divine at the same time. The divine element kept the human element from making any errors. The result is an inerrant or flawless book in the original manuscripts.

A helpful analogy to the *written* Word is the dual nature of the *Living* Word, our Lord Jesus Christ. He is not partly human and partly divine (like some Greek myth) but completely human and completely divine at the same time. The divine nature made it impossible for the human to err or sin in any way.

V. Dates

Unlike the NT, which took only half a century to write (about A.D. 50–100), the OT took at least a millennium to complete (about 1400–400 B.C.).[11] The first books written were either the Pentateuch (about 1400 B.C.) or Job (date unknown, but the contents suggest an era before the law was given).

Other books followed that were written *before* the exile (about 600 B.C.), such as Joshua through Samuel, *during* the exile (such as Lamentations and Ezekiel), or *after* the exile, such as Chronicles, Haggai, Zechariah, and Malachi (about 400 B.C.).

VI. Contents

The contents of the OT, presented in the order of the Protestant versions, may be summarized concisely as follows:

Pentateuch
   Genesis through Deuteronomy
Historical[12]
   Joshua through Esther
Poetic
   Job through Song of Solomon
Prophetic
   Isaiah through Malachi

Separate introductions to these four main sections of the OT will be found in the *Believers Bible Commentary* at the appropriate places.

A Christian who gets a good grasp of these books, along with the later and fuller revelation of the NT, will be "thoroughly furnished for every good work."

It is our prayer that the BBC will greatly aid many believers to be just that.

VII. Languages

1. Hebrew

Except for a few sections in Aramaic, a related Semitic[13] tongue, the OT was originally written in the Hebrew language.

Believers are not surprised that God used a thoroughly suitable vehicle for the earlier portion of His Word, an expressive language rich in color and idiom, well adapted to the inspired narratives, poetry, and laws that constitute the OT. Hebrew is one of the *ancient* languages—but it is the only one that (almost miraculously) has been revived as the *modern*[14] everyday speech of a nation—Israel.

Hebrew is written from right to left, originally in consonants only. The person reading aloud supplied the proper vowel sounds from his knowledge of the language. Providentially, this made it possible for the Hebrew text to remain readable for many centuries, since it is chiefly the vowel sounds that change from century to century, from country to country, and from region to region.[15]

Sometimes what was *written* (called *kethîv*), such as the name of God,[16] was thought too sacred to pronounce and so a marginal note told what to *read aloud* (*qerē*). This was also the case for copyists' errors and for words that, over the centuries, had come to be considered vulgar.

In the earlier Christian centuries Jewish scholars called Masoretes (from the Hebrew word for *tradition*) arose. Seeing that Hebrew was becoming an obsolete language, and desiring to preserve the correct reading of the sacred OT text, they devised a sophisticated phonetic system of dots and dashes above, and in, but chiefly below, the twenty-two Hebrew consonants to indicate the accepted vocalization of the words. Even today this ancient "vowel pointing," as it is called, is more scientific and precise than English, French, or *even* German spelling!

The consonantal text is also the source of disputed readings, since a set of consonants at times can be read with different *vowels*, and therefore different *meanings*. Usually the context will determine which is original, but not always. The variant spellings of names in Chronicles (see commentary there) that differ from Genesis, e.g., are partly due to this phenomenon.

By and large, however, the traditional, or Masoretic Text, is remarkably well-preserved. It is a living witness to the Jews' great reverence for God's Word. Often the ancient versions (Targums, Septuagint, and Vulgate) help us to choose the correct variant where a problem exists. Since the mid-twentieth century the Dead Sea Scrolls have given added information on the Hebrew text—chiefly as a confirmation of the accuracy of the Masoretic Text.

Fortunately for us who read the OT in an English translation, Hebrew translates very nicely into English—much better than it does into Latin, for example, as the great sixteenth century Reformation translator William Tyndale pointed out.

The version on which the BBC is based is a direct descendant of Tyndale's beginnings in the OT. He managed to complete Genesis through Chronicles and some poetic and prophetic sections before the Inquisition had him burned at the stake for his efforts (1536). His OT work was completed by others and updated in the King James Version of 1611 and more recently in the New King James Version of 1982.

2. Aramaic

Like Hebrew, Aramaic is a Semitic language, but a Gentile one, spoken widely in the ancient world for very many centuries. As Hebrew became a dead language for the Jews, the OT had to be interpreted for them into Aramaic, the closely related, but different, language that they had come to adopt. The script that we associate with Hebrew was probably borrowed from Aramaic about 400 B.C. and developed into the artistic square letters that are familiar to Hebrew students today.[17]

Most of the above facts concerning Hebrew are also true for the Aramaic portions of the OT. These passages are few, and understandably, chiefly concern Israel's contacts with her Gentile neighbors, such as in the Babylonian Exile and afterward.[18]

VIII. Translation

English is blessed with many translations (perhaps too many). There are, however, far fewer translations of the OT than of the NT. These translations fall into four general types:

1. Very Literal

J. N. Darby's "New" Translation of 1882 (NT much earlier), the English Revised Version of 1881 and its U.S. variant, the American Standard Version of 1901, are extremely literal. This makes them helpful for careful study but weak for worship, public reading, and memorization. The masses of believers have never abandoned the majesty and beauty of the Tyndale—King James tradition for these useful—but rather wooden—versions.

2. Optimum Equivalence

Versions that are quite literal and follow the Hebrew or Greek closely when English allows it, yet still permit a freer translation where good style and idiom demand it, include the KJV, the RSV, the NASB, and the NKJV. Unfortunately, the RSV, while generally reliable in the NT, is wedded to an OT that plays down many Messianic prophecies. This dangerous trend is seen today even among some previously sound scholars. The BBC was edited to conform to the NKJV as the most viable position between the beautiful (but archaic) KJV and today's usage, yet without using any *thee's* and *thou's*.[19]

3. Dynamic Equivalence

This type of translation is freer than the complete—equivalence type, and sometimes resorts to paraphrase, a valid technique as long as the reader is made aware of it. The NEB, NIV, and the Jerusalem Bible all fall into this category. An attempt is made to put whole thoughts into the structure that Moses and Isaiah might have used if they were writing today—and in English. When done conservatively, this methodology can be a helpful tool. The danger lies in the theological looseness of many translators who use this method.

4. Paraphrase

A paraphrase seeks to transmit the text thought by thought, yet it often takes great liberties in *adding* material. Since it is far removed from the original text in wording there is always the danger of *too much interpre-*

tation. The Living Bible, e.g., while evangelical, makes many interpretive decisions that are *at best* debatable.

It is good to have a Bible from at least three of these categories for purposes of comparison. However, we believe that the complete, or optimum-equivalence translation is safest for the type of detailed Bible study presented in the BBC.

IX. Inspiration

Amid all this welter of historical and technical details we do well to consider the words of the great English Baptist preacher, Charles Haddon Spurgeon:

This volume is the writing of the living God: each letter was penned with an Almighty finger; each word in it dropped from the everlasting lips; each sentence was dictated by the Holy Spirit. Albeit, that Moses was employed to write his histories with his fiery pen, God guided that pen. It may be that David touched his harp, and let sweet Psalms of melody drop from his fingers; but God moved his hands over the living strings of his golden harp. It may be that Solomon sang canticles of love, or gave forth words of consummate wisdom, but God directed his lips, and made the preacher eloquent. If I follow the thundering Nahum, when his horses plow the waters, or Habakkuk, when he sees the tents of Cushan in affliction; if I read Malachi, when the earth is burning like an oven;... it is God's voice, not man's; the words are God's words, the words of the Eternal, the Invisible, the Almighty, the Jehovah of this earth.[20]

ENDNOTES

[1]It appears in the name of the Jewish organization called "B'nai B'rith" ("Sons of the Covenant").

[2]His words (in Latin) have also been translated:

The New is in the Old contained;
The Old is in the New explained.

[3]The order of the twenty-four OT books as found in a Hebrew Bible or a Jewish translation is as follows:

I. The Law *(Tôrāh)*
   Genesis
   Exodus
   Leviticus
   Numbers
   Deuteronomy
II. The Prophets *(Nevî'îm)*
   1. *The Former Prophets*
      Joshua
      Judges
      Samuel
      Kings
   2. *The Latter Prophets*
      Isaiah
      Jeremiah
      Ezekiel
      The Book of the Twelve (Hosea through Malachi)
III. The Writings *(Ketûvîm)*
   Psalms
   Job
   Proverbs
   Ruth
   Song of Songs
   Ecclesiastes
   Lamentations
   Esther
   Daniel
   Ezra-Nehemiah
   Chronicles

[4]Merrill F. Unger, *Introductory Guide to the Old Testament*, p. 59.

[5]*Ibid.*

[6]However, the Russian NT has a somewhat different order after the Gospels, for example.

[7]See the Introduction to the New Revised Standard Version with Apocrypha for books added to the Canon by these groups. (They do not agree

among themselves on all books, either.)

[8]The idea of "spurious" has become associated with this word.

[9]Early editions of the KJV in the seventeenth century contained the Apocrypha, but sandwiched *in between* the OT and NT to indicate their inferior status. It shocks many people who look on the KJV as the only true Bible when (and if) they find out that it actually once contained *whole books* that are not of divine origin!

[10]At the Council of Trent, held between 1545 and 1563 (with intermissions) at Trento, Italy.

[11]Less conservative scholars move the dates later but end up with a similar period of time.

[12]Many Bible students prefer to put these two together (Genesis through Esther) and label them *historical*.

[13]Semitic (or Shemitic) are languages which were or are spoken largely by the descendants of *Shem*. They include Arabic, Phoenician, and Akkadian, as well as Hebrew.

[14]Language experts, using French, English, and freshly-coined words based on ancient Hebrew roots, as well as new constructions, helped to bring this ancient tongue into the twentieth century.

[15]For example, an English-speaking person is aware of the different sounds in a word such as *past*, as pronounced at Oxford, Boston, Dallas, and Brooklyn. The consonant sounds remain the same, but the "a" is pronounced *quite* differently in each city!

[16]For example, where the KJV/NKJV reads LORD (all capitals, representing the publicly *read* Hebrew word *Adōnai*), the *written* form is actually the sacred "tetragrammaton" (four letters, YHWH) that spell the covenant name of God, *Yahweh*, or in English tradition, *Jehovah*.

[17]Unger, *Introduction*, p. 124.

[18]The Aramaic portions are: Ezra 4:8—6:18; 7:12–26; Jeremiah 10:11; Daniel 2:4—7:28.

[19]For example, the similar (but less literary) NASB retains *thee's* and *thou's* in prayer and in some poetry.

[20]Charles Haddon Spurgeon, *Spurgeon's Sermons*, I:28. The word "dictated" should not be taken in the modern secretarial sense. As the rest of the quotation shows, Spurgeon believed in the orthodox teaching of inspiration—dual authorship (human and divine) of each book.

INTRODUCTION TO THE PENTATEUCH

"Modern criticism has ventured to undermine and assail almost all the books of holy scripture, but none with such boldness as the Pentateuch, unless it be the prophecy of Daniel. . . . Let us take our stand on the fact, broad, deep, and conclusive, that the authority of Christ has decided the question for all who own Him to be God as well as man."

—William Kelly

"The Pentateuch is an essential introduction to the entire word of God. It opens up that which is afterwards unfolded, and ever leads us on in hope to a consummation which, though distant, is certain."

—Samuel Ridout

Before commenting on the individual Books of Moses, since this is such a basic part of biblical revelation, we would like to present a few facts on the Pentateuch as a whole.

I. Titles of the Pentateuch

The first five books of the Bible are commonly called "the Pentateuch." In ancient times books were in the form of scrolls rather than bound as pages of a "codex" (book form). These scrolls, called *teuchoi*[1] in Greek, were stored in sheathlike containers. The Greek word for "five-roll" is *pentateuchos*, whence our word "Pentateuch."

Jews refer to the Pentateuch as "the Torah" (Heb. *tôrâ*, "law" or "instruction"), and treat it as the most important part of their Bible.

A third common title of these volumes is "the Books of Moses." It is ironical that the Bibles of certain northern European countries that most widely reject the Mosaic authorship of the Pentateuch label these books not as "Genesis, Exodus," etc., but as "First Book of *Moses*," "Second Book of *Moses*," etc.

Except for *Numbers*, whose name is the English translation of the Greek *Arithmoi* and the Latin *Numeri*, we retain the Greek LXX (Septuagint) titles of these five books, but anglicize the spelling and pronunciation. (See the individual books in the Believers Bible Commentary for their meanings.)

The Jews often call the books by their first few words in the Hebrew text. Thus Genesis is called *Berēshîth* ("In the beginning").

II. Contents of the Pentateuch

The usage of our English word *law* is more restricted than the Hebrew meanings of *tôrâ*, hence the term "Pentateuch" is ideal for Christian usage to express the great importance of this five-volume set.

A. Genesis

Genesis is well-named, as it is the Greek word for *beginning*. The first book of the Bible traces the origins of the universe, the earth, man, marriage, sin, true religion, the nations, diverse languages, and the chosen people. The first eleven chapters recount the broad sweep of human history, but chapters twelve through fifty narrow the story down to the family of Abraham, Isaac, Jacob, and his sons.

B. Exodus

Exodus, Greek for *the way out*, narrates how in four hundred years the family of Abraham grew to a nation under the forced labor of the Pharaohs in Egypt, and their redemption from bondage under Moses. The Law of Moses and the detailed description of the tabernacle make up the rest of the book.

C. Leviticus

Leviticus is a manual for the Levites, hence the name. It describes the rituals necessary for sinful men of that era to have fellowship with a holy God. The book contains pictures and types of the sacrifice of Christ.

D. Numbers

Numbers, as the name suggests, includes a numbering of the people, or census—one at the beginning and another at the end of the book. The Hebrew title for the book, "in the desert" (*Bemidbār*), is more expressive, since Numbers recounts the historical events experienced by the Israelites in their wilderness wanderings.

E. Deuteronomy

Deuteronomy, Greek for *second law*, is more than a mere re-telling of the law to a new generation, though it is that. It is the link with the historical books that follow, since it recounts the death of Moses, and his replacement by Joshua, his successor.

Griffith Thomas, in his usual lucid and concise style, summarizes the contents of the Books of Moses as follows:

> The five books of the Pentateuch record the introduction of the Divine religion into the world. Each book gives one phase of God's plan, and together they constitute a real unity. Genesis speaks of the origin of the religion, and of the people chosen by God as its medium. Exodus records the formation of the people into a nation, and the establishment of God's relationship with it. Leviticus shows the various ways in which this relationship was maintained. Numbers shows how the people were organized for the purpose of commencing the life of the Divine religion in the Promised Land. This book also tells of the nation's failure and the consequent delay, with re-organization. Then Deuteronomy shows how the people were prepared, while on the border of the Promised Land, for the entry which was soon to follow.[2]

III. Importance of the Pentateuch

Since the whole OT, in fact the whole Bible, is based on these first five books, the importance of the Pentateuch for revealed religion can hardly be overstated. If rationalistic, unbelieving scholars can undermine faith in the integrity and authenticity of *these* books, the origins of Judaism become lost in a sea of uncertainty. Christians should not think that *our* faith is unaffected by such attacks either, since the NT and our Lord Himself also quote the Books of Moses as true and trustworthy.

Dr. Merrill Unger put the case very bluntly:

> The foundation of all revealed truth and of God's redemptive plan is based on the Pentateuch. If this foundation is unreliable, the whole Bible is unreliable.[3]

IV. Authorship of the Pentateuch

Except for some who in early Christian times opted for Ezra[4] as the author of the Torah, by and large, Judeo-Christian orthodoxy has maintained Mosaic authorship through the centuries—and still does.

A. Mosaic Authorship

Before examining briefly the documentary theory, which largely *denies* Mosaic authorship, let us note the positive evidence *for* it.

1. Moses' Qualifications

The nineteenth century German critic Hartmann denied Mosaic authorship on the grounds that it was quite literally impossible—writing not having yet been invented. (Or, so many thought then!) Archaeology has shown that Moses could have written in early Hebrew script, Egyptian hieroglyphics, or Accadian cuneiform. Of course Acts 7:22 told believers long before archaeology confirmed it, that Moses was educated "in all the learning of the Egyptians." When we say Moses "wrote" the Pentateuch, this allows for his using previous documents in Genesis. It also allows for inspired editorial updatings as Hebrew script changed through the centuries. Of course, the fact that Moses *could have written* the Pentateuch doesn't prove that he *did*. However, as the father of the Jewish faith

it is inevitable that he would make a permanent record of God's revelation for future generations. And so God had commanded him.

2. Pentateuchal Claims

The text of the Torah says specifically that Moses *did* write down at God's command on occasion. See, e.g., Exodus 17:14; 24:4; 34:27; Numbers 33:2; Deuteronomy 31:19.

3. Later Biblical Claims

The rest of God's Word accepts Mosaic authorship as well. See, e.g., Joshua 1:7 and 1 Kings 2:3; and in the NT, Luke 24:44 and 1 Corinthians 9:9.

4. The Witness of Christ

For Christians the fact that our Lord Himself accepted Mosaic authorship should settle the matter. The notion that in His humanity Jesus was ignorant of science and history, or that He knew better but accommodated Himself to the ignorance and prejudice of His countrymen is unworthy of a believer's consideration.

5. Archaeology and the Pentateuch

Many customs, words, names, and historical and cultural details that liberal critics once said were "too late" to be Mosaic have now been found to *predate* Moses by centuries. While this doesn't "prove" Mosaic authorship, it tallies much better with the traditional view than it does with the theory that "redactors" or editors living many centuries later knew all these (by then largely lost) details and pieced them together so nicely.

B. The Documentary Hypothesis

In 1753 Jean Astruc, a French doctor, set forth the theory that Moses compiled Genesis from two documents. Those passages that used the name *Jehovah* for God came from one source, he wrote, and those using *Elohim* another. These supposed sources he labeled "J" and "E" respectively.

Later, liberal scholars developed the theory much further, eventually putting all their supposed sources much later than Moses. Other proposed documents were "D" ("Deuteronomic") and "P" ("Priestly"). The Pentateuch was viewed as a patchwork of sources built up between the ninth and sixth centuries B.C. Popularly, the hypothesis became known as the "JEDP theory."

Several things made the hypothesis attractive to nineteenth-century scholars. First of all it fitted in well with Darwin's theory of evolution, which was being applied to many fields other than just to biology. Next, the anti-supernaturalistic spirit of the day found delight in trying to put the Bible down on a merely human level. Thirdly, the humanistic trends that replaced divine revelation with man's efforts dovetailed with this theory.

In 1878 Julius Wellhausen popularized the documentary hypothesis in a clever and deceptively plausible way.

In this short Introduction we can only mention a few of the main points against the theory.[5]

Serious problems with the theory include the following:

1. Lack of Manuscript Evidence

There is no manuscript evidence that any of the editorial work proposed in the "JEDP" theory ever occurred.

2. Conflicting and Subjective Fragmentation

Scholars divide the Pentateuch up into fragments quite differently, which exposes the extreme, personal viewpoints and lack of concrete, objective evidence for the theory.

3. Archaeology

Archaeology has tended to support the writing, customs, religious knowledge, etc., of the Pentateuch as being very ancient, and definitely *not* from the much later period of composition proposed by the Wellhausen theory.

4. Linguistics

Supposedly "late" language forms and personal names found in the Pentateuch have been found in sources well before the time of Moses. An example is the recently unearthed "Ebla tablets," which contain many Pentateuchal names.

5. Unity of the Pentateuch

Editorially, the five books of Moses hold together very well and exhibit a unity and coherence that is most difficult to reconcile with the alleged evolutionary "scissors and paste" origins of these books.

6. Spiritual Bankruptcy

Finally, from a spiritual viewpoint, the documentary theories, even as modified by archaeology and other similar theories, are unworthy of the great and beautiful truths enshrined in these books. If these theories were true, the Pentateuch would be, in the words of Dr. Unger, "unauthentic, unhistorical, and unreliable, a fabrication of men, not the work of God."[6]

V. Date of the Pentateuch

The contents of the Pentateuch take us back to creation, but the actual writing, of course, was thousands of years later. Obviously the date for the writing that we choose is dependent upon *who* wrote it.

Liberal scholars date the various theorized stages of the work largely as follows: The so-called "J document" is dated about 850 B.C.; the "E document" about 750 B.C.; the "D document" about 621 B.C.;[7] and the "P document" about 500 B.C.

Conservative scholars generally date the Pentateuch around the time of the Exodus, in the fifteenth century B.C. Some prefer a date for this event of about a century and half later.

Probably the best date to fit all the biblical data is sometime between 1450–1410 B.C. See the individual books in the BBC for more details.

VI. Conclusion

We conclude our Introduction to the Pentateuch with the words of Canada's foremost OT scholar:

The Pentateuch is a homogeneous composition in five volumes, and not an agglomeration of separate and perhaps only rather casually related works. It described, against an accredited historical background, the manner in which God revealed Himself to men and chose the Israelites for special service and witness in the world and in the course of human history. The role of Moses in the formulation of this literary corpus appears pre-eminent, and it is not without good reason that he should be accorded a place of high honor in the growth of the epic of Israelite nationhood, and be venerated by Jews and Christians alike as the great mediator of the ancient Law.[8]

ENDNOTES

[1] The word *teuchos* originally meant a tool or implement, and then a roll of material to write on.

[2] W. H. Griffith Thomas, *The Pentateuch*, p. 25.

[3] Merrill F. Unger, *Unger's Bible Handbook*, p. 35.

[4] The Jewish philosopher Spinoza also chose Ezra as the author.

[5] A Christian approach can be found in R. K. Harrison, *Introduction to the Old Testament* (Grand Rapids: Wm. B. Eerdmans Publishing Co., 1966). The Jewish American novelist Hermann Wouk exposes the theory in *This Is My God* (Garden City, NY: Doubleday & Co., 1959).

[6] Unger, *Handbook*, p. 35.

[7] Many liberals posit such a specific date from the mistaken belief that Josiah conveniently "found" (fabricated) what is now called Deuteronomy in order to promote a central sanctuary in his capital, Jerusalem.

[8] Harrison, *Introduction*, p. 541.

GENESIS

Introduction

"The first book of the Bible is for several reasons one of the most interesting and fascinating portions of Scripture. Its place in the Canon, its relation to the rest of the Bible, and the varied and striking character of its contents combine to make it one of the most prominent in Holy Writ. It is with a real spiritual insight, therefore, that the people of God in all ages have fastened upon this book, and given it their earnest attention."

—W. H. Griffith Thomas

I. Unique Place in the Canon

Genesis (Greek for "Beginning"), called *Bereshîth* by the Jews (Hebrew for "In the beginning"), is well named. This exciting volume gives the only true account of creation by the only One who was there—the Creator!

Through His servant Moses, the Holy Spirit traces the beginnings of man, woman, marriage, the home, sin, sacrifices, cities, trade, agriculture, music, worship, languages, and the races and nations of the world. All this in the first eleven chapters.

Then, from chapters 12—50 we see the beginnings of Israel, God's "test-tube nation," to be a spiritual microcosm of all the peoples of the world. The lives of the patriarchs Abraham, Isaac, Jacob, and his twelve sons—especially the attractively devout Joseph, have inspired untold millions, from young children to advanced OT scholars.

A solid grasp of Genesis is necessary for an understanding of the rest of the sixty-five books of the Bible.

They all build on its beautifully proportioned literary base.

II. Authorship

We accept the ancient Jewish and Christian teaching that Genesis was written and compiled by Moses the man of God and Lawgiver of Israel. Since all the events in Genesis are pre-Mosaic it is virtually certain that Moses used ancient documents and perhaps oral accounts as he was guided by the Holy Spirit. See *Introduction to the Pentateuch* for a discussion of Mosaic authorship.

III. Date

The most conservative scholars generally date the Exodus about 1445 B.C. Hence Genesis would probably have been written between this date and Moses' death about forty years later. It is always possible, of course, that this one book of the Pentateuch was written *before* the Exodus, since all the events in Genesis predate that great event.

See *Introduction to the Pentateuch* for further details.

IV. Background and Themes

Except for those who are extremely biased against the Bible, Judaism, or Christianity, nearly everyone agrees that Genesis is a fascinating account of very ancient times and contains narratives of great beauty, such as the story of Joseph.

But just what is the *background* of this first book of the Bible. In short, what *is* it?

Those who reject a personal God have tended to class Genesis as a collection of *myths* adapted from pagan Mesopotamian myths and "cleaned up" from their worst polytheistic elements for monotheistic Hebrew edification.

Others, not quite as skeptical, see Genesis as a collection of *sagas* or *legends*, with some historical value.

Yet others see the stories as explanations of the origins of things in nature and culture (technically called *etiologies*). There *are* etiologies in the OT, especially in this book of beginnings (the origin of sin, the rainbow, the Hebrew people, e.g.) but this by no means makes the explanations unhistorical.

Genesis is *history*. Like all history, it is interpretive. It is *theological* history, or facts narrated in a framework of the divine plan. It has been well said that "history is His story."

Though Genesis is the first book of the "law" there is very little *legal* material in it. It is *"Law"* (*Torah*, Heb. for instruction) in that it lays the foundation for Exodus through Deuteronomy and God's giving of the Law through Moses. In fact, it lays the foundation of all Bible history— yes, of history itself.

The twin *themes* of blessing and cursing are carefully woven throughout the fabric of Genesis, and indeed, the whole word of God. Obedience brings enrichment of blessing, and disobedience the opposite.

The great *curses* are the penalties of the Fall, the universal Flood, and the confusion of tongues at Babel.

The great *blessings* are the promise of a Redeemer, the salvation of a remnant through the Flood, and the choice of a special nation to be a channel of God's grace, Israel.

If Genesis is factual history, how could Moses have known all the ancient genealogies, conversations, events and correct interpretation of these events?

First, let it be said, that archaeology has supported (not "proved" but confirmed and illustrated) the Genesis account in many areas, especially regarding the patriarchs and their customs.

Some nineteenth century liberals, such as Hartmann,[1] taught that Moses could not have written the Pentateuch because writing had not yet been invented! Now we know that Moses could have written in any one of several ancient scripts, being learned in all the lore of Egypt.

Moses no doubt used accounts left by Joseph, and the tablets, parchments, and oral translations brought from ancient Mesopotamia by Abraham and his descendants. These would include the genealogies, the major sections, known as "the generations of Adam," etc.

In the final analysis this is still not enough. The Holy Spirit of God inspired Moses to choose exactly the right materials and to ignore the rest. He probably supplied details of conversations and other things by direct revelation.

It comes down to a matter of *faith.* Either God is capable of producing such a work through His servants or He is not. Believers of all generations from primeval times to today have set their seal that God is true.

Archaeology can help us reconstruct the culture of the patriarchs to make the Bible accounts more vivid,[2] but only the Holy Spirit can illumi-nate the truth of Genesis to our hearts and daily lives.

As you read the *Believers Bible Commentary* on Genesis—or any of the OT books—you must be dependent on the Spirit's illumination of the *Holy Word itself* to really benefit from the comments. A true commentary is not an independent means, but an arrow, pointing to a "thus says the Lord."

OUTLINE

Commentary

I. EARTH'S EARLIEST AGES (Chaps. 1—11)

A. The Creation (Chaps. 1, 2)

1:1 "In the beginning God...." These first four words of the Bible form the foundation for faith. Believe these words, and you can believe all that follows in the Bible. Genesis provides the only authoritative account of creation, meaningful for people of all ages but exhaustible by no one. The divine record assumes the existence of God rather than seeking to prove it. The Bible has a special name for those who choose to deny the fact of God. That name is *fool* (Ps. 14:1 and 53:1). Just as the Bible begins with God, so He should be first in our lives.

1:2 One of several conservative interpretations of the Genesis account of creation, the creation-reconstruction view, says that between verses 1 and 2 a great catastrophe occurred, perhaps the fall of Satan (see Ezek. 28:11–19).[3] This caused God's original, perfect creation to become **without form and void** (*tōhû wāvōhû*). Since God didn't *create* the earth waste and empty (see Isa. 45:18), only a mighty cataclysm could explain the chaotic condition of verse 2. Proponents of this view point out that the word translated **was** (*hāyethā*) could also be translated "had become."[4] Thus the earth "had become waste and empty."

The Spirit of God was hovering over the face of the waters, preparatory to the great creative and reconstructive acts to follow. The remaining verses describe the six days of creation and reconstruction which prepared the earth for human habitation.

1:3–5 On **the first day God** commanded **light** to shine out of **darkness** and established the **Day** and **Night**

cycle. This act is not to be confused with the establishment of the sun, moon, and stars on the fourth day. In 2 Corinthians 4:6 the Apostle Paul draws a parallel between the original separation of light from darkness and the conversion of a sinner.

1:6–8 Prior to **the second day**, it seems that the earth was completely surrounded by a thick layer of water, perhaps in the form of a heavy vapor. On **the second day** God divided this layer, part covering the earth with water and part forming clouds, with the atmospheric layers (**firmament** or "dome") between. **God called the firmament Heaven**—that is, the expanse of space immediately above the earth (not the stellar heavens, nor the third heaven, where God dwells). Verse 20 makes it clear that the heaven here is the sphere where the birds fly.

1:9–13 Then God caused **the dry land** to **appear** out of the **waters** that covered the face of the planet. Thus were born the **Earth** and the **Seas**. Also on **the third day** He caused vegetation and trees of all kinds to spring up in the earth.

1:14–19 It was not until **the fourth day** that the Lord set the sun, moon, and **stars** in **the heavens** as lightbearers and as means for establishing a calendar.

1:20–23 The fifth day saw **the waters** stocked with fish and the earth stocked with bird-life and insects. The word translated **birds** means "flying ones" and includes bats and probably flying insects.

1:24, 25 On **the sixth day** God first created animals and reptiles. The law of reproduction is repeatedly given in the words **according to its kind**. There are significant variations within "kinds" of biological life, but there is no passing from one kind to another.

1:26–28 The crown of God's work was the creation of **man in His image and according to** His **likeness**. This means that man was placed on earth as God's representative, and that He resembles God in certain ways. Just as God is a Trinity (Father, Son, and Holy Spirit), so man is a tripartite being (spirit, soul, and body). Like God, man has intellect, a moral nature, the power to communicate with others, and an emotional nature that transcends instinct. There is no thought of physical likeness here. In contrast to animals, man is a worshiper, an articulate communicator, and a creator.

There is an allowance for or even an intimation of the Trinity in verse 26: **Then God** [*Elohim*, plural] **said** [singular verb in Hebrew], **"Let Us** [plural] **make man in Our image . . . ."**

The Bible describes the origin of the sexes as a creative act of God. Evolution has never been able to explain how the sexes began. Humanity was commanded to **be fruitful and multiply**.

God gave man a mandate to **subdue** creation and **have dominion over** it—to use it but not abuse it. The modern crises in the earth's environment are due to man's greed, selfishness, and carelessness.

1:29, 30 It is clear from these verses that animals were originally herbivorous and that man was vegetarian. This was changed after the Flood (see 9:1–7).

Were the six days of creation literal 24-hour days, or were they geological ages? Or were they days of "dramatic vision" during which the creation account was *revealed* to Moses? No scientific evidence has ever refuted the concept that they were literal solar days. The expression "the evening and the morning" points to 24-hour days. Everywhere else in the

OT these words mean normal days. Adam lived through the seventh day and died in his 930th year, so the seventh day could not have been a geological age. Wherever the "day" is used with a number in the OT ("first day," etc.) it means a literal day. When God commanded Israel to rest on the Sabbath day, He based the command on the fact that He had rested on the seventh day, after six days of labor (Ex. 20:8–11). Consistent interpretation here requires the same meaning of the word "day."

A difficulty, however, is that the solar day as we know it may not have begun until the fourth day (vv. 14–19).

As far as the Bible is concerned, the creation of the heavens and the earth is undated. The creation of man is undated also. However, genealogies are given, and, even allowing for possible gaps in the genealogies, man could not have been on the earth for the millions of years demanded by evolutionists.

We learn from John 1:1, 14, Colossians 1:16, and Hebrews 1:2 that the Lord Jesus was the active Agent in creation. For the inexhaustible wonders of His creation, He is worthy of endless worship.

1:31 At the end of the six days of creation **God saw everything that He had made, and indeed it was very good**.

2:1–3 God **rested** from His creative activity **on the seventh day**. This is not the rest that follows weariness but the rest of satisfaction and completion of a job well done. Although God did not command man to keep the Sabbath at this time, He taught the principle of one day of rest in seven.

2:4–6 The name Lord **God** (*Jehovah* [*Yahweh*] *Elohim*) appears for the first time in verse 4, but only after the creation of man (1:27). As Elohim, God is the Creator. As Jehovah, He is in covenant relation with man. Failing to see this, some Bible critics have concluded that these different names for God can only be explained by a change in authorship.

This is the history (v. 4) refers to the beginnings described in chapter 1. Verse 5, which reads, **"before any plant of the field was in the earth and before any herb of the field had grown,"** describes conditions on the earth in 1:10, when the dry land appeared but before vegetation appeared. **The earth** was watered by **a mist** rather than by **rain**.

2:7 A fuller account of the creation of **man** is now given. **God formed** his body from **the dust of the ground**, but only the impartation of **the breath** of God made him **a living being**. Adam ("red" or "ground") was named after the red earth from which he was made.

2:8–14 The **garden** that **God planted in Eden** was toward the east, i.e., east of Palestine, the point of reference for Bible directions. It was located in the region of Mesopotamia, near the **Hiddekel** (Tigris) and **Euphrates** Rivers. **The tree of the knowledge of good and evil** provided a test of man's obedience. The only reason it was wrong to eat of that fruit was because God had said so. In different forms, that fruit is *still with us today*.

2:15–23 The penalty for violating the commandment was death (v. 17)—instant spiritual death and progressive physical death. In the process of naming the animals and birds, Adam would have noticed that there were males and females. Each one had a mate that was similar to itself, yet different. This prepared Adam for **a helper** who would be **comparable to**

himself. His bride was formed from **one of his ribs**, taken from his side as **he slept**. So from Christ's side, His Bride was secured as He shed His life's blood in untold agony. **Woman** was taken not from Adam's head to dominate him, nor from his feet to be trodden down, but from under his arm to be protected, and from near his heart to be loved.

God gave headship to man before sin entered. Paul argues this fact from the order of creation (man was created first) and the purpose of creation (woman was made for the man) (1 Cor. 11:8, 9). Also, although it was Eve who sinned first, it is by Adam, the head, that sin is said to have entered the world. He had the position of head and was thus responsible.

Verse 19 is clearer with the English pluperfect tense[5]: **"The LORD God** *had* **formed . . . every beast,"** i.e., before He made man.

2:24 With the words of verse 24 God instituted monogamous marriage. Like all divine institutions, it was established for man's good and cannot be violated with impunity. The marriage bond illustrates the relationship that exists between Christ and the church (Eph. 5:22–32).

2:25 Although Adam and Eve lived in the Garden of Eden without any clothes, they **were not ashamed**.

B. The Temptation and Fall (Chap. 3)

3:1–6 **The serpent** that appeared to Eve is later revealed to be none other than Satan himself (see Rev. 12:9). Those who seek to "demythologize" the Bible believe that this account of the fall is allegorical and not literal. They cite the talking serpent as proof. Can the story of the serpent's deceiving Eve be accepted as factual? The Apostle Paul thought so

(2 Cor. 11:3). So did the Apostle John (Rev. 12:9; 20:2). Nor is this the only instance of a talking animal in Scripture. God gave a voice to Balaam's donkey to restrain the madness of the prophet (Num. 22), and the Apostle Peter accepted this as literal (2 Pet. 2:16). These three apostles were inspired by the Holy Spirit to write as they did. Thus to reject the account of the fall as literal is to reject the inspiration of Holy Scripture. There are allegories in the Bible, but this is not one of them.

Notice the steps that plunged the human race into sin. First Satan insinuated doubt about the Word of God: **"Has God indeed said?"** He misrepresented God as forbidding Adam and Eve to **eat of every tree**. Next, Eve said that they were **not** to **eat** or **"touch the fruit of the tree which is in the midst of the garden."** But God had said nothing about *touching* the tree. Then Satan flatly contradicted God about the inevitability of judgment on those who disobeyed, just as his followers still deny the facts of hell and eternal punishment. Satan misrepresented God as seeking to withhold from Adam and Eve something that would have been beneficial to them. Eve yielded to the threefold temptation: the lust of the flesh (**good for food**), the lust of the eyes (**pleasant to the eyes**), and the pride of life (**a tree desirable to make one wise**). In doing so, she acted independently of Adam, her head. She should have consulted him instead of usurping his authority. In the words **"she took of its fruit and ate"** lie the explanation of all the sickness, sorrow, suffering, fear, guilt, and death that have plagued the human race ever since that time. Someone has said, "The wreckage of earth and a million billion graves attest that God is true and

Satan is the liar." Eve was deceived (1 Tim. 2:14), but Adam acted willfully and in deliberate rebellion against God.

Secular humanism perpetuates Satan's lie, "You will be like God."

3:7–13 The first result of sin was a sense of shame and fear. The aprons of **fig leaves** speak of man's attempt to save himself by a bloodless religion of good works. When called to account by God, sinners excuse themselves. Adam said, **"The woman whom You gave to be with me . . ."** as if blaming God (see Prov. 19:3). Eve said, **"The serpent . . ."** (v. 13).

In love and mercy God searched after His fallen creatures with the question **"Where are you?"** This question proved two things—that man was lost and that God had come to seek. It proved man's sin and God's grace.[6] God takes the initiative in salvation, demonstrating the very thing Satan got Eve to doubt—His love.

3:14 The Lord God cursed the **serpent** to degradation, disgrace, and defeat. The fact that the serpent is **cursed more than all cattle** or any **other beast of the field** suggests that reptiles are primarily in view here rather than Satan.

3:15 But verse 15 switches to the Devil himself. This verse is known as the *protevangelium*, meaning "The First Gospel." It predicts the perpetual hostility **between** Satan **and the woman** (representing all mankind), **and between** Satan's **seed** (his agents) **and her Seed** (the Messiah). The woman's **Seed** would crush the Devil's **head**, a mortal wound spelling utter defeat. This wound was administered at Calvary when the Savior decisively triumphed over the Devil. Satan, in turn, would **bruise** the Messiah's **heel**. The **heel** wound here speaks of suffering and even of physical death,

but not of ultimate defeat. So Christ suffered on the cross, and even died, but He arose from the dead, victorious over sin, hell, and Satan. The fact that He is called the *woman's* **Seed** may contain a suggestion of His virgin birth. Note the kindness of God in promising the Messiah before pronouncing sentence in the following verses.

3:16–19 Sin has inevitable consequences. **The woman** was sentenced to suffering in childbirth. She would be subject to her **husband**. The man was sentenced to earn his livelihood from **ground** that was **cursed** with **thorns and thistles**. It would mean **toil** and **sweat** for him. Then at the end of life, he himself would **return** to **dust**. It should be noted here that work itself is *not* a curse; it is more often a blessing. It is the sorrow, toil, frustration, perspiration, and weariness connected with work that are the curse.

3:20, 21 **Adam** displayed faith in calling **his wife's name Eve . . . the mother of all living**, since no baby had ever been born up to this time. Then **tunics of skin** were provided by God through the death of an animal. This pictures the robe of righteousness which is provided for guilty sinners through the shed blood of the Lamb of God, made available to us on the basis of faith.

3:22–24 There was a shade of truth in Satan's lie that Eve would become like God (v. 5). But she and Adam learned by the hard way of experience to discern between **good and evil**. If they had then eaten of the tree of life, they would have lived forever in bodies subject to sickness, degeneration, and infirmity. Thus it was God's mercy that prevented them from returning to Eden. **Cherubim** are celestial creatures whose function is to "vindicate the holiness of God against the presumptuous pride of fallen man."[7]

Adam and Eve had to decide whether God or Satan was lying. They decided that God was. "Without faith it is impossible to please God." Thus their names are missing from the Honor Roll of Faith in Hebrews 11.

The ideal environment of Eden did not prevent the entrance of sin. A favorable environment is not the answer to man's problems.

C. Cain and Abel (Chap. 4)

4:1 **Adam knew Eve his wife** in the sense that he had sexual relations with her. When **Cain** was born, she acknowledged that this birth was only by the Lord's enablement. In naming him **Cain** ("acquisition"), Eve may have thought that she had given birth to the Promised Seed.

4:2–6 **The process of time** mentioned in verse 3a allows for a considerable increase in the world's population. There must have been a time when **Cain** and **Abel** were instructed that sinful man can approach the holy God only on the ground of the blood of a substitutionary sacrifice. Cain rejected this revelation and came with a bloodless offering of fruits and vegetables. Abel believed the divine decree and offered slain animals, thus demonstrating his faith and his justification by God (Heb. 11:4). He brought **the firstborn of his flock**, saying in effect that **the LORD** deserves the best. Abel's offering points forward to the substitutionary death of the Lamb of God, who takes away the sin of the world.

4:7 Because Cain's jealous anger was incipient murder, God spoke to him in loving warning. Verse 7 may be understood in several ways:

1. "**If you do well** [by repenting], you will be able to look up again in freedom from anger and guilt. **If you do not do well** [by continuing to hate Abel], **sin** is crouching **at** your **door**, ready to destroy you. His [Abel's] **desire is for you** [i.e., he will acknowledge your leadership] and **you** will **rule over** him" [i.e., if you do well].

2. "**If you do well** (or, as the Septuagint reads it, "If you offer correctly") will you not be accepted?" The well-doing had reference to the offering. Abel did well by hiding himself behind an acceptable sacrifice. Cain did badly by bringing an offering without blood, and all his after-conduct was but the legitimate result of this false worship.[8]

3. The RSV says, "If you do well, will you not be accepted? And if you do not do well, sin is crouching at the door; its desire is for you, but you must master it."

4. F. W. Grant says in his *Numerical Bible*, "If you do not well, a sin-offering croucheth or lieth at the door."[9] In other words, provision was made if he wanted it.

4:8–12 Cain's evil attitude of jealous rage was soon translated into evil action, the murder of **his brother**. Though Abel is dead, he still witnesses to us that the life of faith is the life that counts (Heb. 11:4). When the Lord's loving question was met by an unrepentant, insolent reply, He pronounced Cain's judgment—he would no longer be able to make a living from the soil, but would wander as **a fugitive** in the desert.

4:13–16 Cain's whimpering complaint reveals remorse for the consequences of his sin rather than for its guilt. But even then the Lord allayed the fugitive's fears for his life by putting a protective **mark on Cain** and a curse on anyone who killed him. **Cain went out from the presence of the LORD**, the saddest of all departures.

4:17–24 Cain married his sister or other blood relative. As mentioned, Genesis 4:3 allows time for a population increase, and Genesis 5:4 specifically states that Adam had sons and daughters. Marriage of close relatives was not forbidden then (nor was it genetically risky).

Verses 17–24 list Cain's posterity, and a series of firsts: the first **city**, named **Enoch**; the first case of polygamy; the beginning of organized animal husbandry; the beginning of the art of music and of metalcrafts; the first song, concerning violence and bloodshed. In the song, **Lamech** explains **to his wives** that he **killed . . . a young man** in self-defense, but that because it wasn't premeditated, like Cain's murder of his brother, Lamech would be much more immune from reprisal.

4:25, 26 Now in striking relief, the godly line of **Seth** is introduced. It was through this line that the Messiah would eventually be born. When **Enosh** (meaning "frail" or "mortal") was born, men began to use **the name of the LORD** (Jehovah) for God, or perhaps **to call on the name of** Jehovah in public worship.

D. Seth and His Descendants (Chap. 5)

Chapter 5 has been called "The Tolling of the Death Bells" because of the oft-repeated expression "and he died." It records the bloodline of the Messiah from Adam to Noah's son, Shem (compare Luke 3:36–38).

5:1–17 **Adam** was created **in the likeness of God**. **Seth** was born in the **image** of **Adam**. In between, the Fall took place and the image of God in man became marred by sin. Verse 5 records the *physical* fulfillment of what God said would happen in 2:17; the *spiritual* fulfillment took place the day Adam sinned.

5:18–24 The **Enoch** and Lamech mentioned here should not be confused with those in chapter 4. The **Enoch** in verse 18 is the seventh from Adam (Jude 14), not the third. By faith **Enoch walked with God** for 300 years and pleased the Lord (Heb. 11:5). It seems that the birth of his son had a sanctifying, ennobling influence on his life (v. 22a). It is good to start well, but it is even better to continue steadfastly to the end. The word *walk* implies a steady, progressive relationship and not just a casual acquaintance. To walk **with God** is the business of a lifetime, and not just the performance of an hour. **Enoch** was transported to heaven prior to the flood just as the church will be raptured to heaven before the Tribulation begins (1 Thess. 4:13–18; Rev. 3:10).

5:25–32 **Methuselah lived** longer than any other man (**nine hundred and sixty-nine years**). If, as Williams says, the name **Methuselah** means "it shall be sent,"[10] it may be a prophecy, because the flood came in the year of his death. Perhaps Lamech's prediction when he named **Noah** looked forward to the comfort that would come to the world through Noah's greater Son, the Lord Jesus Christ. Noah's name means "rest." As the years passed, man's life expectancy decreased. Psalm 90:10 speaks of seventy years as normal.

An artist's conception of Noah's ark, based on information from an explorer who claimed he saw the ark on Mt. Ararat in 1908.

E. Widespread Sin and the Universal Flood (Chaps. 6—8)

6:1, 2 There are two principal interpretations of verse 2. One is that **the sons of God** were angels who left their proper sphere (Jude 6) and intermarried with women on earth, a form of sexual disorder that was most hateful to God. Those who hold this view point out that the expression "sons of God" in Job 1:6 and 2:1 means angels who had access to the presence of God. Also, "the sons of God" as a term for angels is a standard Semitic expression. The passage in Jude 6, 7 suggests that the angels who left their own abode were guilty of vile sexual behavior. Notice the words "as Sodom and Gomorrah" at the beginning of verse 7, immediately after the description of the fallen angels.

The main objection to this view is that angels don't reproduce sexually, as far as we know. Matthew 22:30 is used to prove that Jesus taught that the angels don't marry. What the verse actually says, however, is that the angels *in heaven* neither marry nor are given in marriage. Angels appeared in human form to Abraham (Gen. 18:1–5), and it seems from the text that the two who went to Sodom had human parts and emotions.

The other view is that **the sons of God** were the godly descendants of Seth, and **the daughters of men** were the wicked posterity of Cain. The argument is as follows: The preceding context deals with the descendants of Cain (chap. 4) and the descendants of Seth (chap. 5). Genesis 6:1–4 describes the intermarriage of these two lines. The word *angels* is not found in the context. Verses 3 and 5 speak of the wickedness of *man*. If it was the *angels* who sinned, why was the race of *man* to be destroyed? Godly men are called "sons of God," though not in exactly the same Hebrew wording as in Genesis

6:2 (see Deut. 14:1; Ps. 82:6; Hos. 1:10; Matt. 5:9).

There are several problems with this view. Why were all the Sethite *men* godly and all the *women* of Cain's lineage ungodly? Also, there is no indication that Seth's line *stayed* godly. If they did, why should they be destroyed? Also, why should such a union between godly men and ungodly women produce giants?

6:3 The LORD warned that His **Spirit** would not **strive with man forever**, but that there would be a delay of **one hundred and twenty years** before the judgment of the flood would occur. God is longsuffering, not willing that any should perish, but there is a limit. Peter tells us that it was Christ who was preaching through Noah to the antediluvians by the Holy Spirit (1 Pet. 3:18–20; 2 Pet. 2:5). They rejected the message and are now imprisoned.

6:4, 5 Regarding the **giants** (Heb. *nephilim*, "fallen ones") Unger explains:

> The Nephilim are considered by many as giant demigods, the unnatural offspring of "the daughters of men" (mortal women) in cohabitation with "the sons of God" (angels). This utterly unnatural union, violating God's created orders of being, was such a shocking abnormality as to necessitate the worldwide judgment of the Flood.[11]

6:6, 7 The Lord's sorrow does not indicate an arbitrary change of mind, though it seems that way to man. Rather, it indicates a different attitude on God's part in response to some change in man's behavior. Because He is holy, He must react against sin.

6:8–22 **Noah found grace in the eyes of the** LORD and was forewarned to build **an ark**. The measurements are given in **cubits** (1 cubit = 18 inches). Thus the ark was 450 feet long, 75 feet wide, and 45 feet high. It had three decks. The **window** in verse 16 was literally "a place of light," probably an opening for light and air which extended the full length of the ark.

Noah was saved by **grace**, an act of divine sovereignty. His response was to do **all that God** had **commanded** (v. 22), an act of human responsibility. Noah built the ark to save his family, but it was *God* who shut and sealed the door. Divine sovereignty and human responsibility are not mutually exclusive, but are complementary.

Noah (v. 9) and **Enoch** (5:22) are the only men in Scripture who are said to have **walked with God**. If Enoch is a symbol of the church raptured to heaven, Noah symbolizes the faithful Jewish remnant preserved through the Tribulation to live on the millennial earth.

Verse 18 gives the first mention of **covenant** in the Bible. Scofield lists eight covenants: Edenic (Gen. 2:16); Adamic (Gen. 3:15); Noahic (Gen. 9:16); Abrahamic (Gen. 12:2); Mosaic (Ex. 19:5); Palestinian (Deut. 30:3); Davidic (2 Sam. 7:16); and the New Covenant (Heb. 8:8). These eight, plus the Solomonic Covenant, are covered in the following essay. Needless to say, a subject as complex as the covenants has been interpreted differently by various schools of theology. The treatment presented here is in the premillennial and dispensational tradition.

THE MAJOR COVENANTS
OF SCRIPTURE

The Edenic Covenant (Gen. 1:28–30; 2:16, 17)

The Edenic Covenant made man, in his innocence, responsible to multiply, populate the earth, and subdue it. He was given authority over all animal life. He was to cultivate the garden and eat of all its produce except the fruit of the tree of the knowledge of good and evil. Disobedience to this latter command would bring death.

The Adamic Covenant (Gen. 3:14–19)

After the fall of man, God cursed the serpent and predicted enmity between the serpent and the woman, and between Satan and Christ. Satan would injure Christ, but Christ would destroy Satan. Woman would experience pain in childbirth and would be under the authority of her husband. The ground was cursed. Man would have to contend with thorns and thistles in cultivating it. His work would involve sweat and weariness, and he would eventually return to dust, from which he came.

The Noahic Covenant (Gen. 8:20—9:27)

God promised Noah that He would not curse the ground again or destroy the entire earth with a flood. He gave the rainbow as a pledge of this. But the covenant also includes the establishment of human government, with the power of capital punishment. God guaranteed the regularity of time periods and seasons, directed man to repopulate the earth, and reaffirmed his dominion over lower creatures. Man could now add meat to his previous vegetarian diet. Concerning Noah's descendants, God cursed Ham's son, Canaan, to be a servant to Shem and Japheth. He gave Shem a place of favor, which we know includes being in the line of the Messiah. Japheth would enjoy great expansion, and would dwell in the tents of Shem.

The Abrahamic Covenant (Gen. 12:1–3; 13:14–17; 15:1–8; 17:1–8)

The Abrahamic Covenant is unconditional. Only God, manifesting Himself as "a smoking oven and a burning torch," passed through the two pieces of the sacrificed animal in Genesis 15:12–21. This is quite significant. When two people made (Heb., "cut") a covenant, they would *both* walk together between the two pieces to show they would abide by the conditions of the covenant. God put no conditions on Abraham; hence the provisions listed below will (and have) come to pass no matter how faithful Abraham's descendants might prove.

Those who see no future for God's ancient people often try to make this covenant appear to be conditional, at least regarding the land. Then they lay claim to all the blessings for the church, leaving Israel with little or nothing.

The covenant includes the following promises to Abraham and his descendants: a great nation (Israel); personal blessings to Abraham; a name of renown; being a source of blessing to others (12:2); divine favor to his friends and a curse on his enemies; blessing to all nations—fulfilled through Christ—(12:3); everlasting possession of the land known as Canaan and later as Israel and Palestine (13:14, 15, 17); numerous posterity, natural and spiritual (13:16; 15:5); a fatherhood of many nations and kings—through Ishmael and Isaac—(17:4, 6); special relationship to God (17:7b).

The Mosaic Covenant (Ex. 19:5; 20:1–31:18)

In its broadest sense, the Mosaic Covenant includes the Ten Commandments, describing duties to God and to one's neighbor (Ex. 20:1–26); numerous regulations concerning the social life of Israel (Ex. 21:1—24:11); and detailed ordinances dealing with religious life (Ex. 24:12—31:18). It was given to the nation of Israel, not to the Gentiles. It was a conditional covenant, requiring man's obedience, and therefore it was "weak through the flesh" (Rom. 8:3a). The Decalogue was never intended to provide salvation, but rather to produce conviction of sin and failure. Nine of the Ten Commandments are repeated in the NT (the Sabbath excepted), not as law with penalty attached, but as behavior suitable for those who have been saved by grace. The Christian is under grace, not law, but he is bound to Christ by love, a higher motivation.

The Palestinian Covenant (Deut. 30:1–9)

This covenant has to do with the still-future occupation of the land which God promised to Abraham "from the river of Egypt [i.e., the Brook of Egypt, not the Nile] to the great river, the River Euphrates" (Gen. 15:18). Israel has never fully occupied the land. During Solomon's reign, countries in the eastern portion paid tribute (1 Kgs. 4:21, 24), but that cannot be counted as possession or occupation.

The Palestinian Covenant foresees the dispersion of Israel among the nations because of disobedience, their return to the Lord, the Lord's Second Advent, their regathering to the land, their prosperity in the land, their change of heart (to love and obey the Lord), and the punishment of their enemies.

The Davidic Covenant (2 Sam. 7:5–19)

God promised David not only that his kingdom would endure forever, but that he would always have a lineal descendant to sit on the throne. It was an unconditional covenant, not dependent in any way on David's obedience or righteousness. Christ is the legal heir to the throne of David through Solomon, as is seen in Joseph's genealogy (Matt. 1).

He is a lineal descendant of David through Nathan, as is seen in Mary's genealogy (Luke 3). Because He lives forever, His kingdom is everlasting. His one-thousand-year reign on earth will merge into the eternal kingdom.

The Solomonic Covenant (2 Sam. 7:12–15; 1 Kgs. 8:4, 5; 2 Chron. 7:11–22)

The covenant with Solomon was unconditional as far as the everlasting kingdom was concerned, but conditional as far as Solomon's descendants sitting on the throne (1 Kgs. 8:4, 5; 2 Chron. 7:17, 18). One of Solomon's descendants, Coniah (also called Jeconiah), was barred from having any physical descendant sit on David's throne (Jer. 22:30). Jesus is not a descendant of Solomon, as pointed out above. Otherwise He would come under the curse of Coniah.

The New Covenant (Jer. 31:31–34; Heb. 8:7–12; Luke 22:20)

The New Covenant is clearly made with the house of Israel and the house of Judah (Jer. 31:31). It was future when Jeremiah wrote (Jer. 31:31a). It is not a conditional covenant, like the Mosaic Covenant, which Israel broke

(Jer. 31:32). In it God unconditionally promises (note the repetition of "I will"): Israel's regeneration (Ezek. 36:25); the indwelling of the Holy Spirit (Ezek. 36:27); a heart that is favorably disposed to do the will of God (Jer. 31:33a); a unique relationship between God and His people (Jer. 31:33b); universal knowledge of the Lord in Israel (Jer. 31:34a); sins both forgiven and forgotten (Jer. 31:34b); and the continuance of the nation forever (Jer. 31:35–37).

Israel as a nation has not as yet received the benefits of the New Covenant, but will at the Lord's Second Advent. In the meantime, true believers do share some of the blessings of the covenant. The fact that the church is related to the New Covenant is seen in the Lord's Supper, where the cup represents the covenant and the blood by which it was ratified (Luke 22:20; 1 Cor. 11:25). Also Paul spoke of himself and the other apostles as ministers of a New Covenant (2 Cor. 3:6).‡

A pair of every living creature was to be brought into the ark, as well as food. Critics claim that the ark was not big enough to hold all the species of animals and enough food for one year and seventeen days. But it is likely that the ark contained only the basic kinds of animal and bird life, and that many variations have resulted since then. The ark was more than large enough for this.

7:1 The word **"come"** appears for the first time in verse 1—a gracious gospel invitation: **"Come into the ark of safety."**

7:2–18 No reason is given why Noah was commanded to **take seven** pairs of **clean** animals into the ark, but only one pair of **unclean**. Perhaps it was for food and in anticipation of the **clean** animals' being needed for sacrifice (see 8:20). The ark was filled with its inhabitants for **seven days** before the **rain** began and the underground reserves of water gushed out. The torrent continued for **forty days and forty nights; forty** is the number of probation or testing in the Bible.

7:19–24 Was this a local flood, as some allege? Consider the following: **All the high hills under the whole heaven were covered** (v. 19). God need not have told Noah to build an **ark** equivalent to 1½ football fields in length and 800 railroad cars in volume to escape a local flood. He could easily have moved eight people and the animals to a different location. Traditions of a universal flood have come from all parts of the world. The mountains of Ararat range up to 17,000 feet. The flood was **fifteen cubits** higher (vv. 19, 20). By what sort of miracle was this water kept in a localized area? In Genesis 9:15 God promised that the water would never again become a flood to destroy **all** flesh. There have been many local floods since then, but never a universal flood. If the flood was local, then God's promise has been broken—an impossible conclusion. Peter uses the destruction of the world by water as a symbol of a still future destruction of the earth by fire (2 Pet. 3:6).

The ark is a picture of Christ. The waters depict God's judgment. The Lord Jesus went under the waters of divine wrath at Calvary. Those who are in Christ are saved. Those who are outside are doomed (see 1 Pet. 3:21).

8:1–19 The chronology of the Flood is as follows:

   1. 7 days—from the time Noah entered the ark until the Flood began (7:10).

2. 40 days and nights—duration of the rain (7:12).
3. 150 days—from the time the rain began until **the waters decreased** (8:3) and **the ark rested** on Mount **Ararat** (compare 7:11 and 8:4).
4. 224 days—from the beginning of the Flood until the mountaintops reappeared (compare 7:11 and 8:5).
5. 40 days—from the time the mountaintops were seen until Noah **sent out a raven** (8:7).
6. 7 days—from the sending of the raven to the first sending forth of **a dove** (8:6–10; v. 10, **"yet another seven days"**).
7. 7 more days—until **the dove** was sent forth a second time (8:10).
8. 7 more days—until the final sending forth of the dove (8:12).
9. 314 days—from the beginning of the Flood until **Noah removed the covering** from **the ark** (compare 7:11 and 8:13).
10. 371 days—from the beginning of the Flood until **the earth was dried** (compare 7:11 and 8:14). At this time, Noah was commanded to **go out of the ark** (v. 16)

The unclean **raven** (v. 7) and the clean **dove** (v. 8) are good illustrations of the believer's old and new natures. The old nature loves to feed on garbage and carrion whereas the new nature cannot find satisfaction in a scene of death and judgment. It finds no rest until it sets its feet on resurrection ground.

8:20–22 **Noah** responded to God's saving grace by building **an altar**. Those of us who have been saved from the wrath to come should likewise bring to God our heartfelt worship. It is as acceptable and pleasing today as it was in Noah's day. **The LORD** made a covenant that He would **never again curse the ground** or **destroy every living thing, as** He had **done**; also, He would provide regular seasons as long as the **earth** endured.

In 6:5 and here in verse 21, God speaks of the intense evil of man's heart. In the first instance, there was *no* sacrifice, and judgment ensued. Here there *is* a sacrifice; and God acts in mercy.

F. Noah after the Flood (Chap. 9)

9:1–7 Verse 3 suggests that after the Flood people were permitted to eat meat for the first time. Eating of **blood** was forbidden, however, because the **blood** is the **life** of the **flesh**, and the life belongs to God.

The institution of capital punishment presupposes the establishment of governmental authority. It would be chaos if anyone and everyone avenged a murder. Only duly appointed governments may do so. The NT perpetuates capital punishment when it says concerning the government, ". . . he does not bear the sword in vain" (Rom. 13:4).

9:8–17 **The rainbow** was given as a pledge that God would **never again destroy the earth** with **a flood**.

9:18–23 In spite of God's grace to Noah, he sinned by becoming **drunk** and then lying naked **in his tent**. When **Ham** saw him and reported the matter to **his brothers**, they **covered** their father's shame without looking on his naked body.

9:24, 25 When he **awoke, Noah** pronounced a curse on **Canaan**. The question arises, "Why did the curse fall on **Canaan** instead of **Ham**?" One possible explanation is that the evil tendency which was manifested in

Ham was even more pronounced in **Canaan**. The curse was thus a prophecy of his immoral conduct and its fitting punishment. Another explanation is that Canaan himself committed some vulgar act against his grandfather, and that Noah later became aware of it. Noah **knew what his younger son had done to him**. It may be that verse 24 refers to Canaan as Noah's *youngest grandson*, rather than to Ham as his *younger son*. In the Bible, "son" often means "grandson" or other descendant. In this event, **Canaan** was not **cursed** for his father's sin, but for his own. Yet another possibility is that God's grace allowed Noah to curse only a small segment of Ham's descendants and not a possible third of the human race.

9:26–29 Canaan was cursed to serve **Shem** and **Japheth**. The Canaanites' servitude to the Israelites may be seen in Joshua 9:23 and Judges 1:28. This passage has been used to suggest the slavery of the black people, but there is absolutely no support for this view. Canaan was the ancestor of the Canaanites, who dwelt in the Holy Land before Israel arrived. There is no evidence that they were black people. **Shem** and **Japheth** were blessed with dominion. Verse 27 may suggest Japheth's sharing in spiritual blessings through Shem's descendants, the Israelites.

There is a dispute as to whether Shem or Japheth was the oldest son of Noah. Chapter 10:21 may read "Shem . . . the brother of Japheth the elder" or "Shem . . . the older brother of Japheth" (NKJV marg.). The latter is the preferred reading. Shem appears first in the genealogies of Genesis 5:32 and 1 Chronicles 1:4.

G. The Table of Nations (Chap. 10)

10:1–32 Shem, Ham, and Japheth became the fathers of the nations.

Shem: The Semitic peoples— Jews, Arabs, Assyrians, Arameans, Phoenicians.

Ham: The Hamitic peoples— Ethiopians, Egyptians, Canaanites, Philistines, Babylonians, possibly the African and Oriental peoples, though many scholars view the Orientals as Japhetic.

Japheth: The Japhetic peoples—the Medes, Greeks, Cypriots, etc. Probably the Caucasian people of Europe and of northern Asia. Many scholars would also include the Orientals here.

The order in this chapter is **the sons of Japheth** (vv. 2–5), **the sons of Ham** (vv. 6–20), and **the sons of Shem** (vv. 21–31). The Spirit of God is going to center on Shem and his descendants during the rest of the OT. The different languages of verse 5 probably look forward to the time after the tower of Babel (11:1–9).

Notice three references in this chapter to the division of the people. Verse 5 describes the division of the Japhetic tribes into their different areas. Verse 25 tells us that the division of the earth (at Babel) took place in the days of **Peleg**. Verse 32 serves as an introduction to the Tower of Babel in chapter 11, when **the families of the** sons of Noah were divided into different **nations** with different languages.

Nimrod (vv. 8–10) means *rebel*. He appears as the first **"mighty one on the earth"** after the flood (v. 8) and as the first to establish a **kingdom** (v.

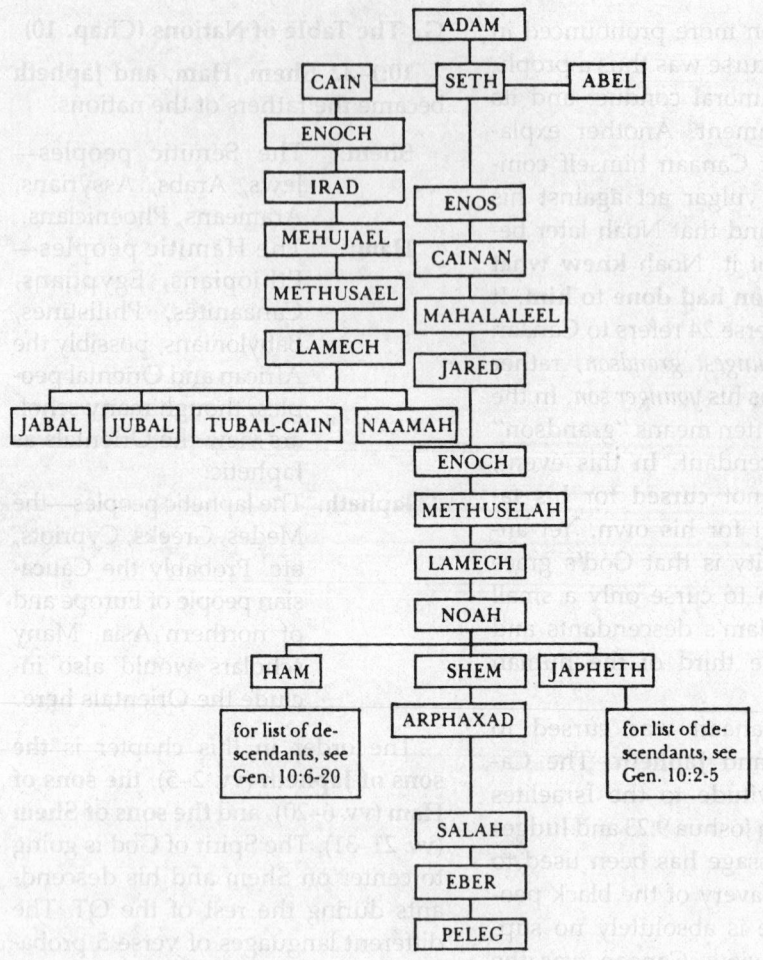

Descendants of Adam

10). He built **Babel** (Babylon) in rebellion against God, and also **Nineveh** in **Assyria** (see v. 11), another inveterate enemy of God's people.

As already mentioned, verse 21 lists **Shem** as the *older* brother of **Japheth**.

It is impossible to identify with certainty the places where the various people settled, but the following will prove helpful in later studies.

Tarshish (v. 4) — Spain
Kittim (v. 4) — Cyprus
Cush (v. 6) — Ethiopia
Mizraim (v. 6) — Egypt
Put or Phut (v. 6) — Libya
Canaan (v. 6) — Palestine

Asshur (v. 11, KJV)— Assyria
Elam (v. 22)   — Persia
Aram (v. 22)   — Syria and
                      Mesopotamia

H. The Tower of Babel (Chap. 11)

11:1-4 In chapter 10, which *chronologically* comes *after* chapter 11, mankind was divided according to languages (vv. 5, 20, 31). Now we learn the cause of the divisions. Instead of dispersing over the earth, as God intended, men built a city and a tower in **Shinar** (Babylon). **They said to one another, "Come, let us build ourselves a city, and a tower whose**

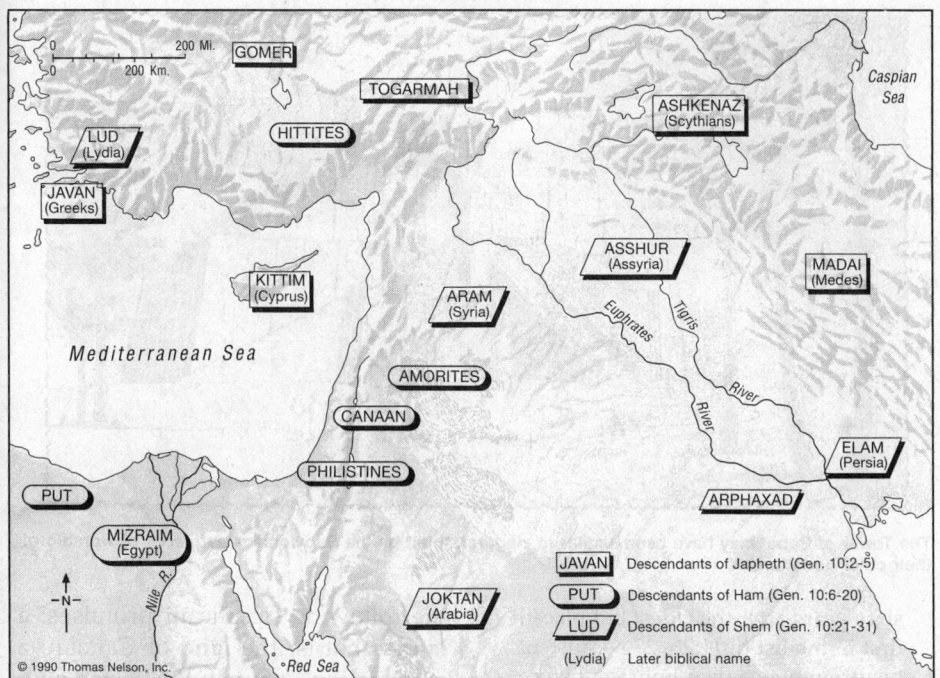

The Nations of Genesis 10

top is in the heavens; let us make us a name for ourselves, lest we be scattered abroad over the face of the whole earth." So it was a policy of pride (to **make a name for** themselves) and defiance (to avoid being **scattered**). To us the **tower** may also picture fallen man's ceaseless effort to reach heaven by his own works instead of receiving salvation as a free gift of grace.

11:5–9 The Lᴏʀᴅ judged the people by confounding **their language**. This was the beginning of the many different languages which we have in the world today. Pentecost (Acts 2:1–11) was the reverse of Babel in the sense that every man heard the wonderful works of God in his own language. Babel means *confusion*, the inevitable result of any union that leaves God out or is not according to God.

11:10–25 These verses trace the line of **Shem** to **Abram**. Thus the historical record narrows from the hu-

man race to one branch of that race (the Semites) and then to one man (**Abram**), who becomes the head of the Hebrew nation. The rest of the OT is largely a history of this nation.

11:26–32 **Abram** was a mighty man of faith and one of the most important men in history. Three world religions— Judaism, Christianity, and Islam—venerate him. He is mentioned in sixteen books of the OT and eleven books of the NT. His name means "exalted father" or, as changed to Abraham, "father of a multitude."

There is a mathematical problem in this passage. Derek Kidner explains:

Terah's age at death presents a difficulty, since it makes his eldest son 135 years old (26), whereas Abram was only 75 (12:4, with Acts 7:4). One solution is to suppose Abram to have been the youngest son, born

The Tower of Babel may have been similar to ziggurats built by the Babylonians as places of worship of their chief god Marduk.

sixty years after the eldest but placed first in the list in 11:26, 27 because of his prominence (like Ephraim before Manasseh). Another is to follow the Samaritan text, which gives Terah's age as 145 at death. This seems preferable, if only because Abram would scarcely have made the exclamation of 17:17 had his own father begotten him at 130.[12]

Ur of the Chaldeans (v. 31), in Mesopotamia, was a center of pagan idolatry. Terah and his family traveled northwest to **Haran**, en route **to the land of Canaan**.

II. THE PATRIARCHS OF ISRAEL (Chaps. 12—50)

A. Abraham (12:1—25:18)

1. The Call of Abraham (12:1–9)

12:1–3 The call of **the LORD** had come to **Abram** when he was still in Ur (compare v. 1 with Acts 7:1,2). Abram was called to leave his **country**, his **family**, and his **father's house**, and to embark on a life of pilgrimage (Heb. 11:9). God made a marvelous covenant with him which included the following significant promises: **a land**—that is, the **land** of Canaan; **a great nation**—namely, the Jewish people; material and spiritual prosperity for Abram and his seed; a **great name** for Abram and his posterity; they would be a channel of **blessing** to others; friends of Israel would be **blessed** and anti-Semites would be cursed; **all the families of the earth** would be **blessed in** Abram, pointing forward to the Lord Jesus Christ, who would be a descendant of Abram. This covenant was renewed and enlarged in 13:14–17; 15:4–6; 17:10–14; and 22:15–18.

12:4–9 After what have been called "the wasted years in Haran," that is, years without progress, Abram moved to Canaan with **his wife Sarai**, his nephew **Lot**, other relatives, and **possessions**. They came first to **Shechem**, where Abram **built an altar to the LORD**. The presence of hostile **Canaanites** was no obstacle to a man who was walking by faith. Abram next relocated between **Bethel** (*house of God*) and **Ai**. True to form, **he** not only **pitched** a **tent** for himself but

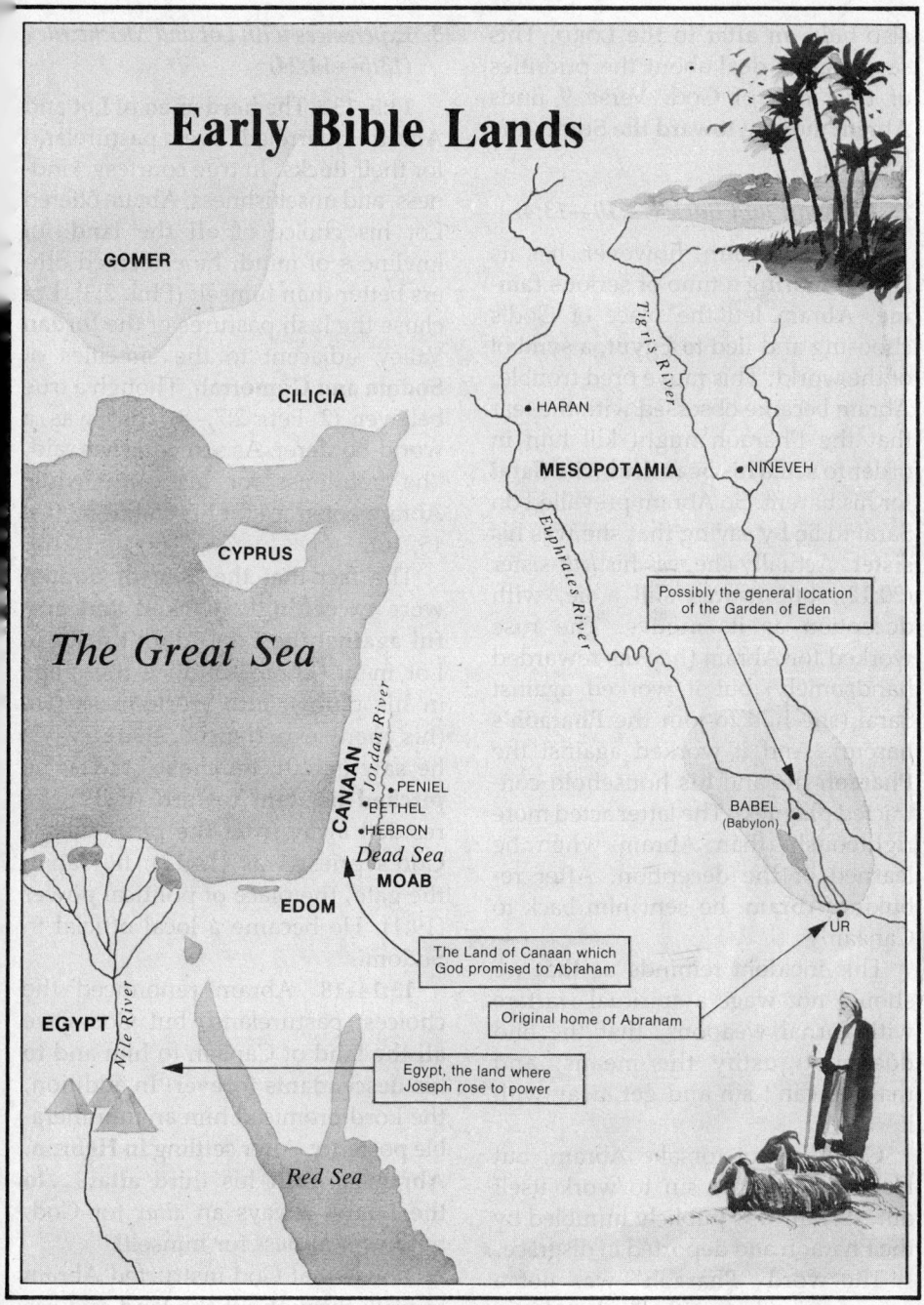

Early Bible Lands

GOMER

CILICIA

CYPRUS

The Great Sea

HARAN

MESOPOTAMIA

NINEVEH

Tigris River

Euphrates River

Possibly the general location of the Garden of Eden

BABEL
(Babylon)

UR

CANAAN

Jordan River

PENIEL
BETHEL
HEBRON

Dead Sea

MOAB

EDOM

The Land of Canaan which God promised to Abraham

Original home of Abraham

EGYPT

Nile River

Egypt, the land where Joseph rose to power

Red Sea

Early Bible Lands

also built **an altar to the** LORD. This says a great deal about the priorities of this man of God. Verse 9 finds **Abram** moving **toward the South** (the Negev).

2. To Egypt and Back (12:10—13:4)

12:10–20 Faith, however, has its lapses. During a time of serious **famine**, **Abram** left the place of God's choosing and fled **to Egypt**, a symbol of the world. This move bred trouble. Abram became obsessed with the fear that the Pharaoh might kill him in order to seize his **beautiful** wife **Sarai** for his harem. So Abram prevailed on Sarai to lie by saying that she was his **sister**. Actually she *was* his *half*-sister (20:12), but it was still a lie, with deception as its motive. The ruse worked for Abram (he was rewarded handsomely) but it worked against Sarai (she had to join the **Pharaoh's** harem). And it worked against the **Pharaoh** (he and **his** household contracted **plagues**). The latter acted more righteously than Abram when he learned of the deception. After rebuking **Abram**, he sent him back to Canaan.

This incident reminds us that we should not wage a spiritual warfare with carnal weapons, that the end does not justify the means, and that we can't sin and get away with it.

God did not forsake Abram, but He did allow the sin to work itself out. Abram was publicly humbled by the Pharaoh and deported in disgrace.

The word "**Pharaoh**" was not a proper name but a title, such as king, emperor, president, etc.

13:1–4 Underlying Abram's return to **Bethel . . . from Egypt** was a return to fellowship with God. "Back to Bethel" is the rallying cry for all who have wandered from the Lord.

3. Experiences with Lot and Melchizedek (13:5—14:24)

13:5–13 The **herdsmen** of **Lot** and **Abram** quarreled over pastureland for their **flocks**. In true courtesy, kindness, and unselfishness, Abram offered Lot his choice of **all** the **land**. In lowliness of mind, he esteemed others better than himself (Phil. 2:3). Lot chose the lush pastures of the **Jordan** Valley, adjacent to the sin-cities of **Sodom and Gomorrah**. Though a true believer (2 Pet. 2:7, 8), Lot was a world-borderer. As someone has said, "he got grass for his cattle while Abram got grace for his children" (vv. 15, 16).

The fact that **the men of Sodom were exceedingly wicked and sinful against the** LORD didn't restrain Lot in his choice. Notice the steps in his plunge into worldliness: He (his men) experienced **strife** (v. 7); he **saw** (v. 10); he **chose** (v. 11); he **pitched his tent** toward (v. 12); he resided away from the place where God's priest was (14:12); he sat in the gate, the place of political power (19:1). He became a local official in Sodom.

13:14–18 Abram renounced the choicest pastureland, but God gave **all the land** of Canaan to him and **to** his **descendants forever**. In addition, the Lord promised him an innumerable posterity. After settling **in Hebron, Abram . . . built** his third **altar . . . to** the LORD—always an *altar* for God, but never a *house* for himself!

Notice that God instructed Abram to walk throughout the land and see his possession. So we are to appropriate God's promises by faith.

14:1–12 Thirteen years before the main events of this chapter, **Chedorlaomer, king of Elam** (Persia), had conquered various kings in the plains

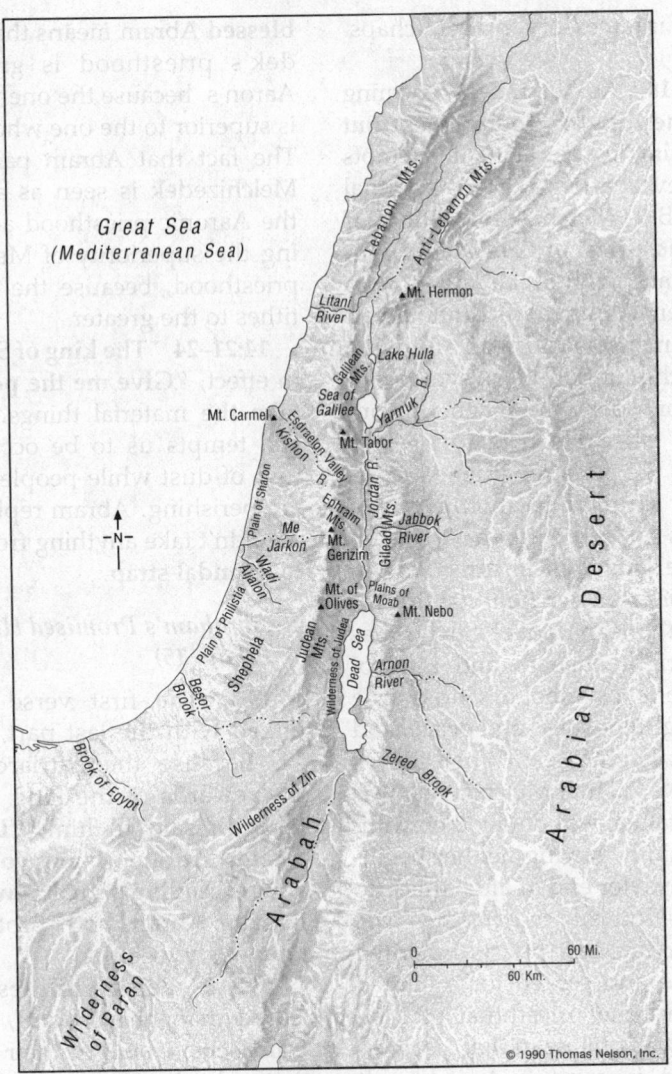

*Great Sea
(Mediterranean Sea)*

Litani
River

Mt. Hermon

Lebanon Mts.

Anti-Lebanon Mts.

Galilee
Mts.

Lake Hula

Sea of
Galilee

Mt. Carmel

Esdraelon Valley

Kishon R.

Mt. Tabor

Yarmuk R.

Mt. Gerizim

Ephraim
Mts.

Jordan R.

Jabbok
River

Me
Jarkon

Wadi
Aijalon

Plain of Sharon

Plain of Philistia

Mt. of
Olives

Plains of
Moab

Mt. Nebo

Shephelah

Judean
Mts.

Wilderness of Judea

Dead Sea

Arnon
River

Besor
Brook

Zered Brook

Brook of Egypt

Wilderness of Zin

Arabah

*Wilderness
of Paran*

Arabian Desert

-N-

0   60 Mi.

0   60 Km.

© 1990 Thomas Nelson, Inc.

The Promised Land

adjacent to the Dead (**Salt**) **Sea. In the thirteenth year**, the five captive kings **rebelled** against Chedorlaomer. So he allied himself with three other kings from the region of Babylon, marched south along the eastern side of the Dead Sea, then north on the western side to **Sodom, Gomorrah**, and the other cities of the plain. The battle took place **in the Valley of Siddim**, which **was full of asphalt pits**. The invaders defeated the rebels and marched north with their booty and captives—including **Lot**, Abram's backslidden nephew.

14:13–16 When **Abram** received the news, he assembled a fighting force of **three hundred and eighteen trained** men and pursued the victors to **Dan**, in the north. He finally defeated them near **Damascus**, in Syria, and rescued **Lot and** all the spoils. Backsliders bring not only misery on themselves but trouble on others. Here Abram delivered Lot by the sword. Later he delivers him through intercessory prayer (chaps. 18, 19).

14:17, 18 As Abram was returning home, **the king of Sodom went out to meet him**, just as Satan often tempts the believer after a great spiritual victory. But **Melchizedek, king of Salem** and **priest of God Most High**, was on hand with **bread and wine** to strengthen Abram. We cannot read this first mention of **bread and wine** without thinking of these symbols of our Savior's passion. When we consider the price He paid to save us from sin, we are strengthened to resist every sinful temptation.

Names in Scripture have meanings. **Melchizedek** means *king of righteousness* and **Salem** (short for Jerusalem) means *peace*. So he was king of righteousness and king of peace. He is a symbol of Christ, true King of righteousness and peace, and our Great High Priest. When it says in Hebrews 7:3 that Melchizedek was "without father, without mother, without genealogy, having neither beginning of days nor end of life," this is to be understood *only in connection with his priesthood*. Most priests inherited their office and served for a limited tenure. But the priesthood of Melchizedek was unique in that, as far as the record is concerned, it wasn't passed on to him from his parents, and it did not have a beginning or an end. Christ's priesthood is "according to the order of Melchizedek" (Ps. 110:4; Heb. 7:17).

14:19, 20 Melchizedek **blessed** Abram, and Abram in turn **gave** to this priest of God **a tithe of all** his captured prizes. In Hebrews 7 we learn that there was a deep spiritual significance to these actions. Because Abram was the progenitor of Aaron, he is seen as representing the Aaronic priesthood. The fact that Melchizedek

blessed Abram means that Melchizedek's priesthood is greater than Aaron's, because the one who blesses is superior to the one who is blessed. The fact that Abram paid tithes to Melchizedek is seen as a picture of the Aaronic priesthood acknowledging the superiority of Melchizedek's priesthood, because the lesser pays tithes to the greater.

14:21–24 **The king of Sodom said**, in effect, "**Give me the persons**; you **take the** material things." So Satan still tempts us to be occupied with toys of dust while people around us are perishing. Abram replied that he wouldn't take anything **from a thread to a sandal strap**.

4. Abraham's Promised Heir (Chap. 15)

15:1 The first verse is closely linked with the last part of chapter 14. Because the patriarch refused the rewards of the king of Sodom, Jehovah said to him, "**Do not be afraid, Abram. I am your shield, your exceedingly great reward,**" thus making Abram both protected and fabulously wealthy.

15:2–6 Being **childless, Abram** feared that their servant, **Eliezer of Damascus**, would be their **heir**, since that was the law at that time. But God promised him a son and **descendants** as numerous as **the stars**. Humanly speaking this was impossible, since Sarai had passed the time when she could bear a child. But Abram **believed** God's promise, and God declared him to be righteous. The truth of justification by faith enunciated here is repeated in Romans 4:3, Galatians 3:6, and James 2:23. In 13:16 God had promised **descendants** as numerous as the dust, and here in 15:5 as numerous as the stars. The *dust* pictures Abram's natural posterity—

those who are Jews by birth. The *stars* depict his spiritual seed—those who are justified by faith (see Gal. 3:7).

15:7–21 To confirm the promise of a seed (vv. 1–6) and of a land (vv. 7, 8, 18–21), God acted out a strange and significant symbolism (vv. 9–21). David Baron explains:

> According to the ancient Eastern manner of making a covenant, both the contracting parties passed through the divided pieces of the slain animals, thus symbolically attesting that they pledged their very lives to the fulfillment of the engagement they made (see Jer. 34:18, 19). Now in Genesis 15, God alone, whose presence was symbolized by the smoking furnace and lamp of fire, passed through the midst of the pieces of the slain animals, while Abram was simply a spectator of this wonderful exhibition of God's free grace.[13]

This signified that it was an *unconditional* **covenant**, dependent for fulfillment on God alone.

According to another view of this passage, the sacrificial **pieces** represent the nation of Israel. The **vultures** speak of the Gentile nations. The **land that is not theirs**, of course, is Egypt. Israel would be delivered from Egyptian bondage and return to Canaan **in the fourth generation**. The **smoking oven** and the **burning torch** describe the national destiny of Israel—suffering and witness-bearing.

Israel's deliverance would not come until **the iniquity of the Amorites** was **complete**. These pagan inhabitants of Canaan must eventually be exterminated. But God often allows evil to run its course, sometimes to the seeming detriment of His people, before He judges it. He is longsuffering, not willing that any should perish—even the depraved **Amorites** (2 Pet.

3:9). He also allows evil to come to fruition so that the awful consequences of wickedness can be clear to all. Thus His wrath is demonstrated to be completely righteous.

Verses 13 and 14 pose a chronological problem. They predict that Abram's people would be in harsh servitude in a foreign **land** for 400 **years**, and that they would leave at the end of that time, carrying **great** wealth with them. In Acts 7:6 this figure of 400 years is repeated.

In Exodus 12:40, 41 we read that the children of Israel, who dwelt in Egypt, were sojourners for 430 years, to the very day.

Then in Galatians 3:17 Paul says that the period from the confirming of the Abrahamic Covenant until the giving of the Law was 430 years.

How can these figures be reconciled?

The 400 years mentioned in Genesis 15:13, 14 and in Acts 7:6 refer to the time of Israel's *harsh affliction* in Egypt. Jacob and his family were not in bondage when they first came to Egypt. On the contrary, they were treated quite royally.

The 430 years in Exodus 12:40, 41 refer to the total time the people of Israel spent in Egypt—to the very day. This is an exact figure.

The 430 years in Galatians 3:17 cover *approximately* the same period as Exodus 12:40, 41. They are reckoned from the time that God confirmed the Abrahamic Covenant to Jacob, just as Jacob was preparing to enter Egypt (Gen. 46:1–4), and they extend to the giving of the Law, about three months after the Exodus.

The four generations of Genesis 15:16 can be seen in Exodus 6:16–20: Levi, Kohath, Amram, Moses. Israel has not yet occupied the land promised in verses 18–21. Solomon had dominion over it (1 Kgs. 4:21, 24), as over vassal states, but his people did not occupy it. The covenant will be fulfilled when Christ returns to reign. Nothing can stop its fulfillment. What God has promised is as sure as if it had already occurred!

The river of Egypt (v. 18) is generally believed to be a small stream south of Gaza now known as Wadi el Arish, and not the Nile.

5. Ishmael, Son of the Flesh (Chaps. 16, 17)

16:1–6 The restlessness of the sin nature is seen here. Instead of waiting on God, **Sarai** persuaded **Abram** to obtain a child **by** her **maid, Hagar,** who was probably acquired during the ill-fated sojourn in Egypt. God is faithful in recording the marital irregularities of His people, even if He never approved them. When **Hagar** became pregnant, she looked down in disdain on **her mistress. Sarai** responded by blaming Abram, then driving Hagar out of the house. This illustrates the conflict between law and grace. They cannot cohabit (Gal. 4:21–31). While some of the behavior in this section may have been culturally acceptable then, it is certainly irregular from a Christian standpoint.

16:7–15 While **Hagar** was in the desert at **Shur,** on the way to Egypt, **the Angel of the LORD** came to her. This was the Lord Jesus in one of His preincarnate appearances, known as a Christophany. (See Judges 6 for an essay on the Angel of the LORD.) He counseled her to **return** and **submit** to Sarai, and promised that her **son** would become head of a great nation. That promise, of course, is fulfilled in the Arab people. The words **"Return . . . and submit"** have marked great turning points in the lives of many who have had dealings with God.

Hagar's exclamation in verse 13 might be paraphrased, "You are a God who may be seen," for she said, **"Have I also here seen Him who sees me?"** She named the **well "Beer Lahai Roi"** (literally, *well of the One who lives and sees me*).[14]

16:16 **Abram was eighty-six** when **Ishmael** was born to **Hagar.** The name **Ishmael** means *God hears.* In this case He heard Hagar's misery. We should remember throughout this narrative that Hagar represents law whereas Sarai represents grace (see Gal. 4).

17:1–14 God's words to Abram in verse 1 may have been a veiled way of saying that he should stop trying to work things out in his own strength and let **Almighty God** work for him. Immediately afterward God renewed His **covenant** and changed the patriarch's **name** from **Abram** (*exalted father*) to **Abraham** (*father of a multitude*). Circumcision was then instituted as a sign of the covenant. This surgical operation, performed on the **male child,** was a physical **sign** that the person belonged to God's chosen earthly people. Although it was already practiced in the Middle East at this time, it took on new meaning for Abraham and his family. Every male in Abraham's house was **circumcised,** and thereafter every male baby was to be circumcised when he was **eight days old** or else **be cut off from his people**—that is, put away from the congregation of Israel (vv. 9–14). The expression "cut off" sometimes means to put to death, as in Exodus 31:14,15. In other places, as here, it seems to mean to ban or ostracize.

The Apostle Paul is careful to point out that Abraham was justified (15:6) *before* he was circumcised. His circumcision was "a seal of the righteousness of the faith which he had while still uncircumcised" (Rom. 4:11).

Believers today are not sealed with a physical mark; they receive the Holy Spirit as a seal at the time of their conversion (Eph. 4:30).

THE SIGN OF CIRCUMCISION

Circumcision was adopted by God as a physical sign of the covenant between Him and His people (Gen. 17:10–14). Thus all descendants of Abraham became known as "the circumcision" (Acts 10:45) and Gentiles were called the "uncircumcision" (Eph. 2:11). It is also the sign and seal of the righteousness which Abraham had by faith (Rom. 4:5).

But then the words "circumcision" and "circumcised" took on a variety of meanings. "Uncircumcised lips" (Ex. 6:12) signified a lack of skill in public speaking. "Uncircumcised ears" and "uncircumcised hearts" spoke of failure to hear, love, and obey the Lord (Lev. 26:41; Deut. 10:16; 30:6; Jer. 6:10; Acts 7:51). "Uncircumcised in flesh" (Ezek. 44:7) meant unclean.

In the NT, "the circumcision of Christ" (Col. 2:11) refers to His death on the cross. Believers are circumcised through their identification with Christ; Paul speaks of it as "the circumcision made without hands, in putting off the body of the sins of the flesh" (Col. 2:11). This circumcision speaks of death to the fleshly nature. It is true positionally of every believer, but should be followed by a practical mortifying of the sinful deeds of the flesh (Col. 3:5). The apostle speaks of believers as the true circumcision (Phil. 3:3), in contrast to a party of Jewish legalists known as "the circumcision" (Gal. 2:12).

In addition to their symbolism, some of God's kindly laws were designed to save His people from the diseases of the Gentiles. Many medical authorities today believe that circumcision tends to prevent certain forms of cancer in both the man and his wife.‡

17:15–17 **God** changed Sarai's name to **Sarah** (*princess*) and promised Abraham that his ninety-year-old wife would have a son. The patriarch **laughed**, but in joyful wonder, not in unbelief. His faith did not waver (Rom. 4:18–21).

17:18–27 When **Abraham** pled that **Ishmael** might have favor **before** God, he was told that the **covenant** would be fulfilled through his son, **Isaac**. However, **Ishmael** would be **fruitful**, would **multiply**, and would become **a great nation**. **Isaac** was a symbol of Christ, through whom the **covenant** receives its ultimate fulfillment.

Notice the promptness of Abraham's obedience: **That very same day Abraham was circumcised, and his son Ishmael**.

6. Sodom and Gomorrah (Chaps. 18, 19)

18:1–15 Shortly after the events of chapter 17, **three men** appeared to Abraham. Actually two of them were angels and the other was the Lord Himself. With typical Middle Eastern hospitality, **Abraham** and **Sarah** entertained the angels unawares (Heb. 13:2) and One who was greater than angels. When **Sarah** overheard the Lord say that she would have a child within a year, her laughter betrayed her unbelief. She was rebuked with the searching question, **"Is anything too hard for the Lord?"** But the promise was repeated in spite of her doubting (vv. 9–15). Hebrews 11:11 indicates that Sarah was basically a woman of faith in spite of this momentary lapse.

18:16–33 After the Lord revealed to **Abraham** that He was going to destroy **Sodom**, and while the two angels were walking toward that city, Abraham's great intercessory countdown began—**fifty ... forty-five ... forty ... thirty ... twenty ... ten.** Even for **ten righteous** people the Lord would **not destroy Sodom!** Abraham's prayer is a wonderful example of effectual intercession. It was based on the righteous character of the Judge of all the earth (v. 25) and evidenced that boldness, yet deep humility which only an intimate knowledge of God can give. Only when Abraham stopped pleading did the Lord close the matter and depart (v. 33). There are many mysteries in life for which the truth of verse 25 is the only satisfying answer.

Don't miss the tribute God paid to Abraham as an outstanding family man (v. 19). Something worth coveting!

19:1–11 The name of **Sodom** has become synonymous with the sin of homosexuality or sodomy. But sexual perversion was not the only cause of the city's fall. In Ezekiel 16:49, 50, the Lord describes the sin of Sodom as "pride, fullness of food, and abundance of idleness."

Lot received the **two angels** and insisted that they **spend the night** in his home, knowing all too well the danger that would face them otherwise. Even then **the men of Sodom** sought to commit homosexual rape against these heavenly visitors. In a desperate effort to save his guests, Lot shamelessly offered his **two daughters.** Only a miracle saved the day; the angels struck the Sodomites **with** a temporary, confusing **blindness.**

HOMOSEXUALITY

Both in the OT (Gen. 19:1–26; Lev. 18:22; 20:13) and in the NT (Rom. 1:18–32; 1 Cor. 6:9; 1 Tim. 1:10), God condemns the sin of homosexuality. He showed His wrath against it by destroying the cities of Sodom and Gomorrah. Under the law of Moses, sodomy was punishable by death. No practicing homosexual will inherit the kingdom of God.

So-called "gays" pay a high price for their immoral lifestyle. Paul says that they receive in themselves "the penalty of their error which was due" (Rom. 1:27b). This includes venereal diseases, pneumocystis, Kaposi's sarcoma (a form of cancer) and AIDS. It also includes haunting guilt, mental and emotional disturbances, and abnormal personality changes.

Like all other sinners, a homosexual or lesbian can be saved if he or she repents of sin and receives the Lord Jesus Christ as personal Savior. God loves the gay person and the lesbian even if He hates their sin.

There is a difference between being a *practicing* homosexual and having a homosexual *tendency*. It is the practice that the Bible condemns, not the orientation. There are many who have an attraction to their own sex but refuse to give in to it. By the power of the Spirit, they have disciplined themselves to resist the temptation and to live in purity. Many Christian persons of homosexual orientation

... have regarded their condition with sorrow and contrition, but, unable to change, have drawn on the Spirit for the power of forbearance and chastity, which is sanctification indeed .... In commitment to Christ, [they] have offered an enduring inner blemish for God's use that divine power may be perfected in human weakness.[15]

Some blame God that they were born with this tendency, but the fault does not lie with God but with human sinfulness. Every fallen child of Adam has evil tendencies. Some have a weakness in one area, some in another. The sin is not in being tempted, but in yielding to the temptation.

There is deliverance from homosexuality or lesbianism, as there is from any form of lust. However, ongoing godly counseling assistance is very important in nearly every case.

Christians should accept gays and lesbians as persons without approving their lifestyle. Because they are people for whom Christ died, believers should seek in every possible way to win them to a life of "holiness, without which no one will see the Lord" (Heb. 12:14).‡

19:12–29 The angels insisted that Lot and his family leave the city. But when he tried to persuade **his sons-in-law** (or perhaps prospective sons-in-law—see RSV), they thought he was **joking**. His backslidden life nullified his testimony when the crisis came. **When the morning dawned, the angels** escorted **Lot**, his **wife**, and **daughters** out of Sodom. Even then Lot temporized, preferring to stay in **Zoar**, one of the satellite sin cities. Not even ten righteous men were found in the city of Sodom, so God destroyed it. But Abraham's prayer was not unanswered, for **God remembered Abraham, and sent Lot out of the midst of the overthrow**.

Though Lot's **wife** left the city, her heart was still in it, and she fell under the judgment of God. In the words "Remember Lot's wife" (Luke 17:32), Christ held her up as a warning to all who trifle with His offer of salvation.

19:30–38 Leaving **Zoar**, Lot fled to a mountain **cave**. There **his daughters made** him drunk and enticed him to commit incest with them. The older daughter subsequently **bore a son** named **Moab**, and the **younger**... **bore a son, Ben-Ammi**. Thus began

the **Moabites** and Ammonites, who became recurring thorns in Israel's side. It was Moabite women who later seduced the men of Israel to commit immorality (Num. 25:1–3) and Ammonites who taught Israel the worship of Molech, including the sacrifice of children (1 Kgs. 11:33; Jer. 32:35). We know from 2 Peter 2:7, 8 that Lot was a just man, but because of his worldliness he lost his testimony (v. 14), his wife (v. 26), his sons-in-law, his friends, his communion (there was none in Sodom), his property (he went in rich but came out poor), his character (v. 35), his life's work, and nearly his life (v. 22). The depraved behavior of his daughters shows that they had been influenced by Sodom's vile standards. There is no escape (Heb. 2:3).

7. Abraham and Abimelech (Chap. 20)

20:1–18 It seems incredible to us that **Abraham** would again try to pass off **Sarah** as his **sister** within twenty years of the same blunder with Pharaoh—incredible, that is, until we remember our *own* perpetual proneness to sin! The incident with **Abimelech** in **Gerar** is almost a replay of Abraham's duplicity in Egypt (12:10–17). God intervened to work out His purposes in the birth of Isaac, which might otherwise have been frustrated. He threatened **Abimelech** with death. He is more than just a spectator on the sidelines of history. He can overrule the evil of His people, even through the lives of the unregenerate. The pagan **Abimelech** acted more righteously in this incident than Abraham, the "friend of God." (*Abimelech* is a title, and not a proper name.) It is shameful when a believer has to be justly rebuked by a man of the world! When a half-truth is presented as the whole truth, it is an untruth. Abraham even tried to shift some of the blame onto God for making him **wander** in the first place. He would have been wiser to humbly acknowledge his guilt. Nevertheless, he was still God's man. And so the Lord sent Abimelech to him so that Abraham would pray that his household be healed of its barrenness.

The expression **"this vindicates you"** (v. 16) is literally "it is a covering of the eyes," meaning a gift given for the purpose of appeasing. Thus it might read, "It is given to you as a payment in satisfaction as evidence to all who are with you and to all men that the wrong has been righted."

8. Isaac, Son of the Promise (Chap. 21)

21:1–10 When the promised son was born to **Abraham** and **Sarah**, the ecstatic parents named him **Isaac** ("laughter"), as commanded by God (17:19, 21). This expressed their own delight and the delight of all who would hear the news. **Isaac** was probably from two to five years old when he **was weaned**. Ishmael would have been between thirteen and seventeen. When **Sarah saw** Ishmael mocking Isaac at the weaning party, she ordered Abraham to **cast out** Hagar **and her son**. Paul interprets this action as evidence that law persecutes grace, that law and grace cannot be mixed, and that spiritual blessings cannot be obtained on the legal principle (Gal. 4:29).

21:11–13 Abraham was grieved to lose Hagar and Ishmael, **but God** consoled him with the promise that Ishmael would become the father of **a great nation**. And yet the Lord made it clear that Isaac was the promised son through whom the covenant would be carried out.

21:14–21 When **Hagar** and **the boy** almost perished from thirst in the desert south of Canaan, God caused them to find a **well**, and they were spared. Ishmael was in his teens at this time; therefore, verse 15 probably means that Hagar pushed him **under one of the shrubs** in his weakness. Ishmael's name, "God hears," is found twice in verse 17—**"God heard"** and **"God has heard."** Children and young people should be encouraged to pray. God hears and answers!

21:22–34 The **Abimelech** in verse 22 is not necessarily the same one as in chapter 20. This chieftain's **servants** had taken a **well of water** from Abraham's men. When **Abimelech** and **Abraham** made a treaty of friendship, the patriarch told Abimelech about the **well** that had been **seized**. The result was a **covenant** granting the well to Abraham. He promptly named it **Beersheba** ("well of the oath"). The place later became a city, marking the southernmost boundary of the land. **Abraham planted a tamarisk tree** as a memorial.

9. The Offering of Isaac (Chap. 22)

22:1–10 Perhaps no scene in the Bible except Calvary itself is more poignant than this one, and none gives a clearer foreshadowing of the death of God's only, well-beloved Son on the cross. The supreme test of Abraham's faith came when God ordered him to **offer up** Isaac **as a burnt offering** in **the land of Moriah**. Actually God had no intention of allowing Abraham to go through with it; He has always been opposed to human sacrifice. **Moriah** is the mountain range where Jerusalem is situated (2 Chron. 3:1) and also where Calvary stood. God's words, **"your only son Isaac, whom you love,"** must have pierced

Abraham's heart like ever-deepening wounds. Isaac was Abraham's **only son** in the sense that he was the **only son** of promise—the unique son, the son of miraculous birth.

The first occurrence of a word in the Bible often sets the pattern for its usage throughout Scripture. **Love** (v. 2) and "worship" (v. 5) are first found here. Abraham's **love** for his **son** is a faint picture of God's love for the Lord Jesus. The sacrifice of Isaac was a picture of the greatest act of worship—the Savior's self-sacrifice to accomplish the will of God.

22:11, 12 "**Abraham, Abraham**" is the first of ten name duplications found in the Bible. Seven are spoken by God to man (Gen. 22:11; 46:2; Ex. 3:4; 1 Sam. 3:10; Luke 10:41; 22:31; Acts 9:4). The other three are Matthew 7:21, 22; 23:37; Mark 15:34. They introduce matters of special importance. **The Angel of the LORD** (v. 11) was **God** (v. 12).

22:13–15 To offer Isaac was surely the supreme test of Abraham's faith. God had promised to give Abraham a numberless posterity through his son. Isaac could have been as much as twenty-five at this time, and he was unmarried. If Abraham slew him, how could the promise be fulfilled? According to Hebrews 11:19, Abraham believed that even if he slew his son, God would raise him from the dead. This faith was remarkable because there was no recorded case of resurrection up to this time in the world's history. Notice his faith also in 22:5: "the lad and I will go yonder and worship, and we will come back to you." Abraham was first justified by faith (15:6), then justified (vindicated) by works here (see James 2:21). His faith was the means of his salvation, while his works were the proof of the reality of his faith. When Isaac asked,

"**Where is the lamb?**", his father replied, "**God will provide for Himself the lamb.**" This promise was not ultimately fulfilled by the **ram** of verse 13 but by the Lamb of God (John 1:29).

There are two outstanding symbols of Christ in this chapter. Isaac is the first: an **only son**, loved by his father, willing to do his father's will, received back from the dead in a figure. The **ram** is the second: an innocent victim died as a substitute for another, its blood was shed, and it was a **burnt offering** wholly consumed for God. Someone has said that, in providing the **ram** as a substitute for Isaac, "God spared Abraham's heart a pang He would not spare His own." **The Angel of the LORD** in verses 11 and 15, as in all the OT, is the Lord Jesus Christ. Abraham named the place **The-LORD-Will-Provide** (Jehovah-jireh) (v. 14). This is one of the seven compound names for God in the OT. The others are:

Jehovah-Rophekha—"The LORD who heals you" (Ex. 15:26).

Jehovah-Nissi—"The LORD my banner" (Ex. 17:8–15).

Jehovah-Shalom—"The LORD our peace" (Judg. 6:24).

Jehovah-Roi—"The LORD my Shepherd" (Ps. 23:1).

Jehovah-Tsidkenu—"The LORD our righteousness" (Jer. 23:6).

Jehovah-Shammah—"The LORD is present" (Ezek. 48:35).

22:16–19 The LORD swore by Himself because He couldn't swear by anyone greater (Heb. 6:13). God's promise here, confirmed by His oath, includes the blessing of the Gentile nations through Christ (see Gal. 3:16). In verse 17c God adds to the already vast blessing promised: Abraham's seed would **possess the gate of** his

enemies. This means that his descendants would "occupy the place of authority over those who would oppose them. The capture of the city gate meant the fall of the city itself."[16]

22:20-24 Abraham's **brother Nahor** had twelve sons, whereas Abraham had only two—Ishmael and Isaac. How this must have tested Abraham's faith concerning God's promise of descendants as the stars of the sky! It may have prompted him to send Eliezer in search of a wife for Isaac (chap. 24). Notice the name **Rebekah** in 22:23.

10. The Family Burial Place (Chap. 23)

23:1-16 When **Sarah died** at **one hundred and twenty-seven years**, Abraham bargained with the Hittite inhabitants of **Hebron** for the purchase of **the cave of Machpelah** as a **burial place**—his only purchase of real estate during his long life of pilgrimage. The passage gives a priceless description of the bargaining that is so typical in Eastern lands. At first, the Hittites suggested that Abraham choose any one of their **burial places**. With overflowing courtesy, Abraham refused and insisted on paying full price for a cave owned by **Ephron**. At first **Ephron** offered not just the **cave** but the entire **field** as an outright gift, but Abraham understood that this was just a polite gesture. The owner really had no intention of giving it away. When Abraham countered by insisting on his desire to purchase it, Ephron suggested a price of **four hundred shekels of silver**, pretending that this was a great bargain. Actually it was an extortionate price, and ordinarily the buyer would have continued to haggle. So it was a surprise to everyone when Abraham agreed to Ephron's first asking price. Abraham

didn't want to be indebted to an unbeliever, and neither should we.

23:17-20 **The cave of Machpelah** later became the **burial place** of Abraham, Isaac, Rebekah, Jacob, and Leah. The traditional location is now the site of a Moslem mosque.

11. A Bride for Isaac (Chap. 24)

24:1-9 Abraham bound his **oldest servant** by an **oath** that in seeking a bride for **Isaac**, he would not allow him to marry a Canaanite or to live in Mesopotamia. The ancient form of oath described in verses 2-4 and 9 is explained by Charles F. Pfeiffer:

> According to Biblical idiom, children are said to issue from the "thigh" or "loins" of their father (cf. Gen. 46:26). Placing the hand on the thigh signified that, in the event that an oath were violated, the children who had issued, or might issue from the "thigh" would avenge the act of disloyalty. This has been called a "swearing by posterity" and is particularly applicable here, because the servant's mission is to insure a posterity for Abraham through Isaac.[17]

24:10-14 **The servant** is a type (symbol) of the Holy Spirit sent by the Father to win a bride for the "heavenly Isaac," the Lord Jesus. The narrative carefully records the preparation for the journey, the gifts carried by the servant, and the sign by which he would know the Lord's chosen woman. Murdoch Campbell elaborates:

> It was a sign that was calculated to throw much light on the character and disposition of the girl worthy of his master's son. He was merely to ask her for "a sip"—as the Hebrew word may be rendered—of water for himself; but the one whom God had chosen to be the mother of a great

people and a remote ancestress of Jesus Christ would reveal her generous nature and her willingness to serve others by offering him not a mere "sip" of water but an abundant "drink." To this she was also to add the astonishing offer of drawing water for the camels also. Now when we consider that these ten beasts, after the toil of the long desert, were prepared to empty at least four barrels of water in all, the spontaneous willingness of the girl of his prayers to serve man and beast would point to a kindly and unselfish disposition and also to a character of the highest order.[18]

24:15–52 It was lovely **Rebekah**, of course, who fulfilled the conditions and who therefore received the servant's gifts. As she led him to her father's home, Abraham's servant knew that his search had ended. When Rebekah explained the situation to her brother, **Laban**, he welcomed the entourage graciously, then heard **the servant** present his request for **Rebekah** as a bride for Isaac. The marvelous convergence of circumstances in answer to the servant's prayer convinced **Laban** and **Bethuel**, Rebekah's father, that **the LORD** had arranged it all.

24:53–61 **The servant** then brought out gifts for **Rebekah**, Laban, and her **mother**, sealing the engagement. In the morning, the family wanted to delay her departure, but Rebekah's willingness to go settled the matter, and she left with their blessing.

24:62–67 The first time we see **Isaac** after his experience on Mount Moriah is when he **went** out to meet Rebekah. So the first time we will see the Savior after His death, burial, resurrection, and ascension is when He returns to claim His chosen bride (1 Thess. 4:13–18). Isaac's meeting

with Rebekah is one of tender beauty. Without ever having seen her before, he married her and **loved her**, and, unlike other patriarchs, he had no other wife besides her.

12. Abraham's Descendants (25:1–18)

25:1–6 In 1 Chronicles 1:32 **Keturah** is called Abraham's concubine. Verse 6 seems to confirm this. Thus she was a *lesser* **wife**, one who did not enjoy the full privileges of a wife in the home. Once again God records marital irregularities that He never approved.

25:7–18 **Abraham breathed his last** at **one hundred and seventy-five years** of age and became the second person to be **buried in the cave** at Hebron. The twelve **sons of Ishmael** listed in verses 12–16 fulfilled God's promise to Abraham: "He shall beget twelve princes" (17:20). With the death of **Ishmael**, **Isaac** moves to center stage in the narrative.

B. Isaac (25:19—26:35)

1. Isaac's Family (25:19–34)

25:19–26 For almost twenty years after her marriage, **Rebekah . . . was barren**. Then, in answer to Isaac's prayer, she **conceived**. The struggle of two sons **within her** perplexed her until she was told that her sons would become the heads of **two rival nations** (Israel and Edom). The firstborn twin was named **Esau** (*hairy*). The other was named **Jacob** (*supplanter*). Even at birth, Jacob tried to gain advantage over his brother by grabbing **hold of Esau's heel**! **Isaac was sixty** when his twin boys were born.

25:27, 28 As **the boys grew** up, Esau turned into an outdoorsman and **a skillful hunter**. Jacob on the other hand was a **mild**, indoor type, **dwelling in tents. Isaac loved Esau**

best, **but Rebekah loved Jacob**. Perhaps he was a "mama's boy."

25:29–34 As the firstborn, **Esau** was entitled to a double portion of his father's possessions—that is, twice as much as any other son might inherit. He also became the tribal or family head. This was known as the **birthright**. In Esau's case, it would also have included being the ancestor of the Messiah. One day, as Esau was returning from a hunting trip, he saw Jacob cooking some **red stew**. He asked for some of the red stuff so imploringly that he got the nickname "Red" (**Edom**), and it stuck to him and to his posterity, the Edomites. When Jacob offered some soup in exchange for Esau's **birthright**, Esau foolishly agreed. "No food except the forbidden fruit was as dearly bought as this broth."[19] The prophecy of verse 23 is partially fulfilled in verses 29–34. God does not condone Jacob's wheeling and dealing, but one thing is apparent—Jacob valued the **birthright** and a place in the godly line, while Esau preferred the gratification of his physical appetite to spiritual blessings.

The chapter closes by emphasizing Esau's treatment of **his birthright** rather than Jacob's treatment of his brother. Esau's descendants were bitter foes of Israel. Their final doom is pronounced in Obadiah.

2. Isaac and Abimelech (Chap. 26)

26:1–6 Isaac reacted to **famine** as his father had done (chaps. 12 and 20). As he journeyed south, the Lord appeared to him at **Gerar** and warned him not to go to Egypt. **Gerar** was sort of a halfway house on the route to Egypt. God told Isaac to stay temporarily[20] in Gerar but instead Isaac **dwelt** there. God also reconfirmed to him the unconditional covenant that He had made with **Abraham**.

26:7–17 **Isaac** reacted to fear as his father had done. He misrepresented his **wife** as his **sister** to the **men of** Gerar. It is the sad story of a father's weakness being repeated in his son. When the deceit was exposed and rebuked, Isaac confessed. Confession leads to blessing. Isaac became wealthy in Gerar—so wealthy that the Abimelech who was then reigning asked him to leave. So Isaac moved from Gerar to the **Valley of Gerar**, not far away.

26:18–25 **The Philistines** had **stopped up** the **wells** which Abraham **had dug**—an unfriendly act signifying that the newcomers were not welcome. Isaac cleaned out the wells. Strife ensued with the Philistines at **Esek** (*contention*) and **Sitnah** (*enmity*). Finally Isaac moved away from the Philistines. This time there was no strife when he **dug** a **well**, so he called it **Rehoboth** (*broad places* or *room*). **He went from there to Beersheba**, where the LORD reassured him with the promise of blessing, and where Isaac **built an altar** (worship), **pitched a tent** (abiding), and **dug a well** (refreshment). Just as water is a basic essential in the physical realm, so is the water of the Word in the spiritual.

26:26–33 Concerning verses 26–31, Williams says:

It is when Isaac definitely separates himself from the men of Gerar that they come to him seeking blessing from God . . . . The Christian best helps the world when living in separation from it. . . . [21]

Isaac's servants . . . found water the same day that Isaac made a nonaggression pact with **Abimelech**. Abraham had previously named the place

Beersheba because he made a covenant there with his contemporary, **Abimelech** (21:31). Now, under similar circumstances, **Isaac** renames it **Shebah** or **Beersheba**.

26:34, 35 Esau's marriage to **Judith** and **Basemath**, two pagan women, caused **grief** to his parents, as have many other unequal yokes since then. It also brought out further his unfitness for the birthright.

C. Jacob (27:1—36:43)

1. Jacob Cheats Esau (Chap. 27)

27:1–22 Approximately thirty-seven years have passed since the events of the previous chapter. **Isaac** is now 137, his sight has failed, and he thinks he is about to die, perhaps because his brother Ishmael had died at that age (Gen. 25:17). But he will live forty-three more years.

When **Isaac** craved some venison from **Esau**, promising a blessing in return, **Rebekah** plotted to deceive her husband and to get the blessing for **Jacob**, whom she loved. Her trickery was unnecessary because God had already promised the blessing to Jacob (25:23b). She cooked goat's meat so that it tasted like **savory** venison, and put the goat's **skins** on Jacob's arms to impersonate the **hairy** Esau. Isaac made the mistake of trusting his feelings; the hairy arm "felt" like Esau's. We should not trust our emotional feelings in spiritual matters. As Martin Luther observed:

Feelings come and feelings go, and
 feelings are deceiving;
Our warrant is the Word of God;
 naught else is worth believing.[22]

Although Rebekah planned the deception, Jacob was equally guilty for carrying it out. And he reaped what

he sowed. C. H. Mackintosh observed that:

> . . . whoever observes Jacob's life, after he had surreptitiously obtained his father's blessing, will perceive that he enjoyed very little worldly felicity. His brother sought to murder him, to avoid which he was forced to flee from his father's house; his uncle Laban deceived him. . . . He was obliged to leave him in a clandestine manner. . . . He experienced the baseness of his son Reuben . . . the treachery and cruelty of Simeon and Levi towards the Shechemites; then he had to feel the loss of his beloved wife . . . the supposed untimely end of Joseph; and to complete all, he was forced by famine to go into Egypt, and there died in a strange land. . . .[23]

27:23–29 Isaac **blessed** Jacob with prosperity, dominion, and protection. It is interesting that the blessings spoken by the patriarchs were prophetic; they came to pass literally because, in a real sense, these men spoke by inspiration.

27:30–40 When Esau returned and learned of the deception, he sought the **blessing** tearfully. But the blessing had been granted to **Jacob** and it couldn't be retracted (Heb. 12:16, 17). However, Isaac did have a word for Esau, as follows:

> Far from rich soil on earth shall you live, far from the dew of heaven on high; you shall live by the sword and serve your brother; but when you grow restive, his yoke you shall break (vv. 39, 40—Moffatt).

This suggests that the Edomites would live in desert places, would be warriors, would be subject to the Israelites, but would one day rebel against this rule. This latter prophecy was fulfilled in the reign of Joram, King of Judah (2 Kgs. 8:20–22).

27:41–46 **Esau** planned to **kill** his **brother Jacob** as soon as his father would die and the period **of mourning** would end. When **Rebekah** learned of this, she told Jacob to head for her brother Laban's home **in Haran**. She feared not only that Jacob would be killed but that Esau would run away or be killed in a blood feud, and she would lose two sons at once. However, to explain Jacob's departure to Isaac, she said she was afraid Jacob might marry a Hittite, as Esau had done. Jacob expected to return soon, but it was not to be for more than twenty years. His father would still be living, but his mother would have passed on.

2. Jacob's Flight to Haran (Chap. 28)

28:1–9 **Isaac called Jacob** and **blessed him**, and sent him to **Paddan Aram**, a district of Mesopotamia, so that he would find a wife among his **mother's** people rather than among the Canaanites. This inspired Esau to try to regain his father's blessing by marrying a **daughter of Ishmael**. It was a case of doing evil (multiplying **wives**) that good might come.

28:10–19 At **Bethel**, **Jacob** had a wonderful dream in which he saw a **ladder** or staircase extending from earth to heaven. This suggested "the fact of a real, uninterrupted, and close communion between heaven and earth, and in particular between God in His glory and man in his solitude."[24] In His encounter with Nathanael, the Lord Jesus made an apparent reference to this incident and connected it with His Second Advent and millennial glory (John 1:51). But believers even now can enjoy moment-by-moment fellowship with the Lord. At this time when Jacob's heart was probably filled with regret for the past, loneliness in the present, and uncertainty about the future, God graciously made a covenant with him as He had with Abraham and Isaac. Notice the promise of *companionship:* **"I am with you"**; *safety:* **"I will keep you wherever you go"**; *guidance:* **"and will bring you back to this land"**; and *personal guarantee:* **"I will not leave you until I have done what I have spoken to you."** Conscious that he had met God there, Jacob changed the name of the place from **Luz** (*separation*) to **Bethel** (*house of God*).

"Prior to Bethel, where Jacob was 'surprised by joy' and 'transfixed by awe,' he had had no personal contact with God. Everything had come to him second-hand" (*Daily Notes of the Scripture Union*).

28:20–22 Next Jacob seems to be bargaining with God. He was actually bargaining for *less* than God had promised (v. 14). His faith was not strong enough to take God at His word, so he had to make his tithe conditional on God's performance of His part of the agreement. Another interpretation, however, is that the **"if"** is simply an inherent part of all Hebrew oaths and that Jacob was binding himself to give a tenth unconditionally (see Num. 21:2; Judg. 11:30,31; 1 Sam. 1:11 for similar Hebrew oaths).

3. Jacob, His Wives, and His Offspring (29:1—30:24)

29:1–14 Jacob was seventy-seven when he left Beersheba for Haran. He would spend twenty years serving his uncle Laban, thirty-three years back in Canaan, and the last seventeen years of his life in Egypt. Arriving in Paddan Aram, he was guided to the very **field** where some shepherds **from Haran** were tending their **flocks**. So perfect was God's timing that **Rachel** was just arriving with her flock when Jacob was talking with the shepherds. Being a good shepherd, Jacob wondered why they were all waiting at the well when there was still daylight for feeding the sheep. They explained that they did not remove the cover from the well until all the herds had arrived. It was an emotion-packed moment for Jacob when he met his cousin Rachel, and for **Laban** a short while later when he met his nephew Jacob.

29:15–35 **Laban** agreed to give Rachel to Jacob in exchange for **seven years** of service. The years **seemed** to Jacob but **a few days because of the love he had for her**. That is how it should be in our service for the Lord.

Leah was weak-eyed and not attractive. **Rachel was beautiful**.

According to custom, it was arranged that the bride should go in to the groom on the wedding night, veiled and perhaps when the room was in darkness. You can imagine how irate Jacob was in the morning when he found that his bride was **Leah**! Laban had tricked him, but excused the trick on the ground that the older daughter should be married first according to the local custom. Then Laban said, **"Fulfill her week** (that is, carry through on the marriage to Leah) **and we will give you this one also** (Rachel) **for the service which you will serve with me still another seven years."** At the end of the week-long wedding feast, Jacob also married Rachel, then served **seven more years** for her. Jacob had sown deceit, and now he was reaping it! When the Lord saw that Leah was hated (that is, loved less than Rachel) He compensated for this by giving her children. This law of divine compensation still operates: People who lack in one area are given extra in another. Leah acknowledged the Lord

when she named her children (vv. 32, 33, 35). From her comes the priesthood (**Levi**), the royal line (**Judah**), and ultimately the Christ. In this chapter we have the first four of the sons of Jacob. The complete list of Jacob's sons is as follows:

The sons born to Leah:

> **Reuben**—(*see, a son*) (29:32)
> **Simeon**—(*hearing*) (29:33)
> **Levi**—(*joined*) (29:34)
> **Judah**—(*praise*) (29:35)
> Issachar—(*hire*) (30:18)
> Zebulun—(*dwelling*) (30:20)

The sons born to Bilhah, the handmaid of Rachel:

> Dan—(*judge*) (30:6)
> Naphtali—(*wrestling*) (30:8)

The sons born to Zilpah, handmaid of Leah:

> Gad—(*a troop* or *good fortune*) (30:11)
> Asher—(*happy*) (30:13)

The sons born to Rachel:

> Joseph—(*adding*) (30:24)
> Benjamin—(*son of the right hand*) (35:18)

30:1–13 In desperation to have a child playing on her knees, **Rachel** gave **her maid, Bilhah,** to Jacob as a wife or concubine. Even though such arrangements were common in those days, they were contrary to God's will. **Bilhah bore** two sons, **Dan** and **Naphtali**. Not to be outdone by Rachel, **Leah** gave **her maid, Zilpah,** to Jacob, and two more sons were born, **Gad** and **Asher**.

30:14–24 The **mandrakes** which **Reuben found** were a sort of love-apple, believed by the superstitious to impart fertility. Since Rachel was barren, she was anxious to have **some of the mandrakes**. In exchange, she agreed to let Leah live as wife with Jacob. (For some unexplained reason, Leah had apparently lost her privileges as wife.) After this, two more sons were born to Leah—**Issachar** and **Zebulun**—and also **a daughter, Dinah**. At last Rachel bore her first **son** and named him **Joseph**, expressing faith that God would give her still **another son**.

4. Jacob Outwits Laban (30:25–43)

30:25–36 When **Jacob** told **Laban** that he wanted to return home to Canaan, his uncle urged him to **stay**. Laban said he had learned by **experience** that the LORD had **blessed** him because of Jacob, and he would meet his wage demands if he would stay. Jacob agreed to continue serving if Laban would give him **all the speckled and spotted sheep** and **goats** and all the dark **lambs**. All other animals in the flock would be acknowledged as Laban's. The latter agreed to the pact, saying, **"Oh, that it were according to your word."** Laban took most of the animals designated for Jacob and gave them to his sons to shepherd, realizing that they would probably reproduce with markings that identified them as belonging to Jacob. Then he entrusted his own animals to Jacob, separated from his own sons by a three-day journey. This made it impossible for the marked animals in the herds tended by Laban's sons to breed with Laban's unmarked animals that were tended by Jacob.

30:37–43 When breeding Laban's herd, Jacob put **rods that he had peeled** in front of them, whether they were of solid color or marked. The lambs or kids were born **streaked, speckled, and spotted**. This, of course, meant that they belonged to Jacob. Did these **rods** actually determine the markings on the animals? There may

or may not have been a scientific basis to the method. (New genetic evidence suggests that there might have been.) How else might the animals have been born with the markings Jacob desired?

First of all, it may have been a miracle (see 31:12).

Or it may have been a clever trick on Jacob's part. There are indications in the narrative that he knew the science of selective breeding. By careful breeding, he not only produced animals with the markings he desired, but he was also able to produce **stronger** animals for himself and **feeble** ones for Laban. Perhaps the peeled rods were just a trick to hide his breeding secrets from others. Whatever the explanation, Jacob's wealth increased during his final six years of serving Laban.

5. Jacob's Return to Canaan (Chap. 31)

31:1–18 After **Jacob** discovered that **Laban** and his **sons** were growing jealous and resentful, the LORD told him that the time had come to **return to** Canaan. First he **called Rachel and Leah** and discussed the matter, rehearsing how Laban had cheated him and **changed** his **wages ten times**, how God had overruled so that the flocks always bred in his favor, how God had reminded him of the vow he had made twenty years earlier (28:20–22), and how the Lord had told him to **return to** Canaan. His wives agreed that their father had not dealt honestly and that they should leave.

Griffith Thomas points out several interesting principles for discerning God's guidance here. First, Jacob had a *desire* (30:25). Secondly, *circumstances* necessitated a change of some sort. Thirdly, *God's word* came strongly to him. And finally, there was *confirming support* from his wives, despite their natural ties to Laban. . . . [25] Note that the Angel of God (v. 11) is the God of Bethel (v. 13).

31:19–21 Before the secret departure, **Rachel** stole her father's **household idols** and hid them in her camel's saddle. Possession of these household gods implied leadership of the family, and, in the case of a married daughter, assured her husband the right of the father's property.[26] Since Laban had sons of his own when Jacob fled to Canaan, they alone had the right to their father's *teraphim*. Rachel's theft was therefore a serious matter, aimed at preserving for her husband the chief title to Laban's estate.

31:22–30 When **Laban** learned of their departure, he and his men **pursued** them **for seven days' journey**, but the Lord warned him **in a dream** not to trouble **Jacob** and his caravan. When he finally overtook them, he only complained that he had been denied the privilege of giving them a royal send-off and that his idols had been stolen.

31:31–35 To the first complaint **Jacob answered** that he left secretly for fear that Laban would **take** his **daughters** (Rachel and Leah) **from** him **by force**. To the second complaint, he denied having stolen the **gods** and rashly decreed death for the culprit. Laban made a thorough search of the caravan, but in vain. **Rachel** was sitting **on them** and excused herself for not getting off the camel's saddle to honor her father because it was her menstrual period— or so she said.

31:36–42 Now it was Jacob's turn to be **angry**. He denounced Laban for accusing him of theft and for treating him so unfairly for **twenty years**, in spite of Jacob's faithful and generous service. This passage reveals that Jacob was a hard worker and that the blessing of the Lord was upon him in all that he did. Are we faithful to our employers? Does the blessing of God rest upon our work?

31:43–50 **Laban** avoided the issue by lamely protesting that he would not harm his own **daughters**, grandchildren, or cattle, then suggested that they should make a pact. It was *not* a gracious, friendly **covenant**, asking the Lord to watch over them while they were separated. Rather, it was a compact between two cheats, asking the Lord to make sure that they did what was right when they were out of sight from one another! It was, in effect, a nonaggression treaty, but it also charged Jacob not to treat Laban's daughters harshly nor to marry other wives. Laban called the **pillar** of **stones** marking the pact **Jegar Sahadutha**, an Aramaic expression. **Jacob called it Galeed**, a Hebrew word. Both words mean "the **heap** of **witness**." Neither man was to pass the stone-heap to attack the other.

31:51–55 **Laban** swore by the **God of Abraham, the God of Nahor, and the God of their father**, Terah. The capitalization of *God* in the NKJV (also Moffatt, NIV, etc.) indicates that the translators felt Laban was referring to the one true God that Abraham came to know. However, since the Hebrew does not have upper and lower case letters, we can't tell if Laban might have been referring to the pagan gods which these men had worshiped in Ur. **Jacob swore by the Fear of his father Isaac**—that is, the God whom Isaac feared. Isaac had never been an idolater. **Jacob** first **offered a sacrifice**, then made a banquet for all those present and camped **all** that **night on the mountain**.

Early in the morning, **Laban kissed** his grandchildren and **daughters** good-bye and left for home.

6. Jacob and Esau Reconciled (Chaps. 32, 33)

32:1–8 En route to Canaan, Jacob met a band of **angels** and called the place **Mahanaim** (*two hosts* or *double camp*). The two camps may be God's army (v. 2) and Jacob's entourage. Or two hosts may be a figurative expression for a great multitude (v. 10). As Jacob neared the land, he remembered his **brother Esau** and feared revenge. Would Esau still be angry at the way he had been cheated out of the blessing? First, **Jacob sent messengers . . . to Esau** with greetings of peace. Then when he heard that Esau was **coming to meet** him with a band of **four hundred men**, he was so terrified that **he divided** his family **into two companies**, so that if the first group was destroyed, the second could flee.

32:9–12 Jacob's prayer was born out of a desperate sense of need for divine protection. It was based on the ground of covenant relationship which the Lord had established with him and his forefathers, and it was prayed in humility of spirit. He based his plea on the word of the Lord and claimed the promises of God.

The best prayer comes from a strong inward necessity. By human security systems, we often protect ourselves from a dynamic prayer life. Why do we do ourselves this wrong?

32:13–21 Jacob next sent three **successive droves** of animals totaling 580 head as gifts for Esau, hoping to **appease him**. Esau would get the gift in three installments. Jacob's maneuvers manifested his unbelief or at least a mixture of faith and unbelief.

32:22–32 After sending his immediate family across the stream **Jabbok**

(*he will empty*), Jacob spent the **night** alone at Peniel for what was to be one of the great experiences of his life. **A Man wrestled with him**. That Man was an angel (Hos. 12:4), the Angel of Jehovah, the Lord Himself. The Lord put **the socket of Jacob's hip . . . out of joint**, causing him to walk with a limp the rest of his life. Although Jacob lost the encounter physically, he won a great spiritual victory. He learned to triumph through defeat and to be strong through weakness. Emptied of self and of confidence in his own cleverness, he confessed he was **Jacob**, a supplanter, a "con man." God then changed his **name** to **Israel** (variously translated as "God rules," "one who strives with God," or "a prince of God"). Jacob called the name of the place **Peniel** (*the face of God*) because he realized he had **seen** the Lord. Pfeiffer points out that verse 32 is still true among Jews today:

> The sciatic nerve, or thigh vein, must be removed from the slaughtered animal before that portion of the animal may be prepared for consumption by orthodox Jews.[27]

33:1–11 As **Esau** drew near, Jacob lapsed back into fearfulness and merely natural behavior, arranging his household in such a way as to afford maximum protection for those he loved most. Jacob **bowed himself to the ground seven times** as he approached **his brother. Esau**, by comparison, was relaxed, warm, and effusive as he met Jacob first, then Jacob's wives and **children**. He protested mildly against the extravagant gift of livestock but finally consented to accept it. Jacob seems to have shown undue servility to his brother, speaking of himself as his **servant**. Some think that he resorted to flattery and exaggeration in telling Esau that seeing his **face** was like seeing **God**. Others think that **the face of God** here means a reconciled face.

33:12–17 When **Esau** suggested that they travel back together, Jacob pretended that this would be impossible because of the slow pace required by the **children** and young animals. Jacob promised to meet Esau **in Seir** (Edom), although he had no intention of doing so. Even when Esau tried to leave behind **some of** his men to travel with Jacob's household, the latter refused the offer without revealing the real reasons—fear and suspicion.

33:18–20 Instead of traveling south to Mount Seir, Jacob went northwest. At length he arrived at **Shechem** and settled there, erecting **an altar** which he (perhaps presumptuously) called **El Elohe Israel** (*God, the God of Israel*). Twenty years earlier, when God had appeared to him at Bethel, Jacob had vowed that the Lord would be his God, that he would give a tenth of his wealth to the Lord, and that he would establish Bethel as God's house (28:20–22). Now, instead of returning to Bethel, he settles thirty miles away in the fertile area of Shechem, probably for the sake of his livestock. (Shechem represents the world.) God does not speak directly to him until several years later, when He calls on Jacob to fulfill his vow (chap. 35). In the meantime, the tragic events of chapter 34 take place.

7. Sins at Shechem (Chap. 34)

34:1–12 The name of God is not mentioned in this chapter. While Jacob and his family were living in Shechem, **Dinah his daughter** mingled socially with the heathen women, a breach of proper separation from the ungodly. On one such occasion, **Shechem, the** son of Hamor, sexually assaulted her, then greatly desired to marry her. Realizing that Jacob and his sons were enraged, **Hamor** proposed a peaceful solution: intermarriage between the Israelites and Canaanites, and full rights for the Israelites as citizens of the land. (Verse 9 can be seen as one of many Satanic attempts to pollute the godly line.) Shechem also offered to pay whatever **dowry and gift** was requested.

34:13–24 The sons of Jacob had no intention of giving **Dinah** to Shechem, but they lied that they would do so if the men of the city would be **circumcised**. The sacred sign of God's covenant was to be used wickedly. In good faith, **Hamor, Shechem, and all** the men of their city met the condition.

34:25–31 But while the Shechemites were recovering from the surgery, Simeon and Levi treacherously murdered them and **plundered** their wealth. When Jacob administered a mild rebuke, **Simeon and Levi** answered that their **sister** should not have been treated **like a harlot**. Actually Jacob seemed to be more concerned about his own welfare than the horrible injustice that had been done to the men of Shechem. Notice his eight uses of the first-person pronoun in verse 30.

8. The Return to Bethel (Chap. 35)

35:1–8 Chapter 35 opens with God's command to Jacob to fulfill the vow made about thirty years earlier (28:20–22). The Lord used the tragic events of the previous chapter to prepare the patriarch to do it. Notice that God is referred to about twenty times in this chapter, in contrast to no references in chapter 34. Before obeying God's command to return **to Bethel**, Jacob first ordered his family to **put away the foreign** household gods and to put on clean clothes. As soon as they did this, they became a **terror** to their heathen neighbors. It was appropriate that Jacob should build an altar at **"El Bethel"** and worship the God who had protected him from his brother, Esau.

35:9–15 Once again God stated that Jacob's **name** was now **Israel** and renewed the covenant He had made with Abraham and Isaac. The patriarch marked the sacred spot with a **pillar** and once again named the place **Bethel**.

35:16–20 As Jacob's family **journeyed** south **from Bethel, . . . Rachel died** in childbirth. She had named the child **Ben-Oni** (*son of my sorrow*), but Jacob named this twelfth son **Benjamin** (*son of my right hand*). These two names pre-picture the sufferings of Christ and the glories that would follow. The traditional (but probably not authentic) site of **Rachel's grave** may still be seen on the road from Jerusalem to **Bethlehem**. Why was she not buried with Abraham, Sarah, and Rebekah in the cave of Hebron? Perhaps it was because she had brought idols into the family.

35:21–29 A brief mention is made of Reuben's sin **with Bilhah his father's concubine**, a sin by which he forfeited the birthright (49:3, 4). The last sentence in verse 22 begins a new paragraph: **Now the sons of Jacob were twelve.** The next two verses list the twelve **sons**. Though it says in verse 26 that these sons were born to Jacob in **Paddan Aram**, **Benjamin** (v. 24) is excepted. He was born in Canaan (vv. 16–19). Jacob returned to **Hebron** in time to see **his father Isaac** before he **died**. His mother, Rebekah, had died some years earlier. Three funerals are recorded in this chapter: that of Deborah, Rebekah's nurse (v.

8); of Rachel (v. 19); and of **Isaac** (v. 29).

9. The Descendants of Jacob's Brother Esau (Chap. 36)

36:1–30 Chapter 36 is devoted to the descendants **of Esau**, who dwelt in the land of **Edom**, southeast of the Dead Sea. **The genealogy** represents the fulfillment of the promise that Esau would be the head of a nation (25:23). Esau had three or possibly four wives, depending on whether some of the women had two names (compare 26:34; 28:9; 36:2, 3). In verse 24 **Anah** found **water** (or "hot springs," NASB).

36:31–43 Moses, the author of Genesis, knew by divine revelation (see 35:11) that Israel would eventually have **a king**. As seven generations of the ungodly line of Cain were given in chapter 4, so seven generations of kings in the ungodly line of Esau are mentioned here in verses 33–39. Seven, the number of completeness, probably indicates the entire line. Not one of Esau's descendants is mentioned in God's registry of the faithful; all are lost in the obscurity of those who depart from the living God. They had temporary riches and the passing fame of this world, but nothing for eternity.

D. Joseph (37:1—50:26)

1. Joseph Sold into Slavery (Chap. 37)

37:1–17 The words **"This is the history of Jacob"** seem abrupt. Jacob's history (chaps. 25—35) is interrupted by the generations of Esau (chap. 36), then continued from chapter 37 to the end of the book, with emphasis on Jacob's son, Joseph.

Joseph is one of the most beautiful types (symbols) of the Lord Jesus Christ in the OT, though the Bible

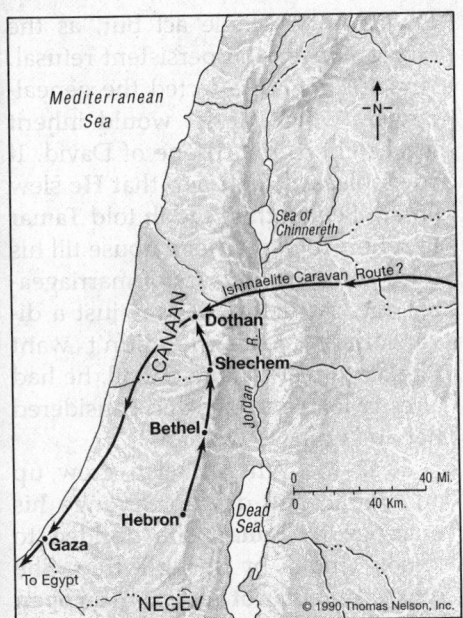

Joseph's Journey into Egypt

never labels him as a type. A. W. Pink lists 101 correspondences between Joseph and Jesus,[28] and Ada Habershon lists 121. For example, Joseph was **loved** by his father (v. 3); he rebuked the sin of his brothers (v. 2); he was **hated** by **his brothers** and sold into the hands of enemies (vv. 4, 26–28); he was punished unjustly (chap. 39); he was exalted and became the savior of the world, for all the world had to come to him for bread (41:57); he received a Gentile bride during his rejection by his brethren (41:45).

The **tunic of many colors** (or a long robe with sleeves, RSV) was a sign of his father's special affection, and it stirred up the jealous hatred of his brothers. In Joseph's first **dream,** eleven **sheaves** of grain **bowed down to** the twelfth **sheaf,** a prophecy that his brothers would one day bow down to him. In the next **dream, the sun, moon, and the eleven stars bowed down to** Joseph. The **sun** and **moon**

represented Jacob and Leah (Rachel had died), and **the eleven stars** were Joseph's **brothers** (vv. 9–11).

37:18–28 When Joseph was sent on an errand to his brothers, they **conspired . . . to kill him,** but at Reuben's suggestion they agreed to **cast him into a pit** near Dothan. As they sat down to eat, they saw **a company of Ishmaelites** bound for **Egypt,** and at Judah's suggestion decided to sell him. In this passage, the Ishmaelites are also called Midianites, as in Judges 8:22–24. As the **Midianite traders passed by,** Joseph's brothers brought Joseph **out of the pit and sold him to the** traders.

37:29–36 **Reuben** was absent when all this was taking place. When he **returned** he was terrified, since he would be responsible to explain Joseph's absence to his father. So the brothers **dipped** Joseph's **tunic in the blood** of a goat and then callously returned it to Jacob, who naturally assumed that Joseph had been killed. Jacob had once deceived his father with a goat, using the skin to impersonate his brother's hairy arms (27:16–23). Now he himself was cruelly deceived by the blood of a goat on Joseph's coat. "The pain of deceit is learned once again." **The Midianites** unwittingly fulfilled God's purposes by providing free transportation for Joseph to Egypt and selling him **to Potiphar, an officer of Pharaoh.** Thus God makes man's wrath to praise Him, and what will not praise Him, He restrains (see Ps. 76:10).

2. Judah and Tamar (Chap. 38)

38:1–11 The sordid story of Judah's sin with **Tamar** serves to magnify the grace of God when we remember that the Lord Jesus was descended from **Judah** (Luke 3:33). **Tamar** is one of five women mentioned in the genealogy in Matthew 1; three of them were guilty of immorality—Tamar, Rahab (v. 5), and Bathsheba (v. 6). The others are Ruth, a Gentile (v. 5) and Mary, a godly virgin (v. 16). Pink notes deeper meanings to this story of moral failure:

> Genesis 37 closes with an account of Jacob's sons selling their brother Joseph unto the Midianites, and they in turn selling him into Egypt. This speaks, in type, of Christ being rejected by Israel and delivered unto the Gentiles. From the time that the Jewish leaders delivered their Messiah into the hands of Pilate, they have as a nation had no further dealings with Him; and God, too, has turned from them to the Gentiles. Hence it is that there is an important turn in our type at this stage. Joseph is now seen *in the hands of the Gentiles.* But before we are told what happened to Joseph in Egypt, the Holy Spirit traces for us, in typical outline, the history of the Jews, while the antitypical Joseph is *absent from the land.*[29]

It is no accident that the story of Joseph is interrupted by chapter 38. The disreputable behavior of other members of Joseph's family makes his conduct, by contrast, shine like a bright light in a sordid world.

Judah's first mistake was in marrying a Canaanite woman, the **daughter of ... Shua**. She bore him three sons—**Er, Onan,** and **Shelah**. Er married a Canaanite woman named **Tamar**, but was slain by **the LORD** for some unspecified wickedness. It was the custom at that time for a brother or other near relative to marry the widow and raise children for the one who had died. **Onan** refused to do this because the first child born as a result would be the legal **heir** of Er, not his own legal child. His sin was not so much sexual as it was selfish.

It was not a single act but, as the Hebrew reveals, a persistent refusal. And the refusal affected the genealogy by which Christ would inherit legal right to the throne of David. It so displeased **the LORD** that **He** slew **Onan**. Seeing this, **Judah** told **Tamar** to return to her father's house till his third son, **Shelah**, was of marriageable age. Actually this was just a diversionary tactic. He didn't want **Shelah** to marry Tamar at all; he had already lost two sons and considered her an "unlucky woman."

38:12–23 When Shelah grew up and Judah still did not arrange his marriage to **Tamar**, she decided to "hook" Judah by laying a trap. She dressed as a **harlot** and **sat in an open place** on the road **to Timnah**, where Judah was going to join his **sheepshearers**. Sure enough, he went in and had illicit relations with her, not knowing it **was his** own **daughter-in-law**. The agreed fee was **a young goat from the flock**, but until he could send it to her, the "harlot" demanded Judah's **signet, cord, and staff**. The **cord** may have been the string by which the seal-ring was suspended. When Judah tried to deliver the kid and have the pledges returned, he couldn't find the "harlot."

38:24–26 Three months later, **Tamar** was accused of playing the **harlot** because she, a widow, was **with child**. **Judah** ordered her to be **burned**. At this point she returned the pledges with the announcement that their owner was the father of her expected **child**. They furnished positive proof that Judah had had sex with her. Walter C. Wright describes the scene vividly:

> The companions of Judah bring him word that his daughter-in-law, Tamar, has played the harlot. His judgment

is quick and decisive: let her be burned. There is neither hesitation nor compromise. As he utters this fearful sentence, we cannot detect even a tremor in his voice. The Israelitish society must be preserved from such folly and wickedness. The word goes out; the day is fixed; the preparations go forward; the stake is planted; the pile is arranged; the procession forms; the crowd gathers; the woman walks to her apparent doom. But she bears in her hands the tokens; the pledges are with her; she carries the staff and the ring. And the staff is the staff of Judah, and the ring is his ring! The pledges become the accusation of her judge. What weight will his sentence have now?[30]

38:27–30 **When** Tamar **was giving birth** and a baby's hand emerged, **the midwife** tied **a scarlet thread** on it, thinking that it would be born **first**. But the **hand** withdrew and another baby was the first to come forth. She named the firstborn **Perez** (*breakthrough*) and the other **Zerah**. Both **twins** are mentioned in Matthew 1:3, though the Messianic line goes through **Perez**. **Zerah** was an ancestor of Achan (Josh. 7:1). "It is simply astonishing" comments Griffith Thomas, "that God could take up the threads of this very tangled skein, and weave them into His own pattern."[31]

Judah's marriage to the Canaanite woman (v. 2) was a first step in the intermingling of God's people with a race that was proverbial for its gross immorality. Israel would become contaminated by the unspeakable enormities of lewd nature worship. God is a God of separation; when we fraternize with the world, we pay an awful price.

3. Joseph's Test and Triumph (Chap. 39)

39:1–19 The story now returns **to Egypt**, where **Joseph** was appointed **overseer** in the **house** of **Potiphar,** . . . **captain of the guard** in Pharaoh's palace. **The LORD was with** him and he became **a successful man** (Tyndale, in 1534, translated it, he was "a lucky fellow," v. 2). Potiphar's **wife** tried repeatedly to seduce Joseph, but he steadfastly **refused**. He would not betray his master's confidence or sin against his God. One day **she caught him by his garment**. He squirmed out of it **and fled,** leaving **her** holding it. He lost his coat but saved his character and eventually gained a crown. She used the coat as "evidence" that Joseph had attempted to rape her.

Believers are taught to flee fornication, idolatry, and youthful lusts. Better to flee than to fall.

39:20–23 Without proper investigation, **Joseph's master** ordered **him** to **prison**; but even there Joseph was blessed by the Lord and was given a position of responsibility. The fact that Joseph was not executed may indicate that Potiphar did not entirely believe his wife; he couldn't help knowing her true character. The truth of Romans 8:28 is wonderfully displayed in this chapter. God was working behind the scenes for Joseph. The latter resisted temptation and sought to avoid occasions for sin (vv. 8–10). Despite this, his would be seducer framed him. And so for a second time Joseph found himself in chains (Ps. 105:17–19). Under the circumstances he should have been upset. But he was not "under the circumstances"; he was above them and saw God's hand in them. His time in prison was "training time for reigning time." So things that were meant by others for evil turned out to be for good.

4. Joseph Interpreting the Butler's and Baker's Dreams (Chap. 40)

40:1–19 Among Joseph's fellow-prisoners were **the butler** (cupbearer) **and the baker of the king of Egypt** (vv. 1–4). When they each **had a dream**, **Joseph** offered to interpret them (vv. 5–8). The butler's **dream** of the **vine** meant that **Pharaoh** would **lift up** his **head** to a position of favor **in three days** (vv. 9–15). But the baker's **dream** of the **three white** cake **baskets** indicated that **within three days Pharaoh** would **lift off** his **head**—by hanging him (vv. 16–19).

Notice that Joseph did not wait for his circumstances to change. He glorified God and served others in the circumstances.

40:20–23 When **the chief butler** was released, he failed to intercede for Joseph, as he had promised (v. 23). But the Lord did not forget. "Remember me, when it is well with you" (v. 14). The Savior spoke similar words on the night of His betrayal, words which we can obey by taking the symbolic bread and wine.

5. Joseph Interpreting Pharaoh's Dreams (Chap. 41)

41:1–13 When none of **the magicians of Egypt** could interpret Pharaoh's **dreams** of the **seven fat** and **seven ugly and gaunt cows,** of the **seven plump and good ears** and **seven thin heads of grain,** then the chief butler remembered Joseph and his ability to interpret **dreams.** The **two full years** mentioned in verse 1 may refer either to the time of Joseph's imprisonment or the time since the chief butler's release.

41:14–32 Called before **Pharaoh, Joseph** explained that there would be **seven years of great plenty** in Egypt, followed by **seven years of famine** which would devastate the land. The repetition or duplication of Pharaoh's **dream** meant that it was **established by God and** that He would **shortly bring it to pass.** We see this also in Joseph's two dreams concerning his future (37:6–9) and in the similar visions of Daniel 2 and 7. In the Bible, *two* is the number of witness. Joseph gave the same reply to Pharaoh in the royal hall as he gave to his servants in the prison house. **"It is not in me; God will give . . . an answer of peace"** (v. 16; cf. 40:8). It is this humility that made it possible for the Lord to entrust Joseph with tremendous responsibility without fear that it would corrupt him.

41:33–36 Joseph counseled **Pharaoh** to set aside reserves of grain during the years of plenty so that there would be sufficient **during the famine** years. His plan was what has since been called "the ever-normal granaries."

41:37–46 Pharaoh was so pleased that he made Joseph second in command, appointed him to administer the program (v. 40), assured him that **without** his **consent** no one would do anything (v. 44), and gave him a new name, **Zaphnath-Paaneah** (v. 45a). The meaning of the name is uncertain. Some suggest *Savior of the world*; others say it probably means *God speaks and He lives.* He also gave **Asenath,** a Gentile, to be Joseph's **wife** (v. 45). How could Pharaoh set a Hebrew prisoner over the land of Egypt on the basis of a dream's interpretation without waiting to see if it was true? The answer is in Proverbs 21:1: "The king's heart is in the hand of the Lord." Cream rises to the surface. Joseph was the first of many godly Jews to rise to prominence in Gentile governments. He **was thirty years old when he** began this ministry (v.

46); it was thirteen years since he was sold by his brothers (cf. 37:2).

41:47–52 The abundance of the first **seven years** was so great that it was impossible to keep an accurate record. It was during those years that **two sons** were born to **Joseph—Manasseh** (*making to forget*) and **Ephraim** (*fruitful*). Forgetting the wrongs committed against him, Joseph became fruitful.

41:53–57 When **the seven years of famine came**, the starving people of **Egypt** and of **all the countries came to Joseph . . . to buy grain**. Here Joseph is a type (symbol) of Christ, through whom all the blessings of God are dispensed to the hungering people of this earth. It was the providence of God that brought Joseph to Egypt to save his people from famine, but it was also to isolate them from the moral pollution of the land of Canaan. Chapter 38 illustrates what was happening to the children of Israel in Canaan. God's remedy was to remove them to Egypt, where they would be virtually cut off from the heathen (43:32).

6. Joseph's Brothers in Egypt (Chaps. 42—44)

42:1–5 The scene switches back to **Jacob** in Canaan, where the famine was very severe. Hearing **that there was** plenty of food (**grain**) in **Egypt**, but knowing nothing of Joseph's being there, Jacob sent ten of **his sons** for supplies. Only **Benjamin** remained at home. So far as Jacob knew, Benjamin was the only living son of his beloved Rachel.

42:6–25 When **Joseph's brothers** appeared before him, he treated them **roughly**, accusing them of being **spies**, putting them **in prison**, then demanding that their **youngest brother**, Benjamin, be brought to him. At last,

Simeon was kept as a hostage in prison while the nine others returned to Canaan for Benjamin, well supplied with **grain**, with **provisions**, and with their **money** refunded secretly in the bags. Shining through the narrative we see Joseph's underlying love and compassion for his brothers (vv. 24a, 25) and their growing conviction of sin for what they had done to their "missing" brother over twenty years earlier (vv. 21, 22). Joseph, of course, was seeking to get them to confess their guilt.

We believe that Joseph is a *type* of Christ dealing with His Jewish brethren during the coming Tribulation Period. The events leading up to the reconciliation of Joseph's brothers form one of the most moving portions in the Bible. Almost no other story is as intimate, detailed, or complete a picture of Christ.

TYPOLOGY

Certain persons, events, and things in the OT are clearly identified as "types" (from the Gk. *tupoi*) or symbols in the NT. Thus, Adam is said to be a type of Christ (Rom. 5:14). Others are not specifically referred to as types, yet the parallels are too many and too obvious to be denied. Joseph, for instance, is never referred to as a type of the Lord Jesus, yet there are *over one hundred* correspondences between Jesus and Joseph.

When the Lord Jesus talked to the two sorrowing disciples on the road to Emmaus, "He expounded to them *in all the Scriptures* [emphasis supplied] the things concerning Himself" (Luke 24:27). The incarnate Christ said, "In the volume of the book it is written of Me. . . ." (Heb. 10:7). Therefore we are justified in looking for Christ in all the Scriptures.

Regarding Israel's experiences in

the OT, Paul tells us that "all these things happened to them as examples (Gk., *tupoi*), and they were written for our admonition, upon whom the ends of the ages have come" (1 Cor. 10:11). This would strongly support the view that not just specifically named types are valid, but many more as well.

Paul reminded Timothy that all Scripture is profitable (2 Tim. 3:16). There are spiritual lessons to be learned, if only we have eyes to see them.

Large sections of the Book of Hebrews are an explanation of the typology of the tabernacle and its furnishings. While it is true that a too narrow view of typology will restrict a believer's spiritual enjoyment of much of the OT, the other extreme of making virtually *everything* a type, or even turning all history into allegory, is to be avoided as well.

Strained or fanciful explanations of the types have brought disrepute on the subject. We should not allow extremism to rob us of the spiritual wealth in the OT. If an interpretation exalts Christ, and/or edifies His people, and/or conveys the gospel to the lost, and is consistent with the entire teaching of the Word, it is at the very least a valid *application* of the truth.‡

42:26–28 On the way home, one of the brothers found his **money** in **his sack**. This threw them into panic, making them fear they might be accused of theft (vv. 26–28).

42:29–38 When they got home and told their story, the rest of them also found their **money**, and their fears multiplied. Jacob was inconsolable. In spite of Reuben's offering the lives of his **two sons** as a guarantee, the patriarch feared to allow **Benjamin** to go to Egypt lest harm **befall him**.

43:1–15 Finally Jacob was forced by the severity of **the famine** to take action. The brothers could not return without Benjamin—that was the condition laid down by the governor, Joseph. So **Judah** agreed to serve as **surety** for Benjamin, and Jacob accepted the offer. In this one respect at least, Judah here reminds us of his descendant, the Lord Jesus, who became our Surety at the cross of Calvary. Jacob sent a **present** to the governor of Egypt, consisting of **balm, honey, gum, spices, myrrh, pistachio nuts, and almonds**—items not affected by the famine. He also insisted they take **double** the amount of **money** in case the refunded money was an **oversight**.

43:16–25 Joseph was deeply moved when he saw his brothers again, but he still did not reveal his identity. He ordered his servants to prepare a banquet. When his brothers were brought to Joseph's **house**, they thought they were on the carpet **because of the money** they found **in** their **sacks**. They made a complete explanation to the chief **steward**, and he in turn assured them there was nothing to worry about. His records showed that they had paid in full. **Simeon** was released from prison and joined them in preparation for the banquet. They got their father's **present ready** to give to Joseph when he arrived **at noon**.

If we ask whether the replaced money was in truth discovered *on the way back to Canaan* (42:27; 43:21) or *when they had arrived* in the presence of Jacob (42:35), the answer is *both*. The discovery was in two stages. One brother discovered his plight *en route*, the others *on arriving home*. It is understandable that in relating the events to Joseph's steward (43:21), a compressed account was given (*Daily Notes of the Scripture Union*).

43:26–34 When Joseph arrived, his brothers **bowed down before him** in fulfillment of his dream (37:7). He was overcome with emotion as he asked for the family and met **Benjamin**. At the banquet, he ate **by himself**; the eleven brothers were served separately; and the **Egyptians** likewise ate **by themselves**. The astonishment of the brothers was caused by their being seated **according to** their ages. How could anyone in Egypt know their order of birth? Special favor was shown to **Benjamin**, Joseph's own full brother.

44:1–13 When the brothers were leaving to return to Canaan, Joseph **commanded** his **silver cup** to be hidden in Benjamin's **sack**. It was not only the **cup** from which he drank, but also the one which he used in **divination**—probably referring to his interpretation of dreams.

Later God's people were forbidden to practice divination (Deut. 18:10–12). But even at this early date, it is unlikely that Joseph practiced the Egyptian forms of fortune-telling. His intuition and foresight came from the Lord, but perhaps by using the cup as a prop, he wished to confirm in his brothers' minds that he was an Egyptian.

Afterwards, when Joseph's brothers were accused of stealing the cup, they protested their innocence, rashly offering the life of anyone who was found with it. Joseph's steward agreed that the guilty one would be his slave. When the cup was found in **Benjamin's sack**, the brothers were crushed and **returned to the city**.

44:14–17 After Joseph had reproached them, **Judah** suggested that they all become his slaves, but Joseph said that Benjamin would do and the rest could return home. His action in hiding the silver cup in Benjamin's sack and in detaining Benjamin was purposely designed to bring his brothers to acknowledge their bloodguiltiness. George Williams writes:

> He acted so as to bring their sin to remembrance, to make them confess it with their own lips . . . . His detention of Simeon, and afterwards of Benjamin, was skillfully designed so as to find out if they were still indifferent to the cries of a captive brother and the tears of a bereaved father. His plan succeeded admirably; his sternness and his kindness both conspired to disquiet them; and his goodness helped to lead them to repentance.[32]

The whole scene foreshadows that coming day when the remnant of Israel will confess its guilt in connection with the death of the Messiah and will mourn for Him as one mourns for an only son (Zech. 12:10).

44:18–34 **Judah** stood **near** Joseph and gave a detailed review of Benjamin's involvement—how Joseph had demanded the presence of the youngest son, how their father, still grieving over the loss of one son, had protested against Benjamin's going to Egypt and how Judah had offered himself as **surety** for Benjamin's safety. Judah said that their **father** would **die** if the brothers went back without Benjamin, so he offered to stay in Egypt and serve **as a slave** in the place of Benjamin.

What a change had been worked in Judah! In chapter 37 he ruthlessly sold Joseph for profit, without concern for his father's heartbreak. In chapter 38 he was involved in deception and immorality. But God was working in his heart, so that in chapter 43 he became surety for Benjamin. Now in chapter 44 he pours out his heart in intercession before Joseph, offering himself as a slave so as not to bring upon his father the crushing sorrow of losing Benjamin. From selling his own brother into slavery to becoming a slave in his brother's stead; from callousness toward his father to sacrificial concern for his well-being—this is the progress of the grace of God in the life of Judah!

7. Joseph Reveals Himself to His Brothers (Chap. 45)

45:1–8 In one of the most moving scenes in all the Bible, Joseph ordered his staff to **go out** of the room while, with an enormous emotional release, he revealed his identity **to his brothers**. He told them not to grieve for the way they had treated him, because **God** had overruled it for good.

45:9–15 They were to **bring** their **father**, their households, and their possessions to **Goshen** in Egypt for the remaining **five years of famine**. "**Tell my father of all my glory in Egypt**"—a command we too can obey when we rehearse before God the glories of His beloved Son. The fountains of the great deep were broken up as **Joseph** embraced **Benjamin** and then **kissed all his brothers**.

This is a happy preview of the joy that awaits the people of Israel when the Christ of Calvary appears to them and reveals Himself as their Messiah-King.

45:16–24 When Pharaoh heard what was going on, he told **Joseph's brothers** to **bring** their **father** and families from Canaan, but not to bother bringing their heavy furniture and **goods** because he would provide everything they needed. So they went back to Canaan with wagons pro-

vided by Pharaoh, and with beautiful **garments**, animals, and provisions from Joseph. **Benjamin** got a gift of money and a special wardrobe. Fearing that his brothers might accuse each other for their guilt in mistreating him years earlier, Joseph warned them not to quarrel on their homeward journey.

45:25–28 On reaching home, they broke the news **to Jacob**. At first it was too much for him. But when he heard the full story and saw the loaded **carts**, he knew it was true—**Joseph** was **still alive** and they would meet again!

Joseph mentions his father five times in this chapter. This reveals his Christlikeness in addition to the free forgiveness he extended to his brothers. It was our Lord's love for His Father and His desire to do the Father's will that brought Him into the world to redeem fallen man. Joseph's love for Jacob is but a faint shadow of that love.

8. Joseph's Reunion with His Family (Chap. 46)

46:1-7 On the way to Egypt, **Israel** stopped the caravan at historic **Beersheba** to worship **the God of his father Isaac**. This was the place where God appeared to Abraham in connection with the offering of Isaac (21:31—22:2). It was also the place where the Lord appeared to Isaac (26:23, 24). Now He appears to **Jacob** to encourage him. This is the last of the Lord's seven appearances to him. The second promise of verse 4 seems to indicate that Jacob would return to Canaan. Actually, of course, he died in Egypt. But the promise was fulfilled in two ways. His body was taken back to Canaan for burial, and, in a sense, he also returned when his descendants went back in the days of

Joshua. The expression **"Joseph will put his hand on your eyes"** predicted a peaceful death. Atkinson explains the idiom beautifully:

> ...Joseph would close his father's eyes at the time of his death. Joseph would be with him when he died. Notice the personal promise graciously made to Jacob, which would compensate him for the long years of sorrow and mourning for Joseph. God cares for the personal needs of His servants (1 Pet. 5:7).[33]

And so **Jacob** reached **Egypt** with **all his descendants**, his **livestock**, and his personal **goods**.

46:8–27 In verses 8–27 we have the family register of **Jacob and his sons**. There were **sixty-six** family members (v. 26) who came **with Jacob to Egypt**. There are admitted difficulties in reconciling this figure with the **seventy** of verse 27 and of Exodus 1:5 and the seventy-five of Acts 7:14. The most obvious explanation is that the numbers expand from direct descendants to wider circles of relatives.

46:28–34 The epic meeting between **Israel** and **Joseph** took place in **Goshen**, the most fertile section of Egypt, near the delta of the Nile. Jacob and his sons preferred to stay there, since it provided the best pasture for their herds. It was agreed that they would **tell Pharaoh** that they were **shepherds**. Since shepherds were despised by **the Egyptians**, Pharaoh would let them live **in the land of Goshen**, far away from the royal palace. There in Goshen they were isolated from social intercourse with the Egyptians, first because of their nationality (43:32) and then because of their **occupation**. God left them in this incubator until they were a strong nation, able to possess the land that He promised to their forefathers.

9. Joseph's Family in Egypt (Chap. 47)

47:1–6 When **five** of Joseph's **brothers** told **Pharaoh** that they were **shepherds**, he responded, as expected, by telling them to settle in the lush pasturelands **of Goshen**. He also asked Joseph to find some **competent** men from among his relatives to tend the royal herds.

47:7–12 **Joseph** arranged for **his father**, then **one hundred and thirty**, to be presented to **Pharaoh**. The fact that **Jacob blessed Pharaoh** means that this aged, obscure Jew was greater than the potentate of Egypt, because the lesser is blessed by the greater (Heb. 7:7). Jacob said that his days had been **few and evil**. Actually he had brought *most* of the evil upon himself! **Joseph** settled his family in the best part of Egypt, and provided all they needed. Theirs was truly the more abundant life.

47:13–26 When the people **of Egypt** and Canaan had spent **all** their **money** for food, Joseph accepted their **livestock** in payment. Then later he **bought all the land**, except that belonging to the Egyptian **priests**, gave the people **seed** with which to plant crops, and charged them **one-fifth** of the crop for **land** rental, a very fair arrangement.

47:27–31 As **Israel** neared the end of his life, he made **Joseph** promise to **bury** him in Canaan. Then he bowed himself **on the head of** his **bed** (or "on the top of his staff," Heb. 11:21). Actually the same Hebrew consonants can be read either "bed" or "staff," depending on which vowels are supplied. The traditional Hebrew text reads **bed**, but here the Septuagint, quoted in the Hebrews passage, reads "staff." Kidner comments:

While both versions have "bed" at 48:2, the present occasion tells of Jacob before his last illness (*cf.* 48:1), and "staff" may well be the right meaning. It would be an appropriate object to mention as the symbol of his pilgrimage (*cf.* his grateful words in 32:10), worthy of the prominence it receives in the New Testament passage.[34]

And thus the ex-supplanter was to end his life in an act of worship. He is the only hero of faith of Hebrews 11 to be commended as a worshiper. He had come a long way by the grace of God, and would soon go out in a blaze of glory.

10. Jacob's Blessing of Joseph's Sons (Chap. 48)

48:1-7 When **Joseph was told** that his **father** was **sick**, he hurried to his bedside with **Ephraim** and **Manasseh**. The dying patriarch **sat up on the bed** and adopted his **two** grandsons as his own. By doing this he arranged that the tribe of Joseph would receive a double portion of the land of Canaan when it would be divided among the tribes years later. Joseph thus received the birthright as far as territory was concerned. Any **offspring** born to Joseph **after them** would be Joseph's, not Jacob's, and would dwell in the territories allotted to Ephraim or Manasseh. Verse 7 explains why Jacob wanted to adopt Joseph's sons as his own. They were his grandsons by his beloved wife, **Rachel**, who he felt had died so prematurely.

48:8-22 Then Jacob **blessed** the grandsons, giving the birthright to **Ephraim**, who was the younger. **Joseph** tried to correct this in favor of **Manasseh, the firstborn,** but Jacob said that he had done this intentionally. What memories must have gone through his mind as he, by faith,

gave the blessing to the **younger**. Years earlier his own father had unknowingly blessed him, the younger. But now he was blessing the younger, not through ignorance, but because he was in touch with the God who holds the future. Israel had faith that his descendants would one day return to the Promised **land**. Jacob gave Joseph a mountain slope which he captured from **the Amorites**. Perhaps this refers to the area containing the well that came to be known as "Jacob's well" (John 4:5).

11. Jacob's Prophecy Concerning His Sons (Chap. 49)

49:1, 2 Jacob's last words were both a *prophecy* (v. 1) and a *blessing* (v. 28).

49:3, 4 **Reuben**, as the **firstborn** son, represented the primacy of his father's manly **strength** in procreation, and held the place of **power** and **dignity**. The birthright, with its double portion, belonged to him. But he forfeited his preeminence because he boiled over with dark passion and sinned with Bilhah, his **father's** concubine (35:22).

49:5-7 Because these **brothers** had cruelly killed the men of Shechem and **hamstrung an ox, Simeon and Levi** would be dispersed **in Jacob** and scattered **in Israel**. By the time of the second census (Num. 26), these were the two smallest tribes. This dispersal was also fulfilled when the tribe of Simeon was largely absorbed by Judah (Josh. 19:1-9), and the tribe of Levi was assigned to 48 cities throughout the land. Jacob **cursed** their **cruel** deception but not the people of these two tribes themselves.

49:8-12 **Judah** (meaning **praise**) would be praised and respected by his **brothers** because of his victories over his **enemies**. He is likened to **a**

lion that goes forth to capture **prey,** then returns to well-deserved rest that no one dares disturb. Just as Joseph inherited the birthright with regard to territory, so Judah inherited it with regard to government. Rulership would continue in this tribe till **Shiloh** (the Messiah) came, and in **Him** it would remain forever. His **people** would give Him willing **obedience** in the day of His power. The meaning of the name **"Shiloh"** is obscure. Some suggested meanings are: *Prince of peace, tranquil, seed* (of Judah), *his descendant, whose it is* (cf. Ezek. 21:27).

49:13 Zebulun would enjoy prosperity from maritime commerce. Since this tribe's territory in OT times was landlocked, this prophecy may look forward to the Millennium.

49:14, 15 Issachar is likened to **a strong donkey,** so content to **rest** in **pleasant** pastoral surroundings that it had no will to fight for independence and so became subject to the enemy's yoke.

49:16–18 Dan, true to the tribe's name, would concern itself with judging the **people.** Verse 17 is difficult. It may allude to Dan's introducing the idolatry which caused the nation's **fall** (Judg. 18:30, 31). Many think that it is a veiled reference to the Antichrist's springing from **Dan,** and that this is why this tribe goes unmentioned in 1 Chronicles 2:3—8:40 and Revelation 7:3–8. In verse 18, Jacob injects a prayer for the final deliverance of his people from their foes or for his own deliverance.

49:19 Gad, unprotected in its territory east of the Jordan, would be subjected to frequent enemy raids. But the tribe would trample the troops of its foes.

49:20 Happily for **Asher** (*happy*), this tribe would have fertile agricul-tural land, producing delicacies fit for a king.

49:21 Naphtali is likened to a doe that has been released from confinement. It springs forth with tremendous speed to carry good news. All the disciples except the traitor came from the territory of **Naphtali,** and much of the Lord's ministry was there (Matt. 4:13–16).

49:22–26 Compassing the territories of Ephraim and Manasseh, **Joseph is a fruitful bough,** sending out blessing far beyond his own borders. He was the object of bitter hostility but he did not yield, because he was strengthened by **the Mighty God of Jacob**—the One from whom **the Shepherd, the Stone of Israel** (that is, the Messiah) comes forth. God blesses Joseph with rain in abundance, wells and gushing springs, and numerous progeny. Jacob humbly felt that he had been blessed more richly than his **ancestors.** Now he wishes that such **blessings** might come to **Joseph,** the one **who was separate from his brothers**.

49:27 Benjamin, a tribe of fighters, would continually conquer and **divide the spoil.** Someone has said that Benjamin proved himself the most spirited and warlike of all the tribes.

49:28–33 In closing, Jacob instructed his sons to **bury** him in the **cave . . . of Machpelah,** near his home in Hebron, the burial place of **Abraham and Sarah, Isaac and Rebekah,** and **Leah.** Then **he drew** himself back **into the bed and breathed his last.**

12. *Death of Jacob and Then of Joseph in Egypt (Chap. 50)*

50:1–14 Even **the Egyptians mourned for . . . seventy days** when Jacob died. His body was **embalmed** by the palace **physicians.** Then **Pharaoh** gave Joseph permission to accompany the body back to Canaan, with a great procession of officials, relatives, and servants. They stopped east of **the Jordan** and mourned for **seven days** so deeply that **the Canaanites . . . called** the place **Abel Mizraim**, the meadow (or **mourning**) of Egypt. Following the burial in the **cave . . . of Machpelah** at Hebron, **Joseph and his** entourage **returned to Egypt**.

50:15–21 Now that Jacob **was dead, Joseph's brothers** feared that he might seek vengeance on them, **They sent** word **to** him, claiming that their **father** Jacob had left word that **Joseph** should **forgive** them. Joseph disclaimed any intent to seek revenge or to judge, since that was God's prerogative. He further relieved their fears with the memorable words, **"You meant evil against me, but God meant it for good. . . ."**

50:22–26 Joseph was apparently the first of the twelve sons of Jacob to die. This was fifty-four years after his father's death. His faith that God would take the people of Israel back to Canaan is eulogized in Hebrews 11:22. He gave instructions that his **bones** be buried in that land.

It has been pointed out that Genesis opens with God's perfect creation and closes with **a coffin in Egypt**. It is a book of biographies. Whereas two chapters are devoted to an account of the creation of the heavens and earth, forty-eight chapters are largely concerned with the lives of men and women. God is interested primarily in people. What a comfort and challenge to those who know Him!

ENDNOTES

[1](Intro) Anton Hartmann (1831). See Merrill F. Unger, *Introductory Guide to the Old Testament*, p. 244.

[2](Intro) See, e.g., Gleason Archer, *Archaeology and the Old Testament*.

[3](1:2) Others put the catastrophe *before* v. 1 and see v. 1 as a summary statement.

[4](1:2) However, the Hebrew verb *hayah* usually is followed by the preposition *le* when it means "become," and that is not the case here.

[5](2:15–23) Hebrew has only two tenses (plus participles): perfect and imperfect. Context determines the precise verb form that is best in translating into English.

[6](3:7–13) C. H. Mackintosh, *Genesis to Deuteronomy*, p. 33.

[7](3:22–24) Merrill F. Unger, *Unger's Bible Dictionary*, p. 192.

[8](4:7) Mackintosh, *Genesis to Deuteronomy*, p. 42.

[9](4:7) F. W. Grant, "Genesis," *The Numerical Bible*, I:38.

[10](5:25–32) George Williams, *The Student's Commentary on the Holy Scriptures*, p. 12.

[11](6:4, 5) Unger, *Bible Dictionary*, p. 788.

[12](11:26–32) Derek Kidner, *Genesis*, p. 112.

[13](15:7–21) David Baron, *The New Order of the Priesthood*, pp. 9–10 footnote.

[14](16:7–15) F. Davidson, *The New Bible Commentary*, p. 90.

[15](Excursus) Bennett J. Sims, "Sex and Homosexuality," *Christianity Today*, February 24, 1978, p. 29.

[16](22:16–19) Charles F. Pfeiffer, *The Book of Genesis*, p. 6.

[17](24:1–9) *Ibid.*, p. 62.

[18](24:10–14) Murdoch Campbell, *The Loveliest Story Ever Told*, p. 9.

[19](25:29–34) D. L. Moody, *Notes From My Bible*, p. 23.

[20](26:1–6) The word *dwell* in v. 3 is a different verb in Hebrew from that in verse 6 and suggests a less settled stay.

[21](26:26–33) Williams, *Student's Commentary*, p. 31.

[22](27:1–22) Martin Luther, further documentation unavailable.

[23](27:1–22) Mackintosh, *Genesis to Deuteronomy*, p. 114.

[24](28:10–19) H. D. M. Spence and J. S. Exell, "Genesis," in *The Pulpit Commentary*, pp. 349–50.

[25](31:1–18) W. H. Griffith Thomas, *Genesis: A Devotional Commentary*, p. 288.

[26](31:19–21) Unger, *Bible Dictionary*, p. 550.

[27](32:22–32) Pfeiffer, *Genesis*, p. 80.

[28](37:1–17) Arthur W. Pink, *Gleanings in Genesis*, pp. 343–408.

[29](38:1–11) Ibid., pp. 343–408.

[30](38:24–26) Walter C. Wright, *Psalms*, II:27.

[31](38:27–30) Griffith Thomas, *Genesis*, p. 366.

[32](44:14–17) Williams, *Student's Commentary*, p. 39.

[33](46:1–7) Basil F. C. Atkinson, *The Pocket Commentary of the Bible, The Book of Genesis*, p. 405.

[34](47:27–31) Kidner, *Genesis*, p. 212.

BIBLIOGRAPHY

Atkinson, Basil F. C. *The Pocket Commentary of the Bible. The Book of Genesis.* Chicago: Moody Press, 1957.

Campbell, Murdoch. *The Loveliest Story Ever Told.* Inverness: Highland Printers Ltd., 1962.

Grant, F. W. *Genesis in the Light of the New Testament.* New York: Loizeaux Bros. Inc., n.d.

———. "Genesis." In *The Numerical Bible*, Vol. 1. Neptune, NJ: Loizeaux Brothers, 1977.

Keil, C. F. and Delitzsch, F. "Genesis." In *Biblical Commentary on the Old Testament*, Vol. 3. Grand Rapids: Wm. B. Eerdmans Publishing Company, 1971.

Kidner, Derek. *Genesis.* The Tyndale Old Testament Commentaries. Downers Grove, IL: InterVarsity Press, 1973.

Pfeiffer, Charles F. *The Book of Genesis.* Grand Rapids: Baker Book House, 1976.

Pink, Arthur W. *Gleanings in Genesis.* Chicago: Moody Press, 1922.

Ross, Allen P. "Genesis." In *The Bible Knowledge Commentary.* Wheaton: Victor Books, 1985.

Spence, H. D. M., and Exell, J. S. "Genesis." In *The Pulpit Commentary, Genesis.* New York: Funk and Wagnalls, n.d.

Thomas, W. H. Griffith. *Genesis: A Devotional Commentary.* Grand Rapids: Wm. B. Eerdmans Publishing Co., 1973.

Yates, Kyle M., Sr. "Genesis." In *The Wycliffe Bible Commentary.* Chicago: Moody Press, 1968.

BIBLIOGRAPHY

Atkinson, Basil F. C. *The Pocket Commentary of the Bible: The Book of Genesis*. Chicago: Moody Press, 1957.

Campbell Murdoch. *The Obedient Story: Far Hills Inverness*. Baptist and First Inverness, 1952.

EXODUS

Introduction

"To those who see theology as essentially the recital of the saving acts of God, Exodus 1—15 gives the supreme example, around which the rest of the biblical narrative can be assembled. To those who see the Old Testament as the product of the worshipping life of the community, at the heart of the book of Exodus lies the account of the institution of the passover, greatest and most characteristic of Israel's festivals . . . To those who see God's tôrâ, His law, as central to the life and thinking of later Israel, Exodus enshrines the law giving and contains the very kernel of the law in the form of the ten commandments."

—R. Alan Cole

I. Unique Place in the Canon

Exodus (*the way out* in Greek) picks up the narrative of the Israelites after the death of Joseph. The foundations of the Jewish religion in the Passover are rooted in Israel's escape from four centuries of slavery in Egypt—but only after stubborn Pharaoh has defied the God of the Hebrews and has had to suffer ten dreadful plagues on his nation, the Bible's picture of the world.

The narrative of the Red Sea crossing, many other marvelous miracles, the giving of the law on Mount Sinai, and the detailed instructions for the tabernacle complete this wonderful book.

II. Authorship

We hold to the traditional Jewish and Christian view that The Second Book of Moses, like the rest of the Pentateuch, is actually by Moses. For a defense of this position see Introduction to the Pentateuch.

III. Date

Bible scholars have set the date of the Exodus from Egypt as early as 1580 B.C. and as late as 1230 B.C. First Kings 6:1 says that the Exodus took place 480 years previous to Solomon's starting to build the temple. Since this was about 960 B.C. it would place the Exodus at 1440 B.C., the more conservative date. Many scholars maintain that archaeology better supports a later date (c. 1290 B.C.) but other archaeological finds seem to fit the early date. We cannot be sure of the exact date, of course, but all things considered, the early date of 1440 for the Exodus event, and the somewhat later date for the Book of Exodus, seems best.

IV. Background and Theme

As Exodus opens we find the Israelites in Egypt where we left them at the end of Genesis. But the *background*

85

has changed completely. It is over four centuries later; the once-favored Hebrews are now slaves, making bricks for Pharaoh's vast building programs.

The *themes* of Exodus are *redemption* and the founding of *the nation of Israel*. For over 3,400 years Jews the world over have celebrated this event— the escape from Egypt by power and by blood, and the beginnings of the people of Israel as an actual nation—in the Passover.

The Christian Lord's Supper, also celebrating the redemption of God's people by power and blood, grows out of the Passover, both historically and theologically. To a certain extent, the bread and wine of the communion hark back to the same elements in the Passover ritual.

After the Exodus from Egypt, the scene changes to the wilderness, where Moses receives God's Law for His people. Nearly half of the book concerns the tabernacle and its priesthood (chaps. 25—40). These details are not merely historical.

To really enjoy the book of Exodus, we need to look for Christ in it. Moses, the Passover lamb, the rock, and the tabernacle are only a few of the types (symbols) of the Lord Jesus, many of which are referred to elsewhere in Scripture (see, for example, 1 Cor. 5:7; 10:4; Heb. chaps. 3—10). May the Lord do for us what He did for the two disciples on the road to Emmaus—interpret to us "in all the Scriptures the things concerning Himself" (Luke 24:27).

OUTLINE

I. ISRAEL'S BONDAGE IN EGYPT (Chap. 1)

II. THE BIRTH, RESCUE, AND TRAINING OF MOSES (Chap. 2)

III. THE CALL OF MOSES (Chaps. 3, 4)

   A. The Revelation of Jehovah to Moses (Chap. 3)

   B. The Reluctance of Moses (4:1–17)

   C. The Return of Moses to Egypt (4:18–31)

IV. MOSES' CONFRONTATIONS WITH PHARAOH (5:1—7:13)

   A. The First Confrontation (5:1—7:6)

   B. The Second Confrontation (7:7–13)

V. THE FIRST NINE PLAGUES (7:14—10:29)

   A. The First Plague—The Nile Turned to Blood (7:14–25)

   B. The Second Plague—Frogs (8:1–15)

   C. The Third Plague—Lice (8:16–19)

   D. The Fourth Plague—Flies (8:20–32)

   E. The Fifth Plague—Pestilence on Livestock (9:1–7)

   F. The Sixth Plague—Boils (9:8–12)

   G. The Seventh Plague—Hail and Fire (9:13–35)

   H. The Eighth Plague—Locusts (10:1–20)

   I. The Ninth Plague—Three Days of Darkness (10:21–29)

6. The Gifted Artisans (31:1–11)
7. The Sign of the Sabbath (31:12–18)
D. An Outbreak of Idolatry (Chaps. 32, 33)
1. The Golden Calf (32:1–10)
2. The Intercession and Anger of Moses (32:11–35)
3. The Repentance of the People (33:1–6)
4. Moses' Tent of Meeting (33:7–11)
5. The Prayer of Moses (33:12–23)
E. The Covenant Renewed (34:1—35:3)
F. Preparation of the Tabernacle Furnishings (35:4—38:31)
1. The People's Gifts and the Gifted People (35:4—36:7)
2. The Curtains Covering the Tabernacle (36:8–19)
3. The Boards for the Three Sides (36:20–30)
4. The Bars Which Held the Boards Together (36:31–34)
5. The Veil Leading to the Most Holy Place (36:35, 36)
6. The Screen Leading to the Holy Place (36:37, 38)
7. The Ark of the Covenant (37:1–5)
8. The Mercy Seat (37:6–9)
9. The Table of Showbread (37:10–16)
10. The Golden Lampstand and Its Accessories (37:17–24)
11. The Altar of Incense (37:25–28)
12. The Anointing Oil and the Incense (37:29)
13. The Altar of Burnt Offering (38:1–7)
14. The Laver (38:8)
15. The Outer Court, Pillars, and Screen (38:9–31)
G. Preparation of the Priests' Garments (Chap. 39)
H. Erection of the Tabernacle (Chap. 40)

Commentary

I. ISRAEL'S BONDAGE IN EGYPT (Chap. 1)

1:1–8 The first words of the book, **"Now these are the names"** (Heb., *weēlleh shemôth*), constitute the title of Exodus in the Jewish tradition. How personal God is! Not numbers or notches in a computer card, but **names**. Jesus said of the Good Shepherd, "He calls his own sheep by name and leads them out" (John 10:3). This is very fitting here. The Israelites came down to Egypt as shepherds—but now they are slaves. But God, the Good Shepherd, has plans "to lead them out."

For explanations of the **seventy persons who were descendants of Jacob**, see the notes on Genesis 46:8–27. The **seventy** people had multiplied to a few million, including 603,550 men of war, by the time the Jewish people were ready to leave Sinai for Canaan (Num. 1:46). Verses 6 and 7 indicate that many years elapsed between the end of Genesis and the events of Exodus. The mean-

ing of verse 8 is that **a new king
. . . arose** who **did not** *look with approval on* the descendants of **Joseph**; Joseph himself was already dead, of course.

1:9–10 The Israelites had so increased in number and in power that the Pharaoh thought they would pose a threat in time of war, so he decided to make slaves of the people and to destroy every male child and thus eventually wipe out the Hebrew race. Three evil rulers in Scripture ordered the slaughter of innocent children: Pharaoh, Athaliah (2 Kgs. 11), and Herod (Matt. 2). These satanically inspired atrocities were aimed at the extinction of the messianic line. Satan had never forgotten God's promise in Genesis 3:15.

1:11–14 **Pharaoh** used the enslaved Jews to build the **supply cities** of **Pithom and Raamses**. But instead of being wiped out by his repression, **they multiplied** all the more! Pharaoh meant the **hard bondage** for evil, but God meant it for good. It helped prepare the Jews for their arduous journey from Egypt to the Promised Land.

1:15–19 When **Shiphrah and . . . Puah**, who were probably the chief **Hebrew midwives**, saw the Jewish mothers bearing children **on the birthstools**, they did not kill the male children, as **Pharaoh** had ordered. They excused their inaction by explaining that the **Hebrew** children were usually born too quickly—that is, **before the midwives could** get to the mothers. This assertion probably had some truth to it.

1:20–22 *The Daily Notes of the Scripture Union* comment on the midwives:

The reward given to the midwives in terms of a flourishing family life (v. 21) was granted them not for their falsehood but for their humanity. This is not to say that the end justified the means, still less that there are no absolute standards of morality. But in a world as charged with sin and its effects as ours has become, it may be that obedience to greater duties is possible only at the cost of obedience to lesser ones. In this as in all else, "the fear of the Lord is the beginning of wisdom."

Foiled by the Hebrew midwives, **Pharaoh** now **commanded his** own **people** to enforce the decree.

II. THE BIRTH, RESCUE, AND TRAINING OF MOSES (Chap. 2)

2:1, 2 The **man of the house of Levi** in verse 1 was Amram, and the **daughter of Levi** was Jochebed (6:20). Thus both of Moses' parents were of the priestly tribe of **Levi**. By faith Moses' parents **hid him** for **three months** (Heb. 11:23). This must mean that they received some revelation that he was a child of destiny, because faith must be based on some revealed word of God.

2:3–8 Jochebed's **ark**, like Noah's, is a picture of Christ. Moses' **sister** was Miriam (Num. 26:59). This chapter is full of seeming coincidences. For example, why did Pharaoh's **daughter** happen to **bathe** right where the ark was floating? Why did **the baby** happen to cry and thus draw out her **compassion**? Why was Moses' **mother** accepted by **Pharaoh's daughter** as his **nurse**?

2:9, 10 Christian parents should take the words of verse 9 as a sacred charge and an unfailing promise. In Egyptian, **"Moses,"** the **name** given

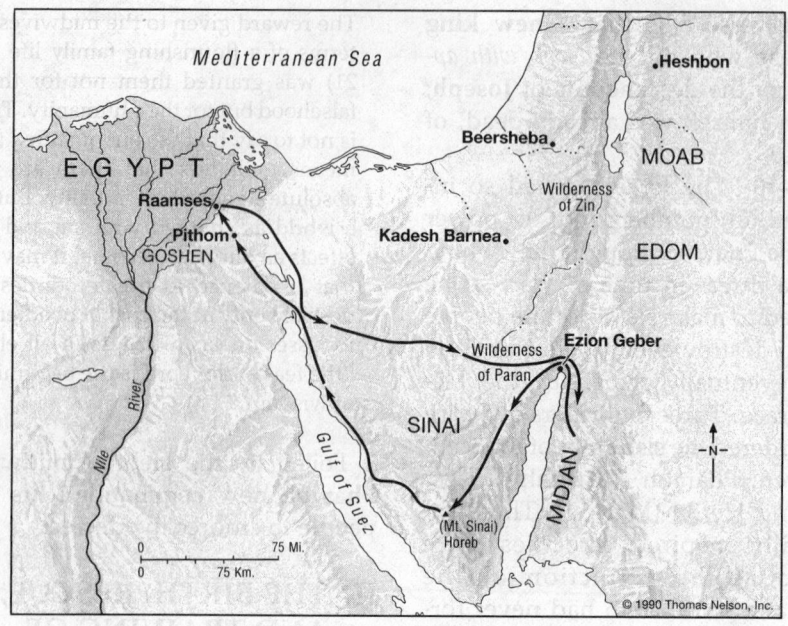

Moses' Flight & Return to Egypt

by **Pharaoh's daughter**, probably means *child* or *son*. In Hebrew the same name means *drawn out*—i.e., drawn out of the water.[1] Mackintosh remarks with his usual insight:

> The devil was foiled by his own weapon, inasmuch as Pharaoh, whom he was using to frustrate the purpose of God, is used of God to nourish and bring up Moses, who was to be His instrument in confounding the power of Satan.[2]

2:11, 12 We know from Acts 7:23 that **Moses** was forty years old when he visited **his** own people. His killing **the Egyptian** was ill-advised; his zeal outran his discretion. God would one day use Moses to deliver his people from the Egyptians, but the time had not yet come. First he must spend forty years on the back side of the desert, learning in the school of God. God had predicted that His people would be in the land of Egypt as slaves for 400 years (Gen. 15:13), so

Moses' actions were forty years premature. He needed more training in the solitude of the desert. And the people needed more training in the brickkiln. The Lord orders all things according to His infinite wisdom. He is not in a hurry, but neither will He leave His people in affliction one moment longer than necessary.

2:13–15a When he went out the second day Moses tried to break up a fight between **two Hebrew men**, but they rejected his leadership, as the Hebrews were later to reject One greater than Moses. When he found out they knew he had **killed the Egyptian**, Moses panicked. **When Pharoah heard** about the killing, he sought to kill Moses, so **Moses fled** to **the land of Midian**—that is, Arabia or the Sinai area.

2:15b–22 At a well in Midian, **Moses helped the seven daughters** of the **priest of Midian** against some surly **shepherds**, and watered their flocks. This **priest of Midian** is given two names—Jethro (3:1) and **Reuel**

(v. 18), which is the same as Raguel (Num. 10:29; NKJV marg.; LXX). The Midianites were distant relatives of the Hebrews (Gen. 25:2). Jethro's **daughter**, **Zipporah**, became Moses' wife, and **a son, . . . Gershom** (meaning *stranger there*), was born to them.

2:23–25 **God** was not oblivious to the plight of His people. When a new **king** ascended to the throne, **God heard** and **remembered** and **looked upon the children of Israel** and **acknowledged** their condition. His response was to bring His servant back to Egypt (chap. 3) to lead His people out of that land in the mightiest display of power since the creation of the world.

III. THE CALL OF MOSES (Chaps. 3, 4)

A. The Revelation of Jehovah to Moses (Chap. 3)

3:1–4 In **tending the flock of Jethro**, **Moses** learned valuable lessons about leading God's people. When he went to **Horeb** (Mount Sinai), the Lord appeared to him in **a bush** that burned **with fire but . . . was not consumed**. The **bush** suggests the glory of God, before which he was told to stand with unshod **feet**. It might also foreshadow Jehovah's dwelling in the midst of His people without their being consumed. And some have even seen in it the destiny of Israel, tried in the fires of affliction but **not consumed**. We should all be like the **burning . . . bush**—burning for God, yet **not consumed**.[3]

3:5 The Lord promised Moses that He would deliver His people from Egypt and bring them into a land of abundance—that is, Canaan—inhabited by the six heathen nations listed in verse 8. The word **"holy"** occurs here for the first time in the Bible. By

removing his **sandals**, Moses acknowledged that **the place** was **holy**.

3:6 God reassures Moses that He is the **God** of his forefathers—**Abraham** and **Isaac** and **Jacob**. Cole shows the importance of this revelation:

Moses brings no new or unknown god to his people, but a fuller revelation of the One whom they have known. Not even Paul's words to the Athenians on the Areopagus are a fair parallel here (Acts 17:23). The only true parallel is the continuing Self-revelation made by God in later centuries, culminating in the coming of Christ. Yet in its day the Mosaic revelation, while a fulfilment of patriarchal promises, was as new and shattering to Israel as the coming of the Messiah was later to prove to be.[4]

3:7–12 Moses protested God's sending him **to Pharaoh**, citing his own inadequacy. But the Lord assured Moses of His presence and promised that he would yet **serve God on this mountain** (Mount Sinai) with a liberated people. J. Oswald Sanders remarks:

His inventory of disqualifications covered lack of capability (3:11), lack of message (3:13), lack of authority (4:1), lack of eloquence (4:10), lack of special adaptation (4:13), lack of previous success (5:23), and lack of previous acceptance (6:12). A more complete list of disabilities would be difficult to conjure up. But instead of pleasing God, his seeming humility and reluctance stirred His anger. "The anger of the Lord was kindled against Moses" (4:14). In point of fact, the excuses Moses advanced to show his incapacity were the very reasons for God's selection of him for the task.[5]

3:13, 14 Moses anticipated questions from the children of Israel when he returned **to them** as the Lord's spokesman, and he wanted to be able to tell them who sent him. It was at this point that God first revealed Himself as Jehovah, the great I AM. Jehovah (more precisely Yahweh) comes from the Hebrew verb "to be," *hāyāh*. This sacred name is known as the *tetragrammaton* ("four letters"). English *Jehovah* comes from the Hebrew *YHWH*, with vowel markings supplied from Elohim and Adonai, other names of God. No one knows for sure the true pronunciation of *YHWH* because the ancient Hebrew spelling used no actual vowels in its alphabet. However, the pronunciation "Yahweh" is probably correct. The Jews consider *YHWH* too sacred to utter. The name proclaims God as self-existent, self-sufficient, eternal,[6] and sovereign. The fuller name I AM WHO I AM may mean I AM BECAUSE I AM or I WILL BE THAT I WILL BE.

3:15–22 Fortified by this revelation that God was really present and ready to come to His people's aid, Moses was told to announce to the people of Israel that they would soon be free. Also, he was to test Pharaoh by requesting that the Israelites be allowed to travel **three days' journey** to **sacrifice to the LORD**. This was not an attempt to deceive but a minimal test of Pharaoh's willingness. It would also prevent the Egyptians from witnessing the slaying of animals that were sacred to them. God knew that Pharaoh wouldn't yield until compelled by divine power. The **wonders** of verse 20 are the plagues that God sent on **Egypt**. By the time God was finished with them, the Egyptians would be glad to give the Jewish women anything they asked! The wealth thus accumulated would only be just compensation for all the slave labor of the Jews under the taskmasters of Egypt. The Israelites did not

"borrow" jewels and clothing (as in the KJV); they "asked" for them (NKJV). No deceit was involved—only the just payment of wages.

B. The Reluctance of Moses (4:1–17)

4:1–9 Moses continued to doubt that the people would accept him as a spokesman of God. Maybe the disillusionment of 2:11–15 had eaten deep into his soul. Therefore God gave him three signs, or miracles, to confirm his divine commission. (1) His **rod**, thrown on the ground, **became a serpent**. Taken **by the tail**, the serpent **became a rod again**. (2) **His hand**, placed **in his bosom**, became **leprous**. The same **hand**, placed **in his bosom again**, became free of leprosy. (3) **Water** of the Nile, poured out on the land, became **blood**.

These signs were designed to convince the people of Israel that Moses was sent by God. They spoke of God's power over Satan (i.e., the **serpent**), and sin (pictured by the **leprosy**) and of the fact that Israel would be redeemed from both of these through **blood**.

4:10–17 Moses was still reluctant to obey the LORD, excusing himself because he was **not eloquent**. After reminding Moses that the Lord **made man's mouth**, and therefore could make him eloquent, God appointed **Aaron**, Moses' **brother**, to **speak** for him. Moses should have obeyed the Lord in simple dependence, knowing that His commands are His enablements. God never asks us to do anything without giving us the power to do it. Because Moses was not satisfied with God's best, he had to take God's second best—that is, having Aaron as his spokesman. Moses thought that Aaron would be a help, but he later proved to be a hindrance in leading the people to worship the golden calf (chap. 32).

C. The Return of Moses to Egypt (4:18–31)

4:18–23 Forty years after fleeing to Midian, Moses returned to Egypt at God's command and with Jethro's blessing. His wife and sons were **Zipporah**, **Gershom**, and **Eliezer** (18:2–4). The staff in verse 2 becomes **the rod of God** in verse 20. The Lord uses ordinary objects to do extraordinary things so that it can be plainly seen that the power is from God. The **wonders** which God commanded Moses to perform **before Pharaoh** were the plagues that followed. God hardened Pharaoh's **heart**, but only after that despotic ruler had first hardened his own heart. **"Firstborn"** sometimes refers to the order in physical birth, but here it means a position of honor normally held by the firstborn son, the inheritor of the birthright. Pharaoh was forewarned that if he did not obey, God would slay his **son**.

4:24–26 But before Moses could deliver the message, he had to learn obedience himself. He had failed to circumcise his own son (Gershom or Eliezer), possibly because of Zipporah's opposition. When God threatened **to kill** Moses, perhaps by serious illness, Zipporah angrily circumcised the son and secured her husband's release. She called him a **"husband (or "bridegroom," NASB) of blood."** This incident, plus Zipporah's apparent lack of faith in the Lord, may have been the reason why Moses sent Zipporah home to her father with her two sons (18:2, 3).

4:27–31 **Aaron** came out to meet Moses as he returned to Egypt. They both stood before the people of Israel, delivered the Lord's message, and confirmed it with the three **signs** which the Lord had given. **So the people believed** and **worshiped** the Lord.

IV. MOSES' CONFRONTATIONS WITH PHARAOH (5:1—7:13)

A. The First Confrontation (5:1–7:6)

5:1 In 3:18 God had told Moses to take the elders when he went before Pharaoh. In the meantime, the Lord had appointed Aaron as Moses' spokesman (4:14–16). So **Aaron went with Moses** in place of the elders. The Lord's message was unequivocal: **"Let My people go."**

5:2–14 When Moses and Aaron delivered their first ultimatum to Pharaoh, he accused them of distracting **the people from their work**. Also, he changed their work load by insisting that henceforth they would have to **gather** their own **straw** for making **bricks**, yet produce the same **quota** as **before**. Pharaoh was making an impossible situation for the Jews, reminding one of the Nazi treatment of the Jews in the concentration camps. They had to go **throughout all the land of Egypt to gather stubble instead of straw**. The Hebrew text indicates the contempt with which these repressed people were treated. Cole points out that stubble is a poor substitute for straw since it is rough and uneven.[7]

5:15–23 Until now the straw had been provided for the Israelites. It was used to reinforce the bricks, and to keep them from sticking to the forms in which they were made. When the Jewish foremen were **beaten**, they protested **to Pharaoh** but received no consideration. Then they blamed **Moses and Aaron**, and Moses in turn blamed **the Lord**. Opposition from *within* the ranks of God's people is often harder to bear than persecution from *without*.

6:1–12 **The Lord** graciously answered Moses' petulant speech first by assuring him that **Pharaoh** would **let** the Israelites **go** because he would be compelled by God's **strong hand**. Then He reminded Moses that He had revealed Himself to the patriarchs as El-Shaddai or **God Almighty**, not primarily as Jehovah (*NKJV* "LORD"), the personal name of the covenant-keeping God. The thought here seems to be that He would now reveal Himself as Lord in a new way— that is, in new power in delivering His people. He had made a covenant and was about to fulfill it by freeing the Israelites from Egypt and bringing them **into the** Promised Land. Notice the seven "I will's" in verses 6–8. The name "Jehovah" (or "LORD") had been used before, but now it took on new significance. Notice twenty-five personal pronouns used by God in these verses, emphasizing what He had done, was doing, and would do. Moses seems to have missed the point, being still occupied with his own inadequacy. After further reassurance, he did obey the word of the Lord (chap. 7). **"Uncircumcised lips"** in verse 12 and 30 means faltering speech. Moses did not consider himself a great speaker.

6:13–30 The genealogies in verses 14–25 are limited to **Reuben**, **Simeon**, and **Levi**, the first three sons born to Jacob. The author did not want to give a complete genealogy but only to trace the line to **Moses and Aaron**. So he quickly passed over Reuben and Simeon to come to the priestly tribe.

7:1–5 At the close of chapter 6, Moses wondered why the mighty Pharaoh would listen to such a poor speaker as he. The Lord's answer was that Moses stood before **Pharaoh** as a representative of **God**. Moses would speak to Aaron, and **Aaron** would convey the message to **Pharaoh. Pharaoh** would **not heed**, but

God would deliver His people anyway!

7:6 Moses and **Aaron** were **eighty** and **eighty-three years old** respectively when their great ministry of deliverance began. Even in what today would be called "old age," God can use men and women for His glory.

B. The Second Confrontation (7:7–13)

Pharaoh was forewarned of coming trouble. When **Aaron cast down his rod** and it became **a serpent**, Pharaoh's **magicians and sorcerers** were able to duplicate the miracle through demonic powers. We learn from 2 Timothy 3:8 that the magicians of Egypt were Jannes and Jambres. They resisted Moses by imitating him and Aaron, but **Aaron's rod swallowed up their rods**. God hardened **Pharaoh's heart**, not arbitrarily, but in response to his stubbornness. It was now time for the first plague.

V. THE FIRST NINE PLAGUES (7:14—10:29)

A. The First Plague—The Nile Turned to Blood (7:14–25)

7:14–18 The LORD told Moses to have a personal confrontation with **Pharaoh** down by the riverside when his majesty went out **to the water**. (He was probably bathing in the "sacred" Nile.) Moses was to warn the king that the **fish** would **die**, the **river** would **stink** and become loathsome to **the Egyptians** after it was **turned to blood by the rod** in Moses' **hand**.

7:19–25 Moses and Aaron did as God commanded. They stretched out the **rod over the waters of Egypt**. The **waters** of the Nile and of **the land of Egypt** were **turned to blood, the fish . . . died**, and **the river stank**. The magicians duplicated this miracle with water found elsewhere than in the Nile. This probably encouraged Pharaoh to resist Moses' demands to let the people go. During the **seven days** when the Nile was polluted, the people obtained water by digging wells.

B. The Second Plague—Frogs (8:1–15)

The plague of **frogs** which covered **the land of Egypt** was so distressing that Pharaoh seemed to relent. When he asked Moses to have the plague lifted, Moses said, **"Accept the honor of saying when I shall intercede for you, for your servants, and for your people, to destroy the frogs from you and your houses, that they may remain in the river only."** The magicians were able to produce **frogs** also—as if there weren't enough already! They probably did this by demonic power, but they dared not *destroy* the frogs because the frog was worshiped as the god of fertility! When the frogs died the next day, there was a tremendous stench from their dead bodies. **Pharaoh** once again **hardened his heart**.

C. The Third Plague—Lice (8:16–19)

In the third plague **the dust of the earth** changed into gnats or **lice**. This time **the magicians**, unable to produce **lice**, warned **Pharaoh** that a power greater than theirs was at work, but the king was obdurate. The more he hardened his **heart**, the more it was hardened by God.

D. The Fourth Plague—Flies (8:20–32)

8:20–24 So God sent the fourth plague—**swarms** *of flies*. As the italics in the NKJV indicate, the Hebrew literally means **swarms** (or "mixed"), and the specific insect (**flies**) is supplied by the translators. Perhaps the **swarms** were a mixture of many species. Since most or all of the plagues

were aimed at the false gods of Egypt (the Nile, and virtually every creature was a deity in Egypt!), it is possible that the beetle is meant. This would be an attack against Khepri, the god of the sacred beetle.[8]

8:25–32 Pharaoh buckled to the extent of allowing the Israelites to **sacrifice to** God **in the land** of Egypt. But this wouldn't do because they would be sacrificing animals worshiped by **the Egyptians** and thus incite a riot. Pharaoh made a further concession: The Jews could go into **the wilderness** to sacrifice but they must **not go . . . far**. This too was unsatisfactory because God had commanded them to go three days' journey. As soon as Egypt got relief from the plague, Pharaoh changed his mind and forbade **the people to go**.

E. The Fifth Plague—Pestilence on Livestock (9:1–7)

After **Pharaoh** had been warned, God sent a **pestilence**, possibly anthrax, that killed **all** the Egyptians' **livestock . . . in the field**. The animals belonging to the Israelites were not affected. So it was a discriminating judgment that cannot be explained by natural phenomena. All attempts to explain the plagues on naturalistic grounds dash themselves against the rocks. Not all the animals of the Egyptians were destroyed, since some are referred to in verse 19 and some were later killed on the Passover night (12:29b). Some fled into the houses (v. 20). So the **"all"** of verse 6a means "all in the field" or "all kinds." The ram, the goat, and the bull were sacred animals in Egypt. Now their decomposing carcasses were polluting the environment.

F. The Sixth Plague—Boils (9:8–12)

When **Pharaoh** steeled himself still further, God caused **ashes** to be turned into **boils** on the men and animals **of Egypt**. Even **the magicians** were affected. The more Pharaoh hardened his heart, the more it became judicially **hardened** by God.

G. The Seventh Plague—Hail and Fire (9:13–35)

"All My plagues" probably indicates the full force of God's plagues. The Lord reminds Pharaoh that He could have destroyed him and the Egyptians with the preceding **pestilence**, but instead He had spared Pharaoh in order to demonstrate His **power** and spread His fame. There is no thought in verse 16 that Pharaoh was predestined to be damned. Reprobation is not a Bible doctrine. The Lord used Pharaoh as an example of what happens to a person who is determined to resist the power of God (see also Rom. 9:16,17).

The next plague consisted of **hail** and lightning or **fire**, accompanied by **thunder**. It destroyed men, beasts, and **the flax and . . . barley**, that were ready for harvest (cf. vv. 31, 32); **but the wheat and the spelt were not struck, for they are late crops**. The Israelites, dwelling in **Goshen**, were untouched. In response to Pharaoh's plea, Moses prayed and the plague stopped. But, as **Moses** expected, **Pharaoh** became even more adamant against letting the Hebrews leave.

H. The Eighth Plague—Locusts (10:1–20)

Moses and Aaron warned Pharaoh of an impending locust plague, but he would agree to **let** only **the men go** to hold a feast to **the Lord**. The women and children had to stay behind. But God would not have the men in the wilderness while their families were still in Egypt. The plague was of unprecedented severity, with **locusts** covering **the land** and eating everything edible. This showed that the god Serapis was powerless to protect from **locusts**. **Pharaoh** seemed willing to yield, but **he** would **not let the children of Israel go**.

I. The Ninth Plague—Three Days of Darkness (10:21–29)

10:21–28 The ninth plague was **three days** of **darkness which could be felt**. Only **the children of Israel had light in their dwellings**, an obvious miracle. The Egyptian sun god, Ra, was unmasked as impotent. Pharaoh told Moses to **go** to the wilderness with the women and children but to leave the **flocks and . . . herds** behind. He thought this would guarantee their return. (Perhaps he also wanted to replenish his own herds.) But in that case, there would be nothing to sacrifice to Jehovah, and **sacrifice** was the reason for their departure from Egypt. When Moses was unwilling to make the demanded compromise, Pharaoh ordered him banished from his presence forever.

10:29 Moses' strong statement, **"You have spoken well. I will never see your face again,"** seems contradicted by 11:8, where it says that Moses "went out from Pharaoh in great anger." Matthew Henry suggests that **"never . . . again"** means "after this time," and 11:8 is included in the same "conference." He writes:

So that, after this interview, Moses came no more, till he was sent for. Note, when men drive God's word from them he justly permits their delusions, and answers them according to the multitude of their idols. When the Gadarenes desired Christ to depart, he presently left them.[9]

VI. THE PASSOVER AND THE DEATH OF THE FIRSTBORN (11:1—12:30)

11:1-10 Moses had not yet departed from Pharaoh's presence. In verses 4-8 he is still speaking to the ruler. The first three verses may be thought of as a parenthesis. In view of the tenth and final plague, God told Moses to have the Israelites **ask** (not "borrow," as in KJV) for **gold and silver articles** from **the Egyptians**. Moses warned Pharaoh that **all the firstborn . . . of Egypt** would be slain at **midnight** of the appointed date (see 12:6), that the Israelites would not be affected by the slaughter, and that Pharaoh's officials would **bow down**, begging the Hebrews to leave at once and en masse. **Then** Moses left the potentate in **great anger**. The warning fell on deaf ears, and **the LORD hardened Pharaoh's heart** still more.

12:1-10 The LORD gave detailed instructions to **Moses and Aaron** on how to prepare for the primary **Passover**. The **lamb**, of course, is a type of the Lord Jesus Christ (1 Cor. 5:7). It was to be **without blemish**, speaking of the sinlessness of Christ; **a male of the first year**, perhaps suggesting our Lord's being cut off in the prime of life; kept **until the fourteenth day of the . . . month**, pointing forward to the Savior's thirty years of private life in Nazareth, during which He was tested by God, then publicly for three years by the full scrutiny of man; killed by **the congregation of Israel**, as Christ was taken by wicked hands and slain (Acts 2:23); killed **at twilight**, between the ninth and eleventh hours, as Jesus was killed at the ninth hour (Matt. 27:45-50). Its **blood** was to be applied to the door, bringing salvation from the destroyer (v.

7), just as the blood of Christ, appropriated by faith, brings salvation from sin, self, and Satan. **The flesh** was to be **roasted** with **fire**, picturing Christ enduring God's wrath against our sins. It was to be eaten **with unleavened bread and with bitter herbs**, symbolizing Christ as the food of His people. We should live lives of sincerity and truth, without the leaven of malice and wickedness, and with true repentance, always remembering the bitterness of Christ's suffering. Not a bone of the lamb was to be broken (v. 46), a stipulation that was literally fulfilled in the case of our Lord (John 19:36).

12:11-20 The first **Passover** was to be observed by a people ready to travel, a reminder to us that pilgrims on a long journey should travel light. The **Passover** was so named because the Lord *passed over* the houses where the blood was applied. The expression "passover" does not mean "pass by." Cole explains:

> Whether it was correct etymology or a pun, *pesah* to Israel meant "a passing-over" or "a leaping over" and was applied to God's act in history on this occasion, in sparing Israel.[10]

The **Passover** was **on the fourteenth day** of Israel's religious calendar year (v. 2). Closely connected with the Passover was **the Feast of Unleavened Bread**. On that first Passover night, the people left Egypt in such a hurry that there was no time for the dough to become leavened (vv. 34, 39). Thereafter, in keeping the Feast **for seven days**, they would be reminded of the speed of their exodus. But since leaven speaks of sin, they would also be reminded that those who have been redeemed by blood should leave sin and the world (Egypt) behind them. **Whoever** ate **leavened** bread would be **cut off**— that is, excluded from the camp and its privileges. In some contexts, the expression "cut off" means condemned to death.

12:21–27 Next we hear **Moses** passing on the instructions to **the elders of** the people. Further details are given about how to sprinkle **the blood** on **the door**. The **hyssop** may picture faith, which makes a personal application of **the blood** of Christ. The **Passover** would provide a springboard for teaching future generations the story of redemption when they would ask the meaning of the ceremony.

12:28–30 At midnight the blow finally fell as threatened. **There was a great cry in Egypt, for there was not a house where there was not one dead.** The Israelites were at last permitted to leave.

VII. THE EXODUS FROM EGYPT (12:31—15:21)

A. Flight toward the Sea (12:31—13:22)

12:31–37 Verse 31 does not necessarily mean that **Moses** met **Pharaoh** face-to-face (see 10:29). What a servant says or does is often ascribed to his master. Moses had predicted that Pharaoh's servants would beg the Israelites to go (11:8).

The Israelites **journeyed...to Succoth**, a district in Egypt, not to be confused with the town of that name in Palestine (Gen. 33:17). **The Egyptians** were only too glad to give their wealth to the Israelites and be rid of them. For the Hebrews, it was only just recompense for all the labor they had given to Pharaoh. It provided them with equipment for the journey and materials for the service of God.

About six hundred thousand men left Egypt, in addition to women and **children**. The exact number of men was 603,550 (38:26). The total number of Israelites was about two million.

12:38, 39 There is considerable dispute concerning the date of the Exodus. A commonly accepted conservative date is c. 1440 B.C. Other scholars place it at 1290 B.C. or even later (see Introduction). **A mixed multitude** (that is, including foreigners) tagged along with the Israelites when they left Egypt. They are referred to as "rabble" in Numbers 11:4 (NASB), where they are seen complaining against the Lord despite His goodness to them.

12:40–42 Concerning the chronology in verse 40, see the commentary on Genesis 15:13, 14. The **four hundred and thirty years** mentioned here cover the total time that the Israelites spent in Egypt. It is an exact figure, to the **very . . . day**. The important thing to see is that the Lord did not forget the promise He had made centuries earlier. In bringing His people out, He fulfilled His Word. God is not slack concerning the promise of *our* redemption either (2 Pet. 3:9). In a coming day, Moses' "antitype," the Lord Jesus, will lead His people out of this world to the eternal Promised Land.

12:43–51 The ordinance of **the** permanent **Passover** specified that only **circumcised** men were allowed to participate, whether aliens, neighbors, or servants. **No foreigner shall eat it . . . a sojourner and a hired servant shall not eat it.**

13:1–15 God had saved **the firstborn** of the Israelites from death in Egypt; therefore, **the firstborn** of humans and of animals were to be **consecrated** to God, as belonging to Him. The firstborn sons became priests

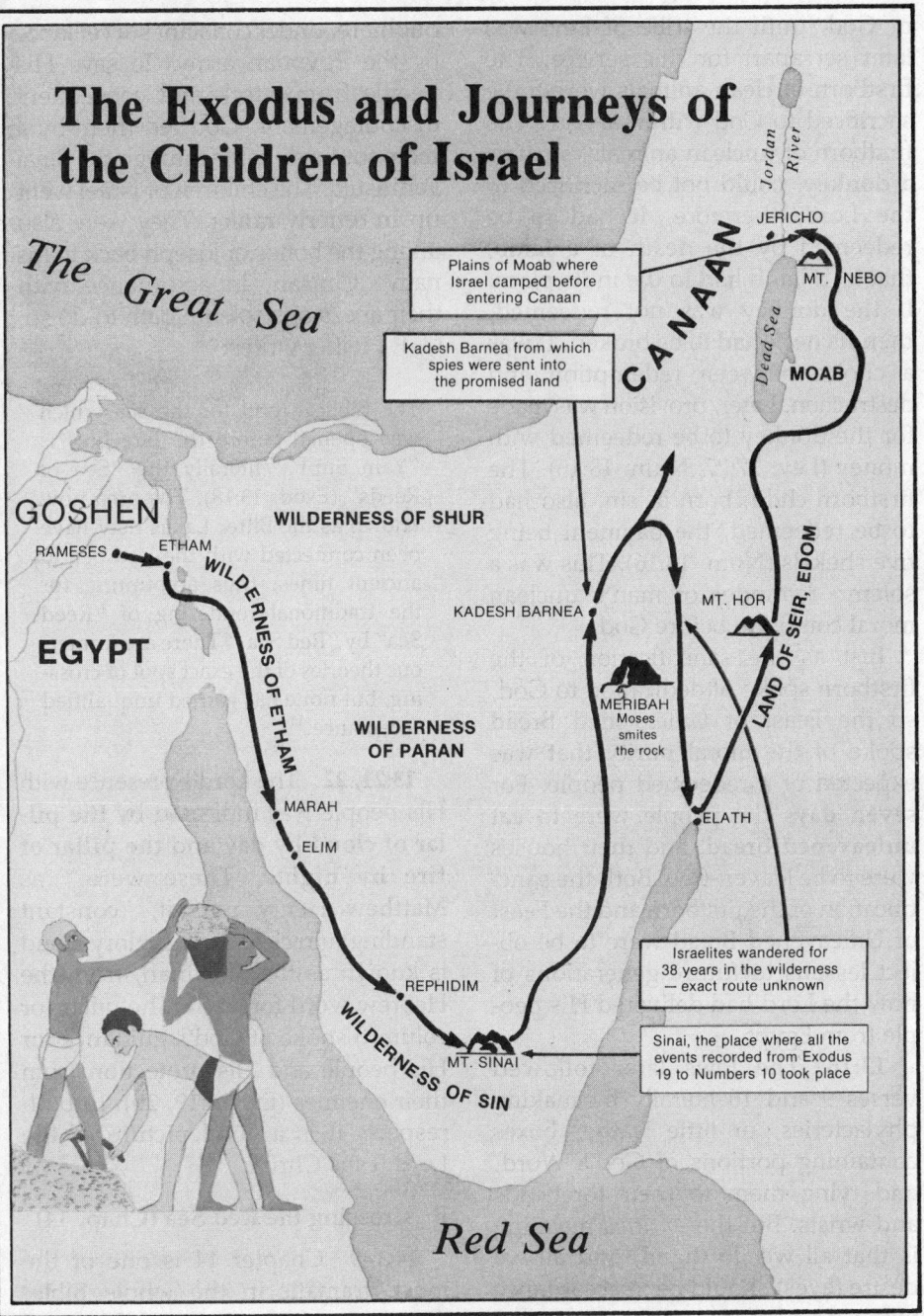

The Exodus and Journeys of the Children of Israel

The Great Sea

GOSHEN

RAMESES • → ETHAM

WILDERNESS OF ETHAM

EGYPT

WILDERNESS OF SHUR

MARAH

ELIM

WILDERNESS OF PARAN

WILDERNESS OF SIN

REPHIDIM

MT. SINAI

Red Sea

KADESH BARNEA

MERIBAH
Moses smites the rock

MT. HOR

LAND OF SEIR, EDOM

ELATH

CANAAN

Jordan River

JERICHO •

MT. NEBO

Dead Sea

MOAB

Plains of Moab where Israel camped before entering Canaan

Kadesh Barnea from which spies were sent into the promised land

Israelites wandered for 38 years in the wilderness — exact route unknown

Sinai, the place where all the events recorded from Exodus 19 to Numbers 10 took place

The Exodus and Journeys of the Children of Israel

of God, until the tribe of Levi was later set apart for this service. The firstborn of clean animals were to be sacrificed to God within a year. The firstborn of unclean animals, such as **a donkey**, could not be sacrificed to the Lord; therefore, **it** had to be redeemed by the death of **a lamb**; that is, a lamb had to die in its place. If the donkey was not redeemed, then **its neck** had to be broken. It was a choice between redemption and destruction. Later, provision was made for the donkey to be redeemed with money (Lev. 27:27; Num. 18:15). The firstborn child, born in sin, also had to be redeemed, the payment being five shekels (Num. 18:16). This was a solemn reminder of man's unclean moral condition before God.

Just as the sanctification of the firstborn spoke of dedication to God, so the Feast of Unleavened Bread spoke of the moral purity that was expected of a redeemed people. For **seven days** the people were to **eat unleavened bread**, and their houses were to be leaven-free. Both the sanctification of the firstborn and the Feast of Unleavened Bread were to be object lessons to future generations of how the Lord had delivered His people from Egypt.

13:16 The Jews later followed verses 9 and 16 literally by making phylacteries, or little leather boxes containing portions of God's Word, and tying them to their foreheads and wrists. But the *spiritual* meaning is that all we do (**hand**) and all we desire (**eyes**) should be in accordance with God's Word.

13:17–20 The most direct route from Egypt to Canaan would have been through Philistine country, a trip of about two weeks along the coastal road known as "The Way of Horus." But this was a busy thor-oughfare, under constant surveillance by the Egyptian army. To save His people from attack and consequent discouragement, **God led** them by a more southerly route through the Sinai Peninsula. The children of Israel went up **in orderly ranks.** They were also taking the bones of Joseph back to his native Canaan, in accordance with their ancestor's solemn oath to do so. C. F. Pfeiffer writes:

The Biblical term for the sea which was opened before the Israelites is "Yam Suph," literally the "Sea of Reeds" (Exod. 13:18). The area now known as the Bitter Lakes may have been connected with the Red Sea in ancient times, thus accounting for the traditional rendering of "Reed Sea" by "Red Sea." There are numerous theories of the exact spot of crossing, but none has gained unqualified acceptance.[11]

13:21, 22 The Lord's presence with His people was indicated by **the pillar of cloud by day** and **the pillar of fire by night**. "These were," as Matthew Henry puts it, "constant standing miracles."[12] This glory cloud is known as the Shekinah, from the Hebrew word for *dwell*. The pillar (or column) spoke of God's guidance for His people and His protection from their enemies (Ex. 14:19, 20). In both respects it is a good picture of the Lord Jesus Christ.

B. Crossing the Red Sea (Chap. 14)

14:1–9 Chapter 14 is one of the most dramatic in the whole Bible. **The LORD** directed **the children of Israel** southward to **Pi Hahiroth**, somewhere west of the Red Sea. This made escape seem impossible, but made the subsequent miracle more marvelous. Pharaoh thought they were trapped and set out after them with his army of **six hundred choice chariots, and all the chariots of Egypt with captains over every one of them**. Pharaoh's overtaking the two million apparently helpless Israelites **camping by the sea** and shut in between the two is probably the origin of the popular idiom for a terrible dilemma: "Between the devil (Pharaoh) and the deep blue (Red!) sea."

14:10–14 When **the children of Israel** raised **their eyes** and saw the Egyptian army marching **after them** they were naturally petrified, but wisely **cried out to the LORD**. Yet they quickly complained to the Lord's leader, Moses, as they had once before (5:21), saying **it would have been better for** them **to serve the Egyptians than** to **die in the wilderness**. This was sheer unbelief on their part, and not the last instance, by any means. No longer timid, Moses told them to **"stand still and see the salvation of the LORD."**

14:15–18 One of the greatest miracles in all history was about to occur:

> The LORD instructed **Moses**, . . . **"Tell the children of Israel to go forward. But lift up your rod, and stretch out your hand over the sea and divide it. And the children of Israel shall go on dry ground through the midst of the sea."**

Regarding God's hardening of **the hearts of the Egyptians**, and gaining **honor over Pharaoh and over all his** military might, Matthew Henry writes:

> It is a righteous thing with God to put those under the impressions of his wrath who have long resisted the influences of his grace. It is spoken in a way of triumph over this obstinate and presumptuous rebel.[13]

14:19–28 The Angel of God (Christ, see Judges 6 for discussion)

took His place as a **pillar of cloud** at the rear of the host of Israel, protecting them from **the Egyptians**. **The pillar of cloud** provided **light** for the Israelites **and darkness** for **the Egyptians**. At Moses' bidding the Red Sea parted, forming two walls of water with a path of **dry land** between. The Israelites passed through safely, but when **Pharaoh's** army tried to follow, **the LORD . . . troubled** them and disabled their chariots **so that they drove them with difficulty**. Before they could retreat, **the sea** closed in on them at Moses' command. **Not so much as one of them remained**. The same faith that opened up the Red Sea enables us to do the impossible when we are moving forward in the will of God.

14:29–31 The crossing of the Red Sea is set forth as the greatest display of God's power *in the OT*, but the greatest power *of all time* is that which raised Christ from the dead.

C. The Song of Moses (15:1–21)

Just as the Passover speaks of redemption by *blood*, the Red Sea tells of redemption by *power*. The song of Moses celebrates the latter. Dr. H. C. Woodring outlined it as follows:[14]

Prelude (v. 1)—The triumph of Jehovah.

Stanza #1 (vv. 2,3)—What *He is*: **strength, song, salvation**.

Stanza #2 (vv. 4–13)—What *He has done*: victory over past enemies, deliverance of His people from Egypt.

Stanza #3 (vv. 14–18)—What *He will do*: victory over future enemies; bring His people into their inheritance.

Postlude (v. 19)—Contrast of the defeat of Egypt and the deliverance of Israel.

Antiphonal response by **Miriam and all the women** (vv. 20, 21).

Nearly three centuries ago the English commentator Matthew Henry expressed his appreciation and understanding of this great spiritual ode as follows:

> We may observe respecting this song, that it is, (1.) An ancient song, the most ancient that we know of. (2.) A most admirable composition, the style lofty and magnificent, the images lively and proper, and the whole very moving. (3.) It is a holy song, consecrated to the honour of God, and intended to exalt his name and celebrate his praise, and his only, not in the least to magnify any man: holiness to the Lord is engraven on it, and to him they made melody in the singing of it. (4.) It is a typical song. The triumphs of the gospel church, in the downfall of its enemies, are expressed in the song of Moses and the song of the Lamb put together, which are said to be sung upon a sea of glass, as this was upon the Red Sea, Rev xv. 2, 3.[15]

VIII. THE JOURNEY TO SINAI (15:22—18:27)

A. The Wilderness of Shur (15:22–27)

Verse 22 begins the record of the journey **from the Red Sea** to Mount Sinai. Each step is filled with spiritual lessons for believers of every age. **Marah**, which means *bitter*, for instance, speaks of the bitter experiences of life. The tree suggests the cross of Calvary, which transmutes the bitter things of life into sweetness. At **Marah** the Lord revealed Himself as *"the LORD who heals you"* (*YHWH Rōphekā*). He promised to deliver Israel from **the diseases** that afflicted the Egyptians. **Elim**, with its **twelve wells of water** and **seventy palm trees**, suggests the rest and refreshment which are ours after we have been to the cross.

B. The Wilderness of Sin (Chap. 16)

16:1–19 Journeying to the southeast, the people **came to the Wilderness of Sin.**[16] There they **complained** bitterly about the lack of food and sighed for the food **of Egypt**, seemingly forgetful of the terrible slavery that accompanied the food. God graciously responded by supplying plenty of **quails** at night and manna **in the morning**. The quails were provided only twice, here and in Numbers 11:31, whereas the manna was provided continuously. "Manna" means **"What is it?"** It was food miraculously provided by God; no attempts to explain it on a natural basis succeed. Manna was **small, round**, white, and sweet (v. 31), picturing the humility, perfection, purity, and sweetness of Christ, the Bread of God (John 6:48–51). Its arrival was somehow connected with the **morning dew**, reminding us that it is the Holy Spirit who ministers Christ to our souls. The Israelites were allowed to **gather . . . one omer** (about three pints) per person. No matter how much or how little they gathered, seeking to approximate an omer, they always had enough and never too much. This suggests the sufficiency of Christ to meet every need of all His people, and the results achieved when Christians share with those who are in need (2 Cor. 8:15). The manna had to be gathered early in the **morning**, before the **sun . . . melted** it. So we should feed on Christ at the start of each day, before the pressures of life crowd in on us. It had to be gathered daily, just as we must feed daily on the Lord. It was to be gathered on the first six days of the week; none was provided on the seventh.

16:20–31 On the sixth day the people were ordered to gather **twice**

as much as on the other days, to tide them over the **Sabbath**. If they **left part of it** on any other day, the manna **bred worms and stank. Manna was like white coriander seed, and the taste of it was like wafers made with honey.** It could be baked or cooked. Moses rebuked those who went out to gather it on the Sabbath.

16:32–34 Some of the **manna** was placed in a golden urn and **kept** as a memorial, later to be placed in the Ark of the Covenant (Heb. 9:4). God rested on the seventh day at creation (Gen. 2:2), but He did not command man to do so at that time. But now He gave the law of the Sabbath to the nation of Israel. Later it became one of the Ten Commandments (20:9–11). It was a sign of the covenant made with Israel at Mount Sinai (31:13) and a weekly reminder of their deliverance from Egyptian bondage (Deut. 5:15). Gentiles were never commanded to keep the Sabbath. Nine of the Ten Commandments are repeated in the NT as instructions in righteousness for the church. The only one that is *not* repeated is the law of the Sabbath. Yet there is a *principle* of one day of rest in seven for all mankind. For the Christian, that day is the first day of the week, the Lord's Day. It is not a day of legal responsibility but a day of gracious privilege, when, released from secular activities, we can give ourselves more wholly to the worship and service of the Lord.

The "Testimony," meaning the "Ark" of the Covenant, is mentioned here before it ever existed. This is an illustration of the law of prior mention. **The "Testimony"** can also mean the Ten Commandments, depending on the context.

16:35, 36 Eating manna for **forty years** is a prediction of the time the Israelites would wander in the wilderness. The manna ceased when they reached Gilgal, just inside **the border of the land of Canaan** (Josh. 5:12).

C. Rephidim (Chap. 17)

17:1–7 At **Rephidim** the people **contended with Moses** because of a shortage of **water**. The Lord instructed Moses to proceed to the general area known as **Horeb** (meaning *the desolate place*) and to **strike the rock** with his **rod**. When he did, water flowed from the rock—a picture of the Holy Spirit, who was given on the day of Pentecost as the fruit of Christ's being struck on Calvary. **Massah** (*tempting* or *testing*) was where they tried or tested God. **Meribah** (*chiding* or *strife*) was where they strove with Moses.

17:8–16 Joshua (*Jehovah is salvation*) now comes on the stage for the first time. As the servant of Moses, he **fought** against **Amalek** in Rephidim. As long as **Moses held up his hand** in intercession and in dependance on God, the Israelites had the margin of victory. But when Moses' hand sagged, Amalek gained the ascendancy. **Amalek**, a descendant of Esau, is a type of the flesh—that is, the evil, corrupt, Adamic nature of man. Observe the following parallels between the flesh and Amalek: (1) It presents itself after the Holy Spirit is given at conversion to fight against the Spirit; (2) **The LORD will have war with** the flesh from generation to generation; (3) It is never eradicated from the believer till death or the Rapture of the church; (4) Two means of triumph over the flesh are suggested—prayer and the Word.

According to the ancient Jewish historian Josephus, **Hur** was the husband of Miriam, Moses' sister. This same Hur was later left with **Aaron** to supervise the people while Moses was on Mount Sinai (24:14).

The-Lord-Is-My-Banner (Heb. *YHWH Nissî*) is a compound name of Jehovah.

D. Moses and Jethro (Chap. 18)

18:1–12 Chapter 18 marks a distinct division in the book of Exodus. Until now we have had the manna, the stricken rock, and the stream—speaking of Christ's incarnation, His death, and the giving of the Holy Spirit. Now we seem to have a foregleam of Christ's future glory. **Moses** is a type of Christ reigning over the earth. We also see the Jews, represented by his **sons**; the Gentiles, pictured by **Jethro**; and the church, typified by Moses' Gentile bride, **Zipporah**. All these will enjoy the blessings of the Millennial Kingdom—the Jews and Gentiles as subjects in it, and the Church reigning with Christ over the earth.

The events are not in chronological order. Jethro is described as coming to Moses at Mount Sinai in verse 5, but the Israelites did not arrive at Mount Sinai until 19:2. One commentator suggests that this arrangement is to clear the way for an uninterrupted account of the meeting with Jehovah and the giving of the Law. Moses had probably left his wife and two sons in Midian when he went back to Egypt. Now **Jethro** brings **Zipporah, Gershom** and **Eliezer** (*my God is help*) to Moses for a joyous reunion. It appears that Jethro had become a convert to the one true **God** here, though some scholars believe he had already been a worshiper of Jehovah.

18:13–27 When Jethro saw the tremendous task that fell to **Moses** in judging **the people**, he advised his son-in-law to **select men** of high character, **such as fear God, men of truth, hating covetousness**, to assist him. Jethro's suggestion included **rulers of thousands, rulers of hundreds, rulers of fifties, and rulers of tens**. This would ease the **burden** on Moses and enable the work to be handled more quickly. Some think that Jethro's counsel was divinely given, that it urged a sensible delegation of authority to others. Others remind us, however, that God never assigns tasks without giving grace for them. Up to this time God had been speaking to Moses as a man speaks with a friend, and had not been using a go-between. Therefore Moses should have carried on until God Himself made other arrangements.

IX. THE GIVING OF THE LAW (Chaps. 19—24)

A. Preparation for Revelation (Chap. 19)

19:1–9 The children of Israel have now arrived at Mount **Sinai**. The rest of the book of Exodus, the entire book of Leviticus, and the first nine chapters of Numbers record events that took place here.

From Adam until this time, there had been no direct law of God. The Lord's dealings with His people had been predominantly in grace. Now He offered them a conditional covenant of law: **If you will indeed obey My voice and keep My covenant, then you shall be a special treasure to Me above all people; . . . you shall be to Me a kingdom of priests and a holy nation.** If they would **obey**, He would bless. Not realizing their own sinfulness and helplessness, the people readily agreed. D. L. Moody comments:

"All that the Lord has spoken we will do." Bold and self-confident language. The golden calf, the broken tablets, the neglected ordinances, the stoned messengers, the rejected and crucified Christ, are overwhelming evidences of man's dishonored vows.[17]

THE DISPENSATIONS

There is a very major break here in the history of God's dealings with mankind, especially with His chosen nation Israel. The change in the Divine ordering of human affairs here and elsewhere indicates a change in *dispensations* or administrations.

Augustine once said, "Distinguish the ages and the Scriptures harmonize." God has divided human history into ages: ". . . by whom also he made the ages" (Heb. 1:2 RV, marg.). These ages may be long or short. What distinguishes them is not their length but the way God deals with mankind in them.

While God *Himself* never changes, His *methods* do. He works in different ways at different times. We call the way God administers His affairs with man during a particular era a *dispensation*. Technically, a dispensation does not mean an age but rather an administration, a stewardship, an order, or an *economy* (our word "economy" comes from *oikonomia*, the NT Greek word for "dispensation" or "administration"). But it is difficult to think of a dispensation without thinking of time. For example, the history of the United States government has been divided into administrations. We speak of the Kennedy administration or the Bush administration. We mean, of course, the way the government was operated while those presidents were in office. The important point is the policies that were followed, but we necessarily link those policies with a particular period of time.

Therefore, we think of *a dispensation as the way God deals with people during any period of history.* God's dispensational dealings may be compared to the way a home is run. When there are only a husband and wife in the home, a certain program

is followed. But when there are young children, an entirely new set of policies is introduced. As the children mature, the affairs of the home are handled differently again. We see this same pattern in God's dealings with the human race (Gal. 4:1–5).

For example, when Cain killed his brother Abel, God set a mark on him, so that anyone finding him would not kill him (Gen. 4:15). Yet after the Flood God instituted capital punishment, decreeing that "Whoever sheds man's blood, by man his blood shall be shed" (Gen. 9:6). The difference is due to the change in dispensations.

Another example is Psalm 137:8, 9, where the writer calls down severe judgment on Babylon: "O daughter of Babylon, who are to be destroyed, happy the one who repays you as you have served us! Happy the one who takes and dashes your little ones against the rock!"

Still later the Lord taught His people: "Love your enemies, bless those who curse you, do good to those who hate you, and pray for those who spitefully use you and persecute you" (Matt. 5:44).

It seems clear that language suitable for the psalmist living under law would no longer be suitable for a Christian living under grace.

In Leviticus 11 *certain foods* were designated as *unclean*. But in Mark 7:19b Jesus declared *all foods* to be *clean*.

In Ezra 10:3 the Jews were told to *put away* their foreign wives and children. In the NT, believers are instructed *not* to put them away (1 Cor. 7:12–16).

Under the law *only the high priest* could enter the presence of God (Heb. 9:7). Under grace *all believers* have access into the Most Holy Place (Heb. 10:19–22).

These changes clearly show that there has been a change of dispensations.

Not all Christians are agreed on the number of dispensations or the names that should be given to them. In fact, not all Christians accept dispensations at all.

But we can demonstrate the existence of dispensations as follows. First of all, there are at least two dispensations—law and grace: "For the law was given through Moses, but grace and truth came through Jesus Christ" (John 1:17). The fact that our Bibles are divided into Old and New Testaments indicates that a change of administrations occurred. Further proof is given by the fact that believers in this age are not required to offer animal sacrifices. This too shows that God has introduced a new order. Hardly any Christians fail to see this major break between the Testaments.

But if we agree that there are *two* dispensations, we are forced to believe that there are *three*, because the Dispensation of Law was not introduced until here in Exodus 19, hundreds of years after Creation. So there must have been at least one dispensation before the law (see Rom. 5:14). That makes three.

And then we should be able to agree on a *fourth* dispensation, because the Scriptures speak of "the age to come" (Heb. 6:5). This is the time when the Lord Jesus Christ will return to reign over the earth, otherwise known as the Millennium.

Paul also distinguishes between the *present age* and *an age to come*. First he speaks of a dispensation that was committed to him in connection with the truth of the gospel and the church (1 Cor. 9:17; Eph. 3:2; Col. 1:25). That is the present age. But then he also points forward to a future age when (Eph. 1:10) he refers to "the dispensation of the fullness of times." It is apparent from his description of it that it has not yet arrived.

So we know that we are not living in the final age of the world's history.

Dr. C. I. Scofield lists seven dispensations, as follows:

1. Innocence (Gen. 1:28). From Adam's creation up to his fall.
2. Conscience or Moral Responsibility (Gen. 3:7). From the fall to the end of the Flood.
3. Human Government (Gen. 8:15). From the end of the Flood to the call of Abraham.
4. Promise (Gen. 12:1). From the call of Abraham to the giving of the Law.
5. Law (Ex. 19:1). From the giving of the Law to the Day of Pentecost.
6. Church (Acts 2:1). From the Day of Pentecost to the Rapture.
7. Kingdom (Rev. 20:4). The thousand-year reign of Christ.[18]

While it is not important to agree on the exact details, it is very helpful to see that there are different dispensations. The distinction between law and grace is especially important. Otherwise we will take portions of Scripture that apply to other ages and refer them to ourselves. While all Scriptures are *profitable for us* (2 Tim. 3:16), not all were written directly *to us*. Passages dealing with other ages have applications for us, but their primary interpretation is for the age for which they were written. We have already noted the dietary restrictions of Leviticus 11. While this prohibition is not binding on Christians today (Mark 7:18, 19), the underlying principle remains—that we should avoid moral and spiritual uncleanness.

God promised the people of Israel that if they obeyed Him, He would make them materially prosperous (Deut. 28:1–6). The emphasis then was on material blessings in earthly places. But this is not true today. God does not promise that He will reward our obedience with financial prosperity. Instead, the blessings of this dispensation are spiritual blessings in the heavenly places (Eph. 1:3).

While there are differences among the various ages, there is one thing that never changes, and that is the gospel. Salvation always has been, is now, and always will be by faith in the Lord. And the basis of salvation for every age is the finished work of Christ on the cross.[19] People in the OT were saved by believing whatever revelation the Lord gave them. Abraham, for example, was saved by believing God when He said that the patriarch's seed would be as numerous as the stars (Gen. 15:5, 6). Abraham probably did not know much, if anything, about what would take place at Calvary centuries later. But the Lord knew. And when Abraham believed God, He put to Abraham's account all the value of the future work of Christ at Calvary.

As someone has said, the OT saints were saved "on credit." That is, they were saved on the basis of the price that the Lord Jesus would pay many years later (that is the meaning of Romans 3:25). We are saved on the basis of the work which Christ accomplished over 1900 years ago. But in both cases salvation is by faith in the Lord.

We must guard against any idea that people in the Dispensation of Law were saved by keeping the law or even by offering animal sacrifices. The law can only condemn; it cannot save (Rom. 3:20). And the blood of bulls and goats cannot put away a single sin (Heb. 10:4). No, God's way of salvation is by faith and faith alone! (See Rom. 5:1.)

Another good point to remember is this: When we speak of the present Church Age as the Age of Grace, we don't imply that God wasn't gracious in past dispensations. We simply mean that God is now testing man under grace rather than under law.

It is also important to realize that the ages do not close with split-second precision. Often there is an overlapping or a transition period. We see this in Acts, for instance. It took time for the new church to throw off some of the trappings of the previous dispensation. And it's possible that there will be a period of time between the Rapture and the Tribulation during which the Man of Sin will be manifested and the temple will be built in Jerusalem.

One final word. Like all good things, the study of dispensations can be abused. There are some Christians who carry dispensationalism to such an extreme that they accept only Paul's Prison Epistles as applicable for the church today! As a result they don't accept baptism or the Lord's Supper,[20] since these are not found in the Prison Epistles. They also teach that Peter's gospel message was not the same as Paul's. (See Gal. 1:8, 9 for a refutation of this.) These people are sometimes called ultradispensationalists or Bullingerites (after a teacher named E. W. Bullinger). Their extreme view of dispensations should be rejected.‡

19:10–20 The people were told to prepare for a revelation from God by washing **their clothes** and refraining from sexual intercourse. This was designed to teach them the necessity for purity in the presence of God. **Mount Sinai** was a forbidding place. Neither mankind nor animals were to **touch** it on penalty of **death**. A transgressor was not to be followed onto the mount but was to be **shot** through **with an arrow** or **stoned** from a distance. Only Moses and Aaron were allowed to ascend (v. 24), and then only **when the** ram's horn sounded. The mount was covered with **a thick cloud; there were thunderings and lightnings, fire** and **smoke; the whole mountain quaked greatly.** All this spoke of the terrors of meeting God, especially on the basis of lawkeeping.

19:21–25 The LORD repeated His warning **to Moses** that the people should not touch the mount. Moses at first thought it unnecessary to remind the people but later obeyed. **The priests** in verses 22 and 24 were probably the firstborn sons.

B. The Ten Commandments (Chap. 20)

The Ten Commandments were divided by the Lord Jesus into two sections, one covering love to God and the other covering love to one's neighbor (Matt. 22:37–40). Some suggest that the first four commandments teach love to God, while others add the fifth. The expression "The LORD your God" is found in the first five commandments.

I.

20:1–3   Have no other gods. This is a prohibition against the worship of many gods (polytheism) or against the worship of any other god except Jehovah.

II.

20:4–6   Use no carved image. Not only the worship of idols but their manufacture is forbidden. This includes pictures, images, and statues used in worship. It does not, however, include all pictures or statues, since the tabernacle contained carved cherubim. Also, God told Moses to make a serpent of brass (Num. 21:8).

Mount Sinai. Viewed from a trail leading to its summit, Jebel Musa (right) is traditionally considered to be the biblical Mount Horeb, or Sinai. It is located on the southern portion of the Sinai Peninsula between the Red Sea and the Gulf of Aqaba.

The commandment undoubtedly refers to pictures or images of deity.

God is **a jealous God**—that is, jealous of the worship and love of His people. He visits **the iniquity of the fathers upon the children to the third and fourth generations**, through inherited weaknesses, poverty, diseases, and shortened lifespan. But God's **mercy** endures **to thousands** (of generations) of **those who love** Him **and keep** His **commandments**.

III.

20:7 Taking God's **name . . . in vain** is forbidden. This means to swear by God's name that a false statement is actually true. It could also include profanity, cursing, minced oaths, or swearing to a promise and failing to fulfill it.

IV.

20:8–11 Remember the Sabbath day. First mentioned in Genesis 2:1–3, and enjoined in connection with the gathering of manna (Ex. 16), the Sabbath was now formally given to the nation of Israel for strict observance. It was a picture of the rest which believers now enjoy in Christ and which a redeemed creation will enjoy in the Millennium. The Sabbath is the seventh day of the week, from sundown on Friday to sundown on Saturday. Nowhere in the NT are Christians commanded to keep the Sabbath.

V.

20:12 Honor **father** and **mother**. To honor here means to obey. The verse teaches that a life of obedience to parents is the type of life which, in general, insures length of days. A life of disobedience and sin often leads to premature death. This is the first commandment with a promise attached (Eph. 6:2). It teaches respect for authority.

VI.

20:13 You shall not murder. This refers specifically to murder and not to capital punishment or to manslaughter. The command teaches respect for human life.

VII.

20:14 You shall not commit adultery. This prohibition teaches respect for marriage, and warns against exploiting another person's body. It *may* cover all forms of unlawful sexual behavior.

VIII.

20:15 You shall not steal. This refers to any act by which a person wrongfully deprives another person of his property. It teaches respect for private property.

IX.

20:16 You shall not bear false witness. This commandment forbids damaging the character of another person by making statements which are not true, and thus possibly causing him to be punished or even executed. It teaches respect for a person's reputation.

X.

20:17 You shall not covet. The tenth commandment passes from acts to thoughts, and it shows that it is sinful to lust after anything that God never intended one to have. Paul states that this commandment produced deep conviction of sin in his life (Rom. 7:7).

20:18–21 After the Ten Commandments were given, **the people** were terrified by the manifestations of the divine Presence. They were afraid they would die if God spoke to them directly, so **Moses** became their mediator.

20:22–26 The purpose of the Law of Moses was to show the people their sinfulness. Next, God graciously gave instructions for the erection of **an altar**, reminding the people that sinners can approach God only on the ground of shed blood. The altar speaks of Christ as the way of approach to God. Man could contribute nothing to the perfection of Christ, either by the tools of personal effort or the steps of human achievement. Priests ascending **steps** in long, flowing garments might accidentally expose themselves in a manner that would be inappropriate for such a solemn occasion.

C. Miscellaneous Laws (Chaps. 21—24)

1. Laws Regarding Slaves (21:1–11)

21:1–6 Following the giving of the Ten Commandments, God delivered many other miscellaneous laws for the conduct of the children of Israel.

A Hebrew could become a slave to pay off a debt, to make restitution for a theft, or by being born to Hebrew slaves. **A Hebrew servant** could be required to work for **six years**, but **in the seventh** year **he** had to be set **free**. If **he** was **married** when he became a slave, **then his wife** was freed with him. But if he married during his servitude, then **the wife and her children** were the **master's** property. In such a case, he could choose to remain a slave by having his ear bored to the doorpost, thus voluntarily identifying himself with his master's house. Henceforth he was "earmarked." This is a beautiful picture of Christ, the perfect Servant, who so loved us that He would not go out free, but rather went to the cross of Calvary. In view of what the

Savior has done for us, we should be His willing bondslaves, saying in the words of Bishop Moule:

> My Master, lead me to the door;
> Pierce this now-willing ear once more.
> Thy bonds are freedom; let me stay
> With Thee to toil, endure, obey.[21]

21:7–11 In the case of **a female** slave, she could **not go out** free in the seventh year if her master had taken her as a wife or concubine and was willing to fulfill his responsibilities to her. If he was not willing, she had to **be redeemed**, but not sold to Gentiles. If he wanted her as a wife for **his son**, then he had to treat her as he would any daughter-in-law. If the master took **another wife**, he was still responsible to provide for the slave girl and to give **her** full **marriage rights**. The latter probably means nothing more than living accomodations. Otherwise, she must be freed **without paying money**. The fact that God gave legislation concerning slavery does not mean that He approved it. He was only protecting the civil rights of the enslaved.

2. Laws Regarding Personal Injury (21:12–36)

21:12–14 Verse 12 states the general rule that to kill another person brings the sentence of **death** upon the offender. An exception is provided in the case of manslaughter; if the death was involuntary, the manslayer could **flee** to the altar of God, or later to special cities of refuge. But in cases of willful murder, the **altar** of God provided no safety for the offender.

21:15–17 Parenthood was especially protected by making the striking of one's **father or . . . mother** a crime punishable by **death**. Kidnapping and cursing one's parents were also capital crimes.

21:18, 19 If a man injured another in a quarrel, he was responsible to pay his **loss of . . . time** at work and also his medical expenses.

21:20, 21 A master could punish a slave, but he did not have the right to kill him. If a servant died immediately after a beating, the master was guilty; but if the slave lived **a day or two**, the master was not punishable because he obviously did not intend to kill a slave who was worth money to him.

21:22 If a pregnant woman was hit as a result of a **fight** between two **men** and **she** gave **birth prematurely**, though there was no serious injury, then her **husband** named the amount of the fine and **the judges** arbitrated the case.

21:23–25 The general rule concerning personal injury was **life for life, eye for eye, tooth for tooth,** etc. *The penalty should suit the crime,* avoiding excessive leniency or extreme severity. In practice, all cases except murder could be settled by paying a fine (see Num. 35:31).

21:26–36 If a man injured his slave's **eye** or **tooth**, the slave was allowed to **go free**. If an ox unexpectedly killed a person, the ox was to **be stoned**, and his **flesh** could **not be eaten**. If the **owner** knew that **the ox** was vicious and had been informed of it, then he too was to be **put to death**. But provision was made for the owner to pay a fine in lieu of **his life**. The fine would be the same for the death of **a son or . . . a daughter**. For the death of a **servant**, the fine was **thirty shekels of silver**, and **the ox** was to **be stoned**. Note: Judas betrayed Jesus for the same cost that was claimed for a slave killed by an ox, thus pricing Him at the value of a

dead slave. **If a man** left **a pit** uncovered, he was responsible for any loss incurred by animals falling into it. **If one man's ox** killed another man's ox, the value of both animals was divided equally. If the owner of the offending animal knew of its dangerous habits, then he had to **pay** for the slain animal, but he himself could take **the dead animal**.

3. Laws Regarding Stealing and Property Damage (22:1–6)

A **thief** had to **make full restitution** for what he had stolen, the amount depending on the nature of the theft. **If a thief** was slain while **breaking in** at night, his killer was not accountable; he had no way of knowing whether the motive was theft or murder. But to kill a thief during daylight hours brought guilt on the killer. If the thief of verse 1 could not make **restitution**, then he was **sold** as a slave. If a stolen animal was **found alive**, the thief had to **restore double**. If a farmer allowed an **animal** to stray into a neighbor's grain **field**, he had to restore the same amount that was **grazed from the best of his own field** or **vineyard**. Anyone who carelessly started a **fire** that destroyed crops had to **make restitution**.

4. Laws Regarding Dishonesty (22:7–15)

22:7–13 Verses 7–9 deal with the theft of **money** or property that was being kept in trust by one person for another. The one who stole it had to **pay double**. **If the thief** could **not be found**, the one holding the money in safekeeping had to appear before **the judges** to see if he himself was the guilty one. In any case of breach of trust, the judges decided whether the accused or accuser was guilty, then required **double** payment. If an **animal**

died, was **hurt, or** was **driven away** while being held in trust, and if the trustee swore **an oath** before **the LORD** that what had happened was beyond his power to prevent, no restitution was necessary. **If** the animal was **stolen** through the trustee's lack of watchfulness, he had to **make restitution.** No restitution was required for a mauled animal if the carcass was produced **as evidence.**

22:14, 15 If a borrowed animal was **injured** or killed, the borrower had to **make it good.** But **if the owner was** present when it happened, and was therefore able to protect it, no restitution was necessary. No restitution was necessary in the case of a **hired** animal, since the risk of loss was included in the price.

5. Laws Regarding Seduction (22:16, 17)

If a man seduced an unengaged **virgin** to sin with him, he was obligated to marry her and to **pay the** regular dowry. **If** the **father** refused **to give** his daughter in marriage, the man still had to pay the **"bride-price"** to the father, since the possibility that the daughter would ever marry was now greatly reduced.

6. Laws Regarding Civil and Religious Obligations (22:18–23:19)

22:18–20 Three capital crimes in addition to murder were sorcery or witchcraft, sexual intercourse **with an animal,** and idolatry.

22:21–24 The Jews were to be compassionate toward strangers in their land, because they too had been **strangers in** a foreign **land.** Humane treatment was also to be accorded to widows and **fatherless** children. The Lord took it upon Himself to enforce this commandment. Men were appointed to punish most other viola-

tions, but in this case, God would punish directly. He hasn't changed in His attitude toward the defenseless. He still cares for **widows** and orphans, and we as believers should do the same.

22:25–27 No interest was to be charged on **money** lent to an Israelite, though it could be charged to Gentiles (Deut. 23:20). Clothing taken **as a pledge** had to be returned **before** nightfall, since the cloak was used as a blanket.

22:28–31 It was forbidden to **revile God** or **curse a ruler** (cf. Acts 23:5). The Lord was to receive His portion, whether of crops or **sons** or animals. **Firstborn** animals were to be offered **on the eighth day.** It was forbidden to **eat meat** that had been **torn by beasts.** In such a case, the blood would not have been drained immediately, and to eat blood was a violation of God's law (Lev. 17). Also, there was the danger of infection from various diseases spread by animals (such as rabies), from which God was protecting His people.

23:1–12 In judicial matters, it was forbidden to **circulate a false report,** to conspire **with the wicked** to defend the guilty, to take sides with an evil **crowd,** or to **show partiality to** the **poor.** No spite was to be shown to an animal belonging to an enemy. If it was lost, it should be returned to its owner; and if it had fallen down with a heavy load, it should be assisted to its feet. Justice was to be shown to the **poor,** and **the innocent and righteous** were not to be condemned through **wicked** legal tricks. It was forbidden to take a **bribe,** or to **oppress** strangers. **The seventh year** was a sabbath, during which **land** was to **lie fallow** (idle). **The poor** were allowed to take what grew by itself that year. **The seventh day** was also to provide **rest** for master, **servant**, and animal. Note that the God of the OT was merciful and just, in spite of the charges made against Him by unbelieving modern critics.

23:13–17 Jews were forbidden to **mention . . . other gods** (idols) except perhaps by way of condemning them, as the prophets did. Three great feasts were to be kept to Jehovah: (1) **The Feast of Unleavened Bread**. It was held at the beginning of the year, immediately after the Passover Feast. It speaks of the importance of purging our lives from malice and wickedness. (2) **The Feast of Harvest**, also called Pentecost and the Feast of Weeks. It speaks of the coming of the Holy Spirit on the Day of Pentecost and the formation of the church. (3) **The Feast of Ingathering**, also called the Feast of Tabernacles. It typifies Israel dwelling securely in the land during the Millennium. Adult **males** were *required* to attend these feasts; for others it was *voluntary*. In the NT we see not only Joseph, but Mary and Jesus the Boy also going up annually to Jerusalem for the Passover Feast (Luke 2:41).

23:18, 19 **Leavened bread** (leaven symbolizes sin) was not to be used in connection with **the blood of** God's **sacrifice**, i.e., the Passover. **The fat** of an offering was the Lord's because it signified the best part; it was **not** to be left **until** the **morning**, but probably was to be burned. The best of **the firstfruits** were to be brought to **the house of the LORD**. An animal was not to be cooked **in its mother's milk**. This was probably aimed against fertility rites practiced by idolaters. Strict Jews today refrain from cooking meat and milk dishes in the same pan. Also, they refrain from eating meats in cream sauces, etc.[22]

7. Laws Regarding Conquest (23:20–33)

Here God promised to **send . . . an Angel** (the Lord Himself) **before** the Israelites, to lead them to the Promised Land and to **drive out** the heathen inhabitants. If the Jews refrained from idolatry and obeyed the Lord, He would do great things for them. Regarding the warning against disobedience, Henry writes:

> We do well to take heed of provoking our protector and benefactor, because if our defence depart from us, and the streams of his goodness be cut off, we are undone.[23]

Their land would extend **from the Red Sea to the sea** of the Philistines (the Mediterranean Sea) and **from the desert** (the Negev south of Canaan) **to the River** (Euphrates).

Notice the command to **drive . . . out** the inhabitants of the land. There were to be **no** treaties, no idolatry, no intermingling. God had already promised to destroy the wicked Canaanites, but Israel had to cooperate. This enshrines an important spiritual principle: God will give us victory over our enemies (the world, the flesh, and the devil), but He expects us to fight the good fight of faith.

Verse 33 finds its counterpart in 2 Corinthians 6:14–18. Separation from the world has always been God's will for His people. Israel's failure to obey this command led to her downfall. It is still true that "bad company corrupts good morals."

8. Ratification of the Covenant (24:1–8)

24:1, 2 Moses was on Mount Sinai when God spoke to him the laws and ordinances contained in Exodus 20–23. Before Moses left the top of the mountain, God told him to return with **Aaron** and his two sons, **Nadab and Abihu, and** with **seventy of the elders**. However, only **Moses** was to draw **near** to **the** LORD; the others were to remain at a distance. Under law, distance must be maintained between the sinner and God. Under grace we have "boldness to enter the Holiest by the blood of Jesus" (Heb. 10:19). Law says, "They shall not come near." Grace says, "Let us draw near" (Heb. 10:22).

24:3–8 **Moses** then descended to **the people** and delivered the law to them. They immediately agreed to keep it, little realizing their powerlessness to do so. To ratify this conditional covenant between God and Israel, Moses first **built an altar** with **twelve pillars** (for the twelve tribes of Israel). He then **took ... blood** from the offerings and **sprinkled ... half ... on the altar** (representing God's part in the covenant) and half **on the people** (signifying their determination to keep their part of the agreement).

9. Revelation of God's Glory (24:9–18)

24:9–11 Following this, **Moses** and the others **went** back **up** on Mount Sinai, as instructed in verses 1 and 2. There **they saw ... God** in His glory. Ordinarily, to see God would be sufficient to kill a person, but it was not so here. They were not destroyed; **they saw God, and they ate and drank.** In other words, they saw God and lived to eat the peace offering.

There is a seeming paradox in the Bible with regard to the matter of seeing God. On the one hand, there are verses which indicate that it is impossible to see God (Ex. 33:20; John 1:18; 1 Jn. 4:12). On the other hand, there are passages which speak of men seeing God, such as Genesis

32:30; Exodus 24:10; 33:23. The explanation is that while God in His unveiled glory is a consuming fire which would vaporize anyone looking at Him, yet He can reveal Himself in the form of a man, an angel, or a glory cloud (Deut. 5:24) which a person could see and still live.

24:12–18 A different ascent to Mount Sinai is apparently described here. This time **Joshua** accompanied Moses for part of the distance. In his absence, he delegated **Aaron and Hur** to serve as judges for the people. For **six days** Moses waited on the side of the mountain while the glory **cloud covered** the summit. Then, at God's invitation, he climbed up to the top and entered **the cloud**, where he was to remain for the next **forty days and forty nights.** Forty is the number of testing or probation. Here the testing was for the people rather than for Moses. They failed the test by plunging into sin. Thus the Lord revealed through the law what was in the heart of man.

The instructions Moses received during this time are recorded up to 31:18.

X. THE TABERNACLE AND THE PRIESTHOOD (Chaps. 25—40)

The next seven chapters deal with instructions for building the tabernacle, setting up the priesthood, and related legislation. Fully fifty chapters in the Bible are devoted to the tabernacle, showing its importance in God's sight.

The tabernacle was a tentlike structure which was to be God's dwelling place among His people. Each part of the tabernacle teaches us spiritual lessons concerning the Person and work of Christ and the way of approach to God. The priesthood reminded the people that sin had created distance between God and themselves, and that they could draw near to Him only through these representatives appointed and made fit by Him.

A. Instructions for Building the Tabernacle (Chaps. 25—27)

1. The Collection of Materials (25:1–9)

Moses was told to take from the people **an offering** of the materials that would be needed in erecting the **tabernacle** (sanctuary). The precious metals, fine fabrics, skins, **oil**, spices, and precious **stones** were no doubt the payment the Israelites received from the Egyptians when they left Egypt. They had worked—yes, slaved—for these things. Now they were giving them sacrificially. God insisted that **the tabernacle** be made strictly according to the divine pattern. If this is true of a physical building, how much more important to build up Christ's congregations (the people) according to the divine NT pattern!

2. The Ark of the Covenant (25:10–16)

The **ark** was a wooden chest, covered **inside and out . . . with pure gold**. On each side were **rings of gold** through which **poles** were placed for carrying it. The ark was to contain **the Testimony**—that is, the two tablets of the Law (v. 16) and later Aaron's rod and a jar of manna (Heb. 9:4).

3. The Mercy Seat (25:17–22)

The lid of the ark was called the **mercy seat**. It was a solid **gold** platform supporting two angel-like figures. These **cherubim**[24] faced **one another** and had **their wings** spread upward to meet each other. God manifested Himself in the glory cloud **between the two cherubim** and **above the mercy seat**. Cherubim are mentioned in at least thirteen books of the Bible. They are connected primarily with the holiness and righteousness of Jehovah, and are often mentioned in association with the throne of God. They are described in Ezekiel chapters 1 and 10.

4. The Table of Showbread (25:23–30)

The **table** of **showbread** was a wooden table covered **with pure gold**. It had an ornamental **molding** around the top (a crown), and **a handbreadth**-wide rim or **frame** with a second ornamental **gold molding**. Like the ark, **the table** was **carried** by **poles** placed through **rings . . . at** the lower **corners that are at its four legs**. On top of the table were placed twelve loaves (v. 30) for the twelve tribes of Israel. Also, there were various **dishes, pans, pitchers, and . . . bowls for pouring**.

5. The Golden Lampstand and Its Accessories (25:31–40)

25:31–39 The **lampstand** was made of solid **gold**. It had seven **branches** or arms at the top, each one holding a small lamp on a swivel with a wick for burning oil. In connection with the **lampstand**, there were **wick-trimmers** and **trays** for holding the pieces that were trimmed off (vv. 38, 39).

25:40 The great single requirement in making these objects was to follow the **pattern** which God gave **on the mountain**. There was no room for human improvising. So it is with all spiritual matters: We must follow divine directives and not deviate from **the pattern** that the Lord in His wisdom has given.

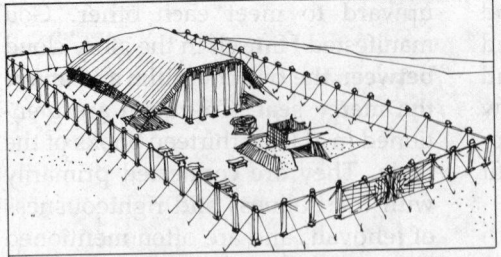

The tabernacle was to provide a place where God might dwell among His people. The term *tabernacle* sometimes refers to the tent, including the holy place and the Most Holy, which was covered with embroidered curtains. But in other places it refers to the entire complex, including the curtained court in which the tent stood.

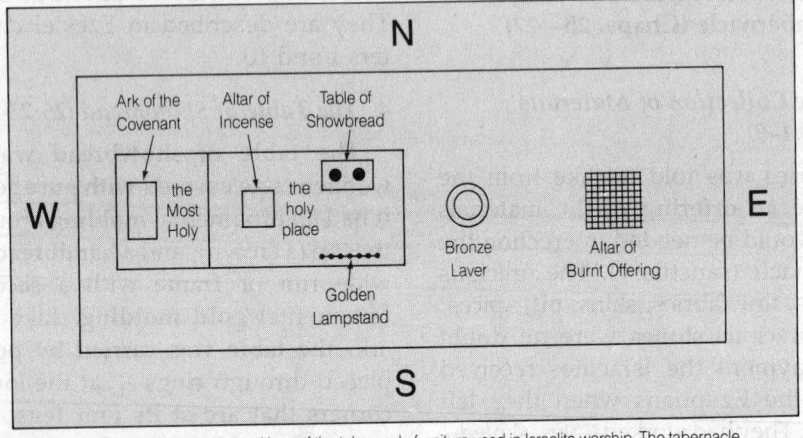

This illustration shows the relative positions of the tabernacle furniture used in Israelite worship. The tabernacle is enlarged for clarity.

The Plan of the Tabernacle

All the furniture of the tabernacle spoke of Christ in glory: the ark symbolized His deity (gold) and humanity (wood). The mercy seat pictured Christ as our mercy seat, or propitiation (Rom. 3:25). The table of showbread represented Christ as the Bread of life. The candlestick portrayed Christ as the Light of the world. The bronze altar (chap. 27) typified Christ as the Burnt Offering, wholly consumed for God. The altar of incense or the golden altar (chap. 30) pictured the fragrance of Christ to God. The laver (chap. 30) symbolized Christ cleansing His people by the washing of water by the Word (cf. Tit. 3:5; John 13:10; Eph. 5:26).

6. The Tabernacle Itself (Chap. 26)

26:1–6 Chapter 26 describes the tabernacle itself. It measured approximately forty-five feet long, fifteen feet wide, and fifteen feet high (assuming a cubit of about 18 inches). The two sides and one end consisted of upright boards, set in sockets and joined together. The other end (the entrance) had pillars.

The first covering, here called **the tabernacle**, was made of **fine woven linen, with artistic designs of cherubim** embroidered in **blue, purple, and scarlet**. It consisted of two sets of **five curtains . . . coupled** together. These two sets were joined by **clasps of gold** that were apparently attached to **fifty . . . loops of blue**. The total covering measured forty-two by sixty feet. It formed the ceiling and covered the sides to within eighteen inches from the ground.

26:7–13 The next covering, called **the tent**, was made of **goats' hair**. A set of **five curtains** was joined to a set

of **six curtains** by **bronze clasps** that
were connected to **fifty loops**. The
total covering, measuring forty-five
by sixty-six feet, overlapped all sides
of the tabernacle except the front.
There a section was folded back.

26:14 The third **covering** was made
of rams' skins, and the fourth was
made **of badger skins** (also translated
seal, porpoise, or dolphin skins).[25]
No measurements are given; these
coverings were probably the same
size as the goats' hair covering.

26:15–30 The **upright . . . boards**
that formed three sides of the tabernacle are described in verses 15–25.
Each **board** was fifteen by two-and-
one-quarter feet. It was made **of acacia wood** covered with gold and had
two tenons at the bottom to fit into
sockets. There were **twenty boards**
on each **side** and **six boards** on the
rear. **Two** special **boards** were made
for the **back corners**. The **boards** were
kept in place by wooden **bars**, covered **with gold**, that passed through
gold rings on the **boards**. **The middle bar** was one continuous piece.
Two shorter **bars** of varying lengths
may have been joined together to
form one bar at the top, and two
others joined to form one bar at the
bottom. Some think that the boards
were trellised frames.

26:31–37 The tabernacle itself was
divided into two rooms—first **the holy
place**, measuring thirty feet by fifteen
feet, and then **the Most Holy** place
(the Holy of Holies), measuring fifteen
feet by fifteen feet. These two rooms
were separated by **a veil** made **of fine
woven linen** and embroidered with
cherubim. The **veil** was hung on **four
pillars**. The **ark** and the **mercy seat**
were to be put **in the Most Holy**
place, whereas **the table** of showbread
and the golden **lampstand** were to be
put in the holy place. The altar of

incense (chap. 30) was the only other
furniture in the holy place; it was
placed in front of the veil. The
lampstand was on **the south** side of
the holy place **and the table on the
north side**. The door of the tabernacle was a woven **screen**, similar to
the veil, but hung on **five pillars of
acacia wood** covered **with gold**, and
standing on bronze bases.

7. The Bronze Altar of Burnt Offering (27:1–8)

The **altar** of burnt offering, also
known as the bronze altar, was made
of acacia wood covered with **bronze**.
It measured seven-and-a-half feet
square and four-and-a-half feet high.
Horns protruded from each of **its
four corners**. It was carried by **poles**
attached to the lower **sides**.

8. The Outer Court, Pillars, and Screen (27:9–19)

Surrounding the tabernacle itself
was a large area known as **the court**.
This was enclosed by **woven linen
. . . hangings** stretched between **bronze
pillars**. The enclosure measured 150
feet long, 75 feet wide, and 7.5 feet
high. The **gate** at the east end was
thirty feet wide. It had a **screen** of
embroidered linen, similar to the curtains of the tabernacle. Unless otherwise designated, **all the utensils of
the tabernacle** were to be made **of
bronze**.

9. The Oil for the Lampstand (27:20, 21)

Oil for the lampstand was to be
pure oil of pressed olives, a symbol
of the Holy Spirit. It was **to burn
continually**—that is, every evening,
"from evening until morning." The
expression **"the tabernacle of meeting"**
or "the tent of meeting" (NASB) is
used here of the tent that would be

This replica of the high priest's breastplate is set with stones representing the 12 tribes of Israel. On each stone the name of one tribe is engraved.

God's dwelling place, but it is used in chapter 33:7 of a provisional tent erected by Moses.

B. The Priesthood (Chaps. 28, 29)

1. The Garments of the Priests (Chap. 28)

28:1, 2 Chapter 28 deals with the **garments** of the high **priest** and of his **sons**. These garments, their colors, the jewels, etc., all speak of the various glories of Christ, our Great High Priest. The family of **Aaron** was the priestly family.

28:3–29 The high **priest** had two sets of **garments**: (1) garments of glory and beauty, richly colored and intricately embroidered; (2) plain white linen garments. The former are described here (vv. 2–4). **The ephod** (vv. 6,7) was similar to an apron, with **two** sections **joined** at the shoulders and open at the sides. **The intricately woven band** (v. 8) was a belt which went around the waist just above the

hem of the ephod. The **settings** (v. 13) were **of gold** filigree to hold precious stones. On each shoulder was placed an **onyx** stone engraved with **the names of . . . six** of the tribes **of Israel** (vv. 9–12). On the front of the ephod rested **the breastplate**, containing twelve precious **stones, each one** bearing the **name** of a tribe. The breastplate was attached to the ephod by gold **chains** (vv. 13–28). Thus the high priest carried the tribes **of Israel** before God on his **shoulders** (v. 12—the place of strength) and **over his heart** (the place of affection; v. 29).

28:30 The breastplate is called **the breastplate of judgment** (vv. 15, 29, 30), probably because **the Urim and Thummim** were in it and were used to determine the judgments of the Lord (Num. 27:21).

The expression **"Urim and Thummim"** means *lights* and *perfections*. We do not know exactly what these were, but we do know (as explained above) that they were connected with the breastplate and that they were used to obtain guidance from the Lord (1 Sam. 28:6).

28:31–35 **The robe of the ephod** was a **blue** garment worn underneath the ephod. It extended below the knees. On the **hem** were small **bells** and **pomegranates**, speaking of testimony and fruit. The **sound** of the bells had to **be heard** when **Aaron** entered or left **the holy place**.

28:36–38 **On the** headcovering, or **turban**, the high priest wore a golden **plate** or miter bearing the words **"HOLINESS TO THE LORD,"** which was **always** to **be on his forehead**. It was for **the iniquity of the holy things**, a reminder that even our most sacred acts are stained with sin. As Archbishop Beveridge once said, "I cannot pray but I sin. . . . My repentance needs to be repented of and my tears need to be washed with the blood of my Redeemer."[26]

28:39–43 The woven **tunic** of checkered work was a **linen** coat which the high priest wore underneath the blue robe. This had a **woven . . . sash**. Aaron's sons wore plain white **tunics, sashes**, and **hats . . . for glory and beauty** (v. 40). As underclothing, they wore **linen trousers**. They were clothed from head to ankles, but there was no covering on their feet. This is because they were on holy ground when they ministered to the Lord (3:5). The word rendered **"consecrate"** (v. 41) literally means *to fill the hand* (that is, with offerings).

2. The Consecration of the Priests (Chap. 29)

29:1–9 God ordained **Aaron and his sons** as the first priests. After that the only way to become a priest was by being born into the priestly tribe and family. In the church the only way to become a priest is by the *new birth* (Rev. 1:5,6). For man to ordain priests is sheer human presumption.

The ritual described here was carried out in Leviticus 8. The consecration of the priests is somewhat similar to the cleansing of lepers (Lev. 14). In both cases, sacrificial blood was applied to the person himself, teaching the necessity for expiation before sinful man can approach God.

The materials for the offerings are introduced in verses 1–3; detailed instructions are given later concerning their use. The first step in the consecration of the priests was the washing of **Aaron and his sons . . . with water** at **the door of the tabernacle** (v. 4). Second, **Aaron** was clothed with the **garments** described in the previous chapter (vv. 5, 6). Then he was anointed with **oil** (v. 7). Next, the sons were clothed in their priestly tunics (vv. 8, 9).

29:10–21 Three offerings followed: a **bull** for **a sin offering** (vv. 10–14); a **ram** for **a burnt offering** (vv. 15–18); another **ram of consecration** (vv. 19–21). Laying **hands on the head of** a sacrificial victim signified identification with it and indicated that the animal was to die in place of the offerer (v. 10). **The blood**, of course, was a picture of the blood of Christ, shed for the forgiveness of sins. **The fat** was considered the choicest part of the animal and was therefore offered to the Lord (v. 13). The first **ram** was completely burned on the altar (vv. 15–18). This speaks of Christ's complete devotion to God and His being completely offered up to God. The **blood** of the second **ram** (the **ram of consecration**) was to be **put . . . on the tip of the right ear of Aaron . . . and . . . his sons, on the thumb of their right hand**, upon the **big toe of their right foot** (v. 20), and sprinkled on their **garments** (v. 21). This signified the need of cleansing from sin in every area of human life—the **ear** for obedience to God's Word, the **hand** for action or service, and the **foot** for walk or deportment. It might seem strange that the priests' beautiful **garments** should be sprinkled with blood; atoning blood might not seem attractive in man's eyes, but it is absolutely necessary in the sight of God.

29:22–34 Next, Moses was ordered to fill the priests' **hands** with the materials necessary for sacrifice and thus authorize them to sacrifice (vv. 22–28). The first offering (vv. 22–25) was to be waved **before the LORD** and then burned **on the altar** of **burnt offering. The breast of the ram was** waved **before the LORD**, perhaps horizontally, and the shoulder or **thigh**

was heaved before the Lord, doubtless vertically. These two portions were then given to the priests for food (vv. 26–28). The waved breast speaks of God's affection for us, and the heaved shoulder symbolizes His power stretched forth in our behalf. Aaron's **garments** became the property of **his sons after him**, since the priesthood was handed down from father to son (vv. 29, 30). The food of the priests and how it was prepared is described in verses 31–34.

29:35–46 The consecration ceremony lasted **seven days**, with the sacrifices repeated **every day** and **the altar** cleansed by blood and anointed with oil (vv. 35–37). From then on, the priests were required to **offer on the altar** of burnt offering **two lambs** which were one **year** old—**one lamb . . . in the morning** and the **other** in the evening of every day **at twilight** (vv. 38–42). God then promised to meet with the people **at the . . . tabernacle**, to **dwell among** them and to **be their God** (vv. 43–46).

C. Further Instructions Concerning the Tabernacle (Chaps. 30, 31)

1. The Altar of Incense (30:1–10)

The **altar** of **incense** was a **gold-plated wooden altar** which stood in the holy place. It was eighteen inches square and three feet high. It was also known as the golden altar. On this altar, **incense** was burned both **morning** and evening, picturing the intercessory work of Christ on our behalf. Although this altar was in the holy place, it was so intimately connected with the Holy of Holies that the writer to the Hebrews possibly mentions it as being behind the second veil (Heb. 9:4, KJV), although the word in Hebrews can also be translated *censer* (NKJV).[27] The altar

was carried on **poles** that were placed through **rings** that were **under the molding** on opposite **sides**.

2. The Redemption Money (30:11–16)

God ordered every male Israelite **twenty years old and above** to pay **half a shekel** as **a ransom for himself**. This payment, the same for **rich** and **poor**, was levied whenever there was a **census** and was used to finance **the service of the tabernacle**. It guaranteed protection against plague (v. 12). At the outset it was used to make silver sockets to support the boards of the tabernacle. Silver speaks of redemption, which is the foundation of our faith. Redemption is needed by all and is available to all on the same terms.

3. The Laver (30:17–21)

The **laver of bronze** stood **between** the entrance to **the tabernacle of meeting and the altar**. It was a basin where the priests could **wash their hands and their feet**. It was made of the bronze mirrors donated by the women (38:8). No dimensions are given. Any priest who handled holy things before washing was sentenced to death. This is a solemn reminder that we must be spiritually and morally clean before entering any service for the Lord (see Heb. 10:22).

4. The Anointing Oil (30:22–33)

A **holy anointing oil** was used to **anoint the tabernacle**, its furniture, and the priests themselves. It was not to be used for any other purpose. **Oil** in Scripture is often a *type of the Holy Spirit*. The anointing of the priests signifies the necessity for enduement of the Spirit in all divine service.

5. The Incense (30:34–38)

The **incense** was a perfume made of various **spices** that was burned on the golden altar of incense morning and evening. Like the oil, it was not to be imitated or used elsewhere.

6. The Gifted Artisans (31:1–11)

God appointed **gifted artisans, Bezalel**[28] and **Aholiab**, to construct **the tabernacle . . . and all** its **furniture**. They supervised other workers in this holy task (v. 6b). The repetition of **"I"** in this paragraph shows that with the divine command there is divine enablement. The Lord appoints His workers, endows them with ability and talent, and gives them a work to do for His glory (v. 6). The work is all the Lord's, but He accomplishes it through human instrumentality, then rewards His agents.

7. The Sign of the Sabbath (31:12–18)

31:12–17 Keeping the **Sabbath** was to be **a sign between** God and Israel. No **work** was to be done **on the seventh day**, not even the building of the tabernacle. Disobedience was punishable by **death**.

31:18 At this point the Lord **gave Moses two tablets of . . . stone** inscribed with the Law **of God**—that is, the Ten Commandments (cf. Deut. 10:4).

THE TABERNACLE: GOD'S PICTURE OF CHRIST

Basically the tabernacle speaks of Christ, the Word who became flesh and "tabernacled" among us (John 1:14, Greek).[29]

It can also be used as picturing God's way of salvation and the subsequent life and ministry of the believer.

But although it pictures the way of salvation, it was given to a people who were already in covenant relationship with God. Rather than providing a way of salvation, the tabernacle offered the means by which the people could be cleansed from outward, ritual defilement and thus be able to approach God in worship.

The tabernacle and the services connected with it were copies of things in the heavens (Heb. 8:5; 9:23, 24). This does not mean that there must be a structural or architectural likeness in heaven, but that the tabernacle pictures spiritual realities in heaven. Notice these correspondences:

The earthly sanctuary (Heb. 9:1–5)	The heavenly sanctuary (Heb. 8:2; 9:11–15)
The Holiest of all (Heb. 9:3b)	The Holiest, God's presence (Heb. 10:19)
The veil (Heb. 9:3a)	The veil, Christ's body (Heb. 10:20)
The blood of animals (Heb. 9:13)	The blood of Christ (Heb. 9:14)
The altar (Heb. 7:13; Ex. 27:1–8)	Christ, our altar (Heb. 13:10)
The high priest (Heb. 5:1–4)	Christ our Great High Priest (Heb. 4:14, 15; 5:5–10; 7:20–28; 8:1; 10:21)
The sacrifices (Heb. 10:1–4, 11)	Christ, our sacrifice (Heb. 9:23–28; 10:12)
The ark (Heb. 9:4)	The throne of grace (Heb. 4:16)
The altar of incense (Heb. 9:4, KJV)	The altar of incense in heaven (Rev. 8:3)

The Linen Curtains Forming the Outer Court (150 ft. x 75 ft.)

The curtains were made of white, fine-twined linen, symbolizing the perfect righteousness of God. They were 7½ feet high, forming a barrier that prevented man from seeing over them. This suggests man's failure to reach God's standard of righteousness (Rom. 3:23) and the sinner's inability to see or understand the things of God (1 Cor. 2:14). The curtains were held upright by 56 pillars that stood in bronze sockets and had silver hooks and bands.

The Gate

To enter the court, a person had to go through the door or gate. There was only one way of entrance, just as Christ is the only way to God (John 14:6; Acts 4:12). The gate was 30 feet wide, picturing the sufficiency of Christ for all mankind (John 6:37; Heb. 7:25).

The curtains forming the gate were made of white linen, embroidered with blue, purple, and scarlet. This typifies Christ as presented in the four Gospels:

Purple	Matthew	The King (Matt. 2:2)
Scarlet	Mark	The lowly Servant, suffering for sins, that are likened to scarlet in Isaiah 1:18
White	Luke	The perfect Man (Luke 3:22)
Blue	John	The heavenly One (John 3:13)

The Bronze Altar of Burnt Offering (7½ ft. sq., 4½ ft. high)

The first object in the inner court was the altar. This was the place of sacrifice. It speaks of the cross of Christ at Calvary (Heb. 9:14, 22). This is where the sinner must begin in approaching God. The altar was made of bronze and acacia wood, the incorruptible wood of the wilderness. Bronze speaks of judgment and the wood pictures Christ's sinless, incorruptible humanity. He who knew no sin bore God's judgment against our sins (2 Cor. 5:21).

The altar was hollow, with a grating halfway down, on which the animal was placed. There were four horns overlaid with bronze, one at each corner (Ex. 27:2). Apparently the sacrifice was tied to these horns (Ps. 118:27b). It was not cords or even nails that bound our Savior to the cross, but His everlasting love for us.

When an Israelite brought a burnt offering, he laid his hand on the head of the victim, identifying himself with it, and saying in this way that the animal would die in his place. It would be a substitutionary sacrifice. The animal was slain and its blood poured out, pointing forward to the blood of Christ, without which there is no forgiveness of sins (Heb. 9:22).

All except the skin was burned on the altar. Here, as so often, the type breaks down because Christ was *totally* devoted to the Father's will at Calvary.

It was a sweet aroma offering, reminding us of God's complete satisfaction with the work of Christ. And it made atonement for the offerer.

The Laver

The laver was made of bronze from the mirrors of the women (Ex. 38:8). J. H. Brown remarks: "They handed over those things that were used for self-gratification, those things that in some measure ministered to the gratification of the flesh." Self-judgment must precede worship (1 Cor. 11:31).

The laver was for the priests. It spoke of the necessity of cleansing for service (Isa. 52:11). The priests were bathed once on entering their office (Lev. 8:6). After that, they were required to wash their hands and feet regularly. One bath—many cleansings. Today all believers are priests (1 Pet. 2:5, 9). We need the bath of regeneration only once (John 3:5; 13:10; Tit. 3:5). But we need to constantly wash our hands (for service) and our feet (for the godly walk) (John 13:10). We do this with the water of the Word (Ps. 119:9–11; John 15:3; Eph. 5:26).

The laver may have had an upper basin for washing the hands and a lower one for washing the feet. The Bible does not describe the exact form or size of the laver.

The Tabernacle Itself (15 ft. x 45 ft.)

The structure itself was outwardly plain but inwardly beautiful. Everything inside was covered with gold or was embroidered work. It suggests Christ, who tabernacled among us (John 1:14); He had no beauty outwardly that we should desire Him (Isa. 53:2b), but inwardly He is altogether lovely.

There were four coverings in the following order from the inside out:

Fine embroidered linen	The righteousness and beauty of Christ.
Goat's hair	The atonement of Christ, who became our Scapegoat (cf. Lev. 16).
Ram's skins, dyed red	The consecration of Christ (cf. the ram of consecration, Ex. 29:19–22).
Badger skins	These are also translated porpoise skins, dolphin skins, and hides of sea cows. They protected the tabernacle from the elements, suggesting Christ's guarding His people from outward evil.

The Boards

Some think these were lattice frames rather than solid boards. In any case, they picture believers, forming a unified habitation of God in the Spirit (Eph. 2:22). They were made of acacia wood overlaid with gold, representing our humanity and our position in Christ. God sees us in Him. The boards were 15 feet high and were joined together by five horizontal bars covered with gold (Ex. 26:26–28). The middle one went through the boards, perhaps a type of the Holy Spirit. Each board was held in place by tenons in two silver sockets. Silver speaks of redemption (cf. Ex. 30:15 where the silver shekel was the atonement money). The believer's foundation is the redemptive work of Christ (1 Pet. 1:18, 19).

The Holy Place

The veil leading to the holy place suggests Christ as the way to communion with God (Eph. 2:18; 3:12).

There was no chair in the holy place because the priests' work was never completed. Contrast the once-for-all work of Christ (Heb. 10:12).

The Table of Showbread (36 in. long, 18 in. wide, 27 in. high; on the north side)

The table was made of acacia wood overlaid with gold, picturing the humanity and deity of our Lord. There were twelve unleavened loaves on the table, symbolizing God's people as they appear before God in association with Christ. The bread was surrounded by two crowns of gold, just as we are kept secure by the crowned, glorified Christ.

The Lampstand (Weighed 75 lbs. No dimensions given; on the south side)

Made of beaten gold, it had a base and a stem rising from it, out from which rose seven arms with an oil lamp on top of each. It was the only source of light in the tabernacle. It may picture the Holy Spirit in His ministry of glorifying Christ (John 16:14) or it may speak of Christ as the One who is the light of heaven (Rev. 21:23) and the source of all spiritual light (John 8:12). The pure gold speaks of deity.

The lamps burned from evening until morning (Ex. 27:21; 1 Sam. 3:3).

The Altar of Incense (18 in. sq. and 36 in. high; before the veil in the center)

It was made of acacia wood and gold, typifying the humanity and deity of Christ. It pictures the glorified Christ interceding for His people (Heb. 7:24–26; Rev. 8:3, 4). The incense speaks of the fragrance of His Person and work. The fire had to come from the altar of burnt offering, the fragrance of Christ's offering of Himself without spot to God.

The incense was made of stacte, onycha, galbanum, and frankincense—all combining to make one fragrance—the sweet aroma of Christ (Eph. 5:2).

The Most Holy Place

The veil leading to the Most Holy Place speaks of the flesh of Christ (Heb. 10:19–22), rent in death at Calvary (Luke 23:45). Whereas only the priests could enter the holy place, and only the high priest could enter the Holiest on only one day of the year, believers now have access to God's presence at any and all times (Heb. 10:19–22).

The Ark (3¾ ft. long, 2¼ ft. wide and high)

This was a chest of acacia wood plated with gold. It spoke of the throne of God. There are two ways of thinking of its contents, one man-centered and somewhat negative, and one Christ-centered, and very positive:

First, it contained three memorials of rebellion (manna, Ex. 16:2, 3; the law, Ex. 32:19; Aaron's rod, Num. 17:1–13) and thus may picture Christ bearing the curse because of our rebellion.

Or the manna may picture *Christ* as the Bread of God; the law as that expression of God's holiness which the Lord magnified and made glorious; and Aaron's rod as Christ in resurrection, a Priest of God's own choosing.

The Mercy Seat

The mercy seat was a lid for the ark. On top were two cherubim, made of beaten gold, guardians of God's throne and defenders of His righteousness. They looked down on the blood that was sprinkled before the ark and on the mercy seat. The blood of Christ satisfies God's righteousness

and hides all our transgressions from view. Thus a judgment seat becomes a mercy seat. Christ is our Mercy Seat (same word as *propitiation*, 1 Jn. 2:2). God meets the sinner in Christ.

The Glory Cloud

When the tabernacle was completed, the Lord appeared on the mercy seat in a glory cloud, also known as the *Shekinah*; from the Hebrew word for *dwell*. This was a visible symbol of His glory.‡

D. An Outbreak of Idolatry (Chaps. 32, 33)

1. The Golden Calf (32:1–10)

Impatient at Moses' delay in returning to them, **the people** asked **Aaron** to **make** an idol for them. He meekly complied by converting their **golden earrings** into a golden **molded calf**, an act that was expressly forbidden (Ex. 20:4). Then they broke out in revelry, worshiping the idol and eating, drinking, and playing immorally. They professed to be worshiping **the Lord** (v. 5), but by means of the calf. God had blessed His people with gold when they left Egypt (12:35, 36), but the blessing turned into a curse through the sinful hearts of the people. God informed **Moses** what was going on at the foot of the mountain (vv. 7, 8) and threatened to destroy **this people** (vv. 9, 10).

2. The Intercession and Anger of Moses (32:11–35)

32:11–13 In his reply, **Moses** stands out as one of the great intercessors of the Bible. Notice the strong arguments he uses: The people were the Lord's **people** (vv. 11, 12). God had cared for them enough to deliver them from **Egypt** (v. 11). **The Egyptians** would gloat if God did to His people what the Egyptians had been unable to do (v. 12). God must be true to the covenants He made with the patriarchs (v. 13).

32:14 "So the LORD relented of the harm..." (v. 14). The word *harm* means punishment in this context. In response to the intercession of Moses, the Lord turned away from the punishment which He otherwise **would** have inflicted on **His people**.

32:15–20 Moses descended the mountain with **the two tablets of the Testimony**, met **Joshua** on the way, and **came** to the people as they were carrying on their sensual, idolatrous feast. In righteous **anger, he ... broke** the tablets of the law as a witness of what the people had already done. He then **ground** the golden **calf ... to powder, scattered it on the water and made the** people **drink it** (v. 20)—perhaps a suggestion that our sins return to us as a bitter potion.

32:21–24 When **Moses** asked Aaron **what** the **people** had done to deserve this treatment, Aaron explained to him what had happened, implying that the golden **calf** had come **out** of **the fire** rather mysteriously (v. 24). It was only because of the intercession of Moses that the Lord did not kill Aaron (Deut. 9:19, 20).

32:25–29 Some of **the people** were still carrying on without restraint. When Moses called for loyal followers, the tribe of **Levi** responded and proceeded to slay with **the sword** those who were "out of control" (NASB). Even close relatives were not spared (vv. 25–29). Here the broken law brought death to **three thousand ... people**. At Pentecost the gospel of grace brought salvation to 3,000 people. The heroic loyalty of the Levites may be why theirs was chosen to be the priestly tribe (see v. 29).

32:30–35 Moses **returned** up the mountain to meet **the** LORD, thinking that he might **make atonement for** the people's **sin** (vv. 30–32). The Lord's answer was twofold: First, He would punish the people who made the calf (He did this by sending a plague—v. 35); second, He would send His **Angel** to **go before** Moses as he led **the people to the** Promised Land. The character of Moses shines out in verse 32—he was willing to die for his people. **"Blot me out of Your book"** is a figurative way of saying "end my life."[30] God spared Moses but He did not spare His beloved Son. How like our Lord who died, the Just for the unjust!

3. The Repentance of the People (33:1–6)

The Lord refused to accompany the sinful Israelites on their journey to Canaan, **lest** He be compelled to destroy them **on the way**. Instead, He would send an **Angel** as His representative. **When the people heard this bad news, they mourned** and **stripped themselves of their ornaments**, such as had been used to make the golden calf, and never wore them from **Mount Horeb** onward.

4. Moses' Tent of Meeting (33:7–11)

The **tent** mentioned in verse 7 was *not* the tabernacle, which had not yet been erected, but a provisional tent **pitched** by **Moses** and called here **"the tabernacle (tent) of meeting."** Individuals who desired to seek the Lord could go there, **outside the camp**. The camp itself had been defiled by the sin of the people, so the tent was situated **outside**. When **Moses entered the** tent, the pillar of cloud descended, indicating God's presence. Verse 11 cannot mean that Moses saw God in His essential being. It simply means that he had direct, **face to face**, unhindered communion with God. It is worth noting that *Joshua*, then **a young man**, did **not depart from** the **tabernacle**. Perhaps this was the secret of his later spiritual success.

5. *The Prayer of Moses (33:12–23)*

33:12–17 Moses asked for God's presence to lead His **people** to Canaan. Then the Lord graciously promised that His **Presence** would **go with** them. Moses insisted that nothing short of this would do. Like Noah, Moses had **found grace in** the Lord's **sight** and received his request. "Safety does not consist in the absence of danger but in the presence of God."

33:18–23 Next Moses asked for a sight of God's **glory**. God replied by promising to reveal Himself as a God of grace and **compassion** (see Ex. 34:6, 7). Moses could not **see** God's **face . . . and live**, but he would be permitted to **stand on** a **rock** while God's **glory** passed **by**, and he would see an appearance of God's **back**. This is figurative language, of course, since God does not have a body (John 4:24). As Hywel Jones put it, "Moses is to see the afterglow which is a reliable indication of what the full splendor is to be."[31]

No one can see God's face and live (v. 20). This means that no one can look upon the unveiled glory of God; He dwells "in unapproachable light, whom no man has seen or can see" (1 Tim. 6:16). In that sense, no one has seen God at any time (1 Jn. 4:12). How then do we explain passages in the Bible where people saw God and did not die? For example, Hagar (Gen. 16:13); Jacob (Gen. 32:30); Moses, Aaron, Nadab, Abihu, and seventy of the elders of Israel (Ex. 24:9–11); Gideon (Judg. 6:22,23); Manoah and his wife (Judg. 13:22); Isaiah (Isa. 6:1); Ezekiel (Ezek. 1:26, cf. 10:20); John (Rev. 1:17).

The answer is that these people saw God as represented by the Lord Jesus Christ. Sometimes He appeared as the Angel of the LORD (see Judges 6 for a discussion of this doctrine), sometimes as a Man, and once manifested Himself as a Voice (Ex. 24:9–11; cf. Deut. 4:12). The only begotten Son, who is in the bosom of the Father, has fully declared God (John 1:18). Christ is the brightness of God's glory and the express image of His Person (Heb. 1:3). That is why He could say, "He who has seen Me has seen the Father" (John 14:9).

E. The Covenant Renewed (34:1—35:3)

34:1–9 Again **Moses** alone was called **up . . . to Mount Sinai**, this time with **two tablets of stone** which he himself had prepared. There the Lord revealed Himself as a **merciful and gracious** God, **longsuffering, and abounding in goodness and truth** (vv. 6, 7).

Three different words are used in verse 7 for wrongdoing. **Iniquity** has to do with perverting the ways of the Lord. **Transgression** means rebellion against God. **Sin** is literally "offense," primarily by missing the mark which God has set. They all convey the idea of falling short of the glory of God (Rom. 3:23). The Israelites should all have died for having broken the law of God, but God spared them in **mercy**. Moses **worshiped** the Lord and pled for His presence and **grace** on the basis of His people's unworthiness (vv. 8, 9).

34:10–17 God then renewed the **covenant**, promising to do marvels for Israel in **driving out** the inhabitants of Canaan. He cautioned them against intermingling with the heathen or adopting their idolatrous practices. Asherim were obscene images, or phallic idols, symbols of fertility.

Because God had made a **covenant** with His people, they were not to **make a covenant with the inhabitants of the land**. It is impossible to be joined to God and to idols at the same time (see 1 Cor. 10:21).

34:18–27 God then repeated instructions concerning **the Feast of Unleavened Bread** (v. 18); the consecration of **the firstborn** (vv. 19, 20); the Sabbath (v. 21); the **Feast of Weeks** and the **Feast of Ingathering** (v. 22). **All** males were to **appear before the LORD** for the **three** annual feasts mentioned in 23:14–17 (vv. 23,24). Note in verse 24 that God promised to control the wills of the Canaanites so that they would not try to seize the property of the Jewish men when the latter went to Jerusalem **three times** a **year**. After repeating other rules (vv. 25, 26), **the LORD** ordered Moses to **write** down the **words** He had just spoken in verses 11–26 (v. 27). Then the Lord Himself **wrote . . . the Ten Commandments . . . on the tablets of stone** (v. 28; cf. v. 1 and Deut. 10:1–4).

34:28–35 After **forty days and forty nights** on the mountain, **Moses came down** with the **two tablets in** his **hand** (vv. 28, 29a). He was unaware that **his face** was shining as a result of being in the Lord's presence (vv. 29b, 30). People **were afraid to come near him**. After delivering the **commandments** of the Lord to **Israel, he put a veil on his face** (vv. 31–33). Verse 33 (NKJV) reads **"And when Moses had finished speaking . . ."** instead of "Till . . ." (KJV). Paul explains in 2 Corinthians 3:13 that Moses veiled his face so the people would not see the fading glory of the law, the legal dispensation.

35:1–3 Then Moses gathered all the congregation . . . together and repeated the law of the **Sabbath** to them.

F. Preparation of the Tabernacle Furnishings (35:4—38:31)

1. The People's Gifts and the Gifted People (35:4—36:7)

35:4–20 Moses gave instructions for a free-will **offering to the LORD** consisting of materials for the building of **the tabernacle** (vv. 4–9). He also called for **gifted artisans** to make the various parts (vv. 10–19). God had two buildings for worship, the tabernacle and the temple. Both were paid for in advance. God moved the hearts of His people to supply what was needed (vv. 5, 21, 22, 26, 29). Our giving and service should likewise be voluntary and ungrudging.

35:21—36:1 Many of the people responded generously with the treasures they had brought from Egypt (vv. 21–29). Those who had given gold for the calf lost it all. Those who invested in the tabernacle had the joy of seeing their wealth used for the glory of Jehovah.

Moses publicly named **Bezalel** and **Aholiab** as the ones whom God had appointed **to work in all manner of artistic workmanship**. They also had **the ability to teach** others (35:30—36:1).

36:2–7 The skilled workers began the task of **making the sanctuary**, but the people brought so much material **each morning** that Moses had to restrain them **from bringing** more.

From verse 8 of chapter 36 to the end of chapter 39 we find a detailed account of the construction of the tabernacle and its furnishings. The repetition of so much detail reminds us that God never tires of those things which speak to Him about His beloved Son.

2. The Curtains Covering the Tabernacle (36:8–19)

The inner **curtains**, made **of fine linen**, were called **"the tabernacle"**

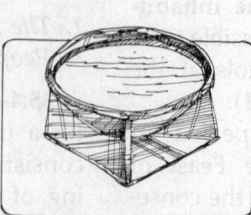

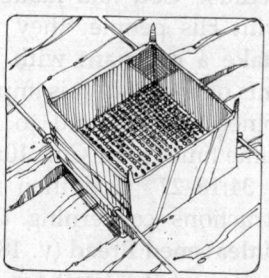

Ark of the Covenant
(Ex. 25:10–22)
The ark was most sacred of all
the furniture in the tabernacle.
Here the Hebrews kept a copy of
the Ten Commandments, which
summarized the whole covenant.

Bronze Laver
(Ex. 30:17–21)
It was to the laver of bronze
that the priests would come
for cleansing. They must be
pure to enter the presence
of God.

Altar of Burnt Offering
(Ex. 27:1–8)
Animal sacrifices were
offered on this altar, located in
the court in front of the
tabernacle. The blood of the
sacrifice was sprinkled on
the four horns of the altar.

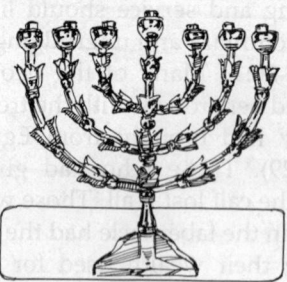

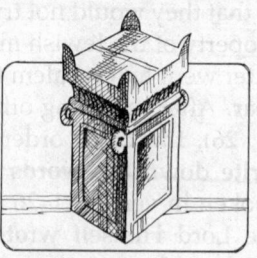

Golden Lampstand
(Ex. 25:31–40)
The gold lampstand stood in
the holy place, opposite the table
of showbread. It held seven
lamps, flat bowls in which a wick
lay with one end in the oil of
the bowl and the lighted end
hanging out.

Table of Showbread
(Ex. 25:23–30)
The table of showbread was
a stand on which the
offerings were placed.
Always in God's presence on
the table were the 12 loaves
of bread representing the 12
tribes.

Altar of Incense
(Ex. 30:1–10)
The altar of incense inside
the tabernacle was much
smaller than the altar of burnt
offering outside. The incense
burned on the altar was a
perfume of a sweet-smelling
aroma.

The Furniture of the Tabernacle

(v. 8). Next were **curtains of goats' hair**, "**the tent**" (v. 14). The curtains **of ram skins** and **badger** skins (or possibly seal or porpoise skins) were called "the **covering**" (v. 19).

3. The Boards for the Three Sides (36:20–30)

These **boards** were made **of acacia wood**, the only kind of wood used in the tabernacle. Acacia trees flourished in dry places, were very beautiful,

and produced wood that was practically indestructible. Likewise, the Lord Jesus was a root out of dry ground (Isa. 53:2), was morally beautiful, and is the Eternal One.

4. The Bars Which Held the Boards Together (36:31–34)

Four of the **bars** were visible, one invisible because it passed **through the** center of the **boards**. The invisible bar is a good picture of the Holy

Spirit, binding believers together into "a holy temple in the Lord" (Eph. 2:21, 22). The four other bars may suggest the life, love, position, and confession that are common to all God's people.

5. The Veil Leading to the Most Holy Place (36:35, 36)

This **veil** represents the flesh of the Lord Jesus (Heb. 10:20), torn on Calvary in order to open the way of approach to God for us. The **cherubim** on the veil are thought to represent guardians of the righteous throne of God.

6. The Screen Leading to the Holy Place (36:37, 38)

This **screen** was made of the same material as the gate of the court and the veil mentioned above, and pictures Christ as the way to God.

7. The Ark of the Covenant (37:1–5)

The ark was a chest made **of acacia wood ... overlaid ... with pure gold**. It pointed to the humanity and deity of our Lord. It contained the tablets of the Law, a golden jar of manna, and Aaron's rod that budded. If applied to Christ, these things speak of Him as the One who said, "Your law is within my heart" (Ps. 40:8b); as the bread of God come down from heaven (John 6:33); and as the Priest of God's choosing, risen from the dead (Heb. 7:24–26). If applied to the people of Israel, they were all memorials of failure and rebellion.

8. The Mercy Seat (37:6–9)

The **mercy seat** was God's throne, the place of His dwelling on earth. As the golden **cherubim** looked down upon it, they did not see the Law (which Israel had broken) or the jar of manna and Aaron's rod, both of which

were associated with rebellions by Israel. Rather, they saw the sprinkled blood, which enabled God to be merciful to rebellious sinners. The mercy seat typifies Christ as the One "whom God set forth as a *mercy seat*" (Rom. 3:25, lit.).[32] . . . The mercy seat was the lid of the ark.

9. The Table of Showbread (37:10–16)

The **table** of showbread held twelve loaves, "typical of Israel's place before God in the acceptability of Christ, who as the true Aaron maintains them even now before God."[33] The loaves may also speak of God's provision for each of the twelve tribes.

10. The Golden Lampstand and Its Accessories (37:17–24)

Some see the **lampstand of pure gold** as a type of Christ, the true Light of the world (John 8:12). Others prefer to view it as picturing the Holy Spirit, whose mission is to glorify Christ, since it illuminates all that speaks of Christ in the holy place. Still others see it as typifying Christ in union with believers. The middle **shaft** is unique because the other **six branches** come out of it, **three branches** on each side; yet they are all made of one piece of gold.

11. The Altar of Incense (37:25–28)

The **altar** of **incense** speaks of Christ being a perpetual sweet aroma of God. It also suggests the present ministry of the Lord Jesus, interceding for us in heaven.

12. The Anointing Oil and the Incense (37:29)

Oil typifies the Holy Spirit, and the **incense** speaks of the ever-fragrant perfections of our Lord, bringing delight to His Father.

13. The Altar of Burnt Offering (38:1–7)

The altar of burnt offering represents the cross, where the Lord Jesus offered Himself to God as a complete sacrifice. There can be no access to God apart from His sacrificial death.

14. The Laver (38:8)

The laver speaks of the present ministry of Christ, cleansing His people by the washing of water with the Word (Eph. 5:26). The priests were required to wash their hands and feet before performing any service. So our actions and our walk must be clean before we can serve the Lord effectively. The laver was made from the bronze mirrors of the serving women. Glorification of self gave way to service for God.

15. The Outer Court, Pillars, and Screen (38:9–31)

38:9–20 The outer **court** around the tabernacle consisted of white **linen hangings**, fifty-six **pillars** with **bronze sockets** and **silver hooks**, and an embroidered **screen** at the **gate**. The white linen speaks of the righteousness which bars the unbelieving sinner from approaching God, but which also separates and protects the believer inside. The only entrance to the court was the **gate**, made of **fine woven linen** and embroidered with **blue, purple, and scarlet thread**. This suggests Christ ("I am the door," John 10:9) here as the only way of approach to God. The fine linen is a picture of His spotless purity; the blue, of His heavenly origin; the purple, of His regal glory; the scarlet, of His suffering for sin.

38:21–23 The names of the skilled workers are repeated. Whenever God has a task to do, He raises up people to do it. For the tabernacle He called and equipped **Bezalel** and **Aholiab**. For the building of the temple He used Hiram to supply materials. For the building of the church, he used His chosen workmen, Peter and Paul.

38:24–31 The materials used in building the tabernacle are carefully tabulated. They would be valued in the millions of dollars in today's currency. We too can dedicate our possessions to the work of the Lord, saying in effect, "Take my silver and my gold; not a mite would I withhold."[34]

G. Preparation of the Priests' Garments (Chap. 39)

39:1–7 Now we come to the preparation of the priests' **garments**. We are struck at the outset by the repetition of the four colors. Some see them as representing the manifold glories of Christ as seen in the four Gospels: **purple**—Matthew—the King; **scarlet**—Mark—the Suffering Servant; **white**—Luke—the sinless Man; **blue**—John—the Son of God come down from heaven. The **gold** threads in the ephod speak of Christ's deity (v. 3). On each shoulder-strap of the **ephod** was an **onyx** stone engraved with the names of six of the tribes of Israel.

39:8–21 The **breastplate** held **twelve** precious **stones**, one for **each** of the **twelve tribes** (vv. 10–14). So it is with our Great High Priest. The gospel preacher Peter Pell expressed it beautifully. "The strength of His shoulders and the love of His heart are thus bearing the names of God's people before the presence of God."

39:22–26 The robe of the ephod was a **blue** garment worn under the ephod. On its **hem** were **bells of pure gold** and **pomegranates of blue, purple, and scarlet**. These speak of spiritual fruit and testimony as they are found in our Great High Priest and as they should be reproduced in us.

39:27–29 The linen **tunics** were the first garments that the priests put on (Lev. 8:7). Then came the garments of glory. God first clothes the repentant sinner with His own righteousness (2 Cor. 5:21). When the Lord Jesus returns, He will clothe His own people in garments of glory (Phil. 3:20, 21). Righteousness must precede glorification.

39:30, 31 The gold **plate** on the high priest's turban was engraved like **a signet** with the words "HOLINESS TO THE LORD" so that he might bear the iniquity of the holy things (Ex. 28:38). All that we do is stained with sin, but our worship and service are purged from all imperfection by our Great High Priest before they reach the Father.

39:32–43 When the people **finished** the work **and brought** the parts of **the tabernacle** to Moses, he inspected them and found that **all the work** had been made exactly according to God's specifications. **And Moses blessed** the people.

H. Erection of the Tabernacle (Chap. 40)

40:1–8 God commanded that **the tabernacle** be **set up** on the first day of the year (vv. 1, 2); this was about a year after the Exodus and eight and a half months after Israel's arrival at Sinai. He also described where each piece of furniture should be placed (see Figure 4 at Ex. 26).

40:9–17 In verses 9–15, instructions were repeated for **anointing . . . the tabernacle**, its furnishings, and the high priest **and his sons**. The instructions were carried out on the first day of the first month, almost one year after the Israelites had left Egypt (vv. 16, 17).

40:18–33 So Moses raised up the **tabernacle . . .** This paragraph tells how the great lawgiver carried out all the detailed instructions **as the LORD had commanded Moses** for each part of the structure itself, as well as for each item of furniture.

Last of all Moses **raised up the court all around the tabernacle**. Then come the climactic words of completion of an important task well done: **So Moses finished the work.**

40:34–38 The glory **cloud** descended on and filled **the tabernacle** so that **Moses was not able to enter.** This cloud was to accompany the people on their journeys. They were to move only when **the cloud** moved. When it stopped, they were to stop also (vv. 34–38). As a member of the tribe of Levi, Moses was apparently qualified to perform priestly functions until Aaron and his sons were invested with this responsibility (Lev. 8).

And so Exodus is the history of God's people during the year between their deliverance from Egypt and the erection of the tabernacle at Mount Sinai. The book is filled with beautiful pictures of Christ and His moral perfections. It is our responsibility to worship this Christ of glory and to live in the light of His holiness.

ENDNOTES

[1] (2:9, 10) The Hebrew *māshāh*, "draw out" may be actually a bilingual play on words. The Hebrews used puns even in serious situations, such as the naming of children. (See, for example, the naming of Jacob's sons in Genesis 29, 30.)

[2] (2:9, 10) C. H. Mackintosh, *Genesis to Deuteronomy*, p. 144.

[3] (3:1–4) Appropriately, the Scottish Covenanters adopted the burning bush

as their emblem, with the Latin motto below: *"Nec consummaretur"* ("Yet it was not consumed").

[4] (3:6) R. Alan Cole, *Exodus: An Introduction and Commentary*, p. 66.

[5] (3:7–12) J. Oswald Sanders, *On to Maturity*, p. 56.

[6] (3:13, 14) Some Bibles, such as the Moffatt Version, translate the name by "the Eternal" (cf. also Louis Segond's French version: "l' éternel").

[7] (5:2–14) Cole, *Exodus*, p. 82. The author attempts to reproduce the contemptuous attitude of the taskmasters in English by the translation "stub themselves stubble" (v. 12).

[8] (8:20–24) The Septuagint, which was produced in Egypt and may reflect local knowledge and Jewish tradition, translates by *dog-fly* (*kynomuia*), a gadfly with a painful bite. See Cole, *Exodus*, pp. 93, 94, for more details.

[9] (10:29) Matthew Henry, "Exodus," in *Matthew Henry's Commentary on the Whole Bible*, I:314.

[10] (12:11–20) Cole, *Exodus*, p. 108.

[11] (13:17–20) C. F. Pfeiffer, *Baker's Bible Atlas*, pp. 73, 74.

[12] (13:21, 22) Henry, "Exodus," I:328.

[13] (14:15–18) Henry, "Exodus," I:332.

[14] (15:1–21) Dr. H. C. Woodring, unpublished notes, Emmaus Bible School.

[15] (15:1–21) Henry, "Exodus," I:335, 336.

[16] (16:1–19) The name is not related to the English word *sin*.

[17] (19:1–9) D. L. Moody, *Notes From My Bible*, pp. 33, 34.

[18] (Essay) *The New Scofield Study Bible, New King James Version*, p. 4.

[19] (Essay) The old charge that dispensationalists believe in "seven different ways to get saved" is totally false.

[20] (Essay) Some do accept one of the ordinances.

[21] (21:1–6) This is the second stanza of Bishop Handley C. G. Moule's hymn, "My Glorious Victor, Prince Divine," *Hymns of Truth and Praise*, #535.

[22] (23:18, 19) Orthodox Jews have two complete sets of china: one for meat products and one for milk products. To discourage Jews from eating meat and milk products in the same meal some cafeterias in Israel force one to go through two lines to have both. One Jerusalem cafeteria visited by the editor of this volume actually had the meat and milk lines on separate floors!

[23] (23:20–33) Henry, "Exodus," I:376.

[24] (25:17–22) The word *cherub* may come from a Semitic root meaning "bless," "praise," or "adore," but it is more commonly held to be from the Hebrew *kārav, draw near*. Thus cherubim are "covering ones" or those who draw near as protectors.

[25] (26:14) The reason for the variety of translations is that we do not know for sure which animal skin the Hebrew word refers to.

[26] (28:36–38) Archbishop Beveridge, further documentation unavailable.

[27] (30:1–10) The Greek word *thumiatērion* literally means "place (or thing) for incense." Hence it could refer to the incense altar or to the censer which was taken behind the veil on the Day of Atonement, filled with incense from the altar.

[28] (31:1–11) It is noteworthy that the national art academy in modern Israel is named after Bezalel.

[29] (Essay) The typology of the tabernacle is widely held among evangelical believers, though obviously there is not complete agreement on all details. Some Christians accept only those types that are mentioned specifically in the NT, chiefly in Hebrews. See Genesis 42 for a brief discussion of typology.

[30] (32:30–35) Some believe that, like Paul fifteen centuries later, Moses was willing to be accursed and lost if it would save his fellow Israelites.

[31] (33:18–23) Hywel R. Jones, further documentation unavailable.

[32] (37:6–9) The same Greek word, *hilastērion*, means both *propitiation (satisfaction by sacrifice)* and *place of propitiation* (i.e., the mercy seat).

[33] (37:10–16) G. Morrish, *New and Concise Bible Dictionary*, p. 754.

[34] (38:24–31) It is much easier to *sing* this line from Frances Ridley Havergal's great spiritual hymn, "Take My Life and Let It Be," than it is to *practice* it!

BIBLIOGRAPHY

Borland, James A. "Exodus." In *Liberty Bible Commentary*. Lynchburg, VA: The Old-Time Gospel Hour, 1982.

Cole, R. Alan. *Exodus: An Introduction and Commentary*. The Tyndale Old Testament Commentaries. Downers Grove, IL: InterVarsity Press, 1973.

Dennett, Edward. *Typical Teachings of Exodus*. Reprint. Denver: Wilson Foundation, n.d.

Henry, Matthew. "Exodus." In *Matthew Henry's Commentary on the Whole Bible*. Vol. 1. *Genesis to Deuteronomy*. McLean, VA: MacDonald Publishing Company, n.d.

Keil, C. F. and Delitzsch, F. "Exodus." In *Biblical Commentary on the Old Testament*. Vols. 1, 2. Grand Rapids: Wm. B. Eerdmans Publishing Co., 1971.

Lange, John Peter. "Exodus." In *Commentary on the Holy Scriptures, Critical, Doctrinal and Homiletical*. Vol. 2. Reprint (24 vols. in 12). Grand Rapids: Zondervan Publishing House, 1980.

Pell, Peter, Jr. *The Tabernacle* (Correspondence Course). Oak Park, IL: Emmaus Bible School, 1957.

Ridout, Samuel. *Lectures on the Tabernacle*. New York: Loizeaux Brothers, Inc., 1973.

Rosen, Moishe and Ceil. *Christ in the Passover*. Chicago: Moody Press, n.d.

Sanders, J. Oswald. *On to Maturity*. Chicago: Moody Press, 1962.

LEVITICUS

Introduction

"There is no book, in the whole compass of that inspired Volume which the Holy Ghost has given us, that contains more of the very words of God than Leviticus. It is God that is the direct speaker on almost every page; His gracious words are recorded in the form wherein they were uttered. This consideration cannot fail to send us to the study of it with singular interest and attention."

—Andrew Bonar

I. Unique Place in the Canon

J. N. Darby once warned of the dire results if believers grow bored with holiness. Holiness is the main theme of Leviticus, and this book certainly is the hardest one for many Christians to read. Of course, if the instructions are merely taken as details of ancient Jewish sacrificial rituals and laws to maintain holiness in everyday life and separation from pagan peoples, the blessing will be limited. Once you see, however, that every detail of the sacrifices pictures the perfection of Christ's person and work, there is much to meditate upon. Further blessing comes from correlating Leviticus with its NT counterpart, The Epistle to the Hebrews.

II. Authorship

Twenty of the twenty-seven chapters in Leviticus and about thirty-five other paragraphs start with "And the Lord spoke to Moses, saying . . ." or a similar, equivalent expression. Until fairly modern times most people who professed Judaism or Christianity accepted these words at face value. Our Lord Himself refers to Leviticus

13:49—a leper showing himself to the priest and making an offering—as "those things which Moses commanded" (Mark 1:44). Today, however, it is fashionable in many circles to deny or at least to question Mosaic authorship, not only of Leviticus, but of the whole Pentateuch.

Since we believe the traditional view is not only true but important as well, the issue is taken up in some detail in our Introduction to the Pentateuch, which should be read carefully.

III. Date

Accepting the Mosaic authorship of Leviticus and the evidence within the Pentateuch, we suggest that the book was revealed to Moses during the fifty-day period after the tabernacle was set up (Ex. 40:17), and before the Israelites left Sinai (Num. 10:11). The exact year of writing is unknown, but somewhere between 1450 and 1410 B.C. is indicated.

IV. Background and Theme

An easy way to remember the contents of Leviticus is to associate its name with the word "Levites" or "priests," and then realize that the book is a manual for the priests. Exodus ended with the setting up of the tabernacle in the wilderness. Now the priests and Levites need instruction on how to carry out the sacrifices associated with that structure and with some other rituals as well (e.g., cleansing "leprous" houses).

In Exodus we saw Israel delivered from Egypt and set apart as God's special possession. In Leviticus we see how they are to be separated from sin and uncleanness in order to approach God in the sanctuary. Holiness becomes the rule of the camp. Both in the OT and the NT God demands that His people be holy because He is holy. This poses a serious problem, since man by nature and by practice is unholy. The solution lies in blood atonement (Lev. 17:11). In the OT there were animal sacrifices that looked forward to the once-for-all sacrifice of the Lamb of God, as revealed in the NT, especially in Hebrews.

OUTLINE

Commentary

I. TYPES OF OFFERINGS (1:1—6:7)

A. The Burnt Offering (Chap. 1)

Leviticus opens with **the LORD** calling **to Moses**, speaking **to him from the tabernacle of meeting**. As Bonar said in our opening quotation, no other book "contains more of the very words of God than Leviticus," which should show that we should study it "with singular interest and attention." At the outset the Lord prescribes the five offerings—burnt, meal, peace, sin, and trespass. The first three were known as sweet-savor offerings, the last two as sin offerings. The first three were voluntary, the last two compulsory.

The first message God has for **the children of Israel** is that they should **bring** their **offerings to the LORD** from their **livestock**—both from the **herd and** from **the flock**.

Chapter 1 deals with the **burnt sacrifice** (Heb. *'ōlāh*[1]). There were three grades, depending on what the offerer could afford: a **bull** from the **herd** (v. 3; cf. v. 5), a **male without blemish**; a **sheep or a goat from the flock** (v. 10), **a male without blemish**; **turtledoves or young pigeons** (v. 14). All were peaceful creatures; nothing wild was offered on the altar of the Lord.

Peter Pell suggests that the bull speaks of our Lord as the patient, unwearied Laborer, always doing the Father's will in a life of perfect service and a death of perfect sacrifice. The sheep represents the Lord as the meek and lowly One, submissive to God's will in unresisting self-surrender. The goat speaks of Christ as our Substitute. The turtledove points to Him as the heavenly One, and also as the Man of sorrows (mourning dove).[2]

> Behold! a spotless Victim dies,
> My Surety on the tree;
> The Lamb of God, the Sacrifice,
> He gave Himself for me!
> —*Author unknown*

Duties of the offerer: He brought the offering to **the door of the tabernacle**, near the bronze altar (v. 3); **he put his** hand on the head of the victim (v. 4) (or, "he leaned his hand as if in reliance"); he killed the bull (v. 5) or the sheep or goat (v. 11); he skinned the animal and cut it into its pieces (vv. 6, 12); he washed the entrails and legs with water (vv. 9, 13). In verse 3, the expression "of his own free will" is translated in some versions "to be accepted." Note verse 4.

Duties of the priests: They sprinkled the blood of the animal all around on the altar (vv. 5, 11); they put the fire and the wood on the altar (v. 7) and then placed the parts of the animal in order on the wood (vv. 8, 12). Everything was burned on the altar except the skin (v. 13; 7:8); in the case of the birds, the priest wrung off its head, pressed out its blood at the side of the altar, put the crop (gullet) with its feathers on the east side of the altar, opened the body of the bird without cutting it in pieces, and burned it on the altar. The word for *burn* is the one used for burning incense; a different word is used in connection with the sin offerings.

Distribution of the offering: All that was burned on the altar belonged to God; the skin was given to the priests (7:8); the offerer received no part of this particular offering.

The person bringing a burnt offering was expressing his complete surrender and devotion to the Lord. We learn elsewhere that this offering was presented on many different occasions. (See a Bible dictionary for details.)

Typically, the burnt offering pictures the offering of Christ without spot to God. On Calvary's altar the Lamb of God was totally consumed by the flames of divine justice. Amelia M. Hull's hymn captures the spirit of this:

I have been at the altar and
  witnessed the Lamb
Burnt wholly to ashes for me;
And watched its sweet savour
  ascending on high,
Accepted, O Father, by Thee.

B. The Grain Offering (Chap. 2)

The grain offering (Heb. *minhāh*) was of meal flour, or grain.[3]

The offering itself: There were various types of grain offerings, as follows: fine flour, with oil and frankincense poured on it (v. 1). This was not cooked, but a handful of it was burned on the altar (v. 2). There were three different types of bread or cakes: (a) baked in the oven (v. 4); (b) baked in a flat pan (v. 5); (c) cooked in a covered pan (v. 7; the KJV and RSV say "frying pan," but some believe this offering was boiled in water, like a dumpling). There were also kernels of grain representing firstfruits of harvest, roasted in fire (v. 14). Verse 12 refers to a special meal offering (23:15–21) which was not to be burned on the altar because it contained leaven.

No leaven or honey was to be used in any of these meal offerings (v. 11). These implied fermentation and natural sweetness. But salt was to be added, as a sign of the covenant between God and Israel. It was called the salt of the covenant (v. 13), signifying that the covenant was unbreakable. See Numbers 18:19; 2 Chronicles 13:5; Ezekiel 43:24 for other references to "the covenant of salt."

Duties of the offerer: He prepared the offering at home and brought it to the priests (vv. 2, 8).

Duties of the priest: The priest presented the offering at the altar (6:14); he then took a handful of the offering and burned this memorial handful on the altar (vv. 2, 9).

Distribution of the offering: The "memorial handful," burned on the altar with *all* the frankincense, was the Lord's; the priests were permitted to take all the rest of the offering as food (vv. 3, 10). The officiating priest was entitled to whatever was baked in the oven or cooked in a pot or pan (7:9). Everything mixed with oil and everything dry was to belong to the rest of the priests (7:10); the offerer received no part of this offering.

The person who brought the meal offering acknowledged the bounty of God in providing the good things of life, represented by flour, frankincense, oil (and wine in the case of the drink offering).

Symbolically this offering speaks of the moral perfection of the life of our Savior (fine flour), untainted by evil (no leaven), fragrant to God (frankincense), and filled with the Holy Spirit (oil). The hymn writer expresses it beautifully:

Life, life of love poured out fragrant
    and holy!
Life, 'mid rude thorns of earth,
    stainless and sweet!
Life, whence God's face of love,
    glorious but lowly,
Shines forth to bow us, Lord, low
    at Thy feet!
                              —*F. Allaben*

C. The Peace Offering (Chap. 3)

3:1–15 The **peace** or fellowship **offering** (Heb. *shelem*[4]) celebrated peace with God that was established on the basis of the efficacy of the atoning blood. It was a feast of joy, love, and communion.

The offering itself: There were three grades of this offering also: an animal from **the herd** (oxen or cattle), **male or female** (vv. 1–5); a **lamb** from **the flock, male or female** (vv. 6–11); a goat from the flock, male or female (vv. 12–17).

Duties of the offerer: He presented the animal **before the Lord** at the gate of the court (vv. 1, 2, 7, 12); he laid **his hand on the head of** the victim (vv. 2, 8, 13); he killed it at the **door of the tabernacle** (vv. 2, 8, 13); he removed certain portions of the animal—**the fat, the kidneys, the whole fat tail**, and **the fatty lobe attached to the liver**—to be burned on the altar (vv. 3, 4, 9, 10, 14, 15).

Duties of the priests: They sprinkled **the blood all around on the altar** (vv. 2, 8, 13); they burned the Lord's portion (the fat, etc.) on top of **the burnt sacrifice** (v. 5).

Distribution of the offering: The Lord's portion, *called* the **food** of the **offering made by fire** (v. 11), was the fat, the kidneys, the caul, and the fat tail; in Leviticus 7:32, 33 we learn that the officiating priest received the right thigh after it had been first presented as a heave offering; the other priests received the animal's breast (7:31). This was first presented as a wave offering before the Lord; the offerer received all the rest (7:15–21). This is the only offering in which the offerer received a portion. He probably made a feast for his family and friends as a kind of fellowship meal. Thus the offering promoted peace between fellow Israelites within the covenant.

The person bringing this offering was expressing his joyful gratitude for the peace he enjoyed in fellowship with Jehovah. A person might also present the peace offering in connection with some vow he was making to the Lord, or in thanksgiving for some special favor.

As to its typical (symbolic) meaning, Peter Pell comments:

The finished work of Christ in relation to the believer is seen in the peace offering. The Lord Jesus is our peace (Eph. 2:14), having made peace through the blood of His cross (Col. 1:20). He preached this peace to those who were afar off and to those who were near (Eph. 2:17), thus breaking down the middle wall of partition between Jew and Gentile. In Christ, God and the sinner meet in peace; the enmity that was ours is gone. God is propitiated, the sinner is reconciled, and both alike are satisfied with Christ and with what He has done.[5]

Lord Adalbert Cecil's hymn exults in what Christ has done for us:

Oh, the peace forever flowing
From God's thoughts of His own Son!
Oh, the peace of simply knowing
On the cross that all was done.
Peace with God! the blood in heaven
Speaks of pardon now to me:
Peace with God! the Lord is ris'n!
Righteousness now counts me free.

3:16, 17 The people of Israel were forbidden to eat **fat** or **blood**, since both belonged to the Lord. In addition to its symbolic meaning, this regulation concerning fat was an early form of preventive medicine. Today doctors recommend a reduction in fat intake to reduce the incidence of hypertension, heart disease, strokes, diabetes, and lung disease.

These first three offerings—burnt, meal, and peace—had a place in the public worship of the nation, but they could also be brought to the Lord by an individual at any time on a voluntary basis. The next two offerings were commanded to be brought when someone had sinned. Thus we have the twin concepts of *voluntary worship* and *compulsory atonement* set forth in the offerings.

D. The Sin Offering (4:1—5:13)

Chap. 4 The **sin offering** (Heb., *hattā'th*[6]) was appointed for a redeemed people. It does not speak of a sinner coming to the Lord for *salvation*, but of an Israelite in covenant relationship with the Lord, seeking *forgiveness*. It has to do with sins committed unconsciously or unintentionally.

The offering itself: There were different grades of offerings, depending upon the person who sinned: **The anointed priest**—that is, the high priest, if he by sinning brought **guilt on the people** (v. 3)—brought **a young bull without blemish; the whole congregation** (v. 13) brought **a young bull** also; **a ruler** (v. 22) brought **a kid of the goats, a male without blemish**; an ordinary person (v. 27) brought a **female** goat, **without blemish** (v. 28), or a **female** sheep, **without blemish** (v. 32). (The Hebrew wording here indicates full-grown animals.)

Duties of the offerer(s): In general, the offerer brought the animal to the gate of the tabernacle court, presented it to the Lord, laid his hand on its head, killed it, and removed the fat, the kidneys, and the fatty lobe above the liver. **The elders** acted for **the congregation** (v. 15). The victim's death was regarded symbolically as the sinner's death.

Duties of the priest: For himself and for the congregation, the high priest carried the blood of the sacrifice into the holy place of the tabernacle, sprinkled it seven times before the veil (vv. 5, 6, 16, 17) and on the horns of the golden altar of incense (vv. 7, 18). Then he poured the rest of the blood at the base of the altar of burnt offering (vv. 7, 18). For a ruler and for common people, a priest sprinkled the blood on the horns of the altar of burnt offering and poured the rest of the blood at the bottom of the altar

(vv. 25, 30, 34). For all classes, he burned the fat, kidneys, fatty lobe above the liver, and fat tail on the altar of burnt offering (vv. 8–10, 19, 26, 31). In the case of the offering for the high priest or for the whole congregation, all the rest of the animal was taken outside the camp and burned (vv. 11, 12, 21).

Distribution of the offering: The Lord's share was the portion that was burned upon the altar—the fat, kidneys, fatty lobe above the liver, etc. The priest was allowed to eat the flesh of the offerings of a ruler or of a commoner because the blood of these offerings was not taken into the sanctuary (7:30), as in the case of the offerings of the high priest and the congregation (4:5, 6, 16, 17). He could also eat the offerings described in 5:6, 7, 11 for the same reason. No part of the above offerings was set aside for the offerer.

The body of any sin offering whose blood was taken into the holy place was burned outside the camp. So our Lord, through His own blood, entered the holy place once for all (Heb. 9:12) after He had suffered outside the city of Jerusalem. We are admonished to "go forth to Him outside the camp, bearing His reproach" (Heb. 13:13).

Note: The expression "sin through ignorance" seems to mean more than lack of knowledge of the sin. It probably means that the sin was not willful, deliberate, or done in defiance or rebellion. There was no sacrifice for willful sin; the death penalty had to be exacted (Num. 15:30).

The person who brought a sin offering was acknowledging that he had sinned unintentionally through weakness or negligence. He sought forgiveness of sins and ceremonial cleansing.

The sin offering points symbolically to Christ, who was "made sin" for us, though He knew no sin, that we might be made the righteousness of God in Him. Some suggest that the sin offering speaks of Christ dealing with *what we are,* whereas the trespass offering pictures Him dealing with *what we have done.*

> The Holy One who knew no sin,
> God made Him sin for us;
> The Savior died our souls to win,
> Upon the shameful cross.
> His precious blood alone availed
> To wash our sins away;
> Through weakness He o'er hell prevailed,
> Through death He won the day.
> —*Hannah K. Burlingham*

5:1–13 The first 13 verses of chapter 5 seem to describe the trespass offering (see v. 6), but it is generally agreed that these verses have to do with two additional grades of sin offering. The reason for not treating them with the trespass offering is that there is no mention of restitution, which was an important part of the trespass offering. (However, it is freely admitted that verses 1–13 are closely linked to both the sin and trespass offerings.)

Instead of dealing with various classes of people, these offerings have to do with differing types of sins: Verse 1 describes a man who has knowledge of a crime, and yet refuses to testify after hearing the high priest or judge put him under **oath**. As a Jew living under the Law, Jesus testified when the chief priest put Him under oath (Matt. 26:63, 64). Verse 2 deals with the defilement which a Jew contracted by touching a dead body, even if he did not know it at the time. Verse 3 describes the uncleanness contracted by touching a person with leprosy, a running sore, etc. Verse 4 has to do with the making of rash oaths or promises which one later finds he cannot fulfill.

The offering itself: There were three types of offerings for these sins, depending upon the ability of the offerer to pay: a **female** lamb or goat—**as a sin offering** (v. 6); **two turtledoves or two young pigeons— one as a sin offering and the other as a burnt offering** (v. 7); the **tenth** part **of an ephah of fine flour** with **no oil** or **frankincense** (v. 11). This put the sin offering within reach of the poorest person. Likewise, no one is excluded from forgiveness through Christ. The question arises in verses 11–13, "How can a meal offering serve as a sin offering to make atonement for sin when we know that without the shedding of blood there is no remission?" (Heb. 9:22). The answer is that it was offered *on top of* a fire offering on the altar (which did have blood), and this gave the meal offering the value of a blood sacrifice.

Duties of the offerer: He first of all confessed his guilt (v. 5), then brought his offering **to the priest** (v. 8).

Duties of the priest: In the case of the female lamb or goat, he offered it in accordance with the instructions for a sin offering in chapter 4. If the offering was two birds, he first offered one bird as a **sin offering**, wringing **its neck**, sprinkling some blood on the side of the altar, and draining out the rest **at the base of the altar** (vv. 8, 9). He next offered the **second** bird **as a burnt offering**, burning it completely on the bronze altar (v. 10). If the offering was **fine flour**, the priest took a **handful of** it and burned it on the altar of burnt offering. He burned it over other offerings involving the shedding of blood, thus giving it the character of a sin offering (v. 12).

Distribution of the offering: The Lord's portion consisted of whatever was burned on the altar. The priest was entitled to whatever was left (v. 13).

E. The Trespass Offering (5:14—6:7)

The **trespass offering** (Heb., *'āshām*[7]) is taken up in 5:14—6:7. The distinctive feature of this offering is that **restitution** had to be made for the sin committed *before* the offering was presented (5:16).

There were several types of sin for which an offering had to be made. *Trespass against God:* Withholding from the Lord that which rightly belonged to Him—tithes and offerings, consecration of firstfruits or of the firstborn, etc. (5:15). Unwittingly committing some act forbidden by the Lord (5:17), and presumably an act that required restitution. "In cases where it was not possible to know whether another had been wronged, the scrupulously devout Israelite would still offer a guilt offering by itself" (*Daily Notes of the Scripture Union*).

Trespass against man: Dealing falsely with one's neighbor in a matter of deposit or bargain or robbery or oppression (6:2). Finding a lost article and swearing to a lie about it (6:3). A trespass offering was also required in the case of immorality with a slave girl who was engaged (19:20–22), the cleansing of a leper (14:10–14), and the defilement of a Nazirite (Num. 6:6–12).

The offering itself: A ram without blemish (5:15, 18; 6:6) or a male lamb in the case of a leper (14:12) or a Nazirite (Num. 6:12).

Duties of the offerer: In the case of a trespass against God, he first brought the restitution to the priest, with twenty percent added. Then he brought the animal to the priest at the entrance to the tabernacle court, presented it to the Lord, placed his hand on its head, and killed it. He also removed the fat, fat tail, kidneys, and fatty lobe above the liver. The procedure was the same in the case of a trespass against a neighbor. In both instances, the offerer had to pay the twenty percent penalty, reminding him that sin is unprofitable and costly.

Duties of the priest: He sprinkled the blood around the bronze altar (7:2); he then burned the fat, the fat tail (rump), the kidneys, and the fatty lobe above the liver on the altar (7:3, 4).

Distribution of the offering: The Lord's portion was that which was burned on the altar (7:5). The officiating priest received the skin of the ram (7:8). All the priests shared the meat of the animal as food (7:6). The offerer had no part in the sin or trespass offerings.

As has been mentioned, the person bringing a trespass offering was seeking to make amends for some action of his that had caused loss or damage to someone else.

Symbolically, the trespass offering points to that aspect of the work of Christ by which He restored that which He took not away (Ps. 69:4b). Through man's sin, God was robbed of service, worship, obedience, and glory. And man himself was robbed of life, peace, gladness, and fellowship with God. As our trespass offering, the Lord Jesus not only restored what had been stolen through man's sin, but He added more. *For God has received more glory through the finished work of Christ than if sin had never entered the world.* And we are better off in Christ than we ever could have been in unfallen Adam.

Aside He threw His most divine array,
And veiled His Godhead in a robe of
  clay;

And in that garb did wondrous love
  display,
Restoring what He never took away.
      —Author unknown

II. LAWS OF THE OFFERINGS (6:8—7:38)

The section from 6:8 to 7:38 presents "the law of the offerings." In many ways, it is very similar to what has gone before. However, it is addressed to the priests whereas the previous instructions were for the children of Israel (1:2).

6:8–13 *The law of the burnt offering:* Additional details are given here concerning the **garments** worn by **the priest**, the manner in which he disposed of **the ashes** from **the burnt offering**, and the care he must exercise to see that **the fire on the altar** never went **out**. The ashes were first placed at the east side of the altar, and then carried **outside the camp to a clean place**.

6:14–17 *The law of the grain offering:* Here we learn that the priests had to **eat** their portion of the offering within **the court of the tabernacle**, and that it was **not** to be leavened because it was **most holy** to the Lord.

6:18 Any male **children of Aaron** could **eat** the grain offering, but they **must be holy**, that is, ceremonially clean. These priests did not become holy by touching the offerings. Holiness was not imparted by touch, but defilement was (Hag. 2:11–13).[8]

6:19–23 These verses describe a special **grain offering** which the high **priest** had to offer **morning** and evening continually. It was **wholly burned** by fire.

6:24–30 *The law of the sin offering:* As explained previously, **the priest** was allowed to **eat** portions of certain sin offerings (those described in Lev. 4:22—5:13, where **the blood** was not carried into the sanctuary). The offerings had to **be eaten . . . in the court of the tabernacle**. Notice that this offering was **most holy**. If a layman touched the **flesh** of the offering, he **must be** holy or consecrated and had to cleanse himself from ceremonial defilement just as the priests did, though he could not exercise priestly functions. If any of the **blood** was **sprinkled on** a **garment**, the garment had to be washed—not because it was unclean but so that the most holy blood might not be carried out of the sanctuary into everyday life, and thus be profaned. An **earthen vessel** used to cook the meat of the sin offering had to **be broken** because the earthenware, being porous, absorbed some of the blood and might later be used for profane purposes. A **bronze pot** had to **be both scoured and rinsed in water** to prevent any portion of the most holy sin offering from ever coming in contact with anything that was common or unclean. **The sin offering**, like the guilt offering, was to be slain **in the place where the burnt offering is killed**. This was the north side of the altar (1:11), the place of shadows.

7:1–7 The first seven verses of chapter 7 review **the law of the trespass offering**, most of which has already been covered in 5:14—6:7.

7:8 Verse 8 refers to the **burnt offering** and provides that the officiating **priest** was entitled to **the skin** of the animal.

7:9, 10 Verse 9 indicates the portion of the **grain offering** that was to go to the *officiating* **priest**, and verse 10 what was to go to the *rest* of the priests.

7:11–18 The law of the **peace** offering is given in 7:11–21. There were

three types of **peace offerings**, depending on the motive or purpose of the offering: **for . . . thanksgiving** (v. 12), praising God for some special blessing; for **a vow** (that is, a votive **offering**) (v. 16), "in fulfillment of a promise or pledge made to God for the granting of some special request in prayer; for example, preservation on a hazardous journey"[9]; **voluntary** or freewill (vv. 16, 17), "This would appear to be in the nature of a spontaneous expression of praise to God in appreciation of what He has revealed Himself to be."[10] The **peace offering** itself was a sacrificial animal (chap. 3), but here we learn that it was accompanied by certain **cakes** or breads. The **cakes** that were required with a thank offering are listed in verses 12 and 13. The offerer was to bring **one** of **each** for **a heave offering**, and this was given to **the** officiating **priest** (v. 14). **The flesh of the . . . thanksgiving** offering was to be eaten **the same day** (v. 15), whereas the votive offering and the freewill offering could be eaten on the first or second **day** (v. 16). Anything remaining after two days had to be **burned** (v. 17); to eat such meat would cause the person to be **"cut off,"** meaning excommunicated or removed from the privileges of the people of Israel. "This shows," John Reid writes, "that communion with God must be fresh and not too far removed from the work of the altar."[11]

7:19–21 If **the flesh** touched **any unclean thing**, it could **not be eaten** but had to **be burned**. Only persons **who** were ceremonially **clean** could **eat** the **clean flesh**. Any **person who** was ceremonially **unclean** and who ate **of the peace offering** would **be cut off**.

The fact that different portions of the peace offering were designated for the Lord, the priests, and the offerer indicates that it was a time of fellowship. But since God can have no fellowship with sin or uncleanness, those who partook of this festive meal had to be clean.

7:22–27 **The fat**, considered the best portion, belonged **to the LORD**. It was burned for Him on the altar, and it was not to be eaten (vv. 22–25). Likewise, the **blood**, being the life of the flesh, belonged to God and was not to be eaten (vv. 26, 27). Today many Jews still seek to comply with these dietary laws. In order for meat to be fit for their consumption, or "kosher," the blood must be removed. In avoiding the consumption of fat, many Jewish households will not use soaps which contain animal fats. They believe that even to use such products in washing dishes would be to make the dishes non-kosher. Besides the spiritual reason for not eating fat there is also a medical reason, as Dr. S. I. McMillen points out:

In the past few years medical science has awakened to the fact that the eating of animal fat is an important cause of arteriosclerosis. This fat forms the tiny, fatty, cholesterol tumors within the walls of the arteries, which hinder the flow of blood. Now, in this decade, magazines, radio and T.V. are broadcasting the good news that we can reduce the ravages from man's greatest killer by cutting down our intake of animal fats. Happy as we are with the fact that medical science has arrived, we may be amazed to discover that our ultramodern research is about thirty-five hundred years behind the Book of books.[12]

7:28–34 The offerer waved **the breast** of the peace offerings **before the LORD**, and it then became the portion of the priests. **The right thigh** was heaved before the Lord, and

then was given to the officiating **priest** as food for himself and his family.

7:35, 36 These verses repeat that the breast and right thigh were the **portion** of **Aaron and his sons** from the day that God first anointed them **as priests**. As previously suggested, the breast speaks of divine affection and the thigh of divine power.

7:37, 38 This paragraph concludes the section on the laws of the offerings, which began in 6:8. God has devoted much space in His Word to the offerings and their ordinances because they are important to Him. Here in beautiful imagery the Person and work of His Son can be seen in minute detail. Like the different facets of a diamond, these types all reflect the resplendent glory of Him "who through the eternal Spirit offered Himself without spot to God" (Heb. 9:14). Miss F. T. Wigram expresses her praise in a hymn:

The person of the Christ,
Enfolding every grace,
Once slain, but now alive again,
In heaven demands our praise.

III. CONSECRATION OF THE PRIESTS (Chap. 8—10)

A. Investiture of the Priests by Moses (Chap. 8)

8:1–5 In Exodus 28 and 29, God gave Moses elaborate instructions for consecrating Aaron and his sons as priests. Now, in Leviticus 8–10, we read how Moses carried out these instructions. He called together the assembly—priests and people—**at the door of the tabernacle**. It was a very public investiture service.

8:6–9 **Moses washed** both **Aaron and his sons with water**. Next **Moses** dressed **Aaron** in the complete vestments of the high priest: **the tunic**, the sash, the robe, the ephod, the band of the ephod, the breastplate, the Urim and the Thummim, the turban and the holy crown. It must have been an impressive sight.

8:10–13 Then Moses . . . anointed the tabernacle and all its contents, and sanctified them.

The fact that he poured (not sprinkled) on Aaron's head is a lovely picture of the Holy Spirit being poured out without measure on the Lord Jesus, our Great High Priest.

Next Moses put tunics and sashes, as well as hats (or head-pieces), on Aaron's sons.

8:14–17 As Aaron and his sons laid their hands on the head of the bull for the sin offering, . . . Moses killed it. Even the highest religious leaders (then as well as now) are merely sinners who need God's atoning sacrifice as well as the least important member of the community.

8:18–21 Moses likewise brought a ram for a burnt offering for Aaron and his sons and carried out the prescribed rites.

8:22–29 The consecration offering for Aaron and his sons was also called the ram of consecration (or, more literally, the ram of the "fill offering"). It differed from the customary peace offerings as to the application of the blood (vv. 23, 24), and also as to the burning of the right thigh and bread cakes, which ordinarily would have been eaten. Since he officiated, Moses received the breast as his part.

The blood was placed on . . . the ear, . . . hand, and . . . foot of Aaron and his sons, reminding us that Christ's blood should affect our *obedience*, *service*, and *walk*.

8:30–36 Moses . . . sprinkled . . . Aaron and his sons with some of the blood and some of the anointing oil from the sacrifice. The priests were instructed to eat of the flesh of the peace offering along with the bread.

The above consecration ritual was repeated for seven days, during which they were not allowed to go outside the door of the tabernacle.

In commenting on this chapter, Matthew Henry discerns the one thing that is missing:

> But after all the ceremonies that were used in their consecration, there was one point of ratification which was reserved to be the honour and establishment of Christ's priesthood, which was this, that they were *made priests without an oath, but Christ with an oath* (Heb. vii.21), for neither such priests nor their priesthood could continue, but Christ's is a perpetual and unchangeable priesthood.[13]

B. Offerings Presented by Aaron (Chap. 9)

9:1-4 Aaron and his sons took up their official duties on the eighth day. First, they were to offer for themselves a young bull for a sin offering and a ram for a burnt offering. Then they were to offer for the people: a he-goat for a sin offering; a yearling calf and a lamb for a burnt offering; a bull and a ram for peace offerings; a grain offering.

9:5–23 All the congregation drew near to the Lord's presence in front of the tabernacle. When Aaron had fully complied with all the instructions of Moses regarding the sin offering, the burnt offering, the people's offering, the grain offering, the peace offerings, and the wave offering (vv. 5–21), he lifted his hand and blessed the people (vv. 22, 23).

9:24 Then a fire came out from

the Most Holy place of the tabernacle **and consumed the burnt offering** which was upon the bronze **altar**. This indicated God's acceptance of the offering. This fire of the Lord was to be kept burning continually on the altar of burnt offering.

C. Nadab and Abihu's Sacrilege (Chap. 10)

10:1–3 Nadab and Abihu, the sons of Aaron, each burned **incense . . . before the** Lord with **profane fire**, perhaps **fire** that was not taken off the brazen altar. Since the altar speaks of Calvary, it was as if they tried to approach God in some way other than through the atoning work of Christ. **Fire went out from** the Most Holy Place and **devoured them** as they stood by the golden altar in the holy place. Moses warned Aaron, in effect, that any complaint would be rebellion against God's righteous dealings.

10:4–7 After **Mishael and Elzaphan** had **carried** the corpses from in front of the tabernacle to a place outside **the camp**, Moses told Aaron and his two remaining sons that they must not mourn but remain within **the tabernacle** while the **the whole house of Israel** mourned the flaring forth of God's wrath.

10:8–11 Some have inferred from the injunction against drinking **wine or intoxicating drink** in **the tabernacle** that Nadab and Abihu may have been drunk when they offered the strange fire.

10:12–18 Moses commanded Aaron and Eleazar and Ithamar, his remaining **sons**, to **eat . . . the grain offering** (vv. 12, 13) and the **breast of the wave offering** (vv. 14, 15). When he looked for **the goat** that had been used as a **sin offering** for the people, he found that **Eleazar and Ithamar,**

. . . sons of Aaron, had **burned** the sacrifice instead of eating it **in a holy place**. (Perhaps they feared God's wrath which had just fallen on their brothers.) The rule was that if the **blood** of the sin offering was **brought** into **the holy place**, then the sacrifice was to be burned (6:30). But if not, it was to be eaten (6:26). Moses reminded them that, in this case, the **blood** had **not** been **brought inside the holy place**; therefore, they should **have . . . eaten** the meat (vv. 16–18).

10:19, 20 In reply to Moses' reprimand, **Aaron** explained that they had carried out the **sin** and **burnt** offerings, as required, but, in view of the Lord's severe chastisement on Nadab and Abihu, he wondered if his eating **the sin offering would have been accepted** by **the** Lord. **Moses** accepted the excuse.

Chapter 10 concludes the section on the priesthood.

IV. THE CLEAN AND THE UNCLEAN (Chaps. 11—15)

The next five chapters deal with matters of ceremonial cleanness and uncleanness. For the Jews there were acts that were not morally wrong but nevertheless barred them from participating in the rituals of Judaism. Those who became defiled were ritually unfit until they were cleansed. A holy people must be holy in every area of life. God used even food to illustrate the difference between what is clean and unclean.

A. Clean and Unclean Foods (Chap. 11)

11:1–8 A *clean* animal was one which had **hooves** that were completely **cloven** and which chewed **the cud**. The expression **"whatever divides the hoof, having cloven hooves"**

seems to say the same thing in two different ways. But the words mean that the **hoof** must be *completely* divided. Clean animals were oxen, cattle, sheep, goats, deer, etc. **Unclean** animals were pigs, camels, rock badgers (hyraxes), rabbits, etc. The spiritual application is that Christians should meditate on the Word of God (chew the cud) and have a separated walk (the cloven hoof).

But God was also protecting the health of His people by prohibiting meat that was likely to transmit disease in days when there was little or no refrigeration and the use of antibiotics in animal husbandry was unknown.

11:9–12 A clean fish was one that had both **fins and scales**. Fish such as mackerel, eels, and shellfish were unclean. Scales are often taken to picture the Christian's armor, protecting him in a hostile world, while the fins typify the divine power which enables him to navigate through the world without being overcome by it.

11:13–19 **Birds** which preyed on other creatures were unclean—e.g., eagles, hawks, vultures, bats. (Bats are not birds, but the Hebrew word translated *birds* is broader than the English word, meaning "flying thing.")

11:20–23 Verses 20–23 deal with certain forms of **flying insects**. Only those which had jointed legs above their feet were clean—namely, locusts, **destroying** locusts, crickets, and grasshoppers.

11:24–28 Touching **the carcass of any** of the foregoing unclean creatures rendered a person **unclean until evening**. Special mention is made of animals which walk **on . . . paws**, such as cats, dogs, lions, tigers, bears, etc.

11:29–38 Other creeping animals are described next—**the mole, the**

mouse, the **large lizard, . . . the gecko**, the **monitor lizard, the sand reptile, the sand lizard, and the chameleon**. A person touching their carcasses became **unclean until evening**. If the **dead** body of one of these creatures fell on any **vessel**, the utensil had to be washed **in water**, and it was **unclean until evening**, except that an **earthen vessel** had to be broken. **Any edible food** in the **earthen vessel** became **unclean** and could not be eaten. Two exceptions are given—**a spring** of running water did not become unclean through contact with the body of one of these animals, nor did **planting seed** used for sowing, if it had not been soaked in **water**.

11:39, 40 Human contact with the carcass of a clean **animal** which had died (rather than being slaughtered) or eating such meat unintentionally made a person **unclean until evening**. **His clothes** had to be washed.

11:41–47 Verses 41–43 refer to worms, snakes, rodents, and insects. Anyone eating them became ritually **unclean**. In giving this law concerning clean and unclean creatures, God was teaching lessons concerning His holiness and the necessity for His people to **be holy** as well (vv. 4–47).

In Mark 7:18, 19, the Lord Jesus declared all foods to be ceremonially clean. And Paul taught that no food should be refused if it is received with thanksgiving (1 Tim. 4:1–5). However, even that would not include foods that are contaminated, culturally unacceptable, or digestively disagreeable to a person.

B. Purification after Childbirth (Chap. 12)

12:1–4 Chapter 12 deals with uncleanness connected with childbirth. A woman giving birth to a boy was **unclean** for **seven days**, just as the days of the **impurity** of her menstruation. **On the eighth day**, the boy was **circumcised** (v. 3). The eighth day was the safest as far as blood clotting was concerned. Today the blood clotting problem is solved by injections of vitamin K. She then remained at home for an additional **thirty-three days** so as **not** to **touch any hallowed thing** or enter **the sanctuary**—i.e., the court surrounding the tabernacle.

12:5 In the case of a baby girl, the mother was **unclean** for **two weeks**, and then remained home for an additional **sixty-six days**.

12:6–8 At the end of the time of **purification**, the mother was commanded to **bring a** yearling **lamb** for **a burnt offering** and **a young pigeon or a turtledove** for **a sin offering**. If she was too poor to afford the **lamb**, **she** could **bring two turtledoves or two young pigeons—one** for the **burnt offering** and **the other** for the **sin offering**. The mother of our Lord brought two birds (Luke 2:22–24), an indication of the poverty into which Jesus was born.

It may seem strange that uncleanness is connected with the birth of a baby, since marriage was instituted before sin entered the world, since the Scriptures teach that marriage is holy, and since God commanded men to reproduce. The uncleanness is probably a reminder that, with the exception of our Lord, we are all brought forth in iniquity and conceived in sin (Ps. 51:5). The extended time of uncleanness in the case of a baby girl was perhaps an intended reminder that man was created before woman, that the woman was created for the man, that the woman is given a place of positional submission (not intrinsic inferiority) to the man, and that the woman was the first to sin.

Williams sees in this legislation the

tender care of God in protecting the mother from visitors during a time when her weakness and the danger of infection were greatest.[14]

C. The Diagnosis of Leprosy (Chap. 13)

Chapter 13 has to do with the diagnosis of leprosy, and chapter 14 with its cleansing. Opinion is divided as to the nature of biblical leprosy. Bible lepers were usually mobile, were not deformed, were harmless when completely leprous, and were sometimes cured.

In some ways the priest filled the role of physician, perhaps a subtle reminder of the close connection between the spiritual and the physical. Man is a tripartite being, and what affects one part affects all.

Chapter 13 is admittedly difficult, dealing as it does with technical descriptions of leprous and non-leprous diseases and with "leprosy" in houses and garments. Dr. R. K. Harrison, who has medical training as well as being a Hebrew scholar, points out that there is "no translation that is satisfactory for all the conditions covered by the Hebrew word, but that it should be broad enough to include the disease we call Hansen's disease."[15]

He summarizes the known facts about the Hebrew term and its Greek translation (whence our English terms *leprosy, leper, leprous*):

The Hebrew term *sāra'at* comes from a root meaning "to become diseased in the skin," and is a generic rather than a specific description. In Old Testament usage it was extended to include mould or mildew in fabrics, as well as mineral eruptions on the walls of buildings, and possibly dry rot in the fabric of such structures.

In the LXX the Hebrew was rendered by the Greek word *lepra*, which itself appears to have been rather indefinite in nature and meaning. The Greek medical authors used the word to describe a disease that made the surface of the skin flaky or scaly, while Herodotus mentioned it in connection with an affliction known as *leukē*, a type of cutaneous eruption which seems to have been the same as the Greek *elephantiasis*, and thus similar to modern clinical leprosy (Hansen's disease).[16]

13:1–3 The opening paragraph describes **the priest** inspecting **a man** for the symptoms of biblical leprosy.

13:4–8 Next the proper procedure in questionable cases is detailed. The person was confined for **seven days**. **If the ... spot** had **not spread**, then he was confined for **another seven more days**. Then if the disease seemed to be checked, **the priest** pronounced the person **clean**. If the eruption in the skin had spread after the second examination, then the priest declared him to be **unclean**.

13:9–11 When the **leprosy** was **old** or chronic, **the priest** pronounced the leper unclean.

13:12, 13 Strangely, when a person had turned **white** all over, the disease was no longer active, and **the priest** pronounced the leper **clean**.

13:14, 15 When **raw flesh** appeared on a person, **the priest** pronounced him **unclean**. It was **leprosy**.

13:16, 17 In a case of leprosy where the **raw flesh** had healed and **turned white**, here again the person was **clean**.

13:18–23 Three possible diagnoses regarding a **boil** are next presented. When it is obvious to **the priest** that the boil is **deeper than the skin, and**

its hair has turned white, he must **pronounce** the patient unclean (vv. 18–20). When in quarantine the sore **spread** during a seven-day test period, it was **leprous** (vv. 21, 22). When it did **not** spread, the person was pronounced **clean** (v. 23).

13:24–28 The case of a possibly leprous **burn** is described. When from its symptoms it was obviously **leprous, the priest** would **pronounce** the person **unclean** (vv. 24, 25). A seven-day period of testing would reveal the condition to be spreading and therefore **leprous** (vv. 26, 27). Where it is merely **a swelling from the burn** it was not leprous (v. 28).

13:29–37 The case of a **scale** of the head or beard is considered next. Where **a man or a woman** obviously had **leprosy** from his or her symptoms, the person had to be declared **unclean** (vv. 29, 30). Where it was not clearly known (vv. 31–37), the person was confined for **seven days**. If the condition had **not spread**, the person shaved off his hair and waited for **another seven days**. If the **scale** had **spread**, the person was **unclean**. **If the scale** had been checked, the person was **clean**.

13:38, 39 **A man or a woman** with **white bright spots on the skin of the body** was declared ceremonially **clean**. According to Harrison's semi-technical translation, it was "a mottling that has arisen in the skin."[17]

13:40–44 Ordinary baldness (alopecia) is differentiated from that which was caused by **leprosy**.

13:45, 46 A **leper** was a miserable person. He was put **outside the camp** of Israel and had to wear **torn ... clothes** and let his **head** be **bare**. Whenever people approached, he had to **cover his** upper lip or **mustache and cry, "Unclean! Unclean!"** Again we have an early example of preventive medicine. Isolation is an accepted medical procedure to prevent the spread of infection.

13:47–59 The case of "leprosy" in a **garment** probably refers to some type of mold or mildew on a **wool or linen** cloth or **leather** garment. Harrison explains the wisdom of destroying garments so tainted:

Moulds are fungous growths on dead or decomposing animal or vegetable matter, and occur in patches of various shades.[18]

He goes on to make a spiritual application:

The fungous growth affects the entire article by its presence, just as the taint of original sin reaches all areas of the human personality.[19]

Jehovah's people must be pure and clean externally as well as internally:

Oh, for a heart to praise my God,
A heart from sin set free;
A heart that's trusting in the blood
So freely shed for me.

A humble, lowly, contrite heart,
Believing, true, and clean,
Which neither death nor life can part
From Him that dwells within.
—*Charles Wesley*

D. The Cleansing of Leprosy (Chap. 14)

14:1–7 Here is given the ritual for cleansing a leper after he had been **healed**: First he was inspected by the **priest** outside **the camp**. If healed, he offered **two living and clean birds**, with **cedar wood, scarlet, and hyssop**. The **cedar wood** and the **hyssop**, coming from a lofty tree and a lowly plant, picture the judgment of God on all men and on all that the world

contains, from the highest to the lowest things. **Scarlet** is associated with sins in Isaiah 1:18, so the thought here may be of God's judgment on sins. **One** bird was **killed . . . over running water**, and the other with the **cedar wood and the scarlet and the hyssop** was dipped **in the blood of the** slain bird. The cleansed leper was sprinkled with the blood **seven times** and pronounced **clean**. Then the **living bird** was allowed to go free.

In many ways, **leprosy** is a type of sin. It rendered a man unclean, it excluded him from the camp of God and the people of God, it made the victim miserable, etc. This is why there needed to be an application of **blood** (the blood of Christ) and the **running water** (the Holy Spirit's regenerating work) in the cleansing of a leper. When a sinner turns to the Lord in repentance and faith today, the death and resurrection of Christ (pictured by the two birds) is reckoned to his account. The **blood** is applied through the power of the Spirit and, in God's sight, the person is **clean**.

Rock of Ages, cleft for me,
Let me hide myself in Thee;
Let the water and the blood,
From Thy riven side which flowed,
Be of sin the double cure,
Cleanse me from its guilt and power.
—*Augustus M. Toplady*

14:8–20 The **cleansed** leper washed **his clothes**, shaved **off all his hair, and** washed his body (v. 8). Then he was allowed to enter **the camp**, but he could not enter **his** own **tent** for **seven** more **days**. Seven days later he again washed and shaved and was pronounced **clean** (v. 9). **On the eighth day**, he brought offerings to **the Lord** (vv. 10, 11): a **trespass offering** (vv. 12–18); a **sin offering** (v. 19); a **burnt**

offering (v. 20). **The priest** applied **the blood** to the leper's **ear, hand,** and **foot** (v. 14). This speaks of *hearing* God's Word, of *doing* God's will, and of *walking* in God's ways.

14:21-32 If the cleansed leper was too **poor** to bring all the required animals, then he was permitted to bring **two turtledoves or two young pigeons, one** for **a sin offering and the other** for **a burnt offering**, but he still had to bring **the lamb** for the **trespass offering.**

A **grain offering** accompanied the trespass, sin, and burnt offerings in each instance.

14:33-53 Finally, laws for the detection of **leprosy ... in a house** are given. These would apply when the people finally reached **Canaan** and dwelt in permanent houses rather than in tents. "Leprosy" in a house was probably some sort of fungus, mildew, or dry rot. The Lord made provision for **the house** to be emptied **before the priest** went **in** so that the contents need **not** become **unclean** or be quarantined (vv. 36, 38). At first only the affected **stones** in a house were removed. But if the leprosy continued to break out, the house was torn down (vv. 39-45). In the event that the leprosy was arrested in the house, the priest followed a ritual of cleansing similar to that for a leper (vv. 48-53).

14:54-57 This paragraph is a summary of chapters 13 and 14.

E. Purification after Bodily Secretions (Chap. 15)

15:1-18 Chapter 15 deals with the **uncleanness** arising from discharges from the human body, either natural or diseased. Verses 1-12 seem to refer to a running **discharge** from a **man,** resulting from disease, such as gonorrhea. The ritual for **cleansing** is

given in verses 13-15. Verses 16-18 refer to the **emission of semen,** involuntary (vv. 16, 17) and voluntary (v. 18).

15:19-33 Verses 19-24 deal with a woman's normal menstrual cycle. This required no offerings. Verses 25-30 describe **a discharge of blood** from **a woman,** but not connected with menstruation—therefore abnormal. Verses 31-33 summarize the chapter.

V. THE DAY OF ATONEMENT (Chap. 16)

The greatest day on the Jewish calendar was the Day of Atonement (Heb., *Yôm Kippur*), when the high priest went into the Most Holy Place with sacrificial blood to make atonement for himself and for the people. It fell on the tenth day of the seventh month, five days before the Feast of Tabernacles. Although the Day of Atonement is usually listed along with the *feasts* of Jehovah, it was actually a time of *fasting* and solemnity (23:27-32).

It will be helpful to remember that in this chapter the Most Holy Place (the "Holy of Holies") is called the Holy Place, and the Holy Place is called the tabernacle of meeting.

16:1-3 The sacrilege of **the two sons of Aaron,** Nadab and Abihu, forms the backdrop for these instructions. A fate similar to theirs would befall the high priest if he entered the Most **Holy Place** on **any** day other than the Day of Atonement. And on that day he must carry **the blood of a young bull** for **a sin offering and of a ram as a burnt offering**.

16:4-10 The order of events is not easy to follow, but the following is a general outline of the ritual. First the high priest bathed and dressed in white **linen ... garments** (v. 4). By way of preliminaries, he brought a bullock and a ram to the tabernacle. He would offer these **for himself and for his** family, the bull for **a sin offering** and the ram for a burnt offering (v. 3). He brought **two . . . goats and one ram** which he would offer for the people, the **goats** for **a sin offering** and the **ram** for **a burnt offering** (v. 5). He presented **the two goats** before **the door of the tabernacle** and **cast lots—one for the LORD** and **the other lot** as **a scapegoat** (vv. 7, 8). The word translated "scapegoat" is *azazel*, meaning "goat of departure."

16:11–22 Then he killed the **bull as the sin offering . . . for himself and for his house** (v. 11). Next **he** took **a censer . . . of burning coals with his hands full of sweet incense** and carried them into the Most Holy Place. There he poured **the incense** over the live coals, causing a **cloud of incense** to **cover the mercy seat** (vv. 12, 13). He returned to the altar of burnt offering for some **blood of the bull**, took it into the Most Holy Place, and sprinkled it **on** top of **the mercy seat** and in front of it **seven times** (v. 14). He killed **the goat** chosen for a **sin offering** (v. 8), and sprinkled **its blood**, as he did the blood of the bull, before and on the **mercy seat** (vv. 9, 15). This made **atonement for the Most Holy Place because of the uncleanness of the children of Israel** (v. 16). By the sprinkling of blood he also made **atonement . . . for the tabernacle** and **for** the **altar** of burnt offering (vv. 18, 19), though the details here are not clear. Atonement started with the Most Holy place, then worked outward to the holy place and finally to the bronze altar (vv. 15–19). After he **laid both his hands on the head of** the scapegoat (v. 8) and confessed the sins of the people (vv. 10, 20, 21), **a** chosen **man** led the **goat** into **the wilderness** (vv. 21, 22). The two goats

symbolized two different aspects of atonement: "that which meets the character and holiness of God, and that which meets the need of the sinner as to the removal of his sins."[20] Aaron's laying his hands on the head of the live goat pictures the placing of the sins of Israel (and of ourselves) on Christ, to be taken away forever (v. 21).

The hymnwriter has expressed it thus:

My sins were laid on Jesus,
The spotless Lamb of God;
He bore them all and freed me
From the accursed load.
My guilt was borne by Jesus;
He cleansed the crimson stains
In His own blood most precious
And not a spot remains.
—*Horatius Bonar, alt.*

16:23–33 The high priest bathed **in a holy place**, perhaps at the laver, then **put on his garments** of glory and beauty (vv. 23, 24a). Jewish tradition says that the white linen garments were never worn again. The high priest next offered two rams as **burnt** offerings, one **for himself** and the other **for the people** (v. 24b). He burned **the fat of the** two **sin** offerings **on the altar** while **their skins, their flesh, and their offal** were being burned **outside the camp** (vv. 25, 27). Even the skin of the burnt offering, which usually went to the priest (7:8), was to be burned. According to the Jewish Talmud, the high priest went into the Holy of Holies after the evening sacrifice to bring out the censer. In the ritual of atonement, the people confessed their sins and refrained from work (v. 29).

From the above it will be seen that the high priest entered the Most Holy Place at least four times. This does not contradict Hebrews 9:7–12, where the thought is that there was only *one day* in the year when the high priest could enter.

16:34 Despite the solemn ceremonies of this day, its failure to adequately deal with sins was written across it in the words **"once a year."** "For it is not possible that the blood of bulls and goats could take away sins" (Heb. 10:4). In vivid contrast is the work of Christ, by which human sins are totally removed instead of being merely covered for a year! Isaac Watts expressed it this way:

> Not all the blood of beasts
> On Jewish altars slain,
> Could give the guilty conscience peace,
> Or wash away its stain.
>
> But Christ, the heavenly Lamb
> Took all our sins away,
> A sacrifice of nobler name
> And richer blood than they.

VI. LAWS CONCERNING SACRIFICE (Chap. 17)

17:1–9 Commentators hold differing views on verses 1–9. (1) The passage prohibited the killing of any animals, even for food, without offering them at the tabernacle. (2) It forbade the offering of sacrificial animals in the fields or in any place other than the tabernacle. (3) It prohibited the slaughter of sacrificial animals for food as long as the people were in the wilderness. This was changed when the people reached the Promised Land (Deut. 12:15). Morgan explains:

> The Hebrew word [translated 'devils' in KJV and 'goatdemons' in ASV] is literally 'hairy ones.' In Isaiah 13:21 and 34:14 it is rendered 'satyr' in the Authorized Version and 'wild-goats' in the American Standard Version. The satyr was an imaginary being,

half-goat, half-man, of demon nature. In Egypt the goat-man, Pan, was worshiped. It would seem as though this word recognized the fact that these people had in Egypt probably worshiped the false god.[21]

17:10–14 The eating of **blood** was likewise forbidden. The blood was for **atonement**, not for nourishment. **"The life of the flesh is in the blood"** (v. 11). The principle behind atonement is life for life. Since the wages of sin is death, symbolized by the shedding of blood, so "without the shedding of blood is no remission." Forgiveness does not come because the penalty of sin is *excused*, but because it is *transferred* to a sacrifice whose lifeblood is poured out. Verse 11 is one of the key verses in Leviticus and should be memorized. When an animal was slaughtered, its blood was drained immediately. An animal that died accidentally was unclean if its blood was not drained right away.

17:15, 16 This refers to a **person who** ignorantly ate the meat of an animal that had not been bled. Provision was made for his cleansing. But if he refused this provision, he was to be punished.

VII. LAWS CONCERNING PERSONAL CONDUCT (Chaps. 18—22)

A. Laws of Sexual Purity (Chap. 18)

18:1–5 Chapter 18 deals with various forms of unlawful marriages with which the Israelites had become familiar in **Egypt** but which they were to completely renounce in **the land of Canaan.**

18:6–18 The expression **"to uncover the nakedness"** here means to have sexual intercourse. Verse 6 states the general principle. Marriage with a close relative was forbidden, whether **mother** (v. 7); stepmother (v. 8); **sister** or half-sister (v. 9); granddaughter (v. 10); the **daughter of** a stepmother (v. 11); aunt (vv. 12, 13); uncle (v. 14a). Modern medicine confirms that in marriages of blood relatives, the physical or mental weaknesses of the parents are sometimes magnified in the children. But the prohibition extended to in-laws and other relatives-by-marriage as well (vv. 14b–16), sometimes known as relationships of affinity. A reason sometimes given for this latter code is that the term "one flesh" in Genesis 2:24 describes a family relationship that is so close and permanent that even the union of relatives-by-marriage is considered to be incest. A man must not marry a **daughter-in-law** or step-granddaughter (v. 17) or take a woman as a rival to her sister (v. 18), as in the case of Hannah and Peninnah (1 Sam. 1:1–8). Verse 16 was later amended by Deuteronomy 25:5: If a man died childless, his brother was obliged to marry the widow. This was known as *levirate* marriage.

18:19–21 Intercourse with **a woman** was forbidden during menstruation. Adultery with a **neighbor's wife** was prohibited. Also banned were the terrible practices sometimes connected with the worship of the idol **Molech**, causing newborn babies to **pass through . . . fire** (2 Kgs. 23:10; Jer. 32:35). Molech was the god of the Ammonites: His idol-image was in the Valley of Hinnom. Francis Schaeffer describes the ritual:

According to one tradition there was an opening at the back of the brazen idol, and after a fire was made within it, each parent had to come and with his own hands place his firstborn child in the white-hot, outstretched

arms of Molech. According to this tradition, the parent was not allowed to show emotion, and drums were beaten so that the baby's cries could not be heard as the baby died in the arms of Molech.[22]

18:22, 23 Sodomy or homosexuality was forbidden, as well as sexual intercourse with **an animal**. In legislating against homosexuality, God may also have been anticipating the modern AIDS epidemic and seeking to save people from it.

18:24–30 Verses 1–23 tell the people *what* not to do; verses 24–30 tell them *why* not to do it. It is no accident that impurity and idolatry are found together in the same chapter (see also chap. 20). A person's morality is the fruit of his theology, his concept of God. The Canaanites were a graphic illustration of the degradation that idolatry produces (vv. 24–27). When the children of Israel took possession of the land, they killed thousands of these people at Jehovah's command. When we consider the moral degradation of the Canaanites, as described in verses 24–30, we can understand why God dealt so harshly with them.

B. Laws of Everyday Life (Chap. 19)

19:1–25 The basis of all holiness is found in the words **"I the LORD your God am holy"** (v. 2). Various laws for the conduct of the people are here laid down, as follows:

Mother and father were to be revered (v. 3)—the fifth commandment.

God's **Sabbaths** were to be observed (v. 3)—the fourth commandment.

Idolatry was prohibited (v. 4)—the second commandment.

Eating of the peace offering on

the third day was forbidden (vv. 5–8).

In harvesting a **field**, the owner was to **leave** some grain in the corners **for the poor and** strangers (vv. 9, 10). Field crops and grapes are mentioned as examples, not as a complete list.

Stealing, cheating, and lying were forbidden (v. 11)—the eighth commandment.

Swearing **by the Name of . . . God** to a false statement was outlawed (v. 12)—the third commandment.

Defrauding, robbing, or withholding wages were prohibited (v. 13).

Cursing **the deaf** or causing **the blind** to stumble were condemned (v. 14). The people were to express their reverence for Jehovah by their respect for one another (25:17). The handicapped (v. 14), the aged (v. 32), and the poor (25:26, 43) were all to be treated with kindness by those who feared the Lord.

Showing partiality **in judgment** was forbidden (v. 15).

Slander and plotting **against the life of** a **neighbor** were prohibited (v. 16).

Hatred of one's **brother** was forbidden: **"You shall surely rebuke your neighbor, and not bear sin because of him"** (v. 17). Matters should be dealt with openly and frankly lest they become the cause of inward animosity leading to outward sin.

Vengeance or bearing of grudges was prohibited (v. 18). The second part of verse 18, loving **your neighbor as yourself**, is the summation of the whole law (Gal. 5:14). Jesus said it was the second-greatest command (Mark 12:31). The greatest command is found in Deuteronomy 6:4, 5.

Verse 19 is generally understood to forbid the interbreeding of animals that results in mules. **Livestock** here means beasts in general.

Also, sowing a **field** with different kinds of **seed**, or wearing a **garment of mixed linen and wool** was forbidden. God is a God of separation, and in these physical examples He was teaching His people to separate themselves from sin and defilement.

If a man had illicit relations with a slave-girl **betrothed to** another **man**, both were scourged and he was required to **bring** a **trespass offering** (vv. 20–22).

When settled in Canaan, the Israelites were not to pick the **fruit** of their **trees** for **three years**. The **fruit** of **the fourth year** was to be offered **to the** Lord, and **in the fifth year** the **fruit** could be eaten (vv. 23–25). Perhaps the fruit of the fourth year went to the Levites or, as one commentator suggests, was eaten before the Lord as part of the second tithe.

19:26–37 Other forbidden practices were: eating of flesh from which the **blood** had not been drained (v. 26a); practicing witchcraft (v. 26b); trimming the hair in accordance with idolatrous practices (v. 27); making **cuttings in** one's **flesh** as an expression of mourning **for the dead** (v. 28a); making **marks on** the body as the heathen did (v. 28b); making one's **daughter** become a **prostitute**, as was common in pagan worship (v. 29); breaking of the Sabbath (v. 30); consulting **mediums** or **familiar spirits** (v. 31). **Honor** was to be shown to the aged (v. 32), and strangers were to be treated with kindness and hospitality (vv. 33, 34). **Honest** business practices were enjoined (vv. 35–37).

C. Punishment for Gross Offenses (Chap. 20)

This chapter gives the punishments for some of the offenses listed in chapters 18 and 19. The person who caused a child to go through the fire in an offering **to Molech** was to be stoned **to death** (vv. 1–3). **If the people failed to kill him, God would destroy him** and **his family** (vv. 4, 5). The death penalty was also pronounced against one who consulted **mediums** and **familiar spirits** (v. 6); one who cursed **his father or his mother** (v. 9); an **adulterer** and an **adulteress** (v. 10); one who committed incest **with his father's wife** (v. 11) or **daughter-in-law** (v. 12); and a **sodomite** (v. 13). (Both parties were to be killed in these cases of unlawful intercourse.) In the case of a man having unlawful sexual intercourse with a **mother** and her daughter, all three offenders were to **be burned** (v. 14). Sexual perversion between humans and animals was a capital crime; both man and beast were to be slain (vv. 15, 16). The death penalty (or, as some think, excommunication) was pronounced against intercourse with a **sister** or half-sister (v. 17) or with a menstruous **woman** (v. 18). Intercourse with an aunt called forth the judgment, **"they shall bear their guilt,"** but no details were given (v. 19). Some think it means that they would die childless, as in verse 20, where a man had intercourse with his uncle's wife, and in verse 21, where the offense was with a sister-in-law.

Verse 21 applied only as long as the brother was alive. If he died without leaving a son to carry on his name, his brother was commanded to marry the widow and name the first son after the deceased (Deut. 25:5). Such unions were known as *levirate* marriages.

The longing of God's heart was to have a holy people, separated from the abominations of the Gentiles and enjoying the blessings of the Promised Land (vv. 22–26). Mediums and people with **familiar spirits** were to be exterminated by stoning (v. 27).

D. Conduct of the Priests (Chaps. 21, 22)

Chapters 21 and 22, along with 16 and 17, are addressed to Aaron and his sons.

21:1–4 **Priests** were not to **defile** themselves by touching **the dead** . . . **except** in the case of **nearest relatives**. Even entering the tent of the dead defiled a person for seven days (Num. 19:14). This would disqualify a priest from serving the Lord during that time, so he was forbidden to make himself unclean for any but his **nearest relatives**. Verse 4 probably means that, because of his high rank, he must **not defile himself** for any reason except those listed in verses 2 and 3.

21:5–9 Practices of the heathen in defacing their bodies with signs of mourning for the dead were forbidden. The priest was not permitted to marry a woman profaned by harlotry or a **divorced** . . . **woman**. However, he could marry a widow. A priest's **daughter** who became a **harlot** was to **be burned** to death.

21:10–15 A **high priest** was not permitted to mourn in the customary ways or leave the **sanctuary** to show honor to the dead. He was to **marry** an Israelite **virgin**, and his married life was to be above reproach.

21:16–24 A physical **defect** barred a man from the service of the priesthood—blindness, lameness, facial deformities, a deformed limb, foot or hand injuries, hunchbackedness, dwarfism, defective eyes, itching diseases, scabs, or injured reproductive organs. Any son **of Aaron** who was defective in any of these ways could share the food of the priests, but he could not actively serve as a priest before the Lord (vv. 22, 23). The **holy** food was the priests' share of the peace offerings. The **most holy** food was their share of other offerings. The priests who offered the sacrifices must be without **defect** because they portrayed Christ as our unblemished High Priest.

22:1–9 If a priest was ceremonially unclean through leprosy, a running **discharge**, contact with something defiled by a dead body, eating meat that had not been drained of its blood, or for any other reason, he was not to partake of the food of the priests. That is what is meant by **"separate themselves from the holy things"** (v. 2). If the priest was a leper or had a running sore, the disqualification probably lasted for a long time. In the other cases mentioned, the following ritual prevailed for the priest: First, he must bathe himself, then wait until the evening, at which time he would **be clean** again.

22:10–13 In general, strangers, visitors, and hired servants were not permitted to **eat** the **holy** food. But a slave who had been purchased by the **priest**, as well as the slave's children, could **eat** it. **If the priest's daughter** got **married** to **an outsider, she** was **not** permitted to **eat** it, but if she were widowed **or divorced** and childless, and living with her father, then she could share the food of the priests.

22:14–16 If **a man** ate some of **the holy** food **unintentionally**, he could make restitution by replacing it and adding **one-fifth**, as in the case of the trespass offering.

22:17–30 **Offerings** brought **to the** Lord had to be **without blemish** (v.

19), whether for **burnt** offerings (vv. 18–20) or **peace** offerings (v. 21). Diseased, disabled, or disfigured animals were forbidden (v. 22). **A bull or a lamb** with an overgrown **limb** or a stunted **limb** could be presented for **a freewill offering** but not for a votive offering (v. 23). Castrated animals or those with damaged reproductive organs were not acceptable (v. 24). Israelites were not to accept any of the above defective animals as an offering from a stranger (v. 25). A sacrificial animal could not be offered until it was at least eight days old (vv. 26, 27). A mother animal and **her young** were **not** to be killed on **the same day** (v. 28). The meat of a **thanksgiving** offering was to **be eaten . . . on the same day** that it was offered (vv. 29, 30).

22:31–33 The final paragraph explains why the Israelites were to **keep** and **perform** all these **commandments of the** Lord. It was because the God **who** had **brought** them **out of the land of Egypt** is holy. Several expressions in this short section stress the message of Leviticus as a whole: **"not profane," "holy name," "I will be hallowed,"** and **"I am the** Lord **who sanctifies."**

VIII. THE FEASTS OF THE LORD (Chap. 23)

A. The Sabbath (23:1–3)

The religious calendar of Israel now becomes the subject of God's legislation. **The** Lord told the **children of Israel** through **Moses** to proclaim the **feasts of the** Lord as **holy convocations.**

After **six days** of labor, **the seventh day**, or **Sabbath**, was to be a day of **rest** from **work**. This was the only weekly holy day.

B. The Passover (23:4, 5)

The LORD's Passover was held on the fourteenth day of the first month (Nisan, or Abib). It commemorated Israel's redemption from slavery in Egypt. The Passover lamb was a type of Christ, the Lamb of God, our Passover (1 Cor. 5:7), whose blood was shed to redeem us from slavery to sin. He did not die at Creation but in the fullness of time (Gal. 4:4–6).

C. The Feast of Unleavened Bread (23:6–8)

The Feast of Unleavened Bread occurred in connection with the Passover. It extended over a period of seven days, beginning with the day after Passover—i.e., from the fifteenth day of Nisan to the twenty-first. The names of these two feasts are often used interchangeably. During this time the Jews were required to put away all leaven from their households. In Scripture, leaven speaks of sin. The feast pictures a life from which the leaven of malice and wickedness has been put away, and a life which is characterized by "the unleavened bread of sincerity and truth" (1 Cor. 5:8). There was no lapse between the Passover (our redemption) and the Feast of Unleavened Bread (our obligation to walk in holiness) . . . Even today the Jews eat unleavened bread during this feast. The bread is called matzo. The preparation of matzo involves piercing the bread, and in the *baking process* it becomes striped. This unleavened bread clearly reminds us of the sinless Messiah. He was pierced for us, and by His stripes we are healed.

D. The Feast of Firstfruits (23:9–14)

The presentation of a wave . . . sheaf of barley took place the second day of the Feast of Unleavened Bread (on the day after the Sabbath—i.e., the first day of the week). This is known as the Feast of Firstfruits. It marked the beginning of the barley harvest, the first grain of the year. A sheaf of barley was waved before the LORD in thanksgiving for the harvest. A burnt offering and a grain offering were also presented. This first harvest was viewed as the promise of the larger harvest to come. This pictures Christ in resurrection—"Christ . . . the firstfruits of those who have fallen asleep" (1 Cor. 15:20). His resurrection is the guarantee that all who put their faith in Him will also gain immortality through resurrection.

E. The Feast of Weeks (23:15–22)

23:15–22 The Feast of Weeks (Heb., *Shāvûôt*) or Pentecost (Gk. for "fifty") was held fifty days . . . after the Passover Sabbath. It was a harvest festival thanking God for the beginning of the wheat harvest. The firstfruits of the wheat harvest were presented at this time, along with a burnt offering, a new grain offering, drink offerings, and a peace offering. According to Jewish tradition, Moses received the law on this day of the year. The Feast is typical of the descent of the Holy Spirit on the Day of Pentecost, when the church was brought into existence. The wave offering consisted of two . . . loaves of bread made from the freshly reaped fine flour. (This was the only offering that was made with leaven.) These loaves represent, in type, the Jews and the Gentiles made into "one new man in [Christ]" (Eph. 2:15).

After Pentecost there was a long interval, about four months, before there was another feast. This span of time may picture the present church age, in which we eagerly await the return of our Savior.

F. The Feast of Trumpets (23:23–25)

The Feast of **Trumpets** took place on the **first day of the ... seventh month**. The blowing of trumpets called the sons of Israel together for a solemn **holy convocation**. At this time there was a period of ten days for self-examination and repentance, leading up to the Day of Atonement. It typifies the time when Israel will be regathered to the land prior to her national repentance. This was the first day of the civil year, today called Rosh Hashanah (Heb. *head of the year*). Some see this feast as picturing another gathering as well—that is, the gathering of the saints to meet the Lord in the air at the Rapture.

G. The Day of Atonement (23:26–32)

The **Day of Atonement** (Heb., *Yôm Kippur*), occurring on **the tenth day of the seventh month**, has been described in detail in chapter 16. It prefigures the national repentance of Israel, when a believing remnant will turn to the Messiah and be forgiven (Zech. 12:10; 13:1). In almost every verse dealing with the Day of Atonement, God repeats the command to **do no work**. The only person who was to be active on this day was the high priest. The Lord reinforced the charge by threatening to **destroy** any **person** who violated it. This is because the salvation which our High Priest obtained for us was "not on the basis of deeds which we have done" (Titus 3:5). There can be no human works involved in the business of removing our sins. Christ's work and His alone is the source of eternal salvation. To **"afflict your souls"** (vv. 27, 29) means to fast. Even today religious Jews observe the day as a time for fasting and prayer. Although the **Day of Atonement** is listed among the feasts of Jehovah, it was actually

a time for *fasting* rather than *feasting*. However, after the sin question was settled, there came a time of rejoicing in the Feast of Tabernacles.

H. The Feast of Tabernacles (23:33–44)

The **Feast of Tabernacles** (Heb., *Sukkôth*, "booths") began on **the fifteenth day of** the **seventh month**. **For seven days** the Israelites dwelt **in booths** (v. 42). It pictured the final rest and final harvest, when Israel will be dwelling securely in the land during the Millennium. This feast is also called the Feast of Ingathering (Ex. 23:16). It was associated with harvesting. In fact several of the feasts mentioned in this chapter have to do with harvesting. The two **Sabbaths** may picture the Millennium and the Eternal Rest. Moishe and Ceil Rosen describe the tradition:

> The Jewish people built booth-like structures and lived in them during this feast as a reminder of the temporary dwellings the Israelites had in the wilderness. Even today many Jewish people build open-roofed, three-sided huts for this festival. They decorate them with tree boughs and autumn fruits to remind them of harvest.
>
> Everyone who was able came up to Jerusalem for this harvest festival every year. The Temple worship for the holiday included the ritual pouring of water from the Pool of Siloam, symbolic of the prayers for the winter rains. It was at this time that Jesus cried out, "... If any man thirst, let him come to Me and drink" (John 7:37–38).
>
> After Israel's final Day of Atonement, the Feast of Booths will be celebrated again in Jerusalem (Zech. 14:16).[23]

One of the things the Lord sought to teach His people through the feasts was the close association between the spiritual and the physical aspects of life. Times of bounty and blessing were to be times of rejoicing **before the Lord**. The Lord was portrayed to them as the One who abundantly provided for their daily needs. Their response as a nation to His goodness found expression in the festivals connected with the harvest.

Notice the repetition of the commandment that the Israelites were to do **no** servile or **customary work** on these solemn occasions (vv. 3, 7, 8, 21, 25, 28, 30, 31, 35, 36).

A definite chronological progression can be traced in the Feasts of Jehovah. The Sabbath takes us back to God's rest after creation. The Passover and the Feast of Unleavened Bread speak to us of Calvary. Next comes the Feast of Firstfruits, pointing to the resurrection of Christ. The Feast of Pentecost typifies the coming of the Holy Spirit. Then looking to the future, the Feast of Trumpets pictures the regathering of Israel. The Day of Atonement foreshadows the time when a remnant of Israel will repent and acknowledge Jesus as Messiah. Finally the Feast of Tabernacles sees Israel enjoying the millennial reign of Christ.

IX. CEREMONIAL AND MORAL LEGISLATION (Chap. 24)

In chapter 23 the yearly feasts were dealt with. Now the daily and weekly ministries before the Lord are taken up.

24:1–9 Pure **oil of pressed olives** was to be burned in the **gold lampstand before the Lord continually**. The **twelve cakes** were to be **set** in **two rows** or piles on the **table** of showbread, and replaced each Sabbath. The **frankincense** mentioned in verse 7 belonged to the **Lord**. It was offered to Jehovah when the old bread was removed and given to the priests for food.

24:10–23 Then there is the abrupt account of **a son of an Israelite woman, whose father was an Egyptian**, who was **stoned** to death for cursing God (vv. 10–16, 23). The incident shows that the law was the same for anyone who lived in the camp of Israel, whether he was a fullblooded Jew or not (v. 22). It shows that blasphemy, like murder, was punishable by **death** (vv. 14, 16, 17, 23). (Verse 16 was probably the law against blasphemy, which the Jews referred to when they said, "We have a law, and according to our law He [the Lord Jesus] ought to die, because He made Himself the Son of God" [John 19:7].) It shows that compensation could be made for some other crimes (vv. 18, 21). Finally the incident shows that:

> ... retribution was a basic principle of law; wrongs had to be righted. Softness brought the law into disrepute. The law of retaliation is scoffed at today in the Western world, but thoughtful people will not dismiss it. (a) In ancient society, punishment was often out of all proportion with the wrong done. Retaliatory punishment was thus a great step toward true justice. (b) Furthermore, rehabilitative punishment—the alternative most frequently suggested—suffers from subjectivism. Who is to decide when a man is rehabilitated, ready to rejoin society? The terms may be lenient today, but what of tomorrow? True justice is an eye (and not more) for an eye. (*Daily Notes of the Scripture Union*)

In verses 1–9 we see a picture of Israel as God intended. In verses 10–16 the cursing man pictures Israel as it actually became, blaspheming the Name and cursing ("His blood be on us, and on our children").

X. THE SABBATICAL YEAR AND THE YEAR OF JUBILEE (Chap. 25)

The legislation in chapters 25—27 was given to Moses on Mount Sinai and not from within the tabernacle (25:1; 26:46; 27:34).

25:1–7 Every **seventh year** was to be observed as **a sabbath. The land** was to lie fallow (uncultivated). **Food** for the people would be provided from the crop that grew **of its own accord**. The owner was not to harvest it, but leave it for free use by the people.

25:8–17 **The fiftieth year** was also a sabbath, known as **the Year of Jubilee**. It began **on the Day of Atonement** following **seven** sabbatic-year cycles (**forty-nine years**). Slaves were to be set free, the **land** was to lie fallow, and was to revert to its original owner. **The price** of a slave or a piece of land decreased as the Year of Jubilee approached (vv. 15–17), and all business transactions were supposed to take this fact into account. The words "Proclaim liberty throughout all the land unto all the inhabitants thereof" (v. 10 KJV) are inscribed on the United States Liberty Bell. Believers today may liken the **Year of Jubilee** to the coming of the Lord. As we get closer to His coming, our material wealth decreases in value. The moment He comes, our money, real estate, and investments will be worthless to us. The moral is to put these things to work for Him *today!*

25:18–22 With regard to the sabbatic year, the people might wonder how they would have enough food to eat that year and the following year. God promised them that if they were obedient, He would give them sufficient crops during the sixth year to last **for three years**.

Once every fifty years, there would be two successive years when there would be no sowing or harvesting, that is, when the regular sabbatic year would be followed by the year of jubilee. Presumably the Lord gave enough crops in the forty-eighth year to last for four years.

Some scholars believe that, by inclusive reckoning, the fiftieth year was actually the forty-ninth. At any rate, this is an ancient example of good ecology: conserving the land's fertility by enforced rest. In modern times man has become concerned about preserving our planet's resources. As so often, God's Word is centuries ahead of the times.

25:23–28 **Land** could **be sold**, but not **permanently**, because Jehovah is the Owner. There were three ways in which land could be "redeemed" (revert to its original Jewish owner): The nearest **relative** could buy it back for the seller (v. 25); the seller (original owner), if he regained financial solvency, could redeem it, paying the purchaser for the years remaining until the Year of Jubilee (vv. 26, 27); otherwise, the land automatically reverted to the original owner in **the Year of Jubilee** (v. 28).

25:29–34 **A house in a walled city** was subject to redemption for one **year**; after that, it became the property of the new owner **permanently**. **Houses** in unwalled **villages** were **counted** as part of the land and therefore reverted to the original owner in **the Year of Jubilee**. **Houses** owned by **the Levites** in the special **cities** assigned to them were always subject to being bought back by the Levites. The **field** assigned to **the Levites** for **common-land** was **not** to be **sold**.

25:35-38 If an Israelite fell **into** debt and **poverty**, his Jewish creditors were not to oppress him. They were not to charge him **interest** on money or demand additional food for **food** that was lent.

25:39-46 If an impoverished Israelite sold **himself** to a Jewish creditor for nonpayment of debt, he was not to be treated **as a slave** but **as a hired servant**, and was to be released in the **Year of Jubilee**, if this came before the end of his six years of service. The Jews were permitted to have slaves from the Gentile nations, and these were considered their own property, to be handed down to their descendants. But Jewish people were **not** to be **slaves** themselves.

25:47-54 If a Jew **sold** himself to a Gentile who happened to be living in the land, the Jew could always be bought back and set free. The redemption **price** was determined by **the number of years** remaining **until the Year of Jubilee**. The relative redeeming the Jew could use him as **a hired servant** until the **Jubilee**. If no relative **redeemed** him, then he automatically went free in **the Year of Jubilee**.

25:55 This verse is a vivid reminder that the Israelites and their land (v. 23) belonged to **the LORD** and that He should be recognized as rightful Owner. Neither God's people nor God's land could be sold permanently.

XI. BLESSINGS AND CURSINGS (Chap. 26)

A. The Blessings for Obedience to God (26:1-13)

Twice as much space is devoted to warning as to blessing in this chapter. Adversity, the promised fruit of disobedience, is a tool which God uses, not to inflict revenge but to lead

His people to repentance (vv. 40-42). National chastisement would be increasingly severe until the people confessed their iniquity. Notice the progression in verses 14, 18, 21, 24, and 28.

After warnings against idolatry (v. 1), sabbath-breaking, and irreverence (v. 2), the Lord promised the following blessings to the nation if it would keep His commandments: **rain**, fertility (v. 4), productivity, security (v. 5), **peace**, safety (v. 6), victory over **enemies** (vv. 7, 8), fruitfulness, and the presence of the Lord (vv. 9-13). Knox's version of verse 13 is especially graphic: "Was it not I ... that ... struck the chains from your necks, and gave you the upright carriage of free men?"

B. The Curses for Disobedience to God (26:14-39)

26:14-33 Disobedience would result in **terror**, **disease**, conquest by **enemies**, drought, barrenness, **wild beasts**, **pestilence**, invasion, and captivity.

Verse 26 describes famine conditions. **Bread** would be so scarce that **ten women** would be able to **bake** their supply **in one oven**, ordinarily big enough for only one family's use. Even more severe famine is pictured in verse 29, where cannibalism prevails (see 2 Kgs. 6:29 and Lam. 4:10 for the historical fulfillment of this warning).

26:34-39 Persistent disobedience on Israel's part would result in their being taken captive by a foreign power. The **land** of Israel would **enjoy** a period of **rest** equal to the number of sabbatic years which the people disregarded. This is what happened in the Babylonian captivity. During the years from Saul to the captivity the people had failed to keep the sabbatic years. Thus they spent seventy years in exile, and the land enjoyed its rest (2 Chron. 36:20, 21).

C. Restoration through Confession and Repentance (26:40–46)

The final section of chapter 26 provided a way of recovery through confession and repentance for the disobedient nation. God would not completely forsake His people, but would **remember** His **covenant** promises to **their ancestors**.

XII. VOWS AND TITHES (Chap. 27)

The last chapter of Leviticus deals with voluntary vows made to the Lord. It seems that in gratitude to the Lord for some blessing, a man could vow to the Lord a person (himself or a member of his family), an animal, a house, or a field. The things vowed were given to the priests (Num. 18:14). Since these gifts were not always of use to the priests, provision was made that the person making the vow could give the priest a sum of money in lieu of the thing vowed.

27:1, 2 A **vow** of consecration was very special.

27:3–7 If a person was vowed to the Lord, then the redemption price to be paid to the priest was as follows:

A man from 20–60 years old	50 shekels
A woman from 20–60 years old	30 shekels
A male from 5–20 years old	20 shekels
A female from 5–20 years old	10 shekels
A male from 1 month to 5 years old	5 shekels
A female from 1 month to 5 years old	3 shekels
A male 60 years old and above	15 shekels
A female 60 years old and above	10 shekels

27:8 If a man was **too poor** to redeem his vow according to this chart, then the **priest** determined some figure **according to** his **ability**.

27:9–13 If the vow was an ani-

mal, the following rules applied: A clean **animal**, suitable for sacrifice, could not be redeemed (v. 9). It was to be offered to the Lord upon the altar (Num. 18:17); nothing could be gained by exchanging one **animal** for another, because both would then become the Lord's (vv. 10, 33); an unclean animal could be redeemed by paying the **value** placed on it by **the priest**, plus **one-fifth** (vv. 11–13).

27:14, 15 If **a man** dedicated **his house to . . . the** LORD, he could change his mind and buy it back by paying the priest's estimate of its value, plus **one-fifth**.

27:16–18 Appraising the value of **a field** was complicated by the fact that it reverted to the original owner **in the Year of Jubilee**.

If it was dedicated by its original owner, that is, if he inherited it, then the rules in verses 16–21 applied. It was valued **according to the seed** sown in it. For example, if a **homer of barley seed** were sown in it, it would be valued **at fifty shekels of silver**.

If the **field** was vowed near or at the **Year of Jubilee**, then the above appraisal was effective. **But if** it was dedicated some years **after the** Year of **Jubilee**, then the value of the field decreased accordingly. In other words, the field would be worth only 30 shekels if it was vowed 20 years after the Year of Jubilee.

27:19–21 If **the field** was redeemed, then an added payment of **one-fifth** was required.

If, after giving the land to the Lord, the owner did **not . . . redeem** it before the Year of Jubilee, or if he secretly **sold** it to someone else, it could no longer **be redeemed** but became the **possession of the priest** at **the** Year of **Jubilee**. The land was then "devoted" or "holy" to the LORD.

27:22–25 If **a field** was dedicated by someone who was not its original owner, that is, by someone who bought it, then verses 22–25 applied. **The priest** set a value on the property, depending on how many crops could be raised on it before the Year of Jubilee. In that year, **the field** went back to its original owner.

27:26, 27 The **firstborn** of a sacrificial animal could not be dedicated to the Lord, because it belonged to Him anyway. The firstborn of **an unclean animal** could be redeemed by paying the priest's **valuation** of it, plus **one-fifth**. Otherwise the priest could sell it.

27:28, 29 Nothing that was under sentence of **death** or **destruction** could **be redeemed**. This is what was meant by a **devoted** or proscribed thing. Thus a son who cursed his parents could not **be redeemed** but must **be put to death**.

It should be noted that there is an important distinction in this chapter between what is consecrated (NASB) or sanctified (KJV) and what is proscribed (NASB) or devoted (NKJV, KJV). Things sanctified by vow—that is, set apart for divine use—could be redeemed. Devoted things were given completely and finally, and could not be redeemed.

27:30, 31 A **tithe** or tenth of the grain and **fruit** belonged to the Lord. If the offerer wanted to keep it, he could pay its value plus **one-fifth**.

27:32, 33 The expression "whatever passes under the rod" refers to the practice of numbering sheep or goats by causing them to pass under the shepherd's rod. Leslie Flynn comments:

With rod in hand, he [the shepherd] would touch every tenth one. He

could in no way contrive to change their order so that a good animal would escape tenth place. If he tried to alter the order, both the real tenth and the attempted switch would be the Lord's.[24]

This first **tithe** was called the levitical tithe, because it was paid to the Levites (Num. 18:21–24). A second tithe, which apparently is a different one, is prescribed in Deuteronomy 14:22–29.

27:34 **The commandments which the LORD commanded Moses** in the last verse of Leviticus probably refer to the whole book. After studying the multitude of detailed rituals and blood sacrifices, we can rejoice with Matthew Henry that

We are not under the *dark shadows* of the law, but enjoy the clear light of the gospel, . . . that we are not under the *heavy yoke* of the law, and the carnal ordinances of it . . . , but under the sweet and easy institutions of the gospel, which pronounces those the *true worshippers that worship the Father in spirit and truth*, by Christ only, and in his name, who is our priest, temple, altar, sacrifice, purification, and all. Let us not therefore think that because we are not tied to the ceremonial cleansings, feasts, and oblations, a little care, time, and expense, will serve to honour God with. No, but rather have our hearts more enlarged with free-will offerings to his praise, more inflamed with holy love and joy, and more engaged in seriousness of thought and sincerity of intention. *Having boldness to enter into the holiest by the blood of Jesus, let us draw near with a true heart, and in full assurance of faith*, worshipping God with so much the more cheerfulness and humble confidence, still saying, *Blessed be God for Jesus Christ!*[25]

ENDNOTES

[1] (Chap. 1) The word *'ōlāh* comes from the root word meaning "to go up." The idea is that the whole animal is brought up to God's altar and offered up as a gift in its entirety.

[2] (Chap. 1) Peter Pell, *The Tabernacle*, pp. 102, 103.

[3] (Chap. 2) The translation "meat" in the KJV meant solid food as opposed to liquid in 1611. What we call *meat* today was called *flesh* in the seventeenth century. Some scholars derive the word *minḥāh* from a root meaning "lead" or "guide." Most suggest a root meaning "gift."

[4] (3:1–15) This word, almost always in the plural form *shelāmîm*, is related to the well-known Hebrew word *shālôm*. The Hebrew concept is broader than merely absence of hostility, but includes prosperity and wholeness as well as peace with God. A second meaning of this word is a sacrifice of communion in God's presence. Usually, though not here, the peace offering is last in order, and some scholars derive the word from the rare meaning "to complete." Carr makes a nice application: "If this sense is correct, the NT references to Christ our Peace (e.g., Eph 2:14) become more meaningful, as he is the final sacrifice for us (cf. Heb. 9:27; 10:12)." G. Lloyd Carr, "Shelem," *Theological Wordbook of the Old Testament*, III:932.

[5] (Chap. 3) Pell, *Tabernacle*, p. 92.

[6] (Chap. 4) Strangely enough to us, this same Hebrew word, occurring almost 300 times in the OT, can mean either "sin" or "sin offering."

[7] (5:14—6:7) The RSV and NEB translate by "guilt offering," but the traditional translation is preferable.

[8] (6:18) Keil and Delitzsch interpret the latter part of this verse to mean that "every layman who touched these most holy things became holy through the contact, so that henceforth he had to guard against defilement in the same manner as the sanctified priests." C. F. Keil and Franz Delitzsch, "Leviticus," in *Biblical Commentary on the Old Testament*, II:319.

[9] (7:11–18) A. G. Clarke, *Precious Seed Magazine*, No. 2, Vol. 11, March-April 1960, p. 49.

[10] (7:11–18) *Ibid.*

[11] (7:11–18) John Reid, *The Chief Meeting of the Church*, p. 58.

[12] (7:22–27) Dr. S. I. McMillen, *None of These Diseases*, p. 84.

[13] (Chap. 8) Matthew Henry, *Matthew Henry's Commentary on the Whole Bible*, I:474.

[14] (Chap. 12) George Williams, *The Student's Commentary on the Holy Scriptures*, p. 71.

[15] (13:Intro) Harrison, *Leviticus*, p. 137. In Appendix A, p. 241 of his commentary he gives a semi-technical translation of chapter 13 that proves helpful for those who are interested in the medical aspects of the conditions mentioned.

[16] (13:Intro) *Ibid.*, pp. 136, 137.

[17] (13:38, 39) *Ibid.*, p. 245.

[18] (13:47–59) *Ibid.*, p. 146.

[19] (13:47–59) *Ibid.*

[20] (16:11–22) G. Morrish, publisher, *New and Concise Bible Dictionary*, p. 91.

[21] (17:1–9) G. Campbell Morgan, *Searchlights from the Word*, p. 38.

[22] (18:19–21) Francis A. Schaeffer, *The Church at the End of the 20th Century*, p. 126.

[23] (23:33–44) Moishe and Ceil Rosen, *Christ in the Passover*, pagination unavailable.

[24] (27:32, 33) Leslie B. Flynn, *Your God and Your Gold*, pp. 30, 31.

[25] (27:34) Henry, "Leviticus," I:562.

BIBLIOGRAPHY

Bonar, Andrew. *A Commentary on the Book of Leviticus*. 1852. Reprint. Grand Rapids: Baker Book House, 1978.

Borland, James A. "Leviticus." In *Liberty Bible Commentary*. Lynchburg, VA: The Old-Time Gospel Hour, 1982.

Coleman, Robert O. "Leviticus." In *Wycliffe Bible Commentary*. Chicago: Moody Press, 1962.

Harrison, R. K. *Leviticus: An Introduction and Commentary*. The Tyndale Old Testament Commentaries. Downers Grove, IL: InterVarsity Press, 1980.

Henry, Matthew. "Leviticus." In *Matthew Henry's Commentary on the Whole Bible*. Vol. 1. McLean, VA: MacDonald Publishing Company, n.d.

Jukes, Andrew. *The Law of the Offerings*. London: The Lamp Press, 1954.

Keil, C. F., and Delitzsch, F. "Leviticus." In *Biblical Commentary on the Old Testament. The Pentateuch, Vol. 4*. Grand Rapids: Wm. B. Eerdmans Publishing Co., 1971.

Lindsey, F. Duane. "Leviticus." In *The Bible Knowledge Commentary*. Wheaton, IL: Victor Books, 1985.

Smith, Arthur E. *Leviticus for Lambs*. Privately Printed, n.d.

Periodicals

Clarke, A. G. "The Levitical Offerings," *Precious Seed Magazine*, 1960.

NUMBERS

Introduction

"Numbers has a unique contribution to the life of the Christian when the broad sequence of its historical setting is seen as a parallel situation to Christian living. The writer of the Epistle to the Hebrews makes this significant application, devoting two chapters to it (Heb. 3 and 4)."

—Irving L. Jensen

I. Unique Place in the Canon

The English name of the fourth book of Moses is a translation of the Septuagint's title, *Arithmoi*, and obviously is so-called because of the census in chapter 1 and again in chapter 26, as well as the many other numerical data given throughout.

The Hebrew title is much more descriptive of the book as a whole: "In the Wilderness" (*Bemidbār*). The narrative of forty years in the wilderness is full of interesting and well-known stories: the spies visiting Canaan, Korah's rebellion, Aaron's rod that budded, the brass serpent, Balaam and his donkey, and other lesser known events.

It should not be thought that this is merely "Hebrew history." All of these things happened for our spiritual edification. We are to learn from the mistakes of the children of Israel, not repeat them. Consequently Numbers is a very important book.

II. Authorship

According to Jewish and Christian teaching, Numbers was written by the great law-giver, Moses. This is widely discounted in liberal circles, but see Introduction to the Pentateuch for a concise defense of the Mosaic authorship.

III. Date

Rationalistic scholars put the Pentateuch very late in Jewish history, but a date of about 1406 B.C. is compatible with conservative and believing scholarship. (See Introduction to the Pentateuch for details.)

IV. Background and Theme

The historical backdrop for the Book of Numbers, as its Hebrew title suggests, is the wilderness. The journeys and wanderings depicted here cover about thirty-eight years, from Israel's departure from Mount Sinai till they reached the Plains of Moab, opposite the Promised Land. The wanderings were due to unbelief, hence God gives no itinerary of them. As Scroggie remarks, "The movements of God's people out of His will are not on His calendar."[1]

As Leviticus stresses worship and spiritual position, the theme of Numbers is *walk* and spiritual *progress* (or lack of it!). Christians should not think that this book is a dry Jewish history book! It is full of applications to modern Christian experience. It would be pleasant to think that all (or most) Christians advance swiftly from salvation to a full entering into God's promises of victory; observation and experience, however, show how much

we resemble the ancient Israelites in complaining, backsliding, and rank unbelief.

The good news is that we do not need to repeat the wanderings of Israel in our spiritual pilgrimage. God has made full provision for spiritual success through faith. (See *Believers Bible Commentary, New Testament*, especially Romans 6—8.)

OUTLINE

Commentary

I. THE LAST DAYS AT SINAI (1:1—10:10)

A. The Census and Arrangement of the Tribes (Chaps. 1, 2)

1:1 As the book of Numbers opens, it is one year and one month after the children of Israel left **Egypt** and one month after the **tabernacle** was erected (Ex. 40:17). As noted, the book received its name because the people are numbered twice (chaps. 1, 26). The census mentioned here is not the same as the one recorded in Exodus 30:11–16. They were taken at different times and for different purposes. The second census (Num. 1) was probably based on the earlier census; hence the similar totals.

1:2, 3 The people of Israel were soon to begin their journey from Mount Sinai to the Promised Land. It was essential that they be arranged as orderly marching **armies**, and for this purpose God commanded that **a census** should be taken. The census would include all men **twenty years old and above—all who were able to go to war**.

1:4–17 One **man** was appointed **from every tribe** to assist Moses with the census. Their names are given in verses 5–16. Verse 17 reads, **"Then Moses and Aaron took these men who had been mentioned by name."**

1:18–46 The results of the census were as follows:

TRIBE	REFERENCE	NUMBER
Reuben	vv. 20, 21	46,500
Simeon	vv. 22, 23	59,300
Gad	vv. 24, 25	45,650
Judah	vv. 26, 27	74,600
Issachar	vv. 28, 29	54,400
Zebulun	vv. 30, 31	57,400
Ephraim	vv. 32, 33	40,500
Manasseh	vv. 34, 35	32,200
Benjamin	vv. 36, 37	35,400
Dan	vv. 38, 39	62,700
Asher	vv. 40, 41	41,500
Naphtali	vv. 42, 43	53,400
TOTAL		603,550

Notice that **Ephraim** is larger than **Manasseh**. This is in accordance with the blessing of Jacob in Genesis 48:19, 20. The tribes are listed beginning with **Reuben**, the firstborn, and his camp (south), then **Judah** and his camp (east), then **Dan** and his camp (north), and finally **Ephraim** and his camp (west).

1:47–54 The Levites were not numbered among the men of Israel who were to be warriors (v. 47). They were charged with the setting **up** and taking **down** of the **tabernacle** and with the ministry connected with it. By positioning themselves around the tabernacle, they protected it from desecration and thus protected the people from punishment (v. 53).

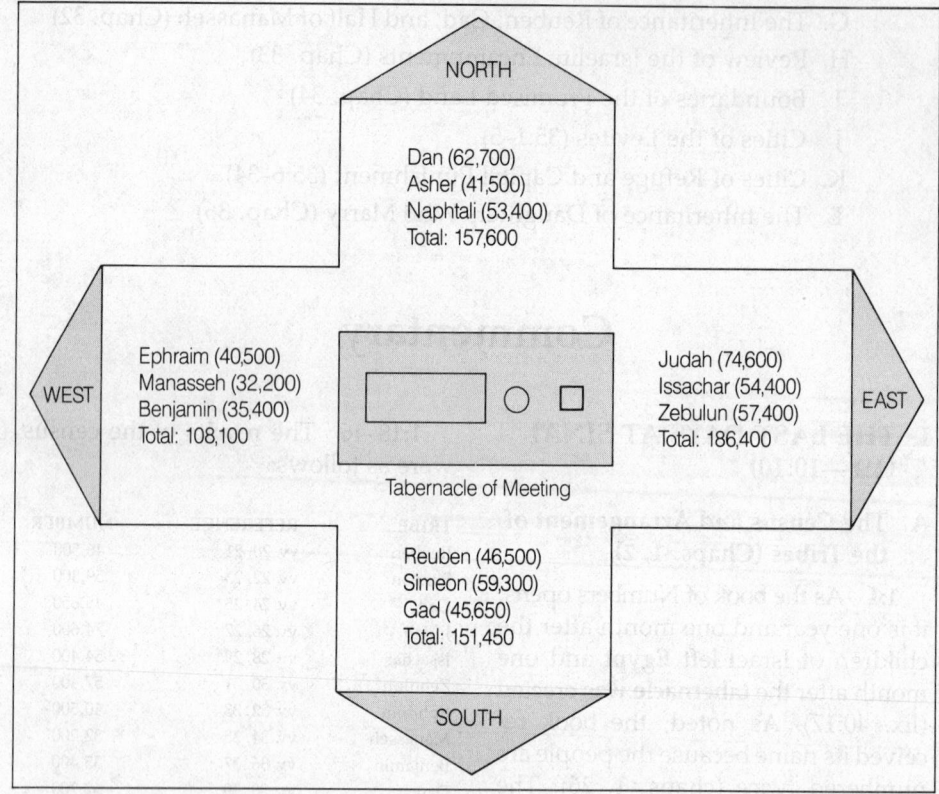

NORTH

Dan (62,700)
Asher (41,500)
Naphtali (53,400)
Total: 157,600

Ephraim (40,500)
Manasseh (32,200)
Benjamin (35,400)
Total: 108,100

WEST

Judah (74,600)
Issachar (54,400)
Zebulun (57,400)
Total: 186,400

EAST

Tabernacle of Meeting

Reuben (46,500)
Simeon (59,300)
Gad (45,650)
Total: 151,450

SOUTH

Placement of the Tribes in the Israelite Encampment

2:1, 2 The tribes of Israel were commanded to pitch their tents in the area around **the tabernacle** (see diagram), three tribes on each side.

2:3–16 On the east side, under the flag of **Judah**, were **Judah, Issachar,** and **Zebulun** (vv. 3–9). Each tribe had its own military **leader**. These tribes totaled **one hundred and eighty-six thousand four hundred. On the south side**, under the flag of **Reuben**, were **Reuben, Simeon,** and **Gad** (vv. 10–16). The camp of Reuben totaled **one hundred and fifty-one thousand four hundred and fifty**.

2:17–31 On the west side, under the flag of **Ephraim**, were **Ephraim, Manasseh,** and **Benjamin** (vv. 18–24). This camp numbered **one hundred and eight thousand one hundred**.

On the north side, under the flag of **Dan**, were **Dan, Asher,** and **Naphtali** (vv. 25–31). These totaled **one hundred and fifty-seven thousand six hundred**. The tribes were to march in the order given—the camp of **Judah** first, etc. **The Levites** marched after **Gad** and before **Ephraim** (v. 17).

2:32–34 The total number of men of war was **six hundred and three thousand five hundred and fifty** (v. 32). The total manpower, including the Levites (3:39), was 625,550. Assuming the men to be a third of the nation, then the total population must have been at least 1,876,650. The number of warriors is a better index of the strength of a church than the number of pewsitters!

B. The Number and Duties of the Levites (Chaps. 3, 4)

Chapters 3 and 4 have to do with the service of the Levites, who were not included in the census of chapters 1 and 2. The tribe of Levi was set aside by God for the service of the sanctuary. Originally, He had selected the firstborn sons to belong to Himself, but later He selected the tribe of Levi in their place for divine service (vv. 12, 13). Levi had three sons—Gershon, Kohath, and Merari. Their descendants were charged with the care of the tabernacle and its fixtures.

3:1–10a The family of **Aaron** (descended from Kohath) was the priestly family (v. 9). All other **Levites** served in connection with the **tabernacle** but were not priests. (The expression "the priests the Levites," found later in the Pentateuch, means the Levitical priests. It does not mean that all Levites were priests but that all priests were descended from **Levi**.) The priestly family is described in verses 1–4. After Nadab and Abihu had been slain for their sacrilege, Aaron was left with two sons—Eleazar and Ithamar. The Levites were servants of the priests (vv. 5–9). No one but **Aaron and his descendants** were to serve in **the priesthood** (v. 10a).

3:10b–13 The mediation of the OT priests could not bring the individual sinner into close communion with God. He had to stay away from the holy things under pain of **death** (v. 10b). But now the mediation of the Lord Jesus Christ, our Great High Priest, gives us not only access to God but also boldness to enter into His very presence (Heb. 4:16). This drastic change stems from that great event which lies between Numbers and Hebrews—the miracle of Calvary.

3:14–39 The Levites were **numbered**, not as warriors but as worshipers (v. 15). Each son of Levi was charged with responsibility for certain parts of the tabernacle:

TRIBE	CHARGE	REFERENCE	NUMBER
Gershon	All the curtains, coverings, and **hangings of the tabernacle** and outer **court**, except the "veil" which was wrapped around the ark.	vv. 18–26	7500
Kohath	The most holy things—**the ark, the table** of showbread, **the utensils, the screen, the altars, the** golden lamp-**stand**, etc.	vv. 27–32	8600
Merari	**The boards,** the **bars**, the **pillars**, the **sockets**, the **pegs, and** the **cords**.	vv. 33–37	6200

The Levites were to pitch their tents immediately outside the tabernacle enclosure, with the **Gershonites** on the west (v. 23), the **Kohathites** on the south (v. 29), and **the families of Merari** on the north (v. 35). **Moses** and **Aaron** and **sons were to camp . . . on the east**, at the entrance to the tabernacle (vv. 38, 39). (See diagram.)

Levi was the smallest tribe in Israel. The total number of Levites a month old and upward was **twenty-two thousand** (v. 39). However, the figures recorded in verses 22, 28, and 34 total 22,300. Various explanations of this discrepancy have been given. Williams suggests that the additional 300 were firstborn sons, born since the Exodus, who would naturally be omitted when the Levites were chosen to replace the firstborn of the other tribes.[2]

3:40–51 The meaning of this passage is as follows: the **Levites** were chosen by God to be His own, **instead of all the firstborn** sons. There were 22,000 Levites and 22,273 firstborn sons (vv. 39, 43). Thus there weren't enough Levites to compensate for all the firstborn of Israel who would have served under the original plan. The Lord commanded that the additional **two hundred and seventy-three** firstborn sons could be redeemed (bought back) by the payment of **five shekels . . . each**. This redemption money (273 x 5 = 1365 shekels) was paid to Aaron and his sons (v. 51). It should be noted that the **firstborn** mentioned in verse 43 might include only those born since the Exodus from Egypt.

4:1–3 The numbering in chapter 4 was to determine the number of Levites who were available for active **service** in connection with **the tabernacle**. These were the men **from thirty . . . to fifty years** of age.

4:4–20 Exodus 25:15 says, "The poles shall be in the rings of the ark; they shall not be taken from it." But verse 6 says that the priests **"shall insert its poles."** A possible solution suggested in Keil and Delitzsch's commentary is that verse 6 might be translated, "adjust its bearing poles."[3]

The duties of **the Kohathites** are taken up first (vv. 4–20). Aaron and his sons were designated to pack the **tabernacle** and the sacred **vessels** (vv. 5–13). **The ark** (vv. 5, 6), **the table of showbread** (vv. 7, 8), the golden **lampstand** (vv. 9, 10), **the golden altar** (v. 11), **the utensils** (v. 12), and the **bronze altar** (vv. 13, 14) were to be draped with **a covering of badger skins**. The other **sons of Kohath** were then appointed to **carry** these covered articles. (The laver isn't mentioned here but they must have carried it

also.) They were **not** allowed to **touch** or even look on them uncovered, lest they die (vv. 15, 17–20). **Eleazar the son of Aaron** was placed in charge of the **tabernacle** and its sacred **furnishings** (v. 16).

The **veil** between the Holiest and the holy place always hid the ark from view (v. 5). Even when Israel was on the move, the ark was covered by this same veil, which pictured the body of our Lord Jesus Christ. No one except the high priest could look upon the throne of God above the ark until Calvary, when the veil was forever torn in two.

4:21–28 **The Gershonites** were to carry **the curtains of the tabernacle**, the **tabernacle of meeting**, **the hangings of the court**, and the **screens. Ithamar the son of Aaron** was in charge of the Gershonites.

4:29–33 **The families of the sons of Merari** were appointed to **carry** the **boards, bars, pillars, sockets, pegs, and cords**.

4:34–49 The results of the census were as follows:

Kohathites	2750
Gershonites	2630
Merarites	3200
TOTAL number of **Levites** from ages 30–50	8580

C. Cleanliness and Confession (5:1–10)

This section deals with precautions the Israelites were to take to keep the camp free from defilement. The reason for the command in verse 3 can be found in Deuteronomy 23:14: God was walking in the midst of the camp.

5:1-4 Lepers, people with running sores, and those who had touched a dead body were to be **put . . . outside the camp**. The camp was composed of the tabernacle area plus that space around it occupied by the tents of Israel.

5:5–10 When a man or woman ... committed **any sin** against another, he or she was required to **confess** the **sin**, to offer a trespass **offering**, to **make restitution**, and to add **one-fifth** part. If the person who was wronged had died or could not be located, and if **no** near **relatives** were available, then payment was to be made to **the priest**.

D. The Law of Jealousy (5:11–31)

5:11–15 This passage describes a lie-detecting ritual known as the trial of **jealousy**. The purpose of this ceremony was to determine the **guilt** or innocence of **a woman** who was suspected of being unfaithful to **her husband**. The woman was required to **drink ... water** mixed with **dust** from **the floor of the tabernacle**. If she was guilty, it would prove a **curse** to her, causing swelling of the **stomach** and rotting of the **thigh**. If she was innocent, no ill effects would follow. It is obvious from verses 12–14 that the **husband** did not know whether his wife had been unfaithful. He first was required to **bring his wife to the priest**, together with **a grain offering**.

5:16–31 The **priest** prepared the mixture of **water** and **dust ... in an earthen vessel**. He brought her to the altar **before the LORD**, unbound the hair of her **head**, and **put** the meal **offering ... in her hands**. Then he made her agree to an **oath** whereby she would be cursed if guilty. After writing **the curses in a book** and scraping **them off into the bitter water**, he waved the **grain offering before the LORD**, burned **a handful of** it **on the altar**, and then made **the woman drink the water**. The statement in verse 24 that he caused the woman to drink the water is repeated in verse 26. She drank only once. If she was guilty, the threatened judgments came

upon her, including sterility. If innocent, then she was pronounced **clean**, was **free** from punishment, and was able to live a normal married life, bearing **children**. Verses 29–31 summarize the trial of jealousy.

Jealousy can destroy a marriage, whether it has justifiable grounds or not. This ritual provided a way to settle the issue once for all. The judgment of God would be upon the guilty, and the innocent would be freed from the suspicion of her partner.

Some Bible students believe that this section will have a special application in a coming day, when the nation of Israel will be tried for its unfaithfulness to Jehovah.

E. The Law of the Nazirite (Chap. 6)

6:1–8 The word "Nazirite" comes from a root meaning **"to separate."** **The vow of a Nazirite** was a voluntary vow which **a man or woman** could make for a specified period of time. The Mishna states that a Nazirite **vow** could last as long as 100 days, but the usual length was thirty days. In some rare cases, people were Nazirites for life—e.g., Samuel, Samson, John the Baptist. The vow contained three provisions: (1) He would **neither ... eat** nor **drink** of the fruit of the **grapevine**—including **vinegar, wine, grape juice, grapes or raisins** (vv. 2–4); (2) he would not cut his hair (v. 5); (3) he would **not go near a dead body** (vv. 6–8).

Wine speaks of human joy. Long hair, being a shame for a man, is a sign of humiliation. A **dead body** causes defilement.

Thus the Nazirite was, and is, an enigma to the children of this world. To be joyful, he withdrew from joy; to be strong, he became weak; and in order to love his relatives, he 'hated' them (Luke 14:26).[4]

6:9–12 This paragraph describes the procedure to be used when a man broke a vow through unintentional contact with a dead body. First he had to go through the seven-day **cleansing** process described in Numbers 19. **On the seventh day he** shaved **his head**, and on the following day he offered **two turtledoves or two young pigeons, one** for **a sin offering and the other** for **a burnt offering**. He also brought a yearling **lamb** for **a trespass offering**. In spite of all the offerings, **the days of his** original **separation were lost**, and he had to begin all over again. Thus although a defiled Nazirite could be reconsecrated, the days of his defilement were lost. For us, this means that a backslidden believer can be restored but the time spent out of fellowship with God is wasted.

6:13–21 Here we have the ceremony required when a man came to the close of the time of his vow. Four offerings were brought—**burnt, sin, peace**, and **meal** (vv. 14, 15). **The Nazirite** shaved **his . . . head** and burned **the hair** in **the fire . . . under . . . the peace offering** (v. 18). The priest's part in the ritual is given in verses 16, 17, 19, and 20. Verse 21 refers to a freewill **offering** which the **Nazirite** could offer upon completion of his vow.

6:22–27 The closing verses of chapter 6 give the lovely and familiar blessing with which **Aaron and his sons** were to **bless** the people. The great evangelist D. L. Moody appreciated it very much:

Here is a benediction that can go all the world over, and can give all the time without being impoverished. Every heart may utter it: it is the speech of God: every letter may conclude with it; every day may begin with it; every night may be sanctified by it. Here is blessing—keeping—shining— the uplifting upon our poor life of all heaven's glad morning. It is the Lord himself who brings this bar of music from heaven's infinite anthems.[5]

F. The Offering of the Princes (Chap. 7)

7:1–9 This chapter takes us back to Exodus 40:17, when the **tabernacle** had been set up. The **leaders of Israel** were **the heads of** the various **tribes**. Their names were already given in Numbers 1:5–16 and in Numbers 2. They first of all brought an offering of **six covered carts and twelve oxen** (v. 3). **Moses** distributed **two carts and four oxen . . . to the sons of Gershon**, and **four carts and eight oxen . . . to the** Merarites to be used in carrying their share of the tabernacle fixtures. No wagons or oxen were given to the Kohathites because they bore the precious burden of the sacred vessels **on their shoulders**.

7:10–83 The tribal **leaders** brought offerings on twelve consecutive days for **the dedication of the altar**. These offerings are described in minute detail, as follows:

Day	Name of Prince	Tribe	Reference
1	Nahshon	Judah	vv. 12–17
2	Nethanel	Issachar	vv. 18–23
3	Eliab	Zebulun	vv. 24–29
4	Elizur	Reuben	vv. 30–35
5	Shelumiel	Simeon	vv. 36–41
6	Eliasaph	Gad	vv. 42–47
7	Elishama	Ephraim	vv. 48–53
8	Gamaliel	Manasseh	vv. 54–59
9	Abidan	Benjamin	vv. 60–65
10	Ahiezer	Dan	vv. 66–71
11	Pagiel	Asher	vv. 72–77
12	Ahira	Naphtali	vv. 78–83

7:84–89 The total of all the gifts is given in verses 84–88. God doesn't forget any service that is done for

Him. He keeps a careful record. At the close of the **offering, Moses went into the** Most Holy Place and **heard the voice of** God **speaking to him from above the mercy seat**, perhaps expressing satisfaction with the gifts of the leaders (v. 89). Although Moses was of the tribe of Levi, he was not a priest. Yet God made an exception in his case, not only authorizing him to enter the Most Holy Place but commanding him to do so (Ex. 25:21, 22).

G. The Services of the Tabernacle (Chap. 8)

8:1–4 **Aaron** was instructed to **arrange the lamps** on the golden **lampstand** in such a way that the light would be cast **in front of the lampstand**. If the light speaks of the testimony of the Holy Spirit and the lampstand speaks of Christ, then it is a reminder that the Spirit's ministry is to glorify Christ.

8:5–13 The consecration of **the Levites** is described next. They were first cleansed by sprinkling with the **water of purification** (explained in Num. 19), by shaving their bodies with a razor, and by washing **their clothes and . . . themselves** (v. 7). Representatives of the people laid **their hands on the** heads of the **Levites** at the door of the tabernacle, **and Aaron** offered **the Levites before the LORD like a wave offering**. This reminds us of Romans 12:1, 2, where today's believers are to present their bodies as a living sacrifice to God. Moses then offered **a burnt offering** and **a sin offering**.

8:14–22 God repeats that He had chosen the **Levites** to belong to Himself **instead of . . . the firstborn** whom He had claimed as His own after the Exodus. The **Levites** were appointed to serve the priests. The consecration of **the Levites** took place as commanded, and they took up their **service** in connection with **the tabernacle**.

8:23–26 **The Levites** were to serve from **twenty-five years** of age to **fifty** (v. 24). In Numbers 4:3, the beginning age was said to be thirty years. Some take the reference in chapter 4 to apply to those who carried the tabernacle through the wilderness. They understand the lower age in chapter 8 to refer to service at the tabernacle after it had been set up in the Promised Land. Others understand the additional five years to be a sort of apprenticeship. Those retiring at **fifty years** of age no longer did heavy **work** but were allowed to continue in a kind of supervisory capacity (vv. 25, 26). These verses distinguish between **"work"** and ministry or attending **to needs**. The former is heavy work; the latter is overseeing.

Someone has pointed out that the Levites are pictures of Christians, who are redeemed, cleansed, and set apart to serve the Lord, having no inheritance on earth.

H. The Passover, the Cloud, and the Silver Trumpets (9:1—10:10)

9:1–14 God's instructions to **keep the Passover** (vv. 1–2) preceded the events in chapter 1. Not all the events in Numbers are chronological. The Passover was kept **on the fourteenth day of** the first **month**. Special provision was made for those who were ceremonially **defiled** (perhaps involuntarily), through contact with **a human corpse**, or were away on a journey, to keep the Passover one month later—**on the fourteenth day of the second month** (vv. 6–12). But anyone else who failed to keep the Passover was **cut off from among his people** (v. 13). **A stranger** (Gentile) was permitted **to keep the LORD's Passover** if he so desired, but on the same terms as the Jews (v. 14).

9:15–23 These verses anticipate the next chapters. They describe the glory cloud which **covered the tabernacle— the cloud . . . by day** and **the appearance of fire by night. Whenever the cloud** lifted off **the tabernacle**, the people **of Israel** were to break camp and march forward. When **the cloud settled**, the people were to stop and **pitch their tents**. The cloud was, of course, a symbol of God guiding His people. Although the Lord does not lead in such a visible way today—we walk by *faith*, not by *sight*—the principle is still valid. Move when the Lord moves, and not before, because "darkness about going is light about staying."

10:1–10 **Moses** was instructed to **make two silver trumpets**. These were to be used to: (a) assemble **the congregation . . . at the door of the tabernacle of meeting** (vv. 3, 7); (b) give the signal for marching forward; (c) assemble the **leaders (only one** trumpet was used for this) (v. 4); (d) **sound an alarm** in time of **war** (v. 9); (e) announce certain special days, such as feast days (v. 10).

Different trumpet calls were used for these different purposes. Sounding **the advance** in verse 5 was the signal to march. The tribes **on the east side** of the tabernacle set out first. **The second sound** of **advance** was the signal for those **on the south side** to start. Presumably those on the west and north followed in that order. The **trumpets** were not only for the wilderness march, but were to be used in the land as well (v. 9). Note the words **"in your land."** God would fulfill His promise made to Abraham. His descendants *would* be given a land, but their disobedience and faithlessness would *delay* their entrance for forty years.

II. FROM SINAI TO THE PLAINS OF MOAB (10:11—22:1)

A. Setting out from the Sinai Wilderness (10:11–36)

10:11 Verse 11 marks a definite division in the book. Up to this point, the people had camped at Mount Sinai. From verse 11 to 22:1 is the record of the journey from Mount Sinai to the plains of Moab, just outside the Promised Land. This journey covered a period of almost forty years. They did not start until **the twentieth day** because of the celebration of the second Passover (see Num. 9:10, 11).

10:12, 13 The first section of the journey was from Mount **Sinai** to **the Wilderness of Paran**. However, there were three stops before they reached this wilderness—Taberah, Kibroth Hattaavah, and Hazeroth. They actually reached the Wilderness of Paran in Numbers 12:16.

10:14–28 The order in which the tribes marched is given next. The leader of each tribe was at its head. The order is the same as in chapter 2, with one exception: in 2:17, it seems that the Levites marched after Gad and before Ephraim. In 10:17, the Gershonites and Merarites are listed after Zebulun, and the Kohathites after Gad. Apparently the Gershonites and Merarites moved on ahead with their equipment so they could have it all set up at the camping site when the Kohathites arrived with the sacred vessels.

10:29–32 **Hobab** was Moses' brother-in-law. **Raguel** (same as Reuel and Jethro) was Hobab's father and therefore **Moses' father-in-law**. Being a **Midianite**, Hobab was probably very familiar with **the wilderness**. Perhaps that is why Moses invited him to accompany the Israelites—**"You**

can be our eyes." Many Bible interpreters believe that this invitation showed a lack of faith on Moses' part, since God had already promised to guide.

Another view is held by Kurtz, who suggests,

The pillar of cloud determined the general route to be taken, the place of encampment, and the length of tarry in each location; yet human prudence was by no means precluded with respect to arranging the encampment so as to combine most advantageously the circumstances of water, pasture, shelter, supply of fuel. In all these particulars, Hobab's experience, and knowledge of the desert, would be exceedingly useful as supplementary to the guidance of the cloud.[6]

10:33, 34 The ark of the covenant was wrapped in the veil that separated the holy place from the Most Holy (Num. 4:5), and was carried by the Kohathites at the front of the procession. The trip from Sinai to Kadesh Barnea lasted three days. The glory **cloud** overshadowed the people as the Lord searched out **a resting place for them**.

10:35, 36 We are not told whether Hobab actually did accompany the Israelites. However, it appears from Judges 1:16 and 4:11 that he did, since his descendants are found among the Israelites. **Whenever the ark set out** in the morning, **Moses** called on the LORD for victory. And when at evening **it rested**, he prayed for **the** LORD **to return to** the people **of Israel**.

B. Rebellion in the Camp (Chap. 11)

11:1–3 The reader is startled by the readiness of **the people** to complain against God after all He had done for them. A clue to the discon-

tent is found in verse 1—**"consumed some in the outskirts of the camp."** The malcontents were at a distance from the ark. **Fire** from God **"consumed" in the** extremity **of the camp**, giving the name **Taberah** ("burning") to the place. The King James and New King James Versions read that the fire **consumed some** of the complainers. The ASV states only that the fire devoured in the uttermost part of the camp. Either way it was a merciful warning to the people as a whole of a judgment that would be severe.

11:4–9 The second complaining took place right in the midst of the camp, but this time the reason can be found in the expression **the mixed multitude** or "rabble." Some unbelievers had come out of **Egypt** with the Israelites, and this **mixed multitude** was a source of continual grief to the Israelites. Their disaffection spread to the Israelites, causing them to long with **intense craving** for the food of **Egypt** and to despise the **manna**. See Psalm 78:17–33 for God's commentary on this.

How strange that souls whom Jesus feeds
  With manna from above
Should grieve Him by their evil deeds,
  And sin against His love.

But 'tis a greater marvel still
  That He from whom they stray
Should bear with their rebellious will,
  And wash their sins away.

11:10–15 **Moses** first cried **to the** LORD concerning his own inability to take care of such a people **alone**; then he described the utter impossibility of providing **meat** for such a multitude. Finally, he asked for death as an escape from such problems.

11:16, 17 The Lord's first reply

was to provide for the appointment of **seventy... elders** to share **the burden of the people** with Moses. Many Bible students question whether this was God's best for Moses. They reason that because God gives strength to do whatever He orders, Moses suffered a decrease of divine enablement when his responsibilities decreased.[7] Earlier, Moses had appointed men to act as civil authorities according to his father-in-law's advice (Ex. 18:25; Deut. 1:9–15). Possibly the **seventy** chosen here were to help bear the *spiritual* burden. These two distinct appointments should not be confused.

11:18–23 As for the people, God said that they would have plenty of **meat to eat**. He would send them enough **meat** to make them sick of it. They would have it **for a whole month**. Moses questioned the possibility of such an event, but the Lord promised to bring it to pass. On the way to Mount Sinai, God had miraculously provided meat for the children of Israel (Ex. 16:13). Moses should have remembered this and not questioned the ability of the Lord. How quickly we forget the Lord's past mercies when circumstances close in around us!

11:24–30 When the **seventy** elders were officially installed, **the Spirit** of **the Lord came ... upon them** and **they prophesied**; that is, they spoke direct revelations from God. Even **two** of the **men** who **had remained in the camp ... prophesied. Joshua** apparently thought that this miracle posed a threat to Moses' leadership and sought to restrain them. But **Moses** showed his largeness of spirit by his noble answer in verse 29.

11:31–35 The promised meat came in the form of a swarm of **quail**. Verse 31 may mean that the quail flew two cubits off the ground or were piled **two cubits** deep on **the ground**. The latter is not impossible; quail that were exhausted by migration have been known to land on a ship in sufficient quantity to sink it.[8] The people went forth to feast on the meat, but many were soon struck by a terrible **plague**. The place was called **Kibroth Hattaavah** ("the graves of lust") because the people's **craving** brought them to the grave. **Hazeroth** is listed as the next place of encampment (v. 35).

C. Rebellion of Aaron and Miriam (Chap. 12)

12:1, 2 The next sad chapter in the history of Israel concerns two of the leaders of the people, **Miriam and Aaron**. Though they were Moses' sister and brother, they spoke against him for marrying **an Ethiopian woman**. At least that was their pretext. But the real reason seems to be given in verse 2: they resented Moses' leadership and wanted to share it— they were jealous. At this time there was no law against marrying **an Ethiopian**, though when they came to the land, the Israelites were forbidden to marry a non-Jew.

12:3 Moses did not try to vindicate himself but trusted God, who had placed him in the position of leadership. His family (chap. 12), the leaders (chap. 16), and ultimately the whole congregation (16:41, 42) disputed his authority. Yet when the judgment of God fell upon his adversaries, Moses did not gloat but interceded for them. He was indeed **very humble, more than all men who were on the face of the earth**. The fact that he wrote this about himself does not deny his humility; rather it illustrates 2 Peter 1:21b; he wrote as he was moved by the Holy Spirit.[9]

12:4–8 God summoned **Moses, Aaron, and Miriam** to the door of **the tabernacle of meeting**, rebuked Miriam and Aaron, and reminded them that **Moses** held a position of nearness to God that no other prophet ever held. He might speak to others indirectly, by visions and dreams, but He spoke to Moses directly, **face to face**. (The word **plainly** in v. 8 means "directly," i.e., without a go-between.) **The form of the LORD** means some manifestation or visible representation. Although **Miriam** herself was a prophetess (Ex. 15:20), the Lord made clear the difference between His relationship with Moses and other prophets. The only other thing recorded about Miriam after this incident is her death (Num. 20:1).

12:9, 10 **The LORD** was angry with **them**, and **He departed**. As punishment for her rebellion, **Miriam** was smitten with leprosy. Since **Aaron** was not punished, some suggest that Miriam was the ringleader. They point out that the verb in verse 1 is feminine singular. Others believe that Aaron's punishment was to see his sister become **a leper**. Aaron was the high priest, and he would have been unable to function on behalf of the people if he had been made leprous. His position might have saved him from the humiliation that Miriam had to go through.

12:11–16 **Aaron** confessed his **sin** to **Moses** and asked that Miriam should not be "like a stillborn child, which comes into the world half decomposed."[10] In response to Moses' intercession, God healed Miriam of the leprosy but insisted that she should go through the usual seven-day period for the cleansing of a leper. The Lord reminded Moses that she would have been barred from **the camp** as unclean **if her father had but spit in her face**.

D. Spying out the Promised Land (Chaps. 13, 14)

13:1–20 In this chapter sending out the spies was ordered by **the LORD**. In Deuteronomy 1:19–22 it was suggested by the people. Doubtless God's instruction was in response to the people's request, even if their attitude was one of unbelief. The names of the twelve spies are given in verses 4–15. Notice particularly **Caleb** (v. 6) and **Hoshea** (v. 8). **Moses called Hoshea** by the name **Joshua** (v. 16). Moses asked the twelve spies to bring back a complete report concerning the land and its inhabitants (vv. 17–20). First they were to go to the Negev in **the South**, then to the hill country in the central part of the land.

13:21–29 The spies searched **the land from the Wilderness of Zin** in the south to **Rehob** in the north (v. 21). Verses 22–24 describe the spying operation in **the South**. At **Hebron** they saw three sons **of Anak**, who were giants, according to Deuteronomy 2:10, 11. Near Hebron they came to a valley of vineyards. They cut down a large **cluster of grapes** and, suspending it **on a pole . . . between two** men, carried it back to the camp of Israel, together with **pomegranates and figs**. **The place was called the Valley of Eshcol**, meaning **"cluster."** The majority report of the spies pictured a beautiful **land** with dangerous inhabitants. The spies doubted the ability of Israel to conquer the inhabitants (in spite of God's promise to drive them out).

13:30–32 Reference to Nephilim (v. 33, Heb.) does not mean that these **giants** survived the Flood. The Israelites had heard about the Nephilim that lived before the Flood, and they identified these giants with them. **Caleb** (speaking for Joshua and him-

The Arabah. Derived from a Hebrew word meaning "steppe" or "desert," *Arabah* is the name given to the southern extension of the Jordan Valley. This depression extends more than 160 km. (100 mi.) from the Dead Sea to the Gulf of Aqaba.

self) expressed confidence that Israel would be victorious. But the others flatly denied this. The expression **"a land that devours its inhabitants"** means that the present inhabitants would destroy any others who tried to settle there.

13:33 Ten of the spies had the wrong perspective. They saw themselves as the inhabitants of Canaan saw them (**like grasshoppers**). Joshua and Caleb saw Israel from God's point of view, **well able to** conquer the land. To the ten unbelieving spies the problem of **giants** was insurmountable. To the two believing spies the presence of giants was insignificant.

14:1–10 **All the congregation** broke out into bitter complaint **against Moses and Aaron**, accused the Lord of delivering them from **Egypt** so they would be slain in the Promised Land, and proposed a new **leader** who would take them back **to Egypt** (vv. 1–3). When **Joshua . . . and Caleb** sought to assure the people that they would be

victorious against the enemy, the Israelites conspired to **stone them** (vv. 6–10).

Verses 3 and 4 demonstrate graphically the stupidity of unbelief. **Return to Egypt**! Return to a land devastated by their God! Return to a land still mourning for its firstborn sons! Return to the land they had plundered on the eve of their exodus! Return by the Red Sea where the Egyptian army had been drowned, pursuing them! And what kind of welcome would Pharaoh give them? Yet this seemed safer than to believe that God would lead them to victory in Canaan. Jehovah had struck Egypt, parted the sea, fed them with bread from heaven, and led them through the wilderness, yet they still could not trust His power to prevail over a few giants! Their actions revealed clearly what they thought about God. They doubted His power; was the Lord really a match for the giants? They had failed to grasp what had been so manifestly revealed to them the past year—namely, the nature and ways of Jehovah. A low concept of God can ruin a person or an entire nation, as is here so painfully illustrated.

14:11–19 The Lord threatened to abandon the Jews and raise up a new **nation** from Moses' descendants (vv. 11, 12). But Moses interceded for them by reminding the Lord that the Gentile nations would then say that **the LORD was not able to bring** His **people** into the Promised Land (vv. 13–19). The honor of God was at stake, and Moses pled that argument with tremendous forcefulness. In Exodus 34:6, 7 the Lord had revealed Himself to Moses. In verse 18 Moses repeats almost verbatim God's description of Himself as the basis of his prayer. How different is the theology of Moses from the theology of the people! His is based on divine revelation; theirs is based on human imagination.

14:20–35 Although God replied that He would not destroy the people, He decreed that of all the men **twenty years** of age or older who came out of Egypt and who were able to go to war (Num. 26:64, 65; Deut. 2:14), only **Joshua** and **Caleb** would **enter** the Promised Land. The people would wander **in the wilderness** for **forty years, until** the unbelieving generation died. The sons had to **bear the brunt of** their fathers' **infidelity** (v. 33). However, they would be permitted after forty years to enter the Promised Land. **Forty years** were specified because the spies had spent **forty days** in **the land** on their expedition (v. 34). Forty years here is a round number; it was actually about thirty-eight years. It was forty years from the time Israel left Egypt till they reached Canaan. The people refused

the good the Lord wanted to give them, so they had to suffer the evil they chose instead. However, the fact that they were excluded from the land does not mean that they were eternally lost. Many of them were saved through faith in the Lord, even though they suffered His governmental punishment in this life because of their disobedience.

There is a great deal of obscurity concerning the exact route followed by the Israelites during their wilderness wanderings. There is also uncertainty concerning how long they stayed in each place. Some believe, for example, that over thirty-seven years were spent at Kadesh and that one year was spent on a journey south to the shore of the Red Sea, now known as the Gulf of Aqaba. Many of the place names on the route between Sinai and the Plains of Moab are no longer identifiable.

The glory of the LORD in verse 21 refers to His glory as righteous Judge, punishing the disobedient people of Israel. The Israelites had tempted God **ten times** (v. 22). These temptings were as follows: at **the Red Sea** (Ex. 14:11, 12), at Marah (Ex. 15:23), in the Wilderness of Sin (Ex. 16:2), two rebellions concerning the manna (Ex. 16:20, 27), at Rephidim (Ex. 17:1), at Horeb (Ex. 32:7), at Taberah (Num. 11:1), at Kibroth Hattaavah (Num. 11:4 ff.), and at Kadesh (the murmuring at the spies' report—Num. 14).

Of the 603,550 men of war who came out of Egypt, only **Joshua** and **Caleb** entered the land (vv. 29, 30; Deut. 2:14).

14:36–38 The ten unbelieving spies **who brought the evil report** were killed **by a plague, but Joshua** and **Caleb** escaped it.

14:39–45 Hearing the doom pronounced upon them, **the people** told

Moses that they would obey God and go into the land, probably meaning directly north from Kadesh Barnea (v. 40). But Moses told them that it was too late, that the Lord had departed from them, and that they would be **defeated** in the attempt. Disregarding Moses' advice, they advanced **to the mountaintop** and were **attacked** and driven **back** by some of the heathen inhabitants of the land (v. 45).

E. Various Legislation (Chap. 15)

15:1, 2 We don't know how much time elapsed between chapters 14 and 15, but the contrast is striking. "... they certainly shall not see the land" (14:23). **"When you have come into the land"** (15:2). God's purposes, though sometimes hindered by sin, are never thwarted. He promised the land of Canaan to Abraham, and if one generation of his descendants was too faithless to receive it, He would give it to the next.

15:3–29 The first 29 verses of this chapter describe offerings which were to be brought by the children of Israel when they were settled in the land. Most of these offerings have already been described in minute detail. Special emphasis is given here to **unintentional** sins **committed by the congregation** (vv. 22–26) or by an individual (vv. 27–29). Verse 24 mentions two offerings for the congregation, a **bull** and a goat. However, Leviticus 4 states that the congregation was only to bring a bullock. But Leviticus 4 also says that a leader, when he sinned, was to bring a goat. Possibly the account here in Numbers mentions these offerings together, whereas in Leviticus they are mentioned separately. In verses 20 and 21 we find an oft-repeated command in Scripture: **"Of the first ... to the Lord."** Whether

the firstborn or the firstfruits, the Lord was to have the best of everything. This also served as a reminder to the people that everything they possessed came from, and ultimately belonged to, Jehovah.

15:30–36 There was no offering for the sin of presumption—that is, for willful, defiant rebellion against the word of the Lord. All who committed such a sin were to be **cut off** (vv. 30, 31). An example of presumptuous sin is given in verses 32–36. **A man** was **found ... gathering sticks on the Sabbath** in clear violation of the Law. It was known that he should **be put to death** (Ex. 31:15), but the mode of execution had never been stated. The Lord now declared that he should be **stoned ... to death outside the camp**.

15:37-41 The Jews were commanded **to make tassels on the corners of their garments** and **to put a blue thread in the tassels of the corners**. **Blue** is the heavenly color, and it was intended to speak to them of the holiness and obedience which suited them as children of **God**.

F. Korah's Rebellion (Chaps. 16, 17)

16:1–3 Korah, a cousin of Aaron (Ex. 6:18–21), was a Levite but not a priest. He apparently resented the fact that the family of Aaron should have exclusive right to the priesthood. **Dathan**, **Abiram**, and **On** were of the tribe of **Reuben**, and they resented Moses' leadership over them. **On** is not mentioned after verse 1, and it is impossible to know if he shared the doom of the others. **Two hundred and fifty** of the princes—**leaders** of Israel—joined in the rebellion against the priesthood and the civil authority (v. 2). They argued that **all the people were holy** and should not be excluded from offering sacrifices (v. 3).

16:4–11 To settle the matter, **Moses** ordered **Korah** and his rebels to appear the following day with **censers** (vv. 6, 7). The burning of **incense** was a priestly function; if God did not recognize them as priests, He would show His displeasure.

16:12–15 **Dathan and Abiram** refused to leave their tents when called by **Moses** but scolded him for his leadership. These men were referring to the earlier promise (Ex. 3:8) that God would bring them into a "a land flowing with milk and honey," and they were complaining here (with sarcasm) that Moses had instead brought them **out of a land flowing with milk and honey** (Egypt) and had **brought** them into a land *not* **flowing with milk and honey** (the desert).

The thought of verse 14 may be that, having failed to fulfill his promise, Moses was now trying to blind the people to his failure or to his true intentions. Moses reminded the Lord that he had not demanded tribute from the people, as rulers usually do.

16:16–22 The following day, **Korah, Aaron**, and the **two hundred and fifty** rebels appeared before the tabernacle with censers. The congregation of Israel also assembled, perhaps in sympathy with Korah. **Then the glory of the LORD appeared to the** whole **congregation. And the LORD** told **Moses and Aaron** to **separate** themselves **from** the **congregation** before He destroyed them. Because Moses and Aaron interceded, the judgment was not executed.

16:23–35 The scene now changes to **the tents** where **Korah, Dathan, and Abiram** lived (v. 24). Moses warned the rest of the people to move away from the vicinity of those tents. Then Moses announced that if **these men** died a natural death, or

were **visited by the common fate of all men, then** Moses himself would be discredited. **But if the LORD** miraculously caused the earth to swallow **them up, then** the people would know **that these men** had been guilty of rebellion (v. 30). No sooner had he uttered **these words** than **the earth opened** up **and swallowed** Dathan and Abiram and their families [**households**], who must have joined in their rebellion (vv. 32, 33). There is considerable question as to when **Korah** died. Some believe that he was swallowed by the earth with Dathan and Abiram (vv. 32, 33). Others suggest that he was destroyed by the same **fire** that killed the **two hundred and fifty** rebels (v. 35). It seems from Numbers 26:10 that he was swallowed up along with Dathan and Abiram. Verse 11 of the same chapter shows that his sons were spared. Israel's next great prophet, Samuel, was a descendant of Korah (1 Chron. 6:22–23, 28). . . . In verse 30 pit (Heb. *Sheol*) means the grave, but it can also mean the disembodied state.

At certain times in history, God has shown His extreme displeasure at certain sins by judging them instantly. He judged Sodom and Gomorrah (Gen. 19:24, 25); Nadab and Abihu (Lev. 10:1, 2); Miriam (Num. 12:10); Korah, Dathan, and Abiram, plus 250 leaders (this chapter); Ananias and Sapphira (Acts 5:5, 10). Clearly He does not do this every time these sins are committed, but He does break in on history on selected occasions as a warning to future generations.

The men with Korah (v. 32) might mean his servants or his followers.

16:36–40 The **holy . . . censers** used by the sinners were converted into **hammered plates** to cover **the altar** of burnt offering. These were a reminder that only the family of **Aaron** had priestly privileges. **The fire** in the censers was scattered abroad.

16:41-50 On the day following these solemn events, the people accused **Moses and Aaron** of killing God's **people**. The Lord, in wrath, threatened to destroy them, but **Moses and Aaron** went **before** the **tabernacle of meeting**, no doubt to intercede for them. The Lord then struck the people with a dreadful **plague**. Only when Aaron rushed **into the midst of** the congregation with **incense** and **made atonement for the people** was the **plague ... stopped**. But even by then, **fourteen thousand seven hundred** had perished. The leaders, along with the congregation, had challenged the priesthood of **Aaron**. Now it was the priestly intercession of **Aaron** which **stopped** the **plague**. Moses and Aaron were not the ones who killed the Lord's people, but the ones who saved them!

17:1-9 In order to emphasize to the people that the priesthood was committed only to the family of Aaron, God commanded that **a rod** for **each** tribe of Israel be placed **in the tabernacle** overnight. **The rod of Levi** had **Aaron's name on** it. The right to the priesthood belonged to the **rod** that blossomed. In the morning, when the rods were examined, it was found that Aaron's **rod ... had sprouted** with **buds, had produced blossoms, and yielded ripe almonds**. Aaron's rod pictures the resurrected Christ as the Priest of God's choosing. Just as the almond tree is the first to blossom in the spring, so Christ is the firstfruits of resurrection (1 Cor. 15:20, 23). The golden lampstand in the holy place was "made like almond blossoms, each with its ornamental knob and flower" (Ex. 25:33, 34). It was a priestly function to take care of the lampstand daily. Aaron's rod corresponded in

design and fruit to the lampstand, thus signifying that the household of Aaron had been divinely chosen to minister as priests.

17:10-13 From now on, **Aaron's rod** was **to be kept** in the ark of the covenant **as a** token **sign against the rebels**. After this, the people were seized with terror and feared to go into the general vicinity of **the tabernacle**.

G. Instructions to the Levites (Chaps. 18, 19)

18:1-7 Chapter 18 is closely linked to the last two verses of the preceding chapter. In order to allay the fears of the people, the Lord repeated the instructions about service at the tabernacle. If these instructions were obeyed, there need be no fear of His wrath. Verse 1 is in two parts. **"You and your sons and your father's house with you"** refers to all the Levites, including the priests. **"You and your sons"** refers to the priests alone. The former bore **the iniquity related to the sanctuary**; the latter bore the **iniquity associated with** their **priesthood**. To **"bear the iniquity"** means to be responsible for any neglect or failure to comply with sacred **duties**. The Levites were assistants to the priests but were not to enter the **tabernacle** on priestly **service ... lest they die**.

18:8-20 The priests were permitted a certain **portion** of various **offerings** as compensation (vv. 8-11). They were also entitled to the **firstfruits** of oil, **wine, grain**, and **fruit** (vv. 12, 13), to things devoted **to the LORD** (v. 14), and to the **firstborn**. In the case of **firstborn** sons and **unclean animals**, the priests received the redemption money in place of the sons or animals. In the case of sacrificial animals, the **firstborn** was sacrificed **to the LORD**, and the priests received their portion (vv. 17–19). **A covenant of salt** (v. 19) means one that is inviolable and permanent. The priests did not receive any **land** because the Lord was to be their special **portion** and **inheritance** (v. 20).

18:21–32 The **Levites** received **tithes** from the people, but they in turn were responsible to give **a tenth** to the priests. This tenth was offered as **a heave offering . . . to the LORD**.

19:1–10 Chapter 19 deals with one of the strongest symbols of cleansing in the OT, the use of the **ashes of** a **red heifer**. This offering had to do particularly with removing defilement caused by coming in contact with a dead person. The children of Israel had just rebelled against the Lord at Kadesh. They were now being sent out into the wilderness to die because of their unbelief. Over 600,000 people would die in a thirty-eight year period, or over forty people a day. One can see the need for the ashes of the red heifer, for who could avoid contact with death on such a journey?

The **heifer** was taken **outside the camp** and **slaughtered** (v. 3). **Eleazar the priest** sprinkled **its blood seven times** before **the tabernacle**, and **then the heifer** was **burned**, skin and all, together with **cedar wood, hyssop** and **scarlet**. These same materials were used in the cleansing of lepers (Lev. 14:4, 6). **The priest** and the man who burned the heifer were **unclean until evening**. **Then a man who** was **clean** carefully gathered **up the ashes** and stored **them outside the camp** for future use (v. 9); then he was **unclean until evening**.

19:11–19 This paragraph tells how the ashes were to be used. If a person had become ceremonially **unclean** through touching a **dead body** or through being **in a tent** where some-

one had died, a **clean person** took **some of the ashes** and mixed them with **running water**. The clean person sprinkled **the water** with **hyssop . . . on the** unclean person or thing **on the third day** and **on the seventh day**. **On the seventh day** the unclean man washed **his clothes**, bathed himself, and was **clean** that **evening** (v. 19).

Williams suggests that the red heifer symbolized Christ: spotless externally and without blemish internally; free from any bondage to sin; and robed with the red earth of manhood.[11] But we must be careful not to press the type too far.

The one historical record of the use of the ashes of a heifer is in Numbers 31. Mantle says that:

> . . . the ashes were regarded as a concentration of the essential properties of the sin offering, and could be resorted to at all times with comparatively little trouble and no loss of time. One red heifer availed for centuries. Only six are said to have been required during the whole of Jewish history; for the smallest quantity of the ashes availed to impart the cleansing virtue of the pure spring water.[12]

The writer of the Epistle to the Hebrews argues that whereas the ashes of a red heifer could do no more than set a person apart from outward, ceremonial defilement, the blood of Christ has infinite power to produce an inward cleansing of the conscience from dead works (Heb. 9:13, 14). An unknown author comments:

> The red heifer is God's provision for inevitable, unavoidable contact with the spiritual death that is around us. It probably has special reference to Israel's bloodguiltiness in connection with the Messiah. It resembles the trespass offering but does not displace it.

Old Testament regulations concerning washing with water, sometimes with running water (Lev. 15:13), are now an accepted medical technique for disinfection.

19:20–22 Punishment was inevitable for an unclean person who did not use **the water of purification**. Also, God decreed that anyone who touched or sprinkled the water was **unclean until evening**, and anyone he touched was also **unclean** for the remainder of the day.

H. The Sin of Moses (20:1–13)

20:1 As this chapter opens, it is forty years since the Israelites left Egypt and thirty-eight years since they sent the spies into the land. The people had wandered for thirty-eight years and had now come back to **Kadesh**, in **the Wilderness of Zin**— the very place from which they had sent the spies. They were no closer to the Promised Land than they had been thirty-eight years earlier! Here **Miriam died...and was buried**. Over 600,000 people had died during the wasted years between chapters 19 and 20. The bitter fruit of unbelief was harvested in silence for an entire generation.

20:2–9 The people who complained to **Moses and Aaron** about the lack of **water** were a new generation, but they acted like their fathers (vv. 2–5). **The LORD** told **Moses** to *speak* to the rock, and **it** would **yield water**. He was to **take the rod** of Aaron which had been deposited in the tabernacle (v. 9; cf. 17:10), though it is **"his rod"** in verse 11. Aaron's rod was the rod of the priesthood; Moses' rod was the rod of judgment and power.

20:10–13 Once before, at a place called Massah (and Meribah), the people had murmured for water. At that time, the Lord told Moses to *strike* the rock (Ex. 17:1–7). But now Moses' patience was exhausted. First, he spoke unadvisedly with his lips, calling the people **rebels** (v. 10). Secondly, he **struck the rock twice** instead of speaking to it. The rock smitten in Exodus 17 was a type of Christ, stricken at Calvary. But Christ was only to be struck once. After His death, the Holy Spirit would be given, of which the water in verse 11 is a type. Because of the sin of **Moses and Aaron** in this matter, God decreed that they would not enter the Promised Land. He called the place **Meribah**, but it is not the same Meribah as in Exodus 17. This is sometimes known as Meribah-Kadesh. G. Campbell Morgan comments:

> By this manifestation of anger, which as we have said was so very natural, the servant of God misrepresented God to the people. His failure was due to the fact that for the moment his faith failed to reach the highest level of activity. He still believed in God, and in His power: but he did not believe in Him *to sanctify Him in the eyes of His people*. The lesson is indeed a very searching one. Right things may be done in so wrong a way as to produce evil results. There is a hymn in which we may miss the deep meaning, if we are not thoughtful—
>
> Lord, speak to me that I may speak In living echoes of Thy tone.
>
> That is far more than a prayer that we may be able to deliver the Lord's message. It is rather that we may do so in His tone, with His temper. That is where Moses failed, and for this failure he was excluded from the Land.[13]

I. The Death of Aaron (20:14–29)

20:14–21 The plan for entering the land was not to go directly north from the wilderness but to travel east through the territory of the Edomites, and then north along the east coast of the Dead Sea. The people would then cross the Jordan. But **the king of Edom . . . refused** safe **passage** to the people of **Israel**—and this in spite of assurances that the Jews would not eat, **drink**, or damage any of Edom's supplies. Later in history, Israel under Saul fought against and defeated the Edomites, descendants of Jacob's brother, Esau.

20:22–29 When the people had **journeyed from Kadesh . . . to Mount Hor**, near **the border of . . . Edom, . . . Aaron died** and was replaced by **Eleazar his son** (vv. 22–29). Matthew Henry writes:

> Aaron, though he dies for his transgression, is not put to death as a malefactor, by a plague, or fire from heaven, but dies with ease and in honour. He is not *cut off from his people*, as the expression usually is concerning those that die by the hand of divine justice, but he is *gathered to his people*, as one that died in the arms of divine grace. . . . Moses, whose hands had first clothed Aaron with his priestly garments, now strips him of them; for, in reverence to the priesthood, it was not fit that he should die in them.[14]

J. The Bronze Serpent (21:1—22:1)

21:1–3 **The king of Arad** lived in the southern portion of the land of promise. When he **heard that** the Israelites were encamped in the wilderness and were planning to invade the land, he attacked but was defeated at a **place . . . called Hormah** (vv. 1–3).

21:4–9 **The Red Sea** (v. 4) does not mean the gulf that the Israelites crossed in their escape from Egypt but the portion of the Red Sea which we know as the Gulf of Aqaba. **The Way of the Red Sea**, however, may be a route name; the Israelites might not have gone to the Gulf of Aqaba at this time.

Once again the people complained about their living conditions, with the result that God **sent fiery serpents among** them. **Many of the people . . . died**, and many more were dying. In answer to the intercession of Moses, God commanded that a **bronze serpent** be lifted **on a pole** and promised that whoever **looked at the bronze serpent** would be healed of the snakebite. This incident was used by the Lord Jesus to teach Nicodemus that Christ must be lifted up on a pole (the cross), so that sinners looking to Him by faith might have everlasting life (John 3:1–16).

The serpent later became a stumbling block to the nation and was finally destroyed in the days of Hezekiah (2 Kgs. 18:4).

21:10–20 The journeys of the children of Israel from Mount Hor to the Plains of Moab can no longer be traced exactly. However, the stops are listed in Numbers 21:10 to 22:1. **The book of the wars of the LORD** (v. 14) was probably a historical record of the early wars of Israel. It is no longer available. At **Beer** (vv. 16–18) the Lord miraculously provided **water** when the princes **dug . . . with their staves** in the arid desert.

21:21–26 When Israel came near the country of **the Amorites**, they sought permission to **pass through** but were refused. In fact, **Sihon, king of the Amorites**, declared war on **Israel** but was thoroughly defeated. This Amorite king, like Pharaoh before him, was hardened by the Lord in order that he and his people might be defeated in battle by Israel (Deut.

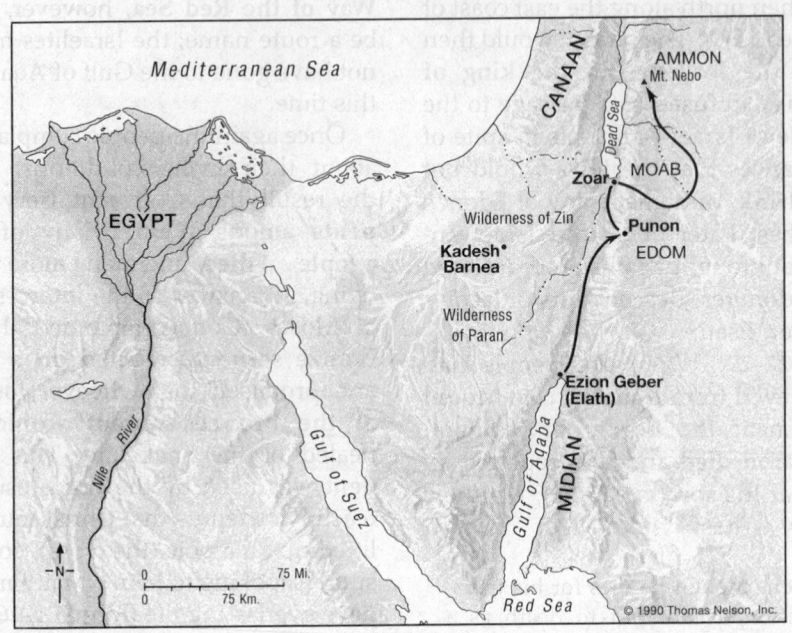

From the Wilderness to Canaan

2:30). "The iniquity of the Amorites" (Gen. 15:16) was complete, and Israel was the instrument of the judgment by Jehovah.

21:27–30 The proverbial song of verses 27–30 seems to say this: **Heshbon** had only recently been captured from the Moabites by the **Amorites**. Now **Heshbon** has fallen to the people of Israel. If those who conquered this city of Moab have themselves been conquered, then **Moab** must be a third-class power. Also, this proverb is probably quoted as evidence that the land was fully in the possession of the Amorite king, Sihon, and no longer a Moabite territory. This fact was important to establish because Israel was forbidden to take any land from **Moab** (Deut. 2:9).

21:31—22:1 The exact route of the Israelites is difficult to reconstruct. It is suggested that they basically moved east from Mount Hor, then north outside the western boundary of Edom to the River Zered. They followed the Zered eastward between Edom and Moab, then north along Moab's eastern boundary to the Arnon, then west to the King's Highway. They conquered Sihon, King of the Amorites, then pushed north to conquer **Bashan**, the Kingdom of **Og**. **Bashan** was rich pastureland east of the Jordan and north of the place where Israel would cross the Jordan into the land. Having conquered **Bashan**, the Israelites returned to **the plains of Moab . . . and camped** there **across from Jericho** (v. 1). These **plains** had been taken from Moab by the Amorites (Num. 21:26), but the name of **Moab** lingered on.

III. EVENTS ON THE PLAINS OF MOAB (22:2—36:13)

A. The Prophet Balaam (22:2—25:18)

1. Balaam Summoned by Balak (22:2–40)

22:2–14 When the Moabites, to the south, heard how the Amorites had been conquered, they became terrified (unnecessarily, see Deut. 2:9). Therefore Balak, the king, sought to hire the prophet Balaam to curse Israel. Though a heathen prophet, Balaam seems to have had some knowledge of the true God. The Lord used him to reveal His mind concerning Israel's separation, justification, beauty, and glory. The first attempt to get Balaam to curse is recorded in verses 7–14. The messengers of Balak came to Balaam with the rewards of divination—that is, with rewards for him if he would successfully pronounce a curse on Israel. But God told him that he must not curse the people because the Lord had blessed them. Balak means "waster." Balaam means "swallower of the people" or "confuser of the people."

22:15–21 Balaam's second try is recorded next. Balaam knew what God's will was, yet he dared to go before the Lord, perhaps in hopes that there would be a change of mind. The Lord told Balaam to go with Balak's men but to do only what the Lord told him. Balaam's reason for going is clearly pointed out in 2 Peter 2:15, 16. He was motivated by his love of "the wages of unrighteousness." He is typical of the "hireling prophet" who prostitutes his God-given ability for money.

22:22–27 The "Angel of the LORD" (v. 22) was Christ in a preincarnate appearance. Three times He stood before Balaam and his donkey to hinder him, because He knew his motives. The first time the donkey saw the Angel and detoured into a field. For this, the poor animal was struck by Balaam. The second time the Angel stood in a narrow path between the vineyards. The terrified donkey crushed Balaam's foot against the wall and again was abused. The third time the Angel confronted them in a narrow pass. The frustrated donkey lay down on the ground and received a third thrashing from Balaam. Even a donkey, the symbol of stubbornness, knew when to quit, but not the stubborn, willful prophet!

22:28–40 The donkey was given the power to speak to Balaam, rebuking him for his inhumane treatment (vv. 28–30). Then Balaam saw the Angel of the LORD with His drawn sword and heard Him explain His mission to hinder Balaam in his disobedience (vv. 31–35). The Angel then permitted the prophet to go to Balak but to speak . . . only the word that God gave him (v. 35). After meeting Balaam, Balak offered sacrifices to his god.

2. Balaam's Oracles (22:41—24:25)

22:41—23:12 The next day Balak took Balaam into a high mountain (Pisgah) where he would look down over the tents of Israel. Later, from this same mountain, Moses would take his only look at the Promised Land, and then die (Deut. 34:1, 5). This chapter and the next chapter contain four memorable utterances by Balaam concerning Israel. The first three were preceded by the offering of seven bulls and seven rams as burnt offerings. The first oracle expressed Balaam's inability to curse a people whom God had not cursed. It predicted for Israel a life of separation from the Gentile nations and a numberless posterity. It pictured Israel as a righteous nation whose eventual destiny was something to be coveted (vv. 7–10). Balak's protest against this blessing availed nothing. The prophet had to speak the word of the LORD.

23:13–15 Balak then took Balaam to a different vantage point in hopes that the prophet would see them in a less favorable light (vv. 13, 14).

23:16–26 The second **oracle** assured **Balak** that God's original blessing on Israel was unchanged (vv. 18–20). The first part of verse 21 describes the nation's position, not its practice. The people were reckoned righteous through faith. So believers today stand before God in all the perfections of His beloved Son. The Lord was with Israel, and the people could **shout** because He reigned as **King** in their midst (v. 21b). He had delivered them from **Egypt** and given them **strength**. No evil pronouncement against them would come to pass. Instead, the victories Israel would soon win would cause the nations to say, **"Oh, what God has done!"** (vv. 22–24). Since **Balaam** refused to **curse** the people, **Balak** ordered him not to **bless them** either (v. 25), but the prophet protested that he could only do what **the LORD** said.

23:27–30 A third time **Balak** tried to wring a **curse** out of **Balaam**, this time from **the top of** Mount **Peor**.

24:1, 2 Realizing that God was determined **to bless Israel**, Balaam did not **seek to** get a message of cursing. He simply looked down over the camp of **Israel**, and **the Spirit of God came upon him**, causing him to say things beyond his own wisdom and will.

24:3–9 The third message spoke of the beauty of the **tents** of **Israel** and predicted tremendous fruitfulness, widespread prosperity, a glorious **king-** dom, and crushing power over all foes. **Agag** (v. 7) was probably a name common to many Amalekites. None would dare to **rouse** this crouching **lion** (v. 9). Those who blessed Israel would be **blessed**, and a curse would only bring cursing. Balaam's prophecy here echoes the covenant given to Abraham: "I will bless them that bless you, and curse him who curses you" (Gen. 12:3).

24:10–14 Thoroughly frustrated by now, **Balak** denounced **Balaam** for his failure to cooperate. But the prophet reminded him that from the beginning he had said that he could only **speak . . . the word of the LORD**. Before leaving Balak to return to his own home, Balaam offered to tell the king what Israel would **do to** the Moabite **people** in **days** to come.

24:15–19 The fourth **oracle** concerns a king ("Star" or "Scepter") who would **rise in Israel** to conquer **Moab** and **all the sons of tumult** (v. 17; cf. Jer. 48:45). **Edom** also would be subjugated by this ruler. This prophecy was partially fulfilled by King David, but will enjoy its complete fulfillment at the Second Coming of Christ.

24:20–25 Similar promises of doom were uttered by Balaam concerning the Amalekites, **the Kenites**, Assyria (**Asshur**), and the people of **Eber** (vv. 20–24). The Amalekites would be utterly destroyed. The Kenites would be gradually depleted in number until the Assyrians would finally take them captive. Even the Assyrians would be captured by armed forces from **Cyprus** (Heb. *Kittim*, which generally means **Cyprus**, but probably represents Greece here and the forces of Alexander the Great). **Eber** probably means the non-Jewish descendants of this postdiluvian patriarch.

Before Balaam left Balak, he set the

wheels in motion for the tragic events of chapter 25.

3. Balaam's Corruption of Israel (Chap. 25)

25:1–3 Although Balaam's name is not mentioned in this chapter, we learn in Numbers 31:16 that he was responsible for the terrible corruption of the children of Israel that is described here. All of Balak's rewards could not induce Balaam to curse Israel, but they finally did persuade him to corrupt **Israel** by causing some of the people to **commit harlotry** and idolatry **with the women of Moab**. Often when Satan cannot succeed in a direct attack, he will succeed in an indirect one.

Balaam's true character emerges here. Up to this point we might think of him as a godly prophet who was loyal to the word of God and an admirer of the people of God. But from Numbers 31:16 and 2 Peter 2:15, 16 we learn that he was a wicked apostate who loved the wages of unrighteousness. Balaam advised Balak how to make the Israelites stumble: get them "to eat things sacrificed to idols, and to commit sexual immorality" (Rev. 2:14). His advice was heeded. This led to gross idolatry at the shrine of **Baal of Peor**.

25:4–8a God commanded that **all the** guilty **leaders** should be hanged **out in the sun**. Before the sentence was carried out, a leader of the tribe of Simeon brought a **Midianite woman** into the camp **of Israel**, to take her **into** his **tent** (v. 14). **Phinehas, the son of** the high priest (**Eleazar**), killed both man and woman with his **javelin**. Samuel Ridout comments:

> Phinehas, "a mouth of brass," is singularly appropriate to him who was so unyieldingly faithful to God,

and by his relentless judgment of sin secured an abiding priesthood for himself and family.[15]

25:8b–13 God sent a **plague** into the camp **of Israel**, killing a total of **twenty-four thousand** of the offenders during the course of the plague (23,000 in one day—1 Cor. 10:8). It was Phinehas' heroic action that **stopped ... the plague**. Because **he was zealous for his God**, the LORD decreed that **an everlasting priesthood** would continue in the family of **Phinehas**.

25:14, 15 Zimri's position of prominence in his tribe and the fact that the woman was a **daughter of** a **Midianite** chief might have stopped the judges from executing judgment upon him, but it did not stop Phinehas. He was jealous for Jehovah's sake.

25:16–18 The LORD ordered **Moses to** war against **the Midianites** (who were mingled with the Moabites at this time). This command was carried out in chapter 31.

B. The Second Census (Chap. 26)

26:1–51 Again **Moses** was instructed to **take a census . . . of the children of Israel**, since they were about to enter the land to war against its inhabitants and to receive their share of the inheritance. There was a decrease of 1,820 people from the first census, as seen in the following numbers:

Tribe	Census (Chap. 1)	Census (Chap. 26)
Reuben (vv. 5–11)	46,500	43,730
Simeon (vv. 12–14)	59,300	22,200
Gad (vv. 15–18)	45,650	40,500
Judah (vv. 19–22)	74,600	76,500
Issachar (vv. 23–25)	54,400	64,300
Zebulun (vv. 26, 27)	57,400	60,500
Joseph (vv. 28–37):		
–Manasseh (v. 34)	32,200	52,700
–Ephraim (v. 37)	40,500	32,500
Benjamin (vv. 38–41)	35,400	45,600
Dan (vv. 42, 43)	62,700	64,400

Tribe (cont'd)	Census (Chap. 1)	Census (Chap. 26)
Asher (vv. 44–47)	41,500	53,400
Naphtali (vv. 48–51)	53,400	45,400
TOTAL	603,550	601,730

Noting the decrease in numbers over the long period of time between the 603,550 of chapter 1 and the 601,730 **children of Israel** here, Moody comments:

> Israel's growth ceased for forty years. So it may be with us as churches, and so forth, if we are unbelieving.[16]

The most striking decrease is seen in the Simeonites, who diminished by almost 37,000. The tribe of Simeon was chiefly involved in the incident at Peor in the previous chapter (Zimri was a leader in that tribe), and perhaps most of the slain were Simeonites. Verse 11 tells us that the sons of Korah did not die with their father.

26:52–56 The land was to be **divided** according to the **number of** people in each tribe, and yet according to **lot**. This can only mean that the *size* of the tribal territory was determined by the **number** in the tribe, but the *location* of the land was determined by lot.

26:57–65 The **Levites** were numbered separately at **twenty-three thousand**. Only **Joshua** and **Caleb** were included in both censuses. All the other men of war listed in the first census had by now perished in the wilderness. Verses 64 and 65 refer to the men who were able to go to war. Levites and women are excluded, though some of these did die during the thirty-eight year journey.

C. Inheritance Rights of Daughters (27:1–11)

The five **daughters of Zelophehad**, of the tribe of **Manasseh**, **came** to Moses to request property in the distribution of the land even though they had no male in the numbered of Israel, among whom Canaan was to be divided (26:53). Their **father** had **died**, but **not** as one of the guilty companions of **Korah. The** LORD answered that they should inherit **their father's** portion. In general, it was God's will that the land be inherited by sons, then daughters, brothers, uncles, or nearest relatives. In this way it would be permanently kept in a family (vv. 1–11).

D. Joshua, Moses' Successor (27:12–23)

27:12–14 God forewarned **Moses** that he would die soon, and He instructed Moses to **go up** to **Mount Abarim** (actually a chain of mountains east of the Dead Sea). Mount Nebo, where Moses died, was a part of this chain [range].

27:15–23 Moses unselfishly thought of a successor to lead the people, and **Joshua the son of Nun** was named in his place. The priesthood and later the kingship in Israel was usually passed on from one generation to the next within the same family. However, Moses' successor was not his son but his servant (Ex. 24:13).

E. Offering and Vows (Chaps. 28—30)

Chaps. 28, 29 In these chapters, the people are reminded of the offerings and feasts which were to be observed in the land.

Daily offerings:
Continual **burnt offering, morning** and **evening**, with a **grain offering** and **drink offering** included (28:3–8).

Every **day** in life, so long as the temple stood, the following sacrifices had to be carried out both **morning** and **evening** (Num. 28:3–8).

Every morning and every evening a one-year-old male **lamb** . . . **without** spot or **blemish** was offered **as a** *burnt offering.* Along with it there was offered **a** *grain offering,* which consisted of **one-tenth of an ephah of fine flour** . . . **mixed with** a quarter **of a hin** of pure **oil.** Also there was a *drink offering,* which consisted of a quarter **of a hin** of wine.

There was an offering of incense before these offerings in the morning, and after them in the evening. Ever since there was a Jewish temple, and so long as the temple continued to exist, this routine of sacrifice went on. There was a kind of priestly tread-mill of sacrifice. Moffatt speaks of "the levitical drudges" who, day in and day out, kept offering these sacrifices. There was no end to this process, and when all was said and done, it still left men conscious of their sin and alienation from God.

Weekly offerings:

Weekly **burnt offering, on** each **Sabbath,** with **grain offering** and **drink offering** (28:9,10).

Monthly offerings:

Burnt offering on the first day of each month, with **grain offering** and **drink offering** (28:11–14).

Sin offering (28:15).

Feasts of Jehovah:

Passover—fourteenth day of first month (28:16).

Feast of **Unleavened Bread—fifteenth day** to twenty-first day of first **month** (28:17–25).

Feast of weeks (28:26–31).

Note: **The** *day* of the firstfruits (v. 26) should not be confused with the *Feast* of Firstfruits (Lev. 23:9–14).

Feast of **Trumpets—first day of seventh month** (29:1–6).

Day of Atonement—**tenth day of seventh month** (29:7–11).

Feast of Tabernacles—**fifteenth day** through twenty-first day **of the seventh month** (29:12–34). There was a special Sabbath observance **on the eighth day** (29:35–39).

30:1–5 Chapter 30 contains special instructions about **vows.** A man making **a vow to the Lord** must carry it out without fail. **If a** young **woman,** still under **her father's** care, made **a vow,** and **her father** heard **her,** he could speak out against the vow—i.e., forbid it—**on the** first **day,** and it would be canceled. If he waited until after the first day or if he did not say anything, the vow was effective and had to be carried out.

30:6–16 Verses 6–8 seem to describe a vow made by a woman before her marriage. Although her husband would not, of course, have heard it on the day it was made, he could **overrule** it **on the day** when he first heard about it. Vows made by **a widow or a divorced woman** were binding (v. 9). Vows made by a married woman could be canceled by the **husband . . . on the** first **day** (vv. 10–15). This maintained the headship of the husband. If a husband canceled her vow after the first day, **he** had to **bear her guilt**—that is, bring the required sacrifice or be punished by the Lord (v. 15).

F. Destruction of the Midianites (Chap. 31)

31:1–11 God commanded **Moses** to destroy **the Midianites** for corrupting His people through fornication and idolatry at Baal of Peor. **Twelve thousand** Israelites marched against the enemy **and they killed all the males**. **Phinehas** went to war (v. 6) rather than his father the high priest, possibly because Phinehas had been the one to turn away the wrath of Jehovah by killing Zimri and the Midianite woman (chap. 25). Now he was to lead the armies of the living God to complete the judgment of the Lord on Midian. **"All the males"** (v. 7) refers to all the Midianite soldiers, and not to all the Midianites in existence, because in the days of Gideon they again become a menace to Israel (Judges 6). **Zur** (v. 8) was probably the father of Cozbi, the Midianite woman slain in the camp of Israel (25:15). (Either **Balaam** never made it all the way back to his home or else he had returned to Midian for some reason, for he too was **killed**.)

31:12–18 Though they had killed all the Midianite soldiers, the children of Israel spared **the women** and children and proudly **brought** them back **to the camp** with a great quantity of **spoil**. Moses was **angry** that they would have spared the very ones who caused Israel to sin and commanded that the **male** children and **every woman who** had lain with **a man** should be slain. The **young girls** were spared, probably for domestic service. This punishment was righteous and necessary to preserve Israel from further corruption.

31:19–54 The warriors and captives were required to undergo the customary **seven days** of purification (v. 19). Also, the spoil had to be cleansed, either by **fire** or by washing with **water** (vv. 21–24). The **spoil** was divided among the warriors and the whole **congregation** (vv. 25–47). **The men of war** were so thankful that **not** one of their number had perished that they brought a large gift to **the LORD** (vv. 48–54).

G. The Inheritance of Reuben, Gad, and Half of Manasseh (Chap. 32)

32:1–15 When the children of **Reuben** and **Gad . . . saw the** rich pasture **land** east of the **Jordan** River, they petitioned that they might settle there permanently (vv. 1–5). **Moses** thought this meant that they did not intend to cross the Jordan and fight against the heathen inhabitants of Canaan with their brethren (vv. 6–15). Their **fathers** had **discouraged** the Israelites at **Kadesh Barnea** from entering the land.

32:16–42 But when Reuben and Gad assured him three times that they intended to fight for the land west of **the Jordan** (vv. 16–32), Moses granted permission. **Gad, Reuben**, and **half the tribe of Manasseh the son of Joseph** acquired **the kingdom of Sihon king of the Amorite and the kingdom of Og king of Bashan**. They **built fortified cities** and sheepfolds and also took over **small towns** and **villages** (vv. 33–42).

Many feel that Reuben and Gad made an unwise choice because, although the land was fertile, the area was exposed to enemy attack. They did not have the protection of the Jordan River. The tribes of **Reuben** and **Gad** (and **half the tribe of Manasseh** which joined them) were the first to be conquered in later years and carried off into captivity. On the other hand, what was to be done with the land east of the Jordan River if none of the children of Israel were to settle in it? God had given this land to them and told them to possess it (Deut. 2:24, 31; 3:2).

H. Review of the Israelite Encampments (Chap. 33)

33:1–49 The journeys of the children of Israel from **Egypt** to **the plains of Moab** are summarized in this chap-

? Exact location questionable

Mediterranean Sea

Tirzah.

.Shechem

.Shiloh

AMMON

Bethel..Ai .Gilgal?
.Jericho. Shittim
Plains
of Moah .Heshbon

Lachish.

.Hebron

.Gaza

Dead Sea

Dibon.

MOAB

.Beersheba

0   30 Mi.
0   30 Km.
Wilderness
of Zin   © 1990 Thomas Nelson, Inc.

Central Canaan's Surroundings

ter. As mentioned previously, it is impossible to locate all the cities with accuracy today. The chapter may be divided as follows: from **Egypt** to Mount **Sinai** (vv. 5–15); from Mount **Sinai** to **Kadesh** Barnea (vv. 16–36); from **Kadesh** Barnea to **Mount Hor** (vv. 37–40); from **Mount Hor** to the plains of Moab (vv. 41–49). This list is not complete, as can be seen by comparing it with other lists of camping spots, as in chapter 21.

33:50–56 God's order to the invading army was to completely exterminate **the inhabitants** of **Canaan**. This may seem cruel to people today, but actually these people were among the most corrupt, immoral, depraved creatures whom the world has ever known. God patiently dealt with them for over 400 years without any change on their part. He knew that if His people did not kill them, Israel would become infected by their immorality and idolatry. Not only were the Israelites to kill the people, but

they were to **destroy** every trace of idolatry (v. 52).

I. Boundaries of the Promised Land (Chap. 34)

34:1–15 The **boundaries** of **the land** which God promised to Israel are given in verses 1–15. In general, the southern boundary extended from the southern tip of the **Salt** (Dead) **Sea** to **the Brook** (not River) **of Egypt** and to **the** Mediterranean **Sea** (vv. 3–5). The **western border** was the **Great** (Mediterranean) **Sea** (v. 6). The **northern border** stretched from the Mediterranean **Sea to Mount Hor** (not the one mentioned in the journeys of Israel) **to the entrance of Hamath** and **Hazar Enan** (vv. 7–9). The **eastern border** extended from **Hazar Enan** south **to the Sea of Chinnereth**[17] (Galilee), **down . . . the Jordan** River to the **Salt** (Dead) **Sea** (vv. 10–12). The **nine** and one-half **tribes** were to inherit the above land, since the **two** and one-half **tribes** had already been promised the land east of the Jordan (vv. 13–15).

34:16–29 The **names of the men who** were appointed to **divide the land** are given in verses 16–29.

J. Cities of the Levites (35:1–5)

Since the tribe of Levi did not inherit with the other tribes, God decreed that forty-eight **cities** should be set apart for the **Levites**. It is difficult to understand the measurements given in verses 4 and 5, but it is at least clear that the cities were surrounded by **common-land** for grazing the livestock. (Perhaps the **two thousand cubits** mentioned in verse 5 were inclusive of the one **thousand cubits** already mentioned in verse 4.)

K. Cities of Refuge and Capital Punishment (35:6–34)

35:6–8 Six of the Levite **cities** were to be designated as **cities of refuge**. A person who had *accidentally* killed another could **flee** to one of these cities and be safe to stand trial. Those tribes which had much territory would donate **cities** for the **Levites** accordingly. Those which had little were not expected to give as many cities.

35:9–21 Of the **cities of refuge**, **three** were to be on each **side of the Jordan** River. A manslayer would ordinarily be pursued by a near relative of the victim, known as **the avenger**. If the **manslayer** reached a city of refuge, he was safe there until his case came up for trial (v. 12). The cities of refuge did not provide sanctuary for a **murderer** (vv. 16–19). Crimes committed through **hatred** or **enmity** were punishable by **death** (vv. 20, 21).

35:22–28 If the homicide appeared to be a case of manslaughter, the man would be tried by **the congregation** (vv. 22–24). If acquitted, the **manslayer** had to stay **in the city of refuge ... until the death of the high priest**. He was then allowed to **return** home (v. 28). If he ventured **outside ... the city** before the death of the high priest, the **avenger of blood** could slay him without incurring guilt (vv. 26–28).

The death of the high priest brought freedom to those who had escaped to the cities of refuge. They could no longer be harmed by the avenger of blood. The death of our Great High Priest frees us from the condemning demands of the Law. How foolish this stipulation would be if one failed to see in it a symbol of the work of our Lord at the Cross!

Unger relates some traditional details:

> According to the rabbis, in order to aid the fugitive it was the business of the Sanhedrin to keep the roads leading to the cities of refuge in the best possible repair. No hills were left,

every river was bridged, and the road itself was to be at least thirty-two cubits broad. At every turn were guideposts bearing the word Refuge; and two students of the law were appointed to accompany the fleeing man, to pacify, if possible, the avenger, should he overtake the fugitive.[18]

As for the symbolic teaching, the people of Israel are the manslayer, having put the Messiah to death. Yet they did it ignorantly (Acts 3:17). The Lord Jesus prayed, "... they know not what they do" (Luke 23:34). Just as the manslayer was displaced from his own home and had to live in the city of refuge, so Israel has been living in exile ever since. The nation's complete restoration to its possession will take place, not at the death of the Great High Priest (for He can never die), but when He comes to reign.

35:29–34 Capital punishment was decreed for murderers; there was no escape or satisfaction (vv. 30, 31). A manslayer could not purchase release from a **city of refuge** (v. 32). **Blood** that was **shed** in murder defiled **the land**, and such blood demanded the death of the murderer (vv. 33, 34). Think of this in connection with the death of Christ!

L. The Inheritance of Daughters Who Marry (Chap. 36)

Representatives of the half-tribe of **Manasseh** who settled in **Gilead**, east of the Jordan, came to Moses with a problem (see Num. 27:1–11). If the **daughters of Zelophehad ... married** men belonging to another **tribe**, their property would pass to the other **tribe**. The Year of **Jubilee** would finalize the transfer to the other tribe (v. 4). The solution was that those women who inherited land should **marry** in their own **tribe**, and thus there would be no transfers of land from one tribe to another (vv. 5–11). The **daughters of Zelophehad** obeyed by marrying in the tribe **of Manasseh** (vv. 10–12). Verse 13 summarizes the section from chapter 26.

Three things stand out in the book of Numbers:

1. The consistent wickedness and unbelief of the human heart.
2. The holiness of Jehovah, tempered with His mercy.
3. The man of God (Moses) who stands as a mediator and intercessor between the sinful people and a holy God.

The human heart has not changed since Numbers was written. Neither has the holiness or mercy of God. But Moses has been replaced by his Antitype, the Lord Jesus Christ. In Him we have strength to avoid the sins that characterized Israel, and thus avoid the displeasure of God which they incurred. In order to profit from what we have studied we must realize that "these things happened to them as examples, and they were written for our admonition" (1 Cor. 10:11).

ENDNOTES

[1](Intro) W. Graham Scroggie, *Know Your Bible, Vol. 1, The Old Testament*, p. 35.

[2](3:14–39) George Williams, *The Student's Commentary on the Holy Scriptures*, p. 80.

[3](4:4–20) C. F. Keil and F. Delitzsch, "Numbers," in *Biblical Commentary on the Old Testament*, III:25.

[4](6:1–8) Williams, *Student's Commentary*, p. 82.

[5](6:24–26) D. L. Moody, *Notes from My Bible*, p. 41.

[6](10:29–32) Quoted by John W. Haley, *Alleged Discrepancies of the Bible*, p. 431.

[7](11:16, 17) In Moses' defense the following points are worth noting: (1) God does not rebuke Moses; (2) God rather encourages Moses, promising him that after the seventy were endued with His Spirit, they would share his burden; (3) God Himself answers his need; (4) Moses was leading up to 2,000,000 complaining and unspiritual people; (5) Verse 17 does not indicate a decrease in Moses' endowment with the Spirit, but rather a distribution of the same Spirit to the seventy.

[8](11:31–35) See *International Standard Bible Encyclopedia* under "Quails," IV:2512.

[9](12:3) It is always possible that an inspired editor (such as Joshua) added these words later.

[10](12:11–16) Keil and Delitzsch, "Numbers," III:81.

[11](19:11–19) Williams, *Student's Commentary*, p. 88.

[12](19:11–19) J. G. Mantle, *Better Things*, p. 109.

[13](20:10–13) G. Campbell Morgan, *Searchlights from the Word*, pp. 47-48.

[14](20:22–29) Matthew Henry, "Numbers," in *Matthew Henry's Commentary on the Whole Bible*, I:662.

[15](25:4–8a) Samuel Ridout, *The Pentateuch*, p. 253.

[16](26:1–51) Moody, *Notes*, p. 43.

[17](34:1–15) Chinnereth (pronounced Kin–) is Hebrew for *harp*, named from the shape of the Sea of Galilee.

[18](35:22–28) Merrill F. Unger, *Unger's Bible Dictionary*, p. 208.

BIBLIOGRAPHY

Harrison, R. K. "Numbers." In the *Introduction to the Old Testament.*

Grand Rapids: Wm. B. Eerdmans
Publishing Co., 1969.

Henry, Matthew. "Numbers." In
*Matthew Henry's Commentary on the
Whole Bible*. Vol. I. McLean, VA:
MacDonald Publishing Company,
n.d.

Jensen, Irving L. *Numbers*. Chicago:
Moody Press, 1964.

Keil, C. F. and Delitzsch, F. "Numbers."
In *Biblical Commentary on the Old
Testament. The Pentateuch*. Vol. 3.
Grand Rapids: Wm. B. Eerdmans
Publishing Co., 1971.

Lange, John Peter. "Numbers." In
*Commentary on the Holy Scriptures,
Critical, Doctrinal and Homiletical*.
Vol. 3. Translated by Philip Schaff.
Reprint. Grand Rapids: Zondervan
Publishing House, 1980.

Merrill, Eugene H. "Numbers." In
the *Bible Knowledge Commentary*.
Wheaton: Victor Books, 1985.

Ridout, Samuel. *The Pentateuch*. New
York: Bible Truth Library, n.d.

Wenham, Gordon J. *Numbers: An Introduction and Commentary*. Downers
Grove, IL: InterVarsity Press, 1981.

DEUTERONOMY

Introduction

"Deuteronomy is one of the greatest books of the Old Testament. Its influence on the domestic and personal religion of all ages has not been surpassed by any other book in the Bible. It is quoted over eighty times in the New Testament and thus it belongs to a small group of four Old Testament books [Genesis, Deuteronomy, Psalms, and Isaiah] to which the early Christians made frequent reference."

—J. A. Thompson

I. Unique Place in the Canon

Our Lord Jesus Christ was tempted by Satan for forty days and nights in the wilderness. Three of these temptations are specifically recounted in the Gospels for our spiritual benefit. Not only did Christ use the OT "sword of the Spirit" three times, but each time He used the same part of the "blade"—Deuteronomy! It is likely that this book was one of Jesus' favorites—and it should be one of ours as well. Deuteronomy has been sadly neglected in many quarters, perhaps due to its somewhat inappropriate title in English, which is from the Greek Septuagint. Its meaning, "Second Law," has given some the false idea that the book is merely a recapitulation of material already presented in Exodus through Numbers. God never repeats just to repeat— there is always a different emphasis or new details. So also with Deuteronomy, a marvelous book worthy of careful study.

II. Authorship

Moses is the author of Deuteronomy as a whole, though the Lord may have used inspired editors to recount and update some details. The last chapter, which records his death, could have been written by him prophetically, or may have been added by Joshua or someone else.

Liberal criticism says confidently that Deuteronomy is the "Book of the Law" that was found in Josiah's time (c. 620 B.C.). They maintain that it was actually a "pious fraud" written at that time *as if by Moses* to unify Jewish worship around a central Jerusalem sanctuary.

Actually there is no such category as a "pious fraud"; if it's a fraud it's not pious, and if it's pious, it's no fraud.

There is also no indication that "the Book of the Law" in 2 Kings 22 does not refer to the *whole Pentateuch*. Josiah's predecessors, Manasseh and Amon, were both wicked kings. They actually perpetuated idolatry in the very temple of Jehovah where the Law of Moses had apparently been hidden by some godly person or persons.

The rediscovery of God's Word and submission to it always bring revival and recovery, as in the great Protestant Reformation.

For a concise defense of Mosaic authorship, see Introduction to the Pentateuch.

III. Date

Deuteronomy was written largely by 1406 B.C., but some material, equally inspired, may have been added after Moses' death, as was noted.

For a more detailed discussion of dating see Introduction to the Pentateuch.

IV. Background and Theme

Deuteronomy is a *re-statement* (not merely a repetition) of the law for the new generation that had arisen during the wilderness journey. They were about to enter the Promised Land. In order to enjoy God's blessing there, they must know the law and obey it.

The book consists first of all of a spiritual interpretation of Israel's history from Sinai onward (chaps. 1–3). The thought is that those who refuse to learn from history are doomed to relive it. The main section is a review of important features of God's legislation for His people (chaps. 4–26). Then follows a preview of God's purposes of grace and government from Israel's entrance into the land until the second advent of the Messiah (chaps. 27–33). The book closes with the death of Moses and the appointment of Joshua as his successor (chap. 34).

The Apostle Paul reminds us that the book has a message for us as well as for Israel. In commenting on Deuteronomy 25:4, he says that it was written "altogether for our sakes" (1 Cor. 9:10).

The book is rich in exhortation, which can be summed up in the verbs of Deuteronomy 5:1: "Hear . . . learn . . . keep and do."

OUTLINE

I. MOSES' FIRST DISCOURSE—APPROACHING THE LAND (Chaps. 1—4)
   A. Introduction (1:1–5)
   B. From Horeb to Kadesh (1:6–46)
   C. From Kadesh to Heshbon (Chap. 2)
   D. Trans-Jordan Secured (Chap. 3)
   E. Exhortation to Obedience (Chap. 4)

II. MOSES' SECOND DISCOURSE—PURITY IN THE LAND (Chaps. 5—28)
   A. Review of the Sinai Covenant (Chap. 5)
   B. Warnings Against Disobedience (Chap. 6)
   C. Instructions on Dealing with Idolatrous Nations (Chap. 7)
   D. Lessons from the Past (8:1—11:7)
   E. Rewards for Obedience (11:8—32)
   F. Statutes for Worship (Chap. 12)
   G. Punishment of False Prophets and Idolaters (Chap. 13)

Commentary

I. MOSES' FIRST DISCOURSE— APPROACHING THE LAND (Chaps. 1—4)

A. Introduction (1:1-5)

1:1, 2 As the Book of Deuteronomy opens, the children of Israel are camped on the plains **of Moab**, which they had reached in Numbers 22:1. In Deuteronomy 1:1 their location is said to be **in the plain opposite Suph**. This means that the wilderness, of which the plains of Moab were an extension, stretched southward to that portion of the Red Sea known as the Gulf of Aqaba. The journey from **Horeb** (Sinai) by way of **Mount Seir to Kadesh Barnea**, on the threshold of Canaan, required only *eleven days*, but now *thirty-eight years* had passed before the Israelites were ready to enter the Promised Land!

1:3-5 Moses delivered his subsequent discourse **to the children of Israel**, preparatory to their entering Canaan **in the fortieth year** after they left Egypt. It was **after** both **Sihon king of the Amorites** and **Og king of Bashan** had been slain (Num. 21).

B. From Horeb to Kadesh (1:6-46)

From Deuteronomy 1:6—3:28 we have a review of the period from Mount Sinai to the plains of Moab. Since most of this has already been covered in Numbers, we shall simply summarize it here: God's command to march to the Promised Land and **possess** it (vv. 6-8); the appointment of **judges** over civil matters (vv. 9-18); the journey from Sinai **to Kadesh Barnea** (vv. 19-21); the sending of the spies and the subsequent rebellion (vv. 22-46). With the exception of

Joshua and **Caleb**, no soldier who had left Egypt was allowed to enter the **land** (vv. 34-38).

C. From Kadesh to Heshbon (Chap. 2)

2:1-23 The journey from **Kadesh Barnea** to the borders of Edom (vv. 1-7) avoided conflict with the Edomites. The journey from the borders of Edom to the **Valley of Zered** (vv. 8-15) avoided conflict with the Moabites. **The LORD commanded the Israelites not to meddle with** the Ammonites because He had **given** this **land to** these **descendants of Lot as a possession** (vv. 16-19). God had already **dispossessed** certain **giants**[1] whom the Ammonites called **Zamzummim, just as He had done for the descendants of Esau** by destroying **the Horites**, the **Avim**, and **the Caphtorim** (vv. 20-23).

2:24-37 The rest of chapter 2 details the smashing defeat of **Sihon the Amorite**, the **king of Heshbon**. Verse 29a indicates that the **descendants** of **Esau**, the Edomites, sold **food** and **water** to the Israelites as the latter skirted the country of Edom. But the record in Numbers 20:14-22 suggests that the king of Edom was completely uncooperative. He was staunch in his refusal to assist Israel, but it seems that some of his people sold **food** and water to the Jews, though this is uncertain. Verses 10-12 and 20-23 were probably added by someone later than Moses, but are nonetheless inspired Scripture.

D. Trans-Jordan Secured (Chap. 3)

3:1-11 **Og king of Bashan** had **sixty cities**, all **fortified with high walls, gates, and bars**, as well as many rural towns. The LORD God **also** delivered these enemies into the **hands** of His people. **Og** is remembered as a **giant**, with a huge **iron bedstead** that was **nine cubits** long and **four cubits** wide (about thirteen or fourteen feet by six feet). Thompson says this **"bedstead"** was his final resting place, not his regular bed:

> On his death he was buried in a massive sarcophagus (lit. *bedstead*, "resting place") made of basalt, called *iron* here because of its colour.... According to the record here the sarcophagus could be seen in Rabbah Ammon (the modern Amman) at the time Deuteronomy was committed to writing.[2]

3:12–20 The captured **land** east of the Jordan was distributed **to the Reubenites**, the **Gadites**, and **to half the tribe of Manasseh** (vv. 12–17). Moses **commanded** their **men of valor to cross over armed** to **aid their brethren** conquer the territory west of the Jordan. Then they could **return** to their own **possession** and their **wives**, **little ones**, **livestock**, and the **cities** they had taken over.

3:21–29 Moses also commanded **Joshua** to remember past victories and trust God for future ones (vv. 21, 22).

But the LORD **was angry with Moses** for his disobedience regarding the children of Israel and would not let him cross over Jordan. He did, however, let him view the Promised Land in every direction from the **top of** Mount **Pisgah** (vv. 23–29).

E. Exhortation to Obedience (Chap. 4)

Chapter 4 introduces Moses' rehearsal of the law. Here he dealt particularly with the worship of the one true God and with the penalties that would follow any turning to idolatry.

4:1–24 **Israel** was commanded to obey **the statutes and the judgments of the LORD God** when they entered Canaan (v. 1). They were **not** to **add to** it **nor take from** it (v. 2). God's punishment of the idolatry practiced at **Baal Peor** should serve as a constant warning (vv. 3, 4). (Perhaps this particular incident of divine wrath against idolatry is mentioned here because it had taken place just a short time earlier and would be fresh in their minds.) Obedience to the **law** would cause Israel to be admired as a **great nation** by the Gentiles (vv. 5–8). Israel should remember from past experiences the blessings of following the Lord (v. 8). They were especially instructed to remember the giving of **the Ten Commandments** at Mount Sinai (**Horeb**) (vv. 9–13). At that time, they did not see the form of God; that is, although they might have seen a manifestation of God, they did not see a physical **form** which could be reproduced by an image or an idol. They were forbidden to **make** an **image** of any kind to represent God, or to worship **the sun**, **the moon**, or **the stars** (vv. 14–19). The Israelites were reminded of their deliverance from **Egypt**, of Moses' disobedience and consequent judgment, and of God's wrath against idolatry (vv. 20–24). **"Only take heed to yourself ... lest you forget"** (v. 9); **"Take careful heed to yourselves ... lest you act corruptly"** (vv. 15, 16); **"Take heed to yourselves, lest you forget"** (v. 23). Moses knew only too well the natural tendency of the human heart, and so he earnestly charged the people to pay close attention.

4:25–40 If the nation in later years should turn to idols, it would be sent away into captivity (vv. 25–28). But even then, if the people repented and turned to **the LORD with all** their **heart**, He would restore them (vv. 29–31). No nation had ever had the privileges of Israel, particularly the miracles connected with the deliverance from **Egypt** (vv. 32–38). Therefore they should be obedient to Him and thus enjoy His continued blessing (vv. 39, 40). It is a sad fact of Jewish history that the nation was subjected to a purging captivity because of their disobedience and failure to take the warning of Jehovah seriously. God's warnings are not idle words. No man and no nation can set them aside with impunity.

4:41–43 Moses set apart **three cities** of refuge on the east **side of the Jordan**—**Bezer**, **Ramoth**-Gilead, **and Golan** (vv. 41–43).

4:44–49 Here begins Moses' second discourse, delivered on the plains of Moab, **east . . . of the Jordan**. Verse 48 is the only instance where Mount **Hermon** is called **Mount Sion**.[3]

II. MOSES' SECOND DISCOURSE—PURITY IN THE LAND (Chaps. 5—28)

A. Review of the Sinai Covenant (Chap. 5)

5:1–6 Chapter 5 reviews the giving of the Ten Commandments at Mount Sinai (**Horeb**). In verse 3, supply the word "only" after "fathers." The covenant *was* made with the **fathers**, but it was intended for *future* generations of Israelites as well.

5:7–21 The Ten Commandments

1. **No other gods** were to be worshiped (v. 7).
2. No **carved image** was to be made or worshiped (vv. 8–10). This commandment does not

repeat the first. People might worship mythical beings, or the sun and moon, without the use of idols. **Children** who thus hate God will suffer the same punishment as their fathers (v. 9).

3. **The name of the LORD** was **not** to be taken **in vain** (v. 11).
4. The **Sabbath** was to be kept **holy** (vv. 12–15). A different reason for keeping the **Sabbath** is given here from the one given in Exodus 20:8–11 (God's rest in Creation). The Jews were to remember that they were slaves in Egypt (v. 15). These two reasons are complementary, not contradictory.
5. Parents were to be honored (v. 16).
6. **Murder** was prohibited (v. 17).
7. **Adultery** was prohibited (v. 18).
8. Stealing was prohibited (v. 19).
9. Bearing **false witness against** a **neighbor** was prohibited (v. 20).
10. Coveting was prohibited (v. 21).

5:22 J. A. Thompson comments on this verse:

The expression *and He added no more* is unusual and may indicate that these commandments were such a complete summary of the fundamental requirements of the covenant that no other law needed to be added. All other law was a mere interpretation and expansion of these basic principles. Alternatively, the expression may refer to a particular occasion when the Lord made known precisely these ten laws. Other laws must have been given on other occasions, since the total volume of law known in Israel and originating from God was considerable.[4]

5:23–33 When the law was given, the people were terrified by the manifestations of the divine Presence and feared for their lives. They sent Moses to speak to the Lord and to assure Him that they would **do** whatever He said. (They did not realize their own sinfulness and powerlessness when they made such a rash vow.) Consequently the rest of the laws and ordinances were given through Moses the mediator. The Ten Words or Ten **Commandments** appear to have been spoken verbally to the whole nation when they were at Mount Sinai (vv. 30, 31).

In verse 28, **the LORD** is not commending them for their promise to keep the law, but rather for their expressions of fear and awe (compare 18:16–18). God knew that they did not have **a heart** to **keep** His **commandments**. He wished that they did, so that He could bless them abundantly (vv. 28–33).

B. Warnings Against Disobedience (Chap. 6)

6:1–9 When the people would enter the Promised Land, God wanted them to be in a right moral condition. In order to enjoy the land as He intended, they must be an obedient people. Therefore, Moses gave them practical instruction to fit them for life in Canaan (vv. 1, 2). The Israelites were to bear testimony to the truth that God is the only true **God** (vv. 3, 4). They were to **love** Him supremely and keep His Word (vv. 5, 6). The commandments of the Lord were to be taught **diligently to** their **children** and to guide them in every department of their lives.

Many Christian parents take this passage as a mandate to teach their own children, not only the faith, but also other so-called secular subjects, rather than sending them to humanistic schools.

In the days of Christ, the Jews actually bound portions of the law to their hands and suspended them **between** their **eyes** (v. 8). But doubtless the Lord intended rather that their actions (**hand**) and desires (**eyes**) should be controlled by the law.

Verses 4–9 are known as the "Shema" (Heb. for "hear") and were recited daily as a creed by devout Jews along with 11:13–21 and Numbers 15:37–41.

The Hebrew word for "one" in verse 4 is significant, viewed in the light of the fuller revelation of the New Testament. It stands, not for absolute unity, but for compound unity, and is thus consistent with both the names of God used in this verse. Jehovah (LORD) emphasizes His oneness. Elohim (God) emphasizes His three persons. The same mysterious hints of trinity in unity occur in the very first verse of the Bible, where "Elohim" is followed by a singular verb (created) and in Genesis 1:26, where the plural pronouns *us* and *our* are followed by the singular nouns *image* and *likeness*. (*Daily Notes of the Scripture Union*)

6:10–15 When the people would enter **the land** and enjoy its great prosperity, there was a danger that they would **forget** the One who gave the law to them or that they would **go after other gods**. Obedience to the law was not so much a means of *gaining favor* with Jehovah as it was of *showing love* to Him. Biblical love is not a warm sentimentality but a calculated pattern of conformity to the revealed will of God. Love is not an option but a necessity for wellbeing. God's jealousy (zeal for His own glory) would **destroy** the people if they broke His covenant through disobedience.

6:16 The Lord Jesus quoted this verse in Matthew 4:7 and Luke 4:12 to answer the tempter's suggestion that He throw Himself down from the pinnacle of the temple. At **Massah**, there was not enough water to drink, and the people questioned that Jehovah was with them (Ex. 17). To doubt God's care and goodness is to **tempt** Him.

6:17–25 Obedience would bring victory over Israel's foes (vv. 17–19). Future generations were to be instructed in God's deliverance of the people from **Egypt** and of His giving of the law **for** their **good** and blessing (vv. 20–25). Compare verse 25 with Romans 3:21, 22. The law says, "**if we are careful to observe**"; grace says, "to all and on all those who *believe*." Today believers are clothed with the righteousness on which the law was based, the righteousness of God (2 Cor. 5:21), and this according to faith, not works (Rom. 4:5).

C. Instructions on Dealing with Idolatrous Nations (Chap. 7)

7:1–5 The people of Israel were strongly warned against mixing with the heathen, idolatrous **nations** which were then inhabiting Canaan. To punish these **seven nations—the Hittites, Girgashites, Amorites, Canaanites, Perizzites, Hivites, and Jebusites**—for their unspeakable sin and to preserve Israel from contamination, God decreed that these Gentiles should be **utterly** exterminated and that every trace of idolatry should be destroyed. Perhaps verse 3 anticipates the failure of the Jews to obey verse 2, because if they destroyed all the inhabitants of the land, obviously there would be no threat of intermarriage.

7:6–11 **God** had **chosen** Israel **to be a people** who were separated to Himself. He did not want them to be like the other nations. He **did not ... choose** them because of their superior numbers (they were the fewest of all peoples). He chose them simply because He loved them, and He wanted them to obey Him in all things. **A thousand generations** means forever. The Lord hated the Canaanite nations because of their evil deeds. He loved the nation of Israel not because of any good but simply because He loved them and **would keep the oath which He swore to** their forefathers. Who can understand the electing grace of a sovereign God!

7:12–26 If God's people would be faithful to Him **in the land**, He would **bless** them with numerous children, abundant crops, large herds, health, and victory over their enemies (vv. 12–16). If they were ever tempted to fear their enemies, they should **remember** God's mighty deliverances in the past, especially the deliverance from **Egypt** (vv. 17–19). As He had done in the past, He would do for them again, sending the **hornet** to **destroy** their foes. **The hornet** may be literal or a figure of speech for a conquering army (vv. 20–24). He would not destroy their enemies all at once lest the land be overrun with wild **beasts** (v. 22). (Unpopulated areas become breeding grounds for wild animals, whereas urban areas serve to control their numbers.) Another reason victory was not to be immediate can be found in Judges 2:21–23: God would use the remaining heathen to test Israel. All idols were to be utterly **destroyed** lest they become a temptation to Israel (vv. 25, 26). The most serious threat to Israel was not the people of Canaan but their idols and the gross immorality associated with these idols. The battles which they needed to prepare for most were spiritual, not physical.

D. Lessons from the Past (8:1—11:7)

Concerning chapters 8 and 9, J. A. Thompson succinctly points out:

Two important lessons from the past are now referred to. First, the experience of God's care in the wilderness period, when the people of Israel were unable to help themselves, taught them the lesson of humility through the Lord's providential discipline. The memory of that experience should keep them from pride in their own achievements amid the security and prosperity of the new land (8:1–20). Secondly, any success they might enjoy in the coming conquest was not to be interpreted as a mark of divine approval for their own righteousness (9:1–6). In fact, both in the incident of the golden calf (9:7–21) and a number of other incidents (9:22–29), Israel had proved herself stubborn and rebellious.[5]

8:1–5 Again Moses urged the people to obey God, using the loving, preserving care of God as a motive. The Lord had allowed trials to come into their lives **to humble** them, prove them, and **test** their obedience. But He also **fed** them with **manna** from heaven, and provided clothes that **did not wear out** and shoes which kept their feet from swelling during the **forty years** of wilderness wanderings.

God knew **what was in** the hearts of the people. He was not trying to learn something by testing Israel **in the wilderness** (v. 2), but He was manifesting to the people themselves their own rebellious nature so that they might more fully appreciate His mercy and grace. Another lesson they were to learn through their wanderings was to fear the Lord.

8:6–20 Moses pled his case not only on the basis of what God had done but on what He was about to do (vv. 6, 7). The blessings of **the good land** of Canaan are described in detail (vv. 7–9). Prosperity might lead to forgetfulness and forgetfulness to disobedience, so the people were to watch against these perils (vv. 10–20). Faithfulness on God's part was to be met by a corresponding faithfulness on the part of Israel. God was keeping His **covenant** with the patriarchs (v. 18); the people needed to keep their word to God in return (Ex. 19:8). **If** the people forgot God's mighty acts on their behalf and attributed their wealth to their own power, Jehovah would destroy them as He destroyed the Gentile **nations** in Canaan.

9:1–3 Chapter 9 opens with a description of the **nations** which **Israel** was soon to face in battle. Israel was not to be afraid, as they had been forty years earlier, because God would fight for them. *"He* will destroy them . . . so *you* shall drive them out and destroy them quickly."* Notice the complementary working of divine sovereignty and human agency. Both were essential for securing the Promised Land.

9:4–7 After . . . God had defeated the Canaanite inhabitants of the land, the Israelites were not to boast. Three times the people are warned about attributing success to their own **righteousness** (vv. 4–6). God would give them the **land . . . because of the wickedness of** the present inhabitants (v. 4), because of His oath to **Abraham, Isaac, and Jacob** (v. 5), and not because of any merit in them. The truth of the matter is that they were **stiff-necked** (stubborn) (v. 6) as well as provocative and **rebellious** (v. 7).

9:8–23 Moses cites as an example the people's behavior at Mount **Horeb**

(Sinai) (vv. 8–21). Verses 22 and 23 mention other places where the people sinned: **Taberah** (Num. 11:3); **Massah** (Ex. 17:7); **Kibroth Hattaavah** (Num. 11:34); **Kadesh Barnea** (Num. 13:31–33). Note how the golden **calf** was destroyed beyond recovery (v. 21).

9:24–29 At Mount Sinai the intercession of Moses was the only thing that saved the people from the wrath of Jehovah. He did not base his plea on the righteousness of the people (which further shows that they had none) but on *possession:* **"Your people and Your inheritance"** (v. 26); *promise:* **"Remember Your servants, Abraham, Isaac, and Jacob"** (v. 27); *power* (God's power would be ridiculed by the Egyptians): **"lest the land from which You brought us should say, 'Because the LORD was not able'"** (v. 28).

In verse 1 of chapter 10, the narrative goes back to the events at Mount Sinai and therefore follows verse 29 of chapter 9. The Bible is not always chronological; often the order of events has a spiritual or moral order that is more important than the mere chronological order. A more appropriate place for the chapter division[6] would seem to be after verse 11, because the first 11 verses deal with events at Mount Sinai (the theme taken up in 10:8) while verses 12 and following are an exhortation to obedience based on God's gracious mercy.

10:1–5 This paragraph records the second giving of the law and the deposit of the **two tablets** in the **ark**. Verse 3 doesn't mean that Moses personally made the ark, but only that he had it made. A person is often said to do what he orders to be done.

10:6–9 Verses 6 and 7 seem to be an abrupt change at this point. Actually they are a parenthesis, recording events that took place at a later date, as the NKJV indicates. But they bring the reader up to the death of **Aaron**. (The NKJV puts vv. 6–9 in parentheses, which makes the passage easier to understand.)

Moserah was probably a district where Mount Hor was located, since that is the mountain **where Aaron died** (Num. 20:25–28). The exact location of Moserah is unknown today. Perhaps this mention of the death of **Aaron** caused Moses to think of the priesthood, and so he reverted to the choosing of **Levi** as the priestly **tribe** (vv. 8, 9). The threefold function of the priesthood is given in verse 8: (1) **to bear the ark of the covenant**; (2) **to stand before the LORD to minister to Him**; (3) **to bless in His name**. Instructions about the priesthood were important for this generation which was about to enter Canaan.

10:10, 11 Moses again reminded them of his second stay on Sinai when for **forty days and forty nights** he interceded for them. God heard, withheld judgment, and told them to **go in and possess the land**.

10:12–22 Jehovah's desire for His people was summed up in the words **"to fear . . . to walk . . . to love . . . to serve . . . to keep"** (vv. 12, 13). All of God's **commandments** were designed **for** their **good** (v. 13b). Moses encouraged them to obey God because of His greatness (v. 14), His sovereign choice of Israel as His special people (v. 15), His righteousness and **justice** (vv. 17–20), and His past favors to the nation (vv. 21, 22). A circumcised **heart** (v. 16) is one that obeys.

11:1–7 Once more Moses reviewed the past history of Israel in order to draw spiritual lessons from it. In verse 2, Moses is speaking to survivors of the older generation as distinguished from those who were born in the desert. Soldiers who were over twenty when they left Egypt were excluded from entering Canaan (2:14; Josh. 5:6). God delivered His people from Egypt and led them through **the wilderness**, but He would not tolerate the rebellion of **Dathan and Abiram**. God's judgment of the idolatrous Egyptians and His vigorous judgment on rebels within the nation itself should serve as lessons on the folly of incurring His displeasure.

E. Rewards for Obedience (11:8–32)

11:8–17 Conversely, the way to **prolong** their **days in the land** (v. 9) was to **keep every commandment** (v. 8). The land which they would enjoy, if obedient, is described in verses 10–12. The expression **"watered it by foot"** may refer to the use of some pedal device for pumping water or perhaps to the opening of sluices with the foot. **Egypt** was a barren land made fruitful by irrigation, but the Promised Land enjoyed the special favor of the God of nature (vv. 11, 12). Abundant **rain** and plentiful harvests would be the reward of obedience (vv. 13–15), but forgetfulness of God or idolatry would be followed by drought and barrenness.

11:18–21 The Word of God was to be the subject of household conversation. It was to be loved and lived. The reward for practicing the Word was that their **days** would **be multiplied in the land**, and also **like the days of the heavens above the earth** (v. 21).

Latterday Jews took 18b literally, and so wore small pouches with portions of Scripture on their foreheads, and put them on their doorposts (as some still do). But verse 19a suggests the truth intended—the Word on the hand means a pair of hands that will not lend themselves to shoddy or unworthy workmanship; the Word between our eyes represents the control of God over our vision—where we look, and what we covet; the Word on the doorpost signifies home and family life under the constraint of responsibility to God, especially for any young lives entrusted to our care. (*Daily Notes of the Scripture Union*)

11:22–25 Those who walked in the ways of the Lord would **drive out** the heathen Canaanites and possess all the land their feet walked on. The rule of possession is given in verse 24. All the land was theirs by promise, but they had to go in and make it their own, just as we have to appropriate the promises of God. The boundaries given in verse 24 have never been realized historically by Israel. It is true that Solomon's kingdom extended from the river (Euphrates) to the border of Egypt (1 Kgs. 4:21), but the Israelites did not actually possess all that territory. Rather, it included states that *paid tribute* to Solomon but maintained their own internal government. Verse 24, along with many others, will find its fulfillment in the Millennial Reign of the Lord Jesus Christ.

11:26–32 So it was to be **a blessing** or **a curse** for Israel—**a blessing** in the event of obedience, and **a curse** for disobedience. Two mountains in Canaan represented this truth—**Mount Gerizim** stood for the **blessing**, and **Mount Ebal** for the **curse**. These two mountains, located near Shechem, had a small valley between them. Half of the tribes were supposed to stand on **Gerizim** while the priests would pronounce the blessings that would follow obedience. The other six tribes were to stand on **Mount Ebal** while the priests recited the curses that would flow from disobedience. In each case, the people were to say "Amen!" See Deuteronomy 27:11–26 for details concerning the significance of these two mountains.

The terebinth trees of Moreh are probably those mentioned in Genesis 35:1–4. There, several centuries earlier, Jacob had purged his house of idolatry. Perhaps this reference was intended to impart not only geographical guidance but spiritual guidance as well.

F. Statutes for Worship (Chap. 12)

12:1–3 When they entered the land, the people of God were to destroy all idols and idol shrines, all places where a false worship had been carried on. The wooden images (Heb. *ashērîm*) were symbols of a female deity. The pillars were symbolic of Baal, the male deity.

12:4–14 God would set apart a place for worship, a place where sacrifices and offerings should be brought. This place was where the tabernacle was pitched at first (Shiloh—Josh. 18:1) and later where the temple was erected (Jerusalem). Only in this appointed place was worship approved. The Christian's center of worship is a Person, the Lord Jesus Christ, the visible manifestation of the invisible Godhead. . . . God had overlooked certain irregularities in the wilderness that must not be practiced in the land of Canaan (vv. 8, 9).

12:15–28 In Leviticus 17:3, 4, God had commanded that when any sacrificial animal such as an ox, sheep, or goat was slain, it had to be brought to the tabernacle. Now that the people were about to settle in Canaan, the law must be changed. Henceforth the Jews could kill and eat domestic animals commonly used for sacrifices, just as they would eat the gazelle and the deer (clean animals that were not

used for sacrifices). This permission was granted to those who were ceremonially unclean as well as to those who were clean. However, they were repeatedly warned not to eat the blood, because the blood is the life of the flesh, and the life belongs to God.

12:29–32 The Israelites were solemnly warned not even to investigate the idolatrous practices of the heathen, lest they be tempted to introduce these wicked practices into the worship of the true God. Verse 31 refers to the horrible practices associated with the worship of Molech and Chemosh. In the NT, Paul tells us that the motivating force behind idolatry is demonic (1 Cor. 10:20). Should we marvel at the cruelty and degradation of idolatry when we realize its true nature? That the human heart gravitates toward this kind of darkness more readily than it seeks the light of the true God is illustrated by the nation to whom Deuteronomy is addressed. Solomon, Israel's third king, actually did build an altar for Chemosh and Molech right in Jerusalem, the city where the Lord had put His Name (1 Kgs. 11:7).

G. Punishment of False Prophets and Idolaters (Chap. 13)

Individuals or groups which might tempt God's people to practice idolatry were to be stoned to death, whether a prophet (vv. 1–5), a near relative (vv. 6–11), or a community (vv. 12–18). A prophet who encouraged people into idolatry was not to be followed, even if some miracle he predicted came to pass. Such a person was a false prophet, and he must be put to death. Even if a close relative enticed his family to practice idolatry, he too was to be slain.

The corrupt men of verse 13 were

base fellows, or "sons of worthlessness" (Heb. *beliyya'al*). Any such gang which led the people **of their city** away from God to idols should be killed, together with **the inhabitants of that city**, and **the city** should be burned.

The same treatment was to be meted out to an idolatrous Israelite **city** as to the Canaanite cities—namely, total destruction. God is not partial; He will deal severely with sin, even among His chosen people. But His motives are different. In the case involving a Jewish city His motive would be fatherly discipline, with a view to correction of the nation as a whole.

H. Clean and Unclean Foods (14:1–21)

14:1, 2 These two verses prohibit the idolatrous practice of disfiguring the body in mourning **for the dead**. The Jews had a higher regard for the body as God's creation than did the Gentiles.

14:3–21a This paragraph reviews the subject of **clean** and **unclean** foods, whether **animals** (vv. 4–8), fishes (vv. 9, 10), flying insects (v. 19), or **birds** (vv. 11–18, 20). (For exceptions to verse 19, see Lev. 11:21, 22.) A similar list is given in Leviticus 11. The two lists are not identical in every detail, nor are they intended to be. Some **animals** were **unclean** for hygienic reasons, and some because they were used in idolatrous rites or venerated by the heathen.

The NT principle concerning foods can be found in Mark 7:15, Romans 14:14, and 1 Timothy 4:3b–5. Gentiles were permitted to eat the flesh of an animal that died by **itself**, whereas Jews were **not** (v. 21a). To do so would violate Deuteronomy 12:23 because the blood had not been properly removed from the animal.

14:21b A **goat** was **not** to be **boiled** in the same pan with **milk** from its mother (v. 21b). (This appears to have been a Canaanite practice. It is forbidden three times in the Pentateuch.) From a natural standpoint, this rule would save the people from the poisoning that is so common when creamed meat dishes spoil. In addition, there is evidence that the calcium value is canceled when both are eaten together. From this restriction the elaborate rabbinical rules about having different sets of dishes for meat and dairy products have evolved.

I. Tithing (14:22–29)

14:22–27 Verses 22–29 deal with the subject of tithes. Some commentators feel that this section does not refer to the first **tithe** (Lev. 27:30–33), which belonged to God alone, was given to the Levites, and was not to be eaten by the Israelites. Rather it may refer to a secondary **tithe**, called the festival tithe, part of which the offerer himself ate. Generally speaking, these secondary tithes were to be brought to **the place** which **God** appointed as the center for worship. However, if the offerer lived so **far from . . . the place** where God placed **His name** that he was **not able to carry** his **tithe** there, he could **exchange** the produce **for money**, carry **the money** to God's sanctuary, and buy food and **drink** there to be enjoyed **before the Lord**. Notice in verse 26 that the Bible does not teach total abstinence. But it does teach moderation, self-control, non-addiction, and abstinence from anything that would cause offense to another. The difference between wine and strong drink is that wine is made from grapes, and strong drink is made from grain, fruit, or honey. For two years the offerer was required to go up with either the tithe or its monetary equivalent.

14:28, 29 In the **third year** he used **the tithe** at home to feed **the Levite, the stranger, the fatherless,** and **the widow**. Once again we see that the poor and needy are a high priority as far as **the LORD** is concerned. "He who has pity on the poor lends to the LORD, and He will pay back what he has given" (Prov. 19:17).

J. Treatment of Debtors and Slaves (Chap. 15)

15:1–3 **At the end of every seven years**, all **debts** among the children of Israel were to be canceled. The seventh year probably coincided with the sabbatic year. The Jews were not required to cancel debts owed to them by foreigners; this law applied only to debts incurred between Jews. Matthew Henry comments:

> Every seventh year was a year of release, in which the ground rested from being tilled and servants were discharged from their services; and, among other acts of grace, this was one that those who had borrowed money, and had not been able to pay it before, should this year be released from it; and though, if they were able, they were afterwards bound in conscience to repay it, yet thenceforth the creditor should never recover it by law.[7]

Seven is the number of fullness or completeness in Scripture. In the fullness of time, God sent forth His Son and through Him proclaimed remission of sins—a "year of release" not only for the Jews (v. 3) but for all men.

15:4–6 Verse 4 seems to conflict with verse 11. Verse 4 suggests a time when there would be **no poor** people **in the land**, whereas verse 11 says that there will always be poor people.

Bullinger's note is helpful on this. He suggests that verse 4 means "that there be no poor among you."[8] In other words, they should release their brethren in debt every seven years *so that* there would be no people in continual poverty. The creditor would not suffer because God would richly **bless** him. The thought in verse 11 is that there will always be poor people, partly as punishment and partly to teach others compassion in sharing.

15:7–11 The fact that all debts were canceled in the seventh year should not cause a person to refuse to **lend** money to **a poor** Israelite as **the year of release** drew near. To refuse is the base or **wicked thought** of verse 9. In this connection, the Jewish people have been deservedly well known for caring for their own throughout history. Paul says the same thing in 2 Corinthians 9:7 that Moses says in verse 10: "God loves a cheerful giver." This verse is not only a command but a promise, for God is no man's debtor. "The generous soul will be made rich, and he who waters will also be watered himself" (Prov. 11:25).

15:12–15 **A Hebrew** slave was also to be released during **the seventh year** (vv. 12–18). But he was **not** to be sent **away** without first providing for **him liberally**. God provided abundantly for His people when He brought them out of slavery in **Egypt** (Ex. 12:35, 36), and for this reason a freed slave should **not . . . go** out **empty-handed**. The Lord's desire is for His people to follow His example or, to rephrase the golden rule, "Do unto your brother as the Lord has done unto you."

15:16–18 On the other hand, the slave could refuse freedom and choose to become "a perpetual love **servant**." He indicated this by having his **ear** pierced with **an awl . . . to the door** of his master's house. A bondservant was **worth** twice as much as a **hired servant**.

15:19–23 Beginning with verse 19 and continuing through 16:17, we have regulations about certain functions which were to be carried out in the place where Jehovah had placed His name:

1. The setting apart of the first-born animals (15:19–23).
2. The Passover and the Feast of Unleavened Bread (16:1–8).
3. The Feast of Weeks, or Pentecost (16:9–12).
4. The Feast of Tabernacles (16:13–17).

The firstborn of clean animals were to be offered **to the LORD**, and the people were allowed to **eat** their share but not the **blood**. The animals had to be without spot or **defect**—nothing but the best for God.

K. Three Apointed Feasts (Chap. 16)

16:1–8 Chapter 16 reviews the three feasts for which the men in Israel were to go to the central sanctuary each year. As to their purpose, Moody writes,

> The holy feasts were (in general) appointed for these ends and uses:—
> 1. To distinguish the people of God from other nations.
> 2. To keep afoot the remembrance of the benefits already received.
> 3. To be a type and figure of benefits yet further to be conferred upon them by Christ.
> 4. To unite God's people in holy worship.
> 5. To preserve purity in holy worship prescribed by God.[9]

The Passover and Feast of **Unleavened Bread** were closely connected. **The Passover** is described in verses 1,

2, 5–7; the Feast of **Unleavened Bread** in verses 3, 4, and 8. These feasts were to remind God's people of His redemptive work on their behalf. The Lord's Supper is a weekly remembrance feast for the NT believer, a memorial of Christ our Passover sacrificed for us. The Feast of **Unleavened Bread** pictures the kind of lives the redeemed should live—full of praise "according to the blessing of the Lord your God" (v. 17) and free from malice and wickedness (1 Cor. 5:8).

The details given concerning the Passover here are different in several respects from the details given in Exodus 12 and 13. For example, what could be offered and where it could be offered are different in each passage.

16:9–12 **The Feast of Weeks** (Pentecost) began with the firstfruits of the wheat harvest, and is a symbol of the gift of the Holy Spirit. It is not to be confused with the Feast of Firstfruits (barley), which was held on the second day of the Feast of Unleavened Bread. The **freewill offering**, as in 2 Corinthians 8 and 9, was to be proportionate to the Lord's blessing on the individual's endeavors, in this case his crops.

16:13–15 **The Feast of Tabernacles** was at the end of the harvest season and looks forward to the time when Israel will be regathered in the land under the rule of Christ.

16:16, 17 **Three times a year** all the Israelite males were to **appear before the LORD** with a gift according to each one's ability. Moody indicates the spiritual meaning of the three feasts they had to attend:

> The Passover, Pentecost, and Feast of Tabernacles typify a completed redemption:
> 1. By the passion of the cross: Suffering.

2. By the coming of the Holy Spirit:
   Grace.
3. By the final triumph of the coming
   King: Glory.[10]

16:18–20 **Judges** must be honest,
righteous, and impartial. They should
not accept **a bribe** because a bribe
makes a man incapable of judging
fairly.

16:21, 22 The **wooden image** (Heb.
'ashērāh) was a pole made from a tree,
and represented a pagan goddess.
Eventually **the altar** of the Lord would
rest in the temple in Jerusalem, where
no trees could easily be planted but
where an idolatrous symbol could be,
and ultimately was, set up (2 Kgs.
23:6).

L. Judges and Kings (Chap. 17)

17:1 Sacrificial animals were to
be without **blemish**. They were a
symbol of the sinless, spotless Lamb
of God.

17:2–7 A person suspected of idolatry was to be tried. **The testimony of
two or three witnesses** was required.
If convicted, he was to be stoned **to
death**.

17:8–13 If legal problems arose
which were **too hard** to be handled
by the elders of a city, they were to be
taken to **the judge**. By comparing
17:9 with 17:12 and 19:17, it appears
that there was a group of **priests** and
a group of judges who heard these
difficult cases. The high **priest** and
the chief **judge** were the respective
leaders, this being implied by the
definite articles used in verse 12. This
tribunal met at **the place** where God's
sanctuary was located. The decision
of this tribunal was final; it was the
Supreme Court of Israel. If the accused refused to **heed the priest . . . or
the judge**, he was to **die** (vv. 12, 13).

17:14–20 God anticipated the de-

sire of the people for **a king** by about
400 years, and He stated the qualifications for such a ruler, as follows: (1)
He must be the man of God's choice
(v. 15). (2) He must be an Israelite—
from among your brethren (v. 15). (3)
He must **not multiply horses**—that
is, depend on such natural means for
victory over his foes (v. 16). His trust
must be in the Lord. (4) He must not
cause the people to return to Egypt,
thinking that the **horses** they could
get there would save them (v. 16). (5)
He must not **multiply wives** (v. 17).
This is not only a prohibition against
polygamy and a warning against the
danger of wives who would lead him
off into idolatry, but also a ban on
marriages designed to form political
alliances (v. 17). (6) He must not
greatly multiply silver and gold, since
these might lure him away from dependence on the Lord (v. 17). (7) He
must **write**, **read**, and obey the **law** of
the Lord, lest he become proud and
willful (vv. 18–20). By continually
spending time in the law the king
was to become a model for the people. (8) He must not be **lifted up** with
pride (v. 20).

Solomon, who ruled Israel in her
golden days, violated almost every
one of these injunctions—to his own
destruction and the ruin of his kingdom (1 Kgs. 10:14–11:10).

M. Priests, Levites, and Prophets (Chap. 18)

18:1–8 Again God's care for **the
priests** and **Levites** is seen. Because
they did not receive a tribal **inheritance**
of land, they were to be supported by
the people. Their part in the offerings
was **the shoulder**, the two **cheeks**
(jawbones), **the stomach**, and **the
firstfruits** of **grain**, **wine**, **oil**, and
fleece. Verses 6–8 describe **a Levite**
who sold his home and moved **to the**

place where God had placed His name to **serve** Him. He was to share in the offerings with the other Levites, and this was in addition to whatever he received **from the sale of his inheritance**. (Levites could own property even though they did not inherit a tribal possession.)

18:9–14 The Israelites were forbidden to have any contact with anyone who claimed to communicate with the unseen world. Eight means of communication with the spirit world are given. They are called **abominations** by God. They include: **one who practices witchcraft** (a witch or a warlock), . . . **a soothsayer** (a seer; a false prophet), . . . **one who interprets omens** (a palm-reader; a fortune-teller; an astrologer), . . . **a sorcerer** (a witch-doctor), . . . **one who conjures spells** (a wizard), . . . **a medium** (spirit medium), . . . **a spiritist** (a séance leader), . . . **one who calls up the dead** (a necromancer). Some of these "professions" overlap.

Tragically, this nearly 3,400 year-old prohibition is just as much needed in "enlightened" modern times as it was long ago. Henry G. Bosch writes:

> Satanism, demons, and the occult are dark, sinister realities, not tricks. One of the signs that we are nearing the close of this age is the widespread interest in witchcraft, astrology, and other forms of the occult. . . . Thousands consult their horoscope each day, attend séances, or seek to communicate with deceased loved ones. There's also a great interest in Satanism and demons. The Bible repeatedly warns against such practices (Lev. 19:31; 20:27; 2 Chron. 33:6; Jer. 10:2; Gal. 5:19, 20).
>
> How urgent and up-to-date are the warnings of Scripture! Let's not play around with something that could become a kiss of death.[11]

To **be blameless** (v. 13) in regard to these forbidden "communications" means to listen to God's voice alone.

18:15–19 In sharp contrast to the evils of the leaders of the occult, verse 15 presents a beautiful prophecy about Christ, the true **Prophet** of God (Acts 3:22, 23). Notice the description in verses 15, 18, and 19: (1) **a Prophet**—that is, one who speaks God's word; (2) **from your midst**—i.e., truly human; (3) **from your brethren** —i.e., an Israelite; (4) **like me**—i.e., like Moses in the sense of being raised up by God; (5) **I . . . will put My words in His mouth**—fullness of inspiration; (6) **He shall speak to them all that I command Him**—fullness of revelation; (7) all are responsible to listen to Him and obey Him.

This section also teaches that this **Prophet** would serve as a Mediator between God and man. The people had been so terrified at Mount Sinai that they asked that God would not speak to them directly anymore and that they might not see the fire anymore lest they die. In response to that request, God promised Christ as the Mediator. That this passage held Messianic hope for the Jews can be seen clearly in the Gospels (John 6:14; 7:40).

18:20–22 False prophets could be detected in various ways. We have previously learned that they were false if they sought to lead the people away from the worship of the true God (13:1–5). Here is another means of detection: If a prediction failed to come to pass, **that prophet** should be put to death, and no one need fear any curse he might pronounce.

N. Criminal Laws (Chap. 19)

19:1–10 Three cities of refuge had already been set up east of the Jordan River. Here Moses reminded the people to set up **three cities** on the other side, conveniently located so that a **manslayer** could **flee there** from **the avenger of blood** (vv. 1–7). To the previous instruction on this subject is added the provision for **three** additional **cities** of refuge, if the people ever possessed the full **territory** originally promised to them (vv. 8–10). No further mention is made of these three extra cities because Israel has never occupied all the land promised in Genesis 15:18. The **three cities** *west* of the Jordan were Kedesh, Hebron, and Shechem (Josh. 20:7).

19:11–13 The **city** of refuge did not provide safety for a murderer. Even though he fled **to one of these cities, the elders** were to weigh the evidence and **deliver him . . . to . . . the avenger** if he was found guilty.

19:14 A **landmark** was a stone placed in a field to indicate the boundary of one's land. These could be moved secretly at night to expand one's own farm, at the same time cheating one's neighbor. Why this one verse is placed in the midst of a passage dealing with judicial practice—i.e., cities of refuge and witnesses false and true—is difficult to say, but its position does not obscure its teaching.

19:15–21 The **witness of one** person was not enough in a legal case. There had to be **two or three witnesses**. **A false witness** was to be tried by **the priests and the judges** (17:8, 9) and punished with the penalty of the crime with which he accused the defendant (vv. 16–21).

The **"eye for eye"** and **"tooth for tooth"** principle is called the *Lex talionis* in Western culture (Latin for "law of retaliation"). It is commonly misrepresented as vindictive, but it is not. This law is not a *license* for cruelty, but a *limit* to it. In the context it refers to

what kind of penalty could be inflicted upon a false witness.

O. Laws Concerning Warfare (Chap. 20)

20:1–8 Chapter 20 is a manual on warfare for God's people. The priests were charged with encouraging the people as they battled **against** the enemy. Various classes were exempt from military service: (1) those who had just **built a new house**; (2) those who had just **planted a vineyard** and had never partaken of the fruit; (3) those whose marriage had not been consummated; (4) those **who** were **fearful and fainthearted**.

The Jewish writers agree that this liberty to return was allowed only in those wars which they made voluntarily . . . not those which were made by the divine command against Amalek and the Canaanites, in which every man was bound to fight.[12]

20:9 Since in any good army there must be organization and rank, the officers appointed **captains of the armies** to **lead the people**.

20:10–20 Unlike other nations, Israel was to make distinctions in her warfare under Jehovah's direction. These distinctions were a further reflection of Israel as a holy people under a loving God. War was necessary, but the Lord would control the evil it caused. One has only to study the cruel practices of other nations, such as the Assyrians,[13] to appreciate these guidelines. Instructions are given as to how war was to be waged. Notice the following distinctions:

1. Cities . . . near and far (10–18). The cities in the land were an immediate danger, totally reprobate and fit for destruction. Cities outside the land but within the

rest of the area promised to Abraham were to be approached first with terms of peace. If they refused, only the men were to be killed; the women and children were to be spared. These cities did not pose so great a threat to contaminate Israel as did the ones within Israel's borders.

2. Fruitful and unfruitful trees (19, 20). The principle here is that Israel was not to practice "desolation warfare." They were to preserve what was useful instead of engaging in wholesale destruction of the land.

P. Various Laws (Chaps. 21—25)

1. Expiation for Unsolved Murder (21:1–9)

If a man was **found slain . . . in the land**, and the slayer could not be located, **the elders of the . . . nearest . . . city** were required to make **atonement**. They brought **a heifer . . . to a valley with flowing water** and killed it **there**. Washing **their hands over the heifer**, they protested their innocence of the crime and asked that no guilt of bloodshed should attach to them. Even when individual **guilt** could not be ascertained, there was still a corporate **guilt** that needed to be taken care of; the land had to be cleansed from the defilement of **blood**. This became the responsibility of the **nearest . . . city**.

Someone has called verses 1–9 "God's Great Inquest Over His Son." Israel is bloodguilty in connection with Christ's death and must be cleansed in a righteous way.

2. Female Prisoners of War (21:10–14)

An Israelite was permitted to marry **a beautiful woman** captured in **war** after she went through a ceremonial cleansing and separation. (But the passage does *not* apply to female inhabitants of the land of Canaan.) The marriage was of a probationary nature; he could subsequently let her leave him if he was not pleased with her. However, he could **not sell her** or **treat her brutally.**

3. Rights of the Firstborn (21:15–17)

The son of an **unloved** wife could not be deprived of the birthright, if he was **the firstborn**. These verses do not prove that God ever approved of bigamy, but simply that He guarded **the right of the firstborn** even in the case of multiple marriages. Sometimes God sovereignly set aside the firstborn of a family to bless the younger—e.g., Jacob and Esau, Ephraim and Manasseh. However, this was the exception, based on the selective choosing of God, and not the rule, which is stated here.

4. Stubborn and Rebellious Sons (21:18–21)

A **rebellious son** was to be stoned **to death**, after having been found guilty by **the elders of** the **city**. Compare this with the reception given to the repentant prodigal son in Luke 15.

5. The Bodies of Hanged Criminals (21:22, 23)

This text definitely points forward to Christ. Though innocent Himself, He was hanged **on a tree**. He was bearing the curse that *we* deserved. **His body** was not allowed to remain **on** the cross **overnight** (see John 19:31).

To Him who suffered on the tree
Our souls at His soul's price to gain,
Blessing and praise and glory be;
Worthy the Lamb, for He was slain!

To Him enthroned by filial right,
All power in heaven and earth proclaim,
Honor, and majesty, and might;
Worthy the Lamb, for He was slain!
—James Montgomery

6. Nine Laws of Behavior (22:1–12)

22:1–3 Chapter 22 expands upon Leviticus 19:18, describing the general command to "Love your neighbor." Even a man's enemies were to be treated with neighborly concern (Ex. 23:4, 5). An Israelite was not allowed to act indifferently toward anything lost by his neighbor (**brother**). Whether it was an animal, a **garment**, or anything else, he was obligated to take **it to** his **own house** and keep it until it was claimed.

22:4 Israelites were also obligated to assist a neighbor's animal which had fallen.

22:5 Men were not to wear women's clothing, or vice versa. God hates transvestism.

22:6, 7 Young birds could be taken from **a bird's nest**, but **the mother** had to be freed, probably so that she could continue reproducing.

22:8 A **parapet** or railing had to be built around the flat **roof** of a house to prevent people from falling off. The roof was the place of fellowship. It is important to guard the communion, especially of the young and careless.

22:9–11 The Jews were forbidden to: (1) **sow** a **vineyard** with **different kinds of seed**; (2) **plow with an ox** (clean) **and a donkey** (unclean) yoked **together**; (3) wear clothes made of a mixture of **wool and linen**. The first prohibition suggests adding to the pure teaching of the Word of God. The second describes the unequal yoke in service. The third speaks of the mixture of righteousness and unrighteousness in the practical life of the believer.

22:12 Jews were supposed to wear **tassels** on the **four corners** of their garments as constant reminders to obey the Lord (Num. 15:37–41). The reason for these **tassels** is given in Numbers 15:37 and following.

7. Offenses Against Chastity (22:13–30)

22:13–21 This paragraph deals with a **man** who married a girl and then suspected that **she was not a virgin**. **Evidence of . . . virginity** probably consisted of marks on the linen of the marriage bed after a woman's first sexual experience.[14] If **the father and mother** could produce evidence of the **young woman's virginity**, the overly suspicious husband was chastised, fined **one hundred shekels of silver**, and required to live with her. If, however, **the young woman** had been immoral before her marriage, then she was to be stoned **to death**.

22:22–30 The remaining verses of this chapter deal with various types of sexual immorality: (1) Both **man** and **woman . . . found** in the act of adultery were to be put to death. (2) If **a man** raped a **betrothed . . . woman . . . in the city**, and **she did not cry out** for help, then both were guilty of adultery and were to be put **to death**. (3) **If a man** raped **a betrothed woman** in a field, where her cries for help could not be heard, then **the man** was to be killed, but **the woman** was innocent. (4) A **man who** had sexual relations with **a virgin** was required to pay **fifty shekels of silver** to her **father** and also to marry her. (5) Verse 30 forbids incest—i.e., sexual relations with a member of the family.

8. Those Barred from Entering the Assembly (23:1–8)

Various persons were barred from entering the **assembly of the LORD**, that is, from full rights as citizens and worshipers: (1) a man whose reproductive organs were damaged or missing; (2) an **illegitimate** person—i.e., one born out of wedlock[15]; (3) **an Ammonite or Moabite**; (4) **an Edomite or Egyptian**. Verse 4 says that Moab did not "meet the Israelites with food and drink," whereas Deuteronomy 2:29 implies that certain Moabites sold food supplies to the Jews. "To **meet . . . with bread and water**" is an idiomatic expression meaning to give a hospitable reception. This the Moabites did not do.

The eunuch was excluded from the congregation. The illegitimate person, the **Moabite**, and the **Ammonite** were barred from **the assembly . . . to the tenth generation**. The **Edomite** and the **Egyptian** could enter after three generations. However, there were exceptions to these general rules when individuals sought Jehovah. Among David's mighty men could be found both an Ammonite and a Moabite (1 Chron. 11:39, 46). Some think that the rules of exclusion applied only to males and therefore did not apply to Ruth, for example. Some think that "**the tenth generation**" is an idiom that means indefinitely.

9. Cleanliness in the Camp (23:9–14)

Verse 9 warns against the temptations that face men who are away from home in military service. (Or perhaps it serves as an introduction to verses 10–14.)

The law on nocturnal emissions shows the sacredness with which the reproduction of life was regarded.

Each soldier was required to carry a shovel with his weapons for sanitation of the camp. All excrement was to be covered immediately with dirt. If all armies down through history had followed this simple regulation, they would have avoided the spread of plagues many times.

10. Social and Religious Laws (23:15–25)

23:15, 16 A foreign **slave** who had **escaped** to freedom was not to be delivered up **to his master**. Thus Israel was to be an asylum for the oppressed.

23:17, 18 Male or female prostitution was not to be tolerated in the land, and money derived from such immoral traffic should never be brought **to the house of the LORD** in payment of a vow. A **"dog"** means a male prostitute.

23:19, 20 Jews were **not** to **charge interest** on **anything** they lent to another Jew, though it was permitted for them to **charge interest . . . to a foreigner**. This is a further expansion of the principle already given in Exodus 22:25, which prohibited exacting usury from the poor.

23:21–23 Vows were voluntary. A man did not have to make **a vow to the LORD**, but once he made it, he was obligated to **pay it**.

23:24, 25 Travelers were allowed to help themselves to **grapes** for their current needs, but they were **not** allowed to **put any** in a **container**. Likewise, they were allowed to take **grain** from a field, but only what they could pick with their hands, not with **a sickle**. In our Lord's day, His twelve disciples made use of this privilege (Mark 2:23).

11. Divorce and Remarriage (24:1–4)

A man could **divorce** his **wife** for **uncleanness** by writing **her a certificate of divorce** and giving it to her. She was then free to marry someone else. But **if** her second **husband** died or divorced **her**, the first **husband** was not allowed to marry her again. Jehovah gave Israel a certificate of divorce (Jer. 3:1–8); yet in a future day

He will take her to Himself again, having purged her of her unfaithfulness. Oh, the depths of the riches of the love of God; how low He stoops to love the unlovable!

12. *Various Social Laws (24:5—25:4)*

24:5 A man who was newly married was **not** required to **go out to war** for the first **year**. This gave him time to cultivate and strengthen the marriage bond and to start a family. If he had to go to war and was killed, his name would be cut off from Israel unless his redeeming relative raised up descendants for him. This "kinsman redeemer"[16] was the nearest relative who was able and willing to marry the widow. The first male born to such a union became the heir of the former husband. This continued the family name and kept the land in the family.

24:6 Since a **millstone** was a person's means of livelihood, it could not be required as a **pledge** in a business transaction. To take either **the lower or the upper millstone** would deprive one of the means of grinding grain.

24:7 A **kidnapper** or a slave trader was to be put to death.

24:8, 9 Special precautions were to be observed in the event of **an outbreak of leprosy**, following previous instructions given **to the Levites**. **Miriam** is cited as a warning.

24:10–13 A man's **house** could not be invaded to obtain a **pledge** from him. If the **man** was so **poor** that he gave his clothing as a **pledge**, it was to be returned to him each night so **that he** could **sleep in** it.

24:14, 15 The **wages** of **a hired servant** should be paid promptly.

24:16 No man was to **be put to death for** another person's sin.

24:17–22 **Justice** was to be shown to **the stranger**, **the fatherless**, and **the widow**. A **field** was not to be completely harvested. Gleanings were to be left for the poor and the helpless. The same applied to the harvesting of **olive trees** and **grapes**. Ronald Sider comments:

> The memory of their own poverty and oppression in Egypt was to prompt them to leave generous gleanings for the poor sojourner, the widow, and the fatherless.[17]

When John Newton was born again, he printed verse 22 in large letters and hung it over his mantlepiece, where he would be constantly reminded of it.

25:1–3 When an offender was found guilty and was sentenced **to be beaten**, he was not to receive more than **forty blows**. The Jews commonly inflicted thirty-nine blows or stripes, lest they miscount and thus transgress this regulation (see 2 Cor. 11:24).

25:4 The **ox** that trod **out the grain** was **not** to be muzzled but rather to be allowed to eat some of the grain. Paul uses this verse in 1 Corinthians 9:9–11 to teach that the man who labors in spiritual things should be taken care of in material things. Thus Paul shows us that there is a spiritual aspect to the law. This does not minimize the literal meaning; it only shows that many times there is a spiritual lesson under the surface. The diligent student will look for and heed this important spiritual lesson.

13. *Law of Levirate Marriage (25:5–10)*

If an Israelite died and left his **widow** without a **son**, there was the danger that his name might perish and his property pass out of the family. Therefore, a **brother** of the dead man was supposed to marry the widow. This practice of "Levirate" marriages existed in many ancient nations. If the brother would not agree to do this, then the widow went to the elders of the city and announced this fact. He was called before the elders and given an opportunity to confirm his unwillingness. If he persisted in his refusal, the widow removed one of his sandals and spat in his face. From then on he was known by a name of reproach because of his unwillingness to perpetuate his brother's house.

Leviticus 20:21 *prohibited* a man from marrying his brother's wife; here he is *commanded* to marry her. The passage in Leviticus no doubt applied when the husband was still living, while Deuteronomy refers to a time when the husband is dead, having left behind no male heir.

14. Three Distinct Laws (25:11–19)

25:11, 12 If a woman interfered by seizing a man immodestly in a fight in which her husband was involved, her offending hand was to be cut off. Her actions might endanger the man's having an heir; thus the severe penalty.

25:13–16 Honest weights and measures were required. Often men had one set of scales for buying and another for selling. This was an abomination to the LORD.

25:17–19 The descendants of Amalek were to be utterly destroyed because of his treachery and cruelty (Ex. 17:8–16). Israel is told not to forget to destroy the Amalekites, but it appears that they did forget. Saul disobeyed the Lord in not exterminating them in his day (1 Sam. 15). In fact, it was not until the days of Hezekiah that "they defeated the rest of the Amalekites who had escaped" (1 Chron. 4:43).

Q. Rituals and Ratifications (Chap. 26)

1. The Ritual for Firstfruits (26:1–11)

After the people were settled in the land, they were supposed to go to God's sanctuary and present the first of all the produce to the priest in joyful recognition of what God had done. Then they were to rehearse the Lord's gracious dealings with them, beginning with their ancestor, Jacob (a wandering Syrian), going on to the slavery in Egypt, God's mighty deliverance, and concluding with their possession of the land flowing with milk and honey. Phillip Keller explains this colorful term:

> In the Scriptures the picture portrayed of the Promised Land, to which God tried so hard to lead Israel from Egypt, was that of a "land flowing with milk and honey." Not only is this figurative language but also essentially scientific terminology. In agricultural terms we speak of a "milk flow" and a "honey flow." By this we mean the peak season of spring and summer, when pastures are at their most productive stages. The livestock that feed on the forage and the bees that visit the blossoms are said to be producing a corresponding "flow" of milk or honey. So a land flowing with milk and honey is a land of rich, green, luxuriant pastures. And when God spoke of such a land for Israel He also foresaw such an abundant life of joy and victory and contentment for His people.[18]

2. The Ritual for the Third Year Tithe (26:12–15)

In addition to the above firstfruits, the Jews were to offer a second tithe, called the festival tithe, which was to be shared with the Levite, the stranger, the fatherless, and the widow every

third year. This tithe was to be distributed to the needy in their own towns. The people then had to testify **before the LORD** that they had **obeyed . . . all** of the commands concerning the tithe.

3. Ratification of the Covenant (26:16–19)

Because the people had agreed to **walk in** the **ways** of the Lord, He in turn acknowledged them as **His** own **special people** and promised to exalt them **above all** other **nations**. They were **a holy people** because God had set them apart from the other **nations**— not because of any intrinsic merit. They were different from any other nation on earth, being the peculiar treasure of Jehovah. Their response to such an honor was supposed to be obedience to His **commands**.

R. Curses and Blessings (Chaps. 27, 28)

27:1–8 After they crossed **the Jordan** River into the Promised Land, the Israelites were to raise up a large monument of **stones, whitewash** it, and **write all the words of** the **law** on it. This monument was to be erected on **Mount Ebal**, together with **an altar** which was to be made with uncut **stones**.

27:9, 10 The Jews had been God's people by His choice for some time, but now that they were about to enter the land, they became His **people** in a special sense. The favor He was showing to them called for loving obedience on their part.

27:11–13 Six tribes were appointed to **stand on Mount Gerizim** in order to "Amen" the blessings. These six tribes were descendants of Leah and Rachel. The other tribes were to **stand on Mount Ebal** to confirm the curses. Notice that Ephraim and Manasseh aren't mentioned separately, but in-

stead the tribe of Joseph is listed. Reuben, Israel's firstborn (who lost his birthright), and Zebulun, Leah's youngest, were on Mount Ebal with the sons of the handmaids. The favored tribes were on Mount Gerizim.

27:14–26 The **Levites** (see v. 9) were to stand in the valley between the two mountains. As they pronounced the curses or blessings, the people were to answer **"Amen!"** The curses are given in verses 15–26. They have to do with idolatry; disrespect of parents (v. 16); dishonesty in removing boundary lines (v. 17); deceiving **the blind** (v. 18); taking advantage of the poor and defenseless (v. 19); various forms of incest (vv. 20, 22, 23); bestiality (v. 21); secret murder of one's **neighbor**; murder of the **innocent** for a **bribe** (v. 25); and disobedience to the **law** of God (v. 26). The historical account of this ceremony can be found in Joshua 8:30 and following. Notice how closely Joshua follows the instructions given by Moses.

It is significant that only the curses are given in Chapter 27. It could not be otherwise because, as Paul reminds us, "For as many as are of the works of the law are under the curse" (Gal. 3:10). It was not merely that the Israelites would *transgress* the law, but that they were under the law *as a principle*.

28:1–14 Verse 1 refers to the end of chapter 26 with the words, **"God will set you high above."** This gives chapter 27 the appearance of being parenthetical. Many Bible students feel that the blessings pronounced in verses 3–6 were not those addressed to the six tribes on Mount Gerizim, but that this entire chapter is a statement by Moses as to what lay ahead for the children of Israel. The first fourteen verses speak of the blessings that would follow obedience, whereas the last fifty-four verses describe the curses that would fall upon the people if they forsook the Lord. The blessings promised include preeminence among **the nations**, material prosperity, fruitfulness, fertility, abundance of crops, victory in battle, and success in international trade.

28:15–37 The curses included scarcity, barrenness, crop failure, pestilence, disease, blight, drought, defeat in battle, madness, fright, adversity, calamity, and powerlessness (vv. 15–32). Verses 33–37 predict captivity in a foreign land, and this was fulfilled by the Assyrian and Babylonian captivities.

Israel would **become an astonishment, a proverb, and a byword** among all **nations**.

28:38–46 The Jews would be cursed with failed crops, **vineyards**, and **olive trees**. Their children would **go into captivity** and **locusts** would **consume** their **trees** and **produce**. The **alien** would **rise higher and higher** and the Israelites would go **down lower and lower**. There is no contradiction between verses 12 and 44. If obedient, the Jews would become international lenders. If disobedient, they would have to borrow from strangers.

28:47–57 The horrors of a **siege** by a foreign invader are described in verses 49–57—so fierce that the people would **eat** one another. This came to pass when Jerusalem was besieged by the Babylonians and later by the Romans. At both times, cannibalism was widespread. People who were normally refined and **sensitive** became **hostile** and cannibalistic.

28:58–68 **Plagues** and **diseases** would greatly reduce the population of Israel. The survivors would be scattered throughout **the earth**, and

there they would live in constant **fear** of persecution. God would even **take** His people **back to Egypt in ships**. According to Josephus, the prophecy that Israel would go **to Egypt** again was partially fulfilled in the time of Titus, when Jews were taken there by ship and sold as **slaves**. But the name **"Egypt"** here may mean servitude in general. God had delivered Israel from literal Egyptian slavery in the past, but if she would not love Him and acknowledge His sovereign right to her obedience, if she would not keep herself pure as His wife, if she would not be His peculiar treasure, choosing instead to be like the other nations, then she would be sold back into slavery. But by then she would be so crushed that **no** one would want her even as a slave.

"To whom much is given, from him much will be required" (Luke 12:48). Israel had been given privileges above all other nations, and therefore her accountability was greater and her punishment more severe.

To meditate on these curses leaves one amazed at the outpouring of Jehovah's wrath. No words are minced, no details are left to the imagination. Moses paints the picture with bold, stark realism. Israel must know what disobedience will bring in order that she may learn to fear **this glorious and awesome name, THE LORD YOUR GOD**.

III. MOSES' THIRD DISCOURSE—COVENANT FOR THE LAND (Chaps. 29, 30)

A. The Covenant Made in Moab (29:1–21)

29:1 The first verse of chapter 29 may logically belong to the previous chapter, as in the Hebrew Bible. Keil and Delitzsch, however, see it as a "heading" for the addresses of chapters 29 and 30.[19]

29:2–9 The people had broken the covenant which God made with them at Mount Sinai. Now **Moses** called on them to ratify the **covenant** contained here in the book of Deuteronomy made on the plains of Moab, just prior to their entrance into the land. The people lacked an understanding of the Lord and His purposes for them. Jehovah longed to give them a **heart to perceive, eyes to see and ears to hear**, but they rendered themselves unfit to receive these things through their continual unbelief and disobedience. Israel had enjoyed manna from heaven and water from the rock; she did not depend on the things manufactured by man for her survival (i.e., bread, wine, strong drink). This was in order that she might come to know the Lord her God in all of His faithfulness and love.

As an incentive to keep **this covenant**, Moses once again reviewed the goodness of God to Israel—the miracles in **Egypt**, the mighty deliverance, the **forty years in the wilderness**, the defeat of **Sihon . . . and Og**, and the distribution of the trans-Jordanian **land** to Reuben, Gad, and the half-tribe **of Manasseh**.

29:10–21 Moses called on all the people to **enter into** the sworn **covenant with the LORD** (vv. 10–13) and reminded them that the **covenant** applied to their posterity as well (vv. 14, 15). Failure to keep the covenant would result in bitter punishment. Rebels should beware of any temptation to **serve** the **idols** of the Gentile **nations** or to think that they would escape God's **anger** if they did so (vv. 16–21). Verse 19 in the RSV reads: "One who, when he hears the words of

this sworn covenant, blesses himself in his heart saying, 'I shall be safe, though I walk in the stubbornness of my heart.' This would lead to the sweeping away of moist and dry alike." No one would escape.

B. Punishment for Breaking the Covenant (29:22–29)

29:22–28 Generations to come, and foreign nations as well, would be amazed at the desolation of Israel and would ask the reason why the **land** should have been treated **like the** cities of the plain—**Sodom and Gomorrah, Admah, and Zeboiim**. The answer would be given, **"Because they have forsaken the covenant of the LORD God of their fathers . . . and served other gods."**

29:29 While there are certain **secret things** that **belong to the LORD**, especially matters concerning His judgments, Moses reminded the people that their responsibility was clearly revealed—to keep the covenant of the Lord. What this is saying is that revelation brings responsibility. Men are accountable to obey, not to sit in judgment on the word of the Lord. This principle can be found many times in the NT also. "To him who knows to do good [revelation] and does not do it [responsibility], to him it is sin" (Jas. 4:17).

C. Restoration for Returning to the Covenant (Chap. 30)

30:1–10 Chapter 30 anticipates that the people would break the covenant and be carried away into exile. This, of course, is exactly what happened. Even then, God would **have compassion** and **restore them if they would turn to** Him in repentance. He would **bring** them back **to the land**. In addition to this physical restoration, there would be a spiritual renewal (**"the**

LORD your God will circumcise your heart"—v. 6). The people would then enjoy the blessings of obedience, whereas their **enemies** would be cursed. The counsels of the Most High will not fail, even though the *objects* of those counsels *do* fail. God would fulfill His word to the patriarchs and give their **descendants...the land** forever. After the exile, which He knew was inevitable, He would restore them and change them. Such is the working of the unconditional love of the great Lover! Verse 6 touches on a theme developed hundreds of years later by the prophets—namely, the New Covenant (Jer. 32:39ff; Ezek. 36:24ff). This covenant, although revealed in the OT, was not ratified until the death of Christ, for His was the blood of the New Covenant (Luke 22:20).

30:11–14 Moses reminded the people that the covenant was not too hard for them to understand (**mysterious**), **nor** was **it far off** (inaccessible). They were not required to do the impossible to find it. The Lord had brought it to them, and their responsibility was to obey it. These verses are used by Paul in Romans 10:5–8 and are applied to Christ and the gospel. The covenant was not easy to keep, but God had made provision in case of failure. The people were then required to repent and to bring the appointed sacrifices. Since the sacrifices were types of Christ, the lesson is that those who sin should repent and put their faith in the Lord Jesus Christ.

30:15–20 The people were called on to choose between **life and good** on the one hand, and **death and evil** on the other—**life** for obedience, but **death** for disobedience. Moses strongly pleaded with them to choose **life and...blessing**. The desired response

brought good results, including **length of...days** and abundant spiritual **life**, implied by the words "**that you may cling to Him.**" The only alternative was one of **cursing**.

IV. MOSES' LAST DAYS— DEATH OUTSIDE THE LAND (Chaps. 31—34)

A. Moses' Replacement (Chap. 31)

31:1–8 Moses was now **one hundred and twenty years old**. He knew God's decree stating that he would **not** be allowed to **cross** the **Jordan** with the people, but he reminded the people that **the LORD** would go **with** them, that **Joshua** would be their captain, and that victory over their enemies was assured. **Moses** next encouraged **Joshua** publicly concerning his new appointment and assured him of the Lord's presence (vv. 7, 8).

31:9–13 The written **law** was entrusted to the Levites. It was to be kept beside **the ark**. The two tablets of the Decalogue were placed *inside* the ark (Ex. 25:16; Heb. 9:4). This copy of the law was placed *beside* the ark. **Every seven years** the **law** was to be **read** in the presence of **all Israel**.

The reading of Holy Scripture is sadly neglected even in doctrinally conservative circles today. The following extended but valuable words from C. H. Mackintosh are unfortunately much more true today than a century ago when they were written:

The Word of God is not loved and studied, either privately or publicly. Trashy literature is devoured in private, and music, ritualistic services, and imposing ceremonies are eagerly sought after in public. Thousands will flock to hear music, and pay for admission, but how few care for a meeting to read the holy Scriptures!

These are facts, and facts are powerful arguments. We cannot get over them. There is a growing thirst for religious excitement, and a growing distaste for the calm study of holy Scripture and the spiritual exercises of the Christian assembly. It is perfectly useless to deny it. We cannot shut our eyes to it. The evidence of it meets us on every hand.

Thank God, there are a few, here and there, who really love the Word of God, and delight to meet, in holy fellowship, for the study of its precious truths. May the Lord increase the number of such, and bless them, "till traveling days are done."[20]

31:14–18 As Moses' death drew near, God called him and **Joshua** to **the tabernacle of meeting** and appeared before them in a **pillar of cloud**. He first revealed **to Moses** that the Israelites would soon give themselves over to idolatry and suffer God's **anger**.

31:19–22 Then He commanded Moses to **write down** a **song** and **teach it to the children of Israel** as a **witness . . . against** them in days to come.

31:23 God personally **inaugurated Joshua** to lead His people **into the** Promised Land and encouraged him to **be** brave and **strong**. Joshua must have been strengthened by these words from Jehovah. He had just heard God speak of a coming national apostasy (v. 16), and he needed to be reassured, rather than discouraged, for the task ahead.

31:24–27 The **Book of the Law**, i.e., Deuteronomy, committed to the Levites, would also serve as **a witness against** the Israelites when they forsook the Lord.

31:28–30 Then **Moses** delivered the following **song** to the **elders of** their **tribes, and** the **officers**, as God had commanded him.

B. Moses' Song (Chap. 32)

32:1–3 The song may be summarized as follows: The universe is summoned to **hear** the word of the Lord. It is refreshing and nourishing, like **the rain** and **the dew**. In verse 3 (which could serve as a title to the song) Moses speaks of ascribing **greatness** to their **God**. The song reveals God's **greatness** in the context of His historical dealings with His people.

32:4–9 In spite of God's greatness, justice, faithfulness, and holiness, the people of Israel forsook Him and sinned against Him. The glory of Jehovah's attributes is displayed here against the dark backdrop of Israel's **perverse** wickedness. It was small thanks He received for being their **Father** and Creator. **When the Most High divided** the earth among **the** Gentile **nations**, He first provided for the needs of His own people. Such was His love and care for them.

32:10–14 The birth and childhood of the nation of Israel are described in verse 10. After the Exodus from Egypt, God guided, **instructed**, and preserved His people with the love of a mother eagle (v. 11). **There was no foreign god** who had a part in Israel's preservation. Why then should the nation turn to idolatry and ascribe the goodness of Jehovah to another? Beginning in verse 13, the song is prophetic. He brought them into the blessings of the Promised Land.

32:15–20 But **Jeshurun** (a poetic name for the people of Israel meaning "upright people") rebelled against Jehovah by turning to idols. They chose to sacrifice **to demons**, many times offering up their own children. They even sank to the stupidity of worshiping **new gods**. Thus they neglected their true **Rock**; they forgot their true Father. As a result, **the**

LORD hid His **face from them**. This hiding of His face was fulfilled in their being sold into captivity.

32:21–33 After setting Israel aside, God acted in grace toward the Gentiles, seeking to **provoke** Israel **to jealousy** (as in the present Church Age). Israel in the meantime would be scattered and persecuted. The people would not be totally destroyed, though, because Jehovah did not want Israel's enemies to misinterpret the nation's downfall. It was not that **their** enemies' **rock** was stronger, but that Israel's **Rock had surrendered them** to slaughter because of their wickedness.

32:34–43 This section has to do with God's **vengeance** upon the nations that were used to punish Israel. **Vengeance** (v. 35) and vindication (v. 36) belong to the Lord. He has sworn by Himself (for there is no one greater) to deal with His **adversaries**. Notice how completely this judgment will be carried out (vv. 41, 42). As a result, God's people and all the nations are to rejoice, because God has avenged Himself and made **atonement for His land and His people**.

32:44–47 The song thus gives a historical and prophetical outline of the nation of **Israel**. Having read the song, Moses solemnly urged the people to follow the Lord with the words: **"For it is not a futile thing for you, because it is your life. . . ."**

32:48–52 Then the LORD called **Moses** to the top of **Mount Nebo**, where he would be allowed to **see the land**. He would not be allowed to enter **Canaan** because of his sin at **Meribah Kadesh**, but would **die on . . . Mount Nebo** and be buried in a valley in Moab (cf. 34:6).

C. Moses' Blessing (Chap. 33)

The Hebrew wording in this chapter is obscure in many places; thus there are various opinions and interpretations offered by different commentators. It is not within the scope of this work to go into detail as to the possible Hebrew renderings; we just suggest a short, prophetical view of each blessing.

33:1–5 As his final official act, **Moses** the **man of God** pronounced a **blessing** on the tribes **of Israel**. Verses 2–5 celebrate God's loving care for His own people. At **Sinai** He gave the **law**. **Seir** and **Mount Paran** were on the route from Sinai to Canaan. In poetic language, Moses describes the Lord as **King in Jeshurun** leading His people on to victory. Then follow the individual blessings:

33:6 *Reuben*. Situated east of the Jordan River and immediately north of Moab, Reuben would be vulnerable to attack; hence the prayer that the tribe would not become extinct but would be populous.

Simeon is not mentioned. It became closely associated with Judah and may be included in that blessing.

33:7 *Judah*. This tribe would be a leader in the conquest of Canaan. The Lord is asked to **help** the warriors and **bring** them back safely to their **people**.

33:8–11 *Levi*. God's **Thummim and** His **Urim** belonged to **Levi**, the tribe criticized by the people at **Massah** and **the waters of Meribah**. Levi was also the tribe that took sides with God against its own people when the latter worshiped the golden calf. Levi was set apart to **teach** the people and to present sacrifices. Moses prays that the LORD will **bless his substance**, find pleasure in his service, and destroy **those who hate him**.

33:12 *Benjamin*. The temple, God's dwelling place on earth, would be located in Benjamin's territory, surrounded by shouldering hills. Therefore **Benjamin** is pictured as a **beloved** tribe, enjoying intimate communion with the Lord.

33:13–17 *Joseph*. The territory of the sons of Joseph would be watered by **dew** from above and springs from **beneath**. It would be unusually fruitful, enjoying the goodwill of the One who revealed Himself **in the** burning **bush**. Majestic and powerful, Joseph's two sons would conquer nations. **Ephraim** got the birthright and is therefore assigned **ten thousands** whereas **Manasseh** is credited with only **thousands**.

33:18, 19 *Zebulun and Issachar*. Successful at home and abroad, they would lead nations to worship at Jerusalem, **the mountain** of the Lord. These tribes would feast on **the abundance of the seas** and of the land. Since there is no record of their leading nations to worship, and since both tribes were landlocked in the past, this blessing must look forward to the Millennium.

33:20, 21 *Gad*. God gave this tribe a large territory east of the Jordan. **Gad** fought like **a lion** to capture and preserve it. It was choice pastureland that he chose for himself—a leader's **portion**. But he also joined **with the heads of the people** to conquer the land west of the Jordan, thus carrying out the Lord's righteous will.

33:22 *Dan* is compared to **a lion's whelp**, ferocious and strong, striking suddenly from ambush. Dan's original territory was in the southwest of Canaan, but the Danites migrated to the northeast and seized additional land adjoining **Bashan**.

33:23 *Naphtali* was located in northeast Canaan and extended **south** to the Sea of Galilee. The tribe was honored with the **favor** and **blessing** of the LORD.

33:24, 25 *Asher* was to be blessed

with a numerous posterity, good relations with the other tribes, and a land flowing with olive **oil**. **Iron and bronze** seem to be strange materials for **sandals**. Keil translates it fortresses. F. W. Grant suggests an interesting alternative translation of the last line of verse 25:

> The moderns against the ancients read "rest" instead of "strength." In these two there would be doubly expressed their abiding security: and though we may not be willing to give up what we are so familiar with, that "as thy days thy strength shall be," it is certainly not unsuited as the close of this wonderful blessing to have "as thy days shall be thy *rest*."[21]

33:26–29 The closing verses celebrate the greatness of God as He acts in behalf of His people. The **God of Jeshurun** is unique **in the heavens to help**. Millions have been fortified by the words in verse 27: **"The eternal God is your refuge, and underneath are the everlasting arms."**

God's future destruction of Israel's enemies and the promise of safety, peace, prosperity, and victory close the Song of Moses.

D. Moses' Death (Chap. 34)

34:1–8 Even if the death of **Moses** here was recorded by someone else, this does not affect the fact that the rest of the Pentateuch was written by Moses.[22] After **Moses** had seen **the land**, he died on **Mount Nebo** and was **buried** by the LORD in a secret **grave**. Doubtless the reason for the secrecy was to prevent men from making a shrine at the lawgiver's tomb and worshiping him there. **Moses was one hundred and twenty years old** at the time of his death, but he was still strong, alert, and keen. This statement is not in contradiction with 31:2. The reason Moses could no longer lead the people was not physical but spiritual. God had told him that because of his sin he would not lead the people into Canaan (31:2), even though physically he was able to do so.

34:9 **Joshua** then assumed his duties as commander-in-chief. **Moses had** confirmed Joshua as his successor according to the word of the Lord in Numbers 27:18–23. Thus his servant became his successor, a further testimony to Moses' humility.

34:10–12 Of few men could the tribute paid to Moses ever be spoken. Of course, when these closing verses were written, the Messiah had not yet appeared. Verse 10 was true only up to the time of Christ's First Advent. "And Moses indeed was faithful in all His house as a *servant*" (Heb. 3:5). Because of his sin he died; his burial place is unknown. But his antitype, the Lord Jesus, "was faithful . . . , as a *Son* over His own house" (Heb. 3:5, 6). It was for *our* sins that *He* died; His burial place is empty because He has ascended to the right hand of the Father in heaven. "Therefore, holy brethren, partakers of the heavenly calling, *consider the Apostle and High Priest of our confession, Christ Jesus. . . .* For this One has been counted worthy of more glory than Moses, inasmuch as He who built the house has more honor than the house" (Heb. 3:1, 3).

ENDNOTES

[1](2:1–23) "Giants" (transliterated *rephā'îm*), were an ancient race of giants from whom Og was descended. The word Rephaim came to mean any people of large stature.

[2](3:1–11) J. A. Thompson, *Deuteronomy: An Introduction and Commentary*, p. 93.

[3](4:4–49) The Syriac Version reads *Sirion*.

[4](5:22) Thompson, *Deuteronomy*, p. 119.

[5](8:Intro) *Ibid.*, p. 134.

[6](10:Intro) The chapter and verse divisions in the Bible were made centuries after the originals were written.

[7](15:1–3) Matthew Henry, "Deuteronomy," *Matthew Henry's Commentary on the Whole Bible*, I:786.

[8](15:4–6) E. W. Bullinger, *The Companion Bible*, p. 259.

[9](16:1–8) D. L. Moody, *Notes from My Bible*, pp. 44, 45.

[10](16:16, 17) *Ibid.*, p. 45.

[11](18:9–14) Henry G. Bosch, *Our Daily Bread*, Grand Rapids: Radio Bible Class, June-July-August 1989, August 31.

[12](20:1–8) Henry, "Deuteronomy," I:806.

[13](20:10–20) See Introduction to Jonah for some details.

[14](22:13–21) Another possible meaning is that "tokens of virginity" should be translated "tokens of adolescence," that is, "that the girl was menstruating regularly. A man who married such a girl would expect to have evidence of this after his marriage unless, of course, she became pregnant by him at once. What was needed was evidence that at the time of marriage the girl was not pregnant and was menstruating. If she had been guilty of sexual misconduct after betrothal, any pregnancy before marriage would eventually show up and a child would be born before nine months had elapsed. The law of verses 13–21 might therefore be concerned with the bride's conduct during her betrothal period prior to marriage and the 'tokens of adolescence' might have been a pregnancy test." (Thompson,

Deuteronomy, p. 236. See also discussion on p. 235.)

[15](23:1–8) The category may refer specifically to offspring of incestuous relations among Jews, or of mixed relations with pagans.

[16](24:5) "Kinsman redeemer" is the older term from the KJV.

[17](24:17–22) Ronald Sider, *Rich Christians in an Age of Hunger*, p. 92.

[18](26:1–11) Phillip Keller, *A Shepherd Looks at Psalm 23*, pp. 46, 47.

[19](29:1) C. F. Keil and F. Delitzsch, "Deuteronomy." In *Biblical Commentary on the Old Testament*, III:446.

[20](31:9–13) C. H. Mackintosh, "Deuteronomy," in *Notes on the Pentateuch*, p. 895.

[21](33:24, 25) F. W. Grant, "Deuteronomy," in *The Numerical Bible*, I:622.

[22](34:1–8) See "Introduction to the Pentateuch" for a defense of the Mosaic authorship of the Pentateuch.

BIBLIOGRAPHY

Grant, F. W. "Deuteronomy." In *The Numerical Bible*. Vol. I. Neptune, NJ: Loizeaux Brothers, 1977.

Henry, Matthew. "Deuteronomy." In *Matthew Henry's Commentary on the Whole Bible*. Vol. I. MacLean, VA: MacDonald Publishing Company, n.d.

Keil, C. F. and Delitzsch, F. "Deuteronomy." In *Biblical Commentary on the Old Testament. The Pentateuch*, Vol. III. Grand Rapids: Wm. B. Eerdmans Publishing Co., 1971.

Kline, Meredith G. "Deuteronomy." In *The Wycliffe Bible Commentary*. Chicago: Moody Press, 1962.

Mackintosh, C. H. "Deuteronomy." In *Notes on the Pentateuch*. Neptune, NJ: Loizeaux Brothers, 1972.

Shultz, Samuel J. *Deuteronomy: The Gospel of Love*. Everyman's Bible Commentary. Chicago: Moody Press, 1971.

Thompson, J. A. *Deuteronomy: An Introduction and Commentary*. The Tyndale Old Testament Commentaries. Downers Grove, IL: InterVarsity Press, 1974.

Towns, Elmer L. "Deuteronomy." In the *Liberty Bible Commentary*. Lynchburg, VA: The Old-Time Gospel Hour, 1982.

INTRODUCTION TO
THE HISTORICAL BOOKS

For the millions of people who love a good story, especially a *true* story, the second main division of the OT is unusually captivating. It picks up the story of God's people where Deuteronomy left off and takes it forward a thousand years to the end of OT history. (The poetical and prophetic books fit into this same framework but they do not advance the *story* any.)

For those who do *not* like "history" (by nature or by faulty exposure to dull history teachers) we can only say that *this* history is unique. First of all Bible history is truly, to use an old saying, "His story" in every sense of the word. It is not a complete account of any period of Hebrew history, but a divinely selected continuous story. Secondly, it is history with a *purpose*— not merely to instruct or entertain, but to make us better believers. To use the Apostle Paul's words in the NT, these things "were written for our learning" (Rom. 15:4).

While all of these events really occurred, the selection and presentation by God's human writers under His Spirit's inspiration was to make it easy for the meditative reader to see the lessons that God wants us to learn, e.g., from David's life, from the division of the Kingdom, or from the return of the Jewish remnant after the Exile.

I. Chronology

The historical books extend from about 1400 B.C. to about 400 B.C., or a full millennium of Hebrew history. This long period divides naturally into three main eras: The Theocratic Period (1405–1043 B.C.), the Monarchical Period (1043–586 B.C. or from Saul to the destruction of Jerusalem), and the Restoration Period (536 to 420 B.C.).

II. The Theocratic Books

Just as a *democracy* (Greek for *people-rule*) is supposed to be a government run by the people, so a *theocracy* is supposed to be a government directly ruled by God. Ancient Israel from Joshua to Saul (1405–1043 B.C.) was such a rule by God.[1]

Three books cover the theocratic era: Joshua, Judges, and Ruth.

A. Joshua

This book continues from the death of Moses and his replacement by Joshua, a military leader who was also a spiritual one. Joshua goes on to challenge the Israelites not only to conquer Palestine but also to follow the Lord. The first half of the book recounts the conquest of the Promised Land and the second half details the division of that land among the twelve tribes of Israel.

B. Judges

Because the Israelites were disobedient to God's orders and left pockets of pagans scattered throughout Palestine, they subsequently experienced wave after wave of Gentile oppressors—seven in all.

The Book of Judges contains some fairly grim—and one or two grisly—stories illustrating what disobedience to God's Word can bring.

C. Ruth

This charming little book does not take place after the time of the book of Judges but during that spiritually dark era, showing that even at a time of great spiritual decline, the godly remnant can serve God in a beautiful and acceptable way.

III. The Monarchical Books

There are also three books covering the era of the monarchy (1043–586 B.C.), but they have been divided into six books for convenience in all modern versions.

A. Samuel

First and Second Samuel can be summarized in three names: Samuel, Saul, and David. They are named after *Samuel*, the prophet who anointed Israel's first king, *Saul*, and also his successor, *David*, whose trials and successes are recounted in some detail.

B. Kings

Solomon, David's son, though a wise and splendid ruler, lost his spiritual power by marrying hosts of pagan women. His son Rehoboam caused the split of the kingdom into Judah in the south (which had good and evil rulers), and Israel in the north (which had only evil rulers). In 722 B.C. the Northern Kingdom went into captivity, and between 605 and 586 the Southern Kingdom was taken captive.

C. Chronicles

In the Hebrew Bible this is the last book, recounting Jewish history from Adam (merely by genealogies) through the downfall of the Southern Kingdom. Since it is a spiritual retelling of Hebrew history, it stresses positive elements (even omitting David's great sin and totally ignoring the rebellious Northern Kingdom).

IV. The Restoration Books

After the seventy-year exile in Babylon, the nation that was once a *theocracy*, then a *monarchy*, became a mere *province* of world Gentile powers—first of Persia, then of Greece, then of Rome. The period covered is 536–420 B.C.

A. Ezra

In 536 B.C. King Cyrus issued a decree allowing the Jews to return to their homeland. About 50,000 Jews (a very small minority) went back under Zerubbabel to rebuild the temple. Ezra the priest took about 2,000 Jews with him in 458 B.C.

B. Nehemiah

In 444 B.C. Nehemiah obtained permission from the king of Persia to rebuild the walls of Jerusalem around the reconstructed temple. When the walls were finished, Ezra and Nehemiah led a reformation and revival in the Jewish state.

C. Esther

This book is not the last of the three Restoration books chronologically, since the events take place in Persia, between chapters 6 and 7 of Ezra. Perhaps the book is put last because it recounts the lives of those who did not bother to return to the Holy Land when they could have done so. Esther illustrates God working behind the scenes (His name is not even mentioned once) to protect His ancient people from antisemitic persecution, indeed from genocide. The instruments that He used were a beautiful and heroic Jewish queen and her shrewd cousin, Mordecai.

ENDNOTES

[1]Calvin's Geneva (1500's) and Puritan New England (1600's) were basically Reformed Protestant attempts at theocracy.

JOSHUA

Introduction

"The sacred canon here presents us with a book of history and historical art, such as our generation, prolific in writing on history, but nevertheless poor in historical feeling and perception, stands in pressing need of."

—Paulus Cassel

I. Unique Place in the Canon

Joshua is an indispensable bridge between the Books of Moses and the history of Israel in the land of Canaan. Both in the Hebrew book order and the modern Christian order Joshua is the sixth book of the OT. To Christians it is the first of the twelve "historical books" (Joshua through Esther); to Jews it is the first of what they call "the Former Prophets" (Joshua through Ezra-Nehemiah, putting Ruth and Chronicles in the "writings" at the end of the Hebrew OT).

Jensen stresses the book's importance in these words:

In a real sense Joshua is the *climax* of a progressive history as well as the *commencement* of a new experience for Israel. Thus its historical nexus gives it a strategic place in the Old Testament Scriptures.[1]

II. Authorship

While the book is anonymous, the ancient tradition that it is largely by Joshua himself, completed after his death by Eleazar the high priest and his son Phinehas, has much to com-

mend it. Joshua contains vivid material, suggesting that the author was an eyewitness. There are also passages in the first person ("I," "we"), such as 5:1, 6. Also the book specifically records that Joshua had some documents written (18:9; 24:26). The fact that Rahab was still alive (6:25) at the time of composition fits well with Joshua's being the main author.

III. Date

The date of Joshua is partly dependent on the date of the Exodus (15th or 13th century B.C.). The facts fit better with the early, more conservative date of the mid–1400's B.C. A date for Joshua between 1400 and 1350 B.C. seems likely for the following reasons: The book has to be earlier than Solomon (cf. 16:10 with 1 Kgs. 9:16) and also before his father David (cf. 15:63 with 2 Sam. 5:5–9). Since Joshua 13:4–6 calls the Phoenicians "Sidonians," it must be before the 1100's B.C. when Tyre subjugated Sidon, and before 1200 B.C. because the Philistines invaded Palestine after that time, yet they are not a problem in Joshua's time.

237

IV. Background and Theme

Just as Exodus is the story of God leading His people out of Egypt, so Joshua is the story of God leading His people into the Promised Land. He would complete the good work He began despite the unbelief of the nation. As we will see, the people hadn't changed; they were still faithless. Nevertheless, the Word of the Lord would be fulfilled and the seed of Abraham would be planted in the covenant land (Gen. 15:13–16) to take root and grow.

The events of this book follow those recorded in the last chapter of Deuteronomy. The people of Israel were encamped on the plains of Moab, east of the Jordan River. Moses had died, and Joshua had become commander-in-chief. He was about to lead the people across the Jordan and into the Promised Land. Law, as represented by Moses, cannot lead God's people into their inheritance. Only Christ in resurrection, pictured by Joshua, can do that.

We should pause to review some important facts about Joshua. Moses had changed his name from Hoshea to Joshua (Num. 13:16). He was an Ephraimite (Num. 13:8) and Moses' personal servant (Joshua 1:1). He was early a man engaged in fighting the Lord's battles. He led the Israelites in their first combat against the Amalekites (Ex. 17) and was the only general they had known since Egypt. But what equipped Joshua to replace Moses at the head of the nation was not his military prowess but his spiritual vitality and faith. As a young man he constantly attended the tent of the Lord (Ex. 33:11). He had been on Mount Sinai with Moses (Ex. 32:17). He and Caleb were the only ones who saw the Promised Land with believing eyes when the people had been at Kadesh Barnea thirty-eight years earlier (Num. 14:6–10). Trained by Moses, he was now commissioned by Jehovah, although he was over ninety years of age.

OUTLINE

Commentary

I. THE OCCUPATION OF THE PROMISED LAND (Chaps. 1—12)

A. Preparations for Crossing the Jordan (Chap. 1)

1:1–9 The LORD first delivered a solemn charge to **Joshua the son of Nun** concerning the task ahead of him. **The land** had been promised to **Israel**, but they must possess it, from the Negev at the south to **Lebanon** in the north, and from the Mediterranean on the west to **the River Euphrates** on the east (see vv. 3, 4). Joshua must **be strong, very courageous**, and obedient. Now, as then, we are assured of **good success** when we fill our hearts and minds with God's Word and obey it (v. 8).

Three times Joshua is told by the Lord to **be strong and very courageous** (vv. 6, 7, 9). The size and duration of the task ahead, the pressures of leading such an obstinate people, and the absence of his spiritual mentor, Moses,

were perhaps heavy on Joshua's mind at this time. But the Lord was not calling him without enabling him. There were good reasons for Joshua to **be strong**: *God's promise* (vv. 5, 6), a sure victory; *God's Word* (vv. 7, 8), a safe guide; *God's presence* (v. 9), a sustaining power.

T. Austin Sparks writes:

> The real battle of faith is joined here. Not what we are, but what He is! Not what we feel, but His facts.[2]

1:10–18 **The people** were to **prepare provisions** for their journey into **the land** of Canaan. As for the two and a half tribes which were settling east of the Jordan, the men were reminded by Joshua that they must help in the conquest of the land; **then** they could **return to** their families (vv. 12–15). To this they readily agreed (vv. 16–18). Any who turned back would **be put to death**.

In some hymns, crossing the Jordan

is likened to death and the land of
Canaan pictures heaven. But there
was conflict in Canaan, whereas there
is no conflict in heaven. Actually the
land of Canaan pictures our present
spiritual inheritance. It is all ours, but
we must possess it by obeying the
Word, claiming the promises, and
fighting the good fight of faith.

B. The Spies at Jericho (Chap. 2)

2:1a In preparation for the invasion, **Joshua the son of Nun sent out
two** spies **from Acacia Grove** to
Jericho. This was not an indication of
lack of faith on his part; rather, it was
a matter of military strategy. They
were not **to spy** out the whole **land**,
as had been done years earlier, but
only to look ahead one step at a time.

2:1b–24 The spies found shelter
in **the house of a harlot named Rahab**.
As Keil and Delitzsch point out, "Their
entering the house of such a person
would not excite so much suspicion."[3]
It is clear from the narrative that
Rahab had **heard** of the marvelous
victories which **the Lord** had **given** to
the Jewish people (vv. 8–11). She concluded that their **God** must be the
true **God**, and so she trusted in Him,
becoming a true convert. She proved
the reality of her faith by protecting
the spies, even though it meant
betraying her country.

The spies promised to spare Rahab
and her family if she hung a **scarlet
cord in the window** of her **home** and
if the **household** remained indoors
during the attack against Jericho (vv.
6–21). The **scarlet cord** makes us think
of a house protected by the blood, as
at the original Passover (Ex. 12).

When messengers from **the king
of Jericho** asked **Rahab** where the
spies were, she told them they had
already left the city (v. 5). While **the
men** of Jericho searched for **them** on

the road to the Jordan, Rahab sent
the spies westward **to the mountain**.
After hiding there for **three days**, the
spies escaped across the Jordan, carrying a confident report **to Joshua**
(vv. 22–24).

Rahab's "works" and not her
"words" justified her (Jas. 2:25). The
Bible does not commend her deceit
(vv. 4, 5) but it does commend her
faith (Heb. 11:31). James also calls her
deed a work of faith (Jas. 2:25). She
risked her life to save the lives of the
spies because she believed in the
power and sovereignty of their God.
So in our Lord's day some outside
the commonwealth of Israel showed
more faith than those who were
eyewitnesses of His glory (Luke 7:2–9).
Great faith, wherever it is found, is
always rewarded (see chap. 6), for it
is pleasing to God (Heb. 11:6).

C. Crossing the Jordan (3:1—5:1)

3:1–13 The time had come to
cross . . . the Jordan River, which was
now in flood stage. **The priests** were
instructed to go forth, carrying **the
ark of the covenant**. (The Kohathites
usually carried the ark, as in Numbers 4:1–15, but **the priests** were to
carry it on this special occasion.) **The
people** were ordered to follow the
ark at a distance, but always keeping
it in view. The ark speaks of Christ.
We should maintain a respectful distance by not irreverently trying to
solve mysteries concerning His Person that are too deep for the human
mind. Some of the worst heresies in
Christian history have arisen because
of brazen attempts to do this. But we
should always keep Christ in view.
This assures us of victory.

3:14–17 When the priests' **feet**
touched **the water** of **the Jordan**, a
miracle occurred. The river was
stopped at **the city** of **Adam**, some

The Jordan River is neither large nor impressive, but it has become the most famous river in the world because of scriptural events associated with it. This is one of the myriad of bends in the Jordan's path from the Sea of Galilee to the Dead Sea. (Photo by Willem Van Gemeren)

miles to the north. **The waters** piled up there **in a heap**, and whatever water was left in the bed of the river below that point drained into **the Salt (Dead) Sea**.

Similar stoppages of the Jordan near where Adam no doubt was located took place in 1267, when the river was dammed for ten hours, and in 1927 for twenty-one hours. Both *times it was due to earthquakes*.[4] However, D. K. Campbell argues that there is much here to suggest not merely perfect timing, but a special miracle:

> Many supernatural elements were brought together: (1) The event came to pass as predicted (3:13, 15). (2) The timing was exact (v. 15). (3) The event took place when the river was at flood stage (v. 15). (4) The wall of water was held in place for many hours, possibly an entire day (v. 16). (5) The soft, wet river bottom became **dry** at once (v. 17). (6) The water returned immediately as soon as the people had crossed over and **the priests** came up out of the river (4:18). Centuries later the Prophets Elijah and Elisha crossed the same river on dry ground to the east (2 Kgs. 2:8). Soon thereafter Elisha crossed back over the river on dry ground. If a natural phenomenon is necessary to explain the Israelites' crossing under Joshua, then one would have to conclude that two earthquakes occurred in quick sequence for Elijah and Elisha, which seems a bit presumptuous.[5]

God, represented by the ark, led the people into the Jordan even as He would lead them to victory west of the Jordan. He was demonstrating that His presence, which caused the waters to flee before Israel, was their hope of triumph, and not anything in themselves.

The priests walked to the middle of the riverbed and stayed there while **all Israel crossed over on dry ground**.

4:1–24 The LORD directed that **twelve men (one man from every tribe)** should **carry** one **stone** apiece **out of the** bed **of the Jordan** and erect **a memorial** marker where **Israel** first camped west of the Jordan. Accordingly, the monument was **set up** at **Gilgal** as a permanent reminder to future generations of God's miraculous stopping of the Jordan so that the Israelites could cross **over . . . on dry land**.

The tribes that received their inheritance east of Jordan—**Reuben, Gad, and half the tribe of Manasseh**—sent **armed** warriors over to help their brethren occupy the land of Canaan. Although the combined strength of the two and a half tribes was over 100,000 men (see Num. 26), only **forty thousand . . . crossed** the Jordan; the rest probably stayed behind to secure their land and protect their families.

After all the people had crossed over, including the men of the two and a half tribes, and after the **twelve stones** had been taken out of the Jordan, **Joshua set up twelve stones in the midst of the Jordan**, **where the . . . priests** were standing. Then as soon as **the priests** marched to the west bank with the ark of the covenant, **the waters of the Jordan** flowed down again in flood tide.

The stones in the riverbed speak of identification with Christ *in death*. Those on the west bank speak of identification with Christ *in resurrection*.

By cutting off the waters of the Jordan, **the Lord exalted Joshua in the sight of all Israel** as He had earlier exalted Moses. Up to now, Joshua had been a servant, humbly serving in Moses' shadow, learning the ways of God. Now was the time of his exaltation, for "he who humbles himself will be exalted" (Luke 14:11).

The people crossed **the Jordan on the tenth day of the first month**, five days short of a full forty years since the Exodus from Egypt, and just in time to prepare for the Passover (see Ex. 12:2, 3).

5:1 The heathen inhabitants of Canaan were seized with panic when they **heard** of the miraculous crossing of the Jordan by the Hebrew army.

D. Ceremonies at Gilgal (5:2–12)

5:2–9 This chapter tells about the events that took place **at Gilgal**, the first encampment Israel made in Canaan. There **the men** were **circumcised** (vv. 2–9). There they kept the Passover, the first in Canaan (v. 10). There the manna ceased (vv. 11, 12), and there Joshua met the Commander-in-chief of the host of the Lord's army, Jesus Christ (vv. 13–15).

The LORD directed **Joshua** to renew the rite of circumcision at this time. All the men **who came out of Egypt . . . had been circumcised**, but **the men of war had** all **died** in the meantime (Deut. 2:16). For **forty years** there had been no circumcision. A new generation had arisen during the **forty years** of wandering, and they now had to undergo this ceremony as a sign of their restoration to the full enjoyment of their covenant blessings. As long as they wandered in the desert, they were ridiculed by the Egyptians for not gaining the Promised Land. But now that they were in the land, **the reproach** was **rolled away** (v. 9). The **"second time"** (v. 2) means the second time that circumcision was practiced by the nation.

5:10 The Passover was **kept** four days after the Jordan was crossed (**on the fourteenth day of the month**). Notice Joshua's faith: Although he

was in enemy territory, he obeyed God by circumcising his soldiers and by keeping the Passover. These have been called "most unmilitary acts."

Through circumcision and the Passover the Lord was calling His people back to the basics of their relationship with Him. Both of these rites had been neglected in the wilderness.

Circumcision was a sign of the covenant between God and Abraham, and God in His faithfulness was keeping His unconditional promise by giving them the land (Gen. 15:18–21). It was also a picture of self-judgment and putting away the filth of the flesh, vitally necessary to victory. The Passover was a reminder of their redemption. Jehovah had bought them and freed them from slavery in Egypt. In observing the Passover the Jews were obeying the word of the Lord given through Moses at the time of the first Passover forty years earlier (Ex. 13:5). Grace was His motive in calling His people and bringing them out. Faithfulness was His guarantee that He would bring them in.

5:11, 12 The manna speaks of Christ in His Incarnation, the bread that came down from heaven as a provision for our wilderness needs. **The produce of the land** illustrates Christ in Resurrection, after entering into the blessings of Canaan. We feed on both. **The manna ceased on** the morning **after they** first ate the **parched grain**. "What a wonderful Time-keeper and Supplier God is!"

E. The Conquest of Jericho (5:13—6:27)

5:13, 14a The **"Man"** in verse 13 was the Angel of Jehovah—the Lord Jesus in one of His preincarnate appearances. He introduced Himself **as Commander of the army of the LORD.** Christ does not come merely to help

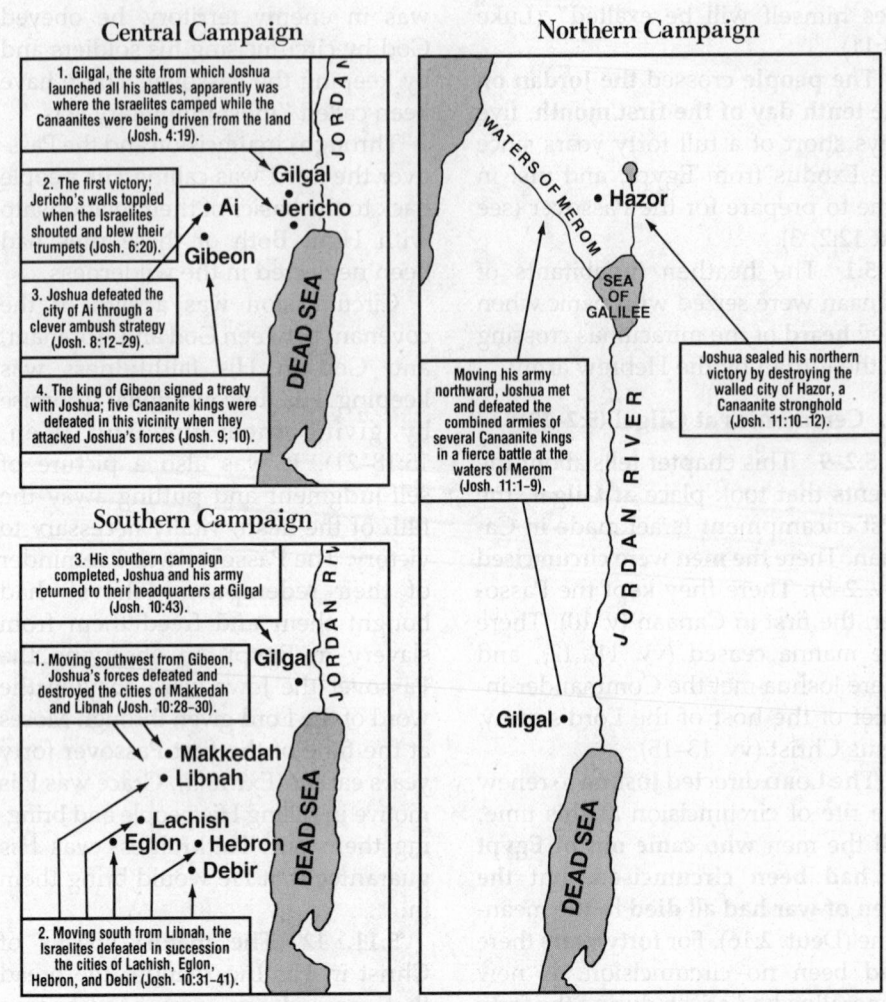

Joshua's Conquest

us, and certainly not to harm us; He comes to take full control.

5:14b, 15 Here is conclusive proof that **Joshua** was in the presence of God, and knew it. Mere angels never accepted worship, but here the Angel of the Lord *commands* worship, thereby proving His divine nature. Joshua must learn firsthand what Moses had to learn at the beginning of his ministry (Ex. 3)—the holiness and supremacy of the Lord.

6:1–21 The conquest of Canaan was accomplished by three military campaigns—central, southern, and northern. The central campaign, designed to divide and conquer, consisted of two major engagements, one at Jericho and the other at Ai.

Jericho was a fortified **city**, but her walls and gates served only to keep her inhabitants inside for judgment; they certainly didn't keep Israel out. It was a low city topographically (over 800 feet below sea level) and morally. It was a doomed city because it stood on God's land and its rightful tenants had come to claim their property. Many things in our lives loom out as Jerichos, impeding our progress in possessing our possessions. Perhaps we've been discouraged with the sheer immensity of our trials. If we will only claim the victory the Lord gives and move ahead in faith, with eyes fixed upon God for success, we too will see miracles.

Fear of the Jews had caused Jericho to be barricaded before the invaders arrived. For **six days** the Israelites **marched around the city**, **once** each day, returning at night to Gilgal. **On the seventh day . . . they marched around** it **seven times. When the priests blew the** rams' horns (**trumpets**), the Israelites let out a great shout. **The** walls **fell down flat**, and **the people** of God were able to enter **the city**.

Some Bible students think that the walls descended into the ground like an elevator, allowing the Israelites to walk across the top of the walls into the city. However it happened, it resulted from the faith of God's people (Heb. 11:30). Notice that **the ark** is mentioned seven times between verses 6 and 12.

Everything in **the city** was "accursed"—that is, **doomed by the Lord to destruction** as the firstfruits of Canaan. The inhabitants (except for **Rahab** and her family) and the livestock were to be **destroyed**, but the **silver, gold, bronze, and iron** were to be put **into the treasury of the Lord**. No one could take anything for himself.

When one realizes the moral perversity of the Canaanites, it is easy to see why God ordered the complete destruction of life within Jericho. Rather than criticize the Lord for administering deserved judgment to the wicked, we should marvel at His grace which preserved Rahab and her family from the same.

6:22–27 The faith that brought the walls down (Heb. 11:30) also **brought . . . Rahab** and **her relatives out** (Heb. 11:31). The grace of God not only made provision for her safety but also elevated her to a place in the ancestry of David and ultimately of the Lord Jesus Christ (Matt. 1:5, 6). Grace not only saves us from destruction but also guarantees our exaltation (Rom. 8:29, 30). Faith is the hand that takes hold of grace.

After **Rahab** and her family were escorted out safely, **the city** was **burned**. **Joshua** pronounced a curse on anyone who sought to rebuild Jericho as a fortress, prophesying that the man's oldest son would die when the **foundation** was laid and **his youngest** son would die when **its gates** were erected. See 1 Kings 16:34 for the fulfillment of this curse.

F. The Campaign at Ai (7:1—8:29)

Chapter 7 deals with the sin question in Canaan. Even though the people had crossed the Jordan, they were still prone to sin. Here is the story of Israel's *defeat* at Ai and Israel's *victory* over sin at Achor.

7:1–5 When **Joshua sent** spies **to Ai**, **they returned** with the confident report that the city was poorly defended and that it would not be necessary to send more than **two or three thousand** soldiers against it. But when an army of **about three thousand men** marched on Ai, they met defeat rather than victory.

7:6–10 Many times defeat comes after victory; that's when we least expect it. That's when we feel strongest in ourselves. The people didn't pray before going against Ai, nor did the Lord command them to go, as He had commanded them to take Jericho. Consequently, they learned painfully that all was not well; something had changed. **The Canaanites** were not any stronger, but Israel was weaker, and the reason was that sin had entered the camp. Although only one man was at fault, the whole nation was guilty (v. 11) and thirty-six men died (v. 5). **The Lord** told **Joshua** that this wasn't a time for prayer but a time for action (v. 10).

7:11–26 Joshua learned that the defeat was caused by sin in the camp. Someone had disobeyed the Lord in the conquest of Jericho by looting. We are not told what method was used to find the culprit; perhaps it was by casting lots. At any rate, the field was narrowed first to **the tribe**, then to **the family**, then to **the household**, and then to **the man—Achan**. He confessed to stealing a **Babylonian garment, two hundred shekels of silver,** and **a wedge of gold**. He also admitted to burying them **in the** floor of his **tent.**

"**When I saw . . . I coveted . . . and took**" (v. 21). The story of Achan provides a vivid illustration of James 1:14, 15: "But each one is tempted when he is drawn away by his own desires and enticed. Then, when desire has conceived, it gives birth to sin; and sin, when it is full-grown, brings forth death."

Achan, by taking something that was under the ban, became accursed himself (Deut. 7:26). It may seem harsh that all of Achan's family shared in his fate, but sin is a serious matter. Rahab's faith saved her entire household. Achan's sin condemned his. Besides, they must have been aware of his activities, since the stolen goods were buried under their tent. Perhaps his children even participated in his sin. The lesson God was teaching

His people was clear: Sin defiles the whole camp, and it must be totally eradicated whenever it surfaces.

As punishment for his crime, **Achan** and his household were **stoned** to death and then **burned**. Also burned were all his possessions, as well as the stolen goods. H. J. Blair comments:

> By Achan's death, the act of sacrilege was expiated, and the scene of the tragedy, the valley of Achor, became a door of hope as the people set their faces once more to the advance.[6]

8:1–29 On the second attempt, Joshua and his army captured **Ai** by the strategy of **ambush**. Although the details of the **ambush** are difficult to understand clearly, the general plan seems to have been as follows: A company of Israelites went past Ai under cover of darkness and hid **on the west side of the city**. In the morning, the rest of the soldiers attacked the city from the north. When the men of Ai counterattacked, Joshua and his men purposely retreated, drawing the inhabitants away from their city. Then **Joshua** stretched **out his spear;** that was the signal for the men lying in ambush to enter **the city** and **set** it **on fire**. Seeing their city on fire, **the men of Ai** panicked. It was then easy for the Israelites to trap Ai's soldiers on both sides, and destroy them.

Verse 3 says that **thirty thousand . . . men** were sent to **ambush . . . the city**, while verse 12 speaks of **five thousand**. There may have been two ambushes. But **thirty thousand** seems an unnecessarily large number for an ambush. Some believe that **thirty thousand** should read **thirty** *captains*, since the Hebrew word for thousand can also be translated chief. Others believe that **thirty thousand** is a copyist's error for **five thousand**. The five thousand men (v. 12) may have been sent to repel any possible attack by the men of **Bethel**, two miles west of **Ai**.

The Jews were allowed to keep the **livestock and the spoil . . . for themselves** in this particular engagement. If Achan had only waited, he might have gotten his booty without losing his life over it!

Israel lost thirty-six men in the first battle; this time they lost none as far as the biblical record mentions. Having purged themselves of defilement, they were once again safe in the midst of war. Victory in the Christian life is not the *absence of* conflict but the presence and protection of God *in the midst of* conflict.

G. The Confirmation of the Covenant at Shechem (8:30–35)

8:30–35 In obedience to the Word of God (Deut. 27:2–6), **Joshua built an altar** on **Mount Ebal** and inscribed upon **stones a copy of the Law of Moses**. The tribes were assembled, **half . . . in front of Mount Gerizim, and half . . . in front of Mount Ebal**. Joshua stood in the valley between them, and he either **read . . . the blessings and the cursings** that are found **written in the Book of the Law** of Moses or else instructed the Levites to read them (Deut. 27:14). "Persons are often said in Scripture to do that which they only command to be done."[7]

H. The Treaty with the Gibeonites (Chap. 9)

9:1–27 News of the military successes of Israel caused **all the kings** in Canaan to unite against **Joshua and Israel** (vv. 1, 2). But **the inhabitants of** the city of **Gibeon** and three other cities, **Chephirah, Beeroth, and Kirjath Jearim** (vv. 3, 17) decided that

it was futile to oppose the invaders. They knew that the Israelites had been ordered **to destroy all the** heathen **inhabitants of the land**. But they also knew that no such orders had been issued concerning nations outside Canaan (Deut. 20:10, 15). If they could persuade Joshua and his army that they had come on a **long journey . . . from a** distant **country**, they would not be killed.

So they disguised themselves in tattered **old garments** and **patched sandals**. Also, they brought with them **dry and moldy bread** and **torn . . . wineskins**. They told Joshua they had **come . . . from a very far country**, and everything about them seemed to support the statement.

The Israelites **did not ask counsel of the** Lord about the matter, but **made a covenant with** the Gibeonites. Three days later the scheme was exposed, and there was agitation among the Jews to kill the tricksters. But **the rulers** decided to honor the treaty by sparing the Gibeonites. However, they would henceforth serve **the congregation** as **woodcutters and water carriers** in connection with the service of **the altar of the Lord**.

Joshua and the princes were wise in keeping their oath, even though they had been **deceived** in the matter. Later Saul tried to exterminate the Gibeonites and was punished for it (2 Sam. 21).

I. The Southern Campaign (Chap. 10)

10:1–6 Chapter 10 records the southern campaign. When the **kings** of five Canaanite **cities . . . heard** that the Gibeonites had defected to the Israelites, they realized that this made the central hilly district vulnerable, and so they decided to **attack Gibeon**.

The Gibeonites **sent** an appeal for military assistance **to Joshua**.

10:7, 8 Once again **Joshua** heard those comforting words from the mouth of **the LORD**, **"Do not fear them."** He had heard them before the victory at Jericho and before the successful ambush of Ai. They guaranteed triumph despite the size of the opposition.

10:9–11 Assured of victory by the Lord, **Joshua** engaged the enemy's forces **at Gibeon**, causing them to flee. Two miracles occurred in the destruction of the enemy. First there was a tremendous hailstorm, which killed **more** men **than** the Israelites had slain. But note that they were discriminating **hailstones**—they killed only the enemies.

10:12–15 Then, at the request of **Joshua**, the **sun** and **moon** "stood **still**" (or "tarried"), prolonging the hours that the Israelites could continue to pursue and destroy the foe before they could escape to the security of their walled cities. It is literally descriptive language to say that the sun and the moon stood still. We use such language when we say that the sun rose or set. Various natural explanations have been given as to what actually happened at this time.[8] But it is enough to know that it was a miracle which resulted in an extended day for fighting. Spurgeon says,

> How He did it is no question for us. . . . It is not ours to try and soften down miracles, but to glorify God in them.[9]

The Book of Jasher (v. 13) may mean "The Book of the Upright." No book of that name can be identified today, and it certainly was not inspired.

The battle was a tremendous undertaking for Israel. They had marched all night and then fought through the longest day in history. They exerted themselves beyond ordinary limits, but still the victory was the Lord's (vv. 10, 11). With his usual insight Matthew Henry observes:

> But why needed Joshua to put himself and his men so much to the stretch? Had not God promised him that without fail He would *deliver the enemies into his hand?* It is true He had; but God's promises are intended, not to slacken and supersede, but to quicken and encourage our endeavours.[10]

10:16–27 The five kings were trapped **in a cave at Makkedah**, then slain and hung **on five trees**, and finally buried in **the cave**.

10:28–39 Following this, Joshua conquered the Canaanite cities of **Makkedah** (v. 28), **Libnah** (vv. 29, 30), **Lachish** (vv. 31, 32), **Gezer** (v. 33), **Eglon** (vv. 34, 35), **Hebron** (vv. 36, 37), and **Debir** (vv. 38, 39). The **king** of **Hebron** in verse 37 was a successor to the one slain in verse 26.

10:40–43 This paragraph summarizes the southern campaign.

The destruction referred to in this chapter must be taken generally, as noted by Haley:

> . . . Joshua swept over this region in too rapid a manner to depopulate it entirely. . . . All whom he pursued he destroyed; but he did not stop to search into every possible hiding place. This was left to be done by each tribe in its own inheritance.[11]

J. The Northern Campaign (Chap. 11)

11:1–9 News of Israel's mounting triumphs caused **the kings** of **the north** to confederate. They gathered **together at the waters of Merom**, north of the Sea of Galilee. **Joshua**

and his army **attacked** and defeated them. Then, in obedience to the Lord, Joshua **hamstrung their horses and burned their chariots**. To hamstring means to cut a tendon in the leg, disabling the horse.

11:10–15 The capital city of **Hazor** was **burned**; the other **cities that stood on their mounds** were **destroyed** but not **burned**. Perhaps Joshua felt that the cities standing on mounds would be useful to the Israelites who would settle there. The inhabitants of all the cities were killed, **and all the spoil was taken by the Israelites**. Complete obedience brings complete victory (v. 15).

11:16–20 These verses review Joshua's conquest of the land from Edom (**Seir**) in **the South** to **Mount Hermon** in the northeast and **the Valley of Lebanon** in the northwest. **Gibeon** escaped destruction. Jerusalem remained unconquered until the time of David. (The **Goshen** mentioned in verse 16 was not in Egypt but was an area to the south of Palestine.)

11:21–23 Special mention is made of the fact that the **Anakim** were **destroyed** in all the **cities** except in **Gaza, in Gath, and in Ashdod**. "The land rested from war" (v. 23) in the sense that the major battles were fought, though there was still a great deal of "mopping up" to be done.

K. Summary of Conquests (Chap. 12)

12:1–6 The first six verses take us back to the victory that God gave Moses over **Sihon, king of the Amorites**, and **Og, king of Bashan**. These victories are considered as part of the total conquest, since the territory was occupied by the two and a half tribes east of the Jordan River.

12:7–24 God had made a promise earlier to Israel before they crossed the Jordan: "He will deliver their

kings into your hand, and you will destroy their name from under heaven; no one shall be able to stand against you until you have destroyed them" (Deut. 7:24). Here are **thirty-one** instances of God's faithfulness (vv. 7–24); **Joshua** defeated **thirty-one . . . kings** on the west side of the **Jordan**.

II. THE SETTLEMENT OF THE PROMISED LAND (Chaps. 13—21)

A. The Lands Yet to Be Possessed (13:1–7)

13:1–6 Joshua was now an **old** man, and the entire **land** promised to the Israelites had not as yet been occupied by them. Verses 2–6 describe portions in the southwest and in the northeast that were still inhabited by the heathen. We know also that the land eastward to the Euphrates had been promised to the Jews, but it has never yet been occupied by them.[12]

13:7 The Lord instructed Joshua to **divide** the **land** which had already been conquered among **the nine tribes and half the tribe of Manasseh**.

B. The Allotment of the Land (13:8—19:51)

1. The Allotment to Reuben, Gad, and Half of Manasseh (13:8–33)

Two and a half tribes had already been assigned land east of **the Jordan**. It is described as follows: the entire territory occupied by the two and a half tribes (vv. 8–13); **Reuben** (vv. 15–23); **Gad** (vv. 24–28); and **half the tribe of Manasseh** (vv. 29–31).

Levi did not receive a tribal **inheritance** (v. 14), since that was the priestly tribe, and **the LORD** was its **inheritance** in a special way (v. 33).

Dropping Levi from the tribes leaves

only eleven tribes. But Joseph's two sons, Ephraim and Manasseh, are included in Joseph's place, and that raises the number to twelve again. The reason Joseph's sons are included is that they were adopted by Jacob as his own sons before his death (Gen. 48:5).

Special mention is made of the fact that **Balaam** was among those slain in Transjordan (v. 22). The Lord had not forgotten the terrible calamity that this wicked prophet caused His people (see Num. 23–25). "Be sure your sin will find you out" (Num. 32:23).

An interesting problem arises in verse 25. The tribe of **Gad** possessed some of **the land of the Ammonites**, which was forbidden in Deuteronomy 2:19. But this land had earlier been taken from the Ammonites by Sihon, king of the Amorites, and made part of his kingdom. So by the time Israel took the land from Sihon, it no longer belonged to the Ammonites.

The **Debir** mentioned in verse 26 is not the same city mentioned in the previous chapter. This city was east of the Jordan, while the one Joshua conquered was west of the river.

2. The Allotment to Judah (Chaps. 14, 15)

14:1–5 This chapter begins the distribution of the land on the west side of Jordan to **the nine tribes and the half-tribe**. The LORD had commanded ...Moses that the distribution be made **by lot**. This probably means that the general location of the tribal portion was determined by lot, but the size of the territory was according to the population of the tribe (Num. 26:53–56).

14:6–15 First in the list of tribes is **Judah** (14:6—15:63). The men of **Judah** led the armies of Israel (see Num. 10:14) and were the largest and most powerful tribe, boasting over 76,000 warriors.

Before giving the territorial boundaries, the Spirit of God records the noble request of **Caleb** for the city of **Hebron**. Though he was then **eighty-five years old**, his faith, courage, and **strength** were unabated. He longed for more spiritual conquests and received **Hebron** for his **inheritance**.

Hebron meant not only the city but the country around it as well (v. 12). The city had been conquered earlier by Joshua (10:36, 37). It later was given to the priests, but **Caleb** kept the surrounding region for his **inheritance**.

Caleb had been spared from the plague that took the lives of the unbelieving spies **forty-five years** earlier (Num. 14:36–38). He had been preserved during the wilderness wanderings. He had survived several years of war in Canaan. He knew that God would not have **kept** him **alive**, promising him a reward for his faith, only to give him over to the **Anakim**. So what if they were giants? They were on his land, and he would **drive them out** by the strength of God. He still saw things through the eyes of faith and not as they appeared outwardly. This was the secret of his abiding **strength** and amazing success. He was not about to retire (although **eighty-five years old**) until he possessed his possessions.

15:1–12 The boundaries of **Judah** are described in verses 1–12. It is almost impossible to trace them with exactness at the present time. This may cause some to wonder why all these details are included in the Bible. The answer is, of course, that these details are important in the sight of God. They are inspired and profitable, full of rich spiritual lessons.

15:13–20 Caleb's conquest of

Hebron is recorded in verse 14. He offered his **daughter**, **Achsah**, to whoever would capture **Kirjath Sepher** (Debir) (v. 16). Caleb's nephew, **Othniel**, was the one who **took** the city and gained the bride (v. 17). He later became the first judge in Israel (Judg. 3:9). **Achsah . . . persuaded** Othniel **to ask her father for a field** (v. 18). Her words **"since you have given me land"** imply that Othniel had done this and obtained **the field**. Then Achsah requested **upper** and **lower springs** to **water** the land.

Some cities, like **Debir** and **Hebron**, had to be taken more than once because of the guerrilla warfare of the Canaanites (see notes on chap. 10). It should also be noted that there was more than one city with the same name (e.g., Debir).

15:21–63 The cities of Judah's territory are listed in verses 21–63. Some of these cities should be familiar to us from our study of the patriarchs: **Hebron** (v. 54) (also called **Kirjath Arba** and Mamre) was familiar to Abraham, Isaac, and Jacob (Gen. 13:18; 35:27), and they were all buried there (Gen. 23:17–20). Perhaps this is what made it so precious to the spiritually discerning Caleb. **Beersheba** (v. 28) means "the well of the oath"; the patriarchs spent much time there. It was a place of renewal, refreshment, and rest (Gen. 21:31; 26:33; 46:1). **Jerusalem** (v. 63) was held by **the Jebusites**. It was not until the time of David that they were finally driven out of Jerusalem (2 Sam. 5:6, 7).

These cities provided a rich heritage for Judah and a powerful stimulus to strengthen their faith. The God of Abraham, Isaac, and Jacob was in the midst of their children to perform His ancient promise.

When we count the cities in verses 21–32, we find that there are thirty-eight, although verse 32 says there are only twenty-nine. Nine of these cities belonged to Simeon, whose inheritance was within the borders of Judah (19:1–9). That leaves **twenty-nine . . . cities** belonging to Judah. There is a similar problem in numbering in verses 33–36; fifteen cities are enumerated, but perhaps **Gederah and Gederothaim** are two names for the same city, leaving the total of **fourteen cities** mentioned in verse 36.[13]

Note the last verse especially. The upper part of the city, Mount Zion, was not taken until the time of David. The lower city, **Jerusalem**, was taken by Judah (Judg. 1:8), then later recaptured by **the Jebusites** (Judg. 1:21). **Jerusalem** is listed as belonging to Benjamin (18:28) as well as to **Judah**; it was located on the border between these two tribes.

3. The Allotment to Joseph (Chaps. 16, 17)

16:1-4 **The tribe of Joseph** is taken up next. To **Joseph** had been given the birthright (i.e., the double portion, 1 Chron. 5:1) which Reuben had forfeited (Gen. 49:4). The general boundaries of Joseph's territory are given in verses 1–4. This was, of course, divided between **Ephraim** and half of the tribe of **Manasseh** which settled west of the **Jordan**.

16:5–10 Ephraim's boundaries are described in verses 5–10. Pay particular attention to verse 10. Failure to **drive out the Canaanites** brought grief to the Israelites in their later history.

17:1-13 The inheritance of **Manasseh** was partly in **Gilead and Bashan**, on the east side of the Jordan (v. 1), and partly on the west side (vv. 7–11). The territory west of the Jordan was flanked **on the north** by six Canaanite fortresses—**Beth Shean**,

Ibleam, Dor, En Dor, Taanach, and Megiddo (vv. 11, 12).

Some of the **cities of Ephraim** were in the territory **of Manasseh**, and some of **Manasseh's towns** were in the territory of **Asher . . . and Issachar** (vv. 7–12).

The **daughters** of **Zelophehad** inherited with the **sons** of **Manasseh**, as God had **commanded Moses** (vv. 3, 4) (Num. 27:1–7). This was done to insure that the house of Zelophehad would have a portion even though there were no male heirs. **The daughters** had to marry within their own tribe so that the land which belonged to Manasseh would not be absorbed by another tribe through intermarriage (Num. 36:1–13).

17:14–18 After Ephraim and Manasseh had received their adjoining allotments west of the Jordan, they complained that they had **only one lot** (v. 14) and that they were hemmed in by fortresses on the north (v. 16). Joshua turned all their arguments against them. When they said they needed more land because they were a numerous **people** (v. 14), he told them to use their manpower to **clear** out **the forest** in their territory and settle there (v. 15). When they complained that there were **Canaanites** within their borders who had **chariots of iron** (v. 16), he assured them that they had superior power to **drive out the Canaanites** (v. 18). The "**one lot**" of verse 14 means the combined territories of Ephraim and Manasseh west of the Jordan. When Joshua said, "**You shall not have only one lot**" (v. 17b), he didn't mean that they would get additional land but that they must occupy all the land that had been given to them.

4. The Allotment to the Rest of the Tribes (Chaps. 18, 19)

18:1 The encampment of **Israel** now changes from Gilgal to **Shiloh**. Here **the tabernacle** is **set up**, and here it remains until the days of Samuel. The division of the land continues here.

18:2–10 **Judah** and **Joseph** had received their inheritance by casting of **lots**, but there were still **seven tribes** west of the Jordan **which had not** been assigned **their inheritance**. Therefore, **Joshua** sent a group of **men**, **three** from **each tribe**, to **survey** the remaining **seven** tribes by lot.

18:11–28 Benjamin's boundaries are given in verses 11–20, and **the cities** in verses 21–28. Benjamin's portion was small, but it was choice. It occupied the heart of the land and possessed within its borders the firstfruits of Israel's labors in Canaan.

Gilgal was in Benjamin's territory, the first campsite west of the Jordan. The memorial stones were there to bear witness to the miraculous crossing of the Jordan. There the people kept the first Passover in Canaan, and began feeding on the produce of the land. There the nation was once again circumcised and the reproach of Egypt was rolled away. There was hardly a more historically significant spot in all of Canaan, because no other place taught so many spiritual lessons.

The ruins of **Jericho** were still visible in Benjamin's land. Her walls, once thought invincible, were now laid low. The portion belonging to Rahab's house remained standing as a testimony to the grace of God, which always responds to faith. A Benjamite could always visit here whenever he needed a fresh reminder that the battle was the Lord's.

Bethel (*the house of God*) caused the Benjamites to remember the faith of their fathers and the faithfulness of Israel's divine Deliverer (Gen. 28:18–22; 35:1–15).

Jerusalem was destined to be the capital city, but it was not until the son of Jesse came that the Jebusites would be driven from their mountain fortress.

Benjamin's land encompassed many evidences and signs of past, present, and future blessings. What a rich lot fell to Jacob's youngest son!

19:1–9 Simeon's inheritance was in the midst of **the inheritance of** the tribe of **Judah**. It seems that Judah's land was so **large** that the tribe could not occupy its portion, so some was assigned to **Simeon**. This is a fulfillment of Jacob's prophetic word concerning Simeon, "I will divide them in Jacob, and scatter them in Israel" (Gen. 49:7).

Beersheba and **Sheba** (v. 2) probably refer to the same place; hence a total of only **thirteen cities** as mentioned in verse 6. Some cities were listed in detailing the borders of individual portions although they were not within the land, so sometimes the number of cities given doesn't match the number stated in the text (e.g., vv. 15, 30, 38).

19:10–39 The borders of the remaining five tribes are given next: **Zebulun** (vv. 10–16); **Issachar** (vv. 17–23); **Asher** (vv. 24–31); **Naphtali** (vv. 32–39); and **Dan** (vv. 40–48). Dan received some of Judah's cities (cf. v. 41 with 15:33).

19:40–48 The original territory allotted to **Dan** was in the southwest, bordering on the Mediterranean Sea,

and included the cities of **Joppa** and **Ekron** (vv. 40–46). Later, when this territory proved too small, some of the tribe migrated to Laish (**Leshem**) in the northeast and changed the name of the city to **Dan** (vv. 47, 48; cf. Judg. 18).

19:49–51 Verse 51 brings to **an end** the division of **the country**. The cities of refuge had to be set apart (chap. 20) and the Levitical cities had yet to be appointed (chap. 21), but Joshua's work was almost done. He received **Timnath Serah, according to the word of the** Lord (v. 50).

C. The Cities of Refuge (Chap. 20)

The next step was to set apart six **cities of refuge**, three **on** each **side of the Jordan** River, where a manslayer might **flee** from **the avenger of blood**. A manslayer was someone who **accidentally** killed another **person**. The **avenger of blood** was usually a close relative of the slain person who sought to avenge the dead. If the manslayer could flee to a city of refuge, he found sanctuary there **until the death of the . . . high priest. Then** he could **return . . . to his** native **city** in safety.

THE CITIES OF REFUGE

The cities of refuge are interesting and of theological importance. MacLear gives traditional details about the cities:

> Jewish commentators tell us how in later times, in order that the asylum offered to the involuntary homicide might be more secure—(a) the roads leading to the cities of refuge were always kept in thorough repair, and required to be about 32 cubits (about 48 feet) broad; (b) all obstructions were removed that might stay the flier's foot or hinder his speed; (c) no hillock was left, no river was allowed over which there was not a bridge;

(d) at every turning there were posts erected bearing the words 'Refuge,' to guide the unhappy man in his flight; (e) when once settled in such a city the manslayer had a convenient habitation assigned to him, and the citizens were to teach him some trade that he might support himself.[14]

These cities picture the nation of Israel and its guilt in connection with the slaying of the Messiah. Christ is the City of Refuge to whom penitent Israel may flee for sanctuary. D. L. Moody noted that "the cities of refuge are a type of Christ, and their names are significant in that connection."[15]

The cities of refuge and the meaning of the names are as follows:

West of Jordan
Kedesh—Holiness
Shechem—Strength
Kirjath-Arba or Hebron—
    Fellowship

East of Jordan
Ramoth-Gilead—Uplifting
Golan—Happiness
Bezer—Safety

Thus Christ provides every blessing suggested by the names of these cities. A glance at the map will show that the cities of refuge were strategically located so that no point in the land was more than thirty miles from one of them. Moody makes the application:

As the cities of refuge were so situated as to be accessible from every part of the land, so Christ is very accessible to needy sinners (1 John 2:1, 2).[16]

Notice the parallels between the temporal salvation offered the manslayer in the cities of refuge and the eternal salvation offered the sinner in Christ. The roads to the city were clear and well-marked, just like the way of salvation, so that none would make a mistake and lose his life. The cities were spread throughout the land and easily accessible to all, even as Christ is accessible to all men. Crisis drove people to the city of refuge, and many times a crisis is needed to drive people to the Lord Jesus for refuge. There was no neutral ground for the guilty person—he was either safe in the city or subject to the wrath of the blood avenger. Each individual is either safe in Christ or under the judgment of God (John 3:36).‡

D. The Levitical Cities (Chap. 21)

21:1–42 Forty-eight cities (v. 41) with their common-lands for pasture, including the cities of refuge, were assigned to **the Levites** as the Lord had commanded (Num. 35:2–8).

Kohathites:

  (a) The sons **of Aaron** (i.e., the priests)—**thirteen cities** out of **Judah,** . . . **Simeon, and** . . . **Benjamin**.

  (b) **The rest of the** Kohathites— **ten cities** out of **Ephraim,** . . . **Dan, and** . . . **the half-tribe of Manasseh**.

Gershonites: **thirteen cities** out of **Issachar,** . . . **Asher,** . . . **Naphtali, and** . . . **the half-tribe of Manasseh**.

Merarites: **twelve cities** out of **Reuben,** . . . **Gad, and** . . . **Zebulun**.

Every tribe gave four cities except Judah and Simeon, which gave nine cities between them, and Naphtali, which gave three cities.

The cities **of refuge**, being cities of **the Levites** (vv. 13, 21, 27, 32, 36, 38), were scattered throughout all the tribes of Israel to fulfill the prophecy of

Jacob (Gen. 49:5–7) and to better facilitate their teaching ministry to the nation.

21:43 This verse must be read in the light of other Scripture. It does not mean that Israel occupied **all the land** from the river of Egypt to the Euphrates; instead, it means that the **land** which Joshua divided was in fulfillment of God's promise that He would give them every place that the sole of their feet walked upon (Josh. 1:3).

21:44 Likewise, verse 44 must be interpreted carefully. There were still **enemies** within the land; not all the Canaanites had been destroyed. But that was not God's fault; He fulfilled His promise by defeating every foe against which the Israelites fought. If there were still undefeated foes and pockets of resistance, it was because Israel did not claim God's promise.

21:45 Note verse 45. **The LORD** had fulfilled every promise. **Not one word failed.** What a tribute to God's faithfulness! But Israel did not appropriate every promise.

E. The Altar East of the Jordan (Chap. 22)

22:1–9 When the land west of the Jordan had been divided, **Joshua** permitted **the Reubenites, the Gadites, and half the tribe of Manasseh** to **return** to their territory east **of the Jordan,** as originally agreed. He also told them to take with them their share of **the spoil** from the battles they had fought.

It was over seven years since they had left their loved ones to fight the Canaanites. They endured the hardships of combat until the land was secured. We too are called upon by our Commander to endure hardships and fight the good fight of faith to further the kingdom of God on earth

(1 Tim. 6:12; 2 Tim. 2:3). This kind of sacrifice is not easy, but it is an essential ingredient in the life that pleases God. Men with fiery zeal are needed on the battlefield today:

> Must I be carried to the skies on
>   flowery beds of ease,
> While others fought to win the prize,
>   and sailed through bloody seas?
>
> Sure I must fight if I would reign;
>   increase my courage, Lord;
> I'll bear the toil, endure the pain,
>   supported by Thy Word.
>   —*Isaac Watts*

22:10, 11 On the way home these men decided to erect **an altar** near the banks of **the Jordan.** When the other nine and a half tribes heard about it, they were highly incensed. They feared that it was a rival altar to the one at Shiloh. They feared too that it might become an idolatrous altar in time to come and that God would punish the entire nation because of it.

22:12–20 Before declaring **war** on the tribes east of the Jordan, **the children of Israel sent** a delegation to interview them and offered them land west of the Jordan if they considered their own territory **unclean** (v. 19).

In dealing with the men who built the altar, **Phinehas** and the others recalled how Israel had suffered because of **the iniquity of Peor** (v. 17; cf. Num. 25) and **the trespass** of **Achan** (v. 20; cf. chap. 7).

They saw this altar as another threat to their welfare; hence their strong reaction to it. As a people they had learned that sin defiled the whole camp, and that God held the nation responsible for the behavior of its individuals.

22:21–29 Then the men **of Reuben, . . . Gad, and half the tribe of Manasseh** explained that this was not an altar of **sacrifice** at all. It was simply a memorial **altar**, testifying to future generations that the tribes east of the Jordan were indeed a part of the nation of Israel.

22:30–34 The other tribes were **pleased** by this explanation, and war was averted. The eastern tribes **called the altar** *Witness*, meaning that it was **a witness between** the tribes on both sides of the Jordan **that the LORD is** the true **God**.

F. Joshua's Farewell Address to the Leaders of Israel (Chap. 23)

This is the first of two farewell addresses by **Joshua**. Here he spoke to the leadership of Israel.

Joshua's command to be both courageous and scriptural (v. 6) echo the words of the Lord to him years earlier (1:7). He had since proven the veracity of them in the crucible of life and was now able to confidently pass them on to the following generation.

He reminded them of the faithfulness of God in fulfilling His promises concerning the land and concerning its heathen inhabitants. God would continue to **drive . . . out** the enemy, but the people would have to be obedient to Him. Above all, they should keep themselves free from the idolatry of the nations or from intermarrying with the Canaanites. Otherwise these pagans would be a continual source of trouble to Israel.

None of God's words had **failed** (v. 14). This does not mean that all of the land was as yet in Jewish hands, for the Lord Himself had said that He would not drive out the inhabitants all at once but gradually (Deut. 7:22). The fact that not one promise of the Lord's had yet failed was the strong encouragement that Joshua was using to urge the leaders to finish the job he had started. To this exhorta-

tion he attached a warning (vv. 5, 16) that Jehovah would be just as faithful in destroying them **from** off **the good land** as He would be in destroying the Canaanites, if they forgot their covenant and turned to idols.

The NT parallel to this chapter is 2 Corinthians 6:14–18. Separation is vital for the man of God. We cannot cleave to the Lord and be bound to His enemies at the same time.

G. Joshua's Farewell Address to the People of Israel (24:1–15)

24:1–14 The second farewell message, this one to the people, was delivered at **Shechem**.

Joshua reviewed the history of the people of God, beginning with **Terah** and continuing on through the time of **Abraham**, **Isaac**, and **Jacob**. He reminded the people of the mighty deliverance from Egypt, the wilderness wandering, and the victory over the Moabites on the east side of Jordan. Then he recounted their entrance into the Promised Land, their victory at **Jericho**, and their destruction of **kings** in Canaan (vv. 2–13). The **darkness** in verse 7 points back to Exodus 14:19, 20, where the cloud produced light for the Israelites and darkness for the Egyptians.

In this succinct summary of history from Genesis to Joshua, one outstanding fact is evident: the sovereignty of God. Notice how He tells the story: **I took** (v. 3), **I gave** (v. 4), **I sent** (v. 5), **I brought** (vv. 6–8), **I would not listen** (v. 10), **I delivered** (v. 11), **I sent** (v. 12), **I have given** (v. 13). Jehovah works according to His eternal purposes, and who can stay His hand? Such a God is to be feared and obeyed (v. 14).

24:15 The choice here was not between **the LORD** and idols: Joshua assumed that the people had *already* decided *against* serving God. So he challenged them to **choose** between **the gods** which their ancestors had served in Mesopotamia and **the gods of the Amorites** that they had found in Canaan. Joshua's noble decision for himself and his household has been an inspiration to succeeding generations of believers: **"But as for me and my house, we will serve the** **Lord."**

H. The Covenant Renewed at Shechem

24:16–28 When the people promised to **serve** Jehovah, **Joshua** said, **"You cannot serve the Lord"** (v. 19). This means that they could not serve Jehovah and worship idols too. Joshua doubtless realized that the people would drift into idolatry, because even then they had **foreign gods** in their tents (v. 23). **The people** persisted in promising allegiance to their **God**, so **Joshua** erected **a large stone** marker **under the oak** as **a witness** of the **covenant** made by Israel. (The **sanctuary of the Lord** mentioned in verse 26 does not refer to the tabernacle, which was at Shiloh, but simply to a holy place.)

Regarding the problem of idols, Carl Armerding writes:

Idolatry seems to have been one of Israel's besetting sins. Their earliest ancestors served other gods, as we have seen (v. 2). When Jacob and his family left Laban, it was Rachel who carried off her father's gods (Gen. 31:30–34). But when they arrived in the land, Jacob ordered his household to put away these "strange gods," and he hid them under an oak tree that was by Shechem (Gen. 35:2, 4). And in the same place Joshua urged his generation to put away the gods which their fathers served (v. 14).[17]

I. The Death of Joshua

24:29–33 **Joshua . . . died** at the age of **one hundred and ten years** and was **buried** in the city **of his inheritance**. The people of **Israel** remained true to **the Lord** as long as the men of Joshua's generation lived. We do not know who penned the last verses of the book, nor is such knowledge necessary, or else it surely would have been included.

The bones of Joseph, which had been carried **out of Egypt** by his request, were now **buried at Shechem** (Gen. 50:24; Ex. 13:19).

Finally, **Eleazar the son of Aaron died** and was **buried in the mountains of Ephraim**.

Three burials are mentioned in the last five verses of this book: Joshua's (vv. 29–31), Joseph's (v. 32), and Eleazar's (v. 33). All three were buried in Joseph's territory. All three had served their God and their country well. Joshua and Joseph were great deliverers during their lives, and Eleazar was a deliverer in his death, for he was the high priest and his death set free all who had fled to a city of refuge (20:6). Like the books of Genesis and Deuteronomy, Joshua closes with the toll of the death bell over great and godly men. "God buries His workmen but continues His work."

ENDNOTES

[1](Intro) Irving L. Jensen, *Joshua, Rest-Land Won*, p. 14.

[2](1:1–9) T. Austin Sparks, *What Is Man?* p. 104.

[3](2:1) C. F. Keil and Franz Delitzsch, "Joshua," in *Biblical Commentary on the Old Testament*, VI:34.

[4](3:14–17) Donald K. Campbell, "Joshua," in *The Bible Knowledge Commentary*, I:335.

[5](3:14–17) *Ibid*.

[6](7:11–26) Hugh J. Blair, "Joshua," *The New Bible Commentary*, p. 229.

[7](8:30–35) R. Jamieson, A. R. Fausset, and D. Brown, *Critical and Experimental Commentary*, II:23.

[8](10:12–15) Three views that recognize that a unique miracle took place and explain (rather than explain away) the text are as follows:

1. That God actually restrained (or halted) the earth's rotation while the sun was above Joshua, making the rotation last forty-eight hours. There are parallels in other ancient cultures that speak of "a long day," which may well have been Joshua's long day.

2. Translating "stand still" (Heb. *dōm*) as "leave off" or "cease" (as in 2 Kgs. 4:6 and Lam. 2:18), some see this as a prayer for relief from the blazing sun on Joshua's troops, the very long hailstorm being God's answer to Joshua's prayer.

3. Since Joshua attacked in the early morning, some believe he was praying for the sun to "hold off" and for semi-darkness to continue. The hailstorm would then have been God's answer to prayer.

The first view seems to fit in best with the text: "So the sun stood still in the midst of heaven, and did not hasten to go down for about a whole day" (v. 13b).

[9](10:12–15) C. H. Spurgeon, *Spurgeon's Devotional Bible*, p. 168. For a brief but helpful treatment of the scientific aspects of the text see Chapter X of *Difficulties in the Bible* by R. A. Torrey (Chicago: Moody Press, 1907).

[10](10:12–15) Matthew Henry, *Matthew Henry's Commentary on the Whole Bible*, II:59.

[11](10:40–43) John Haley, *Alleged Discrepancies of the Bible*, p. 324.

[12](13:1–6) Under Solomon the kingdom did reach to that part of the Euphrates River in the northwest as far as lands under tribute were concerned, but if the entire river is meant as an eastern boundary it must still be a future event.

[13](15:21–63) Keil and Delitzsch maintain that these and similar numerical problems in the OT are simply copyists' errors ("Joshua," pp. 163–64). For further discussion on apparent discrepancies, see the Commentary on 2 Chronicles.

[14](Essay) G.F. MacLear, *The Cambridge Bible for Schools and Colleges, The Book of Joshua*, p. 183.

[15](Essay) D. L. Moody, *Notes from My Bible*, pp. 48, 49.

[16](Essay) *Ibid.*, p. 49.

[17](24:16–28) Carl Armerding, *The Fight for Palestine*, p. 149.

BIBLIOGRAPHY

Blair, Hugh J. "Joshua." In *The New Bible Commentary*. Grand Rapids: Wm. B. Eerdmans Publishing Company, 1953.

Campbell, Donald K. "Joshua." In *The Bible Knowledge Commentary*. Wheaton, IL: Victor Books, 1985.

Freedman, H. "Joshua." In *Soncino Books of the Bible*, Vol. 2. London: The Soncino Press, 1967.

Grant, F. W. "Joshua." In *The Numerical Bible*, Vol. 2. Neptune, N.J.: Loizeaux Bros., 1977.

Henry, Matthew. "Joshua." In *Matthew Henry's Commentary on the Whole Bible*. Vol. 2. McLean, VA: MacDonald Publishing Company, n.d.

Jensen, Irving L. *Joshua: Rest-Land Won*. Everyman's Bible Commentary. Chicago: Moody Press, 1966.

Keil, C. F., and Franz Delitzsch. "Joshua." In *Biblical Commentary on the Old Testament*. Vol. 6. Grand

Rapids: Wm. B. Eerdmans Publishing Company, 1971.

Kroll, Woodrow Michael. "Joshua." In the *Liberty Bible Commentary. Old Testament*. Lynchburg, VA: The Old Time Gospel Hour, 1982.

MacLear, G. F. *The Cambridge Bible for Schools and Colleges, The Book of Joshua*. London: C. J. Clay and Sons, 1888.

Pink, Arthur W. *Gleanings in Joshua*. Chicago: Moody Press, 1964.

JUDGES

Introduction

"There is much in Judges to sadden the heart of the reader; perhaps no book in the Bible witnesses so clearly to our human frailty. But there are also unmistakable signs of the divine compassion and long-suffering. . . . As the lives of these lesser-saviours are considered, there may be a realization of the need in modern times of a greater Saviour, of unblemished life, who is able to effect a perfect deliverance, not only in time but for eternity."

—Arthur E. Cundall

I. Unique Place in the Canon

God bringing strength out of human weakness is uniquely chronicled in this fascinating book. In fact, in a sense, the book of Judges is a commentary on the three verses, "But God has chosen the foolish things of the world to put to shame the wise, and God has chosen the weak things of the world to put to shame the things which are mighty; and the base things of the world and the things which are despised God has chosen, and the things that are not, to bring to nothing the things that are, that no flesh should glory in His presence" (1 Cor. 1:27–29). For example, Ehud was a left-handed Benjamite (3:12–30), the left hand being thought of as weaker than the right. Shamgar used an oxgoad, a rather disreputable weapon, with which to slay 600 enemies (3:31). Deborah was a member of the "weaker sex" (though she herself was not weak!) (4:1—5:31). Barak's 10,000 footsoldiers were a poor match, humanly speaking, for Sisera's 900 iron chariots (4:10, 13). Jael, also a member of the weaker sex, killed Sisera by driv-

ing a tent pin through his skull (4:21). She held the pin with her left hand (5:26, Septuagint). Gideon marched against the enemy with an army which the Lord had reduced from 32,000 to 300 (7:1–8). Barley bread, the food of the poor, suggests poverty and feebleness (7:13). The unconventional weapons of Gideon's army were earthenware pitchers, torches, and trumpets (7:16), and the pitchers had to be smashed (7:19). Abimelech was felled by a woman's hand hurling a piece of millstone (9:53). The name "Tola" means worm (10:1). When we meet Samson's mother, she is a nameless, barren woman (13:2). And Samson killed 1000 Philistines with the jawbone of a donkey (15:15).

II. Authorship

Although Judges is anonymous, the Jewish Talmud and early Christian tradition say that Judges, Ruth, and Samuel were all written by Samuel. This view may be supported by 1 Samuel 10:25, which indicates the prophet was a writer. Also the

261

internal indications of date of writing fit in with Samuel's *time* at the very least.

III. Date

Judges is best dated in the first half-century of the monarchy (1050–1000 B.C.) for the following reasons:

First of all, the repeated phrase "in those days there was no king in Israel" (17:6; 18:1; 19:1; 21:25) suggests that there *was* a king at the time of writing.

Second, since 1:21 shows the Jebusites were still in Jerusalem, a date before David captured that city is needed. Finally, Gezer, mentioned in 1:29, was later given to Solomon by Pharaoh as a wedding present, implying a date before that event. Thus Saul's reign or the early years of David's rule seem very likely.

IV. Background and Theme

The book of Judges takes up the history of the nation of Israel after Joshua's generation had died. The people had failed to drive out the heathen inhabitants of Canaan completely. In fact, they had mingled with the pagans and were practicing idolatry. As a result, God repeatedly delivered His people into the hands of Gentile oppressors. This servitude brought the Jews to the place of repentance and contrition. When they cried out to the Lord to deliver them, He raised up judges. It is from these leaders that the book gets its name.

The events in the book span about 325 years, from Othniel to Samson.

The judges were military leaders rather than simply jurists. By heroic deeds of faith they executed God's judgment or overthrew their oppressors, thereby restoring a measure of peace and freedom to the people. Twelve judges were raised up to deliver Israel. Some are given extensive coverage in the book while others are mentioned in only one or two verses. They came from nine different tribes and delivered their people from the Mesopotamians, Moabites, Philistines, Canaanites, Midianites, and Ammonites. No judge ruled over the entire nation until Samuel.

The book of Judges is not strictly chronological. The first two chapters contain introductory material, both historical and prophetical. The record of the judges themselves (chaps. 3—16) is not necessarily chronological. Some of the judges may have been conquering their enemies at the same time but in different sections of the land. This is important to remember, since the number of years mentioned in the book, if added consecutively, totals over 400, which is more time than the Bible allots for this period (Acts 13:19, 20; 1 Kgs. 6:1).

The closing chapters (17—21) record events that took place during the time of the judges, but they are placed at the end of the book to give a picture of the religious, moral, and civil corruption in Israel during this period. The character of the times is well-described in the key verse (17:6): "In those days there was no king in Israel, everyone did what was right in his own eyes."

If we believe that every word of God is pure and that all Scripture is profitable, then it follows that Judges contains important spiritual themes and lessons for us. Some of these lessons are hidden in the names of the Gentile oppressors and the judges

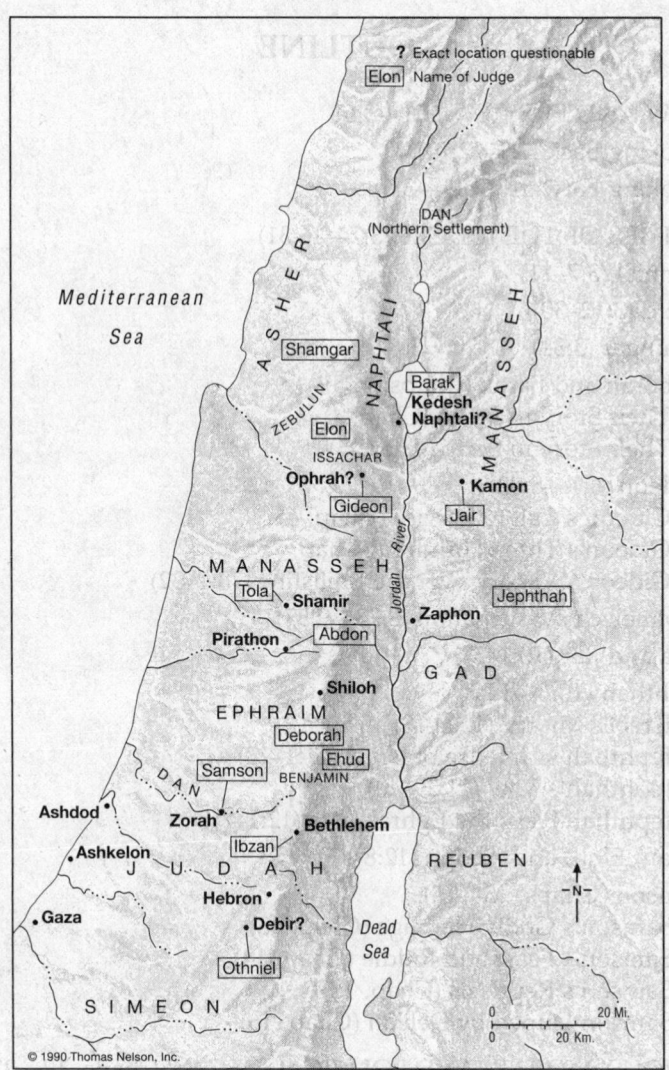

? Exact location questionable

Elon Name of Judge

The Judges of Israel

© 1990 Thomas Nelson, Inc.

who delivered Israel. The oppressors picture the powers of this world that seek to bring God's people into bondage. The judges symbolize the means by which we fight the spiritual warfare.

In our comments we have included some practical applications, many taken from old classic works.[1]

There is always a danger of taking the study of types or figures to an extreme. We have tried to avoid any interpretations that are strained or fanciful. Also, it must be admitted that the meanings of some of the names are uncertain. We have given alternative meanings where such are possible.

OUTLINE

I. REVIEW AND PREVIEW (1:1—3:6)
   A. Looking Back (1:1—2:10)
   B. Looking Forward (2:11—3:6)

II. THE TIMES OF THE JUDGES (3:7—16:31)
   A. Othniel (3:7–11)
   B. Ehud (3:12–30)
   C. Shamgar (3:31)
   D. Deborah and Barak (Chaps. 4, 5)
      1. Their Story in Prose (Chap. 4)
      2. Their Story in Song (Chap. 5)
   E. Gideon (6:1—8:32)
      1. Gideon's Call to Service (Chap. 6)
      2. Gideon's Three Hundred (Chap. 7)
      3. Gideon's Victory over the Philistines (8:1–32)
   F. Abimelech's Usurpation (8:33—9:57)
   G. Tola and Jair (10:1–5)
   H. Jephthah (10:6—12:7)
      1. Israel's Misery (10:6–18)
      2. Jephthah's Defense of Israel (11:1–28)
      3. Jephthah's Vow (11:29–40)
      4. Jephthah Slays the Ephraimites (12:1–7)
   I. Ibzan, Elon, and Abdon (12:8–15)
   J. Samson (Chaps. 13—16)
      1. Samson's Godly Heritage (Chap. 13)
      2. Samson's Feast and Riddle (Chap. 14)
      3. Samson's Reprisals (Chap. 15)
      4. Samson Duped by Delilah (Chap. 16)

III. RELIGIOUS, MORAL, AND POLITICAL DECAY (Chaps. 17—21)
   A. Micah's Religious Establishment (Chap. 17)
   B. Micah and the Danites (Chap. 18)
   C. The Levite and His Concubine (Chap. 19)
   D. The War with Benjamin (Chaps. 20, 21)

Commentary

I. REVIEW AND PREVIEW (1:1—3:6)

A. Looking Back (1:1—2:10)

1:1–3 After the death of Joshua (cf. 2:8), the tribe of **Judah** took the leadership in warring **against the Canaanites** in the south. In spite of God's promise of victory, **Judah** sought the assistance of the tribe of **Simeon**, showing that their faith lacked complete dependence on God's Word.

1:4–7 Their first victory was over the inhabitants of **Bezek**. After slaying **ten thousand men**, they **cut off** the **thumbs and big toes** of the king, as he had done to his foes. He should have been put to death, as the Lord had commanded (Deut. 7:24), but instead he was only maimed. Then he was taken to Jerusalem, where he later died. This foreshadowed Israel's disobedience in dealing with the heathen in their land. Rather than completely crushing them, the Israelites only crippled them. Such partial obedience was disobedience and would cost the Jews dearly in the days ahead.

1:8 **Judah** had a measure of success **against Jerusalem**, putting **the city** to the torch. But neither Judah nor Benjamin could drive the Jebusites out of their fortress (see commentary on Josh. 15:21–63). This was not done until the time of David (2 Sam. 5:6, 7).

1:9–15 The capture of **Hebron** is here credited to **Judah**; Joshua 14 and 15 tell us that Caleb was the one responsible for the conquest of this city. There is no discrepancy here, since **Caleb** was from the tribe of Judah. These verses (9, 10) probably refer to Caleb's conquest of the city (cf. v. 20) and not to a subsequent expedition after Joshua's death, even as the capture of **Kirjath Sepher** by **Othniel** is repeated in verses 11–15, although it took place previously (Josh. 15:16–19).

1:16 The Kenites continued to dwell **with the children of Judah**, though they never were truly converted.

1:17–21 Other conquests of **Judah** include **Hormah, Gaza, Ashkelon, and Ekron**, but the victories were not complete. **The inhabitants of the lowland—had chariots of iron**, and Judah did not have the faith to launch an attack against them. They were unwilling to persevere in difficult circumstances. Verse 21 indicates that Judges was written before David took Jerusalem.

1:22–26 Only the two tribes of **Joseph** are credited with other victories. (These verses perhaps refer to the conquest of **Bethel** while Joshua was still living [Josh. 12:16], just as the previous verses concerning Hebron and Kirjath Sepher hark back to the days of that great general.) They attacked **the city** of Bethel, **formerly** called **Luz**, and destroyed it. But their mistake was in promising safety to a collaborator. He promptly started building another **city** by the **name** of **Luz** in **the land of the Hittites**. Unjudged sin survives and has to be met later.

1:27–36 In the rest of the chapter, seven central and northern tribes are named as having failed to **drive . . . the Canaanites** from their territory: **Benjamin** (v. 21), **Manasseh** (vv. 27, 28), **Ephraim** (v. 29), **Zebulun** (v. 30),

Asher (vv. 31, 32), **Naphtali** (v. 33), and **Dan** (vv. 34–36).

2:1–5   The Angel of the LORD (the Lord Jesus) rebuked the people at **Bochim** (weepers) for their disobedience. Verse 1 says that He **came up from Gilgal** (the place of blessing) **to Bochim** (the place of weeping). Israel had gone from the place of victory to the place of mourning. They had failed to drive out the Canaanites and to destroy their idolatrous altars. Therefore the Lord would refuse to **drive . . . out . . . the inhabitants of** the **land**, but would instead allow them to harass the Israelites. Verses 1–5 thus give the underlying reason for the oppression which followed. No wonder **the people . . . wept** and **called the . . . place Bochim!**

2:6–10 Verses 6–10 review the close of Joshua's life and the generation that outlived him. In Deuteronomy 6 the Lord gave some specific commands to His people. Failure to obey them led to the sad state of affairs described in verse 10, where a lack of spiritual leadership is seen to result in a corresponding lack of obedience on the part of God's people. The previous **generation** had not taught their children to fear **the LORD** and to keep His commandments. The neglect of the fathers led to the apostasy of their sons.

B. Looking Forward (2:11—3:6)

2:11–19 The remaining verses, on the other hand, give a preview of the entire period of the judges. They trace the fourfold cycle which characterized that time:

Sin (vv. 11–13)
Servitude (vv. 14, 15)
Supplication (not stated here, but
     see 3:9; 3:15; 4:3; etc.)
Salvation (vv. 16–18)

This pattern of behavior has also been described as:

Rebellion
Retribution
Repentance
Rest

This synopsis of Judges (vv. 11–19), as Jensen points out, brings into focus the two divergent truths evident throughout the book:

(1) the desperate wickedness of the human heart, revealing its ingratitude, stubbornness, rebellion, and folly; (2) God's longsuffering, patience, love and mercy. No book in the Bible brings these two truths into sharper contrast—the utter failure of Israel and the persistent grace of Jehovah![2]

2:20–23 Because Israel persisted in disobedience, God decided to allow the nations to remain in the land as chastisement upon His people (vv. 20–23). Punishment for disobedience was not the only reason the Lord did not drive out all the Canaanites. He left them *to* **test** Israel (v. 22; 3:4) and *to train* succeeding generations for war (3:1, 2). We can gain insight from this as to why the Lord allows believers to go through problems and trials. He wants to know if **"they will keep the ways of the LORD . . . or not"** (v. 22).

3:1–4 The nations that were **left** as a trial to Israel are listed in verse 3: **five lords of the Philistines, all the Canaanites, the Sidonians, and the Hivites who dwelt in Mt. Lebanon**.

Now the first cycle begins: sin (vv. 5–7); servitude (v. 8); supplication (v. 9a); salvation (vv. 9b–11).

3:5, 6 Six of the seven pagan nations among whom the Israelites lived are given. To the nations listed in verse 3, **the Hittites, the Amorites, the Perizzites, the Hivites, and the**

Jebusites are added here. The seventh was the Girgashites (Josh. 3:10; 24:11).

Dr. Cohen pinpoints the beginning of each downward cycle concisely:

The Israelites ignored the warning of Moses (Deut. vii. 3f.) and intermarried with the natives, the consequence being the adoption of their seductive cults.[3]

II. THE TIMES OF THE JUDGES (3:7—16:31)

A. Othniel (3:7–11)

3:7, 8 The people **did evil in the sight of the Lord** by marrying the heathen and then worshiping their idols. Impurity and immorality (v. 6) lead to idolatry (v. 7). God had warned them earlier of the grave consequences of mingling with the inhabitants of Canaan. They were a holy people and must remain separate from defilement if they would know the blessing of God (Deut. 7:3–6). God punished Israel by delivering the nation **into the hand of Cushan-Rishathaim, king of Mesopotamia**, for **eight years**. His name means *Cush, man of double wickedness*.

3:9–11 In response to the penitent cry of His people, **the LORD** then **raised up ... Othniel**, a nephew of Caleb, to deliver them from their enemy and to usher in **forty years** of peace. **Othniel** (*lion of God*) had previously taken Kirjath Sepher (*city of the book*), turning it into Debir (*a living oracle*). This is what faith does with God's Word.

B. Ehud (3:12–30)

3:12–14 In the second cycle, Israel was subjugated by **Eglon**, the **king of Moab**, for **eighteen years**.

3:15–30 The military leader whom God gave to Israel at this time was **Ehud**, ... a left-handed man of the tribe of Benjamin. He was commissioned by the people to take a gift as **tribute to** King **Eglon**. He also hid a **double-edged ... dagger ... under his clothes**. After the gift had been delivered, the king probably felt at ease concerning the attitude of his Jewish subjects. Then **Ehud** asked for a private audience to discuss **a secret message**. When **all** the attendants had been sent away, **Ehud** assassinated the king and fled. By the time the deed was discovered, Ehud had assembled the men of Israel, marched against Moab, and **killed about ten thousand** retreating soldiers. Israel then enjoyed **rest for eighty years**.

When *meditation* (Gera, v. 15) gives birth to *praise* (Ehud), the *world ruler* (Eglon), is doomed by the sharp, two-edged *sword* (the Bible), even when the Word is used by a left-handed man.

Othniel was from Judah, the mightiest tribe in Israel. Ehud was from Benjamin, now the smallest tribe. God can use the great or the small to gain the victory, since the power is from Him anyway. Men are simply the agents of deliverance, not the originators of it.

C. Shamgar (3:31)

3:31 Only one verse is devoted to this judge. He slew **six hundred men of the Philistines with an oxgoad** (a sharp, pointed instrument used to prod oxen). This is another of the instances in Judges where God used a "weak thing" to accomplish a mighty victory. A *pilgrim* (**Shamgar**) wielding the *Word of God* (oxgoad—see Eccl. 12:11) can put to rout wanderers (**Philistines**) among God's people.

CHART OF THE JUDGES

Oppressor	Meaning or Type	Years of Oppression	Deliverer	Meaning	Years of Rest	Ref.
Chushan-Rishathaim King of Mesopotamia	Cush—man of double wickedness Self-exaltation, pride	8	Othniel	Lion of God (The power of God)	40	3:7–11
Eglon King of Moab	Circle Worldly profession	18	Ehud	Majesty	80	3:12–30
Philistines	Wanderers among God's people or carnal religion		Shamgar	Stranger or pilgrim		3:31
Jabin King of Hazor in Canaan	Understanding or human intellect Settlement	20	Deborah	Honeybee	40	4:1—5:31
Commander-in-Chief Sisera	Battle array Meaning unknown		Barak	Lightning		
Midianites	Contention, strife, the world	7	Gideon (Jerubbaal)	The cutter down Let Baal plead for himself or Baal-fighter	40	6:1—8:35
			Abimelech a Usurper	My father was king	3	9:1–57
			Tola	A worm	23	10:1, 2
			Jair	Light-giver	22	10:3–5
Ammonites	Rationalism or false doctrine	18	Jephthah	He will open	6	10:6—12:7
			Ibzan	Meaning uncertain	7	12:8–15
			Elon	Meaning uncertain	10	
			Abdon	Service	8	
Philistines	Carnal religion	40	Samson	Little sun	20	13:1—16:31

D. Deborah and Barak (Chaps. 4, 5)

1. Their Story in Prose (Chap. 4)

4:1–3 The next oppressor was **Jabin, king of** the Canaanite stronghold of **Hazor. The commander of his army was Sisera**. With his boasted **nine hundred chariots of** war he held the Israelites under his domination **for twenty years**.

4:4–9 God did not raise up a man this time. He raised up a member of the "weaker sex," **a prophetess** named **Deborah**. (It is not the norm for a woman to occupy such a place of spiritual authority, but this was a time of declension. She should not be used as an example of the woman's role in the church today, since she is the exception and not the rule. Also, this was Israel, not the church.) Deborah commissioned **Barak** to **go** north and attack Sisera's forces, but he refused to go unless she accompanied him. Because of his reluctance to lead he was told that the victory over **Sisera** would be given to **a woman** rather than to him.

4:10–16 Deborah took the initiative in calling Barak and ordering him to engage Sisera in battle, as the Lord had commanded. But **Barak**, not Deborah, is commended for his faith in Hebrews 11:32. Though somewhat hesitant at first, he obeyed the Lord by faith and delivered Israel. (According to the NIV, **Hobab** in verse 11 should be listed as *the "brother-in-law of Moses,"* not **father-in-law**, as in the NKJV.)

> Barak openly showed his force of 10,000 on the southern slopes of Mount Tabor. Sisera rose to the bait. He and his chariots crossed the dry Kishon riverbed at the ford just south of Harosheth. They raced southeast along the ancient highway toward Taanach. Israelites from the south, from Ephraim, entered the valley at Jenin (5:14) and joined forces with Barak and his northern troops in the valley below Taanach, south of the Kishon. Deborah called for the attack (14). Footmen against chariots! At the critical moment rain fell, turning the plain into mire, utterly confounding the chariots and horses (5:4). The advantage was now fully with the infantry. . . . Barak pressed the attack. Sisera was separated from his men and fled. The leaderless troops, not used to fighting on foot, ran for their base. The rains continued and the Kishon rose to a torrent. Those who were not slain by the Israelites in pursuit were swept away by the Kishon as they tried to cross the ford to Harosheth . . . [vv. 10–16; cf. 5:20, 21].—*(Daily Notes of the Scripture Union)*

4:17–24 Seeking refuge in **the tent of Jael**, a **Kenite**, **Sisera** was given food and lodging. While he slept, **Jael** hammered **a tent peg . . . into his temple**. As **Barak** passed by in pursuit, **Jael** invited him in to see the corpse of his enemy. Thus was Deborah's prophecy of verse 9 fulfilled. God used a mere honeybee

(Deborah) to cast down human reason (**Jabin**), when it exalted itself against the knowledge of God. The judgment came upon the foe like lightning (**Barak**). **Jael** (climber) used **a tent peg** (the witness of her pilgrim life) to bring down the pretensions of the mighty. The **hammer** speaks of the Word (Jer. 23:29).

2. Their Story in Song (Chap. 5)

5:1–5 The song of **Deborah and Barak** is a classic of inspired literature. After opening with **praise to the LORD**, Deborah recalled the Lord's triumphant march when the Israelites left the borders **of Edom** to move toward the Promised Land. All opposition melted **before** the majesty of **the LORD God of Israel**.

5:6, 7 Then she described conditions **in the days of Shamgar**. The dangers were such that **the highways were deserted**. Travelers used less direct routes in order to avoid robber bands. The villagers dared not venture out of their homes—that is, **until . . . Deborah arose**.

5:8 Because the people had turned to idols, the land was given over to **war** and bloodshed, and **Israel** did not have weapons with which to fight.

5:9–15 But when God raised up **Deborah** and **Barak**, some of the rulers of Israel and some of the people stepped forward gallantly to help. There were men **from Ephraim**, men from **Benjamin**, men **from Machir** (the tribe of Manasseh), and men **from Zebulun** and **Issachar**.

5:16, 17 And then Deborah remembered those who did *not* come to help. **Reuben** had **great searchings of heart** but stayed **among the sheepfolds**. **Gilead** (Gad) did not cross **the Jordan** to join in the battle. **Dan** remained **in ships**, and **Asher** sat idly **at the seashore**.

Scripture notes carefully those who fought in the battle and those who stood passively by, unwilling to risk their safety in Jehovah's cause. And so it is today: The Lord knows who is actively confronting the world and the devil and who is sitting back and simply watching. There is a time of reward coming, but it is also a time of loss (1 Cor. 3:10–15).

5:18–22 **Zebulun** and **Naphtali** were outstanding, risking their lives for Jehovah without pay (**they took no spoils of silver**). They were in the thick of the battle against **the kings of Canaan**. The forces of nature were on their side because they were on the Lord's side.

5:23–27 **Meroz** was singled out for a **curse** for failing to **come to** Jehovah's **help**. The men of this city remained neutral when help was needed against the foe. But **Jael**, living in a tent, was **blessed** for her bravery and cunning in destroying **Sisera**. Our Lord's mother is the only other woman who is specifically called blessed among women (Luke 1:42).

5:28–31 Sisera's **mother**, in the meantime, was looking out **the window**, waiting for her son to return with the spoils of victory. She could not understand his delay. **Her wisest ladies** assured her that he must be **dividing the** booty with his men. But **Sisera** would never return. And let his fate be the same for **all . . . enemies** of Jehovah.

On the other hand, may **those who love** the Lord be as the rising **sun**. The chapter closes with the statement that **the land had rest for forty years** after Sisera's death.

E. Gideon (6:1—8:32)

1. Gideon's Call to Service (Chap. 6)

6:1–6 In the next cycle, the Israelites were oppressed by **the Midia-** nites. These were marauding Bedouin bands who conducted raids on Israel's crops, stripping **the land** like **locusts** and stealing the **livestock**. Israel's backsliding resulted in poverty, slavery, and fear. Those whom Israel had once conquered were now her masters. When we turn from the Lord as Christians, old habits enslave and impoverish us as well.

6:7–16 When **Israel cried out to the Lord** for help, **a prophet** was first **sent** to remind them of their idolatry. Then **the Angel of the Lord**, whom we believe to be the preincarnate Christ (see essay below), **appeared to** a man of Manasseh named **Gideon** as he was secretly threshing **wheat in** a **winepress . . . to hide it from the Midianites**. **The Angel** told this **"mighty man of valor"** that God would use him to deliver **Israel from** Midian. Despite Gideon's protests, the Angel repeated his call to this important task.

THE ANGEL OF THE LORD

The Angel of the Lord (Jehovah) is the Lord Jesus Christ in a preincarnate appearance. A study of the passages in which He is mentioned makes it clear that He is God, and that He is the Second Person of the Trinity.

First, the Scriptures show that He is God. When He appeared to Hagar, she recognized that she was in the presence of God; she referred to Him as "the-God-Who-Sees" (Gen. 16:13). Speaking to Abraham on Mount Moriah, the Angel identified Himself as "the LORD" (Heb. YHWH, or Jehovah; Gen. 22:16). Jacob heard the Angel introduce Himself as the God of Bethel (Gen. 31:11–13). When blessing Joseph, Israel used the names "God" and "the Angel" interchangeably (Gen. 48:15, 16). At the burning bush, it was "the Angel of the LORD" who appeared (Ex. 3:2), but Moses "hid his face, for he was afraid to look upon God" (Ex. 3:6). The Lord who went before Israel in a pillar of cloud (Ex. 13:21) was none other than "the Angel of God" (Ex. 14:19). Gideon feared that he would die because, in seeing the Angel of the LORD, he had seen God (Judg. 6:22, 23). The Angel of the LORD told Manoah that His name was Wonderful (Judg. 13:18), one of the names of God (Isa. 9:6). When Jacob struggled with the Angel, he struggled with God (Hos. 12:3, 4). These are convincing proofs that when the Angel of the LORD is referred to in the OT, the reference is to Deity.

John F. Walvoord (as quoted by Chafer) gives four arguments to support this:

"(a) The Second Person is the Visible God of the New Testament. (b) The Angel of Jehovah of the Old Testament No Longer Appears after the Incarnation of Christ. (c) Both the Angel of Jehovah and Christ Are Sent by the Father. (d) The Angel of Jehovah Could Not Be Either the Father Or the Holy Spirit."[4] As for the fourth evidence, Walvoord goes on to explain that the Father and the Spirit are invisible to man and both have the attribute of immateriality. He concludes, "There is not a single valid reason to deny that the Angel of Jehovah is the Second Person, every known fact pointing to His identification as the Christ of the New Testament."

As the Angel of Jehovah, Christ is distinguished from other angels in that He is uncreated. The words translated *Angel*[5] in both Testaments mean "messenger"; He is the *Messenger* of Jehovah. Thus, as Chafer says, He is an "angel" only by office.[6]‡

6:17–24 Sensing that he was talking to the Lord, **Gideon** asked for **a sign**. Then he **prepared** an **offering** of **a young goat** and of **unleavened bread**. When **the Angel . . . touched** the offering with his **staff** and it was **consumed** by **fire**, Gideon knew he was in the Lord's presence and feared he would **die**. But **the LORD** assured him with the words **"Peace be with you,"** and **Gideon** thereupon **built an altar** and named the place Jehovah-Shalom (**The-Lord-Is-Peace**).

6:25–32 That **night**, in obedience to **the Lord**, **Gideon** destroyed an **altar** which his **father** had erected to **Baal** and **the wooden image . . . beside it**, and instead erected another **altar** to Jehovah. **In the morning . . . the men of the city** were ready to kill him for this bold act. But his father, **Joash**, intervened, saying that if **Baal** were truly **a god**, he should be able to defend himself. **Joash** decreed that anyone who espoused Baal's cause would be executed. Gideon was nicknamed **Jerubbaal**, meaning **"Let Baal plead** (for himself)."

Some people might fault Gideon for tearing down the altar at **night** because of fear. But we must not lose sight of the fact that he did obey **the LORD**. His fear did not stop him from being obedient. All of us have fear, and fear in and of itself is not necessarily wrong. But when it keeps us from obeying the Lord, it has become an obstacle to faith and is sin.

6:33–35 At this time **the Midianites**, the **Amalekites** and **the people of the East gathered together** to make war on Israel as they **crossed** the Jordan **and encamped in the Valley of Jezreel**. **The Spirit of the LORD came upon Gideon** and he assembled an army from the tribes of **Manasseh, Asher, Zebulun, and Naphtali**. Abiezer (v. 34) was an ancestor of Gideon. His name is used here (Hebrew text) as a family name (the Abiezrites, NKJV) for his living descendants. See also 8:2.

6:36–40 Before **Gideon** went into battle, he desired a pledge of victory from **God**. The first pledge came when **dew** fell **on** his **fleece of wool** but not on **the ground** around it. The second came the following night, when the **dew** fell **on . . . the ground** but not on **the fleece**.

Gideon's fleece is often misunderstood by Christians. There are two things about this incident that we should keep in mind: Gideon was not looking to the fleece for *guidance* but for *confirmation*. God had already told him what he was to do. Gideon was just seeking assurance of success. People who talk about putting out a fleece to find the will of the Lord in a certain matter are misapplying the passage. Secondly, Gideon had asked for a *supernatural* sign, not a natural one. Naturally speaking, what Gideon asked for would never have happened without the direct intervention of God. Today people use things as a "fleece" that could happen naturally, without divine intervention. This, too, is a wrong way to use the story. What we see here is God condescending to a man of weak faith to assure him of victory. God can, and does, give such assurances today in answer to prayer.

2. Gideon's Three Hundred (Chap. 7)

7:1–3 In order that victory against Midian might be clearly divine, the Lord first reduced Gideon's army from 32,000 to **ten thousand** by sending the **fearful and** fainthearted home, as the law commanded (Deut. 20:8).

7:4–8 In order to reduce the army still further, God tested the soldiers at the river. Those who took time to get **down on** their **knees** for a **drink**

of **water** were eliminated. Those, on the other hand, who lapped up water like **a dog** and quickly moved on were kept in the army. These numbered **three hundred men**.

7:9–14 The LORD then directed **Gideon** to visit the outskirts of **the camp** of the Midianites by **night**. Accompanied by **Purah his servant**, Gideon went to the outermost part of the enemy's encampment. There he heard a Midianite **telling** his friend of **a dream** he had had in which **a loaf** of barley bread rolled over a Midianite **tent**, crushing it. The friend understood the dream as meaning that the Israelites would defeat **Midian**. **Barley bread** was the food of the common farming people and represented Israel. The **tent** typified the armies of the Midianites.

7:15–20 Perhaps the thought of his diminishing army rekindled Gideon's fears, and justifiably so. God was asking him to face an army of 135,000 with a force of 300 (8:10)! But this word from the mouth of his enemies strengthened his faith. In response, **he** first *worshiped* (v. 15), then *warred*.

Thus assured of victory, Gideon **returned to the camp of Israel** and summoned his men to war. After dividing the army **into three companies** of one hundred each, he armed each man with **a trumpet** and an earthenware pitcher with a lamp or torch **inside**. They marched to the fringe of **the camp** of the Midianites, and then at the appointed signal they all **blew the trumpets**, **broke the** earthenware **pitchers** so that the light of the lamps would be visible, and cried, **"The sword of the LORD and of Gideon!"**

The divine interpretation of this incident is given in 2 Corinthians 4:7. Our bodies are the earthen vessels. It is only as we are constantly delivered unto death for Jesus' sake that the light of the knowledge of the glory of God in the face of Jesus Christ shines forth to others.

7:21–25 In confusion and panic, the Midianites began attacking one another, then **fled**. At first they were chased by men from the tribes of **Naphtali, Asher, and all Manasseh**. But **then all the men of Ephraim** were summoned to join in by taking the fords of **Jordan** and destroying the foe as they sought to escape across the river. The Ephraimites succeeded in capturing and killing **two** of the **princes of** Midian: **Oreb** (*raven*) and **Zeeb** (*wolf*).

There are lessons we can learn about leadership in Gideon's actions. The leader must be thoroughly convinced about what he is doing before he can lead others. He must be a worshiper first of all, giving God His rightful place (v. 15). He must lead by example (v. 17). He must be careful that the credit goes where it belongs— to God first, then to the instruments of His choosing (v. 18).

3. Gideon's Victory over the Philistines (8:1–32)

8:1–3 At first **the men of Ephraim** were angry with Gideon that they had not been invited to help sooner. But when Gideon reminded them that their capture of the two **princes** was more illustrious than anything he had done, they were pacified. As explained previously, **Abiezer** (v. 2) refers to Gideon and his men.

8:4–7 The Jews **of Succoth** refused to give food to **Gideon** and his hungry **three hundred** because they feared reprisal from the Midianites if he were defeated. Gideon threatened to **tear** (Heb. *thresh*) their **flesh** with **thorns** and **briers** when **the LORD** had

delivered Zebah and Zalmunna into his **hand**.

8:8, 9 The men of Penuel answered Gideon's request for food in the negative also. His threat to them was that **when** he came **back in peace** he would **tear down** their **tower**.

8:10–17 Gideon kept his word. He captured the two Midianite kings and **routed the whole army**. With the help of **a young** informer's written list, Gideon **taught** a lesson to the **seventy seven** leading **men of Succoth**. Cohen says:

> This form of punishment "is described in Plato's *Republic* as one inflicted upon the worst offenders."[7]

The learned Rabbis Kimchi and Rashi saw this as an idiom meaning "strike with violence."

> Others explain that he [Gideon] threatened to throw them naked into a bed of thorns and trample them together, like grain on the threshing-floor.[8]

As for **Penuel**, Gideon did tear **down** its **tower** and he also **killed the men of the city**.

"A soft answer turns away wrath, but a harsh word stirs up anger" (Prov. 15:1). The first truth is illustrated in verses 1–3 by Gideon's answer to the Ephraimites. The second truth is illustrated in verses 4–17 by the words of the men of Succoth and Penuel.

8:18–21 **Zebah and Zalmunna had killed** some of Gideon's **brothers** at **Tabor**, so he ordered his oldest son, **Jether**, to slay them. He **was afraid** to **because he was still a youth, . . . so Gideon** finished the job himself.

8:22, 23 **The men of Israel** asked **Gideon** to be their king, so impressed were they by his military exploits.

They gave the glory to man instead of to God (cf. 7:2). But Gideon nobly refused for himself and his sons, pointing out that **the Lord** alone had the right to **rule over** them.

8:24–27 But, after resisting one temptation, Gideon fell into another. He asked for the **golden earrings** which the Israelites had taken from the Midianites (also known as Ishmaelites; cf. Ex. 32:1–6). With these **Gideon made...an ephod**, the apronlike vestment of the priest. When this was **set...up** in **Ophrah**, **it became** an object of idolatrous worship and thus **a snare** to Israel, drawing them away from Shiloh and the tabernacle. "He refused the kingship but wanted the priesthood."

8:28–32 After the conquest of the Midianites, **Israel** enjoyed **quiet for forty years**.

Special mention is made of the fact that **Gideon...had many wives**, and these bore him **seventy sons.** Also, he had a **concubine...in Shechem** who **bore him a son** by the name of **Abimelech.**

Two more characteristics of Gideon's multifaceted personality show themselves in this chapter. His relentless pursuit of the Midianites displayed a thoroughness and completeness in carrying out his orders. Even though he was tired, even though he had already done a great deal, and even though no one would help him, he pressed on until the Ishmaelites were destroyed and their kings were dead at his feet. The Apostle Paul had a similar drive, only it showed itself in spiritual warfare (Phil. 3:12–14).

The second characteristic is a negative one: he requested and accepted **golden earrings from** the **plunder** as a reward for defeating the Ishmaelites (v. 24), and this **became a snare to Gideon**, his family, and his country.

Contrast this with Abraham's behavior in Gen. 14:21–24. We should strive under God to emulate Gideon's virtues and avoid his vices.

F. Abimelech's Usurpation (8:33—9:57)

8:33–35 No sooner had **Gideon** died than **Israel** turned aside to worship of **the Baals**. How quickly the Israelites forgot Gideon's heroic national exploits, even to the point of mistreating his descendants and forgetting God's deliverance! But are we much better at remembering the blessings we have received from the Lord or even from our fellow men? To our shame we tend to forget them.

9:1–6 **Abimelech** (*my father was king*), a **son of** Gideon, was not a judge of Israel but a usurper—one who sought to rule Israel without proper authority. To eliminate any threats to his rule, he murdered all **his brothers** except **Jotham, the youngest**. Working through **worthless and reckless** relatives in **Shechem**, he persuaded the people of that area to recognize him as **king**. Since Gideon had **seventy...sons** (v. 2), and not all were slain, the **seventy** of verse 5 must be a round number.

9:7–15 The Gospels contain many parables, or stories with a deeper meaning. Here is one of the few OT parables. Jensen comments on it as follows:

When Jotham heard of Abimelech's coronation, he hurried to the top of Mount Gerizim at a time when the people were gathered in the valley below. From that vantage point his voice could be heard across the valley, and the people listened intently to the strange parable he related. Using the figure of a republic of trees electing a king, he pictured Israel's conduct. He spoke of Gideon and his sons as the olive tree, the fig tree, and the vine, who wisely refused to leave their God-appointed places of usefulness in order to go and reign over the trees. But he likened Abimelech to a bramble, who not only eagerly accepted the invitation but warned that he would destroy the cedars of Lebanon if the trees did not elect him king.[9]

9:16–21 Jotham then announced boldly to the people that if they had **done** right in destroying his brothers, **then** they could **rejoice in** their new ruler. **But if not, the men of Shechem** and **Abimelech** would become embroiled in civil war and destroy each other.

9:22–33 This is exactly what happened. **Three years** later **God sent a spirit of ill will between Abimelech and the men of Shechem**. God is not the author of evil, but He does allow evil, and even uses it to accomplish His purposes with evil men (cf. 1 Sam. 16:14; 1 Kgs. 22:19–23). **The men of Shechem . . . robbed** those who traveled the trade routes near Shechem, thus depriving Abimelech of the taxes he would ordinarily collect (v. 25). **Gaal the son of Ebed** used the harvest festival as the occasion to call for a rebellion against Abimelech, saying, **"Who is Abimelech, and who are we of Shechem, that we should serve him?"** Zebul, Abimelech's puppet-governor of Shechem, secretly notified **Abimelech** of the conspiracy and advised him to march against the **city . . . in the morning**.

9:34–40 When **Gaal . . . went . . . to the city gate** in the morning, he thought he saw **people** moving **down from the tops of the mountains**. At first **Zebul** pretended that what he saw were just **shadows**, hoping to gain time for **Abimelech**. Finally **Gaal** realized that it was actually **people**,

with a second **company . . . coming from** a different direction. **Then Zebul** challenged him to **go out . . . and fight** the one whose rule he had **despised**. When **Gaal** and his band of outlaws engaged the foe, **many** of his men **fell** and he was soon chased back into the city.

9:41–44 With **Abimelech** camped at nearby **Arumah**, **Zebul** expelled **Gaal and his brothers** from **Shechem**. **The next day . . . people** from Shechem went out into **the field** to work, or perhaps to take spoil from the fallen men. When **Abimelech** heard of this, **he . . . divided** his men **into three companies** and set an ambush. **Two companies** were to rush **upon** them and another was to cut off any retreat back into **the city**. The ambush was successful.

9:45 After a day of fighting, **the city** fell. **The people** were all slain and their **city** was **demolished** and sown . . . **with salt**. (Sowing **with salt** makes the ground sterile. Here it was a symbolic action on the part of Abimelech, expressing his determination that the place be forever a barren salt waste.)

9:46–49 Nearby was **the tower of Shechem**, where there was a **temple of the god Berith. The** people **of the tower** hid in a large room of the temple. **Abimelech** and his men took boughs from the forest of nearby **Mount Zalmon** and made a huge **fire** over **the stronghold. About a thousand men and women** perished in the inferno.

9:50–57 In capturing **Thebez, Abimelech** met his downfall. As he attacked **a . . . tower** where many of **the people** had sought refuge, **a . . . woman dropped an upper millstone on Abimelech's head.** Seriously injured, he asked one of his own men to slay him rather than have it said he was slain by **a woman**. Thus the bramble was devoured, as **Jotham** had predicted.

Justice has its own way of suiting the punishment to the crime. Abimelech had slain his brothers on a stone (v. 5), and a stone crushed his own proud head. Those who live by violence will die by the same.

G. Tola and Jair (10:1–5)

Tola, of the tribe **of Issachar, judged Israel** for **twenty-three years. He** lived **in the mountains of Ephraim**.

The next judge was **Jair, a Gileadite**, who ruled for **twenty-two years** over **Israel**. Mention is made in passing of his **thirty sons**, who ruled over **thirty towns**.

H. Jephthah (10:6—12:7)

1. Israel's Misery (10:6–18)

10:6–9 Again we read the dreary account of how **the children of Israel . . . forsook the** Lord and turned to idolatry. Service to idols brought Israel into slavery to idolaters. **The Philistines** and Ammonites fought **against** the Jews who were **on the** east **side of the Jordan**, and the Ammonites also **crossed over the Jordan to fight against Judah, . . . Benjamin, and . . . Ephraim**.

Israel was powerless before the Philistines and the Ammonites because they abandoned the worship of Jehovah and **served the . . . gods of** these heathen (v. 6).

10:10–16 When the Israelites **cried out to the** Lord, He refused their pleas at first. He cited several instances of past deliverances and reminded them that after each deliverance they had turned away from Him (v. 13). But when they continued to pray and after **they put away** their idols, God listened to their cry. Verse 16 gives us some insight into the

Lord's great heart of tenderness. Like a father, He was moved by the plight of His wayward children. Their **misery** called forth His mercy.

10:17, 18 As the chapter closes, the armies **of Ammon** were camped **in Gilead**, and **Israel** had **assembled . . . in Mizpah**. The men of Gilead were seeking a military leader (vv. 17, 18).

2. Jephthah's Defense of Israel (11:1–28)

11:1–3 The man of the hour was **Jephthah**. He is described as a **Gileadite, a mighty man of valor**, and **the son of a harlot**. Having been rejected by his own countrymen, he had wandered off to **the land of Tob** (probably in Syria), where he became the leader of a band of desperadoes or outlaws.

11:4–11 **The elders of Gilead** now asked **Jephthah** to lead the armies of Israel against the Ammonites, promising to recognize him as their **head** if he defeated the foe.

In some ways Jephthah reminds us of the Lord Jesus: There was a shadow over his birth and he was rejected by his brethren. When they got into bondage they remembered him and called upon him as their savior; and in agreeing to help the Gileadites, Jephthah agreed to be their savior but insisted on being their lord as well.

11:12–28 Jephthah's first action was to send **messengers to the king of . . . Ammon**, giving him an opportunity to explain his aggression. **The king** complained that **Israel** had stolen his **land** from him **when** the nation marched from **Egypt** to Canaan. Jephthah explained clearly that this was not so. The Lord had instructed His people not to meddle with the Edomites (Deut. 2:4, 5), the Moabites

(Deut. 2:9), or the Ammonites (Deut. 2:19)—all distant relatives of the Jews. Therefore, the Israelites **bypassed the land of Edom and the land of Moab**. However, when they came to the territory of the Ammonites, it had already been captured by **the Amorites**, whose **king** was **Sihon. Israel** took **possession of** this **land** by defeating **the Amorites.**

When **the king of ... Ammon** refused to withdraw his claim to the land, **Jephthah** prepared for war.

3. Jephthah's Vow (11:29–40)

Before going into battle, **Jephthah made a** rash **vow** that he would devote to the Lord **whatever** first came **out of** his **doors ... to meet** him if he returned home victorious. **The LORD** gave him victory over the Ammonites, and as he returned to his house **his daughter** came out to meet him. Jephthah therefore offered her to the Lord.

There is considerable disagreement as to what Jephthah actually did to his daughter. One view is that he killed her and offered her as a burnt offering to the Lord. This is perhaps the most obvious meaning of the text, even though the idea of human sacrifice is repulsive and was never approved by God (Deut. 18:9–14). Only animals were sacrificed; human beings were dedicated, then redeemed by money (Ex. 13:12, 13; Lev. 27:1–8).

The other common view is that Jephthah gave his daughter to be a perpetual virgin in the service of Jehovah. Those holding this viewpoint state that Jephthah's **vow** was that **whatever** came forth from **the doors of** his **house ... "shall surely be the LORD's,** or I will offer it up for a burnt offering" (v. 31). The idea of perpetual **virginity** is strongly supported by verses 37–39. In any case,

the lesson is that we should not make rash promises.

4. Jephthah Slays the Ephraimites (12:1–7)

12:1–4 The men of Ephraim were jealous of Jephthah's victory, complaining that they had not been allowed to share in it. **Jephthah** reminded them that he had appealed to them in vain for help. The Ephraimites mocked Jephthah's people, the **Gileadites**, saying that they were nothing but **fugitives** from **Ephraim**. (The Ephraimites were troublemakers. They took issue with Gideon when he defeated the Midianites [chap. 8] and now they quarreled with Jephthah without just cause.)

12:5, 6 Jephthah and his **men** attacked the Ephraimites and cut off their way of escape at **the fords of the Jordan**. Before anyone was allowed to **cross** the Jordan, he was forced to say the password, **"Shibboleth"** (lit. *a flowing stream*). The Ephraimites **could not pronounce** this word correctly; they betrayed their identity by saying **"Sibboleth."**[10] **Jephthah** killed **forty-two thousand** men of Ephraim **at ... the Jordan**—a frightful slaughter of his own countrymen.

This type of infighting among the people of God is a distressing thing to see. The blood of the Ephraimites was now mingled with the blood of the Ammonites. Even the bright spots in Judges are smudged with calamity. Ridout makes a sad observation:

Is it not a fact that ... those who have met and overthrown heresy are those who have then crossed swords with their brethren, and fought over things that were not a vital question of truth?[11]

12:7 Jephthah's service as a judge lasted for **six years**; **then** he **died and**

was buried in Gilead. Jephthah is cited in Hebrews 11:32 along with Gideon, Barak, and Samson. All these men had their faults, but they all, at one time or another, demonstrated great faith.

I. Ibzan, Elon, and Abdon (12:8–15)

12:8–10 Ibzan...judged Israel for seven years. All we know of him is that he was a native of Bethlehem who had thirty sons, all of whom obtained wives from elsewhere (that is, outside his clan).

12:11, 12 Elon was of the tribe of Zebulun. His work as judge lasted for ten years. He was buried at Aijalon.

12:13–15 Abdon the son of Hillel came from the city of Pirathon... in the mountains of the Amalekites, in the land of Ephraim. He judged Israel for eight years. Special mention is made of his forty sons and thirty grandsons.

J. Samson (Chaps. 13—16)

1. Samson's Godly Heritage (Chap. 13)

13:1–3 For the seventh time in Judges we read: "Again the children of Israel did evil in the sight of the LORD." The cycle begins again; this time the Philistines enslaved Israel for forty years. This was the longest oppression the nation had yet undergone. While the Israelites were being oppressed by the Philistines, the Angel of the LORD (Christ) appeared to the wife of Manoah, of the tribe of Dan, and announced that, though she had been barren, she would become the mother of a son. The barren womb is often a starting place in the purposes of God. He calls life out of death and uses the things that "are not" to confound the things that are.

13:4–7 This son was to be a Nazirite from his mother's womb to the day of his death. He was not to drink . . . wine or eat grapes or raisins, nor was his hair to be cut. The mother herself was to abstain from wine or similar drink and from anything unclean.

For the scriptural background of the Nazirite vow, see Numbers 6:2. Ordinarily, Naziriteship was a vow which a person made of his own will. But in Samson's case Naziriteship was to extend from his birth to his death.

13:8–14 Manoah prayed for another visit from the Angel of the LORD and for further instructions. The Angel appeared to the woman again, and she hurriedly brought her husband out to meet this heavenly Visitor. No further instructions were given by the Angel at this time, however.

13:15–18 Then Manoah offered to prepare a meal for the Angel, thinking that he was a mere man. The Angel refused to eat with Manoah merely as one of equal rank. He proposed instead that a kid be offered as a burnt offering . . . to the LORD. When Manoah asked the Angel's name, he was told it was *Wonderful*—one of the names given to the Lord Jesus in Isaiah 9:6.

13:19–23 Then Manoah offered the young goat to the LORD. The Angel ascended to heaven in the flame of the altar, showing clearly that this was an appearance of the LORD Himself. Manoah and his wife then worshiped by falling on their faces—an act that would have been improper if the Angel were less than God. They had seen the LORD, but they would not die as a result, since God had received a burnt offering and a grain offering from them.

13:24, 25 After this the son was born and named Samson (*little sun*).

It soon became obvious that **the Spirit of the LORD** was working powerfully in his life.

Few men in the Bible exhibit such a contrast of strength and weakness. When we think of Samson, we ordinarily think of *his strengths*. He killed a lion with his bare hands (Judg. 14:6). He killed thirty Philistines single-handed (14:19). He broke the cords with which the men of Judah had bound him, and slew 1000 Philistines with the jawbone of a donkey (15:14–16). In escaping from a trap which the Philistines had laid for him, he walked away with the gates of Gaza (16:3). Three times he escaped the treachery of Delilah—once by breaking the seven fresh bowstrings that bound him, once by snapping the new ropes as if they were a thread, and once by pulling out the pin that fastened the seven locks of his hair to a loom (16:6–14). Finally, he pulled down the pillars of the house in which the Philistines were being amused by him, killing more in his death than he did in his life (16:30).

But Samson's *weaknesses* were even more apparent. He had a weakness for women, and was willing to disobey God in order to get a woman who pleased him (14:1–7). He also disobeyed his parents (14:3). He practiced deceit (14:9; 16:7, 11, 13b). He fraternized with thirty Philistines, the enemies of God's people (14:11–18). He gave way to temper and vindictiveness (14:19b; 15:4, 5). He had a cruel streak in his nature (15:4, 5). He consorted with a harlot (16:1, 2). He dallied with evil (16:6–14). He revealed the secret of his strength to the enemy (16:17, 18). He was too cocky and self-confident (16:20b). Last, but not least, he broke his Nazirite vow (14:9).

2. Samson's Feast and Riddle (Chap. 14)

14:1-4 Samson's willfulness soon appeared in his determination to marry a Philistine **woman**—one of the enemies of Israel. **His father and mother** sought to dissuade him, but he insisted. Verse 4 does not mean that **the LORD** approved of Samson's disobedience, but that He permitted it and planned to overrule it for Israel's welfare and for the punishment of the enemy.

14:5–7 En route **to Timnah** (a Philistine city) **with his** parents, Samson was threatened by **a young lion. The Spirit of the LORD came mightily upon him** and enabled him to kill **the lion** unaided. Presumably arrangements for the marriage were made at this time.

14:8, 9 Later, when **Samson** was returning to Timnah to claim his bride, he found **honey . . . in the carcass of the lion** he had slain and shared it with **his father and mother.** He didn't tell them that the honey was defiled by contact with a dead body. (As a Nazirite he broke part of his vow by touching the dead animal.)

14:10–14 At Timnah, **a** great wedding **feast** was arranged, and **Samson** gave **a riddle**, offering each of his **thirty companions** a complete outfit if they could explain it. If not, they would have to give him **thirty linen garments and thirty changes of clothing**. The riddle was:

> **Out of the eater came something to eat,**
> **And out of the strong came something sweet.**

It referred, of course, to his killing of the lion and to his finding the honey in its carcass.

14:15–18 When the men failed to guess the answer, they persuaded **Samson's wife** with threats to obtain the answer from him. **She** did this and **explained** it to the thirty young men. They came to Samson with the answer and demanded the clothing. Samson then realized that they had collaborated with his wife.

14:19, 20 In order to get the clothing to pay the men, Samson angrily **killed thirty... men** of **Ashkelon** and **took their apparel**. On the seventh day, when the marriage should have been consummated, he returned home. His **wife was given to his companion, his best man.**

3. Samson's Reprisals (Chap. 15)

15:1–6 When his father-in-law refused to let Samson have his **wife**, Samson took personal revenge by tying the **tails** of **three hundred foxes** in pairs, putting **a** lighted **torch between each pair of tails**, and releasing the animals in the **grain** fields, **vineyards, and olive groves**. The Philistines learned the cause of this cruel and wasteful act and retaliated by burning to death Samson's wife **and her father**.

15:7–13 Samson's answer was to slay a **great** multitude of Philistines; then he retired to **the cleft of the rock of Etam** in the territory of Judah. But violence triggers more violence. When **the Philistines** marched after him, **the men of Judah** slavishly reminded him that **the Philistines** were their rulers. To save their own skin they agreed to **tie** Samson **securely** and turn him over to the enemy. Samson agreed to this as long as his own countrymen did **not** attempt to **kill** him. They had sunk to a vassal mentality, and chose to betray their own countryman and remain loyal to their oppressors rather than to befriend

Samson and rid themselves of their chains.

15:14–17 Then follows one of the glorious moments of Samson's career. When he was brought out bound, **the Spirit of the Lord came mightily upon him. With the jawbone of a donkey** he proceeded to slay **a thousand** Philistines. He named the **place Ramath Lehi** (*Jawbone Heights*, NKJV marg.). There is a play on words in verse 16, as if to say, "With the jawbone of an ass I have ass-ass-inated them," or "With the jawbone of an ass I have piled them in a mass! With the jawbone of an ass I have assailed assailants" (Moffatt).

One wonders why the Lord gave such a great victory through such an unlikely weapon. Samson was forbidden to touch anything that was unclean, and the jawbone was certainly that, being part of a dead animal. But this unusual weapon made it all the more evident that the victory was a supernatural one, given by God through base means. This is an example of the Lord allowing irregularities during a time of extreme crisis which ordinarily would not be permitted.

15:18–20 In response to Samson's prayer for **water, God** miraculously provided a spring out of "Jawbone Heights." This place was named **En Hakkore**, *Spring of the Caller* (NKJV marg.).

It is at this illustrious period in Samson's career that the Spirit of God records his judging of **Israel** for **twenty years**.

4. Samson Duped by Delilah (Chap. 16)

16:1–3 Toward the end of his rule, Samson's unbridled lust led him to the house of **a harlot** in the Philistine city of **Gaza**. The men of the city thought that at last they had trapped their enemy. But **Samson . . . arose at midnight** and carried off **the doors of the gate of the city**, as well as the **two gateposts, to the top of the hill that faces Hebron**, a distance of almost forty miles.

16:4–10 Next **Samson** fell in love with a Philistine **woman** named **Delilah**. When this became known, **the lords of the Philistines** offered her great reward if she would lure Samson into revealing the secret of **his great strength**.

On her first attempt, Samson said that if he were bound with **seven fresh bowstrings**, he would **become weak**. She thereupon tied **him with . . . seven fresh bowstrings** and suggested that **the Philistines** were about to pounce on him. But Samson broke the cords as if they were **a strand of yarn**.

16:11, 12 On the second attempt, **Delilah** followed Samson's suggestion by binding him **with new ropes** and warning him that **the Philistines** were closing in for the kill. But again Samson **broke** his bonds as if they were **thread**.

16:13, 14 Still playing with fire, Samson told Delilah that he would be helpless if she wove **the seven locks of** his hair and then fastened them **into the web of the loom**. When she woke him up with the warning that **the Philistines** were about to seize him, he left with **the batten and the web**.

16:15–20 Finally Samson broke down and revealed to **Delilah** the secret of his **strength**. His long hair, while not the source of his power, was the outward indication of his being **a Nazirite**—his separation to God. It was his relationship **to God** that made him strong, not his hair. But if his hair were cut off, he would be powerless. Delilah knew now that she had his secret. When he was asleep **on her knees**, she called in **the Philistines**. One of them shaved his head, and **his strength left him**.

C. H. Mackintosh observes:

The lap of Delilah proved too strong for the heart of Samson, and what a thousand Philistines could not do was done by the ensnaring influence of a single woman.[12]

When **Samson . . . awoke**, he tried to summon his strength, **not** knowing that **the Lord had departed from him**.

16:21, 22 The Philistines . . . put out Samson's **eyes** and imprisoned him in **Gaza**, where he was forced to grind grain. Someone has described this threefold degradation as the "binding, blinding, grinding bondage of sin." But slowly his **hair . . . began to grow again**.

16:23–31 When **the lords of the Philistines** held **a great sacrifice** in celebration of **their god, Dagon**, they brought **Samson** forth as an exhibit of what **their god** had done for them. Also, they compelled him to entertain them with his feats. During the feast, **Samson took hold of the two middle pillars** supporting **the temple, called to the Lord** for strength, and then **pushed** down the pillars and demolished the building. **All the people** were **killed**. The melancholy record is that Samson **killed** more in **his death . . . than he had killed in his life**.

Because he consorted with the Philistines so often in his life and found their women irresistible, Samson is *now* found with the Philistines in his death, a corpse among corpses in the rubble of Dagon's temple. Separation would have earned for him a nobler death. Here we are taught a sober lesson, one we should not take lightly.

Loss of separation (sanctification) leads to loss of power and eventual ruin. To yield our members to sin is to pursue self-destruction. Samson's body was removed to the territory of Dan by his relatives and was **buried** there.

III. RELIGIOUS, MORAL, AND POLITICAL DECAY (Chaps. 17—21)

This last section of Judges is almost like an appendix to the book. As far as time is concerned, chapters 17—21 do not advance the narrative. Rather, they give frightening glimpses of the low religious, moral, and political state to which Israel had sunk during the period of the judges. The little book of Ruth likewise does not advance the history of the judges in time but, by way of contrast, does give a charming glimpse of the godly remnant during this dark era in Hebrew history.

A. Micah's Religious Establishment (Chap. 17)

17:1–4 The first narrative is one of religious corruption. **Micah**, a man **of Ephraim**, had stolen **eleven hundred shekels of silver** from **his mother**. She in turn had cursed the thief, not knowing that it was her own son. Apparently he feared the results of the **curse**, so **he returned the silver** to her. She then lifted the curse and **blessed** her son for returning the **silver**. Now she could use it for its intended purpose. She **took two hundred shekels of silver and** ordered two idols to be **made** from them. One was **a graven image . . . carved** from wood and overlaid with silver. The **molded image** was made entirely of silver.

17:5, 6 **Micah** put the **idols** in **a shrine** with his **household** gods (*teraphim*). He also decided to set up a priesthood for his family, so he **made an ephod** (priestly garment) and **consecrated one of his sons** to be **his priest**. This, of course, was contrary to God's law, which forbade an Ephraimite from being a **priest**. In fact, the whole procedure was contrary to the Mosaic Law.

17:7–13 Sometime later **a Levite** who lived in **Bethlehem**, among the people **of Judah**, went into the hill country **of Ephraim** looking for **a place** to stay. (He should have been employed in the service of Jehovah and supported by the tithes of the nation. But since the law was not obeyed he was forced to seek out his own placement.) **Micah** offered him a position as **priest** in his family. Though this man was **a Levite**, he was not of the family of Aaron and therefore not eligible to serve as **a priest**. However, **Micah** offered him a salary, food, and clothing, and the Levite agreed to serve. The Levite should have confronted Micah with the fact that all these arrangements were contrary to God's order. Instead, he gave tacit assent by accepting the salary and other fringe benefits, thereby effectively sealing his lips from declaring the full counsels of God.

The word to describe the state of affairs in this chapter is "confusion": stolen money is used for idols, and the Lord is invoked to bless the thief (v. 2); individual shrines replace worship at the tabernacle; Levites and common people are consecrated as priests; idols are used in the worship of Jehovah. And Micah supposed the Lord would bless him in all of this (v. 13)! This confusion stemmed from the heart of man (v. 6). If the law of

God had been observed at this time in Israel, none of these things would have happened. "There is a way that seems right to a man, but its end is the way of death" (Prov. 14:12), as we shall see in the next chapter.

B. Micah and the Danites (Chap. 18)

18:1–6 At about this same time, the people of **the tribe of the Danites** decided to look for additional territory in which **to dwell**.

(When verse 1 says that Dan did not have **an inheritance**, it does not mean that they weren't given any land when Canaan was originally divided [Josh. 19:40–48], but rather that their portion, the smallest of the twelve, was too little for them.) When some of their spies came **to the house of Micah** in the hill country **of Ephraim, they recognized the voice of the young Levite** and asked him for assurance of the divine blessing on their plans.

18:7–13 Five men of Dan spied out the northern town of **Laish**, finding it **quiet and secure**. What is more, **the town had no ties with anyone**, that is, they were a peace-loving community with "no treaty of mutual aid with any neighbouring people."[13]

Taking their unprotected condition as a gift from **God, six hundred** fully **armed Danites** set out for Laish.

18:14–26 Later, when **the five men** of Dan were marching north to capture **Laish**, they entered **the house of Micah** and seized all **the idols**. After a mild protest, the Levite gladly obeyed their order to serve the tribe of Dan as a priest rather than to serve just the house of Micah. When Micah and some of his townsmen went out to the Danites to protest this theft of his **gods**, he was told to keep quiet and was sent home empty-handed.

18:27–31 The Danites then **struck** the peaceful town of **Laish** and changed **the name of the city** to **Dan**. They set up **the carved image** there and appointed **Jonathan the son of Gershom, the son of** *Moses* (NKJV marg.) **and his sons** as **priests**.

It is generally admitted that, in Judges, for 'Manasseh' (KJV, NASB) we should read 'Moses'—the name having been disguised by Jewish copyists to prevent supposed disgrace to Moses resulting from the idolatry of his grandson.[14]

Presumably, **Jonathan** is the name of the Levite previously mentioned. The city of **Dan** became an idolatrous city from this time onward. It was here that Jeroboam later set up one of the golden calves. It is not known whether the captivity mentioned in verse 30 refers to a Philistine captivity of that area (e.g., 1 Sam. 4:11) or the Assyrian captivity (2 Kgs. 15:29).

Not all the Danites went to **Laish** (v. 11) or sank into idolatry. Some stayed in their land, between Judah and Ephraim. Samson, the most famous member of this tribe, was from this latter group of Danites.

C. The Levite and His Concubine (Chap. 19)

19:1–12 We now come to a story of incredible moral corruption—the account of the **Levite** and **his concubine**. This particular Levite had a concubine who had come **from Bethlehem in Judah**. She forsook him to return to her home and live as a **harlot**. He **went** to her father's house to get her and was entertained there day after day. Each time he tried to leave with **his concubine**, her **father** prevailed on him to stay a little longer. Finally he left, on the evening of the fifth day, with **his servant**, his **two saddled donkeys**, and **his concubine**.

It was late afternoon when they came to **Jebus (that is, Jerusalem)**, but they did not stop because that city was still inhabited by the heathen Jebusites. George Williams observes:

It would have been better for the Levite to have spent the night with the heathen than with the professed children of God, for the latter had already become viler than the former.[15]

19:13–21 At sunset they came to **Gibeah**, in the territory of Benjamin. No one offered to provide lodging for the caravan, so the Levite relaxed temporarily in the street. Then **an old** Ephraimite **man** who was living **in Gibeah** offered to take the party to his home, and the offer was accepted.

19:22–24 That evening a band of sexual perverts **surrounded the house** and demanded that the visiting Levite be brought **out** to them. The only other time we read of such debauched behavior is in the days of Lot (Gen. 19). Unfortunately for the young woman, there were no guardian angels present at Gibeah, as there were in Sodom. Both incidents brought severe consequences on the offenders. The Lord abhors homosexuality. Human depravity can hardly sink lower. The owner sought to satisfy these wicked Benjamites by offering his **virgin daughter and** the Levite's **concubine**. Arthur Cundall comments on their conduct as follows:

In his concern for the accepted conventions of hospitality the old man was willing to shatter a code which, to the modern reader, appears of infinitely more importance, namely, the care and protection of the weak and helpless. Womanhood was but lightly esteemed in the ancient world; indeed it is largely due to the precepts of the Jewish faith, and particularly the enlightenment which has

come through the Christian faith, that women enjoy their present position. The old man was willing to sacrifice his own virgin daughter and the Levite's concubine to the distorted lusts of the besiegers, rather than allow any harm to befall his principal guest.[16]

19:25–30 Finally, fearing for his own skin, the cowardly Levite sent his **concubine** out **to them**. As a result of their vile and harrowing abuse of her, she died during the night. Without excusing the Benjamites, we might point out that if she hadn't given herself to harlotry beforehand (v. 2) she would not have suffered a harlot's death. Sin mercilessly rewards its followers. The Levite found her body at the doorstep in the morning. He was so enraged that such grossness should be practiced in Israel that he cut her body into **twelve pieces . . . and sent** one part to each of the twelve tribes with an account of what had happened.

The nation of Israel was stunned!

D. The War with Benjamin (Chaps. 20, 21)

20:1–14 Chosen warriors from **the tribes of Israel** (except Benjamin) gathered together at **Mizpah** and heard **the Levite** tell what had happened. They decided to fight against **Gibeah**, but first they gave the Benjamites an opportunity to **deliver up** the guilty **perverted men** to them for punishment. When the Benjamites refused, civil war broke out.

20:15–48 This incident took place not long after the death of Joshua and his generation, for **Phinehas** was the high priest at the time (v. 28). The tribe of Benjamin had only 26,700 soldiers, against **four hundred thousand** from the other tribes (vv. 15–17). Yet in the first battle, Benjamin killed twenty-two thousand men (vv. 18–21). In the second encounter, **eighteen thousand** men of **Israel** were slain (vv. 22–25). The reason Israel had such a hard time of it, even though their cause was just, was because they themselves were not walking close to the Lord. In verses 18, 23, and 26–28 we can see the nation being forced to humble itself before the Lord until finally success was promised. In the third engagement, the Israelites used the strategy of **ambush**. They drew the men of Benjamin away from the city of Gibeah, set the city on fire, and then **destroyed** a total of **twenty-five thousand one hundred Benjamites** as they fled to **the wilderness**. Then they burned all of Benjamin's **cities** and killed the women and children (vv. 29–48).

In three battles Benjamin lost 26,100 men (cf. vv. 15, 47). (We must conclude that they lost 1000 in the first two days.) The slain in verses 35 and 44–46 refer to the casualties in the last battle only. **Six hundred** survivors took refuge in **the rock of Rimmon for four months** (v. 47). Were it not for this remnant, the tribe would have been completely wiped out.

21:1–15 Now the eleven tribes of Israel were seized with regret that the tribe of **Benjamin** was almost annihilated. They did not want this tribe to die out. Yet they had made a rash vow in **Mizpah** that they would not give their daughters as wives **to the** men of **Benjamin**. Their first solution was to fight against **Jabesh Gilead**, east of Jordan, because its inhabitants had not helped in the war against Benjamin. All the people were killed except **four hundred young virgins**. These were then taken and given to the men of **Benjamin**.

21:16–24 But it was evident that further provision must be made if the tribe was to prosper. The men of Israel had vowed that they would not give their daughters to Benjamin, and they would not go back on the vow. So they hit on a scheme to allow **the survivors of Benjamin** to take wives for themselves from the young women who danced at an annual feast (perhaps the Feast of Tabernacles) in **Shiloh**. When the men of Shiloh complained, the other tribes explained to them that this was necessary to prevent the loss of one of the tribes of Israel. So Benjamin went back to his land to rebuild for the future.

These last few chapters have given us an intimate look at two tribes in Israel during the early period of the judges. One can imagine what went on unrecorded in the other tribes! And we know that things got worse as time went on! These gruesome stories show how far a people can wander from the Lord. Here we see enough of the fruit of apostasy to revolt us. Better still if what we have read would turn our hearts to seek the Lord our God and to serve Him faithfully all our days.

21:25 Judges closes with the sad theme ringing in our ears: **"In those days there was no king in Israel; everyone did what was right in his own eyes."**

There is one wholesome episode from this dark period, but it is set off by itself so as not to be defiled by too close association with the depravity of Judges. We now turn our attention to the chaste story of Ruth.

ENDNOTES

[1](Intro) These are largely adapted from Grant, Jennings, and Ridout (see Bibliography).

[2](2:11–19) Irving L. Jensen, *Judges/ Ruth*, p. 12.

[3](3:5, 6) A. Cohen, "Joshua • Judges", pp. 176, 177.

[4](Essay) Quoted by Lewis Sperry Chafer in *Systematic Theology*, V:32.

[5](Essay) In Hebrew *mal'āk*, in Greek *angelos* (whence our English word *angel*).

[6](Essay) Chafer, *Systematic Theology*, I:328.

[7](8:10–17) Cohen, "Joshua • Judges," p. 227.

[8](8:10–17) *Ibid.*, p. 225.

[9](9:7–15) Jensen, *Judges/Ruth*, p. 49.

[10](12:5, 6) Some languages (including Greek and Latin) do not have the "sh" sound. Apparently one dialect of Hebrew either couldn't *pronounce* "sh" or couldn't *distinguish* between "s" and "sh," in this word at least. A similar situation existed in World War II when American soldiers in the South Seas chose "lalapalooza" as a password. The Japanese had trouble differentiating between the "l" and "r," and tended to say "raraparooza."

[11](12:5, 6) Samuel Ridout, *Lectures on the Books of Judges and Ruth*, p. 177.

[12](16:15–20) C. H. Macintosh, *Genesis to Deuteronomy*, p. 465.

[13](18:7–13) Cohen, "Joshua • Judges," p. 291.

[14](18:27–31) John Haley, *Alleged Discrepancies of the Bible*, p. 338. In Hebrew the consonants spelling *Moses* and *Manasseh* are nearly the same (*Mshh* and *Mnshh*), so it could be simply a copyist's error.

[15](19:1–12) George Williams, *The Student's Commentary on the Holy Scriptures*, p. 132.

[16](19:22–24) Arthur E. Cundall, *Judges and Ruth*, p. 197.

BIBLIOGRAPHY
(Judges and Ruth)

Atkinson, David. *The Message of Ruth: The Wings of Refuge*. Downers Grove, IL: InterVarsity Press, 1983.

Barber, Cyril J. *Ruth: An Expositional Commentary*. Chicago: Moody Press, 1983.

Campbell, Donald K. *No Time for Neutrality*. Wheaton, IL: Scripture Press Publications, Victor Books, 1981.

Cohen, A. "Joshua • Judges." *Soncino Books of the Bible*. London: The Soncino Press, 1967.

Cundall, Arthur E. and Leon Morris. *Judges and Ruth*. The Tyndale Old Testament Commentaries. Downers Grove, IL: InterVarsity Press, 1968.

Fausset, A. R. *A Critical and Expository Commentary on the Book of Judges*. London: James Nisbet & Co., 1885.

Grant, F. W. "Judges" and "Ruth." In *The Numerical Bible, Vol. 3, Joshua to 2 Samuel*. Neptune, NJ: Loizeaux Brothers, 1977.

Jennings, F. C. *Judges and Ruth*. New York: Gospel Publishing House, 1905.

Jensen, Irving L. *Judges/Ruth*. Chicago: Moody Press, 1968.

Macintosh, C. H. *Genesis to Deuteronomy*. Neptune, NJ: Loizeaux Brothers, 1989.

McGee, J. Vernon. *Ruth and Esther: Women of Faith*. Nashville: Thomas Nelson Publishers, 1988.

Ridout, Samuel. *Lectures on the Books of Judges and Ruth*. New York: Loizeaux Bros., 1958.

RUTH

Introduction

"The little Book of Ruth, the exposition of which usually follows that of the Book of Judges, consists of only eighty-five verses; but these inclose a garden of roses, as fragrant and full of mystic calyxes, as those which the modern traveller still finds blooming and twining about the solitary ruins of Israel and Moab, this side of Jordan and beyond. The significance and beauty of the brief narrative cannot be highly enough estimated, whether regard be had to the thought that fills it, the historical value which marks it, or the pure and charming form in which it is set forth."

—Paulus Cassel

I. Unique Place in the Canon

It is noteworthy that of the two books in the Bible named after women, one was a Jewish girl who married a prominent Gentile (Esther and King Ahasuerus) and the other was a Gentile woman who married a prominent Hebrew (Ruth and Boaz). Another significant thing these two women have in common is that both were part of God's redemptive history. God used Esther to save His people from physical destruction and He used Ruth as an important genealogical link in the messianic line, first to David, and ultimately to Christ, who would save His people from their sins. We are told in Matthew 1:5 that Boaz was a descendant of the Gentile Rahab, almost certainly the Rahab of Jericho. Now Ruth, another Gentile, enters the lineage of Christ as Boaz's wife. Both Rahab and Ruth picture God's grace, since both would have been excluded from the commonwealth of Israel because of their ethnic origin.

"The Book of Ruth," as McGee notes, "is essentially a woman's story, and God has set His seal of approval upon it by its inclusion in the divine library."[1]

The charm and beauty of the book is well illustrated in an incident involving Benjamin Franklin, the American statesman and inventor. When serving at the French court he heard some of the aristocrats "putting down" the Bible as being unworthy of reading, lacking in style, and so forth. Though not personally a believer himself, his youth in the American colonies had exposed him to the excellence of the Bible as literature. So he decided to play a little trick on the French. He wrote out Ruth longhand, *changing all the proper names to French names.* Then he read his manuscript to the assembled elite of France. They all exclaimed on the elegance and simplicity of style of this touching story.

"Charmant! But where did you find this gem of literature, Monsieur Franklin?"

"It comes from that Book you so despise," he answered—*"la sainte Bible!"* There were some red faces in Paris that night, just as there should be in our own biblically illiterate culture today for neglecting God's Word.

II. Authorship

Jewish tradition says that Samuel is the author of Ruth, though the book is anonymous. Since the book ends with David, the author cannot have been written before his time. Samuel, who anointed David as king, may well have provided the book to show the new monarch's pedigree.

III. Date

Since David's name occurs in 4:17, 22 as the culmination towards which the history of Ruth is leading, it is likely that it was written during or soon after his reign (c. 1011–970 B.C.), or at least after Samuel anointed him king.

Jensen writes:

It was probably written before Solomon, David's successor on the throne, or the writer probably would have included Solomon's name in the genealogy. So the author was a contemporary of David.[2]

Some, however, have preferred a little later date, partly since a need was felt by the author to explain the custom of removing the sandal in a business transaction (4:7). This suggests a certain time lapse between this practice and the writing of the book of Ruth.

IV. Background and Theme

The events in the book of Ruth took place during the time of Judges (1:1). While most of the nation of Israel was wandering away from the Lord, there was a Gentile maiden named Ruth whose faith shone out with brilliance.

The key word of the book is *redeem*. Another key word is *kinsman* (KJV) or *relative* (NKJV), occurring twelve times. Boaz is a redeeming relative who buys back the land which belonged to Elimelech and raises up posterity to continue the family name. He is a type of Christ, the true Redeeming Relative. Ruth, the Moabitess, pictures the church as the bride of Christ, redeemed by His wonderful grace.

OUTLINE

Commentary

I. RESIDING IN MOAB (1:1–5)

1:1, 2 As the book opens we meet a Jewish family which left **Bethlehem** (*house of bread*) of **Judah** (*praise*) because of **famine**, and settled in the land **of Moab**, southeast of the Dead Sea. The parents were **Elimelech** (*my God is King*) and **Naomi** (*my pleasant one*). The sons were **Mahlon** (*sickly*) and **Chilion** (*pining*). It would have been better to stay in the land and trust God than to emigrate to **Moab**. *Ephrata* (root of **Ephrathites**), the ancient name of **Bethlehem**, means *fruitfulness*.

The time of the **judges** was characterized by moral decline. So it is not surprising to find the land undergoing **famine**, God's promised chastisement for disobedience. **Elimelech** should not have left the Promised Land, least of all to settle in **Moab**. Had he never read Deuteronomy 23:3–6? Why not settle with his Jewish brethren east of the Jordan River? He led his family from the land of the living to the place of death and barrenness (neither **Mahlon** nor **Chilion** fathered children).

1:3–5 After **Elimelech . . . died**, his **sons** married Moabite wives. **Mahlon** married **Ruth** (4:10) and **Chilion** married **Orpah**. Although Moabites were not specifically named in Deuteronomy 7:1–3 as people whom Israelites should not marry, it is clear from later references that they were included by the law (Ezra 9:1, 2; Neh. 13:23–25). The law also specified that Moabites were not allowed to be received into the congregation of the Lord to the tenth generation (Deut. 23:3). Grace overruled in Ruth's case, as we shall see,

permitting her descendant, David, to become the king of Israel.

After **ten years**, **Mahlon and Chilion...died**, leaving Naomi with two foreign daughters-in-law, **Orpah** and **Ruth**.

II. RETURN TO BETHLEHEM (1:6–22)

1:6–15 Naomi decided to move back to Judah when she heard that there was plenty of food there. **Her two daughters-in-law** started to accompany **her**. But when she urged them to **return . . . to** their homes in Moab, reminding them that she had no more sons to offer to them as husbands, **Orpah kissed her mother-in-law** and went back.

Notice the different attitudes of the three widows: **Naomi** was a *grieving* widow, stripped of the earthly joys of husband and family by divine judgment. **Orpah**, having soberly considered the words of her mother-in-law, proved to be a *leaving* widow, choosing the easiest and most convenient course. But **Ruth** was a *cleaving* widow, clinging to Naomi in spite of the latter's discouragements. When Ruth chose a new life with Naomi, she knew that it wouldn't be easy. There was hard work and poverty ahead since they were without a male provider. There was separation from home and loved ones, too.

1:16, 17 **Ruth**, however, would **not leave** Naomi. In one of the noblest utterances by a Gentile in the OT, she showed that she was making a total commitment (to **Naomi**). She chose Naomi's destination, her dwelling, her **people**, her **God**, and even her burial place.

1:18–22 By divine coincidence, it

was **the beginning of the barley harvest**, the season of firstfruits (typifying Christ's Resurrection), when Naomi and Ruth arrived back in Bethlehem. **All the city was excited** to see **Naomi** once again and greeted her cordially by name.

She said to them, "Do not call me Naomi (*Pleasant*); **call me Mara** (*Bitter*), **for the Almighty has dealt very bitterly with me."** She had gone **out full** (i.e., with her husband and sons), but the Lord had **brought** her back **empty** (i.e., a widow and childless). So it is with us—we can go out by ourselves into paths of backsliding, but the Lord will bring us back empty, and usually through bitter chastening.

III. RUTH IN THE FIELDS OF BOAZ (Chap. 2)

2:1–3 Under the law, Israelites were not allowed to strip the fields clean when harvesting. Instead, they were to leave some of the grain as gleanings for the needy, for strangers, for the fatherless, and for widows (Lev. 19:9; 23:22; Deut. 24:19).

Ruth decided to take advantage of this law by going out to the barley fields to gather up some of these gleanings. It was not good luck but divine arrangement that led her **to the field** owned by **Boaz** (*in him is strength*), a wealthy **relative** of her dead father-in-law.

2:4–12 When **Boaz** arrived **from Bethlehem**, he asked the identity of the **young woman**. Learning that she was Naomi's daughter-in-law, he cordially invited her to continue gleaning in his fields and to share the water provided for his workers. In praising her for the loyal and selfless step that she had taken, Boaz concluded with a little prayer for her:

The LORD repay your work, and a full reward be given you by the LORD God of Israel, under whose wings you have come for refuge (v. 12).

Leon Morris comments:

> In due course, the prayer was answered through him who uttered it. He recognizes the religious aspect of Ruth's change of country by saying that she has *come to trust* (AV) under Yahweh's wings. The imagery is probably that of a tiny bird struggling under the wings of a foster-mother. It gives a vivid picture of trust and security....[3]

She marveled that he, a Jew, should show such undeserved favor to a Gentile. But there was a reason! **Boaz** had, of course, heard of the kindness which Ruth had shown to Naomi, and how she had become a convert to the Jewish faith.

2:13–16 He was so impressed with her that he invited her to **eat** with his workers, and instructed **the reapers** to leave extra **grain** for her on purpose.

2:17 At the end of the day, she **beat out what she had gleaned**, and **she had about an ephah of barley**, which was a very generous amount. We must do this in our study of the Word; that is, we must appropriate the precious truths for ourselves and put them into practice.

In Boaz we see illustrated many of the excellencies of Christ. Boaz was a man of great wealth (v. 1). He was compassionate to the stranger, who had no claim on his favors (vv. 8, 9). He knew all about Ruth, even before she met him (v. 11), even as the Lord knows all about us even before we come to know Him. He served Ruth graciously, and all her needs were satisfied (v. 14). He granted her protection and prosperity for the future (vv. 15, 16). In these acts of grace we see a foreshadowing of our blessed

Redeeming Relative's mercies to us.

2:18–23 When Ruth **brought** the grain home and told Naomi all that had happened, the wise old Jewess knew that the Lord's program was unfolding satisfactorily. She knew that Boaz was a close relative of her dead husband and sensed that the Lord was going to work wonderfully for Ruth and for herself. Therefore she encouraged Ruth to continue to **glean** in the **field** of **Boaz**.

Naomi's counsel to stay in the fields of Boaz was prudent. Since he had shown himself gracious, why should Ruth insult him or spurn his protection by going into another's **field**? We too should not wander from the Lord's promised provision and protection into the fields of worldly pleasures.

IV. RUTH'S REDEEMING RELATIVE (Chap. 3)

3:1–5 Naomi was anxious that Ruth should find **security**—that is, a husband and a home. She therefore relinquished her own prior claim to marriage and property, and instead advised Ruth to **go down to the threshing floor** one night when **Boaz** was **winnowing barley**.

Ruth, being a stranger to Israelite customs, had to be told in detail how she was to make the customary appeal to her kinsman for protection and levirate marriage (*Daily Notes of the Scripture Union*).

3:6, 7 So **after Boaz had** finished his work, **eaten** his meal, and retired, Ruth **lay** . . . at his feet under a corner of his blanket. This may seem very irregular to us in our culture, but actually it was the accepted practice in that day (see Ezek. 16:8), and there was nothing evil or suggestive about it.

3:8–11 Awakened **at midnight**, Boaz found Ruth **at his feet**. Far from rebuking her, he **blessed** her after she had asked him to act as her redeeming relative. The word *wings* in 2:12 is the plural of the same word here translated **"wing."** Boaz had commended Ruth for seeking refuge in Jehovah; how could he refuse her the refuge she sought from him according to Jehovah's laws? Besides, she was **a virtuous woman**, one of those whose worth is far above jewels (Prov. 31:10). He commended her for her loyalty, saying that her latter **kindness** (her personal devotion to him) was better than her first (her leaving home and family to be with Naomi).

The Law of Moses required that when a man died childless, a close relative should marry the widow (Deut. 25:5–10), thus perpetuating the family name and keeping the land in the family. It was especially important that when a man died without a son, someone should marry his widow so that a son would be born and the name carried on.

Now Ruth, of course, had been left childless. Since Boaz was a relative of Elimelech, he was eligible to serve as redeeming relative by marrying her. And not only was he eligible; he was willing.

3:12, 13 But there was a legal complication: There was a **relative closer** than he, and this man had prior claim. If this **closer relative** did not wish to serve as redeeming relative, then Boaz would. The matter would be settled in the **morning**.

3:14–18 Ruth stayed **at his feet** till just before dawn. Boaz filled her **shawl** with **six ephahs of barley**. This assured Ruth of his deep love and gave evidence to Naomi that he would follow through on the matter without delay.

Ruth was a noble woman, intrinsically worthy of Boaz's kindnesses. But we were unworthy sinners. Yet the Lord spread His covering over us and took us as we were. He has loaded us with gifts and encouraged us with His promised return to consummate the marriage. Our salvation is settled, a finished work. But entrance into the full bliss of our union awaits the Bridegroom's return.

When Naomi heard all that had taken place, she told Ruth to **sit still** and wait for the outcome of this complex sequence of events.

This is often the most difficult part of faith—when no more action can be taken and nothing remains but to wait patiently for God to work out His will. It is at this moment that doubts arise and anxiety creeps in (*Daily Notes of the Scripture Union*).

V. REDEMPTION BY BOAZ (4:1–12)

4:1–6 In the morning **Boaz went up to the gate** of the city, where the elders **sat** and where legal matters were settled. It so "happened" —another designed coincidence—that the **close relative** walked by at that very moment. Addressing him as **"friend,"**[4] and asking him to stop for a while, Boaz stood before the **ten . . . elders** and told the story of **Naomi** and Ruth. Then he gave **the close relative** the chance to **buy** back the **land** belonging to **Elimelech**, which had probably been mortgaged when Elimelech went to Moab. Up to this point, the unnamed relative was willing. However, when Boaz told him that whoever bought the land must also marry **Ruth the Moabitess**, he backed away, explaining

that this would **ruin** his **inheritance**.

He would have to devote time and energy to looking after Ruth's property, thus possibly having to neglect his own. Ultimately, the land would go to Ruth's heirs, not his own.[5]

Commenting on the omission of the nearer relative's name, Matthew Poole writes:

Doubtless Boaz knew his name, and called him by it; but it is omitted by the holy writer, partly because it was unnecessary to know it; and principally in way of contempt, as is usual, and as a just punishment upon him, that he who would not preserve his brother's name might lose his own.[6]

The closer relative is widely taken to typify the law. Ten witnesses (the Ten Commandments) confirm its inability to redeem the sinner. "The law can't redeem those whom it condemns. It would be against its own purpose."[7] The law could not redeem because it was weak through the flesh (Rom. 8:3).

The refusal of the closer relative freed Boaz, who was next in line, to marry Ruth.

4:7, 8 In those days, all transactions concerning redemption and exchange were confirmed by one of the parties taking **off his sandal** and handing it to the other. The law actually specified that the widow should take off the sandal of the refusing kinsman and spit in his face (Deut. 25:9). In this case **the closer relative** simply **took off his sandal and gave it to** Boaz.

4:9–12 As soon as **Boaz** received the sandal, he announced that he would purchase **Elimelech's** property and marry **Ruth the Moabitess**. The crowd blessed Boaz, wishing him a posterity as numerous as that of **Rachel and Leah**. The mention of **Perez**, the offspring of **Tamar** by **Judah**, overlooks the sordid aspects of that story and concentrates on the fact that it was another case of levirate marriage involving an Israelite and a foreigner.

VI. THE ROYAL GENEALOGY OF DAVID TRACED BACK TO OBED (4:13–22)

4:13–16 **Boaz** married **Ruth**, and **she bore** him **a son** named Obed (*servant*). **Naomi** took the baby as her own and **became a nurse to him**.

4:17–22 **Obed** later became **the** ancestor **of Jesse, the father of David**. Thus the book closes with a short genealogy of **David** (*beloved*) which was to become part of a greater genealogy—that of David's great Son, the Lord Jesus Christ (Matt. 1). This genealogy is not intended to be complete. **Salmon** lived at the beginning of the period of the judges, and David was not born until the beginning of the period of the kings, a span of almost 400 years. Names are often deliberately omitted in biblical genealogies.

With this little genealogy ending with David, the reader is prepared for the monarchy and the next books in biblical order, 1 and 2 Samuel.

ENDNOTES

[1](Intro) J. Vernon McGee, *Ruth and Esther: Women of Faith*, p. 15.

[2](Intro) Irving L. Jensen, *Judges/Ruth*, p. 80.

[3](2:4–12) Leon Morris (with Arthur E. Cundall), *Judges and Ruth*, pp. 276, 277.

[4](4:1–6) The Hebrew here is colorful. Instead of giving the man's name the text calls him *so and so* (*peloni almoni*, NKJV marg.).

[5](4:1–6) Source unknown.

[6](4:1–6) Matthew Poole, *Matthew Poole's Commentary on the Holy Bible*, p. 511.

[7](4:1–6) Source unknown.

BIBLIOGRAPHY

For Bibliography see Judges.

FIRST SAMUEL

Introduction

"For sheer interest, I Samuel is unsurpassed. Not only does it recount eventful history; it is eventful history interwoven with the biographies of three colourful personalities—Samuel, Saul, David: and it is around these three that the chapters are grouped."

—J. Sidlow Baxter

I. Unique Place in the Canon

Without 1 and 2 Samuel there would be a gaping hole in the OT Canon. Originally one book, Samuel was first divided into two in the Septuagint translation for convenience. Every version of the OT, including printed Hebrew Bibles, has followed suit ever since.

Untold millions of Jewish and Christian children have been charmed and edified by the stories of Samuel, David and Goliath, David and Jonathan, David's flight from Saul, his kindness to Mephibosheth, and his sorrow over his son Absalom's rebellion and death.

On a more doctrinal level, more mature readers have studied the Davidic Covenant and the dreadful parallels to David's sin with Bathsheba that cropped up among his own children.

First and Second Samuel bridge the gap between the judges and the full establishment of the royal line of David. They hold a unique place in the history of Israel.

II. Authorship

While Jewish tradition makes Samuel the author of the book that is now divided into 1 and 2 Samuel, this authorship can only apply to the events *during* his own lifetime (1:1—25:1).[1] Much of the material in these books takes place *after* the prophet's demise.

It is possible that one of the young prophets who studied under Samuel wrote the book, incorporating writings of his teacher. Another possibility is that Abiathar, a priest who would be accustomed to keeping close records, compiled the book. He was closely associated with David's career and even spent time in exile with him.

III. Date

The date of the books of Samuel is impossible to pinpoint. The early part may date from about 1000 B.C. The fact that no reference is made to the captivity of Israel (722 B.C.) certainly demands a date before that event. Some believe that references to "Israel" and "Judah" demand a date after 931 B.C., when the monarchy split into these two parts. Such terms could easily have been used before the political split, however, somewhat as in American history the terms "Yankees" and "Southrons" were used before the secession of 1861.

295

IV. Background and Theme

First and Second Samuel trace God's dealings with Israel from the twelfth to the early tenth centuries B.C. *Samuel* (the prophet-judge), *Saul* (the rejected king), and *David* (the shepherd-king) are the main characters around which the narrative is framed.

Samuel was raised up by God to end the period of the judges and to inaugurate the era of the kings. He lived in a day that saw the failure of the priesthood (represented by Eli and his sons) and the introduction of the prophetic ministry. Samuel himself was the last of the judges, the first of the prophets of this period (not the first prophet in Scripture— Gen. 20:7), and the man to anoint the first kings of Israel. Although a Levite,

he was not of the family of Aaron; yet he served as a priest, apparently with God's approval. His heart was pure and devoted; Eli's was polluted and disobedient.

The theme of Samuel is how God, Israel's true King, at the people's request, delegated royal sovereignty first to Saul, and then to David and his lineage. Eugene Merrill ties the books in nicely with the theme of the whole Bible:

Also through David's royal house his greater Son, Jesus Christ, eventually became incarnate. Christ perfectly exercised kingship in His own life, and provided in His death and resurrection the basis on which all people who believe can reign with and through Him (2 Sam. 7:12–16; Ps. 89:36–37; Isa. 9:7).[2]

OUTLINE

Commentary

I. SAMUEL'S MINISTRY UNTIL THE ANOINTING OF SAUL (Chaps. 1—9)

A. Samuel's Birth and Childhood (Chap. 1)

1:1–10 First Samuel opens by introducing us to **Elkanah** and his **two wives, Hannah** (*grace*) and **Peninnah** (*pearl*). He was a Levite from **Ramathaim Zophim** in **Ephraim**; hence the designation **Ephraimite** in verse 1 (cf. 1 Chron. 6:22–28). As a faithful historical record, the Bible notes the practice of polygamy but never approves it. As was the case with Leah and Rachel, one wife was fruitful while the other was barren. This caused rivalry in the the home because, although **Hannah** was childless, she was more **loved** by her husband. When the family traveled to **Shiloh** . . . **yearly** to celebrate one of the feasts, Hannah would receive **a double portion** of the peace **offering** (vv. 3–5). But

this drew forth stinging taunts from Peninnah. Year after year her barbs cut deeper and deeper, until finally, in desperation, Hannah took the matter before the LORD at the **tabernacle**.

1:11–18 Hannah vowed that if God would **give** her **a male child**, she would **give him** back **to the LORD**. He would be a Nazirite from birth. Bishop Hall counsels:

> The way to obtain any benefit is to devote it in our hearts to the glory of that God of whom we ask it; by this means shall God both please his servant and honor Himself.[3]

The old priest, **Eli**, saw Hannah's **lips** moving and supposed her to be **drunk**. But as soon as she had explained her actions, he perceived her seriousness, blessed her, and sent her on her way **in peace**. Hannah was concerned about her *physical* barrenness. We should mourn our *spiritual* barrenness.

1:19–28 When Hannah's prayer was answered, she named her baby **Samuel** (*heard of God*),[4] because he was **"asked . . . from the LORD."** When Samuel was **weaned**, she **took him . . . to the house of the LORD** and **lent him to the LORD** in a once-for-all act of dedication. From the outset the boy assisted the priests and ministered before the Lord. The last phrase in verse 28 includes Samuel: He was a worshiper, although very young, because his life was devoted to the service of **the LORD**.

B. Hannah's Song (2:1–10)

The devotedness of Elkanah's wife and son stands out against the depravity of Eli's family. After giving her son to the Lord, **Hannah** poured out her heart in thanksgiving. Her words reveal an in-depth knowledge of God, His character, and His deeds. The prayer seems to rebuke Peninnah for the many spiteful things she had said to Hannah, but it prophetically goes beyond this domestic squabble to the triumph of Israel over her foes and to the eventual reign of Christ. Mary's song, often called the *Magnificat* (Luke 1:46–55), was obviously influenced by her knowledge of Hannah's song.

C. Eli and His Wicked Sons (2:11–36)

2:11–17 The narrative now turns to Eli's wicked **sons**. They **did not know the LORD** in the sense that they had not been saved by faith. Three sins are charged to them: They robbed **the people** of their share of the peace offering, not being satisfied with just the breast and thigh (cf. Lev. 7:28–34). They demanded **meat** before the **fat** had been offered to God, thus shirking the law. Third, they wanted to roast the **meat** instead of boiling it, putting

their own carnal appetites first. If anyone tried to protest, they took the **meat . . . by force**. Their **sin . . . was very great** because they treated the Lord's offering with contempt.

2:18–21 In contrast to their wickedness was the devotedness of the child **Samuel**, and the faithfulness of Samuel's parents to the **yearly** feasts. Since the firstfruits of Hannah's womb had been dedicated to the Lord, she was blessed with **three sons and two daughters**. It is a good illustration of our Lord's promise: "Give, and it shall be given to you."

2:22–26 It wasn't until **Eli** heard reports of immorality that he finally reproved **his sons**. But it was far too late for his mild verbal reproof to have any effect. They hardened their hearts and so were judicially hardened, like Pharaoh of old, for God had determined to destroy them. During this time **Samuel** was quietly growing, his purity and goodness pleasing **both . . . the LORD and men**. If we remember that these events took place during the time of the judges, it is not surprising that the priesthood failed to escape the moral decadence of the period.

2:27–36 The Lord's rebuke of Eli was as harsh as Eli's rebuke of his sons had been soft. An unnamed **man of God** appeared and announced the doom of Eli's **priestly . . . house**. The prophet began by reviewing God's call to Aaron's family to be His **priest**, and His generous allowance of sacrificial meats for their sustenance. He then rebuked **Eli** for allowing his sons' appetites to have priority over the claims of God (v. 29). The Lord's previous promise of the perpetuity of the priesthood assumed that the priests would be men of good character. But because of the wickedness of Eli and his **house**, they would no longer be allowed to function in the priestly service; no member of his family would reach old age; the sanctuary at Shiloh would fall into decay; and Eli's posterity would be a grief and a shame. Furthermore, **both . . . Hophni and Phinehas** would **die** on the same **day** as **a sign** that all these judgments would come to pass.

The doom of Eli's house was fulfilled in: The murder of Ahimelech and all his sons (except Abiathar) by Saul (v. 31; 22:16–20); the expulsion of Abiathar from the priesthood by Solomon (vv. 32, 33; 1 Kgs. 2:27); and the death of **Hophni and Phinehas** (v. 34; 4:11). Eli was from the house of Ithamar, and when Abiathar was later removed by Solomon, the priesthood was restored to the house of Eleazar, where it should have been all along. **Phinehas**, the son of Eli, is not to be confused with Phinehas, the grandson of Aaron (Num. 25:7, 8).

The **faithful priest** promised in verse 35 is Zadok, of the house of Eleazar, who ministered in the days of David and Solomon. His priesthood will endure, even during the Millennial Reign of Christ (Ezek. 44:15). But the descendants of Eli would desire the priest's office not in order to serve the Lord, but simply to get something to eat (v. 36). Many see a messianic allusion in the **faithful priest** of verse 35, partly in light of the word **forever**.

D. Samuel's Call (Chap. 3)

3:1–3 At the time that **Samuel** was serving **the LORD** in **the tabernacle** at Shiloh, **the word of the LORD was rare**; that is, the Lord very seldom spoke in visions to men. Williams sees in the first three verses a picture of Israel's moral condition.

Night reigned; the lamp of God was going out in the Temple; the High Priest's eyes were grown dim so that he could not clearly see; and both he and Samuel were asleep.[5]

The lamp of God refers to the lampstand, whose light was extinguished at sunrise.

3:4–9 One night, shortly before morning, **Samuel** heard a voice calling him. He thought it was **Eli**, but the priest had not called. **Samuel did not yet know the LORD** in the sense that he had never previously received a direct, personal revelation from Him (v. 7). After Samuel heard the voice two more times, Eli realized that **the LORD** was calling Samuel. The old priest told the boy to say, **"Speak, LORD, for Your servant hears,"** if he heard the voice again.

3:10–14 When **the LORD . . . called** the fourth time, Samuel replied, **"Speak, for Your servant hears,"** apparently leaving out the word "Lord." The Lord's message confirmed the judgment spoken earlier **against Eli** and **his house**, and the judgment may have included the defeat of Israel and the capture of the ark. The father was as much to blame as the **sons**, because **he did not restrain them** or turn them from their sins. They should have been put to death for their sacrilege instead of just being scolded. **Sacrifice** could not atone for their **iniquity**; their doom was sealed and was confirmed to Eli in the mouth of two witnesses: The man of God (chap. 2) and the boy prophet, Samuel (v. 14).

3:15–18 At first **Samuel was afraid to tell Eli** what the Lord had said, but under a solemn oath he revealed to the priest the impending judgment. Eli took the news submissively. Surely he realized God's justice in the sentence. Could God have struck down the sons of Aaron for their impiety

(Lev. 10) but leave Hophni and Phinehas unjudged?

3:19–21 It soon became known in **all Israel from Dan to Beersheba** that **the LORD was with . . . Samuel**, and all Israel recognized in the young lad a true **prophet of the LORD**.

E. The Ark of God (Chaps. 4—7)

1. The Ark Captured (Chap. 4)

4:1–4 The next three chapters follow the **ark of the covenant of the LORD** on a journey into and back out of enemy territory. God would defend His honor in the midst of **the Philistines** (chap. 5), but He would not defend the Israelites when He was in their midst because they had ceased to honor Him. When they **went out to battle against the Philistines** at **Ebenezer**, they lost **four thousand men**. In an effort to turn the tide, the elders had **the ark of the covenant** brought from **Shiloh . . . into the camp**.

4:5–11 The Israelites rejoiced greatly **when** they saw **the ark**, and **the Philistines** feared greatly because they knew the reputation of Jehovah. But they encouraged themselves and drew near to the battle once more. To their amazement, **Israel . . . fled**, **thirty thousand foot soldiers** were slain, the priests **Hophni and Phinehas** were killed, and **the ark** itself **was captured!**

4:12–22 When a runner went back **to Shiloh** and informed **Eli** that **the ark** had **been captured**, the old priest **fell . . . backward . . . off** his magistrate's **seat**, broke **his neck**, and **died**. The bad news caused **Phinehas' wife** to go into **labor**, and she died in childbirth. Hearing of the death of **her father-in-law and her husband** did not seem to affect her as much as the news that **the ark** had fallen into the hands of the Philistines. As she

died, **she named** her son **Ichabod**, (*inglorious*), **saying, "The glory has departed."**

2. The Ark's Power (Chap. 5)

5:1–5 The **Philistines . . . brought . . . the ark of God . . . from Ebenezer to Ashdod** and **set it** in the temple of **Dagon**, the national god of the Philistines. **Dagon** was supposed to be the father of Baal, another idol we meet often in Scripture. **The Philistines . . . set . . . the ark** beside the image of **Dagon**, thinking them equal. But when they returned to the temple **in the morning**, they found that the Lord had caused Dagon to topple to the foot **of the ark**. Not perceiving the significance of this event, they once again **set** up Dagon by the ark. But **the next morning** there was no doubt as to who was the stronger, for Dagon's **head** and **hands** had been **broken off**. If Dagon were a real god, he could have defended himself. His followers should have faced the facts. Instead, they made a superstitious rule about walking **on the threshold**. Dagon did not fare well in confrontation with the God of Israel. Samson had destroyed his temple in Gaza, God giving him the strength to pull the entire building down on the noblemen of Philistia (Judg. 16). Now Jehovah Himself maimed the image of Dagon, demonstrating that there is no wisdom (**head**) or power (**hands**) to be found in idols.

5:6–9 Not only their idol but **the people of Ashdod** themselves began to feel the displeasure **of the LORD**, suffering confusion, swellings or **tumors**, and death. In desperation the Philistines decided to move **the ark . . . to Gath**, another of their great cities. Here again the men were struck with **tumors**.

5:10–12 When **the ark** was **sent**

...to Ekron, the people were extremely frightened, their fears being justified by a **deadly destruction** that killed many. **The men who did not die** broke out with **tumors.** They begged that **the ark** be sent **back to** Israel.

3. The Ark Restored (Chaps. 6, 7)

6:1-6 In **seven** short **months ... the Philistines** had gained a proper fear of **the ark.** They wanted to **return it** to Israel, but in the proper way so as to avoid further judgment. The heathen **priests and ... diviners** were consulted. They suggested returning the ark with a guilt or **trespass offering** of **five golden tumors** and **five golden rats.** It was common among these people to appease their gods and make indemnity with an offering of whatever had caused destruction among them. The reference to **rats** leads Bible students to think that **the plague** that afflicted the cities was **the** bubonic **plague** carried by fleas on **rats.** The priests further reminded them of Egypt's fate at the hands of Jehovah, and urged them not to **harden** their **hearts as the Egyptians and Pharaoh hardened** theirs, but to make every effort to return **the ark ... to its** proper **place.**

6:7-12 To make sure that the things which had happened to them were judgments of Jehovah, and not mere **chance,** the Philistine priests arranged the details of the return trip in a way that would evidence divine intervention. The **two milk cows** that were used to pull **the cart** had young **calves** and it would violate all natural instincts if they left their calves behind. **The cows** had **never been yoked,** yet they pulled well in a yoke together, turning aside neither **to the right hand** nor **the left.** Without being guided, **the cows headed straight** to-ward **Beth Shemesh,** in the territory of Judah!

6:13-18 **The men of Beth Shemesh were reaping** when **the ark** drew near. What a sight—two unattended cows bringing the ark of God back to Israel! Great rejoicing broke out. **The cart** was used to make a fire, and **the cows** were **offered as a burnt offering** to the Lord. **The ark** and **the chest** containing the **trespass offering** were placed **on** top of a **large stone.**

There is a *spiritual parallel* in the story of **the cows** of **Beth Shemesh.** Christian missionaries leave home and family and carry the message of the Lord to wherever the Lord guides them, turning neither to the right nor to the left. Unbelievers rejoice when they hear about the Lord. The missionaries are prepared for service or for sacrifice.

6:19-21 But **the men of Beth Shemesh** did not treat **the ark of the Lord** as holy; **they had looked into the ark.** As a result, God **struck fifty thousand and seventy of** them. Fearful of having the ark remain in their midst, the people **sent messengers to** the men of **Kirjath Jearim,** and asked them to **take the ark.** (It is doubtful that there were 50,070 men at Beth Shemesh. Josephus,[6] Keil and Delitzsch,[7] and many other authorities say that the text should simply read seventy men, since the 50,000 is lacking in many Hebrew manuscripts.)

7:1-6 **The ark** was **brought** to **the house of Abinadab** in **Kirjath Jearim,** where it **remained** for **twenty years.** Then **Samuel** came forward and urged the people to **return to the Lord** so that God could **deliver** them **from** their Philistine oppressors. Idols were thrown **away** and the nation **gathered** to Samuel **at Mizpah.** There they **fasted** and repented before Jehovah. Their repentance was symbolized by pouring **out . . . water** on the ground.

7:7–14 Hearing that the Israelites were **at Mizpah**, and supposing that a revolt was in the making, **the Philistines** attacked. The Hebrews, unprepared for war, were terrified. When they pleaded with **Samuel** to intercede for them, he offered **a whole burnt offering** (which it seems Levites could do—1 Chron. 23:26–31), and prayed. God subsequently routed the enemy miraculously with **loud thunder**, and Israel won the day. In gratitude **Samuel . . . set . . . up . . . a stone** as a monument and named it **"Ebenezer"** (*stone of help*). Verse 13 refers only to a temporary victory, as is clear from the last part of the verse and from 9:16. Some land was also recovered at this time, and **Israel** enjoyed **peace** with her neighbors for a while.

7:15–17 After this, **Samuel** became a **circuit** judge, traveling through the cities of **Israel** and administering justice according to the law of the Lord. He lived in **Ramah**, **his** father's **home**, and **built an altar . . . there**. We aren't told why he didn't return to the Lord's altar, now at Nob, nor why he allowed the ark to remain in Abinadab's house. But these were days of irregularities, many things being practiced which God allowed even though they weren't according to His original design.

Chapter 7 is a study in revival. God first raised up a man, Samuel, who called the people to repentance, confession, and cleansing. Intercession was made through the blood of a lamb (a type of Calvary's Lamb), and then there was victory. These are the steps to individual as well as national revival.

F. A King Demanded and Chosen (Chaps. 8, 9)

8:1–5 In his **old** age, **Samuel** tried to have **his** two **sons** succeed him as

judges. But they were wicked men who accepted **bribes** and **perverted justice**. Like Eli before him, Samuel did not turn his sons from their evil ways, and so his house was rejected also. **The elders of Israel** refused to accept **Joel** and **Abijah**; they wanted **a king** instead, like **the** other **nations**.

8:6–18 It was God's intention, of course, that He Himself should be the King of Israel. His people were to be holy, and not like any other nation on earth. But they didn't *want* to be different; they wanted to conform to the world. Samuel was grieved by such a request, but **the LORD** told him to do as they said. After all, **they** had **not rejected** the prophet, but the LORD. In agreeing to their wishes, Samuel was to protest **solemnly** and to **forewarn them** as to **the behavior of the king** they would get. In brief, the king would enrich *himself* by impoverishing the people, would draft their young men and women for military and domestic duties, and would make virtual slaves of them. It was true that God had made provisions for the rule of kings in the law (Deut. 17:14–20), but His perfect will was that He Himself should be their King (8:7; 12:12). These laws in Deuteronomy were meant to curb the evil that was sure to follow.

8:19–22 When **the people** persisted in their demand, despite the warning, the Lord again told Samuel to do as they asked **and make them a king**. The prophet then sent the people home. Soon they would have their king.

9:1–14 Now **Saul**, the **son** of **Kish** (**a Benjamite**), enters the picture. While searching for his father's **donkeys**, he and **his servant** decided to inquire as to the animals' whereabouts from **a man of God** in a nearby **city**. With a small gift in hand, they approached the city and found out from **some young women** that **the seer** they were looking for would make an appearance that very day at a religious festival. As they hurried along, they met the man they sought. Little did **Saul** realize that the prophet was also looking for him!

9:15–21 On the preceding day **the LORD had** promised to direct **Samuel** to the **man** who was to be king. Now it was revealed to him that **Saul** was **the man**. But the prophet did not tell Saul immediately. First he invited him to a feast. **The high place** (i.e., a place set apart for worship) was usually connected with the worship of idols, but in this case it was for the worship of Jehovah. Samuel then told the tall, handsome Benjamite that he would have some important news for him in the morning. Apparently without being told of Saul's mission, Samuel told him that the **donkeys** had **been found**, and that he was **not** to **be anxious**. What were a few **donkeys**, anyway? He was soon to possess "all that is desirable in Israel." Saul took this statement with apparent modesty. **Benjamin** was certainly **the smallest . . . tribe** in **Israel**. In the past their numbers had been reduced to 600 because of their wickedness (Judg. 20).

9:22–27 At the banquet **Saul** was given **the place of honor** and was served the choicest cut of meat. In the evening Samuel had a long talk with him. The next day **Samuel** detained **Saul** as he was leaving **the city** and revealed **the word of God** to him.

II. SAUL'S REIGN UNTIL HIS REJECTION (Chaps. 10—15)

A. Anointing and Confirmation (Chaps. 10, 11)

10:1–6 Privately **Samuel** anointed Saul as ruler of Israel by pouring

oil . . . on his head. The priesthood had been inaugurated with anointing (Lev. 8:12), and now the first king was **anointed** in the same manner. A public ceremony would follow later. Three signs were then given to confirm the word of the Lord to Saul: (1) **Two men** would meet him at **Rachel's tomb** and tell him that his father's donkeys had **been found**; (2) **three men** would **meet** him at the oak **of Tabor**, en route to **Bethel**, and would **give** him **two loaves of bread**; (3) when he would **come to "the hill of God"** and would **meet a group of prophets, . . . the Spirit of the LORD** would **come upon** him and he would **prophesy**.

10:7–9 After all **these signs** occurred, Saul was to go **to Gilgal** and wait seven days for Samuel to come and to offer sacrifices. All the signs in verses 2–6 took place that same day; the events in Gilgal occurred later (13:7–15).

It should not be concluded from verse 9 that Saul was genuinely converted. Actually, he was a man after the flesh, as his later history so evidently demonstrates. He was equipped for his official position as ruler of God's people by the Spirit even though he did not know God in a personal, saving way. In other words, he was God's man *officially* even though we believe he was not a true believer.[8]

10:10–16 The **prophets** were dedicated and zealous men, and it surprised **the people** to see Saul **prophesying . . . among them**. This gave rise to the **proverb: "Is Saul also among the prophets?"** It became a common saying expressing surprise that Saul should engage in an activity that was so out-of-character for him. **Saul's uncle** (not his father, as we would expect) quizzed him about his discussion with Samuel. **Saul** mentioned his visit with **Samuel** but did not disclose that he had been privately anointed as king.

10:17–19 Meanwhile, **Samuel** assembled **the people . . . at Mizpah** to announce the appointment of **a king**. Before making the actual announcement, he once again reminded them that their demand for **a king** was a rejection of the **God** who **brought** them **out of Egypt** and into the Promised Land. When Saul was selected he was hiding either because of modesty or fear. Matthew Henry gives four reasons why Saul might have been afraid:

> (1) Because he was conscious to himself of unfitness for so great a trust. . . . (2) Because it would expose him to the envy of his neighbors that were ill-affected towards him. (3) Because he understood, by what Samuel had said, that the people sinned in asking a king, and it was in anger that God granted their request. (4) Because the affairs of Israel were at this time in a bad posture; the Philistines were strong, the Ammonites threatening: and he must be bold indeed that will set sail in a storm.[9]

10:20–27 **Saul** was brought forth and presented to the people as their **king**. A better physical specimen could scarcely be found in all Israel. Several **valiant men** attached themselves to Saul and accompanied him to his **home** in **Gibeah**, but not everyone was solidly behind the new monarch. Saul wisely **held his peace** in front of these **rebels** who **despised him**.

11:1–5 **Jabesh Gilead** was a city on the east side of the Jordan River in the **territory** belonging to Gad. When the Ammonites, the neighbors to the southeast, besieged the city, the inhabitants asked for terms of surrender. But **Nahash** wanted to maim them and make them a **reproach** in **Israel** by gouging out their **right eyes**. Surprisingly, the Ammonites allowed **the elders of Jabesh** to **send** for help. Perhaps **Nahash** was not fully prepared, or was not afraid that the rest of Israel would help Jabesh. **Messengers** were sent **to Gibeah**, where **Saul** was still working in **the field**. It was high time to assert himself as Israel's new king!

11:6–11 With the vividly threatening object lesson of a chopped up yoke of oxen, Saul summoned the nation to arms. **The fear of the LORD** came **on the people**. **Israel** and **Judah** combined mustered 330,000 strong at **Bezek** and marched all night to **Jabesh**, where they thoroughly routed **the Ammonites**.

11:12–15 Flushed with victory, **the people** wanted to kill those who formerly had not accepted Saul's rule. But **Saul** wisely stopped them. The fact that **the LORD** had given the victory was enough for him. **Samuel** then called a solemn assembly at **Gilgal**, and Saul's **kingdom** was renewed on a nationwide scale. There was no opposition this time. Gilgal speaks of spiritual renewal (Josh. 5:9).

B. Rebuke and Charge to the People (Chap. 12)

12:1–13 After the ceremony to renew the kingdom at Gilgal, **Samuel** spoke to **all Israel**. He first of all reminded them of his righteous rule as judge. No one could charge him with injustice. But in asking for a king, Israel had rejected this rule and God's sway over them. The Lord had been gracious in the past, raising up deliverers when they were needed. **"Bedan"** in verse 11 probably refers to Barak (NKJV marg., LXX and Syriac versions).[10] **Samuel** placed himself in the line of deliverers that began with

Moses. But Israel was ungrateful for these past mercies and **cried** out for **a king**. The Lord working through His judges wasn't enough for them, so He gave them Saul.

12:14–18 In demanding a king, they committed a great sin. But **if** they would **obey... the** LORD, even now He would bless them. **If... not**, they would experience His wrath. As solemn proof, **Samuel** prayed down a great thunderstorm, an obvious sign from God because such a storm was unseasonal **during the wheat harvest** and too well-timed to be a fluke of nature.

12:19–25 Stark **fear** gripped **the people** and they implored **Samuel** to **pray for** them. His prayer had brought down judgment; it could also bring down mercy. To this he replied with another appeal to follow **the** LORD; that was the way to avoid judgment. As for him, he couldn't stop praying for them; to do so would have been **sin**. This important statement shows that prayerlessness is *sin* and not just carelessness.

C. Disobedience and Rejection (Chaps. 13—15)

1. Saul's Sinful Sacrifice (Chap. 13)

13:1 There are obvious difficulties with verse 1, as can readily be seen by reading the verse in different versions. The KJV and NKJV read: **"Saul reigned *one* year; and when he had reigned *two* years over Israel..."** The ERV says: "Saul was *thirty* years old when he began to reign, and he reigned two years over Israel..." The RSV states: "Saul was... years old when he began to reign, and he reigned... two years over Israel." The NASB: "Saul was *forty* years old when he began to reign, and he reigned *thirty*-two years over Israel." Some

manuscripts of the Septuagint simply omit the problem verse altogether! The most likely explanation for this confusion is that some letters were dropped out of the Hebrew text by careless copyists in later centuries.[11] We do know that Saul was a mature man when he came to power because his son Jonathan was old enough to go to war.

13:2–5 **Saul** had established a standing army of **three thousand men**. **Jonathan** took his detachment and successfully **attacked** the Philistine **garrison... in Geba**, north of Jerusalem. This incited the Philistines to prepare a huge army for all-out war. (Some translations, following the Syriac and some manuscripts of the Septuagint, read 3,000 chariots in verse 5, a more likely number to accommodate the **six thousand horsemen**.)[12]

13:6–9 **The Hebrews** responded to the challenge with great cowardice; some even fled across **the Jordan**. They had been under the yoke for so long that breaking free seemed almost impossible; the Philistines possessed every advantage. As **Saul** waited for **Samuel** at **Gilgal** (see 10:8), more and more men were missing at each roll call. The seventh day began, **but** still **Samuel** failed to appear. With his forces diminishing and with war impending, Saul was moved by expediency to offer **the burnt offering** himself, even though he had no authority to do so, not being a Levite. Even if Samuel was late, that did not justify Saul's intruding into the priestly office.

13:10–14 Arriving immediately afterward, **Samuel** realized what **Saul** had **done**. What appeared to be valid excuses did not change the fact that Saul had disobeyed God. For this he would lose the **kingdom**. God had already found another **man**, one **after**

His own heart. This was the first of several sins in Saul's life which resulted in his losing the throne of Israel. The others were: his rash vow (chap. 14); sparing Agag and the best of the spoil in the battle with the Amalekites (chap. 15); the murder of Ahimelech and eighty-four other priests (chap. 22); his repeated attempts on David's life (chaps. 18–26); and consulting the witch at En Dor (chap. 28).

13:15–23 **Saul** took his **six hundred men** and joined **Jonathan** at **Gibeah**. **The Philistines**, **encamped** a short distance away at **Michmash**, began sending out **raiders** to the north, west, and east, and Israel seemed helpless to halt them. The Philistines had been in such complete control for so long that they had removed every **blacksmith** from **Israel**. The Hebrews had to come to them to get their farm implements sharpened. Only a few men had **swords**. Things looked grim indeed.

2. Saul's Rash Vows (Chap. 14)

14:1–15 Seeing his father's inactivity, **Jonathan** slipped away with **his armorbearer** to attack **the Philistines**. This was not a brash stunt or a foolish suicide mission. Jonathan was looking to God to provide a great victory. It did not matter that there were only two of them. Jonathan's confidence was: **"For nothing restrains the LORD from saving by many or by few."** Jonathan's faith would be rewarded. God showed him that he would have success when the Philistines would invite him up, perhaps thinking he was a deserter. As soon as the Philistines said **"Come up to us,"** . . . Jonathan climbed up to their **garrison**, and soon laid **twenty** of their number in the dust. As the survivors fled, God sent an earthquake which caused great confusion

in the Philistine camp. The *faith* evidenced by **Jonathan** (v. 6) and **his armorbearer** (v. 7) was all God needed to deal with the Philistines. Too bad that Saul's *foolishness* lessened the fruits of victory!

14:16–23 Saul's **watchmen** noticed the confusion and reported it to him. When **the roll** was **called, Jonathan and his armorbearer were** missing. **Saul** promptly called for **Ahijah** the priest to **bring the ark** so that he could inquire of the Lord. (The NKJV margin, following the Septuagint, reads *ephod* for *ark*.[13] The ark was probably still at Kirjath Jearim.) But Saul quickly changed his mind when the tumultuous **noise** among the enemy increased; he told **the priest** to **withdraw** his **hand**—i.e., to stop seeking the Lord's will (v. 19). He rallied his forces, convinced that he did not need divine guidance to know that the Lord was delivering the Philistines into his hands. Others also noticed that God was fighting for Israel. Those **Hebrews** who had previously defected turned on their Philistine masters, and even **the men . . . who had** been hiding **in the mountains of Ephraim** found new courage to join the battle. Everyone wants to fight when victory is almost won, but where are the Jonathans to make the initial confrontation?

14:24–30 To ensure speedy success, **Saul had** rashly forbidden his soldiers **under oath** to eat anything **until evening**, when the battle was over. He sealed his order with a curse. Hunger caused his men to become fatigued and thus put them at a disadvantage. Not knowing of his father's edict, **Jonathan** ate some **honey** to regain his strength. When he was told about the curse, he mourned that Israel's triumph was to be hindered by such a stupid order.

14:31–42 Saul's restriction not only angered Jonathan, but it endangered the people as well. When the fighting was over, they **rushed on the spoil**, killed the livestock, and **ate** it without draining **the blood**, in violation of Leviticus 17:10–14 and Deuteronomy 12:23–25. When **Saul** heard this, he rebuked them and set up **a large stone** where animals were to be **brought** and slain properly. He also **built an altar**, his **first**. In his zeal, Saul wanted to pursue **the Philistines** into the **night**, so he again talked to **the priest** about consulting **God**. But God **did not answer him**. This led Saul to believe that there was **sin** in the camp. As was done in such cases, the lot was brought out, and to Saul's surprise, **Jonathan was taken**, that is, shown to be the guilty one by the way the lot came out.

14:43–46 Jonathan explained what had happened, and Saul, to save face, ordered him put to death. **But the people** showed more sense than did their king. Hadn't **Jonathan . . . worked with God** to bring this great victory? How could God be displeased with him for breaking Saul's curse, when He had used him so mightily in battle? No, Jonathan would **not die**. Thus the hero was spared an undeserved death. But while Saul was engaged in such unnecessary nonsense, **the Philistines** fled. For the second time his lack of wisdom had diminished his victory.

14:47–52 Verses 47 and 48 summarize some of Saul's military victories. The next three verses give details concerning his family. The last verse is a fulfillment of Samuel's prediction that the king would draft Israel's valiant sons into military service (1 Sam. 8:11).

3. Saul's Incomplete Obedience (Chap. 15)

15:1–3 Saul was on a downward slide and accelerating as he neared the bottom. No matter what he was given to do, he came short of complete obedience. In this chapter he was commanded by God to destroy the Amalekites—the nation that had mercilessly **ambushed** the Hebrew stragglers when they had left **Egypt . . . on the way** to Canaan (Deut. 25:17–19). The order was very clear; everything that breathed was to be destroyed; it was devoted to God. God's longsuffering had put up with the people of **Amalek** for years, but His word against them had not changed (Ex. 17:14–16; Num. 24:20). They were to be blotted out as punishment for their sin.

15:4–12 **Saul gathered** an army and marched south **to a city of Amalek**. Before attacking, he warned **the Kenites** to escape because these nomadic Midianites had shown **kindness to . . . Israel** during the Exodus. This action showed that **Saul** was not just interested in carnage; rather, he was executing the vengeance of the Lord on a wicked people. He thoroughly defeated **the Amalekites** and put everything to **the sword** *except* the **king** and **the best of the** spoil. (A remnant, probably living elsewhere, also survived—see 30:1–6; 2 Sam. 8:12; 1 Chron. 4:43.) Miles away, **the LORD** informed **Samuel** of Saul's disobedience. This greatly disturbed Samuel and drove him to spend the **night** in prayer. By **morning** it was clear what he must do.

15:13–35 On the way **to Gilgal**, Saul stopped and built **a monument**, celebrating his victory. But **Samuel** saw things differently and challenged **Saul** for disobeying. Saul was never short of excuses, but the noise of his failure reached the prophet's ears and left Saul's excuses hanging in midair. *Rejected!* Saul had heard that before (13:14). It came again with stunning force. Saul was constantly redefining the Lord's commands, doing what seemed best to him rather than what God said was best. He made a show of repentance and pleaded with Samuel not to abandon him. He even **tore** the prophet's **robe** when he tried to leave. This too was a sign that **the kingdom** would be **torn . . . from** Saul and **given . . . to** another man.

After accompanying Saul to **worship the** LORD, **Samuel** called for **Agag** to be brought forth. Thinking that he might be spared, **Agag came to him cautiously** saying, "Surely the bitterness of death is past" (v. 32). **Samuel** then **hacked** him **in pieces** with the sword. The aged judge carried a burden the rest of his life because of Saul's failure. In one sense even God **regretted that He had made Saul king over Israel**.

We should memorize verse 22. It is one of the classics in the Word of God. Obedience first, last, and always. It is the watchword of those who would serve and please the Lord. Erdmann comments:

In the following words: **To obey is better than sacrifice**, the thought takes a new turn: apart from what alone is well-pleasing to God, only an obedient disposition of mind is in itself something good, the offering, without such a disposition, is not a good thing, has no moral value. . . . So disobedience and the thence-resulting rebellion and defiant self-dependence is similar in essence to, stands on the same moral plane with the outward wickedness of *witchcraft*, that is, "divination in the service of anti-godly demonic powers" (Keil), and of idolatry.[14]

Verses 29 and 35 seem to be contradictory. The first says that God does not change His mind or **relent**, while the second says that He **regretted** making **Saul king**. Verse 29 describes God in His *essential character*. He is unchanging and unchangeable, the immutable One. Verse 35 means that a change in Saul's *conduct* required a corresponding change in God's *plans and purposes* for him. To be consistent with His attributes, God must bless obedience and punish disobedience.

III. DAVID'S LIFE UNTIL THE DEATH OF SAUL (Chaps. 16—30)

A. Anointing by Samuel (16:1–13)

16:1–3 While **Samuel** was still grieving over **Saul, the** LORD told him bluntly to face the fact that Saul was **rejected**; God had chosen another man to rule His people. **Samuel** was to go to Bethlehem and **anoint . . . one** of the **sons** of **Jesse** to be **king**. Secrecy is not the same as deceit. God was not telling Samuel to lie about his intentions in **Bethlehem**; he really did offer a **sacrifice** there. But the anointing of the new king was a secret affair, not to be made public for many years.

16:4–13 When **Samuel** came to **Bethlehem, the elders . . . trembled**. After inviting **Jesse and his sons . . . to the** sacrificial feast, he looked over the men one by one, confident that the next king was before him. But none was the Lord's choice. **Samuel** should have learned from his experience with Saul that **the outward** man is not nearly as important as the inner man (13:14). God judges **the heart** (v. 7). The principle of verse 7 has always been true: People do judge by looks, dress, and outward things. But today the mass media encourage this faulty outlook by using glamorous people in advertisements, television, and printed matter to such an extent that ordinary-looking people don't seem as satisfactory as they should. Saul was tall, dark, and handsome. Actually, David was **good-looking**, too (v. 12), but still looked too young for major service. Unfortunately the church, especially on television, has often emphasized, not spirituality, but superficial glamor—with disastrous results when these TV idols fall.

David had to be **brought** to the feast. He was so insignificant in his father's eyes that **Jesse** was sure the prophet wouldn't be interested in him. But **the LORD** was very interested in the shepherd boy, and **Samuel**, obeying God's voice, **anointed...David**. **From that** point onward **the Spirit of the LORD came** powerfully **upon David** and left Saul. It would be years before David wore Saul's crown, but from this **day forward** the kingdom was secure for David.

B. Ministering to Saul (16:14–23)

About this time Saul became afflicted with a form of mental disorder caused by an evil spirit. The expression **"a distressing spirit from the LORD"** is explained by the fact that what God *permits* He is often said to *do*. Dr. Rendle Short analyzes the king's problem as follows:

> King Saul would now be diagnosed as a typical example of manic-depressive insanity. The periods of intense gloom with occasional outbreaks of homicidal violence for no particular reason, the delusion that people were plotting against him... are unmistakable.[15]

Saul's servants suggested that the king find someone gifted in music to calm him. David's name was suggested, and Saul sent for him. Verse 18 shows that David had already made quite a name for himself, even before he faced Goliath. Now his music seemed to lift the king out of his depression. Saul liked him so well that he made David **his** personal **armorbearer**.

C. Defeating Goliath (Chap. 17)

17:1–11 **The Philistines gathered their armies** for **battle** near **the Valley of Elah**, southwest of Jerusalem and not far **from Gath**. **Saul and** his army assembled nearby, with **the Valley of Elah** between them. **A champion** by the name of **Goliath** came out of the Philistine camp daily for forty days, defying **the armies of Israel** to send him a worthy opponent. There were no volunteers. This giant was about nine feet nine inches tall and wore at least 175 pounds of armor. **His iron spearhead** alone weighed over fifteen pounds. The heavy weapons were no problem for Goliath, since he himself must have weighed somewhere between 600 and 750 pounds (possibly more, depending on his build). This gave him many times the strength of a normal man.

17:12–30 On one occasion, when **David** was bringing supplies to his three oldest **brothers at the** battlefront, he heard the taunts of the giant and saw the fear on the faces of the Hebrew soldiers. He asked **what** would **be done for the man who** silenced this swaggering brute. **Eliab, his oldest brother,** rebuked him, probably to mask his own cowardice, but David persisted in checking into the prizes that awaited **the man who** would kill the giant.

17:31–40 **Saul** soon got word that a young man had been found to fight for Israel, and **David** was brought before him. When Saul saw David, he had understandable doubts about the lad's ability. But David had known the power of God working through him when he defended his flock against the **lion** and the **bear**. He had proved God in private; now he could rely on God in public. Seeing his courage and determination, **Saul** gave him **his** own **armor**, but **David** discarded it because it was a hindrance to him. Instead, he went forth armed with **five smooth stones**, a **sling**, a **staff**, and the power of **the living God**!

17:41–54 When Goliath saw **David**, who was probably around twenty at this time, he was incensed that Israel should insult him by sending out what in his eyes was a mere child to fight him. But David had no trace of fear as he responded to the giant's curses. He had complete faith that the Lord would give him the victory. As Goliath moved toward him, **David . . . slung** the first **stone**, hitting him **in his forehead**. The giant **fell** forward **on his face**. David then used the Philistine's own **sword** to kill him and **cut off his head**. **When the Philistines saw** this, **they fled**, with **Israel** in hot pursuit.

17:55–58 These verses[16] seem to present a problem: It is strange that Saul did not recognize David when he had already appointed him as his armorbearer (16:21). However, it should be noted that it does not say that Saul did not know who this young hero *was*; it simply says that he asked, **"Whose son is this?"** Saul could have easily forgotten David's family background. Williams comments:

> Saul, having promised exemption of taxation to the family of the victor, and the hand of his daughter in marriage with a handsome dowry, naturally asks Abner for information respecting David's father and his position in society. . . .[17]

This seems to be confirmed by the fact that David later expressed his unworthiness to be the king's son-in-law (18:18). Michael Griffiths makes a good application:

> Both Jonathan (chap. 14) and David initiated action on a small front just where they were, but what they did led to great victories. There is a need for us alike to take the field locally. We cannot hope to take on the whole of the enemy force, but we do not have to do so. There is a work for Jesus ready at your "front." We are called to be bold and to take the initiative where we are. God will take care of the rest when, as a result of our action, the battle spreads along the whole front.[18]

D. Marrying Michal (Chap. 18)

18:1–5 A deep and lasting friendship sprang up between **Jonathan** and **David**. They were kindred souls, each possessing that rare quality of true courage. **Jonathan** was the legitimate successor to his father's throne, but in giving **his robe . . . to David** he indicated that he was willing to forgo his right in order to see David crowned instead.

18:6–16 As **David** continued to win battle after battle, **Saul** became extremely jealous. When he heard the songs of **the women** ascribing to **David** greater exploits than to himself, he became livid with rage. God sometimes uses evil to chastise evil; that is why he allowed Saul to be tormented by **a distressing spirit** (v. 10). **Twice** the king tried to personally kill **David**, **but** both times **David escaped**. Then Saul **made him . . . captain over a thousand** soldiers, perhaps hoping that David would be killed while fighting the Philistines. (It appears that he had formerly held a larger command.) But **the LORD was**

with David, and his exploits attracted the attention of **all Israel**.

18:17–30 The king's **daughter** had been promised to the man who would kill the Philistine giant, so **Merab**, Saul's **older daughter**, was offered to David. However, more victories would have to be won first. **Saul** hoped David would be killed in the process. When David expressed his social unworthiness to be a **son-in-law to the king**, **Merab . . . was given to** another man, which was perhaps Saul's way of trying to humiliate David. But **Saul's** younger **daughter, Michal, loved David**, and **Saul** agreed to give her to him, provided he produced a **dowry** of **one hundred** Philistine **foreskins**. Again Saul hoped to kill **David by the hand of the Philistines**. But David was not to be eliminated so easily. He returned with the bizarre **dowry** in double measure and won **Michal** as his bride. As continual military success made it clear that **the LORD was with David**, Saul's hatred and fear of him continued to grow.

E. Fleeing from Saul (Chaps. 19—26)

1. Jonathan's Loyalty (Chaps. 19, 20)

19:1–7 When **Jonathan** realized that his **father** intended to murder David, he advised David to **hide . . . in the field** while he sought to pacify the king. In reasoning with **Saul** about **David**, **Jonathan** reminded him of David's bravery, loyalty, and success against Israel's enemy. He had done nothing worthy of death. Saul was temporarily conciliated and David was restored to his position in the royal court.

19:8–10 But when **war** broke out again, **David** once more distinguished himself, and Saul's jealousy was kindled afresh. **The distressing spirit** returned and **Saul sought to pin David to the wall with** his **spear**. This was

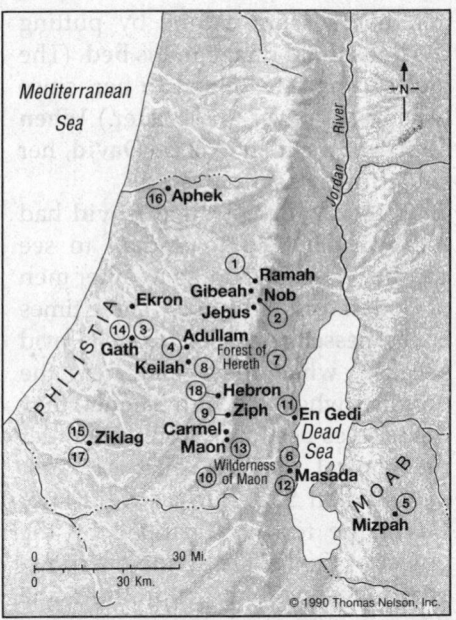

Saul's Pursuit of David

1. David flees Gibeah to Samuel at Ramah (1 Sam. 19:18)
2. David travels to Nob (1 Sam. 21:1-9)
3. David goes to Gath (1 Sam. 21:10)
4. David flees Philistines to Adullam (1 Sam. 22:1)
5. David takes his family to safety in Moab (1 Sam. 22:3)
6. David goes to Moab (1 Sam. 22:4)
7. David moves to the Forest of Hereth (1 Sam. 22:5)
8. David and his men attack Philistines plundering Keilah (1 Sam. 23:5)
9. David retreats to the Wilderness of Ziph (1 Sam. 23:14)
10. David withdraws to the Wilderness of Maon (1 Sam. 23:24)
11. Saul's pursuit drives David to Engedi (1 Sam. 23:29)
12. Sparing Saul's life, David returns to Moab (1 Sam. 24:22)
13. David returns to Carmel Maon, marries Abigail (1 Sam. 25)
14. Sparing Saul's life again, David returns to Gath (1 Sam. 26:1 — 27:2)
15. David is given Ziklag by Achish, Philistine King of Gath (1 Sam. 27)
16. David and his men go to Aphek, joining Philistine forces (1 Sam. 29:1-3)
17. Opposition to David from Philistine commanders forces his return to Ziklag (1 Sam. 30)
18. After Saul's death, David returns to Hebron, where he is crowned King (2 Sam. 1-2).

the third time Saul missed. **David** barely **escaped** with his life.

19:11–17 That same night King Saul **sent messengers** to **kill** David at his **house**. **Michal** knew of the plot and helped him escape by putting the household **image in** his **bed**. (The idol probably belonged to her, since David was never an idolater.) **When Saul sent** the men **to** seize **David**, her subterfuge was discovered.

19:18–23 But by then **David** had **escaped**. He **fled** to **Ramah** to see **Samuel**. Men of God go to other men of God in time of trouble. Three times Saul's **messengers** failed to catch David because, **when they** came near the **prophets** who were with **Samuel, they** themselves began to prophesy under the control of **the Spirit of God**. Later, when Saul himself **went** after **David**, he too was gripped by the power of God. This divine overpowering, however, was not the same thing as conversion.

19:24 Once again the people repeated the proverb about **Saul** being **among the prophets** (10:11, 12). His fluctuating behavior must have been puzzling to them. The word **"naked"** does not mean absolutely nude. It simply means that Saul took off his outer garments, the symbol of his royalty. While **God** held Saul prostrate on the ground **all that day and all that night**, David escaped (20:1).

Verse 24 does not contradict 15:34, 35, which says, "Samuel came no more to see Saul." Here it was *Saul who came to the prophet*, and that unintentionally and quite unexpectedly.

20:1–3 After leaving **Naioth**, **David** came **to Jonathan** and tried to find out why Saul was so intent on his destruction. Apparently Jonathan knew nothing of his father's continued attempts on David's life. David explained that the king would not share his plans with Jonathan because of the friendship that existed between him and David.

20:4–9 A test was proposed that

would make it plain whether **David** was in danger or not. Instead of taking his place at the royal table for the monthly feast, David would remain absent. If Saul inquired as to his absence, **Jonathan** would explain that he had gone to the **yearly sacrifice** at **Bethlehem**. (This might have been true, even though the trip is not recorded in Scripture. If it was a lie, it is simply recorded as a fact that is not approved by God.) **If** Saul didn't object, this would show that David was **safe; but if** the king became **angry** because David had once again slipped out of his hands, then Jonathan would know that David was in grave peril.

20:10–17 **Jonathan** promised to **go . . . into the field** on **the third day** and let **David** know how things had gone by means of a prearranged sign. Perhaps sensing what the outcome would be, Jonathan asked David to **show** the loyal love of **the LORD** to him and to his **house** when he rose to power. It is clear from verses 14–17 that Jonathan believed that David would yet be king; but he reaffirmed his love to David even though he realized the throne rights, vested in him, would be David's. What unselfish devotion!

20:18–23 These verses detail the sign by which David would be notified as to the king's attitude. **Jonathan** would come to the field and **shoot** some **arrows** near a rock where **David** would be hiding. The directions he called **to the lad** who would fetch the **arrows** would tell David to flee for his life or to return to the court in **safety**. We might wonder why Jonathan arranged all this play-acting to communicate with David when he later went and talked with David directly anyway. At this time, however, he might not have known that he would be able to contact David without being seen.

20:24–34 On the first night of **the feast**, **Saul** said nothing about David's absence, reasoning to himself that David was probably ceremonially **unclean**. But on **the second day**, when he quizzed **Jonathan** about David's whereabouts and found that he had gone **to Bethlehem**, Saul flew into a rage, accusing Jonathan of befriending the man who would rob him and his mother of honor. His language was rough and his manner even rougher as he tried to pin his own son to the wall, transferring his hatred for David momentarily to Jonathan.

20:35–42 On **the morning** of the third day, the appropriate sign was given and David's fears were confirmed. The men **wept** in each other's arms; they must now travel separate paths, no longer to enjoy each other's companionship. David went into hiding, a necessary part of God's plan to prepare him for the throne. **Jonathan went** back to the royal court, remaining loyal to his father, yet knowing deep inside that he would not be Israel's next king. Should he have gone with David? Was he right in remaining loyal to his father, even though the Lord had rejected Saul from being king?

2. Ahimelech's Kindness to David (Chap. 21)

Even great men have feet of clay. David is no exception. This sad chapter records his lies before the tabernacle, now situated in Nob (vv. 1–9), and his pretended lunacy before the Philistines (vv. 10–15).

21:1–6 David had gone to Samuel (chap. 19) and to Jonathan (chap. 20), and now he comes to the high **priest** in his flight from Saul. **Ahimelech was afraid** of David, and wondered

why he was traveling alone. (He did have a few companions with him who were waiting elsewhere—v. 2; Matt. 12:3.) David lied by saying that he was on a secret mission for **the king**. Then David asked for some **bread**. But all that was available was showbread, the **holy bread** used in the tabernacle for worship. **The priest** offered it to David, provided that his men were not ceremonially unclean through having sexual relations within the past few days. David said that his **men** were not only clean, but that they were **holy** (set apart) by virtue of their special mission. Shakespeare was right: "Oh what a tangled web we weave when first we practice to deceive!" **The showbread** that **had** just **been taken from** the holy place was given to David.

In Matthew 12:3, 4, the Lord Jesus approved this unlawful use of the showbread, presumably because there was sin in Israel and David represented the cause of righteousness. If David had had his rightful place on the throne, there would have been no need for him to be begging bread. The law, which forbade the profane use of the bread, was not intended to forbid a work of mercy such as this.

21:7–9 **Doeg**, a servant **of Saul**, was **detained before the Lord** in Nob at the time. Though **an Edomite**, he had converted to the Hebrew religion, and was detained by a vow, by uncleanness, or by some other ceremonial requirement. He naturally observed Ahimelech's collaboration with David and carried the report back to Saul. Meanwhile, David made a second request, this time for **weapons**. Again he lied, saying that he was on an urgent mission for the king. Goliath's **sword** was produced and David eagerly took it, exclaiming that there was **none** other **like it**. He had trusted in the Lord to slay the giant, only to lapse into confidence in the **sword** of his slain enemy.

21:10–15 **Then David** left Israel and **fled** to the city **of Gath**, Goliath's hometown. Here he, the anointed king of Israel, sought refuge among the enemies of God's people. When the Philistines became suspicious of him, he was forced to act the **madman** to save his life. DeRothschild notes that David knew well "that the insane were held inviolable, as smitten but protected by the Deity."[19] And so the psalmist of Israel stood drooling in **his beard** as he scribbled **on the doors of the gate**. Because of the callousness of God's people and David's own lapse of faith, he was reduced to this disgraceful behavior.

But David learned some valuable lessons through this ordeal. Before going on to the next chapter, read Psalm 34, which was written about this time. In this psalm we gain new insight into David's character. He possessed a remarkable resilience which enabled him to grow in his knowledge of God despite his failures.

3. David's Escape and Saul's Slaughter of the Priests (Chap. 22)

22:1, 2 When **David** returned to Israel, he found shelter in **the cave of Adullam**, in the territory **of Judah**, southwest of Bethlehem. This became a place for all who were **distressed, discontented**, and **in debt**. David here is a type of Christ in His present rejection, calling the downhearted to Himself for salvation. In a short time, a small army of **about four hundred men** had gathered at Adullam; later it would expand to six hundred men. In the world these men were misfits, but under David they became mighty men of valor (2 Sam. 23).

22:3–5 David's parents had joined

him too. Because of concern for their welfare, he traveled **to . . . Moab** to make arrangements for them to stay there while he was in hiding. Though David was a descendant of Ruth, a Moabitess (Ruth 4:17), he was wrong in putting confidence in the Lord's enemies. (Tradition says that the Moabites eventually killed David's parents.) Soon after David returned, **the prophet Gad** told him to leave Adullam, so he **went** to **the forest of Hereth**, also in **Judah**.

22:6–8 **In Gibeah**, in the land of Benjamin, **Saul** was ranting to the **Benjamites** and **to his servants** against David. He asked them if David would reward them as generously as he had done. David, after all, was not from their tribe. Saul accused them of concealing from him plots **against** his life. By now he was completely paranoid and irrational. He saw everyone as being against him, even his own **son**.

22:9–15 **Doeg the Edomite**, wanting to make the most of his opportunity to impress the king, told Saul how **Ahimelech** the priest had helped David by giving **him provisions** and inquiring **of the Lord for him**. **The priest** and his family were promptly summoned to **the king** and charged with treason. In reply, **Ahimelech** cited David's loyalty to the king and his own innocence in helping a man whom he believed to be **faithful** to Saul. He pointed out that this was not the first time he had inquired of the Lord for David. As for Saul's accusation that David was rebelling against him and lying in wait for him, Ahimelech said he **knew nothing** at all about it.

22:16–19 Saul's actions prove that he was quite insane by now. When his **guards** refused to **kill the priests of the Lord**, **Doeg**, a Gentile "dog" in the true sense of the word, fell on them swiftly, little caring that they were **priests**, and slew **eighty-five** of them. As if that was not enough, he **also** attacked **Nob**, Ahimelech's **city**, and killed all the inhabitants and livestock.

22:20–23 Only **Abiathar** survived; he **fled** to **David** and **told** him what had taken place. Then he stayed with David and served as high priest until he was justly removed from office by Solomon (1 Kgs. 2:27). In one sense **the death** of the priests was the result of David's lying and scheming (v. 22). In another sense it was the judgment of God upon the house of Eli (2:31–36; 3:11–14). But Saul himself must bear the major share of the blame for the massacre, since he ordered it.

Prophet (Gad), priest (Abiathar), and king (David), all in exile together, picture Christ today as He waits until His enemies are made His footstool and His throne is set up on earth.

4. Keilah's Betrayal (Chap. 23)

23:1–5 News came to **David** that the city of **Keilah**, south of Adullam, was under attack by **the Philistines**. Guided by **the LORD**, he fought against the enemy, **saved** the town, and captured a large amount of **livestock**.

23:6–12 When **Saul** heard that **David** was in **Keilah**, he decided to trap him there. But David found out about the plot and asked **the LORD** for guidance as to his next move. Would he be safe in Keilah? Would the inhabitants turn him over to **Saul** despite the favor he had shown them? Through the ephod which Abiathar had brought, and more particularly through the Urim and Thummim, God revealed that when Saul would **come**, the ungrateful people would indeed betray David.

23:13–18 So **David and his men** fled to **the Wilderness of Ziph**, southeast of Hebron. But even there they were relentlessly pursued. It was there that **Jonathan** found **David** and encouraged him in the Lord. What a needed ministry today! The church would greatly benefit if there were more encouragers around. Only those who have experienced the power of a strengthening word spoken in season know the blessing it brings to the soul. Jonathan's love for David was self-abasing. He reassured David that God would fulfill His purpose for him, despite Saul. A man who has a friend like Jonathan is fortunate. Why he failed to stay with David, and always returned home, is an enigma.[20]

23:19–29 The **Ziphites** also betrayed **David**, sending news **to Saul** as to his whereabouts and promising **to deliver** the fugitive **into the king's hand**. When David heard that Saul was coming, he fled to **the Wilderness of Maon** with Saul in hot pursuit. Just when it seemed that he would be surrounded, **the Philistines** attacked Israel and Saul was forced to abandon the chase. Unwittingly, Israel's enemy served as an ally to Israel's rejected king. The son of Jesse then traveled to **En Gedi**, on the western shore of the Dead Sea.

5. Saul Spared (Chap. 24)

24:1–7 After the Philistine threat had been dealt with, **Saul . . . returned** to hunt for **David**. He traced him to the rocky cliffs at **En Gedi**. While there, the king entered one of the caves for a rest stop. The **cave** he chose was not empty. Farther in, the man he ruthlessly hunted was restraining **his men** from taking the monarch's life! They thought God had delivered Saul over to them. But David knew of no command from

God to take the kingdom by force. He was content to await God's time and method. Even when he **cut off a corner of** the king's **robe**, his conscience bothered him. He did not take lightly the fact that Saul had been **anointed** as Israel's king. God must remove this king; David was to respect him until the Lord removed him.

24:8–15 After **Saul** left, **David . . . went out of the cave and called** after him. Bowing to **the king**, David told him that the slanderous reports to which he had listened were untrue. That very day David could have taken his life, but he did not because Saul was **the LORD's anointed**. The portion of the **robe in** David's **hand** was evidence of his kindness. A **wicked** man might want to avenge himself, but David had no such desire. He asked Saul why he should conduct such a relentless campaign against one who was as harmless and insignificant as **a dead dog** and **a flea**.

24:16–22 Temporarily moved to tears by David's words, Saul acknowledged the righteousness of David's behavior and his own wickedness. Surprisingly, he admitted that David would one day **be king** in **Israel**, and he made David take a solemn oath that he would deal kindly with his family. Then Saul left peaceably. But the respite David enjoyed was short. Saul soon forgot his kindness.

In David's words to Saul, he twice called on **the LORD** to act as **Judge**. He was content to leave his case in the hands of God rather than do what might seem right to the natural man. One of the things Peter remembered about our Lord was that "when He was reviled, [He] did not revile in return; when He suffered, He did not threaten, but committed Himself to Him who judges righteously" (1 Pet.

2:23). May God enable us to be as trustingly calm in the face of adversity!

6. Nabal's Folly (Chap. 25)

25:1–9 The death of **Samuel** brought to a close the period of the judges. The nation had now become a monarchy. David's descendants would occupy Israel's throne forever, Christ being the fulfillment of the promise. The deep respect in which Samuel was held is indicated by the grief that swept across the nation when he died.

After the prophet's death, **David . . . went down to the Wilderness of Paran**, in the southern part of Judah, perhaps to get further away from Saul and his murderous schemes. The **Carmel** mentioned in verse 2 was not the *Mount* Carmel which is in the north, but *a town* near **Maon**. **Nabal was shearing his sheep** there, and **David**, according to custom, **sent** some **young men** to ask for a gift in return for the protection he had provided for Nabal's flocks.

25:10–13 But **Nabal answered David's servants** in such a selfish and rude manner that David became enraged and started toward Carmel with **about four hundred men** to punish Nabal and his household.

25:14–22 **Nabal's** beautiful and discerning **wife, Abigail,** learned of the danger that her husband's ill-advised behavior had brought upon them. She quickly gathered a large supply of foodstuffs and went out to meet David. As **David** approached Carmel, he was rehearsing to himself the **good** he had shown Nabal and the contempt Nabal had shown him.

25:23–31 When **Abigail** met **David, she** prostrated herself at his feet and delivered a masterful and successful plea. She first admitted that her husband was true to his name (**Nabal** means *fool* or *cad*). When David's men had come earlier, she had not known about it. As she asked for forgiveness, she reminded him that **the LORD** had restrained him **from . . . bloodshed** and that God would punish his **enemies**—even **Nabal**. She had real spiritual insight into who David was, the anointed of the Lord, and praised him sincerely for fighting **the battles of the LORD**. How much better it would be when he became king if he did not have to look back on a time when he had stretched out his own hand and **avenged himself** instead of leaving his enemies to the vengeance of the Lord!

25:32–35 **David** was deeply impressed by these words of diplomacy and thanked her for preventing him from destroying **Nabal**. The Lord knows how to bring the right people into our lives to direct us and warn us. We should be thankful that He does. Abigail's **advice** was effective; her generous gift was accepted. David left Nabal with the Lord. God wasn't long in acting. Some might argue that Abigail violated God's order by not consulting her husband and by usurping authority over him. Yet the Bible does not suggest that she acted wrongly. On the contrary, she probably saved Nabal and his household from destruction by her emergency action.

25:36–44 When **Abigail** returned home, **Nabal . . . was very drunk**. She waited until the next day to tell him what had happened. When he heard the news, he was probably seized with paralysis, a stroke, or a **heart** attack. **Ten days** later **he died**, leaving behind all the possessions he had selfishly hoarded to himself. Hearing of Nabal's death, **David** soon **sent** a proposal of marriage **to Abigail**, which

she accepted with great humility. David had also acquired another wife, **Ahinoam**, since he had gone into hiding. Meanwhile, **Michal**, his first wife, **had** been **given** to another man.

In this story we see afresh that whoever exalts himself will be humbled (Nabal was killed by God), and she who humbles herself will be exalted (Abigail became the wife of the king) (Luke 14:11).

7. Saul Spared a Second Time (Chap. 26)

26:1–4 Once again **the Ziphites** reported David's whereabouts **to Saul** (cf. 23:19). Saul promptly gathered a force five times larger than David's meager band **and went down to the Wilderness of Ziph**. We are not told what happened to incite Saul anew. When the two men had last parted, they seemed somewhat reconciled (chap. 24). Maybe evil men had stirred up the king's hatred afresh (see v. 19).

26:5–12 **David** spied out Saul's camp, and in the evening he and his relative, **Abishai**, penetrated the camp and came to where Saul was sleeping. An unnatural slumber from the Lord made this possible. **Abishai** wanted to **strike** the king with a quick blow, but David forbade any such action because, although Saul was a wicked man, he was **the LORD's anointed**. It was the Lord's responsibility to deal with him. **David took** Saul's **spear** and **jug of water** and left.

26:13–16 When **David** was safely outside the camp, he raised his voice and taunted **Abner** for his carelessness in guarding **the king**. Such negligence was worthy of death. The **jug** and **spear** which David had taken told of Saul's second deliverance from death at his hand.

26:17–20 What still puzzled David was **why** King **Saul** pursued him so untiringly when he had proven that he meant him no harm. **If the Lord had stirred . . . up** Saul **against** David, then David could satisfy Him by presenting a sacrificial **offering. But if . . . men** had incited Saul's hostility, then **they** should **be cursed** because they were driving David away from the only sanctuary where he could worship God. The expression **"Go, serve other gods"** (v. 19b) was what these evil men were saying by their actions, if not by their words. David asked that he might not die "away from the presence of the Lord," i.e., in a foreign land (v. 20, NASB). Saul was hunting **a flea as . . . one hunts a partridge in the mountains**.

26:21–25 **Saul** apparently repented when he realized that David had spared his **life** again. He acknowledged that David was more righteous than he, for he sought David's life without cause, whereas David spared his life, though he could have killed the king in self-defense. David made a final appeal to **the LORD** to take note of his **righteousness. Then Saul** responded **to David** with a blessing and a prophecy of future greatness for his **"son David."**[21] **David went on his way, and Saul returned to his** city.

F. Living in Philistia (Chaps. 27—30)

1. Ziklag Acquired (Chap. 27)

27:1–4 The pressure of constantly running from place to place one step ahead of death finally took its toll on **David**. In spite of the Lord's miraculous care for him, David's faith wavered. He lost sight of the fact that he was the anointed king of Israel. Would God appoint him king and then allow him to be killed before he could reign? Would God deliver him

from the hand of Goliath only to deliver him into **the hand of Saul?** No, but circumstances have a way of distorting one's outlook. Present danger often obscures the promises of God. David fled **to the land of the Philistines** again and contacted **Achish, . . . king of Gath**. It had been a long time since he was here last, and Achish was probably aware that he was a fugitive. This heathen **king** welcomed him warmly, seeing in him a valiant warrior and an ally against Israel. This is not necessarily the same Achish that David met in 21:10, since "Achish" was a royal name among the Philistines.[22] When **Saul** heard **that David had fled** the country, he stopped hunting for him.

27:5–7 The last time David had been in Gath (chap. 21), the servants of Achish had been suspicious of him and had tried to have him killed. David had not forgotten this. With a show of modesty, he now refused to **dwell** in the capital city and asked for a city of his own. He was given **Ziklag**, a city close to Israel's border that originally **belonged to . . . Judah** (Josh. 15:31).

27:8–12 During his sixteen-month stay with **the Philistines**, **David** made raids against **the Geshurites, the Girzites, and the Amalekites**. These people were heathen inhabitants of Canaan whose destruction had been ordered by God (Ex. 17:14; Josh. 13:13; 1 Sam. 15:2, 3). Even in exile, David was fighting the Lord's battles. This presents quite a paradox: He could trust the Lord to preserve him for victory over Israel's enemies, but he could not trust Him for protection from Saul!

2. Saul's Doom Foretold (Chap. 28)

28:1, 2 Now David's position became extremely difficult. **The**

Philistines were going to war against Israel, and **David** was ordered by the king to join them. To this he seemed to agree, although his words in verse 2 are capable of two meanings—"**You will know what your servant can do** to assist you" or "You will know what your servant can do to double-cross you!" Achish chose the first meaning and made David a member of his personal bodyguard.

28:3–8 The rival armies gathered in the northwest of Israel at the plain of Esdraelon (the valley of Armageddon). **The Philistines encamped ... at Shunem**, and **Israel ... at Gilboa**. When Saul failed to get any response from **the LORD, either by dreams or by Urim or by the prophets**, he sought out **a** spirit **medium**. Earlier he **had** ordered all **the mediums** in Israel killed or exiled, according to the law. Now when **a medium** was located in the nearby town of **En Dor, Saul disguised himself and ... went to** her to seek counsel from the dead.

28:9, 10 The medium's first concern was for her own safety. She reminded her visitor of the king's edict against **mediums and ... spiritists**. How **Saul** could promise protection in the name of **the LORD**, who had decreed the death of such persons, or how the medium could be assured of safety by an oath sworn to that God, is an enigma.

28:11–14 Commentators are disagreed as to what actually happened next. Some feel that an evil spirit *impersonated* **Samuel**, while others believe that God interrupted the séance unexpectedly by allowing the *real* **Samuel** to appear. The latter is preferred for the following reasons: The medium was startled by the sudden appearance of Samuel in place of the familiar spirits with whom she was used to dealing. Also, the text specifies

that **it was Samuel**. Finally, the **spirit** prophesied accurately what would happen the following day.

28:15–19 Saul told **Samuel** why he had summoned him from the realm of the dead. Samuel's rebuke must have cut the king deeply. Did he think Samuel could help him when the *God* whom Samuel served remained silent? Instead, Samuel confirmed Saul's deepest fears. **The kingdom** would be taken from him and **given to** David, as he had been told earlier. **The Philistines** would defeat **Israel** the next day, and Saul . . . **and** his **sons** would join Samuel in death. This does not mean that they shared the same eternal destiny. If we judge them by their fruits, it would appear that Saul was an unbeliever whereas Jonathan was a man of faith.

28:20–25 All Saul's sins would be visited on him before another nightfall. With difficulty he was prevailed upon to **eat** something before he went **on** his **way**. The **fatted calf** was killed, but not for the purpose of celebrating. Shrouded in gloomy silence, the condemned man **ate** his final meal before disappearing into the night.

3. David Discharged by Achish (Chap. 29)

29:1–5 As **the Philistines gathered together** for battle, **David and his men** joined them, marching **with Achish ... at the rear** of the column. Some of **the princes of the Philistines** wisely objected to David's presence. They realized that he might turn on them during the battle. How could he better reconcile himself to King Saul than by producing a row of Philistine heads? Was **this not** the **David** who had been praised as the killer of more Philistines than **Saul** himself?

29:6-11 Their arguments were reasonable, so **Achish** requested **David** to **return** to Ziklag. David's answer seems unworthy of a man of God. He protested that he should be allowed to enter the **fight against "the enemies of my lord the king"**—even though these enemies were his own people. David had lied to Achish before (chap. 27), and this was probably another attempt to deceive the Philistines. If, as seems unlikely, he actually intended to fight against Israel, God prevented it and saved him from the shame of killing his fellow Israelites and strengthening the arm of the Philistines against them. David would not be allowed to use Goliath's sword against Israel.

4. Amalekites Defeated (Chap. 30)

30:1-6 While David had been marching north with the armies of Achish, **the Amalekites had** raided Ziklag and **taken . . . the women and** children **captive**. Thus when **David** returned he found only the smoldering remains of his city. Was this possibly a judgment of God upon him for joining the Philistines? If so, David showed his great insight into the character of God, because he went to Him for comfort when everything and everyone was against him. He knew there was no one to turn to for strength in such an overwhelming crisis except **the LORD**, of whom it is said, "He has torn, but He will heal us; He has stricken, but He will bind us up" (Hos. 6:1).

30:7-15 After inquiring **of the LORD**, **David went** out after the Amalekites, assured of success. **Two hundred** of his **men** (one third) **could** travel no farther than **the Brook Besor** because they were emotionally drained from their recent loss and physically exhausted from their three-day march

to **Ziklag**. David left them there and went south with the remaining **four hundred men**, tired yet pursuing. In a short while **they found** an ailing **Egyptian in the field** who had been **left . . . behind** by his **Amalekite . . . master** to die. He was given food and water and soon regained a measure of **strength**. In return for promised safety, he led David to the Amalekite camp.

30:16-25 The last thing the drunken **Amalekites** expected was a surprise guest at their victory celebration. **David** sprang like a leopard on the revelers and completely overpowered the much larger force. Only **four hundred young men . . . escaped** the sword, riding off **on camels**. The Hebrew captives were freed unharmed and an immense amount of **spoil** was taken, all in less than twenty-four hours. **David** was given the sheep and cattle captured from the Amalekites as his portion; but some of his men didn't want to **share** the rest of the **spoil** with their comrades who had stayed behind at **Besor**. David **made . . . an ordinance** that those who "stayed by the stuff" would **share** equally with those who went out **to the battle** (see also Num. 31:27).

30:26-31 **David** divided his **spoil** into gifts for various friends back in **Judah**. These presents were sent **to all the places where** he was **accustomed to rove**. They evidenced that God had prospered him against his enemies. He might also have been trying to cement his friendships to gain support in his struggle against Saul, not realizing that Saul was now dead.

IV. SAUL'S DEATH (Chap. 31)

31:1-6 Whereas David enjoyed success in battle, **Saul** met defeat.

The Israelites were pushed back and the king's three **sons** were slain. Saul himself was **severely wounded by the archers**. As he lay dying on **Mount Gilboa**, he begged **his armorbearer** to kill him, lest the Philistines find him alive and **abuse** him. But the man **was . . . afraid** to strike the king, so **Saul** took his own life, falling **on . . . a sword**. Shortly thereafter, **his armorbearer** did the same.

31:7–13 **Israel** now became totally demoralized, and they retreated before the invading army. When **the Philistines came to strip** the dead and **found Saul and his three sons** among the **fallen**, **they cut off** Saul's **head** and sent **word throughout** their **land**. **His body** and **the bodies of his sons** were taken to **Beth Shan** and hung on the city's **wall**. **When the** men **of Jabesh Gilead heard** of this, they marched the ten miles to recover **the bodies**. The remains were given a proper burial **under the tamarisk tree at Jabesh**. These men had not forgotten how Saul had saved them from the Ammonites in his first major battle as king (chap. 11). Cremation was not generally practiced in Israel. Perhaps it was used here because the bodies had been so mutilated. Also, it would prevent the Philistines from the possibility of ever dishonoring the bodies still further.

God's judgment on Saul was now complete (see notes on 1 Chron. 10). Many times Saul had tried to arrange for David to be killed by the Philistines, but he himself was the one to eventually fall before them. David received the throne as appointed by God. Saul received the just recompense of his deeds, according to the justice of the Lord to which David often committed him.

ENDNOTES

[1](Intro) The Jewish scholar Abarbanel explained the tradition this way: "All the contents of both books may in a certain sense be referred to Samuel, even the deeds of Saul and David because both, having been anointed by Samuel, were, so to speak, the work of his hands" (quoted by Erdmann, "The Books of Samuel," Lange's *Commentary on the Holy Scriptures*, p. 1).

[2](Intro) Eugene H. Merrill, "1 Samuel," *The Bible Knowledge Commentary*, p. 432.

[3](1:11–18) Bishop Hall, quoted in *Spurgeon's Devotional Bible*, p. 222.

[4](1:19–28) Gesenius and other Hebrew scholars believed the name means *name (Shem) of God*.

[5](3:1–3) George Williams, *The Student's Commentary on the Holy Scriptures*, p. 140.

[6](6:19–21) Flavius Josephus, *The Works of Flavius Josephus (Ant. vi 1:4)*, p. 178.

[7](6:19–21) C. F. Keil and F. Delitzsch, "The Books of Samuel," *Biblical Commentary on the Old Testament*, VII:68.

[8](10:7–9) Some Evangelical scholars consider Saul a believer, but one who became terribly backslidden and then mentally deranged. They argue that it is improbable that God would choose an unregenerate person to be the first king of His chosen people.

[9](10:17–19) Matthew Henry, "I Samuel," in *Matthew Henry's Commentary on the Whole Bible*, II:334, 35.

[10](12:1–13) The names *Bedan* and *Barak* look much alike in the ancient texts. Hebrew "d" (*dalet*) and "r" (*resh*) are often confused in copying, as well as the final forms of "n" (*nun*) and "k" (*kaph*).

[11](13:1) A large part of OT ms.

problems have to do with the Hebrew system of numbers, which were easy to mis-copy. See commentary on Chronicles for more details on this.

[12](13:2–5) See previous note.

[13](14:16–23) The old RV of 1885 reads: "Bring hither the Ephod: for he wore the Ephod at that time before Israel."

[14](15:13–35) Christian F. Erdmann, "The Books of Samuel," in Lange's *Commentary on the Holy Scriptures, Critical, Doctrinal and Homiletical*, III:209.

[15](16:14–23) Arthur Rendle Short, *The Bible and Modern Medicine*, p. 71.

[16](17:55–58) The Septuagint omits these verses.

[17](17:55–58) Williams, *Student's Commentary*, p. 152.

[18](17:55–58) Michael Griffiths, *Take My Life*, p. 128.

[19](21:10–15) DeRothschild, further documentation unavailable.

[20](23:13–18) Perhaps he felt a loyalty to his father's *position* even though he knew that he was *personally* in the wrong.

[21](26:21–25) These may have been mere words. On the other hand, if Saul was sincere it could be an argument that in spite of his sin and his paranoia he did have faith in God.

[22](27:1–4) Keil and Delitzsch, suggesting a fifty-year reign as "not impossible," believe the same Achish is mentioned in both texts, as well as in 1 Kgs. 2:39 ("Samuel," VII:255).

BIBLIOGRAPHY
(1 and 2 Samuel)

Blaikie, William Garden. "The First Book of Samuel." In *The Expositor's Bible*. London: Hodder and Stoughton, 1909.

———. "The Second Book of Samuel." In *The Expositor's Bible*. London: Hodder and Stoughton, 1909.

Erdmann, Christian F. "The Books of Samuel." In Lange's *Commentary on the Holy Scriptures, Critical, Doctrinal and Homiletical*. Vol. 3. Grand Rapids: Zondervan Publishing House, 1960.

Grant, F. W. "Samuel." In *The Numerical Bible*. Vol. 2. New York: Loizeaux Brothers, 1904.

Henry, Matthew. "The Books of Samuel." In *Matthew Henry's Commentary on the Whole Bible*. Vol. 2, Joshua to Esther. McLean, VA: MacDonald Publishing Company, n.d.

Jensen, Irving L. *I & II Samuel*. Chicago: Moody Press, 1968.

Keil, C. F., and Delitzsch, F. "The Books of Samuel." In *Biblical Commentary on the Old Testament*. Vol. 7. Grand Rapids: Wm. B. Eerdmans Publishing Co., 1971.

Laney, J. Carl. *First and Second Samuel*. Everyman's Bible Commentary. Chicago: Moody Press, 1982.

Merrill, Eugene H. "1 and 2 Samuel." In *The Bible Knowledge Commentary. Old Testament*. Wheaton, IL: Victor Books, 1985.

Meyer, F. B. *Samuel*. Chicago: Fleming H. Revell Co., n.d. Reprint. Fort Washington, PA: Christian Literature Crusade, 1978.

Short, Arthur Rendle. *The Bible and Modern Medicine*. Chicago: Moody Press, 1953.

SECOND SAMUEL

"David the king is the great figure of this Book; and, when walking in the Light, presents a rich type of Messiah the King. The first part of the Book records the victories which accompanied his life of faith and conflict; the second part relates the defeats he suffered when prosperity had seduced him from the path of faith and had opened the door to self-will."

—George Williams

For Introduction see 1 Samuel.

OUTLINE

Commentary

I. DAVID'S RISE TO POWER (Chaps. 1—10)

A. Lament over Saul and Jonathan (Chap. 1)

1:1–16 First Samuel 29 records how the Lord kept **David** out of the battle in which Saul and Jonathan lost their lives. Instead, he was busy fighting **the Amalekites**, who had raided Ziklag (1 Sam. 30). After he **had returned** to **Ziklag**, a messenger **came to** him **from** the north with news of Saul's death. The messenger wore **torn . . . clothes** and had **dust on his head**— symbols of mourning. He told how he had found **Saul, leaning** wounded **on his spear** as the enemy's forces drew near. He said that Saul asked him, **an Amalekite**, to administer the death blow, and that he complied with the king's request. This account of Saul's death is obviously in conflict with the one in 1 Samuel 31, where Saul is said to have committed suicide. The most reasonable explanation is that the Amalekite's account was a lie. He thought that David would be pleased to meet Saul's slayer and would reward him handsomely. Instead, David **mourned** deeply all that day, and then at **evening** he ordered the execution of the Amalekite because he had slain the Lord's anointed.

The Amalekites were the inveter-ate enemies of Israel (Ex. 17). One reason Saul lost the kingdom was because he had failed to thoroughly execute the Lord's wrath on them (1 Sam. 15). Some Amalekites had recently been killed by David and his men for their plunder of Ziklag. So when this Amalekite arrived in camp and announced that he had killed Saul, it is little wonder that he received the sword and not a reward.

1:17, 18 It was surely a mark of greatness on David's part that instead of rejoicing over Saul's death, he wept bitterly.

O. von Gerlach sees a parallel between David and Christ here:

> The only deep mourning for Saul, with the exception of that of the Jabeshites (1 Sam. xxxi. 11), proceeded from the man whom he had hated and persecuted for so many years even to the time of his death; just as David's successor wept over the fall of Jerusalem, even when it was about to destroy Himself.[1]

David also composed a moving **lamentation** entitled **"The Song of the Bow." The Book of Jasher**, or the "Book of the Upright," was probably a collection of poems concerning great men of the nation of Israel (see also Josh. 10:13). As far as is known, it is no longer in existence and certainly is not part of inspired Scripture.

1:19–27 David's stirring ode laments the death of **Saul** and **Jonathan**—the beauty of Israel. In majestic poetry, it cautions against letting the cities **of the Philistines** know of the death of the king and his sons **lest** they **rejoice.** The **mountains of Gilboa,** where Saul died, are called upon to suffer drought and barrenness. There **the shield of Saul** was cast down unanointed **with** oil (v. 21); that is, it was discarded and no longer oiled for battle. Tribute is paid to the bravery **of Saul** and **of Jonathan** (v. 22) and their personal virtues. They were together **in their death** as they had been **in their lives** (v. 23), but this should not be pressed to include their eternal destiny. Those who benefited from Saul's reign are called on to **weep** (v. 24). The poem closes with a loving eulogy of **Jonathan,** David's close friend. The refrain "How the mighty have fallen" (vv. 19, 25, 27) has become part of our language.

B. Coronation as King of Judah (2:1–7)

2:1–7 With Saul dead and Israel without a king, **David** sought guidance from **the LORD** and was directed to go **to Hebron,** one **of the cities of** **Judah.** There **the men of Judah . . . anointed** him as their **king.** When they informed him how **the men of Jabesh Gilead** had kindly **buried Saul,** David immediately sent a message of thanks to them and rather indirectly invited them to recognize him as **king,** as the men **of Judah** had done.

C. Conflict with Saul's House (2:8—4:12)

2:8–11 But not all the tribes of Israel wanted to recognize David as their monarch. **Abner,** the **commander**-in-chief of the late Saul and also his uncle, **took** Saul's only surviving son, **Ishbosheth,** and proclaimed **him king.** For **seven years and six months . . .** David reigned **over** the lone tribe of **Judah,** with **Hebron** as his capital. However, it was for only **two** of these **years** that **Ishbosheth . . . reigned** over the other eleven tribes. It may have taken Abner five years to push the Philistines back out of Israel and establish Ishbosheth on his father's throne.

David had never asserted his right to the throne. Neither did he do so now. Rather, he chose to leave the matter in the hands of the Lord. If Jehovah had anointed him as king, Jehovah would subdue his enemies and bring him into the possession of his kingdom. The Lord Jesus similarly awaits the Father's timing to reign over the entire globe. His dominion is recognized only by a minority of mankind now, but there is an appointed day in which every knee will bow and every tongue will confess that Jesus Christ is Lord (Phil. 2:10, 11).

2:12–17 In the course of time, **Abner, the son of Ner,** the captain of the army of Israel (the 11 tribes) met **Joab, the son of Zeruiah,** the military leader of David's soldiers, at **Gibeon.** Seated at opposite sides of a pool, they decided to **let** some of their **young men** engage in a contest to determine who was militarily superior. When **Abner** suggested that **the young men** should **arise** and hold a contest, he did not expect that they would play. It was a military engagement. The **twelve** Benjamites fought the **twelve** men of Judah, and they destroyed each other. Since the result was inconclusive, a **very fierce battle** broke out between the rest of **the men,** with the result that Abner's **men . . . were beaten** and fled in disarray.

2:18–23 One of Joab's brothers, the swift-footed **Asahel**, chased **Abner** with the intent to kill him. At first Abner tried to persuade Asahel to be satisfied with capturing **one of the young men**. It seems that **Abner** realized that he could easily kill **Asahel**, but he did not want to do it because it would further antagonize **Joab**. When Asahel would not listen to Abner's second plea to stop pursuing him, Abner turned on him in self-defense and killed him **with the blunt end of his spear**.

2:24–32 **Joab and** his other brother, **Abishai**, continued to chase until they came to **the hill of Ammah**. There Abner pled with Joab to stop this needless civil war. Joab's reply may be understood in two ways. First, it may mean that if Abner had not issued the original challenge (in verse 14), then the young men would have gone home peaceably. Or it may mean, as in the NIV, that if Abner had not called for a truce, then the young men would have continued chasing **their brethren** until **morning**. In any case, Joab agreed to stop fighting. **Abner and his men . . . crossed over . . . to Mahanaim**, on the east side of **the Jordan** River where Ishbosheth had his capital. He had lost **three hundred and sixty men**. **Joab** and his soldiers **returned** to Hebron, with only **nineteen men . . . missing**.

3:1–5 During David's seven-and-a-half years at Hebron, his kingdom **grew stronger** while Saul's **house**, ruled by Ishbosheth, **grew weaker**. David's family also grew larger. When he first came to **Hebron**, he had two wives, **Ahinoam** and **Abigail**. Contrary to God's will, he married four more—**Maacah, Haggith, Abital**, and **Eglah**. By these six wives he had six sons, three of whom were to be a grief to him—**Amnon, Absalom**, and **Adonijah**. (He had other sons later.)

3:6–11 While professedly serving Ishbosheth, **Abner was** actually **strengthening his** own political position because he saw the balance of power shifting to **David**. **Ishbosheth** accused **Abner** of having relations with **Rizpah**, a **concubine** of **Saul**, and probably interpreted this as an indication that Abner wanted to seize control of the eleven tribes. Whether Abner was guilty of this we do not know; he denied it vigorously and disrespectfully, and announced that he would **transfer** his allegiance and that of the tribes of **Israel** to **David**. **Ishbosheth** was powerless to resist. **"Am I a dog's head that belongs to Judah?"** (v. 8) means "Am I a worthless, contemptible traitor who has been loyal to Judah in the past?"

3:12–16 **Abner** now **sent messengers . . . to David**, offering to turn over **all Israel to** him. Before **David** would agree to Abner's proposal, he demanded that **Michal, Saul's daughter,** be returned to him, hoping thereby to strengthen his claim to Saul's kingdom. **Ishbosheth** meekly assented and **Michal** was brought to **David**—to the great grief of **her husband, Paltiel**. David's personal life thus became further entangled, and another dark chapter was written in his biography.

3:17–21 **Abner** then went to the tribe of **Benjamin** and to the other tribes that had followed Ishbosheth and told them that **David** was God's promised means of saving them **from the** oppression **of the Philistines**. Since their response was apparently favorable, he visited **David** and expressed his readiness to **gather all Israel** together in a great expression of allegiance.

3:22–30 While Abner was leaving David to carry out this plan, **Joab** returned to the royal house and heard of the day's events. After rebuking **the king** for so foolishly entertaining a spy, he secretly **sent** out soldiers to bring Abner **back**. As soon as **Abner . . . returned to Hebron, Joab** pretended he wanted a private interview near **the gate**, but his real purpose was to kill Abner in revenge, which he did by stabbing **him in the stomach**, thus avenging **his brother** Asahel's death and eliminating a potential rival as commander-in-chief. Joab seemed unconcerned that Hebron was a city of refuge, where Abner was at least entitled to a trial (Num. 35:22–25). The expression **"one . . . who leans on a staff"** (v. 29) may mean a cripple. In the NASB it is rendered "one who takes hold of a distaff" (that is, an effeminate man). The RSV similarly translates "one who holds a spindle," meaning unfit for war or heavy work.

3:31–39 **David** proclaimed a great time of mourning **for Abner** but took no action against **Joab** for murdering him. It grieved the king that Abner should have died so ingloriously, since his courage and power deserved a more honorable death. The thought in verse 33 may be, "Did Abner die like an inexperienced fool, who knew not how to defend himself?" And the intended answer is "No, he fell victim to a deceitful, wicked plot."[2] The people knew by the king's sorrow that Joab had acted independently. In fact, David publicly expressed his displeasure at the cruelty of **the sons of Zeruiah** (Joab and Abishai) and called on the Lord to punish them. In chapter 3 we have seen God using the sin and intrigue of men to give the united kingdom to David. He makes even the wrath of men to praise Him (Ps. 76:10).

4:1–7 Abner's death weakened the kingdom of Ishbosheth still further.

As soon as the army had lost its powerful leader, **two** rebels rose up— **Baanah and . . . Rechab**—and assassinated the king. They were able to do this by entering **the house** while **Ishbosheth** was taking his siesta. They pretended that they had come to pick up some **wheat**. The RSV of verse 6, following the Septuagint, reads, "And behold, the doorkeeper of the house had been cleaning wheat, but she grew drowsy and slept; so Rechab and Baanah his brother slipped in." This left only one male heir to the throne of Saul, a crippled lad by the **name** of **Mephibosheth**.

4:8–12 Rechab and Baanah **brought the head of Ishbosheth to David** in hopes of winning his favor. These **wicked men** tried to suggest that **the** Lord had prompted their action. But **David** knew better than that! God would not lead men to break His law in order to enthrone His king. God was well able to fulfill His promises to David without enlisting the aid of murderers. David told them that they were **more** guilty than the one who claimed to have murdered **Saul**, and ordered them to be slain immediately. Their bodies were exposed to the shame of public display, while **the head of Ishbosheth** was honorably **buried in the tomb of Abner**.

D. Coronation as King over All Israel (Chap. 5)

5:1–5 With words of loyalty and allegiance, the eleven **tribes of Israel** now joined Judah in acknowledging **David** as rightful king. Those who came are enumerated in 1 Chronicles 12:23–40. Thus **began** a **reign** over the united nation that was to last **thirty-three years**. In all, David's reign lasted **forty years**.

Verse 3 records David's third

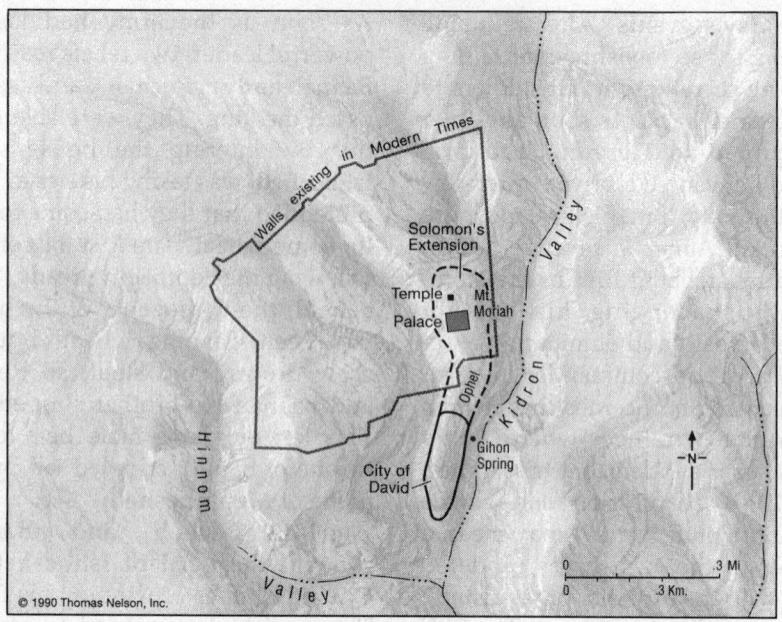

Jerusalem: David's City. David took the fortress called Jebus and renamed it the "City of David." This established his kingship militarily and politically. He then established his religious leadership by moving the ark of the covenant to the City of David. Solomon later expanded northward to Mt. Moriah and built the temple and the royal palace.

anointing. He was first anointed by the prophet Samuel (1 Sam. 16:13). Then he was anointed as king over the house of Judah in Hebron (2:4). Now he was finally **anointed** as rightful **king** by the entire nation.

5:6–10 One of King David's first military acts was to capture the fortress on Mount **Zion** from **the Jebusites**. These heathen warriors considered their city so invincible that it could be defended by **the lame and the blind**. David detected a weak point in the city's **water** system; he ordered his men to climb up through an underground watercourse which the Jebusites used to bring water to the city from a fountain below. The strategy was successful, and Jebus became **Jerusalem**, also called **the City of David**, the capital of the nation of Israel. The latter part of verse 8 looks back to the Jebusite taunt in verse 6, which later became a common saying: **"The blind and the lame shall not come into the house." The Millo** was a part of the fortification of the ancient city. (The parallel account in 1 Chronicles 11 reveals that Joab led the successful attack on the city and thus secured his place as commander of David's forces.)

5:11–16 Hiram, the Gentile **king of Tyre, sent** materials and workmen to build a palace for David in Jerusalem. **David took more concubines and wives** while at **Jerusalem**, in violation of Deuteronomy 17:17, and additional **sons and daughters were born to** him. The royal line of the Messiah is traced through **Solomon**. There are two other lists of the sons born to David **in Jerusalem** (1 Chron. 3:5–8; 14:3–7), with minor variations (mostly in spelling) among the three lists.

5:17–21 Disturbed by news of Israel's unity and strong central government, **the Philistines** decided to attack. They gathered their forces at the **Valley of Rephaim**, south of Jerusalem. Assured of victory by the Lord, **David** attacked the foe and defeated them. **He called** the **place Baal Perazim**, meaning *Baal is broken* or *the master of breakthrough* (NASB and NKJV marg.). The Lord had made breaches in the ranks of the enemy there. The **images** which the Philistines abandoned were seized by **David** (v. 21) and burned (1 Chron. 14:12) so as not to become stumbling blocks to future generations.

5:22–25 Sometime later, **the Philistines** returned to this same **Valley of Rephaim** and threatened Israel. This time **the LORD** told **David** to **circle around behind** the enemy forces, opposite some **mulberry trees**. When he heard **the sound of marching in the tops of the mulberry trees**, he would know that **the LORD** was marching against **the Philistines**. The result was that David destroyed the foe **from Geba** to **Gezer**. **Geba** probably should read *Gibeon* (NKJV marg., LXX, and 1 Chron. 14:16.)[3] Note that David did not assume that God's guidance for one battle (v. 19) would be the same for the next (v. 23). We must constantly seek God's will in everything. God's strategy in the first battle was direct assault; in the second, ambush.

E. The Ark Brought to Jerusalem (Chap. 6)

The events in chapter 6 did not take place immediately after those recorded in chapter 5. Second Samuel does not always follow a strict chronological order.

6:1–7 The last time we read about **the ark of God** was in 1 Samuel 7:1, 2. It had been sent back by the Philistines and was placed in **the house of Abinadab** in Kirjath Jearim. Many years passed. Then **David** decided to bring it to Jerusalem, in order that the city might be the *religious* as well as the *political* capital. So he took **thirty thousand . . . men . . . of Israel** to **Baale Judah** (the same as Kirjath Jearim) to get it. God had instructed that the ark was to be carried on poles, supported on the shoulders of the Kohathites (Num. 7:9). Instead, **David** made **a new cart** and with great jubilation **brought . . . the ark . . . to** the **threshing floor** of Nachon (called Chidon in 1 Chron. 13:9). There **the oxen stumbled**, and the ark was in danger of falling off the cart. So **Uzzah**, a son of **Abinadab**, steadied **the ark** with **his hand**. Since it was forbidden for even the priests to touch the ark (Num. 4:15), **Uzzah** was instantly struck dead by the Lord.

It has frequently been asked why God struck Uzzah for touching the ark when the Philistines often touched it without being destroyed. The answer seems to be that "the nearer a man is to God, the more solemnly and speedily he will be judged for any evil." Judgment must begin at the house of God.

Was God's action too severe? We feel free to judge God because we lack a sense of His awesome holiness and majesty. The Ark was as close to a visible representation of God Himself as men would see until Jesus. Uzzah disregarded this. His death was a lasting lesson to the Israelites to take seriously the glory of their God. Do our language and our actions demonstrate that we mean it when we pray "Hallowed be Thy Name"? (*Daily Notes of the Scripture Union*).

6:8–11 **David** protested to **the LORD** against this solemn judgment and temporarily abandoned his plan to bring **the ark . . . into the City**. Rather, he had it placed in **the house of Obed-Edom**, probably near Jerusalem.

The LORD greatly **blessed** the **household** of **Obed-Edom** during the **three months . . . the ark** was **in** his **house**.

6:12–15 Hearing of this blessing, **King David** decided to bring **the ark of God to** Jerusalem. The account in 1 Chronicles 15:13–15 tells us that during these three months David investigated the Scriptures to see how the ark was to be transported. The new cart was abandoned and the Levites carried the ark on their shoulders. After the bearers moved forward cautiously for **six paces** to make sure the Lord wasn't still displeased, David **sacrificed oxen and fatted sheep**. Then, with dancing in the streets, the ark was brought to a temporary tent in **the City of David**. (It is likely that Psalm 68 was written at this time.) The king himself was so elated that he **danced before the LORD with all his might. David was wearing a linen ephod** instead of his customary royal clothes.

6:16–23 His wife, **Michal, looked through a window and saw** him dressed in an ephod, acting in a manner which she considered unworthy of a king. When he **returned** home, she falsely accused him of indecently dancing in public. ("**Uncovering**" in verse 20 must be understood in the light of verse 14.) He answered that his dancing was an expression of his joy in the Lord and intimated that he did not intend to stifle his enthusiasm for the things of God. He would let himself be even more despised by men and **humble in** his **own sight**, but he would **be held in honor** by the "slave girls" Michal had **spoken** of. Because of her critical attitude, **Michal** suffered the reproach of bearing **no children to the day of her death**. This is a needed reminder that a critical spirit stifles fruitfulness.

F. God's Covenant with David (Chap. 7)

7:1–5 David felt that it was unsuitable for him to be **dwelling in his** fine home while **the ark of God** was kept **inside tent curtains**. So he notified **Nathan the prophet** of his intention to **build a house** for the ark. Nathan at first approved, apparently because he acted without consulting the Lord. Then **the word of the LORD came to** him, informing him that David would not be allowed to build a temple for Jehovah.

7:6–11 The LORD reminded **Nathan** that He had **dwelt in a tent** from **the time** of the Exodus **from Egypt**. The **tent** was suitable for the people of Israel as long as they were on the **move**. The **time** had now come for a settled temple.

7:12–15 Then **the LORD** revealed to Nathan an unconditional covenant which He would make with **David**. This covenant promised that David would have a son (Solomon) who would **build** the temple; that this son's **throne** would be established **forever**; that when he would sin, God would correct **him**, but His **mercy** would **not** cease.

7:16, 17 It further promised that David's **house**, his **kingdom**, and his **throne** would **be established forever**, and that his own descendants would sit upon the **throne**. David's dynasty has been interrupted since the Babylonian captivity, but it will be restored when Christ, the Seed of David, returns to reign over all the earth. Jensen elaborates:

> David wanted to build a temple for God, but Solomon was given the privilege. Undoubtedly the character of David's life work for God was fighting, not building. But even by this fighting he was clearing the way

for another to lay the foundation of that house of worship which his heart had so fondly desired to build. After the warring was over, Solomon erected the temple from materials which David had prepared. David represents Christ in His suffering and victory over the great enemy. Solomon represents Christ in His glory after the suffering and the conflicts are finished. The church, which is the true temple of God, having Christ for its chief cornerstone, will be manifested in the last day. Now in the church's days of suffering and conflict the materials are being prepared for this glorious building for God.[4]

7:18–29 Deeply moved by God's covenant of grace, **David went in** the temporary tent and offered the prayer of thanksgiving recorded here. In it, says Blaikie,

> He expresses wonder at the past, at God's selecting one obscure in family and obscure in person; he wonders at the present: How is it Thou hast brought me thus far? and still more he wonders at the future, the provision made for the stability of his house in all time coming.[5]

"And this is the custom ('law' in margin) of man, O Lord GOD" (v. 19b NASB) means that God had treated David with the same love and condescension that He commanded men to show to one another.

G. Defeat of Israel's Enemies (Chap. 8)

8:1, 2 David's policy as king was to purge out of the kingdom the heathen inhabitants who rebelled against his rule. This policy resulted in the enlargement of the territory of Israel.

For example, **he defeated . . . the Philistines** and seized **Metheg**

Ammah—i.e., Gath (1 Chron. 18:1). He had once played the part of a *madman* in Gath (1 Sam. 21:10–15); now he would serve as *king* there. Also, he conquered **the Moabites** and used a measuring **line** to select two-thirds **to be put to death**. Moab must have shown treachery to Israel.

8:3–8 David's next victory was in the area of Syria. He defeated **Hadadezer, king of** a country named **Zobah**, between Hamath and **Damascus**, capturing **one thousand chariots, seven hundred horsemen**, and **twenty thousand foot soldiers**.

David also hamstrung all of **the chariot horses, except . . . enough of them for one hundred chariots**.[6] This means that a tendon in the leg was cut, making the animals unfit for warfare. **When the Syrians of Damascus came to help Hadadezer, . . . David** destroyed **twenty-two thousand of** them and made **the Syrians** his vassals. Then **David** returned to Jerusalem with the **bronze** and **the shields of gold** which he had captured from **Hadadezer**.

8:9–12 Toi, the neighboring **king of Hamath** congratulated **David** for his military triumph over **Hadadezer** and **sent** gifts **of silver, . . . gold, and . . . bronze**. These precious metals, together **with** all the other **silver and gold** David had won in his wars, were **dedicated . . . to the** LORD and later used in the temple.

8:13 There is an apparent discrepancy here. It says that *David* killed **eighteen thousand** *Syrians* in the Valley of Salt. But 1 Chronicles 18:12 says that *Abishai* killed eighteen thousand *Edomites* in the Valley of Salt. It is true that in some Hebrew manuscripts, as well as in the ancient LXX and Syriac versions, "Edomites" is also found here in 2 Samuel 8:13.[7]

But the fact that **David made him-**

self a name from the victory in 2 Samuel and Abishai is credited with the glory in 1 Chronicles is unusual. First Chronicles is usually very laudatory of David. Perhaps, as so often happens in war, the "top brass," in this case David, got credit for the victory as "commander-in-chief." But the actual direct leading of the battle was under Abishai, and even the chronicler, who seeks to emphasize the Davidic line, was led of the Holy Spirit to draw attention to the leader in the field. To further complicate things, the superscription to Psalm 60 states that *"Joab* [Abishai's brother] killed twelve thousand Edomites in the Valley of Salt."[8]

Eugene Merrill makes the following suggestion:

Perhaps this difference is explainable by noting that the entire campaign was under Abishai's direct command, and that Joab was responsible (with the soldiers in his contingency) for killing two thirds of the Edomites.[9]

8:14 The fact that David **put garrisons throughout all Edom** and made **all the Edomites** become his **servants** probably is further support for the marginal reading "Edomites" in verse 13, and all manuscripts of the parallel passage in Chronicles.

8:15–18 So David's kingdom and power were greatly enlarged, and he ruled with **justice** and equity. Some of his chief officers are listed in verses 16–18: **Joab**—commander-in-chief of **the army**; **Jehoshaphat—recorder**; **Zadok** and **Ahimelech** (perhaps a copyist's error for **Abiathar**, see below) —**priests**; **Seraiah—scribe** or secretary; **Benaiah**—in charge of David's bodyguards; **David's sons—chief ministers**. There is a textual problem in verse 17. There and in 1 Chronicles 18:16 and 24:6 **Ahimelech** is listed as

the son of Abiathar, but in 1 Samuel 22:20 **Abiathar** is said to be "the son of Ahimelech." The simplest solution is that in the verses listing Ahimelech as the son of Abiathar, a copyist may have transposed the names.

However, there is another possibility based on an OT custom by which every other generation had the same name, that is, grandsons were named after their grandfathers. Thus, at any given time the priestly colleague of Zadok would be either Abiathar or Ahimelech. Abiathar and Ahimelech functioned as fellow-priests as Annas and Caiaphas apparently did in the time of our Lord (Luke 3:2). When Saul killed **Ahimelech** and his sons at Nob, **Abiathar** was the only survivor. When David became king, he appointed **Abiathar** as high priest but did not depose **Zadok**.

H. Compassion Shown to Mephibosheth (Chap. 9)

9:1–13 David remembered his covenant with Jonathan (1 Sam. 20:14–17) to **show him kindness** and wanted some opportunity to fulfill it. **Ziba, a servant of** the late King **Saul**, reported that a crippled **son of Jonathan** was living **in Lo Debar**, on the east side of the Jordan River. **David** had him **brought** to Jerusalem, ordered that the family property be returned to him, and arranged for him to **eat** at the royal **table**. **Ziba** and his **sons** were appointed to serve **Mephibosheth**.

Mephibosheth is a picture of an unconverted soul living in a barren land (**Lo Debar** may mean *no pasture*[10]) and sold under sin (**Machir** means *sold*—v. 4). He was an outcast from **the** fallen **house of Saul**. He was unable to come to the king to beg for mercy, being **lame in both his feet**. But the gracious sovereign sought him out in order to bless him. Once found, Mephibosheth was given great riches and a place of fellowship at the king's table. The parallels to salvation are obvious. Like Mephibosheth, we were *helpless* (unable to come to God); our condition was *hopeless* (being part of a fallen race). But by grace we became objects of divine favor. We have been elevated to a place in the family of God and made joint-heirs with Christ.

> Love so amazing, so divine,
> Demands my heart, my life, my all!
> —Isaac Watts

I. Further Conquests (Chap. 10)

10:1–5 Apparently **Nahash, the king of** the Ammonites, had done David a favor at one time. This was the same Nahash whom Saul defeated early in his reign (1 Sam. 11). **Nahash** might have helped David when he was a fugitive, since Saul was their mutual enemy for a time. Now **David** desired to repay that loyalty, so he **sent** messengers **to Hanun the son of Nahash,** who was crowned king when his father **died. The princes of . . . Ammon** suspected David's men of being spies, and so **Hanun** ordered them to be subjected to personal insults and indignities. David was angered when he saw his humiliated messengers.

10:6–8 As soon as the Ammonites learned of this, they prepared for war against Israel by hiring **the Syrians** from the north (see 1 Chron. 19). Thus David's men, under **Joab,** faced two armies—**the Syrians** and the Ammonites.

John Haley gives the following explanation of the apparent inconsistencies between verse 6 and 1 Chronicles 19:6, 7:

Bethrehob was one of the little kingdoms of Mesopotamia, as also were Maacah, Zobah, and Tob petty monarchies of Syria. Thus the names and numbers agree as follows:[11]

2 Samuel

Syrians of Beth Rehob and Zobah	20,000
Syrians of Tob	12,000
Syrians of Maacah	1,000
TOTAL	33,000

1 Chronicles

Syrians from Zobah, etc.	32,000
Syrians of Maacah (number not given)	[1,000]
TOTAL	33,000

10:9–14 **Joab** divided his men into two groups. He himself commanded **some of Israel's best** soldiers in a drive **against the Syrians. His brother . . . Abishai** led the **rest** of the Israelites **against . . . Ammon.** Both generals agreed to send help should the other be threatened. **The Syrians . . . fled** as **Joab and** his men attacked in the open field. Then the frightened Ammonites retreated into their **city** (probably Rabbah).

10:15–19 Shortly thereafter **the Syrians** reorganized their forces and solicited aid from other Syrian states. They marched as far as **Helam,** east of the Jordan (exact location unknown), where David's army met and defeated them. The Israelites destroyed **seven hundred charioteers and forty thousand horsemen.** (In 1 Chron. 19:18 the losses are stated as "seven thousand charioteers and forty thousand foot soldiers." Williams suggests that there was a cavalry brigade of 40,000 men with 700 light chariots, and an infantry brigade of 40,000 with 7,000 heavy chariots.)[12] This battle convinced the Syrians of David's power, so **they made peace with Israel** and refused **to help the** Ammonites **anymore.**

II. DAVID'S FALL (Chaps. 11, 12)

A. Crimes Against Bathsheba and Uriah (Chap. 11)

11:1–5 David's notorious moral lapse was occasioned, writes the venerable commentator Matthew Henry, by three things: (1) "Neglect of his business"; (2) "Love of ease and the indulgence of a slothful temper"; (3) "A wandering eye."[13] Instead of going **to battle** against the Ammonites **in the spring of the year, . . . David sent Joab** against them while he himself **remained** idly at home. Times of idleness are often times of greatest temptation. **One evening . . . he** looked out **from the roof of** his palace and saw **a . . . beautiful . . . woman** bathing. Inquiry revealed that she was **Bathsheba, . . . the wife of Uriah,** one of David's mighty warriors. **David sent** for her and committed adultery **with her**. She purified herself **from her** ceremonial defilement, then **returned to her house**. When she found out she was pregnant, **she sent** the news to **David**.

11:6–13 The king then plotted to hide his sin. First he called **Uriah** back from **the war**, pretending that he wanted to hear of the progress of **Joab** and the army. After **Uriah** had answered his questions, **David** instructed him to return home, hoping that he would have intercourse with Bathsheba. Then when the baby was born, Uriah would think that it was his own child. But Uriah upset David's plans. Instead of returning home, he **slept at the door of the king's house;** he did not feel he could enjoy the comforts of home as long as his nation was at war. In desperation **David . . . made** Uriah **drunk**, but the faithful soldier still refused to **go** home. Uriah's loyalty and faithfulness stand in marked contrast to the king's treachery.

11:14–17 Then **David** stooped to his lowest act of infamy. He ordered **Uriah** to carry **a letter to Joab**—a letter which contained Uriah's death sentence. The king ordered Joab to put **Uriah in the forefront of the hottest battle**, where death would be inevitable. Then Uriah would not be alive to disown the baby that would be born. Joab directed the battle so that Uriah would be sure to be killed. He ordered his troops to advance, then called both flanks to withdraw. As Uriah and his men in the center moved forward, they were easy targets for the Ammonites on the wall. Militarily it was ridiculous, but it succeeded in eliminating **Uriah** as well as many other loyal **servants of David**.

11:18–21 When **Joab sent** news back to **David**, he knew **the king** would be angered by the military defeat. David would say, "**Why did you approach so near to the city**? Didn't you remember how **Abimelech, the son of** Gideon (**Jerubbesheth**) was killed when he did this very thing?" (see Judg. 9:50–55.) So Joab instructed **the messenger** to forestall **the king's wrath** by adding, "**Your servant Uriah the Hittite is dead also.**" This would make David forget about the military reverses of the day.

11:22–25 **The messenger** reported to **David** as instructed. Then he was told to carry back a message **to Joab**, saying that military reverses are inevitable and that Uriah's death should not cause grief because in warfare **the sword devours** indiscriminately. Thus David hypocritically tried to hide his deep guilt "with a fatalistic comment about the inevitability and capriciousness of death."

11:26–27 After the customary time

of **mourning, David sent** for Bathsheba to become **his wife**. Sometime later, the baby was born.

That the Scriptures report this incident from the life of David is an indicator of their faithfulness. They give us an honest and uncut view of God's people the way they really were, warts and all (*Daily Notes of the Scripture Union*).

B. Confession to the Lord (Chap. 12)

12:1–9 It is generally believed that about a year elapsed between chapters 11 and 12. During that time the hand of **the LORD** was heavy upon David; his spiritual struggle is described in Psalms 32 and 51. The prophet **Nathan . . . came to him** with this parable, asking David's judgment on the matter: "A rich man with many sheep was unwilling to use any of his own animals as food when a visitor called on him. Instead, he took the one little ewe lamb belonging to a poor man and slaughtered it." David could judge sin in others more easily than in himself. He angrily declared that the man should restore fourfold and deserved to die for his sin. **Nathan** fearlessly pointed the accusing finger at David, saying, in effect, "You are the man who did it. God dealt graciously with you, making you king, enriching you, giving you everything that your heart could desire. But you took Bathsheba from her husband and then killed him to cover your crime."

12:10–14 The king's solemn sentence was then pronounced: His children would be a grief to him. His family would be torn by bloody conflict. His **wives** would be stolen from him and violated publicly (see 2 Sam. 16:22). His sinful **deed** would become a matter of general knowledge. David then came to the place of repentance

and confessed his sin as being **against the LORD**. Morgan comments:

Note the "also" in verse 13. A man puts away his own sin when in sincerity he confesses it. That makes it possible for God also to put it away.[14]

Nathan immediately assured him that the *penalty* of his **sin** was remitted—he would **not die**. But the *consequences* of his sin would follow him. Actually, he would have to restore fourfold (Ex. 22:1), as he himself had decreed concerning the rich man in the parable: The baby would **die**; Amnon would be murdered (chap. 13); Absalom would be slain (chap. 18); Adonijah would be executed (1 Kgs. 2).

12:15–23 When the baby **became ill, David** prostrated himself in prayer and fasting. He was deeply grieved. But **when** he learned that the baby had **died**, he **arose and ate**, explaining that the baby could not return, but that he, David, would one day join the baby when he died. Verse 23 has been a source of great comfort to believing parents who have lost infants and young children.

Matthew Henry comments:

Godly parents have great reason to hope concerning their children that die in infancy that it is well with their souls in the other world; for *the promise is to us and to our seed*, which shall be performed to those that do not put a bar in their own door, as infants do not.[15]

We can be confident that children who die before they reach the age of accountability go to heaven because Jesus said, "Of such is the kingdom of heaven" (Matt. 19:14).

That David possessed a deep understanding of God's character is evident by the way he responded to God's judgment. Before the blow fell he prayed, knowing that Jehovah was *a God of mercy*. After the blow fell he worshiped, knowing that Jehovah was *a God of righteousness*. He forgot the things that were behind, accepted the divine discipline, and looked ahead to the future. He did not despair because he knew that God would yet bless him. He was right.

12:24, 25 **Bathsheba** gave birth to another **son**, **Solomon**, who was destined to succeed his father as king. Through the prophet **Nathan**, God gave the child the additional **name** of **Jedidiah** (*beloved of Jehovah*).

12:26–30 Now the narrative returns to the attack **against Rabbah** interrupted at 11:1 by David's sin. It seems that **Joab** had captured all but one portion of the city, perhaps the fortress on the top. (Josephus[16] and the NKJV say that Joab captured **the city's water supply**, making surrender imminent.) Then he called for **David** to come and finish the job, thus giving him complete credit for the victory. It was a striking act of selflessness on Joab's part. Joab was at best an unpredictable person. At times he seemed to show a real strength of character. But his overall behavior was that of a clever, ruthless, wicked schemer. David succeeded in capturing **Rabbah** and was rewarded with a **crown . . . of gold** weighing **a talent**, plus much other booty.

12:31 Bible scholars are disagreed as to whether the last verse describes cruel punishment to which David subjected **the people of Ammon** (KJV rendering)[17] or whether it simply describes menial agricultural work or industrial servitude (NKJV rendering). The latter seems more typical of David's way of dealing with his enemies.

III. DAVID'S TROUBLES (Chaps. 13—20)

A. Rape of Tamar by Amnon (13:1–19)

13:1–14 **Absalom** was David's **son** by Maachah, whereas **Amnon** was a son by Ahinoam; thus they were half-brothers. **Amnon** lusted after **Tamar**, the **lovely** full **sister** of Absalom, and therefore his own half-sister. He did not see how he could get near her because of her secluded life and her purity. Then **Jonadab** (David's nephew—v. 3) suggested a solution. By pretending sickness, Amnon lured her into his bedroom to nurse him and then forcibly raped her.

13:15–19 After the crime was committed, **he hated her** more **than . . . he had** ever **loved her**, as is so often the case. Lust and hatred are closely related. He tried to get rid of her, but she would not leave. So he finally had her expelled by force, hoping that "out of sight" would be "out of mind." She wore the symbol of mourning, and this alerted Absalom to what had happened.

B. Absalom's Revenge on Amnon, and Absalom's Flight (13:20–39)

13:20 **Absalom** comforted **Tamar** as if he did not think it was very serious, but actually he was already plotting revenge against Amnon.

Disgraced and unwanted for marriage, through no fault of her own, **Tamar remained desolate in her brother Absalom's house**. This probably means that she lived and died unwed. Lust hurts the innocent as well as the guilty.

13:21 Though David **was very angry**, he did not punish Amnon as he should have done—probably because his own sin was so fresh in everyone's mind.

He knew his duty, but his hands were tied. This is what willful sin does in robbing us of moral freedom, liberty of speech and testimony (*Daily Notes of the Scripture Union*).

The fact that Amnon was his first-born (1 Chron. 3:1) and the natural successor to the throne might also have influenced David.

13:22–29 **Absalom** waited his time for vengeance. It came **after two full years**. A great celebration was planned, as always, at the time of sheepshear-ing near Bethel. Absalom's urgent invitation failed to attract his father, probably because David wanted to spare his son heavy expense. But it did succeed in bringing **all the king's sons**, and most important of all, **Amnon**, who as the eldest son represented his absent father. At a predetermined signal, Absalom's **servants** killed **Amnon**. The rest of the princes **fled** back toward Jerusalem in panic.

13:30–36 In the meantime, **news** reached **David** that **Absalom** had **killed all** of his **sons**! Again David was plunged into mourning. **Jonadab** corrected the false report with the information that it was **only Amnon** who was **dead**, and that **Absalom** had plotted his death since the day that **Tamar** was violated. Shortly there-after David's **sons** returned to Jerusa-lem with great lamentation, confirming Jonadab's report that they were still alive.

13:37–39 **Absalom fled** for his life to **Geshur**, in Syria, where his mother had lived, and where **Talmai**, his maternal grandfather, was **king**. Absalom lived in Geshur for **three years**. Amnon was older than Absalom and until his death was next in line to the throne. With Amnon dead, Absalom had visions of *himself* on the throne. **King David longed to** see **Absalom** again, after his grief over Amnon's death had subsided with the passing of time.

C. Absalom's Return to Jerusalem (Chap. 14)

14:1 **Joab** realized **that the** king longed to have **Absalom** back in Jerusalem. But the people knew that **Absalom** was guilty of murder and should be executed. Thus the fear of public disapproval kept David from bringing Absalom back.

14:2–7 So **Joab** sent a **woman** from **Tekoa** (near Bethlehem) to David with a family situation similar to David's. Pretending to be in deep mourning, she told how one of her **sons** had **killed** the other. Now her **family** was demanding the death of her only heir. This would completely wipe out the family **name** from **the earth**.

14:8–13 At first **the king** told her to return home and await an answer, hoping perhaps to avoid guilt in ex-onerating the murderer. But she wanted an answer immediately so she could trap David by his own decision. She offered to assume any guilt which his decision might in-volve. King David made another gen-eral statement, promising her security. Then she asked him pointblank for assurance that her son would not be killed. As soon as he gave this, she had him trapped. If **the king** would grant this pardon to her son, why would he not restore his own **banished** son, Absalom?

The woman's pretended situation is roughly analogous to David's. One son is dead, and his relatives are calling for the death of the guilty one, as retributive revenge (v. 7). David's decision showed mercy and suspended the usual blood-vengeance that often, in the Middle East, continued through many generations. But the woman presses on to apply the story to David and Absalom, and again, as with Nathan, David is caught in the web of his own moral wisdom. He is bound to restore, with protection, the banished and fearful Absalom (*Daily Notes of the Scripture Union*).

14:14 The woman apparently meant to suggest that, **like water spilled on the ground**, what was past (i.e., the death of Amnon) could not **be gathered up again**, so why dwell on that. Possibly also, that life is too short to be wasted in a prolonged quarrel.[18] The last part of verse 14 seems to mean that **God does not** immediately destroy an offender (as David should well know) **but . . . devises means** by which the sinner might be forgiven and restored. If God acts in this manner, why should not the king do so too?

14:15–23 The woman said that she came to **the king** expecting such Godlike clemency. She had obtained it for her own **son**, and now she was pleading for his **son**. **The king** suspected that **Joab** had engineered the plot, and **the woman** freely admitted it. King David weakly ordered Joab to **bring** Absalom **back** to Jerusalem in spite of the fact that Absalom was unrepentant. It was most unrighteous for David to do this, and he was to pay for it dearly.

14:24–33 For **two full years . . .** Absalom lived **in Jerusalem** without being permitted into his father's presence. (His natural **good looks** and luxurious growth of **hair** are mentioned as factors that would aid him in stealing the hearts of the people of Israel.) After two years Absalom tried to contact Joab for permission to see the king. **Joab** refused to come to him twice, so **Absalom** ordered his **field** of **barley** to be burned. This brought

Joab to his door quickly! Absalom's request for an audience with his father was granted, and the two were reunited.

It had been seven years since Tamar had been raped and five years since the murder of Amnon. For five years Absalom had not seen his father. Though David had forgiven him and brought him back to Jerusalem instead of executing him, he had refused to forget what had happened. But when the two men finally met, Absalom received a complete pardon. He then took the favor his father had shown him and used it as a platform from which to launch a revolution (chaps. 15—18). David spared his son's life, but in response Absalom schemed his father's death.

Joab's actions in all this seemed designed to obtain David's favor and also the favor of Absalom, who was next in line as king.

D. Absalom's Revolt and David's Flight (15:1–18)

15:1–6 Up to this point **Absalom** had concealed his desire to be king. But now he traveled about with an impressive entourage. Also he went boldly up **to the** city **gate** (where legal matters were settled) and acted as if he were the only one in **Israel** who was genuinely interested in the welfare of the people. He practically accused his father of failure to provide adequate legal aid and said that if he were king, the people would receive the **justice** they deserved. He courted the favor of people from the various cities **of Israel**.

15:7–12 After four **years**[19] (according to LXX mss., Syriac, Josephus, NKJV marg.) **Absalom** received permission to **go to Hebron**, ostensibly to fulfill a **vow** he had **made** while in exile. **Hebron** was probably disaffected because David had moved his capital from there to Jerusalem. Also, Hebron was the place of Absalom's birth. The **two hundred men** who accompanied **Absalom** did not know that his real purpose was to announce the formation of a new government, with himself as king! **Ahithophel**, one of David's counselors and Bathsheba's grandfather (cf. 11:3 with 23:34), defected to **Absalom**, and many of **the people** joined Absalom in his **conspiracy** to usurp the throne. Perhaps Ahithophel wanted to get even with David for the latter's sin with his granddaughter.

15:13–18 On hearing the news, **David** decided that the situation was serious and that he should abandon **Jerusalem**, so he gathered **his household** together immediately and fled to **the outskirts** of the city. **But the king left ten . . . concubines** behind **to keep the house**.

E. David's Friends and Foes (15:19—16:14)

15:19–22 Among those who went with David was a group of Philistines who had left **Gath** with him. One of these was **Ittai the Gittite**. When he started out to follow, the king urged him to return. After all, he was not a Jew; he was an exile; he had only recently joined the ranks; and David's cause was at best uncertain. But **Ittai** would not be dissuaded. He resolutely determined to accompany the king, no matter what the cost might be. David rewarded the loyalty of this Gentile by permitting him and his followers to accompany him into exile. **Ittai . . . said: ". . . surely in whatever place my lord the king shall be, whether in death or life, even there also your servant will be."** Believers should have the same devotion to the

King of kings during His rejection as Ittai had to David in his.

15:23 They **crossed over the Brook Kidron**, east of Jerusalem, and headed for the Jordan Valley. Nearly a thousand years later David's Greater Son would retrace his steps, Himself a rejected King (John 18:1). David **crossed** the **Kidron** and fled to *save* his life. Jesus crossed the valley and prayed in Gethsemane, en route to *giving* His life a ransom for many.

15:24–29 **Zadok** and **Abiathar**, the priests, came out of **the city** with **the ark**, intending to follow David into exile. But he sent them **back** with the hope that **the LORD** would allow him to return. Also, he told the priests that they could be more help to him right in **Jerusalem** (as a sort of fifth-column among Absalom's men). He would go as far as the west bank of the Jordan and await **word . . . from** them as to the progress of Absalom's rebellion.

Rather than becoming bitter at his enforced exile, David submitted meekly to what God had allowed. According to its title, Psalm 3 was composed at this time. In this psalm we find that David's trust in the Lord was unshaken as the storm broke over him.

15:30–37 **David** ascended **the Mount of Olives** with his faithful followers in deep mourning, praying that God would **defeat** whatever **counsel** that **Ahithophel** might give to **Absalom**. At the summit of the Mount of Olives, the king was met by **Hushai the Archite**. David asked him to **return to** Jerusalem and pretend loyalty **to Absalom**. In this way he might be able to counteract whatever advice **Ahithophel** might offer. He could relay any important news to **Zadok and Abiathar the priests**, who in turn would send **their two sons** with reports to David. **Hushai** reached **Jerusalem** just as **Absalom** was arriving to take over the government.

16:1–4 After **David** passed the summit of Olivet, **Ziba the servant of Mephibosheth . . . met him with** a large supply of food and **wine**, plus two **donkeys**. When David asked about Mephibosheth, Ziba falsely reported (see 19:27) that the son of Jonathan had stayed **in Jerusalem** in hopes that **the kingdom** would return to **the house of** Saul and thus to him as the next in line. David believed this lie and ordered that Mephibosheth's property should become Ziba's.

16:5–14 At **Bahurim**, on the road to Jericho, a descendant **of Saul** named **Shimei** came out and cursed **David** fiercely, charging him with **the blood of** Saul's **house**. **Abishai**, one of David's officers, wanted to kill **Shimei** on the spot, but the king would not allow it. He suggested that **the LORD** may have **ordered him** to **curse**. He pointed out that, after all, a member of Saul's house had **more** cause to seek his **life** than his own **son**, Absalom. Also, perhaps David remembered the death of Uriah and realized that Shimei's accusations were not entirely without foundation. And David hoped that Shimei's excessive hostility might move God to have mercy. As David and his men headed for the Jordan, **Shimei** followed them, cursing and throwing **dust** and **stones**. Finally **the** exiled **king** reached the river, where he and his party **refreshed themselves**.

F. Absalom's Counselors (16:15—17:23)

16:15–19 The scene now switches back **to Jerusalem**, where **Absalom** had just arrived. **Hushai** made a loud and vigorous display of loyalty **to** **Absalom**. At first he was suspected, but finally he was accepted by the usurper.

16:20–23 **Ahithophel's** first counsel to **Absalom** was that he should **go in to** the ten **concubines** David had **left** behind in Jerusalem. Such an act, disgraceful in itself, would be an unspeakable insult to David, would make reconciliation out of the question, and would constitute a direct claim to the throne. Absalom accepted the **advice** by going in to the royal harem, **in the sight of all Israel**, thus fulfilling Nathan's prophecy in 12:11, 12.

Ahithophel's counsel was highly respected in those days. **Absalom** followed it unquestioningly, as his father had done. But when we remember that Ahithophel was Bathsheba's grandfather, we can see how the desire for revenge might determine his particular counsel.

17:1–4 Having been successful in his first counsel, **Ahithophel** next advised **Absalom** to muster **twelve thousand men**, overtake **David**, kill him unexpectedly, and **bring** his followers **back to Jerusalem**.

17:5–14 **Absalom** was pleased but decided to **call Hushai** for his advice. This was the opportunity **Hushai** had been waiting for. He said that this second bit of **advice** by **Ahithophel** was **not good "at this time."** After all, David **and his men** were **enraged** by the insurrection, and they would fight fiercely. And David was too wise to spend the night with his troops; he would be hiding in a cave somewhere. If Ahithophel's first attack was not successful, then panic would spread throughout the nation, and Absalom's cause would be lost. **Hushai** had an alternative plan, which seemed to indicate his loyalty to Absalom but which in reality was designed to provide additional time for David to escape and to include the possibility of Absalom's death. He suggested a general mobilization of **all** the armies of **Israel**, led by Absalom. Such an army would be invincible. David would be attacked, and escape would be impossible. Absalom decided that Hushai's advice was best, so he rejected Ahithophel's plan, as David had prayed (15:31).

17:15–17 **Hushai** immediately sent word **to Zadok and Abiathar the priests**, and instructed them to notify David to **cross** the Jordan and escape to safety. The priests sent the message by **a female servant** to their sons who were waiting **at En Rogel**, at the outskirts of **the city**.

17:18–22 **Nevertheless a lad saw** this secret meeting and reported the spies to **Absalom**. Accordingly, the two sons of the priests, **Jonathan and Ahimaaz**, hid in **a well** (dry cistern) at **Bahurim** until the search parties had passed. Then they escaped and carried the news to **David**. David **crossed . . . the Jordan**, putting this natural barrier between his forces and those of Absalom. Then David marched to **Mahanaim**, a city in the land of Gilead.

17:23 **Ahithophel** became despondent because his **advice** had been rejected, and because he perceived that David would be victorious. He returned **to his house**, set his **household in order, and hanged himself**. Both in life and in death he was a "type" of Judas Iscariot.

G. Absalom's Death and David's Lament (17:24—19:8)

17:24–26 **Absalom** pursued his father across **the Jordan** to Gilead, having appointed **Amasa** as commander of his forces. Amasa's father was an Ishmaelite by birth (1 Chron. 2:17)

but **an Israelite** by religion. He was David's nephew and a first cousin of Joab.

17:27–29 While **David** was encamped at **Mahanaim**, three men came to him with necessary, nonperishable provisions **for** him **and** his **people**; they were **Shobi, Machir**, and **Barzillai**.

Shobi was a **son of Nahash**, the deceased king of the Ammonites. His brother Hanun had rejected David's goodwill and suffered for it (chap. 10). But **Shobi**, although by birth an alien, cared more for Israel's king than most of the Jews did. Likewise, many Gentiles have received Him who was rejected by "His own" (John 1:11).

Machir had cared for Mephibosheth for many years, until David brought the latter to Jerusalem (9:3–5). He ministered to those in need, whether a lame prince or a dethroned king. Those who give of their substance to aid the cause of Christ through hospitality will have their kindnesses returned a hundredfold when He returns in glory.

Barzillai helped sustain David the entire time he stayed in **Mahanaim**. He was a very wealthy man and his support meant a lot to the king (19:31–39). On his deathbed, David told Solomon to elevate the sons of Barzillai to places in the royal court (1 Kgs. 2:7). Christ won't forget those who have ministered to Him; they will be given positions of honor in His kingdom.

18:1–5 **David** divided his army into three companies, with **Joab, Abishai**, and **Ittai** as the three generals. The king wanted to participate in the coming battle, but **the people** persuaded him to remain **in the city** and send **help** if needed. As the soldiers marched out of the city, David gave public orders to his generals to **deal gently for** his **sake with . . . Absalom**.

18:6–9 **The battle was** fought **in the woods of Ephraim**, east of the Jordan and near Mahanaim. There were **twenty thousand** fatalities that day among Absalom's troops, largely the result of the dense forest which trapped the soldiers. David's army was victorious. As **Absalom** was fleeing through the forest, he was **caught** by **his head** in **a** huge **terebinth tree, . . . and the mule . . . went on** without him. It is a sort of poetic justice that the same part of his body of which he was so proud became the means of his downfall.

18:10–15 The messenger who reported Absalom's helpless position **to Joab** was rebuked for not killing the rebel. He carefully explained that no amount of money would induce him to violate **the king's** instructions. Besides, if he killed Absalom, the news would get back to the king, and Joab would not come to his defense. **Joab** considered all this talk a waste of time. He plunged **three spears through Absalom's heart**, then let his **ten** armorbearers administer the *coup de grâce*. All this was against the king's command, but it was best for the kingdom. David had consistently refused to punish his sons for their crimes, so the task fell to someone else.

18:16–18 As soon as the deed was done, **Joab** wisely called a halt to the fighting, since his major objective had been accomplished. Absalom's body was thrown **into a large pit** and covered with **a very large heap of stones**. This was in marked contrast to the monument which he had erected **for himself** in **the King's Valley**, probably near Jerusalem. Absalom had three sons (14:27), but they must have died

young and left him without an heir. Consequently, he had built **Absalom's monument** to preserve his **name** for posterity.

18:19–23 **Ahimaaz** wanted to carry **the news to** David, but **Joab** did **not** want him to. It seems that Ahimaaz had a reputation for being a bearer of good news (v. 27b), and it would have been out of character for him to bring the news of Absalom's death. So Joab sent a **Cushite** as the official messenger. But after he left, **Ahimaaz** persuaded **Joab** to **let** him go also, even if he would receive no reward for the errand. He succeeded in overtaking **the Cushite** by taking a quicker route.

18:24–30 **David was** on the lookout for **news** from the battle. **The watchman** reported one runner approaching, then **another**. When David heard that **the first** resembled **Ahimaaz**, he prepared himself for **good news** because Ahimaaz had always brought welcome messages in the past. Drawing near, **Ahimaaz** ceremoniously announced that **the LORD** had smitten the rebel army. But when David asked about **Absalom**, Ahimaaz's courage failed, and he gave a vague answer about seeing **a great tumult** but not knowing the details.

18:31–33 By then **the Cushite** had arrived. He announced that David's enemies had been defeated. The inevitable question from the king about Absalom brought the blunt reply that **all** David's **enemies** should **be like that young man**—in other words, *dead*. This news plunged David into very deep mourning. His pathetic lament is recorded in verse 33. This was one of the greatest griefs of his life, and it is doubtful that he ever forgave Joab for it.

19:1–8 So great was the king's sorrow that the people felt ashamed and guilty. They acted as if they were victims rather than victors. **Joab** was impatient with all this and delivered a stern rebuke to the king. He complained that David seemed more interested in his **enemies** than in his faithful followers, and that he was ungrateful to those who had **saved** his **life**. He warned that **if** David did **not** immediately show a kindly interest in his people, they would forsake him that **night**. David complied by taking a position by **the gate** of the city and talking to the people.

H. David's Return from Exile (19:9–43)

19:9, 10 In the meantime confusion reigned in the land of **Israel**. **All the people** were quarreling among themselves. King David, who had **saved** them **from . . . the Philistines**, was in exile, they reasoned, and **Absalom**, their self-appointed ruler, was dead. A movement thus began to restore David to his throne. **"Why do you say nothing about bringing back the king?"** is an appropriate question for a sleeping church today.

19:11–15 When **David** heard that the ten tribes of **Israel** were talking about restoring him to the throne, he **sent** two priests **to the elders of Judah**, asking **why** they, his blood relatives, were **the last to bring** him **back** as **king**. **Judah** had supported Absalom heavily in the rebellion, and doubtless some resentment or fear lingered.

David decided to remove **Joab** as **commander** in chief (probably because Joab had killed Absalom) and to appoint **Amasa** to take his **place**. **Amasa**, a nephew of David, had only recently been Absalom's general. To outsiders it must have looked like David punished loyalty and rewarded rebellion, a government policy unlikely to produce political stability.

But these moves won **the hearts of all the men of Judah** over to David's side, and they sent a unanimous "welcome home" message to him.

19:16–23 **Shimei**, who had **cursed** David previously, **and Ziba**, who had slandered Mephibosheth, **came** rushing down **to the Jordan** River to meet the returning monarch. Shimei's profuse apology was probably insincere; his great desire was to escape punishment now that David was in power again. In the enthusiasm of the moment, the king overruled Abishai's desire to kill Shimei, and instead promised him amnesty. But **David** did not forget Shimei's curses. He later ordered Solomon to deal ruthlessly with the foulmouthed Benjamite (1 Kgs. 2:8, 9).

19:24–30 **Mephibosheth** also **came . . . to meet the king**. It was obvious from his appearance that he had mourned David's exile from the day it began. He had been truly loyal to the king, in spite of Ziba's false charges against him. The king spoke rather roughly to him for not accompanying him into exile. Mephibosheth explained that he had asked his servant Ziba to **saddle a donkey**, and when Ziba had failed to do it, Mephibosheth was helpless, being a cripple. He stated frankly that Ziba had **slandered** him but that injustice did not matter as long as **the king** had returned. When David rather unfairly ruled that **Ziba** and Mephibosheth should **divide the land** between them, the crippled son of Jonathan revealed the true loyalty of his heart: **"Rather, let him take it all, inasmuch as my lord the king has come back in peace to his own house."**

19:31–39 **Barzillai**, the **eighty**-year-**old . . . Gileadite**, was another true friend to David. **He had provided** the king **with supplies at Mahanaim**. Now he accompanied him to **the Jordan**. David invited him to go with him to **Jerusalem**, promising him that he would be well cared for. **But Barzillai** refused to go on the grounds of his short life expectancy, his inability to **discern between** what was pleasant and unpleasant, his loss of **taste**, and his deafness. He would only **be a further burden to . . . the king** if he went. So he agreed to accompany David **a little way** past **the Jordan** and then return to his **own city**. His suggestion that **Chimham** (perhaps his son) should go **with** David was readily accepted.

19:40–43 By now a great procession had formed—**all the people of Judah . . . and half the** men of the other tribes—to bring **the king** back to Jerusalem.

Internal strife broke out because **Judah** had taken such a prominent place in the restoration of the king (i.e., bringing him **across the Jordan**) without inviting the ten tribes to participate. **Judah** explained that David was their **close relative** and that they had not profited in any way above the others by taking the lead. The ten tribes argued that they had **ten** times as much right to participate as Judah. The fierceness of Judah's **words** was an indication of the serious *trouble* that lay ahead.

I. Sheba's Rebellion and Death (Chap. 20)

20:1, 2 A wicked **rebel** named **Sheba**, of the tribe of Benjamin (and possibly related to Saul), took the words **of Judah** (19:42) and turned them into the basis for a rebellion. **The men of Judah** had claimed **David** as their own. **Sheba** now defiantly announced that the ten tribes had **no** part **in David** and were seceding. Only the tribe **of Judah** was left to

David. Later events indicate that Sheba had a relatively small following. The expression **"every man of Israel"** must be understood in a restricted sense, involving only the dissident men of the ten tribes.

20:3 On reaching **Jerusalem, the king** found the **ten . . . concubines whom he had left** there, who had been dishonorably treated by Absalom. David arranged for them to be kept in a house **in seclusion** for the rest of their lives, as if **in widowhood**.

20:4–7 By now Joab had been demoted, and **Amasa**, Absalom's rebel commander, was in charge of David's army. **The king** ordered him to **assemble the** soldiers **of Judah . . . within three days** to **pursue** and capture the rebel leader, **Sheba**. For some unexplained reason, **Amasa** did not complete the job within the **time** given, so **David** ordered **Abishai** to take command and set out with chosen **men** to prevent **Sheba** from getting established in **fortified cities**. Joab was among those who went with Abishai.

20:8–10a As they reached a **large stone** marker in **Gibeon, Amasa came** to meet them. **Joab, . . . dressed in** a soldier's **battle armor**, advanced to meet Amasa, and as he did so his **sword** dropped to the ground. It seems that he did this purposefully. He then picked up his **sword** and moved toward his unsuspecting cousin. With a great show of friendliness, **Joab** grabbed Amasa's **beard** as if **to kiss him**, then killed him with one thrust of the sword.

20:10b–13 When **Joab and Abishai** began to pursue **Sheba**, their followers were immobilized by the sight of **Amasa** wallowing **in his blood** on **the highway**. Not until his body was **removed** did Joab's men follow him.

20:14–22 The hunt for Sheba led

to the far north, to the city of **Abel of Beth Maachah**. This was located north of the waters of Merom. It was a city famous for its **wise** people. As Joab laid **siege** to the city, **a wise woman** called down to him and asked him why he was going **to destroy a mother . . . city in Israel** (i.e., an important city) that had always been proverbial for its wisdom. When **Joab** explained that he was simply after the rebel leader, **Sheba**, who was hiding inside, she agreed to have him killed and **his head . . . thrown over the wall** as proof that he was dead. As soon as this was done, Joab **blew** the **trumpet** and **returned to . . . Jerusalem**, his mission accomplished. Sheba's revolt probably did not last more than a week.

20:23–26 David had demoted **Joab**, appointing first Amasa (19:13) and then Abishai (20:6) in his place. But Joab had regained his position as commander-in-chief.

The list of the king's important officials in verses 23–26 is largely the same as that in 8:15–18. **Joab** headed **the army**; **Benaiah** was in charge of David's bodyguard; **Jehoshaphat . . . was** the **recorder**; **Sheva** (same as Seraiah) **was** the **scribe** or stenographer; **Zadok and Abiathar were the priests**. (**Zadok and** Ahimelech were the priests in the earlier list.) The only other differences were that **Adoram was in charge of revenue** and **Ira the Jairite was** David's priest (or **chief minister**), whereas David's sons had been mentioned in chapter 8.

IV. APPENDIX (Chaps. 21—24)

The remainder of 2 Samuel is really an appendix highlighting various incidents in the reign of David, though not in chronological order. (The chronological order continues again in 1 Kings 1.)

A. The Famine and Its Termination (Chap. 21)

21:1 The first event was the **famine**, which lasted **for three years**. When **David inquired of the LORD** as to the cause, he was told that it was **because . . . Saul** had broken the covenant with **the Gibeonites**. These heathen inhabitants of the land had tricked Joshua into making a treaty with them. **Saul** had broken the treaty by trying to destroy **the Gibeonites**, a fact not mentioned previously in the OT. The term "**bloodthirsty house**" may imply that Saul's descendants had an active part in the slaughter of the Gibeonites, in which case their punishment (vv. 2–9) was just. It may seem harsh that the nation should suffer for the crime of a man now dead, but centuries earlier Israel had sworn a solemn oath to the Gibeonites (Josh. 9:19, 20), and the famine came because that oath had been broken. Time does not dull God's memory or His sense of justice.

21:2–9 David approached **the Gibeonites** to find out what they would accept as satisfaction for Saul's offense. They explained that they didn't want any of Saul's **silver or gold**, and that they had no right to put **any man** to death **in Israel**. Nothing would do but the execution of **seven** of Saul's male descendants, and David consented to this. The seven sons were: **the two sons of Rizpah—Armoni and Mephibosheth** (not Mephibosheth the son of Jonathan)—and **the five sons of** Saul's daughter **Merab** (v. 8, NKJV marg.). Two reasons for rejecting "**Michal**" as the proper reading here are that Michal was married to Palti, not **Adriel** (see 1 Sam. 25:44), and she was childless (2 Sam. 6:23). The **Barzillai** mentioned here is not the same man

HAMATH

(ZOBAH)

PHOENICIA

*Mediterranean
Sea*

Damascus

Tyre
Dan

Megiddo
Beth Shan

Shechem

Joppa
ISRAEL

Bethel
Jericho
Rabbah
(AMMON)

Ashdod
Jerusalem

Ashkelon
Gath

Gaza
Hebron
*Dead
Sea*

Raphia
Beersheba

(MOAB)

Zoar

Bozrah

Kadesh Barnea

(EDOM)

—N—

0   60 Mi.
0   60 Km.

© 1990 Thomas Nelson, Inc.

The Davidic Kingdom. David's military exploits successfully incorporated into the Israelite kingdom the powers of Edom, Moab, Ammon, and Zobah.

who later helped David when he fled from Absalom (17:27).

21:10 **Rizpah**, Saul's loyal concubine, set up a watch by the bodies, day and night, so that neither vultures nor wild **beasts** could touch them. She kept this vigil **from the beginning of harvest until** God sent rain and thus ended the famine which had led to these deaths.

21:11–14 When **David** heard of her devotion, he took steps to give

decent burial to these seven bodies and also to the **bones of Saul** and of **Jonathan**, which had been buried in **Jabesh Gilead. The bones of Saul** and **Jonathan** were laid to rest **in the tomb of Kish** in **Benjamin.**

21:15–22 This passage describes various battles against Philistine giants. In the first one, **David** was almost slain by **Ishbi-Benob**, but **Abishai** rescued him and **killed . . . the Philistine.** From then on the people would not let **David . . . go out with** them **to battle**. In the second battle, **at Gob** (or Gezer), another son of a giant was slain by **Sibbechai**. In the third battle, **Elhanan . . . killed the brother of Goliath the Gittite**, named Lahmi—cf. 1 Chron. 20:5. The fourth battle resulted in the death of a giant **who had six fingers on each hand and six toes on each foot**. Pliny mentions certain six-fingered (*sedigiti*) Romans, and this peculiarity is hereditary in some families.[20]

B. David's Thanksgiving Psalm (Chap. 22)

22:1–51 With **the words of this song David** praises **the LORD** for deliverance from his **enemies** and for the innumerable blessings which had been showered upon him. It was probably penned after David had firmly established himself on the throne. Saul was dead, the kingdom was united under his leadership, and Israel's foes were beaten back. The words are found, with some variations, in Psalm 18 and are quoted in the NT as applying to the Messiah (v. 3, "in whom I will trust," cf. Heb. 2:13; v. 50, cf. Rom. 15:9).

Looking at it as a Messianic psalm, we may outline it as follows:

1. Praise to God for hearing and answering prayer (vv. 2–4)
2. Death closing in on the Savior (vv. 5–7a)
3. God warring against the hosts of hell as they seek unsuccessfully to prevent the Resurrection (vv. 7b–20).
4. Reasons why God raised Messiah from the dead (vv. 21–30).
5. The Messiah's Second Advent, in which He destroys His enemies (vv. 31–43).
6. The glorious kingdom of the Messiah (vv. 44–51).

For a detailed exposition see commentary on Psalm 18.

C. David's Mighty Men (Chap. 23)

23:1–7 The first seven verses give **the** very beautiful **last words of David**—that is, his last inspired utterance in song. He describes the ideal ruler, the Messiah, whose reign shall be a glorious dawn, **a morning without clouds** after a long stormy night.[21] David realized that he did not fit the description, but he took comfort in the fact that God's covenant assured him that the Messiah would be descended from him. Verses 6 and 7 describe Christ's judgment on **the sons of rebellion** when He returns to set up His kingdom.

23:8–12 A catalog of David's mighty men is given in verses 8–39. It is significant that Joab is not honored in this list, probably because he killed Absalom (not to mention Abner and Amasa!). This register is near the end of David's reign, while the parallel list in 1 Chronicles 11:11–47 is placed at the beginning. Although not identical, there are great similarities between the two rosters. More information about these men and their exploits can be found in the commentary on 1 Chronicles 11.

The first three **mighty men** were:

1. **Josheb-Basshebeth**, also **called Adino the Eznite**—**he** slew **eight hundred men at one time**. (1 Chron. says three hundred, but that number is probably a copyist's error.)
2. **Eleazar**—he fought off the Philistines when his fellow soldiers had retreated. They returned only to strip the slain. When the battle was over, **his hand was** so **weary** (probably cramped) that he could not unclasp his fingers from **the sword**.

3. **Shammah**—he stood alone against **the Philistines** when the men of Israel had **fled**. Standing **in** a **field . . . of lentils**, he fought off the enemy and gained **a great victory**.

23:13–17 The **three** unnamed mighty **men** referred to here **came to David** when he was in **the cave of Adullam**, and when **Bethlehem** was in the hands of **the Philistines. David** expressed a **longing** for **a drink of the water from the well of Bethlehem**. At the risk of their lives, these **men broke through** the lines **of the Philistines** and **brought** some **water** back **to David**. He was so overcome by this sacrifice that he **poured it out** as an offering **to the LORD**; he did **not** feel that he could **drink it**. Williams comments:

Those who live close to Jesus hear the longings of His heart for draughts of love from Africa and India and China; and, like these mighty men, they turn their backs on home and wealth, and risk or lay down their lives to win for Christ the affection and service of nations held as hopelessly in the power of Satan as the well of Bethlehem was in the hand of the Philistine.[22]

23:18–23 Two more of David's illustrious heroes were:

1. **Abishai**—he **killed three hundred men** and was commander **of** the **three** mentioned in verse 16, though not one of them.
2. **Benaiah**—he **killed two lion-like heroes of Moab. He** also **. . . killed a lion in . . . a pit on a snowy day**, and **an Egyptian** who was better-armed than he.

23:24–39 The final mighty men of David—**the thirty** (or **thirty-seven**) are given in verses 24–39.

Some numbers in this chapter need to be explained, such as **the thirty** chiefs (vv. 13, 24), the **thirty-seven** (v. 39), etc. **The thirty** may have been an elite military group, but counting all those who had served in it at one time or another, the total was **thirty-seven**. There were three in the first group: Josheb-Basshebeth (or Adino), Eleazar, and Shammah (vv. 8–12). Two were in the second group: Abishai and Benaiah (vv. 18–23). In the third group (vv. 24–39), the number "thirty" may have been a technical term, like "the twelve" for the apostles, even if one or more were not always there. It could also be quite literal, but the extra men beyond thirty may have been replacements for those who died in battle, such as **Uriah the Hittite**, the last valiant man in the list and Bathsheba's husband.

The Lord Jesus has His mighty men (and women!) too. He takes note of them just as surely as David took note of those who valiantly served him. Whatever our rank, let us fight the good fight of faith:

Soldiers of Christ, arise,
And put your armor on,
Strong in the strength which God
   supplies,
Through His eternal Son.

Stand, then, in His great might,
With all His strength endued;
But take, to arm you for the fight,
The panoply of God.
                    —*Charles Wesley*

D. David's Census and Its Consequences (Chap. 24)

William D. Crockett suggests that the events recorded here took place some time after David captured Jerusalem (chap. 5) but before he brought the ark into the holy city (chap. 6).[23]

24:1 It would appear that God in His **anger** told **David** to take a census of **Israel and Judah**. But we learn from 1 Chronicles 21:1 that it was *Satan* who moved David to do this. Satan *precipitated* it, David *performed* it (because of the pride of his heart), and God *permitted* it. The Septuagint rendering of verse 1 reads "and Satan moved David" rather than **"and He moved David."**

24:2–9 When **the king** ordered **Joab** to begin the numbering, David's military **commander** demonstrated better judgment than he did. He realized that the purpose of the census was to cater to David's pride, and he urged **the king** to desist, but in vain. Obedient to David, Joab and his men went throughout the land, numbering the people; they found that there were **eight hundred thousand** soldiers **in Israel** and **five hundred thousand** in **Judah**.

Exodus 30:12, 13 commanded that a half-shekel ransom be collected when a census was taken. There is no record of David's doing so. Pride motivated him to number the people. The census might cause him to depend on the size of his army and not on the arm of the Lord.

24:10–14 **After** the census was finished, the king was convicted of his sin, and cried out **to the LORD** for forgiveness. God sent **the prophet Gad** to him, offering any one of three punishments: (1) **seven years of famine . . . in the land**; (2) **three months** of pursuit by his **enemies**; (3) **three days** of pestilence or **plague**. **David** chose to **fall into the hand of the LORD**, and not into man's.

24:15–25 **The LORD sent** three days of **plague**, killing **seventy thousand men**. **The** destroying **angel** was about to **destroy** the city of **Jerusalem** when God stopped him at **the threshing floor of Araunah** (also called Ornan). David asked the Lord why He was destroying the people of Israel when it was David and his house who were guilty. God's reply, given through **Gad**, was for David to build **an altar . . . on the threshing floor of Araunah**. **So David** the king immediately began to arrange with **Araunah the Jebusite** for the purchase of the site. Although he was a Gentile, Araunah offered not only **the threshing floor** without charge but also **oxen** for sacrifices and the **threshing implements** for firewood. The king's noble answer was, **"nor will I offer burnt offerings to the LORD my God with that which costs me nothing."**

Finally **David bought the threshing floor and the oxen for fifty shekels of silver.** (1 Chron. 21:25 says that David paid 600 shekels of gold for the place, but this undoubtedly included the property surrounding the threshing floor.) **The plague** stopped when **burnt offerings** were offered on the altar (v. 25).

The threshing floor of Araunah, on Mount Moriah, was probably the very same spot where Abraham offered Isaac. It later became the site of Solomon's temple and then of Herod's temple in the time of Christ. Today it is occupied by a Moslem shrine—the Dome of the Rock. It will probably be the location of the temple in the Tribulation and finally of the millennial temple.

The Scriptures are completely honest in their treatment of the heroes of the faith. David had his *faults* and they are mentioned alongside his *faith*. We have followed David from the flock, through exile, into exaltation. Few men walked closer to God; few men fell deeper into sin. But through it all he was sustained by the Lord. We have all benefited from the experiences that David passed through, because he recorded them in his psalms.

Matthew Henry remarks on David as he appears in Samuel and how he appears in Psalms:

> Many things in his history are very instructive; but for the hero who is the subject of it, though in many instances he appears here very great, and very good, and very much the favourite of heaven; yet it must be confessed that his honour shines brighter in his Psalms than in his Annals.[24]

The words of Psalm 40 fitly summarize David's life:

> I waited patiently for the LORD, and He inclined to me, and heard my cry. He also brought me up out of a horrible pit, out of the miry clay, and He set my feet upon a rock, and established my steps. He has put a new song in my mouth—praise to our God; many will see it and fear, and will trust in the LORD (Ps. 40:1–3).

ENDNOTES

[1](1:17, 18) Quoted by Keil and Delitzsch, "The Books of Samuel," in *Biblical Commentary on the Old Testament*," VII: 286, 87.

[2](3:31–39) William Hoste and William Rodgers, *Bible Problems and Answers*, p. 214.

[3](5:22–25) Keil and Delitzsch maintain that Gibeon "is unquestionably the true reading, and *Geba* an error of the pen," because Geba is in the wrong place for this account ("Samuel," VII:326).

[4](7:16, 17) Irving L. Jensen, *I and II Samuel*, p. 92.

[5](7:18–29) William Garden Blaikie,

"The Second Book of Samuel," in the *Expositor's Bible*, p. 105.

[6](8:3–8) There is some confusion when we compare v. 4 with 1 Chronicles 18. Verse 4 says that one thousand chariots (the word *chariots* is supplied by the translators), seven *hundred* horsemen were captured, while 1 Chronicles 18:4 says that seven *thousand* horsemen were taken. The number in 2 Samuel may be from one battle, while the number in 1 Chronicles may be the total taken throughout the conflict. Or this may simply be a copyist's error.

[7](8:13) If "Syrians" (Heb. Aram) is correct here it could mean that the Edomites (Heb. Edom) sought help from them. However, since *Aram* and *Edom* are spelled nearly alike in the Hebrew consonantal text ("r" and "d" being often confused in copying) it is more likely a copyist's error.

[8](8:13) Not all conservative commentators believe the superscriptions of the Psalms are original, but the author and editor of the *BBC* do.

[9](8:13) Eugene H. Merrill, "2 Chronicles," in *The Bible Knowledge Commentary*, p. 608.

[10](9:1–13) However, while "Lo" definitely means "no," the standard vowels for "pasture" are *dō̄ber*, not *debar*. The consonants *dbr* can mean "word" or "thing" in Hebrew. A possible rendering could thus be "no thing" or "nothing."

[11](10:6–8) John Haley, *Alleged Discrepancies of the Bible*, p. 321.

[12](10:15–19) George Williams, *The Student's Commentary on the Holy Scriptures*, p. 166.

[13](11:1–5) Matthew Henry, "The Books of Samuel," *Matthew Henry's Commentary on the Whole Bible*, II:494.

[14](12:10–14) G. Campbell Morgan, *Searchlights from the Word*, p. 91.

[15](12:15–23) Henry, "Samuel," II:504.

[16](12:26–30) Flavius Josephus, *The Works of Josephus*, Peabody, MA: Hendrickson Publishers, 1987, p. 193.

[17](12:31) Keil and Delitzsch believe that the more cruel meaning is correct and that the facts should not be softened by re-translating. However, they see the punishment as meted out either only on the fighting men taken prisoners or referring "at the most to the male population of the acropolis of Rabbah" ("Samuel," VII:396).

[18](14:14) Hoste and Rodgers, *Bible Problems*, p. 215.

[19](15:7–12) Since David's *entire reign* was forty years long the traditional reading here (*forty*) is doubtless a copyist's error. Numbers were especially hard to copy perfectly in ancient Hebrew manuscripts.

[20](21:15–22) Cited by Keil and Delitzsch, "Samuel," VII:446.

[21](23:1–7) A marvelous musical setting of verses 3b and 4 was made by one of America's earliest composers, Richard Billings.

[22](23:13–17) Williams, *Student's Commentary*, p. 309.

[23](Chap. 24: Intro) William D. Crockett, *A Harmony of Samuel, Kings and Chronicles*, pp. 138–40.

[24](24:15–25) Henry, "Samuel," II:446.

BIBLIOGRAPHY

For Bibliography see 1 Samuel.

FIRST KINGS

Introduction

"The history of the nation is recorded from the close of the reign of David to the middle of the reign of Ahaziah. In its highest glory under Solomon, the kingdom foreshadows the millennial kingdom of our Lord. The prosperity of the nation rises or falls according to the character of the ruler and his people, illustrating for us the important principle that obedience is the condition of blessing."

—F. B. Meyer

I. Unique Place in the Canon

The importance of Kings, which was originally only one book, can be seen from a historical perspective in that it spans 400 years of the history of Israel, from the reign of Solomon to the Babylonian Captivity. It records the reigns, not only of Judah (as does Chronicles), but also of the apostate nation called "Israel" or "Ephraim" in the North. However, it is not a mere history book; Kings gives a spiritual analysis of the kings as to whether they served the Lord or idols—or were half-hearted in their loyalty to God.

Perhaps most helpful of all to most Bible readers are the exciting yet edifying ministries of the prophets Elijah and his successor Elisha.

An important lesson of Kings is that God rewards loyalty and punishes apostasy. Hezekiah and Josiah are the clearest examples of the former (2 Kgs. 18:3; 22:2). The obvious examples of the latter—on a national scale—are the exiles, first of the Northern Kingdom (722 B.C.) and then of the Southern (586 B.C.).

II. Authorship

The human author of Kings is unknown. A great deal of the book is apparently compiled from records, but with the guidance of the Holy Spirit. Some have suggested a priestly author, but one wonders what suitable priestly writers would have been available in the apostate Northern Kingdom. A prophetic author seems more likely. The final editor of the book is thought possibly to be Ezra if it was a priest and Ezekiel or Jeremiah if it was a prophet.

III. Date

Second Kings ends on the positive conciliatory note of Babylonian King Evil-Merodach's kindly elevation of King Jehoiachin of Judah after thirty-seven years of prison (c. 560 B.C.). An even more encouraging historical event that is conspicuous by its *absence* is the beginning of the return of the Jews to Palestine (536 B.C.). Since it is unlikely that such a patriotic writer as the author of Kings would neglect to mention this return if it had already started, it seems that the date Kings was finished would be between 560 and 536 B.C.

IV. Background and Themes

The two prominent groups mentioned in Kings are the kings and the prophets. The judgment passed on a king stemmed directly from his obedience or disobedience to the Lord. The prophet's ministry was always one of calling the wandering nation back to Jehovah.

O. J. Gibson summarizes the book as follows:

Two chronological lines of kings are interwoven in the account. Israel, with ten tribes, is sometimes called the northern kingdom because its land was to the north of Jerusalem.

From its first ruler, Jeroboam, to its destruction and captivity by Assyria, it was continuously in disobedience and idolatry before God. The so-called southern kingdom of Judah, centering in Jerusalem, was far from faithful to God, but yet maintained a semblance of obedience among a faithful minority. The most glorious period of the time was that of Solomon's reign. The building of the Temple and its dedication receive more attention than any other period, indicating its importance in God's eyes. Solomon's reign, ending with departure and judgment, is a solemn warning of what will happen when divine privileges and honor are abused and His Word flouted. Only when every appeal of grace had been exhausted by persistent disobedience did God, not heathendom, destroy first the northern and then the southern kingdom.[1]

OUTLINE

Commentary

I. THE LAST DAYS OF DAVID (1:1—2:11)

A. Adonijah's Attempt to Seize the Throne (1:1–38)

1:1–4 **David was** now seventy years **old** and in declining health. He was about to pass off the stage of history. The proposal of **his servants** in verse 2 seems at first glance both puzzling and shocking. However, this practice was accepted at that time as being of value in the case of an illness like David's. It was not an act of doubtful morality and would not create a public scandal. One thing we can be sure of is that David **did not** "**know**" (in the sense of having sexual intercourse with) **Abishag** (v. 4b). And it seems probable from chapter 2 that she was considered a legal wife of David because Solomon interpreted Adonijah's later request for her as a claim to the throne (2:21, 22).

1:5–10 **Adonijah** was apparently David's oldest surviving **son** (2:22) and thus considered himself next in line for the throne. Amnon and **Absalom** were both dead. Chileab was probably dead as well (2 Sam. 3:2–4). Before his father died, Adonijah proclaimed himself as **king**, prepared a great entourage, and enlisted the support of **Joab** and **Abiathar**. Being a **very good-looking** man, he won a great following. Verse 6a indicates that David was an indulgent **father** and Adonijah a spoiled son. When **Adonijah . . . sacrificed** a great many animals near **En Rogel, he . . . invited** to the feast **all** except those whom he knew to be loyal to his father—**Nathan the prophet, Benaiah, the mighty men** of David, and **Solomon**.

1:11–38 God had told David before Solomon was born that Solomon would be Israel's next king (1 Chron. 22:9, 10). **Nathan** had a desire to see the word of the Lord fulfilled. Being concerned about the threat of **Adonijah**, he skillfully brought the issue to David's attention. Coached by **Nathan, Bathsheba** appeared before **the** ailing **king** and notified him of the plot. She also reminded him of a promise he had previously made (though unrecorded) that **Solomon**, her **son**, would be the next king. Just as she finished requesting that he publicly announce Solomon as his successor, **Nathan** arrived and **Bathsheba** withdrew. **Nathan** repeated the news concerning Adonijah's plot to seize the kingdom and asked if this was the king's desire. When **David** called for **Bathsheba**, Nathan withdrew. **David** reassured **Bathsheba** that **Solomon** would indeed be his successor. Then he instructed **Zadok the priest, Nathan the prophet, and Benaiah to take . . . Solomon . . . to Gihon**, a spring located outside the city, on the king's **own mule** and to **anoint him** as **king**.

B. Solomon's Anointing at Gihon (1:39–53)

Since it is widely held that Solomon had a two-year co-regency with his father, for which he would have had to be anointed, this was a second anointing that recognized him as sole ruler. This public anointing by **Zadok the priest** caused **great** rejoicing among David's followers, but consternation among **Adonijah and** those **who were** feasting **with him**. When the latter heard that **Solomon** was now sitting **on the** royal **throne** and that David was grateful to the Lord for this, they realized that Adonijah's plot was a failure. **Adonijah** fled to the tabernacle and **took hold of the horns of the altar**, an act which was supposed to grant him safety from punishment. Solomon decreed that Adonijah would be spared if found **worthy**, but punished if caught in any future wickedness. Then he sent Adonijah home.

C. David's Final Charge to Solomon (2:1–11)

If David in exile typifies Christ in His rejection during this age of grace, Solomon typifies Him as the King reigning in millennial glory. When He returns to set up His kingdom, His first act will be to destroy His foes and to purge out of His kingdom everything that offends. We see this pictured in chapter 2.

Just before his death, **David** delivered a solemn charge to **Solomon**, urging him to be obedient to **the LORD** and instructing him to take appropriate action concerning certain men: **Joab** should be slain for murdering **Abner . . . and Amasa; the sons of Barzillai** should be shown **kindness** because of their father's kindness to David when he was fleeing **from Absalom; Shimei** should be slain eventually because he cursed David, but Solomon could work out the details. The expression "**. . . shed the blood of war in peacetime**" (v. 5b) reads in the NIV, "shedding their blood in peacetime as if in battle."

After a reign of **forty years, David** died and was **buried in** Jerusalem.

II. THE GOLDEN REIGN OF KING SOLOMON (2:12—11:43)

A. Solomon's Purge of the Opposition (2:12–46)

2:12–25 Solomon sat on the **throne**, and **his kingdom was firmly established**. **Adonijah** was grieved that he had been deprived of the throne, although he had to admit that it was Solomon's by the will of God (v. 15b). Whether innocently or insidiously, he made a **petition** of **King Solomon** through **Bathsheba** that **Abishag**, David's nurse, might be given to him for a **wife. Solomon** looked upon this as being the next thing to asking **for . . . the kingdom** itself, so he ordered **Benaiah** to execute **Adonijah**.

2:26–34 The king also expelled **Abiathar** from the priesthood, doubtless because he had supported Adonijah in his abortive plot. This was in partial fulfillment of God's judgment on **the house of Eli** (see 1 Sam. 2:31–35). When **Joab** heard of Abiathar's dismissal, he **fled to the . . . horns of the altar** for refuge. **Benaiah** ordered him to leave the altar, but Joab refused, expressing the determination to **die** there. Benaiah executed him quickly and had him **buried in his own house in the wilderness**. The deaths of **Abner** and **Amasa** were finally avenged. **The altar** of God gave no protection to anyone who broke the law of God.

2:35 **Benaiah** was appointed commander of **the army**, and **Zadok** succeeded **Abiathar** as **priest. Benaiah** had served David since the days of Saul. He was a man of great valor and the captain of David's personal bodyguard (2 Sam. 20:23). His unfailing courage was surpassed only by his undying loyalty to the house of David. Courage and loyalty should also characterize those who serve David's greater Son, the Lord Jesus Christ.

2:36–46 Solomon did not order Shimei's execution immediately. Rather, he put him under a sort of **house** arrest, forbidding him to leave the city. After **three years ... Shimei** left **Jerusalem ... to seek ... two** escaped **slaves ... in Gath**. In so doing he broke **the oath** that Solomon had made him **swear** earlier, and he demonstrated that he was no more faithful to Solomon than he had been to David. When he returned, **the king commanded Benaiah** to put **him** to death.

Thus **Solomon** made his **kingdom** secure by aggressively removing all whose hearts were not with him. Thereafter his reign was one of peace. The Christian will know the peace of God as he puts out of his life the things which oppose the reign of Christ within.

B. The Wisdom of Solomon (Chap. 3)

3:1 **Solomon** married the **daughter** of the **Pharaoh** who was then in power in **Egypt**. Perhaps this shows that his trust was in political alliances. The marriage, although politically expedient, was spiritually disastrous as well as forbidden by the law. From this point onward, Solomon's harem grew until it contained hundreds of foreign women. Solomon thus linked himself with many foreign powers but alienated himself from the Lord (11:1–8).

3:2–4 **High places** were here used for the worship of **the LORD**. This was not strictly in accordance with the law; God was supposed to be worshiped only in the place which He designated. But it is here excused on the ground that **there was no** official **house**, since Shiloh had been destroyed by the Philistines about 1050 B.C. when the ark was carried away (1 Sam. 4). After the temple was built, **high places** continued to be used, but for idolatrous worship. Although the ark was in Jerusalem at this time, the tabernacle was in **Gibeon** (1 Chron.

21:29), about six miles away. It was there that the king **offered a thousand burnt offerings**, probably at the outset of his reign.

3:5–15 God **appeared to Solomon ... at Gibeon** and asked him what he would like most of all. The king requested **an understanding heart** for the great task of judging and ruling **the people** of Israel. The request **pleased the LORD**, and it was granted—together with **riches and honor**, and also long life, if Solomon would **walk in** obedience to God. Today God offers to everyone the greatest gift for which one could possibly ask—the Lord Jesus Christ, "in whom are hidden all the treasures of wisdom and knowledge" (Col. 2:3).

3:16–28 The remainder of chapter 3 gives an example of the king's great wisdom. **Two ... harlots** were quarreling over which one was the **mother** of a baby. When Solomon threatened to **divide** the baby with a **sword** into **two** equal parts, the true **mother** was revealed by her desire to spare the **child** even if she didn't get the baby for herself. Such **wisdom** caused Solomon to be greatly **feared** and respected in all Israel.

C. Solomon's Administrators (4:1–19)

4:1–6 These verses list Solomon's high **officials**, or cabinet: **Azariah**, a grandson **of Zadok**, who seems to have succeeded him as high priest; **Elihoreph and Ahijah**, secretaries of state; **Jehoshaphat, recorder** or chronicler; **Benaiah**, commander of **the army**; **Zadok and Abiathar, the priests**; **Azariah— over the officers**; **Zabud—** the **friend** of Solomon; **Ahishar**, in charge of the palace; **Adoniram**, in charge of the **labor force** (tribute). The name **"Abiathar"** in verse 4 presents a difficulty if it is the same one

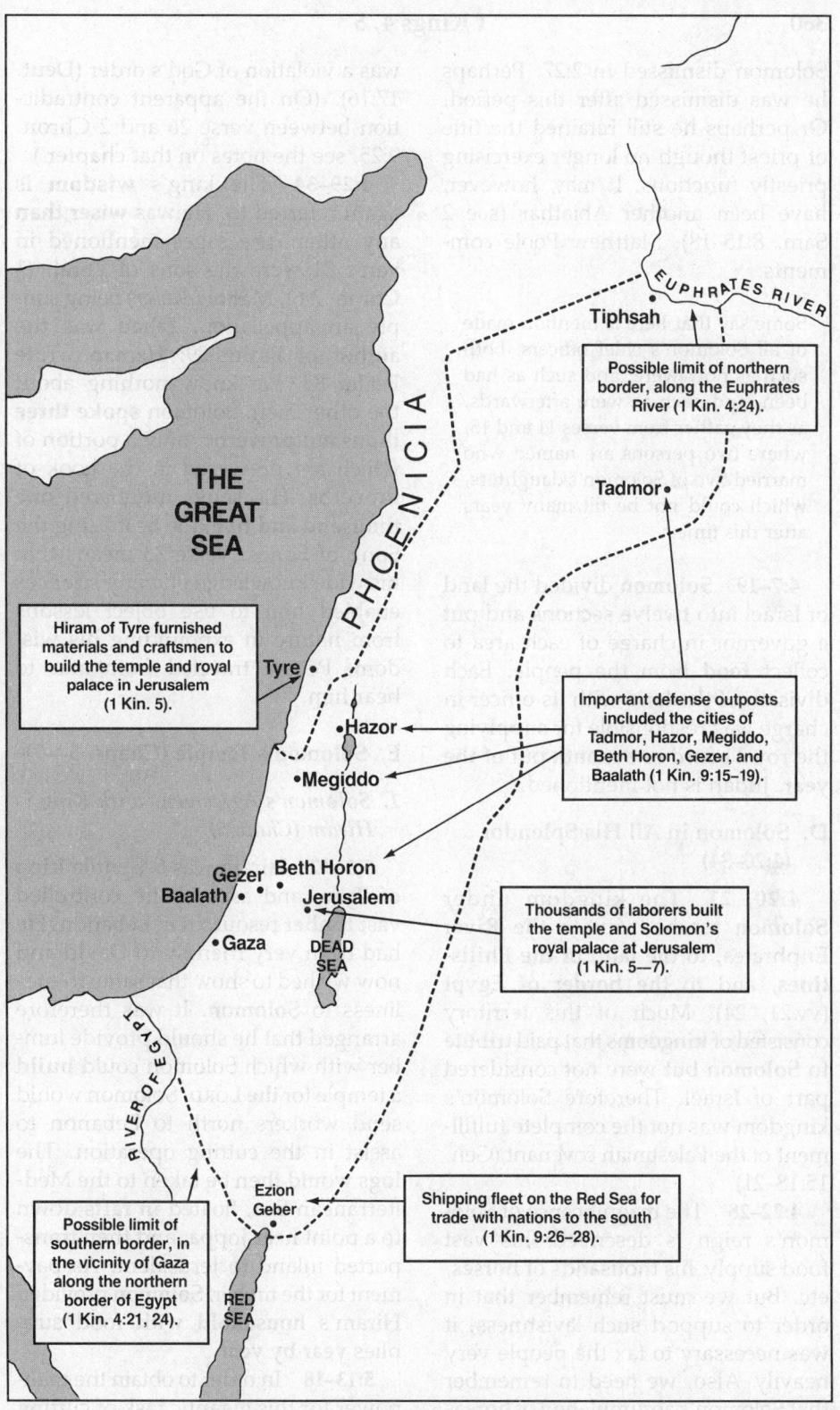

THE
GREAT
SEA

EUPHRATES RIVER

Tiphsah

Possible limit of northern border, along the Euphrates River (1 Kin. 4:24).

Tadmor

PHOENICIA

Hiram of Tyre furnished materials and craftsmen to build the temple and royal palace in Jerusalem (1 Kin. 5).

Tyre

Hazor

Megiddo

Important defense outposts included the cities of Tadmor, Hazor, Megiddo, Beth Horon, Gezer, and Baalath (1 Kin. 9:15–19).

Gezer
Beth Horon
Baalath
Jerusalem
Gaza
DEAD SEA

Thousands of laborers built the temple and Solomon's royal palace at Jerusalem (1 Kin. 5—7).

RIVER OF EGYPT

Ezion Geber

Shipping fleet on the Red Sea for trade with nations to the south (1 Kin. 9:26–28).

Possible limit of southern border, in the vicinity of Gaza along the northern border of Egypt (1 Kin. 4:21, 24).

RED SEA

Solomon's Empire: The Twelve Districts

Solomon dismissed in 2:27. Perhaps he was dismissed after this period. Or perhaps he still retained the title of priest though no longer exercising priestly functions. It may, however, have been another Abiathar (see 2 Sam. 8:15–18). Matthew Poole comments:

Some say that here is mention made of all Solomon's chief officers, both such as now were, and such as had been, and such as were afterwards, as they gather from verses 11 and 15, where two persons are named who married two of Solomon's daughters, which could not be till many years after this time.[2]

4:7–19 **Solomon** divided the land of Israel into **twelve** sections and put a governor in charge of each area to collect **food** from the people. Each division of the land with its officer in charge was responsible for supplying the royal board **one month** out **of the year**. Judah is not mentioned.

D. Solomon in All His Splendor (4:20–34)

4:20, 21 The kingdom under **Solomon** reached out to **the River** Euphrates, **to the land of the Philistines**, and to **the border of Egypt** (vv.21, 24). Much of this territory consisted of **kingdoms** that paid **tribute** to **Solomon** but were not considered part of Israel. Therefore Solomon's kingdom was not the complete fulfillment of the Palestinian covenant (Gen. 15:18–21).

4:22–28 The magnificence of Solomon's reign is described: his vast food supply, his thousands of **horses**, etc. But we must remember that in order to support such lavishness, it was necessary to tax the people very heavily. Also, we need to remember that Solomon's accumulation of **horses**

was a violation of God's order (Deut. 17:16). (On the apparent contradiction between verse 26 and 2 Chron. 9:25, see the notes on that chapter.)

4:29–34 The king's **wisdom** is again referred to. **He was wiser than** any other. The sages mentioned in verse 31 were the sons of Zerah (1 Chron. 2:6), **Mahol** (*dancer*) being simply an appellation. **Ethan** was the author of Psalm 89; **Heman** wrote Psalm 88. We know nothing about the other men. Solomon **spoke three thousand proverbs**, only a portion of which are preserved in the book of Proverbs. **His songs** numbered **one thousand and five**, the best being the Song of Songs. Verse 33 means that his wide knowledge of many sciences enabled him to use object lessons from nature in expounding his wisdom. People traveled from afar to hear him.

E. Solomon's Temple (Chaps. 5—7)

1. Solomon's Agreement with King Hiram (Chap. 5)

5:1–12 **Hiram** was a Gentile **king of Tyre**, and as such he controlled vast **timber** resources in Lebanon. He had been very friendly to **David** and now wished to show that same friendliness to **Solomon**. It was therefore arranged that he should provide lumber with which Solomon could **build** a temple for **the LORD**. Solomon would send workers north to Lebanon to assist in the cutting operation. The **logs** would then be taken to the Mediterranean **Sea**, floated **in rafts** down to a point near Joppa, and then transported inland to Jerusalem. As payment for the timber, **Solomon** provided Hiram's **household** with food supplies **year by year**.

5:13–18 In order to obtain the manpower for this gigantic task of cutting lumber, **Solomon** drafted **thirty thousand men** of **Israel**, requiring them to go **to Lebanon . . . in shifts** of **ten thousand** each **month**. In addition to these men, **the king** had **eighty thousand** Canaanite slaves **(Gebalites)** working in the quarries of Israel, preparing **stones** for **the temple** (cf. v. 15; 2 Chron. 2:17, 18). **He** also **had seventy thousand who carried burdens**.

Solomon's massive building operations involved a great force of slave labor (cf. 9:15–22). But even this proved inadequate, and he was compelled to draft native Israelites (probably excluding Judah), not as slave laborers but as forced laborers. The Israelites, with their tradition for sturdy independence, bitterly resented this, and it became a major cause of the division of the kingdom (12:4). How necessary it is to have divine wisdom in all matters, and not to ride roughshod over the sensitivities and welfare of others! (*Daily Notes of the Scripture Union*).

(See the notes on problems in 2 Chron. 2 for an explanation of the numerical discrepancies between these two chapters.)

2. Description and Construction of the Temple (Chap. 6)

6:1 In verse 1, the work of building the temple is said to have been started 480 years after the exodus from **Egypt**. If Solomon began the construction in 967/66 B.C., this would date the exodus at 1446/47 B.C. It is not possible, however, to fix these dates with absolute certainty. There is much dispute among scholars on this subject, but 1446 B.C. is very close to the early date of the exodus.

6:2–6 Details concerning the plan of **the temple** are given in chapter 6. They are at times technical and in-

volved, making it difficult to get the exact picture. However, we do know that the temple was built somewhat as follows. It was 90 feet long, 30 feet wide, and 45 feet high (v. 2). It was divided into two rooms. The first room was the **sanctuary**, measuring 60 feet long by 30 feet wide by 45 feet high (vv. 2, 17). Latticed **windows**, probably near the top, provided light and an escape for smoke (v. 4). The second room was **the inner sanctuary**, 30 feet long by 30 feet wide by 30 feet high. The **vestibule** added 30 more feet to the length at the east or front end and was elevated 15 feet above ground level. On the north, west, and south sides of the temple were three stories of **side chambers**, or rooms, for the priests. These were **against the wall of the temple** but were not an integral part of it.

6:7–10 All the lumber and **stone** for the temple was **finished at the quarry** to exact specifications so that when brought to Jerusalem, the pieces could be fitted together without **iron** tools (v. 7). Thus **the temple** was erected silently, just as the living temple of God is **being built** today. Verses 8 and 10 describe the **doorway** to the side chambers and the height of each story (7½ feet). Verse 9 describes the roof of the whole temple.

6:11–22 **The word of the** LORD graciously **came to Solomon** during the construction, promising to confirm the Davidic covenant and that God would **dwell** in the temple **among the children of Israel if** the king would be obedient (vv. 11–13). The interior of the building was lined **with cedar boards**, completely **overlaid . . . with pure gold**; **no stone** was **seen**. These stones, so skillfully and precisely cut, were not even visible. Spurgeon makes a spiritual application:

Even the foundation stones were not rugged and rough, but hewn and costly. God would have everything which is done for him done well. He careth not so much for that which meets the eye of man, he delights himself with the beauty of those living stones of his spiritual temple which are hidden away from observation.[3]

6:23–28 Standing on either side of the ark, **in the inner sanctuary**, were **two** carved **cherubim, overlaid ... with gold**. Their outstretched **wings** reached from **one wall** to **the other**. These are not the same as the cherubim on the mercy seat (Ex. 25:18; 37:9).

6:29, 30 Nothing but **gold** was visible inside the temple.

6:31–35 The **folding** or sliding **doors** leading to **the inner sanctuary** are described in verses 31 and 32. The rooms were also separated by a veil which hung inside the doors of the inner sanctuary—2 Chron. 3:14. The main **doors** leading to the **sanctuary** are described in verses 33–35.

6:36 In front of the temple was **the inner court** of the priests. There was a low wall between it and the outer court. This wall consisted of **three rows of hewn stone** and **a row of cedar beams**.

In the inner court were a huge brazen altar for sacrifices, a huge laver used by the priests for cleansing, and ten smaller lavers (chap. 7). The outer court was for the people of Israel.

6:37, 38 The temple was begun **in the fourth year** of Solomon's reign and **was finished ... seven years** later.

3. The Construction of Other Buildings (7:1–12)

7:1 The narrative now turns to the construction of Solomon's **own**

house and other royal buildings included in the great court.

Solomon's **house**, or the royal palace, took **thirteen years to build**. It was located slightly southeast of the temple and just outside the wall of the inner court. Some think that the fact that it took six years longer to build the palace than the temple indicates a greater concern for Solomon's ego than for God's glory. On the other hand, perhaps the temple took only seven years because of Solomon's zeal for God to be given a place, and his thousands of laborers built a "holy temple" (for the LORD) at a greater speed.

7:2–12 The House of the Forest of Lebanon (vv. 2–5) was at the southern portion of the great court. Its outstanding feature was the large number of **cedar pillars** in it. Perhaps this accounted for its name. We do not know definitely the function of this building, but we surmise from 1 Kings 10:17 that it was an armory. Immediately north of the House of the Forest of Lebanon was **the Hall** (or Porch) **of Pillars** (v. 6). It was probably the entrance to **the Hall of Judgment** and **the throne** room (v. 7). Adjoining the royal palace was the House of **Pharaoh's daughter**, where it is likely that the royal harem lived (v. 8). **All** the buildings **were** made **of costly** stone blocks **cut to** exact measurements. Also, the wall around the great court was made of **three rows of** stone blocks covered by **cedar beams**.

Another perspective of these verses sees **the House of the Forest of Lebanon**, **the Hall of Pillars**, and the Hall of the Throne (**the Hall of Judgment**) as all part of the palace. The **hall** made **for Pharaoh's daughter** adjoined the royal residence.

4. Furnishings of the Temple (7:13–51)

7:13, 14 **Huram** (spelled *Hiram* in Heb. and KJV) was not the same as the king of Tyre. He was a master workman of Jewish lineage who lived in **Tyre**.

7:15–22 Next **two** huge **pillars of bronze** which stood at the entrance of the temple are described. One was named **Jachin** (*He shall establish*) and the other **Boaz** (*in Him is strength*). At the top of each pillar was a bowl-like **capital**, highly ornamental. Although the physical details of these **pillars** are given, we are not told the spiritual significance behind them. Someone has well observed that the **pillars** of God's living temple today are believers of holy character (Gal. 2:9). Revelation 3:12 is God's promise that those who overcome will be made **pillars** in His heavenly temple for all eternity.

7:23–26 The **Sea of cast bronze** was the huge laver which stood in the inner court. It was a large basin, supported by **twelve** bronze **oxen** and placed between the temple and the altar, but to the south (2 Chron. 4:10). It supplied water for the priests to wash their hands and feet.

7:27–39 In addition to the large laver, there were **ten** smaller **lavers** resting on **four**-wheeled **carts** or stands. No mention is made of the bronze altar until 8:64, although it too was in the inner court.

7:40–47 **Huram** supervised the construction of all the **burnished bronze** work in connection with the temple area, including **the pots, the shovels, and the bowls** of the temple itself. The **bronze articles** were cast in clay, in much the same manner as is done today (v. 46).

7:48–50 The **furnishings** of the holy place included **the** golden **altar** of incense, **the table of gold**, ten golden tables of showbread (2 Chron. 4:8), ten golden **lampstands of pure gold**, and the golden utensils.

7:51 **David had** made elaborate preparations for the temple that he was not allowed to build. **Solomon brought** these treasures into the temple for use and safekeeping.

Differences between this chapter and 2 Chronicles 2—4 are discussed in the notes on 2 Chronicles.

F. Dedication of the Temple (Chap. 8)

8:1–5 With the temple completed, the next step was to **bring . . . the ark of the covenant from** the section of Jerusalem known as **the City of David**, or **Zion**, to the temple on Mount Moriah. This probably took place almost a year after the building was completed (cf. v. 2 with 1 Kgs. 6:37, 38).

Just before the Feast of Tabernacles, a great national holiday took place, and **the ark, the tabernacle**, and **the holy furnishings** were **brought** to the temple by **the priests and the Levites**. This was accompanied by the sacrifice of a great number of **sheep and oxen**.

8:6–9 **The ark** was put in **the Most Holy Place**. In some way that we do not understand, **the ends of the poles** were visible **from the holy place, but they could not be seen from outside**, on the porch. The **poles** were not removed, as stated in the KJV (v. 8). At this time the only items in **the ark** were **the two tablets of stone**, containing the Ten Commandments. We are not told what happened to the pot of manna or to Aaron's rod that budded (Heb. 9:4).

8:10, 11 As soon as the ark (typical of Christ) was given its proper place, the glory **cloud**, signifying the divine Presence, **filled the** temple. **The priests** were **not** able to carry on their duties because **the glory of the LORD filled the house**.

8:12, 13 When all was finished, **Solomon** addressed **the LORD**. God had said that **He would dwell in** thick darkness. Now Solomon had **built** Him **an exalted house** with a Most Holy Place that had no illumination except the glory of God Himself.

With his usual spiritual insight, Matthew Henry comments:

> He showed himself ready to hear the prayer Solomon was now about to make; and not only so, but took up his residence in this house, that all his praying people might there be encouraged to make their applications to him. But the glory of God appeared in a cloud, a dark cloud, to signify, (1.) The darkness of that dispensation in comparison with the light of the gospel, by which, *with open face, we behold, as in a glass, the glory of the Lord*. (2.) The darkness of our present state in comparison with the vision of God, which will be the happiness of heaven, where the divine glory is unveiled. Now we only say what he is not, but then we shall see him as he is.[4]

8:14–21 Next **the king turned** to the people in blessing. He traced the fulfillment of God's promise to **David** concerning the **temple** and expressed his satisfaction that **the ark** of **the covenant** now had a settled abode.

8:22–26 The prayer of dedication is recorded in verses 22–53. After extolling God for keeping His **covenant** with **David** concerning the temple, he asked Him to fulfill another covenant that He had made with David— the promise that there would never **fail to** be a descendant of David to **sit . . . on the throne**.

8:27–30 Although Solomon real-

ized that no temple on earth was adequate to **contain** the great **God**, yet he asked that the LORD might recognize **this temple** and that when he or any of the **people** of **Israel** addressed God there, He might **hear** and **forgive**.

8:31–53 Then the king listed various specific cases in which the Lord's answer was especially desired.

1. In lawsuits where oaths were taken, presumably because no definite evidence was available, God was asked to punish the guilty and reward the innocent (vv. 31, 32).
2. When defeat came to Israel's army **because** of **sin**, God was asked to **forgive** and restore them **to** their **land** when they confessed their **sin** (vv. 33, 34).
3. In times of drought, God was asked to **send rain . . . when** the **people** humbled themselves before Him in repentance (vv. 35, 36).
4. If **famine** or **pestilence, or blight or mildew**, or insect plagues, or **enemy** siege, or any other calamity should befall them, God was requested to honor any prayers that were **made** to Him **toward** the **temple** and to **forgive . . . the land** (vv. 37–40).
5. If a Gentile converted to Judaism and prayed to God, then He was asked to answer the prayer of such a proselyte (vv. 41–43).
6. Prayers for victory in **battle** were anticipated by Solomon, and he asked the Lord to be mindful of all such supplications (vv. 44, 45).
7. Speaking prophetically, Solomon next envisioned the time when Israel might be carried into cap-

tivity because of **sin**. He asked the Lord to listen to their prayer of repentance and cause their captors to be merciful to them; after all, the Israelites were His **people**, whom He had delivered **out of Egypt**. These verses found fulfillment in the Babylonian captivity and in the subsequent return under the decree of Cyrus (vv. 46–53).

8:54–61 After **praying** to God, **Solomon . . . blessed** the people by pouring out an eloquent request for God's presence, and for power to be **loyal to** Him and to be a witness for Him among the nations **of the earth**.

Solomon's benediction, like the rest of his prayer, shows an immense appreciation of great spiritual truths: 1. *God is utterly reliable.* "Not one word has failed" (56)—what a testimony! 2. *The past guarantees the future* (57). Since God is unchanging (cf. Heb. 13:8), we can build upon the fact that what He has shown Himself to be in times past He will be to us (cf. Josh. 1:5). 3. *Man needs God's help in the life of discipleship* (58), a truth which Jeremiah knew and for which he gave the reason (see Jer. 10:23; 17:9). Even the impulse of man's free will comes from God—a paradox indeed! Compare the activity of the Holy Spirit in John 16:8–11. 4. *We stand in daily need of the assistance of God* ("as each day requires," 59). But then, He neither slumbers nor sleeps (Psa. 121:4)! 5. *God's care for His children is never for their selfish enjoyment, but that others might come to know Him* (60). 6. In view of all this, *can we give less than our absolute loyalty and obedience to Him* (61)? (*Daily Notes of the Scripture Union*)

This prayer is also recorded in 2 Chronicles 6 (see notes), with the only differences being: In 2 Chronicles Solomon ended his prayer with three requests (2 Chron. 6:40–42), omitted in 1 Kings; in 1 Kings Solomon blessed the people (vv. 54–61). This is omitted in 2 Chronicles.

8:62–65 Of the great number of animals that were sacrificed, some were used as food for the huge throng that had assembled (v. 65). Since **the bronze altar** was not large enough **to receive** all **the burnt offerings**, etc., Solomon **consecrated** a place in **the middle of the court** where the rest could be **offered** to the Lord. This great celebration was characterized by joy and worship and thanksgiving. Of the thousands of animals slain, not one was offered as a sin or trespass offering.

At this same **time, Solomon held** the Feast of Tabernacles with Israelites who had come **from** as far as **the entrance of Hamath**, near Dan, in the north and from **the Brook of Egypt** in the south. The Feast of Dedication and the Feast of Tabernacles together lasted for **fourteen days**.

8:66 Then **the people** returned to their homes **joyful and glad of heart**. Second Chronicles 7:9 says that a solemn assembly was held on the "eighth day," while verse 66 says that the people were sent away on the "eighth day." John Haley harmonizes these two accounts as follows:

The feast of tabernacles began on the fifteenth and ended on the twenty-second of the month, closing with a "holy convocation" on the "eighth day" (Lev. 23:33–39), at the end of which Solomon dismissed the people; the dismissal taking effect the next morning, the twenty-third (2 Chron. 7:10).[5]

G. Solomon's Fame (Chaps. 9, 10)

1. His Covenant from God (9:1–9)

9:1–5 God's answer to Solomon's **prayer** was that He would accept the temple as His **house** and would **put His name there forever**. Although Solomon's temple has long since ceased to exist, God will yet dwell in a temple in Jerusalem when the Lord Jesus returns to set up His worldwide kingdom. In the meantime, God dwells in the temple of the believer's body and of the church.

9:6–9 As for Solomon's family, God promised that Solomon and his sons would always have descendants to sit **on the throne** if they would be obedient. **But if** they departed **from** the living God and turned to idolatry, **then** He would send the people into exile, destroy the temple, and make **Israel . . . a proverb and a byword among** the Gentiles. The temple would become a heap of ruins, and visitors would **be astonished** at its desolation.

2. His Gifts to Hiram (9:10–14)

With regard to this paragraph, some commentators suggest that Solomon had borrowed **one hundred and twenty talents of gold** from **Hiram** (v. 14) in order to finance his elaborate building program, and had given **twenty cities . . . of Galilee** to **Hiram** as security. It was because of Hiram's previous help (v. 11a) that Solomon felt free to request the loan. When **Hiram** saw **the cities**, he was dissatisfied and **called them the land of Cabul** (meaning *displeasing, dirty,* or *rubbish;* lit. *Good for Nothing,* NKJV marg.). It appears from 2 Chronicles 8:2 that Solomon may have redeemed the **cities** by paying off the loan.

3. His Subjects and Sacrifices (9:15–25)

9:15–23 Verses 15–22 give the account (rather than **"reason,"** as in KJV and NKJV) of the **forced labor** which **Solomon** used in his construction program. **Hazor, Megiddo, and Gezer** were three cities which Solomon fortified for defense purposes. **Hazor** was in the north and protected the northern door to Palestine. **Megiddo** was:

> . . . an important city of north-central Palestine, overlooking the Plain of Esdraelon. It dominated the intersection of important trade routes and served as the key to the defense of the Jordan Valley (from the south) and the Central Plain (from the north).[6]

Gezer was situated west of Jerusalem on a main trade route from the interior to the coastal land of Philistia. **All the** Gentile captives listed in verse 20 were **forced laborers. The children of Israel** were not reduced to bondage. There were **five hundred and fifty** supervisors established **over Solomon's work.**

9:24 The "Millo" which Solomon **built** was some type of fortification for Jerusalem. It was undertaken after the palace for **Pharaoh's daughter** was completed.

9:25 Solomon sacrificed **to the Lord . . . three times a year** at the three major feasts: Unleavened Bread, Weeks (Pentecost), and Tabernacles (2 Chron. 8:13).

4. His Navy (9:26–28)

King Solomon had **a fleet of ships at Ezion Geber, . . . on the** Gulf of Aqaba, **near Elath. Hiram sent** some of **his servants with the fleet . . . to Ophir** (exact location unknown—some say southern Arabia, some India, and others Africa). **They . . . brought . . . four hundred and twenty talents of gold . . . to King Solomon**.

5. His Visit from the Queen of Sheba (10:1–13)

The purpose of chapter 10 is to emphasize Solomon's glory. From drinking vessels to sailing vessels, from an ivory throne to handcrafted chariots, he possessed everything the human heart could desire in quantities that stagger the imagination. **The queen of Sheba**, that daughter of opulence, was completely overwhelmed by Solomon's **wisdom** and by the splendor of his kingdom. This was in fulfillment of the Lord's promise, to which Solomon owed everything (3:11–13).

The queen of Sheba (probably Saba, in the southern Arabian peninsula) **came to test** Solomon's wisdom by plying him **with hard questions**, but he was able to answer them **all** (v. 3a). **When** she saw the magnificence of his kingdom, she had to acknowledge that the glowing reports she had heard were only partial. She presented him with gifts of **gold** and **spices in great . . . abundance** and then received gifts from him in return before going back **to her own country**.

6. His Riches (10:14–29)

10:14, 15 Hiram's help brought not only **gold** from Ophir for **Solomon** but also great amounts of almug wood and precious stones. Solomon was a genius in trade relationships.

10:16–22 **Gold** was so plentiful that **Solomon** even used it for making **shields** to hang **in the House of the Forest of Lebanon**. His **ivory . . . throne** was **overlaid . . . with pure gold**. At each **side** of **the throne** was a large carved lion. Also **on each side**

of the six steps leading to the throne was a lion. **Silver** was considered as of relatively minor value **in the days of Solomon**. Solomon's **merchant ships** brought not only **gold** and **silver**, but such exotic items as **ivory, apes, and monkeys**.[7]

10:23–25 Solomon's **riches and wisdom** brought him worldwide fame, and gifts poured in to him from admirers who came to visit him.

10:26–29 Mention is made of the fact that Solomon invested heavily in **horses** and **chariots**. **Keveh**[8] (probably Cilicia) was famous for its **horses**. Solomon not only acquired **chariots and horsemen** and **horses** for national defense but also **exported them to** other countries.

Although not mentioned here, the luxury of Solomon's reign required heavy taxation to support it. This was to lead to the disruption of the kingdom (12:3–15).

"The taxation," writes J. R. Lumby, "must have been crushing, and with all this oriental splendor and luxury, there was rottenness within. Solomon was the Jewish Louis XIV."[9]

This multiplication of riches and horses violated God's Word (Deut. 17:16, 17).

H. Solomon's Failures and Death (Chap. 11)

11:1–3 Deuteronomy 17:17 forbade the king of Israel to marry heathen wives. The extent to which Solomon disobeyed this important command is shocking. The result was exactly as predicted: **His wives turned** him to idolatry.

11:4–8 Verse 4 means that King David's **heart** had been wholly true **to the LORD his God** as far as keeping himself from idolatry was concerned, but **Solomon** did not follow **his father** in this matter. He **built** idolatrous shrines on the Mount of Olives, **east of Jerusalem**.

11:9–13 God **had appeared to** Solomon **twice**—in Gibeon (3:5) and in Jerusalem at the dedication of the temple (9:2). Now He announced that, because of Solomon's idolatry, **the kingdom** would be torn **away from** him and given **to** one of **his** servants. However, it would not happen during Solomon's lifetime, and not all twelve tribes would be taken from the house of **David**. **One tribe** (Benjamin; Judah is taken for granted—12:23) would be given to Solomon's **son**.

11:14–22 Three of Solomon's adversaries are now described. The first was **Hadad**, an **Edomite** prince who had escaped **to Egypt** as **a little child** when **Joab** was killing all the males **in Edom**. He was treated well by the **Pharaoh** and was even given **the sister of Queen Tahpenes as** his **wife**. **When Hadad heard . . . that David . . . and Joab** were **dead**, he obtained the Pharaoh's reluctant permission to return to Edom. From there he began military operations against Solomon from the south.

11:23–25 The second **adversary** was **Rezon, who had** escaped **when David killed those of Zobah. He** then **became** the leader of **a band of raiders**. Later he set up an independent kingdom at **Damascus**, and became a military peril to **Solomon** from the north. **Damascus** had worn the yoke of Israel ever since David had captured the city and stationed troops there (2 Sam. 8:5, 6).

Losing Damascus, Syria's chief city-state, was especially significant because the kingdom of Syria would prove to be a thorn in Israel's flesh for centuries to come.

11:26–28 The third adversary was the **servant** of Solomon whom God had mentioned in verse 11: **Jeroboam the son of Nebat**, of the tribe of Ephraim. **Solomon** had given him a position of responsibility in the building of **the Millo**. Perhaps this power gave Jeroboam the desire to reign over all Israel.

11:29–39 One day **Jeroboam** met a **prophet** named **Ahijah**. When they **were alone in the field, Ahijah took hold of** his own **new garment . . . and tore it into twelve pieces**. He gave **ten pieces . . . to Jeroboam** as a sign that **God** would **give** him command over **ten tribes** of Israel. He also explained to Jeroboam that **one tribe** (Benjamin) would be left for Solomon's **son** (Judah understood—12:23) and that **the kingdom** would not be divided until after Solomon's death. **If** Jeroboam would obey the Lord, he would be assured of the Lord's blessing and help. Notice the limitations which God put on Jeroboam: He was to have **ten tribes**, *not* **the whole kingdom**; he was to come to power *only after Solomon's death*; God would make him **an enduring house** *only if* he would obey the Lord and wholly follow Him.

11:40 Apparently **Jeroboam** rebelled while **Solomon** was still alive, so he had to flee **to Egypt** to escape the king's wrath. He remained there **until** Solomon's **death**. Instead of facing his sin and repenting, Solomon tried to thwart the word of God by doing away with Jeroboam. It was foolish to fight against Jeroboam, though, since he was now the divinely appointed heir of the northern tribes. Saul had been unsuccessful in his attempts to kill his successor, David. Solomon was likewise unsuccessful in his attempts to murder Jeroboam.

The tribes over which Jeroboam would rule would be: Reuben, Dan, Naphtali, Gad, Asher, Issachar,

Zebulun, Ephraim, Manasseh, and portions of Levi and Simeon. The tribes over which Solomon's son would reign would be: Judah, Benjamin, and portions of Levi and Simeon. For the most part Levi (2 Chron. 11:13–16) and Simeon were loyal to Judah.

11:41 The book of the acts of Solomon was probably the official chronicle of his reign, but certainly not an inspired part of Scripture.

11:42, 43 After reigning for **forty years**, **Solomon** died **and was buried in** Jerusalem. **Rehoboam his son** succeeded him. Solomon's beginning was better than his ending. A good start does not guarantee a good finish. He had been raised to the pinnacle of greatness, but he plunged off into the abyss of moral degradation and idolatry. If only the king had practiced what he preached in Ecclesiastes 12:13, 14:

Let us hear the conclusion of the whole matter: Fear God and keep His commandments, for this is man's all. For God will bring every work into judgment, including every secret thing, whether good or evil.

III. THE DIVIDED KINGDOM (Chaps. 12—22)

A. King Rehoboam of Judah (12:1–24)

Rehoboam the son of Solomon ruled in Judah for seventeen years (931/30–913 B.C.; 1 Kgs. 12:20–24; 2 Chron. 11 and 12).

12:1–11 Rehoboam **went to Shechem** to be acknowledged as **king**. Having **heard** of the death of Solomon, **Jeroboam** returned from **Egypt** and also went to Shechem, along with **the whole assembly of** men **of Israel**. The Israelites delivered an ultimatum

to Rehoboam—**"Lighten the burdensome service of your father, and his heavy yoke which he put on us, and we will serve you."** To maintain the oriental opulence of his court, Solomon had used forced labor and taxed heavily. So they were saying in effect: "Lower the taxes with which your father oppressed us, and we will serve you. Otherwise we will revolt." Rehoboam asked **for three days** to think it over. During that time he first **consulted** his older counselors. **They** advised **him** to treat the people kindly and **be a servant to** them. His younger advisers, however, suggested the very opposite—they told him to threaten the people with *still* heavier demands! In that sense, Rehoboam's **little finger** would **be thicker than** Solomon's **waist**. If Solomon **chastised** them **with whips**, then Rehoboam would use **scourges** (probably meaning whips with sharp points).

12:12–20 When **Jeroboam and** the congregation of Israel returned for the decision on **the third day**, they were **answered . . . according to the advice of the young men**. Verse 15 points out that this was a **turn of events** brought about by **the** Lord to **fulfill His word . . . spoken** through **Ahijah the Shilonite** (11:30–39). At this point the people of **Israel** revolted against **Rehoboam**, although some of them were still living in the territory **of Judah. Rehoboam sent Adoram**, his unpopular taskmaster over forced labor, to bring these latter Israelites under subjection, but they **stoned** Adoram to death. Then the people of **Israel . . . made . . . Jeroboam** their **king**. Although it says in verse 20 that **only . . . the tribe of Judah . . . followed** Rehoboam, we must remember that Benjamin (v. 21), Simeon (Josh. 19:1b), and most of Levi *belonged to* **Judah**.

12:21–24 Rehoboam planned to

Chart of the Kings and Prophets of Israel and Judah

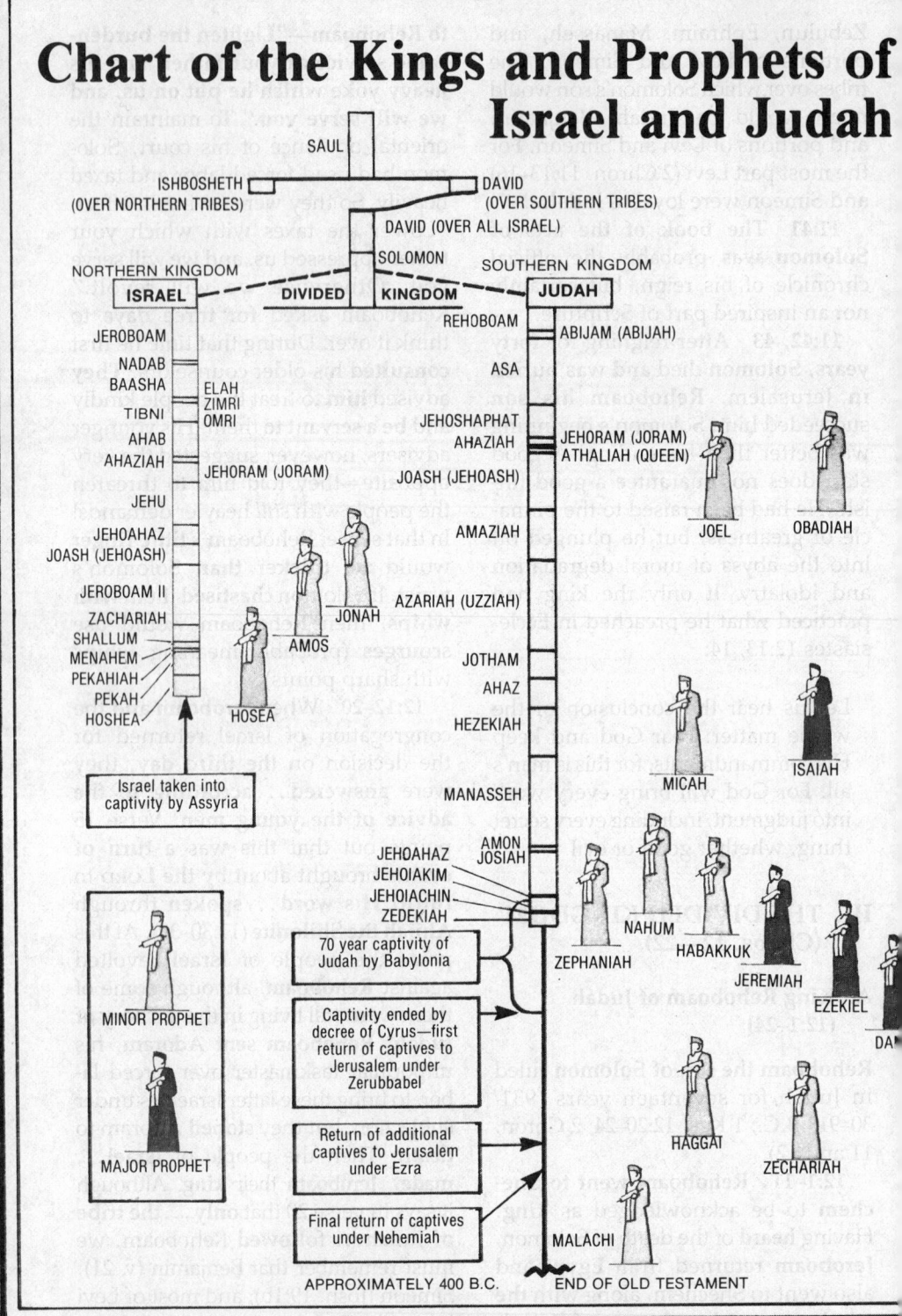

The Kings and Prophets of Israel and Judah

thwart this by declaring war on Israel, but he canceled his plan as a result of a divine command. Having earlier ignored the counsel of his elders, **Rehoboam** now heeded the counsel of **the LORD** and spared the lives of many Israelites. The word of the Lord decreed the split, and the word of the Lord ensured that the division was without bloodshed.

The Division of the Kingdom

The history of the divided kingdom begins here and continues through 2 Kings. Jeroboam reigned over the northern ten tribes, usually known as "Israel" and sometimes referred to in the prophets as "Ephraim." This kingdom had a succession of *nine* dynasties, and *all* the kings were wicked.

Rehoboam reigned over the southern kingdom, known as "Judah." This kingdom had only *one* dynasty. Every king was a descendant of David. It was through this kingdom that Christ's legal title to the throne of David is traced through Joseph, His foster father (see genealogy in Matthew 1). He was also physically a Son of David through the Virgin Mary, who was herself a descendant of David's own son Nathan (see genealogy in Luke 3). A few of these kings were outstanding reformers, though most of them were wicked.

The Kings of Israel and Judah

Dynasty	Israel	Dynasty	Judah—
1	Jeroboam	1	Rehoboam
	Nadab		Abijam (Abijah)
2	Baasha		Asa [good]
	Elah		Jehoshaphat [good]
3	Zimri		Jehoram (Joram)
4	Omri-Tibni		Ahaziah
	Ahab		Athaliah—usurper
	Ahaziah		Jehoash (Joash) [good]
	Joram (Jehoram)		Amaziah [good]
5	Jehu		Uzziah (Azariah) [good]
			Jotham [good]
	Jehoahaz		Ahaz
	Joash (Jehoash)		
	Jeroboam II		Hezekiah [good]
	Zachariah (Zechariah)		Manasseh
6	Shallum		Amon
7	Menahem		Josiah [good]
	Pekahiah		Jehoahaz (Shallum)
8	Pekah		Jehoiakim (Eliakim)
9	Hoshea		Jehoiachin (Jeconiah, Coniah)
			Zedekiah (Mattaniah)

The history of the divided kingdom can be divided into four phases. *First,* there was a time of open conflict, extending from Jeroboam (1 Kgs. 12:1) to Omri (1 Kgs. 16:28). *Secondly,* the two kingdoms settled down to a period of detente, from Omri (1 Kgs. 16:29) to Jehu (2 Kgs. 9). *The third phase,* from Jehu to the captivity of Israel by Assyria (722 B.C.), was one of relative independence (2 Kgs. 9—17). *Finally,* Judah was left as the surviving kingdom, until it was taken into captivity by the Babylonians in 586 B.C. (2 Kgs. 18—25).

The kingdom of Israel never returned to the land as a nation. Judah remained in captivity for seventy years, and then groups returned to Jerusalem in significant numbers, as recorded in Ezra and Nehemiah. The southern tribes thus came back to the land, under Gentile rule, approximately 500 years before the birth of Christ.

At the close of OT history, the Jews in the land were subject to the king of Persia. Later, Persia was conquered by Greece, and the Jews were ruled by this world power. Finally, the Greeks were subjugated by the Roman Empire; it was this empire that was in power when the Lord Jesus appeared.

In studying the divided kingdom, the student frequently comes across seeming contradictions in the dates given. Most of these chronological difficulties can be accounted for by the fact that different methods were used in calculating the length of reigns in Israel and in Judah. Another important factor is that oftentimes two kings served as coregents for a while. The whole subject of the chronology of the kings has been treated capably and in great detail in *The Mysterious Numbers of the Hebrew Kings*, by Edwin R. Thiele.[10]

We shall study the divided kingdom in the order in which the kings are listed, giving the important events in the reign of each. The dates are taken from Thiele's book mentioned above.‡

B. King Jeroboam of Israel (12:25—14:20)

Jeroboam the son of Nebat, of the tribe of Ephraim, was king of Israel for twenty-two years (931/30—910/09 B.C.).

1. Jeroboam's False Religious Centers (12:25–33)

12:25–30 Israel's first king made **Shechem** his capital at the outset, then **built Penuel**, across the Jordan River. Fearing that the **people** of Israel would return to **Jerusalem** to worship on the feast days and then transfer their loyalty **back to** the **king**

of Judah, he set up his own system of religion: He established **Dan** and **Bethel** as new centers of **worship**, setting up a golden calf in each place and declaring *these idols* to be the **gods** which delivered Israel **from the land of Egypt!**

12:31–33 Jeroboam **made** idolatrous **shrines on the high places**. He established a new priesthood from among all the **people**—**not** necessarily from the tribe **of Levi**, as God had ordained. He set up a new religious calendar, with **a** great **feast on the fifteenth day of the eighth month**, replacing the Feast of Tabernacles, which was in the seventh month. He himself usurped the office of the priest by offering sacrifices **on the altar which he had made at Bethel**.

That many of the people of Israel accepted these changes reveals that their hearts were far from the Lord. Their fathers had worshiped a calf before and were punished for it (Ex. 32). Solomon had erected high places and lost most of his kingdom for it (chap. 11). Korah and his followers had tried to usurp the priesthood and lost their lives for it (Num. 16). These innovations by which Jeroboam sought to secure his kingdom only ensured its eventual downfall. Those who had a heart for God fled to Judah (2 Chron. 11:14–16), leaving their brethren to the conveniences—and consequences—of man-made religion. It has been well said that "Jeroboam did not deserve so good a post [as king], but Israel deserved so bad a prince."

2. Jeroboam and the Man of God (13:1–32)

13:1–3 While Jeroboam was offering incense at the altar in Bethel, **a man of God** was sent **from Judah** to denounce the idolatrous **altar**. He predicted that a king named **Josiah** would arise in Judah and would burn **the** idolatrous **priests** on the altar. The fulfillment of the prophecy in verse 2 is found in 2 Kings 23:15, 16. Over 300 years elapsed between the prophecy and its fulfillment. As a token of the certainty of the prophecy, he said that **the altar** would be **split apart** and **the ashes . . . poured out**.

13:4–6 As **Jeroboam** pointed to the prophet and ordered him to be apprehended, the king's **hand** became **withered**. Also, **the altar was split apart and the ashes** spilled **out**—an omen of doom for Jeroboam's religion. In answer to the prophet's gracious prayer, the withered **hand . . . was restored to** normal.

13:7–10 If **the king** could not silence the prophet by threats, he would try by gaining his fellowship. God had issued strict instructions to the prophet that he was to do nothing to indicate the slightest tolerance of Jeroboam's evil reign. Thus, in accordance with the instructions of the Lord, the prophet refused to **eat** or **drink** with Jeroboam. Also, **he** took a different route home from **Bethel**.

13:11–19 On the way he was intercepted by **an old prophet** of **Bethel**. At first **the man of God** refused the hospitality of the **old prophet** lest he show the slightest sympathy with what was going on at **Bethel**. But then the old man said that **an angel** had told him to entertain **the man of God**, and this lie succeeded in persuading the latter to accept the proffered hospitality.

13:20–25 While they were eating together, **the LORD** spoke to the old **prophet** of Bethel, and he in turn delivered the message to the man of God. Because of his disobedience, the man of God would die and would

not be buried with his family. If this seems harsh or severe, we should remember that God deals more strictly with those He loves, with those who are His spokesmen, and with those who are greatly privileged. On his way home, the man of God was **killed** by a **lion**. Contrary to all the laws of nature, **the lion** and the prophet's **donkey stood** watch together over his **corpse on the road**.

13:26–32 When the old **prophet . . . heard** the news, **he** immediately realized that it was the Lord's judgment against disobedience. **He went** to the scene of the tragedy, **brought** the body **back** to Bethel, and buried it in his own tomb. He then instructed **his sons** that he desired to be **buried . . . beside . . . the man of God**; he realized that the idolatrous system of which he was a part was doomed to destruction by God.

3. Jeroboam's False Priesthood (13:33, 34)

King **Jeroboam** persisted in his evil, making **priests from every class of people** and serving as a priest himself. Such **sin** was the eventual cause of destruction to the dynasty **of Jeroboam**.

Irving L. Jensen notes:

King Jeroboam ought to have seen a picture of himself and his own fate if he did not repent, by the fate of the prophet from Judah. Jeroboam, like the prophet, had been chosen by God for a high position. Also like the prophet, he knew perfectly well what God would have him do. But like the prophet, he had disobeyed the word of God.[11]

4. Death of Jeroboam's Son (14:1–20)

14:1–4 When **Abijah the son of Jeroboam became sick**, the king sent **his wife** to the prophet . . . **Ahijah**—

the man of God who had previously told Jeroboam that he **would be king over** the ten northern tribes.

The queen disguised herself, perhaps for several reasons. First, to visit the man of God openly would betray a lack of faith in the idols at Dan and Bethel. Second, Jeroboam realized that Ahijah was opposed to idolatry and would not speak favora-

ble things to her if he knew her identity. Third, perhaps the king thought that by fooling the prophet he might even fool the Lord.

14:5–13 The Lord forewarned the blind prophet of the queen's approach. As soon as she arrived, the prophet exposed her disguise and then sent her back to Jeroboam with a message of doom. Because of the king's diso-

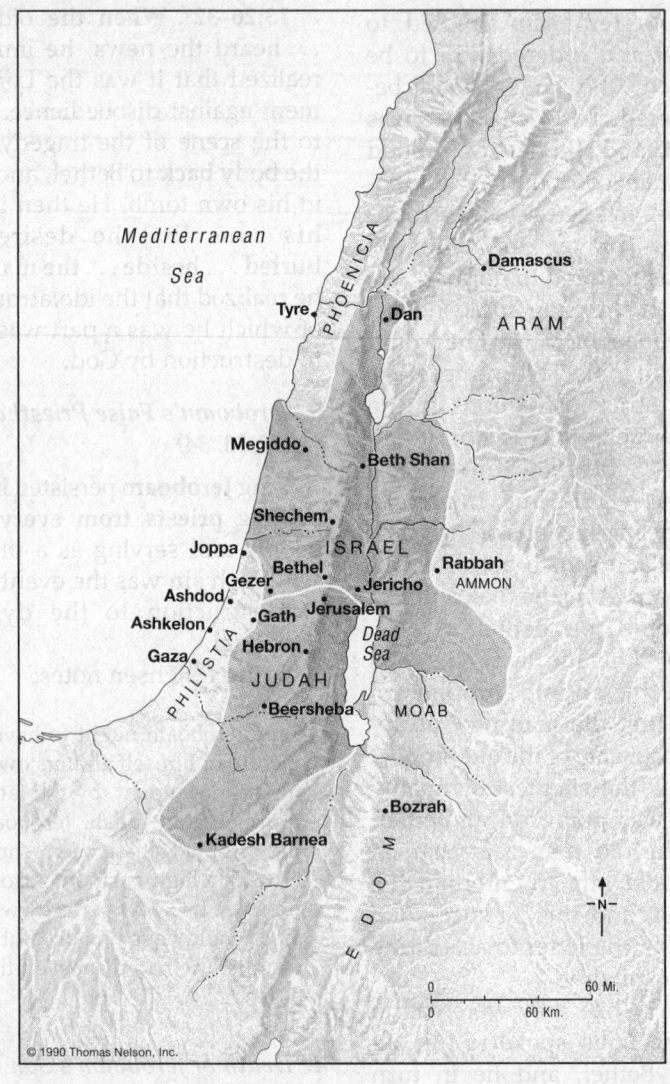

Mediterranean Sea

PHOENICIA

Damascus

Tyre · Dan

ARAM

Megiddo ·

· Beth Shan

Shechem ·

Joppa ·

ISRAEL

Bethel · Rabbah

Gezer · Jericho　AMMON

Ashdod ·

· Gath　Jerusalem

Ashkelon ·

PHILISTIA

Hebron ·

Dead Sea

Gaza ·

JUDAH

· Beersheba

MOAB

· Bozrah

Kadesh Barnea ·

EDOM

—N—

0 ——— 60 Mi.

0 ——— 60 Km.

© 1990 Thomas Nelson, Inc.

A Kingdom Divided. The glory of the united kingdom began to fade at the death of Solomon when his son Rehoboam spoke harshly to Jeroboam and those following him. Their response: "Every man to your tents, O Israel! Now, see to your own house, O David!" Rehoboam reigned over Judah to the south, and Jeroboam became king of Israel to the north.

bedience and idolatry, the Lord would **cut off from** him **every male in Israel**, both **bond and free**, and would utterly consume his house. None of his family would have a decent burial, except the ailing son, Abijah—who would **die** as soon as the queen entered **the city**.

14:14–16 God would **raise up** another **king** (Baasha), who would destroy Jeroboam's family. Eventually the nation of Israel would be led into captivity because **Jeroboam** had inaugurated the worship of Asherim.[12] The Asherim were carved **wooden images** symbolizing fertility.

14:17, 18 It appears from verse 17 that **Tirzah** was now the capital of Israel. As soon as the queen returned there, her son **died**. Israel **buried him** and **mourned**, as predicted by **the prophet**.

14:19, 20 After reigning for **twenty-two years, Jeroboam** died and was succeeded by **his son . . . Nadab. The book of the chronicles of the kings of Israel** does not refer to the book of Chronicles in the Bible but to the official record **of the kings** which was kept as a public national history.

The scene now switches to the kingdom of Judah.

C. King Rehoboam of Judah (cont'd) (14:21–31)

14:21–24 We have already studied the first part of Rehoboam's reign in chapter 12. This section summarizes the significant features of his reign. The fact that the queen mother is mentioned twice as **an Ammonitess** (vv. 21, 31) may be designed to call the reader's attention to an underlying reason for the failure of Rehoboam's rule—his father, Solomon, had married foreign wives, who led him and his family into idolatry. Idolatry was prevalent in **Judah**, and male cult prostitutes (**perverted persons**) carried on their abominable practices at the shrines.

14:25–28 **Jerusalem** was attacked and plundered by **Shishak, king of Egypt. Treasures** were stolen from the temple and the royal palace. **Rehoboam** ordered **bronze shields** to be made in . . . **place** of the **gold** ones that were taken.

Isn't it ironic that Solomon had sought to protect himself from Egypt by marrying Pharaoh's daughter, but within a short time after his death Shishak of Egypt walked off with much of the glitter of Solomon's golden city!

14:29–31 This was a period of warfare between Judah and Israel. It continued for fifty-seven years, through the reign of Asa in Judah and Omri in Israel. The Lord prevented an all-out war between Judah and Israel (12:24), but the sister kingdoms were constantly skirmishing with each other. **Rehoboam** died at the age of fifty-seven, and **his son . . . Abijam** became king in his place.

D. King Abijam of Judah (15:1–8)

Abijam the son of Rehoboam was king of Judah for **three years** (913—911/10 B.C.; 2 Chron. 13:1—14:1a).

15:1 Verse 1 contains a formula that is frequently repeated in the books of Kings. This formula describes the beginning of one reign by naming the king who was reigning in the *other kingdom* and telling how long he had been reigning. Thus this verse explains that **Abijam** began to reign **over Judah** during **the eighteenth year of** Jeroboam's reign over Israel. He is also called Abijah (1 Chron. 3:10; 2 Chron. 12:16).

15:2 Here Abijam's mother is listed as **Maachah the granddaughter of Abishalom**; in 2 Chronicles 11:21 it is

Maachah the daughter of Absalom; in 2 Chronicles 13:2 it is Michaiah the daughter of Uriel. It is possible that his mother had two names, and that she was the daughter of Uriel and the **granddaughter** of Absalom (same as **Abishalom**). ("Son" or "daughter" often simply designates a *descendant* in biblical usage.)

15:3–8 **Abijam** followed **his father** as an idolater and thus failed to follow **David**, who was **loyal** in the sense that he refrained from the worship of carved images. Verses 4 and 5 imply that God would have destroyed the house of Abijam had it not been for His covenant with **David**. Notice at the end of verse 5 how an otherwise exemplary life can be marred by a moment of passion! The **war** with Israel that began in Rehoboam's reign continued through Abijam's reign. In verse 6 **Rehoboam** and **Jeroboam** stand for Judah and Israel. **There was war between** these two kingdoms throughout Abijam's life. He tried to bring Israel back both by persuasion and by force of arms, killing 500,000 Israelites in the attempt (2 Chron. 13:1–20).

E. King Asa of Judah (15:9–24)

Asa the son of Abijam was king of Judah for **forty-one years** (911/10—870/69 B.C.; cf. 2 Chron. 14:1b—16:14).

15:9–15 **Asa** was one of the few good kings of **Judah**. He removed the sodomites (idolatrous homosexuals) from the land and destroyed **all the idols that his fathers had made** (v. 12; cf. 2 Chron. 14:3–5). He deposed **Maachah his grandmother** and destroyed her **obscene image**, though **not . . . the high places** associated with this idol. He enriched the temple with gifts from **his father** and from **himself**.

15:16–22 When **Baasha, king of Israel**, began to fortify **Ramah**, a few miles north of Jerusalem, **Asa** real-

ized that his capital was in peril. However, instead of turning to the Lord, he sought the assistance of **Ben-Hadad, . . . king of Syria**. By making a liberal payment to this foreign monarch, he persuaded him to attack Israel from the north in the region of Galilee. This drew Baasha's forces to the north and enabled **Asa** to disassemble **Ramah** and to build the fortified cities of **Geba** and **Mizpah** along his northern border.

The silver and gold that Asa brought to the temple had been given to the Lord. But when **Baasha** threatened his kingdom, Asa **took all the** treasures and gave them to a heathen king, defrauding God and enriching **Syria**. Christians need to be careful not to take what belongs to God (i.e., their time, money, resources, etc.) and give it to someone else.

15:23, 24 The fact that he was stricken with a disease of the **feet** may be mentioned to indicate God's displeasure that **Asa** had trusted in the king of Syria to deliver him. During his last three or four years, Asa's **son . . . Jehoshaphat** probably **reigned** with him.

F. King Nadab of Israel (15:25–27)

Nadab the son of Jeroboam, of the tribe of Ephraim, was **king** of **Israel** for **two years** (910/09—909/08 B.C.).

Nadab followed **his father** in the practice of idolatry. One of his subjects, **Baasha, conspired against him** and **killed him**. At the same time **Baasha killed all** the remaining members of **the house of Jeroboam,** in fulfillment of the prophecy of **Ahijah** (14:10, 14).

G. King Baasha of Israel (15:28—16:7)

Baasha the son of Ahijah, of the tribe of **Issachar**, was king of Israel for twenty-four years (909/08—886/85 B.C.).

15:28–34 Baasha's reign marks the beginning of the second dynasty in the kingdom of Israel. Conflict between **Judah** and **Israel** continued throughout Baasha's reign. With **Tirzah** as his capital, he continued the idolatrous worship that **Jeroboam** had instituted.

16:1–7 A prophet named **Jehu** announced to **Baasha** that because he followed Jeroboam's idolatry, his **posterity** would suffer a similar fate. They would not be given the customary burial but would be eaten by **dogs** or **birds**. Another reason for Baasha's doom is given at the end of verse 7—**he killed . . . the house of Jeroboam**. Either he was not the one whom God intended to do this or he did it in a cruel and vengeful manner, contrary to God's will.

H. King Elah of Israel (16:8–14)

Elah the son of Baasha, of the tribe of Issachar, was king of Israel for **two years** (886/85—885/84 B.C.).

Elah was a wicked **king**, given over to idolatry and drunkenness. After he had **reigned two years**, he was assassinated by **Zimri, commander of half his chariots**. Also slain were all the rest of Baasha's family, in fulfillment of Jehu's prophecy (16:3). Elah's death ended the second dynasty in Israel.

I. King Zimri of Israel (16:15–20)

Zimri was king of Israel for **seven days**, (885/84 B.C.).

Zimri's wicked reign was the shortest of all the kings, lasting only **seven days**. When he usurped the throne, the army of Israel was trying to capture the city of **Gibbethon** from **the Philistines**. The army proclaimed its **commander**, **Omri**, to be **king**. He

promptly marched against **Tirzah**, the capital, to seize the reins of government. **Zimri** retreated **into the citadel of the** royal palace, set it on **fire**, and perished in the flames.

J. King Tibni of Israel (16:21, 22)

Tibni the son of Ginath was king of Israel for four years (885/84—881/80 B.C.)

Although Israel made Omri, the commander of the army, king over Israel (v. 16), he had a rival in Tibni, and there was civil war for four or five years (cf. v. 15 with v. 23). Half of the Northern Kingdom followed Tibni until his death.

K. King Omri of Israel (16:23–28)

Omri was king of Israel for **twelve years** (885/84—874/73 B.C.).

Omri's reign began the fourth dynasty in the northern kingdom. **Tibni** was defeated in 880 B.C., **and Omri** became the undisputed king. For the first **six years he reigned in Tirzah**. Then he purchased **the hill of Samaria . . . for two talents of silver** and moved his capital there. The **evil** character of his reign is emphasized in verses 25 and 26.

Omri's chronology is somewhat complex. He was proclaimed king in the twenty-seventh year of Asa (with only **half of the people** behind him), after the death of Zimri (v. 15). After the four years of civil war, he became undisputed king over the northern kingdom in Asa's **thirty-first year** (v. 23). He died in the thirty-eighth year of Asa (v. 29). Thus he had about four years of internal strife and about eight years of relative peace.

Omri was a progressive king and brought a measure of peace and prosperity to Israel. Extrabiblical sources mention Omri as the conqueror of Moab. So prominent was he in the view of the Assyrians that they called Israel "the House of Omri" or "the Land of Omri." Archaeologists have found what they believe was Omri's palace in Samaria.

L. King Ahab of Israel and the Prophet Elijah (16:29—22:40)

Ahab the son of Omri was **king** of **Israel** for **twenty-two years** (874/73–853 B.C.).

1. The Sins of Ahab (16:29–34)

Ahab was an exceedingly **evil king,** not only because he followed **Jeroboam** in idolatry, but also because he married **Jezebel,** a **daughter of** the **king of the Sidonians.** This villainous woman was a Baal-worshiper who succeeded in influencing **Ahab** to promote Baal-worship in Israel by building **a temple, an altar,** and **a wooden image.** The godlessness of the times is witnessed by the brazen attempt by **Hiel of Bethel** to rebuild **Jericho** in defiance of God's curse (Josh. 6:26). When **he laid** the **foundation,** his oldest son, **Abiram,** died. As the **gates** were erected, **his youngest son, Segub,** died.

2. Elijah and the Drought (17:1–7)

17:1 In chapter 17 we are introduced to the prophet **Elijah.** His ministry extends through 2 Kings 2:11. God spoke to His people through prophets during times of sin and declension. These prophets were really mouthpieces for Jehovah. They fearlessly cried out against idolatry, immorality, and all other forms of iniquity. They urged the people to repent and return to the Lord, and then warned of dire consequences if they failed to do so. Some prophets ministered primarily to Israel, some to Judah, and some to both. Since Israel was the more wicked of the

two kingdoms, God accompanied the prophet's messages to Israel with miracles and wonders. This left Israel without excuse.

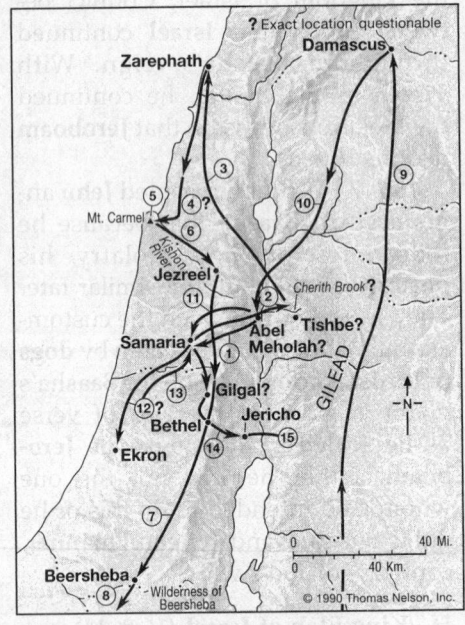

Life of Elijah

1. Elijah the Tishbite Prophesies to Ahab.
2. Elijah hides by the Brook Cherith.
3. Elijah goes to Zarephath.
4. En route to Ahab, Elijah meets Obadiah.
5. Ahab agrees to meet Elijah on Mt. Carmel.
6. Elijah outpaces Ahab to Jezreel.
7. Fearing Jezebel, Elijah goes to Beersheba.
8. Elijah departs into the Wilderness of Beersheba; from there he goes South all the way to Mt. Sinai.
9. Elijah journeys to Damascus by way of the desert to anoint Hazael King of Syria.
10. Elijah finds Elisha.
11. Elijah condemns Ahab's murder of Naboth.
12. Elijah confronts Ahaziah's servants en route to Ekron.
13. Elijah prophesies Ahaziah's death.
14. Elijah and Elisha's last journey.
15. Elijah taken to heaven by a whirlwind.

Elijah is mentioned in the Gospels in connection with the ministry of John the Baptist. John came in the spirit and power of Elijah (Luke 1:17).

Elijah came from Tishbe in **Gilead,** east of the Jordan River, and was thus called a **Tishbite.** His history is recorded only in Kings. We are told nothing about his background, family, or call to the prophetic ministry. But that he was a man sent from God no one could deny. He was God's chosen instrument to bring adulterous and haughty Israel to her knees. His prayers could bring down blessing (rain) or wrath (drought and fire). He served his generation as a fearless, embodied conscience. His first recorded act was to announce **to Ahab** that the land would suffer a drought. This was obviously a divine judgment against idolatry. God chose to use a severe drought to get the people's attention. They did not care that idolatry had brought a spiritual drought upon the land, but they could not ignore the physical drought that typified it.

17:2–7 In obedience to **the LORD**, Elijah went **from** Samaria to **the Brook Cherith**, east of **the Jordan**. There he was sustained by water **from the brook** and by food which was miraculously brought to him morning and evening by **ravens. After a while**, however, due to the drought **the brook dried up**.

3. Elijah and the Widow of Zarephath (17:8–24)

17:8–16 In obedience to **the word of the LORD**, Elijah journeyed **to Zarephath**, on the Mediterranean coast between Tyre and Sidon. There God had arranged that **a** Gentile **widow** would feed him. At first she hesitated because she had only enough meal **for** her **son** and herself. However, the prophet ordered her to **make . . . a small cake for** him **first**. By doing this she was, in effect, giving God the first place. When she obeyed, she learned the precious lesson that those who put God first never lack the necessities of life. Her **bin of flour** and **jar of oil** never failed. Jesus made note of the fact

that Elijah was sent to a *Gentile* **widow** and not to any of the numerous *Israelite* widows (Luke 4:26).

During the drought Jehovah provided for His prophet in most humbling ways—first through unclean birds and then through a Gentile woman, and a poor widow at that. The king in his palace was hard-pressed, but Elijah had all he needed. God's man, obeying God's voice, will always have his needs met, despite the conditions that prevail around him.

17:17–24 Later **the son of the woman** was stricken with a **serious sickness** and died. Immediately the mother suspected that **Elijah** had ordered his death because of some **sin** she had committed. The prophet **took** the lad up to his bedroom, **stretched himself out on the child three times, and cried out to the Lord**. The boy **revived** and was taken **down . . . to his mother** in normal health. This convinced **the woman** that **Elijah** was **a man of God** and that the Lord's **word** was **the truth**. As a Gentile, she showed faith in the God of Israel.

4. Elijah's Challenge to the Priests of Baal (18:1–19)

18:1–6 Three years after Elijah left Israel, and three and a half years after the drought had begun (Luke 4:25), the prophet was instructed to appear before **Ahab**—an action that, humanly speaking, was extremely dangerous. So **severe** was the **famine** that **Ahab** and his steward, **Obadiah** (not the prophet who wrote the book of Obadiah), had searched **the land** for **grass** to feed the animals. (It was this **Obadiah** who had saved **one hundred prophets** of the Lord **when Jezebel** had murdered some and was seeking to exterminate others.)

18:7–15 While **Obadiah was on his** search for grass, **Elijah met him**

and ordered him to notify **Ahab** of Elijah's whereabouts. Obadiah feared that this would result in his death, since Ahab had been searching relentlessly for Elijah in order to silence him once and for all. If Obadiah revealed Elijah's presence, the king would undoubtedly respond. But by then **the Spirit of the LORD** might have carried Elijah away. Then Ahab would **kill** Obadiah for his "false" report. And besides all this, Obadiah's position in the royal court was already precarious because he had protected **the LORD's prophets**. Elijah promised that he would not leave the place, and a meeting was then arranged.

18:16–19 King Ahab went to meet Elijah and accused him of being a **troubler of Israel**, not realizing that the man of God was one of the best friends **Israel** ever had. Not fearing for his own life, Elijah answered Ahab fearlessly and accusingly. He blamed the king for mixing the worship of Jehovah with **Baal**-worship and challenged him to assemble his idolatrous **prophets** for a contest **on Mount Carmel** to determine who was the true God. (**The four hundred and fifty prophets of Baal** went to **Carmel**, but **the four hundred prophets of Asherah** did not; cf. vv. 19, 22.)

5. Elijah's Victory over the Priests of Baal (18:20–40)

18:20–25 Addressing the assembled representatives of Israel, Elijah accused them of wavering between two opinions; they should choose either **the LORD** or **Baal**. Then the contest began. **Two bulls** were to be killed and laid **on** kindling **wood**. **Elijah** would represent **the LORD**, whereas **four hundred and fifty** of Ahab's **prophets** would represent **Baal**. **The God who** answered **by fire** would

be acknowledged as the true **God**.

18:26–29 The prophets of Baal cried out to their god and hopped around **the altar from morning . . . till noon. Elijah mocked them** with "helpful" excuses for Baal's failure to answer. "Perhaps he was such a small, weak god that he could not do two things at once." In desperation, **they . . . cut themselves (as was their custom)** with **knives and lances** and raved on **until the time . . . of the evening sacrifice. But there was no voice; no one answered, no one paid attention.**

18:30–35 Then Elijah . . . **built an altar** of **twelve stones in the name of the LORD**, representing the twelve **tribes of** Israel. Then, to eliminate any possibility that the altar might be ignited in any way other than by a miracle, he saturated the oxen and the wood with twelve barrels of **water** (**four waterpots** emptied three times).

Some wonder how Elijah obtained so much water during a time of drought. But this is not a real difficulty. Twelve barrels of water is not an impossible amount during drought time. The drought had affected farmlands, but drinking water must have been obtainable or else everyone would have died. Another explanation is that this water could have come from the Mediterranean Sea, a few miles away. Williams says:

> The Kishon (v. 40), the sea (v. 43), and a well which still exists could severally or collectively supply the water needed to fill the trench (v. 35).[13]

18:36–40 At the time of . . . the **evening sacrifice, . . . Elijah** prayed that God would reveal himself by sending fire from heaven. Immediately **the fire of the LORD fell** from heaven, consuming not only the **sacrifice** but also **the wood and the stones and the dust, and . . . the water . . . in the trench** around the altar. **The people** were thus compelled to acknowledge **the** LORD as the real **God**. Then they obeyed Elijah's order to slay **the** wicked **prophets of Baal**. Only after the people *acknowledged* that Jehovah was God and *executed* the prophets of Baal could the rain come. Confession of sin and obedience to the Word of God are the steps to blessing.

6. Elijah's Prayer for Rain (18:41–46)

The prophet advised **Ahab** to **eat** a meal because he would soon have to leave Mount Carmel to escape the oncoming **rain**. While **Ahab** sat down **to eat**, **Elijah** rose up to pray. He ascended **to the top of** Mount **Carmel, bowed down on the ground** with **his face between his knees**, and fervently asked the Lord to fulfill His word by sending rain. He continued in prayer until **his servant** reported a tiny **cloud** on the horizon. That was enough for Elijah. He immediately sent word **to Ahab** to make haste for **Jezreel**, a city in Issachar where the royal family lived at times (21:1). As a loyal subject and faithful servant, the prophet **ran** before Ahab's chariot in **a** drenching **rain** twenty miles **to Jezreel**.

7. Elijah's Flight to Horeb (19:1–18)

19:1–4 When **Ahab told Jezebel** of the defeat and death of **the prophets** of Baal on Mount Carmel, she swore that she would slay **Elijah** within a day. Then the prophet whose faith had gained such a mighty victory the previous day lost courage. He **ran for his life** from Jezreel, south across the land **to Beersheba**, about one hundred miles away, at the southern boundary of **Judah**. Leaving **his servant** at **Beersheba**, Elijah contin-

ued south **a day's journey into the wilderness**. At length he rested **under a broom tree**, despondent, defeated, and depressed.

19:5–8 It is interesting to notice God's treatment for this severe depression: rest; food and drink; more rest; more food and drink. Thus fortified, the prophet traveled **in the strength of that food** 200 miles in **forty days and . . . nights** to Mount **Horeb** (Sinai), where God had given the law to Moses.

19:9–14 There in **a cave . . . the** LORD dealt with him. In a self-righteous spirit, Elijah protested his own faithfulness and denounced **the children of Israel**. He said in effect that he was the only one who had remained true to the Lord. God then commanded him to **stand on the mountain** of the law, but Elijah did not obey. We know this because later (v. 13) **he went out and stood in the entrance of the cave**. In rapid succession **the mountains** were visited by **a great . . . wind, an earthquake**, and **a fire**. These violent storms must have reminded Elijah of his harsh, censorious spirit. None of them brought him out of the cave. Finally, **after the fire** the prophet heard **a still, small voice**. It was this gracious voice of the Lord which brought him to **the entrance of the cave**. There he again exalted himself as God's sole remaining witness. George Williams comments:

Had his heart not been occupied with self, he would have learned that tempests, earthquakes and fires cannot accomplish what the gentle voice of love can. He should have recognized that there was no difference between his heart and that of the nation; and, that as coercion failed to make him leave his cave, so it failed, and must fail, to compel men to leave their sins.[14]

19:15–18 It seems that Elijah's usefulness as a servant of God suffered when he adopted this attitude of self-importance. God told him to return north **to the Wilderness of Damascus**, where he would conduct three anointings: (1) He would **anoint Hazael** to be **king over Syria**. The disobedient nation of Israel would be punished by this king. (2) He would **anoint Jehu** to be **king over Israel**. Jehu would execute God's judgment on the house of Ahab. (3) He would **anoint . . . Elisha** as his own successor.[15] This would teach him that he was not indispensable. These three men would execute God's judgment on idolaters in Israel (v. 17), but the Lord would leave **seven thousand** who had **not bowed** the knee **to Baal** or **kissed him**.

8. Elijah's Appointment of Elisha (19:19–21)

19:19 **Elijah** traveled north to Abel Meholah, in the Jordan Valley near Beth Shean. There he **found Elisha**, a farmer **plowing** in the field. The fact that Elisha had **twelve yoke of oxen** indicates that he was not poor. He was probably plowing with one yoke and his servants with the other eleven. **Elijah threw his mantle on** Elisha, a sign that Elisha was to be his successor.

19:20, 21 Elisha asked permission to return home and make a farewell feast for his family. Elijah gave consent but warned him not to forget what had just happened to him—i.e., how Elijah had anointed him. After a sumptuous feast, Elisha **arose and followed Elijah and became his** personal **servant**.

Elisha's request to say goodbye to his parents sounds dangerously like that of a would-be disciple whom Jesus pronounced unfit for the kingdom (Luke 9:61, 62). The difference is

that in Elisha's case it was a no-nonsense decision to sever ties immediately, whereas in the other case it was a delaying tactic and an excuse.

9. Ahab's First Victory over Syria (20:1–22)

20:1–6 **Ben-Hadad, the king of Syria**, was formerly thought to be the son of the Ben-Hadad mentioned in 15:18, 20. But later research has raised the possibility that he was the same person. He formed an alliance of **thirty-two** Aramean **kings** and marched against **Samaria . . . with horses and chariots**. When the city was in a state of siege, he sent surrender terms to Ahab—**"Your silver . . . your gold . . . your loveliest wives and children."** Ahab meekly and weakly agreed. Not satisfied with Ahab's capitulation to his first terms, **Ben-Hadad** next demanded right of entry for his **servants** and the right to seize anything they wanted.

20:7–12 **The elders of** Israel were indignant at this second demand and urged noncompliance. When **Ben-Hadad** was notified of Israel's refusal, he flew into a rage, boasting that he would strip Samaria so bare that there wouldn't be **a handful** of **dust . . . for each of** his soldiers. To this, Ahab replied that a soldier putting **on his armor** should not **boast** as if the victory were already won. This taunt stirred the carousing Syrian and his confederates to action.

20:13–15 At this point **a prophet** of the Lord **approached Ahab**, assuring him of victory. God used a small force of **two hundred and thirty-two** servants of the governors of the districts, followed by **seven thousand** of the people **of Israel**, to defeat the assembled armies from the north. The phrase **"all the children of Israel"** (v. 15b) means all the soldiers in

Samaria. A small number of young servants was chosen to begin the battle, to make it all the more apparent that victory was *from the Lord* and not from the arm of the flesh.

20:16–22 Ahab attacked **at noon**, when **Ben-Hadad and** his allies **were getting drunk**. When Ben-Hadad heard that the 232 men of Israel were advancing, he ordered that they be taken **alive**. This, of course, gave a military advantage to the Israelites and resulted in **a great slaughter** of **the Syrians**. The survivors retreated to their homeland. **The prophet** of the Lord warned Ahab that the Syrian army would return **in the spring**.

10. Ahab's Second Victory over Syria (20:23–34)

20:23–25 Ben-Hadad's **servants** attributed their shameful defeat to two factors: (1) The Israelites had won the battle in hill country. Doubtless **their gods** were **gods of the hills**. But they would be impotent on the plains. So the Syrians should engage them the next time on the plains. (2) The thirty-two kings who fought against Ahab had apparently proved themselves unskilled in warfare. Ben-Hadad's **servants** advised that they be replaced by professional **captains**.

20:26–30a In the spring, . . . Ben-Hadad marched **against Israel** again. The army of Israel looked like **two little flocks of goats** compared to the host of Syria. **A man of God** told Ahab that **the Lord** would show Ben-Hadad that He was the **God of the valleys** as well as **of the hills**. In the battle, Israel killed one hundred thousand foot soldiers. **The Syrians** who escaped tried to take up positions on the walls of the city of **Aphek**, but the walls collapsed, killing **twenty-seven thousand** of them.

20:30b–34 Ben-Hadad hid in an **inner chamber** of Aphek. **His servants** persuaded him to **let them go out to** Ahab, clothed with symbols of surrender and mourning, and to plead for mercy. In the interview, Ahab stupidly referred to the king as his **"brother."** The men of Syria quickly caught that word and said, "Yes, **your brother Ben-Hadad!"** Ahab ordered that the king of Syria be brought to him. Ben-Hadad promised to **restore the cities** which had been taken from Ahab's predecessor (15:20) and to allow Israel to establish **marketplaces . . . in Damascus** (v. 34). **Ahab** made **a treaty** on these terms and let Ben-Hadad escape instead of killing him, as he should have done.

11. Ahab's Disobedience (20:35–43)

20:35, 36 Ahab wanted a strong Syria as a buffer between Israel and the growing menace of Assyria. The incident that follows was an object lesson, acted out by the prophet, to illustrate the folly of Ahab's action.

One **of the sons of the prophets** ordered his fellow **by the word of the Lord** to **strike** him. **The man** disobeyed him and therefore disobeyed **the Lord**. For his failure to obey the Lord's voice, he was destroyed by **a lion**.

> If a good prophet were thus punished for sparing his friend and God's, when God said *Smite*, of much sorer punishment should a wicked king be thought worthy, who spared his enemy and God's, when God said *Smite*.[16]

20:37–43 The prophet **found another man** who obeyed him by striking and wounding him. Then **the prophet . . . disguised himself with a bandage over his eyes** and **waited for** King Ahab. When **the king** was passing by, the prophet told of being in the battle and of being charged with the custody of an enemy prisoner. He had been warned that if the prisoner escaped, he would have to pay either with **his** own **life** or with the exorbitant figure of one **talent of silver**. The disguised prophet told how he had become preoccupied with other things and how the prisoner had escaped. **The king** showed no leniency; he insisted that the original terms of punishment be carried out. Then the prophet sprang the trap. He removed his bandage to reveal himself as a prophet known by Ahab. **Ahab** had had an enemy prisoner, **Ben-Hadad**, in his grasp. Obedience to the Lord required that the Syrian king be killed. For his disobedience Ahab would be slain. Campbell Morgan explains:

> This was the meaning of the parable: Ahab had one thing to do by the command of God, and while he did a hundred things, he neglected the one. What a revelation of a perpetual reason and method of failure! We are given some one responsibility by God, some central, definite thing to do. We start to do it with all good intentions, and then other things, not necessarily wrong in themselves, come in our way. We get "busy here and there" doing many things and we neglect the one central thing.[17]

Like King David before him, Ahab condemned himself by his own words. But unlike David, who repented, Ahab became **sullen** and stormed off to his palace to pout. Instead of asking the Lord for mercy, he continued to incite the Lord to wrath, as we read in the remaining chapters of 1 Kings.

12. Ahab's Crimes against Naboth (Chap. 21)

21:1–4 Chapter 21 traces the events leading up to Ahab's death. The scene is **in Jezreel**, where **Ahab** and Jezebel had a **palace**. Adjoining the palace was **a vineyard** owned by **Naboth the Jezreelite**. **Ahab** desired to annex the **vineyard** so he could plant **a vegetable garden** there. **Naboth** refused to sell or exchange his land, since the law of Israel decreed that property should remain in the family to which it was originally assigned (Lev. 25:23–28; Num. 36:7; Ezek. 46:18).

21:5–16 When **Jezebel** found her husband vexed and **sullen** and learned of Naboth's refusal to sell his **vineyard**, she assured Ahab that the vineyard would soon be his. **She** ordered **a fast** and a court of inquiry. **Two evil men** were appointed to charge Naboth with blasphemy against **God and the king**. Accordingly, **Naboth** was taken **outside** the city and **stoned** to death.

The treacherous Jezebel thus framed Naboth so that it would appear he was being executed for breaking the law of Jehovah. Since the property would pass on to Naboth's sons after his death, Jezebel had them murdered as well (2 Kgs. 9:26). The iniquitous queen was as thorough as she was wicked.

21:17–26 When **Ahab** was on his way to take possession of the vineyard, **Elijah** met him and condemned him for murder and theft. Elijah predicted that **Ahab** himself would be slain, that his **male** descendants would be slain, ending his dynasty, that the body of **Jezebel** would be eaten by **dogs** in **Jezreel**, and that Ahab's descendants would not be given a decent burial (v. 24). The severity of Ahab's punishment is explained by the extremes to which he went in idolatry—**"there was no one like Ahab who sold himself to do wickedness."**

21:27–29 When **Ahab heard** his doom, he **humbled himself before** the Lord. For this, the Lord decreed that the judgments on his wife and family would not take place until after Ahab's death.

If we learn anything from these verses, it is that God is a God of grace and mercy. "'As I live,' says the Lord God, 'I have no pleasure in the death of the wicked, but that the wicked turn from his way and live. Turn, turn from your evil ways! For why should you die?'" (Ezek. 33:11). Even Ahab's superficial repentance brought a respite. But the next chapter proves that his heart was unchanged. Grace was met by pride, so the Lord handed Ahab over to the angel of death, and Jehu was appointed to carry out the bloody decree against the rest of his house according to the prophecy of Elijah (2 Kgs. 9, 10).

13. Ahab's Last Battle (22:1–40)

22:1–6 After **three years** of peace **between Syria and Israel**, Ahab conceived the idea of recapturing **Ramoth Gilead**, on the east of the Jordan, from the Syrians. Ben-Hadad had promised to return Israel's cities when he received amnesty from Ahab (20:34), but he apparently had failed to do so. **Jehoshaphat**, king of Judah, happened to be visiting Ahab at the time and expressed willingness to cooperate in the military venture. But first **Jehoshaphat** suggested that they **inquire** of the Lord through **the prophets**. **Four hundred** prophets in Ahab's court advised in favor of the plan and promised victory. These may well have been the 400 prophets who did not go to Mount Carmel for the showdown with Elijah (18:19, 22).

22:7–12 Jehoshaphat must have felt uneasy because he asked if there were **a prophet of the Lord** who could be consulted. This brought to the fore **Micaiah**, a fearless prophet who was hated by Ahab because of his uncompromising messages. At the time Micaiah was summoned, the 400 prophets were unanimously urging the kings of **Israel** and **Judah** to march against Syria. One of them, **Zedekiah, made horns of iron** to depict the irresistible power of Ahab and Jehoshaphat against **the Syrians**.

22:13–17 Micaiah was informed that his message should agree with that of **the** other **prophets**, but the advice was wasted on him. When Ahab asked if the campaign **against Ramoth Gilead** should be undertaken, Micaiah first said the same thing as the prophets: **"Go and prosper, for the Lord will deliver it into the hand of the king!"** But it is probable that he said it in a mocking manner. The tone of his voice must have dripped with irony and sarcasm.

Ahab sensed this and put Micaiah under oath to **tell . . . the truth** (Lev. 5:1). The prophet then related a vision in which **Israel** was **scattered** because they had **no shepherd**, intimating that Ahab would be killed and his army dispersed.

22:18–23 King Ahab presented this **to Jehoshaphat** as evidence that Micaiah could speak nothing but evil against him. Then the brave prophet spoke up again. He related a vision in which **a lying spirit**, appearing before **the Lord**, agreed to trick Ahab into going against **Ramoth Gilead** and be slain. The **lying spirit** would put this advice into **the mouth of all** the king's **prophets**. This is an example of how God, while not the author of evil, uses it to achieve His ultimate ends. He sent the **lying spirit** only in the sense that He permitted it.

22:24, 25 The point of this parable was not lost upon **Zedekiah**. Realizing that he and the other prophets were being accused of lying, he **struck Micaiah** and asked, **"Which way did**

the spirit from the Lord go from me to speak to you?" In other words, Zedekiah was saying:

> I spoke by the Spirit of God when I advised Ahab to go against Ramoth Gilead. Now you profess to speak by the Spirit, yet you advise the very opposite. How did the Spirit go from me to you?

Micaiah answered calmly that Zedekiah would know the truth when he would hide in terror in a secret place— evidently when Ahab's death would expose Zedekiah to the fate of a false prophet.

22:26–30 The infuriated king of Israel ordered that Micaiah be put . . . in prison and fed with bread . . . and water, . . . until he (Ahab) returned in peace from Ramoth Gilead. Micaiah's parting salute was, "If you ever return in peace, the LORD has not spoken by me." Ahab decided to disguise himself before going into battle, hoping in this way to avoid the disaster predicted by Micaiah. Jehoshaphat, on the other hand, would wear his kingly robes, exposing himself to the very danger that Ahab was trying to escape. Ahab thus attempted to fool the Lord and the king of Syria, but "God is not mocked; for whatever a man sows, that he will also reap" (Gal. 6:7). Ahab was *slain*, but Jehoshaphat was *saved*.

22:31–36 The Syrians had been ordered to kill the king of Israel; this was their prime military objective. At first they mistook Jehoshaphat for Ahab. The king of Judah cried out in terror, perhaps revealing his true identity in this way. Then Ahab was struck between the joints of his armor by a random arrow and was removed from the active fighting. He was propped up in his chariot so that his army would not lose heart. When he died

at sunset, the fact became known, and his soldiers retreated to their homes.

22:37–40 Ahab's body was taken back to Samaria and buried. His blood-stained chariot was washed beside a pool in Samaria, . . . while the harlots bathed. This was only a partial fulfillment of Elijah's prophecy (21:19); it took place in Samaria rather than in Jezreel. Because Ahab had humbled himself (21:29), God compassionately deferred the complete fulfillment to the king's son, Joram (2 Kgs. 9:25, 26).

Ahab received three separate prophetic warnings of his death. One was pronounced by an unnamed prophet when Ahab spared Ben-Hadad (20:42); one was given by Elijah when Ahab took the vineyard of Naboth (21:19); and the third prophecy was uttered by Micaiah on the eve of the eventful battle (vv. 17–23).

M. King Jehoshaphat of Judah (22:41–50)

Jehoshaphat the son of Asa was king of Judah for twenty-five years (873/ 72–848 B.C.).

For the first three or four years, Jehoshaphat co-reigned with his father Asa. We have already been introduced to Jehoshaphat in verses 2–4, where he made a shameful alliance with the wicked king of Israel and nearly lost his life as a result. In general, however, his reign was good. The following are significant features of Jehoshaphat's administration.

1. He followed his father's example in combating idolatry, though he was not successful in eradicating it completely (v. 43).

2. He reigned jointly with his father Asa.

3. He made peace with Ahab, king of Israel (v. 44).

4. He expelled the male cult prostitutes **from the land** (v. 46).

5. His kingdom included the land of **Edom** (2 Sam. 8:14), where he was represented by **a deputy** (v. 47). His son Jehoram later lost Edom through a revolution (2 Kgs. 8:20).

6. He allied himself with **Ahaziah**, Ahab's son, in a shipbuilding project at **Ezion Geber** (2 Chron. 20:35, 36). Their plan was to send the **ships . . . to Ophir for gold**. But **the ships were wrecked** before they ever left port (v. 48), no doubt by a windstorm. The prophet Eliezer told Jehoshaphat that this was because the Lord disapproved of the unholy alliance with Ahaziah (2 Chron. 20:37). When **Ahaziah** suggested renewing the project, **Jehoshaphat** declined (v. 49).

N. King Ahaziah of Israel (22:51–53)

Ahaziah the son of Ahab was **king** of **Israel**, for **two years** (853—852 B.C.; cf. 2 Kgs. 1:1–18).

The reign of **Ahaziah** was one of gross idolatry and wickedness. His mother, Jezebel, no doubt urged him on in ungodliness even as she had pushed **his father. He** worshiped **Baal . . . and provoked the** Lord **God of Israel to anger**. Like father, like son. There is no formal close to 1 Kings, since 1 and 2 Kings were originally one book, and the break was made strictly for convenience. Second Kings continues the narrative from this point.

ENDNOTES

[1](Intro) O. J. Gibson, unpublished notes.

[2](4:1–6) Matthew Poole, *Matthew Poole's Commentary on the Holy Bible*, p. 657.

[3](6:11–22) C. H. Spurgeon, *Spurgeon's Devotional Bible*, p. 305.

[4](8:12, 13) Matthew Henry, "1 Kings," in *Matthew Henry's Commentary on the Whole Bible*, II:614.

[5](8:66) John Haley, *Alleged Discrepancies of the Bible*, p. 223.

[6](9:15–23) *Baker's Bible Atlas*, p. 309.

[7](10:16–22) The word rendered "peacocks" in the KJV is now generally translated *monkeys* (NKJV) or *baboons* (NIV). Ancient kings did indeed favor peacocks, and so that translation (probably a guess) was made by Jerome in the Latin Vulgate.

[8](10:26–29) *Keveh* (also transliterated *Kue*) was translated "linen yarn" in KJV because they did not know in the seventeenth century that it was a place name.

[9](10:26–29) J. R. Lumby, *The Cambridge Bible for Schools and Colleges, The First Book of the Kings*, p. 114.

[10](Essay) See the Bibliography for details.

[11](13:33, 34) Irving L. Jensen, *I Kings with Chronicles*, pp. 80–81.

[12](14:14–16) The word translated *groves* in the KJV is the Hebrew word properly transliterated *Asherim*.

[13](18:30–35) George Williams, *The Student's Commentary on the Holy Scriptures*, p. 195.

[14](19:9–14) *Ibid.*, p. 196.

[15](19:15–18) Elijah must have directed his successor, Elisha, to fulfill the Lord's command to anoint Hazael and Jehu, since these anointings took place after Elijah's homecall (2 Kgs. 8:7ff; 9:1ff). Elisha was the only one of the three whom Elijah would personally anoint.

[16](20:35, 36) Henry, "1 Kings," II:692–93.

[17](20:37–43) G. Campbell Morgan, *Searchlights from the Word*, p. 100.

BIBLIOGRAPHY

Gates, John T. "1 Kings." In *The Wycliffe Bible Commentary*. Chicago: Moody Press, 1962.

Henry, Matthew. "1 and 2 Kings." In *Matthew Henry's Commentary on the Whole Bible*. Vol. 2.

Jamieson, Robert. "I and II Kings." In *A Commentary, Critical, Experimental and Practical on the Old and New Testaments*. 3rd ed. Grand Rapids: Zondervan Publishing House, 1983.

Jensen, Irving L. *I Kings with Chronicles*. Chicago: Moody Press, 1968.

Keil, C. F. "The Books of Kings." In *Biblical Commentary on the Old Testament*. Vol. 8. Grand Rapids: Wm. B. Eerdmans Publishing Co., 1971.

Lumby, J. R. *The Cambridge Bible for Schools and Colleges, The First Book of the Kings*. London: C. J. Clay and Sons, 1890.

McNeely, Richard I. *First & Second Kings*. Everyman's Bible Commentary. Chicago: Moody Press, 1978.

Stigers, Harold. "II Kings." In *The Wycliffe Bible Commentary*. Chicago: Moody Press, 1962.

Thiele, Edwin R. *A Chronology of the Hebrew Kings*. Grand Rapids: Zondervan Publishing House, 1977.

———. *The Mysterious Numbers of the Hebrew Kings*. Rev. ed. Chicago: University of Chicago Press, 1983.

Whitcomb, J. C., Jr. *Solomon to the Exile*. Grand Rapids: Baker Book House, 1975.

SECOND KINGS

Introduction

"The history of the Kings is one of downward progress; things get darker and darker until there is no remedy. . . . The ten tribes are first carried away captive, then the two tribes."

—Samuel Ridout

See 1 Kings for Introduction to both books.

OUTLINE

Commentary

I. THE DIVIDED KINGDOM (Cont'd. from 1 Kings) (Chaps. 1— 17)

A. King Ahaziah of Israel and the Ministry of Elijah (Chap. 1)

1:1 **Moab** had been subjugated by David (2 Sam. 8:2). When Solomon's kingdom was divided into Israel and Judah, Moab came under Israel's sway. **After** Ahab's **death**, the Moabites **rebelled** and won their independence.

1:2 King **Ahaziah fell through the lattice** on the roof of his palace **in Samaria** and **was** seriously **injured**. Instead of appealing to the Lord for healing, **he sent messengers** to **Baal-Zebub, the god of Ekron**, to see if he would **recover**. John C. Whitcomb identifies the pagan god as follows:

> The real name of this Syrian deity was Baal-zebul ('Lord of life'), but the Jews called him Baal-zebub ('Lord of flies') in derision. By the time of Christ, this deity had become a symbol of Satan.[1]

It is pathetic that a king whose name means "whom Jehovah sustains" should turn to Baal for healing!

1:3–8 **A hairy man wearing a leather belt**, Elijah met **the messengers** and sent them back to Ahaziah with a stern rebuke for inquiring **of Baal-Zebub** and with the announcement that his illness would be fatal.

1:9–12 Ahaziah responded by sending **a captain . . . with . . . fifty men** to order **Elijah** to appear before him immediately. When the captain delivered the insolent demand, God vindicated Elijah by causing **fire . . . from heaven** to destroy the captain and his **fifty men**. A second **captain . . . with . . . fifty men** ordered Elijah to

"Come down quickly!" but they met the same fate. With **fire . . . from heaven** God had previously discredited Baal and his priests (1 Kgs. 18). Now that same heavenly flame destroyed the soldiers of Baal who sought to lay unholy hands on Elijah. The prophet took his orders from Israel's true King, not from an idolatrous usurper. We are not told specifically why the two captains and their men were killed; perhaps they shared Ahaziah's determination to destroy Elijah.

1:13–16 Only when the **third captain** humbly acknowledged Elijah's power and **pleaded** for mercy was the prophet instructed by **the angel of the LORD** (Christ in preincarnate appearance) to go and speak with Ahaziah. **Elijah** fearlessly told **the king** that he would **not** recover because he had treated the Lord with contempt by consulting **Baal-Zebub**.

1:17, 18 When **Ahaziah died**, he was succeeded by his brother, **Jehoram** (later referred to as Joram), **because he had no son** to wear the crown. Judah at this time had a co-regency composed of Jehoshaphat (3:1) and his son, who was also named **Jehoram**.

B. The Translation of Elijah (2:1–12a)

This chapter opens with the saintly Elijah being "taken up" (vv. 1–11) and closes with the hooligans of Bethel being "torn up" (vv. 23–25).

2:1–6 The time had now come for **Elijah** to finish his ministry and for **Elisha** to succeed him. But first **Elijah** must visit **Bethel**, **Jericho**, and **Jordan**. Elisha faithfully insisted on going with him to these places. In **Bethel** and **Jericho, the sons of the prophets** told **Elisha** that **the LORD** was going to **take** Elijah **"away from** his head" that day. This refers to the practice of a disciple sitting at his master's feet; in such an arrangement, the master was at the disciple's head, of course. Elisha already knew this and told the prophets to **"keep silent!"** The matter was too sad and sacred to discuss.

2:7–9 From Jericho, Elijah and Elisha went down **to the Jordan** River, followed . . . **at a distance** by **fifty of the . . . prophets**. When **Elijah . . . struck the** Jordan with **his mantle**, the waters **divided** and the two men **crossed over on dry** land. Elijah had come from Gilead, east of the Jordan, during the reign of Ahab, to begin his prophetic work (1 Kgs. 17:1). Now at the close of his ministry he crossed back over Jordan to be taken up into heaven. Encouraged by the departing prophet to make a request, Elisha asked for **a double portion of** his **spirit**. The **double portion** is the right of the firstborn son and may simply mean here that Elisha wanted to be his worthy successor. George Williams says that the fulfillment of the request is seen in the fact that, whereas Elijah performed eight recorded miracles, Elisha performed sixteen.[2]

2:10–12a Elijah said that it was not in his power to grant the request, then added a condition that was also beyond his control: If Elisha would **see** him depart, then his request would be granted. **As they** walked **on and talked**, they were **separated** by **a chariot of fire . . . with horses of fire**. Then **a whirlwind** caught Elijah . . . **up . . . into heaven** in full view of Elisha. **Elisha . . . cried out, "My father, my father, the chariot of Israel and its horsemen!"** This may indicate that Elijah was the strongest weapon of God's power and the best defense of Israel.

C. The Beginning of Elisha's Ministry (2:12b–25)

2:12b–14 After tearing apart **his own clothes** in grief, Elisha returned

to the east **bank of the Jordan**, **struck the water** with Elijah's **mantle**, **and said, "Where is the LORD God of Elijah?"** This question did not express doubt or unbelief but merely afforded opportunity for God to show that He was with **Elisha** as He had been with Elijah. The waters **divided**, permitting the prophet to return to the west bank of the river, where the **fifty** sons of the prophets had been waiting and watching.

2:15–18 After seeing the parting of the Jordan, they acknowledged that **Elisha** was truly the successor of **Elijah**. Against Elisha's better judgment they insisted on sending out a party to **search for** Elijah, but the trip was in vain, of course, as Elisha had warned. Either they had not witnessed Elijah's translation, or, if they had, they thought his absence was temporary.

2:19–22 The ministry of Elisha from this point to 13:20 consists of a series of miracles designed to turn the nation of Israel away from idolatry to the true and living God. The incidents are not necessarily in chronological order. The first of these miracles occurred when **Elisha** threw **salt** into the brackish **water** in the fountain at Jericho; never again did it cause **death or barrenness**.

2:23, 24 En route from Jericho **to Bethel**, one of the centers of calf worship, Elisha was met by some rowdy **youths** who called him a **baldhead** and mockingly challenged him to **go up** to heaven as Elijah had done. After he cursed them **in the name of the LORD, two female bears came out of the woods and mauled forty-two of** them. An insult to God's messenger is an insult to God Himself.

2:25 Elisha retraced Elijah's steps, going to the schools of the prophets in Jericho and Bethel before traveling to Mount Carmel and Samaria. At Jericho the people treated him respectfully and received a blessing. Because of their irreverence for Jehovah, the young people at Bethel treated him shamefully, for which they received a curse.

D. King Jehoram (Joram) of Israel (Chap. 3)

Jehoram the son of Ahab was king of Israel for twelve years (852–841 B.C.; 2 Kgs. 3:1—9:29).

3:1–3 When Jehoram the son of Ahab began to reign as king over Israel, there was a co-regency in Judah (Jehoshaphat and his son Jehoram). That explains how Jehoram, king of Israel, began to reign in the eighteenth year of Jehoshaphat and in the second year of Jehoram, king of Judah (2 Kgs. 1:17).

Jehoram (same name as Joram) was not as evil as his parents; he put away the . . . pillar of Baal which Ahab had erected. However, he clung to the golden calf worship instituted by Jeroboam the son of Nebat.

3:4–9 Under Ahab's reign, the king of Moab had been required to pay annual tribute to Israel. When Ahab died, King Mesha decided that it was a strategic time to rebel. The famous Moabite Stone, discovered by a German missionary in 1868, mentions Israel's subjugation of Moab and Mesha's successful rebellion.[3]

Ahaziah had done nothing about Moab's rebellion. However, when his successor Jehoram came to power he immediately sought to bring Moab back under his control, not wanting to lose her sizable tribute. Jehoram asked Jehoshaphat to join with him in the battle, and once again Jehoshaphat foolishly agreed. (See 1 Kgs. 22, where Jehoshaphat almost lost his life by allying himself with Israel.)

They decided to march down the west side of the Dead Sea, east through Edom, and north to Moab. Since the king of Edom was a vassal of Jehoshaphat at this time, his help was enlisted in the war.

3:10–12 As they approached Moab, the army ran out of water. The insolence of Jehoram in blaming the LORD was answered by Jehoshaphat's suggestion that a prophet of the LORD be consulted. When it became known that Elisha, the servant of Elijah, was nearby, the three kings went down to him.

3:13–19 At first Elisha protested that he had nothing to do with the idolatrous king of Israel and suggested that he go to the idolatrous prophets of his father. Jehoram's reply may have suggested that it wasn't the idols but the LORD who was causing the problem. In deference to Jehoshaphat, Elisha agreed to seek the mind of the Lord. As a musician played, the power of God came upon Elisha and he predicted that the valley would be full of pools not caused by rain, and that the Moabites would be defeated.

3:20–25 The next morning, water flowed in the valley, coming from the direction of Edom. In the light of the sunrise, the water looked like blood to the Moabites, and they decided that the kings of Israel, Judah, and Edom had fought among themselves. As they hurried to the camp of Israel for the spoil, they met a devastating attack. The Israelites filled the arable land with stones, stopped up the wells, and cut down all the good trees.

3:26, 27 The king of Moab, embittered at his former allies, the Edomites, and suspecting that their king would not fight as wholeheartedly as Israel and Judah, sought to break through the lines **of Edom**. When this strategem failed, he offered **his eldest son** as a sacrifice on **the wall** of the city to appease his gods, to incite his men to fiercer battle, and to frighten the enemy. Israel was stunned by this human sacrifice, which was, of course, an abomination. Smitten directly by God or by their own consciences, they withdrew without bringing Moab back into subjection. Harold Stigers comments:

> The author seems to be asking: If Israel was so deeply moved in this case, why was she not shocked enough to forsake her own idolatry? But idolatry continued in Israel and in Judah.[4]

E. The Miraculous Ministry of Elisha (4:1—8:15)

1. Miraculous Provision of Oil (4:1–7)

An impoverished widow of one of **the** godly **prophets** was in danger of losing her sons to slavery because of unpaid debts. She was miraculously supplied with **oil**, the only limit being the number of **vessels** she could borrow to receive it. By selling **the oil** she was able to **pay** her **debt** and support her family. This event illustrates grace for the debtor, enough to meet present needs and to provide for future sustenance. God's grace to needy sinners sets us free from debt and slavery and provides all we need for a new life.

2. Miraculous Birth (4:8–17)

A prominent **woman** of **Shunem** had shown unusual hospitality to **Elisha**, even fitting out **a small upper room** for him in her home. When she was offered a position or favor from **the king** through Elisha's interces-

sion, she humbly expressed her satisfaction at dwelling simply **among** her **own people**. **Gehazi**, the **servant** of the prophet, suggested that she might like a **son**, and this suggestion became a reality at the word of the prophet. The following spring she bore **a son**. Out of death (the barren womb) the Lord brought life, a picture of the spiritual birth of every child of God (Eph. 2:1–10).

3. Raising the Shunammite's Son (4:18–37)

4:18–25a Years later the lad suffered a stroke of some kind while out in the field. He was carried back **to his mother** and **died** in her arms at **noon**. She put his body in the prophet's chamber. **Then**, without revealing the reason, she told **her husband** that she wanted to visit **the man of God** on **Mount Carmel**. He thought it strange to visit the prophet when it was not a religious holiday, but he made the necessary arrangements for transportation. With great speed she rode from Shunem, in the plain of Esdraelon, to Mount Carmel.

4:25b–28 Seeing her approach, Elisha sent **Gehazi** to **meet her** and to inquire as to her welfare. She did not tell Gehazi the purpose of her visit. In fact, she deceived him by saying that all was **well** with herself, her **husband**, and her **son**. She preferred to present her case directly to the prophet. The woman met Elisha with an emotional outburst and would have been dismissed by **Gehazi** if the prophet had not sensed her **deep distress** and permitted her to speak. The LORD had **not** revealed to Elisha the purpose of her visit, and neither did she. But she gave a hint when she said, **"Did I ask a son of my**

lord? Did I not say, 'Do not deceive me'?'' In other words, "I do not want to be deceived by being given a son and then having him taken away from me." Perhaps Elisha surmised from this that the son was seriously ill.

4:29–31 At first the prophet sent **Gehazi** to **lay** his **staff on the** dead **child**, telling him to avoid the usual prolonged Eastern greetings en route. The woman sensed that this would not do and insisted that Elisha himself return with her. As they approached Shunem, **Gehazi** met them with the news that the lad had **not awakened**.

4:32–37 Elisha then went **into** the room where the body lay, closed **the door**, **prayed**, and **stretched himself out on the child—mouth** to **mouth, eyes** to **eyes**, and **hands to hands**. The prophet got up, **walked back and forth**, and then **stretched himself out on** the boy again. This time the lad **sneezed seven times and . . . opened his eyes**. The thankful mother received her son back to life again. In raising the child, Elisha fully identified with the dead youth: mouth to mouth, eye to eye, hand to hand. His staff had effected no change, but when he put himself on the boy and breathed his own life into him, the lad came alive.

4. Detoxifying the Poisonous Stew (4:38–41)

The next recorded miracle took place at **Gilgal**. During a time of **famine** (perhaps the seven-year famine mentioned in chap. 8), Elisha ordered **his servant** to cook some **stew for the sons of the prophets**. By mistake some poisonous **gourds** were put **into the pot**. When the mistake

was detected, Elisha threw **some flour into the pot** and in this way made it safe to **eat**.

5. Miraculous Provision of Bread (4:42–44)

At another time Elisha fed **one hundred men** with **twenty** small, round, flat **loaves of barley bread** and some fresh ears of **grain**. There was enough and to spare, as the Lord had promised there would be. Elisha unselfishly gave to others what rightfully belonged to him. When we share with others and leave the consequences with God, He is able to meet our needs and the needs of others, and to even leave a surplus (Prov. 11:24, 25).

6. Miraculous Cleansing of Naaman the Leper (5:1–19)

5:1–4 Elisha's miracle-working power extended even to the army of the Syrians. A captive Jewish **girl** was a servant in the home of **Naaman**, the **commander of the** Syrian **army**. Knowing that **he was . . . a leper**, she suggested that the **prophet** Elisha **in Samaria** could **heal him**. This girl illustrates how a person of no importance in the eyes of the world, by being in a key place and showing loyalty to God, can influence the course of the history of salvation. D. L. Moody comments:

A little maid said a few words that made a commotion in two kingdoms. God honored her faith by doing for Naaman, the idolater, what he had not done for any in Israel. See Luke 4:24. How often has the finger of childhood pointed grown-up persons in the right direction. The maid boasted of God that he would do for Naaman what he had not done for any in Israel; and God honored her faith.[5]

5:5–7 Naaman obtained **a letter** of introduction from Ben-Hadad, **king of Syria**, to Joram, **king of Israel**, and also took gifts of money and **clothing** with him. Apparently the letter did not mention Elisha but simply requested healing for **Naaman. The king of Israel** was infuriated by such an unreasonable request and suspected that the Syrian king was looking for an excuse to attack Israel.

5:8–12 **Elisha** received word of the king's predicament and asked for Naaman to be sent to him. There was no power in the palace, for they were all idolaters there; but there was **a prophet** of God **in Israel** who had power to cleanse a man and make him whole. Elisha didn't talk to Naaman personally; his word was enough if acted upon by faith. **Elisha sent** word to Naaman to **wash in the Jordan** River **seven times**. Naaman had expected some more dramatic and colorful mode of healing than this, and he protested **in a rage** that **the waters of** his native **Damascus** were superior to the Jordan.

5:13, 14 D. L. Moody analyzed the problem accurately:

Naaman had two diseases—pride and leprosy. The first needed curing as much as the second. Naaman had to get down from his chariot of pride; afterwards, to wash according to the prescribed way.[6]

Finally **his servants** persuaded him to obey the prophet in such a simple matter, and he was thoroughly healed. As has been well said, "He swallowed his pride and lost his leprosy."

5:15–19 Naaman became a convert to the **God** of **Israel** and sought to reward Elisha, but the prophet would accept **nothing** from him. The Syrian general then obtained permission to take **two mule-loads of earth**

back home with him so he could worship the true God on the displaced soil of Israel. He explained that his official duties might require him to go to the **temple of** the idol **Rimmon** with his **master** and even **bow down**, but he hoped that **the LORD** would **pardon** him for **this**. Elisha neither approved nor disapproved this, but simply sent him on his way.

In the story of Naaman we find a classic illustration of the gospel of grace. He was an *enemy* of God, being the captain of the Syrian army. Humanly speaking, his condition was *helpless* and *hopeless*, since he was a leper (cf. Rom. 5:6–10). Being a Gentile, he was a *stranger* to the promises and covenants of God and had no claim on His blessing (Eph. 2:11, 12). But God's grace reached out to touch human need. All Naaman had to do was to humble himself and obey the word of the Lord. He eventually washed himself in obedience to God's word and came up a new man, with new skin and a new heart.

Marvelous grace of our loving Lord,
Grace that exceeds our sin and our
    guilt,
Yonder on Calvary's mount
    outpoured,
There where the blood of the Lamb
    was spilt.
　　　　　　　　　　—Julia H. Johnston

7. The Greed of Gehazi (5:20–27)

But Gehazi coveted the gifts from **Naaman** which Elisha had refused. He told the **Syrian** that Elisha had sent him to collect the gifts for **two young . . . prophets** who had just **come to** him **from the mountains of Ephraim**. Then he took the money and the garments to his own home. As a prophet, Elisha often received special revelations from the Lord. Now he was informed as to what his servant had done, and when Gehazi arrived, Elisha exposed him. He reminded the greedy servant that it was no **time to receive money and** garments or other things that could be bought with money. Gehazi was struck with **the leprosy of Naaman**. He had sinned greatly in giving the Syrians occasion to think that God's free gift of grace was not free at all.

8. Miraculous Recovery of an Axhead (6:1–7)

Some of **the sons of the prophets** were dissatisfied with the cramped quarters where they lived with **Elisha**, probably in Jericho or Gilgal. Therefore, they gained the prophet's permission to move near **the Jordan** and build **a place** there. In the process of building, one of the men lost a borrowed **axhead** in the Jordan. Elisha responded to his distressed plea by casting **a stick** into the river. The **axhead** floated and was retrieved by the grateful builder.

9. Miraculous Military Maneuvers (6:8–23)

Another evidence of Elisha's miraculous powers concerned his knowledge of highly confidential military moves in the **camp** of the enemy. **The** Syrian **king** was nonplussed because all his secret plans repeatedly became known **to the king of Israel**; he suspected that one of his men was a spy for **Israel**. When he learned that the Prophet **Elisha** was revealing his plans to **the king of Israel**, he determined to capture Elisha at all costs. Hearing that **the prophet** was **in Dothan**, a city not far north of Samaria, he sent a band of marauders to surround **the city … by night**. In the morning Elisha's servant was terrified when he saw the enemy host surrounding the city. But in answer to the prophet's prayer, the servant was given miraculous power to **see** a protective host of **horses and chariots of fire** sent by God to guard His people.

Elisha asked **the** Lord **to strike** the Syrians **with blindness**. The prophet was then able to lead them from Dothan **to Samaria** without a struggle. **When the king of Israel** suggested killing them, Elisha reminded him that he **would** not **kill** the captives **whom** he had **taken … with … sword and bow**, so why kill these who were delivered into his hands without any effort on his part? Instead, the king was ordered to feed them and send them home. By this humane treatment he overcame evil with good. Such marauding **bands** conducted no more raids on **Israel**.

Verse 16 reminds us of 1 John 4:4b— ". . . He who is in you is greater than he who is in the world." In our spiritual battle with the forces of evil, we have protection and power given us by our omnipotent Ally. Through the prayer of faith the Lord can open the eyes of our hearts to the reassuring fact that He is defending us and frustrating Satan's destructive intentions.

10. The Famine in Samaria (6:24—7:20)

6:24–31 The incident beginning here is not necessarily in chronological order. **Ben-Hadad, king of Syria**, . . . **besieged Samaria** so successfully that **famine** conditions prevailed **in** the city. (If this siege took place *after* the seven-year famine mentioned in 8:1–2, as some suggest, we can understand how serious the situation really was.) People had to pay exorbitant prices for ceremonially unclean foods (**a donkey's head**) and for herbs or grain. **"Dove droppings"**[7] was the name of a plant with an edible bulb. The plant bears the name "Star of Bethlehem" today. The king of Israel acknowledged that no one but the LORD could help, and he mourned greatly when he found cannibalism being practiced by the people. Blaming Elisha for the terrible conditions and for failing to do anything to relieve the situation, he vowed to kill him before the day was over.

6:32, 33 But Elisha received divine information about the king's intentions and told the elders that a messenger from the king was on the way, followed by the king himself. He ordered them to refuse entrance to the messenger until the king himself arrived. Almost immediately the messenger arrived, and then the king. He felt there was nothing to do but surrender to Syria. Then the king said, "Surely this calamity is from the LORD; why should I wait for the LORD any longer?" The incident reminds us that "The king's heart is in the hand of the LORD, like the rivers of water; He turns it wherever He wishes" (Prov. 21:1).

The king of Israel is not mentioned by name here; in fact, the name of the king is not given in any of the incidents recorded in chapters 4—8. Many commentators hold that Jehoram (Joram) was king during the siege, but it is impossible to be certain since Elisha's ministry, which stretched over half a century under four different kings, is not recorded in chronological order.

7:1, 2 Elisha then made a remarkable prediction to the king. He promised that the next day fine flour and ... barley would be sold at very low prices at the gate of Samaria. When the king's skeptical aide questioned the likelihood of such incredible plenty, Elisha added that he would see it with his eyes, but would not eat of it. "If you would believe," writes Moody, "you must crucify the question, 'how?' "[8] (cf. our Lord's disciples before the feeding of the 4000 in Mark 8:4).

7:3–7 That evening four leprous men who sat at the ... gate of Samaria decided in desperation to desert to the camp of the Syrians in hope of getting food. When they arrived, the Syrian camp was abandoned—the LORD had caused the enemy forces to hear the noise of a mighty onrushing army. Supposing it to be Hittites and Egyptian soldiers hired by the king of Israel, they retreated in pandemonium. Matthew Henry comments:

The Syrians that besieged Dothan had their *sight* imposed upon, *ch.* vi.18. These had their *hearing* imposed upon.... Whether the noise was really made in the air by the ministry of angels, or whether it was only a sound in their ears, is not certain; which soever it was, it was from God.[9]

7:8–16 At first the lepers helped themselves liberally to food, money, and clothing. But realizing that the people would soon find out that the Syrians were gone and would punish them for their silence, they decided to notify the king. He immediately suspected the Syrians of laying an ambush for the Israelites. But a servant suggested sending a few men as scouts, reasoning that if they weren't killed by the Syrians, they would die of starvation anyway like the rest of Israel. The scouts found that the Syrians had actually fled, leaving a trail of abandoned spoil. So the people of Israel plundered the tents of the Syrians, and the famine was over.

7:17–20 In accordance with the prophecy of Elisha, fine flour and barley . . . **sold** at very low prices that day. The king's **officer** who had doubted the prediction saw this, but he did not enjoy it because he was **trampled** to death by the jubilant throng at the city gate. Verses 18–20 reemphasize that the man died according to the word of the Lord because of his unbelief. Unbelief robs its victims of blessing and rewards them with death.

The memorable words of the lepers, **"We are not doing right. This day is a day of good news, and we remain silent"** (v. 9), are a constant challenge to those of us who are entrusted with the gospel of redeeming grace.

11. Restoration of the Shunammite's Property (8:1–6)

Before a seven-year **famine** came to **the land** (perhaps the famine of 4:38), **Elisha** warned **the** Shunammite **woman** (of chap. 4) to leave with her family, including the **son** whom **he had restored to life**. **She went** to **the land of the Philistines** and then **returned** when the famine had ended. At this time **Gehazi** was in the court of **the king** of Israel, a place that would ordinarily have been forbidden to a leper. Just **as he was** relating to **the king how** Elisha **had restored** a lad **to life**, **the woman** arrived to petition that her property be restored to her. **The king** ordered both the property and the produce which had grown on it during the seven years of her absence to be restored to her.

12. Elisha's Prophecy of Hazael's Reign (8:7–15)

8:7–12 When the ailing **Ben-Hadad**, **king of Syria**, heard that **Elisha** had **come . . . to Damascus**, he sent an officer, **Hazael**, with a large gift to **inquire** if he would **recover**.

Since Naaman was captain of the Syrian army under Ben-Hadad, the king would have been aware of Elisha's healing power (chap. 5). Perhaps the prophet would heal him as well. The prophet's vague answer to **Hazael** was, **"Go, say to him, 'You shall certainly recover.' However the LORD has shown me that he will really die."** This meant that the illness itself was not necessarily fatal, but that Ben-Hadad would not recover from it because Hazael was going to murder him. Elisha gazed so intently on Hazael that the latter became **ashamed**. Elisha also foresaw that Hazael would inflict terrible loss and suffering on **the children of Israel**—so terrible that the thought of it caused him to weep.

8:13–15 **Hazael** answered that he was but **a dog**; how could he be expected to do such a **gross thing**? Williams paraphrases it:

> Can it be that I, who am only a dog, should mount the throne of Syria and accomplish such great deeds![10]

But **Elisha** had been told by **the LORD** that Hazael would be **king** of **Syria**. Following this announcement, Hazael returned to Ben-Hadad, told him that he **would . . . recover**, and then treacherously smothered him with **a thick cloth** soaked **in water**.

The following quotation succinctly tells how accurate Elisha's prophecy was:

> Soon after [the murder of Ben-Hadad], Hazael fought against the combined forces of Jehoram and Ahaziah at Ramoth-gilead (8:28, 29; 9:14, 15). He frequently defeated Jehu in battle, devastating all his country east of the Jordan from the Arnon in the south to Bashan in the north (10:32, 33). During the reign of Jehoahaz, Jehu's successor, he repeatedly encroached

upon the territory of Israel, which was kept from complete destruction only by God's mercy (13:3, 22, 23). Hazael also moved into southwest Palestine, taking Gath; he compelled the king of Judah to pay a heavy bribe for sparing Jerusalem (12:17, 18; 2 Chron. 24:23, 24). It was not until the death of Hazael that Israel was able to successfully check the aggression of Syria under Ben-Hadad III, the son of Hazael (2 Kgs. 13:24, 25).[11]

F. King Jehoram (Joram) of Judah (8:16–24)

Jehoram (Joram) **the son of Jehoshaphat** was **king of Judah** for **eight years** (853–841 B.C.; cf. 2 Chron. 21:4–20).

8:16, 17 The chronology in verse 16 needs to be reconciled with that in 1 Kings 22:42, 51; 2 Kings 3:1; and 2 Kings 8:25. One explanation is that **Jehoram** was coregent with his father, **Jehoshaphat**, for five years. Another is that Jehoshaphat shared part of his reign with Asa and that the reigns of Ahaziah and Jehoram are dated from the beginning of Jehoshaphat's sole regency.

8:18, 19 **Jehoram** had married Athaliah, a **daughter of Ahab** and Jezebel. This marriage had doubtless been engineered by his father, Jehoshaphat, as part of his policy of conciliation with Israel. The result of it, however, was to lead the kingdom of **Judah** farther into the idolatrous ways of the northern kingdom. Because of this apostasy, **the LORD** would have destroyed **Judah** had it not been for his promise to **David** (2 Sam. 7:12–16).

8:20–24 During Joram's reign, **Edom revolted against** him. To quell the rebellion, he marched with his army **to Zair** (Edom), south of the Dead Sea. **The Edomites . . . sur-**

rounded him, forcing him to break through their lines to safety. His army **fled** home. From that time, **Edom** was not in complete subjection to Judah. It may have been during the reign of Jehoram that the prophet Obadiah spoke his oracle against Edom.

Mention is made that **Libnah**, near Philistia, also **revolted**, thus calling attention to the inherent weakness of the kingdom of Judah during the evil reign of **Joram**. Libnah was a Levitical city. The reason for her revolt is given in 2 Chronicles 21:10, 11. Judah evidently regained control of the city at a later time (19:8).

G. King Ahaziah of Judah (8:25–29)

Ahaziah the son of Jehoram was **king of Judah** for **one year** (841 B.C., cf. 2 Chron. 22:1–9).

8:25–27 **Ahaziah** is spoken of in verse 26 as the son of **Athaliah, the granddaughter of Omri**. **Ahaziah** is the same as Jehoahaz in 2 Chronicles 21 and is also called Azariah in 2 Chronicles 22:6. Ahaziah was a nephew of Joram, king of Israel. His mother, **Athaliah**, was the daughter of Ahab and the sister of *Israel's* Joram. The names get a bit confusing at this particular point in history! Ahab, king of Israel, had two sons who came to the throne successively, Ahaziah and Jehoram (Joram). Jehoshaphat, king of Judah, had a son named Jehoram who reigned after him. This **Jehoram** was followed on the throne by his **son . . . Ahaziah**. Thus Ahaziah and Jehoram ruled in Israel while **Jehoram** and **Ahaziah** ruled in Judah.

ISRAEL	JUDAH
Ahaziah	Jehoram
Jehoram	Ahaziah

Here **Ahaziah, . . . king of Judah**, is said to have been **twenty-two years**

old when he **began to reign**; in 2
Chronicles 22:2 his age is given as
forty-two years. Most evidence points
to **twenty-two** as the correct age. The
other figure is probably a copyist's
error.

8:28, 29 **Ahaziah** joined his uncle
Joram, king of Israel, in a **war
against . . . Syria at Ramoth Gilead**.
King Joram was wounded in battle
and taken **to Jezreel to recover**. **Ahaziah** visited him there while he was
recovering. Joram's father, Ahab, lost
his life at Ramoth Gilead (1 Kgs.
22). Ahaziah's grandfather, Jehoshaphat, had unwisely joined Ahab there
and was almost killed as a result. But
Ahaziah did not heed history's warning (about allying himself with Israel)
and was later killed as a result (chap.
9).

H. King Jehu of Israel and Elisha's Ministry (Chaps. 9, 10)

1. Jehu's Anointing (9:1–10)

Elisha directed **one of the sons of
the prophets** to **go to Ramoth Gilead**
and secretly anoint **Jehu** as **king** of
Israel to succeed Joram. **Jehu** was **the
son of Jehoshaphat, the son of Nimshi**
(v. 2), *not* the son of Jehoshaphat,
king of Judah. **Jehu** was **commander**
of Joram's **army** and had been
stationed at **Ramoth Gilead** to hold
back the Syrians. In anointing him,
the prophet commissioned him to
destroy **the house of Ahab**, in accordance with the prophecy of Elijah
(1 Kgs. 21:21–24). Elijah had been
told to anoint Jehu (1 Kgs. 19:16), but
it appears that he passed this responsibility on to his successor, Elisha,
who in turn sent an unknown prophet
to Ramoth Gilead that the anointing
might be carried out in secret. This
secrecy gave **Jehu** the element of surprise, which he skillfully used in seizing the throne.

2. Jehu's Executions (9:11—10:17)

9:11–13 When Jehu emerged from
the **inner room**, his fellow officers
wanted to know what the **"madman
of a prophet"** had said to him. Jehu
first tried to evade the question by
suggesting that they already knew.
Perhaps he suspected that they had
sent the prophet to anoint him in
order to overthrow Joram. But at their
insistence, he revealed that he had
just been **anointed . . . king**. In haste,
his men covered **the steps** with their
garments and publicly proclaimed him
as **king** of Israel.

Jehu the son of Jehoshaphat was
king of Israel for twenty-eight years
(841–814/13 B.C.; 2 Kgs. 9:14—10:36).

9:14–26 Jehu's reign began the fifth
dynasty of the northern kingdom.
Before news of his anointing could
get to **Jezreel**, Jehu hurried there to
kill **Joram**. **A watchman . . . saw** the
approach of Jehu's **company** and
notified Joram. Messengers were sent
out twice to learn the identity of the
approaching company, but **Jehu**
prevented them from returning. By
then the watchmen notified the king
that the furious **driving** resembled
that of **Jehu, the "son"** (grandson) **of
Nimshi**. **Joram** then went forth in his
royal **chariot**, accompanied by his
nephew **Ahaziah, king of Judah**, supposing that there was important news
about Ramoth Gilead. He greeted Jehu
with **"Is it peace** (*shālôm*), **Jehu?"**, but
received warlike words in reply. Sensing **treachery, Joram** tried to flee but
was killed by Jehu's **arrow**. In literal
fulfillment of Elijah's prophecy (1 Kgs.
21:19), his body was cast to the **ground**
in Naboth's vineyard.

9:27–29 **Ahaziah** also tried to escape, but he too was hit by an arrow
and died at **Megiddo**. By fraternizing
with the house of Ahab, he fell under
the divine curse that Jehu had been

commissioned to carry out. His body was then returned **to Jerusalem** for burial. Second Chronicles 22:9 says that he died in Samaria, but this could refer to either the kingdom of Samaria or the region. Verse 29 is not in chronological order, being a repetition of 8:25. The discrepancy between the years mentioned (**eleventh** and twelfth) is probably due to different methods of reckoning.

9:30–37 When Jehu reached the city of **Jezreel** itself, **Jezebel** mocked him, shouting, **"Is it peace, Zimri, murderer of your master?"** Zimri too had become king of Israel by murdering his master, but he enjoyed anything but peace. His abortive *coup d'état* lasted only seven days (1 Kgs. 16:9–19). **Jezebel** was intimating to **Jehu** that he would not prosper in his rebellion. **Two eunuchs** in the palace proved their loyalty to Jehu by throwing Jezebel out the window. **Her blood spattered on the wall and on the horses**, and her body was eaten by the **dogs** of **Jezreel** in fulfillment of 1 Kings 21:23—all except **the skull and the feet and the palms of her hands**. Campbell Morgan remarks:

> The very dogs turned from the skull and hands and feet that had designed and executed such abominations; and no tomb but infamy perpetuates her memory.[12]

10:1–11 Jehu's next step was to slay **seventy** descendants (**"sons"**) of **Ahab** who were living **in Samaria**. He first gave their guardians an ultimatum—**choose the best qualified of** Ahab's descendants as kings **and fight** against Jehu and his men. But they remembered how **two kings** (Joram and Ahaziah) had been powerless against **Jehu** at Jezreel, so they **sent** back word that they would be obedient **servants**. He wrote back that

they could demonstrate their loyalty to him by delivering **the heads of** Ahab's seventy male descendants to **Jezreel** the next day. They agreed to this. In the morning Jehu went out to see **the heads**, lying **in two heaps at the entrance of the gate**. Perhaps the assembled people expected him to be angry at this wholesale destruction, not knowing that he had ordered it. Quickly he set their minds at ease, saying in effect:

> You are innocent of this deed. I am innocent too. It is true that I killed my master, Joram, but who killed these? It must have been God, fulfilling what He predicted to His servant Elijah.

In further fulfillment of Elijah's prophecy, **Jehu** proceeded to kill **all** of Ahab's relatives, **great men**, **close acquaintances**, **and his priests** in Jezreel.

10:12–14 On the way to the capital, **Samaria, Jehu met . . . forty-two** of Ahaziah's relatives. **"Brothers"** (v. 13) means cousins, nephews, etc., since Ahaziah's brothers had been slain (2 Chron. 21:17). These people had come from Judah to visit the royal family of Israel. Realizing that they had ties with the house of Ahab, Jehu ordered them to be killed **at the well of Beth Eked**.

10:15–17 Jehu also **met Jehonadab** (also called Jonadab), a Rechabite. On the assurance that **Jehonadab** was loyal to him, Jehu invited him to **ride to Samaria** and witness his **zeal for the** LORD. Jeremiah 35 tells us a little more about Jehonadab. He ordered his descendants to return to the early lifestyle that Israel had known under Moses and Joshua, in an attempt to keep them from following the kingdom into apostasy, the national sin of Israel. Upon hearing of Jehu's purge, he went with the new king, who immediately welcomed him as a great ally in the fight against Baalism. **In Samaria**, **Jehu** slew all the remaining relatives of **Ahab**. Morgan warns:

> He [Jehu] was proud of his own zeal. How subtle the peril! And it is a peril. Wherever it exists it leads to other evil things. While this man was carrying out the judgments of God upon Israel, he was in his own life corrupt.[13]

3. Jehu's Purge of the Baal-Worshipers (10:18–36)

10:18–28 The new king's next assault was aimed at **the worshipers of Baal**. In order to identify them, he ordered **a great** holiday in honor of **Baal**. **The temple of Baal** was filled with **worshipers** from **all** parts of **Israel**, wearing special identifying **vestments**. Care was taken to see that no worshipers of Jehovah were present. **As soon as** Jehu had offered **the burnt offering**, he gave the signal for his **guard and . . . captains** to **kill** all the idolaters. **Eighty men** were stationed **outside** to prevent anyone from escaping. Jehu's men **went into the inner room of the temple of Baal**, removed the **sacred pillars** that were there, **and burned them**. **They tore down the temple of Baal**, converting it into a latrine or **refuse dump**.

10:29, 30 In many ways Jehu was one of the best, perhaps *the* best of the kings of Israel. He executed God's judgment on **the house of Ahab** and purged the land of Baal-worshipers. The Lord rewarded what was praiseworthy by promising that his dynasty would continue **to the fourth generation** (i.e., Jehoahaz, Joash, Jeroboam II, and Zechariah).

10:31–36 However, **Jehu** continued to promote the worship of the golden calves, which **Jeroboam** had inaugurated. Also, he is condemned in Hosea 1:4 for his extreme cruelty in exterminating the house of Ahab. As a result of his failures, **the LORD began to cut off parts of Israel**. **Hazael**, the king of Syria, captured the land east of **the Jordan** that had originally been occupied by the tribes of **Reuben** and **Gad** and the half-tribe of **Manasseh**. Elisha had foreseen the activity of **Hazael** (8:12). The Syrian king was carrying out the judgment of the Lord on the house of Israel even as Jehu had executed judgment on the house of Ahab. Behind the activities of these wicked kings the spiritual eye can see the sovereign hand of Jehovah making the wrath of man accomplish His purposes.

I. Queen Athaliah's Usurpation in Judah (Chap. 11)

Athaliah, the daughter of Ahab, was queen of Judah **for six years** (841–835 B.C.; 2 Chron. 22:10—23:21).

11:1 The scene now changes from Israel to Judah. **Athaliah** seized control when her son **Ahaziah** was slain by Jehu. To prevent any threat to her rule, **she** ordered the deaths of **all** (or so she thought) the sons of Ahaziah. That **Athaliah** could cold-bloodedly order the execution of her own grandchildren shows just how much like her mother (Jezebel) she was. She was also unwittingly carrying out the curse pronounced on the descendants of Ahab, her father (1 Kgs. 21:21, 22).

11:2, 3 **Jehosheba**, the wife of Jehoiada (2 Chron. 22:11) and an aunt of **the** doomed **sons**, courageously entered the royal house **and stole** a lad named **Joash** (same as Jehoash) **from among the . . . sons who were being murdered**. **Athaliah** would have cut off the royal line, but the Lord preserved **Joash** because of the Davidic covenant. The long-range consequences of what she tried to do are staggering. This was a satanic attempt to break the royal Messianic line. Joash was hidden with **his nurse in the bedroom** of the unused temple. He remained there **for six years, while Athaliah reigned over the land**.

11:4–11 In the seventh year, Jehoiada the high **priest** called **the captains of hundreds—of the bodyguards and the escorts—showed them** the heir to the throne, and **made a covenant with them** to overthrow Athaliah and crown Joash as king. Williams comments:

> The steps taken by Jehoiada to bring about the royal revolution (vv. 4–11) may be thus paraphrased. He sent for the officers of the royal bodyguard. One regiment was ordered to surround the king's house, and the two remaining regiments to parade in front of the temple. Any person attempting to force his way through the troops was to be put to death. The guard relieved on that morning (v. 9) was not to return to barracks, but to fall in with the relieving guard and join the main body in defense of the king.[14]

11:12 Then Joash was **brought out** to the people. A **crown** was placed **on** his head and a copy of **the Testimony** (the law) was handed to him. The shout went up from the people, **"Long live the king!"**

11:13–16 When Athaliah was attracted by **the noise** to the court of **the temple** and saw what was going on, she cried, **"Treason! Treason!"** Because **Jehoiada** did not want **her** to **be killed in the** environs of the temple, he ordered that she be taken **outside** between ranks of soldiers and **killed** at **the horses' entrance**.

11:17–21 A covenant was then **made between the** LORD, **the** new **king, and the people, that they** would serve the Lord. In demonstration of this, the people sacked **the temple of Baal**, which Athaliah had promoted, **and killed Mattan the priest of Baal.** The king was escorted to the royal palace in a great procession. **The people of the land rejoiced, and the city was quiet** after **Athaliah** had been executed.

J. King Jehoash (Joash) of Judah (Chap. 12)

Jehoash (Joash), the son of Ahaziah, **king** of Judah, **reigned** for **forty years** (835–796 B.C.; cf. 2 Chron. 23:1—24:27).

12:1–5 John C. Whitcomb comments on the reign of Jehoash:

> The forty-year reign of Joash may be divided into two parts—before and after the death of his spiritual guardian, Jehoiada. The statement that "Joash did that which was right in the eyes of Jehovah *all the days of Jehoiada the priest*" is ominous. Without the moral and spiritual courage of this high priest, Joash was as unstable as Lot without Abram. Therefore, God showed His mercy to the people of Judah by extending Jehoiada's life to an amazing 130 years (2 Chron. 24:15)! Thus Jehoiada lived longer than anyone on record during the previous thousand years, since Amram, an ancestor of Moses, died at 137 (Ex. 6:20).[15]

In general, the reign of **Jehoash** was commendable. However, he failed to stop **the people** from worshiping at **the high places**. His major contribution was his undertaking to **repair . . . the temple**. To do this he issued instructions **to the priests** that certain funds should be laid aside for the purpose of restoring **the house of the**

LORD. According to Williams, these were: (1) the money of everyone who passed the account—that is, the **census** tax of Exodus 30:12; (2) the money that every man is set at—that is, the **assessment money** of Leviticus 27; (3) **all the money that a man** desired **to bring**—that is, the ordinary freewill offerings legislated for in Leviticus.[16]

12:6–16 When no repairs had been made **by the twenty-third year of** the reign of **King Jehoash**, the king **called Jehoiada . . . and the other priests** and announced a new plan for collecting the money and repairing the temple. The priests would no longer collect the funds directly, nor would they supervise the repairs on the temple (v. 7). Instead, **a chest** with **a hole in its lid** was to be placed at **the right side** of **the altar** to receive **money** for the restoration of the temple. **The king's scribe and the high priest** added up the funds and distributed them to **the workmen.** The overseers were honest, so it was not necessary to demand a public accounting of the funds. Verse 13 seems to contradict 2 Chronicles 24:14; however, verse 13 means that these funds were not used to purchase utensils for the temple while it was being restored, whereas 2 Chronicles 12:14 means that after the work on the temple was completed, the surplus funds were used for this purpose. In obedience to God's Word (Lev. 5:16; Num. 5:8, 9), **the money from the sin** and **trespass offerings** continued to be given **to the priests.**

12:17, 18 At this time **Hazael, king of Syria**, captured **Gath** and marched toward **Jerusalem. Jehoash** gave him **sacred things** from the temple and from the **king's house** to dissuade him from attacking the capital of Judah.

12:19–21 After the death of Jehoiada, the princes of Judah turned their king to idolatry. When Zechariah, a son (or grandson) of the high priest, tried to call the people back to the worship of Jehovah, King Jehoash ordered him to be stoned to death (2 Chron. 24).

Jehoash's own **servants** conspired against him **and killed** him **in the house of the Millo.** This was God's judgment on him for the murder of Zechariah.

Jesus referred to the death of Zechariah when He reproved the lawyers (Luke 11:51). He said that the blood of all the prophets, from the blood of Abel to that of Zechariah, would be required of that generation. Thus He included the blood of all martyrs in the OT period, from that of Abel in Genesis to that of Zechariah here and in 2 Chronicles, the last book of the Hebrew Bible. (The Hebrew Bible contains the same books as our OT but in a different order.)

Jehoiada was a godly man who devoted himself to the service of the kingdom and the temple. He received two blessings in return: His son Zechariah followed in his steps, and he was buried with the kings of Judah, a great honor indeed for one born outside the royal family. Joash, on the other hand, got progressively worse after the death of Jehoiada. He plundered the temple he had once repaired and robbed the royal treasury to buy off the Syrians. He was not buried in the tomb of the kings because he died under divine judgment for the murder of Zechariah. It is vital that we persevere in godliness lest we hinder the kingdom of God. Jehoiada, a shining example! Joash, a solemn warning!

K. King Jehoahaz of Israel (13:1–9)

Jehoahaz the son of Jehu was **king** of **Israel** for **seventeen years** (814/13–798 B.C.).

Jehoahaz followed Jeroboam in the mixed worship of Jehovah and the Asherah (v. 6). God punished him by sending the Syrians against Israel. They reduced Jehoahaz's forces to **only fifty horsemen, ten chariots, and ten thousand foot soldiers**. When **Jehoahaz pleaded with the LORD**, He raised up **a deliverer** who rescued Israel **from . . . the hand of the Syrians**. The deliverer might have been Adadnirari III, king of Assyria, who late in the reign of Jehoahaz caused more and more trouble for Syria, leaving her little time to bother Israel. Some commentators suggest that Elisha was the deliverer. Others say that verse 5 refers to either Jehoash (v. 25) or Jeroboam II (14:26, 27). Verse 23 explains why God answered Jehoahaz's prayer: It was because of His covenant with Abraham, Isaac, and Jacob.

Notice that verses 5 and 6 are a parenthesis. The parenthesis is one of grace. Before another century passed, Israel would be swept off the promised land because of her persistence in the sins of Jeroboam. By providing **a deliverer** for the nation, the Lord was seeking to turn her from her destructive course before the final stroke of judgment fell. However, **they did not depart from the sins of the house of Jeroboam . . . but walked in them**.

L. King Jehoash (Joash) of Israel (13:10–13)

Jehoash (Joash) the son of Jehoahaz was **king** of Israel for **sixteen years** (798–782/81 B.C.; 2 Kgs. 13:10—14:16).

13:10–13 This King **Jehoash** is to be differentiated from the king of Judah with the same name who was reigning at this time. The reign of this Jehoash was wicked, patterned after that of **Jeroboam the son of Nebat**. These verses give a condensed ac-

count of his reign: **He became king; he did evil in the sight of the LORD; he rested with his fathers**. His dealings with Amaziah of Judah are recorded in 14:8–16.

M. The Close of Elisha's Ministry (13:14–25)

13:14–19 Verses 14–25 tell of the prophecy and death of **Elisha**, which took place during the rule of Jehoash. When the prophet Elisha was dying, **Joash** (Jehoash) visited him **and wept over** him, saying, **"O my father, my father, the chariots of Israel and their horsemen!"** He meant that men of Elisha's caliber were the truest and best defense of the people of Israel. Elisha had used the same words to lament the passing of Elijah (2:12). He realized that the death of the prophet would be a great loss to the kingdom. From his sickbed, **Elisha** directed Joash to **take a bow and some arrows**, to **shoot** one arrow eastward, and then to **strike the ground** with **the arrows**. The arrow that shot eastward signified victory over the Syrians, who had occupied Israel's land east of the Jordan. Because Joash had **struck** the ground only **three times**, he would strike down **Syria . . . only three times**. If he had **struck five or six times**, the threat of **Syria** would have been eliminated. But he lacked perseverance and endurance. Victory over enemies depends on the measure of obedience. Joash must have known the significance of what he was doing, or else he would not have been held responsible. Elisha's death spelled no good for the northern kingdom.

13:20, 21 In **the spring of** each **year**, marauding **bands** of Moabites **invaded the land**. One day as some men of Israel were taking out a corpse to be buried, they saw one of these marauding bands approaching. Hurriedly they opened **the tomb of Elisha** and threw the corpse in. As soon as **the man . . . touched the bones of Elisha, he revived and stood on his feet**.

13:22–25 Scripture tells us nothing of the last forty-five years of Elisha's ministry, from the anointing of Jehu, in 841 B.C. (chap. 9), until his death in about 795 B.C. His final prophecy (from his deathbed) was one of victory (v. 17). His final miracle (accomplished long after his death—v. 21) was a validation of his message and ministry to Israel and her king. In fulfillment of Elisha's prophecy, **Jehoash . . . recaptured . . . the cities which . . . Hazael . . . had taken** from **Israel**. This was accomplished by **three** successive victories.

N. King Amaziah of Judah (14:1–20)

Amaziah the son of Joash was king of Judah for **twenty-nine years** (796–767 B.C.; 2 Chron. 25).

14:1–7 Amaziah's reign, though good, lacked the excellence of David's reign. It was more like his father's (**Joash**) in that both failed to abolish **the high places**. One of Amaziah's first acts was to kill the conspirators **who had murdered his father** (12:20, 21). However, he spared **the children of** these men, in obedience to Deuteronomy 24:16. Also, he led a brilliant campaign against Edom, killing **ten thousand** of its inhabitants and capturing the rock city of **Selah** (probably the same as Petra). Unfortunately, he brought back Edomite gods and began to worship them (2 Chron. 25:14).

14:8–14 Inflated with pride, **Amaziah** foolishly invited **Jehoash, king of Israel**, to a show of strength. **Jehoash** answered by a parable in which **the thistle** (Judah) said **to the cedar** (Israel), **"Give your daughter to my son as wife"** (a weed making

an impertinent request to a mighty tree). **A wild beast** (the army of Israel) **trampled** down **the thistle** (Judah). Amaziah should be satisfied with his victory over **Edom** and not invite disaster by antagonizing Israel. When **Amaziah** refused to listen, **Jehoash** marched against **Judah**, **broke down the wall of Jerusalem**, and carried away some of its treasures.

14:15–20 The antagonism between Judah and Israel which began at this time continued until the fall of Israel in 722 B.C. **Amaziah . . . fled to Lachish** to escape **a conspiracy but** he was followed **and** slain **there**.

O. King Azariah (Uzziah) of Judah (14:21, 22)

Azariah (same as Uzziah) **the son of Amaziah** was king of Judah for **fifty-two years** (792/91–740/39 B.C.; cf. 15:1–7; 2 Chron. 26).

The ministry of Isaiah, Amos, and Hosea began at this time in OT history (Isa. 1:1; Hos. 1:1; Amos 1:1). The books of Amos and Hosea reveal the social and religious conditions prevalent in Israel. Through these prophets the Lord constantly warned of coming disaster while trying to woo His people back from the precipice of judgment.

Azariah was coregent with his father for the first twenty-four years. **He built Elath**, at the north of the Gulf of Aqaba. A fuller record of his reign is given in chapter 15 and in 2 Chronicles 26.

P. King Jeroboam II of Israel (14:23–29)

Jeroboam II the son of Jehoash was **king of Israel** for **forty-one years** (793/92–753 B.C.).

The first twelve years of Jeroboam's reign overlapped with that of his father, **Joash** (Jehoash). As to his religious policy, this king followed the idolatry of his namesake, **Jeroboam the son of Nebat**. Politically, he recovered for **Israel** the land **from the entrance of Hamath** (Galilee) **to the Sea of the Arabah** (Transjordan), as **Jonah** had prophesied. This particular prophecy is not recorded in the Bible. (Verse 25 pinpoints the time of Jonah's ministry, which is important in studying the book bearing his name. It is startling to realize that the Assyrians carried Israel into captivity only forty to seventy years after the repentance of Nineveh occasioned by Jonah's preaching!) **Jeroboam** II may be the deliverer mentioned in 13:5 (cf. 14:26, 27). Verses 26 and 27 give deep insight into the tender love and patience of **the LORD**. Verse 27 must be understood in context; **Israel**, and later Judah, were subsequently blotted out for a time, but, according to God's promise to the Jewish fathers, the nation will be regathered and replanted in the land.

Q. King Azariah (Uzziah) of Judah, Cont'd (15:1–7)

In general **Azariah** was a good **king**. Part of his failure was his permitting **the high places** to continue in **Judah**. When he insisted on intruding into the priest's office by offering incense in the temple, despite the protests of the priests, he was **struck** with leprosy and had to dwell **in an isolated house** to **the day of his death** (cf. 2 Chron. 26:16–21).

The ministry of Amos ended at this period.

R. King Zechariah of Israel (15:8–12)

Zechariah the son of Jeroboam II reigned over Israel for **six months** (753–752 B.C.).

Like his predecessors, **Zechariah** walked in the steps of **Jeroboam** I, worshiping the golden calves at Dan and Bethel. After a brief reign of **six months**, he was assassinated by **Shallum**. The RSV, following the LXX, says he was killed at Ibleam, a town in the Jezreel Valley close to where Ahaziah had been killed by Jehu (9:27). His death marked the end of the **Jehu** dynasty, **Zechariah** being **the fourth generation** which God had promised Jehu would **sit on the throne of Israel** (v. 12; cf. 10:30).

S. King Shallum of Israel (15:13–15)

Shallum the son of Jabesh was **king** of **Israel** for one **month** (752 B.C.).

Little is recorded about this king. His was the only reign in the sixth dynasty of the ten tribes. **Shallum** had gained the throne by assassination and now lost it the same way one **month** later. He was assassinated by **Menahem**.

T. King Menahem of Israel (15:16–22)

Menahem the son of Gadi was **king** of **Israel** for **ten years** (752–742/41 B.C.).

Menahem proceeded to sack **Tiphsah**—not the city of Tiphsah on the Euphrates but the one near **Tirzah**. When the city refused to **surrender**, he cruelly massacred the people, including the pregnant **women**.

At this time the Syrian kingdom had declined, and Assyria had become Israel's chief enemy. During the reign of Menahem, **Pul**, the **king of Assyria**, invaded **Israel**. **Menahem** gave him **a thousand talents of silver** to appease him and to enlist Pul's support in confirming Menahem's uncertain power. The king of Israel raised this money by taxing all the wealthy men **fifty shekels of silver** apiece

(v. 20). The price of a slave in Assyria at this time was **fifty shekels of silver**. Menahem was voluntarily submitting to the yoke of Assyria because he felt it was to his personal advantage to do so. **Pul** is generally considered to be the same as Tiglath-Pileser III (v. 29).

U. King Pekahiah of Israel (15:23–26)

Pekahiah the son of Menahem was **king** of **Israel** for **two years** (742/41–740/39 B.C.).

All that we know of this king is that his reign was brief and **evil** and that he was slain by **Pekah** and **fifty** Gileadites **in Samaria**. His reign ended the seventh dynasty of Israel. He was the only one of Israel's latter kings who did not take the crown by force, but it wasn't long before it was forcibly taken from him by one of his officials.

V. King Pekah of Israel (15:27–31)

Pekah the son of Remaliah was **king** of **Israel** for **twenty years** (752–732/31 B.C.).

Pekah was captain to Pekahiah, whom he killed. From other Scriptures we learn that he invaded Judah and then enlisted Syrian aid against Judah. But Ahaz, king of Judah, called Assyria to aid him. The king of Assyria first killed Rezin, king of Syria, and then attacked Israel. He conquered the two and a half tribes east of the Jordan and the territory of Galilee, carrying the inhabitants into captivity. This was the first phase of the Assyrian captivity. Pekah's power as captain overlapped with Menahem's (ten years) and Pekahiah's (two years). Supported by Assyria, **Hoshea** seized the throne of Israel by conspiring **against Pekah** and killing him. This ended Israel's eighth dynasty.

W. King Jotham of Judah (15:32–38)

Jotham the son of Uzziah was **king** of **Judah** for a total of twenty **years**, including four years of co-regency with Uzziah (750–732/31 B.C.; cf. 2 Chron. 27).

The first part of Jotham's reign was spent in a coregency with his father Uzziah, the last part with Ahaz. His official reign lasted **sixteen years**. **Jotham** was one of the better kings of Judah, even though he did not abolish **the high places. He built the Upper Gate of the house of the LORD** and sponsored other construction projects in the land. Just before his death, **Rezin** and **Pekah** began their joint attack **against Judah**. The prophet Micah began his ministry during the reign of Jotham.

Second Chronicles 27:6 includes the following editorial comment praising Jotham: "So Jotham became mighty, because he prepared his ways before the LORD his God." This is in stark contrast to the kings of Israel, who ordered their ways after Jeroboam.

Josephus also makes mention of Jotham's godliness.[17]

X. King Ahaz of Judah (Chap. 16)

Ahaz the son of Jotham was **king** of **Judah** for twenty **years** (735–716/15 B.C.; cf. 2 Chron. 28).

16:1–4 Ahaz was coregent with his father for perhaps twelve years. The name Ahaz is a contraction for Jehoahaz. It is by the latter name that the king is known on Assyrian inscriptions. The prefix "Jeho-" stands for Jehovah, and doubtless the Holy Spirit omitted it purposely because Ahaz was an apostate. He followed **the kings of Israel** in his idolatry, even making **his son pass through the fire**. In the worship of Molech, it is believed that children were passed between the red-hot arms of the brass idol, signifying cleansing from evil and dedication to the god. Sometimes the children were actually killed and burned (Jer. 7:31; Ezek. 16:21).

16:5–9 In order to force Judah to join them against Assyria, and to install a vassal king on the throne of Judah (Isa. 7:6), **Syria** and **Israel** united to attack **Jerusalem.** At the same time **Syria captured Elath** and planted a colony of Syrians there. In his distress, **Ahaz** sent a call for help to **Assyria,** accompanying it with **silver and gold** treasures from the temple and the palace. **Tiglath-Pileser** complied by capturing **Damascus** and killing the king of Syria. This was in fulfillment of the prophecy of Isaiah. But God would make the Assyrians a curse to Judah (Isa. 7:17–25).

16:10–16 On a trip **to Damascus** to visit **Tiglath-Pileser, Ahaz ... saw** a heathen **altar** and decided to build one like it in Jerusalem. So he sent a model of it **to Urijah the priest,** and **Urijah** in turn had the **altar ... built ... before King Ahaz** returned. **Ahaz** offered various **offerings on** his new altar (all but sin and trespass-offerings) and then **commanded Urijah** to use it henceforth instead of **the bronze altar.** The last clause in verse 15 seems to suggest that Ahaz would use the **bronze altar** for divination. However, it may also be understood to mean, "As for the bronze altar, it will be for me to enquire (or consider) what I shall do with it."[18] **Urijah the priest** sinfully obeyed **King Ahaz** in his sacrilege instead of fearlessly rebuking him. Uriah (the same as Urijah) is mentioned favorably in Isaiah 8:2, but this was before the attack on Jerusalem. His wicked acquiescence to the demand of Ahaz to build the altar took place at a later date.

16:17–20 Ahaz ... removed certain furnishings from **the temple** area, perhaps for fear that the king of Assyria might take them if he ever captured Jerusalem. Some think he used them to pay tribute. Second Chronicles 28:24 tells how Ahaz closed the temple entirely toward the end of his reign. Like other apostate kings before him, Ahaz was not buried in the royal tombs (2 Chron. 28:27) but **was buried with his fathers in the City of David.**

Y. King Hoshea of Israel (17:1–6)

Hoshea the son of Elah was **king** of **Israel** for **nine years** (732/31–723/22 B.C.).

17:1, 2 We come now to the final king and the ninth and final dynasty of Israel. **Hoshea** killed Pekah (cf. 15:30), perhaps because of his inability to resist Assyria's inroads into Israel, and took the reins of government. He was not as wicked as his predecessors, but the nation had gone too far—his improvements were too late.

17:3–6 Shalmaneser, king of Assyria, marched **against** Samaria and made **Hoshea** pay **tribute.** Hoshea conspired with the **king of Egypt** against **Assyria** and reneged on his payment of **tribute.** Therefore **the king of Assyria** (either Shalmaneser or Sargon, his successor) imprisoned Hoshea, **besieged ... Samaria ... for three years, and carried** some of the people into captivity. We are not told Hoshea's fate; he simply disappears into an Assyrian **prison,** leaving Samaria without a king during her last days. The final fall of Israel took place in 723 or 722 B.C.

Z. The Fall of the Northern Kingdom (17:7–41)

17:7–23 These verses explain the underlying reasons why **God** was displeased with Israel and allowed the nation to be conquered and exiled. **They had feared other gods, . . . walked in the** customs **of the nations, . . . built for themselves high places, . . . sacred pillars,** and **wooden images** (Asherim) everywhere, and multiplied their idolatry. They refused to listen to **His Prophets** but **stiffened their necks** and refused to **believe** the word of **the LORD their God**. They turned their backs on God's **commandments** and adopted the man-made religion of their neighbors. They were zealous in their pursuit of **evil,** offering **their sons and daughters** to false gods.

17:24, 25 The king of Assyria carried the ten northern tribes of Israel away to Mesopotamia and Media. Also, he **brought people from** five other nations which he had conquered and **placed them in the** land of Israel. Earlier, when Israel obeyed the Lord, He drove out the heathen nations and settled His people in Canaan by the hand of Joshua. When they stopped listening to Jehovah, He drove them out and brought the nations back in by the hand of the king of Assyria. These pagan people worshiped their own heathen deities and thus brought themselves under God's displeasure, especially since they were now living in Immanuel's land. The Lord's anger was revealed when He **sent lions among them** which roamed through the land, killing **some of** the people.

17:26–28 Someone notified **the king of Assyria** that the plague of **lions** was caused by the presence of these foreigners who did **not know** the law of **the God of** Israel. **The king of Assyria** then ordered an Israelite **priest** to be returned from captivity for the purpose of instructing the heathen colonists how they should fear the Lord. The priest who returned

was likely one of the idolatrous priests of Israel, not a true priest of Jehovah. He went to Bethel, the seat of calf-worship (although the calf was no longer there), and taught the new inhabitants the polluted religion of Jeroboam, which included, but was in no way limited to, the worship of Jehovah. These foreign colonists intermarried with the Israelites in the land, and this produced the people known as Samaritans—a mixed ethnic group with its own religion and customs.

17:29–34a These verses seem to describe the foreign settlers in the land. Each nationality had **its own . . . gods** and **appointed . . . priests** from among its own people. They also adopted the worship of Jehovah, and the result was a mixed religion, which was worse than out-and-out paganism.[19]

17:34b–40 The section from verse 34b (**"they do not fear the LORD . . ."**) through verse 40 seems to describe the Israelites who remained in the land. They did not heed the repeated warnings of the Lord against idolatry but continued to worship the golden calves.

17:41 This refers back to the foreign settlers in the land. They appeared to be less guilty than Israel. With what little light they had, they **feared the LORD** after a fashion; but the ten tribes, with all the light they had, did **not fear the LORD** (v. 34b).

As far as we know the ten tribes never returned to the land.[20] They are scattered throughout the world. Perhaps they include the black Falasha Jews of Ethiopia, the Chinese Jews of Kaifeng-Fu, and the Cochin Jews of India. Their identity is not hidden from God; He will bring them back to Israel in a coming day.

The prophet Hosea's ministry probably ended at this time—that is, with the fall of Samaria and the captivity of Israel.

II. THE KINGDOM OF JUDAH TO THE CAPTIVITY (Chaps. 18—25)

A. King Hezekiah (Chaps. 18—20)

Hezekiah the son of Ahaz was king of Judah for twenty-nine years (716/15–687/86 B.C.; cf. 2 Chron. 29—32; Isa. 36—39). He is believed to have had a co-regency with Ahaz before that from 729/28 to 716/15.

1. Hezekiah's Righteous Reign (18:1–8)

18:1–6 More space is devoted to Hezekiah in Holy Scripture than to almost any king since the time of Solomon. The parallel accounts in 2 Chronicles 29—32 and Isaiah 36—39 should be read to better understand the spiritual and political victories that Hezekiah gained through his faith in God.

When Hezekiah came to power, Judah was virtually a vassal state under Assyria. His reign was one of great reform. He conducted a campaign against all forms of idolatry, destroying even the high places and the bronze serpent of Numbers 21 (because the children of Israel burned incense to it). He called it Nehushtan, meaning literally "a bronze thing" (NKJV marg.). As far as his trust in the LORD God was concerned, Hezekiah was the greatest of the kings of Judah. Josiah was the greatest of the kings as far as thoroughness in expelling evildoers from the land was concerned (23:24, 25).

18:7, 8 Eventually Hezekiah rebelled against the Assyrian yoke, perhaps because of his military success in driving the Philistines out of the

land from watchtower (country places) to fortified city (thickly inhabited and well-defended places).

2. The Capture of Samaria (18:9–12)

This paragraph reviews the capture of Samaria by the Assyrians, and is perhaps introduced here to emphasize the seriousness of the threat which faced Hezekiah at this time. The seeming contradiction between the dates in verses 9 and 10 is explained by the fact that in Jewish reckoning a part of a year is counted as a year. The siege of Samaria began during the latter part of the fourth year of Hezekiah's reign, continued during the fifth year, and ended in the first part of the sixth year—therefore "three years." This would have been 725–722 B.C., during the co-regency mentioned above.

3. Sennacherib's First Invasion of Judah (18:13–16)

Assyria had been having troubles of her own at this time; Sargon II had died and Babylon was in rebellion. It wasn't until 701 B.C. that Sennacherib, Sargon's successor, was able to march on Palestine and Phoenicia. In his annals Sennacherib claimed to have taken forty-six fortified cities and 200,000 captives from Judah. Hezekiah . . . sent a servile message to him acknowledging that he had been wrong in rebelling. He abjectly paid three hundred talents of silver and thirty talents of gold (a huge sum) to prevent an attack on Jerusalem. At the time, Sennacherib was in Lachish, southwest of Jerusalem, on the way to Egypt.

4. Sennacherib's Second Invasion of Judah (18:17—19:34)

18:17–19 Hezekiah then began to fortify Jerusalem (2 Chron. 32:5). Perhaps it was news of this that caused **the king of Assyria** at a later date to dispatch his army officials to Jerusalem, demanding unconditional surrender. Three Jewish officials went **out to** meet the Assyrian emissaries and to hear their demands. The NIV renders the terms as "supreme commander," "chief officer," and "field commander." The NKJV labels these officials by their original military titles: **the Tartan, the Rabsaris, and the Rabshakeh**. These terms are not proper names.[21]

18:20–25 The Rabshakeh spoke insultingly **to them . . . in** their own **Hebrew** (lit. "Judean") tongue. First, he mocked Hezekiah's **trust** in the fortifications of Jerusalem. Then he revealed his knowledge that **Hezekiah** had sought the help **of Egypt** against Assyria, and ridiculed **Egypt** as a **broken reed** (v. 21). Third, he said that **Judah** could not **trust in the LORD** because **Hezekiah** had destroyed all the **high places and . . . altars**. **Rabshakeh** did not realize that these were *heathen* shrines and not places where the Lord was worshiped! Next he suggested a bet—he would **give . . . two thousand horses** to Judah if Hezekiah could find that number of horsemen. Judah did not have that many cavalrymen, he taunted, and so had to depend on **Egypt for chariots and horsemen**. Finally, **the Rabshakeh** claimed that **the LORD** had sent Assyria to **destroy** Judah.

18:26, 27 The Jewish officials quickly suggested **to the Rabshakeh** that all further discussions be carried on **in Aramaic**, the language of diplomacy, rather than **in Hebrew**. They were secretly fearful that such arrogant talk might be destructive to the morale of **the** Jewish **people** listening **on the wall**. But the Rabshakeh countered that he wanted the people to hear and understand their coming starvation and doom.

18:28–37 Addressing the people directly, **the Rabshakeh** warned them **not** to **let Hezekiah deceive** them into trusting **in the LORD** for deliverance. If they would surrender, they would be granted the privilege of living in Jerusalem temporarily. Then when **the king of Assyria** returned from the Egyptian campaign, he would **take** them to Assyria, **"a land like your own."** No other tribal deities had been able to deliver nations **from . . . Assyria**; how could they expect their God to do it? **The people** on the wall remained silent while the three Jewish officials returned **to Hezekiah**, thoroughly disheartened.

19:1–7 **Hezekiah** was greatly distressed when he heard of the Rabshakeh's taunt. **He sent** messengers **to Isaiah the prophet**, saying that Judah was powerless when it needed strength the most. Further, he asked Isaiah to pray **for the remnant** of Judah and Jerusalem. **Isaiah** sent word back to Hezekiah that he didn't need to fear **the Assyrian king**, that God would put **a spirit** of fear **upon him** and cause him to **hear a rumor and** to **return to his own land**, where he would be slain.

19:8–13 When the **Rabshakeh returned to** Lachish, he **found** that Sennacherib had transferred his assault to the neighboring fortress of **Libnah**.

Sennacherib **heard** that **Tirhakah, king of Ethiopia** in upper (i.e., southern) Egypt, was advancing to attack him. He immediately tried to frighten Jerusalem into quick surrender by sending a blasphemous letter. Some scholars think that the rumor mentioned in verse 7 is explained in verse 9—namely, the rumor of the approach of the Egyptians. Others say that it was a report that the Babylonians were rebelling.

19:14–20 **Hezekiah** wisely took **the letter . . . to the** temple and **spread it before the** LORD. His prayer was a revelation of his deep trust in Jehovah. In reply, God sent **Hezekiah** a twofold answer by way of **Isaiah**.

19:21–28 Verses 21–28 are addressed to Sennacherib. Verses 29–34 are addressed to Hezekiah. The prophecy of **Isaiah** is a taunt song **against . . . Assyria**. It pictures Jerusalem, **the virgin, the daughter of Zion**, as laughing at Assyria's threats. It denounces Sennacherib for blaspheming God's holy name, and for boasting that he would invade Judah (**Lebanon**), destroy her rulers and great men (**tall cedars and . . . cypress trees**), and enter the palaces of Mount Zion (lodging place and **forest**). Sennacherib also boasted of other foreign conquests, including his victory over Egypt. What he didn't realize was that all he had done was what God had already determined to be done. God knew him inside and out and would break his towering arrogance, sending back to Assyria the remnants of his shattered army.

19:29–34 Then, turning to Hezekiah, the Lord gave **a sign** that the Assyrian would not conquer Jerusalem. For two years the people of Judah would not be able to raise normal crops because of the Assyrian presence, but would **eat** things that grew without cultivation. Then, **in the third year**, they would be safe enough from the threat of assault that they could carry on their normal activities. Not only would the people of Jerusalem survive, but **the king of Assyria** would not even be allowed to **come into the city** or to **shoot an arrow there**.

5. Sennacherib's Defeat and Death (19:35–37)

That **night . . . the angel of the Lord**[22] visited the encampment of Assyria **and killed . . . one hundred and eighty-five thousand** soldiers. **When** men **arose early in the morning, the Assyrians** were **corpses**.

Sennacherib returned to his capital, **Nineveh**, where he was slain twenty years later (681 B.C.). (He actually outlived Hezekiah by five years.) Isaiah's prophecy (v. 7) was fulfilled when **two** of Sennacherib's own **sons** murdered him and a third, **Esarhaddon, reigned in his place**.

6. Hezekiah's Sickness and Recovery (20:1–11)

20:1–7 The events of chapter 20 are generally believed to have taken place earlier, probably in the early part of chapter 18, during the first invasion of Sennacherib (see v. 6). When **Hezekiah was** taken seriously ill, **Isaiah** told him to **set** his **house in order** because death was imminent. The king **prayed** earnestly for recovery and was granted **fifteen** additional **years** of life. Whitcomb comments:

What would I do with the remainder of my life if God told me that I had

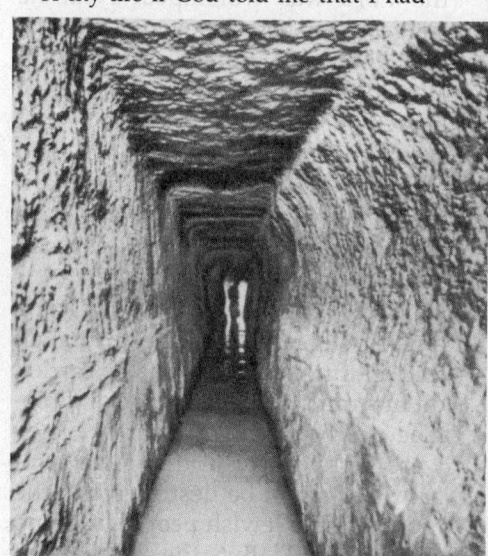

Hezekiah's Tunnel was dug through solid rock from the Pool of Siloam to Jerusalem in order to insure a supply of water for the city in case of an Assyrian attack.

just 15 years to live? What did Hezekiah do with those years? The Bible does not say, for the last event recorded of his reign was the destruction of Sennacherib's army, in 701 B.C. (which probably occurred less than a year after his sickness). It has been suggested that one reason why God prolonged his life was that he had no male heir to the throne (2 Kings 21:1 states that Manasseh was only twelve when he began to reign). However, it is probable that Manasseh was a coregent with his father for nearly ten years, because otherwise it would be impossible to fit the 55 years of his reign into this period of Judah's history, working back from the fixed dates of the Babylonian Captivity.[23]

20:8–11 As a **sign** that Hezekiah would be healed and would return to the temple to worship, God caused **the shadow . . . on the sundial** (or steps, NASB) **of Ahaz** to go back **ten degrees**. (Chronologically, verse 7 follows verses 8–11.)

From 2 Chronicles 32:31 we conclude

that it was a supernatural event, the news of which reached as far as Babylon. The Babylonians worshiped the heavenly bodies and they would certainly notice any irregularities. Word spread quickly that it was on Hezekiah's behalf that this great miracle had taken place.

7. Hezekiah's Foolish Pride (20:12–21)

20:12–18 The **king of Babylon, Berodach-Baladan**, sent congratulations **to Hezekiah** on his recovery. Doubtless his real purpose was to strengthen his ties with Judah against Assyria. **Hezekiah** foolishly **showed** the messengers from Babylon **all . . . his treasures**. (From 2 Chron. 32:31 we learn that God was testing him through this situation to know what was in his heart. The answer: PRIDE!) **Isaiah** rebuked him for this and prophesied that Judah would be taken into captivity by **Babylon** and that **some** of Hezekiah's own **sons** would **be eunuchs** (officials, NASB) **in the palace of the** Babylonian **king**. Before these treasures ended up in Babylon,

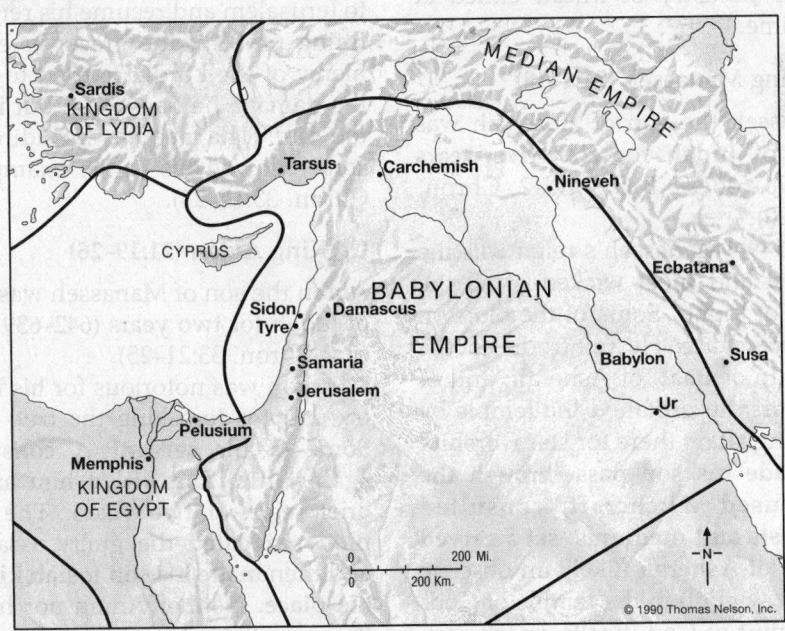

The Babylonian Empire, c. 560 B.C.

many of them would first go to Assyria as part of the tribute that Hezekiah paid to Sennacherib when the Assyrians invaded Palestine shortly after Hezekiah's recovery (18:13–16).

20:19 **Hezekiah** submitted to God's decree and acknowledged its leniency. "For he said, 'Why not, if there will be peace and security in my days?'" (RSV).

20:20, 21 Hezekiah built **a pool and a tunnel** by which **water** could be **brought . . . into** Jerusalem from a well outside the city. Such a hidden source would be especially valuable in a time of siege. It is still possible to wade through Hezekiah's tunnel from the Spring of Gihon to the Pool of Siloam.

In 1880 an inscription made by Hezekiah's workers in the ancient prong-shaped Semitic script was found. It was removed to a museum in Turkey, which was then ruling Palestine as part of the old Ottoman Empire.[24]

The ministry of Micah ended at this time.

B. King Manasseh (21:1–18)

Manasseh the son of Hezekiah was **king** of **Judah** for **fifty-five years** (697/96–643/42 B.C.; cf. 2 Chron. 33:1–20).

21:1–9 Manasseh's reign was the longest and most wicked of all the kings of Judah. Some of the blots on his record are: He reintroduced the worship of **Baal**, of Asherah, and of the stars; he profaned the temple by building **altars** there for star worship; **he made his son pass through the fire; used witchcraft; consulted spiritists and mediums; set a carved image of Asherah** (likely an obscene sexual symbol) in the temple of God. The Spirit of God dwells on the seriousness of this act by rehearsing God's

promise to His people in connection with the temple (1 Kgs. 8:29; 9:3).

21:10–15 **Manasseh** led the people into worse **abominations . . . than** those of **the Amorites.** As a result, God said that He would punish **Judah** as He punished **Samaria** and **the house of Ahab. The measuring line . . . and the plummet** (v. 13) symbolize judgment. Also, He would empty **Jerusalem . . . as** a man empties **a dish** by **turning it upside down** and wiping it out. His people would be led away into captivity because they had provoked the Lord so grievously.

21:16–18 In addition to his idolatry, **Manasseh shed very much innocent blood.** According to "*The Assumption of Isaiah,*" a noncanonical book, Manasseh had the prophet Isaiah sawn in two (cf. Heb. 11:37).

From 2 Chronicles 33 we learn that Manasseh was taken into captivity in Babylon by the king of Assyria (Ashurbanipal). There, while in prison, he repented and turned to the Lord. After this he was permitted to return to Jerusalem and resume his reign—a fitting proof of the grace, love, and mercy of the Lord. He tried to undo the damage he had done, but it was too late. The people, including his son, followed his earlier example (2 Chron. 33:14–23).

C. King Amon (21:19–26)

Amon the son of Manasseh was **king** of Judah for **two years** (642–639 B.C.; cf. 2 Chron. 33:21–25).

Amon was notorious for his idolatry and for forsaking the true **God.** Some of his **servants . . . conspired against him and killed** him after a brief reign of **two years. The people . . . executed** the guilty assassins and then **made his son Josiah king in his place.** Neither Amon nor his father was **buried** in the tombs of the kings of Judah.

D. King Josiah (22:1—23:30)

Josiah the son of Amon was **king** of **Judah** for **thirty-one years** (641–609 B.C.; cf. 2 Chron. 34—35).

1. Josiah's Repairs of the Temple (22:1–7)

Zephaniah (Zeph. 1:1) and Jeremiah (Jer. 25:3) began their prophetic ministries at about this time. Habakkuk may have ministered toward the end of Josiah's time. Josiah's reign was the last era of reform in the kingdom of Judah. He took resolute action against idolatry and encouraged the people to return to the Lord. **In the eighteenth year of** his reign, when he was twenty-six, he instituted a program for the **repair** of the temple. **Money** that had been collected at the temple was turned over to workmen for labor and materials. Because of their honesty, **no accounting** was asked for **the money** which was turned over to them.

2. Josiah's Recovery of the Book of the Law (22:8–20)

22:8–10 While the repairs were going on, **Hilkiah the high priest . . . found** a copy of **the Book of the Law**, perhaps the entire Pentateuch or the book of Deuteronomy. This was taken to King Josiah and **read . . . before** him.

22:11–13 **When the king heard the** Word of God and realized how far the nation had wandered from Him, **he tore his clothes** in penitence. Then he sent five of his officials to **inquire of the** LORD, realizing that **the wrath of** God must be hovering over Judah for its sins.

22:14–20 The officials **went to Huldah, a prophetess** who **dwelt in Jerusalem in the Second Quarter**, a district or suburb of the city. They did not go directly to either Jeremiah or Zephaniah. Huldah was probably Jeremiah's aunt (v. 14; cf. Jer. 32:7). She confirmed Josiah's fears that God was going to punish **Judah** soon because of the corruption of the people. But she added that it would not happen during Josiah's lifetime because he had **humbled** himself and was penitent.

The fact that Josiah later died in battle (23:29) does not contradict verse 20. **"You shall be gathered to your grave in peace"** may mean "before the promised catastrophe of the Babylonian captivity." Or it may mean that Josiah would die at **peace** with God (he certainly did not die at peace with man).

3. Josiah's Renewal of the Covenant (23:1–3)

The king now held a holy convocation at the temple and **read the words of the Book of the Covenant** to all the people. Standing **by** the **pillar**, he **made a covenant** to obey all the words of the law. **The people** also entered into **the covenant** with **the** LORD.

4. Josiah's Reforms (23:4–30)

23:4–9 Then follows a list of the many reforms which Josiah undertook. He cleansed **the temple** of **all the articles** used in idolatry, **burned them**, and took the **ashes to Bethel** (to defile the shrine there). He deposed and probably killed **the idolatrous priests**. He took **the wooden image** (Asherah) out of the temple, **burned it**, and scattered the **ashes on the graves of the common people**. **He tore down the ritual booths** of the male cult prostitutes (sodomites) in the temple area, **where the women wove hangings** for the Asherah **image**. He **defiled the high places**. This means that he desecrated them in such a way that they would not be used again. **He brought all the priests** out of **the cities of Judah, where** they had offered to Jehovah on **the high places**. God had designated Jerusalem as the place where these offerings should be made. Josiah barred these **priests** from further service in the temple, but gave them a share of the **unleavened bread**.

23:10–12 **He** desecrated and ruined **Topheth,** the heathen shrine **in the Valley of the Son of Hinnom**, where child sacrifices had been offered **to Molech. He removed the horses ... dedicated to the sun** and **burned the chariots of the sun ... that the kings of Judah had** used in connection with **sun** worship. He destroyed idolatrous **altars** erected by **Ahaz** and **Manasseh**. Manasseh himself had removed these altars after his conversion (2 Chron. 33:15), but they were undoubtedly pressed back into service by idolatrous Amon. Josiah made sure they would never be used again.

23:13, 14 He **defiled the high places** at the southern end of the Mount of Olives (**Mount of Corruption**), dating from the time of **Solomon. He broke** down **the** idolatrous **sacred pillars and cut down the wooden images** (Asherim), and then defiled their locations **with the bones of men**.

23:15–18 He destroyed **the altar that was at Bethel ... and burned the high place**. Then **he took the bones** from nearby **tombs** and **burned them on** the remains of **the altar**. ("Both Israelites and heathen regarded dead men's bones as a perpetual defilement."[25]) All of this was in fulfullment of the prophecy uttered over 300 years previously by the man of God to **Jeroboam**. Josiah is one of the few men in Scripture named before his birth (1 Kgs. 13:2). He was a chosen vessel, foreordained to fulfill the oracle of the unnamed prophet against **the altar ... at Bethel**.

When King Josiah saw the **grave-stone** of **the man of God who** had testified **against the altar of Bethel**, he ordered that **no one** should **move ... the bones of the prophet**. So they were permitted to remain there **with the bones of the** unnamed **prophet who came** out of **Samaria** (cf. 1 Kgs. 13:30, 31).

23:19, 20 The king's reforms even extended into **Samaria**. Apparently he had won control over this area, largely because the power of Assyria was declining. He destroyed **the high places** and **executed the** idolatrous **priests ... on the altars** where they had offered sacrifices. Also, he defiled these places with the ashes of **men's bones**.

23:21–23 On his return to Jerusalem, Josiah reinstituted **the Passover**, according to the Word of the Lord which he had read (see 2 Chron. 35:1–19 for more details). It was the greatest such observance **since the days of the judges**. Other Passovers had been larger and more elaborate, but this one was particularly pleasing to **the LORD**. Scripture makes mention of only three Passovers during the kingdom years: Solomon's (2 Chron. 8), Hezekiah's (2 Chron. 30), and Josiah's.

23:24 **Josiah** also cleansed the land of **those who consulted mediums and spiritists,** fortune-tellers, and other wizards.

23:25–27 As to the thoroughness of his reforms, he was the greatest of the kings of Judah. Hezekiah held the same honor as far as trust in God was concerned (18:5, 6). Yet in spite of Josiah's good reign, **the LORD did not** change His plan to punish **Judah** by sending the people into captivity and by destroying Jerusalem.

23:28–30 In 609 B.C. **Pharaoh Necho . . . of Egypt** marched north along the coast of Palestine **to . . . aid the Assyrians in their struggle against Babylon.** For political reasons **Josiah** decided to resist Necho's advance and as a result was mortally wounded at **Megiddo. His servants** transported him **to Jerusalem**, where he died and was **buried** (cf. 2 Chron. 35:20–24). **Necho** advanced **to the River Euphrates**, where four years later the Babylonians defeated him in the battle of Carchemish (Jer. 46:2).

E. King Jehoahaz (23:31–33)

Jehoahaz (also called Shallum) the son of Josiah was **king** of Judah for only **three months** (609 B.C.; cf. 2 Chron. 36:1–4).

Jehoahaz disregarded his father's reforms and allowed the people to return to idolatry. **Pharaoh Necho**, king of Egypt, summoned him to **Riblah**, in **Hamath**, a region of Syria where the Egyptians had encamped, and there he put Judah under **tribute**. Later he carried Jehoahaz off to Egypt, where he died (Jer. 22:11, 12).

F. King Jehoiakim (23:34—24:7)

Jehoiakim the son of Josiah was **king** of Judah for **eleven years** (609–598 B.C.; cf. 2 Chron. 36:5–8; Jer. 22:18, 19; 26:21–23; 36:9–32).

23:34–37 Pharaoh Necho made Eliakim, Jehoahaz's brother, **king in** Josiah's **place** and **changed** Eliakim's **name to Jehoiakim. Jehoiakim** was the eldest surviving son of Josiah (cf. vv. 31, 36), but the people had originally placed **Jehoahaz** on the throne instead. **Necho** reversed this and appointed **Jehoiakim** as a vassal king. He was more faithful **to Pharaoh** than he was to Jehovah.

24:1–4 Egypt was defeated by **Babylon** at Carchemish in 605 B.C.,

and Judah came under the control of the Babylonians.

Jehoiakim put Urijah the prophet to death (Jer. 26:23) and burned the Word of God which Jeremiah had written concerning Judah and Israel (Jer. 36:23). He tried to arrest Jeremiah and also Baruch, his scribe, but the Lord hid them (Jer. 36:26). In the third year of Jehoiakim's reign, **Nebuchadnezzar . . . came** against Jerusalem (v. 1), carried some of the inhabitants (including Daniel) to Babylon, and also took some of the vessels from the temple (2 Chron. 36:7; Dan. 1:1, 2). He also bound Jehoiakim in chains to bring him to Babylon. Either he changed his mind or returned the king of Judah to Jerusalem because Jehoiakim subsequently rebelled against the Babylonians (24:1). Whitcomb describes the situation as follows:

> The Chronicler says that Nebuchadnezzar "bound him in fetters to carry him to Babylon" (2 Chron. 36:6); but before the plan was fulfilled something of urgent importance happened that caused Nebuchadnezzar to change his mind. He received word that his father Nabopolassar had died in Babylon on August 15. Realizing that the throne was now in jeopardy, he forced Jehoiakim to promise loyalty as a vassal, then took the short route across the Arabian desert to Babylon.[26]

God sent invasion armies from four nations against **Judah** because of Manasseh's **sins**.

24:5–7 The Lord decreed that the king would have the burial of a donkey—that is, his body would be drawn outside the city and left exposed to the elements and to the creatures of prey (Jer. 22:19). No details of his death are given.

G. King Jehoiachin (24:8–16)

Jehoiachin, also called Jeconiah and Coniah, son of Jehoiakim, was **king** of Judah for **three months** (598–597 B.C.; cf. 25:27–30; 2 Chron. 36:9, 10).

During the short reign of this wicked king, **Nebuchadnezzar . . . besieged** the city of **Jerusalem** and **carried** away a second group of **captives.** Ezekiel was taken to Babylon in this deportation. Also included were the royal family, 7000 soldiers, and the trained **crafts-men.** In fact, only **the poorest people of the land** were left. **Nebuchadnezzar** also took **treasures** from the temple and from **the king's** palace. Verse 14 says that there were **ten thousand captives** in all. Jeremiah says that 4600 captives were taken (Jer. 52:28–30). The number in Kings may include captives taken on other occasions as well. After Jehoiachin had been in captivity for thirty-seven years, Evil-Merodach, the king of Babylon, freed him from prison, set him above the other captive kings, gave him a position of honor in the court, and provided liberally for him (25:27–30).

The prophet Ezekiel began his ministry at this period.

H. King Zedekiah (24:17—25:7)

Zedekiah, Jehoiachin's uncle, was **king** of Judah for **eleven years** (597–586 B.C.; cf. 2 Chron. 36:11–21; Jer. 52:1–30).

24:17–20 The king of Babylon appointed **Mattaniah,** an **uncle** of Jehoiachin, as **king in his place.** The king of Babylon **changed** Mattaniah's **name to Zedekiah.** Zedekiah made a treaty with Nebuchadnezzar, agreeing to serve as his puppet. But then he broke the agreement, **rebelled against the king of Babylon,** and sought the help of Egypt. Zedekiah's treachery in breaking his oath and God's subsequent judgment upon him

are recorded in Ezekiel 17:11–21.

25:1–7 Zedekiah's intrigue with Egypt brought the final blow on the city of **Jerusalem. Nebuchadnezzar . . . besieged** it for eighteen months, causing severe **famine** conditions within the walls. **Zedekiah** and his **men of war** tried to escape from the city **at night** and to flee to the wilderness near the Dead Sea. **The Chaldeans** captured **the king** and **brought him . . . to** Nebuchadnezzar **at Riblah** (in Hamath of Syria). After slaying his **sons . . . before his eyes,** the king of Babylon ordered that his **eyes** should be **put out** and that he should be carried in **bronze fetters to Babylon.** This fulfilled two remarkable prophecies: Jeremiah had predicted that Zedekiah would see the king of Babylon face to face (Jer. 32:4; 34:3). This was fulfilled **at Riblah.** Ezekiel had also prophesied that he would be brought to Babylon but would not see it and would die there (Ezek. 12:13). Zedekiah's **eyes** were **put out** before he ever got **to Babylon.** He died in Babylon.

I. The Fall of Jerusalem (25:8–21)

25:8–12 The final destruction of Jerusalem took place in 586 B.C. by **Nebuzaradan, captain of the** Babylonian **guard. He burned the** temple, the royal palace, and all the great buildings. He **broke down the walls** and **carried** into exile all but the poorest people **of the land.**

25:13–17 These verses describe the wholesale looting of the temple treasures. Those things which were too big to be carried away were cut up into smaller **pieces. The bronze** which was seized **was beyond measure.** In addition, **the Chaldeans . . . took** all **the solid gold and solid silver** they could find.

25:18–21 Nebuzaradan . . . took

about seventy-two of the leading citizens of Jerusalem to King Nebuchadnezzar in **Riblah**, where they were summarily executed.[27]

J. Gedaliah's Governorship (25:22–26)

The king of Babylon appointed **Gedaliah** to be **governor over the people** remaining in . . . **Judah. When** four army **captains . . . heard** this, **they came to** him **at Mizpah**, perhaps to recommend that the people flee to Egypt. **Gedaliah** counseled them to submit to the Babylonian yoke and that all would **be well**. Later **Ishmael**, a member **of the royal family**, attacked **and killed Gedaliah** and his associates. The people were thus left without organized government and fled **to Egypt**.

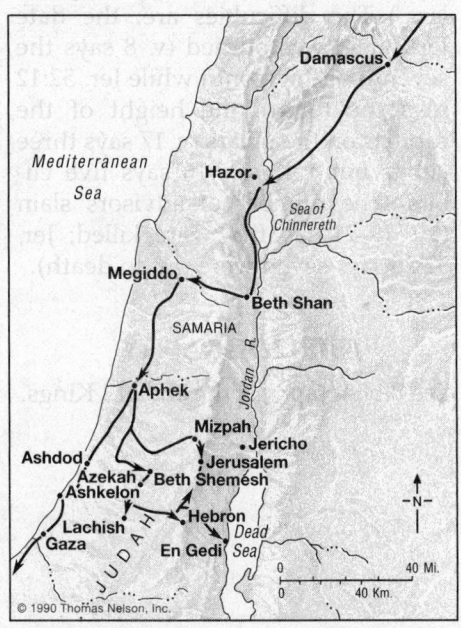

Nebuchadnezzar's Campaigns Against Judah. From 605 to 586 B.C. Judah suffered repeated Babylonian invasions. The final blow came from the southern approach to Jerusalem.

K. King Jehoiachin (25:27–30)

The book closes on an encouraging note. Second Kings and Jeremiah have identical endings (cf. 25:27–30; Jer. 52:31–34). In his **thirty-seventh year** of exile, **Jehoiachin** was afforded honorable treatment **by the king of Babylon**. This gave hope that the rigors of the exile would be eased and later ended completely.

First Kings opens with David's death and 2 Kings closes with Judah's destruction. The nation had failed under Moses, had failed under the judges, and now had failed under the kings. The people refused to listen to God's Word. They refused to be moved by the tears of the prophets. They hardened their hearts and stiffened their necks until God appointed the Assyrians and the Babylonians to teach them that the wages of sin is death. The captivity served its purpose well: it purged the heart of God's chosen people of idolatry.

ENDNOTES

[1](1:2) John C. Whitcomb, Jr., *Solomon to the Exile*, p. 64. *Baal-zebul* is translated "exalted Baal" by many scholars.

[2](2:7–9) George Williams, *The Student's Commentary on the Holy Scriptures*, p. 200.

[3](3:4–9) See *Unger's Bible Dictionary*, pp. 217, 226, 227.

[4](3:26, 27) Harold Stigers, "II Kings," in *The Wycliffe Bible Commentary*, p. 344.

[5](5:1–4) D. L. Moody, *Notes from My Bible*, p. 58.

[6](5:13, 14) *Ibid*.

[7](6:24–31) Some take this to be literal bird excrement, but used for fuel.

[8](7:1, 2) Moody, *Notes*, p. 58.

[9](7:3–7) Matthew Henry, "2 Kings," in *Matthew Henry's Commentary on the Whole Bible*, II:745, 746.

[10](8:13–15) Williams, *Commentary*, p. 207.

[11](8:13–15) Merrill C. Tenney, *The Zondervan Pictorial Encyclopedia of the Bible*, III:49.

[12](9:30–37) G. Campbell Morgan, *Searchlights from the Word*, p. 209.

[13](10:15–17) *Ibid.*, p. 104.

[14](11:4–11) Williams, *Commentary*, p. 210.

[15](12:1–5) Whitcomb, *Solomon*, p. 103.

[16](12:1–5) Williams, *Commentary*, p. 211.

[17](15:32–38) Flavius Josephus, summarized by Matthew Henry, "2 Kings," *Matthew Henry's Commentary*, II:785.

[18](16:10–16) F. C. Cook, ed., *Barnes' Notes on the Old and New Testaments, I Samuel—Esther*, p. 273.

[19](17:29–34a) Such a mixed religion is called "syncretistic."

[20](17:41) However, Luke 2:36 mentions that the prophetess Anna was "of the tribe of Asher," one of the ten tribes. Apparently some from those tribes did return. Also, James sent his Epistle "to the twelve tribes which are scattered abroad" (1:1), so the ten tribes were not totally "lost" from sight, even in the early Christian era.

[21](18:17–19) By omitting the definite articles, the KJV gives the impression that these are proper names.

[22](19:35–37) He is widely believed to be the pre-incarnate Christ (the NKJV footnote with capitalized *Angel* suggests this view).

[23](20:1–7) Whitcomb, *Solomon*, p. 127.

[24](20:20, 21) The text of the inscription can be found in *Unger's Bible Dictionary*, pp. 481, 482, and in *First and Second Kings*, by Richard I. McNeely, p. 145.

[25](23:15–18) Williams, *Commentary*, p. 221.

[26](24:1–4) Whitcomb, *Solomon*, p. 146.

[27](25:18–21) There are three numerical problems in chapter 25, all of them probably copyists' errors, either here in 2 Kings or else in the corresponding verses in 1 Kings and Jeremiah. The accurate copying of numbers in ancient manuscripts posed special problems. (See 2 Chronicles for more details on this type of problem.) The difficulties are: the date Jerusalem was burned (v. 8 says the seventh of the month while Jer. 52:12 says the tenth); the height of the capitals on the pillars (v. 17 says three cubits but 1 Kgs. 7:16 says five cubits); the number of advisors slain (vv. 19–21 say five were killed; Jer. 52:25 says seven were put to death).

BIBLIOGRAPHY

See Bibliography at the end of 1 Kings.

FIRST CHRONICLES

Introduction

"Chronicles has a character and beauty of its own, and a moral propriety, beyond anything, because it takes up and shows that in the ruin of all else the purpose of God stands fast. That is what we have to comfort ourselves with at this present time. There is a ruined state in Christendom; but God's purposes never fail, and those who have faith settle themselves and find their comfort in the sure standing of the purpose of God."

—William Kelly

I. Unique Place in the Canon

Chronicles, originally one large book, occupies the last position in the Hebrew Bible.[1] The Hebrew title means "Journals," or more literally, "Words of the Days." The title in the Greek translation (LXX) is "Omissions" (*Paralipomena*), an unfortunate and misleading title.[2] Our excellent English title traces back to Jerome's Latin Vulgate.

Since, at first glance, 1 Chronicles seems to repeat 1 and 2 Samuel, and 2 Chronicles seems to cover the same material as 1 and 2 Kings, what unique contribution does Chonicles make? Chronicles shows marked differences from Samuel and Kings. Those books emphasize the *historical* side of things whereas Chronicles emphasizes the *spiritual*. Thus Chronicles concentrates on the reign of David and his successors, and on the temple and its worship. It gives details not previously found concerning the priests, Levites, musicians, singers, and doorkeepers. It elaborates on the transporting of the ark to Jerusalem, on preparation for building the temple, and on re-

forms under some of the good kings of Judah. The northern kingdom is mentioned only in its dealings with David's dynasty. The chronicler even passes over the tragic stories of Amnon, Absalom, and Adonijah, and the faithlessness of Solomon. So the books of Chronicles are by no means an unnecessary repetition. Rather, they are a spiritual interpretation of the history in the preceding books.

The affairs of each king's reign were regularly recorded in a book (1 Kgs. 14:29; 15:7; etc.). No doubt it was from this common source that the passages in Samuel and Kings which are identical with those in Chronicles were derived.

Some have criticized Chronicles for not being more complete and well-rounded, for not including important history of the period covered.[3] However, with his usual spiritual perception, William Kelly shows how Chronicles, like all inspired books, reflects just what the Holy Spirit desires:

These collections of testimonies of God that are brought together in the books of Chronicles...are frag-

423

mentary; they are meant to be fragmentary. God could have given a completeness to them if He pleased, but it would have been out of His order. God Himself has deigned and been pleased to mark His sense of the ruin of Israel by giving only fragmentary pieces of information here and there. There is nothing really complete. The two books of Chronicles savor of this very principle. This is often a great perplexity to men of learning, because they, looking upon it merely with a natural eye, cannot understand it. They fancy it altogether corrupted. Not so. It was written, advisedly and deliberately so, by the Spirit of God.[4]

Kelly makes a pertinent application of the situation in Israel to the modern divided and chaotic state of professing Christendom:

So, I am persuaded, the provision by the grace of God for His people at this present time looks very feeble, looks very disorderly, to a man with a natural eye; but when you look into it, you will find that it is according to the mind of God, and that the pretension of having all complete would put us out of communion with His mind—would make us content with ourselves instead of feeling with Him for the broken state of His Church.[5]

First and Second Chronicles are not dull history books. They are a priestly interpretation of sacred history from Adam through Israel's return from the Babylonian Captivity. They are written for us believers and apply to our daily life.

II. Authorship

Most commentators suggest Ezra as the author or compiler of Chronicles. The last two verses of 2 Chronicles are the same as the first two of the book of Ezra, and there are many stylistic similarities. The inspired editor drew on a number of contemporary works for his information, as can be seen from the following list of reference works which he mentions:

1. The book of Samuel the seer (1 Chron. 29:29)
2. The book of Nathan the prophet (1 Chron. 29:29)
3. The book of Gad the seer (1 Chron. 29:29)
4. The prophecy of Ahijah the Shilonite (2 Chron. 9:29)
5. The visions of Iddo the seer (2 Chron. 9:29)
6. The book of Shemaiah the prophet (2 Chron. 12:15)
7. The book of Iddo the seer (2 Chron. 12:15)
8. The annals of the prophet Iddo (2 Chron. 13:22)
9. The book of the kings of Israel and Judah (2 Chron. 20:34; 27:7; 32:32)
10. The story of the book of the kings (2 Chron. 24:27)
11. The vision of Isaiah the prophet (2 Chron. 26:22; 32:32)
12. The sayings of Hozai[6] (2 Chron. 33:19)

III. Date

Chronicles was written after the captivity (2 Chron. 36:22, 23). By using the genealogies we can pinpoint the date more closely. The last person in the Davidic genealogy, Anani (1 Chron. 3:24), is eight generations later than King Jehoiachin (also called Jeconiah [v. 17] or Coniah [v. 17, NKJV marg.]). This was about 600 B.C. Allowing an average of twenty-five years per generation, this brings us up to about 400 B.C. at the earliest. Chronicles can scarcely be much *later* than that, either, since a writer as dedicated to David's line as was the Chronicler would have included any later descendants of the king.

Thus we see that Chronicles is one of the last OT books written, near the time of Malachi.

IV. Background and Theme

The late date of Chronicles also helps us understand its emphasis. The monarchy is no more, but the royal lineage is still traced as far as it has gone, in preparation for the Son of David, the Messiah, who was yet to come.

Although the monarchy no longer exists, the temple services are still central to the spiritual life of the nation. W. Graham Scroggie writes:

> Then, again, all that pertains to worship is here emphasised; the Temple and its services, priests, Levites, singers, and the hatefulness of idolatry. It is shown that the troubles of the nation were due to their disregard of the claims of Jehovah, and their prosperity was due to their return to Him. The KINGS are political and royal, but the CHRONICLES are sacred and ecclesiastical.[7]

It is worth noting that both of these themes—the Messiah and worship—are fundamental to present-day believers as well.

Second Chronicles takes up where 1 Chronicles leaves off. In 1 Chronicles 29 David established Solomon as his successor. Second Chronicles traces the Davidic line from Solomon to the return of the Jewish remnant from the Babylonian Captivity. First and Second Kings cover basically the same time period, but the emphasis in Kings is more on Israel, while in Chronicles the emphasis is on Judah, as we noted earlier. The kings of Israel are mentioned only as they relate to the history of Judah. Although much of the material is the same in both books, Chronicles sometimes contains details not found in Kings, Chronicles having been written at a later date and for a different purpose. We will comment on some of the differences between the two books, but it will be impossible to go into depth about all of them. Other books have been written for this purpose.

OUTLINE

Commentary

I. THE GENEALOGIES (Chaps. 1—9)

The first nine chapters of 1 Chronicles contain genealogical tables, or "family trees," as we like to call them. Genealogies were very important to the Jews in seeking to maintain their tribal distinctions. After the confusion of the captivity, it was also important to establish the kingly and priestly lines once more.

There are several instances in these chapters where names differ from the names given in other parts of the Bible. There are different reasons for these apparent inconsistencies. Sometimes a man had more than one name. It should not surprise us that some names changed in spelling over the centuries. After all, there is a whole millennium between some of the genealogies in Genesis and their counterparts here in Chronicles (1400–400 B.C.). Many cases are copyists' errors. A look at the Hebrew language will show just how easily this could have happened. These "discrepancies" do not stumble the serious student, since most did not exist in the original documents and in no way affect any major doctrine of the faith.[8]

A. From Adam to Abraham (1:1–27)

The book of Genesis appears to have been the source of these genealogies. Verses 1–4 go back to Genesis 5 (**Adam** to **Noah**). Verses 5–23 give the descendants of Noah, as recorded in

Genesis 10. From Genesis 11 comes the genealogy of **Abraham** (vv. 24–27).

B. From Abraham to Israel (1:28–54)

Abraham's natural descendants, listed in Genesis 25, are given in verses 28–33. The descendants of Isaac, the son of promise, are dealt with next. Esau, from Genesis 36, is mentioned in verses 35–54, thus clearing the way for the descendants of Jacob (Israel). Chapters 2 through 9 trace the posterity of Israel.

Here in the first chapter the chronicler is narrowing the focus from Adam, the father of the human race, to Jacob, the father of the twelve tribes of Israel. He quickly clears the stage of all but the chosen nation. Here we also have the beginning of the messianic line (cf. Luke 3:34–38).

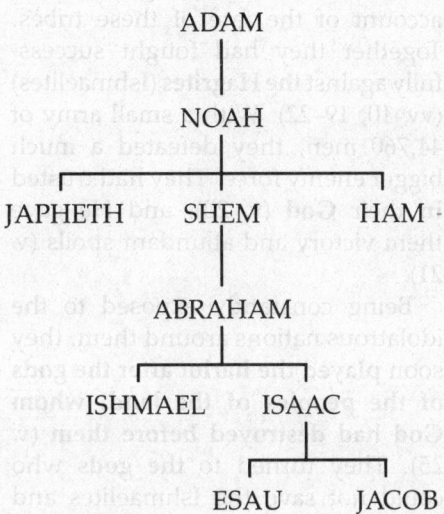

ADAM

NOAH

JAPHETH   SHEM   HAM

ABRAHAM

ISHMAEL   ISAAC

ESAU   JACOB

C. Descendants of Israel (Chaps. 2—8)

1. Judah (2:1—4:23)

Judah was the head of the largest tribe and the foremost in blessing and promise, and thus his genealogy is the first and the longest to be taken up (2:3—4:23). The genealogies of two descendants of **Judah** are devel-

oped more fully—**Caleb**: 2:18–20, 42–55 (this is not the Caleb of Num. 13; see 4:15), and **David**: 3:1–24.

Several historical notes are sprinkled throughout the genealogies. These are things to which the Holy Spirit would draw our attention, points of interest in this panoramic sweep of the history of Israel. In the genealogies of Judah, God's dealings with two wicked men and His blessing of one righteous man are brought to our attention.

"Er, the firstborn of Judah, was wicked in the sight of the LORD, so He killed him" (2:3). He was the offspring of Judah's marriage to **Shua**, a Canaanite woman (Gen. 38:1–10). We are not told what he did, but only that he was evil **in the sight of the LORD**. His wickedness cost him his privileges as the firstborn, his place in the messianic line, and his life. His name became a blot on the family record for all generations to view. Men would do well to ponder the consequences of evil before it is too late. "For evildoers shall be cut off; but those who wait on the LORD, they shall inherit the earth" (Ps. 37:9).

The story of **Achar** (Achan) (2:7) is found in Joshua 7. He "saw," "coveted," and "took" (Josh. 7:21) the things under the ban in Jericho. He troubled **Israel** in that, because of his sin, thirty-six men died in the unsuccessful attack on Ai. He was singled out by the Lord, and he and his family were executed.

"Now Jabez was more honorable than his brothers" (4:9). Here was a man who had a large concept of God and honored Him by seeking His blessing. Jabez was a man of faith, and the Lord took note of it. "But without faith it is impossible to please Him, for he who comes to God must believe that He is, and that He is a rewarder of those who diligently seek Him" (Heb. 11:6). Ironside comments:

His prayer is fourfold. "Bless me indeed." That is, "Give me true happiness." This is only found as one prevails and walks with God. "Enlarge my coast." He was not content to go on only with what he had. He would enter into and enjoy more of the inheritance of the Lord. "That Thine hand may be with me!" He counted on God's protecting care. And lastly, he prayed, "Keep me from evil that it may not make me sorrowful." Sin is the only thing that can rob a child of God of his joy in the Lord.[9]

Jabez sought and was rewarded. May God strengthen us to follow his example!

Bithia (4:18) is one of the few women mentioned in these genealogies. She was a **daughter of Pharaoh** but was now living with the chosen people. Her name means *daughter of Jehovah*.

One apparent discrepancy should be mentioned before we move on. In 2:15 **David** is called **the seventh** son of Jesse while in 1 Samuel 16:10, 11 and 17:12 he is the eighth son. One of Jesse's sons probably died childless or before he married and so is not included by the chronicler.

2. Simeon (4:24—43)

4:24—43 Simeon, Jacob's second born, is taken up next, probably because of the close association of his tribe with Judah. Simeon's portion in the Promised Land was within the territory of Judah (Josh. 19:9). The **cities** listed in 4:28–33 were **their** inheritance. However, later in history they acquired additional land through conquest.

3. Reuben, Gad, and the Half-tribe of Manasseh East of the Jordan (Chap. 5)

Chapter 5 deals with the transjordanian tribes of **Reuben**, **Gad**, and the half-tribe **of Manasseh**. Very little space is devoted to these tribes. They were among the first to go into captivity (5:26).

Verses 1 and 2 explain why the blessing of the **birthright was given to** other tribes instead of to the Reubenites. When Jacob blessed his children before his death (Gen. 49), he took note of Reuben's wickedness (Gen. 35:22) and removed him from having pre-eminence. The double portion of land due the firstborn went to **Joseph** (through Ephraim and Manasseh), and the double portion as far as leadership was concerned went to **Judah**.

The Gadites are listed in verses 11–17, and the leaders of **the half-tribe of Manasseh** are given in verses 23 and 24.

The rest of chapter 5 gives a brief account of the fate of these tribes. Together they had fought successfully against **the Hagrites** (Ishmaelites) (vv. 10, 19–22). With a small army of 44,760 men, they defeated a much bigger enemy force. They had trusted **in** their **God** (v. 20), and He gave them victory and abundant spoils (v. 21).

Being constantly exposed to the idolatrous nations around them, they soon **played the harlot after the gods of the peoples of the land, whom God had destroyed before them** (v. 25). They turned to **the gods** who could not save the Ishmaelites and forsook the one true **God** in whose strength they had conquered. So God gave them into the hand of the Assyrian **king** and they were **carried** away **into captivity**.

4. Levi (Chap. 6)

6:1–53 This chapter takes up the **sons of Levi**, descendants of Jacob's third-born son. Verses 1–15 and 49–53 deal with the most famous family of this tribe, that of **Aaron**. The high priesthood had been given to Aaron and his sons, and thus the importance of an accurate genealogy from **Aaron** to the **captivity**.

Samuel (v. 28) the **son** of **Elkanah** (v. 27) was a great prophet and the last judge in Israel before Saul became king. His ministry is described in 1 Samuel.

Levi had three sons: **Gershom, Kohath, and Merari**. Their genealogies are given in verses 16–30. Verses 31–48 contain three genealogies: **Heman**, a Kohathite (vv. 33–38); **Asaph**, a Gershomite (vv. 39–43); and **Ethan**, a Merarite (vv. 44–47). These were the "songmasters" **whom David appointed** to minister before **the LORD** (vv. 31, 32).

Heman was probably the author of Psalm 88. He was a descendant of the Prophet **Samuel**. There are psalms which bear Asaph's name—e.g., Psalm 50 and Psalms 73—83. **Ethan** may be the author of Psalm 89.

6:54–81 The rest of the chapter is a listing of **the cities** and **commonlands given to** the Levites by the other tribes. This was in accordance with the Lord's command through Moses (Num. 35:1–8). The command was carried out under the supervision of Joshua (Josh. 21).

5. Issachar (7:1–5)

Six tribes are mentioned in chapter 7:

Issachar (vv. 1–5)
Benjamin (vv. 6–12)
Naphtali (v. 13)
Half-tribe of **Manasseh** (west of the Jordan) (vv. 14–19)
Ephraim (vv. 20–29)
Asher (vv. 30–40)

These genealogies are not nearly as complete as those of Judah or Levi,

perhaps because neither the throne nor the priesthood is involved.

6. Benjamin (7:6–12)

Although the tribe of **Benjamin** had at one time been reduced to 600 men because of their folly (Judg. 20), they seem to have regained their strength and size. Benjamin's descendants are listed again in chapter 8. Here in chapter 7 the emphasis is on Benjamin in relation to the people, whereas in the next chapter it is on Benjamin in relation to Saul and Jerusalem.

7. Naphtali (7:13)

The four sons of Naphtali are called **sons of Bilhah** because she was Naphtali's mother. Further descendants of these four are passed over.[10]

8. Half-tribe of Manasseh West of the Jordan (7:14–19)

Manasseh's descendants living east of the Jordan in Gilead and Bashan were recorded in 5:23, 24. This passage deals with the half of the tribe that settled in Canaan, west of the Jordan.

A descendant of Manasseh who stands out in the genealogy is Zelophehad, who had all daughters. They are named in Joshua 17:3 and remembered because they spoke up for the inheritance that the Lord had promised women in such cases (see Num. 27:1–11). Jewish women had rights at a time when most pagan women had few.

9. Ephraim (7:20–29)

The writer goes into greater depth with the tribe of **Ephraim** in order to trace the lineage of **Joshua**, the most famous Ephraimite of ancient history. Men who do exploits for God are a glory to their families and are lovingly remembered and held forth as examples to succeeding generations.

10. Asher (7:30–40)

The four **sons of Asher** and **their sister Serah** coincide with the listing in Genesis 46:17. Their descendants were **choice men, mighty men of valor, chief leaders**.

11. Benjamin (Chap. 8)

8:1–28 **Benjamin**, Judah, and some of the tribes of Simeon and Levi formed the southern kingdom taken into Babylonian captivity. Most of the Israelites who returned to Judah under Nehemiah were from these tribes; hence the larger space devoted to them in these genealogies.

The Benjamites are discussed here more fully than in 7:6–12. When comparing these two lists, as well as those given in Genesis 46:21 and Numbers 26:38–41, the following principles help us to understand the seeming discrepancies.

1. Some men had more than one name.
2. The spelling of some names changed over the years.
3. Some names are omitted because the men died early or childless.
4. The word translated *son* (*ben*) can mean son, grandson, great-grandson, etc.
5. Some names are left out because they don't serve the chronicler's purpose.

8:29–40 **Saul**, a Benjamite, was Israel's first king. His genealogy is given here and in 9:35–44. Only the descendants of his son **Jonathan**, the friend of David, are given here. **Merib-Baal** (v. 34) is another name for Mephibosheth.[11]

The genealogies of Dan and Zebulun are not given. (Dan is also left out

in other portions of Scripture—notably Rev. 7.)

D. Those who Returned from Captivity (9:1–34)

Verses 2–9 mention briefly some of the sons of **Judah** and **Benjamin** who returned to **Jerusalem**, leaders in **their fathers' houses** (v. 9). Verses 10–13 mention **the priests**, while verses 14–34 mention the other **Levites** who returned, describing some of their duties. Another listing of those who returned can be found in Nehemiah 11.

E. The Genealogy of Saul (9:35–44)

The last ten verses of chapter 9, which are virtually the same as 8:29–40, give the lineage of **Saul** and set the stage for the historical part of 1 Chronicles (chaps. 10—29). Saul's history is recorded in 1 Samuel 9—31.

II. THE DEATH OF SAUL (Chap. 10)

10:1–5 A parallel account of the death of Saul and his sons is found in 1 Samuel 31:1–13.

C. H. Spurgeon comments on verse 5:

> While we earnestly condemn the self-destruction, we cannot but admire the faithfulness of the armour-bearer—faithful unto death. He would not survive his master. Shall this man live and die for Saul, and shall we betray our royal master, Jesus the Lord?[12]

10:6–10 In connection with Saul's death, several things should be noticed. **"All his house died together"** (v. 6) refers only to those who fought with Saul (1 Sam. 31:6). Saul had other sons not slain by **the Philistines** (vv. 13, 14; 2 Sam. 2:8; 21:1–9). But even these did not finally escape the fate that overtook their father (2 Sam. 21:1–8).

10:11, 12 Upon hearing the news of Saul and his sons, **the valiant men** of **Jabesh Gilead** marched all night to retrieve their **bodies** from **the Philistines** and then **buried their bones** and **fasted seven days**. Earlier Saul had saved their city from Nahash the Ammonite (1 Sam. 11); these **valiant men** did not forget his kindness.

10:13, 14 These verses give two reasons for Saul's death: **He did not keep the word of the LORD** (see 1 Sam. 13 and 15) and **he consulted a medium** (see 1 Sam. 28).

This brief account of Saul clears the way for the history of David, God's choice to rule over His people Israel.

III. THE REIGN OF DAVID (Chaps. 11—29)

A. David's Army (Chaps. 11, 12)

1. David's Valiant Warriors (Chap. 11)

11:1–3 Chronicles does not mention the short and unsuccessful rule of Ishbosheth (2 Sam. 2—4), but moves on to David's coronation **at Hebron** (cf. 2 Sam. 5).

11:4–9 King David's first order of business was to secure a capital for himself. These verses tell how **Jerusalem** was taken (cf. 2 Sam. 5:6–10).

David's nephew, **Joab the son of Zeruiah**, was also commander of his army. He displayed great courage and bravery in the capture of **Jerusalem**. In accordance with David's promise, he was made **chief** of the armies of Israel. Although a valiant warrior, **Joab** was a ruthless man, not named among David's mighty men, perhaps because of his unscrupulous character.

11:10 This list of David's warriors

is put at the beginning of his reign. In 2 Samuel 23 a similar list is placed at the end of his reign. These **mighty men** came to **David** at different times in his career. Some came to him when he was in the cave at Adullam (vv. 15–19). Some came when he was at Ziklag (12:1–22). Some came when David was made king in Hebron (12:23–40).

Following is a list of some of David's "**mighty men**" and a few of their "mighty deeds":

11:11 Jashobeam: He single-handedly defeated **three hundred** men with nothing but a **spear**. God gave him a supernatural victory against Israel's enemies. Valiant men can still do extraordinary things for God when they trust Him and press the battle against the enemy of men's souls.

11:12–14 Eleazar the son of Dodo: Note first of all that **he was "with David."** He was loyal to David and stood with him when all others **fled**. And for what was he risking himself? A **field . . . of barley**! Principle, not property, was at stake. That land belonged by promise to Israel, and **the Philistines** were not to have so much as one foot of it. Today Christians need to realize that they belong to God and must not allow Satan a foothold in their lives, even in a seemingly insignificant area.

11:15–19 The **three . . . men** at **Adullam**: They were with **David** in his extremity and knew the **longing** of his heart. They risked **their lives** to bring him **water from the well of Bethlehem** which would refresh his spirit. It was not for the honor they would receive, since their names are not mentioned, but for the pleasure it would afford David. Where are the men and women today who dwell close enough to the Lord Jesus to know the longings of His heart? Where are the men and women who will **risk** all to refresh His soul by bringing Him **a drink** from some needy mission field? Those who do so will certainly be reckoned among His valiant ones.

11:20, 21 Abishai the brother of Joab was the most honored of the second **three**.[13] Scripture tells us that **Abishai** was a man of unwavering devotion to David. He went with David into Saul's camp (1 Sam. 26), he was with David when he fled Jerusalem during Absalom's revolt (2 Sam. 16), he crushed the revolt of Sheba (2 Sam. 20), he saved David from the giant Ishbi-Benob (2 Sam. 21), and in many other ways he gave faithful service to his king (2 Sam. 10, 18; 1 Chron. 18). Selfless bravery linked with devoted faithfulness will make anyone a valued friend and servant of the King of kings.

11:22–25 Benaiah: His father was a priest (1 Chron. 27:5) and **a valiant man**. He was the head of David's personal bodyguard. A few of his exploits are listed here. Later he took Joab's place as commander of the armies of Israel (1 Kgs. 2:34, 35). In his victories we see a picture of the overcoming life, where the world (the **Egyptian** giant), the flesh (**Moab**), and the devil (the roaring **lion**) are all confronted and conquered.

11:26–47 Although no deeds are recorded in verses 26–47, the names of those who served David heroically are duly mentioned. Some of the names are very interesting. For example:

Zelek the Ammonite (v. 39) and **Ithmah the Moabite** (v. 46): They were by birth enemies of Israel. But here they are found in the service of Israel's king. We all were born enemies of God, but by His grace we too can find a place in the King's army.

Uriah the Hittite (v. 41): He was a member of a people who were supposed to have been exterminated by the Israelites when they conquered the Promised Land (Deut. 7:1, 2). But here he is, a warrior for David. David proved unworthy of his loyalty, ordering Uriah to be murdered so that he could have his wife, Bathsheba (2 Sam. 11).

2. David's Loyal Followers (Chap. 12)

Chapter 11 dealt with those *individuals* who identified themselves with David. This chapter deals primarily with the *tribes*, along with their **captains**, who allied themselves with the king. Every tribe is listed here in chapter 12, from those **who came to David** when he was in hiding (vv. 1–22) to those who **came to . . . Hebron** after Ishbosheth's death (vv. 23–40). "**. . . and all the rest of Israel were of one mind to make David king. . . . for there was joy in Israel**" (v. 38).

Many who were in trouble or distress had previously come to David to find protection (1 Sam. 22:1, 2). But now these men came to serve David and assist him in obtaining the throne which was his by divine decree. Today the kingdom of God needs men and women who are equipped by God (v. 2), trained and swift (v. 8), strong in faith, able to prevail against overwhelming odds and put the enemy to flight (vv. 14, 15), full of the Spirit, and selflessly dedicated to Jesus (v. 32)—people who have an undivided heart (v. 33)!

David rightly questioned **the sons of Benjamin and Judah** (v. 17) because earlier he had been betrayed by some of them (1 Sam. 23).

The historical events referred to in verses 19–22 can be found in 1 Samuel 29 and 30. God prevented **David** from fighting against Israel while he was **with the Philistines**. He also gave him victory over the Amalekites who had raided **Ziklag** and captured his family.

The eastern tribes came in large numbers (v. 37), while those closer to Hebron were represented by smaller forces—e.g., **Judah**, **Simeon**, etc. (vv. 24, 25 ff.).

Now that Israel was united around their divinely appointed king, there was much rejoicing, feasting, and blessing (v. 40). Division and strife, caused by Saul's disobedience, were past. Israel would now find new prosperity under their godly shepherd-king.

B. David Brings the Ark to Jerusalem (Chaps. 13—16)

13:1–8 Chapter 13 records David's first attempt to **bring the ark** to his newly acquired royal city.

The ark had been neglected during the reign **of Saul**. The Philistines had captured it and held it for seven months, then returned it to **Kirjath Jearim**, where it was kept in **the house of Abinadab**, a Levite (1 Sam. 4—7). Now, at David's instigation, **Uzza and Ahio** put **the ark . . . on a new cart** for the trip to Jerusalem. **Shihor in Egypt** probably refers to the Brook of Egypt (Wady el Arish).

13:9–12 When **the oxen stumbled**, **Uzza put out his hand to** steady **the ark**. Immediately **God . . . struck him** dead. The law forbade anyone to touch the ark, even the priests (Num. 4:15). When the Kohathites carried the ark, they placed the poles on their shoulders, but did not come in contact with the ark itself. The **place** was henceforth **called Perez Uzza** (*outburst against Uzza*). **David became angry** and fearful of bringing **the ark** to Jerusalem.

13:13, 14 So **the ark** was taken aside to **the house of Obed-Edom the Gittite**, where it **remained** for **three months**, bringing great blessing to its host.

14:1, 2 After **David** was established as king over all Israel, **Hiram**, **king of Tyre, sent** men and materials **to build** David **a house**. This was the beginning of a long and close friendship that extended into the reign of Solomon.

14:3–7 **David** sinned against the Lord by "multiplying **wives**"; this was expressly forbidden in Deuteronomy 17:17. Chronicles, while recording the violation, does not mention its sinful implication. The first four **children** mentioned in verse 4 were the sons of Bathsheba (1 Chron. 3:5). 2 Samuel 11 records David's illicit affair with her. However, even here we see the grace of God at work, for the names of two of the **children** of this marriage appear in the genealogy of our Lord: **Nathan** (Luke 3:31), ancestor of Mary, and **Solomon** (Matt. 1:6), ancestor of Joseph.

14:8–17 Upon hearing that **David had been** made **king** in **Israel, the Philistines** came up to attack him. **David inquired of God** (v. 10) and won a spectacular victory. The idols, which could not deliver their worshipers from the living God, were carried away (2 Sam. 5:21) and **burned** (v. 12). When **the Philistines** recovered and returned for a second attack, **David inquired again of** the Lord. He didn't assume that God's guidance would be the same. This time God gave victory through a completely different battle-plan.

These victories struck fear into the hearts of neighboring nations. Note the connection between verses 16 and 17: **"So David did as God commanded him . . . Then the fame of David went out into all lands."**

15:1–3 Three months after the tragedy of Perez Uzza (chap. 13), **David . . . prepared** once again **to bring . . . the ark** to his capital, **Jerusalem**. However, this time he first made diligent search in the law and then proceeded accordingly.

A tent, not a house, was **prepared . . . for the ark** at this time because this was the pattern found in the law. The **tent** was probably made in the same fashion as the one used during Israel's Exodus (Ex. 26). However, **the ark** was the only piece of furniture in David's **tent**, the tabernacle and its furnishings being at Gibeon (16:39) until the days of Solomon.

15:4–15 Then David assembled the heads of the Levitical households. The chief **priests, Zadok and Abiathar** (1 Kgs. 4:4), were also **called** for this occasion (v. 11). The ark was now carried by the right men and in the right way, **as Moses had commanded according to the word of the Lord** (v. 15). Hence, this effort met with success (16:1).

15:16–29 The sweet psalmist of Israel also made elaborate arrangements for joyful **music** of praise to accompany the ark. Some sang, some played musical **instruments**. David was leaping and **making music with stringed instruments and harps**, and all were filled **with joy**. There was one sour note in this happy symphony, however. **Michal**, David's wife, was mocking (v. 29; cf. 2 Sam. 6:16 ff.).

16:1–3 As soon as **the ark** was placed in the tent, sacrifices were **offered**. The **burnt offerings** were the highest expression of worship ceremonially possible (cf. Lev. 1). It was wholly consumed by the flames and it ascended in smoke to be enjoyed by **God** alone.

The other sacrifices offered at this time were the **peace offerings**. These were the only Levitical offerings in which everyone had a part. The fat and the kidneys were offered up to the Lord upon the altar, a portion of the remainder went to the priests, and the rest was given to the offerer to be shared with his family and friends before the Lord (cf. Lev. 3). The peace offering pictured communion with the Lord and a sharing of the good things which came from the Lord. Both **peace** and **burnt offerings** were prominent in the observance of festivals and solemn occasions, and certainly this was a festive day for all Israel. Everyone received a helping of meat before he left for home (v. 3).

16:4–7 David next acted to insure that thanksgiving and rejoicing before the Lord would be carried on daily and not be reserved for special occasions (cf. vv. 37–42). **Levites** were appointed **to commemorate, to thank, and to praise the Lord . . . with . . . instruments** and voices.

16:8–22 The psalm recorded on this occasion has two main parts. Verses 8–22 are addressed to **Israel**, and verses 23–34 are addressed to all **the nations**. Verses 35 and 36 close the psalm. It is a composite of Psalms 105:1–15; 96:1–13; 106:1, 47, 48.

In verses 8–22 the Israelites are exhorted to **sing** the Lord's greatness and to **seek** the Lord's **face**. They are to **remember** His *deeds*, **the marvelous works which He has done** in the past, and they are to **remember His** *covenant*, the unconditional promises He made to their fathers.

16:23–34 Widening the perspectives to **all the earth,** the psalmist urges **all** men to speak of the **glory** of **the Lord**. *Fear* is His due as the God of creation. **Glory** is His due as the God of splendor, **strength**, and **majesty**. *Joy* is His due as the God who sustains and **reigns** over His world.

16:35, 36 This closing prayer is almost identical to Psalm 106:47, 48.

16:37–43 David was careful to appoint Levites to carry on the worship of Jehovah before **the ark** in Jerusalem, and also **at Gibeon** where **the tabernacle** and **the altar of burnt offering** were still located. At Jerusalem he **designated** singers, door-keepers, and trumpeters, all under Abiathar. The priesthood of **Zadok** officiated in **Gibeon**. The chief emphasis in this passage is on the musicians. Two different Obed-Edoms are possibly mentioned in verse 38, and there are two different Jeduthuns in verses 38 and 42. . . . Now that the ark was settled in Zion, all **the people** went home and **David returned** to pronounce a blessing on **his house.**

C. David's Desire to Build the Temple and God's Response (Chap. 17)

Chapter 17 is divided into three parts: David's *desire* to build God a house (vv. 1, 2), God's *determination* to build David a house (vv. 3–15), and David's responsive *prayer* (vv. 16–27). Second Samuel 7 is the parallel passage.

17:1–4 David told **Nathan the prophet** that he was unhappy to be living in a luxurious home while **the ark of the covenant** was in a tent. His desire to **build** a house for **the LORD** met with Nathan's hasty approval. But then the Lord corrected **Nathan**: David was **not** the man chosen for this task.

17:5, 6 The ark of God had never been **in a** permanent **house**, but in a **tent**. Neither had God **commanded** that such **a house** be built up to this time. David later revealed to his son, Solomon, a fact not mentioned here: He was disqualified from building

the temple because he had been involved in so much bloodshed and violence (22:7, 8). It was left for his son, "a man of rest" (22:9), to bring the ark of the Lord to its rest.

17:7–15 As God had spoken in grace to the patriarchs in the past, so now He singles out Israel's shepherd-king for unmerited blessing. These unconditional promises are known as the Davidic covenant. Second Samuel 7:12–16 and Psalm 89 also record the covenant. John Walvoord summarizes its provisions:

> The provisions of the Davidic covenant include . . . the following: (1) David is to have a child, yet to be born, who shall succeed him and establish his kingdom. (2) This son (Solomon) shall build the temple instead of David. (3) The throne of his kingdom shall be established forever. (4) The throne will not be taken away from him (Solomon) even though his sins justify chastisement. (5) David's house, throne, and kingdom shall be established forever.[14]

This covenant, like the other unconditional covenants God made, plays an important part in His dealings with mankind. It is mentioned in several other places in Scripture (e.g., Isa. 9; Jer. 23,33; Ezek. 37; Zech. 14). It will find its complete and total fulfillment in the Lord Jesus Christ, to whom belong the throne and the kingdom forever.

17:16–27 Upon hearing these things, **David** went **before the LORD** and poured out his heart in believing prayer. His response to God shows two of David's outstanding traits: humility and trust in the Lord. Verses 16 and 17 inspired the former slave-trader and later preacher of the gospel, John Newton, to write his famous spiritual song, "Amazing Grace." Like

David he saw his own unworthiness and smallness exalted by God's truly amazing grace.[15]

D. David's Victories (Chaps. 18—20)

The events summarized in the next three chapters (18—20) took place historically after David was made king (chap. 12) and before the ark was brought to Jerusalem (chaps. 13—17).

Many of Israel's hostile neighbors were now brought under her sway as had been originally intended by God. Up till then sin and disobedience had kept her in servitude under those she was meant to conquer. Now, tribute was sent from these Gentile nations to Israel in recognition of her superiority and power.

18:1–6 The Philistines, Moabites, Syrians, and Edomites were all defeated because the Lord preserved ["helped," NASB] David wherever he went.

Verse 4 records another failure on David's part to observe the laws concerning the behavior of Israel's kings (Deut. 17:15–17). First he had multiplied wives for himself (14:3), and now he multiplied horses.

18:7–11 Much wealth was subsequently acquired. For example, all kinds of articles of gold, silver, and bronze, taken from Hadadezer's servants, he dedicated... to the LORD, later to be used by Solomon in building the temple.

18:12, 13 The eighteen thousand who were killed by Abishai are attributed to David in the parallel passage in 2 Sam. 8:13. See the commentary there for a resolution of this apparent discrepancy.

18:14–17 David's enemies felt his wrath, but his people enjoyed his righteousness and justice. He was not only a good general but also an efficient administrator. David's officers and officials are listed here as well as in 2 Samuel 8:16–18. God likes to give recognition for service to Him and His leaders.

19:1–4 Nahash had fought against Israel in the days of Saul (1 Samuel 11). Evidently he had also rendered some unrecorded service to David during Saul's reign. Because of this, messengers were sent... to comfort his son, Hanun, after his father's death. But Hanun followed unwise counsel and treated the ambassadors contemptuously.

19:5–7 Fearing reprisal, the people of Ammon hired mercenaries and prepared for war.

19:8–15 Joab along with his brother... Abishai defeated the combined forces of the Ammonites and Syrians. Joab's exhortation in verse 13 inspired the Israelites and showed that he had the proper perspective as he faced the battle.

19:16–19 The Syrians... sent for their relatives beyond the River and planned to avenge their recent loss. David realized the danger, quickly gathered his forces, and took up the offensive. The surprised army, under Shophach, was no match for Israel, and the proud Syrians... became David's servants.

20:1, 2 Joab had been sent against Rabbah (modern-day Amman) by King David while David himself stayed at Jerusalem (2 Sam. 12:1). The siege probably lasted about two years. During this time David became involved with Bathsheba, the wife of Uriah, one of his thirty "mighty men." Second Samuel 12 tells about David's sin and restoration but, true to the form of Chronicles, the sin is not mentioned here. Joab summoned David when the city was ready to fall, and the crown of the defeated monarch was placed on David's head.

20:3 This verse may refer only to the men of war. Since the Hebrew wording is somewhat obscure in this passage, a possible rendering offered by some commentators is that the people were put under forced labor (see notes on 2 Samuel 12).

20:4–8 Three giants were killed in the course of fighting with Israel's constant enemies, **the Philistines**. **Sibbechai killed Sippai . . . at Gezer**, **Elhanan . . . killed Lahmi** (referred to as Goliath in 2 Sam. 21), and **David's** nephew **Jonathan** (son of his **brother . . . Shimea**, or Shammah) struck down a **giant** who had **six . . . fingers . . . on each hand and six . . . toes . . . on each foot**. Matthew Henry applies the verse for us:

> The servants of David, though men of ordinary stature, were too hard for the giants of Gath in every encounter because they had God on their side. . . . We need not fear great men against us while we have the great God for us. What will a finger more on each hand do, or a toe more on each foot, in contest with Omnipotence?[16]

E. The Census and the Plague (Chap. 21)

When this chapter is compared with 2 Samuel 24, it is not at first clear who was behind David's sin of numbering the people. Second Samuel says that the Lord moved David to number Israel because His anger was kindled against the nation. Here we are told that Satan incited the action. Both statements are, of course, true. God allowed Satan to tempt David. God is not the author of evil, but He permits it and causes it to serve His appointed ends.

For the differences between the figures given in this chapter and those given in 2 Samuel 24, see Endnotes.[17]

21:1–7 **Joab** was against the cen-sus from the start and was not very diligent in carrying out the king's orders. **Levi** was not included per-haps because the tribe was dispersed throughout Israel and Judah, and to number the people would have been difficult. **Benjamin** may have been omitted because the census was inter-rupted before reaching that tribe (1 Chron. 27:24). In numbering the peo-ple no ransom was collected, as commanded in Exodus 30:12. David's disobedience and pride brought grave consequences.

21:8–15 Although **David . . . sinned greatly**, he was quick to con-fess and humble himself before the Lord. When given a choice as to the penalty of his wrongdoing, he chose to **fall into the hand of the LORD** because he knew that He is merciful. **Seventy thousand men** were slain before the pestilence was stopped.

To us the punishment may seem severe. All of us have weaknesses and besetting sins. David was gener-ally humble, but in this instance he fell into the ancient sin of the devil, pride. Matthew Henry makes appli-cation for all of us:

> He was proud of the multitude of his people, but divine Justice took a course to make them fewer. Justly is that taken from us, weakened, or embit-tered to us, which we are proud of.[18]

21:16, 17 When **David** raised **his eyes** he saw a terrifying sight: **the angel of the LORD** with **drawn sword** stretched **out over** his beloved **Jeru-salem**. His response was much better than most believers show when caught in some major sin or disobedience. Henry's four-point summary on how David bore his correction may prove helpful to us all, especially those in a place of leadership.

1. He made a very penitent confession of his sin, and prayed earnestly for the pardon of it, *v.* 8. Now he owned that he had sinned, had sinned greatly, had done foolishly, very foolishly; and he entreated that, however he might be corrected for it, the iniquity of it might be done away. 2. He accepted the punishment of his iniquity: "Let thy hand be *on me, and on my father's house, v.* 17. I submit to the rod, only let me be the sufferer, for I am the sinner; mine is the guilty head at which the sword should be pointed." 3. He cast himself upon the mercy of God (though he knew he was angry with him) and did not entertain any hard thoughts of him. However it be, *Let us fall into the hands of the Lord, for his mercies are great, v.* 13. Good men, even when God frowns upon them, think well of him. *Though he slay me, yet will I trust in him.* 4. He expressed a very tender concern for the people, and it went to his heart to see them plagued for his transgression: *These sheep, what have they done?*[19]

21:18–26 Through **Gad**, the Lord directed David to acquire **the threshing floor of Ornan** (Araunah in 2 Sam.), a **Jebusite**, and to build **an altar** there and offer sacrifices. **Ornan** offered the land **to David** as a gift, but the king insisted on paying for it. Verse 24 is an important spiritual principle: Effective sacrifice is always costly. This **threshing floor** later became the site of the temple (2 Chron. 3:1).

21:27–30 It was on Moriah that Abraham offered up Isaac (Gen. 22). Here the plague was stopped, and when **the LORD commanded the angel,** he **returned his sword to its sheath,** as we read in this chapter. Here the temple stood. And we believe that it was on this same ridge, although not on the same spot, that the Lord Jesus died on the cross for the sins of mankind.

The realization that the site of the **threshing floor** was to be the new center of worship may account for David's fear to go to **Gibeon** for guidance.

F. Preparations for the Temple (Chaps. 22—26)

1. Materials, Men, and Motivation (Chap. 22)

22:1–5 **David** recognized that the threshing floor (21:28) was the future site of the temple and of **the altar of burnt offering**. Therefore he began to **make preparations** for construction, though he knew that **Solomon** was the one who would have the privilege of building the temple. **The aliens** mentioned in verse 2 were the Canaanites who remained **in the land** (1 Kgs. 9:20, 21). **Israel** was supposed to have destroyed them, but, having failed to do this, the Jews now subjected them to forced labor.

22:6–13 In a rather formal address **to Solomon**, **David** rehearsed his own desire to **build** the temple, his disqualification because he had been a man of **blood**, and the Lord's promise that his son **Solomon** would **build** the **house** of God. He requested that **the LORD** would **be with** Solomon, giving him **wisdom and understanding**, and urged Solomon to be obedient to **the law of** God.

22:14–16 Finally, David told Solomon about all **the troubles** he had taken to **prepare** materials and **workmen** for the task. He ended with advice that all Christians would do well to heed: "**Arise and begin working, and the LORD be with you.**"

22:17–19 Then the king urged **the leaders of Israel** to cooperate with **Solomon**. Notice that building for God is first a matter of the heart, then of the hands: "**Set your heart . . . and build the sanctuary.**"

2. Divisions and Duties of the Levites (Chaps. 23—26)

23:1-3 Near the end of David's reign, a census was taken of **the Levites from the age of thirty years and above**, the age at which they could begin their active service.

23:4, 5 The **thirty-eight thousand** men were then divided into four general groups: **twenty-four thousand** overseers in the temple, **six thousand . . . officers and judges**, **four thousand . . . gatekeepers**, and **four thousand** musicians and singers to worship continually before **the LORD**. These instructions were divinely inspired and communicated to David through his prophets (2 Chron. 29:25).

23:6-24 In verses 6-23, the Levitical genealogies are given again: **the Gershonites** (vv. 7-11), Kohathites (vv. 12-20) (including **Moses** and **Aaron**, the most famous Levites of all), and Merarites (vv. 21-23).

Certain priestly functions had been committed exclusively to **Aaron . . . and his sons forever** (v. 13). Burning **incense**, ministry to the Lord in the holy place and Holy of Holies (for the high priest alone), and blessing in the name of Jehovah (Num. 6:23-27) were reserved for the priests.

23:25-27 Next the duties of **the Levites** are spelled out. **They** would **no longer carry the tabernacle** and its furniture as they had been commanded by Moses, since the temple would be a permanent house for God. **David**, with his **last words**, lowered the minimum age to **twenty years old and above** because more manpower would be needed in the service of the temple.

23:28-32 The 6000 judges were probably dispersed throughout Israel while the other Levites served in relation to the temple. The 24,000 overseers of the work in the temple were to

attend to the needs of the priests in the duties enumerated in verses 28-32.

24:1-19 In chapter 24 we are told how the priestly and Levitical **divisions** were formed. There were twenty-four households or divisions of priests (vv. 1-19) and twenty-four divisions of Levites (vv. 20-31). Each division was assigned a **schedule** on a rotating basis to minister in the temple, thus giving everyone the opportunity of serving approximately two weeks each year. Zacharias (Luke 1:5) belonged to **the eighth** course, the course of **Abijah** (v. 10).

The households of Aaron's two surviving **sons**, **Eleazar and Ithamar**, comprised the priesthood, **sixteen** divisions belonging to the former and **eight** divisions going to the latter (v. 4). The **lot** was cast in the presence of **David**, the **leaders** of Israel, and **Zadok** and **Ahimelech** the priests; the results were recorded by **Shemaiah . . . the scribe** with meticulous care.

24:20-31 The Levites also cast their lot before David and the princes. The lot apparently determined the division to which each man was assigned.

25:1-7 In chapter 25 other sons of Levi, the singers and musicians, are set in their courses to perform their sacred service. These are **the sons of Asaph** (v. 2), **Jeduthun** (v. 3), and **Heman** (vv. 4, 5). These **two hundred and eighty-eight** men were appointed to sing **in the house of the LORD**, accompanied by **cymbals, stringed instruments, and harps** (vv. 6, 7).

25:8-31 They were assigned to their **twenty-four** courses or shifts by **lot**, as indicated in verses 8-31.

26:1-19 Details concerning **the gatekeepers** and the gates to which they were assigned by **lot** are given next. Here we find **the Korahites** (v. 1), ". . . their duty being to prevent the presumption of which their father was guilty (Num. 16). Such are the ways of God."[20] Here too is **Obed-Edom**, who sheltered the ark, after the death of Uzza (13:14). God had not forgotten his faithfulness.

Verse 18 means that there were **four** gatekeepers or temple guards at a causeway adjoining one of the gates, and **two** more at the other end of the causeway leading to **Parbar**, probably a court or colonnade extending west of the temple.[21]

26:20–28 Some **Levites** were appointed to guard the temple **treasuries, the spoils**, and the freewill offerings that had been **dedicated** to the Lord.

26:29–32 A third group of Levites was set apart **as officials and judges, one thousand seven hundred . . . west . . . of the Jordan** and **two thousand seven hundred** on the east side of the river in **Gilead**.

G. Military and Governmental Leaders (Chap. 27)

27:1–15 The army, like the Levites, served in **divisions. Twenty-four thousand** men were on duty each **month**. All the commanders are listed among David's mighty men (chap. 11 and 2 Sam. 23).

27:16–22 The tribes are listed in a designed order. First listed are the sons of Leah, in their proper order: **the Reubenites, the Simeonites, the Levites, Judah, Issachar**, and **Zebulun**. Then the sons of Rachel: Joseph (represented by his sons **Ephraim** and **Manasseh**) and **Benjamin**. The children of Bilhah are given (but not in chronological order): **Naphtali** and **Dan**. The sons of Zilpah (Gad and Asher) are not named here.

27:23, 24 Those twenty years old **and under** were **not** recorded in the census that David had ordered. The **census** was never completed because

the **wrath** of the Lord fell before **Joab** finished. **David**, perhaps ashamed of his sin, ordered that the result of the ill-fated census should not be put in the public records.

27:25–34 David had twelve officials who had charge of his domestic affairs. He also had counselors and close friends who advised him. Ahithophel's sad story is given in 2 Samuel 15 and 17. He was, like **Joab**, a man of high privilege but low character. How much nobler was **Hushai, the king's companion. Ahithophel** was a self-seeking opportunist, but **Hushai** was a self-effacing servant. Each one reaped what he had sown (see 2 Sam. 15—17). Both served the king, but each had different motives. The opportunist works for his own glory, but the servant for that of his master.

H. David's Last Days (Chaps. 28, 29)

28:1–8 David assembled at Jerusalem **all the leaders** of the various **divisions** and the **officers of the tribes** and **captains**. Once again he explained his desire **to build a house** for **the LORD** and the reasons why he had not been permitted to do so. But he had been chosen and established as **king** in **Israel**, and his **son Solomon** had been **chosen** to succeed him. Since David's **throne** had been firmly established by God, the people were to obey the Lord through **Solomon** as they had through David.

28:9, 10 Next David addressed his son. Verse 9 contains a command, a promise, and a warning. *The command:* **"As for you, my son Solomon, know the God of your father, and serve Him with a loyal heart and with a willing mind."** *The promise:* **"If you seek Him, He will be found by you."** *The warning:* **"But if you forsake Him, He will cast you off forever."** Since **the LORD** had appointed Solomon to build the temple, he should take courage **and do it**.

28:11–19 But, like Moses before him, **Solomon** must build according to the pattern given **by the Spirit**, perhaps in a vision. There was no room for human imagination or ingenuity, because the temple is a type of Christ. **David gave . . . Solomon the plans** he had drawn up under the inspiration of the **Spirit**. He had even weighed the raw materials to be used for each piece of furniture. (More complete details are given in 2 Chron. 2—4.) **The chariot, that is, the gold cherubim** (v. 18), according to Unger, probably means "the cherubim as the chariot upon which God enters or is throned."[22]

28:20, 21 Solomon now had **the plans**; the materials were collected; the temple servants, **the Levites**, had all been assigned their duties. **God** was **with** him and would not fail him; therefore his father urged him again, **"Be strong . . . and do it."**

29:1–9 Although **King David** had **given** so much already to the work of the temple, yet as a final offering and as an example to the people he dedicated more **silver** and **gold** from his private funds and urged **the people** to give liberally. Their generous response brought rejoicing to their own hearts and to the heart of the king.

29:10–19 David then offered a magnificent prayer of worship and thanksgiving. He eulogized the LORD as worthy of all **honor**, **exalted as head over all**, and as the Source of all **riches and honor**. He acknowledged that he and his **people** were unworthy to give to God, and that what they gave had **come from** Him anyway. He prayed that the present devotion (an *upright* **heart**, v. 17) of his people would become a permanent trait (a **heart** *fixed* on God, v. 18), and

that his **son** would have **a loyal heart** (v. 19) in building **the temple**.

29:20–22a When he called on the congregation to **bless the LORD**, they **bowed** low and **prostrated themselves before the LORD and the king. The next day . . . they** sacrificed 3000 animals, and **they ate and drank before the LORD.**

29:22b–25 Solomon was **made . . . king** a **second time** (v. 22; cf. 23:1); then, after David's death, he **sat on the throne**, enjoying the blessing of the Lord and the allegiance of the people. His glorious kingdom prepictures the splendor of Christ's millennial reign over the entire earth.

29:26–30 First Chronicles closes with a brief summary of David's **reign. He died full of days** (he was seventy), **riches, and honor**.

ENDNOTES

[1](Intro) Thus when our Lord speaks of the blood of Abel (Gen. 4:10, 11) to the blood of Zechariah the son of Berechiah (2 Chron. 24:20, 21), He is saying "from Genesis to Malachi" (or Revelation).

[2](Intro) It would seem to imply that the Chronicler filled in what Samuel and Kings neglected.

[3](Intro) If Chronicles paralleled Samuel and Kings even more it would no doubt be criticized as being redundant.

[4](Intro) William Kelly, *Lectures on the Books of Chronicles*, p. 13.

[5](Intro) *Ibid*.

[6](Intro) The Septuagint translates it *seers*, the Hebrew word for *seers* being close to the name *Hozai*.

[7](Intro) W. Graham Scroggie, *Know Your Bible*, Vol. 1, *The Old Testament*, p. 86.

[8](1:Intro) The New King James Version, which text the *Believers Bible*

Commentary comments upon, foot-notes these variations rather fully in most editions, yet the OT editor as well as the executive editor, translators, and review committees, all hold the position of inerrancy of the original text.

[9](2:1—4:23) H. A. Ironside, *The Continual Burnt Offering*, Reading for March 12.

[10](7:13) *Jahziel* and *Shallum* illustrate names that are slightly different from their Genesis spelling (Jahzeel and Shillem in Gen. 46:24; cf. NKJV footnote).

[11](8:29–40) The "bosheth" part of Mephibosheth's name (cf. Ishbosheth) means *"shame."* Rather than say the name of a pagan deity (here, Baal) devout Jews would replace it with this insult to idolatry.

[12](10:1–5) C. H. Spurgeon, *Spurgeon's Devotional Bible*, p. 265.

[13](11:20, 21) The Syriac version reads "thirty" (see NKJV footnote).

[14](17:7–15) John Walvoord, quoted by J. Dwight Pentecost, *Things to Come*, pp. 101, 102.

[15](17:16–27) Samuel Willoughby Duffield, *English Hymns: Their Authors and History*, p. 166.

[16](20:4–8) Matthew Henry, "1 Chronicles," in *Matthew Henry's Commentary on the Whole Bible*, II:887.

[17](21:Intro) The apparent discrepancies in numbers between 2 Samuel 24 and 1 Chronicles 21 can be reconciled as follows:

2 SAMUEL 24	1 CHRONICLES 21
1. *Census figures*	
800,000 valiant men of Israel who drew the sword (v. 9)	1,100,000—all Israel who drew the sword (v. 5)
500,000 men of Judah (v. 9)	470,000 men of Judah who drew the sword (v. 5)
1,300,000 men	1,570,000 men

But note the different classifications: valiant men vs. *all Israel*; men of Judah vs. men of Judah *who drew the sword*. The figures necessarily include different classes.

2. *Years of famine*

seven years (v. 13)	three years (v. 12)

The seven years may include the three-year famine caused by Saul's slaying of the Gibeonites (2 Sam. 21:1). If David chose three additional years, any part of an intervening year would count as a year, and thus the total famine would be seven.

3. *Price paid to Araunah (Ornan)*

50 shekels (v. 24)	600 shekels (v. 25)

The fifty shekels were for the threshing floor and the oxen. The 600 shekels were for "the place of this threshing floor" (v. 22), the larger area of which the threshing floor was only a part.

[18](21:8–15) Henry, "1 Chronicles," II:889.

[19](21:16, 17) *Ibid.*

[20](26:1–19) George Williams, *The Student's Commentary on the Holy Scriptures*, p. 236.

[21](26:1–19) Another theory is that *Parbar* was a suburb of Jerusalem. The term is uncertain in meaning.

[22](28:11–19) Merrill F. Unger, *Unger's Bible Dictionary*, p. 190.

BIBLIOGRAPHY

Henry, Matthew. "1 Chronicles" and "2 Chronicles." In *Matthew Henry's Commentary on the Whole Bible*. Vol. 2. Reprint. McLean, VA: MacDonald Publishing Company, n.d.

Keil, C. F. "The Books of the Chronicles." In *Biblical Commentary on the Old Testament*. Vol. 9. Grand Rapids: Wm. B. Eerdmans Publishing Co., 1971.

Kelly, William. *Lectures on the Books of Chronicles*. Oak Park, IL: Bible Truth Publishers, 1963.

Payne, J. Barton, "I and II Chronicles." In *The Wycliffe Bible Commentary*. Chicago: Moody Press, 1962.

Sailhamer, John. *First and Second Chronicles. Everyman's Bible Commentary*. Chicago: Moody Press, 1983.

Zöckler, Otto. "The Books of the Chronicles." In *Commentary on the Holy Scriptures, Critical, Doctrinal, and Homiletical*. Vol. 4. Reprint (24 vols. in 12). Grand Rapids: Zondervan Publishing House, 1960.

SECOND CHRONICLES

"The Book of 2 Chronicles outlines God's discipline based on His conditional promises. The period of 427 years covers nineteen kings of Judah. Seven were good kings likened to David; ten were bad kings, likened to Israel or Jeroboam; two were good turning to bad, namely Solomon and Joash. Here we see discipline turning into judgment."

—John Heading

For Introduction see 1 Chronicles.

OUTLINE

    Q. King Jehoahaz (36:1–3)

    R. King Jehoiakim (36:4–8)

    S. King Jehoiachin (36:9, 10)

    T. King Zedekiah (36:11–19)

IV. THE BABYLONIAN CAPTIVITY (36:20, 21)

V. THE DECREE OF CYRUS (36:22, 23)

Commentary

The break between 1 and 2 Chronicles was made strictly for convenience, since they were originally one very large book. Thus 2 Chronicles takes up exactly where 1 Chronicles leaves off. The dividing point is well chosen—between David's and Solomon's reigns.

In 1 Chronicles 29 David established Solomon as his successor. Second Chronicles traces the Davidic line from Solomon to the return of the Jewish remnant from the Babylonian Captivity. First and Second Kings cover basically the same time period, but the emphasis in Chronicles is almost entirely on Judah. The kings of Israel are mentioned only as they relate to the history of Judah. Also, the emphasis of Chronicles is *spiritual* while that of Kings is *historical*. Although much of the material is the same in both books, Chronicles sometimes contains details not found in Kings, Chronicles being written at a later date and for a different purpose. We will comment on some of the differences between the two books, but it will be impossible to go into depth about all of them. (Other books have been written for this purpose.)

I. THE KINGDOM OF SOLOMON (Chaps. 1—9)

A. Solomon's Worship, Wisdom, and Wealth (Chap. 1)

1:1–3 First Kings 1—3 tells what went on between the death of David (1 Chron. 29) and the time when **Solomon** was established as king. Adonijah and Joab were killed in a power struggle as Solomon secured his father's throne in accordance with the word of the Lord (1 Chron. 22:9, 10).

With **his kingdom** secured, **Solomon** called together his subordinates and led them in a solemn procession to **Gibeon**, where **the tabernacle** was located.

1:4–6 **David had** moved **the ark** to **Jerusalem** (1 Chron. 13—15), but the rest of the furniture of **the tabernacle** was at Gibeon, including the **bronze altar**. Upon this **altar** . . . **Solomon** . . . **offered a thousand burnt offerings**, a display of his devotion and loyalty to Jehovah, the God of his father.

1:7–12 **God appeared** to him **that** same **night** in a dream and asked him what he most desired (v. 7; 1 Kgs. 3:5). Solomon's request for **wisdom**

and knowledge in ruling the **people** so pleased the Lord that He also promised him unparalleled **riches, wealth, and honor**. In a sense, God appears to every believer and asks him what he wants. What we want in life largely determines what we get.

1:13–17 **Solomon** returned **to Jerusalem** to a reign of great prosperity. These verses dwell on his **chariots, horsemen, chariot cities, silver, gold**, cedar, and **horses**. But his prosperity contained the seeds of his eventual failure, as is often the case.

B. Solomon's Preparation, Construction, and Dedication of the Temple (Chaps. 2—7)

2:1, 2 In preparation for construction of **the temple, Solomon selected seventy thousand men** to carry the materials, plus **eighty thousand** stonecutters and **three thousand six hundred** supervisors.

2:3–10 Then he **sent** for help to **Hiram, king of Tyre**, who had supplied **cedars** for David's royal palace. After

describing the spiritual significance of the project, **Solomon** asked specifically for a skilled craftsman to work with the artisan **whom David** had hired, and also for the necessary **timber**. Solomon promised to pay handsomely for any help given. There seems to be a discrepancy as to the actual amount.[1]

Apparent Discrepancies

In commenting on 2 Chronicles, we must note that there are some seeming discrepancies between this book and the parallel accounts in 1 and 2 Kings. If we overlook these differences, we do a disservice to our readers. On the other hand, if we overemphasize the differences, we run the risk of undermining confidence in the Word, and we certainly do not want to do this. Our solution is this: We have decided to bring the principal differences out into the open, even if we can't solve them all. At the same time we want to make it clear that they in no way affect the inspiration of the Scriptures. We believe that

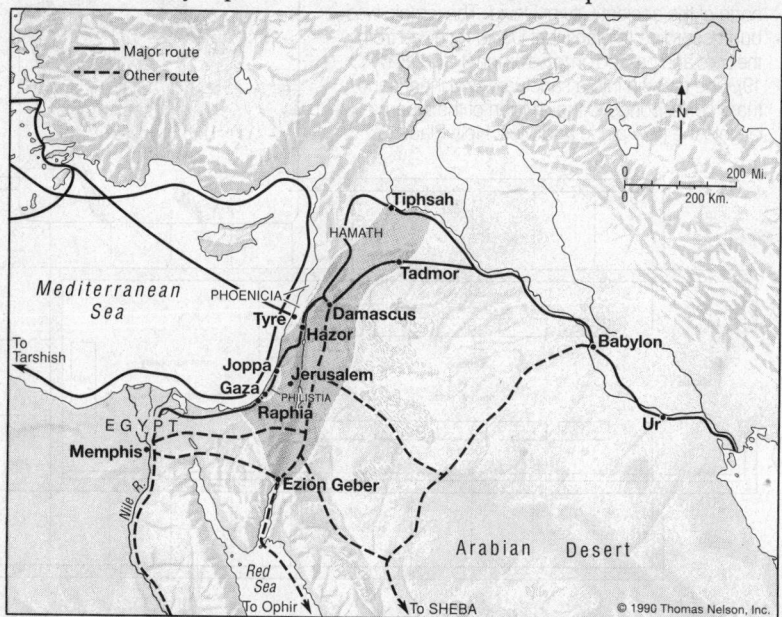

The Spread of Solomon's Fame. Solomon's influence in economic and political affairs was enhanced by the transportation and trade routes that intersected his kingdom.

the Bible, as originally given, is inspired by God, inerrant, and infallible.

We have handled the problems in the Endnotes. In this way the technical discussions of apparently contradictory details will not break up the flow of the commentary. On the other hand, it gives us opportunity to investigate the problems briefly but freely.

Many of the discrepancies are copyists' errors. We should not be surprised if scribes made minor mistakes in copying and recopying the Bible over the course of many centuries. Even today it is almost impossible to publish a book without some typographical errors creeping in.

Someone might ask, "If God could guide the original writers of Scripture to be free from error, why couldn't He cause the scribes to produce error-free copies?" The answer, of course, is that He could have, but in His wisdom He didn't choose to do so.

The important point is that, in spite of minor scribal or copyists' errors (mostly in the spelling of names and in numbers), the Bible as we have it today is the Word of God. Any problems have to do with minor details and not with any Bible doctrine. It is reassuring to remember that when the Lord Jesus was on earth, He used an edition of the OT (not the original manuscripts) and He quoted this text as the Word of God. We can use reputable versions of the Bible today with the same confidence that they are the Word of God.‡

2:11–16   Hiram's reply **in writing, which he sent to Solomon,** seemed to indicate a genuine, spiritual recognition that the undertaking was historic. He said he was sending **Huram,** a **craftsman** with impeccable qualifications.[2] He also promised to send **wood from Lebanon** in exchange for

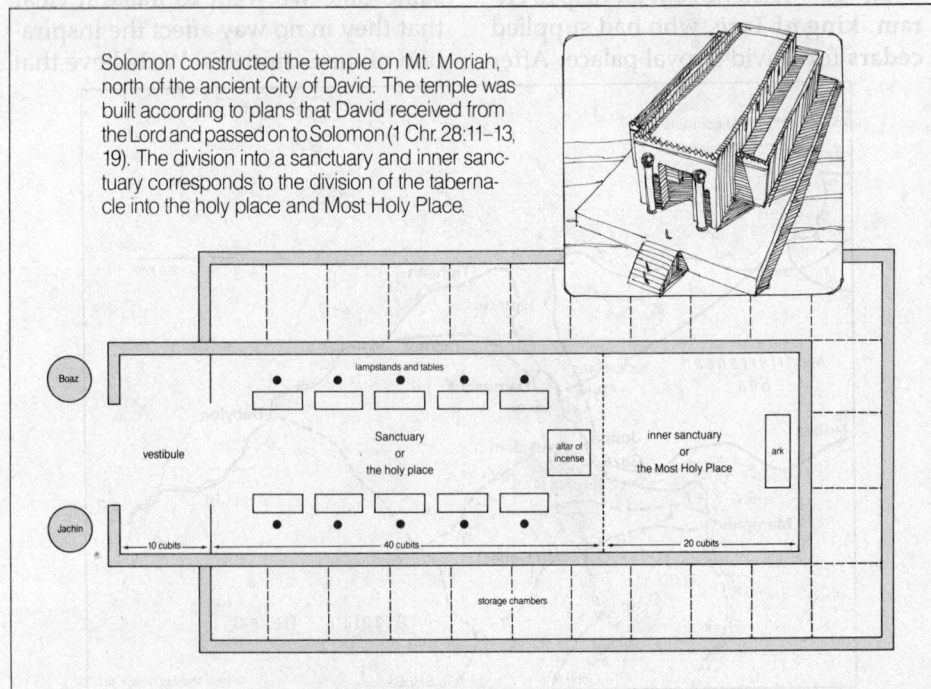

Solomon constructed the temple on Mt. Moriah, north of the ancient City of David. The temple was built according to plans that David received from the Lord and passed on to Solomon (1 Chr. 28:11–13, 19). The division into a sanctuary and inner sanctuary corresponds to the division of the tabernacle into the holy place and Most Holy Place.

Boaz

Jachin

vestibule

Sanctuary
or
the holy place

lampstands and tables

altar of incense

inner sanctuary
or
the Most Holy Place

ark

10 cubits   40 cubits   20 cubits

storage chambers

The Plan of Solomon's Temple

wheat, barley, oil, and . . . wine. The timber would be floated on **rafts** down the Mediterranean Sea **to Joppa**, then transported overland **to Jerusalem**.

2:17, 18 The 153,000 **aliens** or strangers were Canaanites whom the Israelites had failed to destroy. Now they were used as forced laborers.[3]

3:1–4 After much planning and preparation, the construction finally began **in the fourth year of** Solomon's **reign**. With over 150,000 workmen and almost limitless resources, it would still take over seven years to complete this mammoth undertaking.

The foundations were laid **on Mount Moriah**. The temple would be ninety feet long, thirty feet wide, and forty-five feet high (see 1 Kgs. 6, where more details are given). It was roughly twice the size of the tabernacle and had a **vestibule** or porch thirty feet long.[4]

3:5–9 The interior of the temple was divided into two rooms on the main floor. The two rooms were **the larger room** (literally **house**, NKJV marg.) and the **Most Holy Place**. The building was of stone. The interior was **paneled with cypress** wood which was **overlaid with pure gold**, ornamented with various designs, and studded **with precious stones**. All that was visible inside the temple was **gold**, the symbol of deity, picturing the glory of the Lord which was to fill the place.

3:10–13 **Two cherubim** were put into the **Most Holy Place** (in addition to the two cherubim which formed part of the mercy seat atop the ark). Their combined wingspans extended the entire width of the **Most Holy Place**. The ark would later be placed under them (5:7). **Cherubim** are spirit-beings which appear often in Scripture. The walls (v. 7) and the veil (v.

14) were decorated with them, symbolizing their continual waiting on God. The temple and the tabernacle were types of the true dwelling place of God—i.e., heaven, where He is worshiped and glorified day and night by myriad hosts (Heb. 8:5). They were also types of Christ (John 1:14, where "dwelt" is literally "tabernacled"; 2:19).

3:14–17 A **veil** separated the two rooms, just as in the tabernacle. There were also doors (v. 7) between the rooms in the temple. **Two pillars** with capitals and **one hundred** ornamental **pomegranates** were placed in **front of the temple**.[5] The pillar **on the right** side was named **Jachin** (*He shall establish*) and **the one on the left** was called **Boaz** (*in Him is strength*).

4:1–22 The two chief metals used in the temple were **bronze** and **gold**. Chapter 4 briefly lists some of the furnishings made from these metals. **Bronze** was used for the **altar** of burnt offering, **the Sea** and supporting **oxen** (vv. 2–5, 10),[6] **ten lavers** or portable basins (v. 6), overlay for the **doors** of the court (v. 9), various utensils (vv. 11, 14–18), and the **two pillars** and **capitals** (vv. 12, 13). These were all **cast in clay molds between Succoth and Zeredah** (v. 17).

Solomon used **gold** for **ten lampstands** for the holy place (vv. 7, 20), **ten tables** for **the showbread** (vv. 8, 19) a golden **altar** (v. 19), various utensils (vv. 8, 21, 22), and overlay for the holy place and Most Holy Place (v. 22). **Gold** was used primarily for items inside the temple while the **bronze** furnishings were mainly employed outside.

All the furnishings for the temple were made by **Solomon** except the ark of the covenant. That was brought from the tabernacle.

5:1–10 Now the temple **was fin-**

ished (v. 1; cf. 1 Kgs. 8). Verses 2–10 tell about the transporting of the furniture from **the tabernacle of meeting** to the temple. **The ark** was placed in the **Most Holy Place**. Perhaps the other items, like the altar of incense and the table of showbread, were put into the treasury at this time, since they were not used in Solomon's temple.

The Levites who carried **the ark** were **priests** (vv. 4, 7). They set **the ark** in **its place . . . under the wings of the** guarding **cherubim** (vv. 7, 8). Exodus 25:15 required that **the poles** stay with the ark. ("Drew out," v. 9 KJV, is inaccurate.) According to 1 Kings 8:8, **the ends of the poles of the ark could be seen from** the holy place. **The two tablets** of the law were **in the ark** at this time.

5:11–14 Verse 11b, "**all the priests . . . without keeping to their divisions,**" means that **all the priests . . . present** that day participated, not just the course that was assigned the duty.

When **the Levites** and **priests** assembled **at the east end of the altar, praising and thanking the** LORD for His goodness and **mercy, the glory of the** LORD **filled** the temple **so that the priests could not** minister inside.

6:1–11 Before addressing the Lord in his prayer of dedication, Solomon reminded the people how, in Israel's earlier history, the Lord had not **chosen** a **city** as the religious capital or a **man** as **ruler**. (It is true that Samuel and others were leaders, but they did not have the power of a sovereign.) But the time came when God chose **Jerusalem** as His city and **David** as king **over . . . Israel**. **David** desired **to build a temple, but** his good intention was to be carried out by one of his sons. And now here stood **Solomon**, a testimony to the faithfulness of God.

6:12, 13 The central part of chapter 6 is Solomon's prayer of dedication (vv. 12–42). It is the longest prayer recorded in the Bible and is full of praise and petition. Ascending a special **platform** in the temple court, **Solomon . . . spread out his hands** and prayed. He had much for which *to be thankful*. Emboldened by grace, he had much for which *to ask*.

6:14–17 First of all Solomon prayed about **the throne of Israel**. God had **kept** His word thus far concerning His promises to **David**. The king asked that His faithfulness might continue.

6:18–21 These four sentences contain the sum and substance of the entire prayer. All that follows is an expansion of the simple thought expressed by the verbs **hear** and **forgive** (v. 21).

6:22, 23 Next Solomon requests the Lord to **hear . . . and judge** oaths taken **before** His **altar**.

6:24, 25 Then he asks forgiveness for **sin** that might cause **Israel** to be **defeated** by her enemies.

6:26, 27 He requests **rain** after drought caused by **sin**.

6:28–31 He requests deliverance from **famine** or **pestilence** in order that the **people** might learn the **fear** of the Lord.

6:32, 33 He requests that foreigners may see God work when they come to call on His great Name.

6:34, 35 He requests victory in **battle**.

6:36–39 He requests deliverance from **captivity** once the people **repent** and confess their wickedness.

6:40–42 Solomon closed by requesting three things. He asked that his **prayer** might be accepted. He asked for grace and joy for the **priests**, those who serve God in His temple. He prayed for favor for himself based on God's great love for his father **David**.

Lest we think that this prayer consists of petitions only, let us go back through it once more. There is a great deal about the attributes of God here. Solomon mentioned God's: uniqueness (v. 14); lovingkindness (v. 14); transcendence (v. 18); immensity (infinity) (v. 18); omnipresence (v. 18); justice (v. 23); forgiveness (vv. 25, 27, etc.); omniscience (v. 30); grace (v. 33); and mercy (vv. 38, 39).

Besides all these, the Lord's omnipotence and holiness are implied throughout.

7:1–7 As soon as **Solomon had finished praying, fire came down from heaven and consumed the burnt offering** and **the sacrifices, and the glory of the LORD filled the temple**. The people **saw . . . the glory** cloud coming **down . . . on the temple**, and **they bowed . . . on the pavement**, worshiping and praising **the LORD. Solomon** then led **the people** in offering thousands of **bulls** and **sheep** as sacrifices to **the LORD**.

The priests took their positions, **the Levites** played the Lord's musical **instruments, which King David had made** for praising **the Lord. Opposite** the Levites, **the priests sounded their trumpets, while all** the Israelites **stood**.

The bronze altar was too small for the enormous number of sacrifices and **offerings**.

7:8–10 The dedication **feast** lasted for **seven days**, including the Day of Atonement. This was followed by the Feast of Tabernacles, after which Solomon dismissed **the people**.

7:11–16 After **Solomon** had **finished** the temple and his own palace, **the LORD appeared to** him at **night** with promises and warnings. In the event that God sent drought, **locusts**, or **pestilence** on the **people**, they should **humble themselves, . . . pray, . . . seek** His **face, and turn from their**

wicked ways. Then He would **forgive their sin** and restore them.

Verse 14 may very well be the golden text of this entire book. Though originally addressed to the chosen nation of Israel, it has rightly been *applied* to those nations which have a biblical heritage. It is the sure road to restoration and revival for all times. If the conditions are met, the promises are sure of fulfillment.

J. Barton Payne comments:

> This great verse, the best known in all Chronicles, expresses as does no other in Scripture God's requirement for national blessing, whether in Solomon's land, in Ezra's, or in our own. Those who believe must forsake their sins, turn from the life that is centered in self, and yield to God's word and will. Then, and only then, will heaven send revival.[7]

7:17–22 If Solomon would live in obedience **before** God, He would **establish** his **throne** and allow Solomon's descendants to sit upon it. On the other hand, **if** Solomon and his people forsook the Lord for **other gods**, they would be carried into captivity, and God would reject the temple so that it would be an object of derision and a testimony to the nations that Israel had forsaken **the LORD**.

Verse 16 seems to imply that the temple would endure for all time; yet we know that it was destroyed in 586 B.C. The explanation, of course, is that God's promise was conditioned on Israel's faithfulness and obedience. Verses 19 and 20 specifically warn that if the people became idolaters, God would reject the temple.

C. Solomon in All His Splendor (8:1—9:28)

8:1–6 Here we read of Solomon's accomplishments and successes in various areas. First he undertook a vast urban-development program, rebuilding or capturing **storage cities**, **fortified cities**, **chariot cities**, and settlements.

8:7–10 He conscripted Canaanites for his slave **labor** force but used the Israelites as fighting **men**, commanders, and chief **officials**.[8]

8:11 He would not allow his wife, **the daughter of Pharaoh**, to live in the royal palace, saying that it was **holy** because **the ark of the LORD** had entered there. This does not mean that the ark had actually been taken inside the palace, but rather that the palace was **holy** by reason of its proximity to **the ark** in the temple. Unfortunately, the fact that Solomon restricted her to a special residence did not restrict her from leading him off into idolatry (1 Kgs. 11:1–8).

8:12–16 The king was careful to observe the sacrifices and **offerings** connected with the religious calendar. **He** also **appointed . . . the priests** and **Levites** to **serve . . . according to the** schedules prepared by **David his father**.

Thus **all the work of Solomon was** well-ordered from start to finish.

8:17, 18 Finally, we read of Solomon's maritime ventures in partnership with **Hiram**. The **ships** traveled between **Ezion Geber and Elath**—both on the northern tip of the eastern arm of the Red Sea (Gulf of Aqaba)—and **Ophir**.[9] It has been variously conjectured that Ophir was in southern Arabia, eastern Africa, or India.

9:1–9 When the queen of Sheba **heard of the fame of Solomon, she** traveled with **a very great** caravan loaded down with gifts to find out for herself. After seeing the splendor of his kingdom and testing his wisdom with hard **questions**, she was overwhelmed. She confessed that **the half**

had **not** been **told**. She realized that Solomon's prosperity was due to the favor of his **God**.

9:10–12 Verses 10 and 11 interrupt the narrative to explain the source of some of Solomon's wealth and the uniquely beautiful uses to which he put it. When **the queen of Sheba** left, **Solomon gave** her gifts **much** greater in number and value **than** those **she had brought to** him.

9:13–28 **Solomon** received over **six hundred and sixty-six talents of gold** each year and used some of it to make **shields**, to overlay his **throne of ivory**, and to make goblets and tableware. His greatness brought him honor and wealth from **all the kings of the earth**. His trade went all the way to Tarshish, which may have been in Spain.[10] He was rich in the abundance of **horses**,[11] territory, **silver**, and **cedar**. Although he reigned over the territory from **the River** Euphrates westward, it was not incorporated as part of Israel but consisted of vassal states that paid tribute to him.

D. Solomon's Death (9:29–31)

Solomon died after he had **reigned** for **forty years**, and was succeeded by **his son . . . Rehoboam**. The noncanonical books mentioned in verse 29 were probably used as resource materials by the chronicler, but they have since been lost.

II. THE DIVISION OF THE KINGDOM (Chap. 10)

10:1–5 Perhaps to conciliate the northern tribes, **Rehoboam** decided to go **to Shechem** for his inauguration. The people promised to **serve** him if he would **lighten the heavy yoke** which Solomon had placed on them. "**All Israel**" (v. 3) means representatives from all the northern tribes. **Rehoboam** asked for **three days** to consider the people's request.

10:6–11 First **King Rehoboam** checked with **the elders who** had served **his father Solomon**. They told him to listen **to "these" people**. He next turned to **the young men** for **advice**, rejecting the elders' counsel, and heard what was more appealing to him. They urged him to speak roughly to the people.

10:12–19 When **the people** returned after three days and heard the king's threats, they rebelled, under the leadership of **Jeroboam**. The kingdom was divided, fulfilling the word of the Lord through Ahijah (1 Kgs. 11:29 ff.). After the murder of **Hadoram** the tax collector, **Rehoboam** retreated **to Jerusalem**, where he reigned over **Judah** and Benjamin. Williams comments:

> This fulfillment of the prediction of Ahijah affords an instance, similar to many others in the Scriptures, of prophecies being accomplished by the operation of human passions, and in the natural course of events. Men think that they are obeying their own wills and carrying out their own plans, unconscious that the matter is of God, and permitted and overruled by Him for the performance of His Word.[12]

III. THE KINGDOM OF JUDAH (11:1—36:19)

A. King Rehoboam (Chaps. 11, 12)

11:1–4 When Rehoboam returned **to Jerusalem**, **the LORD** intervened through the prophet **Shemaiah** to prevent a civil war. He told Rehoboam to accept the status quo because **"this thing is done from Me."** Rehoboam had not listened to wise counsel before, but he did this time. There was constant strife between the two kingdoms (12:15), but all-out war was avoided. The expression **"all Israel in Judah and Benjamin"** (v. 3) refers to all in the southern kingdom who were loyal to David's dynasty.

11:5–12 Much of the king's time was spent in building **cities** of **defense** for **Judah**. The **fortified cities**, located south of Jerusalem, showed that he feared attack from Egypt.

11:13–17 Meanwhile **Jeroboam** plunged the northern kingdom into gross idolatry (1 Kgs. 12), causing those **priests** and **Levites** who were loyal **to the LORD** to flee **to Judah**. They were followed by all those who had hearts for **God**, and in this way Rehoboam's kingdom was strengthened. It cost them everything to come **to Jerusalem**, for they **left their common-lands**, **possessions**, and friends behind.

11:18–23 **Rehoboam** was a polygamist, although he did not match his father in this regard! **He** had **eighteen wives, sixty concubines, twenty-eight sons, and sixty daughters**. The wives mentioned by name were Israelites from the royal family and not heathen women.

12:1–4 Whereas 1 Kings 14:22–24 mentions some of the details of Rehoboam's apostasy, Chronicles simply says that **"he forsook the law of the LORD"** and "did not prepare his heart to seek the LORD" (v. 14). Now five short years after the powerful monarch Solomon had died, the Egyptians were at Jerusalem's gates to carry away her treasures. Rehoboam's **fortified cities** availed nothing. **Shishak** subdued **Judah** not because of Egypt's military superiority but because of Judah's unfaithfulness to Jehovah.

12:5–8 When **Shemaiah the prophet came to Rehoboam** a second time (see 11:2) and delivered his message of doom, **the king** and the princes of Judah **humbled themselves** before the Lord and acknowledged His righteousness in the coming judgment. Instantly the Lord's mercy and grace provided **deliverance**, but not without a painful lesson on the difference between serving Jehovah and serving their captors.

12:9–12 The people were spared but the kingdom was spoiled. **Rehoboam** tried to adjust as much as possible. He substituted **bronze shields** for **gold**, unwittingly illustrating that God's presence and favor (**gold**) were being replaced by His judgment (**bronze**).[13]

12:13–16 The story of Rehoboam concludes with the statement that **he did evil** and **rested with his fathers**. The difference between Rehoboam and his grandfather David can be seen by comparing Psalm 27:8 with verse 14. David sought the Lord's face. Rehoboam did not.

B. King Abijah (Chap. 13)

13:1–3 Abijah, whose **mother's name was Michaiah,**[14] **became** the next **king** and **reigned three years in Jerusalem**. First Kings 15 mentions his sin in not following after the Lord, as David had done. But Chronicles skips over everything in Abijah's reign except one **battle** with **Jeroboam**.

13:4–12 In his speech before the battle, **Abijah** reminded **Jeroboam** that God had given the kingdom **to David** and to his posterity. **Jeroboam** had **rebelled against** the Davidic dynasty and had mustered a band of **worthless rogues** against Rehoboam when the latter was virtually defenseless. Israel hoped to win the victory because of its superior numbers and **the golden calves**. Israel had set up a counterfeit priesthood which men could enter without divine authorization. Judah, by contrast, clung to the Levitical priesthood, which was still serving the Lord in the prescribed manner. **God** was the Captain of Judah's army, **and His priests** used their **trumpets to sound the alarm against** Israel. It was folly, therefore, for the northern tribes to **fight against the Lord God**.

13:13–18 Instead of listening to Abijah, **Jeroboam** set **an ambush**. When the trap closed on **Judah**, the men **cried out to the Lord** and **the priests** blew **the trumpets**. The Lord answered by giving Judah a great victory. **Five hundred thousand choice men of Israel fell**—a staggering price to pay for turning away from God!

13:19–22 **Abijah** acquired additional territory, although he didn't completely subdue Israel. The loss was devastating for **Jeroboam**, who was later **struck** down by **the Lord**. But **Abijah** became powerful and prosperous.

C. King Asa (Chaps. 14—16)

14:1, 2 The next three chapters give us a brief report of **Asa** and his forty-one year reign. First Kings 15:9–24 should be read along with these chapters. Verse 1 is a bridge from the previous chapter. The Hebrew Bible starts chap. 14 with v. 2.

14:3–8 The source of Asa's peaceful reign was his heart's attitude toward Jehovah. He put away many of the sins of his fathers and urged his people **to seek the Lord**, leading the way himself by zealously purging his kingdom of idolatry.[15] During this time of rest, Asa **fortified** his **cities** and gathered a large **army**.

14:9–15 Judah's peace was shattered by an **Ethiopian . . . army of a million men** with **three hundred chariots**. Judah's smaller force was victorious because of their trust in Jehovah. The enemy was routed decisively.

Asa's prayer in verse 11 is short and to the point. There is no time in battle to be eloquent, but prayers born out of desperate need are very effective if the person praying is in a right relationship with God, as Asa was. Because he followed the Lord in peace, he knew the Lord would care for him in war. The fight began in Mareshah, a city in Judah, and ended around Gerar, a city belonging to the Philistines. Many were slain, including those who owned livestock, and huge amounts of spoil and animals were carried back to Jerusalem.

15:1–6 Asa and his men were jubilant over their recent success against overwhelming odds. As they returned to Jerusalem, the Lord had a lesson for them. First, Azariah reminded them that the LORD was with them because they had sought Him. But . . . He would forsake them if they forsook Him. And history proved more times than not that Israel had forsaken their God. Consequently they had no peace, and they were continually beaten by their enemies. But when the nation sought . . . the LORD, they found Him always ready to forgive and restore.

15:7 Since Asa was seeking after Jehovah, Azariah encouraged him to keep up the good work. Tucked away in this historical narrative, verse 7 is well worth memorizing: "But you, be strong and do not let your hands be weak, for your work shall be rewarded!" The parallel for believers today is 1 Corinthians 15:58.

15:8–15 "Oded" (v. 8) probably refers to Oded's son, Azariah (see NKJV marg.). The king responded to the word of the prophet with real enthusiasm. He stepped up his reformation program immediately, remov-

ing more idols (cf. 14:3), not only from his own land of Judah but from the cities . . . of Ephraim which he had taken in battle. He restored the altar in the temple and consecrated it with sacrifices. He called a solemn assembly at Jerusalem, offered part of the Ethiopian spoil . . . to the LORD on the altar, and bound the people with an oath . . . to seek the LORD. He left no room for dissenters—all who did not obey the covenant were to be executed (v. 13).

15:16–19 Also Asa removed his grandmother (not his mother[16]) from her position as queen mother and destroyed her obscene image. For comment on verse 17 see the note on 14:3–8. Treasures were brought into the temple instead of being taken out. His work was rewarded as the Lord had promised through Azariah, and he had peace.

16:1 Late in the reign of Asa,[17] Baasha king of Israel attempted to prevent his own people from defecting to Asa by fortifying Ramah, a town not far from Jerusalem.

16:2–6 Asa turned to the assistance of man instead of trusting in the arm of the Lord, as he had done earlier when invaded by the Ethiopians. He sent the Lord's treasure to purchase the help of Ben-Hadad. The Syrian king then attacked . . . Israel from the north and forced Baasha to withdraw from Ramah in order to defend his northern border. Asa's scheme apparently worked, but God was displeased.

16:7–10 The end certainly did not justify the means in Jehovah's eyes, so He sent His prophet Hanani to speak to Asa. Hanani boldly accused the king of acting foolishly. Had not the LORD . . . delivered him from the Ethiopians? Was not God continually looking for men through whom He could work? Since Asa had chosen to fight according to the flesh, he would **have wars** from then on. **Asa... was enraged**. Instead of heeding the word of the Lord, as he had done earlier (15:8), he **put** Hanani **in prison**.

16:11–14 Asa chose to work contrary to the way of the Lord, so the Lord afflicted him with a foot **disease**. But he still refused to repent and turn back to Jehovah. He tried **the physicians** instead, and shortly thereafter **died**. Some think that **the physicians** may have been magicians or spiritistic healers.

Despite his sad end, Asa was one of the best kings Judah had (15:17). The people greatly mourned his death. The **very great burning** of verse 14 refers to burning incense, not to the cremation of his body.

D. King Jehoshaphat (Chaps. 17—20)

17:1–5 **Jehoshaphat** succeeded his father and reigned twenty-five years (20:31). Much more space is devoted to him in 2 Chronicles (chaps. 17—20) than in Kings. The material in chapter 17 has no parallel in 1 Kings.

Upon ascending the throne, **Jehoshaphat... strengthened** his kingdom **against Israel**. He *fortified* his **kingdom**, but the secret of his successful reign was that he *followed* **the Lord**, as **David** had done. It is interesting how **David** is constantly used as the standard by which kings were measured. If they **walked** after his example, they prospered and were blessed. If they did not, they failed. The land was at peace under **Jehoshaphat**, and his enemies paid tribute (vv. 10–12).

17:6–9 The Word of God had high priority in Jehoshaphat's life. He was zealous in following its precepts and **took delight** in obeying it. He also made it the rule of his kingdom,

sending a special commission of princes, **Levites**, and **priests** to educate the people **in the ways of the** Lord, thus obeying God's commands in Deuteronomy 6:6ff.

17:10–19 Under Jehovah's blessing, **Jehoshaphat became increasingly powerful**. And what an army he had! Rehoboam started out over sixty years earlier with 180,000 men. Now Judah's militia numbered 1,160,000 men, not counting those stationed **in the fortified cities**. Many of these men had no doubt defected from Israel because they saw that the Lord was with Judah. It is too bad that Jehoshaphat did not use his manpower more wisely, as we shall see in chapter 18.

18:1 Up to this point Israel and Judah had been hostile toward each other. But Jehoshaphat's son married Ahab's daughter (21:5, 6), thus forming an alliance between the two kingdoms.

18:2–7 **Ahab** asked **Jehoshaphat** to help him attack the Syrians, who held some of Israel's territory (cf. 1 Kgs. 22:3, 4). Jehoshaphat immediately consented to help Ahab, but he suggested that they first **inquire for the word of the** Lord. Accordingly Ahab sent for **the prophets**, who with one voice predicted success. However, they must not have been too convincing, because Jehoshaphat, who possessed a measure of spiritual discernment, asked for **"a prophet of the** Lord,**"** as if to imply that the **four hundred men** already assembled were not in touch with Jehovah. It appears that even Ahab knew the difference between his **prophets** and a real **prophet**. But **Micaiah**, the **one man** through whom they could get the word of the Lord, was hated by Ahab because he **always** prophesied **evil** about the king.

18:8–11 When **Micaiah** was being

summoned, **Zedekiah** dramatically portrayed how **the Syrians** would be **destroyed** (perhaps the two **horns** he put on signified the two Jewish kings), while all the king's other prophets chimed in their assent. D. L. Moody comments:

> Ahab had his preachers and proph-
> ets. No man is so corrupt, but he will
> find some one who preaches to suit
> him.[18]

18:12, 13 **Micaiah** meanwhile was being pressured by the king's **messenger** to agree with the other **prophets** in forecasting victory, but **Micaiah** promised only to deliver the word of the Lord. Verse 13 should be the motto of every preacher and every Christian: **"As the LORD lives, whatever my God says, that I will speak."**

18:14–17 At first **Micaiah** pretended to go along with the others, but it was soon apparent that he was not serious. When Ahab made him **swear** to speak **the truth**, he told of Israel's coming defeat and of Ahab's death.

18:18–22 **Micaiah** also explained why Ahab's prophets were giving him false information: They were under the influence of **a lying spirit** which **the LORD** sent because of Ahab's wickedness. Ahab was now the object of judgment, as had been prophesied earlier by Elijah (1 Kgs. 21:19–24). Matthew Henry comments:

> It is not without the divine permis-
> sion that the devil deceives men, and
> even thereby God serves his own
> purposes. . . . Thus Micaiah gave Ahab
> fair warning, not only of the danger
> of proceeding in this war, but of the
> danger of believing those that en-
> couraged him to proceed.[19]

18:23–26 Micaiah suffered for his honesty. **Zedekiah . . . struck** him **on** the cheek and Ahab imprisoned him with only **bread** and **water**, probably intending to kill him. To both men Micaiah responded by saying that the Lord would prove that he was telling the truth. Scripture does not tell us what happened to Zedekiah, but we do know that Ahab was slain in battle, according to the word of Jehovah.

18:27–29 The prophet's words must have had some impact on Ahab, because he tried to **disguise** himself and thus escape God's judgment. He suggested that **Jehoshaphat** wear his kingly **robes** while he (Ahab) donned a soldier's uniform.

18:30–34 But the word of the Lord came to pass. **Jehoshaphat** was delivered from the Syrians, after learning a lesson about the dangers of unholy alliances (2 Cor. 6:14). Ahab was not delivered. God directed a seemingly **random** arrow **between the joints of his armor**, and **about the time of sunset he died**.

19:1–5 When **Jehu, the son of Hanani, the seer**, who was also a prophet, rebuked **Jehoshaphat** for his alliance with Ahab, he responded by repenting.

His relationship with the idolatrous Ahab had set a poor example for his subjects. So the king **went** throughout his kingdom to bring **the people . . . back to the LORD**. He also established a judicial system in accordance with the Mosaic Law (Deut. 16:18–20). This, along with his earlier dispersal of teachers throughout the land (17:7–9), showed Jehoshaphat's tremendous respect for the Scriptures. These actions also displayed his concern for his subjects and his desire to act faithfully as Jehovah's regent.

19:6–11 The king's exhortations were taken from the **law** (v. 10). He reinforced the Lord's original commands to those who would act as

judges among His people. Since they were judging God's covenant people and since He was watching all that was done, the judges were to **fear . . . the Lord** and **"take heed."** Judges were also **appointed** in the capital city of **Jerusalem**, where difficult cases could be brought. **Amariah the chief priest** was in charge of religious cases, **and Zebadiah** the head of the tribe **of Judah** was responsible to handle civil **matters**. **The Levites** served as **officials**.

20:1–6   **A huge army from across the Dead Sea declared war on Judah.** (Some Hebrew manuscripts read "Edom" for "Syria" in v. 2.[20]) **Jehoshaphat** was justifiably alarmed. He **proclaimed a fast** and called the people to the temple, where he prayed to **the Lord**. This is the third "king's prayer" in 2 Chronicles (see also Solomon's prayer, chap. 6, and Asa's prayer, 14:11).

20:7–13   Jehoshaphat reminded the Lord that the Jews were His covenant **people**. The **temple**, where Jehoshaphat was praying, was God's **sanctuary** and the place where He promised to **hear** and answer prayer. Those to whom **Israel** had once shown kindness were now coming to destroy her and take away her land. Jehoshaphat closed his impassioned appeal, and with **all Judah . . . stood before the Lord**, awaiting His answer.

20:14–17   **The Spirit of the Lord** spoke through **Jahaziel**, dispelling the fear that had gripped the nation. **The battle** was **God's**; the people had only to **go** out the next day and **see** what He had done.

20:18–21   By faith the people rejoiced in their victory even before it came to pass. The next **morning** they were up at dawn to see what **the Lord** had done. They marched to the battlefield as though they were going to a festival, the singers leading the way.

20:22–30   God confounded the enemy when He heard His people singing their song of faith. He stirred up the opposition so that they fought and destroyed **one another**. **When Judah** arrived, the only thing left to do was to collect the **spoil**, a task requiring **three days**. **With** unbounded **joy** they praised **the Lord** and returned **to Jerusalem** singing. The neighboring **countries** took notice, and Judah enjoyed peace.

20:31–34   As is customary, a summary of the reign of **Jehoshaphat** is given. Despite his efforts he was unable to stamp out idolatry. But on the whole his had been a good reign. He sought to do good and, even though he was not perfect, he usually did **what was right** in God's **sight**.

20:35–37   This is a postscript concerning Jehoshaphat's partnership **with Ahaziah**, the wicked **king of Israel**. **They made . . . ships** at **Ezion Geber** to travel **to Tarshish**, but **the Lord** wrecked the project, as announced by a prophet named **Eliezer**.

Jehoshaphat was sixty years old when he died. His son Jehoram, who had been his co-regent, succeeded him on the throne of Judah (21:1).

E. King Jehoram (Chap. 21)

21:1–3   Beginning with the reign of **Jehoram**, the history recorded in 2 Chronicles is downhill all the way, ending in calamity and captivity.

Two Azariahs are listed in verse 2 as brothers of Jehoram. The NKJV uses the alternative spelling of one (**Azaryahu**).

21:4–6   Judah's fifth king chose to walk **in the way of the kings of Israel** instead of in the way of **David**. **Jehoram** was a murderer and an idolater. He ruthlessly **killed all his** own

brothers to strengthen his hold on the throne. Scripture leaves us in no doubt as to the evil influence that caused Jehoram to act so wickedly: His **wife** was Ahab's **daughter** (v. 6). Earlier Jehoshaphat had arranged the marriage between the two kingdoms, and now Judah was infected with the same wickedness that was ruining Israel. Ahab's daughter Athaliah was a tool in Satan's hands to bring judgment on God's people.

21:7 But the LORD remembered the Davidic **covenant** and so He did not deal as sternly with Jehoram and Judah as He had dealt with Ahab and Israel. ("A lamp" means a descendant to serve as king.) Still, Judah was to suffer much because of this unholy union.

21:8–15 The Edomites, who had feared Judah during the days of Jehoshaphat (17:10), now **revolted**. **Libnah**, a city in Judah, also rebelled. **Jehoram** made matters worse by leading his people further and further into idolatry. Even the prophecy of **Elijah**, contained in **a letter** to the king, failed to turn him from his course of evil. Jehoram certainly knew of the prophet's powerful ministry in Israel, but he proved as unresponsive to it as **Ahab** had been.

Elijah was taken to heaven sometime during the reign of Jehoshaphat (2 Kgs. 2:11). Since Jehoram reigned with his father for about five years, Elijah may have been alive when this message was delivered. Or the prophet might have written the letter by divine instruction and given it to Elisha to deliver at the appropriate time.

21:16, 17 **The Philistines and the Arabians carried away** Jehoram's **possessions** and his family, **except Jehoahaz, the youngest of his sons** (usually called Ahaziah). Since he had murdered his father's family this punishment would seem to fit his own crime.

21:18–20 Jehoram **died in severe pain** from **an incurable disease** of the **intestines**. He **departed** this life **to no one's** sorrow. Since he had not walked as the other **kings** had in life, he was not **buried** with them in death.

F. King Ahaziah (22:1–9)

22:1–9 The trouble caused by association with the house of Ahab now reached to the third generation. **Ahaziah** (same as Jehoahaz, 21:17, and Azariah, v. 6) became **king** after Jehoram's death. He was twenty-two[21] (NKJV marg.) **years old** at the time.

His mother, Athaliah, a granddaughter of Omri, continued her pernicious influence in Judah after the death of her husband. She was her son's chief counselor to do **evil—"to his destruction."** Ahaziah had been spared (v. 1) so as to leave a son of David on the throne, but he proved himself ungrateful by repeating his father's sins. He joined **with Jehoram (Joram) to war against . . . Syria. Jehu** and his men found Ahaziah **hiding in Samaria** and **killed him**. The king's servants gave him a decent burial (2 Kgs. 9:28) because he was a grandson of the godly Jehoshaphat. Ahaziah left no son old enough to carry on the kingdom.

G. Usurpation of Queen Athaliah (22:10—23:21)

22:10–12 Having lost her husband and now her son, **Athaliah** seized the throne for herself by killing *her own grandchildren!* Satan was the unseen motivator behind this ruthless slaughter of the **royal** family, attempting to cut off the messianic line as he had tried to do earlier and would try to do again. But since the promise of Genesis 3:15 guaranteed the Lord's preserving the line through which the Lord Jesus would eventually come, Jehovah moved **Jehoshabeath** to hide her nephew **Joash**. **He was hidden** in the temple, where Jehoshabeath's husband, **Jehoiada the priest**, took care of him **for six years**.

Second Kings 8—11 gives more details concerning these events and also relates what was going on in Israel at the same time.

23:1–7 Until he felt that Joash was old enough, **Jehoiada** had to bide his time while the usurper sat on David's throne. But **in the seventh year** he called together the princes and **Levites** and plotted Athaliah's overthrow. Word **went** out **throughout** the kingdom and many entered into **a covenant** to set Joash on his father's throne. The words in verse 6b **"all the people shall keep the watch of the LORD"** mean that they were to observe the law forbidding entrance into the temple (see v. 6a). **The Levites** and princes were given their assignments, and a **Sabbath** was chosen as the fateful day.

23:8–11 As new **divisions** came to the temple, the old divisions were **not dismissed**; thus **Jehoiada** was able to gather a large number of men without drawing suspicion. The men were equipped with David's weapons, which **were in the temple**, and when all the preparations were complete, seven-year-old Joash was **brought out** of the temple and crowned. He was given a copy of the law (**the Testimony**) in accordance with the word of Moses (Deut. 17:18–20). Some think this was the original copy of the law which had been placed in the ark (Ex. 25:21; 2 Chron. 5:10).

23:12–15 Queen **Athaliah came to the people in the temple** to investigate the cheering and shouting, only to find a child rival she thought long

dead now wearing a royal crown. But what must have alarmed her even more was the realization that **the people** were solidly behind him. No one listened to her charge of **treason**. After all, she was the usurper, not Joash. **Jehoiada** ordered her killed, but not inside the temple. **She** was taken to **the Horse Gate**, where she was put to death for the atrocities she had committed in Judah.

23:16–19 With Athaliah out of the way, reform was swift. **Jehoiada** and **the people** covenanted to **be the LORD's**. To demonstrate their commitment, they destroyed **the temple of Baal** and **killed Mattan, the priest of Baal**. As a priest, **Jehoiada** was sensitive concerning the temple and divine worship. One of the first things he did was to set the temple service in order, as had been commanded by **Moses** and **David**. **The Levites** and **priests** were **assigned** to their duties. The holiness of the temple was no longer to be treated as a light thing; **gatekeepers** were to keep out ceremonially **unclean** people. Jehoiada knew that reform must begin in **the house of the LORD**.

23:20, 21 Joash was taken **to the king's house**. **The people** looked forward with expectancy to life under Joash, thankful that a son of David sat **on** Judah's **throne** once more.

H. King Joash (Chap. 24)

24:1–3 **Joash was** only **seven years old when he became king, and he reigned forty years**. Joash **did what was right** as long as **Jehoiada the priest** was alive. Even Joash's **two wives** were chosen **for him** by this influential priest of God.

24:4–14 In order to restore the temple, **Joash** ordered **the Levites** to expedite **the collection** of funds from **all Israel**. When **the Levites** failed to respond **quickly**, he became upset with **Jehoiada**. Finally **a** special **chest** was **set** before the temple, and the people were commanded to come and deposit their "temple tax."[22] This was then taken and distributed to **the workmen** who **restored the house of God to its original condition and reinforced it.**[23]

24:15–19 When **Jehoiada ... died**, after a long and fruitful life, he was honored by being **buried** with **the kings**, an unusual honor for one who was not of royalty. But with his godly influence gone, Joash turned to idolaters for advice, to the ruin of his kingdom. Jehovah *sent prophets* to warn him, but rather than repent, the leader of Judah rebelled.

24:20–27 **Zechariah** spoke God's warning to the people, and **the king** ordered him **stoned** for it. **Joash ... did not remember the kindness which Jehoiada**, the father (or grandfather) of Zechariah,[24] **had done to him**. Perhaps in answer to Zechariah's dying prayer, the Lord sent a **small ... army** from **Syria** to plunder **Judah** and to slay the officials and princes. Those who had given wicked counsel to Joash were killed, and Joash himself, **severely wounded**, was then murdered by **his own servants**. Like wicked Jehoram before him, he was denied burial with **the kings** of Judah.

Because Joash forsook the Lord in the latter part of his life, all that he had done earlier was for nothing. He had repaired the temple and had refurnished it, only to hand over its treasures to Hazael the Syrian (2 Kgs. 12:17, 18). It is good to *start* well, but it is far more important to *finish* well. The Apostle John, knowing the tendency people have to "fade in the stretch," warns us to "Look to yourselves, that we do not lose those things we worked for, but that we may receive a full reward" (2 John 8).

Second Kings 12 gives more details about the life and reign of Joash (there called Jehoash); see comments on that chapter.

I. King Amaziah (Chap. 25)

25:1–10 After establishing his throne and dealing with his father's murderers according to **the law**, Amaziah turned his attention to foreign affairs. The Edomites had rebelled against Judah during the reign of Jehoram (21:10), and now perhaps **Amaziah** wanted to bring them back under his rule. So **he ... hired** mercenaries **from Israel**. However, after being warned by **a man of God**, he sent the Israelites home. Although he was concerned about losing the money he had already paid the mercenaries, he accepted the prophet's assurance that **the LORD** was **able to give** him **much more** to make up for his foolish investment.

25:11–13 **Amaziah** and his men **killed ten thousand** Edomites, then **took ten thousand** others **captive**, only to kill them later by hurling them over a precipice. The latter victims may have been guilty of unusual cruelty, or Amaziah may have been following an accepted wartime policy of that day. The mercenaries whom **Amaziah** had sent home to Ephraim angrily **raided the cities of Judah**, killing **three thousand** people and taking **much spoil**.

25:14–21 When **Amaziah** began worshiping idols which he had brought back from Edom, **a prophet** reproved him for thinking that **gods** which could not deliver **their own people** could help *him!* Amaziah interrupted the prophet with a threat, perhaps a veiled allusion to Zechariah, who had lost his life by prophesying against

Amaziah's father (24:20–22). The prophet responded to the king's warning by saying in effect, "I am not going to be struck down. Since you have refused my advice, you are the one who is going to be destroyed." Amaziah did not listen to God's counsel but instead **asked advice** of his own staff. Foolishly he made war with **Joash of Israel**, refusing to heed the prophet's warning.

25:22–28 **Judah was defeated** and **Amaziah** was humiliated and impoverished. **Jerusalem** was invaded and the temple was pillaged. Amaziah's subjects conspired **against him**, and eventually he **fled** from Jerusalem. He was murdered in **Lachish**, then brought back to Jerusalem and **buried**.

J. King Uzziah (Chap. 26)

26:1–5 The reason for Uzziah's success is given early in the chapter. **He did what was right** and **sought God. Zechariah** (not the same as the Prophet Zechariah) was his godly counselor, a man of **understanding**.

26:6–15 Everywhere **Uzziah** turned, he was blessed. He warred successfully **against the Philistines** and **the Ammonites**, and he increased Judah's defenses as well. He assembled **an** elite **army** and built up a powerful armory to equip it. He also **built cities** and encouraged agricultural development (v. 10). The **"devices"** (v. 15) were a form of catapult.

26:16–23 But Uzziah was **lifted up** with pride. He entered **the temple . . . to burn incense** before the LORD, something which only the priests were authorized to do. **Azariah** and **eighty** other **priests**, all **valiant men, went in after** the king. The priests' rebukes angered **Uzziah**, but before he could do anything **the** LORD **struck him** with **leprosy**. He was **hurried . . . out** of the temple, to which he never

returned. He remained **a leper** from that day on, living **in an isolated house** while **Jotham his son** ruled. **Uzziah** was not **buried** in the graves of **the kings**, because he was **a leper**; he was interred **in the field** adjacent to the royal graves.

K. King Jotham (Chap. 27)

27:1–4 Like his father Uzziah, **Jotham** enjoyed peace so that he was able to build and improve his capital and the surrounding **cities**. He followed his father's example, except in the matter of Uzziah's sin. However, the high places were not removed, and Jotham does not appear to have been much of a reformer. He did little to prevent his **people** from acting **corruptly**.

27:5–9 **The Ammonites** had been subdued by Uzziah (26:8), but perhaps his death prompted them to withhold their tribute. **Jotham . . . fought** against them and they were forced to pay tribute once again. His strength lay in the fact that he considered **God** in all he did. They **buried** Jotham **in the city of David** and **Ahaz his son** became Judah's next king.

L. King Ahaz (Chap. 28)

28:1–4 To get the full story of **Ahaz**, one should read 2 Kings 16 and Isaiah 7. He was the most wicked king that Judah had yet known, reigning **sixteen years in Jerusalem**.[25]

After Ahaz became king, he wasted no time plunging into idolatry. He chose **the** evil **kings of Israel** as his pattern instead of **David**. Ahaz revived the abominable ritual of child sacrifice **in the Valley of the Son of Hinnom**, outside Jerusalem. The worship of Molech, of which this was a part, had not been practiced since the days of Solomon (1 Kgs. 11:7), but now all forms of idolatry and **abomi-**

nations were widely practiced and encouraged.

28:5–8 Because of this **the LORD** brought many adversaries against Judah. Isaiah tells us that Rezin, **king of Syria**, and **Pekah**, king of Israel, were allies against Jerusalem. They did not succeed in overthrowing the capital city but they did great damage to **Judah**. The Israelites **killed one hundred and twenty thousand... men... in one day** and **carried** off **two hundred thousand** people **captive**. Many noblemen were slain at this time. It was when Ahaz was threatened by Rezin and Pekah that God in grace gave to the house of Israel through him the promise of the virgin-born Immanuel (Isa. 7:14).

28:9–15 The Israelites intended to enslave their brethren from Judah, which was forbidden in the Law of Moses, **but** the Lord sent **a prophet** to warn them not to do so, for the **fierce wrath of the LORD** was against them. True, Israel had been God's instrument of judgment, but their cruelty had been unwarranted. **Some of the heads of Ephraim** had enough sense to heed **Oded** the prophet and secure the release of **the captives**, who were then fully equipped and fed **from the spoil**, and **returned to** their land.

28:16–27 At this **same time King Ahaz** was also troubled by those nations which his father had subdued, Edom and Philistia. But rather than turn to the Lord in his extremity, Ahaz turned to **the** king **of Assyria, Tiglath-Pileser**. He hired the Assyrians with gold from the temple and the king's **house. The king of Assyria** then attacked Syria and killed Rezin in Damascus (2 Kgs. 16:9). When Ahaz went to Damascus to meet Tiglath-Pileser, he became enamored with the gods of the Syrians (2 Kgs.

16:8–10). Ahaz's alliance with the king of Assyria proved costly, since Assyria deceived him and exacted heavy tribute. But his alliance with the idols **of Syria** proved fatal because it provoked Jehovah to great anger. **King Ahaz** established idolatry so strongly in **Judah** that not even good Hezekiah, his son, would be able to root it out. When Ahaz died, he was **not... buried** in **the tombs of the kings.**[26] **Ahaz** is called the **king of Israel** in verse 19. Sometimes the kings of Judah were given this name (see 2 Chron. 21:2).

M. King Hezekiah (Chaps. 29—32)

29:1–11 The Bible accords several chapters to Hezekiah's reign. Three chapters are devoted to him in 2 Kings (18—20), four in the Book of Isaiah (36—39), and four here. Second Chronicles mentions primarily his religious dealings while 2 Kings relates more of his political and foreign accomplishments. Both books bring out his outstanding character and devotion to the Lord.

Hezekiah started his reformation with the religious leaders. He called together **the priests** and **Levites** and ordered them to consecrate themselves and the temple. Because of unfaithfulness on the part of their fathers, **the wrath of the LORD** was on the land and many people had already been slain or taken captive. The king wanted to get right with God, and he urged the priests and Levites to do the same.

29:12–24 The Levites listed by name in verses 12–14 led their brothers in obeying the king's command. They **cleansed** (v. 18) the courts for eight days, then the temple itself for **eight days** (v. 17). They set the utensils in order for temple-service, then informed **King Hezekiah** that all had been carried out according to his word. Hezekiah offered **a sin-offering** on behalf of **the kingdom**. The blood from the **sin** and **burnt** offerings was used to purge **the altar**.

29:25–36 The priests and Levites were stationed in their places as appointed in the time **of David**, and they **sang** and played the holy **instruments** while the **burnt offering** was being offered. **All** those present **bowed** in worship along with **the Levites**, and those who were so inclined brought **burnt** and **thank offerings**. So much was brought for this freewill gift that **the Levites** had to help **the priests** slaughter the animals because not enough **priests had sanctified themselves**. **The people rejoiced** because of the suddenness of the revival and because it produced a glimmer of hope for a better future for Judah. But this was only the beginning of Hezekiah's reforms.

30:1–5 Chapter 30 is wholly taken up with Hezekiah's reinstatement of **the Passover** Feast, which **had not** been observed in such fashion since before the kingdom was divided (2 Chron. 8:13).

In the first month the king had purified the temple and reestablished its services. **In the second month** he prepared to **keep the Passover** and the Feast of Unleavened Bread. According to Numbers 9:11, **the Passover** could be celebrated **in the second month** if a dead corpse resulted in somebody's uncleanness, or if they were far away on a journey. In Hezekiah's case, observance during the first month, **the regular time**, was not possible **because a sufficient number of priests had not consecrated themselves** (v. 3). Since it was a national feast, the whole nation must be invited. So messengers were sent **throughout** Judah and **Israel** to ask

the people to come to **Jerusalem**. Israel was an Assyrian province at this time, the bulk of the people having been taken into captivity. However, Hezekiah was able to invite the remaining Israelites without opposition from the Assyrians.

30:6–12 Most of the Israelites ridiculed the couriers who exhorted them to **return to the** LORD. However, a small remnant did repent and travel **to Jerusalem** to observe the Passover in the first year of Hezekiah's reign, 716–715 B.C. (2 Chron. 29:3).

30:13–15 The zeal of the **people** shamed **the priests and . . . Levites** and awakened them to a more serious consideration of their duties. The city was cleansed of its heathen filth, and every vestige of idolatry was thrown **into the Brook Kidron**.

30:16–27 **The Levites** aided those who were ceremonially unclean and **Hezekiah prayed** that the Lord would overlook the irregularities and accept the **heart** attitude of the people. **And the** LORD did. **The Feast of Unleavened Bread** was such a joy to all that they decided to celebrate an extra **seven days**. The king and **the leaders** contributed animals for this extended **feast** and **there was great joy in Jerusalem**. **The whole assembly** was blessed; things were as they had been in Israel's golden age, and once more the prayers of Jehovah's priests were heard in **heaven**.

31:1 The first verse of chapter 31 is linked to the closing verse of the previous chapter. **When** the men of **Israel** left Jerusalem, they thoroughly destroyed the idols and idol shrines in **Judah, Benjamin, Ephraim, and Manasseh, then . . . returned to** their homes.

31:2–10 Hezekiah now **appointed the priests and the Levites . . . to their** respective duties, then provided for their **support** through tithes. The people responded so generously that there was **enough to eat and plenty left**.

31:11–19 Special **rooms** had to be set aside in the temple to store the surplus, and capable men were appointed as overseers. These are listed by name, showing how God takes note of each individual who serves His cause.

While the principle of tithing (giving one-tenth) is not commanded in the NT, the practice of systematic, proportionate giving *is* taught.

31:20, 21 Chapter 31 closes with a commendation of **Hezekiah**. Whatever he did for God, **he did . . . with all his heart**. No wonder **he prospered**!

32:1–8 Having carried the northern tribes into captivity (2 Kgs. 17), the Assyrians were now threatening to do the same to **Judah**. **Hezekiah**, who had earlier paid tribute to **Sennacherib** (2 Kgs. 18:13–16), was hard-pressed by the Assyrians to surrender his kingdom as well.

When **Sennacherib** invaded **Judah**, **Hezekiah** responded by cutting off **the water** supply **outside the city**, rebuilding and repairing **the wall** of Jerusalem, providing **weapons** and officers, and encouraging the people to look to Jehovah instead of fearing the army of the Assyrians. G. Campbell Morgan writes:

> It would seem to be a strange answer of God to the faithfulness of His servant that a strong foe should at this moment invade the kingdom. The story needs more details than are found in this record. They may be found in 2 Kings 18:7–16. From that passage we find that Hezekiah had flung off the yoke of the king of Assyria which his father Ahaz had consented to wear. Then Sennacherib had invaded Judah; and in a moment of weakness Hezekiah had paid him

a heavy tribute, and again yielded to his rule in order to buy him off. The result was not what he desired, for Sennacherib now demanded an unconditional surrender. In this hour of crisis, resulting from his own vacillation, his faith and courage were renewed. He took immediate action to embarrass the foe by stopping the supply of water, by strengthening the fortifications, by mobilizing his army, and finally by assuring the people: "There is a Greater with us than with him."[27]

32:9–19 While besieging **Lachish**, the **king of Assyria** taunted Hezekiah and the people, implying that Jehovah was no more powerful than the other **gods** he had already conquered, and suggesting that the wise thing to do was to stop listening to **Hezekiah** and to surrender. Verse 12 shows that even the Assyrians had heard about Hezekiah's reforms. But Sennacherib had not counted on two things: the loyalty of the people to King Hezekiah and the power of Jehovah.

32:20–23 After Sennacherib derided the Lord, **Hezekiah and . . . Isaiah** devoted themselves to prayer, and **the LORD sent an angel who cut down** the Assyrian army. Sennacherib **returned** home in humiliation and was later murdered by **his own** sons in **the temple of his god**.

32:24–26 Hezekiah's illness and recovery probably took place before the siege of Sennacherib. In his sickness he called on **the LORD** and was promised an extension of life, confirmed by **a sign** in which the sun seemed to go backward. When he failed to respond properly to this mercy, the Lord was angry with him, but because he **humbled himself** the punishment **did not come upon** Judah until after his death.

32:27–30 Special mention is made

of his **riches and honor**, and of the **tunnel** he built to bring **water** from a spring in the Kidron Valley to a reservoir inside Jerusalem. (See 2 Kings 20:20 for more details on this water tunnel.)

32:31 **Ambassadors** came from **Babylon**, intrigued by the celestial **wonder** that God had given Hezekiah. They would be especially interested in this since they worshiped the sun and stars. The king foolishly showed them his treasures, arousing their desire to possess them, a desire that was soon to be fulfilled.

32:32, 33 **The rest of the acts of Hezekiah . . . are written . . . in Isaiah**. When **Hezekiah** died, he was buried with full honors. **Manasseh his son reigned in his place**.

N. King Manasseh (33:1–20)

33:1–11 In spite of having such a devout father, **Manasseh** had the most **evil** reign in Judah. It was also the longest, **fifty-five** years. The list of Manasseh's sins is also very lengthy. He polluted God's city and temple with his idols and revived the practice of burning children to Molech **in the Valley of the Son of Hinnom**. He was an inveterate murderer (2 Kgs. 21:16); Josephus states that daily executions were ordered by him. Tradition says that he murdered Isaiah the prophet by having him sawn in two (the reference in Heb. 11:37 to being "sawn in two" may include this tradition). When **Manasseh** refused to **listen** to the LORD and turn from his wickedness, **the LORD** moved **the king of Assyria** to take him away **to Babylon**, which was then under Assyrian control.

33:12–20 Only 2 Chronicles mentions Manasseh's repentance (the reference in verse 18 is not to the canonical books of Kings but to a lost secular chronicle). After serving every kind of detestable idol for years, Manasseh learned that the LORD is **God**, and he was converted. He did what he could to lead the people back to faithfulness to Jehovah and to purge idolatry from his realm. **The high places** mentioned in verse 17 were used for sacrificing **to the LORD** away from Jerusalem. This was forbidden by the law, but went on anyway.

O. King Amon (33:21–25)

After Manasseh's death his son did not follow his reforms but rather his earlier sins. Young King **Amon** lasted only **two years** before he was **killed** by **his** own **servants in his own house**. Then **the people of the land** executed Amon's killers and replaced him with **his son Josiah**.

P. King Josiah (Chaps. 34, 35)

34:1–7 The idolatrous **altars** which Manasseh had removed from the city (33:15) had been brought back by Amon and the people. **In the eighth year of his reign** the teenage King **Josiah . . . began to seek the God of his father David**. Four years later he started his reforms. **Josiah** made sure that the same mistake would not be made again, so he completely destroyed everything connected with idolatry and burned it or ground it to **powder**. He extended his reforms to the farthest reaches of Israel.

34:8–18 Like the great reformers before him, he soon turned his attention to repairing **the temple**. A copy of **the Book of the Law** was subsequently **found** and **read . . . before the king**. Every major or minor revival of true faith has involved a rediscovery of the teaching of the Word of God. The great Reformation of the sixteenth century was no exception.

34:19–28 Josiah took its warnings

The lush Esdraelon Valley as viewed from the site of the ancient city of Megiddo.
(Photo by Howard Vos)

seriously and sent **to Huldah the prophetess** to see if there was still a chance for mercy. Her words only confirmed that God's **wrath** was on the way. However, Josiah would be spared from seeing Judah's day of **calamity because his heart was tender and** he **humbled** himself and believed the Word of the Lord.

34:29–32 Even though Josiah knew that judgment was inevitable, he still **gathered . . . the people** and entered into **a covenant** with **the Lord**. He set the Word of God before the people so that they might understand how grave their situation was and see the deep need for repentance.

34:33 Because of his strong leadership, he was able to promote fidelity to **the Lord** throughout his lifetime. The contents of verse 33 are treated in much greater detail in 2 Kings 23:4–20. The reform that followed the finding of the law and the making of the covenant was even more thorough than Josiah's first purge of his kingdom.

35:1–6 Like Hezekiah before him, **Josiah** encouraged **the priests** and **Levites** to carry out their appointed **service**. They were to **put the holy**

ark back in the temple, organize themselves in their respective **divisions**, take up their station in the temple, and be cleansed and ready to celebrate **the Passover**. There are several suggestions as to why **the ark** had been removed from the temple, and was now to be returned. The priests may have carried it **on** their **shoulders** from place to place to protect it from being profaned. Manasseh or some other idolatrous king may have ordered it to be removed. Josiah may have had it removed elsewhere while the temple was being restored.

35:7–19 Since the land was impoverished by the Assyrians, **Josiah** provided most of the animals for the feast, with other **leaders** and **priests** providing what they could. The Mosaic ordinances **for the Passover** and **the Feast of Unleavened Bread** were followed to the letter. Amid songs of praise, the king and the people celebrated the most notable **Passover . . . since the days of Samuel**. It was not the largest or most elaborate, but it was the most pleasing to Jehovah, perhaps because of the quality of the worship. This **Passover** was held in the same year as the great temple restoration (v. 19; cf. 34:8ff).

35:20–24 Nothing is mentioned about the next thirteen years of Josiah's reign. When he was thirty-nine he went out to fight against **Necho king of Egypt**. The Egyptian army was on its way **to fight** alongside the Assyrians **against** the Babylonians (2 Kgs. 23:29). Josiah could not imagine that God's hand was behind Necho's movements and did not inquire of the Lord to see if the Pharaoh's words were true. Although he **disguised himself**, he was killed in the battle.[28] His people greatly **mourned** his loss, and those who believed the word of the Lord knew that with **Josiah** gone, divine wrath was imminent (34:22–28).

John Whitcomb comments on these events.

> Now came one of the strangest episodes in Old Testament history. The heathen king, Necho II of Egypt, informed Josiah that "God hath commanded me to make haste" and that if Josiah interfered with God's plan, God would destroy him (2 Chron. 35:21). We would immediately dismiss such a statement as propaganda, of course, were it not for the explanation by the Chronicler that Josiah "hearkened not unto the words of Necho from the mouth of God"! Furthermore, Necho must be believed, for Josiah was killed. What does this mean? Did Josiah lose his salvation because of disobedience? No, for Huldah had said he would die "in peace" (2 Chron. 34:28). Was Pharaoh-necho a prophet of Jehovah? No, for God had spoken to pagan kings directly at various times without necessarily transforming their hearts (see Gen. 12:17–20; 20:3–7). We may conclude that God wanted to maneuver the Egyptian army to the Euphrates so that Nebuchadnezzar could de-

stroy it as well as the Assyrian army, and thus fulfill His warning that the Babylonians would conquer and chasten Judah (see Jer. 25:8–11).[29]

35:25–27 **Jeremiah . . . lamented** Josiah's death. The singers remembered him even after the captivity. **Josiah** was a man of one Book; he lived by **the Law of the LORD**, and his faithfulness is forever recorded in the Word of the Lord. In Jeremiah 22:16 we read, " 'He judged the cause of the poor and needy; then it was well. Was not this knowing Me?' says the LORD." Josiah evidenced by his life that he knew God. He started early to seek the Lord (34:3) and carefully obeyed the subsequent light he received. "Now before him there was no king like him, who turned to the LORD with all his heart, with all his soul, and with all his might, according to all the Law of Moses; nor after him did any rise like him" (2 Kgs. 23:25).

Q. King Jehoahaz (36:1–3)

The captivity of Judah took place in stages. In 605 B.C., Nebuchadnezzar entered Jerusalem, made Jehoiakim a vassal, and took captives to Babylon, including Daniel (2 Kgs. 24:1). In 597 B.C., Nebuchadnezzar again invaded Jerusalem, deported Jehoiachin, and took additional captives, including Ezekiel (2 Kgs. 24:10). Finally, in 586 B.C., Nebuchadnezzar destroyed the temple and took captive all but the poorest of the people (2 Kgs. 25:1–10).

Jehoahaz . . . reigned only **three months**, then was **deposed** by **the** Egyptian **king** and forced to pay heavy **tribute**. He was an evil man, not at all like his father Josiah (cf. 2 Kgs. 23:31–34). He was taken **to Egypt**, where he died.

R. King Jehoiakim (36:4–8)

Eliakim, also called **Jehoiakim**, was **Jehoahaz's** older **brother**. He was placed on the throne by **Necho**. His **eleven**-year reign was characterized by wickedness and was ended by **Nebuchadnezzar**, who looted the temple in 605 B.C. Nebuchadnezzar intended **to carry** Jehoiakim **to Babylon** but did not succeed. Although Chronicles does not record the fact, we know that he died ignominiously while still in Jerusalem, as Jeremiah had prophesied (Jer. 22:19; 36:30).

S. King Jehoiachin (36:9, 10)

Jehoiachin was eighteen (NKJV marg.[30]) **when he became king**. After a short reign of **three months and ten days**, **Jehoiachin** surrendered Jerusalem and spent the next thirty-seven years of his life in prison in **Babylon**. After the death of Nebuchadnezzar, he was released and elevated to a place of honor (2 Kgs. 25:27–30).

T. King Zedekiah (36:11–19)

Zedekiah, whose other name was Mattaniah, was yet another son of Josiah. When Jehoiachin proved unfaithful to the Babylonians, they chose Zedekiah as his successor. **He did evil** and refused to **humble himself before Jeremiah the prophet**. **He also** broke his oath to **Nebuchadnezzar** and **rebelled**. **Jerusalem** underwent a terrible siege lasting eighteen months. When 'the **Chaldeans** (Babylonians) took the city in 586 B.C., they **destroyed** it and the temple. Then they took all but the poorest of the land into exile.

IV. THE BABYLONIAN CAPTIVITY (36:20, 21)

The Jewish people had refused to keep the sabbatic year for 490 years; now their **land** would keep an enforced **Sabbath** for **seventy years**. For different ways of computing the seventy-year captivity, see the Introduction to the Commentary on Ezra.

V. THE DECREE OF CYRUS (36:22, 23)

While the people of Judah were in captivity, Babylon was conquered by Medo-Persia. Seventy years after the captivity began, **Cyrus**, **king of Persia**, issued **a proclamation** permitting the Jews to return to their land.

It is noteworthy that in the Hebrew order of the OT books, Chronicles stands last. Instead of ending "with a curse" (Mal. 4:6), the Jewish Bible ends on this positive and encouraging note:

> Thus says Cyrus king of Persia: All the kingdoms of the earth the LORD God of heaven has given me. And He has commanded me to build Him a house at Jerusalem which is in Judah. Who is among you of all His people? May the LORD his God be with him, and let him go up!

ENDNOTES

[1](2:3–10) How much did Solomon pay Hiram? First Kings 5:11 states one amount while 2 Chron. 2:10 gives another. First Kings refers to a personal gift given to Hiram's household while verse 10 refers to the supplies given to Hiram's workmen who were cutting lumber for Solomon.

[2](2:11–16) Who was Huram's mother? Second Chronicles 2:14 says she was a Danite while 1 Kings says she was a widow from the tribe of Naphtali. The answer is that she was a Danite whose first husband was from the tribe of Naphtali; hence she

was a widow of Naphtali. Her second husband was a man of Tyre.

[3](2:17, 18) How many overseers were there on the temple project: 3,600 (2:18) or 3,300 (1 Kgs. 5:16)? There are two other important passages to consider in resolving this problem. Second Chronicles 8:10 says that Solomon had 250 officers who ruled over the work. Add this number to the 3,600 overseers (2:18), and you get 3,850. First Kings 9:23 numbers Solomon's officers at 550. Add this number to the 3,300 overseers mentioned in 1 Kings 5:16 and you get 3,850. The total number of officers and overseers is therefore the same in both books; the proportion is just enumerated differently. The term "officers" refers to military or political personnel, while the term "overseers" refers to industrial personnel (i.e., superintendants or foremen).

[4](3:1–4) Was the porch 120 cubits high (3:4) or 30 cubits (1 Kgs. 6:2) high? Some say this is a copyist's error. Others, like Josephus, maintain that 120 cubits was the actual height. Matthew Poole thinks the 120 cubits refers to a kind of turret.

[5](3:14–17) Were the pillars in front of the temple thirty-five cubits tall (3:15) or eighteen cubits (1 Kgs. 7:15; Jer. 52:21)? Notice that 1 Kings specifically refers to the *height* of one pillar, while the margin of verse 15 says the pillars were thirty-five cubits *long* (i.e., together). In other words, thirty-five cubits was the *total* length of the pillars, which were probably cast in one piece and then cut in two. This would make the two pillars eighteen cubits each (to the nearest cubit).

[6](4:1–22) The measurements given for the Laver in 4:2 are sometimes used to show that the Bible contains error. If the diameter was ten cubits (180"), the circumference would be 180 times pi (π = 3.14), or 565.49 inches, instead of thirty cubits (540"). The difficulty is solved by noting that the Laver was a handbreadth thick (4"). Verse 2 gives the outside diameter and the inside circumference. The inside diameter would have been 180 inches minus two handbreadths (8"), or 172 inches. Multiplying 172 times pi (3.14), we get 540.36 inches, which to the nearest inch equals the thirty cubits of the text.

How much water did the Laver hold—2,000 baths (1 Kgs. 7:26), or 3,000 baths (4:5)? The answer—both. Two thousand baths was probably what the Sea held *normally*, but its brimful capacity was 3,000 baths.

[7](7:11–16) J. Barton Payne, "II Chronicles," *The Wycliffe Bible Commentary*, p. 397.

[8](8:7–10) How many officers were in Solomon's administration—250 (8:10) or 550 (1 Kgs. 9:23)? See Endnotes on 2 Chron. 2:17, 18.

[9](8:17, 18) Did Solomon receive 450 talents of gold from Ophir (8:18), or 420 (1 Kgs. 9:28)? The Hebrew numbers 2 and 5 could very easily be confused by later copyists. Some suggest that the thirty-talent difference went to pay for supplies and wages for the trip.

[10](9:13–28) The name *Tarshish* is used in a generic sense for areas connected with the refining of metals. In the OT it is used for a distant country rich in metals. "Most scholars identify the name with Tartessus, a city in SW Spain, . . . rich in silver, copper, and lead" (*The Revell Bible Dictionary*, p. 1136). "The ships of Tarshish" may have simply referred to deep-sea vessels used to transport refined metals, not necessarily doing business with Spain.

[11](9:13–28) Did Solomon have 4,000 stalls for his horses (v. 25), or 40,000

(1 Kgs. 4:26)? The NASB margin points out that 1 Kings 4:26 reads 4,000 in one ancient manuscript. Since there were only 12,000 horsemen, the very high figure in 1 Kings may well be a copyist's error.

[12](10:12–19) George Williams, *The Student's Commentary on the Holy Scriptures*, p. 246.

[13](12:9–12) Gold is widely recognized by Bible students as symbolic of deity, and bronze (KJV, brass) as symbolic of judgment.

[14](13:1–3) Abijah's mother, Michaiah, was the daughter of Uriel (13:2). But 2 Chronicles 11:20 says she was Maachah the daughter of Absalom. The Jewish historian Flavius Josephus tells us that Uriel was Absalom's son-in-law and the father of Michaiah or Maachah (two names for the same person). This makes Michaiah the daughter of Uriel and the granddaughter of Absalom. (The Hebrew word for *daughter* can also mean *granddaughter*.)

[15](14:3–8) Second Chronicles 14:3 and 14:5 state that Asa removed the high places, but 15:17 says that he did not. Which is right? Both statements are true. Some high places were dedicated to idols, while others were dedicated to Jehovah (e.g., 1 Kings 3:2). Some scholars think that Asa destroyed only the idolatrous shrines.

Keil believes that the second text merely implies that the king did not succeed in carrying his reforms out thoroughly. Rawlinson suggests that the above texts refer to different times; Asa in the early part of his reign, putting down idolatry with a strong hand, but in his later years, when his character had deteriorated, allowing idol-worship to creep in again. See John Haley, *Alleged Discrepancies of the Bible*, p. 323.

[16](15:16–19) The Hebrew word for *mother* can mean *grandmother* in some contexts, as here.

[17](16:1) According to 1 Kings 15:33, Baasha, the third king of the northern tribes, died in Asa's *twenty-seventh* year. But 2 Chronicles 15:19 and 16:1 speak of war between Baasha and Asa in Asa's *thirty-sixth* year. Thiele, an expert in the chronology of the Hebrew kings, maintains that Judah's history and not Asa's sole reign is meant here. The thirty-fifth year of Judah's kingdom, dating from Rehoboam's rebellion, would have been the fifteenth year of Asa's personal reign. This explanation is not without problems, too detailed to go into here. Many simply suggest that a copyist's error is the cause of the discrepancy.

[18](18:8–11) D. L. Moody, *Notes from My Bible*, p. 59.

[19](18:18–22) Matthew Henry, "1 Kings," *Matthew Henry's Commentary on the Whole Bible*, II:703.

[20](20:1–6) In Hebrew the word for *Syria* looks much like the spelling of *Edom*. A copyist's error would be easy to make here.

[21](22:1–9) The Masoretic Text of 2 Chronicles 22:2 says that Ahaziah was *forty*-two years old when he began to reign. However, 2 Kings 8:26 says he was *twenty*-two. This younger age seems likely because his father was only forty when he died. "Forty-two years old" is almost certainly a copyist's error.

[22](24:4–14) Was the chest for the collection of the money placed outside the gate (24:8), or was it located beside the altar (2 Kgs. 12:9)? Some commentators think there were two chests, one outside and one beside the altar. Others think that there was only one box but that it was moved.

[23](24:4–14) Second Kings 12:13 says that no temple vessels were made out of the money collected, but 2 Chroni-

cles 24:14 says that vessels were made with the surplus. Second Kings refers to what went to the workmen for repairing the house, while Chronicles refers to what was done with the surplus afterward.

[24](24:20–27) In 24:20 Zechariah is said to be the son of Jehoiada. However, our Lord referred to him as the son of Berechiah (Matt. 23:25). A different Zechariah, the author of the book by that name, is also said to be the son of Berechiah (Zech. 1:1, 7). A probable explanation is as follows: The Zechariah mentioned in 2 Chronicles 24 was the grandson of Jehoiada and the son of Berechiah; in Hebrew usage, *son* can also mean *grandson*. The Zechariah who wrote the book that bears his name was also the son of Berechiah, but a different Berechiah, of course. Both names were common in OT times.

[25](28:1–4) If Ahaz was thirty-six years old when he died (28:1), that would make him only eleven when Hezekiah was born (29:1), or according to another reconstruction of the data, fifteen. Some think that Ahaz could possibly father a child at eleven; he certainly could at fifteen. Others suggest that a copyist's error may be involved. The simple fact is that we do not have enough information to solve the problem of Ahaz's chronology.

[26](28:16–27) Second Kings 16:20 says that Ahaz was buried with his fathers while 2 Chronicles 28:27 says he was not buried in the tombs of the kings.

Both statements are true. He rested with his fathers and was buried with them (i.e., in the city of Jerusalem), although not in the actual royal tombs.

[27](32:1–8) G. Campbell Morgan, *Searchlights from the Word*, p. 127.

[28](35:20–24) Did Josiah die in Jerusalem (35:24), or in Megiddo (2 Kgs. 23:29)? He was mortally wounded in the battle at Megiddo, and Kings speaks of him as dying there because that is where he received his death wound. Chronicles more specifically states he actually died in Jerusalem. Today we might say a person died in an automobile accident even though he actually died in a hospital a little later. What we mean is that the accident was the cause of death even if it was not the location of the person's last breath.

[29](35:20–24) John C. Whitcomb, Jr., *Solomon to the Exile*, p. 141.

[30](36:9, 10) Verse 9 says Jehoiachin was *eight* years old when he became king while 2 Kings 24:8 says he was *eighteen*. Doubtless verse 9 contains a copyist's error, because Jehoiachin had wives when he surrendered to the Babylonians, only a few months after his ascension to the throne (2 Kgs. 24:15). Some Hebrew manuscripts and the Septuagint and Syriac versions also read *eighteen*.

BIBLIOGRAPHY

See Bibliography at the end of 1 Chronicles.

EZRA

Introduction

> "The Book of Ezra is a work of so simple a character as scarcely to require an 'Introduction'.... It is a plain and straightforward account of one of the most important events in Jewish history—the return of the people of God from the Babylonian captivity.... Very little that is directly didactic occurs in it: the writer tells his story as plainly as he can, and leaves his story to teach its own lesson."
>
> —George Rawlinson

I. Unique Place in the Canon

At one point in history Ezra and Nehemiah were one book in the Hebrew Bible, but being separate books (as in modern Bibles) was no doubt even earlier because Ezra 2 and Nehemiah 7 are virtually the same. Such a repetition would never occur in one book.

Ezra is spiritual, or religious history. It shows that a book which includes many documents from secular sources can by the Holy Spirit's selection and arrangement make them a part of the inspired record.

Of the 280 verses in Ezra we have the following most unusual breakdown for a Bible book:

111 verses:	registers
109 verses:	narrative
44 verses:	letters
10 verses:	prayer
3 verses:	proclamation
3 verses:	excerpt
280 total verses[1]	

II. Authorship

Although the book is anonymous, the inspired compilation of first person memoirs (see 7:27—9:15), genealogies, and documents is probably the work of Ezra. The official documents, logically enough, are in Aramaic, the official Gentile language used as a *lingua franca* during Ezra and Nehemiah's time. About one fourth of Ezra is in this language.[2] The beautiful *form* of the alphabet that we call "Hebrew" was actually borrowed from this semitic sister-tongue, Aramaic.

III. Date

A fifth century B.C. Jewish community living at Elephantine, on the Egyptian Nile, left behind papyri in Aramaic similar to that of Ezra and Nehemiah. This supports the traditional fifth century date of these books rather than the liberal notion of the era of Alexander the Great (about 330 B.C.).

Ezra is believed to have penned his book between the events at the end of chapter 10 (456 B.C.) and Nehemiah's arrival in Jerusalem (444 B.C.). The following chronological chart will aid in understanding the Books of Ezra, Nehemiah, and Esther:

Chronology of Ezra, Nehemiah, and Esther

(Dates are approximate)

538 BC	The decree of Cyrus to rebuild the temple.
538/7 BC	Zerubbabel's expedition to Jerusalem.
536 BC	Foundation of the temple laid.
535 BC	Work on the temple halted.
520 BC	Ministry of Haggai and Zechariah.
520 BC	Decree of Darius to resume work on the temple.
516 BC	Temple completed.
486 BC	Reign of Ahasuerus (Xerxes) begins.
479/8 BC	Esther crowned queen.
464 BC	Reign of Artaxerxes begins.
458 BC	Ezra's expedition to Jerusalem.
444 BC	Nehemiah arrives in Jerusalem.
444 BC	Walls of Jerusalem completed.
420 BC	Nehemiah's second journey to Jerusalem.

IV. Background and Themes

As the book of Ezra opens the Neo-Babylonian Empire is passing away and Jeremiah's prophecy of restoration of the Jews to their land is being fulfilled (Jer. 29:10–14).

In chapters 1—6 the first expedition back to Palestine takes place under Zerubbabel. The first thing the returned exiles do is to build the altar of burnt offering, followed by the house of the Lord. The latter goes up against much opposition from the enemies of God's people, but also with the encouragement of the Prophets Haggai and Zechariah.

Between chapters 6 and 7 there is a period of about fifty-eight years. During that era occur the dramatic story of Queen Esther in sacred history and the famous battles of Marathon, Thermopylae, and Salamis in secular history.[3]

Chapters 7—10 recount Ezra's journey to Jerusalem in about 458 B.C. with a commission from King Artaxerxes Longimanus. Ezra's personal attempts to reform the people are detailed in these chapters.

OUTLINE

B. Register of Those Who Returned (8:1–14)

C. Account of the Trip to Jerusalem (8:15–36)

D. Mixed Marriages and Ezra's Prayer of Confession (Chap. 9)

E. The Jews' Covenant to Put Away Foreign Wives and Children (Chap. 10)

Commentary

I. THE RETURN OF CAPTIVES TO JERUSALEM UNDER ZERUBBABEL (Chaps. 1—6)

A. The Decree of Cyrus (1:1–4)

The first three verses duplicate the last two verses of 2 Chronicles. God used **Cyrus**, **king of Persia**, to issue **a proclamation** permitting the Jews to return to **Judah** and to rebuild the temple **in Jerusalem**. In addition, he commanded their neighbors to contribute generously to the returning remnant. Many years before his birth, **Cyrus** had been named by God and set apart for this high destiny (Isa. 44:28—45:13). He illustrates the truth of Proverbs 21:1: "The king's heart is in the hand of the LORD, like the rivers of water; He turns it wherever He wishes."

The decree ended seventy years of captivity for the Jews. The seventy-year period can be calculated in two ways: from 605 B.C., when Nebuchadnezzar attacked Jerusalem and led off the first deportation, to 535

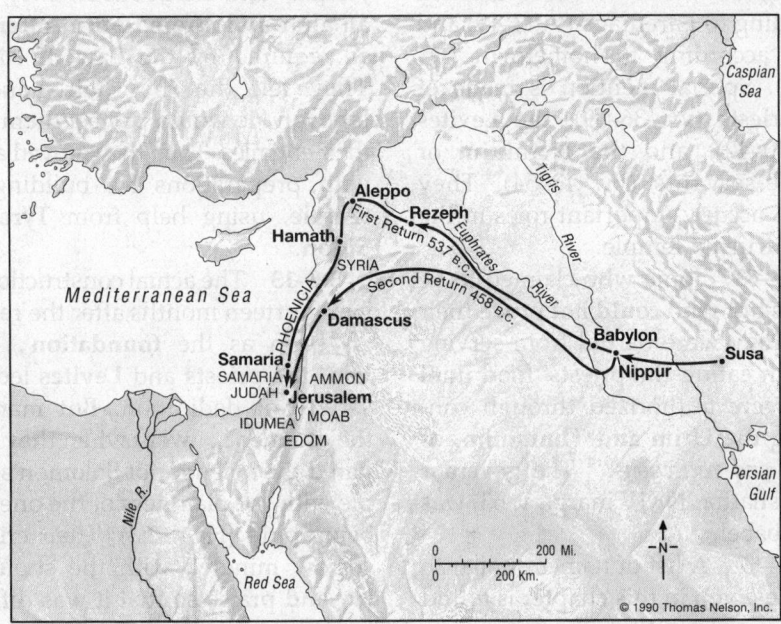

The Return from Exile. When Cyrus the Persian captured Babylon in 539 B.C., the way was opened for captive Judah to begin the return to her homeland. Two major expeditions made the journey, one in 537 B.C. and another in 458 B.C.

B.C., when the foundation of the temple was laid; or from the fall of Jerusalem, in 586 B.C., to the completion of the temple, in 516 B.C.

B. Preparations and Provisions (1:5–11)

In addition to the wealth donated by the neighbors of the Jews, **King Cyrus** gave them **five thousand four hundred** vessels **of gold and silver** that **Nebuchadnezzar had taken from** the temple in **Jerusalem**. **Sheshbazzar** (v. 8) may be the Persian name for Zerubbabel; he may be a totally different person. Notice the mention of **twenty-nine knives** in verse 9. If God cares for such details, how much more does He care for His people!

C. Register of Those Who Returned (Chap. 2)

2:1–58 In verses 1–61 we have a list of those **who returned to . . . Judah** under **Zerubbabel**. Some are recorded according to parentage (vv. 3–19) and some according to hometown (vv. 20–35). Special mention is made of **the priests** (vv. 36–39), **the Levites** (vv. 40–42), and **the Nethinim** or temple-servants (vv. 43–54). They would occupy important roles in the reconstructed temple.

2:59–63 Some who claimed to be **priests** but who **could not** prove their **genealogy** were barred from serving or from eating the priests' food until they were authorized through consulting **the Urim and Thummim**, or "*lights and perfections*."[4] The **governor** (or Tirshatha, NKJV marg., v. 63) was Zerubbabel.

2:64–67 A list of names similar to the one given in this chapter is found in Nehemiah 7. While there are some minor differences in tabulations, both

give the total number of Jews returning to Judah as **forty-two thousand three hundred and sixty** plus **seven thousand three hundred and thirty-seven** servants. Ezra adds 200 singers and Nehemiah adds 245. So the total of the returning remnant was about 50,000—a small fraction of those who had been carried away.

2:68–70 When the Jews reached **Jerusalem, some of the heads of the fathers' houses** contributed **gold** and **silver** for the construction of **the house of God** and **garments** for the priests. Then the **people** settled **in their** respective **cities**.

D. Construction of the Altar and the Temple Foundations (Chap. 3)

3:1–7 In **the seventh month**, which was the beginning of the civil year, the repatriated Jews **gathered** in **Jerusalem** to celebrate **the Feast of Tabernacles**. Under the leadership of **Jeshua**[5] and **Zerubbabel**, they **built an altar** and **offered burnt offerings**, as required by **the Law of Moses**. They felt that by their honoring Jehovah He would protect them from their enemies. Then they moved ahead with preparations for building **the temple**, using help from **Tyre** and **Sidon**.

3:8–13 The actual construction began fourteen months after the return. As soon as the **foundation . . . was laid, the priests** and **Levites** led in a service of dedication. But many of the **old men . . . wept** when they compared the splendor of Solomon's temple with the plainness of the one now being built (Hag. 2:3). Their cries of sorrow mingled with the shouts of **joy** and praise so that it was difficult to distinguish them, **and the sound was heard afar off**.

E. Opposition to Rebuilding the Temple (Chap. 4)

1. In the Reign of Cyrus (4:1-5, 24)

4:1-3 **The adversaries of Judah and Benjamin** mentioned in verse 1 were descendants of colonists from other countries who had been planted in the land when Assyria took the northern kingdom into captivity. These colonists had intermarried with the Jews who remained in the land, and their offspring became known as Samaritans. **They came to Zerubbabel** and pretended that they wanted to assist in the rebuilding of the temple. They, too, worshiped Jehovah, but He was only one of many gods in their idolatrous system of religion. So their offer was refused by Israel's leaders.

4:4-5, 24 The Samaritans then changed their strategy. First they **tried to discourage the people** of Judah. Then **they troubled them in building**. They also **hired counselors** to lobby against Israel at the royal court **to frustrate** the Jews through the use of scare tactics. The work on the temple thus came to a halt.

Verse 24 follows verse 5 chronologically. The enemies of Judah succeeded in having **work** on the temple stopped **until the second year of** Darius's **reign**.

2. In the Reign of Ahasuerus (4:6)[6]

Verse 6 mentions a letter that was written during **the reign of Ahasuerus**, bringing **an accusation against** the Jews. Verses 7-23 describe another letter, written in the days of Artaxerxes, accusing the Jews of rebuilding the city and its walls as an act of rebellion. The king thereupon ordered the work to stop.

3. In the Reign of Artaxerxes (4:7-23)

The rebuilding of the temple was completed during the reign of Darius,

who ruled before Ahasuerus (v. 6) and **Artaxerxes** (v. 7). Therefore, the letters described in verses 6-23 were written *after* the temple was rebuilt. They have to do with attempts to rebuild **the walls** of Jerusalem, not *the temple*. But they are placed here, out of their chronological order, as further illustrations of attempts made to obstruct the work of the returned exiles.

From 4:6 to 6:8, the **language** used is **Aramaic**[7] instead of Hebrew. This was the language used by **Persia** in official decrees.

F. Haggai and Zechariah's Encouragement to Rebuild (5:1, 2)

From **Haggai** 1:1 **and Zechariah** 1:1 we learn that this chapter belongs to the second year of Darius's reign (v. 1, cf. 4:24). These two **prophets** urged the Israelites to resume work on the temple instead of building expensive houses for themselves (Hag. 1:4). **Zerubbabel . . . and Jeshua** obeyed the Lord and ordered construction to begin immediately. Notice here that it was not by the power of the king's decree that the work was resumed, but by the power of *the Holy Spirit* speaking through **the prophets of God** (cf. Zech. 4:6).

G. Opposition During the Reign of Darius (5:3-17)

5:3-5 Opposition arose quickly. The Persian **governor** and his associates **came to** Jerusalem and asked what authority the Jews had to start building and what **the names of the men** were (see vv. 9, 10). They were given **the names** of the Jewish leaders. These Persian officials were more reasonable than those mentioned in chapter 4. They did not stop the work, but sent a **letter . . . to Darius**

to determine its legality. Because the Jews had started to obey God's word, His **eye . . . was upon** them to fulfill it.

5:6–17 In their **letter . . . to Darius**, **Tattenai . . . and Shethar-Boznai** told of their conversation with the Jews and the latter's reply. The **elders** of the people first of all gave their divine authority. They were **servants of** the one true **God**, but they had been delivered up to the Babylonians because of their sins. Now that Jehovah had brought them back to their land, they were to rebuild His temple. As to human authority, they had the **decree** of **Cyrus** which gave them permission to rebuild the temple. **Cyrus** himself had contributed generously to the project. The governor requested that **a search be made** to determine if **King Cyrus** had made such **a decree** and asked Darius to notify him what action should be taken **concerning this matter**.

H. Completion of the Temple through a Favorable Decree of Darius (Chap. 6)

6:1–5 After diligent search, the **decree** of Cyrus **was found** in what used to be his capital city, **Achmetha** (or Ecbatana, NKJV marg.). (The edict was much more detailed than is summarized in chap. 1.) In it, the specifications of **the temple** were given along with an order to return all **the gold and silver articles** taken by **Nebuchadnezzar**.

6:6–12 **Darius** then spelled out to **Tattenai** and his colleagues their responsibilities toward the Jews. They were not to hinder **the work** but were to pay for **the cost** of the temple out of the royal treasury from collected **taxes**. Provisions for the temple service were to be supplied upon **request of the priests** (v. 9) so that the Jews might find favor in the eyes of **God** and hence be effectual in their prayers

for the . . . king and his family. Darius put some teeth into his **edict** by making it a capital offense to hinder the work. He called on **God** to deal with anyone, kings included, who might try to **destroy this house of God** in the future.

6:13–15 The king's orders were quickly obeyed and the work on the temple surged ahead. With encouragement from God's prophets and provisions from Darius's treasury, the temple was completed four years later, but nineteen or twenty years after the laying of the foundation. **Artaxerxes** actually lived later; he contributed to the maintenance of the temple, not to its building.

6:16 The Israelites and their leaders **celebrated the dedication of the** temple with joy. Dennett observes:

> It was but natural that they should rejoice at such a moment, for the house of their God was the expression of all the blessings of the covenant in which they stood. And at length, after weary years of failure, difficulties, disappointments, and sorrow, it stood completed before their eyes. It was for this that they had been brought up out of Babylon, and if any of them had sown in tears they now reaped in joy.[8]

6:17–22 They **offered sacrifices**. If we compare this dedication with Solomon's—22,000 oxen and 120,000 sheep plus innumerable oxen and sheep sacrificed before the ark (2 Chron. 7:5; 5:6), it pales into a poor and feeble event. Fortunately, they did not dwell on this.

Today in many churches, fellowships, denominations, schools, and even whole countries of Christendom, a comparison not unlike the decline from Solomon's time to Ezra's is apparent. Dennett has an encouraging application that is worth quoting at length:

> Faith, however, has to do with unseen things, and it could thus recall to the mind of this feeble remnant that Jehovah was no less mighty and no less merciful for them than for Solomon.
>
> The house might be less glorious, and they themselves but poor subjects of a Gentile monarch, but if God was for them, as He was, the resources available to faith were as unbounded as ever. This truth cannot be too deeply impressed on our minds, that Christ remains the same for His people in a day of difficulty as in a season of prosperity. To be in the power of this raises us, as nothing else can, above our circumstances, and gives us courage to press on, whatever the perils of the path.[9]

Afterward **the Passover** was observed and **the Feast of Unleavened Bread** was **kept . . . with** great **joy**, for the people clearly saw God's hand behind the favors they had obtained from Darius. Darius is called **the king of Assyria** here because he was ruling over the old Assyrian empire.

II. THE RETURN OF CAPTIVES UNDER EZRA (Chaps. 7—10)

A. Generous Authorization by Artaxerxes (Chap. 7)

7:1–5 There is about a fifty-eight-year gap between chapters 6 and 7. (See the chart "CHRONOLOGY OF EZRA, NEHEMIAH, AND ESTHER" in the Introduction.) During that time Darius was succeeded by Ahasuerus (Xerxes). His reign covered the events recorded in the book of Esther. After him, **Artaxerxes** (Longimanus), mentioned in verse 1, came to the throne.

A brief genealogy of **Ezra** is given in verses 1–5 to show his priestly ancestry. G. Campbell Morgan comments:

> As messengers of the will of God, the scribes took the place of the prophets, with this difference: instead of receiving new revelations, they explained and applied the old. Of this new order Ezra was at once the founder and type. . . . He was expert in exposition and application of the Law. The qualifications for such work are very clearly set out in the statement made concerning him in the tenth verse of this chapter. He "set his heart to seek . . . to do . . . to teach."[10]

7:6–10 Besides possessing a distinguished pedigree, **Ezra was . . . a skilled scribe in the Law of Moses**. Certainly **Ezra** was a man of the Book and a living illustration of the first three verses of Psalm 1.[11] Because he meditated on **the Law of the LORD** day and night, he prospered in what he sought to do for God. Jehovah once more directed the heart of a heathen king to carry out His counsels. A decree was issued which made possible a second return **to Jerusalem**, this one under **Ezra**.

7:11–26 **King Artaxerxes** of Persia granted sweeping powers **to Ezra** in this **letter** recorded here. Any Israelites who desired could accompany him **to Jerusalem**, where he was **to inquire** if everything was being done in accordance with **the Law** of Moses. Generous gifts had been donated by **the king and his counselors**. These, along with any temple vessels which were still left **in . . . Babylon**, were committed to his charge. The gifts were to be used to maintain the temple services, and any surplus was to be distributed at Ezra's discretion. If that was not enough, **silver, wheat, wine, oil, and salt** were to be supplied **without prescribed limit** from the royal treasury. The last four items were essential ingredients in the Jewish sacrificial system. Those who served in the temple were granted exemption from taxes. Finally, the edict gave Ezra the political power to appoint **magistrates and judges** for the Jews living west of **the** Euphrates **River**. These **judges** were to **teach** and enforce **the laws of . . . God**.

7:27, 28 In his thanksgiving prayer, Ezra **blessed . . . God** for directing **the king's heart to beautify** the temple and humbly thanked Him for the enabling strength He gave to undertake such an important work. **Encouraged** by the Lord's **hand** on him, Ezra **gathered chief men of Israel to go up with** him to Jerusalem.[12]

B. Register of Those Who Returned (8:1–14)

8:1–14 This first paragraph lists those who went back to Jerusalem **with** Ezra **from Babylon**. Several from these same families had returned under Zerubbabel years earlier (chap. 2). Almost 1500 **males** made up this second expedition.

C. Account of the Trip to Jerusalem (8:15–36)

8:15–20 While stopped **by the river** near **Ahava** (location unknown), Ezra noticed that there were no Levites in his company, so he commissioned eleven of the leading **brethren** to go to **Casiphia**, where he evidently knew that some Levites had settled, to encourage the Levites and temple **servants** to join him. Thirty-eight **Levites** and **two hundred and twenty Nethinim** (servants) responded.

8:21–23 Before the Jews began their 900-mile journey, they camped **at the river of Ahava**, and there Ezra proclaimed **a fast**. He had previously testified of God's goodness and power to the king. **To request** a military escort now would be to deny his words by his actions. Instead he put his faith on the line, trusting in the God who delights to save those who lean hard on Him. He would not be disappointed. **He answered** their **prayer**.

8:24–34 The money and utensils that had been given to Ezra **were weighed** out to **twelve of the leaders of the priests** and twelve **Levites**. Since these things were holy (set apart for sacred use), they had to be kept by men who were holy. After a three-and-a-half-month trek, the entire party reached **Jerusalem** without incident. Upon arrival in Jerusalem **the silver and the gold and the articles** were **weighed** again and given to those in charge of the temple.

8:35, 36 The first order of business for the exiles was to offer **burnt** and **sin** offerings on Jehovah's altar for all Israel. When they had taken care of their spiritual obligations, **they delivered the king's orders** to his officials in the western provinces, who in turn supplied them accordingly.

D. Mixed Marriages and Ezra's Prayer of Confession (Chap. 9)

9:1, 2 Ezra had not been in Jerusalem long when some of **the leaders** approached him with the disturbing news that **the rulers** and **the people** were intermarrying with the heathen. This was one of the sins for which Israel had been punished in days past. The law was clear (Ex. 34:16; Deut. 7:3); God's people must be holy. He wants them to separate themselves from the world and every other form of evil.

9:3, 4 Ezra was **astonished** when he **heard** about these mixed marriages. He was plunged into deep mourning **until the evening sacri-**

fice. With **robe** torn and patches of **hair** missing from his **head and beard**, he **sat** in silence while others who feared the Lord gathered around him.

9:5–15 As the blood of **the evening sacrifice** was being poured out before Jehovah for the **iniquities** of the people, Ezra **fell** to his **knees** and lifted his voice in confession. Making the people's sin his own, he was **humiliated** that they had responded so wickedly to the **grace** which had preserved them **as a remnant** through past judgments **and** had given **them a peg in His holy place** (v. 8). This "peg" speaks of the security of anyone or anything that depends on God. Some, such as Ironside, believe that ultimately it refers to Christ Himself:

> The reference to the "nail" [**peg**, NKJV] is doubtless a recognition of Isaiah's prophecy of the "nail in a sure place," upon which Jehovah's glory was to hang, which is, in the full sense, Christ Himself (Isa. 22:21–25).[13]

The prophets had spoken clearly on mixed marriages, so the men were without excuse, especially in light of the recent favors God had granted them. **"Here we are before You, in our guilt."** There was nothing else to say.

E. The Jews' Covenant to Put Away Foreign Wives and Children (Chap. 10)

10:1–5 Ezra's prayer of confession caused **the people** to weep **bitterly**. Acting as a spokesman, **Shechaniah** confessed their guilt but reminded **Ezra** that there was yet **hope**, if their confession was followed by forsaking the unequal yoke. He suggested that Ezra lead them in making **a covenant . . . to put away** the foreign **wives and** children. **The priests, the Levites,** and all Israel responded to this plea for national repentance and **so they swore an oath**.

10:6–8 All the exiles were summoned to **gather at Jerusalem** for a solemn time of public confession. Those who refused to come **within three days** and face the issues were threatened with loss of **property** and excommunication.

10:9–11 With only **three days** to respond to the command, **all the men of Judah and Benjamin** hurried to **Jerusalem** from the surrounding cities. Adverse weather did not deter them, for the matter to be settled was very grave and caused more consternation than did the rainy weather. **Ezra** spoke to the gathering, pointing out their transgressions.

10:12–17 **All the assembly** was quick to acknowledge that they had disobeyed God's law. But because of the **heavy rain** and the large number of cases involved, they suggested that the individual cases be examined city by city. Four men tried to oppose the plan but were unsuccessful. Judges were appointed, and in less than two weeks the inquiry began. Within three months the probe was complete.

10:18–44 Those indicted are listed in verses 18–43: **priests** first (vv. 18–22), then **Levites** (vv. 23, 24), and finally **others of Israel** (vv. 25–43). Verse 44 reads: **All these had taken pagan wives, and some of them had wives by whom they had children.** Though it is not stated, it is likely that adequate provision was made for the support of these **wives** and **children**. The sorrow created by the disruption of these families must be weighed against the importance of maintaining the solidarity of the nation destined to produce the Messiah.

The unequal yoke is still forbidden (2 Cor. 6:14–18). It should not be found among the children of God. But 1 Corinthians 7:12, 13 is the NT rule for those already bound to an unbeliever at conversion. Under grace, the believer is not required to put away the unbeliever or the children. The latter are set apart in a position of external privilege by the believer.

The book of Ezra is a study in revival. When men read the Word of God and apply its truths to their lives, when intercessory prayers flow for the saints, and when there is confession and separation from known sin, there will be power in the church to do great things for God.

ENDNOTES

[1](Intro) This breakdown is from W. Graham Scroggie, *Know Your Bible*, Vol. I, Old Testament, p. 90. (His total, "880," is no doubt a typographical error.)

[2](Intro) 4:8—6:18 and 7:12–26 are in Aramaic.

[3](Intro) Scroggie, *Know Your Bible*, Vol. I, p. 91.

[4](2:59–63) We do not know for certain exactly what the Urim and Thummim were: "Possibly two precious stones, which were put inside the pouch. They may have been used, like lots, to determine God's will" (*Ryrie Study Bible*, New King James Version, p. 135). See also Ex. 28:30; Lev. 8:8; Num. 27:21; Deut. 33:8; 1 Sam. 28:6; Neh. 7:65.

[5](3:1–7) Jeshua (or "Yeshua") is the Hebrew form of *Jesus*.

[6](4:6) Verses 6–23 belong later in the outline chronologically. See the chart "Chronology of Ezra, Nehemiah, and Esther."

[7](4:7–23) Older books in English often called this language "Chaldee."

[8](6:16) Edward Dennett, *Exposition of the Book of Ezra: Restoration from Babylon*, p. 55.

[9](6:17–22) *Ibid.*, pp. 55, 56.

[10](7:1–5) G. Campbell Morgan, *Searchlights from the Word*, p. 131.

[11](7:6–10) Although Psalm 1 is anonymous, many Bible scholars believe that Ezra is the human author (likewise of Psalm 119, which is about the Word of God).

[12](7:27, 28) In the Bible, going to Jerusalem is always "up," no matter from which direction one is coming. This is partly because the city is up in the mountains of Judea. It probably also has a spiritual application: Going to *God's* house is always "up."

[13](9:5–15) H. A. Ironside, "Notes on the Book of Ezra," in *Notes on Ezra, Nehemiah and Esther*, p. 90.

BIBLIOGRAPHY

Dennett, Edward. *Exposition of the Book of Ezra: Restoration from Babylon*. Oak Park, IL: Bible Truth Publishers, 1956.

Ironside, H. A. "Ezra." In *Notes on Ezra, Nehemiah and Esther*. Neptune, NJ: Loizeaux Brothers, 1972.

Jensen, Irving L. *Ezra/Nehemiah/Esther*. Chicago: Moody Press, 1970.

Keil, C. F. "Ezra." In *Biblical Commentary on the Old Testament*. Vol. 10. Grand Rapids: Wm. B. Eerdmans Publishing Co., 1971.

Kidner, Derek. *Ezra and Nehemiah*. The Tyndale Old Testament Commentaries. Downers Grove, IL: InterVarsity Press, 1979.

Rawlinson, George. "Ezra." In *The Pulpit Commentary*. Vol. 15. Ed. by H.D.M. Spence. New York: Funk and Wagnalls, 1909.

NEHEMIAH

Introduction

"More than half this book is a personal record, punctuated with 'asides' and frank comments which make it (in such parts) one of the liveliest pieces of writing in the Bible. Much of Ezra's story was also told in the first person (Ezra 8:15—9:15), but Ezra was a quieter personality than the formidable, practical Nehemiah; he does not leap out of the page as this man does."

—Derek Kidner

I. Unique Place in the Canon

If you are having any sort of a building program and are having trouble getting people involved, Nehemiah is the book to read, study, teach, or preach. The leadership qualities needed to get a nearly impossible job done are wonderfully exemplified in this 5th century B.C. Hebrew leader.

Whitcomb writes:

No portion of the Old Testament provides us with a greater incentive to dedicated, discerning zeal for the work of God than the book of Nehemiah. The example of Nehemiah's passion for the truth of God's Word—whatever the cost or consequences, is an example sorely needed in the present hour.[1]

II. Authorship

Nehemiah, whose name appropriately means *Jehovah consoles*, writes his memoirs in the first person, but he also includes state documents to which he had access. The Elephantine papyri witness to the historical truth of the book, mentioning Johanan

the high priest (see Neh. 12:22, 23) and the sons of Nehemiah's arch-foe, Sanballat.

All of this supports the traditional authorship by Nehemiah the son of Hachaliah and brother of Hanani (1:1, 2). We know little of Nehemiah's background, but he was probably born in Persia.

The tact, drive, and leadership qualities shown in this book are the type that would be demanded by Nehemiah's position as king's cupbearer, a very important position.

III. Date

Nehemiah probably wrote soon after the events recorded, or about 430 B.C. This would be during the reign of Artaxerxes I (464–424 B.C.).

Josephus says that Jaddua was high priest when Alexander the Great came through Palestine. Since Nehemiah 12:22 mentions a Jaddua, some use this to date the book later than Nehemiah's time. It may be that Jaddua was a very young man when Nehemiah mentioned him (because he was in the priestly line) and was about ninety in Alexander's time. Or, there may have been two high priests with this name. A third possibility is that Josephus, who often was wrong on his chronology of this era, was mistaken here as well!

IV. Background and Theme

Nehemiah was the *third* great leader in the Jewish restoration. Zerubbabel led the *first* group of exiles back to Jerusalem in 538–537 B.C. (Ezra 2) and supervised the building of the temple. Almost eighty years later, Ezra the scribe came to the holy city with a *second* group of Jews, bringing sweeping reforms through his ministry of God's Word. But in time things degenerated in Jerusalem.

Thirteen years after Ezra's expedition, Nehemiah was burdened by God about conditions in Jerusalem. After receiving permission to rectify the situation, he provided the kind of quality leadership the Israelites desperately needed. His roots were deep in God (notice the numerous references to his prayer life); this enabled him to weather the storm of opposition that buffeted him from the outset of his mission. It has been well said that "there are three kinds of people in the world—those who don't know what's happening, those who watch what's happening, and those who make things happen." Nehemiah was a man who made things happen. Whereas the book of Ezra deals with the temple and worship, Nehemiah deals with the walls and everyday work. The book of Nehemiah brings God into the everyday affairs of life.

OUTLINE

C. Elimination of Illegal Activity on the Sabbath (13:15–22)
D. Dissolution of Interracial Marriages (13:23–31)

Commentary

I. NEHEMIAH'S FIRST VISIT: RESTORATION OF JERUSALEM (Chaps. 1—12)

A. Consternation over Jerusalem's Condition (Chap. 1)

1:1–3 Little is given by way of introduction in this first chapter. We are told only two things about **Nehemiah**: his father's name was **Hachaliah** and he himself was the cupbearer to King Artaxerxes, a very influential position. His reaction to the news **concerning Jerusalem** shows that he was a man of spiritual character. J. Alec Motyer comments:

It is rather an uncertain time of history, but it seems very likely that some of the enthusiasm engendered by the mission of Ezra took a political or nationalistic direction; enthusiasm was so roused that it began to flow out into an unauthorized rebuilding of the walls of Jerusalem. Some of the enemies of God's people in the area reported this matter back to . . . Artaxerxes, and he commanded that the building work should cease. The enemies of God capitalized on this by going up to Jerusalem with the royal mandate in their hands, causing the work to cease, and tearing down the city walls. It is very likely that it was the news of this action which came to Nehemiah.[2]

1:4–11 Nehemiah had a burden for the remnant in Judah. Even though he had not experienced their hard-ships, he identified with them, denying himself the luxuries of the palace in order to fast, mourn, and pray. He confessed their **sins** as his own and asked God to **remember** His Word and to be faithful in regathering His people as He had been righteous in scattering them. He also asked the Lord to **grant him** favor **in the sight** of the king, for a bold plan to aid his brethren was taking shape in his mind. For days he pleaded his case before the Most High.

Nehemiah is often used as an example of effective leadership. First, he had a vision of a goal to be achieved. After analyzing the problem, he decided on a proper course of action. Then he motivated others to share his vision and to become actively involved. Next we see him delegating authority and assigning tasks. He supervised the work and checked on performance until the project was satisfactorily completed.

B. Authorization for Jerusalem's Restoration (2:1–8)

2:1–3 It was three or four months before Nehemiah's faith was rewarded in a most unexpected way. One day when he was serving **wine . . . to the king**, his **face** betrayed his **sorrow of heart**. The king's question brought on a wave of fear, for sadness was not allowed in the royal presence (Est. 4:2). George Williams notes:

Eastern monarchs being in daily dread of poison, any appearance of agitation in the cup-bearer would be regarded as especially suspicious.[3]

But Nehemiah meant no harm to the king. The cause of his sorrow was the desolation of Jerusalem, his ancestral home.

2:4, 5 Nehemiah's prayerful dependence upon the Lord was not in vain. Not only did **the king** give him what he requested, he also made him governor of **Judah** (5:14). Artaxerxes' decree fulfilled the word of the Lord to Daniel (Dan. 9:25), even as the earlier decree of Cyrus had fulfilled the prophecy of Jeremiah (Jer. 29:10; Ezra 1).

2:6–8 In answer to the king's question, Nehemiah told him how long he expected to be away. As it turned out, Nehemiah was away from Persia for at least twelve years (5:14). In all of this Nehemiah acknowledged the **good hand of God upon** him.

C. Reconstruction of Jerusalem's Wall (2:9—6:19)

1. Private Inspection and Public Opposition (2:9–20)

2:9–16 Along with the **king's** official **letters**, Artaxerxes sent an armed escort with Nehemiah. Shortly after he **came to Jerusalem**, the new governor surveyed his capital under cover of darkness in order to attract as little attention as possible and to keep his plans secret. He knew it was imperative that **the walls** be repaired if the city was to survive. At one place the rubble was so deep that his mount could not **pass**.

2:17–20 Later he called the leaders together, told them what needed to be done, and encouraged them by relating how **the hand** of the Lord **had been** with him so far, **and also of the king's words**. The Jews were

excited and ready to begin. Their enemies, **Sanballat**, **Tobiah**, and **Geshem**, scoffed and tried to stop the building project by raising the false cry of "rebellion **against the king**." But Nehemiah was not intimidated; the **God** of **heaven** had promised success. The people were united, and that is necessary if God is going to bless (Ps. 133:1–3).

2. The Workers and Their Work (Chap. 3)

The priests were the first to begin the task by repairing **the Sheep Gate**. This gate, located in the northeastern corner of the city, was so named because the sheep destined for the temple altar were brought through it. The gates are mentioned counterclockwise: **the Sheep Gate** (vv. 1, 2); **the Fish Gate** (vv. 3–5); **the Old Gate** (or Corner Gate) (vv. 6–12); **the Valley Gate** (v. 13); **the Refuse** (or Dung) **Gate** (v. 14); **the Fountain Gate** (vv. 15–25); **the Water Gate** (v. 26); **the Horse Gate** (v. 28); **the East Gate** (v. 29); and **the Miphkad Gate** (Inspection Gate, NASB) (v. 31). Verse 32 brings us back full circle to **the Sheep Gate**. Two other gates are mentioned in the book—the Gate of Ephraim (8:16) and the Prison Gate (Gate of the Guard, NASB) (12:39). There were twelve gates in all, even as there will be twelve gates in the New Jerusalem (Rev. 21:12). It is significant that God keeps a careful record of all those who serve Him; this is seen in the listing of those who repaired the walls and gates.

The House of the Mighty (v. 16) may originally have been the headquarters for David's mighty men.

Men and women, artisans and laborers, princes and commoners, all labored side by side. There was only one case of disunity—the **nobles** of

Excavated section of the wall built by Nehemiah in Jerusalem after the Jewish people returned from the Captivity in Babylonia.

Tekoa shirked their responsibility (v. 5). Some who finished their assigned task took on an additional portion of the wall (cf. vv. 4 and 21; 5 and 27). God has given different work assignments to believers today. He has equipped us with various gifts and abilities appropriate to our calling, and He knows who is not really involved and who is doing double duty. "Each one's work will become clear; for the Day will declare it, because it will be revealed by fire; and the fire will test each one's work, of what sort it is" (1 Cor. 3:13).

3. External Hindrances and Special Precautions (Chap. 4)

4:1–6 When **Sanballat** and **Tobiah ... mocked** the early rebuilding efforts, Nehemiah responded by prayer and went on with the work. While the imprecatory language of verses 4 and 5 was acceptable in the Dispen-

sation of Law, it would not be suitable for Christians in this Age of Grace (Rom. 12:19–21). Soon the wall reached **half its** intended **height**.

4:7–14 External pressure from the **Arabs**, the **Ammonites, and the Ashdodites** was not the only threat; at times the immensity of the job almost crushed the Jews. The seemingly unending piles of rubble sapped their **strength** and drive (v. 10). When their countrymen living outside Jerusalem warned of imminent attack, Nehemiah **positioned men behind the lower parts of the wall** and armed the workers, encouraging them to **"Remember the Lord ... and fight."**

4:15–23 With the element of surprise lost, Judah's **enemies** abandoned their plan for a direct attack. **From that time on, half** the Jews **worked at construction, while the other half** stood guard. Even **the builders** carried weapons. Nehemiah kept a trumpeter with him at all times to sound the alarm in case of attack and **rally** the men who were spread out along **the wall**. Those who came from outside the city were ordered to spend the **night in Jerusalem** so as to be readily available if needed. Their strategy was to *pray*, *watch*, and *work*. The people emulated the courage and resoluteness of their indomitable leader. Nehemiah, his relatives, his **servants**, and **the** Persian **guard** that accompanied him gave themselves no leisure as they kept vigil over the city.

4. Internal Problems and Social Reformation (Chaps. 5, 6)

5:1–7 In the midst of rebuilding, an ugly internal problem arose. Food was evidently scarce and expensive. Inflation, plus **the . . . tax** burden placed on the Jews by the king, had reduced many of them to poverty. They were forced to borrow **money** from their wealthier brothers and to mortgage their property. Some even had to sell their **sons** and **daughters** as slaves. And since their land was owned by others, they were left without means to buy back the children. When they told Nehemiah of their sad plight, he called the wealthy to a solemn assembly and **rebuked** them.

5:8–10 Was it not inconsistent to drive their **Jewish brethren . . . into slavery** when Nehemiah and others had been redeeming them from bondage to their heathen neighbors? Was it not imperative for their safety that they maintain a right relationship with **God**? How could they afford to alienate Jehovah by breaking His holy law by charging **usury** (vv. 9, 10; cf. Ex. 22:25)? Even as their leader, Nehemiah, had set an example by not charging interest on loans he made, should they not do the same?

5:11, 12 After Nehemiah urged the rich to return the property gained by usury and to **restore** a measure of the interest exacted on loans of **money**, **grain**, **new wine**, and **oil**, they promised to do so. The **priests** were **called** and they sealed their pledge with **an oath**.

5:13 A vivid warning was then given of what would happen to anyone who reneged. He would **be shaken** off the good land like the dust off a **garment**. With a hearty **"Amen"** the men left the meeting and performed their vow.

5:14–19 A short account of Nehemiah's **twelve**-year tenure as **governor** closes chapter 5. He supported himself rather than charge the people with his maintenance. He did not take advantage of his position to acquire **land** or feather his nest for the future. His time was devoted to making Jerusalem safe for his **brothers**, not to building his own personal fortune. He supplied his own **table** and welcomed strangers to share his hospitality. He did all this because he feared **God**. If **God** kept track of his sacrifices, that was sufficient for Nehemiah.

6:1–4 Having failed to obstruct the Jews by other means, the enemy next tried to destroy Nehemiah. Four times **Sanballat** and **Geshem the Arab** tried to get Nehemiah to leave his work and meet with them **in the plain of Ono**. **Four times** Nehemiah refused, knowing that they were plotting **to do** him **harm**. Such a **great work** must not be stopped.

6:5–9 Still pretending to be his ally, **Sanballat** accused Nehemiah in a **letter** of planning to make himself **king** of **Judah** in rebellion against **the king** of Persia. Sanballat said he wanted to help Nehemiah avoid trouble with the king and suggested that they get **together** to discuss the matter. But Nehemiah refused, knowing all too well that Sanballat did not have his best interests at heart. Besides, the slanderous charges were false. Nehemiah's loyalty spoke for itself.

6:10–14 It was no secret that Nehemiah was a devout **man** and one who feared the Word of the Lord. So false prophets were hired to trick him into sinning and incurring God's displeasure. A Jew named **Shemaiah**, who **was a secret informer** for the enemy, warned Nehemiah about a supposed plot on his life and suggested that the governor accompany him into **the temple** for safety. Nehemiah saw through the prophet's ruse. God's Word forbade any but the priests to enter the temple. Nehemiah would rather lose his life than violate the law. And so Sanballat's third scheme fell harmlessly to the ground.

Verses 9 and 14 are examples of the "arrow prayers"[4] that characterized Nehemiah's life (see also 2:4; 4:9; 5:19). He habitually turned to God in times of crisis. Matthew Henry comments:

> In the midst of his complaint of their malice, in endeavouring to frighten him, and so weaken his hands, he lifts up his heart to Heaven in this short prayer: *Now therefore, O God! strengthen my hands.* It is the great support and relief of good people that in all their straits and difficulties they have a good God to go to, from whom, by faith and prayer, they may fetch in grace to silence their fears and *strengthen their hands* when their enemies are endeavouring to fill them with fears and weaken their hands. When, in our Christian work and warfare, we are entering upon any particular services or conflicts, this is a good prayer for us to put up: "I have such a duty to do,

such a temptation to grapple with; *now therefore, O God! strengthen my hands.*"[5]

6:15–19 Despite continued opposition, **the wall was** completed **in fifty-two days**, a remarkable feat. This evidence of divine blessing demoralized Judah's **enemies**. One further grief Nehemiah endured while the walls were going up is added in verses 17–19. Many of **the nobles** in Jerusalem stayed on friendly terms with the wicked **Tobiah** because they were related to him by marriage. (Tobiah was governor of the Ammonites—2:10.) The nobles **reported** Nehemiah's **words to** Tobiah on the one hand and praised Tobiah in Nehemiah's hearing on the other. We meet Tobiah again in chapter 13.

Although it took only **fifty-two days** to finish the walls, Nehemiah had plenty of other duties to fill up his twelve or more years as governor.

D. Organization of Jerusalem's Guards (7:1–4)

7:1, 2 As soon as the walls and gates were finished and **the gatekeepers, singers, and . . . Levites** were **appointed** to their posts, Nehemiah turned **the charge of** the city over **to** his **brother Hanani and** to **Hananiah.** Both were godly men, well-suited for the responsibility. Hananiah had a deep reverence for **God**, which made him of kindred spirit with Nehemiah.

7:3, 4 Instructions were given to insure Jerusalem's security. **The gates** were to **be opened** only during daylight hours, and **guards** were to be posted around the city, with each man serving by **his own house.** By faith Nehemiah had built the walls where they used to be, even though the enclosed area was too **large** for so **few** inhabitants.

E. Registration of Jerusalem's Population (7:5–73)

7:5, 6 As he planned to repopulate the city with those whose **genealogy** proved their descent as Jews, he **found a register** of those **who** had **returned to Jerusalem and Judah** under Zerubbabel.

7:7–65 This list in verses 7–65 is almost identical with the one given in Ezra 2. The duplication argues against the theory that Ezra and Nehemiah were *originally* one book, even if Jewish tradition put them together at one point.

7:66–69 In these verses we have a recapitulation **of the whole assembly, besides** the **servants, singers**, and animals used for transport.

7:70–72 Donors and their contributions to the work are listed. Verses 70–72 differ significantly from Ezra 2:68, 69. The accounts may refer to two different but overlapping collections. The governor's plan for Jerusalem was not fully carried out until chapter 11.

7:73 The chapter closes peacefully with the **cities** of **the children of Israel** populated and secure.

F. Revitalization of Jerusalem's Religion (Chaps. 8—10)

8:1–8 This important chapter tells of spiritual revival among God's people through the public reading of the Scriptures. Notice that Nehemiah is now referred to in the third person (until 12:31). Ezra is the main character in the next few chapters.

On **the first day of the seventh month, the people gathered together** for a holy convocation, the Feast of Trumpets (Lev. 23:24, 25), typifying the regathering of Israel from among the Gentile nations. Standing **on a** special **platform** and flanked by thirteen Levites, **Ezra read from . . . the**

Law of Moses for several hours. **The people** showed deep respect for God's Word as **the Levites**, mentioned in verse 7, **helped them to understand** (v. 8) what was being read. Since the Aramaic language replaced Hebrew after the captivity, it was necessary to explain many words of the Hebrew Scriptures.[6]

Today, many centuries later, in an entirely different culture and language, preachers and Bible teachers must explain a great deal more. Dr. Donald Campbell emphasizes the importance of this ministry:

> Ezra and his helpers were the first in a long line of expository preachers who explained the Bible. This method of preaching has been blessed by God down through the centuries and continues to be an effective instrument for bringing Christians to spiritual maturity. Topical and textual preaching may often be inspiring and helpful but the spiritual benefits do not compare with those resulting from a preaching ministry like Ezra's. Blessed indeed are the believers who are privileged to sit under expository preaching of the Scriptures.[7]

8:9–12 The people's tears showed that the message was taken seriously (v. 9). They were right in taking the Word of God seriously, but they did not need to be overwhelmed by grief. The feast was not for weeping but for rejoicing. Only one occasion for mourning and fasting was found among Israel's feasts, and that was the Day of Atonement. The rest of the feasts were to be kept with joy and celebration. The fruit of the Spirit was to be visible: love, in sharing with the less fortunate; joy, in eating and drinking before the Lord; peace, in calming their fears and putting their hearts at rest. Their sadness was turned to joy, and **the joy of the** L**ORD** was their **strength**.

8:13–15 **The** next **day** a special time for Bible study was held for the leaders, **the priests, and** the **Levites**. They discovered the ordinances concerning the Feast of Booths (Tabernacles), which was to be observed later that **month**.

8:16–18 This holiday foreshadowed the time when Israel would dwell securely in the Promised Land. They quickly made provisions to keep **the feast**, the first time it had been done by the entire assembly **since the days of Joshua**. (A partial observance of the feast had been kept by the first exiles who returned to Jerusalem under Zerubbabel—Ezra 3:4.) **Booths** were built on rooftops, in courtyards, and in the streets. Joy ran high as the Word **of God** was daily opened to hungry hearts. The feast lasted from the fifteenth through the twenty-second of the month.

9:1–3 After the feast the people **assembled** for a great day of national confession. They **separated themselves from** the **foreigners** in their midst and humbled themselves before **the** L**ORD**. **With fasting** and mourning, **they . . . read** the Scriptures for three hours. Then for three more hours, **they confessed and worshiped**. Confession is the road to revival.

9:4–38 Afterward the **Levites** mentioned in verses 4 and 5 led the people in a great prayer of confession (vv. 6–37) and dedication (v. 38). Some think Ezra led the prayer, although his name is not specifically mentioned. It is one of the longest prayers in the Bible, and its roots go deep into sacred history.

The overriding theme of the prayer is God's faithfulness despite Israel's waywardness. The prayer can be outlined as follows: Creation (v. 6);

the call of **Abraham** and the **covenant** God **made . . . with him** (vv. 7, 8); the exodus from **Egypt** (vv. 9–12); the giving of the law at **Mount Sinai** (vv. 13, 14); God's miraculous provision during the wilderness journey (v. 15); Israel's frequent rebellions **in the wilderness** contrasted with God's unfailing kindness (vv. 16–21); the conquest of Canaan (vv. 22–25); the era of the judges (vv. 26–28); unheeded warnings and ultimate captivity (vv. 29–31); appeal for forgiveness and deliverance from the consequences of the captivity (vv. 32–37); the people's desire to **make a . . . covenant** with God (v. 38).

Another way to outline the prayer is to follow its progress through the books of the Bible: vv. 6–8, Genesis; vv. 9–13, Exodus; v. 14, Leviticus; vv. 15–20, Numbers (except v. 18); vv. 21–23, Numbers and Deuteronomy; vv. 24, 25, Joshua; vv. 26–29, Judges; vv. 30–37, 1 Samuel through 2 Chronicles. That is biblical praying! Events are seen from God's point of view. His faithfulness is acknowledged throughout, and **mercy** and grace are recognized as the only foundation upon which the nation can stand.

In many ways the last verse (38) is the most significant part of the prayer. The Jews realized that the problem was with them, not with the Lord, and they determined to do something about it (see chap. 10 for the details of the **covenant**). Prayer and confession, important as they are, are no substitutes for obedience.

10:1–27 These verses list the men who signed the covenant on behalf of the people (9:38b). Nehemiah's name heads the list (v. 1), followed by **the priests** (vv. 2–8), **the Levites** (vv. 9–13), and **the leaders of the people** (vv. 14–27).

10:28, 29 These two verses form

a preamble to the covenant, stating that the entire population agreed to observe and do all the *commandments* of the LORD their **Lord, and His** *ordinances* **and His** *statutes*.

10:30–38 More specifically, the Jews bound themselves to refrain from foreign marriages (v. 30), to observe **the Sabbath day** and the sabbatical year (v. 31), to make an annual contribution for the temple services (vv. 32, 33), to provide **wood** for **the altar of the LORD** (v. 34), and to bring the redemption money for their **firstborn** and the **firstfruits of** their crops to the temple for the support of **the priests** and **Levites**—i.e., to restore **the tithes** (vv. 35–39).

Concern for their religious life was central in this covenant. With the exception of verses 30 and 31, the covenant deals exclusively with the maintenance of the temple and its servants.

10:39 The words "**we will not neglect the house of our God**" expressed the overriding concern of the postexilic Jews. Out of this genuine care for the externals of their faith would grow the corrupt pharisaical system which so violently opposed the Lord Jesus because He stressed the weightier issues of the law— obedience, mercy, etc. But in its original innocence such devotion must certainly have pleased Jehovah.

G. Repopulation of Jerusalem's Precincts (Chap. 11)

11:1, 2 Chapter 11 is closely related to the last verse of chapter 7. Nehemiah was concerned about the sparse population in **Jerusalem**; more **people** should have been living there to defend the city in case of attack. But fear kept many Jews in the country. Finally, **lots** were **cast** to bring in **one out of** every **ten** residents of the small towns **to dwell in Jerusalem**. Others who volunteered joined them in the city.

11:3–36 Having been enrolled earlier (chap. 7), the families living in Jerusalem are named here (vv. 3–24). There were **four hundred and sixty-eight** men **of Judah**, each the head of a household (vv. 4–6). The Benjamites were **nine hundred and twenty-eight** families strong (vv. 7, 8); **Joel . . . and Judah** were their overseers (v. 9). Three divisions of **priests** are listed in verses 10–14; **Zabdiel** was their leader. The Levites in **the holy city**[8] numbered four hundred and fifty-six, **one hundred and seventy-two** of them being gatekeepers (vv. 15–19). The temple servants, under **Ziha and Gishpa,** lived **in Ophel**, a section of Jerusalem close to the temple (v. 21). A man named **Uzzi** had overall charge **of the Levites**, and **Pethahiah** was **the king's** agent in the city, under Nehemiah, of course (vv. 22–24). The rest of the Jews lived in the neighboring **villages**: **Judah** lived in the **villages** listed in verses 25–30, and **Benjamin** in the **villages** listed in verses 31–35. Some **divisions of Levites** that formerly lived in Judah now moved over to the territory of **Benjamin** (v. 36).

H. Tabulation of Jerusalem's Priests and Levites (12:1–26)

The priests . . . who returned with **Zerubbabel** are named in verses 1–7. **The Levites** who came back are listed in verses 8 and 9. Verses 10 and 11 name the high priests from **Jeshua** (in the days of **Zerubbabel**, v. 1), until **Jaddua**. In verses 12–21 we have **the priests** who served **in the days of Joiakim**, whose son **Eliashib** was the high priest in Nehemiah's day (3:1). Most of them were probably still alive.

The Levites were registered under succeeding high priests from Eliashib until Jaddua. The men mentioned by name in verses 24–26 served before and during Nehemiah's administration as governor.

I. Dedication of Jerusalem's Wall (12:27–47)

12:27–30 For the dedication of the wall, the Levites (particularly the singers) from the surrounding areas were brought to Jerusalem. The priests and Levites ceremonially purified themselves along with the people, the wall, and the gates.

12:31–42 Then Nehemiah assembled the princes of Judah . . . on the wall and divided them into two large thanksgiving choirs. They headed in different directions around the wall, with the singers in front and the people following behind their leaders until they met again at the temple.

12:43–46 Great sacrifices were offered amid loud rejoicing. At the same time some men were appointed to oversee the collection of the offerings, the firstfruits, and the tithes for the support of the priests and Levites, as required by the law. The people contributed joyfully because they were happy to have the divine services resumed. The priests and Levites performed their duties of worship and purification. The singers and . . . gatekeepers also carried on their assigned tasks, tasks that, as far as the singers were concerned, dated back to the time of David and Asaph.

12:47 In the days of Zerubbabel and . . . Nehemiah, the people provided all that was necessary for the support of the singers, gatekeepers, Levites, and priests.

II. NEHEMIAH'S SECOND VISIT: REFORMATION OF JERUSALEM (Chap. 13)

A. Expulsion of Tobiah from the Temple (13:1–9)

13:1–3 After serving for twelve years in Jerusalem, in 433 B.C. Nehemiah returned to Babylon for an unspecified time. Then he obtained permission to visit Jerusalem again, a visit that dealt with the correcting of abuses. "On that day" (v. 1) may refer back to the last chapter, or it may refer to another day during Nehemiah's absence (v. 6). In either case, the Word was read, including the part barring Moabites and Ammonites from the congregation. These Canaanites had not only refused bread and water to God's people, but had hired Balaam to curse them. But God had turned the curse into a blessing. What a wonderful God He is! The people responded by separating the mixed multitude from Israel.

13:4, 5 In expelling the foreigners, they were finishing the job they started in 9:2. Eliashib the priest had made a home for the wicked Tobiah in the forecourt of the house of God, using a storeroom which should have been full of tithes for the Levites and priests.

13:6–9 Upon his return it did not take Nehemiah long to remedy the situation. Other problems had also appeared in his absence, and Nehemiah indignantly campaigned to halt these evils.

B. Restoration of Tithes for the Levites (13:10–14)

Nehemiah rebuked the officials in charge of such matters for their irresponsibility in neglecting the Levites. The Levites who had been forced to work in the fields to make a living were regathered, and **faithful** men were **appointed . . . to distribute** the tithes among them. For this good deed Nehemiah asked his **God** to **remember** him (v. 14).

C. Elimination of Illegal Activity on the Sabbath (13:15–22)

Nehemiah had to rebuke the rulers who allowed the people to work **on the Sabbath**. The foreigners who lived among them tried to make it a market day. But the Sabbath must be kept holy, by force if necessary. Men were sent to secure **the gates**, and **the** greedy **merchants** camping **outside** the city were run off under threat of violence. Illicit activity came to an abrupt halt. For this too Nehemiah asked to be remembered (v. 22).

D. Dissolution of Interracial Marriages (13:23–31)

Several years earlier the foreign **wives** had been put away at the command of Ezra (Ezra 10). The people had since then made a covenant to separate themselves from the heathen (chap. 10) and had done so to a certain extent. But in time the practice of **Jews** marrying **women of Ashdod, Ammon, and Moab** flourished once more, even in the priesthood. Some of the malefactors were physically punished; others were excommunicated. A grandson of **the high priest** was sent away.[9] The heathen were driven away and the Lord was asked to deal with those who had **defiled** their holy offices. Once more Nehemiah asked the Lord that he be remembered (v. 31).

In the church there is no ban on marriage between different ethnic groups, because Christianity is a faith embracing all peoples and tribes. But even in OT times the main reason for the ban was no doubt the corrupt, false religions of the Gentile nations.

Campbell comments on the type of mixed marriages that are destructive to Christianity:

> The New Testament adds its consistent witness against marriages between believers and unbelievers. Paul directed believers to marry "only in the Lord" (1 Cor. 7:39). Yet today as in previous ages, some believers rationalize that they will lead the unsaved mate to the Lord—but it rarely works that way and children more often than not follow the ways of the unregenerate parent.[10]

Throughout his rule Nehemiah was a man of action. Nowhere is that more evident than here, as zeal for the things of God consumed him (Ps. 69:9). Because he was no respecter of persons, his anger was felt equally by all who transgressed the law of the Lord. He warned, admonished, reprimanded, **contended**, **struck**, **pulled out hair**, and generally made things difficult for the ungodly! He was a courageous man and a tenacious general in the front lines of the fight against evil. He was a tireless worker and a great builder for God.

This chapter brings *OT history* to a close. The books that follow Nehemiah fit *chronologically before* this time (except for Malachi, which is contemporary with Nehemiah).[11]

Charles Swindoll closes his commentary on Nehemiah, *Hand Me Another Brick*, with a challenge to us all:

> I think it is significant that the final scene in Nehemiah's book portrays him on his knees asking God for grace. He had fought hard for the right, but he had kept his heart soft before the Lord. What a magnifi-

cent model of leadership! He was a man of honesty, conviction, and devotion.

Can you handle another brick?[12]

ENDNOTES

[1](Intro) John C. Whitcomb, "Nehemiah," *The Wycliffe Bible Commentary*, p. 435.

[2](1:1–3) J. Alec Motyer, *Toward the Mark*, Vol. 6, No. 1, January-February 1977, p. 6.

[3](2:1–3) George Williams, *The Student's Commentary on the Holy Scriptures*, p. 264.

[4](6:10–14) In the terminology of devotion, such are called "arrow prayers," since they are shot swiftly to God's throne.

[5](6:10–14) Matthew Henry, "Nehemiah," in *Matthew Henry's Commentary on the Whole Bible*, II:1087.

[6](8:1–8) Hebrew and Aramaic are closely related Semitic languages. The oral Aramaic "paraphrases" of the Hebrew original text were later written down and called the *Targums*.

[7](8:1–8) Donald Campbell, *Nehemiah: Man in Charge*, p. 75.

[8](11:3–36) This is the first time Jerusalem is called "the holy city."

[9](13:23–31) Josephus says that the exiled rebel went to Samaria, where Sanballat built him a temple which became a refuge for apostate Jews.

[10](13:23–31) Campbell, *Nehemiah*, pp. 116, 117.

[11](13:23–31) The period following Nehemiah is sometimes known as "The Four Hundred Silent Years," although this term is not strictly accurate. Daniel 11, for example, gives a detailed history of the Grecian era, except that it is pre-written history, that is, prophecy. In fact, this section is so accurate in its detail (for those who know the history of the Ptolemies and the Seleucids) that most liberals and their admirers reject Daniel as an actual prophecy. The OT Apocrypha, though uninspired, contains valuable historical information concerning this period.

[12](13:23–31) Charles R. Swindoll, *Hand Me Another Brick*, p. 205.

BIBLIOGRAPHY

Campbell, Donald K. *Nehemiah: Man in Charge*. Wheaton, IL: Victor Books, 1979.

Henry, Matthew. "Nehemiah." In *Matthew Henry's Commentary on the Whole Bible*. Vol. 2. Joshua to Esther. McLean, VA: MacDonald Publishing Company, n.d.

Ironside, H. A. *Notes on Ezra, Nehemiah, Esther*. Neptune, NJ: Loizeaux Brothers, 1972.

Jensen, Irving L. *Ezra/Nehemiah/Esther*. Chicago: Moody Press, 1970.

Keil, C. F. "Nehemiah." In *Biblical Commentary on the Old Testament*. Vol. 10. Grand Rapids: Wm. B. Eerdmans Publishing Company, 1971.

Swindoll, Charles R. *Hand Me Another Brick*. Nashville: Thomas Nelson Publishers, 1978.

ESTHER

Introduction

"The book of Esther gives us a segment of the history of the Jews which is not supplied elsewhere in the Bible. For instance, it is here that we learn about the origin of the Feast of Purim *which, as we all know, is celebrated by the Jewish people to this very day."*

—Carl Armerding

I. Unique Place in the Canon

A Soviet Jew was recently asked by a Westerner what he thought would be the outcome if the USSR stepped up its anti-Semitic policies. "Oh, probably a feast!" Asked for an explanation, the Jewish man said, "Pharaoh tried to wipe out the Hebrews and the result was Passover; Haman tried to exterminate our people and the result was Purim; Antiochus Epiphanes tried to do us in, and the result was Hanukkah!"

Esther explains the origin of the Feast of Purim, a colorful Jewish holiday that today features noisemakers sounding off every time Haman's name occurs in the annual public reading of the book.

Esther is unique in several ways. It tells the story of non-observant[1] Jews who preferred prosperity in Persia[2] to the rigors of the small remnant that returned to Jerusalem under Zerubbabel (Ezra 2). All reference to religion other than fasting is lacking in Esther.

Another remarkable feature of the book is that the name of God[3] is not found in it, a fact that has caused some to question its right to a place in

Scripture. But J. Sidlow Baxter points out that the name *Jehovah* is hidden four times as an acrostic (1:20; 5:4; 5:13; 7:7), always at a crucial point in the story. Also the name *Ehyeh* (I am who I am) is found once in acrostic form (7:5). "This cannot be of chance," writes Scroggie, "and the difficulty of constructing such forms will be apparent to anyone who attempts it."[4]

Since few Christians know Hebrew, and this is a difficult literary form to grasp without examples, we quote two of Arthur T. Pierson's artistic and ingenious attempts to illustrate the acrostics in rhymed English couplets. He uses the word LORD for YHWH. Notice that, as in the original, one example uses *initial* letters and one uses *final* letters. Also, in Pierson's first example, the hidden name "L-O-R-D" is spelled backwards, and in the second example it is in normal order. This parallels the original Hebrew:

Due **R**espect **O**ur **L**adies, all
Shall give their husbands, great and
    small (i. 20).
Il**L** t**O** fea**R** decree**D** I find,
Toward me in the monarch's mind
    (vii. 7).[5]

495

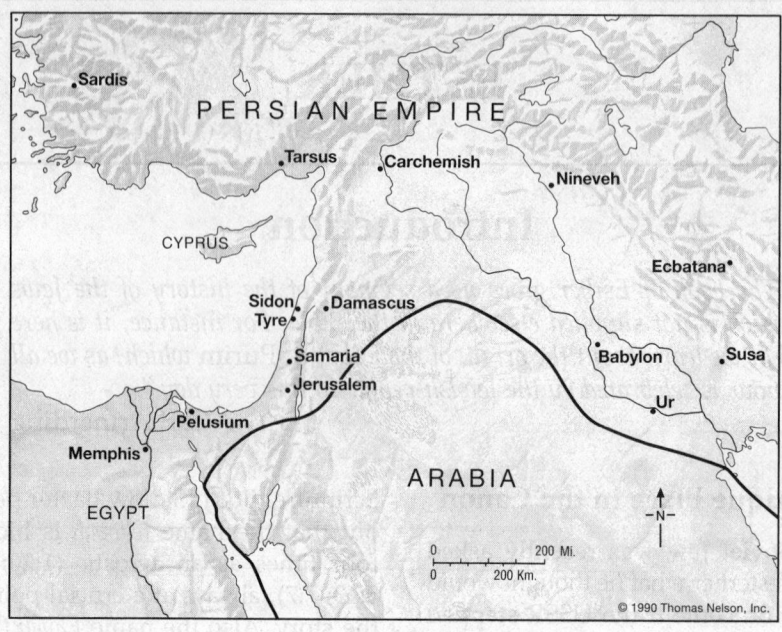

The Persian Empire, c. 500 B.C.

Although God's name is not found explicitly, His presence and power are clearly manifested throughout as He provides deliverance for His people through a series of designed "coincidences." Even if Jehovah's name is not explicitly associated with those who voluntarily stayed in Babylon instead of returning to their own city and land, His care for them cannot be questioned. They were still His people, and He would protect them from the anti-Semitism (inspired by the devil) which sought to exterminate them. God is the Author of all history, even if He does not sign His name at the bottom of every page.

The poetry of James Russell Lowell is a fitting commentary on the Book of Esther:

Careless seems the great avenger:
History's pages but record
One death grapple in the darkness,
　'twixt old systems and the Word.
Truth for ever on the scaffold;

Wrong for ever on the throne:
But that scaffold sways the future;
　and behind the dim unknown
Standeth God, within the shadow,
　keeping watch above His own.

Esther is not quoted in the NT, and so far no fragment has been found in the Dead Sea Scrolls. For these and other reasons, some (even a few Jews) have questioned the canonicity of Esther. However, the book has wonderful lessons on the faithfulness of God even when His people are disobedient.

II. Authorship

The writer of this book was no doubt a Jew who knew Persian customs and the details of the palace. (Archaeology has confirmed some of these special features.) He writes as an eyewitness, using the type of Hebrew of the post-exilic era. Some have suggested Ezra or Nehemiah as author. Jewish tradition points to Mordecai as author. Actually we have no idea who wrote Esther; perhaps the human writer was an unimportant figure historically. Whoever it was, as the Pulpit Commentary put it, "no disbeliever in God could have written it; and no believer in God can read it without finding his faith strengthened thereby."

III. Date

Esther 10:2 implies that King Ahasuerus (Xerxes) was already dead; since he died in 465 B.C., this would date the book after that year. The Persian cultural details, access to court records, and eyewitness vividness all support a date soon after Xerxes' death, sometime during the reign of Artaxerxes I (464–424 B.C.). As usual, unbelieving critics date the book much later (third or second century B.C.).

IV. Background and Theme

The events in this book took place between the sixth and seventh chapters of Ezra, during the reign of Ahasuerus (Xerxes), king of Persia. The book is concerned with those Jews who decided to remain in Babylon rather than go back to Jerusalem with the small remnant that returned to Jerusalem under Zerubbabel (Ezra 2). It derives its name from its principal character, Esther, the orphan girl who became queen. Esther, her Persian name, means "star" and may have been derived from the goddess Ishtar. Hadassah, her Hebrew name, means "myrtle."

Ahasuerus held court in Shushan (Susa, NKJV marg.), one of three principal capital cities in Persia, the others being Achmetha (Ecbatana, NASB), and Babylon. Shushan is the Hebrew name and means "lily."[6] The Prophet Daniel spent time there (Dan. 8). Nehemiah served there after Esther's day (Neh. 1). It is there that our story takes place, beginning in the year 483 BC. (Xerxes came to power in 486 BC; chapter 1 opens in the third year of his reign—v. 3.)

OUTLINE

Commentary

I. THE EXPULSION OF VASHTI DECREED (Chap. 1)

1:1–4 Although not all scholars agree as to the identity of **Ahasuerus**, most modern commentators believe him to be Xerxes (see NKJV, marg.), the son of Darius the Great. Xerxes reigned from 486 to 465 BC.

The first **feast** did not necessarily last *uninterrupted* for **one hundred and eighty days**. Rather, this was the time required to display **the riches of his glorious kingdom**. Probably different nobles came at different times throughout this period since the empire was so vast.

1:5–8 The second **feast** lasted **seven days** and was open to **all the people** of **Shushan**. **Royal wine** flowed freely from **golden vessels** in the elegantly furnished garden court (v. 6 is surely the most colorful verse in the Bible!). Guests were permitted to drink as much or as little as they chose.

1:9–12 The inebriated Xerxes ordered his chamberlains **to bring Queen Vashti**, who was hosting **the women** at a separate banquet. He wanted her at the public celebration so that he could **show her beauty**. Since Persian modesty required women to be veiled in public, it appears that the king was asking her to degrade herself to satisfy his drunken whim. She refused to be displayed, thus greatly angering **the king**.

1:13–20 When **the king** consulted his **wise men**, they told him that Vashti's **behavior** would prove a bad example to the **women** throughout the realm. **Memucan** therefore suggested that Vashti be deposed by **a royal decree** and that the **decree** be circulated in every part of the **empire**. Knowing that the law of the Medes and Persians was unalterable, the wise men might have suggested such a drastic step to ensure that Vashti would not return to power and punish them.

1:21, 22 The king rashly signed their advice into law and ordered it published in every **province** in the **language** of **every people**. Included was the law that every **man should be master in his own house** and that his **language** should be the one used there. Dr. J. Vernon McGee has suggested that Memucan *at home* was a hen-pecked husband, and that he was getting back at his wife with this **decree**.[7]

II. THE ELEVATION OF ESTHER ACCOMPLISHED (Chap. 2)

2:1–4 When the king seemed to have second thoughts over what he had done to **Vashti**, his counselors proposed that a search be made **among all the beautiful young virgins** for a **young woman** to become **queen** in her place.

2:5–7 As potential young women were brought to **Shushan**, **Esther**, one of the capital's maidens, joined them. She had been adopted by her cousin **Mordecai** after the death of her parents. Mordecai was **a Benjamite**, whose ancestor, **Kish**, had been carried into captivity **with Jeconiah** (2 Kgs. 24:14–16).

2:8–11 **Hegai**, the keeper of the harem, showed special favor to **Esther** by **readily** supplying her and her attendants with **beauty preparations, besides her allowance**, and also by giving her **the best place in the house of the women**. In obedience to **Mordecai**, she did not yet reveal her ethnic origin. Although Mordecai could not contact her directly, he had ways of getting news of her progress every day.

2:12–14 The course preparing the young ladies to be brought into the king's bedchamber lasted for **twelve** months. They went through a ceremonial purification program with ointments, spices, and cosmetics. Then, when the **turn** of **each** one **came**, she could request anything in the way of apparel, adornments, or jewels. She then spent one night with **the king**, and would never be with him **again unless** she so pleased him that he asked **for her by name**.

For the Christian, lifetime is training time for reigning time. Soon the Lord will present the church to Himself without spot or wrinkle or any such thing (Eph. 5:27).

2:15–18 Instead of making lavish requests for outward adornments, **Esther** followed Hegai's advice. Perhaps he suggested that she depend on her natural beauty. In any event, **the king loved Esther more than** any of the others, chose **her** as his **queen**, and **made a great feast** in her honor. The **holiday** he made in **the provinces** may have included an amnesty, or a remission of taxes, or it may have been simply a holiday. He also **gave gifts** in keeping with his wealth.

2:19–23 A **second** gathering of **virgins** took place, perhaps to add to the king's harem. **Esther** was still keeping her nationality secret, and **Mordecai** was still positioning himself strategically **at the king's gate**. It was at this time that he overheard a plot to assassinate **King Ahasuerus**. He reported it to **Esther**, who in turn

notified **the king**. The assassins were apprehended, tried, and **hanged**.

The incident was routinely recorded in the official **chronicles** of the kingdom. Mordecai was not rewarded immediately. He had to wait, but it was sure to come. God keeps good records. The ancient Greek historian Herodotus says that hanging was the standard punishment for traitors and rebels in Persia at that time.[8]

III. THE EXTERMINATION OF THE JEWS PLANNED (Chaps. 3, 4)

A. Haman's Talk with the King (Chap. 3)

3:1 The words **"After these things"** indicate a five-year interval between chapters 2 and 3. The last important figure in the drama of Esther comes on stage in verse 1, **Haman, the son of Hammedatha**. We are not told why he was **promoted**, but subsequent history makes it clear that the hand behind the hand of the king was Satan's. Haman was an **Agagite**, a descendant of the kings of the Amalekites (Agag was a royal title). The Lord had declared perpetual war against Amalek (Ex. 17:8–16). The Book of Esther relates the last recorded battle in that war (see also 1 Sam. 15:32; 30:1–10; 1 Chron. 4:43).

3:2–6 By official order **Haman** was now to be **paid homage** as one second only to the king. But **Mordecai** refused to **bow** to a mere man, especially to an Amalekite. The fear of God overcame any fear of man. The law of Moses did not forbid showing due respect to those in authority, but it did forbid the worship of any but God. Eastern monarchs often demanded such worship. Mordecai's fellow workers sought to gain favor in Haman's eyes by pointing out his refusal. Haman was a very egotistical man, and the sight of Mordecai's blatant disrespect infuriated him beyond reason. Instead of dealing with Mordecai alone, he set in motion a plan to annihilate **all the Jews** in **the kingdom**!

3:7–11 Haman's first step was to cast lots **to determine** a suitable date for the mass execution. By a seeming coincidence the date indicated was nearly a year away. As someone has said, "Even superstition was chained to the divine chariot-wheels." God overruled to allow sufficient time to thwart Haman's plan. "The lot is cast into the lap, but its every decision is from the LORD" (Prov. 16:33). **Haman** next approached the king with an inflammatory report about **the Jews**, misrepresenting them as a danger to the **kingdom**. He urged that **a decree** be issued ordering their extinction. According to the law of the Medes and Persians, this decree, once issued, could never be changed or withdrawn. As added incentive, Haman offered to **pay ten thousand talents of silver** into the royal **treasuries**, now badly depleted by the king's losses in Greece. Ahasuerus sealed the death writ **with his signet ring**, sentencing thousands of innocent men, women, and children to be sacrificed at the altar of Haman's pride. Verse 11 might mean that **the money** taken from the slain would belong to Haman.

3:12–15 Copies of the execution order were sent out with great thoroughness, setting **the thirteenth day of the twelfth month** aside for the atrocity. In the palace Ahasuerus and Haman complacently **sat down to drink, but in the city** there was great perplexity. Irving Jensen comments on this:

The last phrase of chapter 3 is significant: "But the city Shushan was perplexed" (KJV). Not only the Jews, but non-Jews reacted to this outrageous example of violent despotism. Sometimes the masses are wrong, but not always. Here was a situation where a king and his high minister were an erring minority with extensive authority. But all people—nations and individuals alike—must reckon with the highest Authority—God. The king's decree was issued and posted, but the King of kings would have the last word.[9]

B. Mordecai's Talk with the Queen (Chap. 4)

4:1–3 The Jewish population was stunned as the news broke throughout the land. There is always sadness where evil reigns. **Mordecai** put on mourner's garb and lamented through **the city** until he came to **the king's gate**, beyond which he could not go because **sackcloth** was not allowed in his majesty's presence. He knew that he was the main object of Haman's hatred. The fate awaiting his nation had been unwittingly prompted by him.

4:4–9 Since custom forbade **Esther** to leave her confinement in the palace, **she sent** a servant to take some **garments to clothe Mordecai** so that he might not be seen in **sackcloth** by the king and lose his life. But Mordecai refused to disguise his anguish. When **Hathach**, Esther's personal servant, came to find out why he continued in mourning, Mordecai told him the whole story. **A copy of the written decree** was sent back to the queen along with an order to use her office to intercede **for her people**.

4:10–12 **Esther** responded to **Mordecai** by reminding him that it was a capital offense to appear before **the king** uninvited, unless he spared the intruder's life by extending **the golden scepter**. She told of a further complication which would make such action doubly dangerous: She had not been summoned by Ahasuerus for **thirty days**, indicating that she may have somehow incurred his displeasure.

4:13, 14 Mordecai's reply to Esther's rationale was to the point: She would not **escape**, when the rest of **the Jews** were slain, even if she was queen. If she refused to act now, someone else would **arise** to deliver His people, but she would be destroyed. And perhaps this opportunity to save her people was the reason she had been exalted to the throne. The words of verse 14 should challenge each of us: **"Yet who knows whether you have come to the kingdom for such a time as this?"** Though few of us will ever be in such a position as Esther's, each believer has an essential role to play in the ongoing plan of God.

4:15–17 Making her decision, **Esther** instructed **all the Jews** to **fast** with her **for three days**. Then she would **go** before **the king**.

Matthew Poole comments on Esther's famous and heroic words, **"If I perish, I perish"**:

> Although my danger be great and evident, considering the expressness of that law, and the uncertainty of the king's mind, and that severity which he showed to my predecessor Vashti, yet rather than neglect my duty to God and to His people, I will go to the king and cast myself cheerfully and resolutely upon God's providence for my safety and success.[10]

The Christian's attitude in difficult and trying circumstances should not be one of fatalism but of optimism, especially when it comes to approaching the heavenly throne for grace to help in time of need. We have bold and confident access; the scepter of

God's forgiveness has been stretched out to us at Calvary. "Let us therefore come boldly to the throne of grace, that we may obtain mercy and find grace to help in time of need" (Heb. 4:16).

IV. THE EXTERMINATION OF THE JEWS THWARTED (Chaps. 5—9)

A. Esther's Supplication and Haman's Rage (Chap. 5)

5:1–3 On the third day, when the fast was completed, **Esther put on her royal robes**, summoned her courage, and appeared before Ahasuerus uninvited. Recognizing that only a very important matter would cause his queen to risk her life, **the king held out to Esther the golden scepter** and granted her safety. He also promised to grant her **request**, **up to half** his **kingdom** (a figure of speech meaning that he would give her anything at all within reason). Christ holds out His scepter of grace to any unbeliever who comes to Him in repentance and faith (see John 6:37b). For the believer the golden scepter is always extended (see Heb. 10:22).

5:4–8 At this point **Esther** simply invited **the king** and his favorite minister, **Haman**, **to the banquet** (the fourth banquet in the book). During the meal the king again tried to find out what the queen wanted. Once more Esther procrastinated and asked Ahasuerus and Haman to return the following day for yet another **banquet**. Then she would make her matter known. Opinions vary as to why Esther planned these two delays before making her request: (1) She wanted time to ingratiate herself with the king, having apparently been out of favor with him (see notes on 4:10–12); (2) her courage failed her both times; (3) she wanted to build up an element of suspense and impress upon the king that her business was vitally important and no mere whim; (4) she wanted to inflate Haman's pride and take him off guard before she exposed him as a vicious murderer. Perhaps elements of all these ideas entered into her strategy.

5:9–14 Filled with pride, **Haman** left the banquet in good spirits. When he met **Mordecai** on the way out of the palace, **he was filled with indignation** but **restrained himself** from violence. Calling **his friends** and **his wife Zeresh** together, he recited all the favorable things that had happened to him. The only cloud on his horizon was that stubborn **Jew! His wife** advised him to make **a gallows** seventy-five feet **high**, then get permission from **the king** to hang **Mordecai . . . on it**. This pleased Haman; **so he had the gallows made**.

B. Haman's Humiliation and Mordecai's Honor (Chap. 6)

6:1–3 While Haman was sleeping, God kept Ahasuerus awake to thwart the evil scheme. In trying to make the best of his insomnia, **the king** had **the chronicles** of his reign **read** to him. By divine "coincidence" the portion that was read contained the account of the attempt on his life which had been foiled by **Mordecai**. Upon inquiry it was learned that **nothing** had ever **been done** to reward **him** for this service.

It is good to notice what J. G. Bellett calls

> . . . the wonderful interweaving of circumstances which we get in this history. There is plot and underplot, "wheels within wheels," circumstances hanging upon circumstances, all formed together to work out the wonderful plans of God.[11]

The Lord is in perfect control.

6:4–11 Probably it was in the morning that **Haman** came **to suggest that the king hang Mordecai**. Strangely enough, it was at the very same time that the king had an impulse to reward the man who had saved him from the assassins. When Haman entered, Ahasuerus asked the general question, **"What shall be done for the man whom the king delights to honor?"** Thinking that *his own* great moment had come, Haman suggested the most elaborate **parade** and the bestowing of honors second only to those of the king himself. Haman further suggested that a public announcement be made as the **parade** moved **through the city**: **"Thus shall it be done to the man whom the king delights to honor!"** Thereupon **the king** ordered **Haman** to **hurry** and bestow all these honors not on Haman, but on **Mordecai the Jew!** Haman went out to proclaim his worst enemy as the man whom the king delighted to honor. Pride went before destruction and a haughty spirit before a fall (Prov. 16:18).

In our day there is a Man whom the King delights to honor—the Lord Jesus Christ. God has decreed that every knee shall bow to Him and every tongue confess Him Lord to the glory of God the Father (Phil. 2:10, 11).

6:12–14 Crestfallen, **Haman** retreated **to his house** and reported these strange developments. **His wife** and **wise . . . friends** saw in the day's events an omen of victory for the Jew and defeat for Haman. But by then it was time for **Haman** to hurry off to Esther's **banquet**.

C. Esther's Accusation and Haman's Execution (Chap. 7)

7:1–4 Esther's second **banquet** turned out to have ramifications which would shake the entire kingdom, starting with Haman's house. At the king's bidding she finally made her appeal. She asked for her own **life** and the lives of her **people**, who had been sentenced to death. If they had only been **sold as . . . slaves** she would **have held** her peace, "for the trouble would not be commensurate with the annoyance to the king" (v. 4b NASB). But the seriousness of their plight impelled her to act.

7:5–7a The king indignantly asked **who** had instigated such a heinous plot against Esther's people. The queen had wisely invited Haman for just this moment. To his face she charged **"this wicked Haman!"** Haman's true character was now fully revealed. Ahasuerus stalked out to **the palace garden** like a raging panther. His conscience might have been bothering him too as he remembered his part in approving the terrible scheme. It was hitting much closer to home than he had anticipated.

7:7b–10 In mortal fear Haman threw himself **before Queen Esther, pleading for his life. The king,** returning to the room, interpreted this as an attempt to assault his wife sexually. Haman's fate was now sealed. Without an express word from the king, the servants **covered** his **face,** a preliminary to execution. **One of** them told **the king** about **the gallows . . . Haman** had built, and Ahasuerus ordered the villain to be hanged **on it.** Thus **Haman** took Mordecai's place **on the gallows.** He reaped what he had sown. **Then the king's wrath subsided.**

D. Mordecai's Promotion and the Jews' Deliverance (Chap. 8)

8:1, 2 Haman's **house** was given to **Esther** and his position was given **to Mordecai.**

8:3–8 Haman was out of the way, but his destructive plot was still in motion. Once again **Esther** appeared before **the king** uninvited, careless of her own life, and tearfully pled for her people. Again **the golden scepter** of grace was extended to her. Verse 3 gives the gist of her plea, verses 5 and 6 the exact words. She asked that the first decree be revoked. But according to the law, no edict signed and sealed by a Persian king could be altered. However, after reminding Esther of what he had already done on her behalf, the king permitted her and Mordecai to **write** another **decree** *counteracting* the first one.

8:9–14 The king's scribes were called and Mordecai dictated an edict which gave **the Jews** the right to **protect their lives.** With great speed the new law was carried to the utmost parts of the kingdom on royal **swift steeds.** How much more should the news of man's redemption from the power of evil be disseminated through Satan's realm with thoroughness and speed!

8:15–17 Having discarded his sackcloth, **Mordecai** left the palace in robes of splendor. **The Jews** were filled with **gladness** when they heard of the sudden turn of events, while the rest of the people were filled with dread. Not wanting to be numbered among their enemies, **many** Gentiles **became** proselytes to the Jewish faith at this time.

E. The Enemy's Destruction and the Inauguration of the Feast of Purim (Chap. 9)

9:1–5 When the fateful **day** arrived— **the thirteenth day** of **the twelfth month**—the Jews gathered together **in their** respective **cities** and destroyed their enemies. Even the princes and rulers **helped the Jews** because they feared **Mordecai**, now the second-most-powerful man in the kingdom.

9:6–15 In the capital alone **five hundred men** were **killed**, along with **the ten sons of Haman**. When it was reported to the king, he realized that the slaughter in the rest of the land must be great as well. **Esther** requested that an additional day be given **the Jews** in **Shushan** to wipe out any remaining pockets of anti-Semitism. As a result **three hundred** more **men** were executed. She also asked that the bodies of **Haman's ten sons be** publicly **hanged**.

9:16 In the king's provinces the Jews killed seventy-five thousand, but had **not** taken any of their foes' **plunder**. This would make it clear to all that they were interested only in protecting themselves, not in growing rich.

9:17–28 The Jews in the provinces held a great feast **on the fourteenth of the month** while those **at Shushan** celebrated **on the fifteenth**. This was the beginning of the feast of Purim. The name **Purim**[12] comes from **"Pur"** —the lot which Haman had cast (3:7). Later Mordecai decreed that both **the fourteenth** and **the fifteenth** should **be observed** by all the Jewish people. Like the feasts of old, it was to be celebrated annually as a reminder to succeeding generations of this marvelous deliverance.

9:29–32 Apparently two **letters** went out **to all the Jews**, charging them to keep the Feast **of Purim**—the first one in verse 20, and the second in verses 29–32. **The book** referred to in verse 32 was probably the chronicles of the kingdom (cf. 2:23; 6:1; 10:2).

V. THE EXALTATION OF MORDECAI (Chap. 10)

10:1, 2 The Book of Esther closes with the exaltation **of Mordecai**. His advancements were recorded alongside the accomplishments of **Ahasuerus . . . in the book of the chronicles of the kings of Media and Persia**. Carl Armerding closes his book on Esther with these words:

> The fact that we have no record of his death is quite remarkable, because the history of most men concludes with some sort of obituary. Not so with Mordecai. Thus the impression is left in our minds of one who lives on and on. "He that doeth the will of God abideth forever" (I John 2:17).[13]

10:3 Mordecai sought the **good of his people**. Spurgeon applies his ministry to Christians:

> Mordecai was a true patriot, and therefore, being exalted to the highest position under Ahasuerus, he used his eminence to promote the prosperity of Israel. In this he was a type of Jesus, who, upon His throne of glory, seeks not His own, but spends His power for His people. It were well if every Christian would be a Mordecai to the church, striving according to his ability for its prosperity. Some are placed in stations of affluence and influence, let them honour their Lord in the high places of the earth, and testify for Jesus before great men. Others have what is far better, namely, close fellowship with the King of kings, let them be sure to plead daily for the weak of the Lord's people, the doubting, the tempted, and the comfortless.[14]

ENDNOTES

[1](Intro) A non-observant Jew is one who is part of the Jewish ethnic community but does not practice his religion or try to keep the Mosaic

Law, such as the dietary rules and traditions.

[2](Intro) Today Persia is called Iran. Their language, Farsi (= Persian) is not related to Arabic but uses a modified Arabic script and many Arabic words from the Muslim religion and culture.

[3](Intro) Thinking to "remedy" this situation, some Jews added many passages (in Greek) to the canonical text of Esther. They did not realize that they were actually ruining the very message of the book—God working in the shadows for His people, even for those who chose to live far from His temple in Jerusalem. These additions will be found in the Apocrypha, and are of a very different character from the Hebrew original. They add a great deal of religious activity along with some almost soap-opera-style content. Jews and Protestants have rightly rejected these apocryphal additions to God's Word.

[4](Intro) W. Graham Scroggie, *Know Your Bible, Vol. I, The Old Testament*, p. 96.

[5](Intro) Quoted by Scroggie, *ibid.*

[6](Intro) Our English names *Susan* and *Susannah* come from this Hebrew word for *lily*.

[7](1:13–20) J. Vernon, McGee, *Ruth and Esther: Women of Faith*, pp. 232, 33.

[8](2:19–23) Cited by Carl Armerding, *Esther: For Such a Time as This*, p. 35.

[9](3:12–15) Irving L. Jensen, *Ezra/Nehemiah/Esther*, p. 88.

[10](4:15–17) Matthew Poole, *Matthew Poole's Commentary on the Holy Bible*, p. 913.

[11](6:1–3) J. G. Bellett, *Witnesses for God in Dark and Evil Times: being Studies and Meditations on the Books of Ezra, Nehemiah, and Esther*, p. 70.

[12](9:17–28) *Pûrîm* is the Hebrew plural, meaning "lots."

[13](10:1, 2) Armerding, *Esther*, p. 128.

[14](10:3) Charles Haddon Spurgeon, *Morning and Evening*, p. 667, reading for November 28, Evening.

BIBLIOGRAPHY

Armerding, Carl. *Esther: For Such a Time as This*. Chicago: Moody Press, 1955.

Baldwin, Joyce G. *Esther*. Tyndale Old Testament Commentaries. Downers Grove, IL: InterVarsity Press, 1984.

Bellett, J. G. *Witnesses for God in Dark and Evil Times: being Studies and Meditations on the Books of Ezra, Nehemiah, and Esther*. Kilmarnock, Scotland: John Ritchie, Publisher of Christian Literature, n.d.

Ironside, H. A. "Esther." In *Notes on Ezra, Nehemiah, and Esther*. Neptune, N.J.: Loizeaux Brothers, 1972.

Keil, C. F. "Esther." In *Commentary on the Old Testament in Ten Volumes*. Vol 10. Grand Rapids: Wm. B. Eerdmans Publishing Co., 1982.

McGee, J. Vernon *Ruth and Esther: Women of Faith*. Nashville: Thomas Nelson Publishers, 1988

INTRODUCTION TO THE POETICAL BOOKS

"Poetry," someone has said, "is that which is lost in translation." Fortunately for us, this is not true, or at best it is a great exaggeration when speaking of OT Hebrew poetry. Classic English or French poetry, on the other hand, being so dependent as a rule on rhyme, strict meter, and special forms, is most difficult to translate into other languages with real success.

Hebrew poetry has meter to a certain extent, uses the techniques of alliteration (words beginning with the same sound), and other devices common to our own poetry.

Though much of the Prophets are written in poetic form, five books in the OT are considered poetical as such: Job, Psalms, Proverbs, Ecclesiastes, and the Song of Songs.[1]

I. The Poetical Books

A. Job

This may be the oldest book in the Bible, since in all its discussions of right and wrong no reference is made to the Law. In dramatic dialogues the greatly suffering yet righteous Job contends with his "friends" about the reason for his affliction, only to be taught at last by the Lord to accept His sovereign will for him. This is Wisdom Literature at its best, recognized even by unbelievers as truly majestic poetry.

B. Psalms

The most popular book in the OT for Christians is the book of Psalms.

We often see it bound together with the NT for convenience when a complete Bible is too unwieldy to carry. Many who love the Psalms are not even aware that it is all poetry.[2]

Psalms is the hymnbook of ancient Israel, consisting of a collection of five books written over a period of about a thousand years, from about 1400 B.C. (Moses) to about 400 B.C. (Ezra).

C. Proverbs

The second most likely OT book to be used by believers on a regular basis is the Book of Proverbs. It is absolutely chock full of wise sayings on how to live a successful life from God's viewpoint (which in the final analysis, is the only one that really counts). It is a marvelous example of Wisdom Literature.

D. Ecclesiastes

This book is the hardest for most people to fit into the framework of Bible teaching. The key to Ecclesiastes is the expression "under the sun," since "the Preacher" is reasoning from the viewpoint of a person without God's revelation. Here is another good example of Wisdom Literature.

E. Song of Songs

All Bible lovers are agreed that this is a beautiful poem of true and pure love, though the interpretations of the story are diverse. The title "Song

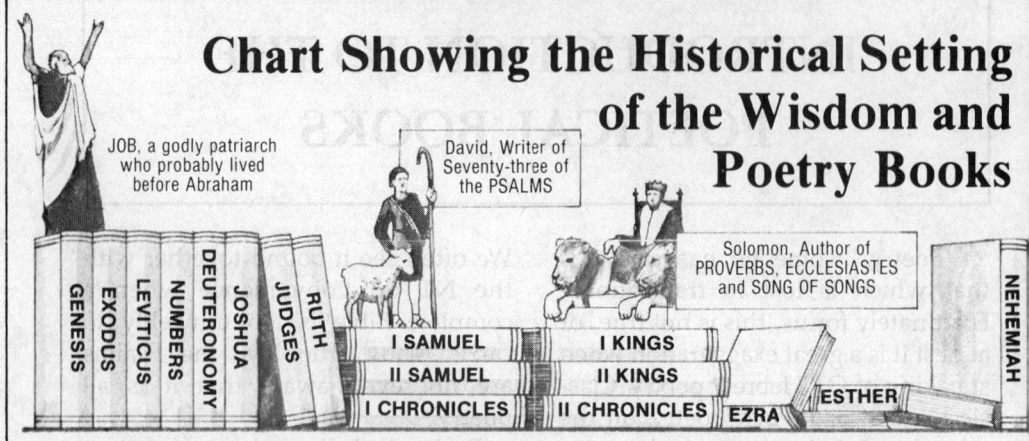

Chart Showing the Historical Setting of the Wisdom and Poetry Books

JOB, a godly patriarch who probably lived before Abraham

David, Writer of Seventy-three of the PSALMS

Solomon, Author of PROVERBS, ECCLESIASTES and SONG OF SONGS

GENESIS | EXODUS | LEVITICUS | NUMBERS | DEUTERONOMY | JOSHUA | JUDGES | RUTH

I SAMUEL | II SAMUEL | I CHRONICLES

I KINGS | II KINGS | II CHRONICLES | EZRA | ESTHER

NEHEMIAH

The Setting of the Books of Wisdom & Poetry

of Songs" is a Hebrew idiom meaning "the most exquisite song." Solomon wrote 1,005 songs (1 Kgs. 4:32); this was his finest.

II. Enjoying OT Poetry

Unfortunately, many people get "turned off" to poetry in school, either by being forced to memorize poems they don't like or don't understand, or by having had teachers who made them dissect poems till all the beauty and freshness was gone. It is somewhat like growing a rose, which anyone can do with little knowledge at all except a desire to experience beauty. A biology class assignment that takes the rose to pieces part by part is no doubt educational, but hardly helpful from an artistic or aesthetic viewpoint.

Enjoying OT poetry is somewhat like a middle ground between experiencing a rose with no knowledge of roses on the one hand, and doing a scientific study on the other. You will enjoy roses more if you know the difference between a tea rose and a floribunda, if you can tell red from

pink and pink from coral and red-orange.

Likewise if you can notice the forms and techniques that lend "color" to poetry, and the techniques of the psalmist or other biblical poet, you will get a great deal more out of Bible poetry. This is true not only in the five books considered poetic, but in the rest of the OT as well—not to mention in the NT.

III. Parallelism

Bible poetry's greatest technique is not to *rhyme sounds*, as in much English poetry, but to "rhyme" *ideas*— that is, to put two or more lines together that somehow match each other. We should be grateful to God that this is the mainstay of biblical poetry because it translates nicely into nearly all languages, and not too much beauty is lost in the translation process. Our Lord Himself also frequently spoke in parallelism. (Carefully reread, e.g., Matthew 5—7 and John 13—17 after studying the following notes.)

We would like to present some examples of the main types of Hebrew parallelism so that the reader can look for similar structures, not only while studying the OT with the help of the *Believers Bible Commentary*, but also while having daily devotions and listening to sermons.

1. Synonymous Parallelism

As the name implies, this type has the second or parallel line saying about the same thing as the first—for emphasis. Proverbs is especially full of these:

In the way of righteousness is life,
And in its pathway there is no death
(Prov. 12:28).

I am the rose of Sharon,
And the lily of the valleys (Song 2:1).

2. Antithetic Parallelism

This type puts two lines "against" each other that form a *contrast:*

For the LORD knows the way of the righteous,
But the way of the ungodly shall perish (Ps. 1:6).[3]

Hatred stirs up strife,
But love covers all sins (Prov. 10:12).

3. Formal Parallelism

This type is parallel in *form* only; the two (or more) lines don't contrast, expand, or emphasize. It is just two lines of poetry put together to express a thought or theme:

Yet I have set My King
On My holy hill of Zion (Ps. 2:6).

4. Synthetic Parallelism

The second line of poetry builds up (*synthesis* is Greek for "putting together") the thought in the first line:

The LORD is my shepherd;
I shall not want (Ps. 23:1).

Keep your heart with all diligence,
For out of it spring the issues of life
(Prov. 4:23).

5. Emblematic Parallelism

A figure of speech in the first *line* of poetry illustrates the content of the second line:

As the deer pants for the water brooks,
So pants my soul for You, O God
(Ps. 42:1).

As a ring of gold in a swine's snout,
So is a lovely woman who lacks discretion (Prov. 11:22).

IV. Literary Figures

We use these every day without realizing it. Such expressions as "She's a real angel" or "He eats like a pig" are figures of speech.

1. Comparisons

Vivid comparisons are often made between one thing and another in the Bible, especially in the five poetical books.

a. Simile

When the comparison uses the word *like* or *as* it is called a *simile:*

For You, O LORD, will bless the righteous;
With favor You will surround him **as** with a shield (Ps. 5:12).

Like an apple tree among the trees of the woods,
So is my beloved among the sons (Song 2:3a).

b. Metaphor

When the comparison is direct, and one thing is called another, without *like* or *as*, it is a *metaphor*. This is a very popular device[4]:

> For the LORD God is a sun and
>   shield;
> The LORD will give grace and glory;
> No good thing will He withhold
> From those who walk uprightly
> (Ps. 84:11).

> A garden enclosed is my sister, my
>   spouse,
> A spring shut up, a fountain sealed
> (Song 4:12).

2. Alliteration

Several words in close proximity beginning with the same letter—often a consonant—give us "apt alliteration's artful aid."[5] For example, the opening verses of the Song of Solomon have many words beginning with the "sh" sound (the letter *shîn* in Hebrew), including the name of the book and the Hebrew form of Solomon. Obviously the alliteration in translation will not and indeed cannot match or be in the same place as in the original language.[6] Nevertheless the KJV and the NKJV have many striking illustrations in translation:

> He frustrates the devices of the
>   crafty,
> So that their hands cannot carry out
>   their plans.
> He catches the wise in their own
>   craftiness,
> And the counsel of the cunning
>   comes quickly upon them
> (Job 5:12, 13).

> Man who is born of woman
>   is of few days and full of trouble.
> He comes forth like a flower and
>   fades away;
> He flees like a shadow and does not
>   continue (Job 14:1, 2).

> He has sent redemption to His
>   people;
> He has commanded His covenant
>   forever:
> Holy and awesome is His name
> (Ps. 111:9).

> A present is a precious stone
>   in the eyes of its possessor;
> Wherever he turns, he prospers
> (Prov. 17:8).

> The words of a talebearer are like
>   tasty trifles,
> And they go down into the inmost
>   body (Prov. 18:8).

3. Anthropomorphism

This means "human form," and describes God, who is spirit, as having human parts:

> The LORD is in His holy temple,
> The LORD's throne is in heaven;
> His **eyes** behold,
> His **eyelids** test the sons of men
> (Ps. 11:4).

4. Zoomorphism

Similarly, God's attributes are compared to *animal forms*:

> He shall cover you with His
>   **feathers**,
> And under His **wings** you shall
>   take refuge;
> His truth shall be your shield and
>   buckler (Ps. 91:4).

5. Personification

An object or abstract quality is treated as a person:

> Let the heavens rejoice, and let the
>   earth be glad;
> Let the sea roar, and all its fullness;
> Let the field be joyful, and all that is
>   in it.

Then all the trees of the woods will
rejoice before the LORD
(Ps. 96:11, 12).

I, wisdom, dwell with prudence,
And find out knowledge and
discretion (Prov. 8:12).

6. Acrostic

This is one device that is almost
impossible to translate,[7] because the
poem is based on the Hebrew alphabet, and successive lines of poetry are
in alphabetical order. Well-known examples are Psalm 119 and four of the
five chapters in Lamentations. The
book of Proverbs ends with the twenty-
two-verse tribute to the ideal woman
based on the letters of the Hebrew
alphabet (Prov. 31:10–31).

There are other figures of speech as
well, some of them overlapping a bit
with those we have presented, but
these will be enough for most believers.

If the reader will be on the lookout
for some of these poetic devices while
studying these five books (and much
of the rest of the Bible as well), a
great deal of fresh interest may be
found in the sacred text—not to mention a deeper appreciation of its beauty.
(See Eccl. 3:11a.)

ENDNOTES

[1]Three of these—Job, Proverbs, and
Ecclesiastes—are also called Wisdom
Literature. While poetic in form their
contents stress wisdom, or the art
and skill of living according to the
fear of God.

[2]Part of the reason for this is that
the KJV traditionally has printed
all forms of Bible literature—laws,
history, poetry, epistles—in exactly
the same format. More modern versions seek to show by the format
itself the type of writing being presented.

[3]The entire first psalm is an anti-
thetical parallelism between the righteous and the ungodly, a masterpiece
of what in art is called "dark against
light and light against dark."

[4]Our Lord used metaphors when
He called Himself "the Door," "the
Vine," "the Bread of Life," and "the
Good Shepherd."

[5]Preachers are especially fond of
this device for sermon outlines, and
when not forced, fanciful, or overdone, alliteration is a real help to the
memory.

[6]In the NT the book of Hebrews
opens with a cluster of words beginning with the "p" sound (Greek *pi*) in
the original.

[7]Ronald Knox's translation of the
Bible makes a rather impressive attempt to do so, but necessarily dropping four lesser-used letters from the
English alphabet, since Hebrew has
only twenty-two letters.

THE BOOK OF JOB

Introduction

"It is our first, oldest statement of the never-ending Problem—man's destiny, and God's way with him here in this earth .... Sublime sorrow, sublime reconciliation; oldest choral melody as of the heart of mankind—so soft, and great; as the summer midnight, as the world with its seas and stars! There is nothing written I think, in the Bible or out of it, of equal literary merit."

—Thomas Carlyle

I. Unique Place in the Canon

Job is the only book of its kind in the whole Word of God: a long, dramatic dialogue in poetic form, set like a large multi-faceted diamond in between a prose historical prologue and epilogue. As originally written in the Hebrew language, the book was entirely in poetry, with the exception of chapters 1, 2, 32:1–6a, and 42:7–17.

Samuel Ridout comments about its place in Holy Scripture:

> From its size, and a rapid glance at its contents, we would judge that the book of Job is a very important part of the word of God. Yet how much it is neglected by most; an intimate familiarity even with its contents is the exception rather than the rule.[1]

The majesty of the language is recognized even (and sometimes especially) by unbelievers. Of course, the rationalists are ever ready with their theories of "sources," "redactions," and "interpolations"—usually with no manuscript evidence whatever to support their destructive theories.

The great Reformer, Martin Luther,

who was himself a gifted writer and translator, said that Job was "more magnificent and sublime than any other book of Scripture." Alfred Lord Tennyson, who as poet laureate of England could be expected to recognize great poetry, called Job "the greatest poem whether of ancient or modern literature."

In light of the book of Job's great style and insight into the human condition, it should prove no surprise that our everyday speech has been greatly enriched by this book. The following expressions are some of the rather clear borrowings. Most of these are direct quotations from the book of Job that have become a part of our everyday speech:

The hair on my body stood up (4:15b). (My hair stood on end.)

My life is a breath (7:7a).

Put my life in my hands (13:14b). (Take my life in my hands.)

"Job's comforters." (These *exact* words are not found, but in 16:2 Job calls his friends "Miserable comforters.")

There is no justice (19:7).

I have escaped by the skin of my teeth (19:20b).

The root of the matter (19:28b).

Put your hand over your mouth (21:5b).

The land of the living (28:13b).

Eyes to the blind . . . feet to the lame (29:15).

Spit in my face (30:10b).

Great men are not always wise (32:9).

Words without knowledge (35:16b).

This far . . . but no farther, and here your proud waves must stop (38:11).

The gates of death (38:17a).

He smells the battle from afar (39:25). (We say, "The smell of battle.")

Repent in dust and ashes (42:6b).

The expression "I know that my Redeemer lives . . ." (19:25) is well-known partly because of Handel's marvelous musical setting of the words in his *Messiah*.

The expression "the patience of Job" (Jas. 5:11, KJV) though not in the book of Job, has become a part of everyday conversation.

As to the content of the book, it has been pointed out that the deep questions that Job poses about life, death, suffering, and life after death are all met in the Mediator he longed for, the Lord Jesus Christ.

II. Authorship

The book of Job is anonymous, though Jewish tradition chooses Moses as the author. Other suggestions are Elihu, Solomon, Hezekiah, Ezra, a nameless Jew living somewhere between 500 and 200 B.C., or Job himself. Since Job lived 140 additional years after the events in the book and experienced all of the events and speeches, perhaps he is the most likely choice.

III. Date

As to the events in the book, it is widely believed that Job lived prior to the birth of Abraham. Thus, the events in the book of Job would fall somewhere in the latter part of Genesis 11. There are several reasons why Job is assigned to this period in history. First of all, there is no undisputable mention in the book of his being a Jew. There is no mention of the Exodus or Law of Moses. In fact, it is clear that Job was the priest for his own family (1:5), and this type of family priesthood belonged to the patriarchal period. The lifestyle characterized by wealth being determined by cattle and other animals is also largely patriarchal. Job lived for more than two hundred years, and this age span was characteristic of the era immediately preceding Abraham. Scholars also notice the musical instruments (21:12) and the forms of money (42:11) which are mentioned in the book of Job, and they assign these to the early part of Genesis chronologically.[2]

As to the time of writing, scholars range all the way from the patriarchal era (c. 2100–1900 B.C.) to the second century B.C.! (This last view is held by extreme liberals, and is virtually impossible to reconcile with Dead Sea Scroll portions of Job coming from the same era.)

The two most likely eras are the patriarchal and Solomonic. It would seem to modern Westerners that such long and complex speeches would be best preserved if written down soon after they were delivered. However, Eastern and Semitic oral transmission is known to be remarkable for its accuracy.

The best argument for the Solomonic age is the content and style of the book: it is Wisdom Literature, not unlike the works of King Solomon. Such conservative OT scholars as Franz Delitzsch and Merrill F. Unger held a Solomonic date for the actual writing of the book, but obviously allowing for a long and accurate oral tradition. Such a literary phenomenon is widely understood in the East but hard for Westerners to relate to.

IV. Background and Theme

Although the author of the book of Job is unknown, there is no question as to its inspiration or historical accuracy. The apostle Paul quotes from Job 5:13 in 1 Corinthians 3:19: "He catches the wise in their own craftiness." In Ezekiel 14:14, Job is spoken of as a historical person, not a fictional character. He is also named in James 5:11: "You have heard of the perseverance of Job and seen the end intended by the Lord—that the Lord is very compassionate and merciful."

The subject of the book is the mystery of human suffering and the problem of pain. Why do all people suffer some, and especially why do the righteous suffer? In Job we see a man who was probably exposed to more catastrophes in one day than any other person who has ever lived, with the exception of the Lord Jesus. The Lord allowed these sufferings to come into Job's life in order to enlarge his capacity for communion with God. Perhaps in a special way, the book is also intended to shadow forth the sufferings of the Jewish people.

If the Jews were to accept a *suffering* Messiah (as over against a heroic "Maccabean" type), it was necessary to show that suffering is not necessarily in return for individual sins.

Christ suffered for us, the just for the unjust.

Several passages in this book can be applied to the Lord Jesus:

1. 9:33—"Nor is there any mediator between us, who may lay his hand on us both." (Christ is the Mediator who can bridge the gap between God and man.)
2. 16:8–19—The sufferings of Job. Many of the expressions in this passage are applied in the Psalms to the sufferings of the Messiah.
3. 16:21—"Oh, that one might plead for a man with God, as a man pleads for his neighbor!" (The Lord Jesus Christ is our Advocate who pleads our case before the Father.)
4. 19:25, 26—"For I know that my Redeemer lives." (Christ's roles as Redeemer and coming King are clearly described.)
5. 33:24—" 'Deliver him from going down to the Pit; I have found a ransom.' " (The word "ransom" here is the same word as "atonement." Through the atonement of Christ, believers are delivered from the pit of hell.)

Several statements in the book of Job are often said to reveal an advanced knowledge of science:

1. The evaporation-precipitation cycle (36:27, 28).
2. Wind and weather directions (37:9, 17).
3. Composition of the human body (33:6).
4. Suspension of the earth (26:7).
5. Ocean-bottom phenomena (38:16).
6. Cloud-lightning relationship (37:11).
7. The orbits of heavenly bodies and their influence upon the earth (38:32, 33).

OUTLINE

Commentary

I. THE PROLOGUE: THE TESTING OF JOB (Chaps. 1, 2)

A. Scene I: The Land of Uz (1:1–5)

1:1–3 **Job** was a wealthy **man** who lived **in the land of Uz**. From Lamentations 4:21 it appears that Uz was located in Edom, southeast of Palestine.[3] The **upright** and God-fearing Job had **seven sons and three daughters**. So vast were his holdings of livestock that he **was the greatest** man in **the East**.

1:4, 5 One of the strong arguments that the events of Job took place in the patriarchal era is the fact that Job, as father of the family, acted as priest and sacrificed **burnt offerings** for his sons. The danger of frivolous and even sacrilegious talk when even generally devout people are **feasting** and making merry is ever present. In his evening meditation for Christmas Day, C. H. Spurgeon makes a good application for us in the Christian dispensation:

> What the patriarch did early in the morning, after the family festivities, it will be well for the believer to do for himself ere he rests tonight. Amid the cheerfulness of household gatherings it is easy to slide into sinful levities, and to forget our avowed character as Christians. It ought not to be so, but so it is, that our days of feasting are very seldom days of sanctified enjoyment, but too frequently degenerate into unhallowed mirth. . . . Holy gratitude should be quite as purifying an element as grief. Alas! for our poor hearts, that facts prove that the house of mourning is better than the house of feasting. Come, believer, in what have you sinned to-day? Have you been even as others in idle words and loose speeches? Then confess the sin, and fly to the sacrifice. The sacrifice sanctifies. The precious blood of the Lamb slain removes the guilt, and purges away the defilement of our sins of ignorance and carelessness.[4]

B. Scene II: Heaven—The Lord's Presence (1:6–12)

As the story unfolds we are told of a scene in heaven when **the sons of God**[5] (angels) appeared **before the Lord. Satan** (the word is Hebrew for "Accuser") **also** was present. When God spoke to Satan concerning the uprightness of His **servant Job**, Satan implied that the only reason Job feared God was that He had been so good to him. According to Satan, if the Lord had not put a protective **hedge around** Job, then he would have cursed his Creator **to His face**.

C. Scene III: The Land of Uz— Calamity to Job's Property and Prosperity (1:13–22)

1:13–19 The Lord, thereupon, granted **Satan** permission to test Job by robbing him of his possessions. However, the devil was *not* permitted to touch Job's **person**.

Then followed a series of dreadful calamities in rapid succession:

1. **The Sabeans** stole **five hundred yoke of oxen** and **five hundred female donkeys**, and **killed the** servants who were in charge of these animals.
2. Lightning destroyed **seven thousand sheep**, as well as **the servants** who were tending them.
3. **The Chaldeans** stole **three thousand camels** and **killed the servants** who cared for them.
4. **A great wind** caused the collapse of **the house** in which Job's **sons and daughters were eating and drinking wine**, killing all of them.

1:20–22 In spite of these terrible losses, **Job** was enabled to worship God, saying, **"Naked I came from my mother's womb, and naked shall I return there. The Lord gave, and the Lord has taken away; blessed be the name of the Lord."**

D. Scene IV: Heaven—The Lord's Presence Again (2:1–6)

In chapter 2, we find **Satan** appearing **before the Lord** once again. This time **Satan** implies that Job's faithfulness to God would soon vanish if he were allowed to **touch his** body. Permission to do so is granted.

E. Scene V: Uz—Calamity to Job's Person (2:7–13)

2:7–10 Job, thereupon, breaks out with **painful boils** from **the sole of his foot to the crown of his head**. So great is his misery that even his **wife** urges him to **"Curse God and die!"** But Job answers her, **"Shall we indeed accept good from God, and shall we not accept adversity?"** Regarding Job's wife, Harold St. John quotes the following paragraph:

I think of all the cruel and one-sided things that masculine commentators have written about Job's wife, and I almost despair of my sex; it takes a woman to understand a woman, and it is reserved for a lady writer (I think that her name was Louise Haughton) to discern that as long as Job's wife could share in his sorrows she bore up bravely, but as soon as he enters a fresh chamber of suffering and leaves her outside, then she breaks down: for her the one intolerable woe is that which she is forbidden to share with him.[6]

2:11–13 Shortly after this, **three** of **Job's friends** hear of his **adversity** and determine to visit him with words of comfort. The friends are **Eliphaz, Bildad, and Zophar**.

However, when they see Job's pitiful and wretched condition, they are so shocked that they are unable to speak to him for **seven days and seven nights**!

II. THE DEBATE BETWEEN JOB AND HIS FRIENDS (Chaps. 3—31)

Chapter 3 begins a series of discourses by Job and his friends, the largest and most complex section of the book. Ridout describes it well:

It has been well named *The Entangle-*

ment, for it is a mass of argument, denunciation, accusation, suspicion, partly correct theories, and withal flashes of faith and hope—all in the language of loftiest poetry, with magnificent luxuriance of Oriental metaphor. To the casual reader there may seem to be no progress, and but little clarity in the controversy. And it must be confessed that God's people at large seem to have gained little from these chapters beyond a few familiar, beautiful and oft-quoted verses.[7]

These discourses may be divided into three series: Job first speaks, then is answered by one of his friends; Job replies to him, only to be answered by another; poor Job seeks to defend himself again—only to be rebuked by the third friend!

The three series of discourses may be shown as follows:

First Round
Job: Chap. 3
Eliphaz: Chaps. 4, 5
Job: Chaps. 6, 7
Bildad: Chap. 8
Job: Chaps. 9, 10
Zophar: Chap. 11

Second Round
Job: Chaps. 12—14
Eliphaz: Chap. 15
Job: Chaps. 16, 17
Bildad: Chap. 18
Job: Chap. 19
Zophar: Chap. 20

Third Round
Job: Chap. 21
Eliphaz: Chap. 22
Job: Chaps. 23, 24
Bildad: Chap. 25
Job: Chaps. 26—31
(Zophar does not speak again.)

The arguments of the three friends may be summarized as follows:

Eliphaz stresses experience or general observation: "I have seen...." (4:8, 15; 5:3; 15:7; 22:19).

Bildad is the voice of tradition and the authority of antiquity (8:8). "His discourses abound in proverbs and pious platitudes which, though true enough, are known to everyone (9:1–3; 13:2)."[8]

Zophar counsels legalism and religiosity (11:14, 15). "He presumes to know what God will do in any given case, why He will do it, and what His thoughts about it are."[9] His ideas are mere assumptions, pure dogmatism.

The remaining portion of the book is taken up with a long speech by a young man named Elihu (Chaps. 32—37), and then by a conversation between God and Job (Chaps. 38—42). Job ends with a prose epilogue that matches the prologue.

A. The First Round of Speeches (Chaps. 3—14)

1. Job's Opening Lament (Chap. 3)

3:1–9 This chapter has been well titled "Unhappy Birthday," because in it Job curses **the day of his birth**, extols the blessings of death, and yet complains that he cannot die! He assigns total **darkness** to the day **a male child**—himself—was **conceived**.

3:10–12 Since he was conceived and born, **why** couldn't he have died **at birth**? (It is worth noting that even in his tremendous bitterness and grief Job does not suggest either abortion or infanticide, which were common evils in the ancient world, and are now so again today in the West.)

3:13–19 Job praises death as a situation where **the weary are at rest, small and great are there, and the servant is free from his master**.

3:20–26 Next he questions why the **light** of life is given to those who are **in misery** (as he was) and **long for death** as if for **hidden treasures**.

Verse 25 is very famous:

> **For the thing I greatly feared has
> come upon me,
> And what I dreaded has happened
> to me.**

Could this indicate that even in Job's
happy and prosperous days he had
fears of losing what he had? This is a
common characteristic of the very
rich: extreme fear of losing wealth
and having to live a frugal life. Riches
give no real security; only *God* can
give that.

2. Eliphaz's First Speech (Chaps. 4, 5)

Chapter four commences the cycle
of speeches of Job's friends and his
responses to them. Ridout summarizes the gist of their message as
follows:

> In the controversy of the three friends
> we have a unity of thought, based on
> a common principle. That principle is
> that all suffering is of a *punitive* rather
> than of an instructive nature; that it
> is based on God's justice rather than
> on His love—though these are ever
> combined in all His ways. Such a
> principle necessarily fails to distinguish
> between the sufferings of the righteous
> and those of the wicked.[10]

In chapters 4 and 5, Eliphaz speaks.
Eliphaz (his name may mean *God is
strength* or *God is fine gold*) was a pious
and prominent person, orthodox in
his views of God's greatness, but
sadly lacking in compassion. He becomes harsher as the series of speeches
progress. It is worth noting that while
the three friends become *less and less*
understanding (in both senses of that
word) throughout the book, Job becomes *more and more* understanding
of God's ways, until, after speeches
by Elihu and a true encounter with
Jehovah, he accepts God's will with
true humility.

4:1–11   Eliphaz says in effect, "You
helped others ('Your words have kept
men on their feet' 4:4, James Moffatt),
but now you cannot help yourself."
(These words are reminiscent of
Christ's mockers at the Crucifixion:
"He saved others; He cannot save
Himself.") The reason he gives for
this is Job's self-righteousness. "Hath
not thy piety been thy confidence,
and the perfection of thy ways thy
hope?" (4:6, JND). Since people suffer for wickedness, it must be that Job
has sinned (vv. 7–9).

4:12–21   Then Eliphaz tells of a
vision which was **secretly brought to**
him at **night**. In this vision **a spirit**
asks the question, **"Can a mortal be
more righteous than God? Can a
man be more pure than his Maker?"**
(v. 17). The meaning of this seems to
be that man has no right to reply
against God. If a person suffers, it is
his own fault, not God's. After all,
God is so great that He cannot trust
His own **servants**, and when compared to Him, **His angels** are guilty
of **error**. Since this is so, **how much
more** untrustworthy and fallible are
mortal men who are as transient as **a
moth**!

5:1–7   Eliphaz challenges Job to
summon men or angels (the **holy
ones**) to disprove that sin is followed
by judgment. The speaker himself
has observed the unalterable link between wickedness and punishment.
Trouble is never causeless. **Man**, being
sinful, is destined **to trouble**, as sure
as the sparks fly upward.

5:8–16   The thing to do is to **seek
God** and to **commit** one's **cause** to
Him, because He is all-wise and all-
powerful. This is seen in His control
of nature and in His providential dealings with mankind. Verse 13 is quoted
by Paul in 1 Corinthians 3:19 to unmask the false wisdom of this world.

5:17–27 By submitting to **the chastening of the Almighty**, says Eliphaz, people experience divine deliverance from **famine**, **war**, slander, civil strife, peril, drought, wild **beasts**, and crop damage. They enjoy domestic **peace**, security, fruitfulness, and longevity.

3. Job's Response (Chaps. 6, 7)

6:1–13 **Job** admits that his **words** have been **rash**, but *there is a reason!* His **grief** and **calamity** are **heavier than the sand of the sea**, and his **spirit** is drinking in the **poison** of **the arrows of the Almighty**. In spite of all the negative and awful things that are expressed in this book, especially by Job, they are so beautifully worded that the sensitive reader is struck by their potency. Job protests that he would not complain so bitterly without cause, any more than animals would **bray** without a reason. Suffering and weeping are linked just like **flavorless food** and seasoning. He wishes he could die because he has no **strength** to endure and no **hope** for the future. Prolonging **life** is useless.

6:14–23 Job's friends (he calls them **brothers**) have failed him and disappointed him when he needed them most. He compares them to brooks or wadis that **vanish** completely when you need them. Though he had sought nothing from them, they had criticized him vaguely without telling him how he had sinned.

6:24–30 Job maintains his integrity in spite of the implications of Eliphaz's speech that he is a secret sinner. He wants to know specifically *where* he has **erred** and desires proof of **injustice on** his **tongue**. Verse 27 is a counter-accusation to the friends; perhaps the **friend** they are undermining is Job himself!

7:1–10 Now Job addresses the Lord directly. It is as natural for him to have the death-wish as for **a servant** to long for rest after a hard day's work. However in Job's case the **night** hours bring no relief to his tortured body, as he tosses **till dawn**. **Like a weaver's shuttle** his life is passing swiftly **without hope**, vanishing from sight like a **cloud**.

7:11–21 He asks the Lord why He should pay so much attention to an insignificant human being, hemming him in, terrifying him with nightmares, until he would rather be strangled. **Is man** so great that God should cause him to suffer continually? Even if Job had **sinned**, is there no **pardon**, since he is going to die soon anyway?

4. Bildad's First Speech (Chap. 8)

The name Bildad may mean *son of contention*, which would be a very appropriate meaning, since this friend of Job seems to love controversy. Ridout compares Bildad to Eliphaz in style and knowledge as follows:

> There is perhaps less of the courtesy and dignity which marked the speech of Eliphaz, together with some harshness toward Job, caused apparently by the bitter charge of the latter against God. With all his ignorance of divine principles, Bildad is jealous of the honor of God, and cannot allow Him to be accused. In this he is surely right, but he fails to convince Job because of the root error in the thoughts, indeed, of them all: God must punish sin, and Job must be a sinner for he is being punished.[11]

8:1–7 Accusing Job of irresponsible and blustery speech, **Bildad** defends the justice of **God** in punishing the wicked and rewarding the **upright**. He says unkindly that Job's **sons** were destroyed because of **their**

transgression. There is no indication of this, and even had there been, it was a cruel thing to say to a man in great sorrow and suffering. But **if** Job would **earnestly** turn **to God**, says Bildad, there was still hope for divine favor.

8:8–22 He next appeals to history to prove the link between evil and retribution. Just as **reeds** wither when there is no **water**, so is the doom of the irreligious and **the hypocrite**. (Verse 16a may be an allusion to the absorption of chlorophyll from sunlight.) God delights to replace **the wicked** with **the blameless**, whom He then proceeds to bless.

5. Job's Response (Chaps. 9, 10)

9:1–13 When **Job** asks, **"How can a man be righteous before God?"**, he is not inquiring as to the way of salvation, but expressing the hopelessness of ever proving his innocence before One who is so great. It is folly **to contend** with God since **one could not answer Him one time out of a thousand**. He is sovereign, all-**wise**, and all-powerful, as seen in His control of **mountains, earth, sun, stars, sea, yes, wonders without number**.

9:14–31 What chance would Job have of defending himself? Could he be sure that God is listening? The Lord is merciless, arbitrary, and unjust, Job says, and therefore a fair trial is impossible. In his despair, Job accuses God of undiscriminatingly destroying the **blameless and the wicked**, of laughing **at the plight of the innocent**, and of causing earth's **judges** to act unrighteously. He says, "I am innocent, but I no longer care. I am sick of living. Nothing matters; innocent or guilty, God will destroy us" (vv. 21, 22 TEV). As his life runs out, he finds no hope in careless self-forgetfulness or self-improvement.

9:32–35 Job sighs for a **mediator between** God and himself, but finds none. We know that the Mediator who could meet his (and our) deepest need is the Lord Jesus Christ (1 Tim. 2:5). Matthew Henry comments:

> Job would gladly refer the matter, but no creature was capable of being a referee, and therefore he must even refer it still to God himself and resolve to acquiesce in his judgment. Our Lord Jesus is the blessed daysman, who has mediated between heaven and earth, has laid his hand upon us both; to him the Father has committed all judgment, and we must. But this matter was not then brought to so clear a light as it is now by the gospel, which leaves no room for such a complaint as this.[12]

10:1–7 In exasperation, Job complains bitterly, asking God to explain His unreasonable behavior to one He had created. Does He act like a mere **man** in judging uncharitably, even when He knows that Job is **not wicked**?

10:8–12 Harold St. John comments on this paragraph as follows:

> We must not miss this amazing passage in which the Clay expostulates with the Potter and reminds God that in creating man He has assumed responsibilities from which he cannot honorably escape. 10:8 Thy hands made and fashioned me. 10:10 The formation of the physical embryo. 10:11 The growth of skin and flesh and the development of bones and sinews. 10:12 (a) The gift of "soul" with its many-sided expressions and (b) The visitation of God by which man's highest part, the "spirit," is conferred and preserved.[13]

10:13–22 **Why** does the Lord inflict severe calamities on Job? Seemingly it makes no difference whether he is **righteous** or **wicked**; his life is filled with divine **indignation**. **Why did God allow him to be born?** But now why not let him have **a little comfort before** he passes off into oblivion, **where even the light is like darkness?**

6. Zophar's First Speech (Chap. 11)

11:1–12 **Zophar the Naamathite** insists that such empty, arrogant **talk** should not go unanswered. Regarding the meaning of Job's third friend's name, Ridout writes:

> Zophar, "a sparrow," from the root verb "to twitter," is the masculine form of Zipporah, Moses' wife, and like her he was an unconscious opponent of God's judgment on the flesh, though he was very zealous in condemning the fancied works of the flesh in Job. His vehement denunciations being utterly out of place, were as harmless as the "twitterings" of the bird for which he was named.[14]

If Job could only see things as *God* does, Zophar contends, he would realize that he is not suffering as much as he really deserves! His ignorance of God's greatness disqualifies him to question His justice. Verse 12 is an especially unkind cut, aimed obviously at Job: **"For an empty-headed man will be wise, when a wild donkey's colt is born a man."**

11:13–20 The best thing for Job to do is **put . . . away** his sins; **then** God will give him security, rest, and comfort. If not, there is no escape from destruction.

7. Job's Response (Chaps. 12—14)

12:1–6 In biting (and now famous) sarcasm, **Job** accuses his friends of intellectual conceit:

No doubt you are the people,
And wisdom will die with you!

Anyone knows that **God** is wise and powerful, but how do they explain the excruciating sufferings of a man who once received answers to his prayers, and the contrasting prosperity of the ungodly? "You have no troubles, and yet you make fun of me; you hit a man who is about to fall" (v. 5 TEV).

12:7–12 Even the world of nature—**the beasts** and **the birds** and **the fish**—shows God's arbitrariness in destroying some and protecting others. If Job's critics tested **words** as carefully as they tasted **food**, they would agree with the ancients, who uniformly agreed with what Job had said.

12:13–25 Now Job launches into a majestic recital of the Lord's sovereignty, **wisdom, and strength**, and how they often produce inexplicable and paradoxical results.

13:1–19 Job scolds his critics. They have not said anything new. He wants to plead his case with God, not with these forgers of lies and worthless physicians. If they kept **silent**, people would think they were wise. Their explanation of God's action was not true; they would be accountable to Him for it. Their arguments were weak and useless. If they would just be quiet, he would plead his **case . . . before** God and commit his **life** to Him. He is confident he will be vindicated, but even if God were to **slay** him he **will** *still* **trust** the Lord.

13:20–28 From 13:20 through 14:22, Job addresses God directly. He begs relief from suffering and demands an explanation of why God is treating him so severely. He wastes away like a rotten thing, a **moth-eaten garment**—scarcely worthy of such notice by God.

Francis Andersen evaluates Job's words as follows:

Here Job shows himself to be a more honest observer, a more exuberant thinker, than the friends. The mind reels at the immensity of his conception of God. The little deity in the theology of Eliphaz, Bildad and Zophar is easily thought and easily believed. But a faith like Job's puts the human spirit to strenuous work.[15]

14:1–6 Job continues to ask why God is so unrelenting with one who is so fleeting, frail, and faulty. Verse 1 is very widely quoted, perhaps because it seems to fit so many occasions:

Man who is born of woman is of few days and full of trouble.

Why not let him live out the rest of his short life with some measure of peace?

14:7–12 **There is** more **hope for a tree** that has been **cut down** than there is for him. There is a terrible finality about human death; a dead person is like a dried-up **river**.

14:13–17 Job wishes that God would **hide** him **in the grave ... until** His anger subsides. Then if the Almighty calls him forth, he will vindicate himself. In the meantime, God takes note of his every sin.

Job does four things in this section: (1) He asks for a revelation of what his sins are; (2) He describes the transitoriness of human life; (3) He despairs over the finality of death (longing for a mediator and grasping at the hope of life beyond); (4) He complains of his present plight.

Verse 14a asks a most important question: **If a man dies, shall he live again?** Our Lord answers the question in John 11:25, 26:

I am the resurrection and the life. He who believes in Me, though he may die, he shall live. And who-

ever lives and believes in Me shall never die.

Harold St. John comments on verses 14 and 15:

In 14:14,15 light dawns on a silent sea, light breaks in, and in a passage of almost incredible daring, Job declares that man is more than matter, that though the heavens will pass and decay, the everlasting hills will crumble, he himself may lie in the grasp of the grave for millennia, yet a day must break when God will feel a hunger round His heart for His friend and will have a desire for the work of His hands.

Then from the deeps of the underworld, Job will answer and, more abiding than the hills, more permanent than the heavens, he will be reunited with the God who had become homesick for His servant.[16]

14:18–22 As inevitable as erosion in nature is man's decay under trials. **His** body returns to dust and **his soul** goes to a place of sadness.

This ends the first round of speeches. The logic of Job's friends has been: God is righteous; He punishes the wicked; if Job is being punished it proves he is wicked. But Job has steadily maintained that he is *not* a wicked person at all.

B. The Second Round of Speeches (Chaps. 15—21)

In the second round of speeches Job's "comforters," no longer appealing for repentance, become more condemning and vehement. Job, meanwhile, becomes more stubborn.

1. Eliphaz's Second Speech (Chap. 15)

15:1–6 It is now the turn of **Eliphaz the Temanite** to reproach Job again for his vanity and his impious, **unprofitable talk**. In a series of rapid-fire questions, **the Temanite** ridicules Job's supposed **knowledge**, calling it **empty**. While Job's bold words challenging God did lay him open to the charge of "casting **off fear**," it was not fair to accuse him of choosing **the tongue of the crafty**. If anything, Job was too open and self-revealing. A hypocrite he was *not!* It is vain for him or for any person to profess righteousness.

15:7–13 Next Eliphaz challenges what he considers Job's arrogance in thinking so highly of his own thoughts: **"Do you limit wisdom to yourself?"** he asks. By Eliphaz's calling the three comforters' words "the **consolations** of God" and "gentle," he shows a complete lack of a heart for genuine compassionate counseling.

15:14–16 Eliphaz repeats his remarks of 4:17–19 on the holiness of **God** and the sinfulness of **man**. But how is Job any more sinful than Eliphaz? Ridout asks:

> Why then apply it to Job as though it proved *him* a sinner above all others? This, surely, is more like crafty speech than all the hot utterances of Job. Let Eliphaz take his place beside Job and confess that he too is "abominable and filthy." The poor sufferer might have responded to that.[17]

15:17–26 Turning to the ancient wisdom **from the fathers**, Eliphaz describes the **pain** that a **wicked man** experiences in life.

15:27–35 A terrible catalog of troubles overtakes **the wicked**, and these calamities are proportionate to the guilt.

2. Job's Response (Chaps. 16, 17)

16:1–5 **Job** rejects Eliphaz's analysis of the situation and fights back by calling his critics **"miserable comforters."** If they were in his **place**, he would at least try to **comfort** them!

16:6–14 But now God has turned against him and tortures him by turning him over **to . . . ungodly** men and persecuting him beyond endurance, **with wound upon wound**. All this is in spite of the fact that he is guilty of no unrighteousness.

16:15–22 The fact that Job had **sewn** (not merely *put* on) **sackcloth** over his **skin** shows he is in permanent mourning. Without **friends** to comfort, or anyone to plead his case, he will soon **go the way of no return**.

Some of the language in verses 9–19 is employed in the Psalms to refer to the Messiah. Therefore we are justified in making an *application* of them to the sufferings of Christ, even if that is not the *primary* meaning.

17:1–12 As Job, **broken** in **spirit**, teeters on the edge of **the grave**, his friends mock him. He wants God alone to try his case because his critics have proven themselves of no use. The Lord has made him an object of contempt. **Upright men** who see his condition will rise **up against** his critics, while he continues to protest his integrity. He cannot find **one wise man among** his three antagonists.

17:13–16 There is nothing left for Job but **the grave** with its **darkness**, **corruption**, and worms.

3. Bildad's Second Speech (Chap. 18)

18:1–4 **Bildad the Shuhite** denounces Job for very strongly scorning the **words** of wisdom spoken by his friends and himself. One good thing that can be said about Bildad: he is *briefer* in his reproaches than his two fellow-comforters. Perhaps his awareness of this virtue of conciseness gave him boldness to suggest that Job **should put an end to words**.

18:5–21 He repeats the now-familiar refrain that **the wicked** person gets caught in the **net** of his own sins.

Then he gives a dreadful list of the calamities that come upon a sinner's house. Bildad was *right* in saying that men suffer for their sins, but he was *wrong* in giving this as an explanation of *Job's* sufferings. Not all suffering is a direct result of sin in one's life.

4. Job's Response (Chap. 19)

19:1–22 Job tells his friends that they ought to be **ashamed** of the way they have **wronged** him. He has been mistreated by **God** and by **relatives, friends**, and servants. His body has wasted away and he has barely **escaped** death. Yet his **friends** join **God** in attacking him pitilessly.

19:23, 24 He wishes that his **words** of defense were **inscribed in a book** and **engraved on a rock with an iron pen and lead, forever**, so that sometime in the future he might obtain justice.

19:25–27 In a rare burst of light, he believes that there is a **Redeemer** who will one day vindicate him and then restore him, even though death and decay intervene.

The great English preacher, Spurgeon, whose own style is not unlike that of the Book of Job, makes a fine application of verse 25:

The marrow of Job's comfort lies in that little word "My"—"My Redeemer," and in the fact that the Redeemer lives. Oh! to get hold of a living Christ. We must get a property in Him before we can enjoy Him . . . So a Redeemer who does not redeem *me*, an avenger who will never stand up for *my* blood, of what avail were such? Rest not content until by faith you can say, "Yes, I cast myself upon my living Lord; and He is mine." It may be you hold Him with a feeble hand; you half think it presumption to say, "He lives as *my* Redeemer;" yet, remember if you have but faith

as a grain of mustard seed, that little faith *entitles* you to say it. But there is also another word here, expressive of Job's strong confidence, "*I know*." To say, "I hope so, I trust so," is comfortable; and there are thousands in the fold of Jesus who hardly ever get much further. But to reach the essence of consolation you *must* say, "I know."[18]

The fact that Job has faith to **see God in** his **flesh after** his **skin is destroyed**, strongly suggests the physical resurrection, a doctrine not widely taught in the OT, but accepted as standard in the time of our Lord by OT—believing Jews.

Again Spurgeon comments in a beautiful way on verse 26:

Mark the subject of Job's devout anticipation—"I shall see God." He does not say, "I shall see the saints" —though doubtless that will be untold felicity—but, "I shall see *God*." It is not—"I shall see the pearly gates, I shall behold the walls of jasper, I shall gaze upon the crowns of gold," but "I shall see God." This is the sum and substance of heaven, this is the joyful hope of all believers.[19]

19:28, 29 In view of this coming vindication, his friends should not **persecute him**, or they will be punished.

5. Zophar's Second Speech (Chap. 20)

20:1–19 Apparently Job's confession of faith fell on deaf ears. **Zophar** was not listening. He says that human history demonstrates that the proud **man . . . will perish** out of sight **forever. His children will** beg from **the poor**, and return what he has taken unjustly. Though still in **youthful vigor**, he will be cut off. No matter how luxuriously he has lived, he will suddenly lose everything he has gained through oppressing **the poor**.

20:20–29 Almost every imaginable calamity will come upon him, including hunger, **distress, misery**, armed attack, **fire**, and loss of tranquility. Heaven **and . . . earth** will conspire **against him**, and his possessions will disappear. This is **the heritage appointed to** the wicked **by God**.

G. Campbell Morgan says concerning this:

> In a passage thrilling with passion, Zophar describes the instability of evil gains. There is a triumph, but it is short. There is a mounting up, but it is followed by swift vanishing. There is a sense of youth, but it bends to dust. There is a sweetness but it becomes remorse; a swallowing down, which issues in vomiting; a getting without rejoicing. The final nemesis of the wicked is that God turns upon him, and pursues him with instruments of judgment. Darkness enwraps him. His sin is set in the light of the heavens, and earth turns against him. Let the history of wickedness be considered and it will be seen how true this is.[20]

6. Job's Response (Chap. 21)

21:1–22 Job now asks for strict attention. His **complaint** is not primarily **against man**, although his pathetic condition should awaken human sympathy. He counters their arguments with the true observation that **the wicked** often prosper in every area of life and die without suffering, even if they have had no place for **God** in their life. **How often**, he asks, do the wicked reap the reward of their sins in their own lifetime? How often are they driven away **like chaff** in **the wind**?

> You claim God punishes a child for the sins of his father. No! Let God

punish the sinners themselves; let Him show that He does it because of their sins. Let sinners bear their own punishment; let them feel the wrath of the Almighty God. When a man's life is over, does he really care whether his children are happy? Can a man teach God who judges even those in high places? (vv. 19–22 TEV)

21:23–34 **One** person **dies** at peace and **in** full **strength**, prosperous. **Another** passes away **in . . . bitterness** and poverty. In death all are alike. If Job's friends insist that the wicked are always punished in this life, he will appeal to those **who travel** extensively to testify that although the wicked may be punished in the afterlife, he often lives quite happily here. No one condemns or punishes him, and he dies just like all others. As a parting shot Job says, "And you! You try to comfort me with nonsense. Every answer you give is a lie!" (v. 34 TEV).

With these words Job ends the second round of speeches between himself and his friends. These "comforters" have about reached the end of their attempts to "convict" Job of sin; they will attempt one more round—minus Zophar.

The problem of the book of Job is still unsolved. Why do the righteous suffer? Job, however, has made some progress and little glimmers of light have begun to shine through the dark enigma of his suffering.

C. The Third Round of Speeches (Chaps. 22—31)

1. Eliphaz's Third Speech (Chap. 22)

In the third round, Eliphaz and Bildad conclude their arguments, using a great deal of repetition. Zophar remains silent. Job answers them and is apparently unaffected by their arguments, since he knows that he is not a secret sinner nor a hypocrite, but, as chapter one reveals, a blameless man (but not sinless or humble). Eliphaz's last speech is full of dignity and literary beauty; he is slightly more polite to the poor sufferer, but unjust nevertheless.

22:1–11 Eliphaz's questions are designed to show that **God** doesn't need Job or anything he has or does, including his **blameless . . . ways**. Then he launches into a prolonged tirade in which he accuses Job of gross **wickedness**— taking wrongful **pledges from** the poor, refusing **water** to **the weary**, **bread** to **the hungry**, taking **land** by force, and oppressing **widows** and orphans. That, according to Eliphaz, accounts for Job's present dilemma. The facts, however, were otherwise; Job had shown great social consciousness and had been generous in his charity.

22:12–20 Job should not think that **God in the height of heaven** doesn't **see** what is going on. If he continues in sin, he will share the fate of the people of Noah's day, when the earth's **foundations were swept away by a flood**—people whom God had previously prospered. **The righteous** rejoice whenever the wicked are punished.

22:21–30 Eliphaz truly has some exquisite words for Job in this his final appeal: **"Now acquaint yourself with Him, and be at peace"** (v. 21a); **"Yes, the Almighty will be your gold and your precious silver"** (v. 25); and **"so light will shine on your ways"** (v. 28b). These words are not only beautiful, but also *true*—for a repentant sinner "returning **to the Almighty**" and "removing **iniquity far from** his **tents**" (v. 23)! The only problem is one of application: Job has not been living in sin! Barnes summarizes Eliphaz's final appeal to Job:

The Almighty would be his defense; he would find happiness in God; his prayer would be heard; light would shine upon his ways; and when others were humbled, he would be exalted.[21]

2. Job's Response (Chaps. 23, 24)

Chapters 23 and 24 are all one speech, merely divided for convenience by the ancient Bible scholars. Job develops three main themes in chapter 23: his longing to present his case at God's throne (vv. 1–9); his defense of his own righteous lifestyle (vv. 10–12); and his fear of God as if He were his adversary (vv. 13–17).

23:1–9 Job's **complaint** is bitter. If only he could **come to** God's throne and **find Him**! Spurgeon comments:

His first prayer is not "O that I might be healed of the disease which now festers in every part of my body!" nor even "O that I might see my children restored from the jaws of the grave, and my property once more brought from the hand of the spoiler!" but the first and uppermost cry is, "O that I knew where I might find HIM, who is my God! that I might come even to His seat!" God's children run home when the storm comes on. It is the heaven-born instinct of a gracious soul to seek shelter from all ills beneath the wings of Jehovah.[22]

Job is confident that if he could approach the Lord He would have to admit that Job was righteous and so he **would be delivered forever from** his **Judge**.

23:10–12 Verse 10 is often quoted to prove the sanctifying effects of trials, but in context it is really Job's confidence in a "not-guilty" verdict. In the meantime God acts in an arbitrary manner, and His fearful judgments leave Job **terrified**. In spite of this, Job believes that if his case were to ever come to trial at God's judgment seat, he would be found to be as pure **as gold** and to have been always obedient to God's **words**, which he has **treasured . . . more than** his **necessary food**. The lovely words of verse 10 are well worth learning by heart for our own lives:

> But He knows the way that I
>   take;
> When He has tested me,
> I shall come forth as gold.

23:13–17 Meanwhile **the unique** and apparently arbitrary God does **whatever His soul desires** and Job **is afraid of Him**, and even **terrified**, because **God** has **made** Job's **heart weak**.

24:1–12 Since nothing is **hidden from the Almighty**, Job can't understand why He doesn't give the solution to the problem of the wicked's prosperity to **those who know Him**. He enumerates in detail the horrible injustice in this world—the crimes of the oppressors and the sufferings of the oppressed.

Ridout comments:

> It is an awful picture of facts only too well-known to them—and to us. How can Eliphaz make such facts fit in with his theory that evil is always punished in this life? But, oh, how can *God* close His eyes to these things, and afflict a faithful man instead of these wrong doers? This is Job's great trouble, and for this he has found no solution.[23]

Job complains of the apparent failure of God's governing of the world (v. 12):

> The dying groan in the city,
> And the souls of the wounded cry
>   out;

Yet God does not charge them with wrong.

24:13–17 Next Job describes the rebellious **murderer, adulterer**, and burglar. All three favor **the night** for their activities; the **morning is the same to them as the shadow of death**.

24:18–25 In spite of the fact that these wicked sinners **should be cursed** in the **earth** and they **should be remembered no more**, **God** apparently **gives them security**. Job maintains that the wicked don't die any more violently than anyone else. He defies anyone to disprove this.

Since Bildad's speech is so short, Zophar has none, and Job's response is so long, some Bible scholars have suggested that verses 18–25 are not really Job at all. Some modern versions even rearrange the text here (and elsewhere) in a very conjectural way. Andersen, who is "not convinced that Job could not have uttered these words,"[24] describes what some have done with them:

> We should not too hastily remove these words from Job's lips, just because they don't sound like what we think he should say. This has been done in three ways: to remove them altogether as a pious gloss which makes Job sound more orthodox than he is; to transfer them to one of the friends, either Bildad (NAB), or Zophar (Pope); to take them as a quotation by Job of what his friends say (RSV, which adds *You say*, and identifies verses 21–24 as Job's rejoinder; or Gordis, who takes all of verses 18–24 as the quotation).[25]

3. Bildad's Third Speech (Chap. 25)

The last of the speeches of Job's comforters turns out to be not by Zophar, but by **Bildad the Shuhite**. Apparently Zophar has depleted his fund of rhetoric. Even Bildad's speech is very short—the briefest in the book of Job:

Judging from the brevity of Bildad's address, and the fact that it contains practically nothing new, it would seem that the friends have exhausted all the arguments that their position permitted them to advance. And this is saying a great deal, for they were men of sober thoughtfulness, with abilities for expression rarely excelled. Their language is noble and elevated, their metaphors of rare beauty and force, but their position and contention were wrong, narrow, and untenable.[26]

Since Bildad has apparently finally comprehended that a multitude of words will not help, he only tries to communicate two themes: the greatness of God (vv. 1–3) and the nothingness of man (vv. 4–6).

25:1-3 God possesses **dominion and fear**, and **His armies** are without **number**.

25:4-6 When even **the moon and the stars are not pure in** God's **sight**, what hope is there for man, a mere **maggot** and **worm**? Bildad's words are true and beautifully stated, but they are spoken without love and comfort, and so they have not ministered to Job's needs.

4. Job's Response (Chap. 26)

26:1-4 First of all Job counters Bildad's argument. Even granting that Job is **without power** and **has no strength** or **wisdom**, **how** has Bildad helped? His words have been futile, insensitive, and a total failure as an answer to Job's arguments.

26:5-13 The rest of the chapter gives a marvelous description of God's power in the universe: the evaporation/

precipitation cycle; the density of the **clouds**; the cycle of **light and darkness**; **the storm** at **sea**; and the stars and constellations **by** which **His Spirit** has **adorned the heavens**.

While Bildad stressed God's glory in the heavens, Job here dwells on His power in the depths: **under the waters**, **Sheol**, and destruction.

Job describes—centuries before science taught it—that God **hangs the earth on nothing** (which is a poetic depiction of the earth's position and movement in the solar system).

How immeasurably above the cosmogonies of the heathen philosophers are these few grand words! In them we have as in germ the discoveries of a Newton and a Keppler. It is a great mistake to think Scripture does not teach scientific truth. It teaches all needed truth, even if not in scientific language, yet with scientific accuracy.[27]

26:14 If these wonders are only the **edges of His ways**, and a mere **whisper we hear of Him**, Job asks, what must the full **thunder of His power** be if not incomprehensible?

5. Job's Closing Monologue (Chaps. 27—31)

Job's "comforters" have not proved their cases—but then neither has Job solved his problem! He is, however, on the right road, and seems to be growing in faith.

Job's monologue has three main themes: Job contrasts his integrity with *the doom of the wicked* (chap. 27); he lauds *the priceless quality of wisdom* (chap. 28); and finally he dwells on *himself* (chaps. 29—31).

27:1-5 The opening words of this chapter, **"Moreover Job continued his discourse, and said,"** suggests a major break. No longer is he merely *answering* Bildad (26:1); he is addressing all, and he is getting many things "off his chest," as we would say. **Job** continues to insist on his own honesty, **integrity**, and **righteousness**. He refuses to admit that his critics might conceivably be right in accusing him of suffering as a result of secret sin.

27:6–23 Job does not defend **the wicked, the unrighteous**, and **the hypocrite**; their calamity is deserved. He **will teach** his three friends about God's dealings with the unrighteous man—truths that they themselves have observed. Disaster will often (but not always) strike his family, his possessions, **his house**, and himself. He will perish while good people rejoice.

28:1–11 This lovely chapter is built around the question voiced in both verses 12 and 20:

> **But where can wisdom be found? And where is the place of understanding?**

Man shows great skill and perseverance in digging for **precious** metals and jewels. Here in the first section of the chapter human cleverness (seen in mining) has been unable *to find wisdom*. In verses 13–19 human riches are incapable *of buying wisdom*, and in verses 21–28 God alone is seen as *the giver of wisdom*.

The description of mining in ancient times is very fascinating, but contains some difficulties for translators. Verse 4 is especially hard: nearly every English version has a different understanding of the text here. Andersen comments that "it is hard to believe that they all had the same Hebrew text in front of them."[28]

Unlike Bildad, who calls man "a maggot," Job admits man's cleverness in mining:

> Man's remarkable success as a miner shows how clever and intelligent he

is; but, for all that, he has failed completely to unearth wisdom.[29]

28:12–19 The path of **wisdom** is not found so easily. It cannot be discovered **in the land** or **the sea**, it cannot **be purchased**, nor can an adequate **price** be placed on it, because its **price . . . is above rubies** and **topaz**, and **cannot** be **valued in pure gold**.

28:20–28 **Wisdom** and **understanding** are **hidden from the eyes of all living** creatures. **Destruction and Death have** only **heard . . . about** them. The same **God** who designed the patterns of nature is the source of wisdom, because **He . . . declared** and **prepared it**. To **fear** Him **is wisdom** and **to depart from evil is understanding**.

This chapter seems to imply that we should submit to God's providential dealings even if we don't always understand them.

29:1–17 **Job** now gives a masterful and nostalgic account of the good old days of his prosperity and honor, and yearns for their return. He enjoyed God's favor and guidance. His **children were** with him. He lived in luxury and was respected in **the city** by **young** and old, by **princes** and **nobles**, because of his deeds of charity, his **righteousness**, and **justice**.

29:18–25 He anticipated long life and a peaceful death **"in his nest,"** as he enjoyed prosperity, vigor, and strength, pictured by **the dew . . . all night on** his **branch**, his **glory . . . fresh within** him, and his **renewed . . . bow**. Others welcomed his advice as a farmer welcomes **the spring rain**. His smiling **countenance** renewed their confidence. His leadership made him like a **chief**, or as a **king in the army, as one who comforts mourners**. It is hard to understand why God would punish such a man as this!

30:1–8 Now, sad to say, Job is scorned by **younger . . . men . . . whose fathers** were outcasts of society, unfitted even to help Job's **dogs** watch the sheep; worn out, weak, and poor; so hungry they fed on desert shrubs; **driven out from among men**; homeless nomads; driven **from the land**.

30:9–15 It is these dregs of humanity who now treat Job with utter contempt. Notice the phrases descriptive of their scorn—"**taunting song**," "**I am their byword**," "**they abhor me**," "they **spit in my face**," "**they push away my feet**" (trip him?), "**they break up** (or block) **my path**," etc. Job's **honor** and **prosperity** have totally vanished.

30:16–23 He is racked with **pains**, disfigured with agony, reduced to **dust and ashes**, and ready to die. God won't **answer** his prayers, cruelly opposes him, tosses him around, and is about to kill him.

30:24–31 Surely He will not afflict in the grave one who has prayed to Him **when** dying. Job had shown mercy to others but he himself was shown no mercy. His intense suffering is compounded by loneliness and rejection. His physical and emotional condition are appalling. Why would a righteous man like Job have to become **a brother of jackals and a companion of ostriches**?

31:1–12 Job insists that he has not been guilty of lustful looks at **a young woman**. He knows that God sees and punishes such sin. He has not acted deceitfully; an **honest** examination would convince **God** of this. He has not strayed **from the way** of righteousness; otherwise he would deserve to lose his **harvest**. He has not coveted his **neighbor's** wife; otherwise his own **wife** should become

another man's, and his possessions and life be destroyed.

31:13–37 Job had been merciful to his servants; charitable to **the poor**, to **the widow**, and to the **fatherless**. He had been free from greed for **gold**; he had not **been secretly enticed** by idolatry (kissing his **hand** toward **the sun** or **the moon**); he was without malice toward his enemies; hospitable to all; free from secret sin; and honest in his real estate dealings. If any charges against him were **written in a book**, he would be proud to **carry it** around and wear it **like a crown**!

31:38–40 At the end of chapter 31 **the words of Job are ended**. Samuel Ridout, for one, is not yet satisfied with Job's finale:

> Job's words will be rightly ended when he is ready to give praise to the One who alone is worthy of it. We are glad to be through with Job's words as uttered here.[30]

III. THE INTERVENTION OF ELIHU (Chaps. 32—37)

A. Elihu's Speech to Job's Three Friends (Chap. 32)

32:1–6 Here the conversation between **Job** and his **three** friends ceases. Normally, as we noted above, it would have been Zophar's turn to speak, but for some reason he chooses not to do so.

A **young** man named **Elihu, the son of Barachel the Buzite**, had been listening to the heated debate between **Job** and **his three** critics. Many Bible students see him as a picture of Christ, our Mediator. He seems the perfect bridge between Job's friends' analysis of his situation and the solution of Jehovah. In short, he is a middleman between men and God, a mediator to prepare for the Lord's coming on the scene.

Other commentators have less favorable views of him, viewing him as a conceited young upstart!

At any rate, Elihu (his name means *my God is He*) became incensed with Job for justifying **himself rather than God**. He was also angry with **his three friends** for failing to **answer** Job adequately. In the following verses, he summarizes twenty-nine chapters of discussions.

32:7–22 In deference to their **age**, he had kept quiet and **paid close attention to** their **words**, but now he can restrain himself no longer.

He says that **great men** (or **men of many years**, NKJV marg.) are **not always wise**, and that God can give insight to a younger man like himself. He blames Job's critics for not coming up with convincing arguments. Because of their failure, he is compelled from **within** to **speak** and he will do so without **partiality** or flattery.

B. Elihu's Speech to Job (Chap. 33)

33:1–7 Elihu, using the word **"please,"** calls for Job's attention because he is going to speak **words** of sincerity and truth. Job had desired the opportunity to vindicate himself before God. Now Elihu, though a mortal **formed out of clay** like himself, is serving as Job's **spokesman before God**, and Job can make his defense, if he wishes, without **fear** of divine wrath.

33:8–18 Elihu rebukes Job for the way in which he had professed absolute innocence, and for blaming God for unjust treatment. **God is greater than man**, and **does not** have to **give an accounting of . . . His** dealings with man. However, **God** does **speak** to people through dreams and nocturnal visions to warn them against evil

and **pride** and to save them from violent death.

33:19–30 The Lord also speaks through **pain** and serious illness, when even **succulent food** seems revolting. **If . . . a messenger** or **a mediator** explains God's way of **uprightness** (and if the sufferer responds in faith), **God** saves **him from going down to the Pit** on the basis of an acceptable **ransom**. Elihu does not explain what he means by a **ransom**, but we are justified in linking it with the One "who gave Himself a ransom for all" (1 Tim. 2:6). When a person responds to the Lord's voice, says Elihu, then he is restored to physical health and spiritual well-being. It is the one who confesses his sin who is redeemed from spiritual and/or physical death.

33:31–33 **If . . . Job** wants to **speak**, he should do so. **If not**, he should continue to **listen** carefully, holding his **peace** while Elihu teaches him **wisdom**.

C. Elihu's Second Speech to Job's Three Friends (Chap. 34)

34:1–15 Elihu next asks the three friends to test his **words** as they would taste **food**. He quotes Job's claim that God was unfair in causing a **righteous** man like him to suffer, and that there is no use being pious in order to please God. He then insists that **God** is never guilty of injustice. **If He** were to withdraw **Himself**, His creatures **would** utterly **perish**.

34:16–30 If it is inappropriate to tell **a king** or a noble that he is **wicked** or **worthless**, how much more unthinkable to condemn the Sovereign of the universe who is completely impartial! No wickedness can be hidden from God; **He strikes** down the evil and delivers the oppressed.

34:31–37 Apparently addressing Job, Elihu next counsels him to confess and forsake his sin, and to stop demanding God to do what he wants. **Job** has been talking ignorance, speaking evil, spewing forth **rebellion**, **sin**, and a multitude of **words against God**.

D. Elihu's Second Speech to Job (Chaps. 35—37)

35:1–8 **Elihu** then reproves Job for claiming to act **more** righteously **than** God and for saying that **righteousness** does not pay. Man's **sin** does not harm the sovereign God, neither does his righteousness benefit God.

35:9–16 Proud oppressors **cry out** in trouble, but they do not acknowledge the **God** who gave them wisdom above that of animals and **birds**; therefore, their prayers are **not** answered. Even if we **do not see Him**, God does see *us*, and we should trust Him and not be arrogant.

36:1–12 In Elihu's fourth speech, he professes to draw from deep truths to defend the **justice** of God and to explain suffering. The Lord is eminently just in dealing with the wicked and the oppressed as well as **the righteous** (vv. 7–9), whether they are **kings . . . on the throne** or prisoners **in fetters**. If **righteous** men **have acted defiantly**, **He seeks to bring them to repentance by convincing them** of **their . . . transgressions**. **If they obey and serve Him**, He prospers them. **If they** don't, **they . . . perish by the sword** and **without** the **knowledge** of God.

36:13–21 If Job had been submissive and contrite, the Lord **would have** delivered him **out of** his **dire distress**, but because he was stubbornly self-righteous, he suffers **the** same **judgment** as **the hypocrites**. Elihu warns him that if he continues, he will suffer a fate from which **a large ransom** will **not** deliver him.

(Verse 18 is a needed warning for sinners in all ages.)

36:22–33 Because **God** is all-wise, Job should **magnify** Him. His greatness is seen in His control of the **rain**, **clouds**, **thunder**, and **lightning**. We cannot fully **understand** the magnitude of His providential dealings, but we know that they portend grace to His people. Andreae wrote long ago:

> The same storm which on the one side is sent upon the lands for punishment and destruction is at the same time appointed on the other side to bless them abundantly, and to make them fruitful. Thus even the severest judgments of God are ever to be regarded as at the same time a source out of which divine grace distils forth.[31]

37:1–13 Elihu continues to delve into various realms of nature to show the wisdom, power, awesome majesty, and golden splendor of **God**. His descriptions of nature, of a thunderstorm with its **heavy rain**, or of the **whirlwind**, **snow**, **gentle rain**, **cold . . . winds of the north**, **thick** and **bright clouds**, or **bright** sunlight, are classic.

37:14–23 Elihu ends with a direct appeal: **"Listen to this, O Job, stand still and consider the wondrous works of God."** He goes on to challenge Job's knowledge of nature: how **the clouds** are **balanced** and why he gets **hot** when the **southwind blows**. These lead up to the similar, but even more challenging, nature questions that the Creator Himself will pose to Job in the next main section of the book. Such **excellent . . . power** surpasses our feeble comprehension. It is best to **fear** the Lord and to submit to His discipline, and not to be like Job, criticizing Him as unfair.

37:24 Elihu's last verse is the application to Job, a concise conclusion to the whole matter. The first line of verse 24 is easy to understand; the second is difficult in the NKJV (and other versions). Francis Andersen translates the second line differently by taking the negative word in Hebrew in this construction as an assertion rather than a negation:

Therefore men fear Him;
Surely all wise of heart fear Him![32]

IV. THE REVELATION OF THE LORD (38:1—42:6)

A. The Lord's First Challenge to Job (38:1—40:2)

1. Introductory (38:1–3)

The LORD Himself now answers **Job out of the whirlwind**, a not uncommon vehicle for an appearance of God in the OT. God's words are a welcome relief after the strife of words in the previous chapters. Job had been darkening **counsel by words without knowledge**, that is, he had been foolishly questioning the justice of God's dealings with him. Now the Lord will do the questioning, and it is time for Job to get ready to **answer**!

In the questions that follow, God does not give a detailed explanation of the mystery of suffering. Instead He ranges through the universe to give glimpses of His majesty, glory, wisdom, and power. He is saying, in effect, "Before you take it on yourself to criticize My ways, you should ask yourself if you could manage the creation as well as I do." This, of course, can only show Job how powerless, ignorant, insignificant, inadequate, incompetent, and finite he is.

We have here, as Ridout points out, the voice of the Lord:

We are no longer listening to the gropings of the natural mind, as in the discourses of the friends; nor to the wild cries of a wounded faith, as in Job; nor even to the clear, sober language of Elihu—we are in the presence of Jehovah Himself, who speaks to us.[33]

As we listen to the Lord's questions, we have a recurring suspicion that they might be *allegorical*, that is, that they might have a deeper spiritual meaning, and that even the order of the questions might have significance. In the meantime, we see through a glass darkly.

Some might proudly say that, thanks to modern science, we know the answers to many of the questions that God asks. In response to that, Baron Alexander Humboldt acknowledged that

what Job could not answer, the men of science cannot answer yet. It is overwhelming to them; because although men of science are very clever about secondary causes, they are always stopped by primary causes. They never can arrive at the great cause, and they do not want the great cause.[34]

2. The Challenge of the Wonders of Inanimate Creation (38:4–38)

38:4–7 In poetic words of unsurpassed beauty, the Lord mentions the creation of the world when He **laid the foundations of the earth**, its measurements, its survey, its support (suspended in space, of course), and the angelic celebration. Then He asks, **"Where were you when** all this took place?"

38:8–11 Moving from cosmology to geography and oceanography, He describes how He restricted **the sea** to its assigned shores, forbade further intrusion, and clothed the waters, as if they were a baby, **with clouds and thick darkness**.

38:12–18 Next He vividly pictures His control of **the morning**—the light of **dawn** streaking across the heavens, illuminating everywhere it goes; unmasking **the wicked** who operate in darkness, as if by shaking them out; revealing the configuration of earth's surface, as if it had been stamped out **like clay under a seal**; and bringing out the colors of the landscape as if it were a beautiful garment. Darkness, which is the preferred "light" of **the wicked, is withheld from** them and their evil plots are frustrated. He challenges Job to tell what he knows about the depths of the ocean, the realm **of death**, and **the breadth** of **the earth**.

38:19–24 God now cross-examines Job on the origin and nature of **light**. The sun is not a sufficient answer, because there was light (Gen. 1:3) before the sun was put in place (Gen. 1:16). Was Job old enough to know the answer? And what does he know about **snow** and **hail**, which God sometimes harnesses in times of trouble and war? How do **light** and **the east wind**, which seem to come from a point, spread **over the** surface of **the earth**?

38:25–30 Next, in a class on weather, Job is quizzed on rainfall and thunder, on how water falls on a desert, causing it to produce luxuriant growth, and on the source of **rain**, **dew**, ice, and **frost**. How is it that water freezes hard as **stone** and solidifies **the surface of the deep**?

38:31–33 No science is so calculated to show man his insignificance as astronomy. So God questions Job on his ability to control the stars and constellations, or keep them in their orbits, or determine their influence **over the earth**.

In light of modern man's supposedly great control over nature through science, Spurgeon's words, based on the KJV text of verse 31, are a healthful counterbalance:

> "Canst thou bind the sweet influences of Pleiades, or loose the bands of Orion? "—Job xxxviii. 31.
>
> If inclined to boast of our abilities, the grandeur of nature may soon show us how puny we are. We cannot move the least of all the twinkling stars, or quench so much as one of the beams of the morning. We speak of power, but the heavens laugh us to scorn. When the Pleiades shine forth in spring with vernal joy we cannot restrain their influences, and when Orion reigns aloft, and the year is bound in winter's fetters, we cannot relax the icy bands. The seasons revolve according to the divine appointment, neither can the whole race of men effect a change therein. Lord, what is man?[35]

38:34–38 Obviously, anyone who can question the wisdom and power of God should be able to bring down rain by shouting **to the clouds**, and command lightning so that it obeys instantly! Can Job tell God how **the mind** operates, how man gets **wisdom** and **understanding** in all these areas?[36] No man has the **wisdom** to **number the clouds**, to say nothing of the particles of moisture by which they are formed. And no one can determine the time when the rain falls on arid ground that has been hardened into **clumps** and **clods**.

3. The Challenge of the Wonders of Animate Creation (38:39—40:2)

38:39–41 God now moves from the *inanimate creation* to the *animate*. By continued questions, He reminds Job of His providence—how He opens His hand and satisfies **the appetite** of every living thing, from kingly **lions in their dens** and **lairs** to the unprepossessing **raven** and **its young ones**.

39:1–8 Job is reminded that no one but God knows fully the gestation periods, the birth habits, and the instincts of **the wild mountain goats** and **the deer**. **The wild donkey** (also called **onager**) scorns restraint, **city** life, and harness, but roams at will over the desert and mountain ranges searching for **every green thing**.

39:9–18 **The wild ox** also rejects a life of service in plowing or transporting. And what about **the ostrich** with her unusual **wings**? In some ways she acts foolishly, laying **her eggs** in places where they are vulnerable, and treating **her young harshly**. Yet she can outrun the race **horse and its rider**!

39:19–25 God next asks Job if he gave **strength** to the war **horse**, or **clothed his neck with thunder** (or a **mane**, NKJV marg.). Majestic and unafraid, devouring **distance with fierceness and rage**, this proud animal eagerly **gallops into** the **battle** in utter disregard of **shouting, trumpet**, or **glittering spears and javelin**.

39:26–30 Did Job give **wisdom** to **the hawk** to migrate **south**? And was he the one who taught **the eagle** to fly, to nest on the high rocky **crag**, to spy out carrion from a great distance, and to train **its young ones** to find their food?

40:1, 2 Again **the LORD** rebukes **Job** for his impertinence in finding fault with **the Almighty**. If he is so wise and powerful, surely he should be able to answer the catalog of questions that he has just heard!

B. Job's Response (40:3–5)

The LORD asks **Job** if he has any right to **correct** or rebuke Him in the realm of providence when he knows so little about the natural creation. With this, **Job** at last takes his proper place, saying, **"Behold, I am vile; what shall I answer You? I lay my hand over my mouth."** Overwhelmed by the wide-ranging knowledge of the Lord, he determines to say no more.

C. The Lord's Second Challenge to Job (40:6—41:34)

1. Job Challenged to Respond Like a Man (40:6–14)

But Job's response comes somewhat short of repentance, so **the LORD** continues to remonstrate with him **out of the whirlwind**. He challenges Job to speak up **like a man**. After all, Job had accused God of injustice, and condemned Him in order to justify himself. Now then, let him play the part of deity by displaying omnipotence and by speaking **in thunder**. Let him take the throne, clothing himself with **majesty, splendor, glory, and beauty**. Let him pour out his **wrath** on the guilty and humble the **proud**. If he can do all these things, then the Lord will acknowledge his power to be his own deliverer.

2. Job Challenged to Consider Behemoth (40:15–24)

Next the Lord challenges Job to consider **behemoth, which** He **made along with** Job. This rules out the notion of some commentators that behemoth and Leviathan are *mythological* creatures well known in ancient time. What challenge can a nonexistent creature be to a created being such as man?

The word behemoth is simply the plural form of the common Hebrew word for cattle (*behēmah*). Meredith Kline explains:

The designation **behemoth**, taken as a plural intensive, "the beast par excellence," would be an epithet like chief of the ways of God (v. 19a). Note the similar supreme claims made for leviathan (41:33, 34).[37]

God presents **the behemoth** as **the first of** His **ways**, that is, as Exhibit A in the animal kingdom. Although we cannot identify it with certainty, we know that it is herbivorous, amphibian, and exceedingly powerful. It rests in shady, marshy areas and is not easily intimidated. The lesson is that if Job can't even control this brute, how can he control the world?

The behemoth is sometimes identified with the hippopotamus,[38] and some translations, such as the Louis Segond translation in French, actually put that animal in the text. But by no stretch of the imagination can the hippopotamus be called "the first of the ways of God"—an elephant or a mammoth might merit that epithet perhaps, but hardly a hippo! When children go to the zoo they squeal with glee at the cute, stubby tail of the hippo—hardly **a tail like a cedar**!

Some Christian scientists are now convinced that the behemoth must be an animal now extinct, or perhaps found in some remote parts of the African jungle. In fact, a reptile of the dinosaur type does fit the description very closely.[39]

3. Job Challenged to Consider Leviathan (Chap. 41)

God has not answered Job's complaints directly. Rather, He has just been saying in effect, "You should be able to trust the wisdom, love, and power of One who is so great, so majestic, so glorious."

41:1–9 Another awesome amphibious creature is **Leviathan**, unique in the creation of God. Can Job harness him? God wants to know. "Touch him once and you'll never try it again; you will never forget the fight" (v. 8 TEV). The term **Leviathan** in ancient Canaanite literature referred to "a seven-headed sea dragon," but as Andersen points out, this "does not prove that Leviathan is still a mythological monster in this poem."[40]

In English we use words like *Thursday*, *January*, and *hell* with no belief whatever in the pagan literary origins of the *words themselves*. Usage must determine meaning, and here God clearly challenges Job to consider a real creature, even if we can't be positive today which one it was. A popular choice is the Nile crocodile, and several parts of the description do fit that reptile well.

While the behemoth is primarily a *land* creature, Leviathan is primarily *aquatic*. Man cannot catch him with **hook** and **line**. Or domesticate him or make him a family pet. He is not considered a **banquet** delicacy. His armor-like exterior resists **harpoons** and **spears**, and **the sight of him** discourages meddling with him.

41:10, 11 God interrupts the description to ask a pertinent question: If men stand in such awe of a mere creature, how much more should they fear Him who created the creature, who is eternal, who is obligated to no one, and who is Owner and Creator of all? Kline comments:

> Here indeed is the point of the passage: Job is to discover from his inability to vanquish even a fellow creature the folly of aspiring to the Creator's throne.[41]

41:12–34 Back to Leviathan. His build is massive and **his mighty power** is enormous. His hide is a tough, protective covering. He cannot be bridled. His mouth and **teeth** are viselike. His skin and **scales** resemble armor with overlapping plates. In poetic terms, the Lord describes his sneezes, **eyes**, **mouth**, and **nostrils** as terrifying when he is aroused. Leviathan's strength is tremendous and his flesh compacted. While he himself is fearless, he fills the stoutest hearts with fear as he thrashes around, and normal weapons bounce off his hide. When he crawls through the mud, he leaves a trail of pointed marks, as if his underside was broken glass. He whips the water into a boiling **pot**, leaving a white phosphorescent **wake**. Even making ample allowance for the Oriental use of great poetic exaggeration (hyperbole), it is hard to see how even the largest crocodile could be called **"king over all the children of pride."**[42]

The descriptions of the wild animals and possibly dinosaurs in these chapters *reflect* the glory, power, and majesty of God Himself. They are His creation, and He purposely uses them to illustrate His own splendor and strength. Therefore, it is not surprising that He begins with harmless creatures such as the deer and the raven and gradually increases in size to the greatest of all creatures, the *behemoth* on land, and the king of all beasts—Leviathan of the sea, which was unbelievably awesome in its reputation.

D. Job's Humble Response (42:1–6)

Job is overwhelmed. He has had enough! He acknowledes the sovereignty of God. He confesses that he has spoken unadvisedly with his lips. Now that he has not only **heard** the Lord but his **eye** has seen Him, he hates himself and repents **in dust and ashes**. He did not see God visually,[43] of course, but he had such

a vivid revelation of His wisdom, power, providence, and sovereignty that it was tantamount to a sight of the great God.

In Job 1:1 Job is called "blameless." Here at the end of the book he abhors himself. This has been the experience of the choicest of God's saints through the ages.[44] The more one grows in grace, writes D. L. Moody, "the meaner he is in his own eyes."[45]

V. EPILOGUE: THE TRIUMPH OF JOB (42:7–17)

A. Job's Friends Rebuked and Restored (42:7–9)

The LORD then reprimands **Eliphaz** and his **two friends**[46] for misrepresenting Him. They had insisted that all suffering is punishment for sin. That was not true in Job's case. In obedience to the divine command, they then offered a huge **burnt offering** (**seven bulls and seven rams**). Job served as mediator by praying **for his friends**, and as a result judgment on them was averted and Job was accepted.

B. Job's Prosperity Restored (42:10–17)

42:10–12 As soon as Job prayed for them, the Lord restored in inverse order twice as much as Job **had before**: **twice as** many **sheep**, **camels**, **oxen**, and **female donkeys**.

42:13–17 He also received **seven sons and three daughters**, which doubled his family, since he presumably still *had* the first ones in heaven. **Job lived** an additional **one hundred and forty years. The LORD blessed the latter days of Job more than his beginning. So Job died, old and full of days**. And in all this, Job had not cursed God as Satan said he would.

It is a lovely touch of God's grace

that Job, who had been so hideously disfigured by his disease, after his restoration had **daughters** who were exceptionally **beautiful** (fathers love to boast of their lovely daughters!). The meanings of their names are instructive[47]: **Jemimah** (*dove*); **Keziah** (*cassia*, a fragrant *cinnamon bark*); and **Keren-Happuch** (*horn of eye-makeup*[48]). Job also gave them an inheritance with their *brothers*, probably not a common practice in the patriarchal era.

VI. CONCLUSION: LESSONS FROM THE BOOK OF JOB

Actually, the mystery of human suffering is not fully explained. As Wesley Baker puts it:

When the end of the Book of Job comes, there is no answer written out. There is nothing there that would satisfy the logical mind![49]

However, we can be sure of these two facts:

First of all, Job's suffering was not a direct result of his personal sin. God testified that he was a perfect and an upright man (1:8). Also, God said that the reasoning of Job's three friends—that God was punishing him because of his sins—was not right (42:8).

Secondly, although Job was not suffering because he had sinned, yet his trials *did reveal* pride, self-justification, and animosity in his heart. He was not delivered until he had a vision of his own nothingness and of God's greatness (42:1–6), and until he prayed for his friends (42:10).

Some of the lessons we learn about suffering from the book of Job are:

1. The righteous are not exempt from suffering.

2. Suffering is not necessarily a result of sin.

3. God has set a protective hedge around the righteous.

4. God does not send sickness or suffering. It comes from Satan (Luke 13:16; 2 Cor. 12:7).

5. Satan has some control in the realm of wicked men (the Sabeans and Chaldeans), supernatural disasters (fire from heaven), weather (a great wind), sickness (the boils on Job), and death.

6. Satan can bring these things on a believer *only by God's permission*.

7. What God permits, He often is said to do. "Shall we indeed accept good from God, and shall we not accept adversity?"

8. We should *view* things as coming from the Lord, by His permission, and not from Satan. "The Lord gave, and the Lord has taken away."

9. God does not always explain the reason for our suffering.

10. Suffering develops endurance.

11. In visiting suffering saints, we should not be judgmental.

12. We should make our visits brief.

13. Human reasonings aren't helpful. Only God can comfort perfectly.

14. At the end of the book of Job we see that "the Lord is very compassionate and merciful" (Jas. 5:11). We also learn that *sometimes*, at least, wrongs are made right in this life.

15. Job's patience in suffering vindicated God.

16. Job's patience proved Satan to be a false accuser and liar.

17. "A man is greater than the things that surround him and,

whatever may befall his possessions or his family, God is just as truly to be praised and trusted as before."

18. We should be careful about making blanket statements that do not allow for exceptions.

19. Satan is neither omnipresent, omnipotent, nor omniscient.

20. In spite of God's allowing unmerited suffering, He is still just and good.

From other parts of the Bible, we get further light on some of the reasons why God allows His saints to suffer:

1. Sometimes it is a result of unjudged sin in the life (1 Cor. 11:32).

2. It is a means by which God develops spiritual graces, such as patience, longsuffering, humility (Rom. 5:3, 4; John 15:2).

3. It purges dross or impurities from the believer's life so that the Lord can see His image reflected more perfectly (Isa. 1:25).

4. It enables the child of God to comfort others with the same type of comfort with which God comforted him or her (2 Cor. 1:4).

5. It enables the saint to share in the non-atoning sufferings of the Savior and thus to be more grateful to Him (Phil. 3:10).

6. It is an object lesson to beings in heaven and on earth (2 Thess. 1:4–6). It shows them that God can be *loved for Himself alone,* and not just because of the favors He bestows.

7. It is an assurance of sonship since God only chastens those whom He loves (Heb. 12:7–11).

8. It causes saints to trust in God alone and not in their own strength (2 Cor. 1:9).

9. It keeps God's people close to Himself (Ps. 119:67).

10. It is a pledge of future glory (Rom. 8:17, 18).

11. God never allows us to be tempted above what we are able to bear (1 Cor. 10:13).

"You have heard of the perseverance of Job and seen the end intended by the Lord—that the Lord is very compassionate and merciful" (Jas. 5:11b).

ENDNOTES

[1](Intro) Samuel Ridout, *Job: An Exposition,* p. 5.

[2](Intro) Genesis 1—11 is generally dated from about 2000 B.C. and much earlier as one traces back through the genealogies.

[3](1:1–3) "Others support an identification with the region E. of Edom in N. Arabia" (*The Revell Bible Dictionary,* ed. by Lawrence O. Richards, p. 1138).

[4](1:4, 5) Charles Haddon Spurgeon, *Morning and Evening,* p. 721.

[5](1:6–12) In the Semitic languages "sons of God" was a standard term for angels.

[6](2:1–10) Harold St. John, *Job, The Lights and Shadows of Eternity,* p. 9.

[7](Chaps. 3—31:Intro) Ridout, *Job,* p. 33.

[8](Chaps. 3—31:Intro) The *New Scofield Study Bible, New King James Version,* p. 595.

[9](Chaps. 3—31:Intro) *Ibid.,* p. 598.

[10](Chaps. 4,5:Intro) Ridout, *Job,* pp. 43, 44.

[11](Chap. 8:Intro) *Ibid.,* p. 64.

[12](9:32–35) Matthew Henry, "Job," in *Matthew Henry's Commentary on the Whole Bible,* III:59.

[13](10:8–12) St. John, *Job*, p. 17.

[14](11:1–12) Ridout, *Job*, p. 31.

[15](13:20–28) Francis I. Andersen, *Job: An Introduction and Commentary*, p. 163.

[16](14:13–17) St. John, *Job*, pp. 17, 18.

[17](15:14–16) Ridout, *Job*, p. 84.

[18](19:25–27) Spurgeon, *Morning and Evening*, Devotion for April 21, Morning.

[19](19:25–27) *Ibid.*, p. 21.

[20](20:20–29) G. Campbell Morgan, *Searchlights from the Word*, p. 145.

[21](22:21–30) Albert Barnes, "Job," in *Notes on the Old Testament*, II:3.

[22](23:1–9) Spurgeon, *Morning and Evening*, Devotion for November 19, Evening.

[23](24:1–12) Ridout, *Job*, p. 124.

[24](24:18–25) Andersen, *Job*, p. 213.

[25](24:18–25) *Ibid.*

[26](Chap. 25:Intro) Ridout, *Job*, p. 127.

[27](26:5–13) *Ibid.*, pp. 133, 134.

[28](28:1–11) Andersen, *Job*, p. 225.

[29](28:1–11) *Ibid.*

[30](31:38–40) Ridout, *Job*, p. 169.

[31](36:22–33) Quoted by Otto Zöckler, "The Book of Job," in *Lange's Commentary on the Holy Scriptures*, IV:596.

[32](37:24) Andersen, *Job*, p. 268.

[33](38:1–3) Ridout, *Job*, pp. 210, 211.

[34](38:1–3) Cited by William Kelly in *Eleven Lectures on the Book of Job*, p. 278.

[35](38:31–33) Spurgeon, *Morning and Evening*, Devotion for March 21, Evening.

[36](38:34–38) Because verse 36 seems to interrupt the discussion of weather phenomena in verses 34–38, many other translations have been suggested. The Hebrew is admittedly difficult.

[37](40:15–24) Meredith G. Kline, "Job," in *Wycliffe Bible Commentary*, p. 488.

[38](40:15–24) For example, Barnes used the following description to make the text fit a hippopotamus: "The huge head of the animal, from the prominency of its eyes, the great breadth of its muzzle, and the singular way in which the jaw is placed in the head, is almost grotesque in its ugliness. When it opens its jaws, its enormously large mouth and tongue, pinkish and fleshly, and armed with tusks of most formidable character, is particularly striking" ("Job," II:247, 248). The problem with this depiction is that while Barnes's description of the *hippopotamus* is good, the tusks, fleshy pink mouth, etc., are not found in *Job*! Also, neither the jaw, head, nor muzzle of the behemoth (ch. 40) is described in Scripture.

[39](40:15–24) See Ken Ham, "What Happened to the Dinosaurs?" *ANSWERS to Some of the Most Asked Questions on Creation/Evolution* (Sunnybank, Australia: Creation Science Foundation Ltd., 1986). See also Henry Morris, *The Remarkable Record of Job* (Grand Rapids: Baker Book House, 1990).

[40](41:1–9) Andersen, *Job*, p. 289.

[41](41:10, 11) Kline, "Job," p. 488.

[42](41:12–34) The description of *Leviathan* in Job 41 brings to mind the plesiosaur, an enormous marine reptile from the age of the dinosaurs and now generally believed to be extinct. This description also resembles the mysterious creatures which have been reportedly sighted in Loch Ness, Scotland.

[43](42:1–6) It is possible that God appeared in a *theophany* to Job, a visible manifestation of God's glory.

[44](42:1–6) Some other biblical figures who sensed their own wretched sinfulness in God's presence include

Moses (Ex. 3:6); Isaiah (Isa. 6:5); Peter (Luke 5:8); Paul (Acts 9:4); and John (Rev. 1:17).

[45](42:1–6) Moody, *Notes from My Bible*, p. 62.

[46](42:7–9) It is interesting to notice that Elihu, the fourth man to address Job, is not rebuked. Furthermore, he is not mentioned again in the book. His advice was apparently correct, and perhaps was used as a "transition" between the friends' bad advice and God's majestic answer to Job. This may also fit in with the afore-mentioned theory that Elihu was a type of Christ.

[47](42:13–17) Ridout believes that the names have "divine significance. . . . These are the fruit of Job's trials. The dove, suggesting the gentleness and love of the bird of sorrow. Cassia, telling of the fragrance that has come from his bruising; and the horn of cosmetic, of the 'beauty for ashes' that is now his. Love, fragrance, beauty—these come of our sorrows. Truly there are no daughters so fair as these" (*Job*, pp. 263, 264).

[48](42:13–17) The ancient women emphasized their eyes with makeup more than their lips. All this illustrates Solomon's words that "There is nothing new under the sun"!

[49](Conclu) Wesley C. Baker, *More Than a Man Can Take: A Study of Job*, p. 128.

BIBLIOGRAPHY

Andersen, Francis I. *Job: An Introduction and Commentary*. London: Inter-Varsity Press, 1976.

Baker, Wesley C. *More Than a Man Can Take: A Study of Job*. Philadelphia: The Westminster Press, 1966.

Delitzsch, F. "The Book of Job." In *Biblical Commentary on the Old Testament*. Vol. 9, 10. Reprint. Grand Rapids: Eerdmans Publishing Co., 1971.

Green, William Henry. *The Argument of the Book of Job*. Reprint. Minneapolis, MN: James & Klock Christian Publishers, 1977.

Ham, Ken. "What Happened to the Dinosaurs?" *Answers to Some of the Most Asked Questions on Creation/Evolution*. Sunnybank, Australia: Creation Science Foundation Ltd., 1986.

Kelly, William. *Eleven Lectures on the Book of Job*. Reprint. Denver: Wilson Foundation, n.d.

Kline, Meredith G. "Job." In *Wycliffe Bible Commentary*. Chicago: Moody Press, 1962.

Minn, H. R. *The Burden of this Unintelligible World* or *The Mystery of Suffering*. Auckland, New Zealand: Whitcombe & Tombs Limited, 1942.

Morris, Henry. *The Remarkable Record of Job*. Grand Rapids: Baker Book House, 1990.

Ridout, Samuel. *The Book of Job: An Exposition*. Seventh Printing. Neptune, NJ: Loizeaux Brothers, 1976.

St. John, Harold. *Job, The Lights and Shadows of Eternity* (pamphlet). New York: Bible Scholar, n.d.

Zöckler, Otto. "The Book of Job." In *Lange's Commentary on the Holy Scriptures*. Vol. 4. Grand Rapids: Zondervan Publishing House, Reprint, 1960.

THE BOOK OF PSALMS

Introduction

"I may truly call this book an anatomy of all parts of the soul, for no one can feel a movement of the spirit which is not reflected in this mirror. All the sorrows, troubles, fears, doubts, hopes, pains, perplexities and stormy outbreaks by which the hearts of men are tossed have been depicted here to the very life."

—John Calvin

I. Unique Place in the Canon

If you were to be marooned on a desert island with only one book of the Bible, which one would you choose?

Frankly, I hope I never have to make this choice, but if I had to, I think I would choose the Psalms! Their range of subjects is so vast, their catalog of life's experiences so full and their worship so exalted that I would be well supplied with rich spiritual food and powerful fuel for praise and prayer for a long time to come.

Our opening quotation shows that Calvin would probably have chosen the Psalms, too.

Graham Scroggie would probably also have cast his vote for the Psalms. He said:

> How full of praise to God are these Psalms! The Keyboard of Creation, Providence and Redemption are all swept by the ecstatic soul; and heaven and earth, sea and sky, things animate and things inanimate are summoned to praise the Lord.[1]

When first studying the Psalms we are often frustrated at our inability to find an orderly flow of thought in certain Psalms. It seems that the continuity is sometimes erratic, sometimes veiled and sometimes completely missing. Two observations by Albert Barnes and C. S. Lewis may help us. Barnes said:

> The Psalms are mostly lyrical poetry, that is, poetry adapted to the harp or lyre; to be used in connection with instrumental music; to be *sung*, not *read*.[2]

Lewis similarly explained:

> Most emphatically the Psalms must be read as poems; as lyrics, with all the licenses and all the formalities, the hyperboles, the emotional rather than logical connections, which are proper to lyric poetry.[3]

These insights can open up a whole new window of understanding for us.

II. Authorship

The Psalms are often called "The Psalms of David," but only about half (seventy-three) are directly attributed to the "sweet singer of Israel." Twelve are attributed to Asaph, ten to the sons of Korah, two to Solomon, and one each to Moses, Ethan, Heman, and Ezra. Forty-nine, or nearly one third, of the Psalms are anonymous.

When we think of the Psalms,

545

Psalm	Portrayal	Fulfilled
2:7	The Son of God	Matthew 3:17
8:2	Praised by children	Matthew 21:15, 16
8:6	Ruler of all	Hebrews 2:8
16:10	Rises from death	Matthew 28:7
22:1	Forsaken by God	Matthew 27:46
22:7, 8	Derided by enemies	Luke 23:35
22:16	Hands and feet pierced	John 20:27
22:18	Lots cast for clothes	Matthew 27:35, 36
34:20	Bones unbroken	John 19:32, 33, 36
35:11	Accused by false witnesses	Mark 14:57
35:19	Hated without cause	John 15:25
40:7, 8	Delights in God's will	Hebrews 10:7
41:9	Betrayed by a friend	Luke 22:47
45:6	The eternal King	Hebrews 1:8
68:18	Ascends to heaven	Acts 1:9–11
69:9	Zealous for God's house	John 2:17
69:21	Given vinegar and gall	Matthew 27:34
109:4	Prays for enemies	Luke 23:34
109:8	His betrayer replaced	Acts 1:20
110:1	Rules over His enemies	Matthew 22:44
110:4	A priest forever	Hebrews 5:6
118:22	The chief stone of God's building	Matthew 21:42
118:26	Comes in the name of the Lord	Matthew 21:9

The Messianic Psalms

however, we usually do so in connection with the life of David. An unknown author expresses this beautifully:

> The harp of David still sounds in our ears, and the Holy Ghost has crystallized for us the prayers and praises of the son of Jesse. Someone said that architecture was music frosted. The Psalms are the music of the heart, sometimes plaintive and sad, sometimes joyous and jubilant, sometimes full of darkness and anguish, sometimes tranquil and happy, the music of David's soul, preserved by the Spirit that, hearing it, we may feel encouraged to draw nigh to God.

III. Date

The Psalms were written over a period of about a thousand years,

from Moses to Ezra (about 1400–400 B.C.). However, most of them were written during the three hundred years from David to Hezekiah (about 1000–700 B.C.). Thus, the Psalter was written over the same period of time as the whole OT (although Job may pre-date Moses).

IV. Background and Themes

The Psalms are divided into five books, each of which closes with a doxology. The doxology for Book 5 is the entire 150th Psalm.

F. W. Grant suggests that the Psalms are grouped according to subject matter.[4] He summarizes each of the five books of the Psalms, found in the Hebrew Bible, as follows:

1. Christ in the counsel of God, the source of all blessing for His people Israel (Pss. 1—41).
2. Their ruin, but redemption in the latter days (Pss. 42—72).
3. The holiness of God in His dealings with them (Pss. 73—89).
4. The failed first man replaced by the Second, and the world established under His hand (Pss. 90—106).
5. The moral conclusion as to the divine ways in which God and man are found at last together (Pss. 107—150).

There may also be a parallel between these five divisions and the books of the Pentateuch. For example, the second division fits the redemption from Egypt; the third matches Leviticus in its emphasis on holiness.

The Psalms themselves may be divided into classifications, although certain Psalms may fit more than one of these classes:

1. Historical—connected with some definite event or events in Israel's history or in the life of the psalmist.
2. Messianic—dealing with the sufferings of Christ and the glories that should follow.
3. Prophetic or Millennial—pointing forward to Israel's future tribulation and the subsequent era of peace and prosperity.
4. Penitential—recording the psalmist's deep confession of sins and his broken-hearted cries for forgiveness.
5. Imprecatory—imploring God to take vengeance on the enemies of His people.

Many other Psalms are expressions of individual or communal praise and worship to God, and still others are

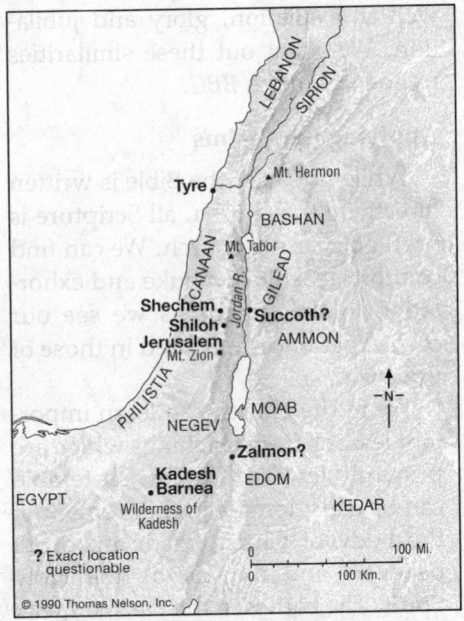

Places Named in the Psalms

narratives of the Lord's dealings with His people.

Interpreting the Psalms

The distinction between Israel and the church is maintained throughout the *Believer's Bible Commentary*. Many of the Psalms, especially the ones which call down curses on the wicked, were entirely appropriate for Jews living under the law but are not suitable language for believers of the Church Age. In this age, we are urged to *love* our enemies and to *do good* to those who despitefully use us. Unless we recognize this important dispensational difference, we will encounter severe problems in interpreting the Psalms.

Every careful reader of the Psalms quickly notices that there is a close parallel between the experiences of the psalmist, the nation of Israel, and the Lord Jesus Christ. All three experienced persecution, suffering, sorrow, hatred and abandonment—as well as exaltation, glory and jubilation. We point out these similarities frequently in the *BBC*.

Applying the Psalms

While not all of the Bible is written directly *to* the church, all Scripture is profitable *for* the church. We can find comfort, teaching, rebuke and exhortation in the Psalms as we see our own experiences mirrored in those of the psalmist.

We in the church can learn important lessons from teachings which are primarily Jewish. The Jewish temple can be considered a prefigurement of the body of Christ, made up of all believers and indwelt by the Holy Spirit. The battles in the Psalms speak to us of our spiritual warfare against principalities and powers, against the forces of darkness in the heavenly places. The material blessings of Israel on earth point us to our spiritual blessings in the heavenlies in Christ—and so forth.

If we use these keys, the Psalms become richly meaningful to us, and many of the problems in interpretation disappear.

Psalm Titles

The titles to the Psalms are very ancient and are probably part of the sacred text. However, the meaning and purpose of many of them are very obscure, and for this reason, we have omitted commenting on most of them. It would not be helpful simply to keep repeating "We do not know what this means!"

OUTLINE

Commentary

I. BOOK 1 (PSALMS 1—41)

Psalm 1: The Good Life

The book of Psalms opens by dispelling the common illusion that the sinful life is the good life. Daily the world is being brainwashed into thinking that true and lasting satisfaction is found by indulging the lusts of the flesh. Television, radio, movies, and magazines all suggest that permissiveness is the road to fulfillment. The life of purity is dismissed as "puritanical." But the psalmist sets the record straight.

1:1 The truly **blessed** person is the one who steers clear of the lifestyle **of the ungodly**. In his contacts with them he avoids complicity with them or even tacit approval of their sin and scoffing. This does not mean that the happy man isolates himself completely from the wicked. Instead he witnesses to them of "sin, righteousness, and judgment," and seeks to introduce them to Christ, the one source of lasting pleasure. The happy man is a real friend to the ungodly, but he is not a partner with them.

1:2 It is impossible to visualize a happy man who is not also a man of God's Book. He has an insatiable hunger for the Word **of the Lord**. He loves the Bible and **meditates** on it **day and night**. By this means his own life is enriched and he becomes a channel of blessing to others.

1:3 The man who is separated from sin and separated to the Scriptures has all the qualities of a strong, healthy, fruitful **tree**:

Planted[5] **by the rivers of water**—he has a never-failing supply of nourishment and refreshment.

It **brings forth its fruit in its season**—he displays the graces of the Spirit, and his words and actions are always timely and appropriate.

Its **leaf also shall not wither**—his spiritual life is not subject to cyclical changes but is characterized by continuous inner renewal. As D. L. Moody put it, "All the Lord's trees are evergreen."[6]

This kind of man **shall prosper** in everything he undertakes. The reason, of course, is that he is living in fellowship with the Lord, and all his service is therefore guided by the Holy Spirit. The only way to be efficient and successful in the Christian life is to be led by the Spirit of God. Self-directed activity is an enormous waste of time, money, and effort!

1:4 The ungodly are not so; that is, they are neither well-planted, fruitful, enduring nor prosperous. **Like chaff**, they lack body or substance. When the storms of life blow, they prove unstable. A strong **wind drives** them **away**.

1:5 The ungodly shall not stand in the judgment. They will, of course, appear before God at the Judgment of the Great White Throne. But the meaning here is that they will have no adequate defense. In idiomatic language, they won't have a leg to stand on! Furthermore, they will never stand **in the congregation of the righteous**; they will be forever excluded from the company of those who are saved by grace through faith in the Lord Jesus Christ.

1:6 What is the reason for all this? **The Lord knows the way of the righteous**. He is not only *aware* of their lives, but He *approves* them as well. What a contrast with the termination of a sinful life—eternal death!

We cannot emphasize too often, however, that a person's destiny is *not* determined by the way he lives. The determining factor is whether he has ever been born again by faith in Jesus Christ. The righteous person is the one who has confessed his sin and received the Lord Jesus Christ as his personal Savior. His righteous life is the *result* of his new life in Christ. **The ungodly** person is the one who refuses to acknowledge his need and to bow his knee to the Lord Jesus. He would rather keep his sin than have the Savior, and thus he seals his doom.

Psalm 2: The Unchanging Decree

To place this Psalm in its proper setting, we must look ahead to the close of the Great Tribulation, immediately prior to the glorious return and reign of our Lord Jesus Christ. At this time a vast federation of rulers and nations will unite in a passionate determination to prevent Christ from taking the reigns of world government.[7]

2:1–3 But such a federation will prove to be an exercise in futility. "Why," asks the psalmist, "**do the** Gentile **nations** and the Jewish **people** enter such a hopeless conspiracy? How do the Gentile **kings** and Jewish rulers think they can ever succeed in rebelling **against** the authority of **the** LORD **and** of **His Anointed**?"

2:4–6 God **in the heavens shall laugh** at their stupid insolence. He will mock their clenched fists and fiery slogans. Their boasts and threats are the squeaks of a mouse against a lion!

Eventually God will break His silence. When He speaks it will be in such **wrath** and fury that His enemies will be terrified. They will hear His irrevocable decision: "**I have** installed **My King on My holy hill of Zion**." Once God pronounces this decision, its fulfillment will be as certain as if it had already taken place.

2:7 Then Christ Himself will add His testimony. He will reveal that in private conversation, the Father had **said** first of all **to** Him, **"You are My Son, today I have begotten You."** This **decree** may be understood in at least four ways. First, there is a real sense in which Christ was the Son of God *from all eternity*. In Acts 13:33, however, the verse is quoted in reference to Christ's *Incarnation*. In a third sense, Christ was begotten in *Resurrection*—"the firstborn from the dead" (Col. 1:18). Finally, some suggest that "this day" refers to the *future day* when Christ will be crowned as King.

2:8 But the Father also added, **"Ask of Me, and I will give You the nations for Your inheritance, and the ends of the earth for Your possession."** In other words, God the Father has promised universal dominion to

His Son. All the earth will submit to His authority, and His rule will extend from shore to shore.

2:9 Finally, God has given Christ the authority to deal with all insubordination and rebellion. He **shall break . . . with a rod of iron** those who rise up against Him, shattering them **like a potter's vessel**. From other Scriptures we learn that Christ will exercise this authority both when He returns to earth and throughout His thousand-year reign. Prior to His inauguration as King, He will destroy those who do not know God and who do not obey the gospel. Then, in the Millennium, Christ will rule with a rod of iron, punishing rebellion wherever it raises its ugly head.

2:10, 11 The voice of the Holy Spirit is heard next. In a moving evangelistic appeal, He urges **kings** and rulers to love and **serve the** LORD. To refuse Him means destruction, whereas to trust Him brings safety and true happiness.

2:12 For man to trust his Creator is the most sane, logical, reasonable thing he can do. On the other hand, to disbelieve and defy the Almighty is about as irrational a thing as a person can do.

Psalm 3: A Study In Moods

If we are subject to rapidly changing moods, we can take courage from the fact that David was too! In this Psalm he sweeps the scale from dark despair to calm confidence.

3:1, 2 At the outset David is overawed by his enemies. Their superior numbers strike terror to his heart. What is one among so many? Then too, he is stung by their taunting jibes. They insinuate that his sin has cut him off from any hope of divine **help**.

Verse 2 closes with the enigmatical word **Selah**. Since this is the first of its seventy-one occurrences in the Psalms, we pause to comment on it. Unfortunately, our remarks will be less an explanation than a confession of ignorance! The simple fact is that *we do not know* what the word means. All we can do is list some of the meanings that have been suggested and let the reader decide which seems best.

Selah may mean to intensify voices or instrumental accompaniment; that is, to sing or play louder. Crescendo!

It may indicate a pause or a rest, as if to say, "Stop and think about that."

"It is rendered in the Septuagint by *diapsalmos*, which either means louder playing, *forte*, or more probably, an instrumental interlude."[8]

Some think it means a repetition, like *da capo*.

It may mean the end of a strophe (a musical section).

It may even mean the bending of the body as an act of reverence or respect.

3:3 The mood of the Psalm changes in verse 3. David gets his eyes off his enemies and on the LORD, and that changes his whole outlook. Immediately he realizes that he has in Jehovah **a shield**, a source of **glory, and the One who lifts up** his **head**. As his **shield**, the Lord gives him complete protection from enemy assaults. As his glory, the Lord gives him honor, dignity and vindication in place of the shame, reproach and slander that were being heaped upon him. As the lifter of his head, the Lord encourages and exalts him.

3:4 Inspired by these great and true thoughts of God, David goes to **the LORD** in prayer and receives immediate assurance that his petition has been heard and answered. God answers **from His holy hill**, that is, from the site of the temple in Jerusalem, the place where He dwelt among His people.

3:5, 6 Assured of Jehovah's protection, the psalmist lies down and goes to sleep. It is the sweetest kind of sleep, a gift of God to those who trust Him in the midst of life's most distressing circumstances.

After a restful night, David awakes with the consciousness that it was the Lord who had calmed the nerves that were taut with fear and foreboding. Now he has courage to face his foes unafraid, even if he is surrounded by **ten thousands of** them!

3:7 But this does not mean that prayer is no longer necessary. The grace that sustained us last night will not do for today. We need a fresh supply of God's grace every day. So David comes to the Lord for continuing deliverance, believing that God will strike his **enemies on the cheekbone** and break their **teeth**.

3:8 As far as David is concerned, Jehovah is the only One who can deliver anyone; **salvation belongs to the LORD** alone. So he asks that God will bless His **people** by continuing to show them His marvelous deliverance.

The swirling emotions of this man of God can perhaps be better understood if we look at the heading of the Psalm once more:

"A Psalm of David, when he fled from Absalom his son."

The commander of David's enemies was *his own son*! It would have been bad enough if the adversaries were foreign invaders, but because they were led by David's rebel son, his grief and bitterness were compounded.

Psalm 4: God's Secret Tranquilizer

4:1 As David enters the Lord's presence, he addresses Him as **God of my righteousness**. This conveys the thought that the God of justice could be depended on to judge David righteously. Men may defame and blackball but God knows the true facts and will see that justice triumphs!

Then David adds, **"You have relieved me in my distress."** In Darby's *New Translation* this reads, "In pressure thou hast enlarged me." Ordinarily we think of pressure as reducing the compass or volume of its object, but God uses pressure to produce spiritual enlargement! Prosperity does little for us, but adversity produces growth and maturity. Spurgeon once said:

> I am afraid that all the grace I have got out of my comfortable and easy times and happy hours might almost lie on a penny. But the good that I have received from my sorrows and pains and griefs is altogether incalculable. What do I not owe to the hammer and the anvil, the fire and the file! Affliction is the best bit of furniture in my house.[9]

Remembering how God had answered his prayers in the past when he was under pressure, David feels free to ask God to **hear** him again.

4:2, 3 The immediate occasion for David's appeal can be deduced from verses 2–5. He was being maligned and slandered by unprincipled men. These carping critics were dragging his name in the mud, assassinating his character, and besmirching his reputation with baseless accusations and downright **falsehood**.

David asks them **how long** their mindless rage against him will continue, then reminds them that their efforts to overthrow him are futile because God Himself is on his side: **"The LORD has set apart for Himself him who is godly."** Those who trust in the Lord are as "the apple of His eye" (Zech. 2:8). Their names are engraved on the palms of His hands (Isa. 49:16). He hears them when they call and hastens to their assistance. David is thus anticipating Paul's argument in Romans 8:31: If God is for us, who can be successfully against us?

4:4 David's enemies should let their passions cool. If they must **be angry**, it should be in a righteous cause. The clause **"Be angry and do not sin"** is quoted in Ephesians 4:26, but there it is addressed to believers, reminding them that it is right to be angry *in God's cause* but never in one's own. Here in Psalm 4, of course, the words are spoken to wicked men to warn them against the overflow of anger into violent action. As they lie awake in the quietness of the night hours, they should search their own hearts and consider the stupidity of fighting against God. Such sober reflections would silence their slanderings and terminate their wicked plans.

4:5 In a bold evangelistic thrust, David counsels the wicked to combine practical **righteousness** with faith **in the LORD**. "Make justice your sacrifice" (Gelineau). But this can only be done by those who have **put** their **trust in the LORD**.

4:6 **There are many who** want prosperity and happiness. They are continually yearning to see some **good**. But the trouble is that they want blessing without the Blesser, and good without God. They want all the benefits of a Christ-filled life but they don't want the Benefactor.

In contrast to them, David goes straight to the Fountainhead of all good with the words, **"LORD, lift up the light of Your countenance upon us."**

4:7 His **gladness** in the Lord far exceeds the joy of the ungodly when their silos bulge with grain and their casks overflow with wine. "Never did rich harvests of corn and wine bring gladness like the gladness Thou puttest into my heart" (Knox).

4:8 Reassured of the Lord's all-sufficiency, the psalmist's inner agitation subsides. He can now **lie down in peace and sleep**, knowing that it is the LORD who makes him **dwell in safety**. What a change prayer has produced in only eight short verses!

Psalm 5: Morning Prayer

The heading of Psalm 5 reads: **To the chief musician; with flutes. A Psalm of David.**

Since many of the Psalms have titles somewhat similar to this, we should mention again that many scholars believe that these superscriptions are part of the inspired text. In some versions of the Bible (following the original Hebrew), the titles are included as verse one. Some scholars think the headings actually belong at the end of each preceding Psalm, but the evidence for this is not convincing. The big problem with these titles is that the meanings are often obscure. In Psalm 5, they indicate the instrumental accompaniment, but in other cases they might indicate the tune of another song to which the Psalm can be sung. Psalm 57, for example, reads in the superscription, "Set to *Do Not Destroy.*" This may

have been the name of a well-known song at that time. Occasionally, the meaning is so doubtful that the NKJ translators decided to transliterate the Hebrew words. Psalm 16, for instance, reads "A *Michtam*[10] of David." Fortunately for us, our enjoyment of a Psalm does not depend on our full understanding of its title.

Psalm 5 is a morning prayer in which David reflects on God's contrasting attitudes toward the righteous and the wicked.

5:1, 2 At the outset he asks God to hear not only **his words** but **consider** his **meditation** as well. It is a valid request. The Holy Spirit can interpret our meditations just as easily as the words we speak.

The psalmist asks God to hear not only his meditations, but also the sound of his **cry**. This may mean more than the mere words; it suggests the very intonation, the deep, earnest pitch of the voice.

In addressing the Lord as **"my King and my God,"** David reveals the warm, personal, intimate relationship he enjoyed with the Lord. In the words, **"for to You I will pray,"** he shows that the true God was the only One to whom he prayed—"to You and to You alone." The relationship was not only possessive, but exclusive as well.

5:3 David's prayers were not spasmodic but regular. Every **morning** the Lord heard his voice. Every **morning** the man of God prepared a sacrifice of praise and prayer and watched for the Lord to reveal Himself during the day. Too often we do not watch for God's responses. "We miss many answers," said F. B. Meyer, "because we get tired of waiting on the docks for the returning ships."

5:4–6 Always aware of his enemies, David's confidence in prayer is strengthened by remembering God's holiness and righteousness. Believers have an inside track to the throne of grace. Not so the ungodly. **God** cannot be tolerantly pleased with any form of **wickedness. Evil** cannot be His overnight guest. **The boastful** are not favored with an audience before this King. He hates all evildoers—a truth that punctures the prevalent myth that God is all love and therefore incapable of hatred! God's holiness demands that He punish all liars and abhor all murderers and deceivers.

5:7 In contrast to his wicked adversaries, David had instant access into the presence of the Lord through **the multitude of** God's unfailing **mercy** or grace. In a spirit of deep reverence, David worshiped, like all godly Jews, facing the **holy temple**. Since the actual temple was not built until after David's death, the word here must refer to the tabernacle, as it does in 1 Samuel 1:9; 3:3 and 2 Samuel 22:7.

5:8 Harassed as he is by **enemies**, David asks the Lord to display His justice by leading him safely through the surrounding danger and making his pathway crystal clear.

5:9 Next the psalmist introduces strong reasons why God should vindicate His righteous servant and punish the wicked enemies. You can't believe a word they say. **Their inward** lives, their thoughts and motives, are utterly corrupt and bent on **destruction. Their throat is** like **an open tomb**, stinking with corruption and ready to devour their victims. They are inveterate and insincere flatterers.

5:10 Their doom is just. They should be made to bear their guilt. Their evil schemes should be made to boomerang on themselves. Their innumerable **transgressions** demand their eviction. Their crowning sin is

that **they have rebelled against** the Lord God.

5:11, 12 But while God deals with His enemies in judgment, may His friends always have reason to **rejoice** and **shout for joy** as they find Him to be their Refuge, strong and sure. May all who love Jehovah magnify Him as their unfailing Defender! No question about it—God does favor the righteous man; He **will surround him** with grace like a protective **shield**.

Psalm 6: Double Trouble

It was bad enough to be racked with a serious illness, but David's grief was compounded by the tormenting pressure of his opponents. Perhaps they were gloating that his condition was hopeless.

6:1 David interpreted his sickness as a stroke of God brought on by some sin. We commonly do this ourselves; often it is the first thought that crosses our mind. And this diagnosis is sometimes correct: some illnesses *are* indeed caused by unconfessed sin in the believer's life (1 Cor. 11:30). But this is by no means always the case. God often permits illness as a springboard for the display of His power and glory (John 9:3; 11:4), or as a means of producing spiritual fruit (Rom. 5:3), or to prevent sin (2 Cor. 12:7), or as a natural result of overwork (Phil. 2:30) or old age (Eccl. 12:3–6).

Whenever sickness strikes, the first thing we should do is to make sure that we have no unconfessed sin in our life. Then we should ask the Lord to work out His purpose in the illness and to heal us. After that it is proper to resort to a physician and to the use of medicine, but we must be careful that our trust is in the Lord and not in the means that He uses (2 Chron.

16:12). All healing is from the Lord, whether miraculous or ordinary. If in any particular case He does not choose to heal, then He will give grace for suffering or for dying. Ordinarily we do not get dying grace until we need it.

6:2, 3 The psalmist was vocal and articulate in his plea for healing. He was wasting away. His **bones** pained him continually. Even his whole inner life—his emotions, intellect and will—were affected. But it seemed that the LORD was slow in responding. **How long** would it be before He would graciously heal the sufferer?

6:4 David asks the **Lord** to turn from what seems to be an attitude of indifference, and to **save** his life from sickness and death. His only claim to deliverance from misery is the steadfast mercy of Jehovah.

6:5 Then follows an unusual argument for healing, namely, that if David should die, it would be no advantage to God. As long as he is alive, he can remember the Lord and praise Him. But if he dies, God would be forgotten. The body without the spirit would not be able to **give** Him **thanks.**

The argument has a certain validity as far as the body is concerned, for a corpse is devoid of memory and of the power to praise. But as far as the spirit and soul are concerned, the argument reflects the limited knowledge which OT saints possessed of life beyond death. Thanks to the fuller revelation which Christ brought, we now know that when a believer dies, he leaves his earthly body and departs to be with Christ, which is far better (Phil. 1:23). He is away from the body and at home with the Lord (2 Cor. 5:8). So the believer does not go into a limbo of soul-sleep, but is consciously in the presence of the Lord, praising and worshiping Him.

It must be said in David's favor that he made wonderful use of the light that he had, weaving it into the fabric of his prayers. If our prayers made as good use of the superior light we have, what paragons of praise and petition they would be!

6:6, 7 We get some idea of the depth of the psalmist's misery by his description of his condition. He was utterly worn out **with** moaning and **groaning. All night** he soaked his pillow **with** his crying and drenched his **couch with** his **tears**. His eyes had become sunken due to his profound **grief**, and vision was fading because of the oppression **of all** his **enemies**. It seemed that his life was filled to overflowing with trouble and that he could stand no more.

6:8–10 But prayer changes things. By the secret, mysterious communication of the Spirit, the assurance comes to him that **the LORD has heard** the sound **of** his **weeping** and that his **prayer** has been answered. Strengthened by this assurance, he orders his **enemies** to disperse. He is no longer cowed by their threat because he realizes that they will go **suddenly** down to shameful defeat when the Lord rises up to punish them.

> Lord, what a change within us one
>   short hour
> Spent in Thy presence will avail
>   to make!
> What heavy burdens from our
>   bosoms take!
> What parched grounds refresh as with
>   a shower!
> We kneel, and all around us seems
>   to lower;
> We rise, and all—the distant and the
>   near—
> Stands forth in sunny outline, brave
>   and clear;

We kneel, how weak; we rise, how
full of power!
Why, therefore, should we do
ourselves this wrong
Or others—that we are not always
strong,
That we are sometimes overborne
with care,
That we should ever weak or
heartless be,
Anxious or troubled, when with us
in prayer,
And joy and strength and courage
are with Thee?
—*Richard Chenevix Trench*

Psalm 7: The Cry of the Oppressed

The Hebrew title identifies this as
a *Shiggaion* **of David, which he sang
to the LORD concerning the words of
Cush, a Benjamite**. F. W. Grant writes
that the word *shiggaion* implies a wandering ode or a loud, enthusiastic
hymn, in which the writer is carried
away with his enthusiasm. **Cush**, the
subject of the ode, was from the same
tribe as Saul and was probably one of
his lieutenants. In any case he was a
malicious foe of David. The NKJV
translates *shiggaion* as **a meditation**.

7:1, 2 In a passionate appeal David
prays for deliverance from his pursuers. Otherwise he will be like a helpless lamb, attacked by **a lion** and
dragged off, limp and lifeless.

7:3–5 Cush was obviously accusing David of a long list of crimes,
probably including attempts on Saul's
life and raids on the king's supply
bases. But David protests his innocence. He was not guilty of the
charges. His **hands** had not **plundered**.
He had not taken vengeance on the
king, even when he had had the
opportunity to do so. If he had actually done these things, then he was
willing to face the music— to be hunted,
captured, struck down and killed.

7:6–8 But since it wasn't so, he
boldly calls on the LORD to **arise in**
His **anger**, punish the **enemies** and
vindicate the innocent. He pictures
God calling a great trial to order. A
huge throng of people are gathered
in the courtroom. Jehovah sits on the
bench and judges **the peoples**. All
David asks is that he be judged **according to** his own **righteousness** and
integrity. This may sound like the
height of conceit, but we must remember that David is not claiming
absolute righteousness in every area
of his life—only in regard to those
accusations that were being hurled
against him.

7:9–11 Verse 9 voices the age-long
cry of God's oppressed people. Every
devout heart pants for the day when
the reign of evil will be ended and **the
just** will inherit the earth. That day
will come when Christ returns to set
up His kingdom. In the meantime,
the righteous God who knows man's
thoughts and motives is the shield or
protector of **the upright** and the righteous **judge** who **is angry with the
wicked every day**.

7:12, 13 God has a well-stocked
armory. Unless the wicked repents,
He will sharpen His sword and tighten
His bow to shoot **arrows** barbed with
fire. All God's weapons are deadly
ones!

7:14–16 In the end, David is confident that his enemy will reap what
he has sowed. His sin will follow the
familiar course of conception, pregnancy, birth, and death. The enemy
first **conceives** a plot to destroy the
psalmist. Soon he is bulging with
wicked ideas. Then he brings to birth
his treacherous scheme. But it back-
fires on himself. He falls into his own
trap, and all the **trouble** and violence
he had mapped out for the psalmist
recoils **on his own crown** (head) by

an inexplicable irony of circumstances.

7:17 This even-handed justice prompts David to lift his heart to **the LORD** in thanksgiving and to **sing praise to the name of the LORD Most High**.

Psalm 8: What Is Man?

God is indescribably great. Man, by contrast, is pathetically tiny. Yet God has conferred tremendous glory and honor upon man. The wonder of this fact brings forth an eloquent gasp from David.

8:1 The majesty of the LORD is evident in all creation, if a person only has eyes to see it. Every area of natural science teems with evidences of the wisdom and power of the Creator. God's **glory** is higher than **the heavens**. The planets, the stars, the limitless universe give only a partial view of how very great God really is. Yet sophisticated men shrug off the evidence as if it didn't exist.

8:2 But **infants** in their innocent faith chant God's greatness in their simple hymns. It is exactly as Christ Himself declared: God has hidden these things from the wise and understanding and has revealed them to babes (Matt. 11:25).

Whether we think of **babes** in a literal way or as those disciples of the Lord who have childlike faith in Him, it is still true that they form a bulwark for the Lord **because of** His **enemies**. They can often silence an enemy of God through an innocent question or a naive observation. Just as it takes only a small pin to prick a large balloon, so these homespun followers of the Lamb often bring low the lofty pretensions of those who deny God's hand in creation and providence!

8:3 No branch of science proclaims God's greatness and man's insignifi-

cance more eloquently than astronomy. The simple fact that distances must be reckoned in light-years (the distance that light travels in a year) illustrates the point. Light travels 186,000 miles per second, and there are 31.5 million seconds in a year, so light travels roughly six trillion miles in a single year! Yet some stars are billions of light-years from the earth. No wonder we call such computation astronomical.

To gaze into **the heavens** at night should give us great thoughts about God. **The moon and the stars** are **the work** of His **fingers**! When we think of the numberless myriads of **stars**, of the vast distances in the universe, and of the power that holds the planets in orbit with mathematical precision, it boggles the mind.

8:4 Relatively speaking, the planet earth is a speck of dust in the universe. If this is so, what is a single **man** perched upon this planet? Yet God is interested in every individual! He has a personal, intimate concern for every human being.

8:5 God **made** man in His own image and after His own likeness. Though **lower** than God,[11] man shares with Him some faculties that are not shared by any other order of creation on earth. Everything God made was pronounced to be good, but the verdict on the Creation of man was *"very good."*

8:6–8 As God's representative on earth, man was given **dominion over** all kinds of animals, **birds, fish**, and reptiles. There was nothing that was not put under him.

But the writer to the Hebrews reminds us that we do not see man enjoying this undisputed sway at the present time (Heb. 2:5–9). Dogs bark at man, snakes bite him, birds and fish elude him. The explanation is that when sin entered the world through Adam, man lost his unqualified sovereignty over the lower creation.

Yet God's purpose still stands. He has decreed that man shall indeed have dominion, and nothing can block God's purposes. So while we do not see all things subject to man right now, we do see Jesus—the one Person by whom man's dominion will eventually be restored. When Christ came to earth, He became temporarily lower than the angels so that as Man He could die for the human race. Now He is crowned with glory and honor at God's right hand. Someday Christ the Son of man will return to earth to reign as King of kings and Lord of lords. In the Millennium, the dominion that was forfeited by the first Adam will be restored by the Last Adam.

8:9 Then God's redeemed people will join to sing with new appreciation, **"O LORD, our Lord, how excellent is Your name in all the earth!"**

Psalm 9: The Day of Retribution

If the inscription in the Chaldee version is correct, **David** is here celebrating his victory over Goliath. But he is obviously looking beyond this triumph to God's final victory over His enemies. The Psalm is an acrostic, based on the first half of the Hebrew alphabet.[12]

9:1, 2 The sweet singer of Israel is ecstatic over **all** God's **marvelous works**. Here he is not thinking so much of His deeds in creation or redemption but of His spectacular feats in crushing the nation's foes. David gives all the glory to God— none to himself and none to man's weapons or skill. With every fiber of his being he honors and magnifies

the **name** of the **Most High**. The example of his love and devotion to the Lord makes many of us realize how cold and unresponsive we often are.

9:3, 4 Then he reminisces about God's epic battle, though the final fulfillment of his words will not come to pass until the Second Coming of our Lord Jesus Christ. One sight of Him will cause the **enemies** to **turn back** and flee. **They shall fall** in panicky disarray **and perish** before they can escape. The righteous will be vindicated in that day by the King on His glorious **throne**. Finally the earth will taste what righteous judgment is really like.

9:5, 6 Gentile oppressors will be sharply **rebuked**, and all Israel's enemies will sink into perpetual oblivion. They will be buried in the ruins of their vaunted civilization. Cities that now seem to be timeless will be completely uprooted. Names like Washington, Moscow, or Ottawa will be forgotten forever.

9:7, 8 The adversaries will all be gone, **but the LORD shall endure forever**, as righteous and trustworthy as He has always been. Resplendent in glory on **His throne**, He will rule **the world** in absolute **righteousness**. Everyone will get a square deal from Him. Paul used the first part of verse 8 in his message at Athens, explaining that the active agent in this future judgment will be the risen Lord Jesus Christ:

Truly, these times of ignorance God overlooked, but now commands all men everywhere to repent, because He has appointed a day on which He will judge the world in righteousness by the Man whom He has ordained. He has given assurance of this to all by raising

Him from the dead (Acts 17:30, 31).

9:9, 10 Earth's **oppressed** masses will find Him to be their high tower and unfailing **refuge**. All **who know** Him **will put their trust in** Him, realizing that He has never disappointed the confidence of His people.

9:11, 12 Israel will not only **sing praises to the LORD** but she will also fulfill a missionary role to the Gentile **people**, rehearsing the wonderful deliverances of the Lord and pointing out that **He** who **avenges** the **blood** of His people was not indifferent to their sufferings after all—that their prayers did not go unanswered.

9:13, 14 But millennial conditions have not yet come. Verses 13 and 14 bring us back with a jolt to the distressing present! David still needs God's **mercy** to protect him from the enemy, so that **the gates** of **Zion** will again echo to his happy songs of praise.

9:15 Then he leaps forward once more to the time when **the** anti-Semitic **nations** will fall into **the pit which they** dug for the Jews and be trampled **in the net which they** intended for God's ancient people. It is history repeating itself—another instance of Haman being hanged on the gallows he made for Mordecai.

9:16 Once again **the LORD** will reveal Himself as the One who evens the score by causing the ungodly to reap what they have sown. God is not mocked. The meaning of **"Selah"** is uncertain. It may mean an intensification (see notes on Psalm 3).

9:17 When David says that **the wicked shall be turned into hell** (Heb., *Sheol*), he does not restrict the word to the disembodied state or to the grave. Here the context demands that it mean **hell** itself. This is the fate of **all the nations that forget God.**

9:18 Equally certain is the fact that **the needy shall not always be forgotten.** As Knox translates, "The patience of the afflicted will not go for nothing." All that they hoped for will be fulfilled in that millennial day.

9:19, 20 David's thoughts of the coming reign of righteousness arouse longings for its arrival. The prayer is born that the LORD will **arise** to foil man's plans and to judge **the nations**. As they stand in the presence of the Almighty Judge, they will realize in terror what puny, mortal **men** they really are.

Psalm 10: Public Enemy Number One

Here the psalmist employs an acrostic based on the second half of the Hebrew alphabet[13] to describe the supreme villain. Since this "Public Enemy Number One" seems to be the very embodiment of sin, we naturally link him with the "Man of Sin" who will arise at the beginning of the seven-year Tribulation. This "son of perdition" will oppose and exalt himself against every so-called god or object of worship. Taking his seat in the temple of God in Jerusalem, he will proclaim himself to be God (2 Thess. 2:3, 4). Those who refuse to worship him will suffer economic sanctions, persecution and even death.

The Silence of God (10:1)

As the Psalm opens we find the question that comes to all of us sooner or later: **Why** does the LORD remain silent while the innocent suffer and the wicked reign unchallenged? It is mysteries like this that call our faith into action, that encourage us to trust when we cannot understand, and that challenge us to endure to the end.

The Prayer of the Oppressed (10:2)

In their insufferable arrogance, **wicked** men relentlessly hunt down the helpless saints. What could be more fitting for them than to suffer the very fate **they** had **devised** for the righteous?

The Profile of the Enemy (10:3–11)

10:3, 4 It is typical for **the wicked** to boast about all the things he plans to do. In his mad craze to get rich he blasphemes **and renounces the LORD**, for to worship gold is to repudiate God. His lifestyle is one of self-sufficiency. He feels no need for **God** and lives as if He never existed.

10:5, 6 Everything seems to go his way; somehow he escapes the troubles that dog the rest of mankind. The guidelines which God has established for His own people are **far** beyond the wicked man; he cannot understand spiritual truths or divine principles. **He** sneers at **all his enemies** with utter contempt; nothing is ever going to disturb his security, he thinks. As long as he lives he will enjoy a trouble-free existence.

10:7, 8 Whenever he is around, you can expect the air to be blue with profanity. If he's not deceiving someone, he's probably browbeating someone else! He never seems to talk about anything constructive; it's always about crime and destruction. Like the other gangsters, he waits in unpatrolled, **lurking places** to ambush **the innocent**; when they walk past, he guns them down. He is always on the lookout for the unsuspecting and the **helpless**.

10:9–11 Like **a lion in his den**, he is poised ready to pounce on his prey. Like a hunter, he lures the victims **into his net**, whether for blackmail, extortion, bribery, servitude, or death. The unfortunate victim is overwhelmed—felled by the enormous power of the criminal. In his despair he feels that **God has forgotten** him, that He is looking in another direction and **will never see** the predicament of His child.

The Cry of the Faithful (10:12–18)

10:12, 13 But now it is time for the LORD to act by lifting His **hand** in judgment on the oppressor and in mercy on the afflicted. Why should the forces of evil be allowed to continue in their godlessness and irreligion? Why should they be encouraged to think that God will never demand **an account** for their crimes?

10:14, 15 God *does* see. He keeps a careful score of every act of injustice and wrong, so that He can **repay** in full in a coming day. So it is not in vain that **the helpless commits himself to** God. Has God not proved Himself to be the orphan's friend? The Lord will hear the cry of the faithful by breaking **the arm of the wicked** and by exposing **his wickedness until** every last vestige is punished.

10:16 That day of vengeance will arrive when the kingdoms of this world become the kingdom of our LORD and of His Christ. Then the wicked and persecuting **nations** will **have perished**, as foretold by Isaiah:

Behold, all those who were incensed against you shall be ashamed and disgraced; they shall be as nothing, and those who strive with you shall perish. You shall seek them and not find them—those who contended with you. Those who war against you shall be as nothing, as a nonexistent thing. For I, the Lord your God, will hold your right hand, saying to you, "Fear not, I will help you" (Isa. 41:11–13).

10:17, 18 We can be fully assured that the LORD will hear and answer the prayers of the **humble**. He will give them grace for every trial and will bend low to see that **justice** is the lot of **the fatherless and the oppressed**. The day is coming, praise God, when **the man of the earth** will **oppress** the poor and defenseless **no more**!

Psalm 11: Why Flee When You Can Trust?

Psalm 11 is an antidote for gloomy headlines. When the news is all bad—wars, violence, crime, corruption and political unrest—**David** reminds us that we can rise above the circumstances of life by keeping our eyes on the Lord.

It seems that when David had opened his front door, a frenzied visitor had burst in. His face was pale and drawn, his eyes were popping with excitement and his lips were quivering. In jerky, breathless gasps he told of imminent disaster and advised David to head for the hills. This Psalm is David's answer to the pessimistic visitor's counsel of despair and discouragement.

11:1–3 David first states his simple **trust in the LORD** as his refuge: "Why *flee* when you can *trust?*" Then he reproaches Calamity Charlie for seeking to disturb his peace. Notice that the text from verse 1b through verse 3 contains the words of the gloom peddler. It begins with **"Flee as a bird to your mountain."** He had said to David, in effect, "You are as insignificant and defenseless as a little bird. The best thing you can do is escape. Criminals now have the upper hand, and they are armed to the teeth, ready to gun down decent, law-abiding citizens. Law and order have vanished and **the foundations** of society are crumbling. This being so, what hope do you think there is for a **righteous** person like you?"

11:4–6 What hope? Why, **the LORD**, or course! **The LORD is in His holy temple**, and nothing can stop the fulfillment of His plans! His **throne is in heaven**, unmoved and unmovable, no matter what kingdoms on earth may rise or fall. Though nothing can disturb God's poise and serenity, He is nevertheless concerned about the doings of **the sons of men**. He not only sees what happens but constantly makes value judgments about **the righteous** and **the wicked**. Although God is infinite love, **His soul hates** men who practice **violence**. He will **rain** down a storm of judgment on them; the rain will be **coals** of **fire and brimstone** and the **wind** will be scorching heat.

11:7 Just as God hates the violent man, so He loves the righteous. God Himself **is righteous** and **He loves righteousness**. The ultimate reward of **the upright** will be to stand in God's presence.

So we need not get all upset over the headlines. The waves of adverse circumstances may seem to be against us at any particular time, but the tide of God's irresistible purpose is sure to win in the end.

> He everywhere hath sway, and all
>   things serve His might;
> His every act pure blessing is, His
>   path unsullied light.
> We comprehend Him not, yet earth
>   and heaven tell
> God sits as sovereign on the throne
>   and ruleth all things well.
> —*Author unknown*

Psalm 12: The Words of Men— and of God

12:1 The general decline of faithfulness among men, especially in their speech, evokes the prayer of verse 1:

> Lord, come to my rescue; piety is dead; in a base world, true hearts have gone rare (Knox).

12:2 Three specific charges are then leveled against the faithless generation:

> **Lies**—They are guilty not only of blatant forms of deceit, but of white lies, half-truths, exaggerations and broken promises.
> **Flattery**—They heap insincere compliments on others. Praise is not the same as flattery; it only becomes flattery when it ascribes virtues to a person which he is known not to possess. And flattery usually has some sinister or selfish motive.
> **Two-facedness**—They think one thing and say something quite different. Like Machiavelli, they practice duplicity and intrigue.

12:3, 4 The age-long sigh of God's true saints is that **the LORD** Himself will silence the ungodly's **flattering lips**—that He will immobilize the tongues of those who boast that their principles **will prevail**, that they have full freedom to say whatever they want, regardless of what anybody thinks.

12:5, 6 In response to the groan of the **poor** and **needy, the LORD** promises to **arise** and "grant them the salvation for which they thirst" (Gelineau). And what He has promised He will surely perform. His promises are **pure . . . , like silver tried in a furnace of earth, purified seven times**—in other words, like the purest **silver** known. There is no deceit, no flattery, no double meaning, no error in God's words. They can be fully trusted.

12:7 So the believer instinctively turns to the **LORD** for protection from **this generation**—protection not only from its attacks but from any form of compromise or complicity with it.

12:8 The last verse is a description of "this generation"—**the wicked** generation which is continually on the prowl, exalting **vileness** and scoffing at virtue. It is the same generation described in Proverbs 30:11–14:

> There is a generation that curses its father, and does not bless its mother. There is a generation that is pure in its own eyes, yet is not washed from its filthiness. There is a generation—oh, how lofty are their eyes! And their eyelids are lifted up. There is a generation whose teeth are like swords, and whose fangs are like knives, to devour the poor from off the earth, and the needy from among men.

Psalm 13: How Long?

Four times the words formed on David's lips—"How long?" Pursued hotly by the enemy (perhaps Saul), **David** wondered what was delaying the chariot of God. Would help never come to free him from the four terrible burdens that were crushing him?

> He felt as if God had forgotten him.
> He considered himself cut off from the Lord's favor.
> He experienced deep depression in his soul daily.
> He suffered the constant humiliation of being on the losing side.

13:1–4 God must take note of David's plight and send help quickly in order to avert two disasters. The first would be David's death and the second would be the jubilant boasting of his **enemy**. Unless the Lord acted quickly to restore the sparkle to David's eyes, they would soon be closed forever in **death**. Unless Jehovah turned the tide, the enemies would soon be boasting that they had won—that David was thoroughly trounced.

13:5, 6 Now there is no doubt as to the outcome. The psalmist believes that the answer is on the way. Trusting in the **mercy** of the Lord, he knows that he will live to celebrate deliverance from his adversary. In anticipation of this **salvation**, he can **sing** praises **to the** LORD for His boundless lovingkindness.

This Psalm is like many of our God-sent testings: they begin with a sigh but end with a song!

Psalm 14: The Fool's Creed

14:1 The creed of the fool is **"There is no God."** He does not *want* there to be a God, therefore he denies the existence of God. It is an irrational position to take. First of all, it is a claim to omniscience; it says, "I know everything. It is not possible that a God could exist beyond the boundaries of my knowledge." Second, this attitude claims omnipresence; it says, "I am present in all places at one and the same time, and it is not possible that God could exist any place in the universe without my knowing it." Again, this position ignores the wonders of God in creation—the immensity of the universe, the amazingly precise movement of the planets, the marvelous suitability of the earth to sustain life, the intricate design of the human body, the fantastic complexity of the human brain and the extraordinary properties of water and soil.

Take for instance the suitability of the earth to sustain life. Henry Bosch has pointed out the following instances of God's careful and marvelous design:

> The earth rotates on its axis at approximately 1000 miles per hour. If that had been 100 miles per hour, our days and nights would be ten times longer, and our planet would alternately burn and freeze. Under such circumstances vegetation could not live!
>
> If the earth were as small as the moon, the power of gravity would be too weak to retain sufficient atmosphere for man's needs; but if it were as large as Jupiter, Saturn, or Uranus, extreme gravitation would make human movement almost impossible. If we were as near to the sun as Venus, the heat would be unbearable; if we were as far away as Mars, we would experience snow and ice every night, even in the warmest regions. If the oceans were half their present dimensions, we would receive only one-fourth the rainfall we do now. If they were one-eighth larger, our annual precipitation would increase fourfold, and this earth would become a vast, uninhabitable swamp.
>
> Water solidifies at 32 degrees above zero [°F]. It would be disastrous if the oceans froze at that temperature, however, for then the amount of thawing in the polar regions would not balance out, and ice would accumulate throughout the centuries! To prevent such a catastrophe, the Lord put salt in the sea to alter its freezing point.[14]

The possibility that all this happened by chance is too small to warrant consideration. That is why the Bible says that atheists are fools. They are *moral* fools. It is not a question of their intelligence quotient but of their morality quotient.

God's verdict on these fools is that **they are corrupt** in themselves and that they act abominably. There is a close connection between a man's creed and his conduct. The lower his conception of God, the lower his morals are apt to be. Either as cause or consequence, atheism and agnosticism are linked with a corrupt life. Barnes writes:

> The belief that there is no God is commonly founded on the desire to lead a wicked life, or is embraced by those who in fact live such a life, with a desire to sustain themselves in their depravity and to avoid the fear of future retribution.[15]

14:2, 3 When **the LORD looks down from heaven** to see if any of Adam's descendants act wisely by seeking after **God**, His findings are dismal. By nature and by practice, man is a sinner. If left to himself, he would never seek after God. It is only through the ministry of the Holy Spirit that men become aware of their need for God and His salvation.

Paul quotes from the first three verses of this Psalm in Romans 3:10–12 to show that sin has affected all mankind and every part of everyone's being. Here in the Psalm, David is not thinking of the whole human race, although the description would certainly be true; rather, he is thinking of outright God-deniers in contrast to the righteous. It is these infidels who have apostatized from the true and living God. They are morally corrupt. God Himself cannot find one of them **who does good, no, not one**.

14:4 Their ignorance is apparent in the way they treat God's **people**. If they realized how God defends the poor and punishes sin, they would never devour believers as if it were a legitimate, everyday thing, like eating **bread**! If they knew the goodness and severity of God, they would not go through life without praying.

14:5, 6 When the Lord takes the

part of the innocent, the unrighteous will be greatly terrified. They had always mocked **the poor** for their simple faith, but now they will see that the God they denied is the **refuge** of His own.

14:7 It will be a great day when the Messiah comes **out of Zion** to deliver His people. Israel's joy will be unbounded when Christ's Jewish saints are fully and finally rescued from **captivity** among the nations that deny the only true God.

Psalm 15: The Man God Chooses

15:1 The individual God chooses as His companion is the subject of Psalm 15. Although it does not say so in this Psalm, the basic qualification for entrance into God's kingdom is to be born again. Apart from the new birth, no one can see or enter the kingdom. This birth from above is experienced by grace, through faith, and takes place completely apart from any meritorious works on man's part.

Taken by itself, the Psalm seems to imply that salvation is somehow connected with a man's righteous character or noble deeds. But taken with the rest of Scripture, it can only mean that the kind of faith that saves is the same kind of faith that results in a life of holiness. Like James in his epistle, David is here saying that genuine faith in the Lord results in the kind of good works described in this Psalm.

Incidentally, the Psalm does not profess to give a complete catalog of the virtues of the citizen of Zion. The portrait is suggestive but certainly not exhaustive.

15:2 First of all, the citizen of Zion **walks** with integrity. The man of integrity is a man of moral soundness. He is complete, well-rounded, and balanced.

Second, the citizen of Zion does what is right. He is careful to maintain a conscience that is void of offense. He would rather go to heaven with a good conscience than stay on earth with a bad one.

You can depend on this man to tell **the truth** from **his heart**. He would rather die than lie. His word is his bond. His yes means yes and his no means no.

15:3 He . . . does not backbite with his tongue. You won't find him gossiping about others. Slander and mud-slinging never get past his lips. He disciplines his tongue to edify instead of assassinate!

He does no **evil to his neighbor**. His whole desire is to help, to encourage and to instruct. When he hears some juicy tidbit of scandal about **his friend**, he lets it die right there. Depend on him not to repeat it to anyone.

15:4 Moral distinctions are not blurred in his vision. He discerns between sin and righteousness, darkness and light, evil and good. He despises **a vile person** in the sense that he outspokenly witnesses against his ungodliness. On the other hand, he identifies himself in open approval with everyone in the household of faith.

Once he has made a promise, he stands by it, even if it results in financial loss. A believer, for example, might agree to sell his house for $85,000. But before the papers are signed, he finds he could have sold the house to a large development company for $90,000. But he has given his word to the first buyer—and he keeps his contract.

15:5 The friend of God **does not put out his money at** interest, that is, to another member of God's family. Under the law of Moses, an Israelite could lend to Gentiles at interest (Deut. 23:19, 20) but was forbidden to do so to a fellow Jew (Ex. 22:25; Lev. 25:35–37).

If Jews living under law were guided by this principle, how much more so should Christians living under grace!

Finally, the righteous man does not **take a bribe against the innocent**. He hates the perversion of justice, and disproves the old saying that "everybody has his price."

This then is the type of person who lives for God in time and for eternity. Come to think of it, no one else would be comfortable in God's presence!

Psalm 16: Christ Arose!

The key to understanding Psalm 16 is found in Acts 2:25–28 where Peter quotes verses 8–11a as referring to the resurrection of Christ. Let us put the key in the door, then, and listen as our wonderful Savior prays to His Father immediately prior to His death.

16:1, 2 As the perfect Man, completely dependent on **God**, Christ cries out for preservation to the One who is His only refuge. Throughout His thirty years of life on earth, the Savior not only acknowledged God as His Lord but joyfully confessed God as the absorbing passion of His life. The words **"My goodness is nothing apart from You"** are not a denial of the Savior's sinlessness, but are simply a moving testimony that Christ found all His sufficiency in God. This testimony is comparable to the worship of Psalm 73:25: "Whom have I in heaven but You? And there is none upon earth that I desire besides You."

16:3 The centrality of God in Messiah's life does not, however, exclude a deep regard for **the saints** in the land. In fact, the two are vitally connected: to love God is to love His people (1 John 5:1, 2). The Lord Jesus considers His saints the nobility of **the earth**, the people **in whom** He finds **all** His **delight**. Consider a similar testimony by an old saint of God:

> From the first day I set off until the present hour, I have been as highly favored as a mortal and sinful being can well be. My fellowship has been with the excellent of the earth, and every one of them striving to the utmost of his power to show me kindness for the Lord's sake.[16]

16:4 Standing in stark contrast to the true worshipers of God are people who worship **another god**. Idolatry inevitably brings a train of **sorrows** into the lives of its devotees. Perhaps one of the greatest judgments on idolaters is that they become like the thing they worship. The holy Son of God disavows any fellowship with **their drink offerings of blood**. He will, in fact, not even mention **their names** in any way that might suggest tolerance toward them or toward their heathen rites.

16:5, 6 As for His personal life, Christ's chosen **portion** and **cup** is the LORD. All His wealth and enjoyment rest in God. It is the Lord who guards the boundaries of His **inheritance**. As He thinks of how wisely and wonderfully the Father has planned every detail of His life, He compares it to a **pleasant** estate in a magnificent setting, and to an **inheritance** that is comprised entirely of **good** things. If we are living in fellowship with God, we too can praise Him for the ordering of our lives. When we complain, we betray a lack of confidence in God's wisdom, love and power.

16:7 Here Christ praises **the LORD** for the faithful way He has provided guidance and **counsel** throughout all His life. Even during hours of sleeplessness, as He prayed and meditated on God's Word, His **heart** had instructed Him. Far from being wasted, the time was sanctified to His comfort and blessing. How often has Christ's experience been duplicated in the lives of God's people!

> For many a rapturous minstrel
> Among those sons of light
> Will say of his sweetest music,
> "I learned it in the night."
> And many a rolling anthem
> That fills the Father's home
> Sobbed out its first rehearsal
> In the shade of a darkened room.
> —*Author unknown*

The remaining verses of Psalm 16 were quoted by Peter on the Day of Pentecost as referring to the resurrection of Christ:

> For David says concerning Him: "I foresaw the Lord always before my face, for He is at my right hand, that I may not be shaken. Therefore my heart rejoiced, and my tongue was glad; moreover my flesh also will rest in hope. For You will not leave my soul in Hades, nor will You allow Your Holy One to see corruption. You have made known to me the ways of life; You will make me full of joy in Your presence."
>
> Men and brethren, let me speak freely to you of the patriarch David, that he is both dead and buried, and his tomb is with us to this day. Therefore, being a prophet, and knowing that God had sworn with an oath to him that of the fruit of his body, according to the flesh, He would raise up the Christ to sit on his throne, he, foreseeing this, spoke concerning the resurrection

of the Christ, that His soul was not left in Hades, nor did His flesh see corruption. This Jesus God has raised up, of which we are all witnesses. Therefore being exalted to the right hand of God, and having received from the Father the promise of the Holy Spirit, He poured out this which you now see and hear (Acts 2:25–33).

Now notice the points that Peter made (most of which we ourselves would never have gathered from the passage):

1. David was speaking of Christ (v. 25). David could not have been speaking about himself, since his body is still in a tomb in Jerusalem.

2. As a prophet, the psalmist knew that God would raise up Christ prior to the time He would reign upon His throne.

3. David therefore predicted that God would not allow Christ's soul to remain in Hades, nor would He allow Christ's body to decompose.

4. God did indeed raise up Christ, and what happened on the Day of Pentecost was the result of His glorification at God's right hand.

With this introduction in mind, let us now look at the closing verses of this Psalm.

16:8 First of all, Messiah asserts without any equivocation that He has kept **the LORD always before** Him. Jehovah has been the One for whom He lived. He has never done anything in self-will; everything has been done in obedience to His Father's will.

Because He is at my right hand, I shall not be moved. In Scripture the **right hand** speaks of:

Power (Ps. 89:13)
Safety (Ps. 20:6)
Honor (Ps. 45:9; 110:1)
Pleasure (Ps. 16:11)
Favor (Ps. 80:17)
Support (Ps. 18:35).

Here it speaks of safety and security.

16:9, 10 Assured of God's constant care and protection, the Savior faces the future with confidence. His **heart is glad**. His soul **rejoices** and His body is safe. He knows that God **will not leave** His **soul in Sheol** or **allow** His body **to see corruption**. In other words, Christ will be raised from the dead.

The reference to **Sheol** needs a word of explanation. It is the word used in the OT for the grave, for the "netherworld," and to describe the disembodied state. It is equivalent to the NT Greek word "Hades." Sheol did not so much indicate a geographical location as the *condition* of the dead—the separation of the personality from the body. It was used to describe the condition of everyone who died, whether believer or unbeliever. On the other hand the NT equivalent, Hades, is used only of *unbelievers*. Sheol was a very indefinite, imprecise word. It did not convey a clear picture of life after death. In fact, it expressed more of uncertainty than of knowledge.

In the NT, all that is changed. Christ has brought life and immortality to light through the gospel (2 Tim. 1:10). Today we know that when an unbeliever dies, his spirit and soul are in a state of suffering called Hades (Luke 16:23), while his body goes to the grave. The spirit and soul of the believer go to be with Christ in heaven (2 Cor. 5:8; Phil. 1:23), while his earthly body goes to the grave.

When the Savior said ". . . **You will not leave my soul in Sheol**," He revealed His foreknowledge that God would not allow Him to remain in the disembodied state. Though He *entered* Sheol, He did not remain there.

God did not allow the usual process of decomposition to take place. By a miracle of preservation, Christ's lifeless body was kept from **corruption** for three days and nights.

16:11 In the final verse, our blessed Lord has complete confidence that God **will show** Him **the path of life— the path** from death back to **life** again. This **path** would ultimately lead Him back to heaven, to God's **presence**. There He would experience **fullness of joy** and **pleasures forevermore**.

Psalm 17: The Perennial Puzzle

When we do wrong and suffer for it, our own consciences tell us that our punishment is just. But it's another story when our suffering is unrelated to any wrong we have done! This kind of suffering—the "suffering for righteousness sake," as Peter calls it—is a perennial puzzle to the child of God.

David knew his share of it. But he also knew what to do about it. He took his case to the Righteous Judge. There he was confident of a fair trial.

At times David seems to be defending himself in a giant ego-trip. He loudly protests his righteousness, integrity and obedience. It almost sounds as if he has reached a state of sinless perfection. But this is really not the case at all. David is not claiming guiltlessness in *all* areas of his life, but simply in *the present circumstances*. He is saying that he did not do anything to provoke the current hostility of his foes.

We might paraphrase David's case as follows:

17:1, 2 "LORD, I ask you to **hear** my **cause** because it is a **just** one.

Listen attentively to what I say, for I am being unjustly persecuted. In my plea for justice I am 'telling it like it is'—no deceit or shading of the truth. Before your tribunal I seek acquittal. **Let your eyes** see every aspect of the case and then decide in favor of the right.

17:3–5 "If **You** test **my heart**, if You check me out in the darkness as well as in the light—no matter how thoroughly you examine me—you will find that the opposition has no valid reason for harassing me the way they do. Honestly—I am telling the truth. As far as the usual wickedness of men is concerned, I have been able to steer clear of violence by staying close to Your **word**, the Bible. Not by depending on my own strength but by Your commands and promises, I have walked in paths of obedience to You. My **footsteps** haven't slipped; I haven't resorted to violence against my enemies when I had plenty of chance to do so.

17:6, 7 "Now I'm committing my cause to You. **I** appeal to **You** for justice, confident that You'll **hear** and answer **me**. You are the Savior of those who seek sanctuary from their enemies at **Your right hand**. As I come running to You now, **show Your marvelous lovingkindness** to me in a spectacular way.

17:8–12 "Protect **me as the apple of Your eye**—I'm thinking of the pupil of the eye and how it is 'protected by the eyelash, lid, brow, bony socket and the swiftly uplifted hand' (F. B. Meyer). **Hide me** in the protective and affectionate **shadow of Your wings**. Then I will be safe **from the wicked who** rob me of everything I have and seek to take my life itself. As You know so well, **their fat hearts** are incapable of pity, and **their mouths** spew out the most frightening boasts of what they are going to do to me. They stealthily track me down. **They have now** hemmed me in. **Their eyes** are intent on the final knockout blow. Savage **as a lion** that is ravenously hungry, and sly as **a young lion lurking** in the bush, they are ready **to tear** me to shreds.

17:13, 14 "LORD, You simply *must* come to my defense. Meet them head on and topple them. **With Your sword** rescue me from the clutches of these **wicked** men who are only concerned with what they can get **in this life**. You have given them more than enough of material things. Even their **children** have an oversupply—enough to **leave** to **their babes**.

17:15 "Well, they can have it all as far as I'm concerned. My interest lies in spiritual rather than material treasures. It is enough for me that I will look upon **Your face** as one who has been declared righteous and not as a guilty sinner. **I shall be satisfied when I awake in Your likeness.**"

E. Bendor Samuel has pointed out that verse 15 contains every element of 1 John 3:2:

Supreme satisfaction:	1 Jn.—It has not yet been revealed ... but
	Ps.—**I shall be satisfied.**
A great transfor-mation:	1 Jn.—We shall be like Him.
	Ps.—I shall **awake in Your likeness.**
An enlarged vision:	1 Jn.—We shall see Him as He is.
	Ps.—**I will see Your face.**[17]

See also 1 Corinthians 15:51–55 and Revelation 22:4.

Psalm 18:
The Power That Raised
Christ From the Dead

We get a clue that this Psalm may be about the Lord Jesus Christ from the fact that verse 49 is quoted in Romans 15:9 as referring to Him.

For this reason I will confess to You among the Gentiles, and sing to Your name.

As we investigate more closely, we find that we were right. The Psalm is indeed all about the Lord Jesus Christ. It describes graphically His death, resurrection, exaltation, Second Coming and glorious kingdom.

Nowhere else in the Bible are we given such a vivid account of the tremendous battle that took place in the unseen world at the time of our Savior's resurrection. But more of that later.

18:1–3 The song opens with praise to **the LORD** for hearing and answering the prayers of His beloved Son. Notice the figures of speech that are used to describe the **strength**, safety, security, and **salvation** that are found in **God: my strength ... my rock ... my fortress ... my deliverer ... my shield and the horn of my salvation, my stronghold**.

18:4–6 **Death** is rapidly closing in on the suffering Savior. In quickly changing pictures, He describes Himself as being bound with ropes, being gradually overwhelmed with waves, being entangled by cords, and being confronted with a host of inescapable **snares**. In such a desperate situation, there is only one resource: prayer to **God**. Christ did not ask to be delivered from dying; that, after all, was His purpose in coming into the world (John 12:27). What He requested was to be delivered out of death. "Who in the days of His flesh, having offered up both supplications and entreaties to Him who was able to save Him out of death, with strong crying and tears ..." (Heb. 5:7, JND).

In His deep **distress** Christ had the assurance that His prayer was heard and answered. The rest of the Psalm reveals how Immanuel's plaintive cries from Gethsemane and Golgotha mobilized all the forces of Omnipotence on His behalf. "The voice is thin and solitary," wrote F. B. Meyer, "but the answer shakes creation."

18:7–15 When you come to verses 7–19, it sounds as if a war has broken out. And that is exactly what happened at the resurrection of Christ. The battle was between God and the hosts of hell. Satan and all his demons encamped at the tomb outside Jerusalem, determined that the Lord Christ would never rise again. Their success in having the Son of God crucified would be completely nullified if He were to rise from the dead. So they massed themselves at the sealed tomb of the Savior.

Then God lowered the heavens and came down in the greatest display of power the world has ever known. The Apostle Paul later spoke of it as "the working of His mighty power which He worked in Christ when He raised Him from the dead" (Eph. 1:19, 20). Greater than the might that created the universe, greater than the strength that delivered Israel from Egypt, God's resurrection power drove back the hosts of principalities, powers, and wicked spirits on that first Easter morning.

At the approach of God **the earth** is convulsed. His rage is fierce, pictured by **smoke** billowing forth **from His nostrils**, intense **fire** issuing in torrents **from His mouth**, and great **coals** of flame hurtling against His enemies. As He descends, riding upon a cloud that resembles **a cherub**, the world is shaken by a violent storm of **darkness**, thunder, **lightnings** and **hailstones** pummeling the enemy in a massive bombing attack. Just as in the crossing of the Red Sea, the waters of the sea and rivers recoil in fear at the titanic display of the wrath of the Almighty.

18:16–19 In striking symbolism God smashes, bruises, crushes, wounds and maims the foe until he retreats in utter defeat. Then He reaches down and takes Christ from the still-sealed tomb. Hallelujah! Christ is risen! Not only does God raise Him from the dead but He gives Him a triumphant ascension through the enemy's realm and glorifies Him at His own right hand. Thus, as Paul says, "Having disarmed principalities and powers, He made a public spectacle of them, triumphing over them in it" (Col. 2:15).

18:20–30 Here we have the rationale or mystique of the Resurrection. There was a certain moral necessity for God to raise the Lord Jesus. This necessity arose from Christ's sinless, spotless life, from His undeviating devotion to the will of His Father, and from the perfection of His work at Calvary's cross. All the righteous attributes of God demanded that He bring the Savior up from the grave in the power of an endless life. This is what is meant by the majestic utterance, "Christ was raised from the dead by the glory of the Father" (Rom. 6:4). The glorious character of God made the Resurrection a moral necessity, the reward of Christ's perfect, personal righteousness.

While David did write verses 20–30, they are really not completely true of him. Instead, he was speaking prophetically through the inspiration of the Holy Spirit about the One who would be both his Son and his Lord (Matt. 22:41–46).

18:31–42 These verses describe Christ's Second Advent. He will come from heaven "with His mighty angels, in flaming fire taking vengeance on those who do not know God, and on those who do not obey the gospel of our Lord Jesus Christ" (2 Thess. 1:7, 8). He will be "clothed with a robe dipped in blood . . . out of His mouth goes a sharp sword, that with it He should strike the nations . . . He Himself treads the winepress of the fierceness and wrath of Almighty God" (Rev. 19:13, 15).

Christ is pictured primarily as a man of war here. This is consistent with the other Scriptures that teach that when He comes back to earth, He will come first of all "to execute judgment on all, to convict all who are ungodly among them of all their ungodly deeds which they have committed in an ungodly way, and of all the harsh things which ungodly sinners have spoken against Him" (Jude 15).

After being equipped for war by **God** the Father (vv. 31–37), Christ pursues and utterly destroys His **enemies** (vv. 37–42).

18:43–45 Following the crushing of His foes, Christ sets up His kingdom on earth and reigns as King of kings and Lord of lords. He is now the **head of** all **the nations** on earth. Both redeemed Israel and redeemed Gentiles serve in willing submission to the righteous rule of the glorified Christ. **Foreigners** yield feigned obedience.

18:46–50 The Psalm closes as it began—with a hymn of praise to **God** for His wonderful vindication of the Lord Jesus. He has given **great** victories to **His king**, and shown **mercy to His anointed**, His Son.

Because of what He has done, we too should extol Him **among the Gentiles, and sing praises to** His **Name**.

Psalm 19: God's Two Books

19:1, 2 **"The heavens declare the glory of God; and the firmament** shows **His handiwork."** And what a story they tell! Think, first of all, what they tell about the immensity of the universe. If we traveled at the speed of light—186,000 miles a *second* or roughly six trillion miles a *year*—it would take us ten billion *years* to reach the farthest point we can see with a telescope. But this would still be far from the outermost limits of space. Now astronomers think that space may have no bounds at all! Our earth is nothing but a tiny speck in a limitless expanse!

Think too of the number of stars and other heavenly bodies. With the naked eye we can see about five thousand stars. With a small telescope we can see about two million. But with the Palomar telescope we can see billions of *galaxies*, to say nothing of individual stars.

Then think about the distances of the heavenly bodies from the earth and from each other. Someone has pictured the distances as follows: if it cost a penny to ride 1000 miles, a trip to the moon would cost $2.38, a trip to the sun would cost $930, but a trip to the *nearest* star would cost $260 million.

It takes light from the most remote stars which can be seen with telescopes ten billion years to reach the earth. So when we look out into space, we are really looking backward in time. For example, we do not see the Andromeda galaxy where it is now but where it was two million years ago!

Although the stars may appear to be crowded in the firmament, the distances between them are so great that they have been likened to lonely lightships a million miles apart, floating in an empty sea.

If creation is so great, how much greater is the Creator! Day and night the heavens are telling the greatness of His power and wisdom. **The firmament** unceasingly proclaims the marvels of His **handiwork**. (In Bible usage "firmament" refers to the expanse of the heavens.) As Isaac Watts wrote, "Nature with open volume stands to spread her Maker's praise abroad."

19:3, 4a There is no speech, no words, no audible voice, yet the sermon of the stars goes **out through all the earth**, and its message **to the end of the world**. Simply by looking up into the heavens man can know that there is a God and can perceive His eternal power (Rom. 1:20). The terrifying dimensions and complexity of the universe confirm Lord Kelvin's observation that "if you think strongly enough, you will be forced by science to believe in God." Kant wrote:

It is impossible to contemplate the fabric of the world without recognizing the admirable order of its arrangement and the certain manifestation of the hand of God in the perfection of its correlations. Reason, when once it has considered and admired so much beauty and so much perfection, feels a just indignation at the dauntless folly which dares ascribe all this to chance and a happy accident. It must be that the Highest wisdom conceived the plan and Infinite power carried it into execution.[18]

19:4b–6 The psalmist sees the vaulted arch of heaven as a vast tent which God prepared **for the sun**. As the sun rises in the morning, it is **like a bridegroom coming out of his chamber**. The sun moves through the arc of the heavens like a **strong man** joyfully running a **race**. The course begins at the eastern end of the heavens and continues on down to the western horizon. We know, of course, that the sun does not actually rise

and set, but that the earth moves in relation to the sun, creating this illusion. But in poetic passages the Bible often uses the language of human appearance, just as we do in our everyday speech.

There is nothing hidden from the heat of the sun. It enjoys universal exposure, pervading every remote corner and crevice of the world.

19:7–9 But creation is only *one* of God's volumes of self-revelation. Verse 7 introduces us to Volume Two of God's revelation—**"the law of the LORD."** Both volumes glorify God and inspire the worship of thoughtful persons. Few commentators on the Psalms can resist quoting Kant's famous dictum:

The starry sky above me and the moral law in me, are two things which fill the soul with ever increasing admiration and reverence.[19]

But there is a difference between the two books of God. Creation reveals God as the Mighty One, the God of Power. But His Word reveals Him as the One who enters into covenant relationship with His people. God's *works* reveal His knowledge and power but His *Word* reveals His love and grace. Scientific truth may stimulate our intellect but spiritual truth convicts our heart and conscience!

In his eulogy of God's Word, David describes it not only as **the law of the LORD** but also as **the testimony of the LORD, the statutes of the LORD, the commandment of the LORD, the fear of the LORD**, and **the judgments of the LORD**. The psalmist attributes eight excellent qualities to the Word of God; it is **perfect, sure, right, pure, clean, enduring, true**, and **righteous**. Then he lists five of its wonderful ministries: it converts **the soul**, makes **wise the simple**, rejoices **the heart**, enlightens **the eyes**, and warns the servant of God.

19:10 The values of the Word cannot be computed in terms of **gold**. But it does have this one thing in common with gold: persons must dig for its treasures. Great wealth is hidden in the pages of God's Book, and our best interests are served by searching for them.

It is the glory of God to conceal a matter,
But the glory of kings is to search out a matter (Prov. 25:2).

I can truly say that no prospector is ever more delighted with the discovery of gold than I am to find nuggets of spiritual treasure in the Bible! Much as I like **honey**, its taste is never as sweet to me as the taste of the good Word of God! No words can ever describe the enrichment and satisfaction I have found in my Bible.

This old book is my guide;
'Tis a friend by my side.
It will lighten and brighten my way.
And each promise I find
Soothes and gladdens my mind
As I read it and heed it each day.
—*Edmund Pillifant*

Incidentally, there is a beautiful touch in the expression **"sweeter also than honey and the** drippings of the **honeycomb."** The purest honey is that which drips from the comb rather than being pressed out.

19:11 Morever, by them Your servant is warned. By the Scriptures the believer is taught to resist the devil, flee from temptation, hate sin and avoid the very appearance of evil. In obeying the precepts of the Word, the Christian finds true fulfillment in

life. Spiritually, physically, and mentally he enjoys the good life! On top of all this, he accumulates **reward** to be bestowed at the Judgment Seat of Christ. "Godliness is profitable for all things, having promise of the life that now is and of that which is to come" (1 Tim. 4:8).

19:12 But when we think of how holy, just and perfect the law of the Lord is, we realize what failures we are, and we exclaim with David, **"Who can understand his errors?"** Barnes writes:

In view of a law so pure, so holy, so strict in its demands, and so extended in its requirements—asserting jurisdiction over the thoughts, the words and the whole life—who can recall the number of times he has departed from such a law? A somewhat similar sentiment is found in Psalm 119:96: "I have seen an end of all perfection; Thy commandment is exceeding broad."[20]

As the Scriptures expose us to ourselves and convict us of sins we were previously unaware of, we are prompted to pray for forgiveness from **secret faults**—faults hidden to ourselves and even to others but not to God. Sin is sin, even if we are ignorant of it. So our confession should always cover hidden sins.

19:13 But the Psalm teaches us to pray not only for clearing from unknown sins, but for preservation **from presumptuous sins**, that is, from **sins** that are born of pride and self-confidence. Pride was the parent sin of the universe. It led to Lucifer's original rebellion against God. More than anything else, the psalmist feared the dominion of such **presumptuous sins** in his own life. If he can escape their domination, he writes, he **shall be innocent of great transgression**—

specifically, the **great transgression** of departing from God and revolting against Him.

19:14 The eulogy is finished. David has extolled the book of creation and the book of revelation. Now he lifts a parting prayer for his **words** and **meditation** to **be acceptable** in the **sight** of the LORD, his **strength** (lit. "Rock") and his **Redeemer**. When God is referred to as a rock, the figure is designed to express **strength**, security, and salvation. As our **Redeemer**, God in Christ is the One who buys us back from sin, servitude, and shame.

Psalm 20: The Name of the God of Jacob

The nation is on the brink of war. Before leading his troops off into battle, King **David** has come to offer sacrifices. A multitude of loyal subjects are there to wish him success. In verses 1–5 we hear them praying that the Lord will protect him and give him victory. Encouraged by his people's prayers, the king expresses confidence that Jehovah will intervene on his behalf (v. 6). His confidence overflows to the people, and their prayers are now mixed with assurance of deliverance (vv. 7–9).

The People's Prayer (20:1–5)

20:1 On the eve of battle the people look to **the LORD** to **answer** the king in the approaching battle by turning back the enemy in crushing defeat. When they chant "**May the name of the God of Jacob defend you**," they remind us that the name of God stands for the Person Himself. Three times in this Psalm we find references to that wonderful name:

May the name of the God of Jacob defend you (v. 1).

In the name of our God we will set up our banners (v. 5).

We will remember the name of the LORD our God (v. 7).

Williams aptly alliterates these allusions as:

The Defending Name.
The Displayed Name.
The Delivering Name.

20:2 The source of the desired aid is specified. The **sanctuary** in **Zion** was the dwelling place of God on earth, and so it was reasonable to expect **help from the sanctuary** and support **out of Zion**.

20:3 The king's faithful obedience in bringing **offerings** and **burnt sacrifice** is presented as a special reason why the Lord should **remember** him with favor.

20:4, 5 The king's **desire** was that the Lord should crown his plans and **purpose** with success. Here his loving people pray that this will indeed be the outcome of the battle. They are already thinking of a great victory celebration, with hilarious joy and excitement as the news is announced and with **banners** whipping and snapping in the breeze in tribute to **the name of** their **God**.

There is a question whether the words "**May the LORD fulfill all your petitions**" are spoken by the people, the priest, or the king. In any case it is a worthy prayer.

The King's Response (20:6)

Buoyed by the prayerful interest of his people, the king rejoices in the knowledge that **the LORD** will indeed send all needed help from **His holy heaven** and intervene with marvelous displays of His infinite **strength**.

The People's Confident Prayer (20:7–9)

20:7, 8 Such confidence is contagious. The devoted people, inspired by the assurance of their leader, are no longer awed by the vaunted military might of the enemy. Let him boast of his invulnerable **chariots** and battle-tested **horses**; Israel will boast in **the name of the LORD**! It is better to trust in Him than in arsenals of stockpiled weapons. At the glance of the Lord even the mightiest armies will crumple to the ground! But those who are on the Lord's side will still **stand upright** when the smoke of battle has cleared away.

20:9 With this peace of mind, the people once again ask the **LORD** to give victory to **the King**, thereby answering their prayers for deliverance.

Application

The historical application of the Psalm may be found in David's defeat of the Ammonites and Syrians (2 Sam. 10:14–19).

But the Psalm may also be applied to the Lord Jesus as a prayer for His Resurrection. His believing people pray that God will indicate His own complete satisfaction with Christ's sacrifice at Calvary by raising Him from the dead. As Messiah engages in conflict with Satan and his armies, He is confident of the final outcome. Psalm 20 anticipates the exultation of the first Easter morning.

The Psalm can also be applied to missionaries moving out into Satan's territory, or to any Christian striving to gain new ground for the Lord.

Psalm 21: Thanksgiving for Victory

There is a close link between this Psalm and the preceding one. There we heard the people praying for victory for the king as he went off to war. Here the prayer has been answered, and these same people rehearse the victory with the Lord. First they review the thrilling way in which God gave success (vv. 1–7). Then they anticipate the final subjugation of all the king's foes (vv. 8–12). Finally they extol the strength and power of Jehovah (v. 13).

The Sweet Taste of Victory (21:1–7)

21:1–4 **The king** rejoices in the way the **LORD** has just revealed His **strength** as the God of battle. He overflows with exultation when he thinks of Jehovah's timely intervention. God has given him the victory he craved, the success for which he prayed. Jehovah went out to **meet him with the blessings** of triumph and prosperity. The Most High **set** an imperishable **crown of pure gold upon his head**. In response to the king's request for preservation God **gave** him **life**—yes, **length of days forever and ever**. This latter expression probably means long life in David's case, but it is literally true of the endless resurrection life of the Messiah.

21:5–7 This passage takes on added beauty when we see them as referring to the Lord Jesus Christ. God's saving help has given Him great **honor**. By raising Him from the dead and seating Him at His own right hand, God has crowned Him with **glory** and **honor** (Heb. 2:9). Yes, the Lord has **made him most blessed forever** and a blessing to all the world! Seated in the highest place, Christ is filled with joy in the presence of His Father. It was His undivided trust **in the LORD** that brought Him to this place of honor. And it is **the mercy of the Most High** that will insure His perpetual exaltation.

The Doom of the King's Enemies (21:8-12)

21:8-10 At this point the people address the king directly. (In the previous section they had been speaking to the Lord.) If we identify the king as the Messiah, the passage describes the doom of Christ's enemies at the time of His Second Advent.

His **right hand will** ferret out **all** His **enemies**; none of those who **hate** Him will escape. The instrument of their destruction will be fire; He will be "revealed from heaven . . . in flaming fire taking vengeance on those who do not know God, and on those who do not obey the gospel of our Lord Jesus Christ" (2 Thess. 1:7, 8). He will also destroy **their offspring from** off the face of **the earth, and their descendants** from the human race.

21:11, 12 This **plot** to thwart Christ from taking the reins of universal government (also described in Ps. 2:2, 3) will fail dismally. The rebels will retreat in terror when God fires at them point-blank!

Praise the Lord (21:13)

In the closing stanza, the LORD is **exalted** because of the way He has revealed His **own strength**. Songs of praise burst forth because of God's **power** unleashed to deliver His own and to put down all His enemies. It is the song of Israel's remnant, praying for the exaltation of the Messiah and acknowledging Him at last as Lord of all.

Psalm 22: Christ in Suffering and Glory

Deserted! God could separate from
  His own essence rather;
And Adam's sins have swept
  between the righteous Son and
  Father;

Yea, once, Immanuel's orphaned
  cry His universe hath shaken—
It went up single, echoless, "My
  God, I am forsaken!"
It went up from His holy lips,
  amid His lost creation
That no believer e'er should use
  those words of desolation.
    —*Elizabeth Barrett Browning*

22:1, 2 Approach this Psalm with the utmost solemnity and reverence, because you have probably never stood on holier ground before. You have come to Golgotha where the Good Shepherd is giving His life for the sheep. For three hours the earth has been enveloped in thick darkness. Now "Immanuel's orphaned cry" echoes through the universe: **"My God, My God, why have You forsaken Me?"**

Behind the poignant question lies an awful reality—the suffering Savior actually *was*, literally and completely, **forsaken** by **God**. The eternal Son who had always been the object of His Father's delight was now abandoned. The Perfect Man who unfailingly did the will of God experienced the terrible desolation of being cut off from God.

The question is, "Why?" Why should the holy, sinless Son of God suffer the concentrated horror of eternal hell in those three long hours of darkness? Scripture gives us the answer. First of all, God is holy, righteous and just, and this means that He must punish sin wherever He finds it. To wink at sin or to overlook it is impossible for God. That brings us to the second point. Although the Lord Jesus had no sins of His own, He took our sins upon Himself. He voluntarily assumed responsibility to pay the penalty of all our iniquities. The debt we owed was charged to

His account, and He willingly became surety for it all. But now what can God do? All His righteous attributes demand that sin be punished. Yet here He looks down and sees His only begotten Son becoming the scapegoat for others. The Son of His love has become our sin-bearer. What will God do when He sees our sins laid on His own beloved Son?

There was never any doubt as to what God would do! He deliberately unleashed all the fury of His righteous wrath on His own beloved Son. The fierce torrent of divine judgment broke upon the innocent Victim. For our sakes, Christ was **forsaken** by **God** so that we might *never* be forsaken.

Thus when we read of Christ's deep, deep suffering, it should always be with the keen awareness that He bore it all for us. We should punctuate each statement with the words *for me*. He was forsaken—*for me*. When I hear Him cry, **"Why are You so far from helping Me, and from the words of My groaning?"** I know that it was for *me*. And it was for my sake that the heavens were silent to Him by day and by **night**.

22:3 In a sense the Savior explained His forsakenness in the words, **"But You are holy, who inhabit the praises of Israel."** The love of God demanded that sin's wages be paid. God's love provided what His holiness demanded. He sent His Son to die as a substitutionary sacrifice. Now "stern justice can demand no more, and mercy can dispense her store."

22:4, 5 But listen again! The Savior is still speaking to His Father, reminding Him that the patriarchs were never forsaken. Their believing cries for help never went unanswered. Not once were they disappointed when **they cried** for deliverance. In spite of their sin and waywardness, God never had occasion to forsake them. *That* sentence was reserved for the spotless Lamb of God!

22:6, 7 Not only was He forsaken by God, but He was **despised** and rejected **by the people**. To the creatures whom His hands had made Christ was hardly even a **man**—just **a worm**. He knew the bitterness of scorn and rejection by the very people He had come to save. Even as Christ hung on the cross, the watching throng ridiculed and mocked the Eternal Lover of their souls! Incredible as it seems, they sang a taunt song in which they mocked His apparent helplessness and the seeming futility of His trust in God.

22:8 **"He trusted in the LORD, let Him rescue Him; let Him deliver Him, since He delights in Him!"** This is exactly what the jeering crowd said at the cross (Matt. 27:39, 43).

22:9–11 **But** now the Son of Man turns away from man to God, and remembers Bethlehem. It was God who had brought Him forth from the virgin's **womb**. It was God who had preserved Him during the fragile days of His infancy. It was God who had sustained Him in His boyhood and young manhood. On the basis of this past relationship of love Christ now appeals to God to draw near in this hour of His crushing, solitary trial.

22:12, 13 **Many** of the hate-filled crowd at Calvary were Israelites. Christ likens them here to **strong bulls of Bashan** and to **a raging and roaring lion**. The district of **Bashan**, east of the Jordan, was known for its rich pasture-land and for its strong, well-fattened animals. Amos later referred to the luxury-loving Israelites as cows of Bashan (Amos 4:1). When Christ speaks here of **bulls of Bashan**, He is referring to His own fellow countrymen, who were even then waiting to close in for the kill. They were not only like goring **bulls** but also like ravening and roaring lions. The Messiah of Israel had come, and they were pouncing on Him like lions on a lamb!

22:14, 15 Christ's physical sufferings were excruciating beyond description. There was His exhaustion; He was **poured out like water**. There was the agony of bone dislocation by hanging on the cross; **all** His **bones** were **out of joint**. There was violent disorder of His internal organs; His **heart**, for instance, was **melted like wax within** His breast. There was His unendurable weakness; His **strength** was **dried up like** a fragment of pottery. There was His unremitting thirst; His **tongue** was clinging **to** His **jaws**. It could only mean that God was laying Him in **the dust of death**.

22:16, 17 Just as He had spoken of His *Jewish* tormentors under the figure of *bulls* and *lions*, so He now compares His *Gentile* executioners to **dogs**. It was a common name for Jews to use in referring to Gentiles (Matt. 15:21–28). Here it refers particularly to the Roman soldiers who **surrounded** Him like a pack of vicious, snarling curs. It was this company of evil-doers who had **pierced** His **hands and** His **feet**. As they gazed upon His half-naked form, they could see His **bones** pressing out against His shrunken skin. This gave them keen pleasure and satisfaction.

22:18 Then, in one of the several wonderful prophecies of this Psalm, the Lord Jesus foresees that the soldiers would **divide** His **garments among them** and **cast lots** for His **clothing**. Here is how it happened hundreds of years later:

Then the soldiers, when they had crucified Jesus, took His garments and made four parts, to each soldier a part, and also the tunic. Now the tunic was without seam, woven from the top in one piece. They said therefore among themselves, "Let us not tear it, but cast lots for it, whose it shall be" (John 19:23, 24).

22:19–21 For the last time in this Psalm the Savior implores God for His presence and assistance. He asks to be delivered **from the sword** and **from the power of the dog**, both references to the Gentiles. **The sword** is the symbol of governmental power (Rom. 13:4). Here, it refers to the Roman government with its power of capital punishment. **The dog**, as explained above, refers to the Gentile soldiers. Then, in verse 21, Christ asks to be saved **from the lion's mouth and from the horns of the wild oxen**. As we saw in verses 12 and 13, this refers to the Jewish people who said to Pilate, "We have a law, and according to our law He ought to die . . ." (John 19:7).

"You have answered Me" makes a distinct and triumphant break between verses 21 and 22. It is the hinge which unites the two sections of the Psalm. The poetry now obviously moves from plaintive pleading to jubilant song. The sufferings of the Lord Jesus are now forever past. His redeeming work has been finished. The cross has been exchanged for the crown!

Between these two verses the psalmist transports us in a moment of time from Christ's First Advent to His Second—from Calvary to Olivet! Although the Psalm does not mention it, we know that the intervening period includes the Savior's death, burial, Resurrection, and Ascension as well as the entire Church Age in which we live.

22:22 By this point in the Psalm Christ has returned to earth to reign as King. The faithful remnant of the nation of Israel has entered the kingdom with all its millennial glories. The Messiah of Israel is ready to testify to His Jewish **brethren** about the faithfulness of God in answering His prayers in the first part of the Psalm. Now Christ praises God **in the midst of the congregation**.

22:23, 24 The next two verses give the substance of what Christ will say to redeemed Israel in that future millennial day. In three majestic parallelisms Christ addresses them as **"you who fear the LORD," "you descendants of Jacob,"** and **"you offspring of Israel."** Then He exhorts them to **praise** the Lord, to **glorify Him** and to **fear Him**. The reason for this reverent response is that God has heard and answered those anguished cries that went up from dark Calvary. God did not despise the sufferings endured by His beloved Son, nor did He permanently hide His face from Him. Instead, "God . . . has highly exalted Him and given Him the name which is above every name, that at the name of Jesus every knee should bow . . . and that every tongue should confess that Jesus Christ is Lord, to the glory of God the Father" (Phil. 2:9–11).

22:25 God is the object of Messiah's **praise**: **"My praise shall be of You in the great congregation. . . ."** In His distress Christ had vowed to praise the Lord publicly, and now He **will pay** those **vows before those who fear** the Lord.

22:26 In the last six verses of the Psalm there is a change of speaker. Now the Holy Spirit speaks, describing the ideal conditions that will prevail during the peace and prosperity of the Millennium.

Poverty will then be banished; **the poor shall eat and be satisfied**. The earth will be full of God's **praise. All who seek Him will praise the LORD.** On all these worshipers the Spirit pronounces the blessing, **"Let your heart live forever!"**

22:27 There will be worldwide revival. **All the ends of the world shall remember** what Christ did at Calvary **and turn to the LORD. All the families of the nations** will unite in one great act of homage and **worship**.

22:28, 29 The Lord Himself will exercise worldwide dominion. The throne rights are His, and He will rule **over the nations**. All the great men of the earth will submit to His rule, and every mortal man **shall bow** down **before Him—all those who go down to the dust** and **who cannot keep** themselves **alive**.

22:30, 31 Christ's fame will endure. One generation after another will **serve Him** and proclaim His excellencies. A special message will be passed down from one **generation** to the next: that Christ has righteously finished the great work of redemption. Psalm 22 begins with the *fourth word* from the cross—the atonement cry. It ends with the words **"that He has done this,"** which have exactly the same meaning as Christ's *seventh word* from the cross: "It is finished!" (John 19:30). Down through the centuries of time the good news will be passed from one generation to another with grateful wonder that Christ **has done** it all.

Psalm 23: The Great Shepherd

The Twenty-Third Psalm is probably the best-loved poem in all literature. Whether sung to the stately measures of Crimond or recited in a Sunday School program, it has a charm that is perennial and a message that is deathless. "Blessed is the day," wrote an old theologian, "when Psalm 23 was born!"

J. R. Littleproud's outline is hard to improve upon:

The secret of a happy life—every need supplied.
The Lord is my shepherd; I shall not want.

The secret of a happy death—every fear removed.
Yea though I walk through the valley of the shadow of death, I shall fear no evil; for You are with me.

The secret of a happy eternity—every desire fulfilled.
Surely goodness and mercy shall follow me all the days of my life, and I will dwell in the house of the Lord forever.[21]

23:1 Despite its worldwide popularity, the Psalm is not for everyone. It is applicable only to those who are entitled to say, **"The Lord is my Shepherd."** It is true that the Good Shepherd died for all, but only those who actually receive Him by a definite act of faith are His sheep. His saving work is *sufficient* for all, but it is *effective* only for those who actually believe on Him. Everything therefore hinges on the personal pronoun *my*. Unless He is *my* Shepherd, then the rest of the Psalm does not belong to me. On the other hand, if He is really mine and I am really His, then I have everything in Him!

23:2 I shall not lack food for my soul or body because **He makes me to lie down in green pastures**.

I shall not lack refreshment either because **He leads me beside the still waters**.

23:3 I shall not lack vitality because **He restores my soul**.

I shall not lack moral direction because **He leads me in the paths of righteousness for His name's sake**.

We smile at the youngster who panicked when reciting this Psalm and came up with the novel version, "The Lord is my shepherd: I should not worry." But he was more right than wrong. He missed the exact words but caught the exact sense. If the Lord is our Shepherd, we need not worry!

23:4 And we need not be afraid of death. In **the valley of the shadow of death** there is no need to **fear**, because the Shepherd is right there **with** us. The sting of death is sin—sin unconfessed and unforgiven. But Christ has robbed death of its sting for the believer. He has put away our sins once for all. Now the *worst* thing that death can do to us is really the *best* thing that can happen to us! Thus we can sing:

O death, O grave, I do not fear your power;
The debt is paid.
On Jesus in that dark and dreadful hour
Our sins were laid.
—*Margaret L. Carson*

It is true that Christians may have a certain foreboding about the suffering that so often accompanies death. As one old saint was overheard to say, "I don't mind the Lord taking down my tent, but I hope He takes it down gently!"

It is also true that we usually do not get dying grace until we need it. But the fact still remains that death has lost its terror for us because we know that dying means going to be with Christ—and this is far better. "To die is gain."

The Shepherd's **rod** and **staff** are sources of **comfort**, protection, and guidance. Whenever necessary He may use the rod for correction also. Most sheep need this ministry from time to time.

23:5 In the meantime, the Shepherd prepares **a table before** us **in the presence of** our **enemies**. On the **table** are spread all the spiritual blessings which He purchased for us with His precious blood. The **table** pictures everything that is ours in Christ. Though surrounded by **enemies**, we enjoy these blessings in peace and security.

J. H. Jowett illustrates:

> Eastern hospitality guarantees the security of the guest. "All the hallowed sanctions of hospitality gather around him for his defense. He is taken into the tent, food is placed before him, while his evaded pursuers stand frowningly at the door."

He also anoints our heads **with oil**. Shepherds anoint the heads of their sheep to soothe the scratches and wounds. For priests the anointing oil speaks of consecration to their work. For kings the anointing oil is associated with coronation. Every believer is anointed with the Holy Spirit the moment he receives the Savior. This anointing guarantees him the teaching ministry of God the Spirit.

When we think of all the riches of grace which we have in Christ Jesus, we burst forth with the grateful acknowledgment, **"My cup runs over!"**

> His love has no limit,
> His grace has no measure,
> His power has no boundary known
>   unto men:
> For out of His infinite riches in Jesus
> He giveth, and giveth, and giveth
>   again.
> —*Annie Johnson Flint*

23:6 Finally there is the secret of a happy eternity. Escorted through **all** of **life** by God's **goodness and mercy**, we reach the Father's **house** at last, our eternal dwelling place. As we think of it all, we have to agree with Guy King when he said, "What lucky beggars we are!"

Psalm 24: Who Is the King of Glory?

The Twenty-Fourth Psalm looks forward to a glorious event which occurs at the end of the Great Tribulation. The thunders of God's judgments have ceased, the Lord Jesus has returned to earth and has put down all His foes, and Christ is now marching to Jerusalem to reign as King of kings and Lord of lords. This is a triumphal procession such as the world has never seen. Even as onlookers were once startled by the depths of the Savior's suffering, so they are now speechless at the height of His glory.

24:1, 2 As the throng nears the city, the announcement rings out that **the earth** and everything in it belong to God. It is a statement of divine ownership and of Christ's full right to reign. Then the reason is given. Christ is the One who made **the world**. It was He who gathered **the waters** together in one place and made the dry land appear. It was He who formed the rivers, some on the surface of the earth and some beneath the ground. So now He is coming to claim what is really His own but has been denied to Him for centuries.

24:3–6 The next four verses describe the kind of people who will enter the kingdom and enjoy the thousand-year reign of peace and prosperity. These are the believing remnant of Israel and the redeemed Gentiles who will go up to the temple in Jerusalem to worship. It might seem that these people qualify for the kingdom by their good character, but this is not the case. Their character is the *result* of their new birth from above, for unless a man is born again he can neither see nor enter the kingdom of God (John 3:3, 5). These people, then, are the noble saints who have come through great tribulation and have made their robes white in the blood of the Lamb.

Four traits of character are specified. They have **clean hands**; in other words, their actions are righteous and blameless. They have **a pure heart**; that is, their motives are sincere and their minds uncorrupted. They do not subscribe to falsehood in any form. And finally, they do not pervert justice by testifying to what is not true. Their **hands**, their **heart**, their **soul**, their lips are all righteous.

These are the kind of people who will be subjects in Christ's Millennial Kingdom. Though formerly ridiculed and despised by the ungodly, they will now be vindicated by the God of their salvation. Yes, these are the citizens of the Millennium—people who seek God's face, people who have received grace from the God who loves the unworthy.

24:7, 8 I like to think that the procession has been singing the words of verses 1–6 as they cross the Valley of the Kidron. But now their singing is interrupted by the clarion call of the herald at the head of the parade. He calls out to the watchmen at the gates of Jerusalem: **"Lift up your heads, O you gates! And be lifted up, you everlasting doors! And the King of glory shall come in."** A sentry on the wall of the city calls back in loud, impressive tones, **"Who is this King of glory?"** The answer comes back in clear, stentorian words, **"The**

LORD strong and mighty, the LORD mighty in battle."

24:9, 10 They are closer to the city now, and the **gates** are still hesitating. So the herald commands again that the doors be opened to **the King of glory**. Again he is asked to identify the King. He responds, **"The LORD of hosts, He is the King of glory."**

Then the King enters the city with His loyal subjects to take the scepter of universal dominion in His nail-pierced hand.

F. B. Meyer says:

This Psalm is accomplished in us when Jesus enters our hearts as our King to reign, and it will have its full realization when the earth and its population welcome Him as its Lord.[22]

Psalm 25: The Secret of the Lord

This is an acrostic Psalm, though one letter of the Hebrew alphabet is omitted, and one is used twice.[23] It is difficult to find a unified theme; instead, the Psalm seems to be a potpourri of prayers and meditations with the only apparent link being the alphabetical one.

25:1–3 First comes a prayer for protection. David's enemies are never far away, it seems. So he looks to the LORD for help, acknowledging **God** as the sole object of his **trust**. David's dual supplication is that he will never be disappointed for having trusted in Jehovah and that his **enemies** will never have occasion to gloat because God has failed His child. This is his prayer for *all* who depend on the Lord. As for those who deliberately deal falsely, he wishes them a full dose of shame.

25:4, 5 In the next section, the psalmist portrays a disciple seeking instruction. He wants to know the ways of the LORD, to walk in His **paths**, and to grow in His **truth**. His motivation arises from love for **the God of** his **salvation**, the One in whom all his expectations are bound up.

25:6, 7 Then David appears as a sinner seeking forgiveness. He appeals to the long-standing **mercies** and **lovingkindness** of the Lord and asks the Lord to remember that He has demonstrated such grace in the past— as if He could ever forget! If such requests betray an imperfect apprehension of God's grace on David's part, we must remember that he lived in an age of shadows while we enjoy the full light of the gospel era. . . . **The sins** of David's **youth** were bedeviling him; they have a way of doing that. The psalmist succinctly asks the Lord to forget these sins but to **remember** him **according to** His **lovingkindness** and for His **goodness' sake**. Such a prayer is irresistible. . . . What release there is in knowing that our sins are under the blood, removed as far as the east is from the west, buried in the sea of God's forgetfulness, forgiven forever!

25:8–10 David now moves from prayer to contemplation. He is lost in admiration as he thinks of the teaching ministry of Jehovah. Because **the LORD** is essentially **good and upright, He teaches sinners in the way of** truth, **justice**, and salvation. The single most important quality which we need to learn from Him is humility—we must be meek enough to admit our ignorance and our need for further instruction. If we are teachable we soon learn what is right, that is, what the will of God is. Far from having to endure an unpleasant life, those who obey the Word of the Lord find that life is filled with tokens of God's steadfast love and faithfulness.

25:11 David now returns briefly to prayer for forgiveness. Thoroughly convicted of the vastness of his guilt, he bases his appeal on **"Your name's sake, O LORD."** Since a person's name often stands for the person himself, the psalmist is here pleading God's own character—and especially His mercy and grace—as his only claim to **pardon**. There is not a word about David's own merit!

25:12, 13 Once again he interrupts his prayer to engage in a spiritual soliloquy. He envisions **the man that fears the LORD** as the one who enjoys God's best. This kind of person will experience:

Unmistakable guidance—God will show him the way to go.
Personal prosperity—he will enjoy abundant provision.
Family security—his children will possess the land.
Divine fellowship—he will be in the inner circle of friends to whom the Lord reveals His mind and ways in an intimate manner.

25:14 This is undoubtedly the golden verse of the Psalm:

The secret of the LORD is with those who fear Him;
And He will show them His covenant.

It was to Daniel, "a man greatly beloved," that God revealed the wonderful visions of Gentile governments superseded by the final kingdom of our Lord and Savior Jesus Christ. And it was to John, the disciple who leaned on Jesus' bosom, that the glorious revelation of Patmos was given.

25:15 David includes himself in this God-fearing group. His **eyes are** looking continually heavenward in trust and expectation, and he is confident that **the LORD** will extricate him from **the net** of trouble and affliction in which he is presently entangled.

25:16–21 The mention of a net causes David to cut short his spiritual reveries and to utter a prayer about his present plight. He is lonely **and afflicted. The troubles of** his **heart** are compounded. So he implores God to turn to him in **mercy**, to relieve his overburdened heart, to **deliver** him from his **distresses**, to take inventory of his afflictions and to **forgive all** his **sins**. David also asks the Lord to protect him from his **enemies** and their vitriolic **hatred**, thereby vindicating him for having trusted in Jehovah. When he prays **"Let integrity and uprightness preserve me"** he is not referring to his own rectitude, but is instead asking God to show His righteousness by delivering the one who put his trust in Him.

25:22 In the final verse, David identifies himself with **Israel** and prays for the nation's redemption. This suggests that a Psalm like this will become the language of the godly Jewish remnant during the coming days of the Tribulation.

Psalm 26: A Psalm of Separation

When we first read Psalm 26 we might conclude that it is the product of a surpassing egotist. More sober consideration, however, will show us that it is really just a factual description of a life that has been separated to God from the world. Reading between the lines, we find that David had been accused of fraternizing with ungodly men and of thus being untrue to Jehovah. Here he pleads his own defense. Nowhere is he claiming sinlessness, but he certainly does plead "not guilty" to the specific charges that were being made against him.

26:1–3 He rests his case with the LORD, asking for divine vindication. Contrary to what his accusers were saying, David had indeed conducted himself with moral **integrity**. He *had* consistently walked in dependence on the Lord. In language borrowed from metallurgy, he submits himself to God to be tested for genuineness and sincerity, to be proved in the smelting furnace for the presence of dross. Both as to his **heart** (affections) and his **mind** (motives), he was confident of acquittal because he had always kept the Lord's **lovingkindness** before him and had walked in paths of faithfulness to God's Word.

26:4, 5 To sit **with idolatrous mortals** means to have approving fellowship with them; this David had not done. To consort **with hypocrites** means to be a willing partner with deceivers and pretenders; David had not been this either. On the contrary, he had **hated** the companionship of criminals and had shown a holy determination to avoid fraternizing **with the wicked**.

26:6–8 But his separation was not merely *from wicked men*; it was *to God*. Before approaching the **altar** of the LORD, David had made sure that his **hands** were cleansed from sin and defilement. Then, as a purged worshiper, he sang a hearty **thanksgiving** and recounted the **wondrous works** of Jehovah. To him worship was not a dreary ritual to be endured stoically; he actually loved the **house** of the Lord where the **glory** cloud symbolized the glorious Presence of God Himself.

26:9–11 Because he had refused to join the gang in this world, David prays to escape their fate in the next. He had shunned the practices of **sinners**, murderers, and payoff men in life; now he pleads to escape their company in death. Because he had lived a righteous life, he now asks to be saved from the doom of the wicked, and to be handled with all the grace of God.

26:12 Standing on the level ground of an unblemished history, David vows to **bless the LORD . . . in the congregations**.

We should note that there is an aspect of separation that is not brought out in this Psalm. Though we should be separate from sinners as far as silent assent or complicity with their evil is concerned, we should not be isolated from them when it comes to telling them about their need of Christ. The Lord Jesus Himself was a friend of sinners; He not only received them but ate and drank with them. But He never compromised His loyalty to God or failed to tell them about their sin and their need of forgiveness. When He visited the house of Simon, says Bishop Ryle:

He carried His "Father's business" with Him to the Pharisee's table. He testified against the Pharisee's besetting sin. He explained to the Pharisee the nature of free forgiveness of sins, and the secret of true love to Himself. He declared the saving nature of faith. If Christians who argue in favor of intimacy with unconverted people will visit their houses in the spirit of our Lord, and speak and behave as He did, let them by all means continue the practice. But do they speak and behave at the tables of their unconverted acquaintances as Jesus did at Simon's table? That is a question they would do well to answer.[24]

This is a question that all of us should ponder.

Psalm 27: The Arrest and Trial of Jesus

Psalm 27 is beautiful in any setting, but it takes on a special attraction if we think of it as expressing our Lord's innermost thoughts during those fateful hours immediately preceding Calvary.

27:1 For example, when the chief priests, the captains of the temple and the elders came to the Garden of Gethsemane to capture Christ, He said to them, "This is your hour, and the power of darkness" (Luke 22:53). But at this very moment He may have been consoling Himself with the thought:

> The LORD is my **light** and my salvation;
> Whom shall I fear?
> The LORD is the strength of my life;
> Of whom shall I be afraid?

God was His **light** as the darkness settled in. God was His **salvation**, that is, His Deliverer from earthly enemies. God was the stronghold of His **life**, a refuge in the time of storm. With such protection, He need not **be afraid** of anyone!

27:2 When men came to arrest the Lord Jesus, He asked them, "Whom are you seeking?" They answered Him, "Jesus of Nazareth." As soon as He said "I am He," they recoiled and fell to the ground (John 18:6). At that moment Christ could well have been meditating on these words:

> When the wicked came against me
> To eat up my flesh
> My enemies and foes,
> They stumbled and fell.

They pounced on Him like birds of prey, but the glory of His deity as the Great I AM shone through His garb of humanity, and His captors were knocked to the ground.

27:3 John tells us that the gang

who came to arrest Jesus in the Garden consisted of a detachment of troops, several officers from the chief priests, and numerous Pharisees. They came with lanterns, torches, and weapons (John 18:3). As He watched them approaching, He could say with perfect composure:

> Though an army should encamp
>   against me,
> My heart shall not fear;
> Though war may rise against me,
> In this I will be confident.

27:4 Poor Peter tried to defend his Master by cutting off the ear of the high priest's slave. But Jesus replied to Peter, "Shall I not drink the cup which My Father has given Me?" His one desire was to dwell with God, and since the pathway to glory led first to the cross, He was prepared to endure its suffering and shame. His language was:

> One thing I have desired of the
>   LORD,
> That will I seek:
> That I may dwell in the house of
>   the LORD
> All the days of my life,
> To behold the beauty of the LORD,
> And to inquire in His temple.

There is something indomitable about "one-thing" people. They know what they want and are determined to get it. Nothing can stand in their way.

27:5 Finally the band of soldiers with their captain and the officers of the Jews seized Jesus and tied Him up (John 18:12). To the onlookers it must have seemed like a lost cause for the Lord Jesus. But at this very moment He may well have been saying:

> For in the time of trouble
> He shall hide me in His pavilion;

> In the secret place of His tabernacle
> He shall hide me,
> He shall set me high upon a rock.

His heart was resting on the protection which God has promised to all those who love Him.

27:6 The soldiers took Christ to Caiaphas, the high priest (Matt. 26:57). It was Caiaphas who had previously given counsel to the Jews that it was expedient for one man to die for the people (John 18:14). Though Christ's enemies planned to have Him lifted up on a cross between heaven and earth, our Lord Himself was anticipating another kind of lifting up:

> And now my head shall be lifted
>   up above my enemies all around
>   me;
> Therefore I will offer sacrifices of
>   joy in His tabernacle;
> I will sing, yes, I will sing
>   praises to the LORD.

Strange optimism, this, for a man on trial for His life and knowing that the outcome would be His execution! Yet even now He was delighting Himself with anticipations of glory. Did He not say to Caiaphas, "Hereafter you will see the Son of Man sitting at the right hand of the Power, and coming on the clouds of heaven" (Matt. 26:64)?

27:7, 8 At this, the high priest exploded with charges of blasphemy. "What do you think?" he demanded of his onlookers. "He is deserving of death," was their reply. Here I can picture the Savior praying silently:

> Hear, O LORD, when I cry with my
>   voice!
> Have mercy also upon me, and
>   answer me.
> When You said, "Seek My face,"
> My heart said to You,
>   "Your face, LORD, I will seek."

27:9 By this time the disciples had all forsaken Him and fled (Matt. 26:56). But God had been His help in the past, and now He pleads that God would not forsake Him at this crucial moment either.

Do not hide Your face from me;
Do not turn Your servant away in
    anger;
You have been my help;
Do not leave me nor forsake me,
O God of my salvation.

27:10 As far as we know, David's parents never forsook him, and neither did our Lord's. J. N. Darby probably translates the verse more accurately as follows:

For had my father and my mother forsaken me, then had Jehovah taken me up.

27:11, 12 At Christ's religious trial the chief priests and the whole council had solicited false testimony against Jesus in a determined effort to put Him to death. But they couldn't seem to concoct anything damaging until two witnesses appeared with the accusation, "This fellow said, 'I am able to destroy the temple of God and to build it in three days'" (Matt. 26:59–61). What Jesus had actually said (referring to the temple of His body) was, "Destroy this temple, and in three days I will raise it up" (John 2:19, 21). But since the whole trial was a sham anyway, the testimony was accepted. Now we can hear the Savior praying:

Teach me Your way, O Lord,
And lead me in a smooth path,
    because of my enemies.
Do not deliver me to the will of
    my adversaries;
For false witnesses have risen
    against me,
And such as breathe out violence.

27:13 Next we hear the frenzied mob outside Pilate's judgment hall screaming, "Let Him be crucified" (Matt. 27:22, 23). The blessed Lord Jesus heard the shouts too, and He knew what they meant. Yet He could have truly said at this very time:

I would have lost heart, unless
    I had believed
That I would see the goodness of
    the Lord
In the land of the living.

27:14 But how about the last verse of the Psalm? How does it fit into our interpretation? Well, I like to think that this verse is His parting word to each of us—a little personal advice from heaven based on the Lord's own experiences in trusting His Father.

Wait on the Lord;
Be of good courage,
He shall strengthen your heart;
Wait, I say, on the Lord!

Psalm 28: The Silence of God

28:1, 2 It's **to You** and You alone that I call, **O Lord**. You are **my Rock**, with all that that name implies of security, strength and stability. I beg You **not** to turn a deaf ear **to me**—if You do, it will be like being united with the wicked in death—utter separation from Yourself. **Hear** my pleading **voice** as I storm Your throne for help—as **I lift up my hands toward Your** inner **sanctuary**, the most **holy** place.

28:3 Never, never abandon **me** to the fate of **the wicked**, who ruthlessly plot **iniquity** against others, **who speak** so smoothly and peaceably **to their neighbors** while planning to do them in.

28:4 Lord, deal with them **according to** what they deserve, taking into account **their deeds** and the exceeding **wickedness of** what they do. Reward **them according to the work of their hands**—that which **they** richly **deserve**.

28:5 And not just because of *their* works, and the work of *their* hands, but because they have no appreciation for *Your* **works** and the **operation** of *Your* **hands**. That is why You will demolish them like a building that can never be rebuilt.

28:6 Lord, while I have been praying, Your Holy Spirit has given me that wonderful, inner assurance that **my supplications** have been **heard** and answered, and I bless You for it. Now I have a song to sing.

28:7, 8 Someone has made a beautiful metrical paraphrase of these verses:

The Lord's my strength; He is my shield
  On Him my heart relies.
So I am helped, my heart exults,
  To Him my thanks arise.
For all His chosen people too,
  The source of strength is He.
And for His blest anointed Son
  His saving strength shall be.

28:9 Lord, now that You have promised to deliver me, I ask one more thing. **Save Your people. Bless** Israel, **Your** heritage. Like the kind and tender Shepherd that You are, feed them well **and bear them up** in Your arms **forever**.

Thank You, Lord!

Psalm 29: The Voice of the Lord

29:1, 2 Do you ever complain about the weather? As David watched a thunderstorm sweep down over Israel it inspired him to praise rather than grumble. In fact he calls upon all the hosts of heaven to **worship the** LORD in full recognition of His **glory and strength** as revealed in the storm.

Oh, worship the Lord in the beauty
  of holiness,
Bow down before Him, His glory
  proclaim;
With gold of obedience, and incense
  of lowliness,
Kneel and adore Him; the Lord is
  His Name.
                              —*J. S. B. Monsell*

29:3, 4 The expression "**the voice of the** LORD" is used seven times. It seems to be applied to the storm in general and to the thunder in particular.

At first the storm **is over the** Mediterranean, moving inland to Lebanon. The thunder reverberates **over many waters** like an advancing cannonade. It is a sound of awesome power and **majesty**.

29:5,6 Now the mountains of **Lebanon** are being bombarded. Tall **cedars** go crashing under the lightning assault. As the wind passes over the forest in sudden, violent gusts, the trees bend in rhythmic waves, creating the impression that the Lebanese range is skipping **like a calf** and Mount **Sirion** (Hermon) **like a young wild ox**.

29:7, 8 The lightning is streaking southward. **The Wilderness of Kadesh** is shaken by the ferocity of nature's onslaught.

29:9 As David sees the storm fade away in the south, he summarizes his admiration in three observations. First he says that **the voice of the** LORD **makes the deer give birth**. It is a scientific fact that weather disturbances have a direct influence on animals that are about to deliver their young.

The psalmist sees the **forests** denuded of leaves. The trees stand gaunt and bare, robbed of their foliage in a matter of minutes.

Then the sweet singer of Israel reminds us that **in** God's **temple everyone** cries "Glory!" **His temple** here quite clearly means the world of nature, especially the area that is being convulsed by the storm. The arrows of lightning, the peals of thunder, the winds of gale velocity, the forests, the wilderness—all join in telling forth the power, **glory** and majesty of God.

29:10, 11 The storm has gone; **the LORD remains.** His throne is unmoved by earth's violent upheavals, including **the** great **Flood.** His sovereignty remains undisturbed by natural cataclysms. In all the tumults of life He is able to **give strength** and **peace** to **His people.** May He be pleased to do so!

Some Bible students believe that this Psalm prefigures a military storm that will sweep down from the north on the nation of Israel during the Tribulation (vv. 3–9). Following that troubled time, the Lord Jesus Christ will reign as King over all the earth and bless His earthly people with strength and peace (vv. 10, 11). The idea deserves serious consideration.

W. E. Vine sees the Psalm as picturing Christ in His Second Advent, appearing first at Har-Magedon (Rev. 16:16), then sweeping down to the wilderness of Kadesh, the center of which is Bozrah (Isa. 63:1).[25] The Psalm thus describes poetically the complete overthrow of the nations that will have invaded Israel at that time.

But then there is always the practical application for today and every day. God's voice is heard in the storms of life as well as in the sunshine. He is working out His purposes. Nothing is beyond His control. For those who know and love Him, He is working all things together for good. Ironside says:

> It is a wonderful picture of the soul that has gone through its exercises, its stress, its trouble, but has learned that God is over all, that He is strong to save. And so the heart rests in Him and is at peace.[26]

Psalm 30: A Song of Healing

Most of us have at one time or another experienced the delicious relief of recovery from a serious illness. We have said goodbye to the sterile world of surgery, anesthesia, intensive care, intravenous feedings, hypodermic injections and the interminable pill parade! It is too easy to think that our recovery was "thanks to modern medicine!" We forget to sing a psalm of thanksgiving to the One who is ultimately responsible for *all* our healing.

But **David** did not forget. It may be that he had just gotten over a critical illness when it came time to dedicate his **house.** In any case, the dedication was the occasion for this hymn of praise to Jehovah, his Healer.

30:1–4 It teaches us first of all to **extol** the LORD with undiluted thanksgiving for the return of good health. David had sunk very low. His life signs were feeble. His **foes** were all but gloating over his imminent demise. Then **he cried out to** the LORD in his extremity and the Lord answered by bringing him back from the brink. It was a narrow escape from the dissolution of Sheol, a close call from going **down to the** grave.

Psalm 30 teaches us that we should not only thank God ourselves, but that we should share our exuberance by inviting the **saints** to join us in **praise;** let the solo become a choir!

The sweet singer of Israel called on all God's people to **sing praise to the LORD** and to **give thanks** to **His holy name**.

30:5   Then he gives the reason for this praise in the form of two extraordinarily beautiful contrasts. Knox's translation of this verse is priceless:

> For a moment lasts His anger,
> for a life-time His love;
> sorrow is but the guest of a night,
> and joy comes in the morning.

Let me pause here with a personal story. There was a time when the MacDonald family was plunged into deep sorrow. Friends trooped in to express their condolences, but nothing seemed to assuage the grief. Their words were well-intentioned but inadequate. Then Dr. H. A. Ironside sent a brief note in which he quoted Psalm 30:5:

**Weeping may endure for a night,
But joy comes in the morning.**

That did it. The bands of sorrow were snapped!

Since then I have had occasion to share this verse with many other believers who were passing through the dark tunnel of grief, and always the verse has evoked a nod of gratitude.

30:6, 7   The next lesson in the Psalm is that we should not rest in material **prosperity** but in God. Before his illness David was prosperous and self-reliant. He thought he was immune from trial and trouble. He was apparently immovable—like a great **mountain**. He had cushioned himself with every conceivable form of protection and security. It seemed he had nothing to fear.

But then something happened. As if overnight, the Lord seemed to hide His **face**; it seemed as if He were angry and had withdrawn His favor. Life became a nightmare.

30:8–10   But the nightmare produced a sudden change in David's prayer life. In his prosperity his prayers had been dull and listless. But now in his illness he prayed intently and sincerely. He reasoned with God that if he died, this would not benefit the Almighty. The lifeless remains of the psalmist could not **praise** Him, nor could his **dust declare** God's faithfulness.

**What profit is there in my blood,
When I go down to the pit?
Will the dust praise You?
Will it declare Your truth?**

To us such an argument does not carry much weight. In fact, it seems grossly deficient from a doctrinal standpoint. But we must be careful not to be too severe on the OT saints. In many ways they saw through a glass darkly. We have two illustrations of this in the Psalm before us.

In verse 5 David had interpreted his illness as a sign of God's anger. We know that God's chastening is a sign of His love, not of His anger (Heb. 12:6). Yet even we ourselves often slip into the fallacious thinking that sickness and suffering are marks of His displeasure.

Then in verse 9 David speaks as though death ends all praise on the part of the believer. As far as praise and witness on this earth are concerned, he is of course correct. But we know from NT teaching that a believer's spirit departs to be with Christ at the time of his death while his body goes into the grave (2 Cor. 5:8; Phil. 1:23). The believer himself is in the conscious presence of the Lord, worshiping Him in a way he never could on earth. The OT saints could not have known this. Christ is the One who brought life and immortality to light through the gospel (2 Tim. 1:10).

But the remarkable thing is this: with their more limited knowledge in many areas, many OT saints seem to have outstripped us in faith, prayer, zeal and devotion!

30:11 Now back to David. Verses 9 and 10 give us his prayer to God when he was in the throes of his illness. Then between verses 10 and 11 the answer comes. He is healed by the Lord. The last two verses of the Psalm celebrate his recovery. For David it was like the difference between the **mourning** of a funeral and the joy of a wedding. Or to change the figure, it was like a new suit of clothes. God had removed his **sackcloth** and dressed him up in garments of **gladness**.

30:12 One result of David's healing was that he could now **praise** the Lord in life rather than lying **silent** in the grave. And that is exactly what he intended to do—to **give thanks to** the Lord **forever**. He says, in effect, "I can never forget what the Lord has done for me, and I'll never cease to praise Him for it."

I don't know what this Psalm does to you, but it makes me feel ashamed. I think of all the times I've been sick, and of the urgent, desperate prayers with which I stormed the gates of heaven, and of how the Lord graciously answered. But then I forgot to come before Him with a thank-offering of praise. I took the healing too much for granted. I neglected to express my thanks.

God has given us David's example not only for us to admire but to follow as well!

Psalm 31: Into Thy Hand

The fifth verse of Psalm 31 alerts us that it has a definite association with the suffering, dying Lamb of God, for these words formed His final cry from the cross:

"Father, 'into Your hands I commend My spirit'" (Luke 23:46).

Of course, the fact that one verse in a Psalm is definitely associated with the Messiah does not require that all the other verses must be. However, in this particular Psalm every verse does seem to have at least some connection with Him.

There is a problem, though, in analyzing this Psalm. Instead of tracing the suffering, death, burial, and resurrection of the Lord Jesus in chronological order, the Psalm alternates back and forth between suffering and resurrection. But we must remember, as C. S. Lewis pointed out, that "the Psalms are poems, and poems intended to be sung; not doctrinal treatises, nor even sermons."[27]

Prayer for Deliverance (31:1–5a)

31:1 In the opening verses the Lord Jesus is praying to His Father from the cross. As the perfect man He has always lived in total dependence on God. Now, in the hour of His deepest anguish, He reaffirms His **trust** in the LORD as His sole and sufficient sanctuary. He asks that He might **never be ashamed** for having relied on God the Father. It is a very powerful prayer, reminding God that the honor of His name is inseparably connected with the Resurrection of His Son. It would be an act of **righteousness** for the Father to raise the Lord Jesus from among the dead. Were He not to do so, the Savior would be exposed as a victim of misplaced confidence and would thus be humiliated.

31:2, 3 In an elegant anthropomorphism, the lonely sufferer asks

God to lean over with His **ear** facing Calvary; then He asks God to hear His urgent plea and to run to His rescue **speedily**. He further asks the Lord to **be** His **rock of refuge**, steadfast and unmovable, and to be a strong bastion in which He can be safe from every peril.

Of course God already *was* His **rock** and **fortress**, His only **defense** and security.

> Other refuge have I none;
> Hangs my helpless soul on Thee.
> Leave, O leave me not alone,
> Still support and comfort me.
> —*Charles Wesley*

Once again Christ bases His appeal on the fact that the honor of God is at stake. **"For Your name's sake lead me and guide me."** Had not God promised to deliver the righteous? Indeed He had! Now He is asked to honor His name by delivering the Lord Jesus Christ out of death to Resurrection and glory.

31:4 A **net** of death had been carefully **laid** to capture and hold the Savior. Here Christ cries to God to **pull** Him **out of** this **net**, to rescue Him from the grave, for Jehovah is His refuge, safe and strong.

31:5a Luke writes that Jesus quoted the words of verse 5a with *a loud voice*. No man took Christ's life from Him; He laid it down voluntarily and in full possession of His faculties. These words have been repeated by dying saints of God down through the centuries since that time—by men like Luther, Knox, Hus and scores of others.

Praise for Resurrection (31:5b–8)

31:5b, 6 There is a distinct break in the middle of verse 5, a transition from death to Resurrection, a change from prayer to praise. True to His Word, God had **redeemed** His Holy One from death and the grave. It was a glorious vindication of His Son for trusting in the living **God**; those who trust in **vain idols** earn nothing but Jehovah's contempt!

31:7, 8 A song of praise now wings its way heavenward for the changeless love that hovered over God's beloved Son in His affliction. This was a love that took full account of all His **adversities**, that refused to abandon Him finally to the power of the enemy, that pulled the Savior out of the pit and **set** His **feet** on the **wide place** which is "Resurrection ground."

Deep Distress (31:9–13)

31:9, 10 But now we are brought back to the life of our Lord prior to His trial and Crucifixion. We are allowed to hear the prayers of the Man of Sorrows as He endured the bitter hatred of sinners. Despised and rejected by men, He turned to Jehovah in His distress and appealed for gracious consideration. His eyes were sunken through excessive grief, and His **soul** and **body** wasted away with weeping. He was worn out with **grief** and exhausted **with sighing**. His misery had sapped away His strength, and His very **bones** seemed fragile.

The only way **"My strength fails because of my iniquity"** can be applied to the sinless Savior is by understanding it to mean *our* **iniquity**, which He took upon Himself as our Sin-bearer. Otherwise the verse cannot have a Messianic connotation.

31:11–13 The patient Sufferer next speaks of Himself as an object of scornful contempt **among all** His **enemies** and a terrifying sight to His **neighbors**. They would cross the street to avoid Him or duck down an alley if they saw Him coming. He was quickly lost to their memory, discarded **like a**

broken dish. He heard the slander campaign that was being carried on against Him. Terror stalked Him day and night as men hatched plots to kill Him.

This picture of abject pathos and misery is sad enough for any man. But what shall we say when we learn that it was written to describe the Maker of the universe, the Lord of life and glory!

Prayer for Deliverance (31:14–18)

31:14–17a Sorrow and sighing give way to believing prayer. The One whom men reject confesses Jehovah as His Hope and the **God** of His life. He finds unspeakable comfort in the fact that His **times are in** the Father's **hand**. This comfort has been shared by God's trusting people as they have sung in sunshine and sorrow:

Our times are in Thy hand;
Father, we wish them there!
Our life, our souls, our all, we leave
Entirely to Thy care.
—*William F. Lloyd*

Following this affirmation of trust and submission, the Lord Jesus prays specifically that God will **deliver** Him **from the** clutches of His persecuting **enemies**. He asks that the Father might look down upon Him in favor. He pleads for salvation out of death, a plea based on the steadfast love of the Lord. Again He asks that He might never be disappointed as He looks to Jehovah alone as His Deliverer. The language is rhetorical, of course, emphasizing style at the expense of literalness. There was no possibility that Christ could ever have been put to shame for trusting in Jehovah. He knew that, and we know it. But we lose something if we insist on strict literalness when we read impassioned prayer or lyrical poetry.

31:17b, 18 Turning to **the wicked**, Christ prays that *they* might be the ones who are put to shame, who go speechless to Sheol. He asks that their **lying lips** might be silenced for their slander of the Holy Son of God. Some sincere people consider these verses sub-Christian in their tone, but the more you think of the ruthlessness of the criminals, the vileness of their crime, and the innocence of the Victim, the more you conclude that the language is not too strong!

God, the Great Refuge (31:19, 20)

Once again the Psalm moves from distress to delight, from petition to praise. In majestic cadence, the Lord Jesus extols His Father as the incomparable Hiding Place. He pictures God as the administrator of an inexhaustible storehouse of **goodness** treasured up for His believing people. To all who seek shelter in Him He waits to pour out these treasures abundantly in the presence of the sons of men. God's presence is a place where His chosen saints can hide from the malicious **plots of man**; He is adequate shelter from what Knox calls "the world's noisy debate."

Personal Gratitude (31:21, 22)

The Lord Jesus had experienced a wonderful demonstration of God's goodness when He was completely surrounded by foes, like a besieged city. In His alarm it seemed to Him as if He had been completely deserted by Jehovah. But though He was forsaken during those three awful hours on the cross, yet God heard His cry and raised Him from the dead.

Love the Lord! (31:23, 24)

Having tasted the love of God, Christ loves Him in return and rightly feels that everyone else should too.

Jehovah can be depended on to protect His believing ones and to mete out adequate punishment to arrogant rebels!

Any believer who is up against seemingly impossible odds can thus be strong and courageous in the assurance that no one can **hope in the LORD** in vain—ever!

Psalm 32: Forgiven!

Happiness is to be forgiven! It is an emotion that defies description. It is the relief of an enormous burden lifted, of a debt canceled, of a conscience at rest. Guilt is gone, warfare is ended, peace is enjoyed. To David it meant the forgiveness of his great transgression, the covering of his sin, the non-imputation of his iniquity, and the cleansing of his spirit from deceit. To the believer today it means more than the mere covering of his sin; that was the OT concept of atonement. In this age the believer knows that his sins have been put away completely and buried forever in the sea of God's forgetfulness.

32:1, 2 In Romans 4:7, 8 the apostle Paul quotes Psalm 32:1, 2 to show that justification was by faith apart from works even in the OT period. But the proof lies not so much in what David says as in what he does not say. He is not speaking about a righteous man who earns or deserves salvation. He is talking about a sinner who has been forgiven. And he makes no mention of works in describing the blessedness of the **forgiven** man. Through the Holy Spirit Paul deduces from this that David is describing the happiness of the one to whom God imputes righteousness apart from works altogether (Rom. 4:6).

32:3, 4 Next David switches to a minor key. After he had committed adultery with Bathsheba and plotted the death of Uriah, he steadfastly refused to confess his sin. He tried to sweep it all under the rug. Perhaps he rationalized that "time heals all things." But in his stubborn refusal to break, he was fighting against God and against his own best interests. He became a physical wreck, and it was all caused by his unrelieved anguish of spirit. He realized that God's **hand was heavy upon** him, blocking him, thwarting him, frustrating him at every turn. Nothing worked out right anymore. The gears of life never meshed. The carefree days had vanished, and continued existence was as unappealing as an arid wilderness.

32:5 After a year of this impenitence, David finally came to the place where he was willing to utter the three words that God had been waiting for—"I have sinned." Then the whole shameful story came out like pus from an abscess. Now there is no attempt to gloss over, to mitigate or to excuse. David finally calls sin by its real name—**"my sin . . . my iniquity . . . my transgressions."** As soon as he confesses, he receives the instant assurance that the Lord has forgiven **the iniquity of** his **sin**.

32:6 His experience of answered prayer moves him to pray that all God's people would prove their Lord in the same way. Those who live in fellowship with the Lord will be delivered in a time of distress. The rush **of great waters** will never reach them.

32:7 The one who had been so hard and impenitent is now contrite and broken. With keen gratitude he acknowledges that God is his **hiding place**, his protection from trouble, and the One who surrounds him **with songs of deliverance**.

32:8, 9 There is a question as to

whether verses 8 and 9 are the words of David or of the Lord. If we interpret them as David's language, then they remind us, in Jay Adam's words, that "the natural response of forgiveness is to help others by sharing one's own experience and specifically by counseling others in trouble."[28] If we adopt the other view, then it is the Lord replying to David's worship with a promise of guidance and a lesson on the need for constant yieldedness. It is the Father spreading a feast for the returned backslider. He offers supervised instruction about the pathway ahead and personal counsel in all the decisions of life. But there is also a word of caution. **Do not be like the horse**, restless to move ahead without command, **or like the mule**, obstinately refusing to go even when directed. Both animals need the bit and bridle in order to make them submissive and obedient. The believer should be so sensitive to the Lord's leading that he does not need the harsher disciplines of life to bring him into line.

32:10, 11 As far as David is concerned, the righteous man has it all over the wicked. There is no comparison. **Many sorrows** are the heritage of **the wicked**. But the humble believer is surrounded by the **mercy** of the Lord. So it is only fitting that the **righteous** should **be glad in the** Lord **and** should **shout for joy**.

Psalm 33: A New Song

There appears to be an unmistakable link between the first verse of this Psalm and the last verse of the preceding one. In both, the writer urges the righteous to rejoice in the Lord. But this Psalm elaborates the theme by telling why it is appropriate for the righteous to praise Him.

We should note that there is no mention here of active enemies, of persecution, of tribulation. It is rather a peaceful scene, with Israel dwelling in safety and the Lord acknowledged as the universal Sovereign. The Psalm thus belongs to the beginning of Christ's kingdom, when Gentile oppression has been smashed and the time of Jacob's trouble is past.

33:1, 2 The call to worship goes out to Israel in the first seven verses, then to the Gentiles as well in verse 8. **Praise** is so **beautiful** and so compelling that the sweetest and finest possible instrumental accompaniment should be utilized—**the harp** and **an instrument of ten strings**.

33:3 The **new song** is the song of redemption. It follows the forgiveness of sins (Ps. 32) and belongs to all who have been cleansed by the precious blood of Christ. But this **song** will be sung in a very special way by redeemed Israel at the outset of the Millennium (Rev. 14:3).

33:4 The new song celebrates **the word of the** Lord and **all His work.** His **word** is absolutely true and righteous, unchanging and trustworthy. **All His works** are **done in** faithfulness. This is seen in creation—"seedtime and harvest, cold and heat, winter and summer, and day and night" (Gen. 8:22). It is seen in providence. "All things work together for good to those who love God, to those who are the called according to His purpose" (Rom. 8:28). And it is seen in redemption—"If we confess our sins, He is faithful and just to forgive us our sins and to cleanse us from all unrighteousness" (1 John 1:9).

33:5 God is not only upright and faithful, upholding **righteousness and justice**, but the evidences **of the goodness of the** Lord are everywhere.

33:6, 7 The greatness of God is

seen in that He created **the heavens** and their starry **host** by no greater expenditure of energy than by speaking the energizing word. Just this easily did He confine the oceans within appointed limits. Some see these two utterances as a poetic veiled reference to Israel as the stars of the heavens (Gen. 15:5) and to the Gentile nations as the raging seas, bottled up at last by the Lord Jesus at His Second Advent.

33:8, 9 In any case, God is so great that all mankind should reverence Him and show Him the deepest respect. His word was the sound energy which became matter. By His command all creation came into being.

33:10, 11 Throughout human history the ungodly **nations** have collaborated to thwart God and to ruin His people. But, as Burns said, "The best-laid schemes o' mice an' men gang aft agley," or, as we would say, they often go haywire! God ultimately frustrates the cleverest plots hatched by His opponents. And nothing can hinder the accomplishment of His purposes. He will always have the last word, and whatever He plans will come to pass.

33:12 So the pathway of blessing lies in cooperating with God. Happy **is the nation** that acknowledges Jehovah as its **God**. This is **the people He has chosen as His own inheritance**.

33:13–17 As **the LORD looks** down **from heaven, He** has a perfect view of all mankind. Nothing escapes Him. He sees all that is done and, what is more, He knows the thoughts and intents of every heart. He sees some who fight with carnal weapons—and He chuckles at their folly. They depend on **army**, navy, and air force rather than on the living God. When will they learn that the finest cavalry can't bring them victory?

33:18, 19 God also sees those who trust in Him for salvation and who depend on His **mercy** for provision. These are the ones who please Him. He looks down on them with keenest favor.

33:20–22 There is no question which class the psalmist and his people belong to. They trust Jehovah as their Helper and Protector. They have found true happiness by putting all their confidence **in His holy name**. All they ask is that they might continue to bask in the sunshine of His steadfast love as they continue to depend on Him alone.

Psalm 34: Psalm of the New Birth

The historical background of this Psalm is found in 1 Samuel 21. In his flight from Saul, **David** had sought refuge with the Philistine king of Gath whose name was Achish, **or Abimelech**, according to the heading of the Psalm. (**Abimelech** may have been a title rather than a personal name.) Fearing that this enemy king might kill him, David had **pretended** to be crazy by making marks on the doors of the gate and letting his saliva drool down over his beard. The trick worked. The king didn't need any more madmen and so he dismissed David, who then escaped to the cave of Adullam. This episode was certainly not one of the more heroic or brilliant chapters in the psalmist's checkered career, but he nevertheless looked back upon it as a dramatic deliverance by the Lord, and so he wrote this Psalm to celebrate that event.

Believers down through the centuries have loved Psalm 34 because it expresses so eloquently their own testimony of salvation by grace through faith in the Lord. Let's look at the Psalm in this light.

34:1 Salvation from sin is a gift of such tremendous value that it should draw unceasing thanks from our hearts to the Giver. If we were to **bless the LORD at all times**, it could hardly be too much. If **His praise** were to **be continually** on our lips, we couldn't begin to exhaust the subject. No human tongue will ever be able to thank God adequately throughout all eternity.

34:2 The converted person boasts **in the LORD**—not in his own character or achievements. When we understand the gospel of grace we realize that *we* did all the sinning and *Christ* did all the saving. So our **boast** must be in Him alone. If those who are still in the grip of sin will hear and heed our testimony of full and free salvation, they too will joyfully awaken to realize that there is hope for them as well.

34:3 The well-saved soul isn't content to enjoy his redemption in isolation. The subject is so superlative that he calls on all his brotherhood to **magnify the LORD with** him **and** to **exalt His name** collectively. Some couples have this reference inscribed on their wedding rings.

34:4 When the Spirit of God begins to brood over the soul of the sinner, He implants in it a divine instinct to seek **the LORD**. Only later does the saved sinner realize that it was the *Lord* who was the original Seeker! It is as the hymn says:

I sought the Lord, and afterward I
  knew
He moved my soul to seek Him,
  seeking me;
It was not I that found, O Savior
  true.
No, I was found of Thee.
—*Anonymous*

Still, when we seek Him He answers, delivering us **from all** our **fears**—the fear of the unknown future, the fear of dying with our sins unconfessed and unforgiven, the fear of standing before the Judgment of the Great White Throne. When we trust Christ as Lord and Savior we hear His words of absolution: "Your sins are forgiven; go in peace!"

34:5 But this is not a private salvation—it is available to all. All those who look to Christ in faith become **radiant**. Frowns are transmuted to smiles of joy, and depression and despair give way to delight. No one who commits his life to the Lord will ever be disappointed; He cannot fail the trusting heart.

34:6 We come to Him in our poverty and rags, our humiliation and helplessness, and gladly confess our inability to procure our own salvation. We put our whole trust in Him. Our language is:

In my hand no price I bring,
Simply to Thy cross I cling.

The LORD hears our cry. Our poverty appeals to His unlimited resources. He stoops down and saves us **out of all** our **troubles**—out of the tangled web of sin which we had woven by our own hands.

34:7 The believer is not only saved, but kept as well. **The angel of the LORD**, that is, the Lord Jesus Christ Himself, serves as an encircling garrison for **those who fear Him**, delivering them from dangers seen and unseen. No sheep of His can ever perish (John 10:28).

34:8, 9 Those who know the Savior long to share Him with others. Like the four lepers in Samaria, they say, "We are not doing right. This is a day of good news, and we are silent and do not speak up" (2 Kings 7:9,

Amplified Bible). And so the evangel rings out, **"Oh, taste and see that the Lord is good; blessed is the man who trusts in Him!"**

This is the authentic, urgent invitation to the unconverted. We may reason, argue, resort to logic and marshal Christian evidences, but when all is said and done, a man must taste and see for himself. Murdoch Campbell writes:

We may argue about God, His existence, and the external evidences which the universe and providence provide. But only when His love and presence touch our hearts can we really know Him in His unspeakable goodness.[29]

Then follows the invitation to the converted. It is the call to the life of faith. The **saints** are invited to walk by faith and not by sight, and to experience God's marvelous, miraculous, and abundant provision. It is the message of Matthew 6:33:

But seek first the kingdom of God and His righteousness, and all these things shall be added to you.

34:10 While **young lions**[30] sometimes **lack** food and **suffer hunger, those who seek the Lord shall not lack any good thing**, for our Lord Jesus Christ is our great, all-sufficient Provider!

34:11 The grace of God not only saves, keeps, and provides but it instructs as well.

For the grace of God that brings salvation has appeared to all men, teaching us that, denying ungodliness and worldly lusts, we should live soberly, righteously, and godly in the present age, looking for the blessed hope and glorious appearing of our great God and Savior Jesus

Christ, who gave Himself for us, that He might redeem us from every lawless deed and purify for Himself His own special people, zealous for good works (Tit. 2:11–14).

So here the psalmist offers practical instruction to his sons on what constitutes the true **fear of the Lord. 34:12–15:**

1. A controlled **tongue**—one that is free **from evil** and **deceit**.
2. A separated walk—separated **from evil** and separated to **good** works.
3. A peaceable disposition—as Paul said, "If it is possible, as much as depends on you, live peaceably with all men" (Rom. 12:18).

Peter states in 1 Peter 3:9, "Knowing that you were called to this [blessing others], that you may inherit a blessing." He then quotes verses 12–16a of this Psalm to reinforce his teaching that we should not return evil for evil or reviling for reviling, but that we should rather bless. The blessing is the favor of the Lord; **His eyes are on the righteous, and His ears are open to their cry** (Ps. 34:15).

34:16 In quoting verse 16, Peter confined himself to the first half:

The face of the Lord is against those who do evil.

He did not quote the rest, which says: **To cut off the remembrance of them from the earth.**

The first part of the verse is true in any age. The second half will be fulfilled when the Lord Jesus Christ returns to the earth as King of kings.

34:17 **The righteous** have the unspeakable privilege of instant audience with **the LORD**. He **hears** them every time they cry and **delivers them out of all their troubles**. Barnes comments here, "No one has ever fully appreciated the privilege of being permitted to call upon God, the privilege of prayer."

Before leaving verse 17 we should note that the Lord does not deliver us *from troubles;* He delivers us *out of them*. Believers are not immune to troubles, but they do have a Mighty Deliverer! That's the crucial difference.

34:18 The LORD knows how to resist the proud, but He cannot resist a **broken** and contrite **heart**. He keeps Himself accessible to the brokenhearted, and is always on hand to rescue the crushed in **spirit**.

34:19 As already mentioned, the righteous do have **many afflictions**. Perhaps we will find someday that we have had more than the ungodly. But at least all our troubles are confined to *this* life. What is more, we do not have to bear them alone, for our eternal Friend is by our side. We have the assurance of complete and final deliverance from afflictions through the Resurrection of the Lord Jesus. Because He has risen from the dead, we too shall rise someday, forever free from sin, sickness, sorrow, suffering, and death!

34:20 But even in death, the Lord protects the bodies of His saints:

He guards all his bones;
Not one of them is broken.

This verse was fulfilled literally at our Lord's death:

But when they came to Jesus and saw that He was already dead, they did not break His legs. For these things were done that the Scripture should be fulfilled, "Not one of His bones shall be broken" (John 19:33, 36).

In this, of course, our Lord was the perfect antitype of the paschal lamb, about which it was written:

Nor shall you break one of its bones (Ex. 12:46).

34:21, 22 The last two verses of the Psalm hinge on the word "**condemned**." As for **the wicked**, calamity shall bring them down in death, and they **shall be condemned**. But the **servants of** Jehovah have One who redeems their soul, **and none of those who trust in Him shall be condemned**. Praise God, there is no condemnation for those who are in Christ Jesus! (See Rom. 8:1.)

Who shall condemn us now?
Since Christ has died, and ris'n, and
  gone above,
For us to plead at the right hand of
  Love,
Who shall condemn us now?
  —*Horatius Bonar*

And so the believer is saved, kept, and abundantly satisfied for time and eternity. It's a wonderful thing to be born again! That is the message of this Psalm.

Psalm 35: Friends Turned Traitors

35:1–3 In an innocent use of his imagination, **David** calls on God to arm Himself with a generous supply of weapons and to thereby deal summarily with those professed friends of the psalmist who turned out to be his cruel adversaries. The psalmist wants to see the LORD reach over for His **shield and buckler** and move into action, hurling His well-aimed **spear**, then saying to David in an aside, "I'll take care of them and be your Savior."

35:4–6 It would be even-handed justice for these would-be murderers to be ashamed and disgraced, and for their devilish plots to be repulsed and foiled. It would be a righteous thing for them to become as helpless and weightless as **chaff** in **the wind**, driven relentlessly by **the angel of the LORD** (the Lord Jesus Christ in one of His pre-incarnate appearances). Yes, it would be fitting retribution for **their way** to **be** as **dark and slippery** as ice, with the **angel of the LORD** in hot pursuit.

35:7, 8 They had no good reason for plotting against the psalmist as they did, for trying to capture him as if he were a wild animal. So now let the Lord lower the boom on them unexpectedly, and let them be caught in their own **net**!

35:9, 10 Then David will **be joyful in the LORD**, celebrating **His salvation.** All his being will join in acknowledging the LORD **as** the incomparable One who saves the defenseless from the superior power of his opponent, the helpless and needy from the spoiler.

35:11–14 To understand the psalmist's deep emotional involvement, we must realize that these people who are now testifying against him were once his friends. Now they malign him and accuse him of things of which he has no knowledge. For all the kindness he has shown to them, he is getting paid with hatred. No wonder he is disconsolate! **When** these same people **were sick**, it was another story. David had grieved over them sympathetically. He couldn't even eat. With his head bowed down in sorrow, he had prayed for them continually—just as he would for an intimate **friend or brother**. His mourning was as deep **as** when **one mourns** the death of **his** own **mother**.

35:15, 16 But when calamity and **adversity** struck David, they were elated. They rose up in a body to accuse him. They brought along railing derelicts from the street to defame him with a continuous tirade. Impertinently they taunted him in a rising crescendo, at the same time baring **their teeth** in hatred. The psalmist's experience makes us think of the Lord Jesus before Pontius Pilate or before Herod; much of the language here applies forcefully to what He endured.

35:17, 18 **How long** can the **Lord look** down **on** the injustice of it all before being moved to action? The time has come to **rescue** the innocent one from the havoc of his foes and to save his **precious life from** these human **lions**.

35:19–21 What a travesty it would be if those who are David's **enemies** for no good reason should have occasion to gloat over his downfall and wink their eyes in apparent triumph. They don't want peace—all they want is to concoct false charges against decent, law-abiding citizens. Whenever they see the slightest slip they say, "Aha, aha! Just as we predicted! We saw you do it."

35:22–25 But **You have seen** too, LORD. You've seen the whole miserable mess. Don't shut Yourself up in silent seclusion. Don't stay so **far from me**. It's time to **awake** and take resolute action to defend me and my righteous cause. I long for You to vindicate me—You always do what is right—and to thwart their desire to celebrate my collapse. Don't ever **let them** exult that they have seen their desires fulfilled, that they have succeeded in devouring me.

35:26 O Lord, see to it that those **who rejoice** to see me fall will be thoroughly disgraced. Dress them with ignominy **and dishonor** for the insolent way they have treated me.

35:27, 28 But may all those who

are hoping for my ultimate acquittal have reason to **shout for joy and be glad**. Let them bear witness that You are truly a great Lord because You take such a keen delight in the welfare of those who serve You. And **my tongue** won't be silent, either; it will be continually telling others about Your justice and Your praiseworthiness!

Psalm 36: Great Sin, Greater God

36:1–4 An **oracle** in the **heart** of David gives a vivid picture of **the transgression of the wicked**. The sinner abandons any **fear of God** that he might have had. **He flatters himself** that his crimes cannot be proved against him and punished. His speech is saturated with **wickedness** and deceit. He scorns a respectable, law-abiding life. When he ought to be sleeping, **he devises** new misdeeds, then deliberately embarks on an evil course, gladly saying "yes" to sinful solicitations.

36:5 In stark contrast to the depravity of such a sinner are the perfections of the LORD. His **mercy**, for instance, extends to **the heavens**. Barnes writes:

It is very exalted: to the very heavens, as high as the highest object of which man can conceive. The idea is not that the mercy of God is manifested in heaven . . . nor that it has its origin in heaven (though that is true) but that it is of the most exalted nature, it is as high as men can conceive.[31]

God's **faithfulness reaches to the clouds**, that is, it is limitless in its dimensions. A. W. Pink says:

What a word is this! "Thy faithfulness extends to the clouds." Far above all finite comprehension is the unchanging faithfulness of God. Everything about God is great, vast, incomparable. He never forgets, never fails, never falters, never forfeits His word. To every declaration of promise or prophecy the Lord has exactly adhered, every engagement of covenant or threatening He will make good, for "God is not a man, that He should lie; neither the son of man, that He should repent: hath He said, and shall He not do it? or hath He spoken, and shall He not make it good?" (Num. 23:19, AV). Therefore does the believer exclaim, "His compassions fail not, they are new every morning: great is Thy faithfulness" (Lam. 3:22, 23, AV).[32]

36:6 God's **righteousness is like the great mountains** He has made—stable, steadfast, immovable, thoroughly dependable. He can always be depended on to do the thing that is right. This was perfectly manifested at the cross. God's righteousness demands that sin be punished. If we were to be punished for our sins we would perish eternally. This is why God's blessed Son took our sins upon Himself. So unbending is God's righteousness that when He saw our sins on His sinless Son, He poured out the torrents of His judgment upon Him. Now God has a righteous basis upon which He can save ungodly sinners—the penalty has been paid by a worthy Substitute.

The perfect righteousness of God
Is witnessed in the Savior's blood.
'Tis in the cross of Christ we trace
His righteousness, yet wondrous grace.

—*Albert Midlane*

God's **judgments are** like the **great deep**. This means that His decrees, decisions, thoughts and plans are wonderfully profound, complex, and wise. When contemplating this attribute of God, Paul exclaimed: "Oh, the depth of the riches both of the wisdom and knowledge of God! How unsearchable are His judgments and His ways past finding out!" (Rom. 11:33).

"O LORD, You preserve man and beast." Here it is a matter of temporal salvation—of the providence of God preserving His creatures. And what a great mercy this is. Think of all that is involved in caring for so many human beings and so many animals, birds, and fish. As for man, God numbers the very hairs of his head; as for the insignificant sparrow, not a single one falls to the ground without your heavenly Father!

36:7 Nothing that enters human life is more precious than the **loving-kindness** of **God**. It is eternal, sovereign, infinite, causeless, and unchanging. And nothing can ever separate the child of God from it. In 1743 John Brine wrote:

No tongue can fully express the infinitude of God's love, or any mind comprehend it: it "passeth knowledge" (Eph. 3:19). The most extensive ideas that a finite mind can frame about Divine love are infinitely below its true nature. The heaven is not so far above the earth as the goodness of God is beyond the most raised conceptions which we are able to form of it. It is an ocean which swells higher than all the mountains of opposition in such as are the object of it. It is a fountain from which flows all necessary good to all those who are interested in it.[33]

This is why **the children of men** find refuge **under the shadow of** His **wings**. Unfortunately, not all men choose to enjoy God's loving protection. But the privilege is available to all, and people from every nation,

class, and culture have found rest, refreshment, and safety under those incomparable wings.

36:8 Not only is there protection, but abundant provision as well. **"They are abundantly satisfied with the fullness of Your house, and You give them drink from the river of Your pleasures."** What food can match that of the house of the Lord for quality and for quantity? And what pleasures also? As F. B. Meyer pointed out, God gives sorrows by cupfuls but pleasure by riverfuls!

36:9 In Christ is **the fountain** or source **of life**. "In Him was life, and the life was the light of men" (John 1:4). **In** that **light we see light**. Just as natural light reveals things in their true form, so the light of God enables us to see things as He does. It enables us to form correct estimates of spiritual realities, of the world, of others, and of ourselves.

Corot, the great landscape painter once said, "When I find myself in one of Nature's beautiful places, I grow angry with my pictures." Pleased with them in his studio, the artist was humbled in sight of Nature's glory. Judging ourselves in the light of the world, we may easily find grounds for personal satisfaction; but to judge ourselves in the light of the Lord, to measure ourselves by the Divine standard, is to put our pride to shame. (*Choice Gleanings*)

36:10, 11 After scaling the Himalayan peaks of the perfections of God, the son of Jesse returns to the valley of human need and prays for continued protection from **the wicked**. Verse 11 explains verse 10. The way in which David asks God to continue His **lovingkindness** and deliverance is by restraining the foot of arrogant men from trampling him down and the hand of the wicked from driving him far away.

36:12 His prayer is answered. Faith enables the psalmist to see the wicked fallen down and powerless to rise again.

Psalm 37: True Peace

David had suffered plenty at the hands of ungodly, unscrupulous men during his lifetime. Now an old man, he shares some advice on how to react when we become a victim of wicked schemes and venomous tongues.

37:1, 2 First, we must not allow ourselves to fret because of evildoers. The danger is that we will lie in bed at night and rehearse the whole outrageous episode. First we think of all they said and did, then we go over how we answered them, then we wish we had thought of some other choice brickbats to hurl at them! Soon our digestive juices have turned to sulfuric acid and we lie and toss and turn, wondering when sleep will ever come! Our fretting is hurting no one but ourselves and accomplishes nothing. We must not do it!

Whatever else we do, we must not be envious of the unrighteous! This earth is the only heaven they're ever going to have. The scythe of retribution will soon mow them down, and their spectacular careers will fade and wither.

37:3 That's the negative side of the picture—don't be agitated over them and don't wish you were like them. On the positive side, the first thing to do is to trust in the LORD, and do good. This trust does not mean an unfounded, breezy optimism that everything will turn out right. Instead, it means a deep, abiding reliance on the God who has promised to punish the ungodly and to reward the righteous. His Word can never fail. The upright will indeed dwell in the land and enjoy security. Despite the fiercest attacks of demons or men, no sheep of Christ will ever perish (John 10:27–29). A dwelling place in the Father's house is guaranteed to all who trust Christ (John 14:1–6).

John Wesley once sent financial help to a preacher-friend named Samuel Bradburn. Enclosing a five-pound note, he wrote: "Dear Sammy: 'Trust in the Lord, and do good; so shalt thou dwell in the land, and verily thou shalt be fed.'" In expressing his thanks, Bradburn said, "I have often been struck with the beauty of the passage of Scripture quoted in your letter, but I must confess that I never saw such a useful expository note on it before."

37:4 But suppose you have had great desires to carry on a certain ministry for the Lord. You feel confident that He has been leading you, and your only desire is to glorify Him. Yet a powerful adversary has opposed, blocked, and thwarted you at every bend in the road. What do you do in a case like this? The answer is that you delight yourself also in the LORD, knowing that in His own time He shall give you the desires of your heart. It is not necessary for you to fight back. "The battle is not yours, but God's" (2 Chron. 20:15). "The Lord will fight for you, and you shall hold your peace" (Ex. 14:14).

37:5, 6 Or it may be that you have been misquoted, falsely accused or slandered. If there were some shred of truth to the charges they wouldn't be so hard to take. But they are absolutely untrue and malicious. What should you do? Commit the entire matter to the LORD. Roll the whole weight of it onto Him. Let Him act on your behalf, and then you will be completely vindicated. It will become clear for all to see that you were innocent after all. Barnes says:

> If you are slandered, if your character is assailed and seems for the time to be under a cloud, if reproach comes upon you from the devices of wicked men in such a way that you cannot meet it—then, if you will commit the case to God, He will protect your character, and will cause the clouds to disperse, and all to be as clear in reference to your character and the motives of your conduct as the sun without a cloud.[34]

37:7, 8 Having committed your way to the Lord, the next step is to **rest in** Him. Since He is carrying your burden, it is not necessary for you to bear it also. Too often that is exactly what we do. We cast our care hesitatingly on Him, then promptly take it back on ourselves.

> It is God's will that I should cast
> On Him my care each day.
> He also bids me not to cast
> My confidence away.
> But oh, I am so foolish
> That when taken unawares,
> I cast away my confidence
> And carry all my cares.
> —T. Baird

"And wait patiently for Him." Notice how the believer's resource is repeatedly said to be in the Lord:

Trust in *the* LORD (*v.* 3).
Delight in *the* LORD (*v.* 4).
Commit your way to *the* LORD (*v.* 5).
Rest in *the* LORD (*v.* 7a).
Wait patiently for *Him* (*v.* 7b).

Sometimes this is the hardest thing for us to do. Waiting is the thing we do least well! But true faith waits, confident that God is able to do what He has promised (Rom. 4:21).

A second time David says, **"Do not fret . . . ."** Why the repetition? For needed emphasis, of course. Even after determining not to get upset over the way we are treated, we often go back and stir up the mud all over again in our minds. But this is both self-defeating and hazardous. Even if the evil person **prospers in his way**— even if he succeeds in carrying out **wicked schemes**—the Christian should not become emotionally disturbed or build up anger, resentment, malice, and hatred. If we allow ourselves to indulge in these attitudes, they can eventually lead to violent words and acts. Then we become offenders ourselves.

37:9–11 The day is coming when all the wrongs of earth will be righted. At that time the **evildoers shall be cut off** and the trusting saints will possess all the blessings He has promised. It will not be very long until **the wicked** vanish from the scene. If you **look diligently for** them in their usual hangouts your search will be in vain! In that day **the meek shall inherit the earth** and thoroughly enjoy its unprecedented prosperity. When will that day come? For the church it will begin when the Savior descends into the clouds to catch away His waiting people and take them to their heavenly home. For the believing remnant of Israel and the nations it will begin when the Lord Jesus returns to earth to decimate His foes and to reign for a thousand years **of peace**. In the Sermon on the Mount, Jesus looked forward to this glorious day in these words:

> "Blessed are the meek; for they shall inherit the earth" (Matt. 5:5).

37:12, 13 In the meantime the cheats, the extortioners and the oppressors lay their plans against God's children. They express the bitterest hostility toward those who love the Lord. But Jehovah is not agitated by the sound of their grinding **teeth**. He knows that the **day** of reckoning is not far away. It is good for us when we can look upon our foes with that same detached nonchalance, when, as someone has suggested, we can leave behind us the world of little men.

37:14, 15 It often seems that "truth is forever on the scaffold, wrong forever on the throne." **The wicked** are well-armed and well-trained. The righteous, by comparison, seem ill-equipped and continually outwitted. But there are certain inflexible laws at work in the moral realm. The way of the transgressor is hard in the end. Sins are sure to come home to roost some day. Men can't get away with their sins forever. The boomerang effect is always at work: **Their sword shall enter their own heart.** When they need them most their weapons will fail: their **bows shall be broken.**

37:16 The few possessions of the **righteous** are **better than the** enormous **riches** of **many wicked** since the saint has the Lord while the sinner does not. The writer of the letter to the Hebrews, after documenting all the incomparable wealth that the believer enjoys in Christ, adds rather wryly: "Be content with such things as you have, for He Himself has said, 'I will never leave you nor forsake you'" (Heb. 13:5).

37:17, 18 **The arms of the wicked** (that is, their strength) **shall be broken.** But not so **the righteous.** They will be upheld by **the LORD** of infinite power. He **knows** the number of **the days of the upright**, all that those days contain, and where they will lead at last. He knows that the heritage of the just will last **forever**—an **inheritance** which is incorruptible, undefiled and unfading, reserved in heaven for all those who by God's power are guarded through faith for a salvation ready to be revealed in the last time (1 Pet. 1:4, 5).

37:19 The saints **shall not be ashamed** of their faith when hard times come. They have the hidden spiritual resources to see them through. In **days of** scarcity they enjoy a special kind of abundance. First of all, they have learned to live sacrificially, so that they do not feel deprived when the meal barrel is low. But also they have the Lord, who is able to spread a table in the wilderness. They have the privilege of seeing God provide for them in miraculous ways, and there is a special, secret-sweet flavor to all such manna from heaven.

37:20 **But the wicked shall perish.** Throughout the Psalm this death bell tolls for **the enemies of the LORD.** They are called **wicked**, wrongdoers, those who prosper in their way, men who carry out evil devices, enemies of the Lord, those cursed by the Lord, children of the wicked, and transgressors. The word "wicked" is mentioned fourteen times in this Psalm and constitutes one of its keynotes.

The Lord's foes are **like the splendor of the** pastures or **meadows.** One day they luxuriate in wild flowers and verdure; the next day they are mowed down by the reaper or withered with the change of season. Insubstantial as **smoke, they shall vanish away.**

37:21 **The wicked borrows and does not repay.** This may mean that he is *careless* about paying back *or cannot.* But with all his money, why can't he **repay**? The answer is that he is always over-extended. In his greed for money he speculates. When he loses, he borrows to cover his losses. It's the old story of borrowing from Peter to pay Paul. He builds his empire on credit and then, when reverses come, he grows desperate to prop up his sagging fortunes. Behind the outward veneer of prosperity lies financial chaos.

Though **the righteous** are often far from affluent, yet they are incredibly generous, always finding it more blessed to give than to receive. They have proved that if a believer really wants to give, he will never lack the means to do it. As Paul taught:

> And God is able to make all grace abound toward you, that you, always having all sufficiency in all things, have an abundance for every good work (2 Cor. 9:8).

37:22 The destiny of the righteous and the wicked hinges on their relationship to the Lord. Those who have been justified by faith are **blessed by** the Lord; they will possess the land. Those who have refused God's offer of salvation have put themselves in the unenviable position of standing under His curse; they will be destroyed.

37:23, 24 The steps of a *good* man are ordered by the Lord . . . . Although the word *good* is not in the original text, the idea is certainly included in verses 23 and 24. God plans and orders the pathways of the man who lives in fellowship with Him. He **upholds** the one whose ways please Him. Though such a man may fall into trials and tribulations, he will never be engulfed by them, for the Lord holds him securely by **His hand**. It is also true that if a righteous man falls into sin, he will not be abandoned by the Lord, though this is not the specific kind of fall that this verse is referring to.

37:25 Throughout David's life—and he was an **old** man when he wrote this—he had never **seen the righteous forsaken** or **his descendants begging bread**. If someone objects that he has known instances where these things have actually happened, we would make two comments. First, David may have meant that he never knew of the righteous man to be *finally* forsaken. Or second, he may have been stating a general principle, without barring the possibility of isolated exceptions. Scripture often does this. It makes sweeping statements describing the normal outworking of spiritual laws. Exceptions do not disprove the overall principles.

37:26 Far from having to send out his children to beg, the righteous man is a generous donor **and lends frequently**. By following God's Word he practices industriousness, thrift and conservation. By working hard, shopping carefully, eliminating waste, and avoiding extravagance, he is able to stretch his funds and thereby to help others who are in need. **His descendants** become a blessing because they have learned these lessons thoroughly at home and follow them throughout their own lives.

37:27 This verse is one of several in the Bible that seem to teach salvation by good works. We know from passages such as Ephesians 2:8–10 and Titus 3:5 that this is not the case. We must conclude that if a man is saved he will produce **good** works, and that such faithful saints are the only ones who will abide forever.

37:28 The Lord loves justice, and it is in keeping with His justice to make **His saints** eternally secure. It is not that the saints deserve eternal life, but that Christ died to purchase it for them, and that God must honor the terms of the purchase.

The psalmist loves to meditate on the security of the believer (see vv. 18, 24, 28 and 33). All who have been born again through faith in the Lord Jesus Christ can know on the authority of the Word of God that they are saved forever. F. W. Dixon wrote:

If you lack assurance there is only one way to gain it or regain it—take the Word of God. Take it and believe it. God says you are His; that you are safe and absolutely secure, and that He will never let you go; take a large dose of that.[35]

But while the righteous will be **preserved forever**, the children **of the wicked shall be cut off**. It is a melancholy business to contemplate the doom of the unsaved. What will it mean to be separated from God, from Christ, and from hope for all eternity?

37:29 Israel's prime hope was to live in **the land** under the reign of the Messiah. Devout Jews admittedly had a heavenly hope as well (Heb. 11:10), but the emphasis in the OT era was upon material blessings in the land of Israel during the golden age of peace and prosperity. When we read that the righteous will dwell upon the land *forever*, we must understand that the earthly kingdom of Christ will last for one thousand years, then merge into His everlasting kingdom. It may be that in the eternal state redeemed Israel will inhabit the new earth mentioned in Revelation 21:1; if that is the case then the promise of possessing the land **forever** can be taken literally.

The contrast between the righteous and the wicked continues.

37:30, 31 The just man's speech is brimful of **wisdom**. What he says is sound, scriptural, and solid. He speaks **justice**—not crookedness and deceit. He meditates continually on the Word

of God, and this keeps **his steps** from slipping into sin and shame. As Spurgeon has mentioned, he has:

the best thing—the law of his God,
in the best place—in his heart,
producing the best result—his steps
do not slip.

37:32, 33 **The wicked watches** for an opportunity to pounce on the innocent and destroy him. But Jehovah will neither abandon the innocent to the power of the foe nor allow him to be declared guilty if a case against him comes to a trial. God is the Guardian and Advocate of all His own people.

37:34 Our best policy is therefore to *trust* (**wait on the LORD**) and *obey* (**keep His way**). There's no other way to be happy in Jesus!

But that is not all. For the sixth time the psalmist promises that all such will **inherit the land**. Then he adds a further assurance. **When the wicked are** destroyed, the believers' only involvement will be that of spectators. They will not take pleasure in this awful event, but will themselves stand free from any form of judgment.

37:35 David was keen and perceptive in observing human life. He had once observed a **wicked**, overbearing man **spreading himself like a** luxuriating **tree** in its **native** soil. Apparently the thought is that this tree had never suffered the setback caused by transplanting. It was still in its **native** soil and thus vigorous and large. The wicked man was correspondingly prosperous and powerful.

37:36 But the next time David was passing through that place, the man was gone. He **sought him but** couldn't find him anywhere. The man prospered for awhile. His power lasted for a short time, but then he himself was gone, and so were his prosperity and power.

37:37, 38 The psalmist counsels us to notice the contrast between the **blameless**, upright **man** and **the transgressors**. There is a posterity for the man of **peace**, whereas **the future** of the **wicked shall be cut off**. *Both the righteous and the unrighteous produce long lines of physical descendants.* Tholuck says of the man of **peace**, "It shall go well at last to such a man." But the wicked has no such promising tomorrow.

37:39, 40 The greatest thing about **the righteous** is their connection with God. He is their Savior and their strength in time of trouble. No wonder Christians turn instinctively to Him in time of need! They find that He helps them, delivers them, and saves them **because they** depend on **Him** completely. Are you in trouble right now? **Trust in Him**. He will see you through!

Psalm 38: Sorrow for Sin

We might think that this Psalm describes the suffering of the Savior were it not for the references to "my sin" (v. 3), "my iniquities" (v. 4), "my foolishness" (v. 5) and "my plague" (v. 11). It might be valid to apply much of the rest of the language to the Lord Jesus as He suffered at the hands of God and of man, but the basic interpretation certainly belongs to David at a time in his life when intense physical and mental distress were admittedly connected to some sin he had committed.

38:1–4 First David thinks of his sufferings as the **rebuke** of an angry God and the chastening of His **hot displeasure**, and he asks the Lord to lift the siege. The **arrows** of the Al-

mighty have found their mark in the psalmist's mind and body, and God's **hand** has come down with crushing pressure upon him. As a result of divine wrath his whole body is sick. The illness has seeped into his very **bones**—and all because of his **sin**. There is no excusing his **iniquities**—he is thoroughly convicted of them. Like gigantic waves, they have dashed over him. Like an enormous weight, they have broken his strength.

38:5–8 Foul and festering wounds have broken out over his body, and he has no doubt why this has happened. He is doubled over in pain, laid low with weakness—a living specter of grief. His body is racked with a high fever, and there is no part of his anatomy that has escaped. He has no more fight left in him. Thoroughly whipped, he can do nothing but **groan** to express how he feels.

38:9–11 It is some comfort to David to realize that the **Lord** knows the anguish of his heart and the emotions he feels but cannot express. But still his **heart** is palpitating wildly, his **strength** rapidly draining away, and all sparkle vanishing from his **eyes**. His **loved ones and** his **friends** avoid him as if he were a leper, and even his **relatives** are reluctant to visit him.

38:12–14 Nor have his would-be assassins given up their plots, threats, and villainy. **But** David is **deaf** to all their threats and remains silent as far as defense, self-vindication, or rebukes are concerned.

38:15–17 Yet no matter how dark the present situation is, he is not without **hope**. He still has the confidence that **God** will answer him. He asks that his adversaries might not have the pleasure of celebrating his complete calamity. But right now he is continually racked with pain and near the limit of human endurance.

38:18 With refreshing candor and brokenness and with no attempt to gloss over his **sin**, David confesses his **iniquity** and says "I'm sorry!" Any man who sincerely takes this position before God will never be denied forgiveness. The Lord has gone on record to state that He will grant mercy to the one who confesses and forsakes his sin (Prov. 28:13). If this were not so, all men would be hopelessly doomed.

38:19, 20 David's thoughts go back to his **enemies** once more. Though he is weak and sickly, they are **vigorous** and **strong**. He then acknowledges the justice of God's chastenings but protests that his **adversaries** have no valid cause for their malice. He has been kind to them but gets only hatred in return. At the bottom of their hostility is the fact that David is a follower of God and of **good**.

38:21, 22 So he appeals to **God** not to **forsake** him, but to stay close by and to hurry to his rescue—to truly be the psalmist's Savior-God!

Paraphrase of Psalm 39: Inner Fire

39:1–3 "I was fiercely determined to keep myself from rebelling or complaining against the Lord in spite of the extremity of my plight. I vowed to muzzle my mouth as long as I was in earshot of unbelievers; I didn't want to give them any excuse for questioning the providence of God. So there I was, dumb and silent, with no outlet for my suppressed emotions. But it was of no use. **My heart was** red **hot** with indignation and perplexity. I couldn't understand why the Lord was allowing me to endure such overwhelming grief. The more I nursed my bitterness of soul, the greater the inward pressure became.

Finally all my pent up feelings burst forth in questioning prayer.

39:4–6 "Lord, how long is this nightmare going to last? Tell me how much time I have left, and when it is going to run out. At best the span of my life is only about the width of my palm; compared to Your eternity, my lifetime isn't worth mentioning. All of us humans are as unsubstantial as a **vapor**. We go through life like phantoms. We rush around in frenzied activity—but what does it all amount to after all? We spend our lives scrimping and saving, and leave it all behind to be enjoyed by ingrates or fools or strangers!

39:7, 8 "So what hope do I have, **Lord? My** only **hope is in You**. Apart from You I have nothing. **Deliver me from all my transgressions**—particularly those sins that might have brought this awful trouble into my life. I can't stand the thought of **foolish** people gloating over my calamity.

39:9, 10 "You know how I have kept quiet since this trouble struck—because I knew it came by Your permissive will. But now I am asking You to **remove Your** chastening hand from me; I am exhausted under Your recurring blows.

39:11 "**When**, Lord, **You correct a man** for his sins with various forms of discipline, he wastes away like a prized garment when it is eaten by moths. It is clear that we are all as transient as a **vapor**!

39:12, 13 "So I come to You, Lord, and ask You to **hear my prayer**. Hear and answer my urgent appeal. Don't be unmoved by my tears. After all, I am like an overnight guest in this world of Yours, a nomad like my ancestors. All I ask is that You stop frowning on me in judgment and let me enjoy a brief period of health and happiness **before I** make my exit from the stage of life, never to be seen on earth again."

Psalm 40: Rescued!

The well-known words "Sacrifice and offering You did not desire" (vv. 6–8) identify this as a Psalm of the Messiah; the words are applied to the Lord Jesus in Hebrews 10:5. But the Psalm poses a difficulty in that the first part deals with His Resurrection while the last part seems to revert to His agony on the cross. To explain this introversion is not easy. Some suggest that in the early verses the Savior is looking forward to His Resurrection and speaking of it as if it had already taken place. Others apply the anguished prayer at the close of the Psalm to the Jewish remnant during the Great Tribulation. In our study we will apply the entire Psalm to the Lord Jesus—first to His Resurrection and then to His sufferings on the cross. If this violation of the chronological order offends our western minds, we may take comfort in the fact that people from the East do not always consider time order to be supremely important.

40:1 The speaker is Messiah Jesus. He **waited patiently for the Lord** to hear His prayer and to deliver Him out of death. Even our blessed Lord did not always receive instant answers to prayer. But He realized that *delays* do not necessarily mean *denials*. God answers prayer at the time that is best suited to the accomplishment of His purposes in our lives.

God's help comes, not too soon,
    lest we should not know
the blessedness of trusting in the
    dark, and not too late,
lest we should know the misery of
    trusting in vain.

40:2 The Savior likens His glorious deliverance out of death to being rescued **out of a horrible pit** and from a **miry** bog. Who can imagine what it meant to the Giver of life to step forth from the tomb as the Victor over sin, Satan, death, and the grave—alive forevermore!

Though Christ's deliverance was unique, in a lesser sense we can all experience the power of God in saving us out of the pits and bogs of life. As we all know, life is full of these deep holes. The unconverted person who is being convicted of his sins by the Holy Spirit is in a particularly **horrible pit**. The backslidden believer also finds himself in a treacherous quagmire. There are the bogs of sickness, suffering and sorrow. Often when we are seeking guidance, we seem to be in a dark dungeon. And of course we sometimes founder in the morass of bereavement, loneliness, or discouragement. These are unforgettable experiences, times when we pray and cry and groan but nothing seems to happen. We need to learn from our Savior's example to wait patiently for the Lord. In God's own time and way He will come to our side, pulling us **up out of** the **pit**, setting our **feet upon a rock** and making our **steps** secure.

40:3 Notice that God is the *source* of our **praise** as well as its *object*. **He** puts the **new song in** our **mouth**—and it is a song of **praise** *to our God.*

Our deliverance results not only in praise to God but in testimony to others: **"Many will see it and fear, and will trust in the Lord."** This was never more true than in connection with the Resurrection of the Lord Jesus. Think of the endless line of faith's pilgrims who have been won to the Living God through the miracle of the empty tomb!

40:4 As He thinks of those who have tasted and seen that the Lord is good, the Risen Redeemer utters one of the greatest, most basic truths in all spiritual life: **"Blessed is that man who makes the LORD his trust. . . ."** True happiness and fulfillment in life come only through faith in God. It could not be otherwise. We have been created in such a way that we can realize our destiny only when we acknowledge God as our Lord and Master. Pascal said it well: "There is a God-shaped vacuum in the human heart!" And Augustine put it this way: "Thou has made us, O Lord, for Thyself, and our heart shall find no rest till it rest in Thee!"

The blessed man not only turns *to* God but he turns *away from* **proud** men and followers of false gods. He is not tricked by two of the greatest delusions of life—the idea that the honor of proud men is important and the concept that the false gods of materialism, pleasure, and sexual indulgence can satisfy the human heart. The blessed man is more concerned with God's approval than with man's, realizing that fullness of joy is found only in God's presence—not in the company of those who worship at idol shrines.

40:5 This leads the Messiah to think of how numberless are the mercies of God. His **works** and His **thoughts** of grace **toward** His people are beyond computation. Who can fully describe the infinite details of His natural creation? Who can exhaust the remarkable interventions of His providence? Who can comprehend the magnitude of His spiritual blessings—election, predestination, justification, redemption, propitiation, pardon, forgiveness, salvation, the new birth, the indwelling Spirit, the seal of the Spirit, the earnest of the Spirit, the anointing, sanctification, sonship, heirship, glorification—**"if I would declare and speak of them, they are more than can be numbered."**

When all Thy mercies, O my God,
My rising soul surveys,
Transported with the view, I'm lost
In wonder, love and praise!
—*Joseph Addison*

40:6 As was mentioned, verses 6–8 identify the Psalm as being distinctly Messianic. In Hebrews 10:5–9 we learn that these words were the language of the Son of God when He came into the world. He was saying, in effect, that although God had instituted **sacrifice and offering** for the nation of Israel, they never represented His ultimate intention. They were designed as types and shadows of something better to come. As temporary stop-gaps, they had their place. But God was never really satisfied with them; to Him they were less than ideal because they did not provide a final solution to the sin problem. Recognizing the inherent weakness of burnt offerings and sin offerings, God instead **opened** the **ears** of His Beloved Son. This simply means that the Savior's ears were open to hear and to obey the will of His Father. It was with this attitude of willing and ready obedience that Christ came into the world.

In the margin of the ERV, the expression **"My ears You have opened"** is rendered "Ears thou hast digged (or pierced) for me." Some interpreters think this refers to the Hebrew slave of Exodus 21:5, 6. If a slave did not desire to be freed in the seventh year, his ear was pierced with an awl at the doorpost and he became indentured to his master forever. Christ, the Antitype, became a willing bond-slave in His Incarnation (Phil. 2:7) and will continue to serve His people when He comes again (Luke 12:37).

When the clause **"My ears You have opened"** is quoted in Hebrews 10:5, it is changed to "a body You have prepared for Me." As to the authority for making such a change, the same Holy Spirit who first inspired the words in Psalm 40 certainly has the right to clarify them when He quotes it in the NT. The literal rendering of the Hebrew expression "to dig an ear" is probably a figure of speech in which a part (here, the ear) is given for the whole (here, the body). (This is called synecdoche.) The NT expands and explains the meaning as a reference to the Incarnation.

40:7, 8 When Christ became Man, it was not with meek resignation but with wholehearted delight. He said at this time, **"Behold, I come; in the scroll of the book it is written of me. I delight to do Your will, O my God, and Your Law is within my heart."** From cover to cover of the OT it was foretold not only that Christ would come into the world but that He would come with an eager, ready spirit to do the will of God. The **will** of God was not just in His head—it was inscribed in His very **heart**.

40:9, 10 These verses describe His earthly ministry. He had **proclaimed the good news** of deliverance **in the great congregation**, that is, to the house of Israel. He had not held back anything that God had given Him to declare. He had not hoarded the great truths of God's saving help, enduring faithfulness, or steadfast love.

40:11 The remaining verses of the Psalm (11—17) seem to carry us back to the cross. We hear the Savior issuing a most compelling and poignant distress call. There is a close link with what He had just said in verse 10.

The connection is this: "I have told the people of Your salvation, Your faithfulness and Your steadfast love. Now do not negate My testimony by withholding these **tender mercies from me**. **Let** them **continually preserve me!"**

40:12 The immediate occasion of His desperate plea was that the calamitous tortures of Calvary were crashing down upon Him. These **innumerable evils** were linked with innumerable sins, as effect is linked with cause. But when He says, **"My iniquities..."** we must be sure to remember that they were actually *our* iniquities—those sins for which He had contracted to pay the awful penalty. So intense were His sufferings that His **heart** was failing. Who of us can ever imagine the depths of agony which He endured that we might be pardoned and forgiven!

40:13 In His extremity, Christ stormed the gates of heaven for help—for immediate help. It is as if He pled, "Please **deliver me** and please *do it now!"* That is the kind of prayer that wins. Divine Omnipotence is moved into action by it.

40:14, 15 As for His enemies, He asks that their punishment be suited to their crimes. For their attempts on His **life** He wishes them disgrace and **confusion**. For wishing Him **evil** He hopes they will be repelled and shamed. For gloating over His misfortune He would like to see them shocked by the depth of their own humiliation. If someone objects that these sentiments are incompatible with a God of love, I would only remind him that in refusing love, man deliberately chooses his own punishment.

40:16 As for the friends of God, Christ prays that they might always find their enjoyment in the Lord. He hopes that **all those who seek** God will **rejoice and be glad in** Him, and that **such as love** His **salvation** will **say continually, "The LORD be magnified!"**

40:17 As for Himself, His strength is small and His need is desperate. But He takes comfort in the fact that the Lord takes thought for Him. As someone has said, "Poverty and need are not barriers to the thoughts of God."

As for God Himself, He is the **help** and **deliverer** of His beloved Son. And so in a final salvo of supplication the Lord Jesus prays, **"Do not delay, O my God."** The answer is not long in coming. On the third day the Father reaches down and delivers Him from the desolate pit, as we saw in the first part of the Psalm.

It seems, then, that in this Psalm we have first the *answer* to prayer and then the *prayer itself*. This vividly suggests the promise, "Before they call, I will answer; and while they are still speaking, I will hear" (Isa. 65:24).

Psalm 41: Prayer From a Sickroom

David was sick, and his enemies hoped it was nothing trivial. They were already rejoicing among themselves that his illness was undoubtedly terminal. An added grief to David was that one of the traitors had been his own close friend at one time.

41:1–3 But the patient is not without comfort. First he remembers that the Lord blesses the person **who considers the poor**. Here **"the poor"** probably means not so much poor financially as poor in health, weakened by sickness. David consoles himself with the thought that he had done just what the Lord did for people in distress—he had assisted, comforted, and cheered all who were in the grip of disease. Now he claims the prom-

ise that **the LORD will deliver** him too **in time of trouble**. Yes, the Lord will keep a protective vigil over him, preserving his life. Because David has earned a good reputation for his consideration of the sick and the suffering, he is confident that God will not desert him to the malicious will of his foes. He will instead give David all needed grace for his time in the sickroom, then raise him up to health and strength once more. The Lord is pictured as a nurse, adjusting the patient's bed so as to make him comfortable.

41:4 But the psalmist did not depend solely on his own past consideration of the ill and infirm. He wisely took his illness to the Lord in prayer, confessing his sin and pleading for healing as something he didn't deserve. Not all sickness is a direct result of sin in a believer's life. Many of the ailments of older people, for example, are part of the normal process of deterioration due to age. Sometimes, however, there is a direct link between sin and sickness, and where the faintest possibility of this exists, the believer should rush into the Lord's presence in heartfelt confession. In all such cases, the Great Physician's forgiveness should precede the local doctor's remedies.

41:5 In the meantime, the psalmist's **enemies** were waiting hopefully for a bulletin from the hospital stating that David had died. **"When will he die?"** they asked each other, "and when will we hear the last of this fellow?"

41:6 Occasionally one of these evil-wishers would show up during visiting hours, but he had no comfort to offer, no words of hope or encouragement. He talked without saying anything. Actually, it seemed he was just looking for some information to use against

David. After he left he broadcast every negative report he could imagine.

41:7, 8 A whispering campaign was going on against the sick man, and the prophets of doom were out-thinking themselves in conceiving calamities for David. They spread the word that a fatal **disease** had attacked him and that his next stop would be the morgue.

41:9 Perhaps the "unkindest cut of all" was the treachery of one who had been an intimate **friend**. Of all the sorrows of life, this is certainly one of the bitterest—to be betrayed by one who has had close associations with you. It is a sorrow the Savior experienced in the betrayal of Judas, and a not-uncommon experience in the lives of those who follow this Captain.

The Lord Jesus quoted verse 9 in connection with Judas. However, it is significant that He omitted the words **"my own familiar friend in whom I trusted."** Knowing in advance that Judas would betray Him, the Lord had never trusted him, so He simply said. "He who eats bread with Me has lifted up his heel against Me" (John 13:18).

41:10 David turns away from the one who had, as it were, stabbed him in the back, and looks instead to the LORD for mercy. When others were deserting him, he counts on the Lord to stand by faithfully. He then makes what might seem to be a strange request: **"and raise me up, that I may repay them."** If at first this seems unworthy of a man of David's stature, we must remember that he was the Lord's anointed ruler of Israel, and it was his duty as king to deal with sedition and betrayal. While as an individual he might have chosen to tolerate villainy and treachery against himself, as the king he was

obliged to suppress any attempts to overthrow the government.

41:11, 12 David sees in the failure of his enemies' plots an indication of the Lord's favor toward him. Then he adds:

> **You uphold me in my integrity,**
> **And set me before Your face**
> **forever.**

If we prefer this translation, it may sound as if David is boasting excessively. But he actually *was* a man of **integrity** in spite of his sins and failures. And compared to his foes he was a paragon of virtue. It is entirely possible that the Lord did **uphold** him because He saw sincerity and righteousness in his life.

Gelineau's translation of the verse presents less difficulty:

> If you uphold me I shall be unharmed
> and set in your presence for evermore.

In this version everything is dependent on the Lord rather than on David's integrity. The Lord's sustaining grace assures safety in this life and a standing in the presence of the heavenly King forever.

41:13 Confident and serene, the psalmist now raises his voice in a parting burst of praise. Jehovah, the covenant-keeping **God of Israel**, is worthy to be worshiped **from everlasting to everlasting**. David could add a double **Amen** to this tribute, and so can we!

II. BOOK 2 (PSALMS 42—72)

Psalm 42: Thirsting for God

Some people hear the voice of David in this Psalm as he wandered in exile during the rebellion of his own son, Absalom.

Others recognize the voice of the Messiah during the time of His rejection and suffering.

Still others detect the plaintive sob of the Jewish remnant during the future Tribulation Period.

Then there are those who like to apply it to the believer as he looks back on the days of his first love and longs for the renewal of that kind of fellowship with the Lord.

Fortunately, it is not necessary to isolate one view, since all of them are legitimate applications. This is typical of the versatility of the Psalms.

42:1 Our inner longing for fellowship with **God** can be compared to the vehement craving of **the deer** as it wanders through the parched countryside, its sides throbbing and its breathing quickened as it longs **for the brooks**. Gamaliel Bradford transferred the picture to himself when he said:

> My one unchanged ambition
> Wheresoe'er my feet have trod
> Is a keen, enormous, haunting,
> Never-sated thirst for God.

42:2 Our thirst is **for God** alone; no one else will do. And it is **for the living God**—not for a dead idol. It is a desire that will only be fully satisfied by a personal appearance before the Lord and the privilege of gazing on His face.

> Show me Thy face, one transient
>   gleam of loveliness divine,
> And I shall never think or dream of
>   other love than thine;
> All lesser lights shall darken quite, all
>   lower glories dim,
> The beautiful of earth will ne'er seem
>   beautiful again.
> —*Author unknown*

42:3 Who can describe the bitterness of separation from the Lord? It is like a continual diet of **tears**, a life of unalleviated misery. As if that were not enough, there is the added grief of the enemies' taunts, **"Where is your God?"** This is what Shimei meant when he said to David, "So now you are caught in your own evil, because you are a bloodthirsty man!" (2 Sam. 16:8). And this is what the chief priests meant when they said of the crucified Messiah, "He trusted in God; let Him deliver Him now if He will have Him . . ." (Matt. 27:43).

42:4 Then, of course, there is the memory of better days. It is the remembrance of how wonderful it was to walk in unbroken fellowship with **God** that makes the absence of this fellowship so intolerable. Knox wonderfully captures the mood in his translation of verse 4:

> Memories come back to me yet, melting the heart; how once I would join with the throng, leading the way to God's house, amid cries of joy and thanksgiving, and all the bustle of holiday.

42:5 The thought of the happy past leads to spiritual depression and activates a ping-pong struggle between pessimism and faith. The **soul** becomes downcast and **disquieted**, but faith challenges the tension of this burdened state of mind.

> **Hope in God; for I shall yet praise Him for the help of His countenance.**

If this were just a pious optimism that "everything will turn out all right," it would be an utterly worthless sentiment. What makes this hope 100% valid is that it is based on the promise of God's Word that His people will see His face (Ps. 17:15; Rev. 22:4).

42:6 The depression recurs in cycles. But faith strikes back with the confident assertion that it **will re-member** God **from the land of the Jordan** and **of Hermon** and **from the Hill Mizar**. Perhaps these three places symbolize three spiritual experiences; we do not know. What does seem clear is that they represent the land of exile, far removed from the house of God in Jerusalem. And the thought seems to be that even when we cannot visit the house of God, we can still remember the God of the house!

42:7 When we come to the seventh verse, our spiritual instincts tell us that in a very special way we are at Calvary, hearing the cries of the Lord Jesus as the **waves and billows** of God's judgment rolled over Him. The cataracts of divine wrath cascaded down upon Him with resounding thunder as He bore our sins in His own body on the cross.

> View that closing scene of anguish:
> All God's waves and billows roll
> Over Him, there left to languish
> On the Cross, to save my soul.
> Matchless love! how vast! how free!
> Jesus gave Himself for me.
> —*J. J. Hopkins*

42:8 Yet, as George Mller said, "Trials are food for faith to feed on." So we hear the confident believer affirm:

The LORD will command His loving-kindness in the daytime, and in the night His song shall be with me—a prayer to the God of my life.

This is the answer to the day-and-night sequence in verse 3. There the psalmist had said, "My tears have been my food day and night. . . ." But now the day is filled with God's steadfast love and the night is filled with song and prayer. So by day and by **night** God's goodness is proven.

42:9, 10 Once again discouragement returns, this time because of the relentless oppression of the enemy. It seems that God has **forgotten** His child. The forlorn believer wanders about like a mourner. He says, "With cries that pierce me to the heart, my enemies revile me" (Gelineau). From all outward appearances it would seem that God has forsaken His child. So the **enemies** taunt him continually with the question, **"Where is your God?"**

42:11 But faith always has the last word. Don't be discouraged. Don't be unsettled. **Hope in God**; you will be delivered from your enemies and from your depression as well. And you'll **praise Him** once again as your Savior and your God. As someone has said:

> The remedy—challenge depression, look up, hope. The Christian life is alertness, upward striving, activity, the running of a race. It is never downcast eyes, folded hands and the acceptance of defeat.

Psalm 43: Send Out Your Light and Your Truth

This is a twin to the preceding Psalm. The connection is so great that the NEB links them together as if they were one composition.

43:1, 2 Here we have the continued prayer of an exile who wants to worship in Zion but is opposed by an apostate **nation** and an **unjust man**. This may picture the oppression of the godly Jewish remnant during the Tribulation by the unbelieving nation of Israel and the Antichrist.

First comes the plea for vindication and for help. The psalmist asks God to defend the **cause** of His people against their unbelieving brethren and the man of sin. It is one of faith's agonies to take refuge in God and yet feel **cast off** by Him; it is one of faith's puzzles to be on the winning side and yet suffer under the heel **of the enemy**.

43:3 Then follows a positive and specific prayer for the return to Zion. The beauty of the language is incomparable:

> Oh, send out Your light and Your truth!
> Let them lead me;
> Let them bring me to Your holy hill
> And to Your tabernacle.

The psalmist wanted an escort consisting of the **light** of God's presence and the **truth** of God's promise. With these to lead him and with goodness and mercy following him (Ps. 23:6), he was assured of a glad return to God's **holy hill**.

43:4 Notice the progression in verses 3 and 4:

> To Your holy hill;
> To Your tabernacle;
> **To the altar of God;**
> **To God my exceeding joy.**

The true worshiper is satisfied with neither a geographical location nor a building nor an altar. He must get through **to God** Himself!

43:5 Brightened by the prospect of appearing before God, the writer once again remonstrates with himself for being disheartened and troubled. Have faith **in God**, he urges, and He will surely bring you to your desired end.

> Be still, my soul: thy best, thy heavenly Friend
> Through thorny ways leads to a joyful end!
> —*Katharina von Schlegel*

Psalm 44: Sheep for the Slaughter

The pain of defeat is made more bitter by the memory of former victories, and we never value our fellowship with God so much as when His face seems to be hidden from us.

44:1–3 Israel's history was replete with soul-thrilling instances of God's intervention on their behalf. He had driven the heathen out of the land of Canaan and had given it to His own people. By subduing the Canaanites He had set Israel free in a country of their own. It certainly wasn't because of any military superiority that the Jews won possession of the pleasant land, nor was it by **their own** strength that they came off victorious. It was by God's powerful **right hand**, by His omnipotent **arm**, by His loving favor showered down on them.

44:4–8 The memory of what the Lord has done inspires our own hearts to praise Him. He is the great **King** and mighty **God** who gives **victories** to the unworthy sons of unworthy **Jacob**. It is through Him that Israel has been able to bulldoze through the ranks of her **enemies** and to walk triumphantly over her attackers. She has learned that the battlebow is not to be trusted for success, nor is the **sword** a sufficient savior. *God* is the One who has delivered His people and thoroughly confused their foes! No wonder the people kept boasting of their connection with Him, kept saying they would never cease to thank Him!

44:9–12 But something has happened in the meantime to change their song to a lament. It seems that the Lord has forsaken His people and made them suffer dishonor. The armies marched out without God's presence and help, and soon they were retreating in panic, with the enemies looting all Israel's wealth. The Lord has abandoned His **sheep** to the butchers and scattered the survivors among the Gentile nations. It all happened like a business deal in which God sold His **people** for next to nothing. And the enemy apparently got away with it all without having to pay the consequences.

44:13–16 Poor Israel became the laughingstock of the other nations, an object of ridicule and **scorn**. Traditional bywords and epithets of **derision** were used to defame these Jews. God's ancient people became the butt of crude jokes **among the nations**. Theirs was a shame from which they could not escape. Their faces were constantly crimsoned by the reproaches and jeers of their enemies, by the very sight of the vengeful foe.

44:17 The puzzling thing about all this defeat and shame was that it was not brought on by any conscious backsliding on Israel's part. At other times in history there *was* a definite connection between suffering and sin. But in this particular case it was not so. It seemed instead that the people's plight was due to the fact that they were God's chosen people. It was a case of suffering for God and for His **covenant**.

44:18, 19 The calamities had come to a people who had **not turned** their backs on God or violated His covenant. They had not abandoned their love for Him or the pathway He had marked out for them. Yet the Lord had shattered them **in the** forsaken land **of jackals, and covered** them **with the shadow of death**.

44:20–22 If they **had forgotten the name of** their **God** or worshiped idols, wouldn't God have known it? He knows the innermost thoughts and motives. No, that was not the cause.

The people were suffering because of their connection with Jehovah. It was for *His* **sake** that they were enduring a living death, abused like animals destined for the slaughterhouse.

Centuries later the apostle Paul found himself in the same situation, and quoted Psalm 44:22 to describe the sufferings of God's people in every age (Rom. 8:36).

44:23–26 The Psalm reaches a peak of bold urgency in verse 23, when the **Lord** is roused from His apparent slumber and asked to intervene for His people. It is more than the psalmist can understand—how God can **hide** His **face** in neglect and indifference while His people lie prostrate in **the dust**. And so he sounds reveille once again:

> **Arise for our help,**
> **And redeem us for Your mercies'**
> **sake.**

Psalm 45: The King of Kings

45:1 It was easy for the psalmist to write this Psalm. In fact, his **heart** was bursting to put in writing the poem he had composed **concerning the King**. The words flowed freely from his pen; he felt himself being literally borne along. His **tongue** was like **the pen of a ready** scribe, and we are not stretching matters if we identify the ready scribe as the Holy Spirit Himself.

45:2 First we are introduced to the King Himself. His beauty is surpassing. He is the chiefest among ten thousand, the altogether lovely One. **Grace is poured upon** His **lips**; His speech is most sweet. Because of His personal excellence, **God has blessed** Him **forever**.

Fairest of all the earth-born race,
Perfect in comeliness Thou art;

Replenished are Thy lips with grace,
And full of love Thy tender heart.
God ever-blest, we bow the knee,
And own all fullness dwells in Thee.
—*Author unknown*

45:3–5 Then almost immediately we are carried forward to Christ's Second Advent, to the time when He returns to earth in power and great glory. This time He comes as a conquering warrior, not as the humble carpenter of Nazareth. With **sword upon** His **thigh**, the **Mighty One** descends in **glory** and **majesty**. In dazzling splendor He rides forth in triumph in the cause of **truth, humility, and righteousness**. His nail-scarred **right hand** is adept in wielding the sword in frightening power against His foes. His **arrows** find their mark **in the heart of the King's enemies; the peoples fall** in waves before Him.

45:6, 7a Now the smoke of battle has passed and the King is seated on the **throne** of His glory in Jerusalem. The voice of God is heard from heaven addressing Him as **God** and certifying His reign as an eternal one. We know it is the voice of God, because Hebrews 1:8, 9 tells us so:

> But to the Son He says: "Your throne, O God, is forever and ever; a scepter of righteousness is the scepter of Your kingdom. You have loved righteousness and hated lawlessness; therefore God, Your God, has anointed You with the oil of gladness more than Your companions."

Notice that God addresses His Son as **God**, one of the clearest proofs of the deity of Christ in the entire Bible. It is true that some translators of Psalm 45:6 render this phrase "Your divine throne endures for ever and ever" instead of "Your throne, O God, is forever and ever." But when they quote this verse in the Hebrews passage, it becomes "Your throne, O God, is forever and ever." So it is not only true that Christ's throne is divine, but also that He Himself is God.

Christ's kingdom will last **forever**. After His reign of one thousand years on earth, His earthly kingdom will merge into "the everlasting kingdom of our Lord and Savior Jesus Christ" (2 Pet. 1:11).

Christ's royal **scepter** is a scepter of equity. A scepter is a staff which symbolizes royal authority. Here the meaning is that the Messiah will rule with absolute justice. And the reign will also be absolutely holy, for the King loves **righteousness** and hates **wickedness**.

45:7b, 8 Because of His righteousness and integrity, God has **anointed** the Lord Jesus **with the oil of gladness more than** all other rulers. **The oil of** joy or **gladness** refers to the holy anointing oil with which priests were inducted into their office (Ex. 30:22–25). Since our Lord is to be a Priest-King, this is the oil to be used. **Myrrh** and **cassia** were the two principal ingredients in this oil, and **aloes** was one of the "chief spices" mentioned in Song of Solomon 4:14. All of these speak of the surpassing fragrance of the Person and work of our Lord. The **myrrh** and **aloes** may have special reference to His sufferings and death, since they were used in preparing His body for burial (John 19:39).

Out of the ivory palaces they make Him **glad**. It is the royal symphony, sounding forth the world's jubilation that man's day of sobbing and sighing has ended and that the golden age has dawned at last!

45:9 The King is not alone in the day of His power. The **daughters** of earth's monarchs are among His royal attendants. **At** His **right** side is **the queen**, decked with jewelry of **gold from Ophir**. And who is **the queen**? Here we must resist the temptation to identify her with the church, since the church is not the subject of OT revelation (Eph. 3:5–9; Col. 1:26). We believe that the queen is the redeemed remnant of the nation of Israel (Ezek. 16:10–14) and that the attendants may represent Gentile nations won to Christ through Israel's testimony.

45:10, 11 The queen is counseled by an unidentified voice, perhaps that of the Holy Spirit, to **forget** her **own people** and her **father's house**. The meaning, of course, is that she should sever the ties which bind her to her pre-conversion life and be totally committed to the King as her Lord. This advice anticipates the words of our Savior in Luke 14:26:

> If anyone come to Me and does not hate his father and mother, wife and children, brothers and sisters, yes, and his own life also, he cannot be My disciple.

Our love for Christ must be so great that all other loves are hatred *by comparison*. The beauty of wholeheartedness is pleasing to Him. Since He is Lord, He deserves all that we are and have.

45:12 The wealthy **daughter of Tyre will come** to the queen **with a gift**. Yes, the richest people in the world will travel to Jerusalem with the choicest presents.

45:13 Then **the royal daughter** is seen in her **palace**, dressed in regal splendor preparatory to her presentation to the King. Once the wearied drudge of sin, she is now seen in her chamber dressed in garments embroidered with **gold**.

45:14, 15 And now **she** is **brought to the King**, arrayed in multi-colored robes and accompanied by a retinue of virgin companions. There is great rejoicing as they move along, eventually entering the **palace** of the King Himself.

> Who can tell of that joy, the joy of the Father, and of the Son, and of the Holy Spirit, and of the holy angels, not to mention their own joy as they enter into the joy of their Lord! Comely in all comeliness, beautiful in all beauty, graceful in all grace, charming in every charm, attractive in every attractiveness, conformed to the image of God's Son (source unknown).

45:16, 17 In the last two verses God the Father is speaking to Christ the King. He promises Him **sons** who will be worthy successors of the patriarchs, who will "divide a world between them for their domain" (Knox).

As for the King Himself, His **name** will be praised **in all generations**. There never will come a time when **the people** will cease to adore Him.

Psalm 46: God With Us

During the First World War in an island community in the highlands of Scotland, young men were being called up in increasing numbers for military service. Each time contingents of them gathered at the pier to sail to the mainland, their relatives and friends assembled there and sang:

> God is our refuge and our strength,
> in straits a present aid;
> Therefore, although the earth remove,
> we will not be afraid:
> Though hills amidst the seas be cast;
> Though waters roaring make,
> And troubled be; yea, though the hills by swelling seas do shake.
>
> A river is, whose streams make glad the city of our God;

The holy place, wherein the Lord
   most high hath his abode.
God in the midst of her doth dwell;
   nothing shall her remove:
The Lord to her an helper will,
   and that right early prove.

Be still and know that I am God:
   among the heathen I
Will be exalted; I on earth
   will be exalted high.
Our God, who is the Lord of hosts,
   is still upon our side:
The God of Jacob our refuge
   for ever will abide.
     —from the Scottish Psalter

This scene is one of thousands in which God's saints have been comforted by this Psalm in times of great crisis. No one can know the hearts that have been lifted as these majestic lines have been read in the sickroom, the house of mourning, the dungeon of persecution and the narrow chamber of suffering and tragedy. It was this Psalm that led a tried and harried former Augustinian monk named Martin Luther to pen his famous Reformation hymn, "A Mighty Fortress Is Our God." Its message is timeless and its encouragement unceasing.

There are three distinct sections to the Psalm, which G. Campbell Morgan has titled as follows:

1–3   Nothing to fear. God is with us.
     The challenge of confidence.

4–7   The Lord enthroned in
     Jerusalem.
     The secret of confidence.

8–11 Peace on earth and worldwide
     dominion.
     The vindication of confidence.

It is generally thought that the historical background of the Psalm is the miraculous deliverance of Jerusalem when it was besieged by the Assyrian wolf, Sennacherib (2 Kgs.

18:13—19:35; Isa. 36:1—37:36). At this time the people of Judah were tremendously conscious of God's presence with them in a unique way. And so the Psalm celebrates the praises of Him who is Immanuel—God with us.

46:1–3 God is our refuge and strength, a very present help in trouble. He is also "abundantly available for help in tight places" (NASB marg.). Blessed are we when we realize that our safety and protection lie not in riches or armies but in Jehovah alone!

Imagine the worst that can happen! Suppose **the earth** itself should melt as if caught in the flow of a gigantic volcano. Suppose an earthquake should toss **the mountains into the midst of the sea**. Suppose a flood of water should **roar** and foam over the land, or that **the mountains** should stagger with wild convulsions of nature.

Or think of **the mountains** as symbols of empires or cities, and the **waters** as nations. The very foundations of society are crumbling; kingdoms are toppling and disintegrating. The nations of the world are churning with political, economic and social confusion and trouble of unprecedented intensity is enveloping the world.

But God . . . ! The worst that can happen is no cause for fear. God Himself is still with us!

46:4 He Himself is the **river whose streams shall make glad the city of God.** Actually the city of Jerusalem has no river. But everything that a river is to an ordinary city, God is to His holy habitation—and more, for He is the fountain of life and refreshment, the river of mercy and goodness!

There the majestic Lord will be for us a place of broad rivers and streams, in which no galley with oars will sail, nor majestic ships pass by (Isa. 33:21).

46:5 It is because **God** is enthroned in Jerusalem that **she shall** never **be moved. God shall help her, just at the break of dawn.** It has been a long dark night for God's people, but soon the morning will dawn and Christ will take His rightful place, showing Himself strong on behalf of His own.

46:6 The nations of the earth may rage in fury; **the kingdoms** may totter. When God speaks in His wrath, **the earth** will melt in subservience to Him.

46:7 These words look forward in a special way to the Great Tribulation when the earth will be racked with violent disturbances of nature, with political upheaval, with wars and pestilences, and with inconceivable distress. Then the Lord will appear from heaven to crush all insubordination and rebellion and reign in righteousness and peace. At that time the believing remnant of the nation of Israel will say, **"The LORD of hosts is with us; the God of Jacob is our refuge."**

The assurance of this verse is inexpressibly sweet. **The LORD of hosts is with us**, that is, **the LORD of** the angelic armies of heaven. But He is also **the God of Jacob**. Now Jacob means "cheat" or "supplanter." Yet God speaks of Himself as **the God of Jacob**. Put the two thoughts together and you learn that the God of the angelic hosts is also the God of the unworthy sinner. The One who is infinitely high is also intimately nigh. He is with us in every step of our way, our unfailing **refuge** in all the storms of life.

46:8 By the time we get to verse 8 the tumult and cataclysms have ended.

Man's day is over. Now the King is seated upon His throne in Jerusalem. We are invited to go out and examine the field of His victory. Everywhere we look we see the wreckage of His defeated foes. Everywhere lies the evidence of the awful judgments which have descended on the world during the Tribulation and at His glorious appearing.

46:9 But now that the Prince of Peace is enthroned, **wars** have ceased throughout the world. What councils and leagues and summits have been helpless to achieve, the Lord Jesus brings about by His iron rod. Disarmament has passed from discussion to actuality. Weaponry is scrapped, and the funds formerly spent on munitions are now diverted into agriculture and other productive channels.

46:10 The voice of God rings out to all the inhabitants of the earth in accents of assurance and supremacy. **"Be still, and know that I am God; I will be exalted among the nations, I will be exalted in the earth!"** Every fear is stilled, every anxiety quieted. His people can relax. He is God. His cause is victorious. He is supreme **among the nations**, supreme over all **the earth**.

It is from verse 10 that Katharina von Schlegel, the author of the hymn "Be Still, My Soul" drew inspiration.

Be still, my soul; thy God doth undertake
To guide the future as He has the past.
Thy hope, thy confidence let nothing shake;
All now mysterious shall be bright at last.
Be still, my soul: the winds and waves still know
His voice who ruled them while He dwelt below.

46:11 No matter what may happen or how dark the hour may be, the believer can still say with confidence and fearlessness, **"The LORD of hosts is with us; the God of Jacob is our refuge."** If the One who directs the armies of heaven is on our side, who can be successfully against us? The God of the unworthy worm **Jacob** is a fortress in which we can all take **refuge** from the storms of this uncertain life!

> Be still, the morning comes,
> The night will end;
> Trust thou in Christ thy Light,
> Thy faithful Friend.
> And know that He is God,
> Whose perfect will
> Works all things for thy good:
> Look up—Be still.
> —*Florence Wills*

Psalm 47: Happy New Year!

Jerusalem: The first New Year of the Golden Age of the Messiah was greeted at sundown by a sacred concert in the National Auditorium. Central in the program were the jubilant strains of Psalm 47, which acquired new meaning in view of recent international developments.

47:1–4 As the Psalm began, the audience realized that the Gentile nations which survived the recent global Tribulation were being summoned to **clap** their **hands** and **shout to God** with loud songs of joy. In an unprecedented display of emotion, the choir itself clapped rhythmically as if to lead the way. When the singers came to the words **"For the LORD Most High is awesome"** the people spontaneously rose to their feet. They remembered the recent coronation of the Lord Jesus Christ, when He was publicly acclaimed **"a great King over all the earth."** Gratitude welled up as the people remembered how He subdued "the goat nations" **under our feet**, those nations which had been implacably hostile to Israel during our time of trouble. Ripples of applause swept through the auditorium as the choir sang:

> He will choose our inheritance for us,
> The excellence of Jacob whom He loves. Selah.

47:5 The Messiah who had come down as a man of war to subdue His foes was now hailed as having **gone up** to His throne in Jerusalem amid the delirious shouts of His people and the trumpets announcing His overwhelming victory.

47:6, 7 It was a moving moment when the choir called Israel to **sing praises to God**, to **sing praises to our King**. No longer was there any hesitancy in acknowledging that King Jesus is God, and that the hands that were pierced on Calvary now hold the reins of universal government! Everyone felt the appropriateness of singing to Him with a skillful Psalm—a *maskil* of **understanding** and contemplation.

47:8 Repeatedly the choir emphasized the deity of the Messiah-King. He is the One who now **reigns over the nations** and whose throne is established on holiness.

47:9 Perhaps a tinge of apprehension was felt by some as the words were sung.

> The princes of the people have gathered together...

So often in the past the princes had gathered to drive Israel into the sea. But as the choir continued, it became clear that they were now assembling as **the people of the God** of Abraham. They were joining with the Israelites in bringing tribute to the King of kings and Lord of lords.

Not everyone might have understood that the shields of the earth meant the rulers, who were appointed as protectors of the people. Now they all belong to God; He is greatly exalted high above all earth's potentates.

At the conclusion of the concert, critics agreed that there had never been such a meaningful Rosh Hashanah in the entire history of the nation!

Psalm 48: What Did They See?

A foreign invader had come up to the very gates of Jerusalem. Inside, the people were expecting the agonies of a long siege. Humanly speaking, the prospects were bleak. Then the Lord worked a miracle. The enemy saw something that threw them into utter panic. They retreated in terror. Jerusalem was preserved from destruction, and a great wave of praise went up to God. Psalm 48 captures something of the ecstasy of that moment.

48:1, 2 The Lord is inexpressibly **great**. He is great in power, in knowledge, in glory, in grace. His love is great, and His mercy, and His compassion. He is great in wisdom and in knowledge. His judgments are unsearchable and His ways inscrutable.

Because God is so **great**, He is **greatly to be praised**. He is worthy to be praised as the great Creator, the great Sustainer, the great Prophet, the great High Priest, the King of all kings, the great Redeemer, and the great Deliverer of His people. Here in Psalm 48 it is His greatness as the Savior and Protector of His city and His people that is especially in view.

The people speak of God and **the city of God** in the same breath. They associate the city with the God who dwelt there in the inner shrine of the temple. To them Jerusalem is the most **beautiful** city in the world, situated on the summit **of His holy mountain**. Like a gem in a handsome crown, it is **beautiful in** its **elevation**—the jewel **of the whole earth**.

Sometimes known as **Mount Zion** (after one of the eminences in the city) Jerusalem is described as being "in the far north" or **"on the sides of the north."** Both Knox and Gelineau translate this phrase as "the true pole of the earth." Jerusalem is truly this in the eyes of God's ancient people; it is the center of magnetic attraction, the place toward which they gravitate as the religious, political and cultural capital of the world. And it is **the city of the great King**, the future capital of the Lord Jesus Christ when He returns to earth to reign as King of kings.

48:3 Inside her walls **God** has proved Himself a trustworthy Defender. Everyone knows how He miraculously rescued the city when her destruction seemed momentary. Here is what happened:

48:4 The enemy forces had massed their troops outside the city. In overwhelming hordes they took up their positions in preparation for the assault. Militarily the city had little hope of holding out against such a concentration of armed strength.

48:5 Then the attackers **saw** something that unnerved them. What did they see?

Was it the city of Jerusalem, as seems indicated in the text? It seems unlikely that the mere sight of such a small city would cause professional military men to panic.

It may be that the curtain between them and the invisible world was drawn back, and that they saw an army of angels poised to defend the city. Or was the mountain filled with horses and chariots of fire (see 2 Kgs. 6:17)? Or did they see the angel of the Lord—the Lord Jesus Christ in one of His preincarnate appearances? (See Isa. 37:36.)

48:6, 7 Frankly, we do not know. But whatever it was, it was an apparition of such terrifying nature that the stout-hearted warriors lost their courage. The sight threw them into panic. Pandemonium broke out in the camp. They beat a hasty retreat, trembling as they went. Their anguish was comparable to that of a **woman in** the **pangs** of childbirth. The chaos and disorder among the enemy invaders was like the scattering of an ocean-going fleet when struck by a hurricane.

48:8 The people inside **the city** are now delirious with joy. What seemed like imminent disaster for them has been turned to miraculous victory. They had always **heard** in the past that God was the Founder and Defender of Jerusalem; now they **have seen** with their own eyes. "We have proved what long has been told us— that God upholds the city forever" (Knox).

48:9–11 So they lift their hearts in praise to **God**. They have had abundant reason to meditate on the **loving-kindness** of the Lord as they went up to the **temple** with their thank-offerings. They reflect that wherever God's **name** is known in **the earth**, there He is praised as the One whose **right hand** is filled with righteous victory. They call on Jerusalem to celebrate and on the lesser cities of **Judah** to **be glad**.

48:12–14 Now they are walking around the city in a sort of post-victory tour. They encourage one another to count the number of **towers** (every one of them is still there), to

consider her **bulwarks** (they are all intact), and to walk through the now-deserted **palaces** (just as undamaged as they were before the enemy arrived). It will be a wonderful story to share with their children and grandchildren—how God supernaturally preserved Jerusalem from the slightest damage! They will teach the new **generation** that the **God** who did this is **"our God for ever and ever. He will be our guide even to death."**

Someone has beautifully suggested that verse 14 could be rendered:

This God is our God from eternity to eternity. He will be our guide even unto death, over death, and beyond death.

Psalm 49: The Wicked and Their Wealth

One of the great riddles of life is how the wicked so often enjoy material prosperity while believers are often poor and dispossessed. But this is not the whole story. The wealth in which the ungodly trust so devoutly will fail them in their hour of greatest need. It cannot save them from dying. They cannot enjoy it forever, nor can it prevent corruption in the grave. They can neither take it with them nor come back to enjoy it. In the long run it is stupid to trust in money rather than in the Lord! That is the gist of the message in Psalm 49.

49:1–4 The message is for **all peoples** and individuals, for small and great, for **rich and poor** alike. It is a message of distilled wisdom that comes from a heart that is full of insight. Korah's sons turn their attention to probe into this common inequality of life; then, when they come up with the answer, they sing it to the accompaniment of the **harp**.

49:5–9 Really, there is no reason for God's people to worry in those dark **days** when oppressors are dogging their heels, when persecutors are surrounding them with their iniquitous plots. Their enemies trust in their gold and in the power it gives; they boast about how affluent they are. But—and this is a very big BUT— all their money cannot save their brother from death (KJV) or their own selves either. The **redemption** of a man's life is tremendously **costly**; attempts to stave off the day of death through financial negotiations must be abandoned **forever**. No one has the means to purchase endless life on earth or to escape the grave.

As the dashes before and after verse 8 indicate, it is parenthetical. Putting verses 7 and 9 together, they read:

> **None of them can by any means redeem his brother, nor give to God a ransom for him . . . that he should continue to live eternally, and not see the Pit.**

49:10 Sooner or later even **wise men die**. Likewise **the** rich **fool** and the unthinking man of affluence die **and leave their wealth to others**. Notice that it does not say that the *wise man* leaves his wealth to other people. It is more probable that his last will and testament reads:

> Being of sound mind, I put my money to work for the Lord while I was still alive.

49:11, 12 It is a strange fact of life that men who are intelligent enough to build up a fortune in this world do not seem to realize that they are mortal. Their inward thoughts tell them **that their houses will continue forever**, that they are going to live on

here indefinitely. They name estates and streets and towns after themselves. But the inescapable truth is that **man** with all his **honor** must **perish**. In that respect **he is like the beasts**. In other respects, of course, man is quite different from the animals. For example, though man's body goes to the grave, his spirit and soul do not perish. And his body will be raised from the grave, either for eternal judgment or for eternal blessing. Man has endless being while the animals do not.

49:13, 14 **This is the** fate **of those who** unwisely trust in their wealth rather than in God—they foolishly live as if they were never going to die. But die they must, and when they do their relatives and friends quote them for their profound wisdom. Destined inevitably to be disembodied, they are **like sheep** being led relentlessly by the shepherd of death to **the grave**. **"The upright shall have dominion over them in the morning"**; that is, the tables will be turned, as with the rich man and Lazarus. Remember that Abraham said to the rich man:

> Son, remember that in your lifetime you received your good things, and likewise Lazarus evil things; but now he is comforted and you are tormented (Luke 16:25).

All the magnificence and **beauty** of the rich man wastes away, and he has no home but Sheol—a striking contrast to the home he enjoyed on earth!

49:15 Here we have one of the few flashes of light about the resurrection found in the OT. Generally speaking, the OT writers reveal very indistinct views of death and beyond. But here the psalmist voices the confidence that **God will redeem** his **soul from the power of the grave,**

that is, that God will deliver his **soul** from the disembodied state and reunite it with his resurrected body. When he says **"for He shall receive me,"** he uses the same word that is used in connection with God's receiving Enoch and Elijah.

49:16–19 So there is really no need for a believer to be disturbed when the ungodly man **becomes rich** and **his house** becomes more and more ornate and lavish. This earth is the only heaven he is ever going to enjoy! **When he dies he shall carry** none of his wealth with him. Empty-handed he will go to the grave, with none of his splendor to accompany him. As long as **he lives** he thinks he can never be robbed of his happiness, and people applaud him for feathering his own nest. But sooner or later he will die like his forefathers and share their long dark night with them.

49:20 There is simply no way that **a man** can hold on to earthly wealth and **honor**. Death is as inevitable for him as for **the beasts that perish**.

Of course someone could object that the righteous die as well as the wicked. This is true. We will all die if the Lord does not come in the meantime. But the point of the Psalm is that the wicked leave all their wealth behind while the righteous go to their eternal reward of infinite wealth.

One final observation. Very often in Scripture a rich man is synonymous with a wicked man. This ought to sober us. While the Bible doesn't say that it is a sin to be rich, it does condemn trusting in riches rather than in the living God (and it is hard to have riches without trusting in them!). The Bible condemns the love of money. It condemns the accumulation of wealth through oppression and dishonesty. And it condemns the hoarding of riches in callous disregard of the needs of a lost and suffering world.

Psalm 50: God's Ongoing Judgment

The setting of this Psalm is a courtroom with God Himself the Judge, Israel the defendant, and heaven and earth the witnesses.

But we should not think of this courtroom scene as some obscure trial that took place long ago in Israel's history; it is instead God's continuing evaluation of His saints throughout the world.

The Court in Session (50:1–6)

50:1 First the Judge is *heard* as He summons all the people in the entire land[36] of Israel—from east to west—to stand before His tribunal. What gives authority to the Judge's voice is the fact that He is **the Mighty One, God the LORD**.

50:2, 3 Next the Judge is *seen* as He leaves His chamber in the temple on Mount **Zion** in the form of a dazzling, brilliant glory cloud—the Shekinah. He will no longer **keep silent** about His people's sin. He comes down as He did at Mount Sinai, with a great jet of **fire** sweeping **before Him** and a great storm with thunder and lightning **all around Him**. But this time He comes not to *present* the law, but to *interpret* its inward, spiritual meaning.

50:4, 5 As He takes His place on the judgment seat He subpoenas **the heavens** and **the earth** to stand by in the witness box. Then He commands His attendants to bring in the defendants. First He is going to try the **saints** of the nation of Israel, whom He describes as **those who have made a covenant with** Him **by sacrifice**. (This refers to the covenant of the law made at Mount Horeb and ratified by the blood of sacrifices—Ex. 24:3–8.) The trial of His faithful ones is found in verses 7–15. Later He has a special session with the wicked (vv. 16–19).

50:6 **The heavens** are called to bear witness to the **righteousness** of God's judgments. The fact that **God Himself is** the **Judge** means that He has perfect knowledge of all the facts, that He is absolutely impartial, and that all His verdicts are wise and equitable.

The Sin of Ritualism (50:7–15)

50:7 God now assumes the position of prosecuting attorney, testifying against His **people, Israel**. In human affairs it would be unthinkable for the judge to also serve as prosecutor, but in this case it is altogether proper, for the Judge is none other than **God** the Most High.

50:8 God makes it clear at the outset that Israel has not been remiss in bringing **sacrifices** to Him. They had been faithful in bringing their **burnt offerings**. But the trouble was that they thought these rituals completely discharged their obligations to Jehovah. They were like girls who treat their mother indifferently throughout the year, then smother her with chocolates on her birthday! Or like sons who never thank their father for all he does for them, then give him a gift tie on Father's Day!

So Jehovah protests that while they had loaded His altar with sacrificial animals, they had treated Him personally with cold neglect. As to the technical details of the offerings, His people had been punctilious. But when it came to a warm, personal relationship with the Lord Himself, they were seriously lacking. F. B. Meyer writes:

The Psalm is a severe rebuke of the hypocrite who contents himself with giving a mere outward obedience to the ritual of God's house, but withholds the love and homage of his heart.[37]

50:9 That is why God says that **He will not take a bull from their house, nor goats out of their folds.** He is not a ritualist, satisfied with religious ceremonies. In instituting the sacrificial system, God had never intended right outward action to serve as a cover for wrong inward attitudes.

50:10–13 If they would only stop to think, God's people would realize that God owns all the creatures in the world anyway—**every beast of the forest . . . the cattle on a thousand hills, . . . the birds** of the air, and everything that moves in **the field**. They would quickly realize that God doesn't need a single thing from men. He doesn't suffer hunger; if He did, He wouldn't have to ask us for anything, because He has a well-stocked pantry! Nor does He derive nourishment or satisfaction from **bulls'** meat or **goats'** blood. In that sense, God is totally self-sufficient.

50:14, 15 What then *does* **God** want from His people? Three things:

Thanksgiving. No gift can ever take the place of simple gratitude. Too often we are like the family that took their queenly mother for granted, then after her death attempted to atone for their thanklessness by dressing her body in a two-thousand-dollar Dior original!

Fulfilled vows. "**Pay your vows to the Most High**"—vows of love, worship, service, and devotion.

Fellowship in prayer. "**Call upon Me in the day of trouble; I will deliver you, and you shall glorify Me.**" Here we have a wonderful insight into the heart of God. He loves to hear His people pray, and He loves to answer those prayers. He cherishes an intimate, tender relationship between His people and Himself.

But to the Wicked . . . (50:16–21)

50:16, 17 It seems clear that the Judge now turns to address a different portion of the nation, those who profess to be religious but whose lives openly contradict the truth. He denies that they have any right to piously quote the Scriptures or to claim the blessings of the Covenant for themselves. Then He levels a series of charges against them.

They hated discipline. Apparently they considered themselves above correction. Instead of welcoming or at least tolerating constructive criticism, these hypocrites resented it bitterly and attacked anyone who tried to offer it—even if it was the Lord.

They treated God's Word with contempt. Instead of profound reverence for the Scriptures, they **cast** God's **words behind** them as a worthless thing.

50:18 *They refused to walk in a path of separation.* By fraternizing with thieves and **adulterers**, they disobeyed the Lord and brought reproach on His name.

50:19, 20 *Their speech was wicked.* Their mouths spewed out **evil** without restraint. They had become experts in lying and **deceit**. Even their closest relatives were not safe from their vicious slander.

50:21 Because God had not punished them immediately, they **thought** He was as careless as they were. They failed to realize that His patience was designed to give them time to repent. But now the Lord

breaks His silence and rebukes them for the charges listed above.

Warning and Promise (50:22, 23)

The Psalm closes with a warning and a promise. The warning is to those **who forget God**, living as if He doesn't matter. If they do not repent, God will pounce on them like a lion and utterly destroy them. But those who come to Him with sacrifices of thanksgiving glorify Him; all who walk in this pathway of obedience will experience God's marvelous deliverances in times of peril.

Psalm 51: Sweet Perfumes of Penitence

Alexander Maclaren once said, "The alchemy of divine love can extract sweet perfumes of penitence and praise out of the filth of sin." We have an illustration of this in Psalm 51. As the heading explains, it was written by **David** after **Nathan the prophet** had boldly exposed him for committing adultery with **Bathsheba** and for murdering Uriah. Utterly convicted of his sin, David pours out this torrent of penitence from his broken and contrite heart.

We might paraphrase his confession as follows:

51:1 Mercy, . . . O God! I ask for Your **mercy!** I deserve to be punished. But You are a God of **lovingkindness** and on that basis I ask that You not treat me the way I deserve. Your **mercies** are super-abounding and because of that I dare to ask that You erase my awful violations of Your holy law.

51:2 Wash me through and through from every instance where I have departed from Your straight line, **and cleanse me from** the frightful ways in which I have missed the mark.

51:3 Oh my God, I publicly **acknowledge** that I have broken Your law. My sin was public and my repentance is public, too. The guilt of **my sin** has been haunting me day and night, and I cannot stand it any more.

51:4 I now see clearly that it was **against You**, and **You** alone that **I sinned**. Oh, I realize that I also sinned against Bathsheba and against her faithful husband, Uriah—God forgive me for my treachery to this valiant general. But I realize that all sin is first and foremost **against You**. Your law has been broken. Your will has been flouted. Your name has been dishonored. So I take sides with You against myself. You are absolutely justified in any sentence You hand down, and no one can find fault with Your decisions.

51:5 Lord, I am no good. **I was** born **in iniquity**, and going back even farther, I was **conceived in sin**. In saying this I don't mean to cast any shame on my mother, or even to extenuate my own guilt. What I mean is that not only have I committed sins but that I am sinful in my very nature.

51:6 But You hate sin and You love faithfulness in a man's **inward** being, so now I am coming to You and asking You to teach me **wisdom** deep in my heart.

51:7 You directed that **hyssop** and running water should be used in the ceremony for cleansing a leper (Lev. 14:1–8). Well, Lord, I take the place of a moral leper. **Purge me with hyssop, and I shall be clean; wash me, and I shall be whiter than snow.**

51:8 When I sinned, I lost my song. It has been so long since I have known what real **joy and gladness** are. Let me hear the music of rejoicing once again. In my backslidden condition, it seemed that You had crippled me by breaking my **bones**. I could no longer dance before You in the holy festivals. Now heal those fractures so that I may join Your people in praising Your name in the dance.

51:9 Oh, my God, I beg You to turn away **Your face** from looking on **my sins** in judgment and punishment. **Blot out** the last vestige of **my** enormous **iniquities**. How they stab me every time I think of them!

51:10 Looking back, I realize that the trouble all started in my mind. My thought-life was polluted. I entertained evil thoughts until at last I committed the sins. So now I ask that You **create in me a clean** mind. I know that if the fountain is clean, the stream flowing from it will be clean as well. Yes, Lord, **renew** my entire inner self so it will be **steadfast** in guarding against future outbreaks of sin.

51:11 Don't give up on me, Lord, or banish me from Your presence. I can't stand the thought of being away from You, or of having **Your Holy Spirit** taken **from me**. In this age in which I live, You do take Your Holy Spirit from men when they walk in disobedience to You. You did it to Saul (1 Sam. 16:14)—I shudder to think of the consequences. Please, Lord, spare me from this fate.

51:12 As I said before, I have lost my song. Not my soul, but my song. Not Your salvation, but **the joy of Your salvation**. Now that I have come to You in repentance, confession, and forsaking of sin, I pray that the "chords that are broken may vibrate once more." And not only do I pray that You will restore to me **the joy of Your salvation**, but also that You will **uphold me by Your generous Spirit**. In other words, I want Your Spirit to make me willing to obey You and to please You in all things. Then I will be maintained in paths of righteousness.

51:13 One by-product of my forgiveness will be that I will aggressively witness to other **transgressors** and tell them **Your ways** of pardon and peace. When they hear of what You have done for me, they will want to return **to You** also.

51:14 Then, too, if You **deliver me from** the guilt of bloodshed, **O God,** the whole world will hear my testimony of Your deliverance. The guilt of Uriah's blood is heavy upon me, O **God of my salvation**. Wipe the slate clean and I'll praise You forever.

51:15 My lips have been sealed shut by my sin. **Open** them by Your forgiveness and **my mouth** will be dedicated to speaking and singing **Your praise**.

51:16, 17 Lord, I am not depending on rituals or ceremonies for forgiveness. I know that You are not a ritualist. If I thought You wanted animal **sacrifice, I would** bring them. But **burnt offering** does **not delight** Your heart. It is true that You instituted sacrifices and offerings, but they never represented Your ultimate ideal. And so I come to You with **a broken heart**—that is the sacrifice You require. **You will not despise** this shattered and **contrite heart** that I bring to You.

51:18 And now, Lord, I want to pray for Your dear people as well as for myself. Be pleased to shower them with good things. Rebuild **the walls of Jerusalem**. My sins have doubtless hindered the progress of Your work. I have brought reproach upon Your name. Now may Your cause move forward without hindrance.

51:19 When we all walk in fellowship with You, confessing and forsaking our sins, **then You shall be pleased with** our **sacrifices of righteousness. Offerings** that speak of complete dedication to Yourself will gladden Your heart. We will **offer bulls on Your altar**—in praise to the God who forgives sin and pardons iniquity.

Psalm 52: The Traitor Unmasked

The historical background of this Psalm is found in 1 Samuel 21, 22. **Doeg the Edomite** was King Saul's chief herdsman. He was present when the fugitive David received food and Goliath's sword from **Ahimelech** the priest. Soon afterward he went and tattled to **Saul**, and was rewarded by being delegated to kill Ahimelech and eighty-four other priests of the Lord. Subsequently he massacred the women and children at Nob and destroyed the village and even the animals.

Doeg's character is delineated in verses 1–4 and his doom in verses 5–7. The psalmist's contrasting character is seen in verses 8 and 9.

52:1–4 David's opening question assails the traitor for taking pride in his extreme **evil** and for "forging wild lies all day against God's loyal servant" (NEB). This treacherous prototype of the Antichrist had a razor-sharp **tongue** that cut people down with its slander. He had a strong bent for **evil more than good**, and would rather lie than tell the truth. The personification of deceit, he reveled in speech that wrecked other lives.

52:5 Divine and human justice agree on the fate which the psalmist foretells for Doeg and all his counterparts. God will break him down to the ground like a building reduced to rubble. The Most High will snatch him out of His tent, and completely **uproot** him **from the** world of **living** men.

52:6, 7 God-fearing people will live to **see** that day, will be struck by the awesome judgment of God, and will chuckle at his reversal, saying:

Here is the man who did not make God his strength, but trusted in the abundance of his riches, and strengthened himself in his wickedness.

52:8, 9 The psalmist's character is in glaring contrast. He compares himself to **a green olive tree in the house of God**—a picture of prosperity and fruitfulness. The olive is, according to F. W. Grant:

> ... the tree in which abides that (oil) which typifies the Spirit of God, green in its freshness of life eternal. It is in the house of God (in contrast to) that "tent" out of which the wicked one is cast.[38]

In contrast to Doeg who would not make God his refuge, David is determined that he will **trust in the mercy of the LORD forever and ever**.

Something else he will do forever is to thank the Lord for what He has done—namely, for punishing the wicked and vindicating the righteous.

Finally, he will magnify the **name of** the Lord in **the presence of** His loyal **saints**, because His name **is good** and all that He is is good.

Psalm 53: The Folly of Atheism

The main difference between Psalm 14 and this one is that the name of God is changed from Jehovah (or Yahweh) to Elohim.[39] In Psalm 14 the fool denies the existence of the covenant-keeping God (Jehovah, LORD) who is deeply interested and involved in the welfare of His people. Here the fool denies the existence of an al-

mighty, sovereign God (Elohim) who sustains and governs the universe.

> God can be denied in both senses: some deny that the Creator has any special interest in any particular race or group of men; others repudiate any possibility of there being a God at all (Daily Notes of the Scripture Union).

53:1   The fool is not necessarily a dunce or stupid. He may be intellectually brilliant as far as contemporary education is concerned, but he does not want to face the evidence as to the person, power and providence of God. He is willfully ignorant. "The Hebrew word has in it the idea of a malicious refusal to acknowledge the truth."

Atheism is linked with depravity and degradation, sometimes as cause, sometimes as effect. Therefore it is not surprising that those who say **"There is no** Elohim" **are corrupt**, doing **abominable iniquity. There is none** of them **who does good.**

53:2 Now the subject seems to glide from atheists in particular to mankind in general. Paul quotes snatches from these verses in Romans 3 to establish the total depravity of all mankind. The indictment is true, of course. As **God looks down from heaven upon** the **race of men,** He cannot find one who, left to himself, would have the wisdom to fear the Lord. Apart from the prior ministry of the Holy Spirit, no one would **seek God**.

53:3 They have all **turned aside** from the living God. **They have** all **become** depraved. Not one **does good** in the sense of something that can gain favor or merit with the Lord.

53:4, 5 Again, there seems to be a switch to a particular class of sinners, namely, those apostates who persecute God's **people**. How can they be so short-sighted? They are cruel and prayerless. They think no more of destroying the faithful remnant than of eating **bread**. And they never feel the need of speaking to **God** in prayer. They seem completely insensible to the fact that one day they will be seized with unprecedented terror. God will scatter **the bones** of those who wage war against His loyal followers.

53:6 In the last verse, David prays for the coming of the Messiah. He is the Deliverer who will **come out of Zion** (Rom. 11:26) and save all believing Israel. In that day Israel will be restored, **Jacob** will **rejoice and Israel will be glad**.

Psalm 54: God Is My Helper

When **David** was fleeing from Saul, **the Ziphites** twice revealed his whereabouts to the king (1 Sam. 23:19; 26:1). These betrayals gave rise to the words of this Psalm, a suitable prayer for God's people in any age when suffering at the hands of men.

54:1 The opening cry for help asks for salvation by God's **name** and vindication **by** His **strength**. His **name** stands for His nature or character and His **strength** for His omnipotence. Salvation here means temporal deliverance from enemies.

54:2, 3 The now-or-never urgency of the psalmist is seen in the importunate plea for **God** to **hear**, to listen to the hissing-hot **words of** his **mouth**. What had happened was that these **strangers** had conspired to double-cross David; bloodthirsty men were out to get him—apostates who cared nothing about **God**.

54:4, 5 **God** is the answer. **The Lord is with those who uphold** the believer's **life**. One day **He will repay**

the **enemies** of His people with calamity and ruin.

The knowledge of what God will do turns quickly into the prayer, "Do it, Lord. In proof of Your faithfulness, bring their wicked careers to an end."

54:6 The saving name of verse 1 will then become the worshiped name. David will bring a freewill **sacrifice** to the Lord, and offer thanksgivings to the **name** of the LORD—the precious name in which all **good** is enshrined.

54:7 In the final verse David speaks as if **all** his **trouble** was past, and as if he had already witnessed the demise of his **enemies**. "Already," writes Morgan, "though perhaps yet in the midst of the peril, he sings the song of deliverance, as though it were already realized."[40] Faith thus "gives substance to our hopes, and makes us certain of realities we do not see" (Heb. 11:1, NEB).

Psalm 55: Cast Your Burden

Ahithophel was one of David's most trusted advisers who later led a defection to the usurping Absalom. In this Psalm, we sense the extreme anguish of David's heart over this bitter blow. We can also read here something of the deep tides of emotion which surged through the Savior's soul in connection with His betrayal by Judas. And the Psalm foreshadows the prayer of the remnant as they suffer under the conspiracy of the coming Antichrist.

55:1, 2a In deep distress the soul does not lack variety or originality in attracting the attention of God. Positively, there is the request to **give ear**. Negatively, the word is **"do not hide Yourself."** There is the appeal for audience, **"Attend to me,"** and the appeal for action, **"and hear me."**

55:2b–5 Then follows a heart-rending catalog of personal grief and of desperate need.

> **Restless** in complaining and moaning.
> Distracted by the shouts **of the enemy**.
> Oppressed by **the wicked**.
> Buried by them under heaps of **trouble**.
> Exposed to furious assaults.
> Heartbroken with anguish.
> Terrified by impending doom.
> Afflicted by uncontrollable **trembling**.
> **Overwhelmed** with **horror**.

55:6–8 His first impulse is to **fly away** from all his troubles. If he **had wings**, he would take off for some quiet spot **in the wilderness**. He would waste no time in escaping from the **tempest** that was swirling around him.

55:9a But now his terror gives way to burning indignation. He is so revolted by the treachery of the conspirators that he calls on the Lord to **destroy**—without specifying whether He should **destroy** the people or their plans. Also he asks God to **divide their tongues**—which may be an allusion to David's prayer at this time that the Lord would turn the counsel of Ahithophel into foolishness (2 Sam. 15:31).

55:9b–11 As the son of Jesse looks at **the city** of Jerusalem which he conquered and chose, he sees it filled with **violence and strife; day and night** these twin evils stalk around **it on its walls**. The city of peace is now a city of mischief and trouble. Ruin is resident. **Oppression and** fraud never leave the marketplace, where there ought to be justice and equity.

55:12–15 At the heart of David's complaint, of course, is his cruel betrayal. The pain would have been more endurable if the culprit had been **an** avowed **enemy**. If the taunts and insults had come from an out-

and-out adversary, then the psalmist could have kept out of his way. But it was one of his own, a **companion**, a loved and trusted friend who had knifed him in the back. It was one with whom the psalmist used to have **sweet** fellowship as they **walked** together in the courts of the tabernacle. The perfidy of this man and his followers deserves sudden death, a quick trip to Sheol, "for wickedness dwells in their homes and deep in their hearts" (Gelineau).

55:16–21 Yet in all his emotional turmoil, David is assured of help in answer to prayer. The sobs and moans that ascend to God **evening and morning and at noon** will reach the Savior's ear. In spite of the numerical superiority of those arrayed against him, David will emerge from **the battle** with **peace** as his portion. Yes, **God will hear, and afflict them**, even **He who** sits eternally enthroned. This is the condemnation of those with whom there is no **change**, i.e., repentance, and who **do not fear God**. This is the condemnation of the traitor—the bosom companion who stretched out his hand to harm his friends and who broke the covenant of friendship and allegiance. His **words** seemed **smoother than butter, . . . yet they were drawn swords**.

55:22 The golden peak of Psalm 55 is reached in verse 22:

> **Cast your burden on the LORD,**
> **And He shall sustain you;**
> **He shall never permit**
> **the righteous to be moved.**

The psalmist came to realize that the best course in time of troubles is not to run away from them, but to **cast** the **burden** of them **on the LORD**. May we learn the lovely lesson set forth by Bishop Horne: "He who once bore the burden of our sins and sorrows requests that we should now and ever permit Him to bear the burden of our cares."

55:23 Men of murder and treachery will die violently and prematurely. Ahithophel did (2 Sam. 17:14, 23) and so did Judas (Matt. 27:5). But God's people can depend on Him to save them.

Psalm 56: God Is For Me!

It was a bitter pill for **David** to have to seek refuge from his own countrymen among the **Philistines** in **Gath** (1 Sam. 21:10–15; 27:4; 29:2–11), but the fierce hostility of King Saul drove him to it—or so he felt. Psalm 56 describes some of the alternating waves of fear and faith which swept over him at that time.

56:1, 2 He begins with a prayer for God's gracious help in view of the constant harassment of his pursuers. Notice the three kinds of terror which were coming upon him **all day** from hostile men:

  . . . **he oppresses me** (v. 1)

My enemies . . . hound me (v. 2)

  . . . they twist my words (v. 5)

His foes were arrogantly attacking him, constantly plotting evil **against** him, federating for greater strength, lurking to pounce upon him, continually spying on him (vv. 2, 5, 6). It seemed like a clear case of overkill.

56:3 But faith breaks through the gloom with the confident declaration, **"Whenever I am afraid, I will trust in You."** This "cheerful courage of a fugitive," as Delitzsch calls it, is based on the character of God and on the faithfulness of His promises. He is more powerful than all our foes combined, and He has promised to protect us from harm. Nothing can penetrate the protective hedge which

He sets up around us except by His permissive will. This is why we can trust in God without a fear.

56:4–6 To the bold challenge **"What can** mere man **do to me?"** reason might answer, "Plenty. Man can persecute, injure, maim, shoot, and kill." But the fact is that the child of God is immortal until his work is done. Also we should understand David's fearlessness in the light of our Savior's words:

> And do not fear those who kill the body but cannot kill the soul. But rather fear Him who is able to destroy both soul and body in hell (Matt. 10:28).

56:7 After rehearsing the studied attempts of his enemies to wipe him out, David calls **on God** to requite them for their treachery by casting them **down in** His **anger.**

56:8 Here is an exquisite description of the tender, personalized care of our Lord. He keeps a count of our **wanderings** or restless tossings during the night, of our fevered turnings from one side to another. He cares so much about the details of our **tears** of sorrow that He can be asked to keep our **tears** in His **bottle.** This may be an allusion to an ancient custom of mourners, namely, preserving their falling tears in a small bottle, which was placed in the tomb of deceased friends, as a memorial of the survivors' affection. In any event, God does keep a record of our **tears in** His **book,** just as Jesus later taught us that He numbers the very hairs of our heads.

56:9 With David we can be confident that God will turn back our **enemies** in answer to our prayers. We know this because God is for us. And if God is for us, who can successfully be against us (Rom. 8:31)?

There is, ultimately, only one question which matters in life; everything else is secondary to this—'Is God *for* us?' David, at *last*, was sure of God; and the man who is sure of God is beyond fear (11) (*Daily Notes of the Scripture Union*).

56:10, 11 The refrain of verse 4 is repeated in verses 10 and 11 but this time using two different names of God:

> In God [Elohim] **(I will praise His word),**
> in the LORD [YHWH, Jehovah] **(I will praise His word),**
> in God [Elohim] **I have put my trust;**
> I will **not be afraid.**
> What can man do to me?

The psalmist praises the promise of the Almighty One and of the covenant-keeping One, in utter assurance of His protecting care, and in cool contempt of frail man's ability to harm him.

56:12, 13 The present assurance of future deliverance puts David under constraint to fulfill the **vows** he **made** to the Lord, and to pay his debt of gratitude to Him. Though still in enemy territory, he is enjoying the blessing of full salvation. His life has been saved, and his **feet** kept from stumbling so that he might continue to **walk** in the presence of **God in the light of** life.

Psalm 57: In the Shadow of His Wings

David was hiding from **Saul** in a **cave** when he wrote this Psalm—either the cave of Adullam or the one at Engedi. There are two ever-present realities before him—the gracious God and the formidable foe. The Psalm see-saws between the two, but faith in the former is greater than fear of the latter and tilts the see-saw in that direction.

The Ever-Present God (57:1–3)

The psalmist does not demand deliverance, as if he had a right to expect it. He asks it as a mercy from **God**, an undeserved blessing stemming from His kindness. Oblivious of his dank, dark surroundings, he reckons himself as sheltered **in the shadow of** God's **wings**, like a chicken snuggled under the wings of the mother hen. And there he will stay **until** the storms of life **have passed by**. From this privileged place of conscious nearness, he cries **to God Most High** with the confidence that no one and nothing can hinder Him from accomplishing His purposes in the lives of His people. When the answer comes **from heaven**, it will mean deliverance for the trusting heart and dishonor for those who walk all over him. It will be an unforgettable demonstration of God's love and dependability.

The Ever-Present Enemy (57:4)

The enemies are formidable—like savage, fiery **lions** that tear and devour; these **sons of men** have **teeth** like **spears and arrows**, and tongues like **sharp** swords. Yet David lies down to rest in the middle of such danger—a truly remarkable feat of faith.

The Ever-Present God (57:5)

In a refrain that is repeated in verse 11, David longs to see God's **glory** manifested in the crushing of His foes and the vindication of His cause. Nothing will do but that His **glory** be astral and global in its dimensions.

The Ever-Present Enemy (57:6)

The adversaries laid careful plans to trap the son of Jesse: his **soul** was bent over with heaviness. Yes, **they** had **dug a pit** to trap him, but **they themselves** fell into it.

The Ever-Present God (57:7–11)

No wonder the psalmist's **heart** is steadfastly determined to **sing** with melody to the **Lord**. No wonder he rouses his soul, and dusts off **the lute and harp**. No wonder he is determined to greet **the dawn** with songs of praise.

Nor will it be a private, provincial songfest. He will thank the Lord **among the peoples**, and **sing** psalms **among the nations**, because God's **mercy** is as infinite as **the heavens** and His **truth** as limitless as **the clouds**.

F. B. Meyer notes that just as David "rose above personal grief in a desire for God's glory" so we should subordinate our own petty griefs in a great passion to see Him **exalted**.

Psalm 58: The Judges Judged

58:1, 2 As the Psalm opens, it is a vigorous protest against unjust judges or rulers. The mighty lords of the earth are put on the spot. Have they been fair in their decisions? Have they dispensed justice to the common people? The obvious answer is **"No."** In their hearts they have concocted all sorts of crookedness. Then their **hands** have dealt out **the violence** that their hearts had planned. The land is filled with perversion of justice.

58:3 The subject broadens from dishonest magistrates to the wider class of **wicked** people to which they belong. Their corruption is not a development of later life; it can be traced right back to their birth. Their law-lessness and rebellion are inborn; as soon as they begin to talk, they begin to lie.

58:4, 5 Their speech is slanderous and malignant **like the** deadly **poison of a serpent**. Their ears are deaf to the voice of God **like the deaf cobra** that will not listen to the charmer, no matter how **skillfully** he plays.

58:6, 7 Just as David drew from the world of nature to describe their wickedness, so he now dips into natural science for fitting metaphors of judgment. Let the **teeth** of these fierce lions be broken, their cruel **fangs** extracted. Let them vanish like **waters** that quickly disappear into the ground, or a stream that mysteriously vanishes underground.

The Hebrew of verse 7b is uncertain. It may mean, "May they be as **arrows** with the heads **cut** off—blunt and harmless."

58:8 Then the world of snails and slugs is invaded. Just as a **snail "melts away"** in a trail of slime, so let these criminals disappear from the haunts of men. Whether snails actually dissolve in slime is an unimportant technicality. No one objects when we say that a burning house "goes up in smoke." Then why quibble over a figurative expression in the Bible?

The next imprecation is that these evildoers might die prematurely, **like a stillborn child** that never sees **the sun**. "The eyes of the wicked have never been opened," says Scroggie, "and their possibilities have never unfolded; the sinner is an abortion, a promise never fulfilled."[41]

58:9 Finally the psalmist asks that they may be suddenly swept **away**, like **burning thorns** are scattered by **a whirlwind** before the pot above them feels the heat. Maclaren says:

The picture before the psalmist seems to be that of a company of travellers round their camp, preparing their meal. They heap brushwood under the pot, and expect to satisfy their hunger; but before the pot is warmed through, not to say before the water boils or the meal is cooked, down comes a whirlwind, which sweeps away fire, pot and all.[42]

58:10 There is nothing uncertain about the Hebrew here. It states unmistakably that the people of God will be elated when **the wicked** are punished, that **he shall wash his feet in the blood of the wicked**. If this sounds vindictive and loveless to our Christian ears, we may justify it by saying, with J. G. Bellett, that while we cannot rejoice in judgment in this age of grace, believers will do so when the Lord vindicates His divine glory by **vengeance**. Or we may consider the words of Morgan that "it is a sickly sentimentality and a wicked weakness that has more sympathy with the corrupt oppressors than with the anger of God."[43]

58:11 In the ongoing judgment of the ungodly, men realize that **the righteous** are rewarded, and that **God** actually does judge men here on **earth**.

Psalm 59: The God Who Comes to Meet Us

Here **David** storms the throne of God in almost breathless haste because Saul has **sent men** to surround **the house** and tighten the noose.

59:1–4 The words come gushing out like a hot torrent—**"Deliver me . . . defend me . . . save me."** The language is vehement, abrupt, urgent. These ungodly men are thirsting for his blood. Relentlessly they wait for their chance to kill him; they unite in a common effort to eliminate him. And yet it is all so unprovoked. The psalmist is not guilty of the treason

and disloyalty with which they charge him. Their feverish preparations were provoked **through no fault of** his. If only God would awaken and come to David's rescue!

59:5 For a moment, the son of Jesse seems to look beyond his immediate foes to all the enemies of **Israel** and calls on God to do a thorough work of punishment. Here he addresses God as *Jehovah, Elohim Sabaoth, Elohe Israel,* a reduplication of the names of God that is intended to express all He is in His essential being and in His special relation to **Israel**.

59:6, 7 Like a pack of wild alley dogs, they return to besiege the psalmist, howling and prowling. Their incessant barking, their snarling growls fill the air. They arrogantly suppose themselves to be immune from detection.

59:8, 9 But they are known to the LORD—and He laughs at their insensate folly, the same God who looks down on the boasting **nations** with cool **derision**. This great **God** is David's **Strength**, the One for whom he watches and his sure **defense**.

59:10 Someone has given us this unforgettable paraphrase of verse 10a: **"My God,** with His lovingkindness, **shall come to meet me** at every corner." What a comfort for storm-tossed souls of every age! Linked with this assurance is the knowledge that **God** will preserve us to **see** this defeat of our **enemies**.

59:11–13 The prayer of verse 11 is unique. David asks the Lord **not** to **slay** the enemy suddenly **lest the people** of Israel entertain light thoughts of the seriousness of sin. If the punishment is gradual, the severity of God will be more indelibly impressed on them. But it is clear from what follows that ultimate destruction is included in the catalog of dire judgments which the psalmist specifies for his persecutors. He prays that they be scattered by God's **power, and** brought **down** by the Lord who guards Israel. He asks that they might be captured while they are showing off their consummate **pride** and brought to account for their sinful, wicked **words**. Finally he prays that they might be utterly destroyed for their **cursing and lying** speech. Then at last the world will **know** from east to west that **God** really does care for the descendants of **Jacob**.

59:14, 15 In the meantime the human dogs **return** to **the city** searching for the psalmist, growling, prowling, and howling for his life, and angry when they don't get it.

59:16, 17 The dogs are growling in the evening, but the son of Jesse is singing **in the morning**. He is extolling the **power** and **mercy** of the Lord because He has proved Himself a **defense and refuge in the day of** deep need. **The morning** is coming for all God's people when their enemies will be gone and when the **power** and love of the Savior will be the theme of endless song.

Psalm 60: Our Hope Is in the Lord

According to the heading, the historical background of this Psalm is **when** David **fought against Mesopotamia and Syria of Zobah, and Joab returned and killed twelve thousand Edomites in the Valley of Salt**. It seems that there was a temporary setback in this war with Syria and Edom (2 Sam. 8:3–14), causing David to storm the gates of heaven with this importunate plea for help.

The outline of the Psalm is as follows:

1. Israel's Defeat Is from the Lord, vv. 1–4.
2. Israel's Hope Is in the Lord, v. 5.
3. Eventual Victory is Promised by the Lord, vv. 6–8.
4. Israel's Need Is for the Lord, vv. 9–11.
5. Israel's Confidence Is in the Lord, v. 12.

Israel's Defeat Is from the Lord (60:1–4)

60:1–3 As he studies reports of casualties inflicted by the Edomite-Syrian alliance, David interprets the disaster as an indication of the Lord's desertion of His people. It can only mean that **God** has rejected Israel. In His anger, He has smashed down the nation's defenses, leaving it helplessly exposed to enemy attack. Now is it not time for the Lord to turn in mercy and restore His battered forces?

It is as if the country has been torn apart by an enormous earthquake. The economic, political, and social foundations of the nation have been **broken** up. The walls of society, weakened by gaping holes, are tottering. If only the Lord would repair the **breaches** and return His people to a measure of normality!

The population has passed through a fiery ordeal. **The wine of** suffering and defeat has caused them to reel like a drunkard.

60:4 This verse is somewhat obscure in the original. It may mean, as in the NKJV, that the Lord unfurls **a banner** for **those who fear** Him, **that it may be displayed because of the truth**. But the margin of the RV gives quite an opposite sense:

Thou hast given a banner to them that fear thee, that they may flee from before the bow.

David would then be complaining, with undisguised sarcasm, that the **banner** God has raised for Israel is not one of victory but of defeat, a flag that signals retreat from before the forces of the enemy.

Israel's Hope Is in the Lord (60:5)

Prayer is born from the ashes of humiliating defeat. Speaking both for himself and his people as **"Your beloved,"** the psalmist implores the Lord for deliverance, victory and the renewal of communion. "O come and deliver Your friends, help with Your right hand and reply" (Gelineau).

Eventual Victory Is Promised by the Lord (60:6–8)

60:6, 7 Verses 6–8 form a divine oracle in which the voice of **God**, heard in the sanctuary, expresses His determination to reoccupy all the land of Israel and to conquer His Gentile foes.

Shechem, Succoth, Gilead, Manasseh, Ephraim, and **Judah** are all Jewish territory. God claims them as His own. He will subdivide **Shechem**, on the west of the Jordan, and the **Valley of Succoth** on the east. He will possess the trans-Jordan land of **Gilead**, and the two territories of **Manasseh**, one on either side of the Jordan.

Ephraim, located centrally in Israel, is His **helmet**, the tribe that will take the lead in national defense. And **Judah** is His scepter; according to Jacob's dying prophecy (Gen. 49:10), it will be the governmental seat.

60:8 Then turning to three of the surrounding nations, the Lord asserts His dominion over them. **Moab**, situated on the southeastern shore of the Dead Sea, will be His **washpot**. He will **cast** His **shoe** upon **Edom**, a figure signifying forcible possession

and servitude and perhaps also contempt. **Philistia** will **shout in triumph because of** God's judgments.

Israel's Need Is for the Lord (60:9–11)

60:9 It seems clear that the speaker changes at this point.[44] It could scarcely be the Lord's voice because He would not need anyone to **bring** Him **to the strong city**. So we understand these to be the words of David, longing for the day when the capital city of Edom (variously called Bozrah, Sela and Petra) will fall into the hands of the Israelites. Of course, the city here stands for the whole country of **Edom**. David wishes that he could be instrumental in fulfilling God's intention to cast His shoe upon it.

60:10 But it is a vain hope at the moment because **God** has hidden His face from His people. He has **cast** them **off**. He no longer accompanies Israel's **armies** as a guarantee of victory.

60:11 So David pleads for God to fight once again on behalf of His troubled people. Divine help is indispensable; **the help of man** is useless.

Israel's Confidence Is in the Lord (60:12)

The Psalm closes on a note of confidence. Given God's aid, Israel's army is assured of an illustrious record. Their **enemies** will be crushed under His heel.

Application

The believer's enemies are the world, the flesh and the devil. In himself he is powerless to conquer them. And the help of other men is insufficient, no matter how well-meaning they might be. But there is victory through the Lord Jesus Christ. Those who trust in Him for deliverance will never be disappointed.

Psalm 60 will have a final fulfillment in the last days when the Jewish remnant, harried and dispirited, looks to the Messiah for salvation and triumph. Then the land of Israel will be apportioned among the tribes and the nation's foes will be brought to bay.

Psalm 61: The Rock That Is Higher Than I

David had a wonderful relationship with the Lord. To him God was:

> . . . a living bright Reality,
> More present to faith's vision keen
> Than any earthly object seen.
> More dear, more intimately nigh
> Than e'en the closest earthly tie.
> —*Author unknown*

Especially in times of danger, when the situation seemed utterly hopeless, he had learned to cast his burden on the Lord and leave it there.

Here he is in another of those cliff-hanging predicaments. The pressure of circumstances wrings from his heart a prayer that has seldom been surpassed for sheer poignancy and articulateness. It has become the timeless language of thousands of God's people as they have passed through persecution, heartache and suffering because it says what they feel but could never express so well.

61:1 Into the throne room of the universe comes the familiar voice of David:

Hear my cry, O God; attend to my prayer.

God's heart is delighted. The childlike faith of His servant assures instant audience with the Sovereign.

61:2 **From the end of the earth I will cry to You,**
    When my heart is overwhelmed.

The psalmist is not literally **at the end of the earth**, but he is literally in a place of extremity where safety and deliverance seem remote, where life ends and death begins. Physically and emotionally he is spent, but he knows that the throne of grace is only a breath away, so he draws near to receive mercy and find grace to help in time of need. "Distance," someone has said, "is meaningless and no extremity of life effective in blocking prayer."

Lead me to the rock that is higher than I.

A true spiritual instinct teaches David that he needs **a rock** for protection, that **the rock** must be **higher than** himself, and that he needs divine guidance to reach it. The Lord, of course, is the Rock (2 Sam. 22:32); the metaphor is never used of any mere man in the Bible.[45] **The rock** must be someone greater than man; otherwise man can never find shelter in it. This points to the deity of Christ. (And incidentally the rock must be cleft to provide a hiding place from the enemy.) Finally, David acknowledges that he does not have the wisdom or strength to direct his own steps, so he asks the Lord to lead him to Himself—the Rock of ages.

61:3 **For You have been a shelter for me,**
    A strong tower from the enemy.

These words confirm that God is the Rock. David had proved Him to be his trustworthy refuge and a **tower** of strength into which the righteous can run for safety (Prov. 18:10). What He has been, He will be.

61:4 **I will abide in Your tabernacle forever;**

**I will trust in the shelter
of Your wings. Selah**

Prayers like this cannot fail to touch
the throne of God! Such tender affection and simple trust could never be
refused. No wonder that God called
David a man after His own heart
(1 Sam. 13:14). The expression **"the
shelter of Your wings"** may be an
allusion to the wings of the cherubim which overshadowed the blood-
sprinkled mercy seat.

**61:5   For You, O God, have heard
my vows;
You have given me the
heritage of those who fear
Your name.**

The word **heritage** or *inheritance* is
applied in the OT to the land of
Canaan (Ex. 6:8), the people of Israel
(Ps. 94:5), the Word of God (Ps.
119:111), children in a family (Ps.
127:3), immunity from harm (Isa.
54:17), and finally to the tabernacle or
temple (Jer. 12:7). The last named is
probably the primary meaning here
since the preceding verse mentioned
God's tent and alluded to the cherubim. Today, we would think of the
heritage of those **who fear** God's **name**
as eternal life (Col. 1:12).

**61:6, 7   You will prolong the king's
life,
His years as many
generations.
He shall abide before God
forever.
Oh, prepare mercy and
truth, which may
preserve him!**

It is interesting that in these two
verses, David slips from the first person to the third. Interesting—because
while he was still no doubt referring
to himself and to the covenant God

made with him (2 Sam. 7), his words
are more appropriate for another King.
If we apply the words to David, they
can only be understood as requesting
long life for himself and the perpetuation of his kingdom. But applied to
the Lord Jesus, they are literally
fulfilled:

- His life was prolonged endlessly,
  in spite of persecution (Heb. 7:16).
- His years will endure to all generations (Heb. 1:12).
- He will be enthroned forever before God (Heb. 1:8).
- Steadfast love and faithfulness
  will watch over Him, like bodyguards (Ps. 91:1–16).

Even the ancient Jewish comment
in the Targum says that the King
Messiah is in view here.

**61:8   So I will sing praise to Your
name forever,
That I may daily perform
my vows.**

And so the Psalm that opened in
extremity closes in serenity. David
has reached the Rock that is higher
than himself, and is so grateful that
he determines to sing the praises of
the Lord continually, paying his **vows**
of worship, love, and service. He will
not be like those who make extravagant vows when the pressure is on,
then quickly forget them when the
crisis is past. He will not be one who
"leaps in prayer but limps in praise."
Psalm 61 inspired this lovely hymn:

O sometimes the shadows are deep,
And rough seems the path to the
    goal;
And sorrows, sometimes how they
    sweep
Like tempests down over the soul!

Refrain:
O then to the Rock let me fly,

To the Rock that is higher than I;
O then to the Rock let me fly,
To the Rock that is higher than I.

O sometimes how long seems the
   day,
And sometimes how weary my feet;
But toiling in life's dusty way,
The Rock's blessed shadow, how
   sweet!

O near to the Rock let me keep,
If blessings or sorrows prevail,
Or climbing the mountain way steep,
Or walking the shadowy vale.
          —Erastus Johnson

Psalm 62: God Alone!

The message of Psalm 62 is that God is the only true refuge. The repetition of the words **only** and **alone** emphasize His exclusive right to our full and undivided trust.

Among the many beautiful ways in which He is presented are:

the source of our **salvation** (vv. 1b, 2a, 6a, 7a)
our **rock** (vv. 2a, 6a, 7b)
our **defense** (vv. 2c, 6c)
the basis of our **expectation** (v. 5b)
our **glory** (v. 7a)
our **refuge** (vv. 7b, 8b)
the source of **power** (v. 11b)
the fountain of **mercy** (v. 12a)

Anyone who makes God the ground of his confidence and strength has the following confidences:

he **shall not be greatly moved** (v. 2b)
he has boldness to rebuke his enemies (v. 3)
he can see through their plans and strategies (v. 4)
he **shall not be moved** (v. 6b)
he will want others to know the joy of trusting **God** (v. 8)

There are five other objects in which people often trust, but such trust is sure to be disappointed. (1) **Men of low degree**, that is, common people, are as substantial and transitory as a **vapor**. (2) **Men of high degree**, whether rulers or wealthy people, are a delusion in that they seem to offer help and security but they are not dependable. Put the rabble or the elite in the scales and they are weightless as far as trustworthiness is concerned. (3) **Oppression** is a foolish method to depend on; "it reeks with God's curse." (4) **Robbery** might seem to be a quick route to power and wealth, but ill-gotten gain is doomed to the judgment of God. (5) *Even riches* gained through honest industry should never take the Lord's place in our affections and service. F. B. Meyer wrote: "How often have we looked for help from men and money in vain—but God has never failed us."

It seems probable that this Psalm was inspired by Absalom's rebellion. The rebels were out to shatter David as if he were a **leaning wall and a tottering fence**. Their goal was to **cast him down from his high position**, that is, from his throne. While pretending loyalty, they were plotting treachery. The fugitive king urges his loyal subjects to maintain their unwavering confidence in the Lord. His enemies were trusting in men and in money, but there was no salvation in either of these. His own trust was in the Lord. Repeatedly the Lord had assured him that He is the fountainhead of power and love; that His power is used to deliver the faithful and to punish the foes; that His love is used to comfort and bless His people. He will see that justice is meted out to all who refuse His grace.

John Donne's comment on the Psalm is memorable:

He is my rock, and my salvation, and
my defense, and my refuge and my
glory.
If my refuge, what enemy can
pursue me?
If my defense, what temptation shall
wound me?
If my rock, what storm shall shake
me?
If my salvation, what melancholy shall
deject me?
If my glory, what calumny shall defame me?

Psalm 63: Better Than Life

Temporarily deposed, **David** is trekking across **the wilderness of Judah**
to his enforced exile east of the Jordan
(2 Sam. 15:23–28; 16:2; 17:16). Even
though the king's political fortunes
are at a low ebb, his spiritual vitality
is high.

63:1 It is magnificent to hear him
claiming God as his own: **"O, God,
You are my God."** The words in
themselves are simple and childlike,
but they contain a world of meaning.
My God—an intimate, personal relationship. **My God**—an abiding treasure when all else is gone. **My God**—a
sufficient resource in every crisis.

And it is humbling to notice the
psalmist's passion for God, especially
when we remember how cold and
diffident we often are. He sought the
Lord **early**—**early** in life and **early**
every day. And he sought him with a
fervor that would not be denied. His
soul thirsted for God, his **flesh** fainted
for God—which means that his entire
being cried out for fellowship with
the Eternal. His longing was as intense as the thirst of a traveler in a
dry, weary, waterless **land**. This, incidentally, is not a bad description of
the world—an arid wasteland.

63:2 In memory he goes back to
those times when he worshiped at

the **sanctuary** in Jerusalem, to those
ineffable moments when, caught up
in an ecstasy of sacred contemplation, he saw God in all His **power**
and **glory**. Now his soul cannot be
satisfied with anything less than a
new unveiling of the Lord in splendor and might. Some call it the be-
atific vision—this view of God in His
divine glory. Whatever it is called, it
is an experience that makes all other
glory seem jaded and dull.

> Be Thou my vision, O Lord of my
>   heart—
> Nought be all else to me, save that
>   Thou art;
> Thou my best thought, by day
>   or by night—
> Waking or sleeping, Thy presence
>   my light.
>   —*8th century Irish hymn*
>   *Trans. by Mary E. Byrne*
>   *Versified by Eleanor H. Hill*

63:3, 4 Then up from the unlikely
wilderness of Judah rises one of the
great rhapsodies of adoration.

**Because Your lovingkindness is
better than life,
My lips shall praise You.
Thus I will bless You while I live;
I will lift up my hands in Your
name.**

The **lovingkindness** of the Lord is
better than anything that **life** can
afford. Human **lips** are best employed
in praising Him. All of life is not too
long to spend in blessing Him. Our
hands pulsate with fulfillment when
lifted **up** to Him in praise and prayer.

63:5–8 No banquet is like this sacred communion. Our souls are fed
with the choicest delights, and **joyful
lips** respond with overflowing thanks
as we redeem the sleepless hours of
night by meditating on our glorious
Lord. What a help He has been to

us—who can ever measure all He has done for us? Shadowed by His **wings**, we raise our joyful song. And as we cling to Him in loving dependence and in conscious need, He preserves us from dangers seen and unseen, and empowers us to press on toward the mark for the prize.

63:9, 10 "Enemies?" did you say. "O yes, I do have enemies, men who are determined to obliterate me. But they are destined to destruction. They will die a violent death and will suffer the disgrace of not having a decent burial.

63:11 "But I will go on enjoying **God**. In fact, **everyone who swears** allegiance to **Him** will share in the jubilation, whereas those who love to lie will be silenced."

Psalm 64: Bows and Arrows

Two archery contests emerge in Psalm 64. The preliminary event is between the wicked and the righteous (vv. 1–6). The main event is between God and the wicked (vv. 7–10).

64:1–6 The first battle seems to be completely one-sided. The righteous **David** is opposed by a multitude of villains. He has no arrows; their quivers are full. But he has the secret weapon of prayer and he uses it to enlist the help of his unseen Partner. First, he raises his **voice** to **God** for preservation **from fear** and for protection **from the secret plots of the wicked**. Then he gives God an intelligence report about **the enemy**. Their tongues are finely honed, as sharp as **a sword**. They **bend their bows to shoot their arrows** of accusation—**bitter words** of reproach. Their attacks come unexpectedly from **secret** hide-outs and without fear of a counterattack. They are inflexible in their

determination to destroy the innocent. As they conspire to trap the psalmist secretly, they imagine that they are immune from detection. "They have thought their plan out well, each with a cunning heart, each in his deep craft" (v. 6, Moffatt).

64:7 Everything seems to be on the side of the villains so far. But the righteous cling to the promise, "The Lord will fight for you while you hold your peace" (Ex. 14:14). "For the battle is not yours but God's" (2 Chron. 20:15).

64:8 So in the second contest we see **God** shooting His **arrow** (singular) at them. It's a bull's-eye. **They** fall **wounded** to the ground. God causes their evil words to recoil on themselves, and all the spectators **flee away** in terror.

64:9, 10 The result is that a sense of awe comes over the populace. Word spreads quickly, and men realize that righteousness has triumphed. This causes **righteous** people to **be glad**, of course, and to **trust in** Jehovah. All those who love what is right will celebrate.

Psalm 65: Millennial Harvest Song

While Psalm 65 is generally used as a classic song of "harvest home," there can be little doubt that its primary interpretation deals with conditions at the Second Advent of the Lord.

65:1 During the long centuries of Israel's estrangement from God, **Zion** was barren as far as **praise** to **God** was concerned. But when God's ancient people are restored to Him, **praise** will await Him there in the silence of awe and reverence. **To Him the vow shall** at last **be performed**. This may mean His own vow that every knee will bow to Him (Isa.

45:23). It may refer to the Messiah's vow of Psalm 22:22: "In the midst of the congregation I will praise You." Or it may mean the vow of love, worship, and service that the persecuted remnant will make during the terrible suffering of the Tribulation.

65:2 Whereas Israel was primarily in view in verse 1, here the subject broadens to include **all** mankind. God is known by the grand and noble title, **"You who hear prayer."** The converted nations will lay hold of Him in believing **prayer**.

65:3 It is important to notice the change of speakers here. In the first clause, the Messiah is rehearsing His vicarious work at Calvary when He was crushed beneath sin's awful load. But the Jewish remnant quickly acknowledges that it was not His sins but **"our transgressions."** They say, "He was wounded for our transgressions, He was bruised for our iniquities; the chastisement for our peace was upon Him; and by His stripes we are healed" (Isa. 53:5). And as soon as Israel makes this confession of guilt, they will have the assurance that their transgressions are all forgiven.

65:4 Again we are aware that the first part of the verse speaks of the Messiah Jesus, whereas the second part is the language of redeemed Israel. God's blessed Son is the One whom God chose, as we read in Isaiah 42:1: "...My elect One in whom My soul delights." Also He is the One whom God caused to **approach** Him—a priest forever according to the order of Melchizedek. He shall **dwell** in the **courts** of the Lord, in the place of special nearness to Him.

Then the remnant expresses its confidence of complete satisfaction **with the goodness** of God's **house**, that is, His **holy temple**. This reference to **the temple** causes some to question the Davidic authorship of the Psalm since the temple was not built until after David's death. However the difficulty vanishes when we realize that the word *temple* was sometimes used to describe the tabernacle before Solomon's temple was erected (1 Sam. 1:9; 3:3; 2 Sam. 22:7).

65:5–7 The remnant is still speaking. In answer to their prayers, the Lord righteously punishes their enemies with **awesome** judgments. Thus He reveals Himself as the **God of** their **salvation** and **the confidence** of people throughout **the earth and** in **far-off seas**. What a great God He is! With omnipotence as His belt, He **established the mountains** firm in their place by an act of super-power. It's nothing for Him to pacify the raging **seas**, the fury of **their waves** (on the Sea of Galilee, for instance). Or to suppress the fury of the Gentile **peoples**, for that matter.

65:8 No wonder that unbelievers **in the farthest** lands **are afraid** of the **signs** and wonders which God visits upon them. Or that believers in the lands of sunrise and sunset **rejoice**.

65:9 While verses 9–13 describe the harvest year from seedtime to harvest, they apply especially to conditions in the Millennium when the curse will be lifted and bumper crops will be the rule.

Springtime is like a visit from God. He sends the showers from His overhead river—the clouds that scud across the sky. Then when the ground has been prepared, He provides the seed to be planted.

65:10 During the growing season, the plowed furrows are irrigated, the rain melting the clods and keeping the ground **soft**. Soon the crops are shooting up in profusion.

65:11–13 God crowns the growth

cycle **with** His **goodness**. Wherever His feet have passed, the stream of plenty flows (Knox). **The pastures** yield rich supplies of fodder. **The little hills** are covered with lush vegetation, as if hilarious with joy. **The pastures** wear a sheepskin coat, **clothed** as they are **with** innumerable **flocks**. Ripened **grain** bends in rhythmic cadence across the floors of **the valleys**. It seems that all nature is celebrating the arrival of the age of the Messiah.

Psalm 66: Come, See, and Hear!

66:1–4 In the first four verses, the psalmist calls on the whole **earth** to join in singing the praises of **God**. It should be a **joyful** song and one that celebrates the excellencies **of His name**. The **praise** should be **glorious** because the Subject is glorious. The very words of the song of universal worship are given. We might paraphrase them as follows:

Lord, Your accomplishments are tremendous. Your power is so devastating that Your enemies cringe before You. At last the whole earth bows before You in worship. Everywhere people praise Your name in song.

This song will no doubt be a favorite when the kingdom age arrives.

66:5–7 The recurrence of *our* and *us* in verses 5–12 leads us to believe that these are the evangelistic sentiments of the Jewish remnant in the last days as they invite the nations to ponder the astounding things that **God** has done for Israel. Two terrific displays of His might come to mind. He made a highway of **dry** land through the Red **Sea**. And when the Israelites came to **the** Jordan **River** forty years later, they were able to cross dry-shod. What rejoicing ex-

ploded in Israel then! The people exulted in their God whose mighty dominion never ends and whose **eyes** keep close watch on **the nations**. It's foolish for anyone to rebel against a God like this.

66:8–12 The Gentiles should also **bless God** for the miraculous way in which He preserved the people of Israel. In a rapidly changing succession of figures Israel is pictured as:

being **refined** like **silver** when it is subjected to intense heat by the smelter (v. 10).

being imprisoned as if in a **net** (v. 11a).

being forced to slave labor (v. 11b).

being downtrodden by wretched men (v. 12a).

being exposed to frightful dangers, as if going **through fire and through water** (v. 12b).

Yet God did not allow them to be finally overthrown. Rather He **brought** them into **rich fulfillment**—a reference to Israel's superabundant prosperity in the Millennium. As Williams puts it:

In spite of the unceasing efforts of Satan and man to utterly destroy Israel, her twelve tribes will appear at Mt. Sion upon the Millennial morn, and so demonstrate the truth of the ninth verse. They will testify that the chastisements justly laid upon them (vv. 10–12) were designed in love and executed in wisdom.[46]

66:13–15 In verses 13–20, the **I** and **my** indicate that the chorus has become a solo. Several sober commentators believe that the speaker is the Lord Jesus, Israel's King and Great High Priest. He comes to God with **burnt offerings** of a life totally devoted to the will of His Father. He pays the **vows** of praise which He had promised when in trouble. This may refer to His own sufferings on the cross, or to the sufferings which He felt in the sufferings of His people, for "In all their affliction He was afflicted" (Isa. 63:9).

When we read here of **burnt offerings**, of the sacrifice of **rams** and of an offering of **bulls** and **goats**, we need not take them with exact literalness, except as the psalmist spoke of his own experience. In association with His people, the Messiah uses these as figures of the spiritual worship which He and the remnant will bring. However, this does not deny that a modified sacrificial system may be reinstituted in the Kingdom.

66:16–19 In verse 5, the invitation was "Come and see." Here in verse 16 it is **"Come and hear."** The works of **God** in history can be seen, but His dealing with the soul can only be heard. The Messiah invites all God-fearing people to hear His testimony of answered prayer. He had **cried to Him** in supplication and in exaltation. The reference is to the days of His flesh when He "offered up both supplications and entreaties to Him who was able to save Him out of death, with strong crying and tears" (Heb. 5:7, JND). If He had regarded **iniquity** in His **heart, the Lord** would not have heard Him. But He was without sin, and so He was heard "because of His piety" (Heb. 5:7, JND).

66:20 And this inspired the closing burst of praise:

> Blessed be God,
> Who has not turned away my
>   prayer,
> Nor His mercy from me!

Psalm 67: Israel's Missionary Call

When God called the nation of Israel, He intended that the nation should have a missionary character. It was to be a witness and a testimony to the surrounding nations of two important truths.

1. The truth of monotheism—that there is only one God (Ex. 20:2, 3; Deut. 6:4; Isa. 43:10–12).
2. The truth that a people living in obedience under the government of Jehovah would be happy and prosperous (Lev. 26:3–12; Deut. 33:26–29; 1 Chron. 17:20; Jer. 33:9).

It was not God's will that Israel should be the *terminal* of His *blessing*, but a *channel*. There are numerous indications throughout the OT that God's salvation was for the Gentiles as well as for the Jews, and that Israel as a kingdom of priests was to serve as mediator between God and the nations.

Unfortunately Israel failed in this aspect of its mission. By lapsing into idolatry, it denied the very truths it was called on to proclaim.

But God's purposes are not so easily defeated. During the Tribulation, a remnant of believing Jews will carry the gospel of the kingdom to all the world (Matt. 24:14). And in the ensuing kingdom, Israel will be the channel of blessing to the nations (Isa. 61:6; Zech. 8:23).

67:1, 2 This Psalm anticipates that time. In it we hear believing Jews praying that **God** will **bless** them so that they can be the means of evangelizing the Gentiles. When we read the words, **"that Your way may be known on earth,"** we should remember that Christ is the way (John 14:6). Only through Him can God's saving power be experienced by **nations** or individuals.

67:3, 4 In an extraordinary burst of missionary enthusiasm, Israel then prays that great torrents of praise will ascend to God from the Gentiles, that **the nations** will enjoy a gala time of celebration as they enjoy Christ's beneficent and equitable rule and His tender, shepherd care.

67:5 Just as Israel yearns to hear **God** praised by **all the peoples** of the world, as F. B. Meyer reminds us, so should "we want crowns for the brow of Christ."

67:6, 7 The last two verses picture the Millennium as having already arrived. The crops have been harvested, and the barns and silos are bursting. This proof of God's blessing to Israel will be a powerful testimony to the nations. The Hebrew scholar Franz Delitzsch summarized: "For it is the way of God, that all the good that He manifests toward Israel shall be for the well-being of mankind."[47]

Psalm 68: Our God Is Marching On!

This is Israel's national processional, in which the journey of the ark of the covenant from Mount Sinai to Mount Zion is seen as symbolizing the march of God to ultimate victory. To the Jewish mind, the ark rightly represented the presence of God; when the ark moved, God moved.

It is quite generally believed that the song was composed to celebrate one particular incident in the history of the ark—the return to Mount Zion after its inglorious capture by the Philistines and after its stay in the house of Obed-Edom (2 Sam. 6:2–18).

We can better enter into the spirit of this marching song if we see that it is divided into the following seven sections:

1. Introductory hymn of praise to God (vv. 1–6).
2. The ark moving from Sinai through the wilderness (vv. 7, 8).

3. The entrance and conquest of the land of Canaan (vv. 9–14).
4. The capture of Jerusalem by David (vv. 15–18).
5. Song praising God for victory over the Jebusites (vv. 19–23).
6. The procession carrying the ark to the sanctuary in Jerusalem (vv. 24–27).
7. The jubilant throng anticipating the final victory of God (vv. 28–35).

In its Messianic setting, the Psalm pictures Christ's Incarnation, His conquest at Calvary, His Ascension, and His Second Advent.

Introductory Hymn (68:1–6)

68:1–3 The first verse gives us a clue that the movements of the ark are the main subject; these are almost the same words which Moses used when the ark first started off from Sinai (Num. 10:35). The sight of the sacred chest under way suggested the time when **God** arises and moves into action. For **His enemies** it means disaster and dispersal; for the righteous, deep-seated joy. His enemies scatter in every direction. They **flee** in pandemonium. As insubstantial as smoke, as unresisting as melting **wax**, they stagger to their doom. But for the righteous it is a time of vindication and reward, of joy and jubilation.

68:4–6 It is a time to **sing** praises **to God** and to clear a way for the Lord in the deserts (MT, see NKJV margin, cf. Isa. 40:3; 62:10). **His name** is **YAH**, the covenant-keeping Jehovah; He is worthy of endless praise. Though He is infinitely high, yet He is intimately near to the friendless and the dispossessed. As the **God** of all grace, He is **father of the fatherless**, **defender of widows**. He provides the warmth and fellowship of a happy home for the lonely, and as for those who have been unjustly condemned to prison, He leads them **into prosperity** with shouts of joy.

With **the rebellious**, it's a different story; they are consigned to a desolate wilderness.

These introductory verses, then, say in the words of the "Battle Hymn of the Republic," "Our God is marching on," and contrast the results of His march on the righteous and on rebels.

Although it is not noticeable in the English version, seven names of God are woven into the texture of this Psalm: *Elohim* (v. 1), *Yah* (v. 4), *Jehovah* (v. 10), *El Shaddai* (v. 14), *Yah Elohim* (v. 18), *Adonai* (v. 19), and *Jehovah Adonai* (v. 20).

The Ark Moves from Sinai through the Wilderness (68:7, 8)

When the Israelites broke camp at Sinai and started the trip toward the Promised Land with the ark in the vanguard, it was an emotion-packed moment. Nature itself seemed to enter into the awesomeness of the event. **The earth** quaked, the **heavens** broke loose with **rain**, and Mount **Sinai** shuddered at the sight.

The Entrance and Conquest of the Land (68:9–14)

68:9, 10 By verse 9, Israel is in Canaan and **God** has produced changes in the weather so that the land is abundantly supplied with **rain**—a welcome change from the irrigation of Egypt and the wilderness drought. The countryside has taken a new lease on life as the drooping vegetation revives and flourishes. The people are at home, richly provisioned by the Lord.

68:11–13 The narrative moves quickly to the conquest of the land. **The Lord** gives **the word**, that is, the command to march against the enemy. Implicit in His word is the assurance of victory. The next thing you know, a great company of women[48] are spreading the news at home: **"Kings of armies flee, they flee!"** In language strongly reminiscent of the Song of Deborah (Judg. 5), we see the women dividing **the spoil** of battle, though they themselves never left **the sheepfolds**. As they try on the beautiful clothes and jewelry, they resemble **the wings of a dove covered with silver**, or, when the light hits at a different angle, they gleam like **feathers** with **yellow gold**.

68:14 For the enemy it was a disastrous rout. God **scattered kings** like **snow in Zalmon**.

The Capture of Jerusalem by David (68:15–18)

68:15, 16 Jerusalem was still held securely by the pagan Jebusites. The first thing David did after he had been anointed king over all Israel was to move against the city. The defenders were smugly satisfied that it was so impregnable that it could be defended by the blind and lame. But David and his men captured the stronghold and called it the City of David (2 Sam. 5:1–9).

This is what the psalmist is referring to here. As the citadel's capture reveals Jerusalem as the chosen city, the high snow-summit of Hermon, located north of **Bashan**, looks enviously at Mount Zion. Hermon is a majestic mountain range with **many** majestic **peaks**, yet **God** passed it by and chose Zion for His permanent dwelling. That is why it looks jealously at Zion.

68:17 David recalls the capture of Jerusalem from the Jebusites. But he has no illusions as to the real source of victory. It was not his clever strategy or the valor of his men. It was **the numberless chariots of God** assaulting the city. The march of God that had begun at **Sinai** had now reached a glorious finale at Zion.

68:18 As David remembered how his soldiers had stormed the heights of Jerusalem, he looked beyond flesh and blood to see God ascending the **high** mount, taking captives in His train and winning spoils of victory for those who were former rebels so that He could **dwell** among these people as their Lord and Savior.

Paul applies verse 18 to the Ascension of Christ (Eph. 4:8–10). When Christ ascended from earth to heaven, **He led captivity captive**, that is, He triumphed gloriously over His foes and gave gifts to men. The **gifts** He **received** *among* men as reward for His finished work on the cross (Ps. 68:18), He turned around and gave these same gifts *to* men for the establishment and expansion of His church (Eph. 4:8).

Song Praising God for Victory over the Jebusites (68:19–23)

68:19, 20 Memories of the capture of Zion inevitably awaken praise to God. The song presents God as both Deliverer and Destroyer. As Deliverer, He "bears our burdens and wins us the victory" (Knox). He is **the God of our salvation**, and He has the power to deliver **from death**.

68:21–23 As Destroyer, He will crush His foes, those rebels whose long hair symbolizes their lawless, wicked careers. He has promised to track them down in the wilds **of Bashan** and from the coasts of the high seas so that Israel can wash its feet **in** their **blood**, and so that Israel's **dogs** can feed on their carcasses. Verse 22 does not refer to the

regathering of Israel, but to the hunting down of Israel's enemies.

The Procession Carrying the Ark to the Sanctuary in Jerusalem (68:24–27)

Not long after David captured Jerusalem, he arranged for the ark to be brought to a tent which had been erected to house it (2 Sam. 6:12–19). The **procession** is described here. As it moves toward **the sanctuary**, "the psalmist says, in effect, 'Look, here He comes.'"[49] The choir is leading, the band brings up the rear, and in between are young women **playing timbrels**. Listen to the words of the song:

> Bless God in the congregations,
> The LORD, from the fountain of
>   Israel.

The tribes are all represented, from those in the south—**little Benjamin** and **Judah**—to those in the north—**Zebulun** and **Naphtali**.

The Jubilant Throng Anticipating the Final Victory of God (68:28–35)

As the ark disappears inside the tabernacle, the people outside join in a final prayer (vv. 28–31) and in a song urging all the earth to praise the Lord (vv. 32–35).

68:28, 29 The prayer first of all calls on **God** to summon His might, to show His **strength** again on behalf of His people, to complete what He has begun for them. This prayer will be finally answered in the Millennium when **the temple** will be the glory of **Jerusalem**, and when **kings will bring presents** of gold and frankincense (Isa. 60:6) to the Great King.

68:30 The Hebrew of verse 30 is obscure, but the overall thought seems to be this: The people call on God to **rebuke the beasts** and **the herd of bulls. The beasts** that live among **the**

reeds, probably crocodiles and hip-popotami, represent the leaders of Egypt. The bulls represent the other rulers who "lord it over the peaceful herd of nations" (Knox).

The clause translated **"Till every-one submits himself with pieces of silver,"** may mean "until those na-tions bow down to You with **silver** as tribute" or "vanquishing those na-tions that have thrived on **silver** trib-ute." The sense is good in either case. And in the same vein the prayer goes up, **"Scatter the peoples who delight in war."** These requests will be fully answered at the Second Advent of Christ when aggressors and warmon-gers will be destroyed.

68:31 In that day, **envoys** from **Egypt** will bring tribute, and **Ethiopia will stretch out her hands** imploringly and adoringly to the King of all the earth.

68:32–35 The closing verses call on the **kingdoms of the earth** to acknowledge the **God** of Israel as worthy of homage and praise. The words carry a tremendous sense of the grandeur and greatness of God. He is the transcendent One, **who rides** in the ancient **heavens**. He is the God of revelation, speaking with **a mighty voice**. He is the omnipotent one, strong on behalf of **Israel**, but almighty beyond **the clouds**.

Awesome as He is in His **holy places**, yet He stoops to give **strength and power to His people**.

There is only one thing left to say—**Blessed be God!**

Psalm 69: Save Me, O God!

Our blessed Redeemer's sufferings and death were, for Him, an immer-sion in the ocean of God's wrath. He Himself spoke of His approaching passion as a baptism:

I have a baptism to be baptized with, and how distressed I am till it is accomplished! (Luke 12:50).

And in Psalm 42:7 we hear Him crying:

Deep calls unto deep at the noise of Your waterfalls;
All Your waves and billows have gone over me.

In His death of bitterest woe, He plumbed the depths of God's judg-ment against our sin.

69:1–3 Here in Psalm 69 we are privileged to hear the deepest exer-cises of His holy soul as He sinks into death. **The waters have come up to His neck** and are about to engulf Him completely. There is nothing to sup-port Him—nothing but **deep mire** under His feet. Now the **floods** are dashing over His head. The waters are very deep—deeper than any of the ransomed will ever know. In a real sense God has gathered all **the waters** together in one place—Calvary—and the Son of His love is enduring that mighty ocean of judg-ment in order to pay the penalty for our sins.

Above the trackless waste of water reverberates His continuous urgent appeal, **"Save me, O God!"** It seems as if He has been pleading for an eternity. His throat is hoarse and parched—worn out **with** His **crying**. His **eyes** are swollen shut, ceaselessly scanning the horizon for some sight of help from **God**. But no help is near.

69:4 The angry mob is milling before the cross, a seething collage of venom, hatred, bitterness and cru-elty. What a scene! The Creator and Sustainer of the universe is hanging on a criminal's cross. His guilty mur-derers are gathered before Him. Who are they? They are men and women who owe their very breath to Him, yet they **hate** Him **without a cause**. They are out to **destroy** Him; they attack Him with lies.

> Why? What hath my Lord done?
> What makes this rage and spite?
> He made the lame to run,
> He gave the blind their sight.
> Sweet injuries!
> Yet they at these
> Themselves displease,
> And 'gainst Him rise.
> —*Samuel Crossman*

Now the poignant sentence crosses the Savior's lips: "What I did not steal, **I still must restore**." Through man's sin, God was robbed of service, worship, obedience, and glory, and man himself was robbed of life, peace, gladness and fellowship with God. In a very real sense Christ came to **restore** what He did not steal.

> Aside He threw His most divine array,
> And veiled His Godhead in a robe of clay
> And in that garb didst wondrous love display,
> Restoring what He never took away.
> —*Author unknown*

In this respect He reminds us of the trespass offering (Lev. 5). The prominent feature of this offering was that restitution had to be made for any loss that the offerer had caused, and an additional fifth part had to be added. As our trespass offering, the Lord Jesus not only restored what had been stolen through man's sin, but He added more. For God has received more glory through the finished work of Christ than if sin had never entered. Through sin He *lost creatures;* through grace He *gained sons.* And we are better off in Christ than we ever could have been in unfallen Adam.

In Him the sons of Adam boast
More blessings than their father lost.

69:5 We must understand verse 5 as referring to *our* **sins** which Jesus voluntarily took upon Himself. He had no folly or wrongs, but "He took our sins and our sorrows, and made them His very own." It was wonderful grace that He would identify Himself so closely with us that He could speak of our sins as His sins.

69:6 Then a fear casts a shadow across His holy mind. He fears that some earnest believers might be stumbled by the fact that His prayers to God go unanswered. He prays that it may not happen—that no one who hopes in **God** might be **ashamed because of** what was happening to Him, and that no one who seeks the God of Israel might be brought to dishonor through His humiliation and abandonment.

69:7, 8 It was, after all, **because** of His obedience to the Father's will that He was bearing **reproach**. It was His delight in pleasing God that allowed men to cover His **face** with unmentionable **shame** and spitting. Part of the cost of obedience was the sorrow of alienation from His own **mother's children**: His own half-brothers looked upon Him as being out of His mind.

69:9 The Lord Jesus was consumed with a **zeal for** His Father's **house**. Whenever He heard men speak insultingly about God, He took it as a personal insult. On that day in Jerusalem when He drove the money changers from the temple courts, His disciples remembered that it was written of Him here in Psalm 69, **"Zeal for Your house has eaten me up"** (John 2:17).

69:10–12 Nothing that He ever did as a perfect man here on earth seemed to please His critics. If He humbled His **soul with fasting**, they found fault with Him—perhaps suggesting, for instance, that He was only trying to appear pious. When He was plunged in the deepest mourning, He **became a byword to them** instead of an object of sympathy. In all strata of society, He was spoken against—from the rulers who sat at **the gate** of the city to **the drunkards** in the local taverns, bawling their coarse songs of derision. This is indeed a strange thing—the Lord of life and glory has come into the world and He is **the song of the drunkards!**

69:13–18 And so once again He retreats into **God**, His only resource. What fervency, what importunity there is in His **prayer!** He storms the bastions of heaven with successive pleas for help. But even then He reserves to God the right to answer at an **acceptable time**. As He sinks into **the mire**, He implores God to rescue Him with His faithful help, to **deliver** Him from His enemies, and to save Him **out of the deep waters, . . . the floodwater** and **the pit**. In His deep extremity, He bases His pleas on God's **lovingkindness** and His abundant **mercies**. His petitions are short and specific. **Hear me, . . . turn to me, . . . do not hide** from me, **draw near to** me, **redeem** me, and **deliver** me. **"Deliver me because of my enemies"** doubtless means "lest they gloat over my unalleviated distress."

69:19, 20 That mention of His enemies recalls all that He has suffered at the hands of men. His pathway through life was strewn with **reproach**, **shame** and **dishonor**. From the time of His infancy, He was pursued by **adversaries**: God knew how numerous they were. His **heart** was **broken** by insults—that **heart** that desires only good for the sons of men. The

grief and **heaviness** of it all plunged Him into despair. There was no one who took **pity** on Him in His sorrow and suffering. He **looked** in vain **for comforters**. Even His disciples forsook Him and fled. He was *all alone*.

69:21 Then in another of those startling prophecies spoken by David but fulfilled only in Jesus, we read:

> They also gave me gall for my
> food,
> And for my thirst they gave me
> vinegar to drink.

The fulfillment is found in Matthew 27:34, 48:

> They gave Him sour wine mingled with gall to drink. But when He had tasted it, He would not drink. . . . Immediately one of them ran and took a sponge, filled it with sour wine and put it on a reed, and gave it to Him to drink.

Gall was a bitter and perhaps poisonous substance which in small quantity might have acted as a sedative. The Lord would not take it because He must suffer as our Substitute in full consciousness. The **vinegar** was a sour wine which might have accentuated His thirst rather than alleviating it.

69:22 The tone of the Psalm changes abruptly at verse 22, and for the next seven verses we hear the dying Savior calling on God to punish the nation which condemned Him to die. At first this seems surprising when we remember that the Lord Jesus also prayed, "Father, forgive them, for they do not know what they do" (Luke 23:34). But actually there is no conflict between the two prayers. Forgiveness was available if they would have repented. But, in the absence of any change of heart, there was nothing left but the judgment described here.

It is important to see that these verses apply particularly to the nation of Israel. Paul applies verses 22 and 23 to Israel in Romans 11:9, 10. Also the mention of "their tents," signifying encampment (v. 25), is a distinctly Jewish allusion.

The verses predict the judgments which would come upon the race of people who had rejected their Messiah and brought about His execution.

Their table would **become a snare**. The **table** speaks of the sum total of the privileges which were conferred on Israel as God's chosen, earthly people. Instead of being a blessing, these privileges would determine the measure of their condemnation.

When they experience **well-being** (*peace*, Heb. *shālôm*), it would become **a trap**. Tribulation would spring forth just as the people think that all is well.

69:23   Their eyes would **be darkened, so that they** would **not** be able to **see**. This refers to the judicial blindness which has actually come on Israel nationally (2 Cor. 3:14). Because they rejected the Light, they have been denied the Light.

Their loins would **shake continually**. Dispersed among the nations, they would find no rest for the sole of their feet, but the Lord would give them "a trembling heart, failing eyes, and anguish of soul" (Deut. 28:65).

69:24   God's **indignation** would be poured out **upon them** and His **wrathful anger** would overtake **them**. We remember with deep, deep sorrow how this has been fulfilled in the awful anti-semitic pogroms, the concentration camps, the gas chambers and the ovens. Though these atrocities were perpetrated by wicked men, there can be no doubt that they were

not prevented by God from coming upon descendants of the people who said, "His blood be on us and on our children" (Matt. 27:25).

69:25   Their **habitation** would become **desolate** and **no one** would **dwell in their tents**. Here we are reminded of the Messiah's words in Matthew 23:38, "See! Your house is left to you desolate." The words were amply fulfilled in A.D. 70 when Titus and the Roman army sacked Jerusalem and destroyed the temple.

69:26   If the punishment seems severe, think of the crime that provoked it.

> For they persecute *him* whom You
> have struck,
> And talk of the grief of those You
> have wounded.

In the parable of the vineyard, the tenants are quoted as saying concerning the son of the householder, "This is the heir. Come, let us kill him and seize his inheritance" (Matt. 21:38). They *knew* He was the Son, and they killed Him nonetheless. The latter part of verse 26 described those followers of the Messiah who would be martyred.

69:27, 28   In view of this, there is no need to apologize for the severity of the Savior's words:

> Add iniquity to their iniquity,
> And let them not come into Your
> righteousness.
> Let them be blotted out of the book
> of the living,
> And not be written with the
> righteous.

And yet we should not forget that even after the crucifixion of God's Son, the Spirit of God still pleaded with the nation of Israel to repent and to turn to Jesus as the Messiah. All through the period of the Acts, you hear the heartbeat of God as He yearns over the nation He loves and tenderly invites to accept His mercy and grace. Even today the gospel goes out to the Jewish people as to the Gentiles. And the only ones who ever have to suffer the judgments described in verses 22–28 are those who deliberately choose that fate by rejecting the Christ of God.

69:29 Now there is a final word from the dying sinner's Friend. Afflicted and in indescribable pain, He asks that the **salvation** of **God** might **set** Him securely **on high**.

And that is exactly what happened. God raised Him from the dead on the third day and set Him at His own right hand, a Prince and a Savior. His sufferings for sin are over forever. And we are glad!

> Never more shall God Jehovah
> Smite the Shepherd with the sword;
> N'er again shall cruel sinners
> Set at nought our glorious Lord.
> —*Robert C. Chapman*

And now we sing:

> The storm that bowed Thy blessed Head
> Is hushed forever now,
> And rest divine is ours instead,
> Whilst glory crowns Thy brow.
> —*H. Rossier*

69:30–33 The speaker in the final seven verses is the risen Redeemer. First He vows to extol God for delivering Him from death and the grave. He **will praise the name of God with a song and will magnify Him with thanksgiving.** This will mean far more to **the LORD** than the most costly sacrifices. And oppressed people everywhere will take heart when they realize that just as **the LORD** heard the Savior's prayers and

delivered Him, so He will hear the needy and free the **prisoners** who call on Him.

69:34–36 And what about the nation of Israel? The last three verses predict a bright tomorrow. Though set aside temporarily, Israel will be restored to the place of blessing. When they look on Him whom they pierced and mourn for Him as one mourns for an only son, when they say, "Blessed is He who comes in the name of the Lord," **God will save Zion and** rebuild **the cities of Judah**. No longer dispersed among the nations, **His servants** shall **dwell** in the land, and their children shall **possess** it. This looks forward, of course, to the Millennium when the Lord Jesus will reign as Messiah-King, and Israel will **dwell** securely in the land.

Psalm 70: Help Quickly!

For the most part, Psalm 70 is a repetition of Psalm 40:13–17. The heading states that it is a **Psalm of David, to bring to remembrance**. Four distinct movements appear.

Help Quickly (70:1)

Morgan calls it "a rushing sob of anxious solicitude." This is certainly the impression we get in verse 1 where David is urging the Lord to **make haste to deliver** him.

Punish Thoroughly (70:2, 3)

The defeat and rout of his foes is of major concern at the moment. He accuses them of trying to kill him, of taking pleasure in harming him, and of jeering at his calamity. He, in turn, asks that they might be thoroughly nonplussed, that they might be **turned back and confused**, and that they might be startled or appalled by the depth of **their** own **shame**.

Be Praised Continually (70:4)

The flow of thought here is that if God comes to the psalmist's rescue, this will result in a great wave of praise to Him. **All those who seek** the Lord will have occasion to exult in His help, and to worship Him as the great **God** of **salvation**.

Help Quickly (70:5)

Again the cry for speedy rescue goes up from the destitute. Although David cannot be said to be soaring in confidence, yet his faith is in the LORD as his **help and** his **deliverer**, and such faith will never go unrewarded.

Psalm 71: Old Age

As is so often the case, we can trace a close parallel between the experiences of the psalmist and those of the nation of Israel. Thus, as Bellett suggests, this Psalm can be studied as a prayer of the afflicted remnant in Israel's old age.[50]

71:1–3 The first three verses are similar to Psalm 31:1–3. The LORD is praised as **refuge, rock** and **fortress**, and is entreated for vindication of the psalmist's **trust**, for deliverance, rescue, salvation, and for His saving help as a **rock** of refuge and a **fortress**.

71:4 As the prayer continues, it is pervaded by a strong sense of gratitude for God's help in the past and confidence in His continued mercy in old age.

If we apply the Psalm to Israel, the **wicked**, unjust and **cruel** man of verse 4 is the Antichrist. His dictatorship of horror will tax the endurance of the saints and wring out from them the most importunate pleas.

71:5, 6 Happy is the man who can say that **God** has been his **hope** and **trust from** childhood. If he has leaned on Jehovah **from** his **birth**, he will not lack support in the sunset years of life. If he can trace God's marvelous grace back to the moment of his **birth**, he will not lack material for **praise** in later years.

71:7, 8 The psalmist had been **a wonder to many** by the depth of his rejection and suffering, and perhaps also by his marvelous deliverances. But through all the changing circumstances of life, God had been his **strong refuge**. And so he wanted every **day** to be crammed with His praise and **glory**.

71:9 **Do not cast me off in the time of old age;**
Do not forsake me when my strength fails.

To grow old gracefully calls for more Grace than Nature can provide. Old age is a new world of strange conflicts and secret fears; the fear of being left alone, the fear of being a burden to loved ones, the fear of becoming a helpless invalid, the fear of losing one's grip, the fear of being imposed upon. These fears are not new. The psalmist is here thinking aloud for the encouragement of all who are in the autumn of life (*Daily Notes of the Scripture Union*).

71:10, 11 Of course, he had the added fear of **enemies** who vilified him and who conspired to kill him. Mistakenly supposing that **God** had **forsaken him**, they prepared their final assault with no fear of opposition.

71:12, 13 This crisis prompted a distress call in which he urges **God** to come to his side and **help**. With no additional trouble, God could also swamp the foes with shame and defeat, **reproach and dishonor**.

71:14–16 But **hope** quickly rises above fear, and praise begins its mighty crescendo. The lyrics recount God's righteous acts and the numberless times He has rescued His beleaguered child. With holy determination the psalmist says, "I will come with the inexhaustible narration of the mighty acts of Jehovah Elohim."[51]

71:17, 18   Once again, as in verses 5–11, he runs the gamut from youth to old age (vv. 17–21) and finds nothing but the faithfulness of **God**. God had **taught** him **from** the days of his **youth** and, as Knox continues, "still I am found telling the tale of Thy wonders." Now he is **old and grayheaded**, but he doesn't feel his work is done. He pleads for time to tell the new **generation** and those **to come** about the mighty miracles of the Lord. This prayer was answered, of course, by the Psalm's being preserved in the sacred Scriptures.

71:19–21   God is really wonderful! His power and His **righteousness** are higher than the heavens. No one can hold a candle to Him, especially when you think of the **great things** He has **done**.

Sometimes God is said to have done what He has permitted. So here, He made the psalmist (and Israel) experience many bitter troubles. For Israel, this suggests the Tribulation Period. But He is the God of recovery, and He will revive His people, and snatch them from the jaws of the grave. That isn't all! He will give them honor in place of reproach and surround them with comfort.

71:22   **The lute** will be pressed into service to sing the **faithfulness** of **God**, and the **harp** enlisted to magnify the **Holy One of Israel**. This name of God—the **Holy One of Israel**—is used two other times in the Psalms—in 78:41 and 89:18.

71:23, 24   But lute and harp will be joined in the chorus by the psalmist's **lips, soul** and **tongue**. His **lips** will be effervescently joyful in song.

His **soul, redeemed** by the blood of the Lamb, will also **greatly rejoice** in song. His **tongue also shall** be unwearied in talking about God's dependability, for all his enemies have been thoroughly **confounded**.

Psalm 72: Messiah's Glorious Reign

This Psalm starts out as a prayer for an earthly monarch, possibly **Solomon**, but before long we realize that the writer is looking beyond Solomon to the glories of the reign of the Lord Jesus Christ. It will be a wonderful time for this weary, warring world. The golden era for which mankind has yearned will then be ushered in. Creation's groan will be hushed, and peace and prosperity will flourish.

72:1   In the first verse, we hear the prayer that rises from the holy convocation as the King is invested. Knox translates it, "Grant to the King Thy own skill in judgment; the inheritor of the throne, may He be just as Thou art just."

Every one of the "He will's" or "He shall's" in the rest of Psalm 72 will become fact when the Redeemer sets up His resplendent reign.

72:2   **He will judge** the **people with righteousness and** the **poor with justice**. Corruption, bribery and oppression will have ceased. Trials will be conducted with strict impartiality, and the **poor** will no longer be disadvantaged.

72:3   **The mountains will** bear a harvest of **peace** and prosperity for **the people**, and justice will cover **the little hills**. **Mountains** are often used in Scripture to signify governmental authorities. So the thought here may be that the subjects of Christ's kingdom can expect equity and justice from all the courts in the land—from the supreme court all the way down to the local magistrate.

72:4 Down through the centuries the poor and needy have been oppressed, underpaid, persecuted and even killed. In the Millennium, the King Himself will be their Advocate. He will emancipate them once for all and punish those who took advantage of them.

72:5, 6 His subjects will respect and **fear** Him **as long as the sun and moon endure, throughout all generations.** His presence shall prove beneficial and refreshing—just **like rain upon the grass** and **showers** on the parched **earth.**

72:7 He will be the true Melchizedek—King of righteousness and King of **peace**. During His reign justice will flourish, and **peace** will abound, **until the moon** ceases to exist. Notice that righteousness precedes peace. "The work of righteousness will be peace, and the effect of righteousness, quietness and assurance forever" (Isa. 32:17). By His righteous work for us on the cross, He bequeathed peace to us. And by His righteous rule He will one day bring peace to the war-torn world.

72:8 The boast of the United Kingdom used to be, "The sun never sets on the British Empire." British colonies were interspersed among the other nations of the world. But Christ's kingdom will be universal. It will not be a matter of scattered colonies. *All* nations will be included. His **dominion** will extend from one **sea to** another **and from the** Euphrates **River to the ends of the earth**.

72:9 The ungovernable nomads of the desert **will bow before Him** at last, and **His enemies** will go down to defeat. To **lick the dust** means to suffer ignoble and shameful subjugation.

72:10, 11 Gentile **kings** will come to Jerusalem with tribute and with **presents** for the King of kings. Here comes the ruler of Spain, there are the heads of states from various island countries, and now you see the rulers of the sheikdoms of Southern Arabia. The airport is crowded with visiting dignitaries because all acknowledge His sway and **all nations** without exception **serve Him**.

"Kings of wealth, and thought, and music, and art have already acknowledged Him, and shall," said Meyer.

72:12–14 The King's tremendous compassion for **the needy** is seen here. **The poor**, the downtrodden and the underdogs will have a Mighty Deliverer. Poverty will vanish and social injustice will be a thing of the past. The weak and **the needy** will have instant access to Him, and will be certain of considerate attention and prompt action. He will rescue them from unjust and cruel treatment, and He will show the world how **precious** their lives are to Him.

72:15 The shout, "Long **live** the King," will rise from His loyal subjects. In their gratitude they will give Him **gold** from the treasures **of Sheba**. Never-ceasing **prayer** will ascend from all over the world **for Him**, and people will bless Him from dawn to dusk.

72:16 The fertility of the land will be indescribable. Barns and silos will bulge with **grain**. Even places never previously cultivated, like **the top of the mountains**, will **wave** with fields of ripened grain, undulating in the breeze **like** the forests of **Lebanon**.

The cities will be richly inhabited with people, as the fields are filled with **grass**. It will be a population explosion of epic proportions, yet there will be no scarcity of food.

72:17 His name shall endure,

loved and revered **forever. As long as the sun** exists, **His** fame **shall continue**. In accordance with the promise God made to Abraham, all **men shall** bless themselves **in Him**, and **all nations shall call Him blessed**.

72:18, 19 The Psalm closes with a doxology. The glorious reign of the Lord Jesus is God's achievement. It is He who brings about these wonderful conditions, as no one else could do. And so it is fitting that **His glorious name** be praised forever, and that **His glory** fill the **whole earth**.

72:20 The prayers of David the son of Jesse are ended. This cannot mean that David's prayers are ended as far as the Book of Psalm is concerned, for many more follow. It might mean that his **prayers are ended** as far as Book II of the Psalms is concerned, Psalm 72 being the last in Book II. But a more plausible explanation is that the predicted reign of the Lord Jesus Christ represents the ultimate fulfillment of his **prayers**. The kingdom described in the preceding verses was the subject of his last words (2 Sam. 23:1–4), and was the event toward which his **prayers** *were directed*. When the Messiah would take His place upon the throne and rule, David's desires would be fully met.

III. BOOK 3 (PSALMS 73—89)

Psalm 73: Faith's Dilemma

73:1 This is **Asaph** speaking. And let me make one point clear at the outset. I know for a fact that **God is good to Israel, to such as are pure in heart**. The truth is so obvious that you'd think no one would ever question it.

73:2, 3 **But** there *was* a time when I actually began to wonder. My stance on the subject became very wobbly, and my faith **almost** took a temporary tumble. You see, I began to think how well off **the wicked** are—lots of money, plenty of pleasure, no troubles—and soon I was wishing I was like them.

73:4–9 Everything seems to be going their way. They don't have as much physical suffering as believers do. Their bodies are healthy and sleek (naturally—they can afford the best of everything). They escape many of the troubles and tragedies of decent people like ourselves. And even if trouble should strike them, they are heavily insured against every conceivable form of loss. No wonder they are so self-confident. They are as proud as a peacock and ruthless as a tiger. Just as their bodies seem to overflow with fatness, so their minds are spilling over with crooked schemes. And are they ever arrogant! They scoff and curse at their underlings and treat them as if they were dirt, threatening them continually. Even God Himself does not escape their malice. Their speech is punctuated with profanity, and they brazenly blaspheme Him. **Their tongue** swaggers and struts **through the earth**, as if to say, "Here I come; get out of my way."

73:10–12 Most of the ordinary **people** think they are great. They bow and scrape and show utmost respect. No matter what the wicked do, the people find no fault with them. And this only confirms the oppressors in their arrogance. They figure that if there is a God, He certainly doesn't **know** what's going on. So they feel safe in pursuing their careers of crookedness. And there they are—cushioned in luxury and getting richer all the time.

73:13, 14 Well, I began to think,

"What good has it done me to live a decent, honest, respectable life?" The hours I've spent in prayer. The time spent in the Word. The distribution of funds to the work of the Lord. The active testimony for the Lord, both public and private. All I've got for it has been a daily dose of suffering and punishment. I wondered if the life of faith was worth the cost.

73:15 Of course, I never shared my doubts and misgivings with other believers. I knew better than to do that. I often thought of the man who said, "Tell me of your certainties; I have doubts enough of my own." So I kept all my doubts to myself, lest I should offend or stumble some simple, trusting soul.

73:16 But still the whole business was a riddle to me: the wicked prosper while the righteous suffer. It seemed so hard to understand. In fact, it wore me out trying to solve the problem.

73:17 Then something wonderful happened. One day **I went into the sanctuary of God**—not the literal temple in Jerusalem but the *heavenly* one. I entered there by faith. As I was complaining to the Lord about the prosperity of the wicked in this life, the question suddenly flashed across my mind, "Yes, but what about the life to come?" The more I thought about their eternal destiny, the more everything came into focus.

73:18–20 So I spoke to the Lord something like this: Lord, now I realize that, despite all appearances, the life of the wicked is a precarious existence. They are walking on the **slippery** edge of a vast precipice. Sooner or later they fall over to their **destruction**. **In a moment** they are cut off—swept away by a wave of **terrors** too horrible to contemplate. They are to me like **a dream when one awakes** in the morning—the things that disturbed the dreamer are seen to be nothing but phantoms.

73:21, 22 I see now that the things that were causing me to be envious were mere shadows. It was stupid of me to become bitter and agitated over the seeming prosperity of the ungodly. In questioning Your justice I was acting more **like a beast** than a man. (Excuse me for behaving as I did.)

73:23, 24 Yet in spite of my ignorant behavior, You have not forsaken me. **I am continually with You**, and **You hold** on to me, like a father holds his child **by the hand**. Throughout all my life, **You** guide me **with Your counsel**, and then at last You will **receive me to glory**.

73:25, 26 It is enough that I have *You* **in heaven**; that makes me fabulously wealthy. And now I have no desire for anything **upon earth** apart from Yourself. Let the ungodly have their wealth. I am satisfied with **You** and find my all-sufficiency in You. My body may waste away and my **heart** may **fail, but God is the strength of my** life and all I'll ever need or want throughout eternity.

73:27, 28 **Those who** try to keep as **far** away **from You** as possible **shall perish** without You. **And all those who desert You** for false gods will be destroyed. As far as I am concerned, I want to be as **near to** You as possible. I have committed myself to You for protection, and I want to **declare all Your** wonderful **works** to anyone who will listen.

Psalm 74: Remember!

This moving lament looks back to the destruction of the temple by the Babylonians under Nebuchadnezzar.

But it also looks forward to three other similar tragedies in Israel:

> The desecration of the sanctuary by Antiochus Epiphanes, 170–168 B.C.
>
> The leveling of the temple by Titus and his Roman legions, A.D. 70.
>
> The still-future desolation of the temple, as prophesied in Matthew 24:15.

When the Babylonian wreckers were finished, it seemed that God had forsaken His people once for all. As they watch smoke arising from the debris, they correctly interpret the catastrophe as a smoking of His anger. But even then they remind the Lord with telling pathos that they are still:

> the sheep of His pasture (v. 1).
> His congregation (v. 2).
> the tribe of His inheritance (v. 2).
> His poor turtledove (v. 19).
> the oppressed (v. 21).
> the afflicted and needy (v. 21).

They also ring the changes on the word "Remember":

> Remember Your congregation (v. 2).
> Remember Mount Zion (v. 2).
> Remember the scoffing of the enemy (v. 18).
> Remember how an impious man sneers and reviles God's name (v. 22).

74:1–4 As if He didn't know what had happened, they call **God** to come and see how completely the Chaldean soldiers had razed the sacred building. Then they give an eyewitness account of how it happened. The foreign invaders stormed right into the middle of the holy place. **They set up their** own **banners for signs,** which means that they introduced heathen rites and idolatrous symbols in place of the scriptural worship of Jehovah.

74:5–8 Just as **thick trees** go down in swift succession under the deft blows of the woodsmen, so the costly **carved work** and wood paneling of the temple was shattered by the **axes and** sledge **hammers** of the pagan warriors. As soon as the place was in shambles, they **set** the ruins on **fire** and thus utterly desecrated God's **sanctuary**. Intent on making complete havoc of Israel and its worship, **they burned up all the meeting places of God in the land**.

74:9 The extreme plight of the nation is summed up in three vacuums and four questions. The vacuums are:

> No **signs**. The miraculous interventions of God which Israel had experienced in the past were conspicuously absent.
>
> No **prophet**. The prophetic voice was silenced at this time (Ezek. 3:26).
>
> No hope of respite. There was no one **who** knew **how long** the misery would continue.

74:10, 11 The four questions are:

> **How long** will **God** allow **the adversary** to ridicule?
>
> Will God allow His **name** to be reviled indefinitely?
>
> **Why** is His **hand** restrained from stopping the destruction?
>
> Why does He keep His **right hand** idly hidden in the folds of His robe?

74:12–17 But the psalmist finds hope and comfort in rehearsing God's mighty power in the past on behalf of His people. As Israel's **King** of long standing, He has distinguished Himself by the fantastic deliverances He wrought in various places. For instance, He **divided the** Red **Sea by** His **strength** to make an easy route for the Jews escaping from Egypt. Then when the Egyptian **sea serpents,** that is, Pharaoh's soldiers, tried to follow, He caused the waters to return to normal and drowned the hosts of the enemy. He crushed **the heads of Leviathan,** the monstrous crocodile that symbolized Egyptian power, and the corpses of the soldiers, washed up on the shores of the sea, became food for the vultures and beasts of the desert. He **broke open** springs and brooks in the wilderness, and **dried up** the Jordan so the people could enter the promised land. **Day** and **night** are under His control, and the **sun,** moon, and stars serve by His appointment. It was He who arranged the geography and topography **of the earth,** and the seasons are controlled by Him.

74:18–21 The psalmist reminds God that He too is involved in the disaster. **The enemy has reproached** His **name**; yes, a vile, **foolish people has** heaped contempt on Him.

But His people's plight is desperate. They implore Him not to abandon them, His **turtledove, to the wild** Babylonian **beast,** or to **forget** His afflicted ones **forever.** They beg Him to **respect the covenant** which He made with Abraham now when **the dark places of the** land of Israel harbored violence and **cruelty.** They beg Him to bring back His **oppressed** people in honor, not in shame, and thus give them ample cause to **praise** His **name** afresh for answered prayer.

74:22, 23 Ultimately it is **God's cause** that is at stake. He must defend the honor of His name, because the impious are mocking Him **daily.** He must **not forget** the swelling deri-

sion of His **enemies** which fills the air **continually** with challenges.

Psalm 75: The Source of Exaltation

The prayer of Psalm 74 is answered in Psalm 75. The Lord *will* arise to plead His own cause (Ps. 74:22) and to quell all insubjection. Ultimately the Psalm looks forward to that moment in history when the Lord Jesus returns to earth to reign in righteousness.

75:1 In anticipation of that event, the Savior leads His people in giving **thanks** to **God.** All God's **wondrous works declare that** He **is near** to deliver His chosen ones and to punish His foes. All His mighty miracles give proof that He cares (LB).

75:2 The same Speaker says, **"When I choose the proper time, I will judge uprightly."** The time has been set by God the Father (Mark 13:32). When it arrives, He will seize it and fulfill Isaiah's prophecy, "A king will reign in righteousness" (32:1).

75:3 At that crucial time when the foundations of human government will be disintegrating, He will **set up** a kingdom that shall never be moved. Though human society becomes utterly corrupt spiritually, politically, and morally, the **pillars** of His government are solid and secure.

75:4, 5 He says **to the boastful,** "Quit your bragging," **and to the wicked,** "Who do you think you are? Don't be so proud, self-confident, and unbending. Don't exalt yourself with conceit."

75:6, 7 "True **exaltation** doesn't come in that way. It doesn't come **from the east** or **west,** or from the wilderness in **the south. . . ."** The fact that the north is not mentioned may be because the invader usually came from the north, and that meant conquest rather than exaltation. Or it may be because the north is sometimes associated with God's dwelling place (Isa. 14:13; Ps. 48:2). In either case, the thought is clear that "lifting up" does not come from any human or earthly source but from the Lord alone. He is the Supreme Ruler, abasing **one** and exalting **another**.

75:8 As the Abaser, He holds **a cup in** His **hand**. The cup contains **the wine** of judgment. It is foaming, **red**, and **fully mixed**, that is, in restive motion and highly potent. When **He pours it out**, the **wicked** inhabitants of the earth will be compelled to **drink** all of it—**down** to the **dregs**.

75:9, 10 In the last two verses, the Lord Jesus is still the Speaker. He **will sing praises** forever **to the God of Jacob**, the God who has exalted His unworthy people. **The horns of the wicked**, that is, their strength and honor, He will cut off, but the power and glory **of the righteous shall be** increased.

Psalm 76: The Wrath of Man Praising God

In 701 B.C. the Assyrian army under Sennacherib threatened to destroy Jerusalem. But before they could even get near the city, the Angel of the Lord visited their encampment by night and slew 185,000 troops.

This Assyrian disaster is memorialized in Byron's epic poem, "The Destruction of Sennacherib," which is quoted in full at the commentary on Isaiah 37:36. If we see Psalm 76 against this historical backdrop, it will come alive in a new and exciting way. It is well worth reading along with this psalm.

76:1 **God** is famous **in Judah** because of His spectacular overthrow of the army that threatened the city and the sanctuary. **His name** is illustrious **in Israel** for this unforgettable chapter in the history of the nation.

76:2–4 He designated Jerusalem, the city of peace, as His capital, the hill of **Zion** as **His dwelling place**. And that is where He smashed the armaments of the foe—the glistening **arrows, the shield, and sword of battle**, and all the other weapons.

This city set upon a hill is **more** majestic **than the mountains of prey**, that is, than the great Gentile governments that have plundered her. And by metonymy this means that the God of Jerusalem is **more glorious** than any power that might lift its hand against Judah.

76:5, 6 This is seen in what happened to the Assyrian army. **The stouthearted** warriors suddenly dropped their weapons. In a moment they became powerless. One word from the **God of Jacob** and **both** riders and horses sank **into** the **sleep** of death.

76:7–9 What a God He is! And how greatly He should **be feared!** All opposition is futile when once His anger has been ignited. As soon as He pronounces **judgment to** come **from heaven, the earth** trembles and becomes **still**—like the lull before the storm. Then God steps forth to make right the wrongs of earth and **to deliver** its **oppressed** people.

76:10 He has a wonderful way of making **the wrath of man** to **praise** Him. And what won't praise Him, He girds on Him like a sword of a conquered general.

> The wrath of men shall praise Thee,
> The rest shalt Thou restrain,
> And out of earth's disasters
> Will bring eternal gain.
> The purpose of man's evil heart
> Works out Thy sovereign will.
> Our God is still upon the throne,
> Therefore, believe, be still.

Be still and know that I am God,
This banishes our fears,
While passing through this scene of
   strife,
Of sorrow and of tears.
The One who rules the heavenly
   hosts
Holds all within His hand,
And none can say, "What doest
   Thou?"
Or can His arm withstand.
                    —*Author unknown*

76:11a In view of the inexpressible greatness and glory of the Lord, the people of Judah are exhorted to **make vows to the LORD their God, and** to **pay them**.

76:11b, 12 Then the Gentile nations surrounding Israel are counseled to **bring presents** as tribute to the Supreme Ruler—this Mighty One who can reduce earth's **princes** to size and cause **awesome** things to happen to the most powerful rulers.

Psalm 77: The Cure for Introspection

In the first ten verses, **Asaph** has a king-sized case of introspection. The personal pronouns *I, me,* and *my* are found *over twenty* times, while the names of God are found only *seven* times, and pronouns referring to God *seven* times. But there is a distinct change at verse 10. In the last ten verses the personal pronouns are found only *three* times whereas nouns and pronouns referring to Deity are used *over twenty* times. "The ministry of Christ through the Holy Spirit does away with *I, me,* and *my*."

Someone has described the flow of thought here in four words:

Sighing (vv. 1–6)
Sinking (vv. 7–10)
Singing (vv. 11–15)
Soaring (vv. 16–20)

77:1–3 First, Asaph pours out his tale of woe **to God**. Some unnamed trouble has come to camp on his doorstep. In his misery, he can think of no one and nothing but himself. In spite of unceasing prayer, he complains that comfort eludes him. He finds himself in the anomalous situation where thoughts of **God** cause him to moan instead of rejoice. The more he meditates, the more melancholy he becomes.

77:4–6 He blames his acute case of insomnia on God alone. Words fail him to express the anguish of his spirit. He seeks comfort in remembering the good old **days** when things went smoothly with him. But the more he is occupied with himself and looks for victory within, the more he begins to doubt the kindness of the Lord. He is assailed by doubts that find expression *in five unbelieving questions.*

77:7–10 *The first* raises the frightening suggestion that perhaps **the Lord** is finished with him for good. The *second* asks if God has **ceased** to love. *Next* he wonders if the Lord has scrapped His promises. *Again,* the impertinent thought crosses his mind that perhaps **God has forgotten to be gracious**. And *finally,* he asks if God's **anger** has cut off the flow of **His** compassion. And he answers himself that this is the case. **The right hand of the Most High** has changed. All his grief can be traced to a change in God's attitude toward him.

77:11–13 But in verse 11 there is a spiritual turning point comparable to the transition from Romans 7 to Romans 8. After introspection had plunged him into the depths of despondency, Asaph turns his eyes heavenward and determines to reflect on God's past interventions for His people when they were in tight spots.

This leads him at once to the acknowledgment that God is holy, that everything He does is perfect, righteous, and good. He makes no mistakes.

77:14, 15 Specifically the psalmist thinks of the marvelous and miraculous display of the **strength** of God that delivered the people of Israel from the bondage of Egypt. By this time he is soaring. The personal pronouns have disappeared entirely from his vocabulary. Self-centeredness has given way to God-centeredness.

77:16–18 With superb literary skill, he pictures **the waters** of the Red Sea as looking up and seeing their Creator, then retreating in terror. All nature exploded in a violent storm. Torrents of rain poured down. Shattering crashes of **thunder** burst overhead. Lightning zigzagged across the sky, lighting up the landscape. A furious whirlwind blitzed the area, and the countryside shook under the fierce assault.

77:19, 20 God Himself made a highway through **the sea**. It was He who opened a **path** so His people could cross dry-shod. Yet no one saw His footprints. As is so often the case, there were abundant evidences of His presence and power, though He Himself was concealed in the shadows.

The Psalm closes on a peaceful note—the Shepherd-God leading Israel through the wilderness to Canaan in the care of **Moses and Aaron**. At the outset, Asaph was a likely prospect for a psychiatric clinic. At the end he is calm and serene. And so the Psalm is an illustration of the well-known saying:

Occupation with self brings distress;
Occupation with others brings discouragement;
Occupation with Christ brings delight.

Psalm 78: A Parable From History

"God's ways in grace and Israel's ways in perverseness"—that is how Bellett sums up the message of this Psalm. It is one of the great songs of Israel's history. Its purpose is to teach us to learn from the past, so that we will not be condemned to relive it.

The Psalmist's Invitation to Learn from History (78:1–4)

The psalmist calls for the attention of his **people** (and of all of us) because he is going to speak **in a parable**, that is, there is going to be a deeper meaning beneath the surface of what he recounts. As he rehearses various chapters from the history of his nation, there will be hidden lessons which he calls **"dark sayings of old."** Just as our parents passed down to us a record of the past, so we are obligated to pass on to the next **generation** an account of the Lord's dealings with His people in grace and government.

God's Gracious Intention in Giving the Law (78:5–8)

Asaph begins his parabolic teaching with the institution of the **law**. God gave it to **Israel** with instructions that it be faithfully transmitted to succeeding **generations**. God's desire in all this was fourfold:

That His people would **set their hope in** Him.
That they would **not forget** His glorious **works**.
That they would be obedient.
That they would learn from the past and not repeat the rebellions of their forefathers.

The People's Disobedience, Rebellion, and Ingratitude (78:9–11)

But what happened? Under the leadership of the tribe of **Ephraim,** the Israelites failed the Lord. **Armed with bows**, they **turned back in the day of battle**. This may refer to their dismal cowardice at Kadesh Barnea when they accepted the pessimistic report of the spies. Or it may allude to their failure in utterly driving out the Canaanites from the land. More probably it is a general description of their characteristic behavior. They repeatedly and willfully broke the **law** of God. They habitually **forgot** all the mighty **wonders that He had** performed for their benefit.

The People's Forgetfulness of Their Deliverance from Egypt (78:12–14)

They forgot **Egypt**—and the marvel of their deliverance from the forced slave-labor in the fields of **Zoan** (Tanis). How could they forget the crossing of the Red **Sea**—when the **waters** stood at attention on both sides of them so they could cross on dry land? There was the miracle of **the** glory **cloud** that led them **in the daytime** and the fiery **light** that went before them at **night**.

The People's Forgetfulness of God's Miraculous Supply of Water in the Wilderness (78:15, 16)

They quickly forgot how God provided water **in abundance** by splitting **rocks in the wilderness**—it came gushing out as if there were a huge fountain. **Rivers** of water in the desert—but their memories were short.

The People's Insolent Demand for Bread and Meat (78:17–22)

They began to provoke the Lord about their diet. Dissatisfied and grumbling, they presented new demands to **the Most High**. They insinuated that God had led them out into **the wilderness** to die of starvation. They doubted His ability to provide. Grud-

gingly admitting that He had provided **water**, they questioned His willingness and ability to provide **bread** and **meat**.

It really infuriated **the LORD** that His people did not trust Him. He was understandably **furious** that **they did not trust** His saving power. He caused the **fire** of His **anger** to blaze forth **against Israel**.

God's Gracious Supply of Manna (78:23–25)

They wanted bread. But there were no supermarkets in the wilderness. Neither were there the ingredients for making bread. So God **opened the doors** of His heavenly granary and **rained down** unfailing supplies of **manna**. The people feasted on something better than bread; it was **angels' food, the bread of heaven**.

God's Gracious Supply of Quail (78:26–31)

They also wanted **meat**. But where could they find meat to feed a multitude in the desert? God solved the problem by harnessing the **east wind** to deliver flocks of quail right into the **camp** of the Israelites. These birds certainly weren't native to the wilderness; they had to be brought from some distance. But they were provided abundantly and freely.

While the people were still gorging themselves, **the wrath of God** blazed out **against them**. He sent a plague that killed off the finest specimens of Israel's manhood.

The People's Continued Sin and God's Unfailing Mercy (78:32–39)

In spite of all the proofs of His love, their hearts were **still** unfaithful. Nothing God did pleased them. Despite His miracles, they were compulsive grumblers. So from time to time Jehovah visited the nation with death and destruction. This seemed to speak to the survivors for a while; they turned to the Lord, repented of their wickedness, and became earnest seekers. They realized what a refuge He had been to them, how He had redeemed them from the terrors of Egypt. But soon again they were living a lie, speaking piously and acting perversely. They were fickle and disobedient.

The Lord showed tremendous restraint. Because of His super-abounding **compassion**, He **forgave** their chronic backsliding and withheld the disaster they deserved. **He remembered that they were** mere men, here today and gone tomorrow.

The People's Rebellions, Provocations, and Ingratitude (78:40, 41)

The psalmist is going to go over the whole sorry history again (vv. 40–58). If *we* as readers grow weary of the repetition, think of how irritating it was to *the Lord!*

Their repeated rebellions **in the desert grieved Him** to the heart. Over and over again they put Him to the test and pained **the Holy One of Israel** by limiting Him.

The People's Forgetfulness of Their Deliverance from Egypt (78:42–53)

78:42 **They did not remember** how He had proved Himself strong on their behalf, how **He** had rescued **them from the enemy**. Their deliverance from Egypt was the greatest display of divine power in human history up to that time. But they took it for granted.

78:43 In verses 43–53 **Egypt** is in retrospect again, this time with emphasis on six of the plagues in the following order:

First plague—*rivers turned to blood* (v.44).
Fourth plague—*flies* (v. 45a).
Second plague—*frogs* (v. 45b).
Eighth plague—*locusts* (v. 46).
Seventh plague—*hail* (vv. 47, 48).
Tenth plague—*death of the firstborn* (vv. 49–51).

78:44 God **turned their rivers into blood**, so **that** the Egyptians **could not drink** from them. The Nile, which they regarded as sacred, suddenly became polluted. But the water supply of the Israelites remained uncontaminated.

78:45 **He sent swarms of flies** into all the houses of the Egyptians. They had worshiped Beelzebub, the "lord of flies," and now this god turned on them to devour them. Interestingly enough, the flies did not invade the land of Goshen where the Israelites were living.

He sent a plague of **frogs** into Egypt. Respected as a symbol of fertility, the frogs **destroyed** the people in the sense that they brought normal life to a standstill. But the plague affected only Egyptians; the Hebrews were protected by the hand of God.

78:46 God sent locusts to cover the land of Egypt. The god Serapis was supposed to protect the people from these destructive insects. But Serapis was powerless. The **crops** were ruined; the harvest wiped out. During all this the Israelites saw neither **caterpillar** nor **locust**.

78:47, 48 The seventh plague involved **hail**, **frost** and **fiery lightning**. It wrought tremendous havoc on man, **cattle**, **flocks**, **vines**, and **trees**. But it was a discriminating judgment. "...In the land of Goshen, where the children of Israel were, there was no hail" (Ex. 9:26).

78:49 Then there was the culminating stroke of God—the death of the **firstborn**. The psalmist speaks of it as a loosing of God's fierce **wrath, indignation, and trouble**, the work of a company of **angels of destruction**. In some Scriptures the Lord Himself is described as passing through the land of Egypt to destroy the firstborn (Ex. 11:4; 12:12, 23, 29), but in Exodus 12:23, there is a reference to a destroyer whom He used as His active agent. The psalmist suggests that it was a band of destroying **angels**.

78:50–53 He made a path for His anger so that it could blaze forth without restraint. In every Egyptian home the firstborn son was struck down by an otherwise unnamed **plague** or pestilence. The flower of Egypt's manhood died that night. But the homes of the Israelites were protected by the blood of the passover lamb, and not one Hebrew son was killed.

All the plagues were so discriminating that no natural explanation could ever account for them. How could the Jews ever cease to be thankful for the wonderful way God had worked in their behalf?

He led them out of Egypt **like a flock** of **sheep, and guided them** through a trackless **wilderness**. "He led them in safety with nothing to fear, while the sea engulfed their foes" (Gelineau). It was a marvelous exhibition of His love and power!

The People's Forgetfulness of God's Kindness in Bringing Them to the Promised Land (78:54, 55)

He brought them to the **border** of the **holy** land, to the **mountain** range **which His right hand had acquired** for them. Of course, it was inhabited by idolatrous pagans at the time, so **He also drove out the nations** and divided the land among **the tribes of Israel**. No shepherd ever cared as tenderly for his sheep as Jehovah did for His!

The People's Treachery and Idolatry in the Land (78:56–58)

Were they grateful to Him? No! During the time of the Judges **they tested** Him to the limit, they rebelled against Him, they disregarded His commandments. **Like fathers**—like sons, they proved utterly faithless and unreliable, just like a warped **bow** that the archer cannot depend on. **They provoked** the Lord by their idolatrous hilltop shrines, and made Him exceedingly jealous **with their carved images**.

God's Wrath, and His Rejection of Israel (78:59–67)

78:59, 60 In poetic language, the psalmist pictures **God** as hearing of their dark ingratitude and exploding in a storm of wrath. Actually it came as no surprise to Jehovah; it was only the last straw in a long series of rebellions. But this time He lowered the boom on Israel, that is, on the northern tribes who were the ringleaders in the provocations and rebellions. He abandoned **Shiloh** as the site of **the tabernacle**—the spot on earth where He had previously chosen to dwell among His people.

78:61–64 At this time God allowed **His strength**, that is, the ark of the covenant, to be taken **into captivity** by the Philistines. The gold-covered symbol of His glory passed into enemy hands (1 Sam. 4:11a). There was a great slaughter among the people of Israel; 30,000 foot soldiers fell in the battle (1 Sam. 4:10). With so many **young men** devoured by war, there were no **marriage** songs, no wedding bells for **their maidens**. The **priests** who **fell by the sword** were Hophni and Phinehas, the corrupt sons of Eli (1 Sam. 4:11b). **Their widows** did not mourn their passing, probably because of their overriding grief that the ark had been captured by the Philistines. They realized that the glory had departed from Israel (1 Sam. 4:19–22).

78:65, 66 For a while it seemed that Jehovah was indifferent to His people's plight. But then He **awoke** with blazing indignation, shouting like a man who has been aroused with **wine**. And what a rout it was for the Philistines! **He beat** them **back** as they turned to flee—a shameful way for them to suffer defeat (1 Sam. 7:10, 11; 13:3, 4; 14:23).

78:67 Yet God stood firm in His decision to reject **the tent of Joseph**; He would **not choose the tribe of Ephraim**. Here both **Joseph** and **Ephraim** are used to signify the ten northern tribes. After Reuben had forfeited the birthright, Joseph inherited the double portion as far as territory was concerned, through his sons, Ephraim and Manasseh.

God's Choice of Judah, Mt. Zion, and David (78:68–72)

78:68, 69 But Ephraim was the leader in rebellion; therefore God bypassed him as far as rule was concerned and gave that honor to **Judah**. It was in Judah's territory that He chose **Mount Zion** as the place to build **His sanctuary**—towering like the high heavens and immoveable as **the earth**.

78:70, 71 And it was from Judah that **He also chose David His servant**. This shepherd-king served his apprenticeship among the **sheepfolds**, caring for **the ewes that had young** and learning spiritual truths from the natural realm. Then Jehovah **brought him to shepherd Jacob His people,**

and Israel His inheritance. And David did this.

78:72   So he shepherded them according to the integrity of his heart, And guided them by the skillfulness of his hands.

And so the Psalm closes on this peaceful, pastoral note. But before leaving it, we must remind ourselves that Israel's history is only a mirror of our own. And if anything, we are more culpable than they because our privileges are so much greater. Living in the full blaze of Calvary's love, why should we ever complain, or rebel, or limit the Lord, or fail to be thankful? Yet we stand condemned. We have provoked the Holy One of Israel times without number. We have grieved Him by a thousand falls. We have murmured and grumbled in spite of countless blessings.

God's patience is not inexhaustible. There comes a time when He allows us to taste the bitterness of our backsliding. If we despise His grace, we will experience His government. If we refuse to serve Him faithfully and loyally, He will find others to do it. We will miss the blessing, and will never find a better master to serve.

Psalm 79: The Groans of the Prisoners

Psalm 79 is a partner to Psalm 74. That one dealt primarily with the destruction of God's real estate—the temple. Although this one refers briefly to the bulldozing of the temple, it is mostly concerned with the ravaging of God's people—the Israelites. The psalmist pleads the cause of the Jews with rare eloquence and asks for respite and revival.

79:1 The pagan aggressors have invaded the land of Israel and have swept, like panzer units, into the capital. The sacred shrine has been defiled by their unsanctified feet, and the beloved city is now reduced to rubble.

79:2-4 The carnage is terrible. The air reeks with the smell of rotting flesh. Jewish **bodies** lie everywhere, suffering the final indignity of being left unburied. The vultures swoop down on them, and the carnivorous **beasts** greedily gobble their prey. **Blood** has flowed **like water all around Jerusalem**, and the invaders haven't bothered to arrange for burial of the slain. Israel's Gentile **neighbors** are gloating over the national calamity.

79:5-7 It is obviously a sign of the Lord's fierce anger and jealous wrath, but how long will His **jealousy burn like fire** against Israel? Isn't it time to turn against the Gentiles for a change? After all, these **nations** do not *want* to **know** Jehovah; they willfully refuse to **call on** His **name**. And now they have crowned their sins with the slaughter of God's people and the devastation of the land.

79:8-10 Everything up to this point has been introductory. The psalmist comes to the crux of the matter now when he recognizes that the nation's sin is the root cause of the disaster. **"Do not remember** the **iniquities** of our forefathers **against us!"** Once that confession has surfaced, he brings out irresistible arguments to move the Almighty to mercy. First he appeals to the compassion of God; the people never needed it more than now. Then he bases his plea on **the glory of** God's own **name**. The Lord has promised forgiveness and deliverance to those who are broken and contrite; now the honor of His name is at stake. And finally, it is important to silence the jeers of the enemy. They are saying that Israel's **God**

doesn't exist. This is His grand opportunity to prove His existence by raining down vengeance upon them to requite **the** outpoured **blood of** His loyal **servants**.

79:11, 12 The psalmist then asks God to listen to the doleful **groaning of the prisoner**, and to rescue **those who are** abandoned **to die** in a way that is worthy of His great **power**. And He asks that the enemies will reap **sevenfold** for all the sacrilegious taunts which they hurled at the **Lord**.

79:13 All this will mean peace for Israel and praise to God. His loving flock will never cease to thank Him. Generation after generation will rise to sing His **praise**.

Psalm 80: The Man of God's Right Hand

The sorrow and sighing which permeate so many of the Psalms are continued here also. First under the figure of a flock, then of a vine, Israel pleads for forgiveness and restoration.

80:1-3 The appeal is addressed to the **Shepherd of Israel**, a name of God which appeared in Jacob's blessing of **Joseph**—"the Shepherd, the Stone of Israel" (Gen. 49:24). It was He who led **Joseph like a flock** from Egypt to Canaan. It was He who in the glory cloud was enthroned **between the cherubim** which overshadowed the mercy seat in the most holy place. But now it seems that He has deserted Israel, and the sanctuary has been destroyed, thus the prayer for Him to **shine forth** in mercy and favor before **Ephraim, Benjamin, and Manasseh**. These were the three tribes that were in the vanguard of the procession when the Kohathites carried the ark. Here they represent all of Israel. They desperately desire God to **stir up** His **strength** (perhaps we would say "to flex His muscles") and to move in to their rescue. They appeal that He **restore** them from captivity. If only His **face** would **shine** on them in compassion, their deliverance would be assured.

80:4–7 Terrible distance has come in between Israel and the LORD God of hosts (*Jehovah Elohim Sabaoth*). He is **angry** not only with their sins but even with their prayers. For food He has given them a diet of weeping, and for drink a torrent of **tears**. He has **made** them **a** cause of **strife** and contention to their Gentile **neighbors**, and they are the butt of cruel jokes among their **enemies**. There is only one solution—that is for the **God of hosts** (*Elohim Sabaoth*) to look down in grace and salvation upon them.

80:8–11 God **brought** Israel **out of Egypt** like a tender **vine**. In order to plant it in the promised land, He **cast out the** Canaanites. As the owner of a vineyard clears the ground and cultivates it, so the Lord took great pains with His people. The transplant was successful. The vine took **deep root** and the population multiplied and **filled the land**. The vine became luxuriant, higher than **the hills** in glory and stronger than **the mighty cedars**. Its tendrils reached out **to the** Mediterranean **Sea** on one side and to **the River** Euphrates on the other. Under the reign of Solomon Israel occupied land as far east as the Euphrates (1 Kgs. 4:21, 24), but this was very temporary.

80:12, 13 But then God lowered His protective wall and allowed the marauding nations to pick away at the vine. **The boar** and other **wild** animals came in and laid it waste— first Egypt, Assyria, and Babylonia, then in later years Persia, Greece, and Rome. In using the figure of a **boar**, the psalmist wrote beyond his

knowledge because centuries later Israel was ravaged by the Roman army with the **boar** proudly displayed as its military ensign.

80:14, 15 Once more the people implore the **God of hosts** to **return** to them in blessing. They want Him to **look down from** the ramparts of **heaven** and take pity on **this vine** which they describe as **"the vineyard which Your right hand has planted, and the branch that You made strong for Yourself."** The Targum, interestingly enough, renders this "and upon the King Messiah, whom You have established for Yourself." In verse 15 it seems more consistent to regard **the vineyard** and **the branch** as referring to Israel. Two verses later the Messiah is unmistakably introduced.

80:16 The vine has been **cut down** and **burned** by the invading armies. **They** deserve to **perish** by a condemning frown from the Lord.

80:17, 18 **"Let Your hand be upon the man of Your right hand, upon the son of man** *whom* **You made strong for Yourself."** The Man of God's right hand is the Lord Jesus Christ (Ps. 110:1; Heb. 1:3; 8:1; 10:12). **The Son of Man** is the title by which He most frequently spoke of Himself in the Gospels. Full and complete blessing will only come to Israel when He is given His proper place. Then Israel will never backslide again. Revived by the Lord, they **will call upon** the **name** of the Lord.

80:19 The familiar refrain closes the Psalm. The Shepherd is urged to **restore** His wandering sheep. One smile from the LORD **God of hosts** and Israel **shall be saved**.

Psalm 81: The Feast of Trumpets

Unger describes this Jewish holiday as follows:

[The Feast of Trumpets] was observed as a feast day, in the strict sense, by resting from all work, and as a memorial of blowing of horns, by a holy convocation. In later times, while the drink offering of the sacrifice was being poured out, the priests and Levites chanted Psalm 81, while at the evening sacrifice they sang Psalm 29. Throughout the day trumpets were blown at Jerusalem from morning to evening. . . . The rabbins [rabbis] believed that on this day God judges all men, and that they pass before him as a flock of sheep pass before a shepherd.[52]

The Feast of Trumpets is a type of the regathering of Israel to its homeland after the out-gathering of the Church.

81:1–5a In the opening verses, the people of Israel are called to join in singing the praises of **God** who is the source of their **strength**, and to **make a joyful shout to the God of Jacob**, that is, the God of all grace. The Levites are invited to join the happy chorus with their musical instruments, and the priests mark the arrival of the seventh **New Moon** by blowing the shophar. It is a holiday instituted by God for the nation of Israel (Lev. 23:23–25; Num. 29:1). **He established it in Joseph** (here **Joseph** stands for all Israel) **when He went throughout the land of Egypt**. Here the meaning seems to be that God ordained this feast after the confrontation with **Egypt** and after His people came out of that **land**.

81:5b At the end of verse 5, we read, **"I heard a language I did not understand,"** and we must consider whether the speaker is the psalmist, Israel, or God.

If it is the psalmist or Israel speaking, the language may refer to:

1. The foreign **language** of the Egyptians (Ps. 114:1).

2. God speaking to Israel in the redemption from Egypt, a new revelation of God to their souls.

3. The oracle of God which is found in the remaining verses of the Psalm.

If God is the Speaker, then the thought may be:

I heard a language (of the Egyptians) that **I did not** know (in the sense of "acknowledge"). As Williams puts it, "He did not acknowledge the Egyptians as His sheep."

In favor of the latter is the fact that the pronoun "I" in the rest of the Psalm always refers to God.

81:6, 7 God had relieved the shoulders of the people **from the burden** of servile work under the Egyptians. Their **hands were freed from** having to carry **baskets** filled with clay and bricks. From all their **trouble** He **delivered** them when they **called**. He **answered** them **in the secret place of thunder**—a reference to the cloud which guided and protected them, or to the giving of the law at Mt. Sinai. He **tested** them **at the waters of Meribah** where Moses struck the rock and incurred God's displeasure.

81:8–10 He had warned them that the pathway of blessing lay in faithfulness to Him as the one true God. His prohibition of idolatry was unmistakable. After reminding them how He had **brought** them **out of the land of Egypt**, He made the marvelous promise that if they would **open** their **mouth wide**, He would **fill it**. This promise has sometimes been wrongly used by lazy preachers to justify any lack of preparation; all they have to do is open their mouth and the Lord will give them a message. But that is not the meaning at all! The thought is that if they came to God with great petitions, He would grant them. There is nothing good that He would not do for an obedient people. Gaebelein puts it well:

Who is able to grasp the full meaning of the sentence! He is the omnipotent Lord; there is nothing too hard for the Lord. Open thy mouth, He says, as wide as you can, and I will fill it. Ask anything in My Name, He says in the New Testament, and I will do it. All He asks is obedience to Him, the yielding of the heart and will.[53]

81:11–16 But God's **people** turned a deaf ear to His **voice, and Israel would** not obey Him. So He let them have their own way, and **gave them over to** the misery of following **their own** advice. But this abandonment was not without a pang in the heart of God. He mourns their continued folly and stubbornness. If only they **would listen** to Him, He **would soon subdue their enemies. Their adversaries** would come cringing in fear before Him, and Israel's prosperity would know no interruption (AV). **He would** feed His people **with the finest of wheat**—that is, the best spiritual and physical nourishment, **and with** the delicious **honey** that comes **from** beehives in the rocks of Palestine.

Psalm 82: Earth's Rulers on Trial

82:1 The court is called to order. The Judge has taken His place at the bench. It is **God** Himself. He has called a special session of the divine council in order to reprove the rulers and judges of the earth. They are called **gods** because they are representatives of God, ordained by Him as His servants in order to maintain an ordered society. Actually, of course, they are only men like ourselves. But

because of their position, they are the anointed of the Lord. Even if they do not know God personally, yet they are God's agents officially and therefore dignified here with the name of **gods**. The basic meaning of the name is *mighty ones*.

82:2 First God rebukes them for malfeasance in office. They have been guilty of graft and corruption. Under their administration, the rich have been favored while the poor have been oppressed. Criminals have escaped unpunished, and the innocent have had to suffer loss without recourse. The scales of justice have become scales of oppression.

82:3, 4 Then the Judge of all the earth reminds them once more of their responsibilities in the area of social justice. They are to champion the rights of **the poor and fatherless, . . . the afflicted and needy**. They should be the helpers of all who are dispossessed and downtrodden.

82:5 But despite all the Lord's warnings, there seems to be no hope of improvement. As if in an aside, He sighs that they fail to act with knowledge and understanding. Since they themselves are groping **about in darkness**, there is scant hope of their helping others who need direction. And as a result of their failure to act righteously and wisely, **the foundations of** society **are unstable**. Law and order have all but vanished.

82:6, 7 Though exalted to heaven in privilege, they shall be cast down in punishment. The fact that God calls them **gods** and **children of the Most High** does not grant them immunity from judgment. They will be subject to the same treatment as other **men, and fall like one of the princes**. Actually the *degree* of their punishment will be greater because of their greater privilege.

Our Lord quoted verse six in one of His confrontations with His foes (John 10:32–36). They had just accused Him of blaspheming because He claimed equality with God.

> Jesus answered them, "Is it not written in your law, 'I said, "You are gods"'? If He called them gods, to whom the word of God came (and the Scripture cannot be broken), do you say of Him whom the Father sanctified and sent into the world, 'You are blaspheming,' because I said, 'I am the Son of God'?"

To the western mind, the argument might not seem clear or convincing, but it obviously had compelling power on His hearers. They understood that Jesus was arguing from the lesser to the greater. The force of the argument is as follows:

In Psalm 82, rulers and judges are addressed by God as gods. Actually they are not divine, but because of their position as God's ministers, they are dignified with the name of gods. Their greatest distinction is that the word of God came to them, that is, they were officially ordained by God as higher powers concerned with government and justice (Rom. 13:1).

If the name *gods* could thus be loosely applied to men like them, how much more fully and accurately can the name God be applied to the Lord Jesus. He had been sanctified and sent into the world by God the Father. This implies that He had lived with God the Father in heaven from all eternity. Then the Father had set Him apart to a mission on earth and had sent Him to be born in Bethlehem.

The Jews understood perfectly that He was claiming equality with God, and they sought to apprehend Him but He eluded them (John 10:39).

82:8 But now back to the last verse of the Psalm:

Arise, O God, judge the earth;
For You shall inherit all nations.

It is Asaph calling on the Lord to intervene in the affairs of men, bringing righteousness and justice to replace corruption and inequity. The prayer will be answered when the Lord Jesus returns to reign over the earth. At that time, as the prophets predicted, "justice will dwell in the wilderness, and righteousness remain in the fruitful field" (Isa. 32:16). The earth will enjoy a time of social justice and freedom from graft and deceit.

Psalm 83: Psalm of the Six-Day War

On May 28, 1967, Gamal Abdel Nasser, President of the United Arab Republic, said, "We plan to open a general assault on Israel. This will be total war. Our basic aim is the destruction of Israel." When war broke out on June 5, the United Arab Republic was joined by Jordan, Syria, Iraq, Algeria, Sudan, Kuwait, Saudi Arabia, and Morocco. The attempt of this confederacy to drive Israel into the sea was unsuccessful. In six days the war was over. Israel was the undisputed victor.

For many Bible lovers, Psalm 83 took on new meaning after the Six-Day War. And perhaps it will have further fulfillments before Israel's claim to the land is irrevocably settled by the coming of the Lord Jesus to reign as King.

83:1–5 The language is obviously that of besieged Israel, calling on **God** to break His silence and to act decisively. Although the people are pleading for their own safety and preservation, they present their case as if it were God's cause as much as their own: "**Your enemies . . . those who hate You . . . Your people . . . Your sheltered ones . . . They form a confederacy against You.**" They will not let Him forget that Israel's enemies are His enemies.

The details are true to life. The enemies are in tumult—a vivid description of the blustering threats of the opposition. They lay crafty plans—assisted behind the scenes by advisors from Soviet Russia. They consult together—in what have now become known as Arab summit meetings. They threaten the annihilation of Israel—as witnessed by the quotation above. They form a formidable federation of nations—mostly of people who are near relatives of the Israelites.

83:6–8 When we try to identify these nations with modern counterparts, we run into difficulty. We do know that **Assyria** is the same as modern-day Iraq, and that **the Ishmaelites**, descended from Abraham and Hagar, were the progenitors of the Arabs. We know that the Edomites and the Amalekites were descended from Esau, and the Moabites and Ammonites from **Lot**, but to trace them today is well-nigh impossible. The Philistines inhabited the area now known as the Gaza strip. The city of **Tyre** was located in what is now Lebanon. **Gebal** is the same as ancient Gubla or Byblos, located in Phoenicia. Some sources list the **Hagrites** as descendants of Hagar, and therefore a segment of the Ishmaelites, but the identification is not positive. Since so much obscurity surrounds these names, it is best not to try to link them with modern countries in the Middle East, but simply to see them as representing Gentile foes of Israel.

How could little Israel stand against such an overwhelming confederacy? Part of the answer is found in the fact that God's people are His "sheltered ones" (v. 3), His "hidden ones" (AV), His "precious ones" (LB), or "those He loves" (Gelineau). In the hour of danger, He miraculously shields them, and makes His strength perfect in their weakness. When the odds are all against them, He sends a victory that defies all human explanations.

83:9, 10 Now the beleaguered people call on Jehovah to **deal with** the current threat as He did with His enemies on three different occasions in the past.

Jabin, king of Canaan, and **Sisera**, his commander in chief, were killed ingloriously at **En Dor** after a disastrous defeat at the **Brook Kishon** (Judg. 4). Their decaying carcasses became fertilizer for Israel's soil.

83:11, 12 **Oreb** and **Zeeb**, two princes of Midian were killed and decapitated (Judges 7:23–25). According to Isaiah (10:26), it was an epic slaughter.

Two kings of Midian, **Zebah and Zalmunna**, had threatened to occupy "**the pastures of God.**" They managed to escape from the Israelites when Oreb and Zeeb were slain, but they were subsequently overtaken and executed by Gideon (Judg. 8).

83:13–18 In its bold plea for God's judgment on His foes, Israel leaves nothing to the divine imagination. The details of the punishment are specified. Let **them** be **like the whirling dust**, or as some translate it, like a tumbleweed. Let them be **like the chaff** driven **before the wind**. Let them be pursued **as** if by a **fire** sweeping through **the woods**, and consumed as if by a raging holocaust. Let them be terrified by the Lord's **storm**. Let them be thoroughly put to **shame** so that men might **seek** the Lord. Let them **perish** in disgrace so that men might learn that Jehovah **alone** is the Sovereign Ruler **over all the earth**.

Strong language? Yes, strong but not unjustified. When the honor of God is at stake, love can be firm. Morgan explains:

> These singers of the ancient people were all inspired supremely with a passion for the honor of God. With them, as with the prophets, selfish motives were unknown. Selfishness sings no song, and sees no visions. On the other hand, a passion for the glory of God is capable of great sternness as well as great tenderness.[54]

Psalm 84: Homesick for Heaven!

There is no question as to the primary *interpretation* of Psalm 84. It breathes out the deep longings of exiled Jews to be back at the temple in Jerusalem once again.

It can also be *applied*, of course, to the Christian today who is somehow prevented from attending the meetings of the local fellowship. He eats his heart out to be back with God's people as they meet to worship the Lord.

But the application I like best is that of a godly pilgrim who is downright homesick for heaven. Let us look at the Psalm from this viewpoint.

84:1, 2 What place can be compared in loveliness to the dwelling place of God! It is a place of unparalleled beauty, unique splendor and unutterable glory. But let us be clear on this point. The *place* is used, by a figure of speech known as metonymy, for the *Person* who lives there. And so when the psalmist says, **"My soul longs, yes, even faints for the courts of the LORD,"** he was really yearning to be with the Lord Himself. He says as much in the next

sentence, **". . . my heart and my flesh cry out for the living God."**

84:3 The pilgrim compares himself to a **sparrow** and a **swallow**. In another Psalm, the sparrow is used as a picture of utter loneliness, **". . . a sparrow alone on the housetop"** (102:7). And anyone who has ever watched a **swallow** knows what a restless creature it is, darting and soaring on the air currents. Both are apt descriptions of God's people sojourning in this wilderness; they are lonely and restless. The only place where they find rest and security for themselves and their families is at the **altars** of the LORD.

There were two **altars** in the tabernacle and the temple. One was the brazen altar and the other the golden altar. The first typified Christ's death and the second His resurrection. Taken together they represent the finished work of our Savior. Here is the place where our souls, like the swallow, can rest, and here we can bring our children to find rest also. "Believe on the Lord Jesus Christ, and you will be saved, *you and your household*" (Acts 16:31).

84:4 Then in an outburst of what we might call sanctified jealousy, the exile says, **"Blessed *are* those who dwell in Your house; they will still be praising You."** When we thus think of the happiness of loved ones who have gone home to be with the Lord, we cannot grieve over them. For us it is loss, but for them eternal gain. They are better off than we are.

84:5 In verses 5–7 we switch back from the blessedness of those who are already in heaven to the lesser blessedness of those who are en route. Several things are mentioned about them. First of all, their **strength is in** the Lord, not in themselves. They are "strong in the Lord and in the power of His might" (Eph. 6:10). Then in their heart are the highways to Zion. The world is not their home. Though *in* it, they are not *of* it. Their **heart** *is* **set on pilgrimage.**

84:6, 7 The third thing is that **as they pass through the Valley of** weeping, for that is what **Baca** means, **they** convert it into **a spring.** These indomitable souls can sing in the midst of sorrow and trace the rainbow through their tears. They transform tragedies into triumphs and use misfortunes as stepping stones to greater things. The secret of their victory over circumstances is found in the next statement, **"the rain also covers it with pools."** The **rain** is commonly taken as a type of the Holy Spirit, and here He is seen in His ministry of refreshment, providing **pools** of cool, clear water for the desert travelers. We take the water to stand for the Word of God (as in Eph. 5:26). This explains how **they go from strength to strength.** Instead of getting weaker as the journey progresses, they get stronger all the time. Though the outer nature is wasting away, the inner nature is being renewed every day (2 Cor. 4:16). And then a wonderful note of assurance: **Each one appears before God in Zion.** No question about it, the trek through the desert will be crowned at last with the joy of seeing the King in His beauty.

84:8 Now the psalmist breaks out into impassioned prayer. It is addressed first to the Lord **God of hosts,** then in the next breath to the **God of Jacob.** As Lord **God of hosts,** He is the sovereign over the vast multitude of angelic beings. As the **God of Jacob,** He is the God of the unworthy one, the God of the cheat. Just think! The God of innumerable angels in festal gathering is also the God of the worm Jacob. The One who is infinitely high

is also intimately nigh. And that is the only reason why you and I will ever enter His presence.

84:9 And what is our title to be there? **O God, behold our shield, and look upon the face of Your anointed.** Our only acceptance is through the Person and work of the Lord Jesus.

> God sees my Savior and then He
>   sees me
> In the Beloved, accepted and free.

84:10 And what is it like, being in heaven? Well, **a day in** His **courts** is **better than a thousand** elsewhere. Which is just another way of saying that there is no comparison. We simply cannot conceive the glory, the joy, the beauty, the freedom of being where Jesus is. And it's a good thing we can't. Otherwise we would probably be unhappy to remain here and to get on with our work.

Better to **be a doorkeeper in the house of** your **God than** to **dwell in the tents of wickedness.** As Spurgeon said, "God's worst is better than the devil's best." And not only better but more enduring. Note the contrast between **the house of our God** and **the tents of wickedness.** One is a permanent dwelling, the other is pitched for a relatively short while.

84:11 The Lord **God is a sun** providing illumination through the darkness, and **a shield** for protection against the scorching heat along the way. **The** Lord **will give grace** along the way for every time of need, and then He **will give glory** at the end of the journey as He welcomes His redeemed children into His eternal home. As a matter of fact the pilgrim has the assurance that he will lack nothing between here and heaven for **no good thing will He withhold from those who walk uprightly.** If it's **good**

for us, He won't **withhold** it; if He withholds it, it isn't good. "He who did not spare His own Son, but delivered Him up for us all, how shall He not with Him also freely give us all things?" (Rom. 8:32).

84:12 No wonder the psalmist ends with the heartfelt exclamation, **"O LORD of hosts, blessed is the man who trusts in You!"** To which my own heart responds, "Yes, Lord, I'm eternally grateful to be a Christian."

Psalm 85: Revive Us Again!

This prayer for revival is divided into four easily discernible sections:

A past instance of revival in Israel (vv. 1–3).

A plea for God to do it again (vv. 4–7).

A pause to hear how the Lord will answer (vv. 8, 9).

A promise of future restoration (vv. 10–13).

It is impossible to pinpoint the particular restoration of Israel that is described here. It could not be the restoration after the Babylonian captivity since this is a Psalm of the sons of Korah, and they lived long before that time. But the identification of the event is not important. What really matters is that God had done it. And if He did it once, He can certainly do it again.

85:1–3 The revival is described as a time when the LORD was **favorable** to the **land** and when He restored the fortunes **of Jacob**. Three actions led up to it. The first was confession of **sin**. Though this is not explicitly stated, confession is an invariable moral necessity before the others can take place. The second was forgiveness of **the iniquity of** His **people** and the third an averting of God's **wrath**.

85:4 This former demonstration of God's pardoning mercy is the basis for a plea that He repeat it. Faith is not satisfied with history; it wants to see God in current events. Although the psalmist does not engage in confession, it is implicit in the prayer, **"Restore us. . . ."** When **God** restores, He first brings His people to repentance, then He forgives their sins, and then He terminates the punishment that resulted from His indignation.

85:5 Any time spent away from the Lord seems like an eternity of misery. But the poignant plea of verse 5 takes on special meaning in the lips of the nation of Israel with its centuries of persecution and dispersion: **"Will You be angry with us forever? Will You prolong Your anger to all generations?"**

85:6 Spiritual declension results inevitably in a loss of joy. Broken fellowship means that the believer's song is gone. Rejoicing cannot co-exist with unconfessed sin. So here the prayer goes winging up to heaven. **"Will You not revive us again, that Your people may rejoice in You?"** The Spirit's renewal sets the joy-bells ringing once again. Every great revival has been accompanied by song.

85:7 When God restores His people it is a gracious demonstration of His **mercy**. But no more than any of His other dealings with us. It is love that chastens us, that disciplines us, that corrects us, and that brings us back at last. And how steadfast is that love that bears with us in all our wanderings, our backslidings, and our disobedience. There is no love like the love of the Lord.

And revival is a granting of **salvation** from the Lord—here not salvation of the soul but deliverance from all the consequences of unfaithfulness—dispersion, captivity, affliction, powerlessness, and unhappiness.

85:8, 9 Having brought His plea for restoration to the throne of grace, the psalmist waits for the answer, confident that it will be an answer of **peace**, and that it will come quickly. His confidence is based on the fact that the covenant-keeping God always speaks **peace** to those who turn to Him in their hearts, and delivers those who fear Him, not turning **back to folly**. And the inevitable result is **that glory** will **dwell in** the **land**. **Glory** here is used to signify the *God* of **glory**, and the thought is that the Lord can be depended on to **dwell** in the midst of His people when they are in fellowship with Him.

85:10 The answer to the prayer for revival is given in the closing verses. They describe the idyllic conditions which will prevail when the Lord Jesus reigns over restored Israel in the coming age of glory. But in a broader poetic sense they tell what it is always like when revival fires are burning.

Mercy and truth have met together. In human affairs strict adherence to the claims of **truth** usually prevent the display of love and **mercy**. But God can shower His steadfast love on His people because all the claims of **truth** were fully met by the Lord Jesus on the cross. In the same sense, **righteousness and peace have kissed.** Believers enjoy peace with God because all the claims of divine justice were met by the substitutionary work of the Savior.

> Our sins were placed on Jesus' head.
> 'Twas in His blood our debt was
>   paid.
> Stern justice can demand no more,
> And mercy can dispense her store.
>   *—Albert Midlane*

85:11–13 Truth, or faithfulness, **shall spring out of the earth, and righteousness shall look down from** the sky. As the believer is true to His Eternal Lover, the heavens respond righteously with multiplied blessing. **The LORD**, ever faithful to His Word, gives **what is good**. He withholds no good thing from those who walk uprightly (Ps. 84:11). Drought and famine conditions cease and **the land** produces a bumper crop. As the Lord visits His land, His route takes Him among a people whose righteous lives are morally prepared for His presence.

Psalm 86: Prayer with Reasons Attached

One of the noteworthy things about this Psalm is that David gives a reason for almost everything he says, whether in petition or adoration. We may illustrate this by the following arrangement:

PETITION	REASON
86:1 For audience with the **LORD**.	The psalmist's helplessness and need.
86:2a For preservation. (Note the recurrence of the title "servant" in vv. 4 and 16.)	His position as a **holy** person.
86:2b For temporal salvation.	No explicit reason is given but it may be implied in the clause **"You are my God."**
86:3 For gracious consideration.	David's persistence in prayer **all day long**.
86:4 For joy and gladness.	His hope is in the **Lord** and in no one else.

86:5

This verse may give an additional reason for the preceding requests. Or it may be mated to the prayer in verse 6.

The goodness, readiness **to forgive**, and **mercy** of the Lord are poured out on **all those who call upon** Him.

86:6 For audience with the Lord.

86:7 For help **in the day of** his **trouble**.

The fact that God does hear and **will answer** prayer.

The psalmist turns to praise in the next verses.

PRAISE

86:8 For the matchlessness of the Lord's Person and **works**.

86:9 For His worthiness to be adored by **all nations**. (This will be fulfilled in the Millennium.)

86:10

REASON

God is **great**. His works are **wondrous**. There is no other **God**.

PETITION

86:11 For instruction in the **way** of the **LORD**.

REASON

In order that the psalmist might **walk** in obedience to God's **truth**.

For a **heart** that is completely dedicated to revere and obey the Lord.

PRAISE

86:12, 13 Here David simply expresses his determination to **praise** the Lord **with all** his being, and to **glorify** His **name forevermore**.

REASON

For God's **great mercy** in delivering him **from the depths of Sheol**. If we apply the Psalm to the Messiah, then this is a reference to His resurrection.

86:14–16 The remaining verses describe the imminent peril of the psalmist. **A mob** of arrogant, **violent** men have conspired to take his **life**. These men have no time for God. **But** David knows the **Lord** and in this crucial moment he comforts himself in the knowledge that **God** is **full of compassion, gracious, longsuffering and abundant in mercy and truth**. Therefore he is confident in asking the Lord to **turn to** him in pity, to strengthen him and to **save** him—**the son of** God's **maidservant**. Some understand the expression **"the son of Your maidservant"** to be a figure of speech meaning "your property" as was the case with the son of a female slave. Those who take the Psalm as Messianic see it as a possible reference to the Virgin Mary.

86:17 Finally, the psalmist asks that the Lord will give him some definite **sign** of His favor. Then his enemies will realize that they have been on the wrong side when they see how God has **helped** David **and comforted** him.

We mentioned at the outset that the Psalm was notable in that it gave reasons for most of its prayers or praises. There are two other unique features that should be mentioned. First, David has quoted prolifically from other Scriptures; he is actually praying or praising with almost a scissors-and-paste collection of Bible verses. Second, the divine name "Adonai" is used seven times (it is translated "Lord" in vv. 3, 4, 5, 8, 9, 12 and 15). God-fearing Jews often used this title rather than Jehovah.

The Sopherim, or ancient custodians of the Sacred Text, changed the name Jehovah to Adonai 134 times when reading aloud, out of what they considered extreme reverence for the ineffable Name "Jehovah."[55]

Regarding *uniting* our hearts to fear God's name (v. 11b) F. W. Grant writes:

This is indeed what is everywhere the great lack among the people of God. How much of our lives is not spent in positive evil, but frittered away and lost in countless petty diversions which spoil effectually the positiveness of their testimony for God! How few can say with the apostle, "This *one* thing I do!" We are on the road . . . but we stop to chase butterflies among the flowers, and make no serious progress. How Satan must wonder when he sees us turn away from the "kingdoms of the world and the glory of them" . . . and yet yield ourselves with scarce a thought to endless trifles, lighter than the thistle-down which the child spends all his strength for, and we laugh at him. Would we examine our lives carefully . . . , how should we realize the multitude of needless anxieties, of self-imagined duties, of permitted relaxations, of "innocent" trifles, which incessantly divert us from that alone in which there is profit! How few, perhaps, would care to face such an examination of the day by day unwritten history of their lives![56]

Psalm 87: Psalm of the Royal Census

The mayor of Jerusalem, Teddy Kollek, and his co-author express natural wonder at the surprising greatness of their 4,000 year old city:

Archaeologists and historians have long wondered why Jerusalem should have been established where it was, and why it should have become great. It enjoys none of the physical features which favored the advancement and prosperity of other important cities in the world. It stands at the head of no great river. It overlooks no great harbour. It commands no great highway and no cross-roads. It is not close to abundant sources of water, often the major reason for the establishment of a settlement, though one main natural spring offered a modest supply. It possesses no mineral riches. It was off the main trade routes. It held no strategic key to the conquest of vast areas prized by the ancient warring empires. Indeed it was blessed with neither special economic nor topographic virtues which might explain why it should have ever become more than a small, anonymous mountain village with a fate any different from that of most contemporary villages which have long since vanished.[57]

87:1–3 The reason for its greatness, of course, is that it was chosen by God. He founded it **in the holy mountains**, and He **loves** its **gates** more than all the other cities or towns in the land. And its greatest glory is still future—when it will be the capital of the Messianic Kingdom, the royal city of the long-awaited King. This Psalm looks forward to that day when **glorious things** will be **spoken** of **Zion**, the **city of God**.

There is a sense in which it will be the spiritual birthplace of many nations:

Now it shall come to pass in the latter days *that* the mountain of the Lord's house shall be established on the top of the mountains, and shall be exalted above the hills; and all nations shall flow to it. Many people shall come and say, "Come, and let us go up to the mountain of the Lord, to the house of the God of Jacob; He will teach us His ways, and we shall walk in His paths" (Isa. 2:2, 3).

87:4 That is what seems to be in

view in verse 4. Zion is personified as saying that among those nations that know her as mother, she can mention **Rahab** (that is, Egypt) to the south and **Babylon** to the north. Also people will speak of **Philistia, Tyre,** and **Ethiopia** as having been **born** in Jerusalem. These will be among the nations that recognize Zion as the spiritual, political, and economic capital of the world, and will go up to worship there and bring their tribute to the Great King (Isa. 60:5–7). The nations that refuse to go up to keep the Feast of Booths will suffer drought and plague (Zech. 14:16–19).

87:5 **Zion** therefore will be reckoned as the place where the nations experience spiritual rebirth, because the **Most High Himself shall establish her** in that place of universal sovereignty.

87:6 And when **the LORD** takes a census of **the peoples**, He will note carefully that certain nations realized their true destiny in becoming citizens of Zion. They visit the capital:

not to admire its architecture, or gaze upon its battlements, or envy the tribes who had come up to worship in the city which is compact together, but to claim its municipal immunities, experience its protection, obey its laws, live and love in its happy society, and hold communion with its glorious Founder and Guardian.[58]

Gaebelein writes:

Jehovah keeps a record as one after another of the nations are brought into the Kingdom through Zion's exaltation and blessing. Then Zion becomes the glorious metropolis of the whole world.[59]

87:7 It will be a time of festival and holiday. **Singers** and **players on instruments** will join in the chorus,

"All my springs are in you." No longer the place of tears and trouble, Jerusalem will be a fountain of blessing, a source of refreshment, and a spiritual home to all the nations of the earth.

But before leaving the Psalm, there is a personal application that should be made. It is this. A time is coming when God is going to register the people. It will be the census of heaven's inhabitants. The great, single qualifying factor will be the new birth. Only those who have been born again will see or enter the kingdom of God (John 3:3–5). So when God writes up the people, He will say, "This man was born again in such and such a place."

Will He be able to say that concerning you?

There is a way in which you can qualify for heavenly citizenship. That way is set forth in John 1:12:

But as many as received Him, to them He gave the right to become children of God, to those who believe in His name.

Psalm 88: The Saddest Psalm

When we come to Psalm 88 we have reached the nadir of human sorrow and suffering. It seems that the psalmist here ransacks the vocabulary of gloom and bitterness to describe his hopeless plight. His is definitely a terminal case, he feels—as if he were on the critical list in the isolation ward of a hospital for incurables. The only thing left is the morgue, and it is only a matter of time before the sheet will be drawn over his face and he will be carted away.

88:1, 2 The only bright spot in the Psalm is the name of **God** with which it begins—**"O LORD, God of my salvation."** Gaebelein calls it the one ray of light that struggles through the gloom, the star that pierces the thick midnight darkness.

But immediately the writer launches into a mournful description of his desperate predicament. **Day and night** he has been crying to the Lord, but still no relief. When will God break the impasse by hearing his **prayer** and doing something about it?

88:3–7 His life is one seething mass **of troubles**, and he is moving irresistibly toward death and **the grave**. He has been given up for dead—already **counted** as a casualty. Any strength he had has ebbed away. Now he is **adrift among the dead**, like an unconscious soldier on a corpse-strewn battlefield, or like a war victim buried with others in a common **grave**. He feels that he is forgotten by God and thus **cut off from** any hope of divine help. Like a captive consigned to a dungeon, so he has been abandoned by God to **the lowest pit**, to the chamber of horrors, dark and ominous. There can be only one explanation, he feels: God is angry with him and he is being submerged by the mountainous **waves** of divine judgment.

88:8, 9 His **acquaintances** have forsaken him as if he were a leper. They treat him as if he were some hideous apparition or "as a thing accursed" (Knox). He is **shut up** in a cell from which there is no escape. His eyes, once bright and full of expression, have lost all their sparkle. And prayer seems unavailing. **Daily** he cries to the LORD with his **hands** raised in earnest entreaty, but nothing happens.

88:10 Then in a series of questions he challenges God to tell what good would come to Him from the psalmist's death. The questions reveal the imperfect knowledge which OT saints had concerning death and the here-

after, and make us unceasingly grateful for the assurance that to die is to be with Christ which is far better (Phil. 1:23). Here then are the questions:

Does God **work wonders for** those who have died? The implied answer is "No." To a Jew living under law, death was a perplexing region of oblivion where nothing constructive ever happens.

Do the "shades" **arise** to **praise** Him? Those who have departed are regarded as ghost-like shadows that have no way of praising the Lord.

88:11, 12 Is God's steadfast love **declared in the grave** or His **faithfulness in** Abaddon, **the place of destruction**?

> Since it was believed that no action or speech was possible in the grey, grim, dusty halls of Sheol, it was surely in God's own interests to keep alive as long as possible those whose earnest praises were always pleasing to Himself.[60]

88:13–18 As if with renewed intensity, the psalmist pleads with the LORD. As surely as he lives, every **morning** hears his passionate **prayer**. He expresses utter perplexity that God should so completely abandon him and hold back any look of pity or of favor. **From** his **youth** his life had been an uninterrupted story of suffering and dying. Now in the vortex of the divine **terrors**, he is **distraught** and helpless. God's **fierce wrath has** overwhelmed him like a tidal wave, and His **terrors** have left him speechless. The furious flood is encircling and unremitting; the waves close in on him in one united assault. It is as if God has caused **loved one and friend** to forsake him. His only companion is **darkness**.

And so ends the saddest Psalm. If we wonder why it is in the Bible, we might listen to the testimony of J. N. Darby. He said that at one time this was the only Scripture that was any help to him because he saw that someone had been as low as that before him. Clarke quotes an unknown source:

> "There is only one Psalm like this in the Bible to intimate the rareness of the experience, but there is one to assure the most desperately afflicted that God will not forsake him."[61]

Psalm 89: God's Covenant with David

89:1, 2 At the outset, **Ethan** declares his personal delight in the steadfast love and **faithfulness** of Jehovah as expressed in the Davidic covenant. He is determined to **sing of the mercies of the LORD forever** because they endure **forever**.

89:3, 4 Faith reverently reminds God of the **covenant** He had made with **David**. Because David was His chosen **servant**, He had **sworn** that he would never lack heirs to sit on his **throne** and that his kingdom would endure **to all generations**. An unbroken dynasty sitting on an everlasting **throne**!

89:5 Then faith rehearses the **wonders** of the LORD who had made the covenant. It is almost as if Ethan is reminding the Lord that the honor of His name is at stake.

89:6–8 He is greater than all the angelic hosts **in the heavens**. The myriads above are called to praise His wonders and His **faithfulness**. No angel **can be compared** to Him; He is supreme above all the heavenly beings. The greatest of them stand in reverential awe of Him; they recognize that He is greater in every way. No one is as mighty as the LORD **God of hosts**, resplendent in robes of **faithfulness**.

89:9, 10 But that is not all. God is great in creation, in providence and in moral perfections (vv. 9–15). One dramatic instance of His greatness in creation is the way in which He rules **the raging of the sea** and makes its **waves** cease. He did this on blue Galilee many years ago, and He does it continually in the storm-tossed lives of His people. As to His greatness in providence, what better example could be adduced than His conquest of Egypt (**Rahab**) at the time of the exodus? He crushed that proud nation like a lion crushes the carcass of its victim; He **scattered** His **enemies** like leaves in the wind.

89:11–13 **The heavens** and **the earth** are His by creatorial right; **the world** and everything in it belongs to Him because it was He who **founded them. The north and the south** owe their origin to Him. Mount **Tabor and** Mount **Hermon** lift up their heads as if joyfully acknowledging Him as their Maker. His **arm** is enormously **mighty** and His **hand** is **strong**. His **right hand** is **high** over all, supreme in the world of power.

89:14 As for His moral perfections, His **throne** is founded on the twin principles of **righteousness and justice. Mercy and truth** are shed abroad wherever He goes.

89:15–18 Having rehearsed the greatness of the covenant-making God, Ethan now describes the blessedness of His **people: "Blessed are the people who know the joyful sound!"** To the pious Jew the **joyful sound** was the festive shouts of the people as they walked to Jerusalem for the high holy days of the religious calendar. To us, it will always be the **joyful sound** of the gospel. Several things are delineated concerning these happy **people. They walk . . . in the light of** His **countenance**; that is, **they walk**

in His favor and are guided by His presence. They find in Him the spring of all their joy and never stop rejoicing in His **righteousness**. They do not boast in their own power but in His alone. It is only through His **favor** that their **horn is exalted**, in other words, that they are made strong. **For our shield belongs to the LORD, and our king to the Holy One of Israel.**

89:19 And that brings Ethan to the covenant which Jehovah made with **David** (vv. 19–37). Many years before, God had spoken to his faithful one **in a vision**. The **holy one** may refer to Samuel (1 Sam. 16:1–12), to Nathan (2 Sam. 7:1–17) or perhaps to the Servant of Jehovah, the Lord Jesus Christ. He made an unconditional covenant of free grace, setting the crown upon a **mighty** one, and exalting **one chosen from the people**. In many of these descriptions of David, we feel almost instinctively that we are seeing beyond David to the coming Messiah-King.

89:20–24 Jehovah had selected **David** from among his brothers and, through Samuel, had **anointed him** with the **holy oil** reserved for king-making. The covenant guaranteed that God's **hand** would forever be upon David and the inheritors of his throne in preservation and protection, and His **arm** would provide all needed strength. The king's enemies would not be able to outfox him, neither would the wicked be able to **afflict him**. The Lord guaranteed to crush **his foes** and **plague those who hate him**. The **faithfulness** and **mercy** of the Lord would never leave him, and the house of David would derive its strength from Him.

89:25 In accordance with the promise made to Abram (Gen. 15:18), the eventual borders of the kingdom would stretch from the Mediterranean to the Euphrates river. In Genesis 15, it says from the river of Egypt to the river Euphrates, but since the river of Egypt flows into the Mediterranean, the boundaries are the same.

89:26, 27 David would acknowledge Jehovah as his **Father**, his **God**, and his **rock** of refuge. God in turn would **make him** His **firstborn, the highest of the kings of the earth**. The phrase **"the firstborn"** sometimes means first in time, as when Mary brought forth her first-born Son (Luke 2:7). But it could not mean that in David's case because he was the *last-born* son of Jesse. Here it means first in rank or honor, as explained in the rest of the verse, **"the highest of the kings of the earth."** This is also what Paul means when he refers to the Lord Jesus as "the firstborn over all creation" (Col. 1:15). It does not mean that Jesus was the first created being, as some cults teach, but that He is preeminent *over all creation*.

89:28, 29 Nothing will ever alter God's love for David, and nothing will affect the **covenant** He has made. There will always be a **throne** of David, and the royal line will be perpetuated **forever**.

89:30–32 The covenant would not exempt David's **sons** from punishment when they sinned. Any infractions of the **law** would be dealt with righteously. Historically, this is what had happened. David's descendants had been unfaithful to Jehovah, and He had chastised them **with the** rod and scourges of Babylonian captivity.

89:33 Nevertheless the covenant still stood, and although the kingdom was in eclipse for a time, and there was no king reigning in Jerusalem, yet God was still miraculously preserving the royal seed and He would re-institute the kingdom in His own time.

89:34–37 In the strongest possible language, God repeats the inviolability of the **covenant** and His determination to keep His promise **to David**. David's line would **endure forever, and his throne** as long as **the sun** and **the moon . . . in the sky**.

89:38, 39 To outward appearances it may have seemed that God had forgotten the Davidic covenant. Judah was invaded by the Babylonians and carried off into exile. No one has sat on the throne of David from that day to this. But God had not forgotten. Almost two thousand years ago, the Lord Jesus was born in David's royal city. He was the adopted son of Joseph, and since Joseph was in the direct line of the kings of Judah, Jesus inherited the *legal right* to the throne of David through him (Matt. 1). Jesus was the *real son* of Mary, and since Mary was a lineal descendant of David through Nathan, our Lord is of the seed of David (Luke 3:23–38). So the covenant is thus fulfilled in the Lord Jesus Christ. David's throne is perpetuated through Him, and since He lives in the power of an endless life, there will always be a descendant of David to sit upon the throne. One day, perhaps soon, He will return to earth to take His rightful place on the throne of David and reign as David's greatest Son.

Ethan could not have seen this, of course. To him it looked as if the covenant had been scrapped. Listen to him as he complains that God has cast off and rejected the royal line, that He has been **furious** against the king whom He had **anointed**. To Ethan there was no other explanation than that God had gone back on His promise to David, and dragged **his crown** in the dust. Ethan knew deep in his heart that God couldn't renege on His promise, and yet from all appearances it had happened.

89:40–45 The walls of Jerusalem had gaping holes in them, and the **strongholds** were shattered. Travelers passing the city helped themselves to the unprotected loot, and unfriendly Gentile **neighbors** sneered at Judah's plight. Israel's **adversaries** held the upper **hand** and chortled over their victory. The weapons of God's people proved useless in **battle**; the soldiers simply were not able to stand against the foe. The king was deposed and **his throne** vandalized. Humiliated and **covered . . . with shame**, he became an old man prematurely.

89:46–48 The LORD who had made the covenant seemed to be hiding from His people. His **wrath** against them was burning **like fire**. The plaintive **"How long?"** goes winging its way to heaven. Ethan asks God to remember **how short** He has made human life anyway, how frail man is, and how insignificant as well. In his day, every **man** could be sure of **death; the power of the grave** would at last win over him. We have a better hope than Ethan; we know that not all will die but that all will be changed when the Lord Jesus returns to take His church home to heaven (1 Cor. 15:51; 1 Thess. 4:13–18). But all this was a secret as far as OT saints were concerned.

89:49–51 Ethan's pleading is very bold and clamant. He asks what has happened to the **lovingkindnesses** which God had guaranteed **to David** in the strongest possible terms. He is keenly sensitive to the taunts and jeers of Israel's enemies, how they insult Ethan himself and mock the exiled king as he moves about.

89:52 But in the closing verse faith triumphs. Though Ethan cannot see the answer to his perplexity, he can still bless Jehovah. It is as if he is saying, "Lord, I can't understand but

I will still trust." So he ends his prayer on the rapturous note, **"Blessed be the** LORD **forevermore! Amen and Amen."**

IV. BOOK 4 (PSALMS 90—106)

Psalm 90: Tolling of the Death Bell

Permit me to use a little sanctified imagination in explaining this Psalm. The scene is the Wilderness of Sinai. It is years since the spies returned to Kadesh-Barnea with their evil report. Now the people are still trekking around the desert but getting nowhere in the process. It is an exercise in futility.

Every morning a reporter comes to Moses' tent with a fresh report of casualties. Deaths, deaths, deaths, and more deaths. Obituaries are the commonest item of news, and the desert seems to be an expanding cemetery. Every time the people break camp, they leave another field of graves behind.

On this particular day, **Moses the man of God** has had all he can take. Overwhelmed by the mounting toll, he retreats into his tent, prostrates himself on the ground and pours out this **prayer** to God.

90:1, 2 In the midst of so much transience and mortality, he first finds relief in the eternity of the LORD. While all else fades and vanishes, God is unchanging, a home and refuge for His people. From all eternity and to all eternity, He is **God**, "infinite, eternal and unchangeable in His being, wisdom, power, holiness, justice, goodness, and truth."

90:3, 4 In stark contrast to God's agelessness is the brevity of human life. It seems that God is constantly issuing the order, **"Return** to dust," and a never-ending line trudges down to the grave. To One who is eternal, fallen man's original life-span of about **a thousand years** is no more than a **past** memory or a fraction of a **night**.

90:5, 6 Even to Moses, human life seems as evanescent as **sleep**. You sleep, you dream, you awake, and yet you are scarcely conscious of the passing of time. Or to change the figure, life is **like grass**—fresh and green in the morning, then faded and withered by **evening**. As Spurgeon said, it is "sown, grown, blown, mown, gone."

90:7–10 While all death is a result of the entrance of sin, Moses realizes that what is happening in the desert is a special visitation from God. All the soldiers who were twenty years or older when they left Egypt will die before they reach Canaan. The tolling of the death bell is a sign that God is angry with His people because they took sides with the unbelieving spies instead of marching into Canaan as Caleb and Joshua had encouraged. Their **iniquities** and **secret sins** are ever **before** Him, a constant irritation and rankling. As a result, the Israelites are living under the somber cloud of His anger, and overwhelmed in the churning waves of His **wrath**. Some, it is true, live their allotted span of **seventy years**, and some even as much as **eighty**. But even in their case, life is a weariness. One ailment follows another. The smallest tasks are an effort. And soon the pulse beat has stopped, and another one becomes "the missing face."

90:11, 12 The man of God stands in awe of **the power** of God that has been awakened in **anger**. Who, he wonders, can reverence Him adequately when one considers the immensity of His **wrath**? This much is sure: it should make us value every day of our lives and spend each one in obedience to Him, and in such a way that it will count for eternity.

90:13, 14 Moses pleads with the LORD to **return** to His people in **mercy**. Will His anger burn forever? Won't He please **have compassion** on them and **satisfy** them **early with** His **mercy** that they might live out their remaining **days** in a measure of tranquility and happiness?

90:15, 16 Now Moses pleads for "equal time," that is, he asks for as many years of gladness for Israel as the years of affliction and trouble they had **seen**. They had already seen His power displayed in works of judgment; now he asks that the Lord show the other side of His countenance; that is, acts of grace.

90:17 Finally, the intercessor asks the Lord to look in favor on His chosen earthly people and to make them fruitful in all their endeavors: **"Yes, establish the work of our hands."**

Traditionally Psalm 90 has been a favorite reading at Christian funerals. And not without reason, because it reminds us of the shortness of life and the need to redeem the time or buy up the opportunities. But the Psalm does not breathe out the comfort and assurance of the NT era. Christ has brought "life and immortality to light through the gospel." We know that to die is gain; it is to be absent from the body and to be at home with the Lord. And so the somber and dark outlook of the Psalm should be replaced by the joy and triumph of the believer's hope in Christ, for now death has lost its sting and the grave has been robbed of its victory. The believer can sing:

> Death is vanquished! Tell it with joy,
>   ye faithful;
> Where is now the victory, boasting
> grave?

> Jesus lives! no longer thy portals are
> cheerless;
> Jesus lives, the mighty and strong to
> save.
> > —*Fanny J. Crosby*

Psalm 91: My Psalm

In 1922, in the Western Hebrides, a five-year-old lad was dying of diphtheria. A mucous membrane was forming across his throat, and breathing was becoming increasingly difficult. His Christian mother turned her back so she would not see him take his last breath. At that very moment there was a knock at the door. It was her brother-in-law from an adjoining village. He said, "I've just come to tell you that you don't have to worry about the child. He is going to recover, and one day God is going to save his soul." She was distracted and incredulous: "Whatever makes you say that?" Then he explained he had been sitting at his fire reading Psalm 91 when God distinctly spoke to him through the last three verses:

> Because on me he set his love,
> I'll save and set him free;
> Because my great name he hath
> known,
> I will set him on high.

> He'll call on me, I'll answer him;
> I will be with him still,
> In trouble to deliver him,
> And honour him I will.

> With length of days unto his mind
> I will him satisfy;
> I also my salvation
> Will cause his eyes to see.
> > —from *The Scottish Psalms In Metre.*

I was that boy. God delivered me from death that night; He saved my soul thirteen years later, and He has satisfied me with long life. So you will understand why I refer to Psalm

91 as *my Psalm*. I usually add, with tongue in cheek, that I am willing to share it with others—but it is definitely *my* Psalm!

Most theologians don't agree with me at all. They say that this is a Messianic Psalm. And of course they are right. Its primary *interpretation* concerns our wonderful Lord Jesus Christ. And we are going to study it from that perspective, but all the while remembering that in a lesser way, we may *appropriate* its precious promises to ourselves:

All the rivers of Thy grace, I claim;
Over every promise write my name.

91:1, 2 Jesus is the One who in a preeminent way dwelt in **the secret place of the Most High**, and abode **under the shadow of the Almighty**. There never was a life like His. He lived in absolute, unbroken fellowship with God, His Father. He never acted in self-will but did only those things that the Father directed. Though He was perfect God, He was also perfect Man, and He lived His life on earth in utter and complete dependence on God. Without equivocation He could look up and say, **"My refuge and my fortress, my God, in Him I will trust."**

91:3 It seems that the Holy Spirit's voice is heard in verses 3–13, assuring the Lord Jesus of the tremendous security that was His because of His life of perfect trust. What are the guarantees of security? There are nine:

Deliverance from hidden dangers. **The snare of the** bird-trapper speaks of the enemy's evil plot to trap the unwary.

Immunity from fatal disease. In our Lord's case, there is no reason to believe that He was ever sick at all.

91:4 *Shelter and refuge* in the Al-

mighty. God's tender, personal care is likened to that of a mother bird with her young.

Protection in the faithfulness of God. His promises are sure. What He has said, He will do. This is the believer's **shield and buckler**.

91:5 *Freedom from fear.* Four types of danger are mentioned that commonly cause apprehension:

Attacks made by an enemy under the cover of **night** are especially terrifying because the source is hard to identify.

The arrow that flies by day may be understood as a literal missile or as a figure for "the evil plots and slanders of the wicked" (Amplified Version).

91:6 **The pestilence that walks in darkness** may also be taken literally or figuratively. Physical disease thrives where it is shielded from the sun's rays, and moral evil also breeds in the dark.

The destruction that lays waste at noonday is unspecified, and perhaps it is best to leave it that way, so that the promise may have a more widespread application.

91:7, 8 *Safety even in the midst of massacre.* Even where there is slaughter on a wholesale basis, the Beloved of the Lord is absolutely safe. When **the wicked** are punished, He will be a spectator only, free from the possibility of harm.

91:9, 10 *Insurance against calamity.* **Because** the Savior made **the Most High** His **refuge** and His **dwelling place**, no disaster would strike Him, no calamity would get near Him.

91:11, 12 *Guarded by angelic escort.* This is the passage which Satan quoted to the Lord Jesus when tempting Him to throw Himself down from the pinnacle of the temple (Luke 4:10, 11). Jesus did not deny that the verses applied to Him, but He did deny that they could be used as a pretext for tempting God. God had not told Him to jump down from the temple. If the Savior had jumped, He would have been acting outside the divine will, and then the promise of protection would not have been valid.

91:13 *Victory over* **the lion and cobra.** It is interesting that Satan stopped before coming to this verse. If he had quoted it, he would have been describing *his own doom!* The devil is presented in Scripture as a roaring lion (1 Pet. 5:8) and as an ancient serpent (Rev. 12:9). As a lion, he is the loud, horrendous persecutor using physical violence. As a serpent, he employs wily stratagems to deceive and to destroy.

And so the Holy Spirit has given nine guarantees of safe-conduct to the Son of Man during His life of perfect trust and obedience on earth. At this point God the Father confirms the guarantees by six tremendous "I wills." In these perhaps there is a suggestion of the entire career of the man Christ Jesus:

91:14 *His spotless life on earth.* **"Because he has set his love upon Me, therefore I will deliver him; I will set him on high, because he has known My name."**

91:15 *His suffering for sins.* **"He shall call upon Me, and I will answer him; I will be with him in trouble."**

His resurrection and ascension. **"I will deliver him and honor him."**

91:16 *His present session at God's right hand and His coming kingdom.* **"With long life I will satisfy him, and show him My salvation."**

So much for what the Psalm says! But wait! You are probably thinking

of what it does not say, of important questions that it does not answer. For example, how can we reconcile all these promises of safe-keeping for the Messiah with the fact that men ultimately *did* put Him to death? And if we apply the Psalm to believers today, how does it square with the fact that some of them do succumb to disease, or fall in battle, or die in plane crashes?

Part of the answer, at least, lies in this: The one who trusts in Jehovah is immortal until his work is done. Jesus said as much to His disciples. When He suggested returning to Judea, the disciples said:

"Rabbi, lately the Jews sought to stone You, and are You going there again?" Jesus answered, "Are there not twelve hours in the day? If anyone walks in the day, he does not stumble, because he sees the light of this world. But if one walks in the night, he stumbles, because the light is not in him" (John 11:7–10).

The Lord knew that the Jews could not touch Him until He had finished His work. And this is true of every believer; he is kept by the power of God through faith.

Then the Lord may speak to a believer in a special, personal way through some verse of this Psalm. If He does, the person can claim the promise and rely on it. The personal incident at the beginning illustrates this.

And finally, it is true in a general way that those who trust the Lord are sure of His protection. We may tend to overemphasize the exceptions. The general rule is still true: there is safety in the Lord.

Psalm 92: A Lesson in Spiritual Botany

92:1–5 No one can deny the fact that **it is** downright **good to give thanks to the** LORD. It **is good** in the sense that the Lord deserves such gratitude, and it **is good** also for the one who offers the **thanks** and for those who hear it. **To sing praises to** the **name** of the **Most High** is about as appropriate an activity as anyone can engage in. And there is no lack of subject matter for praise. His **loving kindness** is an unending theme for **the morning and** His **faithfulness** is sufficient to occupy the nighttime hours—and then some. Enhance the beauty of the song with **an instrument of ten strings, the lute**, and **the harp**, and **with harmonious sound**. No amount of sweet music is enough to praise the Lord for His wonderful **works** of creation, providence, and redemption. Just to think of all He has done makes the heart sing with joy. The marvelous, intricate plans of God, His **deep** designs and wise plans add fuel to the flame of praise.

92:6–9 But don't expect the natural **man** to **understand** the deep things of God. He can't understand them, "because they are spiritually discerned" (1 Cor. 2:14). As far as divine realities are concerned, he is dull and stupid though he may be an intellectual giant as far as the world is concerned. He never comes to grip with the fact that fixed moral laws in the universe prescribe destruction for **the wicked**. Though he may seem to prosper for a while, still his success is as short-lived as **grass**. Just as sure as **the** LORD is enthroned **forevermore**, so surely will His **enemies** be **scattered** and **perish**.

92:10, 11 The other side of the coin is that God exalts the **horn** of the righteous **like** that of the **wild ox**,

that is, He gives strength and honor to His people. And He anoints the faithful ones **with fresh oil**, which typifies the gracious ministry of the Holy Spirit. When the last chapter is written, the saints of God will have witnessed the demise of their **enemies**, and will have heard the long, low wail of their doom.

92:12–15 The prosperity of the **righteous** is comparable to that of **a palm tree** and **a cedar** of **Lebanon**. The **palm tree** symbolizes beauty and fruitfulness while the **cedar** is an emblem of strength and permanence. The reason for the luxuriant growth of believers is that they **are planted in the house of the** LORD and **flourish in the courts of our God**. In other words, they live in daily fellowship with the Lord, drawing their strength and sustenance from Him. Age does not impair their fruit-bearing capabilities. They continue to pulsate with vigorous spiritual life (the sap) and their testimony remains ever green. Their prosperity is an evidence **that the** LORD is upright in fulfilling His promises. **He is** the dependable **rock, and there** is nothing unreliable about **Him**.

The wicked are compared to grass (v. 7), the righteous to an evergreen (v. 14). The wicked wither and fade away, but the righteous go on from strength to strength. This is the order in spiritual botany.

Psalm 93: The Eternal King and His Eternal Throne

93:1, 2 The songs that will be sung when Jesus is crowned LORD are all ready—and this is one of them. It anticipates the glorious day when Israel's Messiah proclaims Himself King. He will be **clothed with majesty**, in contrast to the lowly grace which characterized Him at His First Advent. He will openly clothe Himself **with** the **strength** that is needed to reign over **the world**. And world conditions will then be established on a firm, stable basis, no longer subject to vast moral and political convulsions.

Of course, the **throne** of Jehovah has always existed, but it has not been as clearly manifest as it will be when the Millennium dawns. The King Himself too is eternal, and as His authority had no beginning, so it will have no end.

93:3, 4 When the psalmist speaks of **floods** and **mighty waves**, it seems clear that he is thinking of the Gentile nations which have oppressed His people through the ages and which will conspire against Him when He comes to reign. But their efforts will be futile and short-lived. Though they will **lift up** their voices in terrifying threats and awesome boasts, they will learn that the enthroned Jehovah **is mightier than** all their federations, than all the armed might they can assemble.

93:5 And so it will be seen that God's Word is true after all, and all the promises He made concerning the defeat of His foes and the establishment of His righteous reign will be fulfilled. The temple in Jerusalem will be cleansed from evil, an appropriate purity for the One whose **house** it is.

All will be holy when He reigns; and everything will be characterized by holiness, as predicted in Isaiah 23:18; Zechariah 14:20, 21; Revelation 4:8.[62]

Psalm 94: God of Vengeance

In his splendid work on *The Attributes of God*, A. W. Pink writes:

It is sad to find so many professing Christians who appear to regard the wrath of God as something for which they need to make an apology, or at least they wish there were no such thing. . . . Others harbor the delusion that God's wrath is not consistent with His goodness, and so seek to banish it from their thoughts. . . . But God is not ashamed to make it known that vengeance and fury belong to Him. . . . The wrath of God is as much a Divine perfection as His faithfulness, power or mercy. . . . The very nature of God makes Hell as real a necessity as Heaven is.[63]

94:1–3 In Psalm 94 we hear the faithful remnant of Israel in the last days appealing to the **God** of **vengeance** to reveal Himself in His hatred of evil. The time has come for the righteous **Judge of** all **the earth** to avenge the crimes of evil rulers against His beloved people. The cry **"How long?"** is about to be hushed. The gloating of **the wicked** will soon be silenced.

94:4–7 The condemnation of the proud persecutors is itemized. "Hear their insolence! See their arrogance! How these men of evil boast!" (LB). They grind Jehovah's **people** under their heels; they are unremitting in their harassment of His loyal **heritage**. They victimize the defenseless **widow**, the unsuspecting guests, the helpless orphans. And their attitude is that **the God of Jacob does not understand** or care what is happening.

94:8–11 What stupid **fools** they are to think that God is unaware! If He had the skill to plant **the ear in** man's body, does He **not** have the power also to **hear** what the wicked are saying? Can the Creator of **the eye** be blind Himself as to what is going on? If He has power to chasten **the nations**, as history demonstrates, is He incapable of chastising the Mafia that is oppressing His beloved ones? How can He have less **knowledge** than He imparts to mankind? The fact is that **the LORD knows** everything, He knows what these crooked men are thinking, and He knows that their thoughts are empty wisps of breath.

94:12–15 Faith enables the afflicted psalmist to see his troubles as part of God's education for him. It is a great thing to be thus taught by the LORD, and to be trained **out of** His **law.** God gives **him rest from the days of adversity, until the pit** is being **dug for the wicked.** He can be confident that Jehovah will never forsake **His people** or abandon the **inheritance** He loves. Inevitably justice will be restored to its proper place and honest people will show it to others and receive it in return.

94:16–19 There were times when the psalmist wondered **who** would defend him against the overwhelming power of **evildoers.** But he was never left alone. **The LORD** always came to his **help;** otherwise he would have soon been ushered into the **silence** of the cemetery. Whenever he thought he was about to fall before the onslaughts of men, he found himself wonderfully sustained by the **mercy** of the LORD. When **anxieties** and doubts began to rise in his mind, the Lord soothed and caressed his soul with all kinds of consolations.

94:20–23 Can there be any fellowship between Jehovah and these wicked rulers? Can there be partnership between Christ and Antichrist? Can the Lord approve men who enact ordinances to legalize sin? To ask the question is to answer it. The power-drunk rulers slay **the righteous and condemn** the **innocent. But** the LORD is a fortress for His own,

and **the rock** in which they can hide. He will repay the unjust in full measure. He will wipe them out for all their **iniquity.** Yes, sir, He will wipe them out.

Sic semper tyrannis!
(Thus ever to tyrants!)

Psalm 95: Worship and Warning

The Psalm opens with an exuberant call to worship, and it is difficult to read it without being caught up in the enthusiasm of the writer. (In Heb. 4:7 the Psalm seems to be attributed to David, but the expression "in David" (JND) may simply mean in the book of Psalms, since so many of them were written by him.)

95:1, 2 No doubt we hear the voice of the Holy Spirit in these verses calling Israel back to the worship of Jehovah at the close of her dark days of tribulation. But we must not miss His voice calling to us as well "from each idol that would keep us."

It is interesting to notice the variety of expressions used to describe true worship. It is singing **to the** LORD. It is making a joyful **shout to the Rock of our salvation,** that is, to the cleft Rock of Ages in whom we find eternal refuge. It is coming into **His presence,** confessing with thanksgiving all that He has done for us. It is making the rafters ring with **psalms** of praise to Him.

95:3–5 And just as there is great variety in the manner of our praise, so there is infinite scope in its matter. **The** LORD is to be praised because He **is the great God** (Heb., *El,* i.e., the Omnipotent One). He is a **great King above all** the idolatrous **gods** of the heathen. The **deep places of the earth** are **in His hand** in the sense that He owns them. The mountain peaks **are**

His also because He formed them. He created the mighty oceans, and it was His hands that shaped the continents and the islands.

95:6, 7a But now a second invitation to **worship** rings out, and it becomes even more personal and intimate. We should **worship** and **kneel before the LORD our Maker**, because **He is our God**. He is our God by creation and then by redemption. He is the Good Shepherd who gave His life for us. Now **we are the people of His pasture, and the sheep** who are led, guided, and protected by **His** nail-pierced **hand**.

95:7b–9 In the middle of verse 7 there is an abrupt change from worship to warning. It is the longing, eloquent sighing of the Holy Spirit:

> **Today, if you will hear His voice. . . .**

In the remaining verses we hear the voice of Jehovah Himself warning His people against an evil heart of unbelief. At Meribah near Rephidim the Israelites provoked God by their complaints about the lack of water (this was the same place as Massah—Ex. 17:7). At another Meribah near Kadesh, Moses offended God by smiting the rock instead of speaking to it (Num. 20:10–12). The two events, one at the beginning of the desert journey and the other near the close, form significant terminals expressing in their names (Meribah = **rebellion**; Massah = **trial**) the faithlessness of the people during that time. Even though they had seen God's marvelous **work** in delivering them from Egypt, they **tested** Him and **tried** Him.

95:10, 11 This provocative conduct spanned **forty years**. Finally God said, in effect, "I've had enough. These tiresome **people** have **hearts** that are bent on wandering. They are determined to disregard the pathway that I have mapped for them. So I have made a solemn oath that **they shall not enter** the **rest** that I had planned for them in Canaan."

This poignant appeal, once directed to Israel, is quoted in Hebrews 3:7–11 and directed to any who might be tempted to forsake Christ in order to return to the law. And it will be a warning to Israel in the last days that unbelief will keep them out of God's millennial rest.

Unbelief excludes men from God's rest in every dispensation.

Psalm 96: The King Is Coming

At least seventeen different ways of praising the Lord, given in the form of crisp commands, are found in Psalm 96. Notice the repetition of "sing" (vv. 1, 2), "give" (vv. 7, 8), and "let" (vv. 11, 12).

96:1, 2 The **new song** is the anthem that will swell when the Lord Jesus returns to earth to begin His glorious reign. It will not only be a *new song* but a *universal* one as well; people from all over the earth will blend their voices in it. Men will **bless** the **name** of the Lord and continually bear testimony to His power to save. "Each day (they will) tell someone that he saves" (LB).

96:3–6 What they will do in the future, we should be doing now, namely, declaring **His glory among the nations** and **His wonders among all peoples**. The LORD is **great**, infinitely superior to **all gods**. False **gods** made of wood or stone are powerless; the true God is Jehovah, who **made the heavens**. His attributes are like inseparable attendants, accompanying Him everywhere. Thus **honor and majesty** precede **Him**, and

strength and beauty wait on Him in **His sanctuary**. "Honor and beauty are his escort; worship and magnificence the attendants of his shrine" (Knox).

96:7–9 If we really appreciate the greatness and goodness of **the LORD**, we will want others to magnify His name too. Thus the psalmist calls on the **families of the peoples** to join in telling **the LORD** how majestic and stately and mighty He is. They should ascribe to Him **the glory** that is **due His name**. They should **bring an offering** to lay at His feet. They should **worship** Him **in the beauty of holiness**, or in holy garments (NASB). All the world should pay Him obeisance.

The mention of holy garments reminds us that even the clothes we wear when we worship the Lord should be appropriate to the occasion. While it may be true that reverence is primarily a matter of the heart, it is also true that we can express our reverence by our attire. Slovenly clothes at the communion service, for instance, betray a casualness that is seldom seen at weddings or funerals.

96:10 This verse identifies the occasion of the new song as the investiture of Messiah-King. **The LORD** has begun His reign! The world-system is established on a sound basis so that **it shall not be moved** by wars, depressions, poverty, injustice, catastrophes, or other crises. The clause **"it shall not be moved"** must be understood as meaning "never during the thousand-year reign of Christ." We know that at the end of that time, the heavens and the earth will be destroyed by fire (2 Pet. 3:7–12). The point here is that the Lord will rule over **the peoples righteously**, and will protect them from unsettling influences.

96:11–13 All creation is invited to join in the festal joy as the **LORD** (Jehovah, or Yahweh)[64] arrives to rule **the world**. **The heavens** will be happy. **The earth** will **be glad**. "The sea and all within it will thunder praise" (Gelineau). No field will be silent, and "no tree in the forest but will rejoice to greet its Lord's coming" (Knox). **For He is coming to** rule over the world. He will rule in perfect **righteousness and** in absolute honesty.

"Now therefore, why do you say nothing about bringing back the king?" (2 Sam. 19:10).

Psalm 97: Light Is Sown for the Righteous!

97:1 As the Psalm opens, **the LORD**, Jesus Christ, has taken His throne. The crowning day has come. And there is worldwide rejoicing. The distant **isles** and coastlands have never known such gladness.

97:2 The King's arrival is described in symbolical terms that inspire the deepest reverential awe. First of all, He is swathed in **clouds and darkness**—a reminder that our Lord is often mysteriously hidden from the eyes of men and majestically inscrutable as to His ways. How little we know of Him! Then **righteousness and justice are the foundation of His throne**. His is the ideal government—a beneficent monarchy—where there are no miscarriages of justice, no perversions of the truth.

97:3–5 Great sheets of **fire** sweep **before Him**, consuming those who do not know God and who do not obey the gospel of our Lord Jesus (2 Thess. 1:8). The **lightnings** of His judgments illuminate the countryside. People look on in terror. This is the time when "every mountain and hill shall be brought low" (Isa. 40:4), in other words, when everything that lifts itself against the knowledge of God shall be humbled.

97:6a The heavens declare His righteousness. As He comes in the clouds of heaven (Rev. 1:7) with all His blood-bought saints (1 Thess. 3:13), the world sees that He was righteous after all in restoring Israel as He promised. Also, as Gaebelein explains:

> The many sons He brings with Him to glory make known His righteousness, that great work of righteousness on Calvary's cross by which the redeemed were saved and are now glorified.[65]

97:6b And all the peoples see His glory.

> The King there in His beauty
> Without a veil is seen.
> It were a well-spent journey
> Though seven deaths lay between.
> The Lamb with His fair army
> Doth on Mount Zion stand;
> And glory, glory dwelleth
> In Immanuel's land.
> —*Anne Ross Cousin*

97:7 What will idolaters think then? They will be completely nonplussed, realizing that they had been worshiping empty nothings.

"Worship Him, all you gods" in the Septuagint reads, "Let all God's angels worship him," and it is quoted that way in Hebrews 1:6. The Hebrew word here (Elohim) usually means God but it may also refer to angels, judges, rulers, or even to heathen gods or deities.

97:8, 9 The city of **Zion hears** the news of the King's victories against rebels and idolaters, **and is glad**. The hamlets **of Judah** join in the jubilation. "Glad news for Sion, rejoicing for Judah's townships, when thy judg-

ments, Lord, are made known" (Knox). At last **the LORD** is seen to be what He always was—**most high above all the earth**, and **exalted far above all** other potentates, real or manufactured.

97:10 You who love the LORD, hate evil. The two are moral correlatives—*love* for Jehovah and *hatred* of all that is contrary to Him. Those who pass this test are special objects of His preserving care.

97:11 Light is sown like seed **for the righteous**, that is, the coming of Christ means the diffusion of **light** for the man who does what is right and joy unspeakable for all those whose hearts are honest and sincere.

97:12 So the happy summons rings out to all God's righteous people to join in the rejoicing and **give thanks at the remembrance of His holiness** (NKJV margin). This is a surprise ending for the Psalm. We would have expected it to say "Give thanks at the remembrance of His love—or mercy— or grace—or glory." But no, it is **His holiness**. Once **His holiness** excluded us from His presence. But now, through the redemption accomplished by the Lord Jesus, **His holiness** is on our side instead of being against us, and we can rejoice when we remember it.

Psalm 98: Creation's New Symphony

98:1, 2 The Second Coming of Christ means the final deliverance of Israel from the oppression of the Gentile nations. That glorious emancipation gives rise to this **new song**, celebrating the victory of Messiah over His foes. **"Marvelous"** is the word for all that the Lord **has done** with **His right hand** of power **and His holy arm**.

The Psalm pictures the Kingdom as

having already come. His victory is by now well known. **The nations have seen the faithful fulfillment** of His covenant with Israel.

When Jesus came the first time, Mary sang, "He has helped His servant Israel, in remembrance of His mercy, as He spoke to our fathers . . ." (Luke 1:54, 55). And Zacharias prophesied that He would "perform the mercy promised to our fathers and . . . remember His holy covenant" (Luke 1:72).

98:3 When He comes the second time, Israel will sing:

> He has remembered His mercy
> and His faithfulness to the house
> of Israel;
> All the ends of the earth have seen
> the salvation of our God.

It was the **mercy** of the Lord that prompted Him to make the promises to Israel, and it is His **faithfulness** that now fulfills them.

98:4–6 At first glance it appears that all the Gentile world is being called to rejoice with Israel in verses 4–6. But the **earth** in verse 4 probably means the "land" of Israel, as in F. W. Grant's translation.[66] The saved Israelites are exhorted to break forth in rapturous song. The Levites are encouraged to join with the accompaniment of **the harp**. And in verse 6 the priests complete the harmony **with their trumpets and the sound of a horn**.

98:7–9 Then nature and the nations are welcomed to join the symphony. **The sea** and its numberless inhabitants are imaginatively pictured as roaring with delight. **The world** and its occupants are deliriously happy too. **The rivers clap their hands** as they break upon the rocks. **The hills** lift up their heads as if in songs of ecstasy. All creation reacts with spon-

taneous transport when the King comes to rule over (**judge**) **the earth**— to give this poor, sick, sobbing world a reign of righteousness and of equity. Who wouldn't be happy?

Psalm 99: Holy, Holy, Holy

99:1 The King's *holiness* is the threefold cord that runs through this Psalm (vv. 3, 5, 9). The psalmist sees the Messiah as already having established His kingdom. **He** sits enthroned "above **the cherubim**" (FWG), which probably means that His throne is supported by symbolical cherubs. These are angelic beings with a human body and also with wings. They are assigned to vindicate the holiness of God against the sin of man. The sight of the enthroned Monarch is so moving that the nations might well tremble and the earth quake with fear.

99:2, 3 The LORD **is great** in power and magnificence as He rules from His throne **in Zion**. He is the exalted Ruler over **all the peoples** on earth. They should honor His **great and awesome name** in acknowledgment of the fact that **He is** unimpeachably **holy**.

99:4, 5 This King of power is **also** a lover of **justice**, a rare combination among earth's rulers and great men. "Might and right are wedded at last" (FWG). In His kingdom, graft and corruption are unknown. **Equity, . . . justice, and righteousness** are the rule rather than the exception. How His people should extol Him, prostrating themselves at **His footstool**. In other Scriptures God's footstool is variously defined as the ark of the covenant (1 Chron. 28:2), the sanctuary (Ps. 132:7), Zion (Lam. 2:1), the earth (Isa. 66:1), or even God's enemies (Ps. 110:1). The reference here is probably to the sanctuary in Zion.

99:6, 7 This is the same King who faithfully guided His people in the past. **Moses and Aaron were among His priests, and Samuel was** one of His great intercessors. (Technically neither Moses nor Samuel was a priest, but both performed priestly functions under divine permission.) The point is that when they cried to the Lord, **He answered them**. He communicated with **Moses and Aaron** in the **pillar** of cloud, delivering the law to them at Mt. Sinai. They obeyed His voice, though imperfectly, and **kept** the law, though only partially.

99:8 But **God . . . answered** their prayers then, and the implied assurance is that He will continue to do so now. He was the **God-Who-Forgives**, though He didn't overlook their evil **deeds**. Though the penalty was forgiven, the consequences in this life remained. God's grace, for instance, forgave Moses for his sin at the waters of Meribah, but God's government kept him out of the Promised Land.

It is not improbable that these three heroes represent the believing portion of the nation of Israel, and that what was true of them was true of all God's faithful covenant people. They called upon the Name of the Lord and were saved, and whoever will call upon Him now will also be saved.

99:9 The threefold reference to the holiness of **God** reminds us of Isaiah 6:3 and Revelation 4:8. Also it brings to mind the stately lines of Heber:

Holy, Holy, Holy, Lord God Almighty!
Early in the morning our song shall
  rise to Thee;
Holy, Holy, Holy, Merciful and
  mighty!
God in three persons, Blessed Trinity.
      —*Reginald Heber*

Psalm 100: Old Hundredth

Affectionately known as "Old Hundredth," from its tune in the Geneva Psalter (1551), this Psalm is a call to all the earth to worship Jehovah. Its summons goes beyond the narrow confines of Israel to **all** the Gentile **lands**. Barnes writes:

> The idea is that praise did not pertain to one nation only; that it was not appropriate for one people merely; that it should not be confined to the Hebrew people; but that there was a proper ground of praise for all, there was that in which all nations, of all languages and conditions could unite. The ground of that was the fact that they had one Creator (v. 3).[67]

We learn from these five short verses that worship is simple. The longest words are **thanksgiving**, **everlasting**, and **generations**. The language is neither involved nor flowery. We learn too that the simple recital of facts about God is worship. The words themselves carry cargoes of wonder. The plain facts are more wonderful than fiction.

There is a definite pattern in the Psalm, as follows:

Call to worship (vv, 1, 2).
Why God should be
  worshiped (v. 3).
Call to worship (v. 4).
Why God should be
  worshiped (v. 5).

Seven elements of worship are suggested:

Shout joyfully (v. 1).
Serve the LORD with gladness
(v. 2a).
Come before Him **with singing**
(v. 2b).

Enter into His gates with thanks-giving (v. 4a).
Enter His courts with praise (v. 4b).
Be thankful to Him (v. 4c).
Bless His name (v. 4d).

We should praise Him because of who He is. He is our:

LORD (v. 1).
God (v. 3a).
Creator (v. 3b).
Owner (v. 3c).
Shepherd (v. 3d).

We should praise Him because of His attributes:

He **is good** (v. 5).
His mercy is everlasting (v. 5).
His truth endures to all generations (v. 5).

In the first three verses, God is worshiped as Creator. But in the last two verses, it is not hard to read Calvary into the text because nowhere else do we see so clearly His goodness, His mercy, and His faithfulness.

> All worlds His glorious power confess,
> His wisdom all His works express;
> But O His love!—what tongue can tell?
> Our Jesus hath done all things well!
> —*Samuel Medley*

There is a wonderful conjunction of thoughts in verse 3 that we should not miss. There we learn that **the LORD is God**; this means that He is unapproachably high. But we also read that **we are His**; and this tells us that He is intimately nigh. It is because He is so near to us that the Psalm breathes gladness and singing instead of dread and fear.

The Psalm is a joyful song for the happy God, and its message has been preserved in our hymnology in the well-known paraphrase:

> All people that on earth do dwell,
> Sing to the Lord with cheerful voice;
> Him serve with mirth, His praise forth tell!
> Come ye before Him and rejoice.

> Know that the Lord is God indeed;
> Without our aid He did us make;
> We are His flock, He doth us feed,
> And for His sheep, He doth us take.

> Oh, enter then His gates with praise
> Approach with joy His courts unto;
> Praise, laud, and bless His name always,
> For it is seemly so to do.

> For why? the Lord our God is good,
> His mercy is forever sure;
> His truth at all times firmly stood,
> And shall from age to age endure.
> —*Scottish Psalter*

Psalm 101: Royal Resolutions

David's aspirations for his private and public life were beyond his own achievements. But the goals he set for his house and kingdom will be fully realized by the Lord Jesus when He comes to sit on David's throne. This Psalm is David's manifesto as he entered upon his reign; in it he hitches his wagon to a star.

101:1 He begins by extolling **mercy and justice**, both as they are found in the Lord and as he would like them to be reproduced in himself. Perhaps he is thinking primarily of the *Godward* side—of God's **mercy** toward Israel and of His just judgment on His foes—because he quickly adds, **"To You, O LORD, I will sing praises."**

101:2 Then he turns to some of the features which he desires for his personal life. He is resolved to give heed to the **way** that is blameless, that is, to conduct himself so closely to the teachings of the Lord that there will be no justifiable grounds of reproach. His desires are so ardent and sincere that he interjects the longing sigh, **"Oh, when will You come to me?"** This has been variously interpreted as meaning:

he longs for God to come and to find him living in this upright way;

he yearns for the fulfillment of the covenant which God made with him (2 Samuel 7), the final establishment of God's kingdom on the earth;

he "feels that his resolves require the presence of God Himself to carry them out."[68]

He is determined to walk with integrity of **heart** within his **house**. In his domestic life, he will act righteously and sincerely. No hanky-panky and no two-facedness for him!

101:3, 4 When he says he **will** not **set before** his **eyes** anything that is **wicked**, he means that he will not look with approval on any base person, plan or activity.

As far as **the work of** apostates is concerned, he hates it and is determined to keep free from its contamination. **Those who fall away** from the truth and from righteousness shall have no fellowship with him.

Another characteristic which he intends to stay far away from is **a perverse heart**—one that is inclined to falsehood and depravity. He will not indulge this evil in himself, and he will not have that kind of person among his trusted advisors. The worthy resolve **"I will not know wickedness"** may also refer to his own life or to persons in his court. Thus the KJV renders it, "I will not know a wicked person." The word "know" here means to accept with favor or encourage.

101:5 Anyone who **slanders his neighbor** will be cut off. It scarcely

means that he will be put to death, as in the RSV, but excluded from a position in the king's administration, or put to silence (NASB Margin).

The same goes for the snobbish, **proud** person. He will not be an office-holder in the royal palace.

101:6 The great qualification for service in the kingdom will be moral and spiritual integrity. **The faithful of the land** will be the king's assistants, and those whose lives are clean will be his servants.

101:7, 8 As for crooks, cheats, and liars, they will not be found on the king's payroll. He will have no truck with charlatans and shysters.

Finally, the king is determined to see that all forms of wickedness are dealt with promptly and sternly. Again the word **"destroy"** may mean to punish or to expel them from Jerusalem, **the city of the LORD.** "Wickedness of all kinds must be rooted out of the land, and all vain-doers cut off from the city of Jehovah."[69]

Psalm 102: The Trinity at Calvary

The key to understanding this Psalm lies in detecting the change in speakers.

The Lord Jesus, hanging on the cross, is speaking to God. (vv. 1–11).

The Father replies to His beloved Son; we know this by comparing verse 12 with Hebrews 1:8. (vv. 12–15).

The speaker is unidentified, but we are safe in assuming that it is the Holy Spirit, describing the future restoration of Israel under the Messiah. (vv. 16–21).

The Savior is heard once more as He suffers at the hands of God for our sins. (vv. 23, 24a).

Again by comparing this section with Hebrews 1:10–12, we know that the Father is speaking to His Son. (vv. 24b–28)

Here as nowhere else in the Bible we are enabled to listen in on a conversation that took place between the three Persons of the Trinity when the Lord Jesus was making expiation for the sins of the world.

102:1, 2 As we read the prayer of the afflicted one in verses 1 and 2, we should never lose a sense of wonder that the eternal Son of God would ever humble Himself so low that He would become obedient to death, even death on a cross.

Jesus, the Helper, the Healer, the
    Friend;
Why, tell me why was He there?

We hear Him imploring the LORD to **hear** His **prayer**, to be near Him in distress, and to **answer** Him **speedily**.

102:3–7 Then He describes some of the sufferings which He was called upon to endure as the Man of Sorrows. He was conscious that life was ebbing; His **days** were vanishing **like smoke**. His body was burning with fever. It was as if His vital organs were dried up and **withered**, so much so that appetite had vanished. His torture had been so prolonged that He was now reduced to **skin** and **bones**. **Like a** bird in the **wilderness** or **an owl** in deserted ruins, He was a picture of desolation and melancholia. Sleep was, of course, impossible. Forsaken by God and by man, He was **alone**, **like a sparrow** on a rooftop.

102:8–11 His **enemies** were unremitting in their insults. They used His name for a curse. (Even today the Hebrew name for Jesus, *Yeshua*, is shortened by His foes to *Yeshu*, a curse word meaning "May His name be banished from the earth.") The **ashes** of sorrow were His **bread**, and His **drink** was diluted by tears of grief.

In it all, He realized that He was suffering because of God's **indignation** and **wrath**. Not that God was angry with Him personally, but with our sins which the Lamb of God was bearing in His body on the tree. Forsaken by God, He felt as if He had been picked **up and** thrown **away**. His days were declining like the evening shadows, and His life was withered **like grass**.

102:12–15 God now replies to the Lord Jesus in words of reassurance and encouragement. Addressing the Son as LORD, He reminds Him that He would **endure forever**, and His **name to all generations**. Though He would die, it is true, yet He would **arise** and ascend to heaven. Then He would return to earth as Lion of the tribe of Judah and **have** pity **on Zion**. This would be the time when the nation, now set aside, would be brought back into **favor** again. While waiting for this restoration, the people of Israel hold the **stones** of Zion dear **and show favor to her dust**. This is seen, for example, in the deep regard they have for the Western Wall, formerly called the Wailing Wall, and their tremendous sentimental attachment for the old city of Jerusalem. When Zion welcomes back her King, the Gentile **nations shall fear the name of the LORD, and all** earth's rulers shall pay homage to Him.

102:16–22 In verses 16–22, the first and second personal pronouns are dropped; only the third person is used. And so, as we have suggested, it may be the voice of the Holy Spirit describing the future restoration of Israel under the reign of Christ. The Messiah will return **in** power and great **glory** and will rebuild **Zion**. The prayers of His scattered people will be answered in that day. It will then be seen that their supplications were not in vain. Future generations will be able to read the wonderful saga of how **the LORD** looked down **from heaven**, how He heard the cries of His persecuted, scattered people, and how He brought them back to the land of Israel. When the nations gather **in Jerusalem** to worship **the LORD**, they will rehearse the way in which He freed **the prisoner** and the condemned, and they will **praise** the Lord for His gracious dealings with Israel.

102:23–28 Now the Psalm switches back to the Lord as He expires on the cross. He was a young man at the time—in His early thirties. But already His **strength** was broken in the prime of life. His life was about to end prematurely. And so He prays, **"O my God, do not take me away in the midst of my days."**

The answer comes back from God immediately (v. 24b), "Lord, you live forever" (TEV). We know it is God speaking here, because the words that follow are attributed to God the Father in Hebrews 1:10–12. Notice what God testifies concerning His Son:

He was the Active Agent in creation: He **laid the foundation of the earth, and the heavens are the work of** His **hands**.

Creation **will perish, but** He **will endure**. Creation will wear out and, **like a garment**, be exchanged for something better. But Christ is unchanging and eternal.

And not only is His eternity secure, but also that of His people and of their posterity. **The children of** His **servants** will dwell safely, **and their descendants** in turn will live under His protection.

Psalm 103: Call to Thanksgiving

103:1 One of the reasons we love the Psalms so much is that they verbalize so beautifully what we often feel but cannot find words to express. Nowhere is this more true than in the case of the 103rd. In its majestic cadences of thanksgiving, we read sentiments that mirror our own deepest emotions of gratitude. Here we call on our **soul** to **bless the LORD**—and by our **soul** we mean not just the non-material part of our nature but the entire person. Spirit, soul, and body are cued in to bless the **holy name** of Jehovah.

103:2 The call to worship rings out a second time, with the significant added reminder that we should **forget not all His benefits**. It is a needed reminder because all too often we do forget. We forget to thank Him for soundness of body, soundness of mind, sight, hearing, speech, appetite, and a host of other mercies. We take them too much for granted.

103:3 But above all else, we should be thankful to Him for forgiving **all** our **iniquities**. It is an unspeakable miracle of divine grace that crimson sins can be made whiter than snow. I can empathize with the man who chose one word for his tombstone—FORGIVEN. And also with the Irishman who said, "The Lord Jesus has forgiven me all my sins, and He's never going to hear the end of it." To know that our sins have been put away forever by the precious blood of Christ—well, it's just too much to take in. The second benefit to be remembered is the healing of **all** our **diseases**. Before we get into the problem that this raises, let us notice that healing comes after forgiveness. The physical is closely related to the spiritual. While not *all* sickness is a direct result of sin, *some* of it is. Where the connection exists, forgiveness must precede healing.

But the obvious problem is still there. The verse says "**. . . who heals all your diseases.**" Yet as a matter of practical experience we know that not all diseases are healed, that we will all die sooner or later if the Lord does not come in the meantime. So what does the verse mean? In seeking an answer, we would make the following observations.

First, all genuine healing is from God. If you have been sick, and then have recovered, you can thank God for your recovery because He is the source of all healing. One of the names of God in the Old Testament is *Jehovah Rophi*—the Lord your Healer. Every instance of true healing comes from Him.

Second, the Lord is able to heal *all kinds of diseases*. There is no such thing with Him as an incurable disease.

Third, the Lord can heal by the use of natural means over a period of time or He can heal miraculously and instantly. No limit can be placed on His power to heal.

Fourth, when He was on earth the Lord actually healed all that were brought to Him (Matt. 8:16).

Fifth, during the Millennium He will actually heal all diseases (Isa. 33:24; Jer. 30:17) except in the case of those who rebel against Him (Isa. 65:20b).

But whatever else the verse means, it cannot mean that the believer can claim healing for every disease, be-

cause in other verses of the Psalm we are reminded of the shortness of life and of the certainty of its coming to an end (see vv. 15, 16). What the verse says to me is that whenever a believer is healed, this is a mercy from God, and He should be acknowledged and thanked as the Healer.

103:4 Not only does He heal diseases, He also **redeems** our lives from the Pit, or **destruction**. Of course, this can be applied to His saving us from going down to hell. But I think that the meaning here is rather that He continually delivers us from dangers, accidents, tragedies and thus from going down to the grave. Only when we get to heaven will we realize how often we were protected by the personal intervention of our God from premature death.

The fourth benefit is that He **crowns** us **with lovingkindness and tender mercies**. It is a wonderful diadem for those who were once the loveless and guilty. We are loved with everlasting love and showered day by day with His mercy.

103:5 Then again He **satisfies** us with **good things** as long as we live. The Hebrew here is a bit uncertain. The literal translation is He "satisfies your ornament with good things." From there it is rendered "your prime," "your years" or "as long as you live." But even if we can't agree on the exact words, the truth is there that the Lord **satisfies** the longing heart, and that He does not withhold any good thing from those who walk uprightly.

The result of these five benefits— forgiveness, healing, preservation, coronation, and satisfaction—is that our **youth** is **renewed like the eagle's**. Sickness and violence may affect the body but they cannot touch the spirit.

"Though our outer man is decaying, yet our inner man is being renewed day by day" (2 Cor. 4:16). On earth there is no fountain of eternal youth as far as the body is concerned, but the spirit can go from one degree of strength to another.

> Those who wait on the Lord
>   shall renew their strength;
> They shall mount up with wings
>   like eagles,
> They shall run and not be weary,
> They shall walk and not faint (Isa. 40:31).

The eagle has a reputation for long life and superior strength. Its life is not one of continuous vitality and renewed youth; it too grows old and dies. But what the psalmist is saying is that the man who dwells in God enjoys continuous revival, and goes from strength to strength, like the eagle soaring from one height to the next.

103:6 The mercy and kindness of the LORD are demonstrated in His dealings with the Hebrew people, especially in the exodus from Egypt. That was typical of the way He works vindication **and justice for all who are oppressed**.

103:7, 8 In the trek from Egypt to the Promised Land, God revealed **His ways to Moses** and **His acts to the** people **of Israel**. He took **Moses** into His inner counsels and shared His plans and purposes with him. The people of Israel saw the practical outworking of these plans. The difference between **His ways** and **His acts** is that **His ways** are learned by revelation whereas **His acts** are a matter of observation.

In all His dealings with His people **the** LORD has shown Himself to be **merciful and gracious**. He guides, protects, and provides for every step of the way. His people are wayward, complaining, rebellious and disobedient, yet He puts up with a great deal before His **anger** flares. His **mercy** is steadfast in spite of the ingratitude it meets.

> How utterly unworthy I am, dear
>   Lord, of Thee,
> Yet Thou art always showering Thy
>   wondrous love on me.
> Though oftentimes I wander and fail
>   to do Thy will,
> Thy gracious love constraining abideth
>   with me still.
>
> —*Author unknown*

103:9, 10 There comes a time when the Lord has to chasten His children, but even then His discipline does not last indefinitely. Judgment is His strange work. His mercy rejoices against judgment. If we received what we deserve to receive, we would be in hell forever. But God's mercy is demonstrated in that He does not give us what we deserve. The penalty of **our sins** was paid by another at the cross of Calvary. When we trust the Savior, God can righteously pardon us. And there can be no double jeopardy; Christ has paid the debt once for all, and so we will never be required to pay it.

103:11, 12 God's love in providing this wonderful plan of salvation is immeasurable. It beggars human imagination. If we could measure the distance of **the heavens** from **the earth**, we could get some idea of the magnitude of His love. But we can't. We can't even determine the size of the universe we live in. And talking about infinite distance, that is exactly how **far He has removed our transgressions from us**. Just as "east is east, and west is west, and never the twain shall meet," so the believer and his sins will never meet. Those sins have been put out of God's sight forever by a miracle of love.

103:13, 14 Someone has said that "man's weakness appeals to God's compassion." Just as a human **father** watches with loving understanding as his little fellow struggles with some man-sized load, so the LORD looks down in pity on us in our weakness. He knows what we are—**that we are** made of **dust**—that we are frail and helpless. Too often we forget what God remembers—**that we are dust**. This leads to pride, self-confidence, independence, and breakdowns.

103:15, 16 Not only is man dust, but he soon returns to dust. The primeval edict, "You are dust, and to dust you shall return," finds its inexorable fulfillment. Man is born for one brief day, then like the **flower of the field** he passes away, and his old haunts never see him again.

103:17, 18 With God's **mercy** there is a vivid contrast. It lasts **from everlasting to everlasting** to **those who fear Him**. In duration, as in volume, it is limitless. **And His righteousness** extends **to children's children**. There is great comfort in this. Christian parents often feel concern about their children and grandchildren growing up in a world of mounting wickedness. But we can safely entrust our little ones to One whose love is infinite and whose righteousness is sufficient not only for us but for succeeding generations as well. Of course, the promises necessarily have a condition attached. They are valid for those who **keep His covenant** and **remember His commandments to do them**. But that is only reasonable.

103:19–22 The LORD is King. **His throne** is **in** the heavens. And His authority is universal. As such He should be the object of praise by everyone and everything; so David

steps up to the dais of the universe to lead the massed choir of creation in a mighty diapason of worship. First, he motions to the **angels**, mighty and obedient, to start the rolling anthem. Then he calls on all created beings who serve the Lord to come in with their harmonies of praise. Next he signals all the **works** of God to join the glorious crescendo. And while this great Hallelujah chorus is ringing throughout God's dominion, the choir leader himself adds his voice to **bless the LORD**. Someone has imagined David as saying here:

> "Amidst the praises of creation, let
> my voice sing His praise."

Psalm 104: Creator and Sustainer

Think of what must be involved in running cities like New York or London or Tokyo with their millions of inhabitants. Complex organizations administer the water department, the housing department, the food supplies and all the other essential services.

But then think how infinitely more complex is God's task of managing the world in which we live. There is the problem of supplying water for all His creatures. There is the immense logistical task of providing food for men, beasts, birds and fish. There is the matter of housing and shelter. It can only give us great thoughts of God to meditate on Him as the Creator and Sustainer of this vast world of nature.

104:1–3 After summoning every part of his being to extol **the LORD**, the unnamed psalmist gives one of those great descriptions of God that must have inspired Michelangelo. It has to be understood as figurative language, because how else can you describe the invisible God or capture His infinite greatness with finite words?

As he stands and gazes and wonders, the psalmist exclaims, **"O LORD my God, You are very great!"** Then the details of the theophany (an appearance of God) pour forth. God has robed Himself in garments of inexpressible splendor **and majesty.** He has covered Himself **with light as with a garment**, a symbol of His absolute purity and righteousness. He spreads the stellar and atmospheric **heavens** over the earth **like a curtain—** a work that boggles the mind by its immensity. The watery cloud-cover over the earth forms the foundation on which the pillars of the heavens were set. Scudding across the sky, **the clouds** are the **chariot** of Jehovah, borne along **on the wings of the wind.**

104:4　Who makes His angels spirits, His ministers a flame of fire. Since the Hebrew uses the same word for *wind* and *spirit* and another word means both *angel* and *messenger*, this may be translated: "Who makes winds His messengers, a flame of fire His ministers." This fits the nature context nicely, but the quotation of this verse in the context of Hebrews 1:7 requires the traditional translation. (The Greek language has the same sets of double meanings, so it applies in both Testaments.)

104:5–9　It becomes evident as we move through the Psalm that we are re-living the days of creation in Genesis 1, although some of the days are not as distinctly referred to as others. The psalmist marvels at the providential arrangements of God for His creatures and especially for man.

First, he recalls how God formed the earth on invisible **foundations** so that it would provide a stable, unshakable surface for habitation. At the outset, the entire earth was covered with **waters** so **deep** that even the

mountains were submerged. On the third day God said, "Let the waters under the heavens be gathered together into one place, and let the dry land appear" (Gen. 1:9). Immediately the waters beat a hasty retreat. The **mountains** and **valleys** appeared in the locations which God had prearranged for them. The seas and oceans were formed with distinct boundaries so that they would not invade the dry land.

104:10–13　Then God's marvelous water system began operating. **Springs** began pumping out water in abundance. The streams fought their way downhill to the valleys and lowlands and eventually to the seas. Ever since then the **wild** animals have been quenching **their thirst** in these streams, rivers and lakes. And the **birds have** found nesting places in the trees that grow beside these water courses. Another part of the water department is the rain. As Elihu pointed out, God "draws up drops of water, which distill as rain from the mist, which the clouds drop down and pour abundantly upon man" (Job 36:27, 28). And as the great sprinkling system waters the mountains, **the earth is satisfied with** the results of God's irrigation program.

104:14, 15　Next is the commissary department. He provides **vegetation** in abundance and variety **for the cattle,** and grains for **man** to cultivate, both for himself and as fodder for his livestock. By a slow, silent miracle, **food** comes out of **the earth.** The juice of the grapes is turned into **wine** by a marvelous chemical process, and man is cheered as he drinks it. The olive yields its golden **oil** with a wide variety of uses, both healthful and tasty. And from the grain comes **bread**, the staff of life, to give man strength for his labors.

104:16–18 The great **trees of the** forest suck up tons of water from the ground; **the cedars of Lebanon** grow naturally without human planting. These in turn provide housing facilities for **the birds. The stork**, for instance, nests in the **fir trees** (which may mean junipers or cypresses). The **high** mountains provide ideal sanctuary for **the wild goats**, and the rocks a home for the **badgers**.

104:19–23 Since life moves along in cycles and on schedule, there must be some way to measure time. So God set **the moon** in place to mark the months, and **the sun**, as if conscious, **knows** when to set and thus to mark the end of another day. The regular alternation of day and night is providential for animals and man. Under the cover of **darkness** the **beasts of the forest** go prowling after their food. When morning comes, they slink back to the safety of **their dens**. But **man goes** off **to his work** and utilizes the hours of daylight for productive **labor**.

104:24–26 The variety of God's **works** is staggering. "What wisdom has designed them all" (Knox). **The earth is full of** His creatures, and He cares for each one with amazing attention to detail. The **sea** swarms with life **both small and great**, ranging all the way from the minute plankton to the whales.

The mention of **ships** in verse 26 seems somewhat out of place in a discussion of living creatures. Some understand it to mean sea monsters (Gen. 1:21), but **ships** is the correct reading. **Leviathan** (in the same verse) may refer to the whales or porpoises which find the sea an ideal playground for their sporting antics. (But see comments and endnotes on Job 41.)

104:27–30 Though they may not be conscious of it, all living organisms depend on God for **their food**. As He supplies it, **they gather** it **in**. He opens His **hand** and **they are** abundantly **filled**. In verse 13, the earth is satisfied with the results of God's work in sending the rain. In verse 16 the trees are full of sap. And now **all** creatures are **filled**.

An inescapable fact of God's economy is that death strikes down one generation, and a new one is raised up to take its place. When animals die, either by violence or through age, it is as if God were hiding His **face**. But at the same time that these fall and **return to . . . dust**, God sends **forth** His **Spirit** and repopulates **the earth** with what seems like a fresh creation. On the one hand there is a constant wasting away, on the other hand a continual renewal of **the face of the earth**.

104:31, 32 Just as the Psalm opened with the original creation, now it closes with a passionate prayer for the golden age when the ravages of sin will be suppressed and when **the LORD** will be honored and glorified for His greatness and goodness:

> He (the psalmist) longs to see it all brought back, restored, to find himself and all God's creatures, parts of the mighty harmony, that a new sabbath of creation may dawn, a rest of God, in which He shall rejoice in His works and they in Him, and the universe becomes a temple filled with the anthem of praise.[70]

As for **the LORD**, the psalmist prays that His **glory** will **endure forever**, that He will **rejoice in His works**— this great God whose glance produces an earthquake, whose touch causes volcanic eruptions.

104:33–35 As for himself, the sacred writer is determined to **sing**

forth the excellencies of his God **as long as** he lives. He prays that his **meditation** might **be sweet to** Jehovah in whom he finds his true joy.

As for **sinners** who spoil God's creation, he sees a moral fitness in their being banished **from the earth**. God has already decreed that it shall be so, and thus his prayer is in accord with the divine will.

As for ourselves, we can surely join him in his final doxology:

**Bless the LORD, O my soul.
Praise the LORD!**

Psalm 105: The Covenant with Abraham

In His covenant with Abraham, God promised to his descendants the land from the river of Egypt to the river Euphrates (Gen. 15:18–21; Ex. 23:31; Deut. 1:7, 8; Josh. 1:4). It was an unconditional promise, a covenant of pure grace. Everything depended on God, nothing on man.

This Psalm rehearses with great enthusiasm all that God did from the giving of the covenant to the time when He led the children of Israel into the promised land. The entire emphasis is on what God did. Nothing is said about Israel's sins and backslidings, as in most of the historical Psalms.

Actually Israel has never yet fully occupied all the territory that was promised. The closest she came to it was during the reign of Solomon. Although he ruled over all the kingdoms from the Euphrates to the border of Egypt, the people of Judah and Israel dwelt in the land from Dan to Beersheba (1 Kgs. 4:21–25). But when her Messiah returns in power and glory, Israel's borders will then ex-tend to include all the land which God deeded to Abraham. When that day arrives, believing Israel will sing this song with new spirit and under-standing.

Give Thanks and Praise (105:1–6)

Many of the Psalms open on a low-key, then build up to a crescendo of worship. But this one begins with a veritable explosion of praise that catches up the reader in its eloquent appeal. Notice the variety of impera-tive verbs that are employed to en-courage adoration:

Oh give thanks to the LORD,
Call upon His name;
Make known His deeds among the peoples!
Sing to Him, *Sing* psalms to Him;
Talk of all His wondrous works!
Glory in His holy name:
Let the heart of those *rejoice* who seek the LORD.
Seek the LORD and His strength;
Seek His face evermore!
Remember His marvelous works which He has done,
His wonders, and the judgments of His mouth,
O seed of Abraham His servant,
You children of Jacob, His chosen ones!

His Covenant With Abraham (105:7–11)

105:7, 8 The immediate cause of the psalmist's exhilaration is the Abrahamic **covenant** (Gen. 12:7; 13:14–17; 15:7, 18–21; 17:8; 22:17, 18; Ex. 32:13). It was made by **the LORD our God** whose righteous acts are seen throughout **the earth**. He will never forget His promise, though its fulfillment is delayed **a thousand gen-erations**. Whatever He promises is as certain as if it had already taken place.

105:9–11   The covenant was **made** originally **with Abraham** (Gen. 12:1–20), later confirmed **to Isaac** (Gen. 26:3,4), and then still later **confirmed to Jacob** (Gen. 28:13–15). It was the word of God who cannot lie, guaranteeing **the land of Canaan as the . . . inheritance** of His earthly people.

In the ensuing history of Israel, we see how God removed roadblocks and conquered enemies to bring His word to pass.

The Nation's Infancy (105:12–15)

When they first came to Canaan from Mesopotamia, they were a handful of defenseless immigrants. Those early days were marked by considerable moving about, both within the land and in other countries (Gen. 12:1–13; 20:1–18; 28:1—29:35). But God protected them from danger and oppression, and **rebuked** rulers like Pharaoh (Gen. 12:17–20) and Abimelech (Gen. 20:1–18; 26:6–11), saying, in effect, to these heathen kings, "Don't you dare **touch My** chosen ones, or **do My prophets** any **harm**—these patriarchs to whom I have given direct revelations."

Joseph's Rise to Power in Egypt (105:16–22)

In the process of time, **a** severe **famine** descended on **the land** of Canaan. **Bread** supplies vanished; the main support of life was gone. It was God who summoned the famine and who **destroyed all the provision of bread**, but only in the sense that He permitted these things to happen. God never originates evil, but He does permit it at times and then overrules it for His glory and His people's good. God's man for the crisis was **Joseph**. Hated by his brothers, he **was sold** into Egypt **as a slave**. There he was falsely accused by a seductive

woman and thrown into prison (Gen. 39:20). In verse 18, we have some otherwise unrecorded details concerning his imprisonment: **"They hurt his feet with fetters, he was laid in iron."** During his two years in jail, **the word of the Lord tested** his skill in interpreting dreams and predicting the future. Finally his ability was brought to Pharaoh's attention and he not only **released him**, but promoted him to second in command. He had authority **to bind** Egyptian **princes**, if necessary, and **wisdom** to instruct men who were much older than himself.

Migration of Jacob and Family (105:23–25)

Eventually Joseph's family moved **into Egypt**, and over the years they became numerous, prosperous and strong militarily. But in the providence of God, the Egyptians were allowed to become rabidly anti-semitic and to oppress and cheat the Jews.

Moses and the Plagues in Egypt (105:26–36)

105:26, 27 This time God raised up **Moses and** his lieutenant, **Aaron**, to stand before Pharaoh and demand the release of His enslaved people. Their demands were punctuated with a series of plagues designed to break down the monarch's resistance.

Here the plagues are itemized, not in chronological order, and with two unmentioned—the fifth and the sixth.

105:28 God **sent darkness** over all the land (Plague #9). The psalmist adds the puzzling comment, **"And they did not rebel against His word."** Because of the obvious difficulty, the RSV translators changed it to read, "they rebelled against His words," but they had no manuscript authority to make this change. Barnes explains it as meaning that Moses and Aaron **did not rebel against** the Lord's words, but did as He commanded them. Or it may mean that the darkness was so oppressive that the Egyptians were powerless to resist it.

105:29–31 God **turned their waters into blood** and wiped out the supply of **fish** (Plague #1). It was pollution of the worst kind.

The next mentioned was the plague of **frogs** (Plague #2). There were **frogs** everywhere—**frogs** in the ovens and **frogs** in the beds. Not even the royal suite was proof against these leaping, croaking, slimy creatures!

One word from the Lord and the land was ruined by **swarms of flies** (Plague #4) and by clouds of pesky gnats or **lice** (Plague #3).

105:32–36 Instead of **rain**, He sent destructive **hail** and lightning (Plague #7). As great balls of **fire** careened across the landscape, the **vines**, the **fig trees** and other **trees** were shattered. This plague brought injury and death to men as well (Ex. 9:25).

Then **came** the **locusts**, like an invading army, consuming **all the vegetation** as they advanced, and leaving a wasteland behind (Plague #8).

When none of these plagues succeeded, God **destroyed all the firstborn** of the Egyptians, both of man and beast (Plague #10). That was a night to be remembered—when the pride of every Egyptian home was slain.

The Exodus (105:37, 38)

The Jews left Egypt **with** more **silver and gold** than they had when they arrived; the Egyptians were **glad** to give them anything they wanted just to get rid of them (Ex. 12:33–36). And in spite of the havoc the plagues had wrought on the Egyptians, the Israelites were unaffected. They were

all in good condition for travel. Not one staggered or fell behind.

It was a great relief for the Egyptians **when they departed**; they had developed a deep-seated dread of them.

Wilderness Journey (105:39–42)

God's provision for His people in the wilderness was fantastic. **A cloud** not only kept them on course (Ex. 13:21) but served as a sort of smoke screen to hide them from the enemy (Ex. 14:19, 20). It became a pillar of **fire** at **night** to provide illumination for travel. When they wanted food, He gave them the best—**quails** in great abundance and manna, that wonder **bread** from **heaven**. They needed **water**, so **He** split **the rock, and water gushed out**. After they had used all they wanted, there was still enough to make **a river** in the desert. Why all this painstaking provision by Jehovah? Because He could not forget the **holy promise** which He had made to **Abraham His servant.**

In the Land at Last (105:43–45)

It was a great deliverance, accompanied by indescribable **joy** and singing. Jehovah **brought** them into the land of Canaan and dispossessed **the Gentiles** who were living there. Everything was ready made for them; **they** reaped **the labor of the nations.**

And of course the divine objective was that they might obey Him and **keep His laws.** Actually their tenure of the land was conditional on their obedience (Lev. 26:27–33; Deut. 28:63–68; 30:19, 20).

The last verse of the Psalm forms the intended climax. This was what God had been working toward all the time.

And it is true for us as well. God claimed us for His people in order that we might be living in that last verse:

> That they might observe His
> statutes, and keep His laws.
> Praise the LORD!

Psalm 106: Lessons from History

Cromwell asked, "What is history but God's unfolding of Himself?" The psalmist would have readily agreed because in the history of his people, he saw Jehovah unfolded as a God of goodness, patience and steadfast love.

Although we cannot name the psalmist, we do know that he was a godly Jew who wrote while his people were in captivity (v. 47). The Psalm is primarily a confession of national sin (vv. 6–46) but it also contains elements of praise (vv. 1–3, 48) and petition (vv. 4, 5, 47).

Praise (106:1–3)

106:1 In his approach to God, he begins with worship; he enters the divine gates with thanksgiving, and the sacred courts with praise. **"Praise the LORD,"** the translation of the Hebrew word "Hallelujah," is the first and last note of the song.

Ceaseless thanksgiving should arise **to the LORD**, because **He** has been so **good** to every one of us. **His mercy endures forever**—our continued survival is proof of that. If we received what we deserve, we would be lost forever.

106:2, 3 No human tongue will ever be able to recount all the miraculous interventions of God on behalf of His people. Eternity itself will not be long enough to praise Him adequately for all that He is and all that He has done.

Lord, Remember Me! (106:4, 5)

Praise is followed by personal petition. Looking forward to the restoration of Israel and the glorious reign of the Messiah-King, the writer prays that he might share in the blessedness of that day when God shows favor to His ransomed saints. He longs to see Israel enjoying unbroken prosperity and rejoicing after its long night of sorrow. He desires to share in the glory of God's ancient earthly people. His prayer is not dissimilar to that of the dying thief, "Lord, remember me when You come into Your kingdom" (Luke 23:42).

Red Sea Rebellion (106:6–12)

The Psalm now turns to confession, following much the same order as the Lord's prayer. Both begin with worship, move on to petition ("Give us this day our daily bread") and then ask for forgiveness ("Forgive us our debts . . .").

It is a mark of true spiritual maturity when a man not only confesses his own sins but the sins of his people as well. How hard it is to say from the heart:

> We have sinned with our fathers,
> We have committed iniquity, we
> have done wickedly.

As we consider the sins of the Israelites, we must not look down our theological noses at them. If anything, we are worse than they! Let their backslidings remind us of our own and drive us to our knees in repentance.

Their ingratitude—they did not fully appreciate the **wonders** God performed **in Egypt** to purchase their freedom.

Their forgetfulness—too quickly the memory of God's innumerable **mercies** faded from their minds.

Their rebellion—when they came to **the Red Sea**, they complained that God had led them to die in the wilderness, and that it would have been better to have stayed in Egypt (Ex. 14:11, 12).

But their sin did not quench the Lord's love. He found in their rebellion an opportunity to reveal Himself as their Servant and Savior. True to His name, He delivered them—and what a gigantic exhibition of **power** it was! At the word of His rebuke, the waters of **the Red Sea** parted, leaving a bone-dry causeway for the Jews to cross on. When they were safely on the east side, free from the pursuing enemy, **the waters** returned to their place, conveniently drowning the Egyptian hosts. When they saw this marvelous converging of events, how could the Jews help believing Him and singing **His praise?**

Complaints in the Desert (106:13–15)

But it wasn't long before another cycle of sin began.

Their short memory—**they soon forgot His** miracles for them.

Their self-will—**they** would **not wait for His** guidance.

Their lust—they abandoned self-control in their craving for food (Num. 11:1–35).

Their provocation—they **tested God.**

Well, this time God **gave them** what they wanted, **but sent** a loathsome disease among them (Num. 11:20). Their history teaches us to be careful to pray always in the will of God because, as Matthew Henry said, "What is asked in passion is often given in wrath."

Dathan and Abiram, the Rebels (106:16–18)

Their rejection of God's leadership—**Dathan and Abiram**, together with

Korah and On, were leaders of a rebellion against **Moses and Aaron** (Num. 16:1–30). They **envied** these two men of God. Also they wanted to intrude into the office of the priesthood. In rebelling against God's holy ones, that is, against men who were set apart as God's representatives, they were rebelling against God's rule. As a result, **the earth opened up and swallowed** the leaders and their families. And **fire** burst forth to devour the two hundred and fifty other men who offered incense to the Lord (Num. 16:31–35).

The Golden Calf (106:19–23)

Their idolatry—Before Moses had come down from Mount Sinai with the law of God, the people **made a** golden **calf and worshiped** it (Ex. 32:4). **They** exchanged the **glory** of God for the likeness **of an ox that eats grass.** Instead of acknowledging **God** as their **Savior** from Egypt, they gave all the honor to the lifeless calf. God would have destroyed them in a moment if Moses had not interceded. Like a soldier who covers a break in a wall with his body, so **Moses . . . stood before Him in the breach to turn away** God's **wrath.**

The Evil Report of the Spies (106:24–27)

Their faithlessness at Kadesh Barnea (Num. 14:2, 27, 28)—God had promised them **the pleasant land,** a land that was ideal for location, climate and resources. The promise contained all that was necessary to enter and occupy the land. But they did not believe His promise, and turned up their noses at (**despised**) **the land.** Instead of marching forward in faith, they sulked **in their tents. Therefore** God **raised His** hand in an oath to destroy that generation **in the wilderness** and to disperse **their descendants among the nations** of the world.

Sin with People of Moab (106:28–31)

Their sinful worship of the Baal of Peor—The men of Israel not only committed fornication with the daughters of Moab, they also joined in sacrificing **to the dead** and in other pagan ceremonies involved in the worship of the **Baal of Peor** (Num. 25:3–8). God was so infuriated that He sent a **plague** to slay the people by the thousands. When **Phinehas** saw an Israelite taking a heathen woman to his tent, he slew both of them with his spear. This **stopped** the **plague**, but only after twenty-four thousand had died. This act was a positive proof of his **righteousness**, and was rewarded by a covenant of peace. The Lord said:

> Behold, I give to him My covenant of peace; and it shall be to him and his descendants after him a covenant of an everlasting priesthood, because he was zealous for his God, and made atonement for the children of Israel (Num. 25:12, 13).

Trouble at Meribah (106:32, 33)

The sin of Moses (Num. 20:2–13)—**At the waters of** Meribah (**strife**), the people were blatantly unbelieving. They accused **Moses** of leading them into the wilderness to die of thirst. Instead of speaking to the rock, as God said, Moses struck it twice with his rod. He also **spoke rashly** against the people for their rebellion. As a result God decreed that he would be denied the privilege of leading the people of Israel into the land of promise.

In Canaan—Same Old Story (106:34–39)

The new environment of Canaan did not change the nature of the Israelites, as seen by:

106:34 *Their failure to exterminate the pagan inhabitants.* The debased Canaanites were a gangrenous limb of the human race. After bearing with them for hundreds of years, God decided that the only solution was amputation, and committed the surgery to Israel. But they failed to obey Him (Judg. 1:27–36).

106:35 *Their intermingling with the heathen.* By fraternizing and intermarrying with the pagans, Israel corrupted its own religion and morals.

106:36 *Their idolatry.* Soon the Jews were worshiping **idols** instead of the true and living God.

106:37–39 *Their human sacrifices.* Particularly revolting to the Lord was the sacrifice of **their sons and daughters** to appease the **demons** (2 Kgs. 3:27; 21:6; Ezek. 16:20, 21). Sons and daughters of God's chosen people were sacrificed to the filthy idols of Canaan, **and the land was polluted with** murder.

The Times of the Judges (106:40–46)

"Offended with His people," writes Barnes, "the Lord treated them as if they were an abomination to Him." **He** turned **them** over to **the Gentiles**—Mesopotamians, the Midianites, the Philistines, the Moabites, and others. These ungodly nations lorded it **over** the Jews, oppressing them and persecuting them. In spite of this treatment, the people persisted in their sin and rebellion against Jehovah. But whenever they turned to Him in repentance, He looked down on them in mercy. Mindful of **His covenant**, He turned from judgment to display His steadfast love. Even during the darkest hours of their captivity, the Lord caused **them to be pitied by** their captors—a touching example of mercy triumphing over judgment.

Save and Regather (106:47)

The psalmist prays for the regathering of his people, scattered throughout the nations of the world. This will result in great **thanks** ascending **to** God's **holy name**; His people will make it their glory to **praise** Him. The prayer anticipates the petitions of the remnant of Israel in the future time of the Tribulation, prior to the inauguration of Christ's glorious kingdom.

Doxology (106:48)

With this rapturous note we come not only to the end of the Psalm but to the end of the fourth book of the Psalms. But in coming to the end we must resist the temptation to put this Psalm in a dispensational pigeon-hole, limiting its message to the wicked nation of Israel and failing to see our own history reflected in it. In 1 Corinthians 10:11 we distinctly read:

Now all these things happened to them as examples, and they were written for our admonition, upon whom the ends of the ages have come.

It warns us against *ingratitude*. If Israel should have been grateful for redemption by power from Egypt, how much more grateful should we be for redemption by the blood of Christ from sin and from Satan!

It warns us against *forgetfulness*. How easily we forget the suffering and death of the Lord Jesus. How guilty we are of "the curse of dry-eyed Christianity."

It warns us against *complaining*. It becomes a way of life to complain about the weather, about our living conditions, about minor inconveniences, and even about lumps in the gravy.

It warns us against *self-will*, against putting our will above the will of God. "He gave them their request, but sent leanness into their soul" (v. 15).

It warns us against *criticizing* God's leadership, whether governmental officials, elders in the assembly, or parents in the home.

It warns us against *idolatry*—the worship of money, home, cars, education, pleasure, or worldly success.

It warns us against *disbelief* in the promises of God. This sin caused Israel to wander in the wilderness for thirty-eight years and barred the guilty ones from entering the promised land.

It warns us against *immorality*. The worship of the Baal of Peor involved gross sexual sin. God's attitude toward it is seen in the disaster which He visited upon the culprits.

It warns us against what might seem to be *"trivial" disobedience*. Moses struck the rock instead of speaking to it. That may not seem very serious to us, but no disobedience is trivial.

It warns us against *marrying unbelievers*. God is a God of separation. He hates to see the corruption of His people through the formation of unequal yokes.

Finally, it warns us against the *sacrifice of our children*. Too seldom do Christian parents hold the work of the Lord before their children as a desirable way in which to spend their lives. Too often our children are raised with the ambition to make a name for themselves in business or the professions. We raise them for the world—and for hell.

V. BOOK 5 (PSALMS 107—150)

Psalm 107: Let the Redeemed Say So

There is a common behavior pattern in the lives of God's people which can be summarized by two word series:

Sin or	Rebellion
Servitude	Retribution
Supplication	Repentance
Salvation	Restoration

First of all the people stray from the Lord, walking in disobedience to His Word. Then they suffer the bitter consequences of their backsliding. When they come to themselves, they cry out to the Lord in confession of sin. He then forgives their sin and brings them back into the place of blessing once more. It is the old story of the prodigal son and surely no story is more familiar, more relevant and true to life.

Two basic facts emerge from the contemplation of this ever-recurring cycle. One is the perpetual proneness of the human heart to wander away from the living God. The other is the seemingly inexhaustible mercy of the Lord in restoring His people when they come to Him in repentance.

Here in Psalm 107, the merciful deliverance of the Lord is presented in four different pictures:

Rescue for those lost in the desert (vv. 4–9).

Rescue for those in prison (vv. 10–16).

Recovery for those who are seriously ill (vv. 17–22).

Deliverance for seamen in a terrible storm (vv. 23–32).

Introduction (107:1–3)

First, however, there is an introduction which sounds the theme. It is a call to **give thanks to the LORD**. Two reasons are given—the Lord **is good**, and **His mercy endures forever**. Either reason would be more than enough cause for ceaseless gratitude.

A special class of people is now singled out as particular recipients of His goodness and love, namely, those **whom He has redeemed** from persecution, slavery, oppression and trouble, and brought back to the land from worldwide dispersion. While it is clear that the psalmist has Israel in view, we will not surrender these verses to that nation exclusively because we too have been bought back from the slave market of sin, and as **the redeemed of the LORD** we want to join in the anthem of thanksgiving.

Rescue for Those Lost in the Desert (107:4–9)

This first picture seems clearly to allude to Israel's forty-year trek through the waste, howling **wilderness**. The people were lost. They were **hungry**. They were **thirsty**. They were disheartened and discouraged. **Then they cried out to the LORD.** Suddenly their meanderings ended. The Lord **led them** by a direct route to the Plains of Moab. This proved the jumping-off place for their entrance into Canaan. And there they found **a city** where they could feel at home at last. How they (and all of us) should **give thanks to the LORD** continually for His undying love, and for the **wonderful** care He bestows on His people. For in the Promised Land **He satisfies** the thirsty, and provides the finest food for **the hungry**.

Release for Those in Prison (107:10–16)

107:10–12 The second vignette of Israel's history concerns the Babylonian captivity. The psalmist likens the seventy years to confinement in prison.

Babylon was like a dark, gloomy dungeon. The Israelites felt like chained prisoners condemned to penal servitude (although conditions in Babylon were not as severe as they had been in Egypt). It was because of their rebellion **against the words of God**, their spurning of His Word, that they were sent off into exile. Crushed and beaten by hard **labor, they fell down** under the load, and no one took sides with them.

107:13–16 But when they **cried out to the** Lord, . . . **He saved** them from the land of darkness **and broke** the chains of their captivity. Now the only decent thing for them to do is to **give thanks to the** Lord for His unchanging love and for all the **wonderful works** He has done for them.

> For He has broken the gates of
> bronze,
> And cut bars of iron in two.

This is the verse that leads us to believe that the psalmist is referring to the Babylonian captivity in this section. The identifying link is found in Isaiah 45:2 where the Lord used almost identical words to describe the way in which He would bring the exile to a close. Speaking to Cyrus, He said:

> I will go before you and make the crooked places straight; I will break in pieces the gates of bronze, and cut the bars of iron.

The context makes it clear that He was referring to the termination of the exile in Babylon.

Recovery for Those Who Are Seriously Ill (107:17–22)

107:17–20 This third section may refer to the nation of Israel at the time of Christ's First Advent. The nation was sick at the time. They had just

been through the trying days of the Maccabees. Some were **fools**, suffering God's judgment **because of their iniquities**. They had lost appetite for **food**, and were rapidly drawing **near to the gates of death**. A godly remnant of the nation was praying and waiting for the hope of Israel. God **sent** forth **His word and healed them**. His Word here may refer to the Lord Jesus Christ, the Logos, who came with a healing ministry to the house of Israel. How many times we read in the Gospel records "and He healed them all." Matthew reminds us that in His healing of the sick, the Savior fulfilled what was spoken by the prophet Isaiah, "He Himself took our infirmities and bore our sicknesses" (Matt. 8:17). If it be objected that not all the Israelites were healed, we should remember that not all entered the promised land and not all returned from captivity in Babylon either.

107:21, 22 Again the psalmist calls on men to praise the Lord for His **goodness and for His wonderful works**. The gift of His Son is special cause for sacrifices of thanksgiving and for recital of His deeds in songs of joy.

Deliverance for Seamen in a Terrible Storm (107:23–32)

107:23–27 The last picture is most graphic. It is about seamen who worked on ocean-going **ships**. They knew something about the power of **the** Lord whenever they ran into a storm at sea. First the **wind** would arise to alarming proportions. Then **the waves** would form gargantuan mountains of water. The ship would rise up on the wave, its timbers creaking. At the crest, it would shudder, then crash into the trough. The stoutest ship would be like a matchbox in a swirling, foaming cauldron.

In a storm like that, the toughest sailors lose courage. It is all they can do to **stagger like a drunken man** around the ship to perform their duties. They feel a terrible sense of their own insignificance and **are at their wits' end**.

107:28–30 It is not surprising that cursing, irreligious sailors pray at a time like this. And the Lord is gracious enough to hear those prayers of desperation. **He calms the storm** and the **waves** become **still**. What a relief! The men can navigate once more, and soon they are entering the port toward which they were sailing.

107:31, 32 The relieved seamen should not forget to thank **the LORD** for His unfailing **goodness** and all the **wonderful** answers to prayer He gives. They should pay their vows by joining with His faithful people in extolling Him, by praising **Him in the company of the elders**.

Are we stretching matters by saying that this depicts Israel's final storm and her subsequent entrance into the kingdom of peace? The storm suggests the Great Tribulation. The sea typifies the seething, restless Gentile nations. The seamen represent the nation of Israel, tossed about by the other nations during the Time of Jacob's Trouble. A believing remnant of the nation calls upon the Lord. He then personally intervenes, returning to earth to set up His reign of peace and prosperity.

The Government and Grace of God (107:33–43)

107:33, 34 The remaining verses of the Psalm explain how God reacts when His people are disobedient and then again when they are obedient. By His almighty power, **He** makes **rivers** bone-dry and causes bubbling springs to evaporate. It is nothing for

Him to cause **fruitful land** to turn into salty wasteland when the people turn their backs on Him.

107:35–38 But He can also reverse the process, and this is exactly what will happen when the Prince of Peace returns to rule over the millennial earth. The Negev will be dotted with plentiful **pools of water**. The Sahara and the Mojave will be well-irrigated gardens. Housing settlements will spring up in places that have been uninhabitable for centuries. Modern cities will dot the landscape. The wilderness will suddenly become arable. Grain, vegetables, fruit and berries will grow in profusion. By His blessing there will be bumper crops everywhere, and the **cattle** will be disease-resistant.

107:39–43 The other side of the picture is seen in the way He deals with wicked rulers.

> Tyrants lose their strength and are brought low in the grip of misfortune and sorrow; He brings princes into contempt and leaves them wandering in a trackless waste (vv. 39, 40, NEB).

This was the fate of Pharaoh, Herod, and Hitler, and it will be the termination of the evil triumvirate during the Tribulation.

Yet God lifts **the poor** out of their troubles and blesses them with large families. When good men **see** this, they are profoundly glad. When the ungodly see it, they don't have a word to say (which is unusual for them).

Whoever is wise will see the hand of God behind the changing fortunes of men and of nations and will learn lessons from history and current events. Especially will they consider **the lovingkindness of the LORD** in His dealings with those who obey His Word.

Psalm 108: Help! Quick!

It is not surprising if this Psalm has a familiar ring to it. The first five verses are much the same as Psalm 57:7–11, and the last eight verses are almost identical with Psalm 60:5–12. The Psalm moves successively from praise, to prayer, to promise, to a problem, to prayer again and finally to a bright prospect.

Praise (108:1–5)

108:1, 2 The psalmist **is steadfast** in his determination to **praise** the Lord for His ceaseless love and faithfulness. He is ready and eager to **sing** and make melody to the Most High. While it is still dark, he calls his soul to wake up, and rouses his **lute and harp** from their silent rest in order to greet **the dawn** with songs of thanksgiving. Not a bad idea—to start the day with praise!

108:3 Nor will he confine his song to the privacy of his home or to his own little neighborhood. Wherever he goes, **the peoples** will hear him worshiping the LORD, **the nations** will echo to his songs of praise. This determination should be ours as well.

108:4, 5 Why was David so enthusiastic about the Lord? Because His **mercy** towers in its immensity **above the heavens**, and His **truth** is sky-high. His praise should correspond to His greatness. So may He **be exalted . . . above the heavens**, and may His **glory** be **above all the earth**.

As we listen to David's rapturous songs of adoration, we understand better why someone wrote:

Praise is more divine than prayer;
Prayer points the happy road to heaven.
Praise is already there.

Prayer (108:6)

Now he turns to petition. The country was under attack by enemy forces; the outlook was ominous. The supernatural strokes of success that Israel had so often experienced were strangely absent, therefore he implores the Lord to deliver His **beloved** ones by sending help to turn back the invaders.

Promise (108:7–9)

108:7, 8 Unruffled and majestic in His sanctuary, **God** asserts His sovereign rights over Israel and over the Gentile nations as well. He promises that the Messiah's dominion will include the district of **Shechem**, where Jacob's well is located; **the Valley of Succoth**, where Jacob built booths for his cattle (Gen. 33:17); the lofty plateau of **Gilead**, famous alike for its pastures and medicinal balm; and **Manasseh**, with territory on both sides of the Jordan. **Ephraim** will be His **helmet**, leading the tribes in defending the realm. **Judah** will be His **lawgiver**, the seat of government, as promised in Genesis 49:10.

108:9 Three Gentile nations are mentioned—**Moab**, **Edom** and **Philistia**—as representative of the foreign territory which will also be included in the kingdom. **Moab** will be His **washpot**, a figure expressing contempt and control. He will **cast** His **shoe . . . over Edom**, implying ownership, servitude, and scorn. While **Moab** and **Edom** will be tributary vassals, **Philistia** will be crushed. **"Over Philistia I will triumph."**

Problem (108:10, 11)

The promise of victory over Edom makes David restless to see its fulfillment. Sela, the capital city (also known as Petra), was renowned as being inaccessible and impregnable. He longs for someone to **lead** him **to Edom** that he might shout in triumph over it. But there is a problem—**God** has hidden His face from Israel. His help has been missing, with disastrous results. Israel's **armies** have been marching on to war—and defeat, because the Lord is not with them.

Prayer (108:12)

Without the Lord the situation is hopeless, no one else will do. David had lived long enough to know that man's **help is useless**. He asks the Mighty God to take up Israel's cause again by giving **help** on the battlefield.

Prospect (108:13)

As soon as he leaves the place of prayer, the psalmist is singing a note of triumph. **"Through God we will do valiantly,"** for it is He who will crush the opposition and give victory to His beloved ones. This is the confidence, born of faith, that Paul Gerhardt expressed so eloquently:

> Is God for me? I fear not,
> Though all against me rise;
> When I call on Christ my Savior,
> The host of evil flies.
> My Friend, the Lord Almighty,
> And He who loves me, God;
> What enemy can harm me,
> Though coming like a flood?

> The world may pass and perish,
> Thou, God, wilt not remove;
> No hatred of all devils
> Can part me from Thy love;
> No hungering nor thirsting,
> No poverty nor care,
> No wrath of mighty princes
> Can reach my shelter there.

> My heart with joy upleapeth,
> Grief cannot linger there,
> She singeth high in glory,
> Amidst the sunshine fair.
> The sun that shines upon me
> Is Jesus and His love,
> The fountain of my singing
> Is deep in heaven above.

Psalm 109: The Fate of God's Enemies

Of all the Psalms of imprecation, this one is unrivaled for first place. No other calls down the judgment of God with such distilled vitriol or with such comprehensive detail. The reader cannot fail to be intrigued and fascinated by the sheer ingenuity of the psalmist in the variety of punishments he invokes on his foes!

109:1–3 The Psalm opens with disarming mildness. David pleads for help from the **God of** his **praise**, that is, the God whom he praises. His enemies have been conducting a vicious verbal assault on him, hurling all manner of **lying** charges against him. **Words of hatred** come zeroing in at him from every direction. What makes it especially hard to take is that the attacks are wholly unjustified.

109:4, 5 David has shown **love** and kindness to his assailants, and what does he receive in return? A barrage of false accusations. And all the while he is praying for them. For every kindness, they repay him with insult, and **for love**, they reward him with **hatred**.

109:6, 7 It is at this point that he seems to dip his pen in acid. From now on the imprecations, hot and lethal, shoot out from his wounded soul. From the many foes of verses 1–5, he now turns to concentrate on one in particular.

Eventually this man will be caught and brought to trial. When that happens, let the Lord arrange the circumstances so that **a wicked man** will be his **accuser**, a satanic man his plaintiff. At the conclusion of the trial let the verdict be **"Guilty!"** And if he appeals the sentence, let his request be counted as contempt of court and the penalty increased.

109:8–10 As for his life, may it be

a short one and may someone else **take his office**. This particular imprecation is quoted of Judas and of his office as treasurer of the band of disciples in Acts 1:20:

> For it is written in the book of Psalms, "Let his dwelling place be desolate, and let no one live in it"; and, "Let another take his office."

It will help us to understand the severity of this Psalm if we remember that it refers not only to David and his foe, but also to Messiah and His betrayer, and also perhaps to Israel and the Anti-Christ in a day still future.

As for the foe's family, let **his children** become **fatherless and his wife** be widowed. **Let his children continually be vagabonds** and beggars, evicted from the ruins that used to be their home.

109:11–13 As for his estate, **let the creditor** step in and **seize all that he has**, and let all that he has earned be shared by **strangers**.

Since he showed no mercy, **let no mercy** be shown **to him**, no pity to his **fatherless children**. Let the family name go into oblivion before a **generation** passes. (In eastern reckoning, this is one of the most shameful punishments that could be inflicted.)

109:14, 15 Even his predecessors are not blameless. Let **the LORD** remember **the iniquity of his fathers . . . and let not the sin of his mother be blotted out**. The exact nature of their crimes is not given, but their guilt must have been aggravated since the psalmist goes on to ask that their sins might never be forgotten by the Lord and that **the memory of them** be **cut off . . . from the earth**.

109:16–20 In verse 16 we read the stinging indictment of the wicked man. It was his lifestyle to refrain from showing kindness. Instead he actively and aggressively hunted down **the poor and needy**, and drove the brokenhearted to their death. It is not hard to find Judas in this verse, maliciously hounding the sinless Savior to the cross.

But there is an inexorable law of retribution in the moral realm. Whatever a man sows, that is what he reaps. The harvest is inescapable. There is no getting away with sin. Here the psalmist asks that the law of cause and effect take its full course. This man **loved** to curse others; now may his curses boomerang on himself. He never wanted others to enjoy blessings; now **let** blessings stay **far** away **from him**. He swaggered about **with cursing** as his coat; now let those curses penetrate his life **like water** penetrates a sponge; let them soak into every part of his being, even into the marrow of **his bones**. May cursing cover him like the clothes that he wears, "cling to him like a girdle he can never take off" (Knox).

This then is David's desire for his **accusers** and his calumniators. He has scarcely overlooked one detail in the catalog of judgment. As someone has said, "All is in fact invoked on the wicked that any man could ever desire to see inflicted on an enemy."

109:21–25 The psalmist closes with two prayers and a burst of praise. First, he prays for deliverance from his troubles. He wants **the Lord** to take his part **for** His **name's sake**, that is, in order to glorify Himself as the God of power and justice. In dealing on David's behalf, the Lord will demonstrate once more that His **mercy is good**.

The psalmist's plight is grave. Not only is he **poor and needy**, his **heart** is **wounded within** him. His life is ebbing out **like a** lengthening **shadow**.

He is being **shaken off** from life as easily as a man shakes **a locust** off his hand. **Through** prolonged **fasting**, his **knees** are buckling and his body is reduced to skin and bones. His enemies laugh at him in his pitiable state; they tauntingly **shake their heads** at him.

109:26–29 In his second prayer, he asks the Lord to vindicate him before the foes. When Jehovah comes to his help and rescues him, then the assailants will **know that** it was an act of divine intervention—the **hand** of the Lord. What difference will it make if they **curse**, as long as the Lord blesses. The enemies will **be ashamed**, but the psalmist will **rejoice** at that time. May they be **clothed with shame** and confusion, yes, wrapped in **disgrace as with** a full-cut **mantle**.

109:30, 31 Finally, we hear David planning the **praise** he will offer to the Lord when his prayers are answered. It will not be ordinary praise but great thanks. It will not be private but in the midst of the **multitude**. And the theme will be that Jehovah stands **at the right hand of the poor**, delivering **him from those who** have marked him for execution. It gives great confidence to have the Lord as one's defender. As F. B. Meyer says:

> How brave is the accused if he enters court leaning on the arm of the noblest in the land. How futile is it to condemn when the Judge of all stands beside to justify?[71]

IMPRECATORY PSALMS

So much for what Psalm 109 actually says. But it would not be intellectually honest to pass on without facing up to the problem that is implicit in the imprecatory Psalms. The problem, of course, is how to reconcile the vindictive, judgmental spirit of these Psalms with the spirit of forgiveness and love that is elsewhere enjoined

upon God's people. Since the 109th is the king of the imprecatory Psalms, this seems to be the place to face the problem.

First, I will list some of the explanations which have been put forward but which do not seem entirely convincing to me. Then I will give what I understand to be the true explanation, although it too is not without difficulties.

It is pointed out that these imprecations are not so much invocations of vengeance or of punishment on the wicked as they are predictions of what will happen to God's enemies. Thus Unger says:

> Curses delivered against individuals by holy men are not the expressions of revenge, passion, or impatience; they are predictions and therefore not such as God condemns.[72]

Many of these passages could just as correctly be translated in the future tense as in the imperative.

A second explanation is that David was speaking as God's anointed. Because of his position, he was God's representative. Therefore, he was permitted to pronounce these severe judgments. (Here it should be noted, however, that not all the imprecatory Psalms were written by David.)

Then again some view these passages as a historical record of how these men felt, without approving of their harshness. Concerning this view Barnes writes:

> These expressions are a mere record of what actually occurred in the mind of the psalmist, and are preserved to us as an illustration of human nature when partially sanctified. According to this view the Spirit of inspiration is no more responsible for these feelings on the part of the psalmist than He is for the acts of David, Abraham,

Jacob or Peter. . . . The proper notion of inspiration does not require us to hold that the men who were inspired were absolutely sinless. . . . According to this view the expressions which are used in this record are not presented for our imitation.[73]

And there are other explanations. The imprecatory Psalms are defended by reminding us that because Israel was God's chosen nation, therefore Israel's enemies were God's enemies. That there is something in each one of us which righteously approves of proper punishment for crimes. That the psalmists describe what sinners deserve and do not express any personal desire for revenge.

As I said before, I do not find any of these explanations completely satisfying. The explanation that appeals to me most is that the imprecatory Psalms express a spirit that was *proper for a Jew living under the law, but not proper for a Christian living under grace.* The reason these Psalms seem harsh to us is because we are viewing them in the light of the New Testament revelation. David and the other psalmists did not have the New Testament. As Scroggie points out:

> . . . it will be well to recognize at once the fact that the previous dispensation was inferior to the present one, that while the Law is not contrary to the Gospel it is not equal to it, that while Christ came to fulfill the Law He came also to transcend it. We must be careful not to judge expressions in the Psalter which savor of vindictiveness and vengeance by the standards of the Pauline Epistles.[74]

While the inclusion of a man's family in his judgment seems rather extreme to us, it was justified to the psalmist by the fact that God had threatened to visit the iniquity of the fathers upon the children to the third and fourth generation (Ex. 20:5; 34:7; Num. 14:18; Deut. 5:9). Whether we like it or not, there are laws in the spiritual realm under which sins have a way of working themselves out in a man's family. No man is an island; the consequences of his acts reach out to others as well as affecting himself.

We live today in the acceptable year of the Lord. When this age passes and the day of vengeance of our God begins, language such as that of the imprecatory Psalms will once again be on the lips of God's people. For instance, the Tribulation martyrs will say, "How long, O Lord, holy and true, until You judge and avenge our blood on those who dwell on the earth?" (Rev. 6:10).

One final consideration! The severity of the imprecations in the Psalms prepare our hearts in a feeble way to appreciate the One who bore every curse in His body on the cross so that we might be eternally free from the curse and from cursing. Not all the punishments described in the Psalms put together give a feeble, faint reflection of the avalanche of judgment which He endured as our Substitute.‡

Psalm 110: David's Son and David's Lord

This **Psalm of David** enjoys the distinction of being quoted or referred to more frequently in the NT than any other passage in the OT. It is quite clearly a Psalm of the Messiah— first as the glorified One at God's right hand, then as the King of glory returning to earth to take the scepter of universal government, and also as the eternal Priest according to the order of Melchizedek.

110:1 In the first verse David

quotes the LORD as saying to his **Lord**:

"Sit at My right hand, till I make Your enemies Your footstool."

The key to understanding this lies in identifying the two distinct persons referred to by the name of "Lord." The first use of the word refers unmistakably to Jehovah.[75] The other word "Lord" is the Hebrew *adon* and means "master" or "ruler." It was sometimes used as a name of God and sometimes applied to a human master. Although the word itself does not always indicate a divine person, the words that follow show that David's Lord (*Adon*) was equal with God.

One day when Jesus was speaking to the Pharisees in Jerusalem, He asked them what they believed concerning the identity of the Messiah. From whom would the Promised One be descended? They answered correctly that He would be the son of David. But Jesus showed them that according to Psalm 110 (which they acknowledged to be messianic) the Messiah would also be David's Lord. How could He be David's son and David's Lord at the same time? And how could David, the king, have someone who was his Lord on earth?

The answer of course was that the Messiah would be both God and man. *As God*, He would be *David's Lord*. *As man*, He would be *David's son*. And Jesus Himself, combining in His Person both deity and humanity, was David's Master and David's son.

It was the moment of truth for the Pharisees. Yet in spite of all the evidence, they were unwilling to acknowledge Jesus as the long-awaited Messiah. So we read:

And no one was able to answer Him a word, nor from that day on did anyone dare question Him any-

more (Matt. 22:41–46; cf. Mark 12:35–37; Luke 20:41–44).

The NT writers leave no room for doubt that the One who is seated at God's **right hand** is none other than Jesus of Nazareth (Matt. 26:64; Mark 14:62; 16:19; Luke 22:69; Acts 2:34, 35; 5:31; 7:55, 56; Rom. 8:34; 1 Cor. 15:24ff; Eph. 1:20; Col. 3:1; Heb. 1:3, 13; 8:1; 10:12, 13; 12:2; 1 Pet. 3:22; Rev. 3:21). Therefore verse 1 tells what Jehovah **said to** the LORD Jesus on the latter's ascension day when He sat down **at** God's **right hand**. But He is only there **till** His **enemies** are made His **footstool**.

110:2 Between verses 1 and 2 we have what H. A. Ironside called "the great parenthesis"[76]—the Church Age which extends from the enthronement of Christ to His Second Coming. In verse 2 we see Jehovah sending forth Messiah's royal **rod** from **Zion**; in other words, the Lord establishes Christ as King with Jerusalem as His capital. This scepter is the symbol of royal authority. Christ is given authority to reign over all the earth in the midst of His enemies. **"Rule in the midst of Your enemies."** Prior to this time the Lord Jesus will have destroyed His unreconstructed foes. Here it is not a matter of destroying His foes but of ruling over those foes who have become His friends and who gladly submit to His **rule**.

110:3 This is confirmed by verse 3. His **people** offer themselves willingly on **the day** He leads His army upon the holy mountain. Or as the NKJV states it:

Your people shall be volunteers in the day of Your power; in the beauties of holiness. . . .

Here a willing people greet the King in holy array. "In their lives and conduct," writes Barnes, "they will manifest all the beauty or attractiveness which there is in a holy and pure character."

The last part of verse 3 has been the torture of translators and commentators. Scroggie paraphrases as follows: ". . . as dew is born of its mother the morning, so Thy army shall come to Thee numerous, fresh, bright and powerful."[77]

110:4 One of the extraordinary features of the Kingdom is that the Lord Jesus will combine in His person the dual offices of king and **priest**. It is a combination that is highly dangerous in the case of mere human rulers; the loud, long cry for separation of church and state has not been without valid cause. But the combination is ideal when Jesus is the Ruler. Uncorrupted kingship and spiritual priesthood will give the world an administration such as it has longed for but has never known.

In verse 4 we learn four things concerning the priesthood of the Messiah:

He was made **a priest** by the oath of Jehovah.

This appointment was irrevocable.

His priesthood is eternal.

It is **according to the order of Melchizedek**.

The phrase **"according to the order of Melchizedek"** is interpreted for us in Hebrews 5—7. There the priesthood of Melchizedek is compared and contrasted with the Aaronic or Levitical priesthood.

Under the law God designated the men of the tribe of Levi and the family of Aaron to be priests. Their priesthood was a matter of parentage and it terminated with their death.

The priesthood of that mysterious personage Melchizedek was by sovereign appointment of God. It was

not inherited from his parents ("without father, without mother, without genealogy," Heb. 7:3a) and there is no mention of his priesthood ever beginning or ending ("having neither beginning of days nor end of life," Heb. 7:3b). In these and other ways, the Melchizedek priesthood was superior to that of Levi. Melchizedek was a prototype of the Lord Jesus. Our Lord's priesthood was not a matter of parentage; He was of the tribe of Judah, not Levi. His priesthood was established by the sovereign eternal decree of God, and since He lives in the power of an endless life, His priesthood will never end.

Another way in which **Melchizedek** foreshadowed the Messiah is that he was both king and priest. His name and title signify that he was king of righteousness and king of peace (Heb. 7:2). He was also priest of God Most High (Gen. 14:18).

110:5 The last three verses of the Psalm picture the Lord Jesus as a mighty Conqueror, putting down all lawlessness and rebellion prior to the inauguration of His kingdom. The problem of identifying the personages in these verses is largely solved if we think of them as being addressed to Jehovah and as referring to the Messiah-King. Thus verse 5 would read:

The LORD (Adonai—here the Lord Jesus) **is at Your** (Jehovah's) **right hand; He** (Messiah) **shall execute kings in the day of His wrath**.

110:6 It is the Lord Jesus marching forth against the Gentile nations, as foreseen in Joel 3:9–17; Zechariah 14:3; and Revelation 19:11–21. He executes judgment **among the nations**, strewing the landscape with their corpses. The further statement **"He shall execute the heads of many countries"** could also be translated "He shall strike through the head over a wide land." This could be a reference to the doom of the Man of Sin, "whom the Lord will consume with the breath of His mouth and destroy with the brightness of His coming" (2 Thess. 2:8).

110:7 As He goes forth to deal with His foes, the King **shall drink of the brook by the wayside**. Since water is often a type of the Holy Spirit (John 7:38, 39), this suggests that the Lord is refreshed and reinvigorated by the ministry of the Spirit, and this explains why He subsequently lifts up His **head** in victory.

Psalm 111: The Wonderful Works of the Lord

There are three threads that run through Psalm 111:

the works of Jehovah (vv. 2–4, 6–7).

the words of Jehovah, under such synonyms as covenant (vv. 5, 9), precepts (v . 7).

the everlasting character of all that He is and does (vv. 3, 5, 8–10).

In the Hebrew it is an acrostic Psalm. Each of the first eight verses has two lines. The last two have three lines each. Each of the twenty-two lines begins with a letter of the Hebrew alphabet in proper order.

The subject of the Psalm is the excellencies of the enthroned Christ. Israel is singing the praises of the One who called them out of the darkness of Egypt and of the Babylonian captivity into His marvelous light.

111:1 The song opens with a call to the faithful to **praise the LORD** (Heb., "Hallelujah"), and with the psalmist's own determination to **praise the LORD** without inhibition or distraction. He will do this both in small assemblies of believers and in the great gatherings of the people, or as we might say, both in private and in public.

111:2, 3 The four descriptions of **the works of the LORD** here are true of all He does, but the "Mt. Everest" of all God's works to the OT Jew was the deliverance from Egypt. **The works of the LORD are great**; they form a fruitful study **by all who have pleasure in them**. They are stupendous displays of His glory and majesty, **and His righteousness endures forever**.

111:4, 5 He established the Passover as an enduring memorial of Israel's salvation by the blood of the lamb, a lasting remembrance of His grace and mercy. In the Lord's Supper, He left a memorial of our salvation by the blood of a better Lamb, the unforgettable reminder that He is **gracious and full of compassion**. Perhaps verse 5 refers especially to God's miraculous provision of **food** (lit. "prey") for the Israelites during their wilderness journeys. He never forgot that they were His covenant people. But it is *always* true that He is faithful to the promises He has made.

111:6 He gave His people another demonstration of His mighty works by dispossessing the Canaanite nations and bringing His people safely into the Promised Land, which the psalmist here calls **"the heritage of the nations."**

111:7–9 All God's **works** demonstrate that He is always faithful and just. **All His precepts** are absolutely dependable. He keeps His promises forever, and fulfills them faithfully and honorably. **He sent redemption to His people** at the time of the exodus, then later when He brought them back from the captivity in Babylon. He will do it again when He brings the twelve tribes back to the land of Israel prior to His glorious reign. It is all part of **His covenant**, and it can never fail. **His name** is **holy and awesome**, or reverend, and as His name is, so is He!

111:10 Only the man who reverences Him has started on the road to **wisdom**. The more we obey Him, the more light He gives us. "Obedience is the organ of spiritual knowledge."

He is worthy to be praised **forever**!

Psalm 112: Rewards of the Righteous

112:1 There is a close correspondence between this Psalm and the preceding one, both in its acrostic form and in its spiritual teaching. It takes up where Psalm 111 leaves off—with **the man who fears the Lord** and who practices wisdom. Several of the things that are said about the Lord in the first are applied to the godly man in the second. We see the Sun of Righteousness shining in all His glory in the 111th; here we see the believer, like the moon, reflecting that glory. By beholding the beauty of the Lord, the believer is changed into the same beauty by the Holy Spirit (2 Cor. 3:18).

"Praise the Lord!" These words frequently expressed the psalmist's sentiments, and he has left a good example for the rest of us.

Who is the happy man? It is the one who reverences and submits to **the Lord, who delights greatly in His commandments**, and proves it by obeying them. He reaps the benefits that flow from a life of practical godliness. Such as—

112:2 *Distinguished Posterity.* **His descendants will** occupy positions of power and prestige; they will be honored because of their godly heritage. (In interpreting these blessings for the Church Age, we are wise to transfer them from their earthly, material meaning to the spiritual counterpart.)

112:3 *Prosperity.* It is generally true

that obedience to the Word of God saves men from waste and poverty. The results of his righteousness, that is, of his honesty, diligence, and frugality continue to distant generations.

112:4 *Assured illumination.* There is no guarantee of immunity from darkness, but there is the promise that **light** will rise **in the darkness**. In all the dark times of life the Lord shows Himself to be **gracious, and full of compassion**.

112:5, 6 *Generosity.* Things go better for the man who is generous and who doesn't refuse to lend to others who are in genuine need. This man manages his business **with discretion** and justice. His life is built on a stable foundation, and he will be remembered long after he is gone.

112:7 *Freedom from Fear.* He doesn't have to live in constant fear of bad news, of business reverses, of natural calamities. He is **trusting in the Lord**, and knows that nothing can happen to him apart from God's will.

112:8 *Confidence under Attack.* Even **his enemies** do not upset his poise or calm. He is confident that though they might seem to have the upper hand at the moment, yet their downfall is certain, and he is on the winning side.

112:9 *Lasting Fruitfulness and Honor.* Because he has been generous, the results of his kindness **to the poor** will never cease to be remembered. He won't have to hang **his horn** (symbol of strength) in shame. Rather his head will be crowned with plaudits. Paul quotes this verse in 2 Corinthians 9:9 to show the lasting benefits of generosity.

112:10 *The Envy of the Wicked.* When **the wicked** shall **see** the eventual vindication and permanent honor of the godly, they will be chagrined and envious. They **will gnash** their **teeth** in fury, then become unhinged and evaporate. All that they lived for **shall perish** with them. Barnes notes:

This is in strong contrast to what is said in the Psalm would occur to the righteous. They would be prospered and happy; they would be able to carry out their plans; they would be respected while living, and remembered when dead; they would find God interposing in their behalf in the darkest hours; they would be firm and calm in the day of danger and of trouble; they would put their trust in the Lord, and all would be well. Surely there is an advantage ... in being a friend of God.[78]

Psalm 113: So Great, Yet So Gracious

113:1–6 The first five verses present God as the One who is *infinitely high*, the last four as the One who is *intimately nigh.*

Our God is infinitely high. As such He is worthy to be praised.

By whom?	By all His **servants** (v. 1).
How?	By blessing His **name**, which means by thanking Him for all that He is (v. 2a).
How often?	Continually—now and **forevermore** (v. 2b).
Where?	Everywhere—from lands of sunrise to lands of sunset (v. 3a).
For what?	*For His Greatness.* He **is high above all nations, His glory above the heavens** (v. 4).
	For His matchlessness. No one can be compared to Him, seated on His throne **on high** (v. 5).
	For His limitless vision. There is nothing in heaven or earth that He does not see (v. 6). The text suggests that He has to humble Himself even **to behold the things** in heaven!

But, praise His name, the One who is infinitely high is also intimately nigh.

113:7–9 **The poor** can know this! He **lifts** them from **the dust**.

The **needy** can know this! He elevates them from their low estate and seats them **with princes**, with the excellent of the earth.

The barren woman can know this! **He grants** her **a home** and makes her **like a joyful mother of children**. Barrenness was a fearsome reproach among Jewish women. To be delivered from this curse was the occasion of the most extravagant joy, according to the Prayer Book Commentary.

Application

I was *poor,* but through faith in Christ I have become fantastically wealthy in spiritual things.

I was *needy,* but the Lord Jesus took this beggar from the dunghill and gave him wonderful Christian brothers and sisters, a fellowship that beats anything the world has to offer.

I was *barren,* with no fruit in my life for God. But He has delivered me from empty, wasteful existence to meaningful, productive life.

No wonder I sing with the psalmist: **Praise the LORD!**

> He fills the throne, the throne above,
> He fills it without wrong;
> The object of His Father's love,
> Theme of the ransomed's song.
>
> Though high, yet He accepts the praise
> His people offer here;
> The faintest, feeblest cry they raise
> Will reach the Savior's ear.
> —*Thomas Kelly*

Psalm 114: The Powerful Presence of Lord

114:1 The saga of Israel's redemption from **Egypt**, her wilderness experiences, and her arrival in the land of promise was a tremendous display of the power of God from beginning to end. In fact, to the Jewish mind it was the greatest demonstration of divine power that had ever taken place.

What a historic time that was **when Israel went out of Egypt**, the long years of bondage and oppression over! Who can measure the ecstasy of the people to be emancipated from the Egyptians? No more would they cringe under threats and curses barked out at them in an alien tongue!

114:2 In time the territory assigned to the tribe of **Judah became** God's **sanctuary**. The temple was erected there in Jerusalem. And the entire land of **Israel** became **His dominion**—an area He tended with unwearied care. What was true in a geographic sense of Judah and Israel then is true in a spiritual sense of the church today.

114:3 When the people of Israel came to the Red Sea, the waters took one look and retreated in panic. But be assured that it was not the sight of this ragtag mob of refugees that caused the terror. **The sea** looked up and **saw** its Creator, then quickly **turned back** so that Israel could pass over without even getting their feet wet.

It was the same thing forty years later when they entered the Promised Land. The **Jordan** River halted its flow at the city of Adam, and the last barrier to entering the land became a causeway.

The Red Sea and the Jordan crossings are the two termini of this epic chapter in the nation's history. The Red Sea passage typifies our redemption from the world by God's power through identification with Christ in His death, burial and resurrection. The crossing of the Jordan speaks of deliverance from wilderness wandering and entering into our spiritual inheritance, again through Christ's death, burial and resurrection.

114:4 Between these two events there were other awesome examples of God's power. One of the most spectacular was the giving of the law at Mt. Sinai. Nature was so convulsed that **the mountains skipped like rams, the little hills like lambs**. It seems that the glory of God was so overpowering that the entire area was rocked as if by a cataclysm. So terrifying was the sight that Moses, the man of God, said, "I am exceedingly afraid and trembling" (Heb. 12:21). The writer of the Letter to the Hebrews reminds us that we have not come to that fearful mount of the law but to the throne of grace.

> The terrors of law and of God
> With me can have nothing to do;
> My Savior's obedience and blood
> Hide all my transgressions from view.
> —*Augustus M. Toplady*

114:5, 6 The psalmist is so delighted by these exhibitions of God's power that he teases the **sea**, the **Jordan**, the **mountains** and the **little hills** to explain why they acted as they did. The questions form a mild taunt song, smiling at some of the greatest symbols of power and stability in nature for recoiling at a glance from the Lord.

114:7, 8 The argument follows that the whole **earth** should have the profoundest reverence and respect for such a God. He is the ever-great I AM and at the same time He is the **God of Jacob**, the unworthy one. He **turned the rock into a pool of water, the flint into a fountain of waters.** It happened twice (Ex. 17:6; Num. 20:11). The people of Israel were completely disheartened by thirst. They complained bitterly and even wished they were back in Egypt. God miraculously provided **a pool of water** for them out of a rock, first at Horeb, then at Meribah. Paul tells us that the *rock* was a type of *Christ*, struck for us on Calvary and yielding life-giving water to all who come to Him in faith (1 Cor. 10:4).

Psalm 115: Israel Renounces Idols

The Jews have now returned from their exile in Babylon; they are back in their own land. But they do not take any credit for it to themselves. Their restoration is due solely to Jehovah. He did it because of His unfailing love for His people and because of His faithfulness to His promise.

115:1, 2 For too long the heathen have been taunting the Israelites. **"So where is** your **God?** He doesn't seem to be very interested in you when He leaves you to languish in captivity for seventy years!" But now they can't say this any more. Their scorn and ridicule have been silenced. God has vindicated His name.

115:3 It should be apparent now to all the world that the true **God** is transcendent—**"Our God is in heaven"** and He is sovereign—**"He does whatever He pleases."** The transcendence of God means that He is exalted above the universe, and has His being apart from it. The sovereignty of God means that He is free to do **whatever He pleases**, and what He pleases is always good, just and wise.

115:4–7 It was because of their idolatry that God allowed the Jews to be taken captive by the Babylonians. But now that they have learned the impotence and worthlessness of **idols**, they taunt the heathen for their graven images.

The **idols** are made of **silver and gold**, and therefore their value is determined by conditions in the market place. They are manufactured by men and thus they are inferior to the ones who worship them. **They have mouths but they** cannot teach or predict the future. They have **eyes . . . but they do not see** the problems of their people. **They have ears but** no power to **hear** prayer. They have **noses . . . but they do not smell** the incense that is offered to them. **They have hands but** no power to feel. They have **feet . . . but they do not** move off their

pedestal. They can't even **mutter through their throat**.

115:8 Those who make them are like them. It is a settled principle in the spiritual realm that men become like the object of their worship. Their moral standards are shaped by their god. **Everyone who trusts in** images becomes impure, feeble, obtuse and uncomprehending.

115:9 Only Jehovah is worthy of trust. So now a soloist steps forward and calls **Israel** to a life of unswerving **trust in the Lord**. The choir responds with the confession—**He is their help and their shield.**

115:10, 11 Next the priestly **house of Aaron** is exhorted to put its faith unreservedly **in the Lord**; the choir again responds with the acknowledgment that **He is their** tested and proven **help** and Defender. The third time the precentor widens his appeal to all **who fear the Lord**, possibly including Gentile converts as well. They too know that **He is their** true **help and their shield**.

115:12–15 It sounds as if the priests take up the song next, assuring the people that **the** same **Lord** who **has been mindful** of the nation in restoring their fortunes **will bless** them—the people, the priests, the proselytes, those of every age, rank, class and condition. They pray that God **will bless** His people and their descendants with **increase**—probably thinking of numerical increase for a nation whose ranks were depleted. But the prayer could also include spiritual and material prosperity. In addition they invoke the general blessing of **the Lord**, the One **who made heaven and earth**.

115:16 God made **the heavens** as His own dwelling place, but He assigned **the earth** as a place for **men** to live. And in this place man can worship and serve Him.

115:17, 18 Verse 17 mirrors the common view of OT saints that death ends a man's ability to **praise the LORD**. As far as they knew, **the dead** are in a condition of stony silence. We now know that those who die in faith pass immediately into the presence of the Lord. Though their bodies lie silent in the grave, yet their spirits are unfettered in worship and adoration of the Lord. But the climax of their argument is valid for us—that is, that we should bless the Lord while we are alive. And that is the vow with which the Psalm closes:

We will bless the LORD from this
  time forth and forevermore.
Praise the LORD!

Psalm 116: I Love the Lord!

The joy and gladness of the first Easter morning are singing throughout the Psalm. The garden tomb is empty. Christ has been raised from the dead by the glory of His Father. And now He bursts forth in a song of thanksgiving to God for answered prayer in connection with His Resurrection.

116:1–4 Notice how He begins: **"I love the LORD."** Only four monosyllables, yet the purest worship. To timid souls who mistakenly think that God can only be approached in grandiose language, it should be a tremendous encouragement to know that the simplest statement of love for the Lord is genuine worship.

But we need not stop there. Like the Savior, we can go on to recite the great things that God has done for us. This too is worship. The Lord Jesus overflowed with ceaseless thanks because His Father had **heard** His anguished **supplications** from Gethsemane and Golgotha. When **death** was tightening its ropes around Him, and **the pangs** of physical dissolution

were laying **hold of** Him, when He was enduring agony beyond description, then He called to **the LORD** to **deliver** Him. And the Lord did. He did not save Him from dying, but He did save Him out of death.

116:5, 6 A third element of worship is found in telling out the excellencies of the Lord. The risen Christ here lists some of the virtues of God which were displayed in His Resurrection. God is **gracious**, that is, kind and good. God is **righteous**; all He does is just and fair. **God is merciful**; He is of great compassion. **The LORD preserves the simple**, which in the case of the Lord Jesus on the cross meant that He preserved the sincere, the guileless or the helpless. God saves His people when they are in danger.

116:7 Finally God deals **bountifully** with those who trust in Him—He is not miserly in His benefits. And so the Lord Jesus says, **"Return to your rest, O my soul."** His agitation, His anguish, His agony are over. God has heard Him and delivered Him. Now He enters into well-earned **rest**.

116:8–11 Our Lord next returns to a review of what His Father had done for Him. We learn from this that we need not fear to repeat ourselves in worship. God never tires to hear His children's praise. And the subject is worthy of endless repetition. Christ's heart was full of gratitude to the Father for His threefold deliverance: His **soul** was **delivered from** death; His **eyes** were delivered **from tears**; and His **feet** were delivered **from falling** or defeat. Now He walked **before the LORD in the land of the living**—a victor over sin, death, the grave, and Sheol.

The continuity of thought in verses 10, 11 is admittedly difficult. Perhaps the TEV catches the general meaning:

I kept on believing, even when I said, "I am completely crushed," even when I was afraid and said, "No one can be trusted."

His faith did not falter, even in the moment of His deepest agony, or when men proved how untrustworthy they were. What He said was not born out of distrust but out of deep conviction.

116:12, 13 And then there is a final element of worship, as expressed by the question, **"What shall I render to the LORD for all His benefits toward me?"** In our case, there can be no thought of repaying Him; any repayment we might make would be an insult to His grace. But there is an inborn desire to respond to His grace in some appropriate way. That way is to **take up the cup of salvation and call upon the name of the LORD**. To lift **up the cup of salvation** means to express thanksgiving to the Lord for saving us. Calling **upon the name of the LORD** means to make a special act of devotion in recognition of the greatness of His salvation.

116:14 The risen Savior was determined to **pay** His **vows to the LORD . . . in the presence of all His people**. These were **vows** of praise, worship and thanksgiving which He made before and during His passion. He **now** fulfills those **vows**.

116:15 Once again the flow of thought seems suddenly interrupted by the Lord's observation, **"Precious in the sight of the LORD is the death of His saints."** Even if we have difficulty fitting it into the context, we can still enjoy it as an isolated text. It is true of all **saints**—their death is **precious** to our God because it means they are with Him in glory. But it was never more true than in the case of the Lord Jesus. His death was **precious** to His Father because it provided a righteous basis upon which He could justify ungodly sinners.

116:16, 17 In verse 16, Jesus, the Risen One, is still "the Servant of Jehovah." It is as if He is saying, "I love my master . . . I will not go out free" (Ex. 21:5). And so He indentures Himself as a **servant** forever. As the Son of God's **maidservant**, He vows to serve God just as His mother Mary did, because Jehovah has **loosed** His **bonds**.

116:18, 19 Again He vows to **offer to** the Father **the sacrifice of thanksgiving, and . . . call upon the name of the LORD**. In the congregation of God's **people**, assembled at the temple in Jerusalem, the Lord Jesus **will** yet **pay** His **vows** as He leads them in a resounding chorus of praise **to the LORD**. This will take place when He returns to earth, the great Immanuel, to take the scepter of the universe in His nail-scarred hand.

Psalm 117: The Gentiles Glorify God

In this shortest chapter of the Bible, the **Gentiles** are called to **praise the LORD . . . for His merciful kindness** and enduring **truth**. The Apostle Paul grasped its significance and quoted verse 1 in Romans 15:11 to show that the Gentile nations share with Israel in the mercy of the Messiah. He came not only to confirm the promises given to the patriarchs but also that "the Gentiles might glorify God for His mercy."

The stately paraphrase gives us the message of the Psalm in lines of unusual beauty:

From all that dwell below the skies,
Let the Creator's praise arise;
Let the Redeemer's name be sung
Through every land, by every tongue.

Eternal are Thy mercies, Lord;
Eternal truth attends Thy word;
Thy praise shall sound from shore to shore,
Till suns shall rise and set no more.
—*Isaac Watts*

Psalm 118: Behold Your King!

The occasion of this magnificent chorus of praise is the Second Coming of our Lord and Savior, Jesus Christ. The scene is Jerusalem where the crowds have gathered to celebrate the Advent of Israel's long-awaited Messiah. In the shadow of the temple, a soloist takes his place at the microphone, the choir standing behind him. A hush comes over the audience.

118:1	SOLOIST:	**Oh, give thanks to the LORD, for He is good!**
	CHOIR:	**For His mercy endures forever.**
		(All over the audience heads are nodding in hearty assent.)
118:2	SOLOIST:	**Let Israel now say,**
	CHOIR:	**"His mercy endures forever."**
118:3	SOLOIST:	**Let the house of Aaron now say,**
	CHOIR:	**"His mercy endures forever."**
		(Deep-throated "Amens" rise from the priests who are standing at the temple door.)
118:4	SOLOIST:	**Let those who fear the LORD now say,**
	CHOIR:	**"His mercy endures forever."**
		(At this, a company of God-fearing Gentiles bite their lips and fight back tears of gratitude for the grace that enables them to share in the glory of this moment.)
118:5–9	SOLOIST:	**I called on the LORD in distress;**
		The LORD answered me and set me in a broad place.
		The LORD is on my side; I will not fear.
		What can man do to me?
		The LORD is for me among those who help me;
		Therefore I shall see my desire on those who hate me.
		It is better to trust in the LORD
		Than to put confidence in man.
		It is better to trust in the LORD
		Than to put confidence in princes.
		(The crowd understands that this is the language of the faithful remnant of Israel, marvelously preserved by God during the Tribulation Period. They have learned to trust in God alone, and have lost their fear of men. At last they realize that **it is better to trust in the LORD than** even **in princes,** that is, the best of men.)
118:10	SOLOIST:	**All nations surrounded me,**
	CHOIR:	**But in the name of the LORD I will destroy them.**
118:11	SOLOIST:	**They surrounded me, yes, they surrounded me;**
	CHOIR:	**But in the name of the LORD I will destroy them.**
118:12	SOLOIST:	**They surrounded me like bees;**
		They were quenched like a fire of thorns;
		(Thornbushes make a spectacular blaze but die down quickly.)
	CHOIR:	**For in the name of the LORD I will destroy them.**

118:13, 14   SOLOIST: You pushed me violently, that I might fall, But the LORD helped me.
The LORD is my strength and song.
And He has become my salvation.

(The soloist is referring in verse 13 to the Antichrist and to his bestial treatment of the remnant for their refusal to buckle under to his demands. In the nick of time the Lord intervened and cast the false messiah into the lake of fire [Rev. 19:19, 20].)

118:15, 16   SOLOIST: The voice of rejoicing and salvation
Is in the tents of the righteous;

(All over Israel there is unrestrained jubilation over the triumph of the Messiah. In every home the people are singing the following song of victory.)

CHOIR: The right hand of the LORD does valiantly.
The right hand of the LORD is exalted;
The right hand of the LORD does valiantly.

118:17, 18   SOLOIST: I shall not die, but live,
And declare the works of the LORD.
The LORD has chastened me severely,
But He has not given me over to death.

(Speaking as the remnant, the soloist recalls the many pogroms against the Jews and their close calls with extinction. But the Lord miraculously rescued them from the mouth of the lion, and now they face the future with confidence and security.)

118:19, 20   SOLOIST: Open to me the gates of righteousness;
I will go through them,
And I will praise the LORD.

(Redeemed Israel seeks admission to the temple courts in order to offer sacrifices of thanksgiving to the Lord. The sacrificial system will be partially reinstituted during Christ's reign with the sacrifices looking back to Calvary, that is, they will be commemorative.)

CHOIR: This is the gate of the LORD;
Through which the righteous shall enter.

(These are the words of those Levites who are doorkeepers at the temple. They explain that **this gate** belongs to Jehovah and is for the use of those godly ones who wish to draw near to Him.)

118:21, 22   SOLOIST: I will praise You,
For You have answered me,
And have become my salvation.

(Israel acclaims the Lord Jesus Christ as her Savior.)

CHOIR: The stone which the builders rejected
Has become the chief cornerstone.

(The Lord Jesus is **the stone. The builders** were the

Jewish people, and especially their leaders, who rejected Him at His First Advent. Now the people of Israel confess what Parker calls "the stupidity of the specialists" as they see the despised Nazarene crowned with glory and honor. The rejected stone has become the Headstone of the corner [ASV]. There is some question as to whether the headstone is:

1. the cornerstone of a building.
2. the keystone of an arch.
3. the topmost stone of a pyramid.

Whichever is the correct view, the context demands the thought of highest honor.)

118:23   **This was the Lord's doing;**
            It is marvelous in our eyes.
            (The choir represents Israel as acknowledging that it is Jehovah who has given the Lord Jesus His proper place in the hearts and affections of His people. The crowning day has come at last!)

118:24   **This is the day the Lord has made;**
            We will rejoice and be glad in it.
            (Barnes writes: "As if it were a new day, made for this very occasion, a day which the people did not expect to see, and which seemed therefore to have been created out of the ordinary course, and added to the other days."[79])

118:25   **Save now, I pray, O Lord;**
            O Lord, I pray, send now prosperity!
            (This is the verse which the people of Jerusalem quoted at the time of Christ's so-called triumphal entry; "Hosanna" is the original word for "Save now" [Matt. 21:9]. But they soon changed their welcome to a call for His execution. Now, however, Israel is welcoming the Lord in the day of His power, and their sentiments are both sincere and lasting.)

118:26   SOLOIST: **Blessed is he who comes in the name of the Lord;**
            (As the Lord approaches the temple area, the chief singer chants the blessing of the people in clarion tones. It is an historic moment. Centuries before, Jesus had warned the people of Israel that they would not see Him again until they said, "Blessed is he who comes in the name of the Lord" [Matt. 23:39]. Now at last they gladly acknowledge Him as their Messiah and King.)

            CHOIR: **We have blessed you from the house of the Lord.**
            (Perhaps this is the blessing of the priests, standing inside the door of the temple.)

118:27   God is the LORD, and He has given us light;
          Bind the sacrifice with cords to the horns of the altar.
          (The congregation of Israel worships Jesus as God
          and as the One who has brought light to their
          darkened hearts. As the procession moves toward
          the brazen altar, with Him at the forefront, they call
          for **cords** to **bind the sacrifice**.)

118:28, 29 SOLOIST: You are my God, and I will praise You;
          You are my God, I will exalt You.
          (The Lord Jesus Christ is confessed as God by a
          people who formerly used His name as a by-word.)

          CHOIR: Oh, give thanks to the LORD, for He is good;
          For His mercy endures forever.
          (The song has risen to a crescendo of deep, deep
          praise and worship. The music reverberates through
          the surrounding streets of old Jerusalem. Then as it
          dies away, the people return to their dwellings to
          enjoy the wonderful thousand-year kingdom of the
          glorious Lord whose right it is to reign.)

Psalm 119: All About the Bible

This has been called the golden
alphabet of the Bible. The reason is
that it is divided into twenty-two
sections, one for each letter of the
Hebrew alphabet. Each section has
eight verses and every verse in a
section begins with the corresponding
Hebrew letter. Thus in the Hebrew,
every verse in the first section begins
with Aleph; in the second section every
verse begins with Beth; and so on.

In the NKJV, all but four verses in
this longest Psalm contain some title
or description of the Word of God.
The four exceptions are verses 84,
121, 122 and 132. The names used to
describe God's Word are: law, testimonies, ways, precepts, statutes, commandments, ordinances, word(s),
promise, judgments, faithfulness, appointment, justice and commands.

By using the alphabet in this acrostic form, Ridout feels that the writer
may have been suggesting that "all
the possibilities of human language
are exhausted in setting forth the

fullness and perfection of the Word
of God."[80] We have a similar suggestion in the NT. Our Lord speaks of
Himself as the Alpha and Omega
(Rev. 1:8). These are, of course, the
first and last words of the Greek
alphabet. The thought is that He is
everything of goodness and perfection that can be expressed by every
letter of the alphabet, arranged in
every possible combination.

No two verses in the Psalm say exactly the same thing. There is some different shade of meaning in every one.

Concerning the 119th Psalm, C. S.
Lewis said:

The poem is not, and does not pretend to be, a sudden outpouring of
the heart like, say Psalm 18. It is a
pattern, a thing done like embroi-
dery, stitch by stitch, through long,
quiet hours, for love of the subject
and for the delight in leisurely, disciplined craftsmanship.[81]

The following subject headings for
the various sections of the Psalm are
based primarily on F. W. Grant's notes:

In an eminent sense, the Psalm expresses the love for the Word of God which our Savior experienced as a Man here on earth. Also Bellett suggests that "in its full prophetic character [this Psalm] will be the language of the true Israel on their return to God and His long neglected oracles."[82]

119:1 The **blessed** or happy man is the one whose life is conformed to the Word of **the LORD**. Even if he sins and fails, there is provision in the Word for confession and restoration, and this keeps him in an **undefiled** condition.

119:2 It is obedience to **His testimonies** that counts—not a reluctant, half-hearted, feet-dragging obedience, but a deep, enormous desire to please **Him with the whole heart**!

119:3 Negatively, happiness is found in separation from every form of **iniquity**. Positively it is following the route He has mapped out for us in the Scriptures. The surest way to abstain from evil is to be completely occupied with doing good.

119:4 God's **precepts** are not options but *commandments*, and they are not to be kept haphazardly but **diligently**.

119:5 The psalmist now moves from what is true in general to what he wants to be true in his own life. In moving insensibly from precept to prayer, he acknowledges that the desire as well as the power to be steadfast in obedience must come ultimately from God.

119:6 As long as he keeps all the statutes of the Lord, he will be spared from the shame that tortures the mind, crimsons the cheek and even at times makes the body squirm.

119:7 "From prayer to praise is not a long or difficult journey." Those who **learn** to obey **God's righteous** ordinances have fullness of joy and this leads to spontaneous adoration.

119:8 Firm resolve is coupled with humble dependence. The psalmist is determined to follow hard after the Lord. But he realizes his own inadequacy. The prayer **"Do not forsake me utterly"** is not so much a possible actuality as a statement of what the writer feels he might deserve.

119:9 One of the most crucial problems in the life of every **young man** is how to keep pure. The answer is by practical obedience to the words of the Bible.

119:10 In the matter of holiness, there is a curious merging of human desire (**With my whole heart I have sought You**), and divine empowering (**Oh, let me not wander from Your commandments**).

119:11 He does not make us holy against our will or without our cooperation. Someone has wisely said, "The best book in the world is the Bible. The best place to put it is **in the heart**. The best reason for putting it there is that it saves us from sinning **against** God."

119:12 Because God is so great and so gracious, the renewed nature desires to learn His **statutes** and be molded by them. The love of Christ constrains us!

119:13 Deep delight in the treasures of the Word leads inevitably to the desire to share them with others. It is a law of life that when we really believe something, we want to pass it on.

119:14 No prospector was ever more pleased with his nuggets of gold than the one who searches out the hidden wealth of the Scriptures.

119:15 God's Word provides endless resource material for the most satisfying meditation, but this should never be divorced from the determination to be doers of the Word.

119:16 "His commandments are not burdensome" (1 Jn. 5:3). Whoever is born of God **will delight** in the **statutes** of the Lord and determine to keep them in constant remembrance.

119:17 Without Him we can do nothing. We need His grace for living and also for obeying His **word**. Let us ask for plenteous grace since our need is so great.

119:18 The Bible abounds with **wondrous**, spiritual goodies which are hidden from the casual glance. Our **eyes** need to be opened to see them.

119:19 The Bible is a road map that guides the pilgrim unerringly to his destination.

119:20 It is good when our thirst for the Scriptures is enormous and unflagging. The psalmist's **soul** was eaten up with longing for the Word, and he had this ardent, intense longing **at all times**.

119:21 History teems with instances of how **the proud** and insolent have defied the Lord's **commandments** and soon were brought down by the mighty hand of God.

119:22 The believer is scorned and ridiculed by the world. "They think it strange that you do not run with them in the same flood of dissipation, speaking evil of you" (1 Pet. 4:4). But integrity will be rewarded, and His "well done" will more than compensate for **reproach and contempt**.

119:23 Even when those in positions of authority collaborate in vilifying the Christian, he can find strength and solace in meditating on the Bible, "answering his traducers by not answering them at all."

119:24 Matthew Henry comments:

Was David at a loss what to do when the princes spoke against him? God's statutes were his counsellors, and they counselled him to bear it patiently and commit his cause to God.[83]

119:25 Life has its valleys as well as its mountaintops. Even when we are cast down in sorrow, we can call on the Lord to **revive** us through the restoring power of the **word**.

119:26 When we tell of our **ways**, that is, make open confession of our sins, the Lord answers us by forgiving. This leads to a renewed desire for holiness, as expressed in the prayer, **"Teach me Your statutes!"**

119:27 We need to understand the meaning of God's **precepts** and how to apply them practically in our lives. This will lead to meditation on God's **wonderful works**.

119:28 In the dark spots of life, when our **soul melts** in tears, the God of all comfort bends low and often with a single verse of Scripture lifts us and strengthens us to go on.

119:29 By the Spirit of God and through the Word of God, we can distinguish between truth and error. The Bible inculcates a holy hatred for every form of **lying**. It also teaches us that truth is what God says about a thing (John 17:17).

119:30 No one drifts into holiness. It requires a deliberate choice of **the way of truth** as revealed in the sacred Scriptures. Spurgeon says, "The commands of God must be set before us as the mark to aim at, the model to work by, and the road to walk in."

119:31 The psalmist had adhered to the **testimonies** of God as if he had been glued to them. But he still realizes his proneness to wander, and cries to the LORD in conscious dependence.

119:32 It is when God gives us big hearts, not big heads, that we hasten to keep His commandments. It is more a matter of the affections than of the intellect.

119:33 We should pray for instruction. As students in the school of God, we should be eager to learn how to translate precept into practice, and determine to obey His Word **to the end** of our lives.

119:34 We should pray for **understanding**. It is important to have right views of the Scriptures, of their meaning and obligations. How else can we follow Him with undivided devotedness?

119:35 We should pray for guidance. The spirit is willing but the flesh is weak. So we want the Lord to guide our feet in **the path of** His will, because that is the only way in which we are truly happy.

119:36 We should pray for spiritual rather than material enrichment. "Godliness with contentment is great gain" (1 Tim. 6:6). It is a miracle of grace that takes the love of money from a man and replaces it with a love for the Bible.

119:37 We should pray for divine realities, not shadows. Here is God's commentary on TV: **"Turn away my eyes from looking at worthless things."** TV depicts a never-never land, a world that doesn't exist. God's Word deals with life as it really is.

119:38 We should pray for God to **establish** His promise. "All the rivers of Thy grace I claim; over every promise write my name." Our claim to His promises lies in the fact that we fear Him.

119:39 We should pray to be kept from **reproach**, from anything that would bring shame or dishonor on the name of the Lord Jesus. His **judgments are good**; we need to follow them faithfully.

119:40 We should pray for personal revival. "The parched ground shall become a pool, and the thirsty land springs of water" (Isa. 35:7). As we burn and **long for** His **precepts**, He will **revive** us **in** His **righteousness**.

119:41 We must not take God's **mercies** and **salvation** for granted. We are as dependent on His compassion and protection as when we were first saved. So we claim His promise to care for and keep us day by day.

119:42 Undeniable proofs of the Lord's answers to prayer serve to silence the **reproaches** of unbelievers. Our faith is based on the **word** of God which can never fail.

119:43 May we never be afraid or ashamed to speak **the word of truth**. If we **have hoped in** God's **ordinances**, He will provide continuing opportunities to witness for Him.

119:44 Our response to His love and grace should be an inflexible resolve to **keep** His Word as long as we live. "How can I do less than give Him my best and live for Him completely after all He's done for me?"

119:45 Those who are set free by the Son of God are free indeed (John 8:36). The world thinks of the Christian life as a system of bondage. But those who **seek** His **precepts** are the ones who enjoy perfect **liberty**.

119:46 Faith gives boldness to **speak** for Jesus in the presence of **kings**. How many potentates have heard the Good News from humble and often despised subjects!

119:47 Those who love the Bible find deep personal enjoyment in its pages. It is a fountain of **delight**, a river of pleasure, a never-failing source of satisfaction.

119:48 We revere the Bible in the sense that we stand in awe of its scope, its depths, its power, its treasures and its infinity. We **love** it for what it is and for what it has done. And we **meditate** in it by day and by night.

119:49 It is not possible that God could ever forget His promise, but in the furnace of affliction, when faith has its lapses, we are permitted to pray, "Lord, **remember . . .**" "He cannot have taught us to trust in His name, and thus far have led us to put us to shame."

119:50 Those who have experienced the quickening powers of the **word** find it an unfailing source of **comfort**. The words of well-meaning men are often empty and unavailing but God's Word is always living, relevant and effective.

119:51 If we are faithful to the Lord, we can expect to receive our share of mocking and sneering **derision**, but when we have found divine principles, we should stick with them.

119:52 We are encouraged by the memory of how the Lord has intervened for us in the past. The same mercy that has brought us this far will certainly take us the rest of the way. "His love in times past forbids us to think He'll leave us at last in darkness to sink."

119:53 It causes the believer burning **indignation** to see God's law being dishonored and disobeyed. It was true of the Lord Jesus: "The reproaches of those who reproached You fell on Me" (Rom. 15:3). Any dishonor to the Father was taken as a personal insult by the Son.

119:54 Thanks to the wonderful Word of God, the pilgrim can sing **in the house of** his **pilgrimage**, or, as Knox put it, "in a land of exile." The way may be rough but it cannot be long. The night may be dark but God gives a song.

119:55 The seemingly interminable hours of a sleepless **night** can be redeemed by musing on the Lord as He is revealed in the Word. The more we get to know Him, the more we love Him, and loving Him, we want to **keep** His **law**.

119:56 Obedience is a blessing. "Godliness is profitable for all things, since it holds promise for the present life and also for the life to come" (1 Tim. 4:8).

119:57 The realization of what an incomparable treasure we have in the Lord should make us vow to **keep** His **words**. He is the All-sufficient One. To have Him is to be fabulously wealthy.

119:58 Though He is all-sufficient, we are not. "Our sufficiency is from

God" (2 Cor. 3:5). So we must be people of prayer, entreating God's **favor** and claiming His promise of mercy.

119:59   Guidance is a perennial problem. Which way should we go? Frankly, we don't have the wisdom in ourselves to know. All right, then. Let us turn our **feet** to the paths outlined in the Scriptures.

119:60   We live in a day of instant foods, instant service and instant this and that. Instant obedience to the revealed will of God is something to ponder—and to produce.

119:61   **Wicked** men may conspire to trip up the innocent believer, but that is all the more reason for him to remember the Word for guidance and protection.

119:62   "At midnight Paul and Silas were praying and singing hymns to God" (Acts 16:25). They were being unjustly treated by men but they could still sing about God's **righteous judgments**.

119:63   Those who love God love His people. And those who love the Bible love all Bible-lovers. It is a world-wide fellowship that transcends national, social, and racial distinctions.

119:64   God's steadfast love can be found anywhere in the world, but more than that, **the earth . . . is** *full* **of** it. Our grateful hearts respond by saying, "Lord, keep me teachable by Your Holy Spirit."

119:65   How long is it since I have thanked the Lord for the wonderful way He has treated me **according to** the promise of His **word**? "Count your blessings: name them one by one; and it will surprise you what the Lord has done!"

119:66   We all need to pray for **good judgment** as well as **knowledge**. It is possible to have knowledge without discernment and without balance. From the Word and from the disciplines of life we learn sound judgment.

119:67   God's discipline "yields the peaceable fruit of righteousness to those who have been trained by it" (Heb. 12:11). The memory of what our wanderings cost us serves as a healthy deterrent against repeating them.

119:68   The English words "God" and **"good"** may have a common derivation. God is **good** and everything He does is **good**. To become good we must take His yoke upon us and learn of Him.

119:69   When ungodly men try to ruin our reputation with lies, we can find protection in faithful, unfaltering obedience to the Bible.

119:70   Let the worldling wallow in luxury and pleasure. We find our satisfaction in spiritual instruction rather than in sensual indulgence.

119:71   Sufferings are only for a moment but the benefits of suffering are forever. Men intend their persecution to harm us; God overrules it for good.

119:72   The Bible is the most valuable material possession we have in the world. A computer can add up fantastically large figures but it cannot record the value of the Scriptures.

119:73   Since God has **made** us by such marvelous skill, what is more reasonable than that He should be our Teacher as well. We should find out His purpose in creating us and fulfill it to the hilt.

119:74   There is keen spiritual refreshment in meeting a Christian who is on fire for the Lord Jesus. Those who hope in God's Word become radioactive with the Holy Spirit.

119:75   Sickness, suffering and affliction do not come directly from God, but He permits them under certain circumstances and then harnesses them for His own goals. It is a mark of spiritual maturity when we vindicate Him for His justice and **faithfulness** in them all.

119:76 And yet in ourselves we are weak as dust, and we need His compassionate love to sustain us. "Let us therefore come boldly to the throne of grace, that we may obtain mercy and find grace to help in time of need" (Heb. 4:16).

119:77 Every display of the **tender mercies** of God is like a fresh transfusion of life to the hard-pressed saint. Those who **delight** in His **law** may have confidence that He will **come** alongside to help.

119:78 Gelineau translates verse 78, "Shame the **proud** who harm me with lies, while I ponder **your precepts**." God allows sin to work itself out and the psalmist is merely praying for God to do as He has said He would.

119:79 It is a spiritual instinct to seek the fellowship of **those who know** and love the Word of God. But how often do we ask the Lord to lead **those who fear God** across our pathway?

119:80 There are many reasons why we should desire to **be blameless** in obeying the **statutes** of the Lord. The one singled out by the psalmist here is that we might avoid the searing, scorching shame of falling into sin.

119:81 The believer may be afflicted but not crushed; perplexed but not driven to despair; persecuted but not forsaken; struck down but not destroyed (2 Cor. 4:8, 9). Here he languishes for God's saving help but **hope** is still alive.

119:82 Even though his **eyes** grow dim with **searching** for the fulfillment of God's promise of deliverance, he does not pray "Will you comfort me?" but rather **"When will you comfort me?"**

119:83 **A wineskin in** the **smoke** is shriveled and blackened. The simile explains itself. The harassed believer is wizened, parched, and unsightly through waiting, but he is not hopeless as long as he has the Word to fall back on.

119:84 Life at best is very brief. The **days** of affliction seem to occupy a disproportionate share. It is time for the Lord to act by punishing the oppressors.

119:85 The villains of this verse are godless and lawless; these two characteristics go together. They plot the downfall of the righteous and innocent—it is an evidence that they refuse to conform to God's **law**.

119:86 There is nothing as dependable as God's Word. He has promised to rescue His persecuted people. So when we are attacked by lying accusers, we can confidently use the "golden prayer," **"Help me!"**

119:87 Spurgeon said, "If we stick to the **precepts** we will be rescued by the promises." Even if we reach the place where we despair of life, we should never falter in our obedience. Help will come. Only believe!

119:88 The best prayer comes from a strong, inward necessity. Here the psalmist prays that the Lord will spare his life so that he can go forth to glorify God by obeying His Word.

119:89 Faith is not a leap in the dark. It is based upon the surest thing in the universe—the Bible. There is no risk in believing a word that is fixed firmly and **forever** in **heaven**.

119:90 The **faithfulness** of God is displayed not only in His Word but also in His works. It extends to all generations and is seen in the order and precision of nature.

119:91 Heaven and earth obey His laws. Seedtime and harvest, cold and heat, summer and winter, day and night **are all** God's **servants**. And all are regulated and sustained by His word of power.

119:92 Barnes comments:

"I should have sunk a thousand times," said a most excellent, but much afflicted man to me, "if it had not been for one declaration in the Word of God, 'The Eternal God is thy refuge, and underneath are the ever-lasting arms.'"[84]

119:93 Those who have experienced the power of the Scriptures in their lives are not likely to **forget** them. We were "born again, not of corruptible seed but incorruptible, through the word of God which lives and abides forever" (1 Pet. 1:23).

119:94 Even after we have been saved from the penalty of sin, we still need to be saved day by day from defilement and damage. Acquaintance with God's **precepts** and with our own hearts makes us aware of the need of this present-tense salvation.

119:95 The only way to avoid the attacks of **the wicked** is to lead a petty, inconsequential life. As long as our lives are effective for Him, we can expect opposition. But we find strength and solace when we **consider** God's **testimonies**.

119:96 The very best things in this world fall short of **perfection** and come to an end, but the Word of God is perfect and infinite. The more we get to know the Bible, the more we realize how far short we ourselves come.

119:97 Those who **love** the Lord will certainly love His Word as well. And this love will be manifested in musing on the Bible at every opportunity. It is in moments of meditation that we suddenly discover new beauties and wonders in the Scriptures.

119:98 The humble believer, equipped with the wisdom of the Word, can see more on his knees than his **enemies** can on their tiptoes.

119:99 If the teacher becomes complacent and rests on his laurels, he will soon be surpassed by a younger man who constantly meditates on the Word.

119:100 This may sound like irresponsible boasting, but not so. It is not a person's age or intelligence that matters, but his obedience. So the youth may outstrip the aged if he has a higher OQ (Obedience Quotient).

119:101 Here we have obedience in action. The psalmist restrains his **feet from** paths of sin in order that he might obey to his utmost.

119:102 The sanctifying influence of the Bible is great. **Taught** by the Lord through its pages, we develop a hatred for sin and a love for holiness.

119:103 And then, of course, the Bible is a source of sheer enjoyment. No other book in the world is as pleasurable. **Honey** is **sweet** but God's Word is **sweeter**.

119:104 In order to detect counterfeit money, people study genuine bills. So a deep acquaintance with the truth enables us to detect and despise **every false way**.

119:105 The **word** guides negatively by forbidding certain behavior patterns. And it guides positively by showing the right way. How much we owe to the friendly beams of this **lamp**!

119:106 Here is a holy determination to obey the Holy Scriptures. This is for the glory of God, for the blessing of others, and for our own good as well.

119:107 Spurgeon says:

In the previous verse the psalmist had been sworn in as a soldier of the Lord, and in this verse he is called to suffer hardness in that capacity. The service of the Lord does not screen us from trial, but rather secures it for us.[85]

119:108 We come before the Lord as priests and as pupils. As priests we "offer the sacrifice of praise to God, that is, the fruit of lips, giving thanks to his name" (Heb. 13:15). As pupils, we open our hearts and minds to His divine instruction.

119:109 When our **life** is constantly in danger, there is safety and security in remembering the **law** of the Lord. The tendency to panic, to become hysterical, and to forget God's Word must be avoided at any cost.

119:110 Those who are instructed in the Word are not ignorant of Satan's designs. By simple obedience to the Bible, they avoid his booby-traps.

119:111 The Scriptures are to be chosen as a prized possession, as a **heritage** of vast value. Think of the joy that comes to an heir when he inherits a fortune. How much greater joy should be ours in possessing the Book of books.

119:112 All who realize its worth should determine to obey it **to the very end** of life's day. There should be no vacations, no time off in the school of obedience.

119:113 Moffat translates this verse, "I hate men who are half and half. I love thy law." **Double-minded** people are for God one minute and for the world the next. They can speak out of both corners of their mouth and are traitors to the **law** of God.

119:114 The Lord is our **hiding place** when we are pursued and our **shield** when we are being directly attacked. Those who **hope in** His promise will never be disappointed because He cannot deceive or be deceived.

119:115 We part company with those who do not **keep the commandments of** our **God**. But while we separate from their sinful ways, we still maintain contact with men of the world in order to share the Good News with them.

119:116 The argument of this prayer is: "You have promised to uphold me. Now do as You have said. Otherwise people would say that You have failed me, and I would be disappointed in **my hope.**"

119:117 We are no more able to keep ourselves **safe** than we were to save ourselves in the first place. If God holds us **up**, we **shall be safe**. But our part is to keep His **statutes continually**.

119:118 The Lord spurns those who **stray from** His **statutes**. Their cleverness will one day appear in its true light as stupidity.

119:119 The Word clearly teaches that God will cast **away all the wicked of the earth** like a refiner casts off the scum that rises to the surface of the molten metal. If He did not deal righteously with sin, we could not respect His written Word.

119:120 When we think of God's **judgments** on the wicked, we might well tremble. But also as Barnes says, we are "filled with awe at the strictness, the spirituality, the severity of His law."

119:121 The psalmist's plea that he had done what was just and right must be understood as a general rule and not an invariable one. His righteous life was the fruit of His salvation and therefore a proper basis to ask the Lord **not** to abandon him **to** his **oppressors**.

119:122 A **surety** is one who stands for another, who represents him. He who was our surety at Calvary pleads our cause successfully through all of life and restrains the arrogant oppressor.

119:123 Here is a man who looked for God's deliverance till his **eyes** were sore. He waited till exhausted for the fulfillment of the **righteous** promise that the Lord would intervene for him.

119:124 In spite of what might seem like a plea for justice in verse 121, he here casts himself on the **mercy** or grace of the Lord. One form of His **mercy** is His gracious teaching ministry. **"Teach me Your statutes."**

119:125 The more a **servant** knows about his master, the more useful and effective he can be. So we need **understanding** to **know** the mind of God as it is revealed in His **testimonies**.

119:126 This is an about-face. The servant is now indirectly calling on the Master to **act**, for His **law** has been broken. And this is the cry of God's people in every time of darkness, **"It is time for You to act, O LORD!"**

119:127 One index of how precious the Bible is to us is the amount of time we spend reading it. If we value it above **fine gold**, its cover will be worn and its pages frayed.

119:128 Another proof of our esteem for the Book will be the degree to which we obey it. Unless we do what it says and **hate every false way**, we are deceiving ourselves.

119:129 God's Word is **wonderful** in its timelessness, its purity, its accuracy, its harmony, its universal relevance, its power and its sufficiency. Such a book deserves to be read and heeded.

119:130 **The entrance of** the Word **gives light**, whether to nations, families, or individuals. We little realize the sanctifying influence it has had throughout the world. **It gives understanding to** those who acknowledge themselves to be **simple** and therefore in need of help.

119:131 A deep, enormous thirst for the Word of God is what we all need. "As newborn babes, desire the pure milk of the Word" (1 Pet. 2:2).

119:132 We may tire of these repeated pleas for mercy, but the psalmist didn't, and neither does God. We never get to the place in this life where we are beyond the need of His grace.

119:133 Here are the two sides of the coin of holiness—to be kept going on steadily for the Lord in accordance with His **word**, and to be delivered from the power of indwelling sin.

119:134 The first part of this prayer is not unusual; any of us would want to be delivered from man's **oppression**. But notice the unusual purpose, **"that I may keep Your precepts."**

119:135 In our service for the Lord, we may ask Him for some token of His favor, presence, and power. He knows how to drop encouraging bonuses in answer to our prayer. And we should never lose the desire to be taught more and more.

119:136 Tears flowing like **rivers of water**—a dramatic expression for the deepest anguish and sorrow! And for what? For injustice to the psalmist himself? No, for man's disregard of God's **law** and thus dishonor to His name.

Bendetti, . . . author of "Stabat Mater," one day was found weeping, and when asked the reason of his tears, replied, "I weep because Love goes about unloved."[86]

119:137 The Author of the Book is **righteous**, so it is not surprising that the Book is **upright** too. Most of us know this, but how few of us turn it into an act of praise and worship by thanking the LORD.

119:138 Everything God says is **righteous** and **faithful**, and His Word is completely trustworthy. To believe God's Word is not a meritorious act. It is just common sense.

119:139 Barnes comments with insight:

It is a great triumph in a man's soul when, in looking on the conduct of persecutors, calumniators and slanderers, he is more grieved because they violate the law of God than because they injure him.[87]

119:140 The Bible has been well tried. Thousands have tested its promises and found them true. "It has survived the hatred of men, the fires of spurious priesthood, the sneers of infidels, and the carnal wisdom of modern critics" (Scripture Union).

119:141 In the estimation of his enemies, the psalmist was **small and despised**. But man's scorn did not scare him away from clinging to the Bible.

119:142 God's **righteousness** is not a passing mood but an **everlasting** virtue. It is not enough to say that the Bible contains truth; the Bible **is truth**. Every utterance of God is true.

119:143 The writer had a full cup of **trouble and anguish**, but with the Word of God, he could trace the rainbow through his tears.

119:144 It is not only that God's **testimonies** are righteous now; they always will be. The more we understand them, the greater is our capacity for enjoying life, both now and in heaven.

119:145 The word **"cry"** is the key of this section.[88] Here we have an appeal for help from a trusting heart. Almighty God cannot resist prayers that come from a whole heart and that express a desire to do His will.

119:146 When, like Peter, we begin to sink beneath the waves, we can always send up that short prayer **"Save me."** The Lord then raises us up to go forth and live for Him again.

119:147 Weigle writes, "This is a description of the devotional habits of a pious (man) who rises before dawn to begin his day with meditation and prayer." Our motto should be, "No Bible, no breakfast."

119:148 Even the sleepless hours of the **night** can be utilized for meditation on the Word. Not uncommonly, that is when the Lord gives us "the treasures of darkness."

119:149 We should never get over the wonderful fact that we have instant access to the presence of God in prayer. Like the psalmist, we can plead God's **lovingkindness** and **justice** to preserve our lives.

119:150 The enemy is **near**. They are intent on harm for God's servant. Having rejected the authority of God's **law** over their lives, they will seemingly stop at nothing.

119:151 But the LORD is **near**, and one with God is a majority. "No foe can harm us, no fear alarm us, on the victory side." God's word is true, and He will never forsake His own.

119:152 It is a tremendous comfort to know that God's Word stands forever. "Standing on the promises that cannot fail, when the howling storms of doubt and fear assail; by the living Word of God we shall prevail; standing on the promises of God."

119:153 The Lord really does look on our **affliction**. "In every pang that rends the heart, the Man of Sorrows has a part." And He comes to **deliver** those who cling to Him and to His Word.

119:154 The writer asks God to serve as His advocate and His lifegiver. Grievous charges have been made against him; he needs a defender. He has been persecuted to the point of exhaustion; he needs a new infusion of life.

119:155 God does not save men against their will. He will not populate heaven with people who don't want to be there. There is no **salvation** for those who refuse to listen to the Word.

119:156 No human language could ever be adequate to describe the mercy of God. His **tender mercies** can never be exhausted by our requests. The persecuted psalmist asks for the mercy of life, that is, deliverance from his would-be slayers.

119:157 Many of these verses find their true fulfillment in the Lord Jesus, of course. Surrounded by **persecutors and enemies**, still He remained faithful to the **testimonies** of His Father.

119:158 It is a mark of spiritual maturity to grieve more over insults to God than over wrongs to oneself. Oh, to be thus consumed with zeal for the Lord!

119:159 In verse 153, the psalmist wrote, "Consider my affliction." Here, as Spurgeon points out, he says, in effect, "Consider my affection," that is, affection for the precepts. Also he asks, for the third time in this section, for the preservation of his life (vv. 154, 156).

119:160 God's **word is truth** in its **entirety**. Every promise in it is sure of fulfillment. "Till heaven and earth pass away, one jot or one tittle will by no means pass from the Law till all is fulfilled" (Matt. 5:18).

119:161 Men in places of authority have often oppressed God's servants. But a deep respect and **awe** for the **word** of God preserves the faithful from turning traitor to the Lord.

119:162 The thrill of discovering a hidden cache of **treasure** is experienced by the one who delves into the Bible and finds wonderful spiritual riches.

119:163 Acquaintance with the Word teaches us to **love** what God loves (the **law**) and **hate** what He hates (**lying**). We come to think God's thoughts after Him.

119:164 Since **seven** is the number of perfection or completeness, we understand the psalmist to mean that he praised the Lord continually and wholeheartedly for His **righteous** ordinances.

119:165 The Word gives **peace** in a world of turmoil and safety from the power of temptation. The verse

doesn't mean that believers are immune from sorrow or trouble, but rather that by obeying the law, they avoid the pitfalls of sin.

119:166 Psalm 37:3 says, "Trust in the Lord, and do good." Here the psalmist says he had followed that advice. Faith comes first, then works are the fruit of faith.

119:167 The people in Malachi's day found obedience to be a weariness (Mal. 1:13). Not so the writer. He obeyed the Word and grew to **love** it more and more.

119:168 These last three verses in this section speak of practical obedience to the Bible. If it seems to be stretching a point to attribute them to the average believer, just think of them as the Words of our Savior and the problem vanishes.

119:169 As the Psalm comes to a close, it seems to rise to a crescendo of fervent petition. The word **"let"** is found seven times. First there is the urgent appeal for audience and then for true spiritual **understanding**.

119:170 The enemy never seems far away in these verses, and hence there is the reiterated plea for deliverance in accordance with the promise of the **word**.

119:171 Increased knowledge of God's **statutes** should not lead to pride and exaggerated self-esteem, but to **praise** and adoration of the Lord.

119:172 Instead of talking about trivia and matters of no lasting importance, we should discipline ourselves to talk about spiritual matters. **All** God's **commandments** are **righteousness** and tremendously worthwhile.

119:173 It is a lovely picture—the nail-scarred **hand** of Omnipotence reaching down from heaven to rescue a mere man but one who had deliberately chosen the Lord's **precepts** as his rule of life.

119:174 While enjoying the **salvation** of our souls as an accomplished fact, we long for salvation from the presence of sin when Jesus comes again. In the meantime we find great **delight** in reading and obeying the Bible.

119:175 We are not only saved to serve, but even more directly to **praise**. Every deliverance from sickness or accident should give new momentum to our worship, and new urgency to our prayers for **help**.

119:176 This is one of the few confessions of sin in the Psalm. "The loftiest flights of holy rapture must ever come back to a lowly confession of sin and unworthiness."

Psalm 120: The Helpless Victim of Slander

One of the bitter experiences of a believer's life is to be the victim of lies and slander. It is then he helplessly realizes the truth of Spurgeon's observation that "a lie can go around the world while truth is putting its boots on." He can easily become a twisted mass of humiliation and frustration.

120:1, 2 That was the kind of **distress** that sent the psalmist racing to **the LORD** in this first **"Song of Ascents."**[89] His request was short, simple and specific. He wanted to be delivered from the **lying lips** of his enemies, from the **deceitful tongue** of the pagans.

120:3, 4 Then just as quickly, he turns aside to one particular culprit and predicts severe punishment for him. **What** sentence **shall be** handed down **to** him? **Sharp arrows** shot from the bow of the Master Archer. And what will be done to that deceit-

ful tongue? Will it be washed with soap? No, it will be cauterized **with** glowing **coals of the broom tree**! The root of this desert shrub is used to produce burning charcoal, noted for its intense heat.

120:5 In a moment of self-pity, the peace-loving psalmist laments his enforced stay among the tribes of **Meshech** and **Kedar**. **Meshech** was a son of Japheth (Gen. 10:2), and his descendants became noted as savage, uncivilized people. **Kedar** was the second son of Ishmael (Gen. 25:13), and his posterity was also cruel and merciless. According to the International Standard Bible Encyclopedia, "it is through Kedar that Muslim genealogists trace the descent of Mohammed from Ishmael."

120:6, 7 The psalmist's enforced exile among barbarians who hated **peace** had been **too long** to suit him. His efforts to bring about peaceful co-existence had been repulsed by new acts of war.

Had he lived in NT times, he would have been more prepared to expect slander and strife, and would have been better able to cope with it. He would have the example of the Lord Jesus:

> Who, when He was reviled, did not revile in return; when He suffered, He did not threaten, but committed Himself to Him who judges righteously (1 Pet. 2:23).

He would have the teaching of Peter:

> But when you do good and suffer, if you take it patiently, this is commendable before God (1 Pet. 2:20b).

> Not returning evil for evil or reviling for reviling, but on the contrary blessing, knowing that you were called to this, that you may inherit a blessing (1 Pet. 3:9).

And finally he would have the word of the Lord Jesus:

> Blessed are you when they revile and persecute you, and say all kinds of evil against you falsely for My sake. Rejoice and be exceedingly glad, for great is your reward in heaven, for so they persecuted the prophets who were before you (Matt. 5:11, 12).

Psalm 121: Kept!

121:1, 2 In the KJV, this Psalm begins:

> I will lift up mine eyes unto the hills, from whence cometh my help.
> My help cometh from the LORD, which made heaven and earth.

Later translators thought they detected a pagan heresy here, namely, the idea that help comes from the hills rather than from the Lord (Jer. 3:23). So they punctuated the second clause of verse 1 as a question. The NKJV, for instance, reads:

> **I will lift up my eyes to the hills—**
> **From whence comes my help?**
> **My help comes from the LORD,**
> **who made heaven and earth.**

I still prefer the KJV here, and I'll tell you why. The temple in Jerusalem was the dwelling place of God on earth. The glory cloud in the Holy of Holies signified the Lord's presence among His people. The city of Jerusalem is situated on a mountain and is surrounded by mountains. So when a Jew in other parts of Israel needed divine **help**, he looked toward the **hills**. To him this was the same as looking to the Lord. Since the Creator's dwelling was in the Jerusalem hills, there was a poetic sense in which **all help** came from **the hills**.

In the first two verses, the speaker is the psalmist, expressing his complete reliance on the Maker of **heaven and earth**.

121:3 Beginning with verse 3, there is a change of speaker. In the remaining verses, we hear the Holy Spirit guaranteeing the eternal security of those whose trust is in the Lord. There is the guarantee of unassailable stability. The believer's **foot** will be preserved from being **moved**. Since the foot speaks of foundation or standing, it means that God will keep His trusting child from slipping or failing.

121:4 There is the guarantee of a Guardian who **shall neither slumber nor sleep**. Alexander the Great told his soldiers, "I wake that you may sleep."[90] Throughout the night hours, when we are no longer conscious of the world around us, there is One greater than Alexander who watches over us with constant, unwearied care.

121:5, 6 There is the guarantee that our **keeper** is none other than the **LORD** Himself. The great Sovereign of the universe is personally involved in the security of the most obscure saint.

There is the guarantee that He will protect from every evil influence. When it says that He is **"your shade at your right hand,"** it means that He is alongside as a bodyguard to shield His own from harm day or night. **The sun shall not strike you by day** is usually interpreted by modern day literalists as sunstroke.[91] The allusion to **the moon** is often condescendingly treated as a biblical accommodation to ancient superstition and folklore. To those, however, who have been delivered from demonism, and who realize the important role of the sun and moon in the realm of spiritism, these verses promise welcome protection and freedom from the chains of demon possession.

121:7, 8 There is the guarantee of deliverance **from all evil**. It is a solid fact that nothing can come into the life of a believer apart from God's permissive will. There are no random circumstances, no purposeless accidents, no fatalistic tragedies. Though He is not the author of sickness, suffering, or death, He overrules and harnesses them for the accomplishment of His purposes. In the meantime His trusting child can know that God is working all things together for good to those who love Him, who are called according to His purpose (Rom. 8:28).

Finally there is the guarantee of God's watch-care over all our movements in time and throughout all eternity. He will keep our **going out and** our **coming in from this time forth and even forevermore**.

The words "keep" and "keeper" occur three times in the space of these eight verses. **Preserve** occurs three times.[92] They join to declare that no one is as secure as the person who has received the Lord as his only hope.

> The soul that on Jesus hath leaned
>   for repose,
> He'll never, no never desert to his
>   foes.
> That soul, though all hell should
>   endeavor to shake,
> He'll never, no never, no never forsake!
>   —*Richard Keen (1787)*

Psalm 122: The City of Peace

> Oh, the pure delight of a single hour
> That before Thy throne I spend,
> When I kneel in prayer, and with
>   Thee, my God,
> I commune as friend with friend!
>   —*Fanny J. Crosby*

122:1 David caught the scent of that pure delight when the reminder was passed to him by God-fearing Jews that it was time to **go** to the feast in Jerusalem. He **was glad**. It was no burdensome duty or dreary routine. In going to the temple to worship he found fulfillment and gladness.

122:2 And now faith's pilgrims were actually **standing** inside the city. **"Our feet have been standing within your gates, O Jerusalem!"** As if by a divine homing instinct, they had returned to the place which God had chosen. It was wonderful to be there!

122:3, 4 They stand back to admire the ocher-tinted **city**, built compactly **together**. Within its sun-drenched walls, one mile square, were domed and flat-roofed houses and cluttered alleys. But the one building for which the people had a fierce sentimental attraction was the temple of the Lord. In a real sense it was the temple that made the city for them.

That was the place to which **the tribes of the LORD** made their pilgrimages. It was the one spot on earth where God had decreed for His people to gather and give thanks to His **name**.

122:5 Jerusalem also was the political capital of Israel, of course. It was the seat of the royal **house of David**, and therefore it was the appointed place for the administration of justice.

122:6 Though its name means "the city of peace," the name has been a misnomer so far. Few cities have known the strife, the suffering, the carnage that this city has:

> Jerusalem's stones bear the stigmata of her sanctity and her walls the memory of the crimes committed within them in the name of religion. David and Pharaoh, Sen-

nacherib and Nebuchadnezzar, Ptolemy and Herod, Titus and the Crusaders of Godefrey de Bouillon, Tamerlane and the Saracens of Saladin, all fought and killed there.[93]

In prophecy as well as in history, there is an ocean of meaning in the poignant plea, **"Pray for the peace of Jerusalem!"** Dark days lie ahead. The narrow streets of the city will echo to the tread of Gentile invaders until the Prince of Peace, Israel's Messiah, returns to assume the reins of government (Luke 21:24).

F. B. Meyer notes that there is a graceful alliteration here in verse 6:

Peace in the City of Peace.
May those be at peace who love her.

The benediction of peace rests upon all who love the city of the Great King.

122:7–9 This love is expressed in praying for and promoting tranquility **within** its **walls** and safety within its towers. What the godly Jew desired for Jerusalem, we should desire for the church. How we should endeavor to keep the unity of the Spirit in the bond of peace (Eph. 4:3)! It is through the peace and prosperity of the church that blessing will flow out to the world.

That is the thought in verse 8. **For the sake of** relatives and friends, we should long to see the internal wounds of the church healed, its strifes and divisions ended. Barnes explains:

This expresses the true feelings of piety all over the world; this is one of the grounds of the strong love which the friends of God have for the Church—because they hope and desire that through the Church those most near to their hearts will find salvation.[94]

As already mentioned, the greatest glory of the city is that the house of the Lord is there. Not the city's location, nor its misshapen buildings nor its sad history—no, the central fact is that God chose this city as the site for the temple. The presence of the Lord casts an aura of glory about all that He touches in grace.

Centuries later Jesus was to remind the Pharisees and scribes of this truth. They valued the gold of the temple more than the temple itself, the gift on the altar more than the altar. Jesus pointed out that it is the temple that makes the gold sacred, and the altar that sanctifies the gift (Matt. 23:16–22). And so it is the Lord Himself who set Jerusalem apart from all other cities in the world.

Psalm 123: Eyes that Look for Mercy

There are two key words in this **Song of Ascents**, "eyes" and "mercy." The first is found four times, the second three. The scene is the land of captivity—an all-too-familiar setting for the oppressed people of Israel. They found themselves there in Egypt, in Babylon, in Nazi Germany, in the Warsaw ghetto and more recently in Siberian slave-labor camps. Though the name is not mentioned, the country here is probably Babylon.

123:1 With **eyes** upturned to **the heavens** and straining for some sight of divine mercy, the captives plead with the Lord to end their long, dark night of persecution.

123:2 They compare themselves to **servants** looking **to the hand of their masters**, and as . . . a maid looking **to the hand of her mistress**. This is usually interpreted to mean a readiness to perceive and to obey the will of the master. But that is not the picture here. Rather it indicates the attentiveness and expectancy of the Jews for Jehovah to have **mercy** upon them. And the particular **mercy** which they have in mind is a speedy end to their exile and a return to the land of heart's desire. They are looking to His **hand** for salvation from their oppressors.

123:3, 4 Twice the urgent plea for **mercy** ascends to the throne of God from a people who have had more than their fill of **contempt**. Day after day they have had a diet of **scorn** and hatred, dished out by their Gentile overlords. Too long they have endured the cutting, snide remarks **of those who are at ease** (Zech. 1:15). Too long they have suffered under the arrogance of their **proud** Babylonian captors (Jer. 50:31, 32). Now they are surfeited. Enough is enough! They feel that the breaking time has come.

And so they pour out this compelling prayer to the One who is their only refuge and security in a world of anti-Semitism and discrimination—to the Friend of the oppressed and downtrodden.

Psalm 124: The All—Important "If"

124:1 "If it had not been the LORD who was on our side . . ."

Everything depended on that *if*. It spelled the difference between deliverance and disaster. But the Lord *was* there, and that made all the difference.

Probably no people have had as many narrow escapes as the Jews. According to all natural laws, they should have been extinct long ago. When you think of the sieges, the massacres, the pogroms, the gas chambers, the ovens, the bombs, it is a miracle they have survived. But survive they did—and that for one compelling reason—the LORD **was on** their **side**.

Unfortunately the nation has not always been willing to acknowledge that fact. Too often they have chalked up their victories to their own cleverness and power. But there have always been those godly Jews who realized that apart from the Lord, they would have been exterminated.

124:2–5 The psalmist thinks of times when enemies **rose up against** Israel in overwhelming numbers and with superior armaments. Food supplies dwindled to precarious levels. Medical supplies were gone. Communications were cut off. Necessities had to be improvised out of whatever was available. They were completely surrounded. Their enemies were threatening to drive them into the sea. The outlook was grim.

124:6, 7 Like ferocious beasts, the foe was about to swallow them alive. Or to change the figure, they were about to be engulfed in a great tidal wave of Gentile military might.

But then the unexpected happened. **The LORD** caused the enemy to quarrel among themselves over strategy. Or to get faulty intelligence reports concerning the Jews. Or to panic over the death of a leader. Or to agree to a cease-fire when victory was in their clutch.

On the other hand, the Lord may have led the Jews to unexpected food reserves. Or to hidden caches of weapons. Or He may have brought outside help from the most unlikely source. In either case, the converging of circumstances was so marvelous that it could only be brought about by the hand of God.

Those who have spiritual intelligence give all the glory to the Lord for their mysterious, miraculous deliverance. The carnivorous Gentile beasts have not succeeded in devouring little Israel. God's people have escaped from the trap that was set for them by Gentile summitry. **The snare has been broken**, the ring of steel surrounding the Jews has been snapped, and once again they have **escaped**.

124:8 Their humble and grateful confession is this:

> **Our help is in the name of the** LORD,
> **Who made heaven and earth.**

However, Israel has no monopoly on the God of miracles. The church can appropriate the words of this Psalm in celebrating God's nick-of-time deliverances. And individual believers know that if the Lord had not been on their side, they would have been completely subdued by the world, the flesh and the devil.

Psalm 125: The Way of Peace

125:1 **Mount Zion** is one of the promontories in the city of Jerusalem, and is sometimes used as a figure of speech for the city itself. Here it signifies the ultimate in stability and strength, a citadel that cannot be moved.

The man of faith is like that. His life is built on the solid rock. When the rains fall, and the floods come, and the winds blow and beat upon his house, it does not fall, because it has been built on the rock (Matt. 7:25).

The psalmist says that **Mount Zion . . . abides forever**. As far as the earthly city is concerned, this must be understood as the way it appeared to believers at that time. We know from the NT that the earth will some day be destroyed by fire (2 Pet. 3:7, 10, 12). However, we ourselves use similar expressions. We speak of the everlasting hills and the eternal city (Rome).

The important point is that although Mt. Zion will one day be destroyed, the believer in Christ will never perish. Because he is positionally in Christ, he is as safe as God can make him.

125:2 The psalmist saw another spiritual truth in the topography of **Jerusalem**. It is surrounded by **mountains** from which its army can guard every approach to the city. So **the** LORD Himself forms a protective ring around His children **"from this time forth and forever."** This is the hedge which Satan spoke of as encircling Job.

> Have You not made a hedge around him, around his household, and around all that he has on every side? (Job 1:10).

Which means, of course, that nothing can reach the trusting saint except by the permissive will of God.

125:3 Another gigantic claim is made in verse 3:

> **For the scepter of wickedness shall not rest on the land allotted to the righteous, lest the righteous reach out their hands to iniquity.**

Some might take exception to the first part of this verse by pointing out that the land of Israel has often been invaded and conquered by wicked men. This is true. But the verse must be interpreted in its context. The Psalm is dealing with people who trust in the Lord; its promises are only for that kind of people. It was only when Israel was away from the Lord that its borders were violated and its walls breached. As long as they obeyed the Lord and trusted in Him, **the scepter of wickedness**, that is, the rule of wicked Gentile monarchs, was not allowed to come near them.

An interesting reason is given why God kept back the menacing enemies of Israel during times when the people walked with Him. The reason was that the **righteous** Israelites might be tempted to **reach out their hands to** do wrong. God saves us not only from outside foes but from the inner self and its tendency to sin when unjustly treated.

125:4 The fourth verse must also be understood in the context: **Do good, O Lord, to those who are good, and to those who are upright in their hearts**. The **good** people here are those who have been saved by faith and who walk in obedience to the Lord. Their uprightness is not the basis of their salvation, but is the fruit of their trust and obedience.

125:5 There are others who profess to be members of God's people but who **turn aside to their crooked ways. The Lord shall lead them away** into captivity and dispersion **with the workers of iniquity**.

Peace be upon Israel! The Psalm itself gives the formula for **peace**, both for Israel and everyone else. It is found through trust in the Lord Jesus. When Israel turns to Him whom they pierced and mourns for Him as for an only Son, then the peace that has eluded them for centuries will be theirs at last.

Shalom, shalom!

Psalm 126: Tearful Sowing, Joyful Reaping

126:1 When the announcement reached the Jewish communities in exile, the people were electrified and ecstatic. The Persian King Cyrus had decreed that the captives could return to their land. It seemed almost too good to be true. During the long years in exile, many of them had wondered if they would ever see Jerusalem again. But now at last the news had come. As they gathered their few pitiful belongings together, they were like people walking around in a trance.

126:2 The excited gabble of a normally demonstrative and talkative people was even louder than usual. For the first time in about seventy years, they had something to bring keenest pleasure to them. Something to make them hilarious. They were going home. As their preparations moved into high gear, they laughed and sang—something new for them.

It was a tremendous testimony to the non-Jewish people. They seemed to sense that things happened for the Jews that could not be explained on the natural level. They acknowledged that the God of the Hebrews had intervened for them in miraculous ways. Above the other nations of the earth, Israel appeared to be the special object of Jehovah's love and care.

126:3 And the grateful exiles joyfully concurred with the Gentiles in attributing their deliverance to the Lord alone.

The Lord has done great things for us, and we are glad.

126:4 But they were going back to the land a pathetic remnant with little more than the clothes they wore. They needed manpower, finances and protection. This accounts for their prayer:

Bring back our captivity, O Lord, as the streams in the South.

The South (Heb., Negev) was the desert in the south. Ordinarily it was arid and barren. But after heavy rains, the dry waterbeds became torrential **streams** that made the wilderness blossom. So the returning exiles pray that what is now only a trickle of people may become a multitude until all twelve tribes have been brought back. They pray that the Lord will provide them the means to rebuild and restore. And they ask for everything else that would be needed to make them a happy, fruitful people in the land.

126:5, 6 The first year after their return would be especially difficult. There would be no crops to harvest right away. They would have to make a fresh start by planting their crops and waiting for harvest time. It would be a period of austerity, of doling out the meager food supplies as frugally as possible.

There would be a certain sorrow or frustration about sowing the seed for that first crop. Here is a farmer whose barrel of grain is low. He can use the grain to feed his family now or he can sow most of it in hope of an abundant supply in days to come. He decides to **sow** it, but as he dips his hand into his apron and scatters the seed over the plowed land, his **tears** fall into the apron. He is thinking of his wife and children, of the skimpy bowls of porridge, of how sacrificially they will have to live in the days till harvest. He feels as if he is taking food out of their mouths.

But a cheering word goes out to the returned exiles:

He who continually goes forth weeping, bearing seed for sowing, shall doubtless come again with rejoicing, bringing his sheaves with him.

So they go forth and sow the seed. Their present anguish will be more than compensated by the **joy** of **bringing** their **sheaves** of ripened grain to the barn.

The principle applies also, of course, in the spiritual realm. Those who live sacrificially for the spread of the gospel may endure present privation, but what is that compared to the joy of seeing souls saved and in heaven worshiping the Lamb of God forever and forever?

It is true also in the matter of soul winning. Someone has wisely said, "Winners of souls are first weepers for souls." So our prayer should be:

Let me look on the crowd as my
  Savior did,
Till my eyes with tears grow dim.
Let me view with pity the wandering
  sheep
And love them for love of Him.
—*Author unknown*

Psalm 127: God in Everything

There is a saying, "Little is much if God is in it," but the reverse is also true, "Much is nothing if God is not in it." And that's what this Psalm says: unless our activity is ordered and directed by the Lord, it is a waste of time and energy. We can set out on projects of our own, even in Christian service; we can build vast organizational empires; we can amass statistics to show phenomenal results; but if the projects are not vines planted by the Lord, they are worse than worthless. "Man proposes but God disposes."

The psalmist chooses four common activities of life to illustrate his point. They are house construction, civil defense, general employment, and family building.

127:1 There are two ways to build a **house**. One is to move ahead with plans based on one's own knowledge, skill and financial resources, then ask God's blessing on the completed structure. The other is to wait until the LORD has given unmistakable guidance, then move ahead in conscious dependence on Him. In the first case, the project never rises above flesh and blood. In the second, there is the thrill of seeing God working through the marvelous provision of needed supplies, through the miraculous timing and sequence of events, and through the converging of circumstances that would never happen according to the laws of chance. It makes all the difference in the world to be building with God.

The second illustration of the futility of human effort without God is in the area of security: **Unless the Lord guards the city, the watchman stays awake in vain.** This does not mean we should not have a police force or other protective agencies. Rather it means that ultimately our security lies in the Lord, and unless we are really depending on Him, our ordinary precautions are not enough to keep us safe.

127:2 In our everyday employment, it is futile to work long hours, earning one's living through anxious toil, unless we are in the place of God's choosing. Please don't misunderstand. Throughout the Bible we are taught to work diligently to supply our own needs, the needs of our family, and the needs of others. This Psalm does not encourage people to sit around all day drinking colas and sponging off friends. But the point is this—if we are working in independence of God, we don't really get anywhere. Haggai describes the situation very well:

> You have sown much, and bring in little; you eat, but do not have enough; you drink, but you are not filled with drink; you clothe yourselves, but no one is warm; and he who earns wages, earns wages to put into a bag with holes (Hag. 1:6).

On the other hand, if we are really yielded to the Lord and living for His glory, He can give us gifts while we are sleeping which we could never obtain through long, weary hours of labor without Him. That seems to be the meaning of the clause, **"For so He gives His beloved sleep,"** or as Moffatt translates it, "God's gifts come to His loved ones, as they sleep."

127:3 The fourth and final illustration has to do with building a family. And children are one of the gifts of God. **"Behold, children are a heritage from the Lord; the fruit of the womb is a reward."**

What is said about children presupposes that they have been brought up in a home where the Lord has been honored and obeyed. They have been brought up in the discipline and instruction of the Lord.

127:4 **"Like arrows in the hand of a warrior, so are the children of one's youth."** When parents become old, they can depend on godly children to fight for them as a **warrior**, and also to provide for them as a hunter does with his bow and **arrows**.

127:5 **"Happy is the man who has his quiver full of them!"** In spite of the torrent of modern propaganda against large families, God pronounces a blessing on **the man who has** a **quiver full of** children. But once again it is assumed that they are believing children, members of the household of faith. Otherwise they could be an enormous heartache rather than a blessing.

"They shall not be ashamed, but shall speak with their enemies in the gate." F. B. Meyer reminds us that contending armies of a besieged city would meet at the gate. So the thought here is that a man's children defend him in civil or legal matters so that he does not suffer loss or injury. They see that justice is done.

The Psalm is a tremendous unfolding of the word of the Lord through Zechariah, "Not by might nor by power, but by My Spirit, says the Lord of hosts" (Zech. 4:6). There is such a danger that we depend on the power of the dollar or on human ingenuity. But the Lord's will is not accomplished in that way. It is by His Spirit that we build for eternity. It is not what we do for God through our own resources, but what He does through us by His mighty power. All we can produce is wood, hay, stubble. He can use us to produce gold, silver, precious stones. When we act in our own strength, we are spinning our wheels. When we bring God into everything, our lives become truly efficient. Carnal weapons produce carnal results. Spiritual weapons produce spiritual results.

Psalm 128: The Blessing of the Lord

128:1 The believer who really enjoys life to the hilt is the one who acknowledges **the Lord** in every area of life and who **walks** in practical obedience to the Word of God.

Under the law of Moses this man was rewarded with natural blessings.

128:2 *Longevity.* He did not die prematurely but lived to enjoy the material wealth for which he had labored.

Happiness. He enjoyed freedom from discord and strife, and the joyful contentment of having God's countenance shining upon him.

Prosperity. Things went **well with** him. He was protected from calamity, blight, drought, pestilence and defeat.

128:3 *Productivity.* Like a fruitful vine, his **wife** bore many **children.** There they are, clustered **around** his **table,** like tender **olive plants**—full of vim, vigor and vitality.

128:4 In the Dispensation of Grace, the believer is already blessed in Christ with every spiritual blessing in the heavenly places (Eph. 1:3). But as Williams says, "faith can spiritualize the material blessings of this song and make them real and present." Better than long life on earth is the life of the Lord Jesus energizing us. No happiness can compare with that of the soul set free. Soul prosperity is the best prosperity. And spiritual reproduction surpasses the joys of physical fertility.

128:5, 6 The last two verses of the Psalm may be read as a promise or a prayer. Following the latter, they ask that **the Lord** will **bless** His believing people from His dwelling place in the sanctuary in **Zion** or from His throne in **Jerusalem.** They ask that the godly might **see the** prosperity **of Jerusalem** as long as they live. They ask for long life to enjoy the second generation of offspring. And they pray for **peace upon Israel**.

The Psalm joyfully anticipates the future blessedness of the individual and the nation when Israel's King returns and reigns in righteousness.

Psalm 129: The Harvest of Anti-Semitism

This **Song of Ascents** rehearses Israel's past treatment at the hands of her many foes, then asks the Lord to insure an unpromising future for these cruel aggressors.

129:1, 2 From the early days of nationhood, Israel had been sorely **afflicted**. Their oppression in Egypt, for example, was an unforgettable chapter of servitude and suffering in the nation's **youth**. Yet the enemy never succeeded in exterminating the Jews. God's people were always delivered from captivity. Their survival has been one of the great miracles of history.

129:3 Their sufferings were deep and prolonged. The Gentile taskmasters rode over them like a farmer plowing a field. The **furrows** on their **back** were long welts caused by the lash.

129:4 But **the LORD**, who is **righteous**, intervened in the nick of time by cutting **the cords** or chains with which His people were held captive by their merciless assailants.

129:5–7 May it always be the case that anti-Semites are disgraced and routed. May they never experience a harvest of blessing. Rather let them be like the few odd clumps of **grass** that grow on the flat rooftops in the Middle East. Because they have no depth of soil, these tufts cannot take good root, and they are soon scorched by the blazing sun. Actually the grass **withers before it** has a chance to produce any sizable growth. A **reaper** would never get a handful to cut, let alone **sheaves** to hold in **his arms**.

129:8 Rooftop grass could never produce the happy harvest scene in which onlookers say to the reapers, **"The blessing of the LORD be upon you"** and the reapers call back, **"We bless you in the name of the LORD"** (see Ruth 2:4). So may the enemies of Israel be denied any happy outcome to all the cruel plowing they have done down through the centuries. Rather let them reap what they have sown.

Psalm 130: Out of the Depths

Someone has said that the best prayer comes from a strong, inward necessity. In pleasant, prosperous times of life, meaningful prayer is often the first casualty. But when we are being tossed around by the storms of life, then we really know how to touch the throne of grace in fervent, insistent pleading.

130:1, 2 I am often amazed at the depths of sorrow and suffering that can be endured by the human frame. The psalmist is in one of those dark troughs of life. There is no way to look but up. And so his clamant call goes winging up from **out of the depths** to the throne of heaven.

He urgently pleads that his thin, solitary **voice** be heard, that the LORD will grant him audience. The plea is, of course, answered. Always!

In the suppliant's mind, his trouble was somehow connected with some sin. This may or may not have been true. But in any case it is always a good idea to eliminate unconfessed sin as a possible cause of our calamities.

130:3, 4 If the LORD **should mark iniquities** in the sense of keeping an itemized account and making each of us pay on the line, then the situation would be positively hopeless. But we can be eternally grateful that there is a way in which sins can be forgiven. **There is forgiveness** for the guilty sinner and **there is forgiveness** for the sinning saint.

The first is *judicial* forgiveness, that is, forgiveness from God, the Judge. It is obtained by faith in the Lord Jesus Christ. It covers the penalty of all sins—past, present, and future. It is possible because of the finished work of Christ at Calvary; in His death He paid the penalty for all our sins and God can freely forgive us because all His righteous claims have been met by our Substitute.

The second is *parental* forgiveness— the forgiveness of God, our Father. It is obtained by confessing our sins to Him. It results in a restoration of fellowship with God and with His family. It too is purchased for us by the blood of Jesus, shed on the cross.

One result of His forgiveness is that He should **be feared**. When I think what it cost Him to forgive my sins, and when I realize that His **forgiveness** is full, free, and eternal, it causes me to reverence, trust, love and worship Him forever.

130:5,6 Although the psalmist hasn't asked directly for forgiveness, it is certainly implied in verses 3, 4. But when he says in verse 5 that he **waits for the LORD**, *he does not mean for forgiveness*. That is assured as soon as he confesses. Rather he **waits** for the Lord to deliver him from the depths. Sometimes God answers prayer immediately. Sometimes He teaches us to wait.

God answers prayer; sometimes when
    hearts are weak,
He gives the very gifts His children
    seek,
But often faith must learn a deeper
    rest,
And trust God's silence when He
    cannot speak;
For He whose name is love, will send
    the best;
Stars may burn out, nor mountain
    walls endure,
But God is true, His promises are
    sure
To those who seek.
                    —*Author unknown*

So here he has learned to **wait for the LORD** and to **hope in His word**, that is, in His promise to hear and to answer. **More than** the watchmen wait for the light of dawn, he longs to see the Lord bring light into his darkness.

But verses 5, 6 have a wider application that we must not miss. They express the earnest longing of the believer today as he looks for the coming of Christ to translate His church to heaven. This blessed hope will not be disappointed.

130:7, 8 The last two verses of the Psalm may be thought of as the psalmist's testimony after his prayer for deliverance had been answered. Having proved God's faithfulness for himself, he wants others to share the experience also. It is always this way: if a person really believes something, he is anxious to communicate it to others.

So **Israel** is encouraged to **hope in the LORD**. Three reasons are given. First, His **mercy** is unchanging. Then, His **redemption** is **abundant** in its supply. And finally His willingness to **redeem Israel from all his iniquities** is assured.

The Psalm opened in the depths of gloom. It closes with a vibrant call to trust in the God for whom no problem is too mountainous, no dilemma too complex.

Psalm 131: Intellectual Humility

There are some problems in life that defy explanation. Mysteries too deep to fathom. Strange circumstances that puzzle the keenest intellect.

Who, for example, can say the last word on the problem of human suffering?

Who can answer all the questions that surface in the area of unanswered prayer?

Who can reconcile God's sovereign election and man's free will?

131:1 David didn't profess to know all the answers. His **heart** was not lifted up like that of an insufferable know-it-all. His **eyes** were not raised too high, as if he were the finished intellectual egotist. He recognized his limitations and was not ashamed to say, "I don't know." He was content to know what he could know and leave the mysteries with God. Why occupy himself with things that were too **great** and **too profound** for him? No, he gave God credit for understanding things that he could never understand.

131:2 This attitude of trust in the wisdom, love, and power of God brought peace and quietness to his **soul**. He was **like a weaned child** who is **quieted** at his mother's breasts. At the outset a child may be squalling, restless, impatient. But then feeding time comes and the baby is suddenly silent, relaxed in his mother's arms. And so we can work ourselves into a dither of frustration, trying to understand things that are too high for us. But as soon as we leave the unanswerable questions with God, our souls are loosed from tension.

131:3 The psalmist recommends this attitude of confidence in the Lord to all of **Israel**. So did A. W. Tozer. He wrote: "Never forget that it is a privilege to wonder, to stand in delighted silence before the Supreme Mystery and whisper, 'O Lord God, thou knowest.'"

Psalm 132: Prayer and Promise

There is considerable disagreement as to the author and occasion of this Psalm. One of the possible viewpoints is that it was composed by Solomon when he brought the ark of the covenant to its proper place in the newly-constructed temple in Jerusalem. In that case, the first ten verses are Solomon's prayer that the Lord will descend in the Shekinah (the glory cloud) and dwell above the ark. Verses 11 and 12 reaffirm the covenant God made with David. And the last six verses contain specific promises from

God corresponding to Solomon's specific requests.

132:1–5 The opening request that the LORD should **remember** in David's favor **all** the **afflictions** that he endured does not refer to the general hardships which dogged his steps throughout his life, but rather to the deep emotional and physical experiences he passed through in order to have the temple erected as God's dwelling place on earth. This is explained in the next three verses. On an occasion not otherwise recorded in the Scriptures, David had made a solemn contract with Jehovah that he would **not** enter his own **house**, lie down in his own **bed**, or go to sleep **until** he had arranged a house **for the LORD**, **a place** where **the Mighty One of Jacob** might dwell. The vow must not be understood with precise literalness. It is David's figurative way of saying that he would not rest contentedly until he had established a permanent place for the ark of God. We know that David was not permitted to build the temple because he was a man of war, but he was enabled to make important contributions of materials to Solomon, and God rewarded him for his desire.

132:6 These verses seem to be a reminiscence concerning the location of the ark in Kirjath, and the expressed determination of David's men to bring it to Jerusalem. Verse 6 is especially difficult because it seems to connect the ark with **Ephrathah** (Bethlehem), yet there is no record of the ark's ever having been there. The following are the common attempts to solve the difficulty.

1. The king and his men first heard of the ark's whereabouts when they were in Bethlehem, but they

finally located it in Jaar, i.e., Kirjath-Jearim.

2. Ephrathah may stand for Ephraim, and refer to the residence of the ark in Shiloh.

3. Ephrathah may mean Caleb Ephrathah (see 1 Chron. 2:24) and not Bethlehem. According to this view, Caleb Ephrathah is the same as Jaar (wood) of Kirjath-Jearim, which means "the city of the woods." If this is so, then the two clauses of verse 6 form a parallelism in which the meaning of both is the same.

Behold, we heard of it in Ephrathah; We found it in the fields of the woods.

132:7 As the procession moves with the sacred chest to Jerusalem, the people rejoice that they are going to God's **tabernacle** to **worship at His footstool**. The ark itself is conceived as being God's **footstool** since His presence was in the glory cloud above it.

132:8–10 Next we hear Solomon's prayer when he was dedicating the temple (vv. 8–10; cf. 2 Chron. 6:41, 42). He is asking God to come to dwell in the Sanctuary and thus make real the symbolism of the **ark**. Also he asks for a godly line of **priests**, for a people who are overflowing with **joy**, and for God's continued favor on the king. The phrase **"Your Anointed"** may be understood to refer to Solomon himself, but also ultimately to the Messiah.

132:11–13 The LORD answers the prayer first by making brief reference to the Davidic **covenant**. This covenant was unconditional as far as **David** was concerned; it promised him a **throne forevermore** and a descend-

ant to sit upon it forever. But it was conditional as far as David's offspring were concerned; it depended on their obedience. Thus although the Lord Jesus is a descendant of David, He is not physically a descendant of Solomon but of another son of David, Nathan (Luke 3:31).

132:14–18 Then specific answers are given to Solomon's specific requests. This may be seen from the following comparisons:

Arise, O Lord, to Your resting place; You and the ark of Your strength (v. 8).	**This is My resting place forever; here I will dwell, for I have desired it** (v. 14).
Let Your priests be clothed with righteousness (v. 9a).	**I will also clothe her priests with salvation** (v. 16a).
And let Your saints shout for joy (v. 9b).	**And her saints shall shout aloud for joy** (v. 16b).
For Your servant David's sake, do not turn away the face of Your Anointed (v. 10).	**There I will make the horn of David grow; I will prepare a lamp for My Anointed . . . But upon Himself His crown shall flourish** (vv. 17, 18b).

Actually the Lord answers abundantly above all that Solomon requests. There is the added promise of plentiful provisions and of **bread** for the **poor** (v. 15). There is the promise that the **priests** will be clothed **with salvation**, not just with righteousness (v. 16a). There is the promise that **the saints** will **shout aloud for joy** (v. 16b). There is the promise that the **enemies** will be clothed **with shame** (v. 18a).

The meaning of verse 17 is that in Jerusalem God will make a powerful King to come forth from **David** (see Luke 1:69) and has prepared a **lamp** or Son (see 1 Kgs. 15:4) for David, His **Anointed**. These promises of a perpetual dynasty are fulfilled in the Lord Jesus Christ.

The **enemies** of Christ will be covered **with shame**, but His head will be crowned with glory and honor.

> The head that once was crowned
>   with thorns
> Is crowned with glory now!
> Heaven's royal diadem adorns
> The mighty Victor's brow!
> —*Thomas Kelly*

Psalm 133: In Praise of Unity

Great things come in small packages. This Psalm is short but it is a literary and spiritual gem that makes up in quality what it lacks in quantity.

The psalmist has four main points. First, it is good and pleasant when brothers dwell together in unity. Second, it is fragrant. Third, it is refreshing. Finally, it is the sure guarantee of God's blessing.

133:1 **Unity** among **brethren** is a sight to **behold**. However, **unity** does not require that they see eye to eye on everything. On matters of fundamental importance they agree. On subordinate matters there is liberty for differing viewpoints. In all things there should be a spirit of love. There can be unity without uniformity; we are all different but that does not prevent our working together. All the members of the human body are different, but as they function in obedience to the head, there is a glorious unity. There can be unity without unanimity; God never intended that everyone should agree on matters of minor importance. It is enough to agree on the basics. On everything else we may disagree as long as we can do it without being disagreeable. The real enemies of unity are jealousy, gossip, backbiting, censoriousness and lovelessness.

133:2 Unity is **like the** fragrant perfume that was used in anointing **Aaron** the priest (Ex. 30:22–30). It was poured on his **head**, then ran **down** on his **beard**, and from there to the **edge of his** robe. The pleasing scent was enjoyed not only by the priest himself but by everyone in the vicinity. The holy anointing **oil** pictures the ministry of the Holy Spirit, descending as a sweet-smelling savor on God's people when they live happily together, and diffusing the aroma of their testimony to the surrounding areas.

133:3 Then again unity brings refreshment. **"It is like the dew of Hermon, descending upon the mountains of Zion."** The psalmist sees Mt. **Hermon** as the source of cool, invigorating moisture for distant mountains. Again the dew typifies the Holy Spirit, carrying refreshment from united brethren to the ends of the earth. No one can measure how far-reaching is the influence of believers who walk in fellowship with God and with one another.

The final point is that the LORD commands **the blessing** where brothers and sisters live together in unity. Take Pentecost as an illustration. The disciples were living in harmony and peace, united in prayer and waiting for the promised Holy Spirit. Suddenly the Spirit of God descended upon them in all His fullness and they went forth with the fragrance and refreshment of the gospel to Jerusalem, Judea, Samaria, and the uttermost parts of the earth.

The blessing is explained as being **life forevermore**. This may be understood in two ways. When there is unity among God's people, *they* themselves enjoy **life** in its truest sense. And not only so, they become the channels through which **life** flows out to *others*.

Psalm 134: Come, Bless the Lord!

134:1, 2 After the usual daily schedule of activities at the temple in Jerusalem, the people returned to their homes, but there were priests and Levites who stood watch during the **night** (1 Chron. 9:33), burning incense, giving thanks, and praising the Lord (2 Chron. 29:11; 31:2).

It may be that as the people withdrew, they sang the first two verses of this song to the priests. It is certainly clear that the verses are addressed to **servants of the Lord** on **night** duty in the temple, and that the ministry of these men was to **bless the Lord** and **lift up** their **hands** toward **the sanctuary** in a posture of prayer.

134:3 The response of verse 3 is the blessing of the priests invoking God's blessing on the people individually. Notice four things about the blessing.

The Blesser—**the Lord**, Jehovah, the covenant-keeping God.
His Greatness—He . . . **made heaven and earth**.
The One Blessed—May **the Lord . . . bless you** ("you" here is singular).
The Locale of the Blesser—**Zion**, the place of the sanctuary.

Psalm 135: The Why of Praise

135:1, 2 The first two verses sound out a rather general summons to **"Praise the Lord!"** It is directed quite clearly to the priests and Levites, but probably also to all the people of Israel and to all that fear the Lord (see vv. 19, 20).

135:3 Notice the many reasons that are adduced for praising His name. He **is good**. No created tongue, in time or in eternity, will ever be able to tell how good He is. All we can do is state the fact and adore.

His name is lovely, or **pleasant**. It is amazing grace that saves sinful wretches and destines them to eternal glory.

135:4 **The Lord** chose **Israel** as His own possession. The sovereign election of God leaves the wondering soul asking the perpetual question "Why me?" It is this that makes us worshipers!

135:5 **The Lord is great**. When we contemplate Him as Creator, Sustainer and Redeemer, we sing with deep appreciation "How **great** Thou art!"

Our Lord is supreme **above all gods**, that is, above all rulers and potentates and above all idols. "On His robe and on His thigh He has a name written, *KING OF KINGS, AND LORD OF LORDS*" (Rev. 19:16).

135:6 He is the universal Sovereign (v. 6). He does as He **pleases** in every imaginable realm. As Arthur Pink wrote:

> Divine sovereignty means that God is God in fact, as well as in name, that He is on the Throne of the universe, directing all things, working all things "after the counsel of His own will."[95]

135:7 He holds absolute power over nature. The clouds, the **lightning** and the **wind**—formidable as they are—are directed by His mighty hand. Stephen Charnock says, "God's power is like Himself: infinite, eternal, incomprehensible; it can neither be checked, restrained, nor frustrated by the creature."

135:8, 9 He delivered Israel from **Egypt**. The greatest display of power in Israel's history was the crushing of Pharaoh through the plagues (that were climaxed by the death of **the**

firstborn) and by the parting of the Red Sea.

135:10, 11 He defeated Israel's foes. God graciously gave victory to His people over **Sihon, Og,** and the heathen nations inhabiting **Canaan**.

135:12 He gave Canaan **to Israel**. The land of Canaan was given **as a heritage to** the escapees from Egypt.

135:13 He is eternal. His **name endures forever**, and His name, of course, stands for all that He is.

He has eternal **fame**. He will be lovingly remembered **throughout** eternity.

135:14 He is just and compassionate. We can depend on this—that God will vindicate **His people** and **will have compassion on His servants**. Moses sang it first in Deuteronomy 32:36 but the song will never end.

135:15–18 He is superior to **idols**. The mere description of these false gods is enough to expose their worthlessness. They are **silver and gold**, therefore perishable. They are created by man, therefore inferior to man. They are dumb, blind, deaf and lifeless. And sad to say, **those who make them are like them**—spiritually blind, deaf, dumb, and dead.

135:19, 20 Such a consideration of the greatness of God leads to the desire to **bless** Him, that is, to shower Him with honor, praise, homage, worship and thanksgiving. All the **house of Israel** should **bless** Him. All who minister as priests (**house of Aaron**) should **bless** Him. Those who serve as Levites should **bless** Him. All **who revere the LORD** should **bless** Him, which is another way of saying that all classes of men should praise Him. This is what Israel will sing when the Messiah returns to Zion and reigns from Jerusalem.

135:21   **Blessed be the LORD out of Zion,**
         Who dwells in Jerusalem!
         Praise the LORD!

That is what we should be saying and doing now.

Psalm 136: The Great Hallel!

What makes this Psalm unique is that the second member of each of the twenty-six verses is the same antiphonal response, "for His mercy endures forever." "If one everlasting is not enough," wrote Thomas Goodwin, "there are twenty-six everlastings in this one psalm."

It is known as the Great Hallel, the singing of which was a regular part of the observance of both Pesach and Rosh Hashanah—the Jewish Passover and New Year celebrations. It was also used in their daily worship.

The repetition of the theme is not tiresome; it says to us that the steadfast love of the Lord needs to be constantly before us and that the subject can never be exhausted. His kindness, loyalty and fidelity never fail.

Call to Worship (136:1–3)

The introduction summons us to **give thanks to the LORD** because of who He is, and because of His intrinsic goodness. He is Jehovah—the covenant-keeping Lord. He is **the God of gods**—supreme over all the mighty rulers in the universe. He is **the Lord of lords**—the sovereign over all who hold places of leadership, whether angelic or human. But He is not only great; **He is good** as well—**good** as Creator, Redeemer, Guide, Champion, and Provider for His people.

Creator (136:4–9)

His goodness and mercy are seen first of all in the **great wonders** of creation. **By** His **wisdom** He **made the** marvelous expanse of **the heavens**. He brought forth the continents as if they were enormous floating islands. He placed gigantic light fixtures in the sky—**the sun** providing daylight, and **the moon and stars** as subdued lights for man's bedroom hours.

Redeemer (136:10–15)

The Great Creator is also the Mighty Redeemer. In order to rescue His people from Egyptian tyranny, He cut down the flower of Egypt's manhood, then took His people by His **strong hand** and led them out to freedom. To do this, He had to divide **the Red Sea** into **two** parts with a dry strip of land in between. **Israel** got **through** safely, but the soldiers of **Pharaoh** were engulfed when the waters returned to their place. It was a never-to-be-forgotten display of the steadfast love of Jehovah for His people.

Guide (136:16)

For forty years, God **led** the Israelites **through the** waste, howling **wilderness**. There were no paved highways, no road signs, no maps, but the Lord was all they needed—the Incomparable Guide.

Champion (136:17–22)

He even fought their battles for them. When King **Sihon** and King **Og** blocked their way, He soundly defeated them, **and gave their land** as part of Israel's domain.

Helper, Savior, Provider (136:23–25)

As a sort of summary, the psalmist extols Jehovah for being the wonderful Helper, Savior, and Provider that He is. **He remembered** Israel when the people were few in number, defenseless, and oppressed. He **rescued** them out of the clutches of their **enemies**. He unfailingly provides **food** for **all** living things.

The God of Heaven (136:26)

We take Him too much for granted. Constant awareness of His personal greatness and His ceaseless **mercy** would cause us to **give thanks** to Him more and more.

Psalm 137: If I Forget You, O Jerusalem!

In April, 1948, the Jewish sector of Jerusalem was practically in a state of siege. Food supplies were almost exhausted. The people were existing on a weekly ration of two ounces of margarine, a quarter of a pound of potatoes and a quarter of a pound of dried meat. Then the news spread that a convoy of trucks was arriving from Tel Aviv with supplies. Hundreds of people ran out to welcome the dozens of trucks. They will never forget the first sight they had of the convoy. On the front bumper of the blue Ford leading the procession, someone had painted the words:

If I forget you, O Jerusalem. . . .

And so these words of Psalm 137:5 have become a rallying cry for the Jewish people down through their tumultuous history of captivity and dispersion.

137:1 Written after the return from Babylonian bondage, the Psalm looks back to the bitterness of being exiled from Zion.

Whenever they had free time, perhaps on the Sabbath, they gathered **by the rivers of Babylon** to pray.

Memories would come crowding back and the tears would flow. They **remembered Zion**. To them it was the spiritual center of the whole earth and the center of their lives. They remembered the spiritual joy and exhilaration of being there during the great holy convocations. And now they could no longer go up there to worship, and the holy places were in the unclean hands of the uncircumcised heathen. As they looked into **the rivers of Babylon**, they saw in them a picture of their own rivers of tears and anguish. As Jeremiah had prayed, "My eyes overflow with rivers of water for the destruction of the daughter of my people" (Lam. 3:48). And again:

O that my head were waters, and my eyes a fountain of tears, that I might weep day and night for the slain of the daughter of my people! (Jer. 9:1).

137:2 They had **hung** their **harps upon the willows**, or as we would say, they had put them on the shelf. And why not? There was no use for musical instruments. From the human standpoint, at least, there was nothing to sing about. And without a song to sing, there was no need of accompaniment.

137:3 It often happened that the Babylonian captors **asked** them to sing one of the Hebrew folk songs. As if to rub salt into the wounds, they would say, "**Sing us one of** those happy **songs** you used to sing in your homeland!"

137:4 Ridiculous! The Jews wouldn't sing. Not just because their hearts were breaking, but even more because it would be utterly incongruous to **sing the LORD's song** in a land of heathen idolaters. It would be like forgetting Jerusalem. They saw a moral

impropriety about mixing the things of the Lord and the things of the world. "The land of the stranger and the song of the Lord can never be found together," wrote F. B. Meyer.

137:5, 6 Now that he is back in the land the psalmist expresses the enormous determination of his people to have **Jerusalem** at the center of their life—and we remember here that **Jerusalem** stands for the Lord who dwelt there. Should the time ever come when he no longer has that inexplicable, instinctive attachment to Zion, then a fitting retribution would be that his **right hand** should wither and never again be able to sweep the strings of the harp. Yes, if it should ever happen that Jerusalem doesn't have first place in his heart, then he concurs that his **tongue** should **cling to the roof of** his **mouth** so that he could never sing the sweet old songs of Zion again.

137:7 Having first pronounced these conditional curses on himself, he finds it an easy transition to think next of those who had had a part in the destruction of the Holy City.

Take the **sons of Edom**, for example. They formed a sort of cheering squad, egging the invaders to wreck it completely. "**Raze** it, tear it down!" they yelled, "**to its very foundation!**" May the Lord remember their vicious satisfaction in seeing the city laid low!

137:8 And then there was **Babylon**, of course, the cruel devastator. Though this nation was the instrument in God's hands to punish His people, yet He did not excuse the Babylonians for their merciless atrocities.

I was angry with My people, I have profaned My inheritance, and given them into your hand. You showed them no mercy; on the elderly you laid your yoke very heavily (Isa. 47:6).

I am exceedingly angry with the nations at ease; for I was a little angry, and they helped—but with evil intent (Zech. 1:15).

There was no question in the psalmist's mind as to Babylon's destruction. It had been foretold by the prophets (Isa. 13:1–22; Jer. 50:15, 28; 51:6, 36). Those who accomplished the destruction would have the satisfaction to be used by God as instruments of His judgment.

137:9 The last verse of the Psalm is the one that gives most difficulty:

Happy the one who takes and dashes your little ones against the rock!

To those who have been raised on the non-violent teachings of the NT it seems unusually harsh, vindictive, and unloving. Why should innocent, defenseless children be treated so inhumanely? In answer to the question, we would suggest the following:

First, we begin with the premise that this verse is part of the Word of God, verbally and plenarily inspired. Therefore any problem lies in our understanding rather than in the Word itself. Second, the destruction of Babylon's little ones was clearly predicted by Isaiah:

Their little children also will be dashed to pieces before their eyes; their houses will be plundered and their wives ravished (Isa. 13:16).

So the psalmist is only saying what God had already foretold (except for the part about the happiness of the ones who execute God's sentence).

Then again we know that innocent children are often involved in the consequences of their parents' sin (see Ex. 20:5; 34:7; Num. 14:18; Deut. 5:9). No man is an island. What he does affects others, either for good or for evil. Part of the bitterness of sin is that, in being allowed to work itself out, it engulfs others in its tragic retribution.

In these imprecatory passages, we keep coming back to the fact that conduct and attitudes that were suitable for a person living under the law of Moses are not necessarily suitable for a Christian living under grace. The Lord Jesus said as much in the Sermon on the Mount (see Matt. 5:21–48).

No matter how you interpret the verse, the spiritual application is clear. We must deal radically with little sins in our lives. The little darlings must be destroyed or they will destroy us. C. S. Lewis says, in this connection:

I know things in the inner world which are like babies; the infantile beginnings of small indulgences, small resentments, which may one day become dipsomania, or settled hatred, but which woo us and wheedle us with special pleadings, and seem so tiny, so helpless that in resisting them, we feel we are being cruel to animals. They begin whimpering to us, "I don't ask much, but," or "I had at least hoped," or "you owe yourself *some* consideration." Against all of such pretty infants (the dears have such winning ways) the advice of the Psalm is the best. Knock the little brats' brains out. And "blessed" he who can, for it's easier said than done.[96]

Psalm 138: God's Faithful Word

David was exuberantly thankful for some great answer to prayer. In this expression of his gratitude, he has left us all a worthy example of how we should respond to God's wonderful deliverances. Without doubt this Psalm will realize its fullest application when Israel is finally restored under the aegis of Jesus, the Messiah.

138:1 There is nothing half-hearted about David's thanks. All his powers are employed in blessing Jehovah.

And there is nothing timid or private about his worship. He sings unashamedly **before the gods**, that is, before the kings of the earth. The word "gods" here could also mean angels or idols but the context seems to limit it to the surrounding rulers.

138:2 In accordance with the custom of godly Jews, David bowed down **toward** the **holy** tabernacle when worshiping (the temple had not yet been erected).[97] He extolled the name of Jehovah for His steadfast love and faithfulness. It is His love that prompts Him to give us "His precious and very great promises" and it is His faithfulness that insures that every one of them is fulfilled.

"For You have magnified Your word above all Your name." The context has to do with the faithfulness of God in keeping His **word**, and the meaning seems to be that He has not only done what He said He would, but has done much more in addition. Also there may be the thought that "in the abundant fulfilment of His promise (to David) God had surpassed all previous revelation of Himself."[98] If the verse is applied to the Incarnate Word, then it means, of course, that God has magnified the Lord Jesus above every other manifestation of Himself.

138:3 Verse 3 reveals the immediate occasion for the psalmist's outburst of praise. In a day of desperate need he had **cried out** to the Lord and the answer came immediately. A vast supply of **strength** was poured into his **soul**, casting out fear and emboldening him to meet danger.

138:4–6 God's faithfulness in answering David's prayer is a powerful testimony to **the kings of the earth**. They know what God had promised, and now they see how the prophecy has been fulfilled. So they too acknowledge how **great is the glory of** Jehovah. They realize that though God is the exalted One, yet He takes a special interest in **the lowly** (like David) and keeps tabs on the **proud** (like David's enemies).

138:7 It is a beautiful picture— David is surrounded by all kinds of foes, all kinds of hazards, all kinds of distresses, yet the Lord enables him to **walk** safely through them as if they didn't exist. The same **hand** that strikes out against his adversaries **will save** him from disaster.

138:8 With justified confidence, David affirms, **"The LORD will perfect that which concerns me."** It is the same confidence that Paul expressed in Philippians 1:6, "Being confident of this very thing, that He who began a good work in you will complete it until the day of Christ Jesus."

> The work which His goodness began,
> The arm of His strength will complete;
> His promise is Yea and Amen,
> And never was forfeited yet:
> Things future, nor things that are now,
> Nor all things below nor above,
> Can make Him His purpose forego,
> Or sever our souls from His love.
> —*Augustus M. Toplady*

Yes, His steadfast love endures for ever, and though we are permitted to pray with David, **"Do not forsake the works of Your hands,"** the fact is that He never can or will.

Psalm 139: God Is So Great!

God is so great!
There is nothing He does not know.
There is nowhere He is not present.
There is nothing He cannot do.

If men insist on being the enemies of such a great God, they richly deserve their fate.

That, in brief, is the flow of David's meditation in this magnificent Psalm.

139:1, 2 First, he begins with *the omniscience of God.* God knows everything.

There is nothing He does not know.
Though limitless the universe and
    gloriously grand,
He knows the eternal story of
    every grain of sand.

But here it is His knowledge of the individual life that is particularly in view. In 1988 it was estimated that there were 5,000,000,000 people in the world. Yet God is intimately acquainted with each one. He knows all about every one of us.

He has **searched** us **and known** us! Words and deeds, thoughts and motives, He knows us inside out. He knows when we sit **down** to relax and when we rise **up** to engage in the varied activities of life. He can tell what we are thinking, and even anticipates our thoughts.

139:3 He sees us when we walk and when we lie **down**; in other words, He keeps a constant watch on us. None of our **ways** is hidden from Him.

139:4 He knows what we are going to say before we ever say it. The future as well as the past and present is completely open to Him.

139:5 "And there is no creature hidden from His sight, but all things are naked and open to the eyes of Him to whom we must give account" (Heb. 4:13). And because His knowledge of us is so inconceivably absolute, He can guard us **behind and before**. Ever and always His **hand** is **laid** protectingly **upon** us.

139:6 God's infinite **knowledge** boggles the mind. Our human brains strain under the weight of the idea. It is **too** exalted for us to comprehend. But when we come to the frontier of our capacity to understand and can go no farther, we can still bow in worship at the immensity of the knowledge of God!

139:7, 8 Not only is God omniscient; *He is omnipresent as well.* He is in all places at one and the same time. However, the all-presence of God is not the same as pantheism. The latter teaches that the creation *is* God. The Bible teaches that God is a Person who is separate and distinct from His creation. Is there any place where man can evade the Holy **Spirit** of God? Is there any place **where** he **can** hide from the **presence** of the Lord? Suppose man should **ascend into heaven**, would he elude God there? Of course not; heaven is the throne of God (Matt. 5:34). Even if he made his **bed in** Sheol, the disembodied state, he would find the Lord **there** as well.

139:9, 10 "If I take the wings of the morning, and dwell in the uttermost parts of the sea, even there Your hand shall lead me, and Your right hand shall hold me." The wings of the morning** are an allusion to the rays of the **morning** sun that streak across the heavens from east to west at 186,000 miles per second. Even if we could travel to some remote corner of the universe at the speed of light, we would find the Lord there, waiting to guide and uphold us.

Incidentally verses 9 and 10 are

fantastically appropriate for the age of jet travel in which we live. I shall never forget how the Lord spoke to me through this precious promise as I was about to embark on an extended ministry trip in 1969. The many jet aircraft in which I flew were like the wings of the morning, taking me literally to **the uttermost parts of the** earth. But always there was the sense of the Lord's presence and protection, regardless of speed or distance. So claim this promise for yourself, and share it with Christian friends who travel by air.

139:11, 12 If a person wanted **the darkness** to **hide** him **from** God, he would be trusting a false refuge. **Night** cannot shut out the presence of the Lord. **Darkness** is not dark to Him. **"The night shines as the day; the darkness and the light are both alike to You."**

God is absolutely inescapable. As Pascal said, "His center is everywhere; His circumference is nowhere."

139:13, 14 So much then for the omnipresence of God. David now turns to consider *His power and skill.* And the particular phase of divine omnipotence he chooses is the marvelous development of a baby in his mother's womb. In a speck of watery material smaller than the dot over this i, all the future characteristics of the child are programmed—the color of his skin, eyes and hair, the shape of his facial features, the natural abilities he will have. All that the child will be physically and mentally is contained in germ form in that fertilized egg. From it will develop:

> . . . 60 trillion cells, 100 thousand miles of nerve fiber, 60 thousand miles of vessels carrying blood around the body, 250 bones, to say nothing of joints, ligaments and muscles.[99]

David describes the formation of the fetus with exquisite delicacy and beauty. **"You formed my inward parts; You covered me in my mother's womb."** Yes, God **formed** our **inward parts**; each one a marvel of divine engineering. Think of the brain, for instance, with its capacity for recording facts, sounds, odors, sights, touch, pain; with its ability to recall; with its power to make computations; with its seemingly endless flair for making decisions and solving problems.

And God knit us together in our **mother's womb**. This aptly describes the marvelous weaving of the muscles, sinews, ligaments, nerves, blood vessels and bones of the human frame.

David bursts forth in **praise** to the Lord. As he thinks of man, the crown of God's creation, he can only confess that he is **fearfully and wonderfully made**. The more we think of the marvels of the human body, its orderliness, its complexity, its beauty, its instincts and inherited factors—the more we wonder how anyone trained in natural science can fail to be a believer in an infinite Creator.

139:15 Again the psalmist reverts to the time when his body was being formed in his mother's womb. Notice here that he uses the personal pronouns *I, my, me* to refer to the embryo or fetus. The scriptural view is that human personality exists before birth and that abortion therefore, except in cases of extreme medical necessity, is murder.

David was aware that God knew him through and through from the very beginning. His **frame**, that is, his skeletal structure was **not hidden from** God **when** David **was** being **made in secret, and skillfully wrought in the lowest parts of the earth.** It cannot mean below the surface of the earth; no one is formed there. In the context it can only mean "inside the mother's womb." A similar expression is found in Ephesians 4:9, which speaks of Christ as having descended into the *lower parts of the earth*. Once again in the context it refers to His entering the world through the ante-chamber of the virgin's womb. It is His Incarnation that is in view.

139:16 When the psalmist speaks of his **unformed . . . substance**, he uses a word that means something rolled or wrapped together. Barnes and others think that the word most aptly denotes the embryo, or the fetus, "where all the members of the body are as yet folded up, or undeveloped; that is, before they have assumed their distinct form and proportions." Even in that preliminary phase of his existence, God's **eyes** beheld the sweet singer of Israel.

And in God's **book**, **all the days** of David's life were recorded by the divine Architect before that historic moment when David announced his arrival by that first lusty cry.

139:17, 18a The psalmist thinks of God's careful planning in the creation of his spirit, soul, and body. **How precious . . . are** His **thoughts**—His attention to the minutest details. Andrew Ivy says, "Each cell almost without exception 'knows' its role in carrying out design or purpose for the welfare of the body as a whole."

139:18b "**When I awake, I am still with You.**" It seems to me that the psalmist is here referring to the moment of his birth. In the preceding verses (13–18a) he has been emphasizing God's closeness to him during the nine months prior to his birth. But even after he is born the picture does not change; he is still with the Lord as his Sustainer, Protector, and Guide. He speaks of his birth as an *awaking* just as we speak of it as "first seeing the light of day."

139:19–22 After contemplating the *omniscience*, the *omnipresence* and the *omnipotence* of God, the psalmist thinks of those puny men who dare to turn against Him, and he concludes that their punishment is well-deserved. Inevitably some will raise their eyebrows at David's prayer in verses 19–22 as being something less than Christian in its tone. They will protest that the psalmist's sentiments are judgmental and incompatible with divine love. For my own part I feel that the love of God has been emphasized all out of proportion to His holiness and righteousness. It is *true* that God is love but it is not *all* the truth. That is only *one* of His attributes. And His love can never be exercised at the expense of any other attribute. Furthermore, the fact that God is love does not mean that He is incapable of hating; "the one who loves violence His soul hates" (Ps. 11:5); He hates all evildoers (Ps. 5:5); He hates haughty eyes, a lying tongue, hands that shed innocent blood, a heart that devises wicked plans, feet that make haste to run to evil, a false witness who breathes out lies, and a man who sows discord among brothers (Prov. 6:16–19).

Edward J. Young reminds us:

> Before we proceed to condemn David for this prayer, it is well to note that we ourselves pray for the same thing, whenever we pray the words of the Lord's prayer, "Thy kingdom come, Thy will be done."[100]

The coming of Christ's kingdom will be preceded by the destruction of His foes, so to pray for the one is to pray for the other. David unashamedly longs for the time when God will slay the wicked, and when men of blood will have ceased their harassment of him forever (v. 19). These are the men who maliciously defy the Lord God and who lift themselves up against God with evil intent.

David's hatred of these men was not a matter of personal pique. Rather it was because they hated God and rebelled against the Most High. It was his zeal for the Lord's honor that made him **hate them with perfect hatred** and **count them** as his own **enemies**. In this he reminds us of the Lord Jesus whose zeal for His Father's house prompted Him to drive out the money changers. "The strings of David's harp were the chords of the heart of Jesus." Young explains:

> David hated, but his hatred was like God's hatred; it proceeded from no evil emotion, but rather from the earnest and thoroughly sincere desire that the purposes of God must stand and that wickedness must perish. Had David not hated, he would have desired the success of evil and the downfall of God Himself. It is well to keep these thoughts in mind when we consider the nature of David's hatred.[101]

139:23, 24 The Psalm closes with a prayer that has perennial suitability for all God's people, a prayer that will never die as long as there are sinning saints on earth. It asks the Mighty God to thoroughly **search** and **know** the **heart**, to carefully test and **know** the thoughts or **anxieties**. It asks Him to expose every **wicked way** in order that it might be confessed and forsaken. And finally it asks Him to **lead** him **in the way everlasting**.

It is not the challenge of a person protesting his innocence or righteousness. Rather it is the confession of one who has been in the presence of the Lord and is convicted of his own sinfulness. He realizes that he is not cognizant of all his iniquities and wants the Lord to point them out so they can be dealt with effectively.

Psalm 140: From the Hands of the Wicked

140:1–3 **David** begins with a prayer for deliverance from the defamation of the foe. **Evil men** were slandering him and **violent men** were hatching horrendous plans against him. They weren't happy unless they were stirring up **war**. They had honed **their tongues** to a fine edge, and deadly **poison** came shooting out from **under their lips**.

140:4, 5 But the psalmist also needed protection from the snares of the enemy. These **wicked** men were masters in the art of trapping. They planted devices to trip him up. They put hidden booby-traps in his path. They **spread a net** to get him all fouled up. They dangled baits and lures all along the way.

140:6–8 And then too, he needed protection from their murderous scheming. So he draws near to God.

> In commitment—**"You are my God."**
>
> In petition—**"Hear the voice of my supplications."**
>
> In dependence—**"O GOD the Lord, the strength of my salvation."**
>
> In gratitude—**"You have covered my head"** (as with a helmet) **"in the day of battle."**
>
> In supplication—**"Do not grant, O LORD, the desires of the wicked; do not further his wicked scheme."**

This last supplication means, "Do not let him do the things he wants to do against me. Do not seem to be an accomplice to his evil plot by even allowing it." We know that God would never aid and abet any wickedness, but the thought here is that the mere toleration of it might seem to indicate His approval.

140:9–11   Next the psalmist prays that the tables will be turned on the wicked, that the dire things they had mapped out for him might come crashing down on their own proud heads, that **burning coals** might rain **upon them**, that they might be cast into dungeons without any means of escape. He asks that **a slanderer** might never get a foothold in the land, and that disaster will track down the **violent man** without delay.

140:12, 13   The Psalm closes with quiet confidence in the righteous Lord. Whatever happens, David knows that right will prevail—that **the LORD** is on the side of **the afflicted** and **the poor**. And **the righteous shall** always have reason to thank the Lord for His help. **The upright shall dwell in** His **presence** forever, and that makes all the sufferings of this life seem like pin-pricks.

Psalm 141: Prayer Counted as Incense

141:1   At the outset of the Psalm **David** prays for audience and acceptance. As his plaintive cry wings its way heavenward, he asks that the **LORD** will come to him quickly and listen attentively.

141:2   This verse is extraordinarily beautiful. He asks that his **prayer** might be as pleasing and fragrant to God **as incense**, and that **the lifting up of** his **hands** in supplication might have the same impact with the Lord as **the evening sacrifice**.

141:3, 4   But then he moves from generalities to specifics. His first main concern is that he might be kept from partnership with ungodly men in word

or in deed. He asks for **a guard** to be stationed at his **mouth** to prevent the escape of any wrong word, to keep **the door of** his **lips** from speech that would not be honoring to the Lord. Then too, he asks for a **heart** that is free from any hankering to collaborate with the corrupt men in their **wicked** practices. He does not want to partake of their advantages, however attractive or tempting they might seem.

141:5   The suggestions, criticisms, and rebukes of godly friends are welcomed by sensible people. We often cannot see faults in ourselves as clearly as we can see them in others. Only those who really care for us are willing to point out our defects and "blind spots." It is **a kindness** on their part and should be welcomed like medicine by us.

> For still my prayer is against the deeds of the wicked.

The connection here is abrupt, but the meaning seems to be that David continues to pray that the criminal plans of the wicked men mentioned in verse 4 will fail. Darby translates this clause "for yet my prayer also is [for them] in their calamities." Here the thought is that he prays for those who rebuke him in kindness when trouble comes into their lives. Some take it to mean that he prays for his enemies in their calamities, but such a magnanimous Christian attitude seems to be contradicted by verse 10.

141:6   Their judges are overthrown by the sides of the cliff, and they hear my words, for they are sweet.

Their judges here probably refers to the ring-leaders of the evil Mafia. When they meet their inevitable doom, the rest of the sinners will realize that David's words were true after all.

141:7   Our bones are scattered at

the mouth of the grave, as when one plows and breaks up the earth.

Here the subject seems to shift from the enemies of Israel to the Jewish people themselves. Their persecutions have been as thorough as the plowing of a field. Now it is as if nothing is left but their skeletons, and Sheol waits with open **mouth** to devour the **bones**. This makes us think of Ezekiel's vision of the dry bones, referring, of course, to Israel (Ezek. 37:1–14).

141:8–10 In the last three verses, the psalmist prays for deliverance for himself and retribution for his enemies. His expectation is solely from **the Lord**, and his hope for refuge and defense is in GOD alone. Therefore he asks that he might be delivered from the well-laid traps of the ungodly, and that they themselves may be caught in them.

Psalm 142: No Man Cares

Pursued by his enemies, deserted by his friends, holed up **in a cave**— that is where we find **David** now.

142:1, 2 He is praying out loud— even if he is alone. The cries and supplications of a forsaken man reverberate through the cavern. He pours out his **complaint before** the Lord— not that he is angry or resentful but simply that he wants to tell the Lord all about his **trouble** and grief. It is comforting for him to know that when his strength is all but gone, Jehovah knows what he is going through.

142:3, 4 One major factor in his tale of woe is the constant threat of his enemies; they are always setting a trap where they think he will walk. When he looks to the right, that is, to the place of an advocate or helper, there is no one. Everyone seems indifferent to his desperate need. No

one cares for his life. It is really a haunting cry, **"No one cares for my soul,"** a terrible indictment against a selfish, depersonalized society—and perhaps today against a sleeping church.

142:5–7 But if there is no refuge on the human level, he can turn to the LORD, an unfailing **refuge** and a blessed **portion in the land of the living**. So David asks the Lord to come to his rescue quickly because he is at the end of his rope. Those who are out after him hold the balance of power, so he needs the Lord to tip the scales in his favor. When Jehovah delivers him from this **prison** of exile and trouble, David will show how thankful he is.

Also the believers will crowd around to congratulate him and join in thanksgiving because the Lord has been so good to him. As Clarke says, "Those who cannot protect us in our trouble may yet participate in our triumph."[102]

Psalm 143: The Wide Spectrum of Prayer

It is amazing how many different subjects and moods can be touched in a Psalm of twelve verses. Here we have:

143:1 *General request for audience.* **"Hear . . . give ear . . . answer."** There is no poverty of expression but rather emphatic diversity. David asks God to **answer** him **in** His **faithfulness** (to His promises) and **in** His **righteousness** (i.e., because it is right for Him to defend His defenseless servant).

143:2 *Penitence.* He does **not** want God to give him justice. That would be disastrous. All are sinners. No one is able to produce by himself the perfect righteousness that God demands. So man must cast himself on the grace of God.

When we come to Him as undeserving penitents, acknowledging our sins and accepting Christ as our Savior from sin, then God imputes His own righteousness to us, and in Christ we are made fit for heaven.

143:3 *Acute crisis.* The situation is grim. **The enemy** has been pursuing him relentlessly. He feels as if he has been pummeled **to the ground**. His tormentors have forced him to live in isolation, **darkness**, and hiding, cut off and forgotten like ancient corpses in the tombs.

143:4 *Desperation.* He fears that he can't take much more. His **spirit** is ready to give up, and his **heart** is numb.

143:5 *Reminiscence.* He thinks back to **the days** when God worked mighty deliverances for him, and also for the nation of Israel. Where are those times now?

143:6 *Fervency.* The sincerity and ardor of his prayer is indicated by his **hands** pleadingly **spread out** toward God.

Intensity. He **longs for** God, **like** parched, weary ground thirsts for the refreshing rain.

143:7 *Urgency.* The LORD must hurry to his rescue or he is sure he won't survive much longer.

Request for favor. The hiding of God's **face**, either in anger or disinterest, would be tantamount to death.

143:8 *Plea for lovingkindness.* He longs to hear God speak soon to him in words and tones of steadfast love. "... **In the morning**" means early or without delay.

Prayer for guidance. Someone has said that this is a verse that everyone could take as a life motto, **"Cause me to know the way in which I should walk, for I lift up my soul to You."** Divine guidance is indispensable. We simply do not **know the way**, or what would be best for ourselves. Only the God-directed life is effective and enjoyable.

143:9 *Petition for deliverance.* The threat of his **enemies** causes David to cry to the Lord for rescue and relief. He has not depended on anyone else for protection—only on the LORD, and this singleness of trust now forms the basis of his entreaty.

143:10 *Appeal for instruction.* The psalmist not only wanted to know the will of God (v. 8b), he also wanted a heart trained to obey that **will**. God, after all, was his **God**, and what could be more proper than for the creature to obey his Creator?

Prayer for a level path. Everyone has his ups and downs in life, but not everyone has as rocky a road as David. His desire here is that the Lord's **good Spirit** will **lead** him over smoother terrain, free from the extreme forms of danger and disaster to which he had been exposed.

143:11 *Plea for preservation.* In linking his own continued preservation with the glory of God (**"For Your name's sake"**), the psalmist employs one of the strongest levers to move the hand and heart of Omnipotence. In the same way he pleads the **righteousness** of God as the reason why he should be delivered from **trouble**. This is powerful prayer.

143:12 *Retribution on enemies.* Finally he asks that God search out and destroy his **enemies** as a display of His **mercy**. If these things—destruction and **mercy**—sound irreconcilable to us, we should remember that:

the destruction of the wicked is a favor to the universe; just as the arrest and punishment of a robber is a mercy to society, to mankind, just as every prison is a display of mercy as well as justice:—mercy to society at large; justice to the offenders.[103]

David's last appeal is based on the fact that he is Jehovah's **servant**. He is on the Lord's side. He is serving the Lord. Only through the removal of his foes does he feel he can continue.

Psalm 144: The Happy People

Although this Psalm is largely made up of excerpts from other Psalms, it is not pieced together haphazardly. There is real continuity.

144:1, 2 First, **David** honors God as all he needs in the battles of life. It is the Lord who imparts skill and dexterity to him in his confrontations with the enemy. The LORD is his **Rock**, his **lovingkindness**, his **fortress**, his **high tower**, his **deliverer**, his **shield**, his **refuge** and his victory. What more could he need or desire?

144:3, 4 In the light of the greatness of God, **man** is utterly insignificant. It's a wonder that God ever takes notice of him. He is as evanescent as **a breath** on a cold day, as transient as **a passing shadow**. This is true of all mankind, but perhaps David is thinking especially of his adversaries here.

144:5–8 This leads David to pray for the moment when the invincible God marches forth against His puny enemies. But how can you describe the arrival of the invisible God? The only way is by sketching out one of those majestic theophanies in which all nature is convulsed and the universe is shaken. The **heavens . . . bow down** as God descends. He touches **the mountains** and they become smoking volcanoes. **Lightning** rips across the sky like **arrows** from the Almighty. Then when the enemy has been thoroughly disorganized and repulsed, God reaches down and rescues David from the raging billows of trouble.

He delivers him **from the hand of** foreign invaders who are inveterate liars, who raise their **right hand** to lie rather than to confirm the truth.

144:9–11 As a result of his rescue, the psalmist **will sing a new song** to the Lord. With the ten-stringed **harp** he will extol the One who rescued him **from the deadly sword** of the alien adversaries—these men who are habitual liars even when under oath to tell the truth.

144:12 When the king has been delivered from these subversive elements, then his kingdom will enjoy the ideal conditions described here. Actually these conditions will not be fully realized until the Lord returns, crushes all rebellion, and establishes His Millennial Reign.

First, there will be the blessing of family vitality. The **sons** will be healthy, wholesome and handsome, like strong, vigorous **plants**. The girls will be statuesque and beautiful, like the sculptured **pillars** of a **palace**.

144:13–15 Then there will be agricultural abundance. The **barns** and silos will be filled with **all kinds of** grain and **produce**. The **sheep** will reproduce prolifically till there are herds of **ten thousands in** the **fields**. The cattle will bear without mishap, or it may mean that the **oxen** will be weighted down with immense loads. The expressions **"no breaking in or going out"** and **"no outcry in our streets"** may mean that the country will be free from foreign invaders, that there will be no forced migrations into exile, and no noisy demonstrations or riots **in** the **streets**.

It is a picture of unparalleled happiness, the happiness that belongs to **people** who acknowledge Jehovah as their **God**.

Psalm 145: The Missing Nun

David's "Psalm of Praise" is an acrostic, each verse beginning with a successive letter of the Hebrew alphabet. However, in the traditional (Masoretic) Hebrew text, the letter "nun," corresponding to our "n," is missing between verses 13 and 14. The ancient Greek, Syriac, and Latin versions add the following:

"The Lord is faithful in all His words, and gracious in all His works."

In the twentieth century this same line—the missing "nun" line—was also found in Hebrew in the Dead Sea Scrolls.

145:1–3 The theme of the Psalm is the greatness of the Lord. The psalmist is consumed with a holy determination to **extol, bless** and **praise** his **God** and **King** both in time (**every day**) and in eternity (**forever and ever**). The gist of his endless song will be that God is **great**, that His greatness is worthy of great praise, and that **His greatness** is infinite in its dimensions.

145:4 The **works** and **mighty acts** of God will be extolled from **one generation . . . to another**. The song will never die.

145:5 The psalmist himself **will** gratefully **meditate on the glorious splendor of** God's **majesty** as revealed in His **wondrous works** of deliverance.

145:6 Men shall rehearse the power of God's **awesome acts** of judgment, and David **will** continue to **declare** the Lord's **greatness**.

145:7 People everywhere will enthusiastically pour out the fame of the Lord's **great goodness**. And the greatness of His **righteousness**

will be the theme of joyful singing.

145:8 The Lord's greatness extends to His grace and **compassion**. He is great in His self-control and **great in mercy**.

145:9, 10 His goodness extends **to all**, without discrimination, and He is compassionate toward **all His** creatures, without exception.

All His **works** give thanks to Him, though inaudibly. Their very existence demonstrates His wisdom and power. **And** His **saints** join in blessing Him for His infinite perfections.

145:11–13 Then there is the greatness of His **kingdom**. His is the **power** and **glory**. His own people tell the rest of mankind the greatness of His deeds and the bright-shining perfections of His rule. The **kingdom** is **everlasting**, enduring **throughout all generations**.

145:14 The Lord is great in His preservation of those who are going **down** under the burdens of life. And He **raises up** those who have buckled under the pressures and problems.

145:15, 16 Then too, He is great in His provision. All creatures look to Him in dependence and in expectation, and He provides **them their food** as it is needed—a marvelous organizational feat of growth, preparation, and distribution. With no greater effort than opening His **hand**, He feeds His numberless creatures throughout the universe. What a great God He is!

145:17 He is great in His righteousness and kindness. Nothing He does is wrong or unmerciful. Only in God do these virtues perfectly unite.

145:18 He is great in His condescension and availability—always **near** those who sincerely seek Him.

145:19 He is great in His salvation. No one who approaches Him in contrition and faith is ever turned away.

145:20 He is great in His watch-care over **all who love Him**. He invites them to cast all their cares on Him.

Finally, He is great in His wrath. Eventually, **all the wicked** will be destroyed.

145:21 David's mind was made up—He would **praise** this great God **forever**, and He would exhort everyone else to do the same.

Which leads me to say this about the missing "nun": While all the rest of the universe is praising the Lord, don't you be the missing one!

Psalm 146: Glories of the God of Jacob

146:1 The first verse contains two imperatives in which the psalmist calls upon himself to **"Praise the Lord!"**

146:2 The second verse contains two declaratives in which he responds, in effect, **"While I live I will praise the Lord; I will sing praises to my God while I have my being."** It is a lovely dialogue between a man and his best self.

146:3, 4 The rest of the Psalm explains why God and not man is worthy of our full, confiding trust. It isn't long before most of us learn **not** to **trust in man**—not even **in princes** who are supposed to be superior. The best of men are men at best. They cannot save themselves, let alone others. When man's heart stops beating, he dies, is buried, and his body **returns** to dust. All his grandiose **plans perish**. So we might say of man that he is unreliable, impotent, mortal, and fleeting.

146:5 The way of happiness, help, and hope is to rely on **the God of Jacob**, that is, the God of the undeser-

ving. Here are some of the reasons why He is worthy of all our confidence:

146:6 *Omnipotent Creator*. He **made** the heavens, the **earth, the sea, and all** the creatures in the universe. If He can do that, what can't He do?

Dependable One. **He keeps truth forever**. It is impossible for Him to lie or to go back on His word. There is no risk involved in trusting Him. He cannot fail.

146:7 *Advocate of the helpless*. He sees to it that the righteous are vindicated, that their cause eventually triumphs. The waves may seem to be against them but the tide is sure to win.

Provider. He **gives food to the hungry**, both in a spiritual and physical sense. He brings us into His banqueting house, and what a table He spreads!

Emancipator. He sets the captives free—from human oppression, from the chains of sin, from the grip of the world, from the bondage of the devil, and from selfish living.

146:8 *Sight-Giver*. **The Lord opens the eyes of the blind;** some are **blind** physically, some mentally and spiritually, some by birth, some by accident, and some by choice. No case is too hard for Him.

Uplifter. He lifts the flagging spirits of **those who are bowed down** beneath the burdens of worry, affliction, trouble, and sorrow.

Lover of good men. Barnes writes, "It is a characteristic of God, and a foundation for praise, that He loves those who obey law, who do that which is right."

146:9 *Protector of exiles*. He is interested in the welfare of **strangers**, sojourners, and exiles. Pilgrims find a true paraclete in Jehovah.

Friend of the bereft. He upholds **the fatherless** and the **widow**, and all others who have no human helper.

Judge of the evil. He thwarts the best laid plans of ungodly men and makes **the way of the wicked** end in ruin.

146:10 *Eternal King*. In contrast to man's transiency is the eternity of God. **The Lord shall reign forever—to all generations. Praise the Lord!**

Aren't you glad you know Him?

Psalm 147: Jerusalem Restored— Praise God!

It is generally thought that this song celebrates the restoration of Jerusalem after the Babylonian exile. If it was appropriate then, it will have even fuller meaning when the King comes back and finally restores the fortunes of the city and of the nation.

The continuity of the Psalm is as follows:

The appropriateness of praise (v. 1).
For the restoration of Israel (vv. 2–6).
For God's providence in nature (vv. 7–9).
For His delight in the spiritual rather than in the physical (vv. 10, 11).
For His goodness to Jerusalem (vv. 12–14).
For His control of the elements (vv. 15–18).
For His special favor to Israel (vv. 19, 20).

147:1 The renewed nature of man shows instinctively that **it is good to . . . praise the Lord. It is pleasant** as well and eminently appropriate.

147:2–4 He is the God of restoration. Here He is praised for rebuilding **Jerusalem** and regathering Israel's émigrés from their captivity. The fact that a nation or individual has failed does not mean that God is finished with them. In His gracious ministry

of restoring, **He heals the broken-hearted and binds up their wounds.** And since He numbers **the stars** and **calls** each of **them . . . by name**, it must follow that He numbers His people and knows each one individually and intimately.

The way in which the tender compassion of the Lord is placed beside His infinite knowledge in verses 3 and 4 caused Archibald G. Brown to exclaim:

> O Holy Spirit, with lowly reverence we venture yet to say that never hast Thou collected and put side by side two more exquisite statements than these: "He healeth the broken in heart, and knoweth the number of the stars."[104]

> With His healing hand on a broken heart,
> And the other on a star,
> Our wonderful God views the miles apart,
> And they seem not very far.
> —*M. P. Ferguson*

147:5, 6 He is a **great** Lord—**mighty in power**, and **infinite** in **understanding**. He revives and perks up the oppressed, and throws **down** their **wicked** oppressors.

147:7–9 Then **God** should be thanked and praised for His providence in nature. We should **sing** our gratitude to Him for the **clouds** spread across **the heavens**. We should make melody to Him for the **rain** and all it means to **the earth**. We should praise Him for the **grass** that covers the hills. Whole books could be written about the essential roles played by the **clouds**, the **rain**, and the **grass**.

Though He is so great, yet He is concerned to see that the wild animals get their **food**, and He responds to the plaintive caw of the hungry **young ravens**.

147:10, 11 He should be worshiped for the priority He gives to the spiritual over the physical. He is not awed by the horses in the cavalry unit, or for the strong, muscular **legs** of the infantrymen. Or to change the figure, He doesn't take pleasure in the horses as they race, or the athletes as they contend in the Olympics. But **the LORD** is delighted with **those who** reverence **Him** and **who hope in His mercy**.

147:12–14 Then again He should be adored for His goodness to **Jerusalem**. Four distinct blessings come into view.

Civil security—He makes strong cross-bars to secure the city **gates** against invasion.

Domestic felicity—The inhabitants enjoy a happy, full life.

National tranquility—**He makes peace** along the frontiers.

Agricultural prosperity—He satisfies the people with the **finest** foods.

147:15–18 His control over the elements should not be forgotten when praising Jehovah. When **He sends out His** orders, they produce prompt and dramatic results. The earth becomes covered with **snow**, as if it were a woolen blanket. He dusts the ground with **frost** that looks like white **ashes**. When the **hail** stones come crashing down, who can refrain from scurrying for shelter? Then He changes His orders and the snow and ice melt. The south wind causes the temperature to rise and the spring thaw begins. And so it is in human affairs that the dark, cold winters are followed by the warmth and revival of spring.

147:19, 20 Finally, He is to be honored for His special favor **to Israel**. It was to this nation alone that He delivered His laws and covenants.

No other **nation** has been so favored. The Gentiles were not the recipients of His regulations. Williams writes:

His election of Israel as the depository of His Word, and as the channel of its communication to the world (vv. 19 and 20) moved both Moses and Paul to wonder and worship (Deut. 4:8; Rom. 3:2; 11:33).[105]

Psalm 148: Creation's Choir

I have seen and heard many different choirs but never one like this. It is made up of all creation, animate and inanimate. The universe is the choir loft, endless rows of chairs, tier upon tier.

148:1–6 In the topmost section are the **angels**, praising **the LORD from the heavens**, the **hosts** of heaven singing out the glories of Jehovah. **The sun, moon** and **stars** are next; their part is the music of the spheres. The highest **heavens** and the water-laden clouds are singing "Glory to God in the highest. . . ." All are honoring God as their Creator, the One who spoke and brought the worlds into being. It is He who gave permanence and stability to His creation, and who built into it certain laws and principles which are unvarying.

148:7, 8 Next in descending order are the **great sea creatures** and all the swarming life of the oceans. They too testify that the Hand that made them is divine. **Fire, hail, snow, clouds**, and the **stormy** gale, quick to obey His orders, remind us that Jehovah controls the seasons and the weather and harnesses them to do His will.

148:9, 10 Then there are the **mountains and all the hills**, lifting their heads in adoration. **All** the **trees** are there, those that bear fruit and those that yield lumber; they are lifting up their branches to His name. Wild **beasts** and domestic animals, **creeping things** and birds—all are chanting the wisdom and power of the Lord.

148:11, 12 As we come toward the front rows, we see the great assemblage of mankind—**kings, princes, all** governmental officials, and all the common people. Fellows and girls, **old men and children**—all with heads tilted back and mouths opened wide in worship of Jehovah.

148:13, 14 The massed choir is praising **the name of the LORD** as the **name** above every name and as the One whose **glory** is unsurpassable. And there is a particular theme in the song of the choir—they are magnifying the Lord for what He has done for **Israel**. He has raised up a **horn** for **His people**, that is, the Messiah. In the Second Advent of the Lord Jesus, He has given special occasion for **His saints** to **praise** Him. **The children of Israel**, there at the front of the choir, stand in a place of special nearness **to Him**. Through the restored nation, blessing flows out to all the world. That is why the choir is joining in one grand Hallelujah—**"Praise the LORD!"**

Psalm 149: The High Praises of God

There are two parts to this Psalm. In the first (vv. 1–6a) the saints are singing. In the second (vv. 6b–9) they are reigning. The time in question is when the Lord Jesus returns to the earth and ushers in His long-awaited kingdom.

149:1–3 The **new song** which Israel sings is the song of creation, redemption, and reign. They rejoice in Jehovah as the Author of their natural and spiritual creation and as their glorious Monarch.

They praise Him not only in song but in **the dance** as well. What is this?

Believers dancing? Yes, dancing in holy and pure delight before the Lord. As an expression of true spiritual joy and worship, **the dance** is acceptable to God. But to use this verse to justify dancing as it is practiced today is something else. There is a difference between the use of the dance and its abuse. The psalmist is only speaking about its divinely sanctioned use. The same is true of instrumental music. If timbrels and harps had emotions, they would all aspire to make melody to the Lord. Too often they are debased to sensual employment. Their proper use is good; their abuse is horrendous.

149:4–6a Why all the fuss, all the jubilant music? Because **the LORD takes pleasure in His** restored **people**; He has awarded a garland of victory to the loyal remnant. The Great Tribulation is past, and it is a day of clear shining after rain.

The people have much reason to rejoice **in the glory** which is theirs as they are associated with the King of Glory. They have every reason to raise the rafters with **joyful** song as they sit on their thrones by day or lie **on their beds** at night (the word "beds" in verse 5 may refer to either). It is really appropriate that all their vocal chords be filled with the **high praises of God**.

149:6b–8 As you see, there is an abrupt change in the middle of verse 6. From this point to the end Israel is found in the role of judges, dispensing justice. This may refer to the destruction of her foes at the return of the Messiah. That judgment will be executed by the Lord, but the nation may, in a figure, be thought of as sharing in it. But I rather think it refers to Israel's role as head of the nations during the Millennium. The Lord Jesus will rule with a rod of iron during that period (Rev. 2:27). The apostles will sit on thrones judging the twelve tribes of Israel (Matt. 19:28). And Israel herself will share in the rule over the Gentiles (Dan. 7:22).

So the saints have **two-edged** swords **in their** hands, administering **vengeance and punishments on the peoples** whenever necessary. Rebellious **kings** and **their nobles** will be bound **with chains** and **fetters of iron**. It will be a reign of absolute righteousness, of undeviating justice.

149:9 This is the honored role of Israel in that day—to see that all insubordination and subversion are punished promptly.

It is also true that the *NT* **saints** will share in the coming reign of Christ. We read about that in 1 Corinthians 6:2, 3.

Psalm 150: Praise the Lord!

We have reached the grand finale. And what could be more appropriate than to find a short, pointed appeal for creation to find its true destiny in the worship of God? The Psalm answers four key questions on the subject of praise: Where, What, How, and Who?

The glory of God was the purpose of creation. Therefore man finds the central reason for his existence in praising the Lord. As it is so tersely stated in the Shorter Catechism, "The chief end of man is to glorify God and to enjoy Him forever."

150:1 But *where?* We should **praise** Him **in His sanctuary** and **in His mighty firmament**, which is another way of saying *everywhere*—on earth and in heaven. There is no place where worship is out of place.

150:2 And for *what?* **For His mighty acts** and **according to His excellent greatness**. In other words, we should

praise Him for what He has done for us, and for who He is. But not only *for* His exceeding greatness—also *according to* His exceeding greatness. It is a sin to be unenthusiastic in rehearsing the excellencies of our Creator and Redeemer.

150:3–5 *How?* With an orchestra of every kind of instrument. **The trumpet** with its martial, commanding notes. The **lute** with its dulcet, pastoral tones. The **harp**, gentle and sweet in its strains. **The timbrel,** festive and uninhibited in its accompaniment of the **dance**. **Stringed instruments** of all sorts, the cello, the bass viol, the violin, the mandolin, the guitar—capture every note and chord in the world of music to honor the Great King. Wind instruments—the flute, the oboe, the clarinet—don't miss one in this great philharmonic extravaganza. And the percussion instruments, bless them—especially the crashing, **clashing**, ear-splitting **cymbals**, punctuating the anthem with loud amens.

150:6 But that brings us to the last question. *Who?* And the answer, of course, is, **"Let everything that has breath praise the Lord."** The massed choir of all the voices of earth are given the cue to join in the loud, eternal burst of praise to God. *Hallelujah!* **Praise the Lord!**

ENDNOTES

[1](Intro) Graham Scroggie, *Daily Notes of the Scripture Union.*

[2](Intro) Albert Barnes, *Notes on the Book of Psalms,* I:xix.

[3](Intro) C. S. Lewis, *Reflections on the Psalms,* p. 10.

[4](Intro) F. W. Grant, "Psalms," in *The Numerical Bible,* III:10.

[5](1:3) The word translated "planted"

(*shātûl*) literally means *transplanted* (Koehler-Baumgartner, *Lexicon in Veteris Testamenti Libros*, p. 1015), a fitting image of the born-again person.

[6](1:3) D. L. Moody, *Notes from My Bible*, p. 64.

[7](2:Intro) In Acts 4:25–28, Peter and Paul connected Psalm 2 with the rejection of Christ. It is true that it had a partial fulfillment when Herod, Pontius Pilate, the Gentiles, and the people of Israel united to kill Christ. But the final fulfillment is still future.

[8](3:1, 2) *International Standard Bible Encyclopedia*, III:2096.

[9](4:1) Charles H. Spurgeon, quoted in "Choice Gleanings Calendar."

[10](5:Intro) Koehler and Baumgartner conjecture that *michtām* may be related to the Akkadian word for *cover* and thus may mean "expiation psalm."

[11](8:5) Hebrew has *Elohim* here; see NKJV footnote.

[12](9:Intro) Psalm 10 is built on the second half of the Hebrew alphabet, hence some believe Psalms 9 and 10 were originally one psalm.

[13](10:Intro) See previous note.

[14](14:1) Henry Bosch, *Our Daily Bread*.

[15](14:1) Barnes, *Psalms*, I:114.

[16](16:3) Documentation unavailable.

[17](17:15) E. Bendor Samuel, *The Prophetic Character of the Psalms*, p. 26

[18](19:3, 4a) Immanuel Kant, *General History of Nature*, further documentation unavailable.

[19](19:7–9) Quoted from Wallace's *Kant*, by Alexander Wright in *The Psalms of David and the Higher Criticism, Or Was David "The Sweet Psalmist of Israel"?*, p. 109.

[20](19:12) Barnes, *Psalms*, I:175.

[21](23:Intro) J. R. Littleproud, further documentation unavailable.

[22](24:9, 10) F. B. Meyer, *F. B. Meyer on the Psalms*, p. 35.

[23](25:Intro) The letter for "r" (*resh*) occurs in both verses 18 and 19 whereas one would expect a "q" (*qoph*) in verse 18.

[24](26:12) J. C. Ryle, *Expository Thoughts on the Gospels, Luke*, II:239.

[25](29:10, 11) W. E. Vine, *Isaiah*, p. 205.

[26](29:10, 11) H. A. Ironside, *Studies on the Psalms*, p. 173.

[27](31:Intro) Lewis, *Reflections*, p. 10.

[28](32:8, 9) Jay Adams, *Competent to Counsel*, p. 124.

[29](34:8, 9) Murdoch Campbell, *From Grace to Glory*, p. 66.

[30](34:10) Some scholars believe that "young lions" should be read "deniers of God," but the meaning of the verse remains the same.

[31](36:5) Albert Barnes, *The Bible Commentary, Psalms*, Vol. 1, p. 312.

[32](36:5) Arthur W. Pink, *The Attributes of God*, p. 47.

[33](36:7) John Brine, quoted in *The Attributes of God*, Arthur W. Pink, p. 80.

[34](37:5, 6) Barnes, *Psalms*, I:320.

[35](37:28) F. W. Dixon, further documentation unavailable.

[36](50:1) The same Hebrew word (*eretz*) means both *earth* and *land*.

[37](50:8) Meyer, *Psalms*, p. 63.

[38](52:8, 9) Grant, "Psalms," III:212.

[39](53:Intro) In Psalm 14 the name Jehovah is used four times and Elohim three times. Here the name Elohim is found seven times.

[40](54:7) G. Campbell Morgan, *An Exposition of the Whole Bible*, p. 240.

[41](58:8) W. Graham Scroggie, *Psalms*, p. 50.

[42](58:9) A. Maclaren, quoted in *Psalms* by W. Graham Scroggie, II:49.

[43](58:10) Morgan, *Exposition*, p. 242.

[44](60:9) The NKJV editors show that they agree by ending v. 8 with quotation marks.

[45](61:2) Concerning Matthew 16:18, G. Campbell Morgan says: "Remember,

He was talking to Jews. If we trace the figurative use of the word through Hebrew Scriptures, we find that it is never used symbolically of man but always of God. So here at Caesarea Philippi, it is not upon Peter that the Church is built. Jesus did not trifle with figures of speech. He took up their old Hebrew illustration—rock, always the symbol of Deity, and said, Upon God Himself, Christ, the Son of the living God—I will build my church.'" Perhaps the one exception to Morgan's statement is found in Deuteronomy 32:31: "their rock is not as our Rock." But even here, "rock" is a symbol of deity (although a false god).

[46](66:8–12) Williams, *Student's Commentary on the Holy Scriptures*, p. 67.

[47](67:6, 7) Franz Delitzsch, "Psalms," in *Biblical Commentary on the Old Testament*, XII:240.

[48](68:11–13) The Hebrew word for "those who proclaimed it" (*hamebasserôt*) is feminine plural.

[49](68:24) Lewis, *Reflections*, p. 45.

[50](71:Intro) John G. Bellett, *Short Meditations on the Psalms*, p. 76.

[51](71:14–16) Williams, *Commentary*, p. 72.

[52](81:Intro) Merrill F. Unger, *Unger's Bible Dictionary*, p. 350.

[53](81:8–10) Gaebelein, *Psalms*, p. 316.

[54](83:13–18) Morgan, *Exposition*, p. 252.

[55](86:17) E. W. Bullinger, *The Companion Bible*, Appendix 32, p. 31.

[56](86:17) Grant, "Psalms," III:330.

[57](87:Intro) Teddy Kollek and Moshe Pearlman, *Jerusalem, A History of Forty Centuries*, p. 12.

[58](87:6) Documentation unavailable.

[59](87:6) Gaebelein, *Psalms*, p. 332.

[60](88:11, 12) *The New Bible Commentary*, p. 474.

[61](88:13–18) Quoted by A. G. Clarke, *Analytical Studies in the Psalms*, p. 219.

[62](93:5) Williams, *Student's Commentary*, p. 372.

[63](94:Intro) Pink, *Attributes*, p. 75.

[64](96:11–13) *Jehovah* is the traditional pronunciation of a combination of the consonants *JHWH* (or *YHWH*) and the vowels of *Adonai* (Lord). The Hebrew name was probably originally pronounced *Yahweh*. For fear of profaning the Name of God the Jews said their word for "Lord" (*Adonai*) whenever the sacred letters YHWH appeared in the text. It is noteworthy that the initial letters of the four Hebrew words in the first clause of verse eleven spell out the personal name of God, Yahweh (YHWH). KJV and NKJV indicate the name of God by "LORD" in all capitals, but *quotations* from the Bible generally do not use all capitals.

[65](97:6a) Gaebelein, *Psalms*, p. 363.

[66](98:4–6) See F. W. Grant, "Psalms," III:363. See also previous one on this word. This expression also has been found in the Dead Sea Scrolls of Deuteronomy 32:43 and the LXX there as well. Conceivably the Masoretes (preservers of Jewish tradition) deleted it there because Christians used the verse to support the deity of Christ (as in Heb. 1:6).

[67](100:Intro) Barnes, *Psalms*, III:56.

[68](101:2) Clarke, *Psalms*, p. 247.

[69](101:7, 8) Grant, "Psalms," III:368.

[70](104:31, 32) J. J. Stewart Perowne, *The Book of Psalms*, II:234.

[71](109:30, 31) Meyer, *Psalms*, p. 133.

[72](Essay) Unger, *Bible Dictionary*, p. 231.

[73](Essay) Barnes, *Psalms*, I:xxxvii.

[74](Essay) Scroggie, *The Psalms*, p. 32.

[75](110:1) In the KJV and NKJV "LORD" in all capitals always stands for Jehovah (= *Yahweh*), the personal, covenant name of God. See note 64.

[76](110:2) Ironside used this expres-

sion as a book title: *The Great Parenthesis*, that is, the current dispensation of the Christian church.

[77](110:3) Scroggie, *The Psalms*, p. 85.

[78](112:10) Barnes, *Psalms*, III:149.

[79](118:24) *Ibid.*, pp. 173, 174.

[80](119:Intro) Samuel Ridout, *How to Study the Bible*, p. 73.

[81](119:Intro) Lewis, *Reflections*, p. 52.

[82](119:Intro) Bellett, *Short Meditations*, p. 131.

[83](119:24) Matthew Henry, *Commentary in One Volume*, p. 706.

[84](119:92) Barnes, *Psalms*, III:204.

[85](119:107) Charles H. Spurgeon, *The Treasury of David*, VI:244.

[86](119:136) Quoted by Moody, *Notes*, p. 79.

[87](119:139) Barnes, *Psalms*, III:217.

[88](119:145) Verses 145–152 begin with the letter "qoph," the first letter of the Hebrew word for "cry."

[89](120:1, 2) Psalms 120–134 are called "Songs of Ascents" because the pilgrims sang them as they *went up* to Jerusalem for the annual feasts of the Lord (Passover, etc.).

[90](121:4) Moody, *Notes*, p. 79.

[91](121:5, 6) It must be remembered that this is *poetry*, and it may be a figure of speech that gives both extremes and means everything in between. This is called a *merism*. Another example is "your going out and your coming in" (v. 8), i.e., your whole lifestyle.

[92](121:7, 8) All these forms translate one Hebrew verb, *shāmar*.

[93](122:6) Collins and Lapierre, *O Jerusalem!*, p. 33.

[94](122:7–9) Barnes, *Psalms*, III:238.

[95](135:6) Pink, *Attributes*, p. 27.

[96](137:9) Lewis, *Reflections*, pp. 113, 114.

[97](138:2) The word translated *temple* (*hêkāl*) can also mean a palace or other building, including the tabernacle; the Jewish temple is not always meant.

[98](138:2) Clarke, *Psalms*, p. 337.

[99](139:13, 14) Radmacher, further documentation unavailable.

[100](139:19–22) Edward J. Young, *Psalm 139*, p. 95.

[101](139:19–22) *Ibid.*, p. 105.

[102](142:5–7) Clarke, *Psalms*, p. 343.

[103](143:12) Barnes, *Psalms*, III:314.

[104](147:2–4) Archibald G. Brown, further documentation unavailable.

[105](147:19, 20) Williams, *Student's Commentary*, p. 148.

BIBLIOGRAPHY

Alexander, Joseph A. *The Psalms Translated and Explained*. Grand Rapids, Baker Book House, Reprinted from 1873 Edinburgh edition, 1977.

Barnes, Albert. *Notes on the Old Testament, Psalms*, 3 vols. Grand Rapids: Baker Book House, 1973.

Bellett, J. G. *Short Meditations on the Psalms*. Oak Park, IL: Bible Truth Publishers, 1961.

Bridges, Charles. *Psalm 119*. Edinburgh: The Banner of Truth Trust, Reprinted from 1827 edition, 1977.

Clarke, A. G. *Analytical Studies in the Psalms*. Kilmarnock: John Ritchie, Ltd., 1949.

Delitzsch, Franz. "Psalms." In *Biblical Commentary on the Old Testament*. Vols. 11—13. Grand Rapids: Wm. B. Eerdmans Publishing Co., 1970.

Gaebelein, A. C. *The Book of Psalms*. Neptune, N.J.: Loizeaux Bros., 1939.

Grant, F. W. "Psalms." In *The Numerical Bible*. New York: Loizeaux Bros., 1897.

Ironside, H. A. *Studies on Book One of the Psalms*. Neptune, N.J.: Loizeaux Bros., 1952.

Kidner, Derek. *Psalms 1–72*. Downers Grove, IL: InterVarsity Press, 1973.

———. *Psalms 73—150*. Downers

Grove, IL: InterVarsity Press, 1975.

Lewis, C. S. *Reflections on the Psalms*. London: Collins, Fontana Books, 1969.

Maclaren, A. *The Book of Psalms*. London: Hodder & Stoughton, 1908.

Meyer, F. B. *F. B. Meyer on the Psalms*. Grand Rapids: Zondervan Publishing House, n.d.

Morgan, G. Campbell. *Notes on the Psalms*. Westwood, N.J.: Revell Co., 1947.

Perowne, J. J. Stewart. *The Book of Psalms*. 2 vols. Grand Rapids: Zondervan Publishing House, Reprinted from 1878 edition, 1966.

Samuel, E. Bendor, *The Prophetic Character of the Psalms*. London: Pickering & Inglis, n.d.

Scroggie, W. Graham. *Psalms*. Vol. 2. London: Pickering & Inglis, 1949.

———. *The Psalms*. Old Tappan, N.J.: Fleming H. Revell Co., 1948.

Spence, H.D.M. and Exell, Joseph S., Editors. *Pulpit Commentary*, Vol. 8. Grand Rapids: Wm. B. Eerdmans Publishing Co., 1950.

Spurgeon, C. H. *The Treasury of David*. Grand Rapids: Baker Book House, 1983.

Wright, *The Psalms of David and the Higher Criticism, Or Was David "The Sweet Psalmist of Israel"?* Edinburgh and London: Oliphant Anderson & Ferrier, 1900.

Young, E. J. *Psalm 139*. London: The Banner of Truth Trust, 1965.

PROVERBS

Introduction

"It is not a portrait-album or a book of manners: it offers a key to life. The samples of behaviour which it holds up to view are all assessed by one criterion, which could be summed up in the question, 'Is this wisdom or folly?'"

—Derek Kidner

I. Unique Place in the Canon

The Book of Proverbs is as modern as today. It deals with the problems of life that each of us has to face.

If any book in the Bible could be said to be beamed especially to young people, this one could.

When a young man said to Carlyle that there was nothing in the Book of Proverbs, he replied: "Make a few proverbs and you will think differently of the book."[1]

Proverbs is the world's finest collection of sound, sanctified common sense, written so that young people might not have to make some of the dreary mistakes their elders have made.

The purpose of Proverbs is stated in 1:1–7. In brief, it is to give wisdom and understanding to a young man so that he will find true blessedness in life and escape the snares and pitfalls of sin. The key verse is 9:10, "The fear of the Lord is the beginning of wisdom, and the knowledge of the Holy One is understanding."

Arnot calls the book, "Laws from heaven for life on earth."[2] That describes its contents very concisely.

A proverb is a pithy statement of wisdom, often worded in a clever way to make it easy to remember. Most of the proverbs consist of two clauses, presenting either similarities or contrasts.

There are several varieties of proverbs, as will be seen from the following:

1. Some are single statements, expressing a simple fact:

> When a man's ways please the Lord,
> He makes even his enemies to be at peace with him (16:7).

2. Some consist of two clauses or phrases, in which one thing is compared to another:

> As cold water to a weary soul,
> So is good news from a far country (25:25).

3. Still others have two clauses or phrases, usually connected by *but*, and describing things that are opposite to each other:

> The memory of the righteous is blessed,
> But the name of the wicked will rot (10:7).

This type of proverb is found mostly in Chapters 10—15.

4. There are proverbs with two clauses or phrases in which the same thought is repeated in a slightly different way:

For a harlot is a deep pit,
And a seductress is a narrow
well (23:27).

II. Authorship

This book is sometimes called
"The Proverbs of Solomon," since
most of these sayings were written
by that very wise king (1:1; 10:1;
25:1). 1 Kings 4:32 tells us that Solomon composed 3,000 proverbs, so
these are the several hundred the
Spirit of God inspired to be Holy
Scripture.

Chapter 30 is said to contain "the
words of Agur the son of Jakeh"
(30:1). Chapter 31 is introduced as
"the words of king Lemuel" (31:1).
We have no knowledge today as to
the identity of these two men. Some
think that these were other names
used by Solomon.

III. Date

Since Proverbs 25:1 tells us that
the men of Hezekiah copied out a
section of the Proverbs of Solomon,
the final form of the book has to be at
least as late as 700 B.C. Solomon's
original contributions would be from
the 900's B.C. If Agur and Lemuel are
not poetic names for Solomon himself, and they lived either before 900
B.C. or after 700 B.C., that would
expand the possible period of compilation still further.

IV. Background and Themes

Written by Solomon and others,
the colorfully poetic book of Proverbs
provides a liberal education. It covers
a wide range of subjects—from spanking a child to ruling a kingdom. One
sometimes wonders if there is any

truth that is not found here, at least
in germ form. It speaks of the liquor
problem, installment buying, juven-
ile delinquency, and labor management. You will meet all kinds of
people here—the brawling woman,
the proud fool, the man who does
not like to be told his faults, and the
ideal wife. And best of all, the Lord
Jesus is here, speaking to us as Wisdom personified. "The ideal elements in the book speak of Him; the
actual shortcomings cry out for Him"
(quoted in Daily Notes).

Proverbs is difficult to outline. Instead of presenting a continuity of
thought, like a motion picture, it
presents individual pictures, like colored slides.

As you study it, you will find that
it resembles the book of James in
many ways.

Another valuable study device is
to find illustrations of individual
proverbs from:

1. The Bible Itself
2. History
3. Biography
4. Literature
5. Nature
6. Newspapers and Periodicals
7. Radio and Television
8. Your own Experience

It will be helpful to remember that
while some of the proverbs are statements of *absolute truth*, some are
statements that are *generally true* but
that might have an exception here
and there. For instance, it is always
true that "the name of the Lord is a
strong tower" (18:10), but there may
be exceptions to the statement that "a
friend loves at all times" (17:17).

In studying *The Believers Bible Commentary*, it is essential to read the
corresponding verse or verses first.
Many of the explanations will be

meaningless unless you have read the proverb in question.

Classification of Some of the Subjects in the Book of Proverbs

The Lord

The blessing of (10:22)

Confidence in (3:25, 26)

Creation by (3:19, 20; 16:4; 20:12; 22:2b; 29:13b)

Discipline of (3:11, 12)

The fear of the Lord (1:7, 29; 2:5; 8:13; 9:10; 10:27; 14:26, 27; 15:16, 33; 16:6; 19:23; 22:4; 23:17; 24:21; 28:14)

Guidance of (3:5, 6; 16:3, 9)

Judgment and justice by (15:25a; 17:3; 21:2; 29:26)

Omnipresence of (15:3)

Omniscience of (15:11; 16:2)

Prayer answered by (15:8, 29)

Protection by (15:25b; 18:10)

The rich man and the poor man (10:15; 13:7, 8; 14:20, 21, 31; 15:16; 17:1, 5; 18:23; 19:1, 4, 17; 21:13; 22:2, 7, 16, 22, 23; 28:3, 6, 11, 27; 29:7, 13)

Source of wisdom (2:6–8)

Sovereignty and power of (16:1, 7, 9, 33; 19:21; 20:24; 21:30, 31; 22:12)

To be trusted (29:25b)

Parenting

Instruction in child training (13:24; 19:18; 22:6, 22:15; 23:13, 14; 29:15, 17)

Obedience and disobedience to parents (1:8, 9; 6:20, 22; 13:1, 19–26; 20:20; 23:22; 30:17)

Words of parental advice (1:8–19; 2:1–22; 3:1–35; 4:1–27; 5:1–23; 6:1–35; 7:1–27; 23:19–35; 24:4–22; 31:1–9)

Speech

Appropriate (15:23; 25:11)

Backbiting (25:23)

Belittling (11:12a)

Disturbing (27:14)

Evil (12:13a; 15:28b)

Excessive (10:19a; 13:3b)

Flattering (20:19; 26:28b; 28:23; 29:5)

Foolish (12:23b; 14:3a, 7; 15:2b; 18:6, 7)

Gentle (15:1a, 4a)

Good (10:20a, 21a; 16:21, 23, 24; 23:16)

Harmful (11:9, 11; 12:18a; 15:4b; 16:27; 18:21; 26:18, 19)

Harsh (15:1b)

Hasty (18:13; 29:20)

Healing (12:18b; 15:4a; 16:24; 18:21)

Honest (12:19a; 13:5)

Inappropriate (17:7)

Lying, deceitful (6:17; 10:18a; 12:19b, 22a; 14:25b; 17:4; 26:18, 19, 23–26, 28a)

Perverse (4:24; 10:31b, 32b; 15:4b; 17:20b)

Restrained (10:19b; 11:12b, 13b; 12:23a; 13:3a; 17:27a, 28; 21:23)

Satisfying (12:14; 18:20)

Slanderous (10:18b; 30:10)

Talebearing, gossiping (11:13a; 16:28; 17:9b; 18:8; 20:19; 22:11a; 26:10, 22–26, 28)

Thoughtful (15:28a)

True and false witness (6:19; 12:17; 14:5, 25; 19:5, 9, 28; 21:28; 25:18)

Wise (10:31a; 14:3b; 15:2a; 18:4)

Worthless (14:23b)

Various Themes

Abominations
—to the Lord (3:32; 6:16; 8:7; 11:1, 20; 12:22; 15:8, 9, 26; 16:5; 17:15; 20:10, 23; 21:27; 28:9)
—to others (13:19; 16:12; 24:9; 26:25; 29:27)

Ancient landmarks (22:28; 23:10, 11)

Borrowing and lending (22:7b)

The diligent man (21:5; 22:29; 27:18, 23–27; 28:19a)

The diligent man and the sluggard contrasted (10:4, 5; 12:24, 27; 13:4)

Enemy (16:7; 24:17, 18; 25:21; 27:6)

Envy (3:31; 14:30; 23:17; 24:1, 19; 27:4)

False balances and weights (11:1; 16:11; 20:10, 23)

Friends, neighbors, and friendship (3:27–29; 6:1–5; 11:12; 12:26; 14:21; 16:28; 17:9, 17; 18:17, 24; 21:10; 22:24, 25; 24:17, 19; 25:8, 9, 17, 20, 21, 22; 26:18, 19; 27:6, 9, 10, 14, 17; 28:23; 29:5)

Honey (16:24; 24:13; 25:16, 27; 27:7)

Industriousness (12:9, 11; 14:4, 23a)

The interrelationship between physical, mental, and spiritual health (3:1, 2, 7, 8, 16; 4:10, 22; 9:11; 13:12; 14:30; 15:13, 30; 16:24; 17:22; 18:14; 27:9)

Justice and injustice (13:23; 17:15, 26; 18:5; 21:15; 22:8, 16; 24:23, 24)

The king or ruler (14:28, 35; 16:10, 12–15; 19:12; 20:2, 8, 26, 28; 21:1; 22:11, 29; 23:1; 24:21, 22; 25:2–7, 15; 28:15, 16; 29:2, 4, 12, 14, 26; 30:31; 31:4, 5)

The lot (16:33; 18:18)

Old age (16:31; 17:6; 20:29)

Partiality (18:5; 24:23b–25; 28:21)

Pride and humility (3:34b; 8:13; 11:2; 15:33; 16:5,18, 19; 18:12; 22:4; 29:23)

Reputation (10:7; 22:1)

The righteous man and the wicked man contrasted (3:32, 33; 10:3, 6, 7, 9, 11, 16, 24, 25, 28, 29–32; 11:3–11, 17–21, 23, 27, 31; 12:2, 3, 5–8, 12–14, 20, 21, 26, 28; 13:2, 5, 6, 9, 21, 25; 14:2, 9, 11, 14, 22, 32; 15:8, 9, 26; 24:15, 16; 28:1, 12)

The scorner or scoffer (3:34a; 9:7, 8, 12; 13:1; 14:6; 15:12; 19:25; 21:11, 24; 22:10; 24:9; 29:8a)

Servants and slaves (14:35; 17:2; 19:10; 29:19, 21)

The sluggard (6:6–11; 10:26; 15:19; 18:9; 19:15, 24; 20:4, 13; 21:25; 22:13; 24:30–34; 26:13–16)

Soul-winning (11:30; 24:11, 12)

Strife and contention (10:12; 12:18; 13:10; 15:1–4, 18; 16:27, 28; 18:6–8; 21:9, 19; 28:25)

Suretyship (6:1–5; 11:15; 17:18; 20:16; 22:26, 27; 27:13)

Teachableness (willingness to accept instruction and correction) (1:5; 9:7–9; 10:17; 12:1, 15; 13:1, 10, 18; 15:5, 10, 12, 31, 32; 17:10; 19:20, 25; 21:11; 25:12; 27:5, 6; 28:23; 29:1)

Temper and patience (14:17, 29; 15:18; 16:32; 19:11)

Temperance and self-control (23:1–3; 25:28)

Wine (20:1; 21:17; 23:20, 21, 29–35; 31:4–7)

The wisdom of getting guidance or advice from others (11:14; 12:15; 15:22; 20:18; 24:6)

Wisdom personified (1:20–33; 8:1–36; 9:1–6; 14:1a; 16:16, 22; 19:23)

The wise man and foolish man contrasted (3:35; 10:8, 13, 14, 23; 12:15, 16, 23; 13:16; 14:3, 8, 15, 16, 18, 19, 24, 33; 15:7, 14, 20, 21; 17:11, 12, 16, 21, 24, 25, 28; 18:2, 6–8; 29:8, 9, 11)

The Word and obedience to it (13:13, 14; 16:20; 19:16; 28:4, 7, 9; 29:18; 30:5, 6)

Wealth

Accompanied by trouble (15:6, 16, 17; 16:8; 17:1)

Brings friends (19:4, 6)

Gained by violence (11:16)

Gained dishonestly (10:2; 13:22b; 15:6b; 20:17; 21:6; 22:16; 28:8)

Gained hastily (13:11; 20:21; 28:20b, 22)

Gained honestly (10:16)

Gifts and bribes (15:27; 17:8, 23; 18:16; 19:6; 21:14; 25:14; 29:4)

Inherited (19:14)

Its limited value (11:4)

Less valuable than wisdom (16:16)

Not to be trusted (11:28)

Pretended (13:7)

Protection of (10:15a; 13:8; 18:11)

Stewardship and generosity (3:9, 10, 27, 28; 11:24–26; 19:6; 21:26b; 22:9; 28:27)

Transient (23:4, 5; 27:24)

The Wicked Woman

The wicked woman or harlot (2:16–19; 5:3–23; 6:24–35; 7:5–27; 9:13–18; 22:14; 23:27, 28; 30:20)

Other women

A beautiful woman without discretion (11:22)

A contentious woman (19:13; 21:9, 19; 25:24; 27:15, 16)

A good wife (12:4; 18:22; 31:10–31)

A gracious woman (11:16)

A prudent wife (19:14)

An unloved woman (30:23)

The wife of one's youth (5:18, 19)

OUTLINE

Commentary

I. INTRODUCTION (1:1–7)

1:1 **Solomon the son of David** was the wisest, richest, and most honored of the kings **of Israel** (1 Kgs. 3:12, 13; 4:30, 31). He spoke three thousand **proverbs**, but only some of them are preserved in this book. These extend from 1:1 to 29:27.

1:2, 3 Verses 2–6 tell us why he wrote these proverbs. In brief, they provide practical **wisdom** for the living and management of life.

Here people may learn shrewdness and receive the kind of **instruction** that provides know-how. Here they may learn to **perceive the words of understanding**, to discern between what is good and evil, profitable and worthless, helpful and harmful. Here men are schooled in what is wise, righteous, proper, and honorable.

1:4 By listening to these proverbs **the simple** develop **prudence** or "savvy," and **young** people gain insight and sanctified common sense.

1:5 **Wise** men will grow wiser by heeding these proverbs, and **a man of understanding** will learn how to guide himself and to advise others as well. Is it not significant that a book addressed primarily to youth should announce at the very outset, **"A wise man will hear"**? That is what is meant by a wise person in the book of Proverbs. It is one who is teachable. He is willing to listen and not do all the talking. He is not an insufferable know-it-all.

1:6 The book is designed to enable a person **to understand a proverb and an enigma**, i.e., the lesson which often lies beneath the surface. It helps him to grasp the meaning of **wise** sayings and the hidden truths contained in them.

1:7 Now we come to the key verse of the book (see also 9:10). **The fear of the LORD is the beginning** or chief part **of knowledge**. If a man wants to be wise, the place to begin is in reverencing God and in trusting and obeying Him. What is more reasonable than that the creature should trust his Creator? On the other hand, what is more illogical than for a man to reject God's Word and to live by his own hunches? The wise thing to do is to repent of one's sins, trust Jesus Christ as Lord and Savior, and then live for Him wholeheartedly and devotedly.

Fools despise wisdom and instruction. Just as a wise man in this book is one who is willing and anxious to learn, a fool is one who cannot be told anything. He is intractable and conceited, and only learns lessons the hard way, if at all.

II. PROVERBS OF SOLOMON ON WISDOM AND FOLLY (1:8—9:18)

A. Wisdom's Admonition (1:8–33)

1:8 The first seven chapters are largely addressed to **"My son"**; the expression occurs about 15 times. In these chapters, we hear the heartbeat of a parent who wants the best in life for his child. By heeding this parental advice, a young person will avoid life's booby traps and develop expertise in practical, everyday affairs.

How much we owe to the influence of godly parents, and especially godly mothers! Henry Bosch reminds us:

Many great men of the past have been richly blessed by what they learned at their mother's knee. Consider Moses, Samuel, and Timothy. The maternal care and godly influence experienced by these spiritual leaders bore rich fruit in their lives. Think too of Augustine, John Newton, and the zealous Wesley brothers. Their names would probably never have lighted the pages of history if it hadn't been for the godly women who raised them in homes where the law of love and Christian witness was their daily guide and inspiration.[3]

1:9 When parental advice is followed, it becomes a **graceful** wreath **on** the **head** and ornamental **chains about** the **neck**, which is a poetic way of saying that obedience brings honor and moral beauty to the life of a wise son.

1:10 Often when a young man ruins his life, the explanation is given that he "got in with the wrong crowd." The process is described in verses 10–19 in living color.

First, however, the warning flag is flown. Life is full of enticements to evil. We must have the courage and backbone to say "No" a thousand times a week.

1:11 Here the street-corner gang invites our young friend to participate in an armed robbery. If necessary they will "bump off" the victim. Our friend may be flattered that these toughs would accept him as one of the gang. **"Come with us," they say**. And he may be lured by the excitement of anything so daring.

1:12–14 Perhaps he is bored by a sheltered life, and wants to do something "for kicks." Well, here it is! The perfect crime! Sudden and violent death, then a quick disposal of any tell-tale evidence. And the great incentive, of course, is that they will all be rich overnight. There will be enough loot to **fill** the **houses** of all the ac-

complices. So the word is, "Get with it, and you'll make a bundle. Everyone shares equally. You can't lose."

1:15, 16 But a wiser voice says, "**My son**, don't do it. Stay as far away from them as possible. Have nothing to do with their plans for instant wealth. You can't win."

"What you must realize is that these guys constantly pursue lives of crime, and are quick on the trigger. They commit one murder after another in rapid succession."

1:17, 18 A **bird** has enough sense to avoid any **net** or snare that can be clearly seen. But these men make a trap for **their own lives**, then walk straight into it.

1:19 There is a moral to the story. Those who try to get rich quick pay for their greed with their own lives. **So are the ways of everyone who is greedy for gain; it takes away the life of its owners.**

This particular passage deals with the attempt to get rich through violence. But the application is wider. Any get-rich-quick scheme is included, whether it be gambling, sweepstakes, or stock market speculation.

Next we hear two voices calling out to men as they pass by. One is the voice of Wisdom, the other the voice of the strange woman. Wisdom, though presented here as a woman, actually symbolizes the Lord Jesus Christ.[4] The strange woman is a type of sinful temptation and of the ungodly world.

In verses 20–33 Wisdom pleads with those who foolishly think they can get along without her.

1:20 Notice that **Wisdom** stands and **calls aloud** in strategic places so that everyone may hear her message. **She raises her voice in the city squares.**

1:21 Now **she** is at the noisy intersections, and now at the entrances

of the gates of the city. And so it is that our Lord calls to the race of men wherever they pass by:

> Where cross the crowded ways of
> life,
> Where sound the cries of race and
> clan,
> Above the noise of selfish strife,
> We hear Thy voice, O Son of Man!
>   —*Frank Mason North*

1:22 Wisdom cries to the **simple**, the **scorners**, and **fools**. The **simple** are naive, impressionable people who are open to all kinds of influences, both good and bad; here their instability seems to be leading them in the wrong direction. **Scorners** are those who treat wise counsel with contempt; nothing is sacred or serious to them. **Fools** are those who senselessly refuse instruction; they are conceited and opinionated in their ignorance.

1:23 This verse may be understood in two ways. First, it may mean,

> Since you won't listen to my invitation, now **turn** and listen to **my rebuke. I will pour out my spirit** in words of judgment, and will tell you what lies ahead for **you**.

According to this interpretation, verses 24–27 are the words which describe their fate.

The second possible meaning is this:

> **Turn** and repent when I reprove you. If you do, then **I will pour out my spirit on you** in blessing, and **make my words** of wisdom **known to you.**

The word **"spirit"** here probably means "thoughts" or "mind." While it is true that Christ pours out the Holy Spirit on those who answer His call, this truth was not as clearly stated in the OT as it is in the NT.

1:24 One of the greatest tragedies of life is the crass rejection of Wisdom's gracious entreaties. It **called** forth the lament of lost opportunity from the summit of Olivet, "I would... but you would not."

1:25 Wisdom sorrows over men who brush aside **all** her **counsel** and who will have nothing to do with her constructive criticism.

What makes man's stubborn refusal so irrational is that God's commandments and warnings are for man's good, not for God's. This is illustrated in a story which D. G. Barnhouse told. A small child squeezed past the metal railing that kept spectators six feet from the lions' cage at the Washington Zoo. When her grandfather ordered her to come out, she backed away teasingly. A waiting lion grabbed her, dragged her into the cage, and mangled her to death. According to Barnhouse the lesson is this:

> God has given us commandments and principles that are for our good; God never gives us a commandment because He is arbitrary or because He doesn't want us to have fun. God says, "Thou shalt have no other gods before Me," not because He is jealous of His own position and prerogatives, but because He knows that if we put anything, anything before Him, it will hurt us. If we understand the principle behind this fact, we can also understand why God chastens us. "Whom the Lord loves, He chastens" (Heb. 12:6). He doesn't want us to back into a lion, for there is a lion, the devil, seeking whom he may devour.[5]

1:26 If man persists in his refusal to listen, that rejection will inevitably bring disaster and ruin. Then it will be Wisdom's turn to **laugh**. **"I also**

will laugh at your calamity; I will mock when your terror comes."

Does this mean that the Lord will actually **laugh** when disaster falls on the ungodly, as suggested here and in Psalm 2:4? If we think of the laughter as containing any trace of cruelty, malice, or vindictiveness, then the answer is clearly "No." Rather we should think of this laughter in a figurative way. In idiomatic language, it expresses how ludicrous and ridiculous it is for a mere man to defy the Omnipotent Sovereign, as if a gnat should defy a blast furnace. And there may also be this thought: A man may laugh at Wisdom's commandments or treat them as if they didn't exist; but when that man is reaping the harvest of his folly, the commandments still stand unmoved, and to the scorner, at least, they seem to be having the last laugh—the **laugh** of poetic justice.

1:27 Payday will surely come. The judgment men feared will descend on them **like a storm**. Calamity will roar down like a tornado. **Distress, anguish**, shock, and despair will seize them.

1:28 **Then** men **will call on** Wisdom in vain. They will be desperate to find her, but won't be able to. They will realize too late that light rejected is light denied. They *would not* see; now they *cannot* see. God's Spirit will not always strive with man (Gen. 6:3). This is what gives urgency to the Gospel appeal:

> Be in time! Be in time!
> While the voice of Jesus calls you,
> Be in time!
> If in sin you longer wait,
> You may find no open gate,
> And your cry be just too late.
> Be in time!
> —*Author unknown, 19th Century*

1:29 The condemnation of these scorners is that they **hated** Wisdom's instructions, and stubbornly refused to reverence Jehovah. Perhaps they sneered that the gospel was all right for women and children, but not for them. "Professing to be wise, they became fools" (Rom. 1:22). The hatred of wisdom is also treated in John 3:19–21.

1:30 **They** had no place in their lives for the good **counsel** contained in the Word of God, and laughed when the Scriptures condemned their ungodly words and works. They weren't afraid of God or of His **rebuke**.

1:31 Now they must pay the staggering price of their willfulness, and be glutted with **the** bad **fruit of their own** schemes. It is their own fault, not Wisdom's. They simply would not listen.

1:32 "For heedless folk fall by their own self-will, the senseless are destroyed by their indifference" (Moffatt). Every man is free to make his own choices in life, but he is not free to choose the *consequences* of his choices. God has established certain moral principles in the world. These principles dictate the consequences for every choice. There is no way to put asunder what God has thus joined together.

1:33 On the plus side, the one who heeds Wisdom will live in safety and in freedom from **fear**. Those who are Wisdom's disciples enjoy the good life, escaping the sufferings, sorrows, and shame that dog the footsteps of the willful and the wicked.

B. Wisdom's Ways (Chap. 2)

In chapter 2, Solomon urges his son to walk in the ways of wisdom. The first four verses give the conditions for receiving the knowledge of God; a person must be earnest and sincere in seeking it with all his heart. The rest of the chapter promises that wisdom and discernment will be given. The 22 verses correspond to the 22 letters of the Hebrew alphabet.

2:1 First, the **son** is urged to take to heart his father's teaching and **treasure** up his **commands**. The proverbs were intended to be treasured up **"within you,"** or memorized.

2:2 There must be an open **ear** and an open **heart** or mind. The son must be an attentive listener, not a compulsive talker. He is not told to talk out his problems, as in much of modern counseling; rather he should listen to the wise advice of others.

2:3,4 If he really means business, let him **cry out for discernment**, and send out an appeal for **understanding**. Seriousness of purpose is of primary importance. It is a law of life that we get what we go after.

What we need is the same kind of drive that men have in mining for **silver** or in searching for **hidden treasures**. The tragedy is that too often men show more zeal in acquiring material wealth than spiritual riches.

2:5 But those who seek inevitably **find**. Those who are anxious to come into a right relationship with the Lord and to really know **God** are never disappointed. That is why one of the early church fathers said that the man who seeks God has already found Him. Christ reveals the Father to all who believe on Him. To know Christ is to know God.

2:6 After we have been saved through faith in Christ, we are then in a position to learn divine **wisdom** from the LORD. He teaches us how to think straight, how to evaluate, how to discern truth and error, and how to develop divine insight.

2:7 He provides rich stores of **sound wisdom for the upright**, and a special **shield** of protection for **those who walk** in integrity.

2:8 **He guards the paths of** those who live clean, moral lives. **His saints** escape the pain and bitterness that sin leaves in its trail. "Safe and sound the chosen friends of God come and go" (Knox).

2:9 This verse parallels verse 5. Both begin with **"Then"** and list the benefits of seriously seeking the knowledge of God.

The person who keenly desires to know and do God's will learns how to behave righteously, to act fairly, to conduct himself honestly—in short, to choose the right way **and every good path**.

2:10 The reason this happens is that **wisdom** takes control of one's mind or **heart**, and the **knowledge** of what is right becomes **pleasant** rather than distasteful. To the true believer, God's commands are not irksome. Christ's yoke is easy and His burden is light.

2:11 **Discretion**, or the ability to make wise decisions, saves a person from many a "bad trip." Sound judgment delivers us from involvement with wicked men. None of us realizes the extent to which we are daily preserved from spiritual, moral, and physical perils. The Christian enjoys a well-guarded life, having escaped the corruption that is in the world through lust.

2:12 We are saved from the partnership of **evil** *men* (vv. 12–15) and from the embrace of the loose *woman* (vv. 16–19).

First we are saved from the world of ungodly men who misrepresent facts and distort the truth. Their speech is utterly untrustworthy.

2:13–15 These are men **who leave** the well-lighted streets of **uprightness**

to slink in the dark alleys of crime and crookedness.

They take savage pleasure in **doing evil** and **delight in** the way their sin turns everything topsy-turvy.

They follow **crooked** routes and **their** behavior is sly and **devious**.

2:16 Wisdom saves not only from the company of men like these but also from the clutches of the **immoral woman**. We may understand this woman as a literal prostitute or we may see her as a figure of false religion or of the ungodly world.

Her method is flattery: "You aren't appreciated at home as you should be. You are so handsome, so talented. You have so much to offer. You need love and sympathetic understanding, and I'm the one to give it to you."

2:17 She is unfaithful to **the companion of her youth**, that is, her husband. She **forgets the covenant of her God**, that is, the marriage vows that she made before God. Or "the covenant of her God" may refer to the Ten Commandments and specifically to the seventh commandment, which forbids adultery.

2:18 The first clause of verse 18 may be translated **"For her house leads down to death"** or "she sinketh down unto death, which is her house" (RV margin). The parallel second clause of the verse seems to support the NKJV translation. Putting them together, the thought is: **her house leads down to death**, and therefore those who enter it are sliding toward the grave. Her **paths** lead **to the dead**, and therefore those who follow her will soon be in the realm of departed spirits. Since everybody will die some day, death must be more here than the common lot of all mortals; it must mean moral death leading to eternal death.

2:19 Once a man is ensnared by her, it is almost impossible to escape. The verse actually seems to rule out any hope of a comeback at all. But many statements in the Bible must be understood as general rules, to which there may be a few exceptions. That is the point here. Once a man is initiated into her secrets, it is extremely hard to **regain** the right road.

2:20 Link verse 20 with verse 11. Wisdom preserves not only from evil men and the strange woman, but, on the positive side, it encourages companionship with those who are worthwhile and upright.

2:21, 22 Under the Law of Moses, men of integrity—**the upright** and **the blameless**—were rewarded with a secure place **in the land** of Canaan. When we come over to the NT, these material blessings in earthly places give way to spiritual blessings in the heavenlies. But the fact remains that righteousness and decency are rewarded in this life as well as in the life to come.

It is equally true that **the wicked will be cut off from the** land of blessing. There is no lasting inheritance there for the treacherous.

C. Wisdom's Rewards (3:1–10)

3:1 Like all good parents, Wisdom wants the best for her children. She knows that that can come only through obedience to her teachings, which is another way of saying obedience to the sacred Scriptures. So here she pleads with her **son** to remember with the mind and obey with the **heart**.

3:2 In general, those who are subject to their parents live longer and better lives. Those who kick up their heels against parental discipline invite illness, accidents, tragedies, and premature death. This verse thus corresponds to the fifth commandment (Ex. 20:12) which promises **long life** to those who honor their parents. Jay Adams writes:

The Bible teaches that a peace of mind which leads to longer, happier living comes from keeping God's commandments. A guilty conscience is a body-breaking load. A good conscience is one significant factor which leads to longevity and physical health. And so, in a measure, one's somatic (bodily) welfare stems from the welfare of his soul. A close psychosomatic connection between one's behavior before God and his physical condition is an established physical principle.[6]

3:3, 4 **Mercy** and **truth** should be seen in the outward behavior (**bind them around your neck**) and should be true of the inward life as well (**write them on the tablet of your heart**).

This is the way to **find favor and high esteem** (or success, AV margin) **in the sight of God and man**. What it boils down to is that the satisfying life is the one that is lived in the center of God's will. But that brings up the question, "How can I know God's will in my life?" A classic answer is given in the next two verses.

3:5 First, there must be a full commitment of ourselves—spirit, soul, and body—to **the LORD**. We must **trust** Him not only for the salvation of our souls but also for the direction of our lives. It must be a commitment without reserve.

Next, there must be a healthy distrust of self, an acknowledgment that we do not know what is best for us, that we are not capable of guiding ourselves. Jeremiah expressed it pointedly: "O Lord, I know the way of man is not in himself; it is not in man who walks to direct his own steps" (Jer. 10:23).

3:6 Finally, there must be an acknowledgment of the Lordship of Christ: **"In all your ways acknowledge Him."** Every area of our lives must be turned over to His control. We must have no will of our own, only a single pure desire to know His will and to do it.

If these conditions are met, the promise is that God **shall direct** our **paths**. He may do it through the Bible, through the advice of godly Christians, through the marvelous converging of circumstances, through the inward peace of the Spirit, or through a combination of these. But if we wait, He will make the guidance so clear that to refuse would be positive disobedience.

3:7, 8 Conceit puts us on "hold" as far as divine guidance is concerned. When we **fear the LORD** and **depart from evil**, it means "all systems go." It spells **health to** the body and **strength** (lit. *drink* or *refreshment*) **to** the **bones**. Here again we are brought face to face with the close connection between man's moral and spiritual condition and his physical health.

It has been estimated that fear, sorrow, envy, resentment, hatred, guilt, and other emotional stresses account for over 60% of our illness. Add to that the terrible toll taken by alcohol (cirrhosis of the liver); tobacco (emphysema, cancer, heart disease); immorality (venereal diseases, AIDS). Then we realize that "he shall direct your paths" is more literally "he shall make your paths smooth" or "straight," but guidance is surely included in the promise. Solomon, by divine inspiration, was way ahead of his times in the field of medical science.

3:9 One way in which we can **honor** the lordship of Christ is in our stewardship of **possessions**. All we have belongs to Him. We are stewards, responsible for its management. It is our privilege to choose a modest standard of living for ourselves, put everything above that to work for God, and trust God for the future. Like David Livingston, we should determine not to look upon anything we possess except in relation to the Kingdom of God.

3:10 The generous Jew in the OT was promised bulging **barns** and overflowing **vats** of **wine**. Even though our blessings may be of a more spiritual nature, it is still true that we cannot outgive the Lord.

D. Wisdom as the Prize (3:11–20)

3:11, 12 We can also acknowledge the Lord by submitting to His discipline. Too often we tend to think of discipline as meaning punishment, but it actually includes all that is involved in the proper training of a child, i.e., instruction, warning, encouragement, advice, **correction**, and **chastening**. Everything that God allows to come into our lives is purposeful. We should not **detest** it or **despise** it. Neither should we shrink from it or give up under it. Rather we should be concerned that God's purpose is achieved through the discipline, and thus we reap the maximum profit from it. God's ultimate purpose in the disciplines of life is that we become partakers of His holiness.

Discipline is a proof of love, not anger. **Correction** is a proof of sonship (see Heb. 12:6–8).

Thought: A gardener prunes grapevines but not thistles.

3:13 The **happy** individual is the one **who finds wisdom**, and especially so when we remember that Wisdom here is a veiled presentation of Christ Himself. Let us put Christ

into the following verses and see what happens.

3:14 The benefit of knowing the Lord Jesus far surpasses any **profits** a man might get from **silver** and **gold**. He gives what money can never buy.

> Thou treasure inexhaustible,
> Thou source of true delight.
> What care I for the world's applause
> Or for its diamonds bright?
> More prized by far one smile from Thee
> Than all earth hold more dear
> I want for nothing man can give,
> For I have Jesus here.
> Yes, yes, the Loved One is my own;
> Can any richer be?
> For all He is, and all He has
> All, all belongs to me.
>
> *—Author unknown*

3:15 He is **more precious than rubies**, or any other jewels, more to be desired than any earthly prize.

3:16 With one **hand** He offers long life, in fact, eternal life. With the other, spiritual **riches and honor**.

3:17 All His **ways are ways of pleasantness**, and **all** His **paths are peace**. "Where He guides, journeying is pleasant, where He points the way, all is peace" (Knox, alt.).

3:18 **To those who take hold of** Him, He is like **a tree** whose fruit is **life** worth living. Those who remain close to Him are the **happy** ones.

3:19, 20 These two verses describe the **wisdom** of God in creation, in judgment, and in providence. In creation He **founded the earth** and **established the heavens**. With **understanding**, He opened up the fountains of the great deep at the time of the Flood. By providence, He lifts the water from the ocean into the **clouds**, then distributes it again as rain upon the earth.

And who is the active agent of the Godhead in doing all this? It is Christ, the Wisdom of God (John 1:3; Col. 1:16; Heb. 1:2).

E. Wisdom Practiced (3:21–35)

3:21 The privilege of being instructed by the Wisdom that created and sustains the universe is too great to miss. We shouldn't let **sound wisdom and discretion** out of our sight.

3:22–24 They provide inward vitality (**life to your soul**) and outward beauty (**grace to your neck**).

They enable us to **walk safely in** our **way**, free from danger of tripping or slipping.

They guarantee a good night's **sleep**, with no guilt on the conscience and no fear on the mind.

3:25 They preserve a man from the kind of **sudden terror** that overtakes **the wicked**. Those who envy the apparent prosperity of the ungodly fail to realize the built-in hazards of that kind of life—such as extortion, theft, revenge, payoffs, blackmail, kidnapping, and murder.

3:26 The LORD guards those who walk in His ways. He won't let our **foot** get **caught** in a trap. We are often conscious of God's marvelous interventions and rescues in our lives. But these are only the tip of the iceberg. Some day we will realize more fully all we have been saved from as well as saved to.

3:27 Notice the negatives in verses 27–31: **"Do not withhold** . . . do not say . . . do not devise . . . do not strive . . . do not envy . . . do not choose. . . ."

First, never **withhold** anything **good from those to whom it is due** when you are in a position to give it. This might refer to wages that have been earned, to a debt that is due, to tools that have been borrowed.

But in a wider sense it may mean, "Never withhold a kindness or a good deed from someone who is entitled

to it." This injunction may be introduced here to warn the righteous against becoming so occupied with their proper relationship with God as to neglect their responsibility towards others (see Jas. 4:17).

3:28 Don't put **your neighbor** off till **tomorrow** when you can meet his need today.

Who is my neighbor? Anyone who needs my help.

What does my neighbor need? He needs to hear the good news of salvation.

If the Holy Spirit burdens my heart to witness to someone, I should do it today. Never refuse any prompting of the Spirit.

3:29 Love to our **neighbor** forbids us to **devise evil against** him as he **dwells** trustingly and unsuspectingly in the house next door. This rules out all the mean, sarcastic, and cruel revenge that too often follows neighborhood squabbles.

3:30 Here we are warned against picking a fight **with a man** when he has done nothing to provoke it. There is already enough strife in the world without needlessly going around to stir up more!

3:31, 32 The oppressor may seem to have instant success. But we should **not envy** his prosperity or follow **his ways. The** LORD hates, loathes, despises, and abominates **the perverse person**, but takes the upright into His intimate confidence (see John 14:23).

3:33 God's condemnation or His confidence, His **curse** or His blessing—that is the choice! A dark cloud hovers over **the house of the wicked**. The sunshine of God's favor beams down on **the home of the just**.

3:34 Again the choice is between God's scorn and His **grace. He scorns the** scoffer **but gives grace to the humble**. The importance of this choice is seen in that the verse is quoted twice in the NT (Jas. 4:6; 1 Pet. 5:5).

3:35 Finally the choice is between honor and disgrace. **Wise** men **inherit glory**; **fools** become well-known by falling into disgrace.

F. Wisdom as a Family Treasure (4:1–9)

4:1 In the first nine verses, Solomon rehearses the sound teaching which his father had passed on to him, and urges his **children** to spare no effort in gaining true insight. The book of Proverbs teems with earnest exhortations to the young to listen to **instruction** from a wise **father**.

4:2 It pays to cultivate the friendship of godly, older people. You can learn a lot from them and benefit from their years of experience. Their **doctrine** is **good**, and **not** to be disregarded.

4:3 Here Solomon refers to the time when he was a **son** to his father and **"the only one" in the sight of** his **mother**. Actually he was not an only son, but perhaps the expression **"the only one in the sight of my mother"** means "my mother's darling" (Knox).

4:4 Solomon's father, David, had **taught** his son to **retain** his sound advice and thus **live** a life that counts. A summary of David's instruction is given in verses 4b–9.

4:5, 6 His major concern was for his son to **get wisdom** and **understanding**—which really means to live for the Lord. Whatever else Solomon did, he should never **forget** this, because only the life that's lived for God really counts.

4:7 The first step in getting **wisdom** is to have motivation or determination. We get in life what we go after. We should **get wisdom** at all cost, and in the process **get** good **understanding** and discernment. This means,

among other things, that we will learn to choose between the evil and the good, the good and the best, the soulish and the spiritual, the temporal and the eternal.

4:8 If we give Wisdom first place in our priorities, **she will promote** us handsomely. If we **embrace her** lovingly, **she will bring** us to places of **honor**.

4:9 "She will adorn you with charm and crown you with glory" (Moffatt). Wisdom confers a moral beauty on her children. Contrast, for instance, the repulsiveness of a life abandoned to dissipation and immorality.

G. Wisdom and the Two Paths (4:10–27)

4:10 Having finished quoting his father's counsel, Solomon now resumes his appeal to his own **son**. It is a general rule, though not without exceptions, that a clean life is conducive to a long **life**. Think how tobacco, alcohol, drugs, and sexual sin are directly linked with disease and death.

4:11, 12 A father can be gratified when he has **taught** his son **the way of wisdom** and has been a good example to him. However, the teaching must be combined with the example. A father's actions speak louder than his words.

A son who walks in the **right paths** will **walk** unimpeded and will **run** without stumbling.

The Syriac version reads: "As thou goest step by step, I will open up the way before thee." This teaches two important principles: First, God guides us step by step, rather than revealing the whole plan at once. Second, God guides people when they are moving forward for Him. A ship must be in motion before the skipper can steer it. So must a bicycle; you can only guide it when it is moving. The same is true of us; God guides us when we are in motion for Him.

4:13 We should **take firm hold** of good **instruction**, and **not let** it slip from us. We should guard wisdom as we would guard our life—because it **is** our **life**, especially when we think of Wisdom Incarnate in the person of the Lord Jesus.

4:14 Verses 14–19 warn against evil companions and contrast **the way of** darkness with the way of light.

These exhortations against joining up with unrighteous men do not forbid our witnessing to them but they do forbid any partnership in their plans.

4:15 There is a note of urgent warning in these short, staccato commands. **Avoid** a life of sin. Don't pass by to investigate. **Turn** the other way. Keep going. It might seem interesting, intriguing, and thrilling, but it eventually will destroy you.

4:16, 17 The henchmen of sin **do not sleep** well **unless they have** pulled some shady deal. They get a king-sized case of insomnia **unless they** have lured **someone** to ruin and disaster.

Their diet is **the bread of wickedness** and **the wine of violence**. Or we might say that **wickedness** is their meat and drink.

These verses give a very drastic picture of the sinful nature of man. Since his nature is sin, sinning is for him as meat and drink for the body. This passage does not apply only to criminals. (See *BBC* on Jer. 17:9).

4:18, 19 Not so the life of the righteous person. It is **like the** dawning light which **shines ever brighter** until it reaches the full blaze of noonday. In other words, **the path of the just** grows better and **brighter** all the time.

The wicked stagger on in deep **darkness**, with no idea as to what they're stumbling over.

4:20 Solomon continues to plead with his **son** to pay close **attention to** his instruction in wisdom. In a verse like this, we should hear the voice of the Lord speaking to us.

4:21 It is for our own good that we should **not let** Wisdom's teachings out of our sight, but should rather treasure them **in** our **heart**.

4:22 Wisdom's words **are** life-giving and creative. As Jesus said, "The words that I speak to you are spirit, and they are life" (John 6:63).

And they are **health to** the whole body because they deliver a person from the sins and stresses that cause so much illness.

4:23 Verses 23–27 are the OT counterpart of Romans 12:1. They beseech us to present our entire beings to God—heart, mouth, lips, eyes, and feet. God begins with the inner man, then works outward.

The **heart** is first. It speaks of the inner **life**, the mind, the thoughts, the motives, the desires. The mind is the fountain from which the actions spring. If the fountain is pure, the stream that flows from it will be pure. As a man thinks, so is he. So this verse emphasizes the importance of a clean thought life.

4:24, 25 A **deceitful mouth** signifies dishonest and devious speech. **Perverse lips** refer to conversation that is not straightforward and aboveboard.

Eyes and **eyelids** that **look straight ahead** suggest a walk with singleness of purpose, one that does not turn aside for sin or for anything that is unworthy. In a day when the mass media bombard us with publicity designed to arouse our animal appetites, we must learn to keep our eyes on Jesus (Heb. 12:2).

4:26, 27 If we are careful to **ponder the path** of holiness, **all** our **ways** will be well-ordered and safe.

All along the highway, **to the right** and **to the left**, there are side streets and alleys which lead to the haunts of sin. "Let's be true to Jesus, though a thousand voices from the world may call."

When tempted to go to a questionable place, ask yourself, "Would I like to be found there when Jesus comes back?" **Remove your foot from evil**.

H. The Folly of Immorality (Chap.5)

5:1, 2 Solomon is anxious to warn his **son** against one of the besetting sins of youth. Those who **pay attention** to sound advice and learn from the experience of others develop true **discretion**. Because their speech is pure and true, it protects them from getting into trouble. Nothing but the Word of God is an adequate safeguard against the seduction and delusion running rampant in our day. Therefore, Paul exhorts Timothy to stick to the Word when surrounded by apostasy (2 Tim. 3:13–17).

5:3 The rest of chapter 5 deals with what has been called "the oldest profession"—prostitution. The **immoral woman** is a prostitute, one who hires herself out for debased purposes. She may be thought of as a symbol of sin, of the evil world, of false religion, of idolatry, or of any other seductive temptation that the sons of men meet. Her **lips . . . drip honey**—sweet, smooth, and specious. She is a flatterer, a slick, clever talker.

5:4 At first she seems pleasant and desirable, **but in the end she is bitter as wormwood**. It is the old story—sin is attractive as a prospect but hideous in retrospect.

The price of going to bed with her is enormous—guilty conscience, remorse, scandal, venereal disease, wrecked marriage, broken home, mental disturbance, and a host of other ills.

5:5, 6 She leads her victims down a one-way street **to death** and **hell**. Abandoned woman, she cares nothing for the good life. **Her** character is **unstable** and shifty, and she doesn't realize how low she has fallen. "The high road of Life is not for her, shifty and slippery are her tracks" (Moffatt).

5:7 As he considers all that is at stake, Solomon injects a solemn warning to his **children**, to **hear** him and **not depart from** what he has to say.

5:8 One great safeguard is to stay as **far** away **from** the temptation as possible. There is no use asking God for deliverance if we insist on toying with objects or places that are associated with sin.

In some cases, it is necessary to actually flee. Joseph did this, and although he lost his coat, he maintained his purity and gained a crown.

In order to obey verse 8 we may have to get a new job, move to a different location, or take some other equally decided step.

5:9, 10 Those who visit the brothel squander their manly vigor, and **give** the best of their golden **years to** a **cruel** temptress.

In addition, "respectable" citizens who have secret immoral liaisons—whether literally or through pornography, "x-rated" films, and videotapes—often find themselves the victims of blackmail. If they don't pay "hush money," they are threatened with public exposure.

5:11 The end of such a life is punctuated with a protracted groan, as the **body** is racked with gonorrhea, syphilis, blindness, locomotor ataxia, AIDS, and emotional disturbances.

5:12, 13 There is the added grief of regret and remorse. The burned-out wreck reproaches himself for not having **obeyed** his parents, his Sunday School **teachers**, his Christian friends. He could have avoided oceans of misery, but he was too pig-headed to be warned.

5:14 And there is the possibility of being brought to public disgrace. That seems to be the thought in this verse, although it might also include the idea of being sentenced for his misdeeds.

5:15, 16 In figurative language, Solomon counsels his son to find all his sexual satisfaction with his **own** wife in a life of pure married love.

If we follow the KJV, this verse describes the blessings of a faithful marriage relationship reaching out to family and friends.

The NKJV changes the verse to a question: **"Should your fountains be dispersed abroad, streams of water in the streets?"** This is a picturesque description of the utter waste of one's reproductive powers that is involved in going in to a prostitute.

Knox translates the verse, "Thence let thy offspring abound, like waters from thy own fountain flowing through the public streets." The wife here is the fountain, and the waters are the children, tearing out of the house and playing happily in the streets.

5:17 The true marriage relationship is an exclusive one, and the children enjoy the security of "belonging." So this verse warns against the tragedy of illegitimate children or the doubtful parentage of those who are born as a result of promiscuous sexual union.

5:18 The **fountain** here again refers to a man's own wife. Let him find his joy and companionship in **the wife of** his **youth**. In "forsaking all others" a man finds, as Michael Griffiths expressed it, that "there is no end to the richness that springs out of that exclusive relationship, and the warmth of the welcome that reaches out from his home to bless others."[7]

5:19, 20 Let a man reserve the intimacies of marital union for his wife, treating her as the **loving**, **graceful** woman she is. **Let her breasts** be his satisfying portion, and may he **always be enraptured with her love**.

For **why should** he be **enraptured** by the false charms of **an immoral woman**? Or why fold a **seductress** into his arms?

5:21, 22 Though no human eye may follow him to the brothel, the motel room, or the secret rendezvous, yet God sees **all** that takes place. "Secret sin on earth is open scandal in heaven."

Man cannot **sin** and get away with it. Sin's built-in consequences are inescapable. As Jay Adams counsels:

Sinful habits are hard to break, but if they are not broken, they will bind the client ever more tightly. He is held fast by these ropes of his own sin. He finds that sin spirals in a downward cycle, pulling him along. He is captured and tied up by sin's ever-tightening cords. At length he becomes sin's slave.[8]

5:23 Ellicott calls this verse the final scene in the life of the profligate. He would not exercise self-control. Now he dies as a result. "For lack of sense he dies; his utter folly ruins him" (Moffatt).

The poet Shelley is an illustration of this passage. In his conceit, he ridiculed the idea of monogamous marriage, as if it were a matter of marrying one and disappointing thousands. The results of his approach, according to Griffiths, were desertions, suicides, illegitimate children, and jealousy. G. Sampson questioned "whether in the life of any poet there is such a trail of disasters as that which this 'beautiful but ineffectual' angel left behind him."

I. The Folly of Suretyship, Laziness, and Deception (6:1–19)

6:1 The first five verses are a warning against becoming **surety**, that is, making oneself liable for someone else's debt in case that other person is unable to pay. Suppose **your friend** wants to buy a car on the installment plan but doesn't have much of a credit rating. The loan company demands the signature of someone who can pay in case the borrower defaults. The neighbor comes to you and asks you to cosign the note with him. This means that you will pay if he doesn't.

The **friend** in this verse is your neighbor. The **stranger** is the loan company to which you give your guarantee.

6:2 You are snared by the words of your mouth; you are taken by the words of your mouth. In other words, if you have made a rash promise, you have fallen into a trap. It was a great mistake.

6:3 Now the best thing to do is to get **yourself** released from the agreement. Try to persuade **your friend** to get your signature removed from the note you have been trapped into signing.

6:4, 5 The matter is of such importance that you shouldn't rest until you are released from this liability. You should squirm free **like a gazelle from** its captor, or like **a bird from . . . the fowler**.

But why does the Bible warn against suretyship so sternly? Isn't it a kindness to do this for a friend or neighbor? It might seem to be a kindness, but it might not be at all.

1. You might be helping him to buy something which it is not God's will for him to have.
2. You might be encouraging him to be a spendthrift or even a gambler.
3. If he defaults and you have to pay for something that is not your own, friendship will end and bitterness begin.

It would be better to give money outright if there is a legitimate need. In any case, you should not become surety for him.

6:6, 7 Verses 6–11 are a protest against laziness. **The ant** is an object lesson to us as it scurries back and forth, keeps on the move, and often carries oversized loads. It gets a lot accomplished without benefit of a boss, foreman, or superintendent. When we watch a swarm of ants, they seem to move crazily in every direction, but their activity is purposeful and directed, even though there is no apparent chain of command.

6:8 This little creature diligently and industriously works **in the summer** and **gathers her food in the harvest**. The emphasis here is not on making provision for the future but on hard work now.

This passage should not be used to teach that Christians should make provision for a rainy day. We are forbidden to lay up treasures on earth (Matt. 6:19). It is true that ants do provide for their future, and it is also true that Christians should provide for theirs. But the difference is that an ant's future is in this world, whereas the believer's future is in heaven. Wise Christians, therefore, lay up their treasures in heaven, not on earth.

6:9 The lazy fellow seems to have an endless capacity for **sleep**. His philosophy is, "It's nice to get up in the morning, but it's nicer to lie in bed." He seems to have an infinite deafness to alarm clocks.

6:10, 11 When finally roused, he says, "Just let me have a few more winks, **a little** more **sleep**, a short nap, a quick beauty rest."

Others in the household may wait, but the day of **poverty** won't. **So shall your poverty come on you like a prowler, and your need like an armed man.**

6:12 Verses 12–15 are a classic description of a con man. He is a malicious swindler whose cunning smile masks a treacherous heart. He goes around with falsehood on his lips.

6:13, 14 He uses all kinds of suggestive gestures and sinister motions to signal to his accomplice or to take his victims off guard. He **winks with his eyes**, **shuffles** or scrapes with **his feet**, and beckons **with his fingers**.

His heart is filled with malice and **perversity** as he incessantly plots mischief and **sows discord**.

6:15 "Such men will be overtaken by their doom ere long, crushed all of a sudden beyond hope of remedy" (Knox). If you look hard enough, you can probably find an illustration of this in today's newspaper.

6:16 The **things** which characterize this wicked man (vv. 12–15) are hated by God (vv. 16–19), especially the sowing of discord (compare vv. 14 and 19).

The formula **"six things . . . yes, seven . . ."** may mean that the list is specific but not exhaustive. Or it may indicate that the seventh is worst of all.[9]

6:17 **A proud look.** Pride is dust deifying itself. The valet of an emperor said:

I cannot deny that my master was vain. He had to be the central figure in everything. If he went to a christening, he wanted to be the baby. If he went to a wedding, he wanted to be the bride. If he went to a funeral, he wanted to be the corpse.[10]

A lying tongue. The tongue was created to glorify the Lord. To lie is to pervert its use for that which is ignoble. Is it ever right for a believer to lie? The answer is that God cannot lie, and He cannot give the privilege to anyone else.

Hands that shed innocent blood. Every human life is of infinite value to God. He proved this by paying an infinite price at Calvary for our redemption. The institution of capital punishment (Gen. 9:6) reflects God's attitude toward murder.

6:18 **A heart that devises wicked plans.** This, of course, refers to the mind that is always plotting some evil. The Lord Jesus listed some of these wicked imaginations in Mark 7:21, 22.

Feet that are swift in running to evil. God hates not only the mind that plans the evil but the **feet** that are eager to carry it out.

6:19 **A false witness who speaks lies.** Here it is a matter of public testimony in a court of law. In verse 17b it was more a matter of everyday conversation.

One who sows discord among brethren. The striking thing here is that God ranks the one who causes divisions among **brethren** with murderers, liars, and perjurers!

How many of the seven sins listed above can you associate with the trial and crucifixion of our Lord?

J. The Folly of Adultery and Harlotry (6:20—7:27)

6:20 The subject of adultery or unfaithfulness is taken up again here.

The frequency with which it recurs is not accidental. The words of verse 20 are a sort of formula used to introduce important instruction.

6:21 Some extreme literalists in Jesus' day thought they obeyed this verse by wearing phylacteries, that is, small leather boxes containing Scripture portions. During prayer, these Jews wore one on the left arm (near the **heart**) and one on the head (near the **neck**). Some Jews still use them today.

But what this verse *really* means is that we should make the Word of God so much a part of our lives that it will accompany and direct us wherever we go. It is not just a question of honoring the Scriptures outwardly but of obeying them from the heart.

6:22 Obedience to God's Word affords:

guidance—**When you roam, they will lead you.**
protection—**When you sleep, they will keep** (guard) **you.**
instruction—*When* **you awake, they will speak with you.**

6:23 This verse amplifies the previous one:

the commandment is a lamp—for guidance
the law is **a light**—for protection
reproofs of instruction are the way of life—for teaching.

6:24, 25 One particular ministry of the Word is to save men from the **seductress** with the glib, **flattering tongue**.

No one should be taken in by **her** natural **beauty** or by the come-hither flickers of her eyelashes.

6:26 The interpretation of this verse differs according to different translations.

The thought in the NKJV and the NASB is that a man is **reduced** to poverty (**a crust of bread**) by **a harlot**, and may lose **his precious life** to **an adulteress**. Both kinds of entanglement are costly.

The RSV says, "for a harlot may be hired for a loaf of bread, but an adulteress stalks a man's very life." Here a distinction is made between a harlot, who can be hired, and an adulteress who is not satisfied until she controls the man completely.

6:27, 28 To have illicit relations with another man's wife is like carrying **fire** in one's **bosom**. You can't do it without being **burned**. It is like walking **on hot coals**; you can't do it without burning your **feet**. Griffiths warns:

It is utter folly for all that will commit adultery, for the result will be self-destruction, wounds and dishonor, disgrace, and the unappeased anger of the wronged parties.[11]

6:29 As sure as a man **goes in to his neighbor's wife**, he will be caught and punished. There is a principle in the moral universe by which such sin is generally brought to light. Even, if by some remote chance, his sin is not discovered in this life, it will have to be accounted for in the next.

6:30, 31 These verses may be understood in one of two ways. According to the KJV and the NKJV, **people** have a measure of sympathy **if** a man **steals to** feed **himself** and his hungry family, but even then, **when he is** caught, he has to make restitution, even if it means losing everything he owns.

The RSV, by translating verse 30 as a question, implies that men *do* despise a thief, even if he steals to satisfy his hunger, and that he has to make complete restitution.

In either case, the point is that a thief can make restitution for his crime whereas an adulterer can never fully erase the damage he incurs.

6:32 **Whoever commits adultery lacks** sense because he **destroys** himself socially, spiritually, and morally, and perhaps even physically (Deut. 22:22).

6:33 For one moment of passion, he gets **wounds and dishonor**, perhaps from the enraged husband. He also gets shame and disgrace that will dog him the rest of his life. (Thank God, however, there is forgiveness with the Lord if the man will repent, confess, and forsake his sin.)

6:34 Here we see the **fury** of the jealous husband who returns unexpectedly and finds his wife in the arms of another man. When he starts to take revenge, **he will not** be conciliated by any pleas or excuses.

6:35 Nothing that the offender could pay would appease the husband; no bribe would be sufficient satisfaction for the violation of his marriage.

7:1 Chapter 7 continues to warn young people against ruining their lives by immorality. They should **treasure** these inspired **commands** as more valuable than earthly, material riches.

7:2 Obedience to God's Word is the pathway to abundant living. Therefore, it should be kept **as the apple of the eye**. With regard to this expression, the *International Standard Bible Encyclopedia* says:

> The eyeball, or globe of the eye, with pupil in center, is called "apple" from its round shape. Its great value and careful protection by the eyelids' automatically closing when there is the least possibility of danger made it the emblem of that which was most precious and jealously protected.[12]

7:3 In poetic language, this verse says to let the Word of God control all that we do (**bind them on your fingers**) and become a matter of unquestioning obedience (**write them on the tablet of your heart**).

7:4 We should treat **Wisdom** with the honor and respect due to a **sister**, and make **understanding** one of our **nearest kin**. **Wisdom** in this passage is contrasted with the evil woman, who is to be carefully avoided.

7:5 Those who follow Wisdom and her instructions are preserved from **the immoral woman** and from the flattery of **the seductress**. Two different words are used here to describe this evil woman. **Immoral** means loose and faithless to her marriage vows. **Seductress** means foreigner and adventuress.

7:6 Verses 6–23 give a vivid account of a prostitute plying her trade and of a young man being "taken in" by her. The tragic drama unfolded as the writer **looked through** the venetian blinds on his **window**.

7:7 An empty-headed, aimless **young man** is out on the town. Perhaps he is from a decent home, but now he is out to have a good time. It could be that he is a G.I. who isn't going to be outdone by his boasting pals. He isn't really a hardened sinner, just an inexperienced small-town guy.

7:8 Now he wanders into the red-light district. He crosses **the street near her corner**. He slowly saunters on with the gait of idleness. That's the whole trouble. If he were busy in some constructive, worthwhile activity, he wouldn't be here. If his feet were shod with the preparation of the gospel of peace, he wouldn't have time to waste! There is real protection from sin in a life sold out to God. On the other hand, as Isaac Watts said,

"Satan finds some mischief still, for idle hands to do."

7:9 He has been wandering around all **evening**—from sunset to dusk to midnight blackness—"There is a certain symbolic meaning," writes Barnes, "in the picture of the gathering gloom. Night is falling over the young man's life as the shadows deepen."

He is like a moth flying to the flame. The awful moment of danger approaches when the temptation to sin and the opportunity to sin coincide. We should pray constantly that these two should never come together in our lives.

7:10 The prostitute now makes her appearance, dressed to kill in the latest Hollywood styles, painted, powdered, and perfumed. Beneath her charming exterior lies a sensuous, secretive, subtle **heart**.

7:11, 12 No gracious, modest lady this! She is brash, **loud**, and aggressive. Not for her to be a homemaker! She must prowl the streets for clients.

She is almost ubiquitous. **At times she was outside, at times in the open square, lurking at every corner.** Sin is like that; it is easy to find. The Gospel should be easy to find, but unfortunately we fail to make it widely available.

7:13 The first step in her technique is the shock treatment. She rushes up to him, throws her arms around him and kisses him. Wow! He is swept off his feet by this tremendous display of love. He doesn't know it is lust, not love.

7:14 Next comes the religious pose. She says, **"I have peace offerings with me; today I have paid my vows."** He remembers his mother and the Bible on the living room table, then says to himself, "This woman must be all right. She's religious. I can't go wrong with anyone

who has peace offerings and who pays her vows." The noose is tightening.

There is an added lure in the **peace offerings**. Those who offered them had to eat them that day or the next (Lev. 7:15ff), so she has plenty of good food with which to regale him. She believes that at least one way to a man's heart is through his stomach.

7:15 Then she pretends that he is the one she has been looking for. What a lie! She would have taken the first man who came along. But he is elated to think that he is important; someone really appreciates him, someone really cares.

7:16, 17 She gives more than a hint of her proposal by describing her bed: **"I have spread my bed with tapestry, colored coverings of Egyptian linen. I have perfumed my bed with myrrh, aloes, and cinnamon."** Everything here is designed to appeal to his sensual nature. Even his sense of smell is to be captivated by exotic perfumes.

7:18 Now the mask is torn away. She openly invites him to go to bed with her. With carefully chosen words, she makes it all sound very pleasurable.

7:19, 20 She disarms him by explaining that the man of the house **is not at home** and won't be home for a long time, because **he has gone on a long journey**. He expected to be away for an extended time because he took a good supply of cash **with him**. He wouldn't come home till full moon (v. 20b NASB). The darkness described in verse 9 indicates that the moon wouldn't be full for some time.

7:21 The more she talks, the more his resistance melts. **With** a little more flattery, **she caused him to yield**.

7:22 He makes a snap decision to follow **her** to her house.

As he saunters along with her,

there is all the pathos of **an ox** going unwittingly **to the slaughter**.

The Hebrew text of the last line is very obscure, as will be seen by the variety of translations:

"**or as a fool to the correction of the stocks**" (KJV, NKJV).

"or as one in fetters to the correction of the fool" (ASV).

"or as a stag is caught fast" (RSV).

"like a dog cajoled to the muzzle" (Moffatt).

"or as a frisky lamb" (Knox).

"as in fetters a fool to his punishment" (Berkeley).

But the general sense is clearly that the victim is moving irresistibly toward shackles and punishment.

7:23 The expression "**till an arrow struck his liver**" may mean:

1. The method by which the ox in the preceding verse is killed, i.e., a knife pierces its entrails.

2. The thorough inflaming of the man's passions.

3. The consequences of immorality in the man's body. The young man goes in to the harlot like a bird flies into a net, little realizing what it is going to cost him (e.g., VD or AIDS).

7:24, 25 No wonder then that the writer pleads for an attentive ear from his **children**! They should guard their **heart** against any desire to associate with this type of woman. They should guard their feet from straying **into her paths**.

7:26, 27 Her list of victims is a long one. She has ruined or **slain** a great army.

Anyone who enters **her house** is on the broad road **to hell**. He is marching down **to the chambers of death**.

K. Wisdom Personified (Chap. 8)

8:1 Chapter 8 is in sharp contrast to chapter 7. There the adulteress called out to the sons of men. Here **wisdom** invites them to follow her, and gives strong reasons for doing so. A parallel passage in the NT is John 7:37 where Christ calls men to come to Him and drink.

8:2, 3 These verses tell where Wisdom is found. The list of places indicates that she is readily available to the race of men in their daily travels.

8:4, 5 She issues her **call** to all types of **men**, to those of distinction and those of inferior rank. She calls to the **simple** and the **fools**. She is "the would-be guide of Everyman," says Kidner.

8:6–9 The character of Wisdom's teaching is next described. She speaks **of excellent things, . . . right things, . . . truth,** and **righteousness**. From her **lips** come no evil, **crooked** or **perverse** things. Anyone who has a measure of discernment and understanding will find them straight and just.

8:10, 11 The value of Wisdom's **instruction** is incomparable. It is to be desired above **silver, . . . choice gold, . . . rubies**, or anything else that men prize highly.

8:12, 13 **Wisdom** lives in the same house with **prudence**. They go together, so that, if you have Wisdom, you also have insight. Wisdom gives **knowledge and discretion** for the management of the affairs of life.

There are things that Wisdom does *not* live with. They are moral opposites, and she despises them, namely, all forms of **evil**, whether **pride**, **arrogance**, wicked behavior, or lying speech.

8:14–21 Some of the rewards or benefits of Wisdom are:

Good **counsel** (v. 14a)

Sound judgment (v. 14b)

Understanding (v. 14c)

Moral **strength** to do what is right and to resist evil (v. 14d)

Leadership ability (vv. 15a, 16a)

Judicial skill (vv. 15b, 16b)

Affection and companionship (see John 14:21) (v. 17a)

Ready access to those who mean business (v. 17b)

Enduring riches coupled with **honor** and **righteousness** (v. 18)

Character that is worth more **than fine gold** or **choice silver** (v. 19)

Guidance in paths **of righteousness** and **of justice**, bringing **wealth** in abundance (vv. 20, 21).

We have already mentioned that these passages dealing with Wisdom can be fittingly applied to the Lord Jesus, since the NT refers to Him as Wisdom (Matt. 11:19; Luke 11:49; 1 Cor. 1:24,30; Col. 2:3). Nowhere is the application more clear and beautiful than in the following verses. The Christian Church has consistently regarded this paragraph as referring to the Lord Jesus Christ.

What then do we learn about Christ in "this noble specimen of sacred eloquence?"

8:22 His eternal generation: **"The LORD possessed me at the beginning of His way."** We must not understand the word "possessed" as implying that Christ ever had a beginning. God never existed without the quality or attribute of wisdom, and neither did He ever exist without the Person of His Son. The meaning here is exactly the same as in John 1:1: "In the beginning . . . the Word was with God. . . ."

8:23 His appointment from eternity. **"Established"** means anointed or appointed. Long before creation

took place, He was appointed to be the Messiah of Israel and the Savior of the world.

8:24–26 His pre-existence. The words **"brought forth"** must not be taken to mean that He was ever created and thus had a beginning. They are poetic language describing the Son's eternal existence and His personality as being distinct from that of God the Father.

The primal dust refers to the beginnings of the world.

8:27–29 His presence at creation. He was there when **the heavens** were stretched over the land and sea, when **clouds** were formed, and **fountains** and springs began gushing forth. He was there when the boundaries of the oceans were decided upon, **the waters** being commanded not to pass beyond the limits set. He was there when **the foundations of the earth** were made, including the internal structure that supports the outer crust.

8:30a His activity in creation. Here we learn that the Lord Jesus was the active Agent in creation. The NKJV correctly renders the first part of verse 30, **"Then I was beside Him as a master craftsman. . . ."** This agrees, of course, with John 1:3; Colossians 1:16; and Hebrews 1:2.

8:30b His position of affection and **delight . . . before** God. The eternal and infinite love of the Father for His Son increases the marvel that He would ever send that Son to die for sinners.

8:30c His personal delight before God. This magnifies the grace of our Lord Jesus Christ—that He would ever leave that scene of pure and perfect joy to come to this jungle of shame, sorrow, and suffering.

8:31 His **rejoicing in** the **inhabited world**. It is amazing that out of all the vast universe, He should be especially interested in this speck of a planet.

His special **delight** in **the sons of men**. The final wonder is that He should set His affection upon the rebel race of men.

William Cowper left us this magnificent hymn based on verses 22–31:

Ere God had built the mountains,
  Or raised the fruitful hills;
Before He filled the fountains
  that feed the running rills;
In Thee, from everlasting
  The wonderful I AM
Found pleasures never wasting,
  And Wisdom is Thy Name.

When like a tent to dwell in,
  He spread the skies abroad,
And swathed about the swelling
  Of ocean's mighty flood,
He wrought by weight and measure;
  And Thou wast with Him then:
Thyself the Father's pleasure,
  And Thine, the sons of men.

And could'st Thou be delighted
  With creatures such as we,
Who, when we saw Thee, slighted
  And nailed Thee to a tree?
Unfathomable wonder?
  And mystery divine?
The voice that speaks in thunder
  Says, "Sinner, I am thine!"

8:32–36 This final paragraph sets forth the eternal issues involved in man's response to Wisdom's call. It pronounces a blessing on those who **listen to** her instruction, walking in her **ways**. It promises happiness to those who wait **daily at** her **gates**, who keep faithful vigil **at her doors**. It holds out **life** and divine **favor** to those who find her, but personal loss and death to those who miss her.

Apply these last two verses to Christ. Whoever finds Him receives eternal life and stands in full favor with God (see John 8:51; 17:3; Eph.

1:6; 1 John 5:12). But those who miss Him injure themselves, and **those who hate** Him **love death** (cf. John 3:36b).

L. Invitations from Wisdom and Folly (9:1–18)

9:1 Here Wisdom is seen building **her house** and preparing a great feast for those who will answer her invitation. A feast is especially appropriate as a picture of the joy, fellowship, and satisfaction which she provides for her guests.

Various interpretations have been given for the **seven pillars**. Some commentators refer us to Isaiah 11:2, the sevenfold gifts of the Holy Spirit which rested on the Messiah; but actually only six are clearly listed. An alternative interpretation is found in James 3:17 where the wisdom from above is described as (1) pure, (2) peaceable, (3) gentle, (4) willing to yield, (5) full of mercy and good fruits, (6) without partiality and (7) without hypocrisy.

9:2, 3 **Meat** and **wine** are served in abundance. The **table** is richly **furnished**. The regal hostess sends forth **her maidens** to issue the invitation **from the highest places of the city**. The commission of the maidens should remind us who have come to know the Wisdom of God, i.e., the Lord Jesus, to share this Wisdom with others, inviting them to come, find, and enjoy it for themselves.

9:4–6 The actual words of the invitation are given. It is issued to the **simple**, that is, to impressionable people who are prone to go astray and therefore need help and guidance. It is not issued to the wise because they are already inside the palace.

The menu includes the finest foods and the most exquisite **wine**, **mixed** by Wisdom herself.

Those who come are expected to part company with **foolishness**, and show that a moral change has taken place in their own lives.

9:7–9 The continuity here seems to be broken, but perhaps these verses explain either why the invitation is not sent to scorners, or why Wisdom's guests must forsake them.

If you **correct a scoffer**, you get only abuse for it. If you rebuke **a wicked man**, he will turn on you and assault you.

The way in which a man receives rebuke is an index of his character. A **scoffer** hates you, whereas **a wise man** will thank you. How do you react when parent, teacher, employer, or friend corrects you?

Instead of resenting criticism, a wise man takes it to heart and thus becomes **still wiser. A just man** benefits by increasing his store of useful **learning**.

9:10 Once again we are reminded that the starting point for all true **wisdom** is in **the fear of the LORD**. "To know the Deity is what knowledge means" (Moffatt). Because he knows the Holy, a true believer can see more on his knees than others can see on their tiptoes.

The Holy One (plural) may be the plural of majesty, excellence, and comprehensiveness, or it may modify Elohim (understood), a plural word for God.

9:11 Wisdom leads to **multiplied . . . days** and increased **years**. . . . It provides not only for long **life**, but for good and productive living, and then—beyond that—for the life that never ends.

9:12 It is **for** a man's own best advantage to be **wise**; he benefits himself more than anyone else. On the other hand, **if** he chooses to **scoff**, he will suffer the penalty of his choice, though others may be dragged in as well, of course. In the long run, he **alone** is the winner or loser.

9:13 Those who reject Wisdom's feast are prime prospects for Folly's fast. Notice the obvious contrast between Wisdom's elegant offer (vv. 1–6) and Folly's tawdry proposition (vv. 13–18).

The **foolish woman** is loudmouthed, empty-headed, and brazenfaced.

9:14–16 She sits outside her front **door** or on conspicuous heights **of the city**, not as a gracious lady, but as the shameless harlot she is.

She is out to seduce men who are easily led, **simple** fellows **who** have no sense.

9:17 Her line is, **"Stolen water is sweet, and bread eaten in secret is pleasant."** Basically she means that illicit intercourse is attractive because it is forbidden and because there is the intrigue of secrecy about it.

When fallen human nature is forbidden to do a certain thing, that prohibition stirs up the desire to do it all the more (see Rom. 7:7, 8). The harlot appeals to this depraved instinct in man. She invites the gullible and the "easy touches" in for a visit.

9:18 But she doesn't tell them the other side of the story. Following the moment of pleasure and passion is the lifetime of remorse and the eternity in the **depths of hell**.

Even the world sometimes recognizes the truth of this verse. A very popular French song of the past century, speaking of the world's idea of "love," put it well:

Love's pleasure lasts only for a night;
Love's chagrin lasts for a lifetime.[13]

III. PROVERBS OF SOLOMON ON PRACTICAL MORALITY (10:1—22:16)

Up to this point in the book of Proverbs, there has been a definite continuity of thought and a connection between the verses. Subjects have been dealt with in paragraph form. From 10:1—22:16 we have a series of 375 proverbs, each distinct in itself. Most of them present contrasting statements, separated by the word "but." It may be no coincidence that the numerical value of the letters of Solomon's name in Hebrew is 375, corresponding to the number of proverbs in this section entitled **"The proverbs of Solomon."**

A. Righteous and Wicked Lifestyles Contrasted (10:1—15:33)

10:1 The behavior of **a . . . son** has a direct effect on the emotional health of his parents. Every son may turn out to be a Paul (**a wise son**) or a Judas (**a foolish son**), with all that means by way of joy or grief.

10:2 Wealth obtained illegally doesn't last; it has a way of disappearing. And in the hour of death, it cannot win a moment's reprieve. **Righteousness**, on the other hand, **delivers from death** in at least two ways. It preserves a man from the perils of a sinful life, and, as the outward evidence of the new birth, it shows that he has eternal life.

10:3 It is a general rule that God **will not allow the righteous soul to famish**. David said, "I have been young, and now am old; yet I have not seen the righteous forsaken, nor his descendants begging bread" (Ps. 37:25). But it is equally true that the Lord "thwarts the craving of the wicked" (RSV). Just as they reach out to grasp satisfaction and fulfillment, it eludes them.

10:4 The lazy, careless person reaps poverty. The one who is **diligent** and aggressive succeeds.

10:5 Summertime is reaping time. It is senseless to go to all the labor of plowing, planting, and cultivating, only to sleep when the time comes to **harvest** the crop. Jesus says to all His disciples, "Lift up your eyes and look at the fields, for they are already white for harvest" (John 4:35).

10:6 The law of harvest is that we reap what we sow. If we sow an upright life, we will receive the **blessings** of God and the praise of our fellow men. If we sow the wild oats of sin, our mouth will be covered with **violence**. This is what happened to Haman: his **mouth** was covered and he was led out to a violent death (Est. 7:8–10).

10:7 A holy life lingers long after the person is gone. The **name of the wicked** evokes a stench, not a fragrance. Men still call their sons Paul—but not Judas!

10:8 A wise-hearted person **will receive commands** in the sense that he is willing to listen to sound advice. The loudmouthed **fool**, because of his unwillingness to learn and obey, is hurled down to his ruin.

10:9 There is safety and security in an upright life, but the life that is built on deception will be found out and exposed.

10:10 The contrast in this verse is clearer if we follow the RSV: "He who winks with the eye causes trouble, but he who boldly reproves makes peace." The winking eye indicates subterfuge and cunning. When this form of deceit is frankly rebuked, peace is exchanged for sorrow.

10:11 **The mouth of** a **righteous** person **is a well of life** flowing with words of edification, comfort, and counsel. **The mouth of the wicked** is silenced by his **violence** and malice.

10:12 A hateful spirit isn't satisfied to forgive and forget; it insists on raking up old grudges and quarrels. A heart of **love** draws a curtain of secrecy over the faults and failures of others. These faults and failures must, of course, be confessed and forsaken, but love does not gossip about them or keep the pot boiling.

10:13 The conversation of an intelligent man is helpful to others. A fool helps no one, but only succeeds in bringing punishment on himself.

10:14 **Wise people** value **knowledge** and **store** it **up** for the appropriate moment. "He reserves what he has to say for the right time, place, and persons (cf. Matt. 7:6)," writes Barnes. But you never know what a **foolish** blabbermouth will say next. He is always bringing trouble to others and to himself.

10:15 The **rich** get richer and the **poor** get poorer. Those who have money can make money. The poor man can't get started; his **poverty** is his undoing. The rich can buy quality merchandise that lasts longer. The poor buy worn-out, second-hand things that keep them poor with repair bills. This is the way things are in life, but not the way they should be.

10:16 Wealth obtained by reputable employment is a blessing. Profit from dishonorable work leads **to sin**. Compare a Christian carpenter and a non-Christian bartender. The income of the carpenter represents positive, productive work and is used for beneficial purposes. The work of the barkeeper is destructive. The more he works, the more he sins. The more he sins, the more he makes.

10:17 The one who makes it a practice to listen to godly **instruction** stays on the road **of life**. The one

who turns his back on good advice **goes astray** himself and leads others astray.

10:18 This proverb contrasts the man who **hides** his **hatred** by insincere words and the man who openly reveals it by slandering his neighbor. The first is a hypocrite, the second **is a fool**, and there is not much to choose between them. A third alternative, and one that believers should learn to practice, is not to harbor any hatred at all.

10:19 The more we talk, the greater is the probability of saying something wrong. Compulsive talkers should beware! The lust for incessant conversation often leads to exaggeration, breaking of confidences, and associated sins. Trying to top someone else's joke often mushrooms into off-color stories.

The man who exercises self-control in his speech **is wise**. He saves himself from embarrassment, apologies, and outright sin.

10:20 What a good man says is a reflection of what he is. Because his character is sterling, so is his speech. Since **the heart** (or mind) **of the wicked** man is not worthwhile, neither is the conversation that flows from it.

10:21 Someone has aptly paraphrased this proverb, "Good feeds itself and others. Evil cannot keep itself alive."

Fools here are stubborn, intractable people.

10:22 It is only **the blessing of the LORD** that truly enriches a life.

But is it true that **He adds no sorrow with it**? How does this reconcile with the fact that the most godly people pass through times of deep sorrow?

There are several possible explanations for this second part of the proverb:

1. God doesn't send sorrow. All sorrow, sickness, and suffering come from Satan. God often permits them in the lives of His children but He is not the source.
2. Sorrow is not an ingredient of God's blessing as it is of prosperity apart from God.
3. Another possible translation is "and toil adds nothing to it" (margin of RV and RSV). Here the thought is that toil, apart from God, adds nothing to the blessing. Toil is good, but unless it is God-directed, it is futile (see Ps. 127:1, 2).

10:23 A fool amuses himself by getting into trouble; it's his favorite **sport. A man of understanding** gets his pleasure in conducting himself wisely.

10:24 The calamity which the wrongdoer fears will descend on him. **The desire of the righteous**—the will of God in this life and the presence of God in the next—**will be granted**. In this vein, C. S. Lewis says:

In the end, that Face which is the delight or the terror of the universe must be turned upon each of us either with one expression or the other, either conferring glory inexpressible or inflicting shame that can never be cured or disguised.[14]

10:25 When the whirlwind of God's judgment **passes by, the wicked is** nowhere to be found. **But the righteous** person is established on the Rock of Ages; nothing can ever move him.

10:26 Vinegar sets the **teeth** on edge, and **smoke** irritates the **eyes**. In the same way, a **lazy** messenger who dillydallies on the way proves exasperating, frustrating, and annoying **to those who send him**.

10:27 A devout life leads to longevity. **Wicked** men are cut off prematurely, e.g., gangland slayings, reprisal killings, deaths caused by drunkenness, drugs, and dissipation.

10:28 The things **the righteous** look forward to **will be** realized with **gladness**. Not so **the wicked**—their hopes will be thoroughly disappointed. G. S. Bowes illustrates:

Alexander the Great was not satisfied, even when he had completely subdued the nations. He wept because there were no more worlds to conquer, and he died at an early age in a state of debauchery. Hannibal, who filled three bushels with the gold rings taken from the knights he had slaughtered, committed suicide by swallowing poison. Few noted his passing, and he left this earth completely unmourned. Julius Caesar, "dyeing his garments in the blood of one million of his foes," conquered 800 cities, only to be stabbed by his best friends at the scene of his greatest triumph. Napoleon, the feared conqueror, after being the scourge of Europe, spent his last years in banishment.[15]

Surely **the expectation of the wicked** perishes!

10:29 In His providential dealings **the LORD** proves to be a **tower of strength for the upright, but destruction . . . to** evildoers.

10:30 God guarantees a dwelling place to **the righteous, but the wicked** will be exiles and vagabonds.

The captivity of Israel illustrates this.

10:31 A good man's **mouth** is like a tree that **brings forth** blossoms of **wisdom**. Speech that is crooked and **perverse** will be **cut out**.

10:32 You can depend on a good man to say **what is acceptable. The wicked** man knows only how to distort the facts and to speak **what is perverse**.

11:1 Crooked merchants sometimes had two sets of weights, one for buying and one for selling. The buying weights were heavier than they should have been, so that he got more merchandise than he paid for. The selling weights were lighter than the standard, so that the customer got less than he paid for.

There are dishonest practices in business today that come under this ban on **dishonest scales**, as well as applications in school life, social life, home life, and church life.

11:2 First, **pride**; then a fall; **then comes shame** connected with the fall. But to be **humble** and down-to-earth reduces the danger of stumbling.

11:3 Honesty is the best policy. The **integrity** of **upright** people **will guide them** on the right track; the experience of Joseph is an example. The crookedness **of the unfaithful** is their downfall; Balaam's life testifies to this.

11:4 **Riches** cannot avert the wrath of God in time or in eternity. **Righteousness** is a safeguard against premature **death** in the here and now. And only those who are clothed in the righteousness of God will escape the second death.

11:5 The **blameless** man is directed by **righteousness**, the ideal guide. **The wicked** man **will fall**, a victim of **his own wickedness**.

11:6 **Righteousness** not only guides good men; it **will deliver them** from perils seen and unseen. Apostates, like Judas, **will be caught** in the meshes of **their** own **lust** and greed.

11:7 It has been said that a fool is a man all of whose plans end at the grave. When the coffin lid closes, all his hopes are ended. The things he lived for are no longer his, and **his** expectation of prosperity is gone forever.

11:8 God delivers **the righteous** from **trouble** and sends it upon **the wicked instead**. Thus the three Hebrews were delivered out of the fiery furnace, but their would-be executioners were consumed by the fire (Dan. 3:22–26).

11:9 An apostate or **hypocrite** seeks to undermine the faith of **his neighbor** with doubts and denials. **Knowledge** of the truth enables **the righteous** to detect the counterfeit, and to save himself and others from subversion.

11:10 Two occasions when a **city** breaks out in joyful celebration are **when the righteous** prosper and **when the wicked perish**.

11:11 **The blessing of the upright** may refer to their prayers for **the city** (1 Tim. 2:1, 2), or to the benefits which their presence and godly influence bring to the city (cf. Jesus' description of His followers as the salt of the earth in Matt. 5:13).

The deceit, broken promises, fraud, and profanity of the wicked are enough to ruin any local government.

11:12 **He who is devoid of wisdom despises his neighbor, but a man of understanding holds his peace.** To belittle another man is to insult God, to hurt the man, to invite strife, and to help no one. **A man of understanding** knows that it is better to say nothing if he can't praise or edify.

11:13 **A talebearer** seems to take a malicious delight in spreading scandal, informing on others, and breaking confidences. He doesn't hold anything back, but tells everything he knows.

A **faithful** friend knows how to maintain a confidence and to refrain from talking.

11:14 Without wise leadership and

statesmanship, **the people** are bound to **fall** into trouble. On the other hand, **there is safety** in having the combined judgment of many good **counselors**.

11:15 To be **surety for a stranger** means to guarantee his debt or his promissory note. The person who does this **will suffer** for it, that is, he will pay a stinging penalty. The man who **hates** suretyship saves himself a lot of headaches. See notes on 6:1–5.

11:16 **A gracious woman retains** respect and **honor**, as is seen in the case of Abigail (1 Sam. 25). **Ruthless men** may **retain riches** but they never get a good name.

11:17 A man's disposition affects his own health. The kind person avoids the dyspepsia, apoplexy, gastrointestinal ulcers, and heart trouble which the **cruel** one brings on himself. He **does good for his own soul**.

The *British Medical Journal* once said that there is not a tissue in the human body that is wholly removed from the spirit. A **cruel** disposition takes its toll on the body. One having such a temperament **troubles his own flesh**.

11:18 **The wicked man does deceptive work, but he who sows righteousness will have a sure reward.** It is true that evil people often seem to grow rich overnight, but their wealth is unsatisfying, unenduring, and unable to help them when they need it most. The rewards of a righteous life are real and permanent.

11:19 All conduct leads in one of two directions—either **to life** or **to . . . death**. This proverb does not teach salvation by good works, however. No one can be steadfast in **righteousness** unless he is in right relationship to God. He must first have been born again. A man **who pursues evil** proves thereby that he never was converted.

11:20 As far as **the LORD** is concerned, a **heart** that is false is hateful and loathsome. He really likes the person who is straightforward. No view of God is complete unless it sees that He is capable of hatred as well as of love.

A heart that is **blameless**, on the other hand, is **His delight**.

11:21 **"Though they join forces"** is literally "hand in hand" (NKJV margin). It may refer to two things that are certain in this uncertain world—the punishment of **the wicked** and the deliverance of **the posterity of the righteous**.

11:22 **A ring of gold in a** pig's **snout** is incongruous. The **snout** is as unattractive as the **ring** is lovely. **A lovely woman who lacks discretion** also combines two opposites—physical attractiveness and moral deficiency.

11:23 **Righteous** people aspire **only** for **good** and they get it. **The wicked** seek for evil and they get it in the form of **wrath** or judgment.

This proverb emphasizes the importance of having worthy goals, because ultimately we get what we go after in life. That is why Emerson said, "Hitch your wagon to a star." A British statesman urged his cabinet, "Whatever else you do, buy big maps!"

11:24 Here is a glorious paradox. We enrich ourselves by being generous. We impoverish ourselves by laying up treasures on earth.

What we save, we lose. What we give, we have.

Jim Elliot said, "He is no fool who gives what he cannot keep to gain what he cannot lose." And Dr. Barnhouse observed that everybody tithes, either to the Lord or to the doctor, the dentist, and the garage mechanic.

11:25 **The generous** person reaps dividends that the miser can never know. Whatever we do for others returns to us in blessing.

When a Sunday school teacher prepares diligently and then teaches her class, who do you think benefits from it most—the students or herself?

11:26 The selfish man keeps his **grain** off the market in a time of famine, hoping for greater return as the price is forced up. He is a profiteer, enriching himself by impoverishing and starving others. No wonder **the people will curse** him! They want someone who will meet their desperate need now.

The world is perishing for the bread of life. The bread is free, and always will be. We have it to share with others. What are we waiting for? **Blessing will be on** the one **who sells** the grain, that is, who spreads the good news of the gospel.

11:27 When a man's motives are pure and unselfish, he wins the esteem of others. But the man who is out to cause **trouble** for others will get it for himself.

11:28 The NT counterpart of this proverb is 1 Timothy 6:17–19. **Riches** are uncertain and therefore not worthy of trust. Our confidence should be in the living God who gives us richly all things to enjoy.

"The lust of gold," said Samuel Johnson, "unfeeling and remorseless, is the last corruption of degenerate man."

The righteous, that is, those whose trust is in the Lord, **will flourish** with life and vitality **like foliage**.

11:29 There are several types of men who trouble their **own house**— the drunkard, the crank, and the adulterer, for instance. But here it is probably the man who is greedy of gain (see 15:27), and who loses sight of the worthwhile values of life in his mad quest for wealth. He **will inherit the wind**, that is, end up with nothing tangible to satisfy his greed. His

penalty for thus playing **the fool** will be servitude to a man who acts more wisely.

11:30 A **righteous** life is like a fruit-bearing **tree** that brings nourishment and refreshment to others. The **wise** man **wins** others to a life of wisdom and righteousness.

This is one of the great texts for soul winners in the Bible. It reminds us of the promise which Jesus made to Peter, "You will catch men" (Luke 5:10). What an unspeakable privilege it is to be used of God in doing a work in human lives that will result in eternal blessing! Every soul won to the Lord will be a worshiper of the Lamb of God forever and ever!

11:31 Even **righteous** people are **recompensed** in this life for their misdeeds. Moses was excluded from the Promised Land and David had to restore fourfold. If the righteous reap what they sow, **how much more** do **the ungodly**! Or, as Peter put it, "If the righteous one is scarcely saved, where will the ungodly and the sinner appear?" (1 Pet. 4:18).

12:1 Anyone who is open to discipline and **instruction** shows that he really wants to learn. The man who resents being told anything and refuses **correction is stupid**.

12:2 A moral, ethical person can be sure of the Lord's **favor**. A **man of wicked intentions** can be equally sure of His condemnation. "Think—" wrote Foreman, "the supreme Power in the universe against what a wicked man is doing, determined that he shall fail! The supreme Power leaving man to himself in silent scorn."

12:3 Lives that are dominated by **wickedness** have no stability. They are like the seed which fell on the rocky places (Matt. 13:5, 6); the earth was shallow and because they had no root, the seeds quickly withered away.

A **righteous** man has his **root** deep in God. He is able to stand when the storms of life blow. This man is described in Psalm 1:3.

12:4 An **excellent wife** brings joy and gladness to **her husband**. The one who disgraces her husband gives him a terrible letdown—as if **his bones** rotted away.

12:5 The goals **of the righteous** are honorable, and, just as surely, the plans **of the wicked are deceitful**. In other words, a man's aims are a mirror of his character.

12:6 By their speech sinners seek to lay fatal traps for the innocent and unwary. **Upright** men **deliver** themselves and others by speaking the truth.

12:7 When justice catches up with **the wicked**, that's the end of them. Godly people have a good foundation; they are not swept away by calamity.

12:8 People speak well of one who has insight and acts wisely, but they have nothing but contempt for one who has no principles.

12:9 **Better is the one who is slighted but has a servant, than he who honors himself but lacks bread.** The combination of low rank and food on the table is better than pretended status with starvation.

12:10 **A righteous** man's kindness extends even to dumb animals, but a **wicked** man is **cruel**, even when he thinks he is being most gentle.

Although God is transcendent, He is not too high to care for animals, but legislates concerning them (Ex. 20:10; 23:4, 5). He even legislates concerning a bird's nest (Deut. 22:6).

12:11 A man who engages in positive, constructive work, like farming, **will** have his needs supplied. But the man who spends his time in worthless pursuits not only has an empty cupboard but also an empty head.

12:12 The **catch of evil men** means, by metonymy, what is caught in the net of evil, or what is taken from others unjustly. In other words, **the wicked covet** what belongs to others.

In contrast, **the righteous** are satisfied to provide quietly for their own needs.

12:13 Ungodly people are often trapped by their own words. By failing to tell a consistent story, they trip themselves up. A liar has to have a good memory; otherwise his accounts won't mesh. And to support a lie, he has to build a structure of other lies.

The righteous will come through trouble. God does not promise His people freedom from *all* trouble, but rather that they will **come through** it.

12:14 **Good** speech and **good** behavior carry their own reward with them. Wise, gentle, pure speech is rewarded with love, favor, and respect. **Good** deeds come back to a man in blessing.

12:15 You can't tell **a fool** anything. He knows everything, and will not listen. But a **wise** man will welcome advice. He recognizes that it is impossible for one person to see all sides of a question.

12:16 A fool doesn't restrain his **wrath**. He blows up at the slightest provocation. **A prudent man** knows how to ignore insult and to exercise self-control.

12:17 A witness who tells the **truth** in court gives righteous evidence. **A false witness** tells lies.

12:18 Some people use their tongues like **a sword**; slashing away at others, cutting and causing pain. **The wise** person speaks words of **health** and healing, that is, healing the wounds inflicted by the prattler.

12:19 Truth is eternal. Why? Because truth is what God says about a thing; therefore, it never changes.

A lying tongue lasts as long as a wink.

12:20 Treachery fills **the heart of those who** plan wickedness. **Joy** fills the heart of those who pursue **peace**.

12:21 It is true in a general sense that **no grave trouble** happens to **the righteous**. However, this is not a rule without exception. What is true without exception is that the just are preserved from the evil consequences that follow the behavior of the wicked. **The wicked** get plenty of this type of trouble.

12:22 God hates liars. How careful we should be about shading of the truth, white lies, exaggerations, and half-truths! A sure way of bringing **delight** to His heart is by being absolutely honest and trustworthy.

12:23 A **prudent man** doesn't go around showing off how much he knows. He modestly **conceals** his learning. But you aren't long in the presence **of fools** before they reveal their **foolishness**.

12:24 In the ordinary course of life, dedicated, **diligent** people rise to positions of leadership just as cream rises to the surface. Laziness leads to poverty, and poverty reduces man to the level of **forced labor**.

Oswald Chambers said that slovenliness is an insult to the Holy Spirit; he could have said the same thing about laziness.

12:25 **Anxiety . . . causes depression**. A **good**, encouraging, or sympathetic **word** works wonders in perking someone up again.

12:26 Contrary to appearances, **the righteous** man is actually better off than his unrighteous neighbor. It doesn't seem that way. The sinner seems to have everything going his own way, and this seduces people into believing that forbidden fruit really is sweeter. Therefore the Christian **should choose his friends carefully**.

12:27 This **lazy** loafer either doesn't hunt or he **does not roast what he** has taken **in hunting**. In the first place he lacks the inertia to get started; in the second, he lacks the drive to finish what he began.

The Hebrew of the latter part of the proverb is also obscure, like the first part, but the sense almost surely is that a diligent person values what he has worked for and uses it to the best advantage. Ruth was like that; she beat out what she had gleaned (Ruth 2:17). In our Bible study, we should improve on what we have learned and we can do it through meditation, prayer, and practical obedience:

> Thus on Thy Holy Word we'd feed and live and grow,
> Go on to know the Lord, and practice what we know.

12:28 In the narrow path of **righteousness**, there **is life** along **the way** and life at the close of the journey. **There is no death** in it, as there is on the broad road that leads to destruction. **"Life"** here looks to a future beyond death, to eternal life. The NIV translates the verse, "In the way of righteousness there is life; along that path is immortality."

13:1 Both in physical and spiritual development, there is a normal process of development. A baby, for instance, must crawl before he walks or talks. In the spiritual realm, a convert must listen and learn before he launches forth in service. **A wise son** submits to the discipline of **instruction**. The **scoffer** won't have it; he thinks he has all the answers, and refuses to be corrected.

13:2 Here is **a man** whose speech is edifying, encouraging, and comforting; he himself is rewarded when he sees the beneficial results of the spoken word. By way of contrast, the **unfaithful** man plans **violence** for others, and he is paid in his own coin.

13:3 The man who **guards his** speech controls **his** whole **life** (see Jas. 3:2b). The one who exercises no self-control is in for trouble. The lesson is: be careful what you say—it might be used against you.

13:4 "If wishes were horses, beggars would ride." The **lazy man** has great **desires**, but that isn't enough. "The wish without the exertion is useless." **The diligent** man applies himself to his work and carries home the bacon. This is true in spiritual matters as well as in temporal. Bosch illustrates:

Adam Clark is reported to have spent 40 years writing his commentary on the Scriptures. Noah Webster labored 36 years forming his dictionary; in fact, he crossed the ocean twice to gather material needed to make the book absolutely accurate. Milton rose at 4 o'clock every morning in order to have sufficient hours to compose and rewrite his poetry which stands among the best of the world's literature. Gibbon spent 26 years on his book *The Decline and Fall of the Roman Empire*, but it towers as a monument to careful research and untiring dedication to his task. Bryant rewrote one of his poetic masterpieces 100 times before publication, just to attain complete beauty and perfection of expression. These men enjoyed what they were doing, and each one threw all of his energy into his effort no matter how difficult the job.

The most happy and productive people are those who are diligent in their labors for the betterment of mankind and the glory of God.[16]

13:5 **A righteous man hates** any kind of dishonesty, **but a wicked man** "acts shamefully and disgracefully" (RSV). J. Allen Blair illustrates from the life of a great American:

It is said of Abraham Lincoln that he would accept no case in which the client did not have justice on his side. One time a man came to employ him. Lincoln stared at the ceiling, yet listened intently as the facts were given. Abruptly, he swung around in his chair.

"You have a pretty good case in technical law," he said, "but a pretty bad one in equity and justice. You will have to get someone else to win the case for you. I could not do it. All the time while pleading before the jury, I'd be thinking, Lincoln, you're a liar! I might forget myself and say it out loud."

Lying and all forms of guilt grieve the heart of God. No Christian should lie or deceive, regardless of consequences to himself. If he does, he will never advance in the things of God.[17]

13:6 A righteous life is a protected life. God undertakes to guard the **blameless.** But **the sinner** walks in constant peril, for their **wickedness overthrows** them sooner or later.

13:7 There are two ways of looking at this proverb. First, a man who has nothing in the way of material possessions may try to create the impression that he is wealthy, while one who actually has lots of money may give the appearance of being **poor.**

Or it may mean this. The godless millionaire actually is a spiritual pauper, whereas the humblest believer, though financially poor, is an heir of God and a joint heir with Jesus Christ. Morgan illustrates:

Our age abounds with men who have made themselves rich, and yet have nothing. They have amassed great wealth, and yet it has no purchasing power in the true things of life. It cannot insure health, it brings no happiness, it often destroys peace. On the other hand, there are those who have impoverished themselves, and have by so doing become wealthy in all the highest senses of the word. How is this to be explained? Is not the solution found by laying the emphasis in each of the contrastive declarations, upon the word self. To make self rich, is to destroy the capacity for life. To make self poor, by enriching others is to live. It is impossible to consider this saying of Hebrew wisdom, without thinking of the One who became incarnate Wisdom.[18]

13:8 A rich man is often threatened by those who want his money. He faces robbery, blackmail, and kidnapping for **ransom**, and he has to guard his **life** by hiring protection or by meeting extortionate demands. **The poor** person never has to listen to this kind of threat.

13:9 The testimony **of the righteous** is like a **light** that burns brightly and cheerily. The life and hopes **of the wicked** are a **lamp** that **will be put out**.

13:10 There may be two thoughts in the first line. One is that when contentions come, **pride** is the invariable cause. Or second, "by pride there only cometh contention" (JND), that is, nothing good ever comes from pride: only bitter feuding. C. S. Lewis writes:

It is Pride which has been the chief cause of misery in every nation and every family since the world began. Other vices may sometimes bring people together; you may find good fellowship and jokes and friendli-

ness among drunken people or unchaste people. But Pride always means enmity—it is enmity. And not only enmity between man and man, but enmity to God.[19]

Those who are willing to listen to good advice are wise; they avoid pride and the personality conflicts that go with it.

13:11 **Wealth gained by dishonesty** comes in haste or without exertion. This would include the money won by gambling, sweepstakes, or stock market speculation. This kind of wealth has a way of leaking out of a man's hands.

Wealth gained **by** honest **labor** accumulates instead of dwindling.

13:12 Repeated postponement of one's expectations is disheartening; **but when the desire** is at last fulfilled, it is a source of tremendous satisfaction. Apply this to the coming of the Lord.

13:13 The "word" here is the Word of God. Our attitude toward it is a matter of life and death. Whoever **despises** it pushes the self-destruct button. Whoever trusts and obeys **the commandment** is abundantly **rewarded**.

13:14 The counsel and instruction **of the wise** are a **fountain of life** and refreshment to those who heed. They deliver a person from deadly **snares** along life's pathway.

13:15 **Good understanding** brings a person into **favor** with God and man. "A man with good sense is appreciated" (LB).

In the second part of the proverb, the word translated **"hard"** basically means permanent, enduring, or perennial. But to make good sense it has been taken to mean **hard** or rugged. If it meant permanent, there would have to be a negative, that is, "the way of the unfaithful is not permanent." Perhaps we are best to stick to the traditional text: **"the way of the unfaithful is hard."** Each day's newspaper provides illustrations of that truth!

13:16 A man's conduct reveals his character. If a **man** is **prudent**, it comes out in the responsible way he **acts**. **A fool** displays **his folly** for everyone to see.

13:17 An unreliable **messenger** brings **trouble** to everyone concerned. Better to send **a faithful ambassador**; he accomplishes his mission to the satisfaction of all.

"Now then, we are ambassadors for Christ . . ." (2 Cor. 5:20).

13:18 The one **who disdains correction** and discipline earns **poverty and shame** by his stubbornness. The man **who** listens to **a rebuke will be honored**.

13:19 Good men are pleased when they achieve their goals, but **fools** hate to give up their sin. The contrast seems to be between good men pursuing worthy objects, and sinners unwilling to **depart from evil**.

13:20 We should seek out the companionship of **wise men**; they will lift us up. "Evil company corrupts good habits" (1 Cor. 15:33). A man is often known by the company he keeps. A **companion of fools** is brought to ruin.

13:21 Sinners are dogged by the hounds of misfortune, physical harm, bad reputation, loss of possessions. **The righteous** enjoy a **good** reputation, a **good** life, and a **good** reward.

13:22 **A good man leaves an inheritance** not only **to his** children but to his grandchildren. In the OT, this probably meant that he left *material* wealth for them. But a Christian today is better advised to leave a rich *spiritual* heritage to his descendants.

The wealth of the sinner is stored up for the righteous; "ill-gotten gain has a way of finding better hands."

13:23 **Poor** people cultivate their land intensively and get **much** produce from a small area. They use what they have to the best advantage.

The second part of the verse may mean that: (1) rich men, with bigger farms, often come to ruin because of their injustice, or (2) the tillage of the poor is often swept away by injustice.

13:24 The Bible teaches corporal punishment, whether the modern "experts"agree or not. To withhold punishment from a child when it is deserved is to encourage the child in sin and thus to contribute to his eventual ruin. The parent **who spares his rod** might think he is manifesting love, but God says it is hatred.

For years Dr. Benjamin Spock encouraged parents to be permissive. After living to see a generation of bratty, pesky children, he admitted that he had been wrong. He said, "Inability to be firm is, to my mind, the commonest problem of parents in America today." He placed the blame, at least in part, on the experts—"the child psychiatrists, psychologists, teachers, social workers, and pediatricians, like myself."[20]

The parent **who** genuinely **loves** his child does not condone naughtiness, but **disciplines** the child **promptly**.

13:25 God insures that the needs of **the righteous** will be supplied, but **wicked** men are equally assured of an empty **stomach**.

14:1 A sensible housewife attends to **her house** and her family. **The foolish** woman neglects her husband and children, and wonders why her family goes to ruin.

Is it possible for a woman to tear **down** her home by too much religious activity too?

14:2 A man's conduct is a reflection of his attitude toward **the LORD**. The righteous man is guided by what he knows will please God. The **perverse** man doesn't care what God thinks, and thus reveals his contempt of **Him**. Kidner writes:

> Every departure from God's path is a pitting of one's will, and a backing of one's judgment, against His; but the contempt which it spells is too irrational to acknowledge.[21]

14:3 **In the mouth of a fool is a rod of pride.** He will have to take a beating for his arrogant talk. **Wise** people's speech **will preserve them** from any such punishment.

14:4 A barn can be kept cleanly swept **where** there are **no oxen**, but isn't it better to have some dust and dirt around, knowing that the labor **of an ox** will lead to a bountiful harvest? The rewards of toil more than compensate for its disagreeable aspects.

This proverb is not intended to encourage homes or chapels that look like disaster areas. But it does discourage that passion for order and dustlessness that puts the brakes on progress and productiveness.

14:5 C. H. Mackintosh once said that it is better to go to heaven with a good conscience than stay on earth with a bad one. How careful we should be to be utterly truthful at all times!

14:6 By continued refusal to listen, **a scoffer** loses the capacity to hear. He can never **find** true **wisdom** as long as he rejects the Lord.

The man of understanding perceives the right thing quickly. "For whoever has, to him more will be given, and he will have abundance..." (Matt. 13:12).

14:7 Don't cultivate the friendship **of a foolish man**, "for there you do not meet words of knowledge" (RSV), or "you will not find a word of sense in him" (Moffatt).

14:8 For a **prudent** man **wisdom** means knowing how to behave honestly, conscientiously, and obediently. What a fool considers to be wisdom is actually **folly**, and the essence of that folly is deceiving others, which eventually results in self-inflicted **deceit**.

14:9 Although the Hebrew here is obscure, the NKJV makes good sense.

> Fools make a mock of sin, will not
>   believe;
> It has a fearful dagger up its sleeve;
> "How can it be," they say, "that such
>   a thing,
> So full of sweetness, e'er should wear
>   a sting?"
> They know not that it is the very
>   spell
> Of sin, to make them laugh
>   themselves to hell.
> Look to thyself then, deal with sin
>   no more.
> Lest He who saves, against thee shuts
>   the door.
>   —*John Bunyan*

The upright enjoy the Lord's **favor**, free from the guilt and condemnation of sin.

14:10 There are sorrows in the human **heart** that no other human being can share (though the Lord can and does). There is also **joy** that can be enjoyed only by the person directly involved.

14:11 Notice the contrast between **house** and **tent**. We think of a *house* as permanent and a *tent* as temporary. But it is **the tent of the upright** pilgrim that survives, while **the house of the wicked** earth dweller tumbles.

14:12 The **way** which **seems right**

to men is salvation by good works or good character. More people go down to hell laboring under that misconception than under any other. (See also 16:25.)

In a broader sense, the **way** which **seems right to a man** is his own way, the path of self-will that scorns divine guidance or human counsel. It can **end** only in disaster and spiritual **death**.

14:13 There is no such thing in life as pure, unadulterated joy. **Sorrow** is always mixed to some extent. Knox says, "Joy blends with grief, and laughter marches with tears."

14:14 **The backslider in heart will be filled with his own ways, but a good man will be satisfied from above.** A person who wanders away from the Lord reaps the consequences of his waywardness. Thus Naomi said, "The Almighty has dealt very bitterly with me. I went out full, and the Lord has brought me home again empty" (Ruth 1:20b, 21a). And the prodigal son said, "How many of my father's hired servants have bread enough and to spare, and I perish with hunger!" (Luke 15:17).

The upright man is satisfied with his ways, because they are the Lord's ways. He can say with David, "My cup runs over" (Ps. 23:5c). Or with Paul, "I have fought a good fight, I have finished the race, I have kept the faith" (2 Tim. 4:7).

14:15 A naive, gullible person is susceptible to **every** new idea or fad. **The prudent** man takes a second look and thus preserves **his steps** from error. Faith demands the surest evidence, and finds it in the Word of God. Credulity believes what every passing scientist, philosopher, or psychologist has to say.

14:16 A **wise man fears** in the sense that he is careful and cautious.

Of course, the verse may also mean that he fears the Lord.

The **fool** is arrogant and careless, throws off restraint, and is obviously **self-confident**.

14:17 A **quick-tempered man acts foolishly.** In anger, he does things without stopping to consider the consequences. He slams doors, throws whatever is handy, yells curses and insults, breaks furniture, and walks out in a rage. But if we had to choose, we could tolerate him more easily than **the man of wicked intentions**. Everyone hates this man for his cold-blooded treachery.

14:18 **The simple inherit folly.** If they refuse to listen to sound teaching, they thereby choose to become more stupid.

The prudent are honored and rewarded by acquiring more and more **knowledge**.

14:19 This proverb points to the eventual triumph of good over evil. God will vindicate the cause of the righteous. The day came when Haman had to **bow before** Mordecai. And the day will come when every knee in the universe **will bow before** Jesus Christ as King of kings and Lord of lords.

14:20 **The poor man is hated even by his own neighbor.** It shouldn't be this way, but it often is. Many people form friendships on the basis of self-interest. They avoid the poor and cultivate the rich for selfish ends. We should be interested in people for what we can do for them, not what we can get from them.

In one sense **the rich** man **has many friends**, but in another sense he never knows how many true friends he has, that is, friends who love him for who he is rather than for what he has.

14:21 This verse is obviously connected with the preceding one. It is sin to despise the poor because God has chosen them (Jas. 2:5). The man **who has mercy on the poor** is blessed in the act.

We should never forget that the Lord Jesus came into the world as a poor man. Someone referred to Him as "my penniless friend from Nazareth."

14:22 Those who plot mischief and **devise evil** plans are destined to **go astray**. **Those who devise** the **good** of others are rewarded with **mercy and truth**. This means that God shows kindness to them and is true to His promises of protection and reward. It also means that people repay them with loyalty and faithfulness.

14:23 **All** honorable work is profitable. Nothing but talk **leads only to poverty**. We all know people who talk by the hour about their problems but never lift a little finger to solve them. They talk up a storm about world evangelism but never move from their reclining chair to witness to their neighbor. Without coming up for air, they tell you what they plan to do in the future, but they never do it.

14:24 The glory **of** the **wise is their riches**. They have something to show for their wisdom, whether we think of that wealth as spiritual or material. **Fools** have nothing but **folly** to show for their lives and labors.

14:25 **A true witness** in a court of law **delivers** innocent people from being "framed." **A deceitful witness** misrepresents the facts, with all the ruinous results that flow from such deceit.

The gospel preacher is **a true witness** who **delivers souls** from eternal death. The "liberals" and "cultists" are **deceitful** witnesses who speak **lies** and lead souls astray.

14:26 The man who fears **the Lord** has every reason to have **strong confidence**. If God is for him, no one can be successfully against him (Rom. 8:31). That man's **children will have a place of refuge** under God's wings when evil attacks.

14:27 Trust in God is a source of spiritual strength and vitality, enabling one to avoid **the snares of death**.

14:28 The size, contentment, and loyalty of the populace determine **a king's honor**. There is little prestige for **a prince** to hold the title if he has few or no **people** over whom to rule.

14:29 A man who is patient under provocation shows **great** insight. **He who is impulsive** promotes **folly** and holds it up to public view.

14:30 **A sound heart** here means a satisfied mind. Thus Knox translates, "Peace of mind is health of body."

Envy and passion are bad for a person's health. Dr. Paul Adolph confirms this:

> Some of the most important causes of so-called nervous diseases which psychiatrists recognize are guilt, resentment (an unforgiving spirit), fear, anxiety, frustration, indecision, doubt, jealousy, selfishness, and boredom. Unfortunately, many psychiatrists, while definitely effective in tracing the causes of emotional disturbances which cause disease, have significantly failed in their methods of dealing with these disturbances because they omit faith in God as their approach.[22]

14:31 Whoever takes advantage of **the poor** insults **his** Creator. George Herbert said that man is God's image, but a poor man is Christ's stamp as well.

The second line means that those who have compassion **on the needy** honor God in the process.

14:32 "When the wicked is paid in his own coin, there is an end of him; at death's door, the just still hope" (Knox). Judas is an illustration of the first line, and Paul, of the second.

14:33 The clause, **"Wisdom rests in the heart of him who has understanding"** may mean (1) that wisdom is at home there, or (2) that the man doesn't needlessly parade everything he knows.

The second line is more difficult. It may mean (1) you will soon find out **what is in the heart of fools**; (2) wisdom is not known in the heart of fools (RSV); (3) "wisdom must clamor loudly before being recognized by fools" (Berkeley margin).

14:34 In order for **a nation** to be great, its leaders and people must have upright, moral characters known for their **righteousness**. Corruption, graft, bribery, "dirty tricks," scandal, and all forms of civil unrighteousness bring disgrace to a country.

14:35 A ruler looks with **favor** on a **servant** who acts wisely (compare Joseph, Mordecai, Daniel). **His wrath is** directed **against him who** acts shamefully. "The king favors an able minister; his anger is for the incompetent" (Moffatt).

15:1 Much of chapter 15 is devoted to the subject of speech. A gentle or conciliating **answer** prevents **wrath** from bursting forth or from increasing. If you answer a man with **a harsh word**, it **stirs up** his fleshly nature, and pretty soon you have a violent quarrel on your hands. Spurgeon gives a charming illustration:

> I once lived where my neighbor's garden was divided from me only by a very imperfect hedge. He kept a dog, and his dog was a shockingly bad gardener, and did not improve my plants. So, one evening, while I walked alone, I saw this dog doing mischief and being a long way off, I

threw a stick at him, with some earnest advice as to his going home. This dog, instead of going home, picked up my stick, and came to me with it in his mouth, wagging his tail. He dropped the stick at my feet and looked up to me most kindly. What could I do but pat him and call him a good dog, and regret that I had ever spoken roughly to him?[23]

15:2 A **wise** man's **tongue** pours forth helpful information. He knows what, when, where, and how to speak. **Foolishness** gushes like a torrent from **the mouth of fools**.

15:3 God is omniscient, that is, He knows everything. His **eyes** are **in every place**. Nothing is hidden from Him. He is **keeping watch** over every word, act, thought, and motive, both on **the evil and the good**. This caused David to exclaim, "Such knowledge is too wonderful for me; it is high, I cannot attain it" (Ps. 139:6).

15:4 **Wholesome**, gracious speech refreshes, soothes, and revives. Perverse, malicious talk **breaks the spirit**.

15:5 We have met this **fool** before. He considers his father outdated, his ideas old-fashioned, and his **instruction** worthless. The wise son **receives** parental **correction** and benefits by it. He is **prudent** and becomes even more so.

15:6 Those who were reared in a godly home can testify to the truth of the first line. Even though the parents might not have been affluent, they left their children a spiritual heritage of immense value.

The ill-gotten gain of the unscrupulous man brings **trouble** on himself and his family. A good illustration of this is Achan (Josh. 7).

15:7 A **wise** man's conversation is full of helpful **knowledge**. The foolish man can't edify anyone else because his own mind is empty.

15:8 The first line teaches the worthlessness of ritual without reality. A **wicked** man may bring costly offerings **to the** LORD but God despises them. He wants the man's life to be clean first. "To obey is better than sacrifice" (1 Sam. 15:22). God delights in the humble **prayer of the upright** person; "The sacrifices of God are a broken spirit, a broken and a contrite heart—these, O God, You will not despise" (Ps. 51:17).

15:9 The way of the wicked displeases **the** LORD greatly. **He loves** the person **who** lives in obedience to His Word.

15:10 There are two ways of looking at this proverb. It may be describing two different men—the wayward (**him who forsakes the way**) and the unteachable (**he who hates correction**), and the punishment they earn—**harsh discipline** and death respectively. Or it may be describing the same man in both lines. At first his waywardness brings him severe **harsh discipline**. But he refuses to learn from it and so plunges on to death. Hebrew poetic structure (parallelism) favors the second interpretation.

15:11 Hell and Destruction (Heb., *Sheol* and *Abaddon*) are symbolic of the unseen world beyond the grave. If God knows all about what transpires in death and in the hereafter, **how much more** does He know the thoughts and secrets **of the sons of men** on earth? "All things are naked and open to the eyes of Him to whom we must give account" (Heb. 4:13).

15:12 A scoffer resents being corrected. **Nor will he go to the wise** person for advice, but to someone who he thinks will tell him what he wants to hear. Such a policy is self-defeating; it only confirms him in his obstinacy and leaves him in the grave of stagnation.

15:13 A merry heart is reflected in a smiling face, but a broken **heart** has deeper effects. It causes despondency and despair.

15:14 The most knowledgeable people never stop in their pursuit of **knowledge. The mouths of fools** chew vacantly **on foolishness.** "The wise grow wiser, the foolish more dense."

15:15 This seems to contrast the pessimist and the optimist. The first is always down-in-the-mouth. He is gloomy, fearful, and negative. The optimist always seems to be on top. He enjoys life to the full.

15:16 A poor believer is **better** off than a wealthy worrywart. Wealth has **trouble** attached. The life of faith is the carefree life.

15:17 A plate of vegetables in an atmosphere of **love is . . . better** than a filet mignon roast where there is strife. Moffatt says, "Better is a dish of vegetables, than the best beef served with hatred."

A fatted calf is one that has been raised in a stall and given the best feed; its meat is tender and delicious.

Joseph R. Sizoo says:

In a nearby city I visited one of the most luxurious estates I've ever seen in America. Within the house were Italian fireplaces, Belgian tapestries, Oriental rugs, and rare paintings. I said to a friend, "How happy the people must have been who lived here!" "But they weren't," he replied. "Although they were millionaires, the husband and wife never spoke to each other. This place was a hotbed of hatred! They had no love for God or for one another." (*Our Daily Bread*)

15:18 A hot-tempered **man** is always spreading **strife**. A wiser man knows how to avoid **contention** or cool it down after it has started.

15:19 The way of the lazy man is beset with all kinds of difficulties. Maybe he tries to use these as an excuse for doing nothing. **The way of the upright is a** smooth, well-paved **highway**.

15:20 A clean-living **son** brings great satisfaction to his dad. But the wayward son treats **his mother** with contempt by disobeying her will and disregarding her tears.

15:21 A stupid man enjoys his stupidity. He has never known anything better. The wise man gets his joy out of a life of sobriety and morality.

A pig enjoys wallowing in the mire, whereas a sheep wants the clean pasture.

15:22 When men act singly, **without counsel** of others, their programs often **go awry**. It is safer to get a broad range of information and advice. Men who have had experience can warn against dangers to be avoided, can suggest the best methods, etc.

15:23 There is genuine satisfaction in being able to give an honest, helpful **answer**. Also a timely **word—spoken** at just the right time to meet a particular need—**how good it is!** Compare Isaiah 50:4, ". . . a word in season to him who is weary." Jesus knows how to speak that word.

15:24 **The wise** person's pathway **winds upward** toward **life, that he may** avoid the pathway that leads downward to death and destruction. Once again we are reminded of the two roads and two destinies of the human race.

15:25 **The LORD will destroy the** estate **of the** haughty and highhanded, **but He will** protect **the boundary of the** oppressed widow's little farm.

15:26 **The LORD** detests **the wicked** plans of unscrupulous men, but He is pleased with **the words of the pure**.

15:27 This proverb may refer primarily to a judge or other public officer who swells his bank account by accepting bribes. In so doing he perverts judgment and corrupts his conduct. But even worse—he brings trouble unlimited on **his own** household. The man who refuses to have anything to do with **bribes** is the one who enjoys life.

15:28 A good man thinks before he speaks. He meditates on **how to answer**. An ungodly man opens his **mouth** and out comes a torrent of profanity, filth, and vileness.

15:29 **The LORD is far from the wicked** in the sense that He does not enjoy fellowship with them, and they are not in touch with Him by prayer. Believers have instant audience with the Sovereign of the universe in the throne room of heaven by prayer. "Now we know that God does not hear sinners; but if anyone is a worshiper of God and does His will, He hears him" (John 9:31).

15:30 A person's beaming countenance is contagious. It gladdens **the heart** of everyone he meets. Also, good news **makes** a man's whole being feel good.

15:31 The man who heeds counsel that leads to the true way **of life** takes his place **among the wise** of the earth. The teaching of the Bible in general and the gospel in particular is life-giving counsel.

15:32 If a man won't listen to godly **instruction**, it means that he **despises** himself because he is plunging over the cataract to ruin. **He who heeds rebuke** promotes his own best interests.

15:33 **The fear of the LORD is the** discipline that leads to **wisdom. Humility** is the way to **honor**.

B. The Righteous Lifestyle Exalted (16:1—22:16)

16:1 The name Jehovah (LORD) occurs nine times in the first eleven verses of chapter 16. Man may plan his thoughts in advance, but **the LORD** is sovereign and overrules all man's words for the accomplishment of His purposes. "Man proposes but God disposes."

Balaam, for instance, wanted to curse the people of Israel, but the words came out as a blessing (Num. 22:38; 23:7–10).

Or think of Caiaphas, who spoke beyond his own wisdom (John 11:49–52). Herod and Pilate conspired to do to Jesus what God had already appointed to be done (Acts 4:27, 28).

It may also mean that though God's persecuted people often plan in advance what to say at their trial, God gives the proper words at the suited time (Matt. 10:19).

16:2 A man's **ways** are his outward acts; he judges himself by them and pronounces himself **pure**. But God sees the motives and intentions of the heart. "Who can understand his errors? Cleanse me from secret faults" (Ps. 19:12).

16:3 The best way to insure that our dreams and goals will be achieved is to dedicate our **works to the LORD**. J. Allen Blair advises:

Occasionally we find ourselves disturbed and depressed, even in trying to do the Lord's work. Could anything be further from what God desires? God cannot work through anxious hearts. Whenever a Christian reaches this state, he should stop at once and ask himself, "Whose work is it?" If it's God's work, never forget the burden of it is His, too. You are not the important person. Christ is! He is at work through us. What should we do then when things do not go well? Go to Him! Anything less than this is disobedience.[24]

Prayer: "Give me the eye which sees God in all, and the hand which can serve Him in all, and the heart which can bless Him for all" (Daily Notes).

16:4 This verse does not suggest that God has created certain men to be damned. The Bible nowhere teaches the doctrine of reprobation. Men are damned by their own deliberate choice, not by God's decree.

The proverb means that God has an end, object, or purpose for everything. There is a result for every cause, a reward or punishment for every act. He has ordained a **day** of trouble or evil for **the wicked**, just as He has prepared heaven for those who love Him. "Everything the Lord has made has its destiny; and the destiny of the wicked man is destruction" (TEV).

16:5 Human pride is hateful **to the LORD**. As explained previously, **"though they join forces"** literally reads "hand in hand." In this context it probably suggests the certainty of the proud's being punished.

16:6 The doctrine of this verse must be studied in the light of all other Scriptures on the subject. It cannot mean that a man is saved by being merciful and truthful; salvation is by grace through faith in the Lord. Only to the extent that **mercy and truth** are the signs of saving faith can they be said to purge **iniquity**.

The second part of the proverb is clear on the face of it. By trusting **the LORD**, men escape misfortune and calamity.

16:7 Like so many of the proverbs, this is a general rule, but it does have exceptions. "A righteous life disarms opposition." Or, as Barnes put it, "Goodness has power to charm and win even enemies to itself."

Stanton treated Lincoln with utter contempt. He called him a "low cunning clown" and "the original gorilla." He said there was no need to go to Africa to capture a gorilla when one was available in Springfield, Illinois. Lincoln never retaliated. Instead he made Stanton his war minister, believing that he was the best qualified for the office.

Years later when Lincoln was killed by an assassin's bullet, Stanton looked down on his rugged face and said tearfully, "There lies the greatest ruler of men the world has ever seen."

16:8 It is **better** to have a modest income which is earned honestly than to have **vast revenues without justice** or with fraud.

16:9 As we were reminded in verse 1, man goes to great length to plan his career, **but the LORD** alone determines whether these plans ever come to pass. Saul of Tarsus planned to persecute the Christian saints in Damascus but ended up becoming one of them! Onesimus planned to leave Philemon forever but God brought him back on better terms than ever.

16:10 Because a **king** is a representative of God (Rom. 13:1), his edicts and decisions carry authority and finality. Therefore **his mouth must not transgress in judgment.**

16:11 God maintains a Bureau of Standards. He determines **honest weights and scales**. When men deal in accordance with His standards, He approves and blesses them.

16:12 Actually **it is an abomination for** *anyone* **to commit wickedness**, but especially for **kings**. They represent God in their position, and therefore have greater responsibility. The **throne is established** on a foundation of doing right.

It should be added that the verse may mean that **it is an abomination** to kings for *their subjects* **to commit wickedness**. Lawful, orderly government must be sustained **by righteous-**ness. Where moral standards are abandoned, anarchy prevails.

16:13 Good **kings** don't appreciate those who flatter and speak hypocritically. They want men whose word is trustworthy, who are frank and sincere.

16:14 Once enraged, a king can quickly sentence offenders to **death. A wise man** will not provoke the ruler needlessly but **will** seek to pacify him.

16:15 When the king is joyful, the happiness of his **face** spreads gladness through the realm. **His favor** is as refreshing as the clouds that bring **the latter rain**.

16:16 Earthly riches are not to be compared to **wisdom** and knowledge. Riches often disappear overnight but divine wisdom remains throughout eternity.

16:17 The righteous follow **the highway of** holiness without turning off on the tangents of sin. The one **who keeps** straight on this highway **preserves his** life from damage and misfortune.

16:18 A tall tree attracts lightning. So God puts down those who are conceited. Stuck-up people usually suffer some humiliating experience, designed to deflate their ego. It takes only a small pin to prick a large balloon.

It was **pride** that caused the **fall** of Lucifer—as Marlowe described him, "aspiring pride and insolence for which God threw him from the face of heaven."

16:19 It's **better to be of a humble spirit** yourself and to be a companion of **the lowly, than to** share the seeming advantages of **the proud**.

Would'st thou be chief—then lowly
  serve;
Would'st thou go up—go down;
But go as low as e'er you will,
The Highest has been lower still.
                    —*Author unknown*

16:20 **He who heeds the word wisely will find good, and whoever trusts in the Lord, happy is he.** So the proverb says, "Read your Bible; heed it; and trust the One who wrote it."

16:21 A man who is truly **wise . . . will be** acknowledged for his discernment and insight. In addition, the pleasant manner in which he speaks will make others more willing to listen to him and to learn. "Sweetness of speech increases persuasiveness" (NASB).

16:22 **Understanding** serves as a **wellspring of life** and refreshment **to** its possessor, whereas **folly** is like a whiplash to **fools.** They are punished by their own **folly.** "Folly is the chastisement of fools" (Berkeley).

16:23 The speech of a **wise** man is an index of what is in his **heart.** He displays his knowledge by what he says. And there is a certain persuasiveness about his statements. He speaks with authority.

16:24 Kind, **pleasant words** have the qualities of a **honeycomb**—sweet to the taste **and health to the bones.** As Kidner puts it, "To say nice things when we can is a simple benefit we may bring a person, in mind and thence in body."

Watchman Nee told of a woman whose husband never expressed appreciation for anything she had ever done. She worried constantly that she had failed as a wife and mother. Possibly this is what caused her to develop tuberculosis. When she was dying, her husband said to her, "I don't know what we are going to do. You have done so much and done it well." "Why didn't you say that sooner?" she asked, "I have been blaming myself all along, because you never once said 'Well done.' "[25]

16:25 This repeats 14:12 for emphasis. It seems logical and reasonable that the way to heaven is by being good and doing good. But the true fact is that the only people who will ever get to heaven are sinners saved by grace.

16:26 **The person who labors, labors for himself, for his hungry mouth drives him on.** He knows that if he doesn't work, he won't collect his paycheck, and without money he can't go to the supermarket to buy food. So if he is ever tempted to stop working, his appetite urges him on.

This is also true in the spiritual realm. A realization of our deep spiritual need drives us to the Word and to prayer.

16:27 Verses 27–30 give different portraits of wickedness. First we see **an ungodly man** as one who **digs up evil**, and whose speech is **like a burning fire**, scorching and injuring.

16:28 **A perverse man** is one who distorts the truth. By lying, shading the truth, or withholding the facts, he spreads **strife**. A talebearer **separates** close **friends**.

16:29 **A violent man** seeks to lead **his neighbor** astray, encouraging **him** to be a partner in crime (see Rom. 1:32).

16:30 Facial expressions can have evil connotations. A wink can hint at connivance **to devise** some **perverse things**. Compressed **lips** can express the determination to see it through.

16:31 The "if" should be omitted. **The silver-haired head** stands for long life. It **is a crown of glory** or beauty because it is looked on here as a reward for a righteous life. So this verse is the opposite of Psalm 55:23, "Bloodthirsty and deceitful men shall not live out half their days."

16:32 A man who can control his temper is a greater hero than a military conqueror. Victory in this area is more difficult than in capturing a city. If you don't believe it, try it!

> Peter the Great, although one of the mightiest of the Czars of Russia, failed here. In a fit of temper he struck his gardener, and a few days afterwards the gardener died. "Alas," said Peter, sadly, "I have conquered other nations, but I have not been able to conquer myself!"[26]

16:33 In the OT and even up to the time of Pentecost, the casting of **the lot** was a legitimate way of determining the will of God. The whole process seemed very much a matter of chance, but **the LORD** overruled to reveal His guidance.

Today the complete Word of God gives us a general outline of God's will. When we need specific guidance in matters not covered in the Word, we learn His will through waiting on Him in prayer. Then we find that **every decision is from the LORD**.

17:1 A piece of zwieback or **dry** toast eaten in a relaxed setting is **better** than a sumptuous meal in an elegant **house full of feasting** where there is bickering and unhappiness.

17:2 A capable **servant** often rises higher than **a son who causes shame**. Thus Solomon's servant, Jeroboam, gained control over ten of the tribes of Israel, leaving Solomon's son, Rehoboam, with only two.

The servant often shares the **inheritance** with the sons on an equal basis. In Abram's case it looked for a while as if his servant would be his only heir (Gen. 15:2, 3).

17:3 God can do what no crucible or **furnace** can do. They can test **silver** and **gold** but **the LORD** can test the human heart. In the process of testing, He removes the dross and purifies the life until He sees His own image reflected.

When thro' fiery trials thy pathway
　　shall lie,
My grace, all sufficient, shall be thy
　　supply;
The flame shall not hurt thee; I only
　　design
Thy dross to consume, and thy gold
　　to refine.

—George Keith

17:4 **An evildoer . . . gives heed to** people with **false lips**. They welcome lies, unfounded rumors, false accusations. Liars, in turn, like to listen to scandal, slander, and **a spiteful tongue**. In that sense, the kind of talk a man feeds on is a barometer of what he is at heart.

17:5 We have already seen in 14:31 that whoever **mocks the poor** insults **his Maker** (see Jas. 5:1–4). Whoever takes a heartless satisfaction in **calamity** (which almost invariably makes people poor) **will not go unpunished** by the Lord. The book of Obadiah pronounces doom on Edom for rejoicing when Jerusalem fell.

17:6 A numerous and godly posterity brings honor to **old men** (see Ps. 127:3–5; 128:3). **Children** likewise can be grateful for **their father**. There is no reason for a generation gap here.

17:7 Noble and **excellent speech** seems out of place in the mouth of **a** boorish **fool**. Even more unsuitable are **lying lips to a prince**. You expect more from a prince. The world expects more from those of us who are children of God. They have higher standards for us than they do for themselves.

17:8 A bribe serves like a good luck charm, or so its owner thinks. **Wherever he** uses it, it performs wonders for him, opening doors, obtaining favors and privileges, or getting him out of trouble.

17:9 The man who refuses to remember an offense against him **seeks love** and friendship. The one who insists on digging up past grievances only succeeds in alienating **friends**.

"When we learn to love," Adams writes, "we also learn to cover, to forget, and to overlook many faults in others."

One woman to another: "Don't you remember the mean thing she said about you?"

The other woman: "I not only don't remember; I distinctly remember forgetting!"

George Washington Carver was refused admission to a college because he was black. Years later, when someone asked him for the name of the college, he answered, "It doesn't matter!" Love had conquered.

17:10 A simple **rebuke** makes a deeper impression on **a wise man than a** severe beating **on a fool**. Usually people who are sensitive do not need harsh forms of discipline. But those who are unfeeling and indifferent require the sledgehammer treatment. It is hard for them to think that they are ever wrong.

17:11 An evil man seeks only rebellion. He is unwilling to submit to lawful authority. He is determined to have his own way. The **cruel messenger** who **will be sent against** the rebel may be the arresting officer sent by the king, or it may be the messenger of death sent by God.

17:12 A bear robbed of her cubs is fierce and unmanageable. But she is not nearly as dangerous **as a fool in** a fit of temper. Once he gets some crazy idea into his head, nothing will stop him.

17:13 A curse rests upon the house of any man who repays a kindness with an injury. David repaid his loyal general, Uriah, with treachery, and, as a result, brought misery upon his house (2 Sam. 12:9, 10).

17:14 When a hole develops in a dike, the water rushing through it enlarges the hole rapidly. It is the same with quarrels. Minor disputes have a way of growing to major proportions. So it is better to **stop** while a dispute is still insignificant. Otherwise you may be plunged into a great war soon.

17:15 God hates miscarriages of justice. To acquit the guilty or to condemn the innocent is equally abhorrent to Him. Our law courts are filled with this today, but men will give an account for it all when they stand before God. The dictum "Justice, justice you shall follow" echoes down through the corridors of history.

17:16 A person is **a fool** to go to great expense to get an education if he doesn't really mean business. To be a good learner, one must be highly motivated. He must have "a mind to learn" (Moffatt).

A second and more probable meaning of the proverb is this: a fool should not spend money for wisdom when he doesn't have the ability to grasp things in the first place. "Why is this—a price in the hand of a fool to buy wisdom, when he has no capacity?" (Berkeley). He thinks he can buy wisdom as if it were a loaf of bread. He doesn't realize that he must have an understanding heart.

17:17 A true **friend loves** in adversity as well as in prosperity. Often it takes hard times to show which friends are genuinely loyal. A quaint note from D. L. Moody's Bible says, "A true friend is like ivy—the greater the ruin, the closer he clings."[27]

A brother is born for adversity, that is, one of the great privileges of brotherhood is to be at your side when you need him most.

It is not hard to find the Lord Jesus in this verse.

There's not an hour that He is not
near us,
No, not one! No, not one!
No night so dark but His love can
cheer us,
No, not one! No, not one!
                              —*Johnson Oatman*

17:18 This verse modifies the previous one by showing that love should not be without discernment. It would be a case of bad judgment to agree to guarantee a friend's debts in the event that he should default. Any man who needs a **surety** is a bad credit risk. Why be **surety** for a bad credit risk?

17:19 The man **who loves transgression loves strife**, and vice versa. The man **who exalts his gate** is one who (1) talks arrogantly (Moffatt); (2) loudly proclaims his wealth; or (3) lives luxuriously and perhaps beyond his means. This man courts destruction.

17:20 **A deceitful heart** never wins, and **a perverse tongue** never prospers. They invite mischief and prevent happiness.

17:21 The parent of a senseless dolt (**scoffer**) lives with **sorrow**. There is **no joy** in being **the father** of a "dull thud."

17:22 Here again we learn that a person's mental outlook has a lot to do with recovery from sickness or accident. A cheerful disposition is a powerful aid to healing. **A broken**, disconsolate **spirit** saps a person's vitality.

In a footnote on this verse, the Berkeley Version comments: "Up-to-date therapy, unsurpassed."

Today's doctors tell us that a hearty laugh is great exercise. When you emit an explosive guffaw, they say, your diaphragm descends deep into your body and your lungs expand, greatly increasing the amount of oxygen being taken into them. At the same time, as it expands sideways, the diaphragm gives your heart a gentle, rhythmic massage. That noble organ responds by beating faster and harder. Circulation speeds up. Liver, stomach, pancreas, spleen, and gall bladder are all stimulated—your entire system gets an invigorating lift. All of which confirms what that sage old Greek, Aristotle, said about laughter more than 2000 years ago: "It is a bodily exercise precious to health."[28]

But not all laughter is healthful. Howard Pollis, a psychology professor at the University of Tennessee, reports that when laughter and smiling are used in an aggressive way—to sneer at, to ridicule, to embarrass—they are "nonhealthy" and can really do more harm to the laugher than the one who is laughed at.

A broken spirit dries the bones. Blake Clark agrees:

Emotions can make you ill. They can make hair fall out by the handful, bring on splitting headaches, clog nasal passages, make eyes and nose water with asthma and allergies, tighten the throat with laryngitis, make skin break out in a rash, even cause teeth to drop out. Emotions can plague one's insides with ulcers and itises, give wives miscarriages, make husbands impotent—and much more. Emotions can kill.[29]

17:23 **A wicked man accepts a bribe behind the back** to influence the decision of the judge in his favor.

17:24 A man of **understanding** sets **wisdom** as the goal before his eyes and goes right toward it. **A fool** has no definite ambition. Rather than search for wisdom, which requires discipline, his **eyes** wander in fantasy all over the world.

17:25 One of the great sorrows of

parenthood is to have a child who causes nothing but **grief . . . and bitterness**.

17:26 Also, to punish the righteous is not good, nor to strike princes for their uprightness. Yet this perversion of justice takes place every day.

17:27 He who has knowledge spares his words, and a man of understanding is of a calm spirit. Rash speech and quick temper betray a shallow character.

17:28 You can't tell a fool by his facial appearance; he might look ever so wise. "With closed lips he may be counted sensible" (Moffatt).

"At times," writes James G. Sinclair, "it is better to keep your mouth shut and let people wonder if you're a fool than to open it and remove all doubt."

18:1 The difficulty of this proverb is evident from the widely different interpretations that are given.

A man who isolates himself seeks his own desire; he rages against all wise judgment. This is the nonconformist who is going to have his own way even if it conflicts with tested knowledge or approved methods. He flies in the face of sound wisdom by his self-assertion.

The RSV is quite different: "He who is estranged seeks pretexts to break out against all sound judgment." In other words, the man who becomes alienated looks for excuses to justify all kinds of irresponsible conduct.

Knox's translation is somewhat similar and needs no explanation: "None so quick to find pretexts, as he that would break with a friend; he is in fault continually."

Jewish commentators understand the proverb to commend the life of separation from sin and folly. The man who does this desires his own higher interests and mingles himself

with all true wisdom. But this interpretation is improbable, though true.

18:2 A fool refuses to listen to people with **understanding**; he is interested only **in expressing his own heart**, or in displaying what he is.

18:3 When the wicked comes, contempt comes also; and with dishonor comes reproach. This is another way of saying that outward shame and reproach come on the heels of inward wickedness and baseness.

18:4 Generally speaking, **the words of a man's mouth** don't give him away. They **are deep waters** hiding his true thoughts and motives.

By way of contrast, the fountain **of wisdom is a** gushing, **flowing brook**. In other words, wisdom's message is clear and transparent.

Moffatt understands the verses as saying that the words of a wise man are a deep pool, a flowing stream, and a fountain of life. They are profound, not shallow; flowing, not brackish; refreshing, not insipid.

18:5 God here condemns the reversal of moral judgments. **To show partiality to the wicked** is, in effect, condoning their wickedness. To deprive **the righteous** of justice is what Lowell called putting Truth on the scaffold and Wrong on the throne.

18:6 A loudmouthed fool is always trying to pick a fight or start trouble. A drunkard excels at this, but all he succeeds in doing is bringing black eyes, contusions, and abrasions on himself.

18:7 A fool's speech is his downfall. His reckless and foul language bring about his eventual ruin.

18:8 The words of a talebearer are like delicious tidbits; they are eagerly devoured by the listeners. It is almost as if the listeners say, "Yum, yum. I like that. Tell me more!"

18:9 The lazy or **slothful** man has

much in common with **a destroyer;** they both cause great havoc or devastation. Griffiths warns:

> We know today that it is shoddy workmanship in cars, airplanes, buildings, and the like which is the cause of fatal accidents. This is also true in some offices and leadership in the church, where negligence of responsibility may lead to a breakdown of fellowship. A church may be disintegrated through foolish negligence and laziness as well as by Satanic attack.[30]

18:10 The name of the LORD stands for the Lord Himself. The Lord **is a** place of refuge and protection for those who trust in Him. Therefore, in the moment of fierce temptation, call upon the name of the Lord, and He will preserve you from sinning.

18:11 The **rich** man trusts his **wealth** to protect him. **In his own esteem,** he thinks it will serve **like a high wall** to guard him from danger of every kind. But his riches fail him when he needs them most.

Verse 10 is fact: verse 11 is fiction. The righteous man of verse 10 trusts in fact, the rich man of verse 11 in fiction.

18:12 Pride has one foot in the grave and another on a banana skin. Humility walks securely toward honor. William Law draws the contrast sharply: "Look not at pride only as an unbecoming temper, nor at humility as a decent virtue—one is all hell and the other all heaven."

18:13 A man should get all the facts before giving his opinion. Otherwise he will be embarrassed when the full details are made known. There are two sides to every question: every divorce, every quarrel, etc. Don't agree with a person if you have not heard the other person's side.

18:14 A man's **spirit** can bear up under all kinds of physical infirmities, **but a broken spirit** is far more difficult to endure. Emotional problems are often more serious than physical ailments.

Dr. Paul Adolph tells of an elderly patient who was recovering satisfactorily in the hospital from a broken hip. At her release, she was transferred to an old people's home. Within a few hours, the patient showed general physical deterioration and she died in less than a day—"not of a broken hip but of a broken heart."[31]

A man who had faced the horrors of concentration camp with gallantry discovered after his release that it was his own son who had informed on him. "The discovery beat him to his knees and he died. He could bear the attack of an enemy, but the attack of one whom he loved killed him."

18:15 The wise man never comes to the place where he ceases to learn. His mind is always open to instruction, and his **ear** is receptive to **knowledge**.

18:16 **A man's** bribe or gratuity buys his way into the presence of those whom he wishes to influence.

It is also true, as the proverb is sometimes used, that a man's spiritual gift provides opportunities for him to exercise it. If he can teach or preach the Word, for instance, he will have plenty of openings. But that is not the meaning of this verse.

18:17 When a man tells his side of the story, it seems very convincing and you are apt to believe him. But when **his neighbor comes and** asks him a few leading questions, then it may appear that he was not so right after all.

18:18 When believers in the OT cast **lots,** they were actually appealing to the Lord to settle matters for which they felt themselves inadequate. The lot provided a just and peaceful settlement of matters between powerful contenders who might otherwise have resorted to force.

We too should let the Lord be the final Judge when difficulties arise with others. We can do this, not by casting lots, but by reading and obeying the Bible, by confessing our faults one to another, by prayer, and by the inward witness of the Spirit.

18:19 Quarrels between close relatives are often the hardest to mend. It is easier to conquer a fortified **city** than to effect reconciliation between **offended** brothers. Their **contentions are like the bars of a castle**—cold, straight, and immovable. Civil wars are always the bitterest.

18:20 We sometimes say that a man has to eat his words. If they have been good words, they will yield satisfaction to him. He will be rewarded according to the nature of his speech.

18:21 **The tongue** has great potential for good or evil. **Those who love** to use **it** a lot must be prepared to take the consequences.

18:22 The word "good" is implied before **wife**. A man **who finds a** good **wife finds a** treasure. It is a token of the Lord's favor when he finds a godly, helpful bride.

18:23 **Poor** people often speak softly, humbly, pleadingly. **Rich** people, on the other hand, can respond **roughly** and be overbearing, but not all rich people have bad manners!

18:24 Here again we have a proverb with many interpretations.

A man who has friends must himself be friendly. If we follow the KJV and NKJV, the thought is that friendliness wins friends, and that some friends are closer than others.

The NASB, ASV, NKJV margin, and JND say that a man who has many friends will come to ruin, **but** that **there is a friend who sticks closer than a brother**. This means that it is better to have one true friend than a host of friends who will lead you astray.

The RSV reads, "There are friends who pretend to be friends, but there is a friend who sticks closer than a brother." This presents a contrast between fair-weather friends and those who are loyal through thick and thin.

Happily, most versions agree on the second line—that **there is a friend who sticks closer than a brother**. G. Campbell Morgan writes:

> All consideration of this great verse leads us at last to one place, to One Person. He is the Friend of sinners. There comment ceases. Let the heart wonder and worship.[32]

19:1 The contrast is between a **poor** person **who** is honest and a devious (and perhaps rich) **fool** who distorts the truth. The **poor** person has it all over the **fool**; he is better off.

19:2 **Also, it is not good for a soul to be without knowledge.** This man knows what he wants to do, but he doesn't know how to do it, so he goes off "half-cocked."

Haste only adds to his misery. He is in too much of a hurry to ask for directions or to follow them if given, so he misses the way and goes around in circles.

19:3 When men make a mess of their lives, they turn around and blame the Lord. Thus, Adam tried to put the blame on God with the words "The woman whom You gave to be with me . . ." (Gen. 3:12).

More than we know, apostasy has its seeds in moral failure. A man engages in some form of immorality, then instead of confessing and forsaking the sin, he turns away from the Christian faith and rages **against the LORD**. W. F. Adeney comments, "It is monstrous to charge the providence of God with the consequences of actions that He has forbidden."

19:4 The fact that **wealth makes many friends** is a proof of the innate selfishness of the human heart. **The poor** man is **separated from his friend** because the latter wants only those friendships that will benefit him.

19:5 One who gives **false** testimony or engages in other forms of dishonesty will surely be punished by the Lord, even if he is never caught in this life.

19:6 The nobility here means a generous or powerful person. **Many** try to cultivate his friendship with the hope of getting favors. People tend to befriend those from whom they hope to benefit.

19:7 The relatives **of a poor** man often desert **him. Much more do his friends** give him the cold shoulder. **He** appeals to them pathetically for help and sympathy, **yet they abandon him**.

19:8 It is a form of enlightened self-interest to seek **wisdom** and common sense. And to hold on to **understanding** and insight is a sure road to success.

19:9 We should not be surprised at the frequency with which this is repeated. After all, one of the Ten Commandments deals with perjury (Ex. 20:16).

19:10 Luxury is not fitting for a fool. He doesn't know how to act in the midst of culture and refinement. Neither does a slave know how to act in a position of authority. He treats his former superiors arrogantly.

19:11 A man of good sense knows how to control his temper. He can graciously **overlook** it when some-

body wrongs him. The big-heartedness which David frequently displayed toward Saul illustrates the proverb well.

19:12 The king's wrath, like a lion's **roaring**, warns offenders of danger ahead. **His favor** to those who are obedient subjects **is** as gentle and refreshing as **dew on the grass**.

Romans 13:1–7 sets forth these two aspects of governmental authority and cautions, "Therefore, you must be subject, not only because of wrath but also for conscience' sake" (v. 5).

19:13 Two things that make domestic life miserable are a wayward **son** and a nagging **wife**. The former brings grief to **his father**, and the latter is as annoying as **a continual dripping** of water on metal.

19:14 You can inherit real estate **and** money **from fathers**, but only **the LORD** can provide **a prudent wife**. She is a special gift of God.

This reminds us of Isaac and Rebekah's storybook marriage, of which it is said, "The thing comes from the Lord" (Gen. 24:50). It was a marriage that was arranged in heaven.

19:15 Laziness is like a drug that **casts one into a deep sleep. An idle person** courts poverty and **will suffer hunger**.

This is true in connection with Bible study and prayer.

19:16 The one **who** obeys **the commandment** of the Lord is doing what is best for himself in the long run, both physically and spiritually. The person **who** lives recklessly and carelessly **will die**.

19:17 Giving to **the poor** is lending **to the LORD**. God will not only **pay back** the amount loaned but will pay good interest as well. Even a cup of cold water given in His name will be rewarded (Matt. 10:42). Henry Bosch illustrates:

A father once gave his boy a half dollar, telling him he could do with it as he pleased. Later when he asked about it, the little fellow said he had lent it to someone. "Did you get good security?" inquired his father. "Yes, I gave it to a poor beggar who looked hungry!" "O how foolish you are. You'll never get it back!" "But Dad, I have the best security; for the Bible says, he that giveth to the poor lendeth to the Lord!" Thinking this over, the Christian father was so pleased that he gave his son another half dollar! "See!" said the boy. "I told you I'd get it again, only I didn't think it would come so soon!"[33]

We lose what on ourselves we spend,
We have, as treasures without end,
Whatever, Lord, to Thee we lend,
Who givest all.
—*Christopher Wordsworth*

19:18 Discipline **your son while** he is still young and teachable. Corporal punishment, administered fairly and in an atmosphere of genuine love, will not harm him but, on the contrary, will do him an enormous amount of good.

The second line, **"do not set your heart on his destruction,"** means you should not let his life be ruined by your refusal to punish him. Permissiveness is cruelty. It could *also* mean, of course, "Don't become so angry that you are in danger of overpunishing him."

19:19 A hot-headed **man will suffer punishment** for it. Even **if you rescue him** from the consequences of his vile temper, he will soon be at it again, and **you will have to do it again**.

19:20 Listen to sound advice **and receive instruction** in early life, so **that you may be wise in** later life. As someone has said, "Wisdom is a long-term investment."

19:21 Man makes all kinds of **plans, nevertheless** it is **the Lord's** purposes that come to pass. "Man has his wickedness but God has His way." Ultimately man can do nothing against the truth (2 Cor. 13:8).

19:22 Darby's translation of this verse is priceless: "The charm of a man is his kindness; **and a poor man is better than a liar**." The quality that endears **a man** to you **is kindness**. That's what makes him to be **desired** as a friend. **A poor man** who has nothing but sympathy to offer is better than a rich man who promises help but doesn't deliver it.

19:23 The fear of the Lord is the pathway **to life**. The one **who has it** has every reason to be satisfied. **He will not be** overtaken **with** calamity.

19:24 A lazy man buries his hand in the bowl, and will not so much as bring it to his mouth again. He reaches into the bowl of potato chips but is too **lazy** to lift them to his mouth. They are too heavy.

19:25 Even if you **strike a scoffer**, he won't change, but at least some impressionable onlookers might learn a lesson. This is reminiscent of 1 Timothy 5:20, "Those who are sinning rebuke in the presence of all, that the rest also may fear."

You don't have to strike **one who has understanding**. A word of **rebuke** will make him correct his error and grow wiser in the process.

19:26 A son **who mistreats** or slanders (Berkeley) **his father** and evicts **his mother** from the home is shameful and disgraceful himself **and brings** disgrace and **reproach** to his heartbroken parents. It is small thanks for all his parents have done for him.

19:27 This proverb is like a diamond; every way you turn it, it sparkles with new light. The three most probable interpretations are these:

The KJV means, "Excellent advice for young people in schools and colleges where the Bible is under attack! Better to sacrifice a college career than to subject yourself to a barrage of doubts and denials."

The RSV and Berkeley read: "Cease, my son, to hear instruction only to stray from the words of knowledge." There is no sense in getting good instruction if you are not going to obey it. You are wasting your own time and the teacher's, and increasing your load of guilt. "It is better not to know, than, knowing, to fail to do."

The third interpretation is a warning: **"Cease listening to instruction, my son, and you will stray from the words of knowledge"** (NKJV).

19:28 **A disreputable witness scorns** justice—except when *he* is on trial! He greedily **devours** or spreads **iniquity**. He resembles Eliphaz's description of man, drinking iniquity like water (Job 15:16).

19:29 While **scoffers** and **fools** play to the balconies from the stage of human history, punishment and **judgments** are waiting in the wings. As soon as the curtain is drawn, the inevitable meeting will take place.

20:1 **Wine** does mock men but here the thought is that it causes men to become mockers or scoffers. **Strong drink** converts them into **a brawler**.

Wine is made from grapes, **strong drink** from grain. They both lead men astray. First a man becomes a social drinker, then a heavy drinker, then an alcoholic. He tries to shake off the habit, but he is held as if by chains. Christ gives power to break the chains, but first man must want deliverance.

20:2 When **a king** is angry, fear spreads throughout his court. That fear **is like the roaring of a lion,** warning of danger. **Whoever provokes** the king **to anger** takes **his own life** in his hands.

The lesson for us is found in Romans 13:4: "For he (i.e., the ruler) is God's minister to you for good. But if you do evil, be afraid; for he does not bear the sword in vain; for he is God's minister, an avenger to execute wrath on him who practices evil."

20:3 An **honorable** person makes a point of keeping aloof from strife. **A fool** isn't happy unless he's quarreling with someone.

20:4 Plowing time in Israel is in November and December, when the wind commonly blows from the North. **The lazy man** uses the cold weather to excuse his inaction. Without the plowing there can be no planting, and without the planting no harvest. He'll go out looking for grain in his fields and wonder why it isn't there.

20:5 A man's thoughts and intentions are often hidden deeply in his mind. He will not generally bring them to the surface. **But a** person of discernment knows how to **draw** them **out** by wise questions. For example, a good counselor can help a person bring crooked thinking to the light and thus remedy it.

20:6 It is not hard to find those who *profess* to be loyal, but it is another thing to **find** those who really *are* **faithful**. There is a difference between what men are, and what they want others to think they are. It is the difference between "Person" and "Personality."

20:7 **The righteous man walks in** honesty and **integrity. His children** come into a noble heritage and benefit from his life and example.

20:8 **A king who sits on the throne of judgment** winnows **all evil with his eyes**. When Christ sits upon His throne of judgment, His all-seeing eyes, like flames of fire, will see through pretense and sift all evidence.

20:9 By his own efforts, no one can cleanse himself from sin. **Who can say, "I have made my heart clean, I am pure from my sin"?** If a man thinks he is pure, he is a victim of pure delusion.

But there is cleansing through the precious blood of Christ. True believers have "washed their robes and made them white in the blood of the Lamb" (Rev. 7:14).

> The blood that purchased our release,
> and purged our crimson stains,
> We challenge earth and hell to show
> a sin it cannot cleanse.
> —*Augustus M. Toplady*

20:10 God hates deceitful **weights** and measurements. This includes any dishonest device to benefit self at the expense of others. It includes the butcher's trick of resting his finger on the scales when he is weighing the meat. And it even includes the practice of demanding stricter standards from others than we do from ourselves.

20:11 The basic nature of a person reveals itself early in life. Some children are downright ornery, others are pleasant. "The child is father of the man." He carries his character into adulthood, whether for good or for evil.

20:12 The LORD created **the hearing ear and the seeing eye**. What can this mean but that they belong to Him and should be used for His glory?

20:13 Don't overindulge in **sleep**, **lest you** land in the poorhouse. Get up and go to work. You'll earn money to pay your rent, buy your groceries, and give to the work of the Lord.

20:14 This is an old buyer's trick. As he looks over the used car, he squawks about its dents, its worn tires, its noisy engine, and its hideous color. **"It is good for nothing."** The seller hadn't realized it was such a junk-heap; he naively lowers the price. The buyer gives him the money, **then he** goes and **boasts** to his friends about his tremendous bargain.

20:15 A person may wear **gold** jewelry and precious gems, but the best adornment is wise speech. Wear this!

20:16 **Take the garment of one who is surety for a stranger, and hold it as a pledge when it is for a seductress.** Any man who is foolish enough to make financial guarantees for people he doesn't know is a bad credit risk. If you have any dealings with him, be sure that he puts up plenty of collateral so that you will be protected in case he reneges or goes bankrupt. The advice is especially true if the stranger is an immoral person.

20:17 Any form of wealth **gained** dishonestly might yield momentary satisfaction, **but** eventually it will prove as unpleasant and aggravating as a mouthful of **gravel**. This condemns falsifying tax returns, fudging on expense accounts, bribing inspectors, labeling dishonestly, and advertising product differences that don't exist.

20:18 A pooling of advice is desirable before making any **plans**. No general makes war without consulting with other military experts.

20:19 A gossip betrays confidences. **Therefore, do not associate with** a blabber, because if he talks against others to you, you can be sure that he will talk against you to others.

20:20 Under the law of Moses, cursing one's parents was a capital offense (Ex. 21:17). This should give pause to young people today who are hostile toward their parents. Unless this bitterness is resolved, it will lead to temporal obscurity and eternal perdition.

20:21 The prodigal son got his share of the **inheritance . . . hastily**, but he lost it just as quickly. But this proverb is true also of any get-rich-quick schemes. Easy come, easy go.

20:22 Don't seek vengeance on your enemies. Vengeance is the Lord's. He will repay. **Wait for the LORD. He will** deliver **you** and vindicate you.

20:23 Adam Clarke worked for a silk merchant who suggested that he should stretch the silk when measuring it for a customer. Adam's reply was, "Your silk may stretch, sir, but my conscience won't." God honored Adam Clarke by enabling him years later to write a widely used commentary on the Bible.

20:24 This verse emphasizes God's sovereignty and not man's free will, though both are true. The thought is that God is sovereign over human affairs and He knows what is best for us. Therefore, we ought to look to Him for direction, and not try to be the masters of our fate and manipulate to get our **own way**.

20:25 It is a snare for a man to devote rashly something as holy and afterward to reconsider his vows. It is dangerous to dedicate something to the Lord, and then to have second thoughts about it. Before making a **vow**, a man should be sure that he is able to fulfill it and that he definitely intends to.

20:26 A wise king does not tolerate **the wicked**. He **brings the threshing wheel over them**, that is, he separates them from the righteous, brings them to trial, and punishes them.

20:27 The spirit of a man in this verse is generally taken to refer to the conscience. It is given to us by **the** LORD and serves as a **lamp**, throwing light on our thoughts, motives, affec-

tions, and actions. It approves and reproves the innermost thoughts and intents of our lives (see Rom. 2:14, 15).

20:28 A leader who is characterized by **mercy and truth** will have the respect and support of his subjects. He maintains his position of authority **by lovingkindness**, not by tyranny.

20:29 A prominent **glory of young men is their strength**, while the **gray** hair **of old men** is associated with wisdom and experience. Every church needs both strength for service and age for wise counsel.

20:30 "Blows that hurt cleanse away evil, as do stripes the inner depths of the heart."

The thought seems to be that physical punishment has value in dealing with moral **evil**. A child remembers the pain of the last spanking when he is tempted to steal from his mother's purse.

21:1 Just as a channel or canal directs the flow **of water**, so **the** LORD rules and overrules a **king's** thoughts and actions. This is an encouragement to Christians under oppressive governments or to missionaries taking the gospel to hostile lands.

21:2 A man is not a valid judge of his own life or service; he judges by outward appearances. **The** LORD **weighs** the thoughts and motives of people's **hearts**.

21:3 The LORD is not as pleased with burnt offerings and **sacrifice** as with obedience to His voice (1 Sam. 15:22). God is not a ritualist. What He wants is inward reality.

21:4 This proverb lists three things that are sin in God's sight: **a haughty look**, i.e., the outward expression of conceit; **a proud heart**, i.e., the inward reservoir; and **the plowing of the wicked**, which may mean their prosperity, happiness, life, or hope.

21:5 Those who work diligently for their living are contrasted with those who seek to get rich overnight. The first are assured of **plenty**; the second, of **poverty**.

21:6 Those who seek riches through fraud and **by a lying tongue** are chasing the wind. They are pursuing that which will elude them, and they will perish in the process. Their position is like that of a desert traveler chasing a mirage; it proves to be a snare of **death** for him.

21:7 **The violence of the wicked will destroy them, because they refuse to do justice.** There is a moral principle at work in the universe which guarantees that violence, wickedness, and injustice will never escape unpunished. Never!

21:8 "Very crooked is the way of a guilty man, but as for the pure, his work is upright" (JND). Guilt causes a man to lie, to hide, to masquerade, to fear, and to act deceitfully. The man who has confessed and forsaken his sins has nothing to hide; he can walk in the light.

21:9 Houses in Bible lands had flat roofs. This proverb says that it would be **better to** live alone **in a** cramped **corner of** one of those roofs, exposed to heat, cold, rain, snow, wind, and hail, **than** to live **in a house shared with a** nagging, cantankerous **woman**. The storms from without would be more endurable than the tempest inside.

21:10 **The soul of the wicked** is always plotting some new **evil**, and he shows no mercy to **his neighbor** in perpetrating it. Thus his sin is both deliberate and ruthless. Modern sociological excuses for crime simply won't hold water.

21:11 Even if a **scoffer** might not learn a lesson from the punishment he receives, the naive person will see

it and be warned. A **wise** man doesn't need to be punished; he will learn from simple instruction.

21:12 **The righteous God wisely considers the house of the wicked, overthrowing the wicked for their wickedness**. **God** keeps close watch on all the affairs of ungodly men; at the proper time He throws the switch which brings their doom upon them.

21:13 The rich man of Luke 16:19–31 was quite unconcerned about the desperate need of the beggar at his gate. In the afterlife, he himself cried for relief but his cry went unanswered.

21:14 The Bible often reports facts without approving them. Thus it observes that an angry man will quiet down if the offender slips him **a gift**, and a man who is in a rage is appeased by **a bribe** tucked in his pocket.

21:15 **It is a joy for the just to do justice, but destruction will come to the workers of iniquity.** This is illustrated by the second advent of Christ. It will be a time of ecstasy for the redeemed, but a time of horror for all others (2 Thess. 1:6–9).

21:16 You meet all kinds of people in Proverbs. This **man who wanders** is like a vagrant in the Sahara of sin. When you last see him, he is resting **in the assembly of the dead**.

21:17 Instead of giving the satisfaction and fulfillment they promise, **pleasure** and luxurious living (**wine and oil**) only serve to impoverish **a man**. They drain his financial resources and also reduce him to spiritual poverty.

21:18 In Isaiah 43:3, God says that He gave Egypt as **a ransom for** His people, Israel. The Lord rewarded Cyrus for liberating the Jews by permitting him to possess Egypt and the neighboring kingdoms.

In a broad sense the verse means

that **the wicked** are punished so that the **upright** can go free.

21:19 A touch of sanctified humor! The writer would prefer the discomfort, distance, and loneliness of a desert to being cooped up with an **angry**, quarrelsome **woman**.

21:20 The contrast here is between the cottage **of the wise** man where there is a plentiful supply of all good things, and the home of **a foolish man** where sin, waste, and extravagance lead to scarcity.

We are reminded of the alcoholic who used to sell his furniture and other household goods in order to buy whiskey. After his conversion to Christ, someone said to him, "You don't really believe that stuff about Jesus' turning water into wine, do you?" His answer was, "I don't know about turning water into wine, but I know that in my house He turned whiskey into furniture!"

21:21 The point here seems to be that the one **who** pursues **righteousness and mercy** gets more than he bargained for; in addition to **righteousness** he receives **life** and **honor**.

21:22 The **wise** Christian **brings down the . . . stronghold**, not with artillery and bombs, but with faith, prayer, and the Word of God (see 2 Cor. 10:4). In the spiritual conflict, wisdom can accomplish what armed might is unable to do.

21:23 Whoever can control **his mouth** saves himself **from** stacks of trouble. "Even so the tongue is a little member and boasts great things. See how great a forest a little fire kindles! And the tongue is a fire, a world of iniquity. The tongue is so set among our members that it defiles the whole body, and sets on fire the course of nature; and it is set on fire by hell" (Jas. 3:5, 6).

21:24 If you meet **a proud and**

haughty man, just call him **"Scoffer."** That's **his name**! The **name**, of course, stands for what a person is. "For as his name is, so is he" (1 Sam. 25:25).

21:25, 26 The **lazy man** is torn apart between his craving for riches on the one hand, and his determination not to exert himself on the other. It's a killing impasse! While he spends his time in a dream-world of unfulfilled hopes, the righteous man works hard and earns money so that he can give unsparingly to worthy causes.

21:27 God is "turned off" by the donations of unrepentant sinners but He hates it even more when a gift is intended to "buy Him off" or induce Him to condone, approve, or bless some wicked scheme.

21:28 "A false witness will perish, but the word of a man who hears will endure" (RSV). The false witness swears before God that he will tell the truth, then deliberately perjures himself. The man who listens carefully and answers honestly gives testimony that can never be shaken.

21:29 The brazen **face** of **a wicked man** shows that he is confirmed in his iniquity. He has a forehead of brass. **The upright** man, by being teachable, is safe and **establishes his** behavior.

21:30 Man is powerless to outwit God in **wisdom**, **understanding**, or strategy. None of his plots can avail **against the** LORD. "Every purpose of the Lord shall be performed" (Jer. 51:29).

21:31 Men may go to elaborate plans to insure military success, but victory on **the day of battle** comes from **the** LORD alone. It is better to trust in Him than in horses—or in nuclear weapons—(see Ps. 20:7).

Plumptre summarizes verses 30 and 31 as follows:

Verse 30: Nothing avails against God.

Verse 31: Nothing avails without God.

22:1 **A good name** means a **good** reputation. It is the fruit of a good character. It is better **than great riches** because it is more precious, more powerful, and more enduring.

For the same reasons, **loving favor** is better **than silver and gold**.

22:2 Social distinctions are artificial in the sense that we are all of the same human family, and all come from the same Creator. Class distinctions that survive in life are abolished in death.

22:3 **A prudent man** looks ahead **and hides himself** from coming judgment. The Israelites did this on the Passover night by sprinkling the blood on their door. We do it by finding refuge in Christ.

The thoughtless **pass on** in their folly and "pay for it" (Moffatt).

22:4 **Humility and the fear of the LORD** may seem very dull and commonplace, but don't knock them till you've tried them. They are rewarded with spiritual **riches**, divine **honor**, and abundant **life**.

22:5 All kinds of difficulties and troubles lie **in the way of the perverse** man. The man who keeps himself clean avoids **them**.

22:6 The usual interpretation of this proverb is that if you **train up a child** properly (**in the way he should go**), he will go on well in later life. Of course there are exceptions, but it stands as a general rule. Henry Ward Beecher observes:

It is not hard to make a child or a tree grow right if you train them when they're young, but to make them straighten out after you've allowed

things to go wrong is not an easy matter.[34]

Susannah Wesley, the mother of Charles, John, and 15 other children, followed these rules in training them: (1) Subdue self-will in a child and thus work together with God to save his soul. (2) Teach him to pray as soon as he can speak. (3) Give him nothing he cries for and only what is good for him if he asks for it politely. (4) To prevent lying, punish no fault which is freely confessed, but never allow a rebellious, sinful act to go unnoticed. (5) Commend and reward good behavior. (6) Strictly observe all promises you have made to your child.

The proverb can also be understood as encouraging parents to train their children along the lines of their natural talents, rather than forcing them into professions or trades for which they have no native inclination. Thus Kidner says that the verse teaches respect for the child's individuality and vocation, though not for his self-will.

And the proverb may be a warning that if you train a child in the way that he himself wants to go, he will continue to be spoiled and self-centered in later life. Jay Adams writes:

The verse stands not as a promise but as a warning to parents that if they allow a child to train himself after his own wishes (permissively), they should not expect him to want to change these patterns when he matures. Children are born sinners and, when allowed to follow their own wishes, will naturally develop sinful habit responses. The basic thought is that such habit patterns become deep-seated when they have been ingrained in the child from the earliest days.[35]

22:7 Money is power, and it can be used for good or for evil. Too often **the rich** use it for evil, and perhaps that is why it is called the mammon of unrighteousness.

The borrower is a slave **to the lender**. Debt is a form of bondage. It requires the payment of exorbitant interest rates. It keeps a man's nose to the grindstone. It limits his mobility and his ability to take advantage of opportunities.

22:8 One **who sows iniquity** gains nothing substantial or worthwhile. The attempt to beat others into submission by **anger will** be thwarted.

22:9 The **generous** man is **blessed** in showing benevolence to others. By sharing **his** substance with **the poor**, he gains present happiness and future reward.

22:10 When a **scoffer** fails to respond to instruction, correction, and admonition, the next step is eviction. **Cast** him **out**! When Ishmael was put out of the house, **contention**, quarreling, and abuse ceased (Gen. 21:9, 10).

22:11 The man **who loves purity of heart** and whose speech is gracious will enjoy royal friendships. God may be the **King** referred to here.

A little word in kindness spoken,
A motion, or a tear
Has often healed the heart that's broken,
And made a friend sincere.
                    —*Author unknown*

22:12 The LORD preserves and perpetuates the **knowledge** of the truth so that it will never perish from the earth in spite of the rage of demons and men. The same Lord **overthrows** false teaching and exposes lies.

22:13 If a **lazy man** can't find an excuse for not going to work, he will make one up, no matter how ridiculous it is. Here he says that **there is a lion . . . in the streets** of the city. What would a lion be doing in the city? It's probably nothing more than a cat!

22:14 The seductive words **of an immoral woman** conceal a trap that is difficult to escape from. A man **who** has estranged himself from **the LORD will fall** into that trap. This reminds us that God often abandons men to sin when those men reject the knowledge of God (see Rom. 1:24, 26, 28).

22:15 Mischief and self-will are native to **the heart of a child**, but by applying the board of education to the seat of learning you can rid him of these vices. Matthew Henry counsels:

> Children need to be corrected, and kept under discipline, by their parents; and we all need to be corrected by our heavenly Father (Heb. xii. 6, 7), and under the correction we must stroke down folly and kiss the rod.[36]

22:16 The employer who gets rich by paying starvation wages will himself suffer want. This will also happen to the man **who gives to the rich**, presumably in order to court their favor. We should give to those who can't repay us.

IV. PROVERBS OF THE WISE MEN (22:17—24:34)

A. Words of the Wise (22:17—24:22)

22:17 Verses 17–21 form a section that introduces the proverbs from 22:22 to 24:22. It invites the reader to **incline** his **ear** to **hear the words of the wise**. Perhaps Solomon collected some of these proverbs from others, but the second half of the verse indicates that some of them are his own.

22:18 A person should **keep** these proverbs in his mind (to remember and obey) and **let them all be fixed upon his lips** (to pass them on to others).

22:19 The reason Solomon made known the proverbs was that the readers might truly **trust . . . in the LORD**.

22:20 In the RSV this verse reads, "Have I not written for you thirty sayings of admonition and knowledge?" Some scholars point out that the proverbs that follow (up to 24:22) can be divided into about 30 groupings, as follows:

22:22, 23	23:22–25
24, 25	26–28
26, 27	29–35
28	24:1, 2
29	3, 4
23:1–3	5, 6
23:4, 5	7
6–8	8, 9
9	10
10, 11	24:11, 12
12	13, 14
13, 14	15, 16
23:15, 16	17, 18
17, 18	19, 20
19–21	21, 22

The Berkeley Bible reads, "Have not I written for you previously of counsels and knowledge . . . ?" The word "previously" is in contrast to "this day" in verse 19.

22:21 The writer aimed at imparting **the words of truth** so that his pupils might be able to teach others who sent to him for counsel or so that they might be able to satisfy **those who** sent them for training.

22:22, 23 This begins the section that ends at 24:22. No one should take advantage of **the** defenseless **poor**. Neither should anyone show injustice to **the afflicted at the gate**, that is, at the place of judgment. For God pleads the cause of the poor, and He will punish the rich oppressor and the unjust judge.

22:24, 25 Association with **an an-gry**, hot-tempered **man** is bad business. It often makes a man become like the company he keeps. This can really be a snare because in a moment of passion, a man can ruin his life and testimony.

22:26, 27 Shaking **hands in a pledge** here means to guarantee someone else's debt. It is foolish to do it. If you can't afford to make full payment of the debt, **why** run the risk of having the furniture taken out of your house, and thus expose yourself to discomfort and shame?

22:28 **The ancient landmark** was a series of stones which indicated the boundaries of a person's property. Dishonest people often moved them during the night to increase the size of their farm at their neighbor's expense.

Spiritually, the ancient landmarks would be "the faith which was once for all delivered to the saints" (Jude 3). The fundamental doctrines of Christianity should not be tampered with.

22:29 A **man who excels in his work . . . will** be promoted to a position of honor. **He will not** serve **unknown men**. This is another reminder that cream rises to the surface. We see it in the lives of Joseph, Moses, Daniel, and Nehemiah.

> The heights by great men reached
> and kept
> Were not attained by sudden flight,
> But that while their companions slept
> Were toiling upward through the
> night.
>
> —*Longfellow*

23:1–3 Here we are warned against gluttony and surfeiting. **When** we **eat with** an influential person, we should consider **what** or *who* (JND) **is before** us. Then we should **put a knife to**

our **throat**, that is, exercise restraint in eating and drinking.

Verse 3 suggests that someone might be wining and dining us in order to influence us in some way. It isn't a case of unselfish hospitality but a means of using us for some subtle purpose.

23:4, 5 The ceaseless struggle **to be rich** is a form of "wisdom" to be avoided. It means that you are spending your life pursuing false values and putting your trust in what doesn't last. **Riches** have a way of sprouting **wings** and flying **away like an eagle**.

23:6–8 Another social situation to avoid! Don't be a guest of a man who has an evil eye, **a miser** who begrudges you every bite of the food you eat. It's what **he thinks**, not what he says, that counts. For while he is saying, "Help yourself . . . Have some more, **Eat and drink!**" he is actually counting every spoonful you take.

The LB paraphrases these verses as follows:

> Don't associate with evil men; don't long for their favors and gifts. Their kindness is a trick; they want to use you as their pawn. The delicious food they serve will turn sour in your stomach and you will vomit it, and have to take back your words of appreciation for their "kindness."

23:9 Don't try to teach a dull, stupid **fool**. You are wasting your time on him. **He will despise** your **words** of **wisdom**.

23:10, 11 Don't dishonestly take the property of someone else by secretly moving the **ancient** boundary stones. Don't take advantage of the defenseless by seizing their fields. **For their** Avenger **is mighty**. You will have to deal with *Him*! **He will plead their cause against you.**

23:12 There is no easy way to

gain **instruction**. It requires discipline and application. Disregard the ads that promise it in "three easy lessons."

23:13, 14 It is not a kindness to **a child** to allow him to run wild. The Bible does not condone permissiveness but rather encourages **correction** with **a rod**, and promises that the child **will not die**. This may mean that the beating will not kill him, or that the beating will actually save him from premature and reckless death. It will **deliver his soul from** Sheol.

Instead of disciplining his wicked sons, Eli rebuked them with a mild "Why do you do such things?" (1 Sam. 2:22–25). He fostered a permissiveness that brought ruin on his house, on the priesthood, and on the nation.

David failed in the area of parental discipline, too. He never displeased Adonijah by correcting him (1 Kgs. 1:6). After making two treasonable attempts to seize the throne, Adonijah was killed by Solomon.

23:15, 16 A father rejoices when his son has a **heart** that is **wise** and **lips** that **speak** the truth. The teacher experiences this same joy when his pupil receives wisdom and shares it with others. In a similar vein Paul said, "For now we live, if you stand fast in the Lord" (1 Thess. 3:8). And John said, "I have no greater joy than to hear that my children walk in truth" (3 John 4).

23:17, 18 There is something better than envying the prosperity of the wicked; that is to live in constant fellowship with **the** LORD. Occupation with the wicked brings discouragement; occupation with the Lord brings delight. So the lesson is to make communion with God the aim of our life. Also, to remember that **there is a** future day of reckoning for the wicked and a bright hope of reward for the righteous which shall never be disappointed. The **hereafter** looks past death and resurrection to a glorious future in heaven.

23:19 Whatever others may do, an obedient **son** should heed instruction, **be wise, and guide** his **heart in the** right **way**, that is, the way of God.

23:20, 21 There are two kinds of "drunkards"—those who drink too much and those who eat too much. They both make bad company for anyone who wants the good life.

Intemperance takes its toll. **The drunkard and the glutton** are headed for **poverty**. The stupor which results from surfeiting will clothe a man in rags.

23:22 Young people should welcome advice from their **father**, and not treat their **mother** with contempt. Old folks have years of experience behind them. Young people should recognize this and try to benefit as much as possible from their experience.

23:23 We should be willing to pay a great price for **truth**, but unwilling to **sell it** for any consideration. The same goes for **wisdom and instruction and understanding**. We should spare no pains to acquire them, but never surrender them for anything in this world.

23:24, 25 Modern custom says, "Give father a tie on Father's Day, and give mother a box of chocolates on Mother's Day." But more rewarding to parents is a son who lives wisely and prudently. Hence, the exhortation: **"Let your father and your mother be glad, and let her who bore you rejoice."**

23:26–28 The earnest plea, **"My son, give me your heart..."** introduces solemn warnings against immorality and drunkenness. The writer is saying, "Listen to me carefully and observe the counsel I give you." A prostitute **is** like **a deep**, concealed **pit**, forming a trap for the careless. She **is a narrow well**—easy to fall into but hard to get out of. **She lies in wait** like a robber. She may have a pathological hatred for men, and wreaks her revenge on them by entangling them through deception, like one hooks a fish with a lure. Daily she adds to the list of unfaithful men whose marriages and families are torn apart.

23:29, 30 The rest of chapter 23 is a classic description of a drunkard. He brings all kinds of **woe** upon himself and staggers from one **sorrow** to another. His life is marked by **contentions**, since he is forever trying to pick a fight. He grumbles and complains incessantly, but it never dawns on him that *he* is the cause of all his troubles! He has bruises, **wounds**, a black eye—all from fights that were unnecessary. His **eyes** are bleary and bloodshot. He sits in the tavern all night, consuming one **mixed** drink after another.

23:31, 32 He is warned against being fascinated by the clear **red wine**, by its brilliant sparkle, by the way **it swirls around smoothly**. But he doesn't listen, and so he suffers the consequences, which are like the bite of **a serpent** and the sting of **a viper**—poisonous and painful.

23:33, 34 His **eyes will see strange things**, a possible reference to the horrors of delirium tremens, the violent mental disturbances caused by excessive and prolonged use of liquor. His conversation is thick, garbled, and vile. He reels to and fro unsteadily, as if he were bobbing back and forth in **the sea**, or perched on **top of the mast** as it rocks crazily from one side to the other.

23:35 Someone has clobbered him,

but when he regains consciousness, he says that he **was not hurt**. They mauled him but he **did not feel it**. As soon as he is completely **awake**, he plans to go back to the bar for **another drink**.

24:1, 2   It is not wise **to be envious** of the success **of evil men** or to **desire** their company. They have a way of dragging others down to their own levels. And what is that level? Their minds are always planning **violence** and their conversation centers on **troublemaking**.

24:3, 4   The **house** here may refer to a man's life. A great life is not **built** by wickedness but by godly **wisdom**. Wickedness wrecks a life but **understanding** gives it solidity. Wickedness leaves it empty; true **knowledge** fits it out with **precious and pleasant** furnishings.

24:5, 6   **A wise man** can wield greater power than a strong man, and a man of brains is mightier than a man of brawn. **War** can be waged through **wise** counselors, and the more wise **counselors** there are, the better.

24:7   **Wisdom** seems to be forever beyond the grasp of **a fool**. He can never speak with authority, like the elders at **the gate** of the city do.

24:8, 9   The one who uses his God-given faculties to invent new forms of **evil** earns the title of "master **schemer**." **The devising of foolishness is sin,** and the arrogant **scoffer** who is brazen in his wickedness earns the contempt of others.

24:10   One test of a person's worth is how he behaves under pressure. If he gives up when the going is rough, he doesn't have what it takes.

Christ, if ever my footsteps should falter,
And I be prepared for retreat;
If desert and thorn cause lamenting,

Lord, show me Thy feet.
Thy bleeding feet, Thy nail-scarred feet,
My Jesus, show me Thy feet.
O God, dare I show Thee
My hands and my feet?
—*Amy Carmichael*

24:11, 12   When innocent people are being led off to gas chambers, ovens, and other modes of execution—when unborn babies are destroyed in abortion clinics—it is inexcusable to stand by and not seek to rescue them. It is also useless to plead ignorance. As Dante said, "The hottest places in hell are reserved for those who in a time of great moral crisis maintain their neutrality."

Does this have a voice for those of us who are believers and who are entrusted with the good news of salvation? Men and women are dying without Christ. Jesus said, "Lift up your eyes and look at the fields: for they are already white for harvest" (John 4:35). Dare we remain neutral?

See the shadows lengthen round us,
Soon the day-dawn will begin;
Can you leave them lost and lonely?
Christ is coming—call them in!
—*Anna Shipton*

24:13, 14   **Honey** is used here as a symbol of wisdom. Both are beneficial and **sweet** to the **taste**. **So shall the knowledge of wisdom be to your soul; if you have found it, there is a prospect, and your hope will not be cut off.** In other words, the man who finds wisdom is assured of a bright future and the realization of all his hopes.

24:15, 16   The unscrupulous person is warned against trying to dispossess a **righteous** man of his home. Maybe the latter has been overtaken by temporary hardship, and the wicked man is ready to pounce on his property.

A righteous man may fall into trouble or calamity **seven times**, but he will recover each time. **The wicked** can stumble to his ruin in a single misfortune.

24:17, 18 A man of good character should never **rejoice when** trouble catches up with his adversary, or be happy to see him stumble. If **the LORD** sees anyone harboring a gloating, vindictive spirit, He will consider that spirit more punishable than the guilt of the enemy.

24:19, 20 Once again we are warned not to get all upset over the apparent success of **evildoers**, and not to envy **the wicked**. This time the reason given is that the prospects of the ungodly are very bad. They have nothing good to look forward to. Instead the light of their life will be extinguished.

24:21, 22 This proverb inculcates reverence and respect for **the LORD and** also for **the king** as His representative. It also warns against **those who** are out to **change** divine institutions or to overthrow civil governments. Both types of rebelliousness will bring sudden and unimaginable **calamity** on the guilty ones.

The Christian is taught to obey human government as long as he can do so without compromising his loyalty to the Lord. If a government orders him to disobey the Lord, then he should refuse and humbly take the consequences. Under no circumstances should he join any plot to overthrow the government.

B. Further Sayings of the Wise (24:23–34)

24:23–26 Here begins a new section of sayings **that belong to the wise**, extending through verse 34.

It is a despicable thing **to show partiality** when judging matters of right and wrong. The judge who blurs moral distinctions by acquitting the guilty will be cursed by the people and hated by nations. On the other hand **those** judges **who rebuke** sin will be rewarded by God and blessed by men. Those who render honest and just verdicts will win the kiss of approval from the people.

24:27 Just as a man must clear away the trees and cultivate the land before building a **house**, so he should get his own life in order before having a family. Thus, the proverb may be a warning against rushing into marriage with all its responsibilities before a person is spiritually, emotionally, and financially prepared.

24:28, 29 Under no circumstance should anyone bring false accusations **against** his **neighbor** or spread lies about him. Even if the neighbor has done those very things, there is no excuse for returning evil for evil.

24:30–34 The writer passed by the sluggard's **vineyard** and saw that **it was all overgrown with thorns**. Plants with stinging hairs or **nettles** were everywhere to be seen. The **stone wall was** in ruins. There was an object lesson in this. When anyone asks for just **a little** more **sleep**, a few more winks, a few more yawns, you can be sure that **poverty** will overtake him like a highwayman and like **an armed** robber.

When we succumb to laziness in spiritual matters, our life (vineyard) becomes infested with the works of the flesh (thistles and nettles). There is no fruit for God. Our spiritual defenses (the wall) are down, and the devil gains a foothold. The result of our coldness and backsliding is poverty of soul.

V. PROVERBS OF SOLOMON COMPILED BY HEZEKIAH'S MEN (25:1—29:27)

25:1 The proverbs contained in chapters 25—29 were composed by Solomon but **copied** years later by the men of **Hezekiah, king of Judah**. There are 140 proverbs, corresponding to the numerical value of the letters in the Hebrew form of the name Hezekiah.

25:2 **It is the glory of God to conceal a** thing. Think of all the secrets hidden in His natural creation, in His written Word, and in His providential dealings! "He would not be God," said Thomas Cartwright, "if His counsels and works did not transcend human intelligence."

The glory of kings is to search out a matter. In its context, this probably means that a wise king will keep himself informed of important developments affecting his kingdom and will make full investigation in order to render true judgments and formulate sound policies.

The application for us is that we should be diligent in searching out the spiritual treasures that are concealed in the Bible.

25:3 The **height** of **the heavens** seems to be limitless, and the **depth** of **the earth** seem to be **unsearchable**. Likewise there is something inscrutable about the **heart of** noble **kings**; no one knows exactly what they are thinking.

25:4, 5 When **silver** is melted in a crucible, **the dross** or impurities rise to the surface like scum. When this scum is removed, **the silversmith** has molten metal that is suitable for making **jewelry**. The **dross** here symbolizes **wicked** counselors in the king's court. When they are removed, the kingdom is **established** on a righteous basis.

The first thing Christ will do when He returns to reign will be to cleanse His kingdom of rebellion, lawlessness, and everything else that offends.

25:6, 7 It is a wise policy not to push **yourself** to the forefront **in the** royal court, or to seek a place among celebrities. **It is** far **better** to be invited to a place of honor than to seize it and then be publicly humiliated in the king's presence.

This advice is reminiscent of Jeremiah 45:5, "And do you seek great things for yourself? Do not seek them." Also the words of the Lord Jesus in Luke 14:8–10.

The last clause **"whom** (or "what") **your eyes have seen"** should possibly belong to the next verse, as in the RSV, "What your eyes have seen do not hastily bring into court . . . ."

25:8–10 The Bible condemns the litigious spirit, that is, the desire to rush **to** the law **court** to settle every grievance. A person might tell everything he has seen and yet be **put to shame** when his **neighbor** testifies.

It is better to handle grievances privately (see Matt. 18:15), and not to blab about them to others, as an unknown author advises:

> A little disagreement arises with some friends, and you have not the courage to go and speak about it to that friend alone, but mention it to another. The principle laid down in God's Word is forgotten, and mischief follows. Talking about a thing of this kind does no good, and in the end widens the breach. If we would only take such a passage as our guide, and regulate our conduct by it, we would lay aside many trivial "causes" of offense, and spare ourselves many disturbings of mind.

Verse 10 contemplates the third party's rebuking you for not going directly to the offender, and your gaining a **reputation** as a gossip—or worse!

25:11 An appropriate **word . . . is like apples of gold in settings of silver**. The right **word** is as morally beautiful and suitable as the combination of precious and attractive metals.

25:12 **An earring of gold and an ornament of fine gold** enhance physical beauty; so a **wise rebuker** adds moral beauty to the one who is willing to learn.

25:13 Ordinarily **snow** would be a disaster **in the time of harvest**. Here it means snow added to a drink of water and given to a reaper in the harvest field.

Just as an iced drink refreshes a man on a hot day, so **a faithful messenger . . . refreshes** those who sent him.

25:14 **Whoever** promises a gift but fails to deliver it is **like clouds and wind** which make people think rain is coming but which pass away **without bringing rain**.

Although this proverb does not deal with spiritual gifts, there is a valid application. A man may pretend to be a great teacher or preacher, but it is disappointing when he cannot live up to people's expectations. The Indians used to have a word for it: "Heap big wind—no rain."

25:15 Gentleness and patience will often persuade a prince more than if a person becomes provoked and excited. In the same way, **a gentle tongue** can break **a bone**, that is, it can accomplish more than the crunch of powerful jaws and teeth.

25:16 **Honey** is good when taken in moderation, but too much of a good thing is sickening. We should eat to live, not live to eat. Larry Christenson illustrates:

Some friends of ours have eight children, and they all love ice cream. On a hot summer day, one of the younger ones declared that she wished they could eat nothing but ice cream! The others chimed agreement, and to their surprise the father said, "All right. Tomorrow you can have all the ice cream you want—nothing but ice cream!" The children squealed with delight, and could hardly contain themselves until the next day. They came trooping down to breakfast shouting their orders for chocolate, strawberry, or vanilla ice cream—soup bowls full! Mid-morning snack—ice cream again. Lunch—ice cream, this time slightly smaller portions. When they came in for mid-afternoon snack, their mother was just taking some fresh muffins out of the oven, and the aroma wafted through the whole house.

"Oh goody!" said little Teddy. "Fresh muffins! My favorite!" He made a move for the jam cupboard, but his mother stopped him.

"Don't you remember? It's ice cream day—nothing but ice cream."

"Oh yeah . . . ."

"Want to sit up for a bowl?"

"No thanks. Just give me a one-dip cone."

By suppertime the enthusiasm for an all-ice-cream diet had waned considerably. As they sat staring at fresh bowls of ice cream, Mary—whose suggestion had started this whole adventure—looked up at her daddy and said, "Couldn't we just trade in this ice cream for a crust of bread?"[37]

25:17 Moderation applies not only to honey but to visiting. It is important to know when to leave. You can overstay your welcome.

"How much better is God's friendship than man's!" says Cartwright. "We are the more welcome to God the oftener we come to Him."

25:18 Here are three apt similes for a **man who bears false witness against his neighbor**:

    a club—mauling and smashing to pieces.

    a sword—with its two sharp cutting edges.

    a sharp arrow—piercing and wounding.

25:19 If you bite down hard with a broken tooth, you'll wish you hadn't. If you put your weight on a foot that's out of joint, it will let you down. That's exactly what it's like to put confidence in an unreliable person in time of trouble—painful and disappointing.

25:20 To **sing songs to a heavy heart** is provoking, annoying, unwelcome. It is as unsuitable as taking **away a** man's **garment in cold weather**, or as pouring **vinegar on soda**, causing violent agitation.

Keith Weston told of a fellow minister who was making his first hospital visit. "He found a poor patient with both legs strung up to pulleys, both arms in plaster, and an intravenous in one of them. And he said with his big evangelical smile and taking out his big evangelical Bible, 'Brother, are you rejoicing?' " Weston said, "The minister never told me what the patient said, but it wasn't very polite."[38]

25:21, 22 Paul quotes these verses in Romans 12:20. We can overcome evil with good by repaying every offense or discourtesy with a kindness.

An irate neighbor called a new believer and delivered a violent tirade against the believer's five-year-old daughter for trampled flowers, a broken window, and other offenses. When the neighbor came up for air,

the Christian asked her to come over to discuss the matter.

By the time the neighbor arrived, the table had been set for coffee and sweet rolls. "Oh, I'm sorry—you're having company." "No," replied the believer, "I thought we could talk about my daughter over a cup of coffee." The Christian gave thanks for the food and asked for God's wisdom. When she opened her eyes, the visitor was crying. "It's not your daughter, it's mine," blurted the neighbor. "I don't know why I lashed out at you. I just can't cope with my children, my husband, or my home!"

As soon as the neighbor made this admission, the young believer started sharing Christ. Within six weeks the neighbor and her family had been born again.[39]

25:23 The north wind brings forth rain; likewise **a backbiting tongue** produces **angry** looks. The angry looks almost surely come from the victim of gossip and they should also come from anyone else who hears it. If people would rebuke the backbiter, he would soon go out of business.

25:24 This is almost identical with 21:9, repeated to emphasize the unpleasantness of living with a nagging woman.

25:25 The gospel is God's **good news from a far country**—heaven. Like **cold water to a** thirsty soul, the gospel is refreshing and thirst quenching.

25:26 When good men bow down **before the wicked**, when they compromise, yield, or fail to stand up for the right, it is like a muddied **spring** or **a polluted well**. You go looking for purity and cleanliness and are disappointed.

25:27 It is not good to overindulge in **honey**. "Beyond God's 'enough' lies nausea,'' writes Kidner, ''not ecstasy.''

The Hebrew of the second line is obscure. It may mean, as in the NKJV, **to seek one's own glory is not glory** (the ''not'' is supplied from the first line), or ''to search into weighty matters is itself a weight'' (JND), or again ''to search into weighty matters is glory'' (JND margin). All three make good sense.

25:28 A man who has never learned to discipline his life is like an undefended **city**, open to every kind of attack, exposed to every temptation.

26:1 **Snow** is distinctly unseasonable **in summer, and rain in harvest** is injurious as well. It is equally out of place and injurious to honor fools. It is morally unfitting and only encourages them in their folly.

26:2 The **sparrow** and the **swallow** flit and dart in the air but never alight on us. In the same manner, an undeserved **curse** will never land on a person, no matter what superstition says. Balaam tried to curse Israel but couldn't (Num. 23:8; Deut. 23:5).

26:3 Just as it is necessary to use **a whip** on a **horse**, and **a bridle** on a **donkey**, so sharp correction is the only language a fool seems to understand. ''Do not be like the horse or like the mule, which have no understanding, which must be harnessed with bit and bridle, else they will not come near you'' (Ps. 32:9).

26:4, 5 These two verses present an apparent contradiction. The first says **not** to **answer a fool**, the second says to **answer** him. What is the explanation? The latter part of each verse holds the key.

Do not answer a fool in such a manner that you become a fool in the process. Don't lose your temper, or behave rudely, or speak unadvisedly. But **answer a fool.** Don't let him

off with his folly altogether. Reprove and rebuke him, as **his folly** deserves, so he will not **be wise in his own eyes**.

26:6 To send **a message by the hand of a fool** is to work against your own best interests. It's like cutting **off** your **own** legs or drinking poison. The fool won't deliver the message properly. He will only cause you grief. To cut off the **feet** means to render oneself helpless.

26:7 **The legs of the lame** man **hang limp** and useless. That's the way it is with a **proverb in the mouth of fools**. It is useless to them because they don't know when, where, or how to apply it.

26:8 You shouldn't bind **a stone in a sling**; it should be free for release. It is just as absurd to give **honor to a fool**.

A second possible meaning is that just as a stone is soon parted from a slingshot, so **a fool** will quickly prove himself unworthy of any **honor** that is bestowed upon him.

26:9 When **a drunkard** handles thorns, they are painful and dangerous to himself and others. So a parable **in the mouth of fools** can be misapplied and distorted. He might use it to justify his folly and to draw false conclusions concerning others.

26:10 The Hebrew text of this verse is very obscure, as is seen by the variety of translations:

''A master roughly worketh everyone: he both hireth the fool and hireth passers-by'' (JND).

''Like an archer who wounds everybody is he who hires a passing fool or drunkard'' (RSV).

''The law settles quarrels at last, yet silence the fool, and feud there shall be none'' (Knox).

"A master performs all things, but he who hires a fool hires a passer-by" (Berkeley).

"Like an archer who wounds everyone, so is he who hires a fool or who hires those who pass by" (NASB).

"An employee who hires any fool that comes along is only hurting everyone concerned" (TEV).

"The great God who formed everything gives the fool his hire and the transgressor his wages" (NKJV).

It is impossible to say which meaning is correct.

26:11 **A dog** is no more revolted by its **own vomit** than **a fool** by **his folly**; they both go back to that which is repulsive and disgusting. This verse is applied in 2 Peter 2:22 to people who experience moral reformation but who are never truly born again. Eventually they revert to their old ways.

26:12 A conceited person is above correction or instruction or rebuke. It is hopeless to try to correct him. An ignorant fool can sometimes be helped by a beating, but the conceited man is impervious to advice.

26:13–16 Here is **the lazy man** again and the imaginary **lion** that prevents his going to work. He **turns**, like **a door on its hinges, . . . on his bed**. Now he lies on his back, now on his front. Back and forth he swings with plenty of motion but no progress toward getting up. Later when he is at the table, he **dips his hand in the bowl** but can't muster up enough energy to lift the food **to his mouth**. Even something as pleasurable as eating is an exhausting effort. He **is wiser in his own eyes than seven men who can** give a proper **answer**; that is, seven intelligent men, unanimous in their insistence that he is wrong, wouldn't change his mind a fraction.

26:17 The passer-by who vexes himself or **meddles in a quarrel** that is none of his business is asking for trouble. It's like grabbing **a dog by the ears**; you don't dare hold on and you don't dare let go.

26:18, 19 Like a **madman** who **throws firebrands** and deadly **arrows** is the man who deals treacherously with **his neighbor** and then, when the harm is done, says, "**I was only** kidding." It is like excusing murder as a joke. This proverb could be applied to irresponsible courtship and engagement.

26:20, 21 Just as fuel feeds a fire, so gossip feeds trouble. Unless a troublemaker keeps adding aggravations and gossip and lies, strife will soon die out.

Some years ago the following appeared in the *Atlanta Journal*:

> I am more deadly than the screaming shell of a howitzer. I win without killing. I tear down homes, break hearts, and wreck lives. I travel on the wings of the wind. No innocence is strong enough to intimidate me, no purity pure enough to daunt me. I have no regard for truth, no respect for justice, no mercy for the defenseless. My victims are as numerous as the sands of the sea, and often as innocent. I never forget and seldom forgive. My name is Gossip![40]

26:22 This is a repetition of 18:8. Fallen human nature eats up gossip as if it were **tasty trifles**.

26:23–26 Fervent lips with a wicked heart are like earthenware covered with silver dross. A shining, silvery finish disguises the worthlessness and drabness of the **earthenware** pottery underneath. So lips burning with pretended love often cover a heart full of **hatred**. The pretended affection of Judas, the betrayer, illustrates the point.

The chronic hater tries to hide his enmity with gracious words, at the same time storing **up deceit within**. Though he may speak graciously, you can't trust him. He hides **seven abominations in his heart**, that is, he is full of evil and malice. **Though his hatred** may be hidden for the time **by deceit**, eventually his wickedness will be manifested before all.

26:27 Man's evil recoils upon himself, just as Louis the Strong's workmanship did. He was asked to make chains that would hold the most desperate prisoners during one of the early French wars. He tempered some very fine steel and made chains that were unparalleled for strength.

Later Louis himself was found guilty of treason and sent to prison. He was heard to moan, "These are my own chains! If I had known I was forging them for myself, how differently I would have made them!"

26:28 This proverb castigates the slanderer and the flatterer. The first one **hates** his victims, the second **works ruin** on his.

27:1 No one is sure of **tomorrow**. Therefore, don't **boast** about all you will do, like the rich fool did (Luke 12:16–21). See also Jas. 4:13–15.

27:2 It is in poor taste and very inelegant to **praise** yourself. A truly refined person tries to keep himself in the background, while praising others. "Beware of autobiographies" (Berkeley margin).

27:3 The persistent, provocative remarks of a fool are harder to put up with than a **heavy** physical burden. A man would rather carry **stone** or **sand** than be constantly annoyed by a loud-mouthed fool.

27:4 **Wrath** and anger are **cruel** and overwhelming, yet often they are short-lived. But **jealousy** continually gnaws away at a person and is therefore more grievous. This would apply, for instance, to one whose marriage has been disrupted by a third person.

27:5 A forthright **open rebuke** benefits the recipient but no one benefits from secret **love**, that is, love that refuses to point out a person's failings or is never acknowledged to exist.

27:6 Most people do not want to be honest with you about your faults; they are afraid that you will turn against them. It is a true friend who is willing to risk your goodwill in order to help you by constructive criticism.

The kisses of an enemy are deceitful, or profuse (RSV).

Judas gave a sign to the mob in advance to help them distinguish Jesus from the disciples; the sign was a kiss. The universal symbol of love was to be prostituted to its lowest use.

As he approached the Lord, Judas said, "Hail, Master!" then kissed Him profusely. Two different words for kiss are used (Matt. 26:48,49). The first, in verse 48, is the normal word for kiss. But in verse 49, a stronger word is used, expressing repeated or affectionate kissing.

27:7 A man who is overfed loses his appreciation of the choicest, sweetest foods. A **hungry** person is grateful for the slimmest pickings.

This is true of material possessions and of spiritual privileges.

27:8 **A man who wanders** from his home is one who is discontented and restless. He has the wanderlust. He is **like a bird that** strays **from its nest**, shirking responsibilities and failing to build anything solid and substantial.

27:9 The pleasantness of **ointment and perfume** is compared to the fragrance of loving advice from a **friend**. There is something truly heartwarming about fellowship with a friend.

27:10 Friendships must be cultivated and kept alive. Often the oldest friends are the best. So don't lose touch with your friends or old friends of the family.

"Nor go to your brother's house"— obviously meaning the home of one who has been offended, one who is **far** off. When trouble comes, you will get more help and sympathy from a faithful **neighbor** than from a near relative who is estranged from you.

27:11 A son's behavior reflects on his father's instruction. A disciple brings either joy or shame to his teacher. Berkeley's footnote says it well:

"The teacher's one defense—the success of his students."

27:12 Noah was **a prudent man**, hiding **himself** and his family in the ark. The rest of the people went on their way carelessly and indifferently and suffered for it. (See notes on 22:3.)

27:13 In modern idiom, the first line means that the man **who is surety for a stranger** will "lose his shirt."

The second line reads, **"and hold it in pledge when he is surety for a seductress."** In other words, be sure you have a legal claim on the property of anyone who will guarantee the debts unworthy of strangers, for if the debtor can't pay, the surety will have to.

27:14 A man doesn't appreciate loud, flattering greetings **early in the morning** when he is trying to sleep. They are more of a nuisance than a blessing.

27:15, 16 The **continual** drip, drip, drip of water through the roof **on a** very rainy day has this in common with a scolding, nagging wife. They are both enough to "drive a person up the wall!"

Whoever restrains her restrains the wind, and grasps oil with his right hand. No matter what you say, she will evade, excuse, blame others—and go right on nagging.

27:17 It used to be common to see the host at a table sharpening the carving knife by drawing each side of the cutting edge against a hardened steel rod with fine ridges. Just as the action of **iron** against **iron sharpens**, so the interchange of ideas among people makes them more acute in their thinking. Sharing each other's opinions gives a helpful breadth of view. Asking questions **sharpens** wits. Friendly intercommunication hones the personality.

27:18 **Whoever** takes good care of a **fig tree** is rewarded by a good crop. Diligence in attending to one's occupation insures food in the pantry or deepfreeze.

It is also true that the one **who** faithfully **waits on his** employer **will be honored**. Jesus said, "If anyone serves Me, him My Father will honor" (John 12:26).

27:19 As you look into a clear pool, you see your **face** reflected **in the water**. Even so, as you study other people, you see much that you find in yourself—the same emotions, temptations, ambitions, thoughts, strengths, and weaknesses.

That is why it happens that if a man preaches to himself, he is surprised by how many other people he hits.

27:20 **Hell and Destruction** (Heb. *Sheol* and *Abaddon*), death and the grave never reach the point where they don't claim more victims. **So the eyes of man are never satisfied** by anything the world has to offer. Arthur G. Gish illustrates:

> Tolstoy tells of a farmer who had a lust for more and more land. Finally he heard of cheap land among the Bashkirs. He sold all he had, made a long journey to their territory, and arranged a deal with them. For one thousand rubles he could buy all the land he could walk around in one day. The next morning he set out and walked far in one direction and then turned left. He made many detours to include extra areas of good soil. By the time he made his last turn, he realized he had gone too far. He ran as fast as possible to get back to the starting point before sunset. Faster and faster he ran and finally staggered and fell across the starting point just as the sun set. He lay there dead. They buried him in a small hole, all the land he needed.[41]

Fortunately, the craving of man's heart is fully satisfied in Christ:

> O Christ, He is the fountain,
> The deep sweet well of love!
> The streams on earth I've tasted,
> More deep I'll drink above!
> There, to an ocean fullness,
> His mercy doth expand.
> And glory, glory dwelleth
> In Immanuel's land.
> —Anne Ross Cousin

27:21 As **a refining pot** or crucible tests **silver**, and **a furnace** tests **gold**, so "a man is tried by his praise." This may mean that **a man** is tested by how he reacts to praise. Does it go to his head and ruin him, or does he accept it calmly and humbly?

Or it may mean that a man is tested by the things that he praises (ASV margin). His standards or sense of values are a reflection of his character.

Or again it might mean, as Barnes suggests, "So let a man be to his praise," that is, "let him purify it from all the alloy of flattery and baseness with which it is too probably mixed up."

27:22 You have probably seen **a mortar** and **pestle** on display in a drug store. The **mortar** is a bowl-shaped object. The **pestle** is a short, thick rod with a globular end and is used for pounding or pulverizing things in the mortar.

Even if you could put **a fool in a mortar** with wheat and pound both **with** the **pestle**, you wouldn't be able to separate the fool and **his foolishness**. In other words, you can separate the wheat from the chaff, but folly is too much a part of **a fool** to take it from him.

27:23–27 This paragraph extols the virtues of agricultural life, but puts ample stress on the importance of the farmer's diligence.

Unwearied and unceasing care must be exercised in tending the **flocks** and **herds**. Pastoral prosperity can only be maintained by constant diligence. This applies with equal force to the shepherding of sheep in a local church.

Riches do not last and the honors of royalty soon pass away unless constant care is exercised in attending to one's affairs.

There is tremendous satisfaction for the farmer in seeing the crops appearing, and in harvesting the vegetation from the hills. **The lambs will provide** wool for **clothing**, and by selling **goats** he can buy additional fields. There is plenty of **food for** his family and for his servants.

28:1 A guilty conscience makes a man jump at the slightest noise. People with a clear conscience don't have to drive with one eye on the rearview mirror; the **righteous are as bold as a lion.**

28:2 When **a land** is guilty of widespread **transgression**, it suffers frequent changes of government. When the ruler is a man of integrity and understanding, the country enjoys a settled, stable condition.

The Northern kingdom (Israel) had 19 kings in the space of about 200 years, or an average of only ten years per reign.

28:3 **A poor man who** rises to a position of wealth and power is often more oppressive on **the poor** than people from a higher income level would be. He is **like a driving rain** that levels fields of grain, that destroys the crops instead of helping them to grow.

28:4 People who throw off the restraint of God's **law** and of civil law often **praise the wicked**. This, of course, is an attempt to justify themselves.

Those who **keep the law** oppose the transgressors and speak out for the cause of righteousness.

28:5 **Evil men do not understand justice**; by refusing to practice it, they lose the power to understand it.

Those who seek the Lord's will are given proper powers of discernment. There is a close link between morality and understanding (see Ps. 119:100).

28:6 A **poor** man who lives a clean, honest life is better than a **rich** man who is **perverse in his ways**, who pretends to be living a good life while all the time practicing deceit and treachery.

28:7 A law-abiding **son** is **discerning**. One who associates with **gluttons** and drunkards brings disgrace on **his father**.

28:8 Under the law of Moses, a Hebrew was forbidden to charge **usury** (interest) to another Hebrew. He could charge it to a Gentile but not to a fellow-Jew (Deut. 23:19, 20). Today usury means exorbitant rates of interest.

Those who enrich themselves **by usury** or other forms of illicit revenue will lose their wealth; it will be taken from them and given to someone who knows how to use it better and how to treat **the poor** considerately.

28:9 If **one** will not hear and obey God's **law**, God will not hear **his prayer**. Actually his prayer is hateful to God.

> I may as well kneel down
> And worship gods of stone
> As offer to the Living God
> A prayer of words alone.
> —*John Burton*

28:10 **Whoever** tempts **the upright** to fall into sin **will fall into** a **pit** of punishment. Jesus warned, "Whoever causes one of these little ones who believe in Me to sin, it would be better for him if a millstone were hung around his neck, and he were drowned in the depth of the sea" (Matt. 18:6).

But the blameless will inherit good. Here **the blameless** may mean those who lead others in paths of holiness rather than sin. Or it may mean those who refuse to be victimized by solicitations to sin.

28:11 A **rich man** who glories in his riches thinks he is very clever. Priding himself on his rare financial acumen, he **is wise in his own** conceit. He confuses riches and wisdom.

A **poor** person **who has understanding** can see through such pretension. Charles Lamb once approached one of those swaggering men with the remark, "Excuse me, sire, but are you anybody in particular?"

28:12 **When the righteous** rise to power, there is great rejoicing. **When the wicked** triumph, **men hide themselves** for fear.

28:13 There are two kinds of forgiveness, judicial and parental. When we trust Christ as Lord and Savior, we receive forgiveness from the penalty of sins; that is judicial forgiveness. When we, as believers, confess our sins, we receive parental forgiveness (1 Jn. 1:9); this maintains fellowship with God our Father.

There is no blessing for the person **who covers his sins**, that is, who refuses to drag them out into the light and to confess them to God and to anyone else who has been wronged. But anyone who **confesses and forsakes** his sins has the assurance that God not only forgives but forgets (Heb. 10:17).

28:14 One element of true happiness is to have a tender heart before the Lord. It is the one who becomes hard and unrepentant who falls into trouble. God can resist the proud and brazen but He cannot resist a broken and contrite heart.

28:15 Beast-like and inhumane describes the tyrant who rides herd **over poor**, weak, and defenseless people. He is **like a roaring lion and a charging bear**.

28:16 Apparently the prince described here is one **who lacks understanding** in the sense that he seeks to enrich himself at all costs. This man **is** also **a great oppressor** because he tramples on others to get richer. The ruler **who hates covetousness** and lives unselfishly for the good of his people **will prolong his days**.

28:17 **A man who is burdened with bloodshed will flee into a pit; let no one help him.** The willful murderer is a fugitive, racing toward his doom. No one should seek to obstruct or interfere with justice. God has said, "Whoever sheds man's blood, by man his blood shall be shed" (Gen. 9:6).

28:18 The first line refers to salvation from damage in this life, not from damnation in the next. Eternal salvation from the penalty of sin is not obtained by walking uprightly but by faith in the Lord Jesus Christ. The upright walk is a fruit of that salvation, although **whoever walks blamelessly will be saved** from many a snare in this life.

The man who vacillates from one form of crookedness to another will go down in one fell swoop.

28:19 The contrast here is between **plenty of** food and plenty of **poverty**. The diligent farmer has the former. The one who engages in empty, nonproductive activities has the latter.

28:20 **A faithful man** here is one who is honest and who does not covet great wealth. He will be richly blessed. The man who seeks to enrich himself quickly by unscrupulous means will be punished.

28:21 It is rank injustice for a judge **to show partiality**, and yet a man will often do this **for a piece of bread**, that is, for the most trifling consideration.

28:22 A miserly, grudging, ungenerous man races **after riches**, little realizing **that poverty will** soon overtake **him**.

28:23 When a friend lovingly **rebukes** you, it is hard to take at the time. It hurts your pride. But **afterward** you realize that this friend must really have cared for you to point out your faults, and so you are grateful to him.

Flattery may seem pleasant at the time, but eventually you realize that it wasn't true anyway, and that the person was simply trying to gain your favor. **He** probably **flatters** everyone he meets.

28:24 A son who **robs his** parents might excuse it on the grounds that it will be his eventually, or that he has dedicated it to the Lord in the meantime (Mark 7:11). But God is not deceived; He puts that person in the same class as a robber or murderer.

28:25 The proud, grasping person **stirs up strife**, perhaps by pushing everyone else aside in a futile race for riches or power or preeminence (see Jas. 4:1). It is the God-fearing man who succeeds in finding peace and satisfaction.

28:26 **He who trusts in his own** wisdom to guide him through life **is a fool**. He is casting his anchor inside the boat, and thus will drift incessantly. The one who looks to the Lord for guidance acts **wisely** (see Jer. 9:23,24).

28:27 God will reward those who show mercy **to the poor**. The man who turns away **his eyes** from genuine cases of need **will have many** a sorrow.

28:28 **When the wicked** rise to power, the populace **hides** itself for fear. **But when** wicked rulers are overthrown, **the righteous increase**.

29:1 A man who continues in sin, in spite of repeated warnings, **will suddenly be destroyed, . . . without** hope of any further opportunity. The people who lived before the flood refused to listen to Noah. The flood came and they were destroyed.

An acquaintance of mine who had repeatedly rejected the gospel invitation met a Christian lady who had prayed for him often. She said, "Don't you think it's time you turned to the Lord?" He answered, "What has He ever done for me?" That weekend his life was snuffed out in a mysterious mishap. It was one of those accidents that couldn't happen—but did!

29:2 The character of a nation's rulers affects the morale of the country. **When the righteous are in authority**, that is, in numbers and in

power, **the people rejoice. A wicked** ruler causes widespread mourning.

29:3 A son who **loves wisdom**, who lives a dedicated, separated Christian life, brings joy to **his father**. But the son who lives in immorality **wastes** his father's money. The prodigal son, you remember, squandered his father's substance in riotous living.

29:4 By acting with **justice**, a **king** brings his country to a position of strength. The one who accepts **bribes** to pervert justice is undermining the stability of the government.

29:5 The flatterer imperils **his neighbor** by refusing to tell him the truth or by praising him for things that are not true. Also he encourages pride which leads to a fall.

29:6 **An evil man** is often **snared** in the net of his own sin. **The righteous** man is happy because he does not have to fear the consequences of transgression. **He sings and rejoices.**

29:7 **Righteous** people take an active interest in **the cause of the poor.** **The wicked** are not interested in showing any such concern.

29:8 **Scoffers set a city aflame.** They create turmoil by arousing tempers, agitating the people, and creating divisions. **Wise men** seek to avert discord and promote peace.

29:9 This proverb may have two meanings. The more probable is this: When **a wise man** argues **with a foolish man**, the fool will only rage and laugh (NKJV, RSV, Berkeley). He will never be persuaded, and **there** will be **no peace**.

The other interpretation is that when **a wise man** argues **with a foolish man**, whether *the wise man* uses severity **or** humor, it doesn't make any difference. Nothing positive is accomplished.

29:10 Again there are two possible interpretations. One is set forth in the ASV: "The bloodthirsty hate him that is perfect; and, as for the upright, they seek his life." Here the bloodthirsty are the wicked aggressors in each case.

The other meaning is found in the NKJV, JND, and Berkeley. Here **the bloodthirsty** are found destroying life in the first line, **but the upright** are seen seeking to preserve and protect it, in the second line.

29:11 A fool vents all his feelings, but a wise man holds them back. Adams counsels:

The idea of allowing anger to break out in an undisciplined manner by saying or doing whatever comes into mind without weighing the consequences, without counting ten, without holding it back and quieting it, without hearing the whole story, is totally wrong.[42]

29:12 The thought here seems to be that if **a ruler** wants to be pampered, flattered, and comforted by pleasant news, then **all his servants** will treat him exactly that way. They will lie and flatter.

29:13 There may be a great gulf between **the poor** and **the oppressor** in human society, but they meet on a **common** level before God. It is **the** Lord who **gives light** to their **eyes**.

29:14 In judging a ruler, God is especially interested in whether he treats **the poor** considerately and without prejudice. If so, He promises to establish **his throne . . . forever**. Actually we know only one such ruler; His name is Jesus.

29:15 This proverb flatly contradicts many modern specialists who advocate "permissive democracy." **The rod** is corporal punishment; **rebuke** is verbal correction. These two forms of parental discipline impart **wisdom**. They do not inhibit a

child or warp his personality as the "experts" say.

29:16 When the wicked grow more numerous and powerful, the crime rate rises. **But the righteous will** live to **see their** downfall. Of course there are exceptions, but they are the exceptions that prove the rule.

29:17 A child who has been disciplined properly will bring **delight** and **rest** to his parents instead of anxiety and heartache.

29:18 Where there is no revelation, the people cast off restraint; but happy is he who keeps the law. Here **revelation** means *prophetic* revelation, hence the Word of God (see 1 Sam. 3:1). The thought is that when God's Word is not known and honored, the people run wild. The ones who obey the law, that is, the Word of God, are the truly blessed ones.

29:19 This verse seems to describe the obstinate, intractable attitude of many **a servant**. Oral orders are not always enough. They may understand the master's instructions but they don't always carry them out. They just remain silent and sullen. Jesus said, "Why do you call Me, 'Lord, Lord,' and not do the things which I say?" (Luke 6:46).

29:20 Of all the subjects dealt with in Proverbs, our **words** come in for a lion's share of attention. Here we learn that the man who speaks before he thinks is more hopeless than **a fool**. This puts him in the same class as the man who is wise in his own conceits (26:12).

29:21 If you pamper and spoil a **servant** he will forget his proper position and will soon expect you to treat him like **a son**. Undue familiarity in the employer-employee relationship often breeds contempt.

The word translated **"son"** in the

second line is of very uncertain meaning.

29:22 Most of us have met these two men at one time or another. The **angry man stirs up** all kinds of trouble, and the passionate or **furious man** commits plenty of sins.

29:23 A proud man can be sure of being brought **low**. It is **the humble** man who is elevated to a place of **honor**.

Professor Smith was climbing the Weisshorn. When near the top the guide stood aside to permit the traveler to have the honor of first reaching the top. Exhilarated by the view, forgetful of the fierce gale that was blowing, he sprang up and stood erect on the summit. The guide pulled him down, exclaiming, "On your knees sir; you are not safe there except on your knees." Life's summits, whether of knowledge, of love, or of worldly success, are full of perils. (*Choice Gleanings*)

O Lamb of God, still keep me
Close to Thy pierced side;
'Tis only there in safety
And peace I can abide.

With foes and snares around me,
And lusts and fears within,
The grace that sought and found me,
Alone can keep me clean.
—*James G. Deck*

29:24 An accomplice of **a thief** acts as if he **hates his own life**. Why? Because when **he swears to tell the truth,** that is, when the judge puts him under oath to tell all he knows, he **reveals nothing,** that is, he does not testify, and thus perjures himself. Under the law of Moses, a man who heard the judge putting him under oath and yet refused to testify, was counted guilty and was punished accordingly (see Lev. 5:1). There was no

such thing as "pleading the Fifth Amendment."

29:25 **The fear of man** results in yielding to human pressure to commit evil or to refrain from doing what is right. How many have gone to hell because they were afraid of what their friends would say if they trusted Christ!

The man who **trusts in the LORD** is **safe**, come what may. "We fear man so much," wrote William Gurnall, "because we fear God so little."

29:26 **Many** people look to an earthly ruler as if he were the solution to all their problems, **but** it is **from the LORD** that **justice comes**.

29:27 There is no rapport between **an unjust man** and a **righteous** one. The just one looks with disfavor on the ungodly, and the wicked abominates the upright. Just as a straight stick shows up a crooked one, so the contrast between a clean life and a wicked one is glaring.

The proverbs of Solomon end at this point.

VI. THE WORDS OF AGUR (Chap. 30)

30:1 All we know about **Agur** is found in this chapter. He introduces himself as **the son of Jakeh**.

The words **his utterance** (oracle, NIV) may also be translated "of Massa" (RSV). This would identify Agur as a descendant of Ishmael (Gen. 25:14).

The second line may also read, "The man said, 'I have wearied myself, O God, I have wearied myself, O God, and am consumed'" (ASV margin). This leads naturally into what follows—the impossibility of the infinitesimal comprehending the Infinite.

30:2 Agur begins with a confession of his own inability to attain to **understanding**. Apparently it is a statement of genuine humility—a proper attitude for anyone who would inquire into the works and ways of God.

30:3 He does not profess to have **learned wisdom** or to have found God by human searching. He recognizes that he does not have the power in himself to attain to the **knowledge of the Holy One**.

30:4 By a series of questions, he sets forth the greatness of God as He is revealed in nature.

The first describes God as having access to the heights and depths of the universe where no man can follow Him. The second points out His control over the massive power of the **wind**. Third is His might in containing **the waters**, either in clouds above the earth or in the ocean beds. Next is His establishment of the boundaries of the land masses.

What is His name, and what is His Son's name? The thought is, "Who can ever fully know such a great Being, so incomprehensible, so mysterious, so powerful, so omnipresent?" The answer is "No one can ever understand Him fully." But we do know that His name is the Lord (Jehovah) and His Son's name is the Lord Jesus Christ.

This is a text that surprises most Jewish people, who have been taught that God never had a Son. From this verse OT believers could understand that God has a Son.

30:5 Agur now turns from the revelation of God in nature to His revelation in the Word. He asserts the infallibility of the sacred Scriptures— **"every word of God is pure."** Then he speaks of the security of all who **trust in** the God of the Bible—**"He is**

a **shield to those who put their trust in Him."**

30:6 The absolute sufficiency of the Scriptures is asserted next. No man should dare to **add** his thoughts and speculations to what God has spoken.

This verse condemns the cults which give their own writings and traditions the same authority as the Bible.

30:7–9 These verses contain the only prayer in the book of Proverbs. The prayer is short and to the point. It contains two petitions, one covering the spiritual life and the other covering the physical life.

First Agur wanted his life to be worthwhile and honest. He didn't want it to be wasted on trivia. He didn't want to major on minors, and he didn't want to deceive others or to be deceived.

As to the physical, he asked to be delivered from the extremes of **poverty** and **riches**. He would be satisfied with the provision of His daily needs. He was saying, in effect, "Give me this day my daily bread."

He gives reasons for wanting to avoid the twin extremes of affluence and poverty. If he were **full**, he might become independent of the Lord and **deny** Him by not feeling any great need for Him. He might be emboldened to say, **"Who is the LORD?"**—that is, who is He that I should look to Him for what I need or want?

The peril of poverty would be that he might **steal**, and then, to cover up, he might deny under oath that he had done it.

30:10 In what seems to be an abrupt transition, Agur warns against slandering **a servant to his master**. The penalty would be that the **curse** he pronounces against you would come to pass because God is the Defender of the oppressed.

The NT warns us against judging servants of the Lord; to their own Master they stand or fall (Rom. 14:4).

30:11 The **generation** described here bears striking resemblance to the generation living today and to the one which will exist in the last days (2 Tim. 3:1–7). Notice the following features:

Disrespectful to parents. They curse their **father** and show no gratitude to their **mother**, thus breaking the Fifth Commandment. The hostility of young people toward their parents is one of the chief characteristics of our decadent society.

30:12 *Self-righteous.* These people are vile and unclean, yet they have no sense of shame. Outwardly they appear like whitewashed tombs but inwardly they are full of dead men's bones.

30:13 *Pride and arrogance.* They resemble Rabbi Simeon Ben Jochai who said, "If there are only two righteous men in the world, I and my son are the two. If only one, I am he."

30:14 *Fiercely oppressive.* In their insatiable greed for wealth, they rip, tear, and **devour the poor** by long hours, low wages, miserable working conditions, and other forms of social injustice.

30:15, 16 The greed of the oppressors in the preceding verse leads on to other examples of desires that are never satisfied.

1. The **leech** or vampire (ASV margin) is pictured as having **two daughters** who have an endless capacity for sucking blood. They are both named **"Give."**

2. **The grave** never says "No vacancy." Death never takes a holiday, and the tomb never fails to accommodate its victims.

3. **The barren womb** is never willing to accept its sterility but hopes continually for motherhood.

4. **The earth** is **not satisfied with water**, no matter how much rain falls. It can always absorb some more.

5. **The fire never says "Enough!"** It will devour as much fuel as a person wants to feed it.

The expression **"There are three things . . . yes, four . . ."** is a literary formula used to produce a sense of climax. Grant indicated that **four** is the number of earthly completeness or universality (as in the four corners of the earth), or of the creature in contrast to the Creator.[43]

30:17 This proverb seems to be isolated from the rest, though similar to verse 11. It teaches that a son who **mocks his father** and disobeys **his mother** will die a violent death and will be denied a decent burial. To the Jewish mind, it was a great tragedy and disgrace for a body to be unburied. The fate of the wayward son is for his carcass to be devoured by vultures.

30:18, 19 Agur lists **four** things that were **too wonderful for** him. As we study them, we have a vague suspicion that there is a spiritual analogy beneath the surface, but what is that analogy and what is the common thread that ties them together? Most commentators suggest that these four things leave no trace behind them. This seems to be confirmed by the way the adulterous woman in verse 20 is able to hide her guilt. Kidner says that the common denominator is "the easy mastery, by the appropriate agent, of elements as difficult to negotiate as air, rock, sea—and young woman."[44]

1. **The way of an eagle in the air.** Here we face the marvel of flight.

The gracefulness and speed of the eagle are proverbial.

2. **The way of a serpent on a rock.** The wonder here is the movement of a reptile without benefit of legs, arms, or wings.

3. **The way of a ship in the midst of the sea.** It is possible that the "ship" here may be a poetic name for fish (see also Ps. 104:26), and that Agur is marveling at the navigational finesse of marine life.

4. **The way of a man with a virgin.** The simplest explanation of this expression refers it to the instinct of courtship. Some, however, take a less idyllic view and apply it to the seduction of a virgin.

30:20 A fifth wonder, apparently thrown in for good measure, is the way **an adulterous woman** can satisfy her lust, then wipe **her mouth** and protest her complete innocence.

30:21–23 Four insufferable things are next listed; they are the kind of things that throw the earth into turmoil.

1. **A servant when he reigns**. He becomes arrogant and overbearing, drunk with his new position.

2. **A fool . . . filled with food**. His prosperity causes him to be more insolent than ever.

3. **A hateful woman** who finally succeeds in getting **married**. Her wretched disposition would normally have kept her single, but by some fluke, she lands a husband. Then she becomes imperious and haughty, taunting those who are still unmarried.

4. **A maidservant who succeeds her mistress**. She doesn't know

how to act with refinement and grace, but is coarse, rude, and vulgar.

30:24 Now Agur turns to **four things which** are **wise** out of all proportion to their size.

30:25 1. **The ants** are tiny creatures and seemingly helpless, yet they busy themselves during **the summer** months. Most of the common ant species do not provide for the winter, because, according to the World Book, "Ants cluster together and spend the winter sleeping inside their nests." The harvester ant is an exception, however, since it stores food in warm, dry seasons for later use during cold times. The emphasis in this text, though, is on the ants' busy activity preparing **their food**.

30:26 2. **The rock badgers** are naturally **feeble** and defenseless, yet they have the wisdom to find protection in the rocks. (The **rock badger**, also known as the "hyrax," is not to be confused with the common badger, which is quite a fighter.) Cleft rocks provide the best protection. The spiritual application is found in the hymn, "Rock of Ages, cleft for me."

30:27 3. **The locusts have no** visible ruler, **yet** the order in which they **advance** is remarkable.

30:28 4. **The spider**, or lizard (NASB), is small, yet it succeeds in getting into **king's palaces**. Its access to unlikely and important places is often duplicated by Christians today. God does not leave Himself without a witness, even in courts of royalty.

30:29–31 The final series has to do with **four** examples of stately, **majestic**, or graceful movement.

1. **The lion**, the king of **beasts**, is majestic and unruffled as it walks.

2. There is considerable uncertainty about the second example. It may be a strutting rooster (NIV), a warhorse (JND margin), or **a greyhound**. All these fit the description of lofty dignity, but perhaps the graceful **greyhound** is the best choice.

3. **A ram** or **male goat** is a picture of noble bearing as it strides at the head of a flock.

4. There is also some doubt about the fourth example, whether it should read "a king, against whom there is no rising up" (KJV), "a king striding before his people" (RSV), or **"a king whose troops are with him"** (NKJV). In any case, the point is clear that the king marches with regal dignity.

30:32, 33 The chapter closes with two verses that seem strangely unrelated to what has preceded. Williams paraphrases the verses:

If feeble man in his folly has lifted up himself against God, or even indulged hard thoughts of Him, let him listen to the voice of wisdom and lay his hand upon his mouth; for otherwise there will be a result as surely as there is a result when milk is churned, the nose wrung, or anger excited.[45]

VII. THE WORDS KING LEMUEL'S MOTHER TAUGHT HIM (31:1–9)

31:1 We have no way of knowing who **King Lemuel** was. His name means "dedicated to God" or "belonging to God." The important thing is that he has preserved for us the wise counsel which **his mother** gave him.

31:2 We might fill in the thought here as follows: "**What** shall I say to you, and **what** gems of wisdom will I pass on to you, **my son**, whom I have dedicated to the Lord?"

31:3 First is a warning to avoid a life of dissipation and sensual lust. *The Speaker's Commentary* points out that "the temptations of the harem were then, as now, the curse of all Eastern kingdoms."

31:4–8 Second is a plea to refrain from the excessive use of **wine** and strong **drink**. The danger for kings is that their ability to judge and to make proper decisions might be impaired by drinking. They might **forget** the standards of **justice** demanded by **the law** and fail to uphold the rights of the downtrodden. The medicinal use of wine is sanctioned as a stimulant for the dying and an anti-depressant for the despondent. It is all right for people like these to **drink**, and to **forget** their need and their **misery**.

31:9 The king should be a responsible spokesman for all who cannot defend themselves, and plead the cause of all who are left **to die**. He should speak up on behalf of **the poor and needy**.

VIII. THE IDEAL WIFE AND MOTHER (31:10–31)

The closing section of the book describes the ideal wife. It is written in the form of an acrostic, each verse beginning with a letter of the Hebrew alphabet in proper order. Knox's translation attempts to reproduce this acrostic style in English, using twenty-two of our twenty-six letters.

31:10–12 **A virtuous** or fine **wife** is one who is capable, diligent, worthy, and good. **Her worth** cannot be measured in terms of costly jewels. **Her husband** can have full confidence in **her**, with no need to fear any **lack of** honest **gain**. Her finest efforts are put forth to help him; she never fails to cooperate.

31:13–15 She is always on the lookout for **wool and flax**, and enjoys converting them into cloth. On her shopping trips, **she is like the merchant ships** that return to port laden with produce **from afar**. See her going to the supermarket, loading her shopping cart with the best bargains. **She also rises** before daybreak to prepare **food for her household**. The **portion** she gives to **her maidservants** may include not only their breakfast but their work assignments for the day.

31:16–18 When she hears that some nearby **field** is for sale, she goes out to see it. It is just what she needs, so she **buys it**, then industriously **plants a vineyard** with money she has earned. She prepares herself for her tasks with great vigor and enthusiasm. She is not afraid of strenuous work. She takes a quiet, humble satisfaction in the results of her labor. After the others have gone to bed, she often works late into the **night**.

31:19–22 She stretches out her hands to the distaff, and her hand holds the spindle, that is, she busies herself spinning wool and flax into yarn and thread. In addition to all this, she finds time to help **the needy**. She unselfishly shares with those who are less fortunate. She does not dread the approach of winter because there is plenty of warm clothing in the closets. **She makes tapestry for herself; her** own **clothing is fine linen and purple**.

31:23 **Her husband** is a man of prominence in the community. He sits at the **gates** with **the elders**. He can devote himself to public affairs without worrying about conditions at home.

31:24–27 His wife weaves **linen garments and sells them** at the market. She also earns money by **supply-** ing sashes to **the merchants**. Clothed with industry and dignity, she faces the future with confidence. The instruction she gives to her family is a balance of **wisdom** and **kindness**. She keeps in close touch with the affairs of **her household**, and does not waste time or engage in shallow, unproductive activity.

31:28, 29 **Her children** realize that she is an outstanding mother, and they tell her so. **Her husband also praises her** as a God-given wife. He says, "There are **many** good wives in the world, **but you excel them all**."

31:30, 31 The writer now adds his *amen* to what the husband has just said. It is true. A woman may have **charm** but no common sense. She may be beautiful but impractical. **But a woman who fears the LORD**, as described above, is the best kind. Let her be honored for her diligence and noble character. When the town fathers meet at the civic center, let them **praise** her outstanding accomplishments.

It is noteworthy and fitting that Proverbs should end on this very positive note about women. Three women have been prominent in this book: the personification of *Wisdom*, seen as a woman inviting learners to her banquet, the immoral woman or *seductress*, and finally, the *"woman* (or wife) *of valor,"* as the literal translation reads in 31:10 (NKJV margin).

ENDNOTES

[1](Intro) Quoted by D. L. Moody in *Notes from My Bible*, p. 81.

[2](Intro) Arnot uses this as the title for his commentary on Proverbs (see Bibliography).

[3](1:8) Henry Bosch, ed., *Our Daily Bread*.

[4](1:19) The Hebrew word for wis-

dom (*hokmāh*) is a feminine noun, hence it was natural to personify this virtue as a woman.

[5](1:25) Donald Grey Barnhouse, *Words Fitly Spoken*, p. 239.

[6](3:2) Jay Adams, *Competent to Counsel*, p. 125.

[7](5:18) Michael Griffiths, *Take My Life*, p. 117.

[8](5:22) Adams, *Counsel*, p. 145.

[9](6:16) Derek Kidner, *The Proverbs: An Introduction and Commentary*, p. 73. See similar forms in 30:15, 18.

[10](6:17) J. Oswald Sanders, *On To Maturity*, p. 63.

[11](6:28) Griffiths, *Life*, p. 116.

[12](7:2) *International Standard Bible Encyclopedia*, I:209.

[13](9:18) The French text is as follows: *Plaisir d'amour ne dure qu'une nuit; Chagrin d'amour dure toute la vie.*

[14](10:24) C. S. Lewis, *Weight of Glory*, ed. by Walter Hooper, p. 13.

[15](10:28) G. S. Bowes, quoted in *Our Daily Bread*.

[16](13:4) Bosch, ed., *Daily Bread*,

[17](13:5) J. Allen Blair, further documentation unavailable.

[18](13:7) G. Campbell Morgan, *Searchlights from the Word*, p. 203.

[19](13:10) C. S. Lewis, *Christianity*, pp. 110, 111.

[20](13:24) Benjamin Spock, taken from the Tampa Tribune, Tampa, FL, January 22, 1974.

[21](14:2) Kidner, *Proverbs*, p. 106.

[22](14:30) Paul Adolph, "God in Medical Practice," in *The Evidence of God in an Expanding Universe* by John Clover Monsma, pagination unavailable.

[23](15:1) Charles Haddon Spurgeon, quoted by A. Naismith in *1200 More Notes, Quotes and Anecdotes*, p. 239.

[24](16:3) J. Allen Blair, further documentation unavailable.

[25](16:24) Watchman Nee, *Do All to the Glory of God*, p. 55.

[26](16:32) Henry Durbanville, *Winsome Christianity*, p. 41.

[27](17:17) Moody, *Notes*, p. 83.

[28](17:22) Paul Brock, *Reader's Digest*, September, 1974.

[29](17:22) Blake Clark, *Reader's Digest*, May, 1972.

[30](18:9) Griffiths, *Life*, p. 53.

[31](18:14) Adolph, "God in Medical Practice," pagination unavailable.

[32](18:24) Morgan, *Searchlights*, p. 204.

[33](19:17) Henry Bosch, ed., *Our Daily Bread*.

[34](22:6) Quoted in *A Treasury of Illustrations*, NY: Fleming Revell Co., 1904, pp. 11–12.

[35](22:6) Adams, *Counsel*, p. 158.

[36](22:15) Matthew Henry, *Matthew Henry's Commentary on the Whole Bible*, III:919.

[37](25:16) Larry Christenson, *The Christian Family*, p. 58.

[38](25:20) Keith Weston, *Living in the Light*, p. 122.

[39](25:21, 22) Sarah Anne Jepson, "Preparing Tables of Forgiveness," *Good News Broadcaster*, June 1975, p. 13.

[40](26:20, 21) *Atlanta Journal*, further documentation unavailable.

[41](27:20) Arthur G. Gish, *Beyond the Rat Race*, p. 91.

[42](29:11) Adams, *Counsel*, p. 221.

[43](30:15, 16) F. W. Grant, *The Numerical Bible*, I:15.

[44](30:18, 19) Kidner, *Proverbs*, p. 180.

[45](30:32, 33) George Williams, *The Student's Commentary on the Holy Scriptures*, p. 437.

BIBLIOGRAPHY

Arnot, William. *Laws for Heaven for Life on Earth*. London: James Nisbet & Co., n.d.

Bridges, Charles. *A Commentary on Proverbs*. Reprint. Edinburgh: The Banner of Truth Trust, 1983.

Delitzsch, Franz. "Proverbs." In *Biblical Commentary on the Old Testament*. Vols. 16, 17. Grand Rapids: Wm. B. Eerdmans Publishing Co., 1971.

Harris, R. Laird. "Proverbs." In *The Wycliffe Bible Commentary*. Chicago: Moody Press, 1962.

Henry, Matthew. "Proverbs." In *Matthew Henry's Commentary on the Whole Bible*. Vol. 3. McLean, VA: MacDonald Publishing Company, n.d.

Ironside, H. A. *Notes on the Book of Proverbs*. Neptune, N.J.: Loizeaux Brothers, 1964.

Jensen, Irving L. *Proverbs*. Everyman's Bible Commentary. Chicago: Moody Press, 1982.

Kidner, Derek. *The Proverbs: An Introduction and Commentary*. Downers Grove, IL: InterVarsity Press, 1964.

MacDonald, William. *Listen, My Son*. Kansas City, KS: Walterick Publishers, 1965.

Plumptre, E. H. "Proverbs." In *Commentary on the Holy Bible* (Speaker's Commentary). London: John Murray, 1873.

Spence, H.D.M., and Joseph S. Exell, eds. "Proverbs." In *The Pulpit Commentary*, Vol. 9. Grand Rapids: Wm. B. Eerdmans Publishing Company, 1909.

Weston, Keith. *Living in the Light*. Bromley, Kent, England: STL Books, 1983.

ECCLESIASTES

Introduction

"I know nothing grander in its impassioned survey of mortal pain and pleasure, its estimate of failure and success, none of more noble sadness; no poem working more indomitably for spiritual illumination."

—E. C. Stedman

I. Unique Place in the Canon

Ecclesiastes is one book of the Bible whose *uniqueness*, at least, has never been questioned, even though nearly everything else about it *has* been (e.g., its authorship, date, theme, and theology).

The reason this book seems to clash with the rest of the Word of God is that it presents merely human reasoning "under the sun." This phrase, *under the sun*, forms the most important single key to understanding Ecclesiastes. The fact that it occurs twenty-nine times indicates the general perspective of the author. His search is confined to this earth. He ransacks the world to solve the riddle of life. And his whole quest is carried on by his own mind, unaided by God.

If this key—*under the sun*—is not kept constantly in mind, then the book will present mountainous difficulties. It will seem to contradict the rest of Scripture, to set forth strange doctrines, and to advocate a morality that is questionable, to say the least.

But if we remember that Ecclesiastes is a compendium of human, not divine, wisdom, then we will understand why it is that while some of its conclusions are true, some are only half true, and some are not true at all. Let us take some illustrations.

Ecclesiastes 12:1 is true and dependable advice for young people in all ages; they should remember their Creator in the days of their youth. Verse 4 of chapter 1 is only half true; it *is* true that one generation follows another, but it is *not* true that the earth remains forever (see Ps. 102:25–26 and 2 Pet. 3:7, 10). And the following statements, if taken at face value, are not true *at all:* "Nothing is better for a man than that he should eat and drink, and that his soul should enjoy good in his labor" (2:24); "Man has no advantage over animals" (3:19); and "The dead know nothing" (9:5).

However, if we did not have any revelation from God, we would probably arrive at the same conclusions.

Ecclesiastes and Inspiration

When we say that some of the book's conclusions "under the sun" are only half true and that some are not true at all, what does this do to the inspiration of Ecclesiastes? The answer is that it does not affect the question of inspiration in the slightest.

The book is part of the inspired Word of God. It is God-breathed in the sense that the Lord ordained that it should be included in the canon of Scripture. We hold to the verbal, plenary inspiration of Ecclesiastes as we do of the rest of the Bible. (See Introduction to the Old Testament, page 15.)

But the inspired books of the Bible sometimes contain statements by Satan or by men which are not true. In Genesis 3:4, for instance, Satan told Eve that she would not die if she ate the fruit of the tree in the middle of the garden. It was a lie, but it is quoted in the Scripture to teach us that the devil has been a liar from the beginning. As Dr. Chafer observed:

> Inspiration may record the untruth of Satan (or of men) but it does not vindicate the lie or sanctify it. It secures the exact record of what was said—good or bad.[1]

Misuse of Ecclesiastes

For the very reason that it does present human reasoning "under the sun," Ecclesiastes is one of the favorite books of skeptics and of the false cults. They quote it with great enthusiasm to prove their unbelieving or heretical doctrines, especially doctrines dealing with death and the hereafter. For instance, they use verses from this book to teach soul-sleep after death and the annihilation of the wicked dead. They wrench verses out of context to deny the immortality of the soul and the doctrine of eternal punishment.

But they never put the key in the door. They never tell their victims that Ecclesiastes expounds man's wisdom under the sun and therefore is not a valid source of proof texts for doctrines of the Christian faith.

II. Authorship

Until the seventeenth century most Jews and Christians believed Solomon wrote the book of Ecclesiastes. A century before that, the generally conservative Martin Luther rejected Solomonic authorship, but he was an exception.

It will come as a surprise to some to learn that today most Bible scholars—including conservative ones—believe the book was not written by Solomon but was presented in a Solomonic framework, not to deceive, but as a literary device.

The Problem with Solomonic Authorship

The main argument for rejecting the traditional authorship by King Solomon is *linguistic*. That is, many experts say the book contains words and grammatical constructions that did not exist till the Babylonian Captivity or later.

For most evangelicals, the whole idea of putting words into Solomon's mouth seems to be an illegitimate literary device, at least suggesting deception to Western believers.

The arguments pro and con are lengthy and involved, and we cannot go into them here. It is sufficient to say that none of the objections that have been raised against Solomonic authorship are insuperable. Responsible scholars, such as Gleason Archer, show that to believe that Solomon wrote the book is still a live option.[2]

The Arguments for Solomonic Authorship

Since the traditional view has never been really disproved—no matter how unpopular it may be at present—we feel it is safest to maintain the Solomonic authorship.

The *indirect indications* that Solomon wrote this book include the references in 1:1, 12 to the writer as "son of David, king in Jerusalem." While "son" can refer to a later descendant, these phrases, when coupled with the direct details that dovetail with King Solomon's known biography, have real weight.

Since the writer says he "was" king, many take this as proof that the writer no longer was king. Hence, they say, it could not be Solomon, because he died as king. This is not a necessary inference. Writing in his old age it would be quite possible to refer to the distant past in this way.

The *direct historical references* in Ecclesiastes fit Solomon exactly—and really no one else.

Solomon was a king in Jerusalem: (1) of great *wisdom* (1:16); (2) of great *wealth* (2:8); (3) one who denied himself no *pleasure* (2:3); (4) one who had many *servants* (2:7); and (5) one who was noted for a great *building* and *beautification* program (2:4–6).

Jewish tradition[3] ascribes Ecclesiastes to Solomon, and centuries of Christian scholars have followed suit until fairly modern times.

This evidence, coupled with the fact that the linguistic arguments on which non-Solomonic authorship are largely based have been seriously challenged by specialists in Hebrew, makes us opt for the traditional Judeo-Christian view of authorship.

III. Date

If we accept King Solomon as the human author a date of about 930 B.C. is likely, assuming he wrote in old age when he was disillusioned with his self-seeking life.

If Solomon is rejected as "the Preacher" (*Koheleth*), then "dates assigned for the Book range over nearly a thousand years."[4]

Due to what many scholars consider "late" Hebrew (though Archer classifies it as "unique"), Ecclesiastes is generally dated in the *late post-exilic era* (c. 350–250 B.C.). Some evangelicals prefer the immediately preceding *late Persian period* (c. 450–350 B.C.).

The latest possible date for Ecclesiastes is 250–200 B.C., since the apocryphal book of Ecclesiasticus (c. 190 B.C.) definitely makes use of the book, and the Dead Sea Scrolls (late second century B.C.) contain fragments of the book.

IV. Background and Theme

Building a foundation on the Solomonic authorship of Ecclesiastes makes it easier to trace the historical background and theme of the book with some confidence.

Solomon's Search

At one time in his life, Solomon set out to find the true meaning of human existence. He was determined to discover the good life. Richly endowed with wisdom and comfortably cushioned by wealth (1 Kgs. 10:14–25; 2 Chron. 9:22–24), King Solomon thought that if anyone could find lasting satisfaction, he was the one.

But there was a self-imposed condition to Solomon's search. He was going to do this on his own. He hoped that his own intellect would enable him to discover fulfillment in life, quite apart from divine revelation. It would be the exploration of a man without any help from God. He would search "under the sun" for the greatest good in life.

Solomon's Findings

Solomon's search for meaning ended with the dismal conclusion that life is "vanity and grasping for the wind" (1:14). As far as he was able to determine, life under the sun simply wasn't worth the effort. He wasn't able to find fulfillment or lasting satisfaction. In spite of all his wealth and wisdom, he failed to discover the good life.

And of course his conclusion was right. If one never gets *above* the sun, life is an exercise in futility. It is meaningless. Everything that the world has to offer, put together, cannot satisfy the heart of man. It was Pascal who said, "There is a God-shaped vacuum in the human heart." And Augustine observed, "You have made us, O Lord, for Yourself, and our heart will find no rest until it rests in You."

Solomon's experience anticipated the truth of the words of the Lord Jesus, "Whoever drinks of this water will thirst again" (John 4:13). The water of this world cannot provide lasting satisfaction.

Solomon's search for reality was only a temporary phase, a single chapter in his biography. We do not know how old he was when he embarked on this philosophical quest for truth, but apparently he was an older man when he wrote this diary of it (1:12; 11:9). Eventually Solomon did get his sights above the sun; this seems evident from the fact that the greater part of three books of the Bible are attributed to him. However, the sin and failure which clouded the closing years of his life remind us how seriously a believer can backslide, and how imperfect even the most brilliant types[5] of the Lord Jesus are.

Solomon and God

It is obvious that Solomon believed in God, even during the time when he was searching for fulfillment. He makes no less than forty references to Him in Ecclesiastes. But this does not mean that he was a devout believer at that time. The word for "God" which he uses throughout is *Elohim*, the name which reveals Him as the Mighty Creator. Not once does he refer to God as *Jehovah* (LORD, *Yahweh*), the God who enters into covenant relationship with man.

This is an important observation. Man under the sun can know that there is a God. As Paul reminds us in Romans 1:20:

> For since the creation of the world His invisible attributes are clearly seen, being understood by the things that are made, even His eternal power and Godhead, so that they are without excuse.

The existence of God is obvious from creation. Atheism is not a mark of wisdom but of willful blindness. Solomon, the wisest man who ever lived, groping for truth with his own mind, acknowledged the fact of a Supreme Being.

But while anyone can know that there is a God (*Elohim*) who created all things, God as *Jehovah* can only be known by special revelation. So the repeated references to God (*Elohim*) in this book should not be equated with saving faith. All they prove is that creation witnesses to the existence of God, and that people who deny it are fools (Ps. 14:1; 53:1).

The Need for Ecclesiastes

The question inevitably arises, "Why did God ordain that a book which never rises above the sun should be included in the Holy Bible?"

First of all, the book was included so that no one will ever have to live through Solomon's dismal experience, searching for satisfaction where it cannot be found.

Natural man instinctively thinks he can make himself happy through possessions, pleasure, or travel on the one hand, or through drugs, liquor, or sexual indulgence on the other. But the message of this book is that someone wiser and wealthier than any of us will ever be in this life has tried and failed. So we can save ourselves all the expense, heartache, frustration, and disappointment by looking above the sun to the One who alone can satisfy—the Lord Jesus Christ.

But there is a further value to this unique book for those who are not yet ready to accept the gospel. As Dr. W. T. Davison put it:

There is no need to point at length the contrast between Ecclesiastes and Christ's Gospel. There is perhaps some need to insist on the fact that the appearance of the new Evangel has not made void or useless the Wisdom-Literature of an earlier age. It did its work in its own time, and it has work to do still. There are times in a man's history when he is not ready to sit at the feet of Jesus, and when it is better for him to go to school to Koheleth. The heart must be emptied before it can be truly filled. The modern preacher has often to enforce the lesson, not yet obsolete, nor ever to become obsolete, "Fear God and keep His commandments, for this is the whole duty of man." He must come to Christ to learn how to do this effectively, and to be taught those higher lessons for which this does but prepare the way.[6]

OUTLINE

Commentary

I. PROLOGUE: ALL IS VANITY UNDER THE SUN (1:1–11)

1:1 The author introduces himself as **the Preacher, the son of David, king in Jerusalem**. That word *Preacher* is interesting. The Hebrew equivalent is *Koheleth*, and it means "caller" or "congregator." The Greek is *ekklēsiastēs*, meaning, "one who convenes an assembly." From there it has been variously interpreted as meaning "convener, assembler, speaker, debater, spokesman, and preacher."

The Preacher was **the son of David**. While *son* here could admittedly mean a grandson or an even later descendant, the first sense probably makes the best sense. Solomon was the only descendant of David who was **king** over Israel *in Jerusalem* (v. 12). All the rest were kings over Judah. Those of other dynasties who were kings over Israel used Shechem (1 Kgs. 12:25) or Samaria (1 Kgs. 16:24), and not Jerusalem as their capital.

1:2 Solomon comes to the point right away; we don't have to wait till the last chapter. The result of all of Solomon's investigation and research under the sun is that **all is vanity**. Life is transitory, fleeting, useless, empty, and futile. It has no meaning. Nothing on this earth provides a valid goal of existence.

Is that true? Yes, it is absolutely true! If this life is all, if death draws a final curtain on human existence, then life is nothing but a vapor—unsubstantial and evanescent.

The Apostle Paul reminds us that the whole creation was subjected to vanity or futility as a result of the entrance of sin (Rom. 8:20). And it is not without significance that the first parents named their second son Abel, which means "vanity" or "vapor." Solomon is right. **All is vanity** under the sun.

1:3 Frail man's life is filled with **labor** and activity, but where does it get him when all is said and done? He is on a treadmill, a tiresome round of motion without progress. You ask him why he works, and he replies, "To get money, of course." But why

does he want money? To buy food. And why does he want food? To maintain his strength. Yes, but why does he want strength? He wants strength so he can work. And so there he is, right back where he began. He works to get money to buy food to get strength to work to get money to buy food to get strength, and so on, ad infinitum. As Henry Thoreau observed, he lives a life of quiet desperation.

Seeing a woman crying at a bus stop, a Christian asked her if he could be of any help. "Oh," she replied, "I'm just weary and bored. My husband is a hard worker, but he doesn't earn as much as I want. So I went to work. I get up early every morning, fix breakfast for our four children, pack lunches, and take a bus to my job. Then I return home for more drudgery, a few hours of sleep, and another day just like the one before. I guess I'm just sick of this endless routine."

It was H. L. Mencken who said:

> The basic fact about human experience is not that it is a tragedy, but that it is a bore. It is not that it is predominantly painful, but that it is lacking in any sense.[7]

1:4 The transience of man stands in stark contrast to the seeming permanence of his natural environment. **Generation** succeeds **generation** with irresistible momentum. This is life under the sun.

> Each one dreams that he will be enduring,
> How soon that one becomes the missing face![8]
> —*Will H. Houghton*

Apart from revelation, we might think that **the** present **earth** *will* last for-

ever. That is what Solomon concludes. But Peter tells us that the earth and the works that are upon it will be burned up in the coming Day of the Lord (2 Pet. 3:10).

1:5 Nature moves in a continuous, inexorable cycle. For instance, **the sun . . . rises** in the east, swings through the heavens to set in the west, then **hastens** around the other side of the world to rise in the east again. This seemingly endless pattern, age after age, makes man realize that he is nothing but a passing shadow.

If any are tempted to accuse Solomon of a scientific blunder for describing the sun as moving when actually it is the earth that moves in relation to the sun, they should hold their fire. He was merely using the language of human appearance. The sun *appears* to rise and set. Even scientists use this language all the time, and it is so readily understood that it should not require explanation.

1:6 Solomon continues the thought into verse 6. **The wind** patterns change with the same regularity as the seasons of the year. In the winter, the north winds sweep down over Israel to the Negev, the desert in **the south**. Then when summer comes, the south winds carry warmth on their northward flights. With almost dreary sameness, they follow this **circuit**, and then, with callous disregard for the world of men, pass off the scene.

1:7 Not only the earth, the sun, and the wind, but the water follows its same monotonous routine throughout the centuries. **All the rivers run into the sea** but never to the point where the ocean overflows, because the sun evaporates enormous quantities of water. Then as air cools, the vapor condenses and forms clouds. The clouds in turn scud across the skies and drop the water over the land areas in the form of rain, snow, or hail. And as the rivers are fed with the surplus, they bear the water back to the ocean. The ceaseless activity of nature reminds man of his own unending labor. Perhaps Kristofferson had this verse in mind when he wrote, "I'm just a river that rolled forever and never got to the sea."

1:8 Thus the life that is confined to this earth is full of weariness. Human language is inadequate to describe the monotony, boredom, and futility of it all. Man is never **satisfied**. No matter how much he sees, he still wants more. And his ears never reach the stage where they don't want to hear something new. He travels incessantly and frenetically for new sensations, new sights, new sounds. He is after what an American sociologist calls the fundamental wish for new experience. But he returns dissatisfied and jaded. Man is so constituted that all the world cannot bring lasting happiness to his heart. This does not mean that his case is hopeless. All he needs to do is get above the sun to the One who "satisfies the longing soul, and fills the hungry soul with goodness" (Ps. 107:9).

Worldly joy is fleeting—vanity itself;
Vain the dazzling brightness, vain
  the stores of wealth;
Vain the pomp and glory; only Thou
  canst give
Peace and satisfaction while on earth
  we live.
There is none, Lord Jesus, there is
  none like Thee
For the soul that thirsteth, there is
  none like Thee.[9]

—Author unknown

1:9 An additional feature of Solomon's disillusionment was the discovery that **there is nothing new under the sun**. History is constantly repeating itself. He longed for new thrills, but before long, he found everything was, in its own way, "a bad trip."

1:10 Is it true that there is nothing really **new**? Yes, in a sense. Even the most modern discoveries are developments of principles that were locked into creation at the beginning. Many of man's most boasted achievements have their counterparts in nature. Birds flew long before man did, for instance. Even space travel is not new. Enoch and Elijah were transported through space without even having to carry their own oxygen supplies with them! So those who spend their lives searching for novelties are bound to be disappointed. **It has already** happened **in ancient times**, long **before** we were born.

1:11 Another bitter pill that man has to swallow is the speed with which he forgets and is forgotten. Lasting fame is a mirage. Many of us would have great difficulty in naming our great-grandparents. And fewer, perhaps, could name the last four vice-presidents of the United States. In our self-importance, we think that the world can't get on without us; yet we die and are quickly forgotten, and life on the planet goes on as usual.

II. ALL IS VANITY (1:12—6:12)

A. The Vanity of Intellectual Pursuits (1:12–18)

1:12 So much for Solomon's conclusions. Now he is going to retrace for us the pilgrimage he made in search of the *summum bonum*—the greatest good in life. He reminds us that he **was king over Israel in Jerusalem**, with all that implies of wealth, status, and ability.

When Solomon says **I . . . was king**, he does not mean that his reign had ended. He **was king** and still is king (v. 1).

1:13 Here Solomon begins his search for happiness **under the sun**. First, he decides to travel the intellectual route. He thinks he might be happy if he could just acquire enough knowledge. So he applies himself to get the most comprehensive education possible. He devotes himself to research and exploration, synthesis and analysis, induction and deduction. But he soon becomes disenchanted with learning as an end in itself. In fact, he says that it is an unhappy business with which **God** allows men to occupy themselves—this deep inner drive to find out the meaning of life.

Malcolm Muggeridge, a contemporary sage, reached a similar conclusion:

> Education, the great mumbo-jumbo and fraud of the ages, purports to equip us to live, and is prescribed as a universal remedy for everything from juvenile delinquency to premature senility. For the most part, it only serves to enlarge stupidity, inflate conceit, enhance credulity and put those subjected to it at the mercy of brainwashers with printing presses, radio and television at their disposal.[10]

Recently someone painted this telling graffiti in bold, black letters on the wall of a university library: APATHY RULES. Someone had found what Solomon had learned centuries earlier—that education is not the sure road to fulfillment, but that, taken by itself, it can be a bore.

This does *not* mean that intellectual pursuit cannot play an important role in life. There is a place for it, but that place is at the feet of Christ. It should not be an end in itself but a means of glorifying Him.

The reference to **God** in this verse must not be equated with deep personal faith. The name of *God* is what W. J. Erdman calls His natural name—*Elohim*.[11] As mentioned in the introduction, this name presents Him as the Almighty One who created the universe. But nowhere in this book does Solomon acknowledge Him as the covenant-keeping Jehovah who shows redeeming grace to those who put their trust in Him.

1:14 There can be no doubt that Solomon got the best education that was available in Israel at that time. This is apparent from his unblushing claim to **have seen** everything that is **done under the sun**. What this means is that he became highly knowledgeable in the sciences, philosophy, history, the fine arts, the social sciences, literature, religion, psychology, ethics, languages, and other fields of human learning.

But an alphabet of degrees after his name and a room papered with diplomas didn't give him what he was seeking. On the contrary, he concluded that it was **all a grasping for** something as elusive as **the wind**.

1:15 He was frustrated to discover that book learning doesn't solve all the puzzles of life. There are **crooked** things that **cannot be made straight** and missing things that **cannot be numbered**. Robert Laurin observed:

Life is full of paradoxes and anomalies that cannot be solved; and contrariwise, it is empty of so much that could give it meaning and value.[12]

Man can fly to the moon, but the flight of a bee defies all known laws of aerodynamics. Scientists have delved into the secrets of the atom, but they cannot harness lightning or store its power. Diseases such as polio and tuberculosis have been controlled, but the common cold is still unconquered.

1:16 After he had won all his academic laurels, Solomon took personal inventory. He could boast that he had more **wisdom** than **all** those **who** had ruled **before** him **in Jerusalem** (1 Kgs. 4:29–31; 2 Chron. 1:12). His mind had absorbed an enormous fund of knowledge. And he had **wisdom** as well; he knew how to apply his **knowledge** to the practical, everyday affairs of life, to make sound judgments, and to deal judiciously with others.

1:17 Solomon reminisced about how he had disciplined himself to acquire **wisdom** on the one hand, and to learn about **madness and folly** on the other. In other words, he explored both extremes of human behavior, just in case the true meaning of life was found in either or in both. He ran the gamut of life's experiences, but his disconsolate conclusion was that it was all a **grasping for the wind**.

Centuries later, a young fellow named Henry Martyn sought and won top honors at Cambridge University. Yet in the hour of his academic triumph, he said, "I was surprised to find I had grasped a shadow." It was a blessed disillusionment for, as J. W. Jowett noted, "His eyes were now lifted far above scholastic prizes to the all-satisfying prize of the high calling of God in Christ Jesus our Lord."

1:18 If intellectualism is the key to meaning in life, then our college campuses would be Camelots of peace and contentment. But they are not. Rather they are cauldrons of ferment and unrest. The timeworn caricature of a college student, swathing his head in a turkish towel and washing down aspirin with huge mugs of coffee, fits in well with Solomon's conclusion in verse 18:

For in much wisdom is much grief, And he who increases knowledge increases sorrow.

In other words, "The wiser you are the more worries you have; the more you know, the more it hurts." According to this, there is *some* truth to the adages, "Ignorance is bliss," and "What you don't know won't hurt you."

B. The Vanity of Pleasure, Prestige, and Affluence (Chap. 2)

2:1 Having failed to find fulfillment in intellectual pursuit, Solomon turns next to the pursuit of **pleasure**. *It seems reasonable that one would be happy if one could just enjoy enough pleasure*, he thought. Pleasure, by definition, means the enjoyable sensations that come from the gratification of personal desires. So he decided that he would live it up, that he would try to experience every stimulation of the senses known to man. He would drink the cup of fun to the full, and then, at last, his heart would ask no more.

But the search ended in failure. He concludes that pleasures under the sun are **vanity**. His disappointment is echoed in the verse:

I tried the broken cisterns, Lord,
But ah, the waters failed,
E'en as I stooped to drink they fled
And mocked me as I wailed.[13]
—B. E.

Does this mean that God is opposed to His people having pleasure? Not at all! In fact the reverse is true. God wants His people to have a good life.

But He wants us to realize that this world cannot provide true pleasure. It can only be found above the sun. In His "presence is fullness of joy"; at His "right hand are pleasures forevermore" (Ps. 16:11). In that sense, God is the greatest hedonist or pleasure-lover of all!

The big lie promulgated by the movies, TV, and the advertising media is that man can make his own heaven down here without God. But Solomon learned that all this world can offer are cesspools and cisterns, whereas God offers the fountain of life.

2:2 As he thinks back on all the empty **laughter**, he sees that it was mad, and all his good times actually accomplished nothing. And so it is. Behind all the laughing there is sorrow, and those who try to entertain others are often in great need of personal help.

Billy Graham tells in *The Secret of Happiness* of the disturbed patient who consulted a psychiatrist for help. He was suffering from deep depression. Nothing he had tried could help. He woke up discouraged and blue, and the condition worsened as the day progressed. Now he was desperate; he couldn't go on this way. Before he left the office, the psychiatrist told him about a show in one of the local theaters. It featured an Italian clown who had the audience convulsed with laughter night after night. The doctor recommended that his patient attend the show, that it would be excellent therapy to laugh for a couple of hours and forget his troubles. Just go and see the Italian clown! With a hangdog expression, the patient muttered, "I am that clown." He too could say **of laughter—"Madness!"; and of mirth, "What does it accomplish?"**

How often in life we look at others

and imagine that they have no problems, no hangups, no needs. But E. A. Robinson shatters the illusion in his poem, "Richard Cory":

Whenever Richard Cory went down town,
We people on the pavement looked at him:
He was a gentleman from sole to crown,
Clean favored, and imperially slim.

And he was always quietly arrayed,
And he was always human when he talked;
But still he fluttered pulses when he said,
"Good morning," and he glittered when he walked.

And he was rich—yes, richer than a king—
And admirably schooled in every grace;
In fine, we thought that he was everything
To make us wish that we were in his place.

So on we worked, and waited for the light,
And went without the meat, and cursed the bread;
And Richard Cory, one calm summer night,
Went home and put a bullet through his head.[14]

2:3 Next Solomon, the OT prodigal, turns to **wine**. He would become a connoisseur of the choicest vintages. Perhaps if he could experience the most exquisite taste sensations, his whole being would relax satisfied.

He was wise enough to place a bound on his Epicureanism. It is expressed in the words **while guiding my heart with wisdom**. In other words, he would not abandon himself to intemperance or drunkenness. There was no thought of his becoming *addicted* to strong drink. And nowhere in his search for reality did he suggest that he became hooked on drugs. He was too wise for that!

Another thing he tried was **folly**, that is, harmless and enjoyable forms of nonsense. Just in case **wisdom** didn't hold the answer, he decided to explore its opposite. Sometimes people who are clods seem to be happier than those who are very clever. So he didn't want to leave that stone unturned. He turned his attention to trivia, indulgence, and amusement. It was a desperate ploy to discover the best way for man to occupy himself during his few fleeting **days** under the sun. But he didn't find the answer there.

2:4, 5 So Solomon decided to embark on a vast real estate program. If education, pleasure, wine, or folly didn't hold the key, then surely possessions would. He built luxurious **houses, and planted** for himself **vineyards** by the acre. From what we know of Solomon's building programs, we can be sure that he spared no expense.

He built enormous estates with parks and **gardens**—literal paradises. **Orchards** with **all kinds of fruit trees** punctuated the landscape. It's easy to imagine him taking his friends on guided tours and having his ego inflated by their expressions of awe and enthusiasm.

Probably none of his guests had the courage to say to him what Samuel Johnson said to a millionaire who was taking a similar ego trip. After seeing all the luxury and magnificence, Johnson remarked, "These are the things that make it hard for a man to die."

The world still has its share of the deluded millionaires, like the king in Andersen's tale, *The Emperor's Clothes*.

This king went on parade in what he wanted to believe were stunningly beautiful clothes, but a little child could see that he was stark naked.

2:6 Such vast estates needed irrigation during the hot, dry summers. So Solomon constructed aqueducts, lakes, and ponds, with all the necessary canals, ditches, and ducts to transport the **water**.

If the accumulation of possessions could guarantee peace and happiness, then he had arrived. But like the rest of us, he had to learn that true pleasure comes from noble renunciations rather than from frenzied accumulations. He was spending his money for what is not bread and his wages for what does not satisfy (Isa. 55:2).

2:7 Battalions of **servants** were needed to operate and maintain the king's grandiose estates, so he hired **male and female** slaves. What is more, he had slaves that were **born in** his **house**—an exceptionally important status symbol in the culture of that time.

To Solomon, as to most men, one aspect of greatness lay in being served. To sit at the table was greater than to serve. A greater than Solomon came into the world as a Slave of slaves and showed us that true greatness in His kingdom lies in servanthood (Mark 10:43–45; Luke 9:24–27).

The largest **herds and flocks** ever owned by any resident of **Jerusalem** grazed in the pastures of Solomon's ranches. If prestige was the key to a happy life, then he held the key. But it wasn't, and he didn't. Someone has said, "I asked for all things that I might enjoy life; I was given life that I might enjoy all things."

2:8 And what shall we say about his financial resources! He had **silver and gold** in abundance and the **treasure of kings and of the provinces**.

This may mean the taxes which he collected from those under him or wealth taken from conquered territories, or it may refer to objects of art which were presented to him by visiting dignitaries, such as the Queen of Sheba.

He tried music. Music has power to charm, they say. So he assembled the finest **singers**, both **male and female**. The Jerusalem News probably carried rave reviews of all the public concerts. But of course the king had private performances too—dinner music, chamber ensembles—you name it. Yet I think his disappointment was well expressed by Samuel Johnson in *The History of Rasselas, The Prince of Abyssinia*:

> I likewise can call the lutanist and the singer, but the sounds that pleased me yesterday weary me today, and will grow yet more wearisome tomorrow. I can discover within me no power of perception which is not glutted with its proper pleasure, yet I do not feel myself delighted. Man has surely some latent sense for which this place affords no gratification, or he has some desires distinct from sense which must be satisfied before he can be happy.[15]

And he tried sex. Not just wine (v. 3) and song (v. 8) but women as well. Wine, women, and song! The meaning of the word translated **musical instruments** in NKJV is actually unknown, and this rendering was chosen chiefly by context. The NASB renders the last clause "the pleasures of men—many concubines." The Bible tells us factually (though not approvingly) that Solomon had 700 wives and 300 concubines (1 Kgs. 11:3). And did he suppose this was the way to happiness? Just think of all the jealousy, gossip, and backbiting possible in such a harem!

And yet the delusion persists in our own sick society that sex is a highway to happiness and fulfillment. Within the God-appointed bounds of monogamous marriage, that can be true. But the abuse of sex leads only to misery and self-destruction.

A victim of today's sex-obsession felt afterward that she had been cheated. She wrote:

> I guess I wanted sex to be some psychedelic jackpot that made the whole world light up like a pinball machine, but when it was all over I felt I had been shortchanged. I remember thinking, "Is that all there is? Is that all there *really* is?"[16]

2:9 So Solomon **became great**. He had the satisfaction of outclimbing **all** his predecessors on the prestige ladder— for whatever that satisfaction is worth. And his natural **wisdom** still **remained with** him after all his experiments and excursions. He hadn't lost his head.

2:10 In his search for satisfaction, he had placed no limits on his expenditures. If he saw something he **desired**, he bought it. If he thought he'd enjoy some pleasure, he treated himself to it. He found a certain sense of gratification in this ceaseless round of getting things and doing things. This fleeting joy was all the **reward** he got for his exertions in pursuing pleasure and possessions.

2:11 **Then** he took stock of all that he had done, and of all the energy he had expended, and what was the result? **All was vanity** and futility, a **grasping for the wind**. He hadn't found lasting satisfaction under the sun. He found, like Luther, that "the empire of the whole world is but a crust to be thrown to a dog." He was bored by it all.

Ralph Barton, a top cartoonist, was bored too. He wrote:

> I have few difficulties, many friends, great successes. I have gone from wife to wife, from house to house, and have visited great countries of the world. But I am fed up with devices to fill up twenty-four hours of the day.[17]

The failure of pleasure and possessions to fill the heart of man was further illustrated by a fictional character who only had to wish for something and he got it instantly:

> He wanted a house and there it was with servants at the door; he wanted a Cadillac, and there it was with chauffeur. He was elated at the beginning, but it soon began to pall on him. He said to an attendant, "I want to get out of this. I want to create something, to suffer something. I would rather be in hell than here." And the attendant answered, "Where do you think you are?"[18]

That is where our contemporary society is—in a hell of materialism, trying to satisfy the human heart with things that cannot bring lasting enjoyment.

2:12 Because of the disheartening outcome of all his research, Solomon began **to consider** whether it's better to be a wise man or a fool. He decided to look into the matter. Since life is such a chase after bubbles, does the man who lives prudently have any advantage over the one who goes to the other extreme, having a good time in **madness and folly**?

Being an absolute monarch, and a wise and wealthy one at that, he was in a good position to find out. If he couldn't find out, what chance did anyone succeeding him have? Anyone **who succeeds the king** could scarcely discover any new light on the subject.

2:13 His general conclusion was that **wisdom** is better than **folly** to the same degree that **light excels darkness**. The wise man walks in the light and can see the dangers in the way. The fool, on the other hand, gropes along in darkness and falls into every ditch and trap.

2:14 But even granting that advantage—that **the wise man's eyes** can see where he's going—what final difference does it make? They both die eventually and no amount of wisdom can delay or cancel that appointment. It is the lot of **them all**.

2:15 When Solomon realized that the same fate was awaiting him as awaited **the fool**, he wondered why he had put such a premium on being **wise** all his life. The only redeeming feature of wisdom is that it sheds light on the way. Apart from that, it is no better. And so the pursuit of wisdom is also a great waste of effort.

2:16, 17 He continues this idea into verses 16 and 17. After the funeral, both the wise man and the fool are quickly forgotten. Within a generation or two, it is as if they had never lived. The names and faces that seem so important today will fade into oblivion. As far as lasting fame is concerned, **the wise** man is no better off than **the fool**.

The chilling realization that fame is ephemeral and that man is quickly **forgotten** made Solomon hate **life**. Instead of finding satisfaction and fulfillment in human activity under the sun, he found only grief. It troubled him to realize that everything was **vanity and grasping for the wind**.

A former athlete who had achieved fame said:

The greatest thrill of my life was when I first scored the decisive goal in a big game and heard the roar of the cheering crowds. But in the quiet of my room that same night, a sense of the futility of it swept over me. After all, what was it worth? Was there nothing better to live for than to score goals? Such thoughts were the beginning of my search for satisfaction. I knew in my heart that no one could meet my need but God Himself. Soon after, I found in Christ what I could never find in the world.[19]

2:18 One of the greatest injustices that bothered Solomon was that he would not be permitted to enjoy the wealth which he had accumulated. C. E. Stuart wrote:

Death is a worm at the root of the tree of pleasure. It mars pleasure, it chills enjoyment, for it cuts off man just when he would sit down after years of toil to reap the fruit of his labor.[20]

And he has to **leave it** all to his heir.

2:19 The galling thing is that the heir may not **be wise**. He may be a spendthrift, a dummy, a playboy, a loafer, but he will inherit the estate nevertheless. He will preside over the dissipation of a fortune for which he neither labored nor planned.

This really nettled Solomon. Perhaps he had a premonition that it would happen in his own family. Perhaps Solomon foresaw that his son, Rehoboam, would squander by his folly all that he had **toiled** so hard to accumulate. History tells us that Rehoboam did just that. By refusing to listen to his older counselors, he precipitated the division of the kingdom. When the Egyptians invaded Judah, he bought them off by giving them the temple treasures. The gold shields went to swell the coffers of Egypt, and Rehoboam had to substitute brass shields in their place (see 2 Chron. 12:9–10).

2:20 The prospect of having to leave his life's work and wealth to an unworthy successor plunged the Preacher into gloom and depression. It seemed so senseless and incongruous. It made him feel that all his efforts were for nothing.

2:21 The whole idea distressed him, that a man who builds up financial resources through wise investments, shrewd business decisions, and skillful moves is forced at death to leave it to someone who never did a lick of work for it or expended an ounce of worry. What is this but an absurdity **and a great** calamity?

In spite of Solomon's finding, parents throughout the world still spend the best part of their lives accumulating wealth that will be left to their children. They altruistically describe it as their moral obligation. But Jamieson, Fausset, and Brown suggest, "Selfishness is mostly at the root of worldly parents' alleged providence for their children."[21] Their first thought is to provide luxuriously for their own old age. They are thinking primarily of themselves. That their children inherit what is left is only the result of the parents' death and the laws of inheritance.

From the Christian perspective, there is no reason for parents to work, scrimp, save, and sacrifice in order to leave money to their children. The best heritage to bequeath is spiritual, not financial. Money left in wills has often caused serious jealousy and disunity in otherwise happy and compatible families. Children have been ruined spiritually and morally by suddenly becoming inheritors of large

bequests. Other evils almost inevitably follow.

The spiritual approach is to put our money to work for God *now* and not to leave it to children who are sometimes unworthy, ungrateful, and even unsaved. Martin Luther felt he could trust his family to God as he had trusted himself. In his last will and testament he wrote:

> Lord God, I thank You, because You have been pleased to make me a poor and indigent man upon earth. I have neither house nor land nor money to leave behind me. You have given me wife and children, whom I now restore to You. Lord, nourish, teach and preserve them, as You have me.

2:22 Solomon concludes that **man** has nothing of enduring value as a result of **all his labor** and heartache **under the sun**. He strives, he plods, he frets and fumes—but for what? What difference does it all make five minutes after he dies?

Apart from revelation, we would come to the same conclusion. But we know from God's Word that our lives can be lived for God and for eternity. We know that all that is done for Him will be rewarded. Our labor is not in vain in the Lord (1 Cor. 15:58).

2:23 For the man who has no hope beyond the grave, however, it is true that his days are filled with pain and vexatious **work**, and his nights with tossing and turning. Life is a king-sized frustration, filled with worry and heartache.

2:24 This being the case, a logical philosophy of life for the man whose whole existence is under the sun is to find enjoyment in eating, drinking, and **in his labor**. The Preacher is not advocating gluttony and drunkenness but rather finding pleasure wherever possible in the common things of life.

Even this is **from the hand of God**—that men should enjoy the normal mercies of life, the taste of good food, the refreshment of table beverages, and the satisfaction that comes from honest work. Man does not have the power of enjoyment unless it is given to him by **God**.

A later preacher, the Apostle Paul, confirmed Solomon's outlook. He said that if there is no resurrection of the dead then the best policy is, "Let us eat and drink, for tomorrow we die!" (1 Cor. 15:32).

Solomon adds that the ability to eat and find enjoyment in other ways comes from **God**. Without Him, we cannot enjoy the most ordinary pleasures. We depend on Him for food, appetite, digestion, sight, hearing, smell, memory, health, sanity, and all that makes for normal, pleasurable experiences.

2:25 In verse 25, he adds that he was able to enjoy all these things more than anyone.

John D. Rockefeller had an income of about a million dollars a week, yet all his doctors allowed him to eat cost only a few cents. One of his biographers said that he lived on a diet that a pauper would have despised:

> Now less than a hundred pounds in weight, he sampled everything (at breakfast): a drop of coffee, a spoonful of cereal, a forkful of egg, and a bit of chop the size of a pea.[22]

He was the richest man in the world but did not have the ability to enjoy his food.

2:26 Finally, the Preacher felt that he observed a general principle in life that God rewards righteousness and punishes sin. **To a man** who pleases Him, **God gives wisdom and knowledge and joy. But to the** habitual **sinner, He gives the** burden of hard **work**, accumulating and piling up, only to see it taken over by someone who strikes God's fancy. What could be more fruitless and defeating than that?

C. The Vanity of the Cycle of Life and Death (Chap. 3)

3:1 As a research student of life and of human behavior, Solomon observed that there is a predetermined **season** for **everything** and a fixed **time** for **every** happening. This means that God has programmed every activity into a gigantic computer, and, as Hispanics say, *"Que será, será"*: What will be, will be! It also means that history is filled with cyclical patterns, and these recur with unchangeable regularity. So man is locked into a pattern of behavior which is determined by certain inflexible laws or principles. He is a slave to fatalism's clock and calendar.

In verses 1–8, the Preacher enumerates twenty-eight activities which are probably intended to symbolize the whole round of life. This is suggested by the number twenty-eight, which is the number of the world (four) multiplied by the number of completeness (seven).

The list is made up of opposites. Fourteen are positives and fourteen negatives. In some ways, they seem to cancel out each other so that the net result is zero.

3:2 There is **a time to be born**. The person himself has no control over this, and even the parents must wait out the nine months which form the normal birth cycle.

There is also **a time to die**. Man's allotted span is seventy years, according to Psalm 90:10, but even apart from that, it seems that death is a predetermined appointment that must be kept.

It is true that God foreknows the terminus of our life on earth, but for the Christian this is neither morbid nor fatalistic. We know that we are immortal until our work is done. And though death is a possibility, it is not a certainty. The blessed hope of Christ's return inspires the believer to look for the Savior rather than the mortician. As the preacher Peter Pell put it so colorfully, "I'm not waiting for the *undertaker*—I'm waiting for the *upper-taker!*"

A time to plant, and a time to pluck what is planted. With these words, Solomon seems to cover the entire field of agriculture, linked closely as it is with the seasons of the year (Gen. 8:22). Failure to observe these seasons in planting and harvesting can only spell disaster.

3:3 A time to kill, and a time to heal. Bible commentators go to great lengths to explain that this cannot refer to murder but only to warfare, capital punishment, or self-defense. But we must remember that Solomon's observations were based on his knowledge under the sun. Without divine revelation, it seemed to him that life was either a slaughterhouse or a hospital, a battlefield or a first-aid station.

A time to break down, and a time to build up. First the wrecking crew appears to demolish buildings that are outdated and no longer serviceable, then the builders move in to erect modern complexes and rehabilitate the area of blight.

3:4 A time to weep, and a time to laugh. Life seems to alternate between tragedy and comedy. Now it wears the black mask of the tragedian, then the painted face of the clown.

A time to mourn, and a time to dance. The funeral procession passes by with its mourners wailing in grief. But before long, these same people are dancing at a wedding reception, quickly removed from their recent sorrow.

3:5 A time to cast away stones, and a time to gather stones. Taken at face value, this means that there is a time to clear land for cultivation (Isa. 5:2), then to gather the stones for building houses, walls, or other projects. If we take the words figuratively, as most modern commentators do, there may be a reference to the marriage act. Thus, TEV paraphrases, "The time for having sex and the time for not having it."

A time to embrace, and a time to refrain from embracing. In the realm of the affections, there is a time for involvement and a time for withdrawal. There is a time when love is pure and a time when it is illicit.

3:6 A time to gain, and a time to lose. This makes us think of business cycles with their fluctuating profits and losses. First the markets are bullish with income soaring. Then they become bearish, and companies find themselves in the red.

A time to keep, and a time to throw away. Most housewives are familiar with this curious pattern. For months or even years, they stash things away in closets, basements, and attics. Then in a burst of house-cleaning zeal, they clear them out and call some local charity to cart the gathered items away.

3:7 A time to tear, and a time to sew. Could Solomon have been thinking of the constant changes in clothing fashions? Some noted fashion designer dictates a new trend, and all over the world, hems are let out or shortened. Today the fashions are daring and attention-getting. Tomorrow they revert to the quaint styles of grandmother's day.

A time to keep silence, and a time to speak. The **time to keep silence** is when we are criticized unjustly, when we are tempted to criticize others, or to say things that are untrue, unkind, or unedifying. Because Moses spoke unadvisedly with his lips, he was barred from entering the promised land (Num. 20:10; Ps. 106:33).

The **time to speak** is when some great principle or cause is at stake. Mordecai advised Esther that the **time** had come for her **to speak** (Est. 4:13–14). And he could have added, with Dante, "The hottest places in hell are reserved for those who remain neutral in a time of great moral crisis."

3:8 **A time to love, and a time to hate.** We must not try to force these words into a Christian context. Solomon was not speaking as a Christian but as a man of the world. It seemed to him that human behavior fluctuated between periods of **love** and periods of **hate**.

A time of war, and a time of peace. What is history if it is not the record of cruel, mindless wars, interspersed with short terms **of peace**?

3:9 The question lingering in Solomon's mind was, "**What** lasting gain **has the worker** for all his toil?" For every constructive activity there is a destructive one. For every plus a minus. The fourteen positive works are cancelled out by fourteen negatives. So the mathematical formula of life is fourteen minus fourteen equals zero. Man has nothing but a zero at the end of it all.

3:10 Solomon had conducted an exhaustive survey of all the activities, employments, and pursuits that God has given to man to occupy his time. He has just given us a catalog of these in verses 2–8.

3:11 He concluded that God **has made everything beautiful in its time**, or, better, that there is an appropriate time for each activity. He is not so much thinking here of the beauty of God's creation as the fact that every action has its own designated time, and that in its time it is eminently fitting.

Also God **has put eternity** in man's mind. Though living in a world of time, man has intimations of **eternity**. Instinctively he thinks of "forever," and though he cannot understand the concept, he realizes that beyond this life there is the possibility of a shoreless ocean of time.

Yet God's works and ways are inscrutable to man. There is no way in which we can solve the riddle of creation, providence, or the consummation of the universe, apart from revelation. In spite of the enormous advances of human knowledge, we still see through a glass darkly. Very often we have to confess with a sigh, "How little we know of Him!"

3:12 Because man's life is governed by certain inexorable laws and because all his activities seem to leave him where he started, Solomon decides that the best policy is to be happy and enjoy life as much as possible.

3:13 He did not mean that life should be an orgy of drunkenness, dissipation, and debauchery, but that **it is the gift of God** for man to enjoy his food and drink and find what pleasure he can in his daily work. It is a low view of life, and completely sub-Christian in its outlook, but we must continually remember that Solomon's viewpoint here was thoroughly earthbound.

3:14 He did accurately perceive that God's decrees are immutable. What God has decided will stand and man cannot alter it, either by addition or subtraction. It is foolish for creatures to fight against the arrangements of their Creator. Much better to respect Him and submit to His control.

3:15 Current events are merely a replay of what has happened previously, and nothing will happen in the future but what **has already been**. God arranges everything on a recurring basis so that things will happen over and over again. He brings back again what is past and thus history repeats itself. The expression **"God requires an account of what is past"** is often used to press home the fact that past sins must be accounted for by unbelievers. While this is true, it is hardly the force of this passage. Here God is rather seen as recalling past events to form another cycle of history. R. C. Sproul calls it the theme of eternal recurrence. "This idea maintains that in infinite time, there are periodic cycles in which all that has been is repeated over again. The drama of human life is a play with one encore after another."[23]

3:16 Among other things that pained the Preacher were injustice and **wickedness**. He found crookedness in the law courts where justice should be dispensed and dishonesty in government circles where **righteousness** should be practiced.

3:17 These inequalities of life led him to believe that there has to be **a time** when God will **judge** men, when the wrongs of earth will be made right. Solomon does not say explicitly that this will be in the next life, but it is a foregone conclusion since so many inequities are unrequited in this world. His conclusion mirrors a common emotion in the hearts of righteous people. Decency and fairness demand a time when accounts are settled and when the right is vindicated.

3:18 In the closing verses of chapter 3, the Preacher turns to the subject of death, and sees it as the grim spoilsport, ending all man's best ambitions, endeavors, and pleasures. He views it exactly as we would if we did not have the Bible to enlighten us.

Notice that he introduces his views with the words, **"I said in my heart."** It is not a question of what God revealed to him but of what he concluded in his own mind. It is his own reasoning under the sun. Therefore, this is not a passage from which we can build an adequate doctrine of death and the hereafter. And yet this is precisely what many of the false cults have done. They use these verses to support their erroneous teachings of soul-sleep and the annihilation of the wicked dead. Actually a careful study of the passage will show that Solomon was not advocating either of these views.

Basically what he is saying is that **God tests** man through his short life on earth to show him how frail and transient he is—just **like animals**. But is he saying that man is no better than an animal?

3:19 No, the point is not that man is an animal, but that in *one respect*, he has no advantage over an animal. As death comes **to animals**, so it comes to man. **All have one breath**, and at the time of death, that breath is cut off. So life is as empty for man as for the lower orders of creation.

3:20 **All** share a common end in the grave. They are both going to the same place—the **dust**. They both came from it; they will both go back to it. Of course, this assumes that the body is all there is to human life. But we know that this is not true. The body is only the tent in which the person lives. But Solomon could not be expected to know the full truth of the future state.

3:21 Solomon's ignorance as to what happens at the time of death is evident from his question, **"Who knows the spirit of the sons of men, which goes upward, and the spirit of the animal, which goes down to the earth?"** This must not be taken as a doctrinal fact. It is human questioning, not divine certainty.

From the NT, we know that the spirit and soul of the believer go to be with Christ at the time of death (2 Cor. 5:8; Phil. 1:23), and his body goes to the grave (Acts 8:2). The spirit and soul of the unbeliever go to Hades, and his body goes to the grave (Luke 16:22b–23). When Christ comes into the air, the bodies of those who have died in faith will be raised in glorified form and reunited with the spirit and soul (Phil. 3:20–21; 1 Thess. 4:16–17). The bodies of the unbelieving dead will be raised at the Great White Throne Judgment, reunited with the spirit and soul, then cast into the lake of fire (Rev. 20:12–14).

Strictly speaking, animals have body and soul but no spirit.[24] Nothing is said in the Bible concerning life after death for animals.

3:22 From what he knew about death, and also from what he didn't know, Solomon figures that the best thing a man can do is enjoy his daily activities. That, after all, is his lot in life, and he might as well cooperate with the inevitable. He should find satisfaction in accepting what cannot be changed. But above all, he should enjoy life as it comes to him, because no one can tell him what **will happen** on earth **after** he has passed on.

D. The Vanity of Life's Inequalities (Chap. 4)

4:1 Robert Burns said, "Man's inhumanity to man makes countless thousands mourn!" Sensitive hearts in every age have been grieved to see the **oppression** that is carried out by men against their fellowmen. It tormented Solomon also. He was grieved to see **the tears of the oppressed**, the **power** of **their oppressors**, and the failure of anyone to defend the downtrodden. **Power** was **on the side of** the **oppressors**, and no one dared to defy that power. From this vantage point, it seemed that "Truth [was] forever on the scaffold, Wrong forever on the throne." He could not see that "behind the dim unknown, standeth God within the shadow, keeping watch above His own."[25]

4:2 So in his dejection, he concluded that **the dead** are better off **than the living**. To him, death provided welcome escape from all the persecutions and cruelties of this life. He was not concerned at the moment with the deeper implications of death— that a person who dies in unbelief is doomed to more severe suffering than the worst oppression on earth. For him the question was not, "Is there life after death?", but rather, "Is there life after birth?"

4:3 Solomon's cynicism touched bottom with the observation that though the dead are better off than the living, the unborn are still more enviable. They have never lived to be driven mad by oppressions **under the sun**. They have never had to endure "that ghastly mockery of happiness called life."

4:4 There was something else that drove him up the wall—the fact that human activity and skill are motivated by the desire to outdo one's

neighbor. He saw that the wheel of life was propelled by the competitive spirit. The desire to have better clothes and a more luxurious home—it all seemed so empty and unworthy of men created in God's image and after His likeness.

When Michelangelo and Raphael were commissioned to use their artistic talents for the adornment of the Vatican, a deep spirit of rivalry broke out between them. "Although each had a different job to do, they became so jealous that at last they would not even speak to one another."[26] Some are more adept at concealing their envy than these geniuses were, but this same attitude of rivalry is at the bottom of much contemporary activity.

A modern cynic has written, "I've tried everything that life has to offer, but all I see is one guy trying to outdo another in a futile attempt at happiness."[27]

4:5 In contrast to the one whose motive and reward is envy is **the fool**—the dull, stupid sluggard. He **folds his hands** and lives off what little food he can get without much exertion. Perhaps he is wiser than his neighbors who are driven relentlessly on by their envy and covetousness.

4:6 While those around him are working themselves into a frenzy of competition, the fool's sentiments are: **Better a handful with quietness than both hands full, together with toil and grasping for the wind.** Or as H. C. Leupold paraphrases it, "Rather would I have my ease, though I possess but little, than acquire more and have all the vexation that goes with it."

4:7, 8 There was another kind of folly which blew the Preacher's mind. It was the mindless craze of the man who is alone, to keep working and accumulating wealth. **He has neither son nor brother,** no close relatives. He already has more money than he will ever need. Yet he wears himself out day after day and denies himself the simple amenities of life. It never occurs to him to ask, **"For whom do I toil and deprive myself of good?"** Charles Bridges in his exposition comments, "The miser—how well he deserves the name—the wretched slave of mammon, grown old as a toiling, scraping, griping drudge!" His name is miser and as his name, so is he— miserable. What an empty, wretched way to live, thought Solomon!

Surely Samuel Johnson was right when he said, "The lust for gold, unfeeling and remorseless, is the last corruption of degenerate man."

4:9 The solitariness of the miser leads Solomon to point out the advantages of fellowship and partnership. He uses four illustrations to press home his thesis. First of all, **two** workers are **better than one**, because by cooperation they can produce more efficiently.

4:10 Also if there is an accident on the job, one can help **his companion.** But pity the man who falls off the ladder when he is alone. There is no one around to call for help.

4:11 Two in a bed on a cold night are better than one because they help to keep each other **warm.** We could shoot holes in his argument by mentioning the annoyance caused by the partner who has cold feet or who hogs the covers, or the superior controlled heat that comes from the electric blanket. But the point remains that there are pleasures and benefits from friendship and socializing that are unknowable to the one who lives in isolation.

4:12 The third illustration has to do with protection against attack. A thief can often overpower one victim, but two can usually resist the intruder successfully.

Finally, a rope made with three cords is stronger than a rope with only one or two strands. In fact, three strands twisted together are more than three times as strong as three separate strands.

4:13–16 The follies and vanities of life are not confined to the peons; they are even found in the palaces of kings. Solomon describes **a king** who overcame poverty and a prison record in his rise to the throne; yet now when he is old, he is intractable. He will not listen to his advisers. It would be better to have a young man who is teachable, even though **poor**, to reign in his place. Solomon thought about **all the people** who are subjects of the **king** and about the young man who is second in the chain of command— the heir apparent. Multitudes flock to his banner. They are tired of the **old** ruler and want a change, hoping for a better administration. **Yet** even **those who come afterward will not** be happy with **him**.

This fickleness and craving for novelty made Solomon realize that even the world's highest honors are **vanity**. They too are like **grasping for the wind**.

E. The Vanity of Popular Religion and Politics (5:1–9)

Man is instinctively religious, but that is not necessarily good. In fact, it may be positively bad. His very religiosity may hide from him his need of salvation as a free gift of God's grace. In addition, man's own religion may be nothing more than a charade, an outward show without inward reality. Vanity may seep into religious life just as much as in any other sphere, maybe even more so. So, in chapter

5, Solomon lays down some advice to guard against formalism and externalism in dealing with the Creator.

5:1 First, he advises people to watch their steps **when** they **go to the house of God**. While this may refer to reverence in general, here it is explained to mean being more ready to learn than to engage in a lot of rash talk. Rash promises are the sacrifice of fools. Unthinking people make them without considering that it is **evil**.

5:2 Worshipers should avoid recklessness in prayers, promises, or in professions of devotion to **God**. The presence of the Almighty is no place for precipitate or compulsive talking. The fact that **God is** infinitely high above man, as **heaven** is high above the **earth**, should teach man to curb his speech when drawing near to Him.

5:3 Just as a hyperactive mind often produces wild dreams, so a hyperactive mouth produces a torrent of foolish words, even in a prayer. Alexander Pope wrote that "Words are like leaves, and where they most abound, much fruit of sense beneath is rarely found."

Solomon did not intend verse 3 to be a full, scientific explanation of the origin of dreams; he was merely pointing out what seemed to him to be a connection between the whirring wheels of his mind during the day and the restless dreams that often followed at night.

5:4 In the matter of vows **to God**, simple honesty demands that they be paid promptly. God has no use for the dolt who talks up a storm, then fails to deliver. So the word is, **"Pay what you have vowed."**

5:5 If you don't intend to **pay**, don't **vow** in the first place.

How well the Preacher knew man's propensity to strike a bargain with

God when caught in a tight, desperate situation: "Lord, if you get me out of this, I'll serve you forever." But then the tendency is to forget quickly when the crisis is past.

Even in moments of spiritual exhilaration, it is easy to make a vow of dedication, or celibacy, or poverty, or the like. God has never required such vows of His people. In many cases, such as in the matter of celibacy, it would be better not to make them anyway. But where they are made, they should be kept. Certainly the marriage vow is ratified in heaven and cannot be broken without costly consequences. Vows made before conversion should be kept, except in those cases where they violate the Word of God.

5:6 So the general rule is **not** to **let your mouth** lead you into **sin** through shattered vows. And don't try to excuse yourself before God's **messenger** by saying it was **an error** and that you didn't really mean it. Or don't think that the mechanical offering of a sacrifice before Him will atone for careless breaking of vows.

The messenger of God may refer to the priest, since broken vows were to be confessed before him (Lev. 5:4–6). But this presupposes a knowledge of the Mosaic law, whereas Solomon is speaking here apart from revealed religion. So perhaps we are safer to understand him as meaning anyone who serves as a representative **of God**.

The basic thought is that God is exceedingly displeased by insincerity of speech. Why then say things that are certain to anger Him? This will inevitably cause Him to obstruct, frustrate, and **destroy** everything you try to do.

5:7 Just as there is tremendous unreality **in a multitude of dreams**, so in words spoken unadvisedly there is **vanity** and ruin. The thing to do, says Solomon, is to **fear God**. However, he does not mean the loving trust of Jehovah but the actual fear of incurring the displeasure of the Almighty. G. Campbell Morgan reminds us that this is the fear of a slave, not a son. Unless we see this, we give Solomon credit for a greater burst of spiritual insight than is intended here.

5:8 Next Solomon reverts to the subject of **oppression of the poor** and **perversion of justice**. He counsels against complete despair if we see these evils **in a province**. After all, there are chains of command in government, and those in the higher echelons watch their subordinates with an eagle eye.

But do they really? Too often the system of checks and balances breaks down, and every level of officialdom receives its share of graft and payola.

The only satisfaction that righteous people have is in knowing that God is higher than the highest authorities, and He will see that all accounts are settled some day. But it is doubtful if Solomon refers to this here.

5:9 Verse 9 is one of the most obscure verses in Ecclesiastes. The reason is that the original Hebrew is uncertain. This can be seen from the wide variety of translations:

JND: Moreover the earth is every way profitable: the king (himself) is dependent on the field.

NASB: After all, a king who cultivates the field is an advantage to the land.

TEV: Even a king depends on the harvest.

NKJV: **Moreover the profit of the land is for all; even the king is served from the field.**

The general thought seems to be that even the highest official is dependent on the produce of the field and thus on the providence of God. All are accountable to God.

F. The Vanity of Passing Riches (5:10—6:12)

5:10 People who love money are never **satisfied**; they always want more. Wealth does not buy contentment. Profits, dividends, interest payments, and capital gains whet the appetite for more. It all appears rather empty.

5:11 **When** a man's possessions **increase**, it seems that there is a corresponding increase in the number of parasites who live off his wealth, whether management consultants, tax advisers, accountants, lawyers, household employees, or sponging relatives.

A man can wear only one suit at a time, can only eat so much in a day. So the main benefit of his wealth is to be able to look at his bank books, stocks, and bonds, and to say with other rich fools, "Soul, you have many goods laid up for many years to come; take your ease, eat, drink and be merry" (Luke 12:19).

5:12 When it comes to sound **sleep, a laboring man** has the advantage. Whether he has had a banquet or a snack, he can rest without care or apprehension. Across town, **the rich** man is having a fitful night worrying about the stock market, wondering about thefts and embezzlements, and swallowing antacid to calm the churning sea of dyspepsia that is in his stomach.

5:13 Solomon saw that hoarding **riches** gives rise to disastrous consequences. Here is a man who had vast reserves of wealth, but instead of using them for constructive purposes, he kept them stashed away.

5:14 All of a sudden, there was some calamity such as a market crash, and the money was all gone. Even though the man had **a son**, he had **nothing** to leave to him. He was penniless.

5:15 Empty-handed he had come **from his mother's womb**, and now empty-handed he leaves this world. In spite of all the money he had been able to accumulate during his lifetime, he dies a pauper.

Cecil Rhodes spent years exploiting the natural resources of South Africa. When he was about to die, he cried out in remorse:

> I've found much in Africa. Diamonds, gold and land are mine, but now I must leave them all behind. Not a thing I've gained can be taken with me. I have not sought eternal treasures, therefore I actually have nothing at all.[28]

5:16 Solomon says **this is a severe evil**—a painful calamity—he could have used his money for lasting benefit. Instead of that he leaves as empty as he came, with nothing to show for all his work. He **has labored for the wind**.

5:17 The tragedy is compounded by the fact that the closing days of this man's life are filled with gloom, **sorrow**, worry, **sickness, and anger**. His life has been a reverse Cinderella story—from riches to rags.

Of course, there is a sense in which every man who dies leaves everything. But here the Preacher seems to point up the folly of hoarding money when it could be put to useful purposes, then losing it all, and having nothing to show for a lifetime of work.

5:18 So the best strategy is to enjoy the common activities of daily life—eating, drinking, and working.

Then no matter what happens, nothing can rob one of the pleasures he has already had. **Life** at best is very brief, so why not **enjoy** it while you can?

5:19 Solomon thought that it was ideal when God **gave** a man **riches and wealth** and when at the same time He also gave him the ability to enjoy them, to be satisfied with his lot in life, and to enjoy his work. This combination of circumstances was a special **gift of God**, or as we might say, this was "the real thing."

5:20 Such a man doesn't brood over the shortness **of his life** or its tragedies and inequities because **God keeps** his mind occupied **with the joy of his** present circumstances.

6:1, 2 There is a cruel irony in life that lays a heavy burden on men. It concerns **a man to whom God has given** everything that his heart could desire in the way of **riches and wealth and honor**, but unfortunately **God does not give him the** capacity to enjoy these things. Notice that Solomon blames **God** for depriving him of the enjoyment of his wealth.

Then premature death robs this man of the power to enjoy his riches. He leaves it all to a stranger, not even to a son or a close relative. This certainly makes life look like an empty bubble or a malignant disease.

6:3 Even **if a man** has a big family and lives to a ripe, old age, these superlative mercies mean nothing if he can't enjoy life or if he doesn't have a decent **burial** at the end. In fact, **a stillborn child** is more to be envied than he.

6:4 The untimely birth **comes in vanity and departs in** anonymity. His name is covered in the obscurity of one who was never born and who never died.

6:5 Though the stillborn child never sees **the sun** or gets to know anything, nevertheless he enjoys **more rest** than the miser. He never experiences the maddening perversities of life.

6:6 Even if the miser should live **a thousand years twice** over, what good is it if he **has not** been able to enjoy the good things of life? He shares the same fate as the stillborn child by going to the grave.

6:7 A man's main reason for working is to buy food for himself and his family. But the odd thing is that he is never **satisfied**. The more his income rises, the more he wants to buy. Contentment is the carrot on the stick that forever eludes him.

6:8 So in this futile quest, **the wise man** doesn't have any advantage over **the fool**. And even if a poor man knows how to face life better than the rest of the people, he isn't any further ahead.

6:9 It is far **better** to be content with the meals that are set before one than to be always craving for something additional. This business of always lusting for more is as foolish as **grasping for the wind**. As Leupold said, it's like "lustful straying about from one thing to another in quest of true satisfaction."[29]

6:10, 11 **Whatever one is**, rich or poor, wise or foolish, old or young, **he has already** been given the name of **man**. *Man* here represents the Hebrew word *adam* and means "red clay." How can red clay dispute with the Creator?

6:12 The simple fact, according to the Preacher, is that no one **knows** what is best for him in this **vain life** of shadows. And no one knows **what will happen** on the earth **after** he is gone.

III. ADVICE FOR LIFE UNDER THE SUN (7:1—12:8)

A. The Good and the Better Under the Sun (Chap. 7)

7:1 The sour note at the end of chapter 6 was that man cannot determine what is best for him under the sun. But Solomon does have ideas as to some things that are good and others that are better. That is his subject in chapter 7. In fact, the words *good* and *better* together occur here more times than in any other chapter in the OT.

First, **a good name is better than precious ointment. A good name**, of course, signifies **a good** *character*. **Precious ointment** represents what is costly and fragrant. The thought is that the most expensive perfume can never take the place of an honorable life.

The Preacher says **the day of death is better than the day of one's birth**. This is one of his statements that leaves us guessing. Did he mean this as a general axiom, or was he referring only to a man with **a good name**? When applied to true believers, the observation is quite true. But it is certainly not true of those who die with sins unconfessed and unforgiven.

7:2 Next Solomon decides that it is **better to go to** a funeral parlor than gorge oneself at a banquet. Death **is the end of all men**, and when we come face to face with it, we are brought up short and forced to think about our own departure.

Every thinking person must take into account the fact of death and should have a philosophy of life which enables him or her to confidently face that inevitable appointment. The gospel tells of the Savior, who, through death, destroyed him who has the power of death, that is, the devil, and who delivers all those who, through fear of death, are subject to lifelong bondage (Heb. 2:14–15).

7:3 Another "better": **sorrow is better than laughter**. The Preacher was convinced that seriousness accomplishes more than levity. It sharpens the mind to grapple with the great issues of life, whereas frivolity wastes time and prevents people from coming to grips with what is important.

I walked a mile with Pleasure;
She chattered all the way,
But left me none the wiser
For all she had to say

I walked a mile with Sorrow,
And not a word said she;
But oh, the things I learned from her
When Sorrow walked with me!
—*Robert Browning Hamilton*

For by a sad countenance the heart is made better. It is one of the paradoxes of life that joy can coexist with sorrow. Even heathen philosophers have attributed a therapeutic value to suffering and sadness. But what is only moderately true for the unbeliever is more gloriously true for the child of God. Sorrows and sufferings here are the means of developing graces in his life. They give him a new appreciation of the sufferings of Christ. They enable him to comfort others who are experiencing similar trials. And they are a pledge of future glory (Rom. 8:17).

7:4 The mind of a **wise** person maintains poise and serenity in the presence of death. He can cope with sorrow and pressure because his roots are deep. **Fools** can't stand to face serious crises. They try to drown out the sounds of life as it is with laughter and gaiety. They avoid contact with hospitals and mortuaries because their shallow resources do not equip them to stand up under the pressures of life.

7:5 There is something else that is *better*. **It is better to hear the rebuke of the wise than for a man to hear the song of fools.** Constructive criticism instructs, corrects, and warns. The empty mirth of fools accomplishes nothing of lasting value.

7:6 The laughter of the fool is **like the crackling of thorns under a pot**—showy and noisy but not productive. Burning thorns may snap, crackle, and pop, but they do not make a good fuel. Little heat is generated, and the fire goes out quickly. It is noise without effectiveness, froth without body.

7:7 Even **a wise** person acts foolishly when he becomes a cheating oppressor. He becomes power-mad and loses his sense of balance and restraint. And all those who indulge in bribery and graft corrupt their own minds. Once they stoop to accept payola, they lose the power to make unprejudiced judgments.

7:8 It seemed to Solomon **that the end of a thing is better than its beginning**. Perhaps he was thinking of the tremendous inertia that must often be overcome to begin a project and of the drudgery and discipline that go into its early stages. Then by contrast there is the sense of achievement and satisfaction that accompanies its completion.

But it doesn't take much insight to realize that the rule does not always hold. The end of *righteous* deeds is better than the beginning, but the end of sin is worse. The latter days of Job were **better than** the **beginning** (Job 42:12), but the end of the wicked is indescribably terrible (Heb. 10:31). The Preacher was on firmer ground

when he said that **the patient in spirit is** superior to **the proud in spirit**. Patience is an attractive virtue, whereas pride is the parent sin. Patience fits a man for God's approval (Rom. 5:4), whereas pride fits him for destruction (Prov. 16:18).

7:9 Next we are warned against the tendency to fly off the handle. Such lack of self-control reveals a decided weakness of character. Someone has said that you can judge the size of a man by the size of what it takes to make him lose his temper. And if we nurse grudges and resentments, we expose ourselves as **fools**. Intelligent people don't spoil their lives by such nonsensical behavior.

7:10 Another foolish activity is living in the past. When we constantly harp on "the good old days" and wish they would return because they were so much better, we are living in a world of unreality. Better to face conditions as they are and live triumphantly in spite of them. Better to light a candle than to curse the darkness.

7:11 Solomon's thought with regard to **wisdom** and **an inheritance** may be understood in several ways. First, **wisdom is good with an inheritance** (NKJV; NASB); it enables the recipient to administer his bequest carefully. Second, wisdom is good *as* an inheritance (JND); if one could choose only one heritage, wisdom would be a good choice. Third, wisdom is *as good as* an inheritance; it is a source of wealth. Also it is an advantage **to those who see the sun**, that is, to those who live on earth. How this is so is explained in verse 12.

7:12 Wisdom resembles **money** in that both afford protection and security of sorts. With **money**, one can insure himself against physical and financial losses, whereas **wisdom** provides added protection from moral and spiritual damage. That is why wisdom is superior; it preserves the lives of its possessors, not just their material fortunes.

When we remember that Christ is the wisdom of God and that those who find Him find life, the infinite superiority of wisdom is obvious. In Him are hidden all the treasures of wisdom and knowledge (Col. 2:3).

7:13 One thing a wise person will do is to **consider** God's sovereign control of affairs. If **He has made** something **crooked, who can make** it **straight**? In other words, who can successfully countermand His will? His decrees are immutable and not subject to human manipulation.

7:14 In His ordering of our lives, God has seen fit to permit times of prosperity and times of adversity. When **prosperity** comes, we should be glad and enjoy it. **In the day of adversity**, we should realize that God sends the good and the bad, happiness and trouble, so that man will not know what is going to happen next. This can be both a mercy and a frustration.

There may also be the thought that God mixes the good and the bad so people won't be able to find fault with Him.

In either case, the conclusions are distinctly subsolar. They do not rise above flesh and blood.

7:15 We have an expression "Now I've **seen everything**" when we witness the unexpected, the paradoxical, the ultimate surprise. That seems to be Solomon's meaning here. In the course of his empty life, he had seen every kind of contradiction. He saw **just** people die young and **wicked** ones live to old age.

7:16 Since the Preacher could not detect a fixed relation between righ-teousness and blessing on the one hand and sin and punishment on the other, he decided that the best policy is to avoid extremes. This shallow, unbiblical conclusion is known as "the law of the golden mean."

By avoiding extreme righteousness and excessive wisdom, one might escape premature destruction. This, of course, is untrue. God's standard for His people is that they should not sin (1 Jn. 2:1). And His guarantee for His people is that they are immortal till their work is done.

7:17 The other danger, in Solomon's reckoning, was extreme wickedness. The foolhardy man can also be cut off **before** his **time**. A middle-of-the-road policy is therefore the ideal toward which we should strive, says the Preacher.

It is clear that these are man's reasonings, not God's revelations. God cannot condone sin at all. His standard is always perfection.

7:18 According to the Preacher, the best policy is to **grasp this** fact— the untimely fate of the overrighteous man—and not to let go of the opposite fact—the self-destruction of the profligate. The one **who fears God** (by walking in the middle) **will escape** from both pitfalls.

This advice wrongly puts God in favor of moderation in sin and in unrighteousness. But it arose from Solomon's observations under the sun. Unless we remember that, we will be puzzled by such a worldly philosophy.

7:19 Solomon believes that **wisdom** gives **more** strength and protection to a man **than ten rulers** give to a **city**, which simply means that wisdom is greater than armed might. God is not necessarily on the side of the biggest battalions.

7:20 The fact that this verse begins with **for** shows that it is vitally connected with what precedes. But what is the connection? The connection is that we all need the benefits of the wisdom that the Preacher has been describing, because we are all imperfect. There is no one who is absolutely righteous in himself, **who** invariably **does good** and who never sins.

Generally verse 20 is taken to teach the universality of sin, and that application is legitimate. But in its context, writes Leupold, the verse tells why we stand in need of a closer alliance with that wisdom which has just been described.[30]

7:21 A healthy sense of our own imperfection will help us to take criticisms in stride. If we **hear** a **servant cursing** us, though he is much lower on the social ladder, we can always be glad he doesn't know us better, because then he would have more to curse!

When Shimei cursed David, Abishai wanted to cut off his head, but David's reply implied that perhaps Shimei's cursing was not entirely causeless (2 Sam. 16:5–14).

7:22 And we should always remember that we have been guilty of the same thing. **Many times** we **have cursed others** in our **heart**. We can scarcely expect others to be perfect when we are so far from perfect ourselves.

That is one of the frustrations of a perfectionist. He wants everything and everyone else to be perfect, but he lives in a world of imperfection, and he himself cannot reach the goal he sets for others.

7:23 The Preacher used his extraordinary **wisdom** to probe into all these areas of life. He wanted to be **wise** enough to solve all mysteries and unravel all the tangled skeins. But because he was making all his investigations apart from God, he found that the ultimate answers eluded him. Without special revelation, life remains an insoluble riddle.

7:24 Explanations of things as they exist are remote, inaccessible, **and exceedingly deep**. The world is filled with enigmas. The realm of the unknown remains unexplored. We are plagued by mysteries and unanswered questions.

7:25 In spite of his failure to come up with the answers, Solomon doggedly persevered in his search for greater wisdom and a solution to the human equation. He wanted to understand **the wickedness of folly, even of foolishness and madness**, that is, why people abandon themselves to debauchery and shame.

7:26 In that connection, he thought especially of a loose **woman** or a prostitute—a woman whose influence is **more bitter than death**. Her mind is filled with subtle ways of snaring men, and those in her clutches are bound as if by chains. Anyone whose desire is to please **God shall escape** her traps, but the man who plays around with sin is sure to cross her path and be hooked **by her**.

It is altogether possible that the woman here may be a type of the world or of the wisdom of the world (Col. 2:8; Jas. 3:15).

7:27, 28 Verses 27–29 seem to express Solomon's general disappointment with his fellow human beings. When he first met anyone, he had great expectations, but after he got to know that person better, his hopes were dashed. No one met his ideal. Perhaps he would see someone who was rather attractive. He would think, *I must get to know that person better. I'd like to develop a close personal friendship.* But the more he got to know this new acquaintance, the more disillusioned he became. He found that there is no such person as the perfect stranger, and that familiarity *does* breed contempt.

Solomon decided to total the number of friendships in which he found a measure of real satisfaction and of fulfilled hopes. Out of all the people he had known, how many did he regard as true "soul brothers"?

He had sought repeatedly for a perfect person, but had never been able to find a single one. Everyone he met had some flaws or weaknesses of character.

All that he discovered was that good men are rare and good women rarer still. He found one man in a thousand who came close to his ideal, that is, a man who was a loyal, dependable, selfless friend.

But he couldn't find one woman in a thousand who impressed him as a reasonable approach to excellence. He did not find **a woman among** all those. Such a shocking outburst of male chauvinism is incomprehensible and offensive to us today, but that is because our judgments are based on Christian principles and values. It would not be shocking to the orthodox Jew who thanks God every day that he was not born a woman. Nor would it be shocking to men of some cultures in which women are looked on as slaves or mere property.

Commentators go through interpretive gymnastics to soften the force of Solomon's harsh words here, but their well-intentioned efforts are misdirected. The fact is that the Preacher probably meant exactly what he said. And his conclusion is still shared by men throughout the world whose outlook is earthbound and carnal.

Solomon's view of women was terribly one-sided. G. Campbell Morgan gave a more balanced view when he wrote:

The influence of women is most powerful for good or for ill. I once heard one of the keenest of observers say that no great movement for the uplifting of humanity has been generated in human history but that woman's influence had much to do with it. Whether so superlative a statement is capable of substantiation I do not know; but I believe there is a great element of truth in it. It is equally true that the part that women have taken in corrupting the race has been terrible. When the womanhood of a nation is noble, the national life is held in strength. When it is corrupt, the nation is doomed. Woman is the last stronghold of good or of evil. Compassion and cruelty are superlative in her.[31]

Solomon later redeemed himself by writing one of literature's noblest tributes to womanhood—Proverbs 31. In Ecclesiastes he writes from the earthly plane of human prejudice, but in Proverbs 31 he writes from the lofty peak of divine revelation.

With the advent of the Christian faith, woman has reached the summit in her rise to dignity and respect. The Lord Jesus is her truest Friend and Emancipator.

7:29 As the Preacher pondered his unending disappointment in the people he had met, he correctly concluded that man has fallen from his original condition. How true! **God made man** in His own image and after His likeness. But man **sought out many** sinful **schemes** which marred and distorted the divine image in him.

Even in his fallen condition, man still has an intuitive hunger to find perfection. He goes through life looking for the perfect partner, the perfect job, the perfect everything. But he cannot find perfection in others or in himself. The trouble is that his search is confined to the sphere *under the sun*. Only one perfect life has ever been lived on this earth, that is the life of the Lord Jesus Christ. But now He is above the sun, exalted at the right hand of God. And God satisfies man's hunger for perfection with Christ—no one else, no other thing.

B. Wisdom Under the Sun (Chap. 8)

8:1 In spite of the failure of human wisdom to solve all his problems, Solomon still admired the **wise man** above others. No one else is as qualified to search out the hidden meaning of things. As far as the Preacher-King was concerned, **wisdom** is even mirrored in one's physical appearance. **His face** is radiant, and an otherwise stern visage is softened.

8:2 Wisdom teaches one how to act in the presence of the king, whether that king be conceived of as God or as an earthly monarch. It inculcates obedience first of all. The Hebrew of the latter part of this verse is ambiguous, as is seen by the following translations:

and that in regard of the oath of God (KJV).
because of the oath before God (NASB).
for the sake of your oath to God (NKJV).

The **oath** here may refer to one's pledge of allegiance to the government or to God's oath by which He authorized kings to rule (e.g., see Ps. 89:35).

8:3 The obscurity continues in verse 3. We may understand this verse to advise leaving the king's presence without delay when unpleasantness develops. Or it may advise *against* making a **hasty** exit, either in anger, disobedience, insolence, or in quitting one's job (KJV, NASB, NKJV).

At any rate the thrust of the passage is that it is unwise to cross a king, since he has wide authority to do **whatever pleases him**.

8:4 Whenever **a king** speaks, his word is backed with **power**. It is supreme and is not subject to challenge by his subjects.

8:5 Those who obey the king's **command** need not fear the royal displeasure. Wisdom teaches a person what is appropriate, both as to **time** and procedure in obeying the royal edicts.

8:6 There's a right and wrong way of doing things, and a right and wrong **time** as well. The trouble that lies heavy upon man is that he cannot always discern these moments of destiny.

8:7 There is so much that **he does not know** or do. He cannot know the future—**what** is going to **happen** or **when it will occur**.

8:8 He cannot prevent his **spirit** from departing or determine the exact time of his **death**. He cannot obtain discharge **from that war**—the war that death is relentlessly waging against him. He cannot win a reprieve by any form of **wickedness** that he may give himself over to.

8:9 These are some of the things that the Preacher observed when he studied life **under the sun**, in a world where one man crushes another under his heel, **in which one man** has exercised authority **over another to his own hurt**.

8:10 So much of life is shallow. The **wicked** dies and is **buried**. He once made trips to **the place of** worship. Now that he is gone, people praise him for his piety **in the** very **city** where he used to carry on his crooked schemes. Religion can be a facade to cover up dishonesty. It is all so empty and meaningless.

8:11 Endless delays in the trial and punishment of criminals only serve to encourage lawlessness and create contempt for the judicial system. While it is important to guarantee that every defendant has a fair trial, it is possible to overprotect the criminal at the expense of his victim. Fair, impartial justice meted out promptly serves as a deterrent to crime. On the other hand, interminable postponements make offenders more fixed in their determination to break the law. They reason that they can get away with it or at least get a light sentence.

8:12 Although Solomon had seen some cases that seemed to be exceptions, he believed that **those who fear God** will fare best in the long run. Even if an habitual criminal lives to an old age, that exception doesn't invalidate the fact that righteousness is rewarded eventually and that the way of the transgressor is hard.

8:13 The Preacher was confident that **the wicked** person is an ultimate loser. By his failure to **fear before God**, he dooms himself to a short life. His life is transient **as a shadow**.

8:14 Solomon seems to alternate between general rules and glaring exceptions. Sometimes **just men** seem to be punished as if they were **wicked**. And sometimes **wicked men** seem to be rewarded as if they were decent, **righteous** citizens. These violations of what ought to be caused the Philosopher-King to be disgusted with the **vanity** of life.

8:15 The only logical policy, as far as he was concerned, is to enjoy life while you can. There is **nothing better under the sun than to eat, drink, and** have a good time. **This will** stand by a person as he toils on throughout **his life which God gives him** in this world. No pie-in-the-sky

philosophy for Solomon. He wanted his pie here and now.

8:16 So the Preacher devoted himself to finding all the answers. He trained his mind in the study of philosophy, determined to get to the bottom of the activities of life—a task in which **one sees no sleep day or night**.

8:17 **Then** he found that **God** has so arranged things **that a man cannot** put all the parts of the puzzle together. No matter how hard he tries, he will fail. And no matter how brilliant he is, **he will not be able to find** answers to all the questions.

C. Enjoying Life Under the Sun (Chap. 9)

9:1 In chapter 9, the Preacher **considered** all **this**, taking in as wide and exhaustive a view as possible. He saw that good people and **wise** people and all that they do **are in the hand of God**. But whether what will happen to them is a sign of God's **love** or **hatred**, no one knows. The entire future is unknown and unknowable, and anything can happen.

9:2 What makes it all so enigmatical is that **the righteous and the wicked, the good** and the evil, **the clean and the unclean**, the worshiper and the nonworshiper **all** end in the same place—the grave. As far as escaping death is concerned, **the righteous** person has no advantage over **the wicked**. Those who put themselves under **oath** are in the same predicament as those who shun **an oath**.

9:3 **This is** the great calamity of life—that death eventually claims **all** classes of men. People can live outrageous, insane lives, and after that—death. What is this but gross injustice if death is the end of existence?

9:4 As long as man is alive, **there**

is hope; that is, he has something to look forward to. In that sense, **a living dog is better** off **than a dead lion**. Here the **dog** is spoken of, not as man's best friend, but as one of the lowest, meanest forms of animal life.[32] The **lion** is the king of beasts, powerful and magnificent.

9:5 **The living** at least **know that they will die, but the dead** don't know anything about what's going on in the world.

This verse is constantly used by false teachers to prove that the soul sleeps in death, that consciousness ceases when the last breath is taken. But it is senseless to build a doctrine of the hereafter on this verse, or on this book, for that matter. As has been repeatedly emphasized, Ecclesiastes represents man's best conclusions as he searches for answers "under the sun." It sets forth deductions based on observations and on logic but not on divine revelation. It is what a wise man might think if he did not have a Bible.

What would you think if you saw a person die and watched his body as it was lowered into the grave, knowing that it would eventually return to dust? You might think, *That's the end. My friend knows nothing now; he can't enjoy any activities that are going on; he has forgotten and will soon be forgotten*.

9:6 And so it is, thought Solomon. Once a person has died, there is no more **love, hatred, envy** or any other human emotion. Never again **will he have a share** in any of this world's activities and experiences.

9:7 So once again the Preacher comes back to his basic conclusion—live your life, have a good time, enjoy your food, cheer your heart with **wine**. **God has already** approved what you do. It's all right with Him.

9:8 Wear bright clothing, not mourning attire. And put perfume on **your head** rather than ashes. Some people think the world was made for fun and frolic, and so did Solomon.

9:9 The joys of the marriage relationship should also be exploited to the full as long as possible. It's a vain, empty life anyway, so the best thing is to make the most of it. Enjoy every day because that's all you are going to get out of your toil and trouble.

Verses 7–9 are strikingly similar to the following passage in the Gilgamesh Epic, an ancient Babylonian account of immortality and of the great deluge:

Since the gods created man
Death they ordained for man,
Life in their hands they hold,
Thou, O Gilgamesh, fill indeed thy
    belly.
Day and night be thou joyful,
Daily ordain gladness,
Day and night rage and be merry,
Let thy garments be bright,
Thy head purify, wash with water.
Desire thy children which thy hand
    possesses.
A wife enjoy in thy bosom.[33]

The significance of this is not that one was copied from the other, but that man's wisdom **under the sun** leads to the same conclusion. I was impressed with this fact when I read Denis Alexander's summary of what humanism offers us today:

The humanist model does seem a very big pill to swallow. As a representative of a late twentieth-century generation of under-thirties, I am first asked to believe that I am the result of a purely random evolutionary process. The only prerequisites for this process are the presence of matter, time and chance. Because by some strange whim of fate, I and other men are the only physical structures which happen to have been bestowed with a consciousness of their own existence, I am supposed to think of both myself and others as being in some way more valuable than other physical structures such as rabbits, trees or stones, even though in a hundred years time the atoms of my decayed body may well be indistinguishable from theirs. Furthermore the mass of vibrating atoms in my head are supposed to have more ultimate meaning than those in the head of a rabbit.

At the same time I am told that death is the end of the line. In the time-scale of evolution my life is a vapour which soon vanishes. Whatever feelings of justice or injustice I may have in this life, all my strivings, all my greatest decisions, will be ultimately swallowed up in the on-going march of time. In a few million years' time, a mere drop compared with the total history of the earth, the memory of the greatest literature, the greatest art, the greatest lives will be buried in the inexorable decay of the Second Law of Thermodynamics. Hitler and Martin Luther King, James Sewell and Francis of Assisi, Chairman Mao and Robert Kennedy, all will be obliterated in the unthinking void.

So, I am told, I must make the best of a bad job. Even though I have strong feelings of transcendence, a deep sense that I am more than just a blind whim of evolution, I must nevertheless forget such troubling questions, and concern myself with the real problems of trying to live responsibly in society. Even though my job involves studying man's brain as a machine, like any other of nature's machines, I must still believe that man has some special intrinsic worth which is greater than an animal's worth, and while my emotions tell me that it may be true, I am not given any more objective reason for believing it.[34]

9:10 The maxim in verse 10, one of the best known in the book, is often used by believers to encourage zeal and diligence in Christian service, and the advice is sound. But in its context, it really means to seize every possible pleasure and enjoyment while you can, because you won't be able to work, invent, think, or know anything **in the grave, where** you are irreversibly heading.

The advice given in this verse is excellent, but the reason is utterly bad! And even the advice must be restricted to activities that are legitimate, helpful, and edifying in themselves.

9:11 Another thing that the Preacher observed is that luck and chance play a big part in life. **The race is not** always won by the fastest runner. The bravest soldiers don't always win **the battle**. The wisest don't always enjoy the best meals. The cleverest are not always the richest. And the most capable do not always rise to the presidency. Bad luck dogs everyone's steps. **Time and chance** are factors that play an important role in success and failure. When the billionaire J. Paul Getty was asked to explain his success, he replied, "Some people find oil. Others don't."

9:12 And no one knows when bad luck will strike. **Like fish caught in a net** or **birds in a** trap, man is overtaken by bad fortune or even by death. He never knows which bullet has his name on it.

9:13–15 Still another heartache in life is that **wisdom** is not always appreciated. To illustrate: **There was a little city with few** inhabitants and therefore poorly defended. **A** powerful **king** surrounded it with artillery and prepared to break through the walls.

When the situation seemed hopeless, a **man** who was **poor** but very **wise** came forward with a plan that saved **the city**. At the moment he was a hero, but then he was quickly forgotten.

9:16 It grieved the Preacher that though **wisdom is better than** power, yet the **poor man's** advice was subsequently **despised**. As soon as the crisis was past, no one was interested in what he had to say.

This parable has a definite evangelistic ring to it. The city is like man's soul—small and defenseless. The great king is Satan, bent on invasion and destruction (2 Cor. 4:4; Eph. 2:2). The deliverer is the Savior—poor (2 Cor. 8:9) and wise (1 Cor. 1:24; Col. 2:3). Though He provided deliverance, yet how little He is honored and appreciated! Most people of the world live as if He had never died. And even Christians are often careless about remembering Him in His appointed way, that is, in the Lord's Supper.

9:17 Yet in spite of man's ingratitude and indifference it is still true that the **words of the wise, spoken quietly**, are worth more than the shouting tirades of a powerful **ruler of fools**.

9:18 **Wisdom is** superior to **weapons** and munitions. In 2 Samuel 20:14–22 we read how a wise woman delivered the city of Abel of Beth Maachah when Joab besieged it.

But one sinful dolt can undo a lot of **good** that the wise person accomplishes, just as little foxes can spoil the vines.

D. The Wise and the Foolish Under the Sun (Chap. 10)

10:1 When **flies** get caught in the **perfumer's ointment** and die, they cause it **to give off a foul odor**. And in this, there is an analogy to human behavior. A man may build up a reputation for wisdom and honor, yet he can ruin it all by a single misstep. People will remember one little indiscretion and forget years of worthy achievements. Any person can ruin his reputation by speaking just three words of the wrong kind in public.

10:2 **The right hand** is traditionally viewed as more dexterous, the **left** more awkward. **A wise** man knows the right way to do a thing; **a fool** is an awkward bungler.

10:3 **Even when a fool** does something simple, like walking **along the way**, he betrays a lack of common sense. He **shows everyone that he is a fool**, which may mean that he calls everyone else stupid or that he shows his own ignorance in all he does. The latter is probably the thought.

10:4 If a **ruler** explodes in anger at you, it is best not to quit in a huff. It is better to be meek and submissive. This will be more apt to pacify him and atone for serious **offenses**.

10:5, 6 Another inconsistency which bothered Solomon in this mixed-up world proceeded from unwise decisions and injustices **proceeding from the ruler**. Often men are appointed to positions without suitable qualifications, while capable men waste their talents on menial tasks.

10:7 Thus **servants** often ride **on horses, while princes** have to travel by foot. Such inequities exist in politics, in industry, in the military services, and in religious life as well.

10:8 **He** who **digs a pit** to harm others will be the victim of his own malice. Chickens have a way of coming home to roost.

Whoever breaks down a wall of stones, either for unlawful entry, or mischief, or to change a property line can expect to **be bitten by a serpent** or to pay for it in some other unpleasant way.

10:9, 10 Even legitimate activities

have risks attached. The quarryman is in danger of being **hurt by** stones, and the log-splitter is **endangered by** the ax.

It's a good idea to work with sharp tools. Otherwise it takes a lot more labor to get the job done. The time spent sharpening the ax is more than compensated by the time and effort saved. **Wisdom** teaches shortcuts and labor-saving devices. As Leupold renders it, "Wisdom prepares the way for success."[35]

10:11 What good is a charmer if the **serpent** bites before the charm begins? Or as we might say, why lock the barn after the horse is stolen? Things must often be done on time in order to be valuable and effective.

10:12, 13 The words of a wise man's mouth bring him favor because they **are gracious**. The words **of a fool** prove to be his downfall.

He may begin with harmless nonsense, but by the time he is through, he is engaging in **raving madness**.

10:14 A fool doesn't know when to stop. **Words**, words, words. He talks on and on as if he knew everything, but he doesn't. His endless chatter almost inevitably includes boasts of what he will do in the future. He is like the rich fool who said, "I will do this: I will pull down my barns and build greater, and there I will store all my crops and my goods. And I will say to my soul, 'Soul, you have many goods laid up for many years; take your ease; eat, drink, and be merry'" (Luke 12:18–19). But he does not know what is going to happen next. He would be better advised to say, "If the Lord wills, we shall live and do this or that" (Jas. 4:15).

10:15 He exhausts himself by his inefficient and unproductive work. He can't even see the obvious or find the way to anything as conspicuous as a **city**. Perhaps we could add that he doesn't know enough to come in out of the rain. His ignorance in such simple matters makes his plans for the future all the more ludicrous.

10:16, 17 Pity the **land** whose ruler is immature and impressionable like **a child** and whose legislators carouse **in the morning** instead of attending to their duties.

The fortunate **land** is one in which the **king is** a man of character and nobility, and in which the other leaders manifest propriety and self-control by eating **for strength and not for drunkenness**.

10:18 Continued **laziness** and neglect cause a **house** to fall apart, whether that house represents a government or an individual life. Any roof will leak unless the owner provides regular maintenance.

10:19 Meal time is a happy time. **Wine** adds sparkle to life. **Money answers everything.**

Did Solomon really believe that **money** is the key to all pleasure? Perhaps he simply meant that money can buy whatever man needs in the way of food and drink. Or maybe he was just quoting the drunken rulers of verse 16 when they were warned where their excesses would lead (v. 18). The fact, as someone has said, is that money will buy anything except happiness and is a ticket to everywhere except heaven. A man's life does not consist in the abundance of the things he possesses.

10:20 Be careful **not** to speak evil against **the king** or his **rich** subordinates. You may think that nobody hears. But even the walls have ears, and some unsuspected **bird** will **carry** the message to the royal palace. "Indiscretions have a way of sprouting wings."

E. Spreading the Good Under the Sun (11:1—12:8)

11:1 **Bread** is used symbolically here for the grain from which it is made. To **cast bread upon the waters** may refer to the practice of sowing in flooded areas, or it may mean carrying on grain trade by sea. In any case, the thought is that a widespread and wholesale distribution of what is good will result in a generous return in the time of harvest.

This verse is true of the gospel. We may not see immediate results as we share the bread of life, but the eventual harvest is sure.

11:2 Giving **a serving to seven**, even **to eight** suggests two things— unrestrained generosity or diversifying of business enterprises. If the first is meant, the idea is that we should show uncalculating kindness while we can, because a time of calamity and misfortune may come when this will not be possible. Most people save for a rainy day; this verse counsels to adopt a spirit of unrestricted liberality because of the uncertainties of life.

Or the thought may be: Don't put all your eggs in one basket. Invest in several interests so that if one fails, you will still be able to carry on with the others. This is known as *diversification*.

11:3 Verse 3 carries on the thought of the previous one, especially with regard to the unknown evil which may happen on earth. It suggests that there is a certain inevitability and finality about the calamities of life. Just as surely as rain-laden clouds **empty themselves upon the earth**, so surely do troubles and trials come to the sons of men. And once **a tree** is felled, it remains a fallen monarch. Its destiny is sealed.

A wider application of the verse is given in the poem:

> As a tree falls, so must it lie,
> As a man lives, so must he die,
> As a man dies, so must he be,
> All through the years of eternity.
> —*John Ray*

11:4 It is possible to be too cautious. If you wait till conditions are perfect, you will accomplish nothing. There are usually some **wind** and some **clouds**. If you wait for zero wind conditions, you will never get the seed into the fields. If you wait until there is no risk of rain, the crops will rot before they are harvested. The man who waits for certainty will wait forever.

11:5 Since we don't know everything, we have to muddle along with what knowledge we do have. We don't understand the movements of **the wind** or **how the bones** are formed **in the womb** of an expectant mother. Neither do we understand all that **God** does or why He does it.

11:6 Since we don't know this, the best policy is to fill the day with all kinds of productive work. We have no way of knowing **which** activities **will prosper**. Maybe they all will.

In spreading the Word of God, success is guaranteed. But it is still true that some methods are more fruitful than others. So we should be untiring, versatile, ingenious, and faithful in Christian service.

Then too we should sow **in the morning** of life and not slack off **in the evening**. We are called to unremitting service.

11:7, 8 **The light** may refer to the bright and shining days of youth. It's great to be young—to be healthy, strong, and vivacious. But no matter how many years of vigor and prosperity a man enjoys, he should be aware that **days of darkness** are almost sure to come. The aches and pains of old age are inevitable. It's a dreary, empty time of life.

11:9 It is hard to know whether verse 9 is sincere advice or the cynicism of a disillusioned old man. Do what your **heart** desires and see as much as you can. **But** just remember that eventually **God will bring you into judgment**, that is, the **judgment** of old age, which seemed to Solomon like divine retribution for the sins of early life.

11:10 While you have your **youth**, maximize enjoyment and minimize **sorrow** and trouble. (**Evil** here probably means trouble rather than sin.) **Childhood and youth are vanity** because they are so short-lived.

Nowhere in literature is there a more classic description of old age than in the first half of chapter 12. The meaning does not lie on the surface because it is presented as an allegory. But soon the picture emerges of a doddering old man, a walking geriatric museum, shuffling his way irresistibly to the grave.

12:1 The doleful picture of age and senility is a warning to young people to **remember** their **Creator in the days of** their **youth**. Notice Solomon does not say their Lord or Savior or Redeemer but their **Creator**. That is the only way Solomon could know God from his vantage point under the sun. But even at that, the advice is good. Young people *should* **remember** their **Creator . . . before** the sunset time of life, when the days are **difficult** and cruel and the years are totally lacking in **pleasure** and enjoyment. The aspiration of every young person should be that which is expressed in the following lines:

Lord, in the fullness of my might,
  I would for Thee be strong;
While runneth o'er each dear delight,
  To Thee should soar my song.

I would not give the world my heart,
  And then profess Thy love;
I would not feel my strength depart,
  And then Thy service prove.

I would not with swift winged zeal
  On the world's errands go:
And labor up the heav'nly hill
  With weary feet and slow.

O not for Thee my weak desires,
  My poorer baser part!
O not for Thee my fading fires,
  The ashes of my heart.

O choose me in my golden time,
  In my dear joys have part!
For Thee the glory of my prime
  The fullness of my heart.[36]
                    —*Thomas H. Gill*

12:2 Old age is the time when the lights grow dim, both physically and emotionally. The days are dreary, and the nights are long. Gloom and depression settle in.

Even in earlier years, there was a certain amount of **rain**, that is, trouble and discouragement. But then the sun would emerge and the spirit would quickly bounce back. Now it seems that the sunny days are gone, and after each spell of **rain**, **the clouds** appear with the promise of more.

Youth is the time to remember the Creator because then the **sun, . . . moon, and . . . stars are not darkened, and the clouds do not return after the rain.**

12:3 Now the body of the old man is presented under the figure of a **house. The keepers of the house** are the arms and hands, once strong and active, now wrinkled, gnarled, and trembling with Parkinson's disease.

The strong men are the legs and thighs, no longer straight and athletic, but bowed like parenthesis marks, as if buckling under the weight of the body.

The grinders cease because they are few, that is, the teeth are no longer able to chew because there are too few uppers to meet the remaining lowers. The dentist would say there is inadequate occlusion.

Those that look through the windows grow dim. The eyes have been failing steadily. First they needed bifocals, then trifocals, then surgery for cataracts. Now they can only read extra large type with the use of a magnifying glass.

12:4 The doors on the street **are shut.** This refers, of course, to the ears. Everything has to be repeated over and over. Loud noises, like the **grinding** of the mill, are very **low** and indistinct.

The old man suffers from insomnia; he **rises up** bright and early, when the first **bird** begins to chirp or the rooster crows.

All the daughters of music are brought low; the vocal chords are seriously impaired. The voice is crackling and unsteady, and song is out of the question.

12:5 They develop *acrophobia*, that is, **they are afraid of height**, whether ladders, views from tall buildings, or plane rides.

And **terrors** are **in the way.** They have lost self-confidence, are afraid to go out alone, or to go out at night.

The blossoming **almond tree** is generally taken to picture the white hair, first in rich profusion, then falling to the ground.

The grasshopper may be interpreted in two ways. First, **the grasshopper is a burden**, that is, even the lightest objects are too heavy for the old person to carry. Or, the grasshopper dragging itself along (NASB) carica-

tures the old man, bent over and twisted, inching forward in jerky, erratic movements.

Desire fails in the sense that natural appetites diminish or cease altogether. Food no longer has flavor or zest, and other basic drives peter out. Sexual vigor is gone.

This degenerative process takes place because **man** is going to **his** long-lasting **home** of death and the grave, and soon his funeral procession will be moving down the street.

12:6 And so the advice of the wise man is to **remember** the **Creator before the silver cord** is snapped, **or the golden bowl is broken, or the pitcher** is **shattered at the fountain, or the wheel broken at the** cistern. It is difficult to assign precise meanings to all of these figures.

The snapping of **the silver cord** probably refers to the breaking of the tender thread of life when the spirit is released from the body. The blind poet apparently understood it in this way when she wrote:

Some day the silver cord will break
And I no more as now shall sing
But oh the joy when I shall wake
Within the palace of the King.[37]
—Fanny J. Crosby

The golden bowl has been understood to mean the cranial cavity, and its breaking to be a poetic picture of the cessation of the mind at the time of death.

The broken **pitcher** and **wheel** taken together could be a reference to the circulatory system with the breakdown of systolic and diastolic blood pressure.

12:7 Rigor mortis sets in. Then the body begins its return to **dust**, while **the spirit** returns **to God who gave it.** Or so it seemed to Solomon. In the case of a believer, his conclusion is true. But in the case of an unbeliever, the spirit goes to Hades, there to await the Great White Throne Judgment. Then the spirit will be reunited with the body and the entire person cast into the lake of fire (Rev. 20:12–14).

12:8 And so the Preacher comes full-circle to where he began—with the basic tenet that life under the sun is **vanity**, meaningless, futile, and empty. His pathetic refrain reminds us of the little girl who went to the fair and stayed too long.

> I wanted the music to play on forever—
> Have I stayed too long at the fair?
> I wanted the clown to be constantly
>   clever—
> Have I stayed too long at the fair?
> I bought me blue ribbons to tie up
>   my hair,
> But I couldn't find anybody to care.
> The merry-go-round is beginning to
>   slow now,
> Have I stayed too long at the fair?
>
> I wanted to live in a carnival city,
>   with laughter and love everywhere.
> I wanted my friends to be thrilling
>   and witty.
> I wanted somebody to care.
> I found my blue ribbons all shiny and
>   new,
> But now I've discovered them no
>   longer blue.
> The merry-go-round is beginning to
>   taunt me—
> Have I stayed too long at the fair?
> There is nothing to win and no one
>   to want me—
> Have I stayed too long at the fair?[38]
> —*Billy Barnes*

As we come here to Solomon's last reference to the emptiness of life under the sun, I am reminded of a story which E. Stanley Jones used to tell. On board ship he saw a very corpulent couple, their faces bovine, who

lived from meal to meal. They were retired on plenty—and nothing.

They were angry with the table stewards for not giving them super-service. They seemed to be afraid they might starve between courses. Their physical appetites seemed the one thing that mattered to them. I never saw them reading a book or paper. They sat between meals and stared out, apparently waiting for the next meal. One night I saw them sitting thus and staring blankly, when a bright idea flashed across the dull brain of the man. He went to the mantelpiece and picked up the vases, and looked into them, and then returned to his wife with the news: "They're empty!" I came very near laughing. He was right; "They're empty!" But it wasn't merely the vases! The souls and brains of both of them were empty. They had much in their purses, but nothing in their persons; and that was their punishment. They had security with boredom—no adventure. They had expanding girths and narrowing horizons.[39]

IV. EPILOGUE: THE BEST THING UNDER THE SUN (12:9–14)

12:9 Besides being **wise** himself, **the Preacher** shared his **knowledge** with others. He sought to transmit his wisdom in the form of **proverbs**, after carefully weighing them and testing them for accuracy.

12:10 He chose his **words** carefully, trying to combine what was comforting, pleasant, and true. It was like preparing a nutritious meal, then serving it with a sprig of parsley.

12:11 **The** teachings **of the wise are like** sharp, pointed instruments, plain, direct, and convincing. And the collected sayings from the **one Shepherd are like well-driven nails**

or pins that give stability to a tent. They provide strength and are also pegs on which we may hang our thoughts.

Most Bible versions capitalize the word **Shepherd**, indicating that the translators understood it as referring to God. However, it should also be remembered that in Eastern thought, a king is looked on as a shepherd. Homer said, "All kings are shepherds of the people." So it could be that King Solomon was referring to *himself* as the **one shepherd**. This interpretation fits into the context more smoothly.

12:12 There is no thought that Solomon had exhausted the subject. He could have written more, but he warns his readers that the conclusion would be the same. **There is no end** to the writing and publishing of **books**, and it would be exhausting to read them all. But why bother? All they could reveal would be the vanity of life.

12:13 His final **conclusion** may give the impression that he has at last risen above the sun. He says, "**Fear God and keep His commandments**, because **this is** the whole duty of man, **man's all**." But we must keep in mind that the **fear** of **God** here is not the same as saving faith. It is the slavish terror of a creature before His Creator. And the **commandments** do not necessarily mean the law of God as revealed in the OT. Rather they might mean any commands which God has instinctively written on the hearts of mankind.

In other words, we need not assign a high degree of spiritual insight to Solomon's words. They may be nothing more than what a wise person would conclude from natural intuition and from practical experience.

This is man's all—not just the whole duty but the basic elements that make for a full and happy life.

12:14 The motive for fearing and obeying **God** here is the certainty of coming **judgment**. We can be eternally grateful as believers that the Savior has delivered us from this kind of fear.

"There is no fear in love; but perfect love casts out fear, because fear involves torment. But he who fears has not been made perfect in love" (1 Jn. 4:18).

We do not trust and obey because of fear but because of love. Through His finished work on Calvary, we have the assurance that we will never come into judgment but have passed from death into life (John 5:24). Now we can say:

> There is no condemnation,
> There is no hell for me,
> The torment and the fire
> My eyes shall never see;
> For me there is no sentence,
> For me there is no sting
> Because the Lord who loves me
> Shall shield me with His wing.
> —*Paul Gerhardt*

ENDNOTES

[1](Intro) L. S. Chafer, *Systematic Theology*, I:83.

[2](Intro) See Gleason Archer, *A Survey of Old Testament Introduction*, pp. 478–88.

[3](Intro) *Megillah 7a; Sabbath 30.*

[4](Intro) W. Graham Scroggie, *Know Your Bible*, I:143.

[5](Intro) Solomon is widely held to be a "type" (or picture) of Christ reigning in peace during the Millennial Kingdom.

[6](Intro) Quoted by Scroggie, *Know Your Bible*, I:144.

[7](1:3) H. L. Mencken, quoted by Bill Bright, *Revolution Now*, 1969, p. 15.

[8](1:4) Will Houghton, "By Life or by Death."

[9](1:8) Author unknown. "Thou Alone, Lord Jesus," in *Hymns of Grace and Truth*, no. 220.

[10](1:13) Malcolm Muggeridge, *Jesus Rediscovered*, p. 11.

[11](1:13) For example, this name was used by other Semitic nations, and even in the OT *Elohim* is used for false "gods." It is debated whether Satan's words in Genesis 3:5 should be translated "You shall be like God" (KJV, NKJV) or "You shall be like gods" (NEB, Knox).

[12](1:15) Robert Laurin, "Ecclesiastes," in *The Wycliffe Bible Commentary*, p. 587.

[13](2:1) B. E. "None but Christ Can Satisfy!" in *Hymns of Truth and Praise*, no. 306.

[14](2:2) From *Selected Poems of Edwin Arlington Robinson*. London: The Macmillan Company, 1965, pp. 9, 10.

[15](2:8) Samuel Johnson, *The History of Rasselas, The Prince of Abyssinia*, ed. J. P. Hardy.

[16](2:8) Quoted by David R. Reuben, "Why Wives Cheat on Their Husbands," in *Reader's Digest*, Aug. 1973, p. 123.

[17](2:11) Ralph Barton, quoted by Denis Alexander, *Beyond Science*, p. 123. Used by permission of Lion Publishing.

[18](2:11) E. Stanley Jones, *Growing Spiritually*, p. 4.

[19](2:16, 17) *Choice Gleanings Calendar*. Grand Rapids: Gospel Folio Press.

[20](2:18) C. E. Stuart, *Thoughts on Ecclesiastes*, in Assembly Writers Library, Vol. 5, p. 186.

[21](2:21) Robert Jamieson, A. R. Fausset, and David Brown, *Critical and Experimental Commentary on the Old and New Testament*, III:518.

[22](2:25) Jules Abels, *The Rockefeller Billions*, p. 299.

[23](2:2)*Table Talk*, Vol. 11, No. 4, August 1987, p. 3.

[24](3:21) The same Hebrew word translated *spirit* can also mean *breath*.

[25](4:1) James Russell Lowell, "The Present Crisis," in *Complete Poetical Works*, p. 67.

[26](4:4) Cited by Henry G. Bosch, *Our Daily Bread*, 24 May 1973.

[27](4:4) Quoted by Bill Bright, *Revolution Now*, p. 37.

[28](5:15) *Choice Gleanings Calendar*.

[29](6:9) H. C. Leupold, *Exposition of Ecclesiastes*, p. 141.

[30](7:20) *Ibid.*, p. 167.

[31](7:27, 28) G. Campbell Morgan, *Searchlights from the Word*, p. 217.

[32](9:4) Dogs in the Middle East are often snarling curs that feed on garbage and run wild through the streets, not the beloved pets of Western homes.

[33](9:9) The Gilgamesh Epic, quoted by Leupold, *Ecclesiastes*, p. 216.

[34](9:9) Denis Alexander, *Beyond Science*, pp. 132–33. Used by permission of Lion Publishing.

[35](10:9, 10) Leupold, *Ecclesiastes*, p. 242.

[36](12:1) Thomas H. Gill, "Lord in the Fullness of My Might," in *Hymns*, no. 26.

[37](12:6) Fanny J. Crosby, "Saved by Grace," in *Hymns of Truth and Praise*, no. 621.

[38](12:8) Billy Barnes, "I Stayed Too Long at the Fair." Used by permission.

[39](12:8) E. Stanley Jones, *Is the Kingdom of God Realism?*, pagination unknown.

BIBLIOGRAPHY

Delitzsch, Franz. "Ecclesiastes." In *Biblical Commentary on the Old Testament*. Vol. 18. Grand Rapids: Wm. B. Eerdmans Publishing Co., 1971.

Eaton, Michael A. *Ecclesiastes*. The Tyndale Old Testament Commentaries. Downers Grove, IL: Inter-Varsity Press, 1983.

Erdman, W. J. *Ecclesiastes*. Chicago: B.I.C.A., 1969.

Hengstenburg, Ernest W. *A Commentary on Ecclesiastes*. Reprint. Minneapolis: James and Klock Christian Publishing Co., 1977.

Lange, John Peter, ed. "Ecclesiastes." In *Commentary on the Holy Scriptures*. Vol. 7. Reprint (25 vols. in 12). Grand Rapids: Zondervan Publishing House, 1960.

Laurin, Robert. "Ecclesiastes." In *The Wycliffe Bible Commentary*. Chicago: Moody Press, 1962.

Leupold, H. C. *Exposition of Ecclesiastes*. Grand Rapids: Baker Book House, 1952.

MacDonald, William. *Chasing the Wind*. Chicago: Moody Press, 1975.

Introduction

"In the glorious temple of revelation, a place which the Lord our God has chosen to cause his name to dwell there, even in brighter glory than in the temple of the material world, does this book stand, like one of the apartments in the temple on Mount Zion, small indeed, but exquisitely finished, the walls and ceiling of something richer than cedar, richer than bright ivory overlaid with sapphires, and filled with specimens of truth brought down from heaven by the Holy Spirit, and here deposited for the comfort and delight of those who love the habitation of God's house, and the place where his glory dwelleth."

—George Burrowes

I. Unique Place in the Canon

The title "the Song of Songs" is a Hebrew idiom meaning *The Most Exquisite Song*. The Jewish Midrash calls it "the most praiseworthy, most excellent, most highly treasured among the songs." This song, also called Canticles, is generally considered the hardest book in the Bible to *understand*. Franz Delitzsch wrote, "The Song is the most obscure book in the Old Testament."[1] It is not hard to *enjoy* it if you appreciate poetry, love, and nature, but what *is* it and what does it *mean*?

Scholars are divided as to whether it is an anthology of unrelated love lyrics, a little drama, or a "unified dramatic lyric dialogue of love."[2] In the light of repeated refrains and the flow of the story, plus the too great brevity of the work to be a real "play," the last named is the best choice.

But still, how is one to *interpret* the book? Here the imagination of readers throughout the ages has had a field day. While certain Jews and Christians have prudishly avoided the book

as "sensual," some of the most devout saints throughout history have reveled in its pages.

II. Authorship

Jewish tradition has it that Solomon wrote the Song in his youth, Proverbs in his prime, and Ecclesiastes after he had grown weary of this world. This view has much to commend it. Since the author praises marital fidelity, it has been suggested that Solomon dedicated the book to the first of his many wives, before he got entangled in polygamy and concubinage. The present commentary, however, takes quite a different view.

Seven verses in the Song refer to Solomon by name (1:1, 5; 3:7, 9, 11; 8:11, 12). The first one probably ascribed *authorship* to him (though it could also be translated "The Song of Songs which is *about* Solomon"). The allusions to nature fit in with Solomon's interests (1 Kgs. 4:33). Also, references to royal horses, chariots, and the palanquin tend to support Solomonic authorship. The

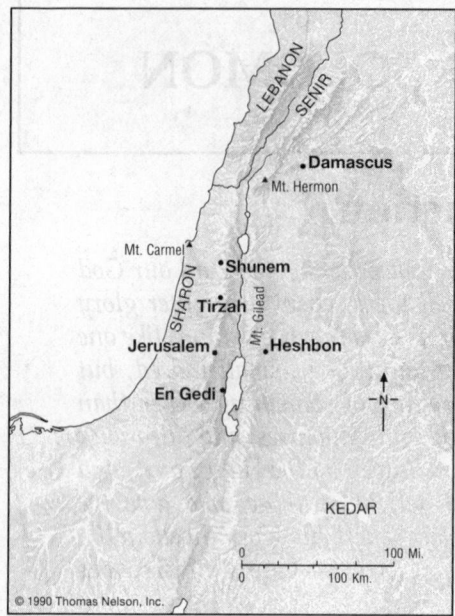

Places Named in the Song of Solomon

geographical references suggest that the places were all in one united kingdom, which was true chiefly during Solomon's reign.

Thus, there is every reason to accept the traditional view of authorship, and contrary arguments are not convincing.

III. Date

King Solomon probably wrote this loveliest of his 1,005 songs (1 Kgs. 4:32) some time during his forty year reign (971–931 BC). The tradition that he was still young and not yet jaded with too many women is logical and attractive.

IV. Background and Theme

The usual Christian interpretation given to this book is that it represents the love of Christ for His church. This interpretation is followed in the chapter headings in many editions of the Bible. According to this view Solomon is a type of Christ and the Shulamite a type of the church. However, the careful student of Scripture will realize that this cannot be the primary interpretation of the book since the church was a secret hidden in God from the foundation of the world and not revealed until the apostles and prophets of the NT (Rom. 16:25, 26; Eph. 3:9). Few Christians will deny that in this song we have a very beautiful picture of the love of Christ for the church, but this is an application and not the interpretation. The primary *interpretation* of the book must be concerned with Jehovah and the nation of Israel.

A second interpretation sees this book as a protest against marital infidelity. Solomon, with his many wives, seeks to woo a young Shulamite maiden. But she has a shepherd-lover to whom she is faithful and true. She does not yield to the blandishments of Solomon. Every time he flatters her, she begins to speak about her own lover. At the close of the book, she is seen united with her shepherd-lover and resting in his love. Those who accept this interpretation point out that most references to Solomon have the city and palace as background whereas references to the shepherd picture him appropriately in a rural setting. This sharp contrast between the city and the country reinforces the idea that there are two male characters in the drama, not just one. This interpretation is not popular because it puts Solomon in an unfavorable light.[3] However, it is true that he was a polygamist, whereas God's order for His people was monogamy. The nation of Israel, of course, had been unfaithful to Jehovah, running after other lovers. In this song, they read of the beauty of faithful love.

A third interpretation sees the Shulamite maiden as a type of the believing remnant of the nation of Israel in a coming day. Solomon is a type of the Lord Jesus. The song pictures the loving fellowship which will be enjoyed by the remnant when they look on Him whom they have pierced and mourn for Him as one mourning for an only son. The fact that Solomon was a polygamist does not bar him from being a type of the Lord. The type is imperfect; the Antitype is perfect.

A fourth view, very popular today, is to see the book as an encouragement to true love and purity within the bonds of matrimony. In light of the world's exploitations of sex without married love, this is a viable option, fitting in well with Genesis 1:27 and 2:20–24.

At any rate, no matter which view one holds, the Song of Songs has been widely, and we believe rightly, used by believing couples on their wedding night and to enhance their marriage.

OUTLINE

Commentary

I. TITLE (1:1)

The song of songs is introduced as **Solomon's**; it could also mean "concerning Solomon."

II. THE SHULAMITE IN SOLOMON'S COURT THINKS OF HER ABSENT SHEPHERD-LOVER AND TELLS THE COURT LADIES ABOUT HIM AND ABOUT HERSELF (1:2–8)

1:2–4 The Shulamite is longing for **the kisses** of her shepherd-lover; then, imagining that he is present, she tells him that his **love is better than wine**. Comparing his virtues to fragrant **ointment**, she sees this as the reason why he is loved by **the** other **virgins**, but she longs for him to come and claim her as his own. The daughters of Jerusalem **will** try in vain to follow. King Solomon **has brought** the Shulamite **into his chambers**, presumably to add her to his harem, but it was quite against her own will. When the daughters of Jerusalem adopt her sentiments concerning her beloved as their own, she

comments that their appreciation of him is justified.

1:5, 6 Unlike the pale court ladies, the rustic Shulamite has spent much time in **the sun** as **a keeper of the vineyards**. Hence she is **tanned** and **dark, but**[4] **lovely**.

1:7, 8 Her thoughts wander to her lover. She wonders **where he** is feeding his **flock, where** he is making **it rest at noon**. And she can't understand **why** she can't be with him instead of being a veiled woman in the presence of others, who were, to her, less worthy men.

The daughters of Jerusalem[5] sarcastically suggest that she could find him by following **the footsteps of the flock**.

III. SOLOMON WOOS THE SHULAMITE MAIDEN BUT SHE IS DEAF TO HIS FLATTERY (1:9—2:6)

1:9, 10 Solomon now begins his courtship of the Shulamite. She reminds him of a caparisoned prize **filly among Pharaoh's chariots**. He sees her **cheeks** adorned with choice **ornaments** and her **neck** draped **with chains of gold**.

1:11 Using the editorial we,[6] he offers to enrich her with golden **ornaments** and **studs of silver**.

1:12–14 The Shulamite is unaffected by the king's flattering words and luring offers. She can think only of her lover. **While the king** sits **at his table**, she has her own source of **fragrance**—a little sachet **of myrrh** that she keeps next to herself as a memento of her shepherd. He is as fragrant to her as **a cluster of henna blooms in the vineyards of En Gedi**.

1:15 Again Solomon tries to woo her, this time extolling her beauty and comparing her **eyes** to those of a dove.

1:16,17 But the Shulamite switches the conversation in her own mind, at least, by telling her lover how **handsome** he is. She pictures the great outdoors as their house, the grass as their **bed**, and the overhanging **cedar** and **fir** branches as their roof. The setting of their romance is uniformly pastoral, not a palace.

2:1 The maiden continues by protesting her own plainness and unworthiness. When she likens herself to **the rose of Sharon** and **the lily of the valleys**,[7] she is not thinking of the cultivated flowers we call "roses" and "lilies" but probably of the common, wild scarlet anemones, or perhaps the crocus.[8]

2:2 Solomon must have heard her protestations of mediocrity because he tells her that she is very special. Compared to other virgins, she is like a **lily among thorns**.

2:3 Switching again to rural scenes, she sees her beloved as a cultivated **apple tree among the** wild **trees of the woods**. To be with him had always been delightful, and fellowship with him was ever so **sweet**.

2:4–6 Just to be with him was like being in a **banqueting house**; always

overhead was **his banner** of **love**. Overcome with thoughts of him she calls for **cakes of raisins** and **apples** to **refresh** and strengthen her. It is as if he were actually with her, holding and embracing her.

IV. THE MAIDEN'S CHARGE TO THE DAUGHTERS OF JERUSALEM (2:7)

Turning to the **daughters of Jerusalem**,[9] the Shulamite strikes the keynote of the book. There is a time for love. It should not be aroused by carnal means (as the king was trying to do). She charges them **by the** graceful **gazelles** that they should **not stir up** or **awaken love until it pleases**. In other words, "love is not a thing to be bought or forced or pretended, but a thing to come spontaneously, to be given freely and sincerely."[10] If Israel had followed this simple rule, it would not have been unfaithful to Jehovah.

V. THE SHULAMITE REMINISCES ABOUT A VISIT FROM HER SHEPHERD-LOVER, INTERRUPTED BY ORDERS FROM HER BROTHERS TO GET TO WORK (2:8–17)

2:8–14 Now the maiden recalls a past visit of her **beloved**. He came **leaping** over **the mountains**, **skipping** over **the hills** in his haste to reach her. He had all the grace of **a gazelle or a young stag**. Soon he was standing **behind** the **wall**, **looking through the windows**, **gazing through the lattice**. She heard his voice, calling to her to leave with him. The dark night of **winter** was **past** and the **rain** was **over**. All the signs of spring were appearing—**the flowers**, **the turtledove**, **the fig tree** with **green figs**, and **the vines with . . . tender grapes**. He urged her to **"Rise up, . . . and come away."** Perhaps there was a delay, because he then asked her to come to the window, so he could **see** her **face** and **hear** her **voice**. Up to now she was hidden from him like a **dove, in the clefts of the rock**, or in the covert of a **cliff**.

2:15 Any possibility of leaving was lost when her brothers appeared and ordered her and her companions (the command is plural in the original)[11] to **catch . . . the little foxes** that were ruining **the vines** at the crucial time when they were bearing **tender grapes**.[12]

2:16,17 This is a great disappointment, but she is consoled by the fact that she and her shepherd-lover belong to each other. So she said to him, in effect, "Come back again sometime in the cool of the evening, when **the shadows** have flown **away**. Return with the speed of **a young stag** over **the mountains of Bether** (or Separation, i.e., the mountains that separate us)."

VI. THE MAIDEN DREAMS OF A RENDEZVOUS WITH HER BELOVED (3:1–4)

Now the maiden is recalling a dream in which she had a rendezvous with her beloved. One **night** she was looking for him, but when she couldn't **find him**, she went into **the city**, searched **the streets** and **squares**, and even asked **the watchmen**. Then almost immediately she **found** him, embraced **him**, and took **him** to her family home.

VII. REPETITION OF CHARGE TO DAUGHTERS OF JERUSALEM (3:5)

She interrupts long enough to repeat her **charge** to the **daughters of** **Jerusalem**—don't **stir up . . . love until it pleases**.

VIII. SOLOMON'S PROCESSION ARRIVES AT JERUSALEM (3:6–11)

The scene changes. We now watch the colorful and grandiose arrival of **Solomon's** procession at Jerusalem. The question implied is, "Who could resist the romantic overtures of such a glorious king?" The implied answer, of course, is "The Shulamite can." She is faithful to her own lover, and deaf to all other voices.

The spectators along the parade route are awed by the king's arrival, with the attendant clouds of **myrrh and frankincense**. They see the **couch** or **palanquin** of Solomon, guarded by **sixty** fully armed soldiers. Inside are the magnificent **pillars of silver, the support of gold, the seat of purple** upholstery, and the carpeting woven lovingly **by the daughters of Jerusalem**. Zion's citizens are summoned to greet **King Solomon**, wearing **the crown** given to him by **his mother . . . on the day of his wedding**.

IX. AGAIN SOLOMON SEEKS TO WIN THE MAIDEN, BUT SHE IS IMPERVIOUS TO HIS CHARMS (4:1–6)

4:1–5 There is a difference of opinion among those who hold the three-character view of the Song of Songs as to whether the speaker in these verses is Solomon or the shepherd. We shall assume that it is the much-married Solomon who has just returned to Jerusalem and is making another attempt to captivate the Shulamite.

He launches into a detailed description of her beauty. Her **eyes**, looking out from **behind** a **veil**, remind him of **doves' eyes**. The rippled sheen of her **hair** resembles a **flock of goats** moving together **down** the side of **Mount Gilead** in the sunshine. Her gleaming white **teeth** make him think of ewes, newly sheared and freshly washed. The teeth are like twin lambs in that every upper has a corresponding lower; not one is missing. **Her lips are like a strand of scarlet**, and the symmetry of her **mouth** is perfect. Her **temples behind** the **veil are** contoured **like a piece of pomegranate**. Her **neck, like the tower of David**, speaks of strength and dignity. Her **two breasts, like** twin **fawns**, suggest delicate and tender beauty.

4:6 The Shulamite interrupts[13] to let Solomon know that she is impervious to his flattery, and that she is looking forward to reunion with her beloved. When **the day** cools and **the shadows** vanish, she **will go . . . to the mountain of myrrh, and to the hill of frankincense**, that is, to her shepherd-lover.

X. THE YOUNG SHEPHERD ARRIVES AND APPEALS TO THE MAIDEN TO LEAVE JERUSALEM FOR THE HOME THEY HAVE PLANNED IN THE COUNTRY, AND SHE EXPRESSES HER WILLINGNESS (4:7—5:1)

4:7–15 Now the shepherd appears[14] and urges his fiancée to **come with** him **from Lebanon**, at the same time praising her for her beauty, **love, lips, the fragrance of** her **garments**, meaning her life, and her chastity. He likens her to **a** well-watered **garden**, bearing the choicest **fruits** and the most **fragrant . . . spices**.

4:16 In poetic language, she tells him to **come** to the **garden** and claim it as his own.

5:1a Now the shepherd responds to the Shulamite's invitation of 4:16, saying that he is coming **to the garden** to gather his spices, to eat **honeycomb**, and to drink **wine** and **milk**.

5:1b The latter part of verse 1 seems to be an anonymous encouragement from interested spectators to these two ardent lovers.[15]

XI. THE SHULAMITE RECALLS A DISTURBING DREAM IN WHICH SHE MISSED SEEING HIM BECAUSE OF HER LETHARGY (5:2–8)

5:2–7 Now the maiden describes a dream in which she heard him knocking at the door, calling for her to **open**. He was wet **with** the **dew** of the evening. When she hesitated to open to him because she had already bathed and retired for the night, he withdrew **his hand** from **the door**. Finally she got up and went to the door. Her **hands** became perfumed **with** the **liquid myrrh** which he had left **on the handles of the lock**. But he **had . . . gone**. She looked for him, **called** for **him, but . . . could not find him. The** city **watchmen**—misunderstanding her character—**struck** her and **took** off her **veil**.

5:8 In her sorrow she charges the **daughters of Jerusalem** to **tell him**, if they should somehow see him, that she still loves him as much as ever.

XII. ON INQUIRY BY THE COURT LADIES, SHE EXTOLS THE BEAUTIES OF HER BELOVED, MAKING THEM WANT TO SEE HIM TOO (5:9—6:3)

5:9 Her constant enthusiasm for a mere shepherd arouses the interest of the daughters of Jerusalem. They can't understand why anyone should refuse the love of a Solomon for some obscure country lad, so they ask her **what** is so special about her **beloved**.

5:10–16 This gives her just the opportunity she wants to extol his physical attractiveness as **"chief among ten thousand."** Using a wealth of poetic metaphors and similes, she raves about his complexion, **head**, **locks**, **eyes**, **cheeks**, **lips**, **hands**, **body**, **legs**, **countenance**, and **mouth**. In short, her **beloved** and her **friend is altogether lovely**.[16]

6:1 By this time **the daughters of Jerusalem** really want to see this paragon of male beauty. They ask **where they might seek him** with her.[17]

6:2,3 The maiden's answer is purposely vague and evasive—he **"has gone to his garden."** Why should she tell *them*? She belongs to him, he belongs to her, and that's the way she intends it to remain!

XIII. SOLOMON RENEWS HIS AMOROUS APPEALS (6:4–10)

Solomon appears again and tries to woo her. Using middle-eastern imagery, he raves over her facial beauty; much of what he says is a repeat of 4:1–3. In his mind, she surpassed **sixty queens**, **eighty concubines**, and numberless **virgins**. Not only was she her mother's **favorite**, but **the queens**, **concubines**, and maidens all **praised her**, saying, "Who is she who looks forth as the morning, fair as the moon, clear as the sun, awesome as an army with banners?"

XIV. SHE EXPLAINS TO THE COURT LADIES THE UNEXPECTED WAY IN WHICH SHE WAS BROUGHT TO THE PALACE (6:11–13)

6:11,12 The Shulamite deflects Solomon's overtures with an obscure explanation, perhaps of how the king's chariot came by while she was in the field checking the fruit and **garden of nuts**. The king's subsequent interest in taking her to the palace in Jerusalem was nothing that she had planned or even desired.

6:13 As she starts to leave, either Solomon and the daughters of Jerusalem or his friends call her back for another **look** at her beauty. But she asks why they would want to look on anyone as ordinary as she. The last line in the verse is difficult. **The two camps** (Heb. *Mahanaim*) that the Shulamite speaks of may well be a dance in which two groups of dancers weave in and out with one another.

XV. SOLOMON'S FINAL APPROACH PROVES TO BE IN VAIN (7:1–10)

7:1–9a Solomon continues his fulsome praise by giving a full-length portrait of her physical charms, comparing her to famous places in his far-flung realm: **Heshbon**, **Bath Rabbim**, **Damascus**, and **Mount Carmel**. Then he sees her as a stately **palm tree**, and would like to embrace her. When he does, her **breasts** would **be like clusters of** fruit, her **breath like apples**, and her kisses **like the best wine**—

7:9b–10 The maiden finishes the sentence by letting him know that her **wine** is not for him but **for** her **beloved**. She belongs to her lover and not to the king. Even as she said it, she knew that the shepherd was longing for her.

XVI. SHE CONVERSES WITH HER SHEPHERD-LOVER WHO HAS ARRIVED TO TAKE HER AWAY (7:11–8:2)

7:11–13 Now the shepherd-lover has arrived in Jerusalem and she is free to **go to the field** and **the villages** with him. She anticipates walking in **the field** with him, going out at daybreak **to the vineyards** to check **the vine . . . and the pomegranates**. In that rural setting where **the mandrakes** are fragrant, she will give him her love and all kinds of **pleasant fruits** which she has stored up for him.

8:1, 2 The Shulamite is still speaking. If the shepherd **were** only her **brother**, she could **kiss** him and **not be** reproached. She would take him to her mother's **house** and serve him the choicest **spiced wine** made of **pomegranate**.

XVII. FINAL CHARGE TO THE DAUGHTERS OF JERUSALEM (8:3, 4)

In an aside **to the daughters of Jerusalem**, the Shulamite sees herself in his arms, then charges them for the last time **not** to **stir up** love **until it pleases**.

XVIII. THE COUPLE ARRIVE IN THEIR COUNTRY VILLAGE, EXCHANGE THEIR VOWS, AND LIVE HAPPILY EVER AFTER (8:5–14)

8:5a In her home village, the local people see her returning **from** Jerusalem and ask **who** it **is, coming up from the wilderness, leaning upon her beloved**.

8:5b Then as the lovers approach, the shepherd points out familiar places— **under the apple tree** where their romance began, and then also her birthplace.

8:6,7 The Shulamite suggests renewing their vows. In words of great beauty that have been widely quoted, she affirms that there is no rival for her **love**. It **is as strong as death**, unquenchable, and beyond price.

8:8, 9 Years ago, when planning the young Shulamite's future, her **brothers** had made this decision. If she proved to be chaste, pure, and faithful, they would give her a **silver** dowry. **If**, however, **she** was promiscuous and accessible as **a door**, they would hide her away in seclusion.

8:10, 11 The maiden assures them that, now of marriageable age, she has been steadfast as **a wall**. Her lover knows that. She tells them of Solomon's **vineyard at Baal Hamon** with its many tenants.

8:12 But she wasn't interested. She had her **own vineyard**—her shepherd-lover. **Solomon** could keep his wealth as far as she was concerned.

8:13 In the presence of witnesses, the shepherd asks her to commit herself to him now in marriage, to say "I do."

8:14 In figurative language, she tells her **beloved** to **make haste** to claim her as his own. And thus the book closes. It has been called

the Old Testament's endorsement of monogamy in the face of the most glaring example of polygamy to be found in the Scriptures. It is a powerful plea to Israel of Solomon's day to return to the God-given ideal of love and marriage.[18]

ENDNOTES

[1](Intro) Franz Delitzsch, "The Song of Songs," in *Biblical Commentary on the Old Testament*, XVI:1.

[2](Intro) Arthur Farstad, "Literary Genre of the Song of Songs," p. 63.

[3](Intro) Clarke's commentary (see

Bibliography) presents the same view as the *Believers Bible Commentary*.

[4](1:5, 6) The little word translated "but" (*we*) can be (and more often is) translated "and." Then a literal translation would be "black and beautiful."

[5](1:7, 8) The translators of the NKJV take verse 8 to be the words of the Beloved, and hence not sarcastic. The Beloved and Solomon are taken as the same person rather than as rivals for the Shulamite's love. It should be stressed that the headings in the NKJV, New Scofield, or any Bible, are editorial, and not part of the text. However, as the note at 1:1 in the NKJV points out, the Hebrew wording is clearer than the English as to gender and number of persons referred to.

[6](1:11) The NKJV takes the "we" literally as referring to the daughters of Jerusalem.

[7](2:1) In prose, poetry, and hymnody our Lord has been likened to the lily of the valley and the rose of Sharon. That comparison is still valid even if it is not the thought in this passage.

[8](2:1) Farstad, "Literary Genre," p. 79, f.n. 6.

[9](2:7) The NKJV takes the address to the daughters to start at v. 4.

[10](2:7) W. Twyman Williams, "The Song of Solomon," *Moody Monthly*, February 1947, p. 398.

[11](2:15) The plural form of "catch" may be explained by the likelihood that these lines (extremely song-like and full of rhymes in the original) are a "vine-dresser's ditty" (Delitzsch, "Song of Songs," p. 53). Otto Zöckler writes that "this verse is a little vintagers' song or at least a fragment of one" and says that all the commentators of his time who are not allegorists are settled on this ("Song of Songs," in *Lange's Commentary on the Holy Scriptures*, V:71).

[12](2:15) Young foxes (the term includes jackals) come out in the spring and destroy the vines by burrowing passages and holes beneath the roots, thus undermining their support. See Delitzsch, "Song of Songs," p. 54.

[13](4:6) The NKJV editors take this verse as part of the Beloved's speech.

[14](4:7–15) The NKJV editors see no indication of a new speaker here and take these verses as part of the Beloved's speech.

[15](5:1b) The NKJV editors agree, calling these people "His friends."

[16](5:10–16) Based on the Christological interpretation of the book, the phrases "chief among ten thousand" and "altogether lovely" have been applied to our Lord in sermon and song. Especially in the spiritual sense, these applications are well warranted, even if not originally meant by the context.

[17](6:1) In the Christological interpretation the bride's (= church's) "witnessing" to the beauties of her beloved (= Christ) causes others to seek Him too.

[18](8:14) Williams, "Song," p. 422.

BIBLIOGRAPHY

Bellett, J. G. *Meditations upon the Canticles*. London: G. Morrish, n.d.

Burrowes, George. *A Commentary on the Song of Solomon*. Philadelphia: William S. & Alfred Martien, 1860.

Clarke, Arthur G. *The Song of Songs*. Kansas City, KS: Walterick Publishers, n.d.

Delitzsch, Franz. "The Song of Songs." In *Biblical Commentary on the Old Testament*, Vol. 16. Grand Rapids: Wm. B. Eerdmans Publishing Company, 1971.

Zöckler, Otto. "The Song of Solomon." *Lange's Commentary on the Holy Scriptures*. Vol. 5. Grand Rapids: Zondervan Publishing House, 1960.

Periodicals

Williams, W. Twyman. "The Song of Solomon," *Moody Monthly*, February 1947.

Unpublished Materials

Farstad, Arthur L. "Literary Genre of the Song of Songs." Th.M. Thesis, Dallas Theological Seminary, 1967.

INTRODUCTION TO THE PROPHETS

The section of the OT from Isaiah through Malachi is often spoken of as "the Prophets." Isaiah, Jeremiah, Ezekiel, and Daniel are known as the *Major* Prophets, simply because their books are longer than most of the others. The twelve shorter prophets are known as the *Minor* Prophets.

I. The Ministry of the Prophets

In the true biblical sense, a prophet is one who speaks for God. These men[1] were raised up in periods of sin and declension to accuse the people of their sin and predict the judgment of God if they did not repent.

In the OT, the prophetic period began in the time of Samuel (about 1100 B.C.), when the priesthood had failed. The prophets continued their ministry through the end of OT history (about 400 B.C.), including the return from captivity and the rebuilding of Jerusalem and the temple.

However, the *writing* prophets of the OT did not come upon the scene until the time of the divided kingdom (about 930 B.C.). Thus, they fit into the events recorded in 1 and 2 Kings and 1 and 2 Chronicles, and also extend through Ezra and Nehemiah.

II. The Methods of the Prophets

It has often been pointed out that the prophets' messages consisted of both forthtelling and foretelling.

By *forthtelling*, we mean that these prophets told forth the Word of God.

They were conscious that they were doing this. They used such expressions as, "Thus says the Lord," or "The word of the Lord came to me" (See Jer. 1:9 and Ezek. 2:7).

As *foretellers*, they peered into the future and told the people what the consequences would be if they obeyed or disobeyed. The prophets did not always understand the messages themselves (Dan. 7:28; 8:15–27; 10:7–15; Rev. 7:13, 14; 17:6). They had particular difficulty when they made prophecies concerning the coming Messiah. When they prophesied of the sufferings of Christ and the glories that should follow (1 Pet. 1:10–13), they could not understand how the Messiah could come as the suffering Servant of Jehovah and at the same time reign as the King over all the earth. They did not realize that there were two distinct comings—His coming to Bethlehem and His coming back again to the Mount of Olives. They did not realize that an interval of time would come between these two comings.

III. The Topics of the Prophets

The topics taken up by the OT prophets may be summarized as follows:

1. The holiness of God.
2. The sin and failure of God's chosen people.
3. A call to repentance.
4. God's judgment on them if they would not repent.

931

5. God's judgment on the surrounding nations.
6. The return of part of the nation from captivity.
7. The coming of the Messiah and His rejection.
8. The Messiah's coming in power and great glory.
9. The restoration of God's chosen people.
10. Christ's universal reign.

It should be noted at this point that the church is not the subject of OT prophecy. We would not expect the church to be found here since we are distinctly told in the NT that it is a mystery which was hidden in God from the foundation of the world (Eph. 3:4–6).

The law of double reference is a helpful key to understanding certain OT passages. The law of double reference simply means that some of the prophecies of the OT had an immediate and partial fulfillment, and yet would some day have a complete fulfillment. For instance, the prophecy in Joel 2:28–32 had a partial fulfillment on the Day of Pentecost (Acts 2:7–21), but it will have a complete fulfillment when the Lord Jesus returns to set up His kingdom on the earth at the close of the Great Tribulation period.

It is good to remember that while some prophecies are crystal clear from the outset, there are others that will not be clear until they actually take place.

We should avoid fanciful interpretations of prophecy. Great harm has been done by stating that certain individuals and events are fulfillments, when it later becomes obvious that they were not.

IV. The Terminology of the Prophets

Some further key terms to help us understand the Prophets are:

1. The name *Israel* ordinarily refers to the Northern Kingdom, the ten tribes. But it sometimes refers to the entire nation—all who are descendants of Abraham.
2. *Judah,* on the other hand, usually refers to the Southern Kingdom, the two tribes of Judah and Benjamin.
3. *Ephraim* is used, especially in Hosea, to describe the ten tribes, or the Northern Kingdom. The house of Joseph also refers to the Northern Kingdom.
4. *Samaria* was the capital of the Northern Kingdom and is mentioned frequently.
5. *Jerusalem,* on the other hand, was the capital of the Southern Kingdom.
6. *Nineveh* was the capital of Assyria.
7. The city of *Babylon* was the capital of the nation of Babylon (also called Babylonia).
8. *Damascus* was the chief city-state of Syria.

In their denunciation of idolatry, the prophets often used words associated with idolatry, such as "wooden images," "high places," "terebinth trees" or "oaks," and "gardens."

"Judgment" is often used by the prophets to mean justice. They denounced the perverting of "judgment," meaning that they condemned judges who took bribes and thus did not dispense justice.

The thought of a remnant of the nation of Israel is prominent in the Prophets. These books predict the return of a believing remnant of the nation in a latter day, just as a remnant returned after the captivity in Babylon.

V. The Classification of the Prophets

The books of the Prophets may be classified in several ways. We have already seen that they are divided into the Major and Minor Prophets. They can also be classified according to the time in which they lived:

Pre-exilic

Isaiah	Jonah
Jeremiah	Micah
Hosea	Nahum
Joel	Habakkuk
Amos	Zephaniah
Obadiah	

Exilic	**Post-exilic**
Ezekiel	Haggai
Daniel	Zechariah
	Malachi

The pre-exilic prophets were those who ministered *before* the nation was taken into captivity. The exilic prophets were those who spoke for God *during* the time of the Babylonian captivity. The post-exilic prophets returned with the people *after* the captivity and urged them to rebuild the city and the temple and to reform their morals.

Then the prophets may also be classified according to the people to whom their messages were primarily directed:

Israel	**The Nations**
Hosea	Nahum
Amos	Obadiah
Jonah	

Judah

Isaiah	Zephaniah
Jeremiah	Ezekiel
Joel	Daniel
Micah	Haggai
Habakkuk	Zechariah
Malachi	

Some of these prophets ministered to more than one of these groups. For instance, Jonah might also be listed as a prophet to the nations. Micah prophesied to Israel as well as to Judah. Nahum spoke to Judah (1:15) as well as to Nineveh. Habakkuk had much to say about the nations.

In several instances, the name of the prophet is hidden in the text of his prophecy. For instance, the name Isaiah means *Jehovah is salvation*. In Isaiah 12:2 we read, "YAH, the Lord has . . . become salvation."

Jeremiah—*Jehovah establishes* or *exalted of Jehovah*—52:31.
Ezekiel—*God strengthens*—34:16.
Joel—*Jehovah is God*—2:13.
Micah—*who is like Jehovah?*—7:18.
Zephaniah—*hidden by Jehovah*—2:3.
Malachi—*My messenger*—3:1.

VI. The Chronology of the Prophets

The following chronology will help the reader to understand various references in the books of the Prophets.

Kingdom of Israel (Northern Tribes)

Syria was the principal foreign foe of Israel after the division of the Kingdom.

Then Assyria rose to power and menaced Israel. The steps by which Assyria conquered Israel are as follows:

1. Jehu paid tribute to Shalmaneser, King of Assyria (842 B.C.).
2. Menahem paid tribute to Tiglath-Pileser. The latter started taking the Israelites away from the land.
3. In the reign of Pekah, Tiglath-Pileser captured cities of Naphtali and carried off inhabitants to Assyria (2 Kgs. 15:29). He also overran the country east of the Jordan and deported the two and one-

half tribes to Mesopotamia, 740 B.C. (1 Chron. 5:26). By his connivance, Pekah was killed, and Hoshea was put on the throne.

4. Hoshea became Shalmaneser's servant and paid tribute to him, but plotted against him by sending gifts to Egypt and seeking an alliance so that the Assyrian yoke could be broken (2 Kgs. 17:3, 4).

5. Shalmaneser besieged Samaria. The city was taken in the first year of Sargon's reign, 722 B.C. or 721 B.C. Many of the people were deported to Mesopotamia and Media (2 Kgs. 17:5, 6, 18). The rest were placed under tribute.

Kingdom of Judah (Southern Tribes)

After conquering the Northern Kingdom, Assyria began to threaten Judah. God assured the Jews that, though the Assyrians would come against them, they would not succeed, but would be destroyed. This happened when Sennacherib came against Jerusalem during Hezekiah's reign.

Then Babylon rose to power and became the great threat to Judah. The political steps that led to the conquest of Judah by Babylon are as follows:

1. Jehoiakim became the puppet of the King of Egypt.

2. Babylon conquered Egypt and Assyria, and thus Judah came under her power (605 B.C.).

3. In 605 B.C. (third or fourth year of Jehoiakim), Nebuchadnezzar came to Jerusalem, took some of the vessels of the temple to Babylon, and carried off certain members of the royal family as captives. The captives included the king (Jehoiakim) and the prophet Daniel (2 Kgs. 24:1–6; 2 Chron. 36:5–8; Jer. 45:1; Dan. 1:1, 2).

4. In 597 B.C., Nebuchadnezzar carried off Jehoiachin (Jeconiah or Coniah) and many others (2 Kgs. 24:10–16). Ezekiel was taken to Babylon in this deportation.

5. In 586 B.C., the armies of Nebuchadnezzar burned the temple, destroyed Jerusalem, and carried off the bulk of the population, leaving only some of the poorest people in the land (2 Kgs. 25:2–21).

6. The people who remained in the land were ruled by a governor, Gedaliah. Jeremiah was in this group. Then Gedaliah was assassinated, and many of the people fled to Egypt, taking Jeremiah with them (2 Kgs. 25:22–26).

Seventy-Year Captivity and Post-Captivity Period

The Babylonian world empire extended to 539 B.C., when Cyrus captured Babylon. It was he who issued the decree permitting the captives to return to the land of Israel. An expedition under Zerubbabel returned in 538 B.C., and another under Ezra in 458 B.C.

Darius the Mede reigned from 538–536 B.C.

The Medo-Persian empire continued until 333 B.C., when the Grecians, under Alexander the Great, gained world dominion.

The seventy-year captivity extended from the fall of Jerusalem in 586 B.C. to the rebuilding of the temple in 516 B.C.

ENDNOTES

[1]There were also some female prophets, or prophetesses, such as Huldah (2 Kgs. 22:14; 2 Chron. 34:22).

ISAIAH

Introduction

"Isaiah . . . is the greatest of the Hebrew prophets and orators. For splendor of diction, brilliance of imagery, versatility and beauty of style, he is unequalled. Correctly he has been called the 'Prince of Old Testament Prophets.'"

—Merrill F. Unger

I. Unique Place in the Canon

Visitors to Ireland's lovely capital who appreciate Christian culture are often shown a private house where one of the greatest musical compositions had its "world premiere." It was in Dublin on April 13, 1742 that Handel's *Messiah* was first performed.[1] No knowledgeable person has ever questioned the excellence of Handel's composition as to the music, but what about the libretto (words) of this most famous of all oratorios? They are all from God's Word, especially from the OT Messianic prophecies. And the prophet who contributed most to the libretto[2] was a Hebrew writer who lived seven centuries before the incarnation of his Messiah—and Handel's, and yours, and mine. His name is Isaiah and he wrote the longest, loveliest, and most Messianic of OT prophecies.

II. Authorship

Isaiah (Hebrew, *Yesha'yāhû, Jehovah is salvation* or *salvation of Jehovah*), the son of Amoz, had a vision which constitutes the Book of Isaiah. Because of the critical theories that have "sawn it asunder," we will give a somewhat fuller introduction to this book than to most.

The Unity of Isaiah

There are several theories of the so-called "higher critics" that have been taught for a century or so, not as hypotheses, but almost as fact. These are virtually taken for granted in many circles. Among them are: Moses did not write the Pentateuch, Daniel did not write Daniel, Peter did not write 2 Peter, Paul (probably) did not write the Pastoral Epistles,[3] and Isaiah only wrote the first part of the sixty-six chapters attributed to him.

Because Isaiah is such a major work, is so replete with messianic prophecies (especially in the parts the critics attribute to others), and is quoted so often in the NT, we feel it is necessary to spend more space on this critical question than we ordinarily would in a book on a popular level for ordinary believers.

Our approach will be to give the *positive arguments* for Isaiah's authorship of the entire book and then answer one by one the arguments presented against that unity.

1. The witness of history and tradition

Until the late 1700's virtually all Jewish and Christian scholars accepted

Isaiah as one long prophecy by one very gifted writer, Isaiah the son of Amoz.

But in 1795 J. C. Doederlein proposed a "Second Isaiah" (or "Deutero-Isaiah") as the author of chapters 40—66. Of course the difference in content and outlook between Isaiah 1—39 and 40—66 had been noted by all careful readers for centuries, but this does not necessitate different authors. In 1892 B. Duhm denied the unity of chapters 40—66, postulating a "Third Isaiah" (or "Trito-Isaiah") for chapters 55—66. Some carried the thing even further, but two or three "Isaiahs" are generally accepted in liberal circles.

No early tradition ever suggested two or more authors; in fact, belief in the unity of Isaiah is early, uniform, and unchallenged.

2. The Witness of the NT

Isaiah is the second most quoted OT book in the NT (after Psalms), and there is always an assumption of unity. Quotations from the second part of the prophecy as being by Isaiah are made by John the Baptist (Matt. 3:3; Luke 3:4; John 1:23); by Matthew (8:17; 12:18–21); by John (12:38–41); and by Paul (Rom. 9:27–33; 10:16–21). This is especially noteworthy in John 12:38–41 because the actual author as a person, and not merely the book, is referred to: "These things Isaiah said when he saw His glory and spoke of Him" (v. 41). The "these things" are Isaiah 53:1, which is from the second part of the book (v. 38) and Isaiah 6:10 (where Isaiah saw Christ's glory) (vv. 39–40) is from the first.

3. Unity of Plan and Development

The book of Isaiah displays a consistent plan and order which does not go well with the theory of a collection of fragments by two or more different authors.

4. The Sheer Grandeur of the Poetry

The outstanding beauty in the second part of the book makes it hard to believe that such a marvelous writer, alleged to live in the 500's B.C., could be completely forgotten. After all, the very short Minor Prophets are all ascribed to their authors by name.

5. Dead Sea Scrolls

The Dead Sea Scrolls of Isaiah (Second Century B.C.) give no hint whatsoever of any split at chapter 40.

Arguments Against Isaianic Unity Answered

Three main arguments are leveled against the unity of the book: Its *historical* viewpoint, the *linguistic* argument, and the *theological* argument.

1. The Historical Viewpoint

That Isaiah falls into two main sections is agreed upon by nearly all (1—39 and 40—66). Chapters 36—39 are a sort of historical interlude. It is interesting how chapters 1—39 mirror the OT and 40—66 parallel the NT—even in the numbers: one chapter per OT and NT book. This may be coincidental, however, since the chapter divisions are not part of the inspired text.

The viewpoint of chapters 1—39 is definitely pre-exilic and that of 40—66 is clearly post-exilic. Could Isaiah project himself into the future and write from a viewpoint in the future? Many critics say no. And yet Jeremiah, Daniel, and even our Lord (Matt. 13) did so on occasion.

If chapters 40—66 were written in the 500's B.C., why is the flavor of the book Palestinian and not Babylonian?

2. Linguistic Argument

The style of "Second Isaiah" is different from that of Isaiah, critics maintain. All have noted the major break in outlook beginning with "Comfort, yes, comfort My people" (40:1). But this can merely prove the versatility of the writer. Plato, Milton, and Shakespeare also could vary their styles amazingly—according to content. The glorious comfort of the Messiah, prominent in 40—66, is enough to explain the difference.

Also, there are many similarities of style between the two (or three) parts of the book. Many details demand a knowledge of Hebrew, but one of Isaiah's phrases that shows up throughout his work is "the Holy One of God"—a divine title.

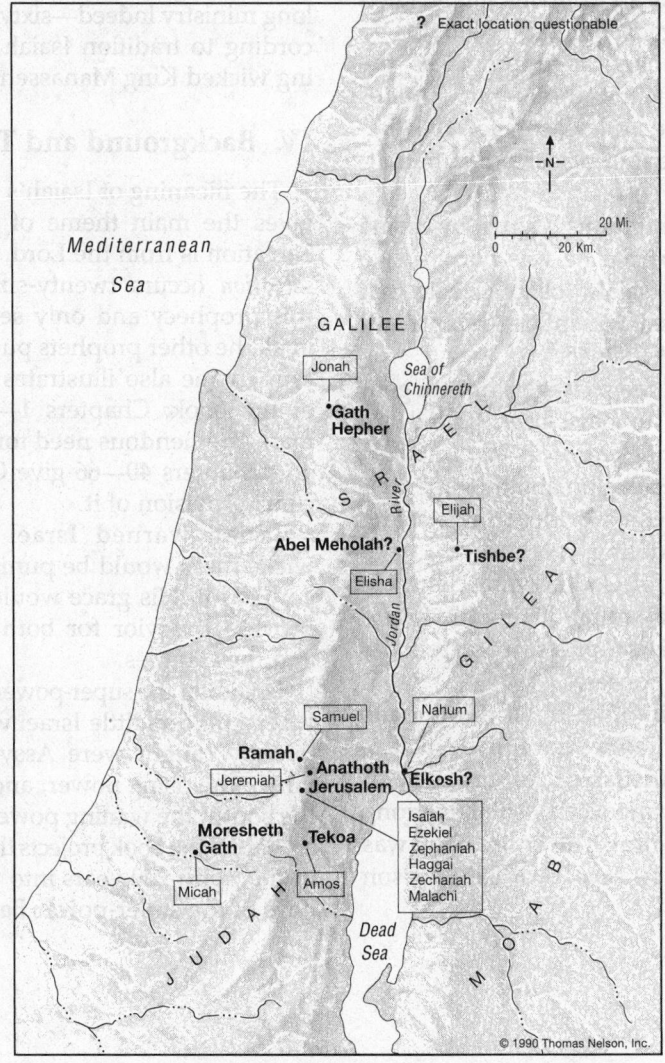

The Prophets of Israel and Judah

3. Theological Argument

Critics do not suggest a contradiction between the theology of "First" and "Second" Isaiah, merely that "Second Isaiah" is more "advanced." (This fits in with the whole unsound theory of evolution as applied to everything, and not merely to biology. Isaiah is said to emphasize God's majesty, "Second Isaiah" His infinity. Actually, Micah, who was a contemporary of Isaiah, contains similar ideas to the alleged "Second Isaiah.")

The theological argument is the weakest of the three, but it does suggest the *real* reason for the theories in the first place: anti-supernaturalism.

Isaiah mentions Cyrus by name centuries before he was born—if we accept one Isaiah. Josephus said that Cyrus himself was influenced by reading this in Isaiah 45.[4]

Many of the passages that are generally said to have been added are mostly *specific prophecies that have been fulfilled.* Here again an anti-supernatural bias seems evident in rejecting their early dating.

After all, if God is omniscient, He has no problem predicting the future through His prophets in as great detail as He chooses.

Hence, in spite of all the inroads that these theories have made in supposedly Christian circles, the ancient, uniform, evangelical position is strong and also logical: The entire book was written, as 1:1 says, by Isaiah, the son of Amoz.

III. Date

Isaiah started his ministry "in the year that King Uzziah died" (6:1; c. 740 B.C.). His years of ministry, chiefly to Judah, extended through the reigns of four kings: Uzziah and Jotham, who were largely good kings; Ahaz, a wicked king; Hezekiah, a very good king and a personal friend of the prophet. Since Isaiah records Sennacherib's death (681 B.C.), he likely lived till at least 680, giving a very long ministry indeed—sixty years! According to tradition Isaiah died during wicked King Manasseh's reign.

IV. Background and Theme

The meaning of Isaiah's name also gives the main theme of the book. Salvation is from the Lord. The word *salvation* occurs twenty-six times in this prophecy and only seven times in all the other prophets put together. This theme also illustrates the unity of the book: Chapters 1—39 depict man's tremendous need for salvation and chapters 40—66 give God's gracious provision of it.

Isaiah warned Israel that her wickedness would be punished, and yet God in His grace would one day provide a Savior for both the Jews and the Gentiles.

Politically, the super-powers between whose pincers little Israel was so frequently caught were Assyria to the north, the rising power, and Egypt to the south, the waning power. The latter part of the book projects the prophet in the Spirit 200 years into the future days of the super-power Babylon.

OUTLINE

III. PROPHECIES OF COMFORT FROM THE VIEWPOINT OF THE FUTURE
    CAPTIVITY (Chaps. 40—66)

    A. The Comfort of Israel's Coming Deliverance (Chaps. 40—48)
       1. Comfort from God's Pardon and Peace (40:1-11)
       2. Comfort from God's Attributes (40:12-31)
       3. Comfort from the Holy One of Israel (Chap. 41)
       4. Comfort from the Servant of the Lord (Chap. 42)
       5. Comfort from Israel's Restoration (Chaps. 43, 44)
       6. Comfort from Cyrus, God's Anointed (Chap. 45)
       7. Comfort from the Fall of Babylon's Idols (Chap. 46)
       8. Comfort from the Fall of Babylon (Chap. 47)
       9. Comfort from Israel's Return after Chastening (Chap. 48)

    B. The Messiah and His Rejection by Israel (Chaps. 49—57)
       1. The Messiah as Servant (Chap. 49)
       2. The Messiah as True Disciple (Chap. 50)
       3. The Messiah as Righteous Ruler (51:1—52:12)
       4. The Messiah as Sin-bearing Sacrifice (52:13—53:12)
       5. The Messiah as Redeemer and Restorer (Chap. 54)
       6. The Messiah as World Evangelist (55:1—56:8)
       7. The Messiah as Judge of the Wicked (56:9—57:21)

    C. Israel's Sin, Judgment, Repentance, and Restoration (Chaps. 58—66)
       1. The Delights of True Spirituality (Chap. 58)
       2. The Iniquities of Israel (Chap. 59)
       3. The Future Glory of Zion (Chap. 60)
       4. The Messiah's Ministries (Chap. 61)
       5. The Future Delights of Jerusalem (Chap. 62)
       6. The Day of Vengeance (63:1-6)
       7. The Prayer of the Remnant (63:7—64:12)
       8. The Lord's Answer to the Prayer of the Remnant (Chap. 65)
       9. The Consummation: Peace Like a River (Chap. 66)

Commentary

I. PROPHECIES OF PUNISHMENT AND BLESSING FROM ISAIAH'S TIME (Chaps. 1—35)

A. Judgments on Judah and Jerusalem with Glimpses of Glory Shining Through (Chaps. 1—5)

1. God's Case Against Israel (Chap. 1)

1:1 The first verse of Isaiah is much like a title; its historical refer-ences are handled in our Introduction.

1:2, 3 The whole universe is summoned to attend a trial with God as the Judge, and with **Judah and Jerusalem** as defendants. The indict-ment charges the people with being intractible sons who **have rebelled against** God and fail to show the natural gratitude and devotion that could be expected of a domestic animal!

1:4–6 The **people** are guilty of aggravated **iniquity** in turning their backs on **the Holy One**. God's chastenings have not succeeded, even though the body is covered with **wounds and bruises and putrefying sores**.

1:7–9 Beginning with verse 7, the prophet describes the future as if it had already taken place.[5] Enemy invaders have made Judah **desolate**. Jerusalem, **the daughter of Zion**, is like a crude, temporary **hut**, standing gauntly amid the wreckage. But for the grace of God in sparing **a very small remnant**, the destruction **would have** been as complete as that of **Sodom** and **Gomorrah**.

1:10–15 The **rulers** and **people of** Jerusalem (**Sodom** and **Gomorrah**) should realize that God despises rituals without reality, **sacrifices** without obedience, gifts without the givers. As long as people are living in sin, their attendance at the temple services is an insulting trampling of His **courts**. The mixing of **iniquity** and solemn assembly is hateful to Him. He will pay no attention to their outstretched **hands** or **many prayers**.

W. E. Vine warns believers of the same danger today:

> Mere external religion is ever a cloak to cover iniquity. The Lord exposed all that in His strong denunciations in Matt. 23. The guilty combination in Judaism has largely developed in Christendom. The conscience of a believer may become so seared that a person can practise religion while yet living in sin.[6]

1:16, 17 What they should do is **wash** themselves through repentance and forsaking of **evil**, then practice righteousness and social **justice**.

1:18–20 If they follow this line of divine reasoning, they will be cleansed from **sins** of deepest dye and enjoy **the good** things that God has provided for them. It is significant that

the first chapter of the evangelical prophet, whose name means "the salvation of Jehovah," should contain the winning gospel invitation:

> **"Come now, and let us reason together,"** says the LORD, **"Though your sins are like scarlet, they shall be as white as snow; though they are red like crimson, they shall be as wool."**

Divine reasoning, accepted by faith, teaches that there is cleansing from sin, that this cleansing is totally apart from human merit or effort, and that it is only through the redemption which the Lord Jesus accomplished by the shedding of His blood on the cross. Who can know the throngs who have answered the invitation of Isaiah 1:18? And it is still sounding out!

But if the people **refuse and rebel**, then war and destruction await them.

1:21–23 Jerusalem is no longer a **city** of faithfulness, **justice**, and **righteousness**. It is now a **harlot** city, a refuge of **murderers**. Its best things have been corrupted and its **princes** are scoundrels. Bribery and injustice are everywhere.

1:24–31 **Therefore**, God **will** vent His wrath on all those who show by their sin that they are His **enemies**. His judgments will **purge** all impurity and restore Jerusalem to its former glory. His **righteousness** will insure the deliverance of those who repent.

The Lord's combined name, **the** LORD **of hosts**, insures the inevitability of the judgments described.

But **sinners** will be destroyed. Idolaters will **be ashamed** of their shrines (**terebinth trees** and **gardens**). They themselves will be like a **terebinth whose leaf fades** and a parched **garden that has no water**. Leaders who rely on their own strength (**the strong**) will be like highly flammable **tinder**, ignited by the **spark** of their own wicked works.

2. Future Blessing Through Cleansing (Chaps. 2—4)

2:1–3 **The son of Amoz** now looks beyond the current chaos to the glorious kingdom of the Messiah. In that day **Jerusalem** will **be established** as the religious and political capital of the world. The Gentile **nations** will make pilgrimages to **Zion** for worship and for divine instruction.

2:4 The King will arbitrate international problems and settle disputes for the **people**. As a result, there will be universal disarmament.[7] The funds formerly spent on munitions will be spent on agricultural equipment. These opening verses resemble Micah 4:1–3, either because they are inspired by the same Holy Spirit or because one prophet could be quoting the other.

2:5 The glorious prospect of Christ's kingdom moves Isaiah to call the people of Judah to repentance immediately.

2:6–9 Then addressing God directly, Isaiah rehearses the sins which led to the nation's calamity. Instead of looking to the Lord, the people consulted diviners from the East and became **soothsayers like the Philistines**. They made forbidden alliances with the heathen. In disobedience to the law of God, they heaped up financial **treasures** and **horses** and **chariots**, trusting in these for security. They worshiped idols which they themselves had made. Those are the reasons God has humbled them, and does **not forgive them**. The expression **"filled with eastern ways"** aptly describes the current popularity of Eastern religion in Western countries.

2:10, 11 Turning now to the people, the seer warns them to seek refuge from the coming **terror of** Jehovah's wrath which will lay low **the lofty looks of man**.

2:12–18 In a sudden transition, Isaiah jumps forward to the judgments of **the day of the LORD** which will precede Christ's reign. **The LORD of hosts** will deal with all human arrogance, whether of individuals (**cedars** and **oaks**), governments (**high mountains** and **hills**), military might (**tower and wall**), or commerce (**ships** and **beautiful sloops**[8]). Man's **loftiness** will be leveled and **the LORD alone will be exalted**. **Idols** will be abandoned.

2:19–22 People will seek for shelter wherever they can hide. It will be clear then that fleeting man is unworthy of trust. Only the Lord is worthy of the undivided confidence of His people.

3:1–5 In that day of which we read in 2:20, **the Lord** will take **away** the responsible leadership that the people had depended on. The loss of **bread and water** may refer to famine conditions, but here **bread and water** probably symbolize essential leaders, as suggested by the following verse. There will be a lack of capable, mature leaders in every walk of life. It will be a time of oppression, anarchy, insolence, disrespect, and insubordination.

3:6–8 People will try to draft a relative to take charge of **"these ruins,"** but the latter will refuse, since he has neither **food nor clothing in** his **house**. And no one is to blame for the calamity, says Isaiah, but the people **themselves**.

3:9–12 In verse 9, the prophet begins a series of eight "woes," two in this chapter and six in chapter 5. The first arraigns the populace for partiality and for shamelessness. The second upbraids them for their wickedness, but promises blessing to **the righteous** remnant. One result of their sin is that they are being led by the inexperienced and immature (**children**), by the weak (**women**), and by deceivers.

3:13–15 In these verses **the Lord** summons Israel to stand trial. The charges are leveled. He takes the rulers to task for enriching themselves at the expense of **the poor** (through bribery and extortion, no doubt). Since the verdict is "guilty," the sentence is announced.

3:16–24 Next comes a scathing denunciation of the women of Judah for their pride, their suggestive mannerisms, and their expensive clothing and jewelry. The faces on which they had spread expensive cosmetics will be encrusted with scabs. Their bodies will be stripped of all the **finery**. Instead of being elegant ladies, they will become bedraggled refugees— reeking of body odor, tied with **rope**, their heads shaved bald, only burlap to wear, branded for identification.

3:25—4:1 An added calamity will be the loss of their **men . . . in war**. The decimation of the male population will lead **seven women** to aggressively propose to **one man**, promising to support themselves as long as they can carry his **name** and thus escape the awful **reproach** of being unmarried and of dying childless.

4:2–6 The rest of chapter 4 looks forward to the **glorious** kingdom of Christ. He is **the Branch** of verse 2, **beautiful and glorious**. Matthew Henry comments:

He is the *branch of the Lord*, the man the branch; it is one of his prophetical names, *my servant the branch* (Zech. iii. 8; vi. 12), the *branch of righteousness* (Jer. xxiii. 5; xxxiii. 15), a *rod out of the stem of Jesse and a branch out of his roots* (*ch.* xi. 1), and this, as some think, is alluded to when he is called a *Nazarene*, Matt. ii. 23. Here he is called *the branch*

of the Lord, because planted by his power and flourishing to his praise. The ancient Chaldee paraphrase here reads it, *The Christ, or Messiah, of the Lord.*[9]

He is also the first **fruit of the land**, in whom the restored Israelites boast. Unbelievers will have been destroyed by the Lord Jesus at His Second Advent. Saved Jews, **recorded** for life **in Jerusalem, will be called holy**. The cleansing of verse 4 is accomplished **by . . . judgment** and not by the gospel. **Mount Zion** will be covered by a canopy of **cloud . . . by day** and **of flaming fire by night**, a symbol of God's care and protection.

3. Israel's Punishment for Sin (Chap. 5)

5:1, 2 In the song which Isaiah sings for his **Well-beloved** (Jehovah, or NKJV Lord), he rehearses the tender care of the Lord for **His vineyard**. God chose the best location, cultivated the land, **planted it with the choicest vine**, protected it, and prepared **a winepress** in hope of a good harvest. Instead of the harvest He expected (obedience, thanksgiving, love, worship, service), He found foul-smelling, **wild grapes** (disobedience, rebellion, idolatry).

5:3–6 Indignantly the Lord asks Judah **what more could** He **have . . . done**, and **why** did He receive such poor returns. He then announces the punishment impending. He will **take away** Judah's **hedge** of protection. The country will be invaded and laid **waste**. It will return to **briers and thorns** and suffer drought. All this looks forward, of course, to the oncoming captivity.

5:7 The cause is clear: when God **looked for justice** and righteousness from Israel and Judah, He got nothing but murder and the **cry** of the downtrodden.

5:8–10 In verses 8–23 we have six

woes, continued from chapter 3. The woes are pronounced as follows:

First Woe: Covetous landowners who try to corner the real estate market till there is an acute shortage of houses and land, yet the owners **dwell** in solitary splendor. The captivity will leave many **houses** empty, and the land will yield only fractional harvests. The grapevines growing on five acres of land will yield only five gallons of wine. Ten bushels **of seed** will produce only **one** bushel of grain.

5:11–17 *Second Woe:* Confirmed alcoholics who imbibe from **morning ... until night**. They feast and carouse in total disregard of God and His works.

It is for this kind of unthinking behavior that the exile is drawing near. The **honorable men** and the **multitude** will suffer famine and then death. No class will escape humiliation. But God will be vindicated by His righteous **judgment** when foreign bedouin shepherds feed their flocks in the ruins of Israel.

5:18, 19 *Third Woe:* Brazen liars and God-defiers who are hitched to sin and drag guilt and punishment after them. They challenge God to **hasten** with the punishment He has threatened on them.

5:20 *Fourth Woe:* Those who obliterate moral distinctions, denying the difference between **good** and **evil**.

5:21 *Fifth Woe:* Conceited men who cannot be told anything.

5:22, 23 *Sixth Woe:* Judges who are heroes at **drinking** and who pervert **justice** through accepting bribes.

5:24, 25 These wicked men who have no respect for the Word of God will be devoured like grass in a prairie **fire**. God will deal with **His people** in judgment, causing **the hills** to shake and **the streets** to be littered with **carcasses**. But there is more!

5:26–30 **He ... will whistle** for the Babylonians to come. See their troops approaching—in top physical condition, perfectly uniformed, well armed. The horses and chariots approach fast and furiously. The troops pounce **like a lion** upon the populace, then carry the people off into exile. It's a dark **day** for Judah!

B. Isaiah's Call, Cleansing, and Commission (Chap. 6)

6:1 In the year that King Uzziah died,[10] Isaiah had a vision of the King of kings. We learn from John 12:39–41 that the King he saw was none other than the Lord Jesus Christ. F. C. Jennings comments:

> He, like John of Patmos, becomes "in the Spirit," and sees Adohn (the name of God as the supreme Lord of all; and here, as in Romans 9:5, "Christ who is *over all*, God, blessed forever") with every accompaniment of majestic splendor, sitting on a Throne, which is itself "high and exalted," for "His Throne ruleth over all;" yet, while sitting on this lofty Throne the hem of His raiment fills that glorious temple.[11]

6:2–5 Attending Him were celestial beings called **seraphim**,[12] with "four wings for reverence and two for service." These celebrate the holiness of God and require that God's servants be cleansed before serving Him. The vision produced deep conviction of sin in the prophet, then brought him to the place of confession.

6:6–8 This was immediately followed by cleansing. Only then did Isaiah hear the call **of the LORD**. He quickly consecrated himself to the Lord and was given his commission.

6:9, 10 He was to declare the Word of the Lord to a **people** who would be judicially blinded and hardened through rejection of the message. Verses 9 and 10 do not describe the *goal* of Isaiah's ministry, but its inevitable *result*. These verses are quoted in the NT to explain Israel's rejection of the Messiah. Vine writes:

> The people had so persistently perverted their ways that they had gone beyond the possibility of conversion and healing. A man may so harden himself in evil as to render his condition irremediable, and this by God's retributive judgment upon him.[13]

6:11–13 The question **"How long?"** means how long would God's judgments continue on His people. The answer was **"Until the cities are laid waste and without inhabitant, the houses are without a man, the land is utterly desolate, the LORD has removed men far away."** God will spare a remnant (**a tenth**), but even this remnant will have to pass through deep tribulation. This **holy seed** is like the living **stump** of a great tree that survives after the rest of the tree has been destroyed.

C. The Book of Immanuel (Chaps. 7—12)

1. Messiah's Miraculous Birth (Chap. 7)

7:1, 2 Chapters 7–12 have been called the Book of Immanuel because of their clear prophecies concerning Christ.

Between chapters 6 and 7 Isaiah passes over the reign of Jotham and takes up the narrative during the time **of Ahaz**. It is the time when **Syria and** Israel (**Ephraim**) have made an alliance **against** Judah and are threatening **Jerusalem**.

7:3 Isaiah and his **son Shear-Jashub**[14] go out to meet King **Ahaz . . . at the end of the aqueduct from the upper pool, on the highway to the Fuller's Field**. Perhaps the king had gone there to secure the safety of

the city's water supply. The Fuller's Field was where the people spread their freshly-washed clothes to bleach in the sun.

7:4–9 The Lord assures Ahaz through the prophet that he need **not fear**. The kings of Syria and Israel (**Rezin** and **Pekah**) are nothing but the **stubs of smoking firebrands** on the verge of being extinguished. Although the confederacy does plan to attack Judah and **set** up some otherwise unknown **son of Tabel** as puppet **king**, the plan will largely fail. (Syria and Israel did invade Judah, but the pressure lifted when the Assyrians advanced.) As sure as Syria's chief city-state is **Damascus** and its **head is Rezin**, so surely will Israel be conquered **within sixty-five years**. (See 2 Kgs. 17 for fulfillment.) As sure as Israel's capital is **Samaria** and its **head** is Pekah, so **surely** will Ahaz be disestablished if he does **not believe** the Word of the Lord.

7:10–13 The LORD instructs **Ahaz** to **ask** for a **sign**, on earth or in the heavens, that the Syria-Israel alliance will not prevail against Judah. Unwilling to abandon his trust in Assyria for protection, Ahaz refuses, with mock piety and humility. The Lord is displeased with the king's attitude but gives the sign anyway. Vine comments:

> As Ahaz refused to ask for a sign, the Lord would give one of His own choosing, and a sign the range of which would extend to circumstances far beyond those of the time of Ahaz, and would bring to a culmination the prophecies and promises relating to "the house of David". Ahaz and men of that sort would have no share in the blessings and glories of the fulfillment of the sign.[15]

7:14 Like many prophecies, this one seems to have had an early fulfillment (in the days of Ahaz) and later, complete fulfillment (in the First Advent of Christ). Verse 14 points irresistibly to Christ—the **Son** of **the virgin**[16] whose name indicates that He is **Immanuel**, God-with-us. Again we quote Vine:

"Behold", in Isaiah, always introduces something relating to future circumstances. The choice of the word *almah* is significant, as distinct from *bethulah* (a maiden living with her parents and whose marriage was not impending); it denotes one who is mature and ready for marriage.[17]

7:15–17 Verses 15 and 16 may refer to Isaiah's second son, Maher-Shalal-Hash-Baz, who is said to be a sign in 8:18. This maiden-born son will live in poverty (eating **curds and honey**) until he reaches the age of accountability. But **before** he reaches that age, the lands of Syria and Israel will be **forsaken by . . . their kings** and thus the alliance that Judah feared will come to nothing. But God will also punish Judah through the incursions of **the king of Assyria**. How?

7:18–22 God **will whistle for the fly** (Egypt) **and for the bee** (Assyria) and they will swarm over Judah. **Assyria** will be God's **hired razor**, bringing shame and disgrace. Jennings notes:

Poor indeed shall Judah be in that day, for the sum-total of a man's wealth shall consist in a calf and two sheep, or goats, yet so abundant shall be the pasture afforded by the uncultivated lands that even these three creatures shall give him all the food he needs, or indeed can get.[18]

7:23–25 Land that formerly yielded bumper crops will be covered by **briers and thorns**. No longer arable, it will be fit only for **oxen** and **sheep**.

2. Messiah's Marvelous Land (Chaps. 8—10)

8:1–4 The Lord instructs Isaiah to write **"Maher-Shalal-Hash-Baz"** on a tablet in clear letters, and to have two **witnesses, Uriah the priest and Zechariah the son of Jeberechiah**, who will later attest the message. The name means "speed the spoil, hasten the booty," and points to the destruction of Syria and Israel by Assyria. **The LORD** interprets the meaning when he directs Isaiah to give this name to his newborn **child**.

8:5–10 **The Lord also** has a word about Israel. Because the **people** of the Northern Kingdom had **refused the waters of Shiloah that flow softly**, they will be inundated by **the River**, i.e., the Euphrates. **Shiloah** (called "Siloam" in John 9:7) was the secret water supply of Jerusalem and is here used as a symbol of God's word of grace or of trust in the Lord. The Euphrates typifies **Assyria** which will conquer Israel and Syria. It will also invade **Judah**, covering the breadth of Immanuel's land, but not with complete success—only **up to the neck**. Judah's enemies will eventually **be shattered** in spite of their plans and preparations.

8:11–15 Isaiah is **instructed** by Jehovah **not** to join **this people** in their fear of the **conspiracy** formed against them, but to trust the Lord alone. **He will be as a sanctuary** to all who rely on Him, **but a stone of stumbling** to all others.

8:16–18 Isaiah commands that the word of the Lord be stored up by faithful disciples until history records its fulfillment. The prophet **will wait** for **the Lord, who** is now estranged **from** His people, **and . . . will hope in Him**. Isaiah (*Jehovah saves*), Shear-jashub (*a remnant shall return*), and

Maher-Shalal-Hash-Baz (*speed the spoil, hasten the booty*) are by their very names **signs and wonders** of God's eventual mercy to **Israel** and judgment on their foes.

8:19 The prophet cautions his people against those who advocate consulting spirit **mediums and wizards**. Men should turn to the living God, not to **the dead on behalf of the living**. Today's devotion to the occult is nothing new:

> Before every great crisis in human affairs there has been an outburst of spiritism. So it was in Judah and Israel just before the captivity. So it was at the time of Christ's Incarnation and atoning Death. So it is today. God has provided all that is requisite for our guidance and spiritual needs in the Scriptures of truth (2 Tim. 3:16, 17).[19]

8:20–22 All teachers must be tested by the **word** of God. If their teaching does not agree with the Scriptures, **"there is no light in them."** All who are thus misguided will wander about, **hard pressed and hungry**, cursing **their God** and **their king** for their plight. They will **look** heavenward and earthward for relief, but will find nothing but **darkness** and **gloom of anguish**.

9:1–5 Now we are carried forward to the coming of the Messiah. The northern territory of Israel, called **the land of Naphtali**, which had been brought into contempt by the invaders, will be made glorious. (**Galilee of the Gentiles** was the Savior's boyhood home and the scene of part of His public ministry.) Christ's First Advent brought **light** to Galilee. His Second Coming will bring **joy** to the nation and put an end to slavery and war.

9:6 The First Advent is described in verse 6a: **"For unto us a Child is born, unto us a Son is given."** The first clause speaks of His humanity, the second of His deity. The next part of the verse points forward to the Second Advent:

the government will be upon His shoulder—He will reign as King of kings and Lord of lords. The rest of the verse describes His personal glories:

His name will be called Wonderful— *this name is a noun*, not an adjective, and speaks of His Person and work.

Counselor—His wisdom in government.

Mighty God—the omnipotent, supreme Ruler.

Everlasting Father—or better, the Father (or "Source") of eternity. Eternal Himself, He confers eternal life on those who believe in Him. Vine comments: "There is a twofold revelation in this: (1) He inhabits and possesses eternity (57:15); (2) He is loving, tender, compassionate, an all wise Instructor, Trainer, and Provider."[20]

Prince of Peace (*Sar-Shālôm*)—the One who will at last bring peace to this troubled world.

9:7 **His government** will be far-flung, peaceful, and endless. Sitting **upon the throne of David**, He will rule with **judgment** and **justice**. How will all this be brought about? The Lord's jealous care for His people **will perform this**.

9:8–12 Again the prophet turns back to the thunders of judgment, dividing his message into four stanzas, each ending with the refrain,

"For all this His anger is not turned away, but His hand is stretched out still" (vv. 12, 17, 21, 10:4).

Unmoved by previous punishment, Israel threatens in pride and arrogance to rebuild more gloriously than ever. But the Lord promises that they will be attacked by the Syrians from the east and the Philistines from the west.

9:13–17 He further warns of the wholesale destruction of the population, from the honored elder to the prophet who teaches lies. Because ungodliness prevails, the Lord's anger is not turned away and His hand is stretched out still—in judgment, not in mercy.

9:18–21 Because of general wickedness, the land is consumed with the fire of civil war, anarchy, famine, looting, and cannibalism.

10:1–4 A woe is pronounced on those rulers who rob the needy, oppress the poor, and write unjust decrees. When the judgment of God falls, they will lose all the wealth they gained through graft and extortion.

10:5–11 God will use Assyria to punish Judah. But the Assyrian has bigger plans than that! His aim is to build a world empire through conquest. He boasts that his princes (or commanders) are all kings, that the cities in his pathway are no greater than those he has conquered, and that the idols of Israel and Judah are not comparable to those of the kingdoms he has captured, or to himself.

10:12–19 But God will punish the pride and arrogance of the king of Assyria. The latter ascribes his success to his own strength and wisdom. The rod and staff in the hands of the Lord should not boast itself against the hands that hold it. A terrible disaster will strike Assyria's stout warriors, who are also called his glory and the glory of his forest and of his fruitful field. The light of Israel is the Lord, and His thorns and His briers are the Assyrian troops. The survivors of those troops will be so few . . . that a child will be able to count them.

10:20–23 In that day . . . the remnant of Israel never again will depend on the Assyrian, as Ahaz did, but rather on the LORD. Much of this prophecy looks forward to the Second Advent.

10:24–27 Though the Assyrian king will march against Jerusalem from the north, the people of Judah need not be afraid, because the LORD of hosts will intervene, as He did against Midian and Egypt, and Judah will be freed from the fear of Assyrian domination.

10:28–34 In the cities mentioned we have a graphic, animated description of the marching route of the Assyrians. Everywhere there is panic and flight as the invaders approach. Finally they come within sight of the hill of Jerusalem. Then the Lord intervenes and destroys the army, officers and men, as if He were cutting down a forest.

3. Messiah's Millennial Kingdom (Chaps. 11, 12)

11:1 Isaiah 11 is one of the greatest passages on the Millennium in either the OT or the NT. In one of the quick transitions, so frequent in the prophets, we are now carried forward to the Second Coming of Christ.

First we see the lineage of the Son of David, a Rod from the stem of Jesse,[21] who was David's father (1 Sam. 17:12).

11:2 Messiah's anointing with the spirit of the LORD is expressed in three pairs of spiritual attributes. W. E. Vine explains them clearly and concisely:

The first, **"the spirit of wisdom and understanding"**, relates to powers of mind: wisdom discerns the nature of things, understanding discerns their differences. The second, **"the spirit of counsel and might"**, relates to practical activity: counsel is the ability to adopt right conclusions, might is the power exercised in carrying them out. The third pair, **"the spirit of knowledge and of the fear of the Lord"**, relates to fellowship with Jehovah; knowledge is here a knowledge of Jehovah (both details of this pair go with "of Jehovah"); Christ Himself said "ye have not known Him (*ginōskō*, i.e., ye have not begun to know Him), but I know Him (*oida*, i.e., I know Him intuitively and fully)", John 8:55.[22]

11:3–5 Next the absolute **equity** of Christ's rule is described in majestic poetry; then His punishment of **the wicked**, His personal **righteousness**, and His reign of peace and safety.

11:6–9a Even wild animals will submit to Messiah's rule, making it possible for a **nursing child** to **play by the cobra's hole**.[23]

11:9b One of the most glorious promises in all of Holy Scripture is the second half of v. 9, giving the reason for the ideal conditions during the Millennial Kingdom. Jennings translates it into rhymed English verse, bringing out the poetic name for the Lord (Jah):

For full of Jah's knowledge shall the land be,
E'en as the waters cover the sea.

11:10–16 The Messiah will be **a banner**, attracting **the Gentiles** to Himself, and the seat of His authority will **be glorious**. The Lord will regather **the remnant of His people** from all directions of the compass. **Judah and** Israel (**Ephraim**) will live together in peace, and will subdue their enemies—the Philistines, Edomites, Moabites, and Ammonites. **The tongue of the Sea of Egypt** (the Red Sea) will be dried up, and **the River** (the Euphrates) will be reduced to **seven streams** so that the Jews can return to the land. **A highway** will connect **Assyria** and **Israel** so that the return from the north will be made easy.

12:1–6 In the glad millennial **day**, Israel will sing songs of thanksgiving and of **trust**. **With joy** the saved remnant will quench its thirst by drawing **water from the wells of salvation**. Israel will also **sing** as God's missionaries to the nations, inviting them to come to Christ for satisfaction.

D. Judgment on the Nations (Chaps. 13—24)

1. Judgment on Babylon (13:1—14:23)

13:1–5 The next eleven chapters contain prophecies against Gentile nations. The first is **Babylon**, the world power that crushed Assyria (about 609 B.C.). In Chapter 13, we see Babylon being conquered by the Medes and Persians (539 B.C.). However, some of the prophecies look beyond that event to the final destruction of Babylon at the close of the Great Tribulation (Rev. 17, 18).

God musters the Medo-Persian army (**"My sanctified ones"**) to **enter the gates of the nobles** (the City of Babylon) and to **destroy the whole land**.

13:6–13 The horrors of the disaster are described next—fear **and sorrows**, terrible celestial disturbances, and an awesome reduction in the population. Some of these verses look beyond the Medo-Persian triumph to **the day of the LORD**, which will affect **the** whole **world** and which will actually involve cataclysms in **the heavens**.

13:14–22 There will be a mass exit from Babylon, foreigners returning to their own lands. Those who remain will suffer unspeakable cruelty. Verses 19–22 have had a partial fulfillment,[24] but the complete unfolding is future.

There are certain difficulties connected with the prophecies of the destruction of Babylon, both the city and the country (Isa. 13:6–22) 14:4–23; 21:2–9; 47:1–11; Jer. 25:12–14; 50; 51). For example, the capture of the city by the Medes (Isa. 13:17) in 539 B.C. did not result in a destruction similar to that of Sodom and Gomorrah (Isa. 13:19); did not leave the city uninhabited forever (Isa. 13:20–22); was not accomplished by a nation from the north—Medo-Persia was to the east—(Jer. 50:3); did not result in Israel or more than a remnant of Judah seeking the Lord or returning to Zion (Jer. 50:4, 5); and did not involve the breaking of the walls and burning of the gates (Jer. 51:58).

When we come to a difficulty like this, how do we handle it? First of all, we reaffirm our utter confidence in the Word of God. If there is any difficulty, it is because of our lack of knowledge. But we remember that the prophets often had a way of merging the immediate future and the distant future without always indicating any time signals. In other words, a prophecy could have a local, partial fulfillment and a remote, complete fulfillment. That is the case with Babylon. Not all the prophecies have been fulfilled. Some are still future.

Babylon is slated to play a prominent role in the Tribulation. But its doom is already painted in vivid colors in Revelation 17 and 18. Before the Second Advent of Christ, all the prophecies concerning the destruction of Babylon will be fulfilled

to a "T." What is unclear to us today will be crystal clear to those living at that time.

14:1, 2 The LORD in His **mercy** will restore Israel to **their own land**. Gentile nations will assist in the return and live peacefully with God's people. Israel's former overlords will be her **servants**.

Jacob and **the house of Israel** represent the Jews in captivity in Babylon. The Lord's choosing them means His delivering them from the country of captivity and settling them back in **their own land**. Those **strangers** who clung to **the house of Jacob** are the proselytes from Babylon. The **people** that **bring them to their place** would consist of the favorable backing of Cyrus and others who helped the Jews in their return.

14:3–11 Free from persecution and **hard bondage**, Israel will sing a taunt song against the **king of Babylon**. **The LORD has broken** his power and ended his tyranny. Now the earth rejoices—even the forests, which will no longer be denuded by his armies. Peace at last! Sheol's inhabitants are there to greet him, delighted that he too has been stripped of power. The **pomp** and pageantry of Babylon's king has passed away. The palace music is ended. He sleeps on a sheet of maggots, and is covered by a blanket of **worms**.

14:12–17 As the taunt song continues, the theme seems to expand from the fall of the king of Babylon to the fall of the one who energized him, Satan (**Lucifer**[25]) himself. Ryrie writes that this is "evidently a reference to Satan, because of Christ's similar description (Luke 10:18) and because of the inappropriateness of the expressions of Isa. 14:13–14 on the lips of any but Satan (cf. 1 Tim. 3:6)."[26] Because this day star, **son of**

the morning, proudly asserted his will above the will of God, he was cast out of heaven. Verses 13, 14 record the notorious "I will's" of Satan in his defiance of God. Eventually he will be consigned to Sheol, an object of astonishment. The denizens of Sheol will marvel that one who exercised such power has been brought so low.

14:18–21 Returning to the king of Babylon, the song mentions that while most **kings** lie in magnificent tombs, he is denied a decent burial. He will have no monument, and the royal line (**his children**) will be cut off.

14:22, 23 The city of Babylon will be depopulated and swept clean by **the broom** of God.

2. Judgment on Assyria (14:24–27)

The subject now switches to the destruction of **the Assyrian**, which had dominion over Babylon at this time. The armies of Assyria will be crushed on the **mountains** of Israel.[27] The complete fulfillment of this prophecy will be in the Tribulation period when the king of the North is defeated as he attempts to sweep down over Immanuel's land.

3. Judgment on Philistia (14:28–32)

14:28–31 Philistia should **not rejoice** in the death of **Ahaz**, the grandson (here called **rod**) of Uzziah, who had **struck** the Philistines (2 Chron. 26:6, 7). Another descendant, Hezekiah, would attack them like **a viper** and **a fiery flying serpent** (see 2 Kgs. 18:8). Then God's **poor** and **needy** would be safe, but the Lord would visit the Philistines **with famine** and **slay** the survivors. The invading Assyrians would come from **the North** like a cloud of **smoke**. However, God's people would be safe in Jerusalem.

14:32 If any Gentile couriers ask what is going on, they will be told that **the LORD** is fulfilling His promises to **Zion**, and protecting the inhabitants of Jerusalem.

4. Judgment on Moab (Chaps. 15, 16)

15:1–7 Isaiah sings an eloquent dirge concerning the doom of **Moab**. Its two strongly fortified cities, **Ar** and **Kir**, are suddenly destroyed. The towns and hamlets are plunged into mourning. Even Isaiah is moved to compassion for the refugees as they **flee** the country. The landscape is **laid waste** and the people stream across the frontier with whatever they can salvage.

15:8, 9 The cry extends to **the borders** of Moab. The name of the town of **Dibon** (pining) in verse 2 becomes **Dimon** in verse 9—perhaps a play on words, since Dimon resembles the Hebrew word *dām* (blood). So **"the waters of Dimon will be full of blood."** Even those who escape will be tracked down as by a lion.

16:1, 2 The description of Moab's devastation continues in chapter 16. The Moabites who have fled to **Sela** (Petra, Edom's capital) for refuge are counseled to send **the** tribute **lamb to the ruler of the land** (the king of Judah) in the mountain **of the daughter of Zion** (Jerusalem) as they had previously sent lambs to Samaria (2 Kgs. 3:4). The people are nervously agitated over their impending calamity.

16:3–5 The Lord counsels **Moab** to **hide** God's Jewish **outcasts**, as if in a dark **shadow**, to provide sanctuary and safety for them. **The spoiler, extortioner**, and oppressor will cease, and the Lord will reign on **the throne . . . of David . . . in mercy, truth, justice**, and **righteousness**.

16:6–12 The downfall of **Moab** is caused by **his pride** and **haughtiness**. There is widespread mourning in the land. **The** fertile **fields of Heshbon**

are bare, and the luxuriant vines **of Sibmah** are ruined. Again the prophet himself mourns over the widespread ruin. When Moab prays to his idols, no help will come.

16:13, 14 To God's previous prophecies concerning the fall of Moab, He now adds the information that it will happen **within three years, as the years of a hired man**—i.e., not a minute longer than the agreed time.

5. Judgment on Damascus (Chap. 17)

17:1–3 The third oracle foretells the leveling of **Damascus**, the chief city-state of Syria, and of its satellite cities. Because of its alliance with **Syria, Ephraim** (Israel) will share a similar downfall. **Ephraim** will be stripped of its defenses, **Damascus** of its **kingdom**, and the surviving Syrians of their **glory**. Damascus was destroyed by the Assyrian armies in 732 B.C., and Samaria fell ten years later.

17:4–6 In the **day** of its judgment, Israel will be disgraced and starved. It will be stripped like harvested fields in **the Valley of Rephaim**—only a small remnant will be left.

17:7–11 Then people will turn **to** the true and living God, their **Maker, the Holy One of Israel**, and will renounce everything that has to do with idolatry. Fortified **cities will** lie waste, like the cities of the Hivites and Amorites after the invading Israelites had conquered them. And why will all this happen? **Because** God's people have **forgotten** Him and have turned to **foreign seedlings**, i.e., foreign alliances, religions, and customs. **The harvest will be** disastrous.

17:12–14 Beginning with verse 12 and continuing throughout chapter 18, we have a short interlude with two movements, each beginning with **"Woe."** The first movement pictures the Gentile nations moving against

Israel with the awesome **noise** of modern warfare. But suddenly they are turned back by the Lord, and the threat to Israel is lifted overnight, as in the destruction of the Assyrian army.

6. Judgment on Unnamed Lands in Africa (Chap. 18)

This is not a **"woe"**[28] but a "ho," calling to an unidentified friendly nation that **sends ambassadors** to the people of Israel (vv. 2, 7). The expression **"shadowed with buzzing wings"** may suggest the desire to protect the Jewish people.

At the same time, other Gentile nations will prey upon God's people while He watches silently. But eventually God will destroy them, leaving their carcasses to the **beasts** and **birds of prey**.

Israel will then come **to Mount Zion** as **a present . . . to the** LORD. Verse 7 may read, "In that day shall a present be brought unto Jehovah *of* a people scattered and ravaged . . ." (JND) rather than "*from* a people. . . ." This speaks of the restoration of Israel at the Second Advent of Christ.

7. Judgment on Egypt (Chaps. 19, 20)

19:1–3 When **the** LORD descends in judgment on **Egypt, the idols . . . will totter** and the people will panic. Civil war will break out and the government's best brains will resort in vain to **idols** and various forms of spiritism (**the charmers**).

19:4–10 A **cruel** despot **will rule** the land. Severe drought will dry up the water supplies, causing crop failure, wiping out the fishing industry, closing up the textile mills, and bringing ruin to all segments of the population, whether leaders or common people.

19:11–15 Pharaoh's best **coun-**

selors, who lived in **Zoan** and **Noph**, will have no wisdom to cope with the situation. In fact, their advice has brought disaster on Egypt, so that the situation is now hopeless.

The first fifteen verses have already been fulfilled. Following the death of Tirhakah, who was ruling Egypt at the time of Isaiah's prophecy, the country was torn by civil strife. Egypt was split up into twelve kingdoms, all subject to Assyria. Finally the country was united again under Psammetichus, the "cruel master" of verse 4. The rest of the chapter is still unfulfilled.

19:16, 17 When God shakes His fist, the populace will shake with **fear**. The mere mention **of Judah** will cause the hearts of the Egyptians to sink.

19:18–20 But **the land of Egypt** is promised restoration also. **Five cities** will become centers for the worship of Jehovah, including Heliopolis (city of the Sun), also called **the City of Destruction**. **There will be an altar to the** LORD **in the midst of the land, and a pillar to the** LORD **at its border**, both of which will be witnesses **to the Lord**. Josephus tells us that the prophecy of verse 19 was fulfilled in 1 B.C. when Onias, the high priest, fleeing from Jerusalem, obtained permission to build an altar in Egypt. But the full meaning of the prophecy is undoubtedly millennial.

19:21, 22 God's judgments on **Egypt** will succeed in bringing the people to worship Him.

19:23 A **highway** will pass **from Egypt** (through Israel) **to Assyria** with unrestricted passage. The nations will unite in the worship of Jehovah.

19:24, 25 Then **Israel will be one of three with Egypt and Assyria**, that is, they will form a triple alliance, enjoying the blessings of Christ's king-

dom. Note the repetition of **"in that day"** (vv. 16, 18, 19, 21, 23, 24).

20:1–6 In 711 B.C., the **Tartan**, or commander-in-chief of **Sargon the king of Assyria**, conquered the Philistine city of **Ashdod. At the same time the** LORD told **Isaiah** to walk **naked** (scantily clad—not completely naked) **and barefoot** as **a sign and a wonder** of the three-year humiliation that would come to **Egypt** and **Ethiopia** when conquered by **Assyria**. Then the people of Judah would see the folly of trusting Egypt for protection against Assyria. (Some commentators suggest that verses 5 and 6 refer to the Philistines or to both Judah and the Philistines, that is, the whole land of Palestine.)[29]

8. Judgment on Babylon (21:1–10)

21:1–4 The three oracles in chapter 21 bring bad news for Babylon, Edom, and Arabia.

The Wilderness of the Sea is Babylon, perhaps that portion of Babylon adjacent to the Persian Gulf. Destruction will roar upon it like **whirlwinds . . . from the desert**. Because it still **plunders** and despoils, it will be laid low by the Persians (**Elam**) and the Medes (**Media**). No more will Babylon cause others, like the Jewish captives, to groan. The vision is so terrible that it causes Isaiah acute anguish.

21:5 While the rulers feast and carouse in supposed security, suddenly the call to arms rings out (**"Anoint the shield!"**). The reference, of course, is to Belshazzar's Feast (Dan. 5).

21:6–10 The **Lord** instructs Isaiah to appoint **a watchman** to describe the attacking hordes, especially the numberless cavalry units. After waiting for days and nights, he reports the advance of riders in pairs. This may suggest the Medes and the Persians. Then, with a lion-like roar, he announces the fall of Babylon and of her idolatrous religion. The announcement is a message of comfort to Israel, a nation that has been threshed and winnowed by Babylon. It is good to remember that this prophecy was made about two hundred years before Babylon's fall.

We too can be watchmen for God's kingdom:

> The watchman is one who stands in God's counsels, knows what is coming and looks out for the event. So now, he who learns from the completed Scriptures what God has foretold, discerning His purposes, not by speculative interpretation, but by comparing Scripture with Scripture, and accepting what is therein made plain, is able to warn and exhort others. He stands upon the watch-tower (verse 7) in fellowship with God.[30]

9. Judgment on Dumah (Edom) (21:11, 12)

Dumah is Idumea, or Edom. An anxious Edomite asks **the watchman** how far gone **the night** is, that is, if the Assyrian menace is almost over. The answer is:

> The night of your present turmoil will end, and a new day will follow, but soon another night will come. If you seek a comforting answer to your anxious inquiries, you must first "return," a word which also means "repent." Only then will the answer be such as you hoped for; the night of your suffering will end, and a new bright morning of deliverance will dawn upon you.[31]

10. Judgment on Arabia (21:13-17)

There is trouble ahead for **Arabia**, too. The caravans **will** hide (**lodge**) in **the forest** from the Assyrian army, and those who escape from the carnage will suffer intense hunger and thirst. **The LORD** has decreed that Arabia's **glory will fail** in **a year**, and only a few of her famous warriors will survive. The expression **"the year of a hired man"** means not one day longer than a year.

11. Judgment on Jerusalem (Chap. 22)

22:1-5 **The Valley of Vision** refers to Jerusalem (see vv. 9-11). The city is in siege. The people are milling about on **the housetops** to see the enemy at the gates. The streets of the once festive city are littered with victims of plague. The rulers and people who attempt escape **are captured** without a struggle. Isaiah himself is inconsolable as he sees the threatened judgment of God on Jerusalem.

22:6-11 **Elam and Kir** are the southern and northern units of the Babylonian army. Their **chariots** and cavalry fill the **valleys** surrounding the city. The Jews make elaborate plans to withstand the siege. They ransack the armory (**the House of the Forest**), they demolish **houses** to get stones for repairing **the wall**, they try to devise a makeshift water supply. They do everything but look to their **Maker** who wrought the disaster and planned it **long** before.

22:12-14 At a time when **the Lord** is calling them to repentance, they live riotously and callously. For this they will not be forgiven.

22:15-19 **Shebna**, the palace administrator in Hezekiah's court, is preparing **himself** an ornate **sepulcher**. God says through Isaiah that his efforts are futile. The Lord **will toss** him into captivity **like a** wadded ball, and he will **die** in a foreign land so that he will be long remembered.

Perhaps Shebna led the party that advocated alliance with Egypt.

22:20–24 After Shebna is demoted, **Eliakim** (God will establish) will take his place. A type of the Lord Jesus, Eliakim will be a responsible and compassionate ruler with full authority. He will be given **the key of the house of David**,[32] controlling the royal chambers and choosing the servants in the royal household. (In Rev. 3:7 the Lord Jesus is said to have the key of the house of David.) Eliakim will be firmly established in his position and will have complete authority in his sphere of service.

22:25 Since Eliakim is clearly **the peg that is fastened in the secure place** (v. 23a), his removal and **fall** may refer to the captivity of the house of Judah, of which he was a representative.

12. Judgment on Tyre (Chap. 23)

23:1–5 Returning from **Tarshish** (probably means Spain here), seamen from **Tyre** receive news of the city's fall when they reach **Cyprus**. With their houses destroyed and **no harbor** to return to, they howl in dismay. The **merchants of Sidon** sit in stunned silence as they remember how their Tyrian neighbors had crossed **the sea**, bringing **grain** from the Upper Nile (**Shihor**), how they had been the merchants of **the nations**. **Sidon**, the mother city of Tyre, is **ashamed** as the waves beating against the ruins of Tyre seem to echo the city's lament. It is as if Tyre never had any **children** to inhabit it! **Egypt**, too, is **in agony at the report** of the loss of her best customer.

23:6–9 The Tyrians are told to seek asylum as far away as Spain (**Tarshish**). Once the **inhabitants** of an ancient prosperous **city**, their **feet** now carry them to **far off** lands. And **who**

brought this horror on **Tyre**, with all its power, riches, and glory? It was **the Lord of hosts**—determined **to dishonor the pride of all** human **glory**.

23:10–17 In view of Nebuchadnezzar's attack on **Tyre**, the people are told to escape to other countries, spreading out **like the River** (i.e., the Euphrates River which flows through many countries). God has roused Babylon to destroy the merchant city (**Canaan**). Even if the refugees flee **to Cyprus**, they will find **no rest**. The prophet is amazed that an obscure nation with humble beginnings, **founded** by **Assyria**, should bring Tyre **to ruin**. **Tyre will be forgotten** during the **seventy years** of the Chaldean monarchy. At the end of that time, it will joyfully resume its commercial **fornication with all the kingdoms of the world**.

23:18 "Tyre's **gain and her pay**" looks forward to the Second Advent of Christ when "the daughter of Tyre will come with a gift" (Ps. 45:12). Her treasures will be a holy offering to the Lord.

13. Judgment on All the Earth (Chap. 24)

24:1–3 The judgments of God seem to start with the land of Israel, but they widen to include the whole earth and even wicked beings in the heavens. **"The earth"** may also be translated "the land," and the reference to **the priest** in verse 2 suggests that the land of Israel is in view in verses 1–3. Notice how the text alternates between the land and **the people**. The destruction is cataclysmic and affects all classes of the populace.

24:4–13 Mention of **"the world"** in verse 4 suggests that the theater of judgment has widened. The cause of worldwide pollution is that men **have broken the everlasting covenant**. Some take this to refer to the Noahic covenant (Gen. 9:16), but that unconditional covenant depended entirely on God. Others think that the Mosaic law is referred to, but that was given only to Israel, and is not said to be an **everlasting covenant**. *The Bible Knowledge Commentary* says it is "the covenant people implicitly had with God to obey His Word."[33] **The city of confusion** could mean Jerusalem, but in a wider sense could include all urban civilization.

24:14–20 A preserved remnant is heard singing the praises of Jehovah (NKJV, LORD) for His saving grace.

Then the prophet mourns the dread horrors of the Great Tribulation. It will be a time of treachery. Escape will be impossible. **The earth** will careen **like a drunkard**, as if struck by a mammoth quake. It falls to rise no more.

24:21–23 The wicked hosts in heavenly places will also be judged. This corresponds to Revelation 19:19, 20; 20:1–3. **Kings of the earth** who have served as their puppets will share in this judgment at the Second Advent of Christ. The Lord's surpassing glory will put **the sun** and **moon** to shame.

E. The Book of Songs (Chaps. 25—27)

1. Israel's Song of Praise for Kingdom Blessings (Chap. 25)

25:1–5 Chapters 25–27 have been called "the Book of Songs." Here the restored Jewish remnant praises the LORD for its deliverance through the Great Tribulation. Enemy cities (not necessarily any particular city) have been pulverized, causing Gentiles to acknowledge Jehovah's power. God has been to His people all that they needed.

25:6–9 On Mount Zion **the Lord** spreads **a feast** of the finest spiritual

delights. He removes the covering of ignorance, **the veil** of satanic blindness that has shrouded **all nations**. He conquers **death** (by raising the tribulation saints who have died), abolishes sorrow, and removes the stigma from the Jewish **people**. The remnant will say **"This is our God; we have waited for Him; we will be glad and rejoice in His salvation."**

25:10–12 Israel's enemies, of whom **Moab** is perhaps representative, will be shamefully **trampled**. God is compared to **a swimmer** in verse 11, spreading out **His hands** in judgment in the midst of the Moabites.

2. Judah's Song to the Rock of Ages (Chap. 26)

26:1–4 Back in the land, the restored remnant celebrates the life of faith and dependence. The **city** of God is in contrast to man's city (24:10). **The righteous nation** (redeemed Israel) experiences the **perfect peace** that comes from leaning hard on Jehovah. Regarding verse 3 the celebrated American Baptist hymnwriter, Philip P. Bliss, used to say "I love this verse more than any other verse in the Bible, 'Thou wilt keep him in perfect peace whose mind is stayed on Thee: because he trusteth in Thee.' "[34]

Moody tied v. 3 with v. 4 in the following words: "The tree of peace strikes its roots into the crevices of the Rock of Ages."[35] They realize at last that **"in YAH, the** LORD (Heb. YAH, a shortened form of YHWH), **is everlasting strength,"** or **"the Rock of Ages"** (NKJV marg.). It was from this expression that Augustus Toplady got the idea for one of the greatest hymns in the English language, "Rock of Ages." Seeking shelter in a cleft in a rocky crag during a violent thunderstorm, he wrote:

Rock of Ages, cleft for me,
Let me hide myself in Thee;
Let the water and the blood,
From Thy riven side which flowed,
Be of sin the double cure,
Cleanse me from its guilt and power.

While I draw this fleeting breath,
When mine eyes shall close in death,
When I soar to worlds unknown,
See Thee on Thy judgment-throne,
Rock of Ages, cleft for me,
Let me hide myself in Thee.

26:5,6 Man's proud civilization has been brought low to the point where **the feet of the poor** and **needy** trample down **the lofty city**.

26:7–15 Verses 7–19 seem to rehearse the prayers of the remnant when passing through the Tribulation. The Lord has smoothed the path for them and they **have waited** earnestly **for** Him to reveal Himself. Only when God acts in judgment will the wicked **learn righteousness**. God's **hand** has been raised in readiness, but when it descends in fury they will **be ashamed**, and then there will be **peace for** Israel. The remnant has been ruled by many Gentile **masters, but** God is their true and **only** Lord. The nations that troubled Israel **will not rise** to trouble God's people again. This verse does not deny the bodily resurrection of the wicked; it merely promises that the Gentile powers will never be restored.

26:16–19 But after Israel goes through travail similar to that of childbirth, which seemingly has accomplished nothing, the nation will enjoy a resurrection. Jehovah answers His people's prayer with a definite promise of national restoration when the refreshing **dew of herbs** (the Holy Spirit) is poured out on the land.

26:20,21 In the meantime, the Lord counsels the faithful remnant of His **people** to **hide** in secret **chambers** while He pours out His wrath on the apostate world.

3. God's Song over Redeemed Israel (Chap. 27)

27:1 In the coming **day** of the LORD, Jehovah **will punish Leviathan the fleeing serpent** (Assyria), **Leviathan that twisted serpent** (Babylon), **and He will slay the reptile that is in the sea** (Egypt). Some commentators understand *all three* monsters as symbolizing Babylon. Still others see them as picturing Satan, who energizes world powers; he is called serpent and dragon (Gen. 3:1; Rev. 12:3; 13:2; 16:13).

27:2–6 **In that day** God will rejoice over His redeemed **vineyard of red wine** (Israel) with singing. He will guard **it night and day**. He has no more **fury** against His people. If any hostile powers were to arise against the remnant, He **would burn them** like **briers and thorns**. It would be better for such powers to turn to the Lord for protection and **peace**. In the Millennium **Israel shall blossom and bud, and fill the face of the world with fruit**.

27:7–9 God has not dealt with **Israel** as with her Gentile overlords! No, His chastisement of Israel has been **in measure** and limited. He drove them off into exile to purge them of the **sin** of idolatry. This objective will be achieved when Israel utterly destroys every last vestige of **images**.

27:10, 11 In the meantime, Jerusalem is seen in ruins, as shown by calves grazing on the bushes, and **women** gathering **boughs** for firewood. All this has come because the people showed no spiritual discernment.

27:12, 13 **In** a coming **day**, the

LORD will thresh the true and the false within the land of Israel. Then He will regather those Jews who are dispersed in such Gentile nations as Assyria and Egypt. Back in the land, they will come to Jerusalem to worship the LORD.

F. The Fall and Rising Again of Israel and Jerusalem (Chaps. 28—35)

1. Woe to Ephraim/Israel (Chap. 28)

28:1–4 Samaria was the crown of pride, the fading flower of the drunkards of Israel (Ephraim). The hilltop city was like a crown looking over the verdant valleys of people overcome with wine, pleasure, materialism, and sex. The Assyrian conquerors stand ready to devour the city as if it were a ripe fig in June.

28:5, 6 The LORD of hosts will be an unfading crown of glory... to the faithful remnant when He returns to set up His Kingdom. He will empower the leaders to execute judgment and to turn back the enemy to his own city gate.

28:7, 8 The prophet turns to Judah. Like Israel, they are drunken and wallowing in their own vomit and filth of the tables. Even the priest and the prophet have become dissolute.

28:9, 10 The religious leaders mock God, complaining that He uses baby talk in speaking to them. Does the Lord think He is dealing with youngsters, teaching them with monosyllables (in the Hebrew)?[36]

28:11–13 "All right," says God, "since you don't want to listen to my simple, understandable language, I will send a foreign invader (Assyria) into your midst." Their alien tongue will be a sign of judgment on a people who refused God when He vainly offered rest to them and the ability to administer rest to others. As for the LORD, He will, as Jennings puts it,

> continue to speak in the simplest, clearest words; but that will be in order that all responsibility for their rejection can only be charged, not to the obscurity of the message, but to those who reject it.[37]

28:14, 15 The rulers of Judah boasted of their covenant with Egypt as making them free from Assyrian attack, but their alliance would mean death...and Sheol for them. They were trusting lies and falsehood. (The covenant with death and the pact with Sheol was not a literal treaty, of course. The thought seems to be that Judah felt that it was on good terms with death and Sheol, and had nothing to fear, because of its alliance with Egypt. Some commentators see this covenant as picturing the still-future alliance between Israel and the Beast [Dan. 9:27].)

28:16, 17 God has established the Messiah as the only worthy object of trust, a sure foundation. Those who rely on Him never need run scared. Under His reign, everything will have to meet the test of justice and righteousness, and judgment will sweep away every false object of trust.

28:18–22 Judah's power politics will fail to protect her when the invader comes. Every enemy incursion will succeed. The people will realize too late the truth of what God had been saying. The bed is too short, the covering too narrow, that is, the covenant fails to provide the desired comfort and protection. God the Lord will rise up in judgment against His people as He had formerly done against their enemies—a judgment that was utterly foreign to Him. If they scoff, they will only increase their bondage.

28:23–29 As Herbert Vander Lugt points out, the prophet illustrates the way God deals with His children by citing three aspects of a farmer's work. First, he declares that the plowman doesn't continue breaking the ground indefinitely, but stops when it is ready for planting (v. 24). Likewise, our trials are brought to an end as soon as they have accomplished His purposes in our lives. Then the prophet says that the farmer sows his seed with discernment, scattering the cummin but putting the wheat in rows (vv. 25, 26). This assures us that the Lord carefully selects the discipline especially suited to our particular need. Finally, Isaiah portrays the laborer threshing his crop. With extreme care he beats out the dill with a light stick, and strikes the cummin with a heavier flail. For the wheat he employs a wheel just heavy enough to avoid crushing the grain (vv. 27, 28). Thus the Almighty uses the gentlest possible touch for our condition, never allowing an affliction to be greater than we can bear.[38]

2. Woe to Ariel/Jerusalem (Chap. 29)

29:1–4 **Ariel** is the privileged city of Jerusalem **where David** had his headquarters. The people there may go through their religious motions **year** after **year**, but God will bring **distress** on the city till it is nothing but an Ariel. The name Ariel has two meanings, "lion of God" and "altar" (see Ezek. 43:15, 16 where *ariel* is translated *altar hearth*). The city that was once the "lion of God" is now a *flaming altar*. Its people are the sacrificial victims.

29:5–8 Yet God will intervene **suddenly** and the enemies will be driven back **like fine dust** and **chaff**. Just when the foes think they will completely devour Jerusalem, they will be foiled as if waking out of a dream.

29:9–12 The people's willful blindness had brought judicial blindness upon them, and they **stagger** as if **drunk**. God's word is unintelligible to them. To some it is a **sealed . . . book**, to others illegible. Everyone has an excuse.

29:13–14 Because their religion is purely external and their only fear of God is a matter of memorized creeds, God will perform a supernatural work of judgment, stripping the keenest minds of wisdom and discernment. The **"marvelous work"** in verse 14 refers to the invasion of Sennacherib. W. E. Vine writes:

> The rulers of Judah sought to rely on Egypt for assistance. That was a piece of political wisdom from the natural point of view; in God's sight it was an act of rebellion; hence God brought the policy to nought, reducing Judah to a condition of helplessness, that they might depend on God alone.[39]

Today the "marvelous work" is accomplished by the gospel (see 1 Cor. 1:18–25).

29:15, 16 A **woe** is pronounced on the deceitful rulers who are making plots with Egypt, as if God does not see them. They have everything topsy-turvy, putting **the clay** in the potter's place and vice versa, thus denying God's power and knowledge.

29:17–21 But a day of deliverance is coming when God will also reverse things. What is now a wild forest (**Lebanon**) will be **a fruitful field**, and what is now counted **a fruitful field** will be looked on as nothing more than an overgrown **forest**. Then **the deaf shall hear, the blind shall see, the humble also shall increase their joy in the LORD**. The oppressor and the scoffer shall be no more— also those nit-pickers who tried to trip up the righteous!

29:22–24 The closing verses describe the believing remnant, here called **Jacob**. Shame and reproach will be a thing of the past. The children of Jacob will realize how God has intervened on their behalf and will honor Him for it. **Those who** misjudged and **complained** will be knowledgeable and teachable.

3. Woe to the Alliance with Egypt (Chaps. 30, 31)

30:1–7 **The rebellious children** are the politicians of Judah who make a league with **Egypt** against Assyria. Since there is no record of such an alliance, we are justified in thinking of this as still future. Judah will learn that **Egypt** is not worthy of trust. Caravans are seen carrying tribute from Judah to Egypt, through dangerous areas in the Negeb (**the South**), but though the Jewish envoys get as far as **Zoan** and **Hanes**, the whole project is doomed to failure. God calls Egypt **"Rahab-Hem-Shebeth"** (Rahab who sits still).

30:8–14 Let it be recorded for posterity that the treaty with Egypt (and all such misplaced trust) is a blatant rejection of **the law of the LORD** through His prophets. Judah will see that Egypt is a poor wall of defense. In fact the **high wall** will **bulge** and crash. It will be smashed as completely as an earthenware vessel, with no **fragments** big enough to use in minor chores.

30:15–17 God has been saying to Judah, "Your salvation lies **in returning** to Me and resting on Me. **Your strength** lies in quiet trust in Me rather than frenzied flight to Egypt." But Judah said, **"No, for we will** fly against the enemy." To which God answers, "You will fly all right, but in retreat and in panic! You will be chased by under-manned forces till you are like a single, scrawny **pole on a hill**."

30:18–25 Still **the LORD will wait** to **be gracious**. "God waits until the disaster of our choice has taught us the foolishness of that choice." When Judah turns to the Lord, He will be their Teacher, Guide, Giver of **rain**, fertility and prosperity, Healer, Rock, and Defender. His people "will throw away their idols like the polluted things they are, shouting after them 'Good riddance!'"

30:26–33 The intensified **light** of verse 26 must be understood as symbolic of glory and righteousness. The godless nations will be sifted in a sieve of destruction. **Assyria will be beaten down** by the Lord, and every stroke **of punishment** will be accompanied by jubilant music from Judah. The burning **fires** of **Topheth** (hell) are ready to welcome **the** wicked **king**.

31:1–3 God is against those who go **to Egypt for help**, who trust in **horses, . . . chariots, . . . and in horsemen** for victory. He **will arise against the house of evildoers** (Judah) **and against the** helpers (Egypt) **of those who work iniquity** (Judah). The helper (Egypt) **will** stumble, **and he who is helped** (Judah) **will fall**.

31:4–9 God is like **a lion** which a **multitude of shepherds** (Assyria) tries to frighten away. Or, to change the figure, He is like a flock of **birds**, hovering over **Jerusalem**; He is ready to defend and **deliver** the city. When **Israel** turns back to the Lord, it will **throw away** its **idols**. The Assyrians will perish by a direct intervention of the Lord. The destruction of Sennacherib did not exhaust the meaning of these verses, so the prophecy has a future fulfillment as well, that is, in the Tribulation.

4. The Reign of the Righteous King (Chap. 32)

32:1–8 The first five verses describe the Millennial **reign** of Christ. He is the **king** who reigns **in righteousness**; the **princes** may be the twelve apostles (see Matt. 19:28). **"A man will be as a hiding place from the wind . . ."**—that Man is the Lord Jesus, providing shelter, protection, refreshment, and shade. No longer will judicial blindness afflict the people, nor will **ears** be closed to listening obediently. Those who now make **rash** decisions will have discernment, and those who now stammer will express themselves without hesitation. Moral distinctions will no longer be blurred. The senseless person will not be honored. The coming of Christ will reveal men in their true light. The fool and the knave will be exposed as such (and punished accordingly). The **generous** man also will be manifested and blessed. Verses 6–8 describe life as Isaiah saw it in his day.

32:9–15 But the kingdom hasn't come yet. The **women** of Judah are still living in luxury, **ease**, and complacency. Soon the blow of judgment will fall—crop failure, depopulation, and desolation. Judah's troubles will continue **until the Spirit is poured** out at the Second Advent of Christ. Then the desert will become **a fruitful field**, and what is now considered **a fruitful field** will be as luxuriant **as a forest**.

32:16–20 Social **justice** and **righteousness** will permeate every aspect of life, resulting in **peace**, **quietness**, safety, and confidence. The enemy (**forest**) shall be leveled by the **hail** of God's judgment and **the city** (its capital) shall be laid low. It will be a happy time, when people can safely sow beside all waters and when the

ox and the donkey can range freely without danger.

5. Woe to the Plunderer/Assyria (Chap. 33)

33:1–6 The destructiveness and treachery of the Assyrian come back on him (vv. 1, 2). Then God's people pray to the LORD for deliverance in their time of trouble. When God moves into action, a thunderous **noise** sends the nations scrambling. It is the Jews' turn to pounce on the loot of the fleeing enemy and pick it over thoroughly. Christ is enthroned, filling **Zion with justice and righteousness**, thus making the **times** stable, and enriching His people with spiritual **treasure**.

33:7–9 These verses revert to the time when Hezekiah sent **ambassadors of peace** to Sennacherib and was told to pay a fine of three hundred talents of silver and thirty talents of gold (2 Kgs. 18:13–16). But even this did not succeed in buying off the Assyrian. He marched against Judah, leaving a trail of havoc and suffering.

The envoys from Judah are weeping bitterly because of the failure of their mission. The Assyrian has broken his word by invading Judah. The most scenic places are scenes of desolation.

33:10–12 In the nick of time **the** LORD arises to deal with the foe. In biting sarcasm, He describes the Assyrian as conceiving **chaff** and bringing **forth stubble**. In other words, his schemes are futile. The same kind of wrath he vented on others will backfire and utterly devour himself. Burning **lime** and **thorns** speak of complete judgment.

33:13–16 A word goes out to godless Gentiles (**you who are afar off**) and to apostate Jews in Zion (**you who are near**). In the fire of God's judgment, the burning of His wrath, the only ones who will survive are those who walk **righteously** and separate themselves from every form of **evil**.

33:17 Then secure and satisfied, the believing remnant **will see the King in His beauty** and **the land** whose borders are greatly expanded. A. J. Gordon adapted this verse for one of his hymns:

> I shall see the King in His beauty,
> In the land that is far away,
> When the shadows at length have lifted,
> And the darkness has turned to day.
>
> I shall see Him in the glory,
> The Lamb that once was slain;
> How I'll then resound the story
> With all the ransomed train!
> Hallelujah, Hallelujah!
> To the Lamb that once was slain;
> Hallelujah, Hallelujah,
> Hallelujah! Amen.

33:18, 19 Only a harmless memory will be those moments of **terror** when the Assyrian weighed out the gold paid in tribute, when his spies counted **the towers** of the city in preparing to attack it, when the Jews heard the foreign language of the Assyrians in their midst.

33:20–22 In the millennial **Zion**, the solemn **appointed feasts** will be held again. The city will be like a tent that is pitched securely and permanently. **The LORD will be** to Zion everything that a river is to a city—protection, refreshment, and beauty. No enemy **galley** or **majestic ships** will ever **pass by**, because **the LORD** is there.

33:23, 24 Commentators are disagreed whether verse 23a refers to Jerusalem or to her enemies. If it refers to Zion's enemies, then it pictures the fate of any ship that would

presume to attack the city. If it refers to Jerusalem, verse 23

> speaks of the weakness and inability of the people themselves, pictured whether as unable to guide the ship of state, or, what is more probable, arrange their tent as their dwelling place, with the necessary cord, tent pole and canvas.[40]

In the kingdom, even **the lame** will be able to **take the prey**. Sickness will be over, and the **iniquity** of **the people** will **be forgiven**.

6. Woe to All Nations (Chap. 34)

34:1–4 In chapter 34 we have God's **indignation against all nations** in general, and against Edom in particular. The latter may be representative of all the other nations. When Jehovah judges the Gentiles (**nations**) the air will reek from the decomposing **corpses**, and **the mountains** will melt away from the torrent of **their blood**. Even **the** stellar **heavens** will be convulsed.

34:5–7 The **sword of the LORD**, "intoxicated **with blood**," will fall in fury **on Edom**, both on the common people (**lambs, goats, rams**) and on the nobles or leaders (**wild oxen, young bulls, mighty bulls**).

34:8 **It is the day of the Lord's vengeance.**

> The word 'vengeance' is of crucial importance. It does not mean getting even with someone, as we use it. It refers to God's action in carrying out the sentence which He as Judge has justly imposed (*Daily Notes of the Scripture Union*).

34:9–17 This passage describes Edom's fate—a blazing inferno, an uninhabited waste, taken over by mysterious birds and **wild beasts**. God will not stop until it is without form and void.[41] There will be no **kingdom**, no king, no **princes** worthy of the name. Its ruins will be overgrown with **thorns** and it will be a sanctuary for strange creatures (which cannot be identified with certainty). Every weird creature will have **a mate**, and thus will reproduce, and God has given them the ruins of Edom to **possess . . . from generation to generation**. **Forever** in this chapter (vv. 10, 17) means **from generation to generation**.

7. The Glory of the Coming Kingdom (Chap. 35)

35:1–7 After the rebellious nations are destroyed, the glorious kingdom of our Lord and Savior, Jesus Christ, is introduced. Features of that period include increased fertility of the land and the personal presence of **the Lord** in **glory** and **excellence**. There will be mutual encouragement among the saints. Every type of disability will be removed, and great rejoicing will celebrate the transformation of **the desert** into well-irrigated fields.

35:8–10 The hundreds of miles of desert route from exile back to Jerusalem will become a **"Highway of Holiness,"** exclusive to God's redeemed people. The **return** of Israel from worldwide dispersion prepictures the **joy** and **gladness** that will accompany the translation of believers to the Father's house when Jesus comes again.

In some editions of the Bible, the supplied summary titles at the tops of the pages of Isaiah will read in substance, "Blessings on the church" and "Curses on Israel." In fact, almost all these predictions are directly aimed at Israel—whether blessings or curses, and the church comes in later or by application. Jennings decries this unjust treatment of Israel by many Christians:

We justly blame those who take all the promises of the Old Testament, and leave only the threatenings for the poor Jew, for in this they do greatly err; yet there is an element of truth in their contention, since "all the promises of God are Yea and Amen in Christ Jesus." Their error is in saying that since God has no further use for Israel, these comforting forecasts apply, and only apply, to Christians, not to Israel as a nation at all! God be thanked that whatever is of a spiritual character does so apply: the material blessings that Israel shall enter into on the basis of the new covenant of grace are, in a spiritual sense, ours by that same grace. But that does not *fulfil* these promises that were given directly to Israel as identified with her Messiah, Jesus, and given her long before the Church of God was revealed at all.[42]

II. HISTORICAL TRANSITION: THE BOOK OF HEZEKIAH (Chaps. 36—39)

Chapters 36 through 39, sometimes called "The Book of Hezekiah," form the historical section of the book of Isaiah. Except for 38:9–20, they are almost an exact repetition of 2 Kings 18:13, 17—20:19.

A. Hezekiah's Deliverance from Assyria (Chaps. 36, 37)

1. Assyria's Defiance of God (Chap. 36)

36:1–3 In chapter 36, **the Rabshakeh** (lit. *chief wine-pourer*, but used of a governor or chief of staff), an envoy of the King of Assyria, meets three delegates of **Hezekiah by the aqueduct from the upper pool, on the highway to the Fuller's Field**. This is the same place where Ahaz had stood when he was bent on trusting Assyria rather than Jehovah to save him from the Syrian-Ephraim alliance (7:3).

36:4–10 The Rabshakeh warns them that it is folly to **trust** in promises from **Egypt** because that base kingdom will wound anyone who **leans** on it. To any claim that they were trusting in Jehovah, he says that Hezekiah had removed the **high places** and **altars** of Jehovah. This was either ignorance or deliberate misrepresentation; **Hezekiah** had removed the **high places** of the idols and strengthened the worship of Jehovah at the temple. The Rabshakeh further taunts that the King of Judah couldn't provide enough **riders** if Sennacherib were to donate **two thousand horses**. Since Judah is so undermanned, how can they hope to defeat the Assyrians, even with Egypt's help? Finally he falsely claims that **the LORD** has commanded the Assyrians **to destroy** Judah.

36:11–20 Hezekiah's envoys fear that the Rabshakeh's insolent boasts and threats, spoken in Hebrew, will undermine the morale of the men of Judah, so they ask him to **speak . . . in Aramaic**. He not only refuses, but begins another **loud** harangue, charging that **Hezekiah** is deceiving the people into false security. He promises the men of Judah plenty of food if they surrender to him, plus eventual relocation in a land of equal fertility. He lists a series of conquered cities (including **Samaria**) whose **gods** had not been able to save them from the Assyrian juggernaut, and pointedly asks what chance **Jerusalem** has. The Rabshakeh arrogantly decides that God's people should surrender.

36:21, 22 Following their **king's commandment** Hezekiah's men do not try to answer him but go and report his words to the king.

2. God's Destruction of Assyria (Chap. 37)

37:1–4 When King Hezekiah hears what the Rabshakeh has said, he is plunged into gloom. After going to the temple, he sends a deputation **to Isaiah** saying, **"Children have come to birth, but there is no strength to bring them forth."** As J. A. Alexander points out, this metaphor is "expressive of extreme pain, imminent danger, critical emergency, utter weakness, and entire dependence on the aid of others."[43] In timidity that surpasses faith, Hezekiah suggests that maybe Jehovah **has heard the** mocking **words of the Rabshakeh**, and **will rebuke** him.

37:5–7 The LORD then assures the king through Isaiah that there is no reason to fear the king of Assyria. The Lord **will send a spirit** (perhaps of apprehension) **upon** Sennacherib so that, hearing **a rumor**, he will **return to his own land** and be killed there.

37:8–13 When **the Rabshakeh** leaves Jerusalem to rejoin Sennacherib, he finds that the latter has redirected his fighting **from Lachish** to **Libnah**, ten miles to the northwest. Another part of the army, of course, is besieging Jerusalem. Then, frustrated by a rumor that **Tirhakah**, an Ethiopian ruling in Egypt, has set out to attack him, Sennacherib sends **messengers to Hezekiah** with a blasphemous letter similar to the diatribe that Rabshakeh had delivered. He cites the folly of trusting in Jehovah by recounting the historic victories of the kings of Assyria.

37:14–20 **Hezekiah** has the good sense to take **the letter** to the temple **and spread it before the Lord**. In a short but moving prayer that demonstrates the king's great faith, he asks God to **save** Judah from the king **of Assyria** so "that all the kingdoms of the earth may know that You are the LORD, You alone."

37:21–29 Jehovah answers through **Isaiah** in a poem that first pictures **Jerusalem** as **a virgin**, taunting **Sennacherib** as he goes down to defeat. Then Jehovah takes the Assyrian to task for mocking **the LORD** Himself and for bragging as if he had already conquered Judah and Egypt. God tells Sennacherib that he is only a pawn in Jehovah's hand, doing what He planned long ago. The same Lord who knows everything about this wicked king will lead him **back** to Assyria like an animal with a **hook in** its **nose**.

37:30–32 Then turning to Hezekiah, the Lord assures him that though food supplies will be limited **this year and the** next because of the Assyrian incursion, crops will return to normal in **the third year**. The people who have holed up in **Jerusalem** in preparation for a siege will emerge and resume normal life. Jehovah's **zeal** for His people will guarantee it.

37:33–35 The LORD assures Hezekiah that **the king of Assyria** will not enter Jerusalem or get near enough to attack it. God **will defend** the **city** and send back the invader **the way that he came**.

37:36 And so it happened. **The angel of the LORD killed one hundred and eighty-five thousand** Assyrian soldiers during the night.

One of the great poems in the English language, written in 1815, dramatizes this event. Since many readers do not have access to an extensive library, we make no apology for reproducing it in full:

THE DESTRUCTION OF SENNACHERIB

The Assyrian came down like the
    wolf on the fold,
And his cohorts were gleaming in
    purple and gold;
And the sheen of their spears was
    like stars on the sea,
When the blue wave rolls nightly on
    deep Galilee.

Like the leaves of the forest when
    Summer is green,
That host with their banners at
    sunset were seen:
Like the leaves of the forest when
    Autumn hath blown,
That host on the morrow lay withered
    and strown.

For the Angel of Death spread his
    wings on the blast,
And breathed in the face of the foe as
    he passed;
And the eyes of the sleepers waxed
    deadly and chill,
And their hearts but once heaved,
    and forever grew still!

And there lay the steed with his
    nostril all wide,
But through it there rolled not the
    breath of his pride;
And the foam of his gasping lay
    white on the turf,
And cold as the spray of the rock-
    beating surf.

And there lay the rider distorted and
    pale,
With the dew on his brow, and the
    rust on his mail:
And the tents were all silent—the
    banners alone—
The lances unlifted—the trumpet
    unblown.

And the widows of Ashur are loud in
    their wail,
And the idols are broke in the temple
    of Baal;

And the might of the Gentile, unsmote
   by the sword,
Hath melted like snow in the glance
   of the Lord![44]
> —*George Gordon, Lord Byron*
> *(1788–1824)*

37:37, 38 **Sennacherib** returned to **Nineveh**, only to be slain by **his sons Adrammelech and Sharezer** in his idol temple.

B. Hezekiah's Sickness and Recovery (Chap. 38)

38:1–8 Chapter 38 does not follow chapter 37 chronologically because in verse 6 Hezekiah is promised deliverance from the Assyrian threat, whereas, at the end of the previous chapter, that threat has already ended.

When **Hezekiah** is taken seriously ill, he earnestly prays for lengthened life, and **the God of David** his **father** grants him **fifteen** more **years**. As a **sign** that he will recover and that Sennacherib will be repulsed, God promises to make **the shadow on the sundial of Ahaz** go **ten degrees backward**. The Hebrew of verse 8 is difficult, but it seems probable that Ahaz had built an obelisk with steps leading up to it for telling time, and that God miraculously caused the shadow to decline **ten degrees** while Hezekiah watched.

38:9–15 To celebrate his recovery, Hezekiah wrote a poem or psalm. This is the unique part of the historical section; it has no parallel in 2 Kings. It opens with the sadness that filled him when he heard that he was going to die **in the prime of** his **life**. He will **not see YAH, the** Lord, that is, experience the goodness of the Lord, and he will be cut off from the rest of mankind. His **life** is ending as if **a shepherd's tent** is being taken down, or a finished fabric **cut off** from the loom. He describes his sense of desolation, his **bitterness**, his earnest supplication, and his helplessness under the stroke of God.

38:16–20 But a change comes in verse 16. Hezekiah acknowledges that **by these** afflictions **men live**, and that they have a beneficial influence on man's character. Now God has delivered him from dying, an indication to the king that the Lord has forgiven his **sins**. Verse 18 reflects the indistinct view of the disembodied state which OT saints had. Now, because he is alive, he can give thanks to the Lord and tell his **children** of the faithfulness of God. He is determined to **praise** Jehovah **all the days of** his **life**.

38:21, 22 These two verses fit chronologically between verses 6 and 7. By placing them here, writes Kelly, "God shows His interest in His own, whatever their infirmity, and explains the means employed, and why the sign was given."[45]

Matthew Henry draws two good lessons on healing from this passage:

> 1. That God's promises are intended not to supersede, but to quicken and encourage, the use of means. Hezekiah is sure to recover, and yet he must *take a lump of figs and lay it on the boil*, v. 21. We do not trust God, but tempt him, if, when we pray to him for help, we do not second our prayers with our endeavours. . . . 2. That the chief end we should aim at, in desiring life and health, is that we may glorify God, and do good, and improve ourselves in knowledge, and grace, and meetness for heaven.[46]

C. Hezekiah's Sin (Chap. 39)

39:1–7 Chapter 39 records Hezekiah's colossal mistake in showing all his resources to a delegation which came from **the king of Babylon**, ostensibly to congratulate him on his recovery. **Hezekiah** probably hoped that the Babylonians would help Judah against the menace of Assyria. When **Isaiah** heard what had happened, he pronounced God's judgment. Judah will be taken into captivity by the Babylonians. The king's **sons** will **be eunuchs in the palace** at **Babylon**. This prediction was made seventy years in advance of the events, when *Assyria*, not Babylon, was the major threat to Judah.

39:8 Hezekiah's response, **"The word of the Lord . . . is good!"** reflects his submission and also his own relief that he personally would not live to see the disaster.

III. PROPHECIES OF COMFORT FROM THE VIEWPOINT OF THE FUTURE CAPTIVITY (Chaps. 40—66)

If the preceding thirty-nine chapters correspond to the books of the OT, then the following twenty-seven chapters, filled with pictures of Jesus the Messiah, certainly correspond to the books of the NT.

In this section of Isaiah (chaps. 40—66), the prophet looks forward to Judah's return from Babylonian captivity and then to the entire nation's future restoration at the Second Advent of Christ.

A. The Comfort of Israel's Coming Deliverance (Chaps. 40—48)

1. Comfort from God's Pardon and Peace (40:1–11)

40:1, 2 Chapter 40 opens with a message of **comfort** for the returning captives. Jerusalem's troubles are over, **her iniquity is pardoned, for she has received . . . double** (that is, full and fitting measure) **for all her sins**. This will be fully realized at the Second

Coming of Christ. In the meantime this old earth and even the church is greatly in need of comfort. Each one of us can do his or her bit to comfort God's people:

Ask God to give thee skill
  In comforts' art;
That thou mayst consecrated be
  And set apart
  Into a life of sympathy.
For heavy is the weight of ill
  In every heart;
And comforters are needed much
  Of Christlike touch.
       —A. E. Hamilton

40:3–5 The call goes out to **"Prepare the way of the Lord."** John the Baptist filled the role of forerunner at Christ's First Advent (Matt. 3:3), and Elijah will fill it at the Second Advent (Mal. 4:5, 6). The preparation for His coming is moral and spiritual, not topographical. Morgan writes:

The faithful among men prepare His way and make straight His highway when they yield to Him their complete loyalty, and confide in Him alone.[47]

Mountains and hills represent the proud and arrogant among men, valleys the people of low degree. All unevenness and roughness of character must be **made smooth. The glory of the Lord** (that is, the Lord Himself) **shall be revealed, and all flesh shall see it together** (see Rev. 1:7).

40:6–8 The Lord instructs the prophet to **"Cry out!"** to men, telling them how transitory they are, and how permanent His **word** is. While these verses describe the transience of all men, they may refer especially to Israel's overlords.

"The word of our God stands forever" has been adopted as the motto of a number of Christian schools, usually in Latin: *Verbum Dei manet in aeternam*. William Kelly wrote that

> as the end draws nearer we do greatly need simplicity to rest upon God's Word. There may be difficulties to such as we are, and the Word seems a weak thing to confide in for eternity, but in truth it is more stable than heaven or earth.[48]

40:9–11 **Zion** herself may be the herald of the **good tidings** of the Messiah's advent or the news may be brought to Zion by some female herald. (The **You** is feminine.) Verses 10 and 11 show the severity and the goodness of God—severity to those who refuse to acknowledge Him, but gentle goodness to His **flock** and **lambs** who have been dispersed among the Gentiles. These verses picture His coming in power and glory.

2. Comfort from God's Attributes (40:12–31)

40:12 Here begins a classic passage on the greatness of God in contrast to the utter vanity of idols. Jehovah has **measured the waters** of the sea **in the hollow of His hand**, and **measured heaven with a span**, the distance from the tip of His thumb to the tip of His little finger. He enclosed **the dust of the earth in a measure** (about a peck).

40:13, 14 No one ever **directed the Spirit of the LORD**. All His works of creation and providence were and are performed without outside help.

40:15–17 **The nations are** as insignificant **as a drop in a bucket** to Him. The forests of **Lebanon** are **not sufficient** for fuel and all its animals inadequate for a worthy **burnt offering** to Him.

40:18–26 What man-made **image** could ever portray a **God** so great? The rich man makes his idol with precious metal and the poor man with wood. Utterly ridiculous! **Have** they **not known** or **heard** of the greatness of Jehovah's Person and power? What image could ever capture the **greatness** of the One who made the stars? When He calls them to come out at night, **not one is missing**.

40:27–31 If any of the people of Judah are discouraged and wonder if God still cares for them, let them realize that those **who wait on the Lord** are assured of renewed **strength**. It is absurd to think that He cares less for His people than for the stars which He guides so unerringly.

3. Comfort from the Holy One of Israel (Chap. 41)

41:1 God summons the nations to a confrontation with Him; they should **renew their strength**, i.e., produce their strongest arguments.

41:2–4 Jehovah first describes His calling of Cyrus, the **one from the east**. The past tense is used to describe the certainty of what is still future. It should be mentioned here that some commentators believe verses 2 and 3 refer to the call of Abraham, but the military victories of the man described here far overshadow Abraham's achievements. This man (Cyrus, King of Persia) has an unbroken record of victories. In the path of his juggernaut, resistance is as weak as dust and stubble. He advances swiftly into places that are new to him. **Who raised up** Cyrus and calls one generation to succeed another? It is Jehovah— **the first; and with the last**, that is, **with the last** generation, He is still the same.

41:5–7 The nations are terrified as they hear of the conqueror's approach. The people try to encourage one another that there is nothing to fear. Then they hastily fashion an idol to save them from destruction. The poor idol has to be nailed into place so it will **not totter**!

41:8–10   Verses 8–20 describe God's personal love and care for His people. The implied question is, "Have idols ever cared for you so tenderly?" God has called them from Ur of the Chaldees to be His **servant**; they are assured of His presence, His relationship, His help, and His sustaining power in what must be one of the loveliest verses in Isaiah:

> **Fear not, for I am with you; be not dismayed, for I am your God. I will strengthen you, yes, I will help you, I will uphold you with My righteous right hand.**

41:11–16   Their enemies **shall perish** and disappear; God is their Helper and **Redeemer**. The Lord will use Israel as His **threshing sledge** against the nations and Israel will **rejoice in the** LORD alone.

41:17–20   **The poor and needy** will be cared for by the Lord. The millennial earth will have **water** in abundance, and the **wilderness** will flourish with a great variety of trees. It will be a lesson to all that **the** LORD really cares for His own.

41:21–24   In verse 21, God switches back to His controversy with the nations. He challenges them to produce idols which can predict **things to come**, or even account for things that already are. Let them prophesy, or let them do **good** or **evil**—anything to show that they can do *something!* But they cannot. They are a fraction of **nothing**—not even complete nothing.[49]

41:25–28   Cyrus comes into view again in verse 25, this time as **one from the north**. He originally came from Persia (the east, v. 2), then he conquered Media (**the north**), and

proceeded on his conquests from there. Cyrus called on God's name in the sense that he acknowledged God as the One who guided and empowered him (Ezra 1:2). No idol had ever predicted the coming of Cyrus. God told it in advance to His people, but He cannot find one among the idols to speak with authority. They are all a delusion, and unworthy of trust.

41:29   The last verse in chapter 41 clearly reveals the contrast between God and worthless "molded images." Vine renders it close to the original as follows:

> Look at them all! Vanity! Their productions are nothingness; wind and desolation are their molten images.[50]

4. Comfort from the Servant of the Lord (Chap. 42)

42:1–4   The name **"Servant"** is applied by Isaiah to the *Messiah*, to the entire *nation of Israel*, to the *godly remnant* of the people (43:10), and to *Cyrus*. Usually the context makes clear which one is intended. In verses 1–4 it is clearly the Lord Jesus—upheld and chosen by God and endued with the Holy **Spirit**. He will **bring forth justice to the Gentiles**, will not be a rabble-rouser, will **not** crush true penitence or **quench** a spark of faith, **will not fail nor be discouraged till He has established** His righteous kingdom.

42:5–9   **God**, the mighty Creator, now addresses the Messiah and tells what He proposes to accomplish through this One whom He has **called . . . in righteousness**. God **will not** share His **glory** with **another**, and least of all with **carved images**. His past predictions **have come to pass**, and now He reveals the future once more.

42:10–13   Israel calls on earth's

remotest nations to join in **praise** to the Messiah as He descends, **a mighty . . . man of war**, to execute vengeance on His **enemies**. The mention of **Kedar** and **Sela** means that Arab voices will join in the **new song**.

42:14–17 Jehovah is speaking here. The time of His self-restraint is past; now He will unloose His fury on His foes, He will deal mercifully with the believing remnant of Israel, and He will utterly shame all idolaters.

42:18–22 In verse 19 the **servant** is no longer the Messiah. It is Israel, **deaf** and **blind** to the words and works of Jehovah. **"Who is blind as he who is perfect?"** may mean **perfect** as to privilege, or may be translated "Who is blind as him whom I have trusted?" (JND), or, "Who is so blind as he that is at peace with Me?" (NASB). Israel was brought into covenant relationship with the Lord, but did not walk worthy of her high calling. The Lord exalted **the law**. It was **honorable** to Him. But Israel despised and disobeyed it, and as a result was given over to robbery, **plunder**, and prison.

42:23–25 The prophet Isaiah asks: **"Who among you will give ear to this? . . . Who gave Jacob for plunder, and Israel to the robbers? Was it not the LORD, He against whom we have sinned?"** God had **poured** out **on** Israel **the fury of His anger** and the **fire** of **battle**, but no one seemed to discern the significance of His chastisement or **take it to heart**.

5. Comfort from Israel's Restoration (Chap. 43, 44)

43:1–7 In tones of tender love, Jehovah assures His people that they need **not . . . fear**, because He who created, formed, redeemed, and called them **will be with** them in the flood and **fire**. **The Holy One of Israel**

gives **Egypt** as their **ransom**, a promise that was fulfilled after the return of the Jews from captivity. Vine writes:

> The Lord rewarded Cyrus the Persian Monarch for liberating them, by permitting him and his son Cambyses to possess Egypt and the neighbouring kingdoms. Seba was the large district between the White and the Blue Nile, contiguous to Ethiopia. The possession of these lands was not merely a gift, it was a ransom price (a *kopher*, or covering), the people on whose behalf payment was made, being covered by it.[51]

Because Israel is **precious, honored**, and **loved**, God **will give men** in exchange **for** her, that is, judgment will fall on the Gentiles in every direction in order that His **sons and** His **daughters** might be restored to the land. Verses 5–7 describe that restoration.

43:8–13 The Lord now summons Israel and **all the nations** to a court test. **Let them bring . . . witnesses** as to the ability of idols to predict future events. Otherwise let them acknowledge that only God is true. **The LORD** calls Israel as His **witnesses**;[52] they should testify that He is the only true **God**, that He is eternal, that **besides** Him **there is no savior** and Deliverer, and that His decrees and acts cannot be thwarted.

43:14–21 **The LORD** is determined to crush **Babylon** for Israel's sake. This will demonstrate that He is **the LORD**, His people's **Holy One, Creator**, and **King**. He is the One who brought them through the Red **Sea**, destroying the pursuing Egyptians at the same time. But the Exodus is forgettable compared to what He is now going to do. He will **make a road** through the desert for His **people** as they return from captivity. In the renewed earth, the waste places will enjoy plentiful water supplies so that the creatures of **the wilderness** will be grateful. God's **people**, too, will be grateful and will **praise** His Name.

43:22–24 These verses revert to Israel's pre-captivity days. The people were prayerless and they grew **weary of** God. Although they **brought** Him **offerings** in a perfunctory way, their hearts were far from God, so it was the same as if they brought no sacrifices. They didn't overload God with gifts—only **with** their **iniquities**!

43:25–28 Yet in His grace He **blots out** their **transgressions** and forgives and forgets their **sins**. Can they cite any merit in themselves why He should do this? No. Their entire history has been one unbroken record of sin and failure—from Adam on. That is why His judgment came upon them.

44:1–5 In these verses we hear the heartbeat of the Lord for His people. His love is unextinguished by all their sin. He calls them **Jacob** (supplanter), **Israel** (prince of God), and **Jeshurun** (upright). He **who made** them, **formed** them, and chose them **will help** them. The promise of the **Spirit** was partially fulfilled at Pentecost but it will have its final and complete fulfillment at the Second Advent. Then the thirsty **ground**, both literal and figurative, will experience **floods** of water. Israel's **offspring** will flourish, and they will not be ashamed to identify themselves **by the name of Israel** and **by the name of Jacob** and by **the Lord's** name. (Or verse 5 *may* mean that *Gentiles* will identify themselves with Jehovah and with His people, see Ps. 87:4, 5.)

44:6–8 The **Lord**, the **King of Israel**, is unique—the only true God. He challenges any so-called god to predict the future as He does, especially with regard to **the ancient peo**ple, Israel. His people need **not fear** any challenge to His supremacy. They are His **witnesses** that He has foretold the future, and that He is the only **God**. He Himself does **not know** of any **other** genuine **Rock**; how then could Israel know of any?

44:9–11 **Those who make an image** are doomed to shame and disappointment. The idols are **useless** and powerless.

44:12–17 Here is a **blacksmith** making an idol for a rich man. He works hard, forming it into the desired shape. But then he has to stop for a break—he needs food, drink, and a rest. If the idol maker runs out of **strength** so quickly, what about the inanimate image which he makes?

Or here is a **craftsman**, making a wooden idol for a poor man. He chisels away at the block of wood until the **figure of a man** appears. Maybe he himself had planted the tree. He uses **some of it** as fuel **to warm himself**, some to bake his food, and some to make **a god**. Then he **falls down** and worships a god of his own creation.

44:18–20 Because of their refusal to see, God **has shut** the **eyes** of the idolaters. They never stop to think that the same tree that is their master is also their servant, that they worship part of it and use part for household chores! They feed **on** what is worthless as **ashes**, they are led astray by a delusion, they **cannot deliver** themselves from their bondage, and they never face up to the fact that the god they hold in their **hand** is **a lie**.

44:21–23 **Israel** is called to **remember** that God is their Creator who never forgets them, and that they are His **servant**. He has **blotted out** the **cloud** of **transgressions** that hid His face from them; He has bought them back from bondage and invites them to **return to** Him. All creation is invited to **sing** and **shout**, because **the LORD has redeemed Jacob**.

44:24–27   God presents Himself to the faithful remnant as **Redeemer**, Jehovah (**the LORD**), Creator, Protector, and Restorer. He **frustrates** the predictions of the Chaldean **babblers and . . . diviners** and the wisdom of the **wise**. He **confirms** the predictions of His own prophets that **Jerusalem** and **Judah** will be restored, and that His people will return from captivity under the decree of Cyrus.

44:28   This prophecy concerning **Cyrus** is remarkable in that it mentions him *by name* 150 to 200 years before he was born. It is also amazing that God calls him **"My shepherd."**

Again Cyrus is named as the one whom God will use to deliver His people from Babylon and to authorize the rebuilding of **the temple**. Josephus, the Jewish historian, wrote:

> Now Cyrus learned this (as to building the Temple) by reading the book that Isaiah had left of his own prophecies 210 years before. . . . These things Isaiah foretold 140 years before the Temple was destroyed. When Cyrus, therefore, had read them, and had admired their divine character, an impulse and emulation seized him to do what was written.[53]

6. Comfort from Cyrus, God's Anointed (Chap. 45)

45:1–6   The LORD calls **Cyrus** His **"anointed"** (the same word as "messiah" in Hebrew) because the Persian monarch was a prototype of the Messiah who would give final deliverance to His people. Jehovah promises to give him victory over **nations**, principally Babylon, to remove all hindrances to his conquests, and to hand over to him tremendous amounts of

hidden riches in **secret places**. Still addressing Cyrus, **the LORD** speaks of Himself as the only true **God**, who calls Cyrus **by name**, who surnames him as **anointed** and shepherd (44:28), and who equips him for his mission. God does all this for the sake of His people, and so that the whole world may know that He alone is **the LORD**.

45:7   Verse 7 does not mean that God creates moral "evil," as some have claimed, based on the King James Version and other early translations.[54]

Delitzsch points out that the early "Christian" heretic Marcion, and the heretical Valentinians and other Gnostic sects, abused this text to teach that the God of the OT was "a different being from the God of the New."[55]

Addressing the problem of evil (including calamity, no doubt), Delitzsch continues, "Undoubtedly, evil as an act is not the direct working of God, but the spontaneous work of a creature endowed with freedom."[56]

In the present context the contrasts are between **light** and its opposite, **darkness**; between **peace** and its opposite, **calamity**. What God permits, He is often said to **create**. Some think that **light** and **darkness** refer to two principles which the Persians practically revered as two gods who were in perpetual conflict. (Others say that there is no evidence that Cyrus followed this religion.) As Cyrus swept forward in his campaigns, there would be **peace** for Israel and **calamity** for Israel's foes, and God was the One who was supervising the entire operation.

45:8   The ideal conditions of abundant **righteousness** (or justice) and **salvation** (or deliverance) described here are those that would result on a small scale from Cyrus's intervention on behalf of Israel. Their *complete* fulfillment awaits the Millennial Kingdom.

45:9–11 A **woe** is pronounced on any who would question Jehovah's right to use a foreigner in redeeming Judah. That is like **clay** talking back to the **potter** and accusing him of having **no hands**—of being powerless. Verse 11 should possibly be read as a question, *"Do you ask **Me** what I purpose far in the future **concerning My sons**, or do you command **Me concerning the work of My hands?"** In other words, "What right do you have to question Me?"

45:12, 13 The same One who **created man and stretched out the heavens** and **the earth raised up** Cyrus to liberate His **exiles**, and **build** His **city** of Jerusalem. While the rebuilding of the city was actually accomplished later through the decree of Artaxerxes (Neh. 2:8b), it was Cyrus's leadership that first laid the groundwork for this project by allowing the Jews to return from Babylon.

45:14–17 Israel's former enemies will one day **come to** her with gifts and tribute, acknowledging that the **God** of the Jews is the true **God** and that **there is no other**. This promise, as well as all God's dealings, causes the saved remnant to praise God for His inscrutable judgments and His ways past finding out. Makers and worshipers of false gods will **be ashamed**, whereas **Israel**, **saved by the Lord**, will never have occasion to **be ashamed** after the Second Coming of the Messiah.

45:18, 19 When **the Lord created** the world, it was not as a chaos or **in vain** (*tōhû*, the same word used in Gen. 1:2). He **formed it to be inhabited** by men, and revealed Himself to men in clear, understandable language. He did not create chaotically, nor did He communicate chaotically. Rather He revealed Himself in truth and **righteousness** as the absolute and supreme God.

45:20, 21 He calls on the Gentiles, toting their idols and praying to powerless gods, to produce evidence that their idols can foretell the future as He has done. Only He can do this—and He is the only **just God and a Savior**.

45:22–25 He invites the Gentiles to come to Him for salvation, and decrees that **every knee shall bow** to Him and **every tongue** confess Him (see Rom. 14:11; Phil. 2:9–11). This will find its fulfillment in the Millennium. Then men will acknowledge the Lord Jesus as the only source of **righteousness and strength**. **All** His enemies will come to Him in contrition, and **Israel shall be justified and shall glory** in Him, not in idols.

7. Comfort from the Fall of Babylon's Idols (Chap. 46)

46:1, 2 The idols of Babylon, **Bel** and **Nebo**, are being carted away by the Persians. As the weary **beasts** plod on, the **idols** topple. The gods they represent cannot save the load; instead they are carried off **into captivity**.

46:3, 4 In contrast to the idols which are carried by the people, the true God **will carry** His people **even to** their **old age**. James Stewart summarizes concisely:

> Ever since Isaiah, men have been aware that one of the vital distinctions between true religion and false is that whereas the latter is a dead burden for the soul to carry, the former is a living power to carry the soul.[57]

46:5–7 What image could ever represent the absolute and exclusive Deity? Yet, deluded people still pay generous amounts to the goldsmith to make **a god** for them. **They prostrate themselves** in **worship**, . . . **they**

carry it, and when they **set it** down, it stays there, unable to **move**. It can neither hear prayer **nor save**.

46:8–11 Any people who are leaning toward idolatry should stop and **remember** that only the true **God** has revealed events before they came to pass with the determination to accomplish all His plans. He will call Cyrus (**a bird of prey from the east**) to deliver His people from the Chaldeans.

46:12, 13 Those who stubbornly refuse to face the evidence now hear God's established purpose to **place salvation in Zion**.

8. Comfort from the Fall of Babylon (Chap. 47)

47:1–4 The city of **Babylon** is pictured as a beautiful young **virgin** queen who is forced to step down from her **throne** and become a servant, doing menial work and wading **through the rivers** into captivity. She will be stripped bare and exposed to public view. God will **take vengeance** and spare no **man**, because He is acting as the **Redeemer, . . . the Holy One of Israel**.

47:5–15 Babylon will be punished for four sins.

1. Although God did appoint her to carry His people into exile, He did *not* order her to be cruel and merciless. She overplayed her part. Now she says, **"I shall be a lady forever,"** but God says, **"You shall no longer be called the Lady of Kingdoms."**

2. She was proud and arrogant, supposing that nothing could ever destroy her prosperity. She will become widowed and childless **in one day**, and none of her **sorceries** will be able to prevent the calamity.

3. She considered herself immune from detection and punishment. But her smugness and proud self-sufficiency will be rewarded with disaster.

4. She trusted in sorcerers and **astrologers**. Jennings writes, "Jehovah counsels her to call all these powers to her aid, for she will need them sorely."[58] God's punishment will be a blazing inferno, not a comfortable **fire** in the fireplace. Those who trafficked with Babylon will go their own way, unable to **save** her.

9. Comfort from Israel's Return after Chastening (Chap. 48)

48:1, 2 God here addresses the captives of **Judah** in Babylon. Most of them are probably apostate; only a few are faithful to Jehovah. He complains that they call themselves by the name of **Israel** (prince of God) but they are not princes. They are descended from **Judah** (praise) but they do not praise Him. They confess the God of Israel but they do not confess their sins. **They call themselves after the holy city** but they are not holy. They **lean on the God of Israel** but they are not godly.

48:3–5 Jehovah had predicted their history well in advance, and it **came to pass** as foretold. Knowing their stubbornness and hardness, God **proclaimed** what He would do so they wouldn't credit it to their idols when it happened.

48:6–8 Now He is going to predict something **new**—the restoration from captivity under Cyrus. He is doing this so that they will not be able to say, **"Of course I knew** it all along."

48:9–11 He will end the exile for Judah, not because of their merit, but **for** His **own sake**. He has **refined**

them, **not** like **silver** in literal fire, but **in the furnace of affliction** (the Babylonian captivity). Now He will restore them for His own **name's sake**—a name that has been **profaned** by them. He will not share the credit for this restoration with their idols.

48:12–16 Presenting Himself as the eternal, absolute God (**the First** and **the Last**), the Creator and Sustainer of the universe, the Arranger of history, the God of prophecy, He announces that He will raise up one whom He loves (Cyrus) to defeat the Babylonians and to deliver the people of Israel. Notice all three Persons of the Trinity in verse 16—**the Lord GOD and His Spirit**, and **Me** (i.e., Christ). Here the subject turns almost imperceptibly from Cyrus to his Antitype, the Lord Jesus, who will deliver the nation from their worldwide dispersion at His Second Advent.

48:17–19 Again **the LORD** appeals to the people of **Israel** as their **Redeemer**, their **God**, their Teacher, and Guide. If they had obeyed Him, they would have enjoyed **peace, righteousness,** fertility, and uninterrupted fellowship with Him.

48:20–22 He calls on the godly remnant to **go forth from Babylon** and joyfully **proclaim** the Lord as their Redeemer (see Rev. 18:4). Verse 21 was fulfilled in the Exodus from Egypt. If Jehovah did it once, He can do it again. **The wicked** Israelites who refuse to obey the Lord by separating themselves from Babylon and all it stands for can never know **peace**.

B. The Messiah and His Rejection by Israel (Chaps. 49—57)

1. The Messiah as Servant (Chap. 49)

In chapters 49 through 53, God is dealing with His people because of their rejection of the Messiah. This is the book of the Suffering Servant of Jehovah.

49:1–6 The **servant** of Jehovah in chapter 49 may seem to be the nation of Israel in verses 1–3, but only the Lord Jesus fully answers to the text. In verse 3 **Israel** is mentioned by name, but it is Christ, the true "Prince of God," and not the nation. In verses 5 and 6 the Servant is distinguished from Israel. The restorations of Israel merge in these verses, first the return under Cyrus, then the future restoration when the Messiah sets up His kingdom.

The Servant calls on the people of the world to **heed** Him as He recounts His birth, the **name** that was given to Him before His birth (Matt. 1:21), His incisive, authoritative message, and His appointment by God as Servant, a Prince of God (**Israel**) in whom Jehovah would **be glorified**. He further intimates the trouble of soul He experienced over His rejection by Israel (see Matt. 11:16–24), but then His satisfaction that God would **reward** (cf. v. 4 with Matt. 11:25, 26).

God called Him not only to bring about the spiritual rebirth of Israel, but also to bring salvation **to the Gentiles**. Verse 6b is quoted in Acts 13:47 as referring to Christ.

49:7 In His First Advent **the LORD** was deeply despised and abhorred by **the nation** of Israel, lower on the social ladder than the Gentile **kings**. But in His Second Advent, earth's monarchs will pay homage to Him. The phrase **"Servant of rulers"** has been true of Israel as well; compare Joseph, Mordecai, Ezra, Nehemiah, and Daniel.

49:8–13 God answered Christ's prayer by raising Him from the dead, then assigning Him to bring Israel back to the land. The Servant of

Jehovah will summon **the people** to return to the land, and provide ideal travel conditions along the way. They will come **from all** over the world, from as far away as **Sinim** (possibly China). It will be a glad day for the world when Israel experiences His comfort and compassion in this way.

49:14–16 In the meantime, the city of **Zion** is portrayed as feeling that her **Lord has forgotten** her. Jehovah's answer is that a mother may **forget her nursing** baby, but He will never **forget** His city. Zion is **inscribed on the palms of** His **hands**, and her **walls are** never out of His mind. We instinctively compare the reference to **the palms** of Jehovah's hands with the lovewounds borne by Christ for us. A great English Christian poet expressed it beautifully:

My name from the palms of His hands
Eternity will not erase;
Imprest on His heart it remains
In marks of indelible grace.
　　　　　　　—Augustus Toplady

49:17, 18 Israel's children are hurrying back to Zion, while the wrecking crew is leaving. The assembling crowds, converging on the city, become like jewels on **a bride**.

49:19–21 The **waste and desolate places** of Israel will experience a population explosion. Zion will wonder where so many Jews come from—after all, she has been widowed a long time!

49:22, 23 At a signal **from the Lord** God, the nations will set up an enormous airlift to carry the exiles back to the land. Gentile monarchs will serve God's people, and Israel will realize that it does pay after all to **wait for** the Lord.

49:24–26 If the **captives** in Babylon have any qualms as to the possibility of their being freed from **the mighty** tyrant, let them know that Jehovah **will contend with** their adversaries and **save their children**. When the oppressors reap what they have sown, then the world will know that the Lord is Israel's **Savior and** their **Redeemer, the Mighty One of Jacob**.

2. The Messiah as True Disciple (Chap. 50)

50:1–3 In a heart-to-heart talk with Israel, Jehovah reminds them that it was not for some trifling whim that He divorced them (though He did divorce them, Jer. 3:8), nor did He deliver them to the Chaldeans because of any debt to that Gentile nation. The cause was their own **iniquities** and **transgressions**. No one in the nation welcomed Him, and no one answered His call. Did they think He was powerless **to deliver** them? Had He not dried up **the** Red **Sea** and the Jordan River? Had He not **clothed the heavens** in mourning?

50:4–9 The Messiah speaks next. The nation that spurned Jehovah in the OT spurned Jesus in the NT. He came as the True Disciple, taught by God to speak the appropriate **word**. Every **morning** His **ear** was **opened** to receive instructions from His Father for that day. He delighted to do the will of God, even if it meant going to the cross. He did not turn **back** but willingly **gave** Himself over to suffering and **shame**. In full confidence that **God** would vindicate Him, He **set** His **face like a flint** to go to Jerusalem. He was vindicated, of course, by His resurrection. Now he challenges the adversary, Satan, to **condemn** Him. (We too can now throw out the same challenge, Rom. 8:31–39.) All His foes will **grow old like a** moth-eaten **garment**.

50:10 The last two verses describe

two classes of people. The first are those who walk in dependence on **the L**ORD. They confess their own need for guidance. For them God's advice is to **trust in the name of the L**ORD **and rely upon** their **God**. Then they will be flooded with illumination.

50:11 The second class are those who try to manufacture their own guidance, feeling no need of divine direction. They can **walk in the light of** their own **sparks** but the Lord will see to it that they will **lie down in torment**.

3. The Messiah as Righteous Ruler (51:1—52:12)

51:1–3 All in Israel who seek deliverance should remember God's care for them since He took them from **the rock** quarry (Mesopotamia). They should be encouraged by the memory of God's gracious dealings with **Abraham . . . and Sarah**, and how He gave them a numerous posterity. And they should be heartened by His promise to **comfort Zion**. Notice three calls to **listen** (vv. 1, 4, 7) and three calls to awake (51:9, 17; 52:1).

51:4–6 The Messiah will rule over **the** Gentile **peoples** as well as Israel during the Millennium. At the close of the kingdom, **the heavens** and **the earth** will be destroyed, and all unbelievers will perish, but God's people will be eternally secure.

51:7, 8 The Lord urges the remnant **not** to **fear** the wrath **of men** during the dark days of the Tribulation period, because the doom of evil men is sealed, and the deliverance of His people is assured.

51:9–11 This prompts the remnant to call on **the L**ORD to deliver His people as He delivered them from Egypt (**Rahab**) and from Pharaoh (**the serpent**, his symbol), drying **up the sea** so **the redeemed** could **cross over**.

The memory of God's intervention in the past causes them to foresee the **ransomed** captives' **return to Zion**. F. C. Jennings describes the event beautifully:

> Their heads are garlanded with joy and gladness which they have vainly pursued hitherto, but have overtaken at last, while the storm through which they have passed rolls off like a thick cloud, taking with it all their sighs and tears![59]

51:12–16 Jehovah speaks a message of comfort to those who fear the tyrant, whether Nebuchadnezzar in that day or the man of sin in the future. They should fear **the L**ORD who **stretched out the heavens and laid the foundations of the earth**; then they would lose their fear of frail **man. The captive exile hastens, that he may be loosed, that he should not die in the pit, and that his bread should not fail.** These captives were **loosed** at that time by Cyrus, and will be **loosed** by the Messiah at His appearing in glory. Jehovah will bring it to pass; He who is infinitely high is also intimately nigh, hiding His people **with the shadow of** His **hand**. He puts His **words in** their **mouth** so that they might be His missionaries to the world. Verse 16 may also be applied to the Lord Jesus. The Father put His **words** in the Messiah's **mouth**, protected and equipped Him that He might **plant the** new **heavens** and new **earth** of the millennial period **and say to Zion, "You are My people."**

51:17–20 **"Awake, awake!"** He bids **Jerusalem** after her dark night of suffering when none of her **sons** could **guide her**, when she was devastated by famine and sword, when her men lay helpless **like an** exhausted **antelope** caught **in a net**.

51:21–23 He will take the **cup of His fury** which has made Jerusalem stagger, and He will give it to her enemies who have gone beyond the limits assigned to them by God by being cruel and merciless.

52:1, 2 Again **Zion** is called to **"Awake, awake!"** from its sleep of captivity and **put on** its **beautiful garments**. Never again will it be invaded by the heathen. This, of course, looks forward to the inauguration of the kingdom; only then will it be true.

52:3–6 Israel had not been **sold** as a slave for monetary gain; she will **be redeemed without money** as well. The Israelites **went down at first into Egypt** as guests; but subsequently they were abused. Later **the Assyrian oppressed them without cause**, but not for monetary gain. **Now** once again God's people are being tyrannized by oppressors who make no payment to the Lord. The overlords are delighted, and God's **name is blasphemed**. But He will show Himself strong on behalf of His own, and they will know that **He** is all that He promised to be.

52:7–10 The next verses picture the return of the Jews from their worldwide dispersion. As the exiles travel over **the mountains . . . to Zion** they are preceded by heralds who proclaim the **good news** of the Messiah's reign. The **watchmen** on the walls of Jerusalem **sing** with joy as they **see . . . the Lord** returning at the head of the multitude. **Jerusalem** itself is summoned to celebrate the Lord's mighty deliverance.

52:11, 12 The exiles are urged to leave behind the pollutions of the land of captivity as they **bear** the temple **vessels** back to Jerusalem. They will not leave in panic or fright; **the God of Israel** will be their protection both **before** and behind.

4. The Messiah as Sin-bearing Sacrifice (52:13—53:12)

The closing verses of chapter 52 really belong to chapter 53. They trace the history of the Servant of Jehovah from His earthly life to the cross and then to His glorious appearing. Adolph Saphir, himself a Hebrew Christian, rhapsodizes on this greatest of all prophecies of the cross:

> Blessed, precious chapter, how many of God's ancient covenant people have been led by thee to the foot of Christ's cross!—that cross over which was written, "Jesus Christ, the King of the Jews!" And oh! what a glorious commentary shall be given of thee when, in the latter days, repentant and believing Israel, looking unto Him whom they have pierced, shall exclaim, "Surely He hath borne our griefs, and carried our sorrows; yet we did esteem Him stricken, smitten of God, and afflicted!"[60]

52:13 Jehovah's **Servant** dealt **prudently** throughout His earthly ministry. He was **exalted** in Resurrection, lifted up in Ascension, and made **very high** in glory at God's right hand.

52:14 At His first coming, **many were astonished** at the depths of His suffering. His face and His body were **marred** beyond recognition as a **man**.

52:15 But when **He** comes again men will be startled (NKJV marg.)[61] at the magnificence of His glory. Gentile **kings** will be speechless when they see His unheard-of splendor. They will understand then that the humble Man of Calvary is the King of kings and Lord of lords:

> Did Thy God e'en then forsake Thee,
> Hide His face from Thy deep need?
> In Thy face, once marred and smitten,
> All His glory now we read.
> —*Miss C. Thompson*

53:1 The repentant remnant of Israel recalls that when the **report** of the Messiah's First Advent went forth, not many **believed**. And consequently the saving power **of the** LORD was not **revealed** to many either.

53:2 The Lord Jesus grew **up before** the delighted gaze of Jehovah like an exotic, **tender plant** in this world of sin. He was like **a root out of dry ground**. Israel was the **dry ground**, a most unlikely soil. The nation of Israel could see **no beauty** in Him, nothing in His appearance to attract them. F. B. Meyer describes the mystery of His humiliation:

> The tender plant; the sucker painfully pushing its way through the crust of the caked ground; the absence of natural attractiveness. Such imagery awaits and receives its full interpretation from the New Testament, with its story of Christ's peasant parentage, his manger-bed, and lowly circumstances—fisherfolk his choice disciples; poverty his constant lot; the common people his devoted admirers; thieves and malefactors on either side of his cross; the lowly and poor the constituents of his Church. This were humiliation indeed, though the irregularities of human lot are scarce distinguishable from the heights whence He came.[62]

53:3 Despised and rejected, He was **a Man of sorrows** who knew what **grief** was. To men He was repulsive; even by Israel He was not appreciated.

> "Man of Sorrows," what a name
> For the Son of God who came
> Ruined sinners to reclaim!
> Hallelujah! what a Saviour!
>
> Bearing shame and scoffing rude,
> In my place condemned He stood;
> Sealed my pardon with His blood;
> Hallelujah! what a Saviour!
> —*Philip P. Bliss*

53:4–6 The remnant now knows and acknowledges the truth about Him. They confess: "It was *our* griefs He bore, *our* sorrows He **carried**, yet as we saw Him on the cross, we thought He was being punished **by God** for *His own* sins. But no! It was for **our** transgressions, for *our* iniquities, and in order that *we* might have **peace**, in order that we might be **healed**. The truth is that *we* were the ones who went **astray** and who walked in self-will, and Jehovah placed our **iniquity on Him**, the sinless Substitute."

Until that time when the remnant acknowledges Him, we who are Christians can confess:

> He was wounded for our
>   transgressions,
> He bore our sins in His body on the
>   tree;
> For our guilt He gave us peace,
> From our bondage gave release,
> And with His stripes, and with His
>   stripes,
> And with His stripes our souls are
>   healed.
>
> He was numbered among
>   transgressors,
> We did esteem Him forsaken by His
>   God;
> As our sacrifice He died,
> That the law be satisfied,
> And all our sin, and all our sin,
> And all our sin was laid on Him.
>
> We had wandered, we all had
>   wandered,
> Far from the fold of "the Shepherd of
>   the sheep";
> But He sought us where we were,
> On the mountains bleak and bare,
> And brought us home, and brought
>   us home,
> And brought us safely home to God.
> —*Thomas O. Chisholm*

Our Lord Jesus suffered all five kinds of wounds known to medical science: *contusions*—blows by a rod; *lacerations*—scourging; *penetrating wounds*—crown of thorns; *perforating wounds*—nails; *incised wounds*—the spear.

53:7, 8 Like **a sheep**, that is, **silent** and uncomplaining **before its shearers**, He endured the cross. He was hurried away **from prison** and a fair trial (or "by oppression and judgment He was taken away"). It seemed impossible that He would have any posterity since **He was cut off** in His prime, slain for the sins of the people.

53:9 **Wicked** men plotted to bury Him with the criminals, but God overruled, and He was **with the rich at His death**—in the new tomb of Joseph of Arimathea. Men plotted a shameful burial for Him although **He had done no** wrong, spoken no lie.

53:10, 11a Yet **the LORD** saw fit **to bruise Him**, to **put Him to grief**. When **His soul** has been made **an offering for sin, He will see His** posterity, that is, all those who believe on Him, **He shall prolong His days**, living in the power of an endless life. All God's purposes shall be realized through Him. Seeing the multitudes of those who have been redeemed by His blood He will **be** amply **satisfied**.

53:11b **"By His knowledge My righteous Servant shall justify many."** This may mean that **His knowledge** of the Father's will led Him to the cross, and it is by His death and resurrection that He can reckon believers to be righteous. Or it may mean "by the **knowledge** of Him," that is, it is by coming to know Him that men are justified (John 17:3). In either case, it is through His bearing their **iniquities** that justification is possible for the **"many."**

The last stanza of Thomas Chisholm's hymn, quoted above, reads triumphantly:

Who can number His generation?
Who shall declare all the triumphs of
  His Cross?
Millions, dead, now live again,
Myriads follow in His train!
Victorious Lord, victorious Lord,
Victorious Lord and coming King!

53:12 Another result of His finished work is that Jehovah will **divide** Him **a portion with the great**, that is, with the saints, whose only greatness lies in their connection with Him. **And He shall divide the spoil with the strong**; here again **the strong** are those believers who are weak in themselves but strong in the Lord.

Four reasons for His glorious triumph are given. (1) **He poured out His soul unto death**; (2) **He was numbered with the transgressors**, that is, the two thieves; (3) **He bore the sin of many**; (4) He **made intercession for the transgressors**. David Baron comments:

The verb . . . *yaph'gia'* ("made intercession") is an instance of the imperfect or indefinite future, and expresses a work begun, but not yet ended. Its most striking fulfilment, as Delitzsch observes, was the prayer of the crucified Saviour, "Father, forgive them, for they know not what they do." But this work of intercession which He began on the cross He still continues at the right hand of God, where He is now seated, a Prince and a Saviour, to give repentance unto Israel and the forgiveness of sins.[63]

On the paradoxes of this great passage as a whole, Moody comments:

Despised, yet accepted and adored. Poor, yet rich. To die, yet to live. The Rabbis said there must be a double Messiah to fulfil this chapter.[64]

5. The Messiah as Redeemer and Restorer (Chap. 54)

54:1–3 It is not a coincidence that chapter 54 should begin with the word "Sing!" Coming immediately after the 53rd chapter with its presentation of Christ's death, burial, resurrection, and exaltation, no word could be more appropriate.

The first verse contrasts Israel in captivity, **barren** and **desolate**, with the restored and redeemed nation, prolific and rejoicing. Paul applied the verse in Galatians 4:21–31 to the heavenly Jerusalem versus the earthly city. The borders of the land will be considerably enlarged to accommodate the population explosion, Israel will be the leader of the **nations**, and God's people will inhabit **cities** that had been abandoned.

54:4–8 All the shame connected with enslavement in Egypt (**youth**) and captivity in Babylon (**widowhood**) shall be forgotten because Jehovah will bring the nation back into fellowship with Himself. The captivity expressed God's momentary **wrath**; the restoration will demonstrate His great compassion and **everlasting kindness**.

54:9, 10 Just as God made a covenant with **Noah**, so He now promises that when Israel enters the Millennium, she will never experience His rebuke or wrath again.

54:11, 12 Though Jerusalem has been **afflicted** and **tossed** with **tempest**, yet God will restore and beautify her. Her **stones** will be set **with colorful gems**, and her **foundations** will be laid **with sapphires**. Her **pinnacles**, **gates**, and **walls** will be **precious stones**—figurative language expressive of extreme beauty. Dean Alford expressed Jerusalem's future in English verse:

Far o'er yon horizon
  Rise the city towers,
Where our God abideth;
  That fair home is ours!
Flash the streets with jasper,
  Shine the gates with gold,
Flows the gladdening river,
  Shedding joys untold.

54:13–15 Divine education will be given to all, and prosperity will abound. **Righteousness** will prevail. No longer will there be **fear** of invasion, exile, or **oppression**. Anyone who causes trouble with Israel will be tried and punished.

54:16, 17 The God who created the munitions-maker (**blacksmith**) and the conqueror (**spoiler**) is well able to control His creatures. Jehovah has decreed that **no weapon formed against** Israel **shall** succeed, and that Israel herself **shall condemn . . . every** accuser. This freedom from condemnation and certain victory are **the heritage of the servants of the LORD**. This is how God will vindicate them in the golden era of peace and prosperity.

6. The Messiah as World Evangelist (55:1—56:8)

55:1 The Spirit of God sends out the evangelistic invitation to Israel to return, and at the same time invites **everyone** everywhere to the gospel feast. All that is necessary is a consciousness of need (thirst). The blessings are the **waters** of the Holy Spirit, the **wine** of joy, and the **milk** of the good Word of God. They are the free gift of grace, **without money and price**.

55:2–5 In its alienation from God, Israel has been wasting its energy and resources. True satisfaction and lasting pleasure are found only in the Lord. If Israel returns to the Lord, they will receive all the **sure mercies**

promised to **David** in the **everlasting covenant** (see Psalm 89:3, 4, 28, 29). These blessings are fulfilled in the Lord Jesus and in His glorious reign. The Gentile **nations**, too, will share in the benefits of the kingdom, and there will be amicable relations between Israel and the nations.

55:6,7 The pathway of blessing lies in seeking **the LORD** and in forsaking sin. Those who thus **return to the Lord** will find Him full of **mercy** and **pardon**.

55:8,9 Men shouldn't judge Jehovah by their own **thoughts** and **ways**. He thinks and acts in **ways** that transcend anything man could ever imagine. This is never more true than in the gospel plan of salvation, which is all of God's grace and allows no glory in self-effort. William Cowper expressed it with his usual elegant English in his poem "Truth":

O how unlike the complex works of man,
Heav'n's easy, artless, unencumber'd plan!
No meretricious graces to beguile,
No clustering ornaments to clog the pile;
From ostentation, as from weakness, free,
It stands like the cerulian arch we see,
Majestic in its own simplicity.
Inscribed above the portal, from afar
Conspicuous as the brightness of a star,
Legible only by the light they give,
Stand the soul-quickening words—
BELIEVE, AND LIVE.

55:10, 11 God's **word** is just as irresistible and effective as **the rain** and **snow**. All the armies in the world cannot stop them, and they **accomplish** their intended purpose. God's Word *never fails* to achieve its aims:

So shall My word be that goes forth from My mouth; it shall not return to Me void, but it shall accomplish what I please, and it shall prosper in the thing for which I sent it.

55:12, 13 Those who seek the Lord will leave the land of captivity **with joy**, and travel home **with peace**. All nature will rejoice in their liberation. The land will enjoy freedom from the curse, with resulting fruitfulness. **Instead of the thorn** and **the brier**, the **cypress**, and **the myrtletree** will **come up**. All the foregoing millennial blessings will bring **the LORD** renown and will **be . . . for an everlasting sign**, that is, an eternal memorial of His grace and goodness.

56:1–8 In anticipation of God's deliverance, the exiles are urged to practice **justice** and **righteousness** and keep **the Sabbath**. Neither **the foreigner** nor **the eunuch** should fear that they will be barred from any of the benefits of Christ's kingdom. In fact, those who obey the Word of the Lord will have preferred positions. The temple will then be **a house of prayer for all nations**, not just Israel. God will gather Gentiles to His fold in addition to the house of Israel.

7. The Messiah as Judge of the Wicked (56:9—57:21)

56:9–12 Verse 9 reverts to Israel in her days of rebellion. The nations (**beasts**) are summoned to chastise a people whose watchmen don't see the danger. They are like **dumb dogs** that don't **bark** and warn the people. They are **slumber**-loving dreamers. They are mercenary, self-seeking, **greedy shepherds**. They invite their friends to **drink** and carouse, saying, "Tomorrow shall be as today was, and braver, braver yet" (Ronald Knox).

57:1, 2 The first two verses of chapter 57 are linked with verses 9–12 of the preceding chapter. In the midst of all the sin and oppression, **the righteous** are swept away by persecution. From the human standpoint **no one** cares. But God cares—He delivers the godly **from evil** and ushers them into **peace** and **rest**.

57:3–6 Even in exile, some of the people are continuing with their idolatrous practices. In this sense they are **offspring of** their unfaithful parents, **the adulterer and the harlot**. Mocking the Lord, they are **children of transgression** and **falsehood**. They burn with lust in the worship of trees, they sacrifice **children** to Baal or Molech **in the valleys**.

57:7–10 It is all an adulterous relationship with idols at the **mountain** shrines. Instead of writing the law of God on the **posts . . . of the doors** (Deut, 6:9; 11:20), they hang idolatrous symbols **behind the doors**, and engage in sex orgies. They bring gifts and offerings **to the king** (Molech means king) and send **messengers to Sheol** in search of new abominations. Even when they become exhausted by their dissipation, they do not give up, but seem to get their second wind and press on to further wickedness.

57:11–13 Without fear of Jehovah, they lie and do not give Him a second thought. Because He holds His **peace**, they lose their respect for Him. But He will expose their self-**righteousness** and sin, and their **idols** will not help them. Their gods will utterly fail them, but those **who . . . trust in** the Lord will enter into blessing.

57:14–19 To the faithful ones in exile, God promises that a highway will be constructed for their return, and every obstruction will be removed. For the God who dwells **in the high**

and holy place also dwells in the **humble** and **contrite** heart. He **will not contend forever** with **the souls** that He has **made**, otherwise they would perish under His anger. God did send forth His wrath against His covetous, **backsliding** people, but His anger has a limit. He will **restore** those who turn from their idolatry, causing them to bring Him **the fruit of** their **lips**.

57:20, 21 Isaiah's marvelous comparison of **the wicked** to **the troubled sea** is rendered nicely into English verse as follows:

> 20: But as to the wicked—they are
> as the sea,
> Storm-tossed, nor able to rest,
> But its waters are ever
> upheaving,
> Upheaving the mire and the
> dirt![65]

It will be peace to the righteous but **no peace . . . for the wicked**.

C. Israel's Sin, Judgment, Repentance, and Restoration (Chaps. 58—66)

The last nine chapters of the book of Isaiah depict the final outcome of both the faithful and the apostate. Alfred Martin summarizes:

> The closing section of the book describes the glorious consummation which God has in store for Israel, the people of the Servant, and God's channel of blessing to the world. There is a strong contrast throughout the section between the rebellious and the faithful, a contrast which is never entirely absent from any extended portion of the Word of God.[66]

1. The Delights of True Spirituality (Chap. 58)

58:1–5 The prophet must loudly proclaim the **transgression** of Judah.

The people seem to take real pleasure in going through the prescribed **daily** rituals, acting as if they are a truly obedient **nation**. In fact they accuse **God** of being indifferent to their fasts and acts of contrition, but God accuses them of self-gratification, of taking advantage of their employees, and of **fist**-fighting in the midst of their fasting. Theirs is not the kind of fasting that counts with God. True fasting is not a matter of physical posture or of outward display of mourning.[67]

58:6–8 God wants **the fast** that is accompanied by the loosing of the shackles **of wickedness**, lifting the **yoke** of oppression, feeding **the hungry**, providing shelter for **the poor**, clothing **the naked**, and helping the needy neighbor. Those who thus practice social justice are assured of guidance, **healing**, and a protective escort. **"Your righteousness"** may mean the abovementioned acts of mercy or it may mean the righteousness of God which is imputed to those who believe. The paraphrase of verses 5–8 in the Scottish Psalter is worth quoting:

Let such as feel oppression's load thy
   tender pity share:
And let the helpless, homeless poor
   be thy peculiar care.
Go, bid the hungry orphan be with
   thy abundance blest;
Invite the wanderer to thy gate and
   spread the couch of rest.
Let him who pines with piercing cold
   by thee be warmed and clad;
Be thine the blissful task to make the
   downcast mourner glad.
Then, bright as morning, shall come
   forth, in peace and joy, thy days;
And glory from the Lord above shall
   shine on all thy ways.

58:9–12 The godly one is assured that whenever he calls, **the LORD will** answer . . . **"Here I am."** If he will eliminate oppression, stop **pointing . . . the finger** in accusation or in scoffing, and cease from mud-slinging and slander, if he will alleviate human need, both spiritual and physical, then God promises that his night will turn to day. He will enjoy guidance, abundant supply of good things, health and strength, beauty and fruitfulness, and national restoration. "Your sons will rebuild the long-deserted ruins of your cities, and you will be known as 'The People who Rebuild their Walls and Cities'" (v. 12, LB).

58:13, 14 If God's people respect the Sabbath[68] by abstaining from business or selfish **pleasure**, if they consider it a delight to honor God's **holy day, then** they will **delight . . . in the LORD** who gave the day, and He will give them a place of leadership in the earth and **the heritage** that God promised to **Jacob**. Nothing can hinder this because **the mouth of the LORD has spoken**.

2. The Iniquities of Israel (Chap. 59)

59:1–8 It is Israel's sin that holds God back from delivering them; the fault cannot be laid at Jehovah's door. Their **hands, fingers, lips,** and **tongue** are all active in murder and lying. There is widespread perversion of **justice** and dishonesty. People **conceive evil and bring forth** crime. Their activities are as dangerous as **vipers' eggs** and as useless as a **spider's web**. Sin controls every area of their lives—what they do, where they go, what they think. They care nothing for **peace** and **justice**, preferring what is **crooked**. What was true of Israel is also true of the entire human race (Rom. 3:15–17).

59:9–15a Speaking for the believing remnant, Isaiah now confesses their sin as his own. He acknowledges their injustice, unrighteousness, blindness, deadness. They **growl** with impatience and **moan** in despondency. There is no **justice** and no deliverance. Their **transgressions** had **multiplied** in God's sight and testified **against** them. They denied the Lord and wandered far from Him. They spoke in the language of **oppression**, rebellion, and **falsehood**. **Justice is** driven **back, righteousness stands afar off**, and **truth** falls a victim **in the street**. Uprightness is refused admission, **truth** is nowhere to be found, and the godly man is assaulted.

59:15b–21 When **the Lord** looks down, He is grieved **that there is no justice**. He marvels that there is **no man** (**intercessor** or mediator) capable of handling the situation, so He steps in and does it Himself. **His own arm** (strength) brings **Him** victory and **His own righteousness** upholds **Him**. He dons the armor and moves out against His foes in **righteousness**, **salvation**, **vengeance**, **zeal**, and **fury**. He gives the Gentiles exactly what they deserve, so that, at last, all the people from east to west are forced to acknowledge that He is Lord, for He (the Messiah) **comes in like a flood**, driven by the breath of Jehovah. He will come as **Redeemer** to the godly remnant in **Zion**. Then God will make a new **covenant with** the house of Israel, as we also read in Jeremiah 31:31–34; Hebrews 8:10–12; 10:16, 17.

3. The Future Glory of Zion (Chap. 60)

60:1–3 Zion's time to **arise** and **shine has come**, for **the glory of the Lord**, that is, the Messiah Himself, has appeared. It is the time of His Second Advent. The world is still in spiritual **darkness** and the darkness

of the Tribulation, but the Lord shines on Israel and through Israel to the rest of the world. Representatives of **the Gentiles**—including kings—flock to Jerusalem to pay their respect to the reborn nation.

60:4–7 As Jerusalem raises her **eyes**, she sees her **sons** and **daughters** returning to the land. Super-abounding **joy** fills her **heart** as she watches **the Gentiles** bringing their gifts and tribute. Camel caravans from far and near come with **gold and incense**, praising Jehovah's name. Great **flocks** arrive in Jerusalem to be used for the sacrifices at the temple, commemorating the Messiah's finished work on Calvary. Note that myrrh is missing in verse 6. Myrrh speaks of suffering. Christ's atoning sufferings are finished forever! At His Second Advent there will only be **gold** (glory) **and incense** (fragrance).

60:8, 9 Plane-loads of Israel's **sons** and exiles return to Israel like flocks of birds, along with large **ships** bringing their accumulated wealth with them.

60:10 **Foreigners** serve as construction crews, and **kings** as servants of God's people. The tables are turned. God is now showing **mercy** to the nation that He has punished.

60:11–14 No need to lock the city **gates** because there is no danger. On the contrary, it is important to keep them **open** because **kings** and caravans of **wealth** are arriving **day** and **night**! Destruction awaits any **nation** that does **not serve** Israel in that day. **Lebanon** sends its finest trees **to beautify** the temple area. The descendants **of those** Gentiles who formerly persecuted Israel now acknowledge Jerusalem as **The City of the Lord, Zion of the Holy One of Israel**.

60:15, 16 Formerly **hated** and **for-**

saken, Zion becomes a city of **excellence**, nourished and supported by the rest of the world. Jehovah's ancient people will know then that He is their **Savior and** their **Redeemer, the Mighty One of Jacob.**

60:17–22 The costliest materials— **gold** and **silver** and **bronze** and **iron**— will be used in building the city, with **peace** serving as superintendents and **righteousness** as the police force. In place of **violence** and **destruction** will be **Salvation** and **Praise**. The light of **the sun** and **moon** will no longer be necessary in Jerusalem, since the glory of **the LORD will** provide all necessary **light**. Darkness will vanish and Israel's **mourning shall be ended.** A **righteous . . . people inherit the land,** planted by God for His glory. The humblest of the people will be blessed with numerous posterity, because **the LORD** has decreed it and **will hasten** to do it.

4. The Messiah's Ministries (Chap. 61)

61:1–4 We know that the Lord Jesus is the speaker here because He quoted verses 1–2a in the synagogue at Nazareth (Luke 4:16–21) and added, "Today this Scripture is fulfilled in your hearing" (v. 21). He was **anointed** with the Holy Spirit at His baptism and His earthly ministry was concerned with bringing the **good tidings** of salvation **to the poor,** binding up **the brokenhearted,** proclaiming **liberty** to sin's **captives,** and **opening . . . the prison** (or eyes, RSV marg.) of **those who** were **bound.** He ended the quotation with the words **"to proclaim the acceptable year of the LORD"** because what follows, **"the day of vengeance of our God,"** will not be fulfilled until His Second Advent. At His glorious appearing He will proclaim **the day of** God's judgment. Then He will **comfort** those **who mourn** in Zion,

granting to them a garland in place of **ashes** on their heads, **the oil of joy** instead of **mourning, praise** instead of a **spirit of heaviness.** His chosen people will then **be called trees of righteousness,** planted by the Lord, and bringing glory to Him. **They** will **rebuild the** cities of the promised land that have lain in **ruins.**

61:5–9 Foreigners will serve the Israelites as farm hands, honoring them as **priests** and **servants of our God.** Gentile **riches** will come to the Jews, and the reproach of the centuries will be ended as the Lord's people enjoy a **double** portion of **honor.** (The **"you"** and **"they"** in verse 7 refer to the same people, that is, the Jews.) Remembering the injustice, **robbery,** and wrong that His chosen ones have suffered, Jehovah will reward them and make **an everlasting covenant . . . with them,** so that the nations will **acknowledge them** as the **blessed** of the **LORD.** This is generally understood to be the new covenant (Jer. 31:31–34; Heb. 8:8–12).

61:10, 11 The Messiah leads the praises of His redeemed remnant. He celebrates the glorious **garments of salvation** and **righteousness** with which God has decked them, and the sprouting forth of practical **righteousness and praise** in Israel before the nations during the Millennium. (The speaker in vv. 10, 11 is variously identified as Isaiah, Zion, or the Messiah Himself. We prefer the last, the same speaker as in vv. 1–3.)

5. The Future Delights of Jerusalem (Chap. 62)

62:1–5 The Lord **will not** keep silent or **rest** satisfied until the blessings promised to Jerusalem are realized. Then **the Gentiles** will **see** Zion vindicated, and Jehovah will give **a new name** to the city. He will handle

Zion admiringly as a king handles his **crown**. The city called **"Forsaken"** will henceforth be called "My delight is in her" (**Hephzibah**) and the land named **"Desolate"** will be renamed **"married" (Beulah)**. These names tell of God's tender affection and marital delight in His city and land. Jerusalem's citizens will be wedded to her, and the Lord will **rejoice over** Zion like a **bridegroom**.

62:6–9 In the meantime, Jehovah has **set watchmen on** the **walls** of **Jerusalem** and has instructed them not to rest in their intercession or to **give Him . . . rest till Jerusalem** becomes the queen city of the world. Never again will Israel's produce be carried off by **enemies**. Rather it will be enjoyed by those who **labored** for it.

62:10–12 Now the exiles are told to **go through the gates** of Babylon and return to Israel over well-paved highways with ensign waving proudly. The announcement has gone out worldwide that Israel's **salvation** has come in the Person of the Messiah, and He will **reward** His people. They will carry the dignified name **"The Holy People"** and Jerusalem will be called **"Sought Out, A City Not Forsaken."** This paragraph looks beyond the return from Babylon to the final restoration of Israel at the Second Coming of Christ.

6. The Day of Vengeance (63:1–6)

When the Lord returns to set up His kingdom, He must first destroy His enemies. That destruction takes place at different times and in different places. One stage occurs in the Valley of Armageddon (Rev. 16:16), another in the Valley of Jehoshaphat (Joel 3:12), and still another in **Edom**. The latter is what we have here in chapter 63. The Messiah is marching up **from Bozrah**, a metropolis of **Edom**, in glorious **garments** that are **red** with the **blood** of Israel's foes. When asked why His **apparel** is **red**, He uses the figure of a **winepress** to describe His trampling of His enemies. The time had come for Him to wreak **vengeance** on them and to redeem His people. In the absence of any merely human deliverer, He stepped in and won the victory.

7. The Prayer of the Remnant (63:7—64:12)

63:7–10 Next the prophet, speaking for the remnant in captivity, seeks deliverance from their pitiable condition. First he rehearses God's past dealings with the nation. Jehovah has displayed nothing but **lovingkindnesses, great goodness**, and **mercies**. God had called them as His **people**. Though He knew in advance exactly what they would do, He is here represented as considering it unthinkable that they would ever forsake Him for other gods. **So He became their Savior.** He also became their partner in all their trials, and particularly **in all their affliction** in Egypt. **The Angel** (same word as *Messenger*) **of His Presence**, that is, the Messiah, **saved them. In His love and in His pity He redeemed them** out of Egypt, and cared for them throughout their wilderness journeys. They repaid His love with rebellion, and so He became their Adversary.

63:11–13 But even remembering the **days of old**, of **Moses and his** generation, would raise the questions: **"Where is He who brought** Israel through **the** Red **Sea with** Moses and Aaron and their other shepherds? **Where is He who put His Holy Spirit** in Moses, then divided the sea so that **Moses** could lead them through, thus bringing **everlasting** honor to

His **name**? Where is Jehovah who brought them through the sea, making the way as smooth as a flat desert where **a horse** never needs to **stumble**?"

63:14 As a beast goes down into the valley to find rest and refreshment, **so** God led His **people** into the land of rest, and in so doing, He earned **a glorious name** for Himself. Note the Trinity: the Lord Jehovah (v. 7); the Angel of Jehovah (v. 9); **the Spirit of the Lord** (vv. 10, 11, 14).

63:15, 16 The recital of past mercies leads the prophet to look ahead to the Babylonian captivity and to intercede for the exiles. It seems that God's **zeal**, **strength**, and **mercies** are being withheld from the remnant. Isaiah pleads that God is still their **Father**, even **though Abraham** and **Israel** were to disown them.

63:17–19 In verse 17, the remnant seems to blame **the Lord** for their backsliding, but the truth is that God only hardens men's hearts after they have first **hardened** their own **heart**. Probably the remnant means to say, "Why did you permit us to err from Your ways?" God is often said to do what He permits. In any case, the exiles cry to Jehovah to **return** to them in grace. Israel had **possessed** the land in peace for only a comparatively short time, and now the **sanctuary** lies in ruins, and the Israelites, God's people, are no better off than the other nations who never had a covenant relationship with the Lord.

64:1–5 The prayer which began in 63:15 now continues and turns to confession. The remnant implores God to **rend the heavens** and **come down** in fury on His **adversaries**. They recall previous interventions of God, unique manifestations of the only true God who **acts for the one who waits for Him**. They remember that God shows favor to those who delight in

practical **righteousness**, but they have incurred His anger by their long-continued sins, and wonder if there is any hope for people like them **to be saved**.

64:6, 7 They confess to personal uncleanness, and admit that their best deeds (**righteousnesses**) **are like filthy rags**.[69] No wonder that they are fading leaves, driven away by **the wind** of their own **iniquities**. There is spiritual deadness in Israel. Intercessors are nowhere to be found, because Jehovah has abandoned them to the consequences of their sins.

64:8, 9 Yet the Lord is still their **Father**, and there is still hope that the **potter** can do something with **the clay**. And so they plead with Him to relax His anger, to forgive and forget their sins, and to acknowledge them as His **people** still.

64:10–12 The devastated condition of the country, and particularly of **Jerusalem** and the **temple**, are strong reasons why God should release His anger and act decisively in behalf of His afflicted people.

8. The Lord's Answer to the Prayer of the Remnant (Chap. 65)

65:1 Here begins Jehovah's answer to the preceding prayer (63:15—64:12).

In context the first verse refers to Israel's failure to **seek** God and her unwillingness to answer His call. But Paul applies it in Romans 10:20 to the call of the Gentiles: "I was found by those who did not seek Me; I was made manifest to those who did not ask for me."

65:2–7 These verses refer unmistakably to Israel. God pleads tirelessly with a **people** who give themselves over to the **abominable things** associated with idolatry and heathenism. Because they have been initiated into secret rites, they consider themselves **holier than** their fellows. Because they are a continual irritation to the Most High, He will **repay** them for all their idolatry and sin.

65:8–12 Jehovah promises to spare a good **cluster** of grapes (the faithful remnant) in an otherwise bad vineyard (the rest of the nation). This preserved remnant will **dwell** in the land. **Flocks** will graze on the Plain of **Sharon** in the west and in **the Valley of Achor** to the east, all for the benefit of the saints. As for the apostate mass, it is a different story. They have forsaken the temple and worship **Gad** (meaning Troop, Fortune) and **Meni** (meaning **number**, Destiny). Therefore God will destine them **for the sword**. Instead of responding to the Lord's entreaties, they **chose** the things that were **evil** and distasteful to the Lord.

65:13–16 The contrast between the lot of the true believers and that of the unbelievers is brought out here. It is the difference between abundant food and hunger, between plentiful drink and thirst, between rejoicing and shame, between singing and wailing, between the curse of an adulteress (Num. 5:21–24) and a blessing. In that day, when the wrongs of earth are righted, people will use the name **"the God of truth"** when they **bless** themselves or when they take an oath. In other words, God will be acknowledged as the One who brings His plans to pass, who does as He says He will do.

65:17 The closing verses of chapter 65 describe millennial conditions. The **new heavens and** the **new earth** here refer to Christ's kingdom on earth; in Revelation 21 they refer to the eternal state. In Isaiah's **new heavens** and **new earth** there is still sin and death; in Revelation 21, these have passed away.

65:18–23 When the kingdom comes, the Lord **will rejoice in Jerusalem** and in the **people** of Israel. The sounds of sorrow and anguish will **no longer be heard**. Infant mortality and premature death will be eradicated. A person who dies at the age of **one hundred years** will be reckoned **a child**. A centenarian who sins outwardly will be cut off. Men will live to enjoy the **fruit** of their labors because the lifespan will extend throughout the Millennium for the faithful. There will be no unproductive **labor**, and young people will not be cut off by war or calamity. Parents and children will enjoy the blessing of **the Lord**.

65:24, 25 There will be no more hindrances to prayer. Wild animals will be domesticated, and poisonous snakes will feed on the **dust** of defeat and humiliation. There will be no more danger in God's **holy mountain** of Zion.

9. The Consummation: Peace Like a River (Chap. 66)

66:1, 2 The opening words of the last chapter of Isaiah were written to the unrepentant people of Israel. They need not think that, in that condition, they can please God by building a temple for Him. After all, He is the universal Creator and Owner, enthroned in **heaven**, with the **earth** as His **footstool**. The dwelling place He desires is the heart of a person who is humble and **contrite**, and **who trembles at** His **word**.

66:3, 4 Those who are impenitent offend God by their religious observances. When divorced from practical holiness, their **sacrifices** and offerings are crimes and **abominations**. They can choose their hypocritical **ways**, but they cannot **choose** the consequences. God will do that.

Those who refuse His call to repentance and who go on in ways that He hates will taste His wrath.

66:5, 6 Those faithful, God-fearing Jews **who tremble at His word** will be persecuted by their own **brethren**. The wicked persecutors will think that they are doing God service, as is evidenced by their pseudo-pious taunt, **"Let the Lord be glorified, that we may see your joy,"** that is, **your joy** at being miraculously delivered. But the Lord will intervene to shame their foes. The work of judgment will begin at **the temple**; there **the voice** of Jehovah will reveal that the time of recompense has come.

66:7–9 In verse 7 Israel brings forth **a male child** (the Messiah) *before* the time of her birth-pangs (the Great Tribulation). In verse 8 she brings forth sons *after* her time of travail. The first birth took place nearly two thousand years ago at Bethlehem. The second is the spiritual rebirth of Israel, which will occur after the Tribulation. Nothing will hinder God from accomplishing this purpose.

66:10–17 The day of Israel's restoration will be a time of great rejoicing in **Jerusalem**. **All . . . who love her** and who have wept with her will share in the ecstasy and jubilation of that moment. Enriched by **the glory of the Gentiles**, she in turn will give prosperity, nourishment, **comfort**, and rejuvenation to all who come to her. Then it will be obvious to all that Jehovah is committed to the welfare of His own and to the punishment of **His enemies**. The Lord's Second Coming will mean the unleashing of His fiery **indignation** against all idolaters and rebels. He sees them going through ceremonies to make themselves ritually clean, only to engage in the most abominable idolatrous practices.

66:18–21 He knows **their works and their thoughts** and when He rains down judgment on them, **they will see** His **glory**. He will give them some supernatural **sign**, which we cannot identify at present. Those **who escape** will go to the ends of the earth with the news of the Lord's power and **fame**. Then the Gentiles will mobilize their transportation facilities to carry dispersed Israelites back to the land, as if they were bringing **an offering** to Jehovah. God will reinstitute the priesthood and the Levitical order for service in the millennial temple.

66:22, 23 Israel's status with God will be as permanent and secure as **the new heavens and the new earth**. Pilgrims **from** all nations will come to Jerusalem at the appointed times **to worship**.

66:24 While there they will walk out to the Valley of Hinnom and see **the corpses** of rebels being cremated in the perpetual **fire** of the city dump.

It is worth noting that our Lord quotes from the last verse in Isaiah as a warning to those who would live in sin and offend Christ's little ones. Three times[70] in Mark 9 Jesus uses Isaiah's solemn words: **"Their worm does not die and their fire is not quenched"** (vv. 44, 46, 48).

The good news is that a person can escape these eternal fires of hell by putting his or her faith in the Savior, the Servant of the Lord that Isaiah has described so winsomely in so many of his prophecies.

For most of our readers, who have already received Christ as their Savior, the book of Isaiah is great prophecy and great poetry—certainly among the finest in the OT. But it would be a shame if that were all. We are meant to *apply* this book to our daily lives and practice God's good pleasure.

We close with a practical exhortation from the devout English Bible scholar, W. E. Vine:

All this brings home the folly, futility and sinfulness of pursuing our own way, carrying out our own designs and turning after that in which God cannot take pleasure, instead of waiting upon Him, listening to His voice and delighting in the fulfilment of His will. Through our walking with God He fulfils, and will fulfil, all the promises of His Word. He responds to delighted confidence in Him, by adding an Amen to His assurance. The peace of an obedient heart and a trusting spirit is that which enjoys the sunshine of His countenance and the calmness of holy communion with Him.[71]

ENDNOTES

[1](Intro) It was a benefit performance "for the relief of Prisoners in the several Gaol's, and for the support of Mercer's Hospital in Stephen Street, and of the Charitable Infirmary on the Inn's Quay." In light of Isaiah's stress of freeing the prisoners, and binding up the wounds of the sick, he no doubt would have been pleased with these charities, which were often associated with early performances of *Messiah*.

[2](Intro) After the Overture, the very beginning of the second part of Isaiah is sung in a tenor solo: "Comfort ye My people" (40:1). Who can read Isaiah 7:14 without hearing the contralto solo of "Behold, a virgin shall conceive," or Isaiah 9:6 without hearing the chorus sing "Unto us a Child a born, unto us a Son is given"? "Surely He hath borne our griefs, and carried our sorrows" is another lesser-known setting with words by

Isaiah (53:4). Also with words by Isaiah are: "O thou that tellest good tidings to Zion" (40:9); "Then shall the eyes of the blind be open'd and the ears of the deaf unstopped" (35:5); "He shall feed His flock like a shepherd" (40:11); and the moving "He was despised and rejected of men" (53:3).

Comparatively little of the text of the oratorio is from the NT, which is unusual, especially when we consider that the subject matter is all about the Messiah.

[3](Intro) See the *Believers Bible Commentary* in the Introductions to the books mentioned for a defense of the traditional and orthodox positions on the authorship.

[4](Intro) Josephus, *Antiquities* XI:1:f.

[5](1:7–9) So sure are the prophecies that they are often expressed in the Hebrew perfect tense, suggesting a completed action.

[6](1:10–15) W. E. Vine, *Isaiah: Prophecies, Promises, Warnings*, p. 14.

[7](2:4) This verse—minus the opening words about God—is inscribed on the United Nations Building in New York City.

[8](2:12–18) A sloop is a kind of ship that generally has one mast.

[9](4:2–6) Matthew Henry, "Isaiah," *Matthew Henry's Commentary on the Whole Bible*, IV:27.

[10](6:1) This would be 740 B.C. Moody writes: "Uzziah's reign was a kind of Victorian era in Jewish history. It was when this passed away into shame and disgrace that Isaiah saw the Eternal King on his throne." *Notes from My Bible*, p. 85.

[11](6:1) F. C. Jennings, *Studies in Isaiah*, p. 61.

[12](6:2–5) The word *seraphim* is from the Hebrew verb *sāraph*, "burn," stressing the burning holiness of God, as in "Our God is a consuming fire" (Heb. 12:29, cf. Deut. 4:24).

[13](6:9, 10) Vine, *Isaiah*, p. 32.

[14](7:3) His son's name means *a remnant shall return.*

[15](7:10–13) Vine, *Isaiah*, p. 35.

[16](7:14) The Hebrew word translated *virgin* (*'ālmāh*) in verse 14 may also mean "young woman." The prophecy may have had an early, partial fulfillment when Isaiah's wife gave birth to Maher-Shalal-Hash-Baz (8:1–4). But the ultimate, complete fulfillment was in the birth of Christ. When Matthew quotes verse 7, he uses the Greek word *parthenos*, which can only mean *virgin* (Matt. 1:23).

[17](7:14) Vine, *Isaiah*, p. 35.

[18](7:18–22) Jennings, *Isaiah*, p. 90.

[19](8:19) Vine, *Isaiah*, p. 41.

[20](9:6) *Ibid.*, p. 43.

[21](11:1) The beautiful old German carol, "Lo, How a Rose E'er Blooming," captured Isaiah's thought here so well. Poetically the author chose a rose as the plant which will grow from Jesse's roots.

[22](11:2) Vine, *Isaiah*, p. 49.

[23](11:6–9a) The self-taught American Quaker artist Edward Hicks loved this passage so much that he painted several very literal canvases called "The Peaceable Kingdom." His charming style far outweighed his knowledge of animal anatomy.

[24](13:14–22) Ryrie writes, "The decline of Babylon occurred in stages. By 20 B.C. Strabo described it as 'a vast desolation.' Even the desert wanderer (*the Arabian*) shunned the site because it became an omen of ill fortune" (*Ryrie Study Bible, New King James Version*, p. 1053).

[25](14:12–17) "Lucifer" is the Latin form of "day-star," meaning "light-bearer."

[26](14:12–17) Ryrie, *Study Bible*, p. 1054.

[27](14:24–27) Ryrie writes that "the fulfillment of this prediction of the destruction of Assyria is recorded in 37:21–38," *ibid.*, p. 1055.

[28](18:1–7) The word is the usual one for *woe*, but here "it differs from ch. xvii. 12 and is an expression of compassion (cf. Isa. 1v.1, Zech. ii.10) rather than of anger," Franz Delitzsch, "Isaiah," in *Biblical Commentary on the Old Testament*, XVII:348.

[29](20:1–6) The name "Palestine" is derived from the word Philistine.

[30](21:6–10) Vine, *Isaiah*, p. 62.

[31](21:11, 12) Victor Buksbazen, *The Prophet Isaiah*, p. 224.

[32](22:20–24) D. L. Moody writes, "The Spanish Jews have a silver key of David, bearing the inscription 'God shall open, the King shall enter'" (*Notes*, p. 85).

[33](24:4–13) John A. Martin, "Isaiah," *The Bible Knowledge Commentary, Old Testament*, p. 1072.

[34](26:1–4) Quoted by Moody in *Notes from My Bible*, p. 86.

[35](26:1–4) *Ibid.*

[36](28:9, 10) These verses are often quoted out of context as the proper way to teach (going from the known to the unknown, a little at a time, for example). While this is no doubt good advice, it is certainly not the meaning of the text within the context.

[37](28:11–13) Jennings, *Isaiah*, p. 333.

[38](28:23–29) H. Vander Lugt, *Our Daily Bread*, Radio Bible Class, further documentation unavailable.

[39](29:12–14) Vine, *First Corinthians*, p. 23.

[40](33:23, 24) Vine, *Isaiah*, p. 83.

[41](34:9–17) The Hebrew for "confusion and emptiness" in v. 11 is the same as those words translated "without form and void" in Gen. 1:2.

[42](35:8–10) Jennings, *Isaiah*, p. 417.

[43](37:1–4) J. A. Alexander, *The Prophecies of Isaiah*, p. 289.

[44](37:36) See *The Literature of England, An Anthology and a History*, p. 726.

[45](38:21, 22) Kelly, *Isaiah*, p. 289.

[46]38:21, 22) Henry, "Isaiah," VI:209.

[47](40:3–5) G. Campbell Morgan, *Searchlights from the Word*, p. 229.

[48](40:6–8) Quoted by Jennings, *Isaiah*, p. 467.

[49](41:21–24) Jennings, *Isaiah*, p. 486, f.n.

[50](41:25–29) Vine, *Isaiah*, p. 105.

[51](43:1–7) *Ibid.*, p. 115.

[52](43:8–13) One of the anti-Trinitarian cults uses this passage "You are My witnesses, says Jehovah," as the origin of their name. Since they witness against so much of the Lord's truth, one fears that they must be called *false* witnesses. The context is far removed from their use of the passage.

[53](44:28) Flavius Josephus, *Antiquities*, xi.2.

[54](45:7) English has a much larger vocabulary than Hebrew. The Hebrew word here translated "evil" in the KJV and "calamity" in the NKJV can mean either of those two things—and several more ("disaster," "badness," etc.). It is unfortunate that the English word that suggests *moral wrong* (*evil*) should have been chosen here in 1611. The rendering *calamity* is much better in context.

[55](45:7) Delitzsch, "Isaiah," in *Biblical Commentary on the Old Testament*, XVIII:220, 21.

[56](45:7) *Ibid.*, p. 221.

[57](46:3, 4) James S. Stewart, further documentation unavailable.

[58](47:5–15) Jennings, *Isaiah*, p. 556.

[59](51:9–11) *Ibid.*, p. 593.

[60](52:11, 12) Quoted by David Baron in *The Servant of Jehovah*, pp. 46, 47.

[61](52:15) The parallel expression "shut their mouths" favors the reading "startle." However, the traditional reading "sprinkle" recalls the sprinkling of sacrificial blood of Leviticus and the global outreach of the message of redemption. Noting the similarity between "astonish" and "startle," Vine writes: "In the degradation and disfigurement which man inflicted on Him many were astonished; in the coming manifestation of His glory He will astonish (cause to leap and tremble in astonishment) many nations; 'startle' is the meaning here, not 'sprinkle' (as the grammatical phraseology makes clear)." *Isaiah*, p. 166.

[62](53:2) F. B. Meyer, *Christ in Isaiah*, p. 126.

[63](53:12) David Baron, *The Servant of Jehovah*, p. 140.

[64](53:12) Moody, *Notes*, p. 87.

[65](57:20, 21) Jennings, *Isaiah*, p. 668.

[66](58:Intro) Alfred Martin, *Isaiah*, p. 107.

[67](58:1–5) Literal fasting can also be a good tool for spiritual discipline. While the NT does not *command* fasting, our Lord did say, "*When* you fast . . ." (not "*If* you fast").

[68](58:13, 14) For a discussion of the Sabbath and how it relates to the Christian, see the NT volume of *The Believers Bible Commentary*, p. 64.

[69](64:6, 7) Literally, menstrual cloths.

[70](66:24) Some Greek mss. lack two of these verses; see the NT volume of the *BBC* under Endnotes to Mark 9 for details.

[71](66:24) Vine, *Isaiah*, pp. 214, 215.

BIBLIOGRAPHY

Alexander, Joseph A. *The Prophecies of Isaiah*. Grand Rapids: Zondervan Publishing House, 1974.

Archer, Gleason L. "Isaiah." In *The Wycliffe Bible Commentary*, Chicago: Moody Press, 1962.

Baron, David. *The Servant of Jehovah: The Sufferings of the Messiah and the Glory that Should Follow*. Reprint. Minneapolis: James Family Publishing, 1978.

Buksbazen, Victor. *The Prophet Isaiah*. West Collingswood, N.J.: The Spearhead Press, 1971.

Delitzsch, Franz. "Isaiah." In *Biblical Commentary on the Old Testament*. Vols. 17, 18. Grand Rapids: Wm. B. Eerdmans Publishing Co., 1971.

Jennings, F. C. *Studies in Isaiah*. New York: Loizeaux Bros., 1935.

Henry, Matthew. "Isaiah." In *Matthew Henry's Commentary on the Whole Bible*, Vol. IV.

Kelly, William. *Exposition of Isaiah*. London: Robert L. Allen, 1916.

Martin, Alfred. *Isaiah: The Salvation of Jehovah*. Chicago: Moody Press, 1967.

Meyer, F. B. *Christ in Isaiah*. Grand Rapids: Zondervan Publishing House, 1952.

Vine, W. E. *Isaiah—Prophecies, Promises, Warnings*. London: Oliphants, Ltd., 1947.

Young, Edward. *Who Wrote Isaiah?* Grand Rapids: Wm. B. Eerdmans Publishing Co., 1958.

JEREMIAH

Introduction

"Most impressive of all ... is the way in which Jesus Christ was associated in the popular mind with Jeremiah. When on one occasion Christ took a sampling of public opinion from His disciples (Matt. 16:13f.), some reports identified Him with the outstanding prophetic figure of the seventh century B.C. It is hardly surprising that some mistook the Man of sorrows for the prophet of the broken heart, for Jeremiah and Christ both lamented and wept over their contemporaries (cf. 9:1 and Luke 19:41)."

—R. K. Harrison

I. Unique Place in the Canon

Jeremiah is best known as "the weeping prophet." This is the key to his writings, for if we remember this and the reason for his weeping, we shall be able to understand his message.

This prophet is unique in that he reveals his heart and personality more than any other OT prophet.[1] By nature he was sensitive and retiring, yet he was divinely called to severely denounce the apostasy of his day. International tension between Babylon, Egypt, and Assyria for world supremacy, severe spiritual decline in Israel after Judah's last revival under Josiah, as well as people who had been raised on God's Word and true religion turning to pagan cults, all remind us of Western Christendom today.

II. Authorship

The prophecy was written by Jeremiah (Heb. *Yirmeyāhû* or *Yirmeyāh*). The name probably means *Jehovah hurls*, or *throws*, perhaps in the sense

of laying down a foundation, hence *Jehovah establishes*. Another possible meaning is *exalted of Jehovah*. The prophet was the son of Hilkiah, a priest from Anathoth, a town less than three miles from Jerusalem, in the territory of Benjamin.

Like most preachers who are faithful to God and are willing to endanger their position and financial security by preaching a message that people do not wish to hear, Jeremiah was slandered and misrepresented by his enemies. There is no evidence that Jeremiah himself ever entered the priesthood.

III. Date

Jeremiah gives many chronological notes scattered throughout his book. He started his ministry about 627 B.C. (Josiah's thirteenth year, 1:2). Jeremiah's ministry was long, extending to the eleventh year of Zedekiah. He was prophesying during the last forty years of Judah, right up to the time when Jerusalem fell and the Jews were deported to Babylon (586

B.C.).[2] After Jerusalem's fall Jeremiah was under the protection of Gedaliah, the governor. When Gedaliah was assassinated by fanatics, the prophet went down to Egypt with some Jews. There he lived out the rest of his days. Apparently he was still ministering as late as 582 B.C. (chaps. 40—44).

In studying Jeremiah it is well to remember that the prophecies are not given in chronological order.

IV. Background and Theme

Jeremiah began his ministry to Judah after the Northern Kingdom of Israel had fallen to the Assyrians, and not many years before the end of the Kingdom of Judah. At the time of his prophecy, there was a three-sided power struggle by Assyria, Egypt, and Babylon. Warned by God that Judah would go into Babylonian captivity, Jeremiah spoke out against any alliance with Egypt, which nation would be a loser. Assyria had made Judah pay tribute, but within twenty years Nineveh, her capital, had fallen after a terrible siege. Necho of Egypt marched north through Palestine to Haran, killing King Josiah (609 B.C.). He and the Assyrian remnant met their match in Nebuchadnezzar, who routed his forces at the famous battle of Carchemish. Judah passed into the hands of Babylon automatically. Necho had previously deposed and replaced Josiah's successor, Jehoahaz, with Jehoiakim in hopes that he would be more favorable to Egypt. Nebuchadnezzar ignored Judah for a while, giving Jehoiakim a chance to try to get Egyptian help to bring about independence for Judah. In 598 B.C. Nebuchadnezzar attacked Jerusalem, captured Jehoiachin, the rebel's son and successor, and took some of the people captive. He put Zedekiah on the throne.

It was probably Psamtik II, Necho's successor, who sought to set up an alliance against Babylon. Jeremiah fought strongly against Judah's part in this (e.g., chap. 28). Jeremiah said those who proposed this were false prophets.

Through Egyptian plotting, Zedekiah broke faith with Babylon, bringing that ruler down to besiege Jerusalem. This was in 588, and Egypt lifted the siege with her armies. The siege was resumed soon, however, and Jeremiah was shown to be correct in his view of Egypt as "a broken reed" to lean on. Much to his personal sorrow, Jeremiah saw his prophecies of destruction and captivity fulfilled.

God revealed to the prophet that Judah's sins would result in that nation's being taken into captivity by the Babylonians and held in exile for seventy years. Jeremiah's unwelcome mission was to announce this fact to his fellow-countrymen and to advise them to submit to the Babylonian power. They accused him of being a traitor and made an attack on his life.

When Jerusalem finally fell to the foreign invaders, Jeremiah was one of those who was permitted to stay in the homeland, while the bulk of the nation was carried away. He now advised the remaining people not to flee to Egypt for help, but they disregarded his counsel and carried him off with them. There the prophet died.

In addition to predicting the Babylonian captivity, Jeremiah also foresaw the destruction of that empire at the end of seventy years and the return of the Jews to their land.

OUTLINE

I. INTRODUCTION: THE PROPHET JEREMIAH'S APPOINTMENT AND COMMISSION (Chap. 1)

II. JEREMIAH'S PUBLIC MINISTRY (Chaps. 2—10)

   A. Sermon against Judah's Willful Infidelity (2:1—3:5)

   B. Judah's Future Conditioned upon Repentance (3:6—6:30)
     1. Past Sin and Future Glory (3:6–18)
     2. The Need for Repentance (3:19—4:4)
     3. Woes of the Judgment from the North (4:5–31)
     4. Judah's Sins to Be Judged (Chap. 5)
     5. Jerusalem's Fall Predicted (Chap. 6)

   C. Jeremiah's Ministry at the Temple Gate (Chaps. 7—10)
     1. Judah's Hypocritical Religion (Chap. 7)
     2. Judah's Insensitivity to Sin (Chap. 8)
     3. The Weeping Prophet's Lament (Chap. 9)
     4. A Satire on Idolatry (10:1–18)
     5. The Weeping Prophet's Prayer (10:19–25)

III. JEREMIAH'S PERSONAL EXPERIENCES (Chaps. 11—19)

   A. Jeremiah and the Men of Anathoth (Chaps. 11, 12)

   B. Jeremiah and the Ruined Sash (Chap. 13)

   C. Jeremiah's Intercession Concerning the Drought (Chaps. 14, 15)

   D. Jeremiah's Solitary Ministry (16:1–18)

   E. Jeremiah's Steadfast Heart (16:19—17:18)

   F. Jeremiah's Sabbath Sermon (17:19–27)

   G. Jeremiah at the Potter's House (Chap. 18)

   H. Jeremiah and the Earthen Flask (Chap. 19)

IV. PROPHECIES AGAINST THE CIVIL AND RELIGIOUS LEADERS OF JUDAH (Chaps. 20—23)

   A. Prophecy against Pashhur (20:1–6)

   B. Jeremiah's Complaint to God (20:7–18)

   C. Prophecy against King Zedekiah (21:1—22:9)

   D. Prophecy against King Shallum (22:10–12)

   E. Prophecy against King Jehoiakim (22:13–23)

   F. Prophecy against King Jehoiachin (22:24–30)

   G. Prophecy of the Righteous King (23:1–8)

   H. Prophecy against Judah's False Prophets (23:9–40)

Commentary

I. INTRODUCTION: THE PROPHET JEREMIAH'S APPOINTMENT AND COMMISSION (Chap. 1)

1:1–10 In the first chapter of the prophecy, **Jeremiah the son of Hilkiah** is presented, called, and instructed. His father is described as one **of the priests of Anathoth**, in **Benjamin**. He was **ordained . . . a prophet . . . before** his birth (v. 5), humanly reluctant (v. 6), divinely empowered (vv. 8, 9), and commissioned to predict destruction and restoration (v. 10). William Kelly nicely summarizes the prophet's person and work:

The different character and style of Jeremiah as compared with Isaiah must strike any careful reader. Here we have not the magnificent unfoldings of the purposes of God for that earth of which Israel was the centre, but we have the prophecy in its moral dealing with the souls of the people of God. No doubt, judgments are pronounced upon the heathen, still the intention was to act upon the conscience of the Jew, and in order to do this we see how much the Spirit of God makes of Jeremiah's own experience. Of all the prophets we have none who so much analysed his own feelings, his own thoughts, his own ways, his own spirit.[3]

1:11–19 Next Jehovah (NKJV, Lord) teaches His prophet through visual aids, namely **an almond tree** and **a boiling pot**. The **almond tree**, a first sign of spring, indicated the nearness of the fulfillment of God's Word (vv. 11, 12). The **boiling pot . . . facing away from the north** was Babylon, ready to boil over into

Judah because the people forsook God for idolatry (vv. 13–16). Jeremiah must prophesy this unpopular message **against the kings of Judah**, her **princes**, her **priests, and** her **people**, but will receive divine help. **They will fight against** him, but God will be **with** him **to deliver** him (vv. 17–19).

II. JEREMIAH'S PUBLIC MINISTRY (Chaps. 2—10)

A. Sermon against Judah's Willful Infidelity (2:1—3:5)

2:1–3 Chapters 2 through 19 give a general denunciation of Judah. Judah was once passionately in **love** with Jehovah. She was holy to Him, and anyone who troubled her experienced **disaster**. Now, however, as Kyle Yates puts it:

The honeymoon is over. God reminds rebellious Israel of the fervor and the warmth and the purity of the love streams in the early days. She was desperately in love with her Lover and the tender love made life full of music and joy and hope. She was pure and clean and holy. No disloyalty or unclean thought marred the beauty of her devotion. But now the picture is heart-rending. God's heart is crushed with grief and disappointment. Israel now is living in open sin. She is unfaithful to the covenant vows. Other gods have stolen her affection. She has ceased to love Yahweh and her conduct is shameful in the extreme.[4]

2:4–19 Now **the Lord** asks why she has changed. The people, **priests, rulers**, and **prophets** have forgotten all God did for them. Unlike such heathen lands as **Cyprus** and **Kedar**, who are loyal to their **gods**, Judah has **forsaken the** LORD her **God** for worthless idols. Why had they forsaken the Lord and thus exchanged their freedom for slavery through alliances with Assyria and Egypt?

2:20–25 Verse 20 reads, **"For of old I have broken your yoke and burst your bonds,"** meaning that God had delivered them from slavery in Egypt. Or it may read, "For long ago you broke your yoke and burst your bonds; and you said, 'I will not serve' " (RSV), in which case the meaning is that Judah threw off the divine restraints imposed by the law. In either case, the passage goes on to describe how degenerate the people became in their idolatry. God had **planted** them as a **noble vine**, but they had become **degenerate** shoots of **an alien vine**; their **iniquity** was ineradicable by **soap**; they were like **a swift dromedary or a wild donkey**, burning for sexual intercourse, hopelessly enamored with **aliens**.

2:26–37 When **the house of Israel's** sin catches up with her and she cries for deliverance, her numberless **gods** will be helpless to save. In the meantime, the Lord remonstrates with her for unresponsiveness to chastening, freedom from divine restraint, forgetfulness of God, exceeding a harlot's skill in sinning, destroying **the poor innocents**, yet all the while protesting innocence. God will punish them with exile for their trust in nations which He has rejected.

3:1–5 According to Deuteronomy 24:1–4, a man could not remarry **his** divorced **wife** if she had married **another** man in the meantime. Judah had had **many lovers**, **yet** the Lord still invites her to **return**. Her promiscuity had brought pollution and drought on the land, yet she was as shameless as a harlot. She spoke to God in words of pretended repentance but He knew her **evil** words and deeds.

B. Judah's Future Conditioned upon Repentance (3:6—6:30)

1. *Past Sin and Future Glory (3:6–18)*

3:6–14 **Israel**, the Northern Kingdom, had practiced gross harlotry, and had refused to **return to** the Lord. **Judah saw** her taken captive by the Assyrians, yet persisted in her sin, refusing to return to the Lord. Thus because the **backsliding** ten tribes of **Israel** were **more righteous than treacherous Judah**, God invites them to return to Him in repentance and confession so that He can **bring** them back to Zion.

Note in verse 8 that God divorced Israel and that it was because of adultery. The Savior's words in Matthew 19:9 are consistent with this. He taught that divorce is permissible for an innocent partner when the spouse has been guilty of immorality. When we read in Malachi 2:16 that God hates divorce, it must mean unscriptural divorce, not all divorce.

3:15–18 These verses anticipate the Millennium. God **will give** them **shepherds according to** His **heart, who will feed** them **with knowledge and understanding**. There will then be no need for **the ark of the covenant** because the Messiah Himself will be there. **Jerusalem will be** the world capital and **called The Throne of the** LORD. **Israel** and **Judah** will be restored from worldwide dispersion and reunited.

2. *The Need for Repentance (3:19—4:4)*

Here we have a future dialogue between Jehovah and His people. He covets the very best for them but their sins have cut them off from blessing. They respond with contrite **weeping**. Once more He calls them to **return**. They confess that idols are a deception, that God **is the** only **salvation**, that their apostasy has cost them dearly, and that they are now covered by **shame** and **reproach**.

3. Woes of the Judgment from the North (4:5–31)

4:5–13 To those who would **return** to **the LORD**, the Messiah would come, and **the nations** would **bless them-selves in Him**. The Lord now warns **the men of Judah and Jerusalem**, again exhorting them to be contrite and to throw away their idols. Other-wise God will send the invader (Babylon) as a **lion**, **a** hot **dry wind**, **clouds**, **a whirlwind**, and **eagles**. Verse 10 expresses Jeremiah's inability to reconcile God's former promises of **peace** with His present threats of judgment. The prophet knew that God is faithful, but he was making the mistake of doubting in the dark-ness what he knew in the light. In times of trouble and discouragement, there is a tendency to question our certainties. A better policy for Chris-tians is to believe our beliefs and doubt our doubts, rather than doubting our beliefs and believing our doubts.

4:14–18 Judah should hasten to turn **from** its **wickedness** because warnings of **affliction** are already com-ing from **Dan** and **Mount Ephraim** in the north. Besiegers are ready to de-scend on Jerusalem because of Judah's **bitter** sin and rebellion.

4:19–22 The prophet's affection for his people is expressed in verses 19–21: **"O my soul, my soul!"** means "My anguish, my anguish." He is over-whelmed when he thinks of the approaching **war**, **destruction upon destruction**, and devastation. The question in verse 21, **"How long will**

I see the standard, and hear the sound of the trumpet?" is answered by the Lord in verse 22, where He says in effect, "Until the people turn from their foolishness and sin."

4:23–31 Jeremiah describes a vi-sion he **beheld** of the coming all-inclusive catastrophe on Judah. **The** LORD warns that the desolation will be thorough, yet it will not be complete and final. God's unalterable purpose to chasten will not be deterred by Jerusalem's cosmetic beauty or by her cry of **anguish** as **of** a woman **who brings forth her first child**.

4. Judah's Sins to Be Judged (Chap. 5)

5:1–9 The Lord would **pardon . . . Jerusalem** if a righteous **man** could be found **in** it. Unable to find one among the **poor** and **foolish**, Jeremiah turned to **the great men**, but was equally unsuccessful. **Therefore** judg-ment, pictured by the rapacious work of **lion**, desert **wolf**, and **leopard**, was inevitable. **How** could the Lord **pardon** a people who had once made a covenant with Him but were now swearing by other **gods** and giving themselves over to **adultery**?

5:10–13 The enemy is ordered to invade and destroy (**but . . . not make a complete end**) because the people were denying **the LORD** and the immi-nence of danger, and **the prophets** were telling lies.

5:14–19 Jeremiah's **words** were like **fire**, consuming the **people**, who were like **wood**. The Babylonians were com-ing to devour and to demolish but not completely. Judah's servitude **in** a foreign **land** would be her recom-pense for serving **foreign gods in** her own **land**.

5:20–31 God marvels at the ob-tuseness of His **foolish people**. **The sea** obeys Him, but they do not. They show no inclination to **fear** the One **who gives rain**, even when the rain is withheld. How can God withhold punishment from a nation **so defiant**, so **rebellious**, so steeped in sin? Kelly remarks:

And the worst phase of the national evil was that not merely a certain portion of the people were guilty, but "a wonderful and horrible thing," he says, "is committed in the land; the prophets prophesy falsely, and the priests bear rule by their means; and My people love to have it so: and what will ye do in the end thereof?" (verses 30, 31).

Thus all the springs of moral rectitude were corrupted; and consequently it was plain that nothing but judgment could come to them from the Lord.[5]

5. Jerusalem's Fall Predicted (Chap. 6)

6:1–8 A warning **trumpet** and **a signal-fire** tell the **children of Benjamin** to **flee from ... Jerusalem** because the Babylonian **shepherds** and **their flocks** (military leaders and soldiers) are preparing to attack. The Chaldeans are heard discussing strategy. God has ordered exile for Judea because of the **oppression, violence,** and **plundering** of the people. Even at this late hour He warns His people to desist.

6:9–15 The Lord of hosts warns that the Babylonians will strip the land as bare as a thorough-going **grape-gatherer** gleans a **vine**. Jeremiah feels frustrated in having to **speak** to people who won't **heed**, but he cannot refrain. Jehovah directs him to **pour ... out** the message of impending doom because of their **covetousness**, the falsehood of the prophets and priests, and their shamelessness. It is characteristic of false prophets to

promise prosperity in a time of spiritual declension.

6:16–21 The people reject God's call for them to **walk in ... the old paths** of righteousness and refuse to be warned. Therefore **calamity will** come in spite of the sweet-smelling **sacrifices** that they bring. The people will stumble and **perish**.

6:22–26 The enemy invasion **from the north country** would cause great **fear, mourning, and bitter lamentation**.

6:27–30 The Lord appoints Jeremiah **as an assayer** and tester of metals. The people of Judah are the metals, **stubborn** as **bronze and iron**, like **lead** from which the dross cannot be removed, **rejected silver**. Yates comments:

Perhaps some day we may see clearly how unattractive, how loathsome, how useless sinful men are in the sight of a holy God. How we need to look objectively at ourselves to see the miserable emptiness that is so clearly visible to God! There is no point in keeping refuse silver. It has no worth. Can it be that God has already marked off as valueless many who consider themselves useful?[6]

C. Jeremiah's Ministry at the Temple Gate (Chaps. 7—10)

1. Judah's Hypocritical Religion (Chap. 7)

7:1–4 Chapter 7 has been called "The Temple Sermon." The men **of Judah** thought they were safe because God would never allow **the temple** to be destroyed. Wrong! They were putting false confidence in the building rather than trusting the One who dwelt there.

7:5–15 Their true safety lay in **thoroughly** turning from sin and living righteously. They thought they could get away with their sins as long as they came to the temple and said **"We are delivered."** Our Lord Himself, whose views of outward religion were like Jeremiah's, used the prophet's words in verse 11 about the temple being **"a den of thieves,"** when He cleansed His Father's house (Matt. 21:13; Mark 11:17; Luke 19:46). Because Judah had polluted and desecrated the temple, it would be destroyed just as the sanctuary **in Shiloh** had been. (The destruction of Shiloh is believed to have taken place during Judges or 1 Samuel.)[7]

7:16–26 Jeremiah should **not pray for . . . Judah**—even then they were worshiping **the queen of heaven**[8] and **other gods . . . in the streets**. The people might as well **eat** their **offerings** and **sacrifices**. What God desires is obedience, not rituals. Verse 22 must be read in the light of verse 23: sacrifice without commitment is worthless.

7:27–34 Because of Judah's persistent refusal to **receive correction**, Jeremiah should lament. Because they polluted the temple and offered human sacrifices, they will be overtaken by a terrible slaughter and **the land shall be** left **desolate**.

2. Judah's Insensitivity to Sin (Chap. 8)

8:1–7 **The bones** of those who **worshiped** the starry **host of heaven** will be dug up by the Babylonians and exposed to the heavens, and the living will wish they could die. Unlike those who **fall and** rise again, who sin and repent, Judah refused **to return** to Jehovah. As far as the law was concerned, the people compared unfavorably with the **stork, the turtledove, the swift, and the swallow**, which are obedient to **their appointed** laws of migration.

8:8–12 The people thought they

were **wise** concerning **the law of the** Lord, but **the scribe, the prophet**, and **the priest** had misinterpreted and **rejected** it. They were covetous and deceitful, and dealt with problems superficially. For their shamelessness they would share in the coming **time** of **punishment**.

8:13–17 God will sweep them away like a fully-picked **vine** or **fig tree**. The people are resigned to perishing in the city. The Babylonian army advances like **vipers which cannot be charmed**.

8:18–22 The brokenhearted prophet seems to hear the exiled Jews asking, "Where is God?" God answers by asking why they had forsaken Him for **images** and **foreign idols**. Again the **people** wail that the deliverance for which they hoped never came. Jeremiah weeps inconsolably over the seemingly hopeless plight of the people. Verse 22 is the source of a well-known spiritual, "There Is a Balm in Gilead":

> There is a balm in Gilead to make
>   the wounded whole;
> There is a balm in Gilead to heal
>   the sin-sick soul.

3. The Weeping Prophet's Lament (Chap. 9)

9:1–11 Jeremiah is the speaker in the first two verses. His title "the weeping prophet" is beautifully expressed in verse 1:

> **Oh, that my head were waters,**
> **And my eyes a fountain of tears,**
> **That I might weep day and night**
> **For the slain of the daughter of my**
>   **people!**

Many preachers and missionaries can relate to Jeremiah's feelings in v. 2. Kyle Yates writes:

> This verse reveals a glimpse of a tired, worn, discouraged prophet in

one of his lowest moments. It might be called "a passing shadow on a great soul." In his hour of vexation he imagines he would like to break away from people who do not deserve anything of him. How sweet to be relieved of all responsibility and all irritations! He was literally sick of watching the empty, godless, formal substitute for religion. All his days he prayed, loved, preached and warned, only to find the sort of unresponsiveness that seared his soul.[9]

He laments the sinfulness and consequent punishment of the people. Then he quotes the Lord as cataloging their sins, arguing the inevitability of judgment, yet **weeping** over God's making **Jerusalem a den of jackals** and the **cities of Judah desolate**.

9:12–22 The calamity is directly linked to Judah's idolatry, and for this sin the people will go into exile. **The LORD** directs that **skillful wailing women** (professional mourners) be called to lament the terrible slaughter and destruction. There is no use in the people's boasting **in . . . wisdom**, **might** or **riches**; what really counts is to know **the LORD**.

9:23, 24 These are two of the most famous verses in Jeremiah. As G. Herbert Livingston remarks, they are

> worthy to be memorized. Humans strive for **wisdom**, **might**, and **riches**, while God delights in **lovingkindness**, **judgment** (justice), and **righteousness**. Blessed is the one who **understands** the Lord so as to delight in what He delights.[10]

9:25, 26 An added bitterness in Judah's cup will be to be punished with Gentile nations, because Judah is **uncircumcised in the heart**. Clipping the hair on the temples [RV and NASB][11] was a heathen practice forbidden to the Jews (Lev. 19:27).

4. A Satire on Idolatry (10:1–18)

10:1–5 This chapter alternates between the vanity of idols and the greatness of God. God's people should **not learn the way of the Gentiles** and their lifeless idols.

Yates comments about the satire on idols:

> Jeremiah is cruel in his treatment of the poor, defenseless idols that men use as substitutes for God. They are unresponsive sticks that have to be decorated so as to conceal the fact that they are only dead wood. Instead of carrying they must be carried. They must be fashioned; God fashions. No speech, no power, no breath, no intelligence, no worth, no influence, and no permanence can be attributed to them. In contrast Yahweh is eternal, living, active, powerful.[12]

10:6–9 God is the **great . . . King of the nations**, worthy of fear. Those who worship idols are **dull-hearted and foolish**, bowing to **the work** of men's **hands**.

10:10–16 The LORD **is the true** and **living God**. Manufactured gods will **perish**. Jehovah is the God of Creation and providence. Idol-makers are **dull-hearted**, and their images **futile**. The God (**Portion**) **of Jacob** is **the Maker**, **the LORD of hosts**.

10:17, 18 **The inhabitants of the land** are told to **gather up** what they can carry because the Lord is sending them into exile.

5. The Weeping Prophet's Prayer (10:19–25)

Speaking for the nation, Jeremiah laments the horrors of the siege and exile, confesses human ignorance, asks God to discipline His people and to **pour out** His **fury on** their enemies because **they have eaten up** His people.

III. JEREMIAH'S PERSONAL EXPERIENCES (Chaps. 11—19)

A. Jeremiah and the Men of Anathoth (Chaps. 11, 12)

11:1–10 The LORD commands **Jeremiah** to remind the people of **the covenant** of the law which He gave at Sinai, of the curse on those who disobeyed and the blessings for those who obeyed. God's unceasing reminders in the past had met with persistent refusal. Now **the men of Judah** are pictured as forming a **conspiracy** to break the **covenant** by forsaking God for **other gods**.

11:11–13 When God's judgment falls, He **will not listen to** their prayers, and Judah's innumerable **gods will** to **save them at all**.

11:14–17 Three times the prophet was told **not** to **pray for this people** (7:16; 11:14; 14:11). The people have no right to come to the temple with offerings as if to hide their guilt or avert their **doom**. Once called a beautiful **Green Olive Tree** by the LORD, Judah is now destined to be burned because of its idolatry.

11:18–23 The LORD informs the **docile** and unsuspecting prophet that **the men of Anathoth** have **devised schemes** to kill him. When he prays, he receives assurance that his adversaries **will** be punished.

12:1–6 Jeremiah asks why **the** LORD, who is Himself **righteous**, allows **the wicked** to **prosper**—such as the men of Anathoth—and permits the righteous, like himself, to suffer. God answers that Jeremiah will meet more bitter opposition than this, including treachery from his own **brothers**. If he found it difficult to cope in relatively calm conditions (running **with the footmen**), what would he do in the severe trials that were coming (contending **with horses**)?

12:7–14 Using many words of endearment to describe **Judah**, God expresses grief over the devastation she has brought upon herself. A bird that is markedly different is often attacked by the others, hence the reference to Judah as a **speckled vulture**. God will punish the Gentile nations and restore **Judah** to the land.

12:15–17 But later the Gentiles will be restored to their lands, and if they turn from idols to God, they will share His blessings **in the midst of** His **people**. Otherwise they will be wiped out.

B. Jeremiah and the Ruined Sash (Chap. 13)

13:1–11 **Judah** is compared to a used **sash** (waist-cloth) which Jeremiah was instructed to take **to the Euphrates** and **hide**. Judah once occupied a place of closest intimacy with Jehovah, but like the **sash**, would be carried away and "hidden." Because of her sin, **Judah** was carried away two hundred and fifty miles and "hidden" near **the Euphrates** (Babylon) in captivity. When Jeremiah retrieved the **sash**, it was **ruined**, **profitable for nothing**. As to whether Jeremiah actually went to the Euphrates, Scofield has this helpful footnote:

Some have questioned the possibility of Jeremiah's having actually buried his girdle, or belt, by the Euphrates, in view of the distance and the war conditions. However, there were periods in Jeremiah's ministry when the whole area was at peace. It is not impossible that Jeremiah may have actually made a visit to Babylon, and if so, this event could easily have taken place at that time, as he might have buried the belt on his way there and might have dug it up on his way back. It is also possible to interpret the Hebrew word as meaning, not the Euphrates but the Wadi Farah, a few miles north of Jerusalem. In this case he could have buried the belt at any time prior to the final Babylonian attack. Thus there is reason to assume that this passage describes an actual event—not a mere vision or imaginary story. Jeremiah's marred girdle served as a symbol indicating Israel's unsatisfactory life and service.[13]

13:12–14 All the people will **be filled with wine**—not literal wine, as they thought, but the wrath of Almighty God, and they will be smashed like bottles. Harrison comments:

Jeremiah stresses that just as alcohol affects judgment and impairs mobility, so in the coming crisis men will behave as though inebriated, being unable to distinguish friend from foe or to defend themselves.[14]

13:15–23 Repentance is urged, or exile is inevitable. If the people don't glorify God, they will get **darkness** and **the shadow of death**. **The king and the queen mother** will be dethroned and **the cities of the South** besieged. The Babylonians will make the land desolate—all because of the iniquity of Judah. Judah and her sins are inseparable.

13:24–27 The words used to describe Judah's apostasy—**adulteries**, **lustful neighings**, **lewdness**, and **harlotry**—all have an immoral connotation.

Harrison explains the illustration:

Like nominal believers in all ages, the people were incredulous that such calamities could overtake them. Jeremiah, however, places the blame firmly on their own shoulders and promises them the shameful public

disgracing associated with prostitutes . . . . The irony of it all is that this will be inflicted by the very people whom Judah once courted. Because of her indulgence in the unfruitful works of darkness Judah would be exposed publicly as the corrupt wanton that she was by the One who had first espoused her in covenant love.[15]

C. Jeremiah's Intercession Concerning the Drought (Chaps. 14, 15)

14:1–6 The messages in chapters 14–39 were given before the fall of Jerusalem. Judah is overtaken by severe **droughts** and famine.

The significance of a drought at this time was very great. It was one of the signs predicted in the Palestinian Covenant (Deut. 28:23–24), and had already been fulfilled in part in the reign of Ahab (1 Ki. 17:1ff.). As that sign had been followed, even though after a long interval, by the Assyrian captivity of the northern kingdom, it should have been received by Judah as a most solemn warning.[16]

14:7–16 The prophet, confessing for the people, asks for relief, but **the LORD** says that there will be no relief; rather, the people will be destroyed **by . . . sword, . . . famine and . . . pestilence**. The false **prophets** promised safety, but they were lying and would **be consumed** along with **the people to whom they** prophesied. Jeremiah was commanded to lament the awful destruction of Judah in **city** and country.

14:17–22 He continues to plead with God for the people, reminding us of the intercessions of Abraham (Gen. 18:23–33), Moses (Ex. 32:11–13), and Samuel (1 Sam. 7:5–9). He acknowledges their **wickedness**, and promises that they **will wail** for the only **God** who can **cause rain** and **showers**.

15:1–4 Intercession for the people is useless; they are destined to **death**, the **sword**, **famine**, and **captivity**. **Even** prime intercessors like **Moses and Samuel** couldn't forestall the judgment. **Manasseh** was the cause; he had promoted gross forms of idolatry **in Jerusalem**, including the worship of Molech (see 2 Kgs. 21:1–16).

15:5–9 The pitiable condition of **Jerusalem** is the result of failure to respond to the chastening of the Lord. A woman with an ideal family would not live to enjoy her children.

15:10–18 Jeremiah is hated by his own people without cause but God promises that he will be vindicated when his adversaries turn to him for help. Judah will not be able to **break iron** from the north (the Chaldeans). Instead the latter will carry off Judah's **treasures**. The prophet is puzzled by his persecution and suffering, especially when he had been so faithful to the Lord. Nevertheless he finds his resource in God's **word**, **the joy and rejoicing of** his **heart**.

15:19–21 God's answer is that the prophet has entertained wrong thoughts about Him, and has given expression to these unworthy thoughts from time to time. They must be purged, as one removes **vile** dross from **precious** metal. His adversaries might **return to** him **but he must not return to them**. G. Campbell Morgan comments:

> Let him purge his heart of such dross, and devote himself only to the gold of truth about God. So and only so would he be fitted to be as the mouth of God in uttering His messages.[17]

God **will make** the prophet **a fortified bronze wall** that his oppressors cannot topple. He **will deliver** and **redeem** His servant.

D. Jeremiah's Solitary Ministry (16:1–18)

16:1–9 Jeremiah is commanded **not** to marry because of the impending destruction. He is the only man in the Bible who was forbidden to marry. **Mourning** and **feasting** are also forbidden because death is so widespread and because the calamity is the Lord's doing.

With reference to v. 7, it was the custom for relatives and friends to gather at the home of one who had died, **break bread** together while rehearsing the admirable qualities of the departed one, and drink a **cup** of wine. In this way they consoled the mourners. Kelly shows how this ancient Jewish tradition was transformed by our Lord:

> This practice of breaking bread in connection with death seems to be the origin of what the Lord Jesus consecrated into the grand memorial of His remembrance. "Neither shall men break bread for them in mourning, to comfort them for the dead; neither shall men give them the cup of desolation." There you have the Supper, in both its parts. It was a familiar custom among the Jews, but the Lord gave a unique significance to it, and stamped new truth upon it. It was connected with the passover, for, as we know, that was the time of its institution. There was a particular reason for its establishment at that and at no other time, because it was to mark the impressive change from the great central and fundamental feast of Israel. A new and different feast was begun for the Christians.[18]

16:10–18 If asked the reason for **all** the **great** disaster God had predicted, Jeremiah should remind them of the disobedience and idolatry of their **fathers** and themselves. God **will bring** the people **back** from captivity some day, but first **fishermen** and **hunters** (the Babylonians) will search them out and carry them into captivity where God will punish them for **their iniquity and their sin**.

E. Jeremiah's Steadfast Heart (16:19—17:18)

16:19–21 The prophet foresees the day when **the Gentiles** will turn from idols to God. In verse 21, the Lord expresses His steadfast determination to make Judah know His **might** through His chastening.

17:1–11 Judah's idolatry, deeply **engraved**, will result in her being sent off into captivity. God's **mountain** is Jerusalem. . . . To trust in **man** brings a curse; to trust **in the** LORD brings blessing. God knows man's **deceitful . . . heart** and will punish **the man who gets riches** dishonestly **"as a partridge**[19] **that broods but does not hatch,"** and then sees the chicks leave.

Verse 9 is an unpopular (but nonetheless very true) estimate of the natural heart of man. R. K. Harrison comments on what is translated "desperately wicked" in the KJV tradition and "gravely ill" by some:

Unregenerate human nature is in a desperate condition without divine grace, described by the term *gravely ill* in verse 9 (RSV *desperately corrupt*, NEB *desperately sick*). *Cf.* 15:18 and 30:12, where the meaning "incurable" occurs. Every generation needs regeneration of soul by the Spirit and grace of God (*cf.* Jn. 3:5f.; Tit. 3:5).[20]

To those who may feel that this is too harsh an indictment of *their* heart, we quote an extended but needed exposé by Matthew Henry:

There is that wickedness in our hearts which we ourselves are not aware of and do not suspect to be there; nay, it is a common mistake among the children of men to think themselves, their own hearts at least, a great deal better than they really are. *The heart*, the conscience of man, in his corrupt and fallen state, *is deceitful above all things*. It is subtle and false; it is apt to *supplant* (so the word properly signifies); it is that from which Jacob had his name, a *supplanter*. It calls evil good and good evil, puts false colours upon things, and cries peace to those to whom peace does not belong. When men say in their hearts (that is, suffer their hearts to whisper to them) that there is no God, or he does not see, or he will not require, or they shall have peace though they go on; in these, and a thousand similar suggestions, the heart is deceitful. It cheats men into their own ruin; and this will be the aggravation of it, that they are self-deceivers, self-destroyers. Herein the heart is *desperately wicked*; it is deadly, it is desperate. The case is bad indeed, and in a manner deplorable and past relief, if the conscience which should rectify the errors of the other faculties is itself a mother of falsehood and a ringleader in the delusion. What will become of a man if that in him which should be *the candle of the Lord* give a false light, if God's deputy in the soul, that is entrusted to support his interests, betrays them? Such is the deceitfulness of the heart that we may truly say, *Who can know it?* Who can describe how bad the heart is.[21]

17:12–18 Jeremiah rejoices that Judah's **place of** security is the **glorious high throne** of God. Then he speaks of the folly of trusting anyone else and prays to **the hope of Israel**, on behalf of the people, for healing and deliverance. The people ask him **where** the judgment is that God had promised. Jeremiah reminds the Lord that he had **not** tried to escape from being **a shepherd** of God, neither had he **desired the woeful day** of Jerusalem's destruction; he had only spoken the words of the Lord. He asks God to vindicate him by punishing those who were scoffing at the word of God.

F. Jeremiah's Sabbath Sermon (17:19–27)

Here the **kings of Judah, and all Judah, and all the inhabitants of Jerusalem** are admonished to **hallow the Sabbath**. They are promised future rulers of David's dynasty and continuance of temple worship if they obey, and are warned of the penalty for refusing to obey (the destruction of **Jerusalem**).

Irving L. Jensen explains why Sabbath observance was so important to Israel:

> The real test of the heart's relation to God is *obedience to His Word*. One of the laws for Israel was the hallowing of the Sabbath by not working on that day (17:21–22). The constant pressure of materialism upon the lives of all, including the people of God, made the keeping of such a commandment difficult, and for this reason this one commandment of the ten was a real test of the priority of the temporal or the eternal in the heart. Was the keeping of the Sabbath law that crucial to Judah? The symbolic action of Jeremiah and the explicit words he was told to speak gave an affirmative answer.[22]

Similar principles apply to the Lord's Day for Christians. It too is for spiritual and physical refreshment, remembrance of the Redeemer and our redemption, worship of the Lord, and commemorating our Lord's first-day-of-the-week Resurrection victory.

G. Jeremiah at the Potter's House (Chap. 18)

18:1–12 The Lord is **the potter**; Judah (here called **Israel**) is **the vessel**. The spoiling of the vessel was not God's fault but Israel's. The **clay** is in God's **hand** to do with it as He wishes—judgment or blessing. God threatens **disaster** if the people don't repent, but their answer is that they will **walk according to** their **own plans**.

18:13–17 The LORD pronounces their behavior as unparalleled and unnatural. By their idolatry they invite destruction that will astonish those who see the **land** made **desolate**. The RSV probably gives the sense of verse 14: "Does the snow of Lebanon leave the crags of Sirion? Do the mountain waters run dry, the cold flowing stream?" You could depend on these things *in nature*, but God couldn't depend on *His people!* "Although the snow does not forsake Lebanon, Israel has forgotten the fountain of living water from which water of life flows to it."[23]

18:18 Hearing this, the people of Jerusalem **devise plans against Jeremiah**, express continued faith in their own priests and prophets, and plot to **attack** him by slander.

18:19–23 Jeremiah expresses regret that he ever asked God to spare them. Such a prayer is scarcely suitable for believers in this age of grace.

H. Jeremiah and the Earthen Flask (Chap. 19)

19:1–9 Jeremiah is told to take an **earthen flask** out to the city dump, and there **proclaim** to the **kings of Judah** and **inhabitants of Jerusalem** that **God** is about to smash Judah because of its idolatry and human sacrifices. **The Valley of the Son of Hinnom** will become **the Valley of**

Slaughter. In **the siege** of Jerusalem cannibalism will be practiced.

19:10–15 In breaking **the flask**, the prophet pictures the havoc and destruction to be caused by the Babylonians. Burial places will be scarce, and the houses where idolatry was practiced will **be defiled**. Jeremiah returns to the temple **court** and repeats the fact that judgment is about to fall because the people refuse to **hear** God's **words** and repent.

IV. PROPHECIES AGAINST THE CIVIL AND RELIGIOUS LEADERS OF JUDAH (Chaps. 20—23)

A. Prophecy against Pashhur (20:1–6)

Pashhur, the **chief** officer in the **house of the LORD**, caused **Jeremiah** to be beaten and **put** into **stocks. The next day**, when the prophet was released, he announced to Pashhur his doom, the doom of his family, and the doom of all Jerusalem and **Judah**. **The king of Babylon** would **carry them** into captivity. Pashhur's name was changed to **Magor-Missabib** (**terror** on every side), which is what he would experience.

B. Jeremiah's Complaint to God (20:7–18)

In verses 7–18, Jeremiah regrets his unpopular ministry. The Lord **persuaded** (deceived) him into it. He wanted to stop delivering the unpopular message of Babylonian captivity, but could not. **The word of the LORD** burned like a fire within him. He overheard his friends plotting against him, but committed his cause to **the LORD**. At times, he is confident, praising **the LORD**, but at other times is so discouraged he wishes he had never been **born**.

C. Prophecy against King Zedekiah (21:1—22:9)

21:1–7 When King Zedekiah sent . . . Pashhur (not the same one as in chap. 20) **and Zephaniah** (not the prophet) to **inquire of the LORD** concerning the approaching Babylonians, Jeremiah sent back word that the Lord would help the invaders against Judah. The **king** and the **people** who would survive would be taken into captivity. Regarding this action taken against the king, Kelly comments:

> Royalty was always the last stem of blessing in the history of Israel. If only the king had been right, though the people and the prophets were ever so wrong, God would still send blessing to Israel. Everything depended upon the king, the seed of David. God might have chastised the prophets and priests and people, but He would have held to them for His servant David's sake. But when not only they went astray but the king himself was the leader of the wickedness, it was utterly impossible to hold to them, and it was the sorrowful task of Jeremiah to pronounce this divine decision.[24]

21:8–14 Those who resisted would perish; those who surrendered to the Babylonians (**Chaldeans**) would **live**. The royal **house** was warned to cease its injustice and oppression. The people of Jerusalem, the inhabitants **of the valley**, are forewarned of their destruction. The terms **"inhabitant of the valley, and rock of the plain"** are probably terms of scorn or derision; they do not seem to be literal descriptions of Jerusalem.

22:1–9 Chapter 22 deals with the last four kings of Judah, though not in chronological order. The historical order was: Jehoahaz, Jehoiakim, Jehoiachin, and Zedekiah; in other words the last king is first and the rest are in order.

Zedekiah, the first king, is warned to dispense justice **and righteousness**; otherwise **Judah**, though magnificent as **Gilead** and **Lebanon**, will be stripped bare and depopulated. The warning is enforced by the history of three kings who met dismal ends.

D. Prophecy against King Shallum (22:10–12)

Shallum, the second king, also called Jehoahaz, was **the son of Josiah**. He was carried **captive** into Egypt and died there without seeing his native **land** any **more**.

E. Prophecy against King Jehoiakim (22:13–23)

22:13–19 **Jehoiakim**, the third king, built his palace with unpaid labor, failed to follow his father's (**Josiah**) example and would therefore be **dragged . . . out of . . . Jerusalem**, to die unlamented. He would **be buried with the burial of a donkey**, that is, tossed into a ditch.

22:20–23 The populace is told to **go up to Lebanon** and **Bashan** and mourn the crushing of their **lovers** (foreign allies) and shepherds (**rulers**) by Nebuchadnezzar. They themselves will groan with the labor **pangs** of captivity.

F. Prophecy against King Jehoiachin (22:24–30)

Coniah (also called Jeconiah and Jehoiachin), the fourth king, would be taken captive by the Babylonians and would **die** in Babylon. **None of his descendants** would ever sit **on the throne of David**. No offspring of Jeconiah succeeded him to the throne. His replacement, Zedekiah, the last king of Judah, was his uncle. Charles H. Dyer comments:

This prophecy also helps explain the genealogies of Christ in Matthew 1 and Luke 3. Matthew presented the legal line of Christ through his stepfather, Joseph. However, Joseph's line came through Shealtiel who was a son of Jehoiachin (Jeconiah, Matt. 1:12; cf. 1 Chron. 3:17). Had Christ been a physical descendant of Joseph and not virgin-born, He would have been disqualified as Israel's King. Luke presented the physical line of Christ through Mary, who was descended from David through the line of his son Nathan (Luke 3:31). In that way Christ was not under the "curse" of Jehoiachin.[25]

G. Prophecy of the Righteous King (23:1–8)

The rulers (**shepherds**) are condemned for failure to care for God's **people**. But God will restore a **remnant** of His people and give them faithful **shepherds**. He **will raise** up the Messiah to be their **King**. A not too popular, but necessary, caution, is given to us Christians on this passage by Kelly:

It is plain this prophecy points to the Messiah, the Lord Jesus. But the Messiah is the Lord Jesus not so much in relation to us as to Israel. This is important to hold fast. We do not lose by doing so. Many persons have the idea that if these prophecies are not applied to Christians and the church we lose something. Honesty is always the best policy. You cannot take something from your neighbour without losing far more than your neighbour loses. No doubt he may have a little loss, but you will have a terrible one. As this is true in natural things so much the more is it true in spiritual things. You cannot defraud Israel of one fraction of their portion, without impoverishing yourself immensely.[26]

In verse 5, the Messiah is called the **Branch** (or Son) of **David**. In Zechariah 3:8, He is "My servant the BRANCH." In Zechariah 6:12, He is presented as "The Man . . . the Branch." And in Isaiah 4:2, He is "The Branch of the Lord." These correspond to the four ways Christ is presented in the Gospels—as King, Servant, Son of Man, and Son of God.

"THE LORD OUR RIGHTEOUS- NESS" or *Jehovah-Tsidkenu* (v. 6) is one of seven compound names of Jehovah.[27] M'Cheyne wrote an excellent hymn based on his increasing appreciation of the Lord under this title:

JEHOVAH TSIDKENU—
The Lord Our Righteousness

I once was a stranger to grace and
to God,
I knew not my danger, and felt not
my load;
Though friends spoke in rapture of
Christ on the tree,
Jehovah Tsidkenu was nothing to
me.

I oft read with pleasure, to soothe
or engage,
Isaiah's wild measure and John's
simple page;
But e'en when they pictured the
blood-sprinkled tree,
Jehovah Tsidkenu seemed nothing
to me.

Like tears from the daughters of
Zion that roll,
I wept when the waters went over
His soul;
Yet thought not that my sins had
nailed to the tree
Jehovah Tsidkenu—'twas nothing
to me.

When free grace awoke me, by light
from on high,
Then legal fears shook me, I
trembled to die;

No refuge, no safety in self could I
see—
Jehovah Tsidkenu my Saviour must
be.

My terrors all vanished before the
sweet name;
My guilty fears banished, with
boldness I came
To drink at the fountain, life-giving
and free—
Jehovah Tsidkenu is all things to
me.

Jehovah Tsidkenu! my treasure and
boast,
Jehovah Tsidkenu! I ne'er can be
lost;
In Thee I shall conquer by flood and
by field—
My cable, my anchor, my breastplate and shield!

Even treading the valley, the shadow
of death,
This watchword shall rally my
faltering breath;
For while from life's fever my God
sets me free,
Jehovah Tsidkenu my death-song
shall be.
                    —*Robert Murray M'Cheyne*

God will be known as the One **who brought** the people back to the **land**.

H. Prophecy against Judah's False Prophets (23:9–40)

23:9–22 The rest of chapter 23 is a solemn denunciation of the lying **prophets**, both of Israel and **of Jerusalem**. The latter continued to promise **peace**, but if they had listened to God's Word, they would have known that His judgment was inevitable and that it would continue until the divine purposes were accomplished. They spoke without a divine commission.

23:23–29 The omnipresent and omniscient God exposes **the prophets**

for **their dreams**, which led **people** into idolatry. Their dreams were **chaff** compared to God's **word**, which is like nutritious **wheat**, and also like **fire and . . . a hammer**.

23:30–32 The LORD is **against** these lying **prophets**. Yates describes them well:

> They were professionals who claimed to be speaking with divine authority but were actually giving utterance to lies and deceit. Jeremiah hurls three charges against them. He says they were actually immoral, that they did not know God, and that they had no message for the people. They were careless of sacred responsibilities and lowered the moral standards of the people by active participation in sin. Their knowledge of God was on a low plane. Not understanding His holy nature they thought and preached that He could not desert Israel.[28]

They are still very much with us.

23:33–40 Apparently the **people** were mocking Jeremiah by asking **"What is the** burden (**oracle**)[29] **of the LORD?"** The prophet should answer that they themselves were His burden and that He was going to cast them off. God forbade them to use the word "burden" (**oracle**) any more in jest. If they disobey, He **will punish** them severely.

V. PROPHECIES CONCERNING THE DESTRUCTION OF JERUSALEM AND THE BABYLONIAN CAPTIVITY (Chaps. 24—29)

A. The Sign of the Figs (Chap. 24)

24:1–7 The LORD showed Jeremiah **two baskets of figs set** in front of **the temple. One basket** contained **very good figs** and **the other** contained **very bad figs**.

The **good figs** pictured the exiles in **Babylon**, who would be brought **back** to the land because they would **return** to God **with their whole heart**.

24:8–10 The bad figs pictured **Zedekiah the king of Judah, his princes**, and the people remaining in the land after the deportation in Jeconiah's reign. The exiles will be brought **back to** the **land**, but the others will be scattered and **consumed** by sword, famine, and pestilence.

B. The Seventy-year Captivity in Babylon Predicted (25:1–11)

Jeremiah had warned **all the people of Judah** for twenty-three years; other men of God had not ceased to call them to repentance. Because they would **not** listen, they would be taken captive by God's **servant, Nebuchadnezzar**, and remain in exile for **seventy years**.

The reason the captivity lasted seventy years and God told the Jews in advance how long it would last is indicated in 2 Chronicles 36:20, 21:

> And those who escaped from the sword he carried away to Babylon, where they became servants to him and his sons until the rule of the kingdom of Persia, to fulfill the word of the LORD by the mouth of Jeremiah, until the land had enjoyed her Sabbaths. As long as she lay desolate she kept Sabbath, to fulfill seventy years.

Leviticus 25:3–5 teaches that the land was to lie fallow every seventh year. The people had disobeyed this law.

C. The Babylonian Captors to Be Judged (25:12–38)

25:12–29 The hope of a speedy return was therefore a lie. After the **seventy years**, God would direct His wrath against the **Chaldeans** (Babylonians). Under the symbol of a **cup of wine**, Jeremiah is told to pronounce God's **fury** on **Judah** and on other **nations** to be crushed by Nebuchadnezzar, and finally upon Nebuchadnezzar himself (**king of Sheshach**). By his prophetic utterances, Jeremiah should tell these nations that they *must* **drink . . . the cup** of God's wrath. If God punishes Jerusalem first, the nations can hardly expect to escape.

25:30–38 These verses amplify the terrors of the cup of God's **fierce anger**, using such descriptive and poetic words as **roar**, **shout**, and **noise** to describe it. **The leaders of the flock** of Jews will wail because **the LORD has plundered their pasture**.

D. Jeremiah's Warning to the People (Chap. 26)

26:1–11 Jeremiah is told to **stand in the** temple **court**, warning the people that if they do not repent, the Lord will forsake the temple as He did **Shiloh**. (Note that the *conditional promises* of God are subject to relenting on God's part if man does not meet the conditions [v. 3]. God can never **relent concerning** His *unconditional promises*.) The priests and false prophets and the people became incensed and threatened the prophet.

26:12–19 Fearlessly Jeremiah repeats his message. Then **the princes and all the people** defend him, and the elders remind the crowd that Micah had prophesied boldly in the days of a good king and had not been put to death.

26:20–24 These verses may be an argument presented by the opposition or they may simply be the record of the fact that **Jehoiakim** ordered the execution of a prophet named **Urijah** who prophesied the same things as Jeremiah. However, **Ahikam the son of Shaphan** prevails to deliver **Jeremiah** from death.

E. The Sign of the Yoke (Chap. 27)

27:1–11 This prophecy is dated in the time of **Jehoiakim** (v. 1) but the rest of the chapter places it in the reign of Zedekiah. Some explain it as a scribal error. The ambassadors of five Gentile kings had come to Jerusalem, perhaps to form an alliance against Babylon. They are told by the object lesson of **bonds and yokes** that the **yoke of . . . Babylon** will come upon them until Babylon is conquered by Medo-Persia, and that if they don't submit to the yoke, they will be destroyed—this in spite of what the seers in these nations were saying.

27:12–22 Ryrie's note on an ancient custom as it applied to the Jewish temple will clarify this passage:

> A conqueror customarily took the idols of a conquered people back to the temple of his own god. Since Judaism was an imageless religion, the vessels of the Temple were taken instead.[30]

Zedekiah is entreated by Jeremiah to submit to the Babylonians and not to believe the lying prophets who predict that **the vessels of the LORD's house will shortly be brought back from Babylon**. Jeremiah suggested that the prophets prove their authority by asking God to prevent **the vessels which are left in** Jerusalem from being taken **to Babylon**. But it would be in vain. These vessels were going to be **carried to Babylon** and remain there till the end of the captivity—seventy years later.

F. Hananiah's False Prophecy and Death (Chap. 28)

28:1–9 **Hananiah the son of Azur the prophet** makes the false prediction that the Babylonian captivity will end in **two . . . years**. Jeremiah replies that he wishes this were true, but implies that the prophecy will not come to pass. The true prophets invariably predicted **disaster**; the false prophets predicted **peace**.

28:10–17 Hananiah **broke** the wooden **yoke** which had been on **Jeremiah's neck**, and made a lying prophecy. **Jeremiah** walked **away** (v. 11). Kelly commends the prophet for his self-restraint:

The servant of the Lord shall not strive. The same man, Jeremiah, who had been like a brazen wall, who had resisted kings and prophets and priests to the face, now refuses to contend with the prophet Hananiah.

The reason for his conduct is plain. Jeremiah did remonstrate and warn while there was hope of repentance or when long-suffering grace called for it, but where there was no conscience at work, where there was a false pretence of the name of the Lord, he simply goes his way. He leaves God to judge between prophet and prophet. If Jeremiah was true, Hananiah was false.[31]

God, however, will put a **yoke of iron on** the **nations** to **serve Nebuchadnezzar king of Babylon. Hananiah** is denounced as a lying **prophet** and told he will **die** that **year**; he died two months later (cf. v. 1, **the fifth month** and v. 17, **the seventh month**).

G. Jeremiah's Message to the Jewish Captives of Babylon (Chap. 29)

29:1–9 This is **the letter that Jeremiah . . . sent** to the captives in **Babylon** advising them to prepare for a long stay, warning them against listening to the false **prophets** and **diviners**.

29:10–14 **The LORD** promises that the captivity in **Babylon** will end in **seventy years** and that the people will return to the land.

Verse 13 is an encouragement to all who have been seeking the Lord, sometimes without apparent success:

God's Word to His people in the day of Jeremiah is still His sure word for men who have sinned and lost touch with the Infinite. No perfunctory gesture of interest can procure the rich treasure that is more valuable than all gold. He is always available. His longing is that all men may look to Him and live. His arms are always open in loving invitation to any who will turn to Him. It is just as true, however, that a diligent search is necessary. One who becomes conscious of his need, senses the satisfying gift of God, and sets out to find Him can be sure of victory if he seeks with his whole heart. Cleansing, peace, joy, victory will be his at the hand of a loving God who delights to welcome His children home.[32]

29:15–32 Contrary to what false **prophets . . . in Babylon** were saying, the king and the people remaining in Jerusalem were to suffer by **the sword, the famine, and the pestilence** because they refused to listen to God's **words**. Doom is pronounced on two lying prophets, **Ahab the son of Kolaiah and Zedekiah the son of Maaseiah**, and on another named **Shemaiah the Nehelamite**, who wrote **letters** rebuking the priest in Jerusalem for not fulfilling his duty by casting **Jeremiah . . . in prison**. **Zephaniah the priest read** the letter to **Jeremiah**. The latter then prophesied that Shemaiah's **family** would be destroyed, and he would not live to **see** the end of the captivity.

VI. PROPHECIES CONCERNING THE RESTORATION (Chaps. 30—33)

Chapters 30—33 contain messages of hope and deliverance and are the bright spot in a book majoring on judgment. Clyde T. Francisco characterizes them as follows:

> No more stirring passages ever were written than those found in this section of Jeremiah. Although most of his messages concerned judgment and doom, when he dreamed of the future he could preach the way he really preferred. All his heart went into these sermons.[33]

The return from captivity was only a partial fulfillment; these chapters look forward to the end times and the final restoration.

This is a very important section, as it contains the famous new covenant passage which predicts the revival of the nation of Israel. This can only take place after "the time of Jacob's trouble" (the Great Tribulation) in 30:4–17. God keeps His covenants, contrary to the views of some. Jeremiah is told to buy a field to show the certainty of the restoration.

A. The Captives to Be Regathered (Chap. 30)

30:1–11 Both **Israel and Judah** will be regathered. First there will be **the time of Jacob's trouble** (the Great Tribulation), then God **will break** the power of the Gentiles over His people. The promise that God **will raise up for them David their king** is generally understood to mean the Lord Jesus, the seed of David. However, some take it to mean the literal David, risen from the dead.

30:12–17 Though the nation's **affliction** now seems **incurable**, God **will . . . heal** their **wounds** and plunder their **adversaries**.

30:18–24 These verses describe the idyllic conditions that will prevail in the Millennium. The last two verses of the chapter depict God's judgment on **the wicked**; this precedes His blessing on Israel, as seen in the next chapter.

B. The Country to Be Restored (31:1–30)

31:1–20 In words of endearment, **the LORD** promises to restore **Israel**, the northern tribes; the people will return from all over the world; they will be filled with singing instead of **mourning**; **Rachel weeping** was a figurative expression signifying the sorrow of seeing captives go into exile. It will cease when Israel repents and God pardons. Matthew quotes verse 15 in connection with the massacre of the infants by Herod (Matt. 2:18). Kelly comments:

> It is beautiful to see that the Holy Spirit . . . applies to that event the passage about sorrow but not that about joy. . . He only referred to what was fulfilled. There was bitter sorrow then, even in the birthplace of royalty. Deep anguish was in the place where there ought to have been the greatest joy. The birth of the Messiah ought to have been the signal for universal joy in the land of Israel. And there would have been if there had been faith in God and His promise, but there was not. Moreover, since the state of the people was one of shameful unbelief so there was an Edomite usurper on the throne. Hence violence and deceit ruled in the land, and Rachel wept for her children and could not be comforted because they were not. . . . So the Holy Spirit applied the first part of the prophecy, but there He stops.[34]

31:21, 22 Repentant **Israel** will return by roads marked by **signposts** and **landmarks**. Her days of unfaithfulness will be over, because the Lord has accomplished something **new**—a **woman** will **encompass** or embrace a **man**. The **woman** here is Israel and the man is Jehovah. "The prediction," writes Williams, "is that the virgin of Israel will cease to go 'hither and thither after idols' and will seek and cleave to Immanuel."[35]

Kelly, a devout scholar of undoubted orthodoxy, explains why a popular interpretation of v. 22b is not valid:

> It has been common among the Fathers as well as the divines . . . to apply this passage to the birth of the Lord of the Virgin Mary, but the prophecy has not the smallest reference to it. A woman compassing a man is not at all the same thing as the Virgin compassing and bearing a son. Compassing a man has no reference whatever to the birth of a child.[36]

31:23–30 **Judah** also will be restored, and her **cities** rebuilt. At this point Jeremiah **awoke** from a pleasant **sleep**. Both Judah and Israel will be repopulated. Men will be punished for their **own iniquity**, not for their fathers' sin.

C. The New Covenant Revealed (31:31–40)

The days are coming when God **will make a new covenant with . . . Israel and . . . Judah**, not like the law, but a covenant of grace. Men will be given a new moral nature, and knowledge of the Lord will be universal (See Heb. 8:8–13; 10:15–17).

God made the new covenant primarily with Israel and Judah (v. 31). Unlike the Mosaic Law, it was unconditional. It emphasized what God will do, not what man must do; notice the occurrences of "I will" in verses 33, 34. Jesus is the Mediator of the new covenant because it is through Him that its blessings are secured (Heb. 9:15). The covenant was ratified by His blood (Luke 22:20). It will not become effective for Israel as a nation until Christ's Second Coming. In the meantime, however, individual believers enjoy some of its benefits; e.g., their obedience is motivated by grace, not law; God is their God and they are His people; God no longer remembers their sins and iniquities. Universal knowledge of the Lord (v. 34a) awaits the Millennium.

Those who would seek to wipe out Israel from the face of the earth would do well to learn verses 35 and 36. **Israel** will **cease from being a nation** only when and if **the ordinances of the sun, moon, stars**, and **sea depart**. Jerusalem will be rebuilt in a future day, and areas now unclean will be **"holy to the LORD."**

D. The City to Be Rebuilt (Chap. 32)

32:1–5 The Babylonians were now besieging the city. **Zedekiah** had imprisoned **Jeremiah . . . in the court of the prison** for predicting success for the Babylonians. In verse 4 is one of three prophecies that were uttered concerning Zedekiah. Here it says that he would **see** the **king of Babylon . . . face to face**. In Ezekiel 12:13 we read that he would not see Babylon and that he would die in Babylon. Here is how these seemingly contradictory prophecies were fulfilled: Nebuchadnezzar put out Zedekiah's eyes in Riblah, in the land of Hamath (2 Kgs. 25:7). Then Zedekiah was taken to Babylon, but he never saw Babylon (his eyes having been put out) and he died there.

32:6–25 In obedience to the Lord, the prophet purchased his cousin

Hanamel's **field . . . in Anathoth** for **seventeen shekels of silver**. (**Hanamel** had come to him with the offer.) This was an assurance to the people that God would bring them back from Babylon. **Both** of the **deeds** were given to **Baruch** for safekeeping in an **earthen vessel**. As he watches the Babylonians besieging Jerusalem, Jeremiah wonders why God told him to **buy the field** in Anathoth.

32:26–44 The Lord's answer **to Jeremiah** is classic: **"Behold, I am the LORD, the God of all flesh. Is there anything too hard for Me?"**

> The Savior can solve every problem,
> The tangles of life can undo.
> There's nothing too hard for Jesus;
> There's nothing that He cannot do.
> —*Author unknown*

Although God will destroy **Jerusalem** because of the idolatry of the people, yet He will later **gather** His own and bless them greatly. Property will be bought and sold again, and thus the deed to the field of Anathoth will still be valid in a coming day.

E. The Covenant Recognized (Chap. 33)

33:1–16 **While . . . Jeremiah . . . was still in the court of the prison**, the Lord gave further glowing promises of restoration to **Israel** and **Judah**— the land will be repopulated with joyful people; the **mountains** will be enriched with **flocks**; and, best of all, the Messiah, **"A Branch of righteousness"** descended from **David**, will come. **Jerusalem . . . will be called THE LORD OUR RIGHTEOUSNESS**. Jehovah gives His name to restored Israel, just as a man does to his bride and just as Christ does to the church (1 Cor. 12:12).

33:17–26 God's promise concern-

ing the perpetuation of the Davidic dynasty and the Levitical priesthood would be as unbreakable as God's **covenant** of **day and night**. Some of the people were accusing God of forsaking His two houses—Israel and Judah, and were thus despising the Jews as being cast-offs, a non-people. The Lord replies that His **covenant** with His **people** is as fixed as the laws of nature. **The descendants of David** would be as innumerable as **the host of heaven** and **the sand of the sea**.

VII. HISTORICAL SECTION (Chaps. 34—45)

A. The Downfall of Judah and Jerusalem (Chaps. 34—39)

1. Zedekiah's Captivity Foretold (Chap. 34)

34:1–7 While the Babylonians were besieging **Jerusalem**, Jeremiah was commanded to tell **the king, Zedekiah**, that he would be carried into exile and would **die** in **Babylon**, though **not . . . by the sword**.

34:8–22 At one time during the fighting, **King Zedekiah** made **the people** agree to set at **liberty** all **Jewish** slaves, perhaps so that they would help defend the city. Later, when the enemy withdrew for a while under pressure from the Egyptian army (37:1–10), the people put all the slaves back **in bondage** again! They thus **profaned** God's **name** by breaking a promise made before Him. God therefore decreed that they would experience the "**liberty**" of **the sword, . . . pestilence, and famine**. Those who had ratified **the covenant** to free the slaves (v. 15) by sacrificing a **calf** in the temple area, and then had broken the covenant, would be delivered to their enemies for slaughter. **Zedekiah . . . and his princes** would be taken captive. The Babylonians would return and **burn** the city **with fire**.

2. The Rechabites' Obedience Rewarded (Chap. 35)

35:1–11 Jeremiah obeyed the Lord by inviting **the Rechabites . . . into the house of the** LORD and by offering **them wine to drink**. **The Rechabites** courteously refused to **drink** it because of instructions their **father** had given them. Also, they had refused to **build a house, sow seed, plant a vineyard**, or own vineyards. (They were forced to live in **Jerusalem** by the advance of **the Chaldeans**.) They maintained a true pilgrim character. What an example!

35:12–19 In marked contrast were the people of **Judah**. They were disobedient to God and would be punished. The Rechabites would be rewarded by always having **a man to stand before** God. The Rechabites were named after Rechab whose son Jonadab was active in aiding Jehu in the expulsion of Baal worship in the Northern Kingdom in 841 B.C. They were a nomadic tribe descended from the Kenites (1 Chron. 2:55) who had attached themselves to Judah and continued to be associated with them but did not identify with their manner of life (*Daily Notes of the Scripture Union*).

Some think that the Rechabites were absorbed into the tribe of Levi and that this is how God's promise is fulfilled. Though we cannot identify the Rechabites today, we believe that their identity will become known in the Millennium.

3. King Jehoiakim Burns the Scroll of Jeremiah (Chap. 36)

36:1–10 In the fourth year of **Jehoiakim**, the Lord commanded **Jeremiah** to **write** down **all the** proph-

ecies which he had delivered; these were dictated to **Baruch** and **read** by him publicly at the temple a year later. No explanation is given why Jeremiah was prevented from going. He was not imprisoned at this time, but was certainly a hunted man.

36:11–19 When Michaiah . . . heard the prophecies, he reported immediately to **the princes**. They in turn called for **Baruch** and asked him to **read** the prophecies to them. **Then** they told **Baruch** that he **and Jeremiah** should **go and hide** and **let no one know where** they were.

36:20–26 When the princes reported the matter to **the king** (Jehoiakim) at **court**, he **sent** for **the scroll**. As **Jehudi** read to him, **the king cut** off portions of **the scroll** (God's Word) and threw them **into the fire**, a perfect picture of what liberals and rationalists have been doing with the Word of God ever since. Eventually, **all the scroll was consumed**, although against the protests of three of the princes. The king looked for **Baruch . . . and Jeremiah . . .** , but the LORD **hid them**.

36:27–32 After the king had burned the scroll, Jeremiah rewrote the prophecies, adding an appropriate section concerning the fearful **doom** of **Jehoiakim**! The fact that Jehoiachin was Jehoiakim's son and his successor (2 Kgs. 24:6) seems to invalidate the curse of verse 30a. The usual explanation is that Jehoiachin reigned for only three months, not long enough to be of significance.

4. Jeremiah Imprisoned and Interviewed by Zedekiah (Chaps. 37, 38)

37:1–10 Though **King Zedekiah**, a vassal ruler under Nebuchadnezzar, **gave** no **heed** to Jeremiah's **words**, still he asked the prophet to **pray . . . for**

him and his followers. When the Egyptian **army** came to assist Judah, the **Chaldeans** (Babylonians) left **Jerusalem** to repel them. Jeremiah sent word to Zedekiah that the Babylonians would **come back** to destroy Jerusalem. Even if Zedekiah could reduce the Chaldean army to a remnant of **wounded men**, they would still succeed in burning **the city**.

37:11-21 As **Jeremiah** was leaving **Jerusalem** on a personal errand, he was arrested and imprisoned in a dungeon on a charge of desertion. After many days, **Zedekiah** called for him to hear what **the LORD** had to say. Jeremiah courageously announced that the Babylonians would capture the city and the king. Then he asked for release from **prison** and the request was granted. He was committed to **the court of the prison**.

38:1-13 Jeremiah was **cast into** a miry **dungeon** because he advised the people to leave the city and turn themselves over to the Babylonians. Zedekiah openly expressed his weakness: he could not thwart the will of the princes by protecting the prophet. An **Ethiopian** eunuch succeeded in having him **pulled . . . out** with **ropes** and **old clothes and rags** and returned to **the court of the prison**.

38:14-20 When King **Zedekiah** sought **advice** from **Jeremiah**, promising him immunity, he was told to **surrender to the** invaders and was assured that **the Jews** who had **defected** would not **abuse** him.

38:21-23 If Zedekiah refused to go over to the invaders, **the** palace **women** would taunt him in the presence of their Babylonian captors, reminding him how his **close friends** had misled him, then had forsaken him. Also the king's **wives**, **children**, and the king himself would **be taken** captive **by the** invaders, and Jerusalem would **be burned**.

38:24-28 **Zedekiah** asked **Jeremiah** not to tell what had been discussed but simply to say that he had requested not to go back to the dungeon. **The princes** did come and ask, and Jeremiah answered as Zedekiah had directed. Obviously there is a question here concerning the ethics of Jeremiah's reply. Was it the truth, a half-truth, or a complete falsehood? What he said was probably true, but he did not feel obligated to tell all that he knew. **Jeremiah remained in the court of the prison** until the fall of **Jerusalem**.

5. The Fall of Jerusalem (Chap. 39)

39:1-10 When **Jerusalem** was taken by the Babylonians (586 B.C.), **Zedekiah**, his **sons**, and his **men of war** tried to flee but were **captured** and taken **to Riblah**. The king's **sons** were **killed**, his own **eyes** were **put out**, and he was taken into captivity. The city was destroyed and only **the poor** of the **people** were **left in the land**.

39:11-14 **Nebuchadnezzar**, the **king of Babylon, gave** instructions through **Nebuzaradan the captain of the guard** that Jeremiah should be well-treated. So the prophet was released from **the court of the prison** and entrusted **to Gedaliah**.

39:15-18 Ebed-Melech,[37] the Ethiopian eunuch, had previously been promised safety by the Lord. Presumably he obtained deliverance at this time. Chronologically verses 15–18 fit after 38:13.

B. Events in Judah After the Fall of Jerusalem (Chaps. 40—42)

1. Jeremiah Dwelling with Governor Gedaliah (Chap. 40)

40:1-6 When **Nebuzaradan** the Chaldean **captain of the guard** gave

Jeremiah the choice of going **to Babylon** or of staying **in the land** under the rule of **Gedaliah**, he hesitated. Noticing this indecision, the captain sent him **back to Gedaliah** and **gave him rations and a gift** for the journey. The captain's use of the name of "**the LORD your God**" may have been a result of his familiarity with Jewish vocabulary, or it may have been by divine dictation.

40:7–10 Then **when all the captains of the armies who were in the fields heard that . . . Gedaliah** had been left in charge of some survivors, **they came to** him **at Mizpah**, which had now become the capital of the Babylonian province of Judah. He urged them to submit to the Chaldean rule and to resume their usual work. He would represent them to **the Chaldeans**.

40:11–16 Other Jewish refugees returned to **Gedaliah** from **Moab**, Ammon, **Edom**, and other **countries** and resumed normal activities. **Johanan and** others warned **Gedaliah** that **Ishmael** was deputized by **Baalis**, **the king of the Ammonites**, to **murder** him, and even offered to **kill Ishmael** secretly. Unfortunately for him, **Gedaliah** merely accused **Johanan** of misrepresenting **Ishmael**.

2. Governor Gedaliah Assassinated (Chap. 41)

41:1–9 Ishmael and . . . ten of his **men struck Gedaliah** and his followers, perhaps because they resented his negotiating with the Babylonians, or perhaps because they wanted to rule, since Ishmael was **of the royal family**. Ishmael, pretending sympathy, also killed seventy mourners who **came from Shechem** to worship at the site of the destroyed temple, then **cast** their bodies into **a pit**. He spared **ten** who had hoarded food supplies

and who bartered them for their lives.

41:10–18 Others, including **the king's daughters**, who were taken **captive** were rescued by **Johanan** and his fighting men, and fled to **Bethlehem**, planning to escape from there **to Egypt** because they feared reprisal by **the Chaldeans**. Ishmael and **eight** of his **men . . . escaped to** Ammon.

3. God Forbids Fleeing to Egypt (Chap. 42)

42:1–6 Johanan and his fearful companions asked **Jeremiah** to find out from **the LORD** what they **should do**. When **the prophet** consented, they promised to obey, no matter what the guidance was.

42:7–22 Ten days later the answer came: Don't flee **to . . . Egypt** but stay in the land. If they stay, God will prosper them. If they flee, all the perils they **feared** in Judah will **overtake** them **in Egypt**. But it seems that the people were already *determined* to flee to **Egypt**, so Jeremiah told them flatly that they would meet disaster there.

Modern Christians often do the same thing: they ask God for guidance—and they often request counsel from parents, Sunday School teachers, elders, pastors, and others—yet their mind is already made up to do what they want. Unfortunately, such "seeking counsel" is all window dressing.

C. Jeremiah and the Remnant in Egypt (Chaps. 43, 44)

43:1–7 Accusing **Jeremiah** of lying and being misled by **Baruch**, **Johanan . . . took all** his people, along with **Jeremiah and . . . Baruch**, and **went to the land of Egypt**.

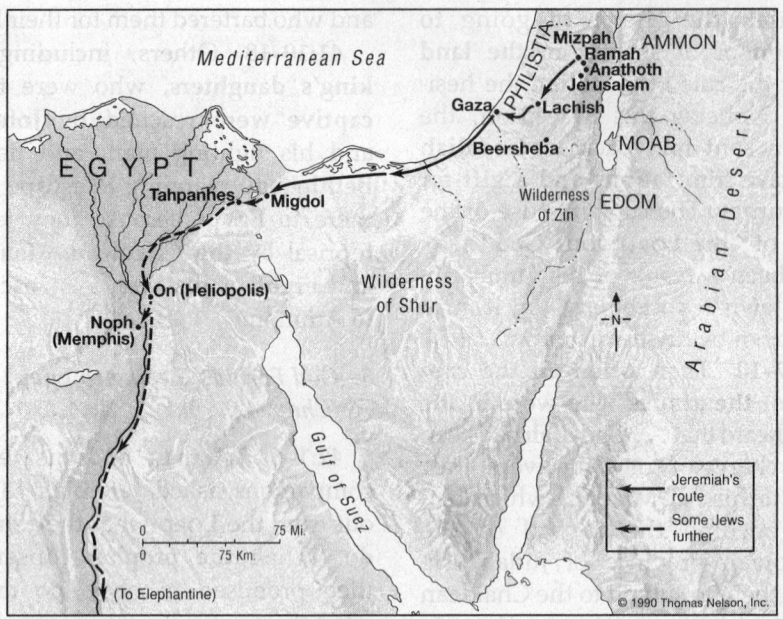

Jeremiah's Journey to Egypt

43:8–13 **In Tahpanhes**, Egypt, **the LORD** commanded **Jeremiah** to **hide** some **large stones** . . . in the clay of the brick courtyard **at the entrance** to **Pharaoh's** palace. He then predicted that **Nebuchadnezzar** would invade **Egypt** and **set his throne above** the **hidden** . . . **stones**. Those who did not die by famine, pestilence, or **the sword** would be led off **to captivity**. The **gods of Egypt** would be destroyed **with fire**.

44:1–14 Chapter 44 is the last record we have of Jeremiah in Egypt. It is presumed that he died there.

Jeremiah reminded his countrymen that **all** their **calamity** came as a result of idolatry; yet they were still worshiping false **gods** in **Egypt**. As a result, they would be utterly destroyed; **none** would **return** to Judah **except** a few refugees.

44:15–30 But the people refused to listen to Jeremiah, claiming that they prospered more when they served **the queen of heaven**. **The men** were involved in this false worship as well as **the women**. Again the prophet told them that idolatry was the cause of their trouble and that, by their sin, they have forfeited the right to call upon the **Name** of **the LORD**. A terrible judgment! They would be sorely punished, and the **king of Egypt** in whom they trusted would be overcome.

D. The Lord's Message to Baruch (Chap. 45)

This chapter was **written** in the reign **of Jehoiakim** and thus precedes chapter 44 chronologically. Perhaps it follows 36:1–8. It is a message of comfort to **Baruch**, who was clearly discouraged because of the threatened judgments on Judah. Perhaps he was also frustrated because his aspirations for a high position were thwarted. God has a right to build up and to tear down. Baruch should **not seek great things for** himself or for Judah, but should be content to escape with his life and do whatever task was assigned to him, no matter how lowly. Kelly comments:

> The great lesson for Baruch was that in a day of judgment the proper feeling for a saint and servant of God is an absence of self-seeking . . . . Lowliness of mind always becomes the saint, but in an evil day, it is the only safety. Humility is always morally right, but it is also the only thing that preserves from judgment. I am speaking now not of God's final judgment, but of that which is executed in this world. Now it seems to me plain that Baruch had not learned this lesson. He had now to learn it. This was the word of the prophet to him at an earlier date—the fourth year of Jehoiakim.[38]

VIII. PROPHECIES AGAINST THE GENTILE NATIONS (Chaps. 46—51)

In this section Jeremiah delivers warnings of destruction and judgment—poetically and beautifully. He prophesies against nine nations: Egypt, Philistia, Moab, Ammon, Edom, Damascus, Arabia (Kedar and Hazor), Elam, and Babylon. The nations are listed geographically, i.e., from west to east. Topically these prophecies fit after 25:13. They were fulfilled after the destruction of Jerusalem. Babylon will be destroyed and desolate, while Israel will be redeemed. This prophecy of Babylon is probably already fulfilled, though some scholars envisage a rebuilding[39] and subsequent overthrow. The rise of the Medes is taken up in 51:1–24.

A. Prophecies against Egypt (Chap. 46)

46:1–12 Chapter 46, a song dealing with **Egypt**, begins a series of prophecies regarding Gentile nations. An **army** is seen preparing for **battle**, then making a hasty retreat. The army is Egypt's, but it is composed mainly of mercenaries—**Ethiopians**, **Libyans**, **and Lydians**. Its defeat took place at Carchemish in 605 B.C.

46:13–19 Next **Egypt** is warned to prepare for invasion and exile. When Nebuchadnezzar invades the land, the **valiant** mercenary soldiers will **fall** against one **another**, then decide to **go back** home. **Pharaoh** will be nicknamed "Empty sound," he is just so much **noise**. The Chaldean's commanding presence, like **Tabor** and **Carmel**, will spell **captivity** for the Egyptians.

46:20–24 The Babylonian gadfly will sting the **very pretty** Egyptian **heifer; her mercenaries, fat** and undisciplined **bulls**, will retreat in disarray. The sound of Egypt "fleeing from the enemy is like the rustling of an escaping **serpent**" (Amplified Version). The invaders approach with battle **axes. They cut down** the Egyptians as if they were a thick **forest. They are . . . more numerous than** a swarm of **grasshoppers. Egypt** is thoroughly disgraced.

46:25–28 The LORD will punish **Amon of No** (the sun god of ancient Thebes), **Pharaoh, and Egypt with their gods and their kings**. But **afterward** they will **be inhabited** again. **Israel**, too, will be restored to her land, and will enjoy quiet and ease.

B. Prophecies against Philistia (Chap. 47)

The **Philistines** will be crushed by the Babylonian invasion from **the north**. They will be **cut off from Tyre and Sidon**, and their great cities, **Gaza** and **Ashkelon**, plunged into mourning, will be struck by the **sword** of the LORD.

C. Prophecies against Moab (Chap. 48)

48:1–10 **Moab**, too, is slated for invasion by Babylon. **Her cities** will be destroyed. The **cry of destruction** is **heard** throughout the land. The people are advised to **flee** from **the plunderer**. They **trusted** their **works and . . . treasures** in vain; now their national god **Chemosh** will **go . . . into captivity** with them. Verse 10 is a curse on the invader if he does not do his work thoroughly. It can also be a warning to us against doing the work of the Lord negligently, and failing to declare all the counsel of God, no matter how unpopular it might be.

48:11–27 **Moab** had had an unruffled history and this did not make for a strong character. It was like new wine that had never **been emptied from vessel to vessel** to strain out the **dregs**, and therefore became unpalatable. Now the Chaldeans will destroy all that the nation trusted. **Moab** will be put to shame because **of Chemosh**, just as **Israel was** put to shame because of the golden calf **of Bethel**. Empty boasts are turned to dirges. The **strongholds** are **destroyed**, the people are fleeing, the country is brought low. **The cities** of the **plain** are in ruins. Because Moab mocked **Israel**, it will be made **drunk** with God's fury.

48:28–39 The once-proud people are exhorted to flee to remote hiding places. Their **haughtiness** and **arrogance** were well-known, but now God sincerely mourns over their ruined crops and their loss of **joy and gladness**. A **cry** of despair goes up from **Moab** as God threatens to put an end to this idolatrous nation. Again the Lord mourns **for the men of Kir Heres**, who have lost their wealth. There is **a general lamentation** by the people of **Moab**.

48:40–47 Babylon will swoop down **like an eagle**, causing terror and destruction. Escape will be impossible. Though the people go into exile, they will be restored **in the latter days**.

D. Prophecies against Ammon (49:1–6)

The Ammonites took possession of the territory of Reuben and **Gad** after these tribes went into captivity. They will be punished for their pride and self-sufficiency, but the nation will not be exterminated.

E. Prophecies against Edom (49:7–22)

Edom prided itself in its **wisdom** and its impregnable position (in **the clefts of the rock**), but God has decreed that it will be without inhabitants. Williams comments: "The first part of verse 12 applies to Israel; the second part to Edom. If God's children must be punished for sin, how much more those who are not His children!"[40] No promise of restoration is held out for Edom.

F. Prophecies against Damascus (49:23–27)

Damascus (Syria) is slated for destruction; **her young men** will **fall in her streets**, **all** her soldiers will be destroyed, and **Damascus** will be burned. Verse 25 may be the words of a citizen within the quotation of the Lord, rather than said by Himself, as the capital "M" of the NKJV would indicate.[41]

G. Prophecies against Kedar and Hazor (49:28–33)

49:28, 29 Kedar's nomadic people (the Arabians) will be defeated by the Babylonians.

49:30–33 Unprotected **Hazor** will be invaded by **Nebuchadnezzar**, will be robbed of its treasures, and left a desolation.

H. Prophecy against Elam (49:34–39)

The Elamites (Persians) will be scattered throughout the earth, but the Lord **will bring** them **back . . . in the latter days**. God will set His throne in Elam in the sense that He will rule there in judgment.

I. Prophecies against Babylon (Chaps. 50, 51)

50:1–16 This and the following chapter deal with the judgment of God **against Babylon**. The prophecies have partial reference to the capture of Babylon by the Medes. But their complete fulfillment is still future.

Babylon is mentioned 164 times in Jeremiah, more than in the rest of God's Word combined. That country will be conquered **from the north**. Six times, after the prophet speaks of judgment on Babylon, he predicts blessing for Israel and Judah; verses 4–7 form the first. Jews in exile are told to lead the return of captives to their own lands because Babylon will be plundered. There will be elements of several nations in the conquering army. Verse 11 is addressed to the Chaldean army. **"Your mother"** is the nation itself. See the *BBC* on Isaiah 13:14–22 for a discussion of certain problems associated with the destruction of Babylon.

50:17–34 The scattered sheep of Israel will be restored to a fertile land and pardoned. God's wrath against Babylon is described in verses 21–32, and then His remembrance of Israel and Judah.

50:35–46 Destruction by the sword awaits the people of Babylon. The invader will leave the city desolate, and the news of its fall will be heard

among the nations. Verses 41–43, and 44–46, previously applied to Judah and Edom respectively (6:22–24; 49:19–21), are here applied to **Babylon**.

51:1–19 God **will send** a destroyer **to Babylon** (*Leb Kamai* is a code word meaning, "The heart [or midst] of those who rise against me.") who will **not spare**; this will be evidence that He has **not forsaken . . . Israel** and **Judah**. God used Babylon as a golden cup of judgment to make the nations stagger; now it will experience **the vengeance of the Lord**. Jewish exiles in Babylon are speaking in verses 9 and 10 in behalf of all the nations which had been conquered by Babylon. God's greatness is contrasted with idols; the true God is the God of Israel and Judah.

51:20–37 Verses 20–23 are addressed to the Medes; verse 24 is probably intended for Judah. Then verse 25 reverts to Babylon again ("the **destroying mountain**"). It is to be a perpetual waste, **without an inhabitant**, **a heap** of ruins, the haunt of wild animals. The inhabitants of Judah and **Jerusalem** are speaking in verses 34 and 35.

51:38–44 These verses had a partial fulfillment in 539 B.C. The Medes captured **Babylon** while Belshazzar and his court were feasting and drinking (Dan. 5). However, the city was not sacked at that time. **The sea** refers to future conquering invaders.

51:45–51 The Jewish captives were forewarned to leave the city before the attack and to return to **Jerusalem** as soon as possible.

51:52–58 The proud city will fall, its **carved images** be destroyed, its boastings be stilled, its leaders be slain, and its **walls** leveled.

51:59–64 Jeremiah commands **Seraiah** to carry these written prophecies against Babylon with him into captivity. After **reading** them, he is to **sink** them in **the Euphrates**—a picture of the doom of **Babylon**. Chronologically, these verses belong to chapter 29.

IX. CONCLUSION: THE FALL OF JERUSALEM (Chap. 52)

The last chapter of Jeremiah is historical, recounting the capture of Jerusalem and the captives.

52:1–16 The account of Zedekiah's closing days is repeated in verses 1–11. The destruction of **Jerusalem** is repeated in verses 12–16.

52:17–23 Then a detailed inventory is taken of the temple **articles** which were seized by the Babylonians and **carried . . . away**.

52:24–27 The captain of the guard brought seventy-four **men . . . out of** Jerusalem **to the King of Babylon**, who, in turn, killed them **at Riblah**.

52:28–34 Others were taken into captivity in three deportations. **In the thirty-seventh year of** his **captivity**, King **Jehoiachin** was taken **out of prison** by the king of **Babylon** and cared for kindly **until the day of his death**.

And thus, a prophetic book steeped in judgment and tears, ends on a kindly note.

We should not think that this is merely "Hebrew history" pre-written as prophecy in many places. It *is* that, to be sure. But the book of Jeremiah is part of the Word of God, ever fresh, ever relevant. Nearly three centuries ago the English commentator Matthew Henry summarized the spiritual lessons from Jeremiah for us:

And now, upon the whole matter, comparing the prophecy and the history of this book together, we may learn, in general, (1.) That it is no new thing for churches and persons highly dignified to degenerate, and become very corrupt. (2.) That iniquity tends to the ruin of those that harbour it; and, if it be not repented of and forsaken, will certainly end in their ruin. (3.) That external professions and privileges will not only amount to an excuse for sin and an exemption from ruin, but will be a very great aggravation of both. (4.) That no word of God shall fall to the ground, but the event will fully answer the prediction; and the unbelief of man shall not make God's threatenings, any more than his promises, of no effect. The justice and truth of God are here written in bloody characters, for the conviction or the confusion of all those that make a jest of his threatenings. Let them *not be deceived, God is not mocked*.[42]

ENDNOTES

[1](Intro) See, e.g., 10:23, 24; 11:18—12:6; 15:10–21; 17:14–18; 18:18–23; 20:7–18.

[2](Intro) This means that he ministered during the reigns of five kings: Josiah, Jehoahaz, Jehoiakim, Jehoiachin (also called Jeconiah and Coniah), and the puppet king, Zedekiah.

[3](1:1–10) William Kelly, *Jeremiah: The Tender-Hearted Prophet of the Nations*, p. 9.

[4](2:1–3) Kyle M. Yates, *Preaching from the Prophets*, p. 139.

[5](5:20–31) Kelly, *Jeremiah*, p. 20.

[6](6:27–30) Yates, *Preaching*, p. 141.

[7](7:5–15) "Excavations reveal that Shiloh was destroyed about 1050 B.C. This would have been at the time when the Philistines captured the ark (1 Sam. 4:11)." (*The Wesley Bible*, New King James Version, ed. by Albert F. Harper, et al., p. 1095). The Mosaic tabernacle survived Shiloh and was later located at Gibeon (2 Chron. 1:2, 3).

[8](7:16–26) After Christendom became the state religion of the Roman Empire, hordes of unconverted heathens flooded into the churches, bringing in their pagan ideas. The application of this pagan title "queen of heaven" to the virgin mother of our Lord, while no doubt thought to be a great honor, would be totally rejected by the lowly "maidservant of the Lord" (Luke 1:38).

[9](9:1–11) Yates, *Preaching*, p. 143.

[10](9:23, 24) G. Herbert Livingston, "Jeremiah," *Wesley Bible*, p. 1100.

[11](9:25, 26) This is an alternative translation of the phrase "all who are in the farthest corners."

[12](10:1–5) Yates, *Preaching*, p. 144.

[13](13:1–11) *New Scofield Reference Bible, New King James Version*, pp. 784, 785.

[14](13:12–14) R. K. Harrison, *Jeremiah and Lamentations*, pp. 99, 100.

[15](13:24–27) *Ibid.*, p. 101.

[16](14:1–6) *New Scofield, NKJV*, p. 785.

[17](15:19–21) G. Campbell Morgan, *Searchlights from the Word*, p. 243.

[18](16:1–9) Kelly, *Jeremiah*, pp. 43, 44.

[19](17:1–11) "The reference to *the partridge* is to the popular belief that it would hatch the eggs of other birds" (Harrison, *Jeremiah*, p. 107). However, in a footnote on the same page Harrison says that it "could refer to some variety of sand grouse."

[20](17:1–11) *Ibid.*, p. 106.

[21](17:1–11) Matthew Henry, "Jeremiah," in *Matthew Henry's Commentary on the Whole Bible*, IV:519, 520.

[22](17:19–27) Irving L. Jensen, *Jeremiah, Prophet of Judgment*, p. 59.

[23](18:13–17) C. F. Keil. "Jeremiah," in *Biblical Commentary on the Old Testament*, XIX:300.

[24](21:1–7) Kelly, *Jeremiah*, p. 47.

[25](22:24–30) Charles H. Dyer, "Jeremiah," in *Bible Knowledge Commentary*, I:1158.

[26](23:1–8) Kelly, *Jeremiah*, p. 48, 49.

[27](23:1–8) The others are: *Jehovah-Jireh* (The-LORD-will-provide—Gen. 22:13, 14); *Jehovah-Ropheka* (The LORD who heals you—Ex. 15:26); *Jehovah-Nissi* (The Lord, my banner—Ex. 17:8–15); *Jehovah-Shalom* (The-LORD-is-peace—Judg. 6:24); *Jehovah-Ro'i* (The Lord, my shepherd—Ps. 23:1); and *Jehovah-Shammah* (THE LORD *IS* THERE—Ezek. 48:35).

[28](23:30–32) Yates, *Preaching*, p. 146.

[29](23:33–40) The same Hebrew word (*massā'*) can mean either "burden" or "oracle." Ryrie calls it "a customary word for a weighty, prophetic message" (cf. Nah. 1:1; Hab. 1:1) in the *Ryrie Study Bible, New King James Version*, p. 1182.

[30](27:12–22) Charles C. Ryrie, ed., *The Ryrie Study Bible, New King James Version*, p. 1187.

[31](28:10–17) Kelly, *Jeremiah*, p. 67.

[32] (29:10–14) Yates, *Preaching*, pp. 146, 147.

[33](Chaps. 30—33:Intro) Clyde T. Francisco, *Studies in Jeremiah*, p. 107.

[34](31:1–20) Kelly, *Jeremiah*, pp. 75, 76.

[35](31:21, 22) George Williams, *The Student's Commentary on the Holy Scriptures*, p. 552.

[36](31:21, 22) Kelly, *Jeremiah*, p. 77.

[37](39:15–18) His name means "servant of the king."

[38](Chap. 45) Kelly, *Jeremiah*, p. 94.

[39](Chaps. 46—51:Intro) At the time of substantive editing of this commentary (1990), Iraq, where ancient Babylon was located, had actually begun the rebuilding of Babylon under Saddam Hussein. Now, however, (1991) that rebuilding has surely been set back by the Allied bombing of Iraq during the UN-sponsored liberation of Kuwait.

[40](49:7–22) Williams, *Student's Commentary*, p. 563.

[41](49:23–27) Since Hebrew does not have capital and lower case letters, all capitalization in English versions must necessarily be decided upon by the translators.

[42](52:28–34) Henry, "Jeremiah," IV:711.

BIBLIOGRAPHY

Dyer, Charles A. "Jeremiah" and "Lamentations." In *The Bible Knowledge Commentary. Old Testament*. Wheaton, IL: Victor Books, 1985.

Feinberg, Charles L. *Jeremiah: A Commentary*. Grand Rapids: Zondervan Publishing House, 1982.

Francisco, Clyde T. *Studies in Jeremiah*. Nashville: Convention Press, 1961.

Harrison, R. K. *Jeremiah and Lamentations*. The Tyndale Old Testament Commentaries. Downers Grove, IL: InterVarsity Press, 1973.

Henry, Matthew. "Jeremiah." In *Matthew Henry's Commentary on the Whole Bible*. Vol. 4. McLean, VA: MacDonald Publishing Company, n.d.

Jensen, Irving L. "Jeremiah and Lamentations." In *Everyman's Bible Commentary*. Chicago: Moody Press, 1974.

Keil, C. F. "Jeremiah—Lamentations." In *Biblical Commentary on the Old Testament*. Vols. 19, 20. Grand Rapids: Wm. B. Eerdmans Publishing Company, 1971.

Kelly, William. *Jeremiah: The Tender-Hearted Prophet of the Nations*. Charlotte: Books for Christians, n.d.

von Orelli, Hans Conrad. *The Prophecies of Jeremiah*. Reprint. Minneapolis: Klock & Klock Christian Publishers, 1977.

LAMENTATIONS

Introduction

"It is a mute reminder that sin, in spite of all its allurement and excitement, carries with it heavy weights of sorrow, grief, misery, barrenness, and pain. It is the other side of the 'eat, drink and be merry' coin."

—Charles R. Swindoll

I. Unique Place in the Canon

This little book is called "Lamentations" in the Greek, Latin, and English versions. The Jews refer to it by the first Hebrew word of chapters 1, 2, and 4, which is translated "How" or "Alas." The book consists of five separate poems united by the common *theme* of Jerusalem's destruction by Nebuchadnezzar in 586 B.C. and by the unique acrostic *structure* of the first four chapters.

Probably to facilitate memorization, the lines of the poems are in Hebrew alphabetical order, one verse beginning with each letter, except in chapter 3 where each letter is assigned three verses in a row starting with the same letter. Chapter 5 has the same number of verses as the Hebrew alphabet (twenty-two) but is not in acrostic form.

In spite of the difficulty of writing in such a rigid framework, the book succeeds in passionately expressing patriotic and heartfelt sorrow.

II. Authorship

The book of Lamentations itself does not name its author, but the tradition that Jeremiah wrote it is ancient and was not challenged until the 18th century.

The Greek translation (the Septuagint) of Lamentations actually gives a preface whose style seems to suggest a Hebrew original: "And it came to pass, after Israel was led into captivity and Jerusalem laid waste, that Jeremiah sat weeping and lamented with this lamentation over Jerusalem, and said . . ." (Here chapter one begins).

The style of the book suggests "the weeping prophet" and 2 Chronicles 35:25 also connects Jeremiah with dirge or lament types of composition. The fact that the author was an eyewitness, and that no other logical candidate comes forth as author, lends support to the traditional Jewish and Christian view that Jeremiah wrote Lamentations.

III. Date

The first-hand descriptions of the devastation of Zion are so vivid and compelling that it is likely they were penned very shortly after the event itself (about 586 or 585 B.C.), and before Jeremiah went to Egypt.

IV. Background and Theme

The fall of Jerusalem was a time of terrible suffering and anguish. It was this fearful catastrophe that brought forth the book of Lamentations, wrung, we believe, from the heart of the prophet Jeremiah.

This book forms a sort of appendix to the prophecies of Jeremiah. It describes the deep mourning of the prophet at the destruction of Jerusalem and of the temple. Instead of being elated over the fact that his prophecies had been fulfilled, he wept bitterly over the miseries of his people.

In addition to being the words of Jeremiah, the book may also be thought of as expressing:

1. The sorrow of the Jewish remnant, for whom Jeremiah was a spokesman, as they witnessed the Babylonian invasion.
2. The anguish of the Messiah when He came to suffer, bleed, and die on the cross of Calvary (see 1:12, for instance).
3. The sorrow of the Jewish remnant in a future day when they will be called upon to go through the Great Tribulation, the Time of Jacob's Trouble.

Sin ⟶ Suffering (1:8)
Sorrow ⟶ Repentance (1:20)
Prayer ⟶ Hope (3:19–24)
Faith ⟶ Restoration (5:21)

The Road to Renewal

OUTLINE

I. THE AWFUL DESOLATION OF JERUSALEM (1:1–11)

II. THE SAD CRY, CONFESSION, AND PRAYER OF THE PEOPLE (1:12–22)

   A. The Cry (1:12–17)

   B. The Confession (1:18, 19)

   C. The Prayer (1:20–22)

III. THE LORD SEEN AS THE ONE WHO PUNISHED JERUSALEM (Chap. 2)

   A. The Effects of God's Wrath (2:1–13)

   B. The Cause of God's Wrath—the False Prophets' Failure to Warn the People (2:14)

   C. The Ridicule of the Onlookers (2:15, 16)

   D. The Fulfillment of God's Threats (2:17)

   E. The Call to Repentance (2:18, 19)

   F. The Prayer for God's Mercy (2:20–22)

IV. THE PROPHET VOICES THE SORROW AND CONFESSION OF THE REMNANT (Chap. 3)

   A. The Judgments of God (3:1–18)

   B. The Mercies of the Lord (3:19–39)

Commentary

I. THE AWFUL DESOLATION OF JERUSALEM (1:1–11)

Here we see the utter desolation of Jerusalem. Verses 1–11 are the language of an onlooker. The once populated city is now a bereaved widow; the princess has become a slave, forsaken by her idols, and betrayed by her allies (vv. 1, 2). The people have gone into captivity because of their sin, and no pilgrims come to worship in Zion (vv. 3–9). The precious vessels of the sanctuary have been taken by the Babylonians (v. 10), and the people suffer famine (v. 11).

II. THE SAD CRY, CONFESSION, AND PRAYER OF THE PEOPLE (1:12–22)

A. The Cry (1:12–17)

This passage speaks of the unique sorrow of Jerusalem. Verse 12 has become "a classic expression of grief"[1] and reminds us of our Lord's lament over the same city for its stiff-necked rejection of Him. The language also fits Christ's condition on the cross, with the hardened soldiers, religious establishment, and general populace callously watching His suffering as a public spectacle.

The Jewish people recognize that it is the LORD (v. 15) who has brought the devastation to pass, and though Zion spreads out her hands in appeal for mercy, no one comforts her; she has become an unclean thing (v. 17).

B. The Confession (1:18, 19)

In the Jews' confession they admit that the LORD is righteous in sending them into captivity; that they had rebelled against His commandment, and that her pagan "lovers"—the Gentile nations—had deceived her.

C. The Prayer (1:20–22)

Judea prays that God will repay the wickedness of her gloating enemies, all the while admitting her transgressions amid her many sighs.

III. THE LORD SEEN AS THE ONE WHO PUNISHED JERUSALEM (Chap. 2)

A. The Effects of God's Wrath (2:1–13)

2:1–7 These verses describe what God has done to Judah—destroyed the temple (footstool) (v. 1), swallowed up the cities (v. 2), refused to hold back the enemy, as if He Himself were Judah's foe (vv. 3–5), treated the temple as if it were a mere **garden**, caused the sacrificial system to cease **in Zion**, and set aside both **king and priest** (vv. 6, 7).

2:8–13 He has laid the city in ruins, the rulers are in exile, the **prophets** receive no word **from the Lord, the elders** mourn, and the maidens hang **their heads** in shame (vv. 8–10). **The children . . . faint** from hunger **in the streets**; they fall and die (vv. 11, 12). The people's calamity is greater than anything the prophet can think of with which to **comfort** them (v. 13). **"Virgin daughter of Zion"** is what the people *should* have been, not what they actually *were*.

B. The Cause of God's Wrath—the False Prophets' Failure to Warn the People (2:14)

Judah's **prophets** had **seen false and deceptive visions**. Rather than exposing the people's **iniquity** they had manufactured **false prophecies and delusions**.

C. The Ridicule of the Onlookers (2:15, 16)

Judah's neighbors gloat over Jerusalem's downfall. They **clap their hands, hiss**, and **say** with sadistic pleasure, **"This is the day we have waited for; we have found it, we have seen it!"**

D. The Fulfillment of God's Threats (2:17)

The Lord had **fulfilled His word**. He had put His own people **down** and **exalted the** power (**horn**, a Hebrew figure of speech) of Judah's **adversaries**.

E. The Call to Repentance (2:18, 19)

Parents are summoned to **cry . . . out to the Lord** unceasingly for their **young children**, who **faint from hunger at every street** corner.

F. The Prayer for God's Mercy (2:20–22)

Women eat their own **offspring** because of the famine. **The streets** are filled with the **slain** because God has **invited** the Babylonians to come **as if to a feast**.

IV. THE PROPHET VOICES THE SORROW AND CONFESSION OF THE REMNANT (Chap. 3)

A. The Judgments of God (3:1–18)

Alternating between **I** and **we**, the prophet draws a parallel between his own experiences and those of his people. God's **wrath** is depicted under the figures of **darkness**, incessant blows from **His hand** (vv. 1–3); premature aging, **broken bones**, confinement in **bitterness, woe**, and a living death (vv. 4–6); inescapable imprisonment, unanswered **prayer** (vv. 7–9); animal-like **ambush**, target-like attack (vv. 10–12); deep wounds, derision, a diet of **bitterness** (vv. 13–15); **broken teeth, ashes for** clothing (v. 16); loss of memory, **peace**, and prosperity, all **hope** of divine help **perished** (vv. 17, 18).

B. The Mercies of the Lord (3:19–39)

With a prayer to God to **remember** his bitter plight, yet with lingering depression over his misery (vv. 19, 20), the prophet gets his eyes off himself and onto the Lord. Hope is revived when he remembers that **the Lord's mercies** and **compassions . . . are new every morning**, and that His **faithfulness** is **great**[2] (vv. 21–24). He cites lessons learned in the school of affliction: it **is good** to **wait** quietly **for** the Lord's deliverance and to submit to His **yoke** early in life (vv. 25–27); to accept divine chastening and human blows and insults without talking back

(vv. 28–30); God's rejection is neither final nor causeless; His **compassion** and **mercies** will always follow (vv. 31–33); **the LORD does not approve** of oppression, injustice, or the denial of rights (vv. 34–36); He is sovereign, His Word prevails, all things serve His will; to **complain** when He punishes sin is senseless (vv. 37–39).

C. The Call for Spiritual Renewal (3:40–42)

The way of blessing is found in self examination, and turning **back to the** LORD. Unconfessed sin is **not pardoned**.

D. The Sorrow of Jeremiah over Jerusalem (3:43–51)

The subject reverts to the sufferings of Jeremiah and his people. God had **pursued** and **slain** without pity, cut Himself off from their prayers, and made them the scum of the earth (vv. 43–45). All their **enemies** mocked while God's people experienced **fear**, danger, and **destruction**. The devastation of his people caused the prophet to weep **without interruption** (vv. 46–51).

E. The Prophet's Prayer for Deliverance from His Foes (3:52–66)

Hunted down like a bird, stoned in a **pit**, engulfed by water, the prophet thought the end had come (vv. 52–54). He prayed earnestly **from the lowest** depths, and God answered, telling him **not** to **fear** (vv. 55–57). Now he asks the LORD to consider how he has been mistreated—the **vengeance**, **schemes**, **reproach**, insults, gossip, and taunts against him—and to judge his case. Righteousness demands that his enemies be punished, cursed, pursued, and destroyed (vv. 58–66). "A **veiled heart**" (v. 65), as in "when

Moses is read, a veil lies on their [the Jews'] heart" (2 Cor. 3:15), probably does not refer to "hardening, but blinding of the heart, which casts into destruction."[3]

V. THE PAST AND PRESENT OF JUDAH CONTRASTED (4:1–20)

The prophet compares the former glory and the present pitiful condition of Jerusalem. The temple is destroyed, mothers desert **their young** (vv. 3, 4), people die of hunger (v. 5), the **punishment** is prolonged (v. 6), the princes are **unrecognized in the streets** (vv. 7, 8), cannibalism prevails even among **compassionate women** (v. 10), and the city that was considered impregnable has fallen (v. 12). It was all caused by **the sins of her prophets, . . . the priests**, and **the people** (vv. 13–16). They looked in vain to Egypt **for** their **help** (v. 17). The Babylonians besieged them suddenly (vv. 18, 19), and King Zedekiah, **the anointed of the** LORD, was captured (v. 20).

VI. THE FUTURE PROSPECT— EDOM TO BE DESTROYED AND JUDAH RESTORED (4:21, 22)

The daughter of Edom rejoiced over the fall of Jerusalem, but she will be punished severely and her **sins** laid bare. **Zion** will be restored.

VII. THE REMNANT APPEALS TO GOD FOR MERCY AND RESTORATION (Chap. 5)

5:1–14 In these verses, the people bewail the terrible conditions that have come upon them—the high cost of necessities (v. 4); the forced **labor**

(v. 5); the oppression (v. 8); the famine and danger (vv. 9, 10); the atrocities committed against **maidens**, **princes**, and **elders** (vv. 11, 12); hardships for **young men**, **boys**, and **elders** (vv. 13, 14).

5:15–18 Because of all these horrors Judah's **joy** had **ceased**, her **dance** had become **mourning**, **the crown** had **fallen from** her **head**, and **Mount Zion** lay **desolate**.

The reason for it all is confessed: "Woe to us, for we have sinned!"

5:19–22 Finally the people ask the LORD to **turn** them **back** to Himself so they can **be restored** and renewed. It is interesting that in many Hebrew manuscripts, verse 21 is repeated after verse 22, apparently so that the book will end with a note of hope rather than gloom.[4] Actually, as Keil notes, a right understanding of verse 22 makes such a repetition unnecessary:

This conclusion entirely agrees with the character of the Lamentations, in which complaint and supplication should continue to the end,—not, however, without an element of hope, although the latter may not rise to the heights of joyful victory, but, as Gerlach expresses himself, "merely glimmers from afar, like the morning star through the clouds, which does not indeed itself dispel the shadows of the night, though it announces

that the rising of the sun is near, and that it shall obtain the victory."[5]

ENDNOTES

[1](1:12–17) R. K. Harrison, *Jeremiah and Lamentations*, p. 210.

[2](3:19–39) If the reader will pardon a personal recollection, verses 22 and 23 have a special meaning to the editor. My father was fond of quoting "Through the LORD's mercies we are not consumed" (v. 22), and my mother's favorite hymn, "Great Is Thy Faithfulness," is based on v. 23. Only after both had gone to be with the Lord did we realize that their sentiments—each characteristic of their personalities—were fittingly "back to back" in Lamentations chapter 3.

[3](3:52–66) C. F. Keil, "Lamentations," in *Biblical Commentary on the Old Testament*, XX:455.

[4](5:19–22) A similar repetition for more suitable synagogue readings occurs at the end of Ecclesiastes, Isaiah, and Malachi.

[5](5:19–22) Keil, "Lamentations," XX:455.

BIBLIOGRAPHY

For Bibliography see Jeremiah.

EZEKIEL

Introduction

"From the first to the last chapter of Ezekiel one supreme thought runs throughout, that of the sovereignty and glory of the Lord God. He is sovereign in Israel and in the affairs of the nations of the world, though the loud and boisterous claims of men seem to have drowned out this truth. In His sovereign will God has purposed that we should glorify Him in life and witness to the ends of the earth."

—Charles Lee Feinberg

I. Unique Place in the Canon

Thanks largely to the famous spirituals "Ezekiel Saw the Wheel" and "Dry Bones," Ezekiel is known as a biblical character by millions of people. Unfortunately, the level of Bible knowledge of his difficult book often doesn't go too much deeper. Certainly Ezekiel is not the first book Christians should read right after conversion, although at least some literary persons have become captivated by the Bible through this prophet's remarkable style.

The unusual thing about Ezekiel (unlike Jeremiah, and to a lesser extent Isaiah and most of the Minor Prophets) is his emphasis, not on judgment, but on *comforting* God's people. From the Chebar Canal, which may have been a kind of ancient concentration camp near Babylon, Ezekiel wrote his prophecies to encourage the Jewish exiles.

II. Authorship

Ezekiel (God strengthens or strengthened by God) was one of those who was taken to Babylonia with the second group of captives, eleven years before Jerusalem was destroyed.

Until the 1920's, Ezekiel's prophecies had largely escaped the "scissors" of rationalistic critics. This situation was lamented by some liberals, who swiftly went to work spinning theories denying the unity, authorship by Ezekiel, and traditional date of writing.

Actually, the ancient and universal Judeo-Christian position that the book was written by a poetic prophet, "Ezekiel the priest, the son of Buzi," is quite defensible and the critical view has been answered well.[1]

We summarize John B. Taylor's six arguments for the unity of the book as having been written by one author as follows:

1. The book has *continuity*, from start to finish, producing a deliberate effect.
2. The book has a *consistent message*: the fall of Jerusalem and the destruction of the temple.
3. The *style and language* are uniform, including special phrases, repeated throughout the work (such as "son of man," "the word of the LORD came to me," "they

shall know that I am the LORD,'' and "the glory of the LORD").

4. Ezekiel has a definite *chronological sequence* unique among the Major Prophets (see Isaiah and Jeremiah).

5. The use of the *first person singular* throughout gives a distinctively autobiographical framework to the book. The writer is identified as Ezekiel in 1:3 and 24:24.

6. Ezekiel's *personality and character* are consistent throughout. These are shown by his earnestness, love of symbolism, concern for detail, and awe at God's glory and transcendence.[2]

III. Date

Ezekiel dated his prophecies precisely. His first prophecy (1:2) came in the fifth year of Jehoiachin's exile (593 B.C.); his last dated prophecy was in 571 B.C. (29:17). Hence his ministry lasted at least twenty-two years. If, as a priest, he started his ministry at the age of thirty, he would have been over fifty when he finished his prophesying.

IV. Background and Themes

Ezekiel ministered to his fellow-exiles immediately before and during the first twenty-some years of the captivity. They falsely expected to return to Jerusalem, so he taught them that they must first return to the Lord.

Ezekiel's prophecy is divided into three parts. First, he rehearses the sins of Judah and warns of God's impending judgment in the captivity of the people and the destruction of the capital. This is all vividly announced in unusual visions and symbolic acts. A bright, shining cloud, a figure of God's presence, is seen

lingering over the temple, then reluctantly departing. This meant that God could no longer dwell among His people because of their sin, and His sword of judgment must soon descend on the polluted temple. The glory of the Lord is one of the key thoughts running throughout the book of Ezekiel.

In the second section, Judah's neighbors are condemned because of their idolatry and their cruel treatment of God's people. These are the Ammonites, Moabites, Edomites, Philistines, Tyrians, Sidonians, and Egyptians.

Finally, in the last section, Ezekiel tells of the restoration and reunion of the entire nation—both Israel and Judah. When the people repent of their sins, God will put His Holy Spirit within them. The Messiah will come to His people and destroy their last enemies. The temple will be rebuilt, and the glory of the Lord will return to it. These prophecies have not yet been fulfilled, but look forward to Christ's one-thousand-year reign on earth, the Millennium.

Like many other prophetic books, Ezekiel is not entirely chronological, though more so than Isaiah and Jeremiah. We should take notice of the dates or time periods that are given at the beginning of many chapters. Albert Barnes puts the prophecies in chronological order as follows:

The prophecies are divided into groups by dates prefixed to various chapters, and we may assume that those prophecies which are without date were delivered at the same time as the last given date, or at any rate, they followed closely upon it.

1. The fifth year of Jehoiachin's captivity.
   Chs. 1—7. Ezekiel's call, and prediction of the coming siege of Jerusalem.

2. The sixth year.
   Chs. 8—19. An inspection of the whole condition of the people, with predictions of coming punishment.
3. The seventh year.
   Chs. 20—23. Fresh reproofs and fresh predictions of the coming ruin.
4. The ninth year.
   Ch. 24. The year in which the siege began. The declarations that the city should be overthrown.
5. The same year.
   Ch. 25. Prophecies against Moab, Ammon and the Philistines.
6. The eleventh year.
   Chs. 26—28. Prophecies against Tyre.
   In this year Jerusalem was taken after a siege of eighteen months and the temple destroyed.
7. The tenth year.
   Ch. 29:1–16. Prophecy against Egypt.
8. The twenty-seventh year.
   Chs. 29:17—30:19. Prophecy against Egypt.
9. The eleventh year.
   Chs. 30:20—31:18. Prophecy against Egypt.
10. The twelfth year.
    Ch. 32. Prophecy against Egypt.
11. The same year.
    Chs. 33—34. Reproof of unfaithful rulers.

12. The same year, or some year between the twelfth and twenty-fifth.
    Ch. 35. Judgment of Mount Seir.
13. The same year.
    Chs. 36—39. Visions of Comfort. Overthrow of Gog.
14. The twenty-fifth year.
    Chs. 40—48. The vision of the temple.[3]

Regarding Ezekiel's ability to communicate God's Word across the many miles between Babylonia and Judea, the *Daily Notes of the Scripture Union* say:

One of the problems of this book is Ezekiel's ministry to those in far off Jerusalem, while he was himself an exile in Babylonia. It must be assumed that those who had been deported were free to maintain communications with the homeland; with the intervening territory unified and pacified by Babylon, this was no doubt more practicable than it had been in earlier times. It was simpler for a messenger to describe in his own words Ezekiel's symbolic act than to bear a verbal message which might have faded in his memory, or a written message which might have invited the attention of the Babylonian authorities.

OUTLINE

I. CALL AND COMMISSION OF EZEKIEL (1:1—3:21)

   A. Ezekiel's Circumstances (1:1–3)

   B. Ezekiel's Vision of God's Glory Riding on a Throne-Chariot (1:4–28a)

   C. Ezekiel's Appointment to Prophesy to the People of Israel (1:28b—3:21)
      1. The Character of the People—Rebellious (1:28b—2:7)
      2. The Nature of the Message—Judgment, as Indicated by the Scroll (2:8—3:3)

Commentary

I. CALL AND COMMISSION OF EZEKIEL (1:1—3:21)

A. Ezekiel's Circumstances (1:1–3)

As the book opens, **Ezekiel** was already in **captivity**, having been carried off in one of the earlier deportations. But he prophesied about the destruction of Jerusalem six or seven years before it happened. Ezekiel was probably thirty years of age at this time ("**in the thirtieth year**"). The first twenty-four chapters were written *before* the fall of Jerusalem, but *after* the first deportations.

B. Ezekiel's Vision of God's Glory Riding on a Throne-Chariot (1:4–28a)

The first chapter is taken up with a vision of the glory of God among the captives. Ezekiel first saw a fierce **whirlwind coming** from **the north.** Then he saw **four living creatures, each** of which **had four faces (lion, ox, eagle, man),**[4] four **wings**, straight feet, and hands under its wings. The creatures symbolize those attributes of God which are seen in creation: His majesty, power, swiftness, and wisdom. Many nations forget about the God above the cloud, who sits on the throne. They worship the creative attributes rather than the Creator Himself.

Above the firmament was **a throne,** with **the LORD** of **glory** seated upon it.

Beside **each** of the living creatures there was **a wheel**, or rather **a wheel** within **a wheel** (perhaps one wheel at right angle to the other like a gyroscope). Thus the vision seems to represent a throne-chariot, with **wheels . . . on the earth**, four living creatures supporting a platform, and the **throne** of God above it. It was this vision of the **glory** of God that preceded Ezekiel's call to the prophetic ministry.

The passage evokes the response in Faber's fine hymn:

My, God, how wonderful Thou art,
Thy majesty how bright,
How beautiful Thy mercy seat,
In depths of burning light!

How dread are Thine eternal years,
O everlasting Lord:
By prostrate spirits day and night
Incessantly adored!

Father of Jesus, love's reward,
What rapture will it be
Prostrate before Thy throne to lie,
And gaze, and gaze on Thee.
—*Frederick William Faber*

Ezekiel explains what he viewed in 43:3 as "the vision which I saw when He[5] [NKJV marg.] came to destroy the city." In other words, the vision depicted God in His glory coming out of the north in judgment on Jerusalem, the Babylonians being the agents of His judgment.

Author's Conception of Throne Car in Ezekiel 1

Ezekiel's Throne Car Vision. This drawing portrays the author's conception of the throne car of Ezekiel 1. In one regard it differs from the text's description, namely that *each* creature has *four* faces, while in this drawing, for the purpose of simplicity, each creature shows only one face.

C. Ezekiel's Appointment to Prophesy to the People of Israel (1:28b—3:21)

1. The Character of the People— Rebellious (1:28b—2:7)

The Spirit entered Ezekiel, **set** him on his **feet**, and told him to prophesy to a rebellious nation, Judah, regardless of the results. He was to be fearless and obedient.

The Lord commissioned Ezekiel, whom He calls **"son of man."**[6] This important expression occurs ninety times in Ezekiel. Taylor explains the usage:

The first words that God addresses to Ezekiel appropriately put the prophet in his rightful place before the majesty which he has been seeing in his vision. The phrase *son of man* is a Hebraism which emphasizes Ezekiel's insignificance or mere humanity. "Son of" indicates "partaking of the nature of" and so when combined with *'adām*, "man," it means nothing more than "human being." In the plural it is a common phrase for "mankind".[7]

By the time of Daniel (7:13, 14) this title had taken on near messianic implications, and in the first century it had become a term for the Messiah:

Our Lord's use of the title seems to have taken advantage of the ambiguity between the simple and the technical meanings, so that in one sense He could not be accused of making any overt claim to Messiahship, while in the other sense He did not debar those with the requisite spiritual insight from accepting the fuller significance of His person.[8]

2. The Nature of the Message— Judgment, as Indicated by the Scroll (2:8—3:3)

2:8–10 Ezekiel was then commanded to **eat . . . a scroll** on which were written the sorrowful judgments that were to fall on the nation.

He was forewarned that his ministry would not be popular. We too are forewarned that a true presentation of the gospel will be offensive to the unsaved. It is known as the offense of the cross. To some people we are a savor of death.

3:1–3 Ezekiel **ate** the **scroll**, as commanded. A later prophet, "John the Revelator," would do the same thing (Rev. 10:8–10). Every prophet or preacher needs to internalize the message, making it a part of his own life (cf. 3:10).

3. The Character of the People— Impudent and Hard-hearted (3:4–11)

Then God repeated that Ezekiel was being **sent to a people** who would **not listen** (Judah is here called **Israel**). Language barriers can be overcome, as many missionaries tell us. But the barrier of a **rebellious** heart cannot be overcome. He was to be fearless . . . in speaking to the Jews in the land and to those in captivity.

True servants of Christ must be tough-minded but not hard-hearted.

4. The Role of the Prophet— Watchman (3:12–21)

3:12–15 The Lord then **took** Ezekiel **to the captives** at **the River Chebar**, and he **sat** with them in silence for **seven days**. Kyle Yates describes Ezekiel's situation:

The call of Ezekiel to leave his comfortable home and go to preach to the captives at Tel-Abib came as an unwelcome interruption. He felt the hand of God upon him and realized a divine compulsion that could not be resisted, but he went in bitterness of spirit to a distasteful task. Fortunately for him and for the people he did not begin preaching immediately but sat among the distraught people for a whole week. That experience gave him a clear understanding of their problems, their miseries and their crying needs. The preacher who is able to see life through the window of his people will be able to help them and provide the leadership so sorely needed.[9]

3:16–21 Ezekiel was appointed **a watchman**, responsible to **speak** God's Word and to **warn the** people solemnly. The solemn fact of bloodguiltiness is taught not only in the OT (vv. 18–20) but in the NT as well (Acts 20:26). However high the responsibility of God's messenger is, Christians should not take this as teaching that they ought to cram the gospel down every throat, or witness in every elevator. Despite his great responsibility, Ezekiel was shut up by God and had to wait for God-given opportunities. We also need to be sensitive to His leading in witnessing. *Sometimes* we need to be silent. However, most of us are silent when we ought to be witnessing.

II. JUDGMENT OF JUDAH AND JERUSALEM DEPICTED (3:22—24:27)

A. Visual Aids Illustrating Coming Judgment (3:22—5:17)

Judgment, wrote Peter, must begin at the house of God (1 Pet. 4:17). And so God starts with the center of revealed religion, the temple at Jerusalem.

1. Ezekiel Commanded to Pretend to Be Mute until Told by God to Speak (3:22–27)

First Ezekiel **went out into the plain** where he beheld **the glory of the LORD**. Then he was commanded to **go** to his **house** where he would be bound and **mute** until God revealed to him what to say.

2. The Siege of Jerusalem Portrayed with a Tile (Chap. 4)

4:1–8 **Jerusalem** was built with stones on a rock foundation. Brick (made of **clay** like tile) is a symbol of Babylon (cf. Gen. 11:3,9). Now Jerusalem has become even worse than Babylon in her morals and idolatry (see 5:7). God therefore commanded Ezekiel to **portray** the **siege** of **Jerusalem**, using a **clay tablet** (tile) to represent the **city** and **an iron**

plate (or pan) to picture the **wall** of **iron** that would cut the city off from help. The prophet is God's representative. This shows that the Lord Himself was besieging Jerusalem. Ezekiel was to **lie . . . on** his **left side . . . three hundred and ninety days** for **Israel** and **on** his **right side . . . forty days** for **Judah**.

Each day represented a year, but no explanation of the totals is completely satisfactory. The Septuagint seeks to solve the problem by changing 390 to 190, but the change lacks Hebrew manuscript support. Another unanswered question is whether Ezekiel actually lay on his side day and night for these two periods of time. Many commentators suggest that he did it only during that part of each day when he would be *seen* by the public, since it was a visual teaching aid.

4:9–17 These verses speak of the famine which resulted from the siege, with **food** and **water** rationed. At first, **human** excrement was to be used as fuel for baking, but later this was changed to the more customary **cow dung**. The chapter is a picture of siege, discomfort, hunger, and defilement—all the result of Judah's sin and departure from God.

3. The People's Fate Predicted by the Use of a Sharp Sword and Hair (Chap. 5)

5:1–9 In an object lesson, Ezekiel showed that **one-third** of the city would die of pestilence (**fire**) or famine (v. 2), **one-third** would fall by **the sword** (knife), and a third would be scattered to other lands (compare v. 2 and v. 12). A remnant would be spared, but even some of these would later perish (vv. 3, 4), perhaps those who were killed at the time Ishmael assassinated Gedaliah. These calamities would come upon **Jerusalem** because the people acted **more** wickedly **than the** surrounding **nations**, in spite of their greater privileges.

We as Christians have even higher privileges than the Jews. May the Lord give us grace not to misuse them and thus bring about our own temporal judgment and loss of eternal rewards!

5:10–17 Cannibalism would be prevalent (v. 10). Because the temple had been **defiled**, God would not **have . . . pity** (vv. 11–13). The Jews would be despised **among the nations** and would suffer violence and **destruction** (vv. 14–17).

B. The Destruction of Idolatry and Preservation of a Remnant of the People (Chap. 6)

6:1–7 **The mountains of Israel** are used here to refer to idolatry, since idol shrines (**high places**) were commonly built on mountains. The land would be punished for its idolatry.

6:8–14 **A remnant** would be spared; these would **remember** the Lord in their captivity and **loathe themselves for . . . their abominations** (vv. 8–10). Idolatry would be punished by **pestilence**, warfare, and **famine** (vv. 11–14).

In every age, God maintains a remnant testimony for Himself—not the moral majority but the *despised minority*.

C. The Imminence and Severity of the Babylonian Invasion (Chap. 7)

7:1–18 The time for God's judgment to fall had **come**, and there would be no question that it was **the LORD** who was striking (vv. 1–13). **No one** would answer the call **to battle**; courage and strength would fail because of the awful destruction (vv. 14–18).

7:19–22 Material possessions would be useless (v. 19). Because the temple (**"the beauty of his ornaments"**) had been polluted with idols, it would be given to **strangers**—the Babylonians. They would **plunder** it and **defile** it (vv. 20–22).

7:23–27 All classes would be affected by the **desolation—the king**, princes, prophets, priests, **elders**, and **common people**. The **common people** should have been a testimony to God, but they totally failed. The only testimony that can be given to God now is through judgment. What a solemn thought. The judgment is complete: all classes and all the land. Any nation that rejects the knowledge of God loses its moral fiber, and has no means of support when trouble comes. This is true of individuals, too.

D. The Vision of Gross Idolatry in the Temple (Chap. 8)

8:1–6 The elders had to witness the judgment, which they had failed to help to avert. This often happens today, too. The Lord carried Ezekiel from Babylon **to Jerusalem . . . in visions**. There he saw some terrible examples of the idolatry of the people. He saw an abominable idolatrous **image . . . in the entrance** of the temple—one which provoked the Lord **to jealousy**.

8:7–15 The second thing the prophet **saw** was in **the court** of the temple. **The elders of** Judah were assembled there **each** with **a censer in his hand**, worshiping vile pictures **portrayed all around on the walls**.

The third sight was at the north gate—the **women were . . . weeping for Tammuz**, a Babylonian deity. The vegetation supposedly dried up when he died.

8:16–18 The fourth instance of idolatry was in **the inner court of the**

temple, where **about twenty-five men**, representing the priests, **were worshiping the sun** and following the lewd practices of that cult. The reference to **the "branch"** or "twig" (v. 17) is obscure. To put **the branch to** the **nose** may have indicated contempt or scorn for God. The branch may have been an obscene phallic symbol.

It is often unsaved religious leaders who grab the headlines by their ungodly behavior and outrageous heresies; but God sees, and He will have the last word.

E. The Removal of God's Presence and the Subsequent Destruction of Idolaters (Chap. 9)

9:1, 2 In this chapter, **six** executioners are seen coming **from** the **north** (the direction from which the Babylonians were to come) to destroy the idolaters of the previous chapter. The man **clothed with linen** may symbolize grace.

9:3 **The glory** cloud (symbol of God's presence) leaves the holy of holies in the temple, grieved away by the idolatry of the people. **The glory** cloud moves **to the threshold of the temple** where its brightness fills the court.

9:4 Those faithful Jews who opposed the idolatry were sealed by **a mark on** their **foreheads** so that they would **not** be killed. This verse should challenge us. How do we react, if some do not follow the Lord? Do we join them? Will they influence us? Do we justify them? Do we show indifference? These faithful men and women sighed and cried; this reaction showed what was in their heart and kept them from judgment.

The sign—or mark on the forehead—was the last letter of the Hebrew alphabet (*tau*), which the rabbis said suggested completeness. It is

also the first letter of *torâ* (law). Feinberg notes a "remarkable similarity between what is stated here and in Revelation 7:1–3."[10] He adds a fascinating parallel from much later times:

> Christian interpreters have seen a somewhat prophetic allusion to the sign of the cross. In the earlier script the last letter of the Hebrew alphabet (*taw*) had the form of a cross. Ezekiel, of course, could not have thought of Christian symbolism nor is the passage a direct prediction of Christ's cross. It is a remarkable coincidence, however.[11]

9:5–7 Then the executioners began to **slay** the idolaters, starting **with the elders** (ancient men). **"Do not come near anyone on whom is the mark,"** says God. We don't know if they were aware of the mark, but believers today can be sure on the basis of the Word that they are safe from judgment. How frightening not to have this assurance!

9:8–11 When Ezekiel interceded for the people, the Lord said that He would **not spare** or **have pity**. The people were saying that because **the LORD** God had **forsaken** them and no longer saw their plight, they owed no loyalty to Him. **"The Lord does not see"** sounds like a very modern quotation!

Judging from this and other texts (cf. Noah and the ark, e.g.), it seems to be characteristic of God to deliver true believers before pouring out judgment on the ungodly.

F. The Vision of God's Glory Visiting Jerusalem with Judgment (Chap. 10)

Chapter 10 is closely linked with Chapter 1, giving further information about the throne-chariot, the living creatures (here identified as cheru-bim), and the glory of the Lord. How-ever, Chapter 1 was addressed to the exiles whereas this is addressed to rebels in Jerusalem.

10:1, 2 The Lord commanded **the man clothed** in **linen** to take burning **coals . . . from** between **the cherubim, and scatter them over** Jerusalem. This signified God's judgment that was to be poured out on **the city**.

10:3–5 These verses are a paren-thesis, repeating the movement of the glory cloud described in 9:3.

10:6–17 A detailed description of **the cherubim** and **the wheels** of the throne-chariot is given in these verses, which are admittedly difficult to visualize. The **cherub . . . face** in verse 14 may be the same as the ox face in 1:10.

10:18, 19 The **glory** cloud next moves **from the threshold** to **the east gate** of the LORD's **house**.

10:20–22 Ezekiel then emphasized that **the cherubim** were the same as **the living creature** he had seen **by the River Chebar** in chapter 1.

This vision teaches us never to lose a sense of the awesome power, wisdom, and majesty of our God.

G. The Repudiation of the Counsel of Wicked Princes (11:1–13)

11:1–3 The **twenty-five men** (rep-resenting the princes) were advising the people of the city that there was nothing to fear. They could carry on their construction projects as usual. They were as secure as **meat** encased in an iron **caldron**. Thus the **twenty-five men** flatly contradicted the word of the Lord, which said: **"The time is not** near to build . . . ." God had given orders through Jeremiah (Jer. 29:4–11) that the captives would build houses in Babylon because Jerusalem would fall. **The men who devise iniquity**

tried to awaken false hopes among the captives by letters. Despite the fire of God's judgment, the princes in Jerusalem felt quite safe there.

In the same way, many nominal Christians feel safe from God's judg-ment despite the sin in their lives, but the Lord will tell them, "I never knew you."

11:4–12 Ezekiel was told to rein-terpret their symbolism quite differ-ently! The **city** of Jerusalem was the **caldron**, and the **slain** people were **the meat**! They themselves would be taken **out of** the city and judged **at the border of Israel** (see 2 Kgs. 25:18–21; Jer. 5:24–27).

11:13 When **Pelatiah** (perhaps the leader of the twenty-five men) dropped dead, seemingly as a result of his evil counsel, Ezekiel interceded to GOD for his people.

H. The Preservation of a Remnant Promised (11:14–21)

11:14, 15 The LORD answered by telling the prophet what **the inhabit-ants of Jerusalem** had been saying, namely, that the exiles had wandered **far . . . from** the LORD and that the land belonged to those remaining in Judah and **Jerusalem**.

11:16–21 But the **Lord GOD** prom-ised that He would be **a little sanctuary** to the exiles, and that He would regather them to **the land of Israel**, completely cleansed of idolatry and with **a heart** to obey the Lord. Yates comments:

Ezekiel follows Jeremiah in urging spiritual religion. It is definitely a heart religion that God wants. The heart is beyond repair. A new one will be provided. Formalism must be left behind. The spiritual emphasis will give them touch with Yahweh that will transform their thinking, their worship, their conduct and their loyalty. A new spirit will be their special gift from their God (Cf. 18:31; 36:26f).[12]

The real hope for the exiles is based on the Lord's promise. The promise of **one heart** (one **of flesh**) and a **new spirit** are unconditional; they are yet to be fulfilled in the New Covenant.

Jesus, before Thy face we fall—
Our Lord, our life, our hope, our all!
For we have nowhere else to flee—
No sanctuary, Lord, but Thee!
    —Samuel Medley

I. The Removal of the Glory Cloud to the Mount of Olives (11:22–25)

At the close of the chapter, **the glory** cloud rises **from the . . . city** and goes to the Mount of Olives, to **the east side of** Jerusalem. George Williams comments:

It retired unwillingly. Its throne was the Most Holy Place, 8:4; it then withdrew to the threshold, 9:3; then, above the threshold, 10:4; then it retired to the Eastern Gate, 10:19; and, finally, to the mountain on the east side of the city, 11:23. Thus did the God of Israel in lingering love forsake His city and temple, not to return till 43:2 (still future).[13]

J. Ezekiel's Signs of the Coming Exile (Chap. 12)

1. His Baggage (12:1–16)

12:1–12 Ezekiel was commanded to move his household goods from one **place . . . to another**, as a sign to the Jews that they would be moving off **into captivity**. By digging **through the wall** at night with his eyes covered, he predicted that Zedekiah (**the prince**) would flee from the city **at twilight** (when he could not **see the ground**).

12:13–16 However, he would be captured and taken **to Babylon**, though he would never **see it . . . with his eyes** (v. 13). This is exactly what happened. Zedekiah was captured as he fled from Jerusalem, his eyes were put out at Riblah, and then he was carried to Chaldea (2 Kgs. 25:7). The people would be scattered among the nations, and many of them would die from **the sword, famine, and . . . pestilence**.

2. His Quaking (12:17–28)

12:17–20 When Ezekiel ate and drank **with trembling** and **quaking**, he gave a pre-picture of the fear **and anxiety** that would precede the exile.

12:21–28 The people had a **proverb** that God's prophecies of doom were never fulfilled. God gave them another proverb, announcing that the day of **fulfillment** was **at hand**, and that **every** prophecy (**vision**) would come to pass. Those who said that the **fulfillment** was yet future would see it in their own day.

The people's tendency to explain the prophecies away or apply them to future generations is still with us. When God speaks to *us* through a message or a book, we immediately seem to know how *our brother or sister* should apply it and change. It is an evil and destructive tendency to apply God's Word to others and not to our own lives.

We should also watch out for glib clichés that contradict God's Word or that deny or postpone His intervention.

K. The Doom of the False Prophets and Prophetesses (Chap. 13)

13:1–3 The subject here is false **prophets** (vv. 1–16) and false prophetesses (vv. 17–23). The former invented prophecies **out of their own heart**;

they would fail the people when most needed. They used the words, **"The Lord says,"** but it was a lie, a **false divination**.

Today we need preachers who don't give us their own thoughts and opinions, but who get their message in the prayer closet, and from God's Word.

Denis Lane gives the following characteristics of the preaching in Ezekiel's day:

> It never rose higher than the preachers' own minds. It deceptively claimed to be God's word. It had no practical or useful effect. It offered cheap grace and a false peace. It simply endorsed the latest world view.[14]

13:4–7 False religious leaders, like **foxes in the deserts**, are always looking for prey in the midst of destruction, filling their own needs and desires. In a situation like this it is the preacher's duty to stand in **the gaps** to intercede and to repair the **wall** by leading people to repentance and a holy life. This is done by preaching God's Word.

13:8–16 They would be destroyed for predicting **peace when there** was **no peace**, for whitewashing **a wall** that was ready to crumble (daubing it **with untempered mortar**). The **wall** represented the rulers' efforts to prevent the divine judgment. Davidson explains the illustration:

> The figure incisively describes the futile projects of the people, and the feeble flattery and approval of the prophets. When a weak man cannot originate anything himself, he acquires a certain credit (at least in his own eyes) by strong approval of the schemes of others, saying, Right! I give it my cordial approval, and indeed would have suggested it. What made the prophets whitewash the wall

which the people built was partly the feeling that from the place they occupied they must do something, and maintain their credit as leaders even when being led; and partly perhaps that having no higher wisdom than the mass they quite honestly approved their policy. Being sharers with them in the spirit of the time they readily acquiesced in their enterprises.[15]

Modern apostate religious leaders are exactly the same—whitewashed walls.[16]

13:17–23 The prophetesses practiced witchcraft, putting **magic charms** on people's wrists and **veils** on their **heads**. They doomed some people to death by magic spells and kept others **alive**. God would **deliver** His **people** and destroy these false prophetesses. The LB paraphrases verses 17–19 as follows:

> Son of dust, speak out against the women prophets too who pretend the Lord has given them his messages. Tell them the Lord says: Woe to these women who are damning the souls of my people, of both young and old alike, by tying magic charms on their wrists and furnishing them with magic veils and selling them indulgences. They refuse to even offer help unless they get a profit from it. For the sake of a few paltry handfuls of barley or a piece of bread will you turn away my people from me? You have led those to death who should not die! And you have promised life to those who should not live, by lying to my people—and how they love it!

L. God's Threat to the Idolatrous Elders (Chap. 14)

14:1–11 When **some of the elders of Israel**—idolaters at heart—visited Ezekiel to get counsel from the Lord, **the Lord** announced that He would answer idolaters directly, not through a **prophet**. If a **prophet** did answer the idolaters, he would be deceived and would be punished together with the inquirers.

14:12–20 Even if **three** righteous **men** like **Noah, Daniel, and Job** should be **in the land**, God would not hearken but would send **famine, wild beasts, the sword**, and **pestilence** on the land. Daniel was living at the court of Nebuchadnezzar when Ezekiel wrote, and yet he was reckoned with God's righteous men of old. It is not true that there cannot be heroes and heroines of the faith today as there have been in former times. Will you be one of them?

14:21–23 If He would severely judge any **land, how much more...** **Jerusalem**, where His temple was located. But **a remnant** would be saved to testify that **the LORD** was justified in doing what He did.

Judah's guilt was too great to be pardoned, even through the intercession of Noah, Daniel, and Job. What about *our* society with its crime, violence, abortion, immorality, idolatry, drugs, and secular humanism?

M. The Parable of the Fruitless Vine (Chap. 15)

A **vine** is good only for bearing fruit; it is not good for making furniture or even a little **peg**. If it has been charred in a **fire**, it is even more useless. In one sense, the **vine** is the people **of Jerusalem** (v. 6). Failing to bear fruit for God, they were charred by the **fire** of the Babylonian invasion. But in a wider sense the vine represents the entire nation, including both Israel and Judah (v. 4). The northern end of the **branch** was charred by the Assyrians. The southern end was charred by the Egyptians. And now the middle, i.e., **Jerusalem**,

would be charred by the Babylonians (see 2 Kgs. 25:9). The second **fire** of verse 7 pictures the captivity of those who escaped. God has determined to **make the land desolate** (v. 8).

As believers we have high privileges, but also the responsibility to produce fruit for God's glory. If we don't glorify Him with our life, our existence is vain and useless. It is like the vine without fruit, and our testimony will be destroyed (cf. John 15:6). As branches in Christ, the True Vine, our chief function is to bear fruit for God. Primarily that means the development of Christian character as seen in the fruit of the Spirit.

N. The Parable of Jerusalem's Marriage (Chap. 16)

16:1–7 The LORD here traces the history of **Jerusalem**, as a type of the people. It began as a foundling child, unwashed and unwanted. The Lord had pity on her and cared for her lovingly, and she **grew, matured, and became very beautiful**.

16:8–22 When she came to young womanhood, Jehovah (NKJV, LORD) betrothed Himself to her, purified her for marriage, lavished kindnesses upon her, and **adorned** her. But because she **trusted in** her **own beauty**, she turned from Him to idols, becoming a **harlot...to everyone who passed by**.

16:23–34 Instead of trusting in the Lord, she played the prostitute to such Gentiles as **the Egyptians, the Assyrians**, and the traders of **Chaldea**. As someone has said, "She outheathened the heathen." She was unlike the usual **harlot** in that *she* **hired** others to sin with her! Who would do something like that? Is it possible that the harlot will pay the man? That she will give her precious possessions away? And yet many who say they follow the Lord give up their precious rewards and inheritance above, spend their money and time on worldly pleasures instead of laying up treasures in heaven. They compromise with the world and lose eternal reward and blessing. This is called spiritual adultery, and whoever is engaged in it pays a high price.

16:35–43 The judgment on her **filthiness** was that she would be destroyed by the Gentile nations which she solicited as **lovers** for hire. Those who turn from God like an unfaithful lover and make compromises with the world will be destroyed by the world they wanted to befriend. This is a solemn warning to us (cf. Jas. 4:4–10).

16:44–52 The abominations committed by Jerusalem (Judah) were worse than those of her heathen predecessors, the Hittites, Amorites, **Samaria**, or **Sodom**. Sexual perversion was only *one* of Sodom's sins. The **iniquity of Sodom** also included **fullness of food and abundance of idleness**. This reads only too much like a description of modern Christendom! Feinberg comments:

> Notice how pride was singled out as the root of Sodom's sin when her abominations were traced to their source. God had blessed her abundantly with fullness of bread (Gen. 13:10), but she monopolized these blessings for her own pleasures and basked in prosperous ease. Provision for her own needs made her insensible to the needs of others; she had no social conscience. Then she committed the abominations and enormities which are linked inseparably with her name. God took her away with a final blow when He saw it (Gen. 18:21).[17]

16:53–58 In grace, God will restore **Sodom** and **Samaria** and Jerusalem in a day yet future. Verse 53 describes the restoration of cities but in no way suggests the eventual salvation of the wicked dead.

16:59–63 He **will establish an everlasting covenant with** His people, and Judah will **be ashamed** that she ever forsook the Lord for idols. This is an unconditional covenant of blessing with the patriarchs which the Lord will fulfill in the future.

John Newton was right when he wrote that the bright glories of God's grace above His other wonders shine.

O. The Parable of the Two Eagles (Chap. 17)

17:1–6 The LORD told Ezekiel to **pose a riddle to the house of Israel**. **A great eagle came to Lebanon**, broke **off the topmost . . . twig** from a **cedar** tree, **and carried it to a** foreign **land**. It also **took . . . the seed of the land and planted it in . . . fertile** soil. There **it grew** into **a spreading vine**.

17:7–10 Then the **vine** began to grow **toward . . . another great eagle**, but it no longer thrived.

17:11–21 The LORD Himself gives the interpretation of the allegory. The first eagle was Nebuchadnezzar, **king of Babylon** (v. 12). He carried off Jehoiachin, **king** of Judah (the topmost twig), from **Jerusalem** (Lebanon) into **Babylon** (land of traffic), and Babylon (city of merchants). He also took Zedekiah, **the king's offspring**, and set him up as his vassal king in Judah (v. 13). For a while, Zedekiah, a **low** spreading vine, flourished in the homeland, but then he turned **to** the king of **Egypt** (another great eagle) for deliverance from Babylon. When Zedekiah broke **the covenant** with Nebuchadnezzar (2 Chron. 36:13), it was the same as if **he broke** it with God (v. 19). As a result, Zedekiah would be carried into **Babylon** and die there; **Pharaoh**-Hophra would not be able to help him (vv. 16–21).

17:22–24 In these verses the coming of the Messiah (the **tender . . . twig**) is promised; He would be descended from the house of David. He would be a fruitful **tree** and afford safety to the people (v. 23). The God of hope does not leave them hopeless, but directs their eyes towards the Messiah. We also should have the future in view and comfort each other with these truths. Carl F. Keil elaborates:

> The cedar, . . . as rising above the other trees, is the royal house of David, and the tender shoot which Jehovah breaks off and plants is not the Messianic kingdom or sovereignty, . . . but the Messiah Himself. . . . The high mountain, described in ver. 23 as the high mountain of Israel, is Zion, regarded as the seat and centre of the kingdom of God, which is to be exalted by the Messiah above all the mountains of the earth (Isa. ii. 2, etc.). The twig planted by the Lord will grow there into a glorious cedar, under which all the birds will dwell. The Messiah grows into a cedar in the kingdom founded by Him, in which all the inhabitants of the earth will find both food (from the fruits of the tree) and protection (under its shadow).[18]

Politics always proves to be a washout. Only the return of Christ offers any hope to this sin-drugged world.

P. The Repudiation of the Parable of the Sour Grapes (Chap. 18)

18:1–4 The people of Judah had a **proverb** which blamed their sins on the failure of their ancestors:

> "The fathers have eaten sour grapes,
> And the children's teeth are set on edge."

God refutes the proverb, stating that individuals are held responsible for their own sins.

18:5–24 He then gives several examples of His principles of judgment:

1. **A man** who shuns sin and lives righteously **shall surely live** (vv. 5–9).
2. A righteous man's wicked **son . . . shall surely die** (vv. 10–13). The Jews during the captivity as well as in the Lord Jesus' time prided themselves on having Abraham as their father (Luke 3:8; John 8:39). God points out that it will do no good to have a righteous father, if their own life is wicked. We also have the tendency to rely on the spirituality of others. But the righteous and holy life of our fathers and godly leaders must become a reality in our own lives.
3. An unrighteous man's righteous **son . . . shall surely live** (vv. 14–17), but the unrighteous **father . . . shall die for his iniquities** (v. 18).
4. **A wicked man** who repents and **turns from his sins** will **live** (vv. 21–23).
5. **A righteous man** who **turns away from his righteousness and commits iniquity . . . shall die** (v. 24).

There is no contradiction between verse 20 and Exodus 20:5. It is true, as taught in Exodus, that children are generally involved in the consequences of their parents' misdeeds. It is also true, as taught here, that each one is personally responsible for his or her actions.

In verse 20, the punishment is *temporal*, not eternal. It is *physical* death because of sin now. The principles stated in verses 5–24 are not dealing with *eternal* life; otherwise we would be forced to conclude that salvation is by works (vv. 5–9) and that the righteous may eventually be lost, two doctrines clearly refuted by our Lord in the NT (e.g., Eph. 2:8, 9; John 10:28).

18:25–32 The people continued to accuse God of injustice, but He shows that there is no injustice because even **a wicked man** can be saved by turning from his sins, and that is what the Lord wants them to do.

When God forgives, He forgets (v. 22). This does not indicate a poor memory but the perfect satisfaction of His justice through the atoning work of Christ. For the believer the case is closed.

Q. Lamentation for the Last Kings of Judah (Chap. 19)

19:1–9 This is a lament for the last kings of Judah. Not all are agreed as to the identity of the kings, but probably they are Jehoahaz, Jehoiachin, and Zedekiah. Judah is the **lioness**. The other nations are **the lions**, and their rulers are **the young lions** (v. 2). The whelp who **became a young lion** (v. 3) is perhaps Jehoahaz, who was captured and taken off **to . . . Egypt** (v. 4). The other whelp (v. 5) is possibly Jehoiachin. Judah was no different than all the other nations, a lioness **among the lions**. The leaders of **the nations** are fierce and selfish, "but among you it shall not be so." The Lord expects His people to be different. If not, they are inviting His judgment.

19:10–14 "Your mother" (v. 10) is Judah or Jerusalem, a **vine in** their **bloodline** that was **fruitful and full of branches**. At one time, she had strong kings (**strong branches**), but she would be destroyed by Babylon (**the east wind**), and the people carried into captivity (**the wilderness**,

vv. 11–13). Zedekiah, the **fire** of verse 14, is regarded as a usurper and the ruin of his people.

Israel had wanted a king like the other nations. Here Ezekiel lowers the curtain on the last act of their monarchy. God wants His people to be different from the world, to be a holy people for Himself, and to acknowledge *Him* as King.

R. Vindication of God's Dealings with Israel (20:1–32)

1. Idolatry in Egypt (20:1–9)

When **the elders . . . came** to Ezekiel **to inquire of the** LORD, He refused to **be inquired of by** them. Instead He recounted their repeated rebellions against Him. The elders were quite conservative and orthodox; they did inquire of the Lord, but their hearts were far from Him. Idols keep us from getting God's answers to our questions. When God recounts our sins and shows us His grace by leading us to repentance, many of us get bored: "We've heard that so often." "The Bible is just full of do's and don'ts." "Is there nothing else but judgment in it?" Instead of reacting properly to God's Word, we are in danger of staying lukewarm.

In spite of their idolatry **in the land of Egypt** (vv. 4–8a), God did not punish them there so that **the Gentiles** would not mock (vv. 8b–9).

2. Defiling God's Sabbaths (20:10–17)

Israel profaned God's **Sabbaths . . . in the wilderness** (vv. 10–13a). Again the Lord restrained His wrath and **spared them from destruction** lest the heathen should laugh (vv. 13b–17).

3. Rebellion in the Wilderness (20:18–26)

The rebellion of the **children** of the original generation **in the wilderness** is recalled (vv. 18–21a); again God held back His **anger against them** (vv. 21b–26).

4. Idolatry (20:27–32)

Their terrible idolatry in **the land** of promise even included making their **sons pass through the fire**, that is, offering them as human **sacrifices**.

S. God's Promise of Eventual Restoration (20:33–44)

20:33–38 In spite of their efforts, God would **never** let them become *permanently* **like the Gentiles . . . serving wood and stone** (v. 32). He would regather them **from the peoples** of captivity, set them in judgment before Him, receive the righteous (v. 37), and **purge** the **rebels from among them** (v. 38).

20:39–44 When the nation is restored to the land **of Israel**, they will no longer worship **idols**, but they will worship **the LORD** in holiness (vv. 39–44).

The apostle John's admonition is timeless: "Little children, keep yourselves from idols."

T. Pictures of the Imminent Invasion (20:45—21:32)

1. The Sign of the Forest Fire (20:45–49)

Verse 45 marks the beginning of chapter 21 in the Hebrew Bible, a more logical place to break, as our outline indicates. In verses 45–49, we have a prophecy **against the South** (Heb. *Negev*, part of Judah); it will be destroyed by the **forest . . . fire** (Babylonian invasion).

2. The Sign of the Drawn Sword (21:1–17)

21:1–7 God expresses His determination to lay waste Judah and **Jerusalem** with His sharpened **sword**. Ezekiel's sighing was to warn the people of the fearfulness of God's **coming** judgment.

21:8–17 The **sword** of Babylon is prepared for the **slaughter** (vv. 8–13) and will satisfy the **fury** of Jehovah (vv. 14–17). Verses 10c and 13 are especially difficult. The thought may be this: It was no time for Judah to **make mirth**. They had despised all previous weapons of affliction, which are spoken of in the NKJV as having been made of **wood**. Now they would experience a **sword** made of steel, and there was the possibility that **the scepter** that despises, i.e., Judah, would be no more.

3. The Sign of the Fork in the Road (21:18–32)

21:18–24 Next, **the king of Babylon** is seen marching toward the **land**. He comes to a **fork** in **the road**: One branch leads **to . . . Jerusalem**, and the other **to Rabbah** (capital of Ammon). Which city shall he attack first? He uses three means of divination: (1) He marks an arrow **for Jerusalem** and one for Rabbah; (2) **He consults** his household gods; (3) **He looks** into **the liver** of some slaughtered animal. The decision? Attack **Jerusalem** *first!*

21:25–27 Zedekiah is the **profane, wicked prince** of verse 25. His kingship is **overthrown** and he will be the last king over God's people **until** the Messiah comes, **whose right it is** to reign. Matthew Henry comments:

> There *shall be no more* kings of the house of David after Zedekiah, till Christ comes, *whose right the kingdom is*, who is that seed of David in

whom the promise was to have its full accomplishment, and *I will give it to him*. He shall have *the throne of his father David*, Luke i. 32. . . . And having the right, he shall in due time have the possession: *I will give it to him;* and there shall be a general overturning of all rather than he shall come short of his right, and a certain overturning of all the opposition that stands in his way to make room for him, Dan. ii. 45; 1 Cor. xv. 25. This is mentioned here for the comfort of those who feared that the promise made in David would fail for evermore. "No," says God, "that promise is sure, for the Messiah's kingdom shall last for ever."[19]

21:28–32   The Ammonites will next be attacked by the king of Babylon; they will be utterly destroyed.

History and current events are full of instances of God overturning human governments until Christ comes, whose right it is to reign.

U. Three Oracles on Jerusalem's Defilement (Chap. 22)

22:1–12   Here is presented a catalog of the sins of Jerusalem—**bloodshed** (v. 9) (perhaps meaning human sacrifices in this context) and idolatry (vv. 3, 4); murder (v. 6); contempt of parents, oppression of strangers, orphans and widows (v. 7); desecrating the temple and breaking the **Sabbaths** (v. 8); **slander**, idolatry and **lewdness** (v. 9); immorality (v. 10); adultery, incest (v. 11); bribery, **usury**, **extortion**, and forgetfulness of **the LORD GOD** (v. 12).

22:13–22   For these sins of **dishonest profit** and **bloodshed**, the people would be scattered **among the nations** (vv. 13–16). Jerusalem would be like a refiner's pot, in which the people, like worthless **dross**, would **be melted** (vv. 17–22).

22:23, 24   **The LORD** tells Ezekiel to **say to** the land that she is in sad shape. Taylor explains what this means for the land:

> The land is described in this oracle as deprived of the blessings of rain. Most commentators prefer to follow LXX in verse 24, which translates not "cleansed" but "rained upon": thus, "a land without rain and without shower."[20]

22:25–31   All classes of society were guilty before the Lord—rulers (v. 25) [**"prophets"** in the KJV and NKJV reads "princes" in the Septuagint];[21] **priests** (v. 26); magistrates (v. 27); **prophets** (v. 28); **people** (v. 29). Not a righteous **man** could be found, not a reformer nor an intercessor to **stand** for God (vv. 30, 31).

God is not looking for new methods or programs; God is always looking for someone to stand in the gap. One person can make a difference.

V. The Parable of the Two Harlot Sisters (Chap. 23)

1. Oholah (23:1–10)

23:1–4   This is the parable of **two** harlot sisters, **Oholah the elder** and **Oholibah her sister**. Oholah was **Samaria**, and **Oholibah** was **Jerusalem**.

23:5–10   **Oholah** means *[she has] her own tent*. Samaria had set up her own center of worship. God's temple was in Jerusalem.[22] **Oholah played the harlot** to the good-looking and macho **horsemen** of Assyria; therefore, she was abandoned to **her lovers** by God, and **they uncovered her nakedness** and **slew her with the sword**.

2. Oholibah (23:11–21)

Oholibah (my tent is in her) went even further in her idolatrous **harlotry**

and immorality. First **she lusted** after the **Assyrians**, just as Israel had done (vv. 12, 13). Then she doted on the **images** of the **men** of Babylon **portrayed in vermilion. She lusted for them and sent messengers to them**, inviting them to her land (2 Kgs. 16:7). Recalling her youthful sins **in the land of Egypt**, she also **multiplied her harlotry** and gave herself over to the Babylonians to commit terrible **immorality**.

3. The Invasion of the Babylonians (23:22–35)

As a result, God would destroy **Oholibah** by her Babylonian **lovers.** Those **desirable young men** she lusted after would treat her **hatefully**. She tried to find satisfaction in the fleshly world, apart from God. Now her sins must be judged. Verses 33 and 34 describe the symptoms of depression and despair, which we find all over today. Only if we drink of God's living water, will we never thirst again.

4. The Judgment of Oholah and Oholibah (23:36–49)

Both sisters were guilty of the same sins: **adultery** (literal and spiritual), murder, offering human sacrifices (v. 37); desecration of the temple, Sabbath-breaking (v. 38); mixing idolatry with worship of God (v. 39); committing spiritual adultery with foreign nations (vv. 40–44). **Righteous men** (nations chosen by God) would **repay** the sisters **for** their **lewdness** with well-deserved destruction (vv. 45–49).

Judah's religion was syncretistic, that is, it combined the worship of Jehovah with idolatry and paganism. Much of modern Christendom, sad to say, combines elements of the Bible with Judaism, paganism, eastern religion, humanism, and psychology.

W. The Parable of the Boiling Pot (24:1–14)

On **the day** the **siege** of **Jerusalem** began, Ezekiel spoke the **parable** of the boiling **pot**. The pot was Jerusalem; the **pieces of meat** were the people. The pot was about to **boil**. It had **scum**, or rust, **in it**—the **lewdness** of idolatry. After the pot was thoroughly emptied, it would be burned to remove the scum. Thus would **the Lord** seek to purge His people of idolatry.

X. The Sign of the Death of Ezekiel's Wife (24:15–27)

24:15–18 Ezekiel was warned that his wife, **the desire of** his **eyes**, would die. She **died** on the **evening** of that day, and, contrary to all normal reactions, he was commanded not to **mourn**.

24:19–24 When **the people** asked the meaning of his strange behavior, he told them that when **the desire of** *their* **eyes** (the temple) would be destroyed and their **sons and daughters** would be killed, they were not to **mourn**.

One purpose of fulfilled prophecy is to let the world **know** who is **the Lord God** (v. 24).

24:25–27 Ezekiel was not to utter any more prophecies to Judah until a fugitive brought him the news that **their stronghold** had fallen. That event is recorded in 33:21, 22. The intervening chapters, 25—32, are prophecies to *Gentile* nations, not to Judah.

III. PROPHECIES AGAINST SEVEN GENTILE NATIONS (Chaps. 25—32)

In these chapters we read of God's judgment on seven heathen nations. These nations are judged for various forms of rebellion against God. They had contact with God's people, knew about Him, but were unwilling to turn to Him. Let us observe this closely, for God's ways always reveal His thoughts, whether in judgment or in grace.

A. Prophecy against Ammon (25:1–7)

The first nation upon which judgment is pronounced is Ammon. Because **the Ammonites rejoiced** at the fall of God's **sanctuary, Israel** and **Judah**, and the Babylonian captivity, they would be destroyed by the Babylonians (**men of the East**). **Rabbah** would become a **stable for camels and Ammon a resting place for flocks**.

B. Prophecy against Moab (25:8–11)

The second nation is **Moab**, which shared with **Seir** a hostile attitude toward **Judah**. The land of Moab would be opened to the Babylonians and would suffer the same fate as Ammon. The **territory** would be cleared of its **cities**, and Moab would know that God is **the LORD**.

C. Prophecy against Edom (25:12–14)

The third nation is **Edom**. Because it took **vengeance** against the **house of Judah**, the Lord GOD said, it would know *His* **vengeance**.

D. Prophecy against Philistia (25:15–17)

The Philistines are the fourth people. Their never-ending **hatred** of Judah would bring upon them **the vengeance of the LORD**.

Just as these nations would learn that if you touch God's people, you touch Him, so those who engage in "Christian-bashing" today will one day learn that believers are the apple of God's eye. This is even true when God's people fall into sin and are judged for it. We should beware of all malicious joy, gloating, or revengeful thoughts. Rather, like Ezekiel, we should mourn, intercede, and confess the sins of other believers as our own.

E. Prophecy against Tyre (26:1—28:19)

1. The Destruction of Tyre (Chap. 26)

26:1, 2 The fifth object of God's judgment is the seacoast city of **Tyre**. Its punishment extends from 26:1 to 28:19. Super-commercial Tyre rejoiced when it heard that its rival city, **Jerusalem**, had fallen, thinking that it would now get *all* the business! Jerusalem had controlled all the overland trade routes, and its fall meant freer traffic for Tyre with Egypt and other southern countries.

26:3–11 God would use **many nations to** chastise this city-state. The predictions of verses 4–6 have been literally fulfilled. First **Nebuchadnezzar**, king of **Babylon, king of kings**,[23] marched **against Tyre from the north** and attacked it (vv. 7–11). The siege was extremely long—about 587 B.C.— 574 B.C. Feinberg gives a vivid picture of the type of siege this renowned city endured:

The forts, the mound and the buckler were all familiar features. The buckler or the testudo or roof of shields was used to protect against missiles thrown from the walls. The battering engines were the battering rams employed to breach the walls. The axes, literally, swords, were used in a figurative manner for all the weapons of warfare. Some have considered the first part of verse 10 a hyperbole, but it is not beyond the range of literal fulfillment. Because of the multitude of the enemy's cavalry, they would cover the city with dust upon entering, at the same time shaking the walls with the noise of the horsemen and chariots. Every street was to be commandeered and the people slain with the sword. The pillars spoken of were actually obelisks, and were probably those mentioned by the historian Herodotus as erected in the temple of Heracles at Tyre. One was of gold and the other of emerald, which shone brilliantly at night, and were dedicated to Melkarth, god of Tyre (cf. I Kings 7:15). These impressive pillars would be demolished by the invader.[24]

26:12–14 But the people fled with their possessions to an offshore island, also called Tyre. They remained secure there for 250 years. Then Alexander the Great built a causeway to the island by scraping clean the original city and throwing the rubble into the sea. This action by Alexander's soldiers (332 B.C.) is described in this paragraph. Over a hundred years ago a traveler described the ruins of Tyre as being exactly as predicted:

The island, as such, is not more than a mile in length. The part which projects south beyond the isthmus is perhaps a quarter of a mile broad, and is rocky and uneven. It is now unoccupied except by fishermen, as "a place to spread nets upon."[25]

26:15–21 News of the fall of Tyre would cause consternation among other nations. All her beauty which they had so admired would be destroyed. But God **shall establish** an everlasting **glory in the land of the living**, which is a part of the same kingdom we belong to.

Tyre has never been rebuilt—a fulfillment of verse 21. In his book, *Science Speaks*, Peter Stoner says that this entire prophecy concerning Tyre, considering all the details, using the principle of probability, had a one-in-four hundred million chance of fulfillment.[26]

2. The Dirge over Tyre (Chap. 27)

27:1–9 **Tyre** is likened to a beautiful ship, luxurious in its construction, with materials in it from all over the world. Tyre was not a military force which conquered the world; the Tyrians were merchants. All kinds of **merchandise** and knowledge were exchanged for the sake of personal gain. This is commonly accepted, but all beauty and knowledge apart from the Lord Jesus is empty. If you gain the whole world, and lose your own soul, what will you give for your soul?

27:10–36 Tyre's army, including soldiers from **Persia, Lydia, and Libya**, is described in verses 10 and 11. The vastness of its commerce in **luxury goods** is seen in verses 12–27a. But it was to be wrecked by an **east wind** (the Babylonians, vv. 26b, 27). The other nations would be convulsed by the fall of the city (vv. 28–36).

3. The Downfall of the Prince of Tyre (28:1–19)

28:1–10 The pride, **wisdom**, and wealth of **the prince of Tyre** are described in verses 1–6, and then his destruction by the Babylonians (vv. 7–10). No doubt this prince foreshadows the Antichrist.

28:11–19 In verse 11 there is a change from the prince of Tyre to **the king of Tyre**. The latter is the spirit that animated the prince. The king of Tyre was noted for his **beauty**, but because of his pride he was destroyed.

The description of the **king of Tyre** as **the seal of perfection, full of wisdom and perfect in beauty**, as having been **in Eden, the garden of God**, as having **every precious stone as a covering**, as being the **anointed cherub**, and as having been **on the holy mountain of God**, taken together seem too impressive for *any* great ruler, even allowing for great use of hyperbole, or literary exaggeration.

For this reason many Bible students see in verses 11–19 a description of Satan and of his fall from heaven. Feinberg explains:

> Ezekiel . . . appeared to have the situation of his day in mind with his attention riveted upon the ruler of Tyre, the embodiment of the people's pride and godlessness. But as he viewed the thoughts and ways of that monarch, he clearly discerned behind him the motivating force and personality who was impelling him in his opposition to God. In short, he saw the work and activity of Satan, whom the king of Tyre was emulating in so many ways. Recall the incident in Matthew 16:21–23 where Peter was rebuked by our Lord Jesus. No sterner words were spoken to anyone in Christ's earthly ministry. But He did not mean that Peter had somehow become Satan himself; He was indicating that the motivation behind Peter's opposition to His going to Calvary was none other than the prince of the demons. This appears to be a similar situation. Some liberal expositors admit that it would appear that Ezekiel had in mind some spirit or genius of Tyre comparable to the angelic powers and princes in the book of Daniel who are entrusted with the affairs of nations.[27]

If pride is deadly enough to destroy a most wise and wise being, how much more should we mortals take heed not to walk independently of the Lord!

F. Prophecy against Sidon (28:20–26)

28:20–23 The sixth object of God's judgment is **Sidon**. It was a seacoast city near Tyre. God warned that it would be subjected to **pestilence** and **sword**, but He did not say it would be destroyed forever. Sidon still stands

today as a town in Lebanon, though biblical Tyre has been wiped out completely (see 26:21).

28:24–26 These verses predict the restoration of Israel when **the Lord GOD** sets up His kingdom on the earth.

G. Prophecy against Egypt (Chaps. 29—32)

The seventh and last nation in this catalog of judgments is Egypt (Chaps. 29—32). These seem to be the most unsparing judgments of all. Without the River Nile, Egypt would be dead, and one would expect its people to cherish life. But no, Egypt is the land of death. Its most famous book is the *Book of the Dead.* Its greatest monuments are the pyramids, which are huge *tombs.* Its kings built small palaces but huge *sepulchers,* and they were embalmed to enjoy their time in the *grave!* The heart of the Egyptian is quite unimpressed facing death, full of self-assertion. Therefore judgment had to come over Egypt, which nation in the Bible is a picture of the world, especially as being without God.

1. General Threat against Pharaoh and His People (Chap. 29)

29:1–12 In verses 1–5, **Pharaoh** is compared to a crocodile in the great **River** Nile. This crocodile is proud, but short-sighted. **The fish** are the people of Egypt. All are to be punished by God. In looking to Egypt for help, Israel had **leaned on** a broken **reed** (vv. 6–9a). Egypt receives the most severe judgment because it was unreliable and untrustworthy. If we as believers have this character flaw, with the Lord's help we need to change. He is in the character-changing business.

Because of Pharaoh's pride, **the land of Egypt** would be **desolate** for **forty years** (vv. 9b–12).

29:13–21 Then God would **gather** the people, but **Egypt** would never be a great **kingdom** again, and **Israel** would **no longer** look to it for help (vv. 13–16). **Nebuchadnezzar** had worked hard besieging **Tyre**, but **received** no **wages** for it (because the people fled to the island fortress with their possessions). Therefore God would **give** him **Egypt** as his **wages** (vv. 17–20). **In** the **day** that Nebuchadnezzar received Egypt as his pay, God caused **the horn of the house of Israel to** bud **forth** (a revival of power of which we have no other mention) and Ezekiel declared God's message to the people (v. 21).

2. Lamentation over the Fall of Egypt (30:1–19)

30:1–12 Egypt and **all** her allies—**Ethiopia**, **Libya**, and **Lydia**—would **fall . . . by the sword** of the Babylonians (vv. 1–9). **Nebuchadnezzar king of Babylon** is named as the one who would **destroy the land** (vv. 10–12).

30:13–19 The leading cities of Egypt are listed as doomed to destruction with their **idols** and **images**: **Noph** (Memphis), **Pathros** (perhaps in the upper southern part of Egypt), **Zoan** (Tanis), **No** (Thebes), **Sin** (Pelusium), **Aven** (Heliopolis), **Pi Beseth** (perhaps Bubastis), **Tehaphnehes**[28] (probably the ancient Daphne, vv. 13–19). The prophecy, **"there shall no longer be princes from the land of Egypt"** (v. 13), has been literally fulfilled. No full-blooded Egyptian of the royal family has reigned in Egypt since that time. King Farouk belonged to a dynasty that was founded by an Albanian in the early 1800's. Farouk was the first member of the dynasty to have even a complete mastery of the Arabic language!

3. The Downfall of Pharaoh (30:20—31:18)

30:20–26 Here the downfall of Egypt is seen in two stages. **One** of Pharaoh's **arms . . . was broken** figuratively when he was defeated in the battle of Carchemish (605 B.C.). The other **was broken** when the Babylonians invaded Egypt and conquered it.

31:1–9 **Whom** was **Pharaoh . . . like** in his **greatness?** He was like the king of **Assyria**, **a** lofty **cedar**. That king grew powerful, so that there was no one else as great as he, a veritable giant tree in whose **shadow all great nations make their home**.

31:10–14 But because his **heart was** lifted up with arrogance, God delivered him over to the Babylonians.

31:15–18 The Assyrian was dashed **down to hell** (Heb., *Sheol*), while other **nations** looked on (vv. 15–17). **The nations . . . were comforted** (v. 16) in the sense that they were gratified to see the humiliation of Assyria, the nation that had formerly despised them. Pharaoh is like the Assyrian in that, although he became great, he too would be delivered **to the depths of the Pit** (v. 18).

4. Lamentation over Pharaoh and Egypt (Chap. 32)

32:1–16 **Pharaoh** thought himself **a young lion,** but God looked upon him as **a monster,** which He would catch in His **net** and destroy. **The king of Babylon** would bring to nothing the **pomp of Egypt,** and **the land** would be left **desolate** and quiet. The nations lamented with tears. **The LORD** ordered Ezekiel to utter **a lamentation** over **Egypt for all her multitude.**

The Lord Jesus also shed tears for a city of murderers that would not accept Him and come under His protective wings. God cares for His creatures and does not enjoy judging them. O Lord, give us tears of compassion for the lost!

32:17–32 In verses 17–31, we have a view of Sheol (**the Pit**) where **Egypt** is sent. **Assyria is there** (vv. 22, 23) and **Elam** (vv. 24, 25), **Meshech and Tubal** (vv. 26, 27), **Edom** (v. 29), and **the Sidonians** (v. 30). Egypt had been great in this world, but in Sheol she is reduced to the same shame as the other nations (vv. 28, 31, 32). This finishes Ezekiel's oracles against seven nations (and city-states).

IV. ISRAEL'S RESTORATION AND THE PUNISHMENT OF HER FOES (Chaps. 33—39)

From chapter 33 to the end of the book, Ezekiel deals primarily with the restoration of Israel and the rebuilding of the temple.

A. The Prophet Recommissioned as a Watchman (Chap. 33)

33:1–9 In this chapter, Ezekiel is compared to a **watchman**. If he warns **the people** faithfully, but they do not hear, then they will be responsible for their own destruction. If he fails to **warn** the people, and they perish, God **will require** their **blood** at the watchman's **hand**.

God held Ezekiel responsible for **the house of Israel**. The question arises for every believer: For whom will God hold us responsible? To whom shall we witness? Whom shall we warn? Our relatives, fellow workers, neighbors, friends? It is a solemn responsibility, and we do harm to our own soul if we do not fulfill it faithfully.

33:10–20 The people ask in despair: **"How can we then live?"** How many people today have lost all hope and are in depression and despair. The Lord's answer is: Repent! There

is hope for the worst sinner, but the only hope is in turning from sin, and not in condoning it. The people complained that God's dealings with them were not just, but He denies this, reminding them that He will pardon a **wicked** man who confesses and forsakes **his sin**; also, He will punish a **righteous man** who turns to **wickedness**.

33:21, 22 Ezekiel's **mouth** was **opened**, and he **was no longer mute** when an escapee **from Jerusalem** came and announced, **"The city has been captured!"** (see 24:27).

33:23–29 These verses apparently refer to the few Jews who were left **in the land of Israel** after the fall of Jerusalem. They argued that if **one** man—**Abraham**—had **inherited the land**, how much more right did such a group as they have to it. But God was interested in quality, not quantity. They were even then committing various forms of idolatry, and **the land** would have to be cleansed from such **abominations**, which testified against them. They were not true (spiritual) descendants of Abraham. Their outward profession would not save them from judgment because God was not interested in mere words, but in life (cf. Jas. 2:14).

33:30–33 The people liked to *listen to* Ezekiel, but they had no intention of *obeying* his **words**! **When** his prophecies were fulfilled, **they** would **know that a prophet** had been in their midst.

We should come to the Word of God with the intention of obeying, and constantly checking our hearts, lest we fail to apply what we hear. The best response to a sermon is not, "That was a fine message," but "God has spoken to me; I must do something."

B. The False Shepherds and the Good Shepherd (Chap. 34)

34:1–6 The **shepherds** (rulers) were interested in **themselves** and not in the welfare of the **sheep** (the people). They **ruled** harshly, and the **sheep** became **scattered**.

To this day many religious leaders have not learned the lesson of *serving* the sheep. They confuse their "service" with a means of *gain*. We can praise God for leaders who serve eagerly, as examples to the flock.

The Lord allowed **the flock** to be **scattered** first in order to prevent further damage (v. 10). Yates describes the situation well:

A heart-rending picture is painted of the unfaithful preachers of Ezekiel's day. The flock are scattered, untended and hungry while selfish shepherds pamper themselves and loll in idleness and luxury without any thought of their responsibility. They are careful to look out for their own food and clothing and comfort but no one else is to be considered for a minute.[29]

34:7–10 Therefore God is determined to rescue His **sheep** from these false **shepherds**. But all the time He has blessing in mind, and so He will gather the sheep and take care of individual needs. The greatest blessing will be the relation between the Lord and His sheep, an intimate fellowship between God and man.

34:11–16 He will be their Shepherd and **will . . . gather them to** the **land** and rule over them (during the Millennium). Evangelist D. L. Moody nicely outlines God's ministry to His sheep:

Notice the "I will's" of the Lord God on behalf of his sheep.
The Shepherd and the sheep:—
v. 11. I will search them and seek them out.

v. 12. I will deliver them.
v. 13. I will bring them out.
v. 13. I will gather them together.
v. 13. I will bring them in.
v. 14. I will feed them.
v. 15. I will cause them to lie down.
v. 16. I will bind up the broken.
v. 16. I will strengthen the sick.

There are a good many lean sheep in God's fold, but none in his pasture.[30]

Some people, including a certain type of preacher, try to suggest that the God of the OT is a harsh and unloving Deity, in contrast to God as He is presented in the NT.[31] John Taylor beautifully ties together the revelations of God as Shepherd in both Testaments for us:

The picture of the shepherd searching out the wanderer, in verse 12, is a remarkable foreshadowing of the parable of the lost sheep (Lk. 15:4ff.), which our Lord doubtless based on this passage in Ezekiel. It illustrates as clearly as anything can do the tender, loving qualities of the God of the Old Testament, and strikes a deathblow at those who try to drive a wedge between Yahweh, God of Israel, and the God and Father of our Lord Jesus Christ. Nor is it the only passage that speaks of the tender shepherd (*cf.* Pss. 78:52f.; 79:13; 80:1; Is. 40:11; 49:9f.; Je. 31:10).[32]

34:17–24 **The Lord GOD** will also save His true **sheep** from the false shepherds, which are selfish and cruel. **"My servant David"** in verses 23 and 24 refers to the Lord Jesus, who is descended from David. The Hebrew Christian, David Baron, explains:

Even the Jews explained the name "David" in these passages as applying to the Messiah—the great Son of David in whom all the promises to the Davidic house are centered. Thus Kimchi, in his comment on Ezekiel

34:23, says: "My servant David—that is, the Messiah who shall spring from his seed in the time of salvation": and in the 24th verse of chapter 37 he observes: "The King Messiah—His name shall be called David because He shall be of the seed of David." And so practically all the Jewish commentators.[33]

34:25–31 The security and prosperity of God's **flock** during the future reign of Christ are described here. Under **a covenant of peace** (v. 25) **there shall be showers of blessing** (v. 26) and **a garden of renown** (v. 29).

The *ideal* form of government is a beneficent, absolute monarchy with Christ as King.

C. The Doom of Edom (Chap. 35)

35:1–7 **Mount Seir** is **Edom**. That country is here denounced by the Lord because of its perpetual **hatred** of the Jews, its rejoicing when Jerusalem fell, its cruelty to the fugitives, and its plan to seize the land **of Israel**. Edom wanted *the blessing*, but they did not want *the Lord*. Apart from the Lord Jesus we cannot be blessed, and this still holds true today. Edom is doomed to perpetual desolation, with all trade cut off (v. 7).

35:8–15 Edom blasphemed the Jews and treated them as enemies. But the Lord still identified Himself with His people. They were under discipline, but not rejected. Edom failed to notice the difference.

As Edom **rejoiced** over the desolation **of Israel**, so **the whole earth will rejoice** over Edom's destruction.

God is displeased when believers secretly rejoice over the downfall of enemies of the faith. Love that is real does not feel even a quiet satisfaction when others are hurt, whether friends or foes.

D. The Restoration of the Land and the People (Chap. 36)

Chapter 36 has been called "the Gospel according to Ezekiel," largely because of verses 25–30.

36:1–7 **The nations** that seized **the land of Israel** and scorned God's people, especially the nation of **Edom**, would be punished by Jehovah.

36:8–15 Israel's **cities** and country places would be **inhabited**, the land would be more fertile and prosperous than ever, and the other **nations** would no longer taunt Israel.

36:16–21 Not only would the **land** be restored, but the people would be restored to the land. The reasons for their exile were bloodshed and idolatry; they caused the **name** of God to be **profaned among the nations wherever they went**.

36:22, 23 Paul quotes verse 22 in Romans 2:24 in his indictment of Jewish inconsistencies in relation to the Gentiles and the law. In order to vindicate His own **name**, and not for Israel's **sake**, God would restore the people to their homeland.

36:24–29a Verses 24–29 describe Israel's spiritual regeneration. God would cleanse them, **give** them **a new heart** and **a new spirit** (the new birth), and save them **from . . . uncleanness**. Keil comments on this important passage:

> Cleansing from sins, which corresponds to justification, and is not to be confounded with sanctification . . . , is followed by renewal with the Holy Spirit, which takes away the old heart of stone and puts within a new heart of flesh, so that the man can fulfill the commandments of God, and walk in newness of life.[34]

When our Lord marveled at Nicodemus's ignorance of the new birth, this passage in Ezekiel is surely one of the main texts that He expected him, as a teacher in Israel, to know (John 3:10).

36:29b, 30 Crops of **grain** and **fruit** would be increased, and they would never suffer **famine** again. All this the Lord would do, not because they deserved it, but for the honor of His Name.

36:31–38 The surrounding **nations** will **know that** God has repopulated and replanted the land. **Men** will then be as plentiful as the **flocks** of animals in **Jerusalem on its feast days**. These prophecies had a partial fulfillment when the Jews returned to the land from Babylon, but the complete fulfillment awaits the future reign of Christ.

Modern Israel achieved statehood in 1948. Jews are even now trickling back to the land in unbelief. It must soon be time for the Lord to come.

E. The Vision of the Valley of Dry Bones (37:1–14)

37:1–8 In the vision of verses 1 and 2, Ezekiel saw the **dry . . . bones** of Israel and Judah in a **valley**. He was ordered to **prophesy to** the **bones** that they would come to life. Yates makes an application to our own need of the breath of life today:

> With weirdness, realism and dramatic force the prophet presents the heartening news that Israel may hope to live. A revival is possible! Even dry bones, without sinew and flesh and blood, can live. The coming of God's Spirit brings life. The same thrilling truth is still needed in a world that has dry bones everywhere. What we need is to have the Holy Spirit come with His quickening power that a genuine revival may sweep the earth. (Cf. also Gen. 2:7; Rev. 11:11.)[35]

The first time he spoke the Word of God, **the sinews, flesh . . . and . . . skin came upon** the bones.

37:9–14 The next time he prophesied **to the** wind or **breath**, and the **breath came into** the bodies. This pictured the national restoration **of Israel** (vv. 11–14), first the restoration of a people spiritually dead, and then their regeneration.

We should notice the parallel in our own regeneration. There must be the word of the Lord (v. 4) and the Spirit (breath) of God (v. 9).

F. The Reunification of Israel and Judah (37:15–28)

37:15–23 Ezekiel was next commanded to **take** two sticks, one representing **Judah** and the other Israel (**Joseph** or **Ephraim**). By holding them end to end, he joined **them . . . into one stick**. This meant that the **two kingdoms**, torn apart in the days of Rehoboam, would be reunited. **One king** (the Messiah) would reign **over them**, and they would be saved, cleansed, and restored.

37:24–28 **David** (here the Lord Jesus) would be the **king**, and the people would obey Him implicitly. God would make an **everlasting covenant . . . of peace** with them, and the temple would be set **in their midst**. This is still future.

This and the following chapter foretell the destruction of Israel's future enemies. Gog is the leader of the foes, and Magog is his land. Bible students do not agree on the identity of Gog. Apparently the time of the events described here is after Israel will return to the land but before the Millennium. The Gog and Magog described in Revelation 20:8, however, belong to the period *after* the Millennium.

G. The Destruction of Israel's Future Enemies (Chaps. 38, 39)

38:1–16 God will lure **Gog** and his allies to muster their **troops** (vv. 1–6). Gog is said to be the **prince of Rosh,**[36] **Meshech, and Tubal,** which some have taken to be the ancient names from which come Russia, Moscow, and Tobolsk. This is a fascinating possibility, but by no means proven. They will move south against the land of Israel. The Jews will be **dwelling** securely in **unwalled villages.** God knows the plans of the enemy even thousands of years ahead of time. He has a plan to deliver His people, which gives great comfort to believers.

38:17–23 Then the forces of **Gog** will swarm over the land. But they will meet the blazing **wrath** and **jealousy** of God. The land will be terribly shaken by **a great earthquake;** Gog's men will be terrified by **pestilence, bloodshed, flooding rain, hailstones, fire, and brimstone** (vv. 17–23).

The destruction of the enemies of God's people reminds us of the Lord's promise in Isaiah 54:17: "No weapon formed against you shall prosper. . . . This is the heritage of the servants of the LORD."

39:1–6 The hordes of **Gog** will meet utter destruction on **the mountains of Israel.** The mention of **bows and arrows** in verse 3 does not necessarily mean that future armies will revert to the use of primitive weapons, although it could mean that. Why would any nation do so?, one may well ask. A possible explanation lies in the fact that for years various military powers have been working on inventions that would totally disable any mechanical weapon, such as

a tank, plane, etc. If this is perfected, it would necessitate using horses and non-mechanical weapons in warfare again.

On the other hand, S. Maxwell Coder maintains that the Hebrew words are sufficiently flexible to include modern, sophisticated hardware. Thus, bows and arrows might mean launching devices and missiles. The "horses" in 38:4 (literally "leapers") could be self-propelled vehicles such as tanks or helicopters. The weapons in 39:9, 10 are not necessarily made of wood. The word could mean military equipment such as fuel oil and rocket propellants, many believe.[37]

39:7, 8 The LORD will vindicate His **holy name** in that **day.**

39:9, 10 The **weapons** of Gog, strewn on the mountains, will provide fuel **for seven years.** The fact that they will not need **wood from the field** or the **forest** with which to make campfires would seem to support the view that the abundant and abandoned weapons are indeed made of wood.

39:11–16 **Burial** of the dead **bodies** will take place in the **Valley of Hamon Gog** (Gog's multitude), **east of the Dead sea.** The task will require **seven months.**

39:17–20 The dead bodies of the **horses and riders** will provide **a great** feast for birds and beasts of prey.

39:21–24 In that day, **the Gentiles shall know that** Israel's captivity was not because God was unable to *prevent* it but **because** their **uncleanness** and **transgressions** *demanded* it.

39:25–29 Israel's restoration will be complete. They will forget **their shame** and acknowledge **the LORD,** who will pour **out** His **Spirit on the house of Israel.**

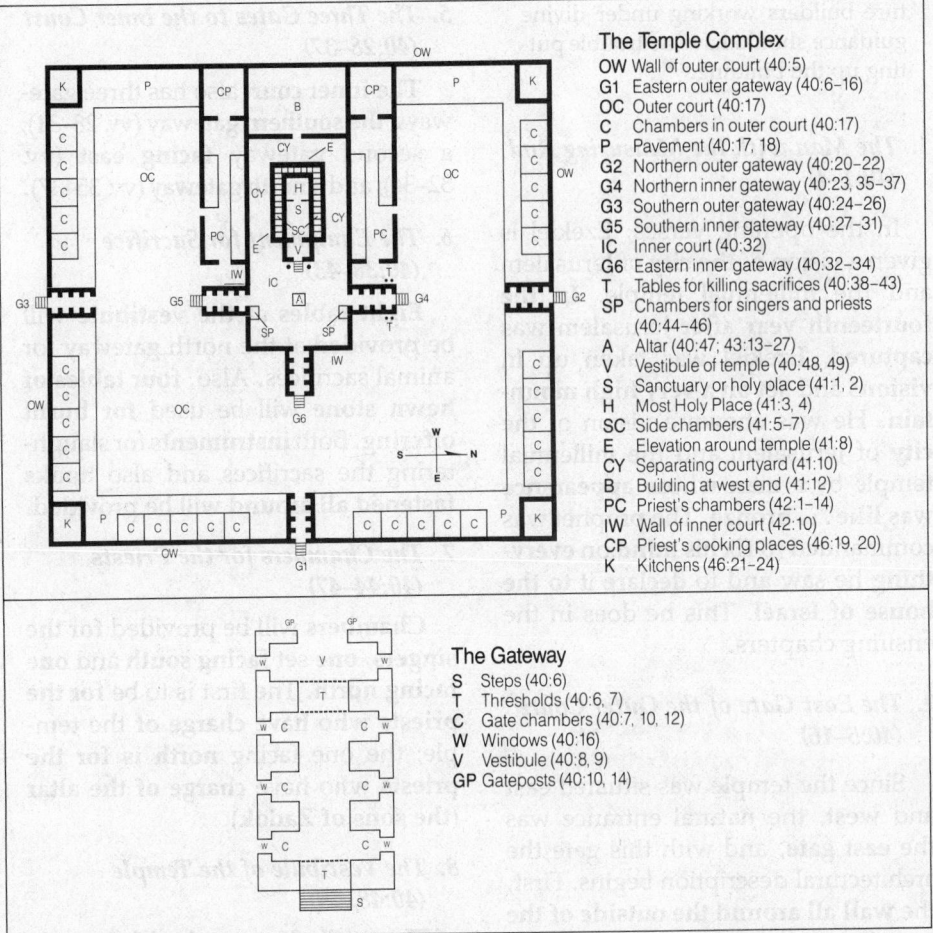

The Temple Complex

OW Wall of outer court (40:5)
G1 Eastern outer gateway (40:6–16)
OC Outer court (40:17)
C   Chambers in outer court (40:17)
P   Pavement (40:17, 18)
G2 Northern outer gateway (40:20–22)
G4 Northern inner gateway (40:23, 35–37)
G3 Southern outer gateway (40:24–26)
G5 Southern inner gateway (40:27–31)
IC Inner court (40:32)
G6 Eastern inner gateway (40:32–34)
T   Tables for killing sacrifices (40:38–43)
SP Chambers for singers and priests (40:44–46)
A   Altar (40:47; 43:13–27)
V   Vestibule of temple (40:48, 49)
S   Sanctuary or holy place (41:1, 2)
H   Most Holy Place (41:3, 4)
SC Side chambers (41:5–7)
E   Elevation around temple (41:8)
CY Separating courtyard (41:10)
B   Building at west end (41:12)
PC Priest's chambers (42:1–14)
IW Wall of inner court (42:10)
CP Priest's cooking places (46:19, 20)
K   Kitchens (46:21–24)

The Gateway

S   Steps (40:6)
T   Thresholds (40:6, 7)
C   Gate chambers (40:7, 10, 12)
W   Windows (40:16)
V   Vestibule (40:8, 9)
GP Gateposts (40:10, 14)

Ezekiel's Temple

V. MILLENNIAL SCENES (Chaps. 40—48)

A. The Millennial Temple in Jerusalem (Chaps. 40—42)

This and the two following chapters give the details of the temple which will be erected in Jerusalem. Many of the descriptions are admittedly difficult to understand, but the general outline can be seen. Paul Lee Tan writes:

Non-literal interpreters maintain that this prophecy is a symbol of the Christian church. However, this major prophecy in the Book of Ezekiel contains descriptions, specifications, and measurements of the millennial Temple which are so exhaustive that one may actually make a sketch of it, just as one might of Solomon's historic temple. In fact, F. Gardiner in Ellicott's *Commentary on the Whole Bible* succeeds in sketching the layout of the millennial Temple—all the while denying it is possible. This has prompted Alva J. McClain to comment that "if an uninspired commentator can make some sense out of the architectural plan, doubtless the future builders working under divine guidance should have no trouble putting up the building."[38]

1. The Man with the Measuring Rod (40:1–4)

In the opening verses, Ezekiel is given a vision of **the city** of Jerusalem and the millennial temple. **In the fourteenth year after** Jerusalem was **captured**, Ezekiel was taken up in **visions** and **set on a very high mountain**. He was shown a vision of **the city** of Jerusalem and the millennial temple by a **man whose appearance was like ... bronze**. The prophet was commanded to **fix** his **mind** on **everything** he saw and to **declare** it **to the house of Israel**. This he does in the ensuing chapters.

2. The East Gate of the Outer Court (40:5–16)

Since the temple was situated east and west, the natural entrance was the **east gate**, and with this gate the architectural description begins. First, the **wall all around the outside of the temple** is measured (v. 5). Then the **east ... gate** of this outer court is described (vv. 6–16).

3. The Outer Court (40:17–19)

Facing **the pavement**, which may well be a mosaic, as in 2 Chronicles 7:3 and Esther 1:6, there are to be **thirty chambers**.

4. The Other Two Gates of the Outer Court (40:20–27)

The **gateway facing north** is to be like the eastern one, with **its archways** and **its palm trees**. The **gateway facing south** had **the same measurements** and structure. There is no gateway facing west.

5. The Three Gates to the Inner Court (40:28–37)

The **inner court** also has three gateways: **the southern gateway** (vv. 28–31); a second gateway **facing east** (vv. 32–34); and a **north gateway** (vv. 35–37).

6. The Equipment for Sacrifice (40:38–43)

Eight tables at the **vestibule** will be provided at the north **gateway** for animal sacrifices. Also, **four tables of hewn stone** will be used **for burnt offering**. Both **instruments** for slaughtering the sacrifices and also **hooks fastened all around** will be provided.

7. The Chambers for the Priests (40:44–47)

Chambers will be provided **for the singers, one** set **facing south and one facing north**. The first is to be **for the priests who have charge of** the temple; the one facing **north is for the priests who have charge of the altar (the sons of Zadok)**.

8. The Vestibule of the Temple (40:48, 49)

The vestibule or porch **of the temple** seems to be planned like the one in Solomon's temple. The pillars remind us of the ones named Jachin and Boaz in that structure (1 Kgs. 7:21).

Chapter 40 deals primarily with the area surrounding the temple; chapter 41 describes the temple itself.

The detailed measurements in chapters 40—43 remind us that in all our service we must build according to God's specifications (see Ex. 25:40). Precise measurements also would seem to be meaningless unless this is to be a literal building. An allegory or type would scarcely be so architecturally precise. Also, no one has given a satisfactory explanation of the several parts if they are merely symbolic.

9. The Sanctuary and Most Holy Place (41:1–4)

The measurements of the sanctuary are to be the same as in Solomon's temple and twice as large as the tabernacle in the wilderness. The man with the appearance of bronze **brought** Ezekiel **into the sanctuary**, but he alone went into the **Most Holy Place**, reminding us of the ancient temple and tabernacle restrictions of entry (see Heb. 9:8, 12; 10:19). The same twofold division of the ancient temple apparently will be continued in the millennial temple.

10. The Side Chambers (41:5–11)

The temple will be very massive and spacious; it will have **three stories** with **thirty chambers in each story**. They will **increase** in size as one ascends, probably by going deeper into the main structure in stair-like fashion (v. 7).

11. A Building West of the Temple (41:12)

Facing the western end of the temple complex is a separate building **seventy** by **ninety cubits**. The purpose of this structure is not given.

12. The Measurements of the Temple (41:13–15a)

Ezekiel's guide to the temple **measured** it at **one hundred cubits long** and **one hundred cubits** wide.

13. The Interior Decoration and Furnishing of the Temple (41:15b–26)

The interior of the temple is to have **galleries** on both sides, **doorposts**, and **beveled window frames**.

Cherubim and **palm trees** will be the decorations, alternating **all around** the building. The cherubim, which speak of God's holiness (see Genesis 3), have **the face of a young lion toward** one **palm tree** and **the face of a man** toward the other **palm tree**. Palm trees are symbolic of victory and righteousness in Scripture.

The altar, which is to be made of **wood**, is called by Ezekiel's guide **"the table that is before the LORD."**

The temple is to have **two doors** of **two panels** each, also **carved** with **cherubim** and **palm trees**.

The vestibule outside will be covered with a **wooden canopy**.

No mention is made of any veil, ark, or high priest. The veil was split apart at Calvary. The symbolism of the ark is fulfilled in Christ. And He is there as Great High Priest.

14. The Priests' Quarters (42:1–14)

The priests will have quarters located both **north** and **south** of the temple. These areas will be where the priests will **eat the most holy offerings**, and in which they will keep their sacred **garments** for ministering.

15. The Measurements of the Outer Court (42:15–20)

The measurements of the outer court are to be **five hundred rods** on each of its four sides. The distinction between **holy** and **common** in verse 20 is the difference between what we might call *sacred* and *secular*. It is the difference between worship and the common affairs of everyday life.

B. The Millennial Worship (Chaps. 43, 44)

43:1–5 Earlier in the book of Ezekiel (11:23) we saw the glory cloud reluctantly leaving the temple at Jerusalem. But **the glory of the God of Israel** will return in the Person of the Lord Jesus when He comes to reign.

43:6–9 He **will dwell... forever
... in the midst of** His people; **no
more** will they practice spiritual **harlotry** (idolatry) and related **abominations** in the shadow of the temple.

43:10–12 When **the House of Israel**
is **ashamed of all that they have
done**, they will see the **pattern, design**, and **arrangement of the** new
temple. As soon as they repent, God
will give them new hope. (We should
also react in this way when someone
repents.) The people were to be told
that **the whole area surrounding the
mountaintop** on which **the temple**
would be built would be **most holy**.

A true sight of the glory of the
Lord makes us ashamed of our iniquities (v. 10):

'Tis the look that melted Peter,
'Tis that face that Stephen saw,
'Tis that heart that wept with Mary,
Can alone from idols draw.
                    —*Author unknown*

43:13–17 **The measurements of the
altar**, apparently like a terraced platform, are given next. The **altar hearth**
is the surface of the altar, where the
fire is built. It will have **four horns
extending upward from the hearth**.
An unusual feature of this altar is the
fact that it has **steps** leading up to it;
this was banned in the previous temples. This one will be so high that it
will need a way to mount up to the
top.

43:18–27 Next is given the ritual
to be followed in consecrating **the
altar** by blood. This will take **seven
days**, and its importance in Israel's
public worship can be seen in several
OT texts: Exodus 29:37; Leviticus
8:11, 15, 19, 33; 1 Kings 8:62-65; and
2 Chronicles 7:4-10. After all these
rites, **on the eighth day**, the regular
offerings will begin.

The chapter ends on an encouraging note: not only would God accept
the people's offerings, but, **"I will
accept you,"** says the Lord GOD.

Note that **the priests** in that day
will be the sons **of Zadok** (v. 19), an
honor probably stemming from Zadok's unwavering loyalty to David
and Solomon.

44:1–3 **The east... gate** of the
outer court must be permanently **shut**
because once **the LORD** returns to the
temple, He will never leave. Only **the
prince** could **sit** in **the vestibule** of
the **gate** and **eat** the sacrificial meal
there. Some think that the prince is
the Messiah Himself, others that he
is a descendant of David who will
serve as a vice-regent under Christ,
the King. However, F. W. Grant points
out that he cannot be the Messiah
because he has sons (46:16) and he
offers a sin offering for himself (45:22).[39]

44:4–9 When the Lord **brought**
Ezekiel **to the front of the temple**, the
prophet was awestruck by **the glory
of the LORD** as it **filled the house**.
Verse 4 should create a passionate
desire for worship meetings where
the glory of the Lord is so manifest
that the worshipers are prostrate before Him.

The Lord instructed him to pay
close attention to **the** new **ordinances
... concerning** the temple, its entrance
and exits (v. 5), and to warn the
people that the use of any **foreigner**
in the service of the temple must
cease (vv. 6–9).

44:10–16 Henceforth, the menial
work would be assigned to **the Levites**,
who had once fallen into idolatry.
Only **the sons of Zadok** could serve
as **priests**, drawing **near** and ministering to God. The sons of Zadok were
faithful in the times of trouble under
David (2 Sam. 15:24; 1 Kgs. 1:32 etc.;
2:26, 27, 35). The Levites might be

suspended from priestly service because of the curse on Eli's family or because of unfaithfulness during the times of the kings. We learn from all this that sin often has bitter consequences, and that faithfulness will be rewarded.

44:17–19 The priests would be required to wear **linen garments**, not woolen. The expression **"in their holy garments they shall not sanctify the people"** (v. 19b) refers to a ritual holiness reserved only for the service of the sanctuary and not for the priests' regular duties (Ex. 29:37; 30:29; Lev. 6:18, 27; Hag. 2:10–12).

44:20–22 Regulations are given concerning well-trimmed haircuts, restrictions on **wine**, and suitable marriages for the priests.

44:23, 24 The sons of Zadok would also serve as teachers and **judges**, making God's **people discern between** what is **holy** and **clean** on the one hand, and **unholy** and **unclean** on the other.

44:25–27 Their necessary contact with **a dead person** would require certain rituals of cleansing.

44:28–31 They will be supported by things **dedicated** to the Lord. The Lord wants to be their inheritance, and they will have nothing on earth. This is true for the servants of God today; He wants us to find our full satisfaction in Him, and thus be free to serve unhindered by worldly attachments. Like Paul we can learn to be content in every state (Phil. 4:11), but we do have to *learn* it because it does not come naturally to anyone. A broken man can say, "There is none upon earth that I desire besides You. . . . God is the strength of my heart and my portion forever" (Ps. 73:25, 26).

C. The Millennial Administration (Chaps. 45, 46)

45:1 In the center of **the land** of Israel, a piece of land will be set apart **for the LORD** as **a holy. . . district**. It will be **twenty-five thousand cubits by ten thousand**.

45:2–5 It will be divided into two strips. The top half will contain the **sanctuary**, and will also be for **the priests**. The lower half will be for **the Levites**.

45:6 At the bottom of the square will be a third strip, a common place, which will include **the city** of Jerusalem.

45:7, 8 All **the land** to **the east** and **west** of this square, as far as the boundaries of the land, will belong to **the prince**.

45:9–12 The **princes of Israel** are to **execute justice** in their dealings (v. 9), using **honest scales** and measures.

45:13–17 In these verses, **all the people** are required to **offer** a certain percentage of their crops to **the prince in Israel** in order to provide for the regular **offerings** and **appointed seasons**.

45:18–20 On the **first day** of **the first month**, **the sanctuary** is to be cleansed, and **on the seventh day of the** same **month**, the people are to be cleansed of sins committed **unintentionally or in ignorance**.

45:21–25 **The Passover** is to be kept **on the fourteenth day of the** first **month** and the Feast of Tabernacles on **the fifteenth day** of **the seventh month**.

No mention is made of the Feast of Pentecost, the Feast of Trumpets, or the Day of Atonement.

In the light of all these rituals and holy days how grateful we should be for the once-for-all substitutionary work of Christ on our behalf!

Millennial Sacrifices

In Ezekiel 43:20, 26; 45:15, 17 some of the offerings that will be presented during the Millennium are distinctly said to be for the purpose of making atonement. How can this be reconciled with Hebrews 10:12: "But this Man, after He had offered one sacrifice for sins forever, sat down at the right hand of God." Or Hebrews 10:18: "Now where there is remission of these, there is no longer an offering for sin?"

As used in the OT, the word "atonement" (lit., covering) never means the putting away of sins. Hebrews 10:4 reminds us that ". . . it is not possible that the blood of bulls and goats could take away sins." Rather the sacrifices were an annual reminder of sins (Heb. 10:3). What then did *atonement* mean? It meant that the sacrifices produced an outward, ceremonial cleanness. They conferred a ritual purification on people, enabling them to draw near as worshipers in fellowship with God. The sacrifices even made atonement for inanimate things, such as the altar (Ex. 29:37), where there could be no thought of remission of sins. All it means is that the altar was cleansed ceremonially and thus made fit for God's service.

When we read of the forgiveness of unintentional sin in connection with atonement (Lev. 4:20), it can only mean the removal of ceremonial defilement so that the person could draw near in worship.

In our day the word *atonement* has acquired a much wider and deeper meaning. It is used, for instance, to describe the entire sacrificial work of Christ by which our sins are put away and we are reconciled to God. But it never has this meaning in the Bible. (In Rom. 5:11 KJV, the word

atonement should be *reconciliation*,[40] as in NKJV and other versions.)

The sacrifices in Israel's history looked forward to the perfect and complete sacrifice of Christ. The sacrifices in the Millennium will commemorate His work on Calvary. They will be memorials for Israel just as the Lord's Supper is for us.

The passages in Hebrews do not rule out any sacrificial ceremony in the future. But they insist that no future sacrifices can ever deal effectively with sins, any more than they did in the past.‡

46:1–8 Verses 1–8 tell how **the prince** is to **stand** in **the east** gate **of the inner court** to **worship** when he brings **his . . . offerings** for the Feast of the Sabbath and of **the New Moon** (v. 6). He cannot enter the inner court. **The people** are to stand behind the prince and **worship** as **the priests** sacrifice. Neither the prince nor the people can enter the inner court.

In the Millennium, Israel will see Christ in the offerings, something the nation as a whole never did in the past.

46:9, 10 **The people** are to leave the outer court by **the opposite gate** to which they entered. They were to follow the movements of the prince.

46:11–18 In verses 11 and 12, the prince's freewill offerings are described; in verses 13–15, the daily sacrifices. Laws with respect to the prince's property prevent him from losing it permanently or from adding to it unjustly.

46:19–24 **Kitchens** are provided for the **priests** and for **the people**.

D. The Millennial Land (Chaps. 47, 48)

1. *The Healing of the Waters (47:1–12)*

Ezekiel saw in a vision a river **flowing** from the door **of the temple**, past **the altar**, through the wall south of the **east** Gate, and down to **the** Dead **Sea**. **The waters** of **the sea...** **will be healed**, and **fish** will abound in it. Yates writes:

> The water of life is a favorite figure in the Old Testament. Desert areas need water that life may be possible. This stream which Ezekiel sees flowing from the Temple makes its way toward the arid regions of the Arabah. In an ever deepening stream it goes on its way to bring life and health and abundant fruit wherever it goes. It is the one remedy that is needed. Jesus took that figure as a basis for his sermon to the woman at the well. (Cf. also Ps. 1:3; 46:4; Joel 3:18; Zech. 14:8; John 4:7–15; 7:38; Rev. 22:1, 2.)[41]

This stream (which will be an actual geographical river) is a striking figure of the blessing, widespread yet incomplete (v. 11), that will flow out during the Millennial Reign of Christ. God will dwell in the temple and therefore a stream of blessing, ever increasing, will go forth to other places. Today God does dwell in our bodies (1 Cor. 6:19) and therefore a stream of blessing should be flowing to others around us (John 7:37, 38). "If a man is filled with the Holy Spirit, and his life touches other lives, something happens for God." What a challenge for us to meet the conditions that will produce a blessing!

The river will bring life wherever it flows—a vivid picture of the life-giving ministry of the Holy Spirit.

2. The Boundaries of the Land (47:13–23)

47:13–20 The future **borders** and divisions of **the land** are next given. The boundaries are described here.

Ezekiel's mention of the Jordan River as a boundary of the land (v. 18)

cannot be a mistake; he certainly knew that the land would stretch east to the Euphrates (Gen. 15:18). Here he may be referring to a preliminary occupation of Palestine itself. Or he may be indicating that the Jordan formed only *part* of the eastern boundary, while the rest reached north-north-east as far as the Euphrates. The second explanation is less popular, but since Ezekiel's description is so detailed and does not mention the Euphrates at all, it merits consideration.

47:21–23 Within each tribal portion, the **land** will be divided **by lot**, **according to the tribes of Israel**, but **strangers** will not be excluded from **an inheritance**.

3. The Division of the Land (Chap. 48)

48:1–7 It seems that the **land** will be divided in horizontal strips, from the Mediterranean to the eastern boundary of the land. The northernmost strip will be **for** the tribe of **Dan** (v. 1). Then below that, **for Asher** (v. 2), **for Naphtali** (v. 3), **for Manasseh** (v. 4), **for Ephraim** (v. 5), **for Reuben** (v. 6), and **for Judah** (v. 7).

48:8–22 **South** of **Judah** will be the portion already assigned to the prince, and including **the sanctuary** and the city of Jerusalem. This **"holy district"** will be a large square area bordering on the northern part of the Dead Sea. It will be divided into three horizontal strips, the northernmost one belonging to the priests, and having the Millennial **temple in** its **center**. The middle strip will be for the Levites, and the southern strip for the common people, with Jerusalem in its center. The remaining territory east and west of the square will belong to **the prince**.

48:23–27 Then south of the holy

district will be **sections** for the tribes of **Benjamin** (v. 23), **Simeon** (v. 24), **Issachar** (v. 25), **Zebulun** (v. 26), and **Gad** (v. 27).

48:28–35 The city of New Jerusalem will have twelve **gates**, three on each **side**, one for each of the twelve tribes of Israel. Its **name** will be: *Jehovah Shammah*—**THE LORD IS THERE**.

This name reminds us of what was always in the heart of God: He loves His creatures so much that He always planned to have them close to Himself. He is ever searching, asking, "Where are you?", calling to repentance and faith. As Son of God He even came down to earth to die for us. His wish will be fulfilled: man will be close to His heart. We can engage in and participate in His search for the lost even now, while living close to His heart here on earth. This is God's desire for us.

We close our commentary on Ezekiel with a summary by the Hebrew Christian OT scholar, Charles L. Feinberg:

> This incomparable prophecy began with a vision of the glory of God and concludes with a description of the glory of the Lord in the glorified city of Jerusalem. Ezekiel concluded, as John in the Revelation, with God dwelling with man in holiness and glory. Beyond this there is no greater goal of history and God's dealings with man.[42]

ENDNOTES

[1](Intro) E.g., by Gleason Archer, in *A Survey of Old Testament Introduction*, under "Ezekiel."

[2](Intro) John B. Taylor, *Ezekiel: An Introduction and Commentary*, Tyndale Old Testament Commentaries, pp. 14–16.

[3](Intro) Albert Barnes, *The Bible Commentary, Proverbs-Ezekiel*, p. 302.

[4](1:4–28a) These four faces have traditionally been linked to the four portraits of our Lord in the Gospels: Matthew—the lion (Christ as King); Mark—the ox (Christ as servant); Luke—man (Christ as the perfect Man); John—eagle (Christ as Son of God). See NT volume of *BBC*, Introduction to the Gospels, p. 13.

[5](1:4–28a) The NKJV, following the Masoretic text, reads "When I came." The New Scofield note on this textual problem reads: "Obviously it was not Ezekiel who came to destroy the city of Jerusalem for her sins, but the LORD Himself. On the basis of the requirements of the context, the reading in some six manuscripts, the version of Theodotion and that of the Vulgate, the best reading is 'when He came to destroy the city.' A possible rendering, and perhaps preferable, would be to read the final letter of the disputed word as a well-known abbreviation for "LORD," thus giving us the reading 'when the LORD came to destroy the city.'" *The New Scofield Study Bible, New King James Version*, p. 995.

[6](1:28b—2:7) The NRSV paraphrases "son of man" as "mortal" to avoid the "masculine-oriented" words *son* and *man*; this obscures the link with Daniel and our Lord's usage.

[7](1:28b—2:7) Taylor, *Ezekiel*, p. 60.

[8](1:28b—2:7) *Ibid.*

[9](3:12–15) Kyle M. Yates, *Preaching from the Prophets*, p. 181.

[10](9:4) Charles Lee Feinberg, *The Prophecy of Ezekiel: The Glory of the Lord*, p. 56.

[11](9:4) *Ibid.*

[12](11:16–21) Yates, *Prophets*, p. 182.

[13](11:22–25) George Williams, *The Student's Commentary on the Holy Scriptures*, p. 579.

[14](13:1–3) Denis Lane, *The Cloud and the Silver Lining*, pp. 53–62.

[15](13:8–16) A. B. Davidson, *The Book of the Prophet Ezekiel*, p. 88.

[16](13:8–16) Our Lord calls the Pharisees by a similar (but worse!) name: "whitewashed tombs" (Matt. 23:27).

[17](16:44–52) Feinberg, *Ezekiel*, p. 91.

[18](17:22–24) Carl F. Keil, "Ezekiel," in *Biblical Commentary on the Old Testament*, XXI:244, 245.

[19](21:25–27) Matthew Henry, "Ezekiel," in *Matthew Henry's Commentary on the Whole Bible*, IV:878, 879.

[20](22:23, 24) Taylor, *Ezekiel*, pp. 168, 169.

[21](22:25–31) *Ibid.*, p. 169. This ancient Greek version sometimes preserves original Hebrew readings other than those in the traditional Hebrew (Masoretic) text. Footnotes to verses 24 and 25 in the NKJV give two examples, as well as readings from other ancient versions.

[22](23:5–10) A rival center of false worship persisted. The Samaritan woman seems to defend their "denominational difference" to our Lord in John 4:20.

[23](26:3–11) Nebuchadnezzar received this title because he had forced many other kings to submit to his rule.

[24](26:3–11) Feinberg, *Ezekiel*, p. 149.

[25](26:12–14) Quoted by W. M. Thomson in *The Land and the Book*, p. 155n.

[26](26:15–21) Peter Stoner, *Science Speaks*, p. 76.

[27](28:11–19) Feinberg, *Ezekiel*, pp. 161, 162.

[28](30:13–19) This is the well-known frontier city to which Jeremiah was taken after Governor Gedaliah's assassination (Jer. 43:7; cf. 44:1).

[29](34:1–6) Yates, *Preaching*, p. 183.

[30](34:11–16) D. L. Moody, *Notes from My Bible*, p. 90.

[31](34:11–16) One liberal Protestant "bishop" of Washington, D.C. in the 1950's blasphemed the God of the OT as a "bully."

[32](34:11–16) Taylor, *Ezekiel*, pp. 220, 221.

[33](34:17–24) David Baron, *The Shepherd of Israel*, pp. 8, 9.

[34](36:24–29a) Keil, "Ezekiel," p. 110.

[35](37:1–8) Yates, *Preaching*, p. 184.

[36](38:1–16) The KJV rendering, which makes the Hebrew *Rosh* an adjective meaning "chief" and modifying "prince," is based on the Latin Vulgate and the Targum, and is not accurate. Surprisingly, this translation was retained in the NIV, perhaps from a fear that people would see Russia in the word *Rosh*. However, taking Rosh as a proper name does not decide the issue as to which area the term will apply. It might refer to Russia, but then again it might not. Most historians and geographers identify Meshech and Tubal as areas in what is now central Turkey.

[37](39:1–6) S. Maxwell Coder, "That Bow and Arrow War," *Moody Monthly*, April 1974, p. 37.

[38](40:Intro) Paul Lee Tan, *The Interpretation of Prophecy*, p. 161.

[39](44:1–3) F. W. Grant, "Ezekiel," in *The Numerical Bible*, IV:273.

[40](Essay) In 1611 *atonement* was "at-one-ment" and *meant* "reconciliation." It was the correct translation in its time, but our language has changed a great deal since the 1600's.

[41](47:1–12) Yates, *Preaching*, p. 184.

[42](48:28–35) Feinberg, *Ezekiel*, p. 239.

BIBLIOGRAPHY

Alexander, Ralph. *Ezekiel*. Everyman's Bible Commentary. Chicago: Moody Press, 1976.

Davidson, A. B. *The Book of the Prophet Ezekiel*. The Cambridge Bible for Schools and Colleges. Cambridge: The University Press, 1900.

Feinberg, Charles Lee. *The Prophecy of Ezekiel: The Glory of the Lord*. Chicago: Moody Press, 1969.

Grant, F. W. "Ezekiel." In *Numerical Bible*. Vol. 4. Neptune, N.J.: Loizeaux Bros., 1977.

Henry, Matthew. "Ezekiel." In *Matthew Henry's Commentary on the Whole Bible*, Vol. IV. McLean, VA: MacDonald Publishing Company, n.d.

Keil, C. F. "Ezekiel." In *Biblical Commentary on the Old Testament*. Vols. 22, 23. Reprint. Grand Rapids:

Wm. B. Eerdmans Publishing Co., 1971.

Mills, Montague S. *Ezekiel: An Overview*. Dallas: 3E Ministries, n.d.

Tatford, Frederick A. *Dead Bones Live: An Exposition of the Prophecy of Ezekiel*. Eastbourne, East Sussex: Prophetic Witness Publishing House, 1977.

Taylor, John B. *Ezekiel: An Introduction and Commentary*. The Tyndale Old Testament Commentaries. Downers Grove, IL: InterVarsity Press, 1969.

DANIEL

Introduction

"I wish to stress . . . that none of the prophets has so clearly spoken concerning Christ as has this prophet Daniel. For not only did he assert that He would come, a prediction common to the other prophets as well, but also he set forth the very time at which He would come. Moreover he went through the various kings in order, stated the actual number of years involved, and announced beforehand the clearest signs of events to come."

—Jerome (A.D. 347–420)

I. Unique Place in the Canon

Daniel is one of the most fascinating and also among the most crucial books in the OT. Due no doubt to its precise predictions, messianic prophecies, and inspiring example of clean-cut separation from apostate world religion, Daniel has come under attacks from rationalist and unbelieving scholarship. No wonder that conservative Bible scholar Sir Robert Anderson titled one of his books *Daniel in the Critic's Den.*

The main thrust of the assault has been as to whether the book was actually written by a *prophet* named Daniel in the sixth century B.C., as conservative Jews and Christians have maintained, or by an unknown second century author writing *history* (especially chap. 11) *as though it were prophecy.*

II. Authorship

Since the traditional authorship of Daniel is so widely rejected and it is

very important for a believer to be well grounded in this great book, we give a fuller treatment here than for most other books.

The first salvo against the orthodox position that Daniel was a real prophet who was divinely endowed with detailed visions of Gentile world empires and the coming of the Messiah was fired in the third century A.D. by the anti-Christian philosopher, Porphyry.

His ideas were later taken up by a handful of Jews in the seventeenth century and then in Christendom in the eighteenth and following centuries. With the spread of rationalism these ideas were further expanded and accepted in liberal and semi-liberal circles.

Merrill F. Unger writes:

Modern criticism views the establishment of a Maccabean date (about 167 B.C.) and the rejection of the traditional Danielic authorship as one of its assured achievements. These views, however, are erected upon a series of highly plausible fallacies, and unsound assumptions.[1]

Before examining the main charges *against* Danielic authorship, let us note several positive evidences *for* this position.

1. Our Lord Jesus Christ specifically quotes the book as by Daniel (Matt. 24:15). This alone is proof enough for the devout Christian.
2. The book sparkles with the local color and customs of ancient Babylon and Medo-Persia, not Maccabean Palestine.
3. Jews and Christians have been edified and blessed for centuries by this book. While this is true of a number of uninspired writings, the Holy Spirit's powerful illumination of the book of Daniel scarcely comports with its being a forgery.
4. A manuscript of Daniel found in Qumran Cave 1 is believed to have been copied during or before the Maccabean era, which fact demands that the original has to be older yet.

The arguments against the authenticity of Daniel are threefold: linguistic, historical, and theological.

The linguistic argument is that Daniel could *not* have been written in the sixth century because the book contains Persian and even Greek words, and the Aramaic is alleged to be a variety from a later date.

Since, however, Daniel lived and served into the Medo-*Persian* period (530's B.C.) the presence of Persian words indicates quite the opposite of the liberal contention. The chances of a second century forger in Palestine knowing Persian are dim.

As to the *Greek* words, most Bible students are shocked when they find

out that there are only *three*—and all names for musical instruments! It is a well-known fact that the names of *objects* from a culture often go into another language long before there is heavy intercultural involvement. While the Greek *Empire* was still in the future when Daniel wrote, Greek culture and inventiveness were already spreading in the ancient world.

As to the *Aramaic*, Kitchen and Kutscher have demonstrated that it does indeed fit the Imperial Period of Daniel.

The historical arguments against the orthodox position on authorship include the contention that the Jews put Daniel in the third section of the OT ("The Writings") and not among the Prophets because that section of the canon was already closed when "Daniel" wrote. It is simpler to realize that Daniel was a prophet not by calling, but by ministry. By vocation he was a statesman. Hence, he was not put with the professional prophets —Isaiah, Jeremiah, etc.

Various alleged historical problems have been raised against the authenticity of Daniel—but all have intelligent answers by conservative scholars of undoubted integrity. For those who wish to pursue this, authors recommended, in chronological order, are: Robert Dick Wilson, Charles Boutflower, John F. Walvoord, R. K. Harrison, and Gleason Archer.

The theological argument against Daniel is that the book has too "advanced" views on angels, the life hereafter (resurrection), and the Messiah. This notion stems from applying the theory of evolution to religion. The *real* protest against Daniel, as a few liberal scholars, such as R. Pfeiffer (*Old Testament Introduction*, p. 755), are honest enough to admit, is prejudice against the supernatural. There are too many miracles, too much precise prediction in Daniel to suit rationalistic criticism. Just as Daniel the prophet escaped unscathed from the lions' den, so does Daniel the prophecy escape from the "critics' den" in the minds and hearts of intelligent believers.

III. Date

Scholars range all the way from the sixth century to the second century B.C. in dating Daniel. Liberals and their admirers nearly all date the book in its present form as being from the Maccabean era. They generally view it as an attempt to encourage the Jews during the horrible anti-Semitic excesses of Antiochus Epiphanes.

Those who believe that God can inspire not only general prophecies of kingdoms not as yet well-known (Greece and Rome) but also minute details of the Grecian period several centuries before they happen (chap. 11), have no trouble accepting the conservative teaching that Daniel wrote his prophecy in the sixth century, probably about 530 B.C.

Even with their "late" date, as Unger points out, the critics have not escaped God's omniscient insight into the future:

It must be remembered that even if the latest date assigned to the composition of the book of Daniel were proved correct, the prophecy yet displays a knowledge of the future which can only be ascribed to divine inspiration.[2]

IV. Background and Theme

Accepting then the orthodox view of authorship and date, we believe

Daniel was one of the intelligent and attractive young Jewish captives carried off to Babylon by Nebuchadnezzar when Jehoiakim was king of Judah (about 604 B.C.). His name means "God is my Judge." His character and behavior show that he lived in the light of that fact.

As to office, Daniel was a statesman high up in the administration of Nebuchadnezzar's and Belshazzar's courts. When Medo-Persia conquered Babylon, Daniel was made the first of three presidents under Darius. He also served under Cyrus. As noted, this is probably why the Hebrew OT has Daniel in the section known as "The Writings," and not with "The Prophets," as in English.

Daniel's *ministry*, however, was that of a prophet, and our Lord so labeled him (Matt. 24:15 and Mark 13:14). Daniel is not unlike those who hold a "secular" job and still give much time to Bible study and preaching. For example, Sir Robert Anderson, himself a scholar of Daniel's prophecy, headed up Scotland Yard's Criminal Investigation Division in the late Victorian era, and yet had a widely blessed biblical ministry.[3]

Since so much of the book has to do with Gentile world powers, it should not surprise us that Daniel 2:4 through chapter 7 is in Aramaic. This is a Gentile tongue related to Hebrew but widely used in international communication in Daniel's time in much the same way that English is today. Some scholars outline Daniel's prophecy by these changes in language.

As to context, Daniel's first six chapters are largely *narrative* with prophetic themes subordinated. The last six chapters are largely *prophetic* with narrative subordinated.

OUTLINE

Commentary

I. THE STEADFAST FIDELITY OF DANIEL AND HIS COMPANIONS (Chap. 1)

1:1–7 The scene is the court of **Nebuchadnezzar** in **Babylon** following his attack on **Jerusalem** in **the third year of** Jehoiakim's **reign**. Nebu-chadnezzar ordered several Jewish **young men** to be prepared **to serve** him as **men** of **wisdom** and **knowl-edge**. Among these were **Daniel, Hananiah, Mishael, and Azariah**. Their Chaldean **names** were **Belte-shazzar, Shadrach, Meshach,** and **Abed-Nego**. As part of their preparation, they were to eat of **the king's delicacies** and drink of his **wine**. These foods probably included meats that were unclean, according to the OT law, or perhaps they were connected with idol worship.

There is a seeming discrepancy between verse 1 and Jeremiah 25:1. Here Nebuchadnezzar is said to have besieged **Jerusalem in the third year** of Jehoiakim's **reign**. The Jeremiah passage says that the fourth year of Jehoiakim was the first year of Nebuchadnezzar. This may be explained by the difference between Jewish and Babylonian reckoning.

1:8–12 **Daniel** nobly refused to eat them. He asked if he and his friends could eat **vegetables** and **drink . . . water** instead. Ashpenaz, **the chief of the eunuchs** (not understanding Jewish customs nor their God), was horrified at this idea, noting that his own **head** would be endangered if the plan didn't work! After all, he was responsible for them.

1:13–21 Daniel's request was nonetheless granted. At the end of the probationary period of **ten days**, they stood **before . . . the king** and proved to be **ten times better than all** the wise men of Babylon. They were therefore accepted by the king. **God** graciously gifted **them** with **knowledge and skill in all literature and wisdom**, and to **Daniel** he granted **understanding in all visions and dreams**.

II. NEBUCHADNEZZAR'S VISION OF THE IMAGE MADE OF FOUR METALS (Chap. 2)

2:1–13 **Nebuchadnezzar had a dream** for which he demanded not merely the interpretation, but the contents of the dream itself—a much harder demand, not to say impossi-

ble. His own wise men, **the Chaldeans**, were not able to tell him **the dream** or its meaning, so he made the sweeping **decision** that **all** the wise men (including **Daniel and his companions**) should be destroyed!

2:14–30 In answer to prayer, **Daniel** learned from the Lord **in a night vision** the nature of the **dream** and **the interpretation** of it. In thanks Daniel **blessed the God of heaven** with a beautiful prayer of praise. Then he **went to Arioch** to prevent further killing **of the wise men of Babylon**. Brought by **Arioch** into **the presence of the king**, Daniel revealed the source of his divinely revealed **secret**.

2:31–35 Daniel made known that the **king** had seen **a great image**, both splendid and **awesome. This image's head was of fine gold, its chest and arms of silver, its belly and thighs of bronze, its legs of iron, its feet partly of iron and partly of clay.** Nebuchadnezzar **watched while a stone . . . cut out without hands** destroyed **the image** and **became a great mountain**, filling **the whole earth**.

2:36–45 The image represented the four Gentile powers that would exercise world dominion, ruling over the Jewish people. Nebuchadnezzar, an absolute monarch (Babylon), was the **head of gold** (v. 38). Persia was the arms of silver, one arm representing Media and the other Persia. Greece, the **third kingdom**, was **the belly and thighs of bronze**. The Roman Empire was the two legs and feet of **iron**, the legs representing the eastern and western wings of the **kingdom. The feet** of **iron** and baked **clay** depict the revived Roman Empire, the toes representing ten kingdoms. Note the decreasing value of the metals and the increasing strength (except in the feet of iron and clay). Note also that man pictures his empires as valuable metals whereas God pictures those same kingdoms as wild beasts (chap. 7). The Lord Jesus is the **stone . . . cut out . . . without hands**. He will destroy the four kingdoms and rule over the whole earth, his **kingdom** standing **forever**.

2:46–49 When **King Nebuchadnezzar** heard Daniel's wisdom, **he made him ruler over the whole province of Babylon, and chief administrator over all the wise men of Babylon**. The three other Jewish youths were made deputies or assistants.

III. NEBUCHADNEZZAR'S GOLDEN IDOL AND THE FIERY FURNACE (Chap. 3)

3:1–7 Nebuchadnezzar . . . **made** an idolatrous **image of gold** ninety feet high **and set it up in the plain of Dura**. He then commanded that when they heard **horn, flute, harp, lyre, and psaltery, in symphony with all kinds of music**, all men were to **fall down** to **worship** it. Any who refused would **be cast . . . into** a **fiery furnace**.

3:8–12 Shadrach, Meshach, and Abed-Nego, as faithful Jews, refused to worship the idol and were reported by certain Chaldeans to the king.

3:13–21 He gave them a chance to change their minds, but they would not. Their confidence in deliverance was magnificent. But even "if not," they would still be true to the Lord. So the king ordered the fiery furnace heated seven times hotter than usual, and then commanded that the three Jews be thrown into it fully clothed.

3:22–25 The **furnace** was so **hot** that the **men** who threw them in were killed, but when the astonished **Nebuchadnezzar** looked into the furnace, he saw **four** men—the **three**

Jews and a **fourth** whose **form** was **like the Son of God** (NKJV) or *a son of the gods* (NKJV marg.). We believe that it was indeed **the Son of God**, no matter how the king viewed Him. The Lord either saves us out of troubles or He is with us in the troubles.

3:26–30 The Jews were unharmed. **The fire** had burned only the cords that bound them. Afflictions succeed in accomplishing God's purposes and setting us free from the things that bind us. **The king** was so impressed that he forbade anyone to speak **against the God of** the Jews and **promoted** the three young men **in the province of Babylon**. All this in spite of the fact that they had **frustrated** his **word**!

IV. NEBUCHADNEZZAR'S DREAM OF THE RUINED TREE AND ITS MEANING (Chap. 4)

4:1–9 Here **Nebuchadnezzar the king** witnesses to the greatness of **the Most High God** and to an experience in his life which led to his conversion (vv. 1–3). He had **a dream** which his own **wise men** were unable to interpret, so he sent for **Daniel** and **told** him **the dream**.

4:10–15b He had seen **a tree**, high, beautiful, and fruitful. **The tree . . . reached to the heavens** and spread out **to the ends of all the earth**. **A watcher, a holy one coming down from heaven**, ordered **the tree** to be chopped **down**, leaving only a **stump and roots in the** ground.

4:15c–18 Then the holy one described **a man** losing his senses and becoming like **a wild beast** of the earth for **seven** years.

4:19–26 Daniel told the king that **the tree** represented him and his worldwide empire. He would lose his throne, and he would become insane for **seven** years, living like an animal in **the field**. (The medical name for his condition is boanthropy.[4]) But **the stump** signified that Nebuchadnezzar would not be destroyed but would be restored.

4:27–37 Daniel also counseled the king to change his ways. However, after **twelve months** of impenitence on the king's part, the vision came to pass. For **seven** years he lived like a beast. **At the end of** that **time**, he turned to God and acknowledged that He is **the Most High . . . who lives forever**. He was then **restored to the glory of** his **kingdom**.

V. BELSHAZZAR'S DOOM ANNOUNCED BY THE HANDWRITING ON THE WALL (Chap. 5)

5:1–4 **Belshazzar** was the son of Nabonidus and the grandson of **Nebuchadnezzar** ("father" in v. 2 may also mean "grandfather"). He **made a great feast**, using the sacred **gold and silver vessels which . . . Nebuchadnezzar had** stolen **from the temple . . . in Jerusalem** for an idolatrous carnival. The king and his entourage drank themselves drunk on wine, and **praised the gods of gold and silver, bronze and iron, wood and stone**.

5:5–9 While he and his lords became drunken and riotous, **the fingers of a man's hand appeared**, writing **on the . . . wall**. The terrified king offered a **purple** robe, a **chain of gold**, and promotion to be one of three rulers (probably with Nabonidus and Belshazzar), to anyone who could interpret the writing.

5:10–16 At the queen's suggestion, **Daniel** was summoned to interpret the **writing**.[5] Even after all these

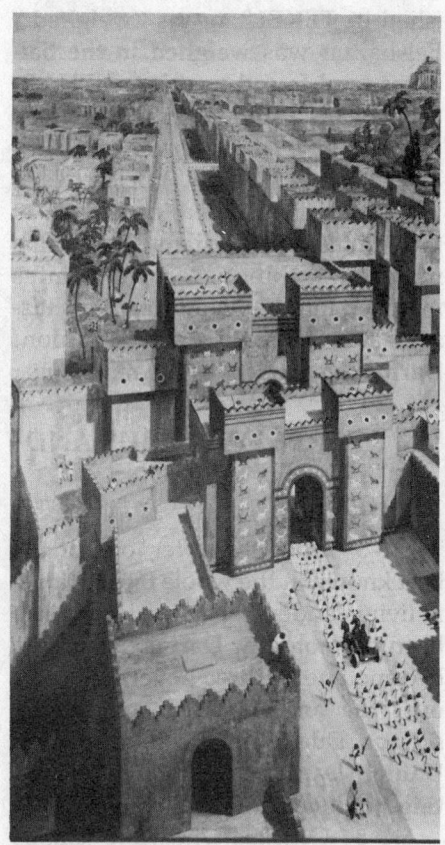

Ishtar Gate. A procession moves along Marduk's Way and enters Nebuchadnezzar's palace through the massive Ishtar Gate in this painting by Maurice Bardin. The famous hanging gardens are pictured in the upper righthand corner, and the city's Ziggurat appears behind them.

years and the changes in government, the **excellent wisdom** and spirituality of Daniel were remembered at least by someone. So **Daniel was brought in before the king**.

5:17–24 After reviewing the experience of **Nebuchadnezzar** and boldly rebuking **Belshazzar** for desecrating **the vessels** of the temple by using them in a drunken, idolatrous feast, Daniel proceeded to reveal the **writing** and its meaning.

5:25–31 The writing was **MENE, MENE, TEKEL, UPHARSIN. MENE** means "numbered." **God** had **numbered** the Babylonian Empire **and fin-**

ished it. **TEKEL**[6] means **"weighed."**
Belshazzar was **weighed in the balances, and found wanting**. **UPHARSIN** means **"divided"** or divisions.
(PHARSIN is the plural of **PERES**.
The **"U"** means "and.") Belshazzar's
kingdom was **divided, and given to
the Medes and Persians**. **That** same
night, the Medo-Persian armies
marched into Babylon, slew **Belshazzar**, and seized world dominion.
Darius the Mede was the new king.

VI. DECREE OF DARIUS AND THE DEN OF LIONS (Chap. 6)

6:1–3 In this chapter, one of the
best known in the whole Bible, Daniel
is living under Persian rule. He has
been promoted by **Darius** the king to
become **one** of **three governors** to be
over the **one hundred and twenty
satraps**. Due to the **excellent spirit** in
Daniel, Darius **gave thought to setting him over the whole realm**.

6:4–8 Officials who were jealous
of **Daniel** and who knew that they
would never **find** him guilty of any
real crime persuaded the **king** to pass
a law forbidding prayer to anyone but
Darius **for thirty days**. Once the **decree**
became **law**, it could not **be changed**.
Daniel's steadfastness is a challenge
to us (1 Pet. 3:13–17).

6:9–13 **King Darius signed the
written decree**, but **Daniel** continued
to pray to **God . . . three times** daily,
and his enemies quickly reported him
to **the king**.[7]

6:14–17 Darius **labored till** sunset to free **Daniel**, but the **decree** was
unalterable, so he was compelled to
have Daniel **cast . . . into the den of
lions**. Nevertheless, this pagan king
encouraged Daniel that the God whom
Daniel served **continually** would
deliver him. It is beautiful to see how

even unbelievers will sometimes pick
up on the faith and morals of consistent believers whom they observe at
close hand. Only too often Christians
fail their unsaved friends and relatives by *not* having as high standards
of faith and practice as the world
expects from God's people.

6:18–28 Rejecting his usual nightly
entertainment, Darius **spent the night
fasting**. **Very early in the morning**,
the worried **king . . . went in haste to
the den** and found the Jewish prophet
unharmed by **the lions**.

In typical fashion the devout
prophet gave the Lord the glory: **"My
God sent His angel and shut the
lions' mouths, so that they have not
hurt me."**

Then Daniel's accusers were **cast**
to the **lions** and devoured. The result
of all this was that **King Darius** issued a decree **to all peoples, nations,
and languages** honoring **the God of
Daniel**.

VII. DANIEL'S DREAM OF FOUR BEASTS DEPICTING FOUR WORLD EMPIRES (Chap. 7)

The first six chapters of Daniel are
mainly historical; the last six are
prophetical. Daniel's **dream and
visions** in chapters 7 and 8 occurred
during the reign of Belshazzar, king
of Babylon, before the Medes and
Persians rose to power.

7:1–4 In chapter 7, we have
Daniel's vision of **four great beasts**
coming **up from the sea**. (The **Great
Sea** is the Mediterranean.) These represent the four world empires.

The **lion** represents *Babylon*. The
eagle's wings suggest swiftness of
conquest.[8] **The wings . . . plucked** may
refer to Nebuchadnezzar's insanity,
and the rest of verse 4 to his recovery
and conversion.

7:5 The **bear** pictures *Medo-Persia*. The Persian section was raised up to greater importance than the Median. The **three ribs** which it held **in its mouth** perhaps represent the three sections of the Babylonian Empire which were sacked by the Medes and Persians under Cyrus—Babylon in the east; Egypt in the south; and the Lydian kingdom in Asia Minor.

7:6 The **leopard** is a type of *Greece*. Its **four wings of a bird** speak of the rapid expansion of the Grecian Empire. **Four** is the number of the world. **Wings** speak of speed. Within thirteen years Alexander conquered the world, marching as far east as India. Then he died at thirty-three—empty handed. The leopard's **four heads** apparently set forth the division of the empire to four of Alexander's generals after his death.

7:7, 8 The **fourth beast**, powerful and destructive, was different from the others but had some of their bestial characteristics. It is described as **dreadful and terrible, exceedingly strong**, with **huge iron teeth**. It speaks of the *Roman Empire*, which would follow the Grecian Empire, would cease, and then, after a considerable space of time, would be revived. It is in this revived form that it would have **ten horns**, that is, ten kings, and a **little . . . horn**, i.e., the future head of the Revived Roman Empire— the Antichrist.

7:9–14 In verse 9, Daniel pictures the fifth and final world empire—the glorious kingdom of the Lord Jesus Christ; He will be given universal dominion. The description of **the Ancient of Days** here resembles that of Christ in Revelation 1. But this identification is somewhat obscured in verse 13 by **One like the Son of Man coming** before **the Ancient of Days**. Then it would read as if Christ were coming

before Himself. Perhaps it is best to think of **the Ancient of Days** here as being God the Father. **One like the Son of Man** would then be the Lord Jesus, coming before the Father to be invested with the kingdom.

The Ancient of Days sits as a Judge in **court** (vv. 10, 26). The little **horn** and his empire are **destroyed** (v. 11). The other world empires also cease, but the nations and people continue (v. 12). The Lord Jesus is **given** universal **dominion, a kingdom, the one which shall** never **be** superseded (v. 14).

7:15–18 When **Daniel** expressed anxious perplexity, an unidentified interpreter explained that the **four . . . great beasts** represented **four** world rulers who would **arise out of the earth**, but who would be succeeded by **the kingdom** of **the Most High** and of His **saints**. Whereas this world's kingdoms will all pass away, **the saints of the Most High** will have an everlasting **kingdom**. In verse 3 the beasts come out of the sea, which usually typifies the Gentile nations. Here in verse 17 they come **out of the earth**; this refers to their moral outlook as being earthbound and their character as being nonspiritual.

7:19–22 Daniel made special inquiry concerning **the fourth beast** which surpassed the others in cruelty and ferocity. He also wanted **to know** about **the ten horns and the other horn before which three fell**. He saw the little **horn . . . making war** with **the saints** of the Tribulation Period **until the Ancient of Days came**, ended their sufferings, and gave them **the kingdom**.

7:23–28 The unnamed interpreter explained **the fourth beast, the ten horns**, and the **pompous** little horn. The latter will blaspheme **the Most High, persecute the saints**, and **in-**

tend to change the Jewish calendar for three and a half years. (This is the Great Tribulation referred to by the Lord Jesus in Matt. 24:21.) But he will be stripped of his power and the glorious, **everlasting kingdom** of our Lord will be ushered in. Daniel responded with alarm and wonderment.

VIII. DANIEL'S VISION OF THE RAM AND GOAT NATIONS (Chap. 8)

8:1–4 Two years later **Daniel** had **a vision** of **a ram** and a male goat. The **ram** was Persia, and the **two horns** the kings of Media and Persia. **One** horn **was higher than the other**, the Persian king being the more powerful. **The ram** was on a rampage of conquest, **westward, northward, and southward**. Seemingly he was irresistible.

8:5–8 Then **a male goat** (Greece) **came from the west** on a blitzkrieg. It **had** one conspicuous **horn** (Alexander the Great). **The goat** defeated **the ram** and went on to tremendous conquests. When Alexander died, his kingdom was divided into **four** parts, depicted by the **four notable** horns which **came up toward the four winds of heaven**.

8:9–14 **One of** these was later ruled by **a little horn** (Antiochus Epiphanes), whose military success took him **south**, **east**, and into Palestine (**the Glorious Land**). Verse 10 describes his persecution of the Jews.[9] He blasphemed the Lord, caused the **sacrifices** to cease in Jerusalem, and desecrated the temple (vv. 11, 12). Daniel learned that this desecration would continue **two thousand three hundred** days. This took place between 171 B.C. and 165 B.C.

8:15–17 **Gabriel** was ordered to explain **the vision** to **Daniel**.

8:18–26 Daniel, although a godly and courageous man, was so overcome by fear in the angel's presence that he fell on his **face** into **a deep sleep**. Perhaps this is to emphasize God's power and holiness which is felt even in the presence of His angels. The explanation of the vision begins in verses 19–22, but at verse 23 we seem to see beyond Antiochus Epiphanes to his future counterpart—a **king** with **fierce features** who will ruthlessly persecute **the holy people** in the Tribulation Period. He will be **cunning**, proud, and deceitful, and **even rise against the Prince of princes** (the Lord Jesus Christ), but he will be destroyed by divine intervention. Daniel **was told** that **the vision** referred to the **future**.

8:27 Daniel became ill **for days**, **astonished** and perplexed.

IX. DANIEL'S VISION OF THE SEVENTY WEEKS OF GENTILE SUPREMACY (Chap. 9)

9:1, 2 This chapter takes place during the reign **of Darius** the Mede. By studying the book of **Jeremiah**, Daniel realized that the **seventy years** of captivity were almost at an end.

9:3–19 He confessed his **sins** and the **sins** of his people (he used the word **our**) and asked the Lord to fulfill His promises concerning **Jerusalem** and the people **of Judah**. In answer to his prayers God granted the prophet the very important revelation of the "seventy weeks," which has been called "the backbone of Bible prophecy."

Daniel's petitions were based on the character of God (His greatness, awesomeness, faithfulness, **righteousness,** forgiveness, **mercies**) and on His interests (**Your people, Your city, Your holy mountain, Your sanctuary**).

9:20–23 While he was . . . **praying, Gabriel, being caused to fly swiftly, reached** Daniel **about the time of the evening sacrifice**. He told him that he was **greatly beloved**, a tremendous tribute, coming as it did from God Himself. He then gave him an outline of the future history of the Jewish nation under the figure of seventy weeks. Each "week"[10] represents seven years. Since the prophecy is so crucial to understanding God's program, we will examine it phrase by phrase.

9:24 Seventy weeks have been decreed **for your people** (Israel) **and for your holy city** (Jerusalem). The historical fulfillment of the first part of the prophecy shows that the weeks are weeks of years. Thus seventy weeks equal 490 years. We will see that the seventy weeks are divided into seven weeks plus sixty-two weeks, and then, after a time gap, one final week. At the end of these **seventy weeks**, the following six things will happen:

To finish the transgression, to make an end of sins. While this may refer in a general sense to all Israel's sinful ways, it has special reference to the nation's rejection of the Messiah. At the Second Advent of Christ, a remnant will turn to Him in faith and the nation's **transgression** and **sins** will be forgiven.

To make reconciliation for iniquity. The basis for **reconciliation** was laid at Calvary, but this refers to the time, still future, when the believing portion of the nation of Israel will come into the benefit and enjoyment of the finished work of Christ.

To bring in everlasting righteousness. This, too, points forward to the

Second Advent and the Millennium, when the King will reign in **righteousness**. It is **everlasting righteousness** in the sense that it will continue on into the eternal state.

To seal up vision and prophecy. The main body of OT **prophecy** centers on the glorious return of Christ to earth, and His subsequent kingdom. Therefore, the bulk of prophecies will be fulfilled at the end of the seventy weeks.

And to anoint the Most Holy Place. At the beginning of the thousand-year reign, the temple described in Ezekiel 40–44 will be anointed or consecrated in Jerusalem. The glory will return in the Person of the Lord (Ezek. 43:1–5).

9:25 So you are to **know and understand that from the** issuing of **the command to restore and** rebuild **Jerusalem**. This was the decree of Artaxerxes in 445 B.C. (Neh. 2:1–8).

Until Messiah the Prince. This refers not merely to the First Advent of Christ, but more particularly to His death (see v. 26a).

There shall be seven weeks (forty-nine years) **and sixty-two weeks** (434 years). The sixty-nine weeks are divided into two periods, **seven weeks** and **sixty-two weeks**.

The city **shall be built again,** with plaza and moat, **even in troublesome times**. Jerusalem would be rebuilt (during the first seven weeks) with public square and protective channel, but not without opposition and turmoil.

9:26 Then **after the sixty-two weeks**—that is, **after the sixty-two** week portion of time, which is really at the end of the sixty-ninth week, **The Messiah shall be cut off**. Here we have an unmistakable reference to the Savior's death on the cross.

A century ago in his book *The*

Coming Prince, Sir Robert Anderson gave detailed calculations of the sixty-nine weeks, using "prophetic years," allowing for leap years, errors in the calendar, the change from B.C. to A.D., etc., and figured that the sixty-nine weeks ended on the very day of Jesus' triumphal entry into Jerusalem, five days before his death.[11]

But not for Himself, or literally *and have nothing*. This may mean that He had received nothing from the nation of Israel, to which He had come. Or it may mean that He died without apparent posterity (Isa. 53:8). Or it may be a general statement of His utter poverty; He left nothing but the clothes that He wore.

And the people of the prince who is to come. This **prince who is to come** is the head of the revived Roman Empire, identified by some as the Antichrist. He will come to power during the Tribulation. His **people**, of course, are the Romans.

Shall destroy the city and the sanctuary. The Romans, under Titus, destroyed Jerusalem and its magnificent gold-trimmed white marble temple in A.D. 70.

The end of it shall be with a flood. The city was leveled as if by a flood. Not one stone of the temple, for instance, was left on another. Titus forbade his soldiers to put Herod's temple to the torch, but in order to get the gold they disobeyed, thus melting down the gold. To retrieve the melted gold successfully from between the stones they had to pry loose the great stones, thus fulfilling Christ's words in Matthew 24:1, 2, as well as Daniel's prophecy.

And till the end of the war desolations are determined. From that time on, the history of the city would be one of war and destruction. **The end** here means the end of the times of the Gentiles.

9:27 We now come to the seventieth week. As mentioned previously, there is a time gap between the sixty-ninth and seventieth weeks. This parenthetical period is the Church Age, which extends from Pentecost to the Rapture. It is never mentioned specifically in the OT; it was a secret hidden in God from the foundation of the world but revealed by the apostles and prophets of the NT period. However, the principle of a gap is nicely illustrated by our Lord in the synagogue at Nazareth (Luke 4:18, 19). Jesus quoted Isaiah 61:1, 2a but cut it short at "the acceptable year of the LORD" (His First Advent), and left off the judgment of His Second Advent: "and the day of vengeance of our God" (Isa. 61:2b). In between was to occur the whole Church Age.

Then he (the Roman prince) **shall confirm a covenant with many** (the unbelieving majority of the nation of Israel) **for one week** (the seven-year Tribulation Period). It may be a friendship treaty, a non-aggression treaty, or a guarantee of military assistance against any nation attacking Israel.

But in the middle of the week he shall bring an end to sacrifice and offering. The Roman prince will turn hostile toward Israel, forbidding further sacrifices and offerings to Jehovah.

And on the wing of abominations. We learn from Matthew 24:15 that he will set up an abominable idolatrous image in the temple and presumably he will command that it be worshiped. Some think that **wing** here refers to a wing of the temple.

Shall be one who makes desolate. He will persecute and destroy those who refuse to worship the image.

Even until the consummation, which is determined, is poured out on the desolate. Terrible persecution of the Jews will continue for the last half of the seventieth week, a period known as the Great Tribulation. Then the Roman prince, "the **one who makes desolate**," will himself be destroyed, as decreed by God, by being cast into the lake of fire (Rev. 19:20).

X. VISION OF GOD'S GLORY INTRODUCING OUTLINE OF COMING EVENTS (Chap. 10)

10:1–9 The events of this chapter took place **in the third year of Cyrus, king of Persia**. Some captives had already gone back to Jerusalem, as permitted by Cyrus's decree, but **Daniel** had remained in exile. After **mourning** for **three weeks**, perhaps because of discouraging reports from those who had returned (the work on the temple had stopped), because of the poor spiritual condition of those still in exile, or because he wanted to know the future of his people, Daniel was standing **by the** banks **of the Tigris** (Heb., *Hiddekel*). There he **saw** a **vision** of a glorious **man clothed in linen**. This description resembles that of the Lord Jesus in Revelation 1:13–16.

10:10–14 Then a voice explained why Daniel's prayers had been delayed. **The prince of the kingdom of Persia** had opposed for **twenty-one days**. Who is this **prince** (or ruler) who **withstood** the answering of Daniel's prayer for so long? Since **Michael** the archangel and protector of Israel is called into the fray, it must be an evil angelic power, one stronger than a merely human "prince." Leon Wood, in his excellent commentary on Daniel, explains:

Because Greece also would have a similar "prince" assigned to her in due time (cf. v. 20), and God's people would be under Greece's jurisdiction following Persia's fall to Greece, the suggestion seems reasonable that Satan often assigns special emissaries to influence

governments against the people of God. Certainly this chapter has much to contribute regarding the nature of struggles between the higher powers in reference to God's program on earth (cf. Eph. 6:11, 12).[12]

But how could the Prince of Persia successfully resist the Lord for twenty-one days, and why would the omnipotent Lord need the help of Michael (v. 13)?[13] One suggestion is that "the certain man" in verses 5 and 6 is *not* the Lord but an angelic being, perhaps Gabriel.

In either case, the voice explained why Daniel's prayers had been hindered; as already mentioned, **the prince of the kingdom of Persia** was responsible. The voice also promised to reveal the things which would **happen to** Daniel's **people**, the Jews, **in the latter days**. This is done in chapters 11 and 12.

10:15–19 There is a question whether the voice was that of the man in linen or the voice of an angelic messenger. Daniel **became** weak and **speechless** by this experience, but was **strengthened** by one with human appearance.

10:20, 21 Then this one whom Daniel addressed as "my lord" **said** that he **must** first **fight with the prince of Persia**, then encounter **the prince of Greece**. He would reveal further to Daniel what is written in **the Scripture of Truth**. **Michael, "your"** (Daniel's and his people's) **prince**, was the only one who stood firmly with him in these battles.

XI. PROPHECIES OF THE IMMEDIATE FUTURE (11:1–35)

A. Greece's Conquest of Medo-Persia (11:1–3)

Though still in the future when written, verses 1–35 are now past history. Verses 36 to 45 are still future. The **him** in verse 1 may refer to Michael, mentioned in the preceding verse, or **Darius**. Verse 2 tells of the power of four **kings** of Persia and the opposition of the last one to **Greece**. The four **kings** were Cambyses, Pseudo-Smerdis, Darius I (Hystaspes), and Xerxes I (Ahasuerus). Alexander the Great was the **mighty king** who wrested world power from Persia to Greece.

B. The Decay of the Grecian Empire (11:4–35)

1. The Wars Between Egypt and Syria (11:4–20)

11:4 When Alexander died, **his kingdom** was **divided** into **four** parts

—Egypt, Syria-Babylon, Asia Minor, and Greece. The ruler of Egypt was the king of the south, while the ruler of Syria-Babylon was the king of the north. Not one of Alexander's successors was from **among his posterity,** but rather they were his generals.

11:5, 6 Verses 5–35 describe warfare lasting about two centuries between these latter two kingdoms. The *first* **king of the South** was Ptolemy I, and the **one** who **shall gain power over him** was Seleucus I of Syria. These two were allies at first, then antagonists.[14] Later Berenice, **the daughter** of Ptolemy II, married Antiochus II, king of Syria, to bring rapprochement between the two nations, but the stratagem failed in a torrent of intrigue and murder.

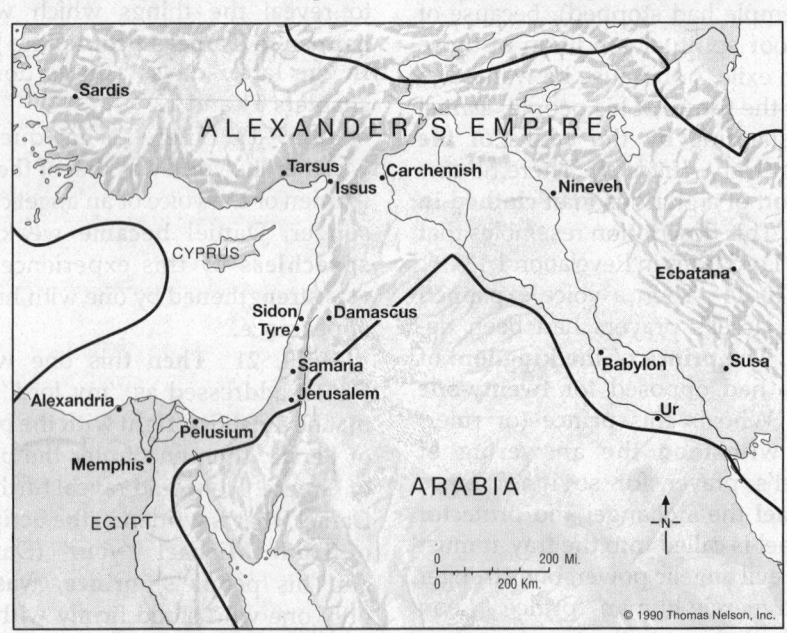

Alexander's Greek Empire

11:7–9 Ptolemy III, a brother of Berenice, successfully attacked the realm of Seleucus Callinicus, returning **to Egypt** with captives and great spoil. Two years later Seleucus launched an unsuccessful attack against Egypt.

11:10–17 **His sons** proved to be more successful, especially Antiochus III. Verses 10–20 describe how the tide of battle seesawed between **the North** and **the South**. Verse 17b tells how Antiochus III made a pact with

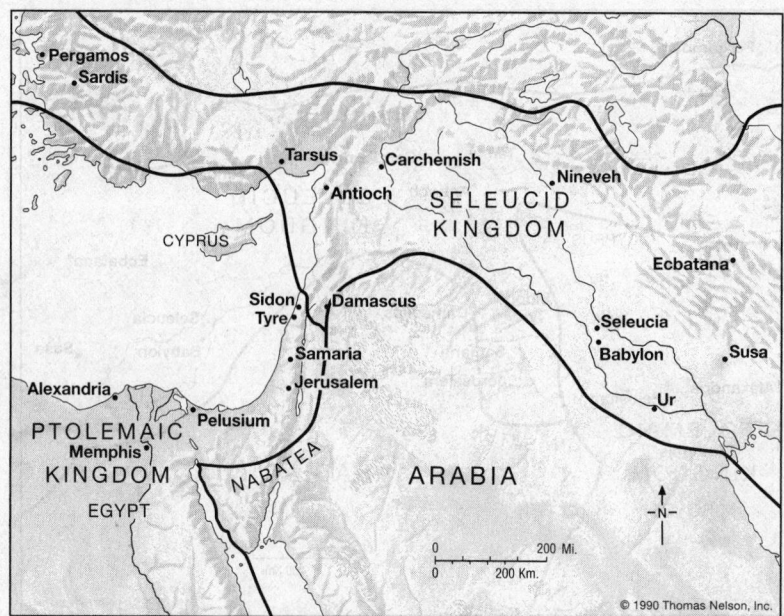

Ptolemaic Control of Palestine

Egypt, giving his **daughter** Cleopatra (not the famous—or notorious—queen of Egypt) in marriage to Ptolemy V, but she defected to side with Egypt.

11:18–20 When Antiochus III attempted to conquer Greece, he was defeated by the Romans at Thermopylae and Magnesia, and returned to his own land to die in an insurrection. His successor, Seleucus Philopater, became infamous for his oppressive **taxes on the glorious kingdom**, Israel. He died mysteriously, perhaps by poisoning.

2. The Reign of Wicked Antiochus Epiphanes (11:21–35)

11:21, 22 Verse 21 brings us to the rise of Antiochus Epiphanes, the "little horn" of Daniel 8. This **vile person** gained by **intrigue** the throne that rightfully belonged to his nephew. Kingdoms were inundated by his military might, and the Jewish high priest, Onias, **the prince of the covenant,** was murdered.

11:23, 24 Antiochus made treaties with various nations, especially Egypt, but always to his own advantage. When he plundered a conquered **province**, he used the wealth to extend his own power.

11:25, 26 His campaign **against** Egypt receives special mention; **the king of the South** was not able to withstand him, partly because of treachery among his own followers.

11:27, 28 Subsequently **both** the kings of Syria and of Egypt engaged in hypocritical and deceitful conferences. When Antiochus was **returning to his** own **land**, he began to direct his hostility against Israel, inflicting great slaughter and destruction.

11:29–31 The next time Antiochus marched against Egypt, he was repulsed by the Romans (**ships of Cyprus**) near Alexandria. Returning through Palestine, he took out his anger against Israel. Some apostate Jews collaborated with him. He discontinued **the daily sacrifices** and

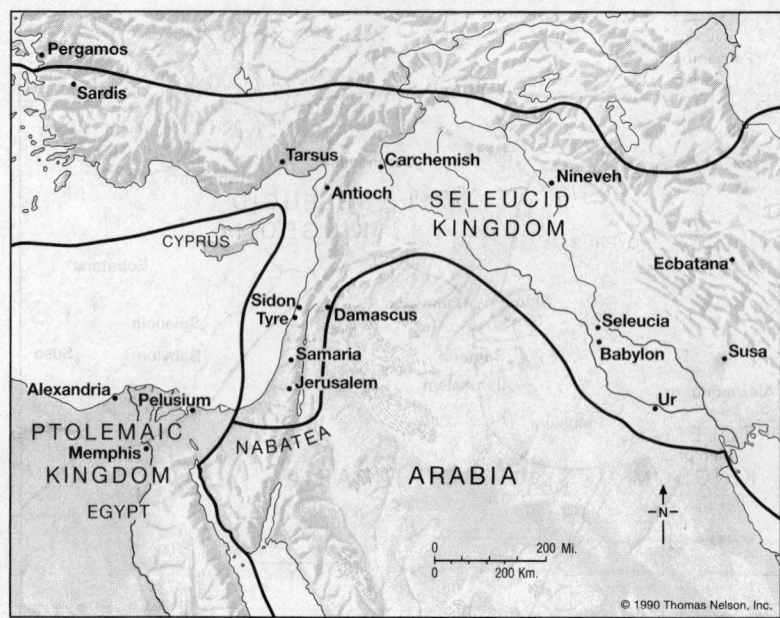

Seleucid Control of Palestine, c. 190 B.C.

ordered an idol to be erected in **the sanctuary**. According to secular history, he polluted the temple by offering a sow upon the altar. **The holy covenant** (vv. 28, 30, 32) refers to the Jewish faith, with particular emphasis on the sacrifical system.

11:32–35 These outrages brought on the Maccabean revolt, led by Judas Maccabaeus ("the hammer") and his

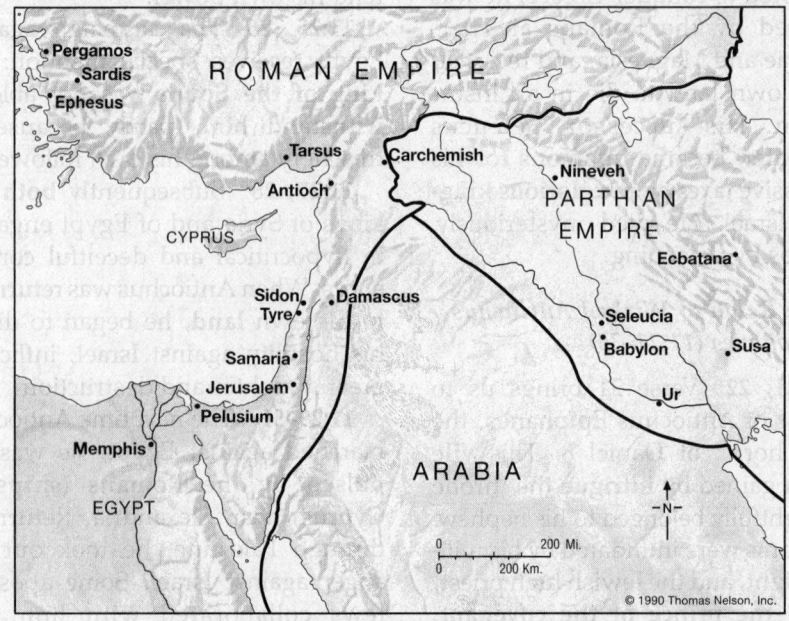

Roman Control of Palestine

family. Apostate Jews sided with Antiochus, but the faithful ones were **strong** and did **great exploits**. It was a terrible time of slaughter on one hand, but of spiritual brilliance and revival on the other.

XII. PROPHECIES OF THE DISTANT FUTURE (11:36—12:13)

A. The Antichrist (11:36–45)

11:36–39 As mentioned, verses 36–45 are still future. Verse 36 introduces the willful **king**, whose description makes him sound very much like the Antichrist. He will **prosper till** God's **wrath** against Israel is **accomplished**. Many believe that he will be a Jew, judging from such expressions as **"the God of his fathers"** and **"the desire of women"** (i.e., the Messiah). The Jews would hardly be deceived by a Gentile messiah. At any rate, he will greatly extend his sway through aggressive militarism.

11:40–45 There is a problem in verses 40–45 as to who is intended by **he** and **him**. One interpretation is as follows: **The king of the South** collides with the willful king in battle. **The king of the North** then swoops down through Palestine and on into Egypt. **But** disturbing **news from the east and** from **the north** causes him to return to Palestine where he encamps between **the seas** (Mediterranean and Dead Seas) and Jerusalem. He will be destroyed, with **no one** coming to **help him**.

B. The Great Tribulation (Chap. 12)

12:1–3 Verse 1 describes the Great Tribulation, the three and one-half years preceding Christ's Second Advent. Some will be raised to enter the Millennium with Christ; the wicked dead will be raised at the end of the

Millennium (v. 2; see Rev. 20:5). **Those** tribulation saints **who** proved themselves **wise** by obeying the Lord and by leading others to faith and **righteousness** will be resplendent in eternal glory.

Some commentators see verse 2 as referring not to *physical resurrection* but to the *national and moral revival* of Israel. After God's ancient people are regathered to the land in unbelief, a remnant will respond to the gospel and will enter the Millennium. These are the ones who awake **to everlasting life**. All the others, who worship the Antichrist, will be condemned **to shame and everlasting contempt**. Buried among the Gentiles for centuries, Israel will be restored nationally, and then the believing remnant will experience the spiritual resurrection described in Isaiah 26:19 and Ezekiel 37.

12:4 **Daniel** was instructed to preserve the prophecies in a **book**. Verse 4b is commonly taken to speak of advances in transportation and scientific knowledge. But it probably doesn't mean this. Darby translates: "many shall diligently investigate." Tregelles renders it, "many shall scrutinize the book from end to end."[15] It teaches that many will study the prophetic Word and **knowledge** of it **shall increase** in the Great Tribulation.

12:5–10 These verses record a discussion between **two** unidentified individuals and a **man clothed in linen** as to **how long** it would be to the time of the end. The time given is three and a half years (**time, times, and half a time**). When Daniel expresses continued failure to **understand**, he is told that the vision will not be completely clear until it occurs. But he can be assured that the righteous will **be purified**, **the wicked** will manifest themselves as such, and only **the wise** will **understand**. From the beginning of the Great Tribulation to its end would be **time, times, half a time** (three and a half years or 1,260 days).

12:11 Perhaps **the abomination of desolation** will be set up in the temple of Jerusalem thirty days before the Great Tribulation begins; this would explain the **one thousand two hundred and ninety days** here.

12:12 As for the **one thousand three hundred and thirty five days**, this has been explained as taking us past the Coming of Christ and the judgment of His foes to the beginning of His reign.

12:13 Daniel would **rest** (in death) and **arise** in resurrection to enjoy his **inheritance**—millennial blessings with his Messiah, the Lord Jesus Christ.

ENDNOTES

[1](Intro) Merrill F. Unger, *Introductory Guide to the Old Testament*, p. 396.

[2](Intro) *Ibid.*, p. 399.

[3](Intro) Anderson first worked out the minutely detailed chronology of Daniel's Seventy Weeks in his classic, *The Coming Prince*.

[4](4:19–26) *Boanthropy* (ox-man), is a rare form of *monomania*. Dr. R. K. Harrison narrates in some detail his meeting a man in a London mental institution with this disease (*Introduction to the Old Testament*, pp. 1114–17).

[5](5:10–16) This probably refers not to Belshazzar's wife, but what we would call the *queen mother*.

[6](5:25–31) *Tekel* is related to the Hebrew word *shekel*. The *words* are in the language of the people present (Aramaic), but the meaning was so cryptic they could not understand the *message*. Also, perhaps the words were in a script other than that used for Aramaic.

[7](6:9–13) In Esther, King Ahasuerus was *also* duped by *his subjects* into making an "unalterable" law condemning God's people. Daniel, threatened by the lion's den, and Esther, facing Ahasuerus, both were in danger of losing their lives. Both depended on their God to save them, facing danger heroically. Both were foreigners in the Persian empire. In each case, a Persian king regretted signing a decree into an irrevocable law. In both accounts, God's people were saved from their enemies.

[8](7:1–4) The winged lion was Babylon's symbol just as a lion is the United Kingdom's and the eagle is the United States' emblem.

[9](8:9–14) Antiochus is in that long line of Jew-haters that includes Haman and Adolf Hitler. He is probably a type of the coming Antichrist. Antiochus liked to be called Epiphanes (Illustrious), but the Jews had another name for him: Epimanes (Madman)! His story is told in the apocryphal books of Maccabees.

[10](9:20–23) The Hebrew word for *week* merely means a unit of seven, and so some prefer to translate with the word *heptad*, a little-used word from the Greek for *seven*.

[11](9:26) April 6, A.D. 32, according to Anderson. In our time, Dr. Harold Hoehner, using a slightly different beginning date (444 B.C.) and ending date (A.D. 33), also comes up with a perfect set of dates for this prophecy. See *Bibliotheca Sacra*, January-March, 1975, pp. 62–64.

[12](10:10–14) Leon Wood, *A Commentary on Daniel*, pp. 272, 273.

[13](10:10–14) Some, like William Kelly, answer these objections by suggesting that the speaker in verse 13 is a person other than the Lord.

[14](11:5, 6) It is important to recognize that the titles "king of the North"

and "king of the South" refer to the leaders of Syria and Egypt ruling at the time of the events described in any verse, and not to the same set of rulers all the way through the text.

[15](12:4) S. P. Tregelles, *The Prophetic Visions in the Book of Daniel*, p. 158.

BIBLIOGRAPHY

Anderson, Sir Robert. *The Coming Prince*. London: Hodder & Stoughton, 1881. Reprint. Grand Rapids: Kregel Publications, 1975.

Baldwin, Joyce G. *Daniel: An Introduction and Commentary*. The Tyndale Old Testament Commentaries. Downers Grove, IL: InterVarsity Press, 1978.

Campbell, Donald K. *Daniel: Decoder of Dreams*. Wheaton, IL: SP Publications, Victor Books, 1977.

Dennett, Edward. *Daniel the Prophet: And the Times of the Gentiles*. Reprint. Denver: Wilson Foundation, 1967.

Gaebelein, Arno C. *The Prophet Daniel.*

A Key to the Visions and Prophecies of the Book of Daniel. New York: "Our Hope," 1911.

Keil, C. F. *Biblical Commentary on the Old Testament*. Vol. 24. Grand Rapids: Wm. B. Eerdmans Publishing Company, 1971.

Luck, G. Coleman. *Daniel*. Chicago: Moody Press, 1958.

Pentecost, J. Dwight. "Daniel." In *The Bible Knowledge Commentary*. Wheaton: Victor Books, 1985.

Tregelles, S. P. *The Prophetic Visions in the Book of Daniel*. London: Samuel Bagster & Sons, 1864.

Walvoord, John F. *Daniel: The Key to Prophetic Revelation*. Chicago: Moody Press, 1971.

Wilson, Robert Dick. *Studies in the Book of Daniel*. Grand Rapids: Baker Book House, 1979.

Wiseman, D. J., et. al. *Notes on Some Problems in the Book of Daniel*. London: Tyndale Press, 1965.

Wood, Leon. *A Commentary on Daniel*. Grand Rapids: Zondervan Publishing House, 1973.

HOSEA

Introduction

"We have in the Book of Hosea one of the most arresting revelations of the real nature of sin, and one of the clearest interpretations of the strength of the Divine love. No one can read the story of Hosea without realizing the agony of his heart. Then, lift the human to the level of the Infinite, and know this, that sin wounds the heart of God."

—G. Campbell Morgan

I. Unique Place in the Canon

While the book of Hosea is not in narrative or story form, it does contain a story, although it is interwoven with the text.[1] Briefly, the story is that Hosea married Gomer and she bore three children—Jezreel, Lo-ruhamah, and Lo-ammi. Gomer was unfaithful, and in spite of this, Hosea sought her in great love, and bought her back from slavery and degradation.

The usual translation of Hosea 1:2 says that God apparently commanded the prophet to marry a woman who was already a harlot.[2]

Many Bible readers see a moral problem here. Would a holy God ask one of his prophets to marry a "wife of harlotry"? And would a morally sensitive prophet obey? At least three solutions have been proposed:

1. The first is that it is a *parable* to illustrate God's love for sinful Israel, and is not to be taken literally. However the style is *narrative*, as in Isaiah 7:3 and Jeremiah 13:11, which also are direct commands from God to prophets—and no one takes them as mere parables. The truth in this view is that the story does beautifully illustrate God's love for sinful Israel; the

error lies in saying it was just a story.

2. A second view says, Yes, God did command it and Hosea obeyed. This certainly seems to be the normal reading of the text. (However, see Endnote 2.) The goal—in this case, salvation—justified the sorrowful means that Hosea had to experience.

Against this view is the fact that if Gomer were a harlot *before* her marriage, this would be a poor type of Israel.

3. A third solution says that Hosea married a pure woman who *later* became an adulteress. This view fits well with the prophet and his wife as being types of Jehovah and His unfaithful wife Israel. It also fits in with the prophet's (and the Bible's) high ideals of marriage. People who hold this view often find it hard to conceive of Hosea suffering so much grief over his wrecked marriage if Gomer had been immoral *to start with*.

A strong argument against this is that Hosea 1:2 calls her "a wife of harlotry" in the very command to take her as wife!

Perhaps our very repugnance against marrying an immoral woman is a further illustration of God's grace in putting up with Israel's sins (and the church's!) when He is much holier than any prophet or preacher ever could be.

Whichever view we may take, the story behind the prophecy vividly illustrates, as words alone could not, the amazing grace of God toward sinful, straying Israel, and by application, to all sinners who turn from their evil ways to a God of love.

II. Authorship

Hosea was the son of Beeri. His name means *salvation* and is basically the same as the name *Joshua* and its Greek form, *Jesus*. Living up to his name, Hosea prophesied concerning the salvation of Jehovah which will come when Christ returns to set up His kingdom. Hosea was a prophet chiefly to Israel, but there are passages that reflect a Judean interest as well.

III. Date

Hosea prophesied when Jeroboam II, the son of Joash, was king of Israel, and also when Uzziah, Jotham, Ahaz, and Hezekiah were kings of Judah. This would be a period of several decades in the eighth century B.C. R. K. Harrison believes Hosea's ministry "extended from about 753 B.C. to a time just before the fall of Samaria in 722 B.C."[3]

IV. Background and Theme

Hosea foretold the Assyrian invasion of the Northern Kingdom and the fall of Samaria.

When his wife Gomer left him to live shamefully in sin, God instructed His servant to buy her on the public market and bring her back in blessing. The purpose of all this, of course, was to picture God's relationship with Israel, (also called Ephraim, Jacob, and Samaria). The nation had proved unfaithful, living in idolatry and moral wickedness. For many years it would be without a king, a sacrifice, or idols. That is its present status.

In the future, however, when Israel returns to the Lord in repentance, He will have mercy. Ephraim will then be forever cured of her idolatrous backsliding and converted to God. Henry Gehman writes:

> Hosea presents the exhaustless mercy of God which no sin of man can bar or wear out. The master thought of Hosea's message is that God's mighty and inextinguishable love for Israel will not rest satisfied until it has brought all Israel into harmony with itself.[4]

Behind the chastening, as G. Campbell Morgan points out, there is a God of love:

> The supreme thing in every one of the prophecies is that the God with Whom these men were intimate was known by them to be a God of tender love, of infinite compassion, angry because He loves, dealing in wrath upon the basis of His love, and proceeding through judgment to the ultimate purpose of His heart. It is the heartbeat of God that throbs through these passages.[5]

OUTLINE

Commentary

I. THE REJECTION OF ISRAEL PICTURED BY THE NAMES OF HOSEA'S THREE CHILDREN (1:1–9)

1:1–5 The LORD directed the prophet **Hosea the son of Beeri** to marry an unfaithful woman. (See Introduction, "Unique Place in the Canon," for a discussion of the ethical question involved in such a marriage.) **He** married **Gomer, the daughter of Diblaim**.

Their first child was named **Jezreel** (God will scatter), an indication of what the Lord was about to do to the nation of Israel. The Assyrian army would **break** the power **of Israel in the Valley of Jezreel**.

1:6, 7 The second child was named **Lo-Ruhamah** (unpitied). This signified that **Israel** would **no longer** be pitied but would be sent into captivity, while **Judah** would be spared from the assaults of the Assyrians.

1:8, 9 The third child was named **Lo-Ammi (not My people). God** no longer recognized Israel as His own. Some also feel the prophet was questioning whether or not this child was *his own.*

II. THE RESTORATION OF ISRAEL PROMISED (1:10—2:1)

1:10, 11 But this judgment on **Israel** was only temporary. God would regather Israel and Judah and acknowledge them as His own. This will take place at the Second Coming of Christ.

In context the latter part of verse 10 clearly applies to *Israel*. But Paul quotes these words in Romans 9:26 and applies them to the call of the *Gentiles*. This illustrates the truth that when the Holy Spirit quotes OT verses in the NT, He is a law unto Himself.

2:1 In chapter 2 Hosea is told to speak to a faithful remnant of the nation. These **brethren** are spoken of as Ammi (**My people**) and Ruhamah (she who has obtained **mercy**).

III. GOD'S WARNING AGAINST ISRAEL'S UNFAITHFULNESS AND HIS THREATENED JUDGMENT (2:2–13)

2:2, 3 The faithful remnant should plead with the mass of the nation of Israel to put away her idolatry and **harlotries** or God will **strip her naked** and bring drought upon **her**.

2:4, 5 The **children** of the sinful nation will also be unpitied because **they are children of** a **harlot** who went **after** false gods and gave these idols credit for supplying her with food, clothing, and luxuries.

2:6, 7 God will put all kinds of roadblocks and obstructions in her way, and cut her off from her idols until she decides to **return** to Him (her **first husband**).

2:8 She did not give God credit for supplying her with necessities and luxuries, including the **gold** and **silver** which she used to make an idol of **Baal**.

2:9, 10 So God **will** cut off from her the food and clothing, and **will** thoroughly **uncover her lewdness**.

2:11–13 Her mirth and her **appointed** religious holidays will be canceled and **her vines and . . . fig trees** will be destroyed (**she** thought **these** were her pay from her idol **lovers**), and she will be punished **for all the days . . . she** served Baal.

IV. A FUTURE OF BLESSING FORETOLD FOR ISRAEL (2:14–23)

2:14–17 After that, He will restore and **comfort** Israel. God **will give her her vineyards** and **she** will **sing** as in the time **when she came up from the land of Egypt. She** will then call Him *Ishi* (**My Husband**), not *Baali* (**My Master**). The people will be cleansed from Baal-worship, even to the degree of forgetting the **names of the Baals**.

2:18–20 The nation will dwell in safety and peace because of the **covenant** God will make **with the beasts of the field** and other animals, rendering all wild animals harmless. Warfare will also be ended. Israel will be married to **the LORD forever**, under terms of **righteousness and justice, in lovingkindness and mercy**, bound by God's **faithfulness**.

2:21–23 In that day, Jezreel (Israel) will no longer mean *scattered*, but *sown*. The people will be sown in their own land; heaven and **earth** will join in blessing them and making them fruitful. Williams helpfully explains this paragraph as follows:

> Jezreel (Israel), as sown by God in the land (v. 23), will cry to the corn, the wine, and the oil to supply her needs; they will cry to the earth to

fructify them; the earth will cry to the heavens for the needed rain in order to produce the fruit; and the heavens will cry to Jehovah to fill them with the required water, and from Him there will be no further appeal, for He is the Great First Cause! In response to the appeal He will fill the heavens with moisture, the heavens will discharge it upon the earth, the earth will produce, as a result, the corn, the wine and the oil, Israel will have ample provision, and the heaven and earth will be bound together with a chain of love. Then God will have pity on Israel, will acknowledge her as His people, and Israel will acknowledge Him as her God.[6]

V. THE REDEMPTION OF HOSEA'S WIFE A TYPE OF ISRAEL'S ULTIMATE RETURN TO JEHOVAH (Chap. 3)

3:1–3 Then the LORD told Hosea to go to the public market and buy back his faithless wife from her sin. The purchase price, **fifteen shekels of silver** and **one and one-half homers of barley**, was that of a female slave. For **many days** after that, there were to be no marital relations; later she would be restored to her full marital status. This pictures the past, present, and future of the nation of Israel. Unfaithful to Jehovah (NKJV, LORD), she ran after other lovers (idols). But God brought her back.

3:4, 5 Her present condition is given in verse 4—**without** a **king**, without a **prince** (or royal family), **without** a **sacrifice** (that is, the Levitical sacrifices have been suspended), without **a sacred pillar** (idol), **without** an **ephod** (symbol of the Levitical priesthood), and without **teraphim** (household gods). Israel's future is given in verse 5—she will **return** to **the** LORD

and will love and **fear** Him in faithfulness.

VI. GOD'S CONTROVERSY WITH HIS PEOPLE (Chaps. 4—10)

A. The Sins of the People (4:1–6)

4:1–3 God contends with Israel because of the people's unfaithfulness, unkindness, irreligion, **swearing**, **lying**, **killing**, **stealing**, **adultery**, and murder. Five of the Ten Commandments are summarized in verse 2. Violations of these commands were the reasons for the condition of **the land**. Even the wildlife would **waste away** because of the coming judgment.

4:4–6 Both **priest** and **prophet** are blamed because of their willful **lack of knowledge**. God's **people** were **destroyed for lack of knowledge**; they had **forgotten the law of** their **God**.

B. The Sins of the Priests (4:7–11)

The more the people **sinned**, the more sin offerings the priests greedily received. So, **like people, like priest**, they were both corrupt. Their punishment would be their enslavement to **harlotry, wine, and new wine**, indulging and never becoming satisfied.

C. The Idolatry of the People (4:12–14)

The idolatry of the people is described next. They sought guidance from **wooden idols**. They worshiped at mountain shrines, in the **shade** of trees. The men set the example, and the women followed.

D. A Special Appeal to Judah (4:15–19)

Judah is warned not to follow Israel's wicked example. Israel is stubborn, refusing to be separated from its idols and loving shame more than glory. In the RSV, verse 16 reads, "Like a stubborn heifer, Israel is stubborn; can the Lord now feed them like a lamb in a broad pasture?"

E. The Evil Behavior of the Priests, the People, and the Royal Family (5:1–7)

The **priests**, the people, and the **king** are alike guilty of idolatry and **Israel is defiled**. **Ephraim** has become a harlot. Both **Israel** and **Judah** shall be punished for their guilt because **they have dealt treacherously with the Lord**; they will take **flocks and herds** as offerings for **the Lord** but will **not** be able to **find Him**.

F. The Promised Judgments of Israel and Judah and God's Intention to Await Their Repentance (5:8–15)

5:8–12 The historical background for this section is found in 2 Kings 16. Israel (**Ephraim**) and Syria had invaded Judah. With the help of Assyria, Judah had counterattacked and captured territory. Three cities of **Benjamin** are warned to prepare for punishment with the words: **"Blow the ram's horn in** Gibeah, the trumpet in Ramah! Cry aloud at Beth Aven (v. 8). God **will be ... like a moth** to Israel and dry rot **to the house of Judah**."

5:13–15 When Ephraim saw his **sickness** he sought help from **Assyria**. But he was not cured because Assyria was hired by Judah (and utilized by God) to fight against him. God determined to **return** to His **place** and wait for Israel and Judah to confess their sins and **seek** His **face**.

G. An Appeal to Israel to Repent (6:1–3)

Verses 1–3 are Israel's response to God's call to repentance (5:15). At first it seems genuine and heartfelt, but upon closer examination, we see that no sin is specifically confessed. The repentance is shallow and insincere. This is apparent from God's continued remonstrance with the nation in the rest of the chapter. True repentance does not come until the last chapter. There the nation repudiates its idolatry and acknowledges its need of God's grace.

Verse 2 may contain an allusion to the resurrection of Christ, which took place **after two days** and **on the third day**. If so, the national restoration of Israel is founded on and foreshadowed by the resurrection of Christ. Or the reference may be to the last three "days" of the Tribulation Period. Israel's repentance and mourning extend over the first two days. Then the nation is reborn on the third day and the Messiah appears.

H. The Sinfulness of Both Israel and Judah (6:4–11)

6:4–6 Because Israel and **Judah** have been faithless, God has condemned **them by the prophets**; He wanted love more than **sacrifice**, and **knowledge of** Himself **more than burnt offerings**.

6:7–11 "But they, like Adam (RV),[7] had **transgressed the covenant**." The wickedness of Israel is pictured in verses 7–10 as **a city of evildoers, bands of robbers**, and a murdering **company of priests**. **Judah**, too, is **appointed** to **a harvest** of suffering (v. 11) before God restores the fortunes of His people. (Some think the harvest here is one of blessing, not judgment.)

I. The Wickedness of Israel Unveiled (Chap. 7)

7:1–7 The corruption of **Ephraim** was great, including **fraud**, robbery, lies, wicked deeds, adultery, and drunkenness. The people and the royal princes were inflamed with lustful passions.

7:8-10 They mixed with foreigners, wasting their substance, and they would not listen to rebuke. The metaphor of Ephraim being a cake unturned suggests a lack of balance. On one side the cake is burnt and overdone; on the other side it is doughy and underdone. In short, Ephraim is completely spoiled.

7:11, 12 Ephraim flew like a silly dove . . . to Egypt and Assyria for help, but God would catch the dove in a net and punish the people.

7:13, 14 They had fled from the Lord and showed no genuine repentance. They wailed to God with their voice but not with their heart. It wasn't the soft sobs of repentance but the howling with pain of a wounded animal.

7:15, 16 The Lord had taught them how to win victories by being disciplined and strengthened; yet they trusted in idols, and so would meet defeat and derision.

J. A Warning to Prepare for Foreign Invasion Because of Idolatry and Foreign Alliances (Chap. 8)

8:1-3 The Assyrian invader is likened to an eagle or a vulture, hovering over Israel. The people had broken the law, and therefore their doom was near. Though they professed to know the Lord, they had spurned Him.

8:4-6 The division of the kingdom into Israel and Judah was without His approval. Their idolatry caused God's anger to burn. God asks, "How long until they attain to innocence?" or, in modern terms, "When will they ever learn?"

8:7-10 The grain crops would fail,

and the nation would be scattered among the Gentiles. Because Ephraim sought help from Assyria and its allies among the nations, God would punish him. This is poetically expressed by "they shall sorrow a little" (or "begin to diminish," NKJV marg.)

8:11-14 Israel's idolatry and Judah's trust in multiplied fortified cities would bring suffering and destruction.

K. The Captivity of Israel Predicted as a Result of Its Iniquity (9:1—10:15)

9:1, 2 Israel should not rejoice. Their idols would not give them the rich harvests they expected. Idolatry is *spiritual adultery*. Francis Shaeffer explains:

> Notice the form of speech God uses. A woman is out harvesting, and there is a freedom in the midst of the harvest. She takes a gift of money from some man to sleep with him on the corn floor in the midst of the harvesting. That is what those who had been God's people had become. The wife of the living God is this in her apostasy.[8]

9:3, 4 Because of their adultery, the people would go into captivity— not literally to Egypt, but to captivity in Assyria similar to the bondage in Egypt. Theirs was a mixed worship— idolatry mixed with the worship of Jehovah, pleasing neither Him nor themselves.

9:5-9 They would not be in the land to observe the appointed feasts; rather, they would be taken into captivity. The tents of Ephraim would be inhabited by nettles and thorns instead of by the people themselves. The exile was near, as well as the doom of false prophets.

9:10-17 Israel had been such

promising fruit at the outset, like **the firstfruits on the fig tree**, but it lapsed into terrible idolatry, and so is appointed to barrenness and loss of **children**. The expression **"to the last man"** (v. 12) must be understood relatively, not absolutely (see v. 17c). The male population would be drastically reduced. Because of exchanging their **glory** for **abomination**, **Ephraim** was given the sentence—**"No birth, no pregnancy, and no conception!"**

10:1, 2 Israel, once a luxuriant **vine**, is now empty, because it only used its prosperity to increase its idolatry. God now accuses them of being double-minded, holding them **guilty** for allowing **their heart** to be **divided**.

10:3, 4 The people disclaimed any need of God or of a **king**. In this we see how far the nation of Israel had fallen. Originally at Mt. Sinai they had pledged themselves to God's rule through Moses and Aaron. A long, continuous, downward apostasy followed, finally leading to a point where they could not even accept a king's rule over them. The progression of their spiritual demise is shown by the successive forms of government they had rebelled against: (1) God (theocracy); (2) Moses (prophet-lawgiver); (3) Joshua (spiritual/military general); (4) judges (judicial government); (5) kings (monarchy); (6) no king (anarchy—no government). They made covenants with empty oaths; therefore **judgment** would cover the land **like** poisonous **hemlock**.

10:5–8 The golden **calf** of **Beth Aven** (Bethel)[9] would **be** captured and **carried** away by the Assyrians. Instead of loving their God, who had saved them many times, the following words suggest with divine sarcasm that Israel was in love with the golden calf: **"Because of the calf . . . its people mourn for it . . . and its priests shriek for it—because its glory has departed."** No wonder God was about to punish them! Samaria's king would perish, the idol shrines would be destroyed, and men would call on **the mountains** and **hills** to fall on them.

10:9, 10 At **Gibeah** the tribes stood together in punishing the tribe of Benjamin for its sin (Judg. 20). But since then, the history of **Israel** has been a record of sin. Now God will use the nations to **chasten** a people united in sin.

10:11 **Ephraim** was once **a trained heifer**, reserved for the light work of threshing **grain**, but now it will be put under the yoke of captivity, and **Judah**, too, will be put to hard labor.

10:12–15 Their only hope of escape would be in repentance and seeking **the LORD**. But Israel must **reap** the fruit of its sinful dependence on chariots and soldiers. The land would be plunged into war, **all their fortresses** would **be plundered**, Samaria would be destroyed, and the king killed. **Shalman** (v. 14) is Shalmaneser III, although some think the name refers to a king of Moab named Salamanu.

VII. IN WRATH, GOD REMEMBERS MERCY (Chaps. 11—13)

It is helpful to distinguish the speakers in the next four chapters—whether it is the Lord or Hosea.

The Lord: 11:1—12:1
Hosea: 12:2–6
The Lord: 12:7–11
Hosea: 12:12—13:1
The Lord: 13:2–14
Hosea: 13:15—14:3
The Lord: 14:4–8

11:1–4 In love, God **called . . . Israel . . . out of Egypt** (Ex. 12). (This is also applied to the Lord Jesus in Matt. 2:15.) The more He **called**, the more **they went** after idols. He dealt tenderly and lovingly with **Ephraim**, but the latter **did not know that** the Lord had **healed** him.

11:5–8 Because of their turning from God, His people would **not** be sent to **Egypt** but would be exiled to Assyria. God's **heart** churned to think of making Israel as desolate as the cities of the plain, **Admah** and **Zeboiim**.

11:9–12 These verses are future. God has planned restoration and blessing for His people, and He will no more **destroy Ephraim**. In the Hebrew Bible, verse 12 is the first verse of chapter 12. It may mean, as in the KJV and NKJV, that while Israel was full of **lies** and **deceit**, **Judah** was **still** trusting in the Lord in Hosea's time. Or it may mean, as in the NASB, that Judah resembled Israel in its unruliness.

12:1, 2 **Ephraim** fed **on the wind** in the sense that he depended for survival on treaties **with the Assyrians** and **Egypt**. God has a controversy with Judah, and although Ephraim's sin was greater, He would **punish Jacob** as well.

12:3 The patriarch Jacob is in view here. Though in some other places he is seen in an unfavorable light, here he is held out as an example of one who won victories through turning to God.

12:4–6 **The Angel** in verse 4 is identified as the LORD **God of hosts** and **the** LORD in verse 5. He is the same as the angel of the Lord who appeared to Hagar (Gen. 16:7–11); Abraham (Gen. 18:1–33; 22:11, 15, 16); and Jacob (Gen. 31:11–13; 48:16). See also Exodus 3:2, 6–15 and Numbers

22:22–35. Evangelicals generally believe that He is the Second Person of the Trinity in a preincarnate appearance.

Ephraim is admonished to imitate Jacob by depending on God's strength rather than his own (see Gen. 32:28).

12:7, 8 But Ephraim is **a cunning Canaanite**[10] (merchantman), a cheater, a self-reliant boaster, who thought himself immune from detection.

12:9 **The** LORD reminds him that he owes all his prosperity to the One who brought him out **of Egypt**. If he would only obey, God would still **make** him **dwell in tents, as in the days of the . . . Feast** (of Tabernacles).

12:10–12 Jehovah had **spoken** repeatedly through **the prophets**, but in vain. **Gilead** and **Gilgal**, the two parts of the Northern Kingdom, divided by the Jordan, will be brought to nothing because of their idolatry. The nation's ancestor, **Jacob**, was a fugitive in **Syria** and a lowly tender of **sheep** in Mesopotamia.

12:13 But God graciously led his descendants **out of** servitude in **Egypt** by Moses the **prophet**.

12:14 Unmindful of this, **Ephraim** has **provoked** the Lord **to anger** by his idolatry and has brought **the guilt of his bloodshed** on himself. God will bring back **his** shame and **reproach upon him**.

13:1 Before Ephraim's idolatrous career, **he exalted himself in Israel when** he **spoke, but when he** turned to **Baal worship, he died**.

13:2, 3 **Now** the people plunge deeper and deeper into idolatry, telling **men** to **kiss the calves**. For this they will be as transient as **the morning** cloud **or the early dew**. They will be **blown** away **like chaff** or **smoke from a chimney**.

13:4–8 It was **the** LORD who saved them from **Egypt** and provided for them **in the wilderness. But they**

forgot Him and turned to idols. Now God will turn on them **like a . . . wild beast**.

13:9–13 When the Lord does this, who **will** then **save** them? Ephraim's sin was **bound up** and kept for the day of judgment. The pains of **childbirth** would **come upon him**, but he did not present himself **where children are born**, that is, at the mouth of the womb for birth. This means that Ephraim did not repent in spite of God's judgments.

13:14 The RSV translates the first part of this verse as questions: "Shall I ransom them from the power of Sheol? Shall I redeem them from death?" The implied answer is "No." Instead, He will call to **Death** for its **plagues**, and to the **Grave** (Sheol) for its **destruction**, because **pity is hidden from** His **eyes**. This verse, however, is quoted in a different sense in 1 Corinthians 15:55.

13:15, 16 The dreadful destruction of Israel and **Samaria** by the cruel Assyrians (**"an east wind"**) is then predicted.

VIII. ISRAEL URGED TO REPENT AND ENJOY GOD'S BLESSING (Chap. 14)

14:1–3 Israel is called to repentance and even given the **words** of confession to use in a day still future. Reliance on **Assyria**, trust in the **horses** of Egypt, and idolatry are the sins mentioned. They acknowledge that God is their only hope.

14:4–7 In truly exquisite nature poetry, the Lord promises healing, **love**, refreshment, attractiveness, revival, and growth.

14:8 The Lord is still speaking in verse 8.[11] He wants the **idols** of His people to be a thing of the past. He reminds them that He is their Protector and Provider.

14:9 The prophet Hosea closes his prophecy by emphasizing that wisdom and prudence lie in obedience to **the ways of the LORD**.

ENDNOTES

[1](Intro) Jonah is the only prophecy in narrative form.

[2](Intro) Morgan, following Ewald and the margin of the ERV and ASV, translates, "When Jehovah spake at the first with (not "by") Hosea." He maintains that the prophet was looking back to his early communion *with* God. Hosea was saying, in effect: "When away back there my ministry began, when, before the tragedy came into my life, Jehovah spoke with me, it was He Who commanded me to marry Gomer. The statement distinctly calls her a woman of whoredom, but it does not tell us that she was that at the time. It certainly does mean that God knew the possibilities in the heart of Gomer, and that presently they would be manifested in her conduct, and knowing, He commanded Hosea to marry her, knowing also what his experience would do for him in his prophetic work. When Hosea married Gomer, she was not openly a sinning woman, and the children antedated her infidelity" (G. Campbell Morgan, *Hosea: The Heart and Holiness of God*, p. 9).

[3](Intro) R. K. Harrison, *Introduction to the Old Testament*, p. 860.

[4](Intro) Henry Snyder Gehman, Editor, *The New Westminster Dictionary of the Bible*, p. 410.

[5](Intro) G. Campbell Morgan, *The Minor Prophets*, p. 6.

[6](2:21–23) George Williams, *The Student's Commentary on the Holy Scriptures*, p. 633.

[7](6:7–11) In Hebrew the same letters spell *man* and *Adam*.

[8](9:1, 2) Francis A. Schaeffer, *The Church at the End of the 20th Century*, p. 124.

[9](10:5–8) *Bethel* means *house of God*; the name *Beth Aven* is a parody of this name, meaning *house of wickedness*.

[10](12:7, 8) The Canaanites were such avid "traffickers" (ERV, ASV) that their name became synonymous with huckstering.

[11](14:8) The punctuation is not part of the original, but most translations agree on this.

BIBLIOGRAPHY

Feinberg, Charles Lee. *The Minor Prophets*. Chicago: Moody Press, 1976.

Keil, C. F. "Hosea." In *Commentary on the Old Testament*. Vol. 25. Grand Rapids: Wm. B. Eerdmans Publishing Co., 1971.

Kelly, William. *Lectures Introductory to the Study of the Minor Prophets*. London: C. A. Hammond Trust Bible Depot, n.d.

Kidner, Derek. *Love to the Loveless: The Message of Hosea. The Bible Speaks Today*. Downers Grove, IL: InterVarsity Press, 1981.

Logsdon, S. Franklin. *Hosea: People Who Forgot God*. Chicago: Moody Press, 1959.

Morgan, G. Campbell. *The Heart and Holiness of God*. Old Tappan, NJ: Fleming H. Revell, 1967.

———. *The Minor Prophets*. Old Tappan, NJ: Fleming H. Revell Company, 1960.

Pfeiffer, Charles F. "Hosea." In *The Wycliffe Bible Commentary*. Chicago: Moody Press, 1962.

Stevenson, Herbert F. *Three Prophetic Voices. Studies in Joel, Amos and Hosea*. Old Tappan, NJ: Fleming H. Revell, 1971.

Tatford, Frederick A. *The Minor Prophets*. Vol. 1. Reprint (3 vols.). Minneapolis: Klock & Klock Christian Publishers, 1982.

JOEL

Introduction

"Joel, . . . was probably the first of the so called writing prophets; so this book provides a valuable insight into the history of prophecy, particularly as it furnishes a framework for the end times which is faithfully followed by all subsequent Scripture. God started a new work with the writing of Joel, that of preparing the human race for the end of this temporal era, and thus gave an outline of His total plan. Later prophets, including even our Lord, would only flesh out this outline, but in keeping with the divine nature of true Scripture, never found it necessary to deviate from this, the initial revelation."

—Montague S. Mills

I. Unique Place in the Canon

The prophecy of Joel is short but certainly not lacking in beauty or interest. The prophet uses many literary devices to produce his vivid style: alliteration, metaphors, similes, and both synonymous and contrasting parallelism (see Introduction to the Psalms for a discussion of parallelism). W. Graham Scroggie praises Joel's literary impact as follows:

The style is elegant, clear, and impassioned, and must be given a high place in Hebrew literature.[1]

A most unusual feature of the Book of Joel is the plague of locusts (Chap. 1). Are they to be taken literally or is this symbolic of invading armies? Probably both. Sometime during the prophet's lifetime—and the date is very much controverted—an all-pervasive plague of locusts invaded Judah and completely devastated the land. This natural phenomenon is a vivid picture of the coming invasion of troops and the great and dreadful Day of the LORD.

A third remarkable feature of the prophecy is the prediction of the outpouring of God's Spirit on all flesh (2:28–32) and the wonders that would follow. Since Peter quotes this passage in his sermon in Acts 2, Joel has also become known as "the prophet of Pentecost."

II. Authorship

Joel is introduced as the son of Pethuel. Apart from that, little is known of him. His name means *Jehovah is God*. He has been called the John the Baptist of the OT.

III. Date

No king is mentioned by Joel and there are few chronological hints in his short prophecy to help place the book in its proper time frame. Dates as varied as the tenth century to the fifth century B.C. have been suggested.

Joel's position in the "Book of the Twelve," as the Jews call the Minor Prophets, indicates that Jewish tradition considered Joel to be an early book. Its style fits the earlier classical period better than the post-exilic era of Haggai, Zechariah, and Malachi. The fact that no king is mentioned may be due to the book having been written when Jehoiada the high priest was regent (in the boyhood years of Joash, who reigned between 835–796 B.C.). Also, Judah's enemies are the Phoenicians and Philistines (3:4) as well as the Egyptians and Edomites (3:19), not her later foes—the Syrians, Assyrians, and Babylonians.

IV. Background and Theme

If we accept the early date, Joel spoke to the nation of Judah from the reign of Joash to that of Ahaz. This would make him the earliest of the *writing* prophets.

The key phrase of the book is "the Day of the Lord," found five times (1:15; 2:1, 11, 31; 3:14).

There is a distinct break or turning point in the book at 2:18. Up to that verse, Joel has been speaking of the *desolation* that would come on Judah. From then on, God tells of the *deliverance* which He will bring to the nation.

OUTLINE

I. DESCRIPTION OF THE LOCUST PLAGUE (Chap. 1)

   A. Its Unprecedented Severity (1:1–4)

   B. Its Effect Upon:

      1. Drunkards (1:5–7)

      2. Priests (1:8–10, 13–16)

      3. Farmers (1:11, 12, 17, 18)

      4. The Prophet Joel (1:19, 20)

II. DESCRIPTION OF THE ENEMY INVASION (2:1–11)

III. DIVINE APPEAL TO JUDAH TO REPENT (2:12–14)

IV. DECLARATION OF A FAST (2:15–17)

V. DIVINE DELIVERANCE PROMISED (2:18—3:21)

   A. Material Prosperity (2:18, 19, 21–27)

   B. Destruction of the Enemy (2:20)

   C. Pouring out of God's Spirit (2:28, 29)

   D. Signs Preceding Christ's Second Advent (2:30–32)

   E. Judgment of Gentile Nations (3:1–16a)

   F. Restoration and Future Blessing of the Jews (3:16b–21)

Commentary

I. DESCRIPTION OF THE LOCUST PLAGUE (Chap. 1)

A. Its Unprecedented Severity (1:1–4)

1:1–4 Under the figure of a locust plague, **Joel the son of Pethuel** here describes the impending invasion of Judah by an army from the north. This prophecy received a partial fulfillment in the Babylonian invasion, but in the future, the invader will be the king of the North (Assyria).

The severity of the locust plague was such that the elders could not remember **anything like** it. The plague was in four stages, the four stages in the growth of the locust: **the chewing locust, the swarming locust, the crawling locust**, and **the consuming locust**.[2] These may refer to the four world empires which ruled over God's people—Babylon, Medo-Persia, Greece, and Rome.

B. Its Effect Upon:

(1) Drunkards (1:5–7);
(2) Priests (1:8–10, 13–16);
(3) Farmers (1:11, 12, 17, 18); and
(4) The Prophet Joel (1:19,20)

The nation is called upon to repent, fast, and pray—from the **drunkards** to the **farmers** (vv. 11, 12, 17, 18), and the **priests** (vv. 8–10, 13–16).

The locusts had so **stripped** the **land** that there was nothing left with which to make offerings and sacrifices to the **LORD** (vv. 8–10).

The prophet saw this as **the day of the Lord and destruction from the Almighty** (v. 15). This expression refers to any time when God steps forth in judgment, putting down evil and rebellion, and triumphing gloriously. In the future, the Day of the Lord includes the Tribulation Period, the Second Advent, the Millennial Reign of Christ, and the final destruction of the heavens and earth with fire.

The prophet, speaking for the people, cries to the LORD for mercy, because **fire has devoured** both **pastures** and **trees**. Even the **beasts of the field cry out to** God because the **brooks are dried up**.

II. DESCRIPTION OF THE ENEMY INVASION (2:1–11)

2:1–3 The people are called to battle by a **trumpet** sounding the **alarm**, for **the day of the Lord . . . is at hand**. The immediate reference was to the Babylonian captivity, but the complete fulfillment is still future. Before the invaders come, **the land** of Judah is like **the Garden of Eden**; afterwards it is a **desolate wilderness**.

2:4–11 The comparison of the locusts to **swift steeds**, climbing **the wall like men of war** marching **in formation**, entering everywhere **like a thief** and blackening the skies with their immense numbers, constitutes some of the most graphic, poetic description in the prophets.

This unendurable invasion is all at the beck and call of **the LORD**, whose **camp is very great**.

III. DIVINE APPEAL TO JUDAH TO REPENT (2:12–14)

Even now, **the LORD** calls the people to repentance. It is not too late to **return to** Him. But it must be more than outward ritual. Their turning was to be with all their heart, with fasting, with weeping, and with mourning.

IV. DECLARATION OF A FAST (2:15–17)

All classes of people are summoned to a sacred assembly and to consecrate a fast. In a future day, the priests will cry to the LORD in a solemn penitential assembly.

V. DIVINE DELIVERANCE PROMISED (2:18—3:21)

A. Material Prosperity (2:18, 19, 21–27)

Then the LORD will be zealous for His land and pity His people. He will send them grain, new wine, and oil to their satisfaction, in addition to removing their reproach from among the nations. The land will be restored to fertility and productiveness. Abundant rain will result in vats overflowing and threshing floors . . . full of wheat. The people will be restored and will never again be put to shame. All the years that the swarming locust had eaten would be restored as well (2:25).

B. Destruction of the Enemy (2:20)

In the remainder of Joel, the Lord tells what He will do for Judah. He will destroy the northern army (the Assyrian) from the eastern sea (Dead Sea) to the western sea (Mediterranean).

C. Pouring out of God's Spirit (2:28, 29)

God will pour out His Spirit on all flesh in that day. The younger generation shall prophesy and see visions and the old men shall dream dreams. This latter prophecy was partially fulfilled in Acts 2:16–21, but Pentecost did not exhaust it. Its complete fulfillment will take place at the outset of Christ's one-thousand year reign.

D. Signs Preceding Christ's Second Advent (2:30–32)

The outpouring of the Spirit will be preceded by wonders in the heavens. Some of these predicted signs are: blood, fire, pillars of smoke, the sun turning into darkness and the moon into blood. All who turn to Jesus as Messiah, calling on His name, will be saved to enter the Millennium with Him.

E. Judgment of Gentile Nations (3:1–16a)

3:1–8[3] God will gather the Gentile nations to the Valley of Jehoshaphat and will judge them there for their treatment of the Jews. Tyre, Sidon, and Philistia will be recompensed for plundering and enslaving God's people. The people in those cities would in turn be sold as slaves—a fitting punishment for their crime.

3:9–16a The Gentiles are told to "Prepare for war!", for the Lord will fight with them in the valley of decision. In the Valley of Jehoshaphat the Lord will sit to judge all the surrounding nations. The sovereign God is currently testing all men and nations, as unfashionable as that concept may be to today's worldly thinkers. Stevenson remarks:

> Men dismiss the Biblical teaching concerning judgment to come, for individuals and nations, as a now outmoded concept. But the people of God have held fast through all the generations to the assurance that, in the "day of the Lord," the Judge of all the earth will do right. That is our confidence, based upon the rock of Holy Scripture.[4]

F. Restoration and Future Blessing of the Jews (3:16b–21)

But the LORD will bless His people with deliverance, safety from invaders, and abundant supplies. The land of Israel would become fruitful and well-watered: **the mountains shall drip with new wine, the hills shall flow with milk, and all the brooks of Judah shall be flooded with water.** **Egypt** and **Edom** will become **a desolate wilderness, . . . but Judah** will be inhabited **forever**. God will also **acquit** her of her **guilt of bloodshed**.

The book ends on a secure note with a reason: **For the LORD dwells in Zion.**

ENDNOTES

[1](Intro) W. Graham Scroggie, *Know Your Bible*, Vol. I, p. 155.

[2](1:1–4) The KJV's "palmerworm, locust, cankerworm, and caterpillar" would suggest four different species of insect. This is not a likely meaning.

[3](3:1–8) In the Hebrew Bible, 2:28–32 constitute chapter 3 and our chapter 3 becomes chapter 4.

[4](3:9–16a) Herbert F. Stevenson, *Three Prophetic Voices. Studies in Joel, Amos and Hosea*, p. 40.

BIBLIOGRAPHY

Feinberg, Charles Lee. *The Minor Prophets*. Chicago: Moody Press, 1976.

Keil, C. F. "Joel." In *Commentary on the Old Testament*. Vol. 25, 26. Grand Rapids: Wm. B. Eerdmans Publishing Co., 1971.

Kelly, William. *Lectures Introductory to the Study of the Minor Prophets*. London: C. A. Hammond Trust Bible Depot, n.d.

Morgan, G. Campbell. *The Minor Prophets*. Old Tappan, NJ: Fleming H. Revell Company, 1960.

Stevenson, Herbert F. *Three Prophetic Voices. Studies in Joel, Amos and Hosea*. Old Tappan, NJ: Fleming H. Revell Company, 1971.

Tatford, Frederick A. *The Minor Prophets*. Vol. 1. Reprint (3 vols.). Minneapolis: Klock & Klock Christian Publishers, 1982.

AMOS

Introduction

"Unlike other prophets, Amos was not a man whose life was devoted to hearing and speaking the Word of the Lord. He was no product of the "schools of prophets," nor a professional "seer." He left his flock for a limited period, at the command of God, to deliver a specific message at Bethel. That done, he presumably returned to his sheep-tending at Tekoa."

—Herbert F. Stevenson

I. Unique Place in the Canon

The book of Amos is written in some of the finest OT Hebrew style. Amos was a sheep-breeder and tender of sycamore trees. Perhaps he illustrates the appearance of God-ordained men throughout history who speak very effectively and even beautifully for the Lord without the traditional "school of the prophets" background or formal education so much sought after today.

II. Authorship

Amos, whose name means *burden*, gives no family pedigree, hence we can assume he was not of noble or prominent stock, like Isaiah or Zephaniah. It has been common for preachers to paint Amos's "country" background too strongly. The word used to describe his regular livelihood is not the usual Hebrew word for "shepherd" but is used elsewhere only of King Mesha, who had a successful sheep-breeding business (2 Kgs. 3:4).[1] Although he belonged to the kingdom of Judah, he was commissioned to go north to Samaria and prophesy against the kingdom of Israel. Amos was a stern prophet of righteousness and uncompromising justice.

III. Date

Amos ministered during the reigns of Uzziah in Judah (790–739 B.C.) and Jeroboam II in Israel (793–753), an age of affluence, luxury, and moral laxity, especially in the Northern Kingdom. Amos mentions that this was "two years before the earthquake." This doesn't necessarily pinpoint the date, but archaeology has unearthed evidence of a violent earthquake in about 760 B.C., which would fit in with the dates of the kings that Amos mentions.

IV. Background and Theme

Assyria under Adad-nirari III had defeated the Syrian confederacy, thus allowing Jehoash and Jeroboam II to appropriate new land. Israel made enormous gains as Samaria became a trade stop-off for caravans. Ivory palaces were built, and businessmen became impatient with Sabbath restrictions. The rich were oppressive and corrupt;

the courts were unjust; the religious services were either a sham or consisted of idolatry. Superstition and immorality abounded. Amos saw that such dreadful conditions could not last and that clouds of judgment were looming. His unpopular commission was to go north to Samaria, denounce the rival kingdom of Israel, and warn of judgment. Israel was a basket of summer fruits whose judgment was on the way.

OUTLINE

Commentary

I. THE THREATENED JUDGMENTS ON EIGHT NATIONS (Chaps. 1—2)

A. Introductory (1:1, 2)

In his first two chapters, Amos pronounces judgment against eight nations.

Each pronouncement of judgment is introduced by the words, "For three transgressions . . . and for four." J. Sidlow Baxter explains this Hebrew idiom for us:

> The phrase is not to be taken arithmetically, to mean a literal three and then four, but idiomatically, as meaning that the measure was full, and more than full; the sin of these people had overreached itself; or, to put it in an allowable bit of modern slang, they had "gone one too many," they had "tipped the scale."[2]

B. Damascus (1:3–5)

The first threat is against **Damascus**, the chief city-state of **Syria**. The Syrians had fought against the two and one-half tribes east of the Jordan (**Gilead**), and had apparently been extremely barbarous and cruel (suggested by **implements of iron**). The punishment for **the people of Syria** was to be carried away **captive to Kir**.

C. Gaza (1:6–8)

The second is against **Gaza**, where the Philistines handed over **captive** Israelites **to** the cruel Edomites. Other Philistine centers to be punished are **Ashdod**, **Ashkelon**, and **Ekron**. The result would be that **the remnant of the Philistines** would **perish**.

D. Tyre (1:9, 10)

The third is against **Tyre**. The Tyrians also **delivered up** captives **to** **Edom** and broke a treaty **of brotherhood** with Israel. "**Fire**" is also predicted for Tyre's **palaces**.

E. Edom (1:11, 12)

The fourth is against **Edom**. The Edomites were perpetual and cruel enemies of their brothers (Esau was a **brother** of Jacob). Because of their merciless dealings and implacable hatred, they would receive a fitting punishment upon the cities of **Teman** and **Bozrah**.

F. Ammon (1:13–15)

The fifth is against **Ammon**. The Ammonites committed terrible atrocities in conquering portions of the land of **Gilead**. **They** even **ripped open** pregnant **women** of **Gilead** in their bloody cruelty. Both **king** and **princes** were destined to **captivity**, **fire**, and a tempestuous battle.

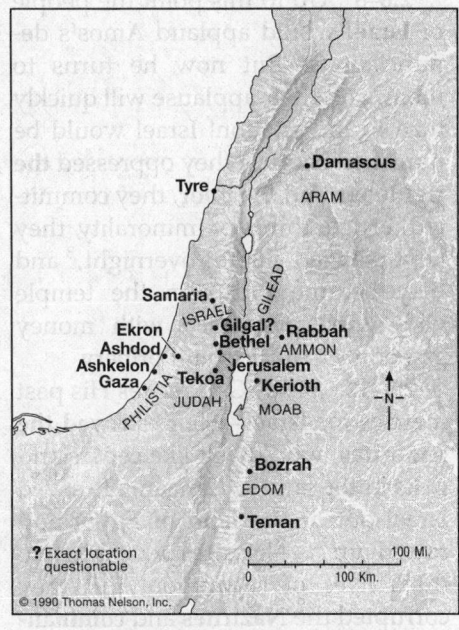

Amos: Places Judged by God

G. Moab (2:1–3)

The sixth judgment is against **Moab**, who deprived **the king of Edom** of a decent burial (See 2 Kgs. 3:26, 27 where "his eldest son" probably refers to the eldest son of the King of Edom, not Moab).

H. Judah (2:4, 5)

Now **the LORD** is getting uncomfortably close to home: The next two nations to be judged are **Judah** and Israel! It is startling that they should be listed along with six Gentile nations. To the Jews of Amos's time, this would have been most degrading! But God points out in this way that, by their sin, Judah and Israel had forfeited all special recognition by Jehovah (NKJV, LORD). Judah would be punished because **they** had **despised the law of the LORD**, they did not keep **His commandments**, and they **followed . . . lies** (idols).

I. Israel (2:6–16)

2:6–8 Up to this point the people of **Israel** would applaud Amos's denunciations. But now he turns to them, and their applause will quickly turn to indignation! Israel would be punished because they oppressed **the righteous** and **the poor**, they committed terrible forms of immorality, they kept pledged **clothes** overnight,[3] and they became drunk in the temple with **wine** purchased with money gained by extortion and bribery.

2:9–12 Next, God recites His past mercies for Israel—He **destroyed the Amorites**, who dwelt like **cedars** and **oaks** in the land of Canaan. He saved Israel out **of the land of Egypt** and **raised up . . . Nazirites** to exhibit to them lives of separation. But they corrupted the **Nazirites** and **commanded the prophets not** to **prophesy**.

2:13–16 As a consequence, God would crush them, prevent their **escape**, and cause their defeat by the Assyrians. Even the **mighty** men will not be able to **deliver** themselves, and **flight shall perish from the swift.**

II. THE GUILT AND PUNISHMENT OF ISRAEL (Chaps. 3—6)

A. The First Summons to Hear (Chap. 3)

3:1, 2 Again **the LORD** threatens judgment on **the children of Israel**. Because they occupied a uniquely close relationship to Jehovah, their sin was all the more serious, and their punishment would be all the more severe. Therefore He would **punish** them **for all** their **iniquities**.

3:3–8 The judgment would not descend without a reason—every effect has a cause. Amos asks seven cause-and-effect questions, culminating with an urban **calamity** caused by **the LORD**. It should not come as a surprise because God had revealed it in advance through His **prophets**.

3:9–12 **Ashdod** (Philistia) and **Egypt** are invited to witness the oppression, injustice, **violence**, and **robbery** in **Samaria**. These sins would bring the Assyrian invader into **the land** of Israel. Only a small remnant, graphically pictured as **remnant** parts of a devoured sheep, would survive.

3:13–15 **The altars** at **Bethel**, where the golden calf was worshiped, would be thoroughly destroyed. The calf itself would be taken to Assyria (Hos. 10:5, 6). The **great houses** of the affluent would **have an end**.

B. The Second Summons to Hear (Chap. 4)

4:1–3 The rich women of Samaria are likened to **cows of Bashan**, well-fed and unmanageable. They were guilty of oppressing **the poor** and living luxuriously. For this they would be carried into Assyrian captivity, leaving the land in confusion and panic. In their exit they and their **posterity** are pictured being led away **with fishhooks** and scrambling **through broken walls**.

Instead of transliterating **Harmon** as a place name (RSV, NASB, NKJV), some versions, including KJV, translate it "palace." Darby notes:

> Some translate "to the mountains"; others, "to the (enemy's) fortress," or "to the palace" [KJV], as in 1:4: the meaning is not ascertained.

4:4–13 God invites them ironically to carry on their idolatrous worship, bringing their **sacrifices** to **Bethel**; there was nothing for Him in it. They had suffered **lack of bread** (v. 6), drought (vv. 7, 8), **blight**, **mildew**, a plague of locusts (v. 9), pestilence, warfare, slaughter (v. 10), and catastrophes (v. 11). Since none of these things caused them to repent, **Israel** should now **prepare to meet ... God** Himself—**the LORD God of hosts**. Verse 12 is not a gospel appeal, but a message of judgment.[4]

C. The Third Summons to Hear (5:1–17)

5:1–7 The prophet laments over Israel's downfall; only one soldier in ten will be spared. Even yet, the people should **not seek** the cities where the idol shrines were (**Bethel, Beersheba, Gilgal**); they should **seek the LORD and live**.

5:8–13 Otherwise the Lord who made the constellations **Pleiades and Orion** and rules the universe will pour out His wrath upon them for their lack of **justice** and righteousness. The sinners of Israel hated a righteous

man who reproved them and abhorred an honest man. Because they had grown rich dishonestly, they would not be permitted to enjoy their wealth.

5:14–17 A call to righteousness and social justice goes forth: **"Seek good and not evil ... establish justice."** However, it is clear from the sudden change—**"There shall be wailing in the streets"**—that the people will not listen and so are doomed to punishment.

D. The First Woe (5:18–27)

5:18–20 The people should not **desire the day of the LORD**; it will be a day of **darkness** and calamity, with one evil overtaking another.

5:21–27 Israel was bringing sacrifices and **offerings** to the Lord on their **feast days**, but their lives were corrupt, so their **offerings** were rejected by God. He would rather have **righteousness** than ritual. Even in the wilderness, when professing to worship Jehovah, they had practiced idolatry with Moloch and other **idols**, such as **Sikkuth** and **Chiun**.

E. The Second Woe (Chap. 6)

6:1–8 Their luxury, ease, complacency, and security would be disturbed by violence. **"Woe"** is pronounced on those **who lie on beds of ivory, stretch out on** their **couches**, eating all they want, **sing idly to the sound of stringed instruments, drink wine** abundantly **from bowls, anoint themselves with the** most expensive perfumes and colognes, **recline at banquets**. God's reaction to their attitude of ease and complacency is: **"I abhor the pride of Jacob, and hate his palaces."** Samaria would be delivered up to the Assyrians.

6:9, 10 These tragic verses are well described by Page H. Kelly:

In the pestilence that will sweep across the land there will be so many victims that normal burial practices will have to be set aside and the survivors will resort to the unusual procedure of burning the corpses. When the relative of a deceased man enters his house to take out his body to be burned, he discovers that there is a lone survivor, hidden in some far corner of the house. When the relative calls out to him, he responds with a Hebrew interjection translated "Hush!" and then adds, "We must not mention the name of the Lord." These men have profaned the name of God in the past but now they dare not pronounce it, lest it loosen some fresh avalanche of His wrath. It is significant that even to this day an orthodox Jew will not pronounce the covenant name of Israel's God.[5]

6:11–14 Their behavior was foolish and futile, and it is compared to **oxen** plowing **on rocks**. They perverted **justice** and scorned **righteousness**. They boasted in their military **strength**, though **Lo Debar** and **Karnaim** were insignificant victories. The Assyrians would **afflict** the land **from the** northern **entrance to Hamath** to the southern boundary, **the Valley of Arabah**.

III. THE SYMBOLS OF APPROACHING JUDGMENT (7:1—9:10)

A. The Plague of Locusts (7:1–3)

In verses 1–9, Amos intercedes for his people. Three threats to Israel are described. The first may typify the attack of Pul, king of Assyria, under the figure of a devouring **locust**. In answer to Amos's prayer, the judgment was averted.

B. The Devouring Fire (7:4–6)

The second may have been the invasion of Tiglath-Pileser, under the symbol of a consuming **fire**. Prayer for little **Jacob** again prevented a catastrophe.

C. The Plumb Line (7:7–9)

The third may refer to the destruction of Samaria by Shalmaneser. The **plumb line** speaks of the absolute uprightness of the judgment. God announced that He would **not pass by**... Israel in mercy **anymore**.

D. Parenthesis: Refusal of Amos to Be Intimidated (7:10–17)

7:10–13 Amaziah, an idolatrous **priest of Bethel**, forbade Amos to **prophesy** against **the king's sanctuary** of **Bethel**, telling him to go back to his home in **Judah** and earn his **bread ... there**.

7:14–17 Amos answered that God had put him into the ministry and that he would not stop. He **was no prophet** in the technical sense, or the **son of a prophet**, but he must speak **the word of the LORD**. So, he told Amaziah of the fearful doom which would come upon him, his **wife**, his **sons and daughters**, and **his land**.

E. The Basket of Summer Fruit (Chap. 8)

8:1–6 The **basket of summer fruit** signified that Israel was ripe for judgment. God would **not pass by** in mercy **anymore**. The rich were oppressing **the poor**; they could not wait for the feast days to end so they could make more money; their business practices were corrupt; they were guilty of **falsifying the scales**.

8:7–12 For all of this, the Lord will punish **the land** with fearful earthquakes. Darkness will cover the earth during the day, and **mourning** will visit every house. People will long to hear **the word of the Lord**, but it will be withheld from them. **Famine** and drought (of God's **word**) will prevail.

8:13, 14　Idolatry will bring severe drought on Israel's most attractive **young** people and destruction on **those who swear by** false gods. Men will seek for a message from their idols but will not receive it.

F.　The Striking of the Lintel (9:1–10)

9:1–4　The LORD is seen beginning His judgment at **the altar**, perhaps the false altar at Bethel. The people find no way of ultimate escape; the sword pursues them wherever they try to flee. Even hypothetical places of "refuge" would elude them: **hell**, **heaven**, **on top of** Mt. **Carmel**, **the bottom of the sea**, **captivity before their enemies**. The seriousness of God's anger against them is seen in the words: **"I will set My eyes on them for harm and not for good."** In no uncertain terms the people of Israel are told that they are in big trouble!

9:5–10　Who can withstand **the Lord GOD of hosts** with His almighty power? The **layers** of earth's atmosphere and the **strata** of rock in the earth itself were **built** and **founded** by the same LORD. Israel is compared here to heathen **Ethiopia** and called **"the sinful kingdom"** by God Himself— strong language indeed! They had forfeited any special place of privilege. He would punish **the sinners** but save a remnant **as grain is sifted in a sieve; yet not the smallest grain** would **fall to the ground**. Although most would be destroyed, those found worthy by the Almighty would be spared.

IV.　THE FUTURE RESTORATION OF ISRAEL (9:11–15)

9:11, 12　The restoration of Israel is described in verses 11–15. God's

promises to **David** will be fulfilled. While some people employ verse 11 to teach that Israel and the church are one and the same, and that the church now is the "repaired" **tabernacle** (lit. "booth," figure of a deposed dynasty, NKJV marg.), it is surely to be taken in context to refer to Israel and **all the Gentiles** in the Millennial Kingdom. Scofield writes:

> The Davidic monarchy, pictured by a tabernacle . . . , was in a degraded condition. Cp. Isa. 11:1. On the basis of this verse the Talmudic rabbis called Messiah *Bar Naphli* ("the son of the fallen"). But He will arise (Mal. 4:2).[6]

9:13–15　Crops such as **grapes**, **wine**, wheat, olives, and **fruit** will grow up with amazing speed, the **cities** will be rebuilt and re-inhabited, and God **will plant** the people, who will never be driven out of **the land** again.

ENDNOTES

[1](Intro) The word for a shepherd is *rō'eh*; the word for a sheep-breeder is *nōgēd*.

[2](1:3–5) J. Sidlow Baxter, *Explore the Book*, p. 130.

[3](2:6–8) A garment given in pledge that a debt would be paid was not to be kept overnight, since it might well be the only blanket that a poor person had (Deut. 24:12, 13).

[4](4:4–13) However, by application it makes a great gospel warning. The evangelist D. L. Moody, for example, found "four things in this text:—*a*. There is one God. *b*. We are accountable to him. *c*. We must meet him. *d*. We need preparation to meet him" (*Notes from My Bible*, p. 92).

[5](6:9, 10) Page H. Kelly, *Amos, Prophet of Social Justice*, p. 97.

[6](9:11, 12) *The New Scofield Study Bible. New King James Version*, p. 1056.

BIBLIOGRAPHY

Feinberg, Charles. *The Minor Prophets*. Chicago: Moody Press, 1976.

Kelly, Page H. *Amos, Prophet of Social Justice*. Grand Rapids: Baker Book House, 1966.

Mills, Montague S. *The Minor Prophets. A Survey*. Dallas: 3E Ministries, n.d.

Stevenson, Herbert F. *Three Prophetic Voices. Studies in Joel, Amos and Hosea*. Old Tappan, NJ: Fleming H. Revell Company, 1971.

Tatford, Frederick A. *The Minor Prophets*. Vol. 1. Reprint (3 vols.). Minneapolis: Klock & Klock Christian Publishers, 1982.

OBADIAH

Introduction

"The prophecy of Obadiah is unique in the character of its contents. It is a book of unmitigated condemnation, unrelieved by any suggestion of compassion or hope."

—Frederick A. Tatford

I. Unique Place in the Canon

"The vision of Obadiah" (1:1) is the shortest book in the OT and the third shortest in the Bible. It has one theme only: the destruction of the descendants of Jacob's twin brother Esau. Throughout history the Edomites had constantly fought against Israel and demonstrated their contempt for the chosen people.

II. Authorship

There are a dozen men in the OT named Obadiah (servant of Jehovah), but none can be identified with this prophet with any likelihood. Actually, we know absolutely nothing about the writer of the book beyond what is revealed by his words.

III. Date

Since we know nothing about the author, the date must be determined by internal considerations.

Liberals, generally, and many conservatives, prefer a late date, soon after 586 B.C., when Jerusalem was destroyed. While similarities to Jeremiah, Lamentations, Psalm 137, and certain vocabulary[1] suggest a late date, the fact that total destruction of the city and temple are not mentioned probably goes better with an earlier date.

The earlier dates suggested are during Jehoram's reign (848–841 B.C.) or Ahaz's reign (731–715 B.C.). Not many hold to the last named period, but those who do tie their argument to 2 Chronicles 28:17, which tells of Edomites attacking Jerusalem and taking prisoners.

If the earliest date is correct, Obadiah is the very first of the *writing* prophets and a contemporary of Elisha. Besides the fact that the book does not suggest the total destruction of 586 B.C., Obadiah vv. 12–14 seem to be a warning to the Edomites not to *repeat* what they had done in the past. If Jerusalem were in ashes, such an admonition would be meaningless.

A Bible-believing Christian can hold any of these three views without compromising a high view of inspiration. A date of about 840 B.C. would seem the most likely, however.

IV. Background and Theme

The prophecy is against the Edomites, who were descendants of Esau and bitter enemies of the people of Israel. They are pictured as having rejoiced over the fall of Jerusalem.

Matthew Henry paints the strong emotions that form the backdrop for Obadiah's short prophecy:

> Some have well observed that it could not but be a great temptation to the people of Israel, when they saw themselves, who were the children of beloved Jacob, in trouble, and the Edomites, the seed of hated Esau, not only prospering, but triumphing over them in their troubles; and therefore God gives them a prospect of the destruction of Edom, which should be total and final, and of a happy issue of their own correction.[2]

As we noted, Bible students are not agreed as to whether this refers to the destruction by Nebuchadnezzar or to an earlier downfall of the city.

In the NT, Edom is known as Idumea. Ruined economically by the Arabs and later conquered by the Romans, the Edomites disappeared from the pages of history about A.D. 70.

OUTLINE

Commentary

I. EDOM'S PRIDE TO BE ABASED (vv. 1–4)

Obadiah opens with a prediction of the downfall of **Edom** by invaders because of its **pride**. An envoy is pictured inciting **the nations** to go to war **against** Edom. Its leading city, Sela or Petra, was carved out of the side of the **high**, rose-red cliffs south of the Dead Sea. It was considered impregnable against attack. However, the Lord would bring them down from their **eagle** heights and their **nest among the stars**.

II. DESTRUCTION OF EDOM (vv. 5–9)

A. The Completeness of the Plunder (vv. 5, 6)

Edom's destruction could not be accounted for as the work of **thieves** or **robbers**; they would only have taken what they wanted. Even marauders **would . . . have left some gleanings** and not stripped it bare. But even Esau's **hidden treasures** would be **sought after!**

B. The Betrayal by Edom's Allies (v. 7)

All the men in Edom's **confederacy** would betray her and **lay a trap for** her.

C. The Destruction of Edom's Leaders (vv. 8, 9)

Her **wise men** and **mighty men**, in whom she gloried, would **be cut off by slaughter**.

III. REASONS FOR EDOM'S DOWNFALL (vv. 10–14)

The Edomites **should not have . . . rejoiced** when they saw **Jerusalem** attacked. They should not have gloated or **spoken proudly** or helped to loot the city or **cut off** the fleeing Jews as they sought to escape or handed over to the enemy **those among them who remained**.

The picture drawn here is one of an utterly cold and heartless lack of restraint in Edom's cruel treatment of God's people. Edom was completely without mercy, showing not one shred of compassion to their **brother Jacob**. Perhaps this betrayed family relationship was one reason why their "doom" was so final.

IV. EDOM'S JUDGMENT IS RETRIBUTIVE (vv. 15, 16)

The day of God's wrath on **the nations** was **near**, and Edom would be punished for her treatment of Judah. Their **reprisal** would bounce back on their **own head**. G. Herbert Livingston explains the illustration of drinking as follows:

The sorrow attending punishment is sometimes depicted by the prophets as comparable to drinking strong wine. See Jer 25:15–28 for an extended application of this analogy. God would not merely pick out Edom for an example but would equally judge all nations for their sins.[3]

V. RESTORATION OF ISRAEL AND JUDAH AND EXTINCTION OF EDOM (vv. 17–21)

vv. 17, 18 Israel's future **deliverance** is foretold in the last section of Obadiah. Israel and Judah shall be **a flame** to **devour . . . the house of Esau** completely. Tatford summarized the history of Edom's demise:

The Edomites were expelled from their country by the Nabateans, but took possession of the Negev, which became known as Idumea, and even temporarily occupied part of Judah, until routed by Judas Maccabeus in 185 B.C. Simon of Gerasa later laid Idumea waste and the Edomites seem to have disappeared altogether in the first century A.D. It is true that Petra became the seat of a Christian patriarchate until the country was taken by the Mohammedans in the 7th century A.D. Today there is no trace of any who could be identified as an Edomite. Obadiah's prediction that there would be no survivor has been fulfilled.[4]

vv. 19–21 The land of Edom will be given to the Israelites dwelling in **the South** (the Negev). Those on the coastal plains (*Shephelah*; **the Lowland**) will be given the land of the Philistines. **The captives** will once more **possess** portions of **the land of the Canaanites**. **Saviors**[5] (or deliverers) will rule **the mountains of Esau**, and the Lord will reign over the entire **kingdom**.

ENDNOTES

[1](Intro) Such as the Hebrew word translated *captives* in v. 20.

[2](Intro) Matthew Henry, "Obadiah," *Matthew Henry's Commentary on the Whole Bible*, IV:1271.

[3](vv. 15, 16) G. Herbert Livingston, "Obadiah," *The Wycliffe Bible Commentary*, p. 841.

[4](vv. 17, 18) Frederick A. Tatford, *Prophet of Edom's Doom*, p. 55.

[5](vv. 19–21) The deliverers or saviors of verse 21 may be the saints who will reign with Christ.

BIBLIOGRAPHY

Feinberg, Charles Lee. *Joel, Amos and Obadiah*. New York: American Board of Missions to the Jews, 1948.

Henry, Matthew. "Obadiah." In *Matthew Henry's Commentary on the Whole Bible*. Vol. IV. McLean, VA: MacDonald Publishing Company, n.d.

Livingston, G. Herbert. "Obadiah." In *The Wycliffe Bible Commentary*. Chicago: Moody Press, 1962.

Mills, Montague S. "Obadiah." In *The Minor Prophets: A Survey*. Dallas: 3E Ministries, n.d.

Tatford, Frederick A. *Prophet of Edom's Doom*. Eastbourne, England: Prophetic Witness Publishing House, 1973.

JONAH

Introduction

"The book is unique in that it is more concerned with the prophet himself than with his prophecy. The condition of his soul, and God's loving discipline of him, instruct and humble the reader."

—George Williams

I. Unique Place in the Canon

Jonah (Heb. for *dove*) is the only one among the prophets whose prophecy does not consist of what he said but rather of his own life and experience. His experience portrays the past, present, and future of the nation of Israel, as follows:

1. Intended to be a witness for God to the Gentiles.
2. Jealous that a message of grace should be extended to the Gentiles.
3. Thrown into the sea (Gentile world) and swallowed by the nations, yet not assimilated by them.
4. Cast upon dry land (restored to the land of Israel) and made a blessing to the nations.

The only part of his experience that does not seem to fit is what is found in chapter 4. Nowhere in the Bible is it ever suggested that Israel will pout and sulk when millennial blessings flow out to the Gentiles!

II. Authorship

Only chapter 2, Jonah's very personal "psalm" from the belly of the great fish, is in the first person (I, me, my). The fact that the other three chapters are *about* Jonah and use the third person (he, him, his), however, does not rule out his having written the whole book (the traditional view). Other Bible writers, including Moses, have done the same from time to time. The authorship of this book should not be made a test of orthodoxy, though, since technically it is anonymous.

III. Date

Jonah's mission to Nineveh took place in the reign of the Northern Kingdom's mightiest monarch, Jeroboam II (2 Kgs. 14:23), who ruled from about 793 to 753 B.C. While Assyrian inscriptions do not mention a great revival during this era, a number of events dovetail with Jonah. It is well known that ancient pagans viewed famines and eclipses as divine portents of coming disaster. The Lord may well have used the Assyrian famines of 765 and 759 B.C. and the total eclipse of June 15, 763 B.C. to prepare the hearts of the Ninevites for Jonah's evangelistic mission. A brief swing toward monotheism in the reign of Queen Semiramis and her co-reigning son Adad-Nirari III (810–782 B.C.) could have been a preparation for Jonah's ministry.

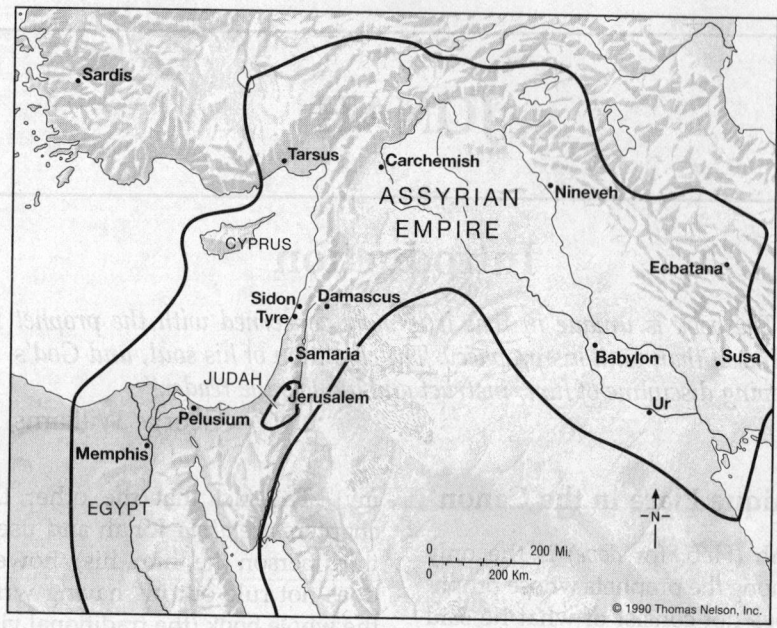

The Assyrian Empire, c. 650 B.C.

© 1990 Thomas Nelson, Inc.

IV. Background and Theme

Jonah was the son of Amittai (true [to God]). In 2 Kings 14:25, we learn that his home was in Gath Hepher, in Galilee.

He prophesied during the days when Assyria was threatening the Northern Kingdom, Israel. God sent him to preach repentance to Nineveh, the capital of Assyria. He was reluctant to do this, fearing that the city would repent and be spared. Assyria was an extremely cruel nation. If their inscriptions are to be believed, they flayed their enemies alive, made heaps of their skulls, and did other dreadful deeds. The haughty and blasphemous words of the Rabshakeh, the Assyrian spokesman of Sennacherib, are recorded in 2 Kings 18:19ff.

Therefore, Jonah fled to go to Tarshish and was swallowed by a great fish en route. After his release, he obeyed the Lord's commission by preaching to Nineveh. The city repented and was spared—much to Jonah's displeasure!

The Lord Jesus used Jonah as a sign of His death, burial, and resurrection (Matt. 12:40; 16:4).

The book is a commentary on Romans 3:29:

> Is He the God of the Jews only? Is He not also the God of the Gentiles? Yes, of the Gentiles also.

It is also an illustration of Romans 11:12, 15. When Jonah was cast into the sea, it resulted in the salvation of a boatload of Gentiles. But when he was cast onto dry land, it resulted in the salvation of a city. So the fall of Israel has resulted in riches to the Gentile world, but how much more blessing will flow to the world through the restoration of Israel!

OUTLINE

Commentary

I. THE DISOBEDIENCE OF THE PROPHET (Chap. 1)

A. Jonah's Missionary Call (1:1, 2)

God sent **Jonah** to preach **to Nineveh**, the capital city of Israel's prime enemy, Assyria. One can understand the prophet's dread of going there from a strictly natural viewpoint (see Background and Theme above).

B. Jonah's Flight to Tarshish (1:3)

In disobedience, **Jonah** took a **ship** for **Tarshish** (probably on the south coast of Spain). H. C. Woodring comments on the prophet's rebellion against his assignment:

God wanted him to go to Nineveh, 500 miles northeast of Palestine. Instead of going east, Jonah went 2000 miles to the west. God wished Jonah to take an overland trip via the Fertile Crescent. Instead he took a distasteful sea voyage (the Jews hated the sea). God sent him to the greatest metropolis of the day. Instead Jonah headed for a remote trading post on the fringes of civilization. The Lord wished to go with His prophet. Instead Jonah tried to flee from the presence and power of God.[1]

C. The Storm at Sea (1:4–10)

The LORD sent out (lit. hurled) **a great wind . . . and a mighty tempest**

that imperiled **the ship** and its occupants. The heathen **mariners**, probably Phoenicians, **cast lots** to see who was responsible for the trouble. **Jonah the Hebrew** was revealed as the culprit; he was fleeing **from the presence of the LORD**.

D. Jonah Thrown Overboard and Swallowed by a Great Fish (1:11–17)

1:11–16 The question, **"What shall we do to you that the sea may be calm for us?"**, shows a typical human attitude of caring for one's own skin at all costs. However, for pagan old salts they displayed a real sense of fair play. Jonah advised them to **throw** him overboard. They were reluctant to do this and **rowed hard to return to land** instead. But finally they were driven to do it as a last resort because **the sea continued to grow more tempestuous against them**.

1:17 A **great fish, prepared** by the LORD, swallowed **Jonah** and kept him a captive for **three days and three nights**. (The miracle was not that a fish could swallow a man, but that the man was not digested.)

II. THE DELIVERANCE OF THE PROPHET (Chap. 2)

A. Jonah's Prayer (2:1–9)

Jonah's prayer to God from the stomach of the fish celebrates his deliverance from drowning and not his escape from the fish. The escape followed his prayer. His prayer is remarkable in that it contains fragments from the book of Psalms. J. Sidlow Baxter analyzes the prayer as follows:

There is not one word of petition in Jonah's prayer. It consists of thanksgiving (verses 2–6), contrition (verses 7, 8) and rededication (verse 9). It is

really a psalm of praise, a "Te Deum," a "doxology." I know of a man who once sang the Doxology with his head in his empty flour barrel, as an expression of faith that God would send a further supply of flour! But the novelty of singing a doxology with your head—and all the rest of you—inside a great fish in mid-ocean, is absolutely without rival.[2]

Jonah's prayer is a foreshadowing of Israel's future repentance. When the nation acknowledges the Messiah as Savior, it will be restored to a place of blessing under Him.

The mention of **the belly of Sheol** in verse 2 has led some to believe that Jonah actually *died* in the fish and was resurrected. However, the Hebrew word *Sheol* can mean *grave*, *afterlife*, and other things. Here it is probably a poetic usage for "the depths," or as modern idiom might put it, "the pits."

Even though it is most unlikely that Jonah literally died and was raised again, our Lord Himself used the prophet as a picture of His own death, burial for three days and nights, and His glorious resurrection (Matt. 12:40). Incidentally, this shows that Christ accepted Jonah as a historical character, and not merely as a "parable," as some modern preachers claim.

B. God's Answer (2:10)

As soon as he acknowledged that salvation is of the LORD, **the fish . . . vomited Jonah** out **onto dry land**.

III. THE DECLARATION OF GOD'S MESSAGE THROUGH THE PROPHET (Chap. 3)

A. The Threat of Judgment (3:1–4)

The LORD recommissioned **Jonah** to go **to Nineveh**,[3] and this time he obeyed. After entering that **great city**, he announced that it would **be overthrown** in **forty days**.

B. The City-Wide Repentance (3:5–9)

The Ninevites, who worshiped the fish god Dagon, apparently knew what had happened to Jonah. Other men who have survived similar experiences in history had such mottled skin from the digestive juices that they would stand out in any crowd. He was a sign to them. The entire city repented and **believed God**, **from the greatest to the least**. **A fast** was **proclaimed** for **man and beast** alike, and **sackcloth** was put on all, from **king** to cattle.

C. The Judgment Averted (3:10)

As a result, Nineveh was spared **from the disaster**. We know from history, however, that the Assyrians returned to their wicked ways, and after over 150 years of grace their capital was destroyed.

IV. THE DISPLEASURE OF THE PROPHET (Chap. 4)

A. Jonah's Petulant Prayer (4:1–3)

Jonah was **angry** that Israel's Gentile enemies had been spared. In despondency, he asked that he might **die**, perhaps fearing that Assyria might again threaten Israel.

Most of Israel's enemies were severely dealt with by God, and the people of Israel expected their enemies' destruction—not their salvation. Even though Jonah, as a preacher, understood that God was **gracious and merciful**, he also knew that countries like Assyria were usually reserved for annihilation by God. For God to show mercy to Assyria (one of the worst of Israel's enemies in the OT economy) seemed totally wrong to the average Israelite.

B. God's Searching Question (4:4)

The LORD pricked the prophet's conscience with the probing query: **"Is it right for you to be angry?"**

C. Jonah Sulking Outside the City (4:5)

By way of answer, **Jonah** passed through Nineveh **and sat on** the **east side of the city** to **see what would become of** it.

D. Object Lesson on God's Sovereign Mercy (4:6–11)

4:6–8 There the LORD God **prepared a** large **plant** to protect him from the sun.[4] Jonah was greatly pleased by this. **The next day**, however, God **prepared a worm** which caused **the plant** to wither. Also, the Lord **prepared a** sultry **east wind** which, together with **the sun**, caused the prophet to **faint** and to **wish** for **death**.

4:9–11 Then God reminded His prophet that if he had **pity on the plant**, how much more reason did the Lord have to show **pity** to a **city** with **more than one hundred and twenty thousand** children alone, to say nothing of **much livestock**.

The lesson of this little book is that God loves the *world*—not just the Jews, but the Gentiles as well.

ENDNOTES

[1] (1:3) H. Chester Woodring, "Easter Challenge" Lectures on Jonah, Emmaus Bible School (now College), 1960.

[2] (2:1–9) J. Sidlow Baxter, *Explore the Book*, p. 169.

[3] (3:1–4) "Nineveh . . . was surrounded by a complex of lesser cities and

villages; so its vast metropolitan area is appropriately described . . . as being so vast that it took three days to journey (50/60 miles) through it." Montague S. Mills, *The Minor Prophets, A Survey*, p. 55.

[4](4:6–8) The Lord *prepared* four things for the unsubmissive prophet: (1) a great fish (1:17); (2) the plant (4:6); (3) a worm (4:7); and (4) a vehement east wind (4:8).

BIBLIOGRAPHY

Banks, William L. *Jonah, the Reluctant Prophet*. Chicago: Moody Press, 1966.

Blair, J. Allen. *Living Obediently: A Devotional Study of the Book of Jonah*. Neptune, N.J.: Loizeaux Brothers, 1963.

Draper, James T., Jr. *Jonah: Living in Rebellion*. Wheaton, IL: Tyndale House Publishers, 1971.

Feinberg, Charles L. *Jonah, Micah, and Nahum*. New York: American Board of Missions to the Jews, 1951.

Gaebelein, Frank E. *Four Minor Prophets: Obadiah, Jonah, Habakkuk, and Haggai*. Chicago: Moody Press, 1977.

Keil, C. F. "Jonah." In *Commentary on the Old Testament*. Vol. 25. Grand Rapids: Wm. B. Eerdmans Publishing Co., 1971.

Kleinert, Paul. "The Book of Jonah." In *Lange's Commentary on the Holy Scriptures*. Reprint (24 vols. in 12). Grand Rapids: Zondervan Publishing House, 1960.

Mills, Montague S. "Jonah." In *The Minor Prophets: A Survey*. Dallas: 3E Ministries, n.d.

Tatford, Frederick A. *The Minor Prophets*. Vol. 2. Reprint (3 vols.). Minneapolis: Klock & Klock Christian Publishers, 1982.

Unpublished Materials

Woodring, H. Chester. "Easter Challenge" Lectures on Jonah. Emmaus Bible School (now College), 1960.

MICAH

Introduction

"It is good to find a worthy champion of the poor who has courage and power to deliver an effective message. Knowing his fellows so intimately Micah was able to present in vivid colors the challenge to justice and consideration. His profound sympathy with the oppressed people came to life in unforgettable words. His spirit burned with righteous indignation as he saw the rank injustice practiced upon his neighbors and friends. The poor peasants of Judah had a strong champion in this powerful young preacher from the country."

—Kyle M. Yates

I. Unique Place in the Canon

Micah is the fourth largest of the minor prophets. It is quoted five times in the NT, once by our Lord. The most famous quotation (Matt. 2:6) is from 5:2, the verse that predicts that the Messiah would be born in Bethlehem Ephrathah (there was another Bethlehem up north).

Another fascinating feature of Micah is the prophet's fondness for "paronomasia," or more popularly, "punning." Many people enjoy making plays on words. In English-speaking cultures this is not generally considered a serious literary form (although Shakespeare used it often). In Hebrew, however, such serious writings as constitute the OT have many plays on words. Micah presents in 1:10–15 a famous example which some have compared with the Latin poet Cicero's oratory. Unfortunately, this is one of the hardest types of literature to translate, since no two languages have the same sets of double meanings. (See footnotes in NKJV and the Moffatt translation quoted below for attempts to express these puns in English.)

II. Authorship

The name Micah—a shorter form of *Mîkāyāh* and *Mîkāyāhû*—(who is like Jehovah) advertises the fact that the prophet was a servant of the one true God, the God of Israel. Like so many prophets he had the name for God (-*el*) or Jehovah (-*yah*) as part of his name. He is probably making a wordplay on his own name in 7:18 when he asks: "Who is a God like You?"

Micah was a contemporary of Isaiah, but from a humbler social class. He came from Moresheth, near Gath, about twenty-five miles southwest of Jerusalem.

III. Date

Micah prophesied from about 740 to about 687 B.C., during the reigns of Jotham, Ahaz, and Hezekiah. Though his main message was to Judah, Micah did predict the captivity of the Northern Kingdom, which occurred in 722/21 B.C. The dates for delivering the messages that constitute his little prophecy may have been some time before he wrote them down.

IV. Background and Theme

By the eighth century B.C. the old agricultural system in Israel and Judah, with its fairly even distribution of wealth, was gradually replaced by a greedy, materialistic, and harsh society that split the people sharply into the "haves" and the "have-nots." The rich land-owners got richer and the poor farmers got poorer. The latter migrated to cities, which were characterized by poverty and vice alongside the upper classes' luxury and also their cruelty to the poor.

Trade with pagan nations also brought in their false religious cults and lower morals.

In short, things were much like Christendom in the Western world today.

Against this dark and worldly background Micah wrote his prophecy, weaving it chiefly around three cities: Samaria, Jerusalem, and Bethlehem.

OUTLINE

Commentary

I. PREDICTION OF WRATH AGAINST ISRAEL AND JUDAH (Chap. 1)

1:1–3 The **peoples** are summoned by **the Lord GOD** to hear His message of judgment as He leaves **His holy temple**, the **place** of blessing, to **witness against** them.

1:4–7 His punishment will be severe on **Samaria** and **Jerusalem** because these cities had become the centers of idolatry. When He arrives in judgment the **mountains will melt under Him, the valley will split like wax before . . . fire, Samaria** will become a **heap of ruins, all her idols** will be **beaten to pieces,** and **her wounds** will be **incurable.**

1:8, 9 Micah's lament that he would **wail and howl,** like the lonely, nocturnal **jackals** and **the ostriches,** and **go stripped and naked** is the ultimate in extreme mourning.

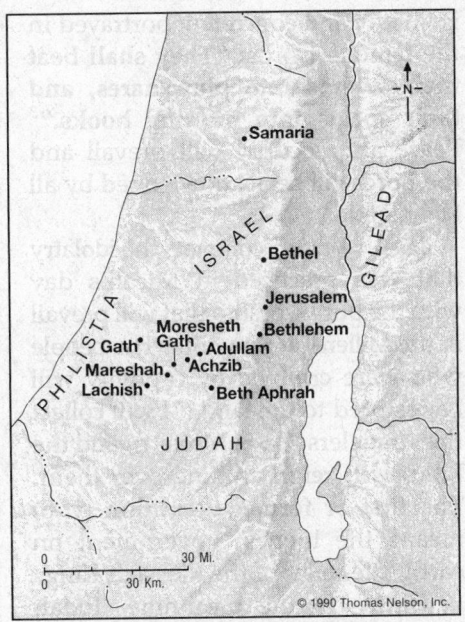

Geographical Puns in Micah

1:10–14 Verses 10–16 are a clever lament, describing the invasion of the land by the Assyrian army. Various cities of Israel and Judah are addressed—**Gath, Beth Aphrah, Shaphir, Zaanan, Beth Ezel, Maroth, Jerusalem, Lachish, Moresheth Gath, Achzib, Mareshah,** and **Adullam**—as the Assyrians draw near. There are many plays on words in this section.[1] Moffatt has translated the passage as follows:

Weep tears at Teartown (Bochim),
grovel in the dust at Dustown
    (Beth-ophrah),
fare forth stripped, O Fairtown
    (Saphir)!
Stirtown (Zaanan) dare not stir,
Beth-êsel....
and Maroth hopes in vain;
for doom descends from the Eternal
to the very gates of Jerusalem.

To horse and drive away,
    O Horsetown (Lakhish),
O source of Sion's sin,
where the crimes of Israel centre!

O maiden Sion, you must part with
Moresheth of Gath;
and Israel's kings are ever balked
at Balkton (Achzib).[2]

1:15, 16 A conqueror would descend on Israel, and the people would flee **to Adullam**. Israel should shave its head **bald** in mourning **because** its **precious children**, that is, the people, would be taken from the land **into captivity**.

II. THE DOOM OF THE WEALTHY OPPRESSORS (2:1–11)

2:1–5 The reasons for the judgment are recited here. The rich people dispossessed the poor of their **houses** and land **by violence**. As a result, this property would be taken from the rich by a foreign invader, and they would have nothing left.

2:6, 7 The people told Micah **not** to **prophesy** such unpleasant things because disgrace would not overtake them. But Micah replied that they should not say, "**Is the Spirit of the** LORD **restricted? Are these** works of judgment **His doings? Do not** His **words do good to him who walks uprightly?**"

2:8–11 By their sins, His **people** had become like **an enemy** of Jehovah— robbing the peaceful of their clothes and driving **women** and **children** out of **their ... houses**. They should **arise and depart** into exile, for the land they polluted would **destroy** them. Any **false** prophet who advocated **wine and** strong **drink** would be quickly accepted by **this people**.

III. THE PROMISE OF RESTORATION (2:12, 13)

After the judgment, God **would gather the remnant of Israel** back from exile. A breaker (the LORD) would break down anything that would hinder their restoration.

IV. DENUNCIATION OF RULERS, FALSE PROPHETS, AND PRIESTS (Chap. 3)

3:1–4 The **rulers of the house of Israel** are condemned for their injustice, unrighteousness, and covetousness. They treated the poor most cruelly. They hated **good** and loved **evil**. Instead of being **shepherds** of the sheep, as rulers are meant to be, these politicians were **wolves**, turning the sheep into **meat for the pot** and **flesh** for **the caldron**. They were the opposite of David, a literal shepherd who came to shepherd a nation (1 Sam. 17:15; 2 Sam. 5:2, 7:7). When their calamity comes, God **will not hear** their cries for help.

3:5–7 The false **prophets** would chant "**Peace**" to those who paid them well and predict **war** to those who would not pay. **Therefore** God would withhold from them the knowledge of His will. They would receive **no answer from God**.

3:8–12 In contrast, Micah was empowered **by the Spirit of the LORD** to declare God's message to **Israel** and Judah (**Jacob**). The mercenary rulers, **priests**, and **prophets** thought that they were safe, but Micah announced that **Jerusalem** would be reduced to **heaps** of rubble.

V. THE GLORY OF CHRIST'S MILLENNIAL REIGN (Chap. 4)

4:1–4 The first eight verses speak of the blessings of Christ's Millennial Reign. Jerusalem will **be exalted**, Gentile **nations** will **come** there to learn about **the LORD**, and He will rule over all nations. Worldwide disarmament is vividly and concretely portrayed in the famous words: "**They shall beat their swords into plowshares, and their spears into pruning hooks.**"[3] Peace and security will prevail and the Lord will be acknowledged by all His people.

4:5–8 Verse 5 contrasts the idolatry that was practiced in Micah's day with the pure worship that will prevail in the Millennial Kingdom. The people who were crippled by captivity will be restored to the land ("I will collect the stragglers," v. 6, Moffatt), and **the LORD will reign** as King over them. The first or **former dominion** (v. 8) means the highest government on earth, the reign of the Messiah King.

4:9–13 In the meantime, Judah must go into captivity **to Babylon**. Also, before the restoration, the Lord will gather the Gentile **nations** together and judge them; Israel will be His instrument to punish them, and their wealth shall be devoted **to the Lord of the whole earth**.

VI. THE PROMISE OF THE MESSIAH'S COMING (Chap. 5)

5:1 Verse 1 seems to describe the status of the nation at the time that Micah was writing. **Israel**, here meaning Judah, is told to prepare for a **siege** by the Babylonians, who will treat the king insolently and rudely. This may refer to Sennacherib's taunting Hezekiah or Nebuchadnezzar's humiliating Zedekiah.

5:2 Verse 2 looks forward to the birth of **the One** who was **to be Ruler in Israel, whose goings forth are from of old, from everlasting**. These words point to the Messiah's eternity, and therefore His deity. Since there were two Bethlehems in the Holy Land, Micah specifies **Bethlehem**

Ephrathah, six miles south of Jerusalem. This verse is intended as a contrast to verse 1. Although Israel's contemporary situation might be discouraging, yet all would be changed when the Messiah came.

5:3 Three stages in the history of Israel are described here: (1) Because of its rejection of the Lord Jesus, it is given up. That describes its present condition in the Age of Grace. (2) Next, a time of travail awaits the nation, that is, the Tribulation. (3) After these pangs, Israel gives **birth**. This refers to the "believing remnant out of the still unbelieving nation" (Scofield). This **remnant** of **Israel** will be regathered to the land, and Christ will rule over His people.

5:4–6 Christ's shepherd care for Israel and His worldwide dominion are set forth in verse 4. **When the** future **Assyrian** army strikes Jerusalem, the Messiah **will raise** up enough capable leaders to drive them back. The expression **"seven shepherds and eight princely men"** should not be taken to mean there would literally be only fifteen leaders raised up to withstand **"the Assyrian."** When one number is followed by the next highest number in a poetic framework,[4] the meaning is that there is an adequate or complete number of whatever occurs in the context.

5:7–9 **Then** Israel will be a channel of blessing to all. The nation will be as invincible **as a lion**—well able to crush God's **adversaries**.

5:10–15 **In that day,** Israel will have been purified. It will no longer trust in **horses** and **chariots** or fortified **cities**. Sorcerers and **soothsayers** will be abolished. **Carved images** and **sacred pillars**—pagan shrines—will be destroyed. Enemy **nations** will be punished with God's **vengeance**.

VII. ISRAEL ON TRIAL (Chap. 6)

6:1–5 **The mountains** are called to serve as judges while **the LORD** (the Prosecutor) states His **case** against **Israel** (the defendant). He rehearses His kindness to them—delivering them **from . . . Egypt** and preventing **Balak** and **Balaam** from cursing them.

6:6–8 **What** does **the Most High** seek in return for this? Not extravagant animal sacrifices! Certainly not *human* sacrifices! But justice, and **mercy**, and humility. Verse 8 describes what God requires; to obey this a person must have divine life. An unconverted person is totally incapable of producing this kind of righteousness.

6:9–12 **The LORD's voice cries to the city,** recounting its sins as the cause of its calamity. The inhabitants used false **weights** and measures, they practiced **violence,** and they spoke **lies**.

6:13–16 Sin brings its own destruction, and the sins of the violent rich people would incur sickness, desolation, **hunger,** dissatisfaction, and frustration. They would not be permitted to enjoy the things they had obtained through dishonesty. **The statutes of Omri** (v. 16) may well refer to the idolatry which **Omri** encouraged (1 Kings 16:25, 26).

VIII. THE NATION BEWAILS ITS SAD STATE (7:1–10)

7:1, 2 Micah here takes his place with the nation and intercedes to God. The city has been stripped of men who are **faithful** and **upright;** violence and murder abound. The sad situation is compared with gleaning **vintage grapes** and finding **no cluster to eat**.

7:3–6 The rulers and judges ask

for bribes; their **punishment** is near. None can be depended on. Friends, neighbors, even relatives betray one another.

7:7–10 Only the LORD can be trusted. The faithful remnant of the nation warn their **enemy . . . not** to **rejoice** much **over** them. The calamity is a result of the people's sins, but the Lord will yet restore His own, to the dismay of their enemies.

IX. FUTURE BLESSING FOR ISRAEL (7:11–20)

7:11–12 Next Jerusalem is addressed. Her **walls** would be **built** again and her boundaries greatly extended. The exiles would return from the lands of their captivity, and the heathen world would be punished for its wickedness.

7:13 This verse seems strange at first reading. The desolation of **the land** probably refers to the results of the judgment of the Gentiles **for the fruit of their deeds**. This takes place just before the promised restoration. It should be noted that the Hebrew word translated "land" (*eretz*) can also mean "earth."[5] Moffatt paraphrases along these lines also: "though all the world lies desolate in retribution for its pagan ways."

7:14–17 Verse 14 is a prayer addressed to the Lord, asking for food and **shepherd** care. The Lord assures His **people** that He will do such wonderful things for them that the Gentile **nations** will **be ashamed** and will bow low before Him.

7:18–20 Micah closes his prophecy with a song of praise to **God**, extolling His **mercy**, forgiveness, **com**passion, faithfulness, and steadfast love.

ENDNOTES

[1] (1:10–14) See the literal renderings in the NKJV margin.

[2] (1:10–14) *The Bible: A New Translation*, by James Moffatt, Micah 1:10–14.

[3] (4:1–4) Although these words are inscribed on the United Nations building in New York City (from the parallel in Isa. 2:2–4, which see in this commentary), since the Prince of Peace is left out, the world cannot expect any lasting peace till He comes.

[4] (5:4–6) This numerical usage is not uncommon in the OT. See, e.g., Job 5:19, Ps. 62:11, 12; Amos 1:3.

[5] (7:13) The NIV so translates it here.

BIBLIOGRAPHY

Carlson, E. Leslie. "Micah." In *The Wycliffe Bible Commentary*. Chicago: Moody Press, 1968.

Feinberg, Charles L. *The Minor Prophets*. Chicago: Moody Press, 1976.

Keil, C. F. "Micah." In *Biblical Commentary on the Old Testament*. Vol. 24. Grand Rapids: Wm. B. Eerdmans Publishing Co., 1971.

Mills, Montague S. *The Minor Prophets: A Survey*. Dallas: 3E Ministries, n.d.

Morgan, G. Campbell. *The Minor Prophets*. Old Tappan, NJ: Fleming H. Revell Company, 1960.

Tatford, Frederick A. *The Minor Prophets*. Vol. 2. Reprint (3 vols.). Minneapolis: Klock & Klock Christian Publishers, 1982.

NAHUM

Introduction

"The descriptions given by Nahum are exceedingly fine and vivid, and the book is deservedly classed among the finest productions of Old Testament literature."

—C. H. H. Wright

I. Unique Place in the Canon

The little prophecy of Nahum, while it is written by a Hebrew against the capital of a Gentile world power (Nineveh), is not a nationalistic treatise, but a denunciation of rampant militarism and tyranny, especially as it affects God's people. Although God uses pagans to punish His people's apostasy and sin, the tool itself is also liable to punishment.

As R. K. Harrison puts it:

In this small prophecy of doom the author demonstrated in vigorous and memorable language that the God of the nation whom the Assyrians had despised was in fact the artificer and controller of all human destiny. To His justice even the greatest world power must submit in humility and shame.[1]

II. Authorship

Nahum was from Elkosh, a town not certainly known, but often identified with Capernaum (Hebrew: *Kāphar Nahûm*, Nahum's town), near the Sea of Galilee. The prophet's name means "Consoler."

III. Date

Although no date is given, it is possible to pin down the period of writing to within half a century. It had to be written *after* the conquest of No-Amon (Thebes) in 663 B.C. since Nahum mentions that event (3:8). It must have been written *before* 612 B.C. when Nineveh was destroyed. This would put the book within the long reign of idolatrous King Manasseh (696–642), probably between about 663 and 654 B.C.

IV. Background and Theme

Nahum the Elkoshite had a message of consolation to Judah since he foretold the doom of the Assyrians and the restoration of God's people. His prophecy supplements the book of Jonah. In Jonah we see Nineveh's repentance, but in Nahum the Ninevites have returned to their old ways and have incurred God's wrath. Our Lord favorably compares the Ninevites in their repentant mode with the unrepentant Pharisees (Matt. 12:41).

The little book is a classic rebuke of militarism. The Assyrians were ruthless with their enemies. Their inscriptions of military victories gloated over hanging the skins of their conquered enemies on their tents and walls. Whether a common practice or not, it reveals their mentality.

They also despised the God of Israel, the God who controls all things— including Nineveh's fall.

Nahum predicts the destruction of Nineveh, the capital of Assyria and the world's largest city of that day. In the literal sense, the prophecy has been fulfilled, but in another sense, it looks forward to the Assyrian of the future who will threaten God's people.

OUTLINE

I. THE CHARACTER OF GOD, THE JUDGE (1:1–8)

II. CERTAINTY OF THE DOOM OF NINEVEH (1:9–15)

III. DESCRIPTION OF THE SIEGE OF NINEVEH (2:1–12)

IV. GOD'S DETERMINATION TO DESTROY THE CITY (2:13—3:19)

Commentary

I. THE CHARACTER OF GOD, THE JUDGE (1:1–8)

1:1–5 The character of **God** is described as **jealous**, avenging, and wrathful on the one hand, and yet **slow to anger** and **great in power** on the other. He controls the universe and all its inhabitants. His jealousy is the righteous jealousy of a husband for the wife he loves, not an envy of others' happiness. Israel is the "wife" of Jehovah (NKJV, LORD; see Hosea).

1:6–8 When He punishes, no one can withstand Him. Yet He **is good** to **those who trust in Him**. His judgment would sweep like **an overflowing flood** through Assyria, destroying Nineveh, her capital.

II. CERTAINTY OF THE DOOM OF NINEVEH (1:9–15)

1:9–11 These words are addressed to the Assyrians. God was about to

destroy them. The **one who** plotted **evil against the LORD** would fall. This probably refers to Sennacherib or to the insolent Rabshakeh.

1:12, 13 Though the Assyrians **are** currently **safe**, they **will be cut down. Though** Israel had been **afflicted**, it will be afflicted **no more**, for God **will break off** the Assyrians' **yoke from** His people.

1:14 Next, **the LORD** addresses the Assyrian king directly. His **name** would be forgotten, his idol-temple would be pillaged, and the Lord would **dig** his **grave**, because he was **vile**.

1:15 This verse describes the messenger **who brings** the **good tidings** of Assyria's destruction and the resulting **peace** in **Judah**. Paul quotes similar words in Romans 10:15, but there they are used in a *gospel* context (Isa. 52:7).

III. DESCRIPTION OF THE SIEGE OF NINEVEH (2:1–12)

2:1 The first ten verses deal with the siege of Nineveh by the Babylonians. **"He who scatters"** may be interpreted as referring to the Lord or to the Babylonians. The frenzied inhabitants of the city are mockingly told to prepare for battle with four commands: **"Man the fort!" "Watch the road!" "Strengthen your flanks!"** and **"Fortify your power mightily."**

2:2 The LORD will restore His people. There will be some restoration of Israel's **excellence**, but it will not necessarily be soon. The Southern Kingdom had not yet been deported, but was paying tribute.

Another totally different meaning to this text is possible from an alternate translation. In his nearly 400-page commentary on Nahum's short prophecy, Walter A. Maier translates "restore" by a word of opposite meaning, "cut off," and renders "excellence" by its frequent translation, "pride." He writes:

> The statement "Yahweh hath cut off the pride of Jacob" describes a past historic punishment which Yahweh has visited upon Judah, the prophet's home, because of its haughty rejection of the Almighty. Nahum may be thinking of the devastation wrought by Sennacherib, who boasted that he had ravaged Judah.[2]

The reference to Israel as a **ruined** and **emptied** vineyard fits in with several OT images (Ps. 80:12ff; Isa. 5:5, 6; Jer. 12:10; Hos. 10:1).

2:3–6 The soldiers of Babylon are pictured in verses 3 and 4, clad in their favorite colors: the Babylonians in **red**, and their allies, the Medes, in their **scarlet** tunics. (The Assyrians' military color was blue.) The stumbling officers of verse 5 have been understood as being the Assyrian defenders, but the context points rather to the Babylonian invaders. The **rivers** pour into the city, undermining

the foundations so that **the palace is dissolved**.

2:7–10 The queen is **led away captive**. The people **flee** from the city, disregarding the order to **"Halt!"** The **wealth** and **treasure** of **Nineveh** are plundered—the **spoil of silver** and the **spoil of gold**. The city is now desolate. Fear reigns on every face.

2:11, 12 These verses will be much better appreciated when we recall that as Great Britain has the lion, and the United States has the eagle as its emblem, the Assyrians were simply mad about lions. Men's heads with lions' bodies (or vice versa) appear regularly in Assyrian art and sculpture. No doubt they thought of themselves as lions and tried to act the part.

Comparing Nineveh to a lion's den, Nahum pushes his ironical knife in deeply to wound Ninevite arrogance by using the words **lions, young lions, lioness, lion's cub**—seven times in two verses!

IV. GOD'S DETERMINATION TO DESTROY THE CITY (2:13—3:19)

2:13 The LORD **of hosts** has decreed Nineveh's utter destruction. Since the Lord has made Himself her enemy, the city does not stand a chance. Her **chariots** will be burned and her **young lions** (warriors) will **be cut off** by the **sword**. The sound of her armies would **be heard no more** and she would have no more victims.

3:1–3 Chapter 3 continues the picture of the fall of Nineveh and gives the underlying reasons: It is a **bloody city** and **full of lies and robbery**, having seized booty from many others. Now the Babylonian **horsemen** are attacking **with bright sword,**

and the streets are full of **countless corpses**.

3:4–7 The nation is being judged for **her harlotries** and **sorceries**, corrupting others with her idolatry and commerce. Jehovah will expose sinfulness and cover her with **shame**, the punishment befitting **a seductive harlot**.

3:8–10 She will not escape any more **than No Amon** (Thebes)[3] did, that great city which symbolized the concentrated might of **Ethiopia and Egypt**.

As allies or **helpers**, Thebes also counted on Put and Lubim for security. These are territories generally associated with Libya,[4] but we cannot be dogmatic. Put may have been as far south as present-day Somaliland.[5]

3:11–13 Nineveh, **also**, would **be drunk** with the cup of God's wrath. Like **ripened figs**, it was ready for judgment. Its defenses would fail when **the gates of** their **land** would swing **wide open for** their **enemies**.

3:14–17 In spite of Nineveh's most elaborate preparations **for the siege**— acquiring extra **water** and fortifying its **strongholds** with new clay bricks where needed—it would fall. Though the **merchants**, **commanders**, and **generals** were as numerous as **the stars of heaven**, yet they would desert the city **like swarming locusts** flying off at sunrise.

3:18, 19 The **shepherds** (leaders) of **Assyria** now **slumber** in death. The nation has suffered a mortal **wound. News of** its fall will cause great rejoicing because many have suffered at its hands. Nineveh fell in 612 B.C.

So thoroughly was Nahum's proph-

ecy fulfilled that, in later times, armies, such as Xenophon's and Alexander the Great's, were totally unaware that they were marching near or over the ruins of great Nineveh.

Not until the nineteenth century was the ancient site of Nineveh even definitely relocated.[6]

ENDNOTES

[1](Intro) R. K. Harrison, *Introduction to the Old Testament*, p. 930.

[2](2:2) Walter A. Maier, *The Book of Nahum, A Commentary*, p. 228.

[3](3:8–10) The Targum and Vulgate read "populous Alexandria" here.

[4](3:8–10) Our word "Libyan" is probably related to "Lubim."

[5](3:8–10) "Put" may be Egyptian "Punt," a country on the Red Sea coast as far south as Somaliland. See Maier, *Nahum*, pp. 321, 322.

[6](3:18, 19) Paul Emile Botta, Austen Henry Layard, and George Smith were pioneer archaeologists among the famed ruins of Nineveh (1840's to 1870's).

BIBLIOGRAPHY

Feinberg, Charles Lee. *The Minor Prophets*. Chicago: Moody Press, 1976.

Keil, C. F. "Nahum." In *Biblical Commentary on the Old Testament*. Vol. 25. Grand Rapids: Wm. B. Eerdmans Publishing Co., 1971.

Maier, Walter A. *The Book of Nahum. A Commentary*. Reprint. Minneapolis: James Family, 1977.

Tatford, Frederick A. *The Minor Prophets*. Vol. 1. Reprint (3 vols.). Minneapolis: Klock & Klock Christian Publishers, 1982.

HABAKKUK

Introduction

"Habakkuk was not a self-centered person concerned only with the comfort and safety of himself and his family. As a true patriot, he was deeply distressed by the moral and spiritual conditions about him. He loved his nation, and knew it was moving ever closer to the precipice of destruction by continuing to break the laws of God. Therefore two anguished questions burst forth from his lips: How long? and Why?"

—Richard W. De Haan

I. Unique Place in the Canon

Habakkuk 2:4 has the distinction of being quoted three times in the NT (see below). In Acts 13:40, 41 the apostle Paul ended his sermon in the synagogue at Antioch, Pisidia, by quoting Habakkuk 1:5, another illustration of how an apparently obscure and short OT book can have rich doctrinal content. Also, compare Habakkuk 3:17, 18 with Philippians 4:4, 10–19. Both the prophet and the apostle could rejoice in their God no matter what the outward circumstances of life might be.

As to style, the Hebrew Christian scholar Charles Feinberg writes:

> All concede to Habakkuk a very high place among the Hebrew prophets. The poetry of chapter 3 has been rightly praised on every hand as the most magnificent Hebrew poetry. The language of the book is very beautiful.[1]

II. Authorship

We know virtually nothing about this prophet. The name Habakkuk[2] may mean *embrace* or *wrestle*.

Since he is one of only a handful to call himself a prophet, some scholars believe that he not only had the *gift* of prophecy, but the *office* as well. (Daniel, for example, was a statesman by calling, but a prophet by gift.) Since Habakkuk refers to musical instruments in chapter 3 it has been suggested that he may have been associated with the temple choir, though this is only a conjecture.

III. Date

Because Habakkuk mentions no kings, his little prophecy is hard to date. It is probably from the 600's B.C., though of course, some rationalistic critics date it much later for reasons of their own. Conservative scholars generally place the prophet during the reigns of either Manasseh, Josiah, or Jehoiakim, all kings of the seventh century B.C. The last named king's reign is perhaps the best choice, with a date near the Battle of Carchemish (605 B.C.), at which Babylon was victorious.

IV. Background and Theme

The religious revival under King Josiah did not last long. Public morals, once more influenced by the licentious Baal and Ashtaroth cults, were very low. Injustice was widespread. These were the deplorable conditions with which Habakkuk had to deal.

This prophet spoke to Judah prior to the Babylonian captivity (586 B.C.). Since his name may mean "wrestler," it is fitting that he wrestled with Jehovah over the sin and punishment of the people of Judah.

Preferring the meaning "to embrace," Feinberg quotes Martin Luther with favor as follows:

Habakkuk signifies an embracer, or one who embraces another, takes him into his arms. He embraces his people, and takes them to his arms, i.e., he comforts them and holds them up, as one embraces a weeping child, to quiet it with the assurance that, if God wills, it shall soon be better.[3]

OUTLINE

Commentary

I. THE PROPHET IS PERPLEXED THAT GOD DOES NOT PUNISH THE INIQUITY OF JUDAH (1:1–4)

The burden (or **oracle**, NKJV marg.) **which the prophet Habakkuk saw** is probably a title for the whole book. In verses 2–4, he complained to the Lord about the terrible **violence**, **iniquity**, robbery, **strife**, and injustice in Judah. He asked **the LORD how long** it would be allowed to go unpunished. Because of this and similar questionings of God, Habakkuk has sometimes been called "the doubting Thomas of the OT."

The first eleven verses of the prophecy are a dialogue between Habakkuk and the Lord.

II. THE LORD REPLIES THAT HE WILL USE THE BABYLONIANS TO PUNISH JUDAH (1:5–11)

God's answer is given in verses 5–11. He would raise up the Chaldean army to punish Judah. The enemy would be **hasty, bitter,** avaricious, violent, dreadful, and proud. The Babylonians were noted for their cavalry, swift in conquest and fiercer **than evening wolves**. They scoffed at captive **kings and princes**, and their might was their **god**. Feinberg comments:

> The success of the Chaldean will be multiplied; he will carry all before him, as the wind sweeps over vast stretches of land. In doing so, the Chaldean conqueror heaps up guilt before God because of his ungodly ambitions and his subjugation of many helpless peoples.[4]

III. HABAKKUK NOW QUESTIONS GOD'S CHOICE OF A MORE WICKED NATION TO PUNISH JUDAH (1:12–17)

When Habakkuk heard this, he was troubled, and his agitation brought forth the second dialogue (1:12—2:20). How could God punish Judah by a nation that was worse than they were? He argues with God based on his knowledge that God is **of purer eyes than to behold evil, and cannot look on wickedness**. And the Babylonians were undoubtedly wicked! However, Judah's wickedness was greater, since the Jews were sinning against much greater light. How could God **look** upon the **wickedness** of the Babylonians as they took men captive by the netful, even by the **hook** and the **net**? They sacrificed to their idols and grew fat. Would there be no end to their slaughter of the **nations**? J. E. Evans explains:

> An analogy was drawn from the life of a fisherman. The men were like fishes whom the fisherman collected in his net, and then paid divine honors to the net by which he has been so enriched. In this comparison, the world was the sea; the nation was the fishes; Nebuchadnezzar was the fisherman; the net was the military might of the Chaldean by which he was able to gain great wealth through the conquest.[5]

IV. GOD'S ANSWER IS THAT THE JUST PEOPLE OF JUDAH WILL SURVIVE, BUT THE UNJUST CHALDEANS WILL BE DESTROYED (Chap. 2)

A. Habakkuk Awaits God's Answer (2:1)

Habakkuk retired to his watchtower to see how the Lord would answer him. He wanted to get alone in order to gain God's perspective. This is a most important principle for believers today as well. Whether we call it our "quiet time," "devotions," or by some other term, daily communion with God is crucial for every Christian.

B. Instructions to Record the Answer and Await Its Fulfillment (2:2, 3)

2:2 The LORD commanded the prophet: **"Write the vision"** (His answer to Habakkuk's question) so that the **one who** read **it** might **run** with the news (of the downfall of Babylon and the restoration of Judah).

2:3 A. J. Pollock says that this verse refers to the hope of the Jew—Christ's coming to earth to subdue His enemies, take out of His kingdom all things that offend, and set up His glorious reign, making Israel the head of the nations because He will be at the head of the Jewish nation.[6] When verse 3 is quoted in Hebrews 10:37, the **"it"** (i.e., **the vision**) becomes "He" (i.e., the Lord), who **will surely come** and **will not tarry**. The NT context refers to the hope of the Christian—the Rapture of the church.

C. The Just Shall Live by Faith, and the Unjust Chaldeans Will Die (2:4)

Because the **soul** of the king of Babylon was lifted up with pride, he would die, but the godly remnant of Israel would **live by . . . faith**. Verse 4c is quoted three times in the NT. The three parts of the verse—the just—shall live—by faith, go well with the emphases of the three contexts where they appear: Romans 1:17 emphasizes "the just"; Gal. 3:11 emphasizes "faith"; Heb. 10:38 emphasizes "shall live." The literal rendering in Habakkuk's context, is "By his faith the just shall live." It could also be paraphrased "the justified-by-faith-one shall live."

D. Catalog of the Chaldean's Sins (2:5–19)

1. Endless Appetite for Conquest (2:5–8)

2:5 **Wine** drinking was a national sin of Babylon, and, no doubt, of Nebuchadnezzar. Keil writes that this addiction "is attested by ancient writers . . ., and it is well known from Dan. [chap.] v. that Babylon was conquered while Belshazzar and the great men of his kingdom were feasting at a riotous banquet."[7] In addition, the latter had an insatiable thirst for conquest.

2:6–8 Verse 6 begins a taunt song, containing five woes against Babylon. The first **woe** is against lust for empire, or aggression. The **many nations** which Nebuchadnezzar had conquered would taunt him for his ill-gotten gain, and would **oppress** and **plunder** Babylon as he had done to them.

2. Greed and Pride (2:9–11)

A second **woe** is pronounced on Nebuchadnezzar for his covetousness and pride. He tried to make his dynasty safe from the reach of **disaster**, but his dishonest **gain** and cruelty would **cry out** against him.

3. Enrichment through Bloodshed (2:12–14)

The third woe against the king was for his lust for magnificence and his bloodshedding tactics. The cities of Babylon, built by slave labor, would merely end up feeding the insatiable fire, and the earth would acknowledge Jehovah as the true God.

But a day is coming when the one true God will be globally acknowledged. This glorious time is predicted in a deservedly famous poetic comparison: **"For the earth will be filled with the knowledge of the glory of the Lord, as the waters cover the sea"** (2:14).

4. Corruption of Neighbors (2:15–17)

The fourth woe is against Nebuchadnezzar for taking a savage delight in corrupting other nations, for shamelessness, and for his destruction of Jerusalem and Judah. In short, Nebuchadnezzar was guilty of promoting two main ingredients of modern television, movies, and "literature"—shameless sexual lifestyles (including forms of perversion) and inordinate violence.

5. Idolatry (2:18, 19)

The fifth and final woe condemns the king for the idolatry of Babylon in vividly sarcastic lines. What good is a gold or silver-plated idol when there is no breath in it at all?

E. Silence Enjoined Before the Storm of God's Judgment (2:20)

A beautiful musical setting of this verse is used in some churches to subdue the congregation to quiet contemplation of the sermon. Unfortunately, while the words fit, the context of the text is that the Lord is about to demonstrate His power in judgment. For that reason **all the earth** should **keep silence before Him**.

V. HABAKKUK PRAYS AND TRUSTS (Chap. 3)[8]

A. He Appeals to God to Act for His People (3:1, 2)

Habakkuk now prays to the Lord. He had heard of the Lord's dealings in the past with the enemies of His people; now he asks Him to revive His work by punishing His foes and saving His people.

B. He Reviews God's Care for Israel from Egypt to Canaan (3:3–15)

3:3–7 In a splendid vision of God's sovereignty that Scroggie calls a "Theophanic Ode"[9] (song about God's manifestation), Habakkuk pictures God marching forth against His foes, crushing them by His power and triumphing gloriously. He makes frequent allusions to the Lord's past punishment of Israel's enemies, the judgment of Egypt at the time of the Exodus, the countries that opposed Israel on the way to the promised land, and the nations that had to be driven out of Canaan by Joshua.

In the first section of the prayer God's glory and brightness are seen in both the *heavens* and the earth.

The geographical details—Teman, Mount Paran, Cushan, and Midian, all speak of enemies of Israel. For example, Teman, a large city in Edom, stands for all of Idumea, and Cushan is probably the same as "Cush," or Ethiopia.

3:8–11 God's power is stressed in these words, especially as manifested over the rivers, the seas, and the mountains.

Verse 11 refers to the famous event at Gibeon during which the Lord worked a mighty miracle in the sky to help Joshua win the battle (Josh. 10:12).

3:12–15 Here God is seen marching **through the land** for Israel and trampling their **enemies** in anger.

The reference in v. 15 is to the crossing of the Red Sea (Ex. 14) when there was a **heap of great waters** on either side of the people of God as they marched through as if on dry land. Habakkuk envisions God as moving **through the sea with** His **horses**.

C. He Waits for the Enemy to Be Punished (3:16)

When the prophet **heard** of the judgment of the Babylonian invaders, he **trembled** and determined to wait quietly for the event to come to pass.

D. No Matter What Happens, He Will Trust in God, His Strength (3:17–19)

In the meantime, whatever trials the prophet Habakkuk and his people might be called upon to endure as a result of the Babylonian invasion— **Though the fig tree may not blossom, . . . and the fields yield no food; . . . and there be no herd in the stalls**—he would **rejoice in the** Lord and **joy in the God of** his **salvation**. Baxter exclaims:

> The literal is "I will jump for joy in the Lord; I will spin around for delight in God." Here is the hilarity of faith!—joy at its best with circumstances at their worst! What a victory! May it be ours![10]

ENDNOTES

[1](Intro) Charles Lee Feinberg, *Habakkuk, Zephaniah, Haggai and Malachi*, p. 12.

[2](Intro) Most people accent the name on the first syllable, but accenting the second syllable is preferred in English. In Hebrew the last syllable is accented (*Ha-ba-KOOK*).

[3](Intro) Feinberg, *Habakkuk*, p. 11.

[4](1:5–11) *Ibid.*, p. 17.

[5](1:12–17) J. E. Evans, further documentation unavailable.

[6](2:3) A. J. Pollock, further documentation unavailable.

[7](2:5) C. F. Keil, "Habakkuk," in *Biblical Commentary on the Old Testament*, Vol. 25, pp. 74, 75.

[8](Chap. 3) This lovely chapter was set to music by the Jews and used in their worship service.

[9](3:3–7) Scroggie, "Habakkuk," in *Know Your Bible*, Vol. 1, The Old Testament, p. 196.

[10](3:17–19) J. Sidlow Baxter, *Explore the Book*, p. 212.

BIBLIOGRAPHY

De Haan, Richard W. *Song in the Night*. Grand Rapids: Radio Bible Class (booklet), 1969.

Feinberg, Charles Lee. *Habakkuk, Zephaniah, Haggai and Malachi*. New York: American Board of Missions to the Jews, 1951.

Kelly, William. *Lectures Introductory to the Study of the Minor Prophets*. London: C. A. Hammond Trust Bible Depot, n.d.

Keil, C. F. "Habakkuk." In *Biblical Commentary on the Old Testament*. Vol. 25. Grand Rapids: Wm. B. Eerdmans Publishing Company, 1971.

Scroggie, W. Graham. "Habakkuk." In *Know Your Bible*. Vol. 1. The Old Testament. London: Pickering & Inglis Ltd., n.d.

Tatford, Frederick A. *The Minor Prophets*. Vol. 3. Reprint (3 vols.). Minneapolis: Klock & Klock Christian Publishers, 1982.

Introduction

"If anyone wishes all the secret oracles of the prophets to be given in a brief compendium, let him read through this brief Zephaniah."
—Martin Bucer (1528)

I. Unique Place in the Canon

Many people are "royalty-watchers" and enjoy following the nobility. As a great grandson of good King Hezekiah,[1] and thus a distant cousin of the currently reigning godly King Josiah, Zephaniah may have been a member of this set. Sad to say, between the reigns of these two righteous kings there had been over half a century of evil rule by Amon and Manasseh. Zephaniah probably had access to the royal court in the capital of the Southern Kingdom, Judah.

II. Authorship

We know very little about Zephaniah the son of Cushi. His name means *Jehovah hides*, i.e., "protects" or "treasures." His genealogy, as noted, traces back to a royal forebear. He liked to put dark against light and light against dark, painting a very gloomy picture of the Day of the Lord, yet giving a very bright foreglimpse of Israel's coming glory and the conversion of the Gentiles to the Lord. As Hewitt points out, the Prophet Zephaniah minced no words:

There is no compromise in the language used. He denounces sin and announces judgment with perfect fearlessness and closes his book with a song full of inspiration and hope looking forward to the inauguration of the Millennial Kingdom.[2]

III. Date

Zephaniah ministered during the reign of Josiah (640–609 B.C.). Believing scholars are divided as to whether he wrote before or after the great revival of 621 B.C. If before, his prophecy likely helped bring about the spiritual awakening. But several details, such as quoting the newly rediscovered law, would suggest a date after 621. Since Zephaniah 2:13 shows that Nineveh was still standing, a date before that city's destruction in 612 B.C. is called for. Hence the book was probably written between 621 and 612 B.C.

IV. Background and Theme

Zephaniah probably prophesied from Jerusalem ("this place," 1:4). The historical background of his prophecy will be found in 2 Kings 21—23 and the early chapters of Jeremiah:

Zephaniah saw the menacing hordes of Scythians, rising over the horizon, swift and terrible in their movements .... The position of Judah was delicate and difficult, for with its small resources it could not hope to prevail over the great powers. When the greater nations to the north and south of Judah strove for the mastery of the world, the weak nations that lay between became involved and were often ravaged. Aware of the seething unrest all around, Zephaniah became a preacher of righteousness and denounced the evils of his age in unsparing terms.[3]

He uses the expression "the Day of the Lord" seven times in his little book. This gives the theme of the book: God's judgment is coming on Judah for disobedience. Other key expressions are "jealousy" and "in the midst." God is jealous in the sense that He resents the idolatry of His people. He is "in the midst" first as a righteous Judge (3:5) and then as Conqueror of their foes (3:15).

OUTLINE

I. GOD'S DETERMINATION TO EXECUTE JUDGMENT (Chap. 1)
    A. On All the Earth (1:1–3)
    B. On Judah and Jerusalem because of Idolatry (1:4–6)
    C. The Day of the Lord under the Figure of a Sacrifice (1:7–13)
       1. Guests—Judah's Enemies (1:7)
       2. Victims—Wicked People of Judah (1:8–13)
    D. The Terror of the Day of the Lord (1:14–18)
II. JUDAH IS CALLED TO REPENT (2:1–3)
III. THE DOOM OF GENTILE NATIONS (2:4–15)
    A. The Philistines (2:4–7)
    B. The Moabites and Ammonites (2:8–11)
    C. The Ethiopians (2:12)
    D. The Assyrians and Especially the City of Nineveh (2:13–15)
IV. WOE PRONOUNCED ON JERUSALEM (3:1–7)
    A. Disobedience, Unresponsiveness, Unbelief, Impenitence (3:1, 2)
    B. Greed of the Princes and the Judges (3:3)
    C. Levity and Treachery of the Prophets and Sacrilege of the Priests (3:4)
    D. The Lord's Presence in Judgment (3:5–7)
V. MESSAGE OF COMFORT TO THE FAITHFUL REMNANT (3:8–20)
    A. Destruction of Wicked Gentiles (3:8)
    B. Conversion of the Remaining Nations (3:9)
    C. Restoration of Dispersed Israel (3:10–13)
    D. Rejoicing over the Second Advent of Christ (3:14–17)
    E. What God Will Do for His People (3:18–20)

Commentary

I. GOD'S DETERMINATION TO EXECUTE JUDGMENT (Chap. 1)

A. On All the Earth (1:1–3)

It is usual for prophets to name their father, and sometimes their grandfather, as the Jews were very "roots"-oriented, as we would say today. But **Zephaniah the son of Cushi** traces back four generations of his ancestors, doubtless to let us know of his regal forebear, King **Hezekiah.**

The chapter as a whole describes the destruction of **the** whole **land**, then specifically of Jerusalem and Judah. God will make **the whole land . . . utterly** desolate.

B. On Judah and Jerusalem because of Idolatry (1:4–6)

The **inhabitants** of **Judah** will be punished for their idolatry—their **Baal**-worship, their star-**worship**, and their worship of **Milcom**, the god of the Ammonites.

C. The Day of the Lord under the Figure of a Sacrifice (1:7–13)

1. Guests—Judah's Enemies (1:7)

The LORD **has prepared a sacrifice**; Judah is the victim, and the Babylonians are the **guests**.

2. Victims—Wicked People of Judah (1:8–13)

God **will punish** Judah for their idolatrous **apparel** and practices, and for their **violence and deceit**. Howls will go up from such various sections of the capital as **the Fish Gate**, **the Second Quarter**, and **the hills**, as the invaders slaughter and take **booty**.

D. The Terror of the Day of the Lord (1:14–18)

The most vivid picture in the Bible of **the day of the** LORD is given here; it is **the day of** God's **wrath** on men because of their wickedness, the men of Judah in particular. It is **a day of** war, **distress**, and slaughter. A classic Latin hymn is based on verses 15 and 16:

> Thomas of Celano in 1250 wrote his famous judgment hymn from verse 15, *Dies irae, dies illa*, meaning "That day is a day of wrath." The day is one of wrath, trouble, distress, wasteness, desolation (the Hebrew

words for wasteness and desolation—*sho'ah* and *umesho'ah*—are alike in sound to convey the monotony of the destruction), darkness, gloominess, clouds, thick darkness, trumpet, alarm against fortified cities and high towers.[4]

God is jealous of the affections of His people and will punish all rivals.

II. JUDAH IS CALLED TO REPENT (2:1–3)

God calls on the **undesirable** (or shameless, NKJV marg.) **nation** to repent. Verse 3 seems to point to a remnant of righteous Jews. If they **seek the** LORD, they **will be hidden in the day of** His fierce **anger**.

III. THE DOOM OF GENTILE NATIONS (2:4–15)

A. The Philistines (2:4–7)

Verses 4–15 foretell judgment on surrounding nations to the west, east, south, and north. First are **the Philistines**, who are also identified by their other name—**the Cherethites**. Their cities—**Gaza**, **Ashkelon**, **Ashdod**—will be **forsaken** and **desolate**. They will be destroyed, and their **land** will be used by **Judah** for pasture.

B. The Moabites and Ammonites (2:8–11)

Next come **Moab** and **Ammon**. God had heard their insolent words and boasts **against** His **people**. They will be left desolate, and the **residue** of God's **people** will dwell there. Verse 11 anticipates millennial conditions, when **the** LORD has reduced **to nothing all the gods of the earth**.

C. The Ethiopians (2:12)

Ethiopia will be punished **by** God's **sword** (the king of Babylon). Some, such as Feinberg, link **"Ethiopians"** here with Egypt:

> The fortunes of Ethiopia were bound up with those of Egypt which was subject to Ethiopic dynasties. Note Jeremiah 46:9 and Ezekiel 30:5, 9. There is reason to believe that Egypt itself is meant under the term Ethiopians.[5]

D. The Assyrians and Especially the City of Nineveh (2:13–15)

Nebuchadnezzar will also **destroy Assyria. Nineveh** will be a refuge for animals and birds, and **everyone who passes by her shall hiss and shake his fist**.

IV. WOE PRONOUNCED ON JERUSALEM (3:1–7)

A. Disobedience, Unresponsiveness, Unbelief, Impenitence (3:1, 2)

The city of Jerusalem, personified as a woman, is condemned as being **rebellious, polluted,** and **oppressing**. She has been disobedient and has **not trusted in the LORD** or **drawn near to her God**.

B. Greed of the Princes and the Judges (3:3)

Her princes . . . are like **roaring lions**, and **her judges** are as greedy as **evening wolves**.

C. Levity and Treachery of the Prophets and Sacrilege of the Priests (3:4)

Her prophets are faithless, and **her priests** profane. Feinberg comments:

> In verse 4 we have the only denunciation of the prophets in this book. They were guilty of levity, trifling with the weightiest matters. There was no gravity or steadfastness in their life or teaching. They were treach-

erous because unfaithful to Him whom they claimed to represent, rather encouraging the people in their apostasy from the Lord. By their unholy deeds they profaned the sanctuary; they made the sacred profane. They did violence to the law by distorting its plain intent and meaning when they were teaching the people.[6]

D. The Lord's Presence in Judgment (3:5–7)

In spite of all this sin and corruption, **the LORD** is **in her midst** to judge righteously. He had punished other **nations**, thinking that this would **surely** cause Judah to **fear** Him, but the people became even more corrupt.

V. MESSAGE OF COMFORT TO THE FAITHFUL REMNANT (3:8–20)

A. Destruction of Wicked Gentiles (3:8)

The faithful remnant of Judah is exhorted to **wait for** God **until** He destroys **all** His foes **with the fire of** His **jealousy**.[7]

B. Conversion of the Remaining Nations (3:9)

The **pure language** of verse 9 probably does not refer to a universal tongue but rather to lips that are undefiled by idolatry, or to speech that is pure with praise to Jehovah. **All peoples** will **serve Him with one accord**.

C. Restoration of Dispersed Israel (3:10–13)

In that Millennial Day the Gentiles will **bring** the dispersed Jews back to the land as an **offering** to the Lord. Wicked men **who rejoice in** their **pride** will be destroyed from Judah, and therefore will no longer cause the believing **remnant of Israel** to be afraid. Those who are left will be humble and meek, trusting in the name of the LORD and living righteously.

D. Rejoicing over the Second Advent of Christ (3:14–17)

Verses 14–20 give the song of restored Israel, praising Jehovah (NKJV, LORD) for His mighty deliverance and celebrating His love for His own. The daughter of Zion has much to sing, shout, and rejoice about! Not only have her enemies been thrown out, but the Messiah-King, the LORD Himself, is right in her midst. There is no need to be weak or fear, because God the Mighty One will quiet her with His love.

E. What God Will Do for His People (3:18–20)

Since judgment was soon to be upon the people, the LORD ends the prophecy with a strong promise of a complete turnabout for the godly remnant. Instead of the reproach and sorrow of missing the appointed assembly, the exiles will be granted praise and fame in every land where they were put to shame.

ENDNOTES

[1](Intro) The "Hizkiah" in 1:1 of KJV is exactly the same spelling as Hezekiah in the original Hebrew.

[2](Intro) J. B. Hewitt, *Outline Studies in the Minor Prophets*, p. 45.

[3](Intro) *Ibid.*, p. 44.

[4](1:14–18) Charles Lee Feinberg, *Habakkuk, Zephaniah, Haggai, Malachi*, p. 50.

[5](2:12) *Ibid.*, p. 59.

[6](3:4) *Ibid.*, p. 64.

[7](3:8) Zephaniah 3:8 is the only verse in the original text of the OT which contains all the letters of the Hebrew alphabet.

BIBLIOGRAPHY

Feinberg, Charles Lee. *Habakkuk, Zephaniah, Haggai and Malachi*. New York: American Board of Missions to the Jews, Inc., 1951.

———. *The Minor Prophets*. Chicago: Moody Press, 1976.

Hewitt, J. B. *Outline Studies in the Minor Prophets*. West Glamorgan, U.K.: Precious Seed Publications, n.d.

Keil, C. F. "Zephaniah." In *Biblical Commentary on the Old Testament*. Vol. 26. Grand Rapids: Wm. B. Eerdmans Publishing Co., 1971.

Kelly, William. *Lectures Introductory to the Study of the Minor Prophets*. London: C. A. Hammond Trust Bible Depot, n.d.

Morgan, G. Campbell. *The Minor Prophets*. Old Tappan, N.J.: Fleming H. Revell Company, 1960.

Tatford, Frederick A. *The Minor Prophets*. Vol. 3. Reprint (3 vols.). Minneapolis: Klock & Klock Christian Publishers, 1982.

HAGGAI

Introduction

"Few prophets have succeeded in packing into such brief compass so much spiritual common sense as Haggai did."

—Frank E. Gaebelein

I. Unique Place in the Canon

The unique thrust of this second shortest book in the OT is simple: Rebuild the temple! The remnant that had returned to Palestine to rebuild had let the work stand idle for sixteen years and so Haggai was commissioned to exhort the lethargic Jews to get to work. Haggai expands his message to include judgment on ungodly nations, as well as future glory for God's people.

II. Authorship

Haggai may have been born on a Jewish holiday since his name means "festal" or "festive." He is the sole character in the OT with this name. Or, perhaps he was named by believing parents in hopes of a future joyful restoration, since he was likely born in exile.

Haggai is the first of three prophets to minister after the return from Babylon, along with Zechariah and Malachi. Ezra mentions Haggai in 5:1 and 6:14 but our knowledge of his life amounts to practically nothing. This points up the importance of the message and the *God* who commissions the prophet, as over against the modern (and age-old) tendency to glorify the preacher.[1]

III. Date

Haggai can be dated precisely at 520 B.C.—"the second year of King Darius" (Darius I).

IV. Background and Theme

As a post-captivity prophet, Haggai returned to the land of Israel when Zerubbabel led the first group back from Babylon. His ministry was to encourage the people to rebuild the temple (Ezra 5:1).

The key expression is, "I am with you, says the LORD" (1:13; 2:4). Other significant expressions are, "Consider your ways" (1:5, 7; 2:15, 18), and, "Be strong" (2:4).

OUTLINE

C. Encouraged by Haggai, the People Resumed Work on the Temple
(1:12–15)

II. SECOND PROPHECY—TWENTY-FIRST DAY OF SEVENTH MONTH
(2:1–9)

A. The Prophet Again Encouraged the People with Assurance of the
Lord's Presence (2:1–5)

B. The Glory of the Future Temple Would Exceed that of the Past (2:6–9)

III. THIRD PROPHECY—TWENTY-FOURTH DAY OF NINTH MONTH (2:10–19)

A. Sacrifices Offered on the Altar Were Unclean as Long as the Temple
Was in Ruins (2:10–14)

B. Before the Foundation of the Temple Was Laid, the People Suffered
from Scarcity (2:15–17)

C. If They Would Resume Work on the Temple, the Lord Would Bless
Them (2:18, 19)

IV. FOURTH PROPHECY—TWENTY-FOURTH DAY OF NINTH MONTH
(2:20–23)

The People Encouraged by Promise of the Overthrow of Gentile Kingdoms
and Establishment of the Messiah's Reign

Commentary

I. FIRST PROPHECY—FIRST DAY OF SIXTH MONTH (Chap. 1)

A. Rebuke for Neglect in Rebuilding the Temple (1:1–4)

This prophecy is dated as being in the second year of King Darius, the Medo-Persian king. The LORD reproved the people of Judah for delay in rebuilding the temple, while they themselves were living comfortably in their paneled houses.

B. Failure to Rebuild Resulted in Scarcity and Drought (1:5–11)

They should have been warned by their recent history. When they neglected the Lord's house, they suffered hunger, thirst, and poverty. Now the LORD commanded them to start work on the temple. As long as

God's **house** lay in ruins, they could expect nothing but **drought**.

C. Encouraged by Haggai, the People Resumed Work on the Temple (1:12–15)

Zerubbabel, the **governor of Judah**, and Joshua . . . , **the high priest**, together **with all the remnant of the people, obeyed** the Word of **the LORD** and began rebuilding twenty-three days after the command to rebuild.

II. SECOND PROPHECY— TWENTY-FIRST DAY OF SEVENTH MONTH (2:1–9)

A. The Prophet Again Encouraged the People with Assurance of the Lord's Presence (2:1–5)

About a month later, **in the seventh month**, the people had become discouraged with the new building, when they thought of the **glory** of the **former . . . temple**. The leaders were told to **"Be strong"** and **not** to **fear** because God's **Spirit** remained **among** them.

B. The Glory of the Future Temple Would Exceed that of the Past (2:6–9)

God encouraged the leaders with the assurance that **the glory of** the **temple** of the future (millennial) would **be greater than** any of its predecessors. **"The Desire of All Nations"** is often taken to refer to the Messiah and His return to the **temple**. However, the context suggests that it might mean the *treasures of the nations* (NKJV marg.).[2] Their **silver** and **gold** would flow into Jerusalem to beautify the temple. Verse 9a reads: **"The glory of this latter temple shall be greater than the former . . . ."** The two temples were viewed as one house. In addition to **glory**, **peace** is also promised for that future time.

III. THIRD PROPHECY— TWENTY-FOURTH DAY OF NINTH MONTH (2:10–19)

A. Sacrifices Offered on the Altar Were Unclean as Long as the Temple Was in Ruins (2:10–14)

The third prophecy was given **on the twenty-fourth day of the ninth month**. The people were told to **ask the priests** two questions: (1) If . . . **holy meat** carried **in the fold of** a **garment** should touch other foods, would those other foods **become holy? The priests** correctly **answered . . . "No."** (2) **If one who** has become **unclean** through touching **a dead body** should touch these foods, would they become **unclean? The priests** correctly **answered** "Yes."

In other words the following was understood: "He that is holy imparts no holiness to anything else, but he that is defiled communicates defilement."[3] Or, to put it another way, "Work and worship do not sanctify sin, but sin contaminates work and worship."[4] This was a reminder to the **people** that their offerings to God were polluted and that they themselves were **unclean** as long as the temple was in ruins.

B. Before the Foundation of the Temple Was Laid, the People Suffered from Scarcity (2:15–17)

Before they had started building **the temple**, they had experienced shortages of grain and **wine**, and their crops had suffered **blight, mildew**, and **hail**. Even since then, their interminable delays in rebuilding had brought the chastisement of God in hardship and deprivation.

C. If They Would Resume Work on the Temple, the Lord Would Bless Them (2:18, 19)

But **from** the **day** on which they would lay **the foundation of the Lord's temple**, God would **bless** them.

IV. FOURTH PROPHECY— TWENTY-FOURTH DAY OF NINTH MONTH (2:20–23)

The People Encouraged by Promise of the Overthrow of Gentile Kingdoms and Establishment of the Messiah's Reign

Zerubbabel is here a type of the Lord Jesus Christ. God would **overthrow** and **destroy** this world's **Gentile kingdoms** and set up Christ's Millennial Kingdom. The **signet ring** indicates that divine authority to rule is committed to the Messiah.

ENDNOTES

[1](Intro) Dr. Howard Hendricks has a colorful phrase for this all-too-common disposition to gush over successful preachers after a sermon: "The glorification of the worm ceremony."

[2](2:6–9) The capitalization in the NKJV goes with this traditional interpretation but the lower case "the desire of all nations" in the margin suggests the alternative view.

[3](2:10–14) William Kelly, *Lectures Introductory to the Study of the Minor Prophets*, p. 427.

[4](2:10–14) Donald Campbell, further documentation unavailable.

BIBLIOGRAPHY

Baldwin, Joyce G. *Haggai, Zechariah, Malachi: An Introduction and Commentary*. The Tyndale Old Testament Commentaries. Downers Grove, IL: InterVarsity Press, 1972.

Feinberg, Charles Lee. *The Minor Prophets*. Chicago: Moody Press, 1976.

Kelly, William. *Lectures Introductory to the Study of the Minor Prophets*. London: C. A. Hammond Trust Bible Depot, n.d.

Keil, C. F. "Haggai." In *Biblical Commentary on the Old Testament*. Vol. 26. Grand Rapids: Wm. B. Eerdmans Publishing Co., 1971.

Tatford, Frederick A. *The Minor Prophets*. Vol. 3. Reprint (3 vols.). Minneapolis: Klock & Klock Christian Publishers, 1982.

ZECHARIAH

Introduction

"The prophecy of Zechariah is profoundly precious to the Christian because of its unique Messianic emphasis and its panoramic unfolding of the events connected with the first and especially the second advent of Christ and the consequent millennial restoration of the nation Israel."

—Merrill F. Unger

I. Unique Place in the Canon

Genesis, Psalms, and Isaiah are the most quoted books in the NT, which, considering their length and crucial contents, is not surprising. Most would be amazed to learn that Zechariah, with only fourteen chapters, is quoted about forty times in the NT. Doubtless this is due especially to the fact that the book is so messianic, certainly the most Christ-centered of the Minor Prophets.

Zechariah's fascinating symbolic visions, plus his messages and revelations, all enhance the importance and interest of this post-exilic book.

II. Authorship

There are about thirty men in the OT named Zechariah (Jehovah remembers), the same name as the NT (Greek) Zacharias and English Zachary.

This prophet and priest was born probably in Babylon during the exile. Nehemiah mentions his arrival at Jerusalem (12:4, 16) and Ezra mentions his ministry (5:1; 6:14). Zechariah took over the short public ministry of the older Haggai to encourage the remnant.

Zechariah had a long ministry and wrote chapters 9–14 probably much later than the dated sections.

III. Date

Zechariah started his prophecies in 520 B.C., the same year that Haggai ministered, but he continued for at least three years.

IV. Background and Theme

Zechariah was the son of Berechiah. Like Haggai, he was a prophet to the people of Judah who had returned to the land after the captivity. He joined with Haggai in encouraging them to rebuild the temple (Ezra 5:1). Zechariah's prophecy began half-way between Haggai's second and third messages.

In eight visions, using highly symbolic language, he predicted the overthrow of Gentile world powers; the judgment of apostate Jews because of their rejection of Christ; the cleansing, restoration, and glory of a remnant; and the future prosperity of Jerusalem. The first five visions are messages of grace; the last three, of judgment.

Zechariah's notable prophecies

concerning the Messiah foretell His entry into Jerusalem (9:9); His betrayal for thirty pieces of silver (11:12, 13); His death as the stricken Shepherd (13:7); His coming again to the Mount of Olives (14:4); and His Millennial Reign as High Priest and King (14:9).

While many of the prophecies had a partial application or fulfillment in Zechariah's day, there are many that are still future.

OUTLINE

Commentary

I. EXHORTATION TO REPENTANCE AND OBEDIENCE, AND WARNING TO PROFIT FROM MISTAKES OF FATHERS (1:1–6)

The first six verses are introductory. They convey a message from the LORD through Zechariah the son of Berechiah to the people, urging them to return to the Lord. Verse 3 strikes the keynote of the book: **"Thus says the LORD of hosts: 'Return to Me,' says the LORD of hosts, 'and I will return to you,' says the LORD of hosts."** He urges the people to profit from the mistakes of their **fathers**, who refused to listen to **the former prophets**, such as Isaiah, Jeremiah, and Hosea. Judgment overtook the people, as the Lord had warned, and then they realized that **the LORD** was dealing with them because of their evil ways.

II. SERIES OF EIGHT VISIONS, DESIGNED TO ENCOURAGE PEOPLE TO REBUILD THE TEMPLE (1:7—6:8)

Zechariah begins his book with a prophetic panorama from his own time to the Millennial Kingdom.

A. Man Riding on a Red Horse (1:7–17)

Meaning: God is displeased with the Gentiles who are at rest while His people suffer. He will punish the nations and restore His people.

1:7–11 In verse 7, the prophet begins his series of eight visions.

In the first vision, the Lord is seen (**man** on the **red horse**, compare **"the Angel of the LORD,"** v. 11) with His agents (probably angels) who patrol **the earth** on **red, sorrel, and white . . . horses. The myrtle trees in the hollow** or low place represent Israel under Gentile subjugation. When the prophet asks the meaning of the riders, an interpreting **angel** promises to explain, but the Lord (**the man** standing **among the myrtle trees**) answers that their function is to patrol **the earth**. The patrols report to the Lord that **all the earth** is **quietly** at rest, probably meaning that the Gentile nations, especially Babylon, are at ease while God's people are being oppressed.

1:12–17 The Angel of the LORD intercedes to **the LORD of hosts** for **Jerusalem and . . . Judah**, which have been desolate for **seventy years**. Given an encouraging reply, **the** interpreting **angel** tells the prophet to **proclaim** that God will intervene for His people. **The nations** had angered God by their cruelty to Judah. God would return **to Jerusalem**, and the temple would be rebuilt. The **surveyor's line** here speaks of reconstruction whereas

in 2 Kings 21:13, it signifies destruction. . . . The prophet should tell the people that God will prosper the **cities** of Judah, **comfort Zion, and will again choose Jerusalem.**

B. Four Horns and Four Craftsmen (1:18–21)

Meaning: Destruction of four Gentile world empires.

The complete fulfillment of this second vision is still future. The **four horns** are identified as the four nations which have **scattered Judah**, Israel, and Jerusalem—in other words, the four Gentile world empires: Babylon, Medo-Persia, Greece, and Rome.[1] The **four craftsmen** are not identified, but they are obviously agencies raised up by God to destroy the Gentile powers which had **scattered Judah**. G. Coleman Luck explains:

> What are these four agents of God? It has been suggested that they may represent the four judgments of God mentioned in Ezekiel 14:21 and Revelation 6:1–8, these being war, famine, wild animals, and pestilence. Another suggestion which seems more probable is that they represent four successive powers that overthrow the four empires pictured in the previous vision: that is, Media-Persia overthrew Babylon, Greece overthrew Media-Persia, Rome overthrew Greece, and the Revived Roman Empire of the last days will be overthrown by the great Messianic kingdom. Certainly the general truth is clearly brought out that every evil power that rises up against the people of God will eventually be overthrown and judged.[2]

C. Man with a Measuring Line (Chap. 2)

Meaning: Future prosperity, populousness, and security of Jerusalem.

2:1–5 The third vision reveals a man with a measuring line. When the prophet asked him where he was going, he answered that he was going to measure the site of Jerusalem, that is, where the city would be rebuilt. The interpreting angel met another angel who told him to assure the young man (either Zechariah or the man with the measuring line) that Jerusalem would yet be thickly populated, and that it would not need walls because the LORD would protect it. This refers ultimately, of course, to Jerusalem during the Millennial Reign of Christ.

2:6–12 Here the Jewish captives remaining in exile are summoned to return to Jerusalem from the land of the north. (Though Babylon is northeast of Jerusalem, yet the captives would come via the route of the Fertile Crescent and thus enter Israel from the . . . north.) This will also have a fulfillment "after glory" has been revealed and established, that is, after the Second Coming of Christ. God will punish the enemies of His people because the latter are what he describes as "the apple of His eye." Singing will break out when Christ comes to the millennial temple, and Gentile nations will join themselves to Him in that day. The term the Holy Land for Palestine is used only here in the entire Bible.

2:13 All flesh is commanded to be silent while the LORD rouses Himself to punish the nations.

D. Joshua the High Priest (Chap. 3)

Meaning: The priesthood, representative of the nation, cleansed and restored.

3:1–3 Joshua the high priest, clothed in filthy garments, pictures the priesthood as representative of Israel. Satan (Heb. for *adversary*) accuses Israel of being unfit to carry out its priestly function. God answers Satan that He has plucked the nation as a brand . . . from the fire, i.e., the captivity.

3:4–7 The Angel promises that the nation will be cleansed and invested with rich robes. At Zechariah's request, a clean turban is placed on Joshua's head, and he is invested while the Angel of the LORD stands by. If the people are faithful and obedient to the Lord, they will rule God's house, and have charge of His courts, and have the right of access among those standing there.

3:8, 9 Joshua and his fellow-priests were a wondrous sign ("men wondered at," that is, men that are for a sign). Unger elaborates:

> . . . men of prophetic portent, men who in their official position shadow forth coming events. . . . Through Christ, Israel will be redeemed and restored and constituted a high-priestly nation, which Joshua and his associate priests prefigure.[3]

In verse 8 Christ is spoken of as "My Servant the BRANCH"; in verse 9 He is referred to under the figure of an engraved stone (cf. Dan. 2:34, 35). Some have suggested that "the Branch" applies to the First Advent, the stone to the Second. Gaebelein says that the engraved stone with seven eyes on it must also mean the redeemed nation, the foundation of the kingdom, filled with His Spirit, for we read in connection with it, "I will remove the iniquity of that land in one day." He speaks of it as "restored Israel as the nucleus of the kingdom of God."[4]

3:10 The chapter closes with a deservedly famous glimpse of the peaceful nature of pastoral life in the Millennium:

"In that day," says the LORD of
hosts, "everyone will invite his
neighbor under his vine and under his fig tree."

E. The Golden Lampstand and the Two Olive Trees (Chap. 4)

Meaning: Israel, God's lightbearer,
will rebuild the temple by the Spirit,
of God (pictured by the oil).

4:1–6 The fifth vision describes a
lampstand of solid gold with **two
olive trees** beside it. It seems that the
golden **lampstand** had a base with a
stem coming up out of it. At the top
of the stem was **a bowl** which served
as a reservoir for oil. Reaching upward out of the stem were **seven
pipes** with **seven** small oil-burning
lamps on top of each. On either side
of the golden lampstand was an olive
tree, apparently supplying oil directly
to **the bowl** of the golden stand, and
then through the **pipes** from **the bowl**
to the **seven lamps**.

The golden **lampstand** may possibly be a picture of Israel as God's
witness in the world. It can only
fulfill its function as a light to the
world by the oil, i.e., by the Holy
Spirit. The immediate interpretation
of the vision is that the temple would
be rebuilt, not by human energy or
power, **but by** the **Spirit** of the Lord.
Difficulties would be removed, and
the hands of Zerubbabel would finish
the rebuilding of the temple, just as
they had laid the foundation. Unger
comments:

The spiritual principle here stated (v.
6) is beautifully illustrated by the
imagery of the vision in which the
automatic and spontaneous supply
of oil for lighting totally apart from
human agency prefigures Israel's millennial testimony conducted in the
fullness of the outpoured Spirit. But
in its context, the promise has direct

application to Zerubbabel, then faced
with the colossal task of completing
the temple.[5]

4:7–10 In spite of mountainous
opposition, the **temple** would be completed and would bring forth excla-
mations **of "Grace, grace . . . !"** to its
beauty. Those **who** have **despised the
day of small things**, that is, those
who mocked the possibility of God's
doing some great thing, would see
**the plumb line in the hand of Zerub-
babel**, that is, would **see . . . the day**
when Zerubbabel would **finish** the
structure.

The seven lamps are **the seven
eyes of the LORD**, signifying His watchful care over the rebuilding and over
the whole earth.

4:11–14 When Zechariah asks
about the **two olive trees** and the **two
olive branches**, the angel explains
that they are **the two anointed ones**
standing by **the LORD**. This is commonly taken to refer to Zerubbabel
and Joshua, representing the offices
of king and priest.

This vision teaches that spiritual
power was necessary for the restoration, just as the previous vision taught
that cleansing was necessary.

F. The Flying Scroll (5:1–4)

Meaning: The curse of God pronounced against perjury and theft
in the land.

5:1, 2 The vision of the **flying
scroll** is the first in a series of three
having to do with administration and
judgment. The **scroll** measured thirty
feet long by fifteen feet wide, the same
size as the portico of Solomon's temple.

5:3, 4 It pronounced a curse on
every thief and **every perjurer**. As
part of this **curse**, the very **house** of
the ones who stole or who swore
falsely would be destroyed, both **tim-**

ber and stones. Perhaps this vision has to do with the worldwide judgments that will precede the setting up of Christ's kingdom. Sins against man (theft) and sins against God (false swearing) will be dealt with at that time. (These may also represent the two tables of the law.)

G. The Woman in a Basket (5:5–11)

Meaning: Idolatry and mercenary religion removed from the land to its ancient home base in Babylon.

The seventh vision shows a woman in a basket (Heb. *ephah*). The ephah was the largest unit of measure used in business, somewhat like a bushel basket. The woman is the personification of "Wickedness." In the land, the lead cover was kept on the ephah, meaning that wickedness was restricted. But two other women flew with the ephah to Shinar (Babylon). This seems to signify the removal of idolatrous and mercenary religion from Israel to its base in Babylon where it originated. Such a removal would, of course, be preparatory to the judgment of Babylon and to the setting up of the kingdom. "House" in verse 11 means "heathen temple."

Israel was cleansed of idolatry after the Babylonian captivity, but it will embrace a worse form of idolatry in the future when it worships the Antichrist as God.

H. The Four Chariots (6:1–8)

Meaning: God's patrols indicate Israel's enemies have been put down.

6:1–4 Zechariah next sees four sets of horses and chariots . . . coming out from between two mountains of bronze. The horses are red, black, white, and dappled or grisled—all strong steeds.

6:5–7 The interpreting angel

identifies the four sets of horses and chariots as the four spirits of heaven, God's agents to bring the Gentile world into subjection to the Messiah. The black horses go to the north, and the dappled ones, to the south. These two directions in the prophetic Scriptures are commonly associated with enemies of Israel (for example, king of the North and king of the South). The white horses go forth after the black ones and apparently the red horses patrol in undesignated areas.

6:8 The interpreting angel points out that the horses which went toward the north country had given rest to His Spirit. This may imply the destruction of the northern army (Babylon) which was a constant source of danger to the land of Israel. Taking the vision as a whole, it seems to indicate the destruction of Israel's enemies by messengers of the Lord. Once again, this is an event that will precede Christ's kingdom on earth.

III. JOSHUA CROWNED AS HIGH PRIEST (6:9–15)

Meaning: A picture of Christ coming as King and High Priest, the ideal combination of church and state.

6:9–13 Now that the visions of judgment are ended, a highly symbolic act takes place. Zechariah was commanded to get gold and silver . . . from three of the returned exiles— from Heldai, Tobijah, and Jedaiah— and to make an elaborate crown for Joshua[6] . . . the high priest, in the house of Josiah. Ordinarily, a crown is made for a ruler, not for a high priest. But this action points forward to the coming of Christ as King and Priest. He is spoken of in verse 12 as the BRANCH who will build the millennial temple, bear royal honor,

and ... sit and rule on His throne. David Baron notes:

> Surely it is in keeping with the Royal Priesthood of Messiah, that the Hebrew word used here (for temple) means both palace and sanctuary. As King He has entered into His palace, and as Priest into His sanctuary.[7]

"The counsel of peace shall be between them both," that is, peaceful understanding will exist between King and Priest (in one Person).

6:14 The ... **crown** was to be kept **in the temple** as **a memorial. Helem** is the same as Heldai and **Hen** is Joshua.

6:15 The restoration of dispersed Israel and the fulfillment of the messianic promise are set before the people as an encouragement to obedience.

IV. JEWS FROM BETHEL INQUIRE CONCERNING CONTINUANCE OF FAST (Chaps. 7, 8)

A. The Question Concerning the Fast (7:1–3)

Chapters 7 and 8 form a division by themselves, dealing with the subject of fasting. A delegation from Bethel (NKJV marg.)[8] came to inquire if they **should** continue to **fast** on the anniversary of the fall of Jerusalem. They had been doing this for over seventy **years**.

B. First Message (7:4–7)

Meaning: The fasts were *their* idea, not *God's*. The Lord wants reality, not just ritual.

The answer to the above question is given in four distinct messages (7:4–7; 7:8–14; 8:1–17; 8:18–23). In the first, God reminds them that the fast **in** both **the fifth and seventh months** had been instituted by themselves,

not by Him. Both their fasting and their feasting were for themselves, not for God. Before the destruction of **Jerusalem, the former prophets** had warned the people that God wants righteousness and reality rather than ritual.

C. Second Message (7:8–14)

Meaning: Judgment had come upon the people because they had refused to practice justice, righteousness, and mercy.

In the second message, God explains why judgment came upon the nation. He had called the people to practice **justice, mercy, and compassion**. But **they refused to heed**. Notice the results of their disobedience: divine **wrath**; unanswered prayer; scattering of the people **among ... the nations**; desolation of **the land**. In other words, the fast about which they were inquiring was a result of their own sinfulness and disobedience. As William Kelly warns:

> Ordinances, whatever they may do, never take the place of practical righteousness, and still less of faith, in the sight of God.[9]

D. Third Message (8:1–17)

Meaning: The Lord will yet pour out His blessings on Judah.

8:1–5 The third message to the delegation from Bethel promises future blessing to Judah. **Great** wrath will go out against the enemies of Judah (v. 2). **Jerusalem** will be restored and **called "the City of Truth,"** its **streets** transformed into a playground for **boys and girls** and a social center for old folks.

8:6–8 If this seemed **marvelous** to **the** numerically tiny **remnant**, was it therefore so hard for *God* to do? He is the One who **will bring ... back**

the exiles and **dwell in** their **midst** as **their God**.

While these verses had an immediate application to the people in Zechariah's time, their complete fulfillment awaits our Lord's Second Advent.

8:9–13 The people who had been hearing the encouragements of Haggai and Zechariah were exhorted to continue building. **Before** they started work on the temple, there had been widespread unemployment, and violence stalked the streets. But now God promises them **peace** and prosperity, and they would **be a blessing** to the Gentiles instead of **a curse**.

8:14–17 **Just as** surely as God had promised calamity to His people in the day of their disobedience, so now He purposes to **do good to** them. In view of that, they are exhorted to live truthfully, justly, and peacefully, avoiding the **things that the** LORD hates (thinking **evil . . . against** one's **neighbor** and loving **a false oath** —dishonesty).

E. Fourth Message (8:18–23)

Meaning: Israel's fasts will be turned to feasts, and Jerusalem will be the world center of worship.

8:18 As an encouragement to the delegation from Bethel, the Lord promises that the mournful fasts would be turned into seasons of **joy and gladness and cheerful feasts**. **The fast of the tenth** month mourned the siege of Jerusalem (2 Kgs. 25:1); **the fourth** month marked its capture (2 Kgs. 25:3); **the fifth** month, its destruction (2 Kgs. 25:8–10); **the seventh** month, the murder of Gedaliah (2 Kgs. 25:25).

8:19–23 The closing verses of the chapter picture **many** Gentile **peoples and strong nations** flocking to **Jerusalem** from all over the world **to seek the** LORD **of hosts**. In that day,

the Jews will be the channel of blessing to the world. Notice the frequent use of the expression **"Thus says the** LORD**"** or **"Thus says the** LORD **of hosts"** in this chapter: vv. 2, 3, 4, 6, 7, 9, 14, 19, 20, 23.

V. THE FIRST ORACLE OR BURDEN, EMPHASIZING MESSIAH'S FIRST ADVENT (Chaps. 9—11)

The remaining chapters contain two oracles or burdens. The first, in chapters 9—11, emphasizes the First Advent of the Messiah, while the second one, chapters 12—14, looks forward to Christ's glorious appearing.

A. Gentile Nations Will Be Judged (9:1–8)

9:1–7 Here in chapter 9, God's judgment is first pronounced **against** Syria (**Hadrach, Damascus, Hamath** —vv. 1, 2a), **Tyre and Sidon** (vv. 2b–4), and Philistia (**Ashkelon, Gaza, Ekron, Ashdod**—vv. 5–7). **Tyre** was proud of its riches and its fortress city, but **the** LORD would **cast her** into the sea. The Philistine cities would be dismayed to **see** the fall of Tyre; they thought it was impregnable. **The Philistines** themselves would be cleansed from idolatry, and they would dwell as a clan in Israel. **Ekron** would be **like** the Jebusites in the sense that they would live among the people of Israel as loyal, peaceful citizens.

9:8 Foreign invaders would no longer threaten the temple or the people. Actually, verses 1–8 had a partial fulfillment when these Gentile powers were conquered by Alexander the Great (see reference to Greece in v. 13).

B. First Coming of Messiah to Zion (9:9)

God's people are next encouraged by the promise of the **coming** of the

Messiah (**King**). Verse 9 describes His First Coming, in **lowly** grace, **on a donkey**. Both Matthew, the most Jewish of the four Gospels, and John, the most universal, quote this verse as referring to the so-called "Triumphal Entry" of our Lord into Jerusalem.

C. Disarmament and Universal Peace at the Second Coming of Christ (9:10)

Verse 10, however, looks forward to His Second Advent, when He will come in power and great glory. Weapons of war will be abolished, and Christ will reign **"from sea to sea, and from the River to the ends of the earth"** (Zechariah is quoting Ps. 72:8). The present Age of Grace is hidden between verses 9 and 10.

D. Return of Captives to Jerusalem from Exile (9:11, 12)

"The blood of your covenant" refers to the **blood** by which a **covenant** was sealed. This expression could refer to the covenant of the law (Ex. 24:8), the covenant guaranteeing the land to Israel (Deut. 30:1–10), the Davidic Covenant (2 Sam. 7:4–17), or the general covenantal relationship of Israel with Jehovah (NKJV, LORD).

Israel's captives will be set **free from the waterless pit** of foreign countries and returned to **the stronghold**, which may mean Jerusalem, Palestine, or God Himself.

E. Triumph of All Israel over Greece (9:13)

Judah and Israel (**Ephraim**) will be conquering nations in that day, subduing **Greece**. This prophecy was partially fulfilled in the War of the Maccabees, 175–163 B.C. It also anticipates the final restoration of Israel from worldwide dispersion.

F. Intervention of Jehovah to Protect His People (9:14–17)

An unknown commentator vividly describes what amounts to a "holy war":

> Not only will God's victors drink full of the blood of their vanquished enemies and be like the sacrificial bowls filled with blood to be sprinkled upon the sides of the altar and its horns, but they shall come through gory triumph bespattered with blood like the corners of the altar.

Merrill Unger depicts the contrast between Israel and her enemies:

> In apparent antithesis to Israel's enemies as *sling-stones* trodden in the mire, in the preceding verse, Zechariah compares Zion's victorious sons (the saved remnant) to *precious stones* of a crown which sparkle over the Lord's land. The figure is evidently of the reward of the faithful martyrs and valiant saints of Israel who enter the kingdom of Messiah.[10]

G. People Exhorted to Ask for Rain from the Lord, Not from Idols (10:1, 2)

The people are exhorted to **ask the LORD for rain** and not to pray to worthless **idols**. Idolatry causes **people** to wander **like sheep** without a **shepherd**.

H. God Will Punish the Leaders of Judah, Raise Up the Messiah, and Give Victory to the People (10:3–5)

10:3 God's **anger is kindled against the shepherds** and leaders (**goatherds**) for leading the people astray. **The LORD ... will visit the flock ... of Judah** and transform it into a war **horse**.

10:4, 5 Many commentators interpret verse 4 as a promise of the Messiah. Coming out of **Judah**, He would be the chief **cornerstone, the tent peg, the battle bow,** and the **ruler**. Others believe that this is a picture of restored Israel. Feinberg says that the last line describes what the Messiah will do, namely, cast foreign oppressors out of the land[11] (see KJV). In any case, the men of Judah will gloriously triumph over **their enemies**.

I. Israel and Judah Will Be Regathered and Restored (10:6–12)

Verses 6–12 predict the regathering of both Israel (**Joseph**) and **Judah** from worldwide dispersion. Israel (**Ephraim**) will **be like a mighty warrior**.

The Lord **will whistle for** His people **and gather them** back **into the land of Gilead and Lebanon . . . from . . . Egypt** and **from Assyria** where He had sown or scattered them. The nations that formerly enslaved them will be punished, and Judah and Israel will glory **in** the **name** of the Lord. The **"He"** in verse 11 is **the** LORD. The **affliction** with which He strikes **the waves of the sea** may well stand for anything that hinders the return, as the Red Sea seemed to hinder the Exodus.

J. Unfaithful Rulers Will Be Punished (11:1–3)

Chapter 11 deals with the rejection of the Messiah and the destruction of Jerusalem by the Romans, and also with the rise of the Antichrist.

The first three verses may be a literal description of the destruction wrought in the forests of Israel (**Lebanon**), both in the highlands and in the lowlands. The **shepherds** howl because the pastures along **the Jordan** are ruined and their sheep have nothing to eat. Some think this points forward to the devastation of the land by the Romans in A.D. 70.

K. Messiah Becomes True Shepherd of the Flock (11:4–8a)

11:4–6 The LORD instructs Zechariah to assume the role of a shepherd whose **flock** is doomed to **slaughter**. In this, Zechariah is a type of the Lord Jesus. The sheep (the Jewish remnant) have been cruelly exploited by their previous **shepherds** (rulers). God has determined to deliver the wicked **inhabitants of the land** into the hands of the Roman emperor whom they will acknowledge as their **king** (John 19:15).

11:7, 8a In carrying out the role of shepherd, Zechariah **took . . . two staffs**—grace (**Beauty**) and union (**Bonds**). They represent God's desire to show grace to His people, and to unite Judah and Israel. Zechariah had to dismiss **three** false **shepherds**, generally taken to refer to the three offices of king, priest and prophet, in order to do his work. (Unger suggests that the three shepherds picture three orders of rulers in the Jewish state—priests, teachers of the law, and civil magistrates. He explains the **one month** as the period of culminating unbelief just before Israel's leaders crucified our Lord.)[12]

L. Messiah Is Rejected by His People (11:8b–14)

11:8b–11 When the people reject the shepherd, he leaves them to their fate. Zechariah then breaks the first **staff** (**Beauty**) **. . . in two,** annulling the covenant that restrained the Gentiles from oppressing God's people. Only **the poor of the flock** understood what God was doing and why.

11:12, 13 When Zechariah asks for his **wages,** they give him **thirty pieces of silver**—the redemption price of a slave who has been gored by an ox. This payment is cast **to the potter,** a prophecy of what Judas would do after his betrayal of the Lord.

11:14 Then Zechariah cuts in two his other staff, (Bonds), indicating that the brotherhood between Judah and Israel was broken, and that there would be disunity and internal strife among the Jews.

M. God Delivers Them Over to the Idol Shepherd (Antichrist) (11:15–17)

Feinberg points out that the Church Age is hidden between verses 14 and 15.[13]

Because Israel rejected the *Good* Shepherd, they would be given a *false* shepherd. Zechariah acts this out by taking the implements of a worthless shepherd. This points to the future Antichrist, who will not care for the sheep but will rob and slay them. His arm will be withered and his right eye ... blinded in battle.

VI. THE SECOND ORACLE OR BURDEN, EMPHASIZING MESSIAH'S SECOND ADVENT (Chaps.12—14)

A. Jerusalem Will Be a Source of Trouble to the Nations (12:1–3)

Here the Gentile nations are seen marching against ... Jerusalem in a future day. All who trouble the city will be greatly troubled. They will hurt themselves in trying to lift this very heavy millstone.

B. The Lord Will Destroy the Enemies of Judah (12:4)

In that day God will strike the invaders, both horse and rider, with madness and panic.

C. The Jews Will Acknowledge God as Their Strength (12:5)

The governors of Judah outside of Jerusalem shall say in their heart that the inhabitants of Jerusalem have strength from the LORD.

D. Outlying Judah Will Devour Its Enemies and Will Be First to Gain the Victory (12:6–9)

In that day, ... the governors of Judah will be like a devouring fire, burning everything they touch. Victory will come first to the inhabitants of outlying Judah so that the men of Jerusalem will not be exalted above them. The inhabitants of Jerusalem will be protected and strengthened, and the invading Gentile nations will be destroyed.

E. The Nation Will Mourn Over Its Rejection of the Messiah (12:10–14)

The people will mourn bitterly when they look on the Messiah whom they had pierced. "Then they shall look on Me whom they pierced. Yes, they will mourn for Him as one mourns for his only son" (v. 10b). Notice "on Me." The One whom they pierced was the Lord Jesus Christ, Jehovah. Mourning for an only son was the deepest form of sorrow for an Israelite. Concerning "the mourning at Hadad Rimmon" (v. 11), see 2 Chronicles 35:20–24. The mourners will include the royal family, the prophets (Nathan), the priests (Levi), the teachers (Shimei), and the people. Some think that Shimei should be Simeon,[14] who, with Levi, was cruel to the men of Shechem (Gen. 34:25). ... Notice the repetition of the words by themselves (vv. 12–14); true confession requires us to be alone with God.

F. Provision Will Be Made for Cleansing from Sin (13:1)

The first verse of chapter 13 is closely connected with the preceding chapter. After the people of Judah and Israel have been brought to the place of repentance for their rejection of the Messiah, then will follow a great national day of atonement. The **fountain** for cleansing was opened at Calvary, but Israel nationally will not enter into the good of it until the Second Advent.

G. Idols and False Prophets Will Be Banished (13:2–6)

13:2 The **land** will be purged of **idols**, and false **prophets** and **unclean** spirits will be banished.

13:3–5 These verses apparently describe the wrath which will come upon false prophets in the day of Israel's restoration. If a man falsely poses as a **prophet**, his own parents will threaten him and stab him. Men will not lightly claim to be prophets if they are not truly sent by God but will rather identify themselves as farmers, or whatever occupation they actually hold.

13:6 If a false prophet has been stabbed or if he has **wounds** which were self-inflicted as part of the cultic practices of the false prophets, he will not give the real reason when asked about them. Rather, he will give some ambiguous answer, such as, **"Those with which I was wounded in the house of my friends."**

Many devout preachers have used verse 6 to refer to our Lord Jesus Christ and to the nail wounds which He received at Calvary. However, it seems difficult to fit such a meaning into the context when a false prophet is clearly in view.[15] In our zeal to protect messianic OT passages from the unbelief of rationalistic critics we must be careful not to press a verse out of its setting.

Such a conservative Bible teacher as G. Coleman Luck agrees with the non-messianic interpretation:

The man being questioned has denied that he ever was a false prophet. His questioner, however, is suspicious and persists in the examination. It was customary for false prophets to inflict cuttings or wounds on themselves (see 1 Kings 18:28; Jer. 16:6, etc.).[16]

Further details in the verse itself fit the false prophet better. In Hebrew the word for *hands* (KJV) refers to the forearms. **These wounds between your arms**, as the NKJV more precisely translates it, could refer to any wounds on one's torso, front or back, such as could be administered in cultic cuttings (or by one's "friends," if the false prophet was telling the truth). Also, our Lord was not wounded in the house of His *friends*, but in that of His cruelest enemies.

H. Messiah Will Be Slain and Israel Scattered (13:7)

Verse 7 starts a section that all believing Bible students consider messianic. Jehovah orders His **sword** to **awake . . . against** the Lord Jesus. **The Shepherd** was struck at Calvary, and **the** Jewish **sheep** have been **scattered** ever since.

I. A Remnant of the Nation Will Return to the Lord (13:8, 9)

Because of their rejection of the Lord Jesus, **two-thirds** of the nation will **die** during the Great Tribulation, yet a remnant of **one-third** will be preserved. This remnant will be refined like **silver** and **gold**. They will acknowledge **God**, and He will acknowledge them as **"My people."**

J. Gentiles Will Gather Against Jerusalem (14:1, 2)

The day of the Lord here refers to the final siege of **Jerusalem** by the nations. The invading armies will divide the **spoil** they have taken inside **the city. Half of the** people will be taken **into captivity** and the other half will remain.

K. The Lord Himself Will Intervene (14:3–5)

Then the LORD Himself will come to **the Mount of Olives. The Mount** will **be split in two, half** to **the north** and **half** to **the south,** with **a very large valley** between. **"Thus the LORD my God will come, and all the saints with You."** Unger explains:

> To demonstrate his ecstasy, the seer passes from indirect to direct address, a phenomenon often met with in animated Hebrew style.[17]

L. Cosmic Changes in Weather and in Illumination (14:6, 7)

The *precise* meaning of this passage is so obscure that many modern versions (such as Moffatt, RSV, NEB, NIV) have adapted one or more of the ancient translations, which convey the idea "that all extremes of temperature will cease."[18] Baldwin gives as an alternative translation of the last clause of verse 6 in the Hebrew text, " 'the splendid ones (stars), congeal,' that is, lose their brightness."[19]

The *general* meaning of the text is clear: the changes predicted will be *cosmic* in scope.

Unger, who rejects the readings supported by the early versions as "obviously wrong," sees the day as a period (the Day of the Lord), not a twenty-four hour interval. He ties this passage in with Isaiah 30:26:

> Moreover the light of the moon will be as the light of the sun, and the light of the sun will be sevenfold, as the light of seven days, in the day that the LORD binds up the bruise of

His people and heals the stroke of their wound.[20]

M. River of Living Water (14:8)

Living waters shall flow from Jerusalem, half to the Dead Sea (**eastern sea**) **and half** to the Mediterranean (**the western sea**) in all seasons.

N. Christ Will Reign as King (14:9)

The LORD **shall be King over all the earth** and He shall be acknowledged as the only true God.

O. Geographical Changes in the Land (14:10)

All the land shall be turned into a plain, with **Jerusalem** elevated above the rest.

P. Jerusalem Inhabited and Secure (14:11)

Jerusalem shall be safely inhabited, and **the people** who **dwell in it** will **no longer** be under the threat of enemy invasion and **utter destruction.**

Q. Plague and Panic Will Afflict the Gentile Foes (14:12–15)

Chronologically these verses belong with 14:3, which describes Christ conquering the enemies of Israel. These enemies will be struck with a terrible plague[21]—**"their flesh shall dissolve while they stand on their feet, their eyes shall dissolve in their sockets, and their tongues shall dissolve in their mouths."** There will be a **great panic from the LORD.** Rural **Judah** will assist in the defense of **Jerusalem,** and the spoil shall be **great.**

R. Gentile Survivors Will Worship at Jerusalem Or Be Under Penalty of the Plague (14:16–19)

Surviving Gentile **nations** will come to **Jerusalem** annually **to worship the King, the LORD of hosts, and to keep** the **Feast of Tabernacles**. Unger explains why:

> The Feast of Tabernacles is the only one of the seven Jewish festivals which is represented in this prophecy as being observed in the kingdom age. Why? It is the only one which at that time will be unfulfilled typically and the only one which will be in process of fulfillment by the kingdom itself.[22]

Those refusing to come and worship will suffer drought. **Egypt** is mentioned specifically as one of the countries that will have **no rain** if they are disobedient.

S. Even Common Utensils and Objects Will Be Sacred to the Lord, and Merchants Will Not Trade in the House of the Lord (14:20–21)

In that day everything will be "HOLINESS TO THE LORD." There will be no difference between "secular" and "sacred." Even **the bells** on **the horses** and the common pots **in Jerusalem and Judah** will be sacred! The **Canaanite**—a derisive term for a huckster or an unclean person—will be banished from the temple, **the house of the LORD of hosts**.

ENDNOTES

[1](1:18–21) Some see the *four* only as representing "the totality of opposition, just as it represents all directions in the eighth vision" (Joyce G. Baldwin, *Haggai, Zechariah, Malachi*, p. 407). However, the specific reference to individual nations is an ancient interpretation.

[2](1:18–21) G. Coleman Luck, *Zechariah*, pp. 26, 27.

[3](3:8, 9) Merrill F. Unger, *Zechariah: Prophet of Messiah's Glory*, pp. 64, 65.

[4](3:8, 9) Arno C. Gaebelein, *Studies in Zechariah*, p. 42.

[5](4:1–6) Unger, *Zechariah*, p. 75.

[6](6:9–13) It is worth noting that *Joshua* and *Jeshua* (Heb. form of Jesus) are really the same name.

[7](6:9–13) David Baron, *The New Order of Priesthood*, p. 30 footnote.

[8](7:1–3) *Bethel* is Hebrew for *house of God*, but the temple is called *the house of the LORD (Jehovah)*, so the city of Bethel is probably meant, contrary to KJV/NKJV tradition. Notice also that *to* is in italics (v. 2), meaning that it is not in the Hebrew (but then neither is *from*). As Baldwin remarks, "The correct way to translate this verse is far from evident." (See Joyce G. Baldwin, *Haggai, Zechariah, Malachi*, pp. 141–143.)

[9](7:8–14) William Kelly, *Lectures Introductory to the Study of the Minor Prophets*, p. 467.

[10](9:14–17) Unger, *Zechariah*, p. 170.

[11](10:4, 5) Charles Lee Feinberg, *God Remembers*, p. 188.

[12](11:7, 8a) Unger, *Zechariah*, p. 195.

[13](11:15–17) Feinberg, *God Remembers*, p. 211.

[14](12:10–14) In Hebrew Simeon is *Shimon*. In the ancient, consonantal text, before the vowels were added, this could very easily be miscopied as *Shimei*.

[15](13:6) Unger, an eminent OT scholar, applies the verse to Christ, but admits that few Bible scholars agree with him:

> The boldness and daring of this Messianic prophecy and the *dramatic abruptness* with which it is introduced have frightened most expositors away from its true import on the supposition that it is inseparably connected with verses 2–5, and therefore, still has the false prophet in mind, and to in-

troduce the Messiah is flagrantly to ignore the context.

Dr. Unger goes on for five columns of his commentary to defend his view (pp. 228–230).

[16](13:6) G. Coleman Luck, *Zechariah*, p. 113.

[17](14:3–5) Unger, *Zechariah*, p. 250.

[18](14:6, 7) Baldwin, *Haggai, Zechariah, Malachi*, p. 203.

[19](14:6, 7) *Ibid*.

[20](14:6, 7) Unger, *Zechariah*, pp. 252, 253.

[21](14:12–15) Many modern readers have noticed how closely this passage resembles the dreadful results of a nuclear attack.

[22](14:16–19) Unger, *Zechariah*, p. 265.

BIBLIOGRAPHY

Baldwin, Joyce G. *Haggai, Zechariah, Malachi: An Introduction and Commentary*. Downers Grove, Ill: Inter Varsity Press, 1972.

Feinberg, Charles Lee. *God Remem-bers*. New York: American Board of Missions to the Jews, Inc., 1965.

Gaebelein, Arno C. *Studies in Zechariah*. New York: Our Hope Publishers, 1904.

Laney, J. Carl. "Zechariah." In *Everyman's Bible Commentary*. Chicago: Moody Press, 1984.

Lindsey, F. Duane. "Zechariah." In *The Bible Knowledge Commentary*. Wheaton: Victor Books, 1985.

Luck, G. Coleman. *Zechariah*. Chicago: Moody Press, 1969.

Mills, Montague S. "Zechariah." In *The Minor Prophets: A Survey*. Distributed by 3E Ministries. Dallas: n.d.

Tatford, Frederick A. *The Minor Prophets*. Vol. 3. Reprint (3 vols.). Minneapolis: Klock & Klock Christian Publishers, 1982.

————. *Prophet of the Myrtle Grove*. Eastbourne, England: Prophetic Witness Publishing House, 1971.

Unger, Merrill F. *Zechariah: Prophet of Messiah's Glory*. Grand Rapids: Zondervan Publishing House, 1962.

MALACHI

Introduction

"Malachi is like a late evening, which brings a long day to a close; but he is also the morning dawn, which bears a glorious day in its womb."

—Nagelsbach

I. Unique Place in the Canon

Malachi (My messenger, possibly a shortened form of *Malā'k-îyyāh*, messenger of Jehovah) has the distinction of being the last of the prophets and the bridge between the two Testaments, looking forward both to John the Baptist and the Lord Jesus Himself.

Strangely enough, some believe the prophecy of Malachi is anonymous, and that the name is merely a title for Ezra or some other writer. Some church fathers even thought the writer was an angel, since in Greek (and Hebrew) the same word can mean *angel* or *messenger*![1]

Malachi also has a special dialectic (question and answer) style that has caused some to call him "the Hebrew Socrates."

II. Authorship

Although Jewish tradition says that Malachi belonged to the "Great Synagogue," and was a Levite from Supha, in Zebulun, we know nothing definite about the prophet apart from his book. There is every reason to accept him as a bold, often severe writer, who with Haggai and Zechariah called the post-exilic Jews back to their covenantal relationship with God.

III. Date

It is clear that Malachi wrote after 538 B.C., since he used an almost exclusively post-exilic word for *governor*.[2] It is also obvious that he wrote later than the other two post-exilic "minor" prophets, Haggai and Zechariah, since in Malachi the temple is finished, the rituals have been reinstituted, and in fact, enough time had elapsed for spiritual declension to set in. Also, the walls of Jerusalem had been rebuilt.

Malachi probably should be dated between about 470 and 460 B.C.

IV. Background and Theme

The problems in Malachi are the same as those in Nehemiah—mixed marriages with pagans, unjust financial practices, withholding of tithes from God's house, and general spiritual apathy. Either they are the identical problems mentioned in Nehemiah or a repetition or continuation of them not too long after his time.

Because of the lackluster religious life of the post-exilic Jews, Malachi sought to stir them up by using his vivid method of dialogue with an unfaithful people.

It has been pointed out that Malachi

is well named "My messenger" or "messenger of Jehovah" (NKJV, LORD), because in these four short chapters, the prophet describes three messengers—the priest of the Lord (2:2); John the Baptist (3:1a); and our Lord Himself (3:16).

Malachi records Jehovah's last pleading with His people in the OT period. After this, the prophetic voice will be silent for four centuries until the coming of John the Baptist.

It is worth noting that no matter how "late" some critics may date Malachi or other prophecies, these writings were definitely written long before the advents of John and the Lord Jesus. Thus they are true *prophecies*, and not "history written *as* prophecy," as some destructive critics claim.

OUTLINE

I. THE LORD'S CHARGES AGAINST ISRAEL, THEIR REPLIES, AND HIS THREATENED JUDGMENTS (1:1—3:15)

    A. Ingratitude (1:1–5)

    B. Sacrilege by the Priests (1:6–14)

    C. Condemnation of the Priests (2:1–9)

    D. Divorce and Mixed Marriages (2:10–16)

    E. Denial of God's Holiness and Justice (2:17)

    F. Parenthesis: Messiah's Coming in Judgment (3:1–6)

    G. The Backsliding of the People (3:7)

    H. Robbing God of Tithes and Offerings (3:8–12)

    I. False Charges Against God (3:13–15)

II. THE BLESSING OF THE REMNANT AND THE JUDGMENT OF THE WICKED (3:16—4:6)

    A. The Restoration of the Faithful Remnant (3:16–18)

    B. The Judgment of the Wicked (4:1)

    C. The Coming of the Messiah to the Remnant (4:2, 3)

    D. Closing Exhortation to Obedience, with Promise of the Coming of Elijah the Prophet (4:4–6)

Commentary

I. THE LORD'S CHARGES AGAINST ISRAEL, THEIR REPLIES, AND HIS THREATENED JUDGMENTS (1:1—3:15)

A. Ingratitude (1:1–5)

In the first chapter, we find the Lord making certain charges against the people, and the people replying with strong denials. First, **the LORD** pleads His love for them, and they ask Him to prove it: **"In what way have You loved us?"** He does so by reminding them of His love for **Jacob** (from whom they were descended), His rejection of **Esau**, and His judgments on Esau's descendants, the Edomites. The **eyes** of **the people** of **Israel** would **see** the desolation of **Edom**, and they would acknowledge the greatness of God.

B. Sacrilege by the Priests (1:6–14)

1:6 Next the Lord charges the **priests** with despising His **name** and failing to **honor** and **reverence** Him. They ask for evidence of their profane behavior.

1:7, 8 The Lord accuses them of bringing **defiled** offerings. They deny this, too, but He reminds them that they acted as if anything was good enough for the Lord. They brought **blind** and **lame** sacrifices, which they would not dare **offer... to** their **governor**.

1:9 The prophet urges them to repent of their sins so that God's wrath might be averted.

1:10 The LORD of hosts wishes that someone would **shut the doors** of the temple so that the sacrifices might stop, because the sacrifices were utterly unacceptable to Him.

1:11 But **the LORD** will vindicate His **name . . . among the Gentiles** even though His own people will not honor Him.

1:12–14 The Jews despised the sacred things of the temple and were wearied of serving God. A curse would rest upon all who brought their **blemished** odds and ends to God for sacrifices. The reason is that **the LORD of hosts** is **a great King**, and His **name is to be feared among the nations**.

C. Condemnation of the Priests (2:1–9)

The **priests** are solemnly warned of dreadful judgment if they do not

repent and change their ways. They are reminded that the priests of old were faithful to God's **covenant with Levi**, but now the priests had become utterly corrupt, and so God had **made** them **contemptible and base before all the people**.

D. Divorce and Mixed Marriages (2:10–16)

2:10–12 Next the subject of divorce and marriage to idolatrous heathen wives is dealt with. The people of **Judah had dealt treacherously** by marrying foreigners, thus destroying their national solidarity. Those who entered mixed marriages would be **cut off**.

2:13–16 The people wept at **the altar** because the Lord no longer accepted their offerings with favor. And why not? **Because the LORD** had **been** a **witness** at their marriages, which they were now breaking so readily. He had intended them to be one pure people, producing **godly offspring** and separated from the corruptions of the heathen. **God . . . hates** unscriptural **divorce** and its resulting **violence**. The link between **divorce** and **violence** is explained by Baldwin as follows:

> He sees divorce to be like *covering one's garment with violence*, a figurative expression for all kinds of gross injustice which, like the blood of a murdered victim, leave their mark for all to see.[3]

E. Denial of God's Holiness and Justice (2:17)

They had **wearied the LORD** by saying that He did not care about the behavior of **everyone who** did **evil**. Hypocritically, they challenged Him to intervene, saying, **"Where is the God of justice?"**

F. Parenthesis: Messiah's Coming in Judgment (3:1–6)

3:1 God next answers the impious challenge of the previous verse. He will **send** His **messenger**, a promise that had an early and partial fulfillment in John the Baptist, but awaits a later and complete fulfillment when Elijah (4:5) will prepare the way of **the Lord, . . . the Messenger of the covenant** whom they desired (irony). The irony here is that when He later arrived (His First Advent), the nation of Israel did *not* **delight in** Him but crucified Him instead.

3:2–4 **The day of His coming** will be the Second Advent. The Lord will come in judgment on sin, and **who** will be able to **stand**? This purifying ministry, pictured by Christ's cleansing of the temple, awaits final fulfillment at His Second Coming. **The sons of Levi** (priests) will be purified so that they can make offerings of holiness and **righteousness** that are **pleasant to the LORD, as in the days of old**.

3:5 The Lord will also punish **sorcerers, adulterers, perjurers**, oppressors of **wage earners, widows, and orphans**, as well as **those who turn away an alien**.

3:6 The fact that **the LORD** is the unchanging One accounts for the preservation of the **sons of Jacob** from destruction.

G. The Backsliding of the People (3:7)

The **LORD** invites the people to **return to** Him, but they deny having **gone away**, asking hypocritically, **"In what way shall we return?"**

H. Robbing God of Tithes and Offerings (3:8–12)

Under the Mosaic Law, the Israelites were required to give a tenth of all produce and livestock to the Lord (or they could redeem it with money and add a fifth part). The tithes were in addition to numerous offerings, and were an acknowledgment that everything belonged to God and that He was the Giver of all possessions.

The NT teaches believers to give systematically, liberally, cheerfully, and as the Lord has prospered them, that is, proportionately. But no mention is made of tithing. Rather, the suggestion is that if a Jew living under law gave a tenth, how much more should a Christian living under grace give!

The reward for faithful tithing in the OT was material wealth; the reward for faithful stewardship in the present age is spiritual riches.

So He reminds them of their failure to bring their **tithes and offerings**, thus robbing **God** and bringing **a curse** on themselves. If they will be faithful with their **tithes**, He will bless them with incredible plenty, so much so **that there will not be room enough to receive it**. He will deliver them from drought, plague, enemies, and locusts, and make them a blessing in the earth.

I. False Charges Against God (3:13–15)

Again **the LORD** charges that they have spoken **harsh** things **against** Him, saying that it does not pay **to serve** God or obey Him. They taught that **the proud**, the wicked, and those who **tempt God** not only prosper but get away with it scot-**free**.

II. THE BLESSING OF THE REMNANT AND THE JUDGMENT OF THE WICKED (3:16—4:6)

A. The Restoration of the Faithful Remnant (3:16–18)

But there was a remnant of people true to Jehovah. These shall be spared and blessed, and acknowledged as God's own possession, being made into His **jewels**.

William Kelly comments:

> The Jews themselves will no longer take the ground of being mere Jews. They will see the vanity of an outward place; they will value what is of God, they will abhor the more those who are wicked because they are Jews (v. 18).[4]

B. The Judgment of the Wicked (4:1)

The day is coming, burning like an oven, when **all the proud** and the wicked shall be destroyed, **root** and **branch**.

C. The Coming of the Messiah to the Remnant (4:2, 3)

The faithful will welcome **the Sun of Righteousness**, who will **arise with healing in His wings**. Those **who fear** God's **name** will triumph over their foes like **ashes under** their **feet**.

D. Closing Exhortation to Obedience, with Promise of the Coming of Elijah the Prophet (4:4–6)

The book closes with an *exhortation* to **remember the Law of Moses** and with a *promise* to **send . . . Elijah** to Israel **before the . . . day of the LORD. He will** bring about reform in the lives of the people, making them resemble their godly forefathers. Otherwise God will have to visit the land[5] (or **earth**) **with a curse**. In reading Malachi in the synagogue the Jews repeat verse 5 after verse 6 so that the book will not end with a curse. However, as Wolf observes, "This attempt to soften the message does not alter the grim reality."[6]

Since we read the Old Covenant in the fuller light of the New, what better way to end the OT volume of the *Believers Bible Commentary* than by quoting the last paragraph of Keil and Delitzsch's devout and scholarly OT commentary,[7] which nicely binds the two together:

> Law and prophets bore witness of Christ, and Christ came not to destroy the law or the prophets, but to fulfil them. Upon the Mount of Christ's Transfiguration, therefore, there appeared both Moses, the founder of the law and mediator of the old covenant, and Elijah the prophet, as the restorer of the law in Israel, to talk with Jesus of His decease which He was to accomplish in Jerusalem . . . for a practical testimony to the apostles and to us all, that Jesus Christ, who laid down His life for us, to bear our sin and redeem us from the curse of the law, was the beloved Son of the Father, whom we are to hear, that by believing in His name we may become children of God and heirs of everlasting life.[8]

ENDNOTES

[1](Intro) Our English word *angel* comes from the Greek word *angelos* (messenger or angel). The name of the book is from the Hebrew word *māla'k*, with the same meanings.

[2](Intro) Joyce Baldwin, *Haggai, Zechariah, Malachi*, p. 241.

[3](2:13–16) *Ibid.*, p. 241.

[4](3:16–18) William Kelly, *Lectures Introductory to the Study of the Minor Prophets*, p. 536.

[5](4:4–6) The same Hebrew word (*eretz*) can mean *land* or *earth*.

[6](4:4–6) Herbert Wolf, *Haggai and Malachi*, p. 126.

[7](4:4–6) It is well worth noting that Keil and Delitzsch's multi-volume work, while over a century old, is still in print and widely used. Whereas rationalistic commentaries are constantly being replaced by ever more

radical unbelief, doctrinally sound and well-written ones can prove valuable for decades and even centuries to come.

[8](4:4–6) C. F. Keil, "Malachi," *Biblical Commentary on the Old Testament*, XXVI:475.

BIBLIOGRAPHY

Baldwin, Joyce G. *Haggai, Zechariah, Malachi: An Introduction and Commentary*. The Tyndale Old Testament Commentaries. Downers Grove, IL: InterVarsity Press, 1972.

Feinberg, Charles Lee. *Habakkuk, Zephaniah, Haggai and Malachi*. New York: American Board of Mission to the Jews, Inc., 1951.

———. *The Minor Prophets*. Chicago: Moody Press, 1976.

Keil, C. F. "Malachi." In *Biblical Commentary on the Old Testament*. Vol. 26. Grand Rapids: Wm. B. Eerdmans Publishing Co., 1971.

Kelly, William. *Lectures Introductory to the Study of the Minor Prophets*. London: C. A. Hammond Trust Bible Depot, n.d.

Logsdon, S. Franklin. *Malachi or Will a Man Rob God?* Chicago: Moody Press, 1961.

Morgan, G. Campbell. *The Minor Prophets*. Old Tappan, N.J.: Fleming H. Revell Company, 1960.

Tatford, Frederick A. *The Minor Prophets*. Vol. 3. Reprint (3 vols.). Minneapolis: Klock & Klock Christian Publishers, 1982.

Wolf, Herbert. *Haggai and Malachi*. Chicago: Moody Press, 1976.

Abels, Jules. *The Rockefeller Billions.* New York: Macmillan, 1965.

Adams, J. *Competent to Counsel.* Grand Rapids: Baker Book House, 1970.

Adolph, Paul Ernest. "God in Medical Practice," a chapter in *The Evidence of God in an Expanding Universe* by John Clover Monsma. Bangalore, India: Thomas Samuel, 1968.

Alexander, Denis. *Beyond Science.* Philadelphia: Holman, 1972.

The Apocrypha. Revised Standard Version. New York: Thomas Nelson & Sons, 1957.

Archer, Gleason. *A Survey of Old Testament Introduction.* Chicago: Moody Press, 1974.

Armerding, Carl. *The Fight for Palestine.* Wheaton, IL: Van Kampen Press, 1949.

Barnes, Albert. *The Bible Commentary, Proverbs-Ezekiel.* Grand Rapids: Baker Book House, 1953.

Barnhouse, Donald Grey. *Words Fitly Spoken.* Wheaton, IL: Tyndale House, 1969.

Baron, David. *The Shepherd of Israel.* London: Morgan and Scott, Ltd., n.d.

Baxter, J. Sidlow. *Explore the Book.* London: Marshall, Morgan and Scott, Ltd., 1958.

Bermant, Chaim, and Michael Weitzman. *Ebla: A Revelation in Archaeology.* New York: Times Books, 1979.

Borland, James A. *Christ in the Old Testament.* Chicago: Moody Press, 1978.

Bright, Bill. *Revolution Now.* San Bernardino, CA: Campus Crusade, 1969.

Bullinger, E. W. *The Companion Bible.* London: Lamp Press, n.d.

Campbell, M. *From Grace to Glory.* London: Banner of Truth Trust, 1970.

Chafer, L. S. *Systematic Theology.* 8 vols. Dallas: Dallas Seminary Press, 1947.

Christenson, Larry. *The Christian Family.* Minneapolis: Bethany Fellowship, 1970.

Collins, Larry, and Dominique Lapierre, *O Jerusalem!* New York: Simon and Schuster, 1972.

Cook, F. C., ed. *Barnes' Notes on the Old and New Testaments.* Reprint. Grand Rapids: Baker Book House, 1973.

Crockett, William D. *A Harmony of Samuel, Kings and Chronicles.* Grand Rapids: Baker Book House, 1961.

Darby, J. N. *The Collected Writings of J. N. Darby.* 34 vols. plus Index. Reprint. Oak Park, IL: Bible Truth Publishers, 1972.

———. *Synopsis of the Books of the Bible.* 5 vols. Reprint. Winschoten, Netherlands: H. L. Heijkoop, 1970.

Davidson, Stibbs and Kevan, eds. *The New Bible Commentary.* Chicago: Inter-Varsity Christian Fellowship, 1953.

Durbanville, Henry. *Winsome Christianity.* Edinburgh: B. McCall Barbour, n.d.

Edersheim, Alfred. *Bible History. Old Testament.* Reprint (7 vols. in 1). Grand Rapids: William B. Eerdmans Publishing Company, 1982.

Falwell, Jerry, ed. *Liberty Bible Commentary. Vol. 1. Old Testament.* Lynchburg, VA: The Old Time Gospel Hour, 1982.

Flynn, Leslie B. *Your God and Your Gold*. Williamsport, PA: Hearthstone Publishers, Inc., 1961.

Gehman, Henry Snyder, ed. *The New Westminster Dictionary of the Bible*. Philadelphia: The Westminster Press, 1976.

Gish, Arthur. *Beyond the Rat Race*. Scottsdale, PA: Herald Press, 1973.

Grant, F. W. *The Numerical Bible*. 7 vols. Neptune, NJ: Loizeaux Bros., 1977.

Gray, James M. *Christian Workers' Commentary on the Whole Bible*. Westwood, NJ: Fleming H. Revell Co., 1953.

Griffiths, Michael. *Take My Life*. Downers Grove, IL: InterVarsity Press, 1967.

Griffith Thomas, W. H. *The Pentateuch*. Grand Rapids: Kregel Publications, 1985.

Haley, John W. *Alleged Discrepancies of the Bible*. Nashville: Gospel Advocate Company, 1967.

Halley, Henry H. *Halley's Bible Handbook*. 24th ed. Grand Rapids: Zondervan Publishing House, 1965.

Harrison, Roland K. *Introduction to the Old Testament*. Grand Rapids: William B. Eerdmans Publishing Company, 1969.

———. Ed. *Major Cities of the Biblical World*. Nashville: Thomas Nelson Publishers, 1985.

Henry, Matthew. *The Matthew Henry Commentary on the Whole Bible*. 6 vols. Grand Rapids: Zondervan, 1974.

Henry, Scott and others. *The Pocket Bible Commentary*. Vol. 4. Chicago: Moody Press, n.d.

Hoste, William, and William Rodgers. *Bible Problems and Answers*. Kilmarnock, Scotland: John Ritchie Ltd., 1957.

Ironside, H. A. *The Continual Burnt Offering*. New York: Loizeaux Bros., 1941.

Jamieson, Fausset, and Brown. *A Commentary, Critical, Experimental, and Practical on the Old and New Testaments*. 6 vols. London: Wm. Collins and Co. Ltd., n.d.

Johnson, Samuel. *The History of Rasselas, Prince of Abyssinia*. ed. J. P. Hardy. London: Oxford University, 1968.

Jones, E. Stanley, *Is the Kingdom of God Realism?* Nashville: Abingdon-Cokesbury, 1940.

———. *Growing Spiritually*. Nashville: Abingdon Press, 1953.

Josephus, Flavius. *The Works of Flavius Josephus*. Trans. William Whiston. Hartford, CT: The S. S. Scranton Co., 1905.

Kautzsch, E. ed. *Gesenius' Hebrew Grammar*. Revised by A. E. Cowley. Reprint. Oxford: Clarendon Press, 1976.

Keil, C. F. *Manual of Historico-Critical Introduction to the Canonical Scriptures of the Old Testament*. 2 vols. Grand Rapids: Wm. B. Eerdmans Publishing Co., 1952.

Keil, C. F. and Franz Delitzsch. *Biblical Commentary on the Old Testament*. 26 vols. Grand Rapids: Wm. B. Eerdmans Publishing Company, 1971.

———. *Lectures Introductory to the Study of the Minor Prophets*. Fifth Edition. London: C. A. Hammond Trust Bible Depot, n.d.

Kitchen, J. Howard. *Holy Fields. An Introduction to the Historical Geography of the Holy Land*. Grand Rapids: Wm. B. Eerdmans Publishing Company, 1955.

Kollek, Teddy and Moshe Pearlman. *Jerusalem, a History of Forty Centuries*. London: Weidenfeld and Nicholson, 1968.

Lange, John Peter. *A Commentary on the Holy Scriptures*. 25 vols. Reprint. Grand Rapids: Zondervan Publishing House, 1960.

Lewis, C. S. *Weight of Glory*. Ed. by Walter Hooper. New York: MacMillan Publishing Company, 1980.

Lockyer, Herbert, Sr., ed. *Nelson's Illustrated Bible Dictionary*. Nashville: Thomas Nelson Publishers, 1986.

MacDonald, William. *Kingdom Divided: A Study of the Books of the Old Testament from Kings to Esther*. Toronto: Everyday Publications, 1974.

————. *16 Men with a Message: The Old Testament Prophets*. Toronto: Everyday Publications, 1972.

Mackintosh, C. H. *Genesis to Deuteronomy*. Neptune, NJ: Loizeaux Bros, 1972.

————. *The Mackintosh Treasury*. Neptune: NJ: Loizeaux Bros., 1976.

Mantle, J. G. *Better Things*. New York: Christian Alliance Publishing Co., 1921.

McMillen, S. I. *None of These Diseases*. Old Tappan, NJ: Fleming H. Revell Co., 1972.

Meyer, F. B. *Through the Bible Day by Day*. 7 vols. Philadelphia: American Sunday-School Union, 1917.

Miller, Rev. H. S. *General Biblical Introduction*. Houghton, NY: The Word-Bearer Press, 1956.

Moody, D. L. *Notes From My Bible*. New York: Fleming H. Revell Company, 1895.

Morgan, G. Campbell. *An Exposition of the Whole Bible*. Westwood, NJ: Fleming H. Revell Company, 1959.

————. *Living Messages from the Books of the Bible, Genesis—Malachi*. New York: Fleming H. Revell Company, 1912.

————. *Searchlights from the Word*. London: Oliphants, 1970.

Muggeridge, Malcolm. *Jesus Rediscovered*. Garden City, NY: Doubleday, 1969.

Naismith, *1200 More Notes, Quotes and Anecdotes*. London: Pickering & Inglis, 1975.

Nee, Watchman. *Do All To The Glory of God*. New York: Christian Fellowship Publishers, Inc., 1974.

A New and Concise Bible Dictionary. London: Central Bible Hammond Trust, 1973.

Orr, James, ed. *International Standard Bible Encyclopedia*. 5 vols. Grand Rapids: Wm. B. Eerdmans Publishing Co., 1939.

Packer, J. I. *Knowing God*. Downers Grove: InterVarsity Press, 1977.

Pentecost, J. D. *Things to Come*. Grand Rapids: Zondervan Publishing House, 1974.

Pfeiffer, Charles F. *Baker's Bible Atlas*. Grand Rapids: Baker Book House, 1966.

————. ed. *The Biblical World*. Grand Rapids: Baker Book House, 1966.

————. *An Outline of Old Testament History*. Chicago: Moody Press, 1960.

Pfeiffer, Charles F., and Everett F. Harrison, eds. *The Wycliffe Bible Commentary*. Chicago: Moody Press, 1962.

Pierson, Arthur T. *Knowing the Scriptures*. Fincastle, VA: Scripture Truth Book Company, 1975.

————. *An Outline of Old Testament History*. Chicago: Moody Press, 1960.

Pilkey, John. *Origin of the Nations*. San Diego, CA: Master Book Publishers, 1984.

Pink, A. W. *The Attributes of God*. Grand Rapids: Baker Book House, 1975.

Poole, Matthew. *Matthew Poole's Commentary on the Holy Bible*. Edinburgh: The Banner of Truth Trust, 1974.

Pritchard, James A. *Archaeology and the Old Testament.* Princeton, NJ: Princeton University Press, 1958.

Reid, John. *The Chief Meeting of the Church.* Waynesboro, GA: Christian Missions Press, 1978.

The Revell Bible Dictionary. Ed. by Lawrence O. Richards. Old Tappan, NJ: Fleming H. Revell Company, 1990.

Ridout, Samuel. *How to Study the Bible.* New York: Loizeaux Brothers, 1947.

Ryrie, Charles C., *The Grace of God.* Chicago: Moody Press, 1975.

———., ed. *The Ryrie Study Bible, New King James Version.* Chicago: Moody Press, 1985.

Sanders, J. Oswald. *On to Maturity.* Chicago: Moody Press, 1969.

Schaeffer, Francis A. *The Church at the End of the 20th Century.* Downers Grove, IL: Inter-Varsity Press, 1970.

Schultz, Samuel J. *The Old Testament Speaks.* New York: Harper & Brothers, Publishers, 1960.

Scofield, C. I., E. Schuyler English, et al., eds. *The New Scofield Study Bible.* New King James Version. Nashville: Thomas Nelson Publishers, 1989.

Scott, Walter. *Handbook to the Bible. Old Testament.* Reprint. Charlotte, NC: Books for Christians, 1977.

Scroggie, W. Graham. *Know Your Bible. A Brief Introduction to the Scriptures. Vol. 1, The Old Testament.* London: Pickering & Inglis Ltd., n.d.

The Serious Christian. Series I. Reprints in 22 vols. Charlotte, NC: Books for Christians, n.d.

The Serious Christian. Series II. Reprints in 13 vols. to date. Charlotte, NC: Books for Christians, n.d.

Sider, Ronald J. *Rich Christians in an Age of Hunger.* Downers Grove: InterVarsity Press, 1978.

Sparks, T. Austin. *What Is Man?* Indianapolis: Pratt Printing Co., n.d.

Spurgeon, C. H. *Morning and Evening.* Grand Rapids: Zondervan Publishing House, 1980.

———. *Spurgeon's Devotional Bible.* Grand Rapids: Baker Book House, 1974.

———. *Spurgeon's Sermons.* Vol. 1. Reprinted. Grand Rapids: Baker Book House, 1984.

Stevenson, Herbert F. *Three Prophetic Voices.* Old Tappan, NJ: Fleming H. Revell Company, 1971.

Stoner, Peter W. *Science Speaks.* Chicago: Moody Press, n.d.

Tan, Paul Lee. *The Interpretation of Prophecy.* Winona Lake, IN: BMH Books, Inc., 1974.

Tenney, Merrill C., gen. ed. and Steven Barabas, assoc. ed. *The Zondervan Pictorial Encyclopedia of the Bible.* 5 Vols. Grand Rapids: Zondervan, 1975.

Thiele, Edwin R. *The Mysterious Numbers of the Hebrew Kings.* 1st ed. Chicago: University of Chicago Press, 1951.

Thomson, W. M. *The Land and the Book; or, Biblical Illustrations Drawn from the Manners and Customs, the Scenes and Scenery of The Holy Land.* London: T. Nelson and Sons, Paternoster Row, 1884.

Unger, M. F. *Introductory Guide to the Old Testament.* Grand Rapids: Zondervan Publishing House, 1951.

———. *Unger's Bible Dictionary.* Chicago: Moody Press, 1965.

———. *Unger's Bible Handbook.* Chicago: Moody Press, 1966.

Vine, W. E. *First Corinthians.* London: Oliphants, Ltd., 1951.

Walvoord, John F. and Roy B. Zuck, eds. *The Bible Knowledge Commentary. Old Testament.* Wheaton, IL: Victor Books, 1985.

Weston, Keith. *Living in the Light*. Bromley, Kent, England: STL Books, 1983.

Westwood, Tom. *Meditations on Elijah and Elisha*. Glendale, CA: The Bible Treasury Hour, Inc., n.d.

Williams, George. *The Student's Commentary on the Holy Scriptures*. 6th ed. Grand Rapids: Kregel Publications, 1971.

Wilson, Robert Dick. *A Scientific Investigation of the Old Testament*. Philadelphia: The Sunday School Times Company, 1926.

Wood, Leon. *A Survey of Israel's History*. Grand Rapids: Zondervan Publishing House, 1970.

Yates, Kyle M. *Preaching from the Prophets*. Nashville: Broadman Press, 1942.

Young, Edward J. *Thy Word Is Truth*. Reprint. Grand Rapids: Wm. B. Eerdmans Publishing Co., 1957, 1970.

Articles and Periodicals

Brock, Paul. "Your Emotions Can Make You Ill." Reader's Digest, Sept. 1974.

Choice Gleanings Calendar. Grand Rapids: Gospel Folio Press, n.d.

Coder, S. Maxwell. "That Bow and Arrow War." *Moody Monthly*, April 1974.

Daily Notes of the Scripture Union. London: C.S.S.M., various dates.

Houghton, Will. "By Life or by Death." Copyright by Hope Publishing Co.

Our Daily Bread. Grand Rapids, Radio Bible Class, various dates.

Reuben, David R. "Why Wives Cheat on Their Husbands," *Reader's Digest*, August 1973.

Sims, Bennett J. "Sex and Homosexuality." *Christianity Today*, February 24, 1978, p. 29.

Toward the Mark. Weston-super-Mare, England: various dates.

Westwood, Tom. *Meditations on David and Joseph*. Denver: Wilson Foundation, n.d.

Unpublished Materials

Gibson, O. J. Unpublished notes, Discipleship Intern Training Program. San Leandro, CA.

Woodring, H. C. Unpublished notes, Emmaus Bible School, Oak Park, IL.

Poetry, Hymns, and Music

Barnes, Billy. "I Stayed Too Long at the Fair." Hollywood: Tylerson Music, 1957. Copyright 1957, Tylerson Music Co.

The Children of the Night.

Duffield, Samuel Willoughby. *English Hymns: Their Authors and History*. New York: Funk & Wagnalls Company, 1886.

Eliot, T. S. "East Coker," *Four Quartets*. New York: Harcourt Brace Jovanovich.

Hymns. Chicago: InterVarsity Press, 1947.

Hymns of Grace and Truth. Neptune: NJ: Loizeaux Bros., n.d.

Hymns of Truth and Praise. Fort Dodge, IA: Gospel Perpetuating Publ., 1971.

Lowell, James R. "The Present Crisis," *Complete Poetical Works*. Boston: Houghton Mifflin, 1897.

Selected Poems of Edwin Arlington Robinson. London: The Macmillan Company, 1965.

Tozer, A. W. *The Christian Book of Mystical Verse*. Harrisburg, PA: Christian Publications, 1963.

THE INTERTESTAMENTAL PERIOD

When God delivered His final message through Malachi, He paused in His communications through man for nearly four hundred years. A deafening silence in divine revelation resulted.

No doubt the silence of God gave rise to many theories about His nature. Some might have demanded that He act as He had always acted. Others might have surmised that man was too sinful to hear from God (this is always an absurdity since *any* sin is an affront to God and apart from grace He would not have communed with any person or generation *before* Malachi's time, let alone after). Still others might have suggested, and quite strongly so, that man's lack of faith was the cause of God's silence and apparent inactivity.

None of these theories would have taken into account the omniscience and sovereignty of Jehovah God. His determined, covenantal love (Hebrew *hesed*) had already set His course. This long silence was part of His eternal plan. He had spoken on numerous occasions and through various people, but He was now preparing to speak His greatest and most powerful Word to mankind: Jesus. A pause—a long and distinct pause—would add emphasis to that monumental revelation.

The ways of God are certainly beyond the complete grasp of man. "For as the heavens are higher than the earth, so are My ways higher than your ways, and My thoughts than your thoughts" (Is. 55:9). But the Architect of this universe is not without order and symmetry in His work, even in His dealings with finite, fickle human beings. Occasionally that order may be discerned.

A brief review of the way God ministered to man during the years chronicled in the Old Testament is very instructive. A consistent pattern of action emerges from the accounts recorded through the Holy Spirit's inspiration. Such consistency in the past sheds light upon the workings of God during what may be called the Intertestamental Period.

Two things stand out. First, God generally designed or allowed a *desperate situation* to arise before presenting His message or providing His deliverance. Secondly, He always called upon a *faithful servant* to "stand in the gap," making intercession to Him on behalf of the people (Ezek. 22:30), and to be His agent through whom He performed His work.

Consider the terrible conditions that prevailed in antediluvian society. God expressed regret that He had even created man (Gen. 6:6). Against the backdrop of this dark, dismal scene, the Bible declares: "But Noah found grace in the eyes of the LORD" (Gen. 6:8). Thus we have a desperate situation, and God's faithful servant.

This pattern was repeated with Abraham in God's calling of a chosen people out of a human race enmeshed in pride and idolatry. It appeared again with Joseph in the sparing of Israel from famine. Moses was another deliverer, who came just in time to rescue God's people from apparently impossible circumstances. The same theme runs through the book of Judges, and continues to appear in such lives as Esther and Nehemiah.

In each of these examples, and others like them, the efforts of man had to be frustrated before divine intervention ensued. The recorded history of the Intertestamental Period points to a similar experience. It seems that God allowed His people to exhaust their resources and to be reduced to another desperate situation before He brought to the scene His most faithful and only perfect Servant, His Son Jesus Christ.

THE PERIOD IN QUESTION

If the book of Malachi was completed in 397 B.C., then the period under consideration begins at that point and continues until the angel's announcement of the birth of John the Baptist (Luke 1:11–17). Throughout this four-hundred-year span of time there were no prophets and no inspired writers of divine revelation.

Six historical divisions are observable. The Persian Era, which actually dates all the way back to 536 B.C. but coincides with the Intertestamental Period from 397 to 336 B.C.; the Greek Era (336–323 B.C.); the Egyptian Era (323–198 B.C.); the Syrian Era (198–165 B.C.); the Maccabean Era

(165–63 B.C.); and the Roman Era (63–4 B.C.). This study will be presented chronologically according to these six divisions. Attention will be given to the historical situation and the religious developments within each segment.

THE PERSIAN ERA (397–336 B.C.)

Historical Situation

As has already been noted, the Persians were the dominating power in the Middle East as far back as 536 B.C. God had used the Persians to deliver Israel from the Babylonian captivity (Dan. 5:30, 31).

Persia's attitude was tolerant toward the Jewish remnant in Palestine, until internal rivalry over the politically powerful office of high priest resulted in partial destruction of Jerusalem by the Persian governor. Otherwise the Jewish people were left undisturbed during this period.

Religious Developments

The Babylonian captivity was used by God to purge idolatry from His people. They returned to Jerusalem with a new reverence for the Scriptures, especially the law of Moses. They also had a firm grasp on the theological concept of monotheism. These two influences carried over into the Intertestamental Period.

The rise of the *synagogue* as the local center of worship can be traced back to this period. *Scribes* became very important for the interpretation of the Scriptures in the synagogue services. By the time Jesus was born, the synagogue was well developed in organization and was widely spread throughout the Jewish communities of the world.

Another development that affected the spread of the gospel during New Testament times had its origin toward the end of the Persian rule. A temple was founded in Samaria, establishing a form of worship that rivaled Judaism. That event encouraged the ultimate social and religious separation between Jew and Samaritan.

THE GREEK ERA (336–323 B.C.)

Historical Situation

Alexander the Great, in many respects the greatest conqueror of all time, was the central figure of this brief period. He conquered Persia, Babylon, Palestine, Syria, Egypt, and western India. Although he died at the age of thirty-three, having reigned over Greece only thirteen years, his influence lived long after him.

Religious Developments

The cherished desire of Alexander was to found a worldwide empire united by language, custom, and civilization. Under his influence the world began to speak and study the Greek language. This process, called Hellenization, included the adoption of Greek culture and religion in all parts of the world. Hellenism became so popular that it persisted and was encouraged even into New Testament times by the Romans.

The struggle that developed between the Jews and Hellenism's influence upon their culture and religion was long and bitter. Although the Greek language was sufficiently widespread by 270 B.C. to bring about a Greek translation of the Old Testament (the Septuagint), faithful Jews staunchly resisted pagan polytheism.

THE EGYPTIAN ERA (323–198 B.C.)

Historical Situation

With the death of Alexander in 323 B.C., the Greek empire became divided into four segments under as many generals: Ptolemy, Lysimachus, Cassander, and Selenus. These were Daniel's "four kingdoms" which took the place of the "large horn" (Dan. 8:21, 22).

Ptolemy Soter, the first of the Ptolemaic dynasty, received Egypt and soon dominated nearby Israel. He dealt severely with the Jews at first, but toward the end of his reign and on into the rule of Ptolemy Philadelphus, his successor, the Jews were treated favorably. It was during this time that the Septuagint was authorized.

The Jews prospered until near the end of the Ptolemaic dynasty when conflicts between Egypt and Syria escalated. Israel was again caught in the middle. When the Syrians defeated Egypt in the Battle of Panion in 198 B.C., Judea was annexed to Syria.

Religious Developments

The policy of toleration followed by the Ptolemies, by which Judaism and Hellenism coexisted peacefully, was very dangerous for the Jewish faith. A gradual infiltration of Greek influence and an almost unnoticed assimilation of the Greek way of life took place.

Hellenism's emphasis on beauty, shape, and movement encouraged Jews to neglect Jewish religious rites which were aesthetically unappealing. Thus worship was influenced to become more external than internal, a notion that had a lasting impact upon Judaism.

Two religious parties emerged: the Hellenizing party, which was pro-Syrian, and the orthodox Jews, in particular the Hasidim or "Pious Ones" (predecessors of the Pharisees). A struggle for power between these two groups resulted in a polarization of the Jews along political, cultural, and religious lines. It was this same conflict that brought about the attack of Antiochus Epiphanes in 168 B.C.

THE SYRIAN ERA (198–165 B.C.)

Historical Situation

Under the rule of Antiochus the Great and his successor Seleucus Philopater, the Jews, though treated harshly, were nonetheless allowed to maintain local rule under their high priest. All went well until the Hellenizing party decided to have their favorite, Jason, appointed to replace Onias III, the high priest favored by the orthodox Jews, and to bring this about by bribing Seleucus's successor, Antiochus Epiphanes. This set off a political conflict that finally brought Antiochus to Jerusalem in a fit of rage.

In 168 B.C. Antiochus set about destroying every distinctive characteristic of the Jewish faith. He forbade all sacrifices, outlawed the rite of circumcision, and canceled observance of the Sabbath and feast days. The Scriptures were mutilated or destroyed. Jews were forced to eat pork and to sacrifice to idols. His final act of sacrilege, and the one that spelled his ultimate ruin, was to desecrate the Most Holy Place by building an altar and offering a sacrifice to the god Zeus. Many Jews died in the ensuing persecutions.

Perhaps a reminder of God's way of working with man is needed at this point. He creates or allows a desperate situation, then calls upon a special, faithful servant.

However, man often attempts to rescue himself and seems to be almost at the point of success only to wind up in worse shape than before. This was about to happen in the life of God's people the Jews. God was simply setting the stage for the coming of the true Deliverer.

Religious Developments

As can be seen by the historical developments of this period, the Jewish religion was divided over the issue of Hellenism. The groundwork was laid for an orthodox party, generally led by the scribes and later called the Pharisees, and for what we may call a more pragmatic faction of Jews which became more or less associated with the office of high priest. The pattern of thinking upon which the latter group was based fostered the rise of the Sadducees at a later date.

THE MACCABEAN ERA (165–63 B.C.)

Historical Situation

An elderly priest named Mattathias, of the house of Hasmon, lived with his five sons in the village of Modein, northwest of Jerusalem. When a Syrian official tried to enforce heathen sacrifice in Modein, Mattathias revolted, killed a renegade Jew who did offer sacrifice, slew the Syrian official, and fled to the mountains with his family. Thousands of faithful Jews joined him, and history records one of the most noble demonstrations of holy jealousy for the honor of God.

After the death of Mattathias three of his sons carried on the revolt in succession: Judas surnamed Maccabeus (166–160 B.C.), Jonathan (160–142 B.C.), and Simon (143–134 B.C.). These men had such success that by December 25, 165 B.C., they had retaken Jerusalem, cleansed the temple, and restored worship. This event is commemorated even today as the Feast of Hanukkah (Dedication).

Fighting continued in the outlying areas of Judea with several futile attempts by Syria to defeat the Maccabeans. Finally, under the leadership of Simon, the Jews received their independence (142 B.C.). They experienced almost seventy years of independence under the reign of the Hasmonaean dynasty, the most notable leaders of which were John Hyrcanus (134–104 B.C.) and Alexander Jannaeus (102–76 B.C.).

Religious Developments

The most significant religious development of this period resulted from a strong difference of opinion concerning the kingship and high priesthood of Judea. For hundreds of years the position of high priest had taken on some very obvious political overtones. Emphasis had not been upon the Aaronite line but upon political strength. Orthodox Jews resented and resisted this development. When John Hyrcanus became governor and high priest of Israel, he conquered Transjordan and Idumaea and destroyed the Samaritan temple. His power and popularity led him to refer to himself as a king. This flew in the face of the orthodox Jews, who by this time were called Pharisees. They recognized no king unless he was of the lineage of David, and the Hasmonaeans were not.

Those who opposed the Pharisees and supported the Hasmonaeans were called Sadducees. These names appeared for the first time during the reign of John Hyrcanus who himself became a Sadducee.

THE ROMAN ERA (63–4 B.C.)

Historical Situation

The independence of the Jews ended in 63 B.C., when Pompey of Rome took Syria and entered Israel. Aristobulus II, claiming to be the king of Israel, locked Pompey out of Jerusalem. The Roman leader in anger took the city by force and reduced the size of Judea. Israel's attempt at freedom from oppression had paid off for a while, but now all hope seemed to be lost.

Antipater the Idumaean was appointed procurator of Judea by Julius Caesar in 47 B.C. Herod, the son of Antipater, eventually became the king of the Jews around 40 B.C.

Although Herod the Great, as he was called, planned and carried out the building of the new temple in Jerusalem, he was a devoted Hellenist and hated the Hasmonaean family. He killed every descendant of the Hasmonaeans, even his own wife Marianne, the granddaughter of John Hyrcanus. Then he proceeded to murder his own two sons by Marianne, Aristobulus and Alexander. This is the man on the throne when Jesus was born in Bethlehem. What a dark and desperate situation for God's people!

Religious Developments

The rise of the Pharisees and Sadducees has already been mentioned. Before moving on to a discussion of three other important parties, some attention needs to be given to these two major groups.

(1) *The Pharisees* were so named early in the reign of John Hyrcanus. The name means "Separatists." They depended heavily upon the scribes and were loyal to the law and religion of Jehovah. Their emphasis upon the strict adherence to the Scriptures led to a strong attachment to the "oral law," or Mishnah, which sought to apply the written law to everyday life.

During the earthly ministry of Jesus, the "oral law" was so rigid with legalistic expansions that it usually had little to do with the original intent of Scripture. What started out to be a very wholesome and much-needed dependence on the Word of God deteriorated to a formalism and legalism that denied the spirit of the Word.

(2) *The Sadducees* derived their name from the word *Zadokites* or maybe from the Hebrew word *tsaddik*, meaning "righteous." Whereas the Pharisees were strongly connected with the scribes, the Sadducees were related to the high priest. The priests seem to have tended toward the more social, political, and earthly aspects of their position. This pattern of thinking was attractive to many of the more socially minded Jewish leaders.

Numerically a much smaller party than the Pharisees, the Sadducees belonged mostly to the wealthy influential priestly families who formed the social aristocracy of the Jewish nation. They felt that God's law and a nation's politics were totally separate. In other words, they saw no relationship between the need for holiness and the destiny of their nation. Religion was religion; politics was politics. They were therefore very skeptical of the Pharisees and seemingly concluded that the latter were old-fashioned, irrelevant, and fanatical.

(3) *The Herodians* emerged during the Roman Era (Matt. 22:16). This was a politi-

cal party whose major aim was to further the cause of Herod's government. They were perhaps motivated by a fear of the Roman government and the possibility of total destruction that could result from an act of rebellion on the part of the Jews. They were strongly inclined toward Hellenism and were opposed to the Pharisees and their constant emphasis on separation.

(4) *The Zealots* (or "Cananaeans," from the Aramaic *kanna'ah*, "zealous"—"Canaanites" in the NKJV New Testament) were also a political party but were in direct opposition to the Herodians. They would not conform to Roman rule, and they did not believe in waiting submissively like the Pharisees until Israel's Messiah would come and overthrow the Romans. In their opinion God only helped those who helped themselves. The Jews must be ready to fight for independence.

To a Pharisee-like fanaticism for the letter of the law, the Zealots added a fiery nationalistic spirit. The teachings of this group stressed a type of man-made, military deliverance rather than divine intervention.

(5) *The Essenes* were also a product of the Roman Era. They are not mentioned in the New Testament but have received considerable attention since the discovery of the Dead Sea Scrolls.

This group of people was religious, not political. They were a type of pseudospiritual cult which felt that they must withdraw from ordinary human society and practice a monastic kind of life and a mystical kind of Judaism.

With a passion for the spirit of the law and a separation to God, the Essenes lost all consciousness of the evangelistic mission of Israel. They were content to lock out the world, ignore its problems, and let it die without hope.

CONCLUSION

The stage was set. Man's futile attempts to deal with the shifting tide of political power and religious belief had produced very little. Israel was in a kind of spiritual bondage that was even worse than her political bondage. The rise of the various parties and movements discussed above was evidence of a sincere search for some final solution to her problem. All seemed to have failed. The stage of history was dark. The situation was indeed desperate.

Amid this setting God broke four hundred years of silence with the announcement of the coming of Christ, the faithful Servant of the Lord, and the Intertestamental Period came to an end.

THE
NEW TESTAMENT

CONTENTS

INTRODUCTION TO THE NEW TESTAMENT

"The value of these Writings, historical and spiritual, is out of all proportion to their number and length, and their influence upon life and history is incalculable. Here is the noontide of the day which began to dawn in Eden. The Christ of Prophecy in the Old Testament becomes the Christ of History in the Gospels; the Christ of Experience in the Epistles; and the Christ of Glory in the Revelation." — W. Graham Scroggie

I. The Name "New Testament"

Before launching out into the deep seas of NT studies, or even the comparatively small area of studying a particular book, it will prove helpful to outline briefly some general facts about the Sacred Book we call "The New Testament."

"Testament" and "covenant" both translate the same Greek word (*diathēkē*), and in one or two places in Hebrews it is debatable which translation is better. In the title of the Christian Scriptures the meaning "covenant" seems definitely preferable because the Book constitutes a pact, alliance, or *covenant* between God and His people.

It is called the *New* Testament (or Covenant) to contrast it with the Old (or "Older") one.

Both Testaments are inspired by God and therefore profitable for all Christians. But naturally the believer in Christ is more often likely to turn to that part of the Bible that specifically tells of our Lord and His church, and how He wishes His disciples to live.

The relationship between the OT and the NT is nicely expressed by Augustine:

The New is in the Old concealed;
The Old is in the New revealed.

II. The NT Canon

The word *canon* (Gk. *kanōn*) refers to a "rule" by which something is measured or evaluated. The canon of the NT is the collection of inspired books. How do we know that these are the *only* books that should be in the canon or that all of these twenty-seven writings should be there? Since there were other Christian epistles and writings (also heretical ones) from early days, how can we be sure these are the right ones?

It is often said that a church council drew up the canonical list in the late 300's of our era. Actually, the books were *canonical* as soon as they were written. Godly and discerning disciples recognized inspired Scriptures from the start, as Peter did Paul's writings (2 Pet. 3:15, 16). However, there was dispute over some of the books (Jude, 2 and 3 John, e.g.) in some churches for a time.

Generally if a book was by an apostle, such as Matthew, Peter, John, or Paul, or one of the apostolic circle, such as Mark or Luke, there was no doubt about that book's canonicity.

The council that officially recognized our canon was actually *confirming* what had been generally accepted for many, many years. The council drew up not an *inspired list* of books, but a list of *inspired books*.

III. Authorship†

The Divine Author of the NT is the Holy Spirit. He inspired Matthew, Mark, Luke, John, Paul, James, Peter, Jude and the anonymous author of Hebrews (see Introduction to Hebrews) to write. The best and correct understanding of this

†See p. i.

question of how the NT books were produced is "dual authorship." The NT is not partly human and partly divine, but totally human and totally divine at the same time. The divine element kept the human element from making any errors. The result is an inerrant or flawless book in the original manuscripts.

A helpful analogy to the written Word is the dual nature of the Living Word, our Lord Jesus Christ. He is not partly human and partly divine (like a Greek myth) but completely human and completely divine at the same time. The divine nature made it impossible for the human to err or sin in any way.

IV. Dates

Unlike the OT, which took about a millennium to complete (c. 1400–400 B.C.), the NT took only half a century to write (c. A.D. 50–100).

The present order of the NT books is best suited for the church for all time. It starts with the life of Christ, then tells of the church, then gives instructions to that church, and finally reveals the future of the church and the world. However, the books do not occur in order of writing. They were written as the need for them arose.

The first books were "Letters to young churches," as Phillips calls the Epistles. James, Galatians, and Thessalonians are probably the first written, near the middle of our first Christian century.

The Gospels are next in order of writing, Matthew or Mark first, Luke next, and John last. Finally comes the Revelation, probably near the end of the first century A.D.

V. Contents

The contents of the NT may be summarized concisely as follows:

Historical
    Gospels
    Acts
Epistolary
    Paul's Epistles
    General Epistles
Apocalyptic
    Revelation

A Christian who gets a good grasp of these books will be "thoroughly furnished for every good work."

It is our prayer that the BBC will greatly aid many believers to be just that.

VI. Language

The NT was written in *everyday language* (called *koinē,* or "common Greek"). This was a nearly universal second language in the first century of the Faith, as well-known and as widely used as English is today.

Just as the Hebrew language's warm and colorful style perfectly fits the prophecy, poetry, and narrative of the OT, so Greek was providentially prepared as a marvelous vehicle for the NT. The Greek language spread far abroad through Alexander the Great's conquests, his soldiers simplifying and popularizing the language for the masses.

The precision of Greek verb tenses, cases, vocabulary, and other details makes it ideal for communicating the important doctrinal truths found in the Epistles — especially in such a book as Romans.

While not an elite literary language, the *koinē* Greek is not "street language" or poor Greek either. A few parts of the NT — Hebrews, James, 2 Peter — do approximate the literary level. Also, Luke, at times, waxes almost classical and even Paul writes with great beauty on occasion (1 Cor. 13, 15, e.g.).

VII. Translation

English is blessed with many (perhaps too many!) translations. These fall into four general types:

1. Very literal

The "New" (in 1871) Translation of J. N. Darby and the English Revised Version (1881) and its U.S. variant, the American Standard Version (1901) are extremely literal. This makes them helpful for study but weak for worship, public reading, and memorization. The masses of Christians have never abandoned the majesty and beauty of the KJV for these versions.

2. Complete Equivalence

Versions that are quite literal and follow the Hebrew or Greek closely when English allows it, yet still permit a freer translation where good style and idiom demand it, include the KJV, and the RSV, the NASB, and the NKJV. Unfortunately, the RSV, while generally reliable in the NT, is wedded to an OT that plays down many Messianic prophecies. This dangerous trend is seen today even among some previously sound scholars. The BBC was edited to conform to the NKJV as the most viable position between the beautiful (but archaic) KJV and today's usage, yet without using any "thee's" and "thou's." It also retains many verses and words eliminated in most modern Bibles (see notes on text throughout the BBC).

3. Dynamic Equivalence

This type of translation is freer than the complete equivalence type, and sometimes resorts to paraphrase, a valid technique as long as the reader is made aware of it. The Moffatt Translation, NEB, NIV, and the Jerusalem Bible all fall into this category. An attempt is made to put whole thoughts into the structure that John and Paul might have used if they were writing

today — and in English. When done conservatively, this methodology can be a helpful tool.

4. Paraphrase

A paraphrase seeks to transmit the text thought by thought, yet it often takes great liberties in *adding* material. Since it is far removed from the original text in wording there is always the danger of *too much interpretation*. The Living Bible, e.g., while evangelical, makes many interpretive decisions that are *at best* debatable.

The paraphrase of J. B. Phillips (he calls it a translation) is very well done from a literary viewpoint. He also usually says in *his* words what he believes Peter and Paul meant in *theirs*.

It is good to have a Bible from at least three of these categories for purposes of comparison. However, we believe that the complete equivalence translation is safest for detailed Bible study, such as is presented in the BBC.

INTRODUCTION TO
THE GOSPELS†

"The Gospels are the firstfruits of all writings." — Origen

I. Our Glorious Gospels

Everyone who has studied literature is familiar with the story, the novel, the play, the poem, and the biography, as well as other literary forms. But when our Lord Jesus Christ came to earth, a whole new category of literature was needed — the *Gospel*. The Gospels are not biographies, though they have strong biographical material. They are not stories, though they contain parables such as the Prodigal Son and the Good Samaritan that are as interesting as any story in all literature. Some parables have even been adapted into novels or short stories. The Gospels are not documentary reports, yet they contain accurate, though obviously condensed, accounts of many conversations and discourses of our Lord.

Not only is the "Gospel" a unique literary category, but after the four evangelists wrote Matthew, Mark, Luke, and John, the canonical mold was broken. Four Gospels and only these four have been recognized by orthodox Christians for nearly two thousand years. Various heretics wrote books they *called* gospels, but these were shabby vehicles to promote some heresy, such as Gnosticism.

But why four Gospels? Why not five, to match the five books of Moses to form a Christian Pentateuch? Or why not just one long Gospel, omitting all repetitions and having room for more miracles and parables? Actually, attempts to "harmonize" or put all four together go as far back as Tatian's second century *Diatessaron* (Greek for "through four").

Irenaeus theorized that there were four Gospels to match the four quarters of the world and the four winds, four being the number of universality.

†*See pp. iii–viii.*

II. The Four Symbols

Many, especially artistic people, appreciate the parallel proposed between the four Gospels and the four symbols of Ezekiel and Revelation: the lion, the ox (or calf), the man, and the eagle. They, however, have been matched up quite differently with the Gospels by different Christians. If there is validity to these *attributes,* as they are called in art, the lion best fits Matthew, the royal Gospel of the Lion of Judah. The ox, as a beast of burden, fits Mark well, the Gospel of the Servant. The man is definitely the key figure of Luke, the Gospel of the Son of Man. Even the *Standard Handbook of Synonyms, Antonyms & Prepositions* says that "the eagle is the *attribute* of St. John as an *emblem* of lofty spiritual vision."[1]

III. The Four Readerships

Probably the best explanation for the fact that there are four Gospels is that the Holy Spirit is seeking to reach four different groups of people — four ancient types that still have clear modern counterparts.

Everyone agrees that Matthew is the most Jewish Gospel. The OT quotations, detailed discourses, genealogy of our Lord, and general Semitic tone are noticed by even a new reader.

Mark, probably writing from the imperial capital itself, is aiming at Romans, and also the millions of similar people who like action more than thought. His Gospel is thus long on miracles and short on parables. This Gospel needs no genealogy, because what Roman would care about Jewish genealogies for an active Servant?

Luke is clearly the Gospel for the Greeks and the many Romans who loved and emulated Greek literature and art. Such people love beauty, humanity, cultural style, and literary excellence. Dr. Luke supplies all of these. Along with the modern Greeks, the most obvious counterparts are the French. It is no surprise that it was a *Frenchman* who said that Luke was "the most beautiful book in the world" (see Introduction to Luke).

Who is left for John? John is the universal Gospel, with something for everyone. It is evangelistic (20:30, 31), yet also cherished by deep Christian thinkers. Perhaps this is the key: John is for "the third race" — a name given by the pagans to the early Christians as being neither Jews nor Gentiles.

IV. Other Fourfold Motifs

There are a few other fourfold motifs in the OT that dovetail beautifully with the emphases of the four Gospels.

"The Branch" as a title of our Lord occurs in the following contexts:
". . . to David a Branch . . . a King" (Jer. 23:5, 6)
"My Servant, the BRANCH" (Zech. 3:8)
"The Man . . . the BRANCH" (Zech. 6:12)
"The Branch of the LORD" (Jehovah) (Isa. 4:2)

There are also four "Beholds" in the OT that exactly match the Gospels' main themes:
"Behold, your King" (Zech. 9:9)
"Behold, my Servant" (Isa. 42:1)
"Behold, the Man" (Zech. 6:12)
"Behold your God" (Isa. 40:9)

A final parallel is one that is a little less obvious but has proved a blessing to many. The four colors of materials in the tabernacle with their symbolic meanings also seem to fit the evangelists' fourfold presentation of the attributes of our Lord:

Purple is an obvious choice for *Matthew,* the Gospel of the King. Judges 8:26 shows the regal nature of this color.

Scarlet dye was derived in ancient times from crushing a cochineal worm. This suggests *Mark,* the Gospel of the bondservant, "a worm and no man" (Ps. 22:6).

White speaks of the righteous deeds of the saints (Rev. 19:8). *Luke* stresses the perfect humanity of Christ.

Blue represents the sapphire dome we call the heavens (Ex. 24:10), an attractive representation of the Deity of Christ, a key note in *John.*

V. Order and Emphasis

In the Gospels, we find the events are not always listed in the order in which they occurred. It is good to know at the outset that the Spirit of God often groups events according to their moral teaching. Kelly says:

It will be proved, as we proceed, that Luke's is essentially a moral order, and that he classifies the facts, conversations, questions, replies, and discourses of our Lord according to their inward connection, and not the mere outward succession of events, which is in truth the rudest and most infantile form of record. But to group events together with their causes and consequences, in their moral order, is a far more difficult task for the historian, as distinguished from the mere chronicler. God can use Luke to do it perfectly.[2]

These different emphases and approaches help explain the variations in the Gospels. While the first three Gospels, the so-called "Synoptics" (meaning "taking a common view") are similar in their approach to the life of Christ, John is different. He wrote later and didn't want to repeat what had already been well covered. His is a more reflective and theological presentation of the life and words of our Lord.

VI. The Synoptic Question

Why there are so many *similarities* — even to almost identical wording of relatively long passages — and yet also so many *differences* among the first three Gospels is usually called the "Synoptic problem." It is much more of a problem for those who deny inspiration than for conservative Christians. Many complex theories have been formulated, often involving theoretical lost documents that have left no trace in manuscript form. Some of these ideas fit in with Luke 1:1 and are at least *possible* from an orthodox standpoint. However, some of these theories have reached the point where they assert that the first century church pieced together "myths" about Jesus Christ. Aside from the infidelity to all Christian Scriptures and church history that these alleged "form-critical" theories represent, it should be pointed out that there is no documentary proof for any of them. Also, *no two scholars agree* on how they categorize and fragment the Synoptic Gospels.

A better solution to the question lies in our Lord's words in John 14:26: "But the Helper, the Holy Spirit, whom the Father will send in My name, He will teach you all things, and bring to your remembrance all things that I said to you."

This takes care of the eyewitness reminicences of Matthew and John, and probably includes Mark as well, assuming he records Peter's remembrances, as church history says. Add to this direct help from the Holy Spirit the written documents mentioned in Luke 1:1, the outstanding verbally accurate *oral tradition* of Semitic peoples, and the Synoptic question is answered. Any necessary truths, details or interpretations beyond these sources can have been directly revealed "(in words) which the Holy Spirit teaches" (1 Cor. 2:13).

Thus, when finding an *apparent* contradiction or differences in details we do well to ask, "Why does *this* Gospel leave out, include, or emphasize *this* event or speech?" For example, twice Matthew records two people being healed (of blindness and from a demon), while Mark and Luke mention only one. Some see this as a contradiction. Better to see Matthew, the Jewish Gospel, mentioning both men, since the law demanded "two or three witnesses," and the others mentioning, for example, the prominent, *named* person (blind Bartimaeus).

The following selections illustrate that some of the seeming duplications in the Gospels actually highlight significant differences:

Luke 6:20–23 seems to duplicate the Sermon on the Mount, but the former is a Sermon on the plain (Luke 6:17). The Beatitudes describe the character of the ideal citizen of the kingdom, whereas Luke traces the lifestyle of those who are Christ's disciples.

Luke 6:40 seems to be the same as Matthew 10:24. But in Matthew, Jesus is the Master and we are His disciples. In Luke, the discipler is the master, and the person he teaches is the disciple. Matthew

7:22 emphasizes service for the King; whereas Luke 13:25–27 describes fellowship with the Master.

Whereas Luke 15:4–7 is a barbed denunciation of the Pharisees, Matthew 18:12, 13 is concerned with children and God's love for them.

When only believers were present, John said, "He will baptize you with the Holy Spirit" (Mark 1:8; John 1:33). When there was a mixed multitude, especially including Pharisees, he said, "He will baptize you with the Holy Spirit and fire" (a baptism of judgment) (Matt. 3:11; Luke 3:16).

The expression "With the measure you use . . ." applies to our *judgmental attitude* toward others in Matthew 7:2, our *appropriation of the Word* in Mark 4:24, and our *liberality* in Luke 6:38.

These differences, then, are not contradictions, but purposeful, suggesting spiritual food for thought to the meditative believer.

VII. The Authorship of the Books[†]

It is standard in discussing who wrote the Gospels — in fact, all of the books of the Bible — to divide the testimonies into *external* and *internal* evidence. This we propose to do in all the twenty-seven New Testament books. Under *external* evidence, writers who lived nearer the times of the books — generally second and third century "church fathers" and a few heretics, or false teachers — are referred to. These men quote, allude to, and sometimes specifically tell us about the books and authors who interest us. For example, if Clement of Rome quotes 1 Corinthians near the end of the first century, it obviously cannot be a second century forgery written under Paul's name. Under *internal* evidence we note the style, vocabulary, history, and contents of a book to see if it supports or contradicts what the outside documents and authors claim. For example, the style of Luke and Acts sustains the view that the author was a cultured Gentile physician.

In many books the "canon" or list of approved books of the second century heretic Marcion is quoted. He only accepted a stripped-down edition of Luke

[†]*See p. i.*

and ten of Paul's Epistles, but he nevertheless is a helpful witness to which books were standard in his time. The Muratorian Canon (named after the Italian Cardinal Muratori, who found the document) is an orthodox, though sometimes fragmentary, list of canonical Christian books.

ENDNOTES

[1]James C. Fernald, ed., "Emblem," *Funk & Wagnalls Standard Handbook of Synonyms, Antonyms, and Prepositions*, p. 175.

[2]William Kelly, *An Exposition of the Gospel of Luke*, p. 16.

THE GOSPEL ACCORDING TO MATTHEW†

Introduction

"In grandness of conception and in the power with which a mass of material is subordinated to great ideas no writing in either Testament, dealing with a historical theme, is to be compared with Matthew."

— Theodor Zahn

I. Unique Place in the Canon

Matthew's Gospel is the perfect bridge between the Old and the New Testaments. Its very first words throw us back to the forefather of the OT people of God, Abraham, and to the first *great* king of Israel, David. In its emphasis, strong Jewish flavor, its many quotations from the Hebrew Scriptures, and its position at the head of the NT books, Matthew is the logical place to start the Christian message to the world.

Matthew has long held this first position in the order of the four Gospels. This is because until very modern times, it was universally believed to be the first Gospel *written*. Also, Matthew's clear, orderly style made it most suitable for congregational reading. Hence it was the most popular Gospel, sometimes vying for that place with John.

It is not necessary to believe that Matthew was the first Gospel written in order to be orthodox. However, the earliest Christians were nearly all of Jewish extraction, and there were many thousands of them. Meeting the needs of the first Christians *first* does seem quite logical.

II. Authorship††

The *external evidence* is ancient and universal that Matthew the tax collector, also called Levi, wrote the First Gospel. Since he was not a prominent member of the apostolic band it would be strange to attribute the First Gospel to him if indeed he had nothing to do with it.

Besides the ancient document known as the "Didache" (*Teaching of the Twelve Apostles*), Justin Martyr, Dionysius of Corinth, Theophilus of Antioch, and Athenagoras, the Athenian quote the Gospel as authentic. Eusebius, the church historian, quotes Papias as saying that "Matthew composed the *Logia* in the Hebrew language, and everyone interpreted them as he was able." Irenaeus, Pantaenus, and Origen basically agree with this. "Hebrew" is widely thought to mean the dialect of Aramaic used by the Hebrews in our Lord's time, as the word is used in the NT. But what are the "*Logia*"? Usually this Greek word means "oracles," as the OT contains the *oracles* of God. It cannot mean that in Papias' statement. There are three main views on his statement: (1) It refers to the *Gospel* of Matthew as such. That is, Matthew wrote an Aramaic edition of his Gospel especially to win the Jews to Christ and edify Hebrew Christians, and only later did a Greek edition appear. (2) It refers to *sayings* of Jesus only, which later became incorporated into his Gospel. (3) It refers to *testimonia*, i.e., citations of OT Scriptures to show that Jesus is the Messiah. Views 1 and 2 are more likely than view 3.

The Greek of Matthew does not read like a mere translation, but such a widespread tradition (with no early dissent) must have some factual basis. Tradition says that Matthew preached for fifteen

†See pp. iii–viii.
††See p. i.

years in Palestine and then left to evangelize in foreign parts. It is possible that about A.D. 45 he left behind for the Jews who had accepted Jesus as their Messiah a first draft of his Gospel in Aramaic (or just the *discourses* of Christ), and later made a *Greek* edition for *universal* use. A similar thing was done by Matthew's contemporary, Josephus. This Jewish historian made an Aramaic first draft of his *Jewish Wars* and then the final form of the book in Greek.

The *internal evidence* of the First Gospel does fit well with a devout Jew who loved the OT and was gifted as a careful writer and editor. As a civil servant of Rome, Matthew would have to be proficient in both the language of his people (Aramaic) and of the ruling authorities. (The Romans used Greek, not Latin, in the East.) The numerical details, parables regarding money, and the monetary terms all fit in with a tax collector. So does the concise, orderly style. Goodspeed, a nonconservative scholar, accepted the Matthaean authorship of this Gospel partly from this corroborating internal evidence.

In spite of such universal external evidence and favorable internal evidence, most nonconservative scholars *reject* the traditional view that Matthew the tax collector wrote this book. They do so on two main grounds.

First of all, *assuming* that Mark was the first Gospel written (taught as "Gospel truth" in many circles today), how could an apostle and eyewitness use so much of Mark's material (93% of Mark occurs also in other Gospels)? To answer this, first of all, it is not *proven* that Mark was first. Ancient testimony says Matthew was first, and since the early Christians were nearly all Jewish, this makes a great deal of sense. But even if we accept the so-called Marcan priority (and many conservatives do so), Matthew could have recognized that Mark's work was largely the reminiscences of the dynamic Simon Peter, Matthew's fellow-apostle, as early church tradition maintains (see Introduction to Mark).

The second argument against the book being by Matthew (or any eyewitness) is that it lacks vivid details. Mark, who no one claims witnessed Christ's ministry, has colorful details that suggest he was there. How could an eyewitness write so matter-of-factly? Perhaps the personality of a tax collector explains it quite well. In order to have room for more of our Lord's discourses, Levi could have cut down on needless details. This would especially be so if Mark wrote first and Matthew saw that Peter's first-hand reminiscences were well represented.

III. Date

If the widespread belief that Matthew made an Aramaic first edition of his Gospel (or at least of the sayings of Jesus) is so, a date for that of A.D. 45, fifteen years after the Ascension, would fit in with ancient tradition. He could have brought out the fuller, canonical Gospel in Greek in 50 or 55, or even later.

The view that the Gospel *must* have been written after the destruction of Jerusalem (A.D. 70) rests largely on disbelief in Christ's ability to predict that future event in detail, and other rationalistic theories that ignore or deny divine inspiration.

IV. Background and Theme

Matthew was a young man when Jesus called him. A Jew by birth, and a tax collector by training and practice, he forsook all to follow Christ. One of his many compensations was that he became one of the twelve apostles. Another was that he was chosen as the writer of what we know as the First Gospel. It is generally believed that Matthew was the same as Levi (Mark 2:14; Luke 5:27).

In his Gospel, Matthew sets out to show that Jesus is the long-expected Messiah of Israel, the only lawful Claimant to the throne of David.

The book does not profess to be a complete narrative of the life of Christ. It begins with His genealogy and early years, then jumps to the beginning of His public ministry when He was about thirty. Guided by the Holy Spirit, Matthew selects those aspects of the Savior's life and ministry which attest Him as God's *Anointed One* (that is what *Messiah* and *Christ* mean). The book moves toward a climax: the trial, death, burial, resurrection, and ascension of the Lord Jesus. And in that climax, of course, is laid the foundation for man's salvation. That is why the book is called a Gospel — not so much because it sets forth the way by which sinful people may receive salvation, but rather because it describes the sacrificial work of Christ by which salvation was made possible.

The Believers Bible Commentary is not intended to be exhaustive or technical, but rather to stimulate independent study and meditation. And most of all it is aimed at creating in the reader's heart an intense longing for the return of the King.

> So even I, and with a heart more burning,
> So even I, and with a hope more sweet,
> Groan for the hour, O Christ! of Thy
>   returning,
> Faint for the flaming of Thine advent feet.
>   – *from St. Paul, by F. W. H. Myers*

OUTLINE

Commentary†

I. GENEALOGY AND BIRTH OF THE MESSIAH-KING (Chap. 1)

A. The Genealogy of Jesus Christ (1:1–17)

A casual reading of the NT may cause a person to wonder why it begins with something as seemingly dull as a family tree. One might conclude that there is little significance to be drawn from this catalog of names and, thus, skip over it to where the action begins.

However, the genealogy is indispensable. It lays the foundation for all that follows. Unless it can be shown that Jesus is a legal descendant of David through the royal line, it is impossible to prove that He is the Messiah-King of Israel. Matthew begins his account where he must — with the documentary evi-

†See p. ix.

dence that Jesus inherited the legal right to the throne of David through His stepfather, Joseph.

This genealogy traces the *legal* descent of Jesus as King of Israel; the genealogy in Luke's Gospel traces His *lineal* descent as Son of David. Matthew's genealogy follows the *royal* line from David through his son, Solomon, the next king; Luke's genealogy follows the *blood* line from David through another son, Nathan. This genealogy concludes with Joseph, of whom Jesus was the *adopted* Son; the genealogy in Luke 3 probably traces the ancestry of Mary, of whom Jesus was the *real* Son.

A millennium earlier, God had made an unconditional agreement with David, promising him a kingdom that would last forever and a perpetually ruling line (Ps. 89:4, 36, 37). That covenant is now fulfilled in Christ: He is legal heir to the throne of David through Joseph and the actual seed of David through Mary. Because He lives forever, His kingdom will last forever and He will reign forever as David's greater Son. Jesus united in His Person the only two bases for claims to the throne of Israel (the legal and the lineal); since He still lives, there can be no other claimant.

1:1-15† The formula **the book of the genealogy of Jesus Christ, the Son of David, the Son of Abraham** is similar to the expression in Genesis 5:1: "This is the book of the genealogy of Adam." Genesis introduces the first Adam; Matthew, the last Adam. The first Adam was head of the first, or physical, creation. Christ, as the last Adam, is Head of the new, or spiritual, creation.

The subject of this Gospel is **Jesus Christ**. The name **Jesus** presents Him as Jehovah-Savior;[1] the title **Christ** ("Anointed"), as the long awaited Messiah of Israel. The title **Son of David** is associated with the roles of both Messiah and King in the OT. The title **Son of Abraham** presents our Lord as the One who is the ultimate fulfillment of the promises made to the progenitor of the Hebrew people.††

The genealogy is divided into three historical sections: from Abraham to Jesse, from David to Josiah, and from Jeconiah to Joseph. The first section leads up to David; the second covers the kingdom period; the third preserves the record of royal descent during the exile (586 B.C. and following).

There are many interesting features in this register. For example, in this paragraph, four women are mentioned: **Tamar, Rahab, Ruth,** and Bathsheba (**her who had been the wife of Uriah**). Since women are seldom mentioned in eastern genealogical tables, the inclusion of these women is all the more astonishing in that two of them were harlots (Tamar and Rahab), one had committed adultery (Bathsheba), and two were Gentiles (Rahab and Ruth). Their inclusion in Matthew's introduction is perhaps a subtle suggestion that the coming of Christ would bring salvation to sinners, grace to Gentiles, and that in Him, barriers of race and sex would be torn down.

Of interest too is the mention of a king named **Jeconiah**. In Jeremiah 22:30 God pronounced a curse on this man:

Thus says the LORD:
"Write this man down as childless,
A man who shall not prosper in
   his days;
For none of his descendants
   shall prosper,
Sitting on the throne of David,
And ruling anymore in Judah."

If Jesus had been the *real* son of Joseph, He would have come under this curse. Yet He had to be the legal son of Joseph in order to inherit the rights to the throne of David. The problem was solved by the miracle of the virgin birth: Jesus was the *legal* heir to the throne through Joseph. He was the *real* Son of David through Mary. The curse on Jeconiah did not fall on Mary or her children since she did not descend from Jeconiah.

1:16 **Of whom** in English could be construed as referring to both Joseph and Mary. However, in the original Greek, **whom** is singular and in the feminine gender, thus indicating that Jesus was born **of Mary**, but not of **Joseph**. But in addition to these interesting features of the genealogy, mention must also be made of the difficulties which it presents.

1:17 Matthew draws special attention to the fact that there are three sections of **fourteen generations** each. However, we know from the OT that

---

certain names are missing from his list. For example, between Joram and Uzziah (v. 8), Ahaziah, Joash, and Amaziah reigned as kings (see 2 Kgs. 8–14; 2 Chron. 21–25).

The genealogies of Matthew and Luke seem to overlap in mentioning two names: Shealtiel and Zerubbabel (Matt. 1:12, 13; Luke 3:27). It is strange that the ancestry of Joseph and Mary should merge in these two men, and separate again. The difficulty is increased when we notice that both Gospels follow Ezra 3:2 in listing Zerubbabel as the son of Shealtiel, whereas in 1 Chronicles 3:19 he is listed as the son of Pedaiah.

A third difficulty is that Matthew counts twenty-seven generations from David to Jesus, while Luke gives forty-two. Even though the evangelists are outlining different family trees, it still seems odd that there should be such a difference in the number of generations.

What attitude should the Bible student take toward these difficulties and seeming discrepancies? First, our foundational premise is that the Bible is the inspired Word of God. Therefore, it cannot contain errors. Second, it is infinite because it reflects the infinity of the Godhead. We can understand the fundamental truths of the Word, but we can never fully comprehend all there is in it.

So, our approach to these difficulties leads us to conclude that the problem lies in our lack of knowledge rather than in the Bible's fallibility. Bible problems should challenge us to study and search for the answers. "It is the glory of God to conceal a matter, but the glory of kings is to search out a matter" (Prov. 25:2).

Careful research by historians and excavations by archaeologists have not been able to demonstrate that the statements of the Bible are false. What seem to us like difficulties and contradictions all have reasonable explanations, and these explanations are filled with spiritual significance and profit.

B. Jesus Christ Is Born of Mary (1:18–25)

1:18 The birth of Jesus Christ was different from any of the births mentioned in the genealogy. There we found the repeated formula: "A begot B." But now we have the record of a birth without a human father. The facts surrounding this miraculous conception are stated with dignity and simplicity. **Mary** had been promised in marriage **to Joseph**, but the wedding had not yet taken place. In NT times, betrothal was a form of engagement (but more binding than engagement today) and it could be broken only by divorce. Although an engaged couple did not live together until the marriage ceremony, unfaithfulness on the part of the betrothed was treated as adultery and punishable by death.

During the time of her betrothal, the Virgin Mary became pregnant by a miracle of **the Holy Spirit**. An angel had previously announced this mysterious event to Mary: "The Holy Spirit will come upon you, and the power of the Highest will overshadow you" (Luke 1:35). A cloud of suspicion and scandal hung over Mary. In all of human history there had never been a virgin birth. When people saw an unwed woman who was pregnant, they had only one possible explanation.

1:19 Even **Joseph** did not yet know the true explanation of Mary's condition. He might have been indignant at his fiancée on two counts: First, her apparent unfaithfulness to him; and second, though innocent, he would almost inevitably be accused of complicity. His love for Mary and desire for justice led him to decide to break the betrothal by a quiet divorce. He wished to avoid the public disgrace which normally accompanied such an action.

1:20 While this gentle and deliberate man was mapping his strategy to protect Mary, **an angel of the Lord appeared to him in a dream**. The salutation, **"Joseph, son of David,"** was doubtless designed to stir up the consciousness of his royal pedigree and to prepare him for the unusual advent of Israel's Messiah-King. He should have no misgivings about marrying **Mary**. Any suspicions concerning her purity were groundless. Her pregnancy was a miracle of **the Holy Spirit**.

1:21 The angel then revealed the unborn Child's sex, name, and mission. Mary would bear **a Son**. He was to be named **JESUS**, (which means "Jehovah is salvation" or "Jehovah, the Savior").

True to His Name, He would **save His people from their sins**. This Child of destiny was Jehovah Himself, visiting earth to save people from the penalty of sin, from the power of sin, and eventually from the very presence of sin.

1:22 As Matthew recorded these events, he realized that a new era had dawned in the history of God's dealings with the human race. The words of a messianic prophecy, long dormant, had now sprung to life. Isaiah's cryptic prophecy was now fulfilled in Mary's Child: **So all this was done that it might be fulfilled which was spoken by the Lord through the prophet**. Matthew claims divine inspiration for the words of Isaiah — the Lord had spoken by the prophet at least 700 years before Christ.

1:23 The prophecy of Isaiah 7:14 included the foretelling of a unique birth ("Behold, the virgin shall conceive"), the sex of the Child ("and bear a Son"), and the name of the child ("and [she] shall call His name Immanuel"). Matthew adds the explanation that **Immanuel** means **God with us**. There is no record of Christ ever being called "Immanuel" while on earth; He was always called "Jesus." However, the meaning of the name *Jesus* (see above on v. 21) implies the presence of **God with us**. Immanuel might also be a designation for Christ which will be used primarily in His Second Advent.

1:24 As a result of the angel's intervention, Joseph abandoned his plan to divorce Mary. He continued to recognize their betrothal until Jesus' birth, after which he married her.

1:25 The teaching that Mary remained a virgin all of her life is disproved by the consummation of their marriage mentioned in this verse. Other references which indicate that Mary had children by Joseph are Matthew 12:46; 13:55, 56; Mark 6:3; John 7:3, 5; Acts 1:14; 1 Corinthians 9:5; and Galatians 1:19.

In taking Mary as his wife, Joseph also took her Child as his adopted Son. This is how Jesus became legal heir to the throne of David. In obedience to the angelic visitor, **he called** the Baby's **name Jesus**.

Thus the Messiah-King was born. The Eternal One entered time. The Omnipotent became a tiny Infant. The Lord

of glory veiled that glory in a human body, and "in Him dwells all the fullness of the Godhead bodily" (Col. 2:9).

II. EARLY YEARS OF THE MESSIAH-KING (Chap. 2)

A. Wise Men Come to Worship the King (2:1–12)

2:1, 2 It is easy to be confused about the chronology of the events surrounding Christ's birth. While verse 1 may appear to indicate that Herod tried to kill Jesus during Mary and Joseph's stay in the stable at Bethlehem,[†] the combined evidence points to a time one or two years later. Matthew says in verse 11 that the wise men saw Jesus in a house. The order by Herod to execute all male children under two years old (v. 16) also is an indication of the passage of an unspecified period of time since the royal birth.

Herod the Great was a descendant of Esau and, therefore, a traditional enemy of the Jews. He was a convert to Judaism, but his conversion was perhaps politically motivated. It was toward the close of his reign that **wise men from the East came** in search of the **King of the Jews**. These men might have been pagan priests whose ritual centered around the elements of nature. Because of their knowledge and predictive powers, they were often chosen as counselors to kings. We do not know where they lived in the East, how many there were, nor how long their journey lasted.

It was the **star in the East** that somehow made them aware of the birth of a **King, whom they came to worship**. Possibly they were familiar with OT prophecies concerning the Messiah's arrival. Perhaps they knew of Balaam's prediction that a Star would come out of Jacob (Num. 24:17) and connected this with the prophecy of seventy weeks which foretold the time of Christ's first coming (Dan. 9:24, 25). But it seems more probable that the knowledge was communicated to them supernaturally.

Various scientific explanations have been offered to account for the star. Some say, for instance, that it was a conjunction of planets. But the course of this star was highly irregular; it went before

---

†See pp. x–xi.

the wise men, leading them from Jerusalem to the house where Jesus was living (v. 9). Then it stopped. In fact, it was so unusual that it can only be accounted for as a miracle.

2:3 **When Herod the king heard** that a Baby had been born who was to be king of the Jews, **he was troubled**. Any such Baby was a threat to his uneasy rule. **All Jerusalem** was troubled **with him**. The city that should have received the news with joy was disturbed by anything that might upset its status quo or risk the displeasure of the hated Roman rulers.

2:4–6 Herod assembled the Jewish religious leaders to find out **where the Christ was to be born**. The **chief priests** were the high priest and his sons (and perhaps other members of his family). The **scribes of the people** were lay experts in the Law of Moses. They preserved and taught the law and served as judges in the Sanhedrin. These priests and scribes promptly quoted Micah 5:2 which identified **Bethlehem of Judea** as the King's birthplace. The text of the prophecy in Micah calls the city "Bethlehem Ephrathah." Since there was more than one town called Bethlehem in Palestine, this identifies it as the one in the district of Ephrathah within the tribal boundaries of Judah.

2:7, 8 **King Herod . . . secretly called the wise men** to determine **what time the star** first **appeared**. This secrecy betrayed his sadistic motive: he would need this information if he was unable to locate the right Child. To cover up his real intention, **he sent** the magi on their **search** and requested that they send **back word** to him of their success.

2:9 As the wise men set out, **the star which they had seen in the East** reappeared. This indicates that the star had not guided them all the way from the East. But now it did guide them to the house **where the young Child was**.

2:10 Special mention is made of the **exceedingly great joy** of the wise men **when they saw the star**. These Gentiles diligently sought for Christ; Herod planned to kill Him; the priests and scribes were (as yet) indifferent; the people of Jerusalem were troubled. These attitudes were omens of the way in which the Messiah would be received.

2:11 **When they entered the house, the magi saw the young Child with Mary His mother. They fell down and worshiped Him,** offering costly gifts of **gold, frankincense, and myrrh**. Notice that they saw Jesus with His mother. Ordinarily mention would be made of a mother first, then her child, but this Child is unique and must be given first place (see also vv. 13, 14, 20, 21). The wise men worshiped Jesus, *not* Mary or Joseph. (Joseph is not even mentioned in this account; he will soon disappear entirely from the Gospel record.) It is Jesus who deserves our praise and worship, not Mary or Joseph.

The treasures they brought spoke volumes. **Gold** is a symbol of deity and glory; it speaks of the shining perfection of His divine Person. **Frankincense** is an ointment or perfume; it suggests the fragrance of the life of sinless perfection. **Myrrh** is a bitter herb; it presages the sufferings He would endure in bearing the sins of the world. The bringing of gifts by Gentiles is reminiscent of the language of Isaiah 60:6. Isaiah predicted that Gentiles would come to the Messiah with gifts, but mentioned only gold and frankincense: ". . . they shall bring gold and incense. And they shall proclaim the praises of the Lord." Why was myrrh omitted? Because Isaiah was speaking of Christ's second advent — His coming in power and great glory. There will be no myrrh then because He will not suffer then. But in Matthew the myrrh is included because His first coming is in view. In Matthew we have the sufferings of Christ; in this passage of Isaiah, the glories that shall follow.

2:12 The wise men were **divinely warned in a dream . . . not to return to Herod,** and so they obediently returned to their homes by another route. No one who meets Christ with a sincere heart ever returns the same way. True encounter with Him transforms all of life.

B. Joseph, Mary, and Jesus Flee to Egypt (2:13–15)

2:13, 14[†] From infancy the threat of death hung over our Lord. It is apparent that He was born to die, but only at the appointed time. Anyone, who walks in God's will is immortal until his work is done. **An angel of the Lord** warned Jo-

†*See p. xvix.*

seph in a dream to flee to Egypt with
his family. Herod was ready to embark
on his "search and destroy" mission.
The family became refugees from the
wrath of Herod. We do not know how
long they stayed, but with the death of
Herod, the coast was clear for their repa-
triation.

2:15 Thus, another OT prophecy became clothed with new meaning. God
had said through the prophet Hosea:
"Out of Egypt I called My Son" (Hos.
11:1). In its original setting this referred
to Israel's deliverance from Egypt at the
time of the exodus. But the statement is
capable of a double meaning — the Messiah's history would closely parallel that
of Israel. The prophecy was fulfilled in
the life of Christ by His return to Israel
from Egypt.

When the Lord returns to reign in
righteousness, Egypt will be one of the
countries sharing in the blessings of the
Millennium (Isa. 19:21–25; Zeph. 3:9, 10;
Ps. 68:31). Why should that nation, a traditional enemy of Israel, be so favored?
Could it be a token of divine gratitude
for its granting sanctuary to the Lord
Jesus?

**C. Herod Massacres the Babies of
Bethlehem (2:16–18)†**

2:16 When the wise men failed to return, **Herod** realized that he had been
deceived in his plot to locate the young
King. In senseless rage, he ordered the
death of **all the male children** under the
age of **two in Bethlehem and in all its
districts**. Estimates vary as to the number slain; one writer suggests about
twenty-six. It is not likely that hundreds
were involved.

2:17, 18 The **weeping** which followed the killing of the children was a
fulfillment of the words of **Jeremiah the
prophet**:

Thus says the Lord:
"A voice was heard in Ramah,
Lamentation and bitter weeping,
Rachel weeping for her children,
Refusing to be comforted for her
   children,
Because they are no more"
   (Jer. 31:15).

In the prophecy, **Rachel** represents
the nation Israel. The grief of the nation
is attributed to Rachel, who was buried

in **Ramah** (near Bethlehem, where the
massacre took place). As the bereaved
parents passed her tomb, she is pictured
as **weeping** with them. In his effort to
eliminate this young Rival, Herod gained
nothing but dishonorable mention in the
annals of infamy.

**D. Joseph, Mary, and Jesus Settle in
Nazareth (2:19–23)**

After Herod's death, **an angel of the
Lord** assured **Joseph** that it was now
safe to return. When he reached **the land
of Israel,** however, **he heard that** Herod's
son **Archelaus** had succeeded **his father**
as king of **Judea.** Joseph was reluctant to venture into this region and
so, after his fears were confirmed **by
God in a dream,** he traveled north to
the region of Galilee and settled in **Nazareth.**

For the fourth time in this chapter,
Matthew reminds us that prophecy was
being **fulfilled.** He mentions none of the
prophets by name, but says that the
prophets had foretold that the Messiah
would **be called a Nazarene.** No OT
verse says this directly. Many scholars
suggest Matthew is referring to Isaiah
11:1: "There shall come forth a Rod from
the stem of Jesse, and a Branch shall
grow out of his roots." The Hebrew
word translated "Rod" is *netzer*, but the
connection seems remote. A more probable explanation is that "Nazarene" is
used to describe anyone who lived in
Nazareth, a town viewed with contempt
by the rest of the people. Nathaniel expresses this by the proverbial question,
"Can anything good come out of Nazareth?" (John 1:46). The scorn heaped
upon this "unimportant" town fell upon
its inhabitants as well. So when verse 23
says **He shall be called a Nazarene,** it
means that He would be treated with
contempt. Although we cannot find any
prophecy that Jesus would be called a
Nazarene, we can find one that says He
would be "despised and rejected by
men" (Isa. 53:3). Another says that He
would be a worm and not a man,
scorned and rejected by people (Ps.
22:6). So while the prophets did not use
the exact words, this was undeniably the
spirit of several prophecies.

It is amazing that when the mighty
God came to earth, He was given a nick-

name of reproach. Those who follow Him are privileged to share His reproach (Heb. 13:13).

III. PREPARATIONS FOR THE MESSIAH'S MINISTRY AND HIS INAUGURATION (Chaps. 3, 4)

A. John the Baptist Prepares the Way (3:1–12)

Between chapters 2 and 3 is an interval of twenty-eight or twenty-nine years which Matthew does not mention. During this time, Jesus was in Nazareth, preparing for the work which lay ahead. They were years in which He performed no miracles, yet in which He found perfect delight in the eyes of God (Matt. 3:17). With this chapter we come to the threshold of His public ministry.

3:1, 2 John the Baptist was six months older than his cousin Jesus (see Luke 1:26, 36). He stepped onto the stage of history to serve as forerunner for the King of Israel. His unlikely parish was **the wilderness of Judea** — an arid area extending from Jerusalem to the Jordan. John's message was, **"Repent, for the kingdom of heaven is at hand!"** The King would soon appear, but He could not and would not reign over people who clung to their sins. They must change directions, must confess and forsake their sins. God was calling them from the kingdom of darkness to **the kingdom of heaven.**

THE KINGDOM OF HEAVEN

In verse 2 we have the first occurrence of the phrase the kingdom of heaven, which is used thirty-two times in this Gospel. Since a person cannot rightly understand Matthew without comprehending this concept, a definition and description of the term are in order here.

The kingdom of heaven is the sphere in which God's rule is acknowledged. The word "heaven" is used to denote God. This is shown in Daniel 4:25, where Daniel said that "the Most High" rules in the kingdom of men. In the next verse he says that "heaven" rules. Wherever people submit to the rule of

God, there the kingdom of heaven exists.

There are two aspects of the kingdom of heaven. In its broadest sense it includes everyone who *professes* to acknowledge God as Supreme Ruler. In its narrower aspect it includes only those who have been genuinely *converted*. We may picture this by two concentric circles.

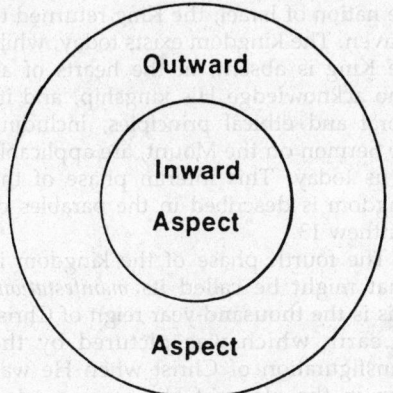

The big circle is the sphere of profession; it includes all who are genuine subjects of the King, and also those who only profess allegiance to Him. This is seen in the parables of the sower (Matt. 13:3–9), the mustard seed (Matt. 13:31, 32), and the leaven (Matt. 13:33). The little circle includes only those who have been born again through faith in the Lord Jesus Christ. The kingdom of heaven in its inward aspect can be entered only by those who are converted (Matt. 18:3).

By putting together all the references to the kingdom in the Bible, we can trace its historical development in five distinct phases:

First, the kingdom was *prophesied* in the OT. Daniel predicted that God would set up a kingdom that would never be destroyed nor yield its sovereignty to another people (Dan. 2:44). He also foresaw the coming of Christ to wield universal and everlasting dominion (Dan. 7:13, 14; see also Jer. 23:5, 6).

Second, the kingdom was described by John the Baptist, Jesus, and the twelve disciples as being *at hand* or *present* (Matt. 3:2; 4:17; 10:7). In Matthew 12:28, Jesus said, " . . . if I cast out demons by the Spirit of God, surely the kingdom of God has come upon you." In Luke 17:21, He said, "For indeed, the kingdom of God is within you" or in your midst. The kingdom was present in the Person of the King. As we shall show later, the terms kingdom of God and kingdom of heaven are used interchangeably.

Third, the kingdom is described in an *interim* form. After He was rejected by the nation of Israel, the King returned to heaven. The kingdom exists today, while the King is absent, in the hearts of all who acknowledge His kingship, and its moral and ethical principles, including the Sermon on the Mount, are applicable to us today. This interim phase of the kingdom is described in the parables of Matthew 13.

The fourth phase of the kingdom is what might be called its *manifestation*. This is the thousand-year reign of Christ on earth which was pictured by the Transfiguration of Christ when He was seen in the glory of His coming reign (Matt. 17:1–8). Jesus referred to this phase in Matthew 8:11 when He said, ". . . many will come from east and west, and sit down with Abraham, Isaac, and Jacob in the kingdom of heaven."

The final form will be the *everlasting* kingdom. It is described in 2 Peter 1:11 as "the everlasting kingdom of our Lord and Savior Jesus Christ."

The phrase "kingdom of heaven" is found only in Matthew's Gospel, but "kingdom of God" is found in all four Gospels. For all practical purposes there is no difference — the same things are said about both. For example, in Matthew 19:23 Jesus said that it would be hard for a rich man to enter the kingdom of *heaven*. Both Mark (10:23) and Luke (18:24) record that Jesus said this about the kingdom of *God* (see also Matt. 19:24 which has a similar maxim using "kingdom of God").

We mentioned above that the kingdom of heaven has an outward aspect and an inner reality. That the same is true of the kingdom of God is further proof that the two terms indicate the same thing. The kingdom of God, too, includes the real and the false. This is seen in the parables of the sower (Luke 8:4–10), the mustard seed (Luke 13:18, 19), and the leaven (Luke 13:20, 21). As to its true, inward reality, the kingdom of God can be entered only by those who are born again (John 3:3, 5).

One final point: the kingdom is not the same as the church. The kingdom began when Christ embarked on His public ministry; the church began on the day of Pentecost (Acts 2). The kingdom will continue on earth till the earth is destroyed; the church continues on earth till the Rapture (the catching away or removal of the church from earth when Christ descends from heaven and takes all believers home with Him — 1 Thess. 4:13–18). The church will return with Christ at His Second Advent to reign with Him as His bride. At present the people who are in the kingdom in its true, inner reality are also in the church. ‡

3:3 To return to the exposition of Matthew 3, note that the preparatory ministry of John had been prophesied by **Isaiah** over seven hundred years before his time:

The voice of one crying in the
　wilderness:
"Prepare the way of the LORD;
Make straight in the desert
A highway for our God" (40:3).

John was **the voice**. The nation of Israel, spiritually speaking, was **the wilderness** — dry and barren. John called on the people to **prepare the way of the LORD** by repenting of, and forsaking, their sins and to **make His paths straight** by removing from their lives anything that would hinder His complete dominion.

3:4 The Baptizer's garment was made of **camel's hair** — not the soft, luxurious camel's hair cloth of our day, but the coarse fabric of an outdoorsman. He also wore a **leather belt**. This was the same attire as that of Elijah (2 Kgs. 1:8) and perhaps served to alert believing Jews to the similarity between John's mission and that of Elijah (Mal. 4:5; Luke 1:17; Matt. 11:14; 17:10–12). John ate **locusts and wild honey**, the subsistence diet of one so consumed by his mission that the normal comforts and pleasures of life were sublimated.

It must have been a convicting, scalding experience to meet John — a man who cared for none of the things that people ordinarily live for. His absorption with spiritual realities must have made others realize how poor they were. His self-renunciation was a stinging rebuke to the worldliness of his day.

3:5, 6 People flocked to hear him from **Jerusalem, all Judea**, and the trans-Jordan area. Some of the people responded to his message and **were baptized by him in the Jordan**, saying in effect that they were ready to give full allegiance and obedience to the coming King.

3:7 With **the Pharisees and Sadducees** it was a different story. When they came to listen to him, John knew that they were not sincere. He recognized their true nature: **the Pharisees** professed great devotion to the law, but they were inwardly corrupt, sectarian, hypocritical, and self-righteous; the **Sadducees** were social aristocrats and religious skeptics who denied such basic doctrines as the resurrection of the body, the existence of angels, the immortality of the soul, and eternal punishment. Therefore he denounced both sects as a **brood of vipers**, who pretended to desire to escape **from the wrath to come**, but exhibited no signs of true repentance.

3:8 He challenged them to prove their sincerity by bearing **fruits worthy of repentance**. True repentance, as J. R. Miller wrote, "amounts to nothing whatever if it produces only a few tears, a spasm of regret, a little fright. We must leave the sins we repent of and walk in the new, clean ways of holiness."

3:9 The Jews should stop presuming on their descent from **Abraham** as a passport to heaven. The grace of salvation is not transmitted in natural birth. God could make the **stones** of the Jordan into **children** of **Abraham** by a less violent process than the conversion of the Pharisees and Sadducees.

3:10 By stating that **the ax is laid to the root of the trees**, John was saying that a work of divine judgment was about to begin. Christ's arrival and presence would test all men. Those found fruitless would be destroyed just as a fruitless **tree . . . is cut down and thrown into the fire**.

3:11, 12 In verses 7–10, John had been speaking exclusively to the Phari-

sees and Sadducees (see. v. 7), but now he apparently addresses his entire audience, which included both the true and the false. He explained that there was a significant difference between his ministry and that of the Messiah who would soon arrive. John baptized **with water unto repentance**: the **water** was ceremonial and had no cleansing power; the **repentance**, though real, did not bring a person to full salvation. John viewed his ministry as preparatory and partial. The Messiah would completely overshadow John. He would be **mightier**, He would be more worthy, His work would reach farther, for He would **baptize . . . with the Holy Spirit and fire.**

The baptism **with the Holy Spirit** is distinct from the baptism with **fire**. The former is a baptism of blessing, the latter of judgment. The former took place at Pentecost, the latter is still future. The former is enjoyed by all true believers in the Lord Jesus, the latter will be the fate of all unbelievers. The former would be for those Israelites whose baptism was an outward sign of inward repentance, the latter would be for the Pharisees, Sadducees, and all who showed no evidence of true repentance.

Some teach that the baptism with the Holy Spirit and the baptism with fire are the same event, i.e., could not the baptism with fire refer to the tongues of fire that appeared when the Spirit was given at Pentecost? In light of verse 12 which equates fire with judgment, it probably does not.

Immediately after his reference to the baptism of fire, John speaks of judgment. The Lord is pictured using a **winnowing fan** to toss the threshed grain into the wind. The **wheat** (true believers) falls directly to the ground and is carried **into the barn. The chaff** (unbelievers) is carried a short distance away by the wind and then gathered and burned **with unquenchable fire**. The fire in verse 12 means judgment, and since this verse is an amplification of verse 11, it is reasonable to conclude that the baptism with fire is a baptism of judgment.

B. John Baptizes Jesus (3:13–17)

3:13 Jesus walked approximately sixty miles **from Galilee** to the lower **Jordan** River **to be baptized by** John. This indicates the importance which He attached to this ceremony and it should indicate the significance of baptism for His followers today.

3:14, 15 Realizing that Jesus had no sins of which to repent, **John** protested against baptizing Him. It was a true instinct that led him to suggest that the proper order would be for Jesus to baptize him. Jesus did not deny this; He simply repeated His request for baptism as a **fitting** way in which **to fulfill all righteousness**. He felt it appropriate that in baptism He identify Himself with those godly Israelites who were coming to be baptized unto repentance.

But there was an even deeper meaning. Baptism for Him was a ritual symbolizing the way in which He would fulfill all the righteous claims of God against man's sin. His immersion typified His baptism in the waters of God's judgment at Calvary. His emergence from the water foreshadowed His resurrection. By death, burial, and resurrection, He would satisfy the demands of divine justice and provide a righteous basis by which sinners could be justified.

3:16, 17† As soon as He came up **from the water**, Jesus **saw the Spirit of God descending** from heaven **like a dove and alighting upon Him**. Just as persons and things in the OT were consecrated to sacred purposes by "the holy anointing oil" (Ex. 30:25–30), so He was anointed Messiah by the Holy Spirit.

It was a hallowed occasion, when all three members of the Trinity were evident. The **beloved Son** was there. The Holy **Spirit** was there in **dove** form. The Father's **voice** was heard **from heaven** pronouncing His blessing on Jesus. It was a memorable event because the voice of God was heard quoting Scripture: **"This is My beloved Son** (from Ps. 2:7) **in whom I am well pleased"** (from Isa. 42:1). This is one of three occasions when the Father spoke from heaven in delighted acknowledgment of His unique Son (the other places are Matt. 17:5 and John 12:28).

C. Jesus Is Tempted by Satan (4:1–11)

4:1 It may seem strange that Jesus should be **led up by the Spirit** into temptation. Why should the Holy Spirit lead Him into such an encounter? The answer

is that this temptation was necessary to demonstrate His moral fitness to do the work for which He had come into the world. The first Adam proved his unfitness for dominion when he met the adversary in the Garden of Eden. Here the last Adam meets the devil in a head-on confrontation and emerges unscathed.

The Greek word translated "tempt" or "test" has two meanings: (1) to test or prove (John 6:6; 2 Cor. 13:5; Heb. 11:17); and (2) to solicit to evil. The Holy Spirit tested or proved Christ. The devil sought to lure Him to do evil.

There is deep mystery connected with the temptation of our Lord. Inevitably the question arises, "Could He have sinned?" If we answer "No," then we must face the further question, "How could it be a real temptation if He could not yield?" If we answer "Yes," we are faced with the problem of how God incarnate could sin.

It is of first importance to remember that Jesus Christ is God and that God cannot sin. It is true that He is also human; however, to say that He could sin as a human but not as God is to build a case without scriptural foundation. The NT writers wrote of the sinlessness of Christ on several occasions. Paul wrote that He "knew no sin" (2 Cor. 5:21); Peter says that He "committed no sin" (1 Pet. 2:22); and John says, "in Him there is no sin" (1 Jn. 3:5).

Like us, Jesus could be tempted from without: Satan came to Him with suggestions contrary to the will of God. But unlike us, He could not be tempted from within — no sinful lusts or passions could originate in Him. Furthermore, there was nothing in Him that would respond to the devil's seductions (John 14:30).

Despite Jesus' inability to sin, the temptation was very real. It was possible for Him to be faced with enticements to sin, but it was morally impossible for Him to yield. He could only do what He saw the Father doing (John 5:19), and it is inconceivable that He would ever see the Father sinning. He could do nothing on His own authority (John 5:30), and the Father would never give Him the authority to yield to temptation.

The purpose of the temptation was not to see if He would sin, but to prove that even under tremendous pressure He could do nothing but obey the Word of God.

If Jesus could sin as a human being, we are faced with the problem of His still being a human in heaven. Could He still sin? Obviously, no.

4:2, 3 After fasting **forty days and forty nights**, Jesus **was hungry**. (The number **forty** in Scripture is frequently used in contexts of testing or probation.) This natural appetite provided **the tempter** with an advantage which in many people he could exploit. He suggested that Jesus use His miraculous power to convert the **stones** of the desert into loaves of **bread**. The introductory words, **"If You are the Son of God,"** do not imply doubt. They actually mean "Since You are the Son of God." The devil is alluding to the words of the Father to Jesus at the baptism, "This is My beloved Son." He uses a Greek construction[2] which assumes the statement to be true and, thereby, he calls on Jesus to exercise His power to appease His hunger.

To fulfill a natural appetite by using divine power in response to Satan's prompting is in direct disobedience to God. The idea behind Satan's suggestion is an echo of Genesis 3:6 ("good for food"). John classifies this temptation as "the lust of the flesh" (1 Jn. 2:16). Our corresponding temptation is to live for the gratification of natural desires, to choose a pathway of comfort instead of seeking the kingdom of God and His righteousness. The devil says, "You have to live, don't you?"

4:4 Jesus **answered** the temptation by quoting the Word of God. Our Lord's example teaches that we *don't* have to live, but we *do* have to obey God! Getting **bread** is *not* the most important thing in life. Obedience to **every word** of **God** is. Since Jesus had received no instructions from the Father to turn stones into bread, He would not act on His own and thus obey Satan, no matter how intense His hunger.

4:5, 6 The second temptation took place in Jerusalem on the **pinnacle of the temple. The devil** challenged Jesus to **throw** Himself **down** as a spectacular display of His divine Sonship. Again, the opening word **if** does not imply doubt,

as is seen in Satan's reference to the protection promised to the Messiah by God in Psalm 91:11, 12.

The temptation was for Jesus to demonstrate that He was Messiah by performing a sensational stunt. He could achieve glory without suffering; He could bypass the cross and still reach the throne. But this action would be outside the will of God. John describes this appeal as "the pride of life" (1 Jn. 2:16). It resembles the "tree desirable to make one wise" (Gen. 3:6) in the Garden of Eden, as both were a means of achieving personal glory in disregard of God's will. This temptation comes to us in the desire to attain religious prominence apart from the fellowship of His suffering. We seek great things for ourselves, then run and hide when difficulties come our way. When we ignore God's will and exalt ourselves, we tempt God.

4:7 Again, **Jesus** resisted the attack by quoting Scripture: **"It is written again, 'You shall not tempt the LORD your God'"** (see Deut. 6:16). God had promised to preserve the Messiah, but that guarantee presupposed living in God's will. To claim the promise in an act of disobedience would be tempting God. The time would come when Jesus would be revealed as Messiah, but the cross must come first. The altar of sacrifice must precede the throne. The crown of thorns must precede the crown of glory. Jesus would await God's time and would accomplish God's will.

4:8, 9 In the third temptation **the devil took** Jesus **up on an exceedingly high mountain, and showed Him all the kingdoms of the world**. He offered them to Jesus in exchange for His **worship**. Although this temptation had to do with **worship**, an exercise of the spirit, it was an effort to induce our Lord to grasp imperial power over the world by worshiping Satan. The reward offered, **all the kingdoms of the world** with their grandeur, appealed to "the lust of the eyes" (1 Jn. 2:16).

In a sense, the kingdoms of the world *do* belong to the devil at present. He is spoken of as "the god of this age" (2 Cor. 4:4), and John tells us that "the whole world lies under the sway of the wicked one" (1 Jn. 5:19). When Jesus appears at the Second Advent as King of kings (Rev. 19:16), then "the kingdoms of this world" become His (Rev. 11:15). Jesus would not violate the divine timetable, and certainly He would never worship Satan!

For us the temptation is twofold: to barter our spiritual birthright for the passing glory of this world, and to worship and serve the creature rather than the Creator.

4:10 For the third time, Jesus resisted temptation by using the OT: **"You shall worship the LORD your God, and Him only you shall serve."** Worship and the service that flows from it are for God alone. To worship Satan would be tantamount to acknowledging him as God.

The order of the temptations as recorded by Matthew varies from that in Luke (4:1–13). Some have suggested that Matthew's order parallels the order of the temptations that Israel faced in the wilderness (Ex. 16; 17; 32). Jesus showed Himself in perfect contrast to Israel's response to hardship.

4:11 When Jesus had successfully rebutted Satan's temptations, **the devil left Him**. Temptations come in waves rather than in a steady flow. "When the enemy comes in like flood, the Spirit of the Lord will lift up a standard against him" (Isa. 59:19). What an encouragement for God's tested saints!

We are told that **angels came and ministered to Him**, but no explanation is given for this supernatural assistance. It probably means that they provided the physical nourishment for Him which He had refused to provide at Satan's suggestion.

From the temptation of Jesus, we learn that the devil can attack those who are controlled by the Holy Spirit, but that he is powerless against those who resist him with the Word of God.

D. Jesus Begins His Galilean Ministry (4:12–17)†

The Judean ministry of Jesus, which lasted almost one year, is not discussed by Matthew. This one year period is covered in John 1–4 and fits between Matthew 4:11 and 4:12. Matthew takes us from the temptation directly to the Galilean ministry.

4:12 When Jesus heard that John the Baptist **had been put in prison**, He rea-

lized that this was an omen of His own rejection. In rejecting the King's forerunner, the people were, for all practical purposes, rejecting the King also. But it was not fear that drove Him north **to Galilee**. Actually He was going right into the center of Herod's kingdom — the same king who had just imprisoned John. In moving to Galilee of the Gentiles, He was showing that His rejection by the Jews would result in the gospel going out to the Gentiles.

4:13†† ** Jesus remained in **Nazareth until the populace tried to kill Him for proclaiming salvation for the Gentiles (see Luke 4:16–30). Then He moved to **Capernaum** by the Sea of Galilee, an area originally populated by the tribes of **Zebulun and Napthali**. From this time, Capernaum became His headquarters.

4:14–16 Jesus' move to Galilee was a fulfillment of **Isaiah** 9:1, 2. The ignorant, superstitious **Gentiles** living in **Galilee** saw **a great light** — that is Christ, the **Light** of the world.

4:17 From then on **Jesus** took up the message which John had preached: **"Repent, for the kingdom of heaven is at hand."** It was a further call for moral renewal in preparation for His kingdom. The kingdom was near in the sense that the King was present.

E. Jesus Calls Four Fishermen (4:18–22)

4:18, 19 This is actually the second time Jesus called **Peter and Andrew**. In John 1:35–42 they were called to salvation; here they are called to service. The first took place in Judea; this one in Galilee. Peter and Andrew **were fishermen**, but Jesus called them to be **fishers of men**. Their responsibility was to **follow** Christ. His responsibility was to **make** them successful fishermen. Their following of Christ involved more than physical nearness. It included their imitation of the character of Christ. Theirs was to be a ministry of character. What they were was more important than what they said or did. Just as with Peter and Andrew, we are to avoid the temptation to substitute eloquence, personality, or clever arguments for true spirituality. In following Christ, the disciple learns to go where the fish are swimming, to use the proper lure, to endure discomfort and

†See p. xii.   ††See p. xx.

inconvenience, to be patient, and to keep out of sight.

4:20 Peter and Andrew heard the call and responded **immediately**. In true faith, they **left their nets**. In true commitment and devotion they **followed** Jesus.

4:21, 22 The call came next to **James** and **John**. They, too, became instant disciples. Leaving not only their means of livelihood but **their father** as well, they acknowledged the priority of Jesus over all earthly ties.

By responding to the call of Christ, these fishermen became key figures in the evangelization of the world. Had they remained at their nets, we would never have heard of them. Recognition of the lordship of Christ makes all the difference in the world.

F. Jesus Heals a Great Multitude (4:23–25)

The ministry of the Lord Jesus was threefold: He taught God's Word **in** the **synagogues**; He preached **the gospel of the kingdom**; and He healed the sick. One purpose of the miracles of healing was to authenticate His person and ministry (Heb. 2:3, 4). Chapters 5–7 are an example of His teaching ministry and chapters 8–9 describe His miracles.

4:23 Verse 23 is the first use of **gospel** in the NT. The term means "good news of salvation." In every age of the world's history there has been only one gospel, only one way of salvation.

THE GOSPEL

The gospel originates in the grace of God (Eph. 2:8). That means that God gives eternal life freely to sinful people who don't deserve it.

The basis of the gospel is the work of Christ on the cross (1 Cor. 15:1–4). Our Savior fulfilled all the claims of divine justice, enabling God to justify believing sinners. Old Testament believers were saved through the work of Christ, even though it was still future. They probably did not know much about the Messiah, but God did — and He imputed the value of Christ's work to their account. In a sense they were saved "on credit." We, too, are saved through the work of Christ, but in our case, the work has already been finished.

The gospel is received by faith alone (Eph. 2:8). In the OT, people were saved by believing whatever God had told them. In this age, people are saved by believing God's testimony concerning His Son as the only way of salvation (1 Jn. 5:11, 12). The ultimate goal of the gospel is heaven. We have the hope of eternity in heaven (2 Cor. 5:6–10), just as OT saints did (Heb. 11:10, 14–16).

While there is only one gospel, there are different features of the gospel in different times. For instance, there is a different emphasis between the gospel of the kingdom and the gospel of the grace of God. The gospel of the kingdom says, "Repent and receive the Messiah; then you will enter His kingdom when it is set up on earth." The gospel of grace says, "Repent and receive Christ; then you will be taken up to meet Him and to be with Him forever." Fundamentally, they are the same gospel — salvation by grace through faith — but they show that there are different administrations of the gospel according to God's dispensational purposes.

When Jesus preached the gospel of the kingdom, He was announcing His coming as King of the Jews and explaining the terms of admission into His kingdom. His miracles showed the wholesome nature of the kingdom.[3] ‡

4:24, 25 **His fame** spread **throughout all Syria** (the territory north and northeast of Israel). **All** the **sick people, demon-possessed**, and disabled felt His healing touch. People thronged to Him from **Galilee**, the **Decapolis** (a confederation of ten Gentile cities in northeastern Palestine), **Jerusalem, Judea** and the region east of **the Jordan** River. As B. B. Warfield wrote: "Disease and death must have been almost eliminated for a brief season from . . . the region." No wonder the public was greatly astonished at the reports they were hearing from Galilee!

IV. THE CONSTITUTION OF THE KINGDOM (Chaps. 5–7)

It is no accident that the Sermon on the Mount is placed near the beginning of the NT. Its position indicates its importance. In it the King summarizes the character and conduct expected of His subjects.

This sermon is *not* a presentation of the plan of salvation; nor is its teaching intended for unsaved people. It was addressed to the disciples (5:1, 2) and was intended to be the constitution, or the system of laws and principles, which was to govern the King's subjects during His reign. It was meant for all — past, present, or future — who acknowledge Christ as King. When Christ was on earth, it had direct application to His disciples. Now, while our Lord reigns in heaven, it applies to all who crown Him King in their hearts. Finally, it will be the code of behavior for Christ's followers during the Tribulation and during His reign on earth.

The Sermon has a distinct Jewish flavor, as seen in allusions to the council (i.e., the Sanhedrin) in 5:22, the altar (5:23, 24), and Jerusalem (5:35). Yet it would be wrong to say that its teaching is exclusively for believing Israelites in the past or future; it is for those of every age who acknowledge Jesus Christ as King.

A. The Beatitudes (5:1–12)

5:1, 2 The sermon opens with the Beatitudes, or blessings. These set forth the ideal citizen of Christ's kingdom. The qualities described and approved are the opposite of those that the world values. A. W. Tozer describes them thus: "A fairly accurate description of the human race might be furnished one unacquainted with it by taking the Beatitudes, turning them wrong side out, and saying, 'Here is your human race.' "

5:3 This first blessing is pronounced on **the poor in spirit**. This does not refer to natural disposition, but to one's deliberate choice and discipline. **The poor in spirit** are those who acknowledge their own helplessness and rely on God's omnipotence. They sense their spiritual need and find it supplied in the Lord. **The kingdom of heaven**, where self-sufficiency is no virtue and self-exaltation is a vice, belongs to such people.

5:4 Those who mourn are blessed; a day of comfort awaits them. This does not refer to mourning because of the vicissitudes of life. It is the sorrow which one experiences because of fellowship

with the Lord Jesus. It is an active sharing of the world's hurt and sin with Jesus. Therefore, it includes, not only sorrow for one's own sin, but also sorrow because of the world's appalling condition, it's rejection of the Savior, and the doom of those who refuse His mercy. These mourners **shall be comforted** in the coming day when "God shall wipe away every tear from their eyes" (Rev. 21:4). Believers do all their mourning in this life; for unbelievers, today's grief is only a foretaste of eternal sorrow.

5:5 A third blessing is pronounced on **the meek**: **they shall inherit the earth**. By nature these people might be volatile, temperamental, and gruff. But by purposefully taking Christ's spirit on them, they become **meek** or gentle (compare Matthew 11:29). Meekness implies acceptance of one's lowly position. **The meek** person is gentle and mild in his own cause, though he may be a lion in God's cause or in defending others.

The meek do not *now* inherit the earth; rather they inherit abuse and dispossession. But they *will* literally **inherit the earth** when Christ, the King, reigns for a thousand years in peace and prosperity.

5:6 Next, a blessing is pronounced on **those who hunger and thirst for righteousness**: they are promised satisfaction. These people have a passion **for righteousness** in their own lives; they long to see honesty, integrity, and justice in society; they look for practical holiness in the church. Like the people of whom Gamaliel Bradford wrote, they have "a thirst no earthly stream can satisfy, a hunger that must feed on Christ or die." These people will be abundantly satisfied in Christ's coming kingdom: **they shall be filled**, for righteousness will reign and corruption will give way to the highest moral standards.

5:7 In our Lord's kingdom, **the merciful** are **blessed . . . for they shall obtain mercy**. To be **merciful** means to be actively compassionate. In one sense it means to withhold punishment from offenders who deserve it. In a wider sense it means to help others in need who cannot help themselves. God showed mercy in sparing us from the judgment which our sins deserved and in demonstrating kindness to us through the saving work of Christ. We imitate God when we have compassion.

The merciful **shall obtain mercy**. Here, Jesus is not referring to the mercy of salvation which God gives to a believing sinner; *that* mercy is not dependent on a person's being merciful — it is a free, unconditional gift. Rather the Lord is speaking of the daily **mercy** needed for Christian living and of **mercy** in that future day when one's works will be reviewed (1 Cor. 3:12–15). If one has not been merciful, that person will not receive mercy; that is, one's rewards will decrease accordingly.

5:8 The pure in heart are given the assurance that **they shall see God**. A pure-hearted person is one whose motives are unmixed, whose thoughts are holy, whose conscience is clean. The expression **they shall see God** may be understood in several ways. First, **the pure in heart see God** now through fellowship in the Word and the Spirit. Second, they sometimes have a supernatural appearance, or vision, of the Lord presented to them. Third, **they shall see God** in the Person of Jesus when He comes again. Fourth, **they shall see God** in eternity.

5:9 A blessing is pronounced on **the peacemakers: they shall be called sons of God**. Notice that the Lord is not speaking about people with a peaceful disposition or those who love peace. He is referring to those who actively intervene to make peace. The natural approach is to watch strife from the sidelines. The divine approach is to take positive action toward creating **peace**, even if it means taking abuse and invective.

Peacemakers are **called sons of God**. This is not how they *become* sons of God — that can only happen by receiving Jesus Christ as Savior (John 1:12). By making peace, believers *manifest* themselves as **sons of God**, and God will one day acknowledge them as people who bear the family likeness.

5:10 The next beatitude deals with those **who are persecuted**, not for their own wrongdoings, but **for righteousness' sake**. **The kingdom of heaven** is promised to those believers who suffer for doing right. Their integrity condemns the ungodly world and brings out its hostility. People hate a righteous life because it exposes their own unrighteousness.

5:11 The final beatitude seems to be a repetition of the preceding one. However, there is one difference. In the previous verse, the subject was persecution because of righteousness; here it is persecution **for** Christ's **sake**. The Lord knew that His disciples would be maltreated because of their association with, and loyalty to, Him. History has confirmed this: from the outset the world has persecuted, jailed, and killed followers of Jesus.

5:12 To suffer for Christ's sake is a privilege that should cause joy. A **great reward** awaits those who thus become companions of **the prophets** in tribulation. Those OT spokemen for God stood true in spite of persecution. All who imitate their loyal courage will share their present exhilaration and future exaltation.

The Beatitudes present a portrait of the ideal citizen in Christ's kingdom. Notice the emphases on *righteousness* (v. 6), *peace* (v. 9), and *joy* (v. 12). Paul probably had this passage in mind when he wrote: "For the kingdom of God is not eating and drinking, but righteousness and peace and joy in the Holy Spirit" (Rom. 14:17).

B. Believers Are Salt and Light (5:13–16)

5:13 Jesus likened His disciples to **salt**. They were to the world what salt is in everyday life: salt seasons food; it hinders the spread of corruption; it creates thirst; it brings out the flavor. So His followers add piquancy to human society, serve as a preservative, and make others long for the righteousness described in the preceding verses.

If the salt loses its flavor, how can its saltiness be restored? There is no way to restore the true, natural taste. Once it has lost its flavor, salt is **good for nothing**. It is discarded on a footpath. Albert Barnes's comment on this passage is illuminating:

The salt used in this country is a chemical compound — and if the *saltiness* were lost, or it were to lose its *savor*, there would be nothing remaining. In eastern countries, however, the salt used was impure, mingled with vegetable and earthly substances; so that it might lose the whole of its saltiness, and a considerable quantity [of salt without flavor] remain. This was good for nothing except that it was used, as it is said, to place in paths, or walks, as we use gravel.[4]

The disciple has one great function — to be **the salt of the earth** by living out the terms of discipleship listed in the Beatitudes and throughout the rest of the Sermon. If he fails to exhibit this spiritual reality, men will tread his testimony under their feet. The world has only contempt for an undedicated believer.

5:14 Jesus also calls Christians **the light of the world**. He spoke of Himself as "the light of the world" (John 8:12; 12:35, 36, 46). The relationship between these two statements is that Jesus is the source of light; Christians are the reflection of His light. Their function is to shine for Him just as the moon reflects the glory of the sun.

The Christian is like **a city that is set on a hill**: it is elevated above its surroundings and it shines in the midst of darkness. Those whose lives exhibit the traits of Christ's teaching **cannot be hidden**.

5:15, 16 People do not **light a lamp and put it under a basket**. Instead, they put it **on a lampstand** so that it will give **light to all who are in the house**. He did not intend that we hoard the light of His teaching for ourselves, but that we share it with others. We should **let** our **light so shine** that as people **see** our **good works**, they will **glorify** our **Father in heaven**. The emphasis is on the ministry of Christian character. The winsomeness of lives in which Christ is seen speaks louder than the persuasion of words.

C. Christ Fulfills the Law (5:17–20)

5:17, 18 Most revolutionary leaders sever all ties with the past and repudiate the traditional, existing order. Not so the Lord Jesus. He upheld the Law of Moses and insisted that it must be fulfilled. Jesus had not come to abolish **the Law or the Prophets**, but **to fulfill** them. He clearly insisted that not **one jot or one tittle** would **pass from the law** until it

was completely fulfilled. The **jot**, or *yod*, is the smallest letter in the Hebrew alphabet; the **tittle** is a small mark or projection that serves to distinguish one letter from another, much as the bottom stroke of a capital *E* distinguishes it from a capital *F*. Jesus believed in the literal inspiration of the Bible, even in what might seem small unimportant details. Nothing in Scripture, even the smallest stroke, is without significance.

It is important to notice that Jesus did *not* say that the law would *never* pass away. He said it would not pass away **till all** was **fulfilled**. This distinction has ramifications for the believer today, and since the believer's relation to the law is rather complicated, we are going to take time to summarize the Bible's teaching on this subject.

THE BELIEVER'S RELATION TO THE LAW

The law is that system of legislation given by God through Moses to the nation of Israel. The entire body of the law is found in Exodus 20-31, Leviticus, and Deuteronomy, though its essence is embodied in the Ten Commandments.

The law was not given as a means of salvation (Acts 13:39; Rom. 3:20a; Gal. 2:16, 21; 3:11); it was designed to show people their sinfulness (Rom. 3:20b; 5:20; 7:7; 1 Cor. 15:56; Gal. 3:19) and then drive them to God for His gracious salvation. It was given to the nation of Israel, even though it contains moral principles which are valid for people in every age (Rom. 2:14, 15). God tested Israel under the law as a sample of the human race, and Israel's guilt proved the world's guilt (Rom. 3:19).

The law had attached to it the penalty of death (Gal. 3:10); and to break one command was to be guilty of all (Jas. 2:10). Since people had broken the law, they were under the curse of death. God's righteousness and holiness demanded that the penalty be paid. It was for this reason that Jesus came into the world: to pay the penalty by His death. He died as a Substitute for guilty lawbreakers, even though He Himself was sinless. He did not wave the law aside; rather He met the full demands of the law by fulfilling its strict requirements in His life and in His death. Thus, the gospel does not overthrow the law; it upholds the law and shows how the law's demands have been fully satisfied by Christ's redemptive work.

Therefore, the person who trusts in Jesus is no longer under the law; he is under grace (Rom. 6:14). He is dead to the law through the work of Christ. The penalty of the law must be paid only once; since Christ paid the penalty, the believer does not have to. It is in this sense that the law has faded away for the Christian (2 Cor. 3:7–11). The law was a tutor until Christ came, but after salvation, this tutor is no longer needed (Gal. 3:24, 25).

Yet, while the Christian is not under the law, that doesn't mean he is lawless. He is bound by a stronger chain than law because he is under the law of Christ (1 Cor. 9:21). His behavior is molded, not by fear of punishment, but by a loving desire to please his Savior. Christ has become his rule of life (John 13:15; 15:12; Eph. 5:1, 2; 1 Jn. 2:6; 3:16).

A common question in a discussion of the believer's relation to the law is, "Should I obey the Ten Commandments?" The answer is that certain principles contained in the law are of lasting relevance. It is always wrong to steal, to covet, or to murder. Nine of the Ten Commandments are repeated in the NT, with an important distinction — they are not given as law (with penalty attached), but as training in righteousness for the people of God (2 Tim. 3:16b). The one commandment not repeated is the Sabbath law: Christians are *never* taught to keep the Sabbath (i.e., the seventh day of the week, Saturday).

The ministry of the law to unsaved people has not ended: "But we know that the law is good if one uses it lawfully" (1 Tim. 1:8). Its lawful use is to produce the knowledge of sin and thus lead to repentance. But the law is not for those who are already saved: "The law is not made for a righteous person" (1 Tim. 1:9).

The righteousness demanded by the law is fulfilled in those "who do not walk according to the flesh but according to the Spirit" (Rom. 8:4). In fact, the teachings of our Lord in the Sermon on the Mount set a higher standard than that set by the law. For instance, the law

said, "Do not murder"; Jesus said, "Do not even hate." So the Sermon on the Mount not only upholds the Law and the Prophets but it amplifies them and develops their deeper implications. ‡

5:19 In returning to the Sermon, we notice that Jesus anticipated a natural tendency to relax God's commandments. Because they are of such a supernatural nature, people tend to explain them away, to rationalize their meaning. But **whoever breaks one** part of the law, and **teaches** other people to do the same, **shall be called least in the kingdom of heaven**. The wonder is that such people are permitted in the kingdom at all — but then, entrance *into* the kingdom is by faith in Christ. A person's position *in* the kingdom is determined by his obedience and faithfulness while on earth. The person who obeys the law of the kingdom — that person **shall be called great in the kingdom of heaven**.

5:20 To gain entrance into the kingdom, our **righteousness** must surpass **the righteousness of the scribes and Pharisees** (who were content with religious ceremonies which gave them an outward, ritual cleansing, but which never changed their hearts). Jesus uses hyperbole (exaggeration) to drive home the truth that external righteousness without internal reality will not gain entrance into the kingdom. The only righteousness that God will accept is the perfection that He imputes to those who accept His Son as Savior (2 Cor. 5:21). Of course, where there is true faith in Christ, there will also be the practical righteousness that Jesus describes in the remainder of the Sermon.

D. Jesus Warns Against Anger (5:21–26)

5:21 The Jews of Jesus' time knew that murder was forbidden by God and that the murderer was liable to punishment. This was true before the giving of the law (Gen. 9:6) and it was later incorporated into the law (Ex. 20:13; Deut. 5:17). With the words, **"But I say to you,"** Jesus institutes an amendment to the teaching on murder. No longer could a person take pride in having never committed murder. Jesus now says, "In My kingdom, you must not even have murderous thoughts." He traces the act of murder to its source and warns against three forms of unrighteous anger.

5:22 The first is the case of a person who **is angry with his brother without a cause**.[5] One accused of this crime would be **in danger of the judgment** — that is, he could be taken to court. Most people can find what they think is a valid cause for their anger, but anger is justified only when God's honor is at stake or when someone else is being wronged. It is never right when expressed in retaliation for personal wrongs.

Even more serious is the sin of insulting a brother. In Jesus' day, people used the word **Raca** (an Aramaic term meaning "empty one") as a word of contempt and abuse. Those who used this epithet were **in danger of the council** —that is, they were subject to trial before the Sanhedrin, the highest court in the land.

Finally, to call someone a **fool** is the third form of unrighteous anger that Jesus condemns. Here the word **fool** means more than just a dunce. It signifies a moral **fool** who ought to be dead and it expresses the wish that he were. Today it is common to hear a person cursing another with the words, "God damn you!" He is calling on God to consign the victim to hell. Jesus says that the one who utters such a curse is **in danger of hell fire**. The bodies of executed criminals were often thrown into a burning dump outside Jerusalem known as the Valley of Hinnom or Gehenna. This was a figure of the fires of hell which shall never be quenched.

There is no mistaking the severity of the Savior's words. He teaches that anger contains the seeds of murder, that abusive language contains the spirit of murder, and that cursing language implies the very desire to murder. The progressive heightening of the crimes demand three degrees of punishment: the *judgment*, the *council*, and *hell fire*. In the kingdom, Jesus will deal with sins according to severity.

5:23, 24 If a person offends another, whether by anger or any other cause, there is no use in his bringing a gift to God. The Lord will not be pleased with it. The offender should first go and make the wrong right. Only then will the gift be acceptable.

Even though these words are written in a Jewish context, that does not mean there is no application today. Paul interprets this concept in relation to the Lord's Supper (see 1 Cor. 11). God receives no worship from a believer who is not on speaking terms with another.

5:25, 26 It is against a litigious spirit and a reluctance to admit guilt that Jesus warns here. It is better to promptly settle with an accuser rather than run the risk of a court trial. If that happens, we are bound to lose. While there is some disagreement among scholars about the identity of the people in this parable, the point is clear: if you are wrong, be quick to admit it and make things right. If you remain unrepentant, your sin will eventually catch up with you and you will not only have to make full restitution but suffer additional penalties as well. And don't be in a hurry to go to court. If you do, the law will find you out, and you will pay the last penny.

E. Jesus Condemns Adultery (5:27–30)

5:27, 28 The Mosaic Law clearly prohibited adultery (Ex. 20:14; Deut. 5:18). A person might be proud that he had never broken this commandment, and yet have his "eyes full of adultery" (2 Pet. 2:14). While outwardly respectable, his mind might be constantly wandering down labyrinths of impurity. So Jesus reminded His disciples that mere abstinence from the physical act was not enough — there must be inward purity. The law forbade the act of adultery; Jesus forbids the desire: **Whoever looks at a woman to lust for her has already committed adultery with her in his heart**. E. Stanley Jones caught the import of this verse when he wrote: "If you think or act adultery, you do not satisfy the sex urge; you pour oil on a fire to quench it." Sin begins in the mind, and if we nourish it, we eventually commit the act.

5:29, 30 Maintaining an undefiled thought life demands strict self-discipline. Thus, Jesus taught that if any part of our body causes us to sin, it would be better to lose that member during life rather than to lose one's soul for eternity. Are we to take Jesus' words literally? Was He actually advocating self-mutilation? The words are literal to this extent: *if it were necessary* to lose a member rather than one's soul, then we should gladly part with the member. *Fortunately it is never necessary*, since the Holy Spirit empowers the believer to live a holy life. However, there must be co-operation and rigid discipline on the believer's part.

F. Jesus Censures Divorce (5:31, 32)

5:31 Under OT law, divorce was permitted according to Deuteronomy 24:1–4. This passage was not concerned with the case of an adulterous wife (the penalty for adultery was death, see Deut. 22:22). Rather, it deals with divorce because of dislike or "incompatibility."

5:32 However, in the kingdom of Christ, **whoever divorces his wife for any reason except sexual immorality causes her to commit adultery**. This does not mean that she automatically becomes an adulteress; it presupposes that, having no means of support, she is forced to live with another man. In so doing she becomes an adulteress. Not only is the former wife living in adultery, **whoever marries a woman who is divorced commits adultery**.

The subject of divorce and remarriage is one of the most complicated topics in the Bible. It is virtually impossible to answer all the questions that arise, but it may be helpful to survey and summarize what we believe the Scriptures teach.

DIVORCE AND REMARRIAGE

Divorce was never God's intention for man. His ideal is that one man and one woman remain married until their union is broken by death (Rom. 7:2, 3). Jesus made this clear to the Pharisees by appealing to the divine order at creation (Matt. 19:4–6).

God hates divorce (Mal. 2:16), that is, unscriptural divorce. He does not hate all divorce because He speaks of Himself as having divorced Israel (Jer. 3:8). This was because the nation forsook Him to worship idols. Israel was unfaithful.

In Matthew 5:31, 32 and 19:9, Jesus taught that divorce was forbidden except when one of the partners had been guilty of sexual immorality. In Mark 10:11, 12 and Luke 16:18, the exception clause is omitted.

The discrepancy is probably best explained as that neither Mark nor Luke record the entire saying. Therefore, even though divorce is not the ideal, it is permitted in the case where one's partner has been unfaithful. Jesus *allows* divorce in this case, but He does not *command* it.

Some scholars see 1 Corinthians 7:12–16 as teaching that divorce is acceptable when a believer is deserted by an unbeliever. Paul says that the remaining person is "not under bondage in such cases," i.e., he or she is free to obtain a divorce (for desertion). The present writer's opinion is that this case is the same exception granted in Matthew 5 and 19; namely, the unbeliever departs to live with someone else. Therefore, the believer can be granted a divorce on the scriptural grounds only if the other party commits adultery.

It is often contended that, although divorce is permitted in the NT, remarriage is never contemplated. However, this argument begs the question. Remarriage is not condemned for the innocent party in the NT — only for the offending person. Also, one of the main purposes of a scriptural divorce is to permit remarriage; otherwise, separation would serve the purpose just as well.

In any discussion of this topic, the question inevitably arises, "What about people who were divorced before they were saved?" There should be no question that unlawful divorces and remarriages contracted before conversion are sins which have been fully forgiven (see, for example, 1 Cor. 6:11 where Paul includes adultery in the list of sins in which the Corinthian believers had formerly participated). Pre-conversion sins do not bar believers from full participation in the local church.

A more difficult question concerns Christians who have divorced for unscriptural reasons and then remarry. Can they be received back into the fellowship of the local church? The answer depends on whether adultery is the initial act of physical union or a continued state. If these people are living in a state of adultery, then they would not only have to confess their sin but also forsake their present partner. But God's solution for a problem is never one that creates worse problems. If, in order to untangle a marital snarl, men or women are driven into sin, or women and children are left homeless and penniless, the cure is worse than the disease.

In the writer's opinion, Christians who have been divorced unscripturally and then remarried can truly repent of their sin and be restored to the Lord and to the fellowship of the church. In the matter of divorce, it seems that almost every case is different. Therefore, the elders of a local church must investigate each case individually and judge it according to the Word of God. If, at times, disciplinary action has to be taken, all concerned should submit to the decision of the elders. ‡

G. Jesus Condemns Oaths (5:33–37)

5:33–36 The Mosaic Law contained several prohibitions against swearing **falsely** by the name of God (Lev. 19:12; Num. 30:2; Deut. 23:21). To swear by God's Name meant that He was your witness that you were telling the truth. The Jews sought to avoid the impropriety of swearing falsely by God's Name by substituting **heaven**, **earth**, **Jerusalem**, or their **head** as that by which they swore.

Jesus condemns such circumvention of the law as sheer hypocrisy and forbids any form of swearing or oaths in ordinary conversation. Not only was it hypocritical, it was useless to try to avoid swearing by God's Name by merely substituting another noun for His Name. To swear **by heaven** is to swear by **God's throne**. To swear **by the earth** is to swear by **His footstool**. To swear **by Jerusalem** is to swear by the royal capital. Even to swear by one's own **head** involves God because He is the Creator of all.

5:37 For the Christian, an oath is unnecessary. His **Yes** should mean **Yes**, and his **No** should mean **No**. To use stronger language is to admit that Satan — **the evil one** — rules our lives. There are no circumstances under which it is proper for a Christian to lie.

This passage also forbids any shading of the truth or deception. It does not, however, forbid taking an oath in a court of law. Jesus Himself testified under oath before the High Priest (Matt. 26:63ff). Paul also used an oath to call God as his witness that what he was writing was true (2 Cor. 1:23; Gal. 1:20).

H. Going the Second Mile (5:38–42)

5:38 The law said, **"An eye for an eye and a tooth for a tooth"** (Ex. 21:24; Lev. 24:20; Deut. 19:21). This was both a command to punish and a limitation on punishment — the penalty must not exceed the crime. However, according to the OT, authority for punishment was vested in the government, *not* in the individual.

5:39–41 Jesus went beyond the law to a higher righteousness by abolishing retaliation altogether. He showed His disciples that, whereas revenge was once legally permissible, now non-resistance was graciously possible. Jesus instructed His followers to offer no resistance to **an evil person**. If they were slapped on one **cheek** by someone, they were to **turn the other to him also**. If they were sued for their **tunic** (an inner garment), they were to surrender their **cloak** (an outer garment used for covering at night) as well. If an official compelled them to carry his baggage for **one mile**, they were to voluntarily carry it **two** miles.

5:42 Jesus' last command in this paragraph seems the most impractical to us today. **Give to him who asks you, and from him who wants to borrow from you do not turn away**. Our obsession with material goods and possessions makes us recoil at the thought of giving away what we have acquired. However, if we were willing to concentrate on the treasures of heaven and be content with only necessary food and clothing, we would accept these words more literally and willingly. Jesus' statement presupposes that the person who asks for help has a genuine need. Since it is impossible to know whether the need is legitimate in all cases, it is better (as someone said), "to help a score of fraudulent beggars than to risk turning away one man in real need."

Humanly speaking, such behavior as the Lord calls for here is impossible. Only as a person is controlled by the

Holy Spirit can he live a self-sacrificing life. Only as the Savior is allowed to live His life in the believer can insult (v. 39), injustice (v. 40), and inconvenience (v. 41) be repaid with love. This is "the gospel of the second mile."

I. Love Your Enemies (5:43–48)

5:43 Our Lord's final example of the higher righteousness demanded in His kingdom concerns the treatment of one's enemies, a topic which grows naturally out of the previous paragraph. The law had taught the Israelites to **love** their **neighbor** (Lev. 19:18). Although they were never explicitly commanded to **hate** their **enemy**, this spirit underlay much of their indoctrination. This attitude was a summary of the OT's outlook toward those who persecuted God's people (see Ps. 139:21, 22). It was a righteous hostility directed against the enemies of God.

5:44–47 But now Jesus announces that we are to **love** our **enemies** and to **pray for those who . . . persecute** us. The fact that **love** is commanded shows that it is a matter of the will and not primarily of the emotions. It is not the same as natural affection because it is not natural to love those who hate and harm you. It is a supernatural grace and can be manifested only by those who have divine life.

There is no reward if we **love those who love us**; Jesus says that even unconverted **tax collectors**[6] do that! That type of love requires no divine power. Neither is there any virtue in greeting our **brethren**[7] **only**, i.e., our relatives and friends. The unsaved can do that; there is nothing distinctively Christian about it. If our standards are no higher than the world's, it is certain that we will never make an impact on the world.

Jesus said that His followers should return good for evil so that they might be **sons of** their **Father in heaven**. He was not saying that this was the way to *become* sons of God; rather, it is how we *show* that we are God's children. Since God shows no partiality to either **the evil** or **the good** (in that both benefit from **sun** and **rain**), so we should deal graciously and fairly with all.

5:48 Jesus closes this section with the admonition: **Therefore you shall be perfect, just as your Father in heaven is perfect**. The word **perfect** must be understood in the light of the context. It does not mean sinless or flawless. The previous verses explain that to be perfect means to love those who hate us, to pray for those who persecute us, and to show kindness to both friend and foe. Perfection here is that spiritual maturity which enables a Christian to imitate God in dispensing blessing to everybody without partiality.

J. Give with Sincerity (6:1–4)

6:1 In the first half of this chapter, Jesus deals with three specific areas of practical righteousness in an individual's life: charitable deeds (vv. 1–4), prayer (vv. 5–15), and fasting (vv. 16–18). The name **Father** is found ten times in these eighteen verses and is the key to understanding them. Practical deeds of righteousness should be done for His approval, not for people's.

He begins this portion of His sermon with a warning against the temptation to parade our piety by performing **charitable deeds** for the purpose of being **seen by** others. It is not the deed that He condemns, but the motive. If public notice is the motivating factor then it is the only **reward**, for God will not reward hypocrisy.

6:2 It seems incredible that **hypocrites** would noisily attract attention to themselves as they gave offerings **in the synagogues** or handouts to beggars **in the streets**. The Lord dismissed their conduct with the terse comment: **"They have their reward"** (i.e., their only reward is the reputation they gain while on earth).

6:3, 4 When a follower of Christ does **a charitable deed**, it is to be done **in secret**. It should be so secret that Jesus told His disciples: **"Do not let your left hand know what your right hand is doing."** Jesus uses this graphic figure of speech to show that our **charitable deed** should be for the **Father**, and not to gain notoriety for the giver.

This passage should not be pressed to prohibit any gift that might be seen by others, since it is virtually impossible to make all one's contributions strictly anonymous. It simply condemns the blatant display of giving.

K. Pray with Sincerity (6:5–8)

6:5 Next Jesus warns His disciples against hypocrisy **when** they **pray**. They should not purposely position themselves in public areas so that others will see them praying and be impressed by their piety. If the love for prominence is the only motive in prayer, then, Jesus declares, the prominence gained is the only **reward**.

6:6 In verses 5 and 7, the Greek pronoun translated **you** is plural. But in verse 6, in order to emphasize private communion with God, *you* switches to singular. The key to answered prayer is to do it in **secret** (i.e., **go into your room** and **shut your door**). If our real motive is to get through to God, He will hear and answer.

It is reading too much into the passage to use it to prohibit public prayer. The early church met together for collective prayer (Acts 2:42; 12:12; 13:3; 14:23; 20:36). The point is not *where* we pray. At issue here is, *why* we pray — to be seen by people or to be heard by God.

6:7 Prayer should not consist of **vain repetitions**, i.e., stock sentences or empty phrases. Unsaved people pray like that, but God is not impressed by the mere multiplication of **many words**. He wants to hear the sincere expressions of the heart.

6:8 Since our **Father knows the things** we **have need of**, even **before** we **ask Him**, then it is reasonable to ask, "Why pray at all?" The reason is that, in prayer, we acknowledge our need and dependence on Him. It is the basis of our communicating with God. Also God does things in answer to prayer that He would not have done otherwise (Jas. 4:2d).

L. Jesus Teaches the Model Prayer (6:9–15)

6:9 In verses 9–13 we have what is generally called "The Lord's Prayer." In using this title, however, we should remember that Jesus never prayed it Himself. It was given to His disciples as a model after which they could pattern their prayers. It was not given as the exact words they were to use (v. 7 seems to rule this out), because many words re-

peated by rote memory can become empty phrases.

Our Father in heaven. Prayer should be addressed to God the Father in acknowledgment of His sovereignty over the universe.

Hallowed be Your name. We should begin our prayers with worship, ascribing praise and honor to Him who is so worthy of it.

6:10 Your kingdom come. After worship, we should pray for the advancement of God's cause, putting His interests first. Specifically, we should pray for the day when our Savior-God, the Lord Jesus Christ, will set up His kingdom on earth and reign in righteousness.

Your will be done. In this petition we acknowledge that God knows what is best and that we surrender our will to His. It also expresses a longing to see His will acknowledged throughout the world.

On earth as it is in heaven. This phrase modifies all three preceding petitions. The worship of God, the sovereign rule by God, and the performance of His **will** are all a reality of **heaven**. The prayer is that these conditions might exist **on earth as** they do **in heaven**.

6:11 Give us this day our daily bread. After putting God's interests first, we are permitted to present our own needs. This petition acknowledges our dependence on God for daily food, both spiritual and physical.

6:12 And forgive us our debts, as we forgive our debtors. This does not refer to judicial forgiveness from the penalty of sin (that forgiveness is obtained by faith in the Son of God). Rather this refers to the parental forgiveness that is necessary if fellowship with our Father is to be maintained. If believers are unwilling to forgive those who wrong them, how can they expect to be in fellowship with their Father who has freely forgiven them for their wrongdoings?

6:13 And do not lead us into temptation. This request may appear to contradict James 1:13, which states that God would never tempt anyone. However, God does allow His people to be tested and tried. This petition expresses a healthy distrust of one's own ability to resist temptations or to stand up under trial. It acknowledges complete dependence on the Lord for preservation.

But deliver us from the evil one. This is the prayer of all who desperately desire to be kept from sin by the power of God. It is the heart's cry for daily salvation from the power of sin and Satan in one's life.

For Yours is the kingdom and the power and the glory forever. Amen. The last sentence of the prayer is omitted in the Roman Catholic and most modern Protestant Bibles since it is lacking in many ancient manuscripts. However, such a doxology is the perfect ending to the prayer and is in the majority of manuscripts.[8] It should, as John Calvin writes, "not only warm our hearts to press toward the glory of God . . . but also to tell us that all our prayers . . . have no other foundation than God alone."

6:14, 15 This serves as an explanatory footnote to verse 12. It is not part of the prayer, but added to emphasize that the parental forgiveness mentioned in verse 12 is conditional.

M. Jesus Teaches How to Fast (6:16–18)

6:16 The third form of religous hypocrisy that Jesus denounced was the deliberate attempt to create an appearance of **fasting. The hypocrites** disfigured **their faces** when they fasted in order to look gaunt, haggard, and doleful. But Jesus says it is ridiculous to attempt to **appear** holy.

6:17, 18 True believers should **fast** in secret, giving no outward appearance of it. **To anoint your head and wash your face** was a means of appearing in one's normal manner. It is enough that **the Father** knows; His **reward** will be better than people's approval.

FASTING

To fast is to abstain from gratifying any physical appetite. It may be voluntary, as in this passage, or involuntary (as in Acts 27:33 or 2 Cor. 11:27). In the NT it is associated with mourning (Matt. 9:14, 15) and prayer (Luke 2:37; Acts 14:23). In these passages fasting accompanied prayer as an acknowledgment of

one's earnestness in discerning the will of God.

Fasting has no merit as far as salvation is concerned; neither does it give a Christian special standing before God. A Pharisee once boasted that he fasted twice a week; however, it failed to bring him the justification he sought (Luke 18:12, 14). But when a Christian fasts secretly as a spiritual exercise, God sees and rewards. While not commanded in the NT, it is *encouraged* by promise of reward. It can aid in one's prayer life by taking away dullness and drowsiness. It is valuable in times of crisis when one wishes to discern the will of God. And it is of value in promoting self-discipline. Fasting is a matter between an individual and God and should be done only with a desire to please Him. It loses its value when it is imposed from outside or displayed from a wrong motive. ‡

N. Lay Up Treasures in Heaven (6:19–21)

This passage contains some of the most revolutionary teachings of our Lord — and some of the most neglected. The theme of the rest of the chapter is how to find security for the future.

6:19, 20 In verses 19–21 Jesus contravenes all human advice to provide for a financially secure future. When He says, **"Do not lay up for yourselves treasures on earth,"** He is indicating that there is no security in material things. Any type of material treasure **on earth** can be either destroyed by elements of nature (**moth or rust**) or stolen by **thieves.** Jesus says that the only investments not subject to loss are **treasures in heaven.**

6:21 This radical financial policy is based on the underlying principle that **where your treasure is, there your heart will be also.** If your money is in a safe-deposit box, then your heart and desire are also there. If your treasures are in heaven, your interests will be centered there. This teaching forces us to decide whether Jesus meant what He said. If He did, then we face the question, "What are we going to do with our earthly treasures?" If He didn't, then we face the question, "What are we going to do with our Bible?"

O. The Lamp of the Body (6:22, 23)

Jesus realized that it would be difficult for His followers to see how His unconventional teaching on security for the future could possibly work. So He used an analogy of the human **eye** to teach a lesson on spiritual sight. He said that **the eye** is **the lamp of the body**. It is through the eye that the body receives illumination and can see. **If** the **eye is good**, the **whole body** is flooded with **light**. **But if** the **eye is bad**, then vision is impaired. Instead of light, there is **darkness**.

The application is this: The good eye belongs to the person whose motives are pure, who has a single desire for God's interests, and who is willing to accept Christ's teachings literally. His whole life is flooded with light. He believes Jesus' words, he forsakes earthly riches, he lays up treasures in heaven, and he knows that this is the only true security. On the other hand, the bad eye belongs to the person who is trying to live for two worlds. He doesn't want to let go of his earthly treasures, yet he wants treasures in heaven too. The teachings of Jesus seem impractical and impossible to him. He lacks clear guidance since he is full of darkness.

Jesus adds the statement that **if therefore the light that is in you is darkness, how great is that darkness!** In other words, if you know that Christ forbids trusting earthly treasures for security, yet you do it anyway, then the teaching you have failed to obey becomes darkness — a very intense form of spiritual blindness. You cannot see riches in their true perspective.

P. You Cannot Serve God and Mammon (6:24)

The impossibility of living for **God** and for money is stated here in terms of **masters** and slaves. **No one can serve two masters. One** will inevitably take precedence in his loyalty and obedience. So it is with **God and mammon**. They present rival claims and a choice must be made. Either we must put God first and reject the rule of materialism or we must live for temporal things and refuse God's claim on our lives.

Q. Do Not Worry (6:25–34)

6:25 In this passage Jesus strikes at the tendency to center our lives around food and clothing, thus missing life's real meaning. The problem is not so much what we eat and wear *today*, but what we shall eat and wear ten, twenty, or thirty years from now. Such worry about the future is sin because it denies the love, wisdom, and power of God. It denies the love of God by implying that He doesn't care for us. It denies His wisdom by implying that He doesn't know what He is doing. And it denies His power by implying that He isn't able to provide for our needs.

This type of worry causes us to devote our finest energies to making sure we will have enough to live on. Then before we know it, our lives have passed, and we have missed the central purpose for which we were made. God did not create us in His image with no higher destiny than that we should consume food. We are here to love, worship, and serve Him and to represent His interests on earth. Our bodies are intended to be our servants, not our masters.

6:26 **The birds of the air** illustrate God's care for His creatures. They preach to us how unnecessary it is for us to worry. They **neither sow nor reap**, yet God **feeds them**. Since, in God's hierarchy of creation, we are **of more value than** the birds, then we can surely expect God to take care of our needs.

But we should not infer from this that we need not work for the supply of our present needs. Paul reminds us: "If anyone will not work, neither shall he eat" (2 Thess. 3:10). Nor should we conclude that it is wrong for a farmer to sow, reap, and harvest. These activities are a necessary part of his providing for his current needs. What Jesus forbids here is multiplying barns in an attempt to provide future security independent of God (a practice He condemns in His story of the rich farmer in Luke 12: 16–21.) The *Daily Notes of the Scripture Union* succinctly summarize verse 26:

> The argument is that if God sustains, *without* their conscious participation, creatures of a lower order, He will all the

more sustain, *with* their active participation, those for whom creation took place.

6:27 Worry about the future is not only a dishonor to God — it is also futile. The Lord demonstrates this with a question: **"Which of you by worrying can add one cubit to his stature?"** A short person cannot worry himself eighteen inches taller. Yet, relatively speaking, it would be far easier to perform this feat than to worry into existence all the provisions for one's future needs.

6:28–30 Next the Lord deals with the unreasonableness of worrying that we will not have enough **clothing** in the future. **The lilies of the field** (probably wild anemones) **neither toil nor spin**, yet their beauty surpasses that of Solomon's royal garments. If God can provide such elegant apparel for wildflowers, which have a brief existence and are then used as fuel in the baking **oven**, He will certainly care for His people who worship and serve Him.

6:31, 32 The conclusion is that we should not spend our lives in anxious pursuit of food, drink, and clothing for the future. The unconverted **Gentiles** live for the mad accumulation of material things, as if food and clothing were the whole of life. But it should not be so with Christians, who have a **heavenly Father** who **knows** their basic needs.

If Christians were to set before them the goal of providing in advance for all their future needs, then their time and energy would have to be devoted to the accumulation of financial reserves. They could never be sure that they had saved enough, because there is always the danger of market collapse, inflation, catastrophe, prolonged illness, paralyzing accident. This means that God would be robbed of the service of His people. The real purpose for which they were created and converted would be missed. Men and women bearing the divine image would be living for an uncertain future on this earth when they should be living with eternity's values in view.

6:33 The Lord, therefore, makes a covenant with His followers. He says, in effect, "If you will put God's interests first in your life, I will guarantee your future needs. If you **seek first the kingdom of God and His righteousness**, then I

will see that you never lack the necessities of life."

6:34 This is God's "social security" program. The believer's responsibility is to live for the Lord, trusting God for the future with unshakable confidence that He will provide. One's job is simply a means of providing for current needs; everything above this is invested in the work of the Lord. We are called to live one day at a time: **tomorrow** can **worry about its own things**.

R. Do Not Judge (7:1–6)

This section on judging immediately follows our Lord's provocative teaching concerning earthly riches. The connection between these two themes is important. It is easy for the Christian who has forsaken all to criticize wealthy Christians. Conversely, Christians who take seriously their duty to provide for the future needs of their families tend to downplay the literalness that some place on Jesus' words in the last chapter. Since no one lives completely by faith, such criticism is out of order.

This command not to judge others includes the following areas: we should not judge motives; only God can read them; we should not judge by appearance (John 7:24; Jas. 2:1–4); we should not judge those who have conscientious scruples about matters that are not in themselves right or wrong (Rom. 14:1–5); we should not judge the service of another Christian (1 Cor. 4:1–5); and, we should not judge a fellow believer by speaking evil about him (Jas. 4:11, 12).

7:1 Sometimes these words of our Lord are misconstrued by people to prohibit all forms of judgment. No matter what happens, they piously say, **"Judge not, that you be not judged."** But Jesus is not teaching that we are to be undiscerning Christians. He never intended that we abandon our critical faculty or discernment. The NT has many illustrations of legitimate judgment of the condition, conduct, or teaching of others. In addition, there are several areas in which the Christian is commanded to make a decision, to discriminate between good and bad or between good and best. Some of these include:

1. When disputes arise between be-

lievers, they should be settled in the church before members who can dècide the matter (1 Cor. 6:1-8).

2. The local church is to judge serious sins of its members and take appropriate action (Matt. 18:17; 1 Cor. 5:9-13).

3. Believers are to judge the doctrinal teaching of teachers and preachers by the Word of God (Matt. 7:15–20; 1 Cor. 14:29; 1 Jn. 4:1).

4. Christians have to discern if others are believers in order to obey Paul's command in 2 Corinthians 6:14.

5. Those in the church must judge which men have the qualifications necessary for elders and deacons (1 Tim. 3:1-13).

6. We have to discern which people are unruly, fainthearted, weak, etc., and treat them according to the instructions in the Bible (e.g., 1 Thess. 5:14).

7:2 Jesus warned that unrighteous judgment would be repaid in kind: **"For with what judgment you judge, you will be judged."** This principle of reaping what we sow is built into all human life and affairs. Mark applies the principle to our appropriation of the Word (4:24) and Luke applies it to our liberality in giving (6:38).

7:3–5 Jesus exposed our tendency to see a small fault in someone else while ignoring the same fault in ourselves. He purposely exaggerated the situation (using a figure of speech known as hyperbole) to drive home the point. Someone with a **plank** in his **eye** often finds fault with the **speck** in the eye of another, not even noticing his own condition. It is hypocritical to suppose that we could help someone with a fault when we ourselves have a greater fault. We must remedy our own faults before criticizing them in others.

7:6 Verse 6 proves that Jesus did not intend to forbid *every* kind of judgment. He warned His disciples not to **give** holy things to **dogs** or to **cast . . . pearls before swine**. Under the Mosaic Law dogs and swine were unclean animals and here the terms are used to depict wicked people. When we meet vicious people who treat divine truths with utter contempt and respond to our preaching of

the claims of Christ with abuse and violence, we are not obligated to continue to share the gospel with them. To press the matter only brings increased condemnation to the offenders.

Needless to say, it requires spiritual perception to discern these people. Perhaps that is why the next verses take up the subject of prayer, by which we can ask for wisdom.

S. Keep Asking, Seeking, Knocking (7:7–12)

7:7, 8 If we think that we can live out the teachings of the Sermon on the Mount by our own strength, we have failed to realize the supernatural character of the life to which the Savior calls us. The wisdom or power for such a life must be given to us from above. So here we have an invitation to **ask** and keep on asking; to **seek** and keep on seeking; to **knock** and keep on knocking. Wisdom and power for the Christian life will be given to all who earnestly and persistently pray for it.

Taken out of context, verses 7 and 8 might seem like a blank check for believers, i.e., we can get anything we ask for. But this is simply not true. The verses must be understood in their immediate context and in light of the whole Bible's teaching on prayer. Therefore, what seems like unqualified promises here are actually restricted by other passages. For example, from Psalm 66:18 we learn that the person praying must have no unconfessed sin in his life. The Christian must pray in faith (Jas. 1:6–8) and in conformity with the will of God (1 Jn. 5:14). Prayer must be offered persistently (Luke 18:1–8) and sincerely (Heb. 10:22a).

7:9, 10 When the conditions for prayer are met, the Christian can have utter confidence that God will hear and answer. This assurance is based on the character of God, our Father. On the human level, we know that if a **son asks for bread**, his father will not **give him a stone**. Neither would he **give him a serpent** if he had asked for **a fish**. An earthly father would neither deceive his hungry son nor give him anything that might inflict pain.

7:11 The Lord argues from the

lesser to the greater. If human parents reward their children's requests with what is best for them, **how much more will** our **Father who is in heaven** do so.

7:12 The immediate connection of verse 12 with the preceding seems to be this: since our Father is a giver of good things to us, we should imitate Him in showing kindness to others. The way to test whether an action is beneficial to others is whether we would want to receive it ourselves. The "Golden Rule" had been expressed in negative terms at least one hundred years before this time by Rabbi Hillel. However, by stating the rule in positive terminology, Jesus goes beyond passive restraint to active benevolence. Christianity is not simply a matter of abstinence from sin; it is positive goodness.

This saying by Jesus **is the Law and the Prophets**, that is, it summarizes the moral teachings of the **Law** of Moses and the writings of the **Prophets** of Israel. The righteousness demanded by the OT is fulfilled in converted believers who thus walk according to the Spirit (Rom. 8:4). If this verse were universally obeyed, it would transform all areas of international relationships, national politics, family life, and church life.

T. The Narrow Way (7:13, 14)

The Lord now warns that the **gate** of Christian discipleship is **narrow** and the **way** is **difficult**.[9] But those who faithfully follow His teachings find the abundant **life**. On the other hand, there is the **wide gate** — the life of self-indulgence and pleasure. The end of such a life is **destruction**. This is not a discussion of losing one's soul, but of a failure to live out the purpose of one's existence.

These verses also have an application to the gospel by depicting the two roads and destinies of the human race. The wide gate and broad way lead to destruction (Prov. 16:25). The narrow gate and difficult way lead to life. Jesus is both the gate (John 10:9) and the way (John 14:6). But while this is a valid *application* of the passage, the *interpretation* is for believers. Jesus is saying that to follow Him would require faith, discipline, and endurance. But this **difficult** life is the only life worth living. If you choose the easy way, you will have plenty of company, but you will miss God's best for you.

U. By Their Fruits You Shall Know Them (7:15–20)

7:15 Wherever the stern demands of true discipleship are taught, there are **false prophets** who advocate the wide gate and easy way. They water down the truth until, as C. H. Spurgeon said, "There is not enough left to make soup for a sick grasshopper." These men who profess to be speaking for God come in **sheep's clothing**, giving the appearance of being true believers. But **inwardly they are ravenous wolves**, i.e., they are vicious unbelievers who prey on the immature, the unstable, and the gullible.

7:16–18 Verses 16–18 deal with the detection of the false prophets: **you will know them by their fruits**. Their licentious lives and destructive teachings betray them. A tree or plant produces **fruit** according to its character. **Thornbushes** cannot bear **grapes**; **thistles** do not bear **figs**. **A good tree** bears **good fruit** and **a bad tree** bears **bad fruit**. This principle is true in the natural world and in the spiritual world. The life and teaching of those who claim to speak for God should be tested by the Word of God: "If they do not speak according to this word, it is because there is no light in them" (Isa. 8:20).

7:19, 20 The destiny of the false prophets is to be **thrown into the fire**. The doom of false teachers and prophets is "swift destruction" (2 Pet. 2:1). They can be known by their fruits.

V. I Never Knew You (7:21–23)

7:21 The Lord Jesus next warns against people who falsely profess to acknowledge Him as Savior, but have never been converted. **Not everyone** who calls Jesus, **"Lord, Lord," shall enter the kingdom of heaven**. Only those who do **the will** of God enter the kingdom. The first step in doing the will of God is to believe on the Lord Jesus (John 6:29).

7:22, 23 On judgment **day** when unbelievers stand before Christ (Rev. 20:11–15), **many will** remind Him that they **prophesied**, or **cast out demons**, or performed **many wonders** — all in His **name**. But their protestation will be in vain. Jesus **will declare to them** that He **never knew** them or acknowledged them as His own.

From these verses we learn that not all miracles are of divine origin and that not all miracle workers are divinely accredited. A miracle simply means that a supernatural power is at work. That power may be divine or satanic. Satan may empower his workers to cast out demons *temporarily*, in order to create the illusion that the miracle is divine. He is not dividing his kingdom against itself in such a case, but is plotting an even worse invasion of demons in the future.

W. Build on the Rock (7:24–29)

7:24, 25 Jesus closes His sermon with a parable that drives home the importance of obedience. It is not enough to hear **these sayings**; we must put them into practice. The disciple who **hears** and **does** Jesus' commands is like **a wise man who built his house on the rock**. His house (life) has a solid foundation and, when it is battered by **rain** and **winds**, it will **not fall**.

7:26, 27 The person who **hears** Jesus' **sayings** and **does not do** them is **like a foolish man who built his house on the sand**. This man will not be able to stand against the storms of adversity: when **the rain descended** and **the winds blew**, the house **fell** because it had no solid base.

If a person lives according to the principles of the Sermon on the Mount, the world calls him a fool; Jesus calls him a **wise man**. The world considers a wise man to be someone who lives by sight, who lives for the present, and who lives for self; Jesus calls such a person a fool. It is legitimate to use the wise and foolish builders to illustrate the gospel. The wise man puts his full confidence in the Rock, Christ Jesus, as Lord and Savior. The foolish man refuses to repent and rejects Jesus as his only hope of salvation. But the interpretation of the parable actually carries us beyond salvation to its practical outworking in the Christian life.

7:28, 29 As our Lord **ended** His message, **the people were astonished**. If we read the Sermon on the Mount and are not astonished at its revolutionary character, then we have failed to grasp its meaning.

The people recognized a difference between Jesus' teaching and that of the scribes. He spoke with authority; their words were powerless. His was a voice; theirs was an echo. Jamieson, Fausset and Brown comment,

> The consciousness of divine authority, as Lawgiver, Expounder and Judge, so beamed through His teaching, that the scribes' teaching could not but appear drivelling in such a light.[10]

V. THE MESSIAH'S MIRACLES OF POWER AND GRACE, AND VARYING REACTIONS TO THEM (8:1–9:34)

In chapters 8–12 the Lord Jesus presents conclusive evidence to the nation of Israel that He was indeed the Messiah of whom the prophets had written. Isaiah, for example, had foretold that Messiah would open the eyes of the blind, unstop the ears of the deaf, heal the lame, and make the mute sing (35:5, 6). Jesus, by fulfilling all these prophecies, proved that He was Messiah. Israel, by referring to her Scriptures, should have had no difficulty in identifying Him as the Christ. But none are so blind as those who will not see.

The events recorded in these chapters are presented according to a thematic scheme, rather than in strict chronological order. This is not a complete account of the Lord's ministry, but a presentation of events selected by the Holy Spirit to portray certain motifs in the Savior's life. Included in this presentation are the following:

1. Christ's absolute authority over disease, demons, death, and the elements of nature.
2. His claim to absolute lordship in the lives of those who would follow Him.
3. The mounting rejection of Jesus by the nation of Israel, particularly by the religious leaders.
4. The ready reception of the Savior by individual Gentiles.

A. Power Over Leprosy (8:1–4)

8:1 Though the teaching of Jesus was radical and extreme, it had a drawing power — so much so that **great multitudes followed Him**. Truth is self-verifying and, though people may not like it, they can never forget it.

8:2 **A leper** knelt before Jesus with a desperate appeal for healing. This leper had faith that the Lord could cure him, and true faith is never disappointed. Leprosy is an appropriate picture of sin because it is loathsome, destructive, infectious, and, in some forms, humanly incurable.[11]

8:3 Lepers were untouchables. Physical contact with them might expose a person to infection. In the case of the Jews, this contact made the person ceremonially unclean, that is, unfit to worship with the congregation of Israel. But when Jesus **touched** the leper and spoke the healing words, the **leprosy** vanished **immediately**. Our Savior has power to cleanse from sin and to qualify the cleansed person to be a worshiper.

8:4 This is the first instance in Matthew's Gospel where it is recorded that Jesus commanded someone to **tell no one** of the miracle done for them or of what they had seen (see also 9:30; 12:16; 17:9; Mark 5:43; 7:36; 8:26). This was probably because He was aware that many people, interested only in deliverance from the Roman yoke, wanted to make Him King. But He knew that Israel was still unrepentant, that the nation would reject His spiritual leadership, and that He must first go to the cross.

Under the Law of Moses, **the priest** also served as physician. When a leper was cleansed, he was obligated to bring an offering and to appear before the priest in order to be pronounced clean (Lev. 14:4–6). It was no doubt a rare event for a leper to be healed, so extraordinary, in fact, that it should have alerted this priest to investigate whether the Messiah had appeared at last. But we read of no such reaction. Jesus told the leper to obey the law in this matter.

The spiritual implications of the miracle are clear: The Messiah had come to Israel with power to heal the nation of its illness. He presented this miracle as one of His credentials. But the nation was not yet ready for her Deliverer.

B. Power Over Paralysis (8:5–13)

8:5, 6 The faith of a Gentile **centurion** is introduced in striking contrast to the unreceptiveness of the Jews. If Israel will not acknowledge her King, the despised pagans will. The centurion was a Roman military officer in charge of about one hundred men, and was stationed in or near Capernaum. He **came to** Jesus to seek healing for his **servant** who had suffered a violent and painful paralysis. This was an unusual display of compassion — most officials would not have shown such concern for a servant.

8:7–9 When the Lord **Jesus** offered to visit the sick servant, **the centurion** showed the reality and depth of his faith. He said, in effect, **"I am not worthy that You should** enter my house. Anyway, it isn't necessary, because You could easily heal him by saying the **word**. I know about **authority**. I take orders from my superiors, and give order to those under me. My commands are obeyed implicitly. How much more would Your words have power over my servant's illness!"

8:10–12 Jesus **marveled** at the faith of this Gentile. This is one of two times when Jesus is said to have marveled; the other time was at the unbelief of the Jews (Mark 6:6). He had **not found such great faith** among God's chosen people, **Israel**. This led Him to point out that in His coming kingdom, Gentiles would flock from all over the world to enjoy fellowship with the Jewish patriarchs while **the sons of the kingdom** would be thrown **into outer darkness** where they would weep and gnash their **teeth. Sons of the kingdom** are those who were Jews by birth, who professed to acknowledge God as King, but who were never truly converted. But the principle applies today. Many children privileged to be born and raised in Christian families will perish in hell because they reject Christ, while jungle savages will enjoy the eternal glories of heaven because they believed the gospel message.

8:13 **Jesus said to the centurion, "Go your way; and as you have believed, so let it be done for you."** Faith is rewarded in proportion to its confidence in the character of God. The **servant was healed** instantly, even though Jesus was some distance away. We may see in this a picture of Christ's present ministry; healing the non-privileged Gentiles from the paralysis of sin, though He Himself is not bodily present.

C. Power Over Fever (8:14, 15)

Entering **Peter's house**, Jesus found the mother-in-law **sick with a fever. He touched her hand, and the fever** vanished. Ordinarily fever leaves a person greatly weakened, but this cure was so instantaneous and complete that she was able to get out of bed and **serve** Him — a fitting expression of gratitude for what the Savior had done for her. We should imitate her, whenever we are healed, by serving Him with renewed dedication and vigor.

D. Power over Demons and Various Sicknesses (8:16, 17)

At **evening**, when the Sabbath was over (see Mark 1:21–34), the people surged to Him with **many** victims of demon-possession. These pathetic individuals were indwelt and controlled by evil spirits. Often they exhibited superhuman knowledge and power; at other times they were tormented. Their behavior sometimes resembled that of insane persons, but the cause was demonic rather than physical or mental. Jesus **cast out the spirits with a word**.

He also **healed all who were sick**, fulfilling the prophecy of Isaiah 53:4: **"He Himself took our infirmities and bore our sicknesses."** Verse 17 is often used by faith-healers to show that healing is in the atonement, and that therefore physical healing is something the believer can claim by faith. But here the Spirit of God applies the prophecy to our Savior's earthly healing ministry and *not* to His work on the cross.

So far in this chapter we have seen four miracles as follows:

1. Healing of the Jewish leper, with Christ present.
2. Healing of the centurion's servant, with Christ at a distance.
3. Healing of Peter's mother-in-law, with Jesus there in the house.
4. Healing of all the demon-possessed and sick, with Jesus present.

Gaebelein suggests that these typify four stages of our Lord's ministry:

1. Christ in His First Advent, ministering to His people Israel.
2. The Gentile dispensation, with Jesus absent.
3. His Second Advent, when He will enter the house, restoring His relations with Israel and heal the sick daughter of Zion.
4. The Millennium when all the demon-possessed and sick will be healed.[12]

This is an intriguing analysis of the progress of teaching in the miracles, and should alert us to the hidden depths of meaning in the sacred Scriptures. We should be warned, however, not to carry this method to extremes by forcing meanings to the point where they are ridiculous.

E. The Miracle of Human Refusal (8:18–22)

We have seen Christ exercising authority over disease and demons. It is only when He comes in contact with men and women that He meets with resistance — the miracle of human refusal.

8:18–20 As **Jesus** prepared to cross the Sea of Galilee from Capernaum to the east side, a self-confident **scribe** stepped forward pledging to follow Him "all the way." The Lord's answer challenged him to count the cost — a life of self-denial. **"Foxes have holes and birds of the air have nests, but the Son of Man has nowhere to lay His head."** In His public ministry, He had no home of His own; however, there were homes where He was a welcome guest and He ordinarily had a place to sleep. The true force of His words seems to be spiritual: this world could not provide Him with true, lasting rest. He had a work to do and could not rest till it was accomplished. The same is true of His followers; this world is not their resting place — or at least, it shouldn't be!

8:21 **Another** well-meaning follower expressed a willingness to follow Him, but had a higher priority: **"Lord, let me first go and bury my father."** Whether or not the father had already died makes little difference. The basic trouble was expressed in the contradictory words: **"Lord . . . me first."** He put self ahead of

Christ. While it is perfectly proper to provide a decent burial for one's father, it becomes wrong when such a worthy act takes precedence over the Savior's call.

8:22 Jesus answered him, in effect: "Your first duty is to **follow Me. Let the** spiritually **dead bury** the physically **dead**. An unsaved person can do that kind of work. But there is a work which you alone can do. Give the best of your life to what really lasts. Don't waste it on trivia." We are not told how these two disciples responded. But the strong implication is that they left Christ to make a comfortable place for themselves in the world and to spend their lives hugging the subordinate. Before we condemn them, we should test ourselves on the two terms of discipleship enunciated by Jesus in this passage.

F. Power Over the Elements (8:23–27)

The Sea of Galilee is noted for sudden, violent storms that whip it into a churning froth. Winds sweep down the valley of the Jordan from the north, picking up speed in the narrow gorge. When they hit the Sea, it becomes extremely unsafe for navigation.

On this occasion, Jesus was crossing from the west side to the east. When the storm broke, **He was asleep** in the boat. The terrified disciples awoke Him with frantic pleas for help. It is to their credit that they went to the right Person. After rebuking them for their puny faith, He **rebuked the winds and the** waves. When **a great calm** descended, the men **marveled** that even the elements obeyed their humble Passenger. How little they comprehended that the Creator and Sustainer of the universe was in the ship that day!

All disciples encounter storms sooner or later. At times it seems we are going to be swamped by the waves. What a comfort to know that Jesus is in the boat with us. "No water can swallow the ship where lies the Master of ocean and earth and skies." No one can quell life's storms like the Lord Jesus.

G. Jesus Heals Two Demon-Possessed Men (8:28–34)

8:28 On the east **side** of the Sea of Galilee was **the country of the Ger-**gesenes.[13] When Jesus arrived, He met **two** unusually violent cases of demon possession. These demoniacs lived in cave-like **tombs** and were so **fierce** they made travel in that area unsafe.

8:29–31 As Jesus approached, the demons **cried out, "What have we to do with You, Jesus, You Son of God? Have You come here to torment us before the time?"** They knew who Jesus was, and that He would finally destroy them. In these respects their theology was more accurate than that of many modern liberals. Sensing that Jesus was going to cast them out of the men, they asked that they might be transfered to **a herd of many swine feeding** nearby.

8:32 Strangely enough Jesus granted their request. But why should the Sovereign Lord accede to the request of demons? To understand His action, we must remember two facts. First, demons shun the disembodied state; they want to indwell human beings, or, if that is not possible, animals or other creatures. Secondly, the purpose of demons is without exception to destroy. If Jesus had simply cast them out of the maniacs, the demons would have been a menace to the other people of the area. By allowing them to go into the swine, He prevented their entering men and women and confined their destructive power to animals. It was not yet time for their final destruction by the Lord. As soon as the transfer took place, the **swine ran violently down the steep place into the sea** and drowned.

This incident demonstrates that the ultimate aim of demons is to destroy, and underlines the terrifying possibility that two men can be indwelt by the number of demons it takes to destroy two thousand swine (Mark 5:13).

8:33, 34 The herdsmen ran back with news of what had happened. The result was that an aroused citizenry came out to Jesus and **begged Him to** leave the area. Ever since then Jesus has been criticized for the needless slaughter of pigs and has been asked to leave because He values human life above animals. If these Gergesenes were Jews, it was unlawful for them to raise pigs. But whether or not they were Jews, their condemnation is that they valued a herd of pigs more than the healing of two demoniacs.

H. Power to Forgive Sins (9:1–8)

9:1 Rejected by the Gergesenes, the Savior recrossed the Sea of Galilee and came to Capernaum, which had become **His own city** after the people of Nazareth attempted to destroy Him (Luke 4:29–31). It was here that He performed some of His mightiest miracles.

9:2 Four men came to Him, carrying **a paralytic** on a crude bed or mat. Mark's account tells us that because of the crowd, they had to tear up the roof and lower the man into Jesus' presence (2:1–12). When **Jesus** saw **their faith,** He **said to the paralytic, "Son, be of good cheer; your sins are forgiven you."** Notice that He saw *their* faith. Faith prompted the men to bring the invalid to Jesus, and the invalid's faith went out to Jesus for healing. Our Lord first rewarded this faith by pronouncing his **sins forgiven**. The Great Physician removed the cause before treating the symptoms; He gave the greater blessing first. This raises the question whether Christ ever healed a person without also imparting salvation.

9:3–5 When **some of the scribes** heard Jesus declare the man's sins forgiven, they accused Him of blasphemy **within themselves**. After all, only God can forgive sins — and they were certainly not about to receive Him as God! The omniscient Lord Jesus read their thoughts, rebuked them for the **evil in** their **hearts** of unbelief, then asked them whether it was **easier to say, "Your sins are forgiven you," or to say, "Arise and walk."** Actually it's as easy to *say* one as the other, but which is easier to *do*? Both are humanly impossible, but the results of the first command are not visible whereas the effects of the second are immediately discernible.

9:6, 7 In order to show the scribes that He had authority **on earth to forgive sins** (and should therefore be honored as God), Jesus condescended to give them a miracle they could *see*. Turning **to the paralytic**, He said, **"Arise, take up your bed and go to your house."**

9:8 When the multitudes saw him walking home with his pallet, they registered two emotions — fear and wonder. They were afraid in the presence of an obviously supernatural visitation. They **glorified God** for giving **such power to men**. But they completely missed the significance of the miracle. The *visible* healing of the paralytic was designed to confirm that the man's sins had been forgiven, an *invisible* miracle. From this they should have realized that what they had witnessed was not a demonstration of God giving authority to men but of God's presence among them in the Person of the Lord Jesus Christ. But they didn't understand.

As for the scribes, we know from later events that they only became more hardened in their unbelief and hatred.

I. Jesus Calls Matthew the Tax-Collector (9:9–13)

9:9 The tense atmosphere building up around the Savior is temporarily relieved by Matthew's simple and humble account of his own call. A tax-collector or custom house officer, he and his fellow officials were hated intensely by the Jews because of their crookedness, because of the oppressive taxes they exacted, and most of all, because they served the interests of the Roman Empire, Israel's overlord. As **Jesus passed** the tax office, **He said to** Matthew, **"Follow Me."** The response was instantaneous; he **arose and followed**; leaving a traditionally dishonest job to become an instant disciple of Jesus. As someone has said, "He lost a comfortable job, but he found a destiny. He lost a good income but he found honor. He lost a comfortable security, but he found an adventure the like of which he had never dreamed." Not the least among his rewards were that he became one of the twelve and was honored to write the Gospel which bears his name.

9:10 The meal described here was arranged by Matthew in honor of Jesus (Luke 5:29). It was his way of confessing Christ publicly and of introducing his associates to the Savior. Necessarily, therefore, the guests were **tax-collectors** and others generally known to be **sinners**!

9:11 It was the practice in those days to eat reclining on couches and facing the table. **When the Pharisees saw** Jesus associating in this way with the social riff-raff, they went to His disciples and charged Him with "guilt by association"; surely no true prophet would eat with **sinners**!

9:12 Jesus overheard and answered,

"Those who are well have no need of a physician, but those who are sick." The Pharisees considered themselves healthy and were unwilling to confess their need for Jesus. (Actually they were extremely ill spiritually and desperately needed healing.) The tax collectors and sinners, by contrast, were more willing to acknowledge their true condition and to seek Christ's saving grace. So the charge was true! Jesus *did* eat with sinners. If He had eaten with the Pharisees, the charge would still have been true — perhaps even more so! If Jesus hadn't eaten with sinners in a world like ours, He would always have eaten alone. But it is important to remember that when He ate with sinners, He never indulged in their evil ways or compromised His testimony. He used the occasion to call men to truth and holiness.

9:13 The Pharisees' trouble was that although they followed the rituals of Judaism with great precision, their hearts were hard, cold, and merciless. So Jesus dismissed them with a challenge to **learn** the meaning of Jehovah's words, **"I desire mercy, and not sacrifice"** (quoted from Hosea 6:6). Although God had instituted the sacrificial system, He did not want the rituals to become a substitute for inward righteousness. God is not a Ritualist, and He is not pleased with rituals divorced from personal godliness — precisely what the Pharisees had done. They observed the letter of the law but had no compassion for those who needed spiritual help. They associated only with self-righteous people like themselves.

In contrast, the Lord Jesus pointedly told them, **"I did not come to call the righteous, but sinners."** He perfectly fulfilled God's desire for mercy as well as sacrifice. In one sense, there are no righteous people in the world, so He came to call all men **to repentance**. But here the thought is that His call is only effective for those who acknowledge themselves to be sinners. He can dispense no healing to those who are proud, self-righteous, and unrepentant — like the Pharisees.

J. Jesus Is Questioned About Fasting (9:14–17)

9:14 By this time **John** the Baptist was probably in prison. His disciples came to Jesus with a problem. They themselves fasted **often, but** Jesus' **disciples** did **not**. Why not?

9:15 The Lord answered with an illustration. He was **the bridegroom** and His disciples the wedding guests. **As long as** He was **with them**, there was no reason to fast as a sign of mourning. But He would be taken **from them; then** His disciples would **fast**. He *was* taken from them — in death and burial, and since His ascension He has been bodily absent from His disciples. While Jesus' words do not *command* fasting, they certainly *approve* it as an appropriate exercise for those who await the Bridegroom's return.

9:16 The question raised by John's disciples further prompted Jesus to point out that John marked the end of one dispensation, announcing the new Age of Grace, and He shows that their respective principles cannot be mixed. To try to mix law and grace would be like using a **piece of** new, **unshrunk cloth** to patch **an old garment**. When washed, the patch would shrink, ripping itself away from the old cloth. The disrepair would be worse than ever. Gaebelein complains rightly:

> A judaistic Christianity which, with a profession of Grace and the Gospel, attempts to keep the law and fosters legal righteousness is a greater abomination in the eyes of God than professing Israel in the past, worshipping idols.[14]

9:17 Or the mixture would be like putting **new wine into old wineskins**. The pressure caused by the fermentation of the new wine would burst the old skins because they had lost their elasticity. The life and liberty of the Gospel ruins the wineskins of ritualism.

The introduction of the Christian era would inevitably result in tension. The joy which Christ brought could not be contained within the forms and rituals of the OT. There must be an entirely new order of things. Pettingill makes this clear:

> Thus does the King warn His disciples against the admixture of the old . . . and the new. . . . And yet this is what has been done throughout Christendom. Judaism has been patched up and adapted everywhere among the churches and the old garment is labelled "Christianity."

The result is a confusing mixture, which is neither Judaism nor Christianity, but a ritualistic substitution of dead works for a trust in the living God. The new wine of free salvation has been poured into the old wineskins of legalism, and with what result? Why, the skins are burst and ruined and the wine is spilled and most of the precious life-giving draught is lost. The law has lost its terror, because it is mixed with grace, and grace has lost its beauty and character as grace, for it is mixed with law-works.[15]

K. Power to Heal the Incurable and Raise the Dead (9:18–26)

9:18, 19 Jesus' discourse on the change of dispensations was interrupted by a distraught **ruler** of the synagogue whose **daughter** had **just died**. He knelt before the Lord, requesting Him to come and restore her to life. It was exceptional that this ruler should seek help from Jesus; most of the Jewish leaders would have feared the scorn and contempt of their associates for doing so. **Jesus** honored his faith by starting out with His disciples toward the ruler's home.

9:20 Another interruption! This time it was **a woman** who had suffered from a hemorrhage **for twelve years**. Jesus was never annoyed by such interruptions; He was always poised, accessible, and approachable.

9:21, 22 Medical science had been unable to help this woman; in fact, her condition was deteriorating (Mark 5:26). In her extremity she met Jesus — or at least she saw Him surrounded by a crowd. Believing that He was able and willing to heal her, she edged through the crowd **and touched the** fringe **of His garment**. True faith never goes unnoticed by Him. He turned and pronounced her healed; instantly **the woman was made well** for the first time in twelve years.

9:23, 24 The narrative now returns to the ruler whose daughter had died. **When Jesus** reached the **house**, the professional mourners were wailing with what someone has called "synthetic grief." He ordered the room cleared of visitors, at the same time announcing that **the girl** was **not dead but sleeping**. Most Bible students believe the Lord was using *sleep* here in a figurative sense for death. Some believe, however, that the girl was in a coma. This interpretation does not deny that Jesus could have raised her had she been dead, but it emphasizes that Jesus was too honest to take credit for raising the dead when actually the girl had not died. Sir Robert Anderson held this view. He pointed out that the father and all the others said she had died, but **Jesus** said she had **not**.

9:25, 26 In any case, the Lord **took** the girl **by the hand** and the miracle occurred — she got up. It didn't take long for the news of the miracle to spread throughout the district.

L. Power to Give Sight (9:27–31)

9:27, 28 As **Jesus departed from** the ruler's neighborhood, **two blind men followed Him**, pleading for sight. Though dispossessed of natural vision, these men had acute spiritual discernment. In addressing Jesus as **Son of David**, they recognized Him as the long-awaited Messiah and rightful King of Israel. And they knew that when the Messiah came, one of His credentials would be that He would give sight to the blind (Isa. 61:1, RSV margin). When Jesus tested their faith by asking if they believed He was **able to do this** (give them sight), they unhesitatingly responded, **"Yes, Lord."**

9:29, 30 Then the Great Physician **touched their eyes** and assured them that because they believed, they would see. Immediately their eyes became completely normal.

Man says, "Seeing is believing." God says, "Believing is seeing." Jesus said to Martha, "Did I not say to you that if you would believe you would see?" (John 11:40). The writer to the Hebrews noted, "By faith we understand . . . " (11:3). The Apostle John wrote, "I have written to you who believe . . . that you may know . . . " (1 Jn. 5:13). God is not pleased with the kind of faith that demands a prior miracle. He wants us to believe Him simply because He is God.

Why did **Jesus sternly** warn the healed men to tell no one? In the notes on 8:4, we suggested that probably He did not want to foment a premature movement to enthrone Him as King. The people were as yet unrepentant; He could not reign over them until they were born again. Also, a revolutionary uprising in favor of Jesus would bring terrible reprisals from the Roman government on the Jews. Besides all this, the Lord Jesus had to go to the cross before He could reign as King; anything that blocked His pathway to Calvary was at variance with the predetermined plan of God.

9:31 In their delirious gratitude for eyesight, the two men **spread the news** of their miraculous cure. While we might be tempted to sympathize, and even to admire their exuberant testimony, the hard fact is that they were crassly disobedient and inevitably did more harm than good, probably by stirring up shallow curiosity rather than Spirit-inspired interest. Not even gratitude is a valid excuse for disobedience.

M. Power to Give Speech (9:32–34)

9:32 First Jesus gave life to the dead; then sight to the blind; now speech to the dumb. There seems to be a spiritual sequence in the miracles here — life first, then understanding, and then testimony.

An evil spirit had stricken this man with dumbness. Someone was concerned enough to bring the demoniac to Jesus. God bless the noble band of the anonymous who have been His instruments in bringing others to Jesus!

9:33 As soon as **the demon was cast out, the mute spoke**. Surely we may assume that he used his restored power of speech in worship and witness for the One who had so graciously healed him. The common people acknowledged that **Israel** was witnessing unprecedented miracles.

9:34 But the Pharisees answered by saying that Jesus cast **out demons by the ruler of demons**. This is what Jesus later labeled the unpardonable sin (12:32). To attribute the miracles which He performed by the Holy Spirit to the power of Satan was blasphemy against the Holy Spirit. While others were being blessed by the healing touch of Christ, the Pharisees remained spiritually dead, blind, and dumb.

VI. APOSTLES OF THE MESSIAH-KING SENT FORTH TO ISRAEL (9:35–10:42)

A. The Need for Harvest Workers (9:35–38)

9:35 This verse begins what is known as the Third Galilean Circuit. **Jesus** traveled throughout **the cities and villages**, preaching the good news of **the kingdom**, namely, that He was the King of Israel, and that if the nation repented and acknowledged Him, He would reign over them. A bona fide offer of the kingdom was made to Israel at this time. What would have happened if Israel had responded? The Bible does not answer the question. We do know that Christ would still have had to die to provide a righteous basis by which God could justify sinners of all ages.

As Christ taught and preached, He healed all kinds of sicknesses. Just as miracles characterized the First Advent of the Messiah, in lowly grace, so they will mark His Second Advent, in power and great glory (cf. Heb. 6:5: "the powers of the age to come").

9:36 As He gazed on Israel's **multitudes**, harassed and helpless, He saw them as **sheep** without a **shepherd**. His great heart of **compassion** went out to **them**. Oh, that we might know more of that yearning for the spiritual welfare of the lost and dying. How we need to pray constantly:

> Let me look on the crowd, as my Savior did,
> Till my eyes with tears grow dim;
> Let me view with pity the wandering sheep,
> And love them for love of Him.

9:37 A great work of spiritual harvest needed to be done, **but the laborers were few**. The problem has persisted to this day, it seems; the need is always greater than the work-force.

9:38 The Lord Jesus told the disciples to ask **the Lord of the harvest to send out laborers into His harvest**. Notice here that the need does not constitute a call. Workers should not *go* until they are *sent*.

Christ, the Son of God has sent me
To the midnight lands;
Mine the mighty ordination
Of the pierced hands.
– *Gerhard Tersteegen*

Jesus did not identify **the Lord of the harvest**. Some think it is the Holy Spirit. In 10:5, Jesus Himself sends out the disciples, so it seems clear that He Himself is the One to whom we should pray in this matter of world evangelization.

B. Twelve Disciples Called (10:1–4)

10:1 In the last verse of chapter 9, the Lord instructed His disciples to pray for more laborers. To make that request sincerely, believers must be willing to go themselves. So here we find the Lord calling **His twelve disciples**. He had previously chosen them, but now He calls them to a special evangelistic mission to the nation of Israel. With the call went authority to cast out unclean spirits and to heal all kinds of diseases. The uniqueness of Jesus is seen here. Other men had performed miracles, but no other man ever conferred the power on others.

10:2–4 The **twelve apostles** were:

1. **Simon, who is called Peter**. Impetuous, generous-hearted, affectionate man that he was, he was a born leader.
2. **Andrew, his brother**. He was introduced to Jesus by John the Baptist (John 1:36, 40), then brought his brother Peter to Him. He made it his business thereafter to bring men to Jesus.
3. **James, the son of Zebedee**, who was later killed by Herod (Acts 12:2) — the first of the twelve to die as a martyr.
4. **John, his brother**. Also a son of Zebedee, he was the disciple whom Jesus loved. We are indebted to him for the Fourth Gospel, three Epistles, and Revelation.
5. **Philip**. A citizen of Bethsaida, he brought Nathanael to Jesus. He is not to be confused with Philip the Evangelist, in the book of Acts.
6. **Bartholomew**. Believed to be the same as Nathanael, the Israelite in whom Jesus found no guile (John 1:47).
7. **Thomas**, also called Didymus, meaning "twin." Commonly known as "Doubting Thomas," his doubts gave

way to a magnificent confession of Christ (John 20:28).

8. **Matthew**. The former tax-collector who wrote this Gospel.
9. **James, the son of Alphaeus**. Little else is definitely known about him.
10. **Lebbaeus, whose surname was Thaddaeus**. He is also known as Judas the son of James (Luke 6:16). His only recorded utterance is found in John 14:22.
11. **Simon, the Canaanite**, whom Luke calls the Zealot (6:15).
12. **Judas Iscariot**, the betrayer of our Lord.

The disciples were probably in their twenties at this time. Taken from varied walks of life and probably young men of average ability, their true greatness lay in their association with Jesus.

C. The Mission to Israel (10:5–33)

10:5, 6 The remainder of the chapter contains Jesus' instructions concerning a special preaching tour to the **house of Israel**. This is not to be confused with the later sending of the seventy (Luke 10:1) or with the Great Commission (Matt. 28:19, 20). This was a temporary mission with the specific purpose of announcing that **the kingdom of heaven** was near. While some of the principles are of lasting value for God's people in all ages, the fact that some were later revoked by the Lord Jesus proves they were not intended to be permanent (Luke 22:35, 36).

First the *route* is given. They were **not** to go to **the Gentiles** or to **the Samaritans**, a mixed race detested by the Jews. Their ministry was limited at this time **to the lost sheep of the house of Israel.**

10:7 The *message* was the proclamation that **the kingdom of heaven** was **at hand**. If Israel refused, there would be no excuse because an official announcement was to be made exclusively to them. The kingdom had drawn near in the Person of the King. Israel must decide whether to accept or reject Him.

10:8 The disciples were given *credentials* to confirm their message. They were to **heal the sick, cleanse the lepers, raise the dead,**[16] and **cast out demons**. The Jews demanded signs (1 Cor. 1:22) so God graciously condescended to give them signs.

As to *remuneration*, the Lord's representatives were to make no charge for their services. They had received their blessings without cost and were to dispense them on the same basis.

10:9, 10 They would not be required to make advance *provision* for the journey. After all, they were Israelites preaching to Israelites, and it was a recognized principle among the Jews that the laborer deserves his food. So it would not be necessary for them to take **gold, silver, copper**, food **bag, two tunics, sandals**, or **staffs**. Probably the meaning is *extra* sandals or an *extra* staff; if they already had a staff, they were permitted to take it (Mark 6:8). The idea is that their needs would be supplied on a day by day basis.

10:11 What arrangements were they to make for *housing*? When they entered a **city**, they were to look for a **worthy** host — one who would receive them as disciples of the Lord and who would be open to their message. Once they found such a host, they were to stay with him as long as they were in the city, rather than moving if they found more favorable living conditions.

10:12–14 If a **household** received them, the disciples were to **greet** the family, showing courtesy and gratitude in accepting such hospitality. If, on the other hand, a house refused to host the Lord's messengers, they were not obligated to pray for God's **peace** on it, that is, they would not pronounce a benediction on the family. Not only so, they were to dramatize God's displeasure by shaking **the dust** off their **feet**. In rejecting Christ's disciples, a family was rejecting Him.

10:15 He warned that such rejection would bring severer punishment **in the day of judgment** than the perversion of **Sodom and Gomorrah**. This proves that there will be degrees of punishment in hell; otherwise how could it be **more tolerable** for some than for others?

10:16 In this section Jesus counsels the twelve concerning their *behavior in the face of persecution.* They would be like **sheep in the midst of wolves**, surrounded by vicious men bent on destroying them. They should **be wise as serpents**, avoiding giving needless offense or being tricked into compromising situations. And they should be **harmless as doves**, protected by the armor of a

righteous character and faith unfeigned.

10:17 They should be on guard against unbelieving Jews who would hale them into criminal courts and flog them **in their synagogues**. The attack against them would be both civil and religious.

10:18 They would be dragged **before governors and kings** for Christ's sake. But God's cause would triumph over man's evil. "Man has his wickedness but God has His way." In their hour of seeming defeat the disciples would have the incomparable privilege of testifying before rulers and **Gentiles**. God would be working all things together for good. Christianity has suffered much from civil authorities, yet "no doctrine was ever so helpful to those appointed to govern."

10:19, 20 They need not rehearse what they would say when on trial. When the time came, **the Spirit** of God would give them divine wisdom to answer in such a way as to glorify Christ and utterly confuse and frustrate their accusers. Two extremes should be avoided in interpreting verse 19. The first is the naive assumption that a Christian never needs to prepare a message in advance. The second is the view that the verse has no relevance for us today. It is proper and desirable for a preacher to prayerfully wait before God for the appropriate word for a specific occasion. But it is also true that in crises, all believers can claim God's promise to give them wisdom to speak with divine intuition. They become mouthpieces for the Spirit of their Father.

10:21 Jesus forewarned His disciples that they would have to face treachery and betrayal. **Brother** would accuse **brother. Father** would betray **his child. Children** would become informers against their **parents**, resulting in the execution of the parents.

J. C. Macaulay put it well:

> We are in good company in enduring the world's hatred. . . . The servant may not expect better treatment at the hands of the enemy than the Lord Himself received. If the world had nothing better than a cross for Jesus, it will not have a royal carriage for His followers: if only thorns for Him, there will not be garlands for us. . . . Only let us see that the world's hatred of us is really "for Christ's

sake," and not on account of anything hateful in us and unworthy of the gracious Lord whom we represent.[17]

10:22, 23 The disciples would **be hated by all** — not by all without exception, but by all cultures, nationalities, classes, etc., of men. **"But he who endures to the end will be saved."** Taken by itself, this could seem to imply that salvation can be earned by steadfast endurance. We know it cannot mean this because throughout the Scriptures salvation is presented as a free gift of God's grace through faith (Eph. 2:8, 9). Neither can the verse mean that those who remain faithful to Christ will be saved from physical death; the previous verse predicts the death of some faithful disciples. The simplest explanation is that endurance is the hallmark of the genuinely saved. Those who endure to the end in times of persecution show by their perseverance that they are true believers. This same statement is found in Matthew 24:13 where it refers to a faithful remnant of Jews during the Tribulation who refuse to compromise their loyalty to the Lord Jesus. Their endurance manifests them as genuine disciples.

In Bible passages dealing with the future, the Spirit of God often shifts from the immediate future to the distant future. A prophecy may have a partial and immediate significance and also a complete and more distant fulfillment. For instance, the two Advents of Christ may be merged in a single passage without explanation (Isa. 52:14, 15; Mic. 5:2–4). In verses 22 and 23 the Lord Jesus makes this kind of prophetic transition. He warns the twelve disciples of the sufferings they will undergo for His sake, then He seems to see them as a type of His devoted Jewish followers during the Great Tribulation. He leaps forward from the trials of the first Christians to those of believers prior to His Second Advent.

The first part of verse 23 could refer to the twelve disciples: But **"when they persecute you in this city, flee to another . . ."** They were not obligated to remain under the tyranny of their enemies if there was an honorable way to escape. "It is not wrong to escape from danger — only from duty."

The latter part of verse 23 carries us forward to the days preceding Christ's coming to reign: **". . . you will not have gone through the cities of Israel before the Son of Man comes."** This could not refer to the mission of the twelve because the Son of Man had already come. Some Bible teachers understand this as a reference to the destruction of Jerusalem in A.D. 70. However, it is difficult to see how this holocaust can be spoken of as "the coming of the Son of Man." It seems far more plausible to find here a reference to His Second Coming. During the Great Tribulation, Christ's faithful Jewish brethren will go forth with the gospel of the kingdom. They will be persecuted and pursued. Before they can reach all the cities of Israel, the Lord Jesus will return to judge His foes and set up His kingdom.

There might seem to be a contradiction between verse 23 and Matthew 24:14. Here it is stated that **not all the cities of Israel** will be reached **before the Son of Man comes**. There it says that the gospel of the kingdom will be preached in all the world before His Second Advent. However, there is no contradiction. The gospel will be preached in all nations though not necessarily to every individual. But this message will meet stiff resistance, and the messengers will be severely persecuted and hindered in Israel. Thus, not all the cities of Israel will be reached.

10:24, 25 The disciples of the Lord would often have occasion to wonder why they should have to endure ill treatment. If Jesus was the Messiah, why were His followers suffering instead of reigning? In verses 24 and 25, He anticipates their perplexity and answers it by reminding them of their relationship to Him. They were the disciples; He was their Teacher. They were servants; He was their Master. They were members of the household; He was the Master of the house. Discipleship means following the Teacher, not being superior to Him. The servant should not expect to be treated better than his Master. If men call the worthy Master of the house **"Beelzebub"** ("lord of flies," an Ekronite god whose name was used by Jews for Satan), they will hurl even greater insults at the members of His **household**. Discipleship involves sharing the Master's rejection.

10:26, 27   Three times the Lord told His followers not to fear (vv. 26, 28, 31). First, they should **not fear** the seeming victory of their foes; His cause would be gloriously vindicated in a coming day. Up to now the gospel had been relatively **covered** and His teachings had been comparatively **hidden**. But soon the disciples must boldly proclaim the Christian message which up to this point had been told them in secret, that is privately.

10:28   Second, the disciples should **not fear** the murderous rage of men. The worst that men can do is **kill the body**. Physical death is not the supreme tragedy for the Christian. To die is to be with Christ and thus far better. It is deliverance from sin, sorrow, sickness, suffering, and death; and it is translation into eternal glory. So the worst men can do is, in a real sense, the best thing that can happen to the child of God.

The disciples should not fear men but should have a reverential **fear** of **Him who is able to destroy both soul and body in hell**. This is the greatest loss — eternal separation from God, from Christ, and from hope. Spiritual death is the loss that cannot be measured and the doom that should be avoided at all cost.

The words of Jesus in verse 28 evoke memories of the saintly John Knox, whose epitaph reads, "Here lies one who feared God so much that he never feared the face of any man."

10:29   In the midst of fiery trials, the disciples could be confident of God's care. The Lord Jesus teaches this from the ubiquitous sparrow. Two of these insignificant birds were **sold for a copper coin**. Yet **not one of them** dies outside the **Father's will**, without His knowledge or His presence. As someone has said, "God attends the funeral of every sparrow."

10:30, 31   The same God who takes a personal interest in the tiny sparrow keeps an accurate count of the **hairs of the head** of each of His children. A strand of hair is of considerably less value than a sparrow. This shows that His people are **of more value** to Him **than many sparrows**, so why should they fear?

10:32   In view of the foregoing considerations, what is more reasonable than that the disciples of Christ should fearlessly **confess** Him **before men**? Any shame or reproach they might bear will be abundantly rewarded in heaven when the Lord Jesus confesses them **before** His **Father**. Confession of Christ here involves commitment to Him as Lord and Savior and the resulting acknowledgment of Him by life and by lips. In the case of most of the twelve, this led to the ultimate confession of the Lord in martyrdom.

10:33   Denial of Christ on earth will be repaid with denial **before** God **in heaven**. To deny Christ in this sense means to refuse to recognize His claims over one's life. Those whose lives say, in effect, "I never knew You" will hear Him say at last, "I never knew you." The Lord is not referring to a temporary denial of Him under pressure, as in Peter's case, but to that kind of denial that is habitual and final.

D. Not Peace But a Sword (10:34–39)

10:34   Our Lord's words must be understood as a figure of speech in which the visible results of His coming are stated as the apparent purpose of His coming. He says He **did not come to bring peace but a sword**. Actually He did come to make peace (Eph. 2:14–17); He came that the world might be saved through Him (John 3:17).

10:35–37   But the point here is that whenever individuals became His followers, their families would turn against them. A converted father would be opposed by his unbelieving son, a Christian mother by her unsaved daughter. A born again mother-in-law would be hated by her unregenerate daughter-in-law. So a choice must often be made between Christ and family. No ties of nature can be allowed to deflect a disciple from utter allegiance to the Lord. The Savior must take precedence over father, mother, son or daughter. One of the costs of discipleship is to experience tension, strife, and alienation from one's own family. This hostility is often more bitter than is encountered in other areas of life.

10:38   But there is something even

more apt to rob Christ of His rightful place than family — that is, the love of one's own life. So Jesus added, **"And he who does not take his cross and follow after Me is not worthy of Me."** The cross, of course, was a means of execution. To take the cross and follow Christ means to live in such devoted abandonment to Him that even death itself is not too high a price to pay. Not all disciples are required to lay down their lives for the Lord, but all are called on to value Him so highly that they do not count their lives precious to themselves.

10:39 Love of Christ must overmaster the instinct of self-preservation. **He who finds his life will lose it, and he who loses his life for** Christ's **sake will find it**. The temptation is to hug one's life by trying to avoid the pain and loss of a life of total commitment. But this is the greatest waste of a life — to spend it in the gratification of self. The greatest use of a life is to spend it in the service of Christ. The person **who loses his life** in devotedness to Him **will find it** in its true fullness.

E. A Cup of Cold Water (10:40–42)

10:40 Not everyone would refuse the disciples' message. Some would recognize them as representatives of the Messiah and receive them graciously. The disciples would have limited ability to reward such kindness, but they need not fret; anything done for them would be reckoned as being done for the Lord Himself and would be rewarded accordingly.

To receive Christ's disciple would be tantamount to receiving Christ Himself, and to receive Him was the same as receiving the Father **who sent** Him, since the one sent represents the sender. To receive an ambassador, who stands in the place of the government that commissions him, is to enjoy diplomatic relations with his country.

10:41 Anyone **who receives a prophet** because he is a **prophet shall receive a prophet's reward**. A. T. Pierson comments:

> The Jews regarded the reward of the prophet as the greatest; because, while kings bore rule in the name of the Lord, and priests ministered in the name of the Lord, the prophet came from the Lord to instruct both priest and king. Christ says

that if you do no more than receive a prophet in the capacity of prophet, the same reward that is given to the prophet will be given to you, if you help the prophet along. Think of that if you are inclined to criticize a speaker! If you help him to speak for God, and encourage him you will get part of his reward; but if you make it difficult for him to discharge his office, you will lose your reward. It is a great thing to help a man who is seeking to do good. You should not regard his dress, his attitude, his manners or his voice; but you should look beyond these things and say, "Is this message of God for me? Is this man a prophet of God to my soul?" If he is, receive him, magnify his word and work, and get part of his reward.[18]

The one **who receives a righteous man** because he is **a righteous man shall receive a righteous man's reward**. Those who judge others by physical attractiveness or material affluence fail to realize that true moral worth is often cloaked in very humble guise. The way a man treats the most homespun disciple is the way he treats the Lord Himself.

10:42 No kindness shown to a follower of Jesus will go unnoticed. Even **a cup of cold water** will be grandly rewarded if it is given to **a disciple** because he is a follower of the Lord.

Thus the Lord closes His special charge to the twelve by investing them with regal dignity. It is true that they would be opposed, rejected, arrested, tried, imprisoned, and perhaps even killed. But let them never forget that they were representatives of the King and that their glorious privilege was to speak and act for Him.

VII. INCREASING OPPOSITION AND REJECTION (Chaps. 11, 12)

A. John the Baptist Imprisoned (11:1–19)

11:1 Having sent the twelve on the special temporary mission to the house of Israel, Jesus **departed from there to teach and to preach in** the **cities** of Galilee where the disciples had previously lived.

11:2, 3 By now **John** had been imprisoned by Herod. Discouraged and lonely, he began to wonder. If Jesus were truly the Messiah, why did He allow His forerunner to languish in prison? Like many great men of God, John suffered a temporary lapse of faith. So **he sent two of his disciples** to ask if Jesus really was the One the prophets had promised, or if they should still be looking for the Anointed One.

11:4, 5 **Jesus answered** by reminding John that He was performing the miracles predicted of the Messiah: **The blind see** (Isa. 35:5); **the lame walk** (Isa. 35:6); **lepers are cleansed** (Isa. 53:4, cf. Matt. 8:16, 17); **the deaf hear** (Isa. 35:5); **the dead are raised up** (not prophesied of the Messiah; it was greater than the predicted miracles). Jesus also reminded John that **the gospel** was being **preached** to **the poor** in fulfillment of the Messianic prophecy in Isaiah 61:1. Ordinary religious leaders often concentrate their attention on the wealthy and aristocratic. The Messiah brought good news to **the poor**.

11:6 Then the Savior added, **"And blessed is he who is not offended because of Me."** On other lips this would be the boast of a supreme egotist. On Jesus' lips, it is the valid expression of His personal perfection. Instead of appearing as a colorful military general, the Messiah had come as a humble Carpenter. His gentleness, lowliness, and humiliation were out of character with the prevailing image of the militant Messiah. Men who were guided by fleshly desires might doubt His claim to kingship. But God's blessing would rest on those who, by spiritual insight, recognized Jesus of Nazareth as the promised Messiah.

Verse 6 should not be interpreted as a rebuke to John the Baptist. Everyone's faith needs to be confirmed and strengthened at times. It is one thing to have a temporary lapse of faith and quite another to be permanently stumbled as to the true identity of the Lord Jesus. No single chapter is the story of a man's life. Taking John's life in its totality, we find a record of faithfulness and perseverance.

11:7, 8 As soon as John's disciples **departed** with Jesus' words of reassurance, the Lord turned **to the multitudes** with words of glowing praise for the Baptist. This same crowd had flocked to the desert when John was preaching

there. Why? **To see** some weak, vacillating **reed** of a man, **shaken** by every passing **wind** of human opinion? Certainly not! John was a fearless preacher, an embodied conscience, who would rather suffer than be silent, and rather die than lie. Had they gone **out to see** a well-dressed palace courtier, luxuriating in comfort? Certainly not! John was a simple man of God whose austere life was a rebuke to the enormous worldliness of the people.

11:9 Had they gone out to see **a prophet**? Well, John was a prophet — in fact, the greatest of the prophets. The Lord did not imply here that he was greater as to his personal character, eloquence, or persuasiveness; he was greater because of his position as forerunner of the Messiah-King.

11:10 This is made clear in verse 10; John was the fulfillment of Malachi's prophecy (3:1) — the **messenger** who would precede the Lord and **prepare** the people for His coming. Other men had prophesied the Coming of Christ, but John was the one chosen to announce His actual arrival. It has been well said, "John *opened the way* for Christ and then he got *out of the way* for Christ."

11:11 The statement that **"he who is least in the kingdom of heaven is greater than he"** proves that Jesus was speaking of John's privilege, not his character. A person **who is least in the kingdom of heaven** does not necessarily have a better character than John, but he does have **greater** privilege. To be a citizen of the kingdom is greater than to announce its arrival. John's privilege was great in preparing the way for the Lord, but he did not live to enjoy the blessings of the kingdom.

11:12 From the opening of John's ministry to his present imprisonment **the kingdom of heaven** had suffered **violence**. The Pharisees and scribes had vigorously opposed it. Herod the king had done his part to buffet the kingdom by seizing its herald.

". . . And the violent take it by force." This statement is capable of two interpretations. First, the foes of the kingdom did their best to take the kingdom in order to destroy it. Their rejection of John foreshadowed the rejection of the King Himself and thus of the kingdom. But it may also mean that those who were ready for the King's advent responded vigorously to the announcement and strained every muscle to enter. This is the meaning in Luke 16:16: "The law and the prophets were until John. Since that time the kingdom of God has been preached, and every one is pressing into it." Here the kingdom is pictured as a besieged city, with all classes of men hammering at it from the outside, trying to get in. A certain spiritual violence is necessary.

Whichever meaning one adopts, the thought is that John's preaching touched off a violent reaction, with widespread and deep effects.

11:13† "For all the prophets and the law prophesied until John." The entire volume from Genesis to Malachi predicted the coming of the Messiah. When John stepped out on the stage of history, his unique role was not just prophecy; it was announcing the fulfillment of all the prophecies concerning Christ's First Advent.

11:14 Malachi had predicted that before Messiah's appearance, Elijah would come as a forerunner (Mal. 4:5, 6). If the people had been **willing to receive** Jesus as Messiah, John would have filled the role of **Elijah**. John was not Elijah reincarnated — he disclaimed being Elijah in John 1:21. But he went before Christ in the spirit and power of Elijah (Luke 1:17).

11:15 Not all appreciated John the Baptist or understood the deep significance of his ministry. Therefore the Lord added, **"He who has ears to hear, let him hear!"** In other words, pay heed. Don't miss the significance of what you are hearing. If John fulfilled the prophecy concerning Elijah, then Jesus was the promised Messiah! In thus accrediting John the Baptist, Jesus was reaffirming His claim to be the Christ of God. To accept one would lead to acceptance of the other.

11:16, 17 But the **generation** to whom Jesus was speaking was not interested in accepting either. The Jews who were privileged to see the Advent of their Messiah-King had no relish for Him or His forerunner. They were a conundrum. Jesus compared them to peevish **children sitting in the marketplaces** who refused to be satisfied with any overtures. If their friends wanted to pipe

so they could **dance**, they refused. If their friends wanted to play-act a funeral, they refused to **lament**.

11:18, 19 **John came** as an ascetic, and the Jews accused him of being demon-possessed. **The Son of Man**, on the other hand, ate and drank in a normal manner. If John's asceticism made them uncomfortable, then surely they would be pleased with Jesus' more ordinary eating habits. But no! They called Him **a glutton**, a drunkard, **a friend of tax-collectors and sinners**. Of course, Jesus never ate or drank to excess; their charge was a total fabrication. It is true that He was **a friend of tax-collectors and sinners**, but not in the way they meant. He befriended sinners in order to save them from their sins, but He never shared or approved their sins.

"But wisdom is justified by her children." The Lord Jesus, of course, is Wisdom personified (1 Cor. 1:30). Though unbelieving men might slander Him, He is vindicated in His works and in the lives of His followers. Though the mass of the Jews might refuse to acknowledge Him as Messiah-King, His claims were completely verified by His miracles and by the spiritual transformation of His devoted disciples.

B. Woes on the Unrepentant Cities of Galilee (11:20–24)

11:20 Great privilege brings great responsibility. No cities were ever more privileged than Chorazin, Bethsaida, and Capernaum. The incarnate Son of God had walked their dusty lanes, taught their favored people, and performed most of His **mighty works** within their walls. In the face of this overwhelming evidence, they had stubbornly refused to **repent**. Little wonder, then, that the Lord should pronounce the most solemn doom upon them.

11:21 He began with **Chorazin** and **Bethsaida**. These cities had heard the gracious entreaties of their Savior-God, yet willfully turned Him away. His mind reverted to the cities of **Tyre and Sidon** which had fallen under the judgment of God because of their idolatry and wickedness. If they had been privileged to see the miracles of Jesus, they would have humbled themselves in deepest repentance. **In the day of judgment**, therefore, **Tyre and Sidon** would fare better than Chorazin and Bethsaida.

11:22 The words **"it will be more tolerable in the day of judgment"** indicate that there will be degrees of punishment in hell, just as there will be degrees of reward in heaven (1 Cor. 3:12–15). The single sin that consigns men to hell is refusal to submit to Jesus Christ (John 3:36b). But the depth of suffering in hell is conditional on the privileges spurned and the sins indulged.

11:23, 24 Few cities had been as favored as **Capernaum**. It became Jesus' home town after His rejection at Nazareth (9:1, cf. Mark 2:1–12), and some of His most extraordinary miracles — irrefutable evidences of His Messiahship — were performed there. Had vile Sodom, the capital of homosexuality, been so privileged, it would have repented and been spared. But Capernaum's privilege was greater. Its people should have repented and gladly acknowledged the Lord. But Capernaum missed its day of opportunity. Sodom's sin of perversion was great. But no sin is greater than Capernaum's rejection of the holy Son of God. Therefore, Sodom will not be punished as severely as Capernaum in the day of judgment. Lifted up **to heaven** in privilege, Capernaum **will be brought down to Hades** in judgment. If this is true of Capernaum, how much truer of places where Bibles abound, where the gospel is broadcast, and where few, if any, are without excuse.

In the days of our Lord, there were four prominent cities in Galilee: Chorazin, Bethsaida, Capernaum, and Tiberias. He pronounced woes against the first three but not Tiberias. What has been the result? The destruction of Chorazin and Bethsaida is so complete that their exact sites are unknown. The location of Capernaum is not positive. Tiberias still stands. This remarkable fulfillment of prophecy is one more evidence of the Savior's omniscience and the Bible's inspiration.

C. The Savior's Reaction to Rejection (11:25–30)

11:25, 26 The three cities of Galilee had neither eyes to see nor heart to love the Christ of God. He knew their attitude was but a foretaste of rejection on a wider scale. How did He react to their impenitance? Not with bitterness, cynicism, or vindictiveness. Rather He lifted His voice in thanks to God that nothing could frustrate His sovereign purposes. **"I thank You, Father, Lord of heaven and earth, because You have hidden these things from the wise and prudent and have revealed them to babes."**

We should avoid two possible misunderstandings. First, Jesus was not expressing pleasure in the inevitable judgment of the Galilean cities. Secondly, He did not imply that God had highhandedly withheld the light from the wise and prudent.

The cities had every chance to welcome the Lord Jesus. They deliberately refused to submit to Him. When they refused the light, God withheld the light from them. But God's plans will not fail. If the intelligentsia will not believe, then God will reveal Him to humble hearts. He fills the hungry with good things and sends the rich away empty (Luke 1:53).

Those who consider themselves too wise and understanding to need Christ become afflicted with judicial blindness. But those who admit their lack of wisdom receive a revelation of Him "in whom are hidden all the treasures of wisdom and knowledge" (Col. 2:3). Jesus thanked the Father for ordaining that if some would not have Him, others would. In the face of titanic unbelief He found consolation in the overruling plan and purpose of God.

11:27 All things had **been delivered to** Christ **by** His **Father**. This would be a presumptuous claim from anyone else, but from the Lord Jesus it is a simple statement of truth. At that moment, with opposition mounting, it did not appear that He was in control; nonetheless it was true. The program of His life was moving irresistibly toward eventual glorious triumph. **"No one knows the Son except the Father."** There is incomprehensible mystery about the Person of Christ. The union of deity and humanity in one Person raises problems that boggle the human mind. For instance, there is the problem of death. God cannot die. Yet Jesus is God and Jesus died. And yet His divine and human natures are inseparable. So although we can know Him and love Him and trust Him, there is a sense in which only the Father can truly understand Him.

But the high myst'ries of Thy Name
The creature's grasp transcend;
The Father only (glorious claim!)
The Son can comprehend.
Worthy, O Lamb of God, art Thou,
That every knee to Thee should bow!
                              – Josiah Conder

"Nor does anyone know the Father except the Son and he to whom the Son wills to reveal Him." The Father, too, is inscrutable. Ultimately, only God is great enough to understand God. Man cannot know Him by his own strength or intellect. But the Lord Jesus can and does reveal the Father to those whom He chooses. Whoever comes to know the Son comes to know the Father also (John 14:7).

Yet, after saying all this, we must confess that in seeking to explain verse 27, we are dealing with truths too high for us. We see in a mirror dimly. Not even in eternity will our finite minds be able to fully appreciate the greatness of God or understand the mystery of the Incarnation. When we read that the Father is revealed only to those whom the Son chooses, we might be tempted to think of an arbitrary selection of a favored few. The following verse guards against such an interpretation. The Lord Jesus issues a universal invitation to all who are weary and heavy laden to come to Him for rest. In other words, the ones to whom He chooses to reveal the Father are those who trust Him as Lord and Savior. As we examine this invitation of infinite tenderness, let us remember that it was issued after the blatant rejection of Jesus by the favored cities of Galilee. Man's hate and obstinacy could not extinguish His love and grace. A. J. McClain said:

Although the nation of Israel is moving toward the ordeal of divine judgment, the King in His final word throws open wide the door of personal salvation. And thus He proves that He is a God of grace, even on the threshold of judgment.[19]

11:28 Come. To come means to believe (Acts 16:31); to receive (John 1:12); to eat (John 6:35); to drink (John 7:37); to look (Isa. 45:22); to confess (1 Jn. 4:2); to hear (John 5:24, 25); to enter a door (John 10:9); to open a door (Rev. 3:20); to touch the hem of His garment (Matt. 9:20, 21); and to accept the gift of eternal

life through Christ our Lord (Rom. 6:23).

to Me. The object of faith is not a church, a creed, or a clergyman, but the living Christ. Salvation is in a Person. Those who have Jesus are as saved as God can make them.

all you who labor and are heavy laden. In order to truly come to Jesus, a person must admit that he is burdened with the weight of sin. Only those who acknowledge they are lost can be saved. Faith in the Lord Jesus Christ is preceded by repentance toward God.

and I will give you rest. Notice that **rest** here is a gift; it is unearned and unmerited. This is the *rest of salvation* that comes from realizing that Christ finished the work of redemption on Calvary's cross. It is the *rest of conscience* that follows the realization that the penalty of one's sins has been paid once for all and that God will not demand payment twice.

11:29 In verses 29 and 30, the invitation changes from salvation to service.

Take My yoke upon you. This means to enter into submission to His will, to turn over control of one's life to Him (Rom. 12:1, 2).

and learn from Me. As we acknowledge His lordship in every area of our lives, He trains us in His ways.

for I am gentle and lowly in heart. In contrast to the Pharisees who were harsh and proud, the true Teacher is meek **and lowly.** Those who take His yoke will learn to take the lowest place.

and you will find rest for your souls. Here it is not the rest of conscience but the rest of heart that is found by taking the lowest place before God and man. It is also the rest that one experiences in the service of Christ when he stops trying to be great.

11:30 "For My yoke is easy and My burden is light." Again there is a striking contrast with the Pharisees. Jesus said of them, "For they bind heavy burdens, hard to bear, and lay them on men's shoulders; but they themselves will not move them with one of their fingers" (Matt. 23:4). Jesus' yoke is easy; it does not chafe. Someone has suggested that if Jesus had had a sign outside His carpenter's shop, it would have read, "My yokes fit well."

His **burden is light.** This does not

mean that there are no problems, trials, labor, or heartaches in the Christian life. But it does mean that we do not have to bear them alone. We are yoked with One who gives sufficient grace for every time of need. To serve Him is not bondage but perfect freedom. J. H. Jowett says:

> The fatal mistake for the believer is to seek to bear life's load in a single collar. God never intended a man to carry his burden alone. *Christ therefore deals only in yokes!* A yoke is a neck harness for two, and the Lord himself pleads to be One of the two. He wants to share the labor of any galling task. The secret of peace and victory in the Christian life is found in putting off the taxing collar of "self" and accepting the Master's relaxing "yoke."[20]

D. Jesus Is Lord of the Sabbath (12:1-8)

12:1 This chapter records the mounting crisis of rejection. The rising malice and animosity of the Pharisees are now ready to spill over. The issue that opens the floodgates is the Sabbath question.

On this particular Sabbath, **Jesus** and His disciples were passing **through the grainfields. His disciples began to pluck heads of grain and to eat** them. The law permitted them to help themselves to grain from their neighbor's field as long as they did not use a sickle (Deut. 23:25).

12:2 But **the Pharisees**, legal nitpickers, charged that the **Sabbath** had been broken. Though their specific charges are not stated it is likely that they accused the disciples of: (1) harvesting (picking the grain); (2) threshing (rubbing it in their hands); (3) winnowing (separating the grain from the chaff).

12:3, 4 Jesus answered their ridiculous complaint by reminding them of an incident in the life of **David**. Once, when in exile, he and his men went into the wilderness **and ate the showbread,** twelve memorial loaves forbidden as food to any but the priests. Neither David nor his men were priests, yet God never found fault with them for doing this. Why not?

The reason is that God's law was never intended to inflict hardship on His faithful people. It was not David's fault

that he was in exile. A sinful nation had rejected him. If he had been given his rightful place, he and his followers would not have had to eat the showbread. Because there was sin in Israel, God permitted an otherwise forbidden act.

The analogy is clear. The Lord Jesus was the rightful King of Israel, but the nation would not acknowledge Him as Sovereign. If He had been given His proper place, His followers would not have been reduced to eating in this way on the Sabbath or on any other day of the week. History was repeating itself. The Lord did not reprove His disciples, because they had done no wrong.

12:5 Jesus reminded the Pharisees that the **priests profane the Sabbath** by killing and sacrificing animals and by performing many other servile duties (Num. 28:9, 10), yet are **blameless** because they are engaged in the service of God.

12:6 The Pharisees knew that the priests worked every Sabbath in the temple without desecrating it. Why then should they criticize the disciples for acting as they did in the presence of *One* who is **greater than the temple**? The italicized word *One* can perhaps better read: "*something* greater than the temple is here." The "something" is the kingdom of God, present in the Person of the King.

12:7 The Pharisees had never understood the heart of God. In Hosea 6:6 He had said, **"I desire mercy and not sacrifice."** God puts compassion before ritual. He would rather see His people picking grain on the Sabbath to satisfy their hunger than observing the day so strictly as to inflict physical distress. If the Pharisees had only realized this, they would not have condemned the disciples. But they valued outward punctiliousness above human welfare.

12:8 Then the Savior added, **"For the Son of Man is Lord even of the Sabbath."** It was He who had instituted the law in the first place, and therefore He was the One most qualified to interpret its true meaning. E. W. Rogers says:

> It seems as if Matthew, here taught by the Spirit, passes in quick review the many names and offices of the Lord Jesus: He

is Son of Man; Lord of the Sabbath; My servant; My beloved; Son of David; greater than the temple; greater than Jonas; greater than Solomon. He does so in order to show the enormity of the sin of refusing to accept Him and accord Him His rights.[21]

Before proceeding with the next incident — Jesus healing the withered hand on the Sabbath — we pause to give a short review of the scriptural teaching concerning the Sabbath.

EXCURSUS ON THE SABBATH

The Sabbath day was, and always will be, the seventh day of the week (Saturday).

God rested on the seventh day, after the six days of creation (Gen. 2:2). He did not command man to keep the Sabbath day at that time, although He may have intended the principle — one day of rest in every seven — to be followed.

The nation of Israel was commanded to keep the Sabbath when the Ten Commandments were given (Ex. 20:8–11). The law of the Sabbath was different from the other nine commandments; it was a ceremonial law while the others were moral. The only reason it was wrong to work on the Sabbath was because God said so. The other commandments had to do with things that were intrinsically wrong.

The prohibition against work on the Sabbath was never intended to apply to: the service of God (Matt. 12:5), deeds of necessity (Matt. 12:3, 4), or deeds of mercy (Matt. 12:11, 12). Nine of the Ten Commandments are repeated in the NT, not as law but as instructions for Christians living under grace. The only commandment Christians are never told to keep is that of the Sabbath. Rather, Paul teaches that the Christian cannot be condemned for failing to keep it (Col. 2:16).

The distinctive day of Christianity is the first day of the week. The Lord Jesus rose from the dead on that day (John 20:1), a proof that the work of redemption had been completed and divinely approved. On the next two Lord's Days, He met with His disciples (John 20:19, 26). The Holy Spirit was given on the first day of the week (Acts 2:1; cf. Lev. 23:15, 16). The early disciples met on that day to break bread, showing forth

the Lord's death (Acts 20:7). It is the day appointed by God on which Christians should set aside funds for the work of the Lord (1 Cor. 16:1, 2).

The Sabbath or seventh day came at the end of a week of toil; the Lord's Day, or Sunday, begins a week with the restful knowledge that the work of redemption has been completed. The Sabbath commemorated the first creation; the Lord's Day is linked with the new creation. The Sabbath day was a day of responsibility; the Lord's Day is a day of privilege.

Christians do not "keep" the Lord's Day as a means of earning salvation or achieving holiness, nor from fear of punishment. They set it apart because of loving devotion to the One who gave Himself for them. Because we are released from the routine, secular affairs of life on this day, we can set it apart in a special way for the worship and service of Christ.

It is not right to say that the Sabbath was changed to the Lord's Day. The Sabbath is Saturday and the Lord's Day is Sunday. The Sabbath was a shadow; the substance is Christ (Col. 2:16, 17). The resurrection of Christ marked a new beginning, and the Lord's day signifies that beginning.

As a faithful Jew living under the law, Jesus kept the Sabbath (in spite of the accusations of the Pharisees to the contrary). As the Lord of the Sabbath, He freed it from the false rules and regulations with which it had become encrusted. ‡

E. Jesus Heals on the Sabbath (12:9–14)

12:9 From the grainfields Jesus **went into** the **synagogue**. Luke tells us that the scribes and Pharisees were there to watch Him so that they might find some charge against Him (Luke 6:6, 7).

12:10 Inside the synagogue **was a man who had a withered hand** — mute testimony to the powerlessness of the Pharisees to help him. Up to now they had treated him with cool disregard. But suddenly he became valuable to them as a means to trap Jesus. They knew that the Savior was always predisposed to alleviate human misery. If He would heal on the Sabbath, then they would catch Him in a punishable offense, they thought. So they began by raising a legal quibble: **"Is it lawful to heal on the Sabbath?"**

12:11 The Savior answered by asking if they would pull one of their **sheep** out of **a pit on the Sabbath**. Of course they would! But why? Perhaps their pretext was that it was a work of mercy — but another consideration might be that the sheep was worth money and they would not want to incur financial loss, even on the Sabbath.

12:12 Our Lord reminded them that a man is of greater **value than a sheep**. If it is right to show mercy to an animal, how much more justified is it **to do good** to a man **on the Sabbath**!

12:13, 14 Having caught the Jewish leaders in the pit of their own greed, Jesus healed the withered hand. In telling **the man** to **stretch out** his **hand**, faith and human will were called into action. Obedience was then rewarded with healing. The hand **was restored as whole as the other** by the wonderful Creator. You would think that the Pharisees would have been happy that the man, whom they had neither the power nor inclination to help, was healed. Instead they went into a white rage against Jesus **and plotted** to kill **Him**. If they had had a withered hand, they would have been glad to be healed on any day of the week.

F. Healing for All (12:15–21)

12:15, 16 When Jesus knew the thoughts of His enemies, **He withdrew**. Yet wherever He went, the crowds gathered; and wherever the sick gathered, **He healed them all**. But He charged them not to publicize His miraculous cures, not to shield Himself from danger, but to avoid any fickle movement to make Him a popular revolutionary Hero. The divine schedule must be kept. His revolution would come, not by the shedding of Roman blood, but by the shedding of His own blood.

12:17, 18 His gracious ministry was in fulfillment of the prophecy of **Isaiah** 41:9; 42:1–4. **The prophet** foresaw the Messiah as a gentle Conqueror. He pictures Jesus as the **Servant whom** Jehovah had **chosen**, the **Beloved** One **in whom** God's **soul** was **well pleased**. God would **put** His **Spirit upon Him** — a prophecy

fulfilled at the baptism of Jesus. And His ministry would reach beyond the confines of Israel; **He** would **declare justice to the Gentiles**. This latter note becomes more dominant as Israel's "NO" grows louder.

12:19 Isaiah further predicted that the Messiah would not wrangle or **cry out** and **His voice** would not be heard **in the streets**. In other words, He would not be a political rabble-rouser, stirring up the populace. McClain writes:

> This King who is God's 'servant' will not reach His rightful place of eminence by any of the usual means of carnal force or political demagoguery; nor yet by means of the supernatural forces at His command.[22]

12:20 He would not break **a bruised reed** or **quench** a **smoking flax**. He would not trample on the dispossessed or underprivileged in order to reach His goals. He would encourage and strengthen the broken-hearted, oppressed person. He would fan even a spark of faith into a flame. His ministry would continue till He would bring **justice to victory**. His humble, loving care for others would not be extinguished by the hate and ingratitude of men.

12:21 And in His name Gentiles will trust. In Isaiah this expression is worded "And the coastlands shall wait for His law," but the meaning is the same. The coastlands refer to the Gentile nations. They are pictured as waiting for His reign so that they might be His loyal subjects. Kleist and Lilly praise this quotation from Isaiah as:

> . . . one of the gems of the Gospel, a picture of Christ of great beauty . . . Isaiah pictures Christ's union with the Father, His mission to instruct the nations, His gentleness in dealing with suffering humanity and His final victory: there is no hope for the world except in His Name. Christ — the Savior of the world — not expressed in dry, scholastic terms, but clothed in rich, oriental imagery.[23]

G. The Unpardonable Sin (12:22–32)

12:22–24 When Jesus healed a **blind and mute** demoniac, the common people began to think seriously that He might be **the Son of David**, the Messiah of Israel. This enraged **the Pharisees**.

Unable to tolerate any suggestion of sympathy with Jesus, they exploded with the charge that the miracle had been performed by the power of **Beelzebub, the ruler of the demons**. This ominous indictment was the first open accusation that the Lord Jesus was demon-empowered.

12:25, 26 When He had read **their thoughts, Jesus** proceeded to expose their folly. He pointed out that no **kingdom, city,** or **house divided against itself** can continue successfully. If He was casting out Satan's demons by the power of Satan, then Satan was working **against himself**. This would be absurd.

12:27 Our Lord had a second devastating answer for the Pharisees. Some of their Jewish associates, known as exorcists, claimed to have the power to cast out demons. Jesus neither admitted nor denied their claim, but used it to point out that if He **cast out demons by Beelzebub**, then the Pharisees' **sons** (i.e. these exorcists) did also. The Pharisees would never admit this, but could not escape the logic of the argument. Their own associates would condemn them for implying that they exorcised as agents of Satan. Scofield said:

> The Pharisees were quick enough to resent any implication of Satanic power as far as they and their sons were concerned, but on the ground they were taking, i.e., that Christ cast out demons by Beelzebub, their own sons would judge them inconsistent; for if the power to cast out demons is Satanic, then whoever exercises that power is in league with the source of that power.[24]

They were not being logical in attributing similar effects to different causes.

12:28 The truth, of course, was that Jesus **cast out demons by the Spirit of God**. His entire life as a Man on earth was lived by the power of the Holy Spirit. He was the Spirit-filled Messiah whom Isaiah had foretold (Isa. 11:2; 42:1; 61:1–3). Therefore He said to the Pharisees, "... **if I cast out demons by the Spirit of God, surely the kingdom of God has come upon you.**" This announcement must have been a crushing blow. They prided themselves on their theological knowledge, yet **the kingdom of God** had **come upon them** because the King was among them and they

hadn't even realized that He was there!

12:29 Far from being in league with Satan, the Lord Jesus was Satan's Conqueror. This He illustrates by the story of **the strong man**. **The strong man** is Satan. His **house** is the sphere in which he holds sway. **His goods** are his demons. Jesus is the One who **binds the strong man**, enters his **house**, and plunders **his goods**. Actually the binding of Satan takes place in stages. It began during Jesus' public ministry. It was decisively guaranteed by the death and resurrection of Christ. It will be true to a more marked degree during the King's thousand-year reign (Rev. 20:2). Finally, it will be eternally true when he is cast into the lake of fire (Rev. 20:10). At the present time the devil does not seem to be bound; he still exercises considerable power. But his doom is determined and his time is short.

12:30 Then Jesus said, "**He who is not with Me is against Me, and he who does not gather with Me scatters abroad.**" Their blasphemous attitude showed that the Pharisees were not **with** the Lord; therefore, they were **against** Him. By refusing to harvest with Him, they were scattering the grain. They had accused Jesus of casting out demons by the power of Satan while actually they themselves were the servants of Satan, seeking to frustrate the work of God.

In Mark 9:40, Jesus said, "... he who is not against us is on our side." This seems a flat reversal of His words here in Matthew 12:30. The difficulty is resolved when we see that in Matthew, it is a matter of *salvation*. A man is either for Christ or against Him; there is no neutrality. In Mark, the subject is *service*. There are wide differences among the disciples of Jesus — differences in local church fellowship, methods, and interpretation of doctrines. But here the rule is that if a man is not against the Lord, he is for Him and should be respected accordingly.

12:31, 32 These verses mark a crisis in Christ's dealings with the leaders of Israel. He accuses them of committing the unpardonable sin by blaspheming against the Holy Spirit, that is, by charging that Jesus performed His miracles by the power of Satan rather than by the power of the Holy Spirit. In effect, this was calling the Holy Spirit Beelzebub, the ruler of demons.

There is forgiveness for other forms of **sin and blasphemy**. A man may even speak **against the Son of Man** and be forgiven. But to blaspheme the Holy Spirit is a sin for which there is no forgiveness **in this age or in the** millennial **age to come**. When Jesus said **in this age**, He was speaking of the days of His public ministry on earth. There is reasonable doubt whether the unpardonable sin can be committed today, because He is not bodily present performing miracles.

The unpardonable sin is not the same as rejecting the gospel; a man may spurn the Savior for years, then repent, believe, and be saved. (Of course, if he dies in unbelief, he remains unforgiven.) Nor is the unforgivable sin the same as backsliding; a believer may wander far from the Lord, yet be restored to fellowship in God's family.

Many people worry that they have committed the unpardonable sin. Even if this sin could be committed today, the fact that a person is concerned is evidence that he is not guilty of it. Those who committed it were hard and unrelenting in their opposition to Christ. They had no qualms about insulting the Spirit and no hesitancy in plotting the death of the Son. They showed neither remorse nor repentance.

H. A Tree Is Known by Its Fruit (12:33–37)

12:33 Even the Pharisees should have admitted that the Lord had done good by casting out demons. Yet they accused Him of being evil. Here He exposes their inconsistency and says, in effect, "Make up your minds. If a **tree** is **good**, its **fruit** is **good** and vice versa." Fruit reflects the quality of the tree that produced it. The fruit of His ministry had been good. He had healed the sick, the blind, the deaf, and the dumb, had cast out demons and raised the dead. Could a corrupt tree have produced such good fruit? Utterly impossible! Why then did they so stubbornly refuse to acknowledge Him?

12:34, 35 The reason was that they were a **brood of vipers**. Their malice against the Son of Man, evidenced by their venomous words, was the outflow of their evil hearts.[25] A heart filled with goodness will be evidenced by words of grace and righteousness. A wicked heart expresses itself in blasphemy, bitterness, and abuse.

12:36 Jesus solemnly warned them (and us) that people **will give account** for **every idle word** they utter. Because the words people have spoken are an accurate gauge of their lives, they will form a suitable basis for condemnation or acquittal. How great will be the condemnation of the Pharisees for the vile and contemptuous words which they spoke against God's Holy Son!

12:37 **"For by your words you will be justified, and by your words you will be condemned."** In the case of believers, the penalty for careless speech has been paid through the death of Christ; however, our careless speech, unconfessed and unforgiven, will result in loss of reward at Christ's Judgment Seat.

I. The Sign of the Prophet Jonah (12:38–42)

12:38 Despite all the miracles Jesus had performed, **the scribes and Pharisees** had the temerity to ask Him for **a sign**, implying that they *would* believe if He would prove Himself to be the Messiah! But their hypocrisy was transparent. If they had not believed as a result of so many wonders, why would they be convinced by one more? The attitude that demands miraculous signs as a condition for belief does not please God. As Jesus said to Thomas, "Blessed are those who have not seen and yet have believed" (John 20:29). In God's economy, seeing follows believing.

12:39 The Lord addressed them as **an evil and adulterous generation; evil** because they were willfully blind to their own Messiah, **adulterous** because they were spiritually unfaithful to their God. Their Creator-God, a unique Person combining absolute deity and perfect humanity, stood in their midst speaking to them, yet they dared to ask Him for a sign.

12:40 He told them summarily that **no sign** would be **given to** them **except the sign of the prophet Jonah**, referring to His own death, burial, and resurrection. Jonah's experience of being swallowed by the fish and then disgorged

(Jon. 1:17; 2:10) prefigured the Lord's passion and resurrection. His rising from among the dead would be the final, climactic sign of His ministry to the nation of Israel.

Just **as Jonah was three days and three nights in the belly of the great fish, so** our Lord predicted that He would **be three days and three nights in the heart of the earth**. This raises a problem. If, as generally believed, Jesus was buried on Friday afternoon and rose again on Sunday morning, how can it be said that He was three days and nights in the tomb? The answer is that, in Jewish reckoning, any part of a day and night counts as a complete period. "A day and a night make an *onah*, and a part of an *onah* is as the whole" (Jewish saying).

12:41 Jesus depicted the guilt of the Jewish leaders by two contrasts. First, the Gentiles **of Nineveh** were far less privileged, yet when they heard the **preaching of** the errant prophet **Jonah, they repented** with deep grief. They **will rise up in the judgment** to condemn the men of Jesus' day for failing to receive Someone **greater than Jonah** — the incarnate Son of God.

12:42 Second, **the queen of** Sheba, a Gentile outside the pale of Jewish privilege, traveled from **the South**, at great effort and expense, for an interview with Solomon. The Jews of Jesus' day did not have to travel at all to see Him; He had traveled from heaven to their little neighborhood to be their Messiah-King. Yet they had no room in their lives for Him — One infinitely **greater than Solomon**. A Gentile queen will condemn them in the judgment for such wanton carelessness.

In this chapter our Lord has been presented as greater than *the temple* (v. 6); greater than *Jonah* (v. 41); and greater than *Solomon* (v. 42). He is "greater than the greatest and far better than the best."

J. An Unclean Spirit Returns (12:43–45)

12:43, 44 Now Jesus gives, in parabolic form, a summary of the past, present, and future of unbelieving Israel.

The **man** represents the Jewish nation, the **unclean spirit** the idolatry which characterized the nation from the time of its servitude in Egypt to the Babylonian captivity (which temporarily cured Israel of its idolatry). It was as if the unclean spirit had gone **out of the man**. From the end of the captivity to the present day, the Jewish people have not been idol-worshipers. They are like a house that is **empty, swept, and put in order**.

Over nineteen hundred years ago, the Savior sought admittance to that empty house. He was the rightful Occupant, the Master of the house, but the people steadfastly refused to let Him in. Though they no longer worshiped idols, they would not worship the true God either.

The **empty** house speaks of spiritual vacuum — a dangerous condition, as the sequel shows. Reformation is not enough. There must be the positive acceptance of the Savior.

12:45 In a coming day, the spirit of idolatry will decide to return to the house, accompanied by **seven spirits more wicked than himself**. Since seven is the number of perfection or completeness, this probably refers to idolatry in its fully developed form. This looks ahead to the Tribulation when the apostate nation will worship the Antichrist. To bow down to the man of sin and to worship him as God is a more terrible form of idolatry than the nation has ever been guilty of in the past. And so **the last state of that man** becomes **worse than the first**. Unbelieving Israel will suffer the awful judgments of the Great Tribulation, and their suffering will far exceed that of the Babylonian Captivity. The idolatrous portion of the nation will be utterly destroyed at Christ's Second Advent.

"So shall it also be with this wicked generation." The same apostate, Christ-rejecting race that spurned the Son of God at His First Advent will suffer severe judgment at His Second Coming.

K. The Mother and Brothers of Jesus (12:46–50)

These verses describe a seemingly commonplace incident in which Jesus' family comes to speak to Him. Why had they come? Mark may give us a clue. Some of Jesus' friends decided He was out of His mind (Mark 3:21, 31–35), and perhaps His family came to take Him away quietly (see also John 7:5). When told that His **mother and brothers** were waiting **outside to speak with Him**, the Lord responded by asking, **"Who is My mother and who are My brothers?"** Then, pointing to **His disciples**, He said **"Whoever does the will of My Father in heaven is My brother and sister and mother."**

This startling announcement is pregnant with spiritual significance; it marks a distinct turning point in Jesus' dealing with Israel. Mary and her sons represented the nation of Israel, Jesus' blood relations. Up to now He had limited His ministry largely to the lost sheep of the house of Israel. But it was becoming clear that His own people would not have Him. Instead of bowing to their Messiah, the Pharisees had accused Him of being controlled by Satan.

So now Jesus announces a new order of things. Henceforth, His ties with Israel would not be the controlling factor in His outreach. Though His compassionate heart would continue to plead with His countrymen according to the flesh, chapter 12 signals an unmistakable break with Israel. The outcome is now clear. Israel will not have Him, so He will turn to those who will. Blood relationships will be superseded by spiritual considerations. Obedience to God will bring men and women, whether Jews or Gentiles, into vital relationship with Him.

Before leaving this incident, we should mention two points concerning the mother of Jesus. First, it is evident that Mary did not occupy any place of special privilege as far as access into His presence was concerned.

Second, the mention of Jesus' brothers strikes a blow at the teaching that Mary was a perpetual virgin. The implication is strong that these were actual sons of Mary and therefore half-brothers of our Lord. This view is strengthened by such other Scriptures as Psalm 69:8; Matt. 13:55; Mark 3:31, 32; 6:3; John 7:3, 5; Acts 1:14; 1 Cor. 9:5; Gal. 1:19.

VIII. THE KING ANNOUNCES A NEW INTERIM FORM OF THE KINGDOM DUE TO ISRAEL'S REJECTION (Chap. 13)

Parables of the Kingdom

We have come to a crisis point in the Gospel by Matthew. The Lord has indicated that earthly relationships are now to be superseded by spiritual ties, that it is no longer a question of Jewish birth but of obedience to God, the Father. In rejecting the King, the scribes and Pharisees have necessarily rejected the kingdom. Now by a series of parables, the Lord Jesus gives a preview of the new form which the kingdom would take during the period between His rejection and His eventual manifestation as King of kings and Lord of lords. Six of these parables begin with the words, "The kingdom of heaven is like. . . ."

In order to see these parables in proper perspective, let us review the kingdom as discussed in chapter 3. The kingdom of heaven is the sphere in which God's rule is acknowledged. It has two aspects: (1) *outward profession*, including all who claim to recognize God's rule; and (2) *inner reality*, including only those who enter the kingdom by conversion. The kingdom is found in five phases: (1) the OT phase in which it was prophesied; (2) the phase in which it was "at hand" or present in the Person of the King; (3) the interim phase, consisting of those on earth who profess to be His subjects following the King's rejection and return to Heaven; (4) the manifestation of the kingdom during the Millennium; and (5) the final, everlasting, kingdom. Every Bible reference to the kingdom fits into one of these phases. It is the third, interim phase which chapter 13 discusses. During this phase the kingdom in its inner reality (true believers) is composed, from Pentecost to the Rapture, of the same people as the church. This is the only identity between the kingdom and the church; they are not otherwise one and the same.

With this background in mind, let us look at the parables.

A. The Parable of the Sower (13:1–9)

13:1 **Jesus went out of the house** where He had healed the demoniac **and sat by the sea** of Galilee. Many Bible students see the house as picturing the nation of Israel and the sea, the Gentiles. Thus the Lord's movement symbolizes a break with Israel; during its interim form, the kingdom will be preached to the nations.

13:2 As **great multitudes gathered** on the beach, **He got into a boat** and began to teach the people by **parables**. A parable is a story with an underlying spiritual or moral teaching which is not always apparent immediately. The seven parables that follow tell us what the kingdom will be like during the time between His First and Second Advents.

The first four were spoken to the multitude; the last three were given only to the disciples. The Lord explained the first two and the seventh to the disciples, leaving them (and us) to interpret the others with the keys He had already given.

13:3 The first parable concerns a **sower** who planted his seed in four different types of soil. As might be expected, the results were different in each case.

13:4–8

SOIL	RESULTS
1. Hard-packed **pathway.**	1. Seeds eaten by the birds.
2. Thin layer of soil over rock deposit.	2. Seed sprouted quickly, but no root; **scorched by the sun** and **withered away.**
3. Ground infested with **thorns**.	3. The seed sprouted, but growth was impossible because of the **thorns.**
4. **Good ground**.	4. The seed sprouted, grew, **and yielded a crop:** some stalks bore **a hundredfold, some sixty, some thirty.**

13:9 Jesus closed the parable with the cryptic admonition, **"He who has ears to hear, let him hear!"** In the parable He was conveying an important message to the multitude, and a different message to the disciples. None should miss the significance of His words.

Since the Lord Himself interpets the parable in verses 18– 23, we will restrain our curiosity until we reach that paragraph.

B. The Purpose of the Parables (13:10–17)

13:10 **The disciples** were puzzled that the Lord should **speak to** the people in the veiled language of **parables**. So they asked Him to explain His method.

13:11 In His reply, Jesus distinguished between the unbelieving crowd and the believing disciples. The crowd, a cross-section of the nation, was obviously rejecting Him, though their rejection would not be complete until the cross. They would not be permitted to know **the mysteries** (secrets) **of the kingdom of heaven**, whereas His true followers would be helped to understand.

A mystery in the NT is a fact never previously known by man, which man could never learn apart from divine revelation, but which has now been revealed. **The mysteries of the kingdom** are hitherto unknown truths concerning the kingdom in its interim form. The very fact that the kingdom would *have* an interim form had been a secret up to now. The parables describe some of the features of the kingdom during the time when the King would be absent. Some people therefore call this "the mystery form of the kingdom" — not that there is anything mysterious about it but simply that it was never known before that time.

13:12 It may seem arbitrary that these secrets should be withheld from the multitude and revealed to the disciples. But the Lord gives the reason: **"For whoever has, to him more will be given, and he will have abundance; but whoever does not have, even what he has will be taken away."** The disciples had faith in the Lord Jesus; therefore, they would be given the capacity for more. They had accepted the light; therefore, they would receive more light. The Jewish nation, on the other hand, had rejected the Light of the world; therefore they were not only prevented from receiving more light, they would lose what little light they had. Light rejected is light denied.

13:13 Matthew Henry compares the

parables to the pillar of cloud and fire which enlightened Israel while confusing the Egyptians. The parables would be revealed to those who were sincerely interested but would prove "only an irritation to those who were hostile to Jesus."

So it was not a matter of whim on the Lord's part, but simply the outworking of a principle which is built into all of life — willful blindness is followed by judicial blindness. That is why He spoke to the Jews in parables. H. C. Woodring put it so: "Because they did not have the love of the truth, they would not get the light of the truth."[26] They professed to see, that is, to be familiar with divine truth, but Truth incarnate stood before them and they resolutely refused to see Him. They professed to hear God's Word, but the living Word of God was in their midst and they would not obey Him. They were unwilling to understand the wonderful fact of the Incarnation; therefore, the capacity to understand was taken from them.

13:14, 15 They were a living fulfillment of the prophecy of Isaiah 6:9, 10. Israel's heart had **grown dull** and their **ears** were insensitive to the voice of God. They deliberately refused to **see with their eyes**. They knew that if they saw, heard, understood, and repented, God would heal them. But in their sickness and need, they refused His help. Therefore, their punishment was that they would **hear** but **not understand**, and **see** but **not perceive**.

13:16, 17 The disciples were tremendously privileged, because they were seeing what no one had seen before. The prophets and righteous men of the OT had longed to be living when the Messiah arrived, but their desire had not been fulfilled. The disciples were favored to live at that crisis moment in history, to see the Messiah, to witness His miracles, and to hear the incomparable teaching which came from His lips.

C. Explanation of the Parable of the Sower (13:18–23)

13:18 Having explained why He used parables, the Lord now proceeds to expound the parable of the four soils. He does not identify **the sower** but we can be sure that it refers either to Himself (v. 37) or to those who preach the message of the kingdom. He defines the seed as the word of the kingdom (v. 19). The soils represent those who hear the message.

13:19 The hard-packed pathway speaks of people who refuse to receive the message. They hear the gospel but do **not understand** it — not because they can't but because they won't. The birds are a picture of Satan; he **snatches away** the seed from the hearts of these hearers. He cooperates with them in their self-chosen barrenness. The Pharisees were hard-soil hearers.

13:20, 21 When Jesus spoke of rocky ground, He had in mind a thin layer of earth covering a ledge of rock. This represents people who hear the word and respond **with joy**. At first the sower might be elated that his preaching is so successful. But soon he learns the deeper lesson, that it is not good when the message is received with smiles and cheers. First there must be conviction of sin, contrition, and repentance. It is far more promising to see an inquirer weeping his way to Calvary than to see him walking down the aisle light-heartedly and exuberantly. The shallow earth yields a shallow profession; there is no depth to the root. But when his profession is tested by the scorching sun of **tribulation or persecution**, he decides it isn't worth it and abandons any profession of subjection to Christ.

13:22 The thorn-infested ground represents another class who hear the word in a superficial way. They appear outwardly to be genuine subjects of the kingdom but in time their interest is choked out by **the cares of this world** and by their delight in **riches**. There is no fruit for God in their lives. Lang illustrates this by a son of a money-loving father with a huge business. This son heard the Word in his youth but became engrossed in the business.

He had soon to choose between pleasing his Lord or his father. Thus the thorns were in the soil when the seed was sown and germinated; the cares of this age and the deceitfulness of riches were already at hand. He fell in with his father's wishes, devoted himself fully to business, rose to be head of the concern, and when well on in life had to acknowledge that he had neglected things heavenly. He was about to retire and he expressed his intention to be more diligent in matters spiritual. But God is not to be mocked. The man retired and died suddenly in only a few months. He left £90,000 and a spiritually wasted life. The thorns had choked the word and it was unfruitful.[27]

13:23 **The good ground** represents a true believer. **He . . . hears the word** receptively and **understands it** through obeying what he hears. Although these believers do not all produce the same amount of fruit, they all show by their fruit that they have divine life. **Fruit** here is probably the manifestation of Christian character rather than souls won to Christ. When the word *fruit* is used in the NT, it generally refers to the fruit of the Spirit (Gal. 5:22, 23).

What was the parable meant to say to the crowds? Obviously it warned against the peril of hearing without obeying. It was calculated also to encourage individuals to receive the Word sincerely, then to prove their reality by bringing forth fruit for God. As for the disciples, the parable prepared them and future followers of Jesus for the otherwise discouraging fact that relatively few of those who hear the message are genuinely saved. It saves Christ's loyal subjects from the delusion that all the world will be converted through the spread of the gospel. The disciples are also warned in this parable against the three great antagonists of the gospel: (1) the devil (the birds — the evil one); (2) the flesh (the scorching sun — tribulation or persecution); and (3) the world (the thorns — cares of the world and the delight in riches).

Finally the disciples are given a vision as to the tremendous returns from investing in human personality. Thirtyfold is 3,000 percent return, sixtyfold is 6,000 percent return, and one hundredfold is 10,000 percent return on the investment. There is actually no way of measuring the results of a single case of genuine conversion. An obscure Sunday school teacher invested in Dwight L. Moody. Moody won others. They in turn won others. The Sunday school teacher started a chain reaction that will never stop.

D. The Parable of the Wheat and Tares (13:24–30)

The preceding parable was a vivid illustration of the fact that the kingdom of heaven includes those who give only lip service to the King as well as those who are His genuine disciples. The first three soils typify the kingdom in its widest circle — outward profession. The fourth soil represents the kingdom as a smaller circle — those who have been truly converted.

13:24–26 The second **parable** — the wheat and the tares — also sets forth the kingdom in these two aspects. The wheat depicts true believers, the tares are mere professors. Jesus compares **the kingdom** to **a man who sowed good seed in his field; but while men slept, his enemy came and sowed tares among the wheat**. Unger says that the most common tare found in grainfields in the Holy Land is bearded darnel, "a poisonous grass, almost indistinguishable from wheat while the two are growing into blade. But when they come into ear, they can be separated without difficulty."[28]

13:27, 28 When **the servants** saw the tares mixed in with the grain, they asked the householder how this happened. He immediately recognized it as the work of **an enemy. The servants** were ready to pull the weeds immediately.

13:29, 30 But the farmer ordered them to wait **until the harvest.** Then reapers would separate the two. The grain would be gathered into barns and the darnel would be burned.

Why did the farmer order this delay in separation? In nature the roots of the grain and darnel are so intertwined that it is virtually impossible to pull up one without the other.

This parable is explained by our Lord in verses 37–43, so we will forego further comment till then.

E. The Parable of the Mustard Seed (13:31, 32)

Next the Savior likens **the kingdom** to **a mustard seed** which He called the smallest of **seeds**, that is, smallest in the experience of His listeners. When a man planted one of these seeds, it grew into **a tree**, a growth that is phenomenal. The normal mustard plant is more like a bush than a tree. The **tree** was large enough for **birds** to **nest in its branches**

The seed represents the humble beginning of the kingdom. At first the kingdom was kept relatively small and pure as a result of persecution. But with the patronage and protection of the state, it suffered abnormal growth. Then the birds came and roosted in it. The same word for birds is used here as in verse 4; Jesus explained the birds as meaning the evil one (v. 19). The kingdom became a nesting place for Satan and his agents. Today the umbrella of Christendom covers such Christ-denying systems as Unitarianism, Christian Science, Mormonism, Jehovah's Witnesses, and the Unification Church (Moonies).

So here the Lord forewarned the disciples that during His absence the kingdom would experience a phenomenal growth. They should not be deceived nor equate growth with success. It would be unhealthy growth. Though the tiny seed would become an abnormal tree, its largeness would become "a dwelling place of demons, a prison for every foul spirit, and a cage for every unclean and hated bird" (Rev. 18:2).

F. The Parable of the Leaven (13:33)

Next the Lord Jesus compared **the kingdom** to **leaven which a woman hid in three measures of meal**. Eventually **all** the meal became **leavened**. A common interpretation is that the meal is the world and the leaven is the gospel which will be preached throughout the world until everyone becomes saved. This view, however, is contradicted by Scripture, by history, and by current events.

Leaven is always a type of evil in the Bible. When God commanded His people to rid their houses of leaven (Ex. 12:15), they understood this. If anyone ate what was leavened from the first till the seventh day of this Feast of Unleavened Bread, he would be cut off from Israel. Jesus warned against the leaven of the Pharisees and Sadducees (Matt. 16:6, 12) and the leaven of Herod (Mark 8:15).

In 1 Corinthians 5:6–8 leaven is defined as malice and evil, and the context of Galatians 5:9 shows that *there* it means false teaching. In general, leaven means either evil doctrine or evil behavior.

So in this parable the Lord warns against the permeating power of evil working in **the kingdom of heaven**. The parable of the mustard seed shows evil in the external character of the kingdom; this parable shows the inward corruption that would take place.

We believe that in this parable the **meal** represents the food of God's people as it is found in the Bible. The **leaven** is evil doctrine. **The woman** is a false prophetess who teaches and beguiles (Rev. 2:20). Is it not significant that women have been the founders of several false cults? Forbidden by the Bible to teach in the church (1 Cor. 14:34; 1 Tim. 2:12), some have defiantly taken the place of doctrinal authorities and have adulterated the food of God's people with destructive heresies.

J. H. Brookes says:

> If the objection is raised that Christ would not liken the kingdom of heaven to that which is evil, it is sufficient to reply that He likens the kingdom to that which includes both tares and wheat, which encloses both good and bad fish, which extends over a wicked servant (Matt. xviii 23–32), which admits into it a man who had not on a wedding garment, and who was lost (Matt. xxii 1–13).[29]

G. The Use of Parables Fulfills Prophecy (13:34, 35)†

Jesus spoke the first four parables **to the multitude**. The use of this teaching method by the Lord fulfilled Asaph's prophecy in Psalm 78:2 that the Messiah would speak **in parables**, uttering **things kept secret from the foundation of the world**. These features of the kingdom of heaven in its interim form, hidden until this time, were now being made known.

H. Explanation of the Parable of the Tares (13:36–43)

13:36 The remainder of the Lord's discourse was spoken to the disciples, inside **the house**. Here **the disciples** may represent the believing remnant of the nation of Israel. The renewed mention of

†See p. xx.

the house reminds us that God has not rejected forever His people whom He foreknew (Rom. 11:2).

13:37 In His interpretation of the wheat and tares parable, Jesus identified Himself as the sower. He sowed directly during His earthly ministry, and has been sowing through His servants in succeeding ages.

13:38 The field is the world. It is important to emphasize that the field is the world, *not the church*. The **good seeds** mean **the sons of the kingdom**. It might seem bizarre and incongruous to think of living human beings being planted into the ground. But the point is that these sons of the kingdom were sown in the world. During His years of public ministry, Jesus sowed the world with disciples who were loyal subjects of the kingdom. **The tares are the sons of the wicked one**. Satan has a counterfeit for every divine reality. He sows the world with those who look like, talk like, and, to some extent, walk like disciples. But they are not genuine followers of the King.

13:39 The enemy is Satan, the enemy of God and all the people of God. **The harvest is the end of the age**, the end of the kingdom age in its interim form, which will be when Jesus Christ returns in power and glory to reign as King. The Lord is not referring to the end of the church age; it leads only to confusion to introduce the church here.

13:40–42 The reapers are the angels (see Rev. 14:14–20). During the present phase of the kingdom, no forcible separation is made of the wheat and the darnel. They are allowed to grow together. But at the Second Advent of Christ, the angels will round up all causes of sin and all evildoers and throw **them into the furnace of fire**, where they will weep and gnash their teeth.

13:43 The righteous subjects of the kingdom who are on earth during the Tribulation will enter **the kingdom of their Father** to enjoy the Millennial Reign of Christ. There they **will shine forth as the sun**; that is, they will be resplendent in glory.

Again Jesus adds the cryptic admonition, "**He who has ears to hear, let him hear!**"

This parable does not justify, as some mistakenly suppose, the toleration of ungodly people in a local Christian church. Remember that the field is the world, not the church. Local churches are explicitly commanded to put out of their fellowship all who are guilty of certain forms of wickedness (1 Cor. 5:9–13). The parable simply teaches that in its mystery form, the kingdom of heaven will include the real and the imitation, the genuine and the counterfeit, and that this condition will continue until the end of the age. Then God's messengers will separate the false, who will be taken away in judgment, from the true, who will enjoy the glorious reign of Christ on earth.

I. The Parable of the Hidden Treasure (13:44)

All the parables so far have taught that there will be good and evil in the kingdom, righteous and unrighteous subjects. The next two parables show that there will be two classes of the righteous subjects: (1) believing Jews during the periods before and after the Church Age; (2) believing Jews and Gentiles during the present age.

In the parable of the **treasure**, Jesus compares **the kingdom** to **treasure hidden in a field. A man** finds it, covers it up, then gladly **sells all he has and buys that field**.

We would suggest that the **man** is the Lord Jesus Himself. (He was the man in the parable of the wheat and tares, v. 37.) The **treasure** represents a godly remnant of believing Jews such as existed during Jesus' earthly ministry and will exist again after the church is raptured (see Psalm 135:4 where Israel is called God's peculiar treasure). They are hidden in the field in that they are dispersed throughout the world and in a real sense unknown to any but God. Jesus is pictured as discovering this treasure, then going to the cross and giving all that He had in order to buy the world (2 Cor. 5:19; 1 Jn. 2:2) where the treasure was hidden. Redeemed Israel will be brought out of hiding when her Deliverer comes out of Zion and sets up the long-awaited Messianic Kingdom.

The parable is sometimes applied to a sinner, giving up all in order to find Christ, the greatest Treasure. But this interpretation violates the doctrine of grace which insists that salvation is without price (Isa. 55:1; Eph. 2:8, 9).

J. The Parable of the Pearl of Great Price (13:45, 46)

The kingdom is also likened to **a merchant seeking beautiful pearls**. When he finds a pearl of unusually **great** value, he sacrifices all he has to buy it.

In a hymn that says, "I've found the Pearl of greatest price," the finder is the sinner and the Pearl is the Savior. But again we protest that the sinner does not have to sell all and does not have to buy Christ.

We rather believe that the **merchant** is the Lord Jesus. The **pearl of great price** is the church. At Calvary He sold all that He had to buy this pearl. Just as a pearl is formed inside an oyster through suffering caused by irritation, so the church was formed through the piercing and wounding of the body of the Savior.

It is interesting that in the parable of the treasure, the kingdom is likened to the treasure itself. Here the kingdom is not likened to the pearl but to the merchantman. Why this difference?

In the preceding parable, the emphasis is on the treasure — redeemed Israel. The kingdom is closely linked with the nation of Israel. It was originally offered to that nation and, in its future form, the Jewish people will be its principal subjects.

As we have mentioned, the church is not the same as the kingdom. All who are in the church are in the kingdom in its interim form, but not all who are in the kingdom are in the church. *The church will not be in the kingdom in its future form but will reign with Christ over the renewed earth.* The emphasis in the second parable is on the King Himself and the tremendous price He paid to woo and win a bride that would share His glory in the day of His manifestation.

As the pearl comes out of the sea, so the church, sometimes called the Gentile bride of Christ, comes largely from the nations. This does not overlook the fact that there are converted Israelites in it, but merely states that the dominant feature of the church is that it is a people called out from the nations for His

Name. In Acts 15:14 James confirmed this as being the grand purpose of God at the present time.

K. The Parable of the Dragnet (13:47–50)

13:47, 48 The final parable in the series likens **the kingdom** to a sieve or **dragnet that was cast into the sea and gathered** fish **of every kind**. The fishermen sorted out the fish, keeping **the good** in containers and discarding **the bad**.

13:49, 50 Our Lord interprets the parable. The time is **the end of the age**; that is, the end of the Tribulation period. It is the time of the Second Advent of Christ. The fishermen are **the angels.** The good fish are the righteous; that is, saved people, both Jews and Gentiles. The bad fish are the unrighteous; namely, unbelieving people of all races. A separation takes place, as we also saw in the parable of the wheat and tares (vv. 30, 39–43). The righteous enter the kingdom of their Father, whereas the unrighteous are consigned to a place of fire where there is **wailing and gnashing of teeth**. This is not the final judgment, however; this judgment takes place at the outset of the Millennium; the final judgment occurs after the thousand years are finished (Rev. 20:7–15).

Gaebelein comments on this parable as follows:

> The dragnet is let into the sea, which, as we have seen before, represents the nations. The parable refers to the preaching of the everlasting gospel as it will take place during the great tribulation (Rev. 14:6, 7). The separating of the good and bad is done by angels. All this cannot refer to the present time nor to the church, but to the time when the kingdom is about to be set up. The angels will be used, as is so clearly seen in the book of Revelation. The wicked will be cast into the furnace of fire and the righteous will remain in the earth for the millennial kingdom.[30]

L. The Treasury of Truth (13:51, 52)

13:51 When He had finished the parables, the Master Teacher asked His disciples if they **understood**. They replied, **"Yes."** This may surprise us, or even make us slightly jealous of them.

Perhaps we cannot answer "yes" so confidently.

13:52 Because they understood, they were obligated to share with others. Disciples are to be channels, not terminals of blessings. The twelve were now scribes trained for the **kingdom of heaven**; that is, teachers and interpreters of the truth. They were **like a householder who brings out of his treasure things new and old**. In the OT they had a rich deposit of what we might call **old** truth. In the parabolic teaching of Christ, they had just received what was completely **new**. From this vast storehouse of knowledge they should now impart the glorious truth to others.

M. Jesus Is Rejected at Nazareth (13:53–58)

13:53–56 Having **finished these parables**, Jesus left the shores of Galilee and went to Nazareth for His last visit there. As **He taught them in their synagogue**, the people **were astonished** at His **wisdom** and His reported miracles. To them He was only **the carpenter's son**. They knew **His mother** was **Mary . . . and His brothers James, Joses, Simon, and Judas . . . and His sisters** — they were still living there in Nazareth! How could one of their own hometown boys say and do the things for which He had become so well known? This puzzled them, and they found it easier to cling to their ignorance than to acknowledge the truth.

13:57, 58 They were offended at Him. This prompted **Jesus** to point out that a genuine **prophet is** generally more appreciated away from home. His own district and His own relatives allowed their familiarity to breed contempt. Unbelief largely hindered the Savior's work in Nazareth. He healed only a few sick folk there (cf. Mark 6:5). It was not because He *could* not do the works; man's wickedness cannot restrain God's power. But He would have been blessing people where there was no desire for blessing, filling needs where there was no consciousness of need, healing people who would have resented being told they were sick.

IX. THE MESSIAH'S UNWEARIED GRACE MET BY MOUNTING HOSTILITY (14:1–16:12)

A. John the Baptist Beheaded (14:1–12)

14:1, 2 News of Jesus' ministry flowed back to **Herod the tetrarch**. This infamous son of Herod the Great was also known as Herod Antipas. It was he who had ordered the execution of John the Baptist. When he heard of Christ's miracles, his conscience began to stab him. The memory of the prophet whom he had beheaded kept coming before him. He told his servants, "It's **John**. He has come back **from the dead**. That explains these miracles."

14:3 In verses 3–12 we have what is known as a literary flashback. Matthew interrupts the narrative to review the circumstances surrounding the death of John.

14:4, 5 Herod had abandoned his wife and had been living in an adulterous, incestuous relationship with **Herodias, his brother Philip's wife**. As a prophet of God, John could not let this pass without rebuke. Indignantly and fearlessly, he pointed his finger at Herod and denounced him for his immorality.

The king was angry enough to kill him but it was not politically expedient. The people acclaimed John **as a prophet**, and would have reacted, perhaps violently, against John's execution. So the tyrant satisfied his rage momentarily by having the Baptizer imprisoned. "The ungodly like religion in the same way that they like lions, either dead or behind bars; they fear religion when it breaks loose and begins to challenge their consciences."[31]

14:6–11 On **Herod's birthday, the daughter of Herodias** so pleased the king by her dancing that he impetuously offered her anything she wanted. Prompted by her wanton mother, she brazenly asked for **John the Baptist's head . . . on a platter!** By now the king's wrath against John had somewhat subsided; perhaps he even admired the prophet for his courage and integrity. But although he was sorry, he felt he had to fulfill his promise. The order was given. John was **beheaded** and the gruesome request of the dancing girl was granted.

14:12 John's **disciples** gave their master's **body** a respectful burial, then **went and told Jesus**. They could not have gone to anyone better to pour out their grief and indignation. Nor could they have left us a better example. In times of persecution, oppression, suffering, and sorrow, we too should go and *tell it to Jesus*.

As for Herod, his crime was finished but the memory lingered on. When he heard of Jesus' activites, the entire episode returned to haunt him.

B. Feeding of the Five Thousand (14:13–21)

14:13, 14 When Jesus heard that Herod was troubled by reports of His miracles, He withdrew **by boat to a** secluded area by the Sea of Galilee. We can be sure He did not go because of fear; He knew that nothing could happen to Him before His time had come. We do not know the main reason for His move, but a lesser reason was that His disciples had just returned from their preaching mission (Mark 6:30; Luke 9:10) and needed a time of rest and quietness.

However, the crowds flocked from the towns and **followed Him on foot**. As He went ashore, they were waiting for Him. Far from being irritated by this intrusion, our compassionate Lord set to work immediately **and healed their sick**.

14:15 When **evening** came, that is, after 3:00 p.m., **His disciples** felt that a crisis was brewing. So many people, and nothing for them to eat! They asked Jesus to send the people **into the villages** where they could get **food**. How little they understood the heart of Christ or discerned His power!

14:16–18 The Lord assured them that there was no **need**. Why should the people leave the One who opens His hand and supplies the desire of every living thing? Then He caught the disciples off guard by saying, **"You give them something to eat."** They were staggered. "Give them something to eat? We have nothing but **five loaves and two fish**." They had forgotten that they also had Jesus. Patiently the Savior said, **"Bring**

them here to Me." That was their part.

14:19–21 We can picture the Lord directing **the multitudes to sit down on the grass**. Taking **the five loaves and the two fish**, He gave thanks, **broke** the loaves, and **gave** them **to the disciples** for distribution. There was plenty for all. When **all** were satisfied, the disciples gathered **twelve baskets** of leftovers. There was more left over when Jesus finished than when He began. Ironically enough there was a basket for each unbelieving disciple. And a multitude of perhaps 10,000 to 15,000 had been fed (5,000 men plus women and children).

The miracle is a spiritual lesson for disciples of every generation. The hungry multitude is always present. There is always a little band of disciples with seemingly pitiful resources. And always there is the compassionate Savior. When disciples are willing to give Him their little all, He multiplies it to feed thousands. The notable difference is that the **five thousand men** who were fed by Galilee had their hunger satisfied only for a short time; those today who feed upon the living Christ are satisfied forever (see John 6:35).

C. Jesus Walks on the Sea (14:22–33)

The previous miracle assured the disciples that they were following One who could abundantly provide for their needs. Now they learn that this One can protect and empower them as well.

14:22, 23 While He was dismissing the multitude, **Jesus** told the **disciples** to **get into the boat** and start back **to the other side** of the lake. Then He went up on a hillside **to pray. When evening came**, i.e., after sunset, **He was alone there**. (In Jewish reckoning there were two "evenings," see Ex. 12:6 RSV margin. One, referred to in v. 15, began in mid-afternoon, and the other, referred to here, at sunset.)

14:24–27 Meanwhile, **the boat was now far** from land and battling a **contrary** wind. As the waves battered the boat, Jesus saw the disciples' plight. **In the fourth watch of the night** (between 3:00 and 6:00 a.m.), He **went to them walking on the sea**. Thinking it was **a ghost** the disciples panicked. But immediately they heard the reassuring voice of their Master and Friend, **"Be of good cheer! It is I; do not be afraid."**

How true to our own experience! We are often storm-tossed, perplexed, in despair. The Savior seems far away. But all the time He is praying for us. When the night seems darkest, He is near at hand. We often mistake Him even then and push the panic button. Then we hear His comforting voice and remember that the waves that caused us to fear are under His feet.

14:28 When **Peter** heard the well-known, well-loved voice, his affection and enthusiasm bubbled over. **"Lord, if it is You, command me to come to You on the water."** Rather than magnify Peter's "if" as a sign of small faith, we should see his bold request as a mark of great trust. Peter sensed that Jesus' commands are His enablements, that He gives strength for whatever He orders.

14:29-33 As soon as Jesus **said, "Come,". . . Peter** jumped out of the boat and began walking toward Him. As long as he kept his eyes on Jesus, he was able to do the impossible; but the minute he became occupied with **the** strong **wind**, he began to sink. Frantically he cried, **"Lord, save me!"** The Lord took him by the hand, gently rebuked his **little faith**, and brought him to the boat. As soon as Jesus went on board, **the wind ceased.** A worship meeting took place in the boat with the disciples saying to Jesus, **"Truly You are the Son of God."**

The Christian life, like walking on water, is humanly impossible. It can only be lived by the power of the Holy Spirit. As long as we look away from every other object to Jesus only (Heb. 12:2), we can experience a supernatural life. But the minute we become occupied with ourselves or our circumstances, we begin to sink. Then we must cry to Christ for restoration and divine enablement.

D. Jesus Heals in Gennesaret (14:34–36)

The boat docked at **Gennesaret**, on the northwest shore of the Sea of Galilee. As soon as the men spotted Jesus, they scoured the area for **all who were sick** and **brought** them **to Him** that the sick **might only touch the hem of His garment; as many** who did **were made perfectly well.** And so the doctors in that area had a holiday. For a while, at least, there were no sick people. The district experienced health and healing through a visit by the Great Physician.

E. Defilement Is From Within (15:1–20)

It is often pointed out that Matthew does not follow a chronological order during the early chapters. But from the beginning of chapter 14 to the end, events are largely given in the sequence in which they occurred.

In chapter 15 a dispensational order also emerges. First, the continued haggling and bickering of the Pharisees and scribes (vv. 1–20) anticipates Israel's rejection of the Messiah. Second, the faith of the Canaanite woman (vv. 21–28) pictures the gospel going out to the Gentiles in this present age. And finally the healing of great crowds (vv. 29–31) and the feeding of 4,000 (vv. 32–39) point to the future millennial age with its worldwide health and prosperity.

15:1, 2 The scribes and Pharisees were unrelenting in their efforts to trap the Savior. A delegation of them came **from Jerusalem**, charging His **disciples** with uncleanness for eating with **their hands** unwashed, therefore violating **the tradition of the elders**.

In order to appreciate this incident, we must understand the references to clean and unclean, and must know what the Pharisees meant by washing. The whole conception of clean and unclean goes back to the OT. The uncleanness with which the disciples were charged was entirely a ceremonial matter. If a person touched a dead body, for instance, or if he ate certain things, he contracted ceremonial defilement — he was not ritually fit to worship God. Before he could approach God, the law of God required him to go through a cleansing ritual.

But the elders had added tradition to the cleansing rituals. They insisted, for instance, that before a Jew ate, he should put his hands through an elaborate cleansing process, washing not just the hands, but also the arms up to the elbows. If he had been in the marketplace, he was supposed to take a ceremonial bath. Thus, the Pharisees criticized the disciples for failing to observe the intricacies of the washings prescribed by Jewish tradition.

15:3–6 The Lord Jesus reminded His critics that *they* transgressed **the commandment of God**, not simply **the tradition** of the elders. The law commanded men to **honor** their parents, including supporting them financially if necessary. But the scribes and Pharisees (and many others) did not want to spend money for the support of their aged parents. So they devised a tradition by which to avoid their responsibility. When asked for help by **father or mother**, all they had to do was recite such words as these: "Any money which I have and which could be used to support you has been dedicated **to God**, and therefore I cannot give it to you," and having recited this formula, they were free from financial responsibility to their parents. Following this devious tradition they had thus nullified the Word **of God** which commanded them to care for their parents.

15:7–9 By their crafty twisting of words they fulfilled the prophecy of **Isaiah** 29:13. They professed to **honor** God **with their lips, but their heart** was **far from** Him. Their worship was worthless because they were giving higher priority to the traditions of men than to the Word of God.

15:10, 11 Turning to **the multitude**, Jesus made a pronouncement of tremendous significance. He declared that **not what goes into the mouth defiles a man, but** rather **what comes out**. We can scarcely appreciate the revolutionary character of this statement. Under the Levitical code, what went into the mouth *did* defile a man. The Jews were forbidden to eat the meat of any animal which did not chew the cud and have cloven hooves. They were not allowed to eat a fish unless it had scales and fins. Minute instructions were given by God as to foods that were clean or unclean.

Now the Law-giver paved the way for the abrogation of the whole system of ceremonial defilement. He said that the food which His disciples ate with unwashed hands did not defile them. But the hypocrisy of the scribes and Pharisees — that was truly defiling.

15:12–14 When **His disciples** brought word **that the Pharisees were offended** by this denunciation, Jesus answered by comparing them to plants which had not been divinely planted. They were tares rather than wheat. They and their teachings would eventually be rooted up; that is, destroyed. Then He added, **"Let them alone. They are blind leaders of the blind."** Though professing to be authorities in spiritual matters, they were **blind** to spiritual realities as were the people they were leading. It was inevitable that **both** leaders and followers would **fall into a ditch**.

15:15 The disciples were undoubtedly shaken by this complete reversal of all they had been taught about clean and unclean foods. It was like a **parable** to them, i.e., an obscure, veiled narrative. **Peter** verbalized their unsettlement when he asked for an explanation.

15:16, 17 The Lord first expressed wonder that they were so slow to understand, then explained that true defilement is moral, not physical. Edible foods are not intrinsically clean or unclean. In fact, no material thing is evil in itself; it is the abuse of a thing that is wrong. The food man eats **enters the mouth, goes into the stomach** for digestion, then the unassimilated residue **is eliminated**. His moral being is not affected — only his body. Today we know that "every creature of God is good, and nothing is to be refused if it is received with thanksgiving; for it is sanctified by the word of God and prayer" (1 Tim. 4:4, 5). The passage is not speaking of poisonous plants, of course, but of foods designed by God for human consumption. All are good and should be eaten thankfully. If a person is allergic to some, or cannot tolerate others, he shouldn't eat them, but in general we can eat with the assurance that God uses food to nourish us physically.

15:18 If food doesn't defile, then *what does*? Jesus answered, **". . . those things which proceed out of the mouth come from the heart, and they defile a man."** Here **the heart** is not the organ that pumps blood, but the corrupt source of human motives and desires. This part of man's moral nature manifests itself by impure thoughts, then by depraved words, then by evil acts.

15:19, 20 Some of the things that

defile a man are **evil thoughts, murders, adulteries, fornications, thefts, false witness,** and **blasphemies,** (this Greek word includes slander of others).

The Pharisees and scribes were extremely careful concerning the ostentatious, punctilious observance of hand-washing ceremonies. But their inner lives were polluted. They majored in minors and overlooked the matters of real importance. They could criticize the disciples' failure to keep uninspired traditions, yet plot to kill the Son of God and be guilty of the whole catalog of sin listed in verse 19.

F. A Gentile Is Blessed For Her Faith (15:21-28)

15:21, 22 Jesus withdrew **to the region of Tyre and Sidon,** on the Mediterranean coast. As far as we know, this was the only time during His public ministry that He was outside Jewish territory. Here in Phoenicia, a Canaanite woman asked Him to heal her **daughter** who was **demon-possessed.**

It is important to realize that this woman was not a Jewess, but a Gentile. She was descended from the Canaanites, an immoral race which God had marked for extinction. Through Israel's disobedience, some had survived the invasion of Canaan under Joshua, and this woman was a descendant of the survivors. As a Gentile, she did not enjoy the privileges of God's chosen earthly people. She was an alien, having no hope. Positionally she had no claim on God or the Messiah.

Speaking to Jesus, she addressed Him as the **Lord,** the **Son of David,** a title which the Jews used in speaking of the Messiah. Although Jesus *was* the **Son of David,** a Gentile had no right to approach Him on that basis. That is why He did not answer her at first.

15:23 His disciples came and urged Him to **send her away;** to them she was a nuisance. To Him she was a welcome example of faith and a vessel in whom His grace would shine. But first He must prove and educate her faith!

15:24, 25 He reminded her that His mission was to the **lost sheep of the house of Israel,** not to Gentiles, and certainly not to Canaanites. She was undismayed by this apparent refusal. Dropping the title, *Son of David,* she

worshiped Him, saying, **"Lord, help me!"** If she couldn't come to Him as a Jew to her Messiah, she would come as a creature to her Creator.

15:26 To further probe the reality of her faith, Jesus told her that it was **not good** for Him to turn aside from feeding the Jewish children in order to give bread to Gentile **dogs.** If this sounds harsh to us, we should remember that, like the surgeon's scalpel, it was not intended to hurt but to heal. She *was* a Gentile. The Jews looked upon the Gentiles as scavenging dogs, prowling the streets for scraps of food. However, Jesus here used the word for **little** pet **dogs.** The question was, "Would she acknowledge her unworthiness to receive the least of His mercies?"

15:27 Her reply was magnificent. She agreed with His description completely. Taking the place of an unworthy Gentile, she cast herself on His mercy, love, and grace. She said, in effect, "You are right! I am only one of the **little dogs** under the table. But I notice that **crumbs** sometimes **fall from** the **table** to the floor. Won't You let me have some crumbs? I am not worthy that You should heal my daughter, but I beseech You to do it for one of Your undeserving creatures."

15:28 Jesus commended her for her **great faith.** While the unbelieving children had no hunger for the bread, here was a self-confessed "doggie" crying out for it. Faith was rewarded; her daughter was **healed** instantly. The fact that our Lord healed this Gentile daughter at a distance suggests His present ministry at God's right hand, bestowing spiritual healing on Gentiles during this age when His ancient people are set aside nationally.

G. Jesus Heals Great Multitudes (15:29-31)

In Mark 7:31 we learn that the Lord left Tyre, traveled north to Sidon, then eastward across the Jordan, south through the region of the Decapolis. There, near the Sea of Galilee,† He healed **the lame,** the **blind,** the **mute,** the **maimed,** and many others. The astonished crowd **glorified the God of Israel.** The presumption is strong that this was a Gentile neighborhood. The people, associating

†*See p. xiv.*

Jesus and His disciples with Israel, correctly deduced that **the God of Israel** was working in their midst.

H. Feeding of the Four Thousand (15:32–39)

15:32 Careless (or critical) readers, confusing this incident with the feeding of the 5,000, have accused the Bible of duplication, contradiction, and miscalculation. The fact is that the two incidents are quite distinct, and supplement rather than contradict each other.

After three days with the Lord, **the multitude** had run out of food. He would not let them go away hungry; they might collapse **on the way**.

15:33, 34 Again **His disciples** became frustrated at the impossible task of feeding such a mob; this time they had only **seven** loaves **and a few little fish**.

15:35, 36 As in the case of the 5,000, Jesus seated the people, **gave thanks, broke** the loaves and fish **and gave them to His disciples** for distribution. He expects His disciples to do what they can; then He steps in and does what they can't.

15:37–39 After the people **were filled**, there were **seven large baskets** of surplus food. The number fed was **four thousand men, besides women and children**.

In the next chapter, we shall see that the statistics relating to the two feeding miracles are significant (16:8–12). Every detail of the Bible narrative is charged with meaning. After dismissing the crowd, our Lord went by **boat** to **Magdala**, on the west shore of the Sea of Galilee.

I. The Leaven of the Pharisees and Sadducees (16:1–12)

16:1 The Pharisees and Sadducees, traditional antagonists in theological matters, represented two doctrinal extremes. But their hostility gave way to cooperation as they united in a common aim to trip up the Savior. To test Him they **asked** Him to demonstrate **a sign from heaven**. In some way not clear to us, they were trying to inveigle Him into a compromising position. In asking for **a sign from heaven**, perhaps they were implying an opposite source for His previous miracles. Or perhaps they wanted

some supernatural sign in the sky. All Jesus' miracles had been performed on the earth. Could He do celestial miracles as well?

16:2, 3 He answered by continuing the theme of **the sky**. When they saw a **red** sky in the **evening**, they forecast **fair weather** for the next day. They also knew that a **red, threatening** sky **in the morning** meant storms for that day.[32] They had expertise in interpreting the appearance of the sky, but they could not interpret **the signs of the times**.

What were these **signs**? The prophet who heralded the advent of the Messiah had appeared in the person of John the Baptist. The miracles prophesied of the Messiah — things no other man had ever done — had been performed in their presence. Another sign of the times was the obvious rejection of the Messiah by the Jews and the movement of the gospel to the Gentiles, all in fulfillment of prophecy. Yet in spite of this incontrovertible evidence, they had no sense of history being made or of prophecy being fulfilled.

16:4 In seeking for a sign when He Himself stood in their midst, the Pharisees and Sadducees exposed themselves as an evil, spiritually **adulterous generation. No sign** would now **be given to** them **except the sign of the prophet Jonah**. As explained in the notes on 12:39, this would be the resurrection of Christ on the third day. **A wicked and adulterous generation** would crucify its Messiah, but God would raise Him from the dead. This would be a sign of the doom of all who refuse to bow to Him as rightful Ruler.

The paragraph closes with the ominous words, **"And He left them and departed."** The spiritual implications of the words should be obvious to all.

16:5, 6 When **His disciples** rejoined the Lord on **the** east **side** of the lake, **they had forgotten to take** food with them. Therefore when Jesus greeted them with a warning to **beware of the leaven of the Pharisees and the Sadducees**, they thought He was saying, "Don't go to those Jewish leaders for food supplies!" Their preoccupation with food caused them to look for a literal, natural explanation where a spiritual lesson was intended.

16:7–10 They were still worrying about a food shortage in spite of the fact that He who fed the 5,000 and the 4,000 was with them. So He reviewed the two miraculous feedings with them. The lesson that emerged concerned divine arithmetic and divine resourcefulness, for *the less Jesus had to work with, the more He fed, and the more food there was left over*. When there were only five loaves and two fish, He fed 5,000 plus and had twelve baskets of food left. With more loaves and fish, He fed only 4,000 plus and had left over only seven basketfuls. If we put our limited resources at His disposal, He can multiply them in inverse proportion to their amount. "Little is much if God is in it."

A different word is used for **baskets**[33] here than in the feeding of the 5,000. The seven baskets in this incident are considered to have been larger than the twelve on the previous occasion. But the underlying lesson remains: Why worry about hunger and want when we are linked with One who has infinite power and resources?

16:11, 12 In speaking of **the leaven of the Pharisees and Sadducees**, the Lord had not referred to bread but to evil doctrine and conduct. In Luke 12:1 the leaven of the Pharisees is defined as hypocrisy. They professed to adhere to the Word of God in minutest details, yet their obedience was external and shallow. Inwardly they were evil and corrupt.

The leaven of **the Sadducees** was rationalism. The freethinkers of their day, they, like the liberals of today, had built a system of doubts and denials. They denied the existence of angels and spirits, the resurrection of the body, the immortality of the soul, and eternal punishment. This leaven of skepticism, if tolerated, will spread and permeate like yeast in meal.

X. THE KING PREPARES HIS DISCIPLES (16:13–17:27)

A. Peter's Great Confession (16:13–20)

16:13, 14 Caesarea Philippi was about twenty-five miles north of the Sea of Galilee and five miles east of the Jordan. When Jesus came to the surrounding villages (Mark 8:27), an incident generally recognized as the apex of His teaching ministry occurred. Up to this time He had been leading His disciples to a true apprehension of His Person. Having succeeded in this, He now turns His face resolutely to go to the cross.

He began by asking **His disciples** what men were saying as to His identity. The replies ran the gamut from **John the Baptist**, to **Elijah**, to **Jeremiah**, to **one of the** other **prophets**. To the average person He was one among many. Good but not the Best. Great but not the Greatest. A prophet but not *the* Prophet. This view would never do. It condemned Him with faint praise. If He were only another man He was a fraud because He claimed to be equal with God the Father.

16:15, 16 So He asked the disciples **who** they believed He was. This brought from **Simon Peter** the historic confession, **"You are the Christ, the Son of the living God."** In other words, He was Israel's Messiah and God the Son.

16:17, 18 Our Lord pronounced a blessing on **Simon**, son of **Jonah**. The fisherman had not arrived at this concept of the Lord Jesus through intellect or native wisdom; it had been supernaturally **revealed** to him by God the **Father**. But the Son had something important to say to Peter also. So Jesus added, **"And I also say to you that you are Peter, and on this rock I will build My church, and the gates of Hades shall not prevail against it."** We all know that more controversy has swirled around this verse than almost any other verse in the Gospel. The question is, "Who or what is the **rock?**" Part of the problem arises from the fact that the Greek words for Peter and for rock are similar, but the meanings are different. The first, *petros*, means a stone or loose rock; the second, *petra*, means rock, such as a rocky ledge. So what Jesus really said was " . . . **you are Peter** (stone), **and on this rock I will build My church.**" He did not say He would build His church on a stone but on a rock.

If Peter is not the rock, then what is? If we stick to the context, the obvious answer is that the rock is Peter's confession that Christ is the Son of the living God, the truth on which the church is founded. Ephesians 2:20 teaches that the church is built on Jesus Christ, the chief cornerstone. Its statement that we are built upon the foundation of the apostles and prophets refers not to them, but to the foundation laid in their teachings concerning the Lord Jesus Christ.

Christ is spoken of as a Rock in 1 Corinthians 10:4. In this connection, Morgan gives a helpful reminder:

Remember, He was talking to Jews. If we trace the figurative use of the word rock through Hebrew Scriptures, we find that it is never used symbolically of man, but always of God. So here at Caesarea Philippi, it is not upon Peter that the Church is built. Jesus did not trifle with figures of speech. He took up their old Hebrew illustration — rock, always the symbol of Deity — and said, "Upon God Himself —Christ, the Son of the living God — I will build my church."[34]

Peter never spoke of himself as the foundation of the church. Twice he referred to Christ as a Stone (Acts 4:11, 12; 1 Pet. 2:4–8), but then the figure is different; the stone is the head of the corner, not the foundation.

"I will build My church." Here we have the first mention of the **church** in the Bible. It did not exist in the OT. The church, still future when Jesus spoke these words, was formed on the Day of Pentecost and is composed of all true believers in Christ, both Jew and Gentile. A distinct society known as the body and bride of Christ, it has a unique heavenly calling and destiny.

We would scarcely expect the church to be introduced in Matthew's Gospel where Israel and the kingdom are the prominent themes. However, consequent to Israel's rejection of Christ, a parenthetical period — the church age — follows and will continue to the Rapture. Then God will resume His dealings with Israel nationally. So it is fitting that God should introduce the church here as the next step in His dispensational program after Israel's rejection.

"The gates of Hades shall not prevail against it" may be understood in two ways. First **the gates of Hades** are pictured in an unsuccessful offensive against the church — the church will survive all attacks upon it. Or the church itself may be pictured as taking the offensive and coming off the victor. In either case, the powers of death will be defeated by the translation of living believers and by the resurrection of the dead in Christ.

16:19 "I will give you the keys of the kingdom of heaven" does not mean that Peter was given authority to admit men to heaven. This has to do with the **kingdom of heaven** *on earth* — the sphere containing all who profess allegiance to the King, all who claim to be Christians. **Keys** speak of access or entrance. The keys which open the door to the sphere of profession are suggested in the Great Commission (Matt. 28:19) — discipling, baptizing, and teaching. (Baptism is not necessary for salvation but is the initiatory rite by which men publicly profess allegiance to the King.) Peter first used the keys on the Day of Pentecost. They were not given to him exclusively, but as a representative of all the disciples. (See Matt. 18:18 where the same promise is given to them all.)

"Whatever you bind on earth will be bound in heaven, and whatever you loose on earth will be loosed in heaven." This and a companion passage in John 20:23 are sometimes used to teach that Peter and his supposed successors were given the authority to forgive sins. We know that this cannot be so; only God can forgive sins.

There are two ways of understanding the verse. First, it may mean that the apostles had power to bind and to loose that we do not have today. For example, Peter bound their sins on Ananias and Sapphira so that they were punished with instant death (Acts 5:1–10), while Paul loosed the disciplined man in Corinth from the consequences of his sin because the man had repented (2 Cor. 2:10).

Or the verse may mean that whatever the apostles bound or loosed on earth must have *already* been bound or loosed in heaven (see NKJV margin). Thus Ryrie says, "Heaven, not the apostles, initiates all binding and loosing, while the apostles announce these things."[35]

The only way in which the verse is true today is in a *declarative* sense. When a sinner truly repents of his sins and receives Jesus Christ as Lord and Savior, a Christian can *declare* that person's sins to be forgiven. When a sinner rejects the

Savior, a Christian worker can *declare* his sins to be retained. William Kelly writes, "Whenever the Church acts in the name of the Lord and really does His will, the stamp of God is upon their deeds."

16:20 Again we find the Lord Jesus commanding **His disciples** to **tell no one** that He was the Messiah. Because of Israel's unbelief, no good could come from such a disclosure. And positive harm might come from a popular movement to crown Him King; such an ill-timed move would be ruthlessly crushed by the Romans.

Stewart, who calls this section the turning point of Jesus' ministry, writes:

The day at Caesarea Philippi marks the watershed of the Gospels. From this point onward the streams begin to flow in another direction. The current of popularity which seemed likely in the earlier days of Jesus' ministry to carry him to a throne has now been left behind. The tide sets toward the Cross. . . . At Caesarea, Jesus stood, as it were on a dividing line. It was like a hilltop from which he could see behind him all the road he had traveled and in front of him the dark, forbidding way awaiting him. One look he cast back to where the afterglow of happy days still lingered and then faced round and marched forward toward the shadows. His course was now set to Calvary.[36]

B. Preparing the Disciples for His Death and Resurrection (16:21–23)

16:21 Now that the disciples had realized that Jesus is the Messiah, the Son of the living God, they were ready to hear His first direct prediction of His death and resurrection. They now knew that His cause could never fail; that they were on the winning side; that no matter what happened, triumph was assured. So the Lord broke the news to prepared hearts. **He must go to Jerusalem**, must **suffer many things from** the religious leaders, must **be killed, and be raised the third day**. The news was enough to spell the doom of any movement — all except that last imperative — **must . . . be raised the third day**. That made the difference!

16:22 Peter was indignant at the thought of his Master's enduring such treatment. Catching hold of Him as if to block His path, he protested, **"Far be it**

from You, Lord; this shall not happen to You!"

16:23 This drew a rebuke from the Lord Jesus. He had come into the world to die for sinners. Anything or anyone who hindered Him from this purpose was out of tune with God's will. So He said to Peter, **"Get behind Me, Satan! You are an offense to Me, for you are not mindful of the things of God, but the things of men."** In calling Peter **Satan**, Jesus did not imply that the apostle was demon-possessed or Satan-controlled. He simply meant that Peter's actions and words were what could be expected of Satan (whose name means *adversary*). By protesting against Calvary, Peter became a hindrance to the Savior.

Every Christian is called to take up his cross and follow the Lord Jesus, but when the cross looms in the pathway ahead, a voice within says, "Far be it from you! Save yourself." Or perhaps the voices of loved ones seek to deflect us from the path of obedience. At such times, we too must say, "Get behind me, Satan! You are a hindrance to me."

C. Preparation for True Discipleship (16:24–28)

16:24 Now the Lord Jesus plainly states what is involved in being His disciple: denial of self, cross-bearing, and following Him. To **deny** self is not the same as self-denial; it means to yield to His control so completely that self has no rights whatever. To **take up** the **cross** means the willingness to endure shame, suffering, and perhaps martyrdom for His sake; to die to sin, self, and the world. To **follow** Him means to live as He lived with all that involves of humility, poverty, compassion, love, grace, and every other godly virtue.

16:25 The Lord anticipates two hindrances to discipleship. The first is the natural temptation **to save** oneself from discomfort, pain, loneliness, or loss. The other is to become wealthy. As to the first, Jesus warned that those who hug their lives for selfish purposes would never find fulfillment; those who recklessly abandon their lives to Him, not counting the cost, would find the reason for their existence.

16:26 The second temptation — that of getting rich — is irrational. "Suppose," said Jesus, "that **a man** became so successful in business that he owned **the whole world**. This mad quest would absorb so much of his time and energy that he would miss the central purpose of his life. What good would it do to make all that money, then die, leave it all behind, and spend eternity empty-handed?" Man is here for bigger business than to make money. He is called to represent the interests of his King. If he misses that, he misses everything.

In verse 24, Jesus told them the worst. That is characteristic of Christianity; you know the worst at the outset. But you never cease discovering the treasures and the blessings. Barnhouse put it well:

> When one has seen all that is forbidding in the Scriptures, there is nothing left hidden that can come as a surprise. Every new thing which we shall ever learn in this life or the next will come as a delight.[37]

16:27 Now the Lord reminds His own of **the glory** that follows the suffering. He points forward to His Second Advent when He will return to earth **with His angels** in the transcendent **glory of His Father. Then He will reward** those who live for Him. The only way to have a successful life is to project oneself forward to that glorious time, decide what will really be important then, and then go after that with all one's strength.

16:28 He next made the startling statement that **there** were **some standing** there with Him **who** would **not taste death** before they saw Him **coming in His kingdom**. The problem, of course, is that those disciples have all died, yet Christ has not come in power and glory to set up His kingdom. The problem is solved if we disregard the chapter break and consider the first eight verses of the next chapter as an explanation of His enigmatic statement. These verses describe the incident on the Mount of Transfiguration. There Peter, James, and John saw Christ transfigured. They were actually privileged to have a preview of Christ in the glory of His kingdom.

We are justified in viewing Christ's transfiguration as a prepicture of His coming kingdom. Peter describes the

event as "the power and coming of our Lord Jesus Christ" (2 Pet. 1:16). The power and coming of the Lord Jesus refer to His Second Advent. And John speaks of the Mount experience as the time when " . . . we beheld His glory, the glory as of the only begotten of the Father" (John 1:14). Christ's First Coming was in humiliation; it is His Second Coming that will be in glory. Thus, the prediction of verse 28 was fulfilled on the Mount; Peter, James, and John saw the Son of Man, no longer as the humble Nazarene, but as the glorified King.

D. Preparing the Disciples for Glory: The Transfiguration (17:1–8)

17:1, 2 Six days after the incident at Caesarea Philippi, **Jesus took Peter, James, and John** up to **a high mountain**, somewhere in Galilee. Many commentators attach significance to the six days. Gaebelein, for instance, says: "Six is a man's number, the number signifying the days of work. After six days — after work and man's day is run out then the day of the Lord, the Kingdom."

When Luke says that the Transfiguration occurred "about eight days" later (9:28), he obviously includes the terminal days as well as the intervening days. Since eight is the number of resurrection and of a new beginning, it is fitting that Luke should identify the kingdom with a new beginning.

Peter, James, and John, who seem to have occupied a place of special nearness to the Savior, were privileged to see Him transfigured. Up to now His glory had been veiled in a body of flesh. But now **His face** and **clothes** became radiant **like the sun** and dazzling bright, a visible manifestation of His deity, just as the glory cloud or Shekinah in the OT symbolized the presence of God. The scene was a preview of what the Lord Jesus will be like when He comes back to set up His kingdom. He will no longer appear as the sacrificial Lamb but as the Lion of the tribe of Judah. All who see Him will recognize Him immediately as God the Son, the King of kings and Lord of lords.

17:3 Moses and Elijah appeared on the Mount and discussed His approaching death at Jerusalem (Luke 9:30, 31). Moses and Elijah may represent OT saints. Or, if we take Moses as representing the Law, and Elijah representing the Prophets, then here we see both sections of the OT pointing forward to the sufferings of Christ and the glories that should follow. A third possibility is that Moses, who went to heaven by way of death, depicts all who will be raised from the dead to enter the Millennium, while Elijah, who was translated to heaven, pictures those who will reach the kingdom by the route of translation.

The disciples Peter, James, and John may represent NT saints in general. They could also foreshadow the faithful Jewish remnant who will be alive at the Second Advent and will enter the kingdom with Christ.

The multitude at the base of the mountain (v. 14, compare Luke 9:37) has been likened to the Gentile nations which will also share in the blessings of Christ's thousand-year reign.

17:4, 5 **Peter** was deeply moved by the occasion; he had a real sense of history. Wanting to capture the splendor, he rashly suggested erecting **three** memorial **tabernacles** or booths — **one for** Jesus, **one for Moses, and one for Elijah**. He was right in putting Jesus first, but wrong in not giving Him the preeminence. Jesus is not one among equals but Lord over all. In order to teach this lesson, God the Father covered them all with a brightly glowing **cloud**, then announced, **"This is My beloved Son, in whom I am well pleased. Hear Him!"** In the Kingdom, Christ will be the peerless One, the supreme Monarch whose word will be the final authority. Thus it should be in the hearts of His followers at the present time.

17:6–8 Stunned by the glory cloud and by the voice of God, **the disciples fell on their faces**. But Jesus told them to get up and **not to be afraid**. As they rose, **they saw no one but Jesus only**. So it will be in the Kingdom — the Lord Jesus will be "all the glory in Immanuel's land."

E. Concerning the Forerunner (17:9–13)

17:9 Descending **from the mountain, Jesus commanded** the disciples to be silent about what they had seen until He had **risen from the dead**. The Jews, overanxious for anyone who might liberate them from the Roman yoke, would have welcomed Him to save them from *Rome*, but did not want Him as a Savior from *sin*. For all practical purposes, Israel had rejected her Messiah, and it was useless to tell the Jews of this vision of Messianic glory. After the resurrection, the message would be proclaimed worldwide.

17:10–13 The disciples had just seen a preview of Christ's coming in power and glory. But His forerunner had not appeared. Malachi had prophesied that **Elijah must come** prior to Messiah's advent (Mal. 4:5, 6), so **His disciples asked** Jesus about this. The Lord agreed that **indeed Elijah** had to come **first** as a reformer, but explained **that Elijah** had **already come**. Obviously He was referring to **John the Baptist** (see v. 13). John was not Elijah (John 1:21), but had come "in the spirit and power of Elijah" (Luke 1:17). Had Israel accepted John and his message, he would have fulfilled the role prophesied of Elijah (Matt. 11:14). But the nation did not recognize the significance of John's mission, and treated him as it pleased. John's death was an advance token of what they would do to the Son of Man. They rejected the forerunner; they would also reject the King. When Jesus explained this, the disciples realized He was referring to **John the Baptist**.

There is every reason to believe that before Christ's Second Advent, a prophet will arise to prepare Israel for the coming King. Whether it will be Elijah personally or someone with a similar ministry is almost impossible to say.

F. Preparation for Service through Prayer and Fasting (17:14–21)

Life is not all a mountain-top experience. After moments of spiritual exhilaration come hours and days of toil and expenditure. The time comes when we must leave the mountain to minister in the valley of human need.

17:14, 15 At the base of the mountain, a distraught father was waiting for the Savior. **Kneeling down** before **Him**, he poured out his impassioned plea that his demon-possessed son might be healed. The son suffered from violent **epileptic** seizures which sometimes caused him to fall **into the fire and often into the water**, so his misery was compounded by burns and near-drownings. He was a classic example of the suffering caused by Satan, the cruelest of all task-masters.

17:16 The father had gone to the **disciples** for help, only to learn that "vain is the help of man." They had been powerless to cure.

17:17 **"O faithless and perverse generation, how long shall I be with you? How long shall I bear with you?"** is addressed to the disciples. They did not have the faith to heal the epileptic, but in that respect, were a cross section of the Jewish people of that day — faithless and perverse.

17:18 As soon as the epileptic was brought to Him, **Jesus rebuked the demon**, and the sufferer **was** instantly **cured.**

17:19, 20 Puzzled by their power-lessness, **the disciples** privately asked the Lord for an explanation. His answer was straightforward: **unbelief**. If they had **faith the** size of **a mustard seed** (the smallest of seeds), they could command a **mountain** to be cast into the sea and it would happen. Of course, it should be understood that true faith must be based upon some command or promise of God. Expecting to perform some spectac-ular stunt in order to gratify a personal whim is not faith but presumption. But if God guides a believer in a certain di-rection or issues a command, the Chris-tian can have utmost confidence that mountainous difficulties will be miracu-lously removed. Nothing is impossible to those who believe.

17:21 **"This kind does not go out except by prayer and fasting"** is omitted in the RSV and most modern Bibles, be-cause it is lacking in many early manu-scripts. However, it is found in the ma-jority of the manuscripts and fits the context of an especially difficult problem.

G. Preparing the Disciples for His Betrayal (17:22, 23)

Again, without drama or fanfare, the Lord Jesus forewarned His disciples that He would be put to death. But again there was that word of vindication and victory — He would **be raised up** on **the third day**. If He had not told them of His death in advance, they would doubt-less have been completely disillusioned when it happened. A death of shame and suffering was not consistent with their expectations of the Messiah.

As it was, they were greatly dis-tressed that He was going to leave them and that He would be slain. They heard His passion prediction but seemed to have missed His resurrection promise.

H. Peter and His Master Pay Their Taxes (17:24–27)

17:24, 25 In **Capernaum** the collec-tors of the **temple tax asked** Peter if his **Teacher** paid the half-shekel used for carrying on the costly temple service. Peter answered, **"Yes."** Perhaps the mis-guided disciple wanted to save Christ from embarrassment.

The omniscience of the Lord is seen in what followed. When Peter came home, Jesus spoke to him first — before Peter had a chance to tell what had hap-pened. **"What do you think, Simon? From whom do the kings of the earth take customs and taxes, from their sons or from strangers?"** The question must be understood in the light of those days. A ruler taxed his subjects for the support of his kingdom and his family, but he didn't tax his own family. Under our form of government, everyone is taxed, including the ruler and his household.

17:26 Peter correctly answered that rulers collected tribute **from strangers**. Jesus then pointed out that **the sons are free**. The point was that the temple was God's house. For Jesus, the Son of God, to pay tribute for the support of this tem-ple would be equivalent to paying tribute to Himself.

17:27 However, rather than cause needless offense, the Lord agreed to pay the tax. But what would He do for money? It is never recorded that Jesus personally carried money. He sent Peter **to the Sea** of Galilee and told him to bring up the first fish he caught. In the mouth of that fish was **a piece of money** or *stater* which Peter used to pay the tribute — one-half for the Lord Jesus and one-half for himself.

This astounding miracle, narrated with utmost restraint, clearly demon-strates Christ's omniscience. He knew which one of all the fish in the Sea of Galilee had a stater in its mouth. He knew the location of that one fish. And he knew it would be the first fish Peter would catch.

If any divine principle had been involved, Jesus would not have made the payment. It was a matter of moral indifference to Him, and He was willing to pay rather than offend. We as believers are free from the law. Yet, in nonmoral matters, we should respect the consciences of others, and not do anything that would cause offense.

XI. THE KING INSTRUCTS HIS DISCIPLES (Chaps. 18–20)

A. Concerning Humility (18:1–6)

Chapter 18 has been called the discourse on greatness and forgiveness. It outlines principles of conduct that are suitable for those who claim to be subjects of Christ the King.

18:1 The disciples had always thought of the kingdom of heaven as the golden age of peace and prosperity. Now they began to covet positions of preferment in it. Their self-seeking spirit found expression in the question, **"Who is greatest in the kingdom of heaven?"**

18:2, 3 Jesus answered with a living object lesson. Placing **a little child** in their midst, He said that men must be **converted and become as little children** to **enter the kingdom of heaven**. He was speaking of the kingdom in its inward reality; in order to be a genuine believer a man must abandon thoughts of personal greatness and take the lowly position of a little child. This begins when he acknowledges his sinfulness and unworthiness and receives Jesus Christ as his only hope. This attitude should continue throughout his Christian life. Jesus was not implying that His disciples were not saved. All except Judas had true faith in Him, and were therefore justified. But they had not yet received the Holy Spirit as an indwelling Person, and therefore lacked the power for true *humility* that we have today (but do not use as we should). Also they needed to be converted in the sense of having all their false thinking changed to conform to the kingdom.

18:4 The greatest person in the kingdom of heaven is the one **who humbles himself as** a **little child**. Obviously the standards and values in the kingdom are exactly opposite those in the world. Our whole mode of thinking must be reversed; we must think Christ's thoughts after Him (see Phil. 2:5–8).

18:5 Here the Lord Jesus glides almost imperceptibly from the subject of a natural child to a spiritual **child**. Whoever receives one of His humble followers **in** His **name** will be rewarded as if he had received the Lord Himself. What is done for the disciple is reckoned as done for the Master.

18:6 On the other hand, anyone who seduces a believer to sin incurs enormous condemnation; **it would be better for him** to have a great **millstone** tied **around his neck and** be **drowned** in the ocean's depths. (The great millstone referred to here required an animal to turn it; a smaller one could be turned by hand.) It is bad enough to sin against oneself, but to cause a believer to sin is to destroy his innocence, corrupt his mind, and stain his reputation. Better to die a violent death than to trifle with another's purity!

B. Concerning Offenses (18:7–14)

18:7 Jesus went on to explain that it is inevitable that **offenses** should arise. The **world**, the flesh, and the devil are leagued to seduce and pervert. But if a person becomes an agent for the forces of evil, his guilt will be great. So the Savior warned men to take drastic action in disciplining themselves rather than to tempt a child of God.

18:8, 9 Whether the sinning member is the **hand or foot** or the **eye**, better to sacrifice it to the surgeon's knife than to let it destroy the work of God in another person's life. **Better to enter into life** without limbs or sight than to be consigned to hell with every member intact. Our Lord does not imply that some bodies will lack limbs in heaven, but merely describes the physical condition at the time a believer leaves this life for the next. There can be no question that the resurrection body will be complete and perfect.

18:10 Next the Son of God warned against despising **one of** His **little ones**, whether children or any who belong to the kingdom. To emphasize their importance, He added that **their angels** are constantly in the presence of God, beholding His **face. Angels** here probably means guardian angels (see also Heb. 1:14).

18:11 While omitted in RSV and most other modern Bibles, this verse about our Savior's mission is a fitting climax to this section, and it has wide manuscript support.[38]

18:12, 13 These little ones are also the object of the tender Shepherd's saving ministry. Even if one out of **a hundred sheep** goes astray, He leaves **the ninety-nine** and searches for the lost one till He finds it. The Shepherd's joy over finding a straying sheep should teach us to value and respect His little ones.

18:14 They are important not only to the angels and to the Shepherd, but also to God the **Father**. **It is not** His **will that one of** them **should perish**. If they are important enought to engage angels, the Lord Jesus, and God the Father, then clearly we should never despise them, no matter how unlovely or lowly they might appear.

C. Concerning Discipline of Offenders (18:15–20)

The rest of the chapter deals with the settlement of differences among church members, and with the need for exercising unlimited forgiveness.

18:15 Explicit instructions are given concerning the Christian's responsibility when wronged by another believer. First, the matter should be handled privately between the two parties. If the offender acknowledges his guilt, reconciliation is achieved. The trouble is that we don't do this. We gossip to everyone else about it. Then the matter spreads like wildfire and strife is multiplied. Let us remember that step number one is to **"go and tell him his fault between you and him alone."**

18:16 If the guilty brother does not listen, then the wronged one should take **one or two** others with him, seeking his restoration. This emphasizes the mounting seriousness of his continued unbrokenness. But more, it provides competent testimony, as required by the Scripture: **"that 'by the mouth of two or three witnesses every word may be established' "** (Deut. 19:15). No one can

measure the trouble that has plagued the church through failure to obey the simple rule that a charge against another person must be supported by the testimony of two or three others. In this respect, worldly courts often act more righteously than Christian churches or assemblies.

18:17 If the accused still **refuses** to confess and apologize, the matter should be taken before **the** local **church**. It is important to notice that the local assembly is the body responsible to hear the case, not a civil court. The Christian is forbidden to go to law against another believer (1 Cor. 6:1–8).

If the defendant refuses to admit his wrong before the church, then he is to be considered **a heathen and a tax collector**. The most obvious meaning of this expression is that he should be looked upon as being outside the sphere of the church. Though he may be a true believer, he is not living as one, and should therefore be treated accordingly. Though still in the universal church, he should be barred from the privileges of the local church. Such discipline is a serious action; it temporarily delivers a believer to the power of Satan "for the destruction of the flesh, that his spirit may be saved in the day of the Lord Jesus" (1 Cor. 5:5). The purpose of this is to bring him to his senses and cause him to confess his sin. Until that point is reached, believers should treat him courteously but should also show by their attitude that they do not condone his sin and cannot have fellowship with him as a fellow believer. The assembly should be prompt to receive him back as soon as there is evidence of godly repentance.

18:18 Verse 18 is linked with what precedes. When an assembly, prayerfully and in obedience to the Word, binds disciplinary action upon a person, that action is honored **in heaven**. When the disciplined person has repented and confessed his sin, and the assembly restores him to fellowship, that loosing action, too, is ratified by God (see John 20:23).

18:19 The question arises, "How large must an assembly be before it can bind and loose, as described above?" The answer is that **two** believers may bring such matters to God in prayer with the assurance of being heard. While verse 19 may be used as a general promise of answers to prayer, in the *context* it refers to prayer concerning church discipline. When used in connection with collective prayer in general, it must be taken in light of all other teaching on prayer. For instance, our prayers must be:

1. In conformity to the revealed will of God (1 Jn. 5:14, 15).
2. In faith (Jas. 1:6–8).
3. In sincerity (Heb. 10:22a), etc.

18:20 Verse 20 should be interpreted in light of its context. It does not refer primarily to the composition of a NT church in its simplest form, nor to a general prayer meeting, but to a meeting where the church seeks the reconciliation of two Christians separated by some sin. It may legitimately be applied to all meetings of believers where Christ is the Center, but a specific type of meeting is in view here.

To meet "in His name" means by His authority, in acknowledgment of all that He is, and in obedience to His Word. No group can claim to be the only ones who meet in His name; if that were so, His presence would be limited to a small segment of His body on earth. Wherever **two or three are gathered in** recognition of Him as Lord and Savior, he is **there in the midst.**

D. Concerning Unlimited Forgiveness (18:21–35)

18:21, 22 At this point **Peter** raised the question of **how often** he should **forgive** a **brother** who sinned against him. He probably thought he was showing unusual grace by suggesting **seven** as an outside limit. **Jesus** answered **"not . . . seven times but up to seventy times seven."** He did not intend us to understand a literal 490 times; this was a figurative way of saying "Indefinitely."

Someone might then ask, "Why bother to go through the steps outlined above? Why go to an offender alone, then with one or two others, then take him to church? Why not just forgive, and let that be the end of it?"

The answer is that there are stages in the administration of forgiveness, as follows:

1. When a brother wrongs me or sins against me, I should forgive him immediately *in my heart* (Eph. 4:32). That frees me from a bitter, unforgiving spirit, and leaves the matter on *his* shoulders.
2. While I have forgiven him in my heart, I do not yet tell him that he is forgiven. It would not be righteous to administer forgiveness publicly until he has repented. So I am obligated to go to him and rebuke him in love, hoping to lead him to confession (Luke 17:3).
3. As soon as he apologizes and confesses his sin, I tell him that he is forgiven (Luke 17:4).

18:23 Jesus then gives a parable of **the kingdom of heaven** to warn against the consequences of an unforgiving spirit by subjects who have been freely forgiven.

18:24–27 The story concerns **a certain king who wanted to** clear his bad debts off his books. One servant, who **owed him ten thousand talents**, was insolvent, so his lord ordered that he and his family be sold into slavery in payment of the debt. The distraught servant begged for time, promising to **pay** him **all** if given the chance.

Like many debtors, he was incredibly optimistic about what he could do if only he had time (v. 26). Galilee's total revenue only amounted to 300 talents and this man owed 10,000! The detail about the vast amount is intentional. It is to shock the listeners and so capture their attention, and also to emphasize an immense debt to God. Martin Luther used to say that we are all beggars before Him. We cannot hope to pay (Daily Notes of the Scripture Union).

When the **master** saw the contrite attitude of his **servant**, he forgave him the entire 10,000 talents. It was an epic display of grace, not justice.

18:28–30 Now that servant had a fellow servant who owed him one **hundred denarii** (a few hundred dollars). Rather than forgive him, he grabbed **him by the throat** and demanded payment in full. The hapless debtor pled for an extension, but it was no use. He was thrown **into prison till he** paid **the debt** — a difficult business at best, since his chance of earning money was gone as long as he was imprisoned.

18:31–34 The other **servants**, outraged by this inconsistent behavior, **told their master**. He was furious with the merciless lender. Having been forgiven a big debt, he was unwilling to forgive a pittance. So he was returned to the jailers' custody till his debt was paid.

18:35 The application is clear. God is the King. All His servants had contracted a great debt of sin which they were unable to pay. In wonderful grace and compassion, the Lord paid the debt and granted full and free forgiveness. Now suppose some Christian wrongs another. When rebuked, he apologizes and asks forgiveness. But the offended believer refuses. He himself has been forgiven millions of dollars, but won't forgive a few hundred. Will the King allow such behavior to go unpunished? Certainly not! The culprit will be chastened in this life and will suffer loss at the Judgment Seat of Christ.

E. Concerning Marriage, Divorce and Celibacy (19:1–12)

19:1, 2 After completing His ministry in **Galilee**, the Lord turned southward to Jerusalem. Though His exact route is unknown, it seems clear that He traveled through Perea, on the east side of the Jordan. Matthew speaks of the area loosely as **the region of Judea beyond the Jordan**. The Perean ministry extends from 19:1 to 20:16 or 20:28; it is not clearly stated when He crossed the Jordan into Judea.

19:3 Probably it was the multitudes that followed Him for healing that alerted **the Pharisees** to the Lord's whereabouts. Like a pack of wild dogs, they began to close in, hoping to trap Him by His words. They asked if **divorce** was legal on any and every ground. No matter how He answered, He would infuriate some segment of the Jews. One school took a very liberal attitude toward divorce; another was extremely strict.

19:4–6 Our Lord explained that God's original intention was that a man have only one living wife. The God who created **male and female** decreed that the marriage relationship should supersede the parental relationship. He also

said that marriage is a union of persons. God's ideal is that this divinely ordained union should not be broken by human act or decree.

19:7 The Pharisees thought they had caught the Lord in a flagrant contradiction of the OT. Hadn't **Moses** made provision for **divorce**? A man could simply give his wife a written statement, then put her out of the house (Deut. 24:1–4).

19:8 Jesus agreed that **Moses** had **permitted** divorce, not as God's best for mankind, but because of Israel's backslidden condition: **"Moses because of the hardness of your hearts permitted you to divorce your wives, but from the beginning it was not so."** God's ideal was that there be no divorce. But God often tolerates conditions that are not His directive will.

19:9 Then the Lord stated with absolute authority that the past leniency on divorce was henceforth discontinued. Hereafter there would be only one valid ground for divorce — unchastity. If a person was divorced for any other reason and remarried, he was guilty of **adultery.**

Although not directly stated, it would seem from the words of our Lord that where a divorce has been obtained on the grounds of adultery, the innocent party is free to remarry. Otherwise divorce would serve no purpose not equally achieved by separation.

Sexual immorality, or fornication, is generally taken to mean adultery. However, many capable Bible students think it refers only to pre-marital immorality which is discovered after marriage (see Deut. 22:13–21). Others believe it refers to Jewish marriage customs only and that is why the "exception clause" is only here in Matthew, the Jewish Gospel.

For a fuller discussion of divorce, see notes on 5:31, 32.

19:10 When the **disciples** heard the Lord's teaching on divorce, they proved themselves creatures of extremes by adopting the absurd position that if divorce is obtainable on only one ground, then to avoid sinning in the married state **it** would be **better not to marry** at all. But that would not save them from sinning in the single state.

19:11 So the Savior reminded them that the ability to remain celibate was not the general rule; only those to whom special grace was given could forego marriage. The dictum, **"All cannot accept this saying, but only those to whom it has been given,"** does not mean that all cannot understand what follows, but that they cannot live a continent life unless they are called to it.

19:12 The Lord Jesus explained that there are three types of **eunuchs**. Some men are **eunuchs** because they were **born** without the power of reproduction. Others are so because they were castrated by men; oriental rulers often subjected the harem attendants to surgery to make them eunuchs. But Jesus especially had in mind those **who have made themselves eunuchs for the kingdom of heaven's sake**. These men could be married, and they have no physical impairment. Yet in dedication to the King and His kingdom, they willingly forego marriage in order to give themselves to the cause of Christ without distraction. As Paul wrote later, "He who is unmarried cares for the things of the Lord — how he may please the Lord" (1 Cor. 7:32). Their celibacy is not physical but a matter of voluntary abstinence.

Not all men can live such a life; only those divinely empowered: "But each one has his own gift from God, one in this manner and another in that" (1 Cor. 7:7).

F. Concerning Children (19:13–15)

It is interesting that children are introduced shortly after the discourse on divorce (see also Mark 10:1–16); often they are the ones who suffer most severely from broken homes.

Parents brought their **little children** to Jesus to be blessed by the Teacher-Shepherd. **The disciples** saw this as an intrusion and annoyance, and **rebuked** the parents. **But Jesus** intervened with those words that have since endeared Him to children of every age, **"Let the little children come to Me, and do not forbid them, for of such is the kingdom of heaven."**

Several important lessons emerge from those words. First, they should impress the servant of the Lord with the importance of reaching children, whose minds are most receptive, with the Word

of God. Second, children who wish to confess their faith in the Lord Jesus should be encouraged, not held back. No one knows the age of the youngest person in hell. If a child truly wishes to be saved, he should not be told that he is too young. At the same time, children should not be pressured into making a false profession. Susceptible as they are to emotional appeals, they should be protected from high-pressure methods of evangelism. Children do not have to become adults to be saved, but adults have to become like children (18:3, 4; Mark 10:15).

Thirdly, these words of our Lord answer the question, "What happens to children who die before they reach the age of accountability?" Jesus said, **" . . . of such is the kingdom of heaven."** That should be adequate assurance to parents who have suffered the loss of little ones.

Sometimes this passage is used to support the baptism of young children in order to make them members of Christ and inheritors of the kingdom. Closer reading will show that the parents brought the children to Jesus, not to the baptistry. It will show that the children were already possessors of the kingdom. And it will show that there is not a drop of water in the passage.

G. Concerning Riches: The Rich Young Ruler (19:16–26)

19:16 This incident provides a study in contrasts. Having just seen that the kingdom of heaven belongs to little children, we will now see how difficult it is for adults to enter.

A rich man intercepted the Lord with an apparently sincere inquiry. Addressing Jesus as **"Good Teacher"** he asked **what** he had to **do** to **have eternal life**. The question revealed his ignorance of the true identity of Jesus and of the way of salvation. He called Jesus **"Teacher,"** putting Him on the same level as other great men. And he spoke of gaining **eternal life** as a debt rather than as a gift.

19:17 Our Lord probed him on these two points. In asking, **"Why do you call Me good? There is no one good but One, that is, God,"** Jesus was not denying His own deity, but was providing the man with an opportunity to say,

"That's why I call You good — You are God."

To test him on the way of salvation Jesus said, **"But if you want to enter into life, keep the commandments."** The Savior was not implying that man can be saved by keeping the commandments. Rather, He was using the law to produce conviction of sin in the man's heart. The man was still under the delusion that he could inherit the kingdom on the principle of *doing*. Therefore, let him obey the law which told him what to *do*.

19:18–20 Our Lord quoted the five commandments dealing primarily with our fellow man, climaxing them by saying, **"You shall love your neighbor as yourself."** Blind to his own selfishness, the man boasted that he had always **kept** these commandments.

19:21 Our Lord then exposed the man's failure to love his neighbor as himself by telling him to **sell** all his possessions **and give** the money **to the poor**. Then he should **come** to Jesus and **follow** Him.

The Lord did not mean that this man could have been saved by selling his possessions and giving the proceeds to charity. There is only one way of salvation — faith in the Lord.

But in order to be saved, a man must acknowledge that he has sinned and fallen short of God's holy requirements. The rich man's unwillingness to share his possessions showed that he did not love his neighbor as himself. He should have said, "Lord, if that's what is required, then I'm a sinner. I cannot save myself by my own efforts. Therefore, I ask You to save me by Your grace." If he had responded to the Savior's instruction he would have been given the way of salvation.

19:22 Instead, **he went away sorrowful**.

19:23, 24 The rich man's response prompted **Jesus** to observe **that it is hard for a rich man to enter the kingdom of heaven**. Riches tend to become an idol. It is hard to have them without trusting in them. Our Lord declared that **"it is easier for a camel to go through the eye of a needle than for a rich man to enter the kingdom of God."** He was using a figure of speech known as hyperbole — a statement made in intensified form to produce a vivid, unforgettable effect.

It is clearly impossible for a camel to go through the eye of a needle! The "needle's eye" has often been explained as the small door in a city gate. A camel could get through it by kneeling down, but only with great difficulty. However, the word used for "needle" in the parallel passage in Luke is the same word used to describe the needle used by surgeons. It seems clear from the context that the Lord was not speaking of difficulty, but of impossibility. Humanly speaking, a rich man simply *cannot* be saved.

19:25 The **disciples** were **astonished** by these remarks. As Jews living under the Mosaic code, by which God promised prosperity to those who obeyed Him, they correctly viewed riches as indicative of God's blessing. If those who thus enjoyed God's blessing couldn't be saved, who *could*?

19:26 The Lord replied, **"With men this is impossible, but with God all things are possible."** Humanly speaking, it is **impossible** for anyone to be saved; only God can save a soul. But it is more difficult for a wealthy man to surrender his will to Christ than for a poor man, as evidenced by the fact that few rich men are converted. They find it almost impossible to replace trust in visible means of support for faith in an unseen Savior. Only God can effect such a change.

Commentators and preachers invariably inject here that it is perfectly all right for Christians to be rich. It is strange that they use a passage in which the Lord denounces wealth as a hindrance to man's eternal welfare, to justify the accumulation of earthly treasures! And it is difficult to see how a Christian can cling to riches in view of the appalling need everywhere, the imminence of Christ's Return, and the Lord's clear prohibition against laying up treasures on earth. Hoarded wealth condemns us as not loving our neighbors as ourselves.

H. Concerning Rewards for Sacrificial Living (19:27–30)

19:27 **Peter** caught the drift of the Savior's teaching. Realizing that Jesus was saying, "Forsake all and follow Me," Peter gloated that he and the other disciples had done exactly that; then he added, **"What shall we have?"** Peter's self-life was showing, the old nature re-asserting itself. It was a spirit each of us must guard against. He was bargaining with the Lord.

19:28, 29 The Lord assured Peter that everything done for Him would be rewarded handsomely. As to the twelve specifically, they would have places of authority in the Millennium. **The regeneration** refers to Christ's future reign on earth; it is explained by the expression, **"when the Son of Man sits on the throne of His glory."** We have previously referred to this phase of the kingdom as the kingdom in *manifestation*. At that time the twelve will **sit on twelve thrones, judging the twelve tribes of Israel**. Rewards in the NT are closely linked with positions of administration in the Millennium (see Luke 19:17, 19). They are *awarded* at the Judgment Seat of Christ, but *manifested* when the Lord returns to earth to reign.

As to believers in general, Jesus added that all who have **left houses or brothers or sisters or father or mother or wife or children or lands for** His **sake shall receive a hundredfold, and inherit eternal life**. In this life, they enjoy a world-wide fellowship of believers that more than compensates for severed earthly ties. For the one house they leave, they receive a hundred Christian homes where they are warmly welcomed. For lands or other forms of wealth forsaken, they receive spiritual riches beyond reckoning.

The future reward for all believers is **eternal life**. This does not mean that we earn eternal life by forsaking all and sacrificing. Eternal life is a gift and cannot be earned or merited. Here the thought is that those who forsake all are rewarded with a greater capacity for enjoying eternal life in heaven. All believers will have that life but not all will enjoy it to the same extent.

19:30 The Lord closed His remarks with a warning against a bargaining spirit. He said to Peter, in effect, "Anything you do for My sake will be rewarded, but be careful that you are not guided by selfish considerations; because in that case, **many who are first will be last, and the last first.** This is illustrated by a parable in the next chapter. This statement may also have been a warning that it isn't enough to start out well on the path of discipleship. It's how we finish that counts.

Before leaving this section we should notice that the expressions "kingdom of heaven" and "kingdom of God" are used interchangeably in verses 23 and 24; therefore, the two terms are synonymous.

I. Concerning Rewards for Labor in the Vineyard (20:1–16)

20:1, 2 This parable, a continuation of the discourse on rewards at the end of chapter 19, illustrates the truth that while all true disciples will be rewarded, the order of rewards will be determined by the spirit in which the disciple served.

The parable describes a **landowner who went out early in the morning to hire laborers** to work in **his vineyard**. These men contracted to work for **a denarius a day**, a reasonable wage at that time. Let us say they began to work at 6:00 a.m.

20:3, 4 At 9:00 a.m. the farmer found some other unemployed laborers **in the market place**. In this case there was no labor-management agreement. They went to work with only his word that he would give them **whatever was right**.

20:5–7 At noon and at 3:00 p.m. the farmer hired more men on the basis that he would give them a fair wage. At 5:00 p.m. he found more unemployed men. They were not lazy; they wanted work but hadn't been able to find it. So he sent them **into the vineyard** without any discussion of pay.

It is important to notice that the first men were hired as a result of a bargaining agreement; all the others left the matter of pay to the landowner.

20:8 At the end of the day, the farmer instructed his paymaster to pay the men, **beginning with the last** hired and working back **to the first**. (In this way the earliest men hired saw what the others received.)

20:9–12 It was the same pay for all — one **denarius**. The 6:00 a.m. men thought they would receive more, but no — they too got one denarius. They were bitterly resentful; after all, they had worked longer and through **the heat of the day**.

20:13, 14 In the farmer's reply to one of them we find the abiding lessons from the parable. First he **said, "Friend, I am doing you no wrong. Did you not agree with me for a denarius? Take what is yours, and go your way. I wish to give to this last man the same as to you."** The first bargained for a denarius a day and got the wage agreed on. The others cast themselves on the farmer's grace and got grace. Grace is better than justice. It is better to leave our rewards up to the Lord than to strike a bargain with Him.

20:15 Then the farmer said, **"Is it not lawful for me to do what I wish with my own things?"** The lesson, of course, is that God is sovereign. He can do as He pleases. And what He pleases will always be right, just, and fair. The farmer added, **"Or is your eye evil because I am good?"** This question exposes the selfish streak in human nature. The 6:00 a.m. men got exactly what they deserved, yet were jealous because the others got the same pay for working fewer hours. Many of us have to admit that it seems a bit unfair to us, too. This only proves that in the kingdom of heaven we must adopt an entirely new kind of thinking. We must abandon our greedy, competitive spirit, and think like the Lord.

The farmer knew that all these men needed money, so he paid them according to need rather than greed. No one received less than he deserved, but all received what they needed for themselves and their families. The lesson, according to James Stewart, is that the person "who thinks to bargain about final reward will always be wrong, and God's loving-kindness will always have the last unchallengeable word."[39] The more we study the parable in this light, the more we realize that it is not only fair but eminently beautiful. Those who were hired at 6:00 a.m. should have counted it an added recompense to serve such a wonderful master all day.

20:16 Jesus closed the parable with the words, **"So the last will be first, and the first last"** (see 19:30). There will be surprises in the matter of rewards. Some who *thought* they would be first will be last because their service was inspired by pride and selfish ambition. Others who served out of love and gratitude will be highly honored.

> Deeds of merit as we thought them,
> He will show us were but sin;
> Little acts we had forgotten,
> He will show us were for Him.
>
> – *Anon*

J. Concerning His Death and Resurrection (20:17–19)

It is apparent that the Lord was leaving Perea for the trip **to Jerusalem** via Jericho (see v. 29). Once again He **took the twelve disciples aside** to explain what would happen after they reached the Holy City. He would **be betrayed to the chief priests and to the scribes** — an obvious reference to the perfidy of Judas. He would be condemned **to death** by the leaders of Jewry. Lacking authority to inflict capital punishment, they would turn **Him** over **to the Gentiles** (the Romans). He would be mocked, scourged, and crucified. But death would not keep its prey — **He** would **rise again** on **the third day.**

K. Concerning Position in the Kingdom (20:20–28)

It is a sad commentary on human nature that, immediately after the third prediction of His passion, His followers were thinking more of their own glory than of His sufferings.

> Christ's first prediction of suffering gave rise to Peter's demur (16:22); the second was soon followed by the disciples' questions, "Who is the greatest . . . ?" So here, we find the third capped with the ambitious request of James and John. They persistently closed their eyes to warnings of trouble, and opened them only to the promise of glory — so getting a wrong, materialistic view of the Kingdom (Daily Notes of the Scripture Union).

20:20, 21 **The mother of** James and John came to the Lord **asking** that her boys might sit on either side of Him **in His kingdom**. It is to her credit that she wanted her sons near Jesus, and that she had not despaired of His coming reign.

But she did not understand the principles upon which honors would be bestowed in the kingdom.

Mark says that the sons made the request themselves (Mark 10:35); perhaps they did it at her direction, or perhaps the three of them approached the Lord together. No contradiction is involved.

20:22 Jesus answered frankly that they did not understand what they were asking. They wanted a crown without a cross, a throne without the altar of sacrifice, the glory without the suffering that leads to it. So He asked them pointedly, **"Are you able to drink the cup that I am about to drink?"** We are not left to wonder what He meant by **the cup**; He had just described it in verses 18 and 19. He must suffer and die.

James and John expressed ability to share in His sufferings, though perhaps their confidence was based more on zeal than knowledge.

20:23 Jesus assured them that they would **indeed drink** of His **cup**. James would be martyred and John persecuted and exiled to the Isle of Patmos. Robert Little said, "James died a martyr's death; John lived a martyr's life."

Then Jesus explained that He could not arbitrarily grant places of honor in the kingdom; the **Father** had determined a special basis on which these positions would be assigned. They thought it was a matter of political patronage, that because they were so close to Christ, they had a special claim to places of preferment. But it was not a question of personal favoritism. In the counsels of God, the places on His right hand and left hand would be given on the basis of suffering for Him. This means that the chief honors in the kingdom are not limited to first century Christians; some living today might win them — by suffering.

20:24 The other **ten** disciples **were greatly displeased** that the sons of Zebedee had made such a request. They were probably indignant because they themselves wanted to be greatest and resented any prior claims being made by James and John!

20:25–27 This gave our Lord the opportunity to make a revolutionary statement concerning greatness in His kingdom. **The Gentiles** think of greatness in terms of mastery and rule. In Christ's kingdom, greatness is manifested by service. Whoever aspires to greatness must become a **servant, and whoever desires to be first** must become a **slave.**

20:28 The Son of Man is the perfect example of lowly service. He came into the world not **to be served, but to serve, and to give His life a ransom for many.** The whole purpose of the Incarnation can be summed up in two words — **serve** and **give**. It is amazing to think that the exalted Lord humbled Himself to the manger and to the cross. His greatness was manifested in the depth of His humiliation. And so it must be for us.

He gave His life **a ransom for many**. His death satisfied all God's righteous demands against sin. It was sufficient to put away all the sins of all the world. But it is effective only for those who accept Him as Lord and Savior. Have you ever done this?

L. Healing of Two Blind Men (20:29–34)

20:29, 30 By now Jesus had crossed the Jordan from Perea and had reached **Jericho**. As He was leaving the city, **two blind men** cried out to Him, **"Have mercy on us, O Lord, Son of David!"** Their use of the title **"Son of David"** means that, though physically blind, their spiritual vision was so acute as to recognize Jesus as the Messiah. They may represent the believing remnant of blinded Israel who will acknowledge Him as the Christ when He returns to reign (Isa. 35:5; 42:7; Rom. 11:25, 26; 2 Cor. 3:16; Rev. 1:7).

20:31–34 The crowd tried to hush them, **but they cried** after Him more insistently. When Jesus asked what they wanted, they didn't indulge in generalities, as we often do when we pray. They came right to the point: **"Lord, that our eyes may be opened."** Their specific request received a specific response. **Jesus had compassion and touched their eyes. And immediately they received their sight, and they followed Him**.

With regard to His touching them, Gaebelein makes a helpful observation:

We have learned before the typical meaning of healing by touch in this Gospel. Whenever the Lord heals by touch it has reference, dispensationally, to His personal presence on the earth and His merciful dealing with Israel. When He heals by His Word, absent in person, . . . or if He is touched in faith, it refers to the time when He is absent from the earth, and Gentiles approaching Him in faith are healed by Him.[40]

There are difficulties in reconciling Matthew's account of this incident with Mark 10:46–52 and Luke 18:35–43; 19:1. Here are *two* blind men; in Mark and Luke, only *one* is mentioned. It has been suggested that Mark and Luke mention the well-known one, Bartimaeus, and Matthew, writing his Gospel especially for Jews, mentions *two* as the minimum number for a valid testimony (2 Cor. 13:1). In Matthew and Mark, the incident is said to have occurred as Jesus left Jericho; in Luke, it is said to have happened as He drew near the city. In fact there were two Jerichos, an old Jericho and a new one, and the miracle of healing probably took place as Jesus was leaving one and entering the other.

XII. PRESENTATION AND REJECTION OF THE KING (Chaps. 21–23)

A. The Triumphal Entry (21:1–11)

21:1–3 On the way up from Jericho, Jesus came to the east side of **the Mount of Olives** where Bethany and **Bethphage** were located. From there the road skirted the south end of Olivet, dipped into the Valley of Jehoshaphat, crossed the Brook Kidron and climbed up to **Jerusalem.**[†]

He **sent two disciples** to Bethany with the foreknowledge that they would **find a** tethered **donkey, and a colt with her**. They were to untie the animals and **bring them to** Jesus. If challenged, they were to explain that **the Lord** needed the beasts. Then the owner would consent. Perhaps the owner knew Jesus and had previously offered to help Him. Or this incident may demonstrate the omniscience and supreme authority of the Lord. Everything happened just as Jesus had predicted.

†See p. xxiv.

21:4, 5 The requisitioning of the animals fulfilled predictions by Isaiah and Zechariah:

"Tell the daughter of Zion,
'Behold, your King is coming to you,
Lowly, and sitting on a donkey,
A colt, the foal of a donkey.' "

21:6 After **the disciples** had spread their garments on the animals, Jesus mounted the colt (Mark 11:7) and rode onward to Jerusalem. It was a historic moment. Sixty-nine weeks of Daniel's prophecy had now run out, according to Sir Robert Anderson (see his computations in the book *The Coming Prince*). Next the Messiah would be cut off (Dan. 9:26).

In riding into Jerusalem in this manner, the Lord Jesus made a deliberate, unveiled claim to being the Messiah. Lange notes:

He fulfills intentionally a prophecy which at His time was unanimously interpreted of the Messiah. If He has previously considered the declaration of His dignity as dangerous, He now counts silence inconceivable. . . . It was hereafter never possible to say that He had never declared Himself in a wholly unequivocal manner. When Jerusalem was afterwards accused of the murder of the Messiah, it should not be able to say that the Messiah had omitted to give a sign intelligible for all alike.[41]

21:7, 8 The Lord rode to the city on a carpet of **clothes** and palm **branches**, with the acclamation of the people ringing in His ears. For a moment, at least, He was acknowledged as King.

21:9 The multitudes shouted, **"Hosanna to the Son of David! Blessed is He who comes in the name of the LORD."** This quotation from Psalm 118:25, 26 obviously applies to the Messiah's advent. **Hosanna** originally meant "save now"; perhaps the people meant, "Save us from our Roman oppressors." Later the term became an exclamation of praise. The phrases, **"Son of David"** and, **"Blessed is He who comes in the name of the LORD,"** both clearly indicate that Jesus was being recognized as the Messiah. He is the Blessed One who comes by Jehovah's authority to do His will.

Mark's account records as part of the

crowd's shouts the phrase, "Blessed is the kingdom of our father David that comes in the name of the Lord" (Mark 11:10). This indicates that the people thought the kingdom was about to be set up with Christ sitting on the throne of David. In shouting, **"Hosanna in the highest,"** the crowd was calling on the heavens to join the earth in praising the Messiah, and perhaps calling on Him to save from the highest heavens.

Mark 11:11 records that, once in Jerusalem, Jesus went to the temple — not inside the temple but into the courtyard. Presumably it was the house of God, but He was not at home in this temple because the priests and people refused to give Him His rightful place. After looking around briefly, the Savior withdrew to Bethany with the twelve. It was Sunday evening.

21:10, 11 Meanwhile, inside **the city** there was bewilderment as to His identity. Those who asked were told only that He was **Jesus the prophet from Nazareth of Galilee.** From this it seems that few really understood He was the Messiah. In less than a week, the fickle crowd would be crying, "Crucify Him! Crucify Him!"

B. Cleansing the Temple (21:12, 13)

21:12 At the outset of His public ministry, Jesus had driven commercialism out of the temple environs (John 2:13–16). But profiteering for an excessive fee had again sprung up in the outer court of the temple. Sacrificial animals and birds were being bought and sold at exorbitant rates. **Moneychangers** converted other currencies into the halfshekel which Jewish men had to pay as temple tribute (tax) — for an excessive fee. Now, as His ministry drew to a close, **Jesus** again **drove out** those who were profiteering from sacred activities.

21:13 Combining quotations from Isaiah and Jeremiah, He condemned desecration, commercialism, and exclusivism. Quoting from Isaiah 56:7, He reminded them that God intended the temple to be **a house of prayer.** They had made it a hangout of **thieves** (Jer. 7:11).

This cleansing of the temple was His first official act after entering Jerusalem.

By it He unmistakably asserted His lordship over the temple.

This incident has a twofold message for today. In our church life, we need His cleansing power to drive out bazaars, suppers, and a host of other money-making gimmicks. In our personal lives, there is constant need for the purging ministry of the Lord in our bodies, the temples of the Holy Spirit.

C. Indignation of the Priests and Scribes (21:14–17)

21:14 The next scene finds our Lord healing **the blind and the lame** in the temple yard. He attracted the needy wherever He went, and never sent them away without meeting their need.

21:15, 16† But hostile eyes were watching. And when these **chief priests and scribes** heard children hailing Jesus as **the Son of David,** they were enraged.

They said, **"Do You hear what these are saying?"** — as if they expected Him to forbid the children from addressing Him as the Messiah! If Jesus had not been the Messiah, this would have been an appropriate time to say so once for all. But His answer indicated that the children were right. He quoted Psalm 8:2 from the Septuagint: **"Out of the mouth of babes and nursing infants You have perfected praise."** If the supposedly knowledgeable priests and scribes would not praise Him as the Anointed, then the Lord would be worshiped by little children. Children often have spiritual insight beyond their years, and their words of faith and love bring unusual glory to the name of the Lord.

21:17 Leaving the religious leaders to ponder this truth, Jesus returned **to Bethany** and spent the night there.

D. The Barren Fig Tree (21:18–22)

21:18, 19 Returning to Jerusalem **in the morning**, the Lord **came to a fig tree**, hoping to find fruit on it to satisfy His hunger. Finding **nothing on it but leaves**, He said, **"Let no fruit grow on you ever again." Immediately the fig tree withered away.**

In Mark's account (11:12–14) the comment is made that it was not the season for figs. Therefore, His condemning the tree because it had no fruit would seem

†*See p. xxi.*

to picture the Savior as unreasonable and petulant. Knowing this cannot be true, how is this difficulty explained?

Fig trees in Bible lands produced an early, edible fruit before the leaves appeared. This was a harbinger of the regular crop. If no early figs appeared, as in the case of this fig tree, it indicated that there would be no regular figs later on.

This is the only miracle in which Christ cursed rather than blessed — destroyed rather than restored life. This has been raised as a difficulty. Such criticism betrays an ignorance of the Person of Christ. He is God, the Sovereign of the universe. Some of His dealings are mysterious to us, but we must begin with the premise that they are always right. In this case, the Lord knew that the fig tree would never bear figs and He acted as a farmer would in removing a barren tree from his orchard.

Even those who criticize our Lord for cursing the fig tree admit it was a symbolic action. This incident is the Savior's interpretation of the tumultuous welcome He had just received in Jerusalem. Like the vine and the olive tree, the fig tree represents the nation of Israel. When Jesus came to the nation there were leaves, which speak of profession, but no fruit for God. Jesus was hungry for fruit from the nation.

Because there was no early fruit, He knew there would be no later fruit from that unbelieving people, and so He cursed the fig tree. This prepictured the judgment which would fall on the nation in A.D. 70.

We must remember that while *unbelieving* Israel will be fruitless forever, a *remnant* of the nation will return to the Messiah after the Rapture. They will bring forth fruit for Him during the Tribulation and during His Millennial Reign.

Although the primary interpretation of this passage relates to the nation of Israel, it has application to people of all ages who combine high talk and low walk.

21:20–22 When **the disciples** expressed amazement at the sudden withering of the tree, the Lord told them that they could do greater miracles than this if they had **faith**. For instance, they

could say to a mountain, **"Be removed and be cast into the sea,"** and it would happen. **"And whatever things you ask in prayer, believing, you will receive."**

Again we must explain that these seemingly unqualified promises concerning prayer must be understood in light of all that the Bible teaches on the subject. Verse 22 does not mean that any Christian can ask anything he wants and expect to get it. He must pray in accordance with the conditions laid down in the Bible.

E. Jesus' Authority Questioned (21:23–27)

21:23 When Jesus **came into** the court outside **the temple** proper, **the chief priests and the elders** interrupted His teaching to ask who gave Him the **authority** to teach, to perform miracles, and to cleanse the temple. They hoped to trap Him, no matter how He answered. If He claimed to have authority in Himself as the Son of God, they would accuse Him of blasphemy. If He claimed authority from men, they would discredit Him. If He claimed authority from God, they would challenge Him. They considered themselves the guardians of the faith, professionals who by formal training and human appointment were authorized to direct the religious life of the people. Jesus had no formal schooling and certainly no credentials from Israel's rulers. Their challenge reflected the age-old resentment felt by professional religionists against men with the power of divine anointing.

21:24, 25 The Lord offered to explain His authority if they would answer a question, "Was John's baptism **from heaven or from men?"** John's **baptism** should be understood as meaning John's ministry. Therefore the question was, "Who authorized John to carry on his ministry? Was his ordination human or divine? What credentials did he hold from Israel's leaders?" The answer was obvious: John was a man sent from God. His power came from *divine enduement*, not from *human endorsement*.

The priests and elders were in a dilemma. If they admitted that John was sent by God, they were trapped. John had pointed men to Jesus as the Messiah. If John's authority was divine, why hadn't they repented and **believed on Christ**?

21:26 On the other hand, if they said that John was not commissioned by God, they adopted a position that would be ridiculed by the people, most of whom agreed that **John** was **a prophet** from God. If they had correctly answered that John was divinely sent, they would have had the answer to their own question: Jesus was the Messiah of whom John had been the forerunner.

21:27 But they refused to face the facts, so they pleaded ignorance. They could not tell the source of John's power. Then Jesus said, **"Neither will I tell you by what authority I do these things."** Why should He tell them what they already knew but were unwilling to admit?

F. Parable of the Two Sons (21:28–32)

21:28–30 This parable is a stinging rebuke to the chief priests and elders for their failure to obey John's call to repentance and faith. It concerns **a man** whose **two sons** were asked to **work in** the **vineyard**. One refused, then changed his mind and went. The other agreed to go, but never did.

21:31, 32 When asked **which** son **did the will of his father**, the religious leaders unwittingly condemned themselves by saying, **"The first."**

The Lord interpreted the parable. **Tax collectors and harlots** were like the first son. They made no immediate pretense of obeying John the Baptist, but eventually many of them did repent and believe in Jesus. The religious leaders were like the second son. They professed to approve the preaching of John, but never confessed their sins or trusted the Savior. Therefore the out-and-out sinners entered the kingdom of God while the self-satisfied religious leaders remained outside. It is the same today. Avowed sinners receive the gospel more readily than those with a veneer of false piety.

The expression **"John came to you in the way of righteousness"** means that he came preaching the necessity of righteousness through repentance and faith.

G. Parable of the Wicked Vinedressers (21:33–46)

21:33–39 Further answering the question about authority, Jesus told the **parable** of **a certain landowner who planted a vineyard and set a hedge around it**, installed **a wine press in it, . . . built a tower**, rented **it to vinedressers**, and **went** away to a distant **country**. At **vintage-time . . . he sent his servants to the vinedressers** to get his share of the crop, but the **vinedressers beat one, killed one, and stoned another**. When **he sent other servants**, they received the same treatment. The third time **he sent his son**, thinking **they** would **respect** him. Knowing full well that he was **the heir**, they **killed him** with the idea of seizing **his inheritance**.

21:40, 41 At this point the Lord asked the priests and elders **what** the owner would **do to those vinedressers**. They answered, **"He will destroy those wicked men miserably, and lease his vineyard to other vinedressers who will render to him the fruits in their seasons."**

The parable is not difficult to interpret. God is the landowner, Israel the vineyard (Ps. 80:8; Isa. 5:1–7; Jer. 2:21). The hedge is the Law of Moses which separated Israel from the Gentiles and preserved them as a distinct people for the Lord. The wine-press, by metonymy, signifies the fruit which Israel should have produced for God. The tower suggests Jehovah's watchful care for His people. The vinedressers are the chief priests and scribes.

Repeatedly God sent His servants, the prophets, to the people of Israel seeking from the vineyard the fruits of fellowship, holiness, and love. But the people persecuted the prophets and killed some of them. Finally, God sent His Son, saying, "They will respect My Son" (v. 37). The chief priests and scribes said, "This is the heir" — a fatal admission. They privately agreed that Jesus was the Son of God (though publicly denying it) and thus answered their own question concerning His authority. His authority came from the fact that He was God the Son.

In the parable they are quoted as saying, "This is the heir. Come, let us kill him and seize his inheritance" (v. 38). In real life they said, "If we let Him alone like this, everyone will believe in Him, and the Romans will come and take away both our place and our nation" (John 11:48). And so they rejected Him, threw Him out, and crucified Him.

21:42 When the Savior asked what the owner of the vineyard would do, their answer condemned them, as He shows in verses 42 and 43. He quoted the words of Psalm 118:22: **"The stone which the builders rejected has become the chief cornerstone. This was the LORD'S doing, and it is marvelous in our eyes."** When Christ, the Stone, presented Himself to the builders — the leaders of Israel, they had no place for Him in their building plans. They threw Him aside as useless. But following His death He was raised from the dead and given the place of preeminence by God. He has been made the topmost stone in God's building: "God also has highly exalted Him and given Him the name which is above every name . . . " (Phil. 2:9).

21:43 Jesus then bluntly announced that **the kingdom of God** would **be taken from** Israel **and given to a nation bearing the fruits of it**. And so it happened. Israel has been set aside as God's chosen people and has been judicially blinded. A hardening has come upon the race that rejected its Messiah. The prophecy that **the kingdom of God** would **be given to a nation bearing the fruits of it** has been understood as referring to: (1) the church, composed of believing Jews and Gentiles — "a holy nation, God's own people" (1 Pet. 2:9); or (2) the believing portion of Israel that will be living at the Second Advent. Redeemed Israel will bring forth fruit for God.

21:44 **"Whoever falls on this stone will be broken; but on whomever it falls, it will grind him to powder."** In the first part of the verse, the **stone** is on the ground; in the second part, it is descending from above. This suggests the two Advents of Christ. When He came the first time, the Jewish leaders stumbled over Him and were broken to pieces. When He comes again, He will descend in judgment, scattering His enemies like dust.

21:45, 46 The chief priests and Pharisees realized these **parables** were aimed directly at them, in answer to their question concerning Christ's authority. They would like to have seized Him then and there, but **they feared the multitudes**, who still **took** Jesus **for a prophet**.

H. Parable of the Wedding Dinner (22:1–14)

22:1–6 Jesus was not through with the chief priests and Pharisees. In a parable of a wedding **dinner** He again pictured favored Israel as set aside and the despised Gentiles as guests at the table. He likened **the kingdom of heaven** to **a certain king who arranged a marriage** feast **for his son**. The invitation was in two stages. First, an advance invitation, personally conveyed by servants, which met a flat refusal. The second invitation announced that the feast was spread. It was treated contemptuously by some, who were too busy with their farms and businesses, and violently by others, who **seized**, abused, and **killed** the servants.

22:7–10 The king was so **furious** that he **destroyed those murderers and burned their city**. Scrapping the first guest list, he issued a general invitation to all who would come. This time there wasn't an empty seat in **the wedding hall**.

22:11–13 Among **the guests**, however, was one **who did not have a wedding garment**. Challenged on his unfitness to attend, **he was speechless**. The king ordered him to be cast out into the night, where there would be **weeping and gnashing of teeth**. The attendants in verse 13 are not the same as the servants in verse 3.

22:14 Our Lord concluded the parable with the words, **"For many are called, but few are chosen."**

As to the meaning of the parable, the king is God and His Son is the Lord Jesus. The wedding feast is an appropriate description of the festive joy which characterizes the kingdom of heaven. Introducing the church as the bride of Christ in this parable unnecessarily complicates the picture. The main thought is the setting aside of Israel — not the distinctive call and destiny of the church.

The first stage of the invitation pictures John the Baptist and the twelve disciples graciously inviting Israel to the wedding feast. But the nation refused to accept. The words, "they were not willing to come" (v. 3), were climactically dramatized in the crucifixion.

The second stage of the invitation suggests the proclamation of the gospel to the Jews in the book of Acts. Some treated the message with contempt. Some treated the messengers with violence; most of the apostles were martyred.

The King, justifiably angry with Israel, sent "his armies," that is, Titus and his Roman legions, to destroy Jerusalem and most of its people in A.D. 70. They were "his armies" in the sense that He used them as His instruments to punish Israel. They were His officially even if they did not know Him personally.

Now Israel is set aside nationally and the gospel goes out to the Gentiles, both bad and good, that is, of all degrees of respectability (Acts 13:45, 46; 28:28). But the reality of each individual who comes is tested. The man without a wedding garment is one who professes to be ready for the kingdom but who has never been clothed in the righteousness of God through the Lord Jesus Christ (2 Cor. 5:21). Actually there was (and is) no excuse for the man without the wedding garment. As Ryrie notes, it was the custom in those days to provide the guests with a garment if they had none. The man obviously did not take advantage of the offered provision. Without Christ, he is speechless when challenged as to his right to enter the kingdom (Rom. 3:19). His doom is outer darkness where there is weeping and gnashing of teeth. The weeping suggests the suffering of hell. Some suggest that the gnashing of teeth signifies continued hatred and rebellion against God. If so, it disproves the notion that the fires of hell exert a purifying effect.

Verse 14 refers to the whole parable and not just to the incident of the man without the wedding garment. **Many are called**, that is, the gospel invitation goes out to many. But **few are chosen**. Some refuse the invitation, and even of those who respond favorably, some are exposed as false professors. All who respond to the good news are chosen. The only way a person can tell whether he is chosen is by what he does with the Lord Jesus Christ. As Jennings put it,

"All are called to enjoy the feast, but not all are willing to trust the Giver to provide the robe that fits for the feast."

I. Rendering to Caesar and to God (22:15–22)

Chapter 22 is a chapter of questions, recording attempts by three different deputations sent to trap the Son of God.

22:15, 16 Here we have an attempt by **the Pharisees** and **Herodians**. These two parties were bitter foes temporarily brought together by a common hatred of the Savior. Their goal was to lure Christ into making a political statement with dangerous implications. They took advantage of the Jews' division over allegiance to Caesar. Some passionately opposed submitting to the Gentile emperor. Others, like the Herodians, adopted a more tolerant view.

22:17 First they insincerely complimented His purity of character, His truthfulness, and His fearlessness. Then they dropped the loaded question, **"Is it lawful to pay taxes to Caesar, or not?"**

If Jesus answered, "No," He would not only antagonize the Herodians, but would be accused of rebellion against the Roman government. The Pharisees would have hustled Him off and pressed charges against Him. If He said, "Yes," He would run afoul of the Jews' intense nationalistic spirit. He would lose much support among the common people — support which so far hindered the leaders in their efforts to dispose of Him.

22:18, 19 Jesus bluntly denounced them as **hypocrites**, trying to trap Him. Then He asked them to show Him a **denarius**, the coin used to pay taxes to the Roman government. Every time the Jews saw the likeness and title of Caesar on the coin it was an annoying reminder that they were under Gentile authority and taxation. The denarius should have reminded them that their bondage to Rome was a result of their sin. Had they been true to Jehovah, the question of paying taxes to Caesar would never have arisen.

22:20, 21 Jesus asked them, **"Whose image and inscription is this?"** They were forced to answer, **"Caesar's."** Then the Lord told them, **"Render therefore to Caesar the things that are**

Caesar's, and to God the things that are God's."

Their question had boomeranged. They had hoped to trap Jesus on the question of tribute to Caesar. He exposed their failure to give tribute to God. Galling as it was, they did give Caesar his due, but they had disregarded the claims of God on their lives. And One stood before them who is the express image of God's Person (Heb. 1:3) and they failed to give Him His rightful place.

Jesus' reply shows that the believer has dual citizenship. He is responsible to obey and financially support human government. He is not to speak evil of his rulers nor work to overthrow his government. He is to pray for those in authority. As a citizen of heaven, he is responsible to obey God. If there is ever a conflict between the two, his first loyalty is to God (Acts 5:29).

In quoting verse 21, most of us emphasize the part about Caesar and skip lightly over the part about God — exactly the fault for which Jesus reprehended the Pharisees!

22:22 When the Pharisees **heard** His answer, they knew they were outdone. All they could do was marvel, then leave.

J. The Sadducees and Their Resurrection Riddle (22:23–33)

22:23, 24 As mentioned previously, the Sadducees were the liberal theologians of that day, denying the resurrection of the body, the existence of angels, and miracles. In fact, their denials were more numerous than their affirmations.

A group of them **came to** Jesus with a story designed to make the idea of resurrection look ridiculous. They reminded Him of the law concerning levirate marriage (Deut. 25:5). Under that law, if an Israelite died without leaving **children, his brother** was supposed to **marry** the widow to preserve the family name in Israel and keep the inheritance within the family.

22:25–28 Their riddle concerned a woman who lost her husband, then married one of his brothers. The second brother died, so she married the third — and so on, down to the seventh. Finally,

the **woman died**. Then came the question designed to humiliate Him who is the resurrection (John 11:25): **"Therefore, in the resurrection, whose wife of the seven will she be? For they all had her."**

22:29 Basically, they argued that the idea of resurrection posed insuperable difficulties, hence it was not reasonable, therefore it was not true. Jesus answered that the difficulty was not in the doctrine but in their minds; they were ignorant of **the Scriptures** and **the power of God.**

First of all, they were ignorant **of the Scriptures.** The Bible never says the husband-wife relationship will be continued in heaven. While men will be recognizable as men, and women as women, they will all be like angels in the sense that they neither marry nor are given in marriage.

Secondly, they were ignorant of **the power of God.** If He could create men from dust, could He not as easily raise the dust of those who had died and refashion it into bodies of glory?

22:30–32 Then the Lord Jesus brought forth an argument from Scripture to show that resurrection is an absolute necessity. In Exodus 3:6 God spoke of Himself as **the God of Abraham, . . . Isaac, and . . . Jacob.** Yet Jesus pointed out, **"God is not the God of the dead, but of the living."** God made covenants with these men, but they died before the covenants were completely fulfilled. How can God speak of Himself as the God of three men whose bodies are in the grave? How can He who cannot fail to keep His promises fulfill those made to men who have already died? There is only one answer — resurrection.

22:33 No wonder **the multitudes** were **astonished at His teaching;** we are too!

K. The Great Commandment (22:34–40)

22:34–36 When the Pharisees **heard** that Jesus **had silenced** their antagonists **the Sadducees,** they came to Him for an interview. Their spokesman, **a lawyer,** asked Jesus to single out **the great commandment in the law.**

22:37, 38 In a masterful way the Lord Jesus summarized man's obligation

to God as the **first and great commandment:** "'You shall love the LORD your
God with all your heart, with all your
soul, and with all your mind.' "** Mark's
account adds the phrase, "and with all
your strength" (Mark 12:30). This means
that man's first obligation is to love God
with the totality of his being. As has
been pointed out: the heart speaks of the
emotional nature, the soul of the volitional nature, the mind of the intellectual
nature, and strength of the physical nature.

22:39, 40 Then Jesus added that
man's second responsibility is to **love** his
neighbor as himself. Barnes says, "Love
to God and man comprehends the whole
of religion: and to produce this has been
the design of Moses, the prophets, the
Savior, and the apostles." We should frequently ponder the words, **"love your
neighbor as yourself."** We should think
of how very much we do love ourselves,
of how much of our activity centers
around the care and comfort of self.
Then we should try to imagine what it
would be like if we showered that love
on our neighbors. Then we should do it.
Such behavior is not natural; it is supernatural. Only those who have been born
again can do it, and then only by allowing Christ to do it through them.

**L. David's Son Is David's Lord
(22:41–46)**

22:41, 42 While the Pharisees were
still awed by Jesus' answer to the lawyer,
He faced them with a provocative problem. **"What** did they **think about the
Christ? Whose Son is He?"**

Most Pharisees did not believe that
Jesus was the Christ; they were still waiting for the Messiah. So Jesus was not
asking them, "What do you think of
Me?" (though that, of course, was involved). He was asking in a general way
whose Son the Messiah would be when
He appeared.

They answered correctly that the
Messiah would be a descendant **of
David.**

22:43, 44 Then the Lord Jesus
quoted Psalm 110:1 where David said,
**"The LORD said to my Lord, 'Sit at My
right hand, till I make Your enemies
Your footstool.' "** The first use of the

word "LORD" refers to God the Father,
and the second to the Messiah. So David
spoke of the Messiah as his Lord.

22:45 Now Jesus posed the question, **"If David then calls Him 'Lord,'
how is He his Son?"** The answer is that
the Messiah is both David's Lord and
David's Son — both God and Man. As
God, He is David's Lord; as Man, He is
David's Son.

Had the Pharisees only been teachable, they would have realized that Jesus
was the Messiah — the Son of David
through the line of Mary, and the Son
of God as revealed by His words, works,
and ways.

22:46 But they refused to see. Completely baffled by His wisdom, they
ceased trying to trick Him with questions. Hereafter they would use another
method — *violence.*

**M. Warning Against High Talk, Low
Walk (23:1–12)**

23:1–4 In the opening verses of this
chapter, the Savior warns the crowds
and **His disciples** against **the scribes
and the Pharisees.** These leaders sat **in
Moses' seat,** or taught the Law of Moses.
Generally, their teachings were dependable, but their practice was not. Their
creed was better than their conduct. It
was a case of high talk and low walk.
So Jesus said, **". . . whatever they tell
you to observe, *that* observe and do, but
do not do according to their works; for
they say, and do not do."**

They made heavy demands (probably
extreme interpretations of the letter of
the law) on the people, but would not
assist anyone in lifting these intolerable
loads.

23:5 They went through religious
observances to be seen by men, not from
inward sincerity. Their use of phylacteries was an example. In commanding Israel to bind His words as a sign upon
their hands and as frontlets between
their eyes (Ex. 13:9, 16; Deut. 6:8; 11:18),
God meant that the law should continually be before them, guiding their activities. They reduced this spiritual
command to a literal, physical sense. Enclosing portions of Scripture in leather
capsules, they bound them to their foreheads or arms. They weren't concerned

about obeying the law as long as, by wearing ridiculously large phylacteries, they appeared super-spiritual. The law also commanded the Jews to wear tassels with blue cords on the corners of their garments, (Num. 15:37–41; Deut. 22:12). These distinctive trimmings were intended to remind them that they were a distinct people, and that they should walk in separation from the nations. The Pharisees overlooked the spiritual lesson and satisfied themselves with making longer fringes.

23:6–8 They showed their self-importance by scrambling for the places of honor **at feasts** and **in the synagogues**. They nourished their ego on **greetings in the marketplaces** and especially enjoyed being called **rabbi** (meaning "my great one," or "teacher").

23:9, 10 Here the Lord warned His disciples against using distinctive titles which should be reserved for the Godhead. We are not to be called rabbi as a distinctive title because there is one **Teacher — the Christ**. We should call no man **father**; God is our **Father**. Weston writes insightfully:

It is a declaration of the essential relations of man to God. Three things constitute a Christian — what he is, what he believes, what he does; doctrine, experience, practice. Man needs for his spiritual being three things — life, instruction, guidance; just what our Lord declares in the ten words of the Gospel — "I am the way, and the truth, and the life". . . . Acknowledge no man as Father, for no man can impart or sustain spiritual life; install no man as an infallible teacher; allow no one to assume the office of spiritual director; your relation to God and to Christ is as close as that of any other person.[42]

The obvious meaning of the Savior's words is that in the kingdom of heaven all believers form an equal brotherhood with no place for distinctive titles setting one above another. Yet think of the pompous titles found in Christendom today: Reverend, Right Reverend, Father, and a host of others. Even the seemingly harmless "Doctor" means teacher in Latin. (This warning clearly applies to *spiritual*, rather than natural, professional or academic relationships. For instance, it does not prohibit a child's calling his parent "Father," nor a patient's addressing his physician as "Doctor.") As far as earthly relationships are concerned, the rule is "respect to whom respect is due, honor to whom honor is due" (Rom. 13:7).

23:11, 12 Once again the revolutionary character of the kingdom of heaven is seen in the fact that true greatness is exactly opposite to what people suppose. Jesus said, **"He who is greatest among you shall be your servant. And whoever exalts himself will be humbled, and he who humbles himself will be exalted."** True greatness stoops to serve. Pharisees who exalt themselves will be brought low. True disciples who humble themselves will be exalted in due time.

N. Woes against the Scribes and Pharisees (23:13–36)

The Lord Jesus next pronounces eight woes on the proud religious hypocrites of His day. These are not "curses," but rather expressions of sorrow at their fate, not unlike the expression, "Alas for you!"

23:13 The first **woe** is directed against their obduracy and obstructionism. They refused to enter **the kingdom** themselves, and aggressively hindered others from **entering**. Strangely, religious leaders are often the most active opponents of the gospel of grace. They can be sweetly tolerant of everything but the good news of salvation. Natural man doesn't want to be the object of God's grace and doesn't want God to show grace to others.

23:14 The second woe[43] lambastes their appropriating of **widow's houses** and covering it up by making **long prayers**. Some modern cults use a similar technique by getting elderly widows, sometimes undiscerning believers, to sign over their property to the "church." Such pretenders to piety **will receive greater condemnation**.

23:15 The third charge against them is misdirected zeal. They went to unimaginable lengths to make one convert, but after he was **won** they made him **twice as** wicked as themselves. A modern analogy is the zeal of false cults. One group is willing to knock on 700 doors to reach one person for their cause; but the final result is evil. As someone has said, "The most converted often become the most perverted."

23:16–22 Fourthly, the Lord denounced them for their casuistry, or deliberate dishonest reasoning. They had built up a false system of reasoning to evade the payment of vows. For instance, they taught that if you swore by **the temple**, you were not obligated to pay, but if you swore **by the gold of the temple**, then you must perform the vow. They said that swearing by the gift on the altar was binding, whereas swearing by the empty altar was not. Thus they valued gold above God (the temple was the house of God), and the gift on the altar (wealth of some form) above the altar itself. They were more interested in the material than the spiritual. They were more interested in getting (the gift) than in giving (the altar was the place of giving).

Addressing them as **blind guides**, Jesus exposed their sophistry. The gold of the temple took on special value only because it was associated with God's abode. It was the altar that gave value to the gift upon it. People who think that gold has intrinsic value are blind; it becomes valuable only as it is used for God's glory. Gifts given for carnal motives are valueless; those given to the Lord or in the Lord's Name have eternal value.

The fact is that whatever these Pharisees swore by, God was involved and they were obligated to fulfill the vow. Man cannot escape his obligations by specious reasonings. Vows are binding and promises must be kept. It is useless to appeal to technicalities to evade obligations.

23:23, 24 The fifth **woe** is against ritualism without reality. The **scribes and Pharisees** were meticulous in giving the Lord a tenth of the most insignificant herbs they raised. Jesus did not condemn them for this care about small details of obedience, but He excoriated them for being utterly unscrupulous when it came to showing **justice, mercy,** and faithfulness to others. Using a figure of speech unsurpassed for expressive-

ness, Jesus described them as straining **out a gnat** and swallowing **a camel**. The gnat, a tiny insect that often fell into a cup of sweet wine, was strained out by sucking the wine through the teeth. How ludicrous to take such care with the insignificant, then bolt down the largest unclean animal in Palestine! The Pharisees were infinitely concerned with minutiae, but grossly blind to enormous sins like hypocrisy, dishonesty, cruelty, and greed. They had lost their sense of proportion.

23:25, 26 The sixth **woe** concerns externalism. The Pharisees, careful to maintain an outward show of religiousness and morality, had hearts filled with **extortion and self–indulgence.**[44] They should **first cleanse the inside of the cup and dish**, that is, make sure their hearts were cleansed through repentance and faith. Then, and only then, would their outward behavior be acceptable. There is a difference between our person and our personality. We tend to emphasize the personality — what we want others to think we are. God emphasizes the person — what we really are. He desires truth in the inward being (Ps. 51:6).

23:27, 28 The seventh **woe** also strikes out against externalism. The difference is that the sixth woe castigates the concealment of avarice, whereas the seventh condemns the concealment of **hypocrisy and lawlessness**.

Tombs were whitewashed so that Jewish people would not inadvertently touch them and thus be ceremonially defiled. Jesus likened the scribes and Pharisees to **whitewashed tombs**, which looked clean on the outside but were full of corruption inside. Men thought that contact with these religious leaders would be sanctifying, but actually it was a defiling experience because they were full of hypocrisy and iniquity.

23:29, 30 The final **woe** was against what we might label outward homage, inward homicide. The **scribes and Pharisees** pretended to honor the OT **prophets** by building and/or repairing their **tombs** and putting wreaths on their monuments. In memorial speeches, they said they **would not have** joined their ancestors in killing **the prophets**.

23:31 Jesus said to them, "Therefore you are witnesses against your-selves that you are sons of those who murdered the prophets." But how did they witness this? It almost seems from the preceding verse that they dissociated themselves from their fathers who killed the prophets. First, they admitted that their fathers, of whom they were physical sons, shed the blood of the prophets. But Jesus used the word **sons** in the sense of meaning people with the same characteristics. He knew that even as they were decorating the prophets' graves, they were plotting His death. Second, in showing such respect for the dead prophets, they were saying, "The only prophets we like are dead ones." In this sense also they were sons of their fathers.

23:32 Then our Lord added, **"Fill up, then, the measure of your fathers' guilt."** The fathers had filled the cup of murder part way by killing the prophets. The scribes and Pharisees would soon fill it to the brim by killing the Lord Jesus and His followers, thus bringing to a terrible climax what their fathers had begun.

23:33 At this point the Christ of God utters those thunderous words, **"Serpents, brood of vipers! How can you escape the condemnation of hell?"** Can Incarnate Love speak such scathing words? Yes, because true love must also be righteous and holy. The popular conception of Jesus as an innocuous reformer, capable of no emotion but love, is unbiblical. Love can be firm, and must always be just.

It is solemn to remember that these words of condemnation were hurled at religious leaders, not at drunkards and reprobates. In an ecumenical age when some evangelical Christians are joining forces with avowed enemies of the cross of Christ, it is good to ponder the example of Jesus, and to remember the words of Jehu to Jehoshaphat, "Should you help the wicked and love those who hate the LORD?" (2 Chron. 19:2).

23:34, 35 Jesus not only foresaw His own death; He plainly told the scribes and Pharisees that they would murder some of the messengers whom He would send — **prophets, wise men, and scribes.** Some who escaped martyr-

dom would be scourged in the **synagogues** and persecuted **from city to city.** Thus the religious leaders of Israel would heap to themselves the accumulated guilt of the history of martyrdom. Upon them would **come all the righteous blood shed on the earth from ... Abel ... to ... Zechariah,** whose murder is recorded in 2 Chronicles 24:20, 21, the last book in the Hebrew arrangement of the Bible. (This is not Zechariah, author of the OT book.)

23:36 The guilt of all the past would come on the **generation** or race to which Christ was speaking, as if all previous shedding of innocent blood somehow combined and climaxed in the death of the sinless Savior. A torrent of punishment would be poured out on the nation that hated its Messiah without a cause and nailed Him to a criminal's cross.

O. Jesus Laments Over Jerusalem (23:37–39)

23:37 It is highly significant that the chapter which, more than almost any other, contains the woes of the Lord Jesus, closes with His tears! After His bitter denunciation of the Pharisees, He utters a poignant lament over the city of lost opportunity. The repetition of the name — **"O Jerusalem, Jerusalem"** — is charged with unutterable emotion. She had killed **the prophets** and stoned God's messengers, yet the Lord loved her, and would often have protectingly and lovingly gathered her children to Himself — **as a hen gathers her chicks** — but she was **not willing.**

23:38 In closing His lament, the Lord Jesus said, **"See! Your house is left to you desolate."** Primarily the house here is the temple, but may also include the city of Jerusalem and the nation itself. There would be an interval between His death and Second Coming during which unbelieving Israel would not see Him (after His resurrection He was seen only by believers).

23:39 Verse 39 looks forward to the Second Advent when a believing portion of Israel will accept Him as their Messiah-King. This acceptance is implicit in the words, **"Blessed is He who comes in the name of the LORD."**

There is no suggestion that those

who murdered Christ will have a second chance. He was speaking of Jerusalem and thus, by metonymy, of its inhabitants and of Israel in general. The next time the inhabitants of Jerusalem would see Him after His death would be when they would look on Him whom they pierced and mourn for Him as one mourns for an only son (Zech. 12:10). In Jewish reckoning there is no mourning as bitter as that for an only son.

XIII. THE KING'S OLIVET DISCOURSE (Chaps. 24, 25)

Chapters 24 and 25 form what is known as the Olivet Discourse, so named because this important pronouncement was given on the Mount of Olives. The discourse is entirely prophetic; it points forward to the Tribulation Period and the Lord's Second Coming. It primarily, though not exclusively, concerns the nation of Israel. Its locale is obviously Palestine; for example, "let those who are in Judea flee to the mountains" (24:16). Its setting is distinctly Jewish; for example, "Pray that your flight may not be . . . on the Sabbath" (24:20). The reference to the elect (24:22) should be understood as God's *Jewish elect*, not the church. The church is not found in either the prophecies or parables of the discourse, as we shall seek to demonstrate.

A. Jesus Predicts the Destruction of the Temple (24:1, 2)

The discourse is introduced by the significant statement that **Jesus went out and departed from the temple** This movement is especially significant in view of the words He had just uttered, " . . . your house is left to you desolate" (23:38). It reminds us of Ezekiel's description of the glory departing from the temple (Ezek. 9:3; 10:4; 11:23).

The disciples wanted the Lord to admire the architectural beauty of the temple with them. They were occupied with the transient instead of the eternal, concerned with shadows rather than substance. Jesus warned that the building would be so completely destroyed that **not one stone** would **be left on** top of **another**. Titus tried unsuccessfully to

save the temple, but his soldiers put it to the torch, thus fulfilling Christ's prophecy. When the fire melted the gold trim, the molten metal ran down between the stones. To get at it, the soldiers had to remove the stones one by one, just as our Lord predicted. This judgment was executed in A.D. 70 when the Romans under Titus sacked Jerusalem.

B. The First Half of the Tribulation (24:3–14)

24:3 After Jesus had crossed over to **the Mount of Olives, the disciples came to Him privately** and asked Him three questions:

1. **When** would **these things** happen; that is, when would the temple be destroyed?
2. **What** would **be the sign of** His **coming**; that is, what supernatural event would precede His return to the earth to set up His kingdom?
3. What would be the sign **of the end of the age**; that is, what would announce the end of the age immediately prior to His glorious reign? (The second and third questions are essentially the same.)

We must remember that these Jewish disciples' thinking revolved around the glorious age of the Messiah on earth. They were not thinking about Christ's coming for the church; they knew little if anything about this phase of His coming. Their expectation was His coming in power and glory to destroy His enemies and rule over the world.

Also we should be clear that they were not talking about the end of the *world* (as in the KJV), but the end of the **age** (Gk., *aiōn*).

Their first question is not answered directly. Rather the Savior seems to merge the siege of Jerusalem in A.D. 70 (see Luke 21:20–24) with a similar siege that will occur in the latter days. In the study of prophecy, we often see the Lord moving almost imperceptibly from an early, partial fulfillment to a later, final fulfillment.

The second and third questions are answered in verses 4–44 of chapter 24. These verses describe the seven year Tribulation Period which will precede

Christ's glorious Advent. The first three and one-half years are described in verses 4–14. The final three and one-half years, known as the Great Tribulation and the Time of Jacob's Trouble (Jer. 30:7), will be a time of unprecedented suffering for those on earth.

Many of the conditions characterizing the first half of the Tribulation have existed to an extent throughout human history, but will appear in greatly intensified form during the period under discussion. Those in the church have been promised tribulation (John 16:33), but this is far different from *the* Tribulation which will be poured out on a world that has rejected God's Son.

We believe that the church will be taken out of the world (1 Thess. 4:13–18) before the day of God's wrath begins (1 Thess. 1:10; 5:9; 2 Thess. 2:1–12; Rev. 3:10).

24:4, 5 During the first half of the Tribulation, many false messiahs will appear who will succeed in deceiving multitudes. The current rise of many false cults may be a prelude to this, but it is not a fulfillment. These false religious leaders will be Jews claiming to be **the Christ**.

24:6, 7 There will be **wars and rumors of wars. Nation will rise against nation, and kingdom against kingdom**. It would be easy to think that we are seeing this fulfilled today, but what we see is mild compared to what will be. Actually the next event in God's time schedule is the Rapture of the church (John 14:1–6; 1 Cor. 15:51–57). There is no prophecy to be fulfilled before then. After the church is removed, God's prophetic clock will begin and these conditions will quickly manifest themselves. **Famines, pestilences, and earthquakes** will occur **in various** parts of the earth. Even today world leaders are alarmed by the specter of famine due to the population explosion. But this will be accentuated by the shortages caused by wars.

Earthquakes are attracting increasing attention — not only those now occurring but also those that are expected. Once again, these are straws in the wind, and not the actual fulfillment of our Savior's words.

24:8 Verse 8 clearly identifies this period as **the beginning of sorrows** — the onset of birth-pangs which will bring forth a new order under Israel's Messiah-King.

24:9, 10 Faithful believers will experience great personal testing during the Tribulation. The nations will conduct a bitter hate campaign against all who are true to Him. Not only will they be tried in religious and civil courts (Mark 13:9), but many will be martyred because they refuse to recant. While such testings have occured during all periods of Christian testimony, this seems to have particular reference to the 144,000 Jewish believers who will have a special ministry during this period.

Many will apostatize rather than suffer and die. Family members will inform against their own relatives and **betray** them into the hands of bestial persecutors.

24:11 Many false prophets will appear **and deceive** hordes of people. These are not to be confused with the false messiahs of verse 5. **False prophets** claim to be spokesmen for God. They can be detected in two ways: their prophecies do not always come to pass, and their teachings always lead men away from the true God. The mention of false *prophets* adds confirmation to our statement that the Tribulation is primarily Jewish in character. **False prophets** are associated with the nation of Israel; in the church the danger comes from false *teachers* (2 Pet. 2:1).

24:12 With wickedness rampaging, human affections will be less and less evident. Acts of unlove will be commonplace.

24:13 **"But he who endures to the end shall be saved."** This obviously does not mean that men's souls will be saved at that time by their enduring; salvation is always presented in the Bible as a gift of God's grace, received by faith in Christ's substitutionary death and resurrection. Neither can it mean that all who endure will escape physical harm; we have already learned that many believers will be martyred (v. 9). It is a general statement that those who stand fast, enduring persecution without apostatizing, will be delivered at Christ's Second Advent. No one should imagine that apostasy will be a means of escape or safety. Only those who have true faith **shall be saved**. Although saving faith may have lapses, it always has the quality of permanence.

24:14 During this period, the **gospel of the kingdom** will be proclaimed worldwide, **as a witness to all nations**. As explained in the notes on 4:23, the **gospel of the kingdom** is the good news that Christ is coming to set up His **kingdom** on earth, and that those who receive Him by faith during the Tribulation will enjoy the blessings of His Millennial Reign.

Verse 14 is often misused to show that Christ could not return for His church at any moment because so many tribes have not yet heard the gospel. The difficulty is removed when we realize that this refers to His coming *with* His saints, rather than *for* His saints. And this refers to the gospel of the *kingdom*, not the gospel of the *grace of God* (see notes on 4:23).

There is a striking parallel between the events listed in verses 3–14 and those of Revelation 6:1–11. The rider on the *white* horse — **false messiah**; the rider of the *red* horse — **war**; the rider of the *black* horse — **famine**; the rider of the *pale* horse — **pestilence** or **death**. The souls under the altar are martyrs. The events described in Revelation 6:12–17 are linked with those in Matthew 24:19–31.

C. The Great Tribulation (24:15–28)

24:15 At this point we have come to the middle of the Tribulation. We know this by comparing verse 15 with Daniel 9:27. Daniel predicted that in the middle of the seventieth week, that is, at the end of three and a half years, an idolatrous image would be set up in the holy place, i.e., the temple in Jerusalem. All men will be ordered to worship this abominable idol. Failure to comply will be punishable by death (Rev. 13:15). **"Therefore when you see the 'abomination of desolation,' spoken of by Daniel the prophet, standing in the holy place" (whoever reads, let him understand)**. . . . The erection of the idol will be the signal to those who know the

Word of God that the Great Tribulation has begun. Note that the Lord wants the one who **reads** the prophecy to **understand** it.

24:16 Those who are in Judea should **flee to the mountains**; in the vicinity of Jerusalem their refusal to bow to the image would be quickly detected.

24:17–19 Utmost haste will be necessary. If a man is sitting **on the housetop**, he should leave all his possessions behind. Time spent in gathering belongings might mean the difference between life and death. The man working **in the field** should not return for **his clothes**, wherever he may have left them. **Pregnant** women and **nursing** mothers will be at a distinct disadvantage — it will be hard for them to make a speedy escape.

24:20 Believers should **pray** that the crisis will not come **in winter** with its added travel hazards, and that it will not come **on the Sabbath**, when the distance they could travel would be limited by law (Ex. 16:29). A Sabbath day's journey would not be enough to take them out of the danger area.

24:21 **"For then there will be great tribulation, such as has not been from the beginning of the world until this time, no, nor ever shall be."** This description isolates the period from all the inquisitions, pogroms, purges, massacres, and genocides of history. This prophecy could not have been fulfilled by any previous persecutions because it is clearly stated that it will be ended by the Second Advent of Christ.

24:22 The tribulation will be so intense that **unless those days were shortened**, nobody would survive. This cannot mean that the Great Tribulation, so often specified as lasting three and a half years, will be shortened. It probably means that God will miraculously shorten the daylight hours — during which most fighting and slaughter occur. **For the elect's sake**, (those who have received Jesus) the Lord will grant the respite of earlier darkness.

24:23–26 Verses 23 and 24 contain renewed warnings against **false** messiahs **and false prophets**. In an atmosphere of crisis, reports will circulate that the Messiah is in some secret location. Such reports could be used to trap those who sincerely and lovingly look for Christ. So the Lord warns all disciples not to believe reports of a local, secret Advent. Even those who perform miracles are not necessarily from God; miracles can be satanic in origin. The Man of Sin will be given satanic power to perform miracles (2 Thess. 2:9, 10).

24:27 Christ's Advent will be unmistakable — it will be sudden, public, universal, and glorious. Like **the lightning**, it will be instantly and clearly visible to all.

24:28 And no moral corruption will escape its fury and judgment. **"For wherever the carcass is, there the eagles will be gathered together."** The carcass pictures apostate Judaism, Christendom, and the whole world system that is leagued against God and His Christ. **The eagles** or vultures typify the judgments of God which will be unleashed in connection with the Messiah's appearing.

D. The Second Advent (24:29–31)

24:29 At the close of the Great Tribulation there will be terrifying disturbances in the heavens. **The sun will be darkened**, and since the moon's light is only a reflection of the sun's, **the moon** will also withhold **its light**. The stars will plunge from heaven and planets will be moved out of their orbits. Needless to say, such vast cosmic upheavals will affect the weather, tides, and seasons on earth.

A faint idea of what it will be like is given in Velikovsky's description of what would happen if a heavenly body came close to the earth and caused it to tilt on its axis:

At that moment an earthquake would make the earth shudder. Air and water would continue to move through inertia; hurricanes would sweep the earth and the seas would rush over continents, carrying gravel and sand and marine animals, and casting them on the land. Heat would be developed, rocks would melt, volcanoes would erupt, lava would flow from fissures in the ruptured ground and cover vast areas. Mountains would spring up from the plains and would travel and climb on the shoulders of other mountains, causing faults and rifts. Lakes would be tilted and emptied, rivers would change their beds; large land areas with

all their inhabitants would slip under the sea. Forests would burn and the hurricane and wild seas would wrest them from the ground on which they grew and pile them, branch and root, in huge heaps. Seas would turn into deserts, their waters flowing away.[45]

24:30 **"Then the sign of the Son of Man will appear in heaven."** We are not told what this **sign** will be. His First Advent was accompanied by a sign in heaven — the star. Perhaps a miracle star will also announce His Second Coming. Some believe **the Son of Man** is Himself **the sign**. Whatever is meant, it will be clear to all when it appears. **All the tribes of the earth will mourn** — no doubt because of their rejection of Him. But primarily the tribes of the *land*[46] will mourn — the twelve tribes of Israel. ". . . then they will look on Me whom they pierced. Yes, they will mourn for Him as one mourns for his only son, and grieve for Him as one grieves for a firstborn" (Zech. 12:10).

Then **"they will see the Son of Man coming on the clouds of heaven with power and great glory."** What a wonderful moment! The One who was spit upon and crucified will be vindicated as the Lord of life and glory. The meek and lowly Jesus will appear as Jehovah Himself. The sacrificial Lamb will descend as the conquering Lion. The despised Carpenter of Nazareth will come as King of kings and Lord of lords. His chariots will be the clouds of heaven. He will come in regal power and splendor — the moment for which creation has groaned for thousands of years.

24:31 When He descends, **He will send His angels** throughout the earth to **gather together His elect** people, believing Israel, to the land of Palestine. From all the earth they will gather to greet their Messiah and to enjoy His glorious reign.

E. The Parable of the Fig Tree (24:32–35)

24:32 **"Now learn this parable from the fig tree."** Again our Lord draws a spiritual lesson from nature. When the branches of the fig tree become green and **tender, you know that summer is near**. We have seen that the fig tree pic-

tures the nation of Israel (21:18–22). For
hundreds of years Israel has been dormant, with no government of its own,
no land, no temple, no priesthood — no
sign of national life. The people have
been scattered throughout the world.

Then, in 1948, Israel became a nation
with its own land, government, currency, stamps, etc. Spiritually, the nation is still barren and cold; there is no
fruit for God. But nationally, we might
say that its branches are green and
tender.

24:33 **"So you also, when you see all
these things, know that it is near, at the
very doors!"** Israel's emergence as a nation means not only that the beginning
of the Tribulation is near, but that the
Lord Himself is near, **at the very doors!**

If Christ's coming to reign is so near,
how much more imminent is the Rapture of the church? If we already see
shadows of events that must precede His
appearing in glory, how much closer are
we to the first phase of His *Parousia*, or
Advent (1 Thess. 4:13–18)?

24:34 After referring to the fig tree,
Jesus added, **"Assuredly, I say to you,
this generation will by no means pass
away till all these things take place."**
"This generation" could not mean the
people living when Christ was on earth;
they have all passed away, yet the
events of chapter 24 have not taken
place. What then did our Lord mean by
"this generation"? There are two plausible explanations.

F. W. Grant and others believe the
thought is: "the very generation that
sees the beginning of these things will
see the end."[47] The same people who see
the rise of Israel as a nation (or who see
the beginning of the Tribulation), will
see the Lord Jesus coming in the clouds
of heaven to reign.

The other explanation is that **"generation"** should be understood as *race*.
This is a legitimate translation of the
Greek word; it means men of the same
stock, breed, or family (Matt. 12:45;
23:35, 36). So Jesus was predicting that
the Jewish race would survive to see all
these things accomplished. Their continued survival, despite atrocious persecution, is a miracle of history.

But I think there is an added thought.

In Jesus' day, "this generation" was a
race that steadfastly refused to acknowledge Him as Messiah. I think He was
predicting that national Israel would continue in its Christ-rejecting condition till
His Second Coming. Then all rebellion
will be crushed, and only those who
willingly submit to His rule will be
spared to enter the Millennium.

24:35 To emphasize the unfailing
character of His predictions, Jesus added
that **heaven and earth** would **pass away
but** His **words** would **by no means pass
away**. In speaking of **heaven** passing
away, He was referring to the stellar and
atmospheric heavens — the blue firmament above us — not to that heaven
which is the dwelling place of God (2
Cor. 12:2–4). The dissolution of the
heaven and the earth is described in 2
Peter 3:10–13 and mentioned again in
Revelation 20:11.

F. The Day and Hour Unknown (24:36–44)

24:36 As to the exact **day and hour**
of His Second Advent, **"no one knows,
not even the angels of heaven,**[48] **but My
Father only."** This should warn against
the temptation to set dates or to believe
those who do. We are not surprised that
angels do not know; they are finite creatures with limited knowledge.

While those living prior to Christ's return will not know its *day* or *hour*, it
seems that those familiar with the
prophecy may be able to know the *year*.
They will know, for instance, that it will
be approximately three and one-half
years after the idol image is set up in the
temple (Dan. 9:27; see also Dan. 7:25;
12:7, 11; Rev. 11:2, 3; 12:14; 13:5).

24:37–39 In those days, however,
most people will be indifferent, just **as
in the days of Noah**. Although the days
before the flood were terribly wicked,
that is not the feature emphasized here.
The people ate, drank, married, gave **in
marriage**; in other words, they went
through the routines of life as if they
were going to live forever. Though
warned that a flood was coming, they
lived as if they were flood-proof. When
it came, they were unprepared, outside
the only place of safety. That is just the
way it will be when Christ returns. Only

those who are in Christ, the ark of safety, will be delivered.

24:40, 41 **Two men will be in the field; one will be taken** away in judgment, **the other** will be **left** to enter the Millennium. **Two women will be grinding at the mill**; they will be instantly separated. One will be swept away by the flood of judgment; the other left to enjoy the blessings of Christ's reign. (Vv. 40 and 41 are often used as a warning to the unsaved, in reference to the Rapture — the first phase of Christ's coming when He takes all believers to heaven and leaves all unbelievers behind for judgment. While that might be a valid *application* of the passage, the context makes it clear that the *interpretation* has to do with Christ's coming to reign.)

24:42–44 In view of the uncertainty as to the day and the hour, men ought to **watch**. If someone knows his house is going to be broken into, he will be ready, even if he doesn't know the exact time. The Son of Man will come when least expected by the masses. Therefore, His people should be on the tiptoes of expectancy.

G. Parable of the Wise and the Evil Servants (24:45–51)

24:45–47 In the closing section of this chapter, the Lord Jesus shows that a **servant** manifests his true character by how he behaves in view of his Master's return. All servants are supposed to feed the household at the proper time. But not all who profess to be Christ's servants are genuine.

The **wise servant** is the one who is found caring for God's people. Such a one will be honored with vast responsibility in the kingdom. The master **will make him ruler over all his goods.**

24:48–51 The **evil servant** represents a nominal believer whose behavior is not affected by the prospect of his Master's soon return. He **begins to beat his fellow servants, and to eat and drink with the drunkards.** Such behavior demonstrates that he is not ready for the kingdom. When the King comes, He will punish him and **appoint him his portion with the hypocrites,** where people weep and gnash their teeth.

This parable refers to Christ's visible return to earth as Messiah-King. But the principle equally applies to the Rapture. Many who profess to be Christians show by their hostility toward God's people and their fraternization with the ungodly that they are not looking for Christ's Return. For them it will mean judgment and not blessing.

H. Parable of the Ten Virgins (25:1–13)

25:1–5 The first word, **Then,** referring back to chapter 24, clearly places this parable in the time preceding and during the King's return to earth. Jesus likens **the kingdom of heaven** at that time **to ten virgins who took their lamps and went to meet the bridegroom. Five of them were wise** and had **oil** for their **lamps**; the others had none. While waiting, all fell asleep.

The five **wise** virgins represent true disciples of Christ in the Tribulation. The **lamps** speak of profession, and **oil** is generally acknowledged to be a type of the Holy Spirit. The **foolish** virgins represent those who profess to hold the Messianic hope but who have never been converted and thus do not have the Holy Spirit. **The bridegroom** is Christ, the King; His delay symbolizes the period between His two Advents. The fact that all ten virgins **slept** shows that outwardly there was not much to differentiate them.

25:6 At midnight the announcement rang out that **the bridegroom** was **coming**. In the previous chapter we learned that His arrival will be heralded by awesome signs.

25:7–9 The **virgins arose and trimmed their lamps** — all wanted to appear ready. The foolish ones, lacking oil, asked the others for some, but were sent to **buy** some. The wise ones' refusal seems selfish, but in the spiritual realm, no one can dispense the Spirit to another. Of course, the Holy Spirit cannot be purchased, but the Bible does use the literary figure of buying salvation without money and without price.

25:10–12 While they were gone **the bridegroom came**. The Syriac and Vulgate versions say that he came *with his bride*. This fits the prophetic picture perfectly. The Lord Jesus will return from the wedding with His bride, the church

(1 Thess. 3:13). (The wedding takes place in heaven [Eph. 5:27] after the Rapture.) The faithful remnant of Tribulation saints will go in with Him to the marriage feast. The marriage feast is a fitting designation of the joy and blessing of Christ's earthly kingdom. The wise virgins **went in with him to the wedding** (or wedding feast, JND); **and the door was closed**. It was too late for anyone else to get into the kingdom. When the **other virgins came** seeking admittance, the bridegroom disavowed knowing them — a clear proof that they had never been born again.

25:13 The lesson, Jesus said, was to **watch**, because **the day** and **hour** of His coming are unknown. Believers should live as if the Lord might come at any moment. Are our lamps trimmed and filled with oil?

I. Parable of the Talents (25:14–30)

25:14–18 This parable also teaches that when the Lord returns, there will be true and false servants. The story revolves around **a man** who, before going on a long journey, assembled **his own servants** and **gave to each** varying amounts of money, **according to his own ability. One** got **five talents**, another got **two**, and the last, **one**. They were to use this money to bring income to the master. The man with **five** earned **another five talents**. The man with **two** doubled his also. But the man with **one** went and **dug** a hole and buried it.

It is not difficult to see that Christ is the master and the long journey is the inter-advent period. The three servants are Israelites living during the Tribulation, responsible to represent the interests of the absent Lord. They are given responsibility according to their individual abilities.

25:19–23 After a long time the lord ... **came back and settled accounts with them**. This depicts the Second Advent. The first two received exactly the same commendation: **"Well done, good and faithful servant; you were faithful over a few things, I will make you ruler over many things. Enter into the joy of your lord."** The test of their service was not how much they earned, but how hard they tried. Each used his ability fully and

earned one hundred percent. These represent true believers whose reward is to enjoy the blessings of the Messianic kingdom.

25:24, 25 The third servant had nothing but insults and excuses for his master. He accused him of being **hard** and unreasonable, **reaping where** he had **not sown, and gathering where** he had **not scattered seed**. He excused himself on the basis that, paralyzed with fear, he buried his **talent**. This servant was doubtless an unbeliever; no genuine servant would entertain such thoughts of his master.

25:26, 27 His lord rebuked him as **wicked and lazy**. Having such thoughts of his master, why hadn't he **deposited his money with the bankers** to earn interest? Incidentally, in verse 26, the master is not agreeing with the charges against him. Rather he is saying, "If that's the kind of master you thought I am, all the more reason to have put the talent to work. Your words condemn, not excuse you."

25:28, 29 If this man had earned one talent with his talent, he would have received the same commendation as the others. Instead, all he had to show for his life was a hole in the ground! His **talent** was **taken** and given to the man with **ten talents**. This follows a fixed law in the spiritual realm: **"To everyone who has, more will be given, and he will have abundance; but from him who does not have, even what he has will be taken away."** Those who desire to be used for God's glory are given the means. The more they do, the more they are enabled to do for Him. Conversely, we lose what we don't use. Atrophy is the reward of indolence.

The mention of **the bankers** in verse 27 suggests that if we cannot use our possessions for the Lord, we should turn them over to others who *can*. The bankers in this case may be missionaries, Bible societies, Christian publishing houses, gospel radio programs, etc. In a world like ours, there is no excuse for leaving money idle. Pierson helpfully recommends:

Timid souls, unfitted for bold and independent service in behalf of the kingdom, may link their incapacity to the capacity and sagacity of others who will make their gifts and possessions of use to the Master and His Church. . . . The steward has money, or it may be other gifts, that can be made of use, but he lacks faith and foresight, practical energy and wisdom. The Lord's **"exchangers"** can show him how to get gain for the Master. . . .The Church partly exists that the strength of one member may help the weakness of another, and that by cooperation of all, the power of the least and weakest may be increased.[49]

25:30 **The unprofitable servant** was cast out — excluded from the kingdom. He shared the anguished fate of the wicked. It was not his failure to invest the talent that condemned him; rather his lack of good works showed that he lacked saving faith.

J. The King Judges the Nations (25:31–46)

25:31 This section describes the Judgment of the Nations, which is to be distinguished from the Judgment Seat of Christ and the Judgment of the Great White Throne.

The Judgment Seat of Christ, a time of review and reward for believers only, takes place after the Rapture (Rom. 14:10; 1 Cor. 3:11–15; 2 Cor. 5:9, 10). The Judgment of the Great White Throne takes place in eternity, after the Millennium. The wicked dead will be judged and consigned to the Lake of Fire (Rev. 20:11–15).

The Judgment of the Nations, or Gentiles (the Greek word can mean either), takes place on earth after Christ comes to reign, as verse 31 clearly states: **"When the Son of Man comes in His glory, and all the holy angels with Him."** If we are right in identifying it with Joel 3, the location is the Valley of Jehoshaphat, outside Jerusalem (3:2). The nations will be judged according to their treatment of Christ's Jewish brethren during the Tribulation (Joel 3:1, 2, 12–14; Matt. 25:31–46).

25:32 It is important to notice that three classes are mentioned — **sheep, goats**, and Christ's brethren. The first two classes, over whom Christ sits in judgment, are Gentiles living during the Tribulation. The third class is Christ's faithful Jewish brethren who refuse to deny His Name during the Tribulation in spite of towering persecution.

25:33–40 The King places **the sheep on His right hand, but the goats on the left**. He then invites the sheep to enter His glorious **kingdom, prepared for** them **from the foundation of the world**. The reason given is that they fed Him when **hungry, gave** Him **drink** when **thirsty**, welcomed Him when **a stranger, clothed** Him when ill-clad, visited Him in sickness, and went to Him **in prison. The righteous** sheep profess ignorance of ever showing such kindnesses to the King; He had not even been on earth in their generation. He explains that in befriending **one of the least of** His **brethren**, they befriended Him. Whatever is done for one of His disciples is rewarded as being done to Himself.

25:41–45 The unrighteous goats are told to **depart from** Him **into the everlasting fire prepared for the devil and his angels** because they failed to care for Him during the terrible Time of Jacob's Trouble. When they excuse themselves by saying they had never seen Him, He reminds them that their neglect of His followers constituted neglect of Himself.

25:46 Thus the goats **go away into everlasting punishment, but** the sheep **into eternal life**. But this raises two problems. First, the passage seems to teach that nations are saved or lost *en masse*. Second, the narrative creates the impression that the sheep are saved by good works, and the goats are condemned through failure to do good. As to the first difficulty, it must be remembered that God *does* deal with nations as such. OT history abounds with instances of nations punished because of their sin (Isa. 10:12–19; 47:5–15; Ezek. 25:6, 7; Amos 1:3, 6, 9, 11, 13; 2:1, 4, 6; Obad. 10; Zech. 14:1–5). It is not unreasonable to believe that nations will continue to experience divine retribution. This does not mean that every single individual in the nation will be involved in the outcome, but that the principles of divine justice will be applied on a national, as well as an individual basis.

The word *ethnē*, translated "nations" in this passage, can equally well be translated "Gentiles." Some believe the passage describes the judgment of individual Gentiles. Whether nations or individuals, there is the problem of how such a vast horde could be gathered before the Lord in Palestine. Perhaps it is best to think of representatives of the nations or individual classes assembled for judgment.

As to the second problem, the passage cannot be used to teach salvation by works. The uniform testimony of the Bible is that salvation is by faith and not by works (Eph. 2:8, 9). But the Bible is just as emphatic in teaching that true faith produces good works. If there are no good works, it is an indication that the person was never saved. So we must understand that the Gentiles are not saved by befriending the Jewish remnant, but that this kindness reflects their love for the Lord.

Three other points should be mentioned. First, the kingdom is said to have been prepared for the righteous from the foundation of the world (v. 34), whereas hell was prepared for the devil and his angels (v. 41). God's desire is that men should be blessed; hell was not originally intended for the human race. But if people willfully refuse life, they necessarily choose death.

The second point is that the Lord Jesus spoke of eternal (same word as "everlasting") fire (v. 41), eternal punishment (v. 46), and eternal life (v. 46). The same One who taught eternal life taught eternal punishment. Since the same word for *eternal* is used to describe each, it is inconsistent to accept one without the other. If the word translated *eternal* does not mean everlasting, there is no word in the Greek language to convey the meaning. But we know that it *does* mean everlasting because it is used to describe the eternality of God (1 Tim. 1:17).

Finally the Judgment of the Gentiles reminds us forcefully that Christ and His people are one; what affects them affects Him. We have vast potential for showing kindness to Him by showing kindness to those who love Him.

XIV. THE KING'S PASSION AND DEATH (Chaps. 26, 27)

A. The Plot to Kill Jesus (26:1–5)

26:1, 2 For the fourth and last time in this Gospel our Lord forewarned His disciples that He must die (16:21; 17:23; 20:18). His announcement implied a close time relationship between the Passover and His crucifixion: **"You know that after two days is the Passover, and the Son of Man will be delivered up to be crucified."** This year the Passover would find its true meaning. The Paschal Lamb had at last arrived and would soon be slain.

26:3–5 Even as He was uttering the words, **the chief priests, the scribes, and the elders** were gathering in the **palace** of **Caiaphas**, the **high priest**, to map out their strategy. They wanted to arrest Him furtively and have Him killed, but did not think it prudent to do it **during the feast; the people** might react violently against His execution. It is incredible that Israel's religious leaders took the lead in plotting the death of their Messiah. They should have been the first to recognize and to enthrone Him. Instead, they formed the vanguard of His enemies.

B. Jesus Anointed at Bethany (26:6–13)

26:6, 7 This incident provides a welcome relief, coming amid the treachery of the priests, the pettiness of the disciples, and the perfidy of Judas. **When Jesus was at the house of Simon the leper in Bethany, a woman came** in and poured out **a flask** of very expensive perfume **on His head**. The costliness of her sacrifice expressed the depth of her devotion for the Lord Jesus, saying, in effect, that there was nothing too good for Him.

26:8, 9 **His disciples**, and Judas in particular (John 12:4, 5), looked upon the act as an enormous **waste**. They thought the money might better have been **given to the poor**.

26:10–12 Jesus corrected their distorted thinking. Her act was not wasteful, but beautiful. Not only so, it was perfectly timed. The poor can be helped at any time. But only once in the world's history could the Savior be anointed for burial. That moment had struck and one lone **woman** with spiritual discernment had seized it. Believing the Lord's predictions concerning His death, she must have realized it was now or never. As it turned out, she was right. Those women who planned to anoint His body after His burial were thwarted by the resurrection (Mark 16:1–6).

26:13 The Lord Jesus immortalized her simple act of love: **"Assuredly, I say to you, wherever this gospel is preached in the whole world, what this woman has done will also be told as a memorial to her."** Any act of true worship fills the courts of heaven with fragrance and is indelibly recorded in the Lord's memory.

C. The Treachery of Judas (26:14–16)

26:14, 15† **Then one of the twelve—** one of the disciples who had lived with the Lord Jesus, traveled with Him, seen His miracles, heard His incomparable teaching, and witnessed the miracle of a sinless life — one whom Jesus could call "my familiar friend . . . who ate my bread" (Ps. 41:9) — it was that one who lifted up his heel against the Son of God. **Judas Iscariot went to the chief priests and** agreed to sell his Master for **thirty pieces of silver**. The priests paid him on the spot — the contemptible total of about fifteen dollars.

It is striking to note the contrast between the woman who anointed Jesus at Simon's home and Judas. She valued the Savior highly. Judas valued Him lightly.

26:16 And so the one who had received nothing but kindness from Jesus went out to arrange his part of the dreadful bargain.

D. The Last Passover (26:17–25)

26:17 It was **the first day of the Feast of the Unleavened Bread** — a time when all leaven was removed from Jewish homes. What thoughts must have flooded the mind of the Lord as He sent **the disciples** into Jerusalem **to prepare for . . . the Passover**. Every detail of the meal would have poignant significance.

26:18–20 Jesus sent the disciples to look for **a certain** unnamed **man** who would lead them to the appointed **house**. Perhaps the vagueness of the instructions was designed to foil the conspirators. At any rate, we note Jesus' full knowledge of individuals, their whereabouts, and their willingness to cooperate. Note His words, **"The Teacher says, 'My time is at hand; I will keep the Passover at your house with My disciples.'"** He faced His approaching death

with poise. With perfect grace, He arranged the meal. What a privilege for this anonymous man to lend his house for this final Passover!

26:21–24 As they were eating, Jesus made the shocking announcement that **one of** the twelve would **betray** Him. The disciples were filled with sorrow, chagrin, and self-distrust. One by one they asked, **"Lord, is it I?"** When all but Judas had inquired, Jesus told them that it was the one **who dipped** with Him **in the dish**. The Lord then took a piece of bread, dipped it in the meat juice, and handed it to Judas (John 13:26) — a token of special affection and friendship. He reminded them that there was a certain irresistibility in what was going to happen to Him. But that did not free the traitor from responsibility; **it would** be better for him **if he had** never **been born**. Judas deliberately chose to sell the Savior and is thus held personally responsible.

26:25 When Judas finally asked point-blank if he were the one, Jesus answered, "Yes."

E. The First Lord's Supper (26:26–29)

In John 13:30 we learn that as soon as Judas received the piece of bread, he went out, and it was night. We therefore conclude that he was not present when the Lord's Supper was instituted (although there is considerable disagreement on this point).

26:26 After observing His last Passover, the Savior instituted what we know as the Lord's Supper. The essential elements — bread and wine — were already on the table as part of the Paschal meal; Jesus clothed them with new meaning. First He **took bread, blessed and broke it**. As He **gave it to the disciples** He **said, "Take, eat, this is My body."** Since His body had not yet been given on the cross, it is clear that He was speaking figuratively, using the bread to symbolize His body.

26:27, 28 The same is true of **the cup**; the container is used to express the thing contained. The cup contained the fruit of the vine, which in turn was a symbol of the **blood of the new covenant**. The **new**, unconditional **covenant** of grace would be ratified by His precious **blood** shed for many for the forgiveness of sins. His blood was *sufficient* to provide forgiveness for all. But here it was **shed for many** in that it was only *effective* in removing the sins of those who believe.

26:29 The Savior then reminded His disciples that He would **not drink** from the **fruit of the vine** with them again **until** He returned to earth to reign. Then the wine would have a new significance; it would speak of the joy and blessedness of His **Father's kingdom**.

The question is often raised whether we should use leavened or unleavened bread, fermented or unfermented wine for the Lord's Supper. There is little doubt that the Lord used unleavened bread and fermented wine (*all* wine in those days was fermented). Those who argue that leavened bread spoils the type (leaven is a picture of sin) should realize that the same is true of fermentation. It is a tragedy when we become so occupied with the *elements* that we fail to see the Lord *Himself*. Paul emphasized that it is the spiritual meaning of the bread, not the bread itself that counts. "For indeed Christ, our Passover, was sacrificed for us. Therefore, let us keep the feast, not with old leaven, nor with the leaven of malice and wickedness, but with the unleavened bread of sincerity and truth" (1 Cor. 5:7, 8). It is not the leaven in the *bread* that matters, but the leaven in our *lives*!

F. The Self-Confident Disciples (26:30–35)

26:30 Following the Lord's Supper, the little band sang **a hymn**, probably taken from Psalms 113–118 — "the Great Hallel." Then they left Jerusalem, crossed the Brook Kidron, and climbed the western slope of Olivet to the Garden of Gethsemane.

26:31 Throughout His earthly ministry the Lord Jesus had faithfully warned His disciples concerning the pathway ahead. Now He told them that they would all dissociate themselves from Him that **night**. Fear would overwhelm them when they saw the fury of the storm breaking. To save their own skins, they would forsake their Master. Zechariah's prophecy would be fulfilled: "Strike the Shepherd, and the sheep will be scattered" (13:7).

26:32 But He did not leave them without hope. Though they would be ashamed of their association with Him, He would never forsake them. After rising from the dead, He would meet them in **Galilee**. Wonderful, never-failing Friend!

26:33, 34 Peter rashly interrupted to assure the Lord that although the others might desert Him, he would **never** do such a thing. Jesus corrected the *"never"* to **"this night . . . three times."** Before **the rooster** crowed, the impetuous disciple would deny his Master **three times**.

26:35 Still protesting his loyalty, **Peter** insisted that he would **die** with Christ rather than **deny** Him. **All the disciples** chimed in their agreement. They were sincere; they meant what they said. It was just that they didn't know their own hearts.

G. The Agony in Gethsemane (26:36–46)

No one can approach this account of the Garden of Gethsemane without realizing that he is walking on holy ground. Anyone who attempts to comment on it feels a tremendous sense of awe and reticence. As Guy King wrote, "The supernal character of the event causes one to fear lest one should in any way spoil it by touching it."

26:36–38 After entering **Gethsemane** (meaning olive vat or olive press), **Jesus** told eight of the eleven **disciples** with Him to **sit** and wait, then took **Peter and the two sons of Zebedee** deeper into the garden. Might this suggest that different disciples have different capacities for empathizing with the Savior in His agony?

He began to be sorrowful and deeply distressed. He frankly told Peter, James, and John that His soul was **exceedingly sorrowful, even to death**. This was doubtless the unspeakable revulsion of His holy soul as He anticipated becoming a sin-offering for us. We who are sinful cannot conceive what it meant to Him, the Sinless One, to be made sin for us (2 Cor. 5:21).

26:39 It is not surprising that He left the three and **went a little farther** into the garden. No one else could share His suffering or pray His prayer: **"O My**

Father, if it is possible, let this cup pass from Me; nevertheless, not as I will, but as You will."

Lest we think this prayer expressed reluctance or a desire to turn back, we should remember His words in John 12:27, 28: "Now My soul is troubled, and what shall I say? Father, save Me from this hour'? But for this purpose I came to this hour. Father, glorify Your name." Therefore, in praying that the **cup** might **pass from** Him, He was *not* asking to be delivered from going to the cross. That was the very purpose of His coming into the world!

The prayer was rhetorical, that is, it was not intended to elicit an answer but to teach us a lesson. Jesus was saying in effect, "My Father, if there is any other way by which ungodly sinners can be saved than by My going to the cross, reveal that way now! But in all of this, I want it known that I desire nothing contrary to Your will."

What was the answer? There was none; the heavens were silent. By this eloquent silence we know that there was no other way for God to justify guilty sinners than for Christ, the sinless Savior, to die as our Substitute.

26:40, 41 Returning to **the disciples, He found them sleeping**. Their spirits were **willing**; their **flesh** was **weak**. We dare not condemn them when we think of our own prayer lives; we sleep better than we pray, and our minds wander when they should be watching. How often the Lord has to say to us as He said to Peter, **"Could you not watch with Me one hour? Watch and pray, lest you enter into temptation."**

26:42 **Again, a second time, He went away and prayed**, expressing submission to the Father's will. He would drink the cup of suffering and death to the dregs.

He was necessarily alone in His prayer life. He taught the disciples to pray, and He prayed in their presence, but He never prayed *with* them. The uniqueness of His Person and work precluded others from sharing in His prayer life.

26:43–45 When He came to the disciples the second time, they were **asleep again**. Likewise the third time: He prayed, they slept. It was then He said

to them, **"Are you still sleeping and resting? Behold, the hour is at hand, and the Son of Man is being betrayed into the hands of sinners."**

26:46 The opportunity of watching with Him in His vigil was gone. The footsteps of the traitor were already audible. Jesus said, **"Rise, let us be going"** — not in retreat but to face the foe.

Before we leave the garden, let us pause once more to hear His sobs, to ponder His sorrow, and to thank Him with all our hearts.

H. Jesus Betrayed and Arrested in Gethsemane (26:47–56)

The betrayal of the sinless Savior by one of His own creatures presents one of the most amazing anomalies of history. Apart from human depravity we would be at a loss to explain the base, inexcusable treachery of Judas.

26:47 While Jesus **was still speaking** to the eleven, **Judas** arrived with a gang armed **with swords and clubs**. Surely the weapons were not Judas's idea; he had never seen the Savior resist or fight back. Perhaps the weapons symbolized the determination of the chief priests and elders to capture Him without any possibility of escape.

26:48 Judas would use a kiss as the sign to help the mob distinguish Jesus from His disciples. The universal symbol of love was to be prostituted to its lowest use.

26:49 As he approached the Lord, Judas said, **"Greetings, Rabbi!"** then **kissed Him** profusely. Two different words for *kiss* are used in this passage. The first, in verse 48, is the usual word for kiss. But in verse 49 a stronger word is used, expressing repeated or demonstrative kissing.

26:50 With poise and convicting penetration, **Jesus** asked, **"Friend, why have you come?"** No doubt the question came with scalding power to Judas, but events were moving fast now. The mob surged in and seized the Lord Jesus without delay.

26:51 One of the disciples — we know from John 18:10 that it was Peter — **drew his sword** and **cut off** the **ear** of the high priest's **servant**. It is unlikely that Peter had aimed for the ear; he had doubtless planned a mortal blow. That his aim was as poor as his judgment must be attributed to divine Providence.

26:52 The moral glory of the Lord Jesus shines radiantly here. First He rebuked Peter: **"Put your sword in its place, for all who take the sword will perish by the sword."** In Christ's kingdom, victories are not won by carnal means. To resort to armed force in spiritual warfare is to invite disaster. Let the enemies of the kingdom use the sword; they will eventually meet defeat. Let the soldier of Christ resort to prayer, the Word of God, and the power of a Spirit-filled life.

We learn from Dr. Luke that Jesus then healed the ear of Malchus — for that was the victim's name (Luke 22:51; John 18:10). Is this not a wonderful display of grace? He loved those who hated Him and showed kindness to those who were after His life.

26:53, 54 If Jesus had desired to resist the mob, He would not have been limited to Peter's puny sword. In an instant He could have asked for and been sent **more than twelve legions of angels** (from 36,000 to 72,000). But that would only have frustrated the divine program. **The Scriptures** predicting His betrayal, suffering, crucifixion, and resurrection had to **be fulfilled**.

26:55 Then **Jesus** reminded the crowds how incongruous it was for them to **come out** after Him with weapons. They had never seen Him resort to violence or engage in plunder. Rather, He had been a quiet Teacher, **daily** sitting **in the temple**. They could easily have captured Him then, but didn't. Why come now **with swords and clubs**? Humanly speaking, their behavior was irrational.

26:56 Yet the Savior realized that man's wickedness was succeeding only in accomplishing the definite plan of God. **"All this was done that the Scriptures of the prophets might be fulfilled."** Realizing there would be no deliverance for their Master, **all the disciples forsook Him and fled** in panic. If their cowardice was inexcusable, ours is more so. They had not yet been indwelt by the Holy Spirit; we have.

I. Jesus Before Caiaphas (26:57–68)[†]

26:57 There were two main trials of the Lord Jesus: a religious trial before the Jewish leaders, and a civil trial before the Roman authorities. Combining the accounts from all four Gospels shows that each trial had three stages. John's account of the Jewish trial shows that Jesus was first brought before Caiaphas' father-in-law, Annas. Matthew's account begins with the second stage at the home of **Caiaphas, the high priest**. The Sanhedrin **were assembled** there. Ordinarily, accused men were given an opportunity to prepare their defense. But the desperate religious leaders hurried Jesus away from prison and justice (Isa. 53:8), in every way denying Him a fair trial.

On this particular night, the Pharisees, Sadducees, **scribes,** and **elders** who comprised the Sanhedrin showed an utter disregard for the rules under which they were supposed to operate. They were not supposed to meet at night nor during any of the Jewish feasts. They were not supposed to bribe witnesses to commit perjury. A death verdict was not to be carried out until a night had elapsed. And, unless they met in the Hall of Hewn Stone, in the temple area, their verdicts were not binding. In their eagerness to get rid of Jesus, the Jewish establishment did not hesitate to stoop to breaking their own laws.

26:58 Caiaphas was the presiding judge. The Sanhedrin apparently served as both jury and prosecution, an irregular combination, to say the least. Jesus was the Defendant. And **Peter** was a spectator — from a safe distance; he **sat with the** guards **to see the end**.

26:59–61 The Jewish leaders had a difficult time finding **false testimony against Jesus**. They would have been more successful had they fulfilled their prior obligation in the judicial process and sought evidence of His innocence. Finally, **two false witnesses** produced a garbled account of Jesus' words: "Destroy this temple, and in three days I will raise it up" (John 2:19–21). According to the witnesses, He had threatened **to destroy the temple** in Jerusalem and then rebuild it. In fact, He had been predicting His own death and subsequent resurrection. The Jews now used that prediction as an excuse for killing Him.

26:62–63 During these accusations the Lord Jesus said nothing: "as a sheep before its shearers is silent, so He opened not His mouth" (Isa. 53:7). The high priest, irritated by His silence, pressed Him for a statement; still the Savior refrained from answering. The high priest then **said to Him, "I put You under oath by the living God: Tell us if You are the Christ, the Son of God!"** The Law of Moses required that a Jew testify when put under oath by the high priest (Lev. 5:1).

26:64 Being an obedient Jew under the law, Jesus answered: **"It is as you said."** He then asserted His Messiahship and deity even more strongly: **"Nevertheless, I say to you, hereafter you will see the Son of Man sitting at the right hand of the Power, and coming on the clouds of heaven."** In essence He was saying, "I am the Christ, the Son of God, as you have said. My glory is presently veiled in a human body; I appear to be just another man. You see Me in the days of My humiliation. But the day is coming when you Jews will see Me as the glorified One, equal in all respects with God, sitting at His right hand and coming on the clouds of heaven."

In verse 64 the first **you**[50] is singular, referring to Caiaphas. The second you is plural (also the third), referring to the Jews as representative of those Israelites living at the time of Christ's glorious appearing, who will clearly see that He is the Son of God.

"The assertion is sometimes made," writes Lenski, "that Jesus never called Himself 'The Son of God.' Here (in v. 64) He *swears* that He is no less."[51]

26:65–67[+] Caiaphas did not miss the point. Jesus had alluded to a Messianic prophecy of Daniel: "I was watching in the night visions, and behold, One like the Son of Man, coming with the clouds of heaven! He came to the Ancient of Days, and they brought Him near before Him" (Dan. 7:13). The high priest's reaction proves that he understood Jesus was claiming equality with God (see John 5:18). He **tore his** priestly **clothes**, a sign that the witness had blasphemed. His in-

flammatory words to the Sanhedrin assumed Jesus was guilty. When asked their verdict, the Council answered, **"He is deserving of death."**

26:68 The second stage of the trial ended with the jurists striking and spitting upon the Accused, then taunting Him to use His power as **Christ** to identify His assailants. The entire proceeding was not only unjuridical, but scandalous.

J. Peter Denies Jesus and Weeps Bitterly (26:69–75)

26:69–72 Peter's darkest hour had now arrived. As he **sat outside in the courtyard**, a young woman came by and accused him of being an associate of Jesus. His denial was vigorous and prompt, **"I do not know what you are saying."** He went **out to the gateway**, perhaps to escape further notice. But there **another girl** publicly identified him as one who had been **with Jesus of Nazareth**. This time he swore that he did not know **the Man**. "The Man" was his Master.

26:73, 74 A little later several bystanders came saying, **"Surely you also are one of them, for your speech betrays you."** A simple denial was no longer sufficient; this time he confirmed it with oaths and curses. **"I do not know the Man!"** With disquieting timing, **a rooster crowed**.

26:75 The familiar sound pierced not only the quiet of the early hours but Peter's heart as well. The deflated disciple, remembering what the Lord had said, **went out and wept bitterly**.

There is a seeming contradiction in the Gospels concerning the number and timing of the denials. In Matthew, Luke, and John, Jesus is reported as saying, "Before the rooster crows, you will deny Me three times" (Matt. 26:34; see also Luke 22:34; John 13:38). In Mark, the prediction is, ". . . before the rooster crows twice, you will deny Me three times" (Mark 14:30).

Possibly there was more than one rooster crowing, one during the night and another at dawn. Also it is possible that the Gospels record at least six different denials by Peter. He denied Christ before: (1) a young woman (Matt. 26:69,

70; Mark 14:66–68); (2) another young woman (Matt. 26:71, 72; Mark 14:69, 70); (3) the crowd that stood by (Matt. 26:73, 74; Mark 14:70, 71); (4) a man (Luke 22:58); (5) another man (Luke 22:59, 60); (6) a servant of the high priest (John 18:26, 27). We believe this last man is different from the others because he said, "Did I not see you in the garden with Him?" The others are not described as saying this.

K. Morning Trial Before the Sanhedrin (27:1, 2)

The third stage of the religious trial took place before the Sanhedrin in the **morning**. No case was to be completed on the same day it was begun unless the defendant was acquitted. A night was supposed to elapse before the verdict was pronounced "so that feelings of mercy might have time to arise." In this case the religious leaders seemed intent on stifling any feelings of mercy. However, since night trials were irregular, they convened a morning session to give legal validity to their verdict.

Under Roman rule the Jewish leaders had no authority to inflict capital punishment. Therefore we now see them hurrying Jesus **to Pontius Pilate, the** Roman **governor**. Though their hatred of everything Roman was intense, they were willing to "use" this power to satisfy a *greater* hatred. Opposition to Jesus unites the bitterest foes.

L. Judas' Remorse and Death (27:3–10)

27:3, 4 Realizing his sin in **betraying innocent blood, Judas** offered the money back to **the chief priests and elders**. These arch conspirators who had co-operated so eagerly a few hours ago now refused to have any further part in the matter. This is one of the rewards of treachery. Judas **was remorseful**, but this was not a godly repentance that leads to salvation. Sorry for the effects which his crime brought on himself, he was yet unwilling to acknowledge Jesus Christ as Lord and Savior.

27:5 In desperation Judas **threw down the pieces of silver in the temple** where only the priests could go, then went out and committed suicide. Comparing this narrative with Acts 1:18, we conclude that he hanged himself on a

tree, that the rope or branch broke, and that his body was hurled over a precipice, causing it to be disemboweled.

27:6 The chief priests, too "spiritual" to put the money **into the** temple **treasury** because it was **the price of blood**, were the guilty ones who paid that money to have the Messiah turned over to them. This didn't seem to bother them. As the Lord had said, they made the outside of the cup clean, but inside it was full of deceit, treachery, and murder.

27:7–10 They used the money to buy **a potter's field** where unclean Gentile strangers might be buried, little realizing how many Gentile hordes would invade their land and splatter their streets with blood. It has been a **Field of Blood** for that guilty nation ever since.

The chief priests unwittingly fulfilled Zechariah's prophecy that the burial money would be used to make a purchase from a potter (Zech. 11:12, 13). Strangely enough, the Zechariah passage has an alternative reading — "treasury" for "potter" (see RSV).

> The priests had scruples about putting blood money into the treasury so they fulfilled the prophecy of the other reading by giving it to the potter in exchange for his field. (Daily Notes of the Scripture Union).

Matthew assigns this prophecy to **Jeremiah**, whereas it obviously comes from the book of Zechariah. He probably labels the citation from Jeremiah because that prophet stood at the head of the prophetic roll he used, according to the ancient order preserved in numerous Hebrew manuscripts and familiar from Talmudic tradition. A similar usage occurs in Luke 24:44 where the book of Psalms gives its name to the entire third section of the Hebrew canon.

M. Jesus' First Appearance Before Pilate (27:11–14)

The Jews' real grievances against Jesus were *religious*, and they tried Him on that basis. But religious charges carried no weight in the court of Rome. Knowing that, when they brought Him before Pilate they pressed three *political* charges against Him (Luke 23:2): (1) He was a revolutionary who posed a threat to the empire; (2) He urged people not to pay taxes, therefore undermining the prosperity of the empire; (3) He claimed to be a King, therefore threatening the power and position of the emperor.

In Matthew's Gospel we hear Pilate interrogating Him on the third charge. Asked if He was **the King of the Jews**, Jesus answered that He was. This brought forth a torrent of abuse and slander from the Jewish leaders. Pilate **marveled greatly** at the Defendant's silence; He would not dignify even one of their charges with an answer. Probably never before had the governor seen anyone remain silent under such attack.

N. Jesus or Barabbas? (27:15–26)

27:15-18 It was customary for the Roman authorities to placate the Jews by **releasing** a Jewish **prisoner** at Passover time. One such eligible convict was **Barabbas**, a Jew guilty of insurrection and murder (Mark 15:7). As a rebel against Roman rule, he was probably popular with his countrymen. So when Pilate gave them a choice between **Jesus** and **Barabbas**, they clamored for the latter. The governor was not surprised; he knew that public opinion had been molded in part by the chief priests, who were envious of Jesus.

27:19 The proceedings were momentarily interrupted by a messenger from Pilate's **wife**. She urged her husband to adopt a hands-off policy with regard to Jesus; she had had a very disturbing **dream** about **Him**.

27:20-23 Behind the scenes **the chief priests and elders** were passing the word for the release of **Barabbas** and the death of Jesus. So when **Pilate** asked the people again which one they wanted freed, they cried for the murderer. Snared in the web of his own indecisiveness, Pilate asked, **"What then shall I do with Jesus who is called Christ?"** They unanimously demanded His crucifixion, an attitude incomprehensible to the governor. Why crucify Him? What crime had He committed? But it was too late to plead for calm deliberation; mob hysteria had taken over. The cry rang out, **"Let Him be crucified!"**

27:24 It was obvious to **Pilate** that the people were implacable and that a riot was beginning. So he **washed his hands** in sight of the mob, declaring his innocence **of the blood** of the Accused. But water will never absolve Pilate's guilt in history's gravest miscarriage of justice.

27:25 The crowd, too frenzied to worry about guilt, was willing to bear the blame: **"His blood be on us and on our children!"** Since then the people of Israel have staggered from ghetto to pogrom, from concentration camp to gas chamber, suffering the awful guilt of the blood of their rejected Messiah. They still face the fearsome Time of Jacob's Trouble — those seven years of tribulation described in Matthew 24 and Revelation 6–19. The curse will remain until they acknowledge the rejected Jesus as their Messiah-King.

27:26 Pilate **released Barabbas to** the crowd, and the spirit of Barabbas has dominated the world ever since. The murderer is still enthroned; the righteous King is rejected. Then, as was customary, the condemned One was **scourged**. A large leather whip with bits of sharp metal embedded in it was brought down across His back, each lash opening up the flesh and releasing streams of blood. Now there was nothing for the spineless governor to do but to turn Jesus over to the soldiers **to be crucified**.

O. The Soldiers Mock Jesus (27:27–31)

27:27, 28 The soldiers of the governor took Jesus into the governor's palace **and gathered the whole garrison around Him** — probably several hundred men. What followed is hard to imagine! The Creator and Sustainer of the universe suffered unspeakable indignities from cruel, vulgar soldiers — His unworthy, sinful creatures. **They stripped Him and put a scarlet robe on Him**, in imitation of a king's robe. But that robe has a message for us. Since scarlet is associated with sin (Isa. 1:18), I like to think that the robe pictures my sins being placed on Jesus so that God's robe of righteousness might be placed on me (2 Cor. 5:21).

27:29, 30 They **twisted a crown of thorns** and pressed it down **on His head**. But beyond their crude jest, we understand that He wore *a crown of* *thorns* that we might wear *a crown of glory*. They mocked Him as the King of Sin; we worship Him as the Savior of sinners.

They also gave Him **a reed** — a mock scepter. They didn't know that the hand that held that reed is the hand that rules the world. That nail-scarred hand of Jesus now holds the scepter of universal dominion.

They knelt **before Him** and addressed Him as **King of the Jews**. Not content with that, **they spat on** the face of the only perfect Man who ever lived, then **took the reed and struck Him on the head** with it.

Jesus bore it all patiently; He didn't say a word. "For consider Him who endured such hostility from sinners against Himself, lest you become weary and discouraged in your souls" (Heb. 12:3).

27:31 Finally they **put His own clothes** back **on Him, and led Him away to be crucified**.

P. The Crucifixion of the King (27:32–44)

27:32 Our Lord carried His **cross** part of the way (John 19:17). Then the soldiers **compelled** a man named **Simon** (from **Cyrene**, in northern Africa) to carry it for Him. Some think he was a Jew; others that he was a black man. The important thing is that he had the wonderful privilege of bearing the cross.

27:33 Golgotha is Aramaic for "skull." Calvary is the anglicized Latin translation of the Greek *kranion*. Perhaps the area was shaped like a skull or received the name because it was a place of execution. The site is uncertain.

27:34 Prior to His being impaled, the soldiers offered Jesus the **sour wine** and **gall** given to condemned criminals as an opiate. Jesus refused to take it. For Him it was necessary to bear the full load of man's sins with no impairment of His senses, no alleviation of His pain.

27:35[†] Matthew describes the crucifixion simply and unemotionally. He does not indulge in dramatics, resort to sensational journalism, or dwell on sordid details. He simply states the fact: **Then they crucified Him**. Yet eternity itself will not exhaust the depths of those words.

As prophesied in Psalm 22:18, the soldiers **divided His garments . . . and . . . cast lots** for the seamless robe. This was His entire earthly estate. Denney said, "The one perfect life that has been lived in this world is the life of Him who owned nothing, and who left nothing but the clothes He wore."

27:36 These soldiers were representatives of a world of little men. They apparently had no sense of history being made. If only they had known, they would not have *sat* down and **kept watch**; they would have *knelt* down and worshiped.

27:37 Over Christ's **head** they had put the title, **THIS IS JESUS THE KING OF THE JEWS.** The exact wording of the superscription varies somewhat in the four Gospels.[52] Mark says, "The King of the Jews" (15:26); Luke: "This is the King of the Jews" (23:38); and John: "Jesus of Nazareth, the King of the Jews" (19:19). The chief priests protested that the title should not be a statement of fact, but the mere claim of the Accused. However, Pilate overruled them; the truth was there for all to see — in Hebrew, Latin, and Greek (John 19:19–22).

27:38 The sinless Son of God was flanked by **two robbers**, because hadn't Isaiah predicted 700 years previously that He would be numbered with the transgressors (53:12)? At first, both robbers hurled insult and invective at Him (v. 44). But one repented and was saved in the nick of time; in just a few hours he was with Christ in Paradise (Luke 23:42, 43).

27:39, 40 If the cross reveals God's love, it also reveals man's depravity. Passers-by paused long enough to jeer at the Shepherd as He was dying for the sheep: **"You who destroy the temple and build it in three days, save Yourself! If You are the Son of God, come down from the cross."** This is the language of rationalistic unbelief. "Let us see and we will believe." It is also the language of liberalism. "Come down from the cross — in other words, remove the offense of the cross and we will believe." William Booth said, "They claimed they would have believed if He had come down; we believe because He stayed up."

27:41–44 The **chief priests, scribes,**

and elders joined the chorus. With unintentional insight they cried, **"He saved others; Himself He cannot save."** They meant it as a taunt; we adapt it as a hymn of praise:

> Himself He could not save,
> He on the cross must die,
> Or mercy cannot come
> To ruined sinners nigh;
> Yes, Christ the Son of God must bleed,
> That sinners might from sin be freed.
> *– Albert Midlane*

It was true in the Lord's life and in ours, too. We can't save others while seeking to save ourselves.

The religious leaders mocked His claim to be the Savior, His claim to be **the King of Israel**, His claim to be **the Son of God. Even the robbers** joined in their cursing. The religious leaders united with criminals in vilifying their God.

Q. Three Hours of Darkness (27:45–50)

27:45 All the sufferings and indignities which He bore at the hands of men were minor compared to what He now faced. **From the sixth hour** (noon) **until the ninth hour** (3:00 p.m.), **there was darkness** not **only over all the land** of Palestine but in His holy soul as well. It was during that time that He bore the indescribable curse of our sins. In those three hours were compressed the hell which we deserved, the wrath of God against all our transgressions. We see it only dimly; we simply cannot know what it meant for Him to satisfy all God's righteous claims against sin. We only know that in those three hours He paid the price, settled the debt, and finished the work necessary for man's redemption.

27:46† At about 3:00 p.m., He **cried out with a loud voice, saying, "My God, My God, why have You forsaken Me?"** The answer is found in Psalm 22:3, " . . .You are holy, enthroned in the praises of Israel." Because God is holy, He cannot overlook sin. On the contrary, He must punish it. The Lord Jesus had no sin of His own, but He took the guilt of our sins upon Himself. When God, as Judge, looked down and saw our sins upon the sinless Substitute, He withdrew from the Son of His love. It was this separation that wrung from the heart of Jesus what Mrs. Browning so beautifully called "Immanuel's orphaned cry":

> Deserted! God could separate from His
>   own essence rather;
> And Adam's sins have swept between the
>   righteous Son and Father:
> Yea, once, Immanuel's orphaned cry
>   His universe hath shaken —
> It went up single, echoless,
>   "My God, I am forsaken!"
> *– Elizabeth Barrett Browning*

27:47, 48 When Jesus cried, **"Eli, Eli . . . ,"** some of those who stood by said He was **calling for Elijah**. Whether they actually confused the names or were simply mocking is not clear. One used a long **reed** to lift a **sponge** soaked with **sour wine** to His lips. Judging from Psalm 69:21, this was not intended as an act of mercy but as an added form of suffering.

27:49 The general attitude was to wait and **see if Elijah** would fulfill the role Jewish tradition assigned to him — coming to the aid of the righteous. But it was not time for Elijah to come (Mal. 4:5); it was time for Jesus to die.

27:50 When He had **cried out again with a loud voice**, He **yielded up His spirit**. The **loud** cry demonstrates that He died in strength, not in weakness. The fact that He **yielded up His spirit** distinguished His death from all others. We die because we have to; He died because He chose to. Had He not said, "I lay down My life that I may take it again. No one takes it from Me, but I lay it down of Myself. I have power to lay it down, and I have power to take it again" (John 10:17, 18)?

> The Maker of the Universe
> As man for man was made a curse;
> The claims of laws which He had made,
> Unto the uttermost He paid.
> His holy fingers made the bough
> Which grew the thorns that crowned His
>   brow.
> The nails that pierced his hands were
>   mined
> In secret places He designed;
> He made the forests whence there sprung
> The tree on which His body hung.
> He died upon a cross of wood,
> Yet made the hill on which it stood.
> The sky that darkened o'er His head
> By Him above the earth was spread;

†See p. xxii.

The sun that hid from Him its face
By His decree was poised in space;
The spear that spilled His precious blood
Was tempered in the fires of God.
The grave in which His form was laid
Was hewn in rock His hands had made;
The throne on which He now appears
Was His from everlasting years;
But a new glory crowns His brow,
And every knee to Him shall bow.

                — *F. W. Pitt*

R. The Torn Veil (27:51–54)

27:51 At the time He expired, the heavy, woven curtain separating the two main rooms of the temple was torn by an Unseen Hand **from top to bottom**. Up to then that **veil** had kept everyone except the high priest from the Holiest Place where God dwelt. Only one man could enter the inner sanctuary, and he could enter on only one day of the year.

In the book of Hebrews we learn that the veil represented the body of Jesus. Its rending pictured the giving of His body in death. Through His death, we have "boldness to enter the Holiest by the blood of Jesus, by a new and living way which He consecrated for us, through the veil, that is, His flesh" (Heb. 10:19, 20). Now the humblest believer can enter God's presence in prayer and praise at any time. But let us never forget that the privilege was purchased for us at tremendous cost — the blood of Jesus.

The death of God's Son also produced tremendous upheavals in nature — as if there was an empathy between inanimate creation and its Creator. There was an earthquake which **split** great **rocks** and **opened** many **graves**.

27:52, 53 But notice that it was not until **after** the **resurrection** of Jesus that the occupants of these tombs **were raised** and **went into** Jerusalem where they **appeared to many**. The Bible does not say whether these risen saints died again or went to heaven with the Lord Jesus.

27:54 The strange convulsions of nature convinced **the** Roman **centurion** and his men that Jesus **was the Son of God** (while there is no definite article in the Greek before Son of God, the word order does make it definite[33]). What did **the centurion** mean? Was this a full con-

fession of Jesus Christ as Lord and Savior, or an acknowledgment that Jesus was more than man? We cannot be sure. It does indicate a sense of awe, and a realization that the disturbances of nature were somehow connected with the death of Jesus, and not with the death of those who were crucified with Him.

S. The Faithful Women (27:55, 56)

Special mention is made of the **women** who had faithfully ministered to the Lord, and who had **followed** Him all the way **from Galilee** to Jerusalem. **Mary Magdalene, Mary the mother of James and Joses**, and Salome, the wife of Zebedee, were there. The fearless devotion of these women stands out with special luster. They remained with Christ when the male disciples ran for their lives!

T. The Burial in Joseph's Tomb (27:57–61)[†]

27:57, 58[††] **Joseph of Arimathea, a rich man** and member of the Sanhedrin, had not concurred in the Council's decision to deliver Jesus to Pilate (Luke 23:51). If up to this point he had been a secret **disciple**, he now threw caution to the wind. Boldly he **went to Pilate** and requested permission to bury his Lord. We must try to imagine the surprise to Pilate, and the provocation to the Jews, that a member of the Sanhedrin would publicly take his stand for the Crucified. In a real sense Joseph buried himself economically, socially, and religiously when he buried the body of Jesus. This act separated him forever from the establishment that killed the Lord Jesus.

27:59, 60 **Pilate** granted permission and **Joseph** lovingly embalmed **the body** by **wrapping it in a clean linen cloth**, placing spices between the wrappings. Then he placed **it in his** own **new tomb**, carved out of solid **rock**. The mouth of the tomb was closed by **a large stone**, shaped like a millstone and standing on its edge in a channel also carved out of stone.

Centuries before, Isaiah had predicted, "And they made His grave with the wicked — but with the rich at His death" (53:9). His enemies had doubtless planned to throw His body into the Valley of Hinnom to be consumed by dump-fires or eaten by foxes. But God overruled their plans and used Joseph to insure that He was buried *with the rich*.

27:61 After Joseph had departed, **Mary Magdalene** and the mother of James and Joses stayed to keep vigil **opposite the tomb**.

U. The Guarded Tomb (27:62–66)

27:62–64 The first day of the Passover, called the **Day of Preparation**, was the day of the crucifixion. **The next day the chief priests and Pharisees** were uneasy. Remembering what Jesus had said about rising again, they went to Pilate and asked for a special guard to be placed at the tomb. This was allegedly to prevent **His disciples** from stealing the body, thus creating the impression that He had risen. Should this happen, they feared, **the last deception** would **be worse than the first**; that is, the report concerning His resurrection would be worse than His claim to be the Messiah and the Son of God.

27:65, 66 Pilate answered, **"You have a guard; go your way, make it as secure as you know how."** This may mean that a Roman guard had already been assigned to them. Or it may mean "Your request is granted. I now assign a guard to you." Was there irony in Pilate's voice as he said **"as secure as you know how?"** They did their best. They sealed the stone and stationed guards, but their best security measures were just not good enough. Unger says:

> The precautions His enemies took to "make the sepulchre sure, sealing it and stationing a guard," 62-64, only resulted in God's overruling the plans of the wicked and offering indisputable proof of the King's resurrection.[54]

XV. THE KING'S TRIUMPH (Chap. 28)[†]

A. The Empty Tomb and the Risen Lord (28:1–10)

28:1–4 Before dawn on Sunday morning the two Marys **came to see the tomb**. As they arrived there **was a great earthquake. An angel . . . descended from heaven, rolled back the stone from** the mouth of the tomb, **and sat on it**. The Roman **guards**, terrified by this radiant being clothed in glistening white, fainted.

28:5, 6 The angel reassured **the women** that there was nothing for them to fear. The One they sought had **risen, as He** had promised. **"Come, see the place where the Lord lay."** The stone had been rolled away, not to let the Lord out, but to let the women see that He had risen.

28:7–10 The angel then deputized the women to **go quickly** to announce the glorious news to **His disciples**. The Lord was alive again and would meet **them in Galilee**. When they were on their way to tell the disciples, Jesus appeared to them, greeting them with a single word, **"Rejoice!"**[55] They responded by falling at His **feet** and worshiping Him. He then personally commissioned them to notify the disciples that they would see Him in **Galilee**.

B. The Soldiers Bribed to Lie (28:11–15)

28:11 As soon as they regained consciousness, **some of the** soldiers sheepishly went **to the chief priests** to break the news. They had failed in their mission! The tomb was empty!

28:12, 13 It is easy to imagine the consternation of the religious leaders. The priests held a conclave with the elders to map out their strategy. In desperation, they bribed **the soldiers** to tell the fantastic yarn that while the soldiers **slept**, the **disciples stole** the body of Jesus.

This explanation raises more questions than it answers. Why were the soldiers sleeping when they should have been on guard? How could the disciples have rolled the stone away without waking them? How could all the soldiers have fallen asleep at the same time? If they were asleep, how did they know that the disciples stole the body? If the story was true, why did the soldiers have to be bribed to tell it? If the disciples had stolen the body, why had they taken time to remove the graveclothes and fold the napkin? (Luke 24:12; John 20:6, 7).

†See p. xvii.

28:14 Actually the soldiers were paid to tell a story incriminating themselves; sleeping on duty was punishable by death under Roman law. So the Jewish leaders had to promise to intervene for them if the story ever got back **to the governor's ears**.

The Sanhedrin was learning that while truth is self-verifying, a lie has to be supported by countless other lies.

28:15 Yet the myth persists **among** many **Jews until this day**, and among Gentiles as well. And there are other myths. Wilbur Smith summarizes two of them:

1. First of all it has been suggested that the women went to the wrong tomb. Think about this for a moment. Would you miss the tomb of your dearest loved one between Friday afternoon and Sunday morning? Furthermore, this was not a cemetery of Joseph of Arimathea. This was his private garden. No other tombs were there.

Now, let's say there were other tombs, which there weren't, and suppose the women with their tear-filled eyes stumbled around and got to the wrong tomb. Well, let's grant that for the women. But hardfisted Simon Peter and John, two fishermen who were not crying, also went to the tomb and found it empty. Do you think they went to the wrong tomb? But more than that, when they got to the tomb and found that it was empty, there was an angel who said, "He is not here. He is risen. Come, see the place where the Lord lay." Do you think the angel went to the wrong tomb too? Yet, don't forget, brainy men have advanced these theories. This is a nonsensical one!

2. Others have suggested that Jesus did not die, but swooned away, and that he was resuscitated somehow in this damp tomb and then came forth. They had a great big stone rolled against this tomb and this was sealed with seals of the Roman government. No man on the inside of that tomb could ever roll back the stone which came down an incline and fitted into a groove. He did not come out of that tomb as an anemic invalid.

The simple truth is that the resurrection of the Lord Jesus is a well-attested fact of history. He presented Himself alive to His disciples after His passion by many infallible proofs. Think of these specific instances when He appeared to His own:

1. To Mary Magdalene (Mark 16:9–11).
2. To the women (Matt. 28:8–10).
3. To Peter (Luke 24:34).
4. To the two disciples on the road to Emmaus (Luke 24:13–32).
5. To the disciples, except Thomas (John 20:19–25).
6. To the disciples, including Thomas (John 20:26–31).
7. To the seven disciples by the Sea of Galilee (John 21).
8. To over 500 believers (1 Cor. 15:7).
9. To James (1 Cor. 15:7).
10. To the disciples on the Mount of Olives (Acts 1:3–12).

One of the great foundation stones, unshakable and unmovable, of our Christian faith, is the historic evidence for the resurrection of the Lord Jesus Christ. Here you and I can stand and do battle for the faith because we have a situation which cannot be contradicted. It can be denied, but it cannot be disproved.[56]

C. The Great Commission (28:16–20)

28:16, 17 In **Galilee** the risen Lord Jesus appeared to His **disciples** at an unnamed mountain. This is the same appearance recorded in Mark 16:15–18 and 1 Corinthians 15:6. What a wonderful reunion! His sufferings were passed forever. Because He lived, they too would live. He stood before them in His glorified body. They worshiped the living, loving Lord — though doubts still lurked in the minds of some.

28:18 Then the Lord explained that **all authority** had **been given to** Him **in heaven and on earth**. In one sense, of course, He always had all authority. But here He was speaking of authority as Head of the new creation. Since His death and resurrection, He had authority to give eternal life to all whom God had given to Him (John 17:2). He had always had power as the firstborn of all creation. But now that He had completed the work of redemption, He had authority as the first-born from the dead — "that in all things He may have the preeminence" (Col. 1:15, 18).

28:19, 20 As Head of the new creation, He then issued the Great Commission, containing "standing orders" for all believers during the present phase of the kingdom — the time between the rejection of the King and His Second Advent.

The Commission contains three commands, not suggestions:

1. **"Go therefore and make disciples of all the nations."** This does not presuppose world conversion. By preaching the gospel, the disciples were to

see others become learners or followers of the Savior — from every nation, tribe, people, and tongue.

2. Baptize **"them in the name of the Father and of the Son and of the Holy Spirit."** The responsibility rests on Christ's messengers to teach baptism and to press it as a command to be obeyed. In believer's baptism, Christians publicly identify themselves with the Triune Godhead. They acknowledge that God is their Father, that Jesus Christ is their Lord and Savior, and that the Holy Spirit is the One who indwells, empowers, and teaches them. **Name** in verse 19 is singular. One **name** or essence, yet three Persons — **Father, Son,** and **Holy Spirit**.

3. Teach **"them to observe all things that I have commanded you."** The Commission goes beyond evangelism; it is not enough to simply make converts and let them fend for themselves. They must be taught to *obey* the commandments of Christ as found in the NT. The essence of discipleship is becoming like the Master, and this is brought about by systematic teaching of, and submission to, the Word.

Then the Savior added a promise of His presence with His disciples until the consummation **of the age**. They would not go forth alone or unaided. In all their service and travel, they would know the companionship of the Son of God.

Notice the four "alls" connected with the Great Commission: **all authority; all nations; all things; always**.

Thus the Gospel closes with commission and comfort from our glorious Lord. Nearly twenty centuries later His words have the same cogency, the same relevance, the same application. The task is still uncompleted.

What are we doing to carry out His last command?

ENDNOTES

[1](1:1) *Jehovah* is the anglicized form of the Hebrew name *Yahweh*, traditionally translated "Lᴏʀᴅ." Compare the similar situation with *Jesus*, the anglicized form of Hebrew *Yeshua*.

[2](4:2, 3) First class condition, using *ei* with the indicative. It may be para-

phrased, "If, and I grant it, You are the Son of God" or "Since You are the Son of God."

[3](Excursus) A "dispensation" is an administration or stewardship. It describes the methods God uses in dealing with the human race at any particular time in history. The word does *not* mean a time period *per se*, but rather the divine program *during* any age. A similar use is seen when we speak of the Reagan administration, indicating the policies President Reagan followed during his years in office.

[4](5:13) Albert Barnes, *Notes on the New Testament, Matthew and Mark*, p. 47.

[5](5:22) The critical text (labeled "NU" in NKJV footnotes) omits *without a cause*, which would rule out even righteous indignation.

[6](5:44–47) The critical (NU) text reads *Gentiles* for *tax collectors*.

[7](5:44–47) The majority text (based on the majority of manuscripts) reads *friends* for *brethren*.

[8](6:13) Some scholars teach that the doxology is adapted from 1 Chronicles 29:11 for liturgical purposes. This is merely a guess. The traditional Protestant (KJV) form of the prayer is completely defensible.

[9](7:13, 14) Both the critical and majority texts have an exclamatory reading here: "How narrow is the gate and difficult is the way which leads to life, and there are few who find it!" When the oldest manuscripts (usually NU) and the vast bulk of manuscripts (M) agree against the traditional text (TR) they are almost certainly correct. In such cases the KJ tradition has weak textual support.

[10](7:28, 29) Jamieson, Fausset & Brown, *Critical and Explanatory Commentary on the New Testament*, V:50.

[11](8:2) Certain forms of leprosy mentioned in the Bible are not the same as the malady we call Hansen's disease. For example, in Leviticus, it includes conditions that can infect a house or a garment.

[12](8:16, 17) Arno C. Gaebelein, *The Gospel of Matthew*, p. 193.

[13](8:28) The NU text reads *Gadarenes*. The names of the town and of the region may overlap somewhat.

[14](9:16) Gaebelein, *Matthew*, p. 193.

¹⁵(9:17) W. L. Pettingill, *Simple Studies in Matthew*, pp. 111, 112.

¹⁶(10:8) The majority of mss. omit "raise the dead" here.

¹⁷(10:21) J. C. Macaulay, *Obedient Unto Death: Devotional Studies in John's Gospel*, II:59.

¹⁸(10:41) Arthur T. Pierson, "The Work of Christ for the Believer," *The Ministry of Keswick, First Series*, p. 114.

¹⁹(11:27) Alva J. Gospel McClain, *The Greatness of the Kingdom*, p. 311.

²⁰(11:30) J. H. Jowett, Quoted in *Our Daily Bread*.

²¹(12:8) E. W. Rogers, *Jesus the Christ*, pp. 65, 66.

²²(12:19) McClain, *Kingdom*, p. 283.

²³(12:21) Kleist and Lilly, *The New Testament rendered from the Original Greek with Expanded Notes*, p. 45.

²⁴(12:27) Ella E. Pohle, *C. I. Scofield's Question Box*, p. 97.

²⁵(12:34,35) Although both critical and majority texts omit "of his heart," it would nevertheless be understood.

²⁶(13:13) H. Chester Woodring, Unpublished class notes on Matthew, Emmaus Bible School, 1961.

²⁷(13:22) G. H. Lang, *The Parabolic Teaching of Scripture*, p. 68.

²⁸(13:24–26) Merrill F. Unger, *Unger's Bible Dictionary*, p. 1145.

²⁹(13:33) J. H. Brookes, *I Am Coming*, p. 65.

³⁰(13:49,50) Gaebelein, *Matthew*, p. 302.

³¹(14:4,5) Source unknown.

³²(16:2,3) Of course, these weather indications are valid for Israel, not North America or Great Britain!

³³(16:7–10) The twelve *kophinoi* of the 5,000 may have held less than the seven *spurides* of the 4,000.

³⁴(16:17,18) G. Campbell Morgan, *The Gospel According to Matthew*, p. 211.

³⁵(16:19) Charles C. Ryrie, ed., *The Ryrie Study Bible, New King James Version*, p. 1506.

³⁶(16:20) James S. Stewart, *The Life and Teaching of Jesus Christ*, p. 106.

³⁷(16:26) Donald Grey Barnhouse, *Words Fitly Spoken*, p. 53.

³⁸(18:11) It is omitted by the NU text, but contained in the majority of mss. (M).

³⁹(20:15) James S. Stewart, *A Man in Christ*, p. 252.

⁴⁰(20:31–34) Gaebelein, *Matthew*, p. 420.

⁴¹(21:6) J. P. Lange, *A Commentary on the Holy Scriptures*, 25 Vols., pagination unknown.

⁴²(23:9, 10) H. G. Weston, *Matthew, the Genesis of the New Testament*, p. 110.

⁴³(23:14) The critical (NU) text omits the second woe.

⁴⁴(23:25, 26) The majority text reads *unrighteousness (adikia)* for *self-indulgence (akrasia)*.

⁴⁵(24:29) I. Velikovsky, *Earth in Upheaval*, p. 136.

⁴⁶(24:30) The same Greek word (*gē*, compare English prefix "geo") means both "land" and "earth."

⁴⁷(24:34) F. W. Grant, "Matthew," *Numerical Bible, The Gospels*, p. 230.

⁴⁸(24:36) The NU text adds "nor the Son."

⁴⁹(25:28, 29) *Our Lord's Teachings About Money* (tract), pp. 3, 4.

⁵⁰(26:64) The Greek singular pronoun *su* is spelled out for emphasis. The second *you* is *humin* (plural) and the third renders the ending on the verb *opsesthe*.

⁵¹(26:64) R. C. H. Lenski, *The Interpretation of St. Matthew's Gospel*, p. 1064.

⁵²(27:37) If all the quoted parts are put together, it reads "This is Jesus of Nazareth, the King of the Jews." Another possibility is that each evangelist is complete but quotes different languages, which could have varied.

⁵³(27:54) In Greek the definite predicate nouns which precede the verb usually lack the article (part of "Colwell's Rule").

⁵⁴(27:65, 66) Merrill F. Unger, *Unger's Bible Handbook*, p. 491.

⁵⁵(28:8) "Rejoice" was the standard Greek greeting; here on Resurrection Morning the literal translation of the NKJV seems most appropriate.

⁵⁶(28:15) Wilbur Smith, "In the Study," *Moody Monthly*, April, 1969.

BIBLIOGRAPHY

Barnhouse, Donald Grey. *Words Fitly Spoken*. Wheaton: Tyndale House Publishers, 1969.

Gaebelein, A. C. *The Gospel of Matthew*. New York: Loizeaux Bros., 1910.

Kelly, William. *Lectures on Matthew*. New York: Loizeaux Bros., 1911.

Lenski, R. C. H. *The Interpretation of Saint Matthew's Gospel*. Minneapolis: Augsburg Publishing House, 1933.

Macaulay, J. C. *Behold Your King*. Chicago: The Moody Bible Institute, 1982.

Morgan, G. Campbell. *The Gospel According to Matthew*. New York: Fleming H. Revell Company, 1929.

Pettingill, W. L. *Simple Studies in Matthew*. Harrisburg: Fred Kelker, 1910.

Tasker, R. V. G. *The Gospel According to St. Matthew, TBC*. Grand Rapids: Wm. B. Eerdmans Publishing Company, 1961.

Thomas, W. H. Griffith. *Outline Studies in Matthew*. Grand Rapids: Wm. B. Eerdmans Publishing Company, 1961.

Weston, H. G. *Matthew, the Genesis of the New Testament*. Philadelphia: American Baptist Publication Society, n.d.

Periodicals and Unpublished Material

Smith, Wilbur. "In the Study," *Moody Monthly*, April, 1969.

Woodring, H. Chester. Class Notes on Matthew, 1961, Emmaus Bible School, Oak Park, IL (now Emmaus Bible College).

THE GOSPEL ACCORDING TO MARK†

Introduction

"There is a freshness and vigor about Mark that grips the Christian reader, and makes him long to serve somewhat after the example of his blessed Lord."
— August Van Ryn

I. Unique Place in the Canon

Since Mark's is the shortest Gospel and about ninety percent of his material also occurs in Matthew, Luke, or both, what contribution does he make that we could not do without?

First of all, Mark's brevity and journalistic simplicity make his Gospel an ideal introduction to the Christian faith. On new mission fields Mark is often the first book translated into a new language.

But it is not merely the direct, active *style* — especially suitable for the Romans and their modern counter-parts — but also the *content* that make Mark's Gospel special.

While Mark handles largely the same events as Matthew and Luke — with a few unique ones — he has colorful details that the others do not. For example, he mentions the way Jesus looked at the disciples, how He was angry, and how He walked ahead on the road to Jerusalem. He no doubt got these touches from Peter, with whom he was associated at the end of Peter's life. Tradition says, and probably correctly, that Mark's Gospel is essentially Peter's reminiscences, which would account for the personal details, the action, and the eyewitness effect of the book.

A common belief is that Mark is the young man who ran away naked (14:51), and that this is his modest signature to the book. (The titles on the Gospels were not originally part of the books themselves.) Since John Mark lived in Jerusa-lem, and there is no reason to tell this little story if the young man is not related to the Gospel in some way, the tradition is likely correct.

II. Authorship††

Most authors accept the early and unanimous opinion of the church that the Second Gospel was written by John Mark. He was the son of Mary of Jerusalem, who owned a house there which the Christians used as a meeting place.

The *external evidence* for this is early, strong, and from various parts of the empire. Papias (about A.D. 110) quotes John the Elder (probably the Apostle John, though conceivably another early disciple) as saying that Mark, the associate of Peter, wrote it. Justin Martyr, Irenaeus, Tertullian, Clement of Alexandria, Origen, and the *Anti–Marcionite Prologue* to Mark all concur.

The *internal evidence* for Marcan authorship, while not extensive, does dovetail with this universal tradition of early Christianity.

The writer obviously knew Palestine well, especially Jerusalem. (The accounts regarding the upper room are more detailed than in the other Gospels — not surprising if it was in his boyhood home!) The Gospel shows some Aramaic background (the language of Palestine), Jewish customs are understood, and the vividness of the narrative suggests close ties with an eyewitness. The outline of the book's contents parallels Peter's sermon in Acts 10.

†See pp. iii–viii.
††See p. i.

The tradition that Mark wrote in Rome is illustrated by the greater number of Latin words in his Gospel than the others (such as *centurion*, *census*, *denarius*, *legion*, and *praetorium*).

Ten times in the NT our author is mentioned by his Gentile (Latin) name, Mark, and three times by his combined Jewish and Gentile name, John Mark. Mark, the "servant" or attendant, first of Paul, then of his cousin Barnabas, and according to reliable tradition, of Peter before his death, was an ideal person to write the Gospel of the Perfect Servant.

III. Date

The date of Mark is debated even by conservative, Bible–believing scholars. While no date can be fixed with certainty, one prior to the destruction of Jerusalem is indicated.

Tradition is divided as to whether Mark penned Peter's preaching on the life of our Lord *before* the death of the apostle (before 64-68) or *after* his passing.

Especially if Mark is the First Gospel written, as most now teach, an early date is necessary in order for Luke to have used Mark's material. Some scholars date Mark in the early 50's, but a date from 57–60 seems quite likely.

IV. Background and Theme

In this Gospel we have the wonderful story of God's Perfect Servant, our Lord Jesus Christ. It is the story of One who laid aside the outward display of His glory in heaven and assumed the form of a Servant on earth (Phil. 2:7). It is the matchless story of One who "did not come to be served, but to serve, and to give His life a ransom for many" (Mark 10:45).

If we remember that this Perfect Servant was none other than God the Son, and that He willingly girded Himself with the apron of a slave, becoming a Servant of men, the Gospel will glow with constant splendor. Here we see the incarnate Son of God living as a dependent Man on earth. Everything He did was in perfect obedience to His Father's will, and His mighty works were all performed in the power of the Holy Spirit.

The author, John Mark, was a servant of the Lord who started well, went into eclipse for a while (Acts 15:38), and was finally restored to usefulness (2 Tim. 4:11).

Mark's style is rapid, energetic, and concise. He emphasizes the deeds of the Lord more than His words, evidenced by the fact that he records nineteen miracles, but only four parables.

As we study the Gospel, we shall seek to discover three things: (1) What does it say? (2) What does it mean? (3) What lesson is there in it for me? For all who wish to be true and faithful *servants of the Lord*, this Gospel should prove a valuable manual of service.

OUTLINE

Commentary†

I. THE SERVANT'S PREPARA-
   TION (1:1–13)

A. The Servant's Forerunner
   Prepares the Way (1:1–8)

1:1 Mark's theme is the good news about **Jesus Christ, the Son of God**. Because his purpose is to emphasize the servant role of the Lord Jesus, he begins not with a genealogy, but with the public ministry of the Savior. This was announced by John the Baptist, the herald of the good news.

1:2, 3 Both Malachi and Isaiah¹ predicted that a **messenger** would precede the Messiah, calling the people to be morally and spiritually prepared for His coming (Mal. 3:1; Isa. 40:3). John the Baptist fulfilled these prophecies. He was the **"messenger, . . . the voice of one crying in the wilderness."**

1:4 His message was that the people should repent (change their minds and forsake their sins) in order to receive **the remission of sins**. Otherwise they would be in no position to receive the Lord. Only holy people are able to appreciate the Holy Son of God.

1:5 When his hearers did repent, John baptized them as an outward expression of their about-face. Baptism separated them publicly from the mass of the nation of Israel who had forsaken the Lord. It united them with a remnant who were ready to receive the Christ. It might seem from verse 5 that the response to John's preaching was universal. This was not the case. There may have been an initial burst of enthusiasm, with multitudes surging out to the desert to hear the fiery preacher, but the majority did not genuinely confess and forsake their sins. This will be seen as the narrative advances.

1:6 What kind of man was **John**? Today he would be called a fanatic and an ascetic. His home was the desert. His clothing, like Elijah's was the coarsest and the simplest. His food was sufficient to maintain life and strength, but was scarcely luxurious. He was a man who subordinated all these things to the glori-

ous task of making Christ known. Perhaps he could have been rich, but he chose to be poor. He thus became a fitting herald of Him who had nowhere to lay His head. We learn here that simplicity should characterize all who are servants of the Lord.

1:7 His message was the superiority of the Lord Jesus. He said that Jesus was greater in power, personal excellence, and in ministry. John did not consider himself worthy to **loose** the Savior's **sandal strap** — a menial duty of a slave. Spirit-filled preaching always exalts the Lord Jesus and dethrones self.

1:8 John's baptism was **with water**. It was an external symbol, but produced no change in a person's life. Jesus would **baptize** them **with the Holy Spirit**; this baptism would produce a great inflow of spiritual power (Acts 1:8). Also it would incorporate all believers into the church, the body of Christ (1 Cor. 12:13).

B. The Forerunner Baptizes the Servant
   (1:9–11)

1:9 The so-called thirty silent years in Nazareth were now at an end. The Lord Jesus was ready to enter upon His public ministry. First He traveled the sixty odd miles **from Nazareth** to the **Jordan** near Jericho. There He was **baptized by John**. In His case, of course, there was no repentance because there were no sins to confess. Baptism for the Lord was a symbolic action picturing His eventual baptism into death at Calvary and His rising from the dead. Thus at the very outset of His public ministry, there was this vivid foreshadow of a cross and an empty tomb.

1:10, 11 As soon as He came **up from the water, He saw the heavens parting and the Spirit descending upon Him like a dove**. The **voice** of God the Father was heard, acknowledging Jesus as His **beloved Son**.

There never was a time in the life of our Lord when He was not filled with the Holy **Spirit**. But now the Holy Spirit came **upon Him**, anointing Him for service and enduing Him with power. It was a special ministry of the Spirit, preparatory to the three years of service that

†See p. ix.

lay ahead. The power of the Holy Spirit is indispensable. A person may be educated, talented, and fluent, yet without that mysterious quality which we call "unction," his service is lifeless and ineffective. The question is basic, "Have I had an experience of the Holy Spirit, empowering me for the service of the Lord?"

C. The Servant Tempted by Satan (1:12, 13)

The Servant of Jehovah was tempted by Satan in **the wilderness** for **forty days**. **The Spirit** of God led Him to this rendezvous — not to see if He would sin, but to prove that He could not sin. If Jesus could have sinned as a Man on earth, what assurance do we have that He cannot now sin as a Man in heaven?

Why does Mark say that He was **with the wild beasts**? Were these animals energized by Satan to seek to destroy the Lord? Or were they docile in the presence of their Creator? We can only ask the questions.

The angels ministered to Him at the end of the forty days (cf. Matt. 4:11); during the temptation He ate nothing (Luke 4:2).

Testings are inevitable for the believer. The closer one follows the Lord, the more intense they will be. Satan does not waste his gunpowder on nominal Christians, but opens his big guns on those who are winning territory in the spiritual warfare. It is not a sin to be tempted. The sin lies in *yielding* to temptation. In our own strength we cannot resist. But the indwelling Holy Spirit is the believer's power to subdue dark passions.

II. THE SERVANT'S EARLY GALILEAN MINISTRY (1:14—3:12)[†]

A. The Servant Begins His Ministry (1:14, 15)

Mark skips over the Lord's Judean ministry (see John 1:1–4:54) and begins with the great Galilean ministry, a period of one year and nine months (1:14–9:50). Then he deals briefly with the latter part of the Perean ministry (10:1–10:45) before moving on to the last week in Jerusalem.

†See p. xii.

Jesus came to Galilee, preaching the good news of the kingdom of God. His specific message was that:

1. **The time** was **fulfilled**. According to the prophetic time-table, a date had been fixed for the public appearing of the King. It had now arrived.
2. **The kingdom of God** was **at hand**; the King was present and was making a bona fide offer of the kingdom to the nation of Israel. **The kingdom** was **at hand** in the sense that the King had appeared on the scene.
3. Men were called on to **repent and believe in the gospel**. In order to be eligible to enter the kingdom, they had to do an about-face regarding sin, and believe the good news concerning the Lord Jesus.

B. Four Fishermen Called (1:16–20)

1:16–18 As **He walked** along the shore of **the Sea of Galilee**,[††] Jesus saw **Simon and Andrew** fishing. He had met them before; in fact, they had become disciples of His at the outset of His ministry (John 1:40, 41). Now He called them to be with Him, promising to make them **fishers of men**. Immediately they gave up their lucrative fishing business to follow Him. Their obedience was prompt, sacrificial, and complete.

Fishing is an art, and so is soul-winning.

1. It requires *patience*. Often there are lonely hours of waiting.
2. It requires *skill* in the use of bait, lures or nets.
3. It requires *discernment* and common sense in going where the fish are running.
4. It requires *persistence*. A good fisherman is not easily discouraged.
5. It requires *quietness*. The best policy is to avoid disturbances and to keep self in the background.

We become **fishers of men** by following Christ. The more like Him we are, the more successful we will be in winning others to Him. Our responsibility is to **follow** Him; He will take care of the rest.

1:19, 20 A little farther on, the Lord Jesus met **James** and **John**, the sons of **Zebedee**, as they were **mending their**

††See p. xiv.

MIRACLE	DELIVERANCE FROM:
1. Healing of man with unclean spirit (1:23–26).	1. The uncleanness of sin.
2. Healing of Simon's mother-in-law (1:29–31).	2. The feverishness and restlessness of sin.
3. Healing of the leper (1:40–45).	3. The loathesomeness of sin.
4. Healing of the paralytic (2:1–12).	4. The helplessness caused by sin.
5. Healing of the man with a withered hand (3:1–5).	5. The uselessness caused by sin.
6. Deliverance of the demoniac (5:1–20).	6. The misery, violence, and terror of sin.
7. The woman with the flow of blood (5:25–34).	7. Sin's power to sap life's vitality.
8. The raising of Jairus' daughter (5:21–24; 35–43).	8. Spiritual death caused by sin.
9. Healing of the Syro-Phoenician's daughter (7:24–30).	9. The thralldom of sin and Satan.
10. Healing of the deaf man with a speech impediment (7:31–37).	10. Inability to hear God's Word and to speak of spiritual things.
11. Healing of blind man (8:22–26).	11. Blindness to the light of the gospel.
12. Healing of the demoniac boy (9:14–29).	12. The cruelty of Satan's dominion.
13. Healing of blind Bartimaeus (10:46–52).	13. The blind and beggarly state to which sin reduces.

nets. As soon as **He called them**, they said goodbye to **their father** and **went after** the Lord.

Christ still calls men to forsake all and follow Him (Luke 14:33). Neither possessions nor parents must be allowed to hinder obedience.

C. An Unclean Spirit Cast Out (1:21–28)

Verses 21–34 describe a typical day in the life of the Lord. Miracle followed miracle as the Great Physician healed the demon-possessed and diseased.

The Savior's healing miracles illustrate how He liberates men from the dread results of sin. This is illustrated in the chart above.

Though the preacher of the gospel is not called upon to perform these acts of physical healing today, he is constantly called upon to deal with their spiritual counterparts. Are these not the greater miracles the Lord Jesus mentioned in John 14:12: "He who believes in Me, the works that I do he will do also; and greater *works* than these he will do"?

1:21, 22 But now let us return to Mark's narrative. At **Capernaum**, Jesus had **entered the synagogue** and had begun to teach **on the Sabbath**. The people realized that here was no ordinary teacher. There was undeniable power connected with His words, unlike **scribes** who droned on mechanically. His sentences were arrows from the Almighty. His lessons were arresting, convicting, challenging. The scribes peddled a second-hand religion. There was no unreality in the teaching of the Lord Jesus. He had the right to say what He did, because He lived what He taught.

Everyone who teaches the Word of God should speak with authority or not speak at all. The Psalmist said, "I believed, therefore I spoke" (Psalm 116:10). Paul echoed the words in 2 Corinthians 4:13. Their message was born of deep conviction.

1:23 **In their synagogue** there was

a man possessed, or inhabited, by a demon. The demon is described as **an unclean spirit**. This probably means that the spirit manifested its presence by making the man physically or morally unclean. Let no one confuse demon-possession with various forms of insanity. The two are separate and distinct. A demon-possessed person is actually indwelt and controlled by an evil spirit. The person is often able to perform supernatural feats and often becomes violent or blasphemous when confronted with the Person and work of the Lord Jesus Christ.

1:24 Notice that the evil spirit recognized **Jesus** and spoke of Him as the Nazarene and **the Holy One of God**. Notice too the change of pronouns from plural to singular: **"What have we to do with You?... Did you come to destroy us?... I know You...."** At first the demon speaks as joined to the man; then he speaks for himself alone.

1:25, 26 **Jesus** would not accept the witness of a demon, even if it was true. So He told the evil spirit to **be quiet**, then commanded him to **come out of** the man. It must have been strange to see the **convulsed** man and to hear the eerie cry of the demon as he left his victim.

1:27, 28 The miracle caused amazement. It was new and startling to the people that with a mere command, a Man could drive out a demon. Was this the beginning of a new school of religious teaching, they wondered? News of the miracle **immediately spread throughout . . . Galilee**. Before leaving this portion, let us note three things:

1. The First Advent of Christ apparently aroused a great outburst of demonic activity on the earth.
2. Christ's power over these evil spirits foreshadows His eventual triumph over Satan and all his agents.
3. Wherever God works, Satan opposes. All who set out to serve the Lord can expect to be opposed every step of the way. "For we do not wrestle against flesh and blood, but against principalities, against powers, against the rulers of the darkness of this age, against spiritual hosts of wickedness in the heavenly places" (Eph. 6:12).

D. Peter's Mother-in-Law Healed (1:29–31)

"Immediately" is one of the characteristic words of this Gospel, and is especially suitable for the Gospel which stresses the servant character of the Lord Jesus.

1:29, 30 From **the synagogue** our Lord went to Simon's house. **As soon as** He arrived, he learned that **Simon's** mother-in-law **lay sick with a fever**. Verse 30 states that **they told Him about her at once.** They wasted no time in bringing her need to the Physician's attention.

1:31 Without a word, Jesus **took her by the hand** and helped her to her feet. She was cured **immediately**. Ordinarily a fever leaves a person in a weakened condition. In this case, the Lord not only cured the fever but gave immediate strength to serve. **And she served them.** J. R. Miller says:

Every sick person who is restored, whether in an ordinary or extraordinary way, should hasten to consecrate to the service of God the life that is given back. . . . A great many persons are always sighing for opportunities to minister to Christ, imagining some fine and splendid service which they would like to render. Meantime they let slip past their hands the very things in which Christ wants them to serve Him. True ministry to Christ is doing first of all and well one's daily duties.[3]

It is noticeable that in each of the healing miracles, the Savior's procedure is different. This reminds us that no two conversions are exactly alike. Everyone must be dealt with on an individual basis.

That Peter had a mother-in-law shows that the idea of a celibate priesthood was foreign to that day. It is a tradition of men which finds no support in the Word of God and which breeds a host of evils.

E. Healing At Sunset (1:32–34)

News of the Savior's presence had spread during the day. As long as it was the Sabbath, the people dared not bring the needy to Him. But **when the sun had set** and the Sabbath had ended, there was a rush to the door of Peter's house. There **the sick and** the **demon-possessed** experienced the power that delivers from every phase and form of sin.

F. Preaching Throughout Galilee (1:35–39)

1:35 Jesus rose **a long while before daylight** and **went out** to a **place** where He would be free from distraction and spend time in prayer. The Servant of Jehovah opened His ear each morning to receive instructions for the day from God the Father (Isa. 50:4, 5). If the Lord Jesus felt the need of this early morning quiet time, how much more should we! Notice too that **He prayed** when it cost Him something; He rose and went out **a long while before daylight**. Prayer should not be a matter of personal convenience but of self-discipline and sacrifice. Does this explain why so much of our service is ineffective?

1:36, 37 By the time **Simon** and the others got up, the crowd was gathered outside the house again. The disciples went to tell the Lord of the rising popular sentiment.

1:38 Surprisingly, He did not go back to the city, but took the disciples into the surrounding **towns**, explaining that He must **preach there also**. Why did He not return to Capernaum?

1. First of all, He had just been in prayer and had learned what God wanted Him to do that day.
2. Secondly, He realized that the popular movement in Capernaum was shallow. The Savior was never attracted by large crowds. He looked below the surface to see what was in their hearts.
3. He knew the peril of popularity and taught the disciples by His example to beware when all men spoke well of them.
4. He consistently avoided any superficial, emotional demonstration that would have put the crown before the cross.
5. His great emphasis was on preaching the Word. The healing miracles, while intended to relieve human misery, were also designed to gain attention for the preaching.

1:39 Thus to the **synagogues throughout all Galilee** Jesus went **preaching** and **casting out demons**. He combined preaching and practicing, saying and doing. It is interesting to see how often He cast out demons in synagogues. Would liberal churches today correspond to the synagogues?

G. A Leper Cleansed (1:40–45)

The account of the **leper** gives us an instructive example of the prayer that God answers:

1. It was earnest and desperate — **imploring Him**.
2. It was reverent — **kneeling down to Him**.
3. It was humble and submissive — **"If You are willing."**
4. It was believing — **"You can."**
5. It acknowledged need — **"make me clean."**
6. It was specific — not "bless me" but **"make me clean."**
7. It was personal — **"make *me* clean."**
8. It was brief — five words in the original.

Notice what happened!

Jesus was **moved with compassion**. Let us never read these words without a sense of exultation and gratitude.

He stretched out His hand. Think of it! The hand of God stretched forth in answer to humble, believing prayer.

He **touched him.** Under the law, a person became ceremonially unclean when he touched a leper. Also, there was of course the danger of contracting the disease. But the Holy Son of Man identified Himself with the miseries of mankind, dispelling the ravages of sin without being tainted by them.

He said, **"I am willing."** He is more willing to heal than we are to be healed. Then **"Be cleansed."** In an instant the skin of the leper was smooth and clear.

He forbade publicizing the miracle until first the man had appeared before **the priest** and had made the required offering (Lev. 14:2ff). This was a test, first of all, of the man's obedience. Would he do as he was told? He did not; he publicized his case, and as a result, he hindered the work of the Lord (v. 45). It was also a test of the priest's discernment. Would he perceive that the long-awaited Messiah had come, performing wonderful miracles of healing? If he was typical of the nation of Israel, he would not.

Again we find that Jesus withdrew from the crowds and ministered **in deserted places**. He did not measure success by numbers.

H. A Paralytic Healed (2:1–12)

2:1–4 Soon after the Lord **entered Capernaum . . . many gathered** around **the house** where He was. Word had spread quickly, and people were anxious to see the Miracle-Worker in action. Whenever God moves in power, people are attracted. The Savior faithfully **preached the word to them** as they clustered round the door. At the rear of the crowd was **a paralytic, carried by four** others on an improvised stretcher. The crowd hindered his getting near the Lord Jesus. There usually are hindrances in bringing others to Jesus. But faith is ingenious. The four carriers climbed the outside stairs to the roof, **uncovered** a portion of **the roof**, and lowered **the paralytic** to the ground floor — perhaps to a courtyard in the middle — bringing him near the Son of God. Someone has nicknamed these good friends Sympathy, Cooperation, Originality, and Persistence. We should each strive to be a friend who displays these qualities.

2:5 Jesus, impressed by **their faith, . . . said to the paralytic, "Son, your sins are forgiven."** Now this seemed to be a strange thing to say. It was a question of paralysis, not sin, wasn't it? Yes, but Jesus went beyond the symptoms to the cause. He would not heal the body and neglect the soul. He would not remedy a temporal condition, and leave an eternal condition untouched. So He said, **"Your sins are forgiven."** It was a wonderful announcement. Now — on this earth — in this life — the man's **sins** were **forgiven**. He didn't have to wait till the Day of Judgment. He had the present assurance of forgiveness. So do all who put their faith in the Lord Jesus.

2:6, 7 The scribes quickly caught on to the significance of the statement. They were well enough trained in Bible doctrine to know that only **God can forgive sins**. Anyone who professed to forgive sins was therefore claiming to be God. Up to this point, their logic was correct. But instead of acknowledging

the Lord Jesus to be God, they accused Him in their hearts of speaking **blasphemies**.

2:8, 9 Jesus read their thoughts, a proof in itself of His supernatural power. He asked them this provocative question: **"Is it easier** to pronounce a man's sins forgiven or his paralysis cured?" Actually it is just as easy to *say* one as the other. But it is equally impossible, humanly speaking, to *do* the one as it is to *do* the other.

2:10–12 The Lord had already pronounced the man's sins forgiven. Yes, but had it really taken place? The scribes could not *see* the man's sins forgiven, therefore they would not believe. In order to demonstrate that the man's sins had really been forgiven, the Savior gave the scribes something they could see. He told the paralytic man to get up, to carry his straw pad, **and walk**. The man responded instantly. The people were **amazed**. They had **never** seen **anything like this** before. But the scribes did not believe, in spite of the most overwhelming evidence. Belief involves the will, and they did not want to believe.

I. The Call of Levi (2:13–17)

2:13, 14 It was while He was teaching **by the sea** that Jesus saw **Levi** collecting taxes. We know Levi as Matthew, who later wrote the first Gospel. He was a Jew, but his occupation was very un-Jewish, considering he collected taxes for the despised Roman government! Such men were not always noted for their honesty — in fact, they were looked down upon, like harlots, as the scum of society. Yet it is to Levi's eternal credit that when he heard the call of Christ, he dropped everything **and followed Him**. May each of us be like him in instant and unquestioning obedience. It might seem like a great sacrifice at the time, but in eternity it will be seen as no sacrifice at all. As the missionary martyr Jim Elliot said, "He is no fool who gives what he cannot keep, to gain what he cannot lose."

2:15 A banquet was arranged at **Levi's house** so he could introduce his friends to the Lord Jesus. Most of his friends were like himself — **tax-collectors and sinners**. Jesus accepted the invitation to be present with them.

2:16 The scribes and Pharisees thought they had caught Him in a serious fault. Instead of going directly to Him, they went **to His disciples** and tried to undermine their confidence and loyalty. **How** was it **that** their Master ate and drank **with tax-collectors and sinners?**

2:17 Jesus heard it and reminded them that healthy people don't need a doctor — only those who are ill. The scribes thought they were **well**, therefore they did not recognize their need of the Great Physician. The tax-collectors and sinners admitted their guilt and their need of help. Jesus came to call sinners like them — not self-righteous people.

There is a lesson in this for us. We should not shut ourselves up in Christianized communities. Rather we should seek to befriend the ungodly in order to introduce them to our Lord and Savior. In befriending sinners, we should not do anything that would compromise our testimony, nor allow the unsaved to drag us down to their level. We should take the initiative in guiding the friendship into positive channels of spiritual helpfulness. It would be easier to isolate oneself from the wicked world, but Jesus didn't do it, and neither should His followers.

The scribes thought they would ruin the Lord's reputation by calling Him a friend of sinners. But their intended insult has become an endearing tribute. All the redeemed gladly acknowledge Him as the friend of sinners, and will love Him eternally for it.

J. Controversy about Fasting (2:18–22)

2:18 The disciples of John the Baptist and of the Pharisees practiced **fasting** as a religious exercise. In the OT, it was instituted as an expression of deep sorrow. But it had lost much of its meaning and had become a routine ritual. They noticed that Jesus' **disciples** did **not fast**, and perhaps there was a twinge of envy and self-pity in their hearts when they asked the Lord for an explanation.

2:19, 20 In reply, He compared His disciples to companions of a **bridegroom**. He Himself was the Bridegroom. **As long as** He was with them, there was no occasion for an outward demonstra-

tion of sorrow. **But the days** were coming when He would **be taken away; then they** would have occasion to **fast**.

2:21 Immediately the Lord added two illustrations to announce the arrival of a New Era which was incompatible with the previous one. The first illustration involved a new patch made of **cloth** that has not been shrunk. If used to repair **an old garment**, it will inevitably shrink and something will have to give. The garment, made of older cloth, will be weaker than the patch and will tear again wherever the patch is sewed to it. Jesus was comparing the Old Dispensation to the old garment. God never intended Christianity to patch up Judaism; it was a new departure. The sorrow of the Old Era, expressed in fasting, must give way to the joy of the New.

2:22 The second illustration involved **new wine** in **old wineskins**. The leather wineskins lost their power to stretch. If **new wine** was put into them, the pressure built up by the fermentation would burst the skins. The **new wine** typifies the joy and power of the Christian faith. The **old wineskins** depict the forms and rituals of Judaism. New wine needs new skins. It was no use for John's disciples and the Pharisees to put the Lord's followers under the bondage of sorrowful fasting, as it had been practiced. The joy and effervescence of the new life must be allowed to express themselves. Christianity has always suffered from man's attempt to mix it with legalism. The Lord Jesus taught that the two are incompatible. Law and grace are opposing principles.

K. Controversy about the Sabbath (2:23–28)

2:23, 24 This incident illustrates the conflict Jesus had just taught between the traditions of Judaism and the liberty of the gospel.

As **He went through the grainfields on the Sabbath, . . . His disciples** picked some **grain** to eat. This didn't violate any law of God. But according to the hair-splitting traditions of the elders, the disciples had broken the Sabbath by "reaping" and perhaps even by "threshing" (rubbing the grain in their hands to remove the husks)!

2:25, 26 The Lord answered them

using an incident in the OT. **David**, though anointed as king, had been rejected, and instead of reigning, was being hunted like a partridge. One day when his provisions were gone, **he went to the house of God and** used **the showbread** to feed his men and himself. Ordinarily this showbread was forbidden to any but the priests, yet David was not rebuked by God for doing this. Why? Because things were not right in Israel. As long as David was not given his rightful place as king, God allowed him to do what ordinarily would be illegal.

This was the case with the Lord Jesus. Though anointed, He was not reigning. The very fact that His disciples had to pick grain as they traveled showed that things were not right in Israel. The Pharisees themselves should have been extending hospitality to Jesus and His disciples instead of criticizing them.

If David had actually broken the law by eating the showbread, yet was not rebuked by God, how much more blameless were the disciples who, under similar circumstances, had broken nothing but the traditions of the elders.

Verse 26 says that David **ate the showbread** when **Abiathar** was **high priest**. According to 1 Samuel 21:1, Ahimelech was priest at the time. Abiathar was his father. It may be that the high priest's loyalty to David influenced him to permit this unusual departure from the law.

2:27, 28 Our Lord closed His discourse by reminding the Pharisees that **the Sabbath** was instituted by God for man's benefit, not for his bondage. He added that **the Son of Man is also Lord of the Sabbath** — He had given the Sabbath in the first place. Therefore He had authority to decide what was permissible and what was forbidden on that day. Certainly the Sabbath was never intended to prohibit works of necessity or deeds of mercy. Christians are not obligated to keep the Sabbath. That day was given to the nation of Israel. The distinctive day of Christianity is the Lord's Day, the first day of the week. However, it is not a day encrusted with legalistic do's and don't's. Rather it is a day of privilege when, free from secular employments, believers may worship, serve, and attend to the culture of their souls. For us it is not a question, "Is it wrong to do this on the Lord's Day?" but rather "How may I best use this day to the glory of God, to the blessing of my neighbor, and to my spiritual good?"

L. The Servant Heals on the Sabbath (3:1–6)

3:1, 2 Another test case arose on the Sabbath. As Jesus **entered the synagogue again**, He met **a man** with **a withered hand**. This raised the question, "Would Jesus **heal him on the Sabbath?**" If He did, the Pharisees would have a case against Him — or so they thought. Imagine their hypocrisy and insincerity. They couldn't do anything to help this man, and they resented anyone who could. They sought some ground on which to condemn the Lord of life. If He healed **on the Sabbath**, they would rush in to the kill like a pack of wolves.

3:3, 4 The Lord told **the man** to **step forward**. The atmosphere was charged with expectancy. **Then He said to** the Pharisees, **"Is it lawful on the Sabbath to do good or to do evil, to save life or to kill?"** His question revealed the Pharisees' wickedness. They thought it was wrong for Him to perform a miracle of healing on the Sabbath, but not wrong for them to plan His destruction on the Sabbath!

3:5 No wonder they didn't answer! After an embarrassed silence, the Savior ordered the man to **stretch out** his **hand**. As he did so, full strength returned, the flesh filled out to normal size, and the wrinkles disappeared.

3:6 That was more than the **Pharisees** could take. They **went out**, contacted **the Herodians**, their traditional enemies, and **plotted with** them to **destroy** Jesus. It was still the Sabbath. Herod had brought about the death of John the Baptist. Perhaps his party would be equally successful in killing Jesus. This was the Pharisees' hope.

M. Great Multitudes Throng the Servant (3:7–12)

3:7–10 Leaving the synagogue, **Jesus withdrew to the Sea** of Galilee. The sea in the Bible often symbolizes the Gentiles. Therefore His action may have depicted His turning from the Jews to the Gentiles. **A great multitude** gathered, not only **from Galilee** but from distant parts as well. The crowd was so great that Jesus asked for **a small boat** so that He could push off from shore to avoid being crushed by those who came for healing.

3:11, 12 When **unclean spirits** in the crowd cried out that He was **the Son of God**, He **sternly warned them** to stop saying this. As already noted, He would not receive the witness of evil spirits. He did not deny that He was the Son of God, but chose to control the time and manner of being revealed as such. Jesus had the power to heal, but His miracles were performed only on those who came for help. So it is with salvation. His power to save is sufficient for all, but efficient only for those who trust Him.

We learn from the Savior's ministry that need does *not* constitute a call. There was need everywhere. Jesus depended on instructions from God the Father as to where and when to serve. So must we.

III. THE SERVANT'S CALL AND TRAINING OF HIS DISCIPLES (3:13–8:38)

A. Twelve Disciples Chosen (3:13–19)

3:13–18 Faced with the task of world evangelization, Jesus appointed **twelve** disciples. There was nothing wonderful about the men themselves; it was their connection with Jesus that made them great.

They were young men. James E. Stewart has this splendid commentary on the youth of the disciples:

> Christianity began as a young people's movement. . . . Unfortunately, it is a fact which Christian art and Christian preaching have too often obscured. But it is quite certain that the original disciple band was a young men's group. It is not surprising then, that Christianity entered the world as a young people's movement. Most of the apostles were probably still in their twenties when they went out after Jesus. . . Jesus himself, we should never forget, went out to his earthly ministry with the "dew of [his] youth" upon him (Ps. 110:3 — this psalm was applied to Jesus first by himself and then by the apostolic Church). It was a true instinct that led the Christians of a later day, when they drew the likeness of their master on

the walls of the Catacombs, to portray Him, not old and weary and broken with pain, but as a young shepherd out on the hills of the morning. The original version of Isaac Watts' great hymn was true to fact:

> When I survey the wondrous cross
> Where *the young Prince* of Glory died.

> And no one has ever understood the heart of youth in its gaiety and gallantry and generosity and hope, its sudden loneliness and haunting dreams and hidden conflicts and strong temptations, no one has understood it nearly so well as Jesus. And no one ever realized more clearly than Jesus did that the adolescent years of life, when strange dormant thoughts are stirring and the whole world begins to unfold, are God's best chance with the soul. . . . When we study the story of the first Twelve, it is a young men's adventure we are studying. We see them following their leader out into the unknown, not knowing very clearly who he is or why they are doing it or where he is likely to lead them; but just magnetized by him, fascinated and gripped and held by something irresistible in the soul of him, laughed at by friends, plotted against by foes, with doubts sometimes growing clamorous in their own hearts, until they almost wished they were well out of the whole business; but still clinging to him, coming through the ruin of their hopes to a better loyalty and earning triumphantly at last the great name the *Te Deum* gives them, "The glorious company of the apostles." It is worth watching them, for we too may catch the infection of their spirit and fall into step with Jesus.[4]

There was a threefold purpose behind the call of the twelve: (1) **that they might be with Him**; (2) **that He might send them out to preach**; and (3) that they **might have power to heal sicknesses and to cast out demons.**

First there was to be a time of training — preparation in private before preaching in public. Here is a basic principle of service. We must spend time **with Him** before we move out as God's representatives.

Secondly, they were sent out **to preach**. Proclamation of the Word of God, their basic method of evangelism, must always be central. Nothing must be allowed to subordinate it.

Finally, they were given supernatural **power.** Casting out **demons** would attest to men that God was speaking through the apostles. The Bible had not yet been completed. Miracles were the credentials of God's messengers. Today men have access to the complete Word of God; they are responsible to believe it *without* the proof of miracles.

3:19 The name of **Judas Iscariot** stands out among the apostles. There is mystery connected with one chosen as an apostle turning out to be the betrayer of our Lord. One of the greatest heart-aches in Christian service is to see one who was bright, earnest, and apparently devoted, later turning his back on the Savior and going back to the world which crucified Him.

Eleven proved true to the Lord, and through them He turned the world up-side down. They reproduced themselves in ever-widening circles of outreach, and in one sense, we today are the continuing fruit of their service. There is no way of telling how far-reaching our influence for Christ may be.

B. The Unpardonable Sin (3:20–30)

3:20, 21 Jesus returned from the mountain where He had called His disciples to a Galilean home. Such a **multitude** gathered that He and His apostles were kept too busy to eat. Hearing of His activities, **His own people** felt that **He** was **out of His mind**, and sought to take Him away. Doubtless they were embarrassed by the zeal of this religious fanatic in the family.

J. R. Miller comments:

> They could account for His unconquerable zeal only by concluding that He was insane. We hear much of the same kind of talk in modern days when some devoted follower of Christ utterly forgets self in love for his Master. People say, "He must be insane!" They think every man is crazy whose religion kindles into any sort of unusual fervour, or who grows more earnest than the average Christian in work for the Master. . . .
>
> That is a good sort of insanity. It is a sad pity that it is so rare. If there were more of it there would not be so many unsaved souls dying under the very shadow of our churches; it would not be so hard to get missionaries and money to send the gospel to the dark continents; there would not be so many empty pews in our churches; so many long pauses in our prayer-meetings; so few to teach in our Sunday schools. It would be a glorious thing if all Christians were beside

themselves as the Master was, or as Paul was. It is a far worse insanity which in this world never gives a thought to any other world; which, moving continually among lost men, never pities them, nor thinks of their lost condition, nor puts forth any effort to save them. It is easier to keep a cool head and a colder heart, and to give ourselves no concern about perishing souls; but we are our brothers' keepers, and no malfeasance in duty can be worse than that which pays no heed to their eternal salvation.[5]

It is always true that a man who is on fire for God seems deranged to his contemporaries. The more like Christ we are, the more we too will experience the sorrow of being misunderstood by relatives and friends. If we set out to make a fortune, men will cheer us. If we are fanatics for Jesus Christ, they will jeer us.

3:22 **The scribes** did not think He was insane. They accused Him of casting out demons by the power of **Beelzebub, the ruler of the demons**. The name **Beelzebub** means "lord of dung flies" or "lord of filth." This was a serious, vile, and blasphemous charge!

3:23 First Jesus refuted it, then pronounced the doom of those who made it. If He were casting out demons by Beelzebub, then Satan would be working against himself, frustrating his own purposes. His aim is to control men through demons, not to free them from demons.

3:24–26 A **kingdom**, a **house**, or a person **divided against** himself cannot endure. Continued survival depends upon internal cooperation, not antagonism.

3:27 The scribes' accusation was therefore preposterous. In fact, the Lord Jesus was doing the very opposite of what they said. His miracles signified the downfall of Satan rather than his prowess. That is what the Savior meant when He said, "**No one can enter a strong man's house, and plunder his goods, unless he first binds the strong man. And then he will plunder his house.**"

Satan is the **strong man**. The **house** is his dominion; he is the god of this age. **His goods** are the people over whom he holds sway. Jesus is the One who binds Satan and plunders **his house**. At Christ's Second Advent, Satan will be bound and cast into the bottomless pit for one thousand years. The Savior's casting out of demons during His ministry on earth was a forecast of His eventual complete binding of the devil.

3:28–30 In verses 28–30, the Lord pronounced the doom of the scribes who were guilty of the unpardonable sin. In accusing Jesus of casting out demons by demonic power, when it was actually by the power of the Holy Spirit that He did it, they in effect called the Holy Spirit a demon. This is blasphemy **against the Holy Spirit. All** kinds of sin can **be forgiven**, but this particular sin has no forgiveness. It is an **eternal** sin.

Can people commit this sin today? Probably not. It was a sin committed when Jesus was on earth performing miracles. Since He is not physically on earth today, casting out demons, the same possibility of blaspheming the Holy Spirit does not exist. People who worry that they have committed the unpardonable sin have not done so. The very fact that they are concerned indicates that they are not guilty of blasphemy against the Holy Spirit.

C. The Servant's True Mother and Brothers (3:31–35)

Mary, the **mother** of Jesus, came with **His brothers** to talk with Him. The crowd prevented their getting to Him, so they sent word that they were waiting **outside** for Him. When the messenger told Him that His **mother and** His **brothers**[6] wanted Him, **He looked around** and announced that His **mother** and **brother** was **whoever does the will of God**.

Several lessons emerge from this for us:

1. First of all, the words of the Lord Jesus were a rebuke to mariolatry (the worship of Mary). He did not dishonor her as His natural mother, but He did say that spiritual relationships take precedence over natural ones. It was more to Mary's credit to do the will of God than to be His mother.

2. Secondly, it disproves the dogma that Mary was a perpetual virgin. Jesus had brothers. He was Mary's firstborn, but other sons and daughters were born to her afterward (see Matt. 13:55; Mark 6:3; John 2:12; 7:3, 5, 10; Acts 1:14; 1 Cor. 9:5;

Gal. 1:19. See also Psalm 69:8).

3. Jesus put God's interests above natural ties. To His followers, He still says today: "If anyone comes to Me and does not hate his father and mother, wife and children, brothers and sisters, yes, and his own life also, he cannot be My disciple" (Luke 14:26).

4. The passage reminds us that believers are bound by stronger cords to fellow-Christians than they are to blood-relations when those relatives are unsaved.

5. Finally, it emphasizes the importance Jesus places on doing the will of God. Do I meet the standard? Am I His mother or brother?

D. The Parable of the Sower (4:1–20)

4:1, 2 **Again** Jesus **began to teach by the sea**. Again the crowd made it necessary for Him to use **a boat** as His pulpit, just a short way from the beach. And again **He taught** spiritual lessons from the world of nature about Him. He could see spiritual truth in the natural realm. It is there for all of us to see.

4:3, 4 This parable has to do with the **sower**, the **seed**, and the soil. The **wayside** soil was too hard for the seed to penetrate. **Birds...came and** ate the seed.

4:5, 6 The **stony ground** had a thin layer of dirt covering a bed of rock. Shallowness of earth prevented the seed from taking deep root.

4:7 The thorny ground had thorn bushes that cut the seed off from nourishment and sunlight, thus choking it.

4:8, 9 The **good ground** was deep and fertile with conditions favorable to the seed. **Some** seeds produced **thirtyfold, some sixty, and some a hundred**.

4:10-12 **When** the disciples were with Him **alone**, they **asked Him** why He spoke in parables. He explained to them that only those with receptive hearts were permitted **to know the mystery of the kingdom of God**. A **mystery** in the NT is a truth hitherto unknown that can only be known through special revelation. **The mystery of the kingdom of God** is that:

1. The Lord Jesus was rejected when He offered Himself as King to Israel.

2. A period of time would intervene before the kingdom would be literally set up on earth.
3. During the interim, it would exist in spiritual form. All who acknowledge Christ as King would be in the kingdom, even though the King Himself was absent.
4. The Word of God would be sown during the interim period with varying degrees of success. Some people would actually be converted, but others would be only nominal believers. All professing Christians would be in the kingdom in its outward form, but only the genuine ones would enter the kingdom in its inner reality.

Verses 11 and 12 explain why this truth was presented in parables. God reveals His family secrets to those whose hearts are open, receptive and obedient, while deliberately hiding truth from those who reject the light given to them. These are the people Jesus referred to as **"those who are outside."** The words of verse 12 may seem harsh and unfair to the casual reader: **"That seeing they may see and not perceive; and hearing, they may hear and not understand; lest they should turn and their sins be forgiven them."**

But we must remember the tremendous privilege which these people had enjoyed. The Son of God had taught in their midst and performed many mighty miracles before them. Instead of acknowledging Him as the true Messiah, they were even now rejecting Him. Because they had spurned the Light of the world, they would be denied the light of His teachings. Henceforth they would see His miracles, yet not understand the spiritual significance; hear His words, yet not appreciate the deep lessons in them.

There is such a thing as hearing the gospel for the last time. It is possible to sin away the day of grace. Men do drift beyond redemption point. There are men and women who have refused the Savior and who will never again have the opportunity to repent and be forgiven. They may hear the gospel but it falls on hardened ears and an insensible heart. We say, "Where there's life, there's hope," but the Bible speaks of some who are alive, yet beyond hope of repentance (Heb. 6:4–6, for example).

4:13 Going back to the parable of the sower, the Lord Jesus asked the disciples how they could expect to **understand** more involved **parables** if they could not understand this simple one.

4:14 The Savior did not identify **the sower**. It could be Himself or those who preach as His representatives. The seed, He said, is **the Word**.

4:15–20 The various types of soil represent human hearts and their receptivity to the Word, as follows:

The **wayside** soil (v. 15). This heart is hard. The person, stubborn and unbroken, says a determined "No" to the Savior. **Satan**, pictured by the birds, snatches away the Word. The sinner is unmoved and untroubled by the message. He is indifferent and insensible to it thereafter.

The **stony ground** (vv. 16, 17). This person makes a superficial response to **the Word**. Perhaps in the emotion of a fervent gospel appeal, he makes a profession of faith in Christ. But it is just a mental assent. There is no real commitment of the person to Christ. He receives the Word **with gladness**; it would be better if he received it with deep repentance and contrition. He seems to go on brightly for a while, but **when tribulation or persecution arises** because of his profession, he decides that the cost is too great and he abandons the whole thing. He claims to be a Christian as long as it is popular to do so, but persecution exposes his unreality.

The thorny ground (vv. 18, 19). These people also make a promising start. To all outward appearances, they seem to be true believers. But then they become preoccupied with business, with worldly worries, with the lust to become rich. They lose interest in spiritual things, until finally they abandon any claim to be Christians at all.

The **good ground** (v. 20). Here there is a definite acceptance of **the Word**, cost what it may. These people are truly born again. They are loyal subjects of Christ, the King. Neither the world, the flesh, nor the devil can shake their confidence in Him.

Even among the good ground hearers, there are varying degrees of fruitfulness. **Some** bear **thirtyfold, some sixty, and some a hundred**. What determines the degree of productivity? The life that is most productive is the one that obeys the Word promptly, unquestioningly, and joyfully.

E. The Responsibility of Those Who Hear (4:21-25)

4:21 The **lamp** here represents the truths which the Lord imparted to His disciples. These truths were not to be put **under a basket or under a bed**, but out in the open for men to see. The bushel **basket** may represent business, which if allowed, will steal time that should be given to the things of the Lord. The **bed** may speak of comfort or laziness, both enemies of evangelism.

4:22 Jesus spoke to the multitudes in parables. The underlying truth was **hidden**. But the divine intention was that the disciples explain those hidden truths to willing hearts. Verse 22 might also mean, however, that the disciples should serve in constant remembrance of a coming day of manifestation when it will be seen if business or self-indulgence were allowed to take precedence over testimony for the Savior.

4:23 The seriousness of these words is indicated by Jesus' admonition: **"If anyone has ears to hear, let him hear."**

4:24 Then the Savior added another serious warning: **"Take heed what you hear."** If I hear some command from the Word of God, but fail to obey it, I cannot pass it on to others. What gives power and scope to teaching is when people see the truth in the preacher's life.

Whatever we measure out in sharing the truth with others comes back to us with compound interest. The teacher usually learns more in preparing a lesson than the pupils. And the future reward will be greater than our puny expenditure.

4:25 Every time we acquire fresh truth and allow it to become real in our lives, we are sure to be given **more** truth. On the other hand, failure to respond to truth results in a loss of what was previously acquired.

F. Parable of the Growing Seed (4:26–29)

This parable is found only in Mark. It can be interpreted in at least two ways.

The **man** may picture the Lord Jesus casting **seed** on the earth during His public ministry, then returning to heaven. The seed begins to grow — mysteriously, imperceptively but invincibly. From a small beginning, a harvest of true believers develops. **When the grain ripens . . . the harvest** will be taken to the heavenly garner.

Or, the parable may be intended to encourage the disciples. Their responsibility is to sow **the seed**. They may **sleep by night and rise by day**, knowing that God's Word will not return to Him void, but will accomplish what He has intended it to do. By a mysterious and miraculous process, quite apart from man's strength and skill, the Word works in human hearts, producing fruit for God. Man plants and waters but God gives the increase. The difficulty with this interpretation lies in verse 29. Only God can put forth **the sickle** at **harvest** time. But in the parable, the same man who sows the seed **puts in the sickle** when the grain is ripe.

G. Parable of the Mustard Seed (4:30–34)

4:30–32 This parable pictures the growth of **the kingdom** from a beginning as small as **a mustard seed** to a tree or bush big enough for **the birds** to roost in. The kingdom began with a small, persecuted minority. Then it became more popular and was embraced by governments as the state religion. This growth was spectacular but unhealthy, much of it representing people who paid lip service to the King but were not truly converted.

As Vance Havner said:

> As long as the church wore scars, they made headway. When they began to wear medals, the cause languished. It was a greater day for the church when Christians were fed to the lions than when they bought season tickets and sat in the grandstand.[7]

The mustard bush therefore pictures professed Christendom, which has become a roosting place for all kinds of false teachers. It is the outward form of the kingdom as it exists today.

4:33, 34 Verses 33 and 34 introduce us to an important principle in teaching. Jesus taught the people **as they were able to hear it**. He built upon their previous knowledge, permitting time for them to assimilate one lesson before giving them the next. Conscious of His hearers' capacity, He did not glut them with more instruction than they could absorb (see also John 16:12; 1 Cor. 3:2; Heb. 5:12). The method of some preachers might make us think Christ had said, "Feed my giraffes" instead of "Feed my sheep"!

Although His general teaching was in parables, He **explained** them **to His disciples** in private. He gives light to those who sincerely desire it.

H. Wind and Wave Serve the Servant (4:35–41)

4:35–37 At **evening** of the **same day**, Jesus and His disciples started across the Sea of Galilee toward the eastern shore. They had not made any advance preparations. **Other little boats** followed. Then suddenly a violent **windstorm arose**. Huge **waves** threatened to swamp **the boat**.

4:38–41 Jesus was sleeping **in the stern** of the boat. The frantic disciples **awoke Him**, rebuking Him for His seeming lack of concern for their safety. The Lord **arose and rebuked the wind** and the waves. The **calm** was immediate and complete. Then Jesus briefly chided His followers for fearing and not trusting. They were stunned by the miracle. Even though they knew who Jesus was, they were impressed afresh by the power of One who could control the elements.

The incident reveals the humanity and the deity of the Lord Jesus. He slept in the stern of the boat; that's His humanity. He spoke and the sea was calm; that's His deity.

It demonstrates His power over nature, as previous miracles showed His power over diseases and demons.

Finally, it encourages us to go to Jesus in all the storms of life, knowing that the boat can never sink when He is in it.

> Thou art the Lord who slept upon the pillow,
> Thou art the Lord who soothed the furious sea,
> What matter beating wind and tossing billow,
> If only we are in the boat with Thee?
> – *Amy Carmichael*

I. The Gadarene Demoniac Healed (5:1–20)

5:1–5 The country of the Gadarenes[8] was on the east side of the Sea of Galilee. There Jesus met an unusually violent, demon-possessed man, a terror to society. Every effort to restrain him had failed. He lived among **the tombs** and on the mountains, yelling continually and gashing **himself with** sharp **stones**.

5:6–13 When the demoniac **saw Jesus**, he first acted respectfully, then complained bitterly. "How true and terrible a picture is this — a man bowed in adoration, petition and faith, and yet hating, defiant and fearing; a double personality, longing for liberty and yet clinging to passion" (Scripture Union Notes).

The exact order of events is unclear, but may have been as follows:

1. The demoniac performed an act of reverence to the Lord Jesus (v. 6).
2. Jesus ordered the **unclean spirit** to **come out** of him (v. 8).
3. The spirit, speaking through the man, acknowledged who Jesus was, challenged His right to interfere, and begged Jesus with an oath to stop tormenting him (v. 7).
4. Jesus **asked** the man's **name**. It was **Legion**, signifying he was indwelt by many demons (v. 9). This apparently does not contradict verse 2 where it says he had an unclean spirit (singular).
5. Perhaps it was the spokesman for the demons who begged permission to **enter** a **herd of swine** (vv. 10–12).
6. Permission was granted with the result that **two thousand** pigs raced down the mountainside **and drowned in the sea** (v. 13).

The Lord has often been criticized for causing the destruction of these pigs. Several points should be noted:

1. He did not cause this destruction; He permitted it. It was Satan's destructive power that destroyed the pigs.
2. There is no record of the owners finding fault. Perhaps they were Jews for whom the raising of pigs was forbidden.
3. The soul of the man was worth more

than all the pigs in the world.

4. If we knew as much as Jesus knew, we would have acted exactly the same way He did.

5:14–17 Those who witnessed the swine's destruction ran back to **the city** with the news. A crowd returned to find the ex-demoniac **sitting** at Jesus' feet **clothed and in his right mind**. The people **were afraid**. Someone has said, "They were afraid when He stilled the tempest on the sea, and now in a human soul." The witnesses recounted the whole story to the newcomers. It was too much for the populace; they pleaded with Jesus **to depart from the region**. This and not the destruction of the pigs is the shocking part of the incident. Christ was too costly a guest!

"Countless multitudes still wish Christ far from them for fear His fellowship may occasion some social or financial or personal loss. Seeking to save their possessions, they lose their souls" (Selected).

5:18–20 As Jesus was about to leave by **boat**, the healed man **begged** to accompany Him. It was a worthy request, evidencing his new life, but Jesus sent him **home** as a living witness of God's great power and mercy. The man obeyed, carrying the good news to **Decapolis**, an area embracing ten cities.

This is a standing order for all who have experienced the saving grace of God: **"Go home to your friends, and tell them what great things the Lord has done for you, and how He has had compassion on you."** Evangelism begins at home!

J. Curing the Incurable and Raising the Dead (5:21–43)

5:21–23 Back on the western shore of blue Galilee, the Lord Jesus was soon in the center of **a great multitude**. A frenzied father came running up to Him. It was **Jairus, one of the rulers of the synagogue**. His **little daughter** was dying. Would Jesus please go and **lay His hands on her** so **that she** might **be healed**?

5:24 The Lord responded and started for the home. A crowd **followed**, thronging **Him**. It is interesting that immediately following the statement of the crowd's *thronging* Him, we have an ac-

count of faith *touching* Him for healing.

5:25–29 A distracted **woman** intercepted Jesus on the way to Jairus' home. Our Lord was neither annoyed nor ruffled by this seeming interruption. How do *we* react to interruptions?

> I think I find most help in trying to look on all interruptions and hindrances to work that one has planned out for oneself as discipline, trials sent by God to help one against getting selfish over one's work. . . . It is not waste of time, as one is tempted to think, it is the most important part of the work of the day — the part one can best offer to God. (Choice Gleanings Calendar)

This woman had suffered with chronic bleeding **for twelve years**. The **many physicians** she went to had apparently used some drastic forms of treatment, drained her finances, and left her **worse** rather than better. When hope of recovery was all but gone, someone told her about Jesus. She lost no time in finding Him. Easing her way through the crowd, she **touched** the border of **His garment**. Immediately the bleeding stopped and she felt completely well.

5:30 Her plan was to slip away quietly, but the Lord would not let her miss the blessing of publicly acknowledging her Savior. He had been aware of an outflow of divine **power** when she touched Him; it cost Him something to heal her. So He asked, **"Who touched My clothes?"** He knew the answer, but asked in order to bring her forward in the crowd.

5:31 His disciples thought the question was silly. Many people were jostling Him continually. Why ask **"Who touched Me?"** But there is a difference between the touch of physical nearness, and the touch of desperate faith. It is possible to be ever so near Him without trusting Him, but impossible to touch Him by faith without His knowing it and without being healed.

5:32, 33 The woman came forward, **fearing and trembling**; she **fell down before Him** and made her first public confession of Jesus.

5:34 Then He spoke words of assurance to her soul. Open confession of Christ is of tremendous importance. Without it there can be little growth in the Christian life. As we take our stand boldly for Him, He floods our souls with full assurance of faith. The words of the Lord Jesus not only confirmed her physical healing, but also no doubt included the great blessing of soul salvation as well.

5:35–38 By this time, messengers had arrived with the news that Jairus' **daughter** had died. There was no need to bring **the Teacher**. The Lord graciously reassured Jairus, then took **Peter, James, and John** to **the house**. They were met by the unrestrained weeping characteristic of eastern homes in times of sorrow, some of it done by hired mourners.

5:39–42 When Jesus assured them that **the child** was **not dead but sleeping**, their tears turned to scorn. Undaunted, He took the immediate family to the motionless child, and taking her **by the hand, said** in Aramaic, **"Little girl, I say to you, arise."** Immediately the twelve-year-old **girl** got up **and walked**. The relatives were stunned, and doubtless delirious with joy.

5:43 The Lord forbade their publicizing the miracle. He was not interested in the popular acclaim of the masses. He must resolutely press on to the cross.

If the girl had actually died, then this chapter illustrates the power of Jesus over demons, disease, and death. Not all Bible scholars agree that she was dead. Jesus said she was not dead but sleeping. Perhaps she was in a deep coma. He could just as easily have raised her from the dead, but He would not take credit for doing so if she were only unconscious.

We should not overlook the closing words of the chapter: **"He . . . said that something should be given her to eat."** In spiritual ministry, this would be known as "follow-up work." Souls that have known the throb of new life need to be fed. One way a disciple can manifest his love for the Savior is by feeding His sheep.

K. The Servant Rejected at Nazareth (6:1–6)

6:1–3 Jesus returned to Nazareth with **His disciples**. This was **His own country**, where He had worked as a Carpenter. On **the Sabbath** He taught **in the synagogue**. The people, **astonished**, could not deny the wisdom of His teaching or the wonder of His miracles. But there was a deep unwillingness to acknowledge Him as the Son of God. They thought of Him as **the carpenter, the Son of Mary**, whose brothers and **sisters** were still there. Had He returned to Nazareth as a mighty conquering Hero, they might have accepted Him more readily. But He came in lowly grace and humility. This **offended** them.

6:4–6 It was then that **Jesus** observed that **a prophet** is generally given a better reception away from home. His relatives and friends are too close to him to appreciate his person or ministry. "No place harder to serve the Lord than at home." The Nazarenes themselves were a despised people. A popular attitude was: "Can anything good come out of Nazareth?" Yet these social outcasts looked down on the Lord Jesus. What a commentary on the pride and unbelief of the human heart! Unbelief largely hindered the work of the Savior in Nazareth. He healed **a few sick people**, but that was all. The unbelief of the people amazed Him. J. G. Miller warns:

> Such unbelief as this has immense consequences for evil. It closes the channels of grace and mercy, so that only a trickle gets through to human lives in need.[9]

Again Jesus tasted the loneliness of being misunderstood and slighted. Many of His followers have shared this sorrow. Often the servants of the Lord appear in a very humble guise. Are we able to look beyond outward appearances and recognize true spiritual worth? Undaunted by His rejection in Nazareth, the Lord **went about the** surrounding **villages, teaching** the Word.

L. The Servant Sends Forth His Disciples (6:7–13)

6:7 The time had come for **the twelve** to launch out. They had been under the matchless tutelage of the Savior; now they would go forth as heralds of a glorious message. He sent **them out two by two**. The preaching would thus be confirmed in the mouths of two witnesses. Also there would be strength and mutual help in traveling together. Finally, the presence of two might be helpful in cultures where moral conditions were low. Next He **gave them power over unclean spirits**. This is worth noting. It is one thing to cast out demons; only God can confer this power on others.

6:8 If our Lord's kingdom were of this world, He would never have given the instructions which follow in verses 8–11. They are the very opposite of what the average worldly leader would give. The disciples were to go forth without provisions — **no bag, no bread, no copper in their money belts**. They were to trust Him to supply these needs.

6:9 They were allowed to take **sandals** and a staff, the latter perhaps for protection against animals, and only one tunic. Certainly no one would envy the disciples' possessions, nor be attracted to Christianity by the prospect of becoming wealthy! And whatever power the disciples would have must come from God; they were totally cast upon Him. They were sent out in the most frugal circumstances, yet representatives of the Son of God, invested with His power.

6:10 They were to accept hospitality wherever it was offered them, and were to **stay there till** they left the area. This instruction prevented their shopping around for more comfortable lodgings. Their mission was to preach the message of One who did not please Himself, who was not self-seeking. They were not to compromise the message by seeking luxury, comfort or ease.

6:11 If a place rejected the disciples and their message, they were not obligated to remain. To do so would be casting pearls before swine. In leaving, the disciples were to **shake off the dust under** their **feet**, symbolizing God's rejection of those who reject His beloved Son.

Although some of the instructions were of a temporary nature and were later withdrawn by the Lord Jesus (Luke 22:35, 36), yet they embody lasting principles for the servant of Christ in every age.

6:12, 13 The disciples **went out and preached** repentance, **cast out many demons, anointed with oil many who were sick, and healed them**. The anointing with **oil**, we believe, was a symbolic gesture, picturing the soothing, alleviating power of the Holy Spirit.

M. The Servant's Forerunner Beheaded (6:14–29)

6:14–16 When news reached **King Herod** that a miracle-worker was traveling through the land, he immediately concluded that it was **John the Baptist . . . risen from the dead**. Others said it was **Elijah** or **one of the** other **prophets**, but Herod was convinced that the man **whom** he had **beheaded** had risen. John the Baptist had been a voice from God. Herod had silenced that voice. Now the terrible pangs of conscience were stabbing Herod for what he had done. He would learn that the way of the transgressor is hard.

6:17–20 The narrative now switches back to the time of John's execution. The Baptizer had reproved Herod for entering into an unlawful marriage with **his brother Philip's wife**. Herodias, now Herod's wife, became furious and vowed to take revenge. But Herod respected John as a **holy man** and thwarted her efforts.

6:21–25 Finally her chance came. At Herod's **birthday** party, with local celebrities attending, **Herodias** arranged for her **daughter** to dance. This so **pleased Herod** that he promised to give the girl anything **up to half** his **kingdom**. Prompted by her mother, she asked for **the head of John the Baptist on a platter**.

6:26–28 The king was trapped. Against his own desires and better judgment, he granted the request. Sin had woven its web around him, and the vassal king was victimized by an evil woman and by a sensual dance.

6:29 When John's faithful **disciples heard** what had happened, they claimed **his corpse** and buried it, then went and told Jesus.

N. Feeding of the Five Thousand (6:30–44)

6:30 This miracle, found in all four Gospels, took place at the beginning of the third year of His public ministry. **The apostles** had just returned to Capernaum from their first preaching mission (see vv. 7–13). Perhaps they were flushed with success, perhaps weary and footsore. Recognizing their need for rest and quiet, the Lord took them by boat to a secluded area on the shore of the Sea of Galilee.

6:31, 32 We often hear, "**Come aside by yourselves to a deserted place and rest a while**" used to justify luxurious vacations for Christians. Kelly wrote:

> It would be well for us if we needed thus to rest more; that is to say, if our labors were so abundant, our self-denying efforts for the blessing of others were so continual, that we could be sure that this was the Lord's word for us.[10]

6:33, 34 A crowd followed the Lord and His disciples by taking the land route along the shore of the lake. **Jesus** had **compassion** on the people. They were wandering around without a spiritual guide, hungry and defenseless. **So He began to teach them**.

6:35, 36 As **the day** wore on, **His disciples** became restless about the crowd — so many people and **nothing to eat**. They urged the Lord to **send them away**. The same crowd that drew out the compassion of the Savior annoyed the disciples. Are people an intrusion to us, or the objects of our love?

6:37, 38 Jesus turned to the disciples and said, **"You give them something to eat."** The whole thing seemed preposterous — five thousand men, plus women and children, and nothing but five loaves and two fish — and God.

6:39–44 In the miracle that followed, the disciples saw a picture of how the Savior would give Himself to be the bread of life for a starving world. His body would be broken that others might have eternal life. In fact, the words used are highly suggestive of the Lord's Supper which commemorates His death: **He had taken**; He **blessed**; He **broke**; He **gave**.

The disciples also learned precious lessons about their service for Him:

1. Disciples of the Lord Jesus should never doubt His power to supply their needs. If He can feed **five thousand men** with **five** loaves **and two fish**, He can provide for His trusting servants under any circumstances. They can labor for Him without worry as to where their food is coming from. If they seek first the kingdom of God and His righteousness, every need will be supplied.

2. How can the perishing world ever be evangelized? Jesus says, **"You give them something to eat!"** If we give Him what we have, however trivial it may seem, He can multiply it in blessing to multitudes.

3. He handled the work in a systematic way by seating the crowd **in** groups of **hundreds and fifties**.

4. He **blessed** and **broke** the loaves and fish. Unblessed by Him, they would never have availed. Unbroken, they would have been utterly insufficient. "The reason we are not more freely given to men is that we are not yet properly broken" (Selected).

5. Jesus did not distribute the food Himself. He allowed **His disciples** to do this. His plan is to feed the world through His people.

6. There was enough for **all**. If believers today would put everything above current necessities into the work of the Lord, the whole world could hear the gospel in this generation.

7. The **fragments** that were left over (**twelve baskets full**) were more than He started with. God is a bountiful Giver. Yet notice that nothing was wasted. The surplus was gathered up. Waste is a sin.

8. One of the greatest miracles would never have happened if the disciples had stuck to their plan to rest. How often that is true with us!

O. Jesus Walks on the Sea (6:45–52)

6:45–50 The Savior can provide not only for His servants' sustenance, but for their safety as well.

After sending the disciples back to the west shore of the lake by **boat**, Jesus went up into a **mountain to pray**. In the darkness of the night, He saw them **rowing** hard against a contrary **wind**. He went to their assistance, **walking on the sea**. At first, they were terrified, thinking **it was a ghost**. Then He spoke reassuringly to them and boarded the boat. **The wind ceased** immediately.

6:51, 52 The account closes with the comment: **"They were greatly amazed in themselves beyond measure, and marveled. For they had not understood about the loaves, because their heart was hardened."** The thought seems to be that even after seeing the power of the Lord in the miracle of the loaves, they still did not realize that nothing was impossible for Him. They shouldn't have been surprised to see Him walking on the water. It was no greater a miracle than the one they had just witnessed.

Lack of faith produced hardness of heart and dullness of spiritual perception.

The church has seen in this miracle a picture of the present age and its close. Jesus on the mountain represents Christ in His present ministry in heaven, interceding for His people. The disciples represent His servants, buffeted by the storms and trials of life. Soon the Savior will return to His own, deliver them from danger and distress and guide them safe to the heavenly shore.

P. The Servant Healing at Gennesaret (6:53–56)

Back on the west side of the lake, the Lord was besieged with **sick** people. **Wherever He** went, people carried needy cases to Him on mats. **Marketplaces** became improvised hospitals. They wanted only to get close enough to Him to **touch the hem of His garment**. All who **touched Him were made well.**

Q. Tradition Versus the Word of God (7:1–23)

7:1 The Pharisees and . . . scribes were Jewish religious leaders who had built up a vast system of rigidly enforced traditions so interwoven with the law of God that they had acquired almost equal authority with the Scriptures. In some cases they actually contradicted the Scriptures or weakened the law of God. The religious leaders delighted in imposing the rules and the people accepted them meekly, satisfied with a system of rituals without reality.

7:2–4 Here we find the Pharisees and scribes criticizing Jesus because **His disciples** ate **with unwashed hands**. This doesn't mean that the disciples didn't wash their hands before they ate, but that they didn't go through the elaborate ritual prescribed by tradition. Unless, for instance, they washed up to the elbows, they were considered ceremonially **defiled**. If they had been in the market place, they were supposed to take a ceremonial bath. This complex system of washing extended even to the dipping of pots and pans. Regarding the Pharisees, E. Stanley Jones writes:

They came all the way from Jerusalem to meet Him, and their life attitudes were so negative and faultfinding that all they saw was unwashed hands. They couldn't see the greatest movement of redemption that had ever touched our planet — a movement that was cleansing the minds and souls and bodies of men. . . . Their big eyes were opened wide to the little and marginal, and blind to the big. So history forgets them, the negative — forgets them except as a background for this impact of the positive Christ. They left a criticism; He left a conversion. They picked flaws, He picked followers.[11]

7:5–8 Jesus quickly pointed out the hypocrisy of such behavior. The people were just what **Isaiah** had predicted. They professed great devotion to the Lord, but were inwardly corrupt. By elaborate rituals, they pretended to worship God, but they had substituted their traditions for the doctrines of the Bible. Instead of recognizing the Word of God as the sole authority in all matters of faith and morals, they evaded or explained away the clear demands of the Scripture by their **tradition**.

7:9, 10 Jesus singled out an example of how **tradition** had made void the law **of God**. One of the Ten Commandments demanded that children **honor** their parents (which included caring for them in their need). The **death** penalty was decreed for anyone who spoke evil of his **father or mother**.

7:11–13 But a Jewish **tradition** had arisen known as **Corban**, which meant "given" or "dedicated." Suppose that certain Jewish parents were in great need. Their son had money to care for them, but didn't want to do it. All he had to do was say "Corban," implying that his money was dedicated **to God** or the temple. This relieved him of any further responsibility to support his parents. He might keep the money indefinitely and use it in business. Whether it ever was turned over to the temple was not important. Kelly remarks:

The leaders had devised the scheme to secure property for religious purposes and to quiet persons from all trouble of conscience about the Word of God. . . . It was God Who called on man to honour his parents, and Who denounced all slight done to them. Yet here were men violating, under cloak of religion, both these commandments of God! This tradition of saying 'Corban,' the Lord treats not only as a wrong done to the parents, but as a rebellious act against the express commandment of God.[12]

7:14–16 Beginning at verse 14, the Lord made the revolutionary pronouncement that it was not what goes into a man's mouth that defiles him (such as food eaten with unwashed hands) but what comes out of man (such as traditions that set aside God's Word).

7:17–19 Even the **disciples** were mystified by this. Brought up under the teachings of the OT, they had always considered that certain foods like pork, rabbit, and shrimp were unclean and would defile them. Jesus now plainly stated that man was not defiled by what went into him. In a sense, this signaled the end of the legal dispensation.

7:20–23 It's what **comes out of** one's heart that defiles a person: **evil thoughts, adulteries, fornications, murders, thefts, covetousness, wickedness, deceit, lewdness, an evil eye, blasphemy, pride, foolishness.** In the context, the thought is that human tradition should be listed here too. The tradition of Corban was tantamount to murder. Parents could die of starvation before this wicked vow could be broken.

One of the great lessons in this passage is that we must constantly test all teaching and all tradition by the Word of God, obeying what is of God and rejecting what is of men. At first a man may teach and preach a clear, scriptural message, gaining acceptance among Bible-believing people. Having gained this acceptance, he begins to add some human teaching. His devoted followers who have come to feel that he can do no wrong follow him blindly, even if his message blunts the sharp edge of the Word or waters down its clear meaning.

It was thus that the scribes and Pharisees had gained authority as teachers of the Word. But they were now nullifying the intent of the Word. The Lord Jesus had to warn the people that it is the Word that accredits men, not men who accredit the Word. The great touchstone must always be, "What does the Word say?"

R. A Gentile Blessed for Her Faith (7:24–30)

7:24, 25 In the preceding incident Jesus showed that all foods are clean. Here He demonstrates that Gentiles are no longer common or unclean. Jesus now traveled northwest **to the region of Tyre and Sidon**, also known as Syro-Phoenecia. He tried to enter **a house** incognito, but His fame had preceded Him and His presence was soon known. A Gentile **woman** came to Him, asking for help for her demon-possessed **daughter**.

7:26 We emphasize the fact that she was **a Greek**, not a Jew. The Jews, God's chosen people, occupied a place of distinct privilege with God. He had made wonderful covenants with them, committed the Scriptures to them, and dwelt with them in the tabernacle, and later in the temple. By contrast, the Gentiles were aliens from the commonwealth of Israel, strangers from the covenants of promise, without Christ, without hope, without God in the world (Eph. 2:11, 12). The Lord Jesus came primarily to the nation of Israel. He presented Himself as King to that nation. The gospel was first preached to the house of Israel. It is important to see this in order to understand His dealings with the **Syro-Phoenician** woman. When she asked **Him to cast the demon out of her daughter**, He seemed to rebuff her.

7:27 Jesus said that **the children** (Israelites) should **be filled first**, and that it was not proper **to take the children's bread and throw it to the little dogs** (Gentiles). His answer was not a refusal. He said, **"Let the children be filled first."** This might sound harsh. Actually it was a test of her repentance and faith. His ministry at that time was directed primarily to the Jews. As a Gentile, she had no claim on Him or His benefits. Would she acknowledge this truth?

7:28 She did, saying in effect, **"Yes, Lord**. I am only a little Gentile dog. But I notice that puppies have a way of eating **crumbs** that children drop **under the table**. That's all I ask for — some crumbs left over from your ministry to the Jews!"

7:29, 30 This faith was remarkable. The Lord rewarded it instantly by healing the girl at a distance. When the woman went home, her **daughter** was fully recovered.

S. A Deaf Mute Healed (7:31–37)

7:31, 32 From the Mediterranean coast, our Lord returned to the east coast of **the Sea of Galilee** — the area known as **Decapolis**. There an incident took

THE FIVE THOUSAND	THE FOUR THOUSAND
1. The people were Jews (see John 6:14, 15).	1. The people were probably Gentiles (they lived in Decapolis).
2. The multitude had been with Jesus one day (6:35).	2. This crowd had been with Him three days (8:2).
3. Jesus used five loaves and two fish (Matt. 14:17).	3. He used seven loaves and a few small fish (8:5, 7).
4. Five thousand men, plus women and children were fed (Matt. 14:21).	4. Four thousand men, plus women and children were fed (Matt. 15:38).
5. The surplus filled twelve hand baskets (Matt. 14:20).	5. The surplus filled seven wicker baskets or hampers (8:8).

place that is recorded only in Mark's Gospel. Interested friends **brought to Him one who was deaf and had an impediment in his speech**. Maybe this **impediment** was caused by a physical deformity or by the fact that, never hearing sounds clearly, he could not reproduce them correctly. At any rate, he pictures the sinner, deaf to the voice of God and therefore unable to speak to others about Him.

7:33, 34 Jesus first **took** the man **aside** privately. He **put His fingers in his ears, and He spat and touched his** tongue, thus by a sort of sign language telling the man that He was about to open his ears and unloose his tongue. Next Jesus looked **up to heaven**, indicating that His power was from God. His sigh expressed His grief over the suffering which sin has brought on mankind. Finally He said **"Ephphatha,"** the Aramaic word for **"Be opened."**

7:35, 36 The man obtained normal hearing and speech **immediately**. The Lord asked the people not to publicize the miracle, but they disregarded His instructions. Disobedience can never be justified, no matter how well-meaning the persons might be.

7:37 The spectators **were astonished** by His wonderful works. They said, **"He has done all things well. He makes both the deaf to hear and the mute to speak."** They did not know the truth of what they said. Had they lived on this side of Calvary, they would have said it with even deeper conviction and feeling.

And since our souls have learned His love,
What mercies has He made us prove,
Mercies which all our praise excel;
Our Jesus hath done all things well.

– *Samuel Medley*

T. Feeding of the Four Thousand (8:1–10)

8:1–9 This miracle resembles the feeding of the five thousand, yet notice the differences in the chart above:

The less Jesus had to work with, the more He accomplished and the more He had left over. In chapter 7, we saw crumbs falling from the table to a Gentile woman. Here a multitude of Gentiles is fed abundantly. Erdman comments:

The first miracle in this period intimated that crumbs of bread might fall from the table for the needy Gentiles; here they may be an intimation that Jesus, rejected by His own people, is to give His life for the world, and is to be the living Bread for all nations.[13]

There is a danger in treating incidents like the feeding of the four thousand as insignificant repetition. We should approach Bible study with the conviction that every word of Scripture is filled with spiritual truth, even if we can't see it at our present state of understanding.

8:10 From Decapolis, Jesus and **His disciples** crossed the Sea of Galilee to the west side, to a place called **Dalmanutha** (Magdala in Matt. 15:39).

U. The Pharisees Seek a Sign From Heaven (8:11–13)

8:11 The **Pharisees** were awaiting Him, demanding **a sign from heaven**. Their blindness and boldness were enormous. Standing in front of them was the greatest Sign of all — the Lord Jesus Himself. He was truly a Sign who had come from heaven, but they had no appreciation for Him. They heard His matchless words, saw His wonderful miracles, came in contact with an absolutely sinless Man — God manifest in the flesh — yet in their blindness asked for **a sign from heaven**!

8:12, 13 No wonder the Savior **sighed deeply**! If any generation in the history of the world was privileged, it was the Jewish **generation** of which those Pharisees were a part. Yet, blind to the clearest evidence that the Messiah had appeared, they asked for a miracle in the heavens rather than on earth. Jesus was saying, "There won't be any more signs. You've had your chance." **Getting into the boat again**, they sailed eastward.

V. The Leaven of the Pharisees and Herod (8:14–21)

8:14, 15 During the journey **the disciples had forgotten to take bread** along. Jesus was still thinking of His encounter with the Pharisees, however, when He warned them against **the leaven of the Pharisees and the leaven of Herod**. Leaven in the Bible is a consistent type of evil, spreading slowly and quietly and affecting everything it touches. **The leaven of the Pharisees** includes hypocrisy, ritualism, self-righteousness and bigotry. The Pharisees made great outward pretensions of sanctity but were inwardly corrupt and unholy. **The leaven of Herod** may include skepticism, immorality and worldliness. The Herodians were conspicuous for these sins.

8:16–21 The disciples completely missed the point. All they could think of was food. So He directed nine rapid questions to them. The first five reproved them for their obtuseness. The last four rebuked them for worrying about the supply of their needs as long as He was with them. Had He not fed **five thousand** with **five** loaves, leaving **twelve baskets** over? Yes! Had He not fed **four thousand** with **seven** loaves, leaving **seven** hampersful over? Yes, He had. Then why did they not understand that He was abundantly able to supply the needs of a handful of disciples in a boat? Didn't they realize that the Creator and Sustainer of the universe was in the boat with them?

W. Healing of the Blind Man at Bethsaida (8:22–26)

This miracle, found only in Mark, raises several interesting questions. First, why did Jesus lead the man **out of the town** before healing him? Why didn't He heal by simply touching the man? Why use such an unconventional means as saliva? Why didn't the man receive perfect sight immediately?[14] (This is the only cure in the Gospels which took place in stages.) Finally, why did Jesus forbid the man to tell about the miracle **in the town**? Our Lord is sovereign and is not obligated to account to us for His actions. There was a valid reason for everything He did, even though we might not perceive it. Every case of healing is different, as is every case of conversion. Some gain remarkable spiritual sight as soon as they are converted. Others see dimly at first, then later enter into full assurance of salvation.

X. Peter's Great Confession (8:27–30)

The last two paragraphs of this chapter bring us to the high water mark of the training of the twelve. The disciples needed to have a deep, personal appreciation of who Jesus is before He could share with them the pathway ahead and invite them to follow Him in a life of devotion and sacrifice. This passage brings us to the heart of discipleship. It is perhaps the most neglected area in Christian thought and practice today.

8:27, 28 Jesus and His disciples sought solitude in the far north. On the way to **Caesarea Philippi**, He opened the subject by asking what public opinion said of Him. In general, men were acknowledging Him to be a great man — equal to **John the Baptist, Elijah** or other **prophets**. But man's honor is actually dishonor. If Jesus is not God, then He is a deceiver, a madman, or a legend. There is no other possibility.

8:29, 30 Then the Lord pointedly asked the disciples for their evaluation of Him. **Peter** promptly declared Him to be **the Christ**, that is, the Messiah, or the Anointed One. Intellectually, Peter had known this. But something had happened in his life so that now there was a profound, personal conviction. Life could never be the same again. Peter could never be satisfied with a self-centered existence. If Christ was the Messiah, then Peter must live for Him in total abandonment.

Y. The Servant Predicts His Death and Resurrection (8:31–38)

Thus far we have watched the Servant of Jehovah in a life of incessant service for others. We have seen Him hated by His enemies and misunderstood by His friends. We have seen a life of dynamic power, of moral perfection, of utter love and humility.

8:31 But the path of service to God leads on to suffering and death. So the Savior now told the disciples plainly that He **must** (1) **suffer**; (2) **be rejected**; (3) **be killed**; (4) **rise again**. For Him the path to glory would lead first to the cross and the grave. "The heart of service would be revealed in sacrifice," as F. W. Grant put it.

8:32, 33 Peter could not accept the idea that Jesus would have to suffer and die; that was contrary to his image of the Messiah. Neither did he want to think that his Lord and Master would be slain by His foes. He rebuked the Savior for suggesting such a thing. It was then that Jesus said to Peter, **"Get behind Me, Satan! For you are not mindful of the things of God, but the things of men."** Not that Jesus was accusing Peter of being Satan, or of being indwelt by Satan. He meant, "You are talking like Satan would. He always tries to discourage us from wholly obeying God. He tempts us to take an easy path to the Throne." Peter's words were Satanic in origin and content, and this caused the Lord's indignation. Kelly comments:

What was it that so roused our Lord? The very snare to which we are all so exposed: the desire of saving self; the preference of an easy path to the cross. Is it not true that we naturally like to escape trial, shame, and rejection; that we shrink from the suffering which doing God's will, in such a world as this, must ever entail; that we prefer to have a quiet, respectable path in the earth — in short, the best of both worlds? How easily one may be ensnared into this! Peter could not understand why the Messiah should go

through all this path of sorrow. Had we been there, we might have said or thought yet worse. Peter's remonstrance was not without strong human affection. He heartily loved the Savior too. But, unknown to himself, there was the unjudged spirit of the world.[15]

Note that Jesus first **looked at His disciples**, then **rebuked Peter**, as if to say, "If I do not go to the cross, how can these, My disciples, be saved?"

8:34 Then Jesus **said to them** in effect, "I am going to suffer and die so that men might be saved. If you desire to **come after Me**, you must deny every selfish impulse, deliberately choose a pathway of reproach, suffering and death, **and follow Me**. You may have to forsake personal comforts, social enjoyments, earthly ties, grand ambitions, material riches, and even life itself." Words like these make us wonder how we can really believe that it is all right for us to live in luxury and ease. How can we justify the materialism, selfishness, and coldness of our hearts? His words call us to lives of self-denial, surrender, suffering, and sacrifice.

8:35 There is always the temptation to **save** our **life** — to live comfortably, to provide for the future, to make one's own choices, with self as the center of everything. There is no surer way of losing one's life. Christ calls us to pour out our lives for His sake and the gospel's, dedicating ourselves to Him spirit, soul, and body. He asks us to spend and be spent in His holy service, laying down our lives, if necessary, for the evangelization of the world. That is what is meant by losing our lives. There is no surer way of saving them.

8:36, 37 Even if a believer could gain all the world's wealth during his lifetime, what good would it do him? He would have missed the opportunity of using his life for the glory of God and the salvation of the lost. It would be a bad bargain. Our lives are worth more than all the world has to offer. Shall we use them for Christ or for self?

8:38 Our Lord realized that some of His young disciples might be stumbled in the path of discipleship by the fear of shame. So He reminded them that those who seek to avoid reproach because of Him will suffer a greater shame when

He returns to earth in power. What a thought! Soon our Lord is coming back to earth, this time not in humiliation, but in His own personal glory and in the glory of His Father, with the holy angels. It will be a scene of dazzling splendor. He will then be ashamed of those who are ashamed of Him now. May His words **"ashamed of Me . . . in this adulterous and sinful generation"** speak to our hearts. How incongruous to be ashamed of the sinless Savior in a world that is characterized by unfaithfulness and sinfulness!

IV. THE SERVANT'S JOURNEY TO JERUSALEM (Chaps. 9, 10)

A. The Servant Transfigured (9:1–13)

Having laid before the disciples the pathway of reproach, suffering, and death which He was to take, and having invited them to follow Him in lives of sacrifice and self-renunciation, the Lord now gives the other side of the picture. Though discipleship would cost them dearly in this life, it would be rewarded with glory by and by.

9:1–7 The Lord began by saying that **some** of the disciples would **not taste death till they** saw **the kingdom of God present with power**. He was referring to **Peter, James, and John**. On the Mount of Transfiguration they saw **the kingdom of God** in **power**. The argument of the passage is that anything we suffer for Christ's sake now will be abundantly repaid when He returns and His servants appear with Him in glory. The conditions which prevailed on the Mount foreshadow the Millennial Reign of Christ.

1. Jesus **was transfigured** — dazzling splendor radiated from His Person. Even **His clothes** were **shining**, whiter than any bleach could make them.

During His First Advent, the glory of Christ was veiled. He came in humiliation, a Man of Sorrows, and acquainted with grief. But He will return in glory. No one will mistake Him then. He will be visibly the King of kings and Lord of lords.

2. **Elijah** and **Moses** were there. They represent: (a) OT saints, or (b) the law (Moses) and the prophets (Elijah), or (c) saints who have died, and those who have been translated.
3. **Peter, James and John** were there. They may represent NT saints in general, or those who will be alive when the kingdom is set up.
4. **Jesus** was the central Person. Peter's suggestion of making **three tabernacles** was rebuked by the **cloud** and the **voice** from heaven. In all things Christ must have the preeminence. He will be the glory of Immanuel's land.
5. The **cloud** may have been the shekinah or glory cloud which stayed in the Holy of Holies in the tabernacle and temple in OT times. It was the visible expression of God's presence.
6. The **voice** was the voice of God the Father, acknowledging Christ as His **beloved Son.**

9:8 When the cloud was lifted the disciples **saw no one anymore, but only Jesus**. It was a picture of the unique, glorious and pre–eminent place He will have when the kingdom comes in power, and which He should have in the hearts of His followers at the present time.

9:9, 10 As they came down from the mountain, He commanded them not to discuss what **they had seen till** after He **had risen from the dead**. This latter point puzzled them. Perhaps they still did not grasp that He was to be slain and rise again. They wondered about the expression **rising from the dead**. As Jews they knew the truth that all would be raised. But Jesus was speaking of a selective resurrection. He would be raised from among the dead ones — not all would be raised when He arose. This is a truth found only in the NT.

9:11 The disciples had another problem. They had just had a preview of the kingdom. But hadn't Malachi predicted **that Elijah must come** as a forerunner of the Messiah, beginning the restitution of all things, and paving the way for setting up His universal reign (Mal. 4:5)? Where was Elijah? Would he **come first**, as **the scribes** said he would?

9:12, 13 Jesus answered in effect,

"Indeed, it is true that **Elijah** must come **first**. But a more important and immediate question is this: 'Don't the OT Scriptures predict that **the Son of Man** is to endure great sufferings and be treated with **contempt**?' As far as Elijah is concerned, **Elijah** did **come** (in the person and ministry of John the Baptist), but men treated him exactly as they wanted to — just as men treated Elijah. The death of John the Baptist was an advance token of what they would do to the Son of Man. They rejected the forerunner; they will reject the King."

B. A Demon-Possessed Boy Healed (9:14–29)

9:14–16 The disciples were not permitted to remain on the mountain-top of glory. In the valley below was groaning, sobbing mankind. A world of need lay at their feet. When Jesus and the three disciples reached the base of the mountain, an animated discussion was going on among **the scribes**, the crowd, and **the** other **disciples**. As soon as the Lord appeared, the conversation broke up and the crowd rushed to Him. **"What are you discussing with** My disciples?" He inquired.

9:17, 18 A distraught father excitedly told the Lord about his **son**, possessed with **a mute spirit**. The demon dashed the child to the ground, made him grind **his teeth** and foam **at the mouth**. These violent convulsions were causing the child to waste away. The father had asked the **disciples** to help, **but they could not**.

9:19 Jesus chided the disciples for their unbelief. Had He not given them power to cast out demons? **How long** would He have to **be with** them before they would use the authority He had given them? **How long** would He have to put up with lives of powerlessness and defeat?

9:20–23 As **they brought** the child to the Lord, the demon induced a particularly serious fit. The Lord **asked his father how long** this had been going on. It was **from childhood**, he explained. These spasms **often** had **thrown** the child **into the fire and into the water**. There had been narrow escapes from death. Then the father asked the Lord to please do something **if** He could — a

heart-rending cry, wrung from years of desperation. **Jesus** told **him** that it was not a question of His ability to heal, but of the father's ability to **believe**. Faith in the living God is always rewarded. No case is too difficult for Him.

9:24 The father expressed the paradox of faith and unbelief experienced by God's people in all ages. **"Lord, I believe; help my unbelief!"** We want to believe, yet find ourselves filled with doubt. We hate this inward, unreasonable contradiction, yet seem to fight it in vain.

9:25–27 When **Jesus** ordered **the unclean spirit** to leave the child, there was another terrible spasm, then the little body relaxed **as if dead**. The Savior raised him up and restored him to his father.

9:28, 29 Later when our Lord was alone with **His disciples** in **the house**, they **asked Him privately** why they hadn't been able to do it. He replied that certain miracles require **prayer and fasting**. Which of us is not faced at times in our Christian service with a sense of defeat and frustration? We have labored tirelessly and conscientiously, yet there has been no evidence of the Spirit of God working in power. We too hear the Savior's words reminding us, **"This kind . . ."** etc.

C. Jesus Again Predicts His Death and Resurrection (9:30–32)

9:30 Our Lord's visit to Caesarea Philippi had ended. Now He **passed through Galilee** — a trip that would lead Him to Jerusalem and the cross. He desired to travel unnoticed. For the most part, His public ministry was over. Now He wanted to spend time with the disciples, instructing and preparing them for what lay ahead.

9:31, 32 He told them plainly that He was going to be arrested and killed, and that **He** would **rise** again **the third day**. They somehow didn't take it in, **and were afraid to ask Him**. We are often afraid to ask too, and thus lose a blessing.

D. Greatness in the Kingdom (9:33–37)

9:33, 34 When they reached the house in **Capernaum** where they would stay, Jesus **asked them what** they had been arguing about along the way. They were ashamed to admit that they had been disputing which of them **would be the greatest**. Perhaps the Transfiguration had revived their hopes for an imminent kingdom, and they were grooming themselves for places of honor in it. It is heartbreaking to realize that at the very time Jesus had been telling them about His impending death, they were esteeming themselves better than others. The heart of man is deceitful and desperately wicked above all things, as Jeremiah said.

9:35–37 Jesus, knowing what they had argued about, gave them a lesson in humility. He said that the way to be first was to voluntarily take the lowest place of service and live for others instead of self. **A little child** was set before them and embraced by the Lord Jesus. He emphasized that a kindness shown **in His name** to the least esteemed, the least renowned, was an act of greatness. It was as if the kindness were shown to the Lord Himself, yes, even to God the Father. "O blessed Lord Jesus, Your teachings probe and expose this carnal heart of mine. Break me of self and let Your life be lived through me."

E. The Servant Forbids Sectarianism (9:38–42)

This chapter seems to be full of failures. Peter spoke clumsily on the Mount of Transfiguration (vv. 5, 6). The disciples failed to cast out the mute demon (v. 18). They argued over who was greatest (v. 34). In vv. 38–40, we find them demonstrating a sectarian spirit.

9:38 It was **John** the beloved who reported to Jesus that they had found a man **casting out demons in** His **name**. The disciples told him to stop because he didn't identify himself with them. The man wasn't teaching false doctrine or living in sin. He simply did not join up with the disciples.

> They drew a circle that shut me out –
> Rebel, heretic, thing to flout;
> But love and I had the wit to win –
> We drew a circle that took them in.

9:39 **Jesus said**, "Don't stop him. If he has enough faith in Me to use My name in casting out demons, he is on My side and is working against Satan. He isn't apt to turn around quickly and **speak evil of Me** or be My enemy."

9:40 Verse 40 seems to contradict Matthew 12:30 where Jesus said: "He who is not with Me is against Me; and he who does not gather with Me scatters abroad." But there is no real conflict. In Matthew, the issue was whether Christ was the Son of God or demon-empowered. On such a fundamental question, anyone who is not with Him is working against Him.

Here in Mark, the question was not the Person or work of Christ, but the matter of one's associates in the service of the Lord. Here there must be tolerance and love. Whoever **is not against** Him in service must be against Satan and therefore **on** Christ's **side**.

9:41 Even the smallest kindness done **in** Christ's **name** will be rewarded. **A cup of water** given to a disciple **because** he belongs **to Christ** will not go unnoticed. Casting out a demon in His name is rather spectacular. Giving a glass **of water** is commonplace. But both are precious to Him when done for His glory. **"Because you belong to Christ"** is the cord that should bind believers together. These words, if kept before us, would deliver us from party spirit, petty bickerings and jealousy in Christian service.

9:42 Constantly the Lord's servant must consider what effect his words and actions will have on others. It is possible to stumble a fellow believer, causing lifelong spiritual damage. **It would be better** to be drowned with a **millstone around** one's **neck** than to cause a **little** one to stray from the path of holiness and truth.

F. Ruthless Self-Discipline (9:43–50)

9:43 The remaining verses of the chapter emphasize the necessity of discipline and renunciation. Those who set out on the path of true discipleship must constantly battle with natural desires and appetites. To cater to them spells ruin. To control them insures spiritual victory.

The Lord spoke of the **hand**, the **foot**, and the **eye**, explaining that it would be better to lose one of these than to be stumbled by it into **hell**. Reaching the goal is worth any sacrifice.

The **hand** might suggest our deeds, the **foot** our walk, and the **eye** the things we crave. These are potential danger spots. Unless they are dealt with severely, they can lead to eternal ruin.

Does this passage teach that true believers can finally be lost and spend eternity in hell? Taken by itself it might suggest that. But taken with the consistent teaching of the NT, we must conclude that anyone who goes to hell was never a genuine Christian at all. A person might *profess* to be born again and appear to go on well for some time. But if that person consistently indulges the flesh, it is clear he was never saved.

9:44–48 The Lord repeatedly[16] speaks of hell as a place **where their worm does not die and the fire is not quenched**. It is tremendously solemn. If we really believed it, we would not live for things but for never-dying souls. "Give me a passion for souls, O Lord!"

Fortunately it is never morally necessary to amputate a hand or foot or to cut out an eye. Jesus did not suggest that we should practice such extremes. All He said was it would be *better* to sacrifice the use of these organs than to be dragged down to **hell** by their abuse.

9:49 Verses 49 and 50 are especially difficult. Therefore we will examine them clause by clause.

"For everyone will be seasoned with fire." The three main problems are: (1) Which **fire** is referred to? (2) What is meant by **seasoned**? (3) Does **everyone** refer to saved, to unsaved, or to both?

Fire may mean hell (as in vv. 44, 46, 48) or judgment of any kind, including divine judgment of a believer's works, and self-judgment.

Salt typifies that which preserves, purifies, and seasons. In eastern lands, it is also a pledge of loyalty, friendship, or faithfulness to a promise.

If **everyone** means the unsaved, then the thought is that they will be preserved in the fires of hell, that is, that they will suffer eternal punishment.

If **everyone** refers to believers, the passage teaches that they must: (1) be purified through the fires of God's chas-

tening in this life; or (2) preserve themselves from corruption by practicing self-discipline and self-renunciation; or (3) be tested at the Judgment Seat of Christ.

"And every sacrifice will be seasoned with salt." This clause[17] is quoted from Lev. 2:13 (see also Num. 18:19; 2 Chron. 13:5). Salt, an emblem of the covenant between God and His people, was intended to remind the people that the covenant was a solemn treaty to be kept inviolate. In presenting our bodies as a living sacrifice to God (Rom. 12:1, 2), we should season the sacrifice with salt by making it an irrevocable commitment.

9:50 "Salt is good." Christians are the salt of the earth (Matt. 5:13). God expects them to exert a healthful, purifying influence. As long as they fulfill their discipleship, they are a blessing to all.

"But if the salt loses its flavor, how will you season it?" Salt without saltiness is valueless. A Christian who is not carrying out his duties as a true disciple is barren and ineffective. It is not enough to make a good start in the Christian life. Unless there is constant and radical self-judgment, the child of God is failing to achieve the purpose for which God saved him.

"Have salt in yourselves." Be a power for God in the world. Exert a beneficial influence for the glory of Christ. Be intolerant of anything in your life that might lessen your effectiveness for Him.

"And have peace with one another." This apparently refers back to verses 33 and 34, where the disciples had argued over which of them was the greatest. Pride must be put away and replaced by humble service for all.

To summarize, verses 49 and 50 seem to picture the believer's life as a sacrifice to God. It is salted with fire, that is, mixed with self-judgment and self-renunciation. It is salted with salt, that is, offered with a pledge of unalterable devotedness. If the believer goes back on his vows, or fails to deal drastically with sinful desires, then his life will be savorless, worthless, and pointless. Therefore he should eradicate anything from his life that would interfere with his divinely-appointed mission, and he should maintain peaceful relations with other believers.

G. Marriage and Divorce (10:1–12)

10:1 From Galilee our Lord traveled southeastward to Perea, the district on the east **side of the Jordan**. His Perean ministry extends through 10:45.

10:2 The Pharisees soon found Him. They were moving in for the kill, like a pack of wolves. In an effort to trap Him, they asked Him if **divorce** was **lawful**. He referred them back to the Pentateuch. **What did Moses command?**

10:3–9 They avoided His question by stating what **Moses permitted**. He **permitted** a man to divorce his wife, provided he gave her a written **certificate of divorce**. But that was not God's ideal; it was permitted only **because of the hardness** of the people's hearts. The divine plan joined a man and woman in marriage as long as they live. This goes back to God's creation of the sexes. A man is to **leave his** parents and be so united in marriage that he and his wife are **one flesh**. Thus **joined** by **God**, they should not be separated by human decree.

10:10 Apparently this was difficult for even **His disciples** to accept. At that time, women did not have a place of honor or security. They were often treated with little more than contempt. A man could divorce his wife if he was displeased with her. She had no recourse. In many cases, she was treated as a piece of property.

10:11, 12 When the disciples questioned the Lord further, He said pointedly that remarriage after divorce was **adultery**, whether the man or the **woman** got the divorce. Taken by itself, this verse would indicate that divorce is forbidden under all circumstances. But in Matt. 19:9, He made an exception. Where one partner has been guilty of immorality, the other is permitted to get a divorce and is presumably free to remarry. It is also possible that 1 Cor. 7:15 permits divorce when an unbelieving partner deserts a Christian spouse.

Assuredly there are difficulties connected with the whole subject of divorce and remarriage. People create marital tangles so involved that it takes the wisdom of a Solomon to extricate them. The best way to avoid these tangles is to avoid divorce. Divorce places a cloud and a question mark over the lives of those involved. When divorced persons seek fellowship in a local church, the elders must review the case in the fear of God. Every case is different and must be considered individually.

This paragraph shows Christ's concern not only for the sanctity of marriage, but also for the rights of women. Christianity gives to women a standing in honor not found in other religions.

H. Blessing the Little Children (10:13–16)

10:13 Now we see the solicitude of the Lord Jesus for **little children**. Parents who **brought** their **children** to be blessed by the Teacher Shepherd were shooed away by the disciples.

10:14–16 The Lord was **greatly displeased and** explained that **the kingdom of God** belongs **to little children**, and to those who have childlike faith and humility. Adults have to become like small children in order to **enter** the kingdom.

George MacDonald used to say that he did not believe in a man's Christianity if boys and girls were never to be found playing around his door. Certainly these verses should impress the servant of the Lord with the importance of reaching little ones with the Word of God. The minds of children are most plastic and most receptive. W. Graham Scroggie said, "Be your best and give your best to the children."

I. The Rich Young Ruler (10:17–31)

10:17 A rich man intercepted the Lord with an apparently sincere inquiry. Addressing Jesus as **"Good Teacher,"** he asked **what** he had to **do to inherit eternal life.**

10:18 Jesus seized on the words **"Good Teacher"**. He did not refuse the title but used it to test the man's faith. Only **God** is good. Was the rich man willing to confess the Lord Jesus as God? Apparently not.

10:19, 20 Next the Savior used the law to produce the knowledge of sin. The man was still under the delusion that he could inherit the kingdom on the principle of *doing*. Then let him obey the law, which told him what to *do*. Our Lord quoted the five commandments which deal primarily with our relations to our fellow man. These five commandments say, in effect, "You shall love your neighbor as yourself." The man professed to have **kept** them from his **youth.**

10:21, 22 But did he really love his neighbor as himself? If so, let him prove it by selling all his property and giving the money **to the poor**. Oh, that was another story. He **went away sorrowful, for he had great possessions**.

The Lord Jesus did not mean that this man could have been saved by selling his possessions and giving the proceeds to charity. There is only one way of salvation — that is faith in the Lord. But in order to be saved a man must acknowledge that he is a sinner, falling short of God's holy requirements. The Lord took the man back to the Ten Commandments to produce conviction of sin. The rich man's unwillingness to share his possessions showed that he did not love his neighbor as himself. He should have said, "Lord, if that's what is required, then I'm a sinner. I cannot save myself by my own efforts. Therefore I ask You to save me by Your grace." But he loved his property too much. He was unwilling to give it up. He refused to break.

When Jesus told the man to sell all, He was *not* giving this as the way of salvation. He was showing the man that he had broken the law of God and therefore needed to be saved. If he had responded to the Savior's instruction, he would have been given the way of salvation.

But there is a problem here. Are we who are believers supposed to love our neighbor as ourselves? Does Jesus say to us, **"Sell whatever you have and give to the poor, and you will have treasure in heaven; and come, take up the cross, and follow Me"**? Each one must answer for himself, but before doing so, he should consider the following inescapable facts:

1. Thousands of people die daily of starvation.
2. More than half the world has never heard the good news.
3. Our material possessions can be used now to alleviate spiritual and physical human need.
4. The example of Christ teaches us that we should become poor that others might be made rich (2 Cor. 8:9).
5. The shortness of life and the imminence of the Lord's coming teach us

to put our money to work for Him now. After He comes it will be too late.

10:23–25 As He saw the rich man fade into the crowd, Jesus remarked on the difficulty of rich people entering **the kingdom of God**. The disciples were amazed by this remark; they linked riches with the blessing of God. So Jesus repeated, **"Children, how hard it is for those who trust in riches**[18] **to enter the kingdom of God!"** "In fact," He continued, **"It is easier for a camel to go through the eye of a needle than for a rich man to enter the kingdom of God."**

10:26, 27 This made the disciples wonder **who then can be saved**. As Jews living under the law, they correctly looked on riches as an indication of God's blessing. Under the Mosaic code, God promised prosperity to those who obeyed Him. The disciples reasoned that if a rich person couldn't enter the kingdom, then no one else could either. Jesus answered that what is humanly **impossible** is divinely **possible**.

What are we to conclude from the teaching of this passage?

First of all, it is especially difficult for rich people to be saved (v. 23) since these people tend to love their wealth more than God. They would rather give up God than give up their money. They put their trust in riches rather than in the Lord. As long as these conditions exist, they cannot be saved.

It was true in the OT that riches were a sign of God's favor. That is now changed. Instead of a mark of the Lord's blessing, riches are a test of a man's devotedness.

A camel can go through a needle's eye more easily than a rich man can go through the door of the kingdom. Humanly speaking, a rich man simply cannot be saved. Someone may object here that humanly speaking, *no one* can be saved. That is true. But it is even more true in the case of a rich man. He faces obstacles that the poor man isn't aware of. The god of mammon must be torn from the throne of his heart, and he must stand before God as a pauper. To effect this change is humanly impossible. Only God can do it.

Christians who lay up treasures on earth generally pay for their disobedience in the lives of their children. Very few children from such families go on well for the Lord.

10:28–30 **Peter** caught the drift of the Savior's teaching. He realized that Jesus was saying, "Forsake all and follow Me." Jesus confirmed this by promising present and eternal reward to those who forsake all for His sake and the gospel's.

1. The present reward is 10,000 per cent return, not in money, but in:
   a. **houses** — homes of other people where he is given accomodations as a servant of the Lord.
   b. **brothers and sisters and mothers and children** — Christian friends whose fellowship enriches all of life.
   c. **lands** — countries of the world which he has claimed for the King.
   d. **persecutions** — these are a part of the present reward. It is a cause of rejoicing when one is found worthy to suffer for Jesus' sake.
2. The future reward is **eternal life**. This does not mean that we earn eternal life through forsaking all. Eternal life is a gift. Here the thought is that those who forsake all are rewarded with a greater capacity for enjoying eternal life in heaven. All believers will have that life but not all will enjoy it to the same extent.

10:31 Then our Lord added a word of warning, "**Many who are first will be last; and the last first.**" It isn't enough to start out well on the path of discipleship. It's how we finish that counts. Ironside said:

Not everyone who gave promise of being a faithful and devoted follower would continue in the path of self-denial for Christ's Name's sake, and some who seemed backward and whose devotedness was questionable would prove real and self-effacing in the hour of trial.[19]

J. Third Prediction of the Servant's Passion (10:32–34)

10:32 The time had now come to go **up to Jerusalem**. For the Lord Jesus this meant the sorrow and suffering of Gethsemane, the shame and agony of the cross.

What were His emotions at such a time? Can we not read them in the words "**Jesus was going before them**"? There was determination to do God's will, knowing fully what the cost would be. There was loneliness — He was out ahead of the disciples, walking alone. And there was joy — a deep, settled joy of being in the Father's will, a joyful prospect of coming glory, the joy of redeeming a bride to Himself. For the joy that was set before Him, He endured the cross, despising the shame.

As we gaze upon Him, striding in the vanguard, we too are **amazed**. Our intrepid Leader, the Author and Finisher of our faith, our glorious Master, Prince divine. Erdman writes:

Let us pause to gaze on that face and form, the Son of God, going with unfaltering step toward the Cross! Does it not awaken us to new heroism, as we follow; does it not awaken new love as we see how voluntary was His death for us; yet do we not wonder at the meaning and the mystery of that death?[20]

Those who followed **were afraid**. They knew that the religious leaders in Jerusalem were bent on His death.

10:33, 34 For the third time Jesus gave His disciples a detailed account of coming events. This prophetic outline shows Him to be more than a mere man:

1. "**Behold, we are going up to Jerusalem**" (11:1–13:37).
2. "**The Son of Man will be betrayed to the chief priests and scribes**" (14:1, 2, 43–53).
3. "**They will condemn Him to death**" (14:55–65).
4. "**And deliver Him to the Gentiles**" (15:1).
5. "**They will mock Him, and scourge Him, and spit on Him, and kill Him**" (15:2–38).
6. "**And the third day He will rise again**" (16:1–11).

K. Greatness Is Serving (10:35–45)

10:35–37 Following this poignant prediction of His approaching crucifixion, **James and John came** with a request that was at once noble and ill-timed. It was noble that they wanted to be near Christ, but it was a poor time to be seeking great things for themselves. They exhibited faith that Jesus would set up His kingdom, but they should have been thinking of His impending passion.

10:38, 39 **Jesus** asked them if they were **able to drink** His **cup**, referring to His suffering, and share His **baptism**, referring to His death. They professed to be **able**, and He said they were right. They would suffer because of their loyalty to Him, and James at least would be martyred (Acts 12:2).

10:40 But then He explained that positions of honor in the kingdom were not bestowed arbitrarily. They would be earned. It is good to remember here that *admission* to the kingdom is by grace through faith, but *position* in the kingdom will be determined by faithfulness to Christ.

10:41–44 **The** other **ten** disciples were **greatly displeased** that **James and John** would try to get ahead of them. But their indignation betrayed the fact that they had the same spirit. This provided the occasion for the Lord Jesus to give a beautiful and revolutionary lesson on greatness. Among the unconverted, great men are those who rule with arbitrary power, who are overbearing and domineering. But greatness in Christ's kingdom is marked by service. **Whoever . . . desires to be first** should become a **slave** to everyone.

10:45 The Supreme Example is **the** Son of Man Himself. **He did not come to be served, but to serve, and to give His life a ransom for many**. Think of it! He came at His miraculous birth. He ministered throughout His life. And in His vicarious death He gave His life.

As mentioned before, verse 45 is the key verse of the entire Gospel. It is a theology in miniature, a vignette of the greatest Life the world has ever known.

L. The Healing of Blind Bartimaeus (10:46–52)

10:46 The scene now shifts from Perea to Judea. The Lord and His disciples had crossed the Jordan and come **to Jericho**. There He met **blind Bartimaeus**, a man with a desperate need, a knowledge of the need, and a determination to have it met.

10:47 Bartimaeus recognized and addressed our Lord as the **Son of David**. It was ironical that while the nation of Israel was blind to the presence of the Messiah, a blind Jew had true spiritual sight!

10:48–52 His persistent pleas for **mercy** did not go unanswered. His specific prayer for sight brought a specific answer. His gratitude was expressed in faithful discipleship, following **Jesus** on His last trip to Jerusalem. It must have cheered the heart of the Lord to find faith like this in Jericho as He moved on toward the cross. It was a good thing that Bartimaeus sought the Lord that day because the Savior never passed that way again.

V. THE SERVANT'S MINISTRY IN JERUSALEM (Chaps. 11, 12)†

A. The Triumphal Entry (11:1–11)

11:1–3 The record of the last week begins here. Jesus had paused on the east slope of the **Mount of Olives**, near **Bethphage** (house of unripe figs) and **Bethany** (house of the poor, humble, oppressed).

The time had arrived to present Himself openly to the Jewish people as their Messiah-King. He would do this in fulfillment of the prophecy of Zechariah (9:9), riding on **a colt**. So He sent **two of His disciples** from Bethany into Bethphage. With perfect knowledge and complete authority, He told them to bring an unbroken **colt** which they would find tethered. If anyone challenged them, they were to say, **"The Lord has need of it."** The omniscience of the Lord, as seen here, has prompted someone to say, "This is not the Christ of modernism, but of history and of Heaven."

11:4–6 Everything happened as Jesus had predicted. They **found the colt** tied at a main intersection in the village. When challenged, the disciples replied as Jesus had told them. Then the people **let them go**.

11:7, 8†† Though the colt had never been ridden before, it did not balk at carrying its Creator into Jerusalem. The Lord rode to the city on a carpet of **clothes** and palm **branches**, with the acclamation of the people ringing in His ears. For a moment, at least, He was acknowledged as King.

11:9, 10 The people cried:

1. **"Hosanna"** — which meant originally "Save, we pray" but which later became an exclamation of

praise. Perhaps the people meant "Save, we pray from our Roman oppressors!"

2. **"Blessed is He who comes in the name of the LORD"** — a clear recognition that Jesus was the promised Messiah (Psalm 118:26).

3. **"Blessed is the kingdom of our father David that comes in the name of the Lord!"** — they thought that **the kingdom** was about to be set up, with Christ sitting on the throne of **David**.

4. **"Hosanna in the highest!"** — a call to *praise* the Lord in the **highest** heavens, or for Him to *save* from the **highest** heavens.

11:11 Once in **Jerusalem**, Jesus went **into the temple** — not inside the sanctuary but into the temple courts. Presumably it was the house of God, but He was not at home in this temple because the priests and people refused to give Him His rightful place. **So when He had looked around** briefly, the Savior withdrew **to Bethany with the twelve** disciples. It was Sunday evening.

B. The Barren Fig Tree (11:12–14)

This incident is the Savior's interpretation of the tumultuous welcome He had just received in Jerusalem. He saw the nation of Israel as a barren **fig tree** — it had leaves of profession but no fruit. The cry of Hosanna would soon turn into the blood-curdling cry, "Crucify Him!"

There is an apparent difficulty in that He condemned the fig tree because it had no fruit, although the record distinctly says that **it was not the season for figs**. This seems to picture the Savior as unreasonable and petulant. We know this is not true; yet how can we explain this curious circumstance?

Fig trees in Bible lands produced an early edible fruit before the leaves appeared. It was a harbinger of the regular crop, here described as the **season for figs**. If no early figs appeared, it was a sign that there would be no regular crop later on. When Jesus came to the nation of Israel, there were leaves, which speak of profession, but there was no fruit for God. There was promise without fulfillment, profession without reality. Jesus was hungry for fruit from the nation. Because there was no early fruit, He knew that there would be no later fruit from that unbelieving people, and so He cursed the fig tree. This prepictured the judgment which was to fall on Israel in A.D. 70.

However, the incident does *not* teach that Israel was cursed to perpetual barrenness. The Jewish people have been set aside *temporarily*, but when Christ returns to reign, the nation will be reborn and restored to a position of favor with God.

This is the only miracle in which Christ cursed rather than blessed, destroyed life rather than restoring it. This has been raised as a difficulty. However, the objection is not valid. The Creator has the sovereign right to destroy an inanimate object in order to teach an important spiritual lesson and thus save men from eternal doom.

Although the primary interpretation of this passage relates to the nation of Israel, it has application to people of all ages who combine high talk and low walk.

C. The Servant Cleanses the Temple (11:15–19)

11:15, 16 At the outset of His public ministry, Jesus had driven commercialism out of the temple environs (John 2:13–22). Now as His ministry drew to a close, He again entered the court of the **temple** and drove out those who were profiteering from sacred activities. He even stopped the carrying of ordinary **wares through the temple area**.

11:17 Combining quotations from Isaiah and Jeremiah, He condemned desecration, exclusivism, and commercialism. God had intended the temple to be **a house of prayer for all nations** (Isa. 56:7), not just for Israel. They had made it a religious market, a hang-out for shysters and racketeers (Jer. 7:11).

11:18 **The scribes and chief priests** were cut deeply by His accusations. They wanted to **destroy Him**, but could not do it brazenly because the common people still looked on Him with a great deal of awe.

11:19 In the **evening . . . He went out of the city**. The tense of the original verb suggests it was His custom, perhaps for safety's sake. He was not afraid for Himself. We must keep in mind that part of His ministry was to preserve the sheep, that is, His own disciples (John 17:6–19) . Furthermore, it would be ludicrous for Him to surrender to His enemies' wishes before the proper time.

D. The Lesson of the Barren Fig Tree (11:20–26)

11:20–23 On the **morning** following the cursing of the fig tree, the disciples passed it on their way to Jerusalem. It had **withered away** from the roots up. When **Peter** mentioned this to the Lord, He simply said, **"Have faith in God."** But what do these words have to do with the fig tree? The following verses show that Jesus was encouraging faith as the means to remove difficulties. If disciples have **faith in God**, they can deal with the problem of fruitlessness, and remove mountainous obstacles.

However, these verses do not give a person authority to pray for miraculous powers for his own convenience or acclaim. Every act of faith must rest on the promise of God. If we know that it is God's will to remove a certain difficulty, then we can pray with utter confidence that it will be done. In fact, we can pray with confidence on any subject as long as we are confident it is according to God's will as revealed in the Bible or by the inner witness of the Spirit.

11:24 When we are really living in touch with the Lord and praying in the Spirit, we can have the assurance of answered prayer before the answer actually comes.

11:25, 26 But one of the basic requirements for answered prayer is a forgiving spirit. If we nurse a harsh, vindictive attitude toward others, we cannot expect God to hear and answer us. We must **forgive** if we are to be forgiven. This does not refer to the judicial forgiveness of sins at the time of conversion; that is strictly a matter of grace through faith. This refers to God's parental dealings with His children. An unforgiving spirit in a believer breaks fellowship with the **Father in heaven** and hinders the flow of blessing.

E. The Servant's Authority Questioned (11:27–33)

11:27, 28 As soon as He reached the temple area, the religious leaders accosted Jesus and challenged His authority by asking two questions: (1) **"By what authority are You doing these things?"** (2) **"And who gave You this authority to do these things?"** (that is, to cleanse the temple, to curse the fig tree, and to ride triumphantly into Jerusalem). They hoped to trap Him, no matter how He answered. If He claimed to have authority in Himself as the Son of God, they would accuse Him of blasphemy. If He claimed authority from men, they would discredit Him. If He claimed to have received authority from God, they would challenge the claim; they considered themselves the God-appointed religious leaders of the people.

11:29–32 But **Jesus** answered by asking a question. Was John the Baptist divinely commissioned or not? (**The baptism of John** refers to his entire ministry.) They couldn't answer without embarrassment. If John's ministry was divinely appointed, they should have obeyed his call to repent. If they disparaged John's ministry, they would risk the anger of the common people, who still considered **John** a spokesman for God.

11:33 When they refused to answer, professing ignorance, the Lord refused to discuss His authority. As long as they were unwilling to acknowledge the credentials of the forerunner, they would hardly acknowledge the higher credentials of the King Himself!

F. Parable of the Wicked Vinedressers (12:1–12)

12:1 The Lord Jesus was not through with the Jewish authorities, even if He had refused to answer their question. He now delivered, in the form of **parables**, a stinging indictment of them for their rejection of God's Son. The **man** who **planted a vineyard** was God Himself. The **vineyard** was the place of privilege then occupied by Israel. The **hedge** was the Law of Moses, which separated Israel from the Gentiles and preserved them as a distinct people for the Lord. The **vinedressers** were the religious leaders, such as the Pharisees, the scribes and the elders.

12:2–5 Repeatedly, God sent His servants, the prophets, to the people of

Israel, seeking fellowship, holiness, and love. But the people persecuted the prophets and **killed** some of them.

12:6–8 Finally God sent His beloved **Son**. Surely they would **respect** Him. But they didn't. They plotted against Him and finally **killed Him**. Thus the Lord predicted His own death and exposed His guilty murderers.

12:9 What would God **do** with such wicked men? He would **destroy** them and give the place of privilege **to others**. The **others** here may refer to the Gentiles, or to the repentant remnant of Israel in the last days.

12:10, 11 All this was in fulfillment of the OT Scriptures. In Psalm 118:22, 23, for example, it was prophesied that the Messiah would be **rejected** by the Jewish leaders in their building plans. They would have no place for this **Stone**. But following His death, He would be raised from the dead and given the place of preeminence by God. He would be made **the chief cornerstone** in God's building.

12:12 The Jewish leaders got the point. They believed that Psalm 118 spoke of the Messiah. Now they heard the Lord Jesus applying it to Himself. **They sought to lay hands on Him**, but His time had not come. **The multitude** would have taken sides with Jesus. **So** the religious leaders **left Him** for the time being.

G. Rendering to Caesar and to God (12:13–17)

Chapter 12 contains attacks on the Lord by the Pharisees and Herodians and by the Sadducees. It is a chapter of questions. (See vv. 9, 10, 14, 15, 16, 23, 24, 26, 28, 35, 37.)

12:13, 14 The Pharisees and the Herodians, bitter foes, were now brought together by a common hatred of the Savior. They desperately tried to inveigle Him into saying something which they could use as a charge against Him. So they asked Him if it was **lawful to pay taxes** to the Roman government.

No Jews particularly *enjoyed* living under Gentile rule. The Pharisees hated it with a passion, whereas the Herodians adopted a more tolerant view. If Jesus openly endorsed paying tribute to **Caesar**, He would alienate many of the Jews. If He spoke against Caesar, they would

hustle Him to the Roman authorities for arrest and trial as a traitor.

12:15, 16 Jesus asked someone to **bring** Him **a denarius**. (Apparently He Himself did not have one.) The coin bore the image of Tiberius Caesar, a reminder to the Jews that they were a conquered, subject people. Why were they in this condition? Because of their unfaithfulness and sin. They should have been humbled at having to admit that the coins they used bore the image of a Gentile dictator.

12:17 Jesus said to them, **"Render to Caesar the things that are Caesar's and to God the things that are God's."** Their great failure had not been in the first area but in the second. They had paid their Roman taxes, though reluctantly, but had disregarded the claims of God on their lives. The coin had Caesar's image on it, and therefore belonged to Caesar. Man has God's image on him — God created man in His own image (Gen. 1:26, 27) — and therefore belongs to God.

The believer is to obey and support the government under which he lives. He is not to speak evil of his rulers or work to overthrow the government. He is to pay taxes and pray for those in authority. If called on to do anything that would violate his higher loyalty to Christ, he is to refuse and to bear the punishment. The claims of God must come first. In upholding those claims, the Christian should always maintain a good testimony before the world.

H. The Sadducees and Their Resurrection Riddle (12:18–27)

12:18 The **Sadducees** were the liberals or rationalists of that day. They scoffed at the idea of bodily **resurrection**. So they came to the Lord with a preposterous story, trying to ridicule the whole idea.

12:19 They reminded Jesus that the Law of **Moses** made special provision for widows in Israel. In order to preserve the family name and to keep the property in the family, the Law stipulated that if a man died childless, **his brother** should marry the widow (Deut. 25:5–10).

12:20–23 Here was a fantastic case in which a woman married **seven brothers**, one after the other. Then **last of all** she **died**. Now for their clever question!

"**Whose wife will she be** in the resurrection?"

12:24 They thought they were smart; the Savior told them they were abysmally ignorant of both **the Scriptures** which teach resurrection and **the power of God** which raises the dead.

12:25 First they should know that the **marriage** relationship does not continue in heaven. Believers will recognize one another in heaven and will not lose their distinctions as men and women, but they will **neither marry nor** give in **marriage**. In that respect, they will resemble the **angels in heaven**.

12:26, 27 Then our Lord took the Sadducees, who valued the books of Moses above the rest of the OT, back to the account of **Moses** at **the burning bush** (Ex. 3:6). There God spoke of Himself as **the God of Abraham, the God of Isaac, and the God of Jacob**. The Savior used this to show that God was **the God of the living, not** of **the dead**.

But how so? Weren't Abraham, Isaac and Jacob dead when God appeared to Moses? Yes, their bodies were in the Cave of Machpelah in Hebron. How then is God the God of the living?

The argument seems to be this:
1. God had made promises to the patriarchs concerning the land and concerning the Messiah.
2. These promises were not fulfilled during their lifetimes.
3. When God spoke to Moses at the burning bush, the bodies of the patriarchs were in the grave.
4. Yet God spoke of Himself as the God of the living.
5. He must fulfill His promises to Abraham, Isaac, and Jacob.
6. Therefore, resurrection is an absolute necessity from what we know of the character of God.

And so the Lord's parting word to the Sadducees was, "**You are therefore greatly mistaken.**"

I. The Great Commandment (12:28–34)

12:28 **One of the scribes**, impressed by our Lord's adroit handling of His critic's questions, **asked** Jesus **which is** the most important **commandment**. It was an honest question, and, in some ways, life's most basic question. He was really asking for a concise statement of the chief aim of man's existence.

12:29 Jesus began by quoting from the *Shema*, a Jewish statement of faith taken from Deuteronomy 6:4: "**Hear, O Israel: The LORD our God, the LORD is one.**"

12:30 Then He summed up man's responsibility to God: **Love** Him with the entirety of one's **heart, soul, mind** and **strength**. God is to have the supreme place in man's life. No other love can be allowed to rival love for God.

12:31 The other half of the Ten Commandments teaches us to **love** our **neighbor as** ourselves. We are to love God *more* than ourselves, and our neighbor *as* ourselves. Thus, the life that really counts is concerned first with God, then with others. Material things are not mentioned. God is important and people are important.

12:32, 33 **The scribe** agreed heartily, stating with commendable clarity that **love** to God and to **one's neighbor** were far more important than rituals. He realized that people could go through religious ceremonies and put on a public display of piety without inward, personal holiness. He acknowledged that God is concerned with what a man is inwardly as well as outwardly.

12:34 **When Jesus** heard this remarkable observation, He told the scribe that he was **not far from the kingdom of God**. True subjects of the kingdom do not try to deceive God, their fellow-men, or themselves with external religion. Realizing that God looks on the heart, they go to Him for cleansing from sin and for power to live in a manner pleasing to Him.

After this, **no one dared** to trap the Lord Jesus by asking Him leading questions.

J. David's Son Is David's Lord (12:35–37)

The scribes had always taught that the Messiah would be a lineal descendant **of David**. Though true, this was not the whole truth. So the Lord Jesus now posed a problem to those gathered around Him in the temple court. In Psalm 110:1, David spoke of the coming Messiah as his **Lord**. How could this be? How could the Messiah be David's *Son* and his *Lord* at the same time? To us the answer is clear. The Messiah would be both Man and God. As David's **Son**, He would be human. As David's **Lord**, He would be divine.

The common people heard Him gladly. Apparently they were willing to accept the fact, even if they might not have understood it fully. But nothing is said of the Pharisees and scribes. Their silence is ominous.

K. Warning against the Scribes (12:38—40)

12:38, 39 The **scribes** were outwardly religious. They loved to parade **in long robes**. This distinguished them from the common herd and gave them a sanctimonious appearance. They loved to be greeted with high sounding titles in public places. It did something for their ego! They sought the places of honor **in the synagogues**, as if physical location had something to do with godliness. They not only wanted religious prominence, but social distinction as well. They wanted **the best places at feasts**.

12:40 Inwardly they were greedy and insincere. They robbed **widows** of property and livelihood in order to enrich themselves, pretending the money was for the Lord! They recited **long prayers** — great swelling words of vanity — prayers of words alone. In short, they loved *peculiarity* (long robes); *popularity* (greetings); *prominence* (best seats); *priority* (best places); *possessions* (widows' houses); *mock piety* (long prayers).

L. The Widow's Two Mites (12:41—44)

In vivid contrast to the scribes' avarice was this widow's devotion. They devoured widows' houses; she gave **all that she had** to the Lord. The incident shows the omniscience of the Lord. Watching the **rich** people dropping sizable gifts into the chest for the temple **treasury**, He knew that their giving did not represent a sacrifice. They **gave out of their abundance**. Knowing also that the two mites she gave was **her livelihood**, He announced that she gave **more than all** the rest put together. As regards monetary value, she gave very little. But the Lord estimates giving by our motive, our means, and by how much we have left. This is a great encouragement to those who have few material possessions, but a great desire to give to Him.

Amazing how we can approve the widow's action and agree with the Savior's verdict without imitating her example! If we really believed what we say we believe, we would do exactly what she did. Her gift expressed her conviction that all belonged to the Lord, that He was worthy of all, that He must have all. Many Christians today would criticize her for not providing for her future. Did this show a lack of foresight and prudence? So men would argue. But this is the life of faith — plunging all into the work of God now and trusting Him for the future. Did He not promise to provide for those who seek first the kingdom of God and His righteousness (Matt. 6:33)?

Radical? Revolutionary? Unless we see that the teachings of Christ are radical and revolutionary, we have missed the emphasis of His ministry.

VI. THE SERVANT'S OLIVET DISCOURSE (Chap. 13)

A. Jesus Predicts the Destruction of the Temple (13:1, 2)

13:1 As the Lord Jesus was leaving **the temple** area for the last time before His death, **one of His disciples** tried to arouse His enthusiasm concerning the magnificence of the temple and the surrounding architecture. The disciples were occupied with the architectural triumphs involved in erecting the enormous stones.

13:2 The Savior pointed out that these things were soon to be destroyed. **Not one stone** would **be left upon another** when the Roman armies would invade Jerusalem in A.D. 70. Why be occupied with things that are only passing shadows?

B. The Beginning of Sorrows (13:3—8)

In His discourse **on the Mount of Olives**, the Lord diverted the disciples' attention to events of greater importance. Some of the prophecies seem to depict the destruction of Jerusalem, A.D. 70; most of them obviously go beyond that date to the Tribulation Period and to the personal Return of Christ in power and glory. The *watchwords* of the discourse, which apply to believers in every dispensation, are: (1) *take heed* (vv. 5, 23, 33); (2) *do not be troubled* (v. 7); (3) *endure* (v. 13); (4) *pray* (vv. 18, 33); (5) *watch* (vv. 9, 33, 35, 37).

13:3, 4 The discourse was introduced by a question from **Peter, James, John, and Andrew**. **When** would the temple be destroyed, and **what** would **be the sign** preceding the prophesied event? The Lord's answer included the destruction of a later temple, which would take place during the Great Tribulation, prior to His Second Advent.

13:5, 6 First, they were to **take heed that no one** deceived them by claiming to be the Messiah. **Many** false Christs would appear, as seen in the rise of so many cults, each with its own anti-Christ.

13:7, 8 Secondly, they should not interpret **wars and rumors of wars** as a sign of the end times. All through the intervening period there would be international strife. In addition, there would be great cataclysms of nature — **earthquakes, famines, and troubles**. These would be but preliminary birth pangs, ushering in a period of unparalleled travail.

C. Persecution of Disciples (13:9–13)

13:9 Thirdly, the Lord predicted great personal testing for those who would be unflinching in their testimony for Him. They would be put on trial before religious and civil courts.

While this section is applicable to all periods of Christian testimony, it seems to have special reference to the ministry of the 144,000 Jewish believers who will carry the gospel of the kingdom to all nations of the earth prior to Christ's coming to reign.

13:10 Verse 10 should *not* be used to teach that **the gospel must . . . be preached to all the nations** *before the Rapture*. It *should be* proclaimed world-wide and perhaps it *will be*, but to say that it *must be* is to state something the Bible doesn't state. No prophecy needs to be fulfilled before Christ's Coming for His saints; He may come at any moment!

13:11 The Lord promised that persecuted believers on trial for His sake would be given divine help in making their defense. They would not need to prepare their case in advance; perhaps

there would not be time. **The Holy Spirit** would give them exactly the right words. This promise should not be used as an excuse for not preparing sermons or gospel messages today, but is a guarantee of supernatural help for crisis times. It is a promise for martyrs, not ministers!

13:12, 13 Another feature of tribulation days will be widespread betrayal of those who are loyal to the Savior. Family members will serve as informers against believers. A great wave of anti-Christian sentiment will sweep the world. It will take courage to remain true to the Lord Jesus, **but he who endures to the end shall be saved**. This cannot mean that they will receive eternal salvation because of their endurance; that would be a false gospel. Neither can it mean that faithful believers will be saved from physical death during the Tribulation, because we read elsewhere that many will seal their testimony with their blood. What it probably means is that endurance to the end will evidence reality, that is, it will *characterize* those who are genuinely *saved*.

D. The Great Tribulation (13:14–23)

13:14–18 Verse 14 marks the middle of the Tribulation Period, the beginning of the *Great* Tribulation. We know this by comparing this passage with **Daniel** 9:27. At that time, a great abominable idol will be set up in the temple in Jerusalem. Men will be compelled to worship it or be slain. True believers will, of course, refuse.

The setting up of this idolatrous image will signal the beginning of great persecution. Those who read and believe the Bible will know that the time has come to flee from **Judea**. There will not be time to gather up personal belongings. **Pregnant** women and **nursing** mothers will be at a distinct disadvantage. If it happens **in winter**, that will add further hazards.

13:19 It will be a time of **tribulation** greater than anything in the past or the future. It is the *Great Tribulation*. The Lord Jesus is not speaking here about the general type of tribulation which believers in every age have encountered. This is a period of trouble unique in its intensity.

Notice that the **tribulation** is primarily Jewish in character. We read of the temple (v. 14, cf. Matt. 24:15) and of Judea (v. 14). It is the time of Jacob's trouble (Jer. 30:7). The church is not in view here. It will have already been taken to heaven before the Day of the Lord begins (1 Thess. 4:13–18; cf. 1 Thess. 5:1–3).

13:20 The bowls of God's wrath will be poured out on the world in those days. It will be a time of calamity, chaos, and bloodshed. In fact, the slaughter will be so great that God will supernaturally shorten the period of daylight; otherwise *no one* would survive.

13:21, 22 The Great Tribulation will again witness the rise of **false** messiahs. People will be so desperate they will turn to anyone who promises them safety. But believers will know that Christ will not appear quietly or unheralded. Even if these **false christs** perform supernatural wonders (as they will), **the elect** will not be deceived. They will realize that these miracles are satanically inspired.

Miracles are not necessarily divine. They represent superhuman departures from the known laws of nature but may represent the work of Satan, angels, or demons. The Man of Sin will be given satanic power to perform miracles (2 Thess. 2:9).

13:23 So believers should **take heed** and be forewarned.

E. The Second Advent (13:24–27)

13:24, 25 **After that tribulation**, there will be startling disturbances in the heavens. Darkness will shroud the earth both by day and by night. **The stars of heaven will fall and the powers in the heavens** (the forces that keep stellar bodies in orbit) **will be shaken**.

13:26, 27 Then the awe-struck world **will see the Son of Man** returning to the earth, not now as the lowly Nazarene but as the glorious Conqueror. He will come **in the clouds**, escorted by myriads of angelic beings and of glorified saints. It will be a scene of overwhelming power and dazzling splendor. He will dispatch His angels to **gather together His elect**, that is, all who have acknowledged Him as Lord and Savior during the Tribulation Period. From one

end of the earth to the other — from China to Colombia — they will come to enjoy the benefits of His wonderful thousand-year reign on earth. His enemies, however, will be destroyed at the same time.

F. Parable of the Fig Tree (13:28–31)

13:28 **The fig tree** is a symbol (or type) of the nation of Israel. Jesus taught here that prior to His Second Advent, the fig tree would put **forth leaves**. In 1948, the independent nation of Israel was formed. Today that nation exerts an influence in world affairs that is out of all proportion to its size. Israel can be said to be "putting forth its leaves." There is no fruit as yet; in fact, there will be no fruit until the Messiah returns to a people who are willing to receive Him.

13:29 The formation and growth of the nation of Israel tell us that the King[21] **is near — at the doors**. If His coming to reign is that near, how much nearer is His coming for the church!

13:30 Verse 30 is often understood to mean that all the things prophesied in this chapter would take place while the men of Christ's day were still living. But it cannot mean that because many of the events, especially verses 24-27, simply did not take place at that time. Others understand it to mean that the **generation** living when the fig tree put forth its leaves, that is, when the nation of Israel was formed in 1948, would be the generation that would see the Second Advent. We prefer a third view. **This generation** may mean "this race." We believe it means "this Jewish race characterized by unbelief and rejection of the Messiah." The testimony of history is that "this generation" has *not* passed away. The nation as a whole has not only survived as a distinct people, but has continued in its deep-seated animosity toward the Lord Jesus. Jesus predicted that the nation and its national characteristic would continue until His Second Advent.

13:31 Our Lord emphasized the absolute certainty of every one of His predictions. The atmospheric **heaven** and the stellar **heaven will pass away. The earth** itself will be dissolved. But every word He spoke will come to pass.

G. The Day and Hour Unknown (13:32–37)

13:32 Jesus said, **"But of that day and hour no one knows, not even the angels in heaven, nor the Son, but only the Father."** It is well known that this verse has been used by enemies of the gospel to prove that Jesus was nothing more than a man with limited knowledge like ourselves. It has also been used by sincere but misguided believers to demonstrate that Jesus emptied Himself of the attributes of deity when He came into the world as a man.

Neither of these interpretations is true. Jesus was and is both God and Man. He had all the attributes of deity and all the characteristics of perfect manhood. It is true that His deity was veiled in a body of flesh, but it was there nonetheless. There was never a time when He was not fully God.

How then can it be said of Him that He does not know the time of His Second Advent? We believe the key to the answer is found in John 15:15: " . . . a servant does not know what his master is doing. . . . " As a perfect Servant, it was not given to the Lord Jesus to know the time of His Coming (John 12:50; 17:8). As God, of course, He does know it. But as Servant, it was not given to Him to know it for the purpose of revealing to others. James H. Brookes explains it thus:

> It is not a denial of our Lord's divine omniscience, but simply an assertion that in the economy of human redemption, it was not for Him "to know the times or seasons, which the Father hath appointed by His own authority," Acts 1:7. Jesus knew that He will come again, and often spoke of His second advent, but it did not fall to His office as Son to determine the date of His return, and hence He could hold it up before His followers as the object of constant expectation and desire.[22]

13:33–37 The chapter closes with an exhortation to watchfulness and prayer in view of the Lord's Return. The fact that we **do not know** the appointed time should keep us on the alert.

A similar situation is common in everyday life. A man goes away from home on a long trip. He leaves instructions with his servant and tells the watchman also to be on the lookout for his return. Jesus likened Himself to the traveling man. He may come back at any hour of the night. His people, serving as night watchmen, should not be found **sleeping**. So He left this word for all His people: **"Watch!"**

VII. THE SERVANT'S PASSION AND DEATH (Chaps. 14, 15)

A. The Plot to Kill Jesus (14:1, 2)

It was now Wednesday of that fateful week. In **two days** it would be **Passover**, ushering in the seven day **Feast of Unleavened Bread**. The religious leaders were determined to destroy the Lord Jesus, but didn't want to do it during the religious holidays because many of the people still considered Jesus a prophet.

Though **the chief priests and the scribes** determined **not** to kill Him **during the feast**, divine Providence overruled them, and the Paschal Lamb of God was killed at that very time (see Matt. 26:2).

B. Jesus Anointed at Bethany (14:3–9)

As a jeweler places a diamond against black velvet, the Holy Spirit and His human writer Mark skillfully highlight the radiance of a woman's love for our Lord between the dark plotting of the religious hierarchy and that of Judas.

14:3 **Simon the leper** held a feast in honor of the Savior, perhaps in gratitude for being healed. An unnamed woman (probably Mary of Bethany, John 12:3) lavishly anointed Jesus' **head** with some **very costly** perfume. Her love for Him was great.

14:4, 5 **Some** of the guests thought this was a tremendous waste. She was reckless, prodigal. Why hadn't she **sold** the perfume and **given** the money **to the poor**? (**Three hundred denarii** was the equivalent of a year's wages.) People still think it a waste to give a year of one's life to the Lord. How much more a waste would they consider it to give one's whole life to the Lord!

14:6–8 **Jesus** rebuked their murmuring. She had recognized her golden opportunity to pay this tribute to the Savior. If they were so solicitous for the poor, they would always be able to help them, because **the poor** are **always** present. But the Lord would soon die and be buried. This woman wanted to show this kindness while she could. She might not be able to care for His **body** in death, so she would show her love while He was still alive.

14:9 The fragrance of that perfume reaches down to our generation. Jesus said that she would be memorialized worldwide. She has been — through the Gospel records.

C. The Treachery of Judas (14:10, 11)

The woman prized the Savior highly. **Judas**, by contrast, valued Him very lightly. Though he had lived with the Lord Jesus for at least a year, and had received nothing but kindness from Him, Judas now sneaked off to the chief priests with a guarantee **to betray** the Son of God into their hands. They seized the offer gladly, offering to pay him for his treachery. All he had to do now was work out the details.

D. Preparations for the Passover (14:12–16)

Although the exact chronology is not certain, we have probably now come to Thursday of Passover Week. The disciples little realized that this would be the fulfillment and climax of all the Passovers that had ever been held. They asked the Lord for directions as to where to hold **the Passover. He sent** them to Jerusalem with instructions to look for a **man . . . carrying a pitcher of water** — a rarity since women usually carried waterpots. This man would lead them to the proper house. They would then ask the owner to show them to a room where **the Teacher** could **eat the Passover with** His **disciples**.

It is wonderful to see the Lord choosing and commanding in this way. He acts as the Sovereign Ruler of men and property. It is also wonderful to see responsive hearts putting themselves and their possessions at His disposal. It is good for us when He has instant, ready access to every room in our lives!

E. Jesus Predicts His Betrayal (14:17–21)

That same **evening He came with the twelve** to the upper room which had been prepared. As they reclined **and ate, Jesus** announced that **one of** the disciples would **betray** Him. They all recognized the evil propensities of their own natures. With a healthy distrust of self, each asked if he were the culprit. Jesus then disclosed the traitor as the one who dipped the bread with Him in the meat-juice, that is, the one to whom He gave the piece of bread. **The Son of Man** was going forward to His death as predicted, He said, but the doom of His betrayer would be great. In fact, **it would have been good . . . if he had never been born.**

F. The First Lord's Supper (14:22–26)

14:22–25 After taking **the bread**, Judas went out into the night (John 13:30). Jesus then instituted what we know as the Lord's Supper. Its meaning is beautifully outlined in the three words: (1) He **took** — humanity upon Himself; (2) He **broke** — He was about to be broken on the cross; (3) He **gave** — He gave Himself for us.

The bread signified His **body** given, **the cup** His **blood** shed. By His **blood** He ratified **the New Covenant**. For Him there would be no more festive joy until He returned to earth to set up His **kingdom**.

14:26 At that point, they sang **a hymn** — probably a portion of the Great Hallel — Psalms 113–118. Then **they went out** from Jerusalem, across the Kidron, **to the Mount of Olives**.

G. Peter's Self-Confidence (14:27–31)

14:27, 28 On the way, the Savior warned the disciples that they would **all** be ashamed and afraid to be known as His followers in the hours ahead. It would be as Zechariah had predicted; **the Shepherd** would be struck and His **sheep** would **be scattered** (Zech. 13:7). But He graciously assured them that He would not disown them; after rising from the dead, He would be waiting for them in **Galilee**.

14:29, 30 Peter was indignant at the thought of denying the Lord. The others might, but he? — Never! Jesus corrected that "Never!" to "Soon." **Before the rooster** crowed **twice**, Peter would have disowned the Savior **three times**.

14:31 "It's preposterous," shouted Peter, "I'll die before I **deny You!**" Peter wasn't the only one to make that noisy boast. **They all** engaged in brash, self-confident assertions. Let us never forget that, for we are no different. We must all learn the cowardice and weakness of our hearts.

H. The Agony in Gethsemane (14:32–42)

14:32 Darkness had settled over the land. It was Thursday night running into Friday morning. When **they came to** an enclosed piece of ground **named Gethsemane**, the Lord Jesus left eight of the disciples near the entrance.

14:33, 34 **He took Peter, James, and John with Him** deeper into the garden. There He experienced an overpowering burden on His holy soul as He anticipated becoming a sin-offering for us. We cannot conceive what it meant to Him, the Sinless One, to be made sin for us. He left the three disciples with instructions to **stay** there and stay awake. **He went a little farther** into the garden — alone. Thus would He go to the cross alone, bearing the awful judgment of God against our sins.

14:35 With wonder and amazement, we see the Lord Jesus prostrate on the ground, praying to God. Was He asking to be excused from going to the cross? Not at all; this was the purpose of His coming into the world. First, **He prayed that if it were possible, the hour might pass from Him**. If there was any other way by which sinners could be saved than by His death, burial, and resurrection, let God reveal that way. The heavens were silent. There was no other way in which we could be redeemed.

14:36 Again, He prayed, **"Abba, Father, all things are possible for You. Take this cup away from Me; nevertheless, not what I will, but what You will."** Notice that He addressed God as His beloved **Father** with whom **all things are possible**. Here it was not so much a matter of physical possibility as of moral. Could the Almighty Father find any other righteous basis upon which He could save ungodly sinners? The silent heavens indicated that there was no other way. The Holy Son of God must bleed that sinners might be freed from sin!

14:37–40 Returning to the three disciples, He **found them sleeping** — a sad commentary on fallen human nature. Jesus warned Peter against **sleeping** in that crucial **hour**. Only recently, Peter had boasted of his undying steadfast-

ness. Now he couldn't even stay awake. If a man cannot pray for **one hour**, it is unlikely that he will be able to resist temptation in the moment of extreme pressure. No matter how enthusiastic his spirit may be, he must reckon with the frailty of his flesh.

14:41, 42 Three times the Lord Jesus returned to find the disciples asleep. Then He said, **"Are you still sleeping and resting? It is enough! The hour has come; behold, the Son of Man is being betrayed into the hands of sinners."** With that, they got up as if to go forth. But they didn't have to go far.

I. Jesus Betrayed and Arrested (14:43–52)

14:43 **Judas** had already entered the garden with a posse. His cohorts were carrying **swords and clubs**, as if they were going to capture a dangerous felon.

14:44, 45 The **betrayer** had a prearranged signal. He would **kiss** the One whom they should **seize**. So he strode up to Jesus, addressed Him as **Rabbi, and kissed Him** effusively. (The emphatic form in the original suggests repeated or demonstrative kissing.) Why did Judas betray the Lord? Was he disappointed that Jesus had not seized the reins of government? Were his hopes dashed for a place of prominence in the kingdom? Was he overcome by greed? All of these might have contributed to his infamous deed.

14:46–50 The armed henchmen of the betrayer stepped forward and arrested the Lord. Peter quickly **drew his sword** and sliced **off** the **ear** of **the servant of the high priest**. It was a natural reaction, not a spiritual one. Peter was using carnal weapons to fight a spiritual warfare. The Lord rebuked Peter and miraculously restored the ear, as we read in Luke 22:51 and John 18:11. Jesus then reminded His captors how incongruous it was for them to take Him by force! He had been **daily with** them **in the temple teaching**. Why hadn't they seized Him then? He knew the answer. **The Scriptures must be fulfilled** which prophesied that He would be betrayed (Ps. 41:9), arrested (Isa. 53:7), manhandled (Ps. 22:12) and forsaken (Zech. 13:7).

14:51, 52 Mark is the only evangelist who records this incident. It is widely believed that Mark himself was the **young man** who, in his frenzy to escape, left his covering in the grasp of the armed men. The **linen cloth** was not a regular garment but a piece of **cloth** which he had picked up quickly for an improvised covering.

Erdman comments: "Probably this picturesque incident is added to show how completely Jesus was forsaken in the hours of His peril and pain. He surely knew what it was to suffer alone."

J. Jesus Before the High Priest (14:53, 54)[†]

The record of the ecclesiastical trial extends from verse 53 to 15:1 and is divided into three parts: (1) Trial before the high priest (vv. 53, 54); (2) Midnight meeting of the Sanhedrin (vv. 55–65); (3) Meeting of the Sanhedrin in the morning (15:1).

14:53 It is generally agreed that Mark here records the trial before Caiaphas. The trial before Annas is found in John 18:13, 19–24.

14:54 **Peter** trailed the Lord Jesus to the **courtyard of the high priest**, following at what he thought would be a safe distance. Someone has outlined his downfall as follows:

1. He first fought — misdirected enthusiasm.
2. He then fled — cowardly withdrawal.
3. Finally he followed afar off — halfhearted discipleship by night.

He sat by **the fire** with the officers, warming **himself** with the enemies of his Lord.

K. Jesus Before the Sanhedrin (14:55–65)

14:55–59[††] Although it is not specifically stated, v. 55 seems to begin the account of a midnight meeting of the Sanhedrin. The body of seventy-one religious leaders was presided over by the high priest. On this particular night, the Pharisees, Sadducees, scribes and elders who comprised the Sanhedrin showed an utter disregard for the rules under which they operated. They were not supposed to meet at night or during any of the Jewish feasts. They were not supposed to bribe witnesses to commit per-

jury. A death verdict was not to be carried out until a night had elapsed. Unless they met in the Hall of Hewn Stone, in the temple area, their verdicts were not binding.

In their eagerness to do away with the Lord Jesus, the religious authorities did not hesitate to stoop to breaking their own laws. Their determined efforts produced a group of **false** witnesses but they failed to produce united testimony. Some misquoted the Lord as threatening to **destroy** the temple **made with hands, and within three days**, to rebuild **another, made without hands**. What Jesus actually said is found in John 2:19. They purposely confused the temple in Jerusalem with the temple of His body.

14:60–62 When **the high priest** first questioned Him, Jesus did not reply. But when asked under oath (Matt. 26:63) whether He was the Messiah, **the Son of the Blessed**, the Savior replied that He was, thus acting in obedience to Leviticus 5:1. Then, as if to remove any doubt as to who He claimed to be, the Lord Jesus told the high priest that he would yet **see the Son of Man sitting at the right hand of the Power, and coming** back to earth **with the clouds of heaven**. By this He meant that the high priest would yet see Him openly manifested as God. During His First Advent, the glory of His deity was veiled in a human body. But when He comes again in power and great glory, the veil will be removed and everyone will know exactly who He is.

14:63, 64 **The high priest** understood what Jesus meant. He **tore his clothes** as a sign of his righteous indignation against this supposed **blasphemy**. The one Israelite who should have been most ready to recognize and receive the Messiah was loudest in his condemnation. But not he alone; the entire Sanhedrin[23] agreed that Jesus had blasphemed, and **condemned Him to be deserving of death**.

14:65 The scene that followed was grotesque in the extreme. Some members of the Sanhedrin **began to spit on** the Son of God, **to blindfold Him**, and to challenge Him to name His assailants. It is almost incredible that the worthy Savior should have to endure such contradiction of sinners against Himself. **The officers** (temple police) joined in the scandal by hitting **Him with the palms of their hands**.

L. Peter Denies Jesus and Weeps Bitterly (14:66–72)

14:66–68 Peter was waiting **below in the courtyard** of the building. **One of the servant girls of the high priest** passed by. She peered intently at him, then charged him with being a follower of the Nazarene, **Jesus**. The pathetic disciple pretended complete ignorance of her charge, then moved to the porch in time to hear **a rooster** crow. It was a ghastly moment. Sin was taking its terrible toll.

14:69, 70 The **girl saw him again** and pointed him out as a disciple of Jesus. Peter made another cold denial, and probably wondered why people didn't leave him alone. Then the crowd said to Peter, **"Surely you are one of them; for you are a Galilean, and your speech shows it."**

14:71, 72 Cursing and swearing, Peter defiantly stated that he did **not know this Man**. No sooner were the words out of his mouth than the **rooster crowed**. The world of nature seemed thus to protest the cowardly lie. In a flash Peter realized that the Lord's prediction had come to pass. **He** broke down and **wept**. It is significant that all four Gospels record Peter's denials. We must all learn the lesson that self confidence leads to humiliation. We must learn to distrust self and to lean completely on the power of God.

M. Morning Trial Before the Sanhedrin (15:1)

This verse describes a **morning** meeting of the Sanhedrin, perhaps convened to validate the illegal action of the night before. As a result, Jesus was **bound** and taken **to Pilate**, the Roman Governor of Palestine.

N. Jesus Before Pilate (15:2–5)

15:2 Up to now, Jesus had been on trial before the religious leaders on a charge of *blasphemy*. Now He was taken before the civil court on a charge of *treason*. The civil trial took place in three stages — first before Pilate, then before Herod, and finally before Pilate again.

Pilate asked the Lord Jesus if He were **the King of the Jews**. If He were, He was presumably dedicated to the overthrow of Caesar, and thus guilty of treason.

15:3–5† **The chief priests** poured out a torrent of charges against Jesus. Pilate couldn't get over His poise in the face of such overwhelming accusations. He asked Him why He didn't defend Himself, but **Jesus** refused to answer His critics.

O. Jesus or Barabbas? (15:6–15)

15:6–8 It was the custom for the Roman Governor to release **one** Jewish **prisoner** at this feast time — sort of a political sop to the unhappy people. One such eligible prisoner was **Barabbas**, guilty of **rebellion** and **murder**. When Pilate offered to **release** Jesus, taunting the envious chief priests, the people were primed to ask for Barabbas. The very ones who were charging Jesus with treason against Caesar were asking the release of a man who was *actually* guilty of that crime! The position of the chief priests was irrational and ludicrous — but sin is like that. Basically they were jealous of His popularity.

15:9–14 Pilate asked what he should do with the One whom they called **the King of the Jews**. The people chanted savagely, **"Crucify Him!"** Pilate demanded a reason, but there was none. Mob hysteria was rising. All they would shout was, **"Crucify Him!"**

15:15 And so the spineless **Pilate** did what they wanted — **he released Barabbas**, flogged Jesus and **delivered** Him over to the soldiers for crucifixion. It was a monstrous verdict of unrighteousness. And yet it was a parable of our redemption — the guiltless One delivered to die in order that the guilty might go free.

P. The Soldiers Mock God's Servant (15:16–21)

15:16–19 The soldiers led Jesus **away into the hall** of the Governor's residence. After assembling **the whole garrison**, they staged a mock coronation for the King of the Jews. If they had only known! It was God the Son they **clothed with purple**. It was their own Creator they crowned with **thorns**. It was the Sustainer of the universe they mocked as

†See p. xxi.

King of the Jews. It was the Lord of life and glory they **struck on the head**. They **spat on** the Prince of peace. They mockingly bowed their knees to the King of kings and Lord of lords.

15:20, 21 When their crude jests were over, **they put His own clothes** back **on Him, and led Him out to crucify Him**. Mark mentions here that the soldiers ordered a passerby, **Simon** of Cyrene (in North Africa), to carry **His cross**. He may have been black but was more probably a Hellenistic Jew. He had two sons, **Alexander and Rufus**, who were probably believers (if **Rufus** is the same one mentioned in Rom. 16:13). In bearing the cross after Jesus, he gave us a picture of what should characterize *us* as disciples of the Savior.

Q. The Crucifixion (15:22–32)

The Spirit of God describes the crucifixion simply and unemotionally. He does not dwell on the extreme cruelty of this mode of execution, or the terrible suffering it entailed.

The exact location is unknown today. Though the traditional site, at the Church of the Holy Sepulcher, is inside the walls of the city, its advocates contend that it was outside the walls at the time of Christ. Another supposed site is Gordon's Calvary, north of the city walls and adjoining a garden area.

15:22 Golgotha is the Aramaic name meaning **skull**. Calvary is the Latin name. Perhaps the area was shaped like a skull or received the name because it was a place of execution.

15:23 The soldiers offered Jesus **wine mingled with myrrh**. This would have acted as a drug, dulling His senses. Determined to bear man's sins in His full consciousness, **He** would **not take it**.

15:24 The soldiers gambled for the clothes of those who were crucified. When they took the Savior's **garments**, they took just about everything material that He owned.

15:25-28† It was 9:00 a.m. when they **crucified Him**. Over His head they had put the title **THE KING OF THE JEWS**. (Mark does not give the full inscription but contents himself with the substance of it; see Matt. 27:37; Luke 23:38; John 19:19.) **Two robbers** were crucified with Him, **one** on each side — just as Isaiah had predicted that He

†*See p. xxii.*

would be associated with criminals in His death (Isa. 53:12).[24]

15:29, 30 The Lord Jesus was mocked by the passers-by (vv. 29, 30), the **chief priests** and **scribes** (vv. 31, 32a), and the two robbers (v. 32b).

The passers-by were probably Jews who were ready to keep the Passover inside the city. Outside they paused long enough to hurl an insult at the Paschal Lamb. They misquoted Him as threatening to **destroy** their beloved **temple** and to rebuild it **in three days**. If He was so great, let Him **save** Himself by coming **down from the cross**.

15:31 The **chief priests** and **the scribes** scorned His claim to save **others**. **"He saved others; Himself He cannot save."** It was viciously cruel, yet unintentionally true. It was true in the Lord's life and in ours, too. We can't save *others* while seeking to save *ourselves*.

15:32 The religious leaders also challenged Him to come down **from the cross** if He were the Messiah, **the King of Israel**. Then they would **believe**, they said. Let us **see** and we will **believe**.[25] But God's order is, "Believe and then you will see."

Even the criminals reproached Him!

R. Three Hours of Darkness (15:33–41)

15:33 Between noon and three o'clock **the whole land** was shrouded in **darkness**. Jesus was then bearing the full judgment of God against our sins. He suffered spiritual desolation and separation from God. No mortal mind can ever understand the agony He endured when His soul was made a sacrifice for sin.

15:34 At the close of His agony, Jesus **cried out with a loud voice** (in Aramaic), **"My God, My God, why have You forsaken Me?"** God had **forsaken** Him because in His holiness He must dissociate Himself from sin. The Lord Jesus had identified Himself with our sins and was paying the penalty in full.

15:35, 36 Some of the cruel mob suggested He was **calling for Elijah** when He said, "Eloi, Eloi." As a final indignity, one of them soaked a **sponge** in **sour wine** and **offered it to Him** on the end of **a reed**.

15:37 Jesus **cried out** with strength and triumph — then **breathed His last**. His death was an act of His will, not an involuntary collapse.

15:38 At that moment, **the veil of the temple was torn in two from top to bottom**. This was an act of God indicating that by Christ's death, access into the sanctuary of God was henceforth the privilege of all believers (see Heb. 10:19–22). A great new era had been ushered in. It would be an era of nearness to God, not of distance from Him.

15:39 The Roman officer's confession, while noble, did not necessarily acknowledge Jesus as equal with God. **The** Gentile **centurion** recognized Him as **the Son of God**. No doubt he had a sense of history being made. But whether his faith was genuine is not clear.

15:40, 41 Mark mentions that certain **women** remained at the cross. It deserves mention that the women shine brightly in the Gospel narratives. Considerations of personal safety drove the men into hiding. The devotion of the women put love to Christ above their own welfare. They were last at the cross and first at the tomb.

S. The Burial in Joseph's Tomb (15:42–47)[†]

15:42 The Sabbath began at sunset on Friday. **The day before the Sabbath** or other festival was known as **the Preparation**.[26]

15:43 The necessity for prompt action probably emboldened **Joseph of Arimathea** to ask Pilate for permission to bury **the body of Jesus**. Joseph was a devout Jew, perhaps a member of the Sanhedrin (Luke 23:50, 51; see also Matt. 27:57; John 19:38).

15:44, 45 Pilate could hardly believe that Jesus **was already dead**. When **the centurion** confirmed the fact, the Governor **granted the body to Joseph**. (Two different words are used for the body of Jesus in this section. Joseph asked for the *body* of the Lord Jesus and Pilate granted the *corpse* to him.)

15:46 With loving care, Joseph (and Nicodemus — John 19:38, 39) embalmed the body, **wrapped Him in the linen**, then put Him **in a** new **tomb** belonging to himself. The tomb was a small room carved **out of the rock**. The door was sealed with a coin-shaped stone which could be rolled into a groove carved out of stone.

15:47 Again the women, that is, the two Marys, are mentioned as being pres-

ent. We admire them for their unflagging and fearless affection. We are told that the preponderance of missionaries today are women. Where are the men?

VIII. THE SERVANT'S TRIUMPH (16:1–20)[††]

A. The Women at the Empty Tomb (16:1–8)

16:1–4 On Saturday evening the two Marys **and Salome** came to the tomb to embalm the body of Jesus with spices. They knew it would not be easy. They knew a huge **stone** had been rolled across the mouth of the tomb. They knew about the Roman seal and the guard of soldiers. But love leaps over mountains of difficulties to reach the object of its affection.

Very early on Sunday morning, they were wondering out loud **who** would **roll away the stone from the door of the tomb. They looked up** and saw that it was already done! How often it happens when we are intent on honoring the Savior that difficulties are removed before we get to them.

16:5, 6[†††] **Entering the tomb, they saw an angel with the appearance of a young man in white**. He quickly dispelled their fears with the announcement that Jesus had **risen**. The tomb was empty.

16:7 The angel then commissioned them as heralds of the resurrection. They were to **tell His disciples — and Peter** — that Jesus would meet them in **Galilee**. Notice that **Peter**, the disciple who had denied His Lord, was singled out for special mention. The risen Redeemer had not disowned him but still loved him and longed to see him again. A special work of restoration needed to be done. The wandering sheep must be brought back into fellowship with the Shepherd. The backslider must return to the Father's house.

16:8 The women **fled from the tomb** with mingled shock and panic. They were too afraid to tell anyone what had happened. This is not surprising. The wonder is that they had been so brave and loyal and devoted up to now.

Because two major ancient manuscripts of Mark lack verses 9–20, many modern scholars believe they are not authentic. However, there are strong argu-

†See p. xvi.   ††See p. xvii. †††See p. xxiii.

ments for their inclusion in the text:

1. Virtually all other Greek manuscripts and many church fathers *do* contain this passage.
2. Verse 8 is a most strange conclusion, especially in the Greek where the last word is (*gar*, for). This word is scarcely ever near the end of a sentence, much less of a book.
3. If, as some teach, Mark's original ending is *lost*, and this is a later summary, then our Lord's words about preservation (Matt. 24:35) apparently have failed.
4. The contents of the passage *are* orthodox.
5. The style, and especially the vocabulary, closely parallel the first chapter of the book.[27] This would illustrate the structure called *chiasm*, in which the beginning and the end of a work are parallel (abcd dcba).

B. The Appearance to Mary Magdalene (16:9–11)

16:9 The Savior's first appearance was **to Mary Magdalene**. The first time she had met Jesus, He had **cast seven demons** out of her. From then on she served Him lovingly with her possessions. She witnessed the crucifixion, and saw where His body was laid.

From the other Gospels we learn that after finding the tomb empty, she ran and told Peter and John. Coming back with her they found the sepulcher empty, as she had told them. They returned to their home but she stayed at the empty tomb. It was then that Jesus appeared to her.

16:10, 11 Again **she went** back to the city to share the good news with the sorrowing disciples. For them it was *too* good to be true. **They did not believe** it.

C. The Appearance to Two Disciples (16:12, 13)

16:12 The full account of this appearance is found in Luke 24:13–31. Here we read that **He appeared in another form to two** disciples on the road to Emmaus. To Mary He had appeared as a gardener. Now He seemed like a fellow-traveler. But it was the same Jesus in His glorified body.

16:13 When the two disciples re-turned to Jerusalem and reported their fellowship with the risen Savior, they met the same disbelief that Mary had encountered.

D. The Appearance to the Eleven (16:14–18)

16:14 This appearance **to the eleven** took place that same Sunday evening (Luke 24:36; John 20:19–24; 1 Cor. 15:5). Although the disciples are referred to as **the eleven**, only ten were present. Thomas was absent on this occasion. Jesus rebuked His own for their refusal to accept the reports of His resurrection from Mary and the others.

16:15 Verse 15 records the commission that was given by the Lord on the eve of His Ascension. There is thus an interval between verses 14 and 15. The disciples were commanded to **preach the gospel to** the whole creation. The Savior's goal was world evangelization. He purposed to accomplish it with eleven disciples who would literally forsake all to follow Him.

16:16 There would be two results of the preaching. Some would believe, be **baptized** and **be saved**; some would disbelieve and **be condemned**.

Verse 16 is used by some to teach the necessity of water baptism for salvation. We know it cannot mean that for the following reasons:

1. The thief on the cross was not baptized; yet he was assured of being in Paradise with Christ (Luke 23:43).
2. The Gentiles in Caesarea were baptized *after* they were saved (Acts 10:44–48).
3. Jesus Himself did not baptize (John 4:1, 2) — a strange omission if baptism were necessary for salvation.
4. Paul thanked God that he baptized very few of the Corinthians (1 Cor. 1:14–16) — an impossible thanksgiving if baptism were essential for salvation.
5. Approximately 150 passages in the NT state that salvation is by faith alone. No verse or few verses could contradict this overwhelming testimony.
6. Baptism is connected with death and burial in the NT, not with spiritual birth.

What then *does* verse 16 mean? We

believe it mentions baptism as the expected outward expression of belief. Baptism is not *a condition* of salvation, but an outward *proclamation* that the person has been saved.

16:17, 18 Jesus here describes certain miracles that would accompany those who believe the gospel. As we read the verses, the obvious question is, "Do these signs exist today?" We believe that **these signs** were intended primarily for the apostolic age, before the complete Bible was available in written form. Most of these signs are found in the Book of Acts:

1. **Cast out demons** (Acts 8:7; 16:18; 19:11–16).
2. **New tongues** (Acts 2:4–11; 10:46; 19:6).
3. Handle **serpents** (Acts 28:5).
4. **Drink** poison without harmful effects — not recorded in Acts but attributed to John and Barnabas by the church historian Eusebius.
5. **Lay hands on the sick** for healing (Acts 3:7; 19:11; 28:8, 9).

What was the purpose of these miracles? We believe the answer is found in Hebrews 2:3, 4. Before the NT was available in completed form, men would ask the apostles and others for proof that the gospel was divine. To confirm the preaching, God bore witness with signs and wonders and various gifts of the Holy Spirit.

The need for these signs is gone today. We have the complete Bible. If men won't believe that, they wouldn't believe anyway. Mark *did not say* that the miracles would continue. The words "to the end of the age" *are not found here* as they are in Matthew 28:18–20.

However, Martin Luther suggested that "the signs here spoken of are to be used according to need. When the need arises, and the Gospel is hard pressed, then we must definitely do these signs, before we allow the Gospel to be maligned and knocked down."

E. The Servant's Ascension to God's Right Hand (16:19, 20)

16:19[†] Forty days after His resurrection, our **Lord** Jesus Christ **was received up into heaven, and sat down at the right hand of God**. This is the place of honor and of power.

[†]*See p. xxiii.*

16:20 In obedience to His command, the disciples **went** forth like flaming fires, preaching the gospel and winning men to the Savior. The power of **the Lord** was **with them**. The promised **signs** accompanied their preaching, **confirming the word** they spoke.

Here the narrative ends — with Christ in heaven, with a few committed disciples on earth burdened for world evangelization and giving themselves entirely to it, and with results of eternal consequences.

We are entrusted with the Great Commission in our generation. Our task is to reach every person with the gospel. One-third of all the people who have ever lived are living today. By the year 2000, one-half of all the people who have ever lived will be living then. As the population explodes, the task increases. But the method is always the same — devoted disciples with unlimited love for Christ who count no sacrifice too great for Him.

The will of God is the evangelization of the world. What are we doing about it?

ENDNOTES

[1](1:2, 3) The critical (NU) text reads "Isaiah the prophet," but the first quote is from Malachi; the traditional reading, "the Prophets," supported by a majority of the mss., is more accurate.

[2](1:14, 15) The NU text omits "of the kingdom."

[3](1:31) J. R. Miller, *Come Ye Apart*, Reading for March 28.

[4](3:13–18) James E. Stewart, *The Life and Teaching of Jesus Christ*, pp. 55, 56.

[5](3:20, 21) Miller, *Come*, Reading for June 6.

[6](3:31–35) Both NU (oldest) and M (majority) of mss. add "and Your sisters." This is no doubt the correct reading.

[7](4:30–32) Quoted by J. Oswald Sanders in *Spiritual Maturity*, p. 110.

[8](5:1–5) The NU text reads Gerasenes.

[9](6:4–6) J. G. Miller, further documentation unavailable.

[10](6:31, 32) William Kelly, *An Exposition of the Gospel of Mark*, p.85.

[11](7:2–4) E. Stanley Jones, *Growing Spiritually*, p. 109.

¹²(7:11–13) Kelly, *Mark*, p. 105.

¹³(8:1–9) Charles R. Erdman, *The Gospel of Mark*, p. 116.

¹⁴(8:22–26) It is possible that the man *did* receive perfect sight in the same way that a baby born with perfect eyes still *has to learn to focus them.*

¹⁵(8:32, 33) Kelly, *Mark*, p. 136.

¹⁶(9:44–48) Three times (vv. 44, 46 and 48) our Lord quotes Isaiah 66:24 to warn of the dangers of hell. This emphatic parallelism of form (found in TR and majority text) is softened, we believe, by the critical (NU) text, which omits the text twice.

¹⁷(9:49) NU text omits this clause.

¹⁸(10:23–25) NU omits "for those who trust in riches," but this is the main emphasis of the passage.

¹⁹(10:31) Harry A. Ironside, *Expository Notes on the Gospel of Mark*, p. 157.

²⁰(10:32) Erdman, *Mark*, p. 147.

²¹(13:29) The subject here in Greek is merely the ending of the verb "is" (*estin*), which in context could be "He" (Christ) or "it" (summer — the events predicted). The resultant meanings are similar.

²²(13:32) James H. Brookes, *"I Am Coming,"* p. 40.

²³(14:63, 64) Joseph of Arimathea and Nicodemus are believed to have been absent from this illegal meeting.

²⁴(15:25–28) The critical (NU) text omits this quotation in Mark.

²⁵(15:32) The majority of mss. add "Him," personalizing the leaders' (probably false) promise.

²⁶(15:42) In modern Greek this word "Preparation" means "Friday."

²⁷(16:8) See further, George Salmon's *Historical Introduction to the Study of the Books of the New Testament*, pp. 144-151.

BIBLIOGRAPHY

Alexander, Joseph Addison. *The Gospel According to Mark*. Edinburgh: The Banner of Truth Trust, 1960.

Coates, C. A. *An Outline of Mark's Gospel and other Ministry*. Kingston-on-Thames: Stow Hill Bible and Tract Depot, 1964.

Cole, Alan. *The Gospel According to St. Mark*. Grand Rapids: Wm. B. Eerdmans Publishing Company, 1961.

Erdman, Charles R. *The Gospel of Mark*. Philadelphia: The Westminster Press, 1917.

Ironside, Harry A. *Expository Notes on the Gospel of Mark*. Neptune, N.J.: Loizeaux Brothers Publishers, 1948.

Kelly, William. *An Exposition of the Gospel of Mark*. London: C. A. Hammond, 1934.

Lenski, R. C. H. *The Interpretation of St. Mark's Gospel*. Minneapolis: Augsburg Publishing House, 1946.

Swete, Henry Barclay. *The Gospel According to St Mark*. London: MacMillan and Company, Limited, 1902.

THE GOSPEL ACCORDING TO LUKE†

Introduction

"Le plus beau livre qu'il y ait" — Ernest Renan.

I. Unique Place in the Canon

"The most beautiful book that exists" is high praise indeed, especially from a skeptic. Yet such was French critic Renan's evaluation of Luke's Gospel. And what sensitive *believer* reading the evangelist's inspired masterpiece would want to contest his words? Luke is probably the only Gentile writer chosen by God to pen His Scriptures, and this may partly explain his special appeal to us Western inheritors of the Greco-Roman culture.

Spiritually we would be much the poorer in our appreciation of the Lord Jesus and His ministry without the unique emphasis of Dr. Luke. Our Lord's love for and offer of salvation to all people, not just to the Jews, His special interest in individuals, yes, and even the poor and the outcasts, are highlighted. Luke also has strong emphasis on praise (giving us examples of the earliest Christian "hymns" in Luke 1 and 2), prayer, and the Holy Spirit.

II. Authorship††

Luke, who was by race an Antiochan and a physician by profession, was long a companion of Paul, and had careful conversation with the other apostles, and in two books left us examples of the medicine for souls which he had gained from them.

This *external evidence* by Eusebius in his *Historia Ecclesiastica*, as to the authorship of the Third Gospel (iii, 4), agrees with universal early Christian tradition. Irenaeus widely quotes the Third Gospel as by Luke. Other early supporters of

Lucan authorship include Justin Martyr, Hegesippus, Clement of Alexandria, and Tertullian. In Marcion's carefully slanted and condensed edition, Luke is the only Gospel accepted by that noted heretic. The fragmentary Muratorian Canon calls this Third Gospel "Luke."

Luke is the only evangelist to write a sequel to his Gospel, and it is from that book, the Acts, that the Lucan authorship is most clearly shown. The so-called "we" sections of Acts are passages in which the writer was personally involved (16:10; 20:5, 6; 21:15; 27:1; 28:16; cf. 2 Tim. 4:11). By the process of elimination, only Luke fits all these periods. It is quite clear from the dedications to Theophilus and the style of writing that Luke and Acts are by the same author.

Paul calls Luke "the beloved physician" and lists him separately from Jewish Christians (Col. 4:14), which would make him the only Gentile writer in the NT. In size, Luke-Acts is larger than all of Paul's epistles combined.

The *internal evidence* strengthens the external documentation and church tradition. The vocabulary (often more precise in medical terms than the other NT writers), along with the educated Greek style, support authorship by a cultured Gentile Christian doctor, but one thoroughly conversant with Jewish themes. Luke's fondness for dates and exact research (1:1–4; 3:1, e.g.) make him the very first church historian.

III. Date

The most likely date for Luke is very early in the 60's of the first century. While some put Luke between 75-85 (or

†See pp. iii–viii.
††See p. i.

even the second century), this is usually due at least partly to a denial that Christ could accurately predict the destruction of Jerusalem. The city was destroyed in A.D. 70, so the Lord's prophecy had to be recorded before that date.

Since nearly all agree that Luke must precede Acts in time, and Acts ends about A.D. 63 with Paul in Rome, a date before that is called for. The great fire of Rome and the resultant persecution of Christians as Nero's scapegoats (A.D. 64) and the martyrdoms of Peter and Paul could scarcely have been ignored by the first church historian if they had occurred already. Hence a date of about A.D. 61–62 is most likely.

IV. Background and Theme

The Greeks were looking for a perfectly divine human being — one with the best characteristics of both men and women but none of their shortcomings. Such is Luke's presentation of Christ as Son of Man — strong, yet compassionate. His humanity is prominent.

His prayer life, for example, is referred to more than in any of the other Gospels. His sympathy and compassion are mentioned frequently. Perhaps this is why women and children occupy such a prominent place. The Gospel of Luke is also known as the missionary Gospel. Here the gospel goes out to the Gentiles, and the Lord Jesus is presented as the Savior of the world. Finally, this Gospel is a discipleship manual. We trace the pathway of discipleship in the life of our Lord, and hear it expounded in His training of His followers. It is this feature we shall follow particularly in our exposition. In the life of the Perfect Man, we shall find the elements that make up the ideal life for all men. In His incomparable words we shall also find the way of the cross to which He calls us.

As we turn to studying Luke's Gospel, may we hear the Savior's call, forsake all, and follow Him. Obedience is the organ of spiritual knowledge. The meaning of the Scriptures becomes clearer and dearer to us as we enter into the experiences described.

OUTLINE

Commentary[†]

I. PREFACE: LUKE'S PURPOSE AND METHOD (1:1–4)

In his preface, Luke reveals himself as a historian. He describes the source materials to which he had access and the method he followed. Then he explains his purpose in writing. From the human standpoint he had two types of source materials — written accounts of the life of Christ and oral reports by those who were eye-witnesses of the events in His life.

1:1 The written accounts are described in verse 1: **Inasmuch as many**

have taken in hand to set in order a narrative of those things which have been fulfilled among us. . . . We do not know who these writers were. Matthew and Mark may have been among them but any others were obviously not inspired. (John wrote at a later date.)

1:2 Luke also depended on oral reports from **those who from the beginning were eyewitnesses and ministers of the word delivered . . . to us**. Luke himself does not claim to be an eyewitness but he had interviews with those who were. He describes these associates of our Lord as **eyewitnesses and ministers of the word**. Here he uses **the word** as a name of Christ, just as John does in his Gospel. **The "beginning"** here means the beginning of the Christian era heralded by John the Baptist. The fact that Luke used written and oral accounts does not deny the verbal inspiration of what he wrote. It simply means that the Holy Spirit guided him in the choice and arrangement of his materials.

James S. Stewart comments:

Luke makes it perfectly clear that the inspired writers were not miraculously freed from the necessity of hard historical research. . . . Inspiration was not God magically transcending human minds and faculties; it was God expressing His will through the dedication of human minds and faculties. It does not supersede the sacred writer's own personality and make him God's machine; it reinforces his personality and makes him God's living witness.[1]

1:3 Luke gives a brief statement of his motivation and of the method he used: **it seemed good to me also, having had perfect understanding of all things from the very first, to write to you an orderly account, most excellent Theophilus**. As to his motivation he simply says, **it seemed good to me also**. On the human level, there was the quiet conviction that he should write the Gospel. We know, of course, that divine constraint was curiously mingled with this human decision.

As to his method, he first traced the course **of all things** accurately **from the** beginning, then he wrote them down in order. His task involved a careful, scientific investigation of the course of events

in our Savior's life. Luke checked on the accuracy of his sources, eliminated all that was not historically true and spiritually relevant, then compiled his materials in order as we have them today. When Luke says that he wrote **an orderly account** he does not necessarily mean in chronological order. The events in this Gospel are not always arranged in the order in which they occurred. Rather they are in a moral or spiritual order, that is, they are connected by subject matter and moral instruction rather than by time. Although this Gospel and the book of Acts were addressed to **Theophilus**, we know surprisingly little about him. His title **most excellent** suggests that he was a government official. His name means *a friend of God*. Probably he was a Christian who held a position of honor and responsibility in the foreign service of the Roman Empire.

1:4 Luke's purpose was to give Theophilus a written account that would confirm the trustworthiness of all that he had been taught concerning the life and ministry of the Lord Jesus. The written message would afford fixity by preserving it from the inaccuracies of continued oral transmission.

And so verses 1–4 give us a brief but enlightening background into the human circumstances under which this book of the Bible was written. We know that Luke wrote by inspiration. He does not mention that here, unless he implies it in the words *from the first* (v. 3) which can also be translated *from above*.[2]

II. ADVENT OF THE SON OF MAN AND HIS FORERUNNER (1:5 – 2:52)

A. Annunciation of the Forerunner's Birth (1:5–25)

1:5, 6 Luke begins his narrative by introducing us to the parents of John the Baptist. They lived at a time when the wicked **Herod** the Great was **king of Judea**. He was an Idumean, that is, a descendant of Esau.

Zacharias (means *the Lord remembers*) was a **priest** belonging to the **division of Abijah**, one of the twenty-four shifts into which the Jewish priesthood had been divided by David (1 Chron. 24:10).

Each shift was called on to serve at the temple in Jerusalem twice a year from Sabbath to Sabbath. There were so many priests at this time that the privilege of burning incense in the Holy Place came only once in a lifetime, if at all.

Elizabeth (means *the oath of God*) was also descended from the priestly family **of Aaron**. She and her husband were devout Jews, scrupulously careful in observing the OT Scriptures, both moral and ceremonial. Of course, they were not sinless, but when they did sin, they made sure to offer a sacrifice or otherwise to obey the ritualistic requirement.

1:7 This couple had *no children*, a reproachful condition for any Jew. Doctor Luke notes that the cause of this was Elizabeth's barrenness. The problem was aggravated by the fact that **they were both well advanced in years**.

1:8–10 One day Zacharias was performing his priestly duties in **the temple**. This was a great day in his life because he had been chosen by lot **to burn incense** in the Holy Place. **The people** had gathered **outside** the temple and were **praying**. No one seems to know definitely the time signified by **the hour of incense**.

It is inspiring to notice that the Gospel opens with **people praying** at the temple and it closes with people praising God at the temple. The intervening chapters tell how their prayers were answered in the Person and work of the Lord Jesus.

1:11–14 With priest and people engaged in prayer, it was an appropriate time and setting for a divine revelation. **An angel of the Lord appeared on the right side of the altar** — the place of favor. At first **Zacharias** was terrified; none of his contemporaries had ever seen an angel. But the angel reassured him with wonderful news. **A son** would be born to **Elizabeth**, to be named **John** (*the favor* or *grace of Jehovah*). In addition to bringing **joy and gladness** to his parents, he would be a blessing to **many**.

1:15 This child would **be great in the sight of the Lord** (the only kind of greatness that really matters). First of all, he would be great in his personal separation to God; he would **drink neither wine** (made from grapes) **nor strong drink** (made from grain).

Secondly, he would be great in his spiritual endowment; he would **be filled with the Holy Spirit, even from his mother's womb**. (This cannot mean that John was saved or converted from birth, but only that God's Spirit was in him from the outset to prepare him for his special mission as Christ's forerunner.)

1:16, 17 Thirdly, he would be great in his role as herald of the Messiah. He would **turn many** of the Jewish people **to the Lord**. His ministry would be like that of **Elijah**, the prophet — seeking to bring the people into right relationship with God through repentance. As G. Coleman Luck points out:

His preaching would turn the hearts of careless parents to a real spiritual concern for their children. Also he would bring back the hearts of disobedient, rebellious children to the "wisdom of the just."[3]

In other words, he would strive to gather out of the world a company of believers who would be ready to meet the Lord when He appeared. This is a worthy ministry for each of us.

Notice how the deity of Christ is implied in verses 16 and 17. In verse 16, it says that John would **turn many of the children of Israel to the Lord their God**. Then in verse 17 it says that John would **go before Him**. To whom does the word *Him* refer? Obviously to the *Lord their God* in the preceding verse. And yet we know that John was the forerunner of *Jesus*. The inference then is clear. Jesus is God.

1:18 The aged **Zacharias** was struck by the sheer impossibility of the promise. Both he and his **wife** were too **old** to become the parents of a child. His plaintive question expressed all the pent-up doubt of his heart.

1:19 The angel answered first by introducing himself as **Gabriel** (*strong one of God*). Though commonly described as an archangel, he is mentioned in the Scripture only as one **who stands in the presence of God** and who brings messages from God to man (Dan. 8:16; 9:21).

1:20 Because Zacharias had doubted, he would lose the power of speech **until** the child was born. Whenever a believer entertains doubts concerning God's word, he loses his testimony and his song. Unbelief seals the lips, and they remain sealed until faith returns and bursts forth in praise and witness.

1:21, 22 Outside, **the people** were waiting impatiently; ordinarily the priest who was burning incense would have appeared much sooner. When **Zacharias** finally **came out, he** had to communicate with them by making signs. Then **they** realized **that he had seen a vision in the temple**.

1:23 After his tour of duty at the temple was **completed**, the priest went back home, still unable to speak, as the angel had predicted.

1:24, 25 When **Elizabeth** became pregnant she went into seclusion in her home for **five months**, rejoicing within herself that **the Lord** had seen fit to free her from the **reproach** of being childless.

B. Annunciation of the Son of Man's Birth (1:26–38)

1:26, 27† **In the sixth month** after his appearance to Zacharias (or after Elizabeth became pregnant), **Gabriel** reappeared — this time **to a virgin** named **Mary** who lived in the **city** of **Nazareth**, in the district **of Galilee**. Mary was **betrothed to a man** named **Joseph**, a lineal descendant **of David**, who inherited legal rights to the throne of David, even though he himself was a carpenter. Betrothal was considered a much more binding contract than engagement is today. In fact, it could be broken only by a legal decree similar to divorce.

1:28 **The angel** addressed Mary as one who was **highly favored**, one whom the Lord was visiting with special privilege. Two points should be noted here: (1) The angel did *not* worship Mary or pray to her; he simply greeted her. (2) He did *not* say that she was "full of grace," but **highly favored**.⁴

1:29, 30 Mary was understandably **troubled** by this greeting; she wondered what it meant. **The angel** calmed her fears, then told her that **God** was choosing her to be the mother of the long-awaited Messiah.

1:31-33†† Notice the important truths which are enshrined in the annunciation:

The real humanity of the Messiah — **you will conceive in your womb and bring forth a Son**.

His deity and His mission as Savior — **and shall call His name JESUS**

(meaning *Jehovah is the Savior*).

His essential greatness — **He will be great**, both as to His Person and His work.

His identity as the Son of God — **and will be called the Son of the Highest**.

His title to the throne of David — **the Lord God will give Him the throne of His father David**. This establishes Him as the Messiah.

His everlasting and universal kingdom — **He will reign over the house of Jacob forever, and of His kingdom there will be no end.**

Verses 31 and 32a obviously refer to Christ's First Advent, whereas verses 32b and 33 describe His Second Coming as King of kings and Lord of lords.

1:34, 35 Mary's question, **"How can this be?"** was one of wonder but not of doubt. How could she bear a child when she had never had relations with **a man**? Although the angel did not say so in so many words, the answer was *virgin birth*. It would be a miracle of **the Holy Spirit**. He would **come upon** her, **and the power of** God would **overshadow** her. To Mary's problem of **"How?"** — it seemed impossible to human reckoning — God's answer is "the Holy Spirit":

"Therefore, also, that Holy One who is to be born will be called the Son of God." Here then we have a sublime statement of the incarnation. Mary's Son would be God manifest in the flesh. Language cannot exhaust the mystery that is shrouded here.

1:36, 37 The angel then broke the news to Mary that **Elizabeth** her **relative**, was in her **sixth month** of pregnancy — she who had been **barren**. This miracle should reassure Mary that **with God nothing will be impossible**.

1:38 In beautiful submission, **Mary** yielded herself to the Lord for the accomplishment of His wondrous purposes. Then **the angel departed from her**.

C. Mary Visits Elizabeth (1:39–45)

1:39, 40 We are not told why **Mary went** to visit **Elizabeth** at this time. It may have been to avoid the scandal which would inevitably arise in Nazareth when her condition became known. If

†*See p. xvix*
††*See p. xviii.*

this is so, then the welcome given by Elizabeth and the kindness shown would have been doubly sweet.

1:41 As soon as **Elizabeth heard** Mary's voice, **the babe leaped in her womb** — a mysterious, involuntary response of the unborn forerunner to the arrival of the unborn Messiah. **Elizabeth was filled with the Holy Spirit,** that is, He took control of her, guiding her speech and actions.

Three persons in chapter 1 are said to be filled with the Holy Spirit: John the Baptist (v. 15); Elizabeth (v. 41); and Zacharias (v. 67).

One of the marks of a Spirit-filled life is speaking in psalms and hymns and spiritual songs (Eph. 5:18, 19). We are not surprised therefore to find three songs in this chapter, as well as two in the next. Four of these songs are generally known by Latin titles, which are taken from the first lines: (1) Elizabeth's Salutation [1:42–45]; (2) The *Magnificat* (it magnifies) [1:46–55]; (3) *Benedictus* (blessed) [1:68–79]; (4) *Gloria in Excelsis Deo* (glory to God in the highest) [2:14]; and (5) *Nunc Dimittis* (now You let depart) [2:29–32].

1:42–45 Speaking by special inspiration, Elizabeth saluted Mary as **"the mother of my Lord."** There was not a trace of jealousy in her heart; only joy and delight that the unborn baby would be her **Lord.** Mary was **blessed among women** in that she was given the privilege of bearing the Messiah. **The fruit of** her **womb** is **blessed** in that He is Lord and Savior. The Bible *never* speaks of Mary as "the mother of God." While it is true that she was the mother of Jesus, and that Jesus is God, it is nevertheless a doctrinal absurdity to speak of God as having a mother. Jesus existed from all eternity whereas Mary was a finite creature with a definite date when she began to exist. She was the mother of Jesus only in His Incarnation.

Elizabeth recounted the seemingly intuitive excitement of her unborn child when Mary first spoke. Then she assured Mary that her faith would be abundantly rewarded. Her expectation would be fulfilled. She had not believed in vain. Her Baby would be born as promised.

D. Mary Magnifies the Lord (1:46–56)

1:46–49 The Magnificat resembles Hannah's song (1 Sam. 2:1–10). First, **Mary** praised **the Lord** for what **He** had done for her (vv. 46b–49). Notice that she said (v. 48) **"all generations will call me blessed."** She would not be one who conferred blessings but one who would *be* blessed. She speaks of **God** as her **Savior,** disproving the idea that Mary was sinless.

1:50–53 Secondly, she praised the Lord for **His mercy on those who fear Him** in every **generation. He** puts **down the proud** and **mighty,** and exalts **the lowly** and **hungry.**

1:54, 55 Finally, she magnified the Lord for His faithfulness to **Israel** in keeping the promises He had made **to Abraham and to his seed.**

1:56 After staying with Elizabeth **about three months,** Mary **returned to her** own **house** in Nazareth. She was not yet married. No doubt she became the object of suspicion and slander in the neighborhood. But God would vindicate her; she could afford to wait.

E. Birth of the Forerunner (1:57–66)

1:57–61 At **Elizabeth's** appointed **time,** she gave birth to **a son.** Her **relatives** and friends were delighted. **On the eighth day,** when **the child** was circumcised, they thought it was a foregone conclusion that he would be named **Zacharias,** after **his father.** When **his mother** told them the child's name would be **John,** they were surprised, because none of his **relatives** had **this name.**

1:62, 63 To get the final decision, they **made signs to** Zacharias. (This indicates that he was not only dumb, but deaf as well.) Calling for **a writing tablet,** he settled the matter — the baby's **name** was **John.** The people **all marveled.**

1:64–66 But it was even more of a surprise when they noticed that the power of speech had returned to Zacharias as soon as he wrote "John." The news spread quickly **throughout all the hill country of Judea,** and people wondered about the future work of this unusual baby. They knew that the special favor **of the Lord was with him.**

F. Zacharias' Prophecy Concerning John (1:67–80)

1:67 Freed now from the fetters of unbelief and **filled with the Holy Spirit, Zacharias** was inspired to utter an eloquent hymn of praise, rich in quotations from the OT.

1:68, 69 *Praise to God for what He had done.* Zacharias realized that the birth of his son, John, indicated the imminence of the coming of the Messiah. He spoke of Christ's advent as an accomplished fact before it happened. Faith enabled him to say **God** had already **visited and redeemed His people** by sending the Redeemer. Jehovah had **raised up a horn of salvation** in the royal **house of . . . David**. (A horn was used to hold the oil for anointing kings; therefore it might mean here a *King* of salvation from the kingly line of David. Or it might be a symbol of power and thus mean "a powerful Savior.")

1:70, 71 *Praise to God for fulfilling prophecy.* The coming of the Messiah had been predicted by the **holy prophets . . . since the world began**. It would mean salvation **from** one's **enemies** and safety from foes.

1:72–75 *Praise to God for His faithfulness to His promises.* The Lord had made an unconditional **covenant** of salvation with **Abraham**. This promise was fulfilled by the coming of Abraham's seed, namely, the Lord Jesus Christ. The salvation He brought was both external and internal. Externally, it meant deliverance **from the hand of** their **enemies**. Internally, it meant serving **Him without fear, in holiness and righteousness**.

G. Campbell Morgan brings out two striking thoughts on this passage.[5] First, he points out the arresting connection between the name of John and the theme of the song — both are the grace of God. Then he finds allusions to the names of John, Zacharias and Elizabeth in verses 72 and 73.

John — the mercy promised (v. 72).

Zacharias — to remember (v. 72).

Elizabeth — the oath (v. 73).

God's favor, as announced by John, results from His remembering **the oath** of **His holy covenant**.

1:76, 77 *The mission of John, the Sav-*

ior's herald. John would be **the prophet of the** Most High, preparing the hearts of the people for the coming of **the Lord**, and proclaiming **salvation to His people** through the forgiveness **of their sins**. Here again we see that references to Jehovah in the OT are applied to Jesus in the New. Malachi predicted a messenger to prepare the way before Jehovah (3:1). Zacharias identifies John as the messenger. We know that John came **to prepare** the way before Jesus. The obvious conclusion is that Jesus is Jehovah.

1:78, 79 *Christ's coming is likened to the sunrise.* For centuries, the world had lain **in darkness**. Now **through the tender mercy of our God**, dawn was about to break. It would come in the Person of Christ, shining on the Gentiles **who** were **in darkness and the shadow of death**, and guiding Israel's feet **into the way of peace** (see Mal. 4:2).

1:80 The chapter closes with a simple statement that **the child grew** physically and spiritually, remaining **in the deserts till the day** of his public appearance **to** the nation of **Israel**.

G. Birth of the Son of Man (2:1–7)

2:1–3[†] **Caesar Augustus** made a **decree that all the world should be registered**, that is, that **a census** should be taken throughout his empire. **This census** was **first** taken **while Quirinius was governing Syria**. For many years the accuracy of Luke's Gospel was called into question because of this reference to Quirinius. Later archaeological discoveries, however, tend to confirm the record. From his standpoint, **Caesar Augustus** was demonstrating his supremacy over the Greco-Roman world. But from God's standpoint, this Gentile emperor was merely a puppet to further the divine program (see Prov. 21:1).

2:4–7[††] The decree of Augustus brought **Joseph and Mary to Bethlehem[†††]** at exactly the right time in order that the Messiah might be born there in fulfillment of prophecy (Mic. 5:2). Bethlehem was crowded when they arrived **from Galilee**. The only place they could find to stay was the stable of an **inn**. That was an omen, a preview of how men would receive their Savior. It was while the couple from **Nazareth** was there that

†*See p. xvix.*
††*See p. xvix.*
†††*See pp. x–xi.*

Mary **brought forth her firstborn Son**. Wrapping **Him in swaddling cloths**, she lovingly **laid Him in a manger**.

Thus did God visit our planet in the Person of a helpless Baby, and in the poverty of an ill-smelling stable. The wonder of it! Darby expressed it nicely:

He began in a manger, and ended on the cross, and along the way had not where to lay His head.[6]

H. The Angels and the Shepherds (2:8–20)

2:8 The first intimation of this unique birth was not given to the religious leaders in Jerusalem, but to contemplative **shepherds** on Judean hillsides, humble men who were faithful at their regular work. James S. Stewart observes:

And is there not a world of meaning in the fact that it was very ordinary people, busy about very ordinary tasks, whose eyes first saw the glory of the coming of the Lord? It means, first, that the place of duty, however humble, is the place of vision. And it means, second, that it is the men who have kept to the deep, simple pieties of life and have not lost the child heart to whom the gates of the Kingdom most readily open.[7]

2:9–11 An angel of the Lord came to the shepherds, and a bright, glorious light **shone** all **around them**. As they recoiled in terror, the angel comforted them and broke the news. It was **good tidings of great joy** for **all** the **people**. That very **day, in** nearby Bethlehem, a Baby had been **born**. This Baby was **a Savior, who is Christ the Lord**! Here we have a theology in miniature. First, He is **a Savior**, which is expressed in His name, Jesus. Then He is **Christ**, the Anointed of God, the Messiah of Israel. Finally, He is **the Lord**, God manifest in the flesh.

2:12 How would the shepherds recognize Him? The angels gave them a twofold **sign**. First the Baby would be **wrapped in swaddling cloths**. They had seen babies in swaddling cloths before. But the angels had just announced that this Baby was the Lord. No one had ever seen the Lord as a little **Babe wrapped in swaddling cloths**. The second part of the sign was that He would be **lying in a manger**. It is doubtful that the shepherds had ever seen a baby in such an unlikely place. This indignity was reserved for the Lord of life and glory when He came into our world. It makes our minds dizzy to think of the Creator and Sustainer of the universe entering human history not as a conquering military hero, but as a little **Babe**. Yet this is the truth of the Incarnation.

2:13, 14 Suddenly heaven's pent-up ecstasy broke forth. **A multitude of the heavenly host** appeared, **praising God**. Their song, known generally today by the title, *Gloria in Excelsis Deo*, catches up the full significance of the birth of the Baby. His life and ministry would bring **glory to God in the highest** heaven, and **peace on earth, good will toward men**, or perhaps to men in whom He is well-pleased.[8] The men in whom God is well-pleased are those who repent of their sins and receive Jesus Christ as Lord and Savior.

2:15–19 As soon as **the angels** departed, **the shepherds** hurried **to Bethlehem** and **found Mary and Joseph**, and Jesus **lying in a manger**. They gave a complete report of the angel's visit, causing considerable surprise among those who had gathered in the stable. **But Mary** had a deeper understanding of what was going on; she treasured **all these things, and** knowingly **pondered them in her heart**.

2:20 The shepherds returned to their flocks, overjoyed at all **they had heard and seen**, and overflowing in their worship of **God**.

I. The Circumcision and Dedication of Jesus (2:21–24)

At least three different rituals are described in this passage:

1. First there was **the circumcision of** Jesus. This took place when He was **eight days** old. It was a token of the covenant that God made with Abraham. On this same day, **the Child** was named, according to Jewish custom. The angel had previously instructed Mary and Joseph to call Him **JESUS**.

2. The second ceremony was concerned with **the purification** of Mary. It took place forty days after the birth of Jesus (see Lev. 12:1–4). Ordinarily

parents were supposed to bring a lamb for a burnt offering and a young pigeon or turtledove for a sin offering.

But in the case of the poor, they were permitted to bring **"a pair of turtledoves or two young pigeons"** (Lev. 12:6–8). The fact that Mary brought no lamb, but only **two young pigeons** is a reflection of the poverty into which Jesus was born.

3. The third ritual was the presentation of Jesus at the temple in **Jerusalem**. Originally, God had decreed that the firstborn sons belonged to Him; they were to form the priestly class (Ex. 13:2). Later, He set aside the tribe of Levi to serve as priests (Ex. 28:1, 2). Then the parents were permitted to "buy back" or "redeem" their firstborn son by the payment of five shekels. This they did when they dedicated him **to the Lord**.

J. Simeon Lives to See the Messiah (2:25–35)

2:25, 26 **Simeon** was one of the godly remnant of Jews who was **waiting for** the coming of the Messiah. It was **revealed to him by the Holy Spirit that he would not** die **before** seeing **the Lord's Christ** or Anointed One. "The secret of the Lord is with those who fear Him" (Ps. 25:14). There is a mysterious communication of divine knowledge to those who walk in quiet, contemplative fellowship with God.

2:27, 28 It so happened that he entered **the temple** area on the very day that Jesus' **parents** were presenting Him to God. Simeon was supernaturally instructed that this Child was the promised Messiah. Taking Jesus **in his arms**, he uttered the memorable song now known as The Nunc Dimittis (*Now you are letting . . . depart*).

2:29–32 The burden of the song is as follows: **Lord, now You are letting** me **depart in peace. I have seen Your salvation** in the Person of this Baby, the promised Redeemer, as You promised me. You ordained Him to provide salvation for all classes of people. He will be **a light to bring revelation to the Gentiles** (His First Advent) and to shine in **glory** on **Your people Israel** (His Second Advent). Simeon was prepared to die

after he had met the Lord Jesus. The sting of death was gone.

2:33 Luke carefully guards the doctrine of the Virgin Birth with his precisely worded **Joseph and His mother**, as read by the King James tradition, following the majority of manuscripts.[9]

2:34, 35 After this initial outburst of praise to God for the Messiah, **Simeon blessed** the parents, then spoke prophetically **to Mary**. The prophecy consisted of four parts:

1. **This Child** was **destined for the fall and rising of many in Israel**. Those who were arrogant, unrepentant, and unbelieving would **fall** and be punished. Those who humbled themselves, repented of their sins, and received the Lord Jesus would rise and be blessed.

2. The **Child** was **destined . . . for a sign which will be spoken against**. There was a special significance connected with the Person of Christ. His very presence on earth proved a tremendous rebuke to sin and unholiness, and thus brought out the bitter animosity of the human heart.

3. **Yes, a sword will pierce through your own soul also.** Simeon was here predicting the grief which would flood Mary's heart when she would witness the crucifixion of her Son (John 19:25).

4. **. . . that the thoughts of many hearts may be revealed.** The way in which a person reacts to the Savior is a test of his inward motives and affections.

Thus Simeon's song includes the ideas of touchstone, stumblingstone, stepping-stone, and sword.

K. The Prophetess Anna (2:36–39)

2:36, 37 **Anna** the **prophetess**, was, like Simeon, a member of the faithful remnant of Israel who was waiting for the advent of the Messiah. She was **of the tribe of Asher** (meaning *happy, blessed*), one of the ten tribes carried into captivity by the Assyrians in 721 B.C. Anna must have been over one hundred years old, having been married for **seven years**, then widowed for **eighty-four years**. As **a prophetess**, she undoubtedly received divine revelations and **served** as a mouthpiece for **God**. She was faithful in her attendance at public services at **the temple**, worshiping **with fastings and** supplications **night and day**. Her **great age** did not deter her from serving the Lord.

2:38 Just as Jesus was being presented to the Lord, and as Simeon was speaking to Mary, Anna came up to this little cluster of people. **She gave thanks to the Lord** for the promised Redeemer, then **spoke** about Jesus **to** the faithful ones **in Jerusalem** who were expecting **redemption**.

2:39 After Joseph and Mary **had performed** the rites of purification and dedication, **they returned to Galilee, to their** home town, **Nazareth**. Luke omits any mention of the visit of the wise men or of the flight into Egypt.

L. The Boyhood of Jesus (2:40–52)

2:40 The normal growth of **the Child** Jesus is set forth as follows: *Physically* He **grew and became strong in spirit**.[10] He passed through the usual stages of physical development, learning to walk, talk, play, and work. Because of this He can sympathize with us in every stage of our growth. *Mentally* He was **filled with wisdom**. He not only learned His ABC's, His numbers, and all the common knowledge of that day, but He grew in **wisdom**, that is, in the practical application of this knowledge to the problems of life. *Spiritually* **the** favor **of God was upon Him**. He walked in fellowship with God and in dependence on the Holy Spirit. He studied the Bible, spent time in prayer, and delighted to do His Father's will.

2:41–44 A Jewish boy becomes a son of the law at the age of twelve. **When** our Lord **was twelve years old**, His family made their annual pilgrimage **up to Jerusalem** for **the Passover**. But when they left to return to Galilee, they didn't notice that **Jesus** was not in the entourage. This may seem strange to us unless we realize that the family probably traveled with a fairly large caravan. They no doubt assumed that Jesus was walking with others of His own age.

Before condemning Joseph and Mary, we should remember how easy it is for us to travel **a day's journey, supposing** Jesus to be **in the company**, when actually we have lost contact with Him

through unconfessed sin in our lives. In order to re-establish contact with Him, we must go back to the place where fellowship was broken, then confess and forsake our sin.

2:45–47 Returning **to Jerusalem**, the distraught parents **found** Jesus **in the temple, sitting** among **the teachers, both listening to them and asking them questions**. There is no suggestion of His acting as a precocious child, disputing with His elders. Rather He took the place of a normal child, learning in humility and quietness from His teachers. And yet in the course of the proceedings, He must have been asked some questions, because the people **were astonished at His understanding and answers**.

2:48 Even His parents **were amazed** when they found Jesus participating so intelligently in a discussion with those who were so many years older than He. Yet **His mother** expressed her accumulated anxiety and irritation by reproving Him. Didn't He know that they had been worried about Him?

2:49 The Lord's answer, His first recorded words, show that He was fully aware of His identity as the Son of God, and of His divine mission as well. **"Why did you seek Me? Did you not know that I must be about My Father's business?"** *She* said, "Your father and I." *He* said, **"My Father's business."**

2:50 At the time, **they did not understand** what He meant by His cryptic remark. It was an unusual thing for a twelve-year old Boy to say!

2:51 At any rate, they were reunited, so they could return **to Nazareth**. The moral excellence of Jesus is seen in the words **"He . . . was subject to them."** Though Creator of the universe, yet He took His place as an obedient Child in this humble Jewish family. **But** all the time, **His mother kept all these things in her heart**.

2:52 Again we have the true humanity and normal growth of our Lord depicted:

1. His mental growth — **increased in wisdom**.
2. His physical growth — **and stature**.
3. His spiritual growth — **in favor with God**.
4. His social growth — in favor with **men**.

He was absolutely perfect in every aspect of His growth. Here Luke's narrative skips silently over eighteen years which the Lord Jesus spent in Nazareth as the Son of a carpenter. These years teach us the importance of preparation and training, the need for patience, and the value of common work. They warn against the temptation to jump from spiritual birth to public ministry. Those who do not have a normal spiritual childhood and adolescence court disaster in their later life and testimony.

III. PREPARATION OF THE SON OF MAN TO MINISTER (3:1–4:30)

A. Preparation by His Forerunner (3:1–20)

3:1, 2 As a historian, Luke identifies the **year** that John began to preach by naming the political and religious leaders who were then in power — one emperor (**Caesar**), one **governor**, three with the title of **tetrarch** and two **high priests**. The political rulers mentioned imply the iron grip with which the nation of Israel was held in subjugation. The fact that there were two high priests in Israel indicate that the nation was in disorder religiously as well as politically. Though these were great men in the world's estimation, they were wicked, unscrupulous men in God's eyes. Therefore when He wanted to speak to men, He by-passed the palace and the synagogue and sent His message **to John the son of Zacharias**, out **in the wilderness**.

3:3† John immediately traveled to **all the region around the Jordan** River, probably near Jericho. There he called upon the nation of Israel to repent of its **sins** in order to receive forgiveness, and thus be prepared for the coming of the Messiah. He also called upon the people to be baptized as an outward sign that they had truly repented. John was a true prophet, an embodied conscience, crying out against sin, and calling for spiritual renewal.

3:4 His ministry was thus in fulfillment of the prophecy in **Isaiah** 40:3–5. He was a **voice of one crying in the wilderness**. Spiritually speaking, Israel was a **wilderness** at this time. As a nation,

it was arid and cheerless, bringing forth no fruit for God. In order to be ready for the coming of the Lord, the people had to undergo a moral change. When a king was going to make a royal visit in those days, elaborate preparations were made to smooth the highways and to make his approach as direct as possible. This is what John called upon the people to do, only it was not a matter of repairing literal roads but of preparing their own hearts to receive Him.

3:5 The effects of Christ's coming are described as follows:

Every valley shall be filled — those who are truly repentant and humble would be saved and satisfied.

Every mountain and hill shall be **brought low** — people like the scribes and Pharisees, who were haughty and arrogant, would be humbled.

The crooked places shall be made straight — those who were dishonest, like the tax collectors, would have their characters straightened out.

The rough ways shall be made **smooth** — soldiers and others with rough, crude temperaments would be tamed and refined.

3:6 A final result would be that **all flesh** — both Jews and Gentiles — would **see the salvation of God**. In His First Advent the offer of salvation went out to all men, though not all received Him. When He comes back to reign, this verse will have its complete fulfillment. Then all Israel will be saved, and the Gentiles too will share in the blessings of His glorious kingdom.

3:7 When **the multitudes came out** to John for baptism, he realized that they were not all sincere. Some were mere pretenders, with no hunger or thirst for righteousness. It was these whom John addressed as offspring **of vipers**. The question, **"Who warned you to flee from the wrath to come?"** implies that John had not done so; his message was addressed to those who were willing to confess their sins.

3:8 If they really meant business with God, they should show that they had truly repented by manifesting a transformed life. Genuine repentance produces **fruits**. They should not start thinking that their descent from **Abraham** was sufficient; relationship to godly

†See pp. xviii, xix.

people does not make men godly. **God was not limited to the physical descendants of Abraham** to carry out His purposes; He could take the **stones** by the river Jordan and **raise up children to Abraham**. *Stones* here are probably a picture of Gentiles whom God could transform by a miracle of divine grace into believers with faith like that of Abraham. This is exactly what happened. The physical seed of Abraham, as a nation, rejected the Christ of God. But many Gentiles received Him as Lord and Savior and thus became the spiritual seed of Abraham.

3:9 **The ax laid to the root of the trees** is a figurative expression, meaning that Christ's coming would test the reality of man's repentance. Those individuals who did not manifest the fruits of repentance would be condemned.

> John's words and phrases went from his mouth like swords: "generation of vipers," "wrath to come," "axe," "hewn down," "cast into the fire." The Lord's prophets were never mealy-mouthed: they were great moralists, and often their words came crashing upon the people as the battle-axes of our forefathers upon the helmets of their foes (Daily Notes of the Scripture Union).

3:10 Stung with conviction, **the people asked** John for some practical suggestions as to how to demonstrate the reality of their repentance.

3:11–14 In verses 11–14, he gave them specific ways in which they could prove their sincerity. In general, they should love their neighbors as themselves by sharing their clothing and **food** with the poor.

As for **tax collectors**, they should be strictly honest in all their dealings. Since as a class they were notoriously crooked, this would be a very definite evidence of reality.

Finally, **soldiers** on active duty were told to avoid three sins common to men in the military — extortion, slander, and discontent. It is important to realize that men were not saved by doing these things; rather these were the outward evidences that their hearts were truly right before God.

3:15, 16a John's self-effacement was remarkable. For a time, at least, he could have posed as the Messiah and attracted a great following. But instead he compared himself most unfavorably with Christ. He explained that his baptism was outward and physical, whereas Christ's would be inward and spiritual. He stated that he was **not worthy to** untie the Messiah's **sandal strap**.

3:16b, 17 Christ's baptism would be **with the Holy Spirit and fire**. His would be a two-fold ministry. First of all, **He** would **baptize** believers **with the Holy Spirit** — a promise of what would take place on the Day of Pentecost when believers were baptized into the body of Christ. But secondly, He would baptize **with fire**.

From verse 17, it seems clear that the baptism of **fire** is a baptism of judgment. There the Lord is pictured as a winnower of grain. As He shovels the grain into the air, **the chaff** is blown to the sides of the threshing floor. Then it is swept up and burned.

When John was speaking to a mixed multitude — believers and unbelievers — he mentioned both the baptism of *the Spirit* and the baptism of *fire* (Matt. 3:11 and here). When, however, he was speaking to believers only (Mark 1:5), he omitted the baptism of fire (Mark 1:8). No true believer will ever experience the baptism of fire.

3:18–20 Luke is now ready to turn the spotlight from John to Jesus. Therefore, in these verses, he summarizes the remainder of John's ministry and carries us forward to the time of his imprisonment by **Herod**. The imprisonment of John actually took place about eighteen months later. He had **rebuked** Herod for living in an adulterous relationship with his sister-in-law. **Herod** then crowned all his other evil deeds by shutting **John up in prison**.

B. Preparation by Baptism (3:21, 22)

As John recedes from our attention, the Lord Jesus moves out into the position of prominence. He opens His public ministry, at about the age of thirty, by being **baptized** in the Jordan River.

There are several points of interest in this account of His baptism:

1. All three Persons of the Trinity are found here: **Jesus** (v. 21); the **Holy Spirit** (v. 22a); the Father (v. 22b).

2. Luke alone records the fact that Jesus **prayed** at His baptism (v. 21). This is in keeping with Luke's aim to

present Christ as the Son of Man, ever dependent on God the Father. The prayer life of our Lord is a dominant theme in this Gospel. He prayed here, at the outset of His public ministry. He prayed when He was becoming well known and crowds were following Him (5:16). He spent a whole night in prayer before choosing the twelve disciples (6:12). He prayed prior to the incident at Caesarea Philippi, the highwater mark of His teaching ministry (9:18). He prayed on the Mount of Transfiguration (9:28). He prayed in the presence of His disciples, and this called forth a discourse on prayer (11:1). He prayed for backsliding Peter (22:32). He prayed in the garden of Gethsemane (22:41, 44).

3. The baptism of Jesus is one of three times when God spoke **from heaven** in connection with the ministry of His own dear **Son**. For thirty years the eye of God had examined that flawless Life in Nazareth; here His verdict was, **"I am well pleased."** The other two times when the Father publicly spoke from heaven were: When Peter suggested building three tabernacles on the Mount of Transfiguration (Luke 9:35), and when the Greeks came to Philip, desiring to see Jesus (John 12:20–28).

C. Preparation by Partaking of Humanity (3:23–28)[†]

Before taking up the public **ministry** of our Lord, Luke pauses to give His genealogy. If Jesus is truly human, then He must be descended from **Adam**. This genealogy demonstrates that He was. It is widely believed that this gives the genealogy of Jesus through the line of Mary. Note that verse 23 does not say that Jesus was the son of Joseph, but **"(as was supposed) the son of Joseph."** If this view is correct, then **Heli** (v. 23) was the father-in-law of Joseph and the father of Mary.

Scholars widely believe that this is the Lord's genealogy through Mary for the following reasons:

1. The most obvious is that Joseph's family line is traced in Matthew's Gospel (1:2–16).

2. In the early chapters of Luke's Gos-

pel, Mary is more prominent than Joseph, whereas it is the reverse in Matthew.

3. Women's names were not commonly used among the Jews as genealogical links. This would account for the omission of Mary's name.

4. In Matthew 1:16, it distinctly states that Jacob begot Joseph. Here in Luke, it does not say that Heli begot Joseph; it says Joseph was the son of Heli. *Son* may mean *son-in-law*.

5. In the original language, the definite article (*tou*) in the genitive form (*of the*) appears before every name in the genealogy *except one*. That one name is Joseph. This singular exception strongly suggests that Joseph was included only because of his marriage to Mary.

Although it is not necessary to examine the genealogy in detail, it is helpful to note several important points:

1. This list shows that Mary was descended from **David** through his son **Nathan** (v. 31). In Matthew's Gospel, Jesus inherited the *legal* right to the throne of David through Solomon. As legal Son of Joseph, the Lord fulfilled that part of God's covenant with David which promised him that his throne would continue forever. But Jesus could not have been the real son of Joseph without coming under God's curse on Jechoniah, which decreed that no descendant of that wicked king would prosper (Jer. 22:30).

As the real Son of Mary, Jesus fulfilled that part of the covenant of God with David which promised him that his *seed* would sit upon his throne forever. And by being descended from David through Nathan, He did not come under the curse which was pronounced on Jechoniah.

2. **Adam** is described as **the son of God** (v. 38). This means simply that he was created by God.

3. It seems obvious that the Messianic line ended with the Lord Jesus. *No one else* can ever present valid legal claim to the throne of David.

D. Preparation by Testing (4:1–13)

4:1 There was never a time in our Lord's life when He was not full of the

Holy Spirit, but it is specifically mentioned here in connection with His temptation. To be **filled with the Holy Spirit** means to be completely yielded to Him and to be completely obedient to every word of God. A person who is filled with the Spirit is emptied of known sin and of self and is richly indwelt by the Word of God. As Jesus was returning **from the Jordan**, where He had been baptized, He **was led by the Spirit into the wilderness** — probably the Wilderness of Judea, along the west coast of the Dead Sea.

4:2, 3 There He was **tempted for forty days by the devil** — **days** in which our Lord **ate nothing**. At the end of the forty days came the threefold temptation with which we are more familiar. Actually they took place in three different places — the wilderness, a mountain, and the temple in Jerusalem. The true humanity of Jesus is reflected by the words **He was hungry**. This was the target of the first temptation. Satan suggested that the Lord should use His divine power to satisfy bodily hunger. The subtlety of the temptation was that the act in itself was perfectly legitimate. But it would have been wrong for Jesus to do it in obedience to Satan; He must act in accordance with the will of His Father.

4:4 **Jesus** resisted the temptation by quoting Scripture (Deut. 8:3). More important than the satisfaction of physical appetite is obedience to God's word. He did not argue. Darby said, "A single text silences when used in the power of the Spirit. The whole secret of strength in conflict is using the word of God in the right way."

4:5–7 In the second temptation, **the devil . . . showed** Jesus **all the kingdoms of the world in a moment of time**. It doesn't take long for Satan to show all he has to offer. It was not the world itself but **the kingdoms of** this **world** he offered. There is a sense in which he *does* have **authority** over the **kingdoms of** this world. Because of man's sin, Satan has become "the ruler of this world" (John 12:31; 14:30; 16:11), "the god of this age" (2 Cor. 4:4), and "the prince of the power of the air" (Eph. 2:2). God has purposed that "the kingdoms of this world" will one day "become the king-

doms of our Lord, and of His Christ" (Rev. 11:15). So Satan was offering to Christ what would eventually be His anyway.

But there could be no short cut to the throne. The cross had to come first. In the counsels of God, the Lord Jesus had to suffer before He could enter into His glory. He could not achieve a legitimate end by a wrong means. Under no circumstances would He **worship** the devil, no matter what the prize might be.

4:8 Therefore, the Lord quoted Deuteronomy 6:13 to show that as a Man He should **worship** and **serve** God alone.

4:9–11 In the third temptation, Satan took Jesus **to Jerusalem**, to **the pinnacle of the temple**, and suggested that He **throw** Himself **down**. Had not God promised in Psalm 91:11,12 that He would preserve the Messiah? Perhaps Satan was tempting Jesus to present Himself as Messiah by performing a sensational stunt. Malachi had predicted that the Messiah would suddenly come to His temple (Mal. 3:1). Here then was Jesus' opportunity to obtain fame and notoriety as the promised Deliverer without going to Calvary.

4:12 For the third time, Jesus resisted temptation by quoting from the Bible. Deuteronomy 6:16 forbade putting **God** to the test.

4:13 Repulsed by the sword of the Spirit, **the devil** left Jesus **until an opportune time**. Temptations usually come in spasms rather than in streams.

Several additional points should be mentioned in connection with the temptation:

1. The order in Luke differs from that in Matthew. The second and third temptations are reversed; the reason for this is not clear.

2. In all three cases, the end held out was right enough, but the means of obtaining it was wrong. It is always wrong to obey Satan, to worship him or any other created being. It is wrong to tempt God.

3. The first temptation concerned the body, the second the soul, the third the spirit. They appealed respectively to the lust of the flesh, the lust of the eyes, and the pride of life.

4. The three temptations revolve around three of the strongest drives of human existence — physical appetite, desire for power and possessions, and desire for public recognition. How often disciples are tempted to choose a pathway of comfort and ease, to seek a prominent place in the world, and to gain a high position in the church.

5. In all three temptations, Satan used religious language and thus clothed the temptations with a garb of outward respectability. He even quoted Scripture (vv. 10, 11).

As James Stewart so aptly points out:

The study of the temptation narrative illuminates two important points. On the one hand, it proves that temptation is not necessarily sin. On the other hand, the narrative illuminates the great saying of a later disciple: "In that He Himself hath suffered being tempted, He is able to succour them that are tempted" (Hebrews 2:18).[11]

It is sometimes suggested that the temptation would have been meaningless if Jesus was not able to sin. The fact is that Jesus is God, and God cannot sin. The Lord Jesus never relinquished any of the attributes of deity. His deity was veiled during His life on earth but it was not and could not be laid aside. Some say that as God He could not sin but as Man He could sin. But He is still both God and Man, and it is unthinkable that He could sin today. The purpose of the temptation was not to see if He *would* sin but to prove that He could *not* sin. Only a holy, sinless Man could be our Redeemer.

E. Preparation by Teaching (4:14–30)

4:14, 15 Between verses 13 and 14 there is a gap of about one year. During this time the Lord ministered in Judea. The only record of this ministry is in John 2–5.

When **Jesus returned in the power of the Spirit to Galilee** to begin the second year of His public ministry,[†] His fame spread **through all the surrounding region**. As **He taught in** the Jewish **synagogues**, He was widely acclaimed.

4:16–21[††] In **Nazareth**, His boyhood town, Jesus regularly went to **the synagogue on the Sabbath day**, that is, Satur-

day. There were two other things which we read that He did regularly. He prayed regularly (Luke 22:39), and He made it a habit to teach others (Mark 10:1). On one visit **to the synagogue**, He rose **to read** from the OT Scriptures. The attendant handed Him the scroll on which Isaiah's prophecy was written. The Lord unrolled the scroll to what we now know as Isaiah 61, and read verse 1 and the first half of verse 2. This passage has always been acknowledged as a description of the ministry of the Messiah. When Jesus said, **"Today this Scripture is fulfilled in your hearing,"** He was saying in the clearest possible manner that He was the Messiah of Israel.

Notice the revolutionary implications of the Messiah's mission. He came to deal with the enormous problems that have afflicted mankind throughout history:

Poverty. **To preach the gospel to the poor**.

Sorrow. **To heal the brokenhearted**.

Bondage. **To proclaim liberty to the captives**.

Suffering. **And recovery of sight to the blind**.

Oppression. **To set at liberty those who are oppressed.**

In short, He came to proclaim the acceptable year of the LORD — the dawning of a new era for this world's sighing, sobbing multitudes. He presented Himself as the answer to all the ills that torment us. And it is true, whether you think of these ills in a physical sense or in a spiritual sense. Christ is the answer.

It is significant that he stopped reading with the words " . . . to proclaim the acceptable year of the Lord." He did not add the rest of the words from Isaiah " . . . and the day of vengeance of our God." The purpose of His First Coming was to preach **the acceptable year of the Lord**. This present age of grace is the accepted time and the day of salvation. When He returns to earth the second time, it will be to proclaim the day of vengeance of our God. Note that **the acceptable** time is spoken of as a **year**, the vengeance time as *a day*.

4:22 The people were obviously impressed. They spoke well of Him, having been attracted to Him by His **gracious words**. It was a mystery to them how **Joseph's son**, the Carpenter, had developed so well.

4:23 The Lord knew that this popularity was shallow. There was no real appreciation of His true identity or worth. To them, He was just one of their own home-town boys who had made good in Capernaum. He anticipated that they would **say** to Him, **"Physician, heal yourself!"** Ordinarily this parable would mean, "Do for yourself what you have done for others. Cure your own condition, since you claim to cure others." But here the meaning is slightly different. It is explained in the words that follow: **"Whatever we have heard done in Capernaum, do also here in Your country,"** that is, Nazareth. It was a scornful challenge for Him to perform miracles in Nazareth as He had done elsewhere, and thus save Himself from ridicule.

4:24–27 The Lord replied by stating a deep-rooted principle in human affairs: great men are not appreciated in their **own** neighborhood. He then cited two pointed incidents in the OT where prophets of God were not appreciated by the people of Israel and so were sent to Gentiles. When **there was a great famine** in Israel, **Elijah** was not sent to any Jewish widows — though there were plenty of them — but he **was sent** to a Gentile **widow** in **Sidon**. And although **many lepers were in Israel** when **Elisha** was ministering, he was not sent to any of them. Instead he was sent to the Gentile **Naaman**, captain of the Syrian army. Imagine the impact of Jesus' words on Jewish minds. They placed women, Gentiles, and lepers at the bottom of the social scale. But here the Lord pointedly placed all three *above* unbelieving Jews! What He was saying was that OT history was about to repeat itself. In spite of His miracles, He would be rejected not only by the city of Nazareth but by the nation of Israel. He would then turn to the Gentiles, just as Elijah and Elisha had done.

4:28 The people of Nazareth understood exactly what He meant. They were infuriated by the mere suggestion of favor being shown to Gentiles. Bishop Ryle comments:

Man bitterly hates the doctrine of the sovereignty of God which Christ had just declared. God was under no obligation to work miracles among them.[12]

4:29, 30 The people **thrust Him out of the city . . . to the brow of the hill**, intending to **throw Him down over the cliff**. Doubtless this was instigated by Satan as another attempt to destroy the royal Heir. But Jesus miraculously walked through the crowd and left the city. His foes were powerless to stop Him. As far as we know, He never returned to Nazareth.

IV. THE SON OF MAN PROVES HIS POWER (4:31–5:26)

A. Power Over An Unclean Spirit (4:31–37)

4:31–34 Nazareth's loss was Capernaum's gain. The people in the latter city recognized that His teaching was authoritative. His words were convicting and impelling. Verses 31–41 describe a typical Sabbath day in the life of the Lord. They reveal Him as Master over demons and disease. First He went to **the synagogue** and there met **a man** with **an unclean demon**. The adjective **unclean** is often used to describe evil spirits; it means that they themselves are impure and that they produce impurity in the lives of their victims. The reality of demon possession is seen in this passage. First there was a cry of terror — **"Let us alone!"** Then the spirit showed clear knowledge that Jesus was **the Holy One of God** who would eventually destroy the hosts of Satan.

4:35 **Jesus** issued a twofold command to the demon, **"Be quiet, and come out of him!"** **The demon** did so, after throwing the man to the ground but leaving him unharmed.

4:36, 37 The people were *amazed!* What was different about the words of Jesus that **unclean spirits** obeyed Him? What was that indefinable **authority and power** with which He spoke? No wonder **the reports about Him** spread throughout **the surrounding region**!

All the physical miracles of Jesus are pictures of similar miracles He performs in the spiritual realm. For instance, the following miracles in Luke convey these spiritual lessons:

Casting out unclean spirits (4:31–37) — deliverance from the filth and defilement of sin.

Healing Peter's mother-in-law of fever (4:38, 39) — relief from the restlessness and debility caused by sin.

Healing of the leper (5:12–16) — restoration from the loathesomeness and hopelessness of sin (see also 17:11–19).

The paralyzed man (5:17–26) — freedom from the paralysis of sin and enablement to serve God.

The widow's son raised to life (7:11–17) — sinners are dead in trespasses and sins, and need life (see also 8:49–56).

The stilling of the storm (8:22–25) — Christ can control the storms that rage in the lives of His disciples.

Legion, the demoniac (8:26–39) — sin produces violence and insanity and ostracizes men from civilized society. The Lord brings decency and sanity and fellowship with Himself.

The woman who touched the hem of His garment (8:43–48) — the impoverishment and depression brought on by sin.

Feeding of the 5,000 (9:10–17) — a sinful world starving for the bread of God. Christ satisfies the need through His disciples.

The demon-possessed son (9:37–43a) — the cruelty and violence of sin, and the healing power of Christ.

The woman with the spirit of infirmity (13:10–17) — sin deforms and cripples, but the touch of Jesus brings perfect restoration.

The man with dropsy (14:1–6) — sin produces discomfort, distress, and danger.

Blind beggar (18:35–43) — sin blinds men to eternal realities. The new birth results in opened eyes.

B. Power Over Fever (4:38, 39)

Next Jesus made a sick-call at **Simon's house**, where **Simon's wife's mother was sick with a high fever**. As soon as the Lord **rebuked the fever, it left her**. The cure was not only immediate but complete, since she was able to get up and serve the household. Usually a great fever leaves a person weak and listless. (Advocates of a celibate priesthood find little comfort in this passage. Peter was a married man!)

C. Power Over Diseases and Demons (4:40, 41)

4:40 As the Sabbath drew to a close, the people were freed from enforced inactivity; they **brought** a great number of invalids and demoniacs **to Him**. None came in vain. He **healed** every one of those who were diseased, and cast out the demons. Many of those who profess to be faith healers today confine their miracles to pre-chosen candidates. Jesus healed *every one* of them.

4:41 The expelled **demons** knew that Jesus was **the Christ, the Son of God**. But He would not accept the testimony of demons. They must be silenced. **They knew that He was the** Messiah, but God had other and better instruments to announce the fact.

D. Power Through Itinerant Preaching (4:42–44)

The next **day**, Jesus retired to **a deserted place** near Capernaum. **The crowd sought** till they found **Him**. They urged Him not to leave. **But He** reminded **them** that He had work to do in **the other cities . . . of Galilee**. So from synagogue to synagogue, He went **preaching** the good news about **the kingdom of God**. Jesus Himself was the King. He desired to reign over them. But first they must repent. He would not reign over a people who clung to their sins. This was the obstacle. They wanted to be saved from political problems but not from their sins.

E. Power Through Training Others: Disciples Called (5:1–11)

Several important lessons emerge from this simple account of the call of Peter.

1. The Lord used Peter's **boat** as a pulpit from which to teach the multitude. If we yield all our property and possessions to the Savior, it is wonderful how He uses them, and rewards us too.

2. He told Peter exactly where to find

plenty of fish — after Peter and the others had toiled **all night** without success. The omniscient Lord knows where the fish are running. Service carried on by our own wisdom and strength is futile. The secret of success in Christian work is to be guided by Him.

3. Though an experienced fisherman himself, Peter accepted advice from a Carpenter, and as a result, the nets were filled. " . . . at Your word I will let down the net." This shows the value of humility, of teachability, and of implicit obedience.

4. It was in **deep** waters that **the nets** were filled to the **breaking** point. So we must quit hugging the shore and launch out on full surrender's tide. Faith has its deep waters, and so do suffering, sorrow, and loss. It is these that fill the nets with fruitfulness.

5. **Their net** began to break and the ships **began to sink** (vv. 6, 7). Christ-directed service produces problems — but what delightful problems they are. They are the kind of problems that thrill the heart of a true fisherman.

6. This vision of the glory of the Lord Jesus produced in **Peter** an overpowering sense of his own unworthiness. It was so with Isaiah (6:5); it is so with all who see the King in His beauty.

7. It was while Peter was engaged in his ordinary employment that Christ called him to be a fisher of **men**. While you are waiting for guidance, do whatever your hand finds to do. Do it with all your might. Do it heartily as to the Lord. Just as a rudder guides a ship only when it is in motion, so God guides men when they too are in motion.

8. Christ called Peter from catching fish to catching **men**, or more literally, "taking men alive." What are all the fish in the ocean compared to the incomparable privilege of seeing one soul won for Christ and for eternity!

9. Peter, **James, and John** pulled their boats up on the beach and **forsook all and followed** Jesus on one of the best business days of their lives. And how much hung on their decision! We would probably never have heard of them if they had chosen to stay by their ships.

F. Power Over Leprosy (5:12–16)

5:12 Doctor Luke makes special mention of the fact that this **man** was **full of leprosy**. It was an advanced case and quite hopeless, humanly speaking. The faith of the leper was remarkable. He said, **"You can make me clean."** He could not have said that to any other man in the world. Yet he had absolute confidence in the power of the **Lord**. When he said, **"If You are willing"** he was not expressing doubt as to Christ's willingness. Rather he was coming as a suppliant, with no inherent right to be healed, but casting himself on the mercy and grace of the Lord.

5:13 To touch a leper was dangerous medically, defiling religiously, and degrading socially. But the Savior contracted no defilement. Instead there surged into the body of the leper a cascade of healing and health. It was not a gradual cure: **Immediately the leprosy left him**. Think what it must have meant to that hopeless, helpless leper to be made completely whole in a moment of time!

5:14 Jesus **charged him to tell no one** about the cure. The Savior did not want to attract a crowd of curiosity-seekers, or to stir up a popular movement to make Him King. Instead the Lord commanded the leper to **go . . . to the priest** and present the **offering** prescribed by **Moses** (Lev. 14:4). Every detail of the offering spoke of Christ. It was the function of **the priest** to examine the leper and to determine if he had actually been healed. The priest could not *heal*; all he could do was *pronounce* a man healed. This priest had never seen a cleansed leper before. The sight was unique; it should have made him realize that the Messiah had at last appeared. It should have been **a testimony to** all the priests. But their hearts were blinded by unbelief.

5:15, 16 In spite of the Lord's instructions not to publicize the miracle, the news traveled quickly, **and great multitudes came** to Him for healing. Jesus **often withdrew into the wilderness** for a time of prayer. Our Savior was a Man of prayer. It is fitting that this Gospel, which presents Him as Son of Man, should have more to say about His prayer life than any other.

G. Power Over Paralysis (5:17–26)

5:17 As the news of Jesus' ministry spread, **the Pharisees and teachers of the law** became increasingly hostile. Here we see them assembling in **Galilee** with the obvious purpose of finding some accusation against Him. **The power of the Lord was present to heal** the sick. Actually Jesus always had the power to heal, but the circumstances were not always favorable. In Nazareth, for instance, He could not do many mighty works because of the unbelief of the people (Matt. 13:58).

5:18, 19 Four **men brought** a paralytic **on a bed** to the house where Jesus was teaching. **They could not** get to Him **because of the crowd**, so they climbed the outside stairs to the roof. Then they lowered the man through an opening that they made by removing some tiles in the roof.

5:20, 21 Jesus took notice of the **faith** that would go to such lengths to bring a needy case to His attention. **When He saw their faith**, that is, the **faith** of the four plus the invalid, **He said to the** paralyzed man, **"Man, your sins are forgiven you."** This unprecedented statement aroused **the scribes and the Pharisees**. They knew that no one but **God** could **forgive sins**. Unwilling to admit that Jesus was God, they raised the cry of blasphemy.

5:22, 23 The Lord then proceeded to prove to them that He had actually forgiven the man's sins. First **He** asked them if it was **easier to say, "Your sins are forgiven you,"** or to say, **"Rise up and walk"?** In one sense it is just as easy to *say* one as the other, but it is another thing to *do* either, since both are humanly impossible. The point here seems to be that it is easier to say **"Your sins are forgiven you,"** because there is no way of telling if it has happened. If you say, **"Rise up and walk,"** then it is easy to see if the patient has been healed.

The Pharisees could not *see* that the man's sins had been forgiven, so they would not believe. Therefore, Jesus performed a miracle which they could *see* to prove to them that He had truly forgiven the man's sins. He gave the paralytic the power to walk.

5:24 **"But that you may know that the Son of Man has power on earth to forgive sins"** — The title, **the Son of Man**, emphasizes the Lord's perfect humanity. In one sense, we are all sons of man, but this title *"the* Son of Man" sets Jesus off from every other man who ever lived. It describes Him as a Man according to God, One who is morally perfect, One who would suffer, bleed, and die, and One to whom universal headship has been given.

5:25 In obedience to His word, the paralyzed man got up, carried his small sleeping pad, and went home, **glorifying God**.

5:26 The crowd was literally **amazed, and they** too **glorified God**, acknowledging that they had **seen** incredible **things** that day, namely the pronouncing of forgiveness and the miracle that proved it.

V. THE SON OF MAN EXPLAINS HIS MINISTRY (5:27–6:49)

A. The Call of Levi (5:27, 28)

Levi was a Jewish **tax collector** for the Roman government. Such men were hated by their fellow-Jews, not only because of this collaboration with Rome, but because of their dishonest practices. One day while Levi was at work, Jesus passed by and invited him to become His follower. With amazing promptness, Levi **left all, rose up, and followed Him**. Think of the tremendous consequences that flowed from that simple decision. Levi, or Matthew, became the writer of the First Gospel. It pays to hear His call and follow Him.

B. Why the Son of Man Calls Sinners (5:29–32)

5:29, 30 It has been suggested that **Levi** had three purposes in arranging this **great feast**. He wanted to honor the Lord, to witness publicly to his new allegiance, and he wanted to introduce his friends to Jesus. Most Jews would not have eaten with a group of **tax collectors**. Jesus ate **with tax collectors and sinners**. He did not, of course, fraternize with them in their sins, or do anything that would compromise His testimony, but He used these occasions to teach, to rebuke, and to bless.

Their scribes and the Pharisees[13] criticized Jesus for associating with these despised people, the dregs of society.

5:31 **Jesus answered** that His action was in perfect accord with His purpose in coming into the world. Healthy people do not need a doctor; only **those who are sick** do.

5:32 The Pharisees considered themselves to be **righteous**. They had no deep sense of sin or of need. Therefore, they could not benefit from the ministry of the Great Physician. But these tax collectors and sinners realized that they were **sinners** and that they needed to be saved from their sins. It was for people like them that the Savior came. Actually, the Pharisees were *not* righteous. They needed to be saved as much as the tax collectors. But they were unwilling to confess their sins and acknowledge their guilt. And so they criticized the Doctor for going to people who were seriously ill.

C. The Non-Fasting of Jesus' Disciples Explained (5:33–35)

5:33 The next tactic of the Pharisees was to interrogate Jesus on the custom of fasting. After all, **the disciples of John** the Baptist had followed the ascetic life of their master. And the followers of the **Pharisees** observed various ceremonial fasts. But Jesus' disciples did not. Why not?

5:34, 35 The Lord answered in effect that there was no reason for His disciples to fast while He was still **with them**. Here He associates fasting with sorrow and mourning. When He would be **taken away from them**, that is, violently, in death, they would **fast** as an expression of their grief.

D. Three Parables on the New Dispensation (5:36–39)

5:36 Three parables follow which teach that a new dispensation had begun, and there could be no mixing of the new and the old.

In the *first* **parable**, the **old** garment speaks of the legal system or dispensation, while the **new garment** pictures the era of grace. They are incompatible. An attempt to mix law and grace results in a spoiling of both. A patch taken from a new garment spoils the new one, and it **does not match the old** one, either in appearance or strength. J. N. Darby states it well: "Jesus would do no such

thing as tack on Christianity to Judaism. Flesh and law go together, but grace and law, God's righteousness and man's, will never mix."

5:37, 38 The *second* parable teaches the folly of putting **new wine into old wineskins**. The fermenting action of the **new wine** causes pressure on the skins which they are no longer pliable or elastic enough to bear. The skins **burst** and the wine is **spilled**. The outmoded forms, ordinances, traditions, and rituals of Judaism were too rigid to hold the joy, the exuberance, and the energy of the new dispensation. The **new wine** is seen in this chapter in the unconventional methods of the four men who brought the paralytic to Jesus. It is seen in the freshness and zeal of Levi. **The old wineskins** picture the stodginess and cold formalism of the Pharisees.

5:39 The *third* parable states that **no one, having drunk old wine, prefers new. He says, "The old is better."** This pictures the natural reluctance of men to abandon the old for the new, Judaism for Christianity, law for grace, shadows for substance! As Darby says, "A man accustomed to forms, human arrangements, father's religion, etc., never likes the new principle and power of the kingdom."

E. The Son of Man Is Lord of the Sabbath (6:1–11)

6:1, 2 Two incidents concerning the Sabbath are now brought before us to show that the mounting opposition of the religious leaders was reaching a climax. The first occurred on "the second-first Sabbath" (literal translation). This is explained as follows: the first Sabbath was the first one after the Passover. The second was the next after that. **On the second Sabbath after the first**, the Lord and His disciples walked **through** some **grainfields**. The disciples **plucked** some **grain**, rubbed the kernels **in their hands**, and **ate them. The Pharisees** could not quarrel about the fact of the grain being taken; this was permitted by the law (Deut. 23:25). Their criticism was that it was done **on the Sabbath**. They sometimes called the plucking of grain a harvesting operation, and the **rubbing** of the grain a threshing operation.

6:3–5 The Lord's answer, using an incident from the life of David, was that the law of the Sabbath was never intended to forbid a work of necessity. Rejected and pursued, **David** and his men were **hungry**. They **went into the house of God** and **ate the showbread**, which ordinarily was reserved for **the priests**. God made an exception in David's case. There was sin in Israel. The king was rejected. The law concerning the showbread was never intended to be so slavishly followed as to permit God's king to starve.

Here was a similar situation. Christ and His disciples were hungry. The Pharisees would rather see them starve than pick wheat on the Sabbath. But **The Son of Man is also Lord of the Sabbath**. He gave the law in the first place, and no one was better qualified than He to interpret its true spiritual meaning and to save it from misunderstanding.

6:6–8 A second incident that **happened on another Sabbath** concerned a miraculous cure. **The scribes and Pharisees watched** Jesus **closely** and maliciously to see **whether He would heal** a **man** with a **withered hand . . . on the Sabbath**. From past experience and from their knowledge of Him, they had good reason to believe that He would. The Lord did not disappoint them. He first asked **the man** to **stand** in the middle of the crowd in the synagogue. This dramatic action riveted the attention of all on what was about to happen.

6:9 **Then Jesus** asked His critics if it was **lawful on the Sabbath to do good or to do evil**. If they answered correctly, they would have to say that it was right to do good on the Sabbath, and wrong to do harm. If it was right to do good, then He was doing good by healing the man. If it was wrong to do **evil** on the Sabbath, then they were breaking the Sabbath by plotting to kill the Lord Jesus.

6:10 There was no answer from the adversaries. Jesus then directed the man to **stretch out** his withered right **hand**. (Only Dr. Luke mentions that it was the right hand.) With the command went the necessary power. As the man obeyed, **his hand was restored** to normal.

6:11 The Pharisees and scribes **were filled with rage**. They wanted to condemn Jesus for breaking the Sabbath. All He had done was speak a few words and

the man was healed. No servile work was involved. Yet they plotted together how they might "get" Him.

The Sabbath was intended by God for man's good. When rightly understood, it did not prohibit a work of necessity or a work of mercy.

F. Twelve Disciples Chosen (6:12–19)

6:12 Jesus spent **all night in prayer** before choosing the twelve. What a rebuke this is to our impulsiveness and independence of God! Luke is the only evangelist who mentions this **night** of **prayer**.

6:13–16 The **twelve** whom **He** chose from among the wider circle of **disciples** were:

1. **Simon, whom He also named Peter**, son of Jonah, and one of the most prominent of the apostles.
2. **Andrew his brother**. It was Andrew who introduced Peter to the Lord.
3. **James** the son of Zebedee. He was privileged to go with Peter and John to the Mt. of Transfiguration. He was killed by Herod Agrippa I.
4. **John** the son of Zebedee. Jesus called James and John "Sons of Thunder." It was this John who wrote the Gospel and the Epistles bearing his name, and the book of Revelation.
5. **Philip**, a native of Bethsaida, who introduced Nathanael to Jesus. Not to be confused with Philip, the evangelist, in the book of Acts.
6. **Bartholomew**, generally understood to be another name for Nathanael. He is mentioned only in the listings of the twelve.
7. **Matthew**, the tax collector, also named Levi. He wrote the First Gospel.
8. **Thomas**, also called Twin. He said he would not believe that the Lord had risen until he saw conclusive evidence.
9. **James the son of Alphaeus**. He may have been the one who held a place of responsibility in the church at Jerusalem after James, the son of Zebedee, had been killed by Herod.
10. **Simon called the Zealot**. Little is known of him, as far as the sacred record is concerned.

11. **Judas the son of James**. Possibly the same as Jude, the author of the Epistle, and commonly believed to be Lebbaeus, whose surname was Thaddaeus (Matt. 10:3; Mark 3:18).

12. **Judas Iscariot**, presumed to be from Kerioth in Judah, and thus the only one of the apostles who was not from Galilee. The betrayer of our Lord, he was called by Jesus "the son of perdition."

The disciples were not all men of outstanding intellect or ability. They represented a cross-section of humanity. The thing that made them great was their relationship to Jesus and their commitment to Him. They were probably young men in their twenties when the Savior chose them. Youth is the time when men are most zealous and teachable and best able to endure hardship. He selected only twelve disciples. He was more interested in quality than quantity. Given the right caliber of men, He could send them out and by the process of spiritual reproduction could evangelize the world.

Once the disciples were chosen, it was important that they should be thoroughly trained in the principles of the kingdom of God. The rest of this chapter is devoted to a summary of the type of character and behavior that should be found in disciples of the Lord Jesus.

6:17–19 The following discourse is not identical with the Sermon on the Mount (Matt. 5–7). That was delivered on a mountain; this was delivered **on a level place**. That had blessings but no woes; this has both. There are other differences — in words, in length, in emphasis.[14]

Notice that this message of stern discipleship was given to the **multitude** as well as to the twelve. It seems that whenever a great multitude followed Jesus, He tested their sincerity by speaking quite bluntly to them. As someone said, "Christ first woos, then winnows."

People had come **from all Judea and Jerusalem** in the south, from **Tyre and Sidon** in the northwest, Gentiles as well as Jews. Diseased people and demoniacs pressed close to touch Jesus; they knew that healing **power** flowed **out from Him**.

It is very important to realize how revolutionary the teachings of the Savior are. Remember that He was going to the cross. He would die, be buried, rise again the third day, and return to heaven. The good news of free salvation must go out to the world. The redemption of men depended on their hearing the message. How could the world be evangelized? Astute leaders of this world would organize a vast army, provide liberal finances, generous food supplies, entertainment for the morale of the men, and good public relations.

G. Beatitudes and Woes (6:20–26)

6:20 Jesus chose twelve **disciples** and sent them out poor, hungry, and persecuted. Can the world be evangelized that way? Yes, and in no other way! The Savior began with four blessings and four woes. **"Blessed are you poor."** Not blessed are *the* poor but blessed are *you* poor. Poverty in itself is not a blessing; it is more often a curse. Here Jesus was speaking about a self-imposed poverty for His sake. He was not speaking of people who are poor because of laziness, tragedy, or reasons beyond their control. Rather He was referring to those who purposely choose to be poor in order to share their Savior with others. And when you think of it, it is the only sensible, reasonable approach. Suppose the disciples had gone forth as wealthy men. People would have flocked to the banner of Christ with the hope of becoming rich. As it was, the disciples could not promise them silver and gold. If they came at all, it would be in quest of spiritual blessing. Also if the disciples had been rich, they would have missed the blessing of constant dependence on the Lord, and of proving His faithfulness. The kingdom of God belongs to those who are satisfied with the supply of their current needs so that everything above that can go into the work of the Lord.

6:21 **"Blessed are you who hunger now."** Once again this does not mean the vast hordes of humanity who are suffering from malnutrition. Rather it refers to disciples of Jesus Christ who deliberately adopt a life of self-denial in order to help alleviate human need, both spiritual and physical. It is people who are willing to get along on a plain, inexpensive diet rather than deprive others of the gospel by their indulgence. All such self-denial will be rewarded in a future day.

"Blessed are you who weep now." Not that sorrow is in itself a blessing; the weeping of unsaved people has no lasting benefit connected with it. Here Jesus is speaking about tears that are shed for His sake. Tears for lost, perishing mankind. Tears over the divided, impotent state of the church. All sorrow endured in serving the Lord Jesus Christ. Those who sow in tears will reap in joy.

6:22 **"Blessed are you when men hate you . . . exclude you . . . revile you, and cast out your name as evil."** This blessing is not for those who suffer for their own sins or stupidity. It is for those who are despised, excommunicated, reproached, and slandered because of their *loyalty to Christ.*

The key to the understanding of these four beatitudes is found in the phrase **"for the Son of Man's sake."** Things that in themselves would be a curse become a blessing when willingly endured for Him. But the motive must be love for Christ; otherwise the most heroic sacrifices are worthless.

6:23 Persecution for Christ is cause for great rejoicing. First it will bring a **great reward in heaven**. Second it associates the sufferer with His faithful witnesses of past ages.

The four blessings describe the ideal person in the kingdom of God — the one who lives sacrificially, austerely, soberly, and enduringly.

6:24 **But**, on the other hand, the four woes present those who are least esteemed in Christ's new society. Tragically, these are the very ones who are counted great in the world today! **"Woe to you who are rich."** There are serious and moral problems connected with hoarding wealth in a world where several thousand die daily of starvation and where every other person is deprived of the good news of salvation through faith in Christ. These words of the Lord Jesus should be pondered carefully by Christians who are tempted to lay up treasures on earth, to hoard and scrimp for a rainy day. To do this is to live for the wrong world. Incidentally, this **woe** on the rich proves quite conclusively that when the Lord said "Blessed are you

poor" in v. 20, He did not mean poor in spirit. Otherwise v. 24 would have to mean "woe to you who are rich in spirit" and such a meaning is out of the question. Those who have wealth and who fail to use it for the eternal enrichment of others **have** already **received** the only reward they will ever get — the selfish, present gratification of their desires.

6:25 **"Woe to you who are full."** These are believers who eat in expensive restaurants, who live on the finest gourmet foods, who spare no expense when it comes to their groceries. Their motto is "Nothing is too good for the people of God!" The Lord says that they will **hunger** in a coming day, that is, when rewards are given out for faithful, sacrificial discipleship.

"Woe to you who laugh now." This **woe** is aimed at those whose lives are a continuous cycle of amusement, entertainment, and pleasure. They act as if life was made for fun and frolic and seem oblivious of the desperate condition of men outside of Jesus Christ. Those who **laugh now** will **mourn and weep** when they look back over wasted opportunities, selfish indulgence, and their own spiritual impoverishment.

6:26 **"Woe to you when all[15] men speak well of you."** Why? Because it is a sure sign you are not living the life or faithfully proclaiming the message. It is in the very nature of the gospel to offend the ungodly. Those who receive their plaudits from the world are fellow-travelers with **the false prophets** of the OT who tickled the people's ears, telling them what they wanted to hear. They were more interested in the favor of men than in the praise of God.

H. The Son of Man's Secret Weapon: Love (6:27–38)

6:27–29a Now the Lord Jesus unveils to His disciples a secret weapon from the arsenal of God — the weapon of **love**. This will be one of their most effective weapons in evangelizing the world. However, when He speaks of **love**, He is not referring to the human emotion of that name. This is *supernatural* love. Only those who are born again can know it or display it. It is utterly impossible for anyone who does not have the indwelling Holy Spirit. A murderer may love his own children, but that is not love as Jesus intended. The one is human affection; the other is divine love. The first requires only physical life; the second requires divine life. The first is largely a matter of the emotions; the second is largely a matter of the will. Anyone can love his friends, but it takes supernatural power to love one's enemies. And *that* is the love (Gk. — *agapē*) of the NT. It means to **do good to those who hate you,** to **bless those who curse you,** to **pray for those who** are nasty to **you,** and ever and always to turn the other **cheek.**

F. B. Meyer explains:

In its deepest sense love is the perquisite of Christianity. To feel toward enemies what others feel toward friends; to descend as rain and sunbeams on the unjust as well as the just; to minister to those who are unprepossessing and repellent as others minister to the attractive and winsome; to be always the same, not subject to moods or fancies or whims; to suffer long; to take no account of evil; to rejoice with the truth; to bear, believe, hope, and endure all things, never to fail — this is love, and such love is the achievement of the Holy Spirit. We cannot achieve it ourselves.[16]

Love like this is unbeatable. The world can usually conquer the man who fights back. It is used to jungle warfare and to the principle of retaliation. But it does not know how to deal with the person who repays every wrong with a kindness. It is utterly confused and disorganized by such other-worldly behavior.

6:29b–31 When robbed of its overcoat, love offers its suit-coat as well. It never turns away from any genuine case of need. When unjustly deprived of its property, it does not ask that it be returned. Its golden rule is to treat others with the same kindness and consideration as it would like to receive.

6:32–34 Unsaved men can **love those who love them.** This is natural behavior, and so common that it makes no impact on the world of unsaved men. Banks and loan companies will *lend* money with the hope of collecting interest. This does not require divine life.

6:35 Therefore Jesus repeated that we should **love** our **enemies, do good,**

and lend, hoping for nothing in return. Such behavior is distinctly Christian and marks out those who are the **sons of the Most High.** Of course, this is not the way men *become* sons of the Most High; that can only happen through receiving Jesus Christ as Lord and Savior (John 1:12). But this is the way true believers *manifest* themselves to the world as sons of God. God treated us in the way described in verses 27–35. **He is kind to the unthankful and** the **evil.** When we act like that, we manifest the family likeness. We show that we have been born of God.

6:36 To be **merciful** means to forgive when it is in our power to avenge. The **Father** showed us mercy by not giving us the punishment we deserved. He wants us to show mercy to others.

6:37 There are two things that love doesn't do — it doesn't **judge** and it doesn't **condemn.** Jesus said, **"Judge not and you shall not be judged."** First of all, we must not judge people's motives. We cannot read the heart and so cannot know why a person acts as he does. Then we must not judge another Christian's stewardship or service (1 Cor. 4:1–5); God is the Judge in all such cases. And in general we must not be censorious. A critical, fault-finding spirit violates the law of love.

There are certain areas, however, in which Christians *must* judge. We must often judge whether other people are true Christians; otherwise we could never recognize an unequal yoke (2 Cor. 6:14). Sin must be judged in the home and in the assembly. In short, we must judge between good and evil, but we must not impugn motives or assassinate character.

"Forgive and you will be forgiven." This makes our forgiveness dependent on our willingness to forgive. But other Scriptures seem to teach that when we receive Christ by faith, we are freely and unconditionally forgiven. How can we reconcile this seeming contradiction? The explanation is that we are speaking of two different types of forgiveness — *judicial* and *parental.* *Judicial forgiveness* is that which is granted by God the Judge to everyone who believes on the Lord Jesus Christ. It means that the penalty of sins has been met by Christ and the believing sinner will not have to pay it. It is unconditional.

Parental forgiveness is that which is granted by God the Father to His erring child when he confesses and forsakes his sin. It results in the restoration of fellowship in the family of God, and has nothing to do with the penalty of sin. As Father, God cannot forgive us when we are unwilling to forgive one another. He doesn't act that way, and cannot walk in fellowship with those who do. It is parental forgiveness that Jesus refers to in the words **"and you will be forgiven."**

6:38 Love manifests itself in giving (see John 3:16; Eph. 5:25). The Christian ministry is a ministry of expenditure. Those who **give** generously are rewarded generously. The picture is of a man with a large apron-like fold in the front of his garment. He uses it for carrying seed. The more widely he broadcasts the seed, the greater his harvest. He is rewarded with **good measure, pressed down, shaken together, and running over**. He receives it **into** his **bosom**, that is, into the fold of his garment. It is a fixed principle in life that we reap according to our sowing, that our actions react upon us, that **the same measure** we **use** to others is **measured back** to us. If we sow material things we reap spiritual treasures of inestimable value. It is also true that what we keep we lose, and what we give we have.

I. Parable of the Blind Hypocrite (6:39–45)

6:39 In the previous section the Lord Jesus taught that the disciples were to have a ministry of giving. Now He warns that the extent to which they can be a blessing to others is limited by their own spiritual condition. **The blind** cannot **lead the blind; both** would **fall into the ditch**. We cannot give what we do not have ourselves. If we are blind to certain truths of God's Word, we cannot help someone else in those areas. If there are blind-spots in our spiritual life, we can be sure that there will be blind-spots in the lives of our understudies.

6:40 **"A disciple is not above his teacher, but everyone who is perfectly trained will be like his teacher."** A person cannot teach what he does not know. He cannot lead his students to a level higher than he himself has attained. The more he teaches them, the more they become like him. But his own stage of growth forms the upper limit to which he can bring them. A student is **perfectly trained** as a disciple when he becomes like his master. Deficiencies in the doctrine or life of the teacher will be carried over into the lives of his pupils, and when the instruction has been completed, the disciples cannot be expected to be above the master.

6:41–42 This important truth is still more strikingly brought out in the illustration of **the speck** and **the plank**. One day a man is walking past a threshing floor where the grain is being beaten out. A sudden gust of wind lifts a tiny **speck** of chaff and lands it squarely in his eye. He rubs the eye to get rid of the irritant, but the more he rubs it, the more irritated it becomes. Just then another man comes along, sees the distress of the first, and offers to help. But this man has a **plank** sticking out of **his own eye**! He can scarcely help because he cannot see what he is doing. The obvious lesson is that a teacher cannot speak to his disciples about blemishes in their lives if he has the same blemishes to an exaggerated degree in his own life, yet cannot see them. If we are to be a help to others, our own lives must be exemplary. Otherwise they will say to us, "Physician, heal yourself!"

6:43–45 The fourth illustration the Lord uses is the **tree** and its **fruit**. A tree bears fruit, **good** or **bad**, depending on what it is in itself. We judge a tree by the kind and quality of fruit it bears. So it is in the area of discipleship. A man who is morally pure and spiritually healthy can bring forth blessing for others **out of the good treasure of his heart**. On the other hand, a man who is basically impure only **brings forth evil**.

Thus in verses 39–45, the Lord is telling the disciples that their ministry is to be a ministry of character. What they are is more important than anything they will ever say or do. The final result of their service will be determined by what they are in themselves.

J. The Lord Demands Obedience (6:46–49)

6:46 **"But why do you call Me**

'Lord, Lord,' and do not do the things which I say?" The word *Lord* means *Master*; it means He has complete authority over our lives, that we belong to Him, and that we are obligated to do whatever He says. To call Him **Lord** and then to fail to obey Him is absurdly contradictory. A mere professed acknowledgment of His lordship is not enough. True love and faith involve obedience. We don't really love Him and we don't really believe on Him if we don't do what He says.

Ye call me the "Way" and walk me not,
Ye call me the "Life" and live me not,
Ye call me "Master" and obey me not,
If I condemn thee, blame me not.
Ye call me "Bread" and eat me not,
Ye call me "Truth" and believe me not,
Ye call me "Lord" and serve me not,
If I condemn thee, blame me not.
— *Geoffrey O'Hara*

6:47–49 To further enforce this important truth, the Lord gives the story of two builders. We commonly apply this story to the gospel; we say the wise man is descriptive of the one who believes and is saved; the foolish man is the one who rejects Christ and is lost. This is, of course, a valid *application*. But if we interpret the story in its context, we find that there is a deeper meaning.

The wise man is the one who **comes to** Christ (salvation), who **hears** His **sayings** (instruction), and who **does them** (obedience). He is the one who builds his life on such principles of Christian discipleship as are laid down in this chapter. This is the right way to build a life. When the house is battered by floods and streams, it stands firm because **it** is **founded on the rock**, Christ and His teachings.[17]

The foolish man is one who hears (instruction) but who fails to follow the teaching (disobedience). He builds his life on what he thinks to be best, following the carnal principles of this world. When the storms of life rage, his **house**, which is **without a foundation**, is swept away. His soul may be saved but his life is lost.

The wise man is the man who is poor, who is hungry, who mourns, and who is persecuted — all for the Son of Man's sake. The world would call such a person foolish. Jesus calls him wise.

The foolish man is the one who is rich, who feasts luxuriously, who lives hilariously, and who is popular with everyone. The world calls him a wise man. Jesus calls him foolish.

VI. THE SON OF MAN EXPANDS HIS MINISTRY (7:1–9:50)[†]

A. Healing of the Centurion's Servant (7:1–10)

7:1–3 At the conclusion of His discourse, Jesus left the multitude and **entered Capernaum**. There He was besieged by the **elders of the Jews**, who had come to ask help for a Gentile **centurion's servant**. It seems that this centurion was especially kind to the Jewish people, even going so far as to build a synagogue for them. Like all the other centurions in the NT, he is presented in a good light (Luke 23:47; Acts 10:1–48).

It is rather unusual for a master to be so kindly disposed toward a slave as this centurion was. When the **servant** took **sick**, the centurion asked the **elders of the Jews** to implore Jesus to heal him. This Roman officer is the only one who sought blessing from Jesus for **a servant**, as far as we know.

7:4–7 It was a strange position for the elders of the people to be in. They did not believe in Jesus, yet their friendship for the centurion forced them to go to Jesus in a time of need. They said concerning the centurion **that he was worthy**. But when the centurion met Jesus, he said, **"I am not worthy,"** meaning "I am not important enough."

According to Matthew, the centurion went directly to Jesus. Here in Luke, he sent the elders. Both are correct. First, he sent the elders, then he himself went out to Jesus.

The humility and faith of the centurion are remarkable. He did **not** consider himself **worthy** that Jesus **should enter** his house. Neither did he consider himself **worthy to come to** Jesus in person. But he had faith to believe that Jesus could heal without being bodily present. A **word** from Him would drive out the sickness.

7:8 The centurion went on to explain that he knew something about **authority** and responsibility. He had considerable experience in this realm. He himself was **under** the **authority** of the Roman government and was responsible to carry out its orders. In addition, he had **soldiers under** him who were instantly obedient to his orders. He recognized that Jesus had the same kind of authority over diseases that the Roman government had over him, and that he had over his subordinates.

7:9, 10 No wonder that **Jesus marveled at** the faith of this Gentile centurion. No one **in Israel** had made such a bold confession of Jesus' absolute authority. **Such great faith** could never go unrewarded. When they got back to the centurion's **house**, they found that **the servant** was completely **well**.

This is one of two times in the Gospels when we read that Jesus **marveled**. He marveled at the faith of this Gentile centurion, and He marveled at the unbelief of Israel (Mark 6:6).

B. Raising of the Widow's Son (7:11–17)

7:11–15 **Nain** was a little town southwest of Capernaum. As Jesus approached, He saw a funeral procession leaving **the city**. It was for **the only son of a widow**. The Lord **had compassion on** the bereft mother. Touching the frame on which the body was **carried** — apparently to stop the procession — Jesus ordered the **young man** to **arise**. Immediately life returned to the corpse, and the lad **sat up**. Thus the One who is Lord over death as well as over disease restored the boy **to his mother**.

7:16, 17 **Fear** seized the people. They had witnessed a mighty miracle. The dead was raised to life. They believed the Lord Jesus was **a great prophet** sent by God. But when they said **"God has visited His people,"** they probably did not understand that Jesus *Himself* was God. Rather they felt that the miracle was evidence that God was working in their midst in an impersonal sort of way. Their **report** of the miracle spread throughout **all the surrounding region**.

Dr. Luke's casebook records the restoration by Jesus of three "only children": the widow's son; Jairus' daughter (8:42); and the child possessed by demons (9:38).

C. The Son of Man Reassures His Forerunner (7:18–23)

7:18–20 News of the miracles of Jesus filtered back to **John** the Baptist in prison in the castle of Machaerus, on the eastern shore of the Dead Sea. If Jesus was truly the Messiah, why didn't He exercise His power in freeing John from Herod's hands? So John sent **two of his disciples** to ask Jesus if He were really the Messiah, or if the Christ was still to come. It may seem strange to us that John should ever question Jesus' Messiahship. But we must remember that the best of men suffer brief lapses of faith. Also, physical distress can lead to severe mental depression.

7:21–23 Jesus answered John's question by reminding him that He was performing miracles such as the prophets predicted would be performed by the Messiah (Isa. 35:5, 6; 61:1). Then He added, as a postscript to John, **"Blessed is he who is not offended because of Me."** This may be understood as a rebuke; John had been **offended** by the failure of Jesus to seize the reins of authority and to manifest Himself in the way people expected. But it may also be interpreted as an exhortation to John not to abandon his faith.

C. G. Moore says:

> I know of no hours more trying to faith than those in which Jesus multiplies evidences of His power and *does not use it* . . . There is need of much grace when the messengers come back saying: "Yes, He has all the power, and is all that you have thought; but He said not a word about taking you out of prison. . . ." No explanation; faith nourished; prison doors left closed; and then the message, "Blessed is he whosoever shall not be offended in me." That is all![18]

D. The Son of Man Praises His Forerunner (7:24–29)

7:24[†] Whatever Jesus might say to John in private, He had nothing but praise for him in public. When the people had flocked out to the desert near Jordan, what had they expected to find? A fickle, spineless, wavering opportun-

†*See p. xx.*

ist? No one could ever accuse John of being **a reed shaken by the wind**.

7:25 Had they then expected to find a Hollywood-style playboy, fashionably dressed, and wallowing in luxury and ease? No, that is the type of person who hangs around **king's courts**, seeking to enjoy all the pleasures of the palace and to make endless contacts for his own profit and gratification.

7:26 It was **a prophet** they went **out to see** — an embodied conscience who declared the word of the living God no matter what the cost to him might be. Indeed, he was **more than a prophet**.

7:27 He himself was the subject of prophecy, and he had the unique privilege of introducing the King. Jesus quoted from Malachi 3:1 to show that John had been promised in the OT, but in so doing, He made a very interesting change in the pronouns. In Malachi 3:1, we read, "Behold, I send My messenger, and he will prepare the way before Me." But Jesus quoted it, **"Behold, I send My messenger before Your face, who will prepare Your way before You."** The pronoun *Me* is changed to **You**.

Godet explains this change as follows:

> In the prophet's view, He who was sending, and He before whom the way was to be prepared, were one and the same person, Jehovah. Hence the *before me* in Malachi. But for Jesus, who, in speaking of Himself, never confounds Himself with the Father, a distinction became necessary. It is not Jehovah who speaks of Himself, but Jehovah speaking to Jesus; hence the form *before Thee*. From which evidence, does it not follow from this quotation that, in the prophet's idea, as well as in that of Jesus, Messiah's appearing is the appearing of Jehovah?[19]

7:28 Jesus continued to praise John by asserting that **among those born of women, there** was **not a greater prophet than John**. This superiority did not refer to his personal character but to his position as forerunner of the Messiah. There were other men who were as great as he in zeal, honor, and devotion. But no one else had the privilege of announcing the coming of the King. In this, John was unique. Yet, the Lord added, the **least one in the kingdom of God** is **greater**

than John. To enjoy the blessings of **the kingdom is greater** than to be the forerunner of the King.

7:29 Jesus is probably still speaking in verse 29, and thus the (supplied) word *Him* should be *him*. He is recalling the reception given to John's preaching. The common **people** and the avowed sinners, like **the tax collectors**, repented and were **baptized** in the Jordan. In believing John's message and acting upon it, they **justified God**, that is, they reckoned God to be righteous in demanding that the people of Israel should first repent before Christ could reign over them. This use of the word *justify* clearly shows that it cannot mean *to make righteous*; no one could *make* God righteous. Rather it means to account God as being right in His decrees and requirements.

E. The Son of Man Criticizes His Own Generation (7:30–35)

7:30–34 **The Pharisees** and teachers of the law refused to submit to John's baptism, and thus **rejected** God's program for their welfare. In fact, it was impossible to please **the generation** of which they were the leaders. Jesus likened them to **children** playing **in the marketplace**. They didn't want to play either wedding or funeral. They were perverse, wayward, unpredictable, and refractory. No matter what ministry God used among them, they took exception to it. **John the Baptist** gave them an example of austerity, asceticism, and self-denial. They didn't like it, but criticized him as demon-possessed. **The Son of Man** ate and drank with **tax collectors and sinners**, that is, He identified Himself with those whom He came to bless. But still the Pharisees were unhappy; they called Him **a glutton** and a tippler. Fast or feast, funeral or wedding, John or Jesus — nothing and no one pleased them!

Ryle admonishes:

> We must give up the idea of trying to please everyone. The thing is impossible, and the attempt is mere waste of time. We must be content to walk in Christ's steps, and let the world say what it likes. Do what we will, we shall never satisfy it, or silence its ill-natured remarks. It first found fault with John the Baptist and then

with his blessed Master. And it will go on cavilling and finding fault with that Master's disciples so long as one of them is left upon earth.[20]

7:35 "**But wisdom is justified by all her children.**" **Wisdom** here represents the Savior Himself. The small minority of disciples who honor Him are wisdom's **children**. Even though the mass of the people reject Him, yet His true followers will vindicate His claims by lives of love, holiness, and devotedness.

F. A Sinner Anoints the Savior (7:36–39)

7:36 In the incident which follows, we have an illustration of wisdom being justified by one of her children, namely the sinful woman. As Dr. H. C. Woodring said so pointedly, "When God cannot get religious leaders to appreciate Christ, He will get harlots to do so." Simon, **the** Pharisee, had **asked** Jesus home **to eat with him**, perhaps through curiosity or perhaps through hostility.

7:37, 38 A sinful **woman** appeared in the room at the same time. We do not know who she was; the tradition that she was Mary Magdalene lacks scriptural support. This woman **brought** a white translucent **flask** of perfume. As Jesus reclined on a couch while eating, with His head near **the table**, she **stood at His feet**. She washed **His feet with her tears, wiped them with** her **hair, and kissed** them repeatedly. Then **she anointed them** with the costly perfume. Such worship and sacrifice revealed her conviction that there was nothing too good for Jesus.

7:39 Simon's attitude was quite different. He felt that prophets, like Pharisees, should be separate from sinners. **If** Jesus **were** truly **a prophet**, he concluded, He would not let **a sinner** bestow such affection on Him.

G. Parable of the Two Debtors (7:40–50)

7:40–43 Jesus read his mind, and courteously asked **Simon** permission to say **something** to him. With consummate skill, the Lord told the story of the **creditor** and the **two debtors. One owed** fifty dollars, the other five. **When** neither

of them could **repay** at all, he cancelled both debts. At this point Jesus asked Simon **which** borrower would **love** the lender **more**. The Pharisee correctly answered, "**I suppose the one whom he forgave more.**" In admitting this, he condemned himself, as Jesus proceeded to show him.

7:44–47 From the time the Lord had **entered** the **house**, the woman had lavished affection upon Him. The Pharisee, by contrast, had given Him a very cool reception, not even attending to the usual courtesies, such as washing the guest's feet, kissing His cheek and giving Him oil for His head. Why was this? The reason was that the woman had the consciousness of having been forgiven much, whereas Simon did not feel he had been a great sinner at all. "**But to whom little is forgiven, the same loves little.**"

Jesus did not suggest that the Pharisee was not a great sinner. Rather He emphasized that Simon had never truly acknowledged his vast guilt and been forgiven. If he had, he would have loved the Lord as deeply as the harlot. We are all great sinners. We can all know great forgiveness. We can all love the Lord greatly.

7:48 Jesus then publicly announced to the woman that her **sins** had been **forgiven**. She had not been forgiven *because of* her love to Christ, but her love was *a result of* her forgiveness. She loved much because she had been forgiven much. Jesus took this occasion to announce publicly the forgiveness of her sins.

7:49, 50 The other guests inwardly questioned Jesus' right to forgive **sins**. The natural heart hates grace. But Jesus again assured **the woman** that her **faith** had **saved** her and that she should **go in peace**. This is something psychiatrists cannot do. They may try to explain away guilt complexes, but they can never give the joy and peace that Jesus gives.

Our Lord's conduct in eating at this Pharisee's table is misused by some Christians in defense of the practice of keeping up intimacy with unconverted people, going to their amusements, and indulging in their pleasures. Ryle gives this warning:

Those who use such an argument would do well to remember our Lord's behavior on this occasion. He carried His "Father's business" with Him to the Pharisee's table. He testified against the Pharisee's besetting sin. He explained to the Pharisee the nature of free forgiveness of sins, and the secret of true love to Himself. He declared the saving nature of faith. If Christians who argue in favor of intimacy with unconverted people will visit their houses in the spirit of our Lord, and speak and behave as He did, let them by all means continue the practice. But do they speak and behave at the tables of their unconverted acquaintances as Jesus did at Simon's table? This is a question they would do well to answer.[21]

H. Certain Women Minister to Jesus (8:1-3)

It is good to remember that the Gospels contain only a few incidents from the life and ministry of our Lord. The Holy Spirit selected those subjects which He chose to include, but passed over many others. Here we have a simple statement that Jesus ministered with His disciples in **every city and village** of Galilee. As He preached and announced the good news **of the kingdom of God**, He was ministered to, probably in the way of food and lodging, by **women** who had been blessed by Him. For instance there was **Mary called Magdalene**. Some think she was a titled lady from Magdala (Migdol). At any rate, she had been wonderfully delivered from **seven demons**. There was **Joanna**, whose husband was **Herod's steward. Susanna** was another, and there were **many others**. Their kindness to our Lord did not go unnoticed or unrecorded. Little did they think as they shared their possessions with Jesus that Christians of all subsequent ages would read of their generosity and hospitality.

The subject of the Lord's ministry was the good news of **the kingdom of God. The kingdom of God** means the realm, visible or invisible, where God's rule is acknowledged. Matthew uses the term "the kingdom of heaven," but the thought is basically the same; it simply means that "the Most High rules in the kingdom of men" (Dan. 4:17) or that "Heaven rules" (Dan. 4:26).

There are various stages of develop-

ment of the kingdom in the NT:

1. First of all, the kingdom was announced by John the Baptist as being at hand (Matt. 3:1, 2).

2. Then the kingdom was actually present in the Person of the King ("the kingdom of God is in the midst of you," Luke 17:21, JND). This was the good news of the kingdom which Jesus announced. He offered Himself as Israel's King (Luke 23:3).

3. Next we see the kingdom of God rejected by the nation of Israel (Luke 19:14; John 19:15).

4. Today the kingdom is in mystery form (Matt. 13:11). Christ, the King, is temporarily absent but His rule is acknowledged in the hearts of some people on earth. In one sense the kingdom today embraces all who even profess to accept the rule of God, even if they are not truly converted. This sphere of outward profession is seen in the parable of the sower and seed (Luke 8:4-15), the wheat and the tares (Matt. 13:24-30), and the fish in the dragnet (Matt. 13:47-50). But in its deeper, truer sense, the kingdom includes only those who have been converted (Matt. 18:3) or born again (John 3:3). This is the sphere of inward reality. (See diagram in Matthew 3:1, 2.)

5. The kingdom will one day be set up in a literal sense here on earth and the Lord Jesus will reign for one thousand years as King of kings and Lord of lords (Rev. 11:15; 19:16; 20:4).

6. The final phase is what is known as the everlasting kingdom of our Lord and Savior Jesus Christ (2 Pet. 1:11). This is the kingdom in eternity.

I. Parable of the Sower (8:4-15)

8:4-8 The **parable** of the **sower** describes the kingdom in its present aspect. It teaches us that the kingdom of God includes profession as well as reality. And it forms the basis for a very solemn warning as to how we **hear** the word of God. It is no light thing to hear the Scriptures preached and taught. Those who hear are made more responsible than they ever were before. If they shrug off the message, or consider obedience an optional matter, they do so to their own loss. But if they hear and obey, they put themselves in a position to receive more light from God. The **parable** was spoken here to **a great multitude**, then explained to the disciples.

The parable told of **a sower, his seed**, four kinds of soil that received the **seed**, and four results.

KIND OF SOIL	RESULT
1. **Wayside**	**Trampled** by men and **devoured** by birds.
2. **Rock**	**Withered away** for lack of **moisture**.
3. **Thorns**	Growth **choked** by thorns.
4. **Good ground**	**Yielded** one hundred grains for each seed.

The Lord ended the parable with the words, **"He who has ears to hear, let him hear!"** In other words, when you hear the word of God, be careful what kind of reception you give to it. The seed must fall into **good ground** in order to become fruitful.

8:9, 10 When **His disciples** inquired concerning the meaning of **this parable**, the Lord Jesus explained that **the mysteries of the kingdom of God** would not be understood by everyone. Because the disciples were willing to trust and obey, they would be **given** the ability to understand the teachings of Christ. But Jesus purposely presented many truths **in** the form of **parables** so **that** those who had no real love for Him would **not understand**; so that **seeing, they** might **not see, and hearing they** might **not understand**. In one sense, they saw and heard. For instance, they knew that Jesus had talked about a sower and his seed. But they did **not understand** the deeper meaning of the illustration. They did not realize that their hearts were hard, impenitent, and thorny soil, and that they did not benefit from the word which they had heard.

8:11–15 Only to the disciples did the Lord expound **the parable**. They had already accepted the teaching they had received, and so they would be given more. Jesus explained that **the seed is the word of God**, i.e. the truth of God — His own teaching.

The **wayside** hearers heard the word but only in a shallow, superficial way. It remained on the surface of their lives. This made it easy for **the devil** (the birds of the air) to snatch it away.

The **rock**-hearers heard the word too, but they did not let the word break them. They remained unrepentant. No

encouragement (moisture) was given to the seed, so it withered away and died. Perhaps they made a bright profession of faith at first, but there was no reality. There seemed to be life, but there was **no root** beneath the surface. When trouble came, they abandoned their Christian profession.

The thorny ground hearers seemed to get along nicely for a while, but they proved that they were not genuine believers by their failure to go on steadfastly. The **cares, riches, and pleasures of life** took control, and the word was stifled and smothered.

The good ground represented true believers whose hearts were **noble and good**. They not only received the word but allowed it to mold their lives. They were teachable and obedient, developing true Christian character and producing **fruit** for God.

Darby summarized the message of this section as follows:

> If, on hearing, I possess that which I hear, not merely have joy in receiving it, but possess it as my own, then it becomes a part of the substance of my soul, and I shall get more; for when the truth has become a substance in my soul, there is a capacity for receiving more.[22]

J. The Responsibility of Those Who Hear (8:16–18)

8:16 At first glance there does not seem to be much connection between this section and what has gone before. Actually, however, there is a continuous flow of thought. The Savior is still emphasizing the importance of what His disciples do with His teachings. He likens Himself to a man who **has lit a lamp**, not to be put under **a vessel or under a bed**, but **on a lampstand** for all to **see the light**. In teaching the disciples the principles of the kingdom of God, He was lighting a lamp. What should they do with it?

First of all, they should not cover it **with a vessel**. In Matthew 5:15, Mark 4:21, and Luke 11:33 (KJV), the vessel is spoken of as a bushel. This of course is a unit of measure used in the world of commerce. So hiding the lamp under a bushel could speak of allowing one's testimony to be obscured or crowded out in the rush of business life. It would be better to put the lamp on top of the bushel, that is, practice Christianity in the marketplace and use one's business as a pulpit for propagating the gospel.

Secondly, the disciple should not hide the lamp **under a bed**. The bed speaks of rest, comfort, sloth, and indulgence. How these can hinder the light from shining! The disciple should put the lamp on a stand. In other words, he should live and preach the truth so that all can see.

8:17 Verse 17 seems to suggest that if we allow the message to be confined because of business or laziness, our neglect and failure will be exposed. Hiding of the truth will **be revealed**, and keeping it a secret will **come to light**.

8:18 Therefore we should be careful **how** we **hear**. If we are faithful in sharing the truth with others, then God will reveal new and deeper truths to us. If, on the other hand, we do not have this spirit of evangelistic zeal, God will deprive us of the truth we think we possess. What we don't use, we lose. G. H. Lang comments:

The disciples listened with a mind eager to understand and ready to believe and obey: the rest heard with either listlessness, or curiosity, or resolute opposition. To the former more knowledge would be granted; the latter would be deprived of what knowledge they seemed to have.[23]

For we must share if we would keep
That good thing from above:
Ceasing to give, we cease to have;
Such is the law of love.
                                    – R. C. Trench

K. Jesus' True Mother and Brothers (8:19–21)

At this point in His discourse, Jesus was told that **His mother and brothers** were waiting to see Him. **Because of the crowd**, they **could not** get near **Him**. The answer of the Lord was that real relationship with Him does not depend on natural ties, but on obedience to the **word of God**. He recognizes as members of His family all who tremble at the word, who receive it with meekness, and who obey it implicitly. No crowd can prevent His *spiritual* family from having audience with Him.

L. The Son of Man Stills the Storm (8:22–25)

8:22 In the remainder of this chapter Jesus is seen exercising His lordship over the elements, over demons, over disease, and even over death. All these obey His word; only man refuses.

Violent storms do rise quickly on the Sea of Galilee, making navigation perilous. Yet perhaps this particular storm was of satanic origin; it might have been an attempt to destroy the Savior of the world.

8:23 Jesus was **asleep** when the storm broke; the fact that *He* slept attests His true humanity. The *storm* went to sleep when Jesus spoke; this fact attests His absolute deity.

8:24 The disciples **awoke** the Savior, expressing anguished fears for their own safety. With perfect poise, He **rebuked the wind** and waves; and all was **calm**. What He did to the Sea of Galilee, He can do to the troubled, storm-tossed disciple today.

8:25 He asked the disciples, **"Where is your faith?"** They should not have worried. They did not need to awaken Him. "No water can swallow the ship where lies the Master of ocean and earth and skies." To be with Christ in the boat is to be absolutely safe and secure.

The disciples did not fully appreciate the extent of the power of their Master. Their understanding of Him was defective. **They marveled** that the elements obeyed Him. They were no different from us. In the storms of life, we often despair. Then when the Lord comes to our aid, we are astonished at the display of His power. And we wonder that we did not trust Him more fully.

M. The Gadarene Demoniac Healed (8:26–39)

8:26, 27 When Jesus and His disciples reached shore, they were in the district **of the Gadarenes**.[24] There they met **a certain man** possessed with **demons**. Matthew mentions two demoniacs, while Mark and Luke speak of only one. Such seeming discrepancies might indicate that they were actually two different occasions, or that one writer gave a fuller account than the others. This particular case of demon-possession caused the victim to discard his **clothes**, shun society, and live **in the tombs**.

8:28, 29 When he saw Jesus, he begged Him to let him alone. Of course, it was **the unclean spirit** who spoke through the pitiful man.

Demon-possession is real. These demons were not mere influences. They were supernatural beings who indwelt the man, controlling his thoughts, speech, and behavior. These particular demons caused the man to be extremely violent — so much so that when he had one of these violent convulsions, **he broke the** chains that were intended to restrain him and ran off **into the wilderness**. This is not surprising when we realize that cooped up within this one man were enough demons to destroy about two thousand pigs (see Mark 5:13).

8:30, 31 The man's **name** was **Legion** because he was possessed by a legion of **demons**. These demons recognized Jesus as the Son of the Most High God. They knew too that their doom was inevitable, and that He would bring it to pass. But they sought a reprieve, begging **Him that He would not command them to** depart at once **into the abyss**.

8:32, 33 They sought permission, when cast out of the man, to enter **a herd of many swine** nearby **on the mountain**. This permission was granted, with the result that the pigs **ran** headlong **down the steep place into the lake and drowned**. The Lord is criticized today for destruction of someone else's property. However, if the swine keepers were Jews, they were engaged in an unclean and illegal business. And whether they were Jews or Gentiles, they should have valued one man more than two thousand pigs.

8:34–39 The news quickly spread throughout that region. When a great crowd gathered, they saw the former demoniac completely restored to normal sanity and to decency. **The Gadarenes** became so upset that they **asked** Jesus **to depart**. They thought more of their swine than of the Savior; more of their sows than of their souls. Darby observes:

> The world beseeches Jesus to depart, desiring their own ease, which is more disturbed by the presence and power of God than by a legion of devils. He goes away. The man who was healed . . . would fain be with Him; but the Lord sends him back . . . to be a witness of the grace and power of which he had been the subject.[25]

Later when Jesus visited Decapolis, a sympathetic crowd met Him (Mark 7:31–37). Could this have been the result of the faithful witness of the healed demoniac?

N. Curing the Incurable and Raising the Dead (8:40–56)

8:40–42 Jesus went back across the Sea of Galilee to its western shore. There another crowd was **waiting for Him. Jairus, a ruler of the synagogue**, was especially anxious to see Him because he had a **twelve** year old **daughter** who **was dying**. He urgently **begged** Jesus to go with him quickly. But **the multitudes thronged Him**, hindering His progress.

8:43 In the crowd was a timid, yet desperate **woman**, who had been afflicted with **a flow of blood for twelve years**. Luke the physician admits that she had **spent all her** life-savings and her income **on physicians** without getting any help. (Mark adds the unprofessional touch that she actually got worse!)

8:44, 45 She sensed that there was power in Jesus to heal her, so she eased her way through the crowd to where He was. Stooping down, she **touched the border of His garment,** the hem or fringe that formed the lower border of a Jew's robe (Num. 15:38, 39; Deut. 22:12). **Immediately** the **blood stopped** flowing and she was completely cured. She tried to steal away quietly, but her escape was blocked by a question from Jesus, **"Who touched Me?" Peter** and the other disciples thought that this was a silly question; all kinds of people were shoving, pushing, and touching Him!

8:46 But Jesus recognized a touch that was different. As someone has said, "The flesh throngs, but faith touches." He knew that faith had **touched** Him, because He sensed an outflow of **power** — the power to heal the woman. He **perceived** that **power** had gone forth **from** Him. Not, of course, that He was any less powerful than He had been before, but simply that it *cost* Him something to heal. There was expenditure.

8:47, 48 The woman . . . came trembling . . . before Him and gave an apologetic explanation of why **she had touched Him**, and a grateful testimony of what had happened. Her public confession was rewarded with a public commendation of her **faith** by Jesus, and a public pronouncement of His **peace** upon her. No one ever touches Jesus by faith without His knowing it, and without receiving a blessing. No one ever confesses Him openly without being strengthened in assurance of salvation.

8:49 The healing of the woman with the issue of blood probably did not delay Jesus very long, but it was long enough for a messenger to arrive with the news that Jairus' **daughter** was **dead**, and that therefore the Teacher's services would no longer be needed. There was faith that He could heal, but none that He could raise the dead.

8:50 Jesus, however, would not be dismissed so easily. He **answered** with words of comfort, encouragement, and promise. **"Do not be afraid; only believe, and she will be made well."**

8:51–53 As soon as He arrived at the home, He went to the room, taking with Him only **Peter, James, and John,** along with the parents. Everyone was wailing in despair, but Jesus told them to stop because the girl was **not dead, but sleeping.** This caused them to ridicule Him, because they were positive **that she was dead**.

Was she really dead, or was she in a deep sleep, like a coma? Most commentators say she was dead. They point out that Jesus referred to Lazarus as being asleep, meaning that he was dead. Sir Robert Anderson says that the girl was not really dead.[26] His arguments are as follows:

1. Jesus said that the girl would "be made well." The word He used is the same word used in verse 48 of this chapter, where it refers to healing, not resurrection. The word is never used in the NT of raising the dead.
2. Jesus used a different word for sleeping in the case of Lazarus.

3. The people thought she was dead, but Jesus would not take credit for raising her from the dead when actually He knew she was sleeping.

Anderson says it is simply a matter of whom you want to believe. Jesus said that she was sleeping. The others thought they knew she was dead.

8:54–56 In any case, Jesus said to her, **"Little girl, arise." She arose immediately.** After restoring her to her parents, Jesus told them not to publicize the miracle. He was not interested in notoriety, in fickle public enthusiasm, in idle curiosity.

Thus ends the second year of Jesus' public ministry. Chapter 9 opens the third year with the sending forth of the twelve.

O. The Son of Man Sends Forth His Disciples (9:1–11)

9:1–2 This incident closely resembles the sending of the **twelve** in Matthew 10:1–15, but there are notable differences. For instance, in Matthew, the disciples were told to go only to the Jews, and they were told to raise the dead, as well as **to cure diseases**. There is obviously a reason for the condensed version in Luke, but the reason is not obvious. The Lord not only *had* power and authority to perform miracles, but He *conferred* this **power and authority** on others. **Power** means strength or ability. **Authority** means the right to use it. The message of the disciples was confirmed by signs and wonders (Heb. 2:3, 4) in the absence of the complete Bible in written form. God can heal miraculously, but whether healing should still accompany the preaching of the gospel is certainly questionable.

9:3–5 Now the disciples would have an opportunity to practice the principles which the Lord had taught them. They were to trust Him for the supply of their material needs — no **bag**, food, or **money**. They were to live very simply — no extra staff or extra tunic. They were to **stay** in the first **house** where they were made welcome — no moving around in hopes of obtaining more comfortable lodging. They were not to prolong their stay or exert pressure on those who rejected the message, but were instructed to **shake off the very dust from** their **feet as a testimony against them**.

9:6 It was presumably in **the towns** of Galilee that the disciples preached **the gospel** and healed the sick. It should be mentioned that their message had to do with the kingdom — the announcement of the King's presence in their midst and His willingness to reign over a repentant people.

9:7 **Herod** Antipas was **tetrarch** in Galilee and Perea at this time. He reigned over one-fourth of the territory included in his father, Herod the Great's, kingdom. Word reached him that Someone was performing mighty miracles in his territory. Immediately his conscience began raising questions. The memory of **John** the Baptist still troubled him. Herod had silenced that fearless voice by beheading John, but he was still haunted by the power of that life. Who was this who made Herod think continually of John? **It was** rumored **by some that John had risen from the dead**.

9:8, 9 Others guessed that it was **Elijah** or **one of the** other **prophets** of the OT. **Herod** tried to quell his anxiety by reminding others that he had **beheaded** the Baptizer. But the fear remained. **Who** was **this** anyway? He **sought to see Him** but he never did until just before the Savior's crucifixion.

The power of a Spirit-filled life! The Lord Jesus, the obscure Carpenter of Nazareth, caused Herod to tremble without ever having met Him. Never underestimate the influence of a person full of the Holy Spirit!

9:10 When **the apostles . . . had returned**, they reported the results of their mission directly to the Lord Jesus. Perhaps this would be a good policy for all Christian workers. Too often the publicizing of work leads to jealousy and division. And G. Campbell Morgan comments that "our passion for statistics is self-centered, and of the flesh, and not of the Spirit." Our Lord **took** the disciples **to a deserted place** adjoining **Bethsaida** (*house of fishing*). It seems that there were two Bethsaidas at this time, one on the west side of the Sea of Galilee and this one on the east. The exact location is unknown.

9:11 Any hopes of a quiet time to-

gether were soon shattered. A crowd of people quickly gathered. The Lord Jesus was always accessible. He did not consider this an annoying interruption. He was never too busy to bless. In fact it specifically states that **He received** (or welcomed) **them**, teaching **them about the kingdom of God** and healing **those who** needed it.

P. Feeding of the Five Thousand (9:12-17)

9:12 As evening drew on, **the twelve** became restless. So many people needing food! An impossible situation. So they asked the Lord to **send the multitude away**. How like our own hearts! In matters concerning ourselves, we say, like Peter, "Command me to come to You. . . ." But how easy it is to say concerning others, **"Send** them **away."**

9:13 Jesus would not send them away to the surrounding villages to get food. Why should the disciples go off on tours to minister to people, and neglect those who were at their own doorstep? Let the disciples feed the crowd. They protested that they had only **five loaves and two fish**, forgetting that they also had the unlimited resources of the Lord Jesus to draw on.

9:14—17 He simply asked the disciples to seat the crowd of **five thousand men** plus women and children. Then after giving thanks, He **broke** the bread and kept on giving it **to the disciples**. They in turn distributed it to the people. There was plenty of food for everyone. In fact, when the meal was over there was more food left than there had been at the outset. The left-overs filled **twelve baskets**, one for each of the disciples. Those who try to explain away the miracle merely fill pages with confusion.

This incident is filled with significance for disciples who are charged with the evangelization of the world. The **five thousand** represent lost humanity, starving for the bread of God. The disciples picture helpless Christians, with seemingly limited resources, but unwilling to share what they have. The Lord's command, "You give them something to eat" is simply a restatement of the great commission. The lesson is that if we give Jesus what we have, He can multiply it to feed the spiritually hungry multitude. That diamond ring, that insurance policy, that bank account, that sports equipment! These can be converted into gospel literature, for instance, which in turn can result in the salvation of souls, who in turn will be worshipers of the Lamb of God throughout eternity.

The world could be evangelized in this generation if Christians would surrender to Christ all that they are and have. That is the enduring lesson of the feeding of the five thousand.

Q. Peter's Great Confession (9:18–22)

9:18 Immediately following the miraculous feeding of the multitude we have Peter's great confession of Christ at Caesarea Philippi. Did the miracle of the loaves and fishes open the eyes of the disciples to see the glory of the Lord Jesus as God's Anointed One? This incident at Caesarea Philippi is commonly acknowledged to be the watershed of the Savior's teaching ministry with the twelve. Up to this point He has been patiently leading them to an appreciation of who He is and what He could do in and through them. Now He has reached that goal, and so He henceforth moves on determinedly to the cross. Jesus prayed **alone**. It is not recorded that the Lord Jesus ever prayed with the disciples. He prayed for them, He prayed in their presence, and He taught them to pray, but His own prayer life was separate from theirs. Following one of His seasons of prayer, He questioned the disciples as to who **the crowds** said **that** He was.

9:19, 20 They reported a difference of opinion: Some said **John the Baptist**; others said **Elijah**; still **others** said **one of the** OT **prophets** in resurrection. But when He asked the disciples, **Peter** confidently confessed Him as **the Christ** (or Messiah) **of God**.

James Stewart's comments concerning this incident at Caesarea Philippi are so excellent that we quote them at length:

He began with the impersonal question — "Whom do men say that I am?" That, at any rate, was not difficult to answer. For on every side men were saying things about Jesus. A dozen verdicts were abroad. All kinds of rumors and opinions were in the air. Jesus was on every tongue. And men were not only saying things about Jesus; they were saying *great* things about Him. Some thought He was John the Baptist back from the dead. Others said He reminded them of Elijah. Others spoke of Jeremiah or another of the prophets. In other words, while current opinions were by no means unanimous as to Jesus' identity, they were unanimous that he was someone great. His place was among the heroes of his race.

It is worth remarking that history here is repeating itself. Once again Jesus is on every tongue. He is being discussed today far beyond the circle of the Christian Church. And great is the diversity of verdicts about Him. Papini, looking at Jesus, sees the Poet. Bruce Barton sees the Man of Action. Middleton Murry sees the Mystic. Men with no brief for orthodoxy are ready to extol Jesus as the paragon of saints and captain of all moral leaders forever. "Even now," said John Stuart Mill, "it would not be easy even for an unbeliever to find a better translation of the rule of virtue from the abstract into the concrete than to endeavor so to live that Christ would approve our life." Like the men of his own day who called him John, Elijah, Jeremiah, so the men of today are agreed that among the heroes and saints of all time Jesus stands supreme.

But Jesus was not content with that recognition. People were saying that he was John, Elijah, Jeremiah. But that meant that he was one in a series. It meant that there were precedents and parallels, and that even if he stood first in rank, he was still only *primus inter pares*, first among his equals. But quite certainly that is not what the Christ of the New Testament claimed. Men may agree with Christ's claim, or they may dissent from it; but as to the fact of the claim itself there is not the shadow of a doubt. Christ claimed to be something and someone unprecedented, unparalleled, unrivaled, unique (for example Matt. 10:37; 11:27; 24:35; John 10:30; 14:6).[27]

9:21, 22 Following Peter's historic confession, the Lord **commanded them** not **to tell** others; nothing must interrupt His pathway to the cross. Then the Savior unveiled His own immediate future to them. He **must suffer**, must **be rejected by the** religious leaders of Israel, must **be killed** and must **be raised the third day**. This was an astounding announcement. Let us not forget that these words were spoken by the only sinless, righteous Man who ever lived on this earth. They were spoken by the true Messiah of Israel. They were the words of God manifest in the flesh. They tell us that the life of fulfillment, the perfect life, the life of obedience to the will of God involves suffering, rejection, death in one form or another, and a resurrection to life that is deathless. It is a life poured out for others.

This of course was the very *opposite* of the popular conception of Messiah's role. Men looked for a saber-rattling, enemy-destroying leader. It must have been a shock to the disciples. But if, as they confessed, Jesus was indeed the Christ of God, then they had no reason for disillusionment or discouragement. If He is the Anointed of God, then His cause can never fail. No matter what might happen to Him or to them, they were on the winning side. Victory and vindication were inevitable.

R. Invitation to Take Up the Cross (9:23–27)

9:23 Having outlined His own future, the Lord invited the disciples to **follow** Him. This would mean denying themselves and taking up their **cross**. To **deny** self means willingly to renounce any so-called right to plan or choose, and to recognize His lordship in every area of life. To **take up** the **cross** means to deliberately choose the kind of life He lived. This involves:
  – The opposition of loved ones.
  – The reproach of the world.
  – Forsaking family and house and lands and the comforts of this life.
  – Complete dependence on God.
  – Obedience to the leading of the Holy Spirit.
  – Proclamation of an unpopular message.
  – A pathway of loneliness.
  – Organized attacks from established religious leaders.
  – Suffering for righteousness' sake.
  – Slander and shame.
  – Pouring out one's life for others.
  – Death to self and to the world.

But it *also* involves laying hold of life that is life indeed! It means finding at last the reason for our existence. And it means eternal reward. We instinctively recoil from a life of cross-bearing. Our minds are reluctant to believe that this could be God's will for us. Yet the words of Christ **"If anyone desires to come after Me"** mean that nobody is excused and nobody is excepted.

9:24 The natural tendency is to **save** our lives by selfish, complacent, routine, petty existences. We may indulge our pleasures and appetites by basking in comfort, luxury, and ease, by living for the present, by trading our finest talents to the world in exchange for a few years of mock security. But in the very act, we **lose** our lives, that is, we miss the true purpose of **life** and the profound spiritual pleasure that should go with it! On the other hand, we may **lose** our lives for the Savior's sake. Men think us mad if we fling our own selfish ambitions to the wind, if we seek first the kingdom of God and His righteousness, if we yield ourselves unreservedly to Him. But this life of abandonment is genuine living. It has a joy, a holy carefreeness, and a deep inward satisfaction that defies description.

9:25 As the Savior talked with the twelve, He realized that the desire for material riches might be a powerful deterrent against full surrender. And so He said, in effect, "Suppose you could stockpile all the gold and silver in **the whole world**, could own all the real estate and property, all the stocks and bonds — everything of material value — and suppose that in your frantic effort to acquire all this you missed the true purpose of life, what good would it do you? You would have it for only a short while; then you would leave it forever. It would be an insane bargain to sell that one, short life for a few toys of dust."

9:26 Another deterrent against total commitment to Christ is the fear of shame. It is completely irrational for a creature to be ashamed of his Creator, for a sinner to be **ashamed** of his Savior. And yet which of us is blameless? The Lord recognized the possibility of shame and solemnly warned against it. If we avoid the shame by leading nominal Christian lives, by conforming to the herd, **the Son of Man will be ashamed** of us **when He comes in His own glory, and in His Father's** glory, and in the glory **of the holy angels**. He emphasizes the triple-splendored glory of His Second Advent as if to say that any shame or reproach we may endure for Him now will seem trifling when He appears in glory compared to the shame of those who now deny Him.

9:27 This mention of His glory forms the link with what follows. He now predicts that **some** of the disciples who were **standing** there would **see the kingdom of God** before they died. His words find their fulfillment in verses 28–36, the incident on the Mount of Transfiguration. The disciples were Peter, James, and John. On the Mount they saw a foreview of what it will be like when the Lord Jesus sets up His kingdom on earth. Peter says this in effect in his Second Epistle:

> For we did not follow cunningly devised fables when we made known to you the power and coming of our Lord Jesus Christ, but were eyewitnesses of His majesty. For He received from God the Father honor and glory when such a voice came to Him from the Excellent Glory: "This is My beloved Son, in whom I am well pleased." And we heard this voice which came from heaven when we were with Him on the holy mountain (1:16–18).

Notice the continuity of the Lord's teaching in this passage. He had just announced His own impending rejection, suffering, and death. He had called His disciples to follow Him in a life of self-denial, suffering, and sacrifice. Now He says in effect, "But just remember! If you suffer with Me, you will reign with Me. Beyond the cross is the glory. The reward is all out of proportion to the cost."

S. The Son of Man Transfigured (9:28–36)

9:28, 29 It was **about eight days** later that Jesus **took Peter, John, and James and went up on the mountain to pray**. The location of this **mountain** is unknown, although high, snow-capped Mt. Hermon is a likely choice. As the Lord was praying, His outward **appearance** began to change. An intriguing truth — that among the things that prayer changes is a man's countenance. **His face** glowed with a bright radiance **and His robe** gleamed with dazzling whiteness. As mentioned above, this prefigured the glory which would be His during His coming kingdom. While He was here on earth, His glory was ordi-narily veiled in His body of flesh. He was here in humiliation, as a Bondslave. But during the Millennium, His glory will be fully revealed. All will see Him in all His splendor and majesty.

Professor W. H. Rogers puts it well:

> In the transfiguration, we have in miniature form all salient features of the future kingdom in manifestation. We see the Lord clothed in glory and not in the rags of humiliation. We behold Moses in a glorified state, the representative of the regenerated who have passed through death into the kingdom. We observe Elijah shrouded in glory, the representative of the redeemed who have entered the kingdom by translation. There are three disciples, Peter, James and John, who are not glorified, the representatives of Israel in the flesh during the millennium. Then there is the multitude at the foot of the mountain, representative of the nations who will be brought into the kingdom after it has been inaugurated.[28]

9:30, 31 **Moses and Elijah talked with** Jesus about **His decease** (lit., *exodus*) **which He was about to accomplish at Jerusalem**. Note that His death is here spoken of as an accomplishment. Also note that death is simply an *exodus* — not cessation of existence but departure from one place to another one.

9:32, 33 The disciples were sleepy while all this was going on. Bishop Ryle says:

> Let it be noted that the very same disciples who here slept during a vision of glory were also found sleeping during the agony in the garden of Gethsemane. Flesh and blood does indeed need to be changed before it can enter heaven. Our poor weak bodies can neither watch with Christ in His time of trial nor keep awake with Him in His glorification. Our physical constitution must be greatly altered before we could enjoy heaven.[29]

When they were fully awake, they saw the bright outshining of Christ's **glory**. In an effort to preserve the sacred character of the occasion, **Peter** proposed erecting **three tabernacles** or tents, **one** in honor of Jesus, **one** of **Moses**, and **one** of **Elijah**. But his idea was based upon zeal without knowledge.

9:34–36 God's **voice came out of the cloud** that enveloped them, acknowledging Jesus as His **beloved Son**, and telling them to **hear** or obey **Him**. As soon as **the voice** was past, Moses and Elijah had disappeared. Jesus **alone** was standing there. It will be like this in the kingdom; He will have the pre-eminence in all things. He will not share His glory.

The disciples left with a sense of awe so profound that they did not discuss the event with others.

T. A Demon-Possessed Boy Healed (9:37–43a)

9:37–39 From the mount of glory, Jesus and the disciples returned **the next day** to the valley of human need. Life has its moments of spiritual exaltation but God balances them with the daily round of toil and expenditure. Out **from the multitude** that **met Him** came a distraught father, pleading for Jesus to help his demon-possessed **son**. It was his **only child** and therefore his heart's delight. What an unspeakable sorrow then it was for that father to see his boy seized with demonic convulsions. These fits came on without warning. The lad would cry out and then foam **at the mouth**. Only after a fearful struggle would the demon depart, leaving him thoroughly bruised.

9:40 The distraught father had previously gone to the **disciples** for help but they were powerless. Why were the disciples unable to help the boy? Perhaps they had become professional in their ministry. Perhaps they thought they could count on a Spirit-filled ministry without constant spiritual exercise. Perhaps they were taking things too much for granted.

9:41 The Lord **Jesus** was grieved by the entire spectacle. Without naming anyone in particular, He said, **"O faithless and perverse generation. . . ."** This may have been addressed to the disciples, the people, the father, or all of them combined. They were all so helpless in the face of human need in spite of the fact that they could draw on His infinite resources of power. **How long** would He have to **be with** them and put up with them? Then He said to the father, **"Bring your son here."**

9:42, 43a As the lad **was still coming** to Jesus, he was seized by **the demon** and thrown to the ground violently. But Jesus was not overawed by this display of the power of an evil spirit; it was the

unbelief of men that hindered Him rather than the power of demonism. He cast out the **unclean spirit, healed the child, and gave him back to his father**. The people **were all amazed**. They recognized that God had worked a miracle. They saw in the miracle a display of **the majesty of God**.

U. The Son of Man Predicts His Death and Resurrection (9:43b–45)

9:43b, 44 The **disciples** might be inclined to think that their Master would continue to perform miracles until at last the whole nation would acclaim Him as King. To disabuse their minds of such a notion, the Lord again reminded them that **the Son of Man** must be **betrayed into the hands of men**, that is, to be killed.

9:45 Why did they **not understand this** prediction? Simply because they lapsed back into thinking of the Messiah as a popular hero. His death would mean defeat for the cause, according to their thinking. Their own hopes were so strong that they were unable to entertain any contrary view. It was not God who concealed the truth from them, but their own determined refusal to believe. **They were** even **afraid to ask** for clarification — almost as if they were afraid to have their fears confirmed!

V. True Greatness in the Kingdom (9:46–48)

9:46 The disciples not only expected the glorious kingdom to be ushered in shortly, but they also aspired to positions of greatness in the kingdom. Already they were arguing among themselves as to who **would be greatest**.

9:47, 48 Knowing the question that was agitating them, **Jesus** brought **a little child** beside Him and explained that anyone who received a **little child in** His **name** received Him. At first glance, this does not seem to have any connection with the question of who was greatest among the disciples. But though not obvious, the connection seems to be this: true greatness is seen in a loving care for the little ones, for those who are helpless, for those whom the world passes by. Thus when Jesus said that the **"least among you all will be great,"** He was referring to the one who humbled himself to associate with believers who are non-descript, insignificant, and despised.

In Matthew 18:4, the Lord said that the greatest in the kingdom of heaven is the one who humbles himself like a little child. Here in Luke, it is a matter of identifying oneself with the lowliest among God's children. In both cases, it involves taking a place of humility, as the Savior Himself did.

W. The Son of Man Forbids Sectarianism (9:49, 50)

9:49 This incident seems to illustrate the behavior which the Lord had just told the disciples to avoid. They had found **someone casting out demons in** Jesus' **name**. They **forbade him** for no better reason than that he was **not** one of their followers. In other words, they had refused to receive a child of the Lord in His name. They were sectarian and narrow. They should have been glad that the demon had been cast out of the man. They should never be jealous of any man or group that might cast out more demons than they did. But then every disciple has to guard against this desire for exclusiveness — for a monopoly of spiritual power and prestige.

9:50 Jesus said to him, **"Do not forbid him, for he who is not against us is on our side."** As far as the Person and work of Christ are concerned, there can be no neutrality. If men are not *for* Christ, they are *against* Him. But when it comes to Christian service, A. L. Williams says:

> Earnest Christians need to remember that when outsiders do anything in Christ's Name, it must, on the whole, forward His cause. . . . The Master's reply contained a broad and far-reaching truth. No earthly society, however holy, would be able exclusively to claim the Divine powers inseparably connected with a true and faithful use of His Name.[30]

VII. INCREASING OPPOSITION TO THE SON OF MAN (9:51–11:54)

A. Samaria Rejects the Son of Man (9:51–56)

9:51 The time of Jesus' Ascension into heaven was now drawing near. He knew this well. He also knew that the cross lay between, so **He** resolutely moved toward **Jerusalem** and all that awaited Him there.

9:52, 53 A Samaritan **village** that lay on His route proved inhospitable to the Son of God. The people knew He was going **to Jerusalem**, and that was enough reason to bar Him, as far as they were concerned. After all, there was intense hatred between the Samaritans and the Jews. Their sectarian, bigoted spirit, their segregationist attitude, their racial pride made them unwilling to **receive** the Lord of Glory.

9:54–56 James and John were so angered by this discourtesy that they offered to call **fire . . . down from heaven** to destroy the offenders. Jesus promptly **rebuked them**. He had **not come to destroy men's lives but to save them**. This was the acceptable year of the Lord, and not the day of vengeance of our God. They should have been characterized by grace and not by vindictiveness.

B. Hindrances to Discipleship (9:57–62)

9:57 In these verses, we meet three would-be disciples who illustrate three of the main hindrances to whole-hearted discipleship. The first man was quite sure he wanted to **follow** Jesus anywhere and everywhere. He did not wait to be called, but impetuously offered himself. He was self-confident, unduly eager, and unmindful of the cost. He did not know the meaning of what he said.

9:58 At first, the answer of Jesus does not seem to be related to the man's offer. Actually, however, there was a very close connection. **Jesus** was saying, in effect, "Do you know what it really means to follow me? It means the forsaking of the comforts and conveniences of life. I do not have a home to call my own. This earth affords no rest to me. **Foxes** and **birds** have more in the way of natural comfort and security than I. Are you willing to follow Me, even if it means forsaking those things which most men consider to be their inalienable rights?" When we read **the Son of Man has nowhere to lay His head** we are apt to pity Him. One commentator remarks: "He does not need your pity. Pity yourself rather if you have a home that holds you back when Christ wants you out upon the high places of the world." We hear no more of the man, and can only assume that he was unwilling to give up the common comforts of life to follow the Son of God.

9:59 The second man heard Christ's call to **follow** Him. He was willing, in a way, but there was something he wanted to do **first**. He wanted to **go and bury** his **father**. Notice what he said. **"Lord, let me first go...."** In other words, **"Lord ... me first."** He called Jesus by the name of **Lord**, but actually he puts his own desires and interests **first**. The words "Lord" and "me first" are totally opposed to each other; we must choose one or the other. Whether the **father** was already dead or whether the son planned to wait at home until he died, the issue was the same — he was allowing something else to take precedence over Christ's call. It is perfectly legitimate and proper to show respect for a dead or dying father, but when anyone or anything is allowed to rival Christ, it becomes positively sinful. This man had something else to do — we might say, a job or an occupation — and this lured him away from a pathway of unreserved discipleship.

9:60 The Lord rebuked his double-mindedness with the words, **"Let the dead bury their own dead, but you go and preach the kingdom of God."** The *spiritually* dead can bury the *physically* dead, but they can't preach the gospel. Disciples should not give priority to tasks that the unsaved can do just as well as Christians. The believer should make sure that he is indispensable as far as the main thrust of his life is concerned. His principal occupation should be to advance the cause of Christ on earth.

9:61 The third would-be disciple resembled the first in that he volunteered to **follow** Christ. He was like the second in that he uttered the contradiction, **"Lord ... me first."** He wanted **first** to say goodbye to his family. In itself, the request was reasonable and proper, but even the common civilities of life are wrong if they are placed ahead of prompt and complete obedience.

9:62 **Jesus** told him that once he **put**

his **hand to the plow** of discipleship, he must not look[31] **back**; otherwise he was not **fit for the kingdom of God**. Christ's followers are not made of half-hearted stuff or dreamy sentimentality. No considerations of family or friends, though lawful in themselves, must be allowed to turn them aside from utter and complete abandonment to Him. The expression not **"fit for the kingdom"** does not refer to salvation but to service. It is not at all a question of *entrance* into the kingdom but of *service* in the kingdom after entering it. Our fitness for entering into the kingdom is in the Person and work of the Lord Jesus. It becomes ours through faith in Him.

And so we have three cardinal hindrances to discipleship illustrated in the experience of these men:

1. Material comforts.
2. A job or an occupation.
3. Family and friends.

Christ must reign in the heart without a rival. All other loves and all other loyalties must be secondary.

C. The Seventy Sent Forth (10:1–16)

10:1–12 This is the only account in the Gospels of the Lord's sending out the **seventy**[32] disciples. It closely resembles the commissioning of the twelve in Matthew 10. However, there the disciples were sent into the northern areas, whereas the seventy are now being sent to the south along the route the Lord was following to Jerusalem. This mission was seemingly intended to prepare the way for the Lord in His journey from Caesarea Philippi in the north, through Galilee and Samaria, across the Jordan, south through Perea, then back across the Jordan to Jerusalem.

While the ministry and office of the seventy was only temporary, nevertheless our Lord's instructions to these men suggest many life principles which apply to Christians in every age.

Some of these principles may be summarized as follows:

1. He sent them out **two by two** (v. 1). This suggests competent testimony. "In the mouth of two or three witnesses every word shall be established" (2 Cor. 13:1).

2. The Lord's servant should constantly **pray** that He will **send out la-**

borers into His harvest field (v. 2). The need is always greater than the supply of workers. In praying for **laborers**, we must be willing to go ourselves, obviously. Notice **pray** (v. 2), **go** (v. 3).

3. The disciples of Jesus are sent forth into a hostile environment (v. 3). They are, to outward appearances, like defenseless **lambs among wolves**. They cannot expect to be treated royally by the world, but rather to be persecuted and even killed.

4. Considerations of personal comfort are not to be permitted (v. 4a). **"Carry neither money bag, knapsack, nor sandals."** The **money bag** speaks of financial reserves. The **knapsack** suggests food reserves. The **sandals** may refer either to an extra pair, or to footgear affording extra comfort. All three speak of the poverty which, though having nothing, yet possesses all things and makes many rich (2 Cor. 6:10).

5. **"Greet no one along the road"** (v. 4b). Christ's servants are not to waste time on long, ceremonious greetings, such as were common in the East. While they should be courteous and civil, they must ultilize their time in the glorious proclamation of the gospel rather than in profitless talk. There is not time for needless delays.

6. They should accept hospitality wherever it is offered to them (vv. 5, 6). If their initial greeting is favorably received, then the host is **a son of peace**. He is a man characterized by **peace**, and one who receives the message of peace. If the disciples are refused, they should not be discouraged; their peace **will return to** them again, that is, there has been no waste or loss, and others will receive it.

7. The disciples should **remain in the same house** that first offers lodging (v. 7). To move **from house to house** might characterize them as those who are shopping for the most luxurious accomodations, whereas they should live simply and gratefully.

8. They should not hesitate to eat whatever food and drink are offered to them (v. 7). As servants of the Lord, they are entitled to their upkeep.

9. Cities and towns take a position either for or against the Lord, just as individuals do (vv. 8, 9). If an area is receptive to the message, the disciples should preach there, accept its hospitality, and bring the blessings of the gospel to it. Christ's servants should **eat such things as are set before** them, not being fastidious about their food or causing inconvenience in the home. After all, food is not the main thing in their lives. Towns which receive the Lord's messengers still have their sin-sick inhabitants healed. Also the King draws very **near to** them (v. 9).

10. A town may reject the gospel and then be denied the privilege of hearing it again (vv. 10–12). There comes a time in God's dealings when the message is heard for the last time. Men should not trifle with the gospel, because it may be withdrawn forever. Light rejected is light denied. Towns and villages which are privileged to hear the good news and which refuse it will be judged more severely than the city of **Sodom**. The greater the privilege, the greater the responsibility.

10:13, 14 As Jesus spoke these words, He was reminded of three cities of Galilee which had been more highly privileged than any others. They had seen Him perform His mighty miracles in their streets. They had heard His gracious teaching. Yet they utterly refused Him. If the miracles He had done in **Chorazin** and **Bethsaida . . . had been done in** ancient **Tyre and Sidon**, those sea-coast cities would have plunged themselves into the deepest repentance. Because the cities of Galilee were unmoved by Jesus' works, their judgment would be more severe than that of **Tyre and Sidon**. As a matter of historical fact, Chorazin and Bethsaida have been so thoroughly destroyed that their exact location is not definitely known today.

10:15 Capernaum became the home town of Jesus after He moved from Nazareth. The city was **exalted to heaven** in privilege. But it despised its most notable Citizen and missed its day of opportunity. So it **will be brought down to Hades** in judgment.

10:16 Jesus closed His instructions to the seventy with a statement that they were His ambassadors. To reject them was to reject Him, and to refuse Him was to refuse God, the Father.

Ryle comments:

> There is probably no stronger language than this in the New Testament about the dignity of a faithful minister's office, and the guilt incurred by those who refuse to hear his message. It is language, we must remember, which is not addressed to the twelve apostles, but to seventy disciples, of whose name and subsequent history we know nothing. Scott remarks, "To reject an ambassador, or to treat him with contempt, is an affront to the prince who commissioned and sent him, and whom he represents. The apostles and seventy disciples were the ambassadors and representatives of Christ; and they who rejected and despised them in fact rejected and despised Him."[33]

D. The Seventy Return (10:17–24)

10:17, 18 As they **returned** from their mission, **the seventy** were elated that **even the demons** had been **subject to** them. Jesus' reply may be understood in two ways. First it may mean that He saw in their success an earnest of the eventual fall of **Satan . . . from heaven**. Jamieson, Fausset, and Brown paraphrase His words:

> I followed you on your mission, and watched its triumphs; while you were wondering at the subjection to you of demons in My Name, a grander spectacle was opening to My view; sudden as the darting of lightning from heaven to earth, lo! Satan was beheld falling from heaven.

This fall of Satan is still future. He will be cast out of heaven by Michael and his angels (Rev. 12:7–9). This will take place during the Tribulation Period, and prior to Christ's Glorious Reign on earth.

A second possible interpretation of Jesus' words is as a warning against pride. It is as if He were saying: "Yes, you are quite heady because even the demons have been subject to you. But just remember — pride is the parent sin. It was pride that resulted in the fall of Lucifer, and in his being cast out of heaven. See that you avoid this peril."

10:19 The Lord had given His disciples **authority** against the forces of evil. They were granted immunity from harm during their mission. It is true of all God's servants; they are protected.

10:20 Yet they were **not to rejoice** in their power over **spirits, but rather in** their own salvation. This is the only recorded instance when the Lord told His disciples not to rejoice. There are subtle dangers connected with success in Christian service, whereas the fact that our **names are written in heaven** reminds us of our infinite debt to God and His Son. It is safe to rejoice in salvation by grace.

10:21 Rejected by the mass of the people, **Jesus** looked upon His humble followers and **rejoiced in the Spirit**, thanking the **Father** for His matchless wisdom. The seventy were not **the wise and prudent** men of this world. They were not the intellectuals or the scholars. They were mere **babes**! But they were babes with faith, devotion, and unquestioning obedience. The intellectuals were too wise, too knowing, too clever for their own good. Their pride blinded them to the true worth of God's beloved Son. It is through babes that God can work most effectively. Our Lord was happy for all those whom the Father had given to Him, and for this initial success of the seventy, which foretold the eventual downfall of Satan.

10:22 **All things** were **delivered to** the Son by His **Father**, whether things in heaven, on earth, or under the earth. God put the entire universe under the authority of His Son. **No one knows who the Son is except the Father**. There is mystery connected with the Incarnation that no one but **the Father** can fathom. How God could become Man and dwell in a human body is beyond the comprehension of the creature. No one knows **who the Father is except the Son, and the one to whom the Son wills to reveal Him**. God too is above human understanding. The Son knows Him perfectly, and the Son has revealed Him to the weak, the base, and the despised people who have faith in Him (1 Cor. 1:26–29). Those who have seen the Son have seen the Father. The only begotten Son who is in the bosom of the Father has fully told forth the Father (John 1:18).

Kelly says, "The Son does reveal the Father; but man's mind always breaks itself to pieces when he attempts to unravel the insoluble enigma of Christ's personal glory."

10:23, 24 **Privately**, the Lord told **His disciples** that they were living in a day of unprecedented privilege. Old Testament **prophets and kings** had **desired to see** the days of the Messiah, but had **not seen** them. The Lord Jesus here claims to be the One to whom the OT prophets looked forward — the Messiah. The disciples were privileged to **see** the miracles and **hear** the teaching of the Hope of Israel.

E. The Lawyer and the Good Samaritan (10:25–37)

10:25 The **lawyer**, an expert in the teachings of the Law of Moses, was probably not sincere in his question. He was trying to trick the Savior, to put Him thoroughly to the test. Perhaps he thought that the Lord would repudiate the law. To him, Jesus was only a **Teacher**, and **eternal life** was something he could earn or merit.

10:26–28 The Lord took all this into consideration when He answered him. If the lawyer had been humble and penitent, the Savior would have answered him more directly. Under the circumstances, Jesus directed his attention to **the law**. What did **the law** demand? It demanded that man **love the LORD** supremely, and his **neighbor as** himself. Jesus told him that if he did **this**, he would **live**.

At first, it might appear that the Lord was teaching salvation by law-keeping. Such was not the case. God never intended that anyone should ever be saved by keeping the law. The Ten Commandments were given to people who were already sinners. The purpose of the law is not to save from sin, but to produce the knowledge of sin. The function of the law is to show man what a guilty sinner he is.

It is impossible for sinful man to love God **with all** his **heart**, and his **neighbor as** himself. If he could do this from birth to death, he would not need salvation. He would not be lost. But even then, his reward would only be long life on earth, not eternal life in heaven. As long as he lived sinlessly, he would go on living. Eternal life is only for sinners who acknowledge their lost condition and who are saved by God's grace.

Thus Jesus' statement, **"Do this and**

you will live," was purely hypothetical. If His reference to the law had had its desired effect on the lawyer, he would have said, "If that's what God requires, then I'm lost, helpless, and hopeless. I cast myself on Your love and mercy. Save me by Your grace!"

10:29 Instead of that, he sought to **justify himself**. Why should he? No one had accused him. There was a consciousness of fault and his heart rose up in pride to resist. He asked, **"Who is my neighbor?"** It was an evasive tactic on his part.

10:30–35 It was in answer to that question that the Lord **Jesus** told the story of the good Samaritan. The details of the story are familiar. The robbery-victim (almost certainly a Jew) lay **half dead** on the road **to Jericho**. The Jewish **priest** and **Levite** refused to help; perhaps they feared it was a plot, or were afraid that they too might be robbed if they tarried. It was a hated **Samaritan** who came to the rescue, who applied first aid, who took the victim to **an inn**, and who made provision for his **care**. To the Samaritan, a Jew in need was his neighbor.

10:36, 37 Then the Savior asked the inescapable question. **Which** of the **three** proved **neighbor** to the helpless man? The one **who showed mercy**, of course. Yes, of course. Then the lawyer should **go and do likewise**. "If a Samaritan could prove himself a true neighbor to a Jew by showing mercy to him, then all men are neighbors."[34]

It is not difficult for us to see in the priest and Levite a picture of the powerlessness of the law to help the dead sinner; the law commanded "Love your neighbor as yourself" but it did not give the power to obey. Neither is it difficult to identify the good Samaritan with the Lord Jesus who came to where we were, saved us from our sins, and made full provision for us from earth to heaven and through all eternity. Priests and Levites may disappoint us but the Good Samaritan never does.

The story of the good Samaritan had an unexpected twist to it. It started off to answer the question "Who is my neighbor?" But it ended by posing the question "To whom do you prove yourself a neighbor?"

F. Mary and Martha (10:38–42)

10:38–41 The Lord now centers His attention on the word of God and prayer as the two great means of blessing (10:38–11:13).

Mary sat at Jesus' feet and heard His word, while **Martha was distracted** by her preparations for the Royal Guest. Martha wanted the **Lord** to rebuke her **sister** for failing to help, but Jesus tenderly rebuked **Martha** for her fretfulness!

10:42 Our Lord prizes our affection above our service. Service may be tainted with pride and self-importance. Occupation with Himself is the **one thing** needful, **that good part which will not be taken away**. "The Lord wants to convert us from Marthas into Marys," comments C. A. Coates, "just as He wants to convert us from lawyers into neighbors."[35]

Charles R. Erdman writes:

> While the Master does appreciate all that we undertake for Him, He knows that our first need is to sit at His feet and learn His will; then in our tasks we shall be calm and peaceful and kindly, and at last our service may attain the perfectness of that of Mary when in a later scene she poured upon the feet of Jesus the ointment, the perfume of which still fills the world.[36]

G. The Disciples' Prayer (11:1–4)

Between chapters 10 and 11, there is a time interval which is covered in John 9:1–10:21.

11:1 This is another of the frequent references by Luke to the prayer life of our Lord. It fits in with Luke's purpose in presenting Christ as the Son of Man, ever dependent upon God His Father. The disciples sensed that prayer was a real and vital force in the life of Jesus. As they heard Him pray, it made them want to pray too. And so **one of His disciples** asked that He would **teach** them **to pray**. He did not say, "Teach us *how* to pray," but **"Teach us to pray."** However, the request certainly includes both the fact and the method.

11:2 The model prayer which the Lord Jesus gave to them at this time is somewhat different from the so-called Lord's prayer in Matthew's Gospel. These differences all have a purpose and

meaning. None of them is without significance.

First of all, the Lord taught the disciples to address God as **Our Father**. This intimate family relationship was unknown to believers in the OT. It simply means that believers are now to speak to God as to a loving heavenly **Father**. Next, we are taught to pray that God's **name** should be **hallowed**. This expresses the longing of the believer's heart that He should be reverenced, magnified, and adored. In the petition, **"Your kingdom come,"** we have a prayer that the day will soon arrive when God will put down the forces of evil and, in the Person of Christ, reign supreme over the **earth**, where His **will** shall **be done as it is in heaven**.

11:3 Having thus sought first the kingdom of God and His righteousness, the petitioner is taught to make known his personal needs and desires. The ever-recurring need for food, both physical and spiritual, is introduced. We are to live in **daily** dependence upon Him, acknowledging Him as the source of every good.

11:4 Next there is the prayer for the forgiveness of **sins**, based on the fact that we have shown a forgiving spirit to others. Obviously this does not refer to forgiveness from the penalty of sin. That forgiveness is based upon the finished work of Christ on Calvary, and is received through faith alone. But here we are dealing with parental or governmental forgiveness. After we are saved, God deals with us as with children. If He finds a hard and unforgiving spirit in our hearts, He will chastise us until we are broken and brought back into fellowship with Himself. This forgiveness has to do with fellowship with God, rather than with relationship.

The plea **"And do not lead us into temptation"** presents difficulties to some. We know that God never tempts anyone to sin. But He does allow us to experience trials and testings in life, and these are designed for our good. Here the thought seems to be that we should constantly be aware of our own proneness to wander and fall into sin. We should ask the Lord to keep us from falling into sin, even if we ourselves might want to do it. We should pray that the opportunity to sin and the desire to do so should never coincide. The prayer expresses a healthy distrust of our own ability to resist temptation. The prayer ends with a plea for deliverance **from the evil one.**[37]

H. Two Parables on Prayer (11:5–13)

11:5–8 Continuing with the subject of prayer, the Lord gave an illustration designed to show God's willingness to hear and answer the petitions of His children. The story has to do with a man who had a guest arrive at his home **at midnight.** Unfortunately he did not have enough food on hand. So he went to a neighbor, knocked on his door, and asked for **three loaves** of bread. At first the neighbor was annoyed by the interruption to his sleep and didn't bother to get up. Yet because of the prolonged banging and shouting of the worried host, he finally did get up **and give him** what he needed.

In applying this illustration we must be careful to avoid certain conclusions. It doesn't mean that God is annoyed by our persistent requests. And it doesn't suggest that the only way to get our prayers answered is to be persistent.

It *does* teach that if a man is willing to help a friend because of his importunity, God is much *more* willing to hear the cries of His children.

11:9 It teaches that we should not grow weary or discouraged in our prayer life. "Keep on asking . . . keep on seeking . . . keep on knocking. . . ."[38] Sometimes God answers our prayers the first time we ask. But in other cases He answers only after prolonged asking.

> God answers prayers:
> Sometimes, when hearts are weak,
> He gives the very gifts believers seek;
> But often faith must learn a deeper rest,
> And trust God's silence when He does
>   not speak;
> For He whose name is love will send
>   the best,
> Stars may burn out, nor mountain walls
>   endure,
> But God is true; His promises are sure.
> He is our strength.   – M.G.P.

The parable seems to teach increasing degrees of importunity — asking to seeking to knocking.

11:10 It teaches that **everyone who asks receives**, everyone **who seeks finds, and** everyone **who knocks** has it **opened** to him. This is a promise that when we pray, God always gives us what we ask or He gives us something better. A "no" answer means that He knows our request would not be the best for us; His denial is then better than our petition.

11:11, 12 It teaches that God will never deceive us by giving us **a stone** when we ask **bread.** Bread in those days was shaped in a round flat cake, resembling a stone. God will never mock us by giving us something inedible when we ask for food. If we ask **for a fish**, He will not give us **a serpent**, that is, something that might destroy us. And if we ask **for an egg**, He will not give us **a scorpion**, that is, something that would cause excruciating pain.

11:13 A human father would not give bad gifts; even though he has a sinful nature, he knows **how to give good gifts to** his **children. How much more** is our **heavenly Father** willing to **give the Holy Spirit to those who ask Him.** J. G. Bellet says, "It is significant that the gift He selects as the one we most need, and the one He most desires to give, is the Holy Spirit." When Jesus spoke these words, the Holy Spirit had not yet been given (John 7:39). We should not pray today for the Holy Spirit to be *given* to us as an indwelling Person, because He comes to indwell us at the time of our conversion (Rom. 8:9b; Eph. 1:13, 14).

But it is certainly proper and necessary for us to pray for the Holy Spirit in other ways. We should pray that we will be teachable by the Holy Spirit, that we will be guided by the Spirit, and that His power will be poured out on us in all our service for Christ.

It is quite possible that when Jesus taught the disciples to ask for **the Holy Spirit**, He was referring to the *power* of the Spirit enabling them to live the other-worldly type of discipleship which He had been teaching in the preceding chapters. By this time, they were probably feeling how utterly impossible it was for them to meet the tests of discipleship in their own strength. This is, of course, true. **The Holy Spirit** is the power that enables one to live the Christian life. So Jesus pictured God as anxious to give this power to those who ask.

In the original Greek, verse 13 does not say that God will give *the* Holy Spirit, but rather He will "give Holy Spirit" (without the article). Professor H. B. Swete pointed out that when the article is present, it refers to the Person Himself, but when the article is absent, it refers to His gifts or operations on our behalf. So in this passage, it is not so much a prayer for the *Person* of the Holy Spirit, but rather for His ministries in our lives. This is further borne out by the parallel passage in Matthew 7:11 which reads, " . . . how much more will your Father who is in heaven give *good things* to those who ask Him!"

I. Jesus Answers His Critics (11:14–26)

11:14–16 Casting out a demon that had caused its victim to be **mute**, Jesus created quite a stir among the people. While **the multitudes marveled**, others became more openly opposed to the Lord. The opposition took two principal forms. **Some** accused Him of casting **out demons by** the power of **Beelzebub, the ruler of the demons. Others** suggested that He should perform a **sign from heaven**; perhaps their idea was that this might disprove the charge that had been made against Him.

11:17, 18 The accusation that He cast out demons because He was indwelt by Beelzebub is answered in verses 17–26. The request for a sign is answered in v. 29. First of all, the Lord Jesus reminded them that **every kingdom divided against itself is** destroyed, **and a house divided against** itself **falls**. If He was a tool of Satan in casting out demons, then **Satan** was fighting against his own underlings. It is ridiculous to think that the devil would thus oppose himself and obstruct his own purposes.

11:19 Secondly, the Lord reminded His critics that some of their own countrymen were at that very time casting out evil spirits. If He did it by the power of Satan, then it necessarily follows that they must be doing it by the same power. Of course, the Jews would never be willing to admit this. And yet how could they deny the force of the argu-

ment? The power to cast out demons came either from God or from Satan. It had to be one or the other; it could not be both. If Jesus acted by the power of Satan, then the Jewish exorcists depended upon the same power. To condemn Him was to condemn them also.

11:20 The true explanation is that Jesus **cast out demons with the finger of God**. What did He mean by **the finger of God**? In the account in Matthew's Gospel (12:28), we read: "But if I cast out demons by the Spirit of God, surely the kingdom of God has come upon you." So we conclude that **the finger of God** is the same as the Spirit of God. The fact that Jesus was casting out demons by the Spirit of God was evidence indeed that **the kingdom of God** had **come upon** the people of that generation. The kingdom had come in the Person of the King Himself. The very fact that the Lord Jesus was there, performing such miracles, was proof positive that God's anointed Ruler had appeared upon the stage of history.

11:21, 22 Up until now, Satan was **a strong man, fully armed**, who held undisputed sway over his court. Those who were possessed by demons were kept in his grip, and there was no one to challenge him. **His goods** were **in peace**, that is, no one had the power to dispute his sway. The Lord Jesus was **stronger than** Satan, came **upon him**, overcame **him**, took **all his armor** from him, and divided **his spoils**.

Not even His critics denied that evil spirits were being cast out by Jesus. This could only mean that Satan had been conquered and that his victims were being liberated. That is the point of these verses.

11:23 Then Jesus added that anyone **who is not with** Him **is against** Him, and anyone **who does not gather with** Him **scatters** abroad. As someone has said, "A man is either on the way or in the way." We have already mentioned the seeming contradiction between this verse and 9:50. If the issue is the Person and work of Christ, there can be no neutrality. A man who is not for Christ is against Him. But when it is a matter of Christian service, those who are not against Christ's servants are for them. In the first verse, it is a matter of salvation; in the second a matter of service.

11:24–26 It seems that the Lord is turning the tables on His critics. They had accused Him of being demon-possessed. He now likens their nation to a man who had been temporarily cured of demon possession. This was true in their history. Prior to the captivity, the nation of Israel had been possessed with the demon of idolatry. But the captivity rid them of that evil **spirit**, and since then the Jews have never been given over to idolatry. Their house has been **swept and put in order**, but they have refused to let the Lord Jesus come in and take possession. Therefore He predicted that in a coming day, the **unclean spirit** would gather **seven other spirits more wicked than himself, and they** would **enter** the house **and dwell there**. This refers to the terrible form of idolatry which the Jewish nation will adopt during the Tribulation Period; they will acknowledge the Antichrist to be God (John 5:43) and the punishment for this sin will be greater than the nation has ever endured before.

While this illustration refers primarily to Israel's *national* history, it also points up the insufficiency of mere repentance or reformation in an *individual's* life. It is not enough to turn over a new leaf. The Lord Jesus Christ must be welcomed into the heart and life. Otherwise the life is open to entrance by more vile forms of sin than ever indulged in before.

J. More Blessed Than Mary (11:27, 28)

A certain woman came **from the crowd** to hail Jesus with the words, **"Blessed is the womb that bore You, and the breasts which nursed You!"** The reply of our Lord was most significant. He did not deny that Mary, His mother, was blessed, but He went beyond this and said that it was even *more* important to **hear the word of God and keep it**. In other words, even the Virgin Mary was more blessed in believing on Christ and following Him than she was in being His mother. Natural relationship is not as important as spiritual. This should be sufficient to silence those who would make Mary an object of adoration.

K. The Sign of Jonah (11:29–32)

11:29 In verse 16, some had tempted the Lord Jesus, asking Him for **a sign** from heaven. He now answers that request by ascribing it to **an evil generation**. He was speaking primarily concerning the Jewish **generation** which was living at that time. The people had been privileged with the presence of the Son of God. They had heard His words and had witnessed His miracles. But they were not satisfied with this. They now pretended that if they could only see a mighty, supernatural work in the heavens, they would believe on Him. The Lord's answer was that **no** further **sign** would **be given to** them **except the sign of Jonah the prophet**.

11:30 He was referring to His own resurrection from the dead. Just **as Jonah** was delivered from the sea, after being in the whale's belly for three days and three nights, so the Lord Jesus would rise from the dead after being in the grave for three days and three nights. In other words, the last and conclusive miracle in the earthly ministry of the Lord Jesus would be His resurrection. **Jonah became a sign to the Ninevites**. When he went to preach to this Gentile metropolis, he went as one who figuratively, at least, had risen from the dead.

11:31, 32 **The queen of the South**, the Gentile Queen of Sheba, traveled a great distance **to hear the wisdom of Solomon**. She did not see a single miracle. If she had been privileged to live in the days of the Lord, how readily she would have received Him! Therefore she **will rise up in the judgment** against those wicked men who were privileged to see the supernatural works of the Lord Jesus and who nonetheless rejected Him. **A greater than Jonah**, and **a greater than Solomon** had stepped on the stage of human history. Whereas **the men of Ninevah repented at the preaching of Jonah**, the men of Israel refused to repent at the preaching of **a greater than Jonah**.

Unbelief today scoffs at the story of Jonah, assigning it to Hebrew legend. Jesus spoke of Jonah as an actual person of history, just as He spoke of Solomon. People who say they would believe if they could see a miracle are mistaken.

Faith is not based on the evidences of the senses but on the living word of God. If a man will not believe the word of God, he will not believe though one should rise from the dead. The attitude that demands a sign is not pleasing to God. That is not faith but sight. Unbelief says, "Let me see and then I will believe." God says, "Believe and then you will see."

L. Parable of the Lighted Lamp (11:33–36)

11:33 At first we might think that there is no connection between these verses and the preceding ones. But on closer examination, we find a very vital link. Jesus reminded His hearers that **no one** puts a lighted **lamp** in the cellar or **under a basket**. He puts it **on a lampstand** where it will be seen and where it will provide light for all who enter.

The application is this: God is the One who has **lit** the **lamp**. In the Person and work of the Lord Jesus, He provided a blaze of illumination for the world. If anyone doesn't see the Light, it isn't God's fault. In chapter 8, Jesus was speaking of the responsibility of those who were already His disciples to propagate the faith and not to hide it under a vessel. Here in 11:33 He is exposing the unbelief of His sign-seeking critics as caused by their covetousness and fear of shame.

11:34 Their unbelief was a result of their impure motives. In the physical realm, **the eye** is that which gives **light** to the **whole body**. If the eye is healthy, then the person can see the light. But if the eye is diseased, that is, blind, then the light cannot get in.

It is the same in the spiritual realm. If a person is sincere in his desire to know whether Jesus is the Christ of God, then God will reveal it to him. But if his motives are not pure, if he wants to cling to his greed, if he continues to fear what others will say, then he is blinded to the true worth of the Savior.

11:35 The men Jesus was addressing thought themselves to be very wise. They supposed that they had a great deal of light. But the Lord Jesus warned them to consider the fact that **the light** that was **in** them was actually **darkness**. Their own pretended wisdom and superiority kept them from Him.

11:36 The person whose motives are pure, who opens His complete being to Jesus, the Light of the world, is flooded with spiritual illumination. His inward life is enlightened by Christ just as his body is illuminated when he sits in the direct rays of a lamp.

M. Outward and Inward Cleanliness (11:37–41)

11:37–40 When Jesus accepted the invitation of **a certain Pharisee** to dinner, His host was shocked **that He had not first washed before dinner**. Jesus read his thoughts and thoroughly rebuked him for such hypocrisy and externalism. Jesus reminded him that what really counts is not the cleanliness of **the outside of the cup** but **the inside**. Outwardly, the Pharisees appeared quite righteous, but inwardly they were crooked and wicked. The same God **who made the outside** of man made the **inside** as well, and He is interested that our inward lives should be pure. "Man looks at the outward appearance, but the LORD looks at the heart" (1 Sam. 16:7).

11:41 The Lord realized how covetous and selfish these Pharisees were, so He told His host first to **give alms of such things as** he had. If he could pass this basic test of love to others, **then indeed all things** would be **clean to** him. H. A. Ironside comments:

> When the love of God fills the heart so that one will be concerned about the needs of others, then only will these outward observances have any real value. He who is constantly gathering up for himself, in utter indifference to the poor and needy about him, gives evidence that the love of God does not dwell in him.[39]

An unknown writer summarizes:

> The severe things said in verses 39–52 against Pharisees and lawyers were said at a Pharisee's dinner table (verse 37). What we call "good taste" is often made a substitute for loyalty to truth; we smile when we should frown; and we are silent when we should speak. Better break up a dinner party than break faith with God.

N. The Pharisees Rebuked (11:42–44)

11:42 The **Pharisees** were externalists. They were punctilious about the smallest details of the ceremonial law, such as tithing tiny **herbs**. But they were careless in their relations with God and with man. They oppressed the poor and failed to love God. The Lord did not rebuke them for tithing **mint and rue** and every herb, but simply pointed out that they should not be so zealous in this particular and neglect the basic duties of life, such as **justice and the love of God**. They emphasized the subordinate but overlooked the primary. They excelled in what could be seen by others but were careless about what only God could see.

11:43 They loved to parade themselves, to occupy positions of prominence **in the synagogues**, and to attract as much attention as possible **in the marketplaces**. They were thus guilty not only of externalism but of pride as well.

11:44 Finally the Lord compared them to unmarked **graves**. Under the Law of Moses, whoever touched a grave was unclean for seven days (Num. 19:16), even if he didn't know at the time that it was a grave. The **Pharisees** outwardly gave the appearance of being devout religious leaders. But they should have worn a sign warning people that it was defiling to come in touch with them. They were **like** unmarked **graves**, full of corruption and uncleanness, and infecting others with their externalism and pride.

O. The Lawyers Denounced (11:45–52)

11:45 The **lawyers** were the scribes — experts in explaining and interpreting the Law of Moses. However, their skill was limited to telling others what to do. They did not practice it themselves. One of the lawyers had felt the cutting edge of Jesus' words, and reminded Him that in criticizing the Pharisees, He was **also** insulting the legal experts.

11:46 The Lord used this as an occasion to lash out at some of the sins of the lawyers. First of all they oppressed the people with all kinds of legal **burdens**, but did nothing to help them bear **the burdens**. As Kelly remarks, "They were notorious for their contempt of the very people from whom they derived their importance."[40] Many of their rules were man-made and were connected with matters of no real importance.

11:47, 48 The lawyers were hypocritical murderers. They pretended to admire the prophets of God. They went so far as to erect monuments over **the tombs of the** OT **prophets**. This certainly seemed to be a proof of their deep respect. But the Lord Jesus knew differently. While outwardly dissociating themselves from their Jewish ancestors who **killed** the prophets, they were actually following in their footsteps. At the very time they were building **tombs** for the prophets, they were plotting the death of God's greatest Prophet, the Lord Himself. And they would continue to murder God's faithful prophets and apostles.

11:49 By comparing verse 49 with Matthew 23:34, it will be seen that Jesus Himself is **the wisdom of God**. Here He quotes **the wisdom of God** as saying, **"I will send them prophets."** In Matthew He does not give this as a quotation from the OT or from any other source, but simply presents it as His own statement. (See also 1 Cor. 1:30 where Christ is spoken of as wisdom.) The Lord Jesus promised that He would **send . . . prophets and apostles** to the men of His generation, and that the latter would **kill and persecute** them.

11:50, 51 He would require **of** that **generation the blood** of all God's spokesmen, beginning with the first recorded case in the OT, that **of Abel**, down to the last instance, that **of Zechariah, who perished between the altar and the temple** (2 Chron. 24:21). Second Chronicles was the last book in the Jewish order of the OT books. Therefore the Lord Jesus ran the entire gamut of martyrs when He mentioned **Abel** and **Zechariah**. As He uttered these words, He well knew that the generation then living would put Him to death on the cross, and thus bring to an awful climax all their previous persecution of men of God. It was because they would murder Him **that the blood of all** previous dispensations would fall upon them.

11:52 Finally the Lord Jesus denounced the **lawyers** for having **taken away the key of knowledge**, that is, for withholding God's Word from the people. Though outwardly they professed loyalty to the Scriptures, yet they stubbornly refused to receive the One of whom the Scriptures spoke. And they

hindered others from coming to Christ. They didn't want Him themselves, and they didn't want others to receive Him.

P. Response of the Scribes and Pharisees (11:53, 54)

The scribes and the Pharisees were obviously angered by the Lord's straightforward accusations. They **began to assail Him vehemently**, and stepped up their efforts to trap Him in His words. By every possible device, they sought to trick Him into saying **something** for which they could condemn Him to death. In doing so, they only proved how accurately He had read their characters.

VIII. TEACHING AND HEALING ON THE WAY TO JERUSALEM (Chaps. 12–16)

A. Warnings and Encouragements (12:1–12)

12:1 An innumerable multitude ... **had gathered together** while Jesus was condemning the Pharisees and lawyers. A dispute or a debate will generally attract a throng, but this crowd was also drawn, no doubt, by Jesus' fearless denunciation of these hypocritical religious leaders. Although an uncompromising attitude toward sin is not always popular, yet it does commend itself to the heart of man as being righteous. Truth is always self-verifying. Turning **to His disciples**, Jesus warned, **"Beware of the leaven of the Pharisees."** He explained that leaven is a symbol or picture of **hypocrisy**. A hypocrite is one who wears a mask, one whose outward appearance is utterly different from what he is inwardly. The Pharisees posed as paragons of virtue but actually they were masters of masquerade.

12:2, 3 Their day of exposure would come. All that they had **covered** up would be **revealed**, and all that they had done **in the dark** would be dragged out into **the light**.

Just as inevitable as the unmasking of hypocrisy is the triumph of truth. Up to then, the message proclaimed by the disciples had been spoken in relative obscurity and to limited audiences. But follow-

ing the rejection of the Messiah by Israel, and the coming of the Holy Spirit, the disciples would go forth fearlessly in the name of the Lord Jesus and proclaim the good news far and wide. Then it would **be proclaimed on the housetops**, comparatively speaking. Godet remarks, "Those whose voice cannot now find a hearing, save within limited and obscure circles, shall become the teachers of the world."[41]

12:4, 5 With the encouraging and warm-hearted words **"My friends,"** Jesus warns His disciples not to be ashamed of this priceless friendship under any trials. The worldwide proclamation of the Christian message would bring persecution and death to the loyal disciples. But there was a limit to what men like the Pharisees could do to them. Physical death was that limit. This they should not fear. God would visit their persecutors with a far worse punishment, namely eternal death in **hell**. And so the disciples were to **fear** God rather than man.

12:6, 7 To emphasize God's protective interest in the disciples, the Lord Jesus mentioned the Father's care for **sparrows**. In Matthew 10:29 we read that two sparrows are sold for a copper coin. Here we learn that **five sparrows** are **sold for two copper coins**. In other words, an extra sparrow is thrown in free when four are purchased. And yet not even this odd sparrow with no commercial value is forgotten in the sight of **God**. If God cares for that odd sparrow, how much more does He watch over those who go forth with the gospel of His Son! He numbers **the very hairs of** their **head**.

12:8 The Savior told the disciples that **whoever confesses** Him now will be confessed by Him **before the angels of God**. Here He is speaking of all true believers. To confess Him is to receive Him as only Lord and Savior.

12:9 Those who deny Him **before men will be denied before the angels of God**. The primary reference here seems to be to the Pharisees, but of course the verse includes all who refuse Christ and are ashamed to acknowledge Him. In that day, He will say, "I never knew you."

12:10 Next the Savior explained to the disciples that there is a difference between criticism of Him and blasphemy **against the Holy Spirit**. Those who speak **against the Son of Man** can **be forgiven** if they repent and believe. But blasphemy **against the Holy Spirit** is the unpardonable sin. This is the sin of which the Pharisees were guilty (see Matt. 12:22–32). What is this sin? It is the sin of attributing the miracles of the Lord Jesus to the devil. It is blasphemy **against the Holy Spirit** because Jesus performed all His miracles in the power of the Holy Spirit. Therefore, it was, in effect, saying that the Holy Spirit of God is the devil. There is no forgiveness for this sin in this age or in the age to come.

This sin cannot be committed by a true believer, though some are tortured by fears that they have committed it by backsliding. Backsliding is not the unpardonable sin. A backslider can be restored to fellowship with the Lord. The very fact that a person is concerned is evidence he has *not* committed the unpardonable sin.

Neither is rejection of Christ by an unbeliever the unforgivable sin. A person may spurn the Savior repeatedly, yet he may later turn to the Lord and be converted. Of course, if he dies in unbelief, he can no longer be converted. His sin then, in fact, does become unpardonable. But the sin which our Lord described as unpardonable is the sin which the Pharisees committed by saying that He performed His miracles by the power of Beelzebub, the prince of demons.

12:11, 12 It was inevitable that the disciples would be brought before governmental **authorities** for trial. The Lord Jesus told them that it was unnecessary for them to rehearse in advance **what** they **should say. The Holy Spirit** would put the proper words in their mouths whenever it was necessary. This does *not* mean that servants of the Lord should not spend time in prayer and study before preaching the gospel or teaching the Word of God. It should not be used as an excuse for laziness! However, it is a definite promise from the Lord that those who are placed on trial for their witness for Christ will be given special help from **the Holy Spirit**. And it is a general promise to all God's people that if they walk in the Spirit, they will be given the suitable words to speak in the crisis moments of life.

B. Warning Against Greed (12:13–21)

12:13 At this point, a man stepped out **from the crowd** and asked the Lord to settle a dispute between his **brother** and himself over an **inheritance**. It has often been said that where there's a will, there are a lot of relatives. This seems to be a case in point. We are not told whether the man was being deprived of his rightful portion, or whether he was greedy for more than his share.

12:14 The Savior quickly reminded him that He had not come into the world to handle such trivial matters. The purpose of His coming involved the salvation of sinful men and women. He would not be deflected from this grand and glorious mission to divide a pitiful inheritance. (In addition, He did not have legal authority to judge matters involving estates. His decisions would not have been binding.)

12:15 But the Lord *did* use this incident to warn His hearers against one of the most insidious evils in the human heart, namely **covetousness**. The insatiable lust for material possessions is one of the strongest drives in all of life. And yet it completely misses the purpose of human existence. **"One's life does not consist in the abundance of the things he possesses."** As J. R. Miller points out:

This is one of the red flags our Lord hung out which most people nowadays do not seem much to regard. Christ said a great deal about the danger of riches; but not many persons are afraid of riches. Covetousness is not practically considered a sin in these times. If a man breaks the sixth or eighth commandment, he is branded as a criminal and covered with shame; but he may break the tenth, and he is only enterprising. The Bible says the love of money is a root of all evil; but every man who quotes the saying puts a terrific emphasis on the word "love," explaining that it is not money, but only the love of it, that is such a prolific root.

To look about, one would think a man's life *did* consist in the abundance of the things he possesses. Men think they become great just in proportion as they gather wealth. So it seems, too; for the world measures men by their bank-account. Yet there never was a more fatal error. A man is really measured by what he *is*, and not by what he *has*.[42]

12:16–18 The **parable** of the **rich fool** illustrates the fact that possessions are *not* the principal thing in life. Because of an exceptionally good crop, this wealthy farmer was faced with what seemed to him a very distressing problem. He did not know what to do with all the grain. All his barns and silos were crammed to capacity. Then he had a brainstorm. His problem was solved. He decided to **pull down** his **barns and build** bigger ones. He could have saved himself the expense and bother of this tremendous construction project if he had just looked on the needy world about him, and used these possessions to satisfy hunger, both spiritual and physical. "The bosoms of the poor, the houses of widows, the mouths of children are the barns which last forever," said Ambrose.

12:19 As soon as his new barns were built, he planned to retire. Notice his spirit of independence: my barns, my fruits, my goods, my soul. He had the future all planned. He was going to **take** his **ease, eat, drink, and be merry**.

12:20, 21 "But when he began to think of time as his, he crashed into God to his eternal ruin." **God** told **him** that he would die that very **night**. Then he would lose ownership of all his material possessions. They would fall to someone else. Someone has defined a fool as one whose plans end at the grave. This man surely was a fool.

"Then whose will those things be?" God asked. We might well ask ourselves the question, "If Christ should come today, whose would all my possessions be?" How much better to use them for God today than to let them fall into the devil's hands tomorrow! We can lay **up treasure** in heaven with them now, and thus be **rich toward God**. Or we can squander them on our flesh, and from the flesh reap corruption.

C. Anxiety Versus Faith (12:22–34)

12:22, 23 One of the great dangers in the Christian life is that the acquisition of food and clothing becomes the first and foremost aim of our existence. We become so occupied with earning money for these things that the work of the Lord is relegated to a secondary place. The emphasis of the NT is that the cause of Christ should have first place in our lives. **Food** and **clothing** should be subordinate. We should work hard for the supply of our current necessities, then trust God for the future as we plunge ourselves into His service. This is the life of faith.

When the Lord Jesus said that we should **not worry about** food and clothing, He did not mean that we were to sit idly and wait for these things to be provided. Christianity does *not* encourage laziness! But He certainly did mean that in the process of earning money for the necessities of life, we were not to let them assume undue importance. After all, there is something more important in life than what we **eat** and what we wear. We are here as ambassadors of the King, and all considerations of personal comfort and appearance must be subordinated to the one glorious task of making Him known.

12:24 Jesus used **the ravens** as an example of how **God** cares for His creatures. They do not spend their lives in a frantic quest for food and in providing for future needs. They live in hourly dependence on God. The fact that **they neither sow nor reap** should not be stretched to teach that men should refrain from secular occupations. All it means is that God knows the needs of those whom He has created, and He will supply them if we walk in dependence on Himself. If **God feeds** the ravens, how much more will He feed those whom He has created, whom He has saved by His grace, and whom He has called to be His servants. The ravens have no barns or storehouses, yet God provides for them on a daily basis. Why then should we spend our lives building bigger barns and storage bins?

12:25, 26 **"Which of you by worrying,"** Jesus asked, **"can add one cubit to his stature?"** This indicates the folly of worrying over things (such as the future) over which we have no control. No one **by worrying can add** to his height, or to the length of his life. (The expression "his stature" can also be translated "the length of his life".) If that is so, why worry about the future? Rather, let us use all our strength and time serving Christ, and leave the future to Him.

12:27, 28 **The lilies** are next introduced to show the folly of spending one's finest talents in the obtaining of clothes. **The lilies** are probably wild scarlet anemones. **They neither toil nor spin, yet** they have a natural beauty which rivals **Solomon in all his glory. If God** lavishes such beauty on flowers which bloom **today** and are burned tomorrow, will He be unmindful of the needs of His children? We prove ourselves to be of **little faith** when we worry, fret, and rush around in a ceaseless struggle to get more and more material possessions. We waste our lives doing what God would have done for us, if we had only devoted our time and talents more to Him.

12:29–31 Actually, our daily needs are small. It is wonderful how simply we can live. Why then give food and clothing such a prominent place in our lives? And why **have an anxious mind**, worrying about the future? This is the way unsaved people live. **The nations of the world** who do not know God as their Father concentrate on food, clothing, and pleasure. These things form the very center and circumference of their existence. But God never intended that His children should spend their time in the mad rush for creature comforts. He has a work to be done on earth, and He has promised to care for those who give themselves wholeheartedly to Him. If we **seek** His **kingdom**, He will never let us starve or be naked. How sad it would be to come to the end of life and realize that most of our time was spent in slaving for what was already included in the ticket home to heaven!

12:32 The disciples formed a **little flock** of defenseless sheep, sent out into the midst of an unfriendly world. They had, it is true, no visible means of support or defense. Yet this bedraggled group of young men was destined to inherit **the kingdom** with Christ. They would one day reign with Him over all the earth. In view of this, the Lord encouraged them **not** to **fear**, because if the **Father** had such glorious honors in store for them, then they need not worry about the pathway that lay between.

12:33, 34 Instead of accumulating material possessions and planning for time, they can put these possessions to work for the Lord. In this way they would be investing for heaven and for eternity. The ravages of age could not af-

fect their possessions. Heavenly treasures are fully insured against theft and spoilage. The trouble with material wealth is that ordinarily you can't have it without trusting it. That is why the Lord Jesus said, **"Where your treasure is, there your heart will be also."** If we send our money on ahead, then our affections will be weaned from the perishing things of this world.

D. Parable of the Watchful Servant (12:35–40)

12:35 Not only were the disciples to trust the Lord for their needs; they were to live in constant expectancy of His coming again. Their **waist** was to be **girded**, and their **lamps burning**. In eastern lands, a belt was drawn around the **waist** to hold up the long, flowing garments when a person was about to walk quickly or run. The girded waist speaks of a mission to be accomplished and the burning lamp suggests a testimony to be maintained.

12:36 The disciples were to live in moment-by-moment expectation of the Lord's return, as if He were a man returning **from** a **wedding**. Kelly comments:

> They should be free from all earthly encumbrances, so that the moment the Lord knocks, according to the figure, they may open to Him immediately — without distraction or having to get ready. Their hearts are waiting for Him, for their Lord; they love Him, they are waiting for Him. He knocks and they open to Him immediately.[43]

The details of the story concerning the man returning **from the wedding** should not be pressed as far as the prophetic future is concerned. We should not identify the wedding here with the Marriage Supper of the Lamb, or the man's return with the Rapture. The Lord's story was designed to teach one simple truth, namely, watchfulness for His return; it was not intended to set forth the order of events at His coming.

12:37 When the man comes back from the wedding, his **servants** are eagerly **watching** for him, ready to swing into action at his command. He is so pleased with their watchful attitude that he turns the tables, as it were. **He girds himself** with a servant's apron, seats them at the table, and serves **them** a meal. This is a very touching suggestion that He who once came into this world in the form of a bondslave will graciously condescend to serve His people again in their heavenly home. The devout German Bible scholar Bengel regarded verse 37 as the greatest promise in all God's word.

12:38 **The second watch** of the night was from 9:00 p.m. to midnight. **The third** was from midnight to 3:00 a.m. No matter what watch it was when the Master returned, his **servants** were waiting for him.

12:39, 40 The Lord changes the picture by alluding to a home owner whose house was **broken into** in an unguarded moment. The coming of **the thief** was entirely unexpected. **If the master of the house had known**, he would **not** have **allowed his house to be broken into**. The lesson is that the time of Christ's coming is uncertain; no one knows the day or the hour when He will appear. When He does come, those believers who have laid up treasures on earth will lose them all, because as someone has said, "A Christian either leaves his wealth or goes to it." If we are really watching for Christ's return, we will sell all that we have and lay up treasures in heaven where no thief can reach them.

E. Faithful and Unfaithful Servants (12:41–48)

12:41, 42 At this point **Peter** asked if Christ's **parable** on watchfulness was intended **only** for the disciples or for **all people**. The Lord's answer was that it was for all who profess to be stewards of God. The **faithful and wise steward** is the one who is set over the Master's household and who gives **food** to His people. The steward's main responsibility here concerns people, not material things. This is in keeping with the entire context, warning the disciples against materialism and covetousness. It is people who are important, not things.

12:43, 44 **When** the Lord **comes** and finds His bondslave taking a genuine interest in the spiritual welfare of men and women, He will reward him liberally. The reward probably has to do with governmental rule with Christ during the Millennium (1 Pet. 5:1–4).

12:45 The **servant** professes to be working for Christ, but actually he is an unbeliever. Instead of feeding the people of God, he abuses them, robs them, and lives in self-indulgence. (This may be a reference to the Pharisees.)

12:46 The coming of the Lord will expose his unreality, and he will be punished **with** all other **unbelievers**. The expression "**cut him in two**" may also be translated "severely scourge him" (AV margin).

12:47, 48 Verses 47 and 48 set forth a fundamental principle in regard to all service. The principle is that the greater the privilege, the greater the responsibility. For believers, it means that there will be degrees of reward in heaven. For unbelievers, it means that there will be degrees of punishment in hell. Those who have come to know God's **will** as it is revealed in the Scriptures are under great responsibility to obey it. **Much** has been **given** to them; **much will be required** of them. Those who have not been so highly privileged will also be punished for their misdeeds, but their punishment will be less severe.

F. The Effect of Christ's First Advent (12:49–53)

12:49 The Lord Jesus knew that His coming to **the earth** would not bring peace at the outset. First it must cause division, strife, persecution, bloodshed. He did not come with the avowed purpose of casting this kind of **fire on the earth**, but that was the result or effect of His coming. Although afflictions and dissensions broke out during His earthly ministry, it was not until the cross that the heart of man was truly exposed. The Lord knew that all of this must take place, and He was willing that the **fire** of persecution should burst forth as soon as necessary against Himself.

12:50 He had **a baptism to be baptized with**. This refers to His **baptism** to the point of death on Calvary. He was under tremendous constraint to go to the cross to accomplish redemption for lost mankind. The shame, suffering, and death were the Father's will for Him, and He was anxious to obey.

12:51–53 He knew very well that His coming would not give **peace on earth** at that time. And so He warned the disciples that when men came to Him, their families would persecute them and drive them out. The introduction of Christianity into an average home of **five** would split the family. It is a curious mark of man's perverted nature that ungodly relatives would often rather have their son a drunkard and dissolute person than have him take a public stand as a disciple of the Lord Jesus Christ! This paragraph disproves the theory that Jesus came to unite all humanity (godly and ungodly) into a single "universal brotherhood of man." Rather, He divided them as they have never been divided before!

G. The Signs of the Times (12:54–59)

12:54, 55 The previous verses were addressed to the disciples. Now the Savior turns **to the multitudes**. He reminds them of their skill in predicting the weather. They knew that when they saw **a cloud** to **the west** (over the Mediterranean), they were in for **a shower**. On the other hand, a **south wind** would bring scorching heat and drought. The people had the intelligence to know this. But there was more than intelligence. There was the will to know.

12:56 In spiritual matters, it was a different story. Though they had normal human intelligence, they did not realize the important **time** which had arrived in human history. The Son of God had come to this earth, and was standing in their very midst. Heaven had never come so near before. But they did not know the time of their visitation. They had the intellectual capacity to know, but they did not have the will to know, and thus they were self-deluded.

12:57–59 If they realized the significance of the day in which they lived, they would be in a hurry to make peace **with** their **adversary**. Four legal terms are used here — **adversary, magistrate, judge, officer** — and they all may refer to God. At that time God was walking in and out among them, pleading with them, giving them an opportunity to be saved. They should repent and put their faith in Him. If they refused, they would have to stand before God as their Judge. The case would be sure to go against them. They would be found guilty and condemned for their unbelief. They would be thrown **into prison**, that is,

eternal punishment. They would not come out **till** they had **paid the very last mite** — which means that they would *never* come out, because they would never be able to pay such a tremendous debt.

So Jesus was saying that they should discern the time in which they lived. Then they should get right with God by repenting of their sins and by committing themselves to Him in full surrender.

H. The Importance of Repentance (13:1–5)

13:1–3 Chapter 12 closed with the failure of the Jewish nation to discern the time in which they lived, and with the Lord's warning to repent quickly or perish forever. Chapter 13 continues this general subject, and is largely addressed to Israel as a nation, although the principles apply to individual people. Two national calamities form the basis of the resulting conversation. The first was the massacre of some **Galileans** who had come to Jerusalem to worship. **Pilate**, the governor of Judea, had ordered them to be slain while they were offering **sacrifices**. Nothing else is known concerning this atrocity. We assume the victims were Jews who had been living in Galilee. The Jews in Jerusalem might have been laboring under the delusion **that these Galileans** must have committed terrible sins, and that their death was an evidence of God's disfavor. However, the Lord Jesus corrected this by warning the Jewish people that **unless** they repented, they would **all likewise perish**.

13:4, 5 The other tragedy concerned the collapse of a **tower in Siloam** which caused the death of **eighteen** persons. Nothing else is known about this accident except what is recorded here. Fortunately, it is not necessary to know any further details. The point emphasized by the Lord was that this catastrophe should not be interpreted as a special judgment for gross wickedness. Rather, it should be seen as a warning to all the nation of Israel that **unless** they repented, a similar doom would come upon them. This doom came to pass in A.D. 70 when Titus invaded Jerusalem.

I. Parable of the Fruitless Fig Tree (13:6–9)

In close connection with the preceding, the Lord Jesus told the **parable** of the **fig tree**. It is not difficult to identify the **fig tree** as Israel, **planted** in God's **vineyard**, that is, the world. God looked for **fruit on** the tree but He **found none**. So He said to the vinedresser (the Lord Jesus) that He had sought in vain for **fruit** from the tree **for three years**. The simplest interpretation of this refers it to the first three years of our Lord's public ministry. The thought of the passage is that the fig tree had been given sufficient time to produce fruit, if it was ever going to do so. If no fruit appeared in three years, then it was reasonable to conclude that none would ever appear. Because of its fruitlessness, God ordered to **cut it down**. It was only occupying **ground** that could be used more productively. The vinedresser interceded for the fig tree, asking that it be given one more year. If at the end of that time, it was still fruitless, then He could **cut it down**. And that is what happened. It was after the fourth year had begun that Israel rejected and crucified the Lord Jesus. As a result, its capital was destroyed and the people scattered.

G. H. Lang expressed it thus:

> The Son of God knew the mind of His Father, the Owner of the vineyard, and that the dread order "Cut it down" had been issued; Israel had again exhausted the Divine forbearance. Neither a nation nor a person has reason to enjoy the care of God if not bringing forth the fruits of righteousness unto the glory and praise of God. Man exists for the honour and pleasure of the Creator: when he does not serve this just end why should not the sentence of death follow his sinful failure, and he be removed from his place of privilege?[44]

J. Healing of the Bent-Over Woman (13:10–17)

13:10–13 The real attitude of Israel toward the Lord Jesus is seen in the ruler of the synagogue. This official objected that the Savior had healed a woman on the Sabbath. The **woman** had suffered from severe curvature of the spine for **eighteen years**. Her deformity was great; she could not straighten **herself up** at all. Without even being asked, the Lord **Jesus** had spoken the healing word, had **laid His hands on her**, and had straightened her spine.

13:14 **The ruler of the synagogue** indignantly told the people that they should come for healing on the first **six days** of the week, but not on the seventh. He was a professional religionist, with no deep concern for the problems of the people. Even if they had come on the first six days of the week, he could not have helped them. He was a stickler about the technical points of the law, but there was no love or mercy in his heart. If he had had curvature of the spine for eighteen years, he would not have minded on which day he was straightened out!

13:15, 16 **The Lord** reproved his hypocrisy and that of the other leaders. He reminded them that they didn't hesitate to **loose** an **ox or donkey from the stall on the Sabbath** in order to let it drink water. If they showed such consideration for dumb animals on the Sabbath, was it wrong for Jesus to perform an act of healing on **this woman** who was **a daughter of Abraham**? The expression "a daughter of Abraham" indicates not only that she was Jewish but also a true believer, a woman of faith. The curvature of the spine was caused by **Satan**. We know from other parts of the Bible that some sicknesses are the result of Satanic activity. Job's boils were inflicted by Satan. Paul's thorn in the flesh was a messenger of Satan to buffet him. The devil is not allowed to do this on a believer, however, without the Lord's permission. And God overrules any such sickness or suffering for His own glory.

13:17 The critics of our Lord were thoroughly **put to shame** by His words. The common people **rejoiced** because a **glorious** miracle had been performed, and they knew it.

K. Parables of the Kingdom (13:18–21)

13:18, 19 After seeing this wonderful miracle of healing, the people might have been tempted to think that the kingdom would be set up immediately. The Lord Jesus disabused their minds by setting forth two parables of **the kingdom of God** which describe it as it would exist between the time of the King's rejection and His return to the earth to reign. They picture the growth of Christendom, and include mere profession as well as reality (see notes on 8:1–3).

First of all He likened **the kingdom of God** to **a mustard seed**, one of the tiniest of seeds. When cast into the ground, it produces a shrub, but not a tree. Therefore when Jesus said that this seed produced **a large tree**, He indicated that the growth was highly abnormal. It was big enough for **birds of the air** to lodge **in its branches**. The thought here is that Christianity had a humble beginning, small as a grain of **mustard seed**. But as it grew, it became popularized, and Christendom as we know it today developed. Christendom is composed of all who profess allegiance to the Lord, whether or not they have ever been born again. **The birds of the air** are vultures or birds of prey. They are symbols of evil, and picture the fact that Christendom has become the resting place for various forms of corruption.

13:20, 21 The second parable likened **the kingdom of God** to **leaven which a woman** placed **in three measures of meal**. We believe that leaven in the Scripture is always a symbol of evil. Here the thought is that evil doctrine has been introduced into the pure food of the people of God. This evil doctrine is not static; it has an insidious power to spread.

L. The Narrow Gate into the Kingdom (13:22–30)

13:22, 23 As Jesus moved **toward Jerusalem**, someone stepped out from the crowd to ask **Him** if only a **few** would be **saved**. It may have been an idle question, provoked by mere curiosity.

13:24 The Lord answered a speculative question with a direct command. He told the questioner to make sure that he himself would **enter through the narrow gate**. When Jesus said **to strive to enter through the narrow gate**, He did not mean that salvation requires effort on our part. **The narrow gate** here is new birth — salvation by grace through faith. Jesus was warning the man to make sure that he entered by this door. **"Many . . . will seek to enter and will not be able"** when once the door is shut. This does not mean that they will seek to enter in by the door of conversion, but rather that in the day of Christ's power and glory, they will want admission to His

kingdom, but it will be too late. The day of grace in which we live will have come to an end.

13:25–27 The Master of the house will rise **up and shut the door**. The Jewish nation is pictured then as knocking **at the door** and asking the **Lord** to **open**. He will refuse on the ground that He never knew them. They will protest at this point, pretending that they had lived on intimate terms with Him. But He will not be moved by these pretensions. They were **workers of iniquity**, and will not be allowed to enter in.

13:28–30 His refusal will cause **weeping and gnashing of teeth**. The **weeping** indicates remorse and the **gnashing of teeth** speaks of violent hatred of God. This shows that the sufferings of hell do not change the heart of man. Unbelieving Israelites will **see Abraham and Isaac and Jacob and all the prophets in the kingdom of God**. They themselves expected to be there, simply because they were related to Abraham, Isaac, and Jacob, but they will be **thrust out**. Gentiles will travel to the brightness of Christ's kingdom from all corners of the earth and enjoy its wonderful blessings. Thus many Jews who were first in God's plan for blessing will be rejected, while the Gentiles who were looked down upon as dogs will enjoy the blessings of Christ's Millennial Reign.

M. Prophets Perish in Jerusalem (13:31–35)

13:31 At this time, the Lord Jesus was apparently in Herod's territory. **Some Pharisees came** and warned Him to **get out** because **Herod** was trying **to kill** Him. The Pharisees seem completely out of character in professing an interest in the welfare and safety of Jesus. Perhaps they had joined in a plot with Herod to frighten Him into going to Jerusalem, where He would most certainly be apprehended.

13:32 Our Lord was not moved by the threat of physical violence. He recognized it as a plot on Herod's part and told the Pharisees to **go** back to **that fox** with a message. Some people have difficulty with the fact that the Lord Jesus spoke of Herod as a she-fox (the form is feminine in the original). They feel that it was in violation of the Scripture which forbids speaking evil of a ruler of the people (Ex. 22:28). However, this was not evil; it was the absolute truth. The gist of the message sent by Jesus was that He still had work to do for a short time. He would **cast out demons and perform** healing miracles during the few remaining days allotted to Him. Then on **the third day**, that is, the final day, He would have finished the work connected with His earthly ministry. Nothing would hinder Him in the performance of His duties. No power on earth could harm Him until the appointed time.

13:33 Further, He could not be slain in Galilee. This prerogative was reserved for the city of **Jerusalem**. It was that city which characteristically had murdered the servants of the Most High God. Jerusalem had more or less a monopoly on the death of God's spokesmen. That is what the Lord Jesus meant when He said that **"it cannot be that a prophet should perish outside of Jerusalem."**

13:34, 35 Having thus spoken the truth concerning this wicked city, Jesus turned in pathos and wept over it. This city that **kills the prophets and stones** God's messengers was the object of His tender love. **How often** He had **wanted to gather** the people of the city **together, as a hen gathers her brood . . . , but** they **were not willing**. The difficulty lay in their stubborn will. As a result, their city, their temple, and their land would be **left desolate**. They would pass through a long period of exile. In fact, they would **not see** the Lord until they changed their attitude toward Him. Verse 35b refers to the Second Advent of Christ. A remnant of the nation of Israel will repent at that **time** and will **say, "Blessed is He who comes in the name of the LORD!"** His people will then be willing in the day of His power.

N. Healing of a Man with Dropsy (14:1–6)

14:1–3 One **Sabbath** day, a ruler **of the Pharisees** invited the Lord to his house for a meal. It was not a sincere gesture of hospitality, but rather an attempt on the part of the religious leaders to find fault with the Son of God. Jesus saw **a certain man** there who was afflicted with **dropsy**, that is, swelling

caused by the accumulation of water in the tissues. The Savior read the minds of His critics by asking them pointedly whether **it** was **lawful to heal on the Sabbath**.

14:4–6 Much as they would like to have said that it was not, they could not support their answer, and so **they kept silent**. Jesus therefore **healed** the man **and let him go**. To Him it was a work of mercy, and divine love never ceases its activities, even on the Sabbath (John 5:17). Then turning to the Jews, He reminded them that if one of their animals fell **into a pit**, they would certainly **pull him out on the Sabbath day**. It was in their own interests to do so. The animal was worth money to them. In the case of a suffering fellow man, they didn't care, and they would have condemned the Lord Jesus for helping him. Although **they could not answer** the reasoning of the Savior, we can be sure that they were all the more incensed at Him.

O. Parable of the Ambitious Guest (14:7–11)

As the Lord Jesus entered the Pharisee's house, He perhaps had seen the guests maneuvering for **the best places** around the table. They sought the positions of eminence and honor. The fact that He too was a guest did not prevent Him from speaking out in frankness and righteousness. He warned them against this form of self-seeking. **When** they were **invited** to a meal, they should take the lower **place** rather than the higher. When we seek a high place for ourselves, there is always the possible **shame** of being demoted. If we are truly humble before God, there is only one direction we can possibly move and that is up. Jesus taught that it is better to be advanced to a place of honor than to grasp that place and later have to relinquish it. He Himself is the living example of self-renunciation (Phil. 2:5–8). He humbled Himself and God exalted Him. **Whoever exalts himself will be humbled** by God.

P. The Guest List God Honors (14:12–14)

The ruler of the Pharisees had undoubtedly invited the local celebrities to this meal. Jesus perceived this at once.

He saw that the underprivileged people in the community were not included. He therefore took occasion to enunciate one of the great principles of Christianity — that we should love those who are unlovely, and who cannot repay us. The usual way for people to act is to invite their **friends, relatives,** and **rich neighbors**, always with the hope of being **repaid** in kind. It does not require divine life to act in this way. But it is positively supernatural to show kindness to **the poor, the maimed, the lame,** and **the blind.** God reserves a special reward for those who show charity to these classes. Although such guests **cannot repay** us, yet God Himself promises to reward **at the resurrection of the just.** This is also known in the Scripture as the first resurrection, and includes the resurrection of all true believers. It takes place at the Rapture, and also, we believe, at the end of the Tribulation Period. That is, the first resurrection is not one single event, but takes place in stages.

Q. Parable of the Excuses (14:15–24)

14:15–18 **One of** the guests who reclined with Jesus at the meal remarked how wonderful it would be to participate in the blessings of **the kingdom of God.** Perhaps he was impressed by the principles of conduct which the Lord Jesus had just taught. Or perhaps it was just a general remark which he made without too much thought. At any rate, the Lord replied that wonderful as it may be to **eat bread in the kingdom of God,** the sad fact is that many of those who are invited make all kinds of foolish excuses for their failure to accept. He pictured God as **a certain man** who **gave a great supper and invited many** guests. When the meal was ready, he asked **his servant** to notify the **invited** guests that everything was **now ready.** This reminds us of the great fact that the Lord Jesus finished the work of redemption on Calvary, and the gospel invitation goes out on the basis of that completed work. One person who had been invited excused himself because he had **bought a** field and he wanted to **go and see it.** Normally he should have gone and seen it before purchasing it. But even then, he was putting the love of material things ahead of the gracious invitation.

14:19, 20 The next one had **bought**

five yoke of oxen, and was **going to test them**. He pictures those who put jobs, occupations, or business ahead of the call of God. The third one said he had **married a wife, and therefore** could not **come**. Family ties and social relationships often hinder men from accepting the gospel invitation.

14:21–23 When **that servant** notified **his master** that the invitation was being rejected right and left, **the master** sent him **out** to **the city** to invite **the poor and the maimed and the lame and the blind**. "Both nature and grace abhor a vacuum," said Bengel. Perhaps the first ones invited picture the leaders of the Jewish people. When they rejected the gospel, God sent it out to the common people **of the city** of Jerusalem. Many of these responded to the call, but **still there** was **room** in the master's house. And so the lord said to the servant to **go out into the highways and** byways, **and compel** people **to come in**. This doubtless pictures the gospel going out to the Gentile people. They were not to be compelled by *force of arms* (as has been done in the history of Christendom), but rather by *force of argument*. Loving persuasion was to be used in an effort to bring them in so **that** the master's **house** might **be filled**.

14:24 Thus the original guest list was no longer useful when the meal was held, because those **who were** originally **invited** did not come.

R. The Cost of True Discipleship (14:25–35)

14:25 **Now great multitudes** followed the Lord Jesus. Most leaders would be elated by such widespread interest. But the Lord was not looking for people who would follow Him out of curiosity, with no real heart interest. He was looking for those who were willing to live devotedly and passionately for Him, and even die for Him if necessary. And so He now began to sift the crowd by presenting to them the stringent terms of discipleship. At times the Lord Jesus *wooed* men to Himself, but after they began to follow Him, He *winnowed* them. That is what is taking place here.

14:26 First of all He told those who followed Him that in order to be true disciples, they must love Him supremely. He did not ever suggest that men should have bitter hatred in their hearts toward **father, mother, wife, children, brothers and sisters**. Rather He was emphasizing that love for Christ must be so great that all other loves are hatred *by comparison* (cf. Matt. 10:37). No consideration of family ties must ever be allowed to deflect a disciple from a pathway of full obedience to the Lord.

Actually, the most difficult part of this first term of discipleship is found in the words **"and his own life also."** It is not only that we must love our relatives less; we must **hate** our **own** lives **also**! Instead of living self-centered lives, we must live Christ-centered lives. Instead of asking how every action will affect ourselves, we must be careful to assess how it will affect Christ and His glory. Considerations of personal comfort and safety must be subordinated to the great task of glorifying Christ and making Him known. The Savior's words are absolute. He said that if we did not love Him supremely, more than our family and more than our own lives, we could not be His disciples. There is no halfway measure.

14:27 Secondly, He taught that a true disciple must **bear his** own **cross and** follow Him. The cross is *not* some physical infirmity or mental anguish, but is a pathway of reproach, suffering, loneliness, and even death which a person voluntarily chooses for Christ's sake. Not all believers **bear** the **cross**. It is possible to avoid it by living a nominal Christian life. But if we determine to be all out for Christ, we will experience the same kind of satanic opposition which the Son of God knew when He was here on earth. *This is the cross.* The disciple must **come after** Christ. This means that he must live the type of life which Christ lived when He was here on earth — a life of self-renunciation, humiliation, persecution, reproach, temptation, and contradiction of sinners against Himself.

14:28–30 Then the Lord Jesus used two illustrations to emphasize the necessity of counting **the cost** before setting out to follow Him. He likened the Christian life to a building project and then to warfare. A man **intending to build a tower** sits **down first** and counts **the cost**. If he doesn't have **enough to finish it**, he doesn't proceed. Otherwise when

the foundation is laid, and the work must stop, the onlookers **begin to mock him, saying, "This man began to build and was not able to finish."** So it is with disciples. They should first count the cost, whether they really mean to abandon their lives wholeheartedly to Christ. Otherwise they might start off in a blaze of glory, and then fizzle out. If so, the onlookers will mock them for beginning well and ending ingloriously. The world has nothing but contempt for half-hearted Christians.

14:31, 32 A **king going to make war against** forces that are numerically superior must consider carefully **whether** his smaller forces have the capacity to defeat the enemy. He realizes full well that it is either absolute committal or abject surrender. And so it is in the life of Christian discipleship. There can be no halfway measures.

14:33 Verse 33 is probably one of the most unpopular verses in the entire Bible. It explicitly states that **"Whoever of you does not forsake all that he has cannot be My disciple."** There is no evading the meaning of the words. They do not say that a person must be *willing* to forsake all. Rather they say that he *must* forsake all. We must give the Lord Jesus credit for knowing what He was saying. He realized that the job would never be done in any other way. He wants men and women who esteem Him more than everything else in the world. Ryle observes:

> The man who does well for himself is the man who gives up everything for Christ's sake. He makes the best of bargains; he carries the cross for a few years in this world, and in the world to come has everlasting life. He obtains the best of possessions; he carries his riches with him beyond the grave. He is rich in grace here, and he is rich in glory hereafter. And, best of all, what he obtains by faith in Christ he never loses. It is "that good part which is never taken away."[45]

14:34, 35 **Salt** is a picture of a disciple. There is something wholesome and commendable about a person who is living devotedly and sacrificially for the Lord. But then we read of **salt** that **has lost its flavor**. Modern table salt cannot lose its savor because it is pure salt. But in Bible lands, the salt was often mixed with various forms of impurity. Therefore it was possible for salt to be wasted away and for a residue to remain in the container. But this residue was worthless. It could not even be used for fertilizing the land. It had to be discarded.

The picture is of a disciple who starts off brilliantly, and then goes back on his vows. The disciple has one basic reason for existence; if he fails to fulfill that reason, then he is a pitiable object. We read concerning the salt that **"men throw it out."** It does *not* say that *God* casts it out; that could never happen. But **men throw it out**, that is, they trample underfoot the testimony of one who began to build and was not able to finish. Kelly notes:

> There is shown the danger of what begins well turning out ill. What is there in the world so useless as salt when it has lost the one property for which it is valued? It is worse than useless for any other purpose. So with the disciple who ceases to be Christ's disciple. He is not suited for the world's purposes, and he has forsaken God's. He has too much light or knowledge for entering into the vanities and sins of the world, and he has no enjoyment of grace and truth to keep him in the path of Christ. . . . Savourless salt becomes an object of contempt and judgment.[46]

The Lord Jesus closed the message on discipleship with the words **"He who has ears to hear, let him hear!"** These words imply that not everyone will have the willingness to listen to the stringent terms of discipleship. But if a person is willing to follow the Lord Jesus, no matter what the cost may be, then he should hear and follow.

John Calvin once said, "I gave up all for Christ, and what have I found? I have found everything in Christ." Henry Drummond commented, "The entrance fee into the kingdom of heaven is nothing: the annual subscription is everything."

S. Parable of the Lost Sheep (15:1–7)

15:1, 2 The teaching ministry of our Lord in chapter 14 seemed to attract the despised **tax collectors**, and others who were outwardly **sinners**. Although Jesus reproved their sins, yet many of them acknowledged that He was right. They took sides with Christ against themselves. In true repentance, they acknowledged Him as Lord. Wherever Jesus found people who were willing to acknowledge their sin, He gravitated toward them, and bestowed spiritual help and blessing upon them.

The Pharisees and scribes resented the fact that Jesus fraternized with people who were avowedly **sinners**. They did not show grace to these social and moral lepers, and they resented Jesus' doing so. And so they hurled a charge at Him, **"This Man receives sinners and eats with them."** The charge was true, of course. They thought it was blameworthy, but actually it was in fulfillment of the very purpose for which the Lord Jesus came into the world!

It was in answer to their charge that the Lord Jesus recounted the parables of the lost sheep, the lost coin, and the lost son. These stories were aimed directly at the scribes and Pharisees, who were never broken before God to admit their lost condition. As a matter of fact, they were as lost as the publicans and sinners, but they steadfastly refused to admit it. The point of the three stories is that God receives real joy and satisfaction when He sees sinners repenting, whereas He obtains no gratification from self-righteous hypocrites who are too proud to admit their wretched sinfulness.

15:3, 4 Here the Lord Jesus is pictured under the symbol of a shepherd. The **ninety-nine** sheep represent the scribes and the Pharisees. The **lost** sheep typifies a tax collector or an acknowledged sinner. When the shepherd realizes that **one** of his sheep **is lost**, he leaves **the ninety-nine in the wilderness** (not in the fold) and goes out **after it until he finds it**. As far as our Lord was concerned, this journey included His descent to earth, His years of public ministry, His rejection, suffering, and death. How true are the lines from the hymn "The Ninety and Nine":

> But none of the ransomed ever knew
> How deep were the waters crossed,
> Nor how dark was the night that
>   the Lord passed through
> Ere He found His sheep that was lost.
> – *Elizabeth C. Clephane*

15:5 Having **found** the sheep, **he**

laid **it on his shoulders** and took it to his home. This suggests that the saved sheep enjoyed a place of privilege and intimacy that it never knew as long as it was numbered with the others.

15:6 The shepherd summoned **his friends and neighbors** to **rejoice with** him over the salvation of the lost **sheep**. This speaks of the Savior's joy in seeing a sinner repent.

15:7 The lesson is clear: **There is joy in heaven over one sinner who repents**, but there is no joy over the ninety-nine sinners who have never been convicted of their lost condition. Verse 7 does not actually mean that there are some persons who need no repentance. All men are sinners, and all must repent in order to be saved. The verse describes those **who**, as far as they see themselves, **need no repentance.**

T. Parable of the Lost Coin (15:8–10)

The **woman** in this story may represent the Holy Spirit, seeking the lost with the **lamp** of the Word of God. The nine **silver coins** speak of the unrepentant, whereas the **one** lost **coin** suggests the man who is willing to confess that he is out of touch with God. In the previous account the sheep wandered away by its own volition. A coin is an inanimate object and might suggest the lifeless condition of a **sinner**. He is dead in sins.

The woman continues to **search carefully** for the coin **until she finds it**. Then **she calls her friends and neighbors** to celebrate with her. The lost coin which she had found brought her more true pleasure than the nine which had never been lost. So it is with God. The **sinner** who humbles himself and confesses his lost condition brings joy to the heart of God. He obtains no such joy from those who never feel their need for repentance.

U. Parable of the Lost Son (15:11–32)

15:11–16 God the Father is here depicted as **a certain man** who **had two sons. The younger son** typifies the repentant sinner, whereas the older son illustrates the scribes and the Pharisees. The latter are sons of God by creation though not by redemption. The younger son is also known as the prodigal son.

A **prodigal** is one who is recklessly extravagant, who spends money wastefully. This son became weary of his father's house and decided he wanted to leave. He could not wait for his father to die, and so asked for his **portion** of the inheritance ahead of time. The father distributed to his sons their proper share. Shortly afterward, the younger son set out **to a far country** and spent his money freely in sinful pleasures. As soon as his funds were gone a severe depression gripped the land, and he found himself destitute. The only employment he could get was as a feeder of **swine** — a job that would have been most distasteful to the average Jew. As he watched the pigs eating their bean **pods**, he envied them. They had more to eat than he had, and **no one** seemed disposed to help **him**. The friends he had when he was spending money freely had all disappeared.

15:17–19 The famine proved to be a blessing in disguise. It made him think. He remembered that his **father's hired servants** were living far more comfortably than he. They had plenty of food to eat, while he was wasting away **with hunger**. As he thought of this, he decided to do something about it. He determined to **go to** his **father** in repentance, acknowledging his sin, and seeking pardon. He realized that he was **no longer worthy to be called** his father's **son**, and planned to ask for a job as a **hired** servant.

15:20 Long before he reached his home, **his father saw him and had compassion**. He **ran and fell on his neck and kissed him**. This is probably the only time in the Bible where haste is used of God in a good sense. Stewart aptly illustrates:

> Daringly Jesus pictured God, not waiting for his shamed child to slink home, nor standing on his dignity when he came, but running out to gather him, shamed and ragged and muddied as he was, to his welcoming arms. The same name "Father" has at once darkened the color of sin and heightened the splendid glory of forgiveness.[47]

15:21–24 **The son** made his confession up to the point where he was going to ask for employment. **But the father** interrupted by ordering the slaves to put the best robe on his son, **put a ring on his hand and sandals on his feet**. He also ordered a great feast to celebrate the return of his **son** who had been **lost and** was now **found**. As far as the father was concerned, he had been **dead** but now was **alive again**. Someone has said, "The young man was looking for a good time, but he did not find it in the far country. He found it only when he had the good sense to come back to his father's house." It has been pointed out that **they began to be merry**, but it is never recorded that their joy ended. So it is with the salvation of the sinner.

15:25–27 When the **older son** returned from **the field** and heard all the merrymaking, he **asked** a servant **what** was going on. He told him that his younger **brother** had returned home and that his **father** was delirious with joy.

15:28-30 The older son was consumed with a jealous rage. He refused to participate in his father's joy. J. N. Darby put it well: "Where God's happiness is, there self-righteousness cannot come. If God is good to the sinner, what avails my righteousness?" When **his father** urged him to participate in the festivities, he refused, whimpering that the father had **never** rewarded him for his faithful service and obedience. He had **never** been given as much as a **young goat**, to say nothing of a fatted calf. He complained that when the prodigal son returned, after spending his father's money on **harlots**, the father did not hesitate to make a great feast. Note that he said **"this son of yours,"** not "my brother."

15:31, 32 The father's answer indicated that there is joy connected with the restoration of a **lost** one, whereas an obstinate, ungrateful, unreconciled son produces no cause for celebration.

The older son is an eloquent picture of the scribes and Pharisees. They resented God's showing mercy to outrageous sinners. To their way of thinking, if not to God's, they had served Him faithfully, had never transgressed His commandments, and yet had never been properly rewarded for all of this. The truth of the matter was that they were religious hypocrites and guilty sinners. Their pride blinded them to their distance from God, and to the fact that He

had lavished blessing after blessing upon them. If they had only been willing to repent and to acknowledge their sins, then the Father's heart would have been gladdened and they too would have been the cause of great celebration.

V. Parable of the Unjust Steward (16:1–13)

16:1, 2 The Lord Jesus now turns from the Pharisees and scribes **to His disciples** with a lesson on stewardship. This paragraph is admittedly one of the most difficult in Luke. The reason for the difficulty is that the story of the unjust steward seems to commend dishonesty. We shall see that this is not the case, however, as we proceed. The **rich man** in this story pictures God Himself. A **steward** is one who is entrusted with the management of another person's property. As far as this story is concerned, any disciple of the Lord is also a steward. This particular **steward** was accused of embezzling his employer's funds. He was called to **account**, and notified that he was being dismissed.

16:3-6 **The steward** did some fast thinking. He realized that he must provide for his future. Yet he was too old to engage in hard physical labor, and he was too proud **to beg** (though not too proud to steal). How then could he provide for his social security? He hit upon a scheme by which he could win friends who would show kindness to him when he was in need. The scheme was this: He went to one of his employer's customers and asked **how much** he owed. When the customer said **a hundred measures of oil**, the steward told him to pay for **fifty** and the account would be considered closed.

16:7 **Another** customer owed **a hundred measures of wheat**. The steward told him to pay for **eighty**, and he would mark the invoice "Paid."

16:8 The shocking part of the story occurs when **the master commended the unjust steward** for acting **shrewdly**. Why would anyone approve of such dishonesty? What the steward did was unjust. The following verses show that the steward was not at all commended for his crookedness, but rather for his foresight. He had acted prudently. He looked to the future, and made provision for it. He sacrificed present gain for future reward. In applying this to our own lives, we must be very clear on this point, however; the future of the child of God is not on this earth but in heaven. Just as the steward took steps to insure that he would have friends during his retirement here below, so the Christian should use his Master's goods in such a way as to insure a welcoming party when he gets to heaven.

The Lord said, **"The sons of this world are more shrewd in their generation than the sons of light."** This means that ungodly, unregenerate men show more wisdom in providing for their future in this world than true believers show in laying up treasures in heaven.

16:9 We should **make friends for ourselves by** *means of* **unrighteous mammon**. That is, we should use money and other material things in such a way as to win souls for Christ and thus form friendships that will endure throughout eternity. Pierson stated it clearly:

> Money can be used to buy Bibles, books, tracts and thus, indirectly, the souls of men. Thus what was material and temporal becomes immortal, becomes nonmaterial, spiritual and eternal. Here is a man who has $100. He may spend it all on a banquet or an evening party, in which case the next day there is nothing to show for it. On the other hand, he invests in Bibles at $1.00 each. It buys a hundred copies of the Word of God. These he judiciously sows as seed of the kingdom, and that seed springs up into a harvest, not of Bibles but of souls. Out of the unrighteous, he has made immortal friends, who when he fails, receive him into everlasting habitations.[48]

This then is the teaching of our Lord. By the wise investment of material possessions, we can have part in the eternal blessing of men and women. We can make sure that when we arrive at the gates of heaven, there will be a welcoming committee of those who were saved through our sacrificial giving and prayers. These people will thank us saying, "It was you who invited me here."

Darby comments:

> Man generally is God's steward; and in another sense and in another way Israel was God's steward, put into God's vineyard, and entrusted with law, promises, covenants, worship. But in all, Israel was

found to have wasted His goods. Man looked at as a steward has been found to be entirely unfaithful. Now, what is to be done? God appears, and in the sovereignty of His grace turns that which man has abused on the earth into a means of heavenly fruit. The things of this world being in the hands of man, he is not to be using them for the present enjoyment of this world, which is altogether apart from God, but with a view to the future. We are not to seek to possess the things now, but by the right use of these things to make a provision for other times. It is better to turn all into a friend for another day than to have money now. Man here is gone to destruction. Therefore now, man is a steward out of place.[49]

16:10 If we are **faithful in** our stewardship of **what is least** (money), then we will be **faithful** in handling **what is much** (spiritual treasures). On the other hand, a man who is unrighteous in using the money which God has entrusted to him is unrighteous when bigger considerations are at stake. The relative unimportance of money is emphasized by the expression **what is least.**

16:11 Anyone who is **not** honest in using **unrighteous mammon** for the Lord can scarcely expect Him to entrust **true riches** to him. Money is called **unrighteous mammon**. It is not basically evil in itself. But there probably wouldn't be any need for money if sin had not come into the world. And money is **unrighteous** because it is characteristically used for purposes other than the glory of God. It is contrasted here with **true riches**. The value of money is uncertain and temporary; the value of spiritual realities is fixed and eternal.

16:12 Verse 12 distinguishes between **what is** another's and **what is your own**. All that we have, our money, our time, our talents — belong to the Lord, and we are to use them for Him. That which is **our own** refers to rewards which we reap in this life and in the life to come as a result of our faithful service for Christ. If we have not been faithful in what is His, how can He give us **what is** our **own**?

16:13 It is utterly impossible to live for things and for **God** at the same time. If we are mastered by money, we cannot really be serving the Lord. In order to accumulate wealth, we must devote our finest efforts to the task. In the very act of doing this we rob God of what is rightfully His. It is a matter of divided loyalty. Motives are mixed. Decisions are not impartial. Where our treasure is, there our heart is also. In the effort to gain wealth, we are serving **mammon**. It is quite impossible to **serve God** at the same time. Mammon cries out for all that we have and are — our evenings, our weekends, the time we should be giving to the Lord.

W. The Greedy Pharisees (16:14–18)

16:14 The **Pharisees** were not only proud and hypocritical; they were greedy as well. They thought that godliness was a way of gain. They chose religion as one would choose a lucrative profession. Their service was not geared to glorify God and help their neighbors, but rather to enrich themselves. As they **heard** the Lord Jesus teach that they should forego wealth in this world and lay up their treasures in heaven, **they derided Him**. To them, money was more real than the promises of God. Nothing would hinder them from hoarding wealth.

16:15 Outwardly the Pharisees appeared to be pious and spiritual. They reckoned themselves to be righteous in the sight of **men**. But beneath this deceptive exterior, **God** saw the greed of their **hearts**. He was not deceived by their pretension. The type of life which they displayed, and which others approved (Psalm 49:18), was **an abomination in the sight of God**. They esteemed themselves successful because they combined a religious profession with financial affluence. But as far as God was concerned, they were spiritual adulterers. They professed love for Jehovah, but actually mammon was their god.

16:16 The continuity of verses 16–18 is very difficult to understand. On first reading, they seem to be quite unrelated to what has gone before, and to what follows. However, we feel they can be best understood by remembering that the subject of chapter 16 is the covetousness and unfaithfulness of the Pharisees. The very ones who prided themselves on the careful observance of the law are exposed as avaricious hypocrites. The spirit of the law is in sharp contrast to the spirit of the Pharisees.

The law and the prophets were until John. With these words, the Lord described the legal dispensation which began with Moses and ended with **John** the Baptist. But now a new dispensation was being inaugurated. From the time of John, the gospel of **the kingdom of God** was being **preached**. The Baptist went forth announcing the arrival of Israel's rightful King. He told the people that if they would repent, the Lord Jesus would reign over them. As a result of his preaching and the later preaching of the Lord Himself and of the disciples, there was an eager response on the part of many.

"Everyone is pressing into it" means that those who did respond to the message literally stormed into the kingdom. The tax collectors and sinners, for instance, had to jump over the roadblocks set up by the Pharisees. Others had to deal violently with the love of money in their own hearts. Prejudice had to be overcome.

16:17, 18 But the new dispensation did not mean that basic moral truths were being discarded. It would be **easier for heaven and earth to pass away than for one tittle of the law to fail**. A **tittle of the law** could be compared to the crossing of a "t" or the dotting of an "i".

The Pharisees thought they were in the kingdom of God, but the Lord was saying in effect, "You cannot disregard the great moral laws of God and still claim a place in the kingdom." Perhaps they would ask, "What great moral precept are we disregarding?" The Lord then pointed them to the law of marriage as a law that would never pass away. Any man who **divorces his wife and marries another commits adultery, and whoever marries** a **divorced** woman **commits adultery** also. This is exactly what the Pharisees were doing spiritually. The Jewish people had been brought into a covenant position with God. But these Pharisees were now turning their backs on God in a mad quest for material wealth. And perhaps the verse suggests that they were guilty of literal adultery as well as spiritual.

X. The Rich Man and Lazarus (16:19–31)

16:19–21 The Lord concludes His discourse on stewardship of material things by this account of two lives, two deaths, and two hereafters. It should be noted that this is *not* spoken of as a parable. We mention this because some critics seem to explain away the solemn implications of the story by waving it off as a parable.

At the outset, it should be made clear that the unnamed **rich man** was not condemned to Hades because of his wealth. The basis of salvation is faith in the Lord, and men are condemned for refusing to believe on Him. But this particular rich man showed that he did not have true saving faith by his careless disregard of the **beggar who was laid at his gate**. If he had had the love of God in him, he could not have lived in luxury, comfort, and ease when a fellow man was outside his front door, begging for a few **crumbs** of bread. He would have entered violently into the kingdom by abandoning his love of money.

It is likewise true that **Lazarus** was not saved because he was poor. He had trusted the Lord for the salvation of his soul.

Now notice the portrait of the rich man, sometimes called Dives (Latin for *rich*). He wore only the most expensive, custom-made clothing, and his table was filled with the choicest gourmet foods. He lived for self, catering to bodily pleasures and appetites. He had no genuine love for God, and no care for his fellow man.

Lazarus presents a striking contrast. He was a wretched **beggar**, dropped off every day in front of the rich man's house, **full of sores**, emaciated with hunger, and plagued by unclean **dogs** that **came and licked his sores**.

16:22 When **the beggar died**, he **was carried by the angels to Abraham's bosom**. Many question whether **angels** actually participate in conveying the souls of believers to heaven. We see no reason, however, for doubting the plain force of the words. Angels minister to believers in this life, and there seems no reason why they should not do so at the time of death. **Abraham's bosom** is a symbolic expression to denote the place of bliss. To any Jew, the thought of enjoying fellowship with Abraham would suggest inexpressible bliss. We take it that **Abraham's bosom** is the same as heaven. When **the rich man died**, his

body **was buried** — the body that he had catered to, and for which he had spent so much.

16:23, 24 But that was not all. His soul, or conscious self, went to **Hades. Hades** is the Greek for the OT word *Sheol*, the state of departed spirits. In the OT period, it was spoken of as the abode of both saved and unsaved. Here it is spoken of as the abode of the unsaved, because we read that the rich man was **in torments**.

It must have come as a shock to the disciples when Jesus said that this rich Jew went to **Hades**. They had always been taught from the OT that riches were a sign of God's blessing and favor. An Israelite who obeyed the Lord was promised material prosperity. How then could a wealthy Jew go to Hades? The Lord Jesus had just announced that a new order of things began with the preaching of John. Henceforth, riches are not a sign of blessing. They are a *test* of a man's faithfulness in stewardship. To whom much is given, of him will much be required.

Verse 23 disproves the idea of "soul sleep," the theory that the soul is not conscious between death and resurrection. It proves that there is conscious existence beyond the grave. In fact, we are struck by the extent of knowledge which the rich man had. **He . . . saw Abraham afar off, and Lazarus in his bosom**. He was even able to communicate with Abraham. Calling him **Father Abraham**, he begged for **mercy**, pleading that **Lazarus** might bring a drop of **water and cool** his **tongue**. There is, of course, a question as to how a disembodied soul can experience thirst and anguish from flame. We can only conclude that the language is figurative, but that does not mean that the suffering was not real.

16:25 **Abraham** addressed him as **son**, suggesting that he was a descendant physically, though obviously not spiritually. The patriarch reminded him of his **lifetime** of luxury, ease, and indulgence. He also rehearsed the poverty and suffering of **Lazarus**. Now, beyond the grave, the tables were turned. The inequalities of earth were reversed.

16:26 We learn here that the choices of this life determine our eternal destiny, and once death has taken place, that destiny is **fixed**. There is no passage from the abode of the saved to that of the damned, or vice versa.

16:27–31 In death, the rich man suddenly became evangelistic. He wanted someone to go to his **five brothers** and warn them against coming **to** that **place of torment**. Abraham's reply was that these five brothers, being Jews, had the OT Scriptures, and these should be sufficient to warn them. The rich man contradicted **Abraham**, stating that **if one** should go **to them from the dead**, they would surely **repent**. However, Abraham had the last word. He stated that failure to listen to the Word of God is final. If people will not heed the Bible, they would not believe if a person rose **from the dead**. This is conclusively proved in the case of the Lord Jesus Himself. He arose from the dead, and men still do not believe.

From the NT, we know that when a believer dies, his body goes to the grave, but his soul goes to be with Christ in heaven (2 Cor. 5:8; Phil. 1:23). When an unbeliever dies, his body likewise goes to the grave, but his soul goes to Hades. For him, Hades is a place of suffering and remorse.

At the time of the Rapture, the bodies of believers will be raised from the grave and reunited with their spirits and souls (1 Thess. 4:13–18). They will then dwell with Christ eternally. At the Judgment of the Great White Throne, the bodies, spirits, and souls of unbelievers will be reunited (Rev. 20:12, 13). They will then be cast into the lake of fire, a place of eternal punishment.

And so chapter 16 closes with a most solemn warning to the Pharisees, and to all who would live for money. They do so at the peril of their souls. It is better to beg bread on earth than to beg water in Hades.

IX. THE SON OF MAN INSTRUCTS HIS DISCIPLES (17:1–19:27)

A. Concerning the Peril of Offending (17:1, 2)

The continuity or flow of thought in this chapter is obscure. It almost seems as if Luke pieces together several disconnected subjects. However, Christ's open-

ing remarks on the peril of offending may be linked with the story of the rich man at the close of chapter 16. To live in luxury, complacency, and ease could very well prove to be a stumblingblock to others who are young in the faith. Especially if a man has the reputation of being a Christian, his example will be followed by others. How serious it is to thus lead promising followers of the Lord Jesus Christ into lives of materialism and the worship of mammon.

Of course, the principle applies in a very general way. **Little ones** can be stumbled by being encouraged in worldliness. They can be stumbled by being involved in sexual sin. They can be stumbled by any teaching that waters down the plain meaning of the Scriptures. Anything that leads them away from a pathway of simple faith, of devotedness, and of holiness is a stumbling block.

Knowing human nature and conditions in the world, the Lord said that it was inevitable that **offenses should come**. But this does not diminish the guilt of those who cause the offenses. **It would be better for** such that **a millstone were hung around** their **neck**, and that they were drowned in the depths of **the sea**. It seems clear that language as strong as this is intended to picture not only physical death but eternal condemnation as well.

When the Lord Jesus speaks of offending **one of these little ones**, He probably included more than children. The reference also seems to be to disciples who are young in the faith.

B. Concerning the Need for a Forgiving Spirit (17:3, 4)

In the Christian life there is not only the peril of offending others. There is also the danger of harboring grudges, of refusing to forgive when an offending person apologizes. That is what the Lord deals with here. The NT teaches the following procedure in connection with this subject:

1. If a Christian is wronged by another Christian, he should first of all forgive the offender in his heart (Eph. 4:32). This keeps his own soul free from resentment and malice.

2. Then he should go to the offender pri-

vately and **rebuke him** (v. 3; also Matt. 18:15). **If he repents**, then he should be told that he is forgiven. Even if he sins repeatedly, then says that he repents, he should be forgiven (v. 4).

3. If a private rebuke does not prove effective, then the person who has been wronged should take one or two witnesses (Matt. 18:16). If he will not listen to these, then the matter should be taken before the church. Failure to hear the church should result in excommunication (Matt. 18:17).

The purpose of rebukes and other disciplinary action is not to get even or to humiliate the offender, but to restore him to fellowship with the Lord and with his brothers. All rebukes should be delivered in a spirit of love. We have no way of judging whether an offender's repentance is genuine. We must accept his own word that he has repented. That is why Jesus says: **"And if he sins against you seven times in a day, and seven times in a day returns to you saying, 'I repent,' you shall forgive him."** This is the gracious way our Father treats us. No matter how often we fail Him, we still have the assurance that "If we confess our sins, He is faithful and just to forgive us our sins, and to cleanse us from all unrighteousness" (1 Jn. 1:9).

C. Concerning Faith (17:5, 6)

17:5 The thought of forgiving seven times in a single day presented a difficulty, if not an impossibility to **the apostles**. They felt they were not sufficient for such a display of grace. And so they asked **the Lord** to **increase** their **faith**.

17:6 The reply of **the Lord** indicated that it was not so much a matter of the quantity of faith but of its quality. Also it was not a question of getting more faith but of using the faith they had. It is our own pride and self-importance that prevent us from forgiving our brothers. That pride needs to be rooted up and cast out. If **faith** the size of **a mustard seed** can root up a **mulberry tree** and plant it **in the sea**, it can more easily give us victory over the hardness and unbrokenness which keep us from forgiving a brother indefinitely.

D. Concerning Profitable Servants (17:7–10)

17:7–9 The true bondslave of Christ has no reason for pride. Self-importance must be plucked out by the roots and in its place there must be a true sense of unworthiness. This is the lesson we find in the story of the bondslave. This **servant** has been **plowing or tending sheep** all day. **When he has come in from the field** at the end of a day of hard work, the master does not tell him to **sit down** for supper. **Rather** he orders **him** to put on his apron and **serve supper**. Only after that is done is the slave allowed to **eat** his own meal. The master does not **thank** him for doing these things. It is expected of a slave. After all, a slave belongs to his master and his primary duty is to obey.

17:10 So disciples are bondslaves of the Lord Jesus Christ. They belong to Him — spirit, soul, and body. In the light of Calvary, nothing they can ever do for the Savior is sufficient to recompense Him for what He has done. So after the disciple has **done** everything that he has been **commanded** in the NT, he must still admit that he is an **unprofitable** servant who has only **done what was** his **duty to do.**

According to Roy Hession, the five marks of a bondservant are:

1. He must be willing to have one thing on top of another put upon him, without any consideration being given him.
2. In doing this, he must be willing not to be thanked for it.
3. Having done all this, he must not charge the master with selfishness.
4. He must confess that he is an unprofitable servant.
5. He must admit that doing and bearing what he has in the way of meekness and humility, he has not done one stitch more than it was his duty to do.[50]

E. Jesus Cleanses Ten Lepers (17:11–19)

17:11 The sin of unthankfulness is another peril in the life of the disciple. This is illustrated in the story of the ten lepers. We read that the Lord Jesus was traveling toward **Jerusalem** along the borders of **Samaria and Galilee.**

17:12–14 As He entered a certain village, . . . ten men who were lepers saw Him. Because of their diseased condition, they did not come near to Him, but they did cry out from a distance, pleading for Him to heal them. He rewarded their faith by telling them to **go** and **show** themselves **to the priests.** This meant that when they reached the priest, they would have been healed from the leprosy. The priest had no power to heal them, but he was designated as the one to *pronounce* them clean. Obedient to the word of the Lord, the lepers started out toward the priests' dwelling, and **as they went, they were** miraculously **cleansed** from the disease.

17:15–18 They all had faith to be healed but only **one** out of the ten turned back to thank the Lord. This **one,** interestingly enough, **was a Samaritan,** one of the despised neighbors of the Jewish people with whom they had no dealings. He **fell down on his face** — the true posture of worship — and **at the feet** of Jesus — the true place of worship. **Jesus** asked if it were **not** true that **ten** had been **cleansed,** but that only one, **"this foreigner,"** had returned to give thanks. **Where** were **the** other **nine?** None of them came back **to give glory to God.**

17:19 Turning to the Samaritan, the Lord Jesus said, **"Arise, go your way. Your faith has made you well."** Only the grateful ten percent inherit Christ's true riches. Jesus meets our turning back (v. 15) and our giving thanks (v. 16) with fresh blessings. **"Your faith has made you well"** suggests that whereas the nine were cleansed from leprosy, the tenth was also saved from sin!

F. Concerning the Coming of the Kingdom (17:20–37)

17:20, 21 It is hard to know whether **the Pharisees** were sincere in the question about **the kingdom,** or just mocking. But we do know that, as Jews, they entertained hopes of a kingdom which would be ushered in with great power and glory. They looked for outward signs and great political upheavals. The Savior told them, **"The kingdom of God does not come with observation,"** that is, in its present form at least, God's realm did **not come with** outward show. It was not a visible, earthly, temporal kingdom which could be pointed out as being **here** or **there.** Rather, the Savior said, **the kingdom of God** was **within** them, or better, *among* them. The Lord Jesus could not have meant that the kingdom was actually inside the hearts of the Pharisees, because these hardened religious hypocrites had no room in their hearts for Christ the King. But He meant that **the kingdom of God** was in their midst. He was the rightful King of Israel and had performed His miracles, and presented His credentials for all to see. But the Pharisees had no desire to receive Him. And so for them, the kingdom of God had presented itself and was completely unnoticed by them.

17:22 Speaking to the Pharisees, the Lord described the kingdom as something that had already come. When He turned **to the disciples,** He spoke about the kingdom as a future event which would be set up at His Second Coming. But first He described the period that would intervene between His First and Second Advents. **The days** would **come when** the disciples would **desire to see one of the days of the Son of Man,** but would **not see it.** In other words, they would long for **one of the days** when He was with them on earth and they enjoyed sweet fellowship with Him. Those days were, in a sense, foretastes of the time He would return in power and great glory.

17:23, 24 Many false christs would arise, and rulers would announce that the Messiah had come. But His followers were not to be deceived by any such false alarms. Christ's Second Advent would be as visible and unmistakable as **the lightning** which streaks from one part of the sky to the other.

17:25 Again the Lord Jesus told the disciples that before any of this could come to pass, **He** Himself would **suffer many things and be rejected by** that **generation.**

17:26, 27 Turning back to the subject of His coming to reign, the Lord taught that **the days** immediately preceding that glorious event would be like **the days of Noah.** People **ate, they drank, they married,** and **were given in mar-**

riage. These things are not wrong; they are normal, legitimate human activities. The evil was that men lived for these things and had no thought or time for God. After **Noah** and his family **entered the ark, the flood came and destroyed** the rest of the population. So the Second Coming of Christ would mean judgment for those who reject His offer of mercy.

17:28–30   Again, the Lord said that the days preceding His Second Advent would be similar to those **of Lot**. Civilization had advanced somewhat by that time; men not only **ate** and **drank**, but **they bought, they sold, they planted, they built**. It was man's effort to bring in a golden era of peace and prosperity without God. **On the** very **day that Lot**, his wife and daughters **went out of Sodom, it rained fire and brimstone from heaven and destroyed** the wicked city. **So will it be in the day when the Son of Man is revealed**. Those who concentrate on pleasure, self-gratification, and commerce will be destroyed.

17:31   It will be a **day** when attachment to earthly things will imperil a man's life. If he is **on the housetop**, he should **not** try to salvage any possessions from his **house**. If he is out **in the field**, he should **not turn back** to his house. He should flee from those places where judgment is about to fall.

17:32   Although **Lot's wife** was taken almost by force out of Sodom, her heart remained in the city. This was indicated by the fact that she turned back. She was out of Sodom, but Sodom was not out of her. As a result, God destroyed her by turning her into a pillar of salt.

17:33   Whoever **seeks to save his life** by caring only for physical safety, but not caring for his soul, **will lose it**. On the other hand anyone who **loses his life** during this period of tribulation because of faithfulness to the Lord **will** actually **preserve it** for all eternity.

17:34–36[51]   The Lord's coming will be a time of separation. **Two men** will be sleeping **in one bed. One will be taken** away in judgment. **The other**, a believer, **will be** spared to enter Christ's kingdom. **Two women will be grinding together; the one**, an unbeliever, **will be taken** away in the storm of God's wrath; **the other**, a child of God, will be spared

to enjoy millennial blessings with Christ.

Incidentally, verses 34 and 35 accord with the rotundity of the earth. The fact that it will be night in one part of the earth and day in another, as indicated by the activities mentioned, displays scientific knowledge not discovered till many years later.

17:37   The disciples fully understood from the Savior's words that His Second Advent would be catastrophic judgment from heaven on an apostate world. So they asked the **Lord where** this judgment would fall. His answer was that **wherever the carcass is, there the eagles will be gathered together. The eagles** or vultures symbolize impending judgments. The answer therefore is that judgments would swoop down on every form of unbelief and rebellion against God, no matter where found.

In chapter 17, the Lord Jesus had warned the disciples that afflictions and persecutions lay ahead. Before the time of His glorious appearing, they would be required to go through deep trials. By way of preparation, the Savior gives further instruction concerning prayer. In the following verses, we find a praying widow, a praying Pharisee, a praying tax-collector, and a praying beggar.

G. The Parable of the Persistent Widow (18:1–8)

18:1   The **parable** of the praying widow teaches **that men always ought to pray and not lose heart**. This is true in a general sense of all men, and of all kinds of prayer. But the special sense in which it is used here is prayer for God's deliverance in times of testing. It is praying without losing **heart** during the long, weary interval between Christ's First and Second Comings.

18:2, 3   The parable pictures an unrighteous **judge** who was ordinarily quite unmoved by fear of **God** or **regard** for his fellow **man. There was** also a **widow** who was being oppressed by some unnamed **adversary**. This **widow came to** the judge persistently, asking him for **justice**, so that she might be delivered from his inhumane treatment.

18:4, 5   The judge was unmoved by the validity of her case; the fact that she was being treated unjustly did not move him to action in her behalf. However, the regularity with which she came before him prompted him to act. Her importunity and persistence brought a decision in her favor.

18:6, 7 Then the Lord explained to the disciples that if an **unjust judge** would act in behalf of a poor widow because of her importunity, how much more will the just **God** intervene in behalf of **His own elect**. The **elect** here might refer in a special sense to the Jewish remnant during the Tribulation Period, but it is also true of all oppressed believers in every age. The reason God has not intervened long ago is because He is longsuffering with men, not willing that any should perish.

18:8 But the day is coming when His spirit will no longer strive with men, and then **He will** punish those who persecute His followers. The Lord Jesus closed the parable with the question, **"Nevertheless, when the Son of Man comes, will He really find faith on the earth?"** This probably means the *kind* of faith that the poor widow had. But it may also indicate that when the Lord returns, there will only be a remnant who are true to Him. In the meantime, each of us should be stimulated to the kind of faith that cries to God night and day.

H. Parable of the Pharisee and the Tax Collector (18:9–14)

18:9–12 The next **parable** is addressed to people who pride **themselves** on being **righteous**, and who despise all **others** as inferior. By labeling the first man as **a Pharisee**, the Savior did not leave any doubt as to the particular class of people He was addressing. Although the Pharisee went through the motions of prayer, he was really not speaking to **God**. He was rather boasting of his own moral and religious attainments. Instead of comparing himself with God's perfect standard and seeing how sinful he really was, he compared himself with others in the community and prided himself on being better. His frequent repetition of the personal pronoun **I** reveals the true state of his heart as conceited and self-sufficient.

18:13 The tax collector was a striking contrast. **Standing** before God, he sensed his own utter unworthiness. He

was humbled to the dust. He **would not so much as raise his eyes to heaven, but beat his breast** and cried to **God** for mercy: **"God be merciful to me a** (literally "the") **sinner!"** He did not think of himself as one sinner among many, but as *the* sinner who was unworthy of anything from God.

18:14 The Lord Jesus reminded His hearers that it is this spirit of self-humiliation and repentance that is acceptable to God. Contrary to what human appearances might indicate, it was the tax collector who **went down to his house justified**. God exalts the humble, but He humbles those who exalt themselves.

I. Jesus and the Little Children (18:15–17)

This incident reinforces what we have just had before us, namely, that the humility of a little child is necessary for entrance into **the kingdom of God**. Mothers crowded around the Lord Jesus with their **infants** in order that they might receive blessing from Him. **His disciples** were annoyed by this intrusion into the Savior's time. But Jesus **rebuked them**, and tenderly **called . . . the little children** to Himself, saying, **"Of such is the kingdom of God."** Verse 16 answers the question, "What happens to little children when they die?" The answer is that they go to heaven. The Lord clearly said **"of such is the kingdom of God."**

Children can be saved at a very tender age. That age probably varies in the case of individual children, but the fact remains that any child, no matter how young, who wishes to come to Jesus should be permitted to do so, and encouraged in his faith.

Little children do not need to become adults in order to be saved, but adults do need the simple faith and humility of **a little child** in order to **enter** God's **kingdom**.

J. The Rich Young Ruler (18:18–30)

18:18, 19 This section illustrates the case of a man who would **not** receive the kingdom of God as a little child. One day **a certain ruler** came to the Lord Jesus, addressing Him as **Good Teacher**, and asking **what** he must **do** in order to **inherit eternal life**. The Savior first of all questioned him on the use of the title *good Teacher*. Jesus reminded him that only **God** is **good**. Our Lord was not denying that He was God, but He was trying to lead the ruler to confess that fact. If He was good, then He must be God, since only God is essentially good.

18:20 Then Jesus dealt with the question, what must I do to inherit eternal life? We know that eternal life is not inherited, and is not gained by doing good works. Eternal life is the gift of God through Jesus Christ. In taking the ruler back to **the ten commandments**, the Lord Jesus was not implying that he could ever be saved by keeping the law. Rather He was using the law in an effort to convict the man of sin. The Lord Jesus recited **the** five **commandments** which have to do with our duty to our fellowman, the second table of the law.

18:21–23 It is apparent that the law did not have its convicting effect in the life of the man, because he arrogantly claimed to **have kept** these commandments **from** his **youth**. Jesus told him that he lacked **one thing** — love for his neighbor. If he had really kept these commandments, then he would have sold **all** his possessions and distributed them **to the poor**. But the fact of the matter was that he did not love his neighbor as himself. He was living a selfish life, with no real love for others. This is proved by the fact that **when he heard** these things, **he became very sorrowful**, because **he was very rich.**

18:24 As the Lord **Jesus** looked upon him, He commented on the difficulty of **those who have riches** entering **the kingdom of God**. The difficulty is in having riches without loving and trusting them.

This whole section raises disturbing questions for Christians as well as unbelievers. How can we be said truly to love our neighbors when we live in wealth and comfort when others are perishing for want of the gospel of Christ?

18:25 Jesus said that **it is easier for a camel to go through the eye of a needle than for a rich man to enter the kingdom of God**. Many explanations have been given of this statement. Some have suggested that the needle's eye is a small inner gate in the wall of a city, and that a camel could enter only by

kneeling down. However, Dr. Luke uses a word that specifically means a surgeon's needle and the meaning of the Lord's statement seems to lie on the surface. In other words, just as it is *impossible* **for a camel to go through the eye of a needle**, so it is *impossible* **for a rich man to enter the kingdom of God**. It is not enough to explain this as meaning that a rich man cannot, by his own efforts, enter the kingdom; that is true of rich and poor alike. The meaning is that it is *impossible* for a man to **enter the kingdom of God** *as a rich man*; as long as he makes a god of his wealth, lets it stand between himself and his soul's salvation, he cannot be converted. The simple fact of the matter is that not many rich people are saved, and those who are must first be broken before God.

18:26, 27 As the disciples thought about all of this, they began to wonder **who then** could **be saved**. To them, riches had always been a sign of God's blessing (Deut. 28:1–8). If rich Jews aren't saved, then who can be? The Lord answered that **God** could do what man cannot do. In other words, God can take a greedy, grasping, ruthless materialist, remove his love for gold, and substitute for it a true love for the Lord. It is a miracle of divine grace.

Again, this whole section raises disturbing questions for the child of God. The servant is not above his Master; the Lord Jesus abandoned His heavenly riches in order to save our guilty souls. It is not fitting for us to be rich in a world where He was poor. The value of souls, the imminence of Christ's return, the constraining love of Christ should lead us to invest every possible material asset in the work of the Lord.

18:28–30 When **Peter** reminded the Lord that the disciples had **left** their homes and families to follow Him, the Lord replied that such a life of sacrifice is rewarded liberally in this life, and will be further rewarded in the eternal state. The latter part of verse 30 (**and in the age to come eternal life**) does not mean that eternal life is gained by forsaking all; rather it refers to increased capacity for enjoying the glories of heaven, plus increased rewards in the heavenly kingdom. It means "the full realization of the life that had been received at the time of conversion, i.e., life in its fulness."

K. Jesus Again Predicts His Death and Resurrection (18:31–34)

18:31–33 For the third time the Lord **took the twelve** and warned them in detail what awaited Him (see 9:22, 44). He predicted His passion as being in fulfillment of what **the prophets** of the OT had **written**. With divine foresight, He calmly prophesied that **He** would **be delivered to the Gentiles**. "It was more probable that He would be privately slain, or stoned to death in a tumult."[52] But the prophets had foretold His betrayal, His being **mocked and insulted and spit upon**, and so it must be. He would be scourged and killed, but **the third day He** would **rise again**.

The remaining chapters unfold the drama which He so wonderfully foreknew and foretold:

We are going up to Jerusalem (18:35–19:45).

The Son of Man **will be delivered to the Gentiles** (19:47-23:1).

He **will be mocked and insulted** (23:1–32).

They **will kill Him** (23:33–56).

The third day He will rise again (24:1–12).

18:34 Amazingly enough, the disciples **understood none of these things**. The meaning of His words **was hidden from them**. It seems hard for us to understand why they were so dull in this matter, but the reason is probably this: Their minds were so filled with thoughts of a temporal deliverer who would rescue them from the yoke of Rome, and set up the kingdom immediately, that they refused to entertain any other program. We often believe what we *want* to believe, and resist the truth if it does not fit into our *preconceived* notions.

L. The Healing of a Blind Beggar (18:35–43)

18:35–37 The Lord Jesus had now left Perea by crossing the Jordan. Luke says the incident that follows **happened as He was coming near Jericho**. Matthew and Mark say that it is when He was *leaving* Jericho (Matt. 20:29; Mark 10:46). Also Matthew says that there were two blind men; Mark and Luke both say there was one. It is possible

that Luke is speaking of the new city whereas Matthew and Mark are referring to the old city. It is also possible that there was more than one miracle of the blind receiving their sight at this place. Whatever the true explanation might be, we are confident that if our knowledge were greater, the seeming contradictions would disappear.

18:38 The blind beggar somehow recognized **Jesus** as the Messiah, because he addressed Him as the **Son of David**. He asked the Lord to **have mercy on** him, that is, to restore his sight.

18:39 In spite of the attempts of some to silence the beggar, he insistently **cried out** to the Lord Jesus. The people were not interested in a beggar. Jesus was.

18:40, 41 So **Jesus stood still**. Darby comments insightfully, "Joshua once bade the sun stand still in the heavens, but here the *Lord* of the sun, and the moon, and the heavens, stands still at the bidding of a blind beggar." At Jesus' command the beggar was **brought to Him**. Jesus **asked** him what he wanted. Without hesitation or generalization, the beggar replied that he wanted his **sight**. His prayer was short, specific, and full of faith.

18:42, 43 Jesus then granted the request **and immediately** the man **received his sight**. Not only so, he **followed** the Lord, **glorifying God**. We may learn from this incident that we should dare to believe God for the impossible. Great faith greatly honors Him. As the poet has written:

> Thou art coming to a King,
> Large petitions with thee bring;
> For His grace and power are such,
> None can ever ask too much.
> – *John Newton*

M. The Conversion of Zacchaeus (19:1–10)

The conversion of Zacchaeus illustrates the truth of Luke 18:27 "The things which are impossible with men are possible with God." Zacchaeus was a rich man, and ordinarily it is impossible for a rich man to enter the kingdom of God. But Zacchaeus humbled himself before the Savior, and did not let his wealth come between his soul and God.

19:1–5 It was when the Lord

passed through Jericho on His third and final trip to Jerusalem that **Zacchaeus sought to see** Him; this was undoubtedly the seeking of curiosity. Although he **was a chief tax collector**, he was not ashamed to do something unconventional in order to see the Savior. Because he was **short**, he knew he would be hindered from getting a good view of Jesus. **So he ran ahead and climbed up into a sycamore tree** alongside the route the Lord was taking. This act of faith did not go unnoticed. As **Jesus** came near, **He looked up and saw** Zacchaeus. He ordered him to **come down** quickly, and invited Himself to the tax collector's **house**. This is the only case on record where the Savior invited Himself to a home.

19:6 Zacchaeus did as he was told, **and received** the Lord **joyfully**. We can almost certainly date his conversion from this time.

19:7 The Savior's critics **all complained** against Him because He went **to be a guest with a man who** was **a** known **sinner**. They overlooked the fact that, coming into a world like ours, He was limited exclusively to such homes!

19:8 Salvation had brought a radical change in the life of the tax gatherer. He informed the Savior that he now intended to **give half** his **goods to the poor**. (Up to this time, he had been gouging as much as possible from the poor.) He also planned to make **fourfold** restitution for any money he had gained dishonestly. This was more than the law demanded (Ex. 22:4, 7; Lev. 6:5; Num. 5:7). It showed that Zacchaeus was now controlled by love whereas formerly he was mastered by greed.

There was little doubt that Zacchaeus had taken things dishonestly. Wuest translates v. 8b: "And since I have wrongfully exacted . . ." No "if" about it.

It almost sounds as if Zacchaeus were boasting of his philanthropy and trusting in this for his salvation. That is not the point at all. He was saying that his new life in Christ made him desire to make restitution for the past, and that in gratitude to God for salvation, he now wanted to use his money for the glory of God and for the blessing of his neighbors.

Verse 8 is one of the strongest in the Bible on restitution. Salvation does not relieve a person from righting the wrongs of the past. Debts contracted during one's unconverted days are not canceled by the new birth. And if money was stolen before salvation, then a true sense of the grace of God requires that this money be repaid after a person has become a child of God.

19:9 Jesus plainly announced that **salvation** had **come to** the **house** of Zacchaeus, because he was **a son of Abraham**. Salvation did not come because Zacchaeus was a Jew by birth. Here the expression, "a son of Abraham" indicates more than natural descent; it means that Zacchaeus exercised the same kind of faith in the Lord that Abraham did. Also, salvation did not come to Zacchaeus's home because of his charity and restitution (v. 8). These things are the effect of salvation, not the cause.

19:10 In answer to those who criticized Him for lodging with a sinner, Jesus said, **"The Son of Man has come to seek and to save that which was lost."** In other words, the conversion of Zacchaeus was a fulfillment of the very purpose of Christ's coming into the world.

N. Parable of the Ten Minas (19:11–27)

19:11 As the Savior neared **Jerusalem** from Jericho, many of His followers **thought the kingdom of God would appear immediately**. In the **parable** of the ten minas,[53] He disabused them of such hopes. He showed that there would be an interval between His First and Second Advents during which His disciples were to be busy for Him.

19:12, 13 The parable of the **nobleman** had an actual parallel in the history of Archelaus. He was chosen by Herod to be his successor but was rejected by the people. He went away to Rome to have his appointment confirmed, then returned, rewarded his servants, and destroyed his enemies.

In the parable, the Lord Jesus Himself is the **certain nobleman** who **went** to heaven to await the time when He would **return** and set up His **kingdom** on earth. The **ten servants** typify His disciples. He gave each one a mina and told them to **do business** with this mina until He came again. While there are differences in the talents and abilities of the servants of the Lord (see the parable of the talents, Matt. 25:14–30), there are some things which they have in common, such as the privileges of sharing the gospel, and representing Christ to the world, and the privilege of prayer. Doubtless the mina speaks of these.

19:14 The **citizens** represent the Jewish nation. They not only rejected Him, but even after His departure, they **sent a delegation after him, saying, "We will not have this man to reign over us."** The embassage might represent their treatment of Christ's servants such as Stephen and other martyrs.

19:15 Here the Lord is seen, in type, returning to set up His **kingdom**. Then He will reckon with those **to whom** He gave **the money**.

Believers in this present age will be reviewed as far as their service is concerned at the Judgment Seat of Christ. This takes place in heaven, following the Rapture.

The faithful Jewish remnant who will witness for Christ during the Tribulation Period will be reviewed at Christ's Second Advent. This is the judgment that seems to be primarily in view in this passage.

19:16 The **first** servant had **earned ten minas** with the one **mina** that had been entrusted to him. He had an awareness that the money was not his own (**"your mina"**) and he used it as best he could in the advancement of his master's interests.

19:17 The master praised him as being **faithful in a very little** — a reminder that after we have done our best we are unprofitable servants. His reward was to **have authority over ten cities**. Rewards for faithful service apparently are linked with rule in Christ's kingdom. The extent to which a disciple will rule is determined by the measure of his devotion and self-expenditure.

19:18, 19 The **second** servant had **earned five minas** with his original mina. His reward was to **be over five cities**.

19:20, 21 The third **came** with nothing but excuses. He returned the **mina**, carefully **kept . . . in a handkerchief**. He had earned nothing with it. Why not?

He as much as blamed the nobleman for it. He said the nobleman was **an austere man** who expected returns without expenditure. But his own words condemned him. If he thought the nobleman was like that, the least he could have done was to turn the mina over to a bank that it might earn some interest.

19:22 In quoting the words of the nobleman, Jesus did not admit that they were true. It was simply the sinful heart of the servant that blamed the master for his own laziness. But if he really believed them he should have acted accordingly.

19:23 Verse 23 seems to suggest that we should either put everything we have to work for the Lord, or turn it over to someone else who will use it for Him.

19:24–26 The nobleman's verdict on the third servant was to **take the mina from him, and give it to** the first **who** had earned the **ten minas**. If we don't use our opportunities for the Lord, they will be taken from us. On the other hand, if we are faithful in a very little, God will see that we will never lack the means to serve Him even more. It may seem unfair to some that the **mina** was given to the man who already had **ten**, but it is a fixed principle in the spiritual life that those who love Him and serve Him passionately are given ever-widening areas of opportunity. Failure to buy up the opportunities results in a loss of all.

The third servant suffered a loss of reward, but no other punishment is specified. There is apparently no question as to his salvation.

19:27 The citizens who would not have the nobleman as their ruler are denounced as **enemies** and doomed to death. This was a sad prediction of the fate of the nation that rejected the Messiah.

X. THE SON OF MAN IN JERUSALEM (19:28–21:38)[†]

A. The Triumphal Entry (19:28–40)

19:28–34 It was now the Sunday before His crucifixion. Jesus had drawn near to the eastern slope of the Mt. of Olives en route **to Jerusalem. When He drew near to Bethphage and Bethany**

[†]See p. xxiv.

... **He sent two of His disciples** into a **village** to get **a colt** for His entrance into Jerusalem. He told them exactly where they would find the animal and what **the owners** would say. After the disciples had explained their mission, the owners seemed quite willing to release their colt for use by Jesus. Perhaps they had been blessed previously by the ministry of the Lord and had offered to be of assistance to Him any time He needed it.

19:35–38 The disciples made a cushion or saddle for the Lord with **their own clothes. Many spread their clothes on the road** before Him as He ascended from the western base of the Mt. of Olives to Jerusalem. Then with one accord the followers of Jesus burst out in **praise for all the mighty works they had seen** Him do. They hailed Him as God's **King,** and chanted that the effect of His coming **was peace in heaven and glory in the highest.** It is significant that they cried **"Peace in heaven"** rather than "Peace on earth." There could not be peace on earth because the Prince of Peace had been rejected and was soon to be slain. But there would be **peace in heaven** as a result of the impending death of Christ on Calvary's cross and His ascension to heaven.

19:39, 40 The Pharisees were indignant that Jesus should be publicly honored in this way. They suggested that He should **rebuke** His **disciples.** But Jesus **answered** that such acclamation was inevitable. **If** the disciples wouldn't do it, **the stones would!** He thus rebuked the Pharisees for being more hard and unresponsive than the inanimate stones.

B. The Son of Man Weeps Over Jerusalem (19:41–44)

19:41, 42 As Jesus **drew near** to Jerusalem, He uttered a lamentation over **the city** that had missed its golden opportunity. If the people had only received Him as Messiah, it would have meant **peace** for them. But they didn't recognize that He was the source of **peace.** Now it was too late. They had already determined what they would do with the Son of God. Because of their rejection of Him, their **eyes** were blinded. Because they *would* not see Him, they *could* no longer see Him.

Pause here to reflect on the wonder of the Savior's tears. As W. H. Griffith Thomas has said, "Let us sit at Christ's feet until we learn the secret of His tears, and beholding the sins and sorrows of city and countryside, weep over them too."[54]

19:43, 44 Jesus gave a solemn preview of the siege of Titus — how that Roman general would **surround** the city, trap the inhabitants, massacre both young and old, and **level** the walls and buildings. **Not one stone** would be left **upon another.** And it was all **because** Jerusalem **did not know the time of** its **visitation.** The Lord had visited the city with the offer of salvation. But the people did not want Him. They had no room for Him in their scheme of things.

C. Second Cleansing of the Temple (19:45, 46)

Jesus had cleansed **the temple** at the outset of His public ministry (John 2:14–17). Now as His ministry rapidly drew to a close, He entered the sacred precincts and cast **out those who** were making **a house of prayer** into **a den of thieves.** The danger of introducing commercialism into the things of God is always present. Christendom today is leavened by this evil: Church bazaars and socials, organized financial drives, preaching for profit — and all in the Name of Christ.

Christ quoted Scripture (Isa. 56:7 and Jer. 7:11) to support His action. Every reformation of abuses in the church is to be built on God's Word.

D. Teaching Daily in the Temple (19:47, 48)

Jesus **was teaching daily in the temple** area — not inside the temple, but in the courts where the public was allowed. The religious leaders longed for some excuse **to destroy Him,** but **the** common **people were** still captivated by the miracle-working Nazarene. His time had not yet come. **But** soon the hour would strike, and then the **chief priests, scribes, and** Pharisees would close in for the kill.

It is now Monday. The next day, Tuesday, which was the last day of His public teaching, is described in 20:1–22:6.

E. The Son of Man's Authority Questioned (20:1–8)

20:1, 2 What a picture! The Master Teacher tirelessly proclaiming the good news in the shadow of **the temple**, and the leaders of Israel insolently challenging His right to teach. To them Jesus was a rude carpenter of Nazareth. He had little formal education, no academic degrees, no accreditation by an ecclesiastical body. What were His credentials? **Who gave** Him **this authority** to teach and preach to others and to cleanse the temple? They wanted to know!

20:3–8 Jesus **answered** by asking them a question; if they had answered correctly, they would have answered their own question. Was **the baptism of John** approved by God, or was it merely of human authority? They were caught. If they acknowledged that John preached with divine unction, then why didn't they obey his message by repenting and receiving the Messiah he proclaimed? But if they said John was just another professional preacher, they would stir up the anger of the masses, who still acknowledged **John** to be **a prophet** of God. **So they** said, "We do **not know where** John got his authority." Jesus said, *"Well, in that case, I won't tell you by whose authority I teach."* If they couldn't tell that much about John, why did they question the authority of One who was greater than John? This passage shows that the great essential in teaching God's word is to be filled with the Holy Spirit. One who has that enduement can triumph over those whose power is wrapped up in degrees, human titles, and honors.

"Where did you get your diploma? Who ordained you?" The old questions, possibly begotten of jealousy, are still being asked. The successful gospel preacher who has not trodden the theological halls of some distinguished university or elsewhere is challenged on the points of his fitness and the validity of his ordination.

F. Parable of the Wicked Vinedressers (20:9–18)

20:9–12 The insistent yearning of the heart of God over the nation of Israel is recounted once again in this **parable** of the **vineyard**. God is the **certain man** who **leased** the **vineyard** (Israel) to **vinedressers** (the leaders of the nation — see Isa. 5: 1–7). He sent servants **to the vinedressers** to get **some of the fruit** for Himself; these servants were the prophets of God, like Isaiah and John the Baptist, who sought to call Israel to repentance and faith. But Israel's rulers invariably persecuted the prophets.

20:13 Finally God sent His **beloved son**, with the express thought that **they** would **respect** Him (although God knew, of course, that Christ would be rejected). Notice that Christ distinguishes Himself from all others. They were servants; He is the Son.

20:14 True to their past history, **the vinedressers** determined to get rid of **the heir**. They wanted exclusive rights as leaders and teachers of the people — **"that the inheritance may be ours."** They would not surrender their religious position to Jesus. If they killed Him, their power in Israel would be unchallenged — or so they thought.

20:15–17 So they cast him out of the vineyard and killed him. At this point Jesus asked His Jewish hearers what **the owner of the vineyard** would **do to** such wicked **vinedressers**. In Matthew, the chief priests and elders condemned themselves by answering that he would kill them (Matt. 21:41). Here the Lord Himself supplied the answer, **"He will come and destroy those vinedressers and give the vineyard to others."** This meant that the Christ-rejecting Jews would be destroyed, and that God would take **others** into the place of privilege. The "others" may refer to the Gentiles or to regenerated Israel of the last days. The Jews recoiled at such a suggestion. **"Certainly not!" they said.** The Lord confirmed the prediction by quoting Psalm 118:22. The Jewish **builders** had **rejected** Christ, **the Stone**. They had no place in their plans for Him. But God was determined that He would have the place of preeminence, by making Him **the chief cornerstone**, a stone which is indispensable and in the place of greatest honor.

20:18 The two comings of Christ are indicated in verse 18.[55] His First Advent is depicted as a **stone** on the ground; men stumbled at His humiliation and lowliness, and they were **broken** to pieces for rejecting Him. In the second part of the verse, the stone is seen falling from heaven and grinding unbelievers to powder.

G. Rendering to Caesar and to God (20:19–26)

20:19, 20 The chief priests and the scribes realized that Jesus had been speaking against them, so they became more intent to lay hands on Him. They sent spies to trick Him into saying something for which He could be arrested and tried by the Roman governor. These spies first praised Him as one who would be faithful to God at any cost and fearless of man — hoping that He would speak against Caesar.

20:21, 22 Then they asked Him if it was right for a Jew to pay taxes to Caesar. If Jesus said no, then they would accuse Him of treason and turn Him over to the Romans for trial. If He said yes, He would alienate the Herodians (and the great mass of the Jews, for that matter).

20:23, 24 Jesus realized the plot against Himself. He asked them for a denarius; perhaps He did not own one Himself. The fact that they possessed and used these coins showed their bondage to a Gentile power. "Whose image and inscription does it have?" Jesus asked. They admitted it was Caesar's.

20:25, 26 Then Jesus silenced them with the command, "Render therefore to Caesar the things that are Caesar's, and to God the things that are God's." They were seemingly so concerned about Caesar's interests but they were not nearly so concerned about God's interests. "The money belongs to Caesar, and you belong to God. Let the world have its coins, but let God have His creatures." It is so easy to quibble over minor matters while neglecting the principal things in life. And so easy to discharge our debts to our fellow-men while robbing God of His rightful dues.

H. The Sadducees and Their Resurrection Riddle (20:27–44)

20:27 Since the attempt to trap Jesus in a political question failed, some of the Sadducees next came to Him with a theological quibble. They denied the possibility of the bodies of the dead ever

being raised again, so they sought by an extreme illustration to make the doctrine of resurrection appear ridiculous.

20:28–33 They reminded Jesus that in the Law of Moses a single man was supposed to marry his brother's widow in order to carry on the family name and preserve the family property (Deut. 25:5). A woman married seven brothers in succession, according to their story. When the seventh died, she was still childless. Then she died also. "In the resurrection, whose wife does she become?" is what they wanted to know. They thought they were so clever in propounding such an unanswerable problem.

20:34 Jesus answered that the marriage relationship was for this life only; it would not be continued in heaven. He did not say that husbands and wives would not recognize each other in heaven, but their relationship there would be on a completely different basis.

20:35 The expression "those who are counted worthy to attain that age" does not suggest that any people are personally worthy of heaven: the only worthiness sinners can have is the worthiness of the Lord Jesus Christ. "Those are counted worthy who judge themselves, who vindicate Christ, and who own that all worthiness belongs to Him."[56] The phrase resurrection from the dead refers to a resurrection of believers only. It literally means resurrection out from (Greek *ek*) the dead ones. The idea of a general resurrection in which all the dead, both saved and unsaved, are raised at one time is not found in the Bible.

20:36 The superiority of the celestial state is further indicated in verse 36. There is no more death; in that respect, men will be equal to the angels. Also they will be manifested as sons of God. Believers are sons of God already, but not to outward observance. In heaven, they will be visibly *manifested* as sons of God. The fact that they participated in the First Resurrection insures this. "We know that when He is revealed, we shall be like Him, for we shall see Him as He is" (1 Jn. 3:2). "When Christ who is our life appears, then you also will appear with Him in glory" (Col. 3:4).

20:37, 38 To prove the resurrection,

Jesus referred to Exodus 3:6 where **Moses** quoted **the Lord** as calling Himself **the God of Abraham, . . . Isaac, and . . . Jacob**. Now if the Sadducees would just stop to think, they would realize that: (1) God **is not the God of the dead but of the living**. (2) **Abraham, Isaac,** and **Jacob** were all dead. The necessary conclusion is that God must raise them from the dead. The Lord did not say "I *was* the God of Abraham . . . ," but "I *am*. . . ." The character of God, as the God of the living, demands the resurrection.

20:39–44 **Some of the scribes** had to admit the force of the argument. But Jesus was not finished; once again He appealed to God's word. In Psalm 110:1 **David** called the Messiah his **Lord**. The Jews generally agreed that the Messiah would be the **Son** of **David**. How could He be David's **Lord** and David's **Son** at the same time? The Lord Jesus Himself was the answer to the question. He was descended from David as Son of Man; yet He was David's Creator. But they were too blind to see.

I. Warning against the Scribes (20:45–47)

Then Jesus publicly warned the crowd against **the scribes**. They wore **long robes**, affecting piety. They loved to be called by distinguished titles as they walked through the **marketplaces**. They maneuvered to get **places** of prominence **in the synagogues** and at banquets. But they robbed defenseless widows of their life savings, covering up their wickedness by **long prayers**. Such hypocrisy would be punished all the more severely.

J. The Widow's Two Mites (21:1–4)

As Jesus watched **the rich putting their gifts into the treasury** of the temple, He was struck by the contrast between **the rich** and **a certain poor widow**. They gave some, but she gave **all**. In God's estimation, she gave **more than all** of them put together. They gave **out of their abundance; she** gave **out of her poverty**. They gave what cost them little or nothing; **she** gave **all the livelihood that she had**. "The gold of affluence which is given because it is not needed, God hurls to the bottomless pit;

but the copper tinged with blood He lifts and kisses into the gold of eternity."[57]

K. Outline of Future Events (21:5–11)

Verses 5–33 constitute a great prophetic discourse. Though it resembles the Olivet Discourse in Matthew 24 and 25, it is not identical. Once again we should remind ourselves that the differences in the Gospels have a deep significance.

In this discourse, we find the Lord speaking alternately of the destruction of Jerusalem in A.D. 70 and then of the conditions that will precede His Second Advent. It is an illustration of the law of double reference — His predictions soon were to have a *partial fulfillment* in the siege of Titus, but they will have a further and *complete fulfillment* at the end of the Tribulation Period.

The outline of the discourse seems to be as follows:

1. Jesus foretold the destruction of Jerusalem (vv. 5, 6).
2. The disciples asked when this would happen (v. 7).
3. Jesus first gave a general picture of events preceding His own Second Advent (vv. 8–11).
4. He then gave a picture of the fall of Jerusalem and the age that would follow (vv. 12–24).
5. Finally, He told of the signs that would precede His Second Coming, and urged His followers to live in expectation of His return (vv. 25-26).

21:5, 6 **As some** of the people were admiring the magnificence of Herod's **temple**, Jesus warned them not to be preoccupied with material **things** that would soon pass away. **The days** were coming when the temple would be completely leveled.

21:7 The disciples immediately became curious to know **when** this would happen **and what sign** would indicate its imminence. Their question undoubtedly referred exclusively to the destruction of Jerusalem.

21:8–11 The Savior's answer first seemed to take them ahead to the end of the age when the temple would again be destroyed prior to the setting up of the kingdom. There would be false messiahs and false rumors, **wars** and uprisings. There would not only be conflict among nations, but great catastrophes of nature — **earthquakes, ... famines and pestilences**, terrors, **and great signs from heaven.**

L. The Period Before the End (21:12–19)

21:12–15 In the preceding section, Jesus had described events immediately preceding the end of the age. Verse 12 is introduced by the expression **"But before all these things. . . ."** So we believe that verses 12–24 describe the period between the time of the discourse and the future Tribulation Period. His disciples would be arrested, persecuted, tried before religious and civil powers, and imprisoned. It might seem like failure and tragedy to them, but actually the Lord would overrule it to make it a **testimony** for His glory. They were not to prepare their defense in advance. In the crisis hour, God would give them special **wisdom** to say things that would completely confound their **adversaries**.

21:16–18 There would be treachery within families; unsaved **relatives** would betray Christians, and **some** would even be killed because of their stand for Christ. There is a seeming contradiction between verse 16, **"and they will put some of you to death,"** and verse 18, **"But not a hair of your head shall be lost."** It can only mean that though some would die as martyrs for Christ, their spiritual preservation would be complete. They would die but they would not perish.

21:19 Verse 19 indicates that those who patiently endure for Christ rather than renouncing Him will thus prove the reality of their faith. Those who are genuinely saved will stand true and loyal at any cost. The RSV reads, "By your endurance you will gain your lives."

M. The Doom of Jerusalem (21:20–24)

Now the Lord clearly takes up the subject of the destruction of **Jerusalem** in A.D. 70. This event would be signaled by the city's being **surrounded by** the Roman **armies**.

The Christian of an early day — the year A.D. 70 — had a specific sign to introduce the destruction of Jerusalem and the

razing of the beautiful marble temple: "When ye shall see Jerusalem compassed with armies, then know that the desolation thereof is nigh." This was to be a positive sign of the destruction of Jerusalem, and at that sign they were to flee. Unbelief might have argued that with a besieging army outside the walls, escape would be impossible; but God's Word never fails. The Roman general withdrew his armies for a short season, thus giving the believing Jews the opportunity to escape. This they did, and went out to a place called Pella, where they were preserved.[58]

Any attempt to re-enter the city would be fatal. The city was about to be punished for its rejection of the Son of God. **Pregnant** women and **nursing** mothers would be at a distinct disadvantage; they would be hindered in escaping from the judgment of God on **the land** of Israel and the Jewish **people**. Many would be slain, and the survivors would be carried off as captives in other lands.

The latter part of verse 24 is a remarkable prophecy that the ancient city of **Jerusalem** would be subject to Gentile rule from that time **until the times of the Gentiles are fulfilled**. It does not mean that the Jews might not control it for brief periods; the thought is that it would be continually subject to Gentile invasion and interference **until the times of the Gentiles are fulfilled**.

The NT distinguishes between the riches of the Gentiles, the fullness of the Gentiles, and the times of the Gentiles.

1. The *riches* of the Gentiles (Rom. 11:12) refers to the place of privilege which the Gentiles enjoy at the present time while Israel is temporarily set aside by God.
2. The *fullness* of the Gentiles (Rom. 11:25) is the time of the Rapture, when Christ's Gentile bride will be completed and taken from the earth and when God will resume His dealings with Israel.
3. The *times* of the Gentiles (Luke 21:24) really began with the Babylonian captivity, 521 B.C., and will extend to the time when Gentile nations will no longer assert control over the city of Jerusalem.

Down through the centuries from the time of the Savior's words, Jerusalem has been largely controlled by Gentile powers. Emperor Julian the Apostate (A.D. 331–363) sought to discredit Christianity by disproving this prophecy of the Lord. He therefore encouraged the Jews to rebuild the temple. They went to the work eagerly, even using silver shovels in their extravagance, and carrying the dirt in purple veils. But while they were working, they were interrupted by an earthquake and by balls of fire coming from the ground. They had to abandon the project.[59]

N. The Second Advent (21:25–28)

These verses describe the convulsions of nature and the cataclysms **on the earth** that will precede Christ's Second Advent. There will be disturbances involving **the sun . . . moon,** and **stars** that will be clearly visible on earth. Heavenly bodies will be moved out of their orbits. This might cause the earth to be tilted off its axis. There will be great tidal waves sweeping over land areas. Panic will seize mankind because of heavenly bodies on a near-collision course with the earth. But there is hope for the godly:

Then they will see the Son of Man coming in a cloud with power and great glory. Now when these things begin to happen, look up and lift up your heads, because your redemption draws near.

O. The Fig Tree and All the Trees (21:29–33)

21:29–31 Another sign indicating the nearness of His return is the **budding** of **the fig tree and all the trees. The fig tree** is an apt picture of the nation of Israel; it would begin to evidence new life in the last days. Surely it is not without significance that after centuries of dispersal and obscurity, the nation of Israel was re-established in 1948, and is now recognized as a member of the family of nations.

The shooting forth of the other trees may symbolize the phenomenal growth of nationalism and the emergence of many new governments in newly developed countries of the world. These signs would mean that Christ's glorious kingdom would soon be set up.

21:32 Jesus said that **this generation** would not **pass away till all things take place**. But what did He mean by "this generation"?

1. Some feel He referred to the generation living at the time He spoke these words, and that all things were fulfilled at the destruction of Jerusalem. But this cannot be so because Christ did not return in a cloud with power and great glory.

2. Others believe that "this generation" refers to the people living when these signs begin to take place, and that those who live to see the beginning of the signs would live to see the return of Christ. All the events predicted would happen within one generation. This is a possible explanation.

3. Another possibility is that "this generation" refers to the Jewish people in their attitude of hostility to Christ. The Lord was saying that the Jewish race would survive, scattered yet indestructible, and that its attitude toward Him would not change through the centuries. Perhaps both numbers 2 and 3 are correct.

21:33 The atmospheric and stellar heavens would **pass away**. So would the **earth** in its present form. But these predictions of the Lord Jesus would not go unfulfilled.

P. Warning to Watch and Pray (21:34–38)

21:34, 35 In the meantime, His disciples should guard against becoming so occupied with eating, drinking, and mundane **cares** that His coming might happen **unexpectedly**. That is the way **it will come on all those who** think of the **earth** as their permanent dwelling place.

21:36 True disciples should **watch** and **pray** at all times, thus separating themselves from the ungodly world which is doomed to experience the wrath of God, and identifying themselves with those who will **stand** in acceptance **before the Son of Man**.

21:37, 38 Each day the Lord taught **in the temple** area, **but at night He** slept **on the** Mt. of Olives, homeless in the world He had made. **Then early in the morning all the people** crowded around **Him** afresh **to hear Him**.

XI. THE SON OF MAN'S PASSION AND DEATH (Chaps. 22, 23)

A. The Plot to Kill Jesus (22:1, 2)

22:1 **The Feast of Unleavened Bread** here refers to the period beginning with the **Passover** and extending for seven more days during which no leavened bread was eaten. The Passover was held on the fourteenth of the month Nisan, the first month of the Jewish year. The seven days from the fifteenth of the month to the twenty-first were known as **the Feast of Unleavened Bread**, but in verse 1, that name takes in the entire feast. If Luke had been writing primarily to Jews, it would not have been necessary for him to mention the connection between **the Feast of Unleavened Bread** and the **Passover**.

22:2 **The chief priests and scribes** were ceaselessly plotting **how they might kill** the Lord Jesus, but they realized that they must do it without causing a tumult, because **they feared the people**, and knew that many still held Jesus in high esteem.

B. The Treachery of Judas (22:3-6)

22:3 **Satan entered Judas, surnamed Iscariot**, one of **the twelve** disciples. In John 13:27, this action is said to have taken place after Jesus had handed him the piece of bread during the Passover meal. We conclude either that this took place in successive stages, or that Luke is emphasizing the fact rather than the exact time when it took place.

22:4-6 At any rate, Judas made a bargain **with the chief priests and captains**, that is, the commanders of the Jewish temple guard. He had carefully worked out a plan by which he could **betray** Jesus into their hands without causing a riot. The plan was entirely acceptable, and they **agreed to give him money** — thirty pieces of silver, as we learn elsewhere. So Judas left to work out the details of his treacherous scheme.

C. Preparations for the Passover (22:7-13)

22:7 There are definite problems in connection with the various time periods mentioned in these verses. **The Day of Unleavened Bread** would normally be thought of as the thirteenth of Nisan when all leavened bread had to be put away from a Jewish home. But here it says it was the day on which **the Passover must be** sacrificed, and that would make it the fourteenth of Nisan. Leon Morris, along with other scholars, suggests that two calendars were used for the Passover, an official one and one followed by Jesus and others.[60] We believe that the events of the final Thursday begin here and continue through verse 53.

22:8-10 The Lord **sent Peter and John** into Jerusalem to make preparations for the celebration of **the Passover** meal. He showed His complete knowledge of all things in His instructions to them. Once inside **the city, a man** would **meet** them **carrying a pitcher of water**. This was an unusual sight in an eastern city; it was ordinarily the women who carried the pitchers of water. The man here makes a good picture of the Holy Spirit, who leads seeking souls to the place of communion with the Lord.

22:11-13 The Lord not only foreknew the location and route of this man, but He also knew that a certain homeowner would be willing to make his **large, furnished upper room** available to Him and His **disciples**. Perhaps this man knew the Lord and had made a total commitment of his person and possessions to Him. There is a difference between the **guest room** and **the large, furnished upper room**. The generous host provided better facilities than the disciples expected. When Jesus was born in Bethlehem, there was no room for Him in the inn (Gk: *kataluma*). Here He told His disciples to ask for **a guest room** (Gk: *kataluma*), but they were given something better — **a large, furnished upper room**.

Everything was as He had predicted, so the disciples **prepared the Passover**.

D. The Last Passover (22:14-18)

22:14 For centuries, the Jews had celebrated the Passover feast, commemorating their glorious deliverance from Egypt and from death through the blood of the spotless lamb. How vividly this must all have come before the mind of the Savior as **He sat down** with His **apostles** to keep the feast for the last time. He was the true Passover Lamb whose blood would soon be shed for the salvation of all who would trust in Him.

22:15, 16 **This** particular **Passover** held inexpressible meaning for Him, and He had ardently **desired** it **before** He was to **suffer**. He would not keep the Passover again till He returned to earth and set up His glorious **kingdom**. The construction **"With fervent desire I have desired"** carries the sense of ardent, passionate longing. These revealing words invite all believers of every time and place to consider how passionately Jesus longs for communion with us at His table.

22:17, 18 When **He took the cup** of wine as part of the Passover ritual, He **gave thanks** for it and passed it to the disciples, reminding them once again that He would **not drink of the fruit of the vine** again **until** His Millennial Reign. The description of the Passover meal ends with verse 18.

E. The First Lord's Supper (22:19–23)

22:19, 20 The last Passover was immediately followed by the Lord's Supper. The Lord Jesus instituted this sacred memorial so that His followers down through the centuries would thus remember Him in His death. He first of all gave them **bread**, a symbol of His **body** which would shortly be **given for** them. Then **the cup** spoke eloquently of His precious **blood** which would be shed on the cross of Calvary. He spoke of it as **the cup** of **the new covenant in** His **blood, which** was **shed for** His own. This means that **the new covenant**, which He made primarily with the nation of Israel, was ratified by His **blood**. The complete fulfillment of the New Covenant will take place during the kingdom of our Lord Jesus Christ on earth, but we as believers enter into the good of it at the present time.

It should go without saying that the bread and wine were typical or *representative of* His body and blood. His body had not yet been given, neither had His blood been shed. Therefore it is absurd to suggest that the symbols were miraculously changed into the realities. The Jewish people were forbidden to eat blood, and the disciples knew therefore that He was not speaking of literal blood, but of that which *typified* His blood.

22:21 It seems clear that Judas was actually present at the last supper. However, in John 13, it appears equally clear that the betrayer left the room after Jesus had handed the piece of bread dipped in the gravy to him. Since this took place before the institution of the Lord's Supper, many believe that Judas was not actually present when the bread and the wine were passed.

22:22 The sufferings and death of the Lord Jesus were **determined**, but Judas betrayed Him with the full consent of his will. That is why Jesus said, **"Woe to that man by whom He is betrayed."** Though Judas was one of the twelve, he was not a true believer.

22:23 Verse 23 reveals something of the surprise and self-distrust of the disciples. They did not know **which of them** would be guilty of **this** dastardly **thing**.

F. True Greatness Is Serving (22:24–30)

22:24, 25 It is a terrible indictment of the human heart that immediately after the Lord's Supper, the disciples should argue **among** themselves **as to which of them** was **the greatest**! The Lord Jesus reminded **them** that in His economy, greatness was the very opposite of man's idea. **The kings** who ruled over **the Gentiles** were commonly thought of as great persons; in fact they were **called "benefactors"**. But it was only a title; actually they were cruel tyrants. They had the name of goodness, but no personal characteristics to match it.

22:26 It was **not** to be **so** of the followers of the Savior. Those who would be great should take the place of **the younger**. And those who would be chief should stoop in lowly service to others. These revolutionary dicta completely reversed the accepted traditions of the younger being inferior to the elder, and the chief manifesting greatness by mastery.

22:27 In men's estimation, it was greater to be a guest at a meal than to serve the meal. But the Lord Jesus came as a servant of men, and all who would follow Him must imitate Him in this.

22:28–30 It was gracious of the Lord to commend the disciples for having **continued with** Him **in** His **trials**. They had just been quarreling among themselves. Very soon they would all forsake Him and flee. And yet He knew that in their hearts, they loved Him and had endured reproach for His name's sake. Their reward would be to **sit on thrones judging the twelve tribes of Israel** when Christ returns to take the throne of David and rule over the earth. Just as surely as the Father had promised this kingdom to Christ, so surely would they reign with Him over renewed Israel.

G. Jesus Predicts Peter's Denial (22:31–34)

Now comes the last in a series of three dark chapters in the history of human faithlessness. The first was the treachery of Judas. The second was the selfish ambition of the disciples. Now we have the cowardice of Peter.

22:31, 32 The repetition **Simon, Simon**, speaks of the love and tenderness of the heart of Christ for His vacillating disciple. **Satan** had **asked** to have all the disciples that he might **sift** them **as wheat**. Jesus addressed Peter as representative of all. **But** the Lord had **prayed for** Simon **that** his **faith** might not suffer an eclipse. (**"I have prayed for you"** are tremendous words.) After he had **returned** to Him, he should **strengthen** his **brethren**. This turning back does not refer to salvation but rather to restoration from backsliding.

22:33, 34 With unbecoming self-confidence, Peter expressed readiness to accompany Jesus **to prison and to death**. But he had to be told that **before** the morning light had fully dawned, he would **deny three times that** he even knew the Lord!

In Mark 14:30, the Lord is quoted as saying that before the rooster crows twice, Peter would deny Him three times. In Matthew 26:34; Luke 22:34; John 13:38, the Lord said that before the rooster crows, Peter would deny Him three times. It is admittedly difficult to reconcile this seeming contradiction. It is possible that there was more than one cock-crowing, one during the night and another at dawn. Also it should be noticed that the Gospels record at least six different denials by Peter. He denied Christ before:

1. A young woman (Matt. 26:69, 70; Mark 14:66–68).
2. Another young woman (Matt. 26:71, 72).
3. The crowd that stood by (Matt. 26:73, 74; Mark 14:70, 71).
4. A man (Luke 22:58).
5. Another man (Luke 22:59, 60).
6. A servant of the high priest (John 18:26, 27). This man is probably different from the others because of what he said — "Did I not see you in the garden with him?" (v. 26).

H. New Marching Orders (22:35–38)

22:35 Earlier in His ministry, the Lord **sent** the disciples out **without money bag, knapsack, and sandals** — the minimum. Bare essentials would be sufficient for them. And so it had proved. They had to confess that they had lacked **nothing**.

22:36 But now He was about to leave them, and they were to enter into a new phase of service for Him. They would be exposed to poverty, hunger, and danger, and it would be necessary for them to make provision for their current needs. They should now take **a money bag**, a **knapsack** or lunch box, and in the absence of a **sword**, they should **sell** their **garment and buy one**. What did the Savior mean when He told the disciples to **buy** a **sword**? It seems clear that He could not have intended them to use the sword as an offensive weapon against other people. This would be in violation of His teaching in such passages as:

"My kingdom is not of this world. If My kingdom were of this world, My servants would fight" (John 18:36).

"All who take the sword will perish by the sword" (Matt. 26:52).

"Love your enemies . . . " (Matt. 5:44).

"Whoever slaps you on your right cheek, turn the other to him also" (Matt. 5:39; see also 2 Cor. 10:4.)

What then did Jesus mean by the sword?

1. Some suggest that He was referring

to the sword of the Spirit which is the Word of God (Eph. 6:17). This is possible, but then the money bag, the knapsack, and the garment should be spiritualized also.

2. Williams says that the sword means the protection of an ordered government, pointing out that in Romans 13:4, it refers to the power of the magistrate.

3. Lange says the sword is for defense against human enemies, but not for offense. But Matthew 5:39 seems to rule out the use of the sword, even for defensive purposes.

4. Some think that the sword was for defense against wild animals only. This is possible.

22:37 Verse 37 explains why it was necessary for the disciples to take money bag, knapsack, and sword now. The Lord had been with them up to this point, providing for their temporal needs. Soon He would be departing from them in accordance with the prophecy of Isaiah 53:12. The things concerning Him had **an end**, that is, His earthly life and ministry would come to a close by His being **numbered with the transgressors**.

22:38 The disciples completely misunderstood the Lord. They brought forth **two swords**, implying that these would surely be enough for any problems that lay ahead. The Lord Jesus ended the conversation by saying **"It is enough."** They apparently thought that they could foil the attempt of His enemies to slay Him by using the swords. This was the farthest thought from His mind!

I. The Agony in Gethsemane (22:39–46)

22:39 The Garden of Gethsemane was situated on the western slope of **the Mount of Olives**. Jesus often went there to pray, and the **disciples**, including the betrayer, of course, knew this.

22:40 At the conclusion of the Lord's Supper, Jesus and the disciples left the upper room and went to the garden. Once they were there, He warned them to **pray that** they should **not enter into temptation**. Perhaps the particular **temptation** which He had in mind was the pressure to abandon God and His Christ when the enemies closed in.

22:41, 42 Then Jesus left the disciples and went further into the garden where He **prayed** alone. His prayer was that **if** the **Father** were willing, **this cup** might pass from Him; **nevertheless** He wanted the **will** of God to be done, **not** His own. We understand this prayer to mean: If there is any other way by which sinners can be saved than by My going to the cross, reveal that way now. The heavens were silent, because there *was* no other way.

We do not believe that Christ's sufferings in the garden were part of His atoning work. The work of redemption was accomplished during the three hours of darkness on the cross. But Gethsemane was in anticipation of Calvary. There the very thought of contact with our sins caused the Lord Jesus the keenest suffering.

22:43, 44 His perfect humanity is seen in the **agony** which accompanied His travail. **An angel appeared to Him from heaven, strengthening Him**. Only Luke records this, as well as the fact that **His sweat became like great drops of blood**. This latter detail caught the interest of the careful physician.

22:45, 46 When Jesus returned to **His disciples**, they were **sleeping**, not from indifference, but rather from sorrowful exhaustion. Once again He urged them to **rise and pray**, because the crisis hour was drawing near, and they would be tempted to deny Him before the authorities.

J. Jesus Betrayed and Arrested (22:47–53)

22:47, 48† By now, **Judas** had arrived with a group of the chief priests, elders, and captains of the temple to arrest the Lord. By prearrangement, the traitor was to mark out Jesus by kissing Him. Stewart comments:

> It was the crowning touch of horror, the last point of infamy beyond which human infamy could not go, when out in the garden Judas betrayed his master, not with a shout or a blow or a stab, but with a kiss.[61]

With infinite pathos, **Jesus** asked, **"Judas, are you betraying the Son of Man with a kiss?"**

22:49–51 The disciples realized

what was going to happen, and were ready to take the offensive. In fact one of them, Peter to be specific, took a sword and cut off the right ear of the servant of the high priest. Jesus rebuked him for using carnal means to fight a spiritual warfare. His hour had come, and God's predetermined purposes must come to pass. Graciously, Jesus touched the ear of the victim and healed him.

22:52, 53 Turning to the Jewish leaders and officers, Jesus asked them why they had come out after Him as if He were a fugitive robber. Had He not taught daily in the temple area, yet they had not tried to take Him then? But He knew the answer, This was their hour, and the power of darkness. It was now about midnight on Thursday.

It seems that the religious trial of our Lord had three stages. First, He appeared before Annas. Then He appeared before Caiaphas. Finally He was arraigned before the Sanhedrin. The events from this point through verse 65 probably took place between 1:00 a.m. and 5:00 a.m. on Friday.

K. Peter Denies Jesus and Weeps Bitterly (22:54–62)

22:54–57 When the Lord was brought into the high priest's house, Peter followed at a distance. Inside, he took his place with those who were warming themselves at a fire in the center of the courtyard. A servant girl looked across at Peter and exclaimed that he was one of the followers of Jesus. Pathetically Peter denied that he knew Him.

22:58–62 Shortly afterwards, someone else pointed the accusing finger at Peter as one of the followers of Jesus of Nazareth. Again Peter denied the charge. After about an hour, someone else recognized Peter as a Galilean, and also as a disciple of the Lord. Peter denied any knowledge of what the man was talking about. But this time his denial was punctuated by the crowing of the rooster. In that dark moment, the Lord turned and looked at Peter, and Peter remembered the prediction that before the rooster crows, he would deny Him three times. The look from the Son of God sent Peter out into the night to weep bitterly.

L. The Soldiers Mock the Son of Man (22:63–65)

It was the officers assigned to the sacred temple in Jerusalem who had apprehended Jesus. Now these supposed guardians of God's holy house began to mock Jesus and to beat Him. After blindfolding Him, they struck Him on the face, then asked Him to identify the one who did it. This is not all they did, but He patiently endured this contradiction of sinners against Himself.

M. Morning Trial Before the Sanhedrin (22:66–71)[†]

22:66–69 At daybreak (5:00–6:00 a.m.), the elders . . . led Jesus away to their council, or Sanhedrin. The members of the Sanhedrin asked Him outright if He was the Messiah. Jesus said, in effect, that it was useless to discuss the matter with them. They were not open to receive the truth. But He warned them that the One who stood before them in humiliation would one day sit on the right hand of the power of God (see Psalm 110:1).

22:70, 71 Then they asked Him plainly if He was the Son of God. There is no question what they meant. To them, the Son of God was One who was equal with God. The Lord Jesus answered "You rightly say that I am" (see Mark 14:62). That was all they needed. Had they not heard Him speak blasphemy, claiming equality with God? There was no need for further testimony. But there was a problem. In their law, the penalty for blasphemy was death. Yet the Jews were under Roman power and they did not have authority to put prisoners to death. So they had to take Jesus to Pilate, and he would not be the least bit interested in a religious charge such as blasphemy. So they had to prefer political charges against Him.

N. Jesus Before Pilate (23:1–7)

23:1, 2 Following His appearance before the Sanhedrin (the whole multitude of them), Jesus was hurried away to be put on civil trial before Pilate, the Roman governor. Three political charges were now brought against Him by the religious leaders. First of all, they accused Him of perverting the nation, that

†See p. xv.

is, of turning the loyalty of the people away from Rome. Secondly, they said that He forbade Jews **to pay taxes to Caesar**. Finally, they accused Him of making Himself **a King**.

23:3–7 When **Pilate asked** Jesus if He was **the King of the Jews, He answered** that He was. **Pilate** did not interpret His claim as any threat to the Roman Emperor. After a private interview with Jesus (John 18:33–38a), he turned **to the chief priests and** to the crowd saying that he could **find no fault** with Him. The mob became more insistent, accusing Jesus of stirring up disloyalty, **beginning** in despised **Galilee** even to Jerusalem. **When Pilate heard** the word **Galilee**, he thought he had found an escape route for himself. Galilee was **Herod's jurisdiction**, and so Pilate tried to avoid any further involvement in this case by turning Jesus over **to Herod**. It so happened that Herod was visiting **in Jerusalem at that** very **time**.

Herod Antipas was the son of Herod the Great, who massacred the infants of Bethlehem. It was Antipas who murdered John the Baptist for condemning his illicit relationship with his brother's wife. This was the Herod whom Jesus called "that fox" in Luke 13:32.

O. Herod's Contemptuous Questioning (23:8–12)

23:8 **Herod** was quite **glad** to have **Jesus** appear before him. **He had heard many things about Him**, and **for a long time** had **hoped to see some miracle** performed **by Him**.

23:9–11 No matter how much Herod **questioned** the Savior, he received no answer. The Jews became more violent in their accusations, but Jesus did not open His mouth. All **Herod** could do, he thought, was to allow his soldiers to manhandle Jesus, and to mock **Him** by clothing **Him in a gorgeous robe** and sending **Him back to Pilate**.

23:12 Previously, **Herod** and **Pilate had been at enmity** between themselves, but now the enmity was changed to friendship. They were both on the same side *against* the Lord Jesus, and this united them. Theophylact mourns in this regard: "It is a matter of shame to Christians that while the devil can persuade

wicked men to lay aside their enmities in order to do harm, Christians cannot even keep up friendship in order to do good."

P. Pilate's Verdict: Innocent but Condemned (23:13–25)

23:13–17 Because he had failed to act righteously in acquitting his royal prisoner, **Pilate** now found himself trapped. He called a hurried meeting of the Jewish leaders and explained to them that neither . . . **Herod** nor he had been able to find any evidence of disloyalty on the part of Jesus. **"Nothing deserving of death has been done by Him."** So he proposed to whip the Lord and then to let Him go. As Stewart points out:

This sorry compromise was, of course, totally unjustifiable and illogical. It was the poor, fear-driven soul's attempt to do his duty by Jesus and to please the crowd at the same time. But it did neither, and it is no wonder that the angry priests would not accept that verdict at any price.[62]

23:18–23† The chief priests and rulers were enraged. They demanded the death of Jesus and the release of **Barabbas**, a notorious criminal **who had been thrown into prison** because of **rebellion** and **murder**. Again Pilate feebly attempted to exonerate the Lord, but the vicious demands of the mob drowned him out. No matter what he said, they persisted in **demanding** the death of the Son of God.

23:24, 25 And although he had already pronounced Jesus innocent, **Pilate** now condemned Him to death in order to please the people. At the same time **he released** Barabbas **to** the multitude.

Q. The Son of Man Led to Calvary (23:26–32)

23:26 It was now approximately 9:00 a.m. on Friday. On the way to the scene of crucifixion, the soldiers commanded a **man** named **Simon, a Cyrenian** to carry **the cross**. Not much is known of this man, but it appears that his two sons afterwards became well-known Christians (Mark 15:21).

23:27–30 A crowd of sympathetic followers wept for Jesus as He was led away. Addressing the **women** in the crowd as **daughters of Jerusalem**, He

†See p. xx.

told them that they should not pity Him but should pity themselves. He was referring to the terrible destruction that would descend on Jerusalem in A.D. 70. The suffering and sorrow of those days would be so great that barren women, hitherto an object of reproach, would be considered especially fortunate. The horrors of the siege of Titus would be such that men would wish for **the mountains** to **fall on** them, and for **the hills** to **cover** them.

23:31 Then the Lord Jesus added the words, **"For if they do these things in the green wood, what will be done in the dry?"** He Himself was the **green** tree, and unbelieving Israel was the **dry**. If the Romans heaped such shame and suffering on the sinless, innocent Son of God, what dreadful punishment would fall on the guilty murderers of God's beloved Son?

23:32 In the procession with Jesus **there were also two others, criminals**, scheduled for execution.

R. The Crucifixion (23:33–38)

23:33 The place of execution was **called Calvary**[63] (from the Latin for "Skull"). Perhaps the configuration of the land resembled a skull, or perhaps it was so named because it was the place of death, and a skull is often used as a symbol of death. The restraint of Scripture in describing the crucifixion is noteworthy. There is no lingering over the terrible details. There is just the simple statement, **"there they crucified Him."** Once again Stewart's remarks are to the point:

That the Messiah should die was hard enough to credit, but that He should die *such* a death was utterly beyond belief. Yet so it was. Everything which Christ ever touched — the cross included — he adorned and transfigured and haloed with splendor and beauty; but let us never forget out of what appalling depths he has set the cross on high.[64]

> O teach me what it meaneth
> That cross uplifted high
> With One, the Man of Sorrows,
> Condemned to bleed and die.
> — *Lucy A. Bennett*

There were three crosses at Calvary that day, the cross of Jesus in the middle, and a criminal's cross on each side

of Him. This fulfilled Isaiah 53:12 — "He was numbered with the transgressors."

23:34[†] With infinite love and mercy, **Jesus** cried from the cross, **"Father, forgive them, for they do not know what they do."** Who knows what a Niagara of divine wrath was averted by this prayer! Morgan comments on the Savior's love:

In the soul of Jesus there was no resentment; no anger, no lurking desire for punishment upon the men who were maltreating Him. Men have spoken in admiration of the mailed fist. When I hear Jesus thus pray, I know that the only place for the mailed fist is in hell.[65]

Then followed the dividing of **His garments** among the soldiers, and the casting of **lots** for His seamless robe.

23:35-38[†] **The rulers** stood before the cross, mocking Him, and challenging Him to **save Himself if He** really was the Messiah, **the chosen of God. The soldiers also mocked Him** . . . **offering Him** sour **wine** and challenging His ability to **save** Himself. Also they put a title at the head of the cross:

THIS IS THE KING OF THE JEWS.

Once again we quote Stewart:

We cannot miss the significance of the fact that the inscription was written in three languages, Greek and Latin and Hebrew. No doubt that was done in order to make sure that everyone in the crowd might read it; but Christ's Church has always seen in it — and rightly — a symbol of the universal lordship of her master. For these were the three great world languages, each of them the servant of one dominant idea. Greek was the language of culture and knowledge; in that realm, said the inscription, Jesus was king! Latin was the language of law and government; Jesus was king there! Hebrew was the language of revealed religion; Jesus was King there! Hence even as he hung dying, it was true that "on his head were many crowns" (Rev. 19:12).[66]

S. The Two Robbers (23:39–43)

23:39-41 We learn from the other Gospel narratives that both robbers reviled Jesus at the outset. If He was **the Christ**, why did He not **save** them all? But then one of them had a change of heart. Turning to his companion, he **rebuked him** for his irreverence. After all they were both suffering for crimes that

[†]*See p. xxii.*

they had committed. Their punishment was deserved. **But this Man** on the middle cross had **done nothing wrong**.

23:42 Turning **to Jesus**, the thief asked the **Lord**[67] to **remember** him **when** He came back and set up His **kingdom** on earth. Such faith was remarkable. The dying thief believed that Jesus would rise from the dead and would eventually reign over the world.

23:43 **Jesus** rewarded his faith with the promise that that very day, they would **be** together **in Paradise. Paradise** is the same as the third heaven (2 Cor. 12:2, 4), and means the dwelling place of God. **Today** — what speed! **With Me** — what company! **In Paradise** — what happiness! Charles R. Erdman writes:

This story reveals the truth to us that salvation is conditioned upon repentance and faith. However, it contains other important messages also. It declares that salvation is independent of sacraments. The thief had never been baptized, nor had he partaken of the Lord's Supper. . . . He did in fact boldly profess his faith in the presence of a hostile crowd and amid the taunts and jeers of rulers and soldiers, yet he was saved without any formal rites. It is further evident that salvation is independent of good works. . . . It is also seen that there is no "sleep of the soul." The body may sleep, but consciousness exists after death. Again it is evident that there is no "purgatory." Out of a life of sin and shame, the penitent robber passed immediately into a state of blessedness. Again it may be remarked that salvation is not universal. There were two robbers; only one was saved. Last of all it may be noted that the very essence of the joy which lies beyond death consists in personal communion with Christ. The heart of the promise to the dying thief was this: "Thou shalt be with me." This is our blessed assurance, that to depart is "to be with Christ" which is "very far better."[68]

From Jesus Christ's side one person may go to heaven and another to hell. Which side of the cross are you on?

T. Three Hours of Darkness (23:44—49)

23:44 **Darkness** covered the whole land (or *earth*, the Greek can mean either) from **the sixth hour until the ninth hour**, that is, from noon to 3:00 p.m. This was a sign to the nation of Israel. They had rejected the light, and now

they would be judicially blinded by God.

23:45 **The veil of the temple was torn in two** from the top to the bottom. This pictured the fact that through the death of the Lord Jesus Christ, a way of approach to God was opened to all who would come by faith (Heb. 10:20–22).

23:46, 47 It was during these three hours of darkness that Jesus bore the penalty of our sins in His body on the tree. At the close of that time, He committed His **spirit** into the **hands** of God, His **Father**, and voluntarily yielded up His life. A Roman **centurion** was so overwhelmed by the scene that **he glorified God, saying, "Certainly this was a righteous Man!"**

23:48, 49 **The whole crowd** was overcome by an awful sense of sorrow and foreboding. Some of Jesus' faithful followers, including **women who followed Him from Galilee, stood . . . watching** this most crucial scene in the history of the world.

U. The Burial in Joseph's Tomb (23:50–56)[†]

23:50–54 Up to this time, **Joseph** had been a secret disciple of the Lord Jesus. Although a **member** of the Sanhedrin, he did not agree with their verdict in the case of Jesus. Joseph now went boldly **to Pilate and asked** if he might have the privilege of removing **the body of Jesus** from the cross and giving it a proper burial. (It was between 3:00 and 6:00 p.m.) Permission was granted, and Joseph promptly **wrapped it in linen, and laid it in a tomb that was hewn out of the rock**, and which had never been used up to this time. This happened on Friday, the **day of the Preparation**. When it says that **the Sabbath drew near**, we must remember that the Jewish Sabbath begins on Friday at sunset.

23:55, 56 **The** faithful **women . . . from Galilee followed** Joseph as he took the **body** to the **tomb** and put it inside. **Then they returned and prepared spices and fragrant oils** so that they could come back and embalm the body of the One they loved. In burying the body of Jesus, Joseph also buried himself, in a sense. That act separated him forever from the nation that crucified the Lord of life and glory. He would never be a

†See p. xvi.

part of Judaism again, but would live in moral separation from it and testify against it.

On Saturday the women rested, in obedience to the commandment concerning the Sabbath.

XII. THE SON OF MAN'S TRIUMPH (Chap. 24)[†]

A. The Women at the Empty Tomb (24:1–12)

24:1 Then on Sunday at **early** dawn they made their way **to the tomb**, carrying **the spices which they had prepared** for the body of Jesus. But how did they expect to get to His body? Did they not know that a huge stone had been rolled against the mouth of the tomb? We are not told the answer. All we know is that they loved Him dearly, and love is often forgetful of difficulties in order to reach its object.

"Their love was early astir (v. 1) and was richly rewarded (v. 6). There is still a risen Lord for the early riser (Prov. 8:17)."

24:2–10 When they arrived **they found the stone** had been **rolled away from** the mouth of **the tomb**. As soon as **they went in**, they saw that **the body of the Lord Jesus** was missing. It is not difficult to imagine their perplexity. While they were still trying to reason it out, **two** angels (see John 20:12), **in shining garments**, appeared and assured them that Jesus was **living**; it was futile to search for Him in the tomb. He had **risen** as He had promised **when He was still** with them **in Galilee**. Had He not foretold them that **the Son of Man** had to be turned over to **sinful men and be crucified, and** that on **the third day** He would **rise again**? (Luke 9:22; 18:33). Then it all came back to them. **They returned** hurriedly to the city **and told** the news **to the eleven** disciples. Among those first heralds of the resurrection were **Mary Magdalene, Joanna,** and **Mary the mother of James**.

24:11, 12 The disciples **did not believe them** at all. It was just an old wive's tale. Incredible! Fantastic! That is what they thought — until **Peter** made a personal visit **to the tomb** and **saw the linen cloths lying** there **by themselves**.

These were the cloths that had been tightly wound around the body. We are not told whether they were unwound, or still in the shape of the body, but we are safe in presuming the latter. It appears that the Lord may have left the grave-clothes as if they had been a cocoon. The fact that the grave-clothes were left behind shows that the body was not stolen; thieves would not take time to remove the coverings. Peter returned to his house, still trying to solve the mystery. What did it all mean?

B. The Walk to Emmaus (24:13–35)

24:13 One of the **two** Emmaus disciples was a man named Cleopas; we do not know the identity of the other. It may have been his wife. One tradition is that it was Luke himself. All we can be sure of is that it was not one of the original eleven disciples (see v. 33). At any rate, the two were sadly[69] rehearsing the death and burial of the Lord as they returned **from Jerusalem** to **Emmaus,** a journey of about **seven miles**.

24:14–18 As they proceeded, a stranger came alongside them; it was the risen Lord but **they did not** recognize **Him**. He asked them what they had been talking about. At first they stopped short, a picture of abject misery. Then **Cleopas** expressed surprise that even a **stranger in Jerusalem** could have been unaware of what had **happened.**

24:19–24 Jesus drew them out further with the question, "Why, **what** did happen?" They answered by first paying tribute to **Jesus,** then reviewing His trial and crucifixion. They told of their dashed hopes, then of reports that **His body** was no longer in the tomb. Indeed some **angels** had given assurance that **He was alive.**

24:25–27 Jesus then lovingly chided them for not realizing that this was exactly the pathway which **the prophets** of the OT had foretold for the Messiah. First, He must suffer, then he would be glorified. **Beginning at** Genesis and continuing through **all the** books of the **Prophets** the Lord reviewed **all the Scriptures** which referred to **Himself,** the Messiah. It was a wonderful Bible study, and how we would love to have been with Him then! But we have the same OT, and we have the Holy Spirit

[†]*See p. xvii.*

to teach us, so we too can discover **in all the Scriptures the things concerning Himself**.

24:28, 29 By now the disciples were nearing their home. They invited their fellow-traveler to spend the night with them. At first, He courteously acted as if He were going to continue His journey; He would not force an entry. But they prevailed on Him to stay with them, and how richly they were rewarded!

24:30, 31 When they sat down for the evening meal, the Guest took the place of Host.

> The frugal meal became a sacrament, and the home became a House of God. That's what Christ does wherever He goes. They who entertain Him will be well entertained. The two had opened to Him their home, and now He opens their eyes (Daily Notes of the Scripture Union).

As He **broke** the **bread** and passed it **to them, they knew Him** for the first time. Had they seen the print of the nails in His hands? We only know that **their eyes** had been miraculously **opened** to recognize Him. As soon as this happened, **He vanished**.

24:32 Then they retraced the day's journey. No wonder their hearts had burned **within** them **while He talked with** them and **opened the Scriptures**. Their Teacher and Companion had been the risen Lord Jesus Christ.

24:33 Instead of spending the night at Emmaus, they raced back **to Jerusalem** where they **found the eleven** and others assembled **together**. "The eleven" here is a general term to indicate the original band of the disciples, excluding Judas. Actually not all eleven were present, as we learn from John 20:24, but the term is used in a collective sense.

24:34 Before the Emmaus disciples could share their joyful news, the Jerusalem disciples jubilantly announced that **the Lord** had really **risen** and had **appeared to Simon** Peter.

24:35 Then it was the turn of the two from Emmaus to say, "Yes, we know, because He walked with us, came into our home, and revealed Himself to us **in the breaking of bread**."

C. The Appearance to the Eleven (24:36–43)

24:36–41 The resurrection body of the Lord Jesus was a literal, tangible body of **flesh and bones**. It was the same body which had been buried, yet it was changed in that it was no longer subject to death. With this glorified body, Jesus could enter a room when the doors were closed (John 20:19).

This is what He did on that first Sunday night. The disciples looked up and saw Him, then heard Him say, **"Peace to you."** They were seized with panic, thinking it was a ghost. Only when He showed them the marks of His passion in **His hands and His feet** did they begin to understand. Even then, it was almost too good to be true.

24:42, 43 Then in order to show them it was really Jesus Himself, He **ate** some **broiled fish** and a piece of **honeycomb**.

D. The Opened Understanding (24:44–49)

24:44–47 These verses may be a summary of the Savior's teaching between His resurrection and His ascension. He explained that His resurrection was the fulfillment of His own **words** to them. Had He not told them that all the OT prophecies **concerning** Him had to **be fulfilled? The Law of Moses and the Prophets and the Psalms** were the three main divisions of the OT. Taken together, they signify the entire OT. What was the burden of the OT prophecies concerning Christ? They were:

1. That He must **suffer** (Psalm 22:1–21; Isa. 53:1–9).
2. That He must **rise** again **from the dead** the third day (Ps. 16:10; Jonah 1:17; Hos. 6:2).
3. **That repentance and remission of sins should be preached in His name to all nations, beginning at Jerusalem.**

Jesus **opened their understanding** to comprehend all these **Scriptures**. In fact, this is a chapter full of opened things: opened *tomb* (v. 12), opened *home* (v. 29), opened *eyes* (v. 31), opened *Scriptures* (v. 32), opened *lips* (v. 35), opened *understanding* (v. 45), and opened *heavens* (v. 51).

24:48, 49 The disciples were **witnesses** of the resurrection. They must go forth as heralds of the glorious message.

But first they must wait for **the Promise of** the **Father**, i.e., for the coming of the Holy Spirit at Pentecost. Then they would be **endued with** divine **power** to bear witness to the risen Christ. The Holy Spirit was promised by the Father in such OT passages as Isaiah 44:3; Ezekiel 36:27; Joel 2:28.

E. The Son of Man's Ascension (24:50–53)

24:50, 51 The Ascension of Christ took place forty days after His resurrection. **He** took His disciples **as far as Bethany**, on the eastern side of the Mt. of Olives, **and He lifted up His hands and blessed them**. While doing so, **He was** taken **up into heaven**.

24:52, 53 They worshiped Him, then **returned to Jerusalem with great joy**. For the next ten days, they spent much time **in the temple praising and blessing God**.

Luke's Gospel **opened** with devout believers at the temple, praying for the long-expected Messiah. It closes at the same place with devout believers **praising and**[70] **blessing God** for answered prayer and for accomplished redemption. It is a lovely climax to what Renan called the most beautiful book in the world. **Amen**.

ENDNOTES

[1](1:2) James S. Stewart, *The Life and Teaching of Jesus Christ*, p. 9.

[2](1:4) The same word (*anōthen*) occurs in John 3:7: "You must be born again" (or "from above").

[3](1:16, 17) G. Coleman Luck, *Luke*, p. 17.

[4](1:28) The Greek word is a *passive* participle, showing she *received* the favor. The Latin *gratia plena* ("full of grace") has been misused to teach that Mary is a *source* of grace. This points up the importance of precisely accurate translation.

[5](1:72–75) G. Campbell Morgan, *The Gospel According to Luke*. pp. 30, 31.

[6](2:7) J. N. Darby, *Synopsis of the Books of the Bible*, III:293.

[7](2:8) Stewart, *Life and Teaching*, p. 24.

[8](2:13, 14) The critical (NU) text reads "to men of good will," which seems to contradict the Bible doctrine of man's depravity. Evangelicals who accept the critical reading generally paraphrase. The KJ tradition is probably best.

[9](2:33) The NU reading "His father and mother" does not *deny* the Virgin Birth, but is less clear. Compare also v. 43 in the traditional and majority texts vs. the NU text.

[10](2:40) The NU text omits "in spirit."

[11](4:13) Stewart, *Life and Teaching*, p. 45.

[12](4:28) John Charles Ryle, *Expository Thoughts on the Gospels, St. Luke*, I:121.

[13](5:30) The NU text reads "the Pharisees and their scribes," meaning those scribes who held the Pharisaic position.

[14](6:17–19) Many scholars, however, believe the "plain" (KJ) was a *flat place* on the mountain side and the differences are merely from condensation, choice of emphasis by Matthew and Luke, and editorial arrangement (inspired by God).

[15](6:26) The majority of mss. omit "all," suggesting that only some would praise compromisers.

[16](6:27–29a) F. B. Meyer, *The Heavenlies*, p. 26.

[17](6:47–49) The critical reading ("well-built") followed in most modern Bibles, misses the point. It is not *how* but on *whom* (Christ) one builds one's life!

[18](7:21–23) C. G. Moore, quoted by W. H. Griffith Thomas, *Outline Studies in the Gospel of Luke*, p. 129.

[19](7:27) F. L. Godet, *Commentary on the Gospel of Luke*, I:350.

[20](7:30–34) Ryle, *St. Luke*, I:230.

[21](7:49, 50) *Ibid.*, p. 239.

[22](8:11–15) J. N. Darby, *The Gospel of Luke*, p. 61.

[23](8:18) G. H. Lang, *The Parabolic Teaching of the Scripture*, p. 60.

[24](8:26, 27) Here and in verse 37 the NU text reads *Gerasenes*.

[25](8:34–39) Darby, *Synopsis*, III:340.

[26](8:51–53) Sir Robert Anderson, *Misunderstood Texts of the New Testament*, p. 51.

[27](9:19,20) Stewart, *Life and Teaching*, pp. 109, 110.

[28](9:28, 29) W. H. Rogers, further documentation unavailable.

[29](9:32,33) Ryle, *Gospels, St. Luke*, I:320.

[30](9:50) A. L. Williams, further documentation unavailable.

³¹(9:62) This probably does not mean a momentary glance back, but the "back to Egypt" mentality of the Israelites in the wilderness.

³²(10:1–12) Here and in v. 17 the NU text reads "seventy-two."

³³(10:16) Ryle, *St. Luke*, I:357, 358.

³⁴(10:36, 37) F. Davidson, ed., *The New Bible Commentary*, p. 851.

³⁵(10:42) C. A. Coates, *An Outline of Luke's Gospel*, p. 129.

³⁶(10:42) Charles R. Erdman, *The Gospel of Luke*, p. 112.

³⁷(11:4) Luke gives a shorter version of the "Disciple's Prayer," which perhaps suggests it is not to be recited word-for-word. The omissions in the critical (NU) text (see NKJV footnotes) are generally considered interpolations from Matthew by the editors of that text.

³⁸(11:9) The Greek *present imperative* suggests continuous action.

³⁹(11:41) Harry A. Ironside, *Addresses on the Gospel of Luke*, p. 390.

⁴⁰(11:46) William Kelly, *An Exposition of the Gospel of Luke*, p. 199.

⁴¹(12:2,3) Godet, *Luke*, II:89.

⁴²(12:15) J. R. Miller, *Come Ye Apart*, reading for June 10.

⁴³(12:36) Kelly, *Luke*, p. 214.

⁴⁴(13:6–9) Lang, *Parabolic Teaching*, p. 230.

⁴⁵(14:33) Ryle, *Gospels, St. Luke*, II:86.

⁴⁶(14:34,35) Kelly, *Luke*, p. 249.

⁴⁷(15:20) Stewart, *Life and Teaching*, pp. 77, 78.

⁴⁸(16:9) *Our Lord's Teachings About Money* (tract), pp. 10, 11.

⁴⁹(16:9) J. N. Darby, *The Man of Sorrows*, p. 178.

⁵⁰(17:10) Roy Hession, *The Calvary Road*, p. 49.

⁵¹(17:34–36) Both the oldest and the majority of mss. lack v. 36, which means it is most likely not authentic.

⁵²(18:31–33) Ryle, *Gospels, St. Luke*, II:282.

⁵³(19:11) A mina (Heb. *minah*, Gk. *mna*) was worth a great deal more than a British "pound," hence the change here from KJV.

⁵⁴(19:41,42) Griffith Thomas, *Luke*, p. 303.

⁵⁵(20:18) Others take the stone to refer to the repentant sinner falling in contrition on Jesus in true brokenness and being saved vs. the Christ-rejecter being smashed to powder at the future judgment.

⁵⁶(20:35) Coates, *Luke's Gospel*, p. 252.

⁵⁷(21:1–4) Dr. Joseph Parker, further documentation unavailable.

⁵⁸(21:20–24) *Christian Truth Magazine*, November 1962, p. 303.

⁵⁹(21:20–24) Edward Gibbon, *The Decline and Fall of the Roman Empire*, II:95-101.

⁶⁰(22:7) Leon Morris, *The Gospel According to Luke*, pp. 302-304.

⁶¹(22:47,48) Stewart, *Life and Teaching*, p. 154.

⁶²(23:13–17) *Ibid.*, p. 161.

⁶³(23:33) This is the only place in the English Bible (KJ tradition) where this beloved name occurs. Even though there are thousands of congregations named "Calvary _____ Church," most modern Bibles have scrapped this traditional rendering.

⁶⁴(23:33) Stewart, *Life and Teaching*, p. 166.

⁶⁵(23:34) Morgan, *Luke*, p. 269.

⁶⁶(23:35–38) Stewart, *Life and Teaching*, p. 168.

⁶⁷(23:42) The traditional and majority text reading, "*Lord*, remember me," is much more impressive than the critical (NU) text "*Jesus*, remember me." The title of respect "Lord" (can also mean "Sir") shows deeper faith than the use of a (then common) personal name.

⁶⁸(23:43) Erdman, *Luke*, pp. 217, 218.

⁶⁹(24:13) The NU text reads, " 'What kind of conversation is this that you have with one another?' And they stood still, looking sad."

⁷⁰(24:52, 53) The critical (NU) text omits "praising and" as well as the final "Amen"

BIBLIOGRAPHY

Coates, C. A. *An Outline of Luke's Gospel.* Kingston on Thames: Stow Hill Bible and Tract Depot, n.d.

Darby, J. N. *The Gospel of Luke.* London: James Carter, n.d.

_____. *The Man of Sorrows.* Glasgow: Pickering and Inglis, n.d.

_____. *Notes of Addresses on the Gospel of Luke.* London: C. A. Hammond, n.d.

Erdman, Charles R. *The Gospel of Luke.* Philadelphia: The Westminster Press, 1921.

Geldenhuys, Norval. *Commentary on the Gospel of Luke,* 2 vols. Grand Rapids: Zondervan Publishing House, 1977.

Ironside, H. A. *Addresses on the Gospel of Luke.* New York: Loizeaux Brothers, 1947.

Kelly, William. *An Exposition of the Gospel of Luke.* London: Pickering and Inglis, n.d.

Luck, G. Coleman. *Luke.* Chicago: Moody Press, 1960.

Morgan, G. Campbell. *The Gospel According to Luke.* New York: Fleming H. Revell Co., 1931.

Morris, Leon. *The Gospel According to St. Luke, TBC.* Grand Rapids: Wm. B. Eerdmans Publishing Company, 1974.

Thomas, W. H. Griffith. *Outline Studies in the Gospel of Luke.* Grand Rapids: Kregel Publications, 1984.

    1947.

THE GOSPEL ACCORDING TO JOHN†

Introduction

"The profoundest book in the world" — A. T. Robertson.

I. Unique Place in the Canon

John specifically tells us that his book is evangelistic — "that you may believe" (20:31). For once the church has followed apostolic precedent: the millions of little pocket Gospels of John given out in the last century witness to that fact.

But John is also one of the favorite Bible books — if not the *very* favorite — of mature and devout Christians. John does not merely give the facts of the life of our Lord, but long discourses and mature reflections of an apostle who has walked with Christ from (probably) late teenage years in Galilee to extreme old age in the Province of Asia. His Gospel contains the best known verse in the NT, what Martin Luther called "the Gospel in a nutshell," John 3:16.

If John's Gospel were the *only* book in the NT, it would still afford enough meat (and milk) of the Word for a lifetime of study and meditation.

II. Authorship††

The authorship of the Fourth Gospel has been widely disputed in the past 150 years. This is undoubtedly because it gives such clear testimony to the deity of our Lord Jesus Christ. The assault has sought to prove that the Gospel was not the work of an eyewitness but the work of an unknown "religious genius" who lived fifty to one hundred years later. Thus it is supposed to reflect the thinking of the church about Christ and not what He Himself actually was, said, or did.

The Gospel itself is anonymous as to

authorship, but there are many good reasons for believing that it was written by the Apostle John, one of the twelve.

Clement of Alexandria recounts that late in John's long life, the Apostle was asked by close friends who came to him at Ephesus, to write a Gospel that would supplement the Synoptic Gospels. Under the influence of the Spirit of God, John thus composed a *spiritual* Gospel. It was not that the others were considered *unspiritual*, but John's emphasis on Christ's words and the deeper meaning of the *signs* do explain why his Gospel especially could be called "spiritual."

External Evidence

Theophilus of Antioch (about A.D. 170) is the first known writer to specifically name John as the author. However, there are earlier allusions to and quotations from the Fourth Gospel in Ignatius, Justin Martyr (probably), Tatian, the Muratorian Canon, and the heretics Basilides and Valentinus.

Irenaeus completes a chain of unbroken discipleship from the Lord Jesus Himself to John, from John to Polycarp, and from Polycarp to himself. This takes us from the dawn of Christianity to near the end of the second century. Irenaeus widely quotes the Gospel as by the apostle, and as already firmly established in the church. From Irenaeus on, the Gospel is very widely attested, including such witnesses as Clement of Alexandria and Tertullian.

Until early in the nineteenth century only an obscure cult called the Alogi rejected Johannine authorship.

The very end of John 21 was probably

---

†See pp. iii–viii.
††See p. i.

written by the church leaders in Ephesus late in the first century, encouraging the faithful to accept John's Gospel. Verse 24 points back to "the disciple whom Jesus loved" in verse 20 and in chapter 13. This has always been taken as referring to the Apostle John.

It used to be commonly taught by liberals that the Fourth Gospel was written even in the *late* second century. In 1920, however, a fragment of John 18 (Papyrus 52, dated by objective methods as from the *first* half of the second century, and, probably about A.D. 125) was discovered in Egypt. The fact that it was found in a provincial town (not Alexandria, e.g.) confirms that the traditional date of writing in the latter part of the first century is sound, since it would take some time to reach from Ephesus to Upper (southern) Egypt. A similar fragment from John 5, Egerton Papyrus 2, also from the early second century, further confirms a date within John's lifetime.

Internal Evidence

In the late nineteenth century the noted Anglican scholar, Bishop Westcott, argued for Johannine authorship in ever-narrowing concentric circles. This may be condensed as follows: (1) The author was *a Jew* — the style of writing, the vocabulary, the familiarity with Jewish customs and characteristics, and the background of the OT reflected in this Gospel all strongly support this. (2) He was *a Jew who lived in Palestine* (1:28; 2:1, 11; 4:46; 11:18, 54; 21:1, 2). He knew Jerusalem and the temple intimately (5:2; 9:7; 18:1; 19:13, 17, 20, 41; also see 2:14–16; 8:20; 10:22). (3) *He was an eyewitness* of what he narrates. There are numerous details of places, persons, time, manner (4:46; 5:14; 6:59; 12:21; 13:1; 14:5, 8; 18:6; 19:31). (4) *He was an apostle* and shows intimate knowledge of the inner circle of the disciples and of the Lord Himself (6:19, 60, 61; 12:16; 13:22, 28; 16:19). (5) Since the author is precise in naming the other disciples and does *not* name himself, it is presumed that the unnamed person of 13:23; 19:26; 20:2; 21:7, 20 *is the Apostle John*. Three important passages for further consideration of the eyewitness character of the author are 1:14; 19:35 and 21:24.

III. Date

Irenaeus definitely states that John wrote his Gospel from Ephesus, so if he is correct, the earliest possible date would be A.D. 69 or 70, when the apostle arrived there. Since John does not mention the destruction of Jerusalem, it is possible that it had not yet happened, which would give a date before that terrible event.

Some quite liberal scholars choose a date for John as early as 45–66 because of possible links with the Dead Sea Scrolls. This is unusual, since it is generally the conservatives who prefer early dates, and nonconservatives the late dates. In this case early church traditions are on the side of the later date.

The arguments for a date late in the first century are quite strong. Most scholars agree with Irenaeus, Clement of Alexandria, and Jerome that John is the last of the four Gospels to be written, partly because he seems to build on and supplement the Synoptics. The fact that the destruction of Jerusalem is not mentioned in John may be because the book was written fifteen to twenty years *later*, when the shock had worn off. Irenaeus writes that John lived until the reign of Emperor Trajan (who started his reign in 98), and a date not too long before that reign is likely. The references to "the Jews" in this Gospel also suggest the later period, when Jewish opposition to the Christian faith had hardened into persecution.

While no precise dating is possible, the decade between A.D. 85 and 95 is the likeliest time frame.

IV. Background and Themes

John builds his Gospel around seven public miracles, or "signs." Each is designed to show that Jesus is God: (1) Turning the water into wine at the wedding in Cana of Galilee (2:9). (2) Healing the nobleman's son (4:46–54). (3) Healing the crippled man at the pool of Bethesda (5:2–9). (4) Feeding the five thousand (6:1–14). (5) Jesus' walking on the Sea of Galilee to rescue His disciples from the storm (6:16–21). (6) Healing the man blind from birth (9:1–7). (7) Raising Lazarus from the dead (11:1–44). In addition to these seven performed in public, there is an eighth sign performed only for His disciples after the resurrection — the miraculous catch of fish (21:1–14).

Charles R. Erdman says that the Fourth Gospel "has induced more persons to follow Christ, it has inspired more believers to loyal service, it has presented to scholars more difficult problems, than any other book that could be named."

The *chronology* of our Lord's earthly ministry is constructed from this Gospel. From the other three Gospels, the ministry of Christ might appear to have lasted only one year. The references to the annual feasts in John give us a duration of approximately three years for His public ministry. Note these references: The first Feast of Passover (2:12, 13); "a feast" (5:1), possibly the Passover or Purim; second (or third) Feast of Passover (6:4); the Feast of Tabernacles (7:2); the Feast of Dedication (10:22); and the last Feast of Passover (12:1).

John is also precise in his references to time. While the other three writers are often content with approximate references, John mentions such specifics as the seventh hour (4:52); the third day (2:1); two days (11:6); and six days (12:1).

The *style* and *vocabulary* of this Gospel are unique except for the Epistles of John. The sentences are short and simple. They are Hebrew in thought although Greek in language. Often the shorter the sentence the weightier the truth! The vocabulary is the most limited of all the Gospels but the most profound in meaning. Note these important words and how often they occur: Father (118), believe (100), world (78), love (45), witness, testify, etc. (47), life (37), light (24).

One marked feature of John is the occurrence of the number seven and its multiples. The ideas of perfection and completion attach to this number throughout Scripture (see Genesis 2:1–3). In this Gospel the Spirit of God perfects and completes the revelation of God in the Person of Jesus Christ, hence patterns based on the number seven are frequent.

The seven "I am's" in John are familiar: "The Bread of Life" (6:35, 41, 48, 51); "The Light of the World" (8:12; 9:5); "The Door" (10:7, 9); "The Good Shepherd" (10:11, 14); "The Resurrection and the Life" (11:25); "The Way, the Truth, and the Life" (14:6); and "The Vine" (15:1, 5). Not so familiar are the seven occurrences of "I am" without a predicate, that is, the simple statement: 4:26; 6:20; 8:24, 28, 58; 13:19; 18:5, 8. The last one is a double one.

In the sixth chapter, which has to do with the Bread of Life, the Greek word translated "bread" and "loaves" occurs twenty-one times, a multiple of seven. Also in the Bread of Life discourse the expression "bread from heaven" occurs precisely seven times; a similar expression "comes down from heaven" occurs seven times as well.

John's purpose in writing, as we have seen, was that his readers might believe "that Jesus is the Christ, the Son of God, and that believing, [they] may have life in His name" (20:31).

OUTLINE

Commentary†

I. PROLOGUE: THE SON OF GOD'S FIRST ADVENT (1:1–18)

John begins his Gospel by speaking about *the Word* — but he does not explain at first who or what the Word is. A word is a unit of speech by which we express ourselves to others. But John is not writing about *speech* but rather about a *Person*. That Person is the Lord Jesus Christ, the Son of God. God has fully expressed Himself to mankind in the Person of the Lord Jesus. By coming into the world, Christ has perfectly revealed to us what God is like. By dying for us on the cross, He has told us how much God loves us. Thus Christ is God's living Word to man, the expression of God's thoughts.

A. The Word in Eternity and Time (1:1–5)

1:1 **In the beginning was the Word**. He did not have a beginning Himself, but existed from all eternity. As far as the human mind can go back, the Lord Jesus was there. He never was created. He had no beginning. (A genealogy would be out of place in this Gospel of the Son of God.) **The Word was with God**. He had a separate and distinct personality. He was not just an idea, a thought, or some vague kind of example, but a real Person who lived **with God. The Word was God**. He not only dwelt **with God**, but He Himself **was God**.

The Bible teaches that there is one God and that there are three Persons in the Godhead — the Father, the Son, and the Holy Spirit. All three of these Persons are God. In this verse, two of the Persons of the Godhead are mentioned — God the Father and God the Son. It is the first of many clear statements in this Gospel that *Jesus Christ is God*. It is not enough to say that He is "a god," that He is godlike, or that He is divine. The Bible teaches that He *is* **God**.

1:2 Verse 2 would appear to be a mere repetition of what has been said, but actually it is not. This verse teaches that Christ's personality and deity were

without **beginning**. He did not become a person for the first time as the Babe of Bethlehem. Nor did He somehow become a god after His resurrection, as some teach today. He is God from all eternity.

1:3 **All things were made through Him**. He Himself was not a created being; rather He was the Creator of **all things**. This includes mankind, the animals, the heavenly planets, the angels — **all things** visible and invisible. **Without Him nothing was made that was made**. There can be no possible exception. If a thing was made, He made it. As Creator, He is, of course, superior to anything He has created. All three Persons of the Godhead were involved in the work of creation: "God created the heavens and the earth" (Gen. 1:1). "The Spirit of God was hovering over the face of the waters" (Gen. 1:2). "All things were created through Him (Christ) and for Him" (Col. 1:16b).

1:4 **In Him was life**. This does not simply mean that He possessed life, but that He was and is the *source* of **life**. The word here includes both physical and spiritual life. When we were born, we received physical life. When we are born again, we receive spiritual life. Both come from Him.

The life was the light of men. The same One who supplied us with life is also **the light of men**. He provides the guidance and direction necessary for man. It is one thing to exist, but quite another to know how to live, to know the true purpose of life, and to know the way to heaven. The same One who gave us **life** is the One who provides us with **light** for the pathway we travel.

There are seven wonderful titles of our Lord Jesus Christ in this opening chapter of the Gospel. He is called (1) the Word (vv. 1, 14); (2) the Light (vv. 5, 7); (3) the Lamb of God (vv. 29, 36); (4) the Son of God (vv. 34, 49); (5) the Christ (Messiah) (v. 41); (6) the King of Israel (v. 49); and (7) the Son of Man (v. 51). The first four titles, each of which is mentioned at least twice, seem to be universal in application. The last three titles, each of which is mentioned only

†See p. ix.

once, had their first application to Israel, God's ancient people.

1:5 **The light shines in the darkness**. The entrance of sin brought **darkness** to the minds of men. It plunged the world into **darkness** in the sense that men in general neither knew God nor wanted to know Him. Into this **darkness** the Lord Jesus came — a **light** shining in a dark place.

The darkness did not comprehend it. This may mean that the darkness did not understand the Lord Jesus when He came into the world. Men did not realize who He really was, or why He had come. Another meaning, however, is given in the NKJV margin: **the darkness did not** *overcome* **it**. Then the thought would be that man's rejection and enmity did not prevent the true **light** from shining.

B. The Ministry of John the Baptist (1:6–8)

1:6 Verse 6 refers to John the Baptist, not the John who wrote this Gospel. **John** the Baptist was **sent from God** as a forerunner of the Lord Jesus. His mission was to announce the coming of Christ and to tell the people to get ready to receive Him.

1:7 **This man came** to testify to the fact that Jesus was truly the **Light** of the world, so **that all** people **might** put their trust in Him.

1:8 If John had tried to attract attention to himself, he would have been unfaithful to his appointed task. He pointed men to Jesus and not to himself.

C. The Son of God's First Advent (1:9–18)

1:9 **That was the true Light**. Other persons down through the ages have claimed to be guides and saviors, but the One to whom John witnessed was the genuine **Light**, the best and the truest **Light**. Another translation of this verse is, "The true Light, which, coming into the world, gives light to every man." In other words, the expression **coming into the world** may describe **the true Light** rather than **every man**. It was by the coming of the **true Light . . . into the world** that every man was given light. This does not mean that every man has received some inward knowledge con-

cerning Christ. Neither does it mean that all men have heard about the Lord Jesus at one time or another. Rather, it means that the **Light** shines on all people, without regard to nationality, race, or color. It also means that by shining on all men, the Lord Jesus has revealed men in their true character. By His coming into the world as the perfect Man, He has shown how imperfect other men are. When a room is in darkness, you do not see the dust on the furniture. But when the light goes on, the room is seen as it actually is. In that same sense, the shining of **the true Light** reveals man as he actually is.

1:10 From the time of His birth in Bethlehem until the day He went back to heaven, **He was in the** very same **world** in which we now live. He had brought the whole world into being and was its rightful Owner. Instead of recognizing Him as the Creator, men thought that He was just another man like themselves. They treated Him like a stranger and an outcast.

1:11[†] **He came to His own** (things or domain, NKJV margin). He was not trespassing on someone else's property. Rather, He was living on a planet which He Himself had made. **His own** (people) **did not receive Him**. In a general sense, this might refer to all mankind, and it is true that most of mankind rejected Him. But in a special sense, the Jewish nation was His chosen, earthly people. When He came into the world, He presented Himself to the Jews as their Messiah, but they would **not receive Him**.

1:12 So now He offers Himself to all mankind again and to those who receive **Him**, He gives **the right** or authority **to become children of God**.

This verse tells us clearly how we can **become children of God**. It is not by good works, not by church membership, not by doing one's best — but by receiving **Him**, by believing **in His Name**.

1:13 To become a child in a physical sense, one must be **born**. So, also, to become a child of God, one must have a second birth. This is known as the new birth, or conversion, or being saved. This verse tells us *three ways* by which the new birth does *not* take place, and the *one way* by which it *does*. First, the three ways by which we are not born again. **Not of blood**. This means that a

†*See p. xx.*

person does not become a Christian through having Christian parents. Salvation is not passed down from parent to child through the **blood** stream. It is not **of the will of the flesh**. In other words, a person does not have the power in his own **flesh** to produce the new birth. Although he must be willing in order to be saved, yet his own **will** is not enough to save him. Not **of the will of man**. No other man can save a person. A preacher, for instance, may be very anxious to see a certain person born again, but he does not have the power to produce this marvelous birth. How, then, does this birth take place? The answer is found in the words **but of God**. This means simply that the power to produce the new birth does not rest with anything or anyone but **God**.

1:14 **The Word became flesh** when Jesus was born as a Baby in the manger at Bethlehem. He had always existed as the Son of God with the Father in heaven, but now chose to come into the world in a human body. He **dwelt among us**. It was not just a short appearance, about which there might be some mistake or misunderstanding. God actually came to this earth and lived here as a Man among men. The word "**dwelt**" means "tabernacled" or "pitched His tent." His body was the tent in which He lived among men for thirty-three years.

And we beheld His glory. In the Bible, "glory" often means the bright, shining light which was seen when God was present. It also means the perfection and excellence of God. When the Lord Jesus was here on earth, He veiled His glory in a body of flesh. But there were two ways in which His glory *was* revealed. First, there was His *moral* **glory**. By this, we mean the radiance of His perfect life and character. There was no flaw or blemish in Him. He was perfect in all His ways. Every virtue was manifested in His life in exquisite balance. Then there was the visible outshining of His **glory** which took place on the Mount of Transfiguration (Matt. 17:1, 2). At that time, Peter, James, and John saw His face shining like the sun, and His garments gleaming like bright light. These three disciples were given a preview of the splendor which the Lord Jesus will have when He comes back to the earth

and reigns for a thousand years.

When John said, "**We beheld His glory**", he was referring primarily, no doubt, to the *moral* **glory** of the Lord Jesus. He and the other disciples beheld the wonder of an absolutely perfect life lived on this earth. But it is likely that John also included the incident on the Mount of Transfiguration as well. The **glory** which the disciples saw indicated to them that He was truly the Son of God. Jesus is **the only begotten of the Father**, that is, Christ is God's unique Son. God did not have any other Son like Him. In one sense, all true believers are sons of God. But Jesus is *the* Son of God — in a class all by Himself. As the Son of God, He is equal to God.

The Savior was **full of grace and truth**. On the one hand, full of undeserved kindness for others, He was also completely honest and upright, and He never excused sin or approved evil. To be completely gracious and at the same time completely righteous is something that only God can be.

1:15 John the Baptist **bore witness** that Jesus was the Son of God. Before the Lord entered upon His public ministry, John had been telling men about Him. When Jesus arrived on the scene, John said, in effect, "This is the One I have been describing to you." Jesus came **after** John as far as His birth and ministry were concerned. He was born six months after John and presented Himself to the people of Israel some time after John had been preaching and baptizing. But Jesus was **preferred before** John. He was greater than John; He was worthy of more honor, the simple reason being that **He was before** John. He existed from all eternity — the Son of God.

1:16 All who believe on the Lord Jesus receive supplies of spiritual strength out **of His fullness. His fullness** is so great that He can provide for all Christians in all countries and in all ages. The expression **grace for grace** probably means "grace upon grace" or "abundant grace." Here **grace** means God's gracious favor which He showers on His beloved children.

1:17 John contrasts the OT period and the NT era. **The law** that was **given through Moses** was not a display of grace. It commanded men to obey and condemned them to death if they failed to do so. It told men what was right but did not give them the power to do it. It was given to show men that they were sinners, but it could not save them from their sins. **But grace and truth came through Jesus Christ**. He did not come to judge the world but to save those who were unworthy, who could not save themselves, and who were His enemies. That is **grace** — heaven's Best for earth's worst.

Not only did **grace** come **through Jesus Christ**, but **truth** came by Him as well. He said of Himself, "I am . . . the truth." He was absolutely honest and faithful in all His words and works. He did not show grace at the expense of **truth**. Although He loved sinners, He did not love their sins. He realized that the wages of sin is death. And so He Himself died to pay the penalty of death that we deserved, in order that He might show undeserved kindness to us in saving our souls and giving us a home in heaven.

1:18 **No one has seen God at any time**. God is Spirit and therefore invisible. He does not have a body. Although He did appear to men in the OT in visible form as an Angel or as a Man, these appearances did not reveal what God is really like. They were merely temporary appearances by which He chose to speak to His people. The Lord Jesus is God's **only begotten Son**;[1] He is God's unique Son; there is no other son like Him. He always occupies a place of special nearness to God the Father. Even when He was here on earth, Jesus was still **in the bosom of the Father**. He was one with God and equal with God. This blessed One has fully revealed to men what God is like. When men saw Jesus, they saw God. They heard God speak. They felt God's love and tenderness. God's thoughts and attitudes toward mankind have been fully **declared** by Christ.

II. THE SON OF GOD'S FIRST YEAR OF MINISTRY (1:19 – 4:54)[†]

A. The Testimony of John the Baptist (1:19–34)

1:19 When news reached **Jerusalem** that a man named **John** was telling the nation to repent because the Messiah

was coming, **the Jews sent** a committee of **priests and Levites** to find out who this was. The **priests** were those who carried on the important services in the temple, while the **Levites** were servants who attended to common duties there. **"Who are you?"** they asked. "Are you the long-awaited Messiah?"

1:20 Other men might have seized this opportunity for fame by claiming to be the Christ. But John was a faithful witness. His testimony was that he was **not the Christ** (the Messiah).

1:21, 22 The Jews expected Elijah to return to the earth prior to the coming of Christ (Mal. 4:5). So they reasoned that if John was not the Messiah, then perhaps he was **Elijah**. But John assured them that he was not. In Deuteronomy 18:15, Moses had said, "The LORD your God will raise up for you a Prophet like me from your midst, from your brethren. Him you shall hear." The Jews remembered this prediction and thought that John might be **the Prophet** mentioned by Moses. But again John said that it was not so. The delegation would have been embarrassed to go back to Jerusalem without a definite **answer**, and so they asked John for a statement as to who he was.

1:23 **He said, "I am 'The voice of one crying in the wilderness.' "** In answer to their query, the Baptist quoted from Isaiah 40:3, where it was prophesied that a forerunner would appear to announce the coming of Christ. In other words, John stated that he was the forerunner who was predicted. He was **the voice**, and Israel was **the wilderness**. Because of their sin and departure from God, the people had become dry and barren, like a desert. John spoke of himself simply as a **voice**. He did not pose as a great man to be praised and admired, but as a **voice** — not to be seen, but only to be heard. John was **the voice** but Christ was the Word. The word needs a voice to make it known and the voice is of no value without a word. The Word is infinitely greater than the voice but it can be our privilege, too, to be a voice for Him.

John's message was, **"Make straight the way of the LORD."** In other words, "The Messiah is coming. Remove everything in your life that would hinder you from receiving Him. Repent of your sins, so that He can come and reign over you as the King of Israel."

1:24, 25 The Pharisees formed a strict sect of the Jews who prided themselves on their superior knowledge of the law and on their efforts to carry out the most minute details of the instructions of the OT. Actually, many of them were hypocrites who tried to appear religious but who lived very sinful lives. They wanted to know what authority John had for baptizing if he was not one of the important persons they named.

1:26, 27 "I baptize with water," said **John**. He did not want anyone to think that *he* was important. His task was simply to prepare men for Christ. Whenever his hearers repented of their sins, he baptized them in water as an outward symbol of their inward change. **"There stands One among you, whom you do not know,"** John continued, referring, of course, to Jesus. The Pharisees did not recognize Him as the long looked-for Messiah. In effect John was saying to the Pharisees, "Do not think of me as a great man. The **One** you should be paying attention to is the Lord Jesus; yet **you do not know** who He really is." He is the One who is worthy. He came after John the Baptist, yet He deserves all the praise and preeminence. It was the duty of a slave or servant to untie his master's sandals. But John did **not** consider himself **worthy** to perform such a humble, lowly service for Christ.

1:28 The exact location of **Bethabara** (or **Bethany**, NKJV margin), is not known. But we do know that it was a place on the east side of **the Jordan** River. If we accept the reading *Bethany*, it cannot be the Bethany near Jerusalem.

1:29 The next day after the visit of the Pharisees from Jerusalem, **John** looked up and **saw Jesus coming toward him**. In the thrill and excitement of that moment, he cried out, **"Behold! The Lamb of God** who bears **the sin of the world!"** The lamb was a sacrificial animal among the Jews. God had taught His chosen people to slay a lamb and to sprinkle its blood as a sacrifice. The lamb was killed as a substitute and its blood shed so that sins might be forgiven.

However, the blood of the lambs slain during the OT period did not put away sin. Those lambs were pictures or types, pointing forward to the fact that God would one day provide a **Lamb** who would actually *take away* the sin. All down through the years, godly Jews had waited for the coming of this **Lamb**. Now at last the time had come, and John the Baptist triumphantly announced the arrival of the true **Lamb of God**.

When he said that Jesus bears **the sin of the world**, he did not mean that everyone's sins are therefore forgiven. The death of Christ was great enough in value to pay for the sins of the whole **world**, but only those sinners who receive the Lord Jesus as Savior are forgiven.

J. C. Jones points out that this verse sets forth the excellency of the Christian atonement:

1. It excels in the NATURE of the victim. Whereas the sacrifices of Judaism were irrational lambs, the sacrifice of Christianity is the Lamb of God.

2. It excels in the EFFICACY of the work. Whereas the sacrifices of Judaism only brought sin to remembrance every year, the sacrifice of Christianity took sin away. "He put away sin by the sacrifice of Himself."

3. It excels in the SCOPE of its operation. Whereas the Jewish sacrifices were intended for the benefit of one nation only, the sacrifice of Christianity is intended for all nations; "it takes away the sin of the world."[2]

1:30, 31 John never grew weary of reminding people that he was only preparing the way for Someone greater than himself who was coming. Jesus was greater than John to the same extent that God is greater than man. John was born a few months before Jesus, but Jesus had existed from all eternity. When John said, **"I did not know Him,"** he did not necessarily mean that he had never seen Him before.

Since they were cousins, it is probable that John and Jesus were well acquainted. But John had not recognized his Cousin as being the Messiah until the time of His baptism. John's mission was to prepare the way of the Lord, and then to point Him out **to** the people of **Israel** when He appeared. It was for this reason that John baptized people in

water — to prepare them for the coming of Christ. It was not for the purpose of attracting disciples to himself.

1:32 The reference here was to the time John baptized Jesus in the Jordan. After the Lord went up out of the water, **the Spirit** of God descended **like a dove** and **remained upon Him** (cf. Matt. 3:16). The writer goes on to explain the meaning of this.

1:33 God had revealed to John that the Messiah was coming and that when He came, **the Spirit** would descend **upon** Him and stay **on Him**. Therefore, when this happened to Jesus, John realized that this was the One who would baptize **with the Holy Spirit. The Holy Spirit** is a Person, one of the three Persons in the Godhead. He is equal with God the Father and God the Son.

Whereas John baptized **with water**, Jesus would baptize **with the Holy Spirit**. The baptism **with the Holy Spirit** took place on the day of Pentecost (Acts 1:5; 2:4, 38). At that time, **the Holy Spirit** came down from heaven to dwell in the body of every believer and also to make each believer a member of the church, the Body of Christ (1 Cor. 12:13).

1:34 On the basis of what he saw at the baptism of Jesus, John **testified** positively to the fact that Jesus of Nazareth was **the Son of God** who was foretold as coming into the world. When John said that Christ was **the Son of God**, he meant that He was God the Son.

B. The Call of Andrew, John, and Peter (1:35–42)

1:35, 36 **The next day** referred to here is the third day that has been mentioned. **John** was **with two of his** own **disciples**. These men had heard John preach and believed what he said. But as yet they had not met the Lord Jesus. Now John bore public witness to the Lord. On the previous day, he had spoken of His Person (the Lamb of God) and His work (who takes away the sin of the world). Now he simply draws attention to His Person. His message was short, simple, selfless, and all about the Savior.

1:37 By his faithful preaching, John lost **two disciples**, but he was glad to see them following **Jesus**. So we should be more anxious for our friends to follow

the Lord than for them to think highly of us.

1:38 The Savior is always interested in those who follow Him. Here He showed His interest by turning to the two disciples and asking, **"What do you seek?"** He knew the answer to the question; He knew all things. But He wanted them to express their desire in words. Their answer, **"Rabbi, where are You staying?"** showed that they wanted to be with the Lord and to get to know Him better. They were not satisfied merely to meet Him. They longed to have fellowship with Him. **Rabbi** is the Hebrew word for **Teacher** (literally "my great one").

1:39 **He said to them, "Come and see."** No one with a genuine desire to learn more of the Savior is ever turned away. Jesus invited the two to the place where He was staying at the time — probably a very poor dwelling, compared to modern homes.

They came and saw where He was staying, and remained with Him that day (now it was about the tenth hour). Never had these men been so honored. They spent that night in the same home as the Creator of the universe. They were among the very first members of the Jewish nation to recognize the Messiah.

The tenth hour is either 10 a.m. or 4 p.m. The earlier time (Roman) is generally preferred.

1:40 **One of the two** disciples was **Andrew. Andrew** is not as well known today as his **brother, Simon Peter**, but it is interesting to notice that he was the first of the two to meet Jesus.

The name of the other was not given to us, but almost all Bible scholars assume that it was John — the one who wrote this Gospel. They reason that humility kept him from mentioning his own name.

1:41 When a person finds Jesus, he usually wants his relatives to meet Him too. Salvation is too good to keep to oneself. So Andrew went quickly **to his own brother Simon** with the thrilling news, **"We have found the Messiah!"** What an astounding announcement this was! For at least four thousand years, men had waited for the promised Christ, God's Anointed One. Now **Simon** hears from the lips of his own brother the startling news that **the Messiah** was nearby. Truly they were living where history was being made. How simple Andrew's message was. It was only five words — **"We have found the Messiah"** — yet God used it to win Peter. This teaches us that we do not have to be great preachers or clever speakers. We need only to tell men about the Lord Jesus in simple words, and God will take care of the rest.

1:42 Andrew **brought** his brother to the right place and to the right Person. He did not bring him to the church, the creed, or the clergyman. **He brought him to Jesus.** What an important act that was! Because of Andrew's interest, Simon later became a great fisher of men, and one of the leading apostles of the Lord. Simon has received more publicity than his brother, but Andrew will doubtless share Peter's reward because it was Andrew who brought him to Jesus. The Lord knew Simon's name without being told. He also knew that Simon had an unstable character. And finally, He knew that Simon's character would be changed, so that he would be firm as a rock. How did Jesus know all this? Because He was and is God.

Simon's name did change to **Cephas** (Aramaic for **stone**), and he did become a man of strong character, especially after the Ascension of the Lord and the Descent of the Holy Spirit.

C. The Call of Philip and Nathanael (1:43–51)

1:43 This is now the fourth **day** we have read about in this chapter. Bosch points out that on the first day we see *John only* (vv.15–28); on the second we see *John and Jesus* (vv. 29–34); on the third we see *Jesus and John* (vv. 35–42); and on the fourth day we see *Jesus only* (vv. 43–51). The Lord walked northward into the region known as **Galilee**. There **He found Philip** and invited him to be a follower. **"Follow Me!"** These are great words because of the One who spoke them and great because of the privilege they offered. The Savior is still issuing this simple, yet sublime, invitation to all men everywhere.

1:44 Bethsaida was a **city** on the shores of the Sea of Galilee. Few cities in the world have ever been so honored. The Lord performed some of His mighty miracles there (Luke 10:13). It was the home of **Philip, Andrew, and Peter**. Yet it rejected the Savior, and as a result it was destroyed so completely that now we cannot tell the exact spot where it was located.

1:45 Philip wanted to share his new-found joy with someone else, so he went and **found Nathanael**. New converts are the best soul-winners. His message was simple and to the point. He told Nathanael that he had **found** the Messiah who had been foretold by **Moses** and **the prophets — Jesus of Nazareth**. Actually his message was not entirely accurate. He described Jesus as being **the son of Joseph**. Jesus, of course, was born of the Virgin Mary and had no human father. **Joseph** adopted Jesus and thus became his legal father, though not His real father. James S. Stewart comments:

> It never was Christ's way to demand a full-fledged faith for a beginning. It never was his way to hold men back from discipleship on the ground of an incomplete creed. And quite certainly that is not his way today. He puts himself alongside his brethren. He bids them attach themselves to him at any point they can. He takes them with the faith that they can offer him. He is content with that as a beginning; and from that he leads his friends on, as he led the first group on, step by step, to the inmost secret of who he is and to the full glory of discipleship.[3]

1:46 Nathanael had problems. **Nazareth** was a despised city of Galilee. It seemed impossible to him that the Messiah would live in such a poor neighborhood. And so he voiced the question that was in his mind. **Philip** did not argue. He felt that the best way to meet objections was to introduce men directly to the Lord Jesus — a valuable lesson for all who are seeking to win others to Christ. Don't argue. Don't engage in prolonged discussions. Just bid men to **come and see**.

1:47 Verse 47 shows that **Jesus** knew all things. Without any previous acquaintance with **Nathanael**, He declared him to be **an Israelite indeed, in whom** there was **no trickery or deceit**. Jacob had gained a reputation for using business methods that were not entirely honest, but Nathanael was an "Israel"-ite in whom there was no "Jacob."

1:48 **Nathanael** was obviously surprised that a total Stranger should speak to him as if He had known him previously. Apparently he had been completely concealed when he was sitting **under the fig tree**. Doubtless the overhanging branches of the trees and the surrounding foliage hid him from view. But Jesus **saw** him, even though he was so hidden.

1:49 Perhaps it was the power of the Lord Jesus to see him when he was shut off from human view that convinced **Nathanael**, or this knowledge was perhaps given to him in a supernatural way. In any event, he now knew that Jesus was **the Son of God** and **the King of Israel**.

1:50 The Lord had given Nathanael two proofs that He was the Messiah. He had described his character, and He had seen Nathanael when no other eyes could have seen him. These two proofs were sufficient for Nathanael, and he believed. But now the Lord Jesus promised that he would **see greater** proofs **than these**.

1:51 Whenever Jesus introduced a saying with the words **Most assuredly** (literally "Amen, amen"[4]), He was always about to say something very important. Here He gave Nathanael a picture of the time in the future when He would come back to reign over all the earth. The world will then know that the carpenter's Son who lived in despised Nazareth was truly the Son of God and Israel's King. In that day, **heaven** will **open**. The favor of God will rest upon the King as He reigns, with Jerusalem as His capital.

It is likely that Nathanael had been meditating on the story of Jacob's ladder (Gen. 28:12). That ladder, with its ascending and descending angels, is a picture of the Lord Jesus Christ Himself, the only access to heaven. **The angels of God** will ascend and descend **upon the Son of Man**. Angels are servants **of God**, traveling like flames of fire on His errands. When Jesus reigns as King, these **angels** will travel back and forth between heaven and earth, fulfilling His will.

Jesus was saying to Nathanael that he had seen only very minor demonstrations of His Messiahship. In the future Reign of Christ, he would see the Lord Jesus fully revealed as God's anointed Son. Then all mankind would know that Someone good did come out of Nazareth.

D. The First Sign: Water Changed to Wine (2:1–11)

2:1 **The third day** doubtless refers to **the third day** of the Lord's stay in **Galilee**. In 1:43 the Savior went into that area. We do not know exactly where **Cana** was situated, but we infer from verse 12 of this chapter that it was near Capernaum and on higher ground.

There was a wedding in Cana on this particular day, **and the mother of Jesus was there**. It is interesting to notice that Mary is spoken of as **the mother of Jesus**. The Savior was not famous because He was the Son of the Virgin Mary, but she was well-known because she was the mother of our Lord. The Scriptures always give the pre-eminent place to Christ and not to Mary.

2:2 **Jesus and His disciples were invited to the wedding**. It was a wise decision on the part of those who arranged the marriage to invite Christ. So it is still a wise decision when people today invite the Lord to their marriage. In order to do this, of course, both bride and groom must be true believers in the Lord Jesus. Then, too, they must give their lives to the Savior and determine that their home will be a place where He loves to be.

2:3 The supply of **wine** had failed. When **the mother of Jesus** realized what had happened, she presented the problem to her Son. She knew that He could perform a miracle in order to provide wine, and perhaps she wanted her Son to reveal Himself to the assembled guests as the Son of God. Wine in the Scriptures often speaks of joy. When Mary said, **"They have no wine,"** she gave a very accurate description of men and women who have never been saved. There is no real, lasting joy for the unbeliever.

2:4 The reply of the Lord to His mother seems cold and distant. But it is not as strong a rebuke as would seem to us. The word **woman** used here is a title of respect, similar to our word "lady." When the Lord asked, **"Woman, what does your concern have to do with Me?"** He indicated that in the performance of His divine mission, He was not subject to instructions from His mother, but acted entirely in obedience to the will of His Father in heaven. Mary had wanted to see Jesus glorified, but He must remind her that the time for this had **not yet come**. Before He would appear to the world as the all-conquering Christ, He must first ascend the altar of sacrifice, and this He did at the cross of Calvary.

Williams points out the following:

The expression "what does your concern have to do with me" occurs several times in the Bible. It means, "What have we in common?" The answer is, "Nothing." David uses it twice with respect to his cousins, the sons of Zeruiah. How impossible it was for them to have anything in common with him in the spiritual life! Elisha uses it in 2 Kings 3 to express how deep was the gulf between him and Jehoram the son of Ahab. Three times the demons, by using the same expression, reveal how Satan has nothing in common with Christ, or Christ with Satan. And lastly the Lord used it to the Virgin Mary to show how impassable is the gulf between His sinless Deity and her sinful humanity, and that only One Voice had authority for His ear.[5]

2:5 Mary understood the meaning of His words, and so she instructed the servants to do **whatever He** commanded them. Her words are important ones for every one of us. Notice that she did not direct men to obey *her*, or any other human being. She pointed them to the Lord Jesus and told them that He was the One who should be obeyed. The teachings of the Lord Jesus are given to us in the pages of the NT. As we read this precious book, we should remember the last recorded words of Mary, **"Whatever He says to you, do it."**

2:6 In the place where the wedding was being held, there were **six** large **stone** vessels, **containing twenty or thirty gallons** of water **apiece**. This water was used by the Jewish people for cleansing themselves from defilement. For instance, if a Jew touched a dead body, he was considered unclean until

he went through a certain ceremony of cleansing.

2:7 Jesus gave instructions to **fill the waterpots with water**. This the servants did immediately. The Lord used the facilities that were available when He was about to perform a miracle. He allowed men to provide **the waterpots**, and to **fill** them **with water**, but then He did what no man could ever do — changed the water into wine! It was the servants and not the disciples who **filled** the vessels with water. In this way, the Lord avoided the possibility of any charge of trickery. Also, the waterpots were filled **to the brim**, so that no one could say that wine had been added to the water.

2:8 The miracle had now taken place. The Lord instructed the servants to **draw some out** from the vessels **and take** the contents **to the master of the feast**. From this it is clear that the miracle had been instantaneous. The water did not become wine over a period of time, but in a second or so. As someone put it poetically, "The unconscious waters saw their God and blushed."

2:9 The master of the feast was the one who had charge of arranging the tables and the food. **When** he **had tasted** it, he realized that something unusual had happened. He **did not know where** the wine **came from**, but he knew that it was of very high quality so he immediately **called the bridegroom**.

What should be the attitude of Christians toward wine today? Wine is sometimes prescribed for medicinal purposes, and this is entirely in accordance with the teaching of the New Testament (1 Tim. 5:23). Regarding its use at the table, Christians ought to act prudently in all situations and in all cultures, seeking before all the glory of the Lord and not the selfish gratification of their own desires. Never rejecting the good gifts of God, the believer should remember the warnings of Scripture specifically against drunkenness (Rom. 13:13; Gal. 5:21; Eph 5:18; 1 Pet. 4:3), and against all lack of moderation in general (1 Cor. 6:12). Finally, the saints should refrain from any behavior that would cause someone else to stumble (Rom. 14:21).

2:10 The ruler of the feast draws attention to the very marked difference between the way the Lord Jesus acts and the way men commonly act. The usual practice at a wedding was to serve the best **wine** first when men could best detect and enjoy its flavor. Later on, having eaten and drunk, they would not be as aware of the quality of their beverage. At this particular wedding, the best wine came last. There is a spiritual meaning in this for us. The world commonly offers people the best it has to offer at the outset. It holds out its most attractive offers to young people. Then when they have wasted their lives in empty pleasure, the world has nothing but dregs for a person's old age. The Christian life is the very opposite. It gets better all the time. Christ keeps the best wine until the last. The feast follows the fast.

This portion of Scripture has a very direct application to the Jewish nation. There was no true joy in Judaism at this time. The people were going through a dreary round of rituals and ceremonies, but life for them was tasteless. They were strangers to divine joy. The Lord Jesus was seeking to teach them to put their faith in Him. He would turn their drab existence into fullness of joy. The water of Jewish ritual and ceremony could be turned into the wine of joyful reality in Christ.

2:11 The statement that **this** was the **beginning of signs** rules out the silly miracles attributed to our Lord in His childhood. These are found in such pseudo-gospels as "The Gospel of Peter." They attribute to our Lord miracles performed allegedly when He was a child and are a little short of blasphemous in character. Foreseeing this, the Holy Spirit safeguarded this period of our Lord's life and His character by this little additional note.

Changing water into wine was a sign, that is, a miracle with a meaning. It was a superhuman act with a spiritual meaning. These miracles also were designed to show that Jesus was indeed the Christ of God. By performing this sign, He **manifested His glory**. He revealed to men that He was indeed God — manifest in the flesh. **His disciples believed in Him**. Of course, in one sense they had believed in Him previously, but now their faith was strengthened, and they

trusted Him more fully. Cynddylan Jones points out:

> Moses' first miracle was to turn water into blood; there was a severe destructive element in it. But Christ's first miracle was to turn water into wine; there was a soothing, solacing element in it.[6]

E. The Son of God Cleanses His Father's House (2:12–17)

2:12 The Savior now left Cana and **went down to Capernaum** with **His mother, His brothers, and His disciples**. They only stayed in Capernaum a few **days**. Soon after, the Lord went up to Jerusalem.

2:13 Beginning at this point, we have the Lord's first witness to the city of **Jerusalem**. This phase of His ministry continues to chapter 3, verse 21. He both began and ended His public ministry by cleansing the temple at **Passover** time (cf. Matt. 21:12, 13; Mark 11:15–18; Luke 19:45, 46). The Passover was an annual feast commemorating the time when the children of Israel were delivered from slavery in Egypt and were led through the Red Sea to the wilderness, and then to the promised land. The first celebration of the Passover is recorded in Exodus 12. Being a devout Jew, the Lord Jesus **went up to Jerusalem** for this important day on the Jewish calendar.

2:14 Coming to **the temple, He found** that it had become a market place. **Oxen and sheep and doves** were sold there, and **the moneychangers** were carrying on their **business** as well. The animals and birds were sold to the worshipers for use as sacrifices. **The moneychangers** took the money of those who came from foreign countries and changed it into the money of Jerusalem so that the pilgrims could pay the tax to the temple. It is known that these moneychangers often took unfair advantage of those who traveled from great distances.

2:15 The **whip** which the Lord made was probably a small lash made **of cords**. It is not recorded that He actually used it on anyone. Instead, it is probable that it was merely a symbol of authority which He held in His hand. Waving the whip before Him, He **drove** the merchants **out of the temple** and **overturned the tables** of the moneychangers.

2:16 The law permitted the poor to offer a pair of doves, since they could not afford the more expensive animals. To **those who sold doves**, the Lord issued a command **to take these things away**. It was not fitting that they should **make** His **Father's house a house of merchandise**. In all ages, God has warned His people against using religious services as a means of getting rich. There was nothing cruel or unjust in any of these actions. Rather, they were simply an indication of His holiness and righteousness.

2:17 When **His disciples** saw what was happening, they were reminded of Psalm 69:9 where it was predicted that when the Messiah came, He would be utterly consumed with a **zeal for** the things of God. Now they saw Jesus manifesting an intense determination that the worship of God should be pure, and they realized that this was the One of whom the Psalmist had spoken.

We should remember that the Christian's body is the temple of the Holy Spirit. Just as the Lord Jesus was anxious that the temple in Jerusalem be kept pure, so we must be careful that our bodies be turned over to the Lord for continual cleansing.

F. Jesus Predicts His Death and Resurrection (2:18–22)

2:18 It seems that the Jewish people were always seeking some sign or miracle. They said in effect, "If You perform some great, mighty work for us, then we will believe." However, the Lord Jesus performed one miracle after another, and yet their hearts were closed to Him. In verse 18 they questioned His authority to cast businessmen out of the temple. They demanded that He should perform some **sign** to support His claim of being the Messiah.

2:19 In answer, the Lord Jesus made an amazing statement concerning His death and resurrection. He told them that they would **destroy** His sanctuary, but **in three days** He would **raise it up**. The deity of Christ is again seen in this verse. Only God could say, **"In three days I will raise it up."**

2:20 **The Jews** did not understand Him. They were more interested in material things than in spiritual truth. The only temple they could think about was Herod's temple which was then standing in Jerusalem. **It had taken forty-six years to build this temple**, and they could not see how any man could possibly rebuild it **in three days**.

2:21 The Lord Jesus, however, **was speaking** about **His** own **body**, which was the sanctuary in which all the fullness of the Godhead dwelt. Just as these Jews had defiled the temple in Jerusalem, so they would put Him to death in a few short years.

2:22 Later on, after the Lord Jesus had been crucified and **had risen from the dead, His disciples remembered that He had** promised to rise again in three days. With such a marvelous fulfillment of prophecy before their eyes, **they believed the Scripture, and the word which Jesus had said**.

We often come across truths which are difficult to understand. But we learn here that we should treasure the Word of God in our hearts. Some day later the Lord will make it plain to us, even though we do not understand it now. When it says that **they believed the Scripture**, it means that they believed the OT predictions concerning the resurrection of the Messiah.

G. Many Profess to Believe in Christ (2:23–25)

2:23 As a result **of the signs** which Jesus performed **in Jerusalem at the Passover, many believed in His name**. This does not necessarily mean that they actually committed their lives to Him in simple trust; rather, they professed to accept Him. There was no reality to their action; it was merely an outward display of following Jesus. It was similar to the condition which we have in the world where many people claim to be Christians who have never truly been born again through faith in the Lord Jesus Christ.

2:24 Although many believed in Him, yet **Jesus did not** believe (same word in Greek) in **them**. That is, He **did not commit Himself to them**. He realized that they were coming to Him out of curiosity. They were looking for something sensational and spectacular. **He**

knew all men — their thoughts and their motives. He knew why they acted the way they did. He knew whether their faith was real or only an imitation.

2:25 No one knew the heart of man better than the Lord Himself. **He had no need that anyone should** teach or enlighten Him on this subject. He had full knowledge of **what was in man** and why man behaved as he did.

H. Jesus Teaches Nicodemus About the New Birth (3:1–21)

3:1 The story of **Nicodemus** contrasts with what had just gone before. Many of the Jews in Jerusalem professed to believe on the Lord, but He knew their faith was not genuine. Nicodemus was an exception. The Lord recognized in him an earnest desire to know the truth. Verse 1 should begin with a connective: *"But⁷* **there was a man of the Pharisees, named Nicodemus, a ruler of the Jews."**

Nicodemus was recognized as a teacher among his people. Perhaps he came to the Lord for instruction, so that he might return to the Jews with this additional learning.

3:2 The Bible does not say *why* Nicodemus **came to Jesus by night.** The most obvious explanation is that he would have been embarrassed to be seen going to Jesus, since the Lord had by no means been accepted by the majority of the Jewish people. However, he did come to Jesus. Nicodemus acknowledged the Lord to be **a teacher** sent by **God,** since no one could perform such miracles without the direct help of **God.** In spite of all his learning, Nicodemus did not recognize the Lord as God manifest in the flesh. He was like so many today who say that Jesus was a great man, a wonderful teacher, an outstanding example. All of these statements fall very far short of the full truth. Jesus *was* and *is* God.

3:3 At first sight, the answer of the Lord Jesus does not seem to be connected with what Nicodemus had just said. Our Lord is saying, "Nicodemus, you have come to Me for teaching, but what you really need is to be **born again.** That is where you must begin. You must be born from above. Otherwise, you can never **see the kingdom of God.**"

The Lord introduced these wonderful words with the expression: **"Most assuredly"** (literally *Amen, amen*). These words alert us to the fact that important truth is being given.

As a Jew, Nicodemus had been looking for a Messiah to come and free Israel from the bondage of Rome. The Roman Empire was then in control of the world, and the Jews were subject to its laws and government. Nicodemus longed for the time when the Messiah would set up His kingdom on earth, when the Jewish people would be chief among the nations, and when all their enemies would be destroyed. Now the Lord informed Nicodemus that in order to enter this kingdom, a man must be **born again.** Just as the first birth is necessary for physical life, so a second birth is necessary for divine life. (The expression **born again** may also mean "born from above.") In other words, Christ's kingdom can only be entered by those whose lives have been changed. Since His reign will be a righteous one, His subjects must be righteous also. He could not reign over people who were going on in their sins.

3:4 Here again we see how difficult it was for men to understand the words of the Lord Jesus. **Nicodemus** insisted on taking everything literally. He could not understand how a grown-up could be **born** again. He pondered the physical impossibility of a man entering **his mother's womb** again in order to **be born.**

Nicodemus illustrates that "the natural man does not receive the things of the Spirit of God, for they are foolishness to him; nor can he know them, because they are spiritually discerned" (1 Cor. 2:14).

3:5 In further explanation, Jesus told Nicodemus that he must be **born of water and the Spirit.** Otherwise, he could never **enter the kingdom of God.**

What did Jesus mean? Many insist that *literal* water is intended, and that the Lord Jesus spoke of the necessity of baptism for salvation. However, such a teaching is contrary to the rest of the Bible. Throughout the Word of God we read that salvation is by faith in the Lord Jesus Christ alone. Baptism is intended for those who have already been saved, but not as a means of salvation.

Some suggest that **water** in this verse refers to the Word of God. In Ephesians 5:25, 26 water is closely associated with the Word of God. Also, in 1 Peter 1:23 and James 1:18, the new birth is said to take place through the Word of God. It is quite possible, therefore, that water in this verse does refer to the Bible. We know that there can be no salvation apart from the Scriptures. It is the message contained in the Word of God that must be appropriated by the sinner before there can ever be the new birth.

But **water** may also refer to the Holy Spirit. In John 7:38, 39 the Lord Jesus spoke of rivers of living water, and we are distinctly told that when He used the word *water* He was speaking of the Holy Spirit. If water means the Spirit in chapter 7, why can it not have the same meaning in chapter 3?

However, there seems to be a difficulty if this interpretation is accepted. Jesus says, **"Unless one is born of water and the Spirit, he cannot enter the kingdom of God."** If **water** is taken to *mean* **the Spirit**, then it would appear that the Spirit is mentioned twice in this verse. But the word translated "and" could just as correctly have been translated "even." Thus, the verse would read: **Unless one is born of water,** *even* **the Spirit, he cannot enter the kingdom of God**. We believe that this is the correct meaning of the verse. Physical birth is not enough.[8] There must also be a spiritual birth if one is to **enter the kingdom of God**. This spiritual birth is produced by the Holy Spirit of God when a person believes on the Lord Jesus Christ. This interpretation is supported by the fact that the expression "born of the Spirit" is found twice in the verses to follow (vv. 6, 8).

3:6 Even if Nicodemus could in some way have entered his mother's womb a second time and been born a second time, that would not have corrected the evil nature in him. The expression **that which is born of the flesh is flesh** means that children born of human parents are born in sin and are hopeless and helpless as far as saving themselves is concerned. On the other hand, **that which is born of the Spirit is spirit**. A spiritual birth takes place when a person trusts in the Lord Jesus.

When a person is born again through the Spirit, he receives a new nature, and is made fit for the kingdom of God.

3:7 Nicodemus was **not** to **marvel** at the teachings of the Lord Jesus. He must realize that one **must be born again** and understand the complete inability of human nature to remedy its own fallen condition. He must realize that in order to be a subject of God's kingdom, a man must be holy, pure, and spiritual.

3:8 As He so often did, the Lord Jesus used nature to illustrate spiritual truth. He reminded Nicodemus that **the wind blows where it wishes**, and a person can **hear the sound of it, but cannot tell where it comes from and where it goes**. The new birth is very much like **the wind**. First of all, it takes place according to the will of God. It is not a power which man holds in his own control. Secondly, the new birth is invisible. You cannot see it taking place, but you can see the results of it in a person's life. When a man has been saved, a change comes over him. The evil things which he formerly loved, he now hates. The things of God which he formerly despised, these things are now the very things which he loves. Just as no one can fully understand the wind, so the new birth is a miraculous work of the Spirit of God which man is not able to comprehend fully. Moreover, the new birth, like **the wind**, is unpredictable. It is not possible to state just when and **where** it will take place.

3:9 Again, **Nicodemus** illustrated the inability of the natural mind to enter into divine things. Doubtless he was still trying to think of the new birth as a natural or physical event, rather than as a spiritual one. And so he asked the Lord Jesus: **"How can these things be?"**

3:10 Jesus **answered** that as **the teacher of Israel**, Nicodemus should have understood **these things**. The OT Scriptures clearly taught that when the Messiah came back to the earth to set up His kingdom, He would first judge His enemies and destroy all things that offend. Only those who had confessed and forsaken their sins would enter the kingdom.

3:11 The Lord Jesus then underlined the infallibility of His teaching, and yet man's unbelief concerning it. From all eternity, He had known the truthfulness of this and had only taught **what** He knew and had **seen**. But Nicodemus and most of the Jews of his day refused to believe His testimony.

3:12 What were the **earthly things** to which the Lord referred in this verse? It was His **earthly** kingdom. As a student of the OT, Nicodemus knew that one day the Messiah would come and set up a literal kingdom here on earth with Jerusalem as His capital. What Nicodemus failed to understand was that in order to enter this kingdom, there must be a new birth. What then were the **heavenly things** to which the Lord referred? They are the truths which are explained in the following verses — the wonderful way by which a person receives this new birth.

3:13 Only one person was qualified to speak about heavenly things, since He was the only One **who** was **in heaven**. The Lord Jesus was not merely a human teacher sent from God, but He was One who lived with God the Father from all eternity, and **came down** into the world. When He said that **no one has ascended to heaven**, He did not mean that OT saints such as Enoch and Elijah had not gone to heaven, but that they had been *taken up* whereas He **ascended to heaven** by His own power. Another explanation is that no human being had access to the presence of God continually in the way which He had. He could ascend to God's dwelling place in a unique way because He had descended out of heaven to this earth. Even as the Lord Jesus stood on earth, speaking with Nicodemus, He said that He was **in heaven**. How could this be? Here is a statement of the fact that, as God, the Lord was in all places at one and the same time. This is what we mean when we say that He is omnipresent. While some modern translations omit the words **who is in heaven**, they are widely supported in the manuscripts and belong to the text.

3:14 The Lord Jesus was now about to unfold heavenly truth to Nicodemus. How can the new birth take place? The penalty of man's sins must be met. People cannot go to heaven in their sins. Just **as Moses lifted up the serpent** of brass on a pole **in the wilderness** when all the children of Israel had been bitten by snakes, **so must the Son of Man be lifted up**. (Read Numbers 21:4–9.) As they wandered through the wilderness to the promised land, the children of Israel became discouraged and impatient. They complained against the Lord. To punish them, the Lord sent fiery serpents among them, and many people died. When the survivors cried to the Lord in repentance, the Lord told Moses to make **a serpent** of brass and put it on a pole. The bitten Israelite who looked to the serpent was miraculously healed.

Jesus quoted this OT incident to illustrate how the new birth takes place. Men and women have been bitten by the viper of sin and are condemned to eternal death. The serpent of brass was a type or picture of the Lord Jesus. Brass, in the Bible, speaks of judgment. The Lord Jesus was sinless and should never have been punished, but He took our place and bore the judgment which we deserved. The pole speaks of the cross of Calvary on which the Lord Jesus was lifted up. We are saved by looking to Him in faith.

3:15 The Savior was made sin for us, He who knew no sin, that we might be made the righteousness of God in Him. **Whoever believes in** the Lord Jesus Christ receives **eternal life** as a free gift.

3:16 This is one of the best known verses in all the Bible, doubtless because it states the gospel so clearly and simply. It summarizes what the Lord Jesus had been teaching Nicodemus concerning the manner by which the new birth is received. **God**, we read, **so loved the world**. **The world** here includes all mankind. God does not love men's sins or the wicked world system, but He loves people and is not willing that any should perish.

The extent of His love is shown by the fact **that He gave His only begotten Son**. God has no other Son like the Lord Jesus. It was an expression of His infinite love that He would be willing to give **His** unique **Son** for a race of rebel sinners. This does *not* mean that everyone is saved. A person must receive what Christ has done for him before God will give him eternal life. Therefore, the words are added, **"that whoever believes in Him should not perish."** There is no need for anyone to perish. A way has been provided by which all might be saved, but a person must acknowledge the Lord Jesus Christ as personal Savior. When he does this, he has eternal **life** as a present possession. Boreham says:

> When the church comes to understand the love with which God loved the world, she will be restless and ill at ease, until all the great empires have been captured, until every coral island has been won.[9]

3:17 God is not a harsh, cruel ruler anxious to pour out His anger on mankind. His heart is filled with tenderness toward man and He has gone to the utmost cost in order to save men. He could have sent **His Son into the world to condemn the world**, but He did **not** do so. On the contrary, He sent Him here to suffer, bleed, and die in order **that the world through Him might be saved**. The work of the Lord Jesus on the cross was of such tremendous value that all sinners everywhere could be saved if they would receive Him.

3:18 Now all mankind is divided into two classes: either believers or unbelievers. Our eternal destiny is determined by the attitude we take toward the Son of God. The one who trusts the Savior **is not condemned, but** the one **who does not** trust Him **is condemned already**. The Lord Jesus has finished the work of salvation, and now it is up to each individual to decide whether he will accept Him or reject Him. It is a terrible thing to reject such a gift of love. If a man will not believe on the Lord Jesus, God can do nothing else but condemn him.

Believing in His **name** is the same as believing in *Him*. In the Bible, the name stands for the person. If you trust His **name**, you trust Him.

3:19 Jesus is **the light** who came **into the world**. He was the sinless, spotless Lamb of God. He died for the sins of all the world. But do men love Him for this? No — they resent Him. They prefer their sins to having Jesus as Savior, and so they reject Him. Just as some creeping things scurry away from the light, so wicked men flee from the presence of Christ.

3:20 Those who love sin hate **the light**, because the light exposes their sinfulness. When Jesus was here in the world, sinful men were made uncomfortable by His presence because He revealed their awful condition by His own holiness. The best way to reveal the crookedness of one stick is to place a straight stick beside it. Coming into the world as a Perfect Man, the Lord Jesus revealed the crookedness of all other men, by comparison.

3:21 If a man is truly honest before God, he will come **to the light**, that is, the Lord Jesus, and realize his own utter worthlessness and sinfulness. Then he will trust the Savior for himself, and thus be born again through faith in Christ.

I. The Ministry of John the Baptist in Judea (3:22–36)

3:22 The first portion of this chapter described the Lord Jesus' witness in the city of Jerusalem. From this verse to the end of the chapter, John describes Christ's ministry in **Judea**, where doubtless He continued to proclaim the good news of salvation. As men came to the light, they were **baptized**. It would appear from this verse that Jesus Himself did the baptizing, but we learn in John 4:2 that it was done by His disciples.

3:23 The **John** referred to in this verse is John the Baptist. He was still preaching his message of repentance in the region of Judea and baptizing those Jews who were willing to repent in preparation for the coming of the Messiah. **John also was baptizing in Aenon . . . because there was much water there**. This does not prove conclusively that he baptized by immersion, but it certainly implies as much. If he baptized by sprinkling or pouring, there would have been no necessity of having **much water**.

3:24 This verse is given in explanation of John's continued ministry and of the continued response of devout Jews to it. In the near future, **John** would be **thrown into prison** and beheaded for his faithful testimony. But in the meantime, he was still diligently carrying out his commission.

3:25 It is clear from this verse that **some of John's disciples** became engaged in **a dispute** with **the Jews about**

purification. What does this mean? **Purification** here probably refers to baptism. The argument was whether the baptism of John was better than that of Jesus. Which baptism had the greater power? Which was of greater value? Perhaps **some of John's disciples** unwisely contended that no baptism could be better than that of their master. Perhaps the Pharisees tried to make John's disciples jealous of Jesus and His current popularity.

3:26 **They came to John** for a decision. They seemed to be saying to him, "If your baptism is the better, why is it that so many men are leaving you and going to Jesus?" (The expression **"He who was with you beyond the Jordan"** refers to Christ.) John bore witness to the Lord Jesus, and as a result of this witness, many of John's own disciples left him and began to follow Jesus.

3:27 If John's reply was referring to the Lord Jesus, it means that any success the Savior received was an indication of God's approval on Him. If John was referring to himself, he was saying that he had never pretended to be anyone great or important. He had never claimed that his baptism was superior to that of Jesus. He simply said here that he did not have anything but what he had received **from heaven**. That is true of all of us, and there is no reason in the world why we should be proud or seek to build up ourselves in men's esteem.

3:28 John reminded his disciples that he had pointed out time and again that he was **not the Christ, but** was simply **sent** to prepare the way for the Messiah. Why should they argue over him? Why should they seek to form a party around him? He was not the important one, but was simply trying to point men to the Lord Jesus.

3:29 The Lord Jesus Christ was **the bridegroom**. John the Baptist was merely **the friend of the bridegroom**, the "best man." **The bride** does not belong to the friend of the bridegroom, but rather to **the bridegroom** himself. Therefore, it was fitting that the people follow Jesus rather than John. **The bride** was used here to refer in a general way to all who would become disciples of the Lord Jesus. In the OT, Israel was spoken of as the wife of Jehovah. Later on in the

NT, those who are members of Christ's church are described under the figure of a bride. But here in John's Gospel, the word was used in a general sense to include those who left John the Baptist when the Messiah appeared. It did not mean either Israel or the church. John was not unhappy to lose followers. It was his great joy to listen to **the bridegroom's voice**. He was satisfied that Jesus receive all the attention. His **joy** was **fulfilled** when Christ was praised and honored by men.

3:30 The entire object of John's ministry is summarized in this verse. He labored ceaselessly to point men and women to the Lord, and to make them realize His true worth. In doing this, John realized that he must keep himself in the background. For a servant of Christ to seek to attract attention to himself is really a form of disloyalty.

Note the three "musts" in this chapter: for the *Sinner* (3:7); for the *Savior* (3:14); and for the *Saint* (3:30).

3:31 Jesus is the One **who comes from above and is above all**. This statement was designed to show His heavenly origin and supreme position. To prove his own inferiority, John the Baptist said that **he** himself was **of the earth** and was **earthly and speaks of the earth**. This simply meant that, as to his birth, he was born a man of human parents. He had not heavenly rank and could not speak with the same authority as the Son of God. He was inferior to the Lord Jesus because **He who comes from above is above all.** Christ is the supreme Sovereign of the universe. It is only proper, therefore, that men should follow Him rather than His messenger.

3:32 But when the Lord Jesus spoke, He spoke with authority. He told men **what** He had **seen and heard**. There was no possibility of error or deceit. Yet strange to say, **no one receives His testimony.** The expression **no one** is not to be taken in an absolute sense. There are individuals who accept the words of the Lord Jesus. However, John was looking at mankind in general and simply stating that the Savior's teachings were rejected by the majority. Jesus was the One who came down from heaven, but comparatively few were willing to listen to Him.

3:33 Verse 33 describes the few who

did accept the words of the Lord as being the very words of God. By their acceptance, they **certified that God is true**. So it is today. When people accept the message of the gospel, they take sides with God against themselves and against the rest of mankind. They realize that if **God** has said something, it must be **true**. Notice how clearly verse 33 teaches the deity of Christ. It says that whoever believes the **testimony** of Christ acknowledges **that God is true**. This is just another way of saying that the testimony of Christ is the testimony of *God*, and to receive the one is to receive the other also.

3:34 Jesus was the One **God has sent**. He spoke **the words of God**. To support this statement, John stated that **God does not give the Spirit by measure**. Christ was anointed by the Holy Spirit of God in a way that was not true of any other person. Others have been conscious of the help of the Holy Spirit in their ministry, but no one else ever had such a Spirit-filled ministry as the Son of God. The prophets received a partial revelation from God but "the Spirit revealed in and by Christ the very wisdom, the very heart of God to man with all its infinitude of love."

3:35 This is one of the seven times in John's Gospel where we are told that **the Father loves the Son**. Here that love is manifested in giving Him control over **all things**. Among these things over which the Savior has complete charge are the destinies of men, as explained in verse 36.

3:36 God has given Christ the power to grant **everlasting life** to all who believe on Him. This is one of the clearest verses in all the Bible on how a person can be saved. It is *simply by believing* **in the Son**. As we read this verse, we should realize that God is speaking. He is making a promise that can never be broken. He says, clearly and distinctly, that anyone **who believes in** His **Son has everlasting life**. To accept this promise is not a leap in the dark. It is simply believing what could not possibly be false. Those who do **not** obey **the Son** of God **shall not see life, but the wrath of God abides on** them already. From this verse we learn that our eternal destiny depends on what we do with the **Son** of

God. If we receive Him, God gives us eternal **life** as a free gift. If we reject Him, we will never enjoy everlasting **life**, and not only so, but God's **wrath** already hangs over us, ready to fall at any moment.

Notice that there is nothing in this verse about keeping the law, obeying the Golden Rule, going to church, doing the best we can, or working our way to heaven.

J. The Conversion of a Woman of Samaria (4:1–30)

4:1, 2 The Pharisees had heard that Jesus was baptizing **more disciples than John** and that John's popularity was evidently declining. Perhaps they had attempted to use this fact to stir up jealousy and contention between the disciples of John and those of the Lord Jesus. Actually, **Jesus Himself did not** perform the act of baptism. This was done by **His disciples**. However, the people were baptized as followers or disciples of the Lord.

4:3 By leaving **Judea** and journeying **to Galilee**, Jesus would prevent the Pharisees from being successful in their efforts to cause divisions. But there is something else of significance in this verse. **Judea** was the headquarters of the Jewish religious establishment, whereas **Galilee** was known as a heavily Gentile region. The Lord Jesus realized that the Jewish leaders were already rejecting Him and His testimony, and so here He turns to the Gentile people with the message of salvation.

4:4 Samaria was on the direct route from Judea to Galilee. But few Jews ever took this direct route. The region of Samaria was so despised by the Jewish people that they often took a very roundabout route through Perea to get north into Galilee. Thus, when it says that Jesus **needed to go through Samaria**, the thought is not so much that He was compelled to do so by geographical considerations, but rather by the fact that there was a needy soul in **Samaria** He could help.

4:5 Traveling into **Samaria**, the Lord Jesus came to a little village **called Sychar**. Not far from that village was a **plot of ground that Jacob** had given **to his son Joseph** (Gen. 48:22). As Jesus journeyed over this territory, all the scenes of its past history were constantly before His mind.

4:6 A spring known as **Jacob's well was there**. This ancient well can still be seen by visitors, being one of the few Biblical sites which can be identified quite positively today.

It was about noon (Jewish time) or 6 p.m. (Roman time) when **Jesus** reached the well. He was **weary** as a result of the long walk He had had, and so He **sat** down **by the well**. Although Jesus is God the Son, He is also a Man. As God, He could never become weary, but as Man, He did. We find difficulty in understanding these things. But the Person of the Lord Jesus Christ can never be fully understood by any mortal mind. The truth that God could come down into the world and live as a Man among men is a mystery which passes our understanding.

4:7 As the Lord Jesus was sitting by the well, **a woman came** out from the village **to draw water**. If, as some scholars say, it was noon, it was a very unusual time for women to go to the well for water; it was the hottest part of the day. But this woman was an immoral sinner, and she may have chosen this time out of a sense of shame because she knew that there would be no other women there to see her. Of course, the Lord Jesus knew all along that she would be at the well at this time. He knew that she was a soul in need, and so He determined to meet her and rescue her from her sinful life.

In this passage, we find the master Soul Winner at work, and we do well to study the methods He used to bring this woman to a sense of her need and to offer her the solution to her problem. Our Lord spoke to the woman just seven times. The woman spoke seven times also — six times to the Lord and once to the men of the city. Perhaps if we spoke to the Lord as much as she did, we might have the success in testimony that she had when she spoke to the men of the city. Jesus opened the conversation by asking a favor. Wearied with His journey, He **said to her, "Give me a drink."**

4:8 Verse 8 explains why, from a human standpoint, the Lord should ask her for a drink. **His disciples had gone away into** Sychar **to buy** some **food**. They ordinarily carried buckets with which to draw water, but they had taken these with them. Thus to all outward appearance, the Lord had no means for getting water from the well.

4:9 The woman recognized Jesus as **a Jew** and was amazed that He would speak to her, **a Samaritan**. The Samaritans claimed descent from Jacob, and looked on themselves as true Israelites. Actually, they were of mixed Jewish and heathen descent. Mount Gerizim had been adopted as their official place of worship. This was a mountain in Samaria, clearly visible to the Lord and to this woman as they talked together. The Jews had a deep dislike for the Samaritans. They considered them half-breeds. That is why this woman said to the Lord Jesus, **"How is it that You, being a Jew, ask a drink from me, a Samaritan woman?"** Little did she realize that she was speaking with her own Creator, and that His love rose above all the petty distinctions of men.

4:10, 11 By asking a favor, the Lord had stirred her interest and curiosity. He now arouses them still further by speaking of Himself as being both God and Man. He was first of all **the gift of God** — the One **God** gave to be the Savior of the world, His only begotten Son. But He was also a Man — the One who, wearied with His journey, asked her for **a drink**. In other words, if she had realized that the One to whom she was talking was God manifest in the flesh, she **would have asked Him** for a blessing, **and He would have given** her **living water**. The woman could only think of *literal* water and of the impossibility of His getting it without the necessary equipment. She completely failed to recognize the Lord, or to understand His words.

4:12 Her confusion deepened when she thought of the patriarch **Jacob, who** had given this **well**. He had used it **himself, as well as his sons and his livestock**. Now here was a weary traveler, centuries later, who asked for a drink from Jacob's well and yet who claimed to be able to give something better than the water which Jacob had given. If He had something better, why should He ask for water from Jacob's well?

4:13 So the Lord began to explain the difference between the literal water of Jacob's well and the water which He would give. **Whoever** drank **of this water** would **thirst again**. Surely the Samaritan woman could understand this. She had been coming out day after day to draw from the well; yet the need was never completely met. And so it is with all the wells of this world. Men seek their pleasure and satisfaction in earthly things, but these things are not able to quench the thirst of the heart of man. As Augustine said in his *Confessions*, "O Lord, You have made us for Yourself, and our hearts are restless till they rest in You."

4:14 **The water** which Jesus gives truly satisfies. **Whoever drinks** of Christ's blessings and mercies **will never thirst** again. Not only do His benefits fill the heart, but they overflow it as well. They are like a bubbling **fountain**, constantly overflowing, not only in this life but in eternity as well. The expression **springing up into everlasting life** means that the benefits of **the water** which Christ gives are not limited to earth, but will go on forever. The contrast is very vivid. All that earth can provide is not sufficient to fill the human heart. But the blessings which Christ provides not only fill the heart, but they are too great for any heart to contain.

> The whole wide world is not enough
> To fill the heart's three corners,
> But yet it craveth still;
> Only the Trinity that made it can
> Suffice the vast, triangled heart of man.
>   — *George Herbert*

The pleasures of this world are for a few short years, but the pleasures which Christ provides go on **into everlasting life.**

4:15 When **the woman** heard of this marvelous water, she immediately wanted to have it. But she was still thinking of *literal* water. She did not want to have **to come** out to the well every day **to draw** the water and to carry it home on her head in a heavy waterpot. She did not realize that the water of which the Lord Jesus had been speaking was spiritual, that He was referring to all the blessings which come to a human soul through faith in Him.

4:16 There is an abrupt change in the conversation here. She had just asked for the water, and the Lord Jesus told her to **go** and **call** her **husband**. Why? Before this woman could be saved, she must acknowledge herself a sinner. She must come to Christ in true repentance, confessing her guilt and shame. The Lord Jesus knew all about the sinful life she had lived, and He was going to lead her, step by step, to see it for herself.

Only those who know themselves to be lost can be saved. All men are lost, but not all are willing to admit it. In seeking to win people for Christ, we must never avoid the sin question. They must be brought face to face with the fact that they are dead in trespasses and sins, need a Savior, cannot save themselves, that Jesus is the Savior they need, and, He will save them if they repent of their sin and trust in Him.

4:17 At first **the woman** tried to withhold the truth without telling a lie. She **said, "I have no husband."** Perhaps in a strictly legal sense, her statement was true. But it was designed to hide the hideous fact that she was then living in sin with a man who was not her husband:

> She chats about religion, discusses theology, uses a little irony, pretends to be shocked — anything to keep Christ from seeing the fugitive soul in full flight from itself (Daily Notes of the Scripture Union).

The Lord Jesus, as God, knew all about this. And so He **said to her, "You have well said, 'I have no husband.'"** Although she might be able to fool her fellow men, she was not able to fool this Man. He knew all about her.

4:18 The Lord never used His complete knowledge of all things to needlessly expose or shame a person. But He did use it, as here, in order to deliver a person from the bondage of sin. How startled she must have been when He recited her past history! She had **had five husbands**, and the man with whom she was now living was **not** her **husband**.

There is some difference of opinion about this verse. Some teach that the woman's five previous husbands had either died or deserted her, and that there was nothing sinful in her relationships with them. Whether or not this is so, it is clear from the latter part of this verse that this woman was an adulteress. **"The one whom you now have is not your husband."** This is the important point. The woman was a sinner, and until she was willing to acknowledge this, the Lord could not bless her with living water.

4:19 When her life was thus laid open before her, **the woman** realized that the One speaking to her was not an ordinary person. However, she did not yet realize that He was God. The highest estimation she could form of Him was that He was **a prophet**, that is, a spokesman for God.

4:20 It seems now that the woman had become convicted of her sins, and so she tried to change the subject by introducing a question concerning the proper place of worship. Doubtless as she said, **"Our fathers worshiped on this mountain,"** she pointed to Mount Gerizim nearby. Then she reminded the Lord (unnecessarily) that **Jews** claimed **Jerusalem** as the proper **place where one ought to worship**.

4:21 **Jesus** did not avoid her comment but used it to impart further spiritual truth. He told her that the time was **coming** when **neither on** Mt. Gerizim **nor in Jerusalem** would be the place of **worship**. In the OT, Jerusalem was appointed by God as *the* city where worship should be offered to Him. The temple in Jerusalem was the dwelling place of God, and devout Jews came to Jerusalem with their sacrifices and offerings. Of course, in the gospel age, this is no longer so. God does not have any certain place on earth where men must go to worship. The Lord explained this more fully in the verses to follow.

4:22 When the Lord said, **"You worship what you do not know,"** He condemned the Samaritan mode of worship. This is in marked contrast to those religious teachers today who say that all religions are good and that they all lead to heaven at last. The Lord Jesus informed this woman that the worship of the Samaritans was not authorized by God, neither was it approved by Him. It had been invented by man and carried on without the sanction of the Word of God. This was not so with the worship

of the Jews. God had set apart the Jewish people as His chosen earthly people. He had given them complete instructions on the way to worship Him.

In saying that **"salvation is of the Jews,"** the Lord was teaching that the Jewish people were appointed by God to be His messengers, and it was to them that the Scriptures had been given. Also, it was through the Jewish nation that the Messiah was given. He was born of a Jewish mother.

4:23 Next Jesus informed the woman that, with His coming, God no longer had a certain place on earth for worship. Now those who believe on the Lord Jesus can worship God at any time and in any place. True worship means that a believer enters the presence of God by faith and *there* praises and worships Him. His body may be in a den, prison, or field, but his spirit can draw near to God in the heavenly sanctuary by faith. Jesus announced to the woman that from now on worship of the Father would be **in spirit and truth**. The Jewish people had reduced worship to outward forms and ceremonies. They thought that by religiously adhering to the letter of the law, and going through certain rituals, they were worshiping the Father. But theirs was not a worship of the spirit. It was outward, not inward. Their bodies might be bowed down on the ground but their hearts were not right before God. Perhaps they were oppressing the poor, or using deceitful business methods.

The Samaritans, on the other hand, had a form of worship, but it was false. It had no scriptural authority. They had started their own religion and were carrying out ordinances of their own invention. Thus, when the Lord said that worship must be **in spirit and truth**, He was rebuking both Jews and Samaritans. But He was also informing them that, now that He had come, it was possible for men to draw near to God through Him in true and sincere worship. Ponder this! **The Father is seeking such to worship Him.** God is interested in the adoration of His people. Does He receive this from me?

4:24 **God is Spirit** is a definition of God's being. He is not a mere man, subject to all the errors and limitations of humanity. Neither is He confined to any one place at any time. He is an invisible Person who is present in all places at one and the same time, who is all-knowing, and who is all-powerful. He is perfect in all His ways. Therefore, **those who worship Him must worship in spirit and truth**. There must be no sham or hypocrisy. There must be no pretense to being religious, when inwardly one's life is corrupt. There must be no idea that in going through a series of rituals, God is thereby pleased. Even if God instituted those rituals Himself, He still insists that man approach Him with a broken and a contrite heart. Two more "musts" are found in this chapter — "must" for the winner of souls (4:4) and "must" for the worshiper (4:24).

4:25 As the woman of Samaria had listened to the Lord, she had been made to think of the coming **Messiah**. The Holy Spirit of God had stirred up within her a desire that the **Messiah** should come. She expressed the confidence that when He did come, He would teach **all things**. In this statement, she showed a very clear understanding of one of the great purposes of Christ's coming.

The expression **"Messiah . . . who is called Christ"** is simply an explanation of the fact that these two words mean the same. **Messiah** is the Hebrew word for God's Anointed One; **Christ** is the Greek equivalent.

4:26 What **Jesus said to her** was literally, **"I who speak to you am."** The word **He** is not a part of the original text. Although the sentence is clearer with the word **He** included, yet there is a deep significance to the actual words of the Lord Jesus. In using the words **"I am"** He used one of the names which God applied to Himself in the OT. He said, "I AM is speaking to you," or, in other words, "Jehovah is the one who is speaking to you." He was announcing to her the startling truth that the One who was speaking to her was the Messiah for whom she had been looking and that He was also God Himself. The Jehovah of the OT is the Jesus of the NT.

4:27 When the **disciples** returned from Sychar they found Jesus talking with this **woman**. They were surprised that He would speak with her, for she was a Samaritan. Also, they could possibly discern that she was a sinful woman. **Yet no one** asked the Lord what he was seeking from the woman or **why** He was **talking with her**. It has been well said, "The disciples marvel that He talks with the woman; they would have been better employed wondering that He talked with them!"

4:28 The woman then left her waterpot! It symbolized the various things in life which she had used in an effort to satisfy her deepest longings. They had all failed. Now that she had found the Lord Jesus, she had no more need for the things which had formerly been so prominent in her life.

> I tried the broken cisterns, Lord,
> But ah! the waters failed!
> E'en as I stooped to drink, they fled,
> And mocked me as I wailed.
>
> Now none but Christ can satisfy,
> None other name for me;
> There's love, and life, and lasting joy,
> Lord Jesus, found in Thee.
> — *B. E.*

She not only **left her waterpot** but she **went her way into the city**. Whenever a person is saved, he or she immediately begins to think of others who are in need of the water of life. J. Hudson Taylor said, "Some are jealous to be successors of the Apostles; I would rather be a successor of the Samaritan woman, who, while they went for food, forgot her waterpot in her zeal for souls."

4:29, 30 Her witness was simple but effective. She invited all the townspeople to **come** and **see a Man who told** her **all things that** she **ever did**. Also, she aroused within their hearts the possibility that this Man might indeed be the Messiah. In her own mind, there could be little doubt because He had already announced Himself to her as **the Christ**. But she raised the question in their minds so that they might go to Jesus and find out for themselves. Doubtless this woman was well known in the village for her sin and shame. How startling it must have been for the people to see her standing in the public places now, bearing public witness to the Lord Jesus Christ! The testimony of the woman was effective. The people of the village left their homes and their work and began to go out to find Jesus.

K. The Son's Delight in Doing His Father's Will (4:31–38)

4:31 Now that the **disciples** were back with the food, they encouraged the Lord to **eat**. Apparently they were not aware of the momentous events that were taking place. At this historic moment when a Samaritan city was being introduced to the Lord of Glory, their thoughts could rise no higher than food for their bodies.

4:32 The Lord Jesus had found **food** and support in winning worshipers to His Father. Compared to this joy, physical nourishment was of little importance to Him. We get what we go after in life. The disciples were interested in food. They went into the village to get food. They came back with it. The Lord was interested in souls. He was interested in saving men and women from sin, and giving them the water of everlasting life. He, too, found what He went after. What are we interested in?

4:33 Because of their earthly outlook, **the disciples** failed to understand the meaning of the Lord's words. They did not appreciate the fact that "the joy and happiness of spiritual success can for the time lift men above all bodily wants, and supply the place of material meat and drink." And so they concluded that someone must have come along and **brought** food to the Lord Jesus.

4:34 Again **Jesus** tried to turn their attention from the material to the spiritual. His **food** was **to do the will of** God, **and to finish** the **work** which God had given Him to do. This does not mean that the Lord Jesus refrained from eating actual food, but rather it means that the great aim and object of His life was not to cater to the body, but rather to do the will of God.

4:35 Perhaps the disciples had been talking together about the coming harvest. Or perhaps it was a common proverb among the Jews, **"Four months** between seed time and **harvest."** At any rate, the Lord Jesus again used the physical fact of **harvest** to teach a spiritual lesson. The disciples should not think that harvest time was still in the distance. They could not afford to spend their lives in quest of food and clothing, with the thought that God's work could be done later on. They must realize that **the fields** were **already white for harvest. The fields** here, of course, refer to the world. At the very moment when the Lord spoke these words, He was in the midst of a harvest field containing the souls of Samaritan men and women. He was telling the disciples that a great work of in-gathering lay before them, and that they should give themselves to it immediately and diligently.

So today, the Lord says to those of us who are believers, **"Lift up your eyes, and look at the fields."** As we spend time contemplating the great needs of the world, the Lord will lay on our hearts a burden for the lost souls around us. Then it will be up to us to go forth for Him, seeking to bring in the sheaves of ripened grain.

4:36 The Lord Jesus was now instructing the disciples concerning the work to which they were called. He had chosen them to be reapers. They would not only earn **wages** in this life, but they would gather **fruit** for eternity as well. Service for Christ has many rewards at the present time. But in a coming day, reapers will have the additional joy of seeing souls in heaven because of their faithfulness in proclaiming the gospel message.

Verse 36 does *not* teach that a person earns life eternal through faithful reaping, but rather that the **fruit** of that work continues on into eternal life.

In heaven, both the sower and the reaper will **rejoice together**. In natural life, the field must first be prepared for the seed, and then the seed must be sown in it. Later on, the grain is harvested. Thus it is in the spiritual life also. First of all, the message must be preached, then it must be watered with prayer. But when the harvest season comes, all who have had a part in the work **rejoice together**.

4:37 **In this**, the Lord saw a fulfillment of **the saying** that was common in that day, **"One sows, and another reaps."** Some Christians are called on to preach the gospel for many years without seeing very much fruit for their labor. Others step in at the end of those years, and many souls turn to the Lord.

4:38 Jesus was sending His disciples into areas that had already been prepared by others. Throughout the OT period, the prophets had foretold the coming of the gospel era and of the Messiah. Then, too, John the Baptist came as a forerunner of the Lord, seeking to prepare the hearts of the people to receive Him. The Lord Himself had sown the seed in Samaria, and prepared a harvest for the reapers. Now the disciples were about to step into the harvest field, and the Lord wanted them to know that, although they would have the joy of seeing many turning to Christ, they should understand that they were entering **into** other men's **labors**.

Very few souls are ever saved through the ministry of a single person. Most people have heard the gospel many times before they ever accept the Savior. Therefore, the one who finally leads a person to Christ should not exalt himself as if he were the only instrument God used in this marvelous work.

L. Many Samaritans Believe in Jesus (4:39–42)

4:39 As a result of the simple and forthright testimony of the woman of Samaria, **many** of her people **believed** on the Lord Jesus. All she said was, **"He told me all that I ever did,"** and yet that was sufficient to bring others to the Savior. This should be an encouragement to each of us to be simple, courageous, and direct in our witness for Christ.

4:40 The reception given to the Lord Jesus by the Samaritans was in marked contrast to that of the Jews. **The Samaritans** seemed to have some real appreciation of this wonderful Person, and **they urged Him to stay with them**. As a result of their invitation, the Lord **stayed there two days**. Just think how privileged this city of Sychar was, that it should entertain the Lord of life and glory during this period of time!

4:41, 42 No two conversions are exactly alike. Some believed because of the testimony of the woman. **Many more believed because of** the words of the Lord Jesus Himself. God uses various means in bringing sinners to Himself. The great essential is that there should be faith in the Lord Jesus Christ. It is wonderful to hear these Samaritans bearing such clear testimony to the Savior. There was no doubt in their minds at all. They had

complete assurance of salvation based not on the word of a woman, but on the words of the Lord Jesus Himself. Having **heard Him** and believed His words, the Samaritans had come to know **that this** was **indeed the Christ,**[10] **the Savior of the world**. Only the Holy Spirit could have given them this insight. The Jewish people apparently thought that the Messiah would be for them alone. But the Samaritans realized that the benefits of Christ's mission would extend to all **the world**.

M. The Second Sign: Healing of the Nobleman's Son (4:43–54)

4:43, 44 **After the two days** which He spent among the Samaritans, the Lord turned His footsteps northward **to Galilee**. Verse 44 seems to present a difficulty. It states that the reason for the Savior's moving from Samaria to Galilee was **that a prophet has no honor in his own country**. And yet Galilee *was* His own country, since Nazareth was a city located in that region. Perhaps what the verse means is that Jesus went into some part of Galilee other than Nazareth. In any case, the statement is certainly true that a person is not usually appreciated as much in his own home town as he is in other places. One's relatives and friends think of him as a mere youngster and one of themselves. Certainly the Lord Jesus was not appreciated by His own people as He should have been.

4:45 When the Lord returned **to Galilee**, He was given a favorable reception because the people had **seen all the things He** had done **in Jerusalem at the feast**. Obviously **the Galileans** referred to here were Jews. They had gone down to **Jerusalem** to worship. There they had seen the Lord and had witnessed some of His mighty works. Now they were willing to have Him in their midst in Galilee, not because they acknowledged Him to be the Son of God, but because they were curiously interested in One who was arousing so much comment everywhere He went.

4:46 Again the village of **Cana** was honored by a visit from the Lord Himself. On the first visit, some of the people had seen Him turn water into wine. Now they were to witness another mighty miracle by Him, the effect of which would extend to **Capernaum**. The **son** of **a certain nobleman . . . was sick at Capernaum**. This man was undoubtedly a Jew employed by Herod, the king.

4:47 He had **heard that Jesus had** been in **Judea** and had now returned to **Galilee**. He must have had some faith in the ability of Christ to heal because he came directly **to Him and implored Him to come down and heal his** dying **son**. In this sense, he seems to have a greater trust in the Lord than most of his fellow countrymen.

4:48 Speaking not only to the nobleman, but to the Jewish **people** in general,[11] the Lord reminded them of a national characteristic, that they desired to see miracles before they would **believe**. In general, we find that the Lord Jesus was not as pleased with a faith that was based on miracles as He was with that which was based on His Word alone. It is more honoring to Him to believe a thing simply because He said it than because He gives some visible proof. It is characteristic of man that he wants to see before he believes. But the Lord Jesus teaches us that we should first believe, and then we will see.

Signs and **wonders** both refer to miracles. **Signs** are miracles that have a deep meaning or significance. **Wonders** are miracles that cause men to be amazed by their supernatural qualities.

4:49 **The nobleman**, with the persistence of true faith, believed that the Lord Jesus could do his son good, and he wanted a visit from the Lord more than anything else. In one sense, his faith was defective. He thought that Jesus would have to be at the boy's bedside before He could heal him. However, the Savior did not rebuke him for this but rewarded him for the measure of faith which he *did* exhibit.

4:50 Here we see the man's faith growing. He exercised what faith he had, and the Lord gave him more. Jesus sent him home with the promise, **"Your son lives."** The son had been healed! Without any miracle or visible proof, **the man believed the word** of the Lord **Jesus** and started for home. That is faith in action!

4:51, 52 **As he was now** nearing home, **his servants** came out to meet him with the happy news that his **son**

was well. The man was not at all shocked by this announcement. He had believed the promise of the Lord Jesus, and having believed, he would now see the evidence. The father **inquired of** the servants as to the time **when** his son **got better**. Their answer revealed that the healing was not gradual; it had taken place instantly.

4:53 There could now be not the slightest doubt about this wonderful miracle. At the seventh hour of the previous day, **Jesus** had **said to** the nobleman in Cana, **"Your son lives." At the** very **same hour** in Capernaum, the son had been healed, and the fever had left him. From this the nobleman learned that it was not necessary for the Lord Jesus to be physically present to work a miracle or answer prayer. This should encourage all Christians in their prayer life. We have a mighty God who hears our requests and who is able to work out His purposes in any part of the world at any time.

The nobleman **himself believed, and his whole household**. It is apparent from this and similar verses in the NT that God loves to see families united in Christ. It is not His will that there should be divided families in heaven. He takes care to record the fact that the **whole household** believed in His Son.

4:54 The healing of the nobleman's son was not the second miracle in the Lord's entire ministry up to this point. It was **the second sign Jesus** performed in **Galilee** after **He had come** from **Judea**.

III. THE SON OF GOD'S SECOND YEAR OF MINISTRY (Chap. 5)[†]

A. The Third Sign: Healing of the Impotent Man (5:1–9)

5:1 As chapter 5 opens, the time had come for one of the Jewish feasts. Many believe this was Passover, but it is impossible to be sure. Born into the world as a Jew, and obedient to the laws which God had made for the Jewish people, **Jesus went up to Jerusalem** for the **feast**. As Jehovah of the OT, the Lord Jesus had been the One who instituted the Passover in the first place. Now as a

Man, obedient to His Father, He obeyed the very laws which He had made.

5:2 **In Jerusalem**, there was **a pool** named **Bethesda**,[12] meaning "house of mercy" or "house of pity." This **pool** was located **by the Sheep Gate**. The exact location is now known and excavated (near the Crusader Church of St. Anne). Around the pool there were **five porches** or large open spaces capable of holding a number of people. Some Bible teachers think that these five porches represent the Law of Moses and speak of its inability to help man out of his deep troubles.

5:3 Apparently the pool of Bethesda was known as a place where miracles of healing occurred. Whether these miracles took place throughout the year, or only at certain times, such as on feast days, we do not know. Surrounding the pool were a large number of **sick people** who had come with the hope of being cured. Some were **blind**, others **lame**, and still others were **paralyzed**. These various types of infirmity picture sinful man in his helplessness, blindness, lameness, and uselessness.

These people, suffering from the effect of sin in their bodies, were **waiting for the moving of the water**. Their hearts were filled with longing to be freed from their sicknesses, and they earnestly desired to find healing. Says J. G. Bellett:

> They lingered round that uncertain, disappointing water, though the Son of God was present. . . . Surely there is a lesson for us in this. The pool thickly populated, and Jesus passing by unheeded! What a witness of man's religion! Ordinances, with all their complicated machinery, sought after, and the grace of God slighted.[13]

5:4 The narrative here is not sufficient to satisfy our curiosity. We are simply told that **an angel went down at a certain time** and **stirred up the water**. The **first** one who was able to get into the water at that time was healed of his sickness. You can imagine what a pathetic sight it was to see so many people in need of help, struggling to get into the water, and yet only one being able to receive healing power.

While in many versions of the Bible, the latter part of verse 3 (beginning with

the words "waiting for the moving of the water") and all of verse 4 are missing, these words are in the majority of manuscripts. Also, the story makes little sense without an explanation of why these sick people were there.

5:5, 6 One of the men who was waiting by the pool had been an invalid for **thirty-eight years**. This means that he had been in this condition even before the Savior was born. The Lord Jesus had complete knowledge of everything. He had never met this man before. Yet He knew that he had been an invalid **a long time**.

In loving compassion, **He said to him, "Do you want to be made well?"** Jesus knew that this was the greatest longing of the man's heart. But He also wanted to draw out from the man an admission of his own helplessness and of his desperate need for healing. It is much the same with salvation. The Lord knows that we desperately need to be saved, but He waits to hear the confession from our own lips that we are lost, that we need Him and accept Him as our Savior. We are not saved by our own will, yet the human will must be exercised before God saves a soul.

5:7 The answer of **the sick man** was rather pathetic. For years he had lain by the pool, waiting to get in, but every time **the water was stirred up**, there was no one to help him. Every time he would try to get in, someone else got there ahead of him. This reminds us how disappointed we are if we depend on our fellow men to save us from our sins.

5:8 The man's **bed** was a pad or light mattress. Jesus told him to **rise**, carry his pad, **and walk**. The lesson here is that when we are saved, we are not only told to rise, but also to walk. The Lord Jesus gives us healing from the plague of sin, and then He expects us to walk in a manner worthy of Him.

5:9 The Savior never tells anyone to do a thing without giving the power to do it. Even as He spoke, new life and power flowed into the body of the invalid. He was healed immediately. It was not a gradual recovery. Limbs that had been useless or weak for years now throbbed with strength. Then there was immediate obedience to the word of the Lord. He **took up his bed and walked**.

What a thrill it must have been for him to do this after thirty-eight years of sickness!

This miracle took place on **the Sabbath**, the seventh day of the week —our Saturday. The Jewish people were forbidden to do any work on the Sabbath. This man was a Jew, and yet at the instruction of the Lord Jesus, he did not hesitate to carry his mattress despite Jewish traditions regarding the day.

B. The Opposition of the Jews (5:10–18)

5:10 When **the Jews** saw the man carrying his mattress on **the Sabbath**, they challenged him. These people were very strict and even cruel in carrying out their religious observances and clung rigidly to the letter of the law, but they themselves often did not show mercy and compassion to others.

5:11 The healed man gave a very simple answer. He said that the One who cured him told him to **take up** his **bed and walk**. Anyone who had the power to heal a man who had been sick for thirty-eight years ought to be obeyed, even if he instructed a person to carry his bed on the Sabbath! The healed man did not really know who the Lord Jesus was at this time. He spoke of Him in a very general way, and yet with real gratitude.

5:12 The Jews were anxious to find out who dared tell this man to break their Sabbath tradition, and so they asked him to identify the culprit. The Law of Moses decreed that one who broke the Sabbath should be stoned to death. The Jews cared little that a paralytic had been healed.

5:13 The **healed** man did not know who had cured him. And it was impossible to point Him out, because **Jesus had** slipped away from the crowd that had gathered.

This incident marks one of the great turning points in the public ministry of the Lord Jesus Christ. Because He performed this miracle on the Sabbath, He stirred up the anger and hatred of the Jewish leaders. They began to pursue Him and to seek His life.

5:14 Some time later **Jesus found** the healed man **in the temple**, where doubtless he was thanking God for the wonderful miracle that had taken place

in his life. The Lord reminded him that because he had been so highly favored, he was therefore under solemn obligation. Privilege always brings with it responsibility. **"See, you have been made well. Sin no more, lest a worse thing come upon you."** It seems clear that the man's sickness had originally come to him as a result of some sin in his life. This is not true of all sickness. Many times illness in a person's life has no direct connection with any sin he has committed. Infants, for instance, may be sick before they are old enough to sin knowingly.

"Sin no more," said Jesus, expressing God's standard of holiness. If He had said, "Sin as little as possible," He would not have been God. God cannot condone sin in any degree. Then the warning was added, **"lest a worse thing come upon you."** The Lord did not indicate what He meant by a worse thing. However, He doubtless intended the man to understand that sin has far more terrible results than physical sickness. Those who die in their sins are condemned to eternal wrath and anguish.

It is a more serious thing to sin against grace than against law. Jesus had shown wonderful love and mercy to this man. Now it would be a poor response if he would go out and carry on in the same kind of sinful life which had originally led to his illness.

5:15 Like the woman of Samaria, this **man** desired to bear public witness to His Savior. He **told the Jews that it was Jesus who had made him well**. He wanted to pay tribute to Jesus, though the Jews were not interested in such tribute. Their chief desire was to apprehend Jesus and punish Him.

5:16 Here is a terrible exposure of the wicked heart of man. The Savior had come and performed a great act of healing and these **Jews** were infuriated. They resented the fact that the miracle took place **on the Sabbath**. They were cold-blooded religionists, more interested in ceremonial observances than they were in the blessing and welfare of their fellow men. They did not realize that it was the very One who set apart the Sabbath in the first place who now performed an act of mercy on this day. The Lord Jesus had not broken the Sabbath. The law forbade menial work on that day, but it did not prohibit the performance of acts of necessity or of mercy.

5:17 Having finished the work of creation in six days, God had rested on the seventh day. This was the Sabbath. However, when sin entered the world, God's rest was disturbed. He would now work ceaselessly to bring men and women back into fellowship with Himself. He would provide a means of redemption. He would send out the gospel message to every generation. Thus, from the time of Adam's fall up to the present time, God **has been working** ceaselessly, and He is still working. The same was true of the Lord Jesus. He was engaged in His Father's business, and His love and grace could not be confined to only six days of the week.

5:18 This verse is very important. It tells us that **the Jews** became more determined than ever **to kill** the Lord Jesus **because He not only** had broken **the Sabbath, but** had claimed equality **with God**! To their narrow minds, it seemed that the Lord had broken the Sabbath although it was not true. They did not realize that God never intended the Sabbath to impose a hardship on man. If a man could be cured of a disease on the Sabbath, God would not require that he should suffer one day longer.

When Jesus spoke of **God** as **His Father**, they realized that He was claiming to be **equal with God**. To them, this was terrible blasphemy. Actually, of course, it was only the truth.

Did the Lord Jesus really claim to be equal with God? If He had not intended this, then He would have explained it to the Jews. Instead of that, He stated in even more positive terms, in the verses that follow, that He was indeed one with the Father. As J. Sidlow Baxter puts it:

He claims equality in seven particulars: (1) Equal in working: "What things soever he (the Father) doeth, these also doeth the Son likewise" (v. 19). (2) Equal in knowing: "For the Father loveth the Son, and showeth him all things that himself doeth" (v. 20). (3) Equal in resurrecting: "For as the Father raiseth up the dead . . . so the Son quickeneth whom he will" (v. 21 with vv. 28, 29). (4) Equal in judging: "For the Father judgeth no man, but hath committed all judgment unto the Son" (v. 22 with v. 27). (5) Equal in hon-

our: "That all men should honour the Son even as they honour the Father" (v. 23). (6) Equal in regenerating: "He that heareth my word, and believeth on him that sent me . . . is passed from death unto life" (vv. 24, 25). (7) Equal in self-existence: "For as the Father hath life in himself; so hath he given to the Son to have life in himself" (v. 26).[14]

C. Jesus Defends His Claim to Be Equal with God (5:19–29)

5:19 The Savior was so vitally linked with God the Father that He could not act independently. He does not mean that He did not have the power to do anything by Himself, but that He was so closely united with God that He could only do the very things which He saw His **Father** doing. For while the Lord claimed equality with the Father, He did not claim independency too. He is not independent of although He is fully equal with Him.

The Lord Jesus clearly intended the Jews to think of Him as equal with God. It would be absurd for a mere man to claim to do the very things which God Himself **does**. Jesus claims to see what the Father is doing. In order to make such a claim, He must have continual access to the Father and complete knowledge of what is going on in heaven. Not only so, but Jesus claims to do the very things which **He sees the Father do**. This is certainly an assertion of His equality with God. He is omnipotent.

5:20 It is a special mark of the Father's love for His **Son** that He **shows Him all things that He Himself does**. These **things** Jesus not only saw; He had the power to perform them as well. Then the Savior went on to say that God would **show Him greater works than these**, so **that** the people might **marvel**. Already they had seen the Lord Jesus performing miracles. They had just seen Him heal a man who had been crippled for thirty-eight years. But they would see **greater** marvels than this. The first such marvel would be the raising of the dead (v. 21). The second was the work of judging mankind (v. 22).

5:21 Here is another clear statement as to the equality of the Son with the Father. The Jews accused Jesus of making Himself equal with God. He did not deny the charge, but rather set forth these tremendous proofs of the fact that He and the Father are one. Just **as the Father raises the dead and gives life to them, even so the Son gives life to whom He will**. Could this ever be said of Him if He were a mere man? To ask the question is to answer it.

5:22 The NT teaches that God **the Father . . . has committed all** the work of **judgment to the Son**. In order for the Lord Jesus to do this work, He must, of course, have absolute knowledge and perfect righteousness. He must be able to discern the thoughts and motives of men's hearts. How strange it was that the Judge of all the earth should stand before these Jews, asserting His authority, and yet they did not recognize Him!

5:23 Here we have the reason God has given authority to His Son to raise the dead and to judge the world. The reason is so **that all should honor the Son just as they honor the Father**. This is a most important statement, and one of the clearest proofs in the Bible of the deity of the Lord Jesus Christ. Throughout the Bible we are taught that God alone is to be worshiped. In the Ten Commandments, the people were forbidden to have any god but the one true God. Now we are taught **that all should honor the Son just as they honor the Father**. The only conclusion we can come to from this verse is that Jesus Christ is God.

Many people claim to worship God, but deny that Jesus Christ is God. They say that He was a good man or more godlike than any other man who ever lived. But this verse puts Him on an absolute equality with God, and requires that men should give Him the *same honor* which they give to *God the Father*. If a person **does not honor the Son**, then he **does not honor the Father**. It is useless to claim a love for God if one does not have the same love for the Lord Jesus Christ. If you have never realized before who Jesus Christ is, then ponder this verse carefully. Remember that it is the Word of God, and accept the glorious truth that Jesus Christ is God manifest in the flesh.

5:24 In the preceding verses, we learned that the Lord Jesus had the power to give life and that, also, the work of judgment had been committed to Him. Now we learn how one may receive spiritual life from Him and escape judgment.

This is one of the favorite gospel verses in the Bible. Multitudes have become possessors of eternal life through its message. Doubtless the reason for its being so greatly loved is the manner in which it sets forth the way of salvation so clearly. The Lord Jesus began the verse with the words **"Most assuredly,"** drawing attention to the importance of what He was about to say. Then He added the very personal announcement, **"I say to you."** The Son of God is speaking to us in a very personal and intimate way.

"He who hears My word." To hear the word of Jesus means not only to listen to it, but also to receive it, to believe it, and to obey it. Many people hear the gospel preached, but do nothing about it. The Lord is saying here that a man must accept His teaching as divine, and believe that He is indeed the Savior of the world.

"And believes in Him who sent Me." It is a matter of believing God. But does that mean that a person is saved simply by believing God? Many profess to believe in God, yet they have never been converted. No, the thought here is that one must believe God, who sent the Lord Jesus Christ into the world. What must he believe? He must believe that God **sent** the Lord Jesus to be our Savior. He must believe what God says about the Lord Jesus, namely, that He is the only Savior and that sins can only be put away through His work on Calvary.

"Has everlasting life." Notice it does not say that he will have eternal life, but that he **has** it right now. **Everlasting life** is the life of the Lord Jesus Christ. It is not only life that will go on forever, but it is a (higher) quality of life. It is the life of the Savior imparted to us who believe in Him. It is the spiritual life received when a man is born again, in contrast to the natural life which he received at his physical birth.

"And shall not come into judgment." The thought here is that he is not condemned now and will never be condemned in the future. The one who believes on the Lord Jesus is free from **judgment** because Christ has paid the penalty for his sins on Calvary. God will not demand the payment of this penalty twice. Christ has paid it as our Substitute, and that is sufficient. He has finished the work, and nothing can be added to a finished work. The Christian will never be punished for his sins.[15]

"But has passed from death into life." The one who has trusted Christ **has passed** out of a state of spiritual **death into** one of spiritual **life**. Before conversion, he was dead in trespasses and in sins. He was dead as far as love for God or fellowship with the Lord was concerned. When he put his faith in Jesus Christ, he was indwelt by the Spirit of God and became a possessor of divine life.

5:25 This is the third time the Lord has used the expression **most assuredly** in chapter 5, and the seventh time so far in this Gospel. When the Lord said that **the hour** was **coming and now is**, He did not refer to a period of sixty minutes, but rather He was saying that the time was coming, and had already arrived. The time referred to was His coming onto the stage of history.

Who are **the dead** spoken of in this verse? Who are they who would **hear the voice of the Son of God** and **live**? This may refer of course to those people who were raised from the dead by the Lord during His public ministry. But the verse has a wider meaning than this. **The dead** referred to are those who are dead in trespasses and sins. They **hear the voice of the Son of God** when the gospel is preached. When they accept the message and receive the Savior, then they pass from death into life.

Supporting the idea that verse 25 refers to spiritual matters and not physical, we list the comparisons and contrasts between it and verses 28, 29:

V. 25 — Life from Death	Vv. 28, 29 — Life after Death
"The hour is coming, and now is"	"the hour is coming"
"the dead"	"all who are in the graves"
"will hear the voice"	"will hear His voice"
"those who hear will live"	"and come forth"

5:26 This verse explains how a person can receive life from the Lord Jesus. Just **as the Father** is the Source and

Giver of **life, so He has** decreed that **the Son**, too, should **have life in Himself** and should be able to give it to others. This again is a distinct statement as to the deity of Christ and as to His equality with the Father. It cannot be said of any man that he has life in himself. Life was given to each one of us, but it was never given to the Father or to the Lord Jesus. From all eternity, They have had life dwelling in Them. That life never had a beginning. It never had a source apart from Them.

5:27 Not only has God decreed that the Son should have life in Himself, but He also **has given Him authority** to be Judge of the world. The power to judge has been given to Jesus **because He is the Son of Man**. The Lord is called both Son of God and **Son of Man**. The title *Son of God* is a reminder to us that the Lord Jesus is one of the Members of the holy Trinity, one of the Persons of the Godhead. As Son of God, He is equal with the Father and with the Holy Spirit, and as Son of God, He gives life. But He is also **the Son of Man**. He came into this world as a Man, lived here among men, and died on the cross as a Substitute for men and women. He was rejected and crucified when He came into the world as a Man. When He comes again, He will come to judge His enemies and to be honored in this same world where He was once so cruelly treated. Because He is both God and Man, He is perfectly qualified to be Judge.

5:28 Doubtless as Christ was making these strong claims as to His equality with God the Father, the Jews who were listening were amazed. He realized, of course, the thoughts that were going through their minds, and so He here told them that they should **not marvel at** these things. Then He went on to reveal to them some even more startling truth. In a time yet future, all of those whose bodies **are lying in the graves will hear His voice**. How foolish it would be for anyone who was not God to predict that bodies lying in the grave would one day hear His voice! Only God could ever support such a statement.

5:29 All the dead will one day be raised. Some will be raised to **life**, and others to **condemnation**. What a solemn truth it is that every person who has ever lived or will ever live falls into one of these two classes![16]

Verse 29 does *not* teach that people who have done good will be saved because of their good deeds, and those who have done evil will be condemned because of their wicked lives. A person is not saved by doing good, but he does good because he has been saved. Good works are not the root of salvation but rather the fruit. They are not the cause, but the effect. The expression **those who have done evil** describes those who have never put their faith and trust in the Lord Jesus, and consequently whose lives have been **evil** in the sight of God. These will be raised to stand before God and to be sentenced to eternal doom.

D. Four Witnesses to Jesus as the Son of God (5:30–47)

5:30 At first, **"I can of Myself do nothing"** seems to say that the Lord Jesus did not have the power to do anything by Himself. However, that was not the case. The thought is that He is so closely united with God the Father that He could not act by Himself. He could not do anything on His own authority. There was no trace of willfulness in the Savior. He acted in perfect obedience to His Father and always in fullest fellowship and harmony with Him.

This verse has often been used by false teachers to support their claim that Jesus Christ was not God. They say that because He could not do anything of His own self, therefore He was just a man. But the verse proves the very opposite. Men can do the things they want, whether they are in accordance with the will of God or not. But because of who He was, the Lord Jesus could not so act. It was not a *physical* impossibility, but a *moral* impossibility. He had the physical power to do all things, but He could not do anything that was wrong: and it would have been wrong for Him to have done anything that was not the will of God the Father for Him. This statement sets the Lord Jesus apart from every other man who ever lived.

As the Lord Jesus listened to His Father and daily received instructions from Him, so He thought, taught, and acted. The word **judge** does not here have the sense of deciding on legal matters but rather of deciding what was proper for Him to do and say.

Because the Savior had no selfish motives, He could decide matters fairly and impartially. His one ambition was to please His Father and to do His will. Nothing was allowed to stand in the way of this. Therefore, His judgment of matters was not influenced by what would be for His own best advantage. Our opinions and teachings are generally affected by what we want to do and what we want to believe. But it was not so with the Son of God. His opinions or judgments were not biased in His own favor. He was without prejudice.

5:31 In the remaining verses of this chapter, the Lord Jesus Christ described the various witnesses to His deity. There was the witness of John the Baptist (vv. 32–35); the witness of His works (v. 36); the witness of the Father (vv. 37, 38); and the witness of the OT Scriptures (vv. 39–47).

First, Jesus made a general statement on the subject of witnessing. He said, **"If I bear witness of Myself, My witness is not true."** This did not mean for a moment that the Lord Jesus could ever say anything that was not true. Rather, He was simply stating a general fact that the witness of a single person was not considered sufficient evidence in a court of law. God's divine decree was that at least two or three witnesses were required before a valid judgment could be formed. And so the Lord Jesus was about to give not two or three, but four witnesses to His deity.

5:32 There is a question as to whether this verse refers to John the Baptist, God the Father, or the Holy Spirit. Some believe that the word **another** describes John the Baptist and that this verse is linked with the three that follow. Others believe that the Lord here was speaking about the **witness** which the Holy Spirit bears concerning Him. We believe that He was referring to the **witness** of the Father (the capitalized **He** shows the NKJV translators see a reference to Deity).

5:33 Having introduced the greatest of all witnesses, His Father, the Lord then turned to the testimony of **John**. He reminded the unbelieving Jews that they **sent** men **to John** to hear what he had to say, and John's testimony was all about the Lord Jesus Christ. Instead of pointing men to himself, he pointed them to the Savior. He bore **witness to** the One who is **the truth**.

5:34 The Lord Jesus reminded His listeners that His claim to be equal with God was not based simply on the **testimony** of human beings. If that was all He had, then His case would indeed be a weak one. But He introduced the testimony of John the Baptist since he was a man sent from God and since he testified that the Lord Jesus was indeed the Messiah and the Lamb of God who takes away the sin of the world.

Then He added, **"But I say these things that you may be saved."** Why was the Lord Jesus speaking to the Jews at such great length? Was He simply trying to show that He was right and that they were wrong? On the contrary, He was bringing before them these wonderful truths in order that they might realize who He was and accept Him as the promised Savior. This verse gives us a clear view of the loving and tender heart of the Lord Jesus. He spoke to those who hated Him and who would soon be seeking in every possible way to take His life. But there was no hatred in His heart toward them. He could only love them.

5:35 Here the Lord paid tribute to John the Baptist as **a burning and shining lamp**. This meant that he was a very zealous man, one who had a ministry that brought **light** to others, and one who was consumed in the process of pointing people to Jesus. At first, the Jewish people had flocked to John the Baptist. He was something of a novelty, a strange figure who had come into their lives, and they went out to listen to him. **For a time**, they accepted him as a popular religious teacher.

Why then, after accepting John so warmly, would they not accept the One of whom John preached? They rejoiced temporarily, but there was no repentance. They were inconsistent. They received the forerunner, but would not receive the King! Jesus paid high tribute to John. For any servant of Christ to be called **a burning and shining lamp** is true praise from the Son of God. May each of us who loves the Lord Jesus desire that we, too, may be flames of fire for Him, burning ourselves out but bringing light to the world in the process.

5:36 The testimony **of John** was not Christ's greatest proof of His deity. The miracles which the Father gave Him to do bore **witness of** Him, that **the Father** had truly **sent** Him. Miracles in themselves are not a proof of deity. In the Bible, we read of men who were given the power to perform miracles, and we even read of evil beings with the power to do supernatural wonders. But the miracles of the Lord Jesus were different from all others. First of all, He had the power *in Himself* to do these mighty works, whereas others were *given* the power. Other men have performed miracles, but they could not confer the power to perform miracles on others. The Lord Jesus not only performed miracles Himself, but He gave His apostles the authority to do likewise. Furthermore, **the works** performed by the Savior were the very ones which were prophesied in the OT concerning the Messiah. Finally, the miracles that the Lord Jesus performed were unique in character, scope, and number.

5:37, 38 Again the Lord spoke of the witness which **the Father** had borne to Him. Perhaps this referred to the time when the Lord Jesus was baptized. Then the voice of God the Father was heard from heaven stating that Jesus was His beloved Son, in whom He was well pleased. But it should be added that in the life, ministry, and miracles of the Lord Jesus, the Father also bore witness to the fact that He was the very Son of God.

The unbelieving Jews had **neither heard** the **voice** of God **at any time, nor seen His form**. This was because they did **not have His word abiding in** them. God speaks to men through His Word, the Bible. These Jews had the OT Scriptures, but they did not allow God to speak to them through the Scriptures. Their hearts were hardened, and their ears were dull of hearing.

They had never seen God's Form or Person because they did **not believe** on the One whom God had **sent**. God the Father does not have a Form or Shape that is visible to mortal eyes. He is Spirit and therefore invisible. But God has revealed Himself to men in the Person of the Lord Jesus Christ. In a very real way, those who believed on Christ saw the Form of God. Unbelievers merely looked upon Him as another man like themselves.

5:39 The first part of this verse may be understood[17] in two ways. First of all, the Lord Jesus may be telling the Jews to **search the Scriptures**. Or He may be simply stating the fact that they did **search the Scriptures** because they thought that in the mere possession of the Scriptures, they had **eternal life**. Either interpretation of the verse is possible. Probably the Lord Jesus was simply stating the fact that the Jews searched **the Scriptures** and thought that in doing so they were receiving **eternal life**. They did not realize that the OT Scriptures telling of the coming Messiah were actually telling about Jesus. It is terrible to think that men with the Scriptures in their hands could be so blind. But it was even more inexcusable that after the Lord Jesus spoke to them in this way, they still refused to accept Him. Notice the latter part of this verse carefully. **"These are they which testify of Me."** This simply means that the main subject of the OT was the coming of Christ. If anyone misses that in studying the OT, he misses the most important part of it.

5:40 The Jews were **not willing to come to** Christ **that** they might **have life**. The real reason people do not accept the Savior is not because they cannot understand the gospel, or find it impossible to believe on Jesus. There is nothing about the Lord Jesus that makes it impossible for them to trust Him. The real fault lies in man's own will. He loves his sins more than he loves the Savior. He does not want to give up his wicked ways.

5:41 In condemning the Jews for their failure to receive Him, the Lord did not want them to think that He was hurt because they had not given Him **honor**. He did not come into the world for the purpose of being praised by the **men** of this world. He was not dependent on their praise, but rather sought the praise of His Father. Even if men rejected Him, that did not detract from His glory.

5:42 Man's failure to receive the Son of God is here traced back to its cause. These men did **not have the love of God in** them, that is, they loved themselves rather than God. If they had loved God, they would have received the One whom God had sent. By their rejection of the Lord Jesus, they showed their utter lack of **love** for His Father.

5:43 The Lord Jesus came **in** His **Father's name**, that is, He came to do His Father's will, to bring glory to His Father, and to obey His Father in all things. If men had really loved God, they would have loved the One who sought to please God in all He said and did.

Jesus now predicted that **another** would **come in his own name** and that the Jews *would* **receive him**. Perhaps in one sense He was referring to many false teachers who arose after Him and sought to be honored by the nation. Perhaps He was referring to leaders of false cults down through the centuries who have claimed to be the Christ. But more probably He was referring here to the Antichrist. In a coming day, a self-appointed ruler will rise among the Jewish people and demand to be worshiped as God (2 Thess. 2:8–10). The majority of the Jewish nation will accept this Antichrist as their ruler, and as a result they will come under severe judgment from God (1 Jn. 2:18).

5:44 Here the Lord gave another reason for the failure of the Jewish people to accept Him. They were more interested in the approval of their fellow men than they were in God's approval. They were afraid of what their friends would say if they left Judaism. They were not willing to endure the reproach and suffering which would be heaped upon them if they became followers of the Lord Jesus. As long as a person is afraid of what others will say or do, he cannot be saved. In order to believe on the Lord Jesus, one must desire God's approval more than anyone else's. He must **seek the honor that comes from the only God**.

5:45 The Lord would **not** need to **accuse** these Jews **to the Father**. Of course, there were many charges He could bring against them. But there would be no need for Him to do it, because the writings of **Moses** would be sufficient to accuse them. These Jews took great pride in the OT and especially in the five books written by **Moses**, the

Torah. They were proud that these Scriptures were given to Israel. But the trouble was that they did not obey the words of Moses, as verse 46 shows.

5:46 The Lord Jesus put the writings of Moses on the same level of authority as His own words. We are reminded that "all Scripture is given by inspiration of God." Whether we read the OT or the New, we are reading the very Word of God. If the Jews had **believed** the words of **Moses**, they would have believed the Lord Jesus Christ also, because Moses **wrote about** the coming of Christ. An example of this is found in Deuteronomy 18:15, 18:

> The Lord Your God will raise up for you a Prophet like me from your midst, from your brethren. Him you shall hear. . . . I will raise up for them a Prophet like you from among their brethren, and will put My words in His mouth, and He shall speak to them all I command Him.

In these verses Moses predicted the coming of Christ, and told the Jewish people to listen to Him and obey Him when He came. Now the Lord Jesus had come, but the Jews failed to receive Him. Thus He said that Moses would accuse them to the Father because they pretended to believe in Moses and yet they did not do what Moses commanded. The words **he wrote about Me** are a clear statement by our Lord that the OT Scriptures contain prophecies about Him. Augustine stated this concisely: "The New is in the Old concealed; the Old is in the New revealed."

5:47 If the Jews would **not believe** the **writings** of Moses, it was not likely that they would believe the **words** of Jesus. There is a very close connection between the OT and the New. If a man doubts the inspiration of the OT Scriptures, it is not likely that he will accept the words of the Lord Jesus as being inspired. If people attack certain parts of the Bible, it won't be long before they cast doubt on the rest of the Book as well. King states:

> The Lord's allusion is, of course, to the Pentateuch, the Five Books of Moses — the portion of the Bible that has been more savagely attacked than any other; and, strangely enough, the portion which, so far as our records go, the Master quoted more than any other. As if,

long before the attacks began, He would set His own imprimatur upon them.[18]

IV. THE SON OF GOD'S THIRD YEAR OF MINISTRY: GALILEE (Chap. 6)

A. The Fourth Sign: Feeding of the Five Thousand (6:1–15)

6:1 The expression **after these things** means that a period of time had elapsed since the events in chapter 5 took place. Just how much time we do not know, but we do know that **Jesus** had traveled from the area around Jerusalem up to the Sea of Galilee. When it says that He crossed the sea, it probably means that He went from the northwestern shore to the northeastern side. **The Sea of Galilee** was also known as **the Sea of Tiberias**, because the city of Tiberias was located on its western bank. This city, the capital of the province of Galilee, was named after the Roman Emperor Tiberius.

6:2, 3 A **great** crowd of people **followed Him**, not necessarily because they believed on Him as the Son of God, but rather **because they saw** the miracles which He had done for **those who were diseased**. A faith founded on miracles is never as pleasing to God as that which is founded on His Word alone. God's Word should not require miracles to verify it. Anything that God says is true. It cannot possibly be false. That should be enough for anyone. The literal translation of verse 3 is **"And Jesus went up on** *the* **mountain"**, but this may merely mean the mountainous (or hilly) region around the Sea.

6:4 It is not clear why John mentioned that the **Passover was near**. Some suggest that the Lord Jesus was probably thinking about the Passover when He gave His wonderful message in this chapter on the true Bread of Life. He had not gone to Jerusalem for the Passover. John spoke of **the Passover** as **a feast of the Jews**. Actually, of course, it had been instituted by God in the OT. He had given it to the Jewish people, and in that sense it was **a feast of the Jews**. But the expression **a feast of the Jews** might also mean that God no longer recognized it as one of His own feasts because the Jewish nation celebrated it as a mere ritual, without any real heart interest. It had lost its real meaning, and was no longer a feast of Jehovah.

6:5 **Jesus** was not annoyed when He saw the **great multitude**, thinking they would disturb His rest or His time with the disciples. His first thought was to provide something for them to **eat**. And so He turned to **Philip** and asked where **bread** could be purchased to feed the multitude. When Jesus asked a question, it was never for the purpose of adding to His own knowledge, but to teach others. He knew the answer, but Philip didn't.

6:6 The Lord was going to teach Philip a very valuable lesson and **test** his faith. Jesus **Himself knew** that He would perform a miracle to feed this great crowd of people. But did Philip realize that He was able to do this? Was Philip's faith great or was it small?

6:7 Apparently Philip's faith did not rise to very great heights. He made some quick calculations and decided that even **two hundred denarii worth of bread** would not be enough to provide even **a little** meal for everyone. We do not know exactly how much bread could be purchased for **two hundred denarii** in that day, but it must have been a very great amount. A denarius was a worker's daily wage.

6:8, 9 **Andrew** was **Simon Peter's brother**. They lived in the vicinity of Bethsaida, along the shore of the Sea of Galilee. Andrew also decided that it would be difficult to feed such a throng. He noticed a little boy with **five barley loaves and two small fish**, but he felt that these would be almost useless in attempting to satisfy the hunger of **so many**. This **lad** did not have very much, but he was willing to put it at the disposal of the Lord Jesus. As a result of his kindness, this story was recorded in each of the four Gospels. He did not do very much, but "little is much if God is in it," and he has become famous throughout the world.

6:10 In making the people **sit down** (literally, recline), the Lord Jesus provided for their comfort. Notice He chose a place where there **was much grass**. It was unusual to find such a place in that region, but the Lord took care that the crowd would eat in a clean, pleasant place.

It is recorded that there were thousands of **men** (Greek: "males"), so this means that there were women and children in addition. The mention of the number **five thousand** is made to indicate what a mighty miracle was about to take place.

6:11 **Jesus took the loaves** and gave **thanks** for them. If He did this before partaking of food or serving it, how much more should we pause to thank God before eating our meals. Next **He distributed** the food **to the disciples**. There is a real lesson for us in this. The Lord Jesus did not do it all Himself. He enlisted the service of others. It has been well said, "You do what you can do; I'll do what I can do; and the Lord will do what we cannot do."

By the time the Lord **distributed** the bread **to the disciples**, it had been wonderfully multiplied. The exact moment when this miracle took place is not recorded, but we know that in a miraculous way those five loaves and two small fish became enough in the Lord's hands to feed this great throng. The disciples went about serving the bread and **the fish to those sitting down**. There was no scarcity because it is distinctly stated that they gave them of the fish **as much as they wanted**.

Griffith Thomas has reminded us that in this story we have a beautiful picture of:

(a) the perishing world; (b) the powerless disciples; (c) the perfect Savior. This miracle involved a true act of creation. No mere man could take five loaves and two small fish and expand them in such a way as to feed so many people as this. It has been well said, "'Twas springtime when He blessed the bread, 'twas harvest when He brake." And it is also true, "Loaves unblessed are loaves unmultiplied."[19]

6:12 This is a very beautiful touch. If Jesus had been a mere man He would never have bothered to think about the remaining **fragments**. Any man who can feed five thousand does not worry about a few leftover crumbs! But Jesus is God, and with God there must be no wasting of His bounties. He does not want us to squander the precious things He has given to us, and so He takes care to instruct that the broken pieces which remained should be gathered up **so that nothing** might be **lost**.

Many people try to explain away this miracle. The crowd, they say, saw the little boy give his five loaves and two fish to Jesus. This made them realize how selfish they were, so they decided to take out their lunches and share them with each other. In this way, there was food for everyone. But no such explanation will fit the facts, as we shall see in the next verse.

6:13 **Twelve baskets** of bread were gathered up after the people had finished eating. It would be a sheer impossibility to gather up as much bread as this if it had just been a matter of each person having his own lunch with him. Man's explanations prove ridiculous. There can be only one conclusion, and that is that a mighty miracle had been performed.

6:14 The people themselves recognized that it was a miracle. They would not have done so if they had simply eaten their own lunches. In fact, they were so convinced that it was a miracle that they were willing to acknowledge that Jesus was **the Prophet who** would **come into the world**. They knew from the OT that a prophet was coming, and they looked for him to deliver them from the control of the Roman Empire. They were waiting for an earthly monarch. But their faith was not genuine. They were not willing to admit that Jesus was the Son of God or to confess their sins and accept Him as Savior.

6:15 As a result of Jesus' miracle, the people wanted **to make Him king**. Again, if Jesus were only a man, He doubtless would have submitted readily to their request. Men are only too anxious to be exalted and to be given a place of prominence. But Jesus was not moved by such appeals to vanity and pride. He realized that He had come into the world to die as a Substitute for sinners on the cross. He would do nothing to interfere with that objective. He would not ascend the throne until first He had ascended the altar of sacrifice. He must suffer, bleed, and die before He would be exalted.

F. B. Meyer writes:

As St. Bernard said, He always fled when they wanted to make Him King, and presented Himself when they wanted to crucify Him. With this clearly in mind let us not hesitate to adopt the noble words of Ittai the Gittite: "As the Lord liveth, and as my lord the King liveth, surely in what place my lord the king shall be, whether in death or life, even there also will thy servant be" (II Samuel 15:21). And He will surely answer, as that same David did to another fugitive who came to identify himself with his cause: "Abide with me, fear not; for he that seeketh my life seeketh thy life, but with me thou shalt be in safeguard."[20]

B. The Fifth Sign: Jesus Walks on the Water and Rescues His Disciples (6:16–21)

6:16, 17 It was **evening**. Jesus had gone to the mountain by Himself. The crowd doubtless returned to their homes, leaving the disciples by themselves. And so the disciples decided to go **down to the sea** and prepare for their trip back across the Sea of Galilee.

As they **went over the sea toward Capernaum, it was already dark. Jesus** was **not** with **them**. Where was He? He was up on the mountain praying. What a picture of Christ's followers today. They are on the stormy sea of life. It is **dark**. The Lord Jesus is nowhere to be seen. But that does not mean that He is unaware of what is going on. He is in heaven praying for those He loves.

6:18 The Sea of Galilee is subject to sudden and violent storms. Winds travel down the valley of the Jordan River at a great speed. When they hit the Sea of Galilee, they cause the waves to rise very high. It is not safe for small boats to be out on **the sea** at such a time.

6:19 The disciples **had rowed about three or four miles**. From a human standpoint, they were in great danger. At the right moment, they looked up and **saw Jesus walking on the sea, and drawing near the boat**. Here is another marvelous miracle. The Son of God was walking on the waters of the Sea of Galilee. The disciples **were afraid** because they did not fully realize who this wonderful Person was.

Notice how simply the story is told. The most amazing facts are being told to us, but John did not use big words to impress us with the greatness of what was taking place. He used great restraint in setting forth the facts.

6:20 Then the Lord Jesus spoke wonderful words of comfort. **"It is I; do not be afraid."** If He were only a man, they might well be afraid. But He is the mighty Creator and the Sustainer of the universe. With such a One close at hand, there was no reason to fear. He who made the Sea of Galilee in the first place could cause its waters to be calm in the second place, and could bring His fearful disciples safely to shore. The words **"It is I"** are literally "I AM." So far this is the second time in John's Gospel where Jesus used this name of Jehovah as applying to Himself.

6:21 When they realized that it was the Lord Jesus, they welcomed **Him into the boat. Immediately** they found themselves at their destination. Here another miracle is stated but not explained. They did not have to row any farther. The Lord Jesus brought them to dry **land** instantly. What a wonderful Person He is!

C. The People Seek a Sign (6:22–34)

6:22 It is now the **day** after the one in which the five thousand were fed. The multitude of **people** are still in the area northeast of the Sea of Galilee. They had watched the disciples get into the small **boat** the previous evening, and they knew that **Jesus had not** gone with them. Only one boat had been available at that time, and **the disciples** had taken it.

6:23 The following day, **boats** had come **from Tiberias, near the place where** the Lord Jesus had fed the multitude. But the Lord could not have departed in one of these because they had just arrived. But perhaps it was in these small boats that the multitude crossed over to Capernaum, as recorded in the following verses.

6:24 **The people** had watched Jesus very carefully. They knew that He had gone up into the mountain to pray. They knew that He had not gone in the boat with the disciples across the lake. Yet on the following day He was nowhere to be found. They decided to cross the sea **to Capernaum**, where the disciples were most likely to be. They could not understand how **Jesus** could be there, but they

decided to go and seek Him anyway.

6:25, 26 Arriving at Capernaum, **they found Him** there. They could not conceal their curiosity, and asked Him **when** He had arrived.

Jesus answered their question indirectly. He realized that they did not seek Him because of who He was but rather because of the food which He gave them. They had seen Him perform a mighty miracle on the day before. This should have convinced them that He was indeed the Creator and the Messiah. But their interest was simply in food. They had eaten of **the** miracle **loaves**, and their hunger had been satisfied.

6:27 So Jesus first advised them **not** to **labor for the food which perishes**. The Lord did not mean that they should not work for their daily living, but He did mean that this should not be the supreme aim in their lives. Satisfying one's physical appetite is not the most important thing in life. Man consists not only of body, but of spirit and soul as well. We should labor **for the food which endures to everlasting life**. Man should not live as if his body were all. He should not devote all his strength and talents to the feeding of his body, which in a few short years will be eaten by worms. Rather, he should make sure that his soul is fed day by day with the Word of God. "Man shall not live by bread alone, but by every word that proceeds out of the mouth of God." We should work tirelessly to acquire a better knowledge of the Word of God.

When the Lord Jesus said that **God the Father** had **set His seal on Him**, He meant that **God** had sent Him and approved Him. When we set our seal to something, it means that we promise that it is true. God sealed the Son of Man in the sense that He endorsed Him as One who spoke the truth.

6:28 The people now asked the Lord what they must do in order to **work the works of God**. Man is always trying to earn his way to heaven. He likes to feel that there is something he can do to merit salvation. If he can somehow contribute to the saving of his soul, then he can find a ground for boasting; and this is very pleasing to him.

6:29 Jesus saw through their hypocrisy. They pretended that they wanted to work for God, and yet they did not want to have anything to do with the Son of God. **Jesus** told them that the first thing they must do is accept the One whom God had **sent**. So it is today. Many are seeking to earn their way to heaven by good works. But before they can do good works for God, they must first **believe** on the Lord Jesus Christ. Good works do not precede salvation; they follow it. The only good **work** a sinner can do is to confess his sins and receive Christ as Lord and Savior.

6:30 This verse was a further proof of the wickedness of the hearts of the people. One day previously, they had seen the Lord Jesus feed five thousand men with five loaves and two fish. On the very next day, they came to Him and asked Him for some **sign** that would prove His claims to be the Son of God. Like most unbelievers, they wanted to see first, and then they would believe. **"That we may see it, and believe You."** But this is not God's order. God says to sinners, "If you believe, then you will see." Faith must always come first.

6:31 Going back to the OT, the Jews reminded Jesus of the miracle of the manna[21] in the wilderness. They seemed to be saying that Jesus had never done anything as wonderful as that. They quoted from Psalm 78:24, 25, where it is written: **"He gave them bread from heaven to eat."** They implied that Moses called down food from heaven; the Lord was not as great as Moses, because He had only multiplied *existing* food!

6:32 The Lord's answer conveys at least two thoughts. First of all, it was *not* **Moses** who gave them the manna, but God. Moreover, the manna was not the true spiritual **bread from heaven**. The manna was literal food, designed for the physical body, but it had no value beyond this life. The Lord Jesus was here speaking about **the true**, ideal, and genuine **bread** which God gives out of heaven. It is bread for the soul and not for the body. The words **My Father** are a claim by Christ to deity.

6:33 The Lord Jesus revealed Himself as **the bread of God** which came **down from heaven and** gives **life**. He was showing the superiority of **the bread of God** to the manna in the wilderness. The manna did not impart life but only

sustained physical life. *It* was not intended for the whole world but only for Israel. The **true bread comes down from heaven and gives life** to men — not just to one nation but **to all the world**.

6:34 The Jews still did not realize that the Lord Jesus was speaking about Himself as the true bread, and so they asked Him for the **bread**. They were still thinking in terms of a literal loaf. Unfortunately, there was no real faith in their hearts.

D. Jesus, the Bread of Life (6:35–65)

6:35 Now **Jesus** stated the truth simply and clearly. He is **the bread of life**. Those who come to Him find enough in Him to satisfy their spiritual hunger forever. Those who believe on Him find their thirst forever quenched. Notice the words **I am** in this verse and recognize that the Lord was making a claim to equality with Jehovah. It would be folly for a sinful man to utter the words of verse 35. No mere man can satisfy his own hunger or thirst, much less satisfy the spiritual appetite of the whole world!

6:36 In verse 30, the unbelieving Jews had asked the Lord for a sign in order that they might see and believe. Here Jesus said that He had already told them that they had **seen** Him — the greatest sign of all — **and yet** they did **not believe**. If the Son of God could stand before them in perfect manhood and not be recognized by them, then it was doubtful that any sign He would perform would convince them.

6:37 The Lord was not discouraged by the unbelief of the Jews. He knew that all the Father's purposes and plans would be fulfilled. Even if the Jews to whom He was speaking would not accept Him, then He knew that all of those who were chosen by God would come to Him. As Pink puts it, "The realization of the invincibility of the eternal counsels of God gives a calmness, a poise, a courage, a perseverance which nothing else can."

This verse is very important because it states in a few words two of the most important teachings in the Bible. The first is that God has given certain ones to Christ and that **all** those whom He has given will be saved. The other is the teaching of man's responsibility. In order to be saved, a man must come to the Lord Jesus and accept Him by faith. God does choose some people to be saved, but the Bible never teaches that He chooses some to be damned. If anyone is saved, it is because of the free grace of God. But if anyone perishes forever, it is his own fault. All men are condemned by their own sinfulness and wickedness. If all men went to hell, they would be receiving only what they deserve. In grace, God stoops down and saves individual people out of the great mass of humanity. Does He have the right to do this? He certainly does. God can do as He chooses, and no man can deny Him this right. We know that God will never do anything that is wrong or unjust.

But just as the Bible teaches that God has elected certain persons to salvation, it also teaches that man is responsible to accept the gospel. God makes a universal offer — that if a man will believe on the Lord Jesus Christ, he will be saved. God does not save men against their will. A person must come to Him in repentance and faith. Then God will save him. No one who comes to God through Christ will be **cast out**.

The human mind cannot reconcile these two teachings. However, we should believe them even if we cannot understand them. They are Biblical teachings and are clearly stated here.

6:38 In verse 37, the Lord Jesus said that all of God's plans would eventually be fulfilled with regard to the salvation of those who were given to Him. Since this was the Father's will, the Lord would personally undertake to bring it to pass, as His mission was to do the will of God. **"I have come down from heaven"** said Christ, clearly teaching that He did not begin His life in the manger at Bethlehem. Rather, He existed from all eternity with God the Father in heaven. Coming into the world, He was the obedient Son of God. He voluntarily took the place of a servant in order to carry out **the will** of His Father. This does not mean that He did not have a will of His own, but rather that His **own will** was in perfect agreement with the will of God.

6:39 The will of the Father was that everyone who was given to Christ would be saved and kept until the resurrection of the just, when they would be raised and taken home to heaven. The words **nothing** and **it** refer to believers. Here He was thinking not of individual believers but of the entire body of Christians who would be saved down through the years. The Lord Jesus was responsible to see that not one member of the body would be lost but that the whole body would be raised **up at the last day**.

As far as *Christians* are concerned, **the last day** refers to the **day** when the Lord Jesus will come in the air, when the dead in Christ will rise first, when the living believers will be changed, and when all will be caught up to meet the Lord in the air, to be forever with the Lord. To the *Jews*, it meant the coming of the Messiah in glory.

6:40 The Lord now went on to explain how a person became a member of the family of the redeemed. God's **will** is **that everyone who sees the Son and believes in Him may have everlasting life**. To *see* **the Son** here means not to see Him with the physical eyes but rather with the eyes of faith. One must see or recognize that Jesus Christ is the Son of God and the Savior of the world. Then, too, he must believe on Him. This means that by a definite act of faith, he must receive the Lord Jesus as his own personal Savior. All who do this receive **everlasting life** as a present possession and also receive the assurance that they will be raised **at the last day**.

6:41 The people were quite unprepared to accept the Lord Jesus, and they showed this by murmuring **against Him**. He had claimed to be **the bread which came down from heaven**. They realized that this was a claim of great importance. To come **down from heaven**, one could not be a mere man or even a great prophet. And **so they complained** about **Him** because they were not willing to believe His words.

6:42 They assumed that **Jesus** was **the son of Joseph**. Here, of course, they were wrong. Jesus was born of the Virgin Mary. Joseph was not His father. Rather, our Lord was conceived of the Holy Spirit. Their failure to believe in the virgin birth led to their darkness and unbelief. So it is today. Those who refuse to accept the Lord Jesus as the Son of God who came into the world through the womb of the virgin find themselves compelled to deny all the great truths concerning the Person and work of Christ.

6:43 Although they had not been speaking directly to Him, yet He knew what they were saying, and here **Jesus** told them **not** to **murmur among** themselves. The following verses explain why their murmuring was useless and profitless. The more the Jews rejected the testimony of the Lord Jesus, the more difficult His teachings became. "Light rejected is light denied." The more they spurned the gospel, the harder it became for them to accept the gospel. If the Lord told them simple things and they would not believe, then He would expound to them more difficult things and they would be thoroughly ignorant of what He was saying.

6:44 Man in himself is utterly hopeless and helpless. He does not even have the strength to come to Jesus by himself. Unless the Father first begins to work in his heart and life, he will never realize his terrible guilt and his need of a Savior. Many people have difficulty with this verse. They suppose that it teaches that a man may desire to be saved and yet might find it impossible. This is not so. But the verse does teach in the strongest possible way that God is the One who first acted in our lives and sought to win us to Himself. We have the choice of accepting the Lord Jesus or refusing Him. But we never would have had the desire in the first place if God had not spoken to our hearts. Again the Lord added the promise that He will **raise** every true believer **up at the last day**. As we have seen before, this refers to the coming of Christ for His saints, when the dead will be raised and the living will be changed. It is a resurrection of believers only.

6:45 Having stated in strong terms that no man could come to Him unless the Father drew him, the Lord goes on to explain how the Father draws men. First of all, He quotes from Isaiah 54:13, **"And they shall all be taught by God."** God not only simply chooses individuals. He does something about it. He speaks to their hearts through the teaching of His precious Word.

Then man's own will is involved. Those who respond to the teaching of God's Word and learn **from the Father** are the ones who come to Christ. Here again we see the two great truths of God's sovereignty and man's choice placed side by side in Scripture. They show us that salvation has a divine side and a human side as well.

When Jesus said, **"It is written in the prophets,"** He meant, of course, the books of the prophets. He meant Isaiah in particular, but the thought He expressed here is found throughout all the prophets. It is by the teachings of God's Word and God's Spirit that men are drawn to God.

6:46 The fact that people are taught by God does **not** mean that they have **seen** Him. The only One who **has seen the Father** is the One who came from God, namely the Lord Jesus Himself.

All those who are taught by God are taught about the Lord Jesus Christ because God's teaching has Christ Himself as its grand Subject.

6:47 Verse 47 is one of the clearest and briefest statements in all the Word of God concerning the way of salvation. The Lord Jesus stated in words that could hardly be misunderstood — that whoever **believes in** Him **has everlasting life**. Notice He introduced these momentous words with His emphatic **"most assuredly."** This is one of many verses in the NT that teaches that salvation is not by works, not by law-keeping, not by church membership, not by obeying the Golden Rule, but simply by believing in the Lord Jesus Christ.

6:48, 49 Now the Lord Jesus states that *He* is the **bread of life** of which He had been speaking. The **bread of life** means, of course, **the bread** which gives **life** to those who eat it. The Jews had previously brought up the subject of the **manna in the wilderness** and challenged the Lord Jesus to produce some food as wonderful as that. Here the Lord reminded them that their **fathers** had eaten the **manna in the wilderness** and were **dead**. In other words, **manna** was for this life only. It did not have any power to give eternal life to those who ate it. By the expression, **"Your fathers,"**

the Lord dissociated Himself from fallen humanity and implied His unique deity.

6:50 In contrast to the manna, the Lord Jesus spoke of Himself as **the bread which comes down from heaven**. If anyone ate this bread, he would **not die**. This did not mean that he would not die physically, but that he would have eternal life in heaven. Even if he did die physically, his body would be raised at the last day, and he would spend eternity with the Lord.

In this and in the following verses, the Lord Jesus spoke repeatedly of men *eating of Him*. What does He mean by this? Does He mean that men must eat of Him in a physical, literal way? Obviously that idea is impossible and repulsive. Some think, however, that He meant to teach that we must eat of Him in the communion service; that in some miraculous way the bread and wine are changed into the body and blood of Christ and that in order to be saved we must partake of those elements. But this is not what Jesus said. The context makes it quite clear that to **eat** of Him means to believe on Him. When we trust the Lord Jesus Christ as our Savior, we appropriate Him by faith. We partake of the benefits of His Person and of His work. Augustine said, "Believe and you have eaten."

6:51 Jesus is **the living bread**. He not only lives in Himself, but is lifegiving. Those who eat **this bread . . . will live forever**. But how can this be? How can the Lord give eternal life to guilty sinners? The answer is found in the latter part of this verse: **"The bread that I shall give is My flesh, which I shall give for the life of the world."** Here the Lord Jesus was pointing forward to His death on the cross. He would give His **life** as a ransom for sinners. His body would be broken, and His blood would be poured out as a sacrifice for sins. He would die as a Substitute. He would pay the penalty that our sins demanded. And why would He do this? He did it **for the life of the world**. He would not die just for the Jewish nation, or even just for the elect. But His death would be of sufficient value for the whole world. This does not, of course, mean that the whole world will be saved, but rather that the work of the

Lord Jesus at Calvary would be sufficient in its value to save the whole world, if all men came to Jesus.

6:52 **The Jews** were still thinking in terms of literal, physical bread and **flesh**. Their thoughts were unable to rise above the things of this life. They did not realize that the Lord Jesus was using physical things to teach spiritual truths. And so they asked among themselves how **this** mere **Man** could possibly give **His flesh** to be eaten by others. A parachute opens only after you jump out of the plane. Faith precedes sight and prepares your soul to understand, your heart to believe, your will to obey. All your questions of "How?" are answered by yielding to the authority of Christ, as Paul did when he cried, "Lord, what do You want me to do?"

6:53 Once again **Jesus**, knowing all things, realized exactly what they were thinking and saying. And so He warned them solemnly that if they did not **eat** His **flesh** and **drink His blood**, they would **have no life in** them. This could not refer to the bread and the wine used at the Lord's Supper. When the Lord instituted His Supper, on the night in which He was betrayed, His body had not yet been broken and His blood had not yet been shed. The disciples partook of the bread and the wine, but they did not literally eat His flesh and drink His blood. The Lord Jesus was simply stating that unless we appropriate to ourselves by faith the value of His death for us on Calvary, we can never be saved. We must believe on Him, receive Him, trust Him, and make Him our very own.

6:54 By comparing this verse with verse 47, it can be definitely shown that to eat His flesh and to drink His blood means to believe on Him. In verse 47 we read that "He who believes in Me has everlasting life." In verse 54, we learn that **whoever eats** His **flesh** and **drinks** His **blood has eternal life**. Now things equal to the same thing are equal to each other. To eat His **flesh** and to drink His **blood** is to believe on Him. All who believe on Him will be raised up **at the last day**. This refers, of course, to the bodies of those who have died trusting in the Lord Jesus.

6:55 The **flesh** of the Lord Jesus is **food indeed**, and His **blood is drink in-**

deed.[22] This is in contrast to the food and drink of this world which is only of temporary value. The value of the death of the Lord Jesus is never-ending. Those who partake of Him by faith receive life that goes on forever.

6:56 A very close union exists between Himself and those who are believers in Him. Whoever **eats** His **flesh and drinks** His **blood abides in** Him, **and** He abides in that person. Nothing could be closer or more intimate than this. When we eat literal food, we take it into our very being; and it becomes a part of us. When we accept the Lord Jesus as our Redeemer, He comes into our lives to abide, and we, too, abide (continually dwell) in Him.

6:57 Now the Lord gave another illustration of the close bond that existed between Himself and His people. The illustration was His own connection with God the Father. **The living Father** had **sent** the Lord Jesus into the world. (The expression **living Father** means the Father who is the Source of life). As a Man here in the world, Jesus lived **because of the Father**, that is, by reason of the Father. His life was lived in closest union and harmony with God the Father. God was the center and circumference of His life. His purpose was to be occupied with God the Father. He was here as a Man in the world, and the world did not realize that He was God manifest in the flesh. Although He was misunderstood by the world, yet He and His Father were one. They lived in closest intimacy. That is exactly the way it is with believers in the Lord Jesus. They are here in the world, misunderstood by the world, hated and often persecuted. But because they have put their faith and trust in the Lord Jesus, they **live because of** Him. Their lives are closely bound up with His life, and this life shall endure forever.

6:58 This verse seems to summarize all that the Lord has said in the previous verses. He **is the bread which came down from heaven**. He is superior to **the manna** which the **fathers ate** in the wilderness. That bread was only of temporary value. It was only for this life. But Christ is the Bread of God who gives eternal life to all who feed on Him.

6:59 The crowd had followed Jesus and His disciples to **Capernaum** from the northeast side of the Sea of Galilee. Apparently the multitude had found Jesus **in the synagogue**[23] and it was there that He delivered the message on the Bread of Life to them.

6:60 By this time, the Lord Jesus had **many** more **disciples** than the original twelve. Anyone who followed Him and professed to accept His teachings was known as a disciple. However, not all who were known as His disciples were real believers. Now **many** of those who professed to be **His disciples** said, **"This is a hard saying."** They meant that His teaching was offensive. It was not so much that it was hard for them to understand, as that it was distasteful for them to receive. When they said, **"Who can understand it"** (literally "hear"), they meant, "Who can stand and listen to such offensive doctrine?"

6:61 Here again we find evidence that the Lord had complete knowledge. **Jesus knew** exactly what the **disciples** were saying. He knew that they were complaining at His claim to have come down from heaven and that they did not like it when He said that men must eat His flesh and drink His blood to have everlasting life. And so He asked them, **"Does this offend you?"**

6:62 They took offense because He said that He had come down from heaven. Now He asked them **what** will they think if they **should see** Him **ascend** back into heaven, which He knew He would do after His resurrection. They were also offended by His saying that men must eat His flesh. What would they think, then, if they should see that body of flesh **ascend where He was before**? How would men be able to eat His literal flesh and drink His literal blood after He had gone back to the Father?

6:63 These people had been thinking in terms of Christ's literal flesh, but here He told them that eternal life was not gained by eating flesh but by the work of the Holy Spirit of God. Flesh cannot give life; only **the Spirit** can do this. They had taken His words literally and had not realized that they were to be understood spiritually. And so here the Lord Jesus explained that **the words that** He spoke were **spirit and they** were **life**; when His sayings about eating His flesh and drinking His blood were understood in a spiritual way, as meaning *belief* in Him, then those who accepted the message would receive eternal life.

6:64 Even as He said these things, the Lord realized that some of His listeners did not understand Him because they would **not believe**. The difficulty lay not so much in their inability as in their unwillingness. **Jesus knew from the beginning** that some of His professed followers would **not believe** on Him and that one of His disciples **would betray Him**. Of course, **Jesus knew** all this from eternity, but here it probably means that He was aware of it from the very start of His ministry on earth.

6:65 Now He explained that it was because of their unbelief that He had previously told them **that no one** could **come to** Him **unless** it were **granted to him** by His **Father**. Such words are an attack on the pride of man, who thinks that he can earn or merit salvation. The Lord Jesus told men that even the power to **come** to Him can only be received from God the **Father**.

E. Mixed Reactions to the Savior's Words (6:66–71)

6:66 These sayings of the Lord Jesus proved so distasteful to **many** who had followed Him that they now left Him and were no longer willing to associate with Him. These disciples were never true believers. They followed the Lord for various reasons, but not out of genuine love for Him or appreciation of who He was.

6:67 At this point **Jesus** turned **to the twelve** disciples and challenged them with the question as to whether they, too, would leave Him.

6:68 Peter's answer is worthy of note. He said in effect, "**Lord**, how could we leave You? **You** teach the doctrines which lead to **eternal life**. If we leave You, there is no one else to whom we could go. To leave You would be to seal our doom."

6:69 Speaking for the twelve, Peter further said that they had **come to believe and know that** the Lord Jesus was the *Messiah*, **the Son of the living God**.[24] Notice again the order of the words "**believe and know**." First of all, they had put their faith in the Lord Jesus Christ, and then they came to **know** that He was

indeed all that He professed to be.

6:70 In verses 68 and 69, Peter had used the word "we" as meaning all twelve of the disciples. Here in verse 70, the Lord Jesus corrected him. He should not say so confidently that all twelve were true believers. It is true that the Lord had **chosen** the **twelve** disciples, but **one of** them was **a devil**. There was one in the company who did not share Peter's views concerning the Lord Jesus Christ.

6:71 The Lord Jesus knew that **Judas Iscariot** was going to **betray Him**. He knew that Judas never really accepted Him as Lord and Savior. Here again we have the all-knowledge of the Lord. Also, we have an evidence of the fact that Peter was not infallible when speaking for the disciples!

In the bread of life discourse, our Lord began with fairly simple teaching. But as He progressed, it was apparent that the Jews were rejecting His words. The more they closed their hearts and minds to the truth, the more difficult His teaching became. Finally He talked about eating His flesh and drinking His blood. That was too much! They said, "This is a hard saying; who can understand it?" and they quit following Him. Rejection of the truth results in judicial blindness. Because they *would* not see, they came to the place where they *could* not see.

V. THE SON OF GOD'S THIRD YEAR OF MINISTRY: JERUSALEM (7:1–10:39)[†]

A. Jesus Rebukes His Brothers (7:1–9)

7:1 There was a lapse of some months between chapters 6 and 7. **Jesus** remained **in Galilee. He did not want** to stay **in Judea**, which was headquarters for **the Jews**, because they **sought to kill Him**. It is generally agreed that **the Jews**[25] referred to in this verse were the leaders or rulers. They were the ones who hated the Lord Jesus most bitterly, and who sought opportunities **to kill Him**.

7:2 The **Feast of Tabernacles** was one of the important events in the Jewish calendar. It came at the time of harvest, and celebrated the fact that the Jews

†See p. xxiv.

lived in temporary shelters or booths after they came out of Egypt. It was a festive, joyous holiday, looking *forward* to the coming day when the Messiah would reign and the saved Jewish nation would dwell in the land in peace and prosperity.

7:3 The Lord's **brothers** mentioned in verse 3 were likely sons born to Mary after the birth of Jesus, (some say cousins or other distant relatives). But no matter how close the relationship to the Lord Jesus was, they were not thereby saved. They did not truly believe on the Lord Jesus. They told Him that He should go to the Feast of Tabernacles in Jerusalem and perform some of His miracles there so **that** His **disciples** might **see** what He was doing. The **disciples** spoken of here were not the twelve, but rather those who professed to be followers of the Lord Jesus in Judea.

Although they did not believe on Him, they wanted Him to manifest Himself openly. Perhaps they wanted the attention that would come to them as relatives of a famous person. Or more probably, they were envious of His fame and were urging Him to go to Judea in hopes that He might be killed.

7:4 Perhaps these words were spoken in sarcasm. His relatives seemed to imply that the Lord was looking for publicity. Why else was He performing all these miracles in Galilee if He did not want to become famous? "Now is Your big opportunity," they say in effect. "You have been seeking to become famous. You should go to Jerusalem for the feast. Hundreds of people will be there, and You will have an opportunity to perform miracles for them. Galilee is a quiet place, and You are practically performing Your miracles in secret here. Why do You do this when we know that You want to become well-known?" Then they added, **"If You do these things, show Yourself to the world."** The thought here seems to be, "If You are really the Messiah, and if You are doing these miracles to prove it, why don't You offer these proofs where they will really count, namely, in Judea?"

7:5 **His brothers** had no sincere desire to see Him glorified. They **did not** really **believe** Him to be the Messiah. Neither were they willing to trust themselves to Him. What they said was said in sarcasm. Their hearts were not right before the Lord. It must have been especially bitter for the Lord Jesus to have His own brothers doubt His words and His works. Yet how often it is that those who are faithful to God find their bitterest opposition from those who are nearest and dearest to them.

7:6 The Lord's life was ordered from the beginning to the end. Each day and every movement was in accordance with a pre-arranged schedule. The opportune **time** for manifesting Himself openly to the world had **not yet come**. He knew exactly what lay before Him, and it was not the will of God that He should go to Jerusalem at this time in order to make a public presentation of Himself. But He reminded His brothers that their **time** was **always ready** or opportune. Their lives were lived according to their own desires and not in obedience to the will of God. They could make their own plans and travel as they pleased, because they were only intent on doing their own will.

7:7 **The world** could **not hate** the Lord's brothers because they belonged to the world. They took sides with the world against Jesus. Their whole lives were in harmony with the world. **The world** here refers to the system which man has built up and in which there is no room for God or for His Christ: the world of culture, art, education, or religion. In fact, in Judea it was particularly the religious world, since it was the rulers of the Jews who hated Christ the most.

The world hated Christ **because** He testified concerning it **that its works were evil**. It is a sad commentary on man's depraved nature that when a sinless, spotless Man came into the world, the world sought to kill Him. The perfection of Christ's life showed how imperfect everyone else's life was. Just as a straight line reveals the crookedness of a zigzag line when they are placed side by side, so the Lord's coming into the world served to reveal man in all his sinfulness. Man resented this exposure of himself. Instead of repenting and crying to God for mercy, he sought to destroy the One who revealed His sin.

F. B. Meyer comments:

Ah, it is one of the most terrible rebukes that Incarnate Love can administer, when it says of any now, as it did of some in the days of his flesh: "The world cannot hate you." Not to be hated by the world; to be loved and flattered and caressed by the world — is one of the most terrible positions in which a Christian can find himself. "What bad thing have I done," asked the ancient sage, "that he should speak well of me?" The absence of the world's hate proves that we do not testify against it that its works are evil. The warmth of the world's love proves that we are of its own. The friendship of the world is enmity with God. Whosoever therefore will be a friend of the world is the enemy of God (John vii. 7; xv. 19; James iv. 4).[26]

7:8 The Lord told His brothers to **go up to this feast**. There was something very sad about this. They pretended to be religious men. They were going to keep the Feast of Tabernacles. Yet the Christ of God was standing in their midst, and they had no real love for Him. Man loves religious rituals because he can observe them without any real heart interest. But bring him face to face with the Person of Christ and he is ill at ease. Jesus said that He was **not yet**[27] **going up to this feast** because His **time** had **not yet fully come**. He did not mean that He would not go to the feast at all, because we learn in verse 10 that He did go. Rather, He meant that He would not go with His brothers and have a great and public manifestation. It was not time for that. When He would go, He would go quietly and with a minimum of publicity.

7:9 So the Lord **remained in Galilee** after His brothers had gone up to the feast. They had left behind the One who could ever impart to them the joy and rejoicing of which the Feast of Tabernacles spoke.

B. Jesus Teaches in the Temple (7:10–31)

7:10 Sometime after **His brothers had gone up** to Jerusalem, the Lord Jesus made a quiet trip there. As a devout Jew, He desired to attend **the feast**. But as the obedient Son of God, He could **not** do so **openly, but as it were in secret**.

7:11 **The Jews** who **sought Him at the feast** were doubtless the rulers who sought to kill Him. When they asked, "Where is He?" they were not interested in worshiping Him, but rather in destroying Him.

7:12 It is clear that the presence of the Lord was creating quite a stir **among the people**. More and more, the miracles which He performed were compelling men to make up their minds as to who He really was. There was an undercurrent of conversation at the feast as to whether He was genuine or a false prophet. **Some said, "He is good"; others said, "No . . . He deceives the people."**

7:13 The opposition of the Jewish rulers to Jesus had become so intense that no one dared to speak **openly** in favor **of Him**. Doubtless many of the common people recognized that He was truly the Messiah of Israel, but they did not dare to come out and say it because they feared the leaders would persecute them.

7:14 **The Feast** of Tabernacles lasted for several days. After it was about half over, **Jesus went up into the** outside area of the **temple** (known as the porch where the people were allowed to gather) **and taught**.

7:15 Those who heard the Savior **marveled**. Doubtless it was His knowledge of the OT that impressed them most. But also the breadth of His learning and His ability to teach attracted their attention. They knew that Jesus had never been to any of the great religious schools of that day, and they could not understand how He could have such an education as He did. The world still expresses amazement and often complains when it finds believers with no formal religious training who are able to preach and teach the Word of God.

7:16 Once again it is beautiful to see how the Lord refused to take any credit for Himself, but simply tried to glorify His Father. **Jesus answered** simply that His teaching was **not** His own, **but** that it came from the One **who sent** Him. Whatever the Lord Jesus spoke and whatever He taught were the things which His Father told Him to speak and to teach. He did not act independently of the Father.

7:17 If the Jews really wanted to know whether His message was true or not, it would be easy for them to find out. If **anyone** really **wills to do** God's **will**, then God will reveal to him whether the teachings of Christ are divine or whether the Lord was simply teaching what He Himself wanted to teach. There is a wonderful promise here for everyone earnestly seeking the truth. If a person is sincere, and truly wants to know what is the truth, God will reveal it to him. "Obedience is the organ of spiritual knowledge."

7:18 Anyone **who speaks from himself**, that is, according to his own will, **seeks his own glory**. But it was not so with the Lord Jesus. He sought **the glory of** the Father **who sent Him**. Because His motives were absolutely pure, His message was absolutely **true. No unrighteousness** was **in Him**.

Jesus was the only One of whom such words could be spoken. Every other teacher has had some selfishness mixed in his service. It should be the ambition of every servant of the Lord to glorify God rather than self.

7:19 The Lord then made a direct accusation against the Jews. He reminded them that **Moses** gave them **the law**. They gloried in the fact that they possessed the law. They forgot that there was no virtue in merely possessing the law. The law demanded obedience to its precepts or commandments. Although they gloried in the law, evidently none of them kept it, for even then they were plotting to kill the Lord Jesus. The law expressly forbade murder. They were breaking the law in their intentions concerning the Lord Jesus Christ.

7:20 **The people** felt the sharp edge of Jesus' accusation but, rather than admitting He was right, they began to abuse Him. They said that He had **a demon**. They challenged His statement that any of them was **seeking to kill** Him.

7:21 **Jesus** now went back to the healing of the impotent man at the pool of Bethesda. It was this miracle that stirred up the hatred of the Jewish leaders against Him, and it was at this point that they began their vicious plot to kill Him. The Lord reminded them that He **did one work**, and they **all** marveled at it. Not that they marveled at it with admiration, but rather they were shocked

that He should do such a thing on the Sabbath.

7:22 The Law of **Moses** commanded that a male child should be circumcised eight days after birth. (Actually, circumcision had **not** originated with **Moses**, but had been practiced by **the 'fathers'**, that is, by Abraham, Isaac, Jacob, etc.) Even if the eighth day fell **on the Sabbath**, the Jews did not consider it wrong to **circumcise** the baby boy. They felt that it was a work of necessity and that the Lord allowed for such a work.

7:23 If they circumcised a child **on the Sabbath**, in order to obey **the law of Moses** regarding circumcision, why should they find fault with the Lord Jesus for making **a man completely well on the Sabbath**? If the law allowed for a work of necessity, would it not also allow for a work of mercy?

Circumcision is a minor surgical operation performed on the male child. Needless to say, it causes pain, and its physical benefits are minor. In contrast with this, the Lord Jesus made a man completely well on the Sabbath. And the Jews found fault with Him.

7:24 The trouble with the Jews was that they judged things **according to** outward **appearance** and not according to inward reality. Their judgment was not righteous. Works which seemed perfectly legitimate when performed by themselves seemed absolutely wrong when performed by the Lord. Human nature always tends to judge according to sight rather than according to reality. The Lord Jesus had not broken the Law of Moses; it was they who were breaking it by their senseless hatred of Him.

7:25 By this time, it had become well-known in **Jerusalem** that the Jewish leaders were plotting against the Savior. Here some of the common people asked if this was not the One whom their rulers were pursuing.

7:26 They could not understand that the Lord Jesus was allowed to speak so openly and **boldly**. If the rulers hated Him as much as the people had been led to believe, why did they allow Him to continue? Is it possible that they had come to find out that He was **truly** the Messiah after all, as He claimed to be?

7:27 The people who did not believe Jesus to be the Messiah thought they knew where He came from. They believed He came from Nazareth. They knew His mother, Mary, and supposed that Joseph was His father. It was commonly believed by the Jews of that day that when the Messiah came, He would come suddenly and mysteriously. They had no idea that He would be born as a Baby and grow up as a Man. They should have known from the OT that He would be born in Bethlehem, but it seemed that they were quite ignorant of the details concerning the coming of the Messiah. That is why they said, **"When Christ comes, no one knows where He is from."**

7:28 At this point **Jesus cried out** to the people who had gathered and were listening to the conversation. They did indeed **know** Him, He said, and knew **where** He came **from**. Here, of course, He was saying that they knew Him simply as a Man. They knew Him as Jesus of Nazareth. But what they did not know was that He was also God. This was what He went on to explain in the rest of the verse.

As to His humanity, He lived in Nazareth. But they should realize, too, that He did **not come** from Himself but that He had been sent from God the Father, whom these people did **not know**. In these words, the Lord Jesus made a direct claim to equality with God. He **did not come of** Himself, that is, of His own authority and to do His own will. Rather, He had been sent into the world by the **true** God, and this God they did **not know**.

7:29 But He knew Him. He dwelt with God from all eternity and was equal in all respects with God the Father. For when the Lord said that He was **from** God, He did not simply mean that He was **sent** from God, but that He always lived with God and was equal with Him in all respects. In the expression **"He sent Me,"** the Lord stated in the clearest possible way that He was the Christ of God, the Anointed One, whom God had sent into the world to accomplish the work of redemption.

7:30 The Jews understood the significance of Jesus' words and realized He

was claiming to be the Messiah. They considered this to be sheer blasphemy, and attempted to arrest Him, but were not able to lay **hands on Him because His hour had not yet come.** The power of God preserved the Lord Jesus from the wicked schemes of men until the time came when He should be offered up as a sacrifice for sin.

7:31 Actually **many of the people believed on** the Lord Jesus. We would like to think that their belief was genuine. Their reasoning was this. What more could Jesus do to prove He was the Messiah? When **the Christ** came, if Jesus was not the Messiah, would He be able to **do more** numerous or more wonderful **signs** than Jesus had done? Obviously from their question they believed the miracles of Jesus proved Him to be the real Messiah.

C. The Enmity of the Pharisees (7:32–36)

7:32 As **the Pharisees** moved in and out among the people, they **heard** this undercurrent of conversation. **The crowd was murmuring** about the Savior, not in the sense of complaining against Him, but secretly revealing their admiration for Him. The Pharisees were afraid that this might enlarge into a great movement to accept Jesus, and so they **sent officers to** arrest **Him**.

7:33 The words of verse 33 were undoubtedly spoken to the officers who came to arrest Him, as well as to the Pharisees and to the people in general.

The Lord Jesus did not weaken His previous claims at all. If anything, He only strengthened them. He reminded them that He would only be with them **a little while longer**, and then He would go back to God the Father **who sent** Him. Undoubtedly this only made the Pharisees the more angry.

7:34 In a coming day, the Pharisees would **seek** Him and would **not** be able to **find** Him. There would come in their lives a time when they would need a Savior, but it would be too late. He would have gone back to heaven, and because of their unbelief and wickedness, they would not be able to meet Him there. The words of this verse are especially solemn. They remind us that there is such a thing as the passing of opportunity. Men may have the opportunity to be saved today; if they reject it, they may never have the opportunity again.

7:35 **The Jews** failed to understand the meaning of the Lord's words. They did not realize He was going back to heaven. They thought that perhaps He was going on a preaching tour, ministering to the Jewish people scattered **among the Greeks**, and also perhaps even teaching the Greeks themselves.

7:36 Again they expressed their wonder at His words. **What did** He mean when **He said** that they would **seek** Him **and** would **not** be able to **find** Him? Where could He go without their being able to follow Him? The Jews here illustrate the blindness of unbelief. There is no heart as dark as the heart that refuses to accept the Lord Jesus. In our own day, we have the expression "there are none so blind as those who will not see." This was exactly the case here. They did not *want* to accept the Lord Jesus, and therefore they *could* not.

D. The Promise of the Holy Spirit (7:37–39)

7:37 Though not mentioned in the OT, the Jews had a ceremony of carrying water from the Pool of Siloam and pouring it into a silver basin by the altar of burnt offering for each of the first seven days of the Feast of Tabernacles. On the eighth day, this was not done, which made Christ's offer of the water of eternal life even more startling. The Jewish people had gone through this religious observance, and yet their hearts were not satisfied because they had not truly understood the deep meaning of the feast. Just before they departed for their homes, **on the last day, that great day of the feast Jesus stood and cried** out to them. He invited them to **come** to Him for spiritual satisfaction. Pay particular attention to the words. His invitation was extended to **anyone**. His gospel was a universal gospel. There was no one who could not be saved if he would simply come to Christ.

But notice the condition. The Scripture says, **"If anyone thirsts."** "Thirst" here speaks of spiritual need. Unless a

person knows he is a sinner, he will never want to be saved. Unless he realizes he is lost, he will never desire to be found. Unless one is conscious of a great spiritual lack in his life, he will never want to go to the Lord to have that need supplied. The Savior invited the thirsting soul to come to Him — not to the church, the preacher, the waters of baptism, or the Lord's Table. Jesus said, **"Let him come to Me."** No one or nothing else will do. **"Let him come to Me and drink."** To **"drink"** here means to appropriate Christ for oneself. It means to trust Him as Lord and Savior. It means to take Him into our lives as we would take a glass of water into our bodies.

7:38 Verse 38 proves that to come to Christ and drink is the same as to *believe* on Him. All who believe on Him will have their own needs supplied and will receive **rivers** of spiritual blessing that will **flow** out from them to others. All through the OT it was taught that those who accepted the Messiah would be helped themselves and would be channels of blessing to others (e.g. Isa. 55:1). The expression **"out of his heart will flow rivers of living water"** means out of the person's inward parts or inner life would flow streams of help to others. Stott points out that we drink in small gulps or sips, but these are multiplied into a mighty confluence of flowing streams. Temple warns: "No one can be indwelt by the Spirit of God and keep that Spirit to himself. Where the Spirit is, He flows forth; if there is no flowing forth, He is not there."

7:39 It is clearly stated that the expression "living water" refers to **the** Holy **Spirit**. Verse 39 is very important because it teaches that all who receive the Lord Jesus Christ also receive the Spirit of God. In other words, it is not true, as some claim, that the Holy Spirit comes to indwell people sometime after their conversion. This verse clearly and distinctly states that all who believe on Christ receive the Spirit. At the time the Lord Jesus spoke these words, **the Holy Spirit** had **not yet** been **given**. It was not until the Lord **Jesus** went back to heaven and **was glorified** that the Holy Spirit descended on the day of Pentecost. From that moment on, every true believer in the Lord Jesus Christ has been indwelt by the Holy Spirit.

E. Divided Opinion Concerning Jesus (7:40–53)

7:40, 41 **Many** who listened were now convinced that the Lord Jesus was **the Prophet** of whom Moses spoke in Deuteronomy 18:15, 18. **Others** were even willing to acknowledge that Jesus was **the Christ**, the Messiah. But some thought this was impossible. They believed that Jesus came from Nazareth in Galilee, and there was no prophecy in the OT that **the Christ** would **come out of Galilee**.

7:42 These Jews were right in believing that **the Christ** would come **from the town of Bethlehem** and be descended from **David**. If they had just taken the trouble to inquire, they would have found that Jesus *was* born in Bethlehem, and that He *was a direct descendant of* David through Mary.

7:43 Because of these differing opinions and because of their general ignorance, **there was a division among the people because of** Christ. It is still the same. Men and women are divided on the subject of Jesus Christ. Some say He was simply a Man like the rest of us. Others are willing to admit that He was the greatest Man who ever lived. But those who believe the Word of God know that "Christ . . . is over all, the eternally blessed God" (Rom. 9:5).

7:44 Efforts were still being made to arrest the Lord Jesus, but no one was successful in taking Him. As long as a person is walking in the will of God, there is no power on earth that can hinder him. "We are immortal until our work is done." The Lord's time had not yet come, and so men were unable to harm Him in any way.

7:45 Now the **Pharisees** and **chief priests** had sent **officers** to take Jesus. **The officers** had returned, but did not have the Lord with them. **The chief priests and Pharisees** were annoyed and asked the officers **why** they had **not brought Him**.

7:46 Here was an instance where sinful men were compelled to speak well of the Savior, even if they did not themselves accept Him. Their memorable words were, **"No man ever spoke like this Man!"** Doubtless these officers had listened to a good many men in their day, but they had never heard anyone speak with such authority, grace, and wisdom.

7:47, 48 In an effort to intimidate the officers, **the Pharisees** accused them of being **deceived** by Jesus. They reminded them that none of **the rulers** of the Jewish nation **believed in Him**. What a terrible argument this was! It was very much to their shame that leading men in the Jewish nation had failed to recognize the Messiah when He came.

These Pharisees were not only unwilling to believe on the Lord Jesus themselves, but it is clear that they did not want others to believe on Him either. So it is today. Many who do not want to be saved themselves do everything in their power to prevent their relatives and friends from being saved also.

7:49 Here the Pharisees spoke of the mass of the Jewish people as ignorant **and accursed**. Their argument was that if the common people knew anything at all about the Scriptures, they would know that Jesus was not the Messiah. The Pharisees could not have been more wrong!

7:50 At this point **Nicodemus** spoke **to them**. It was **he who came to Jesus by night** and who learned that he must be born again. It would appear that Nicodemus had actually trusted the Lord Jesus Christ and been saved. Here he stepped forward, among the rulers of the Jews, to say a word for his Lord.

7:51 Nicodemus' point was that the Jews had not given Jesus a fair chance. The Jewish **law** did not **judge a man before it** heard his case. And yet that was what the Jewish leaders were doing at this very point. Were they afraid of the facts? The answer was obviously that they were.

7:52 Now the rulers turn on one of their own company, that is, on Nicodemus. They asked him with a sneer if he was **also** one of Jesus' followers **from Galilee**? Did he not know that the OT spoke of **no prophet** as coming **out of Galilee**? Here, of course, the rulers showed their own ignorance. Had they never read of the prophet Jonah? He had come from Galilee.

7:53 The Feast of Tabernacles was now over. The men returned to their own homes. Some had met the Savior face to face and trusted in Him. But the majority had rejected Him, and the leaders of the Jewish people were more determined than ever to do away with Him. They considered Him a threat to their religion and way of life.

F. The Woman Taken in Adultery (8:1–11)

8:1 This verse is closely linked with the last verse of chapter 7. The connection is better seen by putting the two verses together as follows: "And everyone went to his own house, **but Jesus went to the mount of Olives.**" The Lord had truly said, "Foxes have holes and birds of the air have nests, but the Son of Man has nowhere to lay His head."

8:2 The Mount of Olives was not far away from the temple. **Early in the morning**, the Lord Jesus walked down the side of Olivet, crossed the Kidron Valley, and climbed back up into the city, where **the temple** was located. **All the people came to Him, and He sat down and taught them.**

8:3 **The scribes** (a group of men who copied and taught the Scriptures) **and** the **Pharisees** were anxious to trick the Lord Jesus into saying something wrong so that they would have some charge to bring against Him. They had just **brought . . . a woman caught** in the very act of **adultery**, and they made her stand in the middle of the crowd, probably facing Jesus.

8:4 The accusation of adultery was made against **this woman**, and it was doubtless true. There is no reason to question that she was **caught** while committing this terrible sin. But where was the man? Too often in life women have been punished when men who were also guilty have gone free.

8:5 The trick was now clear. They wanted the Lord to contradict **the Law of Moses**. If they could succeed in doing that, then they could turn the common people against Jesus. They reminded the Lord that **Moses, in the law commanded** that a person taken in the act of adultery **should be stoned** to death. For their own wicked purposes, the Pharisees hoped the Lord would disagree, and so they asked Him what He had to say on the subject. They thought that justice and the Law of Moses demanded that she should be made an example. As Darby says:

> It comforts and quiets the depraved heart of man if he can only find a person worse than himself: he thinks the greater sin of another excuses himself; and while accusing and vehemently blaming another, he forgets his own evil. He thus rejoices in iniquity.[28]

8:6 They had no real charge against the Lord and were trying to manufacture one. They knew that if He let the woman go free, He would be opposing the Law of Moses and they would **accuse Him** of being unjust. If, on the other hand, He condemned the woman to death, then they might use this to show that He was an enemy of the Roman government, and they might also say that He was not merciful. **Jesus stooped down and wrote on the ground with His finger.** There is absolutely no way of knowing what He wrote. Many people are quite confident that they know, but the simple fact of the matter is that the Bible does not tell us.

8:7 Dissatisfied, the Jews kept insisting that He make some reply. So Jesus simply stated that the penalty of the law should be carried out, but that it should be done by those who had committed no sin. Thus the Lord upheld the Law of Moses. He did not say that the woman should be free from the penalty of the law. But what He did do was to accuse every one of these men of having sinned themselves. Those who wish to judge others should be pure themselves. This verse is often used to excuse sin. The attitude is that we are free from blame because everyone else has done things that are wrong. But this verse does not excuse sin. Rather, it condemns those who are guilty even though they have never been caught.

8:8 Once **again** the Savior **stooped down and wrote on the ground.** These are the only recorded instances of the Lord Jesus writing anything, and what He wrote has long since been erased from the earth.

8:9 **Those who** accused the woman were **convicted by their conscience.**

They had nothing else to say. They began to go away, **one by one**. They were all guilty, from **the oldest** to the youngest. **Jesus was left alone**, with **the woman standing** nearby.

8:10 In wonderful grace, the Lord Jesus pointed out to the woman that all her **accusers** had vanished. They were nowhere to be found. There was not a single person in the entire crowd who dared to condemn her.

8:11 The word **Lord** here probably means "Sir." When the woman **said, "No one,** Sir," the Lord uttered those wonderful words, **"Neither do I condemn you; go and sin no more."** The Lord did not claim to have civil authority in such a matter. This power was vested in the Roman government, and He left it there. He neither condemned nor pardoned her. That was not His function at this time. But He did issue a warning to her that she should refrain from sinning.

In the first chapter of John, we learned that "grace and truth came through Jesus Christ." Here was an example of that. In the words **"neither do I condemn you,"** we have an example of grace; the words **"go, and sin no more"** are words of truth. The Lord did not say, "Go, and sin as little as possible." Jesus Christ is God, and His standard is absolute perfection. He cannot approve of sin in any degree. And so He sets before her the perfect standard of God Himself.[29]

G. Jesus the Light of the World (8:12–20)

8:12 The scene now shifts to the treasury of the temple (see v. 20). A multitude was still following Him. He turned to them and made one of the many grand statements as to His Messiahship. He said, **"I am the light of the world."** Naturally speaking, **the world** is in the darkness of sin, ignorance, and aimlessness. **The light of the world** is Jesus. Apart from Him, there is no deliverance from the blackness of sin. Apart from Him, there is no guidance along the way of life, no knowledge as to the real meaning of life and the issues of eternity. Jesus promised that anyone following Him would **not walk in darkness, but have the light of life**.

To follow Jesus means to believe on Him. Many people have the mistaken idea that they can live as Jesus lived without ever being born again. To follow Jesus means to come to Him in repentance, to trust Him as Lord and Savior, and then to commit one's whole life to Him. Those who do this have guidance in life and clear and bright hope beyond the grave.

8:13 **The Pharisees** now challenged Jesus on a legal point. They reminded Him that He was testifying concerning Himself. A person's own testimony was not considered sufficient because the average human being is biased. The Pharisees did not mind casting doubt on the words of Jesus. In fact they doubted that they were **true** at all.

8:14 The Lord recognized that usually it was necessary to have two or three witnesses. But in His case, His **witness** was absolutely **true** because He is God. He knew that He had come from heaven and was going back to heaven. But they did **not know where** He had **come from and where** He was **going**. They thought He was just another man like themselves and would not believe that He was the eternal Son, equal with the Father.

8:15 The Pharisees judged others by outward appearances and according to merely human standards. They looked upon Jesus as the Carpenter of Nazareth and never stopped to think that He was different from any other man who ever lived. The Lord Jesus said that He judged **no one**. This may mean that He did not judge men according to worldly standards, like the Pharisees did. Or more probably it means that His purpose in coming into the world was not to *judge* people but to *save* them.

8:16 **If** the Lord were to **judge**, His **judgment** would be righteous and **true**. He is God and everything He does is done in partnership **with the Father who** sent Him. Over and over again, the Lord Jesus emphasized to the Pharisees His unity with God **the Father**. It was this that stirred up in their hearts the bitterest antagonism toward Him.

8:17, 18 The Lord acknowledged that **the testimony of two** witnesses was required by the **Law** of Moses. Nothing He had said was intended to deny that fact.

If they insisted on having two witnesses, it was not difficult for Him to produce them. First of all, He bore **wit-**

ness of Himself by His sinless life and by the words that came out of His mouth. Secondly, **the Father** bore **witness** to the Lord Jesus by His public statements from heaven and by the miracles which He gave the Lord to do. Christ fulfilled the prophecies of the OT concerning the Messiah, and yet in face of this strong evidence, the Jewish leaders were unwilling to believe.

8:19 The Pharisees' next question was doubtless spoken in scorn. Perhaps they looked around the crowd as they said, **"Where is Your Father?"** Jesus answered by telling them that they **neither** recognized who He truly was nor did they know His **Father**. Of course, they would have denied vigorously any such ignorance of God. But it was true nonetheless. If they had received the Lord Jesus, they **would have known** His **Father also**. But no one can know God the Father except through Jesus Christ. Thus, their rejection of the Savior made it impossible for them to honestly claim that they knew and loved God.

8:20 Here we learn that the scene of the previous verses was **in the treasury** of **the temple**. Again the Lord is surrounded by divine protection, **and no one** is able to lay **hands on Him** to arrest Him or kill Him. **His hour had not yet come**. **His hour** refers to the time when He would be crucified at Calvary to die for the sins of the world.

H. The Jews' Debate with Jesus (8:21–59)

8:21 Again **Jesus** showed perfect knowledge of the future. He told His critics He was **going away** — referring not only to His death and burial, but to His resurrection and ascension back into heaven. The Jewish people would continue to **seek** for the Messiah, not realizing that He had already visited them and that they had rejected Him. Because of their rejection, they would **die in** their **sin** ("sin" is singular in Greek and in NKJV). This would mean that they would be forever prevented from entering heaven, where the Lord was going. It is a solemn truth! Those who refuse to accept the Lord Jesus have no hope of heaven. How dreadful to die in one's sins, without God, without Christ, without hope forever!

8:22 **The Jews** did not understand that the Lord spoke of going back to heaven. What did He mean by "going away"? Did He mean that He would escape from their plot to kill Him by committing suicide? It was strange that they should think this. If He were to **kill Himself**, there would be nothing to prevent them from doing the same and following Him in death. But it was just another example of the darkness of unbelief. It seems amazing that they could be so dull and ignorant of what the Savior was saying!

8:23 Doubtless thinking of their foolish reference to suicide, the Lord told them that they were **from beneath**. This meant that they had a very low outlook on things. They could not rise above the literal things of time and sense. They had no spiritual understanding. In contrast, Christ was **from above**. His thoughts, words, and deeds were heavenly. All that they did savored of **this world**, whereas His whole life told that He came from a purer land than this world.

8:24 Jesus often used repetition for emphasis. Here He solemnly warned them again that they would **die in** their **sins**. If they steadfastly refused to believe on Him, there was no alternative. Apart from the Lord Jesus, there is no way to obtain forgiveness of sins, and those who **die** with **sins** unforgiven cannot possibly enter heaven at last. The word **He** is not found in this verse in the original, though it may be implied. It reads literally: **"If you do not believe that I am, you will die in your sins."** We see in the words *I am* another claim to deity by the Lord Jesus.

8:25 The Jews were completely perplexed by the teachings of the Lord Jesus. They asked Him pointedly **who** He was. Perhaps they meant this in sarcasm, as if to say, "Who do You think You are, that You should speak to us in this way?" Or perhaps they were really anxious to hear what He would say concerning Himself. His answer is worthy of note: **"Just what I have been saying to you from the beginning."** He was the promised Messiah. The Jews had heard Him say so frequently, but their stubborn hearts refused to bow to the truth. But His answer can have another meaning — the Lord Jesus was exactly what He preached. He did not say one thing and do another. He was the living embodiment of all that He taught. His life agreed with His teaching.

8:26 The meaning of verse 26 is not clear. It seems the Lord was saying that there were **many** additional **things** He could **say** and **judge concerning** these unbelieving Jews. He could expose the wicked thoughts and motives of their hearts. However, He was obediently speaking only those things which the Father had given Him to speak. And since the Father **is true**, He is worthy to be believed and listened to.

8:27 The Jews **did not understand** at this point **that He** was speaking **to them of** God **the Father**. It seems that their minds were becoming more clouded all the time. Previously when the Lord Jesus claimed to be the Son of God, they had realized He was claiming equality with God the Father. But not so anymore.

8:28 Again **Jesus** prophesied what was going to happen. First of all, the Jews would lift up **the Son of Man**. This refers to His death by crucifixion. After they had done that, they would **know that** He was the Messiah. They would know it by the earthquake and by the darkness, but, most of all, by His bodily resurrection from the dead. Notice carefully the words of the Lord, **"Then you will know that** I am." Here, again, the word **He** is not in the original. The deeper meaning is, "Then **you will know that I am** God." Then they would understand He did nothing from Himself, that is, by His own authority. Rather, He came into the world as the dependent One, speaking only those things which the **Father** had **taught** Him to say.

8:29, 30 The Lord's relationship with God the Father was very intimate. Each of these expressions was a claim to equality with God. Throughout all of His earthly ministry, the Father was **with** Him. At no time was Jesus left **alone**. At all times He did the things that were pleasing to God. These words could only be spoken by a sinless Being. No one born of human parents could ever truthfully utter those words, **"I always do those things that please Him."** Too often we do the things that please ourselves.

Sometimes we are prompted to please our fellow men. Only the Lord Jesus was completely taken up with the desire to do the things that were well-pleasing to God.

As He spoke these wonderful **words**, Jesus found that **many** professed to believe on Him. Doubtless some were genuine in their faith. Others might only have been prompted to give lip service to the Lord.

8:31 Then **Jesus** made a distinction between those who are disciples and those who are **disciples indeed**. A disciple is anyone who professes to be a learner, but a **disciple indeed** is one who has definitely committed himself to the Lord Jesus Christ. Those who are true believers have this characteristic — they **abide in** His **Word**. This means that they continue in the teachings of Christ. They do not turn aside from Him. True faith always has the quality of permanence. They are not saved by abiding in His Word, but they abide in His Word because they are saved.

8:32 The promise is made to every true disciple that he **shall know the truth, and the truth shall make** him **free**. The Jews did not know the truth, and they were in a terrible form of bondage. They were in the bondage of ignorance, error, sin, law, and superstition. Those who truly know the Lord Jesus are delivered from sin, they walk in the light, and are led by the Holy Spirit of God.

8:33 Some of the Jews who were standing by heard the Lord's reference to being made free. They resented it immediately. They boasted of their descent from Abraham and said that they had **never been in bondage**. But this was not true. Israel had been in bondage to Egypt, Assyria, Babylon, Persia, Greece, and now Rome. But even more than that, even while they still spoke with the Lord Jesus they were in bondage to sin and to Satan.

8:34 It is evident that the Lord was speaking about the bondage **of sin**. He reminded His Jewish listeners that **whoever** practices **sin is a slave of sin**. These Jews pretended to be very religious, but the truth of the matter was that they were dishonest, irreverent, and soon to be murderers — for even now they were plotting the death of the Son of God.

8:35 Jesus next compared the relative positions **in the house** of **a slave** and **a son**. The **slave** did not have any assurance that he would live there forever; whereas the **son** was at home in the house. Whether the word "Son" applies to the Son of God or whether it applies to those who become children of God by faith in Christ, it is clear that the Lord Jesus was telling these Jews that they were not sons, but slaves who could be put out at any time.

8:36 There is no question that the word **Son** in this verse refers to Christ Himself. Those who are made **free** by Him are made **free indeed**. This means that when a person comes to the Savior and receives eternal life from Him, that person is freed from the slavery of sin, legalism, superstition, and demonism.

8:37 The Lord acknowledged that, as far as physical lineage was concerned, these Jews were **Abraham's descendants** (literally "seed"). But it was evident they were not of the *spiritual* seed of Abraham. They were not godly men like Abraham was. They sought **to kill** the Lord Jesus because His teachings had **no place** in them. This means that they did not allow the words of Christ to take effect in their lives. They resisted His doctrines and would not yield to Him.

8:38 The things Jesus taught them were things He had been commissioned by His **Father** to speak. He and His Father were so completely one that the words He spoke were the words of God the Father. The Lord Jesus perfectly represented His Father while here on the earth. In contrast, the Jews did those things which they had learned from *their* **father**. The Lord Jesus did not mean their literal, earthly father, but rather *the devil*.

8:39 Once again the Jews claimed kinship to **Abraham**. They boasted in the fact that **Abraham** was their **father**. However, the Lord Jesus pointed out that although they were Abraham's descendants [seed] (v. 37), they were not his **children**. Usually children look, walk, and talk like their parents. But not so with these Jews. Their lives were the opposite of Abraham's. Though descendants of Abraham according to the flesh, yet morally they were children of the devil.

8:40 The Lord proceeded to give a very clear example of the difference between them and Abraham. Jesus had come into the world, speaking to them nothing but **the truth**. They were offended and stumbled over His teaching, and so tried **to kill** Him. **Abraham did not do this**. He took his place on the side of truth and righteousness.

8:41 It was very clear who their father was because they acted just like him. They did **the deeds of** their **father**, that is, the devil. The Jews may well have been accusing the Lord of being **born of fornication**. But many Bible students see in the word **fornication** a reference to idolatry. The Jews were saying that they had never committed spiritual adultery. They had always been true to **God**. He is the only One they ever acknowledged as their **Father**.

8:42 The Lord showed the falseness of their claim by reminding them that if they loved God, they **would love** Him whom God had **sent**. It is foolish for anyone to claim to love God and at the same time to hate the Lord Jesus Christ. Jesus said He **proceeded forth . . . from God**. This meant that He was the eternally begotten Son of God. There was no particular time at which He was born the Son of God, but this relationship of Son to the Father existed from all eternity. He also reminded them that He **came from God**. Obviously, He was here stating His pre-existence. He dwelt in heaven with the Father long before He ever appeared on this earth. But the Father **sent** Him into the world to be the Savior of the world, and so He came as the obedient One.

8:43 There is a difference in verse 43 between **speech** and **word**. Christ's **word** referred to the things He taught. His **speech** referred to the words with which He expressed His truths. They could **not** even **understand** His **speech**. When He spoke of bread, they thought only of literal bread. When He spoke of water, they never connected it with spiritual water. Why was it that they could not understand His speech? It was because they were unwilling to tolerate His teachings.

8:44 Now the Lord Jesus came out openly and told them that **the devil** was their **father**. This did not mean that they had been born of the devil in the way believers are born of God. Rather, it meant, as Augustine said, that they were children of the devil *by imitation*. They showed their relationship to the devil by living the way he lived. **"The desires of your father you want to do"** expresses the intention or tendency of their hearts.

The devil was **a murderer from the beginning**. He brought death to Adam and the whole human race. Not only was he **a murderer**, but was **a liar** as well. He did **not stand in the truth, because there is no truth in him. When he** told **a lie, he** was merely speaking **from his own resources**. Lies formed a part of his very existence. **He is a liar and the father** of lies. The Jews imitated the devil in these two ways. They were murderers because the intention of their hearts was to kill the Son of God. They were liars because they said that God was their Father. They pretended to be godly, spiritual men, but their lives were wicked.

8:45 Those who give themselves over to lying seem to lose the capacity for discerning the truth. Here stood the Lord Jesus before these men, and he had always spoken **the truth**. Yet they would **not believe** Him. This showed that their real character was wicked. Lenski puts it well:

> When it meets the truth, the corrupted mind seeks only objections; when it meets what differs from this truth, it sees and seeks reasons for accepting this difference.[30]

8:46 Only Christ, the sinless Son of God, could ever truly utter words like these. There was not a person in the world who could convict Him of a single **sin**. There was no defect in His character. He was perfect in all His ways. He spoke only words of truth, and yet they would **not believe** Him.

8:47 If a man really loves God, he will hear and obey **God's words**. The Jews showed by their rejection of the Savior's message that they did not really belong to **God**. It is clear from verse 47 that the Lord Jesus claimed to speak the very words of God. There could be no misunderstanding of this.

8:48 Once again **the Jews** resorted to abusive language, because they could not answer the words of the Lord Jesus in any other way. In calling Him **a Samaritan**, they senselessly used an ethnic slur. It was as if they said that He was not a pure Jew, but was an enemy of Israel. Also, they accused Him of having **a demon**. By this they doubtless meant that He was insane. To them, only a man out of his mind would ever make the claims which Jesus had been making.

8:49 Notice the even-tempered way in which **Jesus answered** His enemies. His teachings were not the words of one who had **a demon**, but rather of One who sought to **honor** God the **Father**. It was for this they were dishonoring Him, not because He was crazy, but because He was completely taken up with the interests of His Father in heaven.

8:50 They should have known that at no time did he **seek** His **own glory**. All He did was calculated to bring glory to His Father. Even though He accused them of dishonoring Him, that did not mean that He was seeking His **own glory**. Then the Lord added the words, **"There is One who seeks and judges."** This One referred, of course, to God. God the Father would seek glory for His beloved Son, and would judge all of those who failed to give Him this glory.

8:51 Again we have one of those majestic sayings of the Lord Jesus, words which could only be uttered by One who was God Himself. The words are introduced by the familiar emphatic expression **"Most assuredly, I say to you."** Jesus promised that **if anyone keeps** His **Word**, that person **shall never see death**. This cannot refer to *physical death* because many believers in the Lord Jesus die each day. The reference is to *spiritual* **death**. The Lord was saying that those who believe on Him are delivered from eternal **death** and shall never suffer the pangs of hell.

8:52 **The Jews** were now more convinced than ever that Jesus was "mad." They reminded Him that **Abraham and the prophets** were all **dead**. Yet He had said that **if anyone** kept His **Word he** would **never taste death**. How can these things be reconciled?

8:53 They realized the Lord was actually claiming to be **greater than** their **father Abraham** and **the prophets**. Abraham never delivered anyone from death, and he could not deliver himself from death. Neither could the prophets. Yet here was One who claimed to be able to deliver His fellow men from death. He must consider Himself greater than the fathers.

8:54 The Jews thought Jesus was seeking to attract attention to Himself. **Jesus** reminded them that this was not the case. It was the **Father** who was honoring Him, the very **God** they professed to love and serve.

8:55 The Jews said that God was their Father, but actually they did not know Him. Yet here they were speaking with One who *did* know God the Father, One who was equal with Him. They wanted Jesus to deny His equality with the Father, but He said that if He did this, He would be **a liar**. He knew God the Father and obeyed **His word**.

8:56 Since the Jews insisted on bringing Abraham into the argument, the Lord reminded them that **Abraham** had looked forward to the **day** of the Messiah, and he had actually **seen it** by faith, **and was glad**. The Lord Jesus was saying that *He* was the One to whom Abraham looked forward. Abraham's faith rested in the coming of Christ.

When did Abraham see Christ's day? Perhaps it was when he took Isaac to Mount Moriah to offer him as a burnt offering to God. The whole drama of the Messiah's death and resurrection was acted out at that time, and it is possible that Abraham saw it by faith. Thus the Lord Jesus claimed to be the fulfillment of all the prophecies in the OT concerning the Messiah.

8:57 Once again **the Jews** revealed their inability to understand divine truth. Jesus had said, "Abraham rejoiced to see My day," but they answered as though He had said that He had seen Abraham. There is a great difference here. The Lord Jesus claimed for Himself a position greater than Abraham. He was the Object of Abraham's thoughts and hopes. Abraham looked forward by faith to Christ's day.

The Jews could not understand this. They reasoned that Jesus was **not yet fifty years old**. (Actually He was only about thirty-three years of age at this time.) How could He have **seen Abraham**?

8:58 The Lord Jesus here made another clear claim to be God. He did not say, **"Before Abraham was, I** *was*.**"** That might simply mean that He came into

existence before Abraham. Rather, He used the Name of God: **I AM**. The Lord Jesus had dwelt with God the Father from all eternity. There was never a time when He came into being, or when He did not exist. Therefore He said, **"Before Abraham was, I AM."**

8:59 At once the Jews attempted to put Jesus to death, **but He hid Himself and went out of the temple**. The Jews understood exactly what Jesus meant when He said, "Before Abraham was, I AM." He was claiming to be Jehovah! It was for this reason they sought to stone Him, because to them this was blasphemy. They were unwilling to accept the fact that the Messiah was standing in their midst. They would not have Him to reign over them!

I. The Sixth Sign: Healing of the Man Born Blind (9:1–12)

9:1 This incident may have taken place **as Jesus** was leaving the temple area, or it may have occurred some time after the events of chapter 8. It is recorded that the man had been **blind from birth** to show the hopelessness of his condition and the wonder of the miracle that gave him sight.

9:2 The **disciples asked** a rather strange question. They wondered if the blindness had been caused by the man's own sin or by his parents' sin. How could the blindness have been caused by his own sin, when he had been *born* **blind**? Did they believe in some form of reincarnation, the belief that the soul of the dead returned to earth in a new body? Or did they suggest that he might have been born blind because of sins which God knew he would commit after his birth? It is clear that they thought the blindness was directly connected with sin in the family. We know that this was not necessarily so. Although all sickness, suffering, and death came into the world ultimately as a result of sin, it is *not* true that in any particular case a person suffers because of sins which he has committed.

9:3 Jesus did not mean that the man had not sinned, or that his parents had not sinned. Rather, He meant that the blindness was not a direct result of sin in their lives. God had allowed this man to be born blind in order that the man might become a means of displaying the mighty **works of God**. Before the man was born, the Lord Jesus knew He would give sight to those blind eyes.

9:4 The Savior realized that He had about three years of public ministry before He would be crucified. Every moment of that time must be spent in working for God. Here was a man who had been blind from his birth. The Lord Jesus must perform a miracle of healing on him, even though it was the Sabbath. The time of His public ministry would soon be over, and He would no longer be here on earth. This is a solemn reminder to everyone who is a Christian that life's day is swiftly passing, and **the night is coming** when our service on earth will be forever over. Therefore, we should use the time that is given to us to serve the Lord acceptably.

9:5 When Jesus was **in the world** as a Man, He was **the light of the world** in a very direct and special way. As He went about performing miracles and teaching the people, they saw **the light of the world** before their very eyes. The Lord Jesus is *still* the Light of the world, and all who come to Him are promised that they will not walk in darkness. However, in this verse the Lord was speaking particularly of His public ministry on earth.

9:6 We are not told why Jesus mixed **clay** and **saliva** and put it on **the eyes of the blind man**. Some have suggested that the man had no eyeballs and that the Lord Jesus simply created them, giving him eyeballs. Others suggest that in giving sight to the blind, the Lord Jesus commonly used methods that were despised in the eyes of the world. He used weak and insignificant things in working out His purposes. Even today, in giving sight to the spiritually blind, God uses men and women who are made of the dust of the earth.

9:7 The Lord called the faith of the blind man into operation by telling him to **go** and **wash in the pool of Siloam**. Though he was blind, yet he probably knew the location of the pool and was able to do as he was told. The Scripture notes that the word **Siloam** means **Sent**. Perhaps this is a reference to the Messiah (the "Sent" One). The One who was performing this miracle was the One

who had been sent into the world by God the Father. The blind man **went and washed** in the pool, and received his sight. It is not a case that his sight was restored, because he had never seen before at all. The miracle was instantaneous and the man was able to use his eyes immediately. What a delightful surprise it must have been for him to look for the first time upon the world in which he had lived!

9:8, 9 **The neighbors** of the man were startled. They could hardly believe that this was the same man who had **sat and begged** for so long. (It should be this way also when a person is saved. Our neighbors should be able to notice the difference in us.) **Some** insisted it was the same man. **Others**, not quite so sure, were only willing to admit that there was a resemblance. But the man removed all doubt by stating that he was the one who had been born blind.

9:10 Whenever Jesus performed a miracle, it provoked all kinds of questions in the hearts of men. Often these questions gave the believer an opportunity to witness for the Lord. Here people asked the man **how** it all happened.

9:11 His testimony was simple, yet convincing. He recited the facts of his healing, giving credit to the One who had performed the miracle. At this time, the man did not realize who the Lord Jesus was. He simply referred to Him as "**a Man called Jesus**." But later on the man's understanding grew and he came to know who Jesus is.

9:12 When we witness concerning the Lord Jesus Christ, we often create a desire in the hearts of others to come to know Him, too.

J. Increasing Opposition from the Jews (9:13–41)

9:13 Apparently in earnest enthusiasm over the miracle, some of the Jewish people **brought** the **blind** man **to the Pharisees**. They probably did not realize how the religious leaders would resent the fact that this man had been healed.

9:14 Jesus had performed the miracle on **a Sabbath**. The critical Pharisees did not realize that God never intended the Sabbath to prevent an act of mercy or of kindness.

9:15 The man had another opportunity to witness for Jesus. When **the Pharisees also asked him again how he had received his sight**, they heard the simple story once again. The man did not mention the name of Jesus here, probably not because he was afraid to do so, but because he realized that everyone knew who had done this mighty work. By this time, the Lord Jesus was well known in Jerusalem.

9:16 Now another **division** arose over who Jesus was. **Some of the Pharisees** announced boldly that Jesus could not be a godly Man because He had broken **the Sabbath. Others** reasoned that a sinful man could not perform such a wonderful miracle. Jesus often caused divisions among people. Men were forced to take sides and be either for Him or against Him.

9:17 The Pharisees asked **the man** who had been **blind** what he thought of Jesus. As yet, he did not realize that Jesus was God. But his faith had grown to such an extent that he was willing to admit that Jesus was **a prophet**. He believed that the One who had given him sight had been sent by God, and had a divine message.

9:18, 19 Many of **the Jews** were still unwilling to **believe** that a miracle had been performed. And so **they called the parents** of the man to see what they would say.

Who would know better than parents if a child had been born without sight? Surely their testimony would be conclusive. So the Pharisees **asked them** whether this was their **son** and also **how** he received his sight.

9:20, 21 The testimony of **his parents** was very positive. **This** was their **son**, and they knew through years of heartache **that** he had always been **blind**.

Beyond that, they were unwilling to go. They did **not know** how his sight was restored, they said, **or who** the person was who restored it. They directed the Pharisees back to the son himself. He could **speak for himself**.

9:22, 23 Verse 22 explains the timidity of the **parents**. They had heard that any man confessing that Jesus was the Messiah **would be put out of the synagogue**. This excommunication was a very serious matter for any Jew. They

were not willing to pay such a price. It would mean the loss of a means of livelihood, as well as a loss of all the privileges of the Jewish religion.

It was for fear of the Jewish rulers, **therefore**, that **the parents** shifted the testimony back to their son.

9:24 "**Give God the glory!**" may have two meanings. First of all, it may be a form of oath. Perhaps the Pharisees were saying, "Now tell the truth. **We know that this Man is a sinner**". Or it may mean that the Pharisees were demanding that God be given the glory for the miracle, and that no credit be given to Jesus because the Pharisees considered Him to be a sinful man.

9:25 The Pharisees met failure at every turn. Every time they tried to discredit the Lord Jesus, it resulted in bringing more honor to Him. The man's testimony here was beautiful. He did **not know** too much about the Person of Jesus, but he did **know** that **though** once he **was blind, now** he saw. This was a testimony that no one could deny.

So it is in the case of those who have been born again. The world may doubt, scoff, and sneer, but no one can deny our testimony when we say that once we were lost, and now we have been saved by the grace of God.

9:26, 27 **Again** they reopened the questioning, asking him to repeat the details. By now the man who had been blind was obviously annoyed. He reminded them that he had **told** them the facts **already**, and they did **not listen. Why** did they **want to hear it again**? Were they interested in becoming **disciples** of Jesus? Obviously, this was asked in sarcasm. He knew very well that they hated Jesus, and had no desire to follow Him.

9:28 It has been said, "When you have no case, abuse the plaintiff." That is what happened here. The Pharisees had utterly failed to shake the testimony of this man, so they began to abuse him. They accused him of being a **disciple** of Jesus, as if that were the worst thing in the world! Then they professed to be **Moses' disciples**, as if that were the greatest thing possible.

9:29 The Pharisees said **that God spoke to Moses**, but they spoke slightingly of Jesus. If they had believed the writings of Moses, they would have accepted Jesus as their Lord and Savior. Also, if they had thought a little, they would have realized that Moses never gave sight to a man who had been born blind. A greater than Moses was in their midst, and they did not realize it.

9:30 The man's sarcasm now became biting. It was something that the Pharisees didn't expect. The man said to them in effect, "You men are the rulers in Israel. You are the teachers of the Jewish people. And yet here is a Man in your midst who has the power to give sight to blind eyes, and **you do not know where He is from**. Shame on you!"

9:31 The man was now becoming bolder in his witness. His faith was growing. He reminded them that as a general principle, **God does not hear sinners** or work miracles through them. God does not approve of men who are evil, and does not give power to such men to perform mighty works. Worshipers **of God**, on the other hand, receive God's commendation and are assured of God's approval.

9:32, 33 This man realized that he was the first man in all of human history who had been **born blind** and who had received his sight. He could not understand that the Pharisees should witness such a miracle and find fault with the Person who performed it.

If the Lord Jesus **were not from God, He could** never **do** a miracle of this nature.

9:34 Again the Pharisees turned to abuse. They insinuated that this man's blindness was the direct result of **sins**. What right had he to be **teaching** them? The truth is that he had every right in the world, for, as Ryle has said, "The teaching of the Holy Ghost is more frequently to be seen among men of low degree than among men of rank and education." When it says **they cast him out**, this probably refers to more than his being cast out of the temple. It probably means that he was excommunicated from the Jewish religion. And yet what was the ground for the excommunication? A man born blind had been given his sight on the Sabbath. Because he would not speak evil of the One who had performed the miracle, he was excommunicated.

9:35 **Jesus** now sought out this man. It is as if Jesus had said, "If they do not want you, I will take you." Those who are cast out for Jesus' sake lose nothing, but gain a great blessing in His personal welcome and fellowship. See how the Lord Jesus led the man to personal faith in Himself as the Son of God! He simply asked the question, **"Do you believe in the Son of God?"**[31]

9:36 Although he had received his physical sight, the man was still in need of spiritual vision. He asked the Lord **who** the Son of God was, that he might **believe in Him**. In using the word **"Lord"** here, the man was simply saying "Sir."

9:37 **Jesus** now introduced Himself to the man as the Son of God. It was not a mere man who had given him sight and performed the impossible in his life. It was the Son of God, the One whom he had seen and who was now **talking with** him.

9:38 At this the man simply and sweetly placed his faith in the Lord Jesus and fell down and **worshiped Him**. He was now a saved soul as well as a healed man. What a great day this had been in his life! He had received both physical and spiritual sight.

Notice that the blind man did not worship the Lord until he knew that Jesus was the Son of God. Being an intelligent Jew, he would not worship a mere man. But as soon as he learned that the One who healed him was God the Son, **he worshiped Him** — not for what He had done but for who He was.

9:39 At first glance this verse seems to contradict John 3:17, "For God did not send His Son into the world to condemn the world . . . ." But there is no real conflict. The purpose of Christ's coming into the world was not to judge but to save. However, judgment is the inevitable result for all who fail to receive Him.

The preaching of the gospel has two effects. **Those who** admit that they **do not see** are given sight. But **those who** insist that they can **see** perfectly, without the Lord Jesus, are confirmed in their blindness.

9:40 **Some of the Pharisees** realized that the Lord Jesus was speaking of them and of their blindness. So they came to Him and brazenly asked if He meant to

insinuate that they were **blind also**.
Their question expected a negative answer.

9:41 The Lord's answer may be paraphrased as follows: **"If** you admit that
you are **blind** and sinful, and that you
need a Savior, then your sins can be forgiven you, and you can be saved. But
you profess that you are in need of nothing. You claim that you are righteous and
that you have no sin. **Therefore**, there
is no forgiveness of sins for you." When
**Jesus said, " . . . you would have no
sin,"** He did not mean that they would
be absolutely sinless. But He meant that
comparatively speaking, they would be
sinless. If they had only acknowledged
their blindness in failing to recognize
Him as Messiah, their sin would have
been as nothing compared to the enormous sin of professing to see, yet failing
to recognize Him as the Son of God.

K. Jesus, the Door of the Sheep (10:1–10)

10:1 These verses are closely linked
with the latter part of chapter 9. There
the Lord Jesus had been speaking to the
Pharisees, who claimed to be rightful
shepherds of the people of Israel. It was
to them, in particular, that the Lord
Jesus referred here. The solemn character of what He was about to say is indicated by the expression **"Most assuredly, I say to you."**

A **sheepfold** was an enclosure in
which sheep were sheltered at night. It
was an area surrounded by a fence and
having one opening that was used as a
door. Here **the sheepfold** refers to the
Jewish nation.

Many came to the Jewish people, professing to be their spiritual rulers and
guides. They were self-appointed messiahs for the nation. But they did not come
by the way which the OT predicted the
Messiah would come. They climbed up
some other way. They presented themselves to Israel in a manner of their own
choosing. These men were not true
shepherds, but thieves and robbers.
Thieves are those who take what does
not belong to them, and robbers are
those who use violence in doing so. The
Pharisees were thieves and robbers.
They sought to rule over the Jews, and

yet did everything in their power to hinder them from accepting the true Messiah. They persecuted those who followed Jesus, and eventually they would
put Jesus to death.

10:2 Verse 2 refers to Jesus Himself.
He came to the lost sheep of the house
of Israel. He was the true **shepherd of
the sheep**. He entered **by the door**, that
is, He came in exact fulfillment of the OT
prophecies concerning the Messiah. He
was not a self-appointed Savior, but
came in perfect obedience to the will of
His Father. He met all the conditions.

10:3 There is considerable disagreement as to the identity of **the doorkeeper** in this verse. Some think this expression refers to the prophets of the OT
who foretold the coming of the Christ.
Others believe it refers to John the Baptist, since he was the forerunner of the
true Shepherd. Still others are equally
sure that **the doorkeeper** in this verse is
the Holy Spirit who opens the door for
the entrance of the Lord Jesus into hearts
and lives.

The sheep heard the shepherd's
voice. They recognized his voice as that
of the true shepherd. Just as literal sheep
recognize the voice of their own shepherd, so there were those among the
Jewish people who recognized the Messiah when He appeared. Throughout the
Gospel, we have heard the Shepherd
calling **His own sheep by name**. He
called to several disciples in chapter 1,
and they all heard His voice and responded. He called the blind man in
chapter 9. The Lord Jesus still calls those
who will receive Him as Savior, and the
call is personal and individual.

The expression **and leads them out**
may refer to the fact that the Lord Jesus
led those who heard His voice out of the
sheepfold of Israel. There they were shut
up and enclosed. There was no liberty
under the law. The Lord **leads** His sheep
into the freedom of His grace. In the last
chapter, the Jews had cast the man out
of the synagogue. In doing so, they had
been assisting the work of the Lord without knowing it.

10:4 When the true shepherd
brings out His own sheep, he does not
drive them, but He leads **them**. He does
not ask them to go anywhere that He

Himself has not first gone. He is ever out in front of the sheep as their Savior, their Guide, and Example. Those who are true **sheep** of Christ **follow Him**. They do not *become* sheep by following His example, but by being born again. Then when they are saved, they have a desire to go where He leads.

10:5 The same instinct that enables a sheep to recognize the voice of the true shepherd also prompts it to **flee from a stranger**. The strangers were the Pharisees and other leaders of the Jewish people who were only interested in the sheep for their own personal advantage. The man who received his sight illustrates this. He recognized the voice of the Lord Jesus but knew that the Pharisees were strangers. Therefore, he refused to obey them, even though it meant being excommunicated.

10:6 It is distinctly stated now that **Jesus used this illustration** on the Pharisees, **but they did not understand** — the reason being they were not true sheep. If they had been, they would have heard His voice and followed Him.

10:7 Then Jesus used a new illustration. He was no longer speaking about the door of the sheepfold, as in verse 2. Now He was presenting Himself as **the door of the sheep**. It was no longer a question of entering the sheepfold of Israel, but rather the picture was of the elect sheep of Israel passing out of Judaism and coming to Christ, **the door**.

10:8 Others had come **before** Christ, claiming authority and position. But the elect sheep of Israel did not hear them because they knew they were claiming what did not rightfully belong to them.

10:9 Verse 9 is one of those delightful verses which is simple enough for the Sunday School pupil to understand, and yet which can never be exhausted by the most learned scholars. Christ is **the door**. Christianity is not a creed, or a church. Rather it is a Person, and that Person is the Lord Jesus Christ. **"If anyone enters by Me."** Salvation can only be received through Christ. Baptism will not do; neither will the Lord's Supper. We must enter in by Christ, and by the power which He gives. The invitation is for anyone. Christ is the Savior of Jew and Gentile alike. But to be saved, a person must enter in. He must receive Christ by faith. It is a personal act, and without it there is no salvation. Those who do enter in are **saved** from the penalty, the power, and eventually from the very presence of sin.

After salvation, they **go in and out**. Perhaps the thought is that they go into the presence of God by faith to worship, and then they go out into the world to witness for the Lord. At any rate, it is a picture of perfect security and liberty in the service of the Lord. Those who enter **find pasture**. Christ is not only the Savior, and the One who gives freedom, but He is also the Sustainer and Satisfier. His sheep **find pasture** in the Word of God.

10:10 The purpose of **the thief** is **to steal, and to kill, and to destroy**. He comes for purely selfish motives. In order to gain his own desires, he would even **kill** the sheep. But the Lord Jesus does not come to the human heart for any selfish reason. He comes to give, not to get. He comes that people **may have life, and that they may have it more abundantly**. We receive life the moment we accept Him as our Savior. After we are saved, however, we find that there are various degrees of enjoyment of this life. The more we turn ourselves over to the Holy Spirit, the more we enjoy the life which has been given to us. We not only have **life** then, but we **have it more abundantly**.

L. Jesus, the Good Shepherd (10:11–18)

10:11 Many times the Lord Jesus used the expression **"I am,"** one of the titles of Deity. Each time He was making a claim to equality with God the Father. Here he presented Himself as **the good shepherd who** laid down **His life for the sheep**. Ordinarily, the sheep were called upon to lay down their lives for the shepherd. But the Lord Jesus died for the flock.

> When blood from a victim must flow,
> This Shepherd by pity was led,
> To stand between us and the foe,
> And willingly died in our stead.
> — *Thomas Kelly*

10:12 **A hireling** is one who serves for money. For instance, a shepherd might pay someone else to take care of his sheep. The Pharisees were hirelings. Their interest in the people was prompted by the money they received in return. The **hireling** did **not own the sheep**. When danger came, he ran away and left the sheep to the mercy of **the wolf**.

10:13 We do what we do because we are what we are. The hireling served for pay. He did **not care about the sheep**. He was more interested in his own welfare than in their good. There are many hirelings in the church today — men who choose the ministry as a comfortable occupation, without true love for God's sheep.

10:14 Again the Lord speaks of Himself as **the good shepherd. Good** (Gk., *kalos*) here means "ideal, worthy, choice, excellent." He is all of these. Then He speaks of the very intimate relationship that exists between Himself and His **sheep**. He knows His own, and His **own** know Him. This is a very wonderful truth.

10:15 It is unfortunate that this verse is punctuated as a new sentence. Actually, it is better read as follows: ". . . and I know My sheep, and am known by My own, just **as the Father knows Me**, and **I know the Father.**" This is truly a thrilling truth! The Lord compared His relationship with the sheep with the relationship that existed between Himself and His Father. The same union, communion, intimacy, and knowledge that there is between the Father and the Son also exists between the Shepherd and the sheep. **"And I lay down My life for the sheep,"** He said. Again we have one of the many statements of the Lord Jesus in which He looked forward to the time when He would die on the cross as a Substitute for sinners.

10:16 Verse 16 is the key to the entire chapter. The **other sheep** to whom the Lord referred here were the Gentiles. His coming into the world was especially in connection with the sheep of Israel, but He also had in mind the salvation of Gentiles. The Gentile sheep were **not** of the Jewish **fold**. But the great heart of

compassion of the Lord Jesus went out to these sheep as well, and He was under divine compulsion to **bring** them to Himself. He knew that they would be more ready than the Jewish people to **hear** His **voice**.

In the latter part of the verse there is the very important change from the **fold** of Judaism to the **flock** of Christianity. This verse gives a little preview of the fact that in Christ, Jew and Gentile would be made one, and that the former distinctions between these peoples would disappear.

10:17 In verses 17 and 18, the Lord Jesus explained what He would do in order to bring both elect Jews and Gentiles to Himself. He looked forward to the time of His death, burial, and resurrection. These words would be utterly out of place were the Lord Jesus a mere man. He spoke of laying **down** His **life** and taking **it again** by His own power. He could only do this because He is God. The **Father** loved the Lord Jesus **because** of His willingness to die and rise again, in order that lost sheep might be saved.

10:18 **No one** could take the Lord's life **from** Him. He is God, and is thus greater than all the murderous plots of His creatures. He had **power** in Himself **to lay down** His life, **and** He also had **power to take it again**. But did not men kill the Lord Jesus? They did. This is clearly stated in Acts 2:23 and in 1 Thessalonians 2:15. The Lord Jesus allowed them to do it, and this was an exhibition of His **power to lay down** His life. Furthermore, He "gave up His Spirit" (John 19:30) as an act of His own strength and will.

"This command I have received from My Father," He said. The Father had commissioned or instructed the Lord to lay down His life and to rise again from among the dead. His death and resurrection were essential acts in fulfillment of the Father's will. Therefore, He became obedient unto death, and rose again the third day, according to the Scriptures.

M. Division Among the Jews (10:19–21)

10:19 The words of the Lord Jesus

caused **a division again among the Jews**. Christ's entrance into the world, and into homes, and into hearts, produces a sword, rather than peace. Only when men receive Him as Lord and Savior do they know the peace of God.

10:20, 21 The Lord Jesus was the only perfect Man who ever lived. He never said a wrong word or committed an evil deed. Yet such was the depravity of the heart of man that when He came, speaking words of love and wisdom, men said that **He** had **a demon and** was **mad**, and was not worthy to be listened to. This was certainly a dark spot on the record of the human race. **Others** thought differently. They recognized **the words** and works of the Lord Jesus as those of a good Person and not of **a demon**.

N. Jesus Proved to Be the Christ by His Works (10:22–39)

10:22 At this point there is a break in the narrative. The Lord Jesus was no longer speaking to the Pharisees, but to the Jews in general. We do not know what time elapsed between verse 21 and verse 22. Incidentally, this is the only mention in the Bible of **the Feast of Dedication**, or in Hebrew, Hanukkah. It is generally believed that this feast was instituted by Judas Maccabeus when the temple was rededicated after being defiled by Antiochus Epiphanes, 165 B.C. It was a yearly feast, instituted by the Jewish people, and not one of the feasts of the Lord. **It was** not only **winter** according to the calendar, but also spiritually.

10:23, 24 The Lord's public ministry was almost over, and He was about to demonstrate His complete dedication to God the Father by His death on the cross. **Solomon's porch** was a covered area, adjoining Herod's temple. As the Lord walked there, there would have been plenty of room for the Jews to gather around Him.

The Jews surrounded Him and said, "How long do You keep us in doubt (or suspense)**? If You are the Christ, tell us plainly."**

10:25, 26 Jesus again reminded them of His words and His **works**. He had often told them that He was the

Messiah, and the miracles He performed proved that His claim was true. Again He reminded the Jews that He performed His miracles by authority of His Father and for His Father's glory. In doing so, He showed that He was indeed the One whom the Father had sent into the world.

Their unwillingness to receive the Messiah proved that they were **not of** His **sheep**. If they had been set apart to belong to Him, they would have shown a willingness to believe Him.

10:27 These next few verses teach in unmistakable terms that no true sheep of Christ will ever perish. The eternal security of the believer is a glorious fact. Those who are true **sheep** of Christ **hear** His **voice**. They **hear** it when the gospel is preached, and they respond by believing on Him. Thereafter, they **hear** His voice day by day and obey His Word. The Lord Jesus knows His sheep. He knows each one by name. Not even one will escape His attention. No one could be lost through an oversight or carelessness on His part. Christ's sheep **follow** Him, first by exercising saving faith in Him, then by walking with Him in obedience.

10:28 Christ gives **eternal life** to His sheep. This means life that will last forever. It is *not* life that is *conditional* on their behavior. It is **eternal life**, and that means everlasting. But **eternal life** is also a quality of life. It is the life of the Lord Jesus Himself. It is a life that is capable of enjoying the things of God down here, and a life that will be equally suitable to our heavenly home. Note these next words carefully. **"They shall never[32] perish."** If any sheep of Christ ever perished, then the Lord Jesus would have been guilty of failing to keep a promise, and this is not possible. Jesus Christ is God, and He cannot fail. He has promised in this verse that no sheep of His will ever spend eternity in hell.

Does this mean then that a person may be saved and then live the way he pleases? Can he be saved and then carry on in the sinful pleasures of this world? No, he no longer desires to do these things. He wants to follow the Shepherd. We do not live the Christian life in order to become a Christian or in order to retain our salvation. We live a Christian life because *we are* Christians. We desire to live a holy life, not out of fear of losing our salvation, but out of gratitude to the One who died for us. The doctrine of eternal security does not encourage careless living, but rather is a strong motive for holy living.

No one is able to **snatch** a believer out of Christ's **hand**. His hand is almighty. It created the world; and it even now sustains the world. There is no power that can **snatch** a sheep from His grasp.

10:29 Not only is the believer in the hand of Christ; he is in the **Father's hand** as well. This is a twofold guarantee of safety. God the Father **is greater than all; and no one is able to snatch** a believer **out of the Father's hand**.

10:30 Now the Lord Jesus added a further claim to equality with God: **"I and My Father are one."** Here the thought probably is that Christ and the **Father are one** *in power*. Jesus had just been speaking about the power that protects Christ's sheep. Therefore, He added the explanation that His power is the same as the power of God the Father. Of course the same is true of all the other attributes of Deity. The Lord Jesus Christ is God in the fullest sense and is equal with the Father in every way.

10:31 There was no question in the minds of **the Jews** as to what the Savior meant. They realized that He was setting forth His deity in the plainest way. Therefore they **took up stones** in order **to stone Him**.

10:32 Before they had a chance to hurl the stones, **Jesus** reminded them of the **many good works** He had performed by commandment **from** His **Father**. He then asked them **which of those** works so infuriated them that they wanted to **stone** Him.

10:33 **The Jews** denied that it was for any of His miracles that they sought to kill Him. Rather, they wanted to stone Him because they felt He had spoken **blasphemy** by claiming to be equal with **God** the Father. They refused to admit that He was anything more than a man. Yet it was very evident to them that He made Himself **God**, as far as His claims were concerned. They would not tolerate this.

10:34 Here the Lord Jesus quoted to the Jews from Psalm 82:6. He called this a part of their **law**. In other words, it was taken from the OT which they acknowledged to be the inspired Word of God. The complete verse is as follows: "I said, 'You are gods, and all of you are children of the Most High.' " The Psalm was addressed to the judges of Israel. They were called **"gods"** not because they were actually divine, but because they represented God when they judged the people. The Hebrew word for "gods" (*elohim*) is literally "mighty ones" and may be applied to important figures such as judges. (It is clear from the rest of the Psalm that they were only men and not deities because they judged unjustly, showed respect of persons, and otherwise perverted justice.)

10:35 The Lord used this verse from the Psalms to show that God used the word **gods** to describe men **to whom the word of God came**. In other words, these men were spokesmen for God. God spoke to the nation of Israel through them. "They manifested God in His place of authority and judgment, and were the powers whom God had ordained." **"And the Scripture cannot be broken,"** said the Lord, expressing His belief in the inspiration of the OT Scriptures. He speaks of them as infallible writings which must be fulfilled, and which cannot be denied. In fact, the very words of Scripture are inspired, not just its thoughts or ideas. His whole argument is based on the single word **gods**.

10:36 The Lord was arguing from the lesser to the greater. If unjust judges were called "gods" in the OT, how much more right did He have to say He was the Son of God. The word of God *came* to them; He *was* and *is* the Word of God. They were *called* gods; He *was* and *is* God. It could never have been said of them that the **Father** had **sanctified** them **and sent** them **into the world**. They were born into the world like all other sons of fallen Adam. But Jesus was sanctified by God **the Father** from all eternity to be the Savior of the world, and He was **sent into the world** from heaven where He had always dwelt with His Father. Thus Jesus had every right to claim equality with God. He was not blaspheming when He claimed to be **the Son**

of God, equal with the Father. The Jews themselves used the term "gods" to apply to corrupt men who were mere spokesmen or judges for God. How much more could He claim the title because He actually *was* and *is* God. Samuel Green states it well:

> The Jews accused Him of making Himself God. He does not deny that in so speaking He made Himself God. But He does deny that He blasphemed, and this on a ground that might fully justify Him even in claiming the honors of deity; namely, that He was the Messiah, the Son of God, Immanuel. That the Jews did not consider Him as in the least withdrawing His lofty claims, is evident from the continued enmity that was manifested. See verse 39.[33]

10:37 Again the Savior appealed to the miracles which He performed as proof of His divine commission. However, note the expression **"the works of My Father."** Miracles, in themselves, are not a proof of deity. We read in the Bible of evil beings having the power at times to perform miracles. But the miracles of the Lord were **the works of** His **Father**. They proved Him to be the Messiah in a twofold way. First, they were the miracles which the OT predicted would be performed by the Messiah. Second, they were miracles of mercy and compassion, works that benefited mankind and which would not be performed by an evil person.

10:38 Verse 38 has been helpfully paraphrased by Ryle as follows:

> If I do the works of my Father, then, though ye may not be convinced by what I say, be convinced by what I do. Though ye resist the evidence of my words, yield to the evidence of my works. In this way learn to know and believe that I and my Father are indeed one, He in me and I in Him, and that in claiming to be His Son, I speak no blasphemy.

10:39 Again the Jews realized that instead of denying His previous claims, the Lord Jesus had only strengthened them. Thus they made another attempt to arrest Him, but He eluded them once more. The time was not far distant now when He would permit Himself to be taken by them, but as yet, His hour had not come.

VI. THE SON OF GOD'S THIRD YEAR OF MINISTRY: PEREA (10:40–11:57)

A. Jesus' Withdrawal Across the Jordan (10:40–42)

10:40 The Lord **went away again beyond the Jordan to the** very **place where** He began His public ministry. His three years of wondrous words and works were drawing to a close. He ended them where He began them — outside the established order of Judaism, in a place of rejection and loneliness.

10:41 Those who **came to Him** were probably sincere believers. They were willing to bear His reproach, to take their place with Him outside the camp of Israel. These followers paid a glowing tribute to **John** the Baptist. They remembered that John's ministry was not spectacular or sensational, but it was **true**. Everything he said about the Lord Jesus was fulfilled in the ministry of the Savior. This should encourage each one who is a Christian. We may not be able to do mighty miracles or gain public attention, but at least we can bear a true testimony to our Lord and Savior Jesus Christ. This is of great value in God's sight.

10:42 It is lovely to notice that in spite of His rejection by the nation of Israel, the Lord Jesus did find some lowly, receptive hearts. **Many**, we are told, **believed in Him there**. Thus it is in every age. There is always a remnant of the people who are willing to take their place with the Lord Jesus, cast out by the world, hated and scorned, but enjoying the sweet fellowship of the Son of God.

B. The Illness of Lazarus (11:1–4)

11:1 We now come to the last great miracle in the *public* ministry of the Lord Jesus. In some senses, it was the greatest of all — the raising of a dead man. **Lazarus** lived in the little village of **Bethany**, about two miles east of Jerusalem. **Bethany** was also known as the home **of Mary and her sister Martha**. Pink quotes Bishop Ryle:

> Let it be noticed that the presence of God's elect children is the one thing which makes towns and countries famous

in God's sight. The village of Martha and Mary is noticed, while Memphis and Thebes are not named in the New Testament.[34]

11:2 John explains that **it was that Mary** of Bethany **who** had **anointed the Lord with fragrant oil and wiped His feet with her hair**. This singular act of devotion was emphasized by the Holy Spirit. The Lord loves the willing affection of His people.

11:3 When Lazarus took sick, the Lord Jesus was apparently on the east side of the Jordan River. The **sisters sent** word **to Him** immediately that Lazarus, **whom** He loved, was **sick**. There was something very touching in the way these sisters presented their case to the Lord. They appealed to His love for their brother as a special argument why He should come and help.

11:4 When Jesus . . . said, "This sickness is not unto death," He did not mean that Lazarus would not die, but that **death** would not be the final outcome of **this sickness**. Lazarus would die, but he would be raised again from the dead. The real purpose of the sickness was **the glory of God, that the Son of God may be glorified through it**. God allowed this to happen so that Jesus would come and raise Lazarus from the dead, and thus be manifested again as the true Messiah. Men would glorify **God** for this mighty miracle.

There is absolutely no suggestion that Lazarus' sickness was a result of some special sin in his life. Rather, he is presented as a devoted disciple and a special object of the Savior's love.

C. Jesus' Journey to Bethany (11:5–16)

11:5 When sickness enters our homes, we are not to conclude that God is displeased with us. Here sickness was directly linked with His love rather than His anger. "Whom He loves He chastens."

11:6, 7 We would be apt to reason that if the Lord really loved these three believers, then He would drop everything and hurry to their home. Instead, **when He heard** the news, **He stayed two more days . . . where He was**. God's delays are not God's denials. If our prayers are not answered immediately, perhaps He is teaching us to wait, and if we wait patiently, we will find that He will answer our prayers in a much more marvelous way than we ever anticipated. Not even His love for Martha, Mary, and Lazarus could force Christ to act ahead of the proper time. Everything He did was in obedience to His Father's will for Him, and in keeping with the divine timetable.

After two days that might have seemed to be lost time, the Lord Jesus proposed to **the disciples** that they should all **go to Judea again**.

11:8 The disciples were still painfully aware of how **the Jews sought to stone** Christ after He had given sight to the blind man. They expressed surprise that He would even think of going into Judea in the face of such personal danger.

11:9 Jesus answered them as follows: In the ordinary course of events, there are **twelve hours** of light **in the day**, when men can work. As long as a man works during this allotted time, there is no danger of his stumbling or falling **because he sees** where he is going and what he is doing. **The light of this world**, or daylight, keeps him from accidental death through stumbling.

The spiritual meaning of the Lord's words is as follows: The Lord Jesus was walking in perfect obedience to the will of God. There was thus no danger of His being killed before the appointed time. He would be preserved until His work was done.

In a sense this is true of every believer. If we are walking in fellowship with the Lord and doing His will, there is no power on earth that can kill us before God's appointed time.

11:10 The person who **walks in the night** is one who is not faithful to God, but is living in self-will. This man **stumbles** easily **because** he does not have divine guidance to illuminate his pathway.

11:11 The Lord spoke of Lazarus' death as *sleep*. However, it should be noticed that in the NT sleep is *never* applied to the soul but only to the body. There is no teaching in the Scripture that at the time of death, the soul is in a state of sleep. Rather, the believer's soul goes to be with Christ, which is far better. The Lord Jesus revealed His omniscience in this statement. He knew Lazarus had already died, although the report He had heard was that Lazarus was sick. He knew because He is God. While anybody may awaken another out of physical sleep, only the Lord could awaken Lazarus out of death. Here Jesus expressed His intention of doing that very thing.

11:12 **His disciples** did not understand the Lord's reference to sleep. They did not realize that He was speaking of death. Perhaps they believed that sleeping was a symptom of recovery, and they concluded that if Lazarus was able to sleep soundly, then **he** had passed the crisis and would **get well**. The verse might also mean that if physical sleep were the only thing wrong with Lazarus, then there was no need to go to Bethany to help him. It is possible that the disciples were fearful for their own safety and that they seized upon this excuse for not going to the home of Mary and Martha.

11:13, 14 Here it is clearly stated that when **Jesus spoke** of sleep, He was referring to **death** but that His disciples had not understood this. There can be no misunderstanding. **Jesus** notified His disciples **plainly, "Lazarus is dead."** How calmly the disciples received the news! They did not ask the Lord, "How do you know?" He spoke with complete authority, and they did not question His knowledge.

11:15 The Lord Jesus was not glad that Lazarus had died, but He was **glad** He **was not** at Bethany at the time. If He had been there, Lazarus would not have died. Nowhere is it recorded in the NT that a person died in the presence of the Lord. The disciples would see a greater miracle than the prevention of death. They would see a man raised from the dead. In this way, their faith would be strengthened. Therefore, the Lord Jesus said that He was **glad** for their sakes that He had not been at Bethany.

He added, **"that you may believe."** The Lord was not implying that the disciples had not already believed on Him. Of course they had! But the miracle they were about to see at Bethany would greatly strengthen their faith in Him. Therefore, He urged them to **go** with Him.

11:16 **Thomas** reasoned that if the Lord Jesus went into that area, He would be killed by the Jews. If the disciples went with Jesus, he was sure that they too would be killed. And so in a spirit of pessimism and gloom, he urged them all to accompany Jesus. His words are not an example of great faith or courage, but rather of discouragement.

D. Jesus: The Resurrection and The Life (11:17–27)

11:17, 18 The fact of Lazarus' being in the grave for **four days** was added as proof that he was dead. Notice how the Holy Spirit takes every precaution to show that the resurrection of Lazarus was really a miracle. Lazarus must have died shortly after the messengers left to find Jesus. It was a day's journey from Bethany to Bethabara, where Jesus was. After hearing of Lazarus' illness, Jesus stayed two days. Then it was a day's journey to Bethany. This explains the four days Lazarus was in the grave.

As noted previously, **Bethany** was **about two miles** (fifteen stadia) east of **Jerusalem**.

11:19 The nearness of Bethany to Jerusalem made it possible for **many of the Jews** to join **the women around Martha and Mary, to comfort them**. Little did they realize that in a short time their comfort would be entirely unnecessary and that this house of mourning would be turned into a house of great joy.

11:20 **Then Martha, as soon as she heard that Jesus was coming, went** out to meet **Him**. The meeting took place just outside the village. We are not told why **Mary** remained **in the house**. Perhaps she had not received the report of Jesus' arrival. Maybe she was paralyzed with grief, or was simply waiting in a spirit of prayer and trust. Did she sense what was about to happen because of her closeness to the Lord? We do not know.

11:21 It was real faith that enabled **Martha** to believe that Jesus could have prevented Lazarus from dying. Still, her faith was imperfect. She thought He could only do this if He were bodily present. She did not realize that He could heal a man from a distance, still less that He could raise the dead. Often in times of sorrow, we talk like Martha. We think that if such and such a drug or medicine had been discovered, then this loved one would not have died. But all these things are in the hands of the Lord, and nothing happens to one of His own without His permission.

11:22 Again the faith of this devoted sister shone out. She did not know *how* the Lord Jesus would help, but she believed that He would. She had confidence that **God** would grant Him His request and that He would bring good out of this seeming tragedy. However, even now, she did not dare to believe that her brother would be raised from the dead. The word which Martha used for "ask" is the word normally used to describe a creature supplicating or praying to the Creator. It seems clear from this that Martha did not yet recognize the deity of the Lord Jesus. She realized that He was a great and unusual Man, but probably no greater than the prophets of old.

11:23 In order to draw out her faith to greater heights, the Lord Jesus made the startling announcement that Lazarus would **rise again**. It is wonderful to see how the Lord deals with this sorrowing woman and seeks to lead her step by step to faith in Himself as the Son of God.

11:24 Martha realized that Lazarus would **rise** from the dead some day, but she had no thought that it could happen that very day. She believed in **the resurrection** of the dead and understood that it would happen in what she called **"the last day."**

11:25 It is as if the Lord had said, "You do not understand Me, Martha. I do not mean that Lazarus will rise again at the last day. I am God, and I have the power of **resurrection** and of **life** in My hand. I can raise Lazarus from the dead right now, and will do it."

Then the Lord looked forward to the time when all true believers would be raised. This will take place when the Lord Jesus comes back again to take His people home to heaven.

At that time there will be two classes of believers. There will be those who have died in faith, and there will be those who are living at His Return. He comes to the first class as the *Resurrection* and to the second as the *Life.* The first class is described in the latter part of verse 25 — **"He who believes in Me,**

though he may die, he shall live." This means that those believers who have died before Christ's coming will be raised from the dead.

Burkitt remarks:

> O love, stronger than death! The grave cannot separate Christ and His friends. Other friends accompany us to the brink of the grave, and then they leave us. Neither life nor death can separate from the love of Christ.[35]

Bengel comments, "It is beautifully consonant with divine propriety, that no one is ever read of as having died while the Prince of Life was present."

11:26 The second class is described in verse 26. Those who are alive at the time of the Savior's coming and who believe on Him **shall never die**. They will be changed, in a moment, in a twinkling of an eye, and taken home to heaven with those who have been raised from the dead. What precious truths have come to us as a result of Lazarus' death! God brings sweetness out of bitterness and gives beauty for ashes. Then the Lord pointedly asked Martha, to test her faith, **"Do you believe this?"**

11:27 Martha's faith blazed out in noontime splendor. She confessed Jesus to be **the Christ, the Son of God**, whom the prophets had predicted was **to come into the world**. And we should notice that she made this confession *before* Jesus had raised her brother from the dead and not afterwards!

E. Jesus Weeps at Lazarus' Tomb (11:28–37)

11:28, 29 Immediately after this confession, Martha rushed back into the village and greeted **Mary** with the breathless announcement, **"The Teacher has come, and is calling for you."** The Creator of the universe and the Savior of the world had come to Bethany and was **calling for** her. And it is still the same today. This same wonderful Person stands and calls people in the words of the gospel. Each one is invited to open the door of his heart and let the Savior in. Mary's response was immediate. She wasted no time, but **rose quickly** and went to Jesus.

11:30, 31 Now Jesus met Martha

and Mary outside the village of Bethany.

The Jews did not know He was near, since Martha's announcement of the fact to Mary had been a secret one. It was not unnatural that they should conclude that **Mary** had gone out **to the tomb to weep there**.

11:32 Mary . . . fell down at the Savior's **feet**. It may have been an act of worship, or it may have been that she was simply overcome with grief. Like Martha, she uttered the regret that Jesus had not been present in Bethany, for in that case, their **brother would not have died**.

11:33 To see Mary and her friends in sorrow caused Jesus to groan and to be **troubled**. Doubtless He thought of all the sadness, suffering, and death which had come into the world as a result of man's sin. This caused Him inward grief.

11:34 The Lord of course knew **where** Lazarus was buried, but He asked the question in order to awaken expectation, to encourage faith, and to call forth man's cooperation. Doubtless it was with deep earnestness and sincere desire that the mourners led the Lord to the grave.

11:35 Verse 35 is the shortest in the English Bible.[36] It is one of the three instances in the NT where the Lord is said to have **wept**. (He wept in sorrow over the city of Jerusalem and also in the garden of Gethsemane.) The fact that **Jesus wept** was an evidence of His true humanity. He shed real tears of grief when He witnessed the terrible effects of sin on the human race. The fact that **Jesus wept** in the presence of death shows it is not improper for Christians to weep when their loved ones are taken. However, Christians do not sorrow as others who have no hope.

11:36 The Jews saw in the tears of the Son of Man an evidence of His love for Lazarus. Of course, they were correct in this. But He also loved *them* with a deep and undying love, and many of them failed to understand this.

11:37 Again the presence of the Lord Jesus caused questionings among the people. Some of them recognized Him as the same One who had given sight to **the blind** man. They wondered why He could not **also have kept** Lazarus **from dying**. Of course, He could have done so, but instead He was going to perform a mightier miracle, which brought greater hope to believing souls.

F. The Seventh Sign: The Raising of Lazarus (11:38–44)

11:38 It would seem that Lazarus' **tomb** was **a cave** under the earth, into which one would have to descend by means of a ladder or a flight of stairs. **A stone** was placed on top of the mouth of the cave. It was unlike the tomb of the Lord Jesus in that the latter was carved out of rock and a person could doubtless walk into it, as into the side of a hill, without climbing or descending.

11:39 Jesus commanded the onlookers to **take away the stone** from the mouth of the grave. He could have done this Himself by merely speaking the word. However, God does not ordinarily do for men what they can do for themselves.

Martha expressed horror at the thought of opening the grave. She realized that her brother's body had been there for **four days** and feared that it had begun to decompose. Apparently, no attempt had been made to embalm the body of Lazarus. He would have been buried the same day on which he died, as was the custom then. The fact that Lazarus was in the grave for **four days** was important. There was no possibility of his being asleep or in a swoon. All the Jews knew that he was **dead**. His resurrection can only be explained as a miracle.

11:40 It is not clear when **Jesus** had spoken the words of verse 40. In verse 23, He had told her that her brother would rise again. But doubtless what He here said was the substance of what He had previously told her. Notice the order in this verse, **"Believe . . . see."** It is as if the Lord Jesus had said, "If you will just believe, you will see Me perform a miracle that only God could perform. You will **see the glory of God** revealed in Me. But first you must **believe**, and then you will **see**."

11:41 The stone was then removed from the grave. Before performing the miracle, **Jesus** thanked His **Father** for having **heard** His prayer. No previous prayer of the Lord Jesus is recorded in this chapter. But doubtless He had been speaking to His Father continually during this entire period and had prayed that God's Name might be glorified in the resurrection of Lazarus. Here He thanked the Father in anticipation of the event.

11:42 Jesus prayed audibly so that **the people** might **believe that** the Father had **sent** Him, that the Father told Him what to do and what to say, and that He always acted in perfect dependence on God the Father. Here again we have the essential union of God the Father and the Lord Jesus Christ emphasized.

11:43 This is one of the few instances in the NT where the Lord Jesus is said to have **cried with a loud voice**. Some have suggested that if He had not mentioned **Lazarus** by name, then all the dead in the graves would have come forth!

11:44 How did Lazarus come **out**? Some think he hobbled out of the grave; others think that he crawled out on hands and knees; still others point out that his body would have been wrapped tightly in graveclothes and that it would have been impossible for him to have come out by his own power. They suggest that his body came out of the tomb through the air until his feet touched the ground in front of the Lord Jesus. The fact that his **face was wrapped with a cloth** is added as a further proof that he had been dead. No one could have lived for four days with **his face** bound by such **a cloth**. Again the Lord enlisted the participation of the people by commanding them to **loose** Lazarus **and let him go**. Only Christ can raise the dead, but He gives us the task of removing stones of stumbling, and of unwinding the graveclothes of prejudice and superstition.

G. Believing and Unbelieving Jews (11:45–57)

11:45, 46 To **many** of the onlookers, this miracle unmistakably proclaimed the deity of the Lord Jesus Christ, and they **believed in Him**. Who else but God could call forth a body from the grave

after it had been dead for four days?

But the effect of a miracle on a person's life depends on his moral condition. If one's heart is evil, rebellious, and unbelieving, he will not believe even though he were to see one raised from the dead. That was the case here. **Some** of the Jews who witnessed the miracle were unwilling to accept the Lord Jesus as their Messiah in spite of such undeniable proof. And so they **went away to the Pharisees** to report what had happened in Bethany. Was it that they might come and believe on Jesus? Rather, it was probably in order that the Pharisees might be further stirred up against the Lord and seek to put Him to death.

11:47 **Then the chief priests and the Pharisees gathered** their official **council** to discuss what action should be taken. The question **"What shall we do?"** means "What are we going to do about this? Why are we so slow in acting? **This Man** is performing many miracles, and we are doing nothing to stop Him." The Jewish leaders spoke these words to their own condemnation. They admitted that the Lord Jesus was performing **many signs**. Why then did they not believe on Him? They did not *want* to believe because they preferred their sins to the Savior.

Ryle well says:

> This is a marvellous admission. Even our Lord's worst enemies confess that our Lord did miracles, and many miracles. Can we doubt that they would have denied the truth of His miracles, if they could? But they do not seem to have attempted it. They were too many, too public, and too thoroughly witnessed for them to dare to deny them. How, in the face of this fact, modern infidels and skeptics can talk of our Lord's miracles as being impostures and delusions, they would do well to explain! If the Pharisees who lived in our Lord's time, and who moved heaven and earth to oppose His progress, never dared to dispute the fact that He worked miracles, it is absurd to begin denying His miracles now, after eighteen centuries have passed away.[37]

11:48 The leaders felt they could no longer remain inactive. If they did not intervene, the mass of the people would be persuaded by the miracles of Jesus. If the people thus acknowledged Jesus to be their King, it would mean trouble with Rome. The Romans would think that Jesus had come to overthrow their empire; they would then move in and punish the Jews. The expression **"take away both our place and nation"** means that the Romans would destroy the temple and scatter the Jewish people. These very things took place in A.D. 70 — not, however, because the Jews *accepted* the Lord, but rather because they *rejected* Him.

F. B. Meyer put it well:

> Christianity endangers businesses, undermines profitable but wicked trades, steals away customers from the devil's shrines, attacks vested interests, and turns the world upside down. It is a tiresome, annoying, profit-destroying thing.[38]

11:49, 50 Caiaphas was **high priest** from A.D. 26 to 36. He presided at the religious trial of the Lord and was present when Peter and John were brought before the Sanhedrin in Acts 4:6. He was not a believer in the Lord Jesus, in spite of the words which he here uttered.

According to Caiaphas, the chief priests and Pharisees were wrong in thinking that the Jews would die on account of Jesus. Rather, he predicted that Jesus would die for the Jewish nation. He said that it was better that Jesus would **die for the people**, rather than that **the whole nation** should have trouble with the Romans. It almost sounds as if Caiaphas really understood the reason for Jesus' coming into the world. We would almost think that Caiaphas had accepted Jesus as the Substitute for sinners — the central doctrine of Christianity. But unfortunately, that is not the case. What he said was true, but he himself did not believe on Jesus to the saving of his soul.

11:51, 52 This explains why Caiaphas said what he did. **He did not** speak **on his own authority**, that is, he did not make these things up by himself. He did not speak this of his own will. Rather, the message that he uttered was given to him by God, with a deeper message than he intended. It was a divine prophecy **that Jesus would die for the nation** of Israel. It was given to Caiaphas because he was **high priest that year**. God spoke through him because of the office

he held and not because of his own personal righteousness, for he was a sinful man.

The prophecy of Caiaphas was **not that** the Lord would die for the **nation** of Israel **only, but also that He would gather together** His elect among the Gentiles of the earth. Some think that Caiaphas was referring to Jewish people dispersed throughout the earth, but more probably he was referring to Gentiles who would believe on Christ through the preaching of the gospel.

11:53, 54 The Pharisees were not convinced by the miracle at Bethany. Rather, they were even more hostile toward the Son of God. **From that day on they plotted** His **death** with a new intensity.

Realizing the mounting hostility of the Jews, the Lord Jesus went off **to a city called Ephraim**. We do not know today where Ephraim was except that it was in a quiet, secluded area **near the wilderness**.

11:55 The announcement that **the Passover of the Jews was near** reminds us we are coming to the close of the Lord's public ministry. It was at this *very Passover* that He was to be crucified. The people were required to **go up to Jerusalem before the Passover to purify themselves**. For instance, if a Jew had touched a dead body, it was necessary for him to go through a certain ritual in order to be cleansed from ceremonial defilement. This purifying was done through various types of washings and offerings. The sad thing is that the Jewish people were thus seeking to purify themselves, while at the same time planning the death of the Passover Lamb. What a terrible exposure of the wickedness of the heart of man!

11:56, 57 As the people gathered **in the temple**, they began to think about the miracle worker named **Jesus** who had been in their country. A discussion arose as to whether He would **come to the feast**. The reason some thought He would not come is given in verse 57.

Official orders had gone out from **the chief priests and the Pharisees** for the arrest of Jesus. Anyone who knew of His whereabouts was commanded to notify the authorities so that **they might seize Him** and put Him to death.

VII. THE SON OF GOD'S MINIS-
TRY TO HIS OWN
(Chaps. 12–17)

A. Jesus Anointed at Bethany (12:1–8)

12:1 The home in **Bethany** was a place where **Jesus** loved to be. There He enjoyed sweet fellowship with **Lazarus**, Mary, and Martha. In coming **to Bethany** at this time, He was, humanly speaking, exposing Himself to danger because nearby Jerusalem was headquarters for all the forces that were arrayed against Him.

12:2 In spite of the many who were opposed to Jesus, there were still a few hearts which beat true to Him. **Lazarus was one of those who sat at the table with** the Lord, **and Martha served**. The Scripture does not say anything about what Lazarus saw or heard from the time he died until he was raised again. Perhaps he had been forbidden by God to divulge any such information.

12:3 Several instances are recorded in the Gospels where the Lord Jesus was anointed by a woman. No two incidents are exactly alike, but this incident is generally thought to parallel Mark 14:3–9. Mary's devotion to Christ caused her to take this **pound of very costly oil of spikenard** and anoint His **feet**. She was saying in effect that there was nothing too valuable to give to Christ. He is worthy of everything that we have and are.

Each time we meet Mary, she is at the feet of Jesus. Here she is wiping **His feet with her hair**. Since a woman's hair is her glory, she was laying her glory, as it were, at His feet. Needless to say, Mary herself would have carried the fragrance of the perfume for some time after this. Thus when Christ is worshiped, the worshipers themselves carry away something of the fragrance of that moment. No house is so filled with pleasant aroma as the house where Jesus is given His rightful place.

12:4, 5 Here the flesh is seen intruding into this most sacred of occasions. The **one** who was about to **betray** his Lord could not stand to see precious **oil** used in this way.

Judas did not consider Jesus to be worth **three hundred denarii**. He felt that the perfume should have been **sold** and **given to the poor**. But this was sheer hypocrisy. He cared no more for the poor than he did for the Lord. He was about to betray Him, not for **three hundred denarii**, but for a tenth of that amount. Ryle well says:

> That anyone could follow Christ as a disciple for three years, see all His miracles, hear all His teaching, receive at His hand repeated kindnesses, be counted an apostle, and yet prove rotten at heart in the end, all this at first sight appears incredible and impossible! Yet the case of Judas shows plainly that the thing can be. Few things, perhaps, are so little realized as the extent of the fall of man.[39]

12:6 John was quick to add that Judas did **not** say **this** because **he** had any real love **for the poor, but because he was a thief** and was greedy. Judas **had the money box; and he used to take what was put in it.**

12:7 The Lord answered in effect, "Do not prevent her from doing this. **She has kept this** oil **for the day of My burial.**[40] Now she wants to lavish it on Me in an act of affection and worship. She should be permitted to do so."

12:8 There would never be a time when there would not be **poor** people on whom others might lavish their kindness. But the Lord's ministry on earth was swiftly drawing to a close. Mary would *not* **always** have the opportunity to use this oil upon Him. This should remind us that spiritual opportunities are passing. We should never delay doing what we can for the Savior.

B. The Plot Against Lazarus (12:9–11)

12:9 The word quickly spread that Jesus was near Jerusalem. It was no longer possible to keep His presence secret. **Many of the Jews** came to Bethany to see Him, and others came to **see Lazarus, whom He had raised from the dead**.

12:10, 11 The insane hatred of the human heart is again pictured in this verse. **The chief priests plotted to put Lazarus to death also**. One would think that he had committed high treason by being raised from the dead! It was nothing over which he had control, and yet they considered him worthy of death.

Because of Lazarus, **many of the Jews ... believed in Jesus**. Lazarus was therefore an enemy to the Jewish "establishment", and he must be put out of the way. Those who bring others to the Lord are always made the target for persecution and even martyrdom.

Some commentators suggest that because the chief priests were Sadducees, who denied the resurrection, they wanted to get rid of the evidence by destroying Lazarus.

C. The Triumphal Entry (12:12–19)

12:12, 13 We now come to the triumphal entry of **Jesus** into **Jerusalem**. It was the Sunday before His crucifixion.

It is difficult to know exactly what this **multitude** thought about Jesus. Did they really understand that He was the Son of God and the Messiah of Israel? Or did they merely look upon Him as a King who would deliver them from Roman oppression? Were they carried away with the emotion of the hour? Doubtless some in the group were true believers, but the general impression is that most of the people had no real heart interest in the Lord.

Palm branches are a token of rest and peace after sorrow (Rev. 7:9). The word **"Hosanna"** means "Save now, we pray you." Putting these thoughts together, it would seem as if the people were acknowledging Jesus to be the One sent from God to save them from Roman cruelty and to give them rest and peace after the sorrow of their long years of Gentile oppression.

12:14, 15 Jesus rode into the city on **a young donkey**, a common mode of transportation. More than that, however, the Lord was fulfilling prophecy in riding in this manner.

This quotation was taken from Zechariah 9:9. There the prophet predicted that when the **King** came to Israel, He would be **sitting on a donkey's colt**. The **daughter of Zion** is a figurative expression referring to the Jewish people, **Zion** being a hill in the city of Jerusalem.

12:16 The **disciples did not** realize that what was happening was in exact fulfillment of Zechariah's prophecy, that Jesus was actually entering Jerusalem as the rightful King of Israel. **But** after the Lord had gone back to heaven to be **glorified** at the right hand of the Father, it dawned on the disciples that these events were in fulfillment of the Scriptures.

12:17, 18 In the crowd that watched Jesus entering Jerusalem were **people who had seen Him raise Lazarus ... from the dead**. These told the others around them that this One riding on the colt was the same One who had brought Lazarus back to life again. As the report of this notable **sign** spread, a great throng of **people** came out to meet Jesus. Unfortunately, their motive was curiosity rather than true faith.

12:19 As the crowd grew in size, and interest in the Savior mounted, **the Pharisees** were beside themselves. Nothing they could say or do had the slightest effect. With frenzied exaggeration, they cried out that **the** whole **world** had **gone after** Jesus. They did not realize that the interest of the crowd was but a passing thing, and that those who really were willing to worship Jesus as the Son of God were very few.

D. Certain Greeks Wish to See Jesus (12:20–26)

12:20 The **Greeks** who came to Jesus were Gentiles who had become converts to Judaism. The fact that they **came up to worship at the feast** shows that they were no longer carrying on the religious practices of their ancestors. Their coming to the Lord Jesus at this occasion pictures the fact that when the Jews rejected the Lord Jesus, the Gentiles would hear the gospel and many of them would believe.

12:21 No reason is given why **they came to Philip**. Perhaps his Greek name and the fact that he **was from Bethsaida of Galilee** made him attractive to those Gentile proselytes. Their request was a noble one indeed. **"Sir, we wish to see Jesus."** No one who has this sincere desire in his heart is ever turned away unrewarded.

12:22 Perhaps Philip was not too sure as to whether the Lord would see these Greeks. Christ had previously told the disciples not to go to the Gentiles with the gospel, so **Philip** went to **Andrew**, and together they **told Jesus**.

12:23 Why did the Greeks want to see Jesus? If we read between the lines, we can surmise that the wisdom of Jesus appealed to them and that they wanted to exalt Him as their popular philosopher. They knew that He was on a collision course with the Jewish leaders and wanted Him to save His life, perhaps by going to Greece with them. Their philosophy was "Spare yourself," but **Jesus** told **them** that this philosophy was directly opposed to the law of harvest. He would be **glorified** in His sacrificial death and not by a comfortable life.

12:24 Seed never produces grain until first it **falls into the ground and dies**. The Lord Jesus here referred to Himself as **a grain** (or kernel) **of wheat**. If He did not die, He would abide **alone**. He would enjoy the glories of heaven by Himself; there would be no saved sinners there to share His glory. But if He died, He would provide a way of salvation by which many might be saved.

The same applies to us, as T. G. Ragland says:

> If we refuse to be corns of wheat — falling into the ground, and dying; if we will neither sacrifice prospects, nor risk character, and property, and health; nor, when we are called, relinquish home, and break family ties, for Christ's sake; *then we shall abide alone.* But if we wish to be fruitful, we must follow our Blessed Lord Himself, by becoming a corn of wheat, and dying, *then we shall bring forth much fruit.*[41]

12:25 Many people think that the important things in life are food, clothing, and pleasure. They live for these things. But in thus loving their lives, they fail to realize that the soul is more important than the body. By neglecting their soul's welfare, they lose their lives. On the other hand, there are those who count all things loss for Christ. To serve Him, they forego things highly prized among men. These are the people who **will keep** their lives **for eternal life**. To hate one's life means to love Christ more than one loves his own interests.

12:26 To serve Christ, one must **follow** Him. He would have His servants obey His teachings and resemble Him morally. They must apply the example of His death to themselves. All servants are promised the constant presence and

protection of their Master, and this applies not only to the present life but to eternity as well. Service now will receive God's approval in a coming day. Whatever one suffers of shame or reproach here will be small indeed compared to the glory of being publicly commended by God the **Father** in heaven!

E. Jesus Faces Imminent Death (12:27–36)

12:27 Increasingly, the Lord's thoughts were upon the events that lay immediately before Him. He was thinking of the cross, and contemplating the time when He would become the Sin Bearer, and endure the wrath of God against our sins. In thinking of His "hour of heartbreak" (JBP), His **soul** was **troubled**. How should He pray in such a moment? Should He ask His **Father** to **save** Him **from** the **hour**? He could not pray for this because the **purpose** of His coming into the world was to go to the cross. He was born to die.

12:28 Instead of praying that He might be saved from the cross, the Lord Jesus rather prayed that the **name** of His Father might be glorified. He was more interested that honor should come to God than in His own comfort or safety. God now spoke from heaven, saying that He *had* **glorified** His Name and would **glorify it again**. The Name of God was glorified during the earthly ministry of Jesus. The thirty silent years in Nazareth, the three years of public ministry, the wonderful words and works of the Savior — all of these greatly glorified the Name of the Father. But still greater glory would be brought to God through the death, burial, resurrection, and Ascension of Christ.

12:29 Some of those standing by mistook the voice of God for thunder. Such people are always trying to put a natural explanation on spiritual things. Men who are unwilling to accept the fact of miracles try to explain the miracles away by some natural law. Others knew it was not thunder, and yet they did not recognize it as the voice of God. Realizing it must have been superhuman, they could only conclude that it was the voice of **an angel**. God's voice can only be heard and understood by those who are helped by the Holy Spirit. People can listen to the gospel over and over, and yet it might be ever so meaningless to them unless the Holy Spirit speaks to them through it.

12:30 The Lord explained to the listeners that **this voice did not** need to be audible in order for *Him* to hear it. Rather, it was made audible for the sake of those who were standing by.

12:31 **"Now is the judgment of this world,"** He said. The world was about to crucify the Lord of life and glory. In doing so, it would condemn itself. Sentence would be passed upon it for its awful rejection of Christ. That is what the Savior meant here. Condemnation was about to be passed on guilty mankind. **The ruler of this world** is Satan. In a very real sense, Satan was utterly defeated at Calvary. He thought he had succeeded in doing away with the Lord Jesus once for all. Instead, the Savior had provided a way of salvation for men, and at the same time had defeated Satan and all his hosts. The sentence has not yet been carried out on the devil, but his doom has been sealed. He is still going through the world carrying on his evil business, but it is just a matter of time before he will be **cast** into the lake of fire.

12:32 The first part of this verse refers to Christ's death on the cross. He was nailed to a cross of wood and **lifted up from the earth**. The Lord said that if He were thus crucified, He would **draw all peoples to** Himself. Several explanations have been given for this. Some think that Christ draws all people either to salvation or to judgment. Others think that if Christ is lifted up in the preaching of the gospel, then there will be a great power in the message, and souls will be drawn to Him. But probably the correct explanation is that the crucifixion of the Lord Jesus resulted in **all** *kinds* of people being drawn to Him. It does not mean all people without exception, but people from every nation, tribe, and language.

12:33 When the Lord Jesus spoke of being lifted up, He signified the kind of **death He would die**, that is, by crucifixion. Here again we have evidence of the all–knowledge of the Lord. He knew in advance that He would not die in bed or by accident, but that He would be nailed to a cross.

12:34 **The people** were puzzled by this statement of the Lord about being **lifted up**. They knew that He claimed to be the Messiah, and yet they knew from the OT that the Messiah would live forever (see Isa. 9:7; Ps. 110:4; Dan. 7:14; Mic. 4:7). Notice that the people quoted Jesus as saying, **"The Son of Man must be lifted up."** Actually, He had said, "I, if I be lifted up from the earth." Of course, the Lord Jesus had referred to Himself many times as the Son of Man, and perhaps He had even spoken previously of the Son of Man being lifted up, so it was not difficult for the people to put the two thoughts together.

12:35 When the people asked Jesus who the Son of Man was, He spoke of Himself again as **the light** of the world. He reminded them that **the light** would only be with them for a short while. They should come to the Light and walk in the Light; otherwise **darkness** would soon **overtake** them, and they would stumble around in ignorance.

The Lord seemed to liken Himself to the sun and to the daylight it offers. The sun rises in the morning, reaches its peak at noon, and descends over the horizon in the evening. It is only with us for a limited number of hours. We should avail ourselves of it while it is here, because when the night comes, we do not have the benefit of it. Spiritually, the one who believes on the Lord Jesus is the one who walks in the light. The one who rejects Him **walks in darkness and does not know where he is going**. He lacks divine guidance, and stumbles through life.

12:36 Again the Lord Jesus warned His listeners to **believe** on Him **while** there was still opportunity. By doing so, they would **become sons of light**. They would be assured of direction through life and into eternity. After speaking these words, the Lord **departed** from the people and remained in obscurity for a while.

F. Failure of Most Jews to Believe (12:37–43)

12:37[†] John paused at this time to express amazement that **although** the Lord Jesus **had done so many** mighty **signs**, yet the people **did not believe in Him**. As we have mentioned before, their unbelief was not caused by any lack

†*See p. xxi.*

of evidence. The Lord had given the most convincing proofs of His deity, but the people did not want to believe. They wanted a king to rule over them, but they did not want to repent.

12:38 The unbelief of the Jews was in fulfillment of the prophecy in Isaiah 53:1. The question, **"Lord, who has believed our report?"** calls for the answer, "Not very many!" Since the arm in Scripture speaks of power or strength, **the arm of the LORD** speaks of the mighty power of God. God's power is only **revealed** to those who believe the report concerning the Lord Jesus Christ. Therefore, because not many accepted the announcement concerning the Messiah, the power of God was not revealed to many.

12:39 When the Lord Jesus presented Himself to the nation of Israel, they rejected Him. Over and over again, He came back to them with the offer of salvation, but they kept saying "no" to Him. The more men reject the gospel, the harder it becomes for them to receive it. When men close their eyes to the Light, God makes it more difficult for them to see the Light. God causes them to be struck with what is known as judicial blindness, that is, a blindness which is God's judgment on them for refusing His Son.

12:40 This quotation was from Isaiah 6:9, 10. God **blinded** the **eyes** of the people of Israel **and hardened their hearts**. He did not do this at first, but only after they had closed their eyes and hardened their own hearts. As a result of Israel's stubborn and willful rejection of the Messiah, they cut themselves off from sight, understanding, conversion, and healing.

12:41 In Isaiah 6 the prophet was described as seeing the **glory** of God. John now added the explanation that it was *Christ's* **glory** which Isaiah **saw**, and it was of Christ that he **spoke**. Thus, this verse is another important link in the chain of evidence that proves Jesus Christ to be God.

12:42 **Many** of **the rulers** of the Jews became convinced that Jesus was the Messiah. However, they did not dare to share their conviction with the others lest they be excommunicated. We would like to think that these men were genuine believers in the Lord Jesus, but it is doubtful. Where there is true faith, there will be confession of Christ, sooner or later. When Christ is really accepted as Savior, one does not hesitate to make it known, regardless of the consequences.

12:43 It was obvious that these men were more interested in **the praise of** their fellow **men** than they were in **the praise of God**. They thought more of man's approval than of God's. Can a person like this really be a genuine believer in Christ? See chapter 5, verse 44, for the answer.

G. The Peril of Unbelief (12:44–50)

12:44 A paraphrase of verse 44 is as follows: "The one **who believes in Me** actually **believes** not only in Me, **but** also in My Father **who sent Me"**. Here again the Lord taught His absolute union with God the Father. It was impossible to believe in One without believing in the Other. To believe in Christ is to believe in God the Father. One cannot believe in the Father unless he gives equal honor to the Son.

12:45 In one sense, nobody can see God the Father. He is Spirit, and therefore invisible. But the Lord Jesus had come into the world to let us know what God is like. By this we do not mean that He lets us know what God is like physically, but morally. He has revealed the character of God to us. Therefore, whoever has seen Christ has seen God the Father.

12:46 The illustration of **light** was apparently one of our Lord's favorites. Again He referred to Himself **as a light** coming **into the world** in order that those who believe in Him **should not abide in darkness**. Apart from Christ, men are in deepest darkness. They do not have a right understanding of life, death, or eternity. But those who come to Christ in faith no longer grope about for the truth, because they have found the truth in Him.

12:47 The purpose of Christ's First Coming was **not to judge the world but to save**. He did not sit in judgment on those who refused to hear His words or believe on Him. This does not mean that He will not condemn these unbelievers in a coming day, but that judgment was not the object of His First Advent.

12:48 The Lord now looked forward to a coming day when those who rejected His words will stand before the judgment bar of God. At that time, the **words** or teaching of the Lord Jesus will be sufficient to condemn them.

12:49 The things He taught were not things He had made up Himself or learned in the schools of men. Rather, as the obedient Servant and Son, He had only spoken those things which the Father commissioned Him to **speak**. This is the fact that will condemn men at the last day. The word that Jesus spoke was the Word of God, and men refused to hear it. The Father had told Him not only **what** to **say** but **what** He should **speak**. There is a difference between the two. The expression **"what I should say"** refers to the substance of the message; **"what I should speak"** means the very words which the Lord should use in teaching the truth of God.

12:50 Jesus knew the Father had commissioned Him to give **everlasting life** to those who would believe on Him. **Therefore**, Christ delivered the message as it was given to Him by **the Father**.

We now come to a distinct break in the narrative. Up to this point the Lord has presented Himself to Israel. Seven distinct signs or miracles are recorded, each one illustrating an experience which will result when a sinner puts his faith in Christ. The signs are:

1. Changing the water into wine at the wedding in Cana of Galilee (2:1–12). This pictures the sinner who is a stranger to divine joy being transformed by the power of Christ.
2. Healing the nobleman's son (4:46–54). This pictures the sinner as being sick and in need of spiritual health.
3. Healing the cripple at the pool of Bethesda (chap. 5). The poor sinner is without strength, helpless, and unable to do a thing to remedy his own condition. Jesus cures him of his infirmity.
4. Feeding the five thousand (chap. 6). The sinner is without food, hungry, and in need of that which imparts strength. The Lord provides food for his soul so that he never needs to hunger.
5. Calming the Sea of Galilee (6:16–21).

The sinner is seen in a place of danger. The Lord rescues him from the storm.

6. Healing a man blind from birth (chap. 9). This man pictures the blindness of the human heart until it is touched by the power of Christ. Man cannot see his own sinfulness, or the beauties of the Savior, until enlightened by the Holy Spirit.
7. Raising Lazarus from the dead (chap. 11). This, of course, reminds us that the sinner is dead in trespasses and in sins and needs life from above.

All these signs are intended to prove that Jesus is the Christ, the Son of God.

H. Jesus Washes His Disciples' Feet (13:1–11)

In chapter 13, the Upper Room Discourse begins. Jesus was no longer walking among the hostile Jews. He had retired with His disciples to an upper room in Jerusalem for a final time of fellowship with them before going forth to His trial and crucifixion. John 13 through 17 is one of the best-loved sections in the entire NT.

13:1 The day before the crucifixion, the Lord **Jesus knew that** the time **had come** for Him to die, to rise again, and to go back to heaven. He had **loved His own**, that is, those who were true believers. **He loved them to the end** of His earthly ministry, and will continue to love them throughout eternity. But **He** also **loved them to** an infinite degree, as He was about to demonstrate.

13:2 John does not say which **supper** is referred to here — whether the Passover, the Lord's Supper, or an ordinary meal. **The devil** sowed the thought in **the heart of Judas** that the time was now ripe to **betray Jesus**. Judas had plotted evil against the Lord long before this, but he was now given the signal for carrying out his foul plans.

13:3 Verse 3 emphasizes *who* was performing a slave's task — not just a rabbi or teacher, but **Jesus**, who was conscious of His deity. He knew the work that had been committed to Him; He knew **that He had come from God** and that He was already on His journey back **to God**.

13:4 It was the consciousness of

who He was, and of His mission and destiny, that enabled Him to stoop down and wash the disciples' feet. Rising **from supper**, the Lord **laid aside His** long outer **garments**. Then He put a **towel** around Himself as an apron, taking the place of a slave. We might have expected this incident to be in the Gospel of Mark, the Gospel of the Perfect Servant. But the fact that it is in the Gospel of the Son of God makes it all the more remarkable.

This symbolic act reminds us of how the Lord left the ivory palaces above, came down into this world as a Servant, and ministered to those He had created.

13:5 In eastern lands, the use of open sandals made it necessary **to wash** one's **feet** frequently. It was common courtesy for a host to arrange to have a slave wash the feet of his guests. Here the divine Host became the slave and performed this lowly service. "Jesus at the feet of the traitor — what a picture! What lessons for us!"

13:6 **Peter** was shocked to think of the Lord's **washing** *his* **feet**, and he expressed his disapproval that One so great as the Lord should condescend to one so unworthy as he. "The sight of God in the role of a servant is disturbing."

13:7 **Jesus** now taught Peter that there was a spiritual meaning to what He was doing. Foot-washing was a picture of a certain type of spiritual washing. Peter knew that the Lord was performing the physical act, but he did **not understand** the spiritual *significance*. He would **know** it soon, however, because the Lord explained it. And he would **know** it by experience when later he was restored to the Lord after having denied Him.

13:8 **Peter** illustrates the extremes of human nature. He vowed that the Lord would **never wash** his **feet** — and here "never" literally means "not for eternity." The Lord answered Peter that apart from His washing, there could be no fellowship with Him. The meaning of foot-washing is now unfolded. As Christians walk through this world, they contract a certain amount of defilement. Listening to vile talk, looking at unholy things, working with ungodly men inevitably soil the believer. He needs to be constantly cleansed.

This cleansing takes place by the water of the Word. As we read and study the Bible, as we hear it preached, and as we discuss it with one another, we find that it cleanses us from the evil influences about us. On the other hand, the more we neglect the Bible, the more these wicked influences can remain in our minds and lives without causing us any great concern. When Jesus said **"you have no part with Me,"** He did not mean that Peter could not be saved unless He washed him, but rather that fellowship with the Lord can be maintained only by the continual cleansing action of the Scriptures in his life.

13:9, 10 Now **Peter** shifted to the other extreme. A minute ago, he was saying, "Never." Now he said, "Wash me all over."

On the way back from the public bath, a person's feet would get dirty again. He didn't need another bath but did need to have his feet washed. **"He who is bathed needs only to wash his feet, but is completely clean."** There is a difference between the bath and the basin. The *bath* speaks of the cleansing received at the time of one's salvation. Cleansing from the *penalty* of sin through the blood of Christ takes place only once. The *basin* speaks of cleansing from the *pollution* of sin and must take place continually through the Word of God. There is one bath but many footwashings. **"You are clean, but not all of you"** means that the disciples had received the bath of regeneration — that is, all the disciples but Judas. He had never been saved.

13:11 With full knowledge of all things, the Lord **knew** that Judas **would betray Him**, and so He singled out one as never having had the bath of redemption.

I. Jesus Teaches His Disciples to Follow His Example (13:12–20)

13:12 It would seem that Christ **washed** the **feet** of *all* the disciples. Then He put on **His** outer **garments and sat down again** to explain to them the spiritual meaning of what He had done. He opened the conversation by asking a question. The questions of the Savior make an interesting study. They form one of His most effective methods of teaching.

13:13, 14 The disciples had acknowledged Jesus to be their **Teacher and Lord**, and they were right in doing so. But His example showed that the highest rank in the power structure of the kingdom is that of servant.

If the **Lord and Teacher** had **washed** the disciples' **feet**, what excuse could they have for not washing **one another's feet**? Did the Lord mean that they should *literally* wash each other's feet with water?[42] Was He here instituting an ordinance for the church? No, the meaning here was spiritual. He was telling them that they should keep each other clean by constant fellowship over the Word. If one sees his brother growing cold or worldly, he should lovingly exhort him from the Bible.

13:15, 16 The Lord had **given** them **an example**, an object lesson of what they **should do** to one another spiritually.

If pride or personal animosities prevent us from stooping to serve our brethren, we should remember that we are **not greater than** our **Master**. He humbled Himself to wash those who were unworthy and unthankful, and He knew that one of them would betray Him. Would you minister in a lowly way to a man if you knew he was about to betray you for money? Those who were **sent** (the disciples) should not consider themselves too lofty to do anything that the One **who sent** them (the Lord Jesus) had done.

13:17 To **know these** truths concerning humility and unselfishness and service is one thing, but one can know them and never practice them. The real value and blessedness lie *in doing* **them**!

13:18 What the Lord had just been teaching about service did **not** apply to Judas. He was not one of those whom the Lord would send into all the world with the gospel. Jesus knew the Scriptures concerning His betrayal must **be fulfilled** — such Scriptures as Psalm 41:9. Judas was one who had eaten his meals with the Lord for three years, and yet he **lifted up his heel against** Him — an expression indicating that he betrayed the Lord. In Psalm 41 the betrayer is described by the Lord as "my own familiar friend."

13:19 The Lord revealed His betrayal to the disciples in advance so **that when it** came **to pass**, the disciples

would know that Jesus was true deity. The italicized word **He** can be omitted from the end of this verse. **"You may believe that I AM."** The Jesus of the NT is the Jehovah of the Old. Thus, fulfilled prophecy is one of the great proofs of the deity of Christ and also, we might add, of the inspiration of Scriptures.

13:20 Our Lord knew that His betrayal might cause the other disciples to stumble or doubt. So He added this word of encouragement. They should remember that they were being sent on a divine mission. They were to be so closely identified with Him that to receive *them* was the same as receiving *Him*. Also, those who received Christ received God the Father. They were thus to be comforted by their close link with God the Son and God the Father.

J. Jesus Predicts His Betrayal (13:21–30)

13:21, 22 The knowledge that one of His disciples would betray Him caused the Lord to be deeply **troubled**. It seems that Jesus was here giving the betrayer a final opportunity to abandon his evil plan. Without exposing him directly, the Lord revealed His knowledge that **one of** the twelve would **betray** Him. Yet even this did not change the traitor's mind.

The rest of the disciples did not suspect Judas. They were surprised that one of their number would do such a thing and puzzled as to who he could be.

13:23 In those days, people did not sit up at a table for a meal but reclined on low couches. The disciple **whom Jesus loved** was John, the writer of this Gospel. He omitted mentioning his own name, but did not hesitate to mention the fact that he held a place of special affection in the Savior's heart. The Lord loved all the disciples, but John enjoyed a special sense of closeness to Him.

13:24, 25 **Peter therefore motioned** rather than speaking audibly. Perhaps by nodding his head, he asked John to find out the name of the betrayer.

Leaning back on Jesus' breast John asked the fateful question in a whisper and was probably answered in a low voice also.

13:26 **Jesus answered** that He would **give a piece of bread ... dipped** in wine or meat juice to the traitor. Some say that an Eastern host gave the bread to the honored guest at a meal. By making **Judas** the honored guest, the Lord thus tried to win him to repentance by His grace and love. Others suggest that the bread was commonly passed in this way in connection with the Passover supper. If that is true, then Judas left during the Passover supper and before the Lord's Supper was instituted.

13:27 The devil had already put it into Judas' heart to betray the Lord. Now **Satan entered him**. At first, it was merely a suggestion. But Judas entertained it, liked it, and agreed to it. Now the devil took control of him. Knowing the betrayer was now fully determined, the Lord told him to **do** it **quickly**. Obviously, He was not encouraging him to do evil but simply expressing sorrowful resignation.

13:28, 29 This verse confirms that the previous conversation between Jesus and John about the bread was not heard by the other disciples. They still did not know that Judas was about to betray their Lord.

Some thought that Jesus had simply told Judas to go quickly and **buy** something **for the feast**, or because Judas was the treasurer, that the Savior had instructed him to make a donation **to the poor**.

13:30 Judas **received the piece of bread** as a token of special favor, and then left the company of the Lord and of the other disciples. The Scriptures add the meaningful words **and it was night. It was** not only **night** in a literal sense, but **it was night** spiritually for Judas — a night of gloom and remorse that would never end. It is always night when men turn their backs on the Savior.

K. The New Commandment Given (13:31–35)

13:31 As soon as Judas left, **Jesus** began to speak with the disciples more freely and intimately. The tension was gone. **"Now the Son of Man is glorified,"** He said. The Lord was anticipating the work of redemption which He was about to accomplish. His death might have seemed like defeat, yet it was the means by which lost sinners could be saved. It was followed by His resurrection and ascension, and He was

greatly honored in it all. **And God is glorified in** the work of the Savior. It proclaimed Him to be a *holy* God who could not pass over sin, but also a *loving* God who did not desire the death of the sinner; it proclaimed how He could be a *just* God, yet be able to *justify* sinners. Every attribute of deity was superlatively magnified at Calvary.

13:32 **"If God is glorified in Him,"** and He is,[43] **"God will also glorify Him in Himself."** God will see that appropriate honor is given to His beloved Son. **"And glorify Him immediately"** — without delay. God the Father fulfilled this prediction of the Lord Jesus by raising Him from the dead and seating Him at His own right hand in heaven. God would not wait until the kingdom was ushered in. He would **glorify** His Son **immediately**.

13:33 For the first time the Lord Jesus addressed His disciples as **little children** — a term of endearment. And He used it only after Judas had departed. He was only to **be with** them **a little while longer**. Then He would die on the cross. They would **seek** Him then, but would not be able to follow Him, for He would return to heaven. The Lord had told the same thing **to the Jews**, but He meant it in a different sense. For the disciples, His departure would only be temporary. He would come again for them (chap. 14). But for **the Jews**, His leaving them would be final. He was returning to heaven, and they could not follow Him because of their unbelief.

13:34 During His absence, they were to be governed by the **commandment** of **love**. This commandment was not new in point of time because the Ten Commandments taught love to God and to one's neighbor. But this **commandment** was **new** in other ways. It was **new** because the Holy Spirit would empower believers to obey it. It was **new** in that it was *superior* to the old. The old said, "Love your *neighbor*," but the new said, "Love your *enemies*."

It has been well said that the law of love to others is now explained with new clarity, enforced by new motives and obligations, illustrated by a new example, and obeyed in a new way.

Also it was new, as explained in the

verse, because it called for a *higher degree* of love: **"As I have loved you, that you also love one another."**

13:35 The badge of Christian discipleship is not a cross worn around the neck or on the lapel, or some distinctive type of clothing. Anyone could profess discipleship by these means. The true mark of a Christian is **love** for his fellow Christians. This requires divine power, and this power is only given to those indwelt by the Spirit.

L. Jesus Predicts Peter's Denial (13:36–38)

13:36 **Simon Peter** did not understand that Jesus had spoken of His death. He thought He was going on some earthly journey and did not understand why he could not go along. The Lord explained that Peter *would* **follow** Him later, that is, when he died, but could not do so now.

13:37 With typical devotion and enthusiasm, **Peter** expressed willingness to die for the Lord. He thought he could endure martyrdom by his own strength. Later he actually did die for the Lord, but it was because he had been given special strength and courage by God.

13:38 **Jesus** checks his "zeal without knowledge" by telling Peter something he himself did not know — that before the night was ended, he would deny the Lord **three times**. Thus Peter was reminded of his weakness, cowardice, and inability to follow the Lord for even a few hours by his own power.

M. Jesus: the Way, the Truth, and the Life (14:1–14)

14:1 Some link verse 1 to the last verse of chapter 13 and think it was spoken to Peter. Although he would deny the Lord, yet there was a word of comfort for him. But the plural forms in Greek ("ye" in old English) show it was spoken to *all* the disciples, hence we should pause after chapter 13. The thought seems to be: "I am going away, and you will not be able to see Me. But **let not your heart be troubled; you believe in God**, and yet you do not see Him. Now **believe in Me** in the same way." Here is another important claim to equality with God.

14:2 The **Father's house** refers to heaven, where there are many dwelling places. There is room there for all the redeemed. **If it were not so**, the Lord **would have told** them; He would not have them build on false hopes. **"I go to prepare a place for you"** may have two meanings. The Lord Jesus went to Calvary to prepare a place for His own. It is through His atoning death that believers are assured a place there. But also the Lord went back to heaven to prepare a place. We do not know very much about this place, but we know that provision is being made for every child of God — "a prepared place for a prepared people!"

14:3 Verse 3 refers to the time when the Lord **will come** back **again** into the air, when those who have died in faith will be raised, when the living will be changed, and when all the blood-bought throng will be taken home to heaven (1 Thess. 4:13–18; 1 Cor. 15:51–58). This is a personal, literal coming of Christ. As surely as He went away, He **will come again**. His desire is to have His own with Him for all eternity.

14:4, 5 He was going to heaven, and they knew **the way** to heaven, for He had told them many times.

Apparently **Thomas** did not understand the meaning of the Lord's words. Like Peter, he may have been thinking of a journey to some place on the earth.

14:6 This lovely verse makes it clear that the Lord Jesus Christ is Himself **the way** to heaven. He does not merely show the way; He *is* **the way**. Salvation is in a Person. Accept that Person as your own, and you have salvation. Christianity is Christ. The Lord Jesus is not just one of many ways. He is the *only* Way. **No one comes to the Father except through** Him. The way to God is not by the Ten Commandments, the Golden Rule, ordinances, church membership — it is through Christ and Christ alone. Today many say that it does not matter what you believe as long as you are sincere. They say that all religions have some good in them and that they all lead to heaven at last. But Jesus said, **"No one comes to the Father except through Me."**

Then the Lord is **the truth**. He is not just One who teaches the truth; He *is* **the truth**. He is the embodiment of Truth.

Those who have Christ have the Truth. It is not found anywhere else.

Christ Jesus is **the life**. He is the source of life, both spiritual and eternal. Those who receive Him have eternal life because He *is* the Life.

14:7 Once more the Lord taught the mysterious union that exists between the Father and Himself. If the disciples had recognized who Jesus really was, they **would have known** the **Father also**, because the Lord revealed the Father to men. **From now on**, and especially after Christ's resurrection, the disciples would understand that Jesus was God the Son. Then they would realize that to know Christ was **to know** the Father, and to see the Lord Jesus was to see God. This verse does not teach that God and the Lord Jesus are the same Person. There are three distinct *Persons* in the Godhead, but there is only *one God*.

14:8 **Philip** wanted the **Lord** to give some special revelation of **the Father**, and that would be all he would ask. He did not understand that everything the Lord was, and did, and said, was a revelation of the Father.

14:9 **Jesus** patiently corrected him. Philip had been with the Lord for a **long** time. He was one of the first disciples to be called (John 1:43). Yet the full truth of Christ's deity and of His unity with the Father had not yet dawned on him. He did not know that when he looked at Jesus, he was looking at One who perfectly displayed **the Father.**

14:10, 11 The words **"I am in the Father, and the Father in Me"** describe the closeness of the union between **the Father** and the Son. They are separate Persons, yet They are one as to attributes and will. We should not be discouraged if we cannot understand this. No mortal mind will ever understand the Godhead. We must give God credit for knowing things that we can never know. If we fully understood Him, we would be as great as He! Jesus had power to speak the words and to do the miracles, but He came into the world as the Servant of Jehovah and He spoke and acted in perfect obedience to the Father.

The disciples should **believe** that He was one with **the Father** because of His own testimony to that fact. But if not, then they should certainly **believe** because of **the works** He performed.

14:12 The Lord predicted that those who believed on Him would perform miracles like He did, and even **greater works**. In the book of Acts, we read of the apostles performing miracles of bodily healing, similar to those of the Savior. But we also read of greater miracles — such as the conversion of three thousand on the day of Pentecost. Doubtless it was to the world-wide proclamation of the gospel, the salvation of so many souls, and the building of the church that the Lord referred to by the expression **greater works**. It is **greater** to save souls than to heal bodies. When the Lord returned to heaven, He was glorified, and the Holy Spirit was sent to earth. It was through the Spirit's power that the apostles performed these greater miracles.

14:13 What a comfort it must have been to the disciples to know that, even though the Lord was leaving them, they could pray to the Father in His Name and receive their requests. This verse does not mean that a believer can get anything he wants from God. The key to understanding the promise is in the words **in My name — whatever you ask in My name**. To ask in Jesus Name is not simply to insert His Name at the end of the prayer. It is to ask in accordance with His mind and will. It is to ask for those things which will glorify God, bless mankind, and be for our own spiritual good.

In order to ask in Christ's Name, we must live in close fellowship with Him. Otherwise we would not know His attitude. The closer we are to Him, the more our desires will be the same as His are. **The Father** is **glorified in the Son** because the Son only desires those things that are pleasing in God's sight. As prayers of this nature are presented and granted, it causes great glory to be brought to God.

14:14 The promise is repeated for emphasis and as a strong encouragement to God's people. Live in the center of His will, walk in fellowship with the Lord, **ask** for **anything** that the Lord would desire, and your prayers will be answered.

N. The Promise of Another Helper (14:15–26)

14:15 The Lord Jesus was about to leave His disciples, and they would be filled with sorrow. How would they be able to express their **love** to Him? The answer was by keeping His commandments. Not by tears, but by obedience. The **commandments** of the Lord are the instructions which He has given us in the Gospels, as well as the rest of the NT.

14:16 The word translated **pray** that is used here of our Lord is not the same word used to describe an inferior praying to a superior, but of one making request of his equal. The Lord would **pray the Father** to send **another Helper**. The word **Helper** (*Paraclete*) means one called to the side of another to help. It is also translated Advocate (1 Jn. 2:1). The Lord Jesus is our Advocate or Helper, and the Holy Spirit is **another Helper** — not another of a different kind, but another of similar nature. The Holy Spirit would **abide** with believers **forever**. In the OT, the Holy Spirit came upon men at various times, but often left them. Now He would come to remain **forever**.

14:17 The Holy Spirit is called **the Spirit of truth** because His teaching is true and He glorifies Christ who is the truth. **The world cannot receive** the Holy Spirit because it cannot see Him. Unbelievers want to see before they will believe — although they believe in wind and electricity, and yet they cannot see them. The unsaved do not know or understand the Holy Spirit. He may convict them of sin, and yet they do not know that it is He. The disciples knew the Holy Spirit. They had known Him to work in their own lives and had seen Him working through the Lord Jesus.

"He dwells with you, and will be in you." Before Pentecost, the Holy Spirit came upon men and dwelt **with** them. But since Pentecost, when a man believes on the Lord Jesus, the Holy Spirit takes up His abode in that man's life forever. The prayer of David, "Do not take Your Holy Spirit from me," would not be suitable today. The Holy Spirit is never taken from a believer, although He may be grieved, or quenched, or hindered.

14:18 The Lord would **not leave** His disciples as **orphans**, or desolate. He would **come to** them again. In one sense, He came to them after His resurrection, but it is doubtful if that is what is meant. In another sense, He came to them in the Person of the Holy Spirit on the day

of Pentecost. This spiritual coming is the true meaning here. "There was something about Pentecost which made it a coming of Jesus." In a third sense, He will literally come to them again at the end of this age, when He will take His chosen ones home to heaven.

14:19 No unbeliever saw the Lord Jesus after His burial. After He was raised, He was seen only by those who loved Him. But even after His Ascension, His disciples continued to see Him by faith. This is doubtless meant by the words **"but you will see Me."** After the world could no longer see Him, His disciples would continue to see Him. **"Because I live, you will live also."** Here He was looking forward to His resurrection life. It would be the pledge of life for all who trusted Him. Even if they should die, they would be raised again to die no more.

14:20 **"At that day"** probably refers again to the descent of the Holy Spirit. He would instruct believers in the truth that just as there was a vital link between the Son and the Father, so there would be a marvelous union of life and interests between Christ and His saints. It is difficult to explain how Christ is **in** the believer, and the believer is **in** Christ at the same time. The usual illustration is of a poker in the fire. Not only is the poker in the fire, but the fire is in the poker.[44] But this does not tell the full story. Christ is in the believer in the sense that His life is communicated to him. He actually dwells in the believer through the Holy Spirit. The believer is in Christ in the sense that he stands before God in all the merit of the Person and work of Christ.

14:21 The real proof of one's love to the Lord is obedience to His **commandments**. It is useless to talk about loving Him if we do not want to obey Him. In one sense, the Father loves all the world. But He has a special love for those who love His Son. Those are also loved by Christ, and He makes Himself known to them in a special way. The more we love the Savior, the better we shall know Him.

14:22 The **Judas** mentioned here had the misfortune to have the same name as the traitor. But the Spirit of God kindly distinguished him from **Iscariot**. He could not understand how the Lord could appear to the disciples without also being seen by **the world**. Doubtless he thought of the Savior's coming as that of a conquering King or popular Hero. He did not understand that the Lord would **manifest** Himself to His own in a spiritual manner. They would see Him by faith through the Word of God.

By the Spirit of God, we can actually know Christ better today than the disciples knew Him when He was on earth. When He was here, those in the front of the crowd were closer to Him than those in the rear. But today, by faith, each of us can enjoy the closest of fellowship with Him. Christ's answer to Judas' question shows that the promised manifestations to His individual followers is connected with the Word of God. Obedience to the Word will result in the coming and abiding of the Father and the Son.

14:23 If a person truly **loves** the Lord, **he will** want to **keep** all of His teachings, not just isolated commandments. The **Father** loves those who are willing to obey His Son without questions or reservations. Both Father and Son are especially near to such loving and obedient hearts.

14:24 On the other hand, those who do **not love** Him do **not keep** His sayings. And they are not only refusing the words of Christ, but those of the Father as well.

14:25 While He was **with** them, our Lord taught His disciples up to a certain point. He could not reveal more truth to them because they could not have taken it in.

14:26 But **the Holy Spirit** would reveal more. He was sent by **the Father** in the **name** of Christ on the day of Pentecost. The Spirit came in Christ's **name** in the sense that He came to represent Christ's interests on earth. He did not come to glorify Himself but to draw men and women to the Savior. **"He will teach you all things,"** said the Lord. He did this first of all through the spoken ministry of the apostles; then through the written Word of God which we have today. The Holy Spirit brings to **remembrance all** the **things** which the Savior had taught. Actually, the Lord Jesus seems to have presented in germ form

all the teaching which is developed by the Holy Spirit in the rest of the NT.

O. Jesus Leaves His Peace with His Disciples (14:27–31)

14:27 A person who is about to die usually writes a last will and testament in which he leaves his possessions to his loved ones. Here the Lord Jesus was doing that very thing. However, He did not bequeath material things but something that money could not buy — **peace**, inward **peace** of conscience that arises from a sense of pardoned sin and of reconciliation with God. Christ can give it because He purchased it with His own blood at Calvary. It is **not given as the world gives** — sparingly, selfishly, and for a short time. His gift of **peace** is forever. Why then should a Christian **be troubled** or **afraid**?

14:28 Jesus had already told them how He was going to leave them, and then later how He would return to take them home to heaven with Him. **If** they **loved** Him, this would have caused them to **rejoice**. Of course, in a sense they did love Him. But they did not fully appreciate who He was, and thus their love was not as great as it should have been.

"You would rejoice because I said, 'I am going to the Father,' for My Father is greater than I." At first it seems as if this verse contradicts all that Jesus had taught concerning His equality with God the Father. But there is no contradiction, and the passage explains the meaning. When Jesus was here on earth, He was hated and hunted, persecuted and pursued. Men blasphemed Him, reviled Him, and spat on Him. He endured terrible indignities from the hands of His creatures.

God the Father never suffered such rude treatment from men. He dwelt in heaven, far away from the wickedness of sinners. When the Lord Jesus returned to heaven, He would be where indignities could never come. Therefore, the disciples should have rejoiced when Jesus said that He was **going to the Father**, because *in this sense* the **Father** was **greater than** He. The Father was not greater *as God*, but greater because He never came into the world as Man to be cruelly treated. As far as the attributes of deity are concerned, the Son and the Father are equal. But when we think of the lowly place which Jesus took as a Man here on earth, we realize that *in that sense*, God the **Father** was **greater than** He. He was greater as to His *position* but not His *Person*.

14:29 In unselfish concern for the fearful disciples, the Lord revealed these future events to them so that they would not be offended, disheartened, or afraid, but rather **believe**.

14:30 The Lord knew that the time for His betrayal was approaching and that He would not have much more time to **talk** with His own. Satan was even then drawing near, but the Savior knew that the enemy could find no taint of sin in Him. There was nothing in Christ to respond to the devil's evil temptations. It would be ridiculous for anyone else but Jesus to say that Satan could find **nothing** in him.

14:31 We might paraphrase this verse as follows: "The time of my betrayal is at hand. I shall go voluntarily to the cross. This is the Father's will for me. It will tell the world how much **I love** My **Father**. That is why I am now going without offering any resistance." With this, the Lord bade the disciples to **arise** and **go** with Him. It is not clear whether they moved from the upper room at this point. Perhaps the rest of the discourse took place as they walked along.

P. Jesus, the True Vine (15:1–11)

15:1 In the OT, the nation of Israel was depicted as a vine planted by Jehovah. But the nation proved unfaithful and unfruitful, so the Lord Jesus now presented *Himself* as **the true vine**, the perfect fulfillment of all the other types and shadows. God the **Father is the vinedresser**.

15:2 Opinions differ as to what is meant by **the branch in** Him **that does not bear fruit**. Some think that this is a false professor. He pretends to be a Christian but has never really been united to Christ by faith. Others think it is a true Christian who loses his salvation because of his failure to bear fruit. This is clearly impossible because it contradicts so many other passages which teach that the believer has an eternal salvation. Others think that it is a true Christian who becomes a backslider. He gets away from the Lord and becomes interested in the things of this world. He fails to manifest the fruit of the Spirit — love, joy, peace, longsuffering, gentleness, goodness, faith, meekness, temperance.

Exactly what the Lord does to the unfruitful branch depends on how the Greek verb *airo* is translated. It can mean **"takes away"** as in the King James tradition (also translated that way in John 1:29). Then it would refer to the discipline of physical death (1 Cor. 11:30). However, the same word may mean "lifts up" (as in John 8:59). Then it would be the *positive ministry* of encouraging the fruitless branch by making it easier to get light and air, and hopefully, to bear fruit.

The **branch that bears fruit** is the Christian who is growing more like the Lord Jesus. Even such vines need to be pruned or cleansed. Just as a real vine must be cleaned from insects, mildew, and fungus, so a Christian must be cleansed from worldly things that cling to him.

15:3 The cleansing agent is **the word** of the Lord. The disciples had originally been cleansed by **the word** at the time of their conversion. Just as the Savior had been talking to them, His Word had had a purifying effect on their lives. Thus, this verse may refer to justification *and* sanctification.

15:4 To **abide** means to stay where you are. The Christian has been placed in Christ; that is his position. In daily walk, he should stay in intimate fellowship with the Lord. A **branch** abides in a vine by drawing all its life and nourishment from the vine. So we abide in Christ by spending time in prayer, reading and obeying His Word, fellowshiping with His people, and being continually conscious of our union with Him. As we thus maintain constant contact with Him, we are conscious of His abiding in us and supplying us with spiritual strength and resources. **The branch can** only **bear fruit as it abides in the vine**. The only way believers can bear the fruit of a Christ-like character is by living in touch with Christ moment by moment.

15:5 Christ Himself is **the vine**; believers are vine **branches**. It is not a question of the branch living its life for the Vine, but simply of letting the life of the Vine flow out through the branches. Sometimes we pray, "Lord, help me to live my life for You." It would be better to pray, "Lord Jesus, live out Your life through me." **Without** Christ, we **can do nothing**. A vine branch has one great purpose — to bear fruit. It is useless for making furniture or for building homes. It does not even make good firewood. But it *is* good for fruit-bearing — as long as it abides in the vine.

15:6 Verse 6 has caused much difference of opinion. Some believe that the person described is a believer who falls into sin and is subsequently lost. Such an interpretation is in direct contradiction to the many verses of Scripture which teach that no true child of God will ever perish. Others believe that this person is a professor — one who pretends to be a Christian but who was never born again. Judas is often used as an illustration.

We believe that this person is a true believer because it is with true Christians that this section is concerned. The subject is not salvation but abiding and *fruitbearing*. But through carelessness and prayerlessness this believer gets out of touch with the Lord. As a result, he commits some sin, and his testimony is ruined. Through failure to abide in Christ, he is thrown **out as a branch** — not by Christ, but by other people. The branches are gathered and thrown **into the fire, and they are burned**. It is not God who does it, but people. What does this mean? It means that people scoff at this backslidden Christian. They drag his name in the mud. They throw his testimony as a Christian into the fire. This is well illustrated in the life of David. He was a true believer, but he became careless toward the Lord and committed the sins of adultery and murder. He caused the enemies of the Lord to blaspheme. Even today, atheists ridicule the name of David (and of David's God). They cast him, as it were, into the fire.

15:7 Abiding is the secret of a successful prayer life. The closer we get to the Lord, the more we will learn to think His thoughts after Him. The more we get to know Him through His Word, the more we will understand His will. The more our will agrees with His, the more we can be sure of having our prayers answered.

15:8 As the children of God exhibit the likeness of Christ to the world, the **Father is glorified**. People are forced to confess that He must be a great God when He can transform such wicked sinners into such godly saints. Notice the progression in this chapter: fruit (v. 2), more fruit (v. 2), **much fruit** (v. 8).

"So you will be My disciples." This means that we *prove to be* His **disciples** when we abide in Him. Others can then see that we are true disciples, that we resemble our Lord.

15:9 The love which the Savior has for us is the same as the love of **the Father** for the Son. Our hearts are made to bow in worship when we read such words. It is the same in quality and degree. It is "a vast, wide, deep, unmeasurable love, that passeth knowledge, and can never be fully comprehended by man." It is "a deep where all our thoughts are drowned." **"Abide in My love,"** said our Lord. This means we should continue to realize His love and to enjoy it in our lives.

15:10 The first part of verse 10 tells us how we can abide in His love; it is by keeping His **commandments**. "There is no other way to be happy in Jesus, but to trust and obey." The second half of the verse sets before us our Perfect Example. The Lord Jesus **kept** His **Father's commandments**. Everything He did was in obedience to the will of God. He remained in the constant enjoyment of the Father's **love**. Nothing ever came in to mar that sweet sense of loving fellowship.

15:11 Jesus found His own deep **joy** in communion with God His Father. He wanted His disciples to have that joy that comes from dependence upon Him. He wanted *His* **joy** to be theirs. Man's idea of joy is to be as happy as he can by leaving God out of his life. The Lord taught that real joy comes by taking God into one's life as much as possible. **"That your joy may be full,"** or "fulfilled." Their joy would be fulfilled in abiding in

Christ and in keeping His commandments. Many have used John 15 to teach doubts concerning the security of the believer. They have used the earlier verses to show that a sheep of Christ might eventually perish. But the Lord's purpose was not "that your doubts may be full," but **that your joy may be full**.

Q. The Command to Love One Another (15:12–17)

15:12 The Lord would soon leave His disciples. They would be left in a hostile world. As tensions increased, there would be the danger of the disciples' contending with one another. And so the Lord leaves this standing order, **"Love one another, as I have loved you."**

15:13 Their love should be of such a nature that they should be willing to die for one another. People who are willing to do this do not fight with each other. The greatest example of human self-sacrifice was for a man to die **for his friends**. The disciples of Christ are called to this type of devotion. Some lay down their lives in a literal sense; others spend their whole lives in untiring service for the people of God. The Lord Jesus is the Example. He laid down His life for His friends. Of course, they were enemies when He died for them, but when they are saved, they become His friends. So it is correct to say that He died for His friends as well as for His enemies.

15:14 We show that we are His **friends** by doing **whatever** He commands us. This is not the way we become His friends, but rather the way we exhibit it to the world.

15:15 The Lord here emphasized the difference between **servants** and **friends**. **Servants** are simply expected to do the work marked out for them, but **friends** are taken into one's confidence. To the friend we reveal our plans for the future. Confidential information is shared with him. In one sense the disciples would always continue to be servants of the Lord, but they would be more than this — they would be friends. The Lord was even now revealing to them the things which He had **heard from** His **Father**. He was telling them of His own departure, the coming of the Holy Spirit, His own coming again, and

their responsibility to Him in the meantime. Someone has pointed out that as branches, we *receive* (v. 5); as disciples, we *follow* (v. 8); and as friends, we *commune* (v. 15).

15:16 Lest there be any tendency for them to become discouraged and give up, Jesus reminded them that He was the One who **chose** them. This may mean that He **chose** them to eternal salvation, to discipleship, or to fruitfulness. He had appointed the disciples to the work which lay before them. We **should go and bear fruit. Fruit** may mean the graces of the Christian life, such as love, joy, peace, etc. Or it may mean souls won for the Lord Jesus Christ. There is a close link between the two. It is only as we are manifesting the first kind of fruit that we will ever be able to bring forth the second.

The expression **"that your fruit should remain"** leads us to think that fruit here means the salvation of souls. The Lord chose the disciples to go and bring forth *lasting* **fruit**. He was not interested in mere professions of faith in Himself, but in genuine cases of salvation. L. S. Chafer notes that in this chapter we have prayer effectual (v. 7), joy celestial (v. 11), and fruit perpetual (v. 16). **"That whatever you ask . . . ."** The secret of effective service is prayer. The disciples were sent forth with the guarantee that **the Father** would grant them **whatever** they asked in Christ's **name**.

15:17 The Lord was about to warn the disciples about the enmity of the world. He began by telling them to **love one another**, to stick together, and to stand unitedly against the foe.

R. Jesus Predicts the World's Hatred (15:18–16:4)

15:18, 19 The disciples were not to be surprised or disheartened **if the world hates** them. (The **if** does not express any doubt that this would happen; it was certain.) The world **hated** the Lord, and it will hate all who resemble Him.

Men of the world love those who live as they do — those who use vile language and indulge in the lusts of the flesh, or people who are cultured but live only for themselves. Christians condemn them by their holy lives, **therefore the world hates** them.

15:20 Here **servant** literally means "slave." A disciple should not expect any better treatment from the world than **his Master** received. He will be persecuted just as Christ was. His word will be refused just as the Savior's was.

15:21 This hatred and persecution is **"for My name's sake."** It is because the believer is linked to Christ; because he has been separated from the world by Christ; and because he bears Christ's name and likeness. The world is ignorant of God. **They do not know** that the Father **sent** the Lord into the world to be the Savior. But ignorance is no excuse.

15:22 The Lord was not teaching here that if He had not come, then men would not have been sinners. From the time of Adam, all men had been sinners. But their sin would not have been nearly so great as it now was. These men had seen the Son of God and heard His wonderful words. They could find no fault in Him whatever. Yet they rejected Him. It was this that made their sin so great. And so it was a matter of comparison. Compared with their terrible sin of rejecting the Lord of glory, their other sins were as nothing. Now they had **no excuse for their sin**. They had rejected the Light of the world!

15:23 In hating Christ, they hated His **Father also**. The Two are One. They could not say that they loved God, for if they had, they would have loved the One God sent.

15:24 They were not only responsible for having heard the teaching of Christ; they also saw His miracles. This added to their condemnation. They saw **works which no one else** had ever performed. To reject Christ in face of this evidence was inexcusable. The Lord compared all their other sins to this one sin, and said that the former were as nothing when placed alongside the latter. Because they **hated** the Son, they hated His **Father**, and this was their terrible condemnation.

15:25 The Lord realized that man's attitude toward Him was in exact fulfillment of prophecy. It was predicted in Psalm 69:4 that Christ would be **hated . . . without a cause**. Now that it had **happened**, the Lord commented that the very OT which these men prized had predicted their senseless hatred of Him. The fact that it was prophesied did not mean that these men *had to* hate Christ. They hated Him by *their own deliberate choice*, but God foresaw that it would happen, and He caused David to write it down in Psalm 69.

15:26 In spite of man's rejection, there would be a continued testimony to Christ. It would be carried on by **the Helper** — the Holy Spirit. Here the Lord said that *He* would **send** the Spirit **from the Father**. In John 14:16, the *Father* was the One who sent the Spirit. Is this not another proof of the equality of the Son and the Father? Who but God could send One who is God? **The Spirit of truth . . . proceeds from the Father**. This means that He is constantly being sent forth by God, and His coming at the day of Pentecost was a special instance of this. The Spirit testifies concerning Christ. This is His great mission. He does not seek to occupy men with Himself, though He is one of the members of the Trinity. But He directs the attention of both sinner and saint to the Lord of glory.

15:27 The Spirit would testify directly through the disciples. They had **been with** the Lord **from the beginning** of His public ministry and were especially qualified to tell of His Person and work. If anyone could have found any imperfection in the Lord, those who had been with Him the most could have. But they never knew Him to commit a sin of any kind. They could testify to the fact that He was the sinless Son of God and the Savior of the world.

16:1 The disciples probably cherished the hope of the Jewish people generally — that the Messiah would set up His kingdom and that the power of Rome would be broken. Instead of that, the Lord told them that He was going to die, rise again, and go back to heaven. The Holy Spirit would come, and the disciples would go out as witnesses for Christ. They would be hated and persecuted. The Lord told them all this in advance so that they would not be disillusioned, **made to stumble**, or shocked.

16:2, 3 Excommunication from **the synagogues** was considered by most Jews to be one of the worst things that could happen. Yet this would happen to these Jews who were disciples of Jesus. The Christian faith would be so hated that those who sought to stamp it out would **think** they were pleasing **God**. This shows how a person may be very sincere, very zealous, and yet very *wrong*.

Failure to recognize the deity of Christ lay at the root of the matter. The Jews would not receive Him, and in so doing, they refused to receive **the Father**.

16:4 Again the Lord warned the disciples in advance so they would not be moved by these afflictions when they happened. They would **remember** that the Lord had predicted persecution; they would know that it was all a part of His plan for their lives. The Lord had not told them much about this earlier because He was with them. There was no need to trouble them or to cause their minds to wander from the other things He had to teach them. But now that He was leaving them, He must tell them of the path that lay ahead for them.

S. The Coming of the Spirit of Truth (16:5–15)

16:5 Verse 5 seems to express disappointment that the disciples were not more interested in what was ahead for the Lord. Although they had asked in a general way **where** He was **going**, they had not seemed too involved.

16:6 They were more concerned with their own future than with His. Before Him lay the cross and the grave. Before them lay persecution in their service for Christ. They were **filled** with **sorrow** over their own troubles rather than over His.

16:7 **Nevertheless**, they would not be left without help and comfort. Christ would send the Holy Spirit to be their **Helper**. It was **to** the **advantage** of the disciples that the **Helper** should come. He would empower them, give them courage, teach them, and make Christ more real to them than He had ever been before. **The Helper** would not come until the Lord Jesus went back to heaven and was glorified. Of course, the Holy Spirit had been in the world before this, but He was coming in a new way — to convict the world and to minister to the redeemed.

16:8 The Holy Spirit would **convict the world** in respect **of sin, and of righteousness, and of judgment**. This is generally taken to mean that He creates an inward awareness of these things in the life of the individual sinner. While this is true, it is not exactly the teaching in this portion. The Holy Spirit condemns **the world** by the very fact that He is here. He should not be here, because the Lord Jesus should be here, reigning over the world. But the world rejected Him, and He went back to heaven. The Holy Spirit is here in place of a rejected Christ, and this demonstrates the world's guilt.

16:9 The Spirit convicts the world **of** the **sin** of failing to **believe** on Christ. He was worthy of belief. There was nothing about Him that made it impossible for men to believe on Him. But they refused. And the Holy Spirit's presence in the world is witness to their crime.

16:10 The Savior claimed to be righteous, but men said He had a demon. God spoke the final word. He said, in effect, "My Son is righteous, and I will prove it by raising Him from the dead and taking Him back to heaven." The Holy Spirit witnesses to the fact that Christ was right and the world was wrong.

16:11 The presence of the Holy Spirit also convicts the world **of** coming **judgment**. The fact that He is here means that the devil has already been condemned at the cross and that all who refuse the Savior will share his awful judgment in a day yet future.

16:12 There were **still . . . many** other **things** the Lord had to tell the disciples, but they could not take them in. This is an important principle of teaching. There must be a certain progress in learning before advanced truths can be received. The Lord never overwhelmed His disciples with teaching. He gave it to them "line upon line, precept upon precept."

16:13 The work which the Lord began was to be continued by the **Spirit of truth**. **He** would **guide** them **into all truth**. There is a sense in which **all truth** was committed to the apostles in their lifetime. They, in turn, committed it to writing, and we have it today in our NT.

This, added to the OT, completed God's written revelation to man. But it is, of course, true in all ages that the Spirit guides God's people into all the truth. He does it through the Scriptures. **He will** only **speak** the things that are given to Him to say by the Father and the Son. **"He will tell you things to come."** This, of course, is done in the NT, and particularly in the book of Revelation where the future is unveiled.

16:14 His principal work will be to **glorify** Christ. By this we can test all teaching and preaching. If it has the effect of magnifying the Savior, then it is of the Holy Spirit. **"He will take of what is Mine"** means that He will receive of the great truths that concern Christ. These are the things He reveals to believers. The subject can never be exhausted!

16:15 All the attributes of **the Father** belong to the Son as well. It is these perfections that Christ was speaking of in verse 14. The Spirit unveiled to the apostles the glorious perfections, ministries, offices, graces, and fullness of the Lord Jesus.

T. Sorrow Turned to Joy (16:16–22)

16:16 The precise time-frame of verse 16 is uncertain. It may mean the Lord would be away from them for three days, and then He would reappear to them after His resurrection. It may mean He would go back to His Father in heaven, and then after **a little while** (the present Age), He would come back to them (His Second Coming). Or it may mean that for **a little while** they would **not see** Him with their physical eyes, but after the Holy Spirit was given on the day of Pentecost, they would perceive Him by faith in a way they had never seen Him before.

16:17 **His disciples** were confused. The reason for the confusion was that in verse 10, the Savior had said, "I go to My Father and you see Me no more." Now He said, **"A little while, and you will not see Me; and again a little while, and you will see Me."** They could not reconcile these statements.

16:18 They asked each other the meaning of the words **"a little while."** Strangely enough, we have the same problem today. We do not know whether it refers to the three days before His

resurrection, the forty days before Pentecost, or the more than 1900 years prior to His Coming again!

16:19, 20 Being God, the Lord Jesus was able to read their thoughts. By His questions, He revealed His full knowledge of their perplexity.

He did not answer their problem directly but gave further information concerning the "little while." **The world** would **rejoice** because they had succeeded in crucifying the Lord Jesus, but the disciples would **weep and lament**. But it would only be for a short while. Their **sorrow** would be **turned into joy**, and it was — first by the resurrection, and secondly by the coming of the Spirit. Then, for all disciples of all ages, grief will be turned to rejoicing when the Lord Jesus comes back again.

16:21 Nothing is more remarkable than the speed with which a mother forgets the **labor** pains after her **child** is born. So it would be with the disciples. The sorrow connected with the absence of their Lord would be quickly forgotten when they would see Him again.

16:22 Again we must express ignorance as to the time indicated by the Lord's words, **"I will see you again."** Does this refer to His resurrection, His sending of the Spirit at Pentecost, or His Second Advent? In all three cases, the result is rejoicing, and a **joy** that cannot be taken away.

U. Praying to the Father in Jesus' Name (16:23–28)

16:23 Up to now, the disciples had come to the Lord with all their questions and requests. **In that day** (the age ushered in by the descent of the Spirit at Pentecost), He would no longer be with them bodily, so they would no longer be asking Him questions. But did that mean that they would have no one to whom to go? No, **in that day** it would be their privilege to **ask the Father**. He would grant their requests for Jesus' sake. Requests will be granted, not because we are worthy, but because the Lord Jesus is worthy.

16:24 Prior to this, the disciples had never prayed to God the Father in the Lord's **name**. Now they were invited to **ask**. Through answered prayer, their **joy** would **be** fulfilled.

16:25 The meaning of much of the Lord's teaching was not always apparent on the surface. He used parables and **figurative language**. Even in this chapter we cannot always be sure of the precise meaning. With the coming of the Holy Spirit, the teaching **about the Father** became more plain. In Acts and the Epistles the truth is no longer revealed through parables but through direct statements.

16:26 "**That day**" again is the Age of the Holy Spirit, in which we now live. Our privilege is to pray to the Father in the **name** of the Lord Jesus. "**I do not say to you that I shall pray the Father for you**," that is, the Father does not need to be urged to answer our prayers. The Lord will not have to entreat Him. But we should still remember that the Lord Jesus is the Mediator between God and man, and He does intercede on behalf of His people before the throne of God.

16:27 The Father loved the disciples because they had received Christ and **loved** Him and **believed** in His deity. This is the reason why the Lord did not have to plead with the Father. With the coming of the Holy Spirit, they would enjoy a new sense of intimacy with the Father. They would be able to approach Him with confidence, and all because they **loved** His Son.

16:28 Here the Lord repeated His claim to equality with God the Father. He did not say "I came forth from *God*" as if He were just a Prophet sent by God, but "**I came forth from the Father.**" This means He is the eternal Son of the eternal Father, equal with God the Father. He came **into the world** as One who had lived elsewhere before His Coming. At His Ascension, He left the world and returned **to the Father**. This is a brief biographical account of the Lord of glory.

V. Tribulation and Peace (16:29–33)

16:29, 30 Jesus' **disciples** thought that they were now able to understand Him for the first time. He was no longer using figurative language, they **said**.

They thought that they **now** entered into the mystery of His Person. **Now** they were **sure that** He had all-knowledge and **that** He **came forth from** *God*. But He had said that He came forth

from the *Father*. Did they understand the meaning of this? Did they understand that Jesus was one of the Persons of the Godhead?

16:31 Jesus suggested by this question that their belief was still imperfect. He knew they loved and trusted Him, but did they really know that He was God manifest in the flesh?

16:32 In a short while He would be arrested, tried, and crucified. The disciples would all forsake Him and flee to their homes. But He would not be deserted because **the Father** would be **with** Him. It was this union with God the Father that they did not understand. This was the thing that would support Him when they had all escaped for their lives.

16:33 The purpose of this discourse with the disciples was **that** they might **have peace**. When they would be hated, pursued, persecuted, falsely condemned, and even tortured, they could have **peace** *in Him*. He overcame **the world** at the cross of Calvary. In spite of their tribulations, they could rest assured that they were on the winning side.

Also, with the coming of the Holy Spirit, they would have new powers of endurance and new courage to face the foe.

W. Jesus Prays for His Ministry (17:1–5)

We now come to what is known as the High-Priestly prayer of the Lord Jesus. In this prayer, He made intercession for His own. It is a picture of His present ministry in heaven where He prays for His people. Marcus Rainsford puts it well:

> The whole prayer is a beautiful illustration of our blessed Lord's intercession at the right hand of God. Not a word against His people; no reference to their failings, or their shortcomings. . . . No. He speaks of them only as they were in the Father's purpose, as in association with Himself, and as the recipients of the fulness He came down from heaven to bestow upon them. . . . All the Lord's particular petitions for His people relate to spiritual things; all have reference to heavenly blessings. The Lord does not ask riches for them, or honours, or worldly influence, or great preferments, but He does most earnestly pray that they may be kept

from evil, separated from the world, qualified for duty, and brought home safely to heaven. Soul prosperity is the best prosperity; it is the index of true prosperity.[45]

17:1 **The hour** had **come.** Many times His enemies had been unable to take Him because His hour had *not* come. But now the time had arrived for the Lord to be put to death. "**Glorify Your Son,**" the Savior prayed. He was looking ahead to His death on the cross. If He were to remain in the grave, the world would know that He was just another man. But if God glorified Him by raising Him from the dead, that would be proof He was God's Son and the world's Savior. God answered this request by raising the Lord Jesus on the third day and then later by taking Him back to heaven and crowning Him with glory and honor.

"**That Your Son also may glorify You,**" the Lord continued. The meaning of this is explained in the next two verses. Jesus glorifies the Father by giving eternal life to those who believe on Him. It brings great glory to God when ungodly men and women are converted and manifest the life of the Lord Jesus on this earth.

17:2 As a result of His work of redemption at the cross, God has given His Son **authority over all** mankind. This **authority** entitled Him to **give eternal life to** those whom the Father had **given Him.** Here again we are reminded that before the foundation of the world, God marked out certain ones as belonging to Christ. Remember, though, that God offers salvation to anyone who will receive Jesus Christ. There is no one who cannot be saved by trusting the Savior.

17:3 Here is a simple explanation of how **eternal life** is obtained. It is by knowing **God and Jesus Christ. The only true God** is in contrast to idols, which are not genuine gods at all. This verse does not mean that Jesus Christ is not the true God. The fact that His Name is mentioned together with God the Father's as being the joint source of eternal life means that They are equal. Here the Lord called Himself **Jesus Christ. Christ** was the same as Messiah. This verse disproves the charge that Jesus never claimed to be the Messiah.

17:4 As the Lord uttered these words, He was speaking as if He had already died, been buried, and risen again. He had **glorified** the Father by His sinless life, by His miracles, by His suffering and death, and by His resurrection. He had **finished the work** of salvation the Father had **given** Him **to do.** As Ryle puts it:

> The crucifixion brought glory to the Father. It glorified His wisdom, faithfulness, holiness, and love. It showed Him wise, in providing a plan whereby He could be just, and yet the justifier of the ungodly. — It showed Him faithful in keeping His promise, that the seed of the woman should bruise the serpent's head. — It showed Him holy, in requiring His law's demands to be satisfied by our great Substitute. — It showed Him loving, in providing such a Mediator, such a Redeemer, and such a Friend for sinful man as His co-eternal Son.
>
> The crucifixion brought glory to the Son. It glorified His compassion, His patience, and His power. It showed Him most compassionate, in dying for us, suffering in our stead, allowing Himself to be counted sin and a curse for us, and buying our redemption with the price of His own blood. — It showed Him most patient, in not dying the common death of most men, but in willingly submitting to such pains and unknown agonies as no mind can conceive, when with a word He could have summoned His Father's angels, and been set free. — It showed Him most powerful, in bearing the weight of all transgressions of the world, and vanquishing Satan, and despoiling him of his prey.[46]

17:5 Before Christ came into the world, He dwelt in heaven with the Father. When the angels looked upon the Lord, they saw all the glory of Deity. To every eye, He was obviously God. But when He came among men, the glory of Deity was veiled. Though He was still God, it was not apparent to most onlookers. They saw Him merely as the carpenter's Son. Here, the Savior is praying that the visible manifestation of His glory in heaven might be restored. The words **"glorify Me together with Yourself"** mean "glorify Me in Your presence in heaven. Let the original glory which I shared with You before My Incarnation be resumed." This clearly teaches the pre-existence of Christ.

X. Jesus Prays for His Disciples (17:6–19)

17:6 Jesus had **manifested** the Father's **name to the** disciples. The "name" in Scripture means the Person, His attributes, and character. Christ had fully declared the Father's true nature. The disciples had been **given** to the Son **out of the world**. They were separated from the unbelieving mass of mankind and set apart to belong to Christ. "They were the Father's *by election* before the world was, and became Christ's by the gift of the Father, and by purchase of blood," wrote J. G. Bellett.

"They have kept Your word," said the Lord. In spite of all their failures and shortcomings, He credits them with having believed and obeyed His teaching. "Not a word against His people," Rainsford writes, "no allusion to what they had done or were about to do — forsake Him."

17:7, 8 The Savior had perfectly represented His Father. He explained to the disciples that He did not speak or act by His own authority, but only as the Father instructed Him. So they **believed that** the Father had **sent** the Son.

Moreover, Christ did not *originate* His own mission. He came in obedience to the Father's will. He was the perfect Servant of Jehovah.

17:9 As High Priest, He prayed for the disciples; He did **not pray for the world**. This should not be taken to mean that Christ never prayed for the world. On the cross, He prayed, "Father, forgive them; for they do not know what they do."

But here He was praying as the One who represented believers before the throne of God. There His prayer can only be for His own.

17:10 The perfect union between the Father and the Son is shown here. No mere man could truthfully say these words. We might be able to say to God, **"All Mine are Yours,"** but we could not say, **"All Yours are Mine."** It is because the Son is equal with the Father that He could say it. In these verses (6–19), Jesus presents His poor and backward flock, and, robing each lamb in a coat of many colors, declares, **"I am glorified in them."**

17:11 Again the Lord Jesus anticipated His return to heaven. He prayed as if He had already gone. Notice the title **Holy Father. Holy** speaks of One who is *infinitely high*. **Father** speaks of One who is *intimately nigh*.

Jesus' prayer **"that they all may be one"** refers to unity of Christian character. As the Father and Son are One in moral likeness, so believers should be united in this respect — that they are like the Lord Jesus.

17:12 **While** He **was with** the disciples, the Savior **kept them in** the Father's **name**, that is, by His power and authority, and true to Him. **"None of them is lost,"** said Jesus, **"except the son of perdition,"** that is, Judas. But this did not mean that Judas was one of those given to the Son by the Father or that he was ever a genuine believer. The sentence means this: "Those that You gave Me I have kept, and none of them is lost, but the son of perdition is lost, that the Scripture might be fulfilled." The title **"the son of perdition"** means Judas was consigned to eternal ruin or damnation. Judas was not compelled to betray Christ in order to fulfill prophecy, but he chose to betray the Savior and in so doing **the Scripture** was **fulfilled**.

17:13 The Lord explained why He was praying in the presence of His disciples. It was as if He said to them: "These are intercessions which I shall never cease to make in heaven before God. But now I make them **in the world**, in your hearing, so you may more distinctly understand how I am there to be employed in promoting your welfare, so that you may be made in large measure partakers of **My joy**."

17:14 The Lord gave God's **word** to the disciples, and they received it. As a result, **the world** turned on them and **hated them**. They had the characteristics of the Lord Jesus, and so **the world** despised them. They did not fit in with the world's scheme of things.

17:15 The Lord did **not pray that** the Father **should take** believers home to heaven immediately. They must be left here to grow in grace and to witness for Christ. **But** Christ's prayer was that they might be kept **from the evil one**. Not escape, but preservation.

17:16 Christians **are not of the**

world, just as Christ was not of the world. We should remember this when tempted to engage in some worldly pastime or enter into worldly associations where the name of Jesus is unwelcome.

17:17 To **sanctify** means to set apart. The Word of God has a sanctifying effect on believers. As they read it and obey it, they are set apart as vessels suitable for the Master's use. That is exactly what the Lord Jesus was praying for here. He wanted a people who were set apart to God from the world, and usable by God. **"Your word is truth,"** Jesus said. He did not say, as so many do today, "Your word *contains* truth," but **"Your word IS truth."**

17:18 The Father **sent** the Lord Jesus **into the world** to reveal the character of God to men. As the Lord prayed, He realized that He would soon be going back to heaven. But future generations would still need some witness concerning God. This work must be done by believers, through the power of the Holy Spirit. Of course, Christians can never represent God as perfectly as Christ did because they can never be equal with God. But believers are here just the same to represent God to the world. It is for this reason Jesus **sent them into the world**.

17:19 *To sanctify* does not necessarily mean to *make* holy. He *is* holy as to His personal character. The thought is that the Lord *set Himself apart* for the work His Father sent Him to do — that is, His sacrificial death. It may also mean that He set Himself apart by taking His place outside the world and entering into the glory. "His sanctification is the pattern of, and the power for, ours," says Vine. We should be set apart from the world and find our portion with Him.

Y. Jesus Prays for All Believers (17:20–26)

17:20 Now the High Priest extended His prayer beyond the disciples. He prayed for generations yet unborn. In fact, every believer reading this verse can say, "Jesus prayed for me over 1900 years ago."

17:21 The prayer was for unity among believers, but this time it was with the salvation of sinners in view.

The unity for which Christ prayed was not a matter of external church union. Rather it was a unity based on common moral likeness. He was praying that believers might **be one** in exhibiting the character of God and of Christ. This is what would cause **the world** to **believe that** God had **sent** Him. This is the unity which makes the world say, "I see Christ in those Christians as the Father was seen in Christ."

17:22 In verse 11, the Lord prayed for unity in fellowship. In verse 21, it was unity in witness-bearing. Now it is unity in **glory**. This looks forward to the time when saints will receive their glorified bodies. **"The glory which You gave Me"** is the glory of resurrection and ascension.

We do not have this glory yet. It has been **given** to us as far as the purposes of God are concerned, but we will not receive it until the Savior returns to take us to heaven. It will be manifested to the world when Christ returns to set up His kingdom on earth. At that time, the world will realize the vital unity between the Father and the Son, and the Son and His people, and will believe (too late) that Jesus was the Sent One from God.

17:23 **The world** will not only realize that Jesus was God the Son, but it will also know that believers were loved by God just as Christ was loved by God. That we should be so loved seems almost incredible, but there it is!

17:24 The Son desires to have His people with Himself in glory. Every time a believer dies, it is, in a sense, an answer to this prayer. If we realized this, it would be a comfort to us in our sorrow. To die is to go to be with Christ and to **behold** His **glory**. This **glory** is not only the glory of deity which He had with God before the world began. It is also the glory He acquired as Savior and Redeemer. This **glory** is a proof that God **loved** Christ **before the foundation of the world**.

17:25 **The world** failed to see God revealed in Jesus. But a few disciples did, and they believed **that** God had **sent** Jesus. On the eve of His crucifixion, there were only a few faithful hearts in the whole of mankind — and even those were about to forsake Him!

17:26 The Lord Jesus had **declared** the Father's **name** to His disciples when He was with them. This meant that He revealed the Father to them. His words and works were the words and works of the Father. They saw in Christ a perfect expression of the Father. Jesus has continued to **declare** the Father's Name through the ministry of the Holy Spirit. Ever since the day of Pentecost, the Spirit has been teaching believers about God the Father. Especially through the Word of God, we can know what God is like. When men accept the Father as He is revealed by the Lord Jesus, they become special objects of the Father's **love**. Since the Lord Jesus indwells all believers, the Father can look upon them and treat them as He does His only Son. Reuss remarks:

> The love of God which, before the creation of the physical world, had its adequate object in the person of the Son (v. 24), finds it, since the creation of the new spiritual world, in all those who are united with the Son.[47]

And Godet adds:

> What God desired in sending His Son here on earth was precisely that He might form for Himself in the midst of humanity a family of children like Him.[47]

It is because the Lord Jesus is in the believer that God can love him as He loves Christ.

> So dear, so very dear to God,
> I cannot dearer be;
> The love wherewith He loves the Son,
> Such is His love for me!
>
> *– Catesby Paget*

The petitions made by Christ for His people, as Rainsford notes,

> . . . refer to spiritual things, to heavenly blessings. Not for riches, or honor, or worldly influence, but deliverance from evil, separation from the world, qualification for duty, and a safe arrival in heaven.[48]

VIII. THE SON OF GOD'S PASSION AND DEATH (Chaps. 18, 19)

A. Judas Betrays the Lord (18:1–11)

18:1 The words of chapters 13–17 were spoken in Jerusalem. Now **Jesus** left the city and walked eastward toward the Mount of Olives. In doing so, He crossed **the Brook Kidron** and came to the Garden of Gethsemane, which was on the western slope of Olivet.

18:2, 3 **Judas** knew that the Lord spent a great deal of time praying in the garden. He **knew** that the most likely **place** to find the Lord was in the place of prayer.

The **detachment of troops** was probably Roman soldiers; whereas the **officers** were Jewish officials, representing **the chief priests and Pharisees**. They **came with lanterns, torches, and weapons**. "They came to seek the Light of the world with lanterns."

18:4 The Lord **went forward** to meet them, without waiting for them to find Him. This demonstrated His willingness to go to the cross. The soldiers could have left their weapons at home; the Savior would not resist. The question **"Whom are you seeking?"** was designed to draw forth from their own lips the nature of their mission.

18:5 They sought **Jesus of Nazareth**, little realizing that He was their Creator and their Sustainer — the best Friend they ever had. Jesus said, **"I am."** (The **"He"** is not found in the original, but needed in English.) He meant not only that He was Jesus of Nazareth but that He was Jehovah as well. As mentioned previously, I AM is one of the Names of Jehovah in the OT. Did this cause **Judas** to wonder afresh, as he **stood with** the others in the crowd?

18:6 For a brief moment, the Lord Jesus had revealed Himself to them as the I AM, the Almighty God. The revelation was so overpowering that **they drew back and fell to the ground**.

18:7 **Again** the Lord **asked them** to tell Him **whom** they were **seeking**. And again the answer was the same — in spite of the effect which two words of Christ had just had upon them.

18:8, 9 Again **Jesus answered** that He was the One, and that He was Jehovah. **"I have told you that I AM."** Since they sought Him, He told them that they should **let** the disciples **go their way**. It is wonderful to see His unselfish interest in others at a time when His own life was in peril. Thus, too, the words of John 17:12 were fulfilled.

18:10 **Simon Peter** thought the time

had come to use violence in an effort to save his Master from the crowd. Acting without instructions from the Lord, he **drew** his **sword** and **struck the high priest's servant**. Undoubtedly he intended to kill him, but the sword was deflected by an Unseen Hand, so that it **cut off** only **his right ear**.

18:11 Jesus rebuked the ill-advised zeal of **Peter. The cup** of suffering and death had been **given** to Him by His **Father**, and He intended to **drink** it. Luke, the physician, recorded how the Lord touched and healed Malchus' ear at this point (22:51).

B. Jesus Arrested and Bound (18:12–14)

18:12, 13 This was the first time that wicked men had been able to lay hold of **Jesus** and to tie up His arms.

Annas had been high priest previously. It is not clear why Jesus should have been brought to him **first**, rather than to **Caiaphas**, his son-in-law, **who was high priest** at the time. What is important to see is that Jesus was first put on trial before the Jews in an attempt to prove Him guilty of blasphemy and heresy. That was what we might call a *religious* trial. Then He was taken to be tried before the Roman authorities, and here the attempt was made to prove that He was an enemy of Caesar. That was the *civil* trial. Since the Jews were under Roman rule, they had to work through the Roman courts. They could not carry out the death penalty, for instance. This must be done by Pilate.

18:14 John explained that the high priest was the same **Caiaphas** who had prophesied **that one man should die for the** nation (see John 11:50). He was now about to have part in the fulfillment of the prophecy. James Stewart writes:

> This was the man who was the accredited guardian of the nation's soul. He had been set apart to be the supreme interpreter and representative of the Most High. To him was committed the glorious privilege of entering once every year into the holy of holies. Yet this was the man who condemned the Son of God. History provides no more startling illustration of the truth that the best religious opportunities in the world and the most promising environment will not guarantee a man's salvation or of themselves ennoble his

soul. "Then I saw," says John Bunyan, closing his book, "that there was a way to hell, even from the gates of heaven."[49]

C. Peter Denies His Lord (18:15–18)

18:15 Most Bible scholars believe that **the other disciple** mentioned here was John, but that humility prevented him from mentioning his own name, especially in view of Peter's shameful failure. We are not told how John had become so well **known to the high priest**, but it is a fact that gained him admittance **into the courtyard**.

18:16, 17 **Peter** was not able to get in until John went out and spoke to the woman who was the doorkeeper. Looking back, we wonder if it was a kindness for John to use his influence in this way. It is significant that Peter's first denial of the Lord was not before a powerful, terrifying soldier, but before a simple **servant girl who kept the door.** He denied that he was a disciple of Jesus.

18:18 Peter now mingled with the enemies of his Lord and tried to conceal his identity. Like many another disciple, he **warmed himself** at this world's **fire**.

D. Jesus Before the High Priest (18:19–24)†

18:19 It is not clear whether **the high priest** here is Annas or Caiaphas. If it was Annas, as seems most likely, he was probably called high priest out of courtesy because he once held this office. **The high priest then asked Jesus about His disciples and His** teachings, as if these posed a threat to the Mosaic Law and the Roman government. It is obvious that these people had no real case against the Lord, and so they were trying to make one up.

18:20 **Jesus answered him** that His ministry had been carried on **openly**. He had nothing to hide. He had **taught** in the presence of **the Jews**, both **in synagogues and in the temple**. There was no secrecy.

18:21 This was a challenge to bring forth some of the Jews who had listened to Him. Let them bring charges against Him. If He had done or said something wrong, let the witnesses be produced.

18:22 The challenge obviously irritated the Jews. It left them without a

†*See p. xv.*

case. And so they resorted to abuse. **One of the officers** slapped **Jesus** for speaking to **the high priest like that**.

18:23 With perfect poise and unanswerable logic, the Savior showed the unfairness of their position. They could not accuse Him of speaking evil; yet they struck Him for telling the truth.

18:24 The preceding verses describe the questioning before Annas. The trial before Caiaphas is not described by John. It fits in between 18:24 and 18:28.

E. Peter's Second and Third Denials (18:25–27)

18:25 The narrative now turns back to **Simon Peter**. In the cold of the early morning hours, he **warmed himself** by the fire. Doubtless his clothing and accent indicated that he was a Galilean fisherman. The one standing with him asked if he was a disciple of this Jesus. But **he denied** the Lord again.

18:26 Now it was **a relative** of Malchus who spoke to Peter. He had seen **Peter cut off** his relative's **ear. "Did I not see you in the garden with** this Jesus?"

18:27 Peter for the third time **denied** the Lord. **Immediately**, he heard the crowing of **a rooster** and was reminded of the words of the Lord, "The rooster shall not crow till you have denied Me three times." From the other Gospels we know that Peter went out at this point and wept bitterly.

F. Jesus Before Pilate (18:28–40)

18:28 The religious trial was ended, and the civil trial is about to begin. The scene is the hall of judgment or the palace of the governor. The Jews did not want to go into the palace of a Gentile. They felt that they would have been **defiled** and would thus be prevented from eating **the Passover**. It did not seem to bother them that they were plotting the death of the Son of God. It would have been a tragedy for them to enter a Gentile house, but murder was a mere trifle. Augustine remarks:

O impious blindness! They would be defiled, forsooth, by a dwelling which was another's, and not be defiled by a crime which was their own. They feared to be defiled by the praetorium of an alien

judge, and feared not to be defiled by the blood of an innocent brother.[50]

Hall comments:

Woe unto you priests, scribes, elders, hypocrites! Can there be any roof so unclean as that of your own breasts? Not Pilate's walls, but your own hearts, are impure. Is murder your errand, and do you stop at a local infection? God shall smite you, ye white walls! Do you long to be stained with blood — with the blood of God? And do ye fear to be defiled with the touch of Pilate's pavement? Doth so small a gnat stick in your throats, while ye swallow such a camel of flagitious wickedness? Go out of Jerusalem, ye false disbelievers, if ye would not be unclean! Pilate hath more cause to fear, lest his walls should be defiled with the presence of such prodigious monsters of iniquity.[51]

Poole remarks, "Nothing is more common than for persons overzealous about rituals to be remiss about morals."[52] The expression **"that they might eat the Passover"** probably means the feast which *followed* the Passover. The Passover itself had been held on the previous night.

18:29 **Pilate**, the Roman Governor, gave in to the religious scruples of the Jews by going **out** to where they were. He began the trial by asking them to state the charge **against this** Prisoner.

18:30 Their answer was bold and rude. They said, in effect, that they had already tried the case and found Him guilty. All they wanted Pilate to do was to pronounce the sentence.

18:31 **Pilate** tried to evade responsibility and throw it back on the Jews. If they had already tried Jesus and found Him guilty, then why did they not sentence **Him according to** their law? The answer of the Jews was very significant. They said, in so many words: "We are not an independent nation. We have been taken over by the Roman power. Civil government has been taken from our hands, and we no longer have the authority **to put anyone to death."** Their answer was evidence of their bondage and subjection to a Gentile power. Furthermore, they wanted to shift the odium of Christ's death onto Pilate.

18:32 Verse 32 may have two different meanings: (1) In Matthew 20:19, Jesus had predicted that He would be delivered up to the Gentiles to be killed. Here the Jews were doing that very thing to Him. (2) In many places, the Lord said that He would be "lifted up" (John 3:14; 8:28; 12:32, 34). This referred to death by crucifixion. The Jews used stoning in cases of capital punishment; whereas crucifixion was the Roman method. Thus, by their refusal to carry out the death penalty, the Jews unknowingly fulfilled these two prophecies concerning the Messiah (see also Psalm 22:16).

18:33 Pilate now took Jesus into **the Praetorium** for a private interview and asked Him point blank — **"Are You the King of the Jews?"**

18:34 Jesus answered him, in effect, "As governor, have you ever heard that I tried to overthrow the Roman power? Has it ever been reported to you that I proclaimed myself a King who would undermine Caesar's empire? Is this a charge which you know by personal experience, or is it just what you have heard these Jews saying?"

18:35 There was real contempt in Pilate's question, **"Am I a Jew?"** He implied that he was too important to be troubled with such a local Jewish problem. But his answer was also an admission that he knew of no real charge against Jesus. He only knew what the rulers of the Jews had said.

18:36 The Lord then confessed He *was* a King. But not the kind of king the Jews accused Him of being. And not the kind that would threaten Rome. Christ's **kingdom** is not advanced by human weapons. Otherwise His disciples **would fight** to prevent His capture by the Jews. Christ's **kingdom is not from here**, that is, not of this world. It does not receive its power or authority from the world; its aims and objectives are not carnal.

18:37 When **Pilate** asked Him if He was **a king, . . . Jesus answered, "You say rightly that I am a king."** But His kingdom is concerned with **truth**, not with swords and shields. It was to **bear witness to the truth** that He came **into the world. The truth** here means the truth about God, Christ Himself, the Holy Spirit, man, sin, salvation, and all the other great doctrines of Christianity. **Everyone who loves the truth hears** His **voice**, and that is how His empire grows.

18:38 It is difficult to say what **Pilate** meant when he **said to Him, "What is truth?"** Was he puzzled, or sarcastic, or interested? All we know is that the Truth Incarnate stood before him, and he did not recognize Him. Pilate now hurried to the Jews with the admission that he could find **no fault in** Jesus **at all**.

18:39 It was the **custom** among the Jews **at the Passover** to request the release of some Jewish prisoner from the Romans. Pilate seized upon this custom in an effort to please the Jews and at the same time **release** Jesus.

18:40 The scheme failed. The Jews did not want Jesus; they wanted **Barabbas. Barabbas was a robber**. The wicked heart of man preferred a bandit to the Creator.

G. Pilate's Verdict: Innocent but Condemned (19:1–16)

19:1 It was most unjust for **Pilate** to scourge an innocent Person. Perhaps he hoped that this punishment would satisfy the Jews and that they would not demand the *death* of Jesus. Scourging was a Roman form of punishment. The prisoner was beaten with a whip or a rod. The whip had pieces of metal or bone in it, and these cut deep gashes in the flesh.

19:2, 3 The soldiers mocked Jesus' claim to be King. A crown for the King! But it was **a crown of thorns**. This would have caused extreme pain as it was pressed onto His brow. Thorns are a symbol of the curse which sin brought to mankind. Here we have a picture of the Lord Jesus bearing the curse of our sins, so that we might wear a crown of glory. The **purple robe** was also used in mockery. **Purple** was the color of royalty. But again it reminds us of how our sins were placed on Jesus in order that we might be clothed with the robe of God's righteousness.

How solemn it is to think of the eternal Son of God being slapped by the **hands** of His creatures! Mouths which He formed are now being used to mock Him!

19:4 Pilate then went out again to the mob and announced that he was about to bring Jesus **out to** them, but that He was innocent. Thus Pilate condemned himself by his own words. He found no fault in Christ; yet he would not let Him go.

19:5 As **Jesus came out** with **the crown of thorns and the purple robe,** Pilate announced Him as **"the Man."** It is difficult to know whether he said this in mockery, in sympathy, or without any particular emotion.

19:6 **The chief priests** noticed that Pilate was wavering, so they cried out fiercely that Jesus should be crucified. It was *religious* men who were leaders in the death of the Savior. Often, down through the centuries, it has been church officials who have persecuted true believers most bitterly. **Pilate** seemed to be disgusted with them and with their unreasonable hatred of Jesus. He said, in effect: "If that is the way you feel, why don't **you take Him and crucify Him?** As far as I am concerned, He is innocent." Yet Pilate knew that the Jews could not put Him to death because that power could only be exercised by the Romans at that time.

19:7 When they saw that they had failed to prove that Jesus was a threat to Caesar's government, they brought forth their religious charge against Him. Christ claimed equality with God by saying that He was **the Son of God**. To the Jews, this was blasphemy and should be punished by death.

19:8, 9 The possibility of Jesus' being the Son of God troubled **Pilate**. He was already uneasy about the whole affair, but this made him **more afraid**.

Pilate took Jesus **into the Praetorium** or judgment hall and asked Him **where** He came **from**. In all of this, Pilate presented a most tragic figure. He confessed with his own lips that Jesus had done no wrong; yet he did not have the moral courage to let Him go because he feared the Jews. Why did **Jesus** give **him no answer?** Probably because He knew that Pilate was unwilling to act in accordance with the light he had. Pilate had sinned away his day of opportunity. He would not be given more light when he had not responded to the light he had.

19:10 **Pilate** tried to force the Lord to answer by threatening Him. He reminded Jesus that, as Roman governor, he had **power** or authority **to release** Him or to **crucify** Him.

19:11 The self-control of the Lord Jesus was remarkable. He was more calm than Pilate. He answered quietly that whatever **power** Pilate possessed **had been given** to him by God. All governments are ordained by God, and all authority, whether civil or spiritual, is from God.

"The one who delivered Me to you" may refer to: (1) *Caiaphas*, the high priest; (2) *Judas*, the betrayer; or (3) the Jewish *people* in general. The thought is that these Jews should have known better. They had the Scriptures which predicted the coming of the Messiah. They should have recognized Him when He came. But they rejected Him and were even now crying out for His life. This verse teaches us that there are degrees of guilt. Pilate was guilty, but Caiaphas, and Judas, and all the wicked Jews were *more* guilty.

19:12 Just as **Pilate** became determined **to release** Jesus, the Jews used their last and most telling argument. **"If you let this Man go, you are not Caesar's friend."** (Caesar was the official title of the Roman Emperor.) As if they cared for Caesar! They hated him. They would like to destroy him, and free themselves from his control. Yet here they were pretending to protect Caesar's empire from the threat of this Jesus who claimed to be a king! They reaped the punishment of this terrible hypocrisy when the Romans marched into Jerusalem in A.D. 70 and utterly destroyed the city and slaughtered its inhabitants.

19:13 **Pilate** could not afford to have the Jews accuse him of disloyalty to Caesar, and so he weakly submitted to the mob. He now **brought Jesus out** to a public area **called the Pavement,** where such matters were often handled.

19:14 Actually, the Passover feast had been held on the previous evening. The **Preparation Day of the Passover** means the preparation for the feast that followed it. **"About the sixth hour"** was probably 6 a.m. but there are unresolved problems concerning the methods of reckoning time in the Gospels. **"Behold your King!"** Almost certainly, Pilate said this to annoy and provoke the Jews. He doubtless blamed them for trapping him into condemning Jesus.

19:15 The Jews were insistent that Jesus must be crucified. Pilate taunted them with the question, "You mean you want to **crucify your** own **King?**" Then the Jews stooped very low by saying, **"We have no king but Caesar!"** Faithless nation! Refusing your God for a wicked, heathen monarch.

19:16 Pilate was willing to please the Jews, and so he turned Jesus over to the soldiers **to be crucified**. He loved the praise of men more than the praise of God.

H. The Crucifixion (19:17–24)

19:17 The word translated **cross** may refer to a single piece of wood (a stake), or it may have been two cross pieces. At any rate, it was of such size that a man could normally carry it. Jesus carried **His cross** for some distance. Then, according to the other Gospels, it was given to a man named Simon of Cyrene to carry. **The Place of a Skull** may have received this name in one of two ways: (1) The land itself may have resembled a skull, especially if it was a hill with caves in the side of it. Such a site is "Gordon's Calvary" in Israel today. (2) It was the place where criminals were executed; perhaps skulls and bones were found in the area, though in light of the Mosaic Law on burial this is most unlikely.

19:18 The Lord Jesus was nailed to the cross, hands and feet. The cross was then lifted up and dropped into a hole in the ground. The only perfect Man who ever lived, and this was the reception He received from His own! If you have never before trusted Him as your Lord and Savior, will you not do it now, as you read this simple account of how He died for you? Two thieves were crucified with Him, **one on either side**. This was in fulfillment of the prophecy of Isaiah 53:12: "He was numbered with the transgressors."

19:19 It was the custom to put **a title** above the head of the crucified, and to indicate the crime. Pilate ordered that the title **JESUS OF NAZARETH, THE KING OF THE JEWS**, should be placed on the center cross.

19:20 Alexander expresses it eloquently:

In Hebrew, the sacred tongue of patriarchs and seers. In Greek, the musical and golden tongue which gave a soul to

the objects of sense and a body to the abstractions of philosophy. In Latin, the dialect of a people originally the strongest of all the sons of men. The three languages represent the three races and their ideas — revelation, art, literature; progress, war, and jurisprudence. Wherever these three desires of the human race exist, wherever annunciation can be made in human language, wherever there is a heart to sin, a tongue to speak, an eye to read, the Cross has a message.[53]

The place . . . was near the city. The Lord Jesus was crucified outside the city limits. The exact location is no longer known for certain.

19:21 The chief priests did not like the wording. They wanted it to read as a *claim* made by Jesus, but not as a *fact* (which it was).

19:22 Pilate would not change the writing. He had become impatient with the Jews and would not give in to them any more. But he should have shown this determination sooner!

19:23 At such executions, **the soldiers** were allowed to share the personal effects of those who died. Here we find them dividing Christ's **garments** among themselves. Apparently there were five pieces altogether. They divided four, but there was still **the tunic**, which **was without seam** and could not be cut up without making it worthless.

19:24 They **cast lots** for the tunic, and it was handed over to the unnamed winner. Little did they know that in doing this, they were fulfilling a remarkable prophecy written a thousand years previously (Ps. 22:18)! These fulfilled prophecies remind us afresh that this Book is the inspired Word of God, and that Jesus Christ is indeed the promised Messiah.

I. Jesus Commends His Mother to John (19:25–27)

19:25 Many Bible students think that there are four women named in this verse, as follows: (1) Mary, the **mother** of Jesus; (2) Mary's **sister**, Salome, the mother of John; (3) **Mary, the wife of Clopas**; (4) **Mary Magdalene**.

19:26, 27 In spite of His own suffering, the Lord had tender regard for others. Seeing **His mother**, and John, **the disciple**, He introduced John to her as the one who would hereafter take the place of son to her. In calling His mother **"Woman,"** the Lord did not show any lack of respect. But it is noticeable that He did not call her "Mother." Does this have any lesson for those who might be tempted to exalt Mary to the place where she is adored? Jesus here instructed John to care for Mary as if she were his own **mother**. John obeyed and took Mary **to his own home**.

J. The Work of Christ Finished (19:28–30)

19:28 Between verse 27 and 28, we have, no doubt, the three hours of darkness — from noon to 3:00 p.m. It was during this time that Jesus was forsaken by God as He suffered the penalty of our sins. His cry, **"I thirst!"** indicated real, physical thirst, which was intensified by crucifixion. But it also reminds us that, greater than His physical thirst was His spiritual thirst for the salvation of the souls of men.

19:29 The soldiers gave Him **sour wine** to drink. They probably tied **a sponge** to the end of a rod with **hyssop** and pressed it to His lips. (**Hyssop** is a plant, also used at the Passover — Ex. 12:22.) This is not to be confused with the vinegar mixed with gall, which had been offered to Him earlier (Matt. 27:34). He did not drink that because it would have acted as a pain reliever. He must bear our sins in full consciousness.

19:30 **"It is finished!"** The work His Father had given him to do! The pouring out of His soul as an offering for sin! The work of redemption and of atonement! It is true that He had not yet died, but His death, burial, and ascension were as certain as if already accomplished. So the Lord Jesus could announce that the way had been provided whereby sinners could be saved. Thank God today for the finished work of the Lord Jesus on the cross of Calvary!

Some Bible scholars tell us that **bowing His head** may mean that He leaned His head backward. Vine says, "Not the helpless dropping of the head after death, but the deliberate putting of His head into a position of rest."

That **He gave up His spirit** emphasizes the fact that His death was voluntary. He determined the time of His death. In full control of His faculties, **He**

dismissed **His spirit** — an act no mere man could accomplish.

K. Piercing of the Savior's Side (19:31–37)

19:31 Again we see how careful these religious **Jews** were about details when they were committing coldblooded murder. They "strained out a gnat and swallowed a camel." They thought it would **not** be proper to allow the bodies to **remain on the cross on the Sabbath** (Saturday). There would be a religious feast in the city. So they requested Pilate to have the **legs** of the three **broken** to hasten death.

19:32[†] The Scripture does not describe how the legs were broken. However, they must have been broken in many different places, since a single break would not bring on death.

19:33 These soldiers were well experienced in such matters. They knew that **Jesus . . . was already dead**. There was no possibility of His being in a faint or swoon. **They did not break His legs.**

19:34[††] We are not told why **one of the soldiers pierced His side**. Perhaps it was a final outburst of the wickedness of his heart. "It was the sullen shot of the defeated foe after the battle, telling out the deep-seated hatred in man's heart toward God and His Christ." There is no agreement on the significance of the **blood and water**. Some take it as an indication that Jesus died of a ruptured heart — but we have already read that His death was a voluntary act. Others think it speaks of baptism and the Lord's Supper, but this seems farfetched. **Blood** speaks of cleansing from the guilt of sin; whereas **water** typifies cleansing from the defilement of sin through the Word. This is expressed in the verse:

> Let the water and the blood,
> From Thy riven side which flowed
> Be of sin the double cure,
> Save me from its *guilt* and *power*.
> – *Augustus Toplady*

19:35 Verse 35 may refer to the fact that Jesus' legs were not broken, the piercing of Jesus' side, or to the entire crucifixion scene. **He who has seen** undoubtedly refers to John, who wrote the account.

19:36 This verse obviously looks

[†]*See p. xxiii.*
[††]*See p. xxiii.*

back to verse 33 as a fulfillment of Exodus 12:46: "Nor shall you break one of its bones." That verse refers to the Passover lamb. God's decree was that the bones were to be maintained unbroken. Christ is the true Passover Lamb, fulfilling the type with great exactness.

19:37 Verse 37 looks back to verse 34. Although the soldier did not realize it, his action was another wonderful fulfillment of **Scripture** (Zech. 12:10). "Man has his wickedness, but God has His way." Zechariah's prophecy refers to a future day when believing Jews will see the Lord coming back to the earth. "They will look on Me whom they pierced. Yes, they will mourn for Him as one mourns for his only son."

L. The Burial in Joseph's Tomb (19:38–42)†

19:38 This begins the account of the burial of Jesus. Up to now, **Joseph of Arimathea** had been a secret believer. **Fear of the Jews** had kept him from confessing Christ openly. Now he boldly stepped forward to claim **the body of Jesus** for burial. In doing this, he exposed himself to excommunication, persecution, and violence. It is only regrettable that he was not willing to take his stand for a rejected Master while Jesus was still ministering to the masses.

19:39, 40 John's readers are by now familiar with **Nicodemus**, having met him previously when he **came to Jesus by night** (chap. 3) and when he urged that Jesus be given a fair hearing before the Sanhedrin (John 7:50, 51). He now joins Joseph, bringing with him a **hundred pounds** of **myrrh and aloes**. These **spices** were probably in powdered form and were spread on the body. Then **the body** was **bound** with **strips of linen.**

19:41 Almost every detail in this passage was a fulfillment of prophecy. Isaiah had predicted that men would plan to bury the Messiah with the wicked but that He would be with the rich in His death (Isa. 53:9). **A new tomb** in a **garden** would obviously belong to a rich man. In Matthew we learn that it belonged to Joseph of Arimathea.

19:42 The body of **Jesus** was put in the tomb. The Jews were anxious to have the body out of the way because of their feast that began at sunset. But it was all

a part of God's determination that the body should be in the heart of the earth for three days and three nights. In that connection, it should be noted that in Jewish reckoning, any part of a day was counted as a day. So the fact that the Lord was in the tomb for a *part* of three days was still a fulfillment of His prediction in Matthew 12:40.

IX. THE SON OF GOD'S TRIUMPH (Chap. 20)††

A. The Empty Tomb (20:1–10)

20:1 The first day of the week was Sunday. **Mary Magdalene went to the tomb** before dawn. It is probable that the tomb was a small room carved in the side of a hill or cliff. **The stone** was no doubt shaped like a coin — round and flat. It would fit into a groove or gutter along the front of the tomb and could be rolled across the door to close it. When Mary got there, **the stone had been** removed already. This, incidentally, had taken place *after* Christ's resurrection, as we learn in Matthew 28.

20:2 Mary immediately **ran** to **Peter** and John with the breathless announcement that someone had removed the Lord's body **out of the tomb**. She did not say who had done it, but just said **they** to indicate that this was all she knew. The faithfulness and devotion of women at the crucifixion and resurrection of our Lord should be noticed. The disciples had forsaken the Lord and fled. The women stood by without regard for their personal safety. These things are not without meaning.

20:3, 4 It is difficult to imagine what **Peter** and John were thinking as they hurried **out** of the city to the garden near Calvary. John was probably younger than Peter and reached the **tomb first**.

20:5 It is likely that there was a low opening to the tomb, requiring one to stoop to enter or to look in. John **saw the linen cloths lying there**. Had they been unwound from the body, or were they still in the general shape in which they had been wrapped around the body? We suspect that the latter was the case. **Yet he did not go in** the tomb.

20:6, 7 By now **Peter** had caught up and he **went into** the tomb without hesitation. There is something about his impulsive manner that makes us feel a kinship to him. **He too saw the linen cloths lying there**, but the body of the Savior was not there.

The detail about **the handkerchief** was added to show that the Lord's departure was orderly and unhurried. If someone had stolen the body, he would not have carefully **folded** the cloth!

20:8 John entered the tomb and **saw** the orderly arrangement of the linen and the handkerchief. But when it says that **he saw and believed**, it means more than physical sight. It means that he comprehended. Before him were the evidences of Christ's resurrection. They showed him what had happened, **and he . . . believed.**

20:9 Up until now, the disciples did not really understand the OT **Scripture** which stated that the Messiah **must rise again from the dead**. The Lord Himself had told them repeatedly, but they did not take it in. John was the first to understand.

20:10 Then the disciples returned to wherever they were staying — probably in Jerusalem. They doubtless concluded that there was no use waiting by the tomb. It would be better to go and tell the other disciples what they had found.

B. The Appearance to Mary Magdalene (20:11–18)

20:11 The first two words are striking — **But Mary**. The other two disciples went home, *but Mary. . . .* Here again we have the love and devotion of a woman. She had been forgiven much; therefore, she loved much. She kept a lonely vigil outside the tomb, weeping because, as she thought, the body had been stolen, probably by the Lord's enemies.

20:12 This time, as she looked inside, **she saw two angels**, stationed **where the body of Jesus had lain**. It is remarkable how these tremendous facts are stated quietly and without emotion.

20:13 Mary did not seem to have any fear or surprise. She answered their question as if this were quite a normal experience. It is obvious from her answer that she still did not realize that Jesus had risen and was alive again.

20:14 At this point, something caused her to look in back of her. It was **Jesus** Himself, but she did not recognize Him. It was still early in the morning, and perhaps light had not yet dawned. She had been weeping continually, and doubtless her vision was clouded. Also, possibly God prevented her from recognizing the Lord until the proper time had come.

20:15 The Lord knew the answers to these questions; but He wanted to hear them from her own lips. **She** supposed **Him to be the gardener**. The Savior of the world may be very near to men, and yet not recognized. He usually comes in lowly guise, however, and not as one of the great ones of the earth. In her answer, Mary did not name the Lord. Three times she referred to Jesus as **Him**. There was only one Person with whom she was concerned, and she felt it quite unnecessary to identify Him further.

20:16 Mary now heard a familiar voice calling her by name. There was no mistaking the fact — it was **Jesus**! She called Him **Rabboni**, which means "my Great **Teacher**." Actually, she was still thinking of Him as the Great Teacher she had known. She did not realize that He was now more than her Teacher — He was her Lord and Savior. So the Lord prepared to explain to her the newer and fuller way in which she would hereafter know Him.

20:17 Mary had known Jesus personally as a Man. She had seen miracles happen when He was bodily present. So she concluded that if He was not with her in a visible way, then she could have no hope of blessing. The Lord must correct her thinking. He said, **"Do not cling to Me** simply as a Man in the flesh. **I have not yet ascended to My Father**. When I do return to heaven, the Holy Spirit will be sent down to the earth. When He comes, He will reveal Me to your heart in a way you have never known Me before. I will be nearer and dearer to you than was possible during My life here."

Then He told her to **go to** His **brethren** and tell them of the new order that had been ushered in. For the first time, the Lord referred to the disciples as **"My brethren."** They were to know that His

Father was their Father, and His God was their God. Not until now were believers made "sons" and "heirs of God."

The Lord Jesus did not say, "Our Father," but **"My Father and your Father."** The reason is that God is His Father in a different sense than He is ours. God is the **Father** of the Lord Jesus from all eternity. Christ is the Son by eternal generation. The Son is equal with the Father. We are sons of God by adoption. It is a relationship that begins when we are saved and will never end. As sons of God, we are not equal with God and never shall be.

20:18 **Mary Magdalene** obeyed her commission and became what someone has called "the apostle to the apostles." Can we doubt that this great privilege was given to her as a reward for her devotion to Christ?

C. The Appearance to His Disciples (20:19–23)

20:19 It was now Sunday **evening. The disciples were assembled** together, perhaps in the upper room where they had met three nights ago. **The doors were** locked **for fear of the Jews**. Suddenly they saw **Jesus** standing **in the midst,** and they heard His voice saying, **"Peace."** It seems clear that the Lord entered the room without opening the doors. This was a miracle. It should be remembered that His resurrection body was a real body of flesh and bones. Yet He had the power to pass through barriers and otherwise act independently of natural laws. The words **"Peace be with you"** now have new meaning because Christ has made peace by the blood of His cross. Those who are justified by faith have peace with God.

20:20 After announcing peace to them, **He showed them** the marks of His passion, by which peace had been obtained. They saw the print of the nails and the wound cause by the spear. Joy filled their hearts to realize it was truly **the Lord**. He had done as He said He would. He had risen from the dead. The risen Lord is the source of the Christian's joy.

20:21 Verse 21 is very beautiful. Believers are not meant to enjoy His peace selfishly. They are to share it with oth-

ers. So He sends them into the world, **as the Father** had **sent** Him:

Christ came into the world as a poor Person.

He came as a Servant.

He emptied Himself.

He delighted to do the Father's will.

He identified Himself with man.

He went about doing good.

He did everything by the power of the Holy Spirit.

His goal was the cross.

Now He said to the disciples, **"I also send you."**

20:22 This is one of the most difficult verses in the entire Gospel. We read that Jesus **breathed on** the disciples and said, **"Receive the Holy Spirit."** The difficulty is that the Holy Spirit was not given until later, on the day of Pentecost. Yet how could the Lord speak these words without the event taking place immediately?

Several explanations have been offered: (1) Some suggest that the Lord was simply making a promise of what they would receive on the day of Pentecost. This is hardly an adequate explanation. (2) Some point out that what the Savior actually said was, "Receive Holy Spirit," rather than, "Receive the Holy Spirit." They conclude from this that the disciples did not receive the Holy Spirit in all His fullness at this time, but only some ministry of the Spirit, such as a greater knowledge of the truth, or power and guidance for their mission. They say that the disciples received a guarantee or a foretaste of the Holy Spirit. (3) Others state that there was a full outpouring of the Holy Spirit upon the disciples at this time. This seems unlikely in view of such statements as Luke 24:49 and Acts 1:4, 5, 8, where the coming of the Holy Spirit was still spoken of as future. It is clear from John 7:39 that the Spirit could not come in His fullness until Jesus was glorified, that is, until He had gone back to heaven.

20:23 This is another difficult verse, about which there has been a great deal of controversy. (1) One view is that Jesus actually gave His apostles (and their supposed successors) the *power* to forgive sins or to retain sins. This is in direct contradiction of the Bible teaching that only God can forgive sins (Luke 5:21). (2) Gaebelein quotes a second view: "The power promised and authority given is in connection with the preaching of the Gospel, announcing on what terms sins would be forgiven, and if these terms are not accepted, sins would be retained." (3) A third view (which is similar to the second), and the one that we accept, is that the disciples were given the right to *declare* sins forgiven.

Let us illustrate this third view. The disciples go out preaching the gospel. Some people repent of their sins and receive the Lord Jesus. The disciples are authorized to tell them that their **sins** have been **forgiven**. Others refuse to repent and will not believe on Christ. The disciples tell them that they are still in their sins, and that if they die, they will perish eternally.

In addition to this explanation, we should also note that the disciples were given special authority by the Lord in dealing with certain sins. For instance, in Acts 5:1–11, Peter used this power, and it resulted in the death of Ananias and Sapphira. Paul is seen retaining the sin of an evil-doer in 1 Corinthians 5:3–5, 12, 13, and remitting sin in 2 Corinthians 2:4–8. In these cases, it is forgiveness from the punishment of these sins in this life.

D. Doubt Turned to Faith (20:24–29)

20:24 We should not jump to the conclusion that **Thomas** should be blamed for not being present. Nothing is said to indicate the reason for his absence.

20:25 Thomas *is* to be blamed for his unbelieving attitude. He must have visible, tangible proof of the Lord's resurrection; otherwise he **will not believe**. This is the attitude of many today, but it is not reasonable. Even scientists believe many things that they can neither see nor touch.

20:26 One week later the Lord appeared to **His disciples** again. This time **Thomas** was **with them**. Again the Lord Jesus entered the room in a miraculous way and again greeted them with **"Peace to you!"**

20:27[†] The Lord dealt gently and patiently with His faithless follower. He

invited him to prove the reality of His resurrection by putting his **hand** into the spear wound in His **side.**

20:28 **Thomas** was convinced. Whether he ever did put his hand into the Lord's side, we do not know. But he knew at last that Jesus was risen and that He was both **Lord** and **God**. John Boys puts it nicely: "He acknowledged the divinity he did not see by the wounds he did see."

20:29 The important thing to notice is that **Jesus** accepted worship as God. If He were only a man, He should have refused it. But Thomas' faith was not the kind that was most pleasing to the Lord. It was belief based on sight. More **blessed are those who have not seen and yet have believed**.

The surest evidence is the Word of God. If God says a thing, we honor Him by believing it; but we dishonor Him by demanding additional evidence. We should believe simply because He said it and because He cannot lie or be mistaken.

E. The Purpose of John's Gospel (20:30, 31)

Not all the miracles performed by Jesus are recorded in John's Gospel. The Holy Spirit selected those signs which would best serve His purpose.

Here we have John's object in writing the book. It was so that his readers **may believe that Jesus is the** true Messiah and **the Son of God. Believing**, they will **have** eternal **life in His name**.

Have you believed?

X. EPILOGUE: THE RISEN SON WITH HIS OWN (Chap. 21)

A. Christ Appears to His Disciples in Galilee (21:1–14)

21:1 The scene now changes to the **Sea of Tiberias** (Galilee).[††] The disciples had journeyed north to their homes in Galilee. The Lord Jesus met them there. The phrase **in this way He showed Himself** means John is about to describe the manner in which Christ appeared to them.

21:2 Seven of the disciples **were together** at the time — **Peter, Thomas, Na-**

thanael, James and John (**the sons of Zebedee**), **and two others** whose names we do not know.

21:3 **Simon Peter** decided to go **fishing** on the lake, and the others agreed to go with him. This seemed to be a most natural decision, though some Bible students feel that the trip was not in the will of God and that they went without first praying. **That night they caught nothing**. They were not the first fishermen to spend a night fishing without success! They illustrate the uselessness of human efforts apart from divine help, especially in the matter of fishing for souls.

21:4 **Jesus** was waiting for them as they rowed toward **the shore** in **the morning**, although they **did not** recognize Him. Perhaps it was still quite dark, or perhaps they were prevented from knowing Him by God's power.

21:5 It is the same as if the Lord asked, "Young men, have you anything to eat?" Disappointedly **they answered Him, "No."**

21:6 As far as they knew, He was just a stranger, walking along the shore. Yet, in response to His advice, they **cast the net on the right side of the boat**, and lo and behold! A great load **of fish**. So many that they could not pull in the net! This shows that the Lord Jesus had perfect knowledge as to the location of the fish in the lake. It also teaches us that when the Lord directs our service, there are no more empty nets. He knows where there are souls ready to be saved, and He is willing to direct us to them — if we will let Him.

21:7 John was the first to recognize **the Lord** and promptly told **Peter**. The latter **put on his outer garment** and went to the shore. We are not told whether he swam or waded, or walked on the water (as some suggest).

21:8 **The other disciples** transferred from the large fishing boat to a **little** rowboat and dragged **the net** the remaining three hundred feet to land.

21:9 The Savior had their breakfast all ready — broiled **fish** and **bread**. We do not know whether the Lord caught these **fish** or whether He obtained them miraculously. But we do learn that He is not dependent on our poor efforts.

Doubtless in heaven we shall learn that while many people were saved through preaching and personal witness, many others were saved by the Lord Himself without any human help.

21:10 He now instructed them to pull in the net with **the fish** — not to cook them, but to count them. In doing so, they would be reminded that "the secret of success is to work at His command and to act with implicit obedience to His Word."

21:11 The Bible gives the exact number of fish in the net — **one hundred and fifty-three**. Many interesting explanations have been offered as to the meaning of this number: (1) The number of languages in the world at that time. (2) The number of races or tribes in the world, toward which the gospel net would be spread out. (3) The number of different kinds of fish in the sea of Galilee, or in the world. There is no doubt that it speaks of the variety of those who would be saved through the preaching of the gospel — some from every tribe and nation. The fishermen knew that it was remarkable that **the net** had **not broken**. This is further evidence that "God's work carried on in God's way will never lack God's resources." He will see that the net does not break.

21:12 The invitation to **breakfast** is heard, and the disciples gather around the fire of coals to partake of the good things the Lord had provided. Peter must have had his own thoughts as he saw the fire of coals. Was he reminded of the fire at which he warmed himself when he denied the Lord? The disciples felt a strange sense of awe and solemnity in the presence of the Lord. There He stood in His resurrection body. There were many questions they would like to have asked Him. But they did not dare. They knew **it was the Lord** — even if they felt a certain sense of mystery shrouded His Person.

21:13 **Jesus** now served breakfast to them. And they were probably reminded of a similar occasion when He fed the five thousand with a few loaves and fishes.

21:14 **This** was **the third time** mentioned by John that Jesus appeared **to His disciples**. That there were other times is clear from the other Gospels. In this Gospel, He appeared to the disciples on the evening of the day of the resurrection, then one week later, and now by the shore of blue Lake Galilee.

B. The Restoration of Peter (21:15–17)

21:15 The Lord first took care of their physical needs. Then when they were warm and had eaten, He turned to **Peter** and dealt with spiritual matters. Peter had publicly denied the Lord three times. Since then, he had repented and had been restored to fellowship with the Lord. In these verses, Peter's restoration is publicly acknowledged by the Lord.

It has often been pointed out that two different words for **love** are used in these verses. We might paraphrase verse 15 as follows: **"Simon, son of Jonah,**[54] **do you love Me more than these** other disciples love Me?" **He said to Him, "Yes, Lord, you know that I** *am fond of* **You."** Peter would no longer boast that he would never forsake the Lord, even if all the other disciples did. He had learned his lesson.

"Feed My lambs," Jesus said. A very practical way of demonstrating love for Christ is by feeding the young ones in His flock. It is interesting to note that the conversation had changed from fishing to shepherding. The former speaks of the works of evangelism; while the latter suggests teaching and pastoral care.

21:16 For the **second time**, the Lord asked Peter if he loved Him. Peter replied the second time, with genuine distrust of himself, **"You know that I** *am fond of* **You."** This time **He said to him, "Tend My sheep."** There are lambs and sheep in Christ's flock, and they need the loving care of one who loves the Shepherd.

21:17 Just as Peter had denied the Lord thrice, so he was given three opportunities to confess Him.

This time, Peter appealed to the fact that Jesus was God and therefore knew **all things**. He said **the third time, "You know that I** *am fond of* **You."** And for the last time, he was told that he could demonstrate this by feeding Christ's **sheep**. In this passage, the underlying lesson is that love for Christ is the only acceptable motive for serving Him.

C. Jesus Predicts Peter's Death (21:18–23)

21:18 When Peter was **younger**, he had great freedom of movement. He went **where** he **wished**. But the Lord here told him that at the end of his life, he would be arrested, bound, and carried off to execution.

21:19 This explains verse 18. Peter **would glorify God** by dying as a martyr. He who had denied the Lord would be given courage to lay down his life for Him. The verse reminds us that we can glorify God in death as well as in life. Then Jesus exclaimed, **"Follow Me!"** As He said it, He must have started to leave.

21:20 It seems that **Peter** began to follow the Lord, and then **turning around, saw** John **following** too. Here John paused to identify himself as the one **who also had leaned on** Jesus' **breast at the** Passover **Supper**, and had asked the name of the betrayer.

21:21 As **Peter** saw John, the thought probably crossed his mind, **"What about** John? Is he going to die as a martyr too? Or will he still be alive when the Lord comes back again?" He asked the Lord concerning John's future.

21:22 The Lord's answer was that Peter should not be concerned about John's latter days. Even if he were to survive until the Second Coming of Christ, this should not make any difference to Peter. Many failures in Christian service arise from disciples' being more occupied with one another than with the Lord Himself.

21:23 The Lord's words were misquoted. He **did not say** that John would still be alive when He came back again. He only said that even if that were the case, why should that affect Peter? Many see significance in the fact that Jesus here linked John with His Second Advent, and that John was the one who was privileged to write the Revelation of Jesus Christ, describing the end times in great detail.

D. John's Closing Witness to Jesus (21:24, 25)

21:24 John added a word of personal testimony to the accuracy of the things which he had written. Others take this as the attestation of the elders of the church in Ephesus to John's Gospel.

21:25 We have no fear in taking verse 25 literally! Jesus is God and is therefore infinite. There is no limit to the meaning of His words or to the number of His works. While He was here on earth, He was still the Upholder of all things — the sun, moon, and stars. Who could ever describe all that is involved in keeping the universe in motion? Even in His miracles on earth, we have only the barest description. In a simple act of healing, think of the nerves, muscles, blood corpuscles, and other members that He controlled. Think of His direction of germs, fishes, animal life. Think of His guidance in the affairs of men. Think of His control over the atomic structure of every bit of matter in the universe. Could **the world itself** possibly **contain the books** to describe such infinite details? The answer is an emphatic "No."

And so we come to the end of our commentary on John's Gospel. Perhaps we realize a little better why it has come to be one of the best loved parts of the Bible. Certainly one can scarcely read it thoughtfully and prayerfully without falling in love afresh with the blessed Person whom it presents.

ENDNOTES

[1](1:18) The critical text (NU in NKJV margin) reads *only begotten God*. The traditional *only begotten Son* is found in most manuscripts and also in 3:16.

[2](1:29) J. Cynddylan Jones, *Studies in the Gospel According to St. John*, p. 103.

[3](1:45) James S. Stewart, *The Life and Teaching of Jesus Christ*, pp. 66, 67.

[4](1:51) Only John reports the "double amen" (NKJV, *most assuredly*). The other Gospels, apparently *condensing* our Lord's expression, read "amen" (NKJV, *assuredly*).

[5](2:4) George Williams, *The Student's Commentary on the Holy Scriptures*, p. 194.

[6](2:11) Jones, *Studies*, p. 148.

[7](3:1) The little Greek connective *de* can mean *and, now, but*, etc. Modern English Bibles tend to delete these frequently. This is one of the few places

where the KJV did so, and the NKJV followed suit.

[8](3:5) Another valid interpretation that fits the context of contrasting spiritual and physical birth is that the water refers to physical birth and the Spirit refers to the Holy Spirit. The rabbis used "water" for the male seed, and water could also refer to the sack of watery liquid which breaks when a baby is born.

[9](3:16) F. W. Boreham, further documentation unavailable.

[10](4:41, 42) The critical text (NU) omits *the Christ*.

[11](4:48) In Greek there are separate forms for addressing one person (cf. Old English *thou, thee*) and more than one (cf. *ye, you*). The plural is used here.

[12](5:2) The critical text reads *Bethzatha*, but archaeology has confirmed the traditional name used in the majority of manuscripts and the KJV tradition.

[13](5:3) James Gifford Bellett, *The Evangelists*, p. 50.

[14](5:18) J. Sidlow Baxter, *Explore the Book*, V:309.

[15](5:24) There are other verses which teach that a believer will one day stand before the Judgment Seat of Christ (Rom. 14:10; 2 Cor. 5:10). However, the question of his sins will not be brought up at that time for punishment. That question was settled at Calvary. At the Judgment Seat of Christ, the believer's life and service will be reviewed, and he will either receive rewards or suffer loss. It will not be then a question of his soul's salvation, but of his life's fruitfulness.

[16](5:29) If this were the only verse in the Bible on the subject of resurrection, one would think that all the dead will be raised at the same time. However, we know from other portions of Scripture, particularly Revelation 20, that a period of at least one thousand years elapses between the two resurrections. The First Resurrection is the resurrection of those who have been saved through faith in Christ. The Second Resurrection includes all who have died as unbelievers.

[17](5:39) The Greek verb form for *search* is ambiguous. It may be *imperative* ("Search," KJV) or *indicative* ("you search," NKJV). The context favors the NKJV translation.

[18](5:47) Guy King, *To My Son*, p. 104.

[19](6:11) W. H. Griffith Thomas, *The*

Apostle John: His Life and Writings, pp. 173, 74.

²⁰(6:15) Frederick Brotherton Meyer, *Tried By Fire,* p. 152.

²¹(6:31) The manna was a small, round, white food which God miraculously provided for Israel in the wilderness. They had to gather the manna from the ground each morning of the first six days of every week.

²²(6:55) NU text reads "true food . . . true drink," but the meaning is virtually the same (reality).

²³(6:59) A synagogue is a local Jewish religious meeting place, but is not the same as the temple in Jerusalem where alone animal sacrifices could be made.

²⁴(6:69) The critical text (NU) reads "You are the Holy One of God."

²⁵(7:1) It is helpful to know that the Greek word for "Jew" (*Ioudaios*) can mean (1) a *Judean* (as opposed to a Galilean); (2) a Jewish person of any sort (including one who accepts Christ); (3) or an opponent of Christianity, especially a religious leader. John uses it mostly in the last sense, though he himself was a Jew in the second sense.

²⁶(7:7) Meyer, *Tried,* p. 129.

²⁷(7:8) The critical (NU) text's omission of "yet" is unfortunate. It seems to imply deception on our Lord's part.

²⁸(8:5) J. N. Darby, further documentation unavailable.

²⁹(8:11) 7:53 through 8:11 does not appear in the most ancient mss. of John, but is found in over 900 Greek mss. (the vast majority). There is some question as to whether these verses form a part of the original text. We believe that it is proper to accept them as part of the inspired text. All that they teach is in perfect agreement with the rest of the Bible. Augustine writes that some excluded this passage for fear it would promote loose views on morality.

³⁰(8:45) R. C. H. Lenski, *The Interpretation of Colossians, Thessalonians, Timothy, Titus, Philemon,* pp. 701, 02.

³¹(9:35) The NU text reads "Son of Man" here, which does not fit the context of worship nearly as well as the majority reading.

³²(10:28) The Greek has a double negative for emphasis (not permitted in standard English).

³³(10:36) Samuel Green, "*Scripture Tes-*timony to the Deity of Christ," p. 7.

³⁴(11:1) Arthur W. Pink, *Exposition of the Gospel of John,* III:12.

³⁵(11:25) Burkitt, further documentation unavailable.

³⁶(11:35) The shortest verse in the Greek NT is on the opposite side of the emotional spectrum, "Rejoice always" (*Pantote chairete,* 1 Thess. 5:16).

³⁷(11:47) J. C. Ryle, *Expository Thoughts on the Gospels, St. John,* II:295.

³⁸(11:48) Meyer, *Tried,* p. 112.

³⁹(12:5) Ryle, *John,* II:309, 10.

⁴⁰(12:7) The critical text's reading "that she may keep" instead of "she has kept" seems to contradict both this context and Mary's absence at the tomb on Easter morning. NIV solves the problem by paraphrasing.

⁴¹(12:24) T. G. Ragland, further documentation unavailable.

⁴²(13:13, 14) Of course, there are times, especially in Eastern lands, when one would literally wash someone else's feet, but this is only one example of humble service.

⁴³(13:32) The Greek grammar (first class condition plus *ei* with the indicative) assumes it to be true.

⁴⁴(14:20) Other popular illustrations include the bird in the air with the air in the bird, and the fish in water with the water in the fish.

⁴⁵(17:1) Marcus Rainsford, *Our Lord Prays for His Own,* p. 173.

⁴⁶(17:4) Ryle, *John,* III:40, 41.

⁴⁷(17:26) F. L. Godet, *Commentary on the Gospel of John,* II:345.

⁴⁸(17:26) Rainsford, *Our Lord Prays,* p. 173.

⁴⁹(18:14) Stewart, *Life and Teaching,* p. 157.

⁵⁰(18:28) Augustine, Quoted by Ryle, *John,* III:248.

⁵¹(18:28) Bishop Hall, *Ibid.*

⁵²(18:28) Poole, *Ibid.*

⁵³(19:20) Alexander, further documentation unavailable.

⁵⁴(21:15) The critical (NU) text names Peter's father John instead of Jonah (also vv. 16, 17).

BIBLIOGRAPHY

Godet, F. L. *Commentary on the Gospel of John.* Grand Rapids: Zondervan Publishing House, 1969 (Reprint of 1893 ed., 2 vols. in one).

Hole, F. B. *The Gospel of John Briefly Expounded*. London: The Central Bible Truth Depot, n.d.

Ironside, H. A. *Addresses on the Gospel of John*. New York: Loizeaux Bros., 1956.

Jones, J. Cynddylan. *Studies in the Gospel according to St. John*. Toronto: William Briggs, 1885.

Kelly, William. *An Exposition of the Gospel of John*. London: C. A. Hammond Trust Bible Depot, 1966.

Lenski, R. C. H. *The Interpretation of St. John's Gospel*. Minneapolis: Augsburg Publishing House, 1942.

Macaulay, J. C. *Obedience Unto Death: Devotional Studies in John's Gospel*. Grand Rapids: Wm. B. Eerdmans Publishing Co., 1942.

Pink, Arthur W. *Exposition of the Gospel of John. Vol. III*. Swengel, Pennsylvania: Bible Truth Depot, 1945.

Rainsford, Marcus. *Our Lord Prays for His Own*. Chicago: Moody Press, 1955.

Ryle, J. C. *Expository Thoughts on the Gospels: St. John*. London: James Clarke and Co., Ltd., 1957.

Tasker, R. V. G. *The Gospel According to St. John*. Grand Rapids: Wm. B. Eerdmans Publishing Company, 1968.

Tenney, Merrill C. *JOHN: The Gospel of Belief*. Grand Rapids: Wm. B. Eerdmans Publishing Company, 1948.

Thomas, W. H. Griffith. *The Apostle John: Studies in His Life and Writings*. Grand Rapids: Wm. B. Eerdmans Publishing Company, 1968.

Van Ryn, A. *Meditations in John*. Chicago: Moody Press, 1949.

Vine, W. E. *John, His Record of Christ*. London: Oliphants, 1957.

Westcott, B. F. *The Gospel According to St. John*. Grand Rapids: Wm. B. Eerdmans Publishing Co., 1954.

THE ACTS OF THE APOSTLES

Introduction

"Christ is the theme, the church is the means, and the Spirit is the power."
— W. Graham Scroggie

I. Unique Place in the Canon

The Acts of the Apostles is the only *inspired* church history; it is also the *first* church history, and the only primary church history to cover the earliest days of the faith. All others merely draw on Luke's work with a few traditions (and many conjectures!) added. We would be at a total loss without this book. To go from the life of our Lord in the Gospels right into the Epistles would be a tremendous leap. Who were the congregations being addressed and how did they come to be? Acts answers these and many other questions. It is a bridge not only between the life of Christ and the Christ-life taught in the Epistles, but is also a transitional link between Judaism and Christianity, between Law and Grace. This constitutes one of the main difficulties in interpreting Acts, that is, the gradual widening of horizons from a small Jewish movement centered in Jerusalem to a worldwide faith that has made inroads in the imperial capital itself.

II. Authorship†

The authorship of Luke and Acts is the same, as nearly all agree. If the Third Gospel is by Luke, so is Acts, and vice versa (see Introduction to Luke).

The *external evidence* that Luke wrote Acts is early, strong, and widespread. The anti-Marcionite Prologue to Luke (c. 160–180), the Muratorian Canon (c. 170–200), and the early church fathers Irenaeus, Clement of Alexandria, Tertullian, and Origen all concur on Lucan authorship of Acts. So do nearly all who follow them in church history, including such authorities as Eusebius and Jerome.

The *internal evidence* in Acts itself that Luke wrote it is threefold. In the beginning of Acts, the writer specifically refers to an earlier work, also dedicated to Theophilus. Luke 1:1–4 shows that the Third Gospel is the account that is meant. The style, compassionate outlook, vocabulary, apologetic emphasis, and many small details tie the two works together. Were it not for a desire to have Luke with the other three Gospels, no doubt the two would have been together like 1 and 2 Corinthians.

Second, from the text of Acts it is clear that the author was a travel companion of Paul. This appears in the famous "we" passages (16:10–17; 20:5–21:18; 27:1–28:16), where the author is actually present at the events recorded. Skeptical attempts to explain these as a "fictional" touch are not convincing. If they were just added to make the work look more authentic, why so *seldom* and *subtly* introduced — and why is no *name* given to the "I" implied in the "we"?

Finally, when other companions of Paul who are mentioned by the author in the third person are eliminated, as well as companions known *not* to have been with Paul during the "we" sections, Luke is the only viable person left.

III. Date

While the date of some NT books is not crucial, it is more important in Acts, which is specifically a church *history*, and the very first one at that.

Three dates have been proposed for Acts, two accepting Lucan authorship and one denying it:

1. A second century date, of course,

rules out Luke as author; he could hardly have lived beyond A.D. 80 or 85 at the latest. While some (liberal) scholars feel that the author used Josephus' *Antiquities* (c. A.D. 93), the parallels that they allege regarding Theudas (Acts 5:36) do not agree, and the similarities are not strong in any event.

2. A commonly held view is that Luke wrote Luke-Acts between 70–80. This would allow for Luke to have used Mark in his Gospel (probably from the 60's).

3. A strong case can be made that Luke ended Acts where he did soon after the time the book's history ends — during Paul's first imprisonment in Rome.

It is *possible* that *Luke* was planning a third volume (but it was apparently not in God's will), and so Luke did not yet mention the devastating events (to Christians) between A.D. 63 and 70. However, the following omissions suggest the early date: Nero's ferocious persecution of Christians in Italy after the burning of Rome (64); the Jewish war with Rome (66–70); the martyrdom of Peter and Paul (later 60's); and most traumatic for Jews and Hebrew Christians, the destruction of Jerusalem. It is most likely, therefore, that Luke wrote Acts while Paul was in prison in Rome, about A.D. 62 or 63.

IV. Background and Themes

The Acts of the Apostles throbs with life and action. In it we see the Holy Spirit at work, forming the church, empowering the church, and expanding her outreach. It is the magnificent record of the Sovereign Spirit using most unlikely instruments, overcoming most formidable obstacles, employing most unconventional methods, and achieving most remarkable results.

Acts takes up the narrative where the Gospels leave off, then carries us by swift, dramatic descriptions over the early, turbulent years of the infant church. It is the record of the great transition period when the NT church was throwing off the graveclothes of Judaism, and displaying its distinctive character as a new fellowship in which Jews and Gentiles are one in Christ. For this reason, Acts has been aptly called the story of "the weaning time of Isaac."

As we read, we feel something of the spiritual exhilaration that is present when God is at work. At the same time, we sense the tension that arises when sin and Satan oppose and obstruct.

In the first twelve chapters the Apostle Peter occupies a key role, as he courageously preaches to the nation of Israel. From chapter 13 on, the Apostle Paul comes to the forefront as the zealous, inspired, and tireless apostle to the Gentiles.

Acts covers a period of about thirty-three years. J. B. Phillips has pointed out that in no comparable period of human history has "any small body of ordinary people so moved the world that their enemies could say, with tears of rage in their eyes, that these men 'have turned the world upside down!' "[1]

OUTLINE

I. THE CHURCH IN JERUSALEM (Chaps. 1–7)
    A.   The Risen Lord's Promise of the Spirit (1:1–5)
    B.   The Ascending Lord's Mandate to the Apostles (1:6–11)
    C.   The Prayerful Disciples Waiting in Jerusalem (1:12–26)
    D.   The Day of Pentecost and the Birth of the Church (2:1–47)
    E.   The Healing of a Lame Man, and Peter's Charge to Israel (3:1–26)
    F.   The Persecution and Growth of the Church (4:1–7:60)

II. THE CHURCH IN JUDEA AND SAMARIA (8:1–9:31)
    A.   The Ministry of Philip in Samaria (8:1–25)
    B.   Philip and the Ethiopian Eunuch (8:26–40)
    C.   The Conversion of Saul of Tarsus (9:1–31)

Commentary†

I. THE CHURCH IN JERUSALEM (Chaps. 1–7)††

A. The Risen Lord's Promise of the Spirit (1:1–5)

1:1 The Book of Acts opens with a reminder. Luke, the beloved physician, had written to **Theophilus** previously — a writing which we now know as The Gospel According to Luke (see Luke 1:1–4). In the last verses of that Gospel, he had told Theophilus that immediately prior to His Ascension, the Lord Jesus had promised His disciples that they would be baptized with the Holy Spirit (Luke 24:48–53).

Now Luke is going to continue the narrative, so he goes back to this thrilling promise as a starting point. And it is fitting that he should do so, because in that promise of the Spirit lay concealed in germ form all the spiritual triumphs unfolded in the Book of the Acts. Luke describes his Gospel as **the former account**, or the first book. In it he had recorded the things **that Jesus** *began* **both to do and teach**. In Acts he carries on the record by recounting the things that Jesus *continued* to do and teach through the Holy Spirit after His Ascension.

Notice that the Lord's ministry was one of both *doing* and *teaching*. It was not doctrine without duty, or creed without conduct. The Savior was the living embodiment of what He taught. He practiced what He preached.

1:2 Theophilus would remember that Luke's previous book ended with the account of the Savior's Ascension, here described as His being **taken up**.

He would also remember the tender last instructions the Lord had given the eleven **apostles** before He left.

1:3 For the **forty days** between His resurrection and Ascension, the Lord had appeared to His disciples, offering the strongest possible **proofs** of His bodily resurrection (see John 20:19, 26; 21:1, 14).†††

During this time, He had also discussed with them the affairs of **the kingdom of God**. His primary concern was not with the kingdoms of this world, but with the realm or sphere where God is acknowledged as King.

The kingdom is not to be confused with the church. The Lord Jesus offered Himself to the nation of Israel as King but was rejected (Matt. 23:37). His literal kingdom on earth was therefore postponed until Israel repents and receives Him as Messiah (Acts 3:19–21).

At the present time, the King is absent. However, He does have an invisible kingdom on earth (Col. 1:13). It is made up of all who profess allegiance to Him (Matt. 25:1–12). In one sense it consists of everyone who claims to be a Christian; that is its outward aspect (Matt. 13:1–52). But in its inward reality it includes only those who have been born again (John 3:3, 5). **The kingdom** in its present condition is described in the parables of Matthew 13.

The church is something entirely new. It was not the subject of OT prophecy (Eph. 3:5). It is composed of all believers from Pentecost to the Rapture. As the Bride of Christ, the church will reign with Him in the Millennium and share

His glory forever. Christ will return as King at the end of the Great Tribulation, destroy His foes, and set up His reign of righteousness over all the earth (Ps. 72:8).

Although His reign from Jerusalem lasts for only one thousand years (Rev. 20:4), yet **the kingdom** is everlasting in the sense that all of God's foes will have been finally destroyed, and He will reign eternally in heaven without opposition or hindrances (2 Pet. 1:11).

1:4 Luke now relates a meeting of the Lord with His disciples as they **assembled together** in a room in **Jerusalem**. The risen Redeemer **commanded them** to remain in **Jerusalem**. But why in **Jerusalem**, they might well wonder! To them it was a city of hatred, violence, and persecution!

Yes, **the** fulfillment of that **Promise of the Father** would occur in **Jerusalem**. The coming of the Spirit would take place in the very city where the Savior had been crucified. The presence of the Spirit there would bear testimony to man's rejection of the Son of God. The Spirit of truth would reprove the world of sin, righteousness, and judgment — and this would take place first in **Jerusalem**. And the disciples would receive the Holy Spirit in the city where they themselves had forsaken the Lord and had fled to save their own skins. They would be made strong and fearless in the place where they had shown themselves to be weak and cowardly.

This was not the first time the disciples had heard of **the Promise of the Father** from the Savior's lips. Throughout His earthly ministry, and especially in His Upper Room Discourse, He had told them of the Helper who would come (see Luke 24:49; John 14:16, 26; 15:26; 16:7, 13).

1:5 Now, in His last meeting with them, He repeats the promise. Some, if not all of them had already been **baptized** by **John with water**. But John's baptism was outward and physical. Before many days would pass,[2] they would be **baptized with the Holy Spirit**, and this baptism would be inward and spiritual. The first baptism identified them outwardly with the repentant portion of the nation of Israel. The second would incorporate them into the church, the

Body of Christ, and would empower them for service.

Jesus promised that they would **be baptized with the Holy Spirit not many days from now**, but there is no mention of the baptism in fire (Matt. 3:11, 12; Luke 3:16, 17). The latter is a baptism of judgment for unbelievers only and is still future.

B. The Ascending Lord's Mandate to the Apostles (1:6–11)

1:6 Perhaps the incident recorded here took place on the Mount of Olives, over against Bethany. This was the spot from which the Lord Jesus went back to heaven (Luke 24:50, 51).

The disciples had been thinking about the coming of the Spirit. They remembered that the prophet Joel spoke of the outpouring of the Spirit in connection with the Messiah's glorious reign (Joel 2:28). They therefore concluded that the Lord would set up His **kingdom** soon, since He had first said that the Spirit would be given "not many days from now." Their question revealed that they still expected Christ to set up His literal earthly **kingdom** immediately.

1:7 The Lord did *not* correct them for expecting His literal reign on earth. Such a hope was and is justified. He simply told them they could not **know** when His kingdom would come. The date had been fixed by the Father's sole **authority**, but He had not chosen to reveal it. It was information that belonged exclusively to Himself.

The expression **times or seasons** is used in the Bible to refer to various events foretold by God that are yet to come to pass in connection with the nation of Israel. Being of Jewish background, the disciples would understand the expression here to refer to the crucial days prior to and including the establishment of Christ's thousand-year reign on earth.

1:8 Having suppressed their curiosity as to the future date of this kingdom, the Lord Jesus directed their attention to what was more immediate — the nature and sphere of their mission. As to its nature, they were to **be witnesses**; as to its sphere, they were to witness **in Jerusalem, and in all Judea and Samaria, and to the end of the earth**.

But first they must **receive power** — the **power** of **the Holy Spirit**. This **power** is the grand indispensable of Christian witness. A man may be highly talented, intensively trained, and widely experienced, but without spiritual **power** he is ineffective. On the other hand, a man may be uneducated, unattractive, and unrefined, yet let him be endued with the **power** of **the Holy Spirit** and the world will turn out to see him burn for God. The fearful disciples needed **power** for witnessing, holy boldness for preaching the gospel. They would receive this **power** when **the Holy Spirit** came **upon** them.

Their witness was to begin **in Jerusalem**, a meaningful prearrangement of the grace of God. The very city where our Lord was crucified was first to receive the call to repentance and faith in Him.

Then **Judea**, the southern section of Palestine with its strong Jewish population, and with **Jerusalem** as its chief city.

Then **Samaria**, the region in the center of Palestine, with its hated, half-breed population with whom the Jews had no dealings.

Then **the end** of the then-known world — the Gentile countries which had hitherto been outside the pale as far as religious privilege was concerned. In this ever widening circle of witness, we have a general outline of the flow of history in Acts.

1. The *witness* in **Jerusalem** (Chaps. 1–7)
2. The *witness* in **Judea** and **Samaria** (8:1–9:31)
3. The *witness* to **the end of the earth** (9:32–28:31)

1:9 As soon as the Savior had commissioned His disciples, **He was taken up** into heaven. This is all the Scripture says — **He was taken up, and a cloud received Him out of their sight**. Such a spectacular event, yet it is described so simply and quietly! The restraint which the writers of the Bible used in telling their story points to the inspiration of the Word; it is not customary for men to handle such unusual events with such reserve.

1:10 Again without any expression of shocked surprise, Luke narrates the appearance of **two men . . . in white apparel**. These were obviously angelic beings who were enabled to appear on earth in the form of **men**. Perhaps these were the same angels who appeared at the tomb following the resurrection (Luke 24:4).

1:11 The angels first addressed the disciples as **men of Galilee**. As far as we know, all the disciples except Judas Iscariot came from the region west of the Sea of Galilee.

Then the angels awoke them from their reverie, as they looked into heaven. Why were they **gazing up into heaven**? Was it sorrow, or worship, or wonder? Doubtless it was a mixture of all three, though primarily sorrow. So a word of comfort was given. The ascended Christ would come again.

Here we have a clear promise of the Lord's Second Advent to set up His kingdom on the earth. It is not the Rapture, but the coming to reign that is in view.

1. He ascended from the Mount of Olives (v.12).	1. He will return to the Mount of Olives (Zech. 14:4.)
2. He ascended personally.	2. He will return personally (Mal. 3:1).
3. He ascended visibly.	3. He will return visibly (Matt. 24:30).
4. He was received up in a cloud. (v. 9)	4. He will come on the clouds of heaven (Matt. 24:30).
5. He ascended gloriously.	5. He will return with power and great glory (Matt. 24:30).

C. The Prayerful Disciples Waiting in Jerusalem (1:12–26)

1:12 In Luke 24:52 the disciples returned to Jerusalem *with great joy*. "Light from the love of God kindled these men's hearts and made their faces shine in spite of the sea of troubles that surrounded them."

It was a short trip of about three quarters of a mile **from the mount called Olivet**, down through the Kidron Valley, and up to the city. This was the greatest distance a Jew might travel on the **Sabbath** in NT times.

1:13 Once inside the city, **they went up into the upper room where they were staying**.

The Spirit of God here lists the names

of the disciples for the fourth and last
time (Matt. 10:2–4; Mark 3:16–19; Luke
6:14–16). But now there is a notable
omission: the name of Judas Iscariot is
absent from the roll call. The traitor had
gone to his deserved doom.

1:14 As the disciples gathered together, it was **with one accord**. This expression, occurring eleven times in Acts,
is one of the keys that unlocks the secret
of blessing. Where brethren dwell together in unity, God commands the
blessing — life for evermore (Ps. 133).

A second key is given in the words,
continued ... in prayer. Now, as then,
God works when people pray. Ordinarily we would rather do anything than
pray. But it is only when we wait before
God in desperate, believing, fervent, unhurried, united **prayer** that the reviving,
energizing power of the Spirit of God is
poured out.

It cannot be emphasized too strongly
that *unity and prayer were the prelude to
Pentecost.*

Gathered **with** the disciples were certain unnamed **women** (probably those
who had followed Jesus), also **Mary the
mother of Jesus, and** . . . **His brothers**.
There are several points of interest here.

1. This is the last mention of **Mary**
by name in the NT — doubtless "a silent protest against Mariolatry." The
disciples were not praying *to* her, but
with her. She was waiting with them
to receive the gift of the Holy Spirit.

2. **Mary** is called **the mother of Jesus**
but not "the mother of God." Jesus is
the name of our Lord in His humanity.
Since, as man, He was born of **Mary**,
it is proper that she should be called
the mother of Jesus. But never in the
Bible is she called "the mother of
God." Although Jesus Christ is truly
God, it is doctrinally inaccurate and absurd to speak of God as having a
human mother. As God, He existed
from all eternity.

3. The mention of the **brothers** of
Jesus, coming after the reference to
Mary, makes it likely that these were
actual sons of **Mary** and half-brothers
of Jesus. Several other verses in addition to this refute the idea, held by
some, that **Mary** was a perpetual virgin and never bore any children after
the birth of Jesus (see, for instance,
Matt. 12:46; Mark 6:3; John 7:3, 5;

1 Cor. 9:5; Gal. 1:19. See also Psa. 69:8).

1:15 One day, when **about a hundred and twenty disciples** were gathered
together, **Peter** was led to remind them
of OT Scriptures which dealt with the
one who would betray the Messiah.

1:16, 17 At the outset, Peter mentioned that a certain prophecy written by
**David concerning Judas ... had to be
fulfilled**. But before quoting **this Scripture** he reminded them that although
Judas had been one of the twelve and
had shared in their apostolic ministry,
yet he served as **guide to those who arrested Jesus**. Notice the moderation
Peter uses in describing this dastardly
act. Judas became a traitor by his own
deliberate choice, and thus he fulfilled
the prophecies that someone would sell
the Lord to His enemies.

1:18, 19 These two verses are treated as a parenthesis written by Luke and
not a part of Peter's message. They complete the historical facts concerning
Judas through the time of his death and
thus pave the way for the appointment
of his successor.

There is no contradiction between the
mode of Judas' death as given here, and
that which is found in Matthew 27:3–10.
Matthew states that after he had given
the thirty pieces of silver to the chief
priests and elders, he went out and
hanged himself. The chief priests then
took the money and bought a burial
ground.

Here in Acts, Luke says that Judas
purchased a field with the money, that
he fell **headlong ... and all his entrails
gushed out**.

Putting the two accounts together, it
appears that the actual purchase transaction concerning the field was arranged
by the chief priests. However, Judas
bought the **field** in the sense that it was
his money and they merely acted as his
agents. He hanged himself on a tree in
the cemetery, but the rope probably
broke, pitching his body forward and
causing it to **burst open**.

As this incident became known **in Jerusalem**, the potter's field came to be
called **Akel Dama, that is, Field of Blood**
or "bloody field" in Aramaic.

1:20 Peter's message now continues, after Luke's explanatory parenthesis. First, he explains that David was referring to the betrayer of Jesus in Psalm

69:25: **"Let his dwelling place be desolate, and let no one live in it."**[3]

Then he comes to the particular prophecy which must now be fulfilled: **"Let another take his office"** (Ps. 109:8). The Apostle Peter understood this to mean that after Judas' defection, a replacement must be appointed to fill **his office**. It is good to see his desire to obey the word of God.

1:21, 22 Whoever was to be chosen had to fulfill two requirements:

1. He had to be one who had **accompanied** the disciples during the three years of Christ's public ministry — **from** His **baptism** by **John** to His ascension.
2. He had to be able to bear responsible **witness** to the **resurrection** of the Lord.

1:23–26 The names of two men were put forward as possessing the necessary qualifications, **Joseph . . . surnamed Justus**, and **Matthias**. But which one was to be chosen? The apostles committed the matter to the Lord, asking for a revelation of His choice. Then **they cast lots** and **Matthias** was indicated as the proper successor to Judas, who had gone **to his own place**, i.e., eternal doom.

Two questions invariably arise here:

1. Were the disciples acting properly when they named **Matthias**? Should they have waited until God raised up the Apostle Paul to fill the vacancy?
2. Was it proper for them to **cast lots** in order to discern the mind of the Lord?

With regard to the first question, there is nothing in the record to indicate the disciples acted wrongly. They had been spending much time in prayer; they were seeking to obey the Scriptures; and they seemed to be of one mind in selecting a successor to Judas. Furthermore, the ministry of Paul was quite distinct from that of the twelve, and there is no suggestion that he was ever intended to replace Judas. The twelve were commissioned by Jesus on earth to preach to Israel, whereas Paul was called to the ministry by Christ in glory and sent to the Gentiles.

As far as casting lots was concerned, this method of discerning the divine will was recognized by the OT: "The lot is cast into the lap, but its every decision is from the LORD" (Prov. 16:33).

Apparently the choice of Matthias by lot was sanctioned by the Lord, because the apostles are thereafter called *"the twelve"* (see Acts 6:2).

PRAYER IN THE BOOK OF ACTS

Acts is a study in successful prayer. Already in chapter 1 we have seen the disciples praying on two different occasions. Their prayer in the upper room following the Ascension was answered by Pentecost. Their prayer for guidance in choosing a successor to Judas was answered by the lot's falling on Matthias. And so it is throughout the book.

Those who were converted on the day of Pentecost continued steadfastly in prayer (2:42). The succeeding verses (43–47) describe the ideal conditions which prevailed in this prayerful fellowship.

Following the release of Peter and John, the believers prayed for boldness (4:29). As a result, the place was shaken, they were all filled with the Holy Spirit, and they spoke the word of God with boldness (4:31).

The twelve suggested that seven men be chosen to handle financial matters so they themselves might devote their time more fully to prayer and the ministry of the Word (6:3, 4). The apostles then prayed and laid hands on the seven (6:6). The next verses record thrilling new triumphs for the gospel (6:7, 8).

Stephen prayed as he was about to be martyred (7:60). Chapter 9 records an answer to that prayer — the conversion of an onlooker, Saul of Tarsus.

Peter and John prayed for the Samaritans who believed, with the result that they received the Holy Spirit (8:15–17).

Following his conversion, Saul of Tarsus prayed in the house of Judas; God answered the prayer by sending Ananias to him (9:11–17).

Peter prayed at Joppa, and Dorcas was raised to life (9:40). As a result, many believed on the Lord (9:42).

The Gentile centurion Cornelius prayed (10:2); his prayers went up as a memorial before God (10:4). An angel appeared to him in a vision, instructing him to send for a man named Simon Peter (10:5). The next day Peter prayed

(10:9). His prayer was answered by a heavenly vision that prepared him to open the doors of the kingdom to Cornelius and other Gentiles (10:10–48).

When Peter was imprisoned, the Christians prayed for him earnestly (12:5). God answered by miraculously delivering him from jail — much to the astonishment of those who were praying (12:6–17).

The prophets and teachers at Antioch fasted and prayed (13:3). This launched the first missionary journey of Paul and Barnabas. It has been said that "this was the mightiest outreach of prayer ever seen; for it touched the ends of the earth, even to us, through Paul and Barnabas, the missionaries."

On a return trip to Lystra and Iconium and Antioch, Paul and Barnabas prayed for those who had believed (14:23). One of these was Timothy. Was it an answer to these prayers that Timothy joined Paul and Silas on their second missionary journey?

In prison at Philippi, the midnight prayers of Paul and Silas were answered by an earthquake and by the conversion of the jailer and his family (16:25–34).

Paul prayed with the Ephesian elders at Miletus (20:36); this brought a touching demonstration of their affection for him and of their grief that they would not see him again in this life.

The Christians at Tyre prayed with Paul on the beach (21:5), and these prayers doubtless followed him to Rome and to the executioner's block.

Prior to his shipwreck, Paul publicly prayed, giving thanks to God for the food. This brought cheer to the forlorn crew and passengers (27:35, 36).

On the island of Malta, Paul prayed for the governor's sick father. The result was that the patient was miraculously healed (28:8).

So it seems clear that prayer was the atmosphere in which the early church lived. And when Christians prayed, God worked! ‡

D. The Day of Pentecost and the Birth of the Church (2:1–47)

2:1 The Feast of **Pentecost**, typifying the pouring out of the Holy Spirit, was fifty days after the Feast of Firstfruits, which spoke of the resurrection of Christ. On this particular **Day of Pentecost** the disciples **were all with one accord in one place**. A fitting subject for their conversation might have been the OT passages dealing with the Feast of Pentecost (see Lev. 23:15, 16, for example). Or perhaps they were singing Psalm 133, "Behold, how good and how pleasant it is for brethren to dwell together in unity!"[4]

2:2 The coming of the Spirit involved a sound to hear, a sight to see, and a miracle to experience. The **sound**, which was **from heaven** and **filled the whole house**, was like **a rushing mighty wind**. **Wind** is one of several fluid types of the Holy Spirit (oil, fire, water), speaking of His sovereign, unpredictable movements.

2:3 The sight to see was **divided tongues, as of fire**, resting **upon each of** the disciples. It does not say they were tongues of fire, but **tongues as of fire**.

This phenomenon is not to be confused with the baptism of fire. Although the baptism of the Spirit and the baptism of fire are spoken of together (Matt. 3:11, 12; Luke 3:16, 17), they are two separate and distinct events. The first is a baptism of blessing, the second of judgment. The first affected believers, the second will affect unbelievers. By the first, believers were indwelt and empowered, and the church was formed. By the second, unbelievers will be destroyed.

When John the Baptist was addressing a mixed group (repentant and unrepentant, see Matt. 3:6, 7) he said Christ would baptize them with the Holy Spirit and fire (Matt. 3:11). When he was speaking only to those who were truly repentant (Mark 1:5), he said Christ would baptize them with the Holy Spirit (Mark 1:8).

What then is the meaning, in Acts 2:3, of the **divided tongues, as of fire**? The **tongues** doubtless refer to speech, and probably to the miraculous gift of speaking in other languages which the apostles were to receive at this time. The **fire** may refer to the Holy Spirit as the source of this gift, and may also describe the bold, burning, enthusiastic preaching which would follow.

The thought of enthusiastic utterance seems especially fitting, because enthusiasm is the normal condition of a Spirit-filled life, and witness is its inevitable outcome.

2:4 The miracle to experience, connected with Pentecost, was the filling of **the Holy Spirit**, followed by the speaking **with other tongues**.

Up to now, the Spirit of God had been *with* the disciples, but now He took up His residence *in* them (John 14:17). Thus the verse marks an important turning point in the Spirit's dealings with men. In the OT, the Spirit came upon men, but not as an abiding Resident (Ps. 51:11). Beginning with the Day of Pentecost, the Spirit of God indwelt people permanently: He came to stay (John 14:16).

On the Day of Pentecost, the believers were not only indwelt by the Holy Spirit, but they were filled with Him as well. We are indwelt by God's Spirit the moment we are saved, but to be filled with the Spirit we must study the Word, spend time in meditation and prayer, and live in obedience to the Lord.[5] If the filling of the Spirit were automatically guaranteed today, we would not be exhorted, "Be filled with the Spirit" (Eph. 5:18).

The coming of the Holy Spirit on the Day of Pentecost also formed believers into the church, the Body of Christ.

For by one Spirit we were all baptized into one body — whether Jews or Greeks, whether slaves or free — and have all been made to drink into one Spirit (1 Cor. 12:13). Henceforth, believing Jews and Gentiles would become one new man in Christ Jesus and members of the same Body (Eph. 2:11–22).

The disciples who were **filled with the Holy Spirit began to speak with other tongues, as the Spirit gave them utterance**. From the following verses, it is clear they were given the miraculous power to speak *actual foreign languages* which they had never studied. It was not gibberish or ecstatic utterances but definite languages then in use in other parts of the world. This gift of **tongues** was one of the signs or wonders which God used to bear witness to the truth of the message which the apostles preached (Heb. 2:3, 4). At that time, the NT had not been written. Since the complete word of God is now available in written form, the need for the sign gifts

has largely passed (though, of course, the sovereign Spirit of God could still use them if He so desired).

The occurrence of **tongues** on the Day of Pentecost should not be used to prove that **tongues** are the invariable accompaniment of the gift of the Spirit. If that were the case, why is there no mention of tongues in connection with:

1. The conversion of the 3,000 (Acts 2:41)?
2. The conversion of the 5,000 (Acts 4:4)?
3. The reception of the Holy Spirit by the Samaritans (Acts 8:17)?

In fact, the only other occurrences of the gift of **tongues** in the Book of Acts are:

1. At the conversion of the Gentiles in the house of Cornelius (Acts 10:46).
2. At the rebaptism of John's disciples in Ephesus (Acts 19:6).

Before leaving verse 4, we should mention that there is considerable difference among Bible students concerning the whole subject of the baptism of the Holy Spirit, both as to the number of times it has taken place, and the results flowing from it.

As to its frequency, some believe that:

1. It took place only once — at Pentecost. The Body of Christ was formed at that time, and all believers since then have entered into the good of the baptism.
2. It took place in three or four stages — at Pentecost (chap. 2); at Samaria (chap. 8); at the house of Cornelius (chap. 10); at Ephesus (chap. 19).
3. It takes place every time a person is saved.

As to its effect in the lives of individuals, some hold that it is a "second work of grace," commonly taking place after conversion, and resulting in a more or less complete sanctification. This view lacks scriptural support. As has already been mentioned, the baptism of the Holy Spirit is that operation by which believers were:

1. Incorporated into the church (1 Cor. 12:13).
2. Endued with power (Acts 1:8).

2:5–13 Jews, devout men had gathered **in Jerusalem** from all over the then-known world to observe the Feast of

Pentecost. When they heard the rumor of what had happened, they assembled at the house occupied by the apostles. Then, as now, men were attracted when the Spirit of God was at work.

By the time **the multitude** reached the house, the apostles were already speaking in tongues. Much to their amazement, the visitors heard these Galilean disciples speaking in a great variety of foreign languages. The miracle, however, was with those who spoke, not with those who heard. Whether those in the audience were Jews by birth or converts to Judaism, whether they were from east or west, north or south, each one heard **the** mighty **works of God** described **in his own language.** The word, **language,** used in verses 6 and 8 is the one from which we get our word, "dialect."

It is widely believed that one purpose of the gift of tongues at Pentecost was to proclaim the gospel to people of different languages simultaneously. For instance, one writer says, "God gave His law in one language to one nation, but He gave His gospel in all languages to all nations."

But the text does not bear this out. Those who spoke in tongues were declaring **the wonderful works of God** (2:11). This was a sign to the people of Israel (1 Cor. 14:21, 22), intended to excite amazement and marvel. Peter, by contrast, preached the gospel in a language that most, if not all, of his audience could understand.

The response to the tongues among the visitors was varied. Some seemed deeply interested, whereas others accused the apostles of being **full of new wine**. The disciples were indeed under an influence outside their own power, but it was the influence of the Holy Spirit, not of **wine**!

Unregenerate men are always ready to offer a natural explanation for spiritual phenomena. Once when God's voice was heard from heaven, some said it thundered (John 12:28, 29). Now unbelievers mockingly explained the exhilaration caused by the coming of the Spirit in terms of **new wine**. "The world," said Schiller, "likes to tarnish shining objects, and to drag those that are exalted down to the dust."

2:14 The disciple who had denied his Lord with oaths and curses now steps forward to address the throng. No longer the timid and vacillating follower, he has become lion-like and forceful. Pentecost has made the difference. **Peter** is now filled with the Spirit.

At Caesarea Philippi, the Lord had promised to give Peter the keys of the kingdom of heaven (Matt. 16:19). Here in Acts 2 we see him using the keys to open the door to the Jews (v. 14) as later, in chapter 10, he will open it to the Gentiles.

2:15 First the apostle explains that the unusual events of the day were not the result of new wine. After all, **it** was **only** 9:00 a.m., and it would be virtually unheard of for so many to be **drunk** at that early hour. Also, Jews engaged in the exercises of the synagogue on a feast day abstained from eating and drinking until 10:00 a.m., or even noon, depending on when the daily sacrifice was offered.

2:16–19 The true explanation was that the Spirit of God had been poured out, as **spoken by the prophet Joel** (Joel 2:28ff).

Actually, the events of Pentecost were not a complete fulfillment of Joel's prophecy. Most of the phenomena described in verses 17–20 did not take place at this time. But what did happen at Pentecost was a foretaste of what would happen **in the last days**, prior to **the great and awesome day of the LORD**. If Pentecost fulfilled Joel's prophecy, why is a promise given later (3:19) that if there was national repentance and Israel received the One they had crucified, He would come back and bring in the day of the Lord?

The quotation from Joel is an example of the Law of Double Reference, by which a Bible prophecy has a partial fulfillment at one time and a complete fulfillment at a later time.

The Spirit of God *was* poured out at Pentecost but not literally on *all* flesh. The final fulfillment of the prophecy will take place at the end of the Tribulation Period. Prior to the glorious return of Christ, there will be **wonders** in the heavens, and **signs** on the earth (Matt. 24:29, 30). The Lord Jesus Christ will then appear on the earth to put down

His enemies and to establish His kingdom. At the beginning of His thousand-year reign, the Spirit of God will be poured out **on all flesh**, Gentiles as well as Jews, and this condition will prevail, for the most part, throughout the Millennium. Various manifestations of the Spirit will be given without regard to sex, age, or social status. There will be **visions** and **dreams**, which suggest the reception of knowledge; and prophecy, which suggests its impartation to others. Thus, the gifts of revelation and communication will be in evidence. All this will occur in what Joel described as **the last days** (v. 17). This, of course, refers to the last days of Israel and not of the church.

2:20 The supernatural signs in the heavens are distinctly said to occur **before the coming of the . . . day of the LORD**. In this context, **the day of the LORD** refers to His personal return to the earth to destroy His foes and to reign in power and great glory.

2:21 Peter closes the quotation from Joel with the promise that **whoever calls on the name of the LORD shall be saved**. This is the good news for all ages, that salvation is offered to all people on the principle of faith in the Lord. **The name of the LORD** is an expression that includes all that the Lord is. Thus, to **call on** His **name** is to **call on** Himself as the true object of faith and as the only way of salvation.

2:22–24 But who is the Lord? Peter will next announce the startling news that this Jesus whom they had crucified is both Lord and Christ. He does so first by speaking of the life of Jesus, then His death, resurrection, ascension, and finally His glorification at **the right hand of God** the Father. If they had any illusions that **Jesus** was still in a Judean tomb, Peter will soon disabuse their minds! They must be told that the One they had murdered is in heaven, and they must still reckon with Him.

Here then is the flow of the apostle's argument: **Jesus of Nazareth** was demonstrated to be **a Man** from **God by** the many **miracles** He performed in the power of **God** (v. 22). In His **determined purpose and foreknowledge**, **God delivered Him** into the hands of the Jewish people. They, in turn, turned Him over to the Gentiles (men without the law) to

be **crucified and put to death** (v. 23). However, **God raised** Him **up** from among the dead, **having loosed the pains**[6] **of death**. **It was not possible** for death to hold Him a prisoner **because**:

1. The character of God demanded His resurrection. He had died, the Sinless for the sinful. God must raise Him as proof of His complete satisfaction with the redemptive work of Christ.

2. The prophecies of the OT demanded His resurrection. This is the particular point which Peter presses in the following verses.

2:25–27 In Psalm 16 David had written prophetically concerning the Lord's life, death, resurrection, and glorification.

As to His life, **David** described the unbounded confidence and assurance of One who lived in uninterrupted fellowship with His Father. **Heart**, **tongue**, and **flesh** — His whole being was filled with joy and **hope**.

As to His death, David **foresaw** that God **would not leave** His **soul in Hades, nor** would He allow His **Holy One to see corruption**. In other words, the **soul** of the Lord Jesus would not be left in the disembodied state, neither would His body be permitted to disintegrate. (This verse should not be used to prove that the Lord Jesus went to some prison house of departed spirits in the lowest parts of the earth at the time of His death. His soul went to heaven[7] — Luke 23:43 — and His body was placed in the tomb.)

2:28 As to the resurrection of the Lord, David expressed confidence that God would show Him the path of life. In Psalm 16:11a, David wrote, "You will show me the path of life." In Acts 2:28a, Peter quoted it, **You have made known to me the ways of life**. Peter changed the future tense to the past tense. The Holy Spirit obviously directed him to do this since the resurrection was now past.

The present glorification of the Savior was predicted by David in the words, **You will make me full of joy in Your presence**, or as Psalm 16:11 puts it, "In Your presence is fullness of joy; at Your right hand are pleasures forevermore."

2:29 Peter argues that **David** could not have been saying these things about himself, because *his body had seen corrup-*

tion. **His tomb** was well known to the Jews of that day. They knew he had not been raised.

2:30, 31 When he wrote the Psalm, **David** was speaking as **a prophet**. He remembered that **God** had promised to **raise up** One of his descendants **to sit on his throne** forever. **David** realized that this One would be the Messiah, and that though He would die, His **soul** would not be **left in** the disembodied condition, and His body would not decay.

2:32, 33 Now Peter repeats an announcement that must have shocked his Jewish audience. The Messiah of whom **David** prophesied was **Jesus** of Nazareth. **God** had **raised** Him from among the dead, as the apostles could all testify because they were eyewitnesses to His resurrection. Following His resurrection, the Lord Jesus was **exalted to the right hand of God**, and now **the Holy Spirit** had been sent as promised by **the Father**. This was the explanation of what had happened in Jerusalem earlier in the day.

2:34, 35 Had not **David** also predicted the exaltation of the Messiah? He was not speaking of himself in Psalm 110:1. Instead he was quoting Jehovah as saying to the Messiah, **"Sit at My right hand, till I make Your enemies Your footstool."** (Note carefully that verses 33–35 predict a waiting time between the glorification of Christ and His return to punish His enemies and set up His kingdom.)

2:36 Now, once again, the announcement comes crashing down upon the Jewish people. GOD HAS MADE BOTH LORD AND CHRIST — THIS JESUS WHOM YOU CRUCIFIED (Gk. word order). As Bengel said, "The sting of the speech is put at the end" — **THIS JESUS, whom you crucified**. They had **crucified** God's Anointed One, and the coming of the Holy Spirit was evidence that Jesus had been exalted in heaven (see John 7:39).

2:37 So mighty was the convicting power of the Holy Spirit that there was an immediate response from the audience. Without any invitation or appeal from Peter, they cried out, **"What shall we do?"** The question was prompted by

a deep sense of guilt. They now realized that the Jesus whom they had slain was God's beloved Son! This Jesus had been raised from the dead and was now exalted in heaven. This being so, how could these guilty murderers possibly escape judgment?

2:38 Peter's answer was that they should **repent and be baptized in the name of Jesus Christ for the remission of sins**. First, they were to **repent**, acknowledging their guilt, and taking sides with God against themselves.

Then they were to **be baptized for** (or unto) **the remission of** their **sins**. At first glance, this verse seems to teach salvation by baptism, and many people insist that this is precisely what it *does* mean. Such an interpretation is impossible for the following reasons:

1. In dozens of NT passages, salvation is said to be by faith in the Lord Jesus Christ (John 1:12; 3:16, 36; 6:47; Acts 16:31; Rom. 10:9, for example). No verse or two could conceivably contradict such overwhelming testimony.

2. The thief on the cross had the assurance of salvation apart from baptism (Luke 23:43).

3. The Savior is not stated to have baptized anyone, a strange omission if baptism is essential to salvation.

4. The Apostle Paul was thankful that he baptized only a few of the Corinthians — a strange cause for thankfulness if baptism has saving merit (1 Cor. 1:14–16).

It is important to notice that only Jews were ever told to be baptized for the forgiveness of sins (see Acts 22:16). In this fact, we believe, is the secret to the understanding of this passage. The nation of Israel had crucified the Lord of glory. The Jewish people had cried out, "His blood be on us and on our children" (Matt. 27:25). The guilt of the Messiah's death was thus claimed by the people of Israel.

Now, some of these Jews had come to realize their mistake. By repentance they acknowledged their sin to God. By trusting the Lord Jesus as their Savior they were regenerated and received eternal forgiveness of sins. By public water baptism they dissociated themselves from *the nation* that crucified the Lord and identified themselves with *Him*. Baptism thus became the outward sign that their sin in connection with the rejection of Christ (as well as all their sins) had been washed away. It took them off Jewish ground and placed them on Christian ground. But baptism did not save them. Only faith in Christ could do that. To teach otherwise is to teach another gospel and thus be accursed (Gal. 1:8, 9).

An alternative interpretation of baptism **for the remission of sins** is given by Ryrie:

> This does not mean in order that sins might be remitted, for everywhere in the New Testament sins are forgiven as a result of faith in Christ, not as a result of baptism. It means be baptized because of the remission of sins. The Greek preposition *eis*, for, has this meaning "because of" not only here but also in such a passage as Matthew 12:41 where the meaning can only be "they repented because of [not in order to] the preaching of Jonah." Repentance brought the remission of sins for this Pentecostal crowd, and because of the remission of sins they were asked to be baptized.[8]

Peter assured them that if they repented and were **baptized**, they would **receive the gift of the Holy Spirit**. To insist that this order applies to us today is to misunderstand God's administrative dealings in the early days of the church. As H. P. Barker has so ably pointed out in *The Vicar of Christ*, there are four communities of believers in the Book of Acts, and the order of events in connection with the reception of the Holy Spirit is different in each case.

Here in Acts 2:38 we read about *Jewish* Christians. For them, the order was:
1. Repentance.
2. Water baptism.
3. Reception of the Holy Spirit.

The conversion of *Samaritans* is recorded in Acts 8:14–17. There we read that the following events occurred:
1. They believed.
2. They were baptized in water.
3. The apostles prayed for them.
4. The apostles laid their hands on them.
5. They received the Holy Spirit.

In Acts 10:44–48 the conversion of *Gentiles* is in view. Notice the order here:
1. Faith.
2. Reception of the Holy Spirit.
3. Water baptism.

A final community of believers is made up of *disciples of John the Baptist*, Acts 19:1–7:
1. They believed.
2. They were rebaptized.
3. The Apostle Paul laid his hands on them.
4. They received the Holy Spirit.

Does this mean there were four ways of salvation in the Book of Acts? Of course not. Salvation was, is, and always will be on the basis of faith in the Lord. But during the transition period recorded in Acts, God chose to vary the events connected with the reception of the Holy Spirit for reasons which He knew but did not choose to reveal to us.

Then which of these patterns applies to us today? Since Israel nationally has rejected the Messiah, the Jewish people have forfeited any special privileges they might have had. Today God is calling out of the Gentiles a people for His Name (Acts 15:14). Therefore, the order for *today* is that which is found in Acts 10:
Faith.
Reception of the Holy Spirit.
Water baptism.

We believe this order applies to all today, to Jews as well as to Gentiles. This may sound arbitrary at first. It might be asked, "When did the order in Acts 2:38 cease to apply to Jews and the order in Acts 10:44–48 begin?" No definite date can be given, of course. But the Book of Acts traces a gradual transition from the gospel's going out primarily to Jews, to its being repeatedly rejected by the Jews, to its going out to the Gentiles. By the end of the Book of Acts the nation of Israel had been largely set aside. By unbelief it had forfeited any special claim as God's chosen people. During the Church Age it would be reckoned with the Gentile nations, and God's order for the Gentiles, outlined in Acts 10:44–48, would apply.

2:39 Peter next reminds them that **the promise** of the Holy Spirit **is to them and to** their **children** (the Jewish people) **and to all who are afar off** (the Gentiles), even **as many as . . . God** would **call**.

The very people who had said, "His blood be on us and on our children," are now assured of grace for themselves and their children if they will trust the Lord.

This verse has often been used mistakenly to teach that children of believing parents are thereby assured of covenant privileges, or that they are saved. Spurgeon answers this effectively:

> Will not the Church of God know that "that which is born of the flesh is flesh, and that which is born of the Spirit is Spirit?" "Who can bring a clean thing out of an unclean?" The natural birth communicates nature's filthiness, but it cannot convey peace. Under the new covenant, we are expressly told that the sons of God are "born, not of blood, nor of the will of the flesh, nor of the will of man, but of God."[9]

The important thing to notice is that **the promise** is not only **to you and to your children** but **to all who are afar off, as many as the Lord our God will call**. It is as inclusive as the "whosoever" of the gospel invitation.

2:40 Not all of Peter's message is recorded in this chapter, but the gist of the remainder was that the Jewish hearers should save themselves from the crooked, **perverse generation** that rejected and murdered the Lord Jesus. They could do this by receiving Jesus as their Messiah and Savior and by publicly disclaiming any further connection with the guilty nation of Israel through Christian baptism.

2:41 There was a great forward surge of people, desiring to be baptized as outward evidence that they had **gladly**[10] **received** Peter's **word** as the word of the Lord.

There **were added** to the company of believers that day **about three thousand souls**. If the best proof of a Holy Spirit ministry is the conversion of souls, then surely Peter's was that kind of ministry. Doubtless this Galilean fisherman was reminded of the words of the Lord Jesus, "I will make you fishers of men" (Matt. 4:19). And perhaps of the Savior's saying, "Most assuredly, I say to you, he who believes in Me, the works that I do he will do also; and greater works than

these he will do; because I go to My Father" (John 14:12).

It is instructive to notice the care with which the number of converts is recorded — *about* **three thousand souls.** All servants of the Lord might exercise similar caution in tabulating so-called decisions for Christ.

2:42 The proof of reality is in continuance. These converts proved the reality of their profession by continuing **steadfastly in**:

1. **The apostles' doctrine**. This means the inspired teachings of the apostles, delivered orally at first, and now preserved in the NT.

2. **Fellowship**. Another evidence of new life was the desire of the new believers to be with the people of God and share things in common with them. There was a sense of being separated to God from the world, and a community of interests with other Christians.

3. **The breaking of bread**. This expression is used in the NT to refer both to the Lord's Supper and to eating a common meal. The meaning in any particular case must be determined by the sense of the passage. Here it obviously refers to the Lord's Supper, since it would be quite unnecessary to say that they continued steadfastly eating their meals. From Acts 20:7 we learn that the practice of the early Christians was to break bread on the first day of the week. During the early days of the church, a love feast was held in connection with the Lord's Supper as an expression of the love of the saints for one another. However, abuses crept in, and the "agape" or love feast was discontinued.

4. **Prayers**. This was the fourth principal practice of the early church, and expressed complete dependence on the Lord for worship, guidance, preservation, and service.

2:43 A sense of reverential awe came over the people. The mighty power of the Holy Spirit was so evident that hearts were hushed and subdued. Astonishment filled their souls as they saw **the apostles** performing **many wonders and signs. Wonders** were miracles which excited wonder and amazement. **Signs**

were miracles designed to convey instruction. A miracle could be both a *wonder* and a *sign*.

2:44, 45 The believers continually assembled together and held **all things in common** trust. So mightily was the love of God shed abroad in their hearts that they did not look upon **their** material **possessions** as their own (4:32). Whenever there was a genuine case of **need** in the fellowship, they sold personal property and distributed the proceeds. Thus there was an equality.

> Among those who believed was manifested a unity of heart and interest, in which the natural selfishness of the fallen condition was swallowed up in the fulness of a love which the sense of the divine love had begotten. They were together in such sort that all they had was held in common; not by any law or outward constraint, which would have spoiled it all, but in the consciousness of what they were all to Christ, and what Christ was to each and all of them. Enriched by Him with a blessing which nothing could diminish, but the more they ministered it, the more they had it, "they sold their possessions and goods, and distributed them to all, as any one had need."[11]

Many argue today that we need not follow the early believers in this practice. One might just as well contend that we should not love our neighbors as ourselves. This sharing of all one's real estate and personal property was the inevitable fruit of lives that were filled with the Holy Spirit. It has been said, "A real Christian could not bear to have too much when others have too little."

2:46 This verse gives the effect of Pentecost on religious life and home life.

As to *religious life*, we must remember that these early converts were of Jewish background. Although the church was now in existence, the ties with the Jewish temple were not severed immediately. The process of throwing off the graveclothes of Judaism continued throughout the period of the Acts. And so the believers continued to attend the services **in the temple**,[12] where they heard the OT read and expounded. In addition, of course, they met together in homes for the functions listed in verse 42.

As to their *home life*, we read that they broke **bread**, taking **their food with gladness and simplicity of heart**. Here it seems clear that the **breaking** of **bread** refers to the eating of regular meals. The joy of their salvation overflowed into every detail of life, gilding the mundane with an aura of glory.

2:47 Life became an anthem of praise and a psalm of thanksgiving for those who had been delivered from the power of darkness and translated into the Kingdom of the Son of God's love.

At the outset, the believers had **favor with all the people**. But this was not to last. The nature of the Christian faith is such that it inevitably stirs up the hatred and opposition of the human heart. The Savior warned His disciples to beware of popularity (Luke 6:26), and promised them persecution and tribulation (Matt. 10:22, 23). So this **favor** was a momentary phase, soon to be replaced by unrelenting opposition.

And the Lord added to the church daily those who were being saved. The Christian fellowship grew by conversions each day. Those who heard the gospel were responsible to accept Jesus Christ by a definite act of the will. The Lord's electing and adding does not rule out human responsibility.

In this chapter, then, we have had the account of the outpouring of the Holy Spirit, Peter's memorable address to the assembled Jews, the conversion of a great multitude, and a brief description of life among the early believers. An excellent resume of the latter was given in the *Encyclopaedia Brittanica*, 13th edition, in the article on "Church History":

> The most notable thing about the life of the early Christians was their vivid sense of being a people of God, called and set apart. The Christian Church in their thought was a divine, not a human, institution. It was founded and controlled by God, and even the world was created for its sake. This conception . . . controlled all the life of the early Christians, both individual and social. They regarded themselves as separate from the rest of the world and bound together by peculiar ties. Their citizenship was in heaven, not on earth, and the principles and laws by which they strove to govern themselves were from above. The present world was but temporary, and their true life was in

the future. Christ was soon to return, and the employments and labors and pleasures of this age were of small concern. . . . In the everyday life of Christians the Holy Spirit was present, and all the Christian graces were the fruits. A result of this belief was to give their lives a peculiarly enthusiastic or inspirational character. Theirs were not the everyday experiences of ordinary men, but of men lifted out of themselves and transported into a higher sphere.

Just to read this article is to realize in some measure how far the church has drifted from its original vigor and solidarity!

THE HOUSE CHURCH AND PARACHURCH ORGANIZATIONS

Since the first use of the word *church* (Gk. *ekklēsia*) in Acts is found here[13] (2:47), we pause to consider the centrality of the church in the thinking of the early Christians.

The church in the Book of Acts and in the rest of the NT was what is often called a house church. The early Christians met in houses rather than in special ecclesiastical buildings. It has been said that religion was loosed from specially sacred places and centered in that universal place of living, the home. Unger says that homes continued to serve as places of Christian assembly for two centuries.[14]

It might be easy for us to think that the use of private homes was forced by economic necessity rather than being the result of spiritual considerations. We have become so accustomed to church buildings and chapels that we think they are God's ideal.

However, there is strong reason to believe that the first century believers might have been wiser than we are.

First, it is inconsistent with the Christian faith and its emphasis on love to spend thousands of dollars on luxurious buildings when there is such appalling need throughout the world. In that connection, E. Stanley Jones wrote:

I looked on the Bambino, the child Christ in the Cathedral at Rome, laden with expensive jewels, and then walked out and looked upon the countenance of hungry children and wondered whether Christ, in view of this hunger, was enjoying His jewels. And the thought persisted that if He was, then I could no longer enjoy the thought of Christ. That bejeweled Bambino and the hungry children are a symbol of what we have done in putting around Christ the expensive livery of stately cathedrals and churches while leaving untouched the fundamental wrongs in human society whereby Christ is left hungry in the unemployed and the dispossessed.[15]

Not only is it inhumane; it is also uneconomical to spend money on expensive buildings that are used for no more than three, four, or five hours during the week. How have we ever allowed ourselves to drift into this unthinking dream world where we are willing to spend so much in order to get so little usage in return?

Our modern building programs have been one of the biggest hindrances to the expansion of the church. Heavy payments on principal and interest cause church leaders to resist any efforts to hive off and form new churches. Any loss of members would jeopardize the income needed to pay for the building and its upkeep. An unborn generation is saddled with debt, and any hope of church reproduction is stifled.

It is often argued that we must have impressive buildings in order to attract the unchurched to our services. Aside from being a carnal way of thinking, this completely overlooks the NT pattern. The meetings of the early church were largely for believers. The Christians assembled for the apostles' teaching, fellowship, breaking of bread, and prayer (Acts 2:42). They did not do their evangelizing by inviting people to meetings on Sunday but by witnessing to those with whom they came in contact throughout the week. When people did get converted, they were then brought into the fellowship and warmth of the house church to be fed and encouraged.

It is sometimes difficult to get people to attend services in dignified church buildings. There is a strong reaction against formalism. Also there is a fear of being solicited for funds. "All the church wants is your money," is a common complaint. Yet many of these same people are willing to attend a conversational Bible class in a home. There they do not have to be style-conscious, and they enjoy the informal, unprofessional atmosphere.

Actually the house church is ideal for every culture and every country. And probably if we could look over the entire world, we would see more churches meeting in homes than in any other way.

In contrast to today's imposing cathedrals, churches, and chapels — as well as a whole host of highly organized denominations, mission boards, and *parachurch* organizations, the apostles in the Book of Acts made no attempt to form an organization of any kind for carrying on the work of the Lord. The local church was God's unit on earth for propagating the faith and the disciples were content to work within that context.

In recent years there has been an organizational explosion in Christendom of such proportions as to make one dizzy. Every time a believer gets a new idea for advancing the cause of Christ, he forms a new mission board, corporation, or institution!

One result is that capable teachers and preachers have been called away from their primary ministries in order to become administrators. If all mission board administrators were serving on the mission field, it would greatly reduce the need for personnel there.

Another result of the proliferation of organizations is that vast sums of money are needed for overhead, and thus diverted from direct gospel outreach. The greater part of every dollar given to many Christian organizations is devoted to the expense of maintaining the organization rather than to the primary purpose for which it was founded.

Organizations often hinder the fulfillment of the Great Commission. Jesus told His disciples to teach all the things He had commanded. Many who work for Christian organizations find they are not permitted to teach all the truth of God. They must not teach certain controversial matters for fear they will alienate the constituency to whom they look for financial support.

The multiplication of Christian institutions has too often resulted in factions, jealousy, and rivalry that have done great harm to the testimony of Christ.

Consider the overlapping multiplicity of Christian organizations at work, at home, and abroad. Each competes for limited personnel and for shrinking financial resources. And consider how many of these organizations really owe their origin to purely human rivalry, though public statements usually refer to God's will (Daily Notes of the Scripture Union).

And it is often true that organizations have a way of perpetuating themselves long after they have outlived their usefulness. The wheels grind on heavily even though the vision of the founders has been lost, and the glory of a once dynamic movement has departed. It was spiritual wisdom, not primitive naivete, that saved the early Christians from setting up human organizations to carry on the work of the Lord. G. H. Lang writes:

An acute writer, contrasting the apostolic work with the more usual modern missionary methods, has said that "we found missions, the apostles founded churches." The distinction is sound and pregnant. The apostles founded churches, *and they founded nothing else*, because for the ends in view nothing else was required or could have been so suitable. In each place where they laboured they formed the converts into a local assembly, with elders — always elders, never an elder (Acts 14:23; 15:6, 23; 20:17; Phil. 1:1) — to guide, to rule, to shepherd, men qualified by the Lord and recognized by the saints (1 Cor. 16:15; 1 Thess. 5:12, 13; 1 Tim. 5:17–19); and with deacons, appointed by the assembly (Acts 6:1–6; Phil. 1:1) — in this contrasted with the elders — to attend to the few but very important temporal affairs, and in particular to the distribution of the funds of the assembly. . . . All they (the apostles) did in the way of organizing was to form the disciples gathered into other such assemblies. No other organization than the local assembly appears in the New Testament, nor do we find even the germ of anything further.[16]

To the early Christians and their apostolic leadership, the congregation was the divinely ordained unit on earth through which God chose to work, and the *only* such unit to which He promised perpetuity was *the church.* ‡

E. The Healing of a Lame Man, and Peter's Charge to Israel (3:1–26)

3:1 It was 3:00 p.m. when **Peter and John went up together to the temple** in

Jerusalem. As mentioned previously, the early Jewish Christians continued to attend the temple services for some time after the church was formed. This was a period of adjustment and transition, and the break with Judaism was not made instantaneously. Believers today would not be justified in following their example in this, since we have the full revelation of the NT and are told to "go forth to Him, outside the camp, bearing His reproach" (Heb. 13:13. See also 2 Cor. 6:17, 18).

3:2 As they approached the temple, they saw men carrying a crippled beggar to his customary spot at the **gate . . . called Beautiful**. The helpless condition of this man, **lame** since birth, is in marked contrast to the beauty of the architecture of the temple. It reminds us of the poverty and ignorance which abound in the very shadow of great cathedrals, and of the helplessness of mighty ecclesiastical systems to assist those who are physical and spiritual cripples.

3:3 The lame man had obviously given up hope of ever being cured, so he contented himself to ask for a handout.

3:4 Instead of looking on this man as a helpless wretch, **Peter** saw him as one in whom the mighty power of God might be demonstrated! "If we are led by the Spirit, we will fix our eyes on those whom God intends to bless, instead of firing blank cartridges and beating the air" (Selected).

Peter's command, **"Look at us,"** was not intended to attract publicity to John and himself, but merely to insure the undivided attention of the beggar.

3:5, 6 Still **expecting** nothing more than financial help, the cripple **gave them his attention**. Then he heard an announcement that was both disappointing and thrilling to him. As far as a handout was concerned, Peter had nothing to give. But he had something better to give. By the authority **of Jesus Christ of Nazareth**, he commanded the lame man to **rise up and walk**. A witty old preacher said, "The crippled beggar asked for *alms* and he got *legs*."

It is said that Thomas Aquinas visited the pope at a time when large sums of money were being counted. The pope boasted, "We need no longer say with Peter, 'Silver and gold I do not have!' " Aquinas replied, "Neither can you say with Peter, 'Rise up and walk!' "

3:7 As Peter helped the man to his feet, **strength** flowed into the hitherto useless **feet and ankle bones**. Here we are reminded again that in the spiritual life, there is a curious mingling of the divine and the human. Peter helps the man to his feet; then God performs the cure. We must do what we can do; then God will do what we cannot do.

3:8 The miracle of healing was immediate, not gradual. Notice how the Spirit of God multiplies words of action and movement: **leaping up, stood . . . walked and entered . . . walking, leaping**.

When we remember the slow, painful process an infant goes through in learning to walk, we realize how wonderful it was for this man to walk and leap right away, for the first time in his life.

This miracle, performed in the Name of Jesus, was a further testimony to the people of Israel that the One they had crucified was alive and was willing to be their Healer and Savior.

3:9, 10 The fact that the beggar had lain daily at the door of the temple made him a familiar sight. Now that he was healed, the miracle was necessarily generally known. **The people** could not deny that a mighty miracle had taken place, but what was the meaning of it all?

3:11 As the **healed** man **held on to Peter and John**, as to his physicians, **all the people ran together** at **Solomon's porch**, a portion of the temple area. Their amazement and wonder provided the opportunity for Peter to preach to them.

3:12 **Peter** first diverts the attention of the people from the cured man, and from the apostles. The explanation of the miracle was not to be found in any of them.

3:13–16 Quickly he brings them to the true Author of the miracle. It was Jesus, the One they had rejected, denied, and **killed**. **God raised** Him **from the dead** and **glorified** Him in heaven. Now, **through faith in** Him, **this man**

had been cured of his helplessness.

Peter's holy boldness in accusing the men of Israel is remarkable. His charges against them are:

1. They **delivered up** Jesus (to the Gentiles for trial).
2. They **denied** Him **in the presence of Pilate, when he was determined to release Him**.
3. They **denied the Holy One and the Just, and asked for** the release of **a murderer** (Barabbas).
4. They **killed the Prince** (or Author) **of life**.

Notice, by contrast, God's treatment of Jesus:

1. He **raised** Him **from the dead** (v. 15).
2. He **glorified His Servant Jesus** — not His Son Jesus, as in the 1611 Version (v. 13).

Notice finally the emphasis on **faith** in Christ as the explanation of the miracle of healing (v. 16). In this verse, as elsewhere, the **name** stands for the person. Thus, **faith in His name** means **faith in** Christ.

3:17 There is a distinct change in Peter's tone in this verse. Having charged the men of Israel with the death of the Lord Jesus, he now addresses them as his Jewish **brethren**, graciously allowing that they **did it in ignorance**, and urging them to repent and be converted.

It almost seems contradictory to hear Peter say that the Jews crucified the Lord Jesus in ignorance. Did He not come with the full credentials of the Messiah? Did He not perform wondrous miracles in their midst? Did He not infuriate them by claiming to be equal with God? Yes, this is all true. And yet they were ignorant of the fact that Jesus Christ was God incarnate. They expected the Messiah to come, not in lowly grace, but rather as a mighty military deliverer. They looked upon Jesus as an impostor.

They did not know He was truly the Son of God. They probably thought they were doing God a service in killing Him. Thus the Savior Himself said at the time of the crucifixion, "They do not know what they do" (Luke 23:34), and Paul later wrote, "Had they [the princes of this age] known, they would not have

crucified the Lord of glory" (1 Cor. 2:8).

All this was designed to assure the men of Israel that their sin, however great, was still subject to the forgiving grace of God.

3:18 Without excusing their sin, Peter shows that **God** overruled it to fulfill His own purposes. The **prophets** of the OT had predicted that the Messiah **would suffer**. The Jewish people were the ones who inflicted the suffering on Him. But now He offered Himself to them as Lord and Savior. Through Him they could receive forgiveness of their sins.

3:19 The people of Israel should **repent** and make an about-face. When they would do this, their **sins** would **be blotted out, so that times of refreshing may come**.

It must be remembered that this message is addressed to the men of Israel (v. 12). It emphasizes that national repentance must precede national restoration and blessing. The **times of refreshing . . . from the presence of the Lord** refer to the blessings of Christ's future kingdom on earth, as mentioned in the next verse.

3:20[†] Following Israel's repentance, God will **send** the Messiah, **Jesus**. As mentioned previously, this refers to the Second Advent of Christ to set up His thousand-year reign on the earth.

3:21 The question inevitably arises at this point, "If Israel had repented when Peter was speaking, would the Lord Jesus have returned to earth?" Great and godly men have differed on this subject. Some insist He would have returned; otherwise, they say the promise was not a bona fide one. Others take the passage as being prophetic, as showing the order of events that would actually take place. The question is a purely hypothetical one. The facts are that Israel did not repent, and the Lord Jesus has not returned.

It is clear from verse 21 that **God** foresaw that the nation of Israel would reject Christ, and that the present age of grace would intervene before His Second Coming. **Heaven must receive** Christ **until the times of restoration of all things**. **The times of restoration of all things** point forward to the Millennium.

[†]*See p. xx.*

They do not indicate universal salvation, as some have suggested; such a teaching is foreign to the Bible. Rather they point to the time when creation will be delivered from the bondage of corruption and Christ will reign in righteousness as King over all the earth.

These **times of restoration** had been foretold by the **prophets** of the OT period.

Verse 21 has been used in an effort to disprove the pretribulation Rapture. The argument is that if the heavens must receive Jesus until the beginning of the Millennium, then He cannot come before then to take the church home to heaven. The answer, of course, is that Peter is speaking here to the men of Israel (v. 12). He is discussing God's dealings with Israel nationally. *As far as the nation of Israel is concerned*, the Lord Jesus will remain in heaven until He comes to reign at the end of the Tribulation. But individual Jews who believe on Him during this Church Age will share with believing Gentiles in the Rapture of the church, which could take place at any moment. Also, in the Rapture, the Lord does not leave the heavens; we go to Him in the air.

3:22 As an example of an OT prophecy looking forward to Christ's glorious reign, Peter quotes Deuteronomy 18:15, 18, 19. The passage pictures the Lord Jesus as God's **Prophet** in Israel's golden age, announcing God's will and law.

When Moses said, **"The LORD your God will raise up for you a Prophet like me,"** he did not mean likeness as to character or ability, but likeness in the sense that both were *raised up by God.* "He will raise Him up as He raised me up."

3:23 During Christ's reign on earth, those who refuse to **hear** and obey Him will **be utterly destroyed**. Of course, those who reject Him today suffer eternal judgment also, but the primary thought of this passage is that Christ will yet rule with a rod of iron and that those who disobey Him and rebel against Him will be promptly executed.

3:24 To further emphasize that the times of restoration were well predicted, Peter adds that **all the prophets from** Samuel and his successors spoke of **these days**.

3:25 Peter now reminds his Jewish hearers that the promise of these times of blessing was made to them as **sons of the prophets** and descendants of Abraham. After all, **God** had **made** a **covenant** with **Abraham** to bless **all the families of the earth** in his **seed**. All the promises of millennial blessing center in the **Seed**, i.e., in Christ. They should therefore accept the Lord Jesus as Messiah.

3:26   God had already **raised up His Servant** (3:13), and had **sent Him** first to the nation of Israel. This refers to the Incarnation and life of our Lord rather than to His resurrection. If they would receive Him, He would turn **away every one of** them **from** their **iniquities**.

In this sermon by Peter, delivered to the people of Israel, we notice that it is *the kingdom* that is in view rather than *the church*. Also the emphasis is national rather than individual. The Spirit of God is lingering over Israel in longsuffering mercy, pleading with God's ancient people to receive the glorified Lord Jesus as Messiah and thus hasten the advent of Christ's kingdom on earth.

But Israel would not hear.

F. The Persecution and Growth of the Church (4:1–7:60)

4:1–4 The first persecution of the infant church was about to break out. True to pattern, it arose from the religious leaders. **The priests, the captain of the temple, and the Sadducees** rose up against the apostles.

Scroggie suggests that **the priests** represent religious intolerance; **the captain of the temple**, political enmity; and **the Sadducees**, rationalistic unbelief. **The Sadducees** denied the doctrine of resurrection. This brought them into open conflict with the apostles, since **the resurrection** was the keynote of apostolic preaching! Spurgeon sees a parallel:

> The Sadducees, as you know, were the Broad School, the liberals, the advanced thinkers, the modern-thought people of the day. If you want a bitter sneer, a biting sarcasm, or a cruel action, I commend you to these large-hearted gentlemen. They are liberal to everybody, except to

those who hold the truth; and for those they have a reserve of concentrated bitterness which far excels wormwood and gall. They are so liberal to their brother errorists that they have no tolerance to spare for evangelicals.[17]

These leaders resented the fact that the apostles were teaching the people; they felt this was their sole prerogative. Then, too, they were angered by the proclamation **in Jesus** of **the resurrection** *from* **the dead**. If **Jesus** had risen **from** among **the dead**, then the Sadducees were discredited.

In verse 2, the expression **resurrection** *from* **the dead** is important because it disproves the popular idea of a general resurrection at the end of the world. This passage and others speak of resurrection *out from among* dead ones. In other words, some will be raised while others (unbelievers) will remain in the grave until a later time.

The leaders decided to hold the apostles under a sort of house arrest until the next day, since it was getting late. (The miracle of healing in chapter 3 had been performed around 3:00 p.m.)

In spite of official opposition, many people turned to the Lord. About **five thousand** men (Gk. *andres*, "males") are mentioned as entering the Christian fellowship. Commentators are disagreed whether this included the three thousand saved at Pentecost. It does not include women and children.

4:5, 6 **The next day**, the religious council, known as the Sanhedrin, sat as a court of inquiry, intending to put a stop to the activities of these public nuisances. All they succeeded in doing was to give the apostles another chance to witness for Christ!

Together with **their rulers, elders, and scribes** were:

1. **Annas the high priest,** before whom the Lord had been first taken. He formerly was high priest but perhaps was allowed to retain the title as a courtesy.
2. **Caiaphas**, the son-in-law of Annas, who presided at the trial of the Lord.
3. **John and Alexander**, about whom nothing else is known.
4. All who **were of the family of the high priest,** men of high-priestly descent.

4:7 The trial opened by their asking the apostles **by what power or by what name** they had performed the miracle. **Peter** stepped forward to deliver his third successive public confession of Christ in Jerusalem. It was a priceless opportunity to preach the gospel to the religious establishment, and he seized it eagerly and fearlessly.

4:8–12 First he reminded them that they were unhappy because the apostles had performed **a good deed . . . to a helpless man**. Though **Peter** didn't say it, the healed man had begged at the gate of the temple, and the rulers had never been able to heal him. Then the apostle delivered a thunderbolt by announcing **that** it was in **the name of Jesus . . . whom** they had **crucified** that the man was cured. **God** had **raised** Jesus **from the dead**, and it was by His power that the miracle had been performed. The Jews did not have any place for **Jesus** in their building scheme, so they **rejected** and **crucified** Him. But **God raised** Him **from the dead** and exalted Him in heaven. The **rejected stone** thus became **the chief cornerstone**, the indispensable stone that completes the structure. And He *is* indispensable. There is no **salvation** without Him. He is the exclusive Savior. **No other name under heaven** has been **given among men** for **salvation**, and it is by this **name** alone that **we must be saved**.

As we read verses 8–12, let us remember that these words were spoken by the same man who had denied the Lord three times with oaths and curses.

4:13 Dry, formal religion is ever intolerant of enthusiastic, vital evangelism that produces results in hearts and lives. Its leaders are nonplussed to see **uneducated and untrained men** making an impact on the community while they with all their wisdom "fail to rise above flesh and blood."

In the New Testament there is no distinction between clergy and laity. This distinction is a relic brought over from Romanism. John Huss fought and died in Czechoslovakia for the doctrine of the priesthood of all believers, and the Hussite symbol to this present day is the communion cup stand-

ing upon the open Bible. It was this truth
of a royal priesthood and every believer
a witness that was the dynamic force in
the early Church. Without the aid of any
modern equipment, or transportation, or
translation and publication of the Word,
the Gospel of God's grace shook the
whole Empire until there were saints even
in Caesar's household. God is calling us
back to primitive Christianity.[18]

The Sanhedrin was struck by **the
boldness of Peter and John**. They would
like to have brushed them aside as **uneducated and** ignorant fishermen from Galilee. But there was something about their
self-control, their empowered lives, their
fearlessness that made them think of
Jesus when he was on trial. They attributed the boldness of the apostles to the
fact **that they had been with Jesus** in the
past, but the real explanation was that
they were filled with the Holy Spirit *now*.

4:14–18 Then, too, it was embarrassing to have the healed cripple there
in the courtroom. There was no denying
that a miracle had taken place.

J. H. Jowett writes:

Men may more than match you in subtlety of argument. In intellectual argument you may suffer an easy defeat. But
the argument of a redeemed life is unassailable. "Seeing the man that was healed
standing with them, they could say nothing against it."[19]

In order to discuss their strategy,
they sent Peter and John outside the
room temporarily. Their dilemma was
this: they could not punish the apostles
for performing an act of kindness; yet if
they did not stop these fanatics, their
own religion would be seriously threatened by loss of members. So they decided to forbid Peter and John to talk to
the people about **Jesus** in private conversation, or to preach Him publicly.

4:19, 20 Peter and John could not
agree to such a restriction. Their first loyalty and responsibility was **to God**, not
to man. If they were honest, the rulers
would have to admit this. The apostles
had witnessed the resurrection and ascension of Christ. They had sat under
His teaching day after day. They were
responsible to bear witness to their Lord
and Savior, Jesus Christ.

4:21, 22 The weakness of the rulers'
position is seen in the fact that they

could not punish the apostles; all **the
people** knew that a gracious miracle had
taken place. The healed man, **over forty
years old**, was well known, because his
sad plight had been displayed publicly
for a long time. So all the Sanhedrin
could do was to dismiss the accused
apostles with further threats.

4:23 With an instinct of freeborn
sons of God, the apostles **went** directly
to their fellow believers as soon as they
were **let go** by the authorities. They
sought and found their fellowship with
"the panting, huddled flock whose only
crime was Christ." So in all ages one test
of a Christian's character is where he
finds fellowship and companionship.

4:24–26 As soon as the saints **heard**
what had happened, they cried to the
Lord in prayer. Addressing **God** with a
word meaning "Absolute Master," a
word seldom used in the NT, they
praised Him first as the Creator of **all**
things (and therefore superior to the
creatures who were now opposing His
truth). Then they adopted the words of
David in Psalm 2, which he spoke by the
Holy Spirit in connection with the opposition of governmental powers **against
His Christ**. Actually, the Psalm points
forward to the time when Christ will
come to set up His kingdom and when
kings and **rulers** will seek to thwart that
purpose. But the early Christians realized that the situation in their day was
similar, so they applied the words to
their own circumstances. As has been
said, they showed true spirituality by the
divine skill with which they wove Holy
Scripture into the body of their prayers.

4:27, 28 Their application of the
quotation from the Psalm is given next.
Right there in Jerusalem the Romans and
the Jews had leagued **together** against
God's **holy Servant,**[20] **Jesus. Herod** represented the Jews, and **Pilate** acted for the
Gentiles. But there is a surprise ending
in verse 28. One would expect it to say
that these rulers had gathered together
to do whatever their wicked hearts had
planned. Instead, it says that they had
gathered together to do whatever *God's*
hand and purpose had **determined before**.

Matheson explains:

The idea is that their effort of opposition
to the divine will proved to be a stroke

of alliance with it. . . . They met together in a council of war against Christ; unconsciously to themselves they signed a treaty for the promotion of Christ's glory. . . . Our God does not beat down the storms that rise against Him; He rides upon them; He works through them.[21]

4:29, 30 Having expressed confidence in God's overruling power, the Christians made three specific requests:

1. **Look on their threats**. They did not presume to dictate to God how to punish these wicked men, but simply left the matter with Him.

2. **Grant to Your servants . . . all boldness**. Their own personal safety was not the important thing. Fearlessness in preaching the word was paramount.

3. **Stretching out Your hand to heal**. The early preaching of the gospel was attested by God through **signs and wonders** performed **through the name of . . . Jesus**. Here God is petitioned to continue confirming the ministry of the apostles in this way.

4:31 When they had prayed, the place . . . was shaken — a physical expression of the spiritual power that was present. **They were all filled with the Holy Spirit**, indicating their obedience to the Lord, their walking in the light, their yieldedness to Him. They continued to speak **the word of God with boldness**, a clear answer to their prayer in verse 29.

There are several times in the Book of Acts when men are said to be filled with or full of the Holy Spirit. Notice the purposes or the results:

1. For speaking (2:4; 4:8; and here).
2. For serving (6:3).
3. For shepherding (11:24).
4. For rebuking (13:9).
5. For dying (7:55).

4:32–35 When hearts are aflame with love for Christ, they are also kindled with love for one another. This love manifests itself in giving. Thus the early believers expressed the reality of their common life in Christ by practicing a community of goods. Instead of selfishly holding on to personal possessions, they looked upon their property as belonging to all the fellowship. Whenever there was a **need**, they would sell **lands or houses** and bring **the proceeds** to the apostles for distribution. It is important to see that **they distributed** whenever a **need** arose; it was not an arbitrary equal division at one particular time.

F. W. Grant explains:

There was therefore no general renunciation of personal title but a love that knew no holding back from the need of another. It was the instinct of hearts that had found their real possessions in that sphere into which Christ had risen.[22]

Somewhat sarcastic but sadly too often true is F. E. Marsh's modern parallel:

One has said, in contrasting the early Church with the Christianity of today, "Is it not a solemn thought, that if the evangelist Luke were describing modern instead of primitive Christianity, he would have to vary the phraseology of Acts 4:32–35 somewhat as follows: . . . 'And the multitude of them that professed were of hard heart and stony soul, and every one said that all the things which he possessed were his own: and they had all things in the fashion. And with great power gave they witness to the attractions of this world, and great selfishness was upon them all. And there were many among them that lacked love, for as many as were possessors of lands bought more, and sometimes gave a small part thereof for a public good, so their names were heralded in the newspapers, and distribution of praise was made to every one according as he desired.'"[23]

There is mysterious power connected with lives that are utterly dedicated to the Lord. Thus it is not a coincidence that we read in verse 33, **And with great power the apostles gave witness to the resurrection of the Lord Jesus. And great grace was upon them all**. It seems that when God finds people who are willing to turn their possessions over to Him, He gives their testimony a remarkable attractiveness and force.

Many argue that this sharing of goods was a temporary phase of life in the early church and was not intended to be an example to us. Such reasoning only exposes our own spiritual poverty. If we had the power of Pentecost in our hearts, we would have the fruits of Pentecost in our lives.

Ryrie points out:

This is not "Christian communism." The sale of property was quite voluntary (v.

34). The right of possession was not abolished. The community did not control the money until it had voluntarily been given to the Apostles. The distribution was not made equally but according to need. These are not communistic principles. This is Christian charity in its finest display.[24]

Note two marks of a great church in verse 33 — **great power** and **great grace**. Vance Havner lists four other marks, as follows: great fear (5:5, 11); great persecution (8:1); great joy (8:8; 15:3); a great number who believed (11:21).

4:36, 37 These verses are an introductory link with chapter 5. The generosity of **Barnabas** is set forth in striking contrast to the hypocrisy of Ananias. As a **Levite, Joses ... named Barnabas** would not ordinarily have owned land. The Lord was to be the portion of the Levites. How or why he obtained the land, we do not know. But we do know that the law of love worked so powerfully in the life of this **Son of Encouragement** that he **sold** the **land** and **laid** the money **at the apostles' feet.**

5:1–4 When God is working in power, **Satan** is on hand to counterfeit, corrupt, and contend. But where there is real spiritual power, deceit and hypocrisy will be readily exposed.

Ananias and **Sapphira** were apparently moved by the generosity of Barnabas and others. Perhaps they desired to receive the praise of men for some similar act of kindness, so **they sold a possession** and gave a portion of the proceeds to the apostles. Their sin was in professing to give all, while only giving some. No one had asked them to sell the property. **After it was sold**, they were not obligated to give all. But they *pretended* a total dedication, while actually they held some back.

Peter charged **Ananias** with lying **to the Holy Spirit** and **not** just **to men.** In lying **to the Holy Spirit**, he **lied to God**, since **the Holy Spirit** *is* **God.**

5:5, 6 At this point, **Ananias fell down** dead, and was carried out by **the young men** to be buried. This was a solemn act of God's chastening hand on the early church. It does not at all affect the question of Ananias' salvation, of his eternal security. Rather, it was a case of

God showing His displeasure at this first eruption of sin in His church. "As one commentator put it," quotes Richard Bewes, " 'Either Ananias or the Spirit must go.' " Such was the white-hot purity of that early Christian fellowship that a lie of that kind couldn't live within it."

5:7–11 About **three hours later, when** Sapphira appeared, **Peter** charged her with collaborating with her husband in putting **the Spirit of the Lord** to the test. He told her of her husband's fate and predicted the same for her. **Immediately she** collapsed and died, and was carried out for burial.

Peter's ability to pronounce judgment on this couple is an example of the special miraculous powers given to the apostles. Perhaps it was a fulfillment of the Lord's promise, "If you retain the sins of any, they are retained" (John 20:23). It is further seen by Paul's ability to deliver an offending Christian to Satan for the destruction of the flesh (1 Cor. 5:5). There is no reason to believe that this power continued after the time of the apostles.

One can imagine the sense of awe that swept over the church, indeed over all who heard the news of these two deaths.

5:12–16 After the death of Ananias and Sapphira, the **apostles** continued to perform miracles as the people gathered around them **in Solomon's Porch**. So vivid was the sense of God's presence and power that men did not lightly associate with them or make glib professions of faith. And yet the common **people esteemed them highly**, many taking their place as **believers** in the Lord Jesus. The **people** carried their **sick out into the streets on beds** and mattresses so that Peter's **shadow might fall on some of them** as he passed by. Anyone could see that there was reality and power in the lives of the apostles, and that they were channels through whom God was blessing others. From the suburbs came the sick and the demon-possessed, **and they were all healed**.

It is clear from Hebrews 2:4 that miracles like these were God's method of bearing witness to the ministry of the apostles. With the completion of the NT in written form, the need for such **signs** largely passed away. As far as modern "healing campaigns" are concerned, it should be enough to note that *of those brought to the apostles*, **they were all healed**. This is not true of so-called faith healers.

5:17–20 True Holy Spirit ministry invariably leads to conversion on the one hand and bitter opposition on the other. So it was here. **The high priest** (probably Caiaphas) and his Sadducean friends were furious that these fanatical disciples of Jesus were wielding such influence among the people. They resented any threat to their exclusive role as religious leaders, and especially despised preaching concerning bodily resurrection, which they, of course, utterly denied.

Unable to cope with **the apostles** other than by force, they had them arrested and imprisoned. That **night an angel of the Lord** led the apostles out of **the prison** and told them to return to **the temple and speak to the people all the words of this life**. Luke records the miraculous intervention of the **angel** without any expression of surprise or wonder. If the apostles themselves were shocked, there is no indication in the narrative.

The **angel** aptly referred to the Christian faith as **this life**. It is not just a creed or set of doctrines, but a *Life* — the resurrection **life** of the Lord Jesus imparted to all who trust Him.

5:21 At daybreak the apostles were teaching at **the temple**. In the meantime, **the high priest** met in solemn conclave with **the council** (the Sanhedrin) and the senate (**all the elders**), and waited for the prisoners to be **brought** before them.

5:22–25 The bewildered **officers** had to report to the court that everything at **the prison** was in good order — except that the prisoners were gone! **The doors** were properly locked, **and the guards** were all at their stations, but the occupants were missing. A distressing report indeed! "Where will it all end?" mused **the captain of the temple and the chief priests**. "How far will this popular movement go?" Then their questions were interrupted by a messenger announcing that the escaped prisoners were back at their old stand **in the temple — teaching the people**! We must

admire their courage, and we must regain the capacity of the early church to suffer for our convictions at any cost.

5:26 The officers used no **violence** in bringing the apostles to the council. **They feared the people** would stone them if they were openly rough to these followers of Jesus, now held in high regard by many of **the** common **people**.

5:27, 28 The high priest served as spokesman. **"Did we not strictly command you not to teach in this name?"** He purposely avoided using the name of the Lord Jesus Christ. **"You have filled Jerusalem with your doctrine."** This was an unintentional compliment to the effectiveness of the apostles' ministry. "You **intend to bring this Man's blood on us."** But the Jewish leaders had already done this when they cried, "His blood be on us and on our children" (Matt. 27:25).

5:29–32 Previously the apostles had prayed for boldness to speak the word. Now with courage from above, they insist that their obligation is **to obey God rather than men**. They flatly declare that **Jesus** had been **raised up** by **God**, that Israel had **murdered** Him **by hanging** Him **on a tree**, but that **God** had **exalted** Him **to His right hand** — a **Prince and Savior**. As such He was willing **to give repentance to Israel and forgiveness of sins**. As a final thrust, the apostles add that they **are His witnesses to these things, and so also is the Holy Spirit whom God** gives **to those who obey Him** by believing on His Son.

God raising **up Jesus** (v. 30) may refer to His Incarnation or His resurrection. The probable meaning here is that **God raised** Him **up**, in Incarnation, to be the **Savior**.

5:33–37 Deep conviction accompanied the words of these embodied consciences — so deep that the rulers of the Jews **plotted to kill them**. At this juncture Gamaliel intervened. He was one of the most distinguished of Israel's rabbis, and the **teacher** of Saul of Tarsus. His advice does not indicate that he was a Christian or that he was even pro-Christian. It was simply worldly wisdom.

After having **the apostles** taken from the room, he first reminded the Sanhedrin that if this movement were not **of God**, it would soon collapse. Two illustrations of this principle were offered: (1) **Theudas**, a self-styled leader with **about four hundred** revolutionaries, who **was slain** and whose men **were scattered**; (2) **Judas of Galilee**, another fanatic, who stirred up an abortive sedition among the Jews, but who **also perished**, and whose followers **were dispersed**.

5:38, 39 If this Christian religion were not **of God**, the best thing would be to leave it **alone**, and it would soon fade out. To combat it would only make it more determined to survive. (This argument is not altogether true. Many godless institutions have flourished for centuries. In fact, they have gained more adherents than the truth. But the argument is true in God's time, if not in man's.)

On the other hand, Gamaliel continued, **if** the movement were **of God**, they would not be able to **overthrow it**, and they would **be found** in the awkward position of fighting **against God**.

5:40 This logic appealed to the rulers, so **they called for the apostles**, ordered them to be **beaten**, forbade them to **speak in the name of Jesus, and let them go**. The beating was senseless and unrighteous, the unreasonable reaction of bigoted hearts to the truth of God.[25] The command that accompanied the beating was foolish and futile; they might as well have ordered the sun not to shine as to command the disciples to keep silent concerning **the name of Jesus**!

5:41, 42 The beating inflicted on the apostles had two unexpected results. First, it caused them deep joy **that they were counted worthy to suffer shame for** the **name**[26] they loved. Second, it sent them forth with renewed zeal and persistence, **daily in the temple** and in homes, **teaching and preaching Jesus as the** Messiah.

So once again Satan outwitted himself.

THE CHRISTIAN AND GOVERNMENT

As the early Christians moved forward with the gospel, it was inevitable that they would run into opposition from governmental authorities, especially from the religious leaders who at that time had considerable jurisdiction in civil affairs. The believers were prepared for this and reacted with poise and dignity.

In general their policy was to respect and obey their rulers, since the latter are ordained by God and are servants of God to promote the common good. Thus, when Paul unknowingly rebuked the high priest, and was called to account, he immediately apologized, quoting Exodus 22:28: "You shall not speak evil of a ruler of your people" (Acts 23:5).

However, when men's laws ran afoul of the commandments of God, then the Christians' policy was to disobey the government and suffer the consequences, whatever they might be. For instance, when Peter and John were forbidden to preach the gospel, they answered, "Whether it is right in the sight of God to listen to you more than to God, you judge. For we cannot but speak the things which we have seen and heard" (4:19, 20). And when Peter and the apostles were arraigned for continuing to teach in Christ's Name, Peter replied, "We ought to obey God rather than men" (5:29).

There is no suggestion that they ever did or would join in any attempt to overthrow the government. In spite of persecution and oppression, they wished only good for their rulers (26:29).

It goes without saying that they would never stoop to any form of dishonesty to gain favors from the government. The governor, Felix, for instance, waited in vain to receive a bribe from Paul (24:26).

They did not consider it inconsistent with their Christian calling to use their rights of citizenship (16:37; 21:39; 22:25–28; 23:17–21; 25:10, 11).

Yet they themselves did not engage in the politics of this world. Why? No explanation is given. But this much is clear: they were people of one purpose — to preach the gospel of Christ. They gave themselves to this task without distraction. They must have believed that the gospel is the answer to man's problems. This conviction was so strong that they could not be satisfied with subordinate approaches, such as politics.‡

6:1 If the devil cannot destroy by attacks from without, he will seek to overthrow by dissension within. This is illustrated in these verses.

In the early days of the church, it was customary to make daily disbursements to the poor widows of the church who had no other means of support. Some of the believers who had been Greek-speaking Jews complained **because their widows** were not receiving the same treatment as the widows of **Hebrews** (those from Jerusalem and Judea).

6:2, 3 **The twelve** apostles realized that with the increasing growth of the church, some provision would have to be made for handling these business matters. They themselves did not want to forsake the ministry of **the word of God** in order to handle financial matters, so they counseled that the church should designate **seven** spiritual **men** to handle the temporal affairs of the church.

Although these men are not designated deacons in the Bible, it is not unreasonable to think of them as such. In the expression, **serve tables**, the word **serve** is the verb form of the noun from which we get the English word *deacon*, so their function literally was to "deacon" tables.

Their qualifications here are threefold:

1. **Of good reputation** — Reputable
2. **Full of the Holy Spirit** — Spiritual
3. Full of **wisdom** — Practical

More detailed qualifications are given in 1 Timothy 3:8–13.

6:4 The apostles would **give** themselves **continually to prayer and to the ministry of the word**. The order here is significant — first **prayer**, then **the ministry of the word**. They made it a point to speak to God about men before speaking to men about God.

6:5, 6 Judging from the names of the seven men who were chosen, most of them were Greek-speaking Jews before their conversion. This was certainly a most gracious concession to the very group that had made the complaint. Hereafter there could be no charge of favoritism from that quarter. When the love of God fills men's hearts, it triumphs over pettiness and selfishness.

Only two of the deacons are well-known to us — **Stephen**, who became the first martyr of the church; and **Philip**, the evangelist who later carried the gospel to Samaria, won the Ethiopian eunuch to Christ, and entertained Paul at Caesarea.

After praying, the apostles expressed their fellowship with the choice of the church by laying **hands on** the seven.

6:7 If verse 7 is read with the preceding verses, it seems to indicate that the provision of deacons to care for business affairs resulted in a great forward thrust for the gospel. As **the word of God spread**, many **disciples** were added to the fellowship **in Jerusalem**, **and a great many of the** Jewish **priests** became followers of the Lord Jesus.

6:8 The narrative now centers on one of the deacons, **Stephen**,[27] who was mightily used by God in performing miracles and in preaching the word. He is the first man other than an apostle who is said to have performed miracles in the Book of Acts. Was this promotion to higher service a result of his faithfulness as a deacon? Or was it simply an additional ministry which he carried on at the same time? It is impossible to decide from the text.

6:9 Opposition to Stephen's powerful ministry arose from the synagogue. These were places where Jews gathered together on the Sabbath for instruction in the law. The synagogues were named according to the people who met there. The **Freedmen** were perhaps Jews who had been freed from slavery by the Romans. Cyrene was a city in Africa, some of whose Jews had apparently settled in Jerusalem. The Alexandrian Jews had come from the seaport of Egypt by that name. **Cilicia** was the southeastern province of Asia Minor, and **Asia** was a province of Asia Minor made up of three territories. Apparently communities of Jews from all of these places had synagogues in or near Jerusalem.

6:10–14 These zealous Jews proved no match for Stephen as they disputed with him. The words which he spoke and the power with which he spoke them were irresistible. In a desperate move to silence them, **they secretly induced** false witnesses to accuse Stephen of blasphemy **against Moses and God**.[28]

Soon he was standing before the Sanhedrin, charged with speaking **against** the temple **and the law**. They falsely quoted him as saying that **Jesus** would **destroy** the temple and **change** the whole system **which Moses delivered** to Israel.

6:15 The Sanhedrin heard the charges, but as they looked at Stephen, they **saw** not the face of a demon, but **the face of an angel**. They saw the mysterious beauty of a life that is fully surrendered to the Lord, determined to proclaim the Truth, and more concerned with what God thinks than with what men may say. They saw something of the glory of Christ reflected in the radiant face of His devoted follower.

In chapter 7 we have Stephen's masterful defense. It begins quietly with what seems to be a review of Jewish history. As it progresses, it concentrates on two individuals, Joseph and Moses, who were raised up by God, rejected by Israel, then exalted as deliverers and saviors. Though Stephen does not compare their experiences directly with Christ's, the analogy is unmistakable. Then at length, Stephen launches into a scathing attack on Israel's leaders, charging them with resisting the Holy Spirit, murdering the Righteous One, and failing to keep the law of God.

Stephen must have known that his life was at stake. To spare himself, all he had to do was deliver a compromising, placating speech. But he would rather die than betray his sacred trust. Admire his courage!

7:1–8 This first section of the message takes us back to the beginning of the Hebrew nation. It is not exactly clear why Abraham's history is dealt with at such length, unless it is:

1. To show Stephen's familiarity with and love for the nation of Israel.

2. To lead up to the story of Joseph and Moses, both types of the rejection of Christ.

3. To show that Abraham worshiped God acceptably even though his worship was not confined to a specific locality. (Stephen had been accused of speaking against the temple — "this holy place.")

The salient points in Abraham's biography are:

1. His call by God **in Mesopotamia** (vv. 2, 3).

2. His journey to **Haran**, then to Canaan (v. 4).

3. God's promise of the land to Abraham, though the patriarch himself was not given any of it — as was proved by his purchase of the cave of Machpelah as a burial place (v. 5). The fulfillment of that promise is still future (Heb. 11:13–40).

4. God's prediction of Israel's bondage in Egypt and of eventual deliverance (vv. 6, 7). Both parts of this prediction were accomplished by men who had been rejected by the nation: Joseph (vv. 9–19); Moses (vv. 20–36). The **four hundred years** mentioned in verse 6 and in Genesis 15:13 refer to the time when the Jewish people were afflicted in Egypt. The four hundred and thirty years cited in Exodus 12:40 and Galatians 3:17 cover the period from the arrival of Jacob and his family in Egypt to the Exodus and the giving of the law. The Israelites were not persecuted during their first thirty years in Egypt; in fact, they were treated quite royally.

5. **The covenant of circumcision** (v. 8a).

6. The birth of **Isaac**, then **Jacob**, then **the twelve patriarchs** (v. 8b). This, of course, brings the history up to Joseph, one of Jacob's twelve sons.

7:9–19 Of all the types of Christ in the OT, **Joseph** is one of the clearest and most precious, although he is never specifically stated to be. Surely the Jews of Stephen's day must have felt the sharp arrows of conviction as they heard Stephen review the steps of Joseph's career, then remembered what they had done to Jesus of Nazareth!

1. **Joseph sold into Egypt** by his brothers (v. 9).

2. The rejected one raised to power and glory in **Egypt** (v. 10).

3. Joseph's brothers driven to **Egypt** by **famine**, but failed to recognize their brother (vv. 11, 12).

4. **The second time Joseph was made known to** them. Then the rejected one became the savior of his family (vv. 13, 14). Note: There seems to be a contradiction between the

seventy–five souls given in verse 14 and the seventy mentioned in Genesis 46:27. Stephen followed the Greek translation of Genesis 46:27 and Exodus 1:5, which has seventy-five. The Hebrew text has seventy, indicating nothing more serious than a different way of numbering Jacob's family.[29]

5. The death of the patriarchs, and their burial in the land of Canaan (vv. 15, 16). Another difficulty appears in this verse. Here it says that **Abraham bought** a burial place from **Hamor**. Genesis 23:16, 17 says that *Abraham* bought the cave of Machpelah in Hebron from the sons of Heth. *Jacob* bought land in Shechem from the children of Hamor (Gen. 33:19). There are several possibilities: (1) Abraham may have bought land in Shechem as well as in Hebron. Later Jacob could have repurchased the plot in Shechem. (2) Stephen could have used Abraham's name for Abraham's descendant, Jacob. (3) Stephen may have condensed the purchases by Abraham and Jacob into one for brevity.[30]

6. The growth of Jacob's family **in Egypt** and their slavery after Joseph's death (vv. 17–19). This, of course, prepares us for the next step in Stephen's argument — the treatment which Moses received at the hands of his people.

7:20–43 Stephen is showing with incisive boldness that the Jewish people were guilty on at least two previous occasions of rejecting saviors whom God had raised up to deliver them. His second proof is **Moses**.

Stephen had been charged with speaking blasphemous words against Moses (6:11). He proves that the nation of Israel is the guilty party — guilty of refusing this man of God's choice.

Stephen reviews the life of Moses, as follows:

1. Birth, early life, and education in Egypt (vv. 20–22). The phrase, **mighty in words**, may refer to his writings, since he disclaimed being eloquent (Ex. 4:10).

2. His first rejection by **his brethren** when he defended one of them against an **Egyptian** (vv. 23–28). Note verse 25! How it reminds us of Christ's rejection by His own!

3. His exile **in the land of Midian** (v. 29).

4. God's appearance **to him in** the burning **bush**, sending him back **to Egypt to deliver** his people (vv. 30–35).

5. He became the savior of the nation (v. 36).

6. His prophecy concerning the coming Messiah (v. 37). (**Like me** means "as He raised me.")

7. His role as law-giver to **the congregation in the wilderness** (v. 38).

8. Moses rejected a second time by the people, as they worshiped the golden **calf** (vv. 39–41). The idolatry of Israel is elaborated in verses 42 and 43. While professing **to offer . . . sacrifices** to the Lord, the people **took up the tabernacle of Moloch**, one of the most loathsome of all ancient forms of idolatry, and bowed to **Remphan**, a stellar deity. For this sin God warned that they would be carried off into Babylonian captivity. In verses 42 and 43 Stephen quotes from the Septuagint version of Amos 5:25–27. That is why the captivity is said to be **beyond Babylon** instead of "beyond Damascus." Both are, of course, true.

History repeats itself. In every generation we can find the same pattern. *People are the same.* When confronted with God's message, they do not understand (25). When urged to live at peace, they refuse to listen (27). When given a God-sent deliverer, they reject him (39). When rescued from an evil situation, they prefer useless idols to the merciful God (41). Such is human nature — rebellious, ungrateful, foolish. *God is the same.* The God who spoke to Moses was the same God who had spoken to his ancestors (32). This God hears when people are troubled (34). He comes to deliver (34). He leads His people from death to life (36). He surrenders to their own desires those who willfully reject Him (42). Such is our great God — merciful, powerful, holy. He is always the same, whatever happens (Mal. 3:6). For Stephen's hearers it was a warning not to trifle with God. It is also an assurance that every promise of God stands firm forever.[31]

7:44–46 Stephen had been charged with speaking against the temple. He replies by going back to the days when Israel had **the tabernacle** (tent) **of witness**

in the wilderness. It was during this same time that the people were also worshiping the host of heaven. When Joshua led the Israelites into the land of Canaan, and the heathen inhabitants were expelled, the tabernacle was brought into the land and continued until the days of David. The fathers had asked to find a dwelling for the God of Jacob and had thus found favor before God.

7:47–50 David's desire to build the temple was not granted, but Solomon built Him a house.

Although the temple was the dwelling place of God among His people, God was not confined to that building. Solomon stated this clearly when the temple was dedicated (1 Kgs. 8:27). Also Isaiah had warned the people that buildings are not what really count with God but rather the moral and spiritual condition of men's lives (Isa. 66:1, 2). He looks for a broken and contrite heart, for a man who trembles at His word.

7:51–53 The Jewish leaders had charged Stephen with speaking against the law. He now answers the accusation with a brief, finely worded denunciation.

It was they who were stiff-necked and uncircumcised in heart and ears. "He rebukes them, not as the Israel of God, but as stubborn and uncircumcised Gentiles in heart and ears." They were sons of their fathers in habitually resisting the Holy Spirit. Their fathers had persecuted the prophets who foretold the coming of Christ. Now they had betrayed and murdered this Just One. They were the people who had failed to keep the law — the very people to whom it was given by the direction of angels.

Nothing more needed to be said! Indeed, nothing more could be said! They had sought to put Stephen on the defensive. But he became the prosecutor and they the guilty defendants. His message was one of God's final words to the Jewish nation before the gospel started moving out to the Gentiles.

7:54–60 As soon as Stephen bore public testimony to seeing the heavens opened, the mob refused to listen to him further; they cried fiercely, charged upon him, dragged him outside the city walls and stoned him.

As if incidentally, the Spirit records the name of a young man who stood guard over the clothes of the perspiring executioners. The name was Saul. It is as if the Spirit would say to us, "Remember that name. You will hear it again!"

Stephen's death resembled that of our Lord:

1. He prayed, "Lord Jesus, receive my spirit" (v. 59). Jesus had prayed, "Father, into Your hands I commit My spirit" (Luke 23:46).

2. He prayed, "Lord, do not charge them with this sin" (v. 60). Jesus had prayed, "Father, forgive them, for they do not know what they do" (Luke 23:34).

Does it not suggest that through occupation with the Lord, Stephen had been "transformed into the same image from glory to glory, just as by the Spirit of the Lord" (2 Cor. 3:18)?

Then, having prayed, he fell asleep. When the word "sleep" is used in connection with death in the NT, it refers to the body, not the soul. The believer's soul goes to be with Christ at the time of death (2 Cor. 5:8); the body is pictured as sleeping.

Ordinarily the Jews were not allowed to carry out the death penalty; this was reserved for their Roman overlords (John 18:31b). But the Romans seem to have made an exception when the temple was threatened. Stephen had been accused of speaking against the temple, and though the charge was unfounded, he was executed by the Jews. The Lord Jesus had been accused of threatening to destroy the temple (Mark 14:58), but the testimony of the witnesses conflicted.

II. THE CHURCH IN JUDEA AND SAMARIA (8:1–9:31)

A. The Ministry of Philip in Samaria (8:1–25)

8:1 Again the Spirit of God introduces the name of Saul. Great strivings of soul were being born within him. Outwardly his reign of terror would continue, but his days as a foe of Christianity were numbered. Saul was consenting to Stephen's death, but in so doing he was paving the way for his own undoing as an arch-persecutor.

A new era begins with the words, "At that time". Stephen's death seemed to trigger a widespread assault **against the church**. Believers **were scattered throughout . . . Judea and Samaria**.

The Lord had instructed His followers to begin their witness in Jerusalem, but then to branch out to Judea, Samaria, and the end of the earth. Up to this time their witness had been confined entirely to **Jerusalem**. Perhaps they had been timid about branching out. Now they are forced to do it by persecution.

The apostles themselves remained in the city. As Kelly dryly observed, "Those who stayed would naturally be the most obnoxious of all."

From the human standpoint, it was a dark day for the believers. The life of a member of their fellowship had been laid down. They themselves were being chased like rabbits. But from the divine standpoint, it was not dark at all. A grain of wheat had been planted in the ground, and much fruit would inevitably result. The winds of affliction were scattering the seeds of the gospel to distant places, and who could estimate the extent of the harvest?

8:2 The **devout men** who buried Stephen are not identified. Perhaps they were Christians who had not yet been driven out of Jerusalem. Or perhaps they were pious Jews who saw something in the martyr which made them esteem him worthy of a decent burial.

8:3 Again the name of **Saul**! With unbounded energy he is harassing **the church**, **dragging** his hapless victims from their homes, and **committing them to prison**. If only he could forget Stephen — such poise — such unshakable conviction — the face of an angel! He must drown out the memory, and he seeks to do it by stepping up his attacks on Stephen's fellow-believers.

8:4–8 The dispersal of the Christians did not silence their testimony. **Everywhere** they **went** they carried the good news of salvation. **Philip**, the "deacon" of chapter six, headed north to **the city of Samaria**.[32] He not only proclaimed Christ but performed many **miracles**. **Unclean spirits** were driven out and the **paralyzed and lame were healed**. The people gave heed to the gospel, and, as might be expected, **great joy** resulted.

The primitive church obeyed the explicit commands of Jesus Christ:

It went out as Christ had gone (John 20:21; cf. Acts 8:1–4).

It sold its goods and gave to the poor (Luke 12:33; 18:22; cf. Acts 2:45; 4:34).

It left father, mother, houses, and lands to go everywhere preaching the Word (Matt. 10:37; cf. Acts 8:1–4).

It made disciples and taught them to work and obey (Matt. 28:18, 19; cf. 1 Thess. 1:6).

It took up its cross and followed Christ (Acts 4; 1 Thess. 2).

It rejoiced in tribulation and persecution (Matt. 5:11, 12; cf. Acts 16; 1 Thess. 1:6–8).

It left the dead to bury their dead and went and preached the gospel (Luke 9:59, 60).

It shook the dust from off its feet and moved on when men refused to hear (Luke 9:5; cf. Acts 13:51).

It healed, exorcised, raised the dead, and bore lasting fruit (Mark 16:18; Acts 3–16).[33]

8:9–11 Among the most notable of those who heard Philip was a sorcerer **called Simon**. He himself had **previously** made a big impression on **Samaria** by his amazing feats of **sorcery**. He pretended to be very important, and some of the people were actually convinced that he was **"the great power of God."**

8:12, 13 When many of the people **believed** the preaching of **Philip** and **were baptized**, **Simon also** professed to be a believer,[34] **was baptized**, and followed **Philip**, fascinated by **the miracles** he performed.

From what follows it seems that Simon had not been born again. He was a professor but not a possessor. Those who teach salvation by baptism are faced with a dilemma here. Simon had been baptized, but he was still in his sins.

Notice that **Philip preached** good news **concerning the kingdom of God and the name of Jesus Christ**. **The kingdom of God** is the sphere where the rule of God is acknowledged. At the present time, the King is absent. Instead of a literal, earthly kingdom, we have a spiritual, invisible kingdom in the lives of all who are loyal to Him. In the future the King will return to the earth to set up a literal kingdom with Jerusalem as His capital. In order to truly enter the kingdom, in any of its forms, a person must be born again. Faith in **the name of Jesus Christ** is the means of experiencing the new birth. This, then, was doubtless the gist of Philip's preaching.

8:14–17 When news **that Samaria had** avidly **received the word** reached **the apostles . . . at Jerusalem, they sent Peter and John to them**. By the time they arrived, the believers **had been baptized in the name of the Lord Jesus**, but they had not received **the Holy Spirit**. Obviously acting in accordance with divine guidance, the apostles **prayed** that these believers **might receive the Holy Spirit** and **laid** their **hands on them**. As soon as this was done, **they received the Holy Spirit**.

This immediately raises the question, "Why the difference between the order of events here and on the day of Pentecost?" At Pentecost the Jewish people:

1. Repented.
2. Were baptized.
3. Received the Holy Spirit.

Here the Samaritans:

1. Believed.
2. Were baptized.
3. Had the apostles pray for them and lay their hands on them.
4. Received the Holy Spirit.

Of one thing we can be sure: they were all saved in the same way — by faith in the Lord Jesus Christ. He is the only Way of Salvation. However, during this transitional time, bridging Judaism and Christianity, God chose to act sovereignly in connection with various communities of believers. Jewish believers were asked to dissociate themselves from the nation of Israel by baptism before they received the Spirit. Now the Samaritans must have special prayer and the apostles' hands laid on them. But why?

Perhaps the best answer is that it was intended to give expression to the unity of the church, whether made up of Jews or Samaritans. There was a real danger that the church in Jerusalem might retain ideas of Jewish superiority, and that they might continue to have no dealings with their Samaritan brethren. To avoid the possibility of schism, or the thought of two churches (one Jewish and one Samaritan), God sent the apostles to lay their hands on the Samaritans. This expressed full fellowship with them as believers in the Lord Jesus. They were all members of one body, all one in Christ Jesus.

When verse 16 says that **they had only been baptized in** (or into) **the name of the Lord Jesus** (see also 10:48 and 19:5), this does not mean that it was different from being baptized "in the name of the Father and of the Son and of the Holy Spirit" (Matt. 28:19). "Luke is not recording a formula used," writes W. E. Vine, "but is simply stating an historical fact." Both expressions signify allegiance and identification, and all true believers gladly acknowledge their loyalty to a union with the Trinity and the Lord Jesus.

8:18–21 **Simon** the sorcerer was deeply impressed by the fact that **the Holy Spirit was given** when the apostles laid their **hands** on the Samaritans. He had no deep sense of the spiritual implications of this, but rather looked on it as a supernatural power which would serve him well in his trade. So he offered money to the apostles in an effort to buy the power.

Peter's answer indicates that **Simon** was not a truly converted man:

1. **"Your money perish with you."** No believer will ever *perish* (John 3:16).
2. **"You have neither part nor portion in this matter"**; in other words, he was not in the fellowship.
3. **"Your heart is not right in the sight of God."** This is a fitting description of an unsaved person.
4. **"You are poisoned by bitterness and bound by iniquity."** Could these words be true of a regenerate person?

8:22–24 Peter urged **Simon** to **repent** of his great sin, and **pray** that his wicked plan might be forgiven. Simon's reply was to ask Peter to serve as a mediator between God and himself. He was the forerunner of those who would rather go to a human mediator than to the Lord Himself. That there was no true repentance on Simon's part is indicated by the words, **"Pray to the Lord for me, that none of these things which you have spoken may come upon me."** He was not sorry for his sin, but only for the consequences which it might bring on him.

It is from this man, **Simon**, that we

get the modern word, "simony" — making a business out of that which is sacred. It includes the sale of indulgences and other supposed spiritual benefits, and all forms of commercialism in divine matters.

8:25 After Peter and John **had testified and preached the word of the Lord, they returned to Jerusalem**. But now that a beachhead had been established, they continued to preach **in many villages of the Samaritans**.

B. Philip and the Ethiopian Eunuch (8:26–40)

8:26 It was during this great spiritual awakening in Samaria that **an angel of the Lord** directed **Philip** to a new field of labor. He was to leave the place where many were being blessed, and minister to one man. An angel could direct **Philip** but could not do Philip's work of preaching the gospel. That privilege was given to men, not to angels.

In unquestioning obedience, **Philip** journeyed south from Samaria to **Jerusalem**, and then to one of the routes that led **to Gaza**.[35] It is not clear whether the words, **"This is desert"** refer to the route or to Gaza itself. However, the effect is the same: **Philip** left a place of habitation and spiritual fertility for a barren area.

8:27–29 Somewhere along the route he caught up with a caravan. In the main chariot was the treasurer of **Candace**[36] **the queen of the Ethiopians, a eunuch**[37] **of great authority**. (Ethiopia was the southern part of Egypt and the Sudan.) This man had apparently become a convert to Judaism, since he had been **to Jerusalem to worship** and was now returning home. As the chariot rolled along, **he was reading Isaiah the prophet**. With split-second timing, **the Spirit** directed **Philip** to **overtake this chariot**.

8:30, 31 **Philip** opens the conversation with a friendly question, **"Do you understand what you are reading?"** The eunuch readily admits his need of someone to guide him, and invites **Philip** to **sit with him** in the **chariot**. The utter lack of racial prejudice here is refreshing.

8:32, 33 How wonderful it was that the eunuch "happened" to be reading Isaiah 53, with its unsurpassed description of the suffering Messiah! Why did

Philip approach at that particular time in his reading?

The passage in Isaiah pictures One who was meek and **silent** before His enemies; One who was hurried away from **justice** and a fair trial; and One who had no hope of posterity because He was killed in the prime of manhood and while unmarried.

8:34, 35 **The eunuch** wondered whether Isaiah was speaking **of himself or of some other man**. This, of course, gave **Philip** the desired opportunity to tell how these Scriptures were perfectly fulfilled in the life and death of Jesus of Nazareth. No doubt while he was in Jerusalem the Ethiopian had heard reports about a man named **Jesus**, but these reports would, of course, have cast Him in an unfavorable light. Now **the eunuch** learns that **Jesus** of Nazareth is the suffering Servant of Jehovah, of whom Isaiah wrote.

8:36 It seems probable that Philip had explained to the Ethiopian the privilege of Christian baptism, identifying oneself with Christ in His death, burial, and resurrection. Now as they near a body of **water, the eunuch** signifies his desire to be **baptized**.

8:37 Verse 37 of the KJV and NKJV is omitted from most Greek manuscripts of the NT. Not that its teaching is at all inconsistent with the rest of Scripture; belief in **Jesus Christ** is certainly prerequisite to baptism. But the verse is simply not supported by the major NT documents.[38]

8:38 **The chariot** is stopped, and **Philip** baptizes **the eunuch**. That the baptism was by immersion is evident by the expressions, they **went down into the water** and **they came up out of the water**.[39]

One is impressed by the simplicity of the ceremony. Out on a desert route a believer baptized a new convert. The church was not present. None of the apostles was there. Doubtless only the retinue of servants in the caravan witnessed the baptism of their master; they would understand that he was now a follower of Jesus of Nazareth.

8:39 As soon as the baptism was over, **the Spirit of the Lord caught Philip away**. This suggests more than mere guidance to another location. Rather, it speaks of miraculous and sudden removal. Its purpose was **that the eunuch** would not become occupied with the human instrument of his conversion, but with the Lord Himself.

> May His beauty rest upon me,
> As I seek the lost to win,
> And may they forget the channel,
> Seeing only Him.
> — *Kate B. Wilkinson*

The eunuch **went on his way rejoicing**. There is a joy that comes from obedience to the Lord that surpasses all other pleasurable emotions.

8:40 Philip, in the meantime, resumes his evangelistic ministry **at Azotus** (OT Ashdod), north of Gaza and west of Jerusalem, near the coast. From there he works his way north along the coast **to Caesarea**.

And what of the eunuch? There was no opportunity for what we call "follow-up work" by Philip. All the evangelist could do was to commit him to God and to the OT Scriptures. Yet with the power of the Holy Spirit this new disciple doubtless returned to Ethiopia[40] witnessing to all of the saving grace of the Lord Jesus Christ.

EXCURSUS ON BELIEVER'S BAPTISM

The baptism of the eunuch which we have just considered is one of many indications that Christian baptism was taught and practiced by the early church (2:38; 22:16). It was not the same as John's baptism, which was a baptism indicating repentance (13:24; 19:4). Rather, it was a public confession of identification with Christ.

It invariably followed conversion (2:41; 8:12; 18:8) and was for women as well as men (8:12) and Gentiles as well as Jews (10:48). Households are said to have been baptized (10:47, 48; 16:15; 16:33), but in at least two of these cases it is implied that all the members of the household had *believed*. It is *never* stated that infants were baptized.

Believers were baptized very soon after their conversion (8:36; 9:18; 16:33). Apparently it was on the basis of their profession of faith in Christ. No probationary period was required to manifest the reality of their profession. Of course,

the threat of persecution probably restrained people from making professions lightly.

That baptism did not have saving value is seen in the case of Simon (8:13). Even after professing faith and being baptized, he was "poisoned by bitterness and bound by iniquity" (8:23). His "heart" was "not right in the sight of God" (8:21).

As has been mentioned, the mode of baptism was immersion (8:38, 39) — "both Philip and the eunuch went down into the water . . . when they came up out of the water. . . ." Even many present-day advocates of sprinkling and pouring admit that immersion was the practice of the first century disciples.

Twice baptism seems to be linked with the forgiveness of sins. On the day of Pentecost Peter said, "Repent, and let every one of you be baptized in the name of Jesus Christ for the remission of sins . . ." (2:38). And later Ananias said to Saul, "Arise and be baptized, and wash away your sins, calling on the name of the Lord . . ." (22:16). In both instances the instructions were given to Jews; no Gentile was ever told to be baptized for the remission of sins. In believer's baptism a Jew publicly repudiated his connection with the nation that rejected and crucified its Messiah. The basis of his forgiveness was faith in the Lord Jesus. The purchase price of his forgiveness was the precious blood of the Lord. The way in which his forgiveness was administered was through water baptism, because his baptism publicly removed him from Jewish ground and put him on Christian ground.

The baptismal formula, "in the name of the Father and of the Son and of the Holy Spirit" (Matt. 28:19), does not appear in the Book of Acts. The Samaritans were baptized in the name of the Lord Jesus (8:16), and the same was true of John's disciples (19:5). However, this does not necessarily mean that the triune formula was not used. The phrase, "in the name of the Lord Jesus," may mean "by the authority of the Lord Jesus."

John's disciples were baptized twice — first with John's baptism unto repentance, then at the time of their conversion, with believer's baptism (19:3, 5).

This provides a precedent for the "re-baptism" of those who were christened or baptized before they were saved. ‡

C. The Conversion of Saul of Tarsus (9:1–31)

9:1, 2 Chapter 9 marks a distinct turning point in Acts. Up to now, Peter has held a position of prominence as he preached to the nation of Israel. From now on, the Apostle Paul will gradually become the foremost figure, and the gospel will increasingly go out to the Gentiles.

Saul of Tarsus was perhaps in his early thirties at this time. He was generally regarded by the rabbis as one of the most promising young men in Judaism. As to zeal, he outstripped all of his fellows.

As he watched the growth of the Christian faith, known as **the Way**,[41] he saw in it a threat to his own religion. Therefore, with seemingly unbounded vigor, he set out to destroy this pernicious sect. For instance, he had obtained official authorization from **the high priest** to search **Damascus** in Syria for disciples of Jesus to **bring them bound to Jerusalem** for trial and punishment.

9:3–6 His traveling party drew **near Damascus. Suddenly a** great **light shone around him from heaven**, causing Saul to fall **to the ground**. He **heard a voice saying to him, "Saul, Saul, why are you persecuting Me?"** When Saul inquired, **"Who are You, Lord?"** he was told, **"I am Jesus, whom you are persecuting."**

In order to appreciate Saul's emotions at this time, it is necessary to remember that he was convinced that **Jesus** of Nazareth was dead and buried in a Judean grave. Since the leader of the sect had been destroyed, all that was now necessary was to destroy his followers. Then the earth would be free of this scourge.

Now with crushing force, Saul learns that Jesus is not dead at all, but that He has been raised from the dead and has been glorified at the right hand of God in heaven! It was this sight of the glorified Savior that changed the entire direction of his life.

Saul also learned that day that when he had been persecuting the disciples of Jesus, he had been **persecuting** the Lord

Himself. Pain inflicted on the members of the Body on earth was felt by the Head of the Body in heaven.

For Saul it was first doctrine, then duty. First, he was properly instructed as to the Person of Jesus. Then he was sent into Damascus where he would receive his marching orders.

9:7–9 The men who journeyed with him were in a thorough daze by this time. They had heard a sound from heaven, but not the articulate words which **Saul** had heard (22:9). They had not seen the Lord; only **Saul** had seen Him and had been called to apostleship at this time.

The proud Pharisee was now **led by the hand ... into Damascus** where he remained **three days without sight**. During that time he **neither ate nor drank**.

9:10–14 One can picture the effect of the news on the Christians in **Damascus**. They knew that Saul had been on his way to capture them. They had prayed for divine intervention. Perhaps they had even dared to pray for Saul's conversion. Now they hear that the archenemy of the Faith has become a Christian. They can hardly believe their ears.

When the Lord instructed **Ananias**, one of the **Damascus** believers, to visit **Saul**, **Ananias** poured out all the forebodings of his heart concerning this man. But when assured that **Saul** was now **praying** instead of persecuting, **Ananias** went to **the house of Judas** on **Straight** Street.

9:15, 16 The Lord had wonderful plans for Saul: **". . . he is a chosen vessel of Mine to bear My name before Gentiles, kings, and the children of Israel. For I will show him how many things he must suffer for My name's sake."** Primarily Saul was to be the apostle to the **Gentiles**, and this commission would bring him before **kings**. But he would also preach to his countrymen according to the flesh, and here he would experience the keenest persecution.

9:17, 18 In a touching display of Christian grace and love, **Ananias** expresses full fellowship with the new convert by **laying his hands on him**, calling him **"Brother Saul,"** and explaining the purpose of his visit. It was that **Saul** might **receive** his **sight and** that he might **be filled with the Holy Spirit**.

It should be noted here that **the Holy Spirit** was given to **Saul** through the laying on of hands of a simple disciple. **Ananias** was what the commentators call a "layman." That the Lord should use one who was not an apostle should certainly be a rebuke to those who seek to confine spiritual prerogatives to the "clergy."

When a person is truly converted, certain things always happen. There are certain marks which show the reality of that conversion. This was true of Saul of Tarsus. What were these marks? Francis W. Dixon lists a few of them:

1. He met the Lord and heard His voice (Acts 9:4–6). He received a divine revelation, and only that could have convinced him and made him the humble inquirer and devoted follower that he became.
2. He was filled with a longing to obey the Lord and to do His will (Acts 9:6).
3. He began to pray (Acts 9:11).
4. He was baptized (Acts 9:18).
5. He united in fellowship with God's people (Acts 9:19).
6. He began to testify powerfully (Acts 9:20).
7. He grew in grace (Acts 9:22).

"LAY" MINISTRY

One of the most important lessons we can learn from Acts is that Christianity is a lay movement, and that the work of witnessing was not committed to a special class, such as priests or clergymen, but to all believers.

Harnack claimed that

when the church won its greatest victories in the early days in the Roman Empire, it did so not by teachers or preachers or apostles, but by informal missionaries.[42]

Dean Inge wrote:

Christianity began as a lay prophetic religion. . . . It is on the laity the future of Christianity depends. . . .[43]

Bryan Green says:

The future of Christianity and the evangelization of the world rest in the hands of ordinary men and women and not primarily in those of professional Christian ministers.[44]

Leighton Ford says:

A church which bottlenecks its specialists . . . to do its witnessing is living in violation of both the intention of its Head and the consistent pattern of the early Christians. . . .Evangelism was the task of the whole church, not just the "name characters."[45]

And finally, J. A. Stewart writes:

Each member of the local assembly went out to win souls for Christ by personal contact and then brought these newborn babes back into these local churches where they were indoctrinated and strengthened in the faith of the Redeemer. They, in turn, went out to do likewise.[46]

The simple fact is that in the apostolic church there was no such person as a clergyman or minister who presided over a local congregation. The normal local church consisted of saints, bishops, and deacons (Phil. 1:1). *The saints were all ministers*, in the NT sense. The bishops were the elders, overseers, or spiritual guides. The deacons were servants who carried on duties in connection with the finances of the local church, etc.

No one bishop or elder occupied a place as clergyman. There was a body of elders working together as shepherds of the assembly.

But someone may ask, "What about the apostles, prophets, evangelists, pastors, and teachers? Weren't they the clergymen of the early churches?" This is answered in Ephesians 4:12. These gifts were given to build up the saints in order that they (the saints) might carry on the ministry and, thus, build up the body of Christ. Their goal was not to settle themselves as permanent officials over a local congregation, but to work toward the day when the local church could carry on by itself. Then they could move on to establish and strengthen *other* assemblies.

According to church historians, the clerical system arose in the second century. It was not known in the Acts period. It has served as a hindrance to world evangelization and the expansion of the church, because it makes *too much* depend on *too few*.

Believers in the NT are not only ministers; they are priests as well. As holy priests, they have constant access by faith into the presence of God to worship

Him (1 Pet. 2:5). As royal priests, they are privileged to tell about the One who called them out of darkness into His marvelous light (1 Pet. 2:9). The priesthood of all believers does not mean that everyone is qualified to preach or teach publicly; it deals primarily with worship and witness. But it does mean that in the church there is no longer a special class of priests who have control of worship and service. ‡

9:19–25 The disciples in **Damascus** opened their hearts and homes to **Saul**. He soon made his way to **the synagogues**, proclaiming boldly that Jesus **is the Son of God**. Consternation resulted among his Jewish hearers. They had understood that he hated the name of Jesus. Now he was teaching that Jesus is God! How could it be?

How long he stayed **in Damascus** on this first visit we do not know. From Galatians 1:17 we do, however, learn that he left Damascus, went to Arabia for an unspecified length of time, then returned to Damascus. Where does the trip to Arabia fit into the record in Acts 9? Possibly between verses 21 and 22.

Many of God's most used servants have had an Arabian or wilderness experience before being sent out to preach.

In Arabia **Saul** had opportunity to meditate on the great events that had taken place in his life, and especially on the gospel of the grace of God, which had been committed to him. When he returned to **Damascus** (v. 22), he was able to confound **the Jews** in the synagogues, **proving that this Jesus is the** Messiah of Israel. This so infuriated them that they **plotted** against the life of this one who had once been their champion but who was now an "apostate," a "renegade," a "turncoat." **Saul** escaped by being lowered **by night . . . through** a hole in **the** city **wall in a large basket**. It was an ignominious exit, but **Saul** was now a broken man anyway, and broken men can endure reproach for Christ's sake that others would shun.

9:26–30 From the human standpoint, **Jerusalem** was the most dangerous place **Saul** could visit. However, assurance that one is in the will of God permits him to make proper allowance for his personal safety.

Whether this was Saul's first visit to **Jerusalem** as a Christian, the same one that took place three years after his conversion (Gal. 1:18), is debated. On his first visit to **Jerusalem** he met Peter and James, but none of the other apostles. Here, in verse 27, it says that **Barnabas . . . brought him to the apostles**. This could, of course, mean Peter and James, or it could mean all of the apostles. If the latter is intended, then this is a second visit to **Jerusalem**, not mentioned elsewhere.

At first **the disciples** in **Jerusalem were afraid** to receive **Saul**, doubting the sincerity of his profession as a believer. **Barnabas** proved true to his name as a *son of consolation* by befriending **Saul**, recounting his conversion, and telling of his fearless testimony for Christ **at Damascus**. The believers soon realized that **Saul** was genuine when they saw him preaching **boldly in the name of the Lord Jesus** in **Jerusalem**. He provoked the strongest opposition among **the Hellenists**. When **the brethren** saw that his life was in danger from these Jews, they escorted **Saul** to the seaport of **Caesarea**. From there he went to his home town of **Tarsus**, near the southeast coast of Asia Minor.

9:31 Then followed a breathing spell for **the churches** in Palestine. It was a time of consolidating the gains they had made, and of seeing the fellowship grow numerically and spiritually.

III. THE CHURCH TO THE END OF THE EARTH (9:32–28:31)

A. Peter's Preaching of the Gospel to the Gentiles (9:32–11:18)

9:32–34 As the narrative now reverts to **Peter**, we find him visiting believers in various parts of Judea. At length he comes to **Lydda** (Lod), northwest of Jerusalem, on the road to Joppa (modern Jaffa, or Yafo). There he finds a paralytic **who had been bedridden eight years**. Calling him by name, **Peter** announces that **Jesus the Christ** is his Healer. Aeneas **immediately** arises and carries his pallet. It is highly probable that Aeneas received spiritual life and physical healing at the same time.

9:35 The healed paralytic proved to

be a testimony for the Lord in the city of **Lydda and** in the entire coastal Plain of **Sharon**. Many **turned to the Lord** as a result.

9:36–38 **Joppa** was the major seaport of Palestine, located on the Mediterranean about thirty miles northwest of Jerusalem. Among the Christians there was a kindhearted lady named **Dorcas**,[47] who was well-known for making clothes for the poor. When **she** suddenly **died**, the disciples **sent** an urgent message to **Lydda**, asking **Peter** to come without **delay**.

9:39–41 Upon his arrival, he found **all the widows . . . weeping** pathetically as they showed the **garments which Dorcas had made** for them. He asked them to leave, then **knelt down and prayed**, and commanded **Tabitha** to **arise**. Immediately she was restored to life, and rejoined her Christian friends.

9:42 This miracle of resurrection **became** widely **known,** so that **many believed on the Lord**. However, comparing verse 42 with verse 35, it seems that more were converted through the healing of Aeneas than through the raising of Dorcas.

9:43 Peter **stayed many days in Joppa**, staying in the house of **Simon, a tanner**. The mention of Simon's trade here is significant. The Jews considered tanning a disreputable business. Constant contact with the bodies of dead animals caused ceremonial defilement. The fact that Peter lived with **Simon** showed he was no longer bound by this particular Jewish scruple.

It has often been pointed out that in three successive chapters we have the conversion of a descendant of one of Noah's sons. The Ethiopian eunuch (chap. 8) was undoubtedly of the line of Ham. Saul of Tarsus (chap. 9) was a descendant of Shem. Now here in chapter 10, in Cornelius, we see one of Japheth's posterity. It is a striking witness to the fact that the gospel is for all races and all cultures, and that in Christ all these natural distinctions are abolished. As Peter used the keys of the kingdom in opening the door of faith to the Jews in chapter 2, he is seen doing the same to the Gentiles in chapter 10.

10:1, 2 The chapter opens **in Caesarea**, about thirty miles north of Joppa. **Cornelius** was a Roman military officer. As **a centurion** he commanded about one hundred men. He was attached to **the Italian Regiment**. Even more remarkable than his military prominence was his piety. He was a **devout**, Godfearing **man, who gave alms generously** to impoverished Jewish **people, and prayed** consistently. Ryrie suggests he was probably "a proselyte of the gate; that is, he believed in the God of Judaism and His government, but had not yet taken any of the steps to become a full-fledged proselyte."[48]

Whether he was a saved man is open to question. Those who say he was saved refer to verse 2 and 35, where Peter says with obvious reference to **Cornelius**, that "whoever fears Him (God), and works righteousness is accepted by Him." Those who teach **Cornelius** was not saved point to 11:14, where the angel is quoted as promising him that Peter would tell him words whereby he might be saved.

Our view is that **Cornelius** is an example of a man who lived up to the light which God gave him. While this light was not sufficient to save him, God insured that he was given the additional light of the gospel. Before Peter's visit, he did not have the assurance of salvation, but he did feel a kinship with those who worshiped the true God.

10:3–8 At **about** 3:00 p.m. one day **Cornelius** had a clear **vision** in which **an angel of God** appeared to him and addressed him by name. Being a Gentile, he was not as aware of the ministry of angels as a Jew would be, and so he was afraid and mistook the angel for the Lord. The angel spoke reassuringly of God's appreciation of his **prayers** and **alms**, then told him to **send** south **to Joppa** for a man named **Simon Peter**, then **lodging with Simon, a tanner . . . by the sea**.[49] With unquestioning obedience, the centurion **sent** off **two of his household servants** and a military attaché who was also a God-fearing man.

10:9–14 **The next day**, at **about** noon, **Peter went up on** the flat roof of Simon's house in Joppa **to pray. He** was **hungry** at the time and would like to have eaten, but the meal was still being prepared down below. His hunger, of course, provided a fitting preparation for what was to follow. Falling into a trance, he saw a sheet . . . let down from heaven by its four corners, with all kinds of four-footed animals . . . , birds, and reptiles in it, clean and unclean. A voice from heaven directed the hungry apostle to "Rise, . . . kill and eat!" Remembering the Law of Moses which forbade a Jew to eat any unclean creature, Peter uttered the historic contradiction, "Not so, Lord!" Scroggie comments, "Whoever says 'not so' should never add 'Lord,' and whoever truly says 'Lord' will never say 'Not so.' "

10:15, 16 When Peter explained his past unbroken record in the matter of eating only kosher food, the voice from heaven said, "What God has cleansed you must not call common." Three times this dialogue took place, then the sheet returned to heaven.

It is clear that the vision had deeper significance than the mere matter of eating foods, clean and unclean. True, with the coming of the Christian faith, these regulations concerning foods were no longer in effect. But the real significance of the vision was this: God was about to open the door of faith to the Gentiles. As a Jew, Peter had always looked upon the Gentiles as unclean, as aliens, as strangers, as far off, as godless. But now God was going to do a new thing. Gentiles (represented by the unclean beasts and birds) were going to receive the Holy Spirit the same as the Jews (clean beasts and birds) had already received Him. National and religious distinctions were to be dissolved, and all true believers in the Lord Jesus would be on the same level in the Christian fellowship.

10:17–23a While Peter was pondering this vision in his heart, the servants of Cornelius arrived at the gate and inquired for him. Directed by the Spirit, he went down from the housetop to greet them. When he learned the purpose of their visit, he invited them in and gave them accommodations for the night. The servants paid high tribute to their master as "a just man, one who fears God and has a good reputation among all the nation of the Jews."

10:23b–29 On the next day Peter set out for Caesarea with the three servants of Cornelius and some brethren from Joppa. They apparently journeyed all day, because it was on the following day that they reached Caesarea.

In anticipation of their arrival Cornelius . . . had called together his relatives and close friends. When Peter arrived, the centurion fell down at his feet as an act of reverence. The apostle refused such worship, protesting that he was only a man himself. It would be fitting if all self-appointed "successors" of Peter would imitate his humility by forbidding people to kneel before *them*!

Finding a crowd assembled inside the house, Peter explained that as a Jew he would not ordinarily have come into a Gentile house like this one, but that God had revealed to him that he should no longer think of the Gentiles as being untouchables. Then he asked for what reason they had sent for him.

10:30–33 Cornelius readily described the vision he had seen four days before when an angel assured him that his prayer had been heard and directed him to send for Peter. The hunger of the Gentile heart for the word of God is praiseworthy. He said, "Now therefore, we are all present before God, to hear all the things commanded you by God." Such an open and teachable spirit is sure to be rewarded with divine instruction.

10:34, 35 Peter prefaced his message with a frank admission. Up to now he had believed that God's favor was limited to the nation of Israel. Now he realized that God did not respect a man's person because of his nationality, but was interested in an honest, contrite heart, whether in a Jew or a Gentile. "In every nation whoever fears Him and works righteousness is accepted by Him."

There are two principal interpretations of verse 35:

1. Some think that if one truly repents and seeks after God, he is saved even if he has never heard about the Lord Jesus. The argument is that although the man himself might not know about Christ's substitutionary sacrifice, yet God knows about it and saves the man on the basis of that sacrifice. He reckons the value of the work

of Christ to the man whenever He finds true faith.

2. The other view is that even if a man fears God and works righteousness, he is not thereby saved. Salvation is only by faith in the Lord Jesus Christ. But when God finds a man who has lived up to the light he has received about the Lord, He makes sure that the man hears the gospel and thus has the opportunity to be saved.

We believe that the second view is the proper interpretation.

10:36–38 Peter next reminds his hearers that although the gospel message was sent to the Jews first, yet **Jesus Christ . . . is Lord of all** — Gentile as well as Jew. His audience must have heard the story of **Jesus of Nazareth**; it had begun in **Galilee**, at the time **John** was baptizing, and had spread **throughout all Judea**. This **Jesus**, **anointed** by the **Spirit**, had lived a life of selfless service for others, **doing good and healing all who were oppressed by the devil**.

10:39–41 The apostles were **witnesses** to the truth **of all** Jesus **did**. They traveled with Him in all Judea **and in Jerusalem**. In spite of His perfect life, men **killed** Him **by hanging** Him **on a** stake. **God raised** Him from among the dead **on the third day**, and He was seen by **witnesses chosen before by God**. As far as we know, the Lord Jesus was not seen by any unbelievers after His resurrection. But the apostles not only saw Him; they **ate and drank with Him**. This, of course, shows that the Savior's resurrection body was tangible, material, and physical.

10:42 In resurrection, the Lord commissioned the apostles to proclaim Him as **Judge of the living and the dead**. This agrees with many other Scriptures which teach that the Father has committed all judgment to the Son (John 5:22). This means, of course, that as Son of Man He will judge Jews and Gentiles alike.

10:43 But Peter does not linger on a note of judgment. Instead he introduces a grand statement of evangelical truth, explaining how the judgment can be avoided. As **all the prophets** of the OT had taught, **whoever believes** in the name of the Messiah **will receive remission of sins**. It is not an offer to Israel alone, but takes in all the world. Would you like to know the forgiveness of sins? Then believe in Him!

10:44–48 While Peter was still speaking . . . , the Holy Spirit was **poured out on the Gentiles**. They all spoke **with tongues**, praising **God**. This was a sign to those present that Cornelius and his household had indeed **received the Holy Spirit**. The Jewish-born visitors from Joppa **were astonished** to think that **Gentiles** could receive **the Holy Spirit** as such, without becoming Jewish proselytes. But **Peter** was not bound to the same extent by Jewish prejudices. He sensed immediately that God was making no distinction between Jew and Gentile, so he proposed that the household of Cornelius should **be baptized**.

Notice the expression, **who have received the Holy Spirit just as we have**. These Gentiles had been saved in the same way as the Jews — simple faith. There was no suggestion of law-keeping, circumcision, or any other ordinance or ritual.

Notice, too, the order of events in connection with the reception of the Holy Spirit by the Gentiles:

1. They **heard the word**, that is, they believed (v. 44).
2. They **received the Holy Spirit** (v. 44, 47).
3. They were **baptized** (v. 48).

This is the order of events that prevails for Jew and Gentile alike in this dispensation, when God is calling out of the nations a people for His Name.

It is not surprising that after this gracious work of God's Spirit in Caesarea, the believers prevailed on Peter **to stay** with them **a few days**.

11:1–3 Word quickly got back to **Judea** that Peter had preached to **the Gentiles** and that they had been saved. Therefore, **when Peter** returned **to Jerusalem**, he was challenged by **those of the circumcision** for eating with Gentiles. **The circumcision** here refers to Christians of Jewish birth who were still bound by their former ways of thinking. For instance, they believed that a Gentile must be circumcised in order to obtain full blessing from the Lord. They still thought it was wrong for Peter to eat with Gentiles.

11:4–14 In defending his action, **Peter** gave a simple recital of all that had happened — his **vision** of the **sheet let down from heaven**, the appearance of **an angel** to Cornelius, the arrival of the messengers from Cornelius, the Spirit's command to accompany them, and the pouring out of **the Holy Spirit** on the Gentiles. Since **God** had worked in so many definite and yet distinct ways, to resist or oppose would obviously have been to oppose the Lord.

In his message, **Peter** added several interesting details not given in the previous chapter:

1. He said that the **sheet . . . from heaven . . . came** right down to where he was (v. 5).
2. He spoke of observing it **intently** (v. 6).
3. Peter adds the detail that **six brethren** accompanied him from Joppa to Caesarea (v. 12).
4. In verse 14 we are informed that the angel promised Cornelius that Peter would **tell** him **words by which** he **and all** his **household** would **be saved**. This verse is one of the principal evidences that Cornelius was not a saved man before Peter's arrival.

11:15 According to Peter's account, **the Holy Spirit fell upon** the Gentiles **as** he **began to speak**. In Acts 10:44 it appears that he had already been speaking some time. Apparently he had begun to speak but was interrupted before he had proceeded very far.

11:16 When **the Holy Spirit** fell on the Gentiles, Peter thought immediately of Pentecost. Then his mind went back further to the Lord's promise that His disciples would **"be baptized with the Holy Spirit."** He realized that the promise had been fulfilled in part at Pentecost and was now being fulfilled again.

11:17 Then Peter faced the circumcision party with this question: **If therefore God** chose to pour out the Spirit on the Gentiles, **as** He had done previously on the Jews who **believed . . . , who was** Peter that he should **withstand God?**

11:18 It is to the credit of these He-

brew Christians that when they had heard Peter's account, they recognized the hand of **God** in it all and did a complete about-face. All their objections were gone. In their place was praise to **God** for granting **to the Gentiles repentance to life**.

B. The Planting of the Church at Antioch (11:19–30)

11:19 The narrative now goes back to the time of **the persecution** following the martyrdom of **Stephen**. In other words, the events described in the next verses took place *before* the conversion of Cornelius.

Those who were scattered after the persecution carried the gospel to:

1. **Phoenicia**, the narrow coastland along the northeast Mediterranean, and including the ports of Tyre and Sidon (modern Lebanon).
2. **Cyprus**, a large island in the northeast Mediterranean.
3. **Cyrene**, a port city on the north coast of Africa (modern Libya).

However, they preached the gospel **to no one but the Jews.**

11:20, 21 But there were certain of the believers **from Cyprus and Cyrene** who went **to Antioch** and there proclaimed the good news to **the Hellenists.**[50] Blessing accompanied their preaching **and a great number believed and turned to the Lord**. F. W. Grant says: "It is remarkable how officialism is discredited in all this. We do not know the name of a single person used in the work."

The introduction of Christianity to Antioch was an important step in the forward march of the church. Antioch was located on the river Orontes in Syria, north of Palestine. It was considered the third city of the Roman Empire, and has been dubbed "the Paris of the ancient world." From here, Paul and his companions later went forth on their missionary journeys, taking the good news to the Gentiles.

11:22–24 When **news** of great spiritual awakening reached **the church in Jerusalem**, it was decided to send warmhearted, kindly **Barnabas** to **Antioch**. This dear man saw at a glance that the Lord was working mightily among these

Gentiles, so he **encouraged them** to **continue with the Lord** with great determination. How good it was that this infant church should be visited by such **a good man, full of the Holy Spirit and of faith**! While he was there, **a great many people** came **to the Lord**. Also, unity with the church at Jerusalem was preserved.

11:25, 26 Then **Barnabas** remembered **Saul** of **Tarsus**! It was he who had introduced **Saul** to the apostles at Jerusalem. Then **Saul** had been whisked out of the city to rescue him from the plots of the Jews. Since then he had been in his home town, **Tarsus**. Anxious to encourage **Saul** in the ministry and to give the church in **Antioch** the benefit of his teaching, **Barnabas departed for Tarsus** and **brought** Saul **to Antioch. For a whole year** this splendid team worked with the church there, teaching **a great many people**.

It was **in Antioch** that **the disciples were first called Christians**. Doubtless it was a term of reproach at that time, but since then it has been welcomed by all who love the Savior.

J. A. Stewart comments:

> Saintly F. B. Meyer has said: "Antioch will ever be famous in Christian annals, because a number of unordained and unnamed disciples, fleeing from Jerusalem in the face of Saul's persecution, dared to preach the Gospel to Greeks and to gather the converts into a church in entire disregard of the initial rite of Judaism."
>
> If these believers had gone from a modern congregation in which the ministry was designated to the sole responsibility of one man, this triumphant period of the Church's history could never have been written. How tragic that in the average church the ministry gifts of the Holy Spirit lie dormant and latent, because the average believer has no opportunity to minister. *As long as every little group of believers has a paid pastor to take care of them, there is one thing certain, and that is, the world will never be evangelized.* Thank God for all the voluntary Sunday school superintendents, Sunday school and Bible class teachers and so-called laymen. If they all had to be paid for their services very few churches would be able to function financially.[51]

11:27–30 Although **Antioch** became the center from which the gospel went out to the *Gentiles*, it always main-

tained full and hearty fellowship with the church in **Jerusalem**, which was the center for *Jewish* evangelism. The following incident illustrates this fact.

Certain **prophets came from Jerusalem to Antioch** at about this time. These **prophets** were believers who had been gifted by the Holy Spirit to speak as mouthpieces of God. They received revelations from the Lord and delivered them to the people. **One of them, named Agabus**, predicted that **a great famine** would sweep over the inhabited earth. The **famine** did come **in the days of Claudius Caesar. The disciples** at **Antioch** promptly decided **to send relief to** their Christian **brethren dwelling in Judea**. This was certainly a touching testimony that the middle wall of partition between Jew and Gentile was tumbling down, and that ancient antagonisms were obliterated by the cross of Christ. The grace of God was manifest in these **disciples** who gave unanimously, spontaneously, and proportionately. They gave, **each according to his ability**. F. W. Grant sadly noted, "Today it seems to be 'every one a little of his superfluity, and the richest in proportion least of all.' "

The money was **sent to the elders by the hands of Barnabas and Saul**. This is the first mention of **elders** in connection with the church. The idea of **elders** was familiar to Jews, however, since there were elders in the synagogue. No information is given as to how these men in Jerusalem became **elders**. In the Gentile churches, **elders** were appointed by apostles or their representatives (14:23; Titus 1:5). The qualifications of elders are given in 1 Timothy 3:1–7 and Titus 1:6–9.

C. The Persecution by Herod and His Death (12:1–23)

12:1, 2 Satan's relentless attacks on the church continued. This time the persecution came from **Herod the king**. This was Herod Agrippa I, a grandson of Herod the Great. He was appointed king over Judea by the Roman Emperor, Claudius. An observer of the Law of Moses, he went to great lengths to please the Jews. It was in pursuance of this policy that **he** harassed **some from**

the church and **killed James the brother of John with the sword**.

It was this **James** who had been with Peter and John on the Mount of Transfiguration with our Lord; and it was his mother who had requested that her two sons might sit beside Christ in His kingdom.

This chapter affords an interesting study of God's ways in connection with His people. **James** was put to death by the enemy, yet Peter was miraculously delivered. Human reason would ask why such preference should be shown to Peter. Faith rests on the love and wisdom of God, knowing that:

Ill that God blesses is our good,
And unblest good is ill,
And all is right that seems most wrong,
If it be His good will.
– *Frederick W. Faber*

12:3, 4 **The Jews** responded so enthusiastically to the execution of James that Herod was encouraged to do the same with **Peter**. However, it was by then **the Days of Unleavened Bread**, and executions were not exactly appropriate during religious holidays. Also the Jews would be too busy with their ceremonies to appreciate the favor, so Herod ordered **Peter** to jail during the interim. The apostle was guarded by sixteen soldiers in **four squads** of four soldiers each.

12:5 **The church** in Jerusalem prayed earnestly for **Peter**, especially as the death of James was so vivid in their minds. G. C. Morgan comments, "That force of earnest, halting prayer was mightier than Herod, and mightier than hell."

12:6–11 **That night . . . when Herod** planned **to bring him out**, **Peter was sleeping** soundly, manacled **between two soldiers**. Someone has called his slumber a triumph of faith. He probably remembered the Lord's promise that he would live to be an old man (John 21:18), and so he knew that Herod could not kill him prematurely. Suddenly **an angel of the Lord** appeared, and the cell was flooded with **light**. Tapping **Peter on the side**, **the angel** ordered him to get up **quickly**.

Immediately the handcuffs **fell off**.

Then with short, crisp sentences, **the angel** told **Peter** to dress, to **tie on** his **sandals**, to throw his cloak around him, and to **follow**. Though in a daze, **Peter followed** the angel **past the first and second guard posts** of the prison. When **they came to the iron gate**, it **opened** automatically, as if by an electric eye. It was only after they had passed through **one street** of the city, and **the angel** had vanished, that **Peter** came **to himself** and realized it was not a dream, but **that the Lord** had miraculously **delivered** him **from the hand of Herod** and of the Jews.

12:12 When he stopped long enough to consider, Peter realized that the disciples would be **praying** at **the house of Mary, the mother of John . . . Mark**. It must have been an all-night prayer meeting, since Peter's escape from prison probably took place during the early morning hours.

12:13–15 **Peter knocked at the door of the gate** and waited. **A girl named Rhoda** (Gk., "Rose") **came to answer**, but was so excited when she heard **Peter** that she failed to **open the gate**! She **ran** back to announce the good news to those who were praying. They thought she was crazy, and did not hesitate to tell her so, **yet she kept insisting that** the apostle was really at **the gate**. They said, "It must be **his** guardian **angel**," but she stated positively that it was Peter.

These believers have often been chided for their unbelieving prayers; they were actually surprised when their prayers were answered. But any such criticism is probably influenced by our own nervous self–consciousness. Instead of chiding others, we should be greatly comforted that God answers such faithless prayers. We all tend to be unbelieving believers.

12:16, 17 **Peter**, in the meantime, had been standing on the doorstep, **knocking. When they** finally **opened the door** and he stepped in, all their doubts vanished, and they broke out into great expressions of joy. He quickly quieted them down, gave a brief account of his miraculous deliverance, asked them to convey the news **to James** (probably the son of Alphaeus) **and to the brethren, and then departed**. It is impossible to know where he went at this time.

12:18, 19 When morning came and **Peter** was missing, **the** hapless **soldiers** were thrown into a state of panic. For **Herod**, too, it was a traumatic experience to be so outwitted. Nothing that **the soldiers** could say sounded at all convincing. In fact, the lameness of their testimony probably infuriated the king all the more. So he ordered them to be executed. He then left for **Caesarea** to nurse his wounded pride.

12:20 For some unknown reason, **Herod had** become **very angry with the people of Tyre and Sidon**, two commercial ports on the Mediterranean. **The people** of these cities took advantage of his holiday in Caesarea to ingratiate themselves with him, because they depended on importing grain from Judea. So they befriended **Blastus the king's personal aide**, and through him requested restoration of diplomatic relations.

12:21-23 One day **Herod** came forth in all his **royal** finery to address the people. They shouted deliriously, **"The voice of a god and not of a man!"** He made no effort to refuse such divine honors, or to **give glory to God**. Therefore, **an angel of the Lord struck Him** with a fearful disease **and** he **died**. This was in A.D. 44.

Thus, the one who had executed James to please the Jews is himself slain at the hands of Him who is able to destroy both body and soul in hell. **Herod** reaped what he sowed.

D. Paul's First Missionary Journey: Galatia (12:24–14:28)[†]

12:24 Meanwhile, the gospel expands its outreach continually. God makes the wrath of man praise Him, and the remainder of wrath He restrains (Ps. 76:10). He makes the devices of the people of no effect, but the counsel of the Lord stands forever (Ps. 33;10, 11).

12:25 After they had **fulfilled** their mission in **Jerusalem** by delivering the gift from Antioch, **Barnabas and Saul returned** to Antioch,[52] taking **with them Mark**, a cousin of **Barnabas** (Col. 4:10), who later wrote the Second Gospel.

It is impossible to know whether **Barnabas and Saul** were in **Jerusalem** at the time of the death of James, the imprisonment of Peter, or the death of Herod.

Many Bible commentators feel that chapter 13 marks a distinct break in the Book of Acts. Some even go so far as to call it Volume II of Acts. The Apostle Paul has now definitely come into the place of prominence, and Antioch in Syria becomes the center from which the gospel radiates to the Gentiles.

13:1 A **church** had been formed in **Antioch**, as we learned in chapter 11. Instead of having one man designated as the minister or pastor, this assembly had a plurality of gifts. Specifically, there were at least five **prophets and teachers**. As mentioned previously, a prophet was a man specially gifted by the Holy Spirit to receive revelations directly from God and to preach them to others. In a real sense, the **prophets** were mouthpieces for the Lord, and could often foretell coming events. **Teachers** were men to whom the Holy Spirit had given the ability to expound or explain the Word of God to others in a simple and understandable manner.

The names of the **prophets and teachers** are given as follows:

1. **Barnabas**. We have already been introduced to this splendid servant of Christ and Paul's faithful co–worker. Here he is mentioned first, perhaps because he was the oldest in the faith, or in service for Christ.

2. **Simeon who was called Niger** (nye-jer). We judge from his name that he was a Jew by birth, perhaps from an African Jewish community. Or perhaps he adopted the name **Niger** (black or swarthy) for convenience in working with Gentiles. Of course, he may have been black, as the name would suggest. Nothing else is known of him.

3. **Lucius of Cyrene**. He was probably one of the men of **Cyrene** who came to **Antioch** first, preaching the Lord Jesus (11:20).

4. **Manaen** (same as the OT name Menahem). He is listed as one **brought up with Herod the tetrarch**. It is interesting to think of one who had lived in such close relationship with the wicked **Herod** Antipas being one of the earliest converts to the Christian faith. The title, **tetrarch**, indicates that **Herod** ruled over a fourth part of his father's kingdom.

5. **Saul**. Although mentioned last in this list, **Saul** was to become a living embodiment of the truth, "The last shall be first."

These five men illustrate that the early church was integrated and color-blind as far as man's skin is concerned. "A new measuring stick has been brought into being: it is not *who* you are but *whose*."

13:2 These prophets and teachers had gathered together for a time of prayer and fasting, probably with the entire church. From the context, it appears clear that the expression, **they ministered to the Lord**, means they spent time in prayer and intercession. By fasting, they denied the legitimate claims of the body so as to give themselves more undistractedly to spiritual exercises.

Why had they come together to pray? Is it unreasonable to believe that they convened this meeting because of a deep burden for the evangelization of the world? The record does not indicate that it was an all–night prayer meeting, but the implication certainly is that it was of more serious and prolonged nature than the usual "prayer meeting" of today.

As they prayed, **the Holy Spirit** definitely instructed them to **separate** . . . **Barnabas and Saul for the** specific **work** which He had in mind. This, incidentally, is a very definite proof of the personality of **the Holy Spirit**. If He were nothing but an influence, it would be inconceivable that such language as this could be used. How did **the Holy Spirit** convey this message to the prophets and teachers? Although no definite answer is given, it is likely that He spoke through one of these men who were prophets — either Simeon, Lucius, or Manaen.

Barnabas is mentioned first here, then **Saul**. But when they returned to Antioch, the order was reversed.

This verse is of tremendous practical importance in emphasizing the role of **the Holy Spirit** in the guidance of the early church, and the sensitivity of the disciples to His leading.

13:3 After the Holy Spirit had thus revealed His will, the men continued to fast and pray. Then the three (Simeon, Lucius, and Manaen) **laid hands on** Barnabas and Saul. This was not an official act of "ordination" such as is practiced

in Christendom today where a church official confers ecclesiastical status on a subordinate. It was simply an expression of their fellowship with these two men in the work to which the Holy Spirit had called them. The idea of ordination as a rite which confers exclusive authority to administer the "sacraments" and perform other ecclesiastical duties is unknown in the NT. Barnhouse comments:

> A great error in our modern way of doing things is to expect one man to possess all the necessary gifts for leadership. Thus, a church may have several hundred members but only one pastor. He is supposed to be able to preach, comfort and so on. In fact, of the eight gifts mentioned in our text (Romans 12:6–8) seven are usually considered to be the functions of the ordained minister, while the eighth is the function of the congregation. And what one gift is left to the congregation? It is that of paying the bills. Something is out of order here.
>
> Someone may ask if I am suggesting that laymen should preach. Without question, when a layman has a grasp of the Scriptures he should exercise his gift and preach at every opportunity. The growth of laymen's movements is significant and is a step in the right direction — back to the New Testament way of doing things.[53]

It should be remembered that Barnabas and Saul had already been in the work of the Lord for about eight years before this time. They were not novices in the service of Christ. They had already experienced the "ordination of the Pierced Hands." Now their fellow-servants at Antioch were simply expressing their identification with them in this special commission to take the gospel to the Gentiles.

The words, **they sent them away**, are more literally, "they let them go" or "set them free" for the work.

13:4 With this verse begins what has commonly been known as Paul's First Missionary Journey. The record of this journey extends to 14:26. It was concerned chiefly with evangelizing Asia Minor. The Second Missionary Journey carried the gospel to Greece. The Third Missionary Journey included return visits to the churches of Asia Minor and Greece, but it was chiefly concerned with the Province of Asia and the city of Ephesus. Paul's missionary labors covered a period of about fifteen years.

(In tracing Paul's journeys, we shall indicate the places visited by printing the entire name in capital letters the first time it is mentioned on any particular journey.)

From Antioch in Syria the two intrepid servants of Christ first **went down to SELEUCIA** (pronounced sel-you'-shi-a), a seaport about sixteen miles from Antioch. From there **they sailed to** the island of **CYPRUS.**

13:5 After landing at **SALAMIS** (sal'-a-mis), on the east coast of Cyprus, they visited various **synagogues** and **preached the word** there. It was a custom in the synagogues for any Jewish man to be given the opportunity to read or expound the Scriptures. **John Mark,** at this time, was serving **as their assistant** (not "minister," as in the KJV). In going to the synagogue first, Barnabas and Saul were fulfilling the divine injunction that the gospel should go to the Jew first, then to the Gentiles.

13:6 From Salamis they worked their way across the entire length of **the island to PAPHOS** on the west coast. Salamis was the chief commercial city of the island. **Paphos** was the capital.

13:7, 8 There they met a Jewish **false prophet** and **sorcerer** named **Bar-Jesus** (meaning *Son of Jesus* or *of Joshua*). Somehow this **sorcerer** had become closely associated with **Sergius Paulus,** the Roman **proconsul**[54] or administrative officer of the island. The latter is described as **an intelligent man.** When **this man . . . called for Barnabas and Saul** to come to him so he could be instructed in **the word of God,** the **sorcerer** tried to interfere; he was probably satanically inspired to hinder the gospel.

In verse 8 his name is given as **Elymas,** meaning "wise man." It was, of course, a dreadful misnomer.

13:9, 10 Realizing that Sergius Paulus was an earnest seeker after truth, and that the sorcerer was an enemy of the truth, **Saul** openly rebuked him in unsparing terms. Lest anyone might suspect that **Saul** was speaking in the energy of the flesh, it is explicitly stated that he was **filled with the Holy Spirit** at the time. Fixing his eyes **intently** on the sorcerer, **Saul** accused him of being **full of all** guile **and all fraud.** Nor was

Saul deceived by the name Bar-Jesus; he tore away that mask and labeled Elymas as a **son of the devil.** The magician was an **enemy of all righteousness,** working ceaselessly to distort the truth of God.

13:11 Then, speaking with the special disciplinary authority vested in him as an apostle, Saul announced that Elymas would be stricken with blindness **for a time.** Because he had tried to keep others, such as the proconsul, in spiritual darkness, he himself would be punished with physical blindness. **Immediately a dark mist fell on him,** and he groped his way around, trying to find **someone** willing **to lead him by the hand.**

Elymas might be taken as a picture of the nation of Israel, not only unwilling to accept the Lord Jesus, but seeking to prevent others from doing so as well. As a result, Israel has been judicially blinded by God, but only **for a time.** Eventually a repentant remnant of the nation will turn to Jesus as Messiah and be converted.

13:12 **The proconsul** was obviously impressed by the miraculous stroke from God, but he was even more impressed by **the teaching** which had been given to him by Barnabas and Saul. He became a true believer in the Lord Jesus, the first trophy of grace on the first missionary journey.

Note that in this narrative (v. 9) Luke begins using Saul's Gentile name, Paul, rather than his Jewish name, Saul. The use of the name, *Paul*, signals the increasing outflow of the gospel to the Gentiles.

13:13 The fact that **Paul** has now taken the place of prominence is indicated by the words, **Paul and his party. From Paphos** they sailed northwest to **PERGA in PAMPHYLIA** (pam-fil'-i-a). **Pamphylia** was a Roman province on the southern coast of Asia Minor. **Perga** was its capital, and was located seven miles inland on the River Cestrus (Kestros).

It was when they reached **Perga** that **John** Mark left them and **returned to Jerusalem.** Maybe he didn't relish the thought of taking the gospel to the Gentiles. **Paul** considered his withdrawal such a defect in service that he refused to allow Mark to accompany him on the second journey. This caused a sharp cleavage between **Paul** and Barnabas, resulting in their taking separate paths as far as future Christian service was concerned (cf. 15:36–39). Eventually, Mark regained the confidence of the Apostle **Paul** (2 Tim. 4:11).

No further details are given as to the visit to **Perga.**

13:14, 15 The next stop was **ANTI-OCH in PISIDIA** (pi-sid'-i-a). This was approximately one hundred miles north of **Perga**. Once again the two heralds of the cross made their way to **the synagogue on the Sabbath**. After the Scriptures had been read, **the rulers of the synagogue** recognized these visitors as Jewish and invited them to speak, **if** they had **any word of exhortation for the people**. This liberty of proclaiming the truth of the gospel in synagogues was not to continue long.

13:16 Never being one to miss an opportunity to preach the gospel, **Paul stood up** and addressed the synagogue. His general plan of attack was to lay a foundation of Jewish history, then to bring his hearers up to the events connected with the life and ministry of Christ, then to proclaim the resurrection of Christ with considerable emphasis, announce remission of sins through the Savior, and warn of the peril of rejecting Him.

13:17 The message begins with God's choice of the nation of **Israel** as His earthly people. It moves quickly on to the time when they were **strangers in the land of Egypt**, and magnifies His grace in delivering them from the oppression of Pharaoh **with** His **uplifted arm.**

13:18 **Forty years** God **put up with** the **ways** of the people of Israel **in the wilderness**. The verb translated **put up with**, while it means just that by usage, is derived from a word that may suggest a more positive note, namely, taking care of somebody's needs. This the Lord certainly did for Israel in spite of all their complaining.

13:19–22 **The four hundred and fifty years** that Paul mentions is probably meant to go back to the time of the patriarchs and so would be inclusive of that period up to the judges.[55]

Following their entrance into Canaan, God **gave** the people **judges . . . until** the time of **Samuel the prophet**. When **they asked for a king** like the other nations, **God gave them Saul the son of Kish, a man of the tribe of Benjamin**; he ruled over them **for forty years**. Because of his disobedience, **Saul** was **removed** from the throne, and **David** was **raised up** to replace him. God paid high tribute to **David** as **a man after** His **own heart, who** would **do all** His **will**. Verse 22 combines quotations from Psalm 89:20 and 1 Samuel 13:14.

13:23 From the subject of David, Paul made an easy and swift transition to **Jesus**, David's **seed**. As someone has well said, "All roads in Paul's preaching led to Christ." It is perhaps difficult for us to appreciate the courage involved in announcing to the people of **Israel** that **Jesus** was a **Savior** whom **God** according to promise had brought to them. This was not exactly the light in which they had been accustomed to view **Jesus!**

13:24 After this brief introduction, Paul went back to the ministry of **John** the Baptist. Prior to Christ's **coming** (that is His public ministry), **John** had **preached . . . the baptism of repentance to all the people of Israel**. This means he had announced the **coming** of the Messiah, and told **the people** to repent in preparation for that **coming**. They were to signify their **repentance** by being baptized in the Jordan River.

13:25 Not for one minute did **John** permit the suggestion that he might be the promised Messiah. Up to the time when he **was finishing his** ministry, he kept insisting he was **not** the **One** of whom the prophets had spoken. In fact, he was **not worthy to loose** the **sandals** of the **One** whose coming he announced.

13:26 Addressing his audience as **brethren** and **sons of the family of Abraham**, Paul reminded them that **the word of this salvation** was **sent** first to the nation of Israel. It was to the lost sheep of the house of Israel that Jesus came. It was to them that the disciples were instructed to first preach the message.

13:27, 28 But the people **in Jerusalem, and their rulers** did not recognize Jesus as the long-sought Messiah. They did not realize He was the One of whom **the Prophets** had written. When they heard predictions concerning the Messiah from the Scriptures each **Sabbath**, they did not link them with Jesus of Nazareth. Instead, they themselves were the means of fulfilling those very Scriptures by **condemning Him. And though they found no cause of death in Him**, they turned Him over to **Pilate** to **be put to death**.

13:29 In the first part of the verse, **they** refers to the Jewish people who fulfilled the Scriptures by rejecting the Messiah. In the latter part of the verse, **they** refers to Joseph of Arimathea and Nicodemus, who lovingly buried the body of the Lord Jesus.

13:30, 31 The fact that Jesus rose **from the dead** was well attested. **Those who came up with** Jesus **from Galilee to Jerusalem** were still alive, and their witness could not be denied.

13:32–33 The apostle next announced that **the promise** of the Messiah **which was made to the fathers** in the OT had been **fulfilled** in Jesus. It was **fulfilled** first in His birth in Bethlehem. Paul saw the birth of Christ as a fulfillment of Psalm 2:7, where God says, "You are My Son, today I have begotten You." This verse does not mean that Christ began to be the Son of God when He was born in Bethlehem. He was God's Son from all eternity, but He was manifested to the world as the Son of God through His Incarnation. Psalm 2:7 should not be used to deny the eternal Sonship of Christ.

13:34 The resurrection of the Lord Jesus comes into view in verse 34. God **raised Him from the dead, no more to return to corruption**. Paul then quoted Isaiah 55:3: **"I will give you the sure mercies of David."** This quotation presents a difficulty to the average reader. What connection can there possibly be between this verse in Isaiah and the resurrection of Christ? How is the resurrection of the Savior linked with God's covenant with **David**?

God promised **David** an everlasting throne and kingdom, and a seed to sit upon that throne forever. In the meantime **David** had died, and his body had returned to dust. The kingdom had continued for some years after David, but then for over four hundred years Israel had been without a king. The line of **David** continued down through the

years to Jesus of Nazareth. He inherited legal right to the throne of **David** through Joseph. Joseph was His legal father, though not His real father. The Lord Jesus was a lineal descendant of **David** through Mary.

Paul is emphasizing that the **sure** blessings promised to **David** find their fulfillment in Christ. He is the seed of **David** who will yet sit on the throne of **David**. Since He has risen **from the dead**, and lives in the power of an endless life, the eternal aspects of God's covenant with **David** are made certain in Christ.

13:35 This is further emphasized in verse 35, where the apostle quotes Psalm 16:10, **"You will not allow Your Holy One to see corruption."** In other words, since the Lord Jesus has risen from the dead, death has no more power over Him. He will never die again, nor will His body ever **see corruption**.

13:36, 37 Although **David** uttered the words of Psalm 16:10, he could not have been speaking about himself. **After he had served his own generation by the will of God**, he died, **was buried**, and his body returned to dust. But the Lord Jesus was **raised** from the dead the third day, before his body could experience **corruption**.

13:38 On the basis of the work of Christ, of which His resurrection was the divine seal of approval, Paul was now able to announce remission **of sins** as a present reality. Notice his words: **"Through this Man is preached to you the forgiveness of sins."**

13:39 But there was more to it than that. Paul could also now announce full and free justification from all things. This was something **the law of Moses** could never offer.

Justification is the act of God by which He reckons or declares to be righteous those ungodly sinners who receive His Son as Lord and Savior. It is a legal act which takes place in the mind of God, and by which the sinner is cleared of every charge against him. God can righteously acquit the guilty sinner, because the penalty for his sins has been fully met by the substitutionary work of the Lord Jesus Christ on the cross.

On first reading, it might appear that **the law of Moses** could justify from some things, but through Christ a person can receive justification from many other things. But that is not the teaching at all. **The law** could never justify anyone; it could only condemn. What Paul is saying here is that through faith in Christ a man can **be justified from** every charge of guilt that might be brought against him — a clearance that could never be obtained under **the law of Moses.**

13:40, 41 The apostle then closes his message with a solemn warning to those who might be tempted to refuse God's great offer of present salvation. He quotes from Habakkuk 1:5 (and perhaps segments of Isa. 29:14 and Prov. 1:24–31), where God warned those **despisers** of His word that He would bring wrath upon them of such magnitude that they wouldn't even **believe** it if He told them in advance. In Paul's day this might have applied to the destruction of Jerusalem in A.D. 70, but it would also include God's eternal judgment of those who reject His Son.

13:42, 43 When the service in **the synagogue** was over, **many of the Jews and devout** converts to Judaism **followed Paul and Barnabas** with deepest interest. These two servants of the Lord gave them a hearty word of encouragement **to continue in the grace of God.**

13:44 One week later Paul and Barnabas returned to the synagogue to continue where they had left off. **Almost the whole city** gathered **to hear the word of God.** The ministry of these two devoted preachers had made a deep impression on many of the people.

13:45 However, the popularity of this "alien message" **filled the Jews with envy** and rage. They openly contradicted Paul's message and used strong, intemperate language against him.

13:46, 47 **Paul and Barnabas** were not easily intimidated. They explained that they were under obligation to declare the message first of all to the Jewish people. However, since they had rejected the message, and had thus condemned themselves as **unworthy of everlasting life**, the preachers announced they were turning **to the Gentiles** with the gospel. If any authorization were needed for such a break with Jewish tradition, then the words of Isaiah

49:6 would do. Actually, in this verse God is speaking to the Messiah when He says, **"I have set you as a light to the Gentiles, that you should be for salvation to the ends of the earth."** But the Spirit of God permits the servants of the Messiah to apply these words to themselves, since they were His instruments in bringing **light** and **salvation** to the Gentile nations.

13:48 If this announcement of salvation for **the Gentiles** infuriated the Jews, it caused great rejoicing among **the Gentiles** who were present. **They glorified the word of the Lord** which they had heard. All who were **appointed to eternal life believed.** This verse is a simple statement of the sovereign election of God. It should be taken at its face value and believed. The Bible teaches definitely that God chose some before the foundation of the world to be in Christ. It teaches with equal emphasis that man is a free moral agent and that if he will accept Jesus Christ as Lord and Savior, he will be saved. Divine election and human responsibility are both scriptural truths, and neither should be emphasized at the expense of the other. While there seems to be a conflict between the two, this conflict exists only in the human mind, and not in the mind of God.

Men are damned by their own choice and not by any act of God. If all mankind received what is its just due, then all would be lost. But God in grace stoops down and saves some. Does He have a right to do this? Of course He does. The doctrine of the sovereign election of God is a teaching that gives God His proper place as the Ruler of the universe who can do as He chooses and who will never choose to do anything unrighteous or unkind. Many of our difficulties with this subject would be solved if we would remember the words of Erdman:

> The sovereignty of God is absolute; yet it is never exercised in condemning men who ought to be saved, but rather has resulted in the salvation of men who deserved to be lost.[56]

13:49, 50 In spite of the opposition of the Jews, **the word of the Lord was being spread throughout all the** surrounding **region**. This further aroused the opposition party to hinder and obstruct. **The Jews stirred up** some **devout . . . women** who had become converts to Judaism and were **prominent** in the community to agitate against the missionaries. Also they used **the chief men of the city** to further their wicked purposes. Such a storm of **persecution** was **stirred up** that **Paul and Barnabas** were forcibly evicted from the area.

13:51, 52 In accordance with the instructions of the Lord (Luke 9:5; 10:11), **they shook off the dust from their feet** and moved on **to ICONIUM**. However, the incident was not interpreted by the Christians as a defeat or a retreat, for we read that they **were filled with joy and with the Holy Spirit**. Iconium, located east and south of Antioch in Asia Minor, today is called Konya.

14:1, 2 In **Iconium**, as in other places where there was a **synagogue**, Paul and Barnabas were permitted to preach, in accordance with the custom prevailing among the Jews at that time. The Spirit of God accompanied the word with such power that a **great** number of **Jews and** Gentile proselytes accepted the Lord Jesus. This aroused the ire of those **Jews** who refused to obey the gospel, and they in turn **stirred up the Gentiles . . . against the brethren**. In the Book of Acts the unbelieving Jews were the instigators of much of the persecution of the apostles, though they themselves did not necessarily administer the punishment. They were masters at persuading the *Gentiles* to carry out their wicked purposes.

14:3 Although they knew trouble was brewing, the preachers continued to speak **boldly in** the name of **the Lord**, who confirmed the divine nature of the message by empowering them to perform **signs and wonders**. **Signs and wonders** are two different words for miracles. The word "sign" simply means that the miracle conveys a lesson, whereas the word "wonder" suggests that the miracle creates a sense of awe.

14:4–7 As tension built up in the city, sides were naturally formed. Some **sided with the Jews, and** some **with the apostles**. Finally the unbelieving **Gentiles and Jews** made a determined rush

to assault **the apostles**.[57] To escape stoning, they fled **to LYSTRA** (lis'-tra) **and DERBE**, both **cities of LYCAONIA** (lye-kay-own'-ia), a district in the center of Asia Minor. With no lessening of ardor, they continued **preaching the gospel** in that entire region.

When Paul and Barnabas were threatened with stoning, **they fled** to **Lycaonia**. At other times in their missionary labors, they seemed to remain in a place in spite of danger. Why did they escape at some junctures and stand their ground at others? There does not seem to be any neat explanation. The great controlling principle in Acts is the guidance of the Holy Spirit. These men lived in close, intimate communion with the Lord. Abiding in Him, they received marvelous communications of the divine mind and will. To them, this was the important thing, rather than a well-arranged set of rules of conduct.

14:8, 9 In **Lystra** the missionaries came in touch with a man who had been **a cripple** from birth. As he listened to **Paul speaking**, he evidenced an unusual interest. **Paul** somehow realized that this man **had faith to be healed**. Although we are not told how **Paul** knew this, we do believe that a true evangelist is given the ability to discern the state of souls with whom he deals. He is able to tell whether they are only mildly curious, or whether they are in actual soul trouble because of conviction of sin.

14:10–12 As soon as **Paul** commanded the man to get **up on** his **feet, . . . he leaped and walked**. Since the miracle had been performed openly, and since Paul had undoubtedly attracted considerable attention by speaking **with a loud voice**, **the people** were greatly impressed. In fact a popular movement began with the purpose of worshiping **Barnabas as Zeus**, and **Paul as Hermes**.[58] **The people** actually believed that their **gods** had paid them a visit in the person of the two missionaries. For some reason not stated, they looked on **Barnabas** as being the chief god. Because **Paul** had done the speaking, they designated him as **Hermes**, the messenger of **Zeus**.

14:13 Even **the priest of Zeus** became convinced that a divine visitation had taken place; he rushed out of the temple that **was** at the gateway **of their city** with **oxen and garlands** for a great sacrifice. This entire movement was a more subtle form of danger to the Christian faith than all the other forms of opposition recorded. For a successful Christian worker a greater peril than persecution is the tendency for people to center their spiritual attention, not on Christ, but on His servant.

14:14, 15a At first **Barnabas and Paul** did not realize what the crowd was up to, because they didn't understand the Lycaonian vernacular. As soon as it became clear to the missionaries that the people were about to worship them as gods, **they tore their clothes** as a public expression of protest and sorrow. Then they **ran in among the multitude**, and with impassioned words they warned them against such folly. Instead of being gods, they were **men with the same nature as** the Lycaonians. Their object was simply to bring the good news that the people **should turn from** lifeless idols **to the living God**.

14:15b–17 It is noticeable that Paul and Barnabas did not quote the OT to these Gentiles, as they did to the Jews. Rather, they began with the story of creation, a subject of immediate interest to Gentile peoples in all countries and in all ages. The missionaries explained that **in bygone generations** God **allowed all nations to walk in their own ways**. Even then, however, they had evidence of the existence of God in creation and in providence. It was **He** who lovingly provided **rain . . . and fruitful seasons** for them, **filling** their **hearts with food and gladness**. This latter expression is a figurative way of saying that in providing **food** for their bodily means, **God** filled their **hearts with** the **gladness** that comes from the enjoyment of **food**.

14:18 The message had its desired result. The people reluctantly desisted from their intention of **sacrificing to** these servants of the Lord.

14:19, 20 **Jews from** Pisidian **Antioch and Iconium** caught up with **Paul** and Barnabas in Lystra. They succeeded in turning the Gentile populace against the missionaries. The same crowd that wanted to reverence them as gods now **stoned Paul and dragged him out of the city, supposing** that they had killed him.

Kelly's comments on this section are most apropos:

> And why? That very refusal of homage, which the Lystrans were ready to pay, is most offensive to man, and disposes him to believe the most odious misrepresentations of those he was about to worship. Men exalt themselves by human adoration; and to be balked of it soon turns to the hatred and perhaps death of those who seek the honour of the only God. So it was here. Instead of changing their minds like the Maltese (who from a murderer regarded Paul as a god, Acts 28:6), they listen to Jewish calumny though ordinarily despised, and stone as a false prophet him to whom they had been so lately wishing to sacrifice, leaving him dragged without the city as a dead man.[59]

Was Paul actually **dead** as a result of the stoning? If this is the incident referred to in 2 Corinthians 12:2, he himself did not know. The best we can say is that his restoration was miraculous. As **the disciples gathered around him, he rose up and went** back **into the city** with them. **The next day he departed with Barnabas to DERBE**.

14:21 Considerations of personal safety were not uppermost in the minds of the missionaries. This is seen in the fact that **when they had preached the gospel** at Derbe, **they returned to LYSTRA**, the scene of Paul's stoning. This illustrates what has been called "the power of comeback and quick recovery."

Although Timothy is not mentioned here, he may have been saved at this time through the preaching of Paul. When the apostle next visited **Lystra**, Timothy was already a disciple, and was highly regarded by the brethren (Acts 16:1, 2). However, the fact that Paul later spoke of him as his true child in the faith (1 Tim. 1:2) does not *necessarily* mean that Paul had won him to Christ. He may have been a "true child" by following the example of Paul's life and service.

When their work at **Lystra** was completed, the missionaries revisited **ICONIUM and** PISIDIAN **ANTIOCH**, where churches had already been established. Their purpose at this time was what we call "follow-up work." They were never satisfied merely to preach the gospel and see souls won to the Savior. For them, this was only the beginning. They then sought to build up the believers in their most holy faith, especially by teaching them the truth of the church and its importance in God's program.

Erdman points out:

A proper missionary program has as its aim the establishing on the field of self-governing, self-sustaining, self-propagating churches. This was ever the purpose and the practice of Paul.[60]

14:22 The exact nature of their follow-up work was **strengthening the souls of the disciples** and establishing the Christians **in the faith** by instructing them from the word of God. Paul described the process in Colossians 1:28, 29: "We warn everyone we meet, and we teach everyone we can, all that we know about him, so that, if possible, we may bring every man up to his full maturity in Christ Jesus. This is what I am working at all the time, with all the strength that God gives me" (JBP).

Second, they exhorted **them to continue in the faith**, an exhortation especially timely in view of the widespread persecution then prevalent. With this exhortation went a reminder that **we must through many tribulations enter the kingdom of God**. This refers to **the kingdom of God** in its future aspect, when believers will share Christ's glory. A person enters **the kingdom of God** in the first place through the new birth. Persecutions and **tribulations** do not have any saving value. However, those who **enter the kingdom of God** by faith at the present time are promised that the pathway to future glory is filled with **tribulations**. "If indeed we suffer with Him, that we may also be glorified together" (Rom. 8:17b).

14:23 At this time, the missionaries also **appointed elders in every church**. In this connection, several observations should be made:

1. New Testament elders (presbyters) were godly, mature men who exercised spiritual leadership in the local church. They are also spoken of as bishops and overseers.

2. In the Book of Acts, elders were not appointed when a church was first founded. Rather, it was when the apostle *revisited* the churches that this was done. In other words, during the intervening time there was opportunity for those who had been made elders by the Holy Spirit to become manifest.

3. Elders were appointed by the apostles and by their delegates. At this time the NT was not yet written to give explicit instructions concerning the qualifications of elders. The apostles knew what these qualifications were, however, and they were able to single out the men who met the scriptural requirements.

4. We do not have apostles today to appoint elders. However, we do have the qualifications of elders in 1 Timothy 3 and Titus 1. Therefore each local assembly should be able to recognize those men in it who meet God's requirements as undershepherds of the sheep.

After Paul and Barnabas had **prayed with fasting, they commended** the believers **to the Lord**. It seems extraordinary to us that assemblies could be started in such a short time, that they should receive such brief periods of instruction from the missionaries, and yet that they should go on brightly for the Lord, functioning as autonomous churches. The answer ultimately lies in the mighty power of the Holy Spirit of God. However, the power was manifest in the lives of men like Paul and Barnabas. Everywhere they went they exerted a mighty influence for God. People detected reality in their lives. Their public preaching was backed up by the example of their own lives, and the influence of this twofold testimony was incalculable.

Verses 21 to 23 give the apostolic pattern — preaching the gospel, teaching the converts, and establishing and strengthening churches.

14:24–26 **After they had passed through** the district of **Pisidia, they** traveled south **to PAMPHYLIA**. There they revisited **PERGA**, then **they went down to** the seaport city of **ATTALIA** where they boarded a ship and **sailed to ANTIOCH** in SYRIA. This brought them to the end of their first missionary journey. It was from **Antioch** that **they had been**

commended to the grace of God for the work which they had just completed.

14:27 What a joyful time it must have been when **they gathered the church** at Antioch **together** to hear an account of the missionary labors of these two great men of God. With becoming Christian modesty, **they reported all that God had done with them, and that He had opened the door of faith to the Gentiles**. It was not what they had done for God, but what He had been pleased to accomplish through them.

14:28 **They stayed** in Antioch **a long time with the disciples**. Estimates vary between one and two years.

MISSIONARY STRATEGY

It is thrilling to see how a small group of nondescript disciples living in an obscure corner of the world were imbued with a glorious vision for the evangelization of the world and how they carried it out. Each one felt directly involved in this task and gave himself or herself to it without reserve.

Much of the evangelism was carried on by local believers in connection with their everyday duties. They "gossiped" the gospel in their own neighborhoods.

In addition, the apostles and others traveled from country to country, preaching the gospel and planting churches. They went out by twos or in larger companies. Sometimes a younger man went out with an older; for instance, Timothy with Paul.

Basically there were two methods — personal evangelism and mass evangelism. In connection with the latter, it is interesting to notice that most of the preaching was impromptu, and arose from some local situation or crisis.

Nearly all the preachings that took place as recorded there (in Acts) were under circumstances which precluded any possibility of the preacher preparing his discourse; every one of these occasions was unexpected.[61]

As E. M. Bounds has said, their preaching was not the performance of an hour but rather the overflow of a life.

The apostles and their associates were guided by the Holy Spirit, but this guidance was often confirmed by their local church. Thus we read that the prophets and teachers at Antioch laid their hands on Barnabas and Paul and sent them off on the First Missionary Journey (13:2). Again we read that Timothy had the confidence of the brethren at Lystra and Iconium before he set out with Paul (16:2). And Paul and Silas were recommended to the grace of God by the church at Antioch prior to the Second Missionary Journey (15:40).

It is commonly taught that their geographical strategy was to go into large cities and plant churches so that those churches would then evangelize the surrounding territory. This is perhaps an oversimplification. Basically their strategy was to follow the guidance of the Holy Spirit, whether to a large city or a small one. The Holy Spirit led Philip from revival in Samaria to a single man on the road to Gaza (8:26–40). And He led Paul to Berea (17:10), which Cicero called an "out-of-the-way city." Frankly, we do not see a fixed, inflexible geographical strategy in the Book of Acts. Rather we see the sovereign Spirit moving in accordance with His own will.

Local churches were established wherever people responded to the gospel. These assemblies gave permanence and stability to the work. They were self-governing, self-financing, and self-propagating. The apostles revisited the congregations to strengthen and encourage the believers (14:21, 22; 15:41; 20:1, 2) and to appoint elders (14:23).

In their missionary travels the apostles and their associates were sometimes self-supporting (18:3; 20:34); sometimes they were supported by gifts from churches and individuals (Phil. 4:10, 15-18). Paul worked to provide not only for himself but for those who were with him (20:34).

Though they were *commended* to the grace of God by their local church, and *supported* by local churches, yet they were not *controlled* by local churches. They were the Lord's free agents in declaring all the counsel of God and in holding back nothing that was profitable (20:20).

At the conclusion of their missionary journeys, they returned to their home church and gave a report of how the Lord had worked through them (14:26-28; 18:22, 23). This is a good pattern for all missionaries to follow in every age of the church.‡

E. The Council at Jerusalem (15:1–35)

15:1 The dispute which arose over circumcision in the church at Antioch is also described in Galatians 2:1–10. Taking the two accounts together, we get the following picture: **Certain** false brethren **from** the church in **Jerusalem** traveled to Antioch and began preaching in the assembly there. The substance of their message was that Gentiles must be **circumcised** in order to **be saved**. It was not enough that they should believe on the Lord Jesus Christ; they must also put themselves under the Law **of Moses**. This, of course, was a frontal attack on the gospel of the grace of God. The true gospel of grace teaches that Christ finished the work necessary for salvation on the cross. All a sinner needs to do is receive Him by faith. The moment human merit or works are introduced, then it is no longer of grace. Under grace, all depends on God and not on men. If conditions are attached, then it is no longer a gift but a debt. And salvation *is* a gift; it is not earned or merited.

15:2, 3 **Paul and Barnabas** vigorously opposed these Judaizers, knowing that they had come to rob the Gentile believers of their liberty in Christ Jesus.

Here in Acts 15 we learn that the brethren in Antioch decided to send **Paul and Barnabas and certain others . . . to Jerusalem, to the apostles and elders** there. In Galatians 2:2 Paul says that he went to Jerusalem by revelation. There is no contradiction, of course. The Spirit of God revealed to Paul that he should go, and also revealed to the church in Antioch that the brethren should send him. En route **to Jerusalem** the group stopped at various points in **Phoenicia and Samaria**, giving an account of **the conversion of the Gentiles**, and causing **great joy** wherever the story was told.

15:4 **When** he first arrived in **Jerusalem**, Paul went to **the apostles and the elders** privately and gave them a full account of the gospel which he had been preaching to the Gentiles. They had to admit that it was the same gospel which they had been preaching to the Jews.

15:5 Apparently it was in an open meeting of the entire church that certain **of the Pharisees who** were believers **rose up** and contended that Gentiles must be circumcised and must **keep the law of Moses** in order to be disciples in the truest sense.

15:6 From verse 6 it might appear that only **the apostles and elders** were present when the final decision was made. However, verse 12 seems to indicate that the entire church was there as well.

15:7–10 As **Peter rose** to his feet, perhaps the opposition felt he would support their position. After all, **Peter** was the apostle to the circumcision. However, their hopes were doomed to disappointment. **Peter** reminded the audience that some years previously **God** had ordained that **the Gentiles should** first **hear . . . the gospel** from his lips. This took place in the house of Cornelius. When **God** saw that the hearts of those **Gentiles** were reaching out to Him in faith, He gave **them the Holy Spirit, just as He did** to the Jews on the Day of Pentecost. At that time, **God** did not require these **Gentiles** to be circumcised. The fact that they were **Gentiles** made no difference; He cleansed **their hearts by faith**. Since **God** had accepted **the Gentiles** on the principle of **faith** and not of law-keeping, **Peter** asked the assembly why they should now think of **putting** the Gentiles under the **yoke** of the law — a yoke . . . **which neither** their **fathers nor** they had been **able to bear**. The law never saved anyone. Its ministry was condemnation, not justification. By the law is the knowledge of sin, not salvation from sin.

15:11 Peter's final decision is worthy of special notice. He expressed the deep conviction that **through the grace of the Lord Jesus** (and not through law-keeping) **we** (the Jews) **shall be saved in the same manner as they** (the Gentiles). One would have expected Peter, as a Jew, to say that the Gentiles would be saved the same as the Jews. But **grace** is here seen triumphing over ethnic distinctions.

15:12 After Peter had finished, **Bar-**

nabas and Paul gave an account of how God had visited the Gentiles, and had accompanied the preaching of the gospel with miracles and wonders.

15:13, 14 Peter had told how the Lord had opened the door of faith to the Gentiles at the first through him. Paul and Barnabas added their testimony as to how the Lord had worked through them in evangelizing the Gentiles. James now stated authoritatively that God's present purpose for this age is to call out of the Gentiles . . . a people for His name. This was, in substance, what Simon (Peter) had just related.

15:15–19 Then James quoted from Amos 9:11, 12. Notice that he did not say that the calling out of the Gentiles was in fulfillment of the prophecy of Amos, but rather that it agreed with the words of the prophets. The assembly should not think it a strange thing that God should visit the Gentiles with salvation, because this had been clearly predicted in the OT. God had foretold that Gentiles would be blessed as such, and not as believing Jews.

The quotation from Amos looks forward to the Millennium, when Christ will sit upon the throne of David and when the Gentiles will seek after the LORD. James did not intimate that this prophecy was being fulfilled at the time he spoke. Rather, he said that the salvation of Gentiles which was then taking place was in harmony or agreement with what Amos said would take place later.

James' argument was this: First God would visit the Gentiles to take out of them a people for His name. This is what was then happening (and is still happening). Converted Gentiles were included in the church with converted Jews. What was then happening on a small scale (the salvation of the Gentiles) would later happen on a larger scale. Christ would return, restore Israel nationally, and save all the Gentiles who would be called by His name.

James looked on contemporary events as God's first visitation of the Gentiles. He felt this first visitation was in perfect harmony with what Amos predicted — the future visitation of the Gentiles when Christ returns as King. The two events agree though they are not identical.

Notice, then, the order of events:
1. The taking out of the Gentiles a people for His name (v. 14) during this present Age of Grace.
2. The restoration of the believing portion of the nation of Israel at Christ's second advent (v. 16).
3. The salvation of Gentile nations following the restoration of Israel (v. 17). These Gentiles are referred to as all the Gentiles who are called by My name.

James' quotation of Amos 9:11, 12 is quite different from the rendering in the OT. Part of this difference is explained by the fact that James apparently quoted in Greek. However, the quotation is quite different even from the Septuagint. One explanation is that the same Holy Spirit who originally inspired the words now permitted them to be changed in order to meet the problem at hand. Another is that the Hebrew manuscripts have several readings in Amos 9. Alford believes James must have quoted from a translation close to a received Hebrew text, otherwise the Pharisees would never have accepted the quotation as proof.

After this I will return (v. 16). James had already stated that God's program for this present age was to open the door of faith to the Gentiles. Not all of them would be saved, but He would take out of them a people for His name. Now James added that after this, that is, after the church has been called out from the nations, God would return and rebuild the tabernacle of David, which is fallen and in ruins. The tabernacle of David is a figurative expression describing his house or family. Its restoration is a type of the future restoration of the royal family and the re-establishment of the throne of David with Christ sitting upon it as King. Israel will then become the channel of blessing to the world. The rest of mankind will seek the LORD, even all the Gentiles who are called by His name.

The quotation from Amos closes with the statement that these are the words of the LORD who does all these things.

Therefore, because God's present purpose is to call out from the Gentiles a people for Himself, James cautioned against troubling the Gentiles by putting them under the Law of Moses. As far as salvation is concerned, all that was needed was faith.

15:20 However, he suggested that in writing to the church at Antioch the saints there be advised **to abstain from things polluted by idols, from sexual immorality, from things strangled, and from blood**. It might seem at first that James was here reversing himself. Was this not a form of legalism? Was he not now putting them back under the law? The answer is that this advice did not have to do with the subject of salvation at all. That issue had already been settled. But this advice had to do with *fellowship* between Jewish and Gentile believers. While obedience to these instructions was not a condition of salvation, it was certainly of great importance in avoiding sharp cleavages in the early church.

The things prohibited were:

1. **Things polluted by idols**. In verse 29 this is explained as foods offered to idols. If Gentile believers went on eating these foods, then their Jewish brethren might seriously wonder whether they had given up idolatry. Although Gentile Christians might have liberty to eat such foods, it might prove a stumbling block to weak Jewish brethren, and would therefore be wrong.

2. **Sexual immorality.**[62] This was the cardinal sin of the Gentiles. It was therefore especially important for James to include this with the other subjects mentioned. Nowhere in the Bible is the command to abstain from **sexual immorality** ever revoked. It is of standing application for all ages.

3. **Things strangled**. This prohibition goes back to the covenant which God made with Noah after the flood (Gen. 9:4). Thus it is a standing order for the human race and not just for the nation of Israel.

4. **Blood**. This too goes back to Genesis 9:4 and thus precedes the Law of Moses. Since the Covenant with Noah was never abrogated, we take it that these regulations are still in effect today.

15:21 This explains why the advice of verse 20 was given. There were Jews **in every city** who had always been taught that it was wrong to do these things that James warned against. It was wrong not only to commit immorality but also to eat food offered to idols, meat from strangled animals, and blood. Why then should the Gentiles offend God by committing immorality, or offend man by doing the other things?

15:22 It was thus definitely decided that Gentiles did not need to be circumcised in order to be saved. The next step was **to send** official notice of this in writing **to** the church at **Antioch**. **The apostles and elders** in Jerusalem, **with the whole church**, designated **Judas**, called **Barsabas, and Silas**, both **leading men among the brethren**, to go back **to Antioch with Paul and Barnabas**. This **Silas** is the one who later became a traveling companion of **Paul**, and who is referred to as Silvanus in the Epistles.

15:23–29 The substance of the letter is given here. Notice that the false brethren who went from Jerusalem to Antioch originally had never received the authorization or approval of the church in Jerusalem (v. 24).

The moment by moment reliance of the disciples on **the Holy Spirit** is suggested in verse 28: **For it seemed good to the Holy Spirit, and to us . . . .** Someone has spoken of this as "the senior partnership of the Holy Spirit."

15:30, 31 When **the letter** from Jerusalem was **read** in the church at **Antioch**, it proved to be a great **encouragement**. The disciples there now knew that God saved them as Gentiles, and not by their becoming Jews.

15:32, 33 **Judas and Silas** remained for some ministry meetings, in which they **exhorted and** built up **the brethren** in the faith. After a prolonged time of happy fellowship and service in Antioch, they went back to Jerusalem.

15:34 Verse 34 in the King James tradition does not appear in either the oldest or majority of manuscripts (see NKJV footnote). Apparently some copyists thought it would be helpful to supply this information in order to explain the apparent contradiction between verses 33 and 40. In verse 33 Silas is pictured as returning to Jerusalem. But then in verse 40 he is seen accompanying Paul on his Second Missionary Journey. The obvious solution is that Silas did return to Jerusalem, but was then contacted by

Paul with an invitation to accompany him on his travels.

15:35 **Paul and Barnabas** stayed **in Antioch** at this time, **teaching and preaching the word of the Lord**. There were **many** other servants of the Lord who ministered to the assembly. The events described in Galatians 2:11–14 probably occurred at this time.

F. Paul's Second Missionary Journey: Asia Minor and Greece (15:36–18:22)†

15:36–41 The time had come to begin the Second Missionary Journey. **Paul** broached the subject **to Barnabas**, suggesting that they revisit the cities where they had previously **preached the word**. When **Barnabas** insisted that his cousin, **Mark**, accompany them, **Paul** strongly opposed the plan. He remembered vividly how Mark **had departed from them in Pamphylia**, and doubtless feared he would do it again. **The contention** between **Barnabas** and **Paul became so sharp** that these two honored servants of the Lord **parted from one another. Barnabas took Mark and sailed to Cyprus**, the place of his birth, and also the first stop on the First Missionary Journey. **Paul chose Silas** and **went through SYRIA and CILICIA, strengthening the churches**.

Verses 36 and 41 give us additional insight into the true pastoral spirit of **Paul**. His loving care for the people of God was once mirrored by an eminent teacher who said he would rather perfect one saint to the work of ministering than call hundreds of people to the beginnings of Christian life.

At this point the question inevitably arises, "Who was right, **Paul** or **Barnabas**?" There was probably fault on both sides. Perhaps **Barnabas** allowed his judgment to be swayed by his natural affection for **Mark**. Verse 39 indicates that there was **sharp contention** between **Paul** and **Barnabas**. "By pride comes nothing but strife" (Prov. 13:10). Therefore they were both guilty of pride in the matter. Those who think **Paul** was right point out that **Barnabas** disappears from the story at this point. Also, **Paul** and **Silas** were **commended by the brethren to the grace of God**, but this is *not* said in the case of Barnabas and John Mark. In any event, it is heartening to remember that Mark finally did win his colors, and was completely restored to the confidence of Paul (2 Tim. 4:11).

THE AUTONOMY OF THE LOCAL CHURCH

The council at Jerusalem might appear at first sight to be a sort of denominational supreme court. But the facts are otherwise.

Every local assembly in the early days of Christianity was autonomous — that is, self-governing. There was no federation of churches with a centralized authority over them. There were no denominations and therefore no denominational headquarters. Each local church was directly responsible to the Lord. This is pictured in Revelation 1:13 where the Lord is seen standing in the middle of the seven golden lampstands. These represent the seven churches of Asia. The point is that there was no governing agency between the individual churches and the great Head of the church Himself. Each one was governed *directly* by Him.

Why is this so important? First, it hinders the spread of error. When churches are linked together under a common control, the forces of liberalism, rationalism, and apostasy can capture the entire ground simply by seizing the central headquarters and denominational schools. Where churches are independent, the struggle must be waged by the enemy against a host of separate units.

Second, the autonomy of the local church is an important protection when a hostile government is in power. When churches are federated, a totalitarian government can control them all by controlling the few leaders at headquarters. When churches refuse to recognize any centralized authority, they can more readily go underground in times of oppression.

Many governments today, whether democratic or dictatorial, try to bring about the union of small, independent churches. They say they do not want to deal with a large number of local units but with a central committee representing them all. Free governments try to bring about this union by the offer of certain favors and benefits. Other governments try to force the union by edict,

†See p. xxix.

as Hitler did during the Third Reich. In either case, the churches which yield to the pressure lose their scriptural character as well as their ability to resist modernism and to carry on secretly in time of persecution.

Some may object that the churches in Acts did have a central authority, namely, the council in Jerusalem which we have just considered. However, a careful study of the passage will show that this was not an official body with regulatory powers. It was simply a gathering of apostles and elders acting in an advisory capacity.

The council did not summon the men to come from Antioch; the latter decided to consult the men in Jerusalem. The decision of the council was not binding on the churches; it was simply offered as the combined judgment of the group.

The history of the church speaks for itself. Wherever there has been federation of churches under a central organization, there has been an acceleration of decline. The purest testimony for God has been maintained by churches which are free from outside human domination. ‡

16:1, 2 Memories must have come back to Paul like swallows to a barn when **he** returned **to DERBE and LYSTRA**. The memory of his stoning at **Lystra** might conceivably have raised misgivings about ever returning. But the apostle knew that God had people in this area, and no consideration of personal safety could deter him.

As suggested previously, **Timothy** may have been converted through Paul's ministry during the apostle's first visit to **Lystra** (apparently Timothy's home town. Timothy's mother, Eunice, and grandmother, Lois, were both **Jewish** believers (2 Tim. 1:5). **His father was Greek** and may have died by this time.

It rejoiced Paul's heart to learn from **the brethren . . . at Lystra and Iconium** that **Timothy** was progressing well in the Christian faith. **Paul** invited him to go along on this missionary trip. We do well to notice that the early apostles not only worked in pairs, but also took along younger brethren (Mark and Timothy) for training in practical aspects of the Christian ministry. What a privilege it

was for these young men to be yoked together with seasoned veterans in Christian missionary enterprise.

16:3 Before **Paul** departed, he **circumcised** Timothy. Why did he do this, when he had steadfastly refused to have Titus circumcised some time previously (Gal. 2:1–5)? The answer is simply this: in the case of Titus it was a question of fundamental Christian doctrine, whereas here it was not. The false teachers were insisting that a full-blooded Gentile, like Titus, had to be circumcised in order to be saved. Paul recognized this as a denial of the sufficiency of Christ's atoning work, and would not allow it. Here the case was entirely different. The people of the area knew that Timothy was Jewish from his mother. **Paul**, Silas, and Timothy were going forth on evangelistic work. Their first contacts would frequently be with the Jews. If these **Jews** knew that Timothy was not circumcised, they might refuse to listen; whereas if he were, there would be no possibility of offense on this score. Since it was entirely a matter of moral indifference and not of doctrinal importance, **Paul** submitted Timothy to this Jewish ordinance. He was made all things to all men that he might by all means save some (1 Cor. 9:19–23).

The interpretation that Paul's circumcising of Timothy was in order to gain an audience for the gospel with the Jews seems to be strongly implied by the words, **and circumcised him because of the Jews . . . for they all knew that his father was Greek.**

16:4–5 As the three missionaries traveled **through the cities** of Lycaonia, **they delivered to** the churches **the decrees** which had been drawn up **by the apostles and elders at Jerusalem**. These **decrees** were, in brief, as follows:

1. As far as salvation is concerned, faith alone is necessary. Circumcision or law-keeping should not be added to faith as a condition for being saved.

2. Sexual immorality was forbidden for all believers and for all time, but this reminder was probably addressed primarily to converted Gentiles, since this was (and is) their besetting sin.

3. Meats offered to idols, meat from animals that had been strangled, and blood were forbidden as food, not as

matters essential to salvation, but to facilitate fellowship between Jewish and Gentile believers. Some of these instructions were subsequently revised (see 1 Cor. 8–10; 1 Tim. 4:4, 5).

As a result of the ministry of these men, **the churches were strengthened in the** Christian **faith, and increased in number daily.**

16:6–8 These verses are of vital importance because they show the superintendence and guidance of **the Holy Spirit** in the missionary strategy of the apostles. After revisiting the churches in **PHRYGIA** and **GALATIA**, they had thought of going into the province of **Asia**, in western Asia Minor, but **the Holy Spirit** forbade them. We are not told why; some have suggested that perhaps in the divine counsels this region was allocated to Peter (see 1 Pet. 1:1). At any rate they traveled northwest into the district of **MYSIA**. This was actually included in the province of **Asia**, but apparently they did not preach there. When they attempted next **to go** northeast **into Bithynia**, along the coast of the Euxine (Black) Sea, **the Spirit did not permit them**. So they went directly west to the coastal city of **TROAS**. From there the missionaries could look across the Aegean Sea toward Greece, the threshold of Europe. Ryrie writes:

> Asia needed the Gospel, but this was not God's time. Need did not constitute their call. They had just come from the east; they had been forbidden to go south or north, but they did not presume that the Lord was leading them to the west — they waited His specific directions. Logic alone is not the basis for a call.[63]

16:9 During a night **vision** Paul saw **a man of MACEDONIA** calling to him to **come over** and **help. Macedonia** was the northern part of Greece, due west of Troas. Whether consciously or not, **Macedonia** (and all Europe!) needed the gospel of redeeming grace. The Lord had been closing doors in Asia so His servants would carry the good news to Europe. Stalker paints the picture:

> [The man of Macedonia] represented Europe, and his cry for help Europe's need of Christ. Paul recognized in the vision a divine summons; and the very next sunset which bathed the Hellespont in its gold light shone upon his figure seated on

the deck of a ship, the prow of which was moving toward the shore of Macedonia.[64]

16:10 There is a significant change here in the personal pronoun from *he* to *we*. It is generally believed that Luke, the writer of Acts, joined Paul, Silas, and Timothy at this time. From here on he records the events as an eyewitness.

DIVINE GUIDANCE

In order to function effectively on earth, the early church depended on the guidance of its Head in heaven. But how did the Lord Jesus make known His will to His servants?

He had left His *general strategy* with them before He ascended, when He said, "You shall be witnesses to Me in Jerusalem, and in all Judea and Samaria, and to the end of the earth" (Acts 1:8).

After His Ascension, He made known His will to them in several ways.

Peter and the other disciples were guided by the OT *Scriptures* (Ps. 69:25) to choose a successor for Judas (1:15–26).

On at least five occasions the Lord guided men through *visions* — Ananias (9:10–16); Cornelius (10:3); Peter (10:10, 11, 17); Paul (twice — 16:9, 10; 18:9).

Twice He guided through *prophets* (11:27–30; 21:10–12).

At other times the Christians were guided by *circumstances*. For instance, they were scattered or driven by persecution (8:1–4; 11:19; 13:50, 51; 14:5, 6). Civil authorities asked Paul and Silas to leave Philippi (16:39, 40). Later Paul was taken from Jerusalem to Caesarea by the authorities (23:33). The circumstance of Paul's appeal to Caesar determined his trip to Rome (25:11), and the later shipwreck affected the timing and sequence of moves (27:41; 28:1).

Sometimes guidance came through the *counsel and initiative of other Christians*. The church in Jerusalem sent Barnabas to Antioch (11:22). Agabus prophesied a famine, and this moved the church in Antioch to send relief to the saints in Judea (11:27–30). The brethren at Antioch sent Paul and Barnabas to Jerusalem (15:2). Judas and Silas were sent out by the church at Jerusalem with Barnabas and Paul (15:25–27). Paul and Silas were commended by the brethren to the grace of God as they set out on the Second Missionary Journey (15:40). Paul took Timothy with him when he left Lystra (16:3). The brethren in Thessalonica sent Paul and Silas to Berea because of the threat of violence (17:10). The brethren in Berea, in turn, sent Paul away for the same reason (17:14, 15). Finally, Paul sent Timothy and Erastus to Macedonia (19:22).

In addition to the above methods of guidance, there are several instances where men seem to have received communications of the divine will *directly*. An angel of the Lord guided Philip to the Ethiopian eunuch (8:26). The Holy Spirit spoke to the prophets and teachers at Antioch as they fasted and prayed (13:1, 2). Paul and Timothy were forbidden by the Holy Spirit to preach the word in Asia (16:6). Later they tried to go to Bithynia, but the Spirit did not permit them to go (16:7).

To summarize then, the early Christians received guidance:

1. Through the Scriptures.
2. Through visions and prophecies.
3. Through circumstances.
4. Through the advice and initiative of other Christians.
5. Through direct communication, possibly in an inward, subjective manner. ‡

16:11, 12 **Sailing** northwest **from Troas**, the tireless ambassadors of Christ first anchored for a night off the island of **SAMOTHRACE**. They **next** reached the mainland at the port of **NEAPOLIS**, over 120 miles from **Troas**, then journeyed inland a few miles **to PHILIPPI, which** was **the foremost city of that part of Macedonia, a colony.**

16:13–15 Apparently there was no synagogue in Philippi, but Paul and his companions heard that some Jewish people gathered **on the Sabbath** outside **the city** by **the riverside**. Reaching the spot, they found a group of **women** praying, including one **named Lydia**. She was probably a convert to Judaism. Originally **from the city of Thyatira**, in the district of Lydia, in western Asia Minor, she had moved to Philippi, where **she was a seller of purple**-dyed cloth. **Thyatira** was famous for its dyes.

Not only was her ear open to the gos-

pel; **her heart** was open as well. After receiving the Lord Jesus, **she and her household were baptized.** The members of **her household** had, of course, been converted also before they **were baptized**. There is no mention of Lydia's being married; **her household** could have consisted of servants.

Lydia was not saved by good works, but she was saved in order to do them. She proved the reality of her faith by opening her home to Paul, Silas, Luke, and Timothy.

16:16–18 Another day, when **Paul** and his companions were going to the place of **prayer**, they met **a slave girl** who had **a spirit of divination**. Possessed by a demon, she was able to foretell the future and to make other astounding revelations. In this way she **brought** considerable income to **her masters**.

When she **met** the Christian missionaries, and **for many days** thereafter, she **followed** them, crying out, **"These men are the servants of the Most High God, who proclaim to us the way of salvation."** What she said was *true*, but **Paul** knew better than to accept testimony from demons. Also he was grieved because of the wretched condition of this enslaved girl. So, **in the** all-powerful **name of Jesus Christ**, he commanded the demon **to come out of her**. Immediately she was freed from this dreadful bondage, and became a sane, rational person.

MIRACLES

Miracles are woven throughout the narrative of the Book of Acts. The following are some of the more prominent ones:

The miraculous gift of tongues (2:4; 10:46; 19:6).

The healing of the lame man at the gate of the temple (3:7).

The sudden judgmental death of Ananias and Sapphira (5:5, 10).

The deliverance of the apostles from prison (5:19).

Saul's encounter with the glorified Christ (9:3–6).

The healing of Aeneas by Peter (9:34).

The restoration to life of Dorcas (9:40).

Peter's vision of the sheet let down from heaven (10:11).

Peter's deliverance from prison (12:7–10).

The slaying of Herod by an angel (12:23).

The judgment of blindness on Elymas, the sorcerer (13:11).

The healing of the crippled man at Lystra by Paul (14:10).

Paul's restoration after being stoned at Lystra (14:19, 20).

Paul's vision of the man of Macedonia calling for help (16:9).

Paul's casting out the evil spirit from the girl in Philippi (16:18).

The deliverance of Paul and Silas from prison in Philippi (16:26).

Paul's raising Eutychus to life (20:10, 11).

The prophecy of Agabus (21:10, 11).

Paul's deliverance from a viper at Malta (28:3–6).

The healing of Publius' father of fever (28:8).

The healing of others' diseases (28:9).

In addition to these, it is said that the apostles worked wonders and signs (2:43); Stephen performed great wonders and signs among the people (6:8); Philip worked miracles and signs (8:6, 13); Barnabas and Paul worked signs and wonders (15:12); and God worked miracles by the hands of Paul (19:11).

In studying Acts, the question naturally arises, "Should we expect these same miracles today?" There are two extremes to be avoided in answering the question. The first is the position that since Jesus Christ is the same yesterday, today, and forever, we should be seeing the same miracles that were found in the early church.

The opposite extreme is that miracles were only for the early days of the church and that we have no right to look for them today.

It is true that Jesus Christ is the same yesterday, today, and forever (Heb. 13:8). But that does not mean that the divine methods never change. The plagues God used in Egypt, for instance, have never been repeated. His power is the same. He can still perform any kind of miracles. But that does not mean He *must* perform the same miracles in every

age. He is a God of infinite variety.

On the other hand, we should not wave miracles aside as not being for the Church Age. It is all too easy to assign miracles to dispensational pigeonholes and content ourselves with lives that never rise above flesh and blood.

Our lives should be charged with supernatural power. We should be constantly seeing God's hand in the marvelous converging of circumstances. We should be experiencing His guidance in a miraculous, mysterious way. We should experience events in our lives that lie beyond the laws of probability. We should be aware that God is arranging contacts, opening doors, overruling opposition. Our service should crackle with the supernatural.

We should be seeing direct answers to prayer. When our lives touch other lives, we should see something happening for God. We should see His hand in breakdowns, delays, accidents, losses, and seeming tragedies. We should experience extraordinary deliverances and be aware of strength, courage, peace, and wisdom beyond our natural limits.

If our lives are lived only on the natural level, how are we any different from non-Christians? God's will is that our lives should be supernatural, that the life of Jesus Christ should flow out through us. When this takes place, impossibilities will melt, closed doors will open, and power will surge. Then we will be supercharged with the Holy Spirit, and when people get near us, they will feel the sparks of the Spirit.‡

16:19–24 Instead of being grateful that this young woman was no longer demon-possessed, **her masters** bitterly resented the resulting loss **of profit. They** therefore **dragged . . . Paul and Silas** before **the magistrates** (praetors), and trumped up charges against them. Basically, they accused them of being troublemaking **Jews** who were trying to upset the Roman way of life. The mob reacted violently, **and the magistrates tore off** the **clothes** of Paul and Silas **and commanded them to be beaten**. After a thorough beating, the missionaries were sent to jail, with special instructions to **the jailer to keep them securely**. He responded by putting **them into the inner**

prison and fastening **their feet in the stocks**.

In this passage we see two of Satan's chief methods. First, he tried false friendship — the testimony of the demon-possessed girl. When this failed, he resorted to open persecution. Grant says: "Alliance or persecution — these are the alternatives: false friendship or open war." A. J. Pollock comments:

How the Devil must have triumphed as he thought he had brought the career of these devoted servants of Christ to an abrupt close. His triumphing was premature as it ever must be. In this case it turned out to his utter discomfiture, and to the furtherance of the work of the Lord.[65]

16:25 The **midnight** hour found **Paul and Silas . . . praying and singing**. Their joy was completely independent of earthly circumstances. The source of all their **singing** was high in heaven above. Morgan admits:

Any man can sing when the prison doors are open, and he is set free. The Christian soul sings in prison. I think that Paul would probably have sung a solo had I been Silas: but I nevertheless see the glory and grandeur of the Spirit that rises superior to all the things of difficulty and limitation.[66]

16:26 As the other prisoners were listening to their prayers and hymns of praise to God, the prison was rocked by an unusual **earthquake**. It **opened . . . all the doors** and unloosed the stocks and **chains**, but it did not demolish the building.

16:27, 28 When the jailer awoke and saw the **prison** wide **open**, he assumed that **the prisoners had** made their escape. Aware that his own life would be forfeited, he **drew his sword** to commit suicide. **But Paul** assured him there was no need for him to do that, because **all** the prisoners were still present and accounted for.

16:29, 30 Now a new emotion swept over the jailer. His fears of losing his job and perhaps his life gave way to deep conviction of sin. He was now afraid to meet God in his sins. He cried, **"Sirs, what must I do to be saved?"**

This question must precede every

genuine case of conversion. A man must know he is *lost* before he can be *saved*. It is premature to tell a man how to be saved until first he can say from his heart, "I truly deserve to go to hell."

16:31 The only people in the NT who were ever told to believe on the Lord Jesus Christ were convicted sinners. Now that the jailer was thoroughly broken up over his sins, he was told: **"Believe on the Lord Jesus Christ, and you will be saved, you and your household."**

There is no suggestion here that his family would be saved automatically if *he* trusted Christ. The meaning is that if he believed **on the Lord Jesus Christ**, he would **be saved**, and his **household** would **be saved** in the same way. "Believe . . . and you will be saved, and let your household do the same."

Many people today seem to have difficulty knowing what it means to believe. However, when a sinner realizes he is lost, helpless, hopeless, hell-bound, and when he is told to believe on Christ as Lord and Savior, he knows exactly what it means. It is the only thing left that he *can* do!

16:32–34 After Paul and Silas had a teaching session with the household, the jailer demonstrated the genuineness of his conversion by washing their wounds, and by being **baptized** without delay. Also he **brought them into his house** and fed them, rejoicing all the time **with all his household** that they had all come to know the Lord.

Again we would mention that there is no support for believing there were infants or very young children in the household who were baptized. They were all old enough to believe **in God**.

16:35 Apparently **the magistrates** had a change of heart during the night, because in the morning they **sent the officers** (lictors) with instructions to release the two prisoners.

16:36, 37 When the jailer announced the good news **to Paul**, the apostle refused to leave under such circumstances. After all, Silas and he, though Jews by birth, were citizens of Rome. They had been tried and **beaten** unfairly. Now did the magistrates think they would slink away as if guilty and in disgrace? **No indeed!** Let the magistrates **come** and release the prisoners.

16:38–40 **The magistrates** did come, and rather apologetically at that! They urged Paul and Silas **to depart from the city** without further disturbance. With the dignity of sons of the King, the Lord's servants **went out of the prison**, but they did not leave the city immediately. First they went to Lydia's **house**, conferred with **the brethren**, and **encouraged them**. How wonderful! The ones who should have been comforted were encouraging others.

When their mission in Philippi was accomplished, they **departed** with full colors flying.

17:1 After leaving Philippi, Paul and Silas traveled thirty-three miles southwest to **AMPHIPOLIS** (am-fip'-o-lis). Their next stop was **APOLLONIA** (ap-o-lo'-ni-a), another thirty miles southwest. From there they moved in a westward direction thirty-seven miles **to THESSALONICA** (thes-a-lo-nye'-ka). This city was strategically located on trade routes, and was thus an excellent center of commerce. The Holy Spirit chose it as a base from which the gospel would radiate in many directions. In our day, the city is known as Saloniki.

Luke may have remained at Philippi when Paul and Silas left there to claim new territory for the Lord. This is suggested by the narrative changing from the first person plural (we) to the third person (**they**).

17:2, 3 As **was** their **custom**, the missionaries located a Jewish synagogue and preached the gospel there. **For three Sabbaths**[67] Paul opened the OT and showed convincingly that it was predicted **that the** Messiah **had to suffer and rise again from the dead**. Having established this **from the Scriptures**, Paul went on to declare that **Jesus** of Nazareth was the long awaited Messiah. Had He not suffered, and died, and risen from the dead? Did this not prove that He was **the Christ** of God?

17:4–7 **Some** of the Jews **were persuaded**, and took their place with **Paul and Silas** as Christian believers. Also many of the Greek proselytes **and not a few of the leading women** of the city were converted. This provoked the unbe-

lieving **Jews** to decisive action. They rounded up some of the hoodlums **from the marketplace**, incited a riot, and besieged **the house of Jason** where **Paul and Silas** had been guests. **When they did not find** Paul and Silas in the house, **they dragged Jason and some** of his fellow believers before **the rulers of the city** (politarchs). Without meaning to, they paid a genuine tribute to Paul and Silas when they described them as men who had **turned the world upside down**. Then they charged them with plotting to overthrow the government **of Caesar** by preaching about **another king — Jesus**. It was, to say the least, a strange thing for **Jews** to be so zealous in safeguarding the government **of Caesar**, because they had little or no love for the Roman Empire.

But was their charge true? Doubtless they had heard Paul proclaim the Second Coming of Jesus to reign as king over all the earth. But this did not pose an immediate threat to Caesar, since Christ would not return to reign until Israel had repented nationally.

17:8, 9 The politarchs were **troubled** by these reports. They required **Jason** and those with him to post bail, probably adding instructions for his guests to leave the city. Then **they let them go**.

17:10–12 **The brethren** in Thessalonica decided it would be well for the preachers to leave, so they **sent them away by night to BEREA**. These indomitable and irrepressible evangelists **went** straight to **the synagogue of the Jews**. As they preached the gospel there, the Jews showed their open-mindedness by searching, checking, and comparing **the** OT **Scriptures**. They had a simple and teachable attitude and a determination to test all teaching by **the** Sacred **Scriptures**. **Many of** these Jews **believed**. And there were also a good number of converts from **prominent** Gentile **women as well as men**.

17:13, 14 **When** word trickled back to **Thessalonica** that **Paul and Silas** were carrying on their ministry in **Berea**, **the** Thessalonian **Jews** made a special trip to **Berea and stirred up the crowds** against the apostle. **The brethren** thereupon **sent Paul** toward the seacoast, accompanied by an escort of believers. They probably went as far as DIUM and sailed from there to PIRAEUS, the port city of ATHENS. **Silas and Timothy remained** in Berea.

17:15 It was a long journey from Berea **to Athens**. It showed the true devotion of the Christians there that some of the brethren were willing to accompany **Paul** all the way. When it came time for them to leave **Paul in Athens**, he sent word by them **for Silas and Timothy to** join **him with all speed**.

17:16 While waiting **for them at Athens, Paul** was deeply burdened by the idolatry of **the city**. Although **Athens** was the center of culture, education, and fine arts, **Paul** was interested in none of these things. He did not occupy his time with sightseeing trips. Arnot comments:

> It was not that he valued marble statues less, but living men more. . . . He is not the weak but the strong man who regards immortal souls as transcendently more important than fine arts. . . . Paul did not consider idolatry picturesque and harmless, but grievous.[68]

17:17, 18 He reasoned in the synagogue **with the Jews and with the Gentile worshipers**, whereas **in the marketplace** he preached to all who would listen. It was in this way that he came in touch with some **Epicurean and Stoic philosophers**. The Epicureans were followers of a philosopher named Epicurus, who taught that pleasure and not the pursuit of knowledge is the chief end of life. The Stoics were pantheists who believed that wisdom lay in being free from intense emotion, unmoved by joy or grief, willingly submissive to natural law. When these two schools of philosophy heard Paul, they considered him a **babbler** (Greek, "seed-picker") and **a proclaimer of foreign gods, because he preached to them Jesus and the resurrection.**

17:19–21 They took him and brought him to the Areopagus, a judicial body like a supreme court that met on the hill of Mars. In this particular case, it was not exactly a trial, but simply a hearing in which Paul would be given an opportunity to set forth his teaching before the members of the court and the multitude. This is somewhat explained in verse 21. **The Athenians** loved to stand around and talk, and to listen to others. They seemed to have an unlimited amount of time for this.

17:22 Standing **in the midst** of the court, **Paul** delivered what has come to be known as the Mars Hill Address. It must be remembered in studying this address that he was speaking to Gentiles, not Jews. They did not have a background in the OT, so he had to find some subject of common interest with which to begin. He began with the observation that the Athenians were **very religious**. That Athens was indeed a **religious** city was well attested by the fact that it was reputed to have more idols in it than men!

17:23 When he thought of the idols he had seen, **Paul** was reminded of **an altar with this inscription: TO THE UNKNOWN GOD.** He found in that **inscription** a point of departure for his message. The apostle saw in the **inscription** the recognition of two important facts. First, the fact of the existence of **God**, and second, the fact that the Athenians were ignorant of **Him**. It was then a very normal and natural transition for **Paul** to enlighten them concerning **the** true **God.** As someone has said, he turned the wandering stream of their piety into the right channel.

17:24, 25 Missionaries tell us that the best place to begin in teaching pagans about God is the account of creation. This is exactly where Paul began with the people of Athens. He introduced **God** as the One **who made the world and everything in it.** As he looked around on the numerous idol temples nearby, the apostle reminded his hearers that the true **God does not dwell in temples made with hands. Nor is He** dependent on the service of **men's hands.** In idol temples, the priests often bring food and other "necessities" to their gods. But the true **God** does not need anything from man, because **He** is the source of **life, breath, and all things**.

17:26–28a Paul next discussed the origin of the human race. All nations came from the common ancestor, Adam. Not only were the nations brought forth by God, but **He** also arranged the years, and **determined** the countries in which the various peoples would dwell. **He** showered innumerable mercies on them in order that they might **seek** Him. **He** wanted them to **grope for Him and find Him**, even though in actuality **He is not far from each one**. It is **in** the true God that **we live and move and have our being**. **He** is not only our Creator but our environment as well.

17:28b To further emphasize the relationship of the creature to the Creator, Paul quoted from **some** of their Greek **poets**, who **said, "For we are also His offspring."** This is not to be interpreted as teaching the brotherhood of man and the fatherhood of God. We are the **offspring** of God in the sense that He created us, but we only become *sons* of God through faith in the Lord Jesus Christ.

17:29 But Paul's argument continues. If men **are the offspring of God**, then it is impossible to think of God as a **gold or silver or stone** idol. These are **shaped by art and man's devising**, and therefore are not as great as men. These idols are, in a sense, the offspring of human beings, whereas the truth is that human beings are the creation of God.

17:30 Having exposed the folly of idolatry, Paul goes on to state that for many centuries **God overlooked** the **ignorance** of the Gentiles. But now that the revelation of the gospel has come, He **commands all men everywhere to repent**, that is, to do an about-face.

17:31 This is an urgent message, **because** God **has appointed a day on which He will judge the world in righteousness by** the Lord Jesus Christ, **the Man whom He has ordained**. The judgment referred to here will take place when Christ returns to earth to put down His enemies and begin His Millennial Reign. The positive assurance that this will take place is found in the fact that God raised the Lord Jesus **from the dead**. Thus Paul leads up to his favorite theme, the resurrection of Christ.

17:32, 33 Perhaps Paul did not finish his message. It may be that he was interrupted by the scorn of those who **mocked** at the idea of a **resurrection of the dead. Others** did not mock, but hesitated. They delayed taking any action by saying, **"We will hear you again on this**

matter." "They counted the time of closing with Christ an evil day. They couldn't say 'Never' but 'Not Now.' ''

17:34 However, it would not be right to say that Paul's message was a failure. After all, **Dionysius** believed, and he was an **Areopagite**, a member of the court. **A woman named Damaris** also believed **and others** whose names are not given.

So Paul departed from among them. "We hear no more of Athens. To centers of persecution Paul returned again, but to intellectual flippancy, there was nothing more to be said" (Selected).

Some people criticize this sermon because it seems to praise the Athenians for their religiosity when actually they were gross idolaters; it supposes a recognition of the true God from an inscription that might have been intended for an idol; it seems to accommodate itself too much to the manners and customs of the Athenians; and it does not present the gospel as clearly and forcibly as some other messages by the apostle. These criticisms are unjustified. We have already sought to explain that Paul first sought a point of contact, then by easy steps he led his hearers first to the knowledge of the true God, then to the necessity of repentance in view of Christ's coming as judge. It is sufficient vindication of Paul's preaching that souls were genuinely converted through it.

UNCONVENTIONAL PULPITS

Paul's preaching on Mars Hill is an illustration of the *unconventional places* in which the early believers preached the word.

The *open air* was a favorite. At Pentecost the message may have been preached out of doors, judging from the number who heard and were saved[69] (Acts 2:6, 41). Other general instances of open-air preaching are found in 8:5, 25, 40; 13:44; 14:8–18.

The environs of *the temple* echoed with the message on at least three occasions (3:1–11; 5:21, 42). Paul and his associates spoke the Word *by the riverside* in Philippi (16:13). Here in Athens he preached *in the marketplace* (17:17) before the address on Mars Hill.[†] In Jerusalem

†*See p. xxvi.*

he addressed an angry mob *from the stairs* of the fortress of Antonia (21:40–22:21).

At least four times the message was declared before the Jewish *Sanhedrin*: by Peter and John (4:8, 19); by Peter and the other apostles (5:27–32); by Stephen (7:2–53); and by Paul (22:30–23:10).

Paul and his associates habitually preached the gospel *in the synagogues* (9:20; 13:5, 14; 14:1; 17:1, 2, 10, 17; 18:4, 19, 26; 19:8).

Private homes were used repeatedly. Peter preached in Cornelius' house (10:22, 24). Paul and Silas witnessed in the home of the Philippian jailer (16:31, 32). In Corinth Paul preached in the house of Crispus, the ruler of the synagogue (18:7, 8). He preached till midnight in a private house in Troas (20:7). He taught from house to house in Ephesus (20:20) and in his own hired house in Rome (28:30, 31).

Philip preached to an Ethiopian eunuch *in a chariot* (8:31–35), and Paul preached on *board a ship* (27:21–26). At Ephesus he reasoned daily *in a schoolroom* (19:9).

Paul preached *in civil courts* before Felix (24:10), Festus (25:8), and Agrippa (26:1–29).

In 8:4 we read that the persecuted believers went *everywhere* preaching the word.

It shows that they did not think the proclamation of the message should be confined to some specially "consecrated" building. Wherever there were people, there was both reason and opportunity for making Christ known. A. B. Simpson agrees:

The early Christians regarded every situation as an opportunity to witness for Christ. Even when brought before kings and governors, it never occurred to them that they might evade the issue and avoid identifying themselves with Christ because of being fearful of the consequences. It was simply an occasion to preach to kings and rulers whom otherwise they could not reach. It is probable that God allows every human being to cross our path in order that we may have the opportunity to leave some blessing in his path, and drop into his heart and life some influence that will draw him nearer to God.[70]

The Lord Jesus had commissioned them to "Go into all the world and preach the gospel to every creature" (Mark 16:15). The Book of Acts shows them carrying out the command.

We might add that most of the preaching in Acts was spontaneous and extemporaneous. Usually there wasn't time to prepare a message. "It was not the performance of an hour but the preparation of a lifetime." It was the preachers who were prepared, not the sermons.‡

18:1 Some believe **Paul departed from Athens** because of the meager results of his preaching there. We prefer to believe that he was led by the Holy Spirit to journey westward **to CORINTH**, the capital of ACHAIA. Here, in this city noted for immorality, the gospel must be preached and a church established.

18:2, 3 At Corinth, Paul formed a friendship with a couple named **Aquila** and **Priscilla** which was to continue through his life. **Aquila** was **a Jew** from **Pontus**, the northeastern province of Asia Minor. He and his wife had been living in **Rome**, but they had been driven out by an anti-semitic decree of **Claudius** Caesar. Since Corinth was located on the main route from **Rome** to the East, they had stopped here and set up shop as **tentmakers**. Paul was also a tentmaker by trade, and he became acquainted with them.

Life's best revelations flash upon us while we abide in the fields of duty. Keep to your daily breadwinning and amid your toils you shall receive great benedictions and see glad visions. . . . The shop or office or warehouse may become as the house of God. Do thy work and do it diligently: In it, thou mayest find rare soul fellowships, as did Aquila and Priscilla.[71]

It is not clear from the narrative whether **Aquila** and **Priscilla** were already Christians when Paul met them, or whether they were saved through his ministry. Perhaps the burden of evidence is on the side of their being believers when they came to Corinth.

18:4 Paul **reasoned in the synagogue every Sabbath, and persuaded both Jews and** Gentile proselytes that

Jesus was indeed the Christ of God.

18:5 **Paul** had left **Silas and Timothy** in Berea when he moved on to Athens. At Athens he had sent word for them to join him. They caught up with him in Corinth.

After their arrival, **Paul was compelled by the Spirit**. This may mean that the burden of the Lord was upon him to preach the message with great diligence, testifying **to the Jews that Jesus is the Christ**. There might be a suggestion that the apostle no longer spent time making tents here, but gave himself entirely to preaching the gospel.

It was at approximately this time in his history that Paul wrote 1 Thessalonians (about A.D. 52).

18:6 The unbelieving Jews **opposed** Paul **and blasphemed** or railed. To reject the gospel is ultimately to oppose *oneself*. The unbeliever harms no one so much as himself.

Paul **shook** out **his garments and said to them, "Your blood be upon your own heads; I am clean. From now on I will go to the Gentiles."** The shaking of his clothing was an expressive act, signifying his dissociation from them. However, this did not prevent his going to the synagogue in another city, namely, Ephesus (19:8).

The apostle's words are a solemn reminder to every believer that there is such a thing as blood-guiltiness. The Christian is a debtor to all men. If he fails to discharge that debt by proclaiming the gospel, God will hold him responsible. If, on the other hand, he faithfully witnesses for Christ and meets with stubborn refusal, then he himself is free from guilt, and the responsibility rests with the Christ-rejecter.

This verse represents another step in the setting aside of the nation of Israel, and the proclamation of the gospel to the Gentiles. God had decreed that the good news should go to the Jews first, but throughout Acts, as the nation of Israel rejects the message, the Spirit of God sorrowfully turns aside from that people.

18:7, 8 Following the outburst of the Jews, the apostle went to the home of **Justus**, a Gentile convert to Judaism who lived **next door to the synagogue**. As he carried on his ministry from this base, the Apostle Paul had the joy of seeing **Crispus, the ruler of the synagogue, . . . with all his household** come to the Lord. **Many** other Corinthians trusted in the Savior **and were baptized**. Paul baptized Crispus and a few others (1 Cor. 1:14–16), but his usual practice was to have some other believer do the baptizing. Paul feared that people would form a party around himself, instead of being undistracted in their love and loyalty to the Lord Jesus.

18:9, 10 **The Lord** graciously **spoke to Paul in the night by a vision**, assuring him that there was nothing to **be afraid** of. The apostle should continue to preach the word, assured of God's presence and protection. There were **many people in** the **city** who belonged to the Lord in the sense that He was working in their lives and they would ultimately be saved.

18:11 Paul stayed in Corinth eighteen months, **teaching the word of God**. Valuable background material concerning this period is found in 1 and 2 Corinthians.

18:12–16 It was probably toward the end of Paul's stay in Corinth that **Gallio** was appointed **proconsul of Achaia** (approximately A.D. 53). Thinking the new **proconsul** would be friendly to them, **the Jews brought Paul** before him at **the judgment seat** (*bēma*) in the marketplace at Corinth. The accusation was that **Paul** was persuading them **to worship God contrary to the** Jewish **law**. Before the apostle had an opportunity to testify, **Gallio** dismissed the matter with utter contempt. He told the Jews that this was strictly a matter of their **own law** and not one that came under his jurisdiction. **If it were a matter of wrongdoing or wicked crimes**, then it would be reasonable for **Gallio** to **bear** patiently **with** the Jews, but actually it was only **a question of words and names and** the Jewish **law**. The **proconsul** had no intention of becoming **a judge of such matters**, so he dismissed the case.

18:17 Some think that **the Greeks** punished **Sosthenes** for bringing Paul before **Gallio** on such an empty charge. When it says that **Gallio took no notice of these things**, it does not mean he was uninterested in the gospel, although that was probably true. He evidently did not want to become involved in Jewish laws and customs.

18:18 After these incidents, **Paul remained** in Corinth **a good while**. Perhaps it was during this time that he wrote 2 Thessalonians.

When he finally **took leave of** Corinth with **Priscilla and Aquila**, he sailed for Syria, his object being to return to Antioch. Commentators are divided as to whether it was **Paul** or **Aquila** who **had his hair cut off at Cenchrea**, the eastern harbor of Corinth.[72]

Some feel that the manner of the **vow** was strongly Jewish, and not fitting for a man of Paul's spiritual maturity. There is probably no way to decide the matter finally.

18:19, 20 When the ship landed at **EPHESUS**, Priscilla and Aquila disembarked with the intention of staying there. Paul took advantage of the vessel's brief stay to go to **the synagogue and** reason **with the Jews**. Surprisingly enough, they wanted him to remain longer, but he could not do so.

18:21 The ship was leaving. But he promised to **return** to **Ephesus, God willing**, after keeping the **coming feast in Jerusalem**.

18:22 The ship's next stop was **CAESAREA**. From there, the apostle went **up and greeted the church** in Jerusalem. Then **he went down to ANTIOCH** for what was to be his final visit.

Thus ends Paul's Second Missionary Journey.

G. Paul's Third Missionary Journey: Asia Minor and Greece (18:23–21:26)[†]

18:23 **After** a fairly lengthy visit at Antioch, Paul was ready to set out on another extended missionary itinerary. The record of this journey extends from verse 23 through 21:16.

The first regions to be visited were **GALATIA and PHRYGIA**. The apostle went to the churches there, one by one, **strengthening all the disciples.**

18:24–26 The scene now shifts back to **Ephesus** where we left **Aquila and Priscilla. An eloquent** preacher **named Apollos** arrived there, one who was **mighty in the** OT **Scriptures**. He was **a Jew** by birth, and came from **Alexandria**, the capital of northern Egypt. Al-

though his preaching was accompanied by much power, and although he was very zealous, yet he was somewhat deficient in his knowledge of the Christian faith. He had apparently been well schooled in the ministry of **John** the Baptist, and knew how **John** had called the nation of Israel to repentance in preparation for the coming of the Messiah. Apparently he did not know about Christian baptism or some other matters of Christian doctrine. **When Aquila and Priscilla heard him speak . . . in the synagogue**, they recognized that he needed further instruction, so **they** lovingly **took him aside and explained to him the way of God more accurately**. It is to the credit of this **eloquent** preacher that he was willing to be taught by a tentmaker and his wife.

18:27, 28 As a result of his teachable spirit, **the brethren** at Ephesus encouraged him in his desire to go to Corinth in order to preach the word. In fact they **wrote** a letter of commendation for him. As a result **he** was a great help to the believers in Corinth and **vigorously refuted the Jews** there **publicly, showing that Jesus** is indeed **the Christ** of God.

19:1 When Paul originally visited **Ephesus**, he promised the Jews in the synagogue that he would return, in the will of God. In fulfillment of that promise, he journeyed from the regions of Galatia and Phrygia along the inland route, over mountainous terrain **to EPHESUS** on the western coast of proconsular Asia. Arriving there he met about twelve men who professed to be **disciples**. As he talked with them, he realized that their knowledge of the Christian faith was very imperfect and defective. He wondered if they had ever really received the Holy Spirit.

19:2 Therefore he asked them, **"Did you receive the Holy Spirit when you believed?"** In the KJV Paul's question reads, "Have ye received the Holy Ghost since ye believed?" This wrongly implies that the reception of the Holy Spirit takes place *subsequent* to salvation.

The thought of this verse is not that the reception of the Holy Spirit is a work of grace which follows salvation. As soon as a sinner trusts the Savior, he receives the Holy Spirit.

The reply of the disciples was, **"We have not so much as heard whether**

†See p. xxx.

there is a Holy Spirit," or as it is rendered in the ASV, "We did not so much as hear whether the Holy Spirit was given." Since these men were disciples of John the Baptist, as we learn in the next verse, they should have known about the existence of **the Holy Spirit** from the OT. Not only so, but John had taught his disciples that the One who came after him would baptize them with the Holy Spirit. What these disciples did not know was that **the Holy Spirit** had already been given on the Day of Pentecost.

19:3, 4 When the apostle raised the question of baptism, he found out that these men knew only about **John's baptism**. In other words, the extent of their knowledge was that the Messiah was at hand, and they had signified their **repentance** by **baptism** as a necessary preparation for receiving Him as King. They did not know that **Christ** had died, had been buried, and had risen from the dead and ascended back to heaven, and that He had sent the Holy Spirit. **Paul** explained all this to them. He reminded them that when **John** baptized with the **baptism of repentance**, he urged them to **believe . . . on Christ Jesus**.

19:5 When they heard this, they were baptized in the name of the Lord Jesus. Throughout the Book of Acts the emphasis is distinctly on the lordship of Jesus. Therefore, the disciples of John here **were baptized** by the authority **of the Lord Jesus** and as a public acknowledgment that in their lives they accepted Jesus Christ as Lord (Jehovah).

19:6, 7 Paul then **laid** his **hands on them**, and they received **the Holy Spirit**. This is the fourth distinct time in Acts when **the Holy Spirit** was given. The first was in chapter 2, on the Day of Pentecost, and involved the Jews primarily. The second was in Acts 8, when the Spirit was given to the Samaritans through the laying on of the hands of Peter and John. The third time was in Acts 10, at the household of the Gentile, Cornelius, in Joppa. We have previously pointed out that the order of events leading up to the reception of **the Holy Spirit** is different in each case.

Here in Acts 19 the order is:

Faith.

Re-baptism.

Laying on of the apostle's **hands**.

Reception of **the Holy Spirit**.

By giving **the Holy Spirit** to John's disciples through the laying on of Paul's **hands**, the Lord forestalled the possibility of a charge being made later that Paul was inferior to Peter, John, or the other apostles.

When the disciples of John received **the Holy Spirit they spoke with tongues and prophesied**. Such supernatural powers were God's method of working in the days before the NT was given. Today we know that we receive **the Holy Spirit** at the time of conversion, not by signs and wonders, or even by feelings, but by the testimony of the NT Scriptures.

The moment a person believes on the Lord Jesus Christ, he is indwelt by the Holy Spirit; he is sealed by the Holy Spirit; he receives the earnest of the Spirit; he receives the anointing of the Spirit; and he is baptized by the Spirit into the Body of Christ. However, this does not deny that in a believer's life there are subsequent *crises* of the Spirit. There is no denying that the Holy Spirit often comes on individuals in a sovereign manner, empowering them for special ministries, giving them great boldness in the faith, and pouring out upon them a passion for souls.

19:8 For three months Paul visited the synagogue in Ephesus,[†] **reasoning and persuading concerning the things of the kingdom of God**. By **reasoning**, we understand that he spoke to the intellects of the people. By **persuading**, he sought to influence their wills, especially with regard to faith in Jesus as the Christ. The subject of his discourses was **"The Things of the Kingdom of God."**

C. E. Stuart clarifies:

> Not, be it observed, that he preached the *Gospel* of the Kingdom: that would have been dispensationally out of place. The Lord preached that. It, however, fell into abeyance on His death, to be revived in a coming day (Matthew 24:14; Revelation 14:6, 7). But Paul reasoned about the Kingdom of God, for that now exists on earth.[73]

19:9, 10 When some of the Jews were **hardened** (as to their intellects) and disobedient (as to their wills), when they began to agitate **the multitude** against **the Way**, Paul left the synagogue and

†See p. xxvii.

withdrew his **disciples** from the Jews there. He took them to **the school of Tyrannus**, where he had freedom to teach them **daily**. It is generally thought that **Tyrannus** was a Greek who conducted classes in philosophy or rhetoric. **For two years** the apostle made disciples and then sent them out to teach others also. As a result the whole province of **Asia heard the word of the Lord Jesus, both Jews and Greeks**. Thus a great door and effectual was opened to Paul, even though there were many adversaries (1 Cor. 16:9).

19:11, 12 As an apostle of Jesus Christ, **Paul** had the power to perform signs and wonders. These were proofs of his apostleship, and authenticated the message he preached. So great was the power that flowed through him **that even handkerchiefs or aprons** which he touched would be carried away to **the sick** or demon-possessed, and healing would result. The question arises whether these **miracles** can be duplicated today. The Holy Spirit of God is sovereign, and He can do as He pleases. However, it must be admitted that the apostles and their delegates had supernatural powers conferred upon them. Since we do not have apostles today in the full sense of the word, it is futile to insist that their miracles have been perpetuated.

19:13, 14 Whenever God works in power, Satan is invariably on hand to obstruct and oppose. While Paul was preaching and performing miracles, there were certain wandering Jews in Ephesus who were **exorcists**. These men commanded **evil spirits** (using **the name of the Lord Jesus** as a magic formula) to come out of **those who** were possessed. That certain of the Jews actually had the power to expel demons was acknowledged by the Lord Jesus (Luke 11:19).

Among the Jewish magicians practicing this were seven sons of Sceva (pronounced see'-vah). This man was made **chief priest**, or the priest in charge of the twenty-four courses. One day his sons were trying to expel an evil spirit from a demoniac. They said to the demon, **"We adjure you by the Jesus whom Paul preaches."**

19:15, 16 They uttered the words, but they did not have the power, and the demon did not obey. In fact, the reply of **the evil spirit** was most illuminating. He said, **"Jesus I know, and Paul I know; but who are you?"**

F. B. Meyer has an amusing comment on this, which is worth quoting:

> When the sons of Sceva started on the demon, he turned on them, and said, "You little dwarfs, you lilliputians, who are you? I know Paul! I don't know you, I have never heard about you before; your name has never been talked about down in Hell. No one knows you, nor about you outside of this little bit of a place called Ephesus."
>
> Yes, and there is the question that was put to me today: "Does anyone know of me down in Hell?" Do the devils know about us? Are they scared about us? Are they frightened by us? Or do they turn upon us? When we preach on Sunday, or when we visit in the streets, or take our Sunday School Class, the devil says, "I don't know you, you are not worth my powder and shot; you can go on doing your work. I am not going to upset Hell to stop you."[74]

It is interesting how the Scripture distinguishes between **the evil spirit** (v. 15) and **the man in whom the evil spirit** dwelt (v. 16). In verse 15 the demon spoke. But in verse 16 the demoniac himself **leaped on** the sons of Sceva, **overpowered them**, stripped them, and wounded them.

19:17 When news of this defeat of the forces of Satan became known in the surrounding area, a deep sense of awe **fell on** the people, **and the name of the Lord Jesus was magnified**. It was not Paul's name that received the glory, but **the name of** Paul's Savior.

19:18, 19 So mightily did the Spirit of God work among those who had practiced various forms of magical art that a great number turned to Christ, **confessing . . . their deeds**. After doing so, they made a public demonstration of their faith by gathering up **their books** that dealt with magic and burning them in a great bonfire. The original cost of the books would have been **fifty thousand pieces of silver**. It is difficult to determine exactly how much that would be in our currency — perhaps between eight and ten thousand dollars.

19:20 This well-publicized renunciation of pagan practices caused **the word of the Lord** to grow **mightily** and to prevail. Perhaps if modern Christians would burn their trashy books and magazines, the word would prevail much more.

19:21 As Paul's time at Ephesus began to draw to a close, he determined **to go** back **to Jerusalem** via **Macedonia and Achaia**, and after that he would **also see Rome**. His great heart of love and compassion was always reaching out to centers where the gospel could be planted, and from which it could spread.

19:22 He sent Timothy and Erastus on ahead to **Macedonia**, but **he** lingered **in Asia for a time**. It was probably at this time that he wrote 1 Corinthians (about A.D. 56).

19:23–27 As a result of Paul's ministry, many Ephesians turned to the Lord from their idols. The spiritual awakening in the city was so widespread that it caused a business recession among the idol-makers. **Demetrius, a silversmith**, was one of those seriously affected. He **made silver shrines of Diana**.[75] Serving as a spokesman for the **trade, Demetrius** gathered together all his fellow craftsmen and sought to stir them up to take some resolute action. He reminded them how **Paul** had been so successful in persuading **many people** that there are no **gods which are made with** human **hands**. He revealed his real motive when he said that their **trade** was **in danger**, but he sought to give it a religious coloring by pretending great reverence for **Diana** and her **temple**.

19:28–31 The meeting of silversmiths soon developed into a mob scene in which **the whole city** became involved. Chanting **"Great is Diana of the Ephesians!"**, the crowd **rushed into the theater** (arena or coliseum), and **seized Gaius and Aristarchus**, two of **Paul's traveling companions**, doubtless with the purpose of killing them. **Paul** himself **wanted** to step in and speak to the mob, but he was prevented by **the disciples**, and also by the Asiarchs (officers elected by the cities who at their own expense furnished festivals in honor of the gods). These civic benefactors who had befriended **Paul** told him that it would be most unwise for him to enter the arena.

19:32 By this time the mob was completely out of control. Many did not know why they were there. Conflicting voices were heard on every hand.

19:33, 34 A Jew named **Alexander** sought to step forward and address the mob. Doubtless his purpose was to defend the Jews as being completely innocent in the matter. **But when** the crowd **found out that he was a Jew**, they put up a tremendous protesting roar. **For about two hours** they chanted, **"Great is Diana of the Ephesians!"**

19:35 At this crucial moment, **the city clerk** succeeded in quieting **the crowd**. His speech was as successful as it was lame. He said in effect that the Ephesians had nothing to fear. After all, everyone knew that Ephesus had been appointed **the city** to serve as **temple guardian of the great goddess Diana**. Although thirteen cities in Asia had an interest in the temple, yet that sacred building was the solemn charge of the Ephesians. Also to them fell the privilege of guarding an **image** of **Diana** which was supposed to have fallen from heaven.

19:36–40 Implying that their religious foundations were secure, and that nothing could ever topple the worship of Diana, he told the people that they were foolish to make such a fuss. After all, the men against whom they were crying out had not been **robbers of temples** or **blasphemers of** Diana. **If Demetrius and his fellow craftsmen** had a just complaint, the regular **courts** of law were **open** to them, with **proconsuls** ready to hear their **charges**. If they had anything else to say, there was always the possibility of gathering together **in the lawful assembly**. But they had been gathering as a **disorderly** mob. The Roman Empire took a very dim view of any such proceedings. If they were ever **called . . . to account for this** mob scene, they would not be able to justify themselves. Also the city clerk knew that his job and possibly his life would be in danger if news of a riot got back to Rome.

19:41 By this time the mob had been quieted, and they now hastened away to their homes.

Strange to say, it was the action of the town clerk in the interests of civil order, and not the uproar, that ended Paul's ministry there. As long as there was healthy opposition, Paul felt the door of opportunity was widely open in Ephesus (1 Cor. 16:8, 9). But it appears that when municipal protection was extended to him, he moved on (Selected).

The word, **assembly** (vv. 32, 39, 41), translates the Greek word, *ekklēsia*, meaning a called out company of people. It is the same word translated *church* in other parts of the NT. Whether the word refers to a heathen mob, as here, or the congregation of Israel, as in Acts 7:38, or the NT church, must be determined from the context. The word, *assembly*, is a better translation of *ekklēsia* than the word, *church*. The word, *church*, comes from a Greek word meaning "belonging to the Lord" (*kuriakē*, cf. Scottish "kirk"). In modern usage, it commonly refers to a religious building. That is why many Christians prefer the word *assembly*; it expresses the fact that the church is a called out group of people, not a building or even a denomination.

20:1 From verse 1 it would appear that the apostle traveled directly from Ephesus to **Macedonia**. However, from 2 Corinthians we learn that he first went to TROAS. There he found an open door to preach the gospel but was anxious to see Titus and to learn from him how the Corinthians had received his First Epistle. When he did not find Titus in Troas, he crossed over the northeastern corner of the Aegean Sea **to MACEDONIA**. Undoubtedly he landed at NEAPOLIS, then traveled inland to PHILIPPI. While in **Macedonia**, probably at Philippi, he met Titus and was greatly encouraged by the news from Corinth. It was probably at this time that he wrote 2 Corinthians (A.D. 56?). (See 2 Cor. 1:8, 9; 2:12–14; 7:5–7.)

20:2, 3a After ministering for some time in Macedonia, he journeyed south **to GREECE** or ACHAIA. Most of the **three months** there were undoubtedly spent in CORINTH, and it was during this period that he wrote Romans. Some also believe that Galatians was written at this time.

20:3b Originally, Paul had planned to travel straight from Corinth across the Aegean **to Syria**. However, when he learned that **the Jews** were plotting to destroy him somewhere along that route, he changed his plans and went northward again **through MACEDONIA**.

20:4 At this time we are introduced to some of Paul's traveling companions. It is stated that they **accompanied him** as far as **Asia**, but we know that certain of them even went with him to Rome:

Sopater of Berea was possibly the same as Sosipater, a relative of Paul mentioned in Romans 16:21.

Aristarchus of Thessalonica nearly lost his life in the riot at Ephesus (Acts 19:29). We later read of him as being a fellow prisoner with Paul in Rome (Phmn. 24; Col. 4:10).

Secundus, also a native of Thessalonica, accompanied Paul as far as Asia, probably Troas or Miletus.

Gaius of Derbe is not to be confused with the Macedonian who was seized by the mob at Ephesus (Acts 19:29). Another Gaius is mentioned as being an inhabitant of Corinth and Paul's host while there (Rom. 16:23). John's Third Epistle is addressed to a man named Gaius, probably living in some city near Ephesus. Gaius was a very common name.

Timothy not only **accompanied** Paul **to Asia** but was with him in Rome during his first imprisonment. Subsequently he traveled with Paul through proconsular Asia. In his Second Letter to Timothy, Paul expressed the desire to see him again, but we do not know whether this wish was ever fulfilled.

Tychicus, a native **of Asia** Minor, probably journeyed as far as Miletus with the apostle. Later he rejoined Paul in Rome and is mentioned as laboring with him up to and during the time of his second imprisonment.

Trophimus was apparently a Gentile whose home was in Ephesus, in **Asia** Minor. He went with Paul to Jerusalem and unwittingly was the cause of the apostle's arrest. He is also mentioned in 2 Timothy 4:20.

20:5, 6 It appears that the above seven brethren traveled on ahead to **Troas**, while Paul and Luke visited **PHILIPPI**. (We believe that Luke was with the apostle because of the use of the first person pronoun, **us** in verse 5, **we** in verse 6, etc.) **After the Days of Unleavened Bread**, or the Passover, Paul and Luke sailed from Macedonia to **TROAS**. The journey would not ordinarily have taken **five days**. No explanation is given here for the delay.

20:7–9 Comparing verses 6 and 7, it appears that the apostle purposely waited in Troas for seven days so he could be there for the breaking of **bread** on the Lord's Day. It is certainly clear from verse 7 that it was the practice of the early Christians to gather together **on the first day of the week** in order to observe the Lord's Supper.

That **Paul** should have spoken **until midnight** should cause us no shocked surprise. When the spiritual temperature of a church is high, the Spirit of God is free to work without being fettered by the bondage of timepieces. As the night wore on, it became hot and stuffy **in the upper room**. Perhaps the **many lamps** contributed to this, as well as the number of people present. **A certain young man named Eutychus**, sitting in an open **window**, fell asleep and plummeted to the ground below. It was a fall of three stories, and he was killed by it.

20:10 But Paul went down and stretched himself over the body of the young man, as the prophets did of old. He then announced to the people that they should not make any more fuss about the matter since Eutychus was now alive. It might seem from Paul's words that their concern was unnecessary because the young man had not died; **his life** was still **in him**. But it is clear from verse 9 that he was actually dead. Acting with the power of an apostle, **Paul** had miraculously restored him to life.

20:11, 12 When Paul returned upstairs, they broke **bread** (v. 11), i.e., they observed the Lord's Supper, for which they had come together (v. 7). Then they ate a common meal, perhaps the *agapē* or love feast. This fellowship meal was held in conjunction with the Lord's Supper in the early days of the church, but abuses crept in (1 Cor. 11:20–22), and it was gradually discontinued.

After an all-night meeting, never to be forgotten, the apostle bade farewell to the believers in Troas.

20:13–15 Paul left Troas **on foot**, and walked twenty miles across the neck of a promontory of land **to ASSOS**. His traveling companions went by **ship** around the promontory, then picked him up on the southern side. Perhaps he wanted time to be alone and to meditate on the word of God.

Sailing south along the western coast of Asia Minor, they first came **to MITYLENE** (pronounced mit-i-le'-ne), the chief city of the island of LESBOS. The following night they apparently anchored off the island of **CHIOS** (pronounced key'-os). Another day's journey brought them to the island of **SAMOS, and** they **stayed at TROGYLLIUM**. Finally the travelers put in at **MILETUS**, a port on the southwest coast of Asia Minor, thirty-six miles south of Ephesus.

20:16 Paul intentionally bypassed **Ephesus**, because he feared that a visit there would occupy too much time, and **he was hurrying to** get to **Jerusalem** for **the Day of Pentecost**.

20:17 Upon landing at **Miletus**, Paul sent word to **the elders in Ephesus,**[†] asking them to come for a meeting. Undoubtedly it took considerable time for the message to reach them, and for them to make the journey south. However, they were well rewarded by the magnificent message they heard from the lips of the great apostle. In it we have a valuable portrait of an ideal servant of the Lord Jesus Christ. We see a man who was fanatically devoted to the Savior. He labored in season, out of season. He was tireless, indomitable, indefatigable. He was marked by true humility. No cost was too great for him to pay. His ministry was the result of deep exercise of soul. He had a holy boldness and fearlessness. Whether he lived or died was not important; but it was important that the will of God should be carried out and that men should hear the gospel. He was unselfish in all that he did. He would rather give than receive. He was undaunted by difficulties. He practiced what he preached.

20:18, 19 The apostle reminded the elders of Ephesus of his **manner** of life when he **lived among** them. **From the first day that** he set foot in **Asia**, and all the time he was there, he served **the Lord with** true **humility** and self-denial.

[†]See p. xxvii.

In connection with his ministry, there was a constant strain on his emotional system; there were **tears** of sorrow and **trials**. Constantly he suffered persecution as a result of **the plotting of the Jews**. Yet in spite of all the adverse circumstances, his ministry was bold and fearless.

20:20, 21 **Paul** held **back nothing** from the Ephesians that would be for their spiritual welfare. He **taught** them **publicly and from house to house**, constrained by the love of Christ. To him, it was not a matter of holding meetings at stated intervals, but rather of buying up every opportunity to encourage growth among the believers. Without discrimination as to nationality or religious background, he preached the necessity of **repentance toward God and faith toward our Lord Jesus Christ**. These are two fundamental elements of the gospel. In every genuine case of conversion, there are both **repentance** and **faith**. They are the two sides of the gospel coin. Unless a person were duly repentant, saving **faith** would be impossible. On the other hand, **repentance** would be of no avail unless it was followed by **faith** in the Son of God. **Repentance** is an about-face by which the sinner acknowledges his lost condition and bows to God's judgment as to his guilt. **Faith** is commitment of one's self to Jesus Christ as Lord and Savior.

In many NT passages, **faith** alone is stated to be the condition of salvation. However, **faith** presupposes **repentance**. How could a person truly accept Jesus Christ as Savior unless he realized that he needed a Savior? This realization, brought about by the convicting ministry of the Holy Spirit, is **repentance**.

20:22, 23 Having reviewed his past conduct among the Ephesians, the apostle now looks ahead to the sufferings that await him. He was constrained **in his spirit to go to Jerusalem**. It was an inner compulsion, which he was apparently unable to throw off. Although he did not know exactly what the turn of events would be in Jerusalem, he did know **that chains and tribulations** would be a regular part of his life. **The Holy Spirit** had been making this fact known to him **in every city**, perhaps through

the ministry of prophets, or perhaps by the mysterious, inner communication of divine intelligence.

20:24 As the apostle weighed this outlook in his mind, he did not think that his own **life** was the great consideration. His ambition was to obey God and to please Him. If in doing this, he would be called upon to offer up his **life**, he was willing to do so. No sacrifice he could make would be too great for the One who died for him. All that mattered was that he **finish** his **race** and complete **the ministry which** he **received from the Lord Jesus, to testify to the gospel of the grace of God**. No title could better express the good news which Paul preached — **the gospel of the grace of God**. It is the thrilling message of God's undeserved favor to guilty, ungodly sinners who deserve nothing but everlasting hell. It tells how the Son of God's love came from heaven's highest glory to suffer, bleed, and die on Calvary in order that those who believe on Him might receive forgiveness of sins and everlasting life.

20:25–27 Paul was sure he would never see his beloved Ephesian brethren again, but his conscience was clear in leaving them, because he knew he had not held back from declaring to them **the whole counsel of God**. He had instructed them not only in the fundamentals of the gospel, but in all the truths that were vital for godly living.

20:28 Since he would never again meet them on earth, he delivered a solemn charge to the elders that they should first of all **take heed** to their own spiritual condition. Unless they were living in fellowship with the Lord, they could not expect to be spiritual guides in **the church**.

Their function as elders was to **take heed . . . to all the flock, among which the Holy Spirit** had **made** them **overseers**. As mentioned previously, **overseers** in the NT are also called bishops, elders, and presbyters. This verse emphasizes that elders are not appointed or elected by the local assembly. They are **made overseers** by **the Holy Spirit**, and should be recognized by the believers among whom they labor.

Among other things they were responsible **to shepherd the church of God**. The importance of such a charge is seen in the words which follow: **which He purchased with His own blood**. This latter expression has been the cause of considerable discussion and disagreement among Bible scholars. The difficulty is that **God** is here pictured as shedding **His blood**, whereas **God** is Spirit. It was the Lord Jesus who shed His blood, and although Jesus is God, yet nowhere else does the Bible speak of **God** bleeding or dying.

The majority of manuscripts read "the church of the Lord and God which He purchased with His own blood," apparently suggesting that Person of the Godhead (the Lord) who actually shed His blood.

Perhaps J. N. Darby comes closest to the correct sense of the passage in his New Translation: "The assembly of God, which He has purchased with the blood of His own." Here God is the One who purchased the church, but He did it with the blood of His own Son, the blessed Lord Jesus.

20:29, 30　Paul was well aware **that after** his **departure**, the church would be attacked from without and from within. False teachers, **wolves** in sheep's clothing, would prey upon the flock, showing no mercy. From within the fellowship, men would aspire to places of prominence, speaking perversions of the truth, and trying **to draw away the disciples after themselves**.

20:31　In view of these imminent perils, the elders should be on their guard, and constantly **remember** how **for three years** the apostle had warned them **night and day with tears**.

20:32　Paul's great resource now was to **commend** them **to God and to the word of His grace**. Notice that he did not **commend** them to other human leaders, or to supposed successors of the apostles. Rather he entrusted them **to God and** the Bible. This is an eloquent testimony to the sufficiency of the inspired Scriptures. It is they which are **able to build up** the believers and to **give** them **an inheritance among all those who are sanctified**.

20:33–35　In closing his message, the Apostle Paul once again set before the elders the example of his own life and ministry. He could say in all honesty that he had **coveted no one's silver or gold or apparel**. It was not the hope of financial gain that motivated him in the work of the Lord. He was essentially a poor man, as far as material things were concerned, but he was rich toward God. Holding out his hands before them, he could remind them that those **hands** had labored in order to provide for the **necessities** of life, both for himself **and for those who were with** him. But he went beyond that also. He labored as a tentmaker in order that he might have means to help **the weak** — those physically ill, or **weak** as far as moral scruples are concerned, or **weak** in spiritual matters. The elders should remember this, and seek in all things the good of others, remembering **the words of the Lord Jesus, ". . . It is more blessed to give than to receive."** Interestingly enough, these words of our Lord are not found in any of the Gospels. They do represent the sum of much of His teaching, but here they are given as an inspired addition to His words in the Gospels.

20:36–38　At the conclusion of his message, Paul **knelt** on the ground **and prayed with** the elders. For them it was a time of deep sorrow. They showed their affection for the beloved apostle by falling **on** his **neck** and kissing **him**. The thing that particularly grieved them was his statement **that they would see his face no more**. Heavyhearted, they **accompanied him to the ship** for the voyage to Jerusalem.

21:1–4a　After the tender and affectionate farewell at Miletus, Paul and his companions sailed to the island of **COS**, where they spent the night. **The following day** they continued southeast **to** the island of **RHODES**. Leaving the northern tip of the island, they sailed eastward **to PATARA**, a seaport of Lycia on the southern coast of Asia Minor. At **Patara** they transferred to **a ship** that was **sailing over to Phoenicia**, the coastal strip of **Syria**, of which **Tyre** was one of the principal cities. As they sailed southeast across the Mediterranean, they skirted south of the island of **Cyprus**, leaving **it on the left** hand. The first port of call on the mainland of Palestine was **TYRE**. Since **the ship was to unload her cargo** there, Paul and the others looked up the Christian believers and **stayed** with them **seven days**.

21:4b It was during this time that these disciples **told Paul through the Spirit** that he should not set foot in **Jerusalem**. This raises the age-old question as to whether **Paul** was deliberately disobedient in going **to Jerusalem**, whether he unwittingly failed to discern the mind of the Lord, or whether he was actually in the will of God in going. A casual reading of verse 4b might seem to indicate that the apostle was willful and headstrong, acting in deliberate defiance of the Spirit. However, a more careful reading might indicate that **Paul** did not actually know that these warnings were given **through the Spirit**. Luke, the historian, tells his readers that the advice of the Tyrian disciples was Spirit-inspired, but he does not say that the apostle knew this as a definite fact. It seems far more probable that **Paul** interpreted the advice of his friends as calculated to save him from physical suffering or even death. In his love for his Jewish countrymen, he did not feel that his physical well-being was the important consideration.

21:5, 6 When the seven **days** had expired, the believers of Tyre turned out *en masse* to accompany the missionaries to the beach in an eloquent demonstration of their Christian love. After a time of prayer and affectionate goodbys, **the ship** pulled out and those left on shore **returned home**.

21:7 The next stop was **PTOLEMAIS** (pronounced tol-e-may'-is), a seaport approximately twenty-five miles south of Tyre, and now known as Akko (Acre), near Haifa. It was named after Ptolemy. A stopover of one day permitted the Lord's servants to visit the local **brethren**.

21:8 **On the next day** they took the final portion of their voyage — a thirty-mile sail south **to CAESAREA**, on the Plain of Sharon. There they stayed **in the house of Philip the evangelist** (not to be confused with the apostle by that name). It was this **Philip** who was chosen to be a deacon by the church in Jerusalem and who carried the gospel to Samaria.

Through his instruction, the Ethiopian eunuch had been saved.

21:9 Philip **had four virgin daughters who prophesied**. This means they were gifted by the Holy Spirit to receive messages directly from the Lord and to convey them to others. Some have inferred from this verse that it is permissible for women to preach and teach in the church. However, since it is *expressly forbidden* for women to teach, speak, or have authority over the men in the assembly (1 Cor. 14:34, 35; 1 Tim. 2:11, 12), it can only be concluded that the prophetic ministry of these **four virgin daughters** was carried on in the home or in other non-church gatherings.

21:10, 11 During Paul's stay in Caesarea, **a certain prophet named Agabus came down from Judea**. It was the same **prophet** who came to Antioch from Jerusalem and predicted the famine which took place during the reign of Claudius (Acts 11:28). Now **he took Paul's belt** and **bound his own hands and feet with it**. By this dramatic action, like many of the prophets before him, he was acting out his message. Then he gave the meaning of the object lesson. Just as he had **bound** himself, **hands and feet, so** would **the Jews** of **Jerusalem bind** the hands and feet of Paul **and deliver him** over to the Gentile authorities. Paul's service for the Jews (symbolized by the **belt**) would result in his being captured by them.

21:12–14 When the apostle's companions and the Christians in Caesarea heard this, they **pleaded with him not to go up to Jerusalem**. But he could not sympathize with their concern. Their tears only served to break his **heart**. Should the fear of chains and imprisonment restrain him from doing what he considered to be God's will? He would have them know that he was **ready not only to be bound, but also to die at Jerusalem for the name of the Lord Jesus**. All their arguments proved of no value. He was determined to go, and so they simply said, **"The will of the Lord be done."**

It is difficult to believe that Paul's parting words were spoken by a man who was knowingly disobeying the guidance of the Holy Spirit. We know that the disciples in Tyre told him through the Spirit that he should not go to Jerusalem (v. 4). But did Paul *know* they spoke through the Spirit? And did not the Lord later seem to approve his trip to Jerusalem when He said, "Be of good cheer, Paul; for as you have testified for Me in Jerusalem, so you must also bear witness at Rome" (23:11)? Two things are clear: First, *Paul* did not think his personal safety was the main consideration in serving the Lord. Second, the Lord overruled all these events for His glory.

21:15, 16 From Caesarea **to Jerusalem** was an overland journey of more than fifty miles, a long trip in those days of slow transportation. The apostle's traveling party had been increased by the addition of **some of the disciples from Caesarea** and also by a Christian brother named **Mnason** (pronounced nay'-son). Originally from **Cyprus**, he had been one of the earliest disciples there. Now he was living in **Jerusalem**, and was privileged to be host to the apostle and those who journeyed with him during Paul's last visit to **Jerusalem**.

Paul's missionary journeys really end with his arrival in **Jerusalem**. The remainder of the Book of Acts is occupied with his arrest, trial, journey to Rome, trial, and imprisonment there.

21:17, 18 Upon arrival in **Jerusalem**, the apostle and his friends were cordially received by **the brethren**. The next day a meeting was arranged with **James and all the elders**. There is no way of knowing for sure which **James** is referred to here. It could be James, the brother of our Lord, James, the son of Alphaeus, or some other person with that name. The first is the most likely.

21:19, 20a Paul took the lead by telling **in detail** what **God had done among the Gentiles through his ministry**. This caused considerable rejoicing.

21:20b–22 However, the Jewish brethren were apprehensive. Word had traveled around that the Apostle Paul had preached and taught against Moses and the law. This could mean trouble in Jerusalem.

The specific charge being made against Paul was that he taught **all the Jews** in foreign lands **to forsake Moses**, by telling them **not to circumcise their children nor to walk according to the** Jewish **customs**. Did Paul actually teach this or did he not?

He did teach that Christ was the end of the law for righteousness to those who believe. He did teach that once the Christian faith had come, believing Jews were no longer under the law. He taught that if a man received circumcision as a means of obtaining justification, then such a man cut himself off from salvation in Christ Jesus. He taught that to return to the types and shadows of the law, after Christ had come, was dishonoring to Christ. In view of this, it is not hard to see why the Jews should think of him as they did.

21:23, 24 But the Jewish brethren in Jerusalem had a scheme which they thought would placate their countrymen, both saved and unsaved. They suggested that Paul should take upon himself a Jewish **vow**. **Four men** were already in the process of doing this. Paul should join them, purify himself with them, **and pay their expenses**. F. W. Grant explains:

> Let him take these four men, who being believers like himself could yet bind themselves with the Nazirite vow, and presenting himself with them in the Temple purified, take upon him the expenses necessary for the completion of it, and that publicly, that all might recognize clearly his own relation to the law.[76]

We do not know much about what this **vow** involved. The details are veiled in obscurity. But all we need to know is that it was a *Jewish* **vow**, and that if the Jews saw the apostle going through the ritual connected with it, they would **know** assuredly that he was not turning others away from **the law** of Moses. It would be an indication to the Jews that the apostle himself kept **the law**.

The action of the apostle in taking on himself this Jewish **vow** has been defended and criticized. In *defense* of Paul it has been argued that he was acting according to his own principle to be all things to all men, if by any means he might save some (1 Cor. 9:19–23). On the other hand, Paul has been *criticized* for going too far in an effort to conciliate the Jews, and thus creating the impression that he was under the law. In other words, Paul has been charged with being

inconsistent with his view that the believer is not under the law, either for justification or as a rule of life (Gal. 1 and
2). We tend to agree with this criticism,
but we also feel that one should be careful in judging the apostle's motives.

21:25 The Jerusalem brethren advised Paul that no rules need be imposed
on Gentile believers other than those
proposed by the council in Jerusalem,
namely, **the Gentiles . . . should** abstain
**from things offered to idols, from
blood, from things strangled, and from
sexual immorality**.

21:26 The steps taken by **Paul** are
not clear to us today. Many commentators think this was the Nazirite vow. But
even if this were the case, we still do not
understand the various steps in the ceremony as described in this section.

H. Paul's Arrest and Trials
(21:27–26:32)

21:27–29 When the seven days of
the vow **were almost ended**, Paul's attempt to pacify **the Jews** proved futile.
When some of **the** unbelieving **Jews
from** proconsular **Asia** saw him **in the
temple**, they incited a riot against him.
Not only did they charge him with
teachings that were contrary to **the** Jewish **people** and to **the law**, but they also
accused him of defiling **the temple** by
taking Gentiles into the inner courts.
What actually happened was this: **they
had previously seen Paul** with **Trophimus in the city** of Jerusalem. **Trophimus**
was a Gentile convert from Ephesus. Because they saw them together, **they supposed that Paul had** taken his Gentile
friend **into the** inner courts of **the temple**.

21:30–35 Although the charge was
obviously false, it served its purpose. **All
the city was** thrown into an uproar. The
mob **seized Paul, and dragged him out
of the temple** area, closing the gates of
the inner courts behind them. As they
proceeded **to kill him**, word reached the
chiliarch, a military **commander** in
charge **of the garrison** of Antonia. He
came in a hurry with some of his **soldiers** and **took** Paul from the infuriated
mob, **bound** him **with two chains**, and
**asked who he was and what he had
done**. The mob was, of course, incoher-
ent and confused. **Some . . . cried one
thing and some another**. The frustrated

officer **commanded** the soldiers to bring
the prisoner **into the barracks** so he
could find out more definitely what was
going on. Even in the attempt to do this,
the mob surged forward with such determination that Paul **had to be carried by
the soldiers** up the stairs.

21:36 As they did so, they heard
words ringing out from **the multitude** —
words that perhaps some of them had
heard before — **"Away with him!"**

21:37–39 Just as they were about to
take **Paul into the barracks**, he asked the
officer if he could say something. The officer was startled to hear **Paul** speaking
Greek. He apparently thought he had
arrested an **Egyptian** who had **stirred
up a rebellion and led four thousand**
men called **assassins out into the wilderness**. **Paul** quickly assured him that he
was **a Jew from** the city of **Tarsus, in Cilicia**. As such, he was **a citizen of no
mean city**; it was famous as a place of
culture, education, and commerce, and
had been declared a "free city" by Augustus. With characteristic fearlessness,
the apostle requested permission **to
speak to the people**.

21:40 Permission was granted, and
as **Paul stood** there, flanked by Roman
soldiers, he quieted the crowd by mo-
tioning **with his hand**. The **silence** was
as **great** as the tumult had been. He was
now ready to give his testimony to the
Jerusalem Jews.

The Hebrew language here probably means Aramaic (a closely related
tongue) as spoken by the Hebrews at
that time.

22:1, 2 In addressing the Jewish
mob, the apostle wisely used Aramaic
rather than Greek. As soon as **they
heard** their mother tongue, they were
pleasantly surprised, and their shouts
subsided, at least for the moment.

22:3–5 Paul began with his roots as
a Jew, born in Tarsus of Cilicia; his education **at the feet of** the well-known Jewish teacher, **Gamaliel**; and his instruction in Judaism. He then gave special
emphasis to his zeal as a Jew. He had
persecuted the Christian faith, filling the
prisons with those who believed in
Jesus. The **high priest** and the Sanhedrin
could bear **witness** to the thoroughness
of his methods. It was **from** them that
he **received letters** authorizing him to go
to Damascus and **bring** back Christians

from **there to Jerusalem to be punished**.

22:6–8 Up to this point in Paul's message the Jews could understand perfectly, and, if they were honest, they would have to agree that what had been said was true. Now the apostle is going to tell them of an event which changed the entire direction of his life. It will be up to them to decide whether this event was of God.

As Paul **journeyed** to **Damascus ... a great light from heaven shone around** him. The fact that it happened **about noon**, here recorded for the first time, indicates that the **light** was more brilliant and glorious than the sun at its height. Struck to the ground by the intensity of the **light**, the persecutor heard **a voice** from heaven **saying, "Saul, Saul, why are you persecuting Me?"** Upon inquiry, he learned that it was **Jesus of Nazareth** who was speaking to him from heaven. The Nazarene had risen from the dead and was glorified above.

22:9 The men who traveled with him **saw the light**, and heard the sound of **the voice** (9:7), but they did **not hear** the actual words that were spoken. In other words, they were conscious of noise, but not of articulate speech.

22:10, 11 Having had this private audience with the Lord of Life and Glory, Paul made a complete commitment of his spirit, soul, and body to the Savior. This is indicated by his question, **"What shall I do, Lord?"** The Lord Jesus directed him to **go into Damascus, and there** he would receive his instructions. Blinded by the **light** of Christ's **glory**, he was **led by the hand** into the city.

22:12 In Damascus he was visited by **Ananias**. Paul describes him to his Jewish audience as **a devout man according to the law, having a good testimony with all the Jews who dwelt there**. The **testimony** of such a man was important in corroborating the account of Paul's conversion.

22:13 Addressing Paul as **"Brother Saul,"** Ananias commanded him to **receive** his **sight**. It was then that Paul first **looked up at him**.

22:14–16 In verses 14–16 we learn for the first time that Ananias said to Paul,

"The God of our fathers has chosen you that you should know His will, and see

the Just One, and hear the voice of His mouth. For you will be His witness to all men of what you have seen and heard. And now why are you waiting? Arise and be baptized, and wash away your sins, calling on the name of the Lord."

Several points of interest and importance should be noted in these verses. First, Ananias stated that it was **the God of our fathers** who had ordered the events on the road to Damascus. If the Jews were to oppose and resist what had happened, they were really fighting against **God**. Second, Ananias told Paul that he would be a **witness** for the Lord **to** all men. This should have prepared the Jewish crowd for Paul's announcement that he had been sent to the Gentiles. Finally, Paul was told to **arise and be baptized, and wash away** his **sins**.

Verse 16 has been misused to teach baptismal regeneration. It *is* possible that the verse only applies to Paul as a Jew who needed to dissociate himself from his Christ-rejecting nation by water baptism (see comments on 2:38).

A simpler solution, based on the grammatical construction of the original is as follows: Unlike the KJV, which punctuates as if there are four items in a row on the same level, the NKJV, following the original, pairs the first two items and the second two items. In the Greek there is a finite verb modified by a participle in each half of the verse. A literal rendering would be: "Having arisen be baptized, and have your sins washed off (by) calling on the name of the Lord."[77] This last clause is supported by general biblical teaching (cf. Joel 2:32; Acts 2:21; Rom. 10:13).

22:17–21 Now, for the first time, we learn of an experience Paul had toward the close of his first visit **to Jerusalem** after conversion. While he **was praying in the temple**, he fell into **a trance** and heard the Lord commanding him to **get out of Jerusalem quickly**, because the people would **not receive** his **testimony concerning** Christ. It seemed incredible to the apostle that his own people would refuse to listen to him. After all, they knew what a zealous Jew he had been, how he had **imprisoned** and beaten the disciples of Jesus, and how he had even been an accomplice to the murder of **Stephen**. But the Lord repeated

His command, "Depart, for I will send you far from here to the Gentiles."

22:22, 23 Up to this point, the Jews had been listening to Paul quietly. But his mention of going to the Gentiles with the gospel aroused insane jealousy and hatred. Chanting furiously in wild disorder, they cried out for Paul's life.

22:24, 25 When the commander saw them in their mad frenzy, he concluded that Paul must have been guilty of some very serious crime. Apparently he could not understand Paul's message since it was given in Aramaic, so he determined to extract a confession from the apostle by torturing him. He therefore ordered his prisoner to be brought into the barracks and bound with thongs in order to be scourged. As these preparations for the scourging were moving ahead deliberately, Paul quietly asked the centurion if it was legal to scourge a Roman citizen when he was uncondemned. As a matter of fact, it was unlawful even to tie up a Roman citizen before his guilt had been proved! To scourge him was a very serious offense.

22:26 The centurion quickly went and told the commander to take care what he did to Paul, because this man was a Roman citizen.

22:27, 28 This brought the commander to Paul in a hurry. On inquiry, he learned that the apostle was indeed a Roman citizen. There were three ways to become a Roman in those days. *First*, citizenship was sometimes granted by imperial decree as a reward for services rendered, etc. *Second*, it was possible to become a Roman by birth. This was the case with Paul; he was born in Tarsus, a free city of the Roman Empire, and his father was a Roman citizen. *Finally*, it was possible to purchase citizenship, often at a very high price. Thus the commander had obtained his citizenship by paying a large sum.

22:29 Disclosure of Paul's Roman citizenship cancelled all plans to scourge him, and caused fear among the authorities.

22:30 The commander was obviously anxious to know for certain why Paul had been accused by the Jews. At the same time he was determined to carry out the proceedings in a legal and orderly manner. Therefore, on the day after the mob scene in Jerusalem, he had

Paul taken out of prison and brought before the chief priests and the Sanhedrin.

23:1, 2 Standing before the Sanhedrin, Paul prefaced his remarks with a statement that throughout his life he had lived in all good conscience. The high priest, Ananias, was infuriated by this statement. He doubtless looked on Paul as an apostate from the Jewish religion, a renegade, a turncoat. How could one who had turned from Judaism to Christianity claim such innocence? Accordingly the high priest ordered that the prisoner be slapped on the mouth. This order was extremely unjust, since the case had hardly gotten underway.

23:3 Paul snapped back to Ananias that God would strike him for being such a whitewashed wall! Outwardly the high priest seemed righteous and just; inwardly he was corrupt. Professing to judge others according to the law, here he commanded Paul to be struck contrary to the law.

23:4 The attendants were shocked by the apostle's scathing rebuke. Did he not know that he was speaking to the high priest?

23:5 For some reason unknown to us, Paul had not actually realized that Ananias was the high priest. The Sanhedrin had been assembled on short notice, and perhaps Ananias was not wearing his official robes. It may even be that he was not occupying the seat customarily assigned to the high priest. Or perhaps Paul's weak eyesight was the cause. Whatever the reason, Paul had not intentionally spoken evil of the duly constituted ruler. He quickly apologized for his words, quoting Exodus 22:28: "You shall not speak evil of a ruler of your people."

23:6 Sensing from the conversation in the courtroom that there was lack of agreement between the Sadducees and Pharisees, the apostle decided to widen the rift by declaring himself to be a Pharisee who was on trial because he believed in the resurrection of the dead. The Sadducees, of course, denied the resurrection, as well as the existence of spirits or angels. The Pharisees, being very orthodox, believed in both (see 23:8).

Paul has been criticized here for using what might seem to be a carnal expedient to divide his audience. "We cannot avoid feeling," writes A. J. Pollock, "that Paul was wrong in claiming to be a Pharisee, and thus snatch a strategical advantage by setting the rival Sadducees and Pharisees at variance."

23:7–9 Whether or not he was justified, his words did provoke **a dissension . . . between the Pharisees and the Sadducees**, and caused **a loud outcry**. Some of **the scribes of the Pharisees** defended Paul's innocence, and said in effect, "What does it matter anyway, **if a spirit or an angel has spoken to him?"**

23:10 The controversy between the opposing factions became so heated that **the commander** ordered **the soldiers** to escort the prisoner out of the hall and back to **the barracks**.

23:11 The following night the Lord Jesus made a personal appearance to **Paul** in the prison, and said, **"Be of good cheer, Paul; for as you have testified for Me in Jerusalem, so you must also bear witness at Rome."** It is remarkable that in a passage where the apostle's actions have been subject to considerable criticism, **the Lord** should personally praise him for having borne faithful witness **in Jerusalem**. There was not a word of criticism or reproach from the Savior. Rather, it was a message of sheer praise and promise. Paul's service was not over yet. As he had been faithful in his ministry **in Jerusalem**, so he would **also bear witness** for Christ **at Rome.**

23:12–15 The next **day, some of the Jews banded together** to kill the Apostle Paul. In fact, **more than forty of** them **bound themselves under an oath that** they would **eat nothing until** they had **killed** "this imposter." Their scheme was as follows: they went **to the chief priests and elders**, suggesting that a meeting of the Sanhedrin be announced in order to hear Paul's case more thoroughly. The Sanhedrin would ask **the commander** to bring the prisoner to them. But the **forty** assassins would lie in ambush somewhere between the prison and the council hall. When **Paul** came near them, they would pounce on him and **kill him.**

23:16–19 In the providence of God, a nephew of the apostle overheard the plot and reported it to **Paul**. The latter believed in availing himself of legitimate

means to insure his safety; therefore, he reported the matter to **one of the centurions**. The centurion personally escorted the **young man to the commander.**

23:20, 21 Paul's nephew not only gave a complete account of the plot, but made a fervent plea to the commander not to **yield to** the demand of **the Jews** that **Paul** be brought to them.

23:22 When **the commander** had heard the story, he dismissed **the young man** with instructions not to tell anyone else of their meeting together. He now realized that he had to take prompt and decisive action to deliver his prisoner from the burning wrath of the Jews.

23:23–25 The commander quickly **called for two centurions** and arranged for a military escort to take the apostle **to Caesarea**. The guard was made up of **two hundred soldiers, seventy horsemen, and two hundred spearmen**. The trip was to be made under cover of darkness — at nine o'clock at **night**.

The great size of the military escort was not intended to be a tribute to this faithful messenger of Christ. Rather, it was an expression of the determination of the commander to maintain his reputation with his Roman superiors; if the Jews succeeded in killing Paul, a Roman citizen, then the officer in charge would be required to answer for his laxness.

23:26–28 The commander identifies himself as **Claudius Lysias** in the letter which he wrote to the Roman **governor Felix**. The purpose of the letter was, of course, to explain the situation with regard to Paul. It is rather amusing to see how **Lysias** sought to portray himself as a hero and a defender of public righteousness. He probably was extremely fearful lest it be reported to **Felix** that he had tied up an uncondemned **Roman** citizen. Fortunately for **Claudius Lysias**, Paul did not tattle.

23:29, 30 The commander explained that his investigation showed Paul to be innocent of any charge **deserving of death or chains**. Rather, the tumult seemed to be concerned with **questions of Jewish law**. Because of a plot against Paul, he felt it advisable to send Paul to Caesarea so that **his accusers** could come there also, and the whole matter could be aired in Felix's presence.

23:31–35 The trip **to Caesarea** was broken briefly at **Antipatris**, a city about thirty-nine miles from Jerusalem and twenty-four miles from **Caesarea**. Since there was little or no more danger of ambush from the Jews from this point on, **the soldiers** returned to Jerusalem, leaving **the horsemen** to escort **Paul to Caesarea**. Upon arrival, they delivered **Paul** to Felix, together with **the letter** from Lysias. When preliminary inquiry satisfied Felix as to the apostle's Roman citizenship, he promised to hear his case **when** his **accusers** had **come** down from Jerusalem. In the meantime **Paul** was **commanded to be kept in Herod's** palace or **Praetorium**.

The Roman governor, Felix, had enjoyed a meteoric rise from slavery to a position of political prominence in the Roman Empire. As to his personal life, he was grossly immoral. At the time of his appointment to be governor of the province of Judea, he was husband of three royal ladies. While in office, he fell in love with Drusilla, who was married to Azizus, king of Emesa. According to Josephus, a marriage was arranged through Simon, sorcerer from Cyprus.

He was a cruel despot, as is evidenced by the fact that he arranged the assassination of a high priest named Jonathan, who criticized him for his misrule.

It was this Felix before whom Paul had to appear.

24:1   Five days after **Paul** had left Jerusalem for Caesarea, **Ananias the high priest** arrived with certain members of the Sanhedrin. They hired a Roman **named Tertullus** to be their prosecuting attorney. His duty was to stand before Felix and press the charges **against Paul**.

24:2–4 **Tertullus** opened the case for the prosecution by showering the governor with flattery. Of course, there was a measure of truth to what he said. **Felix** had maintained rule and order by suppressing riots and insurrections. But Tertullus' words went beyond a mere acknowledgment of that fact, in an obvious effort to ingratiate his cause with the governor.

24:5–8 He then proceeded to specify four distinct charges against the Apostle Paul:

1. He was **a plague**, that is, a pest or a nuisance.

2. He was **a creator** of revolt **among all the Jews**.

3. He was **a ringleader of the sect of the Nazarenes**.

4. He **tried to profane the temple.**

24:9 After Tertullus had expressed confidence in Felix's ability to determine the accuracy of the charges against Paul, **the Jews** who were present added their voice in support of Tertullus' charges.

24:10 **Paul**, in response to a nod from **the governor**, rose to his own defense. First he expressed satisfaction at being permitted to appear before a man who, because of **many years** of experience, had familiarity with the customs and manners of the Jewish people. This might sound like flattery, but actually it was merely a courteous statement of the truth.

The apostle then answered the charges that were made against him, one by one.

24:11 As to his being a public nuisance, he replied that only **twelve days** had passed since he **went up to Jerusalem**, and that his purpose in going was **to worship**, not to cause a disturbance.

24:12, 13 Next he denied the charge that he incited the Jews to rebel. At no time, either **in the temple**, . . . **the synagogues or in the city**, had he disputed with the people or attempted to stir them up. These were the facts, and no one could disprove them.

24:14–17 Paul did not deny the third charge, namely, that he was a ringleader of the **sect** of the Nazarenes. But what he did say was that in this capacity he served **the God of** the Jews, **believing all things which are written in the** OT. He shared the expectation of all orthodox Jews, especially the Pharisees, **that there** would **be a resurrection of the dead, both of the just and the unjust**. In the light of that coming **resurrection**, he sought to preserve an unclouded relationship with the Lord and with his fellow men at all times. Far from stirring the Jews up to insurrection, Paul had come to Jerusalem **to bring alms** to the Jewish people. He was referring, of course, to the collection from the churches of Macedonia and Achaia, earmarked for the needy Hebrew Christian saints in Jerusalem.

24:18, 19 With regard to the fourth charge, namely, that he had profaned **the temple**, Paul made this reply: While he was in the act of bringing offerings to **the temple**, in the performance of a Jewish vow, certain **Jews from Asia found** him and accused him of taking unclean Gentiles into **the temple**. This, of course, was not true. The apostle was alone at the time, and had been **purified** from ceremonial defilement. These accusing **Jews from Asia** who caused the riot against him in Jerusalem **ought to have** come to Caesarea to accuse him, **if they had anything against** him.

24:20, 21 Paul then challenged **those** Jews **who** were present to state clearly what crimes he had been proved guilty of when he **stood before the council** in Jerusalem. They could not do it. All they would be able to say was that Paul **cried out, "Concerning the resurrection of the dead I am being judged by you this day."** In other words, those things in the accusation that were criminal were not true, and those things that were true were not criminal.

24:22 **When Felix heard** the case, he was faced with a dilemma. He knew enough about the Christian faith to realize who was right. The prisoner before him was obviously innocent of any crime against Roman law. Yet if he were to acquit Paul, he would incur the wrath of the Jewish people. From a political standpoint, it was important that he should curry their favor. So he adopted the expedient of continuing the case. He announced he would wait until **Lysias the commander** could come to Caesarea. Actually this was just a delaying tactic. We have no record that **the commander** ever did arrive.

24:23 In concluding the case, Felix **commanded** that although **Paul** should be retained in custody, he should be permitted reasonable **liberty**, and that **his friends** should be allowed to **visit him** and **provide** him food and clothing. This certainly indicates that the governor did not consider **Paul** a desperate criminal.

24:24, 25a **Some days** after the public trial, **Felix** and **his wife Drusilla** arranged a private interview with the apostle in order that they might hear more **concerning the** Christian **faith**.

With consummate fearlessness, **Paul reasoned** with this profligate governor and his adulterous wife **about righteousness, self-control, and the judgment to come**. They knew little of personal **righteousness**, either in their public or personal life. They were strangers to **self-control**, as was witnessed by their present evil marriage. They needed to be warned concerning **the judgment to come**, because unless their sins were pardoned through the blood of Christ, they would perish in the lake of fire.

24:25b, 26 **Felix** seemed to be more moved than Drusilla. Although he **was afraid**, he did not trust the Savior. He deferred making a decision for Christ with the words, **"Go away for now; when I have a convenient time I will call for you."** Sadly enough, this **convenient time** never came, as far as the Bible record is concerned. Yet this was not Paul's last testimony to **Felix**. The governor called him repeatedly during the next two years, while the apostle was a prisoner in Caesarea. Actually, **Felix** hoped that some of Paul's friends would pay him a handsome bribe in order to have him released.

24:27 **After two years**, in A.D. 60, **Porcius Festus succeeded Felix. Felix, wanting to do the Jews a favor, left Paul** as a manacled prisoner in Caesarea.

25:1 Porcius **Festus** was appointed Roman governor of Judea by the Emperor Nero in the autumn of A.D. 60. **Caesarea** was the political center for the Roman province of Syria, of which Judea was a part. **After three days** Festus **went up from Caesarea to Jerusalem**, the religious capital of his jurisdiction.

25:2, 3 Although it was now two years since **Paul** was imprisoned in Caesarea, **the Jews** had not forgotten him, neither had their murderous hatred subsided. Thinking that they might be able to obtain a political **favor** from the new governor, **the high priest and** principal **men of the Jews** filled his ear with charges **against Paul** and asked for him to be sent **to Jerusalem** for trial. Probably they meant that he should be tried before the Sanhedrin, but their real plan was to waylay him on the journey and **kill him.**

25:4, 5 **But Festus** had doubtless

been informed of their previous plan to kill **Paul**, and of the elaborate preparations taken by the commander in Jerusalem to spirit him away to Caesarea. He therefore refused their request, but promised them that he would permit them an opportunity to state their case against **Paul** if they could come to **Caesarea**.

25:6–8 After a stay of **more than ten days** in Jerusalem, Festus returned **to Caesarea** and convened the court **the next day**. The Jews hastened to the attack, bringing **many serious** charges **against Paul**, but failing to **prove** any of them. Sensing the poverty of their case, the apostle contented himself with a simple denial of any crime **against the law**, **against the temple**, or **Caesar**.

25:9–11 For a moment it seemed as if **Festus** was willing to accede to the request of **the Jews** that **Paul** be sent **to Jerusalem** for trial before the Sanhedrin. However, he would not do this without the prisoner's permission. **Paul** obviously realized that if he agreed, he would never reach **Jerusalem** alive. He therefore refused by stating that the court in Caesarea was the proper place for a trial. If he had **committed** a crime against the Roman Empire, he was not unwilling to die for it. But if he was not guilty of such a sin, then on what legal ground could he be handed over to **the Jews**? Taking full advantage of his rights as a Roman citizen, the Apostle Paul then uttered the memorable words, **"I appeal to Caesar."**

Was **Paul** justified in appealing **to Caesar**? Should he not have committed his cause entirely to God, and refused to stoop to dependence on his earthly citizenship? Was this one of the "mistakes of Paul?" We cannot say with finality. All we know is that his appeal **to Caesar** hindered his being set free at this time, and that even if he hadn't appealed, he would have reached Rome some other way.

25:12 **Festus** briefly **conferred** with his legal advisors concerning the procedure in such matters. He then said to Paul, perhaps in a defiant tone, **"You have appealed to Caesar? To Caesar you shall go!"**

25:13 Some time **after** this, **King** Herod **Agrippa II** and his sister **Bernice**

came to Caesarea to congratulate **Festus** on his new appointment. **Agrippa** was the son of Herod Agrippa I, who murdered James and imprisoned Peter (Acts 12). His sister was a woman of unusual beauty. While historians ascribe an unsavory reputation to her, including her relations with her brother, the NT is silent as to her personal character.

25:14–16 During their rather long stay in Caesarea, **Festus** decided to tell Agrippa about a problem he was facing with a prisoner named Paul. First he recounted the crude demand **of the Jews** that sentence be passed against Paul without a formal trial. Portraying himself as the upholder and protector of proper judicial processes, he told how he had insisted on a trial at which the defendant could meet his **accusers face to face** and be given the opportunity to defend himself.

25:17–19 When the case came to trial, Festus found that the prisoner was not guilty of any crime against the empire. Rather, the case revolved around **"some questions about their own religion and about a certain Jesus, who had died, whom Paul affirmed to be alive."**

25:20–22 Festus then reviewed his offer to **Paul to go to Jerusalem**, and of Paul's appeal to the **Augustus** (a *title* for Caesar here, not a *name*). This, of course, raised a problem. In sending his prisoner to Rome, what charge would he make against him? Since **Agrippa** was a Jew, and therefore conversant with matters involving Judaism, Festus hoped he would get some help in drawing up a suitable charge.

In speaking of the Savior of the world, Festus used the expression, **a certain Jesus**. Bengel's comment on this is worth repeating: "Thus speaks this miserable Festus of Him to Whom every knee shall bow."

25:23 **The next day** a formal hearing was arranged. **Agrippa and Bernice** arrived **with great pomp**. They were accompanied by **the commanders and the prominent men of the city**. Then **Paul was brought in.**

25:24–27 Once again, **Festus** set forth the history of the case — the insistent demands **of the Jews** for Paul's death, the inability of **Festus** to find the apostle guilty of any crime **deserving of**

death, and then Paul's appeal to Caesar. Festus' dilemma, of course, was this: he was forced by Paul's appeal to send him to Nero, yet there was no adequate *legal basis* for a trial. **Festus** plainly stated that he hoped **Agrippa** would be able to help him; after all, it did seem rather **unreasonable to send a prisoner and not to specify the charges against him**. These proceedings were more in the nature of a hearing than a trial. The Jews were not present to accuse the apostle, and **Agrippa** was not expected to render a binding decision.

26:1–3 The scene before us has been well described as "an enslaved king and an enthroned prisoner." From the spiritual standpoint, **Agrippa** was a pitiable figure, whereas the apostle soared on wings of faith, superior to his circumstances.

When given his cue by **Agrippa**, **Paul stretched out his hand and** began a stirring recital of his Christian experience. First, he expressed gratitude that he was permitted to present his case before one who, being a Jew, was conversant with the **customs and questions which** prevailed among the Jewish people. His introduction was not mere flattery; it was a statement of Christian courtesy and simple truth.

26:4, 5 As to his early **life**, the apostle was an exemplary Jew. **The Jews** would have to admit, if only they **were willing to testify**, that Paul had followed a pathway of **the strictest** orthodoxy, being a consistent **Pharisee.**

26:6 Now he was on trial for no greater crime than the fact that he clung to **the hope of the promise made by God to** the Jewish **fathers** in the OT. The flow of Paul's argument here seems to be as follows: In the OT God made various covenants with the leaders of Israel, such as Abraham, Isaac, Jacob, David, and Solomon. The principal covenant had to do with the promise of the Messiah, His coming to deliver the nation of Israel and to reign over the earth. The patriarchs of the OT died without seeing the fulfillment of this promise. Does this mean that God would not carry out the terms of the covenants? He would most assuredly do so! But how could He do it when the fathers were already dead? The answer is, "By raising them from

the dead." Thus, in a very direct way, the apostle links the promises made to the OT saints with the resurrection of the dead.

26:7 The apostle pictured the **twelve tribes** of Israel as **earnestly** and ceaselessly **serving God**, hoping to see the **promise** fulfilled. This reference to the **twelve tribes** is important in view of the current teaching that ten of the tribes of Israel have been "lost" since the captivity. Though they were scattered among the Gentile nations, the Apostle Paul saw them as a distinct people, **serving God** and looking for the promised Deliverer.

26:8 This then was Paul's crime! He believed **that God** would fulfill His promise to the fathers by raising them from **the dead**. What was so **incredible** about this? Paul asked Agrippa and all those who were with him.

26:9–11 Reverting to the story of his life, Paul recounted the savage and unremitting campaign he waged against the followers of the Christian faith. With all his strength he opposed **the name of Jesus of Nazareth**. With **authority from the chief priests**, he imprisoned **many of** the Christians in Jerusalem. When they stood trial before the Sanhedrin, he cast his vote against them consistently. Over and over again he arranged punishment for those whom he found in **every synagogue**, and he did all he could to force them to deny their Lord. (When it says that he **compelled**[78] them to blaspheme, it does not mean he was successful, but *he tried to* do it.) Paul's hate campaign against the disciples of **Jesus** had overflowed from Jerusalem and Judea **to foreign cities**.

26:12–14 It was while he was on one of these foreign expeditions that a great transforming experience occurred in his life. He was en route **to Damascus**, equipped with official papers authorizing him to arrest the Christians and bring them back to Jerusalem for punishment. **At midday** he was overcome by a vision of glory. **A light from heaven** shone upon him, **brighter than the** midday sun. After he **had fallen to the ground**, he **heard a voice** asking this probing question: **"Saul, Saul, why are you persecuting Me?"** The **voice** also added the revealing words, **"It is hard**

for you to kick against the goads."
Goads were sharply pointed instruments
used to force stubborn animals to move
ahead. Paul had been kicking against the
goad of his own conscience, but even
more important, against the convicting
voice of the Holy Spirit. He had never
been able to forget the poise and grace
with which Stephen had died. He had
been fighting against God Himself.

26:15 Paul asked, "Who are You,
Lord?" The voice replied, "I am Jesus
whom you are persecuting." Jesus? How
could that be? Hadn't Jesus been crucified and buried? Hadn't His disciples
stolen His body and laid it away in some
secret place? How then could Jesus be
speaking to him now? The truth quickly
dawned on Paul's soul. Jesus had indeed
been buried, but He had risen from the
dead! He had ascended back to heaven,
from where He was now speaking to
Paul. In persecuting the Christians, Paul
had been persecuting their Master. And
in persecuting Him, he had been persecuting the Messiah of Israel, the very
Son of God.

26:16 Next Paul gives a condensed
summary of the commission which was
given him by the risen Lord Jesus Christ.
He was told by the Lord to rise and
stand on his feet. He had had this special revelation of Christ in glory because
he was appointed to be a servant of the
Lord and a witness of all he had seen
that day, and of all the great truths of
the Christian faith which would yet be
made known to him.

26:17 The promise that Paul would
be delivered from the Jewish people and
the Gentiles must be understood as
meaning deliverance in general until his
work was done.

26:18 Paul would be sent especially
to the Gentiles to open their eyes, in
order to turn them from darkness to
light, and from the power of Satan to
God. Through faith in the Lord Jesus,
they would receive forgiveness of sins
and an inheritance among those who are
sanctified. H. K. Downie shows how
verse 18 is an excellent summary of what
the gospel does:

1. It relieves from darkness.
2. It releases from the power of Satan.
3. It remits sins.
4. It restores a lost inheritance.

26:19–23 Having been thus commissioned, Paul explains to Agrippa that
he was not disobedient to the heavenly
vision. Both in Damascus and in Jerusalem, and throughout all . . . Judea, and
then to the Gentiles he preached to men
that they should repent and turn to
God, doing works that prove the reality
of their repentance. This is what he was
doing when the Jews seized him in the
temple and tried to kill him. But God
had given him protection and help, and
he continued to testify to all with whom
he came in contact, preaching the message which the prophets and Moses
preached in the OT. The message was
that the Messiah would suffer, that He
would be the first to rise from the dead,
and that He would show light both to
the Jewish people and to the Gentiles.

26:24–26 Being a Gentile, Festus
had probably failed completely to follow
the flow of the apostle's argument. Thoroughly unable to appreciate a man who
was filled with the Holy Spirit, he impetuously accused Paul of being crazy as
the result of his much learning. With no
trace of irritation or temper, the apostle
quietly denied the charge and emphasized that his words were those of truth
and reason. He then expressed confidence that the king knew the truth of
what he had been saying. Paul's life and
testimony had not been a secret. The
Jews knew all about it, and doubtless the
reports had reached Agrippa.

26:27 Addressing the king directly,
Paul asked, "King Agrippa, do you believe the prophets?" Then Paul answered his own question, "I know that
you do believe." The force of the argument is unmistakable. Paul was saying
in effect, "I believe all that the prophets
said in the OT. You, too, believe their
testimony, don't you, Agrippa? How
then can the Jews accuse me of a crime
deserving of death? Or how could you
condemn me for believing what you
yourself believe?"

26:28 That Agrippa felt the force of
the argument is indicated by his words,
"You almost persuade me to become a
Christian." However, there is consider-
able disagreement as to exactly what
Agrippa meant. Those who follow the
King James tradition feel that the king
had actually been brought to the thresh-

old of decision for Christ. They feel that Paul's answer in verse 29 substantiates this. Others think that **Agrippa** was using irony, asking Paul, as it were, "Do you think that with a little persuasion you can make me a Christian?" In other words, he was evading the pressure of the apostle's words with a joke.

26:29 Whether Agrippa was speaking in sincerity or in jest, **Paul** answered with deadly earnestness. He expressed the fervent wish that, whether with little persuasion or with much, both Agrippa and **all** the others present might enter into the joys and blessings of the Christian life, that they might share all Paul's privileges, that they **might become** like him, **except for** the **chains**. Morgan writes:

> He would die to save Agrippa, but he would not put his chains upon Agrippa. That is Christianity. Magnify it, multiply it, apply it. The sincerity that persecutes is not Christian. The sincerity that dies to deliver, but will not impose a chain, is Christianity.[79]

26:30–32 **The king**, the **governor**, **Bernice**, and the other officials left the room to confer privately. They were all forced to admit that Paul had **done nothing deserving of death or chains**. Perhaps with a tinge of regret, **Agrippa said to Festus** that if Paul **had not appealed to Caesar**, he **might have been set free**.

We naturally wonder why the appeal to Caesar could not be cancelled. Whether or not such an appeal was unalterable, we do know that it was God's purpose that the apostle to the Gentiles should go to Rome for trial before the Emperor (23:11), and there find the fulfillment of his desire to be made conformable to the death of his Lord.

I. Paul's Voyage to Rome and Shipwreck (27:1–28:16)[†]

This chapter presents the thrilling saga of the apostle's voyage from Caesarea to Malta, en route to Rome. If Paul had not been a passenger, we would never have heard of the trip, or of the shipwreck. The passage is full of nautical terms, and is therefore not always easy to follow.

27:1 The journey began at Caesarea. **Paul** was placed in the custody of

an officer **named Julius**. This **centurion** was attached to the **Augustan Regiment**, a distinguished legion of the Roman army. Like all the other centurions mentioned in the NT, he was a man of superior character in kindness, justice, and consideration for others.

27:2 There were other prisoners on board, who, like Paul, were being taken to Rome for trial. Also on the passenger list were the names of **Aristarchus** and Luke, both traveling companions of the apostle on earlier journeys. The **ship** on which they embarked was from **Adramyttium**, a city of Mysia in the northwest corner of Asia Minor. It was scheduled **to sail** north and west, making stops at ports **along the coasts of** proconsular **Asia**, the western province of Asia Minor.

27:3 The ship sailed north along the coast of Palestine, putting in **at Sidon**, seventy miles from Caesarea. **Julius**, the centurion, **kindly** permitted **Paul to go** ashore and visit **his friends and receive care.**

27:4, 5 From Sidon, the route cut across the northeast corner of the Mediterranean, passing **Cyprus** on the left, and thus taking advantage of the side of the island sheltered from the wind. In spite of **the winds** being **contrary**, the ship crossed over to the southern coast of Asia Minor, then **sailed** westward past **Cilicia and Pamphylia** till it arrived at **Myra, a** port **city of Lycia**.

27:6 **There the centurion** transferred his prisoners to another **ship**, since the first one would not take them any closer **to Italy**; it would rather sail up the western coast of Asia Minor to its home port.

The second **ship** was from Alexandria, on the northern coast of Africa. It carried 276 people, both crew and passengers, and a cargo of wheat. From Alexandria it had sailed due north across the Mediterranean to Myra, and was now heading west for **Italy**.

27:7, 8 For **many days** travel was slow, due to adverse winds. It was **with difficulty** that the crew brought the ship over against the harbor of **Cnidus** (pronounced nigh'-dus), a port on the extreme southwest corner of Asia Minor. Since **the wind** was against them, they headed south and sailed along the shel-

†See p. xxxi.

tered east side of the island of **Crete**. Rounding Cape **Salmone**, they turned westward and bucked heavy winds until they came to **Fair Havens**, a harbor **near the city of Lasea**, on the south central coast of **Crete**.

27:9, 10 By **now** considerable **time** had been lost due to unfavorable **sailing** conditions. The approach of winter weather made further travel **dangerous**. It must have been late September or early October, since **the Fast** (the Day of Atonement) **was already over. Paul** warned the crew that navigation was unsafe and that if **this voyage** were continued, there would be the danger of losing **the cargo and ship,** and even the **lives** of some on board.

27:11, 12 However, **the helmsman and the owner of the ship** wanted to proceed. **The centurion** accepted their judgment, and most of the others agreed with them too. It was felt that **the harbor was not** as **suitable** as **Phoenix** would be as a place to spend the **winter. Phoenix** was located forty miles west of Fair Havens, at the southwest tip of **Crete**. Its **harbor** opened **toward the southwest and northwest.**

27:13–17 When the south wind blew softly, the mariners thought they could make the extra distance to Phoenix. They weighed anchor, and sailed westward, hugging the shore. Then a violent northeaster (**Euroclydon**[80]) beat down upon them from the cliffs along the coast. Unable to steer the desired course, the crew was forced to let **the ship** be driven by the gale. They were driven southwest to a small **island called Clauda**,[81] twenty to thirty miles from Crete. When they reached the protected side of the **island**, they had **difficulty** securing **the skiff** which they had been towing. But finally they were able to hoist **it on board**. Then they tied **cables** around the hull of **the ship** to keep it from being torn apart by the heavy seas. They greatly feared they would be driven south to **Syrtis**, a gulf on the coast of Africa noted for its dangerous shoals. To prevent this, **they struck sail and so were driven.**

27:18, 19 After a day of drifting at the mercy of the storm, they began to throw the cargo overboard. On the third day they threw **the ship's tackle overboard**. Doubtless **the ship** had been tak-

ing a lot of water, and it was therefore necessary to lighten its load to prevent it from sinking.

27:20 For many days they were tossed about helplessly without sight of **sun** or **stars**, and thus without the ability to take bearings and find out where they were. **Hope** of survival **was finally given up.**

27:21–26 Despair was accentuated by hunger. The men had not eaten for many days. Doubtless they spent their time working for the preservation of the ship and bailing out water. Perhaps there were no facilities for cooking. Sickness, fear, and discouragement probably robbed them of appetite. There was no shortage of food, but neither was there an inclination to eat.

Then P**a**ul stood in the midst of them with a message of hope. First he gently reminded them that they **should . . . not have sailed from Crete**. Then he assured them that though **the ship** would be lost, there would **no loss of life**. How did he know? **An angel** of the Lord had appeared to him that **night**, assuring him that he would yet stand **before Caesar** in Rome. **God** had **granted** the apostle **all those who** sailed **with** him, in the sense that they, too, would be preserved. Therefore they should cheer up. **Paul** believed that all would be well, even though they would be shipwrecked **on a certain island**.

A. W. Tozer writes insightfully:

> When the "south wind blew softly," the ship that carried Paul sailed smoothly enough and no one on board knew who Paul was or how much strength of character lay hidden behind that rather plain exterior. But when the mighty tempest, Euroclydon, burst upon them, Paul's greatness was soon the talk of everyone on the ship. The apostle, though himself a prisoner, quite literally took command of the vessel, made decisions and issued orders that meant life or death to the people. And I think the crisis brought to a head something in Paul that had not been clear even to him. Beautiful theory was quickly crystallized into hard fact when the tempest struck.[82]

27:27–29 Fourteen days had elapsed since they left Fair Havens. They were now drifting helplessly in a part of the Mediterranean known as the Ionian, the **sea** between Greece, Italy, and Africa. **About midnight the sailors**

sensed that they were drawing near some land; perhaps they could hear the breakers dashing against the shore. When they first measured the depth, they **found it** was **twenty fathoms** (120 feet), then a little later it was **fifteen fathoms**. To prevent running the ship aground, **they dropped four anchors from the stern, and prayed for** daylight.

27:30–32 Fearing for their lives, some of **the sailors** plotted to get ashore in the small boat. They were in the process of lowering **the skiff** from the bow of **the ship** — pretending they were **putting out** more **anchors** — when **Paul** reported their plot **to the centurion. Paul** warned that **unless** the sailors remained on board, the rest would not **be saved. Then the soldiers cut away the ropes** attached to **the skiff and let it fall off. The sailors** were thus compelled to try to save their own lives on board **the ship**, as well as the lives of the others.

27:33, 34 Phillips titles verses 33–37 "Paul's sturdy common sense." To appreciate the drama of the moment, we should really know something of the terror of a violent storm at sea. Then too, we should remember that Paul was not the captain of the ship but only a captive passenger.

Shortly before daybreak **Paul implored** the people to eat, reminding them that they had gone two weeks **without food**. The time had come to eat; their well-being depended on it. The apostle assured them that **not a hair** of anyone's head would be lost.

27:35 Then he set the example for them by taking **bread**, giving **thanks to God** publicly for it, and eating. How often we shrink from praying in front of others! Yet how often such prayer speaks louder than our preaching.

27:36, 37 Thus **encouraged**, they **took food themselves**. There **were two hundred and seventy-six persons on the ship.**

27:38–41 After eating, **they lightened the ship** by throwing **out the wheat into the sea. Land** was nearby, **but they** could **not recognize it**. The decision was made to beach **the ship**, as far on shore as **possible. They let go the anchors**, leaving **them in the sea**. Then they untied the rudders that had previously been raised, and lowered them into position. Hoisting **the mainsail**, they **made**

for shore and drove the ship aground at **a place where two seas met** — probably in a channel between two islands. The bow **stuck fast** in the sand, **but the stern** soon began to break apart **by the violence of the waves.**

27:42–44 The soldiers' plan was to kill the prisoners to prevent **escape, but the centurion, wanting to save Paul**, overruled. He ordered all **who could swim** to make for shore. **The rest** were told to float in **on boards** or other **parts of the ship**. In this way, every one of the crew and passengers **escaped safely to land.**

28:1, 2 As soon as the crew and passengers reached shore, they learned that they were on the **island** of **Malta**. Some of **the natives** of the island saw the shipwreck and witnessed the victims struggling through the water to get to shore. They very graciously built **a fire** for the new arrivals, who were thoroughly drenched and **cold**, both from the sea and from **the rain.**

28:3 While **Paul** was helping with **the fire**, he was bitten by a poisonous snake. Apparently the snake had lain dormant among some of the driftwood. When the wood was placed **on the fire**, the **viper** quickly revived and struck out against the apostle. It **fastened on his hand**, not just in the sense of coiling on it, but actually biting it.

28:4–6 At first the local citizens concluded the apostle must be **a murderer**. Although he had **escaped** from the shipwreck, **yet justice** was tracking him down and he would soon **swell up or suddenly fall down dead.** However, when Paul showed no ill effects from the snake bite, **they changed their minds** and decided **he was a god**! This is another vivid illustration of the fickleness and changeableness of the human heart and mind.

28:7 The leading citizen of the island of Malta at that time **was Publius**. He owned considerable land in the vicinity of the beach where the shipwrecked party landed. This wealthy Roman official **received** Paul and his friends **courteously**, and provided accommodations for them **for three days**, that is, until permanent quarters could be arranged in which they would spend the winter.

28:8 The kindness of this Gentile did not go unrewarded. At about that time, his **father** took **sick** with **fever and dysentery. Paul went in to him and prayed, and he laid his hands on him and healed him.**

28:9, 10 News of this healing miracle spread quickly throughout **the island.** During the next three months the sick were brought to Paul and were all cured. The people of Malta showed their appreciation to the apostle and to Luke[83] when they left by showering them with many honors, and bringing many gifts that would be helpful on the trip to Rome.

28:11 After the **three months** of winter had passed, and navigation was safe again, the centurion, with his prisoners, embarked on **an Alexandrian ship . . . which had wintered at the island.** The figurehead of this **ship was the Twin Brothers,** that is, Castor and Pollux. These were supposed, by heathen sailors, to be the patron gods of mariners.

28:12–14 From Malta they sailed about eighty miles to **Syracuse,** the capital of Sicily, located on its east coast. The ship stopped there for **three days,** then proceeded to **Rhegium,** on the southwest corner of Italy, at the toe. **After one day** a favorable **south wind blew,** enabling the crew to sail 180 miles northward along the west coast of Italy **to Puteoli,** on the northern shore of the Bay of Naples. **Puteoli** was about 150 miles southeast of **Rome.** There the apostle **found** Christian **brethren,** with whom he was permitted to enjoy fellowship for **seven days.**

28:15 We are not told how news reached Rome of the arrival of Paul in Puteoli. However, two different groups **of brethren** set out **to meet** him. One group traveled forty-three miles southeast of Rome to The Market of Appius. The other group traveled thirty-three miles southeast to the **Three Inns. Paul** was greatly cheered and encouraged by this touching demonstration of the love of the saints in Rome.

28:16 Upon arrival in **Rome,** he **was permitted to dwell** in a private home, **with the soldier who guarded him.**

J. Paul's House-Arrest and Witness to the Jews in Rome (28:17–31)[†]

28:17–19 In accordance with his policy of witnessing to **the Jews** first, Paul sent an invitation to their religious leaders. **When they had come together** in his rented house, he explained his case **to them.** He told them that although he had **done nothing against** the Jewish **people, or** their **customs,** yet **the Jews of Jerusalem** had **delivered** him **into the hands of the Romans** for trial. The Gentile authorities could find no fault in him, and wanted to free him, **but when the Jews** cried out **against it,** the apostle **was compelled to appeal to Caesar.** In making this appeal, it was not for the purpose of bringing any charge against the Jewish **nation.** Rather, it was that he might defend himself.

28:20 It was because he was innocent of any crime against the Jewish people that he had **called** the chief Roman Jews together. Actually it was **because** of **the hope of Israel** that he **was bound with** a **chain. The hope of Israel,** as explained previously, refers to the fulfillment of the promises made to the Jewish patriarchs, especially the promise of the Messiah. Inherent in the fulfillment of these promises was the resurrection of the dead.

28:21, 22 The Jewish leaders professed to know nothing about the Apostle Paul. They had not **received** any **letters from Judea concerning** him, and none of their fellow Jews had brought reports to them against him. However, they did want to hear more from Paul, because they knew that the Christian faith with which he was associated was **spoken against everywhere.**

28:23 Some time later a great number of these Jews came to Paul's **lodging** to hear more from him. He availed himself of the opportunity to testify to them concerning **the kingdom of God,** and to persuade them **concerning Jesus.** In so doing he quoted to them from **the Law of Moses and the Prophets, from morning till evening.**

28:24 Some believed the message he brought, **and some disbelieved.** (Disbelieving is stronger than a simple failure to accept the message. It indicates a positive rejection.)

28:25–28 When **Paul** saw that once again the gospel was being, on the whole, rejected by the Jewish nation, he quoted Isaiah 6:9 and 10, where the

[†]See p. xxxi.

prophet was commissioned to preach the word to a **people** whose **hearts** were **dull**, whose **ears** were deaf, and whose **eyes** were blinded. The apostle felt again the heartbreak of preaching good news to those who did not want to hear it. In view of this rejection by the Jews, **Paul** announced that he was taking the gospel **to the Gentiles**, and he expressed the assurance that **they** would **hear it.**

28:29 The unbelieving **Jews departed**, arguing **among themselves**. As Calvin points out, Paul's quoting a prophecy against them irritated the ungodly element who rejected the Messiah. It whipped them into a fury against those Jews who accepted Him. The reformer makes a helpful application:

> Finally, it will be in vain for anyone to object from this that the Gospel of Christ causes contentions, when it is obvious that these spring only from the stubbornness of men. And indeed, in order to enjoy peace with God, it is necessary for us to wage war with those who treat Him with contempt.[84]

28:30 Then **Paul** remained in Rome for **two whole years**, living **in his own rented house**, and ministering to a continual line of visitors. It was probably during this time that he wrote the Epistles to the Ephesians, Philippians, Colossians, and Philemon.

28:31 He enjoyed a considerable measure of liberty, **preaching the kingdom of God and teaching the things which concern the Lord Jesus Christ with all confidence, no one forbidding him**.

Thus the Book of Acts closes. Some think it ends with a strange abruptness. However, the pattern outlined at the outset had now been fulfilled. The gospel had reached out to Jerusalem, Judea, Samaria, and now the Gentile world.

The events in the life of Paul after the close of Acts can only be inferred from his later writings.

It is generally believed that after his two years in Rome, his case came before Nero and the verdict was acquittal.

He then embarked on what has come to be known as his Fourth Missionary Journey. Places which he probably visited on this trip, though not necessarily in this order were:

1. COLOSSE and EPHESUS (Phmn. 22).
2. MACEDONIA (1 Tim. 1:3; Phil. 1:25; 2:24).
3. EPHESUS (1 Tim. 3:14).
4. SPAIN (Rom. 15:24).
5. CRETE (Titus 1:5).
6. CORINTH (2 Tim. 4:20).
7. MILETUS (2 Tim. 4:20).
8. Winter spent in NICOPOLIS (Titus 3:12).
9. TROAS (2 Tim. 4:13).

We have no information as to why, when, or where he was arrested, but we do know he was brought to Rome as a prisoner a second time. This imprisonment was much more harsh than the first (2 Tim. 2:9). He was deserted by most of his friends (2 Tim. 4:9–11), and knew that the time of his death was at hand (2 Tim. 4:6–8).

Tradition says he was beheaded outside Rome in A.D. 67 or 68. For Paul's eulogy, read his own words in 2 Cor. 4:8–10, 6:4–10, and 11:23–28 along with our commentary on these inspiring summaries.

THE MESSAGE OF ACTS

After reading the Book of Acts, it is good to review the principles and practices of the early Christians. *What characterized the individual believers and the local churches of which they were members?*

First, it is obvious that the first century Christians lived first and foremost for the interests of the Lord Jesus. Their whole outlook was Christ-centered. The primary reason for their existence was to witness for the Savior, and they gave themselves to this task with vigor. In a world which was engaged in a mad struggle for survival, there was a hard core of zealous Christian disciples who sought first the kingdom of God and His righteousness. To them, everything else was subordinated to this glorious calling.

Jowett notes with admiration:

> The disciples had been baptized with . . .the holy, glowing enthusiasm caught from the altar of God. They had this central fire, from which every other purpose and faculty in life gets its strength. This fire in the apostles' soul was like a furnace fire in a great liner, which drives her through the tempests and through the en-

vious and engulfing deep. Nothing could stop these men! Nothing could hinder their going . . . A strong imperative rings throughout all their doings and all their speech. They have heat and they have light because they were baptized by the power of the Holy Ghost.[85]

The message they preached centered around the resurrection and glory of the Lord Jesus Christ. They were witnesses to a risen Savior. Men had slain the Messiah, but God had raised Him from among the dead and given Him the place of highest honor in heaven. Every knee must bow to Him — the glorified Man at God's right hand. There is no other way of salvation.

In an environment of hate, bitterness, and greed, the disciples manifested love to all. They repaid persecution with kindness, and prayed for their assailants. Their love toward other Christians forced their enemies to exclaim, "See how these Christians love one another!"

We get the distinct impression that they lived sacrificially for the spread of the gospel. They did not look upon material possessions as their own, but as a stewardship from God. Wherever there was genuine need, there was a prompt flow of funds to meet the need.

The weapons of their warfare were not carnal, but mighty through God to the pulling down of strongholds. They realized that they were not fighting against religious or political leaders, but rather against evil powers in heavenly places. So they went forth armed with faith, prayer, and the word of God. Unlike Islam, Christianity did not grow through the use of force.

These early Christians lived in separation from the world. They were in it but not of it. They maintained active contact with unbelievers as far as their witness was concerned, but never compromised their loyalty to Christ by engaging in the world's sinful pleasures. As pilgrims and strangers, they traveled through a foreign land seeking to be a blessing to all without partaking of its defilement.

Did they engage in politics or seek to remedy the social evils of the day? Their outlook was that all the ills and abuses in the world arise from man's sinful nature. In order to remedy the evils, one must get at the cause. Political and social reforms treat the symptoms without affecting the disease itself. Only the gospel can get at the heart of the matter, changing man's evil nature. And so they were not distracted by second-best remedies. They preached the gospel in season, out of season. Everywhere the gospel went, the festering sores were eliminated or reduced.

They were not surprised when they ran into persecution. They had been taught to expect it. Instead of retaliating or even vindicating themselves, they committed their cause to God, who judges righteously. Instead of seeking escape from trials, they prayed for boldness to proclaim Christ to all with whom they came in contact.

The goal before the disciples was world evangelization. To them there was no distinction between home and foreign missions. The field was the world. Their evangelistic activity was not an end in itself, that is, they were not content to lead souls to Christ and then let them flounder on by themselves. Rather, the converts were gathered into local Christian assemblies. Here they were taught the word, nurtured in prayer, and otherwise strengthened in the faith. Then they were challenged to go out with the message to others.

It was the establishment of local churches that gave permanence to the work and provided for evangelical outreach in the surrounding areas. These congregations were indigenous, that is, they were self-governing, self-propagating, and self-financing. Each assembly was independent of other churches, yet there was the fellowship of the Spirit between them. Each assembly sought to reproduce other assemblies in adjacent territory. And each one was financed from within. There was no central treasury or parent organization.

The assemblies were primarily spiritual havens for believers rather than centers for reaching the unsaved. Church activities included the breaking of bread, worship, prayer, Bible study, and fellowship. Gospel meetings were not held in the assemblies as such but rather wherever there was opportunity to address the unsaved — in synagogues, in marketplaces, on the streets, in prisons, and from house to house.

The churches did not meet in special

buildings erected for the purpose but in the homes of believers. This gave great mobility to the church in times of persecution, permitting it to "go underground" quickly and easily.

At the outset, there were certainly no denominations. All believers were recognized as members of the body of Christ and every local church as an expression of the church universal.

Neither was there a distinction between clergy and laity. No one man had exclusive rights in an assembly with regard to teaching, preaching, baptizing, or administering the Lord's Supper. There was a recognition of the fact that every believer had some gift, and there was liberty for the exercise of that gift.

Those who were gifted as apostles, prophets, evangelists, pastors, and teachers did not seek to establish themselves as indispensable officials in a church. Their function was to build up the saints in the faith so that they, too, might be able to serve the Lord daily. The gifted men of the NT period were equipped for their work by a special anointing of the Holy Spirit. This accounts for the way in which unlearned and homespun men exercised such an influence on their age. They were not "professional" in the sense we think of the term today, but lay preachers with unction from on high.

The proclamation of the message in the Book of Acts was often accompanied by miracles — signs and wonders and various gifts of the Holy Spirit. While these miracles seem more prominent in the early chapters, they continue to the end of the book.

After a local church was in operation, the apostles or their representatives appointed elders — men who were spiritual overseers. These men shepherded the flock. There were several elders in each church.

The noun, "deacon," is not specifically applied to a church officer in the Book of Acts. However, the verb form of the word is used to describe service carried on for the Lord, whether spiritual or temporal.

The early believers practiced baptism by immersion. The general impression is that believers were baptized soon after their conversion. On the first day of the week the disciples gathered together to remember the Lord in the breaking of bread. This service was probably not as formal as it is today. It seems to have been observed in connection with a common meal or a love feast.

The early church was addicted to prayer. It was the lifeline with God. The prayers were earnest, believing, and fervent. The disciples also fasted in order that all their powers might be concentrated on spiritual matters without distraction or drowsiness.

It was after prayer and fasting that the prophets and teachers at Antioch commended Barnabas and Saul to a special missionary program. Both of these men had been serving the Lord for some time prior to this. The commendation was not an official ordination, therefore, but an acknowledgment by the leaders at Antioch that the Holy Spirit had really called them. It was also an expression of the whole-hearted fellowship of the assembly in the work which Barnabas and Saul were undertaking.

Those who went out in evangelistic service were not controlled by their home assembly in this service. They were apparently free to serve as the Holy Spirit guided them. But they did report back to their home church as to the blessing of God on their labors.

In this connection, the church was not a highly organized complex, but a living organism which moved in constant obedience to the leading of the Lord. The Head of the church, Christ in heaven, directed the members, and they sought to keep themselves teachable, mobile, and responsive. Thus instead of finding an inflexible pattern of service in the Book of Acts, we find a fluidity, a refreshing absence of rigidity. For instance, there was no hard and fast rule as to how long an apostle spent in one place. In Thessalonica Paul may have stayed three months, but in Ephesus he remained three years. It all depended on how long it took to build up the saints so that they could carry on the Christian ministry by themselves.

There are some who feel that the apostles concentrated their attention on the large cities, depending on the churches established there to fan out into the suburbs. But is this true? Did the apostles have any such fixed and finalized strategy? Or did they follow or-

ders from the Lord from day to day —
whether to important centers or to trivial
hamlets?

Certainly one of the outstanding im-
pressions we get from the Book of Acts
is that the early believers expected and
depended on the guidance of the Lord.
They had forsaken all for Christ's sake.
They had nothing and no one but the
Lord Himself. So they looked to Him for
daily directions and were not disappointed.

It seems to have been the practice for
itinerant Christian workers to travel in
pairs. The partner would often be a
younger worker who would thus serve
his apprenticeship. The apostles were
constantly looking for faithful younger
men whom they could disciple.

At times the Lord's servants were
self-supporting, e.g., Paul working as a
tentmaker. At other times they were
supported by love gifts from individuals
or churches.

Another notable impression is that
those who were spiritual leaders were
recognized as such by the saints who
worked with them. It was the Holy Spirit
who empowered them to speak with authority. And it was the same Holy Spirit
who gave other believers the true spiritual instinct to submit to this authority.

The disciples obeyed human governments up to a point. That point was
reached when they were forbidden to
preach the gospel. Then they obeyed
God rather than man. When punished
by civil authorities, they bore it un-
resistingly, without ever conspiring
against the government.

The gospel was preached first to the
Jews, then after Israel's national refusal
of the message, the good news went out
to the Gentiles. The command, "to the
Jew first," was fulfilled historically in the
Book of Acts. Jews today are on the same
basis as Gentiles before God — there is
no difference, "for all have sinned and
fall short of the glory of God."

There was tremendous power in connection with the ministry of the early
church. Through fear of God's displeasure, people did not lightly make professions of being Christians. Sin in the
church came to light quickly and was severely punished by God in some cases,
e.g., Ananias and Sapphira.

A final and lasting conviction that
flows from studying Acts is this: If *we*
were to follow the example of the early
church in faith, sacrifice, devotedness,
and tireless service, the world could be
evangelized in our generation. ‡

ENDNOTES

[1](Intro) J. B. Phillips, *The Young
Church in Action*, p. vii.

[2](1:5) Between Christ's resurrection
and ascension were forty days. Ten additional days elapsed before Pentecost. But
the Lord did not say exactly how many
days, perhaps to keep the disciples in a
state of expectation.

[3](1:20) This is not an exact quotation
from the Psalm as we have it in our
Bible. There are two possible reasons for
this. (1) The writers of the NT often
quoted OT Scriptures from the Septuagint Version (LXX) while our translations
were made from the original Hebrew
text; this would make for some variation
in the words. (2) As is often the case,
the Holy Spirit, who inspired the OT, exercises the liberty of adapting it somewhat when quoting it in a NT context.

[4](2:1) The same words are used for
"dwell together" in the Greek Version of
Psalm 133:1 (132:1 in the LXX) as are
used here in Acts for "in one place" (*epi
to auto*).

[5](2:4) Other ministries of the Holy
Spirit which become ours at *conversion*
are: the anointing (1 John 2:27), the sealing (Eph. 1:13), and the guarantee (Eph.
1:14). Other ministries of the Spirit
which are *conditional* upon our obedience
and surrender are: guidance (Acts 8:29),
joy (1 Thess. 1:6), and power (Rom.
15:13).

[6](2:22–24) The word translated *pains*
usually refers to labor pangs. The resurrection of Christ is likened to a birth
from death to life. The sufferings connected with the entire process were intense but temporary. In Psalm 18:5 the
same expression is rendered "the sorrows of Sheol."

[7](2:25–27) Paradise is the same as the
third heaven (2 Cor. 12:2, 4).

[8](2:38) Charles C. Ryrie, *The Acts of
the Apostles*, p. 24.

[9](2:39) Charles H. Spurgeon, *The Treasury of the New Testament*, I:530.

¹⁰(2:41) The critical (NU) text omits "gladly."

¹¹(2:44, 45) F. W. Grant, "Acts," *The Numerical Bible: Acts to 2 Corinthians,* VI:25, 26.

¹²(2:46) Whenever we read of Paul and others going into the temple, it means into the temple *courts,* not into the sanctuary. Only the priests could enter there. Gentiles were permitted to go only into the outer court; to venture further was punishable by death.

¹³(Excursus) In the critical text "church" doesn't occur till 5:11.

¹⁴(Excursus) Merrill F. Unger, *Unger's Bible Handbook,* p. 586.

¹⁵(Excursus) E. Stanley Jones, *Christ's Alternative to Communism,* p. 78.

¹⁶(Excursus) G. H. Lang, *The Churches of God,* p. 11.

¹⁷(4:1–4) Charles Haddon Spurgeon, further documentation unavailable.

¹⁸(4:13) James A. Stewart, *Evangelism,* p. 95.

¹⁹(4:14–18) J. H. Jowett, *The Redeemed Family of God,* p. 137.

²⁰(4:27, 28) Here "Servant" is the preferred translation of *pais,* rather than "child," as in 3:13, 26; 4:30.

²¹(4:27, 28) George Matheson, *Rest By the River,* pp. 75-77.

²²(4:32–35) Grant, "Acts," p. 34.

²³(4:32–35) F. E. Marsh, *Fully Furnished,* p. 74.

²⁴(4:32–35) Ryrie, *Acts,* p. 36.

²⁵(5:40) Ryrie suggests that the beating might have been for their disobedience to the previous command of the Sanhedrin (cf. Deut. 25:2,3).

²⁶(5:41) There are three intriguing variations in the ms. traditions here: TR: "His name"; NU: "the name"; M: "the name of Jesus".

²⁷(6:8) Stephen (Gk., *Stephanos*) means "garland" or "victory wreath."

²⁸(6:10–14) The word order may indicate that they were more jealous of Moses' honor than of God's!

²⁹(7:9–19) "The original and the Greek version might both be true; the latter reckoning in five sons of Manasseh and Ephraim born in Egypt (1 Chron. vii. 14–27), according to a latitude of various forms, by no means uncommon in such lists." Kelly, *Acts,* p. 84.

³⁰(7:9–19) For further reverent treatment of this and the previous problem, see Kelly, *Acts,* pp. 84, 85.

³¹(7:20–43) Daily Notes of the Scripture Union, May 31, 1969.

³²(8:4–8) It is *down* from Jerusalem in altitude.

³³(8:4–8) Homer L. Payne, "What Is A Missionary Church?" *The Sunday School Times,* February 22, 1964, p. 129.

³⁴(8:12, 13) Since the text says Simon "believed" and he asks Peter to pray for him (v. 24), an argument has been made that he was saved but very carnal.

³⁵(8:26) An ancient Philistine city on the Mediterranean coast southwest of Jerusalem, en route from Palestine to Egypt.

³⁶(8:27–29) *Candace* (or *Kandake*) is probably a title, like Pharaoh, rather than a personal name.

³⁷(8:27–29) Male servants of female dignitaries were sometimes castrated. Eunuchs were barred from first class citizenship in Judaism (Deut. 23:1). They were limited to the status of "proselytes of the gate." But here a eunuch becomes a full-fledged member of the Christian church.

³⁸(8:37) Both the oldest (NU) and the majority (M) of manuscripts lack this verse. It is thought to be a baptismal formula used in Rome in the early second century, being found in Western mss., including the Latin translation. Those who teach baptismal regeneration obviously do not want to lose this verse.

³⁹(8:38) That the ancient mode of baptism was immersion is admitted by most Roman Catholic scholars, Calvin, and many who practice pouring or sprinkling. In all fairness, however, it should be mentioned that "into" and "out of" can also be translated "to" and "from," though the NKJV is quite literal and accurate.

⁴⁰(8:40) Ethiopia is the only country in Africa with a continuous Christian tradition from earliest times to today. Philip's faithfulness was perhaps the key that unlocked the door for the church there.

⁴¹(9:1, 2) See also 19:9, 23; 22:4; 24:14, 22.

⁴²(Excursus) Harnack, Quoted by Leighton Ford, *The Christian Persuader,* p. 46.

⁴³(Excursus) Dean Inge, Quoted by E. Stanley Jones, *Conversion,* p. 219.

⁴⁴(Excursus) Bryan Green, *Ibid.*

[45](Excursus) Leighton Ford, Quoted by Jones, *Conversion*, p. 46.

[46](Excursus) James A. Stewart, *Pastures of Tender Grass*, p. 70.

[47](9:36–38) Tabitha is Aramaic and Dorcas is Greek for *gazelle*.

[48](10:1, 2) Ryrie, *Acts*, p. 61.

[49](10:3–8) It was expedient for a tanner to operate outside the city limits. To be close to the sea was ideal for sanitary disposal of animal carcasses.

[50](11:20, 21) In the NT, "Hellenists" usually means Grecian Jews, but here it can only mean Greeks, i.e., Gentiles. Note the context: Verse 19, "preaching the word to no one but the Jews only." Verse 20, "to Greeks also" (in contrast to Jews).

[51](11:25, 26) James A. Stewart, *Evangelism*, pp. 100, 101.

[52](12:25) Both Alexandrian (NU) and Majority (M) texts read "*to* Jerusalem." Since Barnabas and Saul are again at Antioch in 13:1, it is possible that copyists "corrected" the reading to "from."

[53](13:3) Donald Grey Barnhouse, *The Measure of Your Faith*, Book 69, p. 21.

[54](13:7, 8) In the KJV of verse 7, Sergius Paulus is called a "deputy," but more accurately his title was "proconsul" (NKJV). Luke showed exact knowledge of the names of offices which were then common in the Roman Empire. Thus, in Greek he called the magistrates at Philippi *stratēgoi*, Latin, *praetors* (16:20), and identified the officers as *rhabdouchoi*, Latin, *lictors* (16:35). He correctly named the rulers of Thessalonica as *politarchs* (17:6), whereas in Ephesus he correctly distinguished them as *asiarchs* (19:31).

"All these were the local authorities in the different cities, the Roman governor, or proconsul, being over them as ruling in each province. Luke then, by giving each his correct title in these different cities, shows that he knew well what he was about and this mark of accuracy should increase confidence in him as a faithful historian" — C. E. Stuart, *Tracings from the Acts of the Apostles*, p. 272.

[55](13:19–22) See Kelly, *Acts*, pp. 185, 186 for a discussion of the chronological and textual problem.

[56](13:48) Charles R. Erdman, *The Epistle of Paul to the Romans* p. 109.

[57](14:4–7) Here the word practically equals "missionaries."

[58](14:10–12) These Greek names are used in the original text. The 1611 text uses Jupiter and Mercury, the more common Latin names of these gods.

[59](14:19, 20) Kelly, *Acts*, p. 202.

[60](14:21) Erdman, *Acts*, p. 109.

[61](Excursus) C. A. Coates, *An Outline of Luke's Gospel*, p. 254.

[62](15:20) Some think that the four forbidden practices refer back to Leviticus 17 and 18, as follows: things polluted by idols (17:8, 9); sexual immorality — not only adultery and polygamy (18:20), homosexuality (18:22), and bestiality (18:23), but also marrying blood relatives (18:6–14) and even relatives by marriage, that is, in-law relatives (18:15, 16); eating things strangled or improperly butchered (17:15); eating blood (Lev. 17:10–12). Jewish believers would be offended if they saw Gentile believers violating these codes (Acts 15:21).

[63](16:6–8) Ryrie, *Acts*, pp. 88, 89.

[64](16:9) James Stalker, *Life of St. Paul*, p. 78.

[65](16:19–24) A. J. Pollock, *The Apostle Paul and His Missionary Labors*, p. 56.

[66](16:25) G. Campbell Morgan, *The Acts of the Apostles*, pp. 389, 390.

[67](17:2, 3) Some believe Paul spent about three months in Thessalonica, though he taught in the synagogue for only three Sabbaths.

[68](17:16) William Arnot, *The Church in the House: A Series of Lessons on the Acts of the Apostles*, pp. 379ff.

[69](Excursus) Some scholars believe the preaching took place in the temple courts.

[70](Excursus) A. B. Simpson, further documentation unavailable.

[71](18:2, 3) Dinsdale T. Young, *Neglected People of the Bible*, pp. 232, 233.

[72](18:18) The participle for cutting of the hair is right after "Aquila," and far removed from "Paul" in the original (v. 18 is all one sentence in Greek).

[73](19:8) Stuart, *Tracings*, p. 285.

[74](19:15, 16) F. B. Meyer, quoted by W. H. Aldis, *The Keswick Convention 1934*, p. 60.

[75](19:23–37) *Diana* is the Latin for the Greek *Artemis*, a many-breasted fertility goddess.

[76](21:23, 24) Grant, "Acts," p. 147.

[77](22:14–16) The supplied "by" is commonly understood in such a construction (participle of means). Paraphrased: "Get up (*anastas*) and get baptized (*baptisai*); get your sins washed away (*apolousai*) by means of calling on (*epikalesamenos*) the name of the Lord."

[78](26:9–11) The Greek tense here is no doubt a *conative* imperfect: "I tried to compel them . . ."

[79](26:29) Morgan, *Acts*, p. 528.

[80](27:13–17) The NU text reads *Euraquilon*.

[81](27:13–17) The NU text reads *Cauda*.

[82](27:21–26) A. W. Tozer, *That Incredible Christian*, p. 134.

[83](28:9, 10) It is at least possible that Luke used his medical skills alongside Paul's gift of healing. If God disapproved of the medical profession He would hardly have chosen a physician to write 28% of the NT (Luke-Acts)!

[84](28:29) John Calvin, *The Acts of the Apostles*, II:314. The NU text omits verse 29.

[85](Excursus) J. H. Jowett, *Things that Matter Most*, p. 248.

BIBLIOGRAPHY

Arnot, William. *The Church in the House: A Series of Lessons on the Acts of the Apostles*. New York: Robert Carter & Brothers, 1873.

Blaiklock, E. M. *The Acts of the Apostles, TBC*. Grand Rapids: Wm. B. Eerdmans Publishing Company, 1959.

Calvin, John. *The Acts of the Apostles*, 2 vols. Grand Rapids: Wm. B. Eerdmans Publishing Company, 1977.

Erdman, Charles R. *The Acts*. Philadelphia: The Westminster Press, 1919.

Kelly, William. *An Exposition of the Acts of the Apostles*. London: C. A. Hammond, 1952.

Martin, Ralph. *Understanding the New Testament: Acts*. Philadelphia: A. J. Holman Company, 1978.

Morgan, G. Campbell. *The Acts of the Apostles*. New York: Fleming H. Revell Co., 1924.

Rackham, R. B. *The Acts of the Apostles*. London: Methuen, 1901.

Ryrie, Charles Caldwell. *Acts of the Apostles*. Chicago: Moody Press, 1961.

Stuart, C. E. *Tracings from the Acts of the Apostles*. London: E. Marlborough and Company, n.d.

THE EPISTLE TO THE ROMANS

Introduction

"The cathedral of the Christian faith." — Frédéric Godet

I. Unique place in the Canon

Romans has always stood at the head of Paul's letters, and rightly so. Since Acts ends with Paul's arrival in Rome, it is logical to have the Epistle section of the NT begin with the apostle's letter to the Roman church, written before he visited the Christians there. More decisively, Romans is the most important book theologically in the whole NT, being as close to a systematic presentation of Christian theology as will be found in God's word.

Historically, Romans is the most influential of Bible books. Augustine was converted through reading Romans 13:13 and 14 (A.D. 380). The Protestant Reformation was launched when Martin Luther finally understood the meaning of God's righteousness, and that "the just shall live by faith" (1517).

John Wesley received assurance of salvation through hearing the preface to Luther's commentary on Romans read in a Moravian house church on Aldersgate Street in London (1738). John Calvin wrote, "When anyone understands this Epistle, he has a passage opened to him to the understanding of the whole Scripture."

II. Authorship†

Heretics and even radical negative critics for once accept a universal orthodox position — that the author of Romans was the apostle to the Gentiles. In fact, the heretic Marcion is the first known writer to *specifically* name Paul as author. The book is quoted by such orthodox Christians as Clement of Rome, Ignatius, Justin Martyr, Polycarp, Hippolytus, and Irenaeus. The Muratorian Canon also lists the letter as Pauline.

The *internal evidence* for Pauline authorship is very strong as well. The theology, vocabulary, and spirit are all distinctively Paul's. Of course, the fact that the letter *says* it is from Paul (1:1) is not enough to convince skeptics, but this is further borne out by other references, such as 15:15–20. What is most convincing, perhaps, is the large number of casual coincidences with the book of Acts that have no appearance of being contrived. For example, references to the collection for the saints, to Gaius, Erastus, and a long-planned trip to Rome, all point to Paul as the author. Tertius was his amanuensis (16:22).

III. Date

Romans was written after 1 and 2 Corinthians, because the collection being formed when those letters were written is now ready and about to be taken to the poor saints at Jerusalem. References to Cenchrea, the port city for Corinth (16:1), and other details make most scholars opt for Corinth as the city of origin. Since Paul was there only three months (at the close of his Third Missionary Journey) before he was chased away due to plots against him, it must be during this short period that the Epistle was penned. This makes the date about A.D. 56.

IV. Background and Themes††

How did Christianity first reach Rome? We cannot be positive, but it may be that Jews from Rome who were converted in Jerusalem on the Day of Pentecost (see Acts 2:10) carried back the good news. That was in A.D. 30.

†*See p. ii.*
††*See p. i.*

Paul had never been in Rome when he wrote this letter from Corinth about twenty-six years later. But he knew quite a few of the Christians there, as is seen in chapter 16. Christians in those days were people on the move, whether as a result of persecution or as heralds of the gospel or in the ordinary course of their work. These Christians in Rome were from both Jewish and Gentile backgrounds.

Paul finally did reach Rome around A.D. 60, but not in the way he expected. He came as a prisoner for Christ Jesus.

Romans is a classic. To the unsaved it offers a clear exposition of their sinful, lost condition and God's righteous plan for saving them. New believers learn of their identification with Christ and of victory through the power of the Holy Spirit. Mature believers find never-ending delight in its wide spectrum of Christian truth: doctrinal, prophetical, and practical.

An excellent way to understand the Epistle to the Romans is as a dialogue between Paul and some unnamed objector. As Paul sets forth the gospel, he seems to hear this objector raising all kinds of arguments against it. The apostle replies to his opponent's questions one by one. By the time he is finished, Paul has answered every major attitude that man can take regarding the gospel of the grace of God.

Sometimes the objections are clearly stated; sometimes they are only implied. But whether stated or implied, they all revolve around the gospel — the good news of salvation by grace through faith in the Lord Jesus Christ, apart from the works of the law.

We will think of Romans as dealing with eleven main questions: (1) What is the subject of the Letter? (1:1, 9, 15, 16);

(2) What is the gospel? (1:1–17); (3) Why do men need the gospel? (1:18–3:20); (4) According to the gospel, how can ungodly sinners be justified by a holy God? (3:21–31); (5) Does the gospel agree with the OT Scripture? (4:1–25); (6) What are the benefits of justification in the believer's life? (5:1–21); (7) Does the teaching of salvation by grace through faith permit or even encourage sinful living? (6:1–23); (8) What is the relationship of the Christian to the law? (7:1–25); (9) How is the Christian enabled to live a holy life? (8:1–39); (10) Does the gospel, by promising salvation to both Jews and Gentiles, mean that God has broken His promises to His earthly people, the Jews? (9:1–11:36); (11) How should those who have been justified by grace respond in their everyday lives? (12:1–16:27).

An acquaintance with these eleven questions and their answers will give a working knowledge of this important Epistle. The answer to the first question, "What is the subject of Romans?" is, of course, "the gospel." Paul wastes no time in getting to the point. Four times in the first sixteen verses he mentions it (vv.1, 9, 15, 16).

This gives rise to the second question, "What is the gospel?" The word itself means *good news*. But in vv. 1–17 the apostle tells us six important facts about the good news: (1) Its source is God (v. 1); (2) It was promised by the prophetic OT Scriptures (v. 2); (3) It is the good news concerning God's Son, the Lord Jesus Christ (v. 3); (4) It is God's power for salvation (v. 16); (5) It is for all men, Gentiles as well as Jews (v. 16); (6) It is by faith alone (v. 17). With that as an introduction, let us take a more detailed look at these verses.

OUTLINE

Commentary

I. DOCTRINAL: THE GOSPEL OF GOD (Chaps. 1–8)

A. Introduction to the Gospel (1:1-15)

1:1 **Paul** introduces himself as one who was *purchased* (implied in the designation **a bondservant of Jesus Christ**), *called* (on the road to Damascus he was **called to be an apostle**, a special emissary of the Savior), and **separated** (set apart **to** take **the gospel** to the Gentiles [see Acts 9:15; 13:2]). We too have been purchased by the precious blood of Christ, called to be witnesses to His saving power, and set apart to tell the good news wherever we go.

1:2 Lest any of Paul's Jewish readers think the gospel is completely new and unrelated to their spiritual heritage, he mentions that the OT **prophets** had **promised** it, both in clear-cut statements (Deut. 18:15; Isa. 7:14; Hab. 2:4) and in types and symbols (e.g., Noah's ark, the serpent of brass, and the sacrificial system).

1:3 The gospel is the good news concerning God's **Son, Jesus Christ our Lord, who** is a descendant **of David according to the flesh** (that is, as far as His humanity is concerned). The expression **according to the flesh** implies that our Lord is more than a man. The words mean as to His *humanity*. If Christ were only a man, it would be unnecessary to single out this feature of His being, since there would be no other. But He is more than a man, as the next verse shows.

1:4 The Lord Jesus is marked out as **the Son of God with power**. The Holy Spirit, here called **the Spirit of holiness**, marked Jesus out at His baptism and throughout His miracle-working ministry. The Savior's mighty miracles, performed in the power of the Holy Spirit,[1] bore witness to the fact that He is the Son of God. When we read that He is **declared to be the Son of God with power ... by the resurrection from the dead**, we naturally think of His own resurrection. But a literal reading here is "by resurrection of dead persons," so the apostle may also be thinking of Christ's raising of Jairus' daughter, the widow of Nain's son, and Lazarus. However, there is little question that it is the Lord's own resurrection that is primarily in view.

When we say that Jesus is **the Son of God**, we mean that He is a Son like no one else is. God has many sons. All believers are His sons (Gal. 4:5–7). Even angels are spoken of as sons (Job 1:6; 2:1). But Jesus is God's Son in a *unique* sense. When our Lord spoke of God as His Father, the Jews rightly understood Him to be claiming equality with God (John 5:18).

1:5 It was **through** Jesus Christ our Lord that Paul **received grace** (the undeserved favor that saved him) **and apostleship**. When Paul says **we have received grace and apostleship**, he is almost certainly using the editorial *we*, referring to himself alone. His linking of **apostleship** with the **nations** or Gentiles points to him and not to the other apostles. Paul was commissioned to call men of all nations to obedience of faith — that is, to obey the message of the gospel by repenting and believing on the Lord Jesus Christ (Acts 20:21). The goal of this worldwide proclamation of the message was for His name, to please and to bring glory to Him.

1:6 **Among** those who had responded to the gospel were those Paul dignified with the title **the called of Jesus Christ**, emphasizing that it was God who took the initiative in their salvation.

1:7 The Letter is addressed **to all** believers **in Rome**, and not (as in other Epistles) to a single church. The final chapter of the letter indicates that there were several gatherings of believers in the city, and this salutation embraces them all.

Beloved of God, called to be saints. These two lovely names are true of all who have been redeemed by the precious blood of Christ. These favored ones are objects of divine love in a special way, and are also called to be set apart to God from the world, for that is the meaning of **saints**.

Paul's characteristic greeting combines **grace** and **peace**. **Grace** (*charis*) is a Greek emphasis, and **peace** (*shalom*) is the traditional Jewish greeting. The combination is especially appropriate because Paul's message tells how believing Jews and Gentiles are now one new man in Christ.

The **grace** mentioned here is not the grace that saves (Paul's readers were already saved) but the **grace** that equips and empowers for Christian life and service. **Peace** is not so much peace with God (the saints already had that because they were justified by faith) but rather the **peace** of God reigning in their hearts while they were in the midst of a turbulent society. **Grace** and **peace** came **from God our Father and the Lord Jesus Christ**, strongly implying the equality of the Son with the Father. If Jesus were

only a man, it would be absurd to list Him as equal with the Father in bestowing **grace** and **peace**. It would be like saying, "Grace and peace from God the Father and from Abraham Lincoln."

1:8 Whenever possible, the apostle began his letters by expressing appreciation for whatever was commendable in his readers. (A good example for all of us!) Here he thanks **God through Jesus Christ**, the Mediator, that the **faith** of the Roman Christians was proclaimed **throughout the whole world**. Their testimony as Christians was talked about throughout the Roman Empire, which then constituted the **whole world** from the perspective of those living in the Mediterranean area.

1:9 Because the Roman Christians let their light shine before men, Paul was constrained to pray for them **without ceasing**. He calls **God** as his **witness** to the constancy of his **prayers**, because no one else could know this. But **God** knows — the God whom the apostle served with his **spirit in the gospel of His Son**. Paul's service was with his **spirit**. It was not that of a religious drudge, going through endless rituals and reciting prayers and liturgies by rote. It was service bathed in fervent, believing prayers. It was willing, devoted, tireless service, fired by a spirit that loved the Lord Jesus supremely. It was a flaming passion to make known the good news about God's Son.

1:10 Coupled with Paul's thanksgiving to God for the Roman saints was his prayer that he might visit them in the not-too-distant future. As with everything else, he wanted his journey to be according to **the will of God**.

1:11 The apostle's impelling desire was to help the saints spiritually so that they might be further **established** in the faith. There is no thought here of his conferring some "second blessing" on them, nor did he intend to impart some spiritual gift by the laying on of his hands (though he did this for Timothy in 2 Tim. 1:6). It was a matter of helping their **spiritual** growth through the ministry of the word.

1:12 He goes on to explain that there would be **mutual** blessing. He would **be encouraged** by their **faith**, and they by his. In all edifying society, there is spiritual enrichment. "As iron sharpens iron, so a man sharpens the countenance of his friend" (Prov. 27:17). Note Paul's humility and graciousness — he was not above being helped by other saints.

1:13 He had **often planned to** visit Rome **but** had been **hindered**, perhaps by pressing needs in other areas, perhaps by the direct restraint of the Holy Spirit, perhaps by the opposition of Satan. He desired to **have some fruit among** the Gentiles in Rome **as** he had **among the other Gentiles**. Here he is speaking of **fruit** in the gospel, as the next two verses show. In verses 11 and 12 his aim was to see the Roman Christians built up in their faith. Here he desires to see souls won for Christ in the capital of the Roman Empire.

1:14 Anyone who has Christ has the answer to the world's deepest need. He has the cure to the disease of sin, the way to escape the eternal horrors of hell, and the guarantee of everlasting happiness with God. This puts him under solemn obligation to share the good news with people of all cultures — **barbarians** — and people of all degrees of learning — **wise and unwise**. Paul felt the obligation keenly. He said **"I am a debtor"**.

1:15 To discharge that debt, he was **ready to preach the gospel to** those **in Rome** with all the power God gave him. It was surely not to the believers in Rome, as this verse might seem to suggest, for they had already responded to the glad tidings. But he was ready to preach to the unconverted Gentiles in the metropolis.

B. The Gospel Defined (1:16, 17)

1:16 Paul was **not ashamed** to take God's good news to sophisticated Rome, even though the message had proved to be a stumbling block to the Jews and foolishness to the Greeks, for he knew that **it is the power of God to salvation** — that is, it tells how God by His power saves everyone who believes on His Son. This power is extended equally to Jews and Greeks.

The order **for the Jew first and also for the Greek** was fulfilled historically during the Acts period. While we have an enduring obligation to God's ancient people, the Jews, we are not required to evangelize them before going to the Gentiles. Today God deals with Jews and Gentiles on the same basis, and the message and timing are the same to all.

1:17 Since the word **righteousness** occurs here for the first time in the Letter, we will pause to consider its meaning. The word is used in several different ways in the NT, but we shall consider only three uses.

First, it is used to describe that characteristic of God by which He always does what is right, just, proper, and consistent with all His other attributes. When we say that God is righteous, we mean that there is no wrong, dishonesty, or unfairness in Him.

Secondly, the righteousness of God can refer to His method of justifying ungodly sinners. He can do this and still be righteous because Jesus as the sinless Substitute has satisfied all the claims of divine justice.

Finally, the righteousness of God refers to the perfect standing which God provides for those who believe on His Son (2 Cor. 5:21). Those who are not in themselves righteous are treated as if they were righteous because God sees them in all the perfection of Christ. Righteousness is imputed to their account.

Which is the meaning in verse 17? While it could be any of the three, the righteousness of God seems to refer especially to His way of justifying sinners by faith.

The righteousness of God is revealed in the gospel. First the gospel tells us that God's righteousness demands that sins be punished, and the penalty is eternal death. But then we hear that God's love provided what His righteousness demanded. He sent His Son to die as a Substitute for sinners, paying the penalty in full. Now because His righteous claims have been fully satisfied, God can righteously save all those who avail themselves of the work of Christ.

God's righteousness **is revealed from faith to faith**. The expression **from faith to faith** may mean: (1) from God's faithfulness to our faith; (2) from one degree of faith to another; or (3) by faith from start to finish. The last is the probable meaning. God's righteousness is not im-

puted on the basis of works or made
available to those who seek to earn or
deserve it. It is revealed on the principle
of faith alone. This is in perfect agreement with the divine decree in Habakkuk 2:4, **"The just shall live by faith,"**
which may also be understood to mean
"The justified-by-faith ones shall live."

In the first seventeen verses of Romans, Paul has introduced his subject
and stated briefly some of the principal
points. He now addresses the third main
question, "Why do men need the gospel?" The answer, in brief, is because
they are lost without it. But this raises
four subsidiary questions: (1) Are the
heathen who have never heard the gospel lost? (1:18–32); (2) Are the self-
righteous moralists, whether Jews or
Gentiles, lost? (2:1–16); (3) Are God's ancient earthly people, the Jews, lost?
(2:17–3:8); (4) Are all men lost? (3:9–20).

C. The Universal Need for the Gospel (1:18–3:20)

1:18 Here we have the answer to
the question "Why do men need the
gospel?" The answer is that they are lost
without it, and that **the wrath of God is
revealed from heaven against** the wickedness **of men who suppress the truth**
in an unrighteous manner and by their
unrighteous lives. But how is God's
wrath **revealed**? One answer is given in
the context. God gives men over to uncleanness (1:24), to vile affections (1:26),
and to a reprobate mind (1:28). But it is
also true that God occasionally breaks
through into human history to show His
extreme displeasure at man's sin — for
example, the flood (Gen. 7); the destruction of Sodom and Gomorrah (Gen. 19);
and the punishment of Korah, Dathan,
and Abiram (Num. 16:32).

1:19 "Are the heathen who have
never heard the gospel lost?" Paul shows
that they are, not because of knowledge
they don't have, but **because** of the light
which they do have, yet refuse! Those
things which **may be known of God** in
creation have been revealed **to them**.
God has not left them without a revelation of Himself.

1:20 Ever **since the creation of the
world**, two **invisible** characteristics of
God have been on display for all to see:
His eternal power and His divinity or
Godhead. The word Paul uses here
means *divinity* or *godhood*. It suggests the
character of God rather than His essential being, His glorious attributes rather
than His inherent deity. His deity is assumed.

The argument here is clear: Creation
demands a Creator. Design demands a
Designer. By looking up at the sun,
moon, and stars, anyone can know there
is a God.

The answer to the question "What
about the heathen?" is this: **they are
without excuse**. God has revealed Himself to them in creation, but they have
not responded to this revelation. So people are not condemned for rejecting a
Savior they have never heard of, but for
being unfaithful to what they could
know about God.

1:21 Although they knew God by His
works, **they did not glorify Him** for who
He is or thank Him for all He has done.
Rather, they gave themselves over to **futile** philosophies and speculations about
other gods, and as a result lost the capacity to see and think clearly. "Light rejected is light denied." Those who don't
want to see lose the capacity to see.

1:22 As men grew more conceited
over their self-styled knowledge, they
plunged deeper into ignorance and nonsense. These two things always characterize those who reject the knowledge of
God — they become insufferably conceited and abysmally ignorant at the
same time.

1:23 Instead of evolving from lower
forms, "early man" was of a high moral
order. By refusing to acknowledge the
true, infinite, **incorruptible God**, he *de-*
volved to the stupidity and depravity
that go with idol worship. This whole
passage gives the lie to evolution.

Man is instinctively religious. He
must have some object to worship.
When he refused to worship the living
God, he made his own gods of wood
and stone representing **man, birds, animals, and creeping things**, or reptiles.
Notice the downward progression —
man, birds, animals, creeping things.
And remember that man becomes like
what he worships. As his concept of
deity degenerates, his morals degenerate

also. If his god is a reptile, then he feels free to live as he pleases. Remember too that a worshiper generally considers himself inferior to the object of worship. Created in the image and after the likeness of God, man here takes a place lower than that of serpents!

When man worships idols, he worships demons. Paul states clearly that the things which the Gentiles sacrifice to idols they sacrifice to demons and not to God (1 Cor. 10:20).

1:24 Three times it is said that **God gave** man **up**. He **gave them up to uncleanness** (1:24), to vile passions (1:26), and to a reprobate mind (1:28). In other words, God's wrath was directed against man's entire personality.

In response to the evil lusts of their hearts, God abandoned them to heterosexual uncleanness — adultery, fornication, lewdness, prostitution, harlotry, etc. Life became for them a round of sex orgies in which **to dishonor their bodies among themselves**.

1:25 This abandonment by God was because they first abandoned **the truth** about Him **for** the **lie** of idolatry. An idol is a lie, a false representation of God. An idolater worships the image of a **creature**, and thus insults and dishonors **the Creator, who is** eternally worthy of honor and glory, not of insult.

1:26 For this same reason **God gave** people **up to** erotic activity with members of their own sex. **Women** became lesbians, practicing unnatural sex and knowing no shame.

1:27 Men became sodomites, in total perversion of their natural functions. Turning away from the marriage relationship ordained by God, they **burned** with **lust for** other **men** and practiced homosexuality. But their sin took its toll in their bodies and souls. Disease, guilt, and personality deformities struck at them like the sting of a scorpion. This disproves the notion that anyone can commit this sin and get away with it.

Homosexuality is being passed off today by some as a sickness and by others as a legitimate alternative lifestyle. Christians must be careful not to accept the world's moral judgments but to be guided by God's word. In the OT, this

sin was punishable by death (Lev. 18:29; 20:13), and here in the NT those who practice it are said to be worthy of death (Rom. 1:32). The Bible speaks of homosexuality as a very serious sin, as evidenced by God's obliteration of Sodom and Gomorrah, where militant "gays" ran riot (Gen. 19:4–25).

The gospel offers pardon and forgiveness to homosexuals, as it does to all sinners who repent and believe in the Lord Jesus Christ. Christians who have fallen into this heinous sin can find forgiveness and restoration through confessing and forsaking the sin. There is complete deliverance from homosexuality to all who are willing to obey God's word. Ongoing counseling assistance is very important in most cases.

It is true that some people seem to have a natural tendency toward homosexuality. This should not be surprising, since fallen human nature is capable of just about any form of iniquity and perversion. The gross sin does not consist in the inclination toward it but in yielding to and practicing it. The Holy Spirit gives the power to resist the temptation and to have lasting victory (1 Cor. 10:13). Some of the Christians in Corinth were living proofs that homosexuals need not be irrevocably bound to that lifestyle (1 Cor. 6:9–11).

1:28 Because of men's refusal to retain God in their knowledge, either as Creator, Sustainer, or Deliverer, **God gave them over to a debased mind to** commit a catalog of other forms of wickedness. This verse gives deep insight into why evolution has such enormous appeal for natural men. The reason lies not in their intellects but in their wills. They do not want **to retain God in their knowledge**. It is not that the evidence for evolution is so overwhelming that they are compelled to accept it; rather, it is because they want some explanation for origins that will eliminate God completely. They know that if there is a God, then they are morally responsible to Him.

1:29 Here, then, is the dark list of additional sins which characterize man in his alienation from God. Notice that he is *full* of them, not just an occasional dabbler in them. He is trained in sins which are not fitting for a human being: **unrighteousness** (injustice); **sexual immorality**[2] (fornication, adultery, and other forms of illicit sex); **wickedness** (active evil); **covetousness** (greed, the incessant desire for more); **maliciousness** (the desire for harm on others; venomous hatred); **full of envy** (jealousy of others); *full of* **murder** (premeditated and unlawful killing of another, either in anger or in the commission of some other crime); *full of* **strife** (wrangling, quarreling, contentiousness); *full of* **deceit** (trickery, treachery, intrigue); *full of* **evil-mindedness** (ill-will, spite, hostility, bitterness); **whisperers** (secret slanderers, gossips);

1:30 backbiters (open slanderers, those who bad-mouth others); **haters of God** (or hateful to God); **violent** (despiteful, insulting); **proud** (haughty, arrogant); **boasters** (braggarts, self-paraders); **inventors of evil things** (devisers of mischief and new forms of wickedness); **disobedient to parents** (rebellious to parental authority);

1:31 undiscerning (lacking moral and spiritual discernment, without conscience); **untrustworthy** (breaking promises, treaties, agreements, and contracts whenever it serves their purposes); **unloving** (acting in total disregard of natural ties and the obligations that go with them); **unforgiving**[3] (irreconcilable or implacable); **unmerciful** (cruel, vindictive, without pity).

1:32 Those who abuse sex (1:24), who pervert sex (1:26, 27), and who practice the other sins listed (1:29–31) have an innate knowledge not only that these things are wrong but also that they themselves are **deserving of death**. They know this is God's verdict, however much they seek to rationalize or legalize these sins. But this does not deter them from indulging in these forms of ungodliness. In fact they unite with others to promote them, and feel a sense of camaraderie with their partners-in-sin.

THE UNREACHED HEATHEN

What then, is God's answer to the question "Are the heathen who have never heard the gospel lost?" The condemnation of the heathen is that they did not live up to the light which God gave them in creation. Instead they become idolaters, and as a result abandoned themselves to lives of depravity and vileness.

But suppose an individual heathen *does* live up to the light God gives him. Suppose he burns his idols and seeks the true God. What then?

There are two schools of thought among evangelical believers on this subject.

Some believe that if a pagan lives up to the light of God in creation, God will send him the gospel light. Cornelius is cited as an example. He sought God. His prayers and alms came up as a memorial before God. Then God sent Peter to tell him how to be saved (Acts 11:14).

Others believe that if a man trusts the one true and living God as He is revealed in creation, but dies before he hears the gospel, God will save him on the basis of the work of Christ at Calvary. Though the man himself knew nothing about the work of Christ, God reckons the value of that work to his account when he trusts God on the basis of the light he has received. Those who hold this view point out that this is how God saved people before Calvary and how He still saves morons, imbeciles, and also children who die before they reach the age of accountability.

The first view can be supported by the case of Cornelius. The second view lacks scriptural support for the era following the death and resurrection of Christ (our present era), and it also weakens the necessity for aggressive missionary activity. ‡

Paul has shown that the pagans are lost and need the gospel. Now he turns to a second class of people, whose exact identity is somewhat in dispute. We believe that the apostle is talking here to self-righteous moralists, whether Jews or Gentiles. The first verse shows that they are self-righteous moralists by the way they condemn the behavior of others (yet commit the same sins themselves). Verses 9, 10, 12, 14, and 15 show that Paul is speaking to both Jews and Gentiles. So the question before the court is: *Are the self-righteous moralists, whether Jews* or *Gentiles, also lost?* And the answer, as we shall see, is, "Yes, they are lost too!"

2:1 This second class consists of those who look down their noses at the heathen, considering themselves more civilized, educated, and refined. They condemn the pagans for their gross behavior, yet are equally guilty themselves though perhaps in a more sophisticated way. Fallen man can see faults in others more readily than in himself. Things hideous and repulsive in the lives of others seem quite respectable in his own. But the fact that he can **judge** sins in others shows that he knows the difference between right and wrong. If he knows that it is wrong for someone to steal his wife, then he knows that it is wrong for him to steal someone else's wife. Therefore, when someone commits the very sins he condemns in others, he leaves himself without excuse.

The sins of cultured people are essentially the same as those of the heathen. Although a moralist may argue that he has not committed every sin in the book, he should remember the following facts:

1. he is capable of committing them all.
2. by breaking one commandment, he is guilty of all (Jas. 2:10).
3. he has committed sins of thought which he may never have committed in actual deed, and these are forbidden by the word. Jesus taught that the lustful look, for instance, is tantamount to adultery (Matt. 5:28).

2:2 What the smug moralist needs is a lesson on **the judgment of God**. The apostle proceeds to give that lesson in verses 2–16. The first point is that **the judgment of God is according to truth**. It is not based on incomplete, inaccurate, or circumstantial evidence. Rather, it is based on the truth, the whole truth, and nothing but the truth.

2:3 Secondly, **the judgment of God** *is inescapable* on those who condemn others for the very sins they practice themselves. Their capacity to **judge** others does not absolve them from guilt. In fact, it increases their own condemnation.

The judgment of God is inescapable unless we *repent and are forgiven*.

2:4 Next we learn that *the judgment of God is sometimes delayed*. This delay is an evidence of **His goodness, forbearance, and longsuffering. His goodness** means that He is kindly disposed to sinners, though not to their sins. His **forbearance** describes His holding back punishment on man's wickedness and rebellion. His **longsuffering** is His amazing self-restraint in spite of man's ceaseless provocation.

The goodness of God, as seen in His providence, protection, and preservation, is aimed at leading men **to repentance**. He is "not willing that any should perish but that all should come to repentance" (2 Pet. 3:9).

Repentance means an about-face, turning one's back on sin and heading in the opposite direction. "It is a change of mind which produces a change of attitude, and results in a change of action."[4] It signifies a man's taking sides with God against himself and his sins. It is more than an intellectual assent to the fact of one's sins; it involves the conscience too, as John Newton wrote: "My conscience felt and owned my guilt."

2:5 The fourth thing we learn about the judgment of God is that *it is graduated according to the accumulation of guilt*. Paul pictures hardened and unrepentant sinners **treasuring up** judgment **for** themselves, as if they were building up a fortune of gold and silver. But what a fortune that will be in the day when God's **wrath** is finally revealed at the **judgment** of the Great White Throne (Rev. 20:11–15)! In that day **the judgment of God** *will be seen to be absolutely* **righteous**, without prejudice or injustice of any kind.

2:6 In the next five verses Paul reminds us that *the judgment of God will be* **according to** *one's* **deeds**. A man may boast of great personal goodness. He may rely heavily on his racial or national origin. He may plead the fact that there were men of God in his ancestry. But he will be judged by *his own conduct*, and not by any of these other things. His works will be the determining factor.

If we took verses 6–11 by themselves, it would be easy to conclude that they teach salvation by works. They *seem* to say that those who do good works will thereby earn eternal life.

But it should be clear that the passage

cannot mean that, because then it would flatly contradict the consistent testimony of the rest of Scripture to the effect that salvation is by faith apart from works. Chafer points out that about 150 passages in the NT condition salvation solely on faith or believing.[5] No one passage, when rightly understood, can contradict such overwhelming testimony.

How then are we to understand this passage? First we must understand that good works do not begin until a person has been born again. When the people asked Jesus, "What shall we do, that we may work the works of God?" He replied, "This is the work of God, that you believe in Him whom He sent" (John 6:28, 29). So the first good work that anyone can do is to believe on the Lord Jesus Christ, and we must constantly remember that *faith is not a meritorious work* by which a person earns salvation. So if the unsaved are judged by their works, they will have nothing of value to present as evidence. All their supposed righteousness will be seen as filthy rags (Isa. 64:6). Their condemning sin will be that they have not believed on Jesus as Lord (John 3:18). Beyond that, their works will determine the degree of their punishment (Luke 12:47, 48).

If *believers* are judged according to their works, what will be the outcome? Certainly they cannot present any good works by which they might earn or deserve salvation. All their works before salvation were sinful. But the blood of Christ has wiped out the past. Now God Himself cannot find any charge against them for which to sentence them to hell. Once they are saved, they begin to practice good works — not necessarily good works in the world's eyes, but good works as God sees them. Their good works are the result of salvation, not the meritorious cause. At the Judgment Seat of Christ, their works will be reviewed and they will be rewarded for all faithful service.

But we must constantly remember that this passage does not deal with believers — only with the ungodly.

2:7 In explaining that judgment will be according to works, Paul says that God will render **eternal life to those who by patient continuance in doing good**

seek for glory, honor, and immortality. As already explained, this does *not* mean that these people are saved **by patient continuance in doing good**. That would be another gospel. No one would naturally live that kind of life, and no one could live it without divine power. Anyone who really fits this description has already been saved by grace through faith. The fact that he seeks **for glory, honor, and immortality** shows that he has already been born again. The whole tenor of his life shows that he has been converted.

He seeks for the **glory** of heaven; the **honor** that comes only from God (John 5:44); the **immortality** that characterizes the resurrection body (1 Cor. 15:53, 54); the heavenly inheritance, which is imperishable, undefiled, and unfading (1 Pet. 1:4).

God will award **eternal life** to all who manifest this evidence of a conversion experience. **Eternal life** is spoken of in several ways in the NT. It is a present possession which we receive the moment we are converted (John 5:24). It is a future possession which will be ours when we receive our glorified bodies (here and in Rom. 6:22). Although it is a gift received by faith, it is sometimes associated with rewards for a life of faithfulness (Mark 10:30). All believers will have **eternal life**, but some will have a greater capacity for enjoying it than others. It means more than endless existence; it is a quality of **life**, the more abundant **life** which the Savior promised in John 10:10. It is the very **life** of Christ Himself (Col. 1:27).

2:8 **Those who are self-seeking and do not obey the truth, but** rather **obey unrighteousness**, will be awarded **indignation and wrath**. They **do not obey the truth**; they have never answered the gospel call. Rather, they have chosen to obey unrighteousness as their master. Their lives are characterized by strife, wrangling, and disobedience — sure proof that they were never saved.

2:9 Now the apostle repeats God's verdict concerning the two kinds of workers and works, except that this time he does it in inverse order.

The verdict will be **tribulation and anguish** to everyone **who does evil**. Here again we must stress that these evil works betray an evil heart of unbelief. The works are the outward expression of a person's attitude toward the Lord.

The expression **of the Jew first, and also of the Greek** shows that *the judgment of God will be according to privilege or light received*. The Jews were **first** in privilege as God's earthly chosen people; therefore, they will be **first** in responsibility. This aspect of God's judgment will be developed further in verses 12–16.

2:10 The verdict will be **glory, honor, and peace to everyone**, Jew or Gentile, **who works what is good**. And let us not forget that no one can work good, as far as God is concerned, unless he has first placed his faith and trust in the Lord Jesus Christ.

The expression **to the Jew first, and also to the Greek** cannot indicate favoritism, because the next verse points out that God's judgment is impartial. So the expression must indicate the historical order in which the gospel went out, as in 1:16. It was proclaimed first to Jews, and the first believers were Jews.

2:11 Another truth concerning the judgment of God is that *it is without respect of persons*. In human courts of law, preference is shown to the good-looking, wealthy, and influential; but **God** is strictly impartial. No considerations of race, place, or face will ever influence Him.

2:12 As mentioned above, verses 12–16 expand the point that the judgment of God will be according to the measure of light received. Two classes are in view: those who do not have the law (the Gentiles) and those who are under the law (the Jews). This includes everyone except those who are in the church of God (see 1 Cor. 10:32, where the human race is divided into these three classes).

Those who **have sinned without law will also perish without law**. It does not say "will be *judged* without law" but **will also perish without law**. They will be judged according to whatever revelation the Lord gave them, and, failing to live up to that revelation, they will **perish**.

Those who **have sinned** under **the law will be judged by the law**, and if they have not obeyed it, they too will

perish. The law demands total obedience.

2:13 Mere possession of the law is not enough. The law demands perfect and continuous obedience. No one is accounted righteous simply because he knows what the law says. The only conceivable way of obtaining justification under the law would be to keep it in its entirety. But since all men are sinners, it is impossible for them to do this. So this verse is really setting forth an ideal condition rather than something that is capable of human attainment.

The NT teaches emphatically that it is impossible for man to be justified by law-keeping (see Acts 13:39; Rom. 3:20; Gal. 2:16, 21; 3:11). It was never God's intention that anyone be saved by the law. Even if a person could keep it perfectly from this day forward, he still would not be justified, because God requires that which is past. So when verse 13 says that **doers of the law** will be **justified**, we must understand it as meaning that the law demands obedience, and if anyone could produce perfect obedience from the day he was born, he would be justified. But the cold, hard fact is that no one can produce this.

2:14 Verses 14 and 15 are a parenthesis, looking back to verse 12a, where we learned that Gentiles who sin without the law shall perish without the law. Now Paul explains that although the law was not given to the Gentiles, yet they have an innate knowledge of right and wrong. They know instinctively that it is wrong to lie, steal, commit adultery, and murder. The only commandment they would not know intuitively is the one concerning the Sabbath; that one is more ceremonial than moral.

So what it boils down to is that the **Gentiles, who do not have the law, . . . are a law to themselves**. They form their own code of right and wrong behavior from their moral instincts.

2:15 They **show the work of the law written in their hearts**. It is not the *law itself* which is written in their hearts, but **the work of the law**. The work which the law was designed to do in the lives of the Israelites is seen in some measure in the lives of Gentiles. The fact that they know that it is right to respect their parents, for example, shows **the work of the law written in their hearts**. They also know that certain acts are basically wrong. **Their conscience**, serving as a monitor, confirms this instinctive knowledge. And their thoughts are constantly deciding the rightness or wrongness of their actions, **accusing or excusing**, forbidding or allowing.

2:16 This verse is a continuation of the thought in verse 12. It tells *when* those without law and those under the law will be judged. And in doing so it teaches one final truth about the judgment of God — namely, that *it will take into account* **the secrets of men**, *not just their public sin*. Sin which is secret at the present time will be open scandal at the Judgment of the Great White Throne. The Judge at that solemn time will be **Jesus Christ**, since the Father has committed all judgment to Him (John 5:22). When Paul adds, **according to my gospel**, he means "so my gospel teaches." **My gospel** means the gospel Paul preached, which was the same one which the other apostles preached.

2:17 The apostle has a third class to deal with, so now he turns to the question: *Are the Jews, to whom the law was given, also lost?* And of course the answer is, "Yes, they are lost too!"

There is no doubt that many Jews felt they were immune from God's judgment. God would never send **a Jew** to hell, they thought. The Gentiles, on the other hand, were fuel for the flames of hell. Paul must now destroy this pretension by showing that under certain circumstances Gentiles may be closer to God than Jews.

First he reviews those things which a Jew prized as giving him an inside track with God. He bore the name of **a Jew** and thus was a member of God's chosen earthly people. He rested **on the law**, which was never designed to give rest but rather to awaken the conscience to a sense of sinfulness. He gloried **in God**, the only true God, who had entered into a unique covenant relationship with the nation of Israel.

2:18 He knew God's **will**, because a general outline of that will is given in the Scriptures. He approved the **things that are excellent**, because the **law**

taught him how to assess moral values.

2:19 He prided himself on being **a guide to the** morally and spiritually **blind, a light to those who** were in the **darkness** of ignorance.

2:20 He felt qualified to correct the **foolish** or untaught and to teach **babes**, because the **law** gave him an outline of **knowledge** and of the **truth.**

2:21 But these things in which the Jew boasted had never changed his life. It was simply pride of race, religion, and knowledge without any corresponding moral transformation. He taught others but did not take the lessons to heart himself. He preached against stealing but did not practice what he preached.

2:22 When he forbade **adultery**, it was a case of "Do as I say, not as I do." While he did loathe and **abhor idols**, he didn't hesitate to **rob temples**, perhaps by actually looting heathen shrines.

2:23 He gloried in the possession of **the law**, but dishonored the **God** who gave it by **breaking** its sacred precepts.

2:24 This combination of high talk and low walk caused **the Gentiles** to blaspheme **the name of God**. They judged the Lord, as men always do, by those who professed to be His followers. It was true in Isaiah's day (Isa. 52:5) and it is still true today. Each of us should ask:

> If of Jesus Christ their only view
> May be what they see of Him in you,
> (Insert your name), what do they see?

2:25 In addition to the law, the Jew prided himself on the rite of **circumcision**. This is a minor surgical operation performed on the foreskin of the Jewish male. It was instituted by God as a sign of His covenant with Abraham (Gen. 17:9–14). It expressed the separation of a people to God from the world. After a while the Jews so prided themselves on having had the operation that they contemptuously called the Gentiles "the uncircumcision."

Here Paul links **circumcision** with the **Law** of Moses and points out that it was only valid as a sign when it was combined with a life of obedience. God is not a mere ritualist; He is not satisfied with external ceremonies unless they are accompanied by inward holiness. So a circumcised Jew who transgresses the law might just as well be uncircumcised.

When the apostle speaks about keepers or doers of the law in this passage, we must not take the words in an absolute sense.

2:26 Thus, if a Gentile adheres to the morality prescribed by **the law**, even if he isn't under the law, **his uncircumcision** is more acceptable than the circumcision of a Jewish transgressor. In such a case the Gentile's heart is circumcised, and that is what counts.

2:27 The superior behavior of the Gentile condemns the Jew, who, **with his written code and circumcision** does not keep the **law** or live the circumcised life, the life of separation and sanctification.

2:28 In God's reckoning, a true **Jew** is not simply a man who has Abraham's blood flowing in his veins or who has the mark of circumcision in his body. A person may have both these things and be the scum of the earth morally. The Lord is not swayed by external considerations of race or religion; He looks for inward sincerity and purity.

2:29 A real **Jew** is the one who is not only a descendant of Abraham but who also manifests a godly life. This passage does not teach that all believers are Jews, or that the church is the Israel of God. Paul is talking about those who are born of Jewish parentage and is insisting that the mere fact of birth and the ordinance of circumcision are not enough. There must also be inward reality.

True **circumcision is** a matter **of the heart** — not just a literal cutting of the body but the spiritual reality of surgery on the old, unregenerate nature.

Those who thus combine the outward sign and the inward grace receive God's praise, if not man's. There is a play on words in this last verse that is not apparent in the English. The word "Jew" comes from "Judah," meaning **praise. A** real **Jew** is one whose character is such as to receive **praise from God**.

3:1 Paul continues the subject of the guilt of the Jews in the first eight verses of this chapter. Here a Jewish objector appears and begins to cross-examine the apostle. The questioning proceeds as follows:

OBJECTOR: If all you have said in 2:17–29 is true, then **what** is the **advantage** of being a **Jew** and what **profit** is there from **circumcision?**

3:2 *PAUL:* The Jews have had many special privileges. The most important is that they were entrusted with **the oracles of God**. The OT Scriptures were given to Jews to write and to preserve, but how have the people of Israel responded to this tremendous privilege? On the whole, they have demonstrated an appalling lack of faith.

3:3 *OBJECTOR:* Well, granted that not all Jews have believed, but does this mean that God will go back on His promises? After all, He did choose Israel as His people and He made definite covenants with them. Can the **unbelief** of some cause **God** to break His word?

3:4 *PAUL:* **Certainly not!** Whenever there is a question whether God or man is right, always proceed on the basis that **God** is right and **every man** is **a liar**. This is what David said, in effect, in Psalm 51:4: "The complete truthfulness of all You say must be defended, and You must be vindicated every time You are called into question by sinful man." Our sins only serve to confirm the truthfulness of God's words.

3:5 *OBJECTOR:* If that's the case, why does God condemn us? **If our unrighteousness** causes **the righteousness of God** to shine more gloriously, how can **God** visit us with **wrath**? (Paul notes here that in quoting these words, he is using a typically human argument.)

3:6 *PAUL:* Such an argument is unworthy of serious consideration. If there were any possibility of God's being unrighteous, then how could He be fit to **judge the world?** Yet we all admit that He *will* judge the world.

3:7 *OBJECTOR:* But if my sin brings glory to God, if **my lie** vindicates His **truth**, if He causes man's wrath to praise Him, then how can He consistently find fault with me **as a sinner?**

3:8 Why wouldn't it be logical to say —

PAUL: Let me interrupt to say that **some** people actually accuse us Christians of using this argument, but it is a slander.

OBJECTOR: Why wouldn't it be logical to say, **"Let us do evil, that good may come"?**

PAUL: All I can say is that the **condemnation** of people who talk like that is well-deserved.

(Actually this last argument, stupid as it seems, is constantly leveled against the gospel of the grace of God. People say, "If you could be saved just by faith in Christ, then you could go out and live in sin. Since God's grace superabounds over man's sin, then the more you sin, the more His grace abounds." The apostle answers this objection in chapter 6.)

3:9 *OBJECTOR:* Are you saying, **then**, that **we** Jews are **better than** those sinful Gentiles? Or the question may be, according to some versions, "Are we Jews worse than the Gentiles?" The answer in either case is that the Jews are no better and no worse. All are sinners.

That leads up to and parallels the next question in Paul's presentation. He has shown that the heathen are lost; the self-righteous moralists, whether Jews or Gentiles, are lost; the Jews are lost. Now he turns to the question: *Are all men lost?*

The answer is, "Yes, **we have** already **charged** that **all** people **are under** the power of **sin.**" This means that Jews are no different from Gentiles in this respect.

3:10 If further proof is needed, that proof is found in the OT. First we see that sin has affected everyone born of human parents (3:10–12) and then we see that sin has affected every part of a man (3:13–18). We might paraphrase it as follows: "There is **not** a single **righteous** person" (Ps. 14:1).

3:11 "There is no one who has a right understanding of God. **There is** no one **who seeks after God**" (Ps. 14:2). If left to himself, fallen man would never seek God. It is only through the work of the Holy Spirit that anyone ever does.

3:12 "**All** have gone astray from God. All mankind has become corrupt. There is not one who lives a good life, **no, not one**" (Ps. 14:3).

3:13 "Men's throats are like **an open tomb**. Their speech has been consistently deceitful" (Ps. 5:9). "Their conversation flows from poisonous lips" (Ps. 140:3).

3:14 "Their mouths are **full of cursing** and hatred" (Ps. 10:7).

3:15 "**Their feet are swift to** carry them on missions of murder" (Isa. 59:7).

3:16 "They leave a trail of ruin **and misery**" (Isa. 59:7).

3:17 "They have never **known** how to make **peace**" (Isa. 59:8).

3:18 "They have no respect for **God**" (Ps. 36:1).

This, then, is God's X-ray of the human race. It reveals universal unrighteousness (3:10); ignorance and independence toward God (3:11); waywardness, unprofitableness, and lack of any goodness (3:12). Man's throat is full of rottenness, his tongue is deceitful, his lips are venomous (3:13); his mouth is full of swearing (3:14); his feet are bent on murder (3:15); he leaves behind trouble and destruction (3:16); he doesn't know how to make peace (3:17); and he has no regard for God (3:18). Here we see the total depravity of man, by which we mean that sin has affected all of mankind and that it has affected every part of his being. Obviously every man has not committed every sin, but he has a nature which is *capable* of committing them all.

If Paul had wanted to give a more complete catalog of sins, he could have mentioned *the sins of sex:* adultery, homosexuality, lesbianism, perversion, bestiality, prostitution, rape, lewdness, pornography, and smut. He could have mentioned *the sins associated with war:* destruction of innocents, atrocities, gas chambers, ovens, concentration camps, torture devices, sadism. He could have mentioned *sins of the home:* unfaithfulness, divorce, wifebeating, mental cruelty, child abuse. Add to these the crimes of murder, mutilation, theft, burglary, embezzlement, vandalism, graft, corruption. Also *the sins of speech:* profanity, suggestive jokes, sensual language, cursing, blasphemy, lies, backbiting, gossip, character assassination, grumbling, and complaining. *Other personal sins* are: drunkenness, drug addiction, pride, envy, covetousness, ingratitude, filthy thought-life, hatred, and bitterness. The list is seemingly endless — pollution, littering, racism, exploitation, deceit, betrayal, broken promises, and on and on. What further proof of human depravity is needed?

3:19 When God gave the law to Israel, He was using Israel as a sample of the human race. He found that Israel was a failure, and He correctly applied this finding to all of humanity. It is the same as when a health inspector takes a test-tube of water from a well, tests the sample, finds it polluted, and then pronounces the entire well polluted.

So Paul explains that when **the law** speaks, it speaks **to those who are under the law** — the people of Israel — in order **that every mouth,** *Jew and Gentile,* **may be stopped, and all the world** be brought in **guilty before God.**

3:20 **No** one can **be justified by** keeping **the law.** The law was not given to justify people but to produce **the knowledge of sin** — not the knowledge of *salvation,* but **the knowledge of sin.**

We could never know what a crooked line is unless we also knew a straight line. The law is like a straight line. When men test themselves by it, they see how crooked they are.

We can use a mirror to see that our face is dirty, but the mirror is not designed to wash the dirty face. A thermometer will tell if a person has a fever, but swallowing the thermometer will not cure the fever.

The law is good when it is used to produce conviction of sin, but it is worthless as a savior from sin. As Luther said, its function is not to justify but to terrify.

D. The Basis and Terms of the Gospel (3:21–31)

3:21 We now come to the heart of the Letter to the Romans, when Paul answers the question: *According to the gospel, how can ungodly sinners be justified by a holy God?*

He begins by saying that **the righteousness of God** has been revealed **apart from the law.** This means that a plan or program has been **revealed** by which God can righteously save unrighteous sinners, and that it is not by requiring men to keep the law. Because God is holy, He cannot condone sin or overlook it or wink at it. He must punish it. And the punishment for sin is death. Yet God loves the sinner and wants to save him; there is the dilemma. God's righteousness demands the sinner's death, but His love desires the sinner's eternal happiness. The gospel reveals how God can save sinners without compromising His righteousness.

This righteous plan is **witnessed by the Law and the Prophets.** It was foretold in the types and shadows of the sacrificial system that required the shedding of blood for atonement. And it was foretold by direct prophecies (see, e.g., Isa. 51:5, 6, 8; 56:1; Dan. 9:24).

3:22 Verse 21 told us that this righteous salvation is *not* obtained on the basis of law-keeping. Now the apostle tells us how it *is* obtained — **through faith in Jesus Christ.** Faith here means utter reliance on the living Lord Jesus Christ as one's only Savior from sin and one's only hope for heaven. It is based on the revelation of the Person and work of Christ as found in the Bible.

Faith is not a leap in the dark. It demands the surest evidence, and finds it in the infallible word of God. Faith is not illogical or unreasonable. What is more reasonable than that the creature should trust his Creator?

Faith is not a meritorious work by which a man earns or deserves salvation. A man cannot boast because he has believed the Lord; he would be a fool *not* to believe Him. Faith is not an attempt to earn salvation, but is the simple acceptance of the salvation which God offers as a free gift.

Paul goes on to tell us that this salvation is **to all and on all**[6] **who believe.** It is **to all** in the sense that it is available to all, offered to all, and sufficient for all. But it is only **on** those **who believe;** that is, it is effective only in the lives of those who accept the Lord Jesus by a definite act of faith. The pardon is for all, but it becomes valid in an individual's life only when he accepts it.

When Paul says that salvation is available to all, he includes Gentiles as well as Jews, because now **there is no difference.** The Jew has no special privilege and the Gentile is at no disadvantage.

3:23 The availability of the gospel is as universal as the need. And the need is universal because **all have sinned**[7] **and fall short of the glory of God.** Everybody **sinned** in Adam; when he sinned, he acted as the representative for all his descendants. But men are not only sinners by nature; they are also sinners by *practice*. They **fall short**, in themselves, of the glory of God.

EXCURSUS ON SIN

Sin is any thought, word, or deed that falls short of God's standard of holiness and perfection. It is a missing of the mark, a coming short of the target. An Indian whose arrow fell short of its target was heard to say, "Oh, I sinned." In his language,[8] the same word was used to express sinning and falling short of the target.

Sin is lawlessness (1 Jn. 3:4), the rebellion of the creature's will against the will of God. Sin is not only doing what is wrong but the failure to do what one knows to be right (Jas. 4:17). Whatever is not of faith is sin (Rom. 14:23). This means that it is wrong for a man to do anything about which he has a reasonable doubt. If he does not have a clear conscience about it, and yet goes ahead and does it, he is sinning.

"All unrighteousness is sin" (1 Jn. 5:17). And the thought of foolishness is sin (Prov. 24:9). Sin begins in the mind. When encouraged and entertained, it breaks forth into an act, and the act leads on to death. Sin is often attractive when first contemplated, but hideous in retrospect.

Sometimes Paul distinguishes between sins and sin. Sins refer to wrong things that we have done. Sin refers to our evil nature — that is, to what we are. What we *are* is a lot worse than anything we have ever done. But Christ died for our evil nature as well as for our evil deeds. God forgives our sins, but the Bible never speaks of His forgiving our sin. Instead, He *condemns* or *judges* sin in the flesh (Rom. 8:3).

There is also a difference between sin and transgression. Transgression is a violation of a known law. Stealing is basically sinful; it is wrong in itself. But stealing is also a transgression when there is a law that forbids it. "Where there is no law there is no transgression" (Rom. 4:15).

Paul has shown that all men have sinned and continually come short of God's glory. Now he goes on to present the remedy. ‡

3:24 Being justified freely by His grace. The gospel tells how God justifies sinners as a free gift and by an act of unmerited favor. But what do we mean when we speak of the act of justifying?

The word *justify* means to reckon or declare to be righteous. For example, God pronounces a sinner to be righteous when that sinner believes on the Lord Jesus Christ. This is the way the word is most often used in the NT.

However, a man can justify God (see Luke 7:29) by believing and obeying God's word. In other words, he declares God to be righteous in all that God says and does.

And, of course, a man can justify himself; that is, he can protest his own righteousness (see Luke 10:29). But this is nothing but a form of self-deception.

To justify does not mean to actually *make* a person righteous. We cannot *make* God righteous; He already *is* righteous. But we can *declare* Him to be righteous. God does not *make* the believer sinless or righteous in himself. Rather, God puts righteousness to his account. As A. T. Pierson put it, "God in justifying sinners actually calls them righteous when they are not — does not impute sin where sin actually exists, and does impute righteousness where it does not exist."[9]

A popular definition of justification is *just as if I'd never sinned*. But this does not go far enough. When God justifies the believing sinner, He not only acquits him from guilt but clothes him in His own righteousness and thus makes him absolutely fit for heaven. "Justification goes beyond acquittal to approval; beyond pardon to promotion."[10] Acquittal means only that a person is set free from a charge. Justification means that positive righteousness is imputed.

The reason God can declare ungodly sinners to be righteous is because the Lord Jesus Christ has fully paid the debt of their sins by His death and resurrection. When sinners accept Christ by faith, they are justified.

When James teaches that justification is by works (Jas. 2:24), he does not mean that we are saved by good works, or by faith plus good works, but rather by the kind of faith that results in good works.

It is important to realize that justification is a reckoning that takes place in the mind of God. It is not something a believer feels; he knows it has taken place because the Bible says so. C. I. Scofield expressed it this way: "Justification is that act of God whereby He declares righteous all who believe in Jesus. It is something which takes place in the mind of God, not in the nervous system or emotional nature of the believer."

Here in Romans 3:24 the apostle teaches that we are **justified freely**. It is not something we can earn or purchase, but rather something that is offered as a gift.

Next we learn that we are **justified . . . by** God's **grace**. This simply means that it is wholly apart from any merit in ourselves. As far as we are concerned, it is undeserved, unsought, and unbought.

In order to avoid confusion later on, we should pause here to explain that there are six different aspects of justification in the NT. We are said to be justified by grace, by faith, by blood, by power, by God, and by works; yet there is no contradiction or conflict.

We are justified by grace — that means we do not deserve it.

We are justified by faith (Rom. 5:1) — that means that we have to receive it by believing on the Lord Jesus Christ.

We are justified by blood (Rom. 5:9) — that refers to the price the Savior paid in order that we might be justified.

We are justified by power (Rom. 4:24, 25) — the same power that raised the Lord Jesus from the dead.

We are justified by God (Rom. 8:33) — He is the One who reckons us righteous.

We are justified by works (Jas. 2:24) — not meaning that good works earn justification, but that they are the evidence that we have been justified.

Returning to 3:24, we read that we are justified **through the redemption that is in Christ Jesus. Redemption** means buying back by payment of a ransom price. The Lord Jesus bought us back from the slave market of sin. His precious blood was the ransom price which was paid to satisfy the claims of a holy and righteous God. If someone asks, "To whom was the ransom paid?" he misses the point. The Scriptures nowhere suggest that a specific payment was made either to God or to Satan. The ransom was not paid to anyone but was an abstract settlement that provided a righteous basis by which God could save the ungodly.

3:25 God set forth Christ Jesus **as a propiation. A propitiation** is a means by which justice is satisfied, God's wrath is averted, and mercy can be shown on the basis of an acceptable sacrifice.

Three times in the NT Christ is spoken of as **a propitiation**. Here in Romans 3:25 we learn that those who put their faith in Christ find mercy by virtue of His shed blood. In 1 John 2:2 Christ is described as the propitiation for our sins, and for those of the whole world. His work is sufficient for the whole world but is only effective for those who put their trust in Him. Finally, in 1 John 4:10, God's love was manifested in sending His Son to be the propitiation for our sins.

The prayer of the publican in Luke 18:13 was literally "God be propitious to me, the sinner." He was asking God to show mercy to him by not requiring him to pay the penalty of his aggravated guilt.

The word **propitiation** also occurs in Hebrews 2:17: "Therefore, in all things He had to be made like His brethren, that He might be a merciful and faithful High Priest in things *pertaining* to God, to make propitiation for the sins of the people." Here the expression "to make propitiation" means to put away by paying the penalty.

The OT equivalent of the word *propitiation* is *mercy-seat*. The mercy-seat was the lid of the ark. On the Day of Atonement the high priest sprinkled the mercy-seat with the blood of a sacrificial victim. By this means errors of the high priest and of the people were atoned for or covered.

When Christ made propitiation for our sins, He went much further. He not only *covered them* but *did away with them completely*.

Now Paul tells us in 3:25 that **God set** Christ **forth as a propitiation by His blood, through faith**. We are not told to put our faith in His blood; *Christ Himself* is the object of our faith. It is only a resurrected and living Christ Jesus who can save. He is the propitiation. **Faith** in Him is the condition by which we avail ourselves of the **propitiation**. **His blood** is the price that was paid.

The finished work of Christ declares God's **righteousness** for the remission of **sins** that are past. This refers to sins committed before the death of Christ. From Adam to Christ, God saved those who put their faith in Him on the basis of whatever revelation He gave them. Abraham, for example, believed God, and it was reckoned to him for righteousness (Gen. 15:6). But how could God do this righteously? A sinless Substitute had not been slain. The blood of a perfect Sacrifice had not been shed. In a word, Christ had not died. The debt had not been paid. God's righteous claims had not been met. How then could God save believing sinners in the OT period?

The answer is that although Christ had not yet died, God knew that He *would* die, and He saved men on the basis of the still-future work of Christ. Even if OT saints didn't know about Calvary, *God* knew about it, and He put all the value of Christ's work to their account when they believed God. In a very real sense, OT believers were saved on credit. They were saved on the basis of a price still to be paid. They looked forward to Calvary; we look back to it.

That is what Paul means when he says that the propitiation of Christ declares God's **righteousness because He had passed over the sins that were previously committed**. He is not speaking, as some wrongly think, of sins which an individual person has committed before his conversion. This might suggest that the work of Christ took care of sins before the new birth, but that a man is on his own after that. No, he is dealing with the seeming leniency of God in apparently overlooking the sins of those who were saved before the cross. It might seem that God excused those sins or pretended not to see them. Not so, says Paul. The Lord knew that Christ would make full expiation, and so He saved men on that basis.

So the OT period was a time of the **forbearance** of God. For at least 4000 years He held back His judgment on sin. Then in the fullness of time He sent His Son to be the Sin-bearer. When the Lord Jesus took our sins upon Himself, God unleashed the full fury of His righteous, holy wrath on the Son of His love.

3:26 Now the death of Christ declares God's **righteousness**. God is **just** because He has required the full payment of the penalty of sin. And He can justify the ungodly without condoning their sin or compromising His own righteousness because a perfect Substitute has died and risen again. Albert Midlane has stated the truth in poetry:

> The perfect righteousness of God
> Is witnessed in the Savior's blood;
> 'Tis in the cross of Christ we trace
> His righteousness, yet wondrous grace.
>   God could not pass the sinner by,
>   His sin demands that he must die;
>   But in the cross of Christ we see
>   How God can save, yet righteous be.
>   The sin is on the Savior laid,
>   'Tis in His blood sin's debt is paid;
>   Stern justice can demand no more,
>   And mercy can dispense her store.
>   The sinner who believes is free,
>   Can say, "The Savior died for me";
>   Can point to the atoning blood,
>   And say, "That made my peace
>   with God."

3:27 Where is boasting then in this wonderful plan of salvation? **It is excluded**, shut out, banned. **By what** principle is boasting **excluded**? By the principle **of works**? **No.** If salvation were by works, that would allow room for all kinds of self-congratulation. But when salvation is on the principle **of faith**, there is no room for **boasting**. The justified person says, "I did all the sinning; Jesus did all the saving." True faith disavows any possibility of self-help, self-improvement, or self-salvation, looking only to Christ as Savior. Its language is:

> In my hand no price I bring,
> Simply to Thy cross I cling;
> Naked, come to Thee for dress,
> Helpless, look to Thee for grace.
> Foul, I to the fountain fly;
> Wash me, Savior, or I die.
> — *Augustus M. Toplady*

3:28 As the reason why boasting is

excluded, Paul reiterates **that a man is justified by faith apart from the deeds of the law**.

3:29 How does the gospel present God? Is He the exclusive **God of the Jews**? No, He is **also the God of the Gentiles**. The Lord Jesus Christ did not die for one race of mankind but for the whole world of sinners. And the offer of full and free salvation goes out to whosoever will, Jew or Gentile.

3:30 There aren't two Gods — one for the Jews and one for the Gentiles. There is only **one God** and only one way of salvation for all mankind. He justifies **the circumcised by faith and the uncircumcised through faith**. Whatever the reason for the use of different prepositions here (**by** and **through**[11]), there is no difference in the instrumental cause of justification; it is **faith** in both cases.

3:31 An important question remains. When we say that salvation is by faith and not by law-keeping, do we imply that the law is worthless and should be disregarded? Does the gospel wave the law aside as if it had no place? **On the contrary**, the gospel establishes **the law**, and this is how:

The law demands perfect obedience. The penalty for breaking the law must be paid. That penalty is DEATH. If a lawbreaker pays the penalty, he will be lost eternally. The gospel tells how Christ died to pay the penalty of the broken law. He did not treat it as a thing to be ignored. He paid the debt in full. Now anyone who has broken the law can avail himself of the fact that Christ paid the penalty on his behalf. Thus the gospel of salvation by faith upholds the law by insisting that its utmost demands must be and have been fully met.

E. The Harmony of the Gospel with the Old Testament (Chap. 4)

The fifth main question that Paul takes up is: *Does the gospel agree with the teachings of the OT?* The answer to this question would be of special importance to the Jewish people. Therefore the apostle now shows that there is complete harmony between the gospel in the NT and in the Old. Justification has always been by faith.

4:1 Paul proves his point by refer-

ring to two of the greatest figures in Israel's history: Abraham and David. God made great covenants with both these men. One lived centuries before the law was given, and the other lived many years afterward. One was justified before he was circumcised, and the other after.

Let us first consider **Abraham**, whom all Jews could call their forefather. What was his experience **according to the flesh**?[12] What did he find concerning the way in which a person is justified?

4:2 If **Abraham was justified by works**, then he would have reason for boasting. He could pat himself on the back for earning a righteous standing **before God**. But this is utterly impossible. No one will ever be able to boast before God (Eph. 2:9). There is nothing in the Scriptures to indicate that Abraham had any grounds for boasting that he was justified by his works.

But someone may argue, "Doesn't it say in James 2:21 that Abraham was justified by works?" Yes it does, but there the meaning is quite different. Abraham was justified by faith in Genesis 15:6 when he believed God's promise concerning a numberless posterity. It was thirty or more years later that he was justified (vindicated) by works when he started to offer Isaac as a burnt offering to God (Gen. 22). This act of obedience proved the reality of his faith. It was an outward demonstration that he had been truly justified by faith.

4:3 **What does the Scripture say** concerning Abraham's justification? It says "he believed in the Lord, and He accounted it to him for righteousness" (Gen. 15:6). God revealed Himself to Abraham and promised that he would have a numberless posterity. The patriarch believed in the Lord, and God put **righteousness** to his account. In other words, Abraham was justified by faith. It was just as simple as that. Works had nothing to do with it. They aren't even mentioned.

4:4 All of this brings us to one of the sublimest statements in the Bible concerning the contrast between works and faith in reference to the plan of salvation.

Think of it this way: when a man

works for a living and gets his paycheck at the end of the week, he is entitled to his **wages**. He has earned them. He does not bow and scrape before his employer, thanking him for such a display of kindness and protesting that he doesn't deserve the money. Not at all! He puts the money in his pocket and goes home with the feeling that he has only been reimbursed for his time and labor.

But that's not the way it is in the matter of justification.

4:5 Shocking as it may seem, the justified man is the one **who**, first of all, **does not work**. He renounces any possibility of earning his salvation. He disavows any personal merit or goodness. He acknowledges that all his best labors could never fulfill God's righteous demands.

Instead, he **believes on Him who justifies** *the ungodly*. He puts his faith and trust in the Lord. He takes God at His word. As we have seen, this is not a meritorious action. The merit is not in his faith, but in *the Object of his faith*.

Notice that he **believes on Him who justifies** *the ungodly*. He doesn't come with the plea that he has tried his best, that he has lived by the Golden Rule, that he has not been as bad as others. No, he comes as an **ungodly**, guilty sinner and throws himself on the mercy of God.

And what is the result? **His faith is accounted** to him **for righteousness**. Because he has come believing instead of working, God puts **righteousness** to his account. Through the merits of the risen Savior, God clothes him with **righteousness** and thus makes him fit for heaven. Henceforth God sees him in Christ and accepts him on that basis.

To summarize, then, justification is for the ungodly — not for good people. It is a matter of grace — not of debt. And it is received by faith — not by works.

4:6 Next Paul turns to **David** to prove his thesis. The words **just as** at the beginning of this verse indicate that David's experience was the same as Abraham's. The sweet singer of Israel said that the happy man is the sinner whom God reckons righteous **apart from works**. Although David never said this

in so many words, the Apostle derives it from Psalm 32:1, 2, which he quotes in the next two verses.

4:7 Blessed are those whose lawless deeds are forgiven,
And whose sins are covered;
4:8 Blessed is the man to whom the LORD shall not impute sin.

What did Paul see in these verses? First of all, he noticed that David said nothing about works; forgiveness is a matter of God's grace, not of man's efforts. Second, he saw that if God doesn't **impute sin** to a person, then that person must have a righteous standing before Him. Finally, he saw that God justifies the ungodly; David had been guilty of adultery and murder, yet in these verses he is tasting the sweetness of full and free pardon.

4:9 But the idea may still lurk in some Jewish minds that the chosen people had a corner on God's justification, that only those who were circumcised could be justified. The apostle turns again to the experience of **Abraham** to show that this is not so. He poses the question, "Is righteousness imputed to believing Jews only, or to believing Gentiles as well?" The fact that Abraham was used as an example might seem to suggest that it was only to Jews.

4:10 Here Paul seizes on a historical fact that most of us would never have noticed. He shows that Abraham was justified (Gen. 15:6) before he was ever **circumcised** (Gen. 17:24). If the father of the nation of Israel could be justified **while he was** still **uncircumcised**, then the question arises, "Why can't other uncircumcised people be justified?" In a very real sense, Abraham was justified while still on Gentile ground, and this leaves the door wide open for other Gentiles to be justified, entirely apart from circumcision.

4:11 Circumcision, then, was not the instrumental cause of Abraham's justification. It was merely an outward **sign** in his flesh that he had been justified by faith. Basically, circumcision was the external token of the covenant between God and the people of Israel; but here its meaning is expanded to indicate the righteousness which God imputed to Abraham through faith.

In addition to being a sign, circumcision was a seal — **a seal of righteousness of the faith which he had while still uncircumcised**. A **sign** points to the existence of that which it signifies. A **seal** authenticates, confirms, certifies, or guarantees the genuineness of that which is signified. Circumcision confirmed to Abraham that he was regarded and treated by God as righteous through faith.

Circumcision was **a seal of the righteousness of** Abraham's **faith**. This may mean that his **faith** was righteous or it may mean that he obtained righteousness through **faith**. The latter is almost certainly the correct meaning; **circumcision** was **a seal of the righteousness** which belonged to his **faith** or which he obtained on the basis of **faith**.

Because Abraham was justified before he was circumcised, **he** can **be the father of** other **uncircumcised** people — that is, of believing Gentiles. They can be justified the same way he was — by faith.

When it says that Abraham is **the father** of believing Gentiles, there is no thought of physical descent, of course. It simply means that these believers are his children because they imitate his faith. They are not his children by birth but by following him as their pattern and example. Neither does the passage teach that believing Gentiles become the Israel of God. The Israel of God is composed of those *Jews* who accept Jesus, the Messiah, as their Lord and Savior.

4:12 Abraham received the sign of **circumcision** for another reason also — namely, that he might be **the father of** those Jews who are not only circumcised **but who also** follow his footsteps in a path of **faith**, the kind of **faith which he had while still uncircumcised**.

There is a difference between being Abraham's descendants and Abraham's children. Jesus said to the Pharisees, "I know that you are Abraham's descendants" (John 8:37). But then He went on to say, "If you were Abraham's children, you would do the works of Abraham" (John 8:39). So here Paul insists that physical circumcision is not what counts. There must be **faith** in the living God. Those **of the circumcision** who believe in the Lord Jesus Christ are the true Israel of God.

To summarize, then, there was a time in Abraham's life when he had **faith** and was **still uncircumcised**, and another time when he had faith and was circumcised. Paul's eagle eye sees in this fact that both believing Gentiles and believing Jews can claim Abraham as their father and can identify with him as his children.

4:13 "The argument continues relentlessly on as Paul chases every possible objector down every possible alleyway of logic and Scripture."[13] The apostle now must deal with the objection that blessing came through the law and that therefore the Gentiles who did not know the law were cursed (see John 7:49).

When God promised **Abraham** and **his seed** that he would be **heir of the world**, He did not make the promise conditional on adherence to some legal code. (The law itself wasn't given until 430 years later — Gal. 3:17.) It was an unconditional **promise** of grace, to be received by **faith** — the same kind **of faith** by which we obtain God's **righteousness** today.

The expression **heir of the world** means that he would be the father of believing Gentiles as well as of Jews (4:11, 12), that he would be the father of many nations (4:17, 18) and not just of the Jewish nation. In its fullest sense the promise will be fulfilled when the Lord Jesus, Abraham's seed, takes the scepter of universal empire and reigns as King of kings and Lord of lords.

4:14 If those who seek God's blessing, and particularly the blessing of justification, are able to inherit it on the basis of lawkeeping, then **faith is made void and the promise made of no effect**. Faith is set aside because it is a principle that is completely opposite to law: **faith** is a matter of *believing*, while **law** is a matter of *doing*. The promise would then be worthless because it would be based on conditions that no one would be able to meet.

4:15 The law brings about God's **wrath**, not His blessing. It condemns those who fail to keep its commandments perfectly and continuously. And since none can do that, all who are under the law are condemned to death. It is impossible to be under the law without being under the curse.

But **where there is no law there is no transgression. Transgression** means the violation of a known **law**. Paul does not say that where there is no law, there is no *sin*. An act can be inherently wrong even if there is no law against it. But it becomes **transgression** when a sign goes up saying "Speed Limit 20 MPH."

The Jews thought they inherited blessing through having the law, but all they inherited was **transgression**. God gave the law so that sin might be seen as **transgression**, or to put it another way, so that sin might be seen in all its sinfulness. He never intended it to be the way of salvation for sinful transgressors!

4:16 Because law produces God's wrath and not His justification, God determined that He would save men by **grace** through **faith**. He would give eternal life as a free, undeserved gift to ungodly sinners who receive it by a simple act of **faith**.

In this way **the promise** of life is **sure to all the seed**. We should mention two words here — *sure* and *all*. First, God wants **the promise** to be *sure*. If justification depended on man's law-works, he could never be sure because he could not know if he had done enough good works or the right kind. No one who seeks to *earn* salvation enjoys full assurance. But when salvation is presented as a gift to be received by believing, then a man can be sure that he is saved on the authority of the word of God.

Second, God wants **the promise** to be **sure to** *all* **the seed** — not just to the Jews, to whom **the law** was given, **but also to** Gentiles who put their trust in the Lord in the same way that **Abraham** did. **Abraham is the father of us all** — that is, of **all** believing Jews and Gentiles.

4:17 To confirm Abraham's fatherhood over all true believers, Paul injects Genesis 17:5 as a parenthesis: **"I have made you a father of many nations."** God's choice of Israel as His chosen, earthly people did not mean that His grace and mercy would be *confined* to them. The apostle ingeniously quotes

verse after verse from the OT to show that it always was God's intention to honor faith wherever He found it.

The phrase **in the presence of Him whom he believed** continues the thought from 4:16: ". . . Abraham, who is the father of us all." The connection is this: Abraham is the father of us all in the sight of Him (God) whom he (Abraham) believed, even **God who gives life to the dead** and speaks of **things** that **do not** yet **exist as** already existing. To understand this description of God, we have only to look at the verses that follow. **God gives life to the dead** — that is, to Abraham and Sarah, for although they were not dead physically, they were childless and beyond the age when they could have children (see 4:19). God **calls those things which do not yet exist as** already existing — that is, a numberless posterity involving many nations (see 4:18).

4:18 In the preceding verses Paul has emphasized that the promise came to Abraham by faith and not by law that it might be by grace and that it might be sure to all the seed. That leads quite naturally to a consideration of Abraham's faith in the God of resurrection. God promised Abraham posterity as numberless as the stars and the sand. Humanly speaking, the chances were all but hopeless. But **contrary to** human **hope**, Abraham **believed, in hope** that he would **become the father of many nations**, just as God had promised in Genesis 15:5: **"So shall your descendants be."**

4:19 When the promise of a great posterity was first made to Abraham, he was seventy-five years old (Gen. 12:2–4). At that time he was still physically able to become a father, because after that he begot Ishmael (Gen. 16:1–11). But in this verse Paul is speaking of the time when Abraham was about 100 years old and the promise was renewed (Gen. 17:15–21). By now the possibility of creating new life apart from the miraculous power of God had vanished. However, God had promised him a son, and Abraham believed God's promise.

Without **being weak in faith**, he **did not**[14] **consider his own body**, which was **already dead**, nor **the deadness of Sarah's womb**. Humanly speaking, it was utterly hopeless, but Abraham had faith.

4:20 The apparent impossibility that **the promise** would ever be fulfilled didn't stagger him. God had *said* it; Abraham *believed* it; that *settled* it. As far as the patriarch was concerned there was only one impossibility, and that was for God to lie. Abraham's faith was strong and vibrant. He gave **glory to God**, honoring Him as the One who could be depended on to fulfill His promise in defiance of all the laws of chance or probability.

4:21 Abraham did not know *how* God would fulfill His word, but that was incidental. He knew God and had every confidence that God **was** fully **able** to do **what He had promised**. In one way it was wonderful faith, but in another way it was the most reasonable thing to do, because God's word is the surest thing in the universe, and for Abraham there was no risk in believing it!

4:22 God was pleased to find a man who took Him at His word; He always is. And so He credited **righteousness** to Abraham's account. Where once there had been a balance of sin and guilt, now there was nothing but a righteous standing before God. Abraham had been delivered from condemnation and was justified by a holy God through faith.

4:23 The historical narrative of his justification by faith **was not written for his sake alone**. There was a sense, of course, in which it *was* written for his sake — a permanent record of his acquittal and his now-perfect standing before God.

4:24 But it was written **also for us**. Our faith is likewise reckoned for righteousness when we **believe** on God, **who raised up Jesus our Lord from the dead**. The only difference is this: Abraham believed that God *would* give life to the dead (that is, to his weak body and Sarah's barren womb). We believe that God *has* given life to the dead by raising the Lord Jesus Christ. C. H. Mackintosh explains:

Abraham was called to believe in a promise, whereas we are privileged to believe in an accomplished fact. He was called to look forward to something which was to be done; we look back on something that

is done, even an accomplished redemption, attested by the fact of a risen and glorified Savior at the right hand of the majesty in the heavens.[15]

4:25 The Lord Jesus **was delivered up because of our offenses, and was raised because of our justification**. Although the preposition **because of** (Gk. *dia*) is used here in connection with both our offenses and our justification, the context demands a different shade of meaning in each case. He **was delivered up** not only **because of our offenses** but in order to put them away. **He was raised up because of our justification** — that is, in order to demonstrate God's complete satisfaction with the work of Christ by which we are justified. In the first instance, **our offenses** were the problem that needed to be dealt with. In the second instance, **our justification** is the result that is assured by Christ's resurrection. There could have been no justification if Christ had remained in the tomb. But the fact that He rose tells us that the work is finished, the price has been paid, and God is infinitely satisfied with the sin-atoning work of the Savior.

F. The Practical Benefits of the Gospel (5:1–11)

The apostle carries his case for justification forward another step by taking up the question: *What are the benefits of justification in the believer's life?* In other words, does it really work? His answer is a resounding *yes*, as he enumerates seven major blessings that every believer possesses. These blessings flow to the believer through Christ. He is the Mediator between God and man, and all God's gifts are channeled through Him.

5:1 The first great benefit enjoyed by those of us who have **been justified by faith** is **peace with God through our Lord Jesus Christ**. The war is over. Hostilities have ceased. Through the work of Christ all causes of enmity between our souls and God have been removed. We have been changed from foes to friends by a miracle of grace.

5:2 Also we enjoy **access** *into an indescribable position of favor with God*. We are accepted in the Beloved One; therefore we are as near and dear to God as

His own Beloved Son. The Father extends the golden scepter to us and welcomes us as sons, not strangers. **This grace**, or standing in favor, embraces every aspect of our position before God, a position that is as perfect and permanent as Christ's because we are in Him.

As if that were not enough, *we also* **rejoice in hope of the glory of God**. This means that we joyfully look forward to the time when we will not only gaze on the splendor of God, but will ourselves be manifested in glory (see John 17:22; Col. 3:4). We cannot comprehend the full significance of that hope here on earth, nor will we get over the wonder of it through all eternity.

5:3 The fourth blessing that flows from justification is that **we also glory in tribulations** — not so much in their present discomforts as in their eventual results (see Heb. 12:11). It is one of the delightful paradoxes of the Christian faith that joy can coexist with affliction. The opposite of joy is sin, not suffering. One of the by-products of **tribulation** is that it produces **perseverance** or steadfastness. We could never develop **perseverance** if our lives were trouble-free.

5:4 Paul now goes on to explain that **perseverance** works **character**. When God sees us bearing up under our trials and looking to Him to work out His purposes through them, He awards us His Good Endurance Seal of Approval. We have been tested and approved. And this sense of His approval fills us with **hope**. We know He is working in our lives, developing our character. This gives us confidence that, having begun a good work in us, He will see it through to completion (Phil. 1:6).

5:5 **Hope does not disappoint**. If we were to hope for something but then later find that we were never going to get it, our hope would be put to shame or disappointed. But the hope of our salvation will never be put to shame. We will never be disappointed or find that we have rested on a false confidence. How can we be so sure? **Because the love of God has been poured out in our hearts. The love of God** could mean either our love for God or His love for us. Here it means the latter because verses 6–20 rehearse some of the great proofs

of God's love for us. **The Holy Spirit, given to us** the moment we believe, floods our hearts with these expressions of God's eternal love, and by these we are assured that He will see us safely home to heaven. After you receive the Spirit, you will sense that God loves you. This is not a vague, mystical feeling that "Somebody up there" cares about humanity, but the deep-seated conviction that a personal God really loves *you* as an individual.

5:6† In verses 6–20, Paul argues from the lesser to the greater. His logic is that if God's love went out to us when we were His ungodly enemies, will He not much more preserve us now that we belong to Him? This brings us to the fifth benefit of our justification; *we are eternally secure in Christ.* In developing this theme, the apostle introduces five "much mores."

The "much more" of deliverance from wrath (5:9).

The "much more" of preservation by His resurrection life (5:10).

The "much more" of the gift of grace (5:15).

The "much more" of the believer's reign in life (5:17).

The "much more" of abounding grace (5:20).

In verses 6, 7, and 8 Paul emphasizes what **we were (without strength, ungodly,** sinners) when **Christ died for** us. In verses 9 and 10 he emphasizes what we are now (justified by Christ's blood, reconciled by His death) and the resulting certainty of what the Savior will do for us (deliver us from wrath, preserve us by His life).

First we are reminded that we were weak, helpless, **without strength**, and unable to save ourselves. But at the predetermined time the Lord Jesus Christ visited our planet and died for men. And He did not die for good men, as some might suppose, but **for the ungodly**. There was no virtue, no excellence in us to commend us to God. We were utterly unworthy, but **Christ died for** us anyway.

5:7 This act of divine love was unique and unparalleled by anything in human experience. The average man's life is precious to him, and he would not

†*See p. xxii.*

think of throwing it away for an unworthy person. For example, he would not die for a murderer, an adulterer, or a mobster. In fact, he would be reluctant to **die** even **for a "righteous" man**, one who is honest and dependable but not especially warmhearted. It is possible, in an extreme case, that he would die for a **"good" man**, meaning one who is kind, friendly, loving, and lovable.

5:8 The **love** of **God** is completely supernatural and otherworldly. He demonstrated **His** marvelous **love toward us** by sending His beloved Son to die **for us while we were still sinners**. If we ask why He did it, we must look for the answer in the sovereign will of God Himself. There was no good in us to call forth such love.

5:9 Now a new set of conditions exists. We are no longer reckoned as guilty sinners. At the enormous cost of the Savior's **blood**, shed for us at Calvary, we have been counted righteous by God. Since He went to such tremendous cost to justify us when we were sinners, will He not **much more** save us **from wrath through** Christ? If He has already paid the greatest price to bring us into His favor, is it likely that He would allow us to perish in the end?

Saved from wrath could mean either "saved out of wrath" or "delivered from any contact with wrath." Here we believe the preposition (Gk. *apo*) means the latter — saved away from any contact with the wrath of God, either in time or in eternity.

5:10 Going back to what we were and what we now are, think of it this way. It was **when we were enemies** that **we were reconciled to God through the death of His Son**. We were hostile toward the Lord and quite content to have it so. Left to ourselves, we felt no need of being reconciled to Him. Think of it — **enemies** of God!

God did not share our attitude in the matter. He intervened in a display of pure grace. The substitutionary death of Christ removed the cause of our hostility toward God — namely, our sins. By faith in Christ we have been **reconciled to God.**

If God purchased our reconciliation so dearly, will He ever let us go? If **we were reconciled through the death of His Son**, which is a symbol of utter weakness, shall we not be preserved to the end by the present life of Christ at the right hand of God, a life of infinite power? If His **death** had such power to save us, how much more will **His life** have power to keep us!

5:11 And now we come to the sixth benefit of justification: **we also rejoice in God through our Lord Jesus Christ**. We not only rejoice in His gifts but in the Giver Himself. Before we were saved we found our joys elsewhere. Now we exult whenever we *remember* Him, and are sad only when we *forget* Him. What has produced this marvelous change, so that we can now be glad in God? It is the work of the **Lord Jesus Christ**. Like all our other blessings, this joy comes to us **through** Him.

The seventh benefit enjoyed by the justified is found in the words **We have now received the reconciliation.**[16] **Reconciliation** refers to the establishment of harmony between God and man through the sacrificial work of the Savior. The entrance of sin had brought estrangement, alienation, and enmity between man and God. By putting away sin, which had caused the alienation, the Lord Jesus restored those who believe on Him to a state of harmony with God. We should note, in passing, that *God* did not need to be reconciled. It was *man* who needed it, because he was at enmity with God.

G. The Triumph of Christ's Work over Adam's Sin (5:12–21)

5:12 The rest of chapter 5 serves as a bridge between the first part of the letter and the next three chapters. It is linked with the first part by picking up the subjects of condemnation through Adam and justification through Christ, and by showing that the work of Christ far outweighs in blessing what the work of Adam did in misery and loss. It is linked with chapters 6–8 by moving from justification to sanctification, and from acts of sin to the sin in human nature.

Adam is portrayed in these verses as the federal head or representative of all those who are in the old creation. Christ is presented as the Federal Head of all those who are in the new creation. A federal head acts for all those who are under him. For example, when the President of a country signs a bill into law, he is acting for all the citizens of that country.

That is what happened in Adam's case. As a result of his **sin**, human **death** entered **the world**. Death became the common lot of all Adam's descendants because they had **all sinned** in him. It is true that they all committed individual acts of sin as well, but that is not the thought here. Paul's point is that Adam's sin was a *representative act*, and all his posterity are reckoned as having **sinned** in him.

Someone might object that it was Eve and not Adam who committed the first sin on earth. That is true, but since Adam was the first to be created, *headship* was given to him. So he is seen as acting for all his descendants.

When the Apostle Paul says here that **death spread to all men**, he is referring to *physical* **death**, even though Adam's sin brought spiritual death as well. (Vv. 13 and 14 show that physical death is in view.)

When we come to this passage of Scripture, certain questions inevitably arise. Is it fair that Adam's posterity should be constituted sinners just because he sinned? Does God condemn men for being born sinners, or only for those sins which they have actually committed? If men are born with a sinful nature, and if they therefore sin because they are born sinners, how can God hold them responsible for what they do?

Bible scholars have wrestled with these and a host of similar problems and have come up with a surprising variety of conclusions. However, there are certain *facts* that we can be *sure* of.

First, the Bible does teach that all men are sinners, both by nature and by practice. Everyone born of human parents inherits Adam's sin, and also sins by his own deliberate choice.

Second, we know that the wages of sin is death — both physical death and eternal separation from God.

But no one has to pay the penalty of sin unless he wants to. This is the important point. At enormous cost, God sent His Son to die as a Substitute for sinners.

Salvation from sin and its wages is offered as a free gift through faith in the Lord Jesus Christ.

Man is condemned on three grounds: He has a *sinful nature*, Adam's *sin is imputed* to him, and he is a *sinner by practice*. But his crowning guilt is his rejection of the provision which God has made for his salvation (John 3:18, 19, 36).

But someone will ask, "What about those who have never heard the gospel?" This question is answered in part, at least, in chapter 1. Beyond that we can rest in the assurance that the Judge of all the earth will do right (Gen. 18:25). He will never act unjustly or unfairly. All His decisions are based on equity and righteousness. Although certain situations pose problems to our dim sight, they are not problems to Him. When the last case has been heard and the doors of the courtroom swing shut, no one will have a legitimate basis for appealing the verdict.

5:13 Paul will now demonstrate that Adam's sin affected the whole race. He first points out that **sin was in the world** during the period from Adam to the giving of the **law** at Mount Sinai. But during that time there was no clearly revealed law of God. Adam had received a clear oral commandment from the Lord, and many centuries later the Ten Commandments were a distinct written revelation of divine law. But in the intervening period men did not have a legal code from God. Therefore, although there was **sin** during that time, there was *no transgression*, because transgression is the violation of a known law. **But sin is not imputed** *as transgression* **when there is no law** forbidding it.

5:14 Yet **death** did not take a holiday during the age when there was no law. With the single exception of Enoch, **death** held sway over all mankind. You could not say that these people died because they had transgressed a clear command of God, as Adam did. Why then did they die? The answer is implied: they died because they had sinned in Adam. If this seems unfair, remember that this has nothing to do with salvation. All those who put their faith in the Lord were saved eternally. But they died *physically* just the same, and the reason they died was because of the sin of their federal head, Adam. In his role as federal head, Adam was **a type** (symbol) **of Him who was to come** — that is, the Lord Jesus Christ. In the succeeding verses Paul will develop the subject of these two federal heads, but more by contrast than by similarities. He will show that:

> In Christ the sons of Adam boast
> More blessings than their father lost.

5:15 The first contrast is between **the offense** of Adam and **the free gift** of Christ. By the trespass of the first man, the **many died**. The **many** here refers, of course, to Adam's descendants. Death here may include spiritual as well as physical death.

The free gift abounds much more **to the many**. The free gift is the marvelous manifestation of **the grace of God** abounding to a race of sinners. It is made possible **by the grace of the one Man, Jesus Christ**. It was amazing grace on His part to die for His rebellious creatures. Through His sacrificial death, the gift of eternal life is offered **to the many**.

The two *manys* in this verse do not refer to the same people. The first **many** includes all who became subject to death as a result of Adam's trespass. The second **many** means all who become members of the new creation, of which Christ is the Federal Head. It includes only those to whom God's grace has **abounded** — that is, true believers. While God's mercy is showered on all, His grace is appropriated only by those who trust the Savior.

5:16 There is another important contrast between Adam's sin and Christ's **gift**. The **one offense** of Adam brought inevitable **judgment**, and the verdict was "Condemned." The **free gift** of Christ, on the other hand, dealt effectively with **many offenses**, not just one, and resulted in the verdict "Acquitted." Paul highlights the differences between Adam's sin and Christ's gift, between the terrible havoc wrought by one sin and the tremendous deliverance wrought from many sins, and finally between the verdict of **condemnation** and the verdict of **justification**.

5:17 By the one man's offense, death reigned as a cruel tyrant. But by the gracious **gift of righteousness**, a gift of overflowing grace, all believers **reign in life through the One, Jesus Christ**.

What grace this is! We are not only delivered from death's reign as a tyrant over us, but we reign as kings, enjoying life now and eternally. Do we really understand and appreciate this? Do we live as the royalty of heaven, or do we grovel among the muckheaps of this world?

5:18 The **offense** of Adam brought **condemnation** to all men, but the **righteous act** of Christ brought **justification of life** to all. **The righteous act** was not the Savior's life or His keeping of the law, but rather His substitutionary death on Calvary. This is what brought **justification of life** — that is, the **justification** that results in **life** — and brought it **to all men**.

The two *alls* in this verse do not refer to the same people. The first **all** means **all** who are in Adam. The second **all** means **all** who are in Christ. This is clear from the words in the preceding verse "those who *receive* abundance of grace and of the gift of righteousness. . . ." *The gift must be received by faith.* Only those who trust the Lord receive **justification of life**.

5:19 Just **as by** Adam's **disobedience** to God's command **many were made sinners, so also by** Christ's **obedience** to the Father many who trust Him are declared **righteous**. Christ's obedience led Him to the cross as our Sinbearer.

It is futile for universalists to use these verses to try to prove that all men will eventually be saved. The passage deals with two federal headships, and it is clear that just as Adam's sin affects those who are "in him," so Christ's righteous act benefits only those who are "in Him."

5:20 What Paul has been saying would come as a jolt to the Jewish objector who felt that everything revolved around the law. Now this objector learns that sin and salvation center not in the law but in two federal heads. That being the case, he might be tempted to ask, "Why then was the law given?" The apostle answers, **The law entered that**

the offense might abound. It did not originate sin, but it revealed sin as an **offense** against God. It did not save from sin but revealed sin in all its awful character.

But God's grace proves to be greater than all man's sin. **Where sin abounded, God's grace** at Calvary **abounded much more!**

5:21 Now that the reign of sin, inflicting death on all men, has been ended, **grace** reigns **through righteousness,** giving **eternal life through Jesus Christ our Lord.** Notice that grace reigns **through righteousness.** All the demands of God's holiness have been met, and the penalty of the law has been paid, so God can now grant eternal life to all who come pleading the merits **of Christ,** their Substitute.

Perhaps we have in these verses a partial answer to the familiar question, "Why did God allow sin to enter the world?" The answer is that God has received more glory and man has received more blessings through Christ's sacrifice than if sin had never entered. We are better off in Christ than we ever could have been in an unfallen Adam. If Adam had never sinned, he would have enjoyed continued life on earth in the Garden of Eden. But he had no prospect of becoming a redeemed child of God, an heir of God, or a joint-heir with Jesus Christ. He had no promise of a home in heaven or of being with Christ and like Him forever. These blessings come only **through** the redemptive work of **Jesus Christ our Lord.**

H. The Gospel's Way to Holy Living (Chap. 6)

What Paul had said at the close of chapter 5 — that grace superabounded over all man's sin — raises another question, and a very important one. *Does the teaching of the gospel (salvation by grace through faith) permit or even encourage sinful living?*

The answer, an emphatic denial, extends over chapters 6–8. Here in chapter 6 the answer centers around three key words: *know* (vv. 3, 6), *reckon* or *consider* (v. 11), and *present* (v. 13).

It will help us to follow Paul's argument in this chapter if we understand the difference between the believer's position and his practice. His position is his standing in Christ. His practice is what he is or should be in everyday life.

Grace puts us into the position, then teaches us to walk worthy of it. Our position is absolutely perfect because we are *in Christ.* Our practice should increasingly correspond to our position. It never will correspond perfectly until we see the Savior in heaven, but we should be becoming more and more conformed to His image in the meantime.

The apostle first sets forth the truth of our identification with Christ in death and resurrection, and then exhorts us to live in the light of this great truth.

6:1 The Jewish objector comes forward with what he thinks is a clinching argument. If the gospel of grace teaches that man's sin provides for an even greater display of God's grace, then doesn't it suggest that **we** should **continue in sin that grace may** be all the more abundant?

A modern version of this argument is as follows: "You say that men are saved by grace through faith, apart from the law. But if all you have to do to be saved is believe, then you could go out and live in sin." According to this argument, grace is not a sufficient motivation for holy living. You must put people under the restraints of the law.

It has been helpfully suggested that there are four answers in the chapter to the initial question, **Shall we continue in sin?**

1. You *cannot,* because you are united to Christ. Reasoning (vv. 1–11).
2. You *need not,* because sin's dominion has been broken by grace. Appealing (vv. 12–14).
3. You *must not,* because it would bring sin in again as your master. Commanding (vv. 15–19).
4. You *had better not,* for it would end in disaster. Warning (vv. 20–23).[17]

6:2 Paul's first answer, then, is that we cannot continue in sin because we have **died to sin.** This is a positional truth. When Jesus died to sin, He died as our Representative. He died not only as our *Substitute* — that is, *for* us or *in our place* — but He also died as our *Representative* — that is, *as* us. Therefore, when He died, we died. He died to the whole question of sin, settling it once and for all. All those who are in Christ are seen by God as having died to sin.

This does not mean that the believer is sinless. It means that he is identified with Christ in His death, and in all that His death means.

6:3 The first key word in Paul's presentation is **KNOW**. Here he introduces the subject of baptism to show that it is morally incongruous for believers to go on in sin. But the question immediately arises, "To which baptism is he referring?" So an introductory word of explanation is necessary.

When a person is saved, he is **baptized into Christ Jesus** in the sense that he is identified with Christ in **His death** and resurrection. This is not the same as the baptism in (or of) the Spirit, though both occur simultaneously. The latter baptism places the believer in the body of Christ (1 Cor. 12:13); it is not a baptism **into** death. The baptism **into Christ** means that in the reckoning of God, the believer has died with Christ and has risen with Him.

When Paul speaks of baptism here, he is thinking both of our spiritual identification with Christ and of its portrayal in water baptism. But as the argument advances, he seems to shift his emphasis in a special way to water baptism as he reminds his readers how they were "buried" and "planted together" in the "likeness" of Christ's death.

The NT never contemplates the abnormal situation of an unbaptized believer. It assumes that those who are converted submit to baptism right away. Thus our Lord could speak of faith and baptism in the same breath: "he who believes and is baptized will be saved" (Mark 16:16). Though baptism is not a requirement for salvation, it should be the invariable public sign of it.

6:4 Water **baptism** gives a visual demonstration of **baptism** into Christ. It pictures the believer being immersed in death's dark waters (in the person of the Lord Jesus), and it pictures the new man in Christ rising to walk in newness of life. There is a sense in which a believer attends the funeral of his old self when he is baptized. As he goes under the water he is saying, "All that I was as a sinful son of Adam was put to death at the cross." As he comes up out of the water he is saying, "It is no longer I who live, but Christ lives in me" (see Gal. 2:20).

Conybeare and Howson state that "this passage cannot be understood unless it be borne in mind that the primitive baptism was by immersion."

The apostle moves on to state that the resurrection of Christ makes it possible for us to **walk in newness of life**. He states that **Christ was raised from the dead by the glory of the Father**. This simply means that all the divine perfections of God — His righteousness, love, justice, etc. — demanded that He raise the Lord. In view of the excellence of the Person of the Savior, it would not have been consistent with God's character to leave the Savior in the tomb. God *did* raise Him, and because we are identified with Christ in His resurrection, **we** can and **should walk in newness of life.**

6:5 Just as **we have been united together** with Christ **in the likeness of His death, certainly we also shall be** united with Him **in the likeness of His resurrection**. The words **the likeness of His death** refer to the believer's being put under the water in baptism. The actual union with Christ in His death took place nearly 2000 years ago, but baptism is a "likeness" of what happened then.

We not only go under the water; we come up out of the water, a **likeness of His resurrection**. While it is true that the phrase **in the likeness** is not part of the original text in the second part of this verse, it must be supplied to complete the meaning.

Just as we **have been united** with Christ **in the likeness of His death** (immersion in water), so **we** are united with Him **in the likeness of His resurrection** (being raised out of the water). The clause **we shall be** does not necessarily indicate futurity. Hodge says:

> The reference is not to what is to happen hereafter, but to the certainty of sequence, or causal connection. If the one thing happens, the other shall surely follow.[18]

6:6 We confess in baptism **that our old man was crucified with** Christ. **Our old man** refers to all that we were as children of Adam — our old, evil, unregenerate selves, with all our old habits and appetites. At conversion we put off the **old man** and put on the new man, as if exchanging filthy rags for spotless clothing (Col. 3:9, 10).

The crucifixion of **the old man** at Calvary means **that the body of sin** has been put out of commission. **The body of sin** does not refer to the physical body. Rather, it means indwelling sin which is personified as a tyrant, ruling the person. This body of sin **is done away with**, that is, *annulled* or *rendered inoperative as a controlling power*. The last clause shows that this is the meaning: **that we should no longer be slaves of sin**. The tyranny of sin over us has been broken.

6:7 For he who has died has been freed from sin. Here is a man, for example, who is sentenced to die in the electric chair for murdering a police officer. As soon as he dies, **he** is **freed** (literally "justified") **from** that sin. The penalty has been paid and the case is closed.

Now we have died with Christ on the cross of Calvary. Not only has our penalty been paid, but sin's stranglehold on our lives has been broken. We are no longer the helpless captives of sin.

6:8 Our death **with Christ** is one side of the truth. The other side is **that we shall also live with Him**. We **died** to sin; we live to righteousness. Sin's dominion over us has been shattered; we share Christ's resurrection life here and now. And we shall share it for all eternity, praise His name!

6:9 Our confidence is based on the fact that the risen Christ will never die again. **Death no longer has dominion over Him**. Death did have dominion over Him for three days and nights, but that dominion is forever passed. Christ can never die again!

6:10 When the Lord Jesus **died, He died to** the whole subject of **sin once for all. He died** to sin's claims, its wages, its demands, its penalty. He finished the work and settled the account so perfectly that it never needs to be repeated. Now that **He lives, He lives to God**. In one sense, of course, He always lived to God. But now **He lives to God** in a new relationship, as the Risen One, and in a new sphere, where sin can never enter.

Before going on, let us review the first ten verses. The general subject is *sanctification* — God's method for holy living. As to our standing before God, we are seen as having died with Christ and having risen with Him. This is pictured in baptism. Our death with Christ ends our history as men and women in Adam. God's sentence on our old man was not reformation but death. And that sentence was carried out when we died with Christ. Now we are risen with Christ to walk in newness of life. Sin's tyranny over us has been broken, because sin has nothing to say to a dead person. Now we are free to live for God.

6:11 Paul has described what is true of us *positionally*. Now he turns to the *practical outworking* of this truth in our lives. We are to **RECKON** ourselves **to be dead to sin, but alive to God in Christ Jesus our Lord**.

To **reckon** here means to accept what God says about us as true and to live in the light of it. Ruth Paxson writes:

> [It means] believing what God says in Romans 6:6 and knowing it as a fact in one's own personal salvation. This demands a definite act of faith, which results in a fixed attitude toward "the old man." We will see him where God sees him — on the Cross, put to death with Christ. Faith will operate continuously to keep him where grace placed him. This involves us very deeply, for it means that our hearty consent has been given to God's condemnation of and judgment upon that old "I" as altogether unworthy to live and as wholly stripped of any further claims upon us. The first step in a walk of practical holiness is this reckoning upon the crucifixion of "the old man."[19]

We **reckon** ourselves **dead to sin** when we respond to temptation as a dead man would. One day Augustine was accosted by a woman who had been his mistress before his conversion. When he turned and walked away quickly, she called after him, "Augustine, it's me! it's me!" Quickening his pace, he called back over his shoulder, "Yes, I know, but it's no longer me!"[20] What he meant was that he was **dead to sin** and **alive to God**. A dead man has nothing to do with immorality, lying, cheating, gossiping, or any other sin.

Now we are **alive to God in Christ Jesus**. This means that we are called to holiness, worship, prayer, service, and fruitbearing.

6:12 We saw in 6:6 that our old man

was crucified so that sin as a reigning tyrant might be knocked out, so that we would no longer be the helpless captives of sin. Now the practical exhortation is based on what is true positionally. We should **not let sin reign in** our **mortal** bodies by obeying its evil desires. At Calvary the reign of sin was ended by death. Now we must make it so practically. Our cooperation is needed. Only God can make us holy, but He will not do it without our willing involvement.

6:13 That brings us to the third key word in this chapter — **PRESENT**. We must **not present** the **members** of our body **to sin**, to be used as weapons or tools of wickedness. Our obligation is to turn control of our members **to God**, to be used in the cause of **righteousness**. After all, we have been raised to life from death; and, as we are reminded in 6:4, we should walk in newness of life.

6:14 Now another reason is given why **sin shall not have dominion over** us as believers. The first reason was that our old man was crucified with Christ (6:6). The second reason is that we **are not under law but under grace**.

Sin does have the upper hand over a person who is under law. Why? Because the law tells him what to do but doesn't give him the power to do it. And the law stirs up dormant desires in fallen human nature to do what is forbidden. It's the old story that "forbidden fruit is sweet."

Sin does **not have dominion over** the person who is under grace. The believer has died to sin. He has received the indwelling Holy Spirit as the power for holy living. And he is motivated by love for the Savior, not by fear of punishment. **Grace** is the only thing that really produces holiness. As Denney says, "It is not restraint but inspiration that liberates from sin; not Mount Sinai but Mount Calvary which makes saints."[21]

6:15 Those who are afraid of **grace** insist that it gives license for sinning. Paul meets this error head-on by asking the question, then flatly denying it. We are free from the law but not lawless. **Grace** means freedom to serve the Lord, not to sin against Him.

In 6:1 the question was, "Shall we continue in sin?" Here the question is, **"Shall we sin"** just a little?" The answer in both cases is a horrified **"Certainly**

not!"** God cannot condone any sin at all.

6:16 It is a simple fact of life that when we submit ourselves to someone as our master we become that person's slave. Likewise, if we sell out to sin, we become **slaves** of sin, and eternal **death** lies waiting at the end of that road. If, on the other hand, we choose to obey God, the result is a holy life. Sin's slaves are bound by guilt, fear, and misery, but God's servants are free to do what the new nature loves. So why be a slave when you can be free?

6:17 "Thank God that you, who were at one time the servants of sin, honestly responded to the impact of Christ's teaching when you came under its influence" (JBP). The Roman Christians had given wholehearted obedience to the gospel of grace to which they had been committed, including all the **doctrine** Paul teaches in this Letter.

6:18 Correct doctrine should lead to correct duty. Responding to the truth that they had **been set free from sin** as master, they **became slaves of righteousness**. The phrase **free from sin** does not mean that they no longer had a sinful nature. Neither does it mean that they no longer committed acts of sin. The context shows that it is referring to freedom from sin as the dominating power in life.

6:19 In verse 18 the apostle spoke of slaves of righteousness, but he realizes that those who live righteously are not actually in bondage. "Practical righteousness is not slavery, except when we speak after the manner of men."[22] Those who practice sin are slaves of sin, but those whom the Son sets free are free indeed (John 8:34, 36).

Paul explains that, in using the simile of **slaves** and master, he is speaking **in human terms**; that is, he is using a familiar illustration from everyday life. He does this **because of the weakness of** their **flesh** — in other words, because of their intellectual and spiritual difficulty in understanding truth when it is stated in general terms. Truth often needs to be illustrated in order to become intelligible.

Before their conversion the believers had surrendered their bodies **as slaves of** all kinds of **uncleanness** and to one kind of wickedness after another. Now they should dedicate those same bodies **as** slaves of righteousness, so that their lives would be truly holy.

6:20 When they were slaves of sin, the only freedom they knew was freedom from righteousness. It was a desperate condition to be in — bound by every evil and free from every good!

6:21 Paul challenges them (and us) to inventory the fruits of an unsaved life, fruits in those activities of which believers are now ashamed. Marcus Rainsford has drawn up such an inventory, as follows:

1. Faculties abused. 2. Affections prostrated. 3. Time squandered. 4. Influence misused. 5. Best friends wronged. 6. Our best interests violated. 7. Love outraged — especially the love of God. Or to sum it up in one word — SHAME.[23]

The end of those things is death. "Every sin," writes A. T. Pierson, "tends to death, and, if persisted in, ends in death as its goal and fruit."[24]

6:22 Conversion changes a man's position completely. Now he is free from sin as his master, and he becomes a willing slave to God. The result is a holy life now and everlasting life at the end of the journey. Of course the believer has eternal life now too, but this verse refers to that life in its fullness, including the glorified resurrection body.

6:23 The apostle summarizes the subject by presenting these vivid contrasts:

Two masters — sin and God.

Two methods — wages and free gift.

Two aftermaths — death and eternal life.

Notice that eternal life is in a Person, and that Person is Christ Jesus our Lord. All who are in Christ have eternal life. It's as simple as that!

I. The Place of the Law in the Believer's Life (Chap. 7)

The apostle now anticipates a question that will inevitably arise: *What is the relationship of the Christian to the law?* Perhaps Paul had Jewish believers especially in mind in answering this question, since the law was given to Israel, but the principles apply just as much to Gentile believers who foolishly want to put themselves under the law as a rule of life after they have been justified.

In chapter 6 we saw that death ended the tyranny of the sin nature in the life of the child of God. Now we will see that death likewise ends the dominion of the law over those who were under it.

7:1 This verse is connected with 6:14: "You are not under law but under grace." The connection is, "You should know that you are not under law — or are you ignorant of the fact that the law has dominion over a man only when he is alive?" Paul is speaking to those who are familiar with fundamental principles of law, and who therefore should know that the law has nothing to say to a dead man.

7:2 To illustrate this, Paul shows how death breaks the marriage contract. A woman is bound by the marriage law to her husband as long as he lives. But if he dies, she is released from that law.

7:3 If a woman marries another man while her husband is living, she is guilty of adultery. If, however, her husband dies, she is free to marry again without any cloud or guilt of wrongdoing.

7:4 In applying the illustration, we must not press each detail with exact literalness. For example, *neither* the husband *nor* the wife represents the law. The point of the illustration is that just as death breaks the marriage relationship, so the death of the believer with Christ breaks the jurisdiction of the law over him.

Notice that Paul does *not* say that the law is dead. The law still has a valid ministry in producing conviction of sin. And remember that when he says "we" in this passage, he is thinking of those who were Jews before they came to Christ.

We have been made dead to the law through the body of Christ, the body here referring to the giving up of His body in death. We are no longer joined to the law; we are now joined to the risen Christ. One marriage has been broken by death, and a new one has been formed. And now that we are free from the law, we can bear fruit to God.

7:5 This mention of fruit brings to mind the kind of fruit we bore when we were in the flesh. The expression in the flesh obviously doesn't mean "in the body." In the flesh here is descriptive of our standing before we were saved. Then the flesh was the basis of our standing before God. We depended on what we were or what we could do to win acceptance with God. **In the flesh** is the opposite of "in Christ."

Prior to our conversion we were ruled by **sinful passions which were aroused by the law**. It is not that the law *originated* them, but only that by naming and then forbidding them it stirred up the strong desire to *do* them!

These **sinful passions** found expression in our physical members, and when we yielded to temptation we produced poison fruit that results in **death**. Elsewhere the apostle speaks of this fruit as the works of the flesh: "adultery, fornication, uncleanness, lewdness, idolatry, sorcery, hatred, contentions, jealousies, outbursts of wrath, selfish ambitions, dissensions, heresies, envy, murders, drunkenness, revelries" (Gal. 5:19–21).

7:6 Among the many wonderful things that happen when we are converted is that we are **delivered from the law**. This is a result of our having died with Christ. Since He died as our Representative, we **died** with Him. In His death He fulfilled all the claims of the law by paying its awful penalty. Therefore we are free from the law and from its inevitable curse. There can be no double jeopardy.

> Payment God will not twice demand —
> First at my bleeding Surety's hand
> And then again at mine.
> *– Augustus M. Toplady*

We are now set free to **serve in the newness of the Spirit and not in the oldness of the letter**. Our service is motivated by love, not fear; it is a service of freedom, not bondage. It is no longer a question of slavishly adhering to minute details of forms and ceremonies but of the joyful outpouring of ourselves for the glory of God and the blessing of others.

7:7 It might seem from all this that Paul is *critical* of the law. He had said that believers are dead to sin and dead to the law, and this might have created the impression that the law is evil. But this is far from the case.

In 7:7–13 he goes on to describe the important role which the law played in his own life before he was saved. He emphasizes that the law itself is not sinful, but that it *reveals sin in man*. It was the law that convicted him of the terrible depravity of his heart. As long as he compared himself with other people, he felt fairly respectable. But as soon as the demands of God's law came home to him in convicting power, he stood speechless and condemned.

The one particular commandment that revealed sin to him was the tenth: **You shall not covet**. Coveting takes place in the mind. Although Paul may not have committed any of the grosser, more revolting sins, he now realized that his thought life was corrupt. He understood that evil thoughts are sinful as well as evil deeds. He had a polluted thought life. His outward life may have been relatively blameless, but his inward life was a chamber of horrors.

7:8 **Sin, taking opportunity by the commandment, produced in me all manner of evil desire. Evil desire** here means coveting. When the law forbids all kinds of evil coveting, man's corrupt nature is inflamed all the more to do it. For example, the law says, in effect, "You must not conjure up all sorts of pleasurable sexual encounters in your mind. You must not live in a world of lustful fantasies." The law forbids a dirty, vile, suggestive thought-life. But unfortunately it doesn't give the power to overcome. So the result is that people under law become more involved in a dream-world of sexual uncleanness than ever before. They come to realize that whenever an act is forbidden, the fallen nature wants to do it all the more. "Stolen water is sweet, and bread eaten in secret is pleasant" (Prov. 9:17).

Apart from the law sin is dead, relatively speaking. The sinful nature is like a sleeping dog. When the law comes and says "Don't," the dog wakes up and goes on a rampage, doing excessively whatever is forbidden.

7:9 Before being convicted by the law Paul was **alive**; that is, his sinful nature was *comparatively* dormant and he was blissfully ignorant of the pit of iniquity in his heart.

But when the commandment came — that is, when it came with crushing conviction — his sinful nature became thoroughly inflamed. The more he tried to obey, the worse he failed. He **died** as far as any hope of achieving salvation by his own character or efforts was concerned. He **died** to any thought of his own inherent goodness. He **died** to any dream of being justified by law-keeping.

7:10 He found that **the commandment, which was to bring life** actually turned out to **bring death** for him. But what does he mean that the commandment **was to bring life**? This probably looks back to Leviticus 18:5, where God said, "You shall therefore keep My statutes and My judgments, which if a man does, he shall live by them: I *am* the Lord." *Ideally* the law promised life to those who kept it. The sign outside a lion's cage says, "Stay back of the railing." If obeyed, the commandment brings life. But for the child who disobeys and reaches in to pet the lion, it brings death.

7:11 Again Paul emphasizes that the law was not to blame. It was indwelling **sin** that incited him to do what the law prohibited. Sin tricked him into thinking that the forbidden fruit wasn't so bad after all, that it would bring happiness, and that he could get away with it. It suggested that God was withholding pleasures from him that were for his good. Thus sin **killed** him in the sense that it spelled death to his best hopes of deserving or earning salvation.

7:12 **The law** itself **is holy, and** each **commandment is holy and just and good**. In our thinking we must constantly remember that there is nothing wrong with the law. It was given by God and therefore is perfect as an expression of His will for His people. The weakness of the law lay in the "raw materials" it had to work with: it was given to people who were already sinners. They needed the law to give them the knowledge of sin, but beyond that they needed a Savior to deliver them from the penalty and power of sin.

7:13 **What is good** refers to the law, as is specifically stated in the preceding verse. Paul raises the question "Did the law **become death to me?**" which means "Is the law the culprit, dooming Paul (and all the rest of us) to death?" The answer, of course, is **"Certainly not!"**

Sin is the culprit. The law didn't originate sin, but it showed sin in all its exceeding sinfulness. "By the law *is* the knowledge of sin" (3:20b). But that is not all! How does man's sinful nature respond when God's holy law forbids it to do something? The answer is well-known. What may have been dormant desire now becomes a burning passion! Thus **sin through the commandment** becomes **exceedingly sinful**.

There might seem to be a contradiction between what Paul says here and in 7:10. There he said he found the law to bring death. Here he denies that the law became death to him. The solution is this: The law by itself can neither improve the old nature on the one hand nor cause it to sin on the other. It can reveal sin, just as a thermometer reveals the temperature. But it cannot *control* sin like a thermostat controls the temperature.

But what happens is this. Man's fallen human nature instinctively wants to do whatever is forbidden. So it uses the law to awaken otherwise-dormant lusts in the sinner's life. The more man tries, the worse it gets, till at last he is brought to despair of all hope. Thus sin uses the law to cause any hope of improvement to die in him. And he sees the exceeding sinfulness of his old nature as he never saw it before.

7:14 Up to this point the apostle has been describing a past experience in his life — namely, the traumatic crisis when he underwent deep conviction of sin through the law's ministry.

Now he changes to the present tense to describe an experience he had since he was born again — namely, the conflict between the two natures and the impossibility of finding deliverance from the power of indwelling sin through his own strength. Paul acknowledges **that the law is spiritual** — that is, holy in itself and adapted to man's spiritual benefit. But he realizes that he is **carnal** because he is not experiencing victory over the power of indwelling sin in his life. He is **sold under sin**. He feels as if he is sold as a slave with sin as his master.

7:15 Now the apostle describes the struggle that goes on in a believer who does not know the truth of his identification with Christ in death and resurrection. It is the conflict between the two natures in the person who climbs Mount Sinai in search of holiness. Harry Foster explains:

> Here was a man trying to achieve holiness by personal effort, struggling with all his might to fulfill God's "holy and righteous and good" commandments (v.12), only to discover that the more he struggled, the worse his condition became. It was a losing battle, and no wonder, for it is not in the power of fallen human nature to conquer sin and live in holiness.[25]

Notice the prominence of the first-person pronouns — I, me, my, myself; they occur over forty times in verses 9–25! People who go through this Romans 7 experience have taken an overdose of "Vitamin I." They are introspective to the core, searching for victory in self, where it cannot be found.

Sadly, most modern Christian psychological counseling focuses the counselee's attention on himself and thus adds to the problem instead of relieving it. People need to know that they have died with Christ and have risen with Him to walk in newness of life. Then, instead of trying to improve the flesh, they will relegate it to the grave of Jesus.

In describing the struggle between the two natures, Paul says, **what I am doing, I do not understand**. He is a split personality, a Dr. Jekyll and Mr. Hyde. He finds himself indulging in things that he doesn't want to do, and practicing things that he hates.

7:16 In thus committing acts which his better judgment condemns, he is taking sides **with the law** against himself, because the law condemns them too. So he gives inward assent that the law is **good**.

7:17 This leads to the conclusion that the culprit is not the new man in Christ, but the sinful, corrupt nature that dwells in him. But we must be careful here. We must not excuse our sinning by passing it off to indwelling **sin**. *We* are responsible for what we do, and we must not use this verse to "pass the buck." All Paul is doing here is tracking down the source of his sinful behavior, not excusing it.

7:18 There can be no progress in holiness until we learn what Paul learned here — **that in me (that is, in my flesh) nothing good dwells**. The **flesh** here means the evil, corrupt nature which is inherited from Adam and which is still in every believer. It is the source of every evil action which a person performs. There is nothing good in it.

When we learn this, it delivers us from ever looking for any good in the old nature. It delivers us from being disappointed when we don't find any good there. And it delivers us from occupation with ourselves. There is no victory in introspection. As the saintly Scot, Robert Murray McCheyne said, for every look we take at ourselves, we should take ten looks at Christ.

To confirm the hopelessness of the flesh, the apostle mourns that although he has the desire to do what is right, he doesn't have the resources in himself to translate his desire into action. The trouble, of course, is that he is casting his anchor inside the boat.

7:19 Thus the conflict between the two natures rages on. He finds himself failing to do **the good** he wants to do, and instead doing **the evil** that he despises. He is just one great mass of contradictions and paradoxes.

7:20 We might paraphrase this verse as follows: **"Now if I** (the old nature) **do what I** (the new nature) don't want **to do, it is no longer I** (the person) **who do it, but sin that dwells** within **me."** Again let it be clear that Paul is not excusing himself or disclaiming responsibility. He is simply stating that he has not found deliverance from the power of indwelling sin, and that when he sins, it is not with the desire of the new man.

7:21 He finds a principle or **law** at work in his life causing all his good intentions to end in failure. When he wants to do what is right, he ends up by sinning.

7:22 As far as his new nature is concerned, he delights **in the law of God**. He knows that the law is holy, and that it is an expression of the will of God. He wants to do God's will.

7:23 But he sees a contrary principle at work in his life, striving against the new nature, and making him a captive **of** indwelling **sin**. George Cutting writes:

> The law, though he delights in it after the inward man, gives him no power. In other words, he is trying to accomplish what God has declared to be an utter impossibility — namely, making the flesh subject to God's holy law. He finds that the flesh minds the things of the flesh, and is very enmity itself to the law of God, and even to God Himself.[26]

7:24 Now Paul lets out his famous, eloquent groan. He feels as if he has a decomposing body strapped to his back. That **body**, of course, is the old nature in all its corruption. In his wretchedness he acknowledges that he is unable to deliver himself from this offensive, repulsive bondage. He must have help from some outside source.

7:25 The burst of thanksgiving which opens this verse may be understood in at least two ways. It may mean **"I thank God** that deliverance comes **through Jesus Christ our Lord"** or it may be an aside in which Paul thanks God **through** the Lord **Jesus** that he is no longer the wretched man of the preceding verse.

The rest of the verse summarizes the conflict between the two natures before deliverance is realized. **With the** renewed **mind**, or the new nature, the believer serves **the law of God, but with the flesh** (or old nature) **the law of sin.** Not till we reach the next chapter do we find the way of deliverance explained.

J. The Holy Spirit as the Power for Holy Living (Chap. 8)

The subject of holy living continues. In chapter 6 Paul had answered the question, "Does the teaching of the gospel (salvation by faith alone) permit or even encourage sinful living?" In chapter 7 he faced up to the question, "Does the gospel tell Christians to keep the law in order to lead a holy life?" Now the question is: *How is the Christian enabled to live a holy life?*

We notice right away that the personal pronouns that were so prominent in chapter 7 largely disappear, and that the Holy Spirit becomes the dominant Person. This is an important key to understanding the passage. Victory is not in ourselves but in the Holy Spirit, who indwells us. A. J. Gordon lists seven helps of the Spirit: freedom in service (v. 2); strength for service (v. 11); victory over sin (v. 13); guidance in service (v. 14); the witness of sonship (v. 16); assistance in service (v. 26); assistance in prayer (v. 26).

8:1 From the valley of despair and defeat, the apostle now climbs the heights with the triumphant shout, **There is therefore now no condemnation to those who are in Christ Jesus**! This may be understood in two ways.

First, there is **no divine condemnation** as far as our sin is concerned, because we are in Christ. There was condemnation as long as we were in our first federal head, Adam. But now we are in Christ and therefore are as free from condemnation as He is. So we can hurl out the challenge:

> Reach my blest Savior first,
>   Take Him from God's esteem;
> Prove Jesus bears one spot of sin,
>   Then tell me I'm unclean.
>   – *W. N. Tomkins*

But it may also mean that there is no need for the kind of self-condemnation which Paul described in chapter 7. We may pass through a Romans 7 experience, unable to fulfill the law's requirements by our own effort, but we don't have to stay there. Verse 2 explains why there is **no condemnation**.[27]

8:2 The Spirit's law of **life in Christ Jesus has made us free from the law of sin and death**. These are two opposite laws or principles. The characteristic principle of the Holy Spirit is to empower believers for holy living. The characteristic principle of indwelling sin is to drag a person down to death. It is like the law of gravity. When you throw a ball into the air, it comes back down because it is heavier than the air it displaces. A living bird is also heavier than the air it displaces, but when you toss it up in the air, it flies away. The law of *life* in the bird overcomes the law of gravity. So the Holy Spirit supplies the risen life of the Lord Jesus, making the believer **free from the law of sin and death.**

8:3 The law could never get people

to fulfill its sacred requirements, but grace has succeeded where law failed. Let us see how!

The law could not produce holy living because **it was weak through the flesh**. The trouble was not with the law but with fallen human nature. The law spoke to men who were already sinners and who were without strength to obey. But God intervened **by sending His own Son in the likeness of sinful flesh**. Take careful notice that the Lord Jesus did not come in sinful flesh itself but in **"the likeness of" sinful flesh**. He did no sin (1 Pet. 2:22), He knew no sin (2 Cor. 5:21), and there was no sin in Him (1 Jn. 3:5). But by coming into the world in human form, He resembled sinful humanity. As a sacrifice for sin, Christ **condemned sin in the flesh**. He died not only for the sins which we commit (1 Pet. 3:18) but also for our sin nature. In other words, He died for what we *are* just as much as for what we have *done*. In so doing, **He condemned sin in the flesh**. Our sin nature is never said to be forgiven; it is **condemned**. It is the sins that we have *committed* that are forgiven.

8:4 Now **the righteous requirement of the law** is **fulfilled in us who do not walk according to the flesh but according to the Spirit**. As we turn over the control of our lives to the Holy Spirit, He empowers us to love God and to love our neighbor, and that, after all, is what the law requires.

In these first four verses the apostle has gathered together the threads of his argument from 5:12 to 7:25. In 5:12–21 he had discussed the federal headships of Adam and of Christ. Now in 8:1 he shows that the condemnation which we inherited from our identification with Adam is removed by our identification with Christ. In chapters 6 and 7 he discussed the horrendous problem of sin in the nature. Now he announces triumphantly that the Spirit's law of life in Christ Jesus has made us free from the law of sin and death. In chapter 7 the whole subject of the law was brought up. Now we learn that the law's requirements are met by the Spirit-controlled life.

8:5 Those who live according to the flesh — that is, those who are

unconverted — are concerned with **the things of the flesh**. They obey the impulses of the flesh. They live to gratify the desires of the corrupt nature. They cater to the body, which in a few short years will return to dust.

But those who live according to the Spirit — that is, true believers — rise above flesh and blood and live for those things that are eternal. They are occupied with the word of God, prayer, worship, and Christian service.

8:6 To be carnally minded — that is, the mental inclination of the fallen nature — **is death**. It is death as far as both present enjoyment and ultimate destiny are concerned. It has all the potential of death in it, just like an overdose of poison.

But **to be spiritually minded is life and peace**. The Spirit of God is the guarantee of life that is life indeed, of peace with God, and of a life of tranquility.

8:7 The mind-set of the flesh is death because it **is enmity against God**. The sinner is a rebel against God and in active hostility to Him. If any proof were needed, it is seen most clearly in the crucifixion of the Lord Jesus Christ. The mind of the flesh **is not subject to the law of God**. It wants its own will, not God's will. It wants to be its own master, not to bow to His rule. Its nature is such that it cannot be subject to God's law. It is not only the *inclination* that is missing but the *power* as well. The flesh is dead toward God.

8:8 It is no surprise, therefore, that **those who are in the flesh cannot please God**. Think of that! There is nothing an unsaved person can do to **please God** — no good works, no religious observances, no sacrificial services, absolutely nothing. First he must take the guilty sinner's place and receive Christ by a definite act of faith. Only then can He win God's smile of approval.

8:9 When a person is born again, he is no longer **in the flesh but in the Spirit**. He lives in a different sphere. Just as a fish lives in water and a man lives in the air, so a believer lives in the Spirit. He not only lives in the Spirit, but the Spirit lives in him. In fact, if he is not indwelt by the Spirit of Christ, he does not belong to Christ. Though there is a question whether **the Spirit of Christ** here is the same as the Holy Spirit, the assumption that they are the same seems to fit best in the context.

8:10 Through the ministry of the Spirit, **Christ is** actually **in** the believer. It is amazing to think of the Lord of life and glory dwelling in our bodies, especially when we remember that these bodies are subject to death **because of sin**. Someone may argue that they are not dead yet, as the verse seems to say. No, but the forces of death are already working in them, and they will inevitably die if the Lord doesn't return in the meantime.

In contrast to the body, **the spirit**[28] **is life because of righteousness**. Though once dead toward God, it has been made alive through the righteous work of the Lord Jesus Christ in His death and resurrection, and because the righteousness of God has been credited to our account.

8:11 But the reminder that the body is still subject to death need cause no alarm or despair. The fact that **the** Holy **Spirit** indwells our bodies is a guarantee that, just as He **raised Christ from the dead**, so He **will also give life to** our **mortal bodies**. This will be the final act of our redemption — when our bodies are glorified like the Savior's body of glory.

8:12 Now when we see the stark contrast between the flesh and the Spirit, what conclusion do we draw? We owe nothing **to the flesh, to live according to** *its* dictates. The old, evil, corrupt nature has been nothing but a drag. It has never done us a bit of good. If Christ had not saved us, **the flesh** would have dragged us down to the deepest, darkest, hottest places in hell. Why should we feel obligated to such an enemy?

8:13 Those who **live according to the flesh** must **die**, not only physically but eternally. To **live according to the flesh** is to be unsaved. This is made clear in 8:4, 5. But why does Paul address this to those who were already Christians? Does he imply that some of them might eventually be lost? No, but the apostle often includes words of warning and self-examination in his Letters, realizing that in every congregation there may be some people who have never been genuinely born again.

The rest of the verse describes what is characteristically true of genuine believers. By the enablement of **the** Holy **Spirit** they **put to death the deeds of the body**. They enjoy eternal life now, and will enter into life in its fullness when they leave this earth.

8:14 Another way of describing true believers is to say that they **are led by the Spirit of God**. Paul is not referring here to spectacular instances of divine guidance in the lives of eminent Christians. Rather, he is speaking of what is true of all **sons of God** — namely, that they **are led by the Spirit of God**. It is not a question of the degree in which they are yielded to the Holy Spirit, but of a relationship which takes place at the time of conversion.

Sonship implies reception into God's family, with all the privileges and responsibilities of adult sons. A new convert does not have to wait a certain time before he enters into his spiritual inheritance; it is his the moment he is saved, and it applies to all believers, men and women, boys and girls.

8:15 Those living under law are like minor children, bossed around as if they were servants, and shadowed by the fear of punishment. But when a person is born again, he is not born into a position of servitude. He is not brought into God's household as a slave. Rather, he receives **the spirit of adoption**; that is, he is placed in God's family as a mature son. By a true spiritual instinct he looks up to God and calls Him **"Abba, Father."** **Abba** is an Aramaic word which suffers in translation. It is an intimate form of the word *father* — such as "papa" or "daddy." While we may hesitate to use such familiar English words in addressing God, the truth remains that He who is infinitely high is also intimately nigh.

The phrase **the Spirit**[29] **of adoption** may be a reference to the Holy Spirit as the One who makes the believer aware of his special dignity as a son. Or it may mean the realization or attitude of adoption in contrast to **the spirit of bondage**.

Adoption is used in three different ways in Romans. Here it refers to the consciousness of sonship which the Holy Spirit produces in the life of the believer. In 8:23 it *looks forward* to that time when the believer's body will be redeemed or glorified. In 9:4 it *looks back* to that time when God designated Israel as His son (Ex. 4:22).

In Galatians 4:5 and Ephesians 1:5, the word means "son-placing" — that is, the act of placing all believers as mature, adult sons with all the privileges and responsibilities of sonship. Every believer is a child of God in that he is born into a family of which God is the Father. But every believer is also a son — a special relationship carrying the privileges of one who has reached the maturity of manhood.

In the NT **adoption** *never* means what it means in our society — to take a child of other parents as one's own.

8:16 There is a spiritual instinct in the newborn believer that he is a son of God. The Holy **Spirit** tells him that it is so. **The Spirit Himself bears witness with** the believer's **spirit that** he is a member of God's family. He does it primarily through the word of God. As a Christian reads the Bible, the Spirit confirms the truth that, because he has trusted the Savior, he is now a child of God.

8:17 Membership in God's family brings privileges that boggle the mind. All God's **children** are **heirs of God**. An heir, of course, eventually inherits his father's estate. That is just what is meant here. All that the Father has is ours. We have not yet come into the possession and enjoyment of all of it, but nothing can prevent our doing so in the future. **And** we are **joint heirs with Christ**. When He returns to take the scepter of universal government, we will share with Him the title deeds to all the Father's wealth.

When Paul adds, **if indeed we suffer with Him, that we may also be glorified together**, he is not making heroic suffering a condition for salvation. Neither is he describing some elite inner circle of overcomers who have endured great afflictions. Rather, he sees all Christians as being co-sufferers and all Christians as **glorified** with Christ. The **if** is equivalent to "since." Of course, there are some who suffer more than others in the cause of Christ, and this will result in differing degrees of reward and glory. But all who acknowledge Jesus as Lord and Savior are seen here as incurring the hostility of the world, with all its shame and reproach.

8:18 The greatest shame we may endure for Christ here on earth will be a mere trifle when He calls us forth and publicly acknowledges us before the hosts of heaven. Even the excruciating pain of the martyrs will seem like pinpricks when the Savior graces their brows with the crown of life. Elsewhere Paul speaks of our present sufferings as light afflictions which are only for a moment, but he describes the glory as an exceeding and eternal weight (2 Cor. 4:17). Whenever he describes the coming glory, his words seem to bend under the weight of the idea.[30] If we could only appreciate **the glory** that is to be ours, we could count **the sufferings** along the way as trivia!

8:19 Now in a bold literary figure Paul personifies the whole **creation** as **eagerly** looking forward to the time when we will be revealed to a wondering world as **the sons of God**. This will be when the Lord Jesus returns to reign and we return with Him.

We are already **the sons of God**, but the world neither recognizes nor appreciates us as such. And yet the world is looking forward to a better day, and that day cannot come until the King returns to reign with all His saints. "The whole creation is on tiptoe to see the wonderful sight of the sons of God coming into their own" (JBP).

8:20 When Adam sinned, his transgression affected not only mankind, but all **creation**, both animate and inanimate. The ground is cursed. Many wild animals die violent deaths. Disease afflicts birds and animals as well as fish and serpents. The results of man's sin have rippled like shockwaves throughout all creation.

Thus, as Paul explains, **the creation was subjected to futility**, frustration, and disorder, **not** by its own choice, **but** by the decree of God because of the disobedience of man's first federal head.

The words **in hope** at the end of verse 20 may also be connected with the following verse: "in hope that the creation itself also will be set free" (NASB).

8:21 Creation looks back to the ideal conditions that existed in Eden. Then it surveys the havoc that was caused by the entrance of sin. Always there has been the hope of a return to an idyllic state, when **creation itself also will be delivered from the bondage of corruption** to enjoy the freedom of that golden era when we as God's **children** will be revealed in glory.

8:22 We live in a sighing, sobbing, suffering world. **The whole creation groans** and suffers pain like that of childbirth. Nature's music is in the minor key. The earth is racked by cataclysm. The blight of death is on every living thing.

8:23 Believers are not exempt. Although they **have the firstfruits of the Spirit**, guaranteeing their eventual deliverance, they still **groan** for that day of glory. **The** Holy **Spirit** Himself is **the firstfruits**. Just as the first handful of ripened grain is a pledge of the entire harvest to follow, so the Holy Spirit is the pledge or guarantee that the full inheritance will be ours.

Specifically, He is the guarantee of **the** coming **adoption, the redemption of** the **body** (Eph. 1:14). In one sense we have already been adopted, which means that we have been placed into God's family as sons. But in a fuller sense our **adoption** will be complete when we receive our glorified bodies. That is spoken of as **the redemption of our body**. Our spirits and souls have already been redeemed, and our bodies will be redeemed at the time of the Rapture (1 Thess. 4:13–18).

8:24 We were saved in this attitude of **hope**. We did not receive all the benefits of our salvation at the moment of conversion. From the outset we looked forward to full and final deliverance from sin, suffering, disease, and death. If we had already received these blessings, we wouldn't be hoping for them. We only hope for what is in the future.

8:25 Our hope for deliverance from the presence of sin and all its baneful results is based on the promise of God, and is therefore as certain as if we had already received it. So **we eagerly wait for it with perseverance**.

8:26 Just as we are sustained by this glorious hope, so **the Spirit** sustains us **in our weaknesses**. We are often perplexed in our prayer life. **We do not know** how to **pray as we** should. We

pray selfishly, ignorantly, narrowly. But once again the Spirit comes alongside to assist us in our weakness, interceding **for us with groanings which cannot** find expression. In this verse it is the Spirit who groans and not we who groan, though that is also true.

There is mystery here. We are peering into the unseen, spiritual realm where a great Person and great forces are at work on our behalf. And although we cannot understand it all, we can take infinite encouragement from the fact that a groan may sometimes be the most spiritual prayer.

8:27 If God **searches the hearts** of men, He can also interpret **the mind of the Spirit**, even though that mind finds expression only in groans. The important thing is that the Holy Spirit's prayers for us are always **according to the will of God**. And because they are always in accordance with God's will, they are always for our good. That explains a lot, as the next verse reveals.

8:28 God is working **all things together for good to those who love** Him, **to those who are called according to His purpose**. It may not always seem so! Sometimes when we are suffering heartbreak, tragedy, disappointment, frustration, and bereavement, we wonder what good can come out of it. But the following verse gives the answer: whatever God permits to come into our lives is designed to conform us to the image of His Son. When we see this, it takes the question mark out of our prayers. Our lives are not controlled by impersonal forces such as chance, luck, or fate, but by our wonderful, personal Lord, who is "too loving to be unkind and too wise to err."

8:29 Now Paul traces the majestic sweep of the divine program designed to bring many sons to glory.

First of all, God **foreknew** us in eternity past. This was not a mere intellectual knowledge. As far as knowledge is concerned, He knew *everyone* who would ever be born. But His foreknowledge embraced only those whom He foreordained or **predestined to be conformed ... to the image of His Son**. So it was knowledge with a purpose that could never be frustrated. It is not enough to say that God **foreknew** those whom He realized would one day repent and believe. Actually it is His foreknowledge that insures eventual repentance and belief.

That ungodly sinners should one day be transformed into the image of Christ by a miracle of grace is one of the most astounding truths of divine revelation. The point is not, of course, that we will ever have the attributes of deity, or even that we will have Christ's facial resemblance, but that we will be *morally* like Him, absolutely free from sin, and will have glorified bodies like His.

In that day of glory **He** will **be the firstborn among many brethren. Firstborn** here means first in rank or honor. He will not be One among equals, but the One who has the supreme place of honor among His brothers and sisters.

8:30 Everyone who was **predestined** in eternity is **also called** in time. This means that he not only hears the gospel but that he responds to it as well. It is therefore an effectual call. All are called; that is the general (yet also valid) call of God. But only a few respond; that is the effectual (conversion-producing) call of God.

All who respond are **also justified** or given an absolutely righteous standing before God. They are clothed with the righteousness of God through the merits of Christ and are thereby fit for the presence of the Lord.

Those who are **justified** are **also glorified**. Actually we are *not* glorified as *yet*, but it is so sure that God can use the past tense in describing it. We are as certain of the glorified state as if we had already received it!

This is one of the strongest passages in the NT on the eternal security of the believer. For every million people who are foreknown and **predestined** by God, *every one* of that million will be **called**, **justified**, and **glorified**. Not one will be missing! (Compare the "all" in John 6:37.)

8:31 When we consider these unbreakable links in the golden chain of redemption, the conclusion is inevitable! **If God is for us**, in the sense that He has marked us out for Himself, then no one **can be** successful **against us.**[31] If Omnipotence is working on our behalf, no lesser power can defeat His program.

8:32 He who did not spare His own Son, but delivered Him up for us all. What marvelous words! We must never allow our familiarity with them to dull their luster or lessen their power to inspire worship. When a world of lost mankind needed to be saved by a sinless Substitute, the great God of the universe did not hold back His heart's best Treasure, but gave Him over to a death of shame and loss on our behalf.

The logic that flows from this is irresistible. If God has already given us the greatest gift, is there any lesser gift that He will not give? If He has already paid the highest price, will He hesitate to pay any lower price? If He has gone to such lengths to procure our salvation, will He ever let us go? **How shall He not with Him also freely give us all things?**

"The language of unbelief," Mackintosh said, "is, 'How shall He?' The language of faith is 'How shall He not?' "[32]

8:33 We are still in a courtroom setting, but now a remarkable change has taken place. While the justified sinner stands before the bench, the call goes out for any accusers to step forward. But there is none! How could there be? If God has already justified His elect, **who** can **bring a charge?**

It greatly clarifies the argument of this verse and the following one if we supply the words "No one, because . . ." before each answer. Thus this verse would read, **Who shall bring a charge against God's elect?** *No one, because* **it is God who justifies.** If we do not supply these words, it might sound as if God is going to bring a charge against His elect, the very thing that Paul is denying!

8:34 Another challenge rings out! Is there anyone here to condemn? *No one, because* **Christ** has **died** for the defendant, has been raised from the dead, is now **at the right hand of God** interceding for him. If the Lord Jesus, to whom all judgment has been committed, does not pass sentence on the defendant but rather prays for him, then there is no one else who could have a valid reason for condemning him.

8:35 Now faith flings its final challenge: is there anyone here who can banish the justified **from the love of Christ?** A search is made for every adverse circumstance that has been effective in causing separations in other areas of human life. But none can be found. Not the threshing flail of **tribulation** with its steady pounding of **distress** and affliction, nor the monster of anguish, bringing extreme pain to mind and body, nor the brutality of **persecution**, inflicting suffering and death on those who dare to differ. Nor can the gaunt specter of **famine** — gnawing, racking, and wasting down to the skeleton. Nor can **nakedness**, with all it means in the way of privation, exposure, and defenselessness. Nor can **peril** — the threat of imminent and awful danger. Nor can the **sword** — cold, hard, and death-dealing.

8:36 If any of these things could separate the believer from the love of Christ, then the fatal severance would have taken place long ago, because the career of the Christian is a living death. That is what the psalmist meant when he said that, because of our identification with the Lord, **we are killed all day long**, and are like **sheep** that are doomed to **slaughter** (Ps. 44:22).

8:37 Instead of separating us from Christ's love, these things only succeed in drawing us closer to Him. We are not only **conquerors**, but **more than conquerors**.[33] It is not simply that we triumph over these formidable forces, but that in doing so we bring glory to God, blessing to others, and good to ourselves. We make slaves out of our enemies and stepping stones out of our roadblocks.

But all of this is not through our own strength, but only **through Him who loved us**. Only the power of Christ can bring sweetness out of bitterness, strength out of weakness, triumph out of tragedy, and blessing out of heartbreak.

8:38 The apostle has not finished his search. He ransacks the universe for something that might conceivably separate us from God's love, then dismisses the possibilities one by one —

death with all its terrors;

life with all its allurements;

angels nor principalities, supernatural in power and knowledge;

powers, whether human tyrants or angelic adversaries;

things present, crashing in upon us;

things to come, arousing fearful forebodings;

8:39 **height nor depth**, those things that are in the realm of dimension or space, including occult forces.[34] Then, to make sure that he is not missing anything, Paul adds:

nor any other created thing.

The outcome of Paul's search is that he can find nothing that can **separate us from the love of God which is in Christ Jesus our Lord**.

No wonder these words of triumph have been the song of those who have died martyr's deaths and the rhapsody of those who have lived martyr's lives!

II. DISPENSATIONAL: THE GOSPEL AND ISRAEL (Chaps. 9–11)

A. Israel's Past (Chap. 9)

In chapters 9–11 we hear Paul's answer to the Jewish objector who asks: *Does the gospel, by promising salvation to Gentiles as well as Jews, mean that God has broken His promises to His earthly people, the Jews?* Paul's answer covers Israel's past (chap. 9), its present (chap. 10), and its future (chap. 11).

This section contains a great emphasis on divine sovereignty and human responsibility. Romans 9 is one of the key passages in the Bible on the sovereign election of God. The next chapter sets forth the balancing truth — the responsibility of man — with equal vigor.

DIVINE SOVEREIGNTY AND HUMAN RESPONSIBILITY

When we say that God is sovereign, we mean that He is in charge of the universe and that He can do as He pleases. In saying that, however, we know that, because He is God, He will never do anything wrong, unjust, or unrighteous. Therefore, to say that God is sovereign is merely to allow God to be God. We should not be afraid of this truth or apologize for it. It is a glorious truth and should cause us to worship.

In His sovereignty, God has elected or chosen certain individuals to belong to Himself. But the same Bible that teaches God's sovereign election also teaches human responsibility. While it is true that God elects people to salvation, it is also true they must choose to be saved by a definite act of the will. The divine side of salvation is seen in the words, "All that the Father gives Me will come to Me." The human side is found in the words that follow: "and the one who comes to Me I will by no means cast out" (John 6:37). We rejoice, as believers, that God chose us in Christ before the foundation of the world (Eph. 1:4). But we believe just as surely that whoever will may take of the water of life freely (Rev. 22:17). D. L. Moody illustrated the two truths this way: When we come to the door of salvation, we see the invitation overhead, "Whosoever will may come." When we pass through, we look back and see the words "Elect according to the foreknowledge of God" above the door. Thus the truth of man's responsibility faces people as they come to the door of salvation. The truth of sovereign election is a family truth for those who have already entered.

How can God choose individuals to belong to Himself and at the same time make a *bona fide* offer of salvation to all people everywhere? How can we reconcile these two truths? The fact is that we cannot. To the human mind they are in conflict. But the Bible teaches both doctrines, and so we should believe them, content to know that the difficulty lies in our minds and not in God's. These twin truths are like two parallel lines that meet only in infinity.

Some have tried to reconcile sovereign election and human responsibility by saying that God foreknew who would trust the Savior and that those are the ones whom He elected to be saved. They base this on Romans 8:29 ("whom He foreknew He also predestined") and 1 Peter 1:2 ("elect according to the foreknowledge of God"). But this overlooks the fact that God's foreknowledge is *determinative*. It is not just that He *knows* in advance who will trust the Savior, but that He *predetermines* this result by drawing certain individuals to Himself.

Although God chooses some men to be saved, He never chooses anyone to be damned. To put it another way, though the Bible teaches election, it never teaches divine reprobation. But someone may object, "If God elects some to blessing, then He necessarily elects others to destruction." But that is not true! The whole human race was doomed to destruction by its own sin and not by any arbitrary decree of God. If God allowed everyone to go to hell — and He could justly have done that — people would be getting exactly what they deserved. The question is, "Does the sovereign Lord have a right to stoop down and select a handful of otherwise-doomed people to be a bride for His Son?" The answer, of course, is that He does. So what it boils down to is this: if people are lost, it is because of their own sin and rebellion; if people are saved, it is because of the sovereign, electing grace of God.

To the man who is saved, the subject of God's sovereign choice should be the cause of unceasing wonder. The believer looks around and sees people with better characters, better personalities, and better dispositions than his own, and asks, "Why did the Lord choose me?"

> Why was I made to hear Thy voice,
> And enter while there's room,
> When thousands make a wretched choice,
> And rather starve than come?
> — *Isaac Watts*

The truth of election should not be used by the unsaved for excusing their unbelief. They must not say, "If I'm not elect, there's nothing I can do about it." The only way they can ever know they are elect is by repenting of their sins and receiving the Lord Jesus Christ as Savior (1 Thess. 1:4–7).

Neither should the truth of election be used by Christians to excuse a lack of evangelistic zeal. We must not say, "If they're elect, they'll be saved anyway." Only God knows who the elect are. We are commanded to preach the gospel to all the world, for God's offer of salvation is a genuine invitation to all people. People reject the gospel because of the hardness of their hearts, and not because God's universal invitation is insincere.

There are two dangers to be avoided in connection with this subject. The first is to hold only one side of the truth — for example, to believe in God's sovereign election and to deny that man has any responsible choice in connection with his salvation. The other danger is to overemphasize one truth at the expense of the other. The scriptural approach is to believe in God's sovereign election and to believe with equal force in human responsibility. Only in this way can a person hold these doctrines in their proper biblical balance. ‡

Now let us turn to Romans 9 and follow the beloved apostle as he unfolds this subject.

9:1 In insisting that salvation is for Gentiles as well as for Jews, Paul gave the appearance of being a traitor, a turncoat, a renegade as far as Israel was concerned. So he here protests his deep devotion to the Jewish people by using a solemn oath. He speaks **the truth**. He is **not lying**. His **conscience**, in fellowship with **the Holy Spirit**, attests the truth of what he is saying.

9:2 When he thinks first of Israel's glorious calling, and now of its rejection by God because it rejected the Messiah, his **heart** is filled with **great sorrow and continual grief**.

9:3 He **could** even **wish** himself **accursed** or cut off from Christ if through the forfeiting of his own salvation his Jewish brothers might be saved. In this strong statement of self-abnegation, we sense the highest form of human love — that which constrains a man to lay down his life for his friends (John 15:13). And we feel the enormous burden which a converted Jew experiences for the conversion of his **countrymen**. It reminds us of Moses' prayer for his people: "Yet now, if You will forgive their sin — but if not, I pray, blot me out of Your book which You have written" (Ex. 32:32).

9:4 As Paul weeps over his people, their glorious privileges pass in review. They **are Israelites**, members of God's ancient chosen people.

God had *adopted* that nation to be His son (Ex. 4:22) and delivered His people out of Egypt (Hos. 11:1). He was a father to Israel (Deut. 14:1), and Ephraim was His firstborn (Jer. 31:9). (*Ephraim* is used here as another name for the nation of Israel.)

The Shekinah or **glory** cloud symbolized God's presence in their midst, guiding and protecting them.

It was with Israel, not with the Gentiles, that God made the **covenants**. It was with Israel, for example, that He made the Palestinian Covenant, promising them the land from the River of Egypt to the Euphrates (Gen. 15:18). And it is with Israel that He will yet ratify the New Covenant, promising "the perpetuity, future conversion, and blessing of a repentant Israel (Jer. 31: 31-40)."[35]

It was to Israel that **the law** was given. They and they alone were its recipients.

The elaborate rituals and **service of God** connected with the tabernacle and the temple were given to Israel, as well as the priesthood.

In addition to the covenants mentioned above, God made innumerable **promises** to Israel of protection, peace, and prosperity.

9:5 The Jewish people rightfully claim the patriarchs as their own — Abraham, Isaac, Jacob, and the twelve sons of Jacob. These were the forefathers of the nation. And they had the greatest privilege of all — the Messiah is an Israelite, as far as His human descent is concerned, though He is also the Sovereign of the universe, **the eternally blessed God**. Here we have a positive statement of the deity and humanity of the Savior. (Some Bible versions weaken the force of this verse. For example, the RSV reads, ". . . and of their race, according to the flesh, is the Christ. God who is over all be blessed for ever. Amen." The Greek does not rule out the RSV here from a strictly grammatical viewpoint, but spiritual discernment in comparing Scripture with Scripture favors the reading in the KJV, NKJV, and other conservative translations.)[36]

9:6 The apostle now faces up to a serious theological problem. If God made promises to Israel as His chosen earthly people, how can this be squared with Israel's present rejection and with the Gentiles being brought into the place of blessing? Paul insists that this does not indicate any breach of promise on God's part. He goes on to show that God has always had a sovereign election process based upon promise and not just on lineal descent. Just because a person is born into the nation **of Israel** does not mean that he is an heir to the promises.

Within the nation **of Israel**, God has a true, believing remnant.

9:7 Not **all** Abraham's offspring are counted as his **children**. Ishmael, for example, was of **the seed of Abraham**. But the line of promise came through Isaac, not through Ishmael. The promise of God was, **"In Isaac your seed shall be called"** (Gen. 21:12). As we pointed out in the notes on 4:12, the Lord Jesus made this same interesting distinction when talking with the unbelieving Jews in John 8:33–39. They said to Him, "We are Abraham's descendants . . . " (v. 33). Jesus admitted this, saying, "I know you are Abraham's descendants" (v. 37). But when they said, "Abraham is our father," the Lord replied, "If you were Abraham's children, you would do the works of Abraham" (v. 39). In other words, they were descended from Abraham, but they didn't have Abraham's faith and therefore they were not his spiritual children.

9:8 It is not physical descent that counts. The true Israel consists of those Jews who were selected by God and to whom He made some specific **promise**, marking them out as His **children**. We see this principle of sovereign election in the cases of Isaac and Jacob.

9:9 God appeared to Abraham, promising that He would return **at the** appointed **time** and that **Sarah** would **have a son**. That son, of course, was Isaac. He was truly a child of **promise** and a child of supernatural birth.

9:10 Another case of sovereign election is found in the case of Jacob. **Isaac** and **Rebecca** were the parents, of course. But **Rebecca** was carrying *two* babies, not one.

9:11 A pronouncement was made before **the children** were ever **born**. This pronouncement could not, therefore, have had anything to do with works of merit by either child. It was entirely a matter of God's choice, based on His own will and not on the character or attainments of the subjects. **The purpose of God according to election** means His determination to distribute His favors according to His sovereign will and good pleasure.

This verse, incidentally, disproves the idea that God's choice of Jacob was based on His foreknowledge of what

Jacob would do. It specifically says that it was **not** made on the basis **of works!**

9:12 God's decision was that **the older** would **serve the younger**. Esau would have a subservient place to Jacob. The latter was chosen to *earthly glory and privilege*. Esau was the firstborn of the twin brothers and ordinarily would have had the honors and privileges associated with that position. But God's selection passed him by and rested on Jacob.

9:13 To further enforce God's sovereignty in choosing, Paul quotes Malachi 1:2, 3: **"Jacob I have loved, but Esau I have hated."** Here God is speaking of the two nations, Israel and Edom, of which **Jacob** and **Esau** were heads. God marked out Israel as the nation to which He promised the Messiah and the messianic kingdom. Edom received no such promise. Instead, its mountains and heritage were laid waste for the jackals of the wilderness (Mal. 1:3; see also Jer. 49:17, 18; Ezek. 35:7–9).

Although it is true that the quotation from Malachi 1:2, 3 describes God's dealings with nations rather than individuals, it is used to support His sovereign right to choose individuals as well.

The words **Jacob I have loved, but Esau I have hated** must be understood in the light of the sovereign decree of God that stated, **The older shall serve the younger**. The preference for Jacob is interpreted as an act of love, whereas bypassing Esau is seen as hatred *by comparison*. It is not that God hated Esau with a harsh, vindictive animosity, but only that He loved Esau less than Jacob, as seen by His sovereign selection of Jacob.

This passage refers to *earthly blessings*, and not to eternal life. God's hatred of Edom doesn't mean that individual Edomites *can't* be saved, any more than His love of Israel means that individual Jews *don't* need to be saved. (Note also that Esau *did* receive some earthly blessings, as he himself testified in Gen. 33:9.)

9:14 The apostle correctly anticipated that his teaching on sovereign election would stir up all kinds of objections. People still accuse God of unfairness. They say that if He chooses some, then He thereby necessarily damns the rest. They argue that if God has settled everything in advance, then there's nothing anyone can do about it, and God is unrighteous for condemning people.

Paul hotly denies any possibility of **unrighteousness** on God's part. But instead of watering down God's sovereignty in order to make it more palatable to these objectors, he proceeds to restate it more vigorously and without apology.

9:15 He first quotes God's word to Moses, **"I will have mercy on whomever I will have mercy, and I will have compassion on whomever I will have compassion"** (see Ex. 33:19). Who can say that the Most High, the Lord of heaven and earth, does not have the right to show **mercy** and **compassion**?

All people are condemned by their own sin and unbelief. If left to themselves, they would *all* perish. In addition to extending a genuine gospel invitation to all people, God chooses some of these condemned people to be special objects of His grace. But this does not mean that He arbitrarily chooses the others to be condemned. They are already condemned because they are lifelong sinners and have rejected the gospel. Those who are chosen can thank God for His grace. Those who are lost have no one to blame but themselves.

9:16 The conclusion, then, is that the ultimate destiny of men or of nations does not rest in the strength of their will or in the power of their exertions, but rather in the **mercy** of **God**.

When Paul says that **it is not of him who wills**, he does not mean that a person's will is not involved in his salvation. The gospel invitation is clearly directed to a person's will, as shown in Revelation 22:17: "Whoever desires, let him take the water of life freely." Jesus exposed the unbelieving Jews as being *unwilling* to come to Him (John 5:40). When Paul says, **nor of him who runs**, he does not deny that we must strive to enter the narrow gate (Luke 13:24). A certain amount of spiritual earnestness and willingness are necessary. But man's will and man's running are not the primary, determining factors: salvation is of the Lord. Morgan says:

> No willing on our part, no running on our own, can procure for us the salvation we need, or enable us to enter into the blessings it provides. . . . Of ourselves we shall have no will for salvation, and shall

make no effort toward it. Everything of human salvation begins in God.[37]

9:17 God's sovereignty is seen not only in showing mercy to some but in hardening others. **Pharaoh** is cited as an example.

There is no suggestion here that the Egyptian monarch was doomed from the time of his birth. What happened was this. In adult life he proved to be wicked, cruel, and extremely stubborn. In spite of the most solemn warnings he kept hardening his heart. God could have destroyed him instantly, but He didn't. Instead, God preserved him alive in order that He might display His **power** in him, and that through him God's name might be known worldwide.

9:18 Pharaoh repeatedly hardened his own heart, and *after* each of these times God *additionally* hardened Pharaoh's heart as a judgment upon him. The same sun that melts ice hardens clay. The same sun that bleaches cloth tans the skin. The same God who shows mercy to the brokenhearted also hardens the impenitent. Grace rejected is grace denied.

God has the right to show **mercy** to whomever He wishes, and to harden whomever He wishes. But because He is God, He never acts unjustly.

9:19 Paul's insistence on God's right to do what He pleases raises the objection that, if that is so, **He** shouldn't **find fault** with anyone, since no one **has** successfully **resisted His will**. To the objector, man is a helpless pawn on the divine chessboard. Nothing he can do or say will change his fate.

9:20 The apostle first rebukes the insolence of any creature who dares to find fault with his Creator. Finite **man**, loaded down with sin, ignorance, and weakness, is in no position to talk back to **God** or question the wisdom or justice of His ways.

9:21 Then Paul uses the illustration of **the potter** and **the clay** to vindicate the sovereignty of God. **The potter** comes into his shop one day and sees a pile of formless clay on the floor. He picks up a handful of clay, puts it on his wheel, and fashions a beautiful **vessel**. Does he have a right to do that?

The potter, of course, is God. **The**

clay is sinful, lost humanity. If **the pot-ter** left it alone, it would all be sent to hell. He would be absolutely just and fair if He left it alone. But instead He sover-eignly selects a handful of sinners, saves them by His grace, and conforms them to the image of His Son. Does He have the right to do that? Remember, He is not arbitrarily dooming others to hell. They are already doomed by their own willfulness and unbelief.

God has the absolute **power** and au-thority to make a **vessel for honor** with some of the clay **and another for dis-honor** with some. In a situation where everyone is unworthy, He can bestow His blessings where He chooses and withhold them whenever He wishes. "Where all are undeserving," Barnes writes, "the utmost that can be de-manded is that He should not treat any with injustice."[38]

9:22 Paul pictures **God**, the great Potter, as facing a seeming conflict of in-terests. On the one hand, He wishes to **show His wrath** and exhibit **His power** in punishing sin. But on the other hand He desires to bear patiently with **vessels of wrath prepared for destruction**. It is the contrast between the righteous severity of God in the first place, and His merciful **longsuffering** in the second. And the argument is, "If God would be justified in punishing the wicked imme-diately but, instead of that, shows great patience with them, who can find fault with Him?"

Notice carefully the phrase **vessels of wrath prepared for destruction**. **Vessels of wrath** are those whose sins make them subject to God's **wrath**. They are **prepared for destruction** by their own sin, disobedience, and rebellion, and not by some arbitrary decree of God.

9:23 Who can object if God wishes to **make known the riches of His glory** to people to whom He desires to show **mercy** — people whom **He had** selected **beforehand for** eternal **glory**? Here C. R. Erdman's comment seems especially helpful:

> God's sovereignty is never exercised in condemning men who ought to be saved, but rather it has resulted in the salvation of men who ought to be lost.[39]

God does not prepare vessels of wrath for destruction, but He does pre-pare **vessels of mercy** for **glory**.

9:24 Paul identifies the vessels of mercy as those of us who are Christians, whom God **called** from both Jewish and Gentile worlds. This lays the foundation for much that is to follow — the setting aside of all but a remnant of the nation of Israel and the call of **the Gentiles** to a place of privilege.

9:25 The apostle quotes two verses from Hosea to show that the call of the Gentiles should not have come as a sur-prise to the Jews. The first is Hosea 2:23: **"I will call them My people, who were not My people, and her beloved, who was not beloved."** Now actually in Hosea these words refer to Israel and not to the Gentiles. They look forward to the time when Israel will be restored as God's people and as His beloved. But when Paul quotes them here in Romans he applies them to the call of the Gen-tiles. What right does Paul have to make such a radical change? The answer is that the Holy Spirit who inspired the words in the first place has the right to reinterpret or reapply them later.

9:26 The second verse is Hosea 1:10: **"And it shall come to pass in the place where it was said to them, 'You are not My people,' There they shall be called sons of the living God."** Once again, in its OT setting this verse is not speaking about the Gentiles but describ-ing Israel's future restoration to God's favor. Yet Paul applies it to God's ac-knowledgment of the Gentiles as His sons. This is another illustration of the fact that when the Holy Spirit quotes verses from the OT in the NT, He can rightfully apply them as He wishes.

9:27 The rejection of all but a rem-nant of Israel is discussed in 9:27–29. **Isa-iah** predicted that only a minority of the children of **Israel** would **be saved**, even though the nation itself might grow to tremendous numbers (Isa. 10:22).

9:28 When Isaiah said, **"He will finish the work and cut it short in right-eousness because the LORD will make a short work upon the earth"** (Isa. 10:23), he was referring to the Babylonian inva-sion of Palestine and Israel's subsequent exile. The **work** was God's work of judg-ment. In quoting these words Paul is saying that what had happened to Israel in the past could and would happen again in his day.

9:29 As Isaiah said before (in an earlier part of his prophecy): **Unless the LORD of** the armies of heaven **had left** some survivors, Israel would have been wiped out **like Sodom** and **Gomorrah** (Isa. 1:9).

9:30 **What**, Paul asks, is the conclusion of all this as far as this present Church Age is concerned? The first conclusion is **that Gentiles, who** characteristically **did not pursue righteousness** but rather wickedness, and who certainly didn't pursue a righteousness of their own making, **have** found **righteousness** through **faith** in the Lord Jesus Christ. Not all Gentiles, of course, but only those who believed in Christ were justified.

9:31 Israel, on the other hand, which sought justification on the basis of law-keeping, never found a **law** by which they might obtain **righteousness.**

9:32 The reason is clear. They refused to believe that justification is **by faith** in Christ, **but** went on stubbornly trying to work out their own righteousness by personal merit. **They stumbled** over the **stumbling stone**, Christ Jesus the Lord.

9:33 This is exactly what the Lord foretold through Isaiah. The Messiah's coming to Jerusalem would have a twofold effect. To some people He would prove to be **a stumbling stone and rock of offense** (Isa. 8:14). Others would believe **on Him** and find no reason for **shame**, offense, or disappointment (Isa. 28:16).

B. Israel's Present (Chap. 10)

10:1 Paul's teachings were most distasteful to the unconverted Jews. They considered him a traitor and an enemy of Israel. But here he assures his Christian **brethren** to whom he was writing that the thing that would bring the greatest delight to his heart and the thing for which he prays **to God** most earnestly **for Israel is that they may be saved**.

10:2 Far from condemning them as godless and irreligious, the apostle gives his testimony **that they have a zeal for God**. This was apparent from their careful observance of the rituals and ceremonies of Judaism, and from their intoler-

ance of every contrary doctrine. But **zeal** is not enough; it must be combined with truth. Otherwise it can do more harm than good.

10:3 This is where they failed. They were **ignorant of God's righteousness**, **ignorant** of the fact that God imputes **righteousness** on the principle of faith and not of works. They went about trying to produce a **righteousness** of **their own** by law-keeping. They tried to win God's favor by their own efforts, their own character, their own good works. They steadfastly refused to submit to God's plan for reckoning righteous those ungodly sinners who believe on His Son.

10:4 If they had only believed on **Christ**, they would have seen that He **is the end of the law for righteousness**. The purpose of the law is to reveal sin, to convict and condemn transgressors. It can never impart righteousness. The penalty of the broken law is death. In His death, Christ paid the penalty of the law which men had broken. When a sinner receives the Lord Jesus Christ as his Savior, the law has nothing more to say to him. Through the death of his Substitute, he has died to the law. He is through with the law and with the futile attempt to achieve righteousness through it.

10:5 In the language of the OT, we can hear the difference between the words of the law and the words of faith. In Leviticus 18:5, for example, **Moses writes** that the man who achieves the **righteousness** which the **law** demands **shall live by** doing so. The emphasis is on his achieving, his doing.

Of course, this statement presents an ideal which no sinful man can meet. All it is saying is that if a man could keep the law perfectly and perpetually, he would not be condemned to death. But the law was given to people who were *already* sinners and who were *already* condemned to death. Even if they could keep the law perfectly from that day forward, they still would be lost because God requires payment for those sins which are past. Any hopes that men may have for obtaining righteousness by the law are doomed to failure from the outset.

10:6 In order to show that the language of faith is quite different from that of the law, Paul first quotes from Deuteronomy 30:12, 13, which reads:

> It is not in heaven, that you should say,
> "Who will ascend into heaven for us and bring it to us, that we may hear and do it?"
> Nor is it beyond the sea, that you should say,
> "Who will go over the sea for us and bring it to us, that we may hear it and do it?"

The interesting thing is that, in their setting in Deuteronomy, these verses are not referring to faith and the gospel at all. They are speaking about the law, and specifically the commandment to "turn to the LORD your God with all your heart and with all your soul" (Deut. 30:10b). God is saying that the law is not hidden, distant, or inaccessible. A man doesn't have to go up to **heaven** or cross the sea to find it. It is near at hand and waiting to be obeyed.

But the Apostle Paul takes these words and reapplies them to the gospel. He says that the language of **faith** doesn't ask a man to climb to **heaven to bring Christ down**. For one thing, that would be utterly impossible; but it would also be quite *unnecessary*, because Christ has already come down to earth in His Incarnation!

10:7 When the apostle quotes Deuteronomy 30:13, he changes it from "Who will go over the sea" to **Who will descend into the abyss**. His point is that the gospel does not ask men to **descend into** the grave **to bring Christ up from** among **the dead**. This would be impossible, but it would also be unnecessary, because Christ has already risen from the dead. Notice that in 10:6, 7 we have the two doctrines concerning Christ which were hardest for a Jew to accept — His Incarnation and His Resurrection. Yet he must accept these if he is to be saved. We will see these two doctrines again in 10:9, 10.

10:8 If the gospel doesn't tell men to do the humanly impossible, or to do what has already been done by the Lord, **what** then **does it say?**

Again Paul adapts a verse from Deuteronomy 30 to say that the gospel is **near**, accessible, intelligible, and easily obtained; it can be expressed in familiar conversation (**in your mouth**); and it can be readily understood in the mind (**in your heart**) (Deut. 30:14). It is the good news of salvation by faith which Paul and the other apostles preached.

10:9 Here it is in a nutshell: First you must accept the truth of the Incarnation, that the Babe of Bethlehem's manger is the Lord of life and glory, that the **Jesus** of the NT is the **Lord** (Jehovah) of the OT.

Second, you must accept the truth of His resurrection, with all that it involves. **God has raised Him from the dead** as proof that Christ had completed the work necessary for our salvation, and that God is satisfied with that work. Believing this with the **heart** means believing with one's mental, emotional, and volitional powers.

So **you confess with your mouth the Lord Jesus and believe in your heart that God has raised Him from the dead**. It is a personal appropriation of the Person and work of the Lord Jesus Christ. That is saving faith.

The question often arises, "Can a person be saved by accepting Jesus as Savior without also acknowledging Him as Lord?" The Bible gives no encouragement to anyone who believes with mental reservations: "I'll take Jesus as my Savior but I don't want to crown Him Lord of all." On the other hand, those who make submission to Jesus as Lord a *condition of salvation* face the problem, "To what degree must He be acknowledged as Lord?" Few Christians would claim to have made an absolute and complete surrender to Him in this way. When we present the gospel, we must maintain that *faith is the sole condition of justification*. But we must also remind sinners and saints constantly that Jesus Christ *is* Lord (Jehovah-God), and should be acknowledged as such.

10:10 In further explanation, Paul writes that **with the heart one believes unto righteousness**. It is not a mere intellectual assent but a genuine acceptance with one's whole inward being. When a person does that, he is instantly justified.

Then **with the mouth confession is made unto salvation**; that is, the believer publicly confesses the salvation he has already received. Confession is *not a condition* of salvation but the inevitable outward expression of what has happened: "If on Jesus Christ you trust, speak for Him you surely must." When a person really believes something, he wants to share it with others. So when a person is genuinely born again, it is too good to keep secret. He confesses Christ.

The Scriptures assume that when a person is saved he will make a public confession of that salvation. The two go together. Thus Kelly said, "If there be no confession of Christ the Lord with the mouth, we cannot speak of salvation; as our Lord said, 'He that believeth and is baptized shall be saved.' "[40] And Denney comments,

"A heart believing unto righteousness, and a mouth making confession unto salvation, are not really two things, but two sides of the same thing."[41]

The question arises why confession comes first in 10:9, then belief, whereas in 10:10 belief comes first, then confession. The answer is not hard to find. In verse 9 the emphasis is on the Incarnation and the resurrection, and these doctrines are mentioned in their chronological order. The Incarnation comes first — Jesus is Lord. Then the resurrection — God raised Him from the dead. In verse 10 the emphasis is on the order of events in the salvation of a sinner. First he **believes**, then he makes a public **confession** of his **salvation.**

10:11 The apostle now quotes Isaiah 28:16 to emphasize that **whoever believes on Him will not be put to shame**. The thought of public confession of Christ might arouse fears of shame, but the opposite is true. Our confession of Him *on earth* leads to His confession of us *in heaven*. Ours is a hope that will never be disappointed.

The word **whoever** forms a link with what is to follow — namely, that God's glorious salvation is for all, Gentiles as well as Jews.

10:12 In Romans 3:23 we learned that there is no difference between Jew and Gentile as far as the need for salvation is concerned, for all are sinners. Now we learn that there is **no distinction** as far as the availability of salvation is concerned. The Lord is not an exclusive God, but is **Lord over all** mankind. He

is rich in grace and mercy **to all who call upon Him**.

10:13 Joel 2:32 is quoted to prove the universality of the gospel. One could scarcely wish for a simpler statement of the way of salvation than is found in these words: **"Whoever calls on the name of the LORD shall be saved." The name of the LORD** stands for the LORD Himself.

10:14 But such a gospel presupposes a universal proclamation. Of what use is a salvation offered to Jews and Gentiles if they never hear about it? Here we have the heartbeat of Christian missions!

In a series of three "how's" (**how shall they call . . . believe . . . hear without a preacher**), the apostle goes back over the steps that lead to the salvation of Jews and Gentiles. Perhaps it will be clearer if we reverse the order, as follows:

God sends out His servants.

They preach the good news of salvation.

Sinners hear God's offer of life in Christ.

Some of those who hear believe the message.

Those who believe call on the Lord.

Those who call on Him are saved.

Hodge points out that this is an argument founded on the principle that if God wills the end, He also wills the means to reach that end.[42] This, as we have said, is the basis of the Christian missionary movement. Paul is here vindicating his preaching the gospel to the Gentiles, a policy which the unbelieving Jews considered inexcusable.

10:15 God is the One who sends. We are the ones who **are sent**. What are we doing about it? Do we have **the beautiful feet** which Isaiah ascribed to Him **who** brought **glad tidings of good things** (Isa. 52:7)? Isaiah writes of **the beautiful feet** of *Him* — that is, the Messiah. Here in Romans 10:15 the "him" becomes "them." *He* came with **beautiful feet** 1900 years ago. Now it is *our* privilege and responsibility to go with **beautiful feet** to a lost and dying world.

10:16 But Paul's ever-present grief is that the people of Israel did **not all** listen to **the gospel**. Isaiah had prophesied as much when he asked, **"Lord, who has believed our report?"** (Isa. 53:1). The question calls for the answer, "Not many." When the announcement of the Messiah's First Advent was heralded, not many responded.

10:17 In this quotation from Isaiah, Paul notices that the belief spoken of by the prophet springs from the message that is heard, and that the message comes through the **word** about the Messiah. So he lays down the conclusion that **faith comes by hearing, and hearing by the word of God. Faith** comes to men when they hear our preaching concerning the Lord Jesus Christ, which is based, of course, on the written **word of God**.

But hearing with the ears is not enough. A person must hear with an open heart and mind, willing to be shown the truth of God. If he does, he will find that the word has the ring of truth, and that the truth is self-authenticating. He will then believe. It should be clear, of course, that the **hearing** alluded to in this verse does not involve the ears exclusively. The message might be *read*, for example. So "to hear" means to receive the word by whatever means.

10:18 What then has been the problem? Haven't both Jews and Gentiles **heard** the gospel preached? Yes. Paul borrows the words of Psalm 19:4 to show that they have. He says, **Yes, indeed:**
"Their sound has gone out to all the earth,
And their words to the ends of the world."
But the surprising thing is that these words from Psalm 19 are not speaking of the gospel. Rather, they describe the universal witness of the sun, moon, and stars to the glory of God. But as we said, Paul borrows them and says, in effect, that they are equally true of the worldwide proclamation of the gospel in his own day. By inspiration of the Spirit of God, the apostle often takes an OT passage and applies it in quite a different way. The same Spirit who originally gave the words surely has the right to reapply them later on.

10:19 The call of the Gentiles and the rejection of the gospel by the *majority*

of Jews should not have come as a surprise to the nation of **Israel**. Their own Scriptures foretold exactly what would happen. For example God warned that He would **provoke** Israel **to jealousy** by a non-nation (the Gentiles), and **anger** Israel **by a foolish**, idolatrous **nation** (Deut. 32:21).

10:20 In even bolder language, **Isaiah** quotes the Lord as being **found by** the Gentiles, who weren't really looking for Him, and being **made manifest to those who** weren't inquiring for Him (Isa. 65:1). Taken as a whole, the Gentiles didn't seek after God. They were satisfied with their pagan religions. But many of them *did respond* when they heard the gospel. Relatively speaking, the Gentiles responded more than the Jews.

10:21 Against this picture of the Gentiles flocking to Jehovah, Isaiah portrays the Lord standing all day long with outstretched, beckoning **hands to** the nation of **Israel**, and being met with disobedience and stubborn refusal.

C. Israel's Future (Chap. 11)

11:1 What about the future of Israel? Is it true, as some teach, that God is through with Israel, that the church is now the Israel of God, and that all the promises to Israel now apply to the church?[43] Romans 11 is one of the strongest refutations of that view in all the Bible.

Paul's opening question means, **"Has God cast away His people** *completely*? That is, has every single Israelite been cast off?" **Certainly not!** The point is that although God **has cast** off **His people**, as is distinctly stated in 11:15, this does not mean that He has rejected *all* of them. Paul himself is a proof that the casting away has not been complete. After all, he was an **Israelite, of the seed of Abraham**, and **of the tribe of Benjamin**. His credentials as a Jew were impeccable.

11:2 So we must understand the first part of this verse as saying, **"God has not** *completely* **cast away His people whom He foreknew,"** The situation was similar to that which existed in the time of **Elijah**. The mass of the nation had turned away from God to idols. Conditions were so bad that Elijah prayed **against Israel** instead of for it!

11:3 He reminded the LORD how the people had silenced the voice of the **prophets** in death. They had **torn down** God's **altars**. It seemed to him that his was the only faithful voice for God that was left, and his **life** was in imminent danger.

11:4 But the picture wasn't as dark and hopeless as Elijah feared. God reminded the prophet that He had **reserved** for Himself **seven thousand men** who had steadfastly refused to follow the nation in worshiping **Baal**.

11:5 What was true **then** is true now: God never leaves Himself without a witness. He always has a faithful **remnant** chosen by Himself as special objects of His **grace**.

11:6 God doesn't choose this remnant on the basis **of** their **works**, but **by** His sovereign, electing **grace**. These two principles — **grace** and **works** — are mutually exclusive. A gift cannot be earned. What is free cannot be bought. What is unmerited cannot be deserved. Fortunately, God's choice was based on **grace**, not on **works**; otherwise no one could ever have been chosen.

11:7 The conclusion, then, is that **Israel** failed to obtain righteousness because they sought it through self-effort instead of through the finished work of Christ. The remnant, chosen by God, succeeded in obtaining righteousness through faith in the Lord Jesus. The nation suffered what might be called judicial blindness. Refusal to receive the Messiah resulted in a decreased capacity and inclination to receive Him.

11:8 This is exactly what the OT predicted would happen (Isa. 29:10; Deut. 29:4). **God** abandoned them to a state of **stupor** in which they became insensitive to spiritual realities. Because they refused to see the Lord Jesus as Messiah and Savior, now they lost the power to **see** Him. Because they would not hear the pleading voice of God, now they were smitten with spiritual deafness. That terrible judgment continues **to this very day**.

11:9 **David**, too, anticipated the judgment of God on Israel. In Psalm 69:22, 23 he described the rejected Savior as calling on God to turn **their table** into **a snare and a trap**. The **table** here means the sum total of the privileges and blessings which flowed through Christ. What should have been a blessing was turned into a curse.

11:10 In the Psalms passage, the suffering Savior also called on God to **let their eyes be darkened** and their bodies bent over as by toil or in old age (or, their loins made to shake continually).

11:11 Paul now raises another question. **Have they stumbled that they should fall?** Here we must supply the word *finally* or *forever*. Did they stumble that they might fall and never be restored? The apostle denies such a suggestion emphatically. God's purpose is restorative. His purpose is that as a result of their fall, **salvation** might **come to the Gentiles**, thus provoking Israel **to jealousy**. This **jealousy** is designed to bring Israel back to God eventually.

Paul does not deny the fall of Israel. In fact, he admits it in this very verse — **Through their fall, ... salvation has come to the Gentiles** — and in the next verse — "If their *fall* is riches for the world." But he vigorously opposes the idea that God is through with Israel forever.

11:12 As a result of Israel's rejection of the gospel, the nation was set aside and the gospel went out to **the Gentiles**. In this sense the **fall** of the Jews has meant **riches for the world**, and Israel's loss has been the Gentiles' gain.

But if that is true, **how much more** will Israel's restoration result in rich blessing for all the world! When Israel turns to the Lord at the close of the Great Tribulation, she will become the channel of blessing to the nations.

11:13 The apostle here addresses the **Gentiles** (11:13–24). Some think he is speaking to the Gentile Christians in Rome, but the passage demands a different audience — that is, the Gentile nations as such. It will greatly assist one to understand this passage if he sees Paul as speaking of Israel nationally and of **the Gentiles** as such. He is not speaking of the church of God; otherwise we face the possibility of the church's being cut off (11:22), and this is unscriptural.

Since Paul was **an apostle to the Gentiles**, it was quite natural for him to speak to them very candidly. In doing so, he was only fulfilling his **ministry**.

11:14 He sought by every **means** to **provoke to jealousy those who** were his countrymen, so that he might be used to **save some of them**. He knew and we know that he himself couldn't save anyone. But the God of salvation identifies Himself so closely with His servants that He permits them to speak of their doing what only He can do.

11:15 This verse repeats the argument of 11:12 in different language. When Israel was set aside as God's chosen, earthly people, the Gentiles were brought into a position of privilege with God and thus in a figurative sense were reconciled. When Israel is restored during the Millennial Reign of Christ, it will be like worldwide regeneration or resurrection.

This may be illustrated in the experience of Jonah, who was a figure of the nation of Israel. When Jonah was cast out of the boat during the storm, this resulted in deliverance or salvation for a boatload of Gentiles. But when Jonah was restored and preached to Nineveh, it resulted in salvation for a city full of Gentiles. So Israel's temporary rejection by God has resulted in the gospel going out to a handful of Gentiles, comparatively speaking. But when Israel is restored, vast hordes of Gentiles will be ushered into the kingdom of God.

11:16 Now Paul employs two metaphors. The first has to do with **the firstfruit** and **the lump**, the second with **the root** and **the branches**. **The firstfruit** and **the lump** speak of dough, not of fruit. In Numbers 15:19–21 we read that a piece of dough was consecrated to the Lord as a heave offering. The argument is that if the piece of dough is set apart to the Lord, so is all the dough that might be made from it.

As for the application, the **firstfruit** is Abraham. He was **holy** in the sense that he was set apart by God. If this was true of him, it is true of his chosen posterity. They are set apart to a position of external privilege before God.

The second metaphor is **the root** and **the branches**. **If the root is** set apart, **so are the branches**. Abraham is **the root** in the sense that he was the first to be set apart by God to form a new society, distinct from the nations. If Abraham

was set apart, so are those who are descended from him in the chosen line.

11:17 The apostle continues the metaphor of **the root** and **the branches**.

The branches that **were broken off** picture the unbelieving portion of the twelve tribes of Israel. Because of their rejection of the Messiah, they were removed from their place of privilege as God's chosen people. But only **some of the branches were** removed. A remnant of the nation, including Paul himself, had received the Lord.

The **wild olive tree** refers to the Gentiles, viewed as one people. They were **grafted in** to the olive tree.

With them the Gentiles partook of the root and fatness of **the olive tree**. The Gentiles share the position of favor that had originally been given to Israel and is still held by the believing remnant of Israel.

In this illustration it is important to see that the main trunk of **the olive tree** is *not Israel*, but rather God's line of *privilege* down through the centuries. If the trunk were Israel, then you would have the bizarre picture of Israel being broken off from Israel and then grafted back into Israel again.

It is also important to remember that **the wild olive** branch is *not the church* but the Gentiles viewed collectively. Otherwise you face the possibility of true believers being cut off from God's favor. Paul has already shown that this is impossible (Rom. 8:38, 39).

When we say that the trunk of the tree is the line of privilege down through the centuries, what do we mean by "line of privilege"? God decided to set apart a certain people to occupy a special place of nearness to Himself. They would be set apart from the rest of the world and would have special privileges. They would enjoy what we today might call the "favored-nation status." In the different ages of history, He would have a special inner circle.

The nation of Israel was the first to be in this line of privilege. They were God's ancient, chosen, earthly people. Because of their rejection of the Messiah, **some of** these **branches were broken off** and thus lost their position of "favorite son." The Gentiles **were grafted** into the olive tree and became partakers with believing Jews **of the root and fatness. The root** points back to Abraham, with whom the line of privilege began. The **fatness** of an olive tree refers to its productivity — that is, to its rich crop of olives and oil derived from them. Here the **fatness** signifies the privileges that flowed from union with **the olive tree**.

11:18 But the Gentiles should **not** take a holier-than-thou attitude toward the Jews, or **boast** of any superiority. Any such boasting overlooks the fact that they didn't originate the line of privilege. Rather, it is the line of privilege that put them where they are, in a place of special favor.

11:19 Paul anticipates that the imaginary Gentile with whom he has been conversing **will say**, "Jewish **branches were broken off** so **that I** and other Gentile branches **might be grafted in."**

11:20 The apostle admits that the statement is partially true. Jewish branches **were broken off**, and the Gentiles were grafted **in**. But it was because of the **unbelief** of Israel and not because the Gentiles had any special claim on God. The Gentiles were grafted in because, as a people, they stood **by faith**. This expression, **you stand by faith**, seems to indicate that Paul is speaking about true believers. But that is not necessarily the meaning. The only way in which the Gentiles stood **by faith** was that, comparatively speaking, they demonstrated more faith than the Jews did. Thus Jesus said to a Gentile centurion, "I have not found such great faith, not even in Israel" (Luke 7:9). And Paul later said to the Jews at Rome, "Therefore let it be known to you that the salvation of God has been sent to the Gentiles, and they will hear it!" (Acts 28:28). Notice, "they will hear it." As a people they are more receptive to the gospel today than Israel. To **stand** here is the opposite of to *fall*. Israel had fallen from its place of privilege. The Gentiles had been grafted into that place.

But let him who stands beware lest he fall. Gentiles should not be puffed up with pride **but** should rather **fear.**

11:21 **If God did not** hesitate to cut off **the natural branches** from the line of privilege, there is no reason to believe that **He** would **spare** the wild olive branches under similar circumstances.

11:22 So in the parable of the olive tree, we see two great contrasting facets of God's character — His **goodness and** His **severity**. His **severity** is manifest in the removal of Israel from the favored-nation status. His **goodness** is seen in His turning to the Gentiles with the gospel (see Acts 13:46; 18:6). But that **goodness** must not be taken for granted. The Gentiles too could **be cut off** if they do not maintain that relative openness which the Savior found during His earthly ministry (Matt. 8:10; Luke 7:9).

It must be constantly borne in mind that Paul is not speaking of the church or of individual believers. He is speaking about the Gentiles as such. Nothing can ever separate the Body of Christ from the Head, and nothing can separate a believer from the love of God, but the Gentile peoples can be removed from their present position of special privilege.

11:23 And Israel's severance need not be final. **If they** abandon their national **unbelief**, there is no reason why God cannot put them back into their original place of privilege. It would not be impossible for God to do this.

11:24 In fact, it would be a much less violent process for God to reinstate Israel as His privileged people than it was to put the Gentiles into that place. The people of Israel were the original branches in the tree of God's favor, and so they are called **natural branches**. The Gentile branches came from a **wild** olive tree. To graft a **wild** olive branch **into a cultivated olive tree** is an unnatural graft, or, as Paul says, it is **contrary to nature**. To graft natural branches **into** their original **cultivated olive tree** is a very natural process.

11:25 Now the apostle reveals that the future restoration of Israel is not only a possibility but is an assured fact. What Paul now reveals is a **mystery** — a truth hitherto unknown, a truth that could not be known by man's unaided intellect, but a truth that has now been made known. Paul sets it forth so that Gentile believers will not be **wise in** their **own opinion**, looking down their nationalistic noses at the Jews. **This mystery** is as follows:

Blindness in part has happened to Israel. It has not affected all the nation, but only the unbelieving segment.

That **blindness** is temporary. It will continue only **until the fullness of the Gentiles** arrives. **The fullness of the Gentiles** refers to the time when the last member will be added to the church, and when the completed Body of Christ will be raptured home to heaven. **The fullness of the Gentiles** must be distinguished from the *times* of the Gentiles (Luke 21:24). **The fullness of the Gentiles** coincides with the Rapture. The phrase "times of the Gentiles" refers to the entire period of Gentile domination over the Jews, beginning with the Babylonian captivity (2 Chron. 36:1–21) and ending with Christ's return to earth to reign.

11:26 While Israel's judicial blindness is removed at the time of the Rapture, that does not mean that all Israel will be saved right away. Jews will be converted throughout the Tribulation Period, but the entire elect remnant will not be saved until Christ returns to earth as King of kings and Lord of lords.

When Paul says that **all Israel will be saved**, he means **all** *believing* **Israel**. The unbelieving portion of the nation will be destroyed at the Second Advent of Christ (Zech. 13:8, 9). Only those who say "Blessed is He who comes in the name of the Lord" will be spared to enter the kingdom.

This is what Isaiah referred to when he spoke of the Redeemer coming to **Zion** and turning transgression away **from Jacob** (Isa. 59:20). Notice that it is not Christ's coming to Bethlehem, but His coming to **Zion** — that is, His Second Coming.

11:27 It is the same time referred to in Isaiah 27:9 and Jeremiah 31:33, 34, when God shall take away their sins under the terms of the New **Covenant**.

11:28 So we might summarize Israel's present status by saying first that **concerning the gospel they are enemies for your sake**. They are enemies in the sense of being cast off, set aside, alienated from God's favor so that the gospel might go forth to the Gentiles.

But that is only half the picture. **Concerning the election they are beloved for the sake of the fathers** — that is, Abraham, Isaac, and Jacob.

11:29 The reason they are still beloved is that God's **gifts** and **calling** are

never rescinded. God does not take back His gifts. Once He has made an unconditional promise, He never goes back on it. He gave Israel the special privileges listed in 9:4, 5. He called Israel to be His earthly people (Isa. 48:12), separate from the rest of the nations. Nothing can change His purposes.

11:30 The Gentiles were **once** an untamed, **disobedient** people, but when Israel spurned the Messiah and the gospel of salvation, God turned to the Gentiles in **mercy**.

11:31 A somewhat similar sequence of events will occur in the future. Israel's disobedience will be followed by **mercy**, when they are provoked to jealousy **through the mercy shown** to the Gentiles. Some teach that it is through the Gentiles' showing mercy to the Jews that they will be restored, but we know that this is not so. Israel's restoration will be brought about by the Second Advent of the Lord Jesus (see 11:26, 27).

11:32 When we first read this verse, we might get the idea that God arbitrarily condemned both Jews and Gentiles to unbelief, and that there was nothing they could do about it. But that is not the thought. The unbelief was their own doing. What the verse is saying is this: having found both Jews and Gentiles disobedient, God is pictured as imprisoning them both in that condition, so that there would be no way out for them except on His terms.

This **disobedience** provided scope for God to **have mercy on all**, both Jews and Gentiles. There is no suggestion here of universal salvation. God has shown **mercy** to the Gentiles and will yet show **mercy** to the Jews also, but this does not insure the salvation of everyone. Here it is **mercy** shown along national lines. George Williams says:

> God having tested both the Hebrew and the Gentile nations, and both having broken down under the test, He shut them up in unbelief so that, being manifestly without merit, and having by demonstration forfeited all claims and all rights to divine favor, He might, in the unsearchable riches of His grace, have mercy upon them all.[44]

11:33 This concluding doxology looks back over the entire Epistle and the divine wonders that have been unfolded.

Paul has expounded the marvelous plan of salvation by which a just God can save ungodly sinners and still be just in doing so. He has shown how Christ's work brought more glory to God and more blessing to men than Adam lost through his sin. He has explained how grace produces holy living in a way that law could never do. He has traced the unbreakable chain of God's purpose from foreknowledge to eventual glorification. He has set forth the doctrine of sovereign election and the companion doctrine of human responsibility. And he has traced the justice and harmony of God's dispensational dealings with Israel and the nations. Now nothing could be more appropriate than to burst forth in a hymn of praise and worship.

Oh, the depth of the riches both of the wisdom and knowledge of God!

The **riches** of God! He is rich in mercy, love, grace, faithfulness, power, and goodness.

The **wisdom** of God! His **wisdom** is infinite, unsearchable, incomparable, and invincible.

The **knowledge of God**! "God is omniscient," writes Arthur W. Pink, "He knows everything: everything possible, everything actual; all events, all creatures, of the past, the present, and the future."[45]

His decisions are **unsearchable**: they are too deep for mortal minds to fully understand. The **ways** in which He arranges creation, history, redemption, and providence are beyond our limited comprehension.

11:34 No created being can know **the mind of the LORD,** except to the extent that He chooses to reveal it. And even then we see in a mirror, dimly (1 Cor. 13:12). No one is qualified to advise God. He doesn't need our counsel, and wouldn't profit by it anyway (see Isa. 40:13).

11:35 No one has ever made God obligated to him (see Job 41:11). What gift of ours would ever put the Eternal in a position where He had to repay?

11:36 The Almighty is self-contained. He is the source of every good, He is the active Agent in sustaining and controlling the universe, and He is the Object for which everything has been created. Everything is designed to bring **glory** to Him.

Let it be so! **To** Him **be glory forever. Amen.**

III. DUTIFUL: THE GOSPEL LIVED OUT (Chaps. 12–16)

The rest of Romans answers the question: *How should those who have been justified by grace respond in their everyday lives?* Paul takes up our duties toward other believers, toward the community, toward our enemies, toward the government, and toward our weaker brothers.

A. In Personal Consecration (12:1, 2)

12:1 Serious and devout consideration of **the mercies of God**, as they have been set forth in chapters 1–11, leads to only one conclusion — we should **present** our **bodies** as **a living sacrifice, holy, acceptable to God**. Our **bodies** stand for all our members and, by extension, our entire lives.

Total commitment is our **reasonable service**. It is our **reasonable service** in this sense: if the Son of God has died for me, then the least I can do is live for Him. "If Jesus Christ be God and died for me," said the great British athlete C. T. Studd, "then no sacrifice can be too great for me to make for him."[46] Isaac Watts' great hymn says the same thing: "Love so amazing, so divine, demands my heart, my life, my all."

Reasonable service may also be translated "spiritual worship." As believer-priests, we do not come to God with the bodies of slain animals but with the spiritual sacrifice of yielded lives. We also offer to Him our service (Rom. 15:16), our praise (Heb. 13:15), and our possessions (Heb. 13:16).

12:2 Secondly, Paul urges us **not to be conformed to this world**, or as Phillips paraphrases it: "Don't let the world around you squeeze you into its own mold." When we come to the kingdom of God, we should abandon the thought-patterns and lifestyles of the world.

The **world** (literally *age*) as used here means the society or system that man has built in order to make himself happy without God. It is a kingdom that is antagonistic to God. The god and prince of this world is Satan (2 Cor. 4:4; John 12:31; 14:30; 16:11). All unconverted people are his subjects. He seeks to attract and hold people through the lust of the eyes, the lust of the flesh, and the pride of life (1 Jn. 2:16). The world has its own politics, art, music, religion, amusements, thought-patterns, and lifestyles, and it seeks to get everyone to conform to its culture and customs. It hates nonconformists — like Christ and His followers.

Christ died to deliver us from **this world**. The world is crucified to us, and we are crucified to the world. It would be absolute disloyalty to the Lord for believers to love the world. Anyone who loves the world is an enemy of God.

Believers are not of the world any more than Christ is of the world. However, they are sent into the world to testify that its works are evil and that salvation is available to all who put their faith in the Lord Jesus Christ. We should not only be separated from the world; we should **be transformed by the renewing of** our **mind**, which means that we should think the way God thinks, as revealed in the Bible. Then we can experience the direct guidance of God in our lives. And we will find that, instead of being distasteful and hard, His **will** is **good and acceptable and perfect**.

Here, then, are three keys for knowing God's will. The *first* is a yielded body, the *second* a separated life, and *third* a transformed mind.

B. In Serving through Spiritual Gifts (12:3–8)

12:3 Paul speaks here **through the grace** that was **given to** him as an apostle of the Lord Jesus. He is going to deal with various forms of straight and crooked thinking.

First he says that there is nothing in the gospel that would encourage anyone to have a superiority complex. He urges us to be humble in exercising our gifts. We should never have exaggerated ideas of our own importance. Neither should we be envious of others. Rather, we should realize that each person is unique and that we all have an important function to perform for our Lord. We should be happy with the place **God has dealt**

to us in the Body, and we should seek to exercise our gifts with all the strength that God supplies.

12:4 The human **body** has **many members**, yet each one has a unique role to play. The health and welfare of the body depend on the proper functioning of each member.

12:5 That is how it is in the **body of Christ**. There is unity (**one body**), diversity (**many**), and interdependency (**members of one another**). Any gifts we have are not for selfish use or display but for the good of the **body**. No gift is self-sufficient and none is unnecessary. When we realize all this, we are thinking soberly (12:3).

12:6 Paul now gives instructions for the use of certain **gifts**. The list does not cover all the **gifts**; it is meant to be suggestive rather than exhaustive.

Our **gifts** differ **according to the grace that is given to us**. In other words, God's **grace** deals out differing **gifts** to different people. And God gives the necessary strength or ability to use whatever **gifts** we have. So we are responsible to use these God-given abilities as good stewards.

Those who have the gift of **prophecy** should **prophesy in proportion to** their **faith**. A prophet is a spokesman for God, declaring the word of the Lord. Prediction may be involved, but it is not a necessary element of prophecy. In the early church, writes Hodge, the prophets were "men who spoke under the immediate influence of the Spirit of God, and delivered some divine communication relative to doctrinal truths, to present duty, to future events, as the case may be."[47] Their ministry is preserved for us in the NT. There can be no inspired, prophetic additions to the body of Christian doctrine today since the faith has been once for all delivered to the saints (see Jude 3). Thus a prophet today is simply one who declares the mind of God as it has been revealed in the Bible. Strong says:

All modern prophecy that is true is but the republication of Christ's message — the proclamation and expounding of truth already revealed in Scripture.[48]

Those of us who have the gift of

prophecy should **prophesy in proportion to our faith.** This may mean "according to the rule or norm of the faith" — that is, in accordance with the doctrines of the Christian faith as they are found in the Scriptures. Or it may mean "according to the proportion of our faith" — that is, to the extent that God gives us faith. Most versions supply the word "our" here, but it is not found in the original.[49]

12:7 Ministry is a very broad term meaning service for the Lord. It does not mean the office, duties, or functions of a clergyman (as commonly used today). The person who has the gift of **ministry** has a servant-heart. He sees opportunities to be of service and seizes them.

A *teacher* is one who is able to explain the word of God and apply it to the hearts of his hearers. Whatever our gift is, we should give ourselves to it wholeheartedly.

12:8 Exhortation is the gift of stirring up the saints to desist from every form of evil and to press on to new achievements for Christ in holiness and in service.

Giving is the divine endowment which inclines and empowers a person to be aware of needs and to help meet them. He should do so **with liberality**.

The gift of *leading* is almost certainly connected with the work of elders (and perhaps also deacons) in a local church. The elder is an undershepherd who stands out in front of the flock and leads **with** care and **diligence**.

The gift of **mercy** is the supernatural capacity and talent of aiding those who are in distress. Those who have this gift should exercise it **with cheerfulness**. Of course, we should all show mercy and do it cheerfully.

A Christian lady once said, "When my mother became old and needed someone to care for her, my husband and I invited her to come and live with us. I did all I could to make her comfortable. I cooked for her, did her washing, took her out in the car, and generally cared for all her needs. But while I was going through the motions outwardly, I was unhappy inside. Subconsciously I resented the interruption of our usual schedule. Sometimes my mother would say to me, 'You never smile anymore.

Why don't you ever smile?' You see, I was showing mercy, but I wasn't doing it with cheerfulness."

C. In Relation to Society (12:9–21)

12:9 Next Paul lists some characteristics that every believer should develop in his dealings with other Christians and with the unconverted.

Love should **be without hypocrisy**. It should not wear a mask, but should be genuine, sincere, and unaffected.

We should **abhor** all forms of **evil** and **cling to** everything **good**. In this setting **evil** probably means all attitudes and acts of unlove, malice, and hatred. **Good**, by contrast, means every manifestation of supernatural love.

12:10 In our relations with those who are in the household of faith, we should demonstrate our love by tender affection, not by cool indifference or routine acceptance.

We should prefer to see others honored rather than ourselves. Once a beloved servant of Christ was in a side room with other notables before a meeting. Several had already moved onto the platform before it was his turn. When he appeared at the door, thunderous applause broke out for him. He quickly stepped aside and applauded so that he would not share the honor that he sincerely thought was intended for others.

12:11 Moffatt's colorful translation of this verse is: "Never let your zeal flag, maintain the spiritual glow, serve the Lord." Here we are reminded of the words of Jeremiah 48:10: "A curse on him who is slack in doing the LORD'S work!" (NEB).

> 'Tis not for man to trifle; life is brief
> And sin is here.
> Our age is but the falling of a leaf,
> A dropping tear.
> We have not time to sport away
> the hours;
> All must be earnest in a world like
> ours.
>
> *– Horatius Bonar*

12:12 No matter what our present circumstances may be, we can and should rejoice **in** our **hope** — the coming of our Savior, the redemption of our bodies, and our eternal glory. We are exhorted to be **patient in tribulation** — that is, to bear up bravely under it. Such all-conquering endurance is the one thing which can turn such misery into glory. We should continue **steadfastly in prayer**. It is **in prayer** that the work is done and victories are won. **Prayer** brings power in our lives and peace to our hearts. When we pray in the Name of the Lord Jesus, we come the closest to omnipotence that it is possible for mortal man to come. Therefore we do ourselves a great disservice when we neglect to pray.

12:13 Needy **saints** are everywhere — the unemployed, those who have been drained by medical bills, forgotten preachers and missionaries in obscure places, and senior citizens whose resources have dwindled. True Body-life means sharing with those who are in need.

"Never grudging a meal or a bed to those who need them" (JBP). **Hospitality** is a lost art. Small homes and apartments are used as excuses for not receiving Christians who are passing through. Perhaps we do not want to face the added work and inconvenience. But we forget that when we entertain God's children, it is the same as if we were entertaining the Lord Himself. Our homes should be like the home in Bethany, where Jesus loved to be.

12:14 We are called to show kindness toward our persecutors instead of trying to repay them in kind. It requires divine life to repay unkindness and injury with a courtesy. The natural response is to curse and retaliate.

12:15 Empathy is the capacity for sharing vicariously the feelings and emotions of others. Our tendency is to be jealous when others rejoice, and to pass by when they mourn. God's way is to enter into the joys and sorrows of those around us.

12:16 To **be of the same mind toward one another** does not mean that we must see alike on nonessential matters. It is not so much uniformity of mind as harmony of relationships.

We should avoid any trace of snobbishness and should be as outgoing toward **humble**, lowly folk as toward those of wealth and position. When an illustrious Christian arrived at the terminal he was met by leaders from the church where he was to speak. The limousine

pulled up to take him to a plush hotel. "Who usually entertains visiting preachers here?" he asked. They mentioned an elderly couple in a modest home nearby. "That's where I would prefer to stay," he said.

Again, the apostle warns against a believer being **wise in** his **own opinion**. The realization that we have nothing that we did not receive should keep us from an inflated ego.

12:17 Repaying **evil for evil** is common practice in the world. Men speak of giving tit for tat, of repaying in kind, or of giving someone what he deserves. But this delight in vengeance should have no place in the lives of those who have been redeemed. Instead, they should act honorably in the face of abuse and injury, as in all the circumstances of life. To **have regard** means to *take thought for* or *be careful to do*.

12:18 Christians should not be needlessly provocative or contentious. The righteousness of God is not worked out by belligerence and wrath. We should love peace, make peace, and be at peace. When we have offended others, or when someone has offended us, we should work tirelessly for a peaceful resolution of the matter.

12:19 We must resist the tendency to avenge wrongs that are done to us. The expression **give place to wrath** may mean to allow *God* to take care of it for you, or it may mean to submit passively in a spirit of nonresistance. The rest of the verse favors the first interpretation — to stand back and let the **wrath** of God take care of it. **Vengeance is** God's prerogative. We should not interfere with what is His right. He will repay at the proper time and in the proper manner. Lenski writes:

God has long ago settled the whole matter about exacting justice from wrongdoers. Not one of them will escape. Perfect justice will be done in every case and will be done perfectly. If any of us interfered, it would be the height of presumption.[50]

12:20 Christianity goes beyond non-resistance to active benevolence. It does not destroy its enemies by violence but converts them by love. It feeds the **enemy** when he **is hungry** and satisfies his thirst, thus heaping live **coals of fire**

on his head. If the live **coal** treatment seems cruel, it is because this idiomatic expression is not properly understood. To heap live **coals** on a person's head means to make him ashamed of his hostility by surprising him with unconventional kindness.

12:21 Darby explains the first part of this verse as follows: "If my bad temper puts you in a bad temper, you have been overcome of evil."[51]

The great black scientist, George Washington Carver, once said, "I will never let another man ruin my life by making me hate him."[52] As a believer he would not allow evil to conquer him.

But overcome evil with good. It is characteristic of Christian teaching that it does not stop with the negative prohibition but goes on to the positive exhortation. **Evil** can be overpowered **with good**. This is a weapon we should use more frequently.

Stanton treated Lincoln with venomous hatred. He said that it was foolish to go to Africa in search of a gorilla when the original gorilla could be found in Springfield, Illinois. Lincoln took it all in stride. Later Lincoln appointed Stanton as war minister, feeling that he was the most qualified for the office. After Lincoln was shot, Stanton called him the greatest leader of men. Love had conquered![53]

D. In Relation to Government (13:1–7)

13:1 Those who have been justified by faith are obligated to **be subject** to human government. Actually the obligation applies to everyone, but the apostle here is concerned especially with believers. God established human government after the flood when He decreed, "Whoever sheds man's blood, by man his blood shall be shed" (Gen. 9:6). That decree gave authority to men to judge criminal matters and to punish offenders.

In every ordered society there must be authority and submission to that authority. Otherwise you have a state of anarchy, and you cannot survive indefinitely under anarchy. Any government is better than no government. So God has instituted human government, and no government exists apart from His

will. This does not mean that He approves of all that human rulers do. He certainly does not approve of corruption, brutality, and tyranny! But the fact remains that **the authorities that exist are appointed by God**.

Believers can live victoriously in a democracy, a constitutional monarchy, or even a totalitarian regime. No earthly government is any better than the men who comprise it. That is why none of our governments is perfect. The only ideal government is a beneficent monarchy with the Lord Jesus Christ as King. It is helpful to remember that Paul wrote this section on subjection to human government when the infamous Nero was Emperor. Those were dark days for Christians. Nero blamed them for a fire which destroyed half the city of Rome (and which he himself may have ordered). He caused some believers to be immersed in tar, then ignited as living torches to provide illumination for his orgies. Others were sewn up in animal skins, then thrown to ferocious dogs to be torn to pieces.

13:2 And yet it still holds that anyone who disobeys or rebels against the government is disobeying and rebelling against what God has ordained. **Whoever resists** lawful **authority** earns and deserves punishment.

There is an exception, of course. A Christian is not required to obey if the government orders him to sin or to compromise his loyalty to Jesus Christ (Acts 5:29). No government has a right to command a person's conscience. So there are times when a believer must, by obeying God, incur the wrath of man. In such cases he must be prepared to pay the penalty without undue complaint. Under no circumstances should he rebel against the government or join in an attempt to overthrow it.

13:3 As a rule, people who do what is right need not fear the authorities. It is only those who break the law who have to fear punishment. So if anyone wants to enjoy a life free from tickets, fines, trials, and imprisonments, the thing to do is to be a law-abiding citizen. Then he will win the approval of the authorities, not their censure.

13:4 The ruler, whether president,

governor, mayor, or judge, is a **minister** of God in the sense that he is a servant and representative of the Lord. He may not know God personally, but he is still the Lord's man officially. Thus David repeatedly referred to the wicked King Saul as the Lord's anointed (1 Sam. 24:6, 10; 26:9, 11, 16, 23). In spite of Saul's repeated attempts on David's life, the latter would not allow his men to harm the king. Why? Because Saul was the king, and as such he was the Lord's appointee.

As servants of God, rulers are expected to promote the **good** of the people — their security, tranquility, and general welfare. If any man insists on breaking the law, he can expect to pay for it, because the government has the authority to bring him to trial and punish him. In the expression **he does not bear the sword in vain** we have a strong statement concerning the power which God vests in the government. **The sword** is not just an innocuous symbol of power; a scepter would have served that purpose. **The sword** seems to speak of the ultimate power of the ruler — that is, to inflict capital punishment. So it will not do to say that capital punishment was for the OT era only and not for the New. Here is a statement in the NT that implies that the government has the authority to take the life of a capital offender. People argue against this by quoting Exodus 20:13 in the KJV: "Thou shalt not kill." But that commandment refers to murder, and capital punishment is not murder. The Hebrew word translated "kill" in the KJV specifically means "murder" and is so translated in the NKJV: "You shall not murder."[54] Capital punishment was prescribed in the OT law as the required punishment for certain serious offenses.

Again the apostle reminds us that the ruler is **God's minister**, but this time he adds, **an avenger to execute wrath on him who practices evil**. In other words, in addition to being a **minister** of God to us **for good**, he also serves God by dispensing punishment to those who break the law.

13:5 What this means is that we should be obedient subjects of the government for two reasons — the fear of punishment and the desire to maintain a good **conscience**.

13:6 We owe the government not only obedience but financial support by paying **taxes**. It is to our advantage to live in a society of law and order, with police and fire protection, so we must be willing to bear our share of the cost. Government officials are giving their time and talents in carrying out God's will for the maintenance of a stable society, so they are entitled to support.

13:7 The fact that believers are citizens of heaven (Phil. 3:20) does not exempt them from responsibility to human government. They must pay whatever **taxes** are levied on their income, their real estate, and their personal property. They must pay required **customs** on merchandise being transported from one country to another. They must demonstrate a respectful **fear** of displeasing those who are charged with enforcing the laws. And they must show **honor** for the *names and offices* of all civil servants (even if they can't always respect their *personal* lives).

In this connection, Christians should never join in speaking in a derogatory way of the President or the Prime Minister. Even in the heat of a political campaign they should refuse to join in the verbal abuse that is heaped upon the head of state. It is written, "You shall not speak evil of a ruler of your people" (Acts 23:5).

E. In Relation to the Future (13:8–14)

13:8 Basically, the first part of this verse means "Pay your bills on time." It is not a prohibition against any form of debt. Some kinds of debt are inevitable in our society: most of us face monthly bills for telephone, gas, light, water, etc. And it is impossible to manage a business without contracting some debts. The admonition here is not to get into arrears (overdue accounts).

But in addition there are certain principles which should guide us in this area. We should not contract debts for nonessentials. We should not go into debt when there is no hope of repaying. We should avoid buying on the installment plan, incurring exorbitant interest charges. We should avoid borrowing to buy a product that depreciates in value. In general, we should practice financial responsibility by living modestly and within our means, always remembering that the borrower is slave to the lender (see Prov. 22:7).

The one debt that is always outstanding is the obligation to **love**. The word used for *love* in Romans, with only one exception (12:10), is *agapē*, which signifies a deep, unselfish, superhuman affection which one person has for another. This otherworldly **love** is not activated by any virtue in the person loved; rather, it is completely undeserved. It is unlike any other love in that it goes out not only to the lovable but to one's enemies as well.

This love manifests itself in giving, and generally in sacrificial giving. Thus, God so loved the world that He gave His only begotten Son. Christ loved the church and gave Himself for it.

It is primarily a matter of *the will* rather than the emotions. The fact that we are *commanded* **to love** indicates that it is something we can choose to do. If it were an uncontrollable emotion that swept over us at unexpected moments, we could scarcely be held accountable. This does not deny, however, that the emotions can be involved.

It is impossible for an unconverted person to manifest this divine love. In fact, it is impossible even for a believer to demonstrate it in his own strength. It can only be exhibited by the power of the indwelling Holy Spirit.

Love found its perfect expression on earth in the Person of the Lord Jesus Christ.

Our love to God manifests itself in obedience to His commandments.

The man **who loves** his neighbor **has fulfilled the law**, or at least that section of the law which teaches love for our fellowmen.

13:9 The apostle singles out those **commandments** which forbid acts of unlove against one's neighbor. They are **the commandments** against **adultery**, **murder**, theft, perjury, and coveting. Love doesn't exploit another person's body; immorality does. Love doesn't take another person's life; **murder** does. Love doesn't **steal** another person's property; theft does. Love doesn't deny justice to others; **false witness** does.[55]

Love doesn't even entertain wrong desires for another person's possessions; coveting does.

And if there is any other commandment. Paul could have mentioned one other: "Honor your father and your mother." They all boil down to the same dictum: **Love your neighbor as yourself**. Treat him with the same affection, consideration, and kindness that you treat yourself.

13:10 **Love** never seeks to **harm** another. Rather, it actively seeks the welfare and honor of all. Therefore the man who acts in love is really fulfilling the requirements of the second table of the **law**.

13:11 The rest of the chapter encourages a life of spiritual alertness and moral purity. The **time** is short. The Dispensation of Grace is drawing to a close. The lateness of the hour demands that all lethargy and inactivity be put away. **Our salvation is nearer than** ever. The Savior is coming to take us to the Father's house.

13:12 The present age is like a **night** of sin that has just about run its course. The **day** of eternal glory is about to dawn for believers. This means that we should **cast off** all the filthy garments of worldliness — that is, everything associated with unrighteousness and evil. And we should **put on the armor of light**, which means the protective covering of a holy life. The pieces of armor are detailed in Ephesians 6:14–18. They describe the elements of true Christian character.

13:13 Notice that the emphasis is on our practical Christian walk. Since we are children of the **day**, we should **walk** as sons of light. What does a Christian have to do with wild parties, drunken brawls, sex orgies, vile excesses, or even with bickering and envy? Nothing at all.

13:14 The best policy we can follow is, first of all, **to put on the Lord Jesus Christ**. This means that we should adopt His whole lifestyle, live as He lived, accept Him as our Guide and Example.

Secondly, we should **make no provision for the flesh, to fulfill its lusts**. The **flesh** here is the old, corrupt nature. It incessantly cries to be pampered with comfort, luxury, illicit sexual indulgence, empty amusements, worldly pleasures, dissipation, materialism, etc. We **make**

provision for the flesh when we buy things that are associated with temptation, when we make it easy for ourselves to sin, when we give a higher priority to the physical than to the spiritual. We should not indulge the flesh even a little. Rather, we should "give no chances to the flesh to have its fling" (JBP).

This was the very passage that God used in converting the brilliant but carnal Augustine to Christ and purity. When he reached verse 14 he surrendered to the Lord. He has been known in history ever since as "Saint" Augustine.

F. In Relation to Other Believers (14:1–15:13)

14:1 Romans 14:1–15:13 deals with important principles to guide God's people in dealing with matters of secondary importance. These are the things that so often cause conflict among believers, but such conflict is quite unnecessary, as we shall see.

A **weak** Christian is one who has unfounded scruples over matters of secondary importance. In this context, he was often a converted Jew who still had scruples about eating nonkosher foods or working on Saturday.

The first principle is this: a **weak** Christian should be received into the local fellowship, but **not** with the idea of engaging him in **disputes** about his ultra-scrupulousness. Christians can have happy fellowship without agreeing on nonessentials.

14:2 A believer who walks in full enjoyment of Christian liberty has faith, based on the teachings of the NT, that **all** foods are clean. They are sanctified by the word of God and prayer (1 Tim. 4:4, 5). A believer with a weak conscience may have qualms about eating pork, or any other meat, for that matter. He may be a vegetarian.

14:3 So *the second principle* is that there must be mutual forbearance. The mature Christian must not **despise** his weak brother. Neither should the weak brother **judge** as a sinner someone who enjoys ham, shrimp, or lobster. **God has received him** into His family, a member in good standing.

14:4 *The third principle* is that each believer is a **servant** of the Lord, and we have no right to sit in judgment, as if

we were the master. It is before **his own Master** that each one stands approved or disapproved. One may look down on someone else with icy condescension, sure that he will make shipwreck of the faith because of his views on these matters. But such an attitude is wrong. **God** will sustain those on both sides of the question. His power to do so is adequate.

14:5 Some Jewish Christians still looked on the Sabbath as a day of obligation. They had a conscience about doing any work on Saturday. In that sense, they esteemed **one day above another**.

Other believers did not share these Judaistic scruples. They looked on **every day alike**. They did not look upon six days as secular and one as sacred. To them all days were sacred.

But what about the Lord's Day, the first day of the week? Does it not have a special place in the lives of Christians? We see in the NT that it was the day of our Lord's resurrection (Luke 24:1–9). On the next two Lord's days, Christ met with His disciples (John 20:19, 26). The Holy Spirit was given on the Day of Pentecost, which was on the first day of the week; Pentecost occurred seven Sundays after the Feast of Firstfruits (Lev. 23:15, 16; Acts 2:1), which symbolizes Christ's resurrection (1 Cor. 15:20, 23). The disciples gathered to break bread on the first day of the week (Acts 20:7). Paul instructed the Corinthians to take a collection on the first day of the week. So the Lord's Day does stand out in the NT in a special way. But rather than being a day of *obligation*, like the Sabbath, it is a day of *privilege*. Released from our ordinary employment, we can set it apart in a special way for worshiping and serving our Lord.

Nowhere in the NT are Christians ever told to keep the Sabbath. And yet at the same time we recognize the principle of one day in seven, one day of rest after six days of work.

Whatever view one holds on this subject, the principle is this: **let each be fully convinced in his own mind**. Now it should be clear that such a principle applies only to matters that are morally *neutral*. When it comes to *fundamental* doctrines of the Christian faith, there is no room for individual opinions. But in this area where things are neither right nor wrong in themselves, there is room for differing views. They should not be allowed to become tests of fellowship.

14:6 The one **who observes the day**, in this verse, is a Jewish believer who still has a bad conscience about doing any work on Saturday. It is not that he looks upon Sabbath-keeping as a means of obtaining or retaining salvation; it is simply a matter of doing what he thinks will please **the Lord**. Likewise, a person **who does not observe the day** does so to honor Christ, the substance, rather than the mere shadow of the faith (Col. 2:16, 17).

One who has liberty to eat nonkosher foods bows his head and **gives God thanks** for them. So does the believer with the weak conscience, who eats only kosher foods. Both ask the blessing from God.

In both cases **God** is honored and thanked, so why should this be made the occasion of strife and conflict?

14:7 The lordship of Christ enters into every aspect of a believer's life. We don't live to ourselves but to the Lord. We don't die to ourselves but to the Lord. It is true that what we do and say affects others, but that is not the thought here. Paul is emphasizing that the Lord should be the goal and object of the lives of His people.

14:8 Everything we do in life is subject to Christ's scrutiny and approval. We test things by how they appear in His presence. Even in death we aspire to glorify the Lord as we go to be with Him. Both in life and in death we belong to Him.

14:9 One of the reasons for which **Christ died and rose and lived again** is **that He might be** our **Lord**, and that we might be His willing subjects, gladly rendering to Him the devotion of our grateful hearts. His lordship continues even in death, when our bodies lie in the grave and our spirits and souls are in His presence.

14:10 Because this is true, it is folly for an overscrupulous Jewish Christian to condemn the **brother** who doesn't keep the Jewish calendar and who doesn't limit himself to kosher foods. Likewise, it is wrong for the strong brother to **show contempt** to the weak **brother**. The fact is that every one of us is going to **stand before the judgment seat of Christ**,[56] and that will be the only evaluation that really counts.

This judgment has to do with a believer's service, not his sins (1 Cor. 3:11–15). It is a time of review and reward, and is not to be confused with the Judgment of the Gentile nations (Matt. 25:31–46) or the Judgment of the Great White Throne (Rev. 20:11–15). The latter is the final judgment of all the wicked dead.

14:11 The certainty of our appearance before the *bēma* of Christ is reinforced by a quotation from Isaiah 45:23, where Jehovah Himself makes a strong affirmation that **every knee shall bow** before Him in acknowledgement of His supreme authority.

14:12 **So then** it is clear that we will all **give** an **account of** *ourselves*, not of our brothers, **to God**. We judge one another too much, and without the proper authority or knowledge.

14:13 Instead of sitting in judgment on our fellow Christians in these matters of moral indifference, we should **resolve** that we will never do anything to hinder a brother in his spiritual progress. None of these nonessential matters is important enough for us to cause a brother to stumble or **to fall.**

14:14 Paul knew, and we know, that no foods are ceremonially **unclean** any longer, as they were for a Jew living under the law. The food we eat is sanctified by the word of God and prayer (1 Tim. 4:5). It is sanctified by the word in the sense that the Bible distinctly sets it apart as being good. It is sanctified by prayer when we ask God to bless it for His glory and for the strengthening of our bodies in His service. But if a weak brother thinks it is wrong for him to eat pork, for example, then it is wrong. To eat it would be to violate his God-given conscience.

When Paul says here **that there is nothing unclean of itself**, we must realize that he is speaking *only* of these *indifferent* matters. There are plenty of things in life that are unclean, such as pornographic literature, suggestive jokes, dirty movies, and every form of immorality. Paul's statement must be understood in the light of the context. Christians do not contact ceremonial defilement by eating foods which the Law of Moses branded unclean.

14:15 When I sit down to eat with a weak **brother**, should I insist on my legitimate right to eat Crab Louis or Lobster Thermidor, even if I know he thinks it is wrong? If I do, I am not acting **in love**, because love thinks of others, not of self. Love foregoes its legitimate rights in order to promote the welfare of a brother. A dish of food isn't as important as the spiritual well-being of **one for whom Christ died**. And yet if I selfishly parade my rights in these matters, I can do irreparable damage in the life of a weak brother. It isn't worth it when you remember that his soul was redeemed at such a towering cost — the precious blood of the Lamb.

14:16 So the principle here is that we should not allow these secondary things, which are perfectly permissible in themselves, to give occasion to others to condemn us for our "looseness" or "lovelessness." It would be like sacrificing our good name for a mess of pottage.

14:17 What really counts in **the kingdom of God** is not dietary regulations but spiritual realities. **The kingdom of God** is the sphere where God is acknowledged as Supreme Ruler. In its widest sense, it includes all who even *profess* allegiance to God. But in its inward reality it includes only those who are born again. That is its usage here.

The subjects of the kingdom are not intended to be food faddists, gourmets, or wine connoisseurs. They should be characterized by lives of practical **righteousness**, by dispositions of **peace** and harmony, and by mind-sets of **joy in the Holy Spirit**.

14:18 It isn't what a man eats or doesn't eat that matters. It is a holy life that wins God's honor and man's approval. Those who put the emphasis on righteousness, peace, and joy serve **Christ** by obeying His teachings.

14:19 Thus *another principle* emerges. Instead of bickering over inconsequential matters, we should make every effort to maintain **peace** and harmony in the Christian fellowship. Instead of stumbling others by insisting on our rights, we should strive to build up others in their most holy faith.

14:20 **God** is doing a **work** in the life of each one of His children. It is frightening to think of hindering that work in the life of a weak brother over such secondary matters as **food**, drink, or days. For the child of God, all foods are now clean. But it would be wrong for him to eat any specific food if, in doing so, he would offend a brother or stumble him in his Christian walk.

14:21 It is a thousand times better to refrain from **meat** or **wine** or **anything** else than to offend a **brother** or cause him to decline spiritually. Giving up our legitimate rights is a small price to pay for the care of one who is **weak**.

14:22 I may have complete liberty to partake of every kind of food, knowing that God gave it to be received with thanksgiving. But I should not needlessly flaunt that liberty before those who are weak. It is better to exercise that liberty in private, when no one could possibly be offended.

It is good to walk in the full enjoyment of one's Christian liberty, not being fettered by unwarranted scruples. But it is better to forego one's legitimate rights than have to condemn oneself for offending others. One who avoids stumbling others is the **happy** person.

14:23 As far as the weak brother is concerned, it is wrong for him to eat anything about which he has conscientious scruples. His eating is not an act of **faith**; that is, he has a bad conscience about it. And it is a **sin** to violate one's conscience.

It is true that a person's conscience is not an infallible guide; it must be educated by the word of God. But, writes Merrill Unger, "Paul lays down the law that a man should follow his conscience, even though it be weak; otherwise moral personality would be destroyed."[57]

15:1 The first thirteen verses of chapter 15 continue the subject of the previous chapter, dealing with matters of moral indifference. Tensions had arisen between the converts from Judaism and those from paganism, so Paul here pleads for harmonious relations between these Jewish and Gentile Christians.

Those **who are strong** (that is, with full liberty regarding things that are morally indifferent) are **not to please** themselves by selfishly asserting their rights.

Rather, they should treat their **weak** brothers with kindness and consideration, making full allowance for their excessive **scruples**.

15:2 Here the principle is this: don't live to please self. Live to **please** your **neighbor**, to do him **good**, to build him up. This is the Christian approach.

15:3[†] **Christ** has given us the example. He lived to please His Father, not Himself. He said, **"The reproaches of those who reproached You fell on Me"** (Ps. 69:9). This means that He was so completely taken up with God's honor that when men insulted God He took it as a personal insult to Himself.

15:4 This quotation from the Psalms reminds us that the OT Scriptures **were written for our learning**. While they were not written directly *to* us, they contain invaluable lessons **for** us. As we encounter problems, conflicts, tribulations, and troubles, the Scriptures teach us to be steadfast, and they impart **comfort**. Thus, instead of sinking under the waves, we are sustained by the **hope** that the Lord will see us through.

15:5 This consideration leads Paul to express the wish that **the God** who gives steadfastness and **comfort** will enable the strong and the weak, Gentile and Jewish Christians, to live harmoniously **according to** the teaching and example of **Christ Jesus**.

15:6 The result will be that the saints will be united in the worship of **the God and Father of our Lord Jesus Christ**. What a picture! Saved Jews and saved Gentiles worshiping the Lord with **one mouth**!

There are four mentions of the **mouth** in Romans, forming a biographical outline of a "well-saved soul." At the beginning, his mouth was full of cursing and bitterness (3:14). Then his mouth was stopped, and he was brought in guilty before the Judge (3:19). Next he confesses with his mouth Jesus as Lord (10:9). And finally his **mouth** is actively praising and worshiping the Lord (15:6).

15:7 One more principle emerges from all this. In spite of any differences that might exist concerning secondary matters, we should **receive one another, just as Christ also received us**. Here is the true basis for reception in the local assembly. We do not receive on the basis

of denominational affiliation, spiritual maturity, or social status. We should **receive** those whom **Christ** has **received**, in order to promote the **glory of God**.

15:8 In the next six verses the apostle reminds his readers that the ministry of **Jesus Christ** includes Jews and Gentiles, and the implication is that our hearts should also be big enough to include both. Certainly Christ came to serve **the circumcision** — that is, the Jewish people. God had repeatedly promised that He would send the Messiah to Israel, and Christ's coming confirmed the truth of those **promises**.

15:9 But Christ brings blessings to **the Gentiles** also. God purposed that the nations should hear the gospel, and that those people who believe should **glorify God for His** great **mercy**. This should not come as a surprise to Jewish believers, because it is frequently foretold in their Scriptures. In Psalm 18:49, for example, David anticipates the day when the Messiah will **sing** praise to God in the midst of a host of Gentile believers.

15:10 In Deuteronomy 32:43 the Gentiles are pictured as rejoicing in the blessings of salvation **with His people** Israel.

15:11 In Psalm 117:1 we hear Israel calling on the **Gentiles** to **praise the LORD** in the Millennial Reign of the Messiah.

15:12 Finally **Isaiah** adds his testimony to the inclusion of **the Gentiles** in the dominion of the Messiah (Isa. 11:1, 10). The particular point here is that **the Gentiles** would share in the privileges of the Messiah and His gospel.

The Lord Jesus is **a root of Jesse** in the sense that He is Jesse's Creator, not that He sprang from Jesse (though that *also* is true). In Revelation 22:16 Jesus speaks of Himself as the Root and Offspring of David. As to His deity, He is David's Creator; as to His humanity, He is David's descendant.

15:13 So Paul closes this section with a gracious benediction, praying that **the God** who gives good **hope** through grace will fill the saints **with all joy and peace** as they believe on Him. Perhaps he is thinking especially of Gentile believers here, but the prayer is suitable for all. And it is true that those who **abound in hope by the power of the Holy Spirit**

†See p. xxii.

have no time to quarrel over nonessentials. Our common hope is a powerful unifying force in the Christian life.

G. In Paul's Plans (15:14–33)

15:14 In the rest of chapter 15 Paul states his reason for writing to the Romans and his great desire to visit them.

Though he has never met the Roman Christians, he is **confident** that they will welcome his admonitions. This confidence is based on what he has heard of their **goodness**. In addition, he is assured of their **knowledge** of Christian doctrine, which qualifies them **to admonish** others (NKJV mg.).

15:15 In spite of his confidence in their spiritual progress, and in spite of the fact that he was a stranger to them, Paul didn't hesitate to remind them of some of their privileges and responsibilities. His frankness in writing as he did arose from **the grace given to** him **by God** — that is, **the grace** that appointed him as an apostle.

15:16 He was appointed by God to be a sort of serving-priest **of Jesus Christ to the Gentiles**. He looked upon his work of **ministering the gospel of God** as a priestly function in which he presented saved **Gentiles** as an **acceptable offering** to God because they had been set apart **by the Holy Spirit** to God through the new birth. G. Campbell Morgan exults:

> What a radiant light this sheds on all our evangelistic and pastoral effort! Every soul won by the preaching of the gospel is not only brought into a place of safety and of blessing; he is an offering to God, a gift which gives Him satisfaction, the very offering He is seeking. Every soul carefully and patiently instructed in the things of Christ, and so made conformable to His likeness, is a soul in whom the Father takes pleasure. Thus we labor, not only for the saving of men, but for the satisfying of the heart of God. This is the most powerful motive.[58]

15:17 If Paul engages in boasting, it is not in his own person that he glories, but **in Christ Jesus**. And it is not in his own accomplishments but in what **God** has been pleased to do through him. A humble servant of Christ does not engage in unseemly boasting, but rather he is conscious of the fact that God is using him to accomplish His purposes. Any temptation to pride is tempered by the realization that he is nothing in himself, that he has nothing except what he has received, and that he can do nothing for Christ except by the power of the Holy Spirit.

15:18 Paul does **not** presume **to speak of** what **Christ** had done through the ministry of others. He confines himself to the way the Lord had used *him* to win **the Gentiles** to obedience, both by what he said and by what he did — that is, by the message he preached and by the miracles he performed.

15:19 The Lord confirmed the apostle's message by miracles that taught spiritual lessons and that inspired amazement, and by various manifestations of the Spirit's power. The result was that he had **fully preached the gospel**, beginning at **Jerusalem** and extending in a circle **to Illyricum** (north of Macedonia, on the Adriatic Sea). **From Jerusalem . . . to Illyricum** describes the *geographical* extent of his ministry and not the chronological order.

15:20 In following this route, Paul's **aim** was **to preach the gospel** in virgin territory. His audiences were composed primarily of Gentiles who had never heard of **Christ** before. Thus he was not building on anyone else's **foundation**. Paul's example in pioneering in new areas does not necessarily bind other servants of the Lord to this exact activity. Some are called to move in and teach, for example, after new churches have been planted.

15:21 This foundational work among the Gentiles was a fulfillment of Isaiah's prophecy (52:15) that the Gentiles who had never previously been evangelized would **see**, and that those who had never previously **heard** the good news would **understand** and respond in true faith.

15:22, 23 In his desire to plow untilled territory, Paul had been too occupied to get to Rome in the past. **But now** the foundation had been laid in the region described in 15:19. Others could build on the foundation. Paul was therefore free to fulfill his long-standing **desire** to visit Rome.

15:24 His plan was to stop off at Rome en route **to Spain**. He would not be able to stay long enough to enjoy all the fellowship with them that he would like, but his desire to **enjoy** their **company** would be partially satisfied at least. Then he knew that they would give whatever help was needed to complete his trip to Spain.

15:25 But in the meantime he was **going to Jerusalem** to deliver the funds which had been collected among Gentile churches for **the** needy **saints** in Judea. This is the collection that we read about in 1 Corinthians 16:1 and 2 Corinthians 8 and 9.

15:26, 27 The believers in **Macedonia and Achaia** had gladly contributed to a fund to relieve the distress among the **poor** Christians. This collection was completely voluntary on the part of the donors, and also quite appropriate for them to give. After all, they had benefited spiritually by the coming of the gospel to them through Jewish believers. So it was not too much to expect that they would share with their Jewish brethren **in material things**.

15:28, 29 As soon as Paul had **performed this** mission, delivering the funds as promised, he would visit Rome on his way **to Spain**. He had every confidence that his visit to Rome would be accompanied by **the fullness of the blessing of the gospel** which **Christ** always pours out when God's word is preached in the power of the Holy Spirit.

15:30 The apostle closes this section with a fervent appeal for their **prayers**. The basis on which he appeals is their mutual union with **the Lord Jesus Christ** and their **love** which came from **the** Holy **Spirit**. He asks them to agonize **in prayers to God for** him. As Lenski says, "This calls for prayers into which one puts his whole heart and soul as do the contestants in the arena."[59]

15:31 Four specific prayer requests are given. *First*, Paul asks for prayer that he will **be delivered from** zealots **in Judea who** were fanatically opposed to the gospel, just as he himself had once been.

Second, he wants the Romans to pray that the Jewish **saints** will accept the relief funds in good grace. Strong religious prejudices remained against Gentile believers and against those who preached to the Gentiles. Then there is always the possibility of people being offended at

the idea of receiving "charity." It often takes more grace to be on the receiving end than on the giving end!

15:32 The *third* request was that the Lord might see fit to make the visit to Rome a joyful one. The words **by the will of God** express Paul's desire to be led by the Lord in all things.

Last of all, he asks that his visit might be one in which he **may be refreshed** in the midst of a tumultuous and fatiguing ministry.

15:33 And now Paul closes the chapter with the prayer that **the God** who is the source **of peace** might be their portion. In chapter 15 the Lord has been named *the God of patience* and *consolation* (v. 5), *the God of hope* (v. 13), and now the **God of peace**. He is the source of everything good and of everything a poor sinner needs now and eternally. **Amen.**

H. In Appreciative Recognition of Others (Chap. 16)

At first glance the closing chapter of Romans seems to be an uninteresting catalog of names that have little or no meaning for us today. However, upon closer study this neglected chapter yields many important lessons for the believer.

16:1 Phoebe is introduced as **a servant**[60] **of the church in Cenchrea**. We need not think of her as belonging to some special religious order. Any sister who serves in connection with a local assembly can be a "deaconess."

16:2 Whenever the early Christians traveled from one church to another, they carried letters of introduction. This was a real courtesy to the church being visited and a help to the visitor.

So the apostle here introduces Phoebe and asks that she be welcomed as a true believer **in a manner worthy of** fellow-believers. He further asks that she be assisted in every way possible. Her commendation is that she has given herself to the ministry of helping others, including Paul himself. Perhaps she was the tireless sister who was forever showing hospitality to preachers and other believers in Cenchrea.

16:3 Next Paul sends greetings to **Priscilla and Aquila**, who had been such valiant **fellow workers** of his **in** the service of **Christ Jesus**. How we can thank God for Christian couples who pour themselves out in sacrificial labor for the cause of Christ!

16:4 On one occasion Priscilla and Aquila actually **risked their** lives **for** Paul — a heroic act of which no details are given. But the apostle is grateful, and so are the **churches of** converted **Gentiles** to whom he ministered.

16:5 **Greet the church that is in their house**. This means that an actual congregation of believers met in their house. Church buildings were unknown until the late second century. Earlier, when Priscilla and Aquila lived in Corinth, they had a church in their house also.

Epaenetus means "praiseworthy." No doubt this first convert in the province of Achaia[61] was true to his name. Paul speaks of him as **my beloved**.

16:6 The prominence of women's names in this chapter emphasizes their wide sphere of usefulness (vv. 1, 3, 6, 12, etc.). **Mary** worked like a Trojan for the saints.

16:7 We do not know when **Adronicus and Junia** were **fellow prisoners** with Paul. We cannot be sure whether the word **countrymen** means that they were close relatives of the apostle or simply fellow Jews. Again, we do not know whether the expression **of note among the apostles** means that they were respected *by* the **apostles** or that they themselves were outstanding **apostles**. All we can know for certain is that they became Christians **before** Paul.

16:8 Next we meet **Amplias, beloved** by the apostle. We would never have heard of any of these people except for their connection with Calvary. That is the only greatness about any of us.

16:9 **Urbanus** wins the title **fellow worker**, and **Stachys** is called **my beloved**. Romans 16 is like a miniature of the Judgment Seat of Christ, where there will be praise for every instance of faithfulness to Christ.

16:10 **Apelles** had come through some great trial with flying colors and had won the seal of **approved in Christ**.

Paul greets **the household of Aristobulus**, probably meaning Christian slaves belonging to this grandson of Herod the Great.

16:11 **Herodion** was probably a slave also. A **countryman** of Paul, he may have been the only *Jewish* slave belonging to the household of Aristobulus.

Then some of the slaves belonging to **Narcissus** were also believers, and Paul includes them in his greetings. Even those who are lowest on the social ladder are not excluded from the choicest blessings of Christianity. The inclusion of slaves in this list of names is a lovely reminder that in Christ all social distinctions are obliterated because we are all one in Him.

16:12 **Tryphena** and **Tryphosa** had names that meant "dainty" and "luxurious," but they were veritable workhorses in their service for the Lord. **The beloved Persis** was another of those women workers that are so needed in local churches but seldom appreciated until they are gone.

16:13 **Rufus** may be the son of Simon, who carried the cross for Jesus (Matt. 27:32). He was **chosen in the Lord** not only as to his salvation but also as to his Christian character; that is, he was a choice saint. The **mother** of Rufus had shown maternal kindness to Paul, and this earned his affectionate title "my mother."

16:14, 15 Perhaps **Asyncritus, Phlegon, Hermas, Patrobas**, and **Hermes** were active in a house church, like the one in the house of Priscilla and Aquila (16:3, 5). **Philologus and Julia, Nereus and his sister, and Olympas** may have been the nucleus of another house church.

16:16 The **holy kiss** was the common mode of affectionate greeting among the saints then and is still practiced in some countries today. It is designated as a **holy kiss** to guard against impropriety. In our culture, the **kiss** is generally replaced by the handshake.

The churches in Achaia, where Paul was writing, joined in sending their greetings.

16:17 The apostle cannot close the letter without a warning against ungodly teachers who might worm their way into the church. The Christians should be on their guard against any such who form parties around themselves and set traps to destroy the faith of the unwary. They should be on the lookout for any whose teaching is **contrary to the** sound **doctrine** which the Christians had **learned**, and should **avoid them** completely.

16:18 These false teachers are not

obedient to **our Lord Jesus Christ**. They obey **their own** appetites. And they are all too successful in hoodwinking the unsuspecting by their winsome and **flattering speech.**

16:19 Paul was **glad** that his readers' **obedience** to the Lord was well-known. But still he wanted them to be able to discern and obey **good** teaching and to be unresponsive to **evil**.

16:20 In this way, **the God** who is the source **of peace** would give them a swift victory over **Satan**.

The apostle's characteristic benediction wishes all needed enablement for the saints as they journey toward glory.

16:21 We know **Timothy**, Paul's son in the faith and faithful co-worker. We know nothing of **Lucius** except that he, like Paul, was of Jewish parentage. We may have previously met **Jason** (Acts 17:5) and **Sosipater** (Acts 20:4), also Jews.

16:22 Tertius was the one to whom Paul had dictated **this epistle**. He takes the liberty of adding his personal well-wishes to the readers.

16:23 There are at least four men by the name of **Gaius** in the NT. This is probably the same one spoken of in 1 Corinthians 1:14. He was noted for his hospitality, not only to Paul but to any Christians who needed it. **Erastus** was **treasurer of the city** of Corinth. But was he the same person mentioned in Acts 19:22 and/or 2 Timothy 4:20? We cannot be sure. **Quartus** is mentioned simply as **a brother**, but after all, what an honor, what a dignity!

16:24 The grace of our Lord Jesus Christ be with you all is Paul's typical closing benediction. It is the same as v. 20b with the addition of **all**. As a matter of fact, in most manuscripts of Romans, this is the last verse, and the doxology in vv. 25-27 comes *after chapter 14*. The Alexandrian (NU) text omits v. 20. Both the benediction and the doxology are beautiful ways to end the book. And both end with **Amen**.

16:25 The Epistle closes with a doxology. It is addressed to the God **who is able** to make His people stand firm in accordance with the **gospel** which Paul preached and which he calls **my gospel**. There is only one way of salvation, of course; but it was entrusted to him as

"the Apostle to the Gentiles", whereas Peter, for example, preached it to the Jews. It is the public heralding of the message about **Jesus Christ** concerning **the revelation** of a marvelous truth **kept secret since the world began**. A **mystery**, in the NT is a truth never previously known, and a truth which human intellect could never discover, but one which has now been made known.

16:26 The particular mystery spoken of here is the truth that believing Jews and believing Gentiles are made fellow heirs, fellow members of the Body of Christ, and fellow partakers of His promise in Christ by the gospel (Eph. 3:6).

It **now has been made manifest** by the writing of the prophets — not the prophets of the OT but those of the NT period. It was unknown in the OT Scriptures but has been revealed in **the prophetic Scriptures** of the NT (see Eph. 2:20; 3:5).

It is the gospel message which God **has** commanded to be **made known to all nations** in order that people might obey **the faith** and be saved.

16:27 God alone is the source and display of pure wisdom, and to Him belongs **glory through Jesus Christ**, our Mediator, **forever**.

And so ends Paul's magnificent Epistle. How indebted we are to the Lord for it! And how poor we would be without it! **Amen.**

ENDNOTES

[1](1:4) Some commentators take "the Spirit of holiness" to refer to Christ's own holy being, i.e., His own human spirit.

[2](1:29) It is easy to see how some mss. copyists could delete *sexual immorality* by mistake: in the Greek the word *porneia* looks so much like the next word *ponēria* (evil).

[3](1:31) Verse 31 contains five negative words beginning with "alpha-privative" (cf. a-theist, "no God"), similar in word structure to our English words beginning with "un-". NU omits *unforgiving* (*aspondous*) which looks much like *unloving* (*astorgous*).

[4](2:4) A. P. Gibbs, *Preach and Teach the Word*, p. 12/4.

⁵(2:6) Lewis S. Chafer, *Systematic Theology*, III:376.

⁶(3:22) NU text omits "and on all."

⁷(3:23) Literally "sinned" (aorist, not perfect).

⁸(Excursus) The same is true in Hebrew and Greek.

⁹(3:24) Arthur T. Pierson, *Shall We Continue in Sin?* p. 23.

¹⁰(3:24) Paul Van Gorder, in *Our Daily Bread*.

¹¹(3:30) Cranfield points out (*Romans*, I: 222) that attempts to find a very subtle difference are not convincing. Augustine was probably correct in ascribing the change to rhetorical variety.

¹²(4:1) Or the experience of "Abraham our (fore)father according to the flesh."

¹³(4:13) *Daily Notes of the Scripture Union*, (further documentation unavailable).

¹⁴(4:19) While some manuscripts omit "not," the resultant meaning is much the same.

¹⁵(4:24) C. H. Mackintosh, *The Mackintosh Treasury: Miscellaneous Writings by C. H. Mackintosh*, p. 66.

¹⁶(5:11) The KJV rendering "atonement" was correct in 1611, when it meant "at-one-ment" or reconciliation.

¹⁷(6:1) J. Oswald Sanders, *Spiritual Problems*, p. 112.

¹⁸(6:5) Charles Hodge, *The Epistle to the Romans*, p. 196.

¹⁹(6:11) Ruth Paxson, *The Wealth, Walk, and Warfare of the Christian*, p. 108.

²⁰(6:11) C. E. Macartney, *Macartney's Illustrations*, pp. 378, 379.

²¹(6:14) James Denney, "St. Paul's Epistle to the Romans," *The Expositor's Greek Testament*, II:635.

²²(6:19) Charles Gahan, *Gleanings in Romans, in loco.*

²³(6:21) Marcus Rainsford, *Lectures on Romans VI*, p. 172.

²⁴(6:21) Pierson, *Shall We Continue in Sin?* p. 45.

²⁵(7:15) Harry Foster, article in *Toward the Mark*, p. 110.

²⁶(7:23) George Cutting, "The Old Nature and the New Birth" (booklet), p. 33.

²⁷(8:1) The words "who do not walk according to the flesh, but according to the Spirit" are widely thought to be miscopied from v. 4. However, they do occur in most mss., and may simply give further description of those in Christ.

²⁸(8:10) The NKJV translators took *pneuma* to refer to the *Holy* Spirit, hence the capital "S". The original mss. were in all "capitals" (uncials), so it is a matter of interpretation. We take it as referring to the believer's (human) spirit.

²⁹(8:15) See note 28. Here the alternative meaning of Spirit is not the *human* spirit, but an attitude that is the opposite of slavery.

³⁰(8:18) In Hebrew, the word for *glory* is derived from the verb *to be heavy*, hence the Jews would see a play on words, even though veiled by the Greek.

³¹(8:31) This was John Calvin's life verse.

³²(8:32) C. H. Mackintosh (further documentation unavailable).

³³(8:37) A very literal rendering is "we super-conquer" (*hupernikōmen*).

³⁴(8:39) These words were used in astrology, for example.

³⁵(9:4) *The New Scofield Reference Bible*, p. 1317.

³⁶(9:5) See Hodge, *Romans*, pp. 299–301 for a detailed exposition of this question.

³⁷(9:16) G. Campbell Morgan, *Searchlights from the Word*, pp. 335, 336.

³⁸(9:21) Albert Barnes, *Barnes's Notes on the New Testament*, p. 617.

³⁹(9:23) Charles R. Erdman, *The Epistle of Paul to the Romans*, p. 109.

⁴⁰(10:10) William Kelly, *Notes on the Epistle to the Romans*, p. 206.

⁴¹(10:10) James Denney, quoted by Kenneth Wuest in *Romans in the Greek New Testament*, p. 178.

⁴²(10:14) Hodge, *Romans*, p. 545.

⁴³(11:1) It is sad to note that many who appropriate Israel's blessings for the church are quite satisfied to leave them the predicted curses!

⁴⁴(11:32) George Williams, *The Student's Commentary on the Holy Scriptures*, p. 871.

⁴⁵(11:33) Arthur W. Pink, *The Attributes of God*, p. 13.

⁴⁶(12:1) Norman Grubb, *C. T. Studd, Cricketer and Pioneer*, p. 141.

⁴⁷(12:6) Hodge, *Romans*, p. 613.

⁴⁸(12:6) A. H. Strong, *Systematic Theology*, p. 12.

⁴⁹(12:6) However, the definite article, used here in the original, practically

equals a pronoun in some contexts.

⁵⁰(12:19) R. C. H. Lenski, *St. Paul's Epistle to the Romans*, p. 780.

⁵¹(12:21) J. N. Darby, from footnote on Romans 12:21 in his *New Translation*.

⁵²(12:21) George Washington Carver (further documentation unavailable).

⁵³(12:21) Quoted by Charles Swindoll in *Growing Strong in the Seasons of Life*, pp. 69, 70.

⁵⁴(13:4) The usual Hebrew verbs for "kill" and "slay" are *qātal* and *hārag*. The specific verb "murder" (*rāhats*) is used in the Ten Commandments, and the Greek translation is equally clear.

⁵⁵(13:9) NU text omits this commandment here.

⁵⁶(14:10) Some ancient mss. (NU) read "judgment seat of God" rather than "of Christ" (TR and M texts). But we know that *Christ* will be the Judge, since the Father has committed all judgment to Him (John 5:22).

⁵⁷(14:23) Merrill F. Unger, *Unger's Bible Dictionary*, p. 219.

⁵⁸(15:16) Morgan, *Searchlights*, p. 337.

⁵⁹(15:30) Lenski, *Romans*, p. 895.

⁶⁰(16:1) The feminine form of *diakonos* ("servant," "deacon") would probably have been used if a specific office for women had been meant.

⁶¹(16:5) NU text reads *Asia* here (but Corinth, from which Paul was probably writing, was in *Achaia*).

BIBLIOGRAPHY

Cranfield, C. E. B. *The Epistle to the Romans, Vol. I (ICC)*, Edinburgh: T. & T. Clark Ltd., 1975.

Denney, James. "St. Paul's Epistle to the Romans," *The Expositor's Greek Testament, Vol. II*. Grand Rapids: Wm. B. Eerdmans Publishing Company, 1961.

Erdman, C. R. *The Epistle of Paul to the Romans*. Philadelphia: The Westminster Press, 1925.

Gahan, Charles. *Gleanings in Romans*. Published by author.

Hodge, Charles. *Commentary on the Epistle to the Romans*. New York: George H. Doran Company, 1886.

Kelly, William. *Notes on the Epistle to the Romans*. London: G. Morrish, 1873.

Lenski, R. C. H. *St. Paul's Epistle to the Romans*. Minneapolis: Augsburg Publishing House, 1961.

Newell, William R. *Romans Verse by Verse*. Chicago: Moody Press, 1938.

Rainsford, Marcus. *Lectures on Romans VI*. London: Charles J. Thynne, 1898.

Shedd, William G. T. *A Critical and Doctrinal Commentary on the Epistle of St. Paul to the Romans*. Grand Rapids: Zondervan, 1967.

Stifler, James M. *The Epistle to the Romans: A Commentary Logical and Historical*. Chicago: Moody Press, 1960.

Wuest, Kenneth S. *Romans in the Greek New Testament*. Grand Rapids: Wm. B. Eerdmans Publishing Company, 1964.

THE FIRST EPISTLE TO THE CORINTHIANS

Introduction

"A fragment of ecclesiastical history like no other." — Weizäcker

I. Unique Place in the Canon

First Corinthians is the "problem book" in the sense that Paul handles the problems ("Now concerning . . .") that faced the congregation in the wicked city of Corinth. As such it is most needed by today's problem-racked churches. The divisions, hero-worship of leaders, immorality, legal battles, marital problems, doubtful practices, and regulation of spiritual gifts, are all handled here.

It would be wrong, however, to think it was all problems! This is the Epistle that contains 1 Corinthians 13, the most beautiful essay on love, not just in the Bible, but in *all* literature. The remarkable teaching on the resurrection — both Christ's and ours (chap. 15), the regulation of the Lord's Supper (chap. 11), the command to take part in the collection (chap. 16), are all here.

We would be very much the poorer without 1 Corinthians. It is a treasure trove of practical Christian teaching.

II. Authorship†

All scholars agree that what we call 1 Corinthians is an authentic product of Paul's pen. Some (chiefly liberal) writers think they see some "interpolations" in the letter, but these are subjective conjectures with no supporting manuscript evidence. 1 Corinthians 5:9 apparently implies a previous (uncanonical) letter from Paul that the Corinthians misunderstood.

The *external evidence* for 1 Corinthians is very early, the book being specifically referred to by Clement of Rome (c. A.D. 95) as "the Epistle of the blessed Apostle Paul." Other early church writers quoting the book are Polycarp, Justin Martyr, Athenagoras, Irenaeus, Clement of Alexandria, and Tertullian. It is listed in the Muratorian Canon and comes after Galatians in the heretic Marcion's own "canon," the *Apostolicon.*

The *internal evidence* is very strong as well. Besides the author's references to himself as Paul in 1:1 and 16:21, the argument in 1:12–17; 3:4, 6, 22 also supports Pauline authorship. Coincidences with Acts and with other letters of Paul, plus the strong flavor of genuine apostolic concern rule out a forgery and make the arguments for authenticity overwhelming.

III. Date

Paul tells us he is writing from Ephesus (16:8, 9, cf. v. 19). Since he ministered there for three years, 1 Corinthians was most likely written in the latter half of that extended ministry, or about A.D. 55 or 56. Some scholars date it even earlier.

IV. Background and Theme††

Ancient Corinth was (and is) in southern Greece, west of Athens, strategically situated on the trade routes in Paul's day. It became a great center for international commerce, and immense quantities of traffic came to this city. Because of the depraved religion of the people, it soon became the center also for the grossest forms of immorality, so that the name Corinth was a byword for

†See p. i.
††See p. ii.

all that was impure and sensual. So lewd was the city's reputation, there was even a verb coined, *korinthiazomai*, which meant *to lead a debased life*.

The Apostle Paul first visited Corinth on his Second Missionary Journey (Acts 18). At first he labored among the Jewish people, together with Priscilla and Aquila, his fellow tentmakers. When most Jews rejected his message, he turned to the Gentiles in Corinth. Souls were saved through the preaching of the gospel, and a church was formed.

About three years later, when Paul was preaching in Ephesus, he received a letter from Corinth, telling of serious difficulties in the assembly there and also asking various questions as to matters of Christian practice. It was in answer to this letter that the First Epistle to the Corinthians was written.

The theme of the Epistle is how to set right a worldly and carnal church that regards lightly the attitudes, errors, and actions that the Apostle Paul viewed with such alarm. As Moffatt put it so succinctly, "The Church was in the world, as it had to be, but the world was in the Church, as it ought not to be."

Since such a situation is still common in many congregations, the relevance of 1 Corinthians is lasting.

OUTLINE

Commentary

I. INTRODUCTION (1:1–9)

A. Salutation (1:1–3)

1:1 Paul was **called to be an apos-**tle of Jesus Christ on the Damascus road. This call did not come from or through men, but directly from the Lord Jesus. **An apostle** is literally "a sent one." The first apostles were witnesses of Christ in resurrection. They also could perform miracles to confirm that the message they preached was divine. Paul could truly say in the language of Gerhard Tersteegen:

Christ the Son of God has sent me
To the midnight lands;
Mine the mighty ordination
Of the piercèd hands.

When Paul wrote, a **brother** named **Sosthenes** was with him, so Paul includes his name in the salutation. It cannot be known for sure whether this is the same Sosthenes as in Acts 18:17, the ruler of the synagogue who was publicly beaten by the Greeks. Possibly this leader had been saved through Paul's preaching and was now helping him in the work of the gospel.

1:2 The letter is addressed first of all **to the church of God which is at Corinth**. It is encouraging that there is no place on earth too immoral for an assembly belonging to God to be established. The Corinthian congregation is further described as **those who are sanctified in Christ Jesus, called . . . saints. Sanctified** here means set apart to God from the world, and describes the *position* of all who belong to Christ. As to their *practical condition*, they should set themselves apart day by day in holy living.

Some people contend that sanctification is a distinct work of grace whereby a person obtains the eradication of the sin nature. Such a teaching is contradicted in this verse. The Corinthian Christians were far from what they should have been in practical holiness, but the fact remains that they were positionally **sanctified** by God.

As saints they were members of a great fellowship: **called to be saints, with all who in every place call on the name of Jesus Christ our Lord, both theirs and ours**. Although the teachings of this Epistle were first addressed to the saints in Corinth, they are also intended for all those of the worldwide fellowship who acknowledge the lordship of Christ.

1:3 First Corinthians is in a very special way the letter of His lordship. In discussing the many problems of assembly and personal life, the apostle constantly reminds his readers that Jesus Christ is Lord and that all we do should be done in acknowledgment of this great truth.

Paul's characteristic greeting is given in verse 3. **Grace and peace** summarize his entire gospel. **Grace** is the source of every blessing, and **peace** is the result in the life of a man who accepts the grace of God. These great blessings come **from God our Father and the Lord Jesus Christ**. Paul does not hesitate to mention **the Lord Jesus** in the same breath with **God our Father**. This is one of hundreds of similar expressions in the NT implying the equality of the Lord Jesus with God the Father.

B. Thanksgiving (1:4–9)

1:4 Having concluded his salutation, the apostle now turns to thanksgiving for the Corinthians and for the wonderful work of God in their lives (vv. 4–9). It was a noble trait in Paul's life that always sought to find something thankworthy in the lives of his fellow believers. If their practical lives were not very commendable, then he would at least **thank** his **God** for what He had done for them. This is exactly the case here. The Corinthians were not what we would call spiritual Christians. But Paul can at least give thanks **for the grace of God which was given to** them **by Christ Jesus**.

1:5 The particular way in which God's grace was manifested to the Corinthians was in their being richly endowed with gifts of the Holy Spirit. Paul specifies gifts of **utterance and all knowledge**, presumably meaning that the Corinthians had been given the gifts of tongues, interpretation of tongues, and knowledge to an extraordinary degree. **Utterance** has to do with outward expression and **knowledge** with inward comprehension.

1:6 The fact that they had these gifts was a confirmation of God's work in their lives, and that is what Paul means when he says, **even as the testimony of Christ was confirmed in you**. They heard **the testimony of Christ**, they received it by faith, and God testified that they were truly saved by giving them these miraculous powers.

1:7 As far as the possession of gifts was concerned, the Corinthian church was not inferior to any other. But the mere possession of these gifts was not in itself a mark of true spirituality. Paul was really thanking the Lord for something for which the Corinthians themselves were not directly responsible. Gifts are given by the ascended Lord without regard to a person's own merit. If a person has some gift, he should not be proud of it but use it humbly for the Lord.

The fruit of the Spirit is another matter entirely. This involves the believer's own surrender to the control of the Holy Spirit. The apostle could not commend the Corinthians for evidence of the fruit of the Spirit in their lives, but only for what the Lord had sovereignly bestowed on them — something over which they had no control.

Later in the Epistle the apostle will have to reprove the saints for their abuse of these gifts, but here he is content to express thanks that they had received these gifts in such unusual measure.

The Corinthians were **eagerly waiting for the revelation of our Lord Jesus Christ**. Bible students are not agreed as to whether this refers to Christ's coming for His saints (1 Thess. 4:13–18), or the Lord's coming with His saints (2 Thess. 1:6–10), or both. In the first case it would be a revelation of Christ only to believers, whereas in the second it would be His Revelation to the whole world. Both the Rapture and the glorious appearing of Christ are **eagerly** awaited by the believer.

1:8 Now Paul expresses the confidence that the Lord **will also confirm** the saints **to the end, that** they might be **blameless in the day of our Lord Jesus Christ**. Once again it is striking that Paul's thanksgiving is concerned with what God will do rather than with what the Corinthians have done. Because they have trusted Christ, and because God confirmed this fact by giving the gifts of the Spirit to them, Paul was confident that God would keep them for Himself until Christ's coming for His people.

1:9 Paul's optimism concerning the Corinthians is based on the faithfulness of **God** who called them **into the fellowship of His Son**. He knows that since God had gone to such tremendous cost

to make them sharers of the life of **our Lord**, He would never let them slip out of His hands.

II. DISORDERS IN THE CHURCH (1:10–6:20)

A. Divisions among Believers (1:10–4:21)

1:10 The apostle is now ready to take up the problem of **divisions** in the church (1:10–4:21). He begins with a loving exhortation to unity. Instead of commanding with the authority of an apostle, he pleads with the tenderness of a brother. The appeal for unity is based on **the name of our Lord Jesus Christ**, and since the name stands for the Person, it is based on all that the Lord Jesus is and has done. The Corinthians were exalting the name of men; that could only lead to divisions. Paul will exalt the name of the Lord Jesus, knowing that only in this way will unity be produced among the people of God. To **speak the same thing** means to be of **the same mind and** of one accord. It means to be united as to loyalty and allegiance. This unity is produced when Christians have the mind of Christ, and in the verses to follow, Paul will tell them in a practical manner how they can think Christ's thoughts after Him.

1:11 News concerning the **contentions** in Corinth had come to Paul from **Chloe's household**. In naming his informers, Paul lays down an important principle of Christian conduct. We should not pass on news about our fellow believers unless we are willing to be quoted in the matter. If this example were followed today, it would prevent most of the idle gossip which now plagues the church.

1:12 Sects or parties were being formed within the local church, each one claiming its distinctive leader. Some acknowledged preference for **Paul**, some for **Apollos**, some for **Cephas** (Peter). Some even claimed to belong to **Christ**, probably meaning that they *alone* belonged to Him, to the exclusion of others!

1:13 Paul's indignant rebuke of sectarianism is found in verses 13–17. To form such parties in the church was to deny the unity of the body of **Christ**. To follow human leaders was to slight the One who had been crucified for them. To take the name of a man was to forget that in baptism, they had acknowledged their allegiance to the Lord Jesus.

1:14 The rise of parties in Corinth made Paul thankful **that** he **had baptized** only a few in the assembly there. He mentions **Crispus and Gaius** as among those whom he had baptized.

1:15, 16 He would never want anyone to **say that** he **had baptized in** his **own name**. In other words, he was not trying to win converts to himself or to make a name for himself. His sole aim was to point men and women to the Lord Jesus Christ.

On further reflection Paul remembered that he had **also baptized the household of Stephanas**, but he could **not** think of **any other**.

1:17 He explains that **Christ did not send** him primarily **to baptize, but to preach the gospel**. This does not mean for a moment that Paul did not believe in baptism. He has already mentioned the names of some whom he *did* baptize. Rather, it means that his main business was not to baptize; he probably entrusted this work to others, perhaps to some of the Christians in the local church. This verse, however, does lend its testimony against any idea that baptism is essential to salvation. If that were true, then Paul would be saying here that he was thankful that he saved none of them except Crispus and Gaius! Such an idea is untenable.

In the latter part of verse 17, Paul is making an easy transition to the verses that follow. He did not **preach the gospel** by using **wisdom of words, lest the cross of Christ should be made of no effect**. He knew that if men were impressed by his oratory or rhetoric, then to that extent he had defeated himself in his efforts to set forth the true meaning of **the cross of Christ**.

It will help us to understand the section that follows if we remember that the Corinthians, being Greeks, were great lovers of human wisdom. They regarded their philosophers as national heroes. Some of this spirit had apparently crept

into the assembly at Corinth. There were those who desired to make the gospel more acceptable to the intelligentsia. They did not feel that it had status among scholars, and so they wanted to intellectualize the message. This worship of intellectualism was apparently one of the issues that was causing the people to form parties around human leaders. Efforts to make the gospel more acceptable are completely misguided. There is a vast difference between God's wisdom and man's, and there is no use trying to reconcile them.

Paul now shows the folly of exalting men, and emphasizes that to do this is inconsistent with the true nature of the gospel (1:18–3:4). His first point is that the message of the cross is the opposite of all that men consider to be true wisdom (1:18–25).

1:18 **The message of the cross is foolishness to those who are perishing**. As Barnes so aptly stated:

> The death on the cross was associated with the idea of all that is shameful and dishonorable; and to speak of salvation only by the sufferings and death of a crucified man was fitted to excite in their bosoms only unmingled scorn.[1]

The Greeks were lovers of wisdom (the literal meaning of the word "philosophers"). But there was nothing in the gospel message to appeal to their pride of knowledge.

To those **who are being saved**, the gospel **is the power of God**. They hear the message, they accept it by faith, and the miracle of regeneration takes place in their lives. Notice the solemn fact in this verse that there are only two classes of people, those who perish and those who are saved. There is no in-between class. Men may love their human wisdom but only the gospel leads to salvation.

1:19 The fact that the gospel would be offensive to human wisdom was prophesied by Isaiah (29:14):

"I will destroy the wisdom of the wise, and bring to nothing the understanding of the prudent."

S. Lewis Johnson in *The Wycliffe Bible Commentary* notes that in context these "words are God's denouncement of the policy of the 'wise' in Judah in seeking an alliance with Egypt when threatened by Sennacherib."[2] How true it is that God delights to accomplish His purposes in ways that seem foolish to men. How often He uses methods that the wise of this world would ridicule, yet they achieve the desired results with wonderful accuracy and efficiency. For example, man's wisdom assures him that he can earn or merit his own salvation. The gospel sets aside all man's efforts to save himself and presents Christ as the only way to God.

1:20 Paul next hurls out a defiant challenge: **"Where is the wise? Where is the scribe? Where is the disputer of this age?"** Did God consult them when He devised His plan of salvation? Could they ever have worked out such a plan of redemption if left to their own wisdom? Can they rise to disprove anything that God ever said? The answer is an emphatic "No!" **God has made foolish the wisdom of this world.**

1:21 Man cannot by his own **wisdom** come to the knowledge of God. For centuries God gave the human race this opportunity, and the result was failure. Then **it pleased God** by the preaching of the cross, a **message** that seems foolish to men, **to save those who believe**. The foolishness of the thing preached refers to the cross. Of course, we know that it is not foolishness, but it seems foolish to the unenlightened mind of man. Godet says that verse 21 contains a whole philosophy of history, the substance of entire volumes. We should not hurry over it quickly, but ponder deeply its tremendous truths.

1:22 It was characteristic of the **Jews** to **request a sign**. Their attitude was that they would believe if some miracle were shown to them. The **Greeks** on the other hand searched for **wisdom**. They were interested in human reasonings, in arguments, in logic.

1:23 But Paul did not cater to their desires. He says, **"We preach Christ crucified."** As someone has said, "He was not a sign-loving Jew, nor a wisdom-loving Greek, but a Savior-loving Christian."

To the Jews, Christ crucified was **a stumbling block**. They looked for a mighty military leader to deliver them from the oppression of Rome. Instead of that, the gospel offered them a Savior nailed to a cross of shame. **To the Greeks**, Christ crucified was **foolishness**. They could not understand how One who died in such seeming weakness and failure could ever solve their problems.

1:24 But strangely enough, the very things that the Jews and the Gentiles sought are found in a wonderful way in the Lord Jesus. To those who hear His call and trust in Him, **both Jews and Greeks, Christ** becomes **the power of God and the wisdom of God**.

1:25 Actually there is neither foolishness nor weakness with God. But the apostle is saying in verse 25 that what seems to be **foolishness** on God's part, in the eyes of men, is actually **wiser than men** at their very best. Also, what seems to be **weakness** on God's part, in the eyes of men, turns out to be **stronger than** anything that **men** can produce.

1:26 Having spoken of the gospel itself, the apostle now turns to the people whom God calls by the gospel (vv. 26–29). He reminds the Corinthians that **not many wise according to the flesh, not many mighty, not many noble are called**. It has often been pointed out that the text does not say "not any" but **not many**. Because of this slight difference, one English lady of noble blood used to testify that she was saved by the letter "m."

The Corinthians themselves had not come from the upper intellectual crust of society. They had not been reached by high-sounding philosophies but by the simple gospel. Why, then, were they putting such a premium on human wisdom and exalting preachers who sought to make the message palatable to the worldly-wise?

If men were to build a church, they would want to enroll the most prominent members of the community. But verse 26 teaches us that the people men esteem so highly, God passes by. The ones He calls are not generally the ones the world considers great.

1:27 **God has chosen the foolish things of the world to put to shame the wise, and God has chosen the weak things of the world to put to shame the things which are mighty.** As Erich Sauer says:

The more primitive the material, the greater — if the same standard of art can be reached — the honor of the Master; the smaller the army, the mightier — if the same great victory can be won — the praise of the conqueror.[3]

God used trumpets to bring down the walls of Jericho. He reduced Gideon's army from 32,000 to 300 to rout the armies of Midian. He used an oxgoad in the hand of Shamgar to defeat the Philistines. With the jawbone of a donkey He enabled Samson to defeat a whole army. And our Lord fed over 5,000 with nothing more than a few loaves and fishes.

1:28 To make up what someone has called "God's five-ranked army of fools," Paul adds **the base things of the world and the things which are despised** and **the things which are not**. Using such unlikely materials, God brings **to nothing the things that are**. In other words, He loves to take up people who are of no esteem in the eyes of the world and use them to glorify Himself. These verses should serve as a rebuke to Christians who curry the favor of prominent and well-known personages and show little or no regard for the more humble saints of God.

1:29 God's purpose in choosing those of no account in the eyes of the world is that all the glory should accrue to Himself and not to man. Since salvation is entirely of Him, He alone is worthy to be praised.

1:30 Verse 30 emphasizes even further that all we are and have comes from Him — not from philosophy, and that there is therefore no room for human glory. First of all, Christ **became for us wisdom**. He is the wisdom of God (v. 24), the One whom God's wisdom chose as the way of salvation. When we have Him we have a positional wisdom that guarantees our full salvation. Secondly, He is our **righteousness**. Through faith in Him we are reckoned righteous by a holy God. Thirdly, He is our **sanctification**. In ourselves we have nothing in the way of personal holiness, but in Him we are positionally sanctified, and by His power we are transformed from one degree of sanctification to another. Finally, He is our **redemption**, and this doubtless speaks of redemption in its final aspect when the Lord will come and take

us home to be with Himself, and when we shall be redeemed — spirit, soul, and body.

Traill delineated the truth sharply:

> Wisdom out[side] of Christ is damning folly — righteousness out[side] of Christ is guilt and condemnation — sanctification out[side] of Christ is filth and sin — redemption out[side] of Christ is bondage and slavery.[4]

A. T. Pierson relates verse 30 to the life and ministry of our Lord:

> His deeds and His words and His practices, these show Him as the wisdom of God. Then come His death, burial, and resurrection: these have to do with our righteousness. Then His forty days' walk among men, His ascension up on high, the gift of the Spirit, and His session at the right hand of God, have to do with our sanctification. Then His coming again, which has to do with our redemption.[5]

1:31 God has so arranged it that all these blessings should come to us **in the Lord**. Paul's argument therefore is, "Why glory in men? They cannot do any one of these things for you."

2:1 The apostle now reminds the saints of his ministry among them and how he sought to glorify God and not himself. He came to them proclaiming **the testimony of God**, not **with excellence of speech or of wisdom**. He was not at all interested in showing himself off as an orator or philosopher. This shows that the Apostle Paul recognized the difference between ministry that is soulish and that which is spiritual. By soulish ministry, we mean that which amuses, entertains, or generally appeals to man's emotions. Spiritual ministry, on the other hand, presents the truth of God's word in such a way as to glorify Christ and to reach the heart and conscience of the hearers.

2:2 The content of Paul's message was **Jesus Christ and Him crucified. Jesus Christ** refers to His Person, while **Him crucified** refers to His work. The Person and work of the Lord Jesus form the substance of the Christian evangel.

2:3 Paul further emphasizes that his personal demeanor was neither impressive nor attractive. He was with the Corinthians **in weakness, in fear, and in much trembling**. The treasure of the gospel was contained in an earthen vessel that the excellence of the power might be of God and not of Paul. He himself was an example of how God uses weak things to confound the mighty.

2:4 Neither Paul's **speech** nor his **preaching** were in **persuasive words of human wisdom, but in demonstration of the Spirit and of power**. Some suggest that his **speech** refers to the material he presented and his **preaching** to the manner of its presentation. Others define his **speech** as his witness to individuals and his **preaching** as his messages to groups. According to the standards of this world, the apostle might never have won an oratorical contest. In spite of this, **the Spirit** of God used the message to produce conviction of sin and conversion to God.

2:5 Paul knew that there was the utmost danger that his hearers might be interested in himself or in his own personality rather than in the living Lord. Conscious of his own inability to bless or to save, he determined that he would lead men to trust in **God** alone rather than **in the wisdom of men**. All who proclaim the gospel message or teach the word of God should make this their constant aim.

2:6 First of all, the **wisdom** shown in the gospel is divine in its origin (vv. 6, 7). **We speak wisdom among those who are mature** or full-grown. **Yet** it is **not the wisdom of this age**, nor would it be wisdom in the eyes of **the rulers of this age**. Their wisdom is a perishable thing which, like themselves, is born for one brief day.

2:7 **We speak the wisdom of God in a mystery**. **A mystery** is a NT truth not previously revealed, but now made known to believers by the apostles and prophets of the early Church Age. This mystery is the **hidden wisdom which God ordained before the ages for our glory**. The mystery of the gospel includes such wonderful truths as the fact that *now* Jews and Gentiles are made one in Christ; that the Lord Jesus will come and take His waiting people home to be with Himself; and that not all believers will die but all will be changed.

2:8 **The rulers of this age** may refer to demonic spirit beings in the heavenlies or to their human agents on earth.

They didn't understand the hidden wisdom of God (Christ on a cross) or realize that their murder of the Holy Son of God would result in their own destruction. **Had they known** the ways of God, **they would not have crucified the Lord of glory**.

2:9 The processes of revelation, inspiration, and illumination are described in verses 9–16. They tell us how these wonderful truths were made known to the apostles by the Holy Spirit, how they in turn passed on these truths to us by inspiration of the Holy Spirit, and how we understand them by the illumination of the Holy Spirit.

The quotation in verse 9 from Isaiah 64:4 is a prophecy that God had treasured up wonderful truths which could not be discovered by the natural senses but which in due time He would reveal to **those who love Him**. Three faculties (**eye** and **ear** and **heart**, or mind) by which we learn earthly things, are listed, but these are not sufficient for the reception of divine truths, for there the Spirit of God is necessary.

This verse is commonly interpreted to refer to the glories of heaven, and once we get that meaning in our minds, it is difficult to dislodge it and accept any other meaning. But Paul is really speaking here about the truths that have been revealed for the first time in the NT. Men could never have arrived at these truths through scientific investigations or philosophical inquiries. The human mind, left to itself, could never discover the wonderful mysteries which were made known at the beginning of the gospel era. Human reason is totally inadequate to find the truth of God.

2:10 That verse 9 does not refer to heaven is proven by the statement that **God has revealed them to us through His Spirit**. In other words, these truths foretold in the *OT* were made known to the apostles of the *NT* era. The **us** refers to the writers of the NT. It was by the **Spirit** of God that the apostles and prophets were enlightened, because **the Spirit searches all things, yes, the deep things of God**. In other words, the Spirit of God, one of the members of the Godhead, is infinite in wisdom and understands all the truths of God and is able to impart them to others.

2:11 Even in human affairs no one

knows what a **man** is thinking but he himself. No one else can possibly find out unless the man himself chooses to make it known. Even then, in order to understand a man, a person must have **the spirit of** a **man**. An animal could not fully understand our thinking. So it is with God. The only one who can understand the things of God is **the Spirit of God.**

2:12 The **we** of verse 12 refers to the writers of the NT, although it is equally true of all the Bible writers. Since the apostles and prophets had received the Holy Spirit, He was able to share with them the deep truths of God. That is what the apostle means when he says in this verse: **"Now we have received, not the spirit of the world, but the Spirit who is from God, that we might know the things that have been freely given to us by God."** Apart from **the Spirit who is from God**, the apostles could never have received the divine truths of which Paul is speaking and which are preserved for us in the NT.

2:13 Having described the process of revelation by which the writers of Sacred Scripture received truth from God, Paul now goes on to describe the process of inspiration, by which that truth was communicated to us. Verse 13 is one of the strongest passages in the word of God on the subject of verbal inspiration. The Apostle Paul clearly states that in conveying these truths to us, the apostles did **not** use **words** of their own choosing or words dictated by **man's wisdom**. Rather, they used the very words **which the Holy Spirit** taught them to use. And so we believe that the actual words of Scripture, as found in the original autographs, were the very words of God (and that the Bible in its present form is entirely trustworthy).

A howl of objection arises at this point since to some people what we have said implies *mechanical dictation*, as if God did not allow the writers to use their own style. Yet we know that Paul's writing style is quite different from Luke's, for example. How, then, can we reconcile verbal inspiration with the obvious individual style of the writers? In some way which we do not understand, God gave the very words of Scripture, and yet He clothed those words with the individual style of the writers, letting

their human personality be part of His perfect word.

The expression **comparing spiritual things with spiritual** can be explained in several ways. It may mean (1) teaching spiritual truths with Spirit-given words; (2) communicating spiritual truths to spiritual men; or (3) comparing spiritual truths in one section of the Bible with those in another. We believe that the first explanation fits the context best. Paul is saying that the process of inspiration involves the conveying of divine truth with words that are especially chosen for that purpose by the Holy Spirit. Thus we could paraphrase: "presenting spiritual truths in spiritual words."

It is sometimes objected that this passage cannot refer to inspiration because Paul says we **speak**, not "we write." But it is not uncommon to find the verb "to speak" used of inspired writings (e.g., John 12:38, 41; Acts 28:25; 2 Pet. 1:21).

2:14 Not only is the gospel divine in its revelation and divine in its inspiration, but now we learn that it can only be received by the power of **the Spirit of God**. Unaided, **the natural man does not receive the things of the Spirit of God. They are foolishness to him.** He cannot possibly understand them **because they** can only be **spiritually** understood.

The colorful Vance Havner advises:

> The wise Christian wastes no time trying to explain God's program to unregenerate men; it would be casting pearls before swine. He might as well try to describe a sunset to a blind man or discuss nuclear physics with a monument in the city park. The natural man cannot receive such things. One might as well try to catch sunbeams with a fishhook as to lay hold of God's revelation unassisted by the Holy Spirit. Unless one is born of the Spirit and taught by Him, all this is utterly foreign to him. Being a Ph. D. does not help, for in this realm it could mean 'Phenomenal Dud!'[6]

2:15 On the other hand, the man who is illuminated by the Spirit of God can discern these wonderful truths even though **he himself** cannot be **rightly judged** by the unconverted. Perhaps he is a carpenter, or plumber, or fisherman; yet he is an able student of the Holy Scriptures. "The Spirit-controlled Christian investigates, inquires into, and scrutinizes the Bible and comes to an appreciation and understanding of its contents" (KSW). To the world he is an enigma. He may never have been to college or seminary, yet he can understand the deep mysteries of the word of God and perhaps even teach them to others.

2:16 The apostle now asks with Isaiah the rhetorical question: **"Who has known the mind of the Lord that he may instruct Him?"** To ask the question is to answer it. God cannot be known through the wisdom or power of men. He is known only as He chooses to make Himself known. However, those who have **the mind of Christ** are able to understand the deep truths of God.

To review then, first there is *revelation* (vv. 9–12). This means that God revealed previously unknown truths to men by the Holy Spirit. These truths were made known supernaturally by the Spirit of God.

Secondly, there is *inspiration* (v. 13). In transmitting these truths to others, the apostles (and all other writers of the Bible) used the very words which the Holy Spirit taught them to use.

Finally, there is *illumination* (vv. 14–16). Not only must these truths be miraculously *revealed* and miraculously *inspired*, but they can only be *understood* by the supernatural power of the Holy Spirit.

3:1 When Paul first visited Corinth, he had fed the believers with the elementary milk of the word because they were weak and young in the faith. The teaching which had been given to them was suitable to their condition. They could not receive deeply spiritual instruction because they were new believers. They were mere **babes in Christ**.

3:2 Paul had taught them only the elementary truths concerning Christ, which he speaks of as **milk**. They were not able to take **solid food** because of their immaturity. In the same vein, the Lord Jesus said to His disciples, "I still have many things to say to you, but you cannot bear them now" (John 16:12). With regard to the Corinthians, the tragic thing was that they still had not improved sufficiently to receive deeper truth from the apostle.

3:3 The believers were **still** in a **carnal** or fleshly state of soul. This was evidenced by the fact that there was **envy**

and **strife** among them. Such behavior is characteristic of the men of this world, but not of those who are led by the Spirit of God.

3:4 In forming parties around human leaders, such as **Paul** and **Apollos**, they were acting on a purely human level. That is what Paul means when he asks, "Are you not . . . behaving like mere men?"

Up to this point, the Apostle Paul has been showing the folly of exalting men by a consideration of the true nature of the gospel message. He now turns to the subject of the Christian ministry and shows from this standpoint also, it is sheer foolishness to exalt religious leaders by building parties around them.

3:5 **Apollos** and **Paul** were *servants* (*minister* is Latin for "servant") **through whom** the Corinthians had come to believe in the Lord Jesus. They were simply agents and not the heads of rival schools. How unwise then of the Corinthians to raise servants to the rank of master. Ironside quaintly comments at this point, "Imagine a household divided over servants!"

3:6 Using a figure from agriculture, Paul shows that the servant is after all very limited in what he can do. **Paul** himself could plant and **Apollos** could water, but only **God** could give **the increase**. So today, some of us can preach the word and all of us can pray for unsaved relatives and friends, but the actual work of salvation can only be done by the Lord.

3:7 Looking at it from this point, we can readily see that the planter and the waterer are really not very important, relatively speaking. They have not the power in themselves to bring forth life. Why then should there be any envy or rivalry among Christian workers? Each should do the work that has been allotted to him, and rejoice when the Lord shows His hand in blessing.

3:8 **He who plants and he who waters are one** in the sense that they both have the same object and aim. There should be no jealousy between them. As far as service is concerned, they are on the same level. In a coming day, **each one will receive his own reward according to his own labor**. That day is the Judgment Seat of Christ.

3:9 God is the One to whom all are

responsible. All His servants are **fellow workers**, laboring together in **God's** tilled harvest **field**, or, to change the picture, working together on the same **building**. Erdman renders the thought as follows: "We are fellow-workers who belong to God and are working with one another."[7]

3:10 Continuing with the idea of building, the apostle first of all acknowledges that anything he has been able to accomplish has been due to **the grace of God**. By this he means the undeserved ability from God to do the work of an apostle. Then he goes on to describe his part in the beginning of this assembly at Corinth: **"As a wise master builder, I have laid the foundation."** He came to Corinth preaching Christ and Him crucified. Souls were saved and a local church was planted. Then he adds: **"And another builds on it."** By this, he doubtless refers to other teachers who subsequently visited Corinth and built on the foundation which had already been established there. However, the apostle cautions: **"But let each one take heed how he builds on it."** He means that it is a solemn thing to exercise a teaching ministry in the local church. Some had come to Corinth with divisive doctrines and with teachings contrary to the word of God. Paul was doubtless conscious of these teachers as he penned the words.

3:11 Only one foundation is required for a building. Once it is laid, it never needs to be repeated. The Apostle Paul had laid the foundation of the church at Corinth. That **foundation** was **Jesus Christ**, His Person and Work.

3:12 Subsequent teaching in a local church may be of varying degrees of value. For instance, some teaching is of lasting worth, and might be likened to **gold, silver**, or **precious stones**. Here **precious stones** probably do not refer to diamonds, rubies, or other gems but rather to the granite, marble, or alabaster used in the construction of costly temples. On the other hand, teaching in the local church might be of passing value or of no value at all. Such teaching is likened to **wood, hay,** and **straw**.

This passage of Scripture is commonly used in a general way to refer to the lives of all Christian believers. It is true that we are all building, day by day, and the results of our work will be mani-fested in a coming day. However, a careful student of the Bible will want to note that the passage does not refer primarily to all believers but rather to preachers and teachers.

3:13 In a coming day, **each one's work will become clear. Day** refers to the Judgment Seat of Christ when all service for the Lord will be reviewed. The process of review is likened to the action of **fire**. Service that has brought glory to God and blessing to man, like gold, silver, and precious stones, will not be affected by the fire. On the other hand, that which has caused trouble among the people of God or failed to edify them will be consumed. **The fire will test each one's work, of what sort it is.**

3:14 Work in connection with the church may be of three types. In verse 14 we have the first type — service that has been of a profitable nature. In such a case, the servant's life work **endures** the test of the Judgment Seat of Christ and the worker **will receive a reward**.

3:15 The second type of work is that which is useless. In this case, the servant **will suffer loss**, although **he himself will be saved, yet so as through fire**. E. W. Rogers points out: "Loss does not imply the forfeiture of something once possessed."[8] It should be clear from this verse that the Judgment Seat of Christ is not concerned with the subject of a believer's sins and their penalty. The penalty of a believer's sins was borne by the Lord Jesus Christ on the cross of Calvary, and that matter has been settled once for all. Thus the believer's salvation is not at all in question at the Judgment Seat of Christ; rather it is a matter of his service.

Through failure to distinguish between salvation and rewards, the Roman Catholic Church has used this verse to try to support its teaching of purgatory. However, a careful examination of the verse reveals no hint as to purgatory. There is no thought that the fire purifies the character of a man. Rather, the fire tests a man's work or service, of what sort it is. The man is saved despite the fact that his works are consumed by the fire.

An interesting thought in connection with this verse is that the word of God is sometimes likened to fire (see Isa. 5:24 and Jer. 23:29). The same word of God which will test our service at the Judgment Seat of Christ is available to us now. If we are building in accordance with the teachings of the Bible, then our work will stand the test in that coming day.

3:16 Paul reminds the believers **that** they **are the temple** (Gk., the inner shrine or sanctuary) **of God and that the Spirit of God dwells in** them. It is true that every individual believer is also a temple of God indwelt by the Holy Spirit, but that is not the thought here. The apostle is looking at the church as a collective company, and wishes them to realize the holy dignity of such a calling.

3:17 A third class of work in the local church is that which may be spoken of as destructive. Apparently there were false teachers who had come into the church at Corinth and whose instruction tended more to sin than to holiness. They did not think it a serious matter to thus cause havoc in a temple of God, so Paul thunders out this solemn declaration: **"If anyone defiles the temple of God, God will destroy him."** Viewed in its local setting, this means that if any man enters a local church and wrecks its testimony, **God will destroy him**. The passage is speaking of false teachers who are not true believers in the Lord Jesus. The seriousness of such an offense is indicated by the closing words of verse 17: **"For the temple of God is holy, which temple you are."**

3:18 In Christian service, as in all of Christian life, there is always the danger of self-deception. Perhaps some of those who came to Corinth as teachers posed as men of extreme wisdom. Any who have an exalted view of their own worldly wisdom must learn that they must become fools in the eyes of the world in order to **become wise** in God's estimation. Godet helpfully paraphrases at this point:

If any individual whatever, Corinthian or other, while preaching the gospel *in your assemblies* assumes the part of a wise man and reputation of a profound thinker, let him assure himself that he will not attain true wisdom until he has passed through a crisis in which that wisdom of his with which he is puffed up will perish and after which only he will receive the wisdom which is from above.[9]

3:19 **The wisdom of this world is foolishness with God.** Man by searching could never find out God, neither would human wisdom ever have devised a plan of salvation by which God would become Man in order to die for guilty, vile, rebel sinners. Job 5:13 is quoted in verse 19 to show that God triumphs over the supposed wisdom of men to work out His own purposes. Man with all his learning cannot thwart the plans of the Lord; instead, God often shows them that in spite of their worldly wisdom, they are utterly poor and powerless.

3:20 Psalm 94:11 is quoted here to emphasize that **the LORD knows** all the reasonings **of the wise** men of this world, and He further knows **that they are futile**, empty, and fruitless. But why is Paul going to such pains to discredit worldly wisdom? Simply for this reason — the Corinthians were placing a great premium on such wisdom and were following those leaders who seemed to exhibit it in a remarkable degree.

3:21 In view of all that had been said, **no one** should **boast in men**. And as far as true servants of the Lord are concerned, we should not boast that we belong to them but rather realize that they all belong to us. **All things are yours.**

3:22 Someone has called verse 22 "an inventory of the possessions of the child of God." Christian workers belong to us, whether **Paul** the evangelist, or **Apollos** the teacher, or **Cephas** the pastor. Since they all belong to us, it is folly for us to claim that we belong to any *one* of them. Then **the world** is ours. As joint heirs with Christ, we will one day come into possession of it, but in the meantime it is ours by divine promise. Those who tend its affairs do not realize that they are doing so for us. **Life** is ours. By this we do not mean merely existence on earth but life in its truest, fullest sense. And **death** is ours. For us it is no longer a dread foe that consigns the soul to the dark unknown; rather it is now the messenger of God that brings the soul to heaven. **Things present** and **things to come — all are** likewise ours. It has been truly said that all things serve the man who serves Christ. A. T. Robertson once said: "The stars in their courses fight for the man who is partner with God in the world's redemption."

3:23 All Christians belong to Christ. Some in Corinth were claiming to belong to Him to the exclusion of all others. They formed the "Christ-party." But Paul refutes any such contention. We are all **Christ's, and Christ is God's**. By thus showing the saints their true and proper dignity, Paul reveals in bold relief the folly of forming parties and divisions in the church.

4:1 In order that they might properly appraise Paul and the other apostles, he says that the saints should look upon them **as servants** or assistants **of Christ and stewards of the mysteries of God**. A steward is a servant who cares for the person or property of another. **The mysteries of God** were the previously hidden secrets which God revealed to the apostles and prophets of the NT period.

4:2 A major requirement **in stewards** is to **be found faithful**. Man values cleverness, wisdom, wealth, and success; but God is looking for those who will be faithful to Jesus in all things.

4:3 The faithfulness that is required in stewards is a difficult thing for people to evaluate. That is why Paul says here that **with** him **it is a very small thing that** he **should be judged by** the Corinthians **or by a human court**. Paul realizes how utterly unable man is to form a competent judgment of true faithfulness to God. He adds: **"In fact, I do not even judge myself."** He realized that he was born into the human family with a judgment that was constantly biased in his own favor.

4:4 When the apostle says **"I know of nothing against myself,"** he means that in the matter of Christian service, he is not conscious of any charge of unfaithfulness that might be brought against him. He does not mean for a moment that he does not know of any sin in his life or any way in which he falls short of perfection! The passage should be read in the light of the context, and the subject here is Christian service and faithfulness in it. But even if he did not know anything against himself, **yet** he was **not justified by this**. He simply was not competent to judge in the matter. After all, the Lord is the Judge.

4:5 In view of this, we should be ex-tremely careful in our appraisal of Christian service. We tend to exalt the spectacular and sensational, and depreciate that which is menial or inconspicuous. The safe policy is to **judge nothing before the time**, but to wait **until the Lord comes**. He will be able to judge, not only what is seen by the eye, but also the motives of the hearts — not only what was done, but *why* it was done. He will **reveal the counsels of the hearts**, and, needless to say, anything that was done for self-display or self-glory will fail to receive a reward.

That **each one's praise will come from God** is not to be taken as a flat promise that every believer's service will show up in a favorable way in that day. The meaning is that everyone who *deserves* praise will receive praise **from God** and not from men.

In the next eight verses, the apostle states quite clearly that pride is the cause of the divisions that have come into the church at Corinth.

4:6 He first explains that in speaking about the Christian ministry and the tendency to follow human leaders (3:5–4:5), he used himself and **Apollos** as the examples. The Corinthians were not forming parties around Paul and Apollos alone, but also around other men who were then in their church. However, out of a sense of Christian courtesy and delicacy, Paul **transferred** the entire matter **to** himself **and Apollos** so that by their example the saints would learn not to have exaggerated opinions of their leaders or to gratify their pride by the formation of parties. He wanted the saints to evaluate everything and everyone by the Scriptures.

4:7 If one Christian teacher is more gifted than another, it is because God made him so. Everything he has, he received from the Lord. In fact it is true of all of us that everything we have has been given to us by God. That being the case, why should we be proud or puffed up? Our talents and gifts are not the result of our own cleverness.

4:8 The Corinthians had become self-sufficient; they were **already full**. They prided themselves on the abundance of spiritual gifts in their midst; they were **already rich**. They were living in luxury, comfort, and ease. There was no sense of need. They acted as if they were already reigning, but they were doing so without the apostles. Paul states that he **could wish** that the time to reign had already come so that he **might reign with** them! But in the meantime, "lifetime is training time for reigning time," as someone has said. Christians will reign with the Lord Jesus Christ when He comes back and sets up His kingdom on earth. In the meantime, their privilege is to share the reproach of a rejected Savior. H. P. Barker warns:

> It is positive disloyalty to seek our crown before the King gets his. Yet this is what some of the Christians at Corinth were doing. The apostles themselves were bearing the reproach of Christ. But the Corinthian Christians were "rich" and "honorable." They were seeking a good time where their Lord and Master had such a hard time.[10]

At coronations, peers and peeresses never put on their coronets until the sovereign has been crowned. The Corinthians were reversing this; they were already reigning while the Lord was still in rejection!

4:9 In contrast to the self-satisfaction of the Corinthians, Paul describes the lot of **the apostles**. He pictures them as thrown into the arena with wild beasts while **men** and **angels** look on. As Godet has said: "It was not time for the Corinthians to be self-complacent and boasting, while the church was on the throne and the apostles were under the sword."

4:10 While the apostles were treated as **fools for Christ's sake**, the saints enjoyed prestige in the community as **wise** Christians. The apostles were **weak, but** the Corinthians suffered no infirmity. In contrast to the dishonor of the apostles was the eminence of the saints.

4:11 It did not seem to the apostles that the hour of triumph or of reigning had come. They were suffering from **hunger and thirst** and nakedness and persecution. They were hunted, pursued, and **homeless**.

4:12 They supported themselves by **working with** their **own hands**. For reviling, they returned blessing. When they were **persecuted**, they did not fight back, but patiently endured.

4:13 When **defamed**, they entreated men to accept the Lord Jesus. In short, they were **made as the filth of the world, the** scum **of all things**. This description of suffering for the sake of Christ should speak to all our hearts. If the Apostle Paul were living today, could he say to us, as he said to the Corinthians, "You have reigned as kings without us"?

4:14 In verses 14–21, Paul gives a final admonition to the believers on the subject of divisions. Conscious of the fact that he has been using irony, he explains that he has **not** done so **to shame** the Christians, **but** rather to **warn** them **as** his **beloved children**. He was not inspired by bitterness to speak as he had done, but rather by a sincere interest in their spiritual welfare.

4:15 The apostle reminds them that **though** they **might have ten thousand instructors in Christ, yet** they have only one father in the faith. Paul himself had led them to the Lord; he was their spiritual father. Many others might come along to teach them, but no others could have the same tender regard for them as the one who pointed them to the Lamb. Paul does not at all intend to depreciate the ministry of teaching, but is simply stating what we all know to be true, namely, that many can be engaged in Christian service without the personal interest in the saints that is characteristic of one who has pointed them to Christ.

4:16 Paul **therefore** urges them to be imitators of himself, that is, in his unselfish devotion to Christ and in his tireless love and service for his fellow believers, such as he has described in verses 9–13.

4:17 In order to help them reach this goal, Paul **sent Timothy to** them, his **beloved and faithful son in the Lord**. Timothy was instructed to **remind** them **of** Paul's **ways in Christ**, ways which he taught in all the churches. Paul is saying that he practiced what he preached, and this should be true of everyone who engages in Christian service.

4:18 When Paul explained that he was sending Timothy to them, perhaps some of his detractors in Corinth would rise quickly to suggest that Paul was afraid to come himself. These men were **puffed up** in suggesting that Paul was **not coming** personally.

4:19 But he promises that he **will**

come in the near future, **if the Lord wills**. When he does, he will expose the pride of those who can talk so freely, but have no spiritual **power**.

4:20 After all, it is **power** that counts, **for the kingdom of God is not** concerned principally with words but with action. It does not consist of profession, but of reality.

4:21 The manner in which Paul comes to them will depend on themselves. If they show a rebellious spirit, he will **come to** them **with a rod**. If, on the other hand, they are humble and submissive, he will come **in love and a spirit of gentleness**.

B. Immorality among Believers (Chap. 5)

Chapter 5 deals with the necessity for disciplinary action in a church when one of the members has committed serious sin of a public nature. Discipline is necessary for the church to retain its holy character in the eyes of the world and also so that the Holy Spirit may work ungrieved in its midst.

5:1 Apparently it had become widely **reported** that one of the men in the fellowship at Corinth had committed **sexual immorality**. Here it was a very extreme form of sin, one that was **not even** practiced **among the** ungodly **Gentiles**. Specifically, the sin was **that** this **man** had had illicit intercourse with **his father's wife**. The man's own mother had no doubt died and the father had married again. So his father's wife, in this case, would then refer to his stepmother. She was probably an unbeliever, because nothing is said about taking action against her. The church did not have jurisdiction in her case.

5:2 How had the Corinthian Christians reacted to all this? Instead of plunging into deep mourning, they were proud and haughty. Perhaps they were proud of their tolerance in not disciplining the offender. Or perhaps they were so proud of the abundance of spiritual gifts in the church that they did not give serious thought to what had taken place. Or perhaps they were more interested in numbers than in holiness. They were not sufficiently shocked by sin.

You are puffed up, and have not rather mourned, that he who has done this deed might be taken away from among you. This implies that if the believers had taken the proper attitude of humiliation before the Lord, He Himself would have acted in the matter, taking some form of disciplinary action on the offender. Erdman says:

> They should have understood that the true glory of the Christian church consists not in the eloquence and gifts of its great teachers, but in the moral purity and the exemplary lives of its members.[11]

5:3 In contrast to their indifference, the apostle states that even though he was **absent**, yet he had **already judged** the matter as if he were present.

5:4 He pictures the church being assembled to take action against the offender. Although he is not present bodily, yet he is there in **spirit** as they meet **in the name of our Lord Jesus Christ**. The Lord Jesus had given authority to the church and to the apostles to exercise discipline in all such cases. Thus Paul says he would act with the **power** (or authority) **of our Lord Jesus**.

5:5 The action he would take would be to **deliver such a one to Satan for the destruction of the flesh, that his spirit may be saved in the day of the Lord Jesus**. Commentators disagree on the meaning of this expression. Some feel that it describes the act of excommunication from the local church. Outside the church is the sphere of Satan's dominion (1 Jn. 5:19). Therefore, "to deliver to Satan" would be simply to excommunicate from the church. Others feel that the power to deliver to Satan was a special power granted to apostles but no longer in existence today.

Again, there is disagreement as to the meaning of the expression **the destruction of the flesh**. Many feel that it describes physical suffering that would be used by God to break the power of sinful lusts and habits in the man's life. Others feel that **the destruction of the flesh** is a description of slow death, which would give a man time to repent and be spared.

In any case, we should remember that the discipline of believers is always calculated to bring about their restoration to fellowship with the Lord. Excommunication is never an end in itself, but always a means toward an end. The ultimate purpose is **that his spirit may be saved in the day of the Lord Jesus**. In other words, there is no thought of the man's eternal damnation. He is disciplined by the Lord in this life because of the sin he has committed, but he is **saved in the day of the Lord Jesus.**

5:6 Paul now reproves the Corinthians for their **glorying** or boasting. Maybe they excused themselves by saying that it happened only once. They should have known **that a little leaven leavens the whole lump. Leaven** here is a picture of moral sin. The apostle is saying that if they tolerate a little moral sin in the church, it will soon grow and expand until the whole fellowship is seriously affected. Righteous, godly discipline is necessary in order to maintain the character of the church.

5:7 Thus they are commanded to **purge out the old leaven**. In other words, they should take stern action against evil so that they might be a **new**, in the sense of a pure **lump**. Then Paul adds: **Since you truly are unleavened**. God sees them in Christ as holy, righteous, and pure. Now the apostle is saying that their state should correspond with their standing. As to *position* they were unleavened. Now as to their *practice* they should also be unleavened. Their natures should correspond with their name, and their conduct with their creed.

For indeed Christ, our Passover, was sacrificed for us. In thinking about the unleavened bread, Paul's mind goes back to the Passover Feast where, on the eve of the first day of the Feast, the Jew was required to remove all leaven from his house. He went to the kneading trough and scraped it clean. He scrubbed the place where the leaven was kept till not a trace remained. He searched the house with a lamp to make sure that none had been overlooked. Then he lifted up his hands to God and said, "Oh God, I have cast out all the leaven from my house, and if there is any leaven that I do not know of, with all my heart I cast it out too." That pictures the kind of separation from evil to which the Christian is called in this day.

The slaying of the Passover lamb was a type or picture of the death of our Lord Jesus Christ on the cross. This verse is one of many in the NT that establishes the principle of *typical* teaching. By this we mean that persons and events of the OT were *types* or shadows of things that were to come. Many of them pointed forward directly to the coming of the Lord Jesus to put away our sins by the sacrifice of Himself.

5:8 **The feast** here does not refer to the Passover or to the Lord's Supper but rather is used in a general way to describe the whole life of the believer. Our entire existence is to be a festival of joy, and it is to be celebrated **not with** the **old leaven** of sin **nor with the leaven of malice and wickedness**. As we rejoice in Christ, we must have no evil thoughts in our hearts toward others. From this we see that the Apostle Paul was not speaking about literal leaven, such as the yeast that is used in making bread, but rather he was using leaven in a spiritual sense to describe the manner in which sin defiles that with which it comes into contact. We are to live our lives **with the unleavened bread of sincerity and truth.**

5:9 Now Paul explains to them that he had previously written in a letter that they were **not to keep company with sexually immoral people**. The fact that such an epistle is lost does not affect the inspiration of the Bible at all. Not every letter Paul wrote was inspired, but only those which God has seen fit to include in the Holy Bible.

5:10 The apostle now goes on to explain that in warning them to have no company with **sexually immoral people**, he did not mean to imply that they should separate themselves from any contact at all with ungodly men. As long as we are in the world, it is necessary for us to do business with unsaved people and we have no way of knowing the depths of sin to which they have descended. In order to live a life of complete isolation from sinners, **you would need to go out of the world**.

So Paul says that he did not at all mean complete separation from **the sexually immoral people of this world, or** the **covetous, or extortioners, or idolaters. Covetous** people are those who are convicted of dishonesty in business or financial affairs. For instance, anyone who is found guilty of tax fraud is subject to excommunication for covetousness. **Extortioners** are those who enrich themselves by using violent means, such as threats of harm or death. **Idolaters** are those who are given over to the worship of anyone or anything other than the true God, and who practice the terrible sins of immorality that are almost always connected with idolatry.

5:11 What Paul really wants to warn them against is having fellowship with a professing **brother** who engages in any of these terrible sins. We might paraphrase his words as follows:

> What I meant to say and what I now repeat is that you should not even eat a common meal with any professing Christian who is sexually immoral, or a covetous man, or an idolater, or a reviler, or a drunkard, or an extortioner.

It is often necessary for us to have contact with the unsaved, and we can often use these contacts in order to witness to them. Such contact is not as dangerous to the believer as having fellowship with those who profess to be Christians and yet live in sin. We should never do anything that such a person might interpret as condoning his sin.

To the list of sinners mentioned in verse 10, Paul adds revilers and drunkards in verse 11. **A reviler** is a man who uses strong, intemperate language against another. But we would add a word of caution here. Should a man be excommunicated from the church if on one occasion only he should lose his temper and use unguarded words? We would think not, but would suggest that this expression refers to habitual practice. In other words, **a reviler** would be one who is known as being characteristically abusive toward others. At any rate, this should be a warning to us to exercise control of our language. As Dr. Ironside has mentioned, many people say that they are just *careless* with their tongue, but he points out that they might just as well say that they are careless with a machine gun.

A drunkard is one given to excess in the use of alcoholic beverages.

Does the Apostle Paul mean that we are **not even to eat with such a** Christian who engages in these practices? That is exactly what the verse teaches! We are not to eat with him at the Lord's Supper,

nor are we to enjoy a social meal with him. There may be exceptional cases. A Christian wife, for instance, would still be obligated to eat with her husband who had been disfellowshiped. But the general rule is that professing believers who are guilty of the sins listed should be subjected to social ostracism in order to impress on them the enormity of their transgression and to bring them to repentance. If it is objected that the Lord ate with publicans and sinners, we would point out that these men did not profess to be His followers, and in eating with them He did not recognize them as His disciples. What this passage teaches is that we should not fellowship with *Christians* who are living wicked lives.

5:12 Paul's two questions in verse 12 mean that Christians are not responsible for the judgment of the unsaved. Wicked men in the world about us will be brought into judgment by the Lord Himself in a coming day. But we do have a responsibility as far as judging **those who are inside** the confines of the church. It is the duty of the local church to exercise godly discipline.

Again, if it is objected that the Lord taught, "Judge not that you be not judged," we would reply that there He is speaking about motives. We are not to judge men's motives because we are not competent for that type of judgment. But the word of God is equally clear that we are to judge known sin in the assembly of God so as to maintain its reputation for holiness and so as to restore the offending brother to fellowship with the Lord.

5:13 Paul explains that **God** will take care of the judgment of **those who are outside**, that is, of the unsaved. In the meantime, the Corinthians should exercise the judgment which God has committed to them by putting away **the evil person** from among themselves. This calls for a public announcement in the church that this brother is no longer in fellowship. The announcement should be made in genuine sorrow and humiliation and should be followed by continual prayer for the spiritual restoration of the wanderer.

C. Lawsuits among Believers (6:1–11)

The first eleven verses of chapter 6 have to do with lawsuits among believers. News had come to Paul that some Christians were going to law against their fellow believers — before the judges of this world. So he lays down these instructions of lasting value for the church. Note the repetition of the expression "Do you not know" (vv. 2, 3, 9, 15, 16, 19).

6:1 The opening question expresses shocked surprise that any of them would think of taking a brother **to law before the unrighteous**, that is, before unsaved judges or magistrates. He finds it rather inconsistent that those who know true righteousness should go before men who are not characterized by righteousness. Imagine Christians looking for justice from those who have none to give!

6:2 A second glaring inconsistency is that those who one day **will judge the world** should be incapable of judging trivial matters that come up among themselves. The Scriptures teach that believers will reign with Christ over the earth when He returns in power and glory, and that matters of judgment will be committed to them. If Christians are going to **judge the world**, should they not be able to handle petty differences that plague them now?

6:3 Paul reminds the Corinthians that they will **judge angels**. It is almost astounding to consider the manner in which the apostle injects such a momentous statement into the discussion. Without fanfare or build-up, he states the tremendous fact that Christians will one day **judge angels**. We know from Jude v. 6 and 2 Peter 2:4, 9 that angels will be judged. We also know that Christ will be the Judge (John 5:22). It is because of our union with Him that we can be spoken of as judging angels in a coming day. If we are considered qualified to judge angels, we should be able to handle the everyday problems that arise in **this life.**

6:4 If then **you have judgments concerning things pertaining to this life, do you appoint those who are least esteemed by the church to judge?** Unsaved judges are not given places of honor or esteem by the local church. They are, of course, respected for the work they are doing in the world, but as far as church matters are concerned they do not have any jurisdiction. Thus

Paul is asking the Corinthians:

> When matters arise between you requiring the impartial judgment of some third party, do you go outside the confines of the church and set men to judge you who are not recognized by the church for spiritual discernment?

6:5 Paul asks this question to move them to **shame**. Is it true that in an assembly that boasted of its wisdom and of the rich bestowment of gifts on its members, **not** one **wise man** could be found to settle these quarrels **between his brethren?**

6:6 Apparently not one such wise man was available, since a Christian **brother** was going **to law against** his own **brother** in Christ, taking family matters before the unbelieving world. Truly a deplorable situation!

6:7 The expression **"Now therefore, it is already an utter failure for you"** shows they were entirely wrong in this thing. They shouldn't even think of going to law against one another. But perhaps one of the Christians would object at this point: "Paul, you don't understand. Brother so-and-so cheated me in business dealings." Paul's answer is: **"Why do you not rather accept wrong? Why do you not rather let yourselves be cheated?"** This would be the truly Christian attitude to take. It is much better to receive a wrong than to commit one.

6:8 But this was not the attitude among the Corinthians. Instead of being willing to accept wrong and be cheated, they were actually committing **wrong** against others, even their own brothers in Christ.

6:9 Had they forgotten that people whose lives are characteristically **unrighteous will not inherit the kingdom of God**? If they have forgotten, then he will remind them of a list of sinners who will have no part in God's **kingdom**. He does not mean to imply that Christians can practice such sins and be lost, but rather he is saying that people who practice such sins are not Christians.[12]

In this list, **fornicators** are distinct from **adulterers**. Here fornication means illicit sexual intercourse on the part of an unmarried person, whereas adultery would mean such conduct on the part of a married person. **Idolaters** are mentioned again, as in the two previous lists in chapter 5. **Homosexuals** here means those who allow their bodies to be used in a perverted way, while **sodomites** are those who practice sodomy on others.

6:10 To the list are added **thieves, covetous, drunkards, revilers,** and **extortioners. Thieves** are those who take what does not belong to them. Notice that the sin of covetousness is always listed among the most wicked vices. Though men might excuse it and think lightly of it, God condemns it vigorously. A **covetous** man is one with an inordinate desire for possessions that often drives him to use unjust means of acquiring the same. **Drunkards,** as has been said, are primarily those who are addicted to the use of alcohol. **Revilers** are those who use abusive speech against others. **Extortioners** are those who take advantage of others' poverty or necessities to secure exorbitant gain.

6:11 Paul does not imply that these sins were practiced by the Corinthian believers, but he is warning them that such things characterized them before they were saved — **such were some of you. But** they had been **washed** and **sanctified** and **justified.** They had been **washed** from their sin and impurity through the precious blood of Christ, and they were being continually washed from defilement through the word of God. They were **sanctified** by the operation of the Spirit of God, being set apart to God from the world. They had been **justified in the name of the Lord Jesus Christ and by the Spirit of God;** that is, they had been reckoned righteous before God on the basis of the work of the Lord Jesus on the cross for them. What is Paul's argument here? It is simply this, as so aptly expressed by Godet: "Such a fathomless depth of grace is not to be recrossed."

D. Moral Laxness among Believers (6:12–20)

6:12 In the concluding verses of this chapter, the apostle lays down some principles for judging between right and wrong. The first principle is that a thing may be lawful and yet not helpful. When Paul says, **"All things are lawful for me,"** he does not mean all things in an absolute sense. For instance, it would

not be lawful for him to commit any of the sins mentioned above. He is here speaking only about those things that are morally indifferent. For example, the question as to whether a Christian should eat pork was a very real issue among believers in Paul's time. Actually, it was a matter of moral indifference. It did not really matter to God whether a man ate pork. Paul is simply saying that certain things might be legitimate and yet not profitable. There might be certain things which would be permissible for me to do and yet if someone else saw me doing them, he might be stumbled by my action. In such a case, it would not be at all suitable for me.

The second principle is that some things might **be lawful** and yet they might be enslaving. Paul states: **"I will not be brought under the power of any."** This would have a very direct message today with regard to the subjects of liquor, tobacco, and drugs. These things, as well as many others, are enslaving and the Christian should not allow himself to be thus put in bondage.

6:13 A third principle is that some things are perfectly lawful for the believer and yet their value is temporary. Paul says: **"Foods for the stomach, and the stomach for foods, but God will destroy both it and them."** This means that the human **stomach** has been so constructed that it can receive **foods** and digest them. Likewise, God has wonderfully designed **foods** so they can be received by the human **stomach.** And yet we should not live for foods, because they are only of temporary value. They should not be given an undue place in the life of the believer. Don't live as if the greatest thing in life is to gratify your appetites.

Although the body is wonderfully designed by God for the reception and assimilation of food, there is one thing that is certain; **the body is not for sexual immorality** but **for the Lord, and the Lord for the body.** In planning the human body, God never intended that it should be used for vile or impure purposes. Rather He planned that it should be used for the glory of the Lord and in His blessed service.

There is something amazing in this verse which should not escape notice.

Not only is **the body for the Lord**, but even more wonderful is the thought that **the Lord is for the body**. This means that the Lord is interested in our bodies, their welfare, and their proper use. God wants our bodies to be presented to Him a living sacrifice, holy, and acceptable (Rom. 12:1). As Erdman says: "Without the Lord, the body can never attain its true dignity and its immortal destiny."[13]

6:14 The fact that the Lord is for the body is further explained in this verse. **God** has not only **raised up the Lord** Jesus from among the dead, but He **will also raise us up by His power**. His interest in our bodies does not end at the time of death. He is going to **raise** the body of every believer to fashion it like the glorious body of the Lord Jesus. We will not be disembodied spirits in eternity. Rather, our spirit and soul will be reunited with our glorified body, thus to enjoy the glories of heaven forever.

6:15 To further emphasize the need for personal purity in our lives and for guarding our bodies from impurity, the apostle reminds us that our **bodies are members of Christ**. Every believer is a member of the body of Christ. Would it be proper, then, to **take the members of Christ and make them members of a harlot?** To ask the question is to answer it, as Paul does with an indignant **Certainly not!**

6:16 In the act of sexual union, two bodies become **one**. It was so stated at the dawn of creation: **For "the two," He says, "shall become one flesh"** (Gen. 2:24). This being so, if a believer should be **joined to a harlot**, it would be the same as making a member of Christ a member of a harlot. The two would become **one body**.

6:17 Just as in the physical act there is a union of two into one, so when a person believes on the Lord Jesus Christ and is **joined to** Him, the believer and Christ become so united that they can henceforth be spoken of as **one spirit**. This is the most perfect merging of two persons that is possible. It is the closest type of a union. Paul's argument, therefore, is that those who are thus **joined to the Lord** should never tolerate any type of union that would be in conflict with this spiritual wedlock.

A. T. Pierson writes:

> The sheep may wander from the shepherd, and the branch be cut off from the vine; the member be severed from the body, the child alienated from the father, and even the wife from the husband; but when two spirits blend in one, what shall part them? No outward connection or union, even of wedlock is so emphatically expressive of perfect merging of two lives in one.[14]

6:18 And so the apostle warns the Corinthians to **flee sexual immorality**. They are not to dabble with it, trifle with it, study it, even talk about it. They are to **flee** from it! A beautiful Bible illustration of this is found in the account of Joseph when he was tempted to sin by Potiphar's wife (Gen. 39). While there may be safety in numbers, sometimes there is more safety in flight!

Then Paul adds: **"Every sin that a man does is outside the body; but he who commits sexual immorality sins against his own body."** Most sins have no direct effect on one's **body**, but **sexual immorality** is unique in the sense that it does *directly* affect one's body: a person reaps the consequences of this sin in his own body. The difficulty is that the verse says that *every* sin that a man commits is outside the body. But we believe that the apostle is speaking here in a comparative sense. While it is true that gluttony and drunkenness, for example, affect a person's body, most sins do not. And not even gluttony or drunkenness affect the body as directly, as extensively, or as destructively as immorality. Sex outside marriage inevitably and irresistibly works havoc on the offender.

6:19 Again Paul reminds the Corinthians that theirs was a holy and dignified calling. Had they forgotten that their bodies were a **temple of the Holy Spirit**? That is the solemn truth of Scripture, that every believer is indwelt by the Spirit of God. How could we ever think of taking a body in which the *Holy* Spirit dwells and using it for *vile* purposes? Not only is our body the shrine of the Holy Spirit, but in addition, **we are not** our **own**. It is not for us to take our bodies and use them the way we desire. In the final analysis, they do not belong to us; they belong to the Lord.

6:20 We are the Lord's both by creation and redemption. Here the latter is particularly in view. His ownership of us dates back to Calvary. We **were bought at a price**. At the cross, we see the price tag which the Lord Jesus put on us. He thought us to be of such value that He was willing to pay for us with the price of His own precious blood. How greatly Jesus must have loved us to bear our sins in His body on the cross!

That being the case, I can no longer think of my body as my own. If I am to take it and use it in the way I desire, then I am acting as a thief, taking that which does not belong to me. Rather I must use my **body** to **glorify God**, the One to whom it belongs.

Bates exclaimed:

Head! Think of Him whose brow was thorn-girt. Hands! Toil for Him whose hands were nailed to the cross. Feet! Speed to do His behests whose feet were pierced. Body of mine! Be His temple whose body was wrung with pains unspeakable.[15]

We should also glorify God **in** our **spirit**, since both material and immaterial parts of man **are God's**.[16]

III. APOSTOLIC ANSWERS TO CHURCH QUESTIONS (Chaps. 7–14)

A. Concerning Marriage and Celibacy (Chap. 7)

7:1 Up to this point, Paul has been dealing with various abuses in the church at Corinth which he had heard of by direct report. Now he is about to answer questions which the saints at Corinth sent to him. The first has to do with marriage and the single state. He therefore first lays down the broad principle that **it is good for a man not to touch a woman**. "**To touch**" a woman, in this case, means to have a physical relationship. The apostle does *not* imply that the unmarried state is holier than marriage, but simply that it is better to be unmarried if one desires to give oneself to the service of the Lord without distraction. This will be explained in later verses.

7:2 Paul recognizes, however, that the single state carries with it tremendous temptations to impurity. Thus he qualifies the first statement by saying: "**Because of sexual immorality, let each man have his own wife, and let each woman have her own husband.**" For **each man** to **have his own wife** means monogamous marriage. Verse 2 establishes the principle that God's order for His own people continues to be what it always was, namely, that a person should have only one spouse.

7:3 In the married state, each one should **render to** his partner the obligations of married life, since there is a mutual dependence. When it says: "**Let the husband render to his wife the affection due her,**" it means, "Let him carry out his obligations to her as a husband." She should, of course, **do likewise** to him. Note the delicacy Paul uses on this topic. There is no coarseness or vulgarity. How different from the world!

7:4 In marital union there is a dependence of **the wife** upon the **husband** and vice versa. In order to carry out God's order in this holy union, both husband and wife must recognize their interdependence.

7:5 Christenson writes:

In plain language this means that if one partner desires the sexual relationship, the other should respond to that desire. The husband and wife who adopt this down-to-earth approach to sex will find it a wonderfully satisfying aspect of their marriage — for the simple reason that the relationship is rooted in reality, and not in some artificial or impossible ideal.[17]

Perhaps when some of these Corinthians were first saved, they began to think that the intimacies of married life were not consistent with Christian holiness. Paul will disabuse their minds of any such idea. Here he firmly tells them that Christian couples are **not** to **deprive one another**, that is, to deny one's partner's rights as far as the other partner's body is concerned. There are only two exceptions. First of all, such an abstinence should only be by mutual **consent** so that the husband and wife **may give** themselves to **fasting and prayer**. The second condition is that such abstinence should only be temporary. Husband and wife should **come together again**, lest Satan tempt them for their **lack of self-control**.

7:6 Verse 6 has given rise to a great deal of speculation and controversy. Paul says: **"But I say this as a concession, not as a commandment."** Some have taken this to mean that the apostle did not consider the foregoing words to be inspired by God. Such an interpretation is untenable, since he claims in 1 Corinthians 14:37 that the things which he was writing to the Corinthians were the commandments of the Lord. We feel rather that the apostle was saying that under certain circumstances, it was all right for a married couple to abstain from the marriage act, but that this abstinence is a permission, **not a commandment**. Christian people do not have to refrain from this act in order to give themselves undividedly to prayer. Others feel that verse 6 refers to the whole idea of marriage, that is, that Christians are permitted to marry but are not commanded to do so.

7:7 Paul now begins advice to the unmarried. It is clear, first of all, that he considered the unmarried state preferable, but he recognized that it could be followed only as God enabled. When he says: **"For I wish that all men were even as I myself,"** it is obvious from the context that he means "unmarried." There is much diversity of opinion as to whether Paul had always been a bachelor, or whether he was a widower at the time he wrote this. However, for present purposes, it is not necessary to settle the debate, even if we could. Where Paul says: **"But each one has his own gift from God, one in this manner, and another in that,"** he means that God gives grace to some to remain unmarried whereas He definitely calls others to the married state. It is an individual matter, and no general legislation can be adopted which can be applicable to all.

7:8 Therefore he advises **the unmarried and the widows** to **remain even as** he is himself.

7:9 However, if they lack the power of **self-control** in the unmarried state, then they are permitted to **marry. For it is better to marry than to burn with passion.** This passionate burning involves the very grave danger of falling into sin.

7:10 The next two verses are addressed to **married** couples, where both partners are believers. **Now to the mar-**ried I command, yet not I, but the Lord simply means that what Paul was teaching here had already been taught by **the Lord** Jesus *when He was on earth*. Christ had already given an explicit command on this subject. For instance, He had forbidden divorce except on the ground of unfaithfulness (Matt. 5:32; 19:9). The overall instruction that Paul gives is that **a wife is not to depart from her husband.**

7:11 However, he recognizes that there are extreme cases where it might be necessary for a wife to leave her husband. In such a case, she is obligated to **remain unmarried, or be reconciled to her husband**. Separation does not break the marriage tie; rather it gives opportunity for the Lord to heal the differences that have come between and to restore both parties to fellowship with Him and with one another. The **husband** is commanded **not to divorce his wife**. No exception is made in his case.

7:12 Verses 12–24 deal with the problem of a marriage where only one party is a believer. Paul prefaces his remarks with the statement: **"But to the rest I, not the Lord, say."** Again, we strongly emphasize that this does not mean that what Paul is saying represents his own viewpoints and not the Lord's. He is simply explaining that what he is about to say had **not** been previously taught by **the Lord** Jesus when He was here on earth. There is no instruction in the Gospels similar to this. The Lord Jesus simply did not take up the case of a marriage where only one member was a believer. But now Christ has instructed His apostle in this matter and so what Paul says here is the inspired word of God.

But to the rest means to those whose partners are not believers. This passage does *not* condone a Christian's marrying an unsaved person. It probably has in view the situation where one of the partners was saved after marriage.

"If any brother has a wife who does not believe, and she is willing to live with him, let him not divorce her." In order to appreciate this passage of Scripture properly, it is helpful to remind ourselves of God's commandment to His people in the OT. When Jews married heathen wives and had children by them, they were commanded to put both the wives and the children away. This is clearly seen in Ezra 10:2, 3 and Nehemiah 13:23–25.

Now the question has arisen in Corinth as to what a wife who had been converted should do about her husband and children, or what a man who has an unbelieving wife should do with her. Should he put her away? The answer is obviously negative. The OT commandment no longer applies to the people of God under grace. If a Christian has a non-Christian wife, **and she is willing to live with him**, he should not leave her. This does not mean that it is all right for a man to marry a non-believer, but simply that being married to her when he was converted, he should not leave her.

7:13 Likewise, **a woman who has a** non-Christian **husband** who **is willing to live with her** should stay with her husband. Perhaps by her meek and godly testimony before him, she will win him to the Lord.

7:14 Actually the presence of a believer in a non-Christian home has a sanctifying influence. As mentioned before, to *sanctify* means to set apart. Here it does not mean that the unbelieving husband is saved by his wife, neither does it mean that he is made holy. Rather it means that he is set apart in a position of external privilege. He is fortunate to have a Christian wife who prays for him. Her life and testimony are an influence for God in the home. Speaking from a human point of view, the likelihood of that man being saved is greater when he has a godly, Christian wife than if he had an unbelieving wife. As Vine puts it: "He receives a spiritual influence holding the possibility of actual conversion."[18] The same would hold true, of course, in the case of an **unbelieving wife** and a Christian **husband. The unbelieving wife** would be **sanctified** in such a case.

Then the apostle adds: **"otherwise your children would be unclean; but now they are holy."** We have already mentioned that in the OT the children were to be put away as well as the heathen wife. Now Paul explains that in the dispensation of grace, children born of a marriage where one partner is a believer and the other is not **are holy**. The

word **holy** comes from the same root word translated **sanctified** in this verse. It does not at all mean that the children are made holy in themselves, that is, that they necessarily live clean and pure lives. Rather it means that they are set apart in a place of privilege. They have at least one parent who loves the Lord, and who tells them the gospel story. There is a strong possibility of their being saved. They are privileged to live in a home where one of the parents is indwelt by the Spirit of God. In this sense, they are sanctified. This verse also includes the assurance that it is not wrong to have children when one parent is a Christian and the other is not. God recognizes the marriage, and the children are not illegitimate.

7:15 But what should be the attitude of a Christian if the unsaved partner desires to leave? The answer is that he or she should be allowed to **depart**. The expression **"a brother or a sister is not under bondage in such cases"** is very difficult to explain with finality. Some believe that it means that if the unbeliever deserts the believer, and there is every reason to believe that the desertion is final, then the believer is free to obtain a divorce. Those who hold this view teach that verse 15 is a parenthesis, and that verse 16 is connected with verse 14 as follows:

1. Verse 14 states that the ideal situation is for a believer to remain with an unbelieving partner because of the sanctifying influence of a Christian in the home.

2. Verse 16 suggests that through staying in the home, the believer may win the unbeliever to Christ.

3. Verse 15 is a parenthesis, allowing the believer to be divorced (and possibly to remarry) if he or she is deserted by the unbeliever.

The hope of eventual salvation is connected with continued union rather than with the unbeliever's leaving the home.

But other Bible students insist that verse 15 deals only with the subject of separation and not with divorce and remarriage. To them, it simply means that if the unbeliever departs, he should be allowed to do so peacefully. The wife is not under any obligation to keep the marriage together beyond what she has already done. **God has called us to peace**, and we are not required to use emotional displays or legal processes to prevent the unbeliever from departing.

Which is the right interpretation? We find it impossible to decide definitely. It does seem to us that the Lord taught in Matthew 19:9 that divorce is permitted where one party has been guilty of unfaithfulness (adultery). We believe that in such a case, the innocent party is free to remarry. As far as 1 Corinthians 7:15 is concerned, we cannot be positive that it permits divorce and remarriage where an unbeliever has deserted his Christian partner. However, anyone who is guilty of this form of desertion will almost inevitably enter into a new relationship very soon, and thus the original union will be broken anyway. J. M. Davies writes:

> The unbeliever who departs would very soon be married to another, which would automatically break the marriage bond. To insist that the deserted party remain unmarried would put a yoke upon him/her which in the majority of cases, they would not be able to bear.[19]

7:16 One's understanding of verse 16 varies somewhat depending on the interpretation of verse 15.

If a person believes that verse 15 does not sanction divorce, he points to this verse as proof. He argues that the believer should permit separation but should not divorce the unbeliever because that would prevent the possibility of the restoration of the marriage union and the likelihood of the unbeliever's being saved. If, on the other hand, a person believes that divorce is permitted when a believer has been deserted, then this verse is linked with verse 14, and verse 15 is considered as a parenthesis.

7:17 There is sometimes a feeling among new converts that they must make a complete break with every phase of their former life, including institutions such as marriage which are not in themselves sinful. In the newfound joy of salvation, there is the danger of using forcible revolution to overthrow all that one has previously known. Christianity does not use forcible revolution in order to accomplish its purposes. Rather, its changes are made by peaceful means. In verses 17–24, the apostle lays down the general rule that becoming a Christian need not involve violent revolution against existing ties. Doubtless he has marriage ties primarily in view, but he also applies the principle to racial and social ties.

Each believer is to walk in accordance with the calling of the Lord. If He has called one to married life, then he should follow this in the fear of the Lord. If God has given grace to live a celibate life, then a man should follow that calling. In addition, if at the time of a person's conversion, he is married to an unsaved wife, then he need not overturn this relationship, but should continue to the best of his ability to seek the salvation of his wife. What Paul is stating to the Corinthians is not for them alone; this is what he taught **in all the churches**. Vine writes:

> When Paul says, "and so ordain I in all the churches," he is not issuing decrees from a given center, but is simply informing the Church at Corinth that the instructions he was giving them were what he gave in every church.[20]

7:18 Paul deals with the subject of racial ties in verses 18 and 19. If a man was a Jew at the time of his conversion, and bore in his body the mark of circumcision, he need not take a violent revulsion at this and seek to obliterate all physical marks of his former way of life. Likewise, if a man were a heathen at the time of his new birth, he does not have to seek to hide his heathen background by taking on the marks of a Jew.

We might also interpret this verse to mean that if a Jew were converted, he should not be afraid to live on with his Jewish wife, or if a Gentile were converted he should not try to flee from that background. These external differences are not what really count.

7:19 As far as the essence of Christianity is concerned, **circumcision is nothing and uncircumcision is nothing**. What really counts is **keeping the commandments of God**. In other words, God is concerned with what is inward, not with what is outward. The relationships of life need not be violently forsaken by the entrance of Christianity. "Rather," Kelly says, "by the Christian faith, the believer is raised to a position where he is superior to all circumstances."[21]

7:20 The general rule is that **each one** should **remain** with God in that state **in which he was called**. This, of course, only refers to callings that are not in themselves sinful. If a person were engaged in some wicked business at the time of conversion, he would be expected to leave it! But the apostle here is dealing with things not wrong in themselves. This is proved in the following verses where the subject of slaves is discussed.

7:21 What should **a slave** do when he is saved? Should he rebel against his owner and demand his freedom? Does Christianity insist that we go around seeking our "rights"? Paul gives the answer here: **"Were you called while a slave? Do not be concerned about it."** In other words, "Were you a slave at the time of your conversion? Do not be needlessly concerned about that. You can be a slave and still enjoy the highest blessings of Christianity."

But if you can be made free, rather use it. There are two interpretations of this passage. Some feel that Paul is saying, "If you can become free, by all means avail yourself of this opportunity." Others feel that the apostle is saying that even if a slave could become free, Christianity does not require him to avail himself of that freedom. Rather he should use his bondage as a testimony to the Lord Jesus. Most people will prefer the first interpretation (and it is probably correct), but they should not overlook the fact that the second would be more nearly in accord with the example left to us by the Lord Jesus Christ Himself.

7:22 **He who is called in the Lord while a slave is the Lord's freedman.** This does not mean a man who was freeborn but rather one who was made free, that is, a slave who obtained his freedom. In other words, if a man was a slave at the time of his conversion, he should not let that worry him, because he **is the Lord's freedman**. He has been set free from his sins and from the bondage of Satan. On the other hand, if a man were **free** at the time of his conversion, he should realize that from now on

he is a **slave**, bound hand and foot to the Savior.

7:23 Every Christian has been **bought at a price**. He henceforth belongs to the One who bought him, the Lord Jesus. We are to be Christ's bondslaves and **not become slaves of men**.

7:24 Therefore, no matter what one's social state was, he can consistently **remain with God** in that state. These two words *with God* are the key which unlocks the whole truth. If a man is **with God**, then even slavery can be made true freedom. "It is that which ennobles and sanctifies any position in life."

7:25 In verses 25–38, the apostle is addressing himself to the unmarried, whether male or female. The word **virgins** can be used to apply to either. Verse 25 is another verse that some have used to teach that the contents of this chapter are not necessarily inspired. They even go to such extremes as to say that Paul, being a bachelor, was a male chauvinist and that his personal prejudices are reflected in what he says here! To adopt such an attitude, of course, is to deal a vicious attack on the inspiration of Scriptures. When Paul says he has **no commandment from the Lord** about **virgins**, he simply means that during the Lord's earthly ministry He did not leave any explicit instruction on this subject. Therefore Paul gives his own **judgment, as one whom the Lord in His mercy has made trustworthy**, and this judgment is inspired of God.

7:26 In general, it **is good** to be unmarried, **because of the present distress. The present distress** refers to the sufferings of this earthly life in general. Perhaps there was a special time of distress at the time Paul wrote this letter. However, distress has continued to exist and will last until the Lord comes.

7:27 Paul's advice is that those who are already married should **not seek** to be separated. On the other hand, if a man **is loosed from a wife**, he should **not seek a wife**. The expression **loosed from a wife** here does not only mean widowed or divorced. It simply means free from the marriage bond, and could include those who never married.

7:28 Nothing Paul says should be

construed to indicate that it is a sin to marry. After all, marriage was instituted by God in the Garden of Eden before sin ever entered the world. It was God Himself who decreed: "It is not good that man should be alone" (Gen. 2:18). "Marriage is honorable among all, and the bed undefiled" (Heb. 13:4). Paul elsewhere speaks of those who forbid to marry as being a sign of latter-day apostasy (1 Tim. 4:1–3).

Thus Paul states, **"But even if you do marry, you have not sinned; and if a virgin marries, she has not sinned."** New converts to Christianity should never think that there is anything wrong in the marriage relationship. Yet Paul adds that those women who do marry **will have trouble in the flesh**. This may include the travail connected with childbirth, etc. When Paul says **"But I would spare you,"** he may mean (1) **I would spare you** the physical suffering which accompanies the marriage state, particularly the troubles of family life, or (2) **I would spare** the reader the enumeration of all these troubles.

7:29 Paul would like to emphasize that because **the time is short** we should subordinate even these legitimate relationships of life in order to serve the Lord. Christ's coming is near, and although husbands and wives should perform their mutual duties with faithfulness, they should seek to put Christ first in all their lives. Ironside expresses it in this way:

> Everyone is to act in view of the fact that the time is indeed fleeting, the Lord's return is nearing, and no consideration of personal comfort is to be allowed to hinder devotion to the will of God.[22]

W. E. Vine says:

> The meaning is not, of course, that a married man is to refrain from behaving as a husband should, but that his relationship to his wife should be entirely subservient to his higher relationship with the Lord . . . who is to have the first place in the heart; he is not to permit a natural relation to obstruct his obedience to Christ.[23]

7:30 The sorrows and joys and possessions of life should not be given a place of undue consideration in our lives. All these must be subordinated in our endeavor to buy up the opportunity to serve the Lord while it is still day.

7:31 In living our lives on earth, it is inevitable that we have a certain amount of contact with mundane things. There is a legitimate use of these things in the life of the believer. However, Paul warns that while we may **use** them, we should not *misuse* them. For instance, the Christian should not live for food, clothes, and pleasure. He may use food and clothes as essentials but they should not become the god of his life. Marriage, property, commerce, or political, scientific, musical, and artistic activity have their place in the world, but all may prove a distraction to spiritual life if allowed to do so.

The expression **the form of this world is passing away** is borrowed from the theater and refers to the changing of scenes. It speaks of the transience of all that we see about us today. Its short-lived character is well expressed in Shakespeare's famous lines: "All the world's a stage, and all the men and women merely players. They have their exits and their entrances, and one man in his time plays many parts."

7:32 Paul wants the Christians **to be without care**. He means the cares that would unnecessarily hinder them from serving the Lord. And so he goes on to explain that **he who is unmarried cares for the things of the Lord — how he may please the Lord**. This does not mean that all unmarried believers actually do give themselves undistractedly to the Lord, but it means that the unmarried state provides the opportunity for so doing in a way that the married state does not.

7:33 Again this does not mean that a **married** man cannot be very attentive to the things of the Lord, but it is a general observation that married life requires that a man **please his wife**. He has additional obligations to think of. As Vine has pointed out: "In general, if a man is married, he has limited his range of service. If he is unmarried, he can go on to the ends of the earth and preach the gospel."[24]

7:34 The unmarried woman cares about the things of the Lord, that she may be holy both in body and in spirit. But she who is married cares about the

things of the world — how she may please her husband. A word of explanation is needed here also. **The unmarried woman,** or the **virgin,** is able to give a greater portion of her time to **the things of the Lord.** The expression **"that she may be holy both in body and in spirit"** does not mean that the unmarried state is more holy, but simply that she can be more *set apart* **in both body and spirit** to the work of the Lord. She is not essentially purer, but her time is freer.

Again, **she who is married cares about the things of the world.** That does not mean that she is more worldly than the unmarried woman, but that her day must necessarily be devoted in part to mundane duties such as care of the home. These things are legitimate and right, and Paul is not criticizing them or depreciating them; he is merely stating that an unmarried woman has wider avenues for service and more time than a married woman.

7:35 Paul is not setting forth this teaching in order to put people under a rigid system of bondage. He is merely instructing them for their own **profit** so that when they think of their lives and of the service of the Lord, they may judge His guidance in the light of all this instruction. His attitude is that celibacy is good, and enables a person to **serve the Lord without distraction.** As far as Paul is concerned, man is free to choose either marriage or celibacy. The apostle does not want to **put a leash** on anyone or to put them into bondage.

7:36 Verses 36–38 are perhaps the most misunderstood verses in this chapter, and perhaps in the entire Epistle. The common explanation is this: In Paul's day a man exercised rigid control over his home. It was up to him whether his daughters married or not. They could not do so without his permission. Thus these verses are taken to mean that if a man refuses to allow his daughters to marry, that is a good thing, but if he allows them to marry, then he is not sinning.

Such an interpretation seems almost meaningless as far as instruction for the people of God in this day is concerned. The interpretation does not fit in with the context of the rest of the chapter, and seems hopelessly confusing.

The RSV translates virgin as "betrothed." The thought would then be that if a man marries his betrothed or fiancée, he does not sin; but if he refrains from marrying her, it is better. Such a view is loaded with difficulties.

In his commentary on 1 Corinthians, William Kelly presents an alternate view which seems to have great merit. Kelly believes that the word **virgin** (*parthenos*) may also be translated "virginity."[25] Thus the passage is not speaking about a man's virgin daughters, but about *his own virginity.* According to this interpretation, the passage is saying that if a man maintains the unmarried state he does well, but if he decides to get married, **he does not sin.**

John Nelson Darby adopts this same interpretation in his New Translation:

> But if anyone think that he behaves unseemly to his virginity, and if he is beyond the flower of his age, and so it must be, let him do what he will, he does not sin: let them marry. But he who stands firm in his heart, having no need, but has authority over his own will, and has judged this in his heart to keep his own virginity, he does well. So that he that marries himself does well: and he that does not marry does better.

Looking at verse 36 in greater detail then, we take it as meaning that if a man has come to full manhood, and if he does not feel that he has the gift of continence, **he does not sin** in marrying. He feels that the need requires him to do so, and so **he** should **do what he wishes** in this case, that is, get married.

7:37 **Nevertheless,** if a man has determined to serve the Lord undistractedly, and if he has sufficient self-control so that there is **no necessity** for his marrying, if he has determined to maintain the unmarried state, and this with a view to glorifying God in service, then he **does well.**

7:38 The conclusion is that **he who gives** himself[26] **in marriage** does well, **but he who** maintains the unmarried state for greater service for the Lord **does better.**

7:39 The last two verses of the chapter contain advice to widows. **A wife is bound by law** to her husband **as long as** he **lives.** The **law** referred to here is the marriage law, instituted by God.

If a woman's **husband dies, she is at liberty to be married to** another man. This same truth is enunciated in Romans 7:1–3, namely, that death breaks the marriage relationship. However, the apostle adds the qualification that she is free to marry **whom she wishes, only in the Lord**. This means, first of all, that the person she marries must be a Christian, but it means more than this. **In the Lord** means "in the will of the Lord." In other words, she might marry a Christian and still be out of the will of the Lord. She must seek the guidance of the Lord in this important matter and marry the believer whom the Lord would have for her.

7:40 Paul's frank judgment is that a widow **is happier if she remains** unmarried. This does not contradict 1 Timothy 5:14 where Paul expresses his judgment that younger widows should marry. Here he is stating his general idea — in 1 Timothy a specific exception.

Then he adds, **"I think I also have the Spirit of God."** Some misunderstand these words to mean that Paul was not sure of himself in stating these things! Again we protest vigorously against any such interpretation. There can be no question as to the inspiration of what Paul wrote in this portion. He is using irony here. His apostleship and his teaching had been under attack by some at Corinth. They professed to have the mind of the Lord in what they were saying. Paul is saying in effect, "Whatever else others may say of me, I think that I also have the Spirit of God. They profess to have Him but surely they do not think that they have a monopoly on the Holy Spirit."

We know that Paul did indeed **have the Spirit** in all that he wrote to us, and that the path of happiness for us is to follow his instructions.

B. Concerning Eating Meats Offered to Idols (8:1–11:1)

The question of eating meat offered to idols is taken up in 8:1–11:1, a real problem to those recently converted to Christ from heathenism. Perhaps they would be invited to a social event at a temple where a great feast would be spread with meat previously offered to idols. Or perhaps they would go to the market to buy meat and find that the butcher was selling meat that had been offered to idols. This would not affect the quality of the meat, of course, but should a Christian buy it? In another scenario, a believer might be invited to a home and be served food that had been offered up to some idol deity. If he knew that this had been the case, should he partake of the food? Paul addresses himself to these questions.

8:1 The apostle begins by stating that **concerning things offered to idols**, both the Corinthians and he himself had **knowledge**. It was not a subject about which they were completely ignorant. They **all** knew, for instance, that the mere act of offering a piece of meat to an idol had not changed it in any sense. Its flavor and nutritional value remained the same. However, Paul points out that **knowledge puffs up, but love edifies**. By this he means that knowledge in itself is not a sufficient guide in these matters. If knowledge were the only principle that were applied, then it might lead to pride. Actually in all such matters the Christian must use not only knowledge but also love. He must not only consider what is lawful for himself, but what would be best for others.

8:2, 3 Vine paraphrases verse 2 as follows: "If a man imagines he has fully acquired knowledge, he has not even begun to know how it ought to be gained." Without love there can be no true knowledge. On the other hand, **if anyone loves God, this one is known by Him** in the sense that God approves him. In one sense, of course, God knows everybody, and in another sense He knows especially those who are believers. But here the word "know" is used to denote favor or approval. If anyone makes his decisions in such matters as meats offered to idols out of love to God and man and not out of mere knowledge, that person wins the smile of God's approval.

8:4 As far as things **offered to idols** are concerned, believers understand that **an idol is** not a real god with power, knowledge, and love. Paul was not denying the existence of idols themselves; he knew that there were such things as images carved out of wood or stone. Later on he acknowledges that behind these idols there are demon-powers. But what he emphasizes here is that the gods which these idols purport to represent do not exist. **There is no other God but one**, that is, the God and Father of our Lord Jesus Christ.

8:5 Paul admits that there were many **so-called gods** in heathen mythology, such as Jupiter, Juno, and Mercury. Some of these gods were supposed to live **in heaven**, and others, such as Ceres and Neptune, here **on earth**. In this sense **there are many gods and many lords**, that is, mythological beings which people worshiped and were in bondage to.

8:6 Believers know that **there is one** true **God, the Father, of whom are all things, and we for Him**. This means that God, our Father, is the Source or Creator of **all things** and that **we** were created **for Him**. In other words, He is the purpose or goal of our existence. We also know that there is **one Lord**, namely **Jesus Christ, through whom are all things, and through whom we live**. The expression **through whom are all things** describes the Lord Jesus as the Mediator or Agent of God, whereas the expression **through whom we live** indicates that it is through Him that we have been created and redeemed.

When Paul says that **there is one God, the Father**, and **one Lord Jesus Christ**, he does not mean that the Lord Jesus Christ is not God. Rather he simply indicates the respective roles which these two Persons of the Godhead fulfilled in creation and in redemption.

8:7 However, not all Christians, especially new converts, understand the liberty which they have in Christ Jesus. Having come from backgrounds of idolatry and being used to idols, they think they are committing idolatry when they eat meat that has been **offered to an idol**. They think that the idol is a reality **and** therefore **their conscience, being weak, is defiled**.

The expression **weak** here does not mean physically weak or even spiritually weak. It is a term describing those who are unduly scrupulous in matters of moral indifference. For instance, as far as God is concerned, it is not wrong for a believer to eat pork. It would have been wrong for a Jew to do so in the OT, but

a Christian is at perfect liberty to partake of such food. However, a Jew converted to Christianity might still have scruples about this. He might feel that it is wrong to eat a roast pork dinner. He is what the Bible calls a weak brother. It means that he is not living in the full enjoyment of his Christian liberty. Actually, as long as he thinks that it is wrong to eat pork, he would sin if he went ahead and did it. That is what is meant by the expression **their conscience, being weak, is defiled**. If my conscience condemns a certain act and I go ahead and commit it, then I have sinned. ''Whatever is not from faith is sin'' (Rom. 14:23).

8:8 **Food** in itself is not a matter of great consequence **to God**. Refraining from certain foods does not give us favor with God, nor does partaking of such foods make us better Christians.

8:9 But although there is nothing to gain by eating these foods, there might be much to lose if in so doing I cause a **weak** Christian to stumble. This is where the principle of love must come in. A Christian has liberty to eat meat that has been previously offered in sacrifice to idols, but it would be utterly wrong for him to eat if in so doing he offends a **weak** brother or sister.

8:10 The danger is that the weak brother might be encouraged to do what his conscience condemns, if he **sees** another doing something which to him is questionable. In this verse, the apostle condemns **eating in an idol's temple** because of the effect it would have on others. Of course, when Paul speaks here of **eating in an idol's temple**, he is referring to some social event or some general celebration, such as a wedding. It would never be right to eat in such a temple if the meal involved participation in idol-worship in any way. Paul later condemns that (10:15–26). The expression **for if anyone sees you who have knowledge** means if anybody sees you, who have a full measure of Christian liberty, who know that meat offered to idols is not unclean or impure, etc. The important principle here is that we must not only consider what effect such an action would have on ourselves, but even more important, what effect it would have on others.

8:11 A man may so parade his

knowledge of what is legitimate for a Christian as to cause a brother in Christ to stumble. The word **perish** does not mean that he would lose his eternal salvation. It means not the loss of *being* but the loss of *well-being*. This weak brother's testimony would be hurt and his life would be adversely affected as far as usefulness for God is concerned. The tremendous seriousness of so offending a weak brother in Christ is indicated by the words **for whom Christ died**. Paul's argument is that if the Lord Jesus Christ loved this man so much that He was willing to die for him, we should not dare to hinder his spiritual progress by doing anything that would stumble him. A few slices of meat are not worth it!

8:12 It is not just a matter of sinning against a brother in Christ, or of wounding his **weak conscience**. It constitutes sin **against Christ** Himself. Whatever we do to the least of His brethren we do to Him. What hurts one of the members of the Body hurts the Head as well. Vine points out that in dealing with each subject, the apostle leads his readers to view it in the light of the atoning death of Christ. Barnes says, "It is an appeal drawn from the deep and tender love, the sufferings, and the dying groans of the Son of God."[27] **Sin against Christ** is what Godet calls "the highest of crimes." Realizing this, we should be very careful to examine all our actions in the light of their effect on others, and to refrain from doing anything that would cause a brother to be offended.

8:13 Because it is sin against Christ to make one's **brother stumble**, Paul states that he **will never again eat meat** if in so doing he makes his **brother stumble**. The work of God in the life of another person is far more important than a tender roast! Although the subject of meats offered to idols is not a problem for most Christians today, the *principles* which the Spirit of God gives us in this section are of abiding value. There are many things today in the Christian life, which, while not forbidden in the word of God, would yet cause needless offense to weaker Christians. While we might have the right to participate in them, a greater right is to forego that right for the spiritual welfare of those we love in Christ, our fellow-believers.

At first glance, chapter 9 might seem to indicate a new subject. However, the question of meats offered to idols continues for two more chapters. Paul is merely turning aside here to give *his own example* of self-denial for the good of others. He was willing to forego his right to financial support as an apostle in accordance with the principle set forth in 8:13. Thus this chapter is closely linked with chapter 8.

9:1 As we know, there were those in Corinth who questioned Paul's authority. They said that he was not one of the twelve, and therefore not a genuine apostle. Paul protests that he was free from human authority, a genuine **apostle** of the Lord Jesus. He bases his claim on two facts. First of all, he had **seen Jesus Christ our Lord** in resurrection. This took place on the road to Damascus. He also points to the Corinthians themselves as proof of his apostleship by asking the question, **"Are you not my work in the Lord?"** If they had any doubt as to his apostleship, they should examine themselves. Were they saved? Of course they would say they were. Well, who pointed them to Christ? The Apostle Paul did! Therefore, they themselves were proof of the fact that he was a genuine apostle of the Lord.

9:2 **Others** may not recognize him as **an apostle**, but surely the Corinthians themselves should. They were **the seal of** his **apostleship in the Lord.**

9:3 Verse 3 probably refers to what has gone before (and not to what follows, as the NKJV punctuates it). Paul is saying that what he has just said is his **defense to those who examine** him, or who question his authority as an apostle.

9:4 In verses 4–14, the apostle discusses his **right** to financial support as an apostle. As one who had been sent by the Lord Jesus, Paul was entitled to financial remuneration from the believers. However, he had not always insisted on this right. He had often worked with his hands, making tents, in order that he might be able to preach the gospel freely to men and women. No doubt his critics took advantage of this, suggesting that the reason that he did not take support was that he knew he was not a real apostle. He introduces the subject by asking a question: **"Do we have no right to eat and drink?** — that is — without having to work for it? Are we not entitled to be supported by the church?"

9:5 **Do we have no right to take along a believing wife, as do also the other apostles**, and **the brothers of the Lord, and Cephas?** Perhaps some of Paul's critics suggested that Paul did not marry because he knew that he and his wife would not be entitled to the support of the churches. Peter and the other apostles were married, as were also **the brothers of the Lord**. Here the apostle is stating that he would have just as much right to be married and enjoy the support of the Christians for both his wife and himself. The expression **"to take along a believing wife"** refers not only to the right to marry, but also to the right of support for both husband and wife. **The brothers of the Lord** probably means His actual half-brothers, or possibly His cousins. This text alone does not solve the problem, although other Scriptures indicate that Mary did have other children after Jesus, her Firstborn (Luke 2:7; see Matt. 1:25; 12:46; 13:55; Mark 6:3; John 2:12; Gal. 1:19).

9:6 It appears that **Barnabas**, like Paul, had worked to provide for his material needs while preaching the gospel. Paul asked if they both did not have the **right to refrain from working** and to be cared for by the people of God.

9:7 The apostle based his first claim to financial support on the example of the other apostles. He now turns to an argument from human affairs. A soldier is not sent to war **at his own expense**. Whoever **plants a vineyard** is never expected to do so without receiving some recompense from **its fruit**. Finally, a shepherd is not expected to keep **a flock** without being given a right to partake **of the milk**. Christian service is like warfare, agriculture, and pastoral life. It involves fighting against the enemy, caring for God's fruit trees, and serving as an under-shepherd for His sheep. If the right of support is recognized in these earthly occupations, how much more should it be in the service of the Lord!

9:8 Paul next turns to the OT for further proof of his point. Does he have

to base his argument merely on these mundane things of life, such as warfare, agriculture, and shepherding? **Does not the** Scripture **say the same** thing?

9:9 It is clearly stated in Deuteronomy 25:4 that **an ox** should **not** be muzzled **while it treads out the grain**. That is, when an animal is used in a harvesting operation, it should be allowed to partake of some of the harvest. **Is it oxen God is concerned about?** God does care for oxen, but He didn't cause these things to be written in the OT merely for the sake of dumb animals. There was a spiritual principle involved to be applied to our life and service.

9:10 **Or does He say it altogether for our sakes?** The answer is "yes," our welfare was in His mind when these words were **written**. When a man **plows**, he **should plow** with the expectation of some remuneration. So likewise, when a man **threshes**, he should be able to look forward to some of the harvest in recompense. Christian service resembles plowing and threshing, and God has decreed that those who engage in these aspects of His service should not do so at their own expense.

9:11 Paul speaks of himself as having **sown spiritual things for** the Christians at Corinth. In other words, he came to Corinth preaching the gospel to them and teaching them precious spiritual truths. That being so, is it asking too much if in return they should minister to him of their finances or other **material things**? The argument is that "the wages of the preacher are greatly inferior in value to what he has given. Material benefits are small compared with spiritual blessings."

9:12 Paul was aware that the church at Corinth was supporting **others** who were preaching or teaching there. They recognized this obligation to other men but not to the Apostle Paul, and so he asks: **"If others are partakers of this right over you, are we not even more?"** If they recognized the right of others to financial support, why should they not then recognize that he, their father in the faith, had this right? Doubtless some of those who were being supported were the Judaizing teachers. Paul adds that, although he had **this right**, he did not use it with the Corinthians but endured all things lest he **hinder the gospel of Christ**. Rather than insist on his right to receive support from them, he bore all sorts of privations and hardships so that the gospel would not be hindered.

9:13 Paul next introduces the argument from the support of those who served in the Jewish temple. Those who had official duties in connection with the temple service were supported from the income the temple received. In this sense they lived off **the things of the temple**. Also, the priests themselves **who** served **at the altar** were given a certain portion **of the offerings** that were brought to **the altar**. In other words, both the Levites, who had the ordinary duties around the temple, and the priests, to whom were entrusted the more sacred duties, were alike supported for their service.

9:14 Finally, Paul introduces the definite command of **the Lord** Himself. He **commanded that those who preach the gospel should live from the gospel**. This would be conclusive proof alone of Paul's right to support from the Corinthians. But this raises the question of why he did not insist on being supported by them. The answer is given in verses 15–18.

9:15 He explains that he **used none of these things**, that is, he did not insist on his rights. Neither was he writing **these things** at the present time in order that they might send money to him. He would rather **die than that anyone should** be able to rob him of his **boasting**.

9:16 Paul is saying that he cannot **boast** in the fact that he preaches the gospel. A divine compulsion **is laid upon** him. It is not a vocation that he chose for himself. He received the "tap on the shoulder" and he would have been a most miserable man if he had not obeyed the divine commission. This does not mean the apostle was not willing to preach the gospel, but rather that the decision to preach did not come from himself, but from the Lord.

9:17 If the Apostle Paul preached the gospel **willingly**, he would **have** the **reward** that goes with such service, namely, the right of maintenance. Throughout the Old and New Testaments, it is clearly taught that those who serve the Lord are entitled to support

from the Lord's people. In this passage, Paul does not mean that he was an unwilling servant of the Lord, but is simply stating that there was a divine compulsion in his apostleship. He goes on to emphasize this in the latter part of the verse. **If** he preached **against** his **will**, that is, if he preached because there was a fire burning within him and he could not refrain from preaching, then he had **been entrusted with a stewardship** of the gospel. He was a man acting under orders, and therefore he could not boast in that.

Verse 17 is admittedly difficult, and yet the meaning seems to be that Paul would not claim his right of maintenance from the Corinthians because the ministry was not an occupation which he chose by himself. He was placed in it by the hand of God. The false teachers in Corinth might claim their right to be supported by the saints, but the Apostle Paul would seek his reward elsewhere.

Knox's translation of this verse is as follows: "I can claim a reward for what I do of my own choice; but when I act under constraint, I am only executing a commission."

Ryrie comments:

> Paul could not escape his responsibility to preach the gospel, because a stewardship (responsibility) had been committed to him and he was under orders to preach even though he was never paid (cf. Luke 17:10).[28]

9:18 If then he could not boast in the fact that he preached the gospel, of what would he boast? Of something that was a matter of his own choice, namely, that he presented **the gospel of Christ without charge**. This is something he could determine to do. He would preach the gospel to the Corinthians, at the same time earning his own living, so as not to use to the full his right for maintenance **in the gospel**.

To summarize the apostle's argument here, he is making a distinction between what was obligatory and what was optional. There is no thought of any reluctance in his preaching the gospel. He did that cheerfully. But in a very real sense, it was a solemn obligation that rested upon him. Therefore in the discharge of that obligation there was no reason for his boasting. In preaching the gospel, he could have insisted on his right to financial support, but he did not do this; rather he decided to give the gospel **without charge** to the Corinthians. Since this was a matter of his own will, he would glory in this. As we have suggested, Paul's critics claimed that his working as a tentmaker indicated that he did not consider himself to be a true apostle. Here he turns his self-support in such a way as to prove that his apostleship was nonetheless real; in fact, it was of a very high and noble character.

In verses 19–22, Paul cites his example of the waiving of legitimate rights for the gospel's sake. In studying this section, it is important to remember that Paul does not mean that he ever sacrificed important principles of the Scripture. He did not believe that the end justified the means. In these verses he is speaking about matters of moral indifference. He accommodated himself to the customs and habits of the people with whom he worked in order that he might gain a ready ear for the gospel. But never did he do anything which might compromise the truth of the gospel.

9:19 In one sense he was **free from all men**. No one could exercise jurisdiction or compulsion over him. Yet he brought himself under bondage **to all** people in order **that** he **might win the more**. If he could make a concession without sacrificing divine truth he would do it in order to win souls to Christ.

9:20 **To the Jews** he **became as a Jew, that** he **might win Jews**. This cannot mean that he put himself back under the Law of Moses in order to see Jews saved. What it does mean might be illustrated in the action which Paul took in connection with the circumcision of Timothy and Titus. In the case of Titus, there were those who insisted that unless he was circumcised, he couldn't be saved. Realizing that this was a frontal attack on the gospel of the grace of God, Paul stoutly refused to have Titus circumcised (Gal. 2:3). However, in the case of Timothy it seems that no such issue was involved. Therefore, the apostle was willing that Timothy should be circumcised if this would result in a wider hearing of the gospel (Acts 16:3).

To those who are under the law, as under the law,[29] **that I might win those who are under the law. Those who are under the law** refers to the Jewish people. But Paul had already spoken of his dealings with the Jews in the first part of the verse. Why does he then repeat the subject here? The explanation that has often been offered is that when he speaks of Jews in the first part of the verse, he is referring to their national customs, whereas here he is referring to their religious life.

At this point a brief word of explanation is necessary. As a Jew, Paul had been born under the law. He sought to obtain favor with God by keeping the law, but found that he was unable to do so. The law only showed him what a wretched sinner he was, and utterly condemned him. Eventually he learned that the law was not a way of salvation, but only God's method of revealing to man his sinfulness and his need of a Savior. Paul then trusted in the Lord Jesus Christ, and in so doing he became free from the condemning voice of the law. The penalty of the law which he had broken was paid by the Lord Jesus on the cross of Calvary.

After his conversion, the apostle learned that the law was not the way of salvation, nor was it the rule of life for one who had been saved. The believer is not under law but under grace. This does not mean that he can go out and do as he pleases. Rather, it means that a true sense of the grace of God will prevent him from even wanting to do these things. Indwelt by the Spirit of God, the Christian is raised to a new level of behavior. He now desires to live a holy life, not out of fear of punishment for having broken the law, but out of love for Christ, who died for him and rose again. Under law the motive was fear, but under grace the motive is love. Love is a far higher motive than fear. Men will do out of love what they would never do from terror.

Arnot says:

God's method of binding souls to obedience is similar to His method of keeping the planets in their orbits — that is, by flinging them out free. You see no chain keeping back these shining worlds to prevent them from bursting away from their center. They are held in the grip of an invisible principle. . . . And it is by the invisible bond of love — love to the Lord who bought them — that ransomed men are constrained to live soberly and righteously and godly.[30]

With that brief background in mind, let us now get back to the latter half of verse 20. **To those who are under the law, as under the law, that I might win those who are under the law.** When he was with Jewish people, Paul behaved as a Jew in matters of moral indifference. For instance, he ate the foods which the Jewish people ate and refrained from eating such things as pork which were forbidden to them. Perhaps Paul also refrained from working on the Sabbath day, realizing that if he did this, the gospel might gain a more ready hearing from the people.

As a born-again believer in the Lord Jesus, the Apostle Paul was not under the law as a rule of life. He merely adapted himself to the customs, habits, and prejudices of the people in order that he might win them to the Lord.

9:21 Ryrie writes:

Paul is not demonstrating two-facedness or multi-facedness, but rather he is testifying of a constant, restrictive self-discipline in order to be able to serve all sorts of men. Just as a narrowly channeled stream is more powerful than an unbounded marshy swamp, so restricted liberty results in more powerful testimony for Christ.[31]

To **those who are without law**, Paul acted **as** one **without law** (although he himself was **not without law toward God, but under law toward Christ**). **Those who are without law** does not refer to rebels or outlaws who do not recognize any law, but is a general description of Gentiles. The law, as such, was given to the Jewish nation and not to the Gentiles. Thus when Paul was with the Gentiles he complied with their habits and feelings as far as he could possibly do so and still be loyal to the Savior. The apostle explained that even while he thus acted as **without law**, he was nevertheless **not without law toward God**. He did not consider that he was free to do as he pleased, **but** he was **under law toward Christ**. In other words, he was bound to love, honor, serve, and please the Lord Jesus, not now by the Law of Moses, but by the law of love. He was "enlawed" to Christ. We have an expression "When in Rome, do as the Romans do." Paul is saying here that when he was with the Gentiles, he adapted himself to their manner of living as far as he could consistently do so and still be loyal to Christ. But we must keep in mind that this passage deals only with cultural things and not with doctrinal or moral matters.

9:22 Verse 22 speaks of those who are **weak** or overscrupulous. They were excessively sensitive about matters that were really not of fundamental importance. **To the weak**, Paul **became as**[32] **weak, that** he **might win** them. He would be a vegetarian if necessary rather than offend them by eating meat. In short, Paul became **all things to all men, that** he **might by all means save some**. These verses should never be used to justify a sacrifice of scriptural principle. They merely describe a readiness to accommodate to the customs and habits of the people in order to win a hearing for the good news of salvation. When Paul says **that I might by all means save some**, he does not think for a moment that he could save another person, for he realized that the Lord Jesus was the only Person who could save. At the same time it is wonderful to notice that those who serve Christ in the gospel are so closely identified with Him that He even allows them to use the word **save** to describe a work in which they are involved. How this exalts and ennobles and dignifies the gospel ministry!

Verses 23–27 describe the peril of losing one's reward through lack of self-discipline. To Paul the refusal of financial help from the Corinthians was a form of rigid discipline.

9:23 **Now this I do for the gospel's sake, that I may be partaker of it with you.** In the preceding verses Paul had been describing how he submerged his own rights and desires in the work of the Lord. Why did he do this? He did it **for the gospel's sake**, in order **that** he might share in the triumphs of the gospel in a coming day.

9:24 Doubtless as the apostle wrote the words found in verse 24, he was reminded of the Isthmian games that were held not far from Corinth. The Corinthian believers would be well-acquainted with those athletic contests. Paul reminds them that while many **run in a race**, not all receive **the prize**. The Christian life is like a race. It requires self-discipline. It calls for strenuous effort. It demands definiteness of purpose. The verse does not, however, suggest that in the Christian race only one can win the prize. It simply teaches that we should all run as winners. We should all practice the same kind of self-denial that the Apostle Paul himself practiced. Here, of course, the prize is not salvation, but a reward for faithful service. Salvation is nowhere stated to be the result of our faithfulness in running the race. Salvation is the free gift of God through faith in the Lord Jesus Christ.

9:25 Now Paul changes the figure from running to wrestling. He reminds his readers that **everyone who competes** in the games, that is, wrestles, exercises self-control **in all things**. A wrestler once asked his coach, "Can't I smoke and drink and have a good time and still wrestle?" The coach replied, "Yes, you can, but you can't win!" As Paul thinks of the contestants at the games, he sees the winner stepping up to receive his prize. What is it? It is **a perishable crown**, a garland of flowers or a wreath of leaves that will soon wither away. But in comparison he mentions **an imperishable crown** which will be awarded to all those who have been faithful in their service to Christ.

> We thank Thee for the crown
>   Of glory and of life;
> 'Tis no poor withering wreath of earth,
>   Man's prize in mortal strife;
> 'Tis incorruptible as is the Throne,
>   The kingdom of our God and
>   His Incarnate Son.
>   – *Horatius Bonar*

9:26 In view of this imperishable crown, Paul states that he therefore runs **not with uncertainty**, and fights **not as one who beats the air**. His service was neither purposeless nor ineffectual. He had a definite aim before his eyes, and his intention was that his every action should count. There must be no wasted time or energy. The apostle was not interested in wild misses.

9:27 Instead, he disciplined his **body, and** brought **it into subjection, lest when** he had **preached to others**, he

himself might be rejected or **disqualified**. In the Christian life, there is a necessity for self-control, for temperance, for discipline. We must practice self-mastery.

The Apostle Paul realized the dread possibility that after he had **preached to others**, he himself might be **disqualified**. Considerable debate has centered on the meaning of this verse. Some hold that it teaches that a person can be saved and then subsequently lost. This, of course, is in conflict with the general body of teaching in the NT to the effect that no true sheep of Christ will ever perish.

Others say that the word translated **disqualified**[33] is a strong word and refers to eternal damnation. However, they interpret the verse to mean that Paul is not teaching that a person who was ever saved could be disqualified, but simply that one who failed to exercise self-discipline had never been really saved in the first place. Thinking of the false teachers and how they indulged every passion and appetite, Paul sets forth the general principle that if a person does not keep his body in subjection, this is proof that he never really was born again; and although he might preach to others, he himself will be disqualified.

A third explanation is that Paul is not speaking here of salvation at all but of service. He is not suggesting that he might ever be lost, but that he might not stand the test as far as his service was concerned and might be rejected for the prize. This interpretation exactly fits the meaning of the word *disqualified* and the athletic context. Paul recognizes the awful possibility that, having **preached to others**, he himself might be *put on the shelf* by the Lord as no longer usable by Him.

In any event, the passage is an extremely serious one and should cause deep heart-searching on the part of everyone who seeks to serve the Lord Christ. Each one should determine that by the grace of God he will never have to learn the meaning of the word by experience.

As Paul has been thinking of the necessity for self-control, the example of the Israelites comes before his mind. In chapter 10, he remembers how they became self-indulgent and careless in the discipline of their bodies, and thus became disqualified and disapproved.

First of all, he speaks of the privileges of Israel (vv. 1–4); then the punishment of Israel (v. 5); and finally the causes of Israel's downfall (vv. 6–10). Then he explains how these things apply to us (vv. 11–13).

10:1 The apostle reminds the Corinthians **that all** the Jewish **fathers were under the cloud** and **all passed through the sea**. The emphasis is on the word **all**. He is thinking back to the time of their deliverance from Egypt and how they were miraculously guided by a pillar of **cloud** by day and pillar of fire by night. He is thinking back to the time when they passed through the Red Sea and escaped into the wilderness. As far as privilege was concerned, they all enjoyed divine guidance and divine deliverance.

10:2 Not only that, but **all were baptized into Moses in the cloud and in the sea.** To be **baptized into Moses** means to be identified with him and to acknowledge his leadership. As Moses led the children of Israel out of Egypt toward the Promised Land, all the nation of Israel pledged allegiance to Moses at first and recognized him as the divinely appointed savior. It has been suggested that the expression "under the cloud" refers to that which identified them with God, and the expression "through the sea" describes that which separated them from Egypt.

10:3 They **all ate the same spiritual food**. This refers to the manna which was miraculously provided for the people of Israel as they journeyed through the wilderness. The expression **spiritual food** does not mean that it was nonmaterial. It does not mean that it was invisible or unreal. Rather, **spiritual** simply means that the material food was a type or picture of spiritual nourishment, and that the spiritual reality is what the writer had primarily in mind. It may also include the idea that the food was supernaturally given.

10:4 All through their journeyings, God wonderfully provided water for them to drink. It was real water, but again it is called **spiritual drink** in the sense that it was typical of spiritual refreshment, and miraculously provided.

They would have died from thirst many times had not the Lord given them this water in a miraculous way. The expression **they drank of that spiritual Rock that followed them** does not mean that a literal, material rock journeyed behind them as they traveled. The Rock signifies the river that flowed from it and followed the Israelites. **That Rock was Christ** in the sense that He was the One who provided it and the One it represents, providing living water to His people.

10:5 After enumerating all these marvelous privileges that were theirs, the apostle must now remind the Corinthians that **with most of** the Israelites **God was not well pleased, for their bodies were scattered in the wilderness**. Although all Israel left Egypt and all professed to be one in heart and soul with their leader, Moses, yet the sad truth is that although their bodies were in the wilderness, yet their hearts were still back in Egypt. They enjoyed a physical deliverance from the bondage of Pharaoh, but they still lusted after the sinful pleasures of that country. Of all the warriors over twenty years of age who left Egypt, only two, Caleb and Joshua, ever won the prize — they reached the Promised Land. The carcasses of the rest of them fell **in the wilderness** as an evidence of God's displeasure.

Note the contrast between the word "all" in the first four verses and the word **most** in verse 5. They were all privileged, but **most of them** perished. Godet marvels:

> What a spectacle is that which is called up by the apostle before the eyes of the self-satisfied Corinthians: all those bodies, sated with miraculous food and drink, strewing the soil of the desert![34]

10:6 In the events that happened in the time of the Exodus, we see teaching that applies to us. The children of Israel were actually **examples** for us, showing us what will happen to us if we also **lust after evil things as they** did. As we read the OT, we should not read it merely as history, but as containing lessons of practical importance for our lives today.

In the verses to follow, the apostle is going to list some of the specific sins into which they fell. It is worth noticing that many of these sins are concerned with the gratification of bodily appetites.

10:7 Verse 7 refers to the worship of the golden calf and the feast that followed it, as recorded in Exodus 32. When Moses came down from Mount Sinai, he found that the people had made a golden calf and were worshiping it. We read in Exodus 32:6 how **the people sat down to eat and drink, and rose up to play**, that is, to dance.

10:8 The sin mentioned in verse 8 refers to the time when the sons of Israel intermarried with the daughters of Moab (Num. 25). Seduced by Balaam the prophet, they disobeyed the word of the Lord and fell into immorality. We read in verse 8 that **in one day twenty-three thousand fell**. In the OT, it says that twenty-four thousand died in the plague (Num. 25:9). Critics of the Bible have often used this to try to show a contradiction in the Sacred Scriptures. If they would read the text more carefully, they would see that there is no contradiction. Here it simply states that *twenty-three thousand* fell *in one day*. In the OT, the figure of *twenty-four thousand* describes the entire number that died *in the plague*.

10:9 Paul next alludes to the time when the Israelites complained about the food and expressed doubt as to the goodness of the Lord. At that time God sent **serpents** among them and many perished (Num. 21:5, 6). Here again it is noticeable how food gratification was their downfall.

10:10 The sin of Korah, Dathan, and Abiram is referred to here (Num. 16:14–47). Again there was complaining against the Lord because of the food situation (Num. 16:14). The Israelites did not practice self-control with regard to their bodies. They did not discipline their bodies or put them in a place of subjection. Rather, they made provision for the lusts of the flesh, and this proved to be their downfall.

10:11 The next three verses give the practical application of the events. First of all, Paul explains that the meaning of these events is not limited to their historical value. They have a significance for us today. **They were written** as a warning to us who are living after the close

of the Jewish age and during the gospel age, "to us to whom the revenues of the past ages have descended," as Rendall Harris put it so well.

10:12 They constitute a warning to the self-confident: **Let him who thinks he stands take heed lest he fall**. Perhaps this refers especially to the strong believer who thinks he can dabble with self-gratification and not be affected by it. Such a person is in greatest danger of falling under the disciplinary hand of God.

10:13 But then Paul adds a marvelous word of encouragement for those who are tempted. He teaches that the testings, trials, and temptations which face us are **common** to all. However, **God is faithful, who will not allow** us **to be** tested **beyond what** we **are able**. He does not promise to deliver us from temptation or testing, but He does promise to limit its intensity. He further promises to provide **the way of escape, that** we **may be able to bear it**. Reading this verse, one cannot help but be struck by the tremendous comfort it has afforded to tested saints of God through the centuries. Young believers have clung to it as to a life-line and older believers have reposed on it as upon a pillow. Perhaps some of Paul's readers were being fiercely tempted at the time to go into idolatry. Paul would comfort them with the thought that God would not allow any unbearable temptation to come their way. At the same time they should be warned that they should not expose themselves to temptation.

10:14 The section from 10:14 through 11:1 returns to deal more specifically with the subject of meat offered to idols. First of all, Paul takes up the question as to whether believers should participate in feasts in idol temples (vv. 14–22).

Therefore, my beloved, flee from idolatry. Perhaps it was a real test for the believers at Corinth to be invited to participate in an idol feast at one of the temples. Some might feel that they were above temptation. Perhaps they would say that surely it would not hurt to go just once. The apostle's inspired advice is to **flee from idolatry**. He does not say to study about it, to become better acquainted with it, or to trifle with it in any way. They should run in the opposite direction.

10:15, 16 Paul knows that he is addressing himself to intelligent people who can understand what he is saying. In verse 16 he makes reference to the Lord's Supper. He says first of all: **"The cup of blessing which we bless, is it not the communion of the blood of Christ?"** **The cup of blessing** refers to the **cup** of wine which is used at the Lord's Supper. It is a **cup** which speaks of the tremendous **blessing** which has come to us through the death of Christ; therefore it is called **the cup of blessing**. The clause **which we bless** means "for which we give thanks." When we take that cup and press it to our lips, we are saying in effect that we are participants in all the benefits that flow from the blood of Christ. Therefore we might paraphrase this verse as follows:

> The cup which speaks of the tremendous blessings which have come to us through the blood of the Lord Jesus, and the same cup for which we give thanks, what is it but a testimony to the fact that all believers are partakers of the benefits of the blood of Christ?

The same thing is true of **the bread which we break**, the communion loaf. As we eat the bread, we say, in effect, that we have all been saved through the offering of His body on the cross of Calvary and that we are therefore members of His body. In short, the cup and the loaf speak of fellowship with Christ, of participating in His glorious ministry for us.

The question has been raised as to why the blood should be mentioned first in this verse whereas in the institution of the Lord's Supper, the bread is mentioned first. A possible answer is that Paul is speaking here of the order of events when we come into the Christian fellowship. Usually a new convert understands the value of the blood of Christ before he recognizes the truth of the one body. Thus this verse might give the order in which we understand salvation.

10:17 All believers, **though many, are one body in Christ**, represented by **that one** loaf of **bread. All partake of**

that one bread in the sense that all have fellowship in the benefits that flow from the giving of the body of Christ.

10:18 What Paul is saying in these verses is that eating at the Lord's Table signifies fellowship with Him. The same was true of those Israelites who ate **of the sacrifices**. It meant that they had fellowship with **the altar**. The reference, no doubt, is to the peace offering. The people brought their sacrifices to the temple. A portion of the offering was burnt on the altar with fire; another portion was reserved for the priests; but the third part was set aside for the offerer and his friends. They ate of the offering on the same day. Paul is emphasizing that all who ate of the offering identified themselves with God and with the nation of Israel and, in short, with all of which **the altar** spoke.

But how does this fit in with the portion of the Scripture that we are studying? The answer is quite simple. Just as partaking of the Lord's Supper speaks of fellowship with the Lord, and just as the Israelites, partaking of the peace offering, spoke of fellowship with the altar of Jehovah, so eating at an idol feast in the temple speaks of fellowship with the idols.

10:19 **What am I saying then? That an idol is anything, or that what is offered to idols is anything?** Does Paul mean to imply by all this that meat offered to idols changes its character or quality? Or does he mean to say that an idol is real, that it hears, sees, and has power? Obviously the answer to both of these questions is "No."

10:20 What Paul does want to emphasize is that **the things which the Gentiles sacrifice** are offered **to demons**. In some strange and mysterious way, idol worship is linked with demons. Using the idols, the demons control the hearts and minds of those who worship them. There is one devil, Satan, but there are many demons which are his messengers and agents. Paul adds: **"I do not want you to have fellowship with demons."**

10:21 **You cannot drink the cup of the Lord and the cup of demons; you cannot partake of the Lord's table and of the table of demons.** In this verse **the cup of the Lord** is a figurative expression to describe the benefits which come to us through Christ. It is a figure of speech known as metonymy, where the container is used to denote the thing contained. The expression **the Lord's table** is likewise a figurative expression. It is not the same as the Lord's Supper, although it might include the latter. A table is an article of furniture where food is set out and where fellowship is enjoyed. Here the **table** of the Lord means the sum total of the blessings which we enjoy in Christ.

When Paul says that **you cannot drink the cup of the Lord and the cup of demons**, that **you cannot partake of the Lord's table and of the table of demons**, he does not mean that it is a physical impossibility. It would be a physical possibility, for instance, for a believer to go to an idol temple and to participate in a feast there. But what Paul means here is that it would be morally inconsistent. It would be an act of treachery and disloyalty to the Lord Jesus to profess adherence or allegiance to Him, on the one hand, and then to go and have fellowship with those who sacrifice to idols. It would be morally improper and utterly wrong.

10:22 Not only that, it would not be possible to do this without provoking **the Lord to jealousy**. As William Kelly said, "Love cannot but be jealous of wandering affections, it would not be love if it did not resent unfaithfulness."[35] The Christian should fear to thus displease the Lord, or to provoke His righteous indignation. Do we think that we are **stronger than He**? That is, do we dare to grieve Him and risk an exhibition of His disciplinary judgment upon us?

10:23 The apostle turns from the subject of participation in idol feasts and takes up some general principles that should govern Christians in their daily life. When he says **all things are lawful**, he does not mean all things in an absolute sense. For instance, he is not implying for a moment that it would be lawful for him to commit murder or to get drunk! Here again we must understand the expression as referring only to matters of moral indifference. There is a great area in Christian life where things are perfectly legitimate in themselves and yet where for other reasons it would

not be wise for a Christian to participate. Thus Paul says: **"All things are lawful for me, but all things are not helpful."** For instance, a thing might be quite lawful for a believer and yet might be equally unwise in view of the national customs of the people where he dwells. Also, things that are lawful in themselves might not be edifying. That is, a thing might not result in building up a brother in his most holy faith. Should I then be high-handed in demanding my own rights or should I consider what would help my brother in Christ?

10:24 In all the decisions we make, we should not be selfishly thinking of what will benefit ourselves, but we should rather think of what would be for our neighbor's **well-being**. The principles we are studying in this section could very well be applied to matters of dress, food and drink, standards of living, and the entertainments in which we participate.

10:25 If a believer went to **the meat market** to buy some meat, he was not required to ask the merchant whether that meat had been previously offered to idols. The meat itself would not be affected in one way or another, and there would be no question of loyalty to Christ involved.

10:26 In explanation of this advice, Paul quotes from Psalm 24:1: **"The earth is the LORD'S, and all its fullness."** The thought here is that the food that we eat has been graciously provided by the Lord for us and is specifically intended for our use. Heinrici tells us that these words from Psalm 24 are commonly used among the Jews as a thanksgiving at the table.

10:27 Now Paul takes up another situation which might cause the believers to ask questions. Suppose an unbeliever **invites** a believer to his home for **dinner**. Would a Christian be free to accept such an invitation? Yes. If you are invited to a meal in an unbeliever's home and you are disposed to go, you are at liberty to **eat whatever is set before you, asking no question for conscience' sake**.

10:28 If, during the course of the meal, another Christian should be present who has a weak conscience and informs you that the meat you are eating has been **offered to idols**, should you eat it? No. You should not indulge, because in so doing you might be stumbling him and hurting his conscience. Neither should you eat if an unbeliever would be hindered from accepting the Lord through this action. At the end of verse 28, Psalm 24:1 is once again quoted : **"The earth is the LORD'S, and all its fullness."**[36]

10:29 In the case just cited you would not refrain from eating because of *your own* conscience. You would have perfect liberty, as a believer, to eat the meat. But the weak brother sitting by has a **conscience** about it, and so you refrain from eating out of respect to his conscience.

The question, **"For why is my liberty judged by another man's conscience?"** could perhaps be paraphrased as follows:

Why should I selfishly display my freedom to eat the meat and in so doing be condemned by the other man's conscience? Why should I expose my freedom to the condemnation of his conscience? Why should I let my good be evil spoken of? (see Rom. 14:16).

Is a piece of meat so important that I should cause such an offense to a fellow-believer in the Lord Jesus Christ? (However, many commentators believe that here Paul is quoting the objection of the Corinthians, or asking a rhetorical question, before answering it in the following verses.)

10:30 What the apostle seems to be saying is that to him it seems very contradictory to give **thanks** to God on the one hand, when by so doing he is wounding a brother. It is better to deny oneself a legitimate right than to give thanks to God for something which will cause others to speak **evil** of you. William Kelly comments that it is "better to deny one's self and not allow one's liberty to be condemned by another or incur evil speaking for that for which one gives thanks." Why make such a use of freedom as to give offense? Why let my giving of thanks be exposed to misconstruction or be called sacrilege or scandal?

10:31 There are two great rules to guide us in all our Christian lives. The first is **the glory of God**, and the second is the welfare of our fellow men. Paul gives the first of these here: **"Therefore, whether you eat or drink, or whatever you do, do all to the glory of God."** Christian young people are often faced with decisions as to whether a certain course of action would be right or wrong for them. Here is a good rule to apply: Is there any **glory** for **God** in it? Can you bow your head before you participate in it and ask the Lord that He will be magnified by what you are about to do?

10:32 The second rule is the welfare of our fellow men. We should **give no offense** or occasion for stumbling, **either to the Jews or to the Greeks or to the church of God**. Here Paul divides all mankind into three classes. **The Jews**, of course, are the nation of Israel. **The Greeks** are the unconverted Gentiles, whereas **the church of God** includes all true believers in the Lord Jesus Christ, whether of Jewish or Gentile stock. In one sense we are bound to offend others and excite their wrath if we faithfully witness to them. However, that is not what is spoken of here. Rather, the apostle is thinking of *needless* **offense**. He is cautioning us against using our legitimate rights in such a way as to stumble others.

10:33 Paul can honestly say that he seeks to **please all men in all things, not seeking** his **own profit, but the profit of many**. Probably few men have ever lived so unselfishly for others as the great Apostle Paul.

11:1 Verse 1 of chapter 11 probably goes better with chapter 10. Paul had just been speaking of how he tried to gauge all his actions in the light of their effect on others. Now he tells the Corinthians to **imitate** him, **just as** he **also** copied **Christ**. He renounced personal advantages and rights in order to help those about him. The Corinthians should do likewise, and not selfishly parade their freedoms in such a way as to hinder the gospel of Christ or offend the weak brother.

C. Concerning Women's Head-Coverings (11:2–16)

Verses 2–16 of chapter 11 are devoted to the subject of women's head-coverings. The remaining verses deal with abuses in connection with the Lord's Supper (vv. 17–34). The first section of the chapter has been much disputed. Some think that the instruction given here was applicable only to Paul's day. Some even go so far as to contend that these verses reflect Paul's prejudice against women, since he was a bachelor! Still others simply *accept* the teaching of this portion, seeking to *obey* its precepts even if they do not understand them all.

11:2 The apostle first of all commends the Corinthians for the way in which they remembered him **in all things**, and held fast **the traditions just as** he had **delivered them. Traditions** refer not to habits and practices that have arisen in the church down through the years, but rather, in this case, to the inspired instructions of the Apostle Paul.

11:3 Paul now introduces the subject of women's head coverings. Behind his instruction is the fact that every ordered society is built on two pillars — authority and subjection to that authority. It is impossible to have a well-functioning community where these two principles are not observed. Paul mentions three great relationships involving authority and subjection. First, **the head of every man is Christ**; Christ is Lord and man is subject to Him. Secondly, **the head of woman is man**; the place of headship was given to the man, and the woman is under his authority. Third, **the head of Christ is God**; even in the Godhead, One Person has the place of rule and Another takes the place of willing subordination. These examples of headship and submission were designed by God Himself and are fundamental in His arrangement of the universe.

At the outset it should be emphasized that subjection does *not* mean inferiority. Christ is subject to God the Father but He is not inferior to Him. Neither is woman inferior to man, though she is subordinate to him.

11:4 **Every man** who prays or prophesies with **his head covered dishonors his head**, that is, Christ. It is saying, in effect, that the man does not acknowledge Christ as **his head**. Thus it is an act of gross disrespect.

11:5 **Every woman who prays or prophesies with her head uncovered dishonors her head**, that is, the man. She is saying, in effect, that she does not recognize man's God-given headship and will not submit to it.[37]

If this were the only verse in the Bible on the subject, then it would imply that it is all right for a woman to pray or prophesy in the assembly as long as she has a veil or other covering on her head. But Paul teaches elsewhere that women should be silent in the assembly (1 Cor. 14:34), that they are not permitted to teach or to have authority over the man but to be in silence (1 Tim. 2:12).

Actually meetings of the assembly do not come into view until verse 17, so the instructions concerning the head-covering in verses 2–16 cannot be confined to church meetings. They apply to whenever a woman prays or prophesies. She prays silently in the assembly, since 1 Timothy 2:8 limits public prayer to the men (lit., males). She prays audibly or silently at other times. She prophesies when she teaches other women (Titus 2:3–5) or children in the Sunday school.

11:6 **If a woman is not covered**, she might as well **be shorn. But if it is shameful for a woman to be shorn or shaved**, then she should be **covered**. The unveiled head of a woman is as shameful as if her hair were cut off. The apostle is *not* commanding a barber's operation but rather telling what moral consistency would require!

11:7 In verses 7–10, Paul teaches the subordination of the woman to the man by going back to creation. This should forever lay to rest any idea that his teaching about women's covering was what was *culturally* suitable in his day but not applicable to us today. The headship of man and the subjection of woman have been God's order from the very beginning.

First of all, man **is the image and glory of God** whereas **woman is the glory of man**. This means that man was placed on earth as God's representative, to exercise dominion over it. Man's uncovered head is a silent witness to this fact. The woman was never given this place of headship; instead she **is the glory of man** in the sense that she "renders conspicuous the authority of man," as W. E. Vine expresses it.[38]

Man indeed ought not to cover his head in prayer; it would be tantamount to veiling the **glory of God**, and this would be an insult to the Divine Majesty.

11:8 Paul next reminds us that **man** was **not** created **from woman but woman** was created **from man**. The man was first, then the woman was taken from his side. This priority of the man strengthens the apostle's case for man's headship.

11:9 The purpose of creation is next alluded to in order to press home the point. **Nor was man created** primarily **for the woman, but** rather **woman for the man**. The Lord distinctly stated in Genesis 2:18, "It is not good that man should be alone; I will make him a helper comparable to him."

11:10 Because of her position of subordination to man, **the woman ought to have a symbol of authority on her head. The symbol of authority** is the head-covering and here it indicates *not* her own authority but subjection to the authority of her husband.

Why does Paul add **because of the angels**? We would suggest that **the angels** are spectators of the things that are happening on earth today, as they were of the things that happened at creation. In the first creation, they saw how woman usurped the place of headship over the man. She made the decision that Adam should have made. As a result of this, sin entered the human race with its unspeakable aftermath of misery and woe. God does not want what happened in the first creation to be repeated in the new creation. When the angels look down, He wants them to see the woman acting in subjection to the man, and indicating this outwardly by a covering on her head.

We might pause here to state that the head-covering is simply an outward sign and it is of value only when it is the outward sign of an inward grace. In other words, a woman might have a covering on her head and yet not truly be submissive to her husband. In such a case, to wear a head-covering would be of no value at all. The most important thing is to be sure that the heart is truly subordinate; then a covering on a woman's head becomes truly meaningful.

11:11 Paul is not implying that man is at all independent of the woman, so he adds: **"Nevertheless, neither is man independent of woman, nor woman independent of man, in the Lord."** In other words, man and woman are mutually dependent. They need one another and the idea of subordination is not at all in conflict with the idea of mutual interdependence.

11:12 **Woman came from man** by creation, that is, she was created from Adam's side. But Paul points out that **man also comes through woman**. Here he is referring to the process of birth. The woman gives birth to the man child. Thus God has created this perfect balance to indicate that the one cannot exist without the other.

All things are from God means that He has divinely appointed **all** these **things**, so there is no just cause for complaint. Not only were these relationships created by **God**, but the purpose of them all is to glorify Him. All of this should make the man humble and the woman content.

11:13 The apostle now challenges the Corinthians to **judge among** themselves if it is **proper for a woman to pray to God with her head uncovered**. He appeals to their instinctive sense. The suggestion is that it is not reverent or decorous for a woman to enter into the presence of God unveiled.

11:14 Just how does **nature itself teach** us that it is a shame for **a man** to have **long hair** is not made clear. Some have suggested that a man's hair will not naturally grow into as long tresses as a woman's. For a man to have long hair makes him appear effeminate. In most cultures, the male wears his hair shorter than the female.

11:15 Verse 15 has been greatly misunderstood by many. Some have suggested that since a woman's **hair is given to her for a covering**, it is not necessary for her to have any other covering. But such a teaching does grave violence to this portion of Scripture. Unless one sees that *two* coverings are mentioned in this chapter, the passage becomes hopelessly confusing. This may be demonstrated by referring back to verse 6. There we read: "For if a woman is not covered, let her also be shorn." According to the interpretation just mentioned, this would mean that if a woman "does not have her hair on," then she might just as well be shorn. But this is ridiculous. If she does not "have her hair on," she could not possibly be shorn!

The actual argument in verse 15 is that there is a real analogy between the spiritual and the natural. God gave woman a natural covering of **glory** in a way He did not give to man. There is a spiritual significance to this. It teaches that when a woman prays to God, she should wear a covering on her head. What is true in the natural sphere should be true in the spiritual.

11:16 The apostle closes this section with the statement: **"But if anyone seems to be contentious, we have no such custom, nor do the churches of God."** Does Paul mean, as has been suggested, that the things he has just been saying are not important enough to contend about? Does he mean that there was no such custom of women veiling their heads in the churches? Does he mean that these teachings are optional and not to be pressed upon women as the commandments of the Lord? It seems strange that any such interpretations would ever be offered, yet they are commonly heard today. This would mean that Paul considered these instructions as of no real consequence, and he had just been wasting over half a chapter of Holy Scripture in setting them forth!

There are at least two possible explanations of this verse which fit in with the rest of the Scripture. First of all, the apostle may be saying that he anticipates that certain ones will **be contentious** about these matters, but he adds that **we have no such custom**, that is, the custom of contending about this. We do not argue about such matters, but accept them as the teaching of the Lord. Another interpretation, favored by William Kelly, is that Paul was saying that **the churches of God** did not have any such custom as that of women praying or prophesying without being covered.

D. Concerning the Lord's Supper (11:17–34)

11:17 The apostle rebukes the Corinthians for the fact that there were divisions among them as they gathered together (vv. 17–19). Note the repetition of the expression "when you come together" or related words (11:17, 18, 20, 33, 34; 14:23, 26). In 11:2 Paul had had occasion to praise them for keeping the traditions which he had delivered to them, but there was one matter in which he could **not praise** them, and that is the matter about which he is to speak. When

they gathered together for public meetings, they came **together not for the better but for the worse**. This is a solemn reminder to us all that it is possible to go away from meetings of the church and to have been harmed rather than benefited.

11:18 The **first** cause of rebuke was the existence of **divisions** or schisms. This does not mean that parties had broken away from the church and formed separate fellowships, but rather that there were cliques and factions within the congregation. A schism is a party inside, whereas a sect is a different party outside. Paul could **believe** these reports of divisions because he knew that the Corinthians were in a carnal state, and he had previous occasion in this Epistle to rebuke them because of their divisions.

F. B. Hole writes:

Paul was prepared to give at least partial credence to the reports of the divisions at Corinth, since he knew that, owing to their carnal state, there were bound to be these opinionated factions in their midst. Here Paul reasons forward from their state to their actions. Knowing them to be carnal and walking as men, he knew that they would certainly fall victims to the inveterate tendency of the human mind to form its strong opinions, and the factions founded in those opinions, ending in the schisms and divisions. He knew, too, that God could overrule their folly and take occasion to make manifest those that were approved of Him, walking according to the Spirit and not as man; and consequently eschewing the whole of this divisive business.[39]

11:19 Paul foresaw that the schisms already begun in Corinth would increase until they became more serious. Although in general this would be detrimental to the church, yet one good thing would come out of it, that is, that those who were truly spiritual and who were **approved** of God would **be recognized among** the Corinthians. When Paul says in this verse: **"there must also be factions[40] among you,"** this does not mean that it is a *moral*[41] necessity. God is not condoning splits in the church here. Rather, Paul means that because of the carnal conditions of the Corinthians, it was inevitable that **factions** would result. Divisions are proof that some have failed to discern the mind of the Lord.

11:20 Paul now directs his second rebuke against abuses in connection with the Lord's Supper. When the Christians gathered together, ostensibly to celebrate **the Lord's Supper**, their conduct was so deplorable that Paul says they could not possibly remember the Lord in the way in which He appointed. They might go through the outward motions, but their entire deportment would preclude any true remembrance of the Lord.

11:21 In the early days of the church, Christians celebrated the "aga-pē," or love feast along with the Lord's Supper. The love feast was something like a common meal, shared in a spirit of love and fellowship. At the end of the love feast, the Christians often had the remembrance of the Lord with the bread and wine. But before very long, abuses crept in. For instance, in this verse it is implied that the love feast lost its real meaning. Not only did the Christians not wait for one another, but the rich ones shamed their poorer brethren by having lavish meals and not sharing them. Some went away **hungry**, whereas others were actually **drunk**! Since the Lord's Supper often followed the love feast, they would still be drunk when they sat down to partake of the Lord's Supper.

11:22 The apostle indignantly rebukes such disgraceful conduct. If they insist on carrying on in such a way, then they should at least have the reverence not to do it in a **church** meeting. To practice intemperance at such a time and to **shame** one's poorer brethren is most inconsistent with the Christian faith. Paul cannot but withhold **praise** from the saints for acting in this way; and in withholding **praise**, he thereby condemns them strongly.

11:23 To show the contrast between their conduct and the real meaning of the Lord's Supper, he goes back to its original institution. He shows that it was not a common meal or a feast, but a solemn ordinance of the Lord. Paul **received** his knowledge concerning this directly **from the Lord** and he mentions this to show that any violation would be actual disobedience. What he is teach-

ing, then, he received by revelation.

First of all, he mentions how **the Lord Jesus on the** very **night in which He was betrayed took bread**. The literal rendering is "while He was being betrayed." While the foul plot to deliver Him up was going on outside, **the Lord Jesus** gathered in the upper room with His disciples and **took** the **bread**.

The fact that this occurred at **night** does not necessarily mean that the Lord's Supper must thereafter be observed only at night. At that time, sundown was the beginning of the Jewish day. Our day begins at sunrise. Also it has been remarked that there is a difference between apostolic *example* and apostolic *precepts*. We are not obligated to do all that the apostles *did*, but we are most certainly obligated to obey all that they *taught*.

11:24 The Lord Jesus took the bread, first of all, and gave **thanks** for it. Since the bread was typical of His body, He was, in effect, thanking God that He had been given a human body in which He might come and die for the sins of the world.

When the Savior said, **"This is My body,"** did He mean that the bread actually *became* His body in some real sense? The Roman Catholic dogma of *transubstantiation* insists that the bread and the wine are literally changed into the body and the blood of Christ. The Lutheran doctrine of *consubstantiation* teaches that the true body and blood of Christ are in, with, and under the bread and wine on the table.

In answer to these views, it should be sufficient to remember that when the Lord Jesus instituted this memorial, His body had not yet been given, nor had His blood been shed. When the Lord Jesus said, **"This is My body,"** He meant, "This is symbolic of My body" or "This is a picture of My body which is broken for you." To eat the bread is to remember Him in His atoning death for us. There is inexpressible tenderness in our Lord's expression "in remembrance of Me."

11:25 **In the same manner** the Lord Jesus **also took the cup after** the Passover **supper, saying, "This cup is the new covenant in My blood. This do, as**

often as you drink it, in remembrance of Me." The Lord's Supper was instituted immediately after the Passover Feast. That is why it says that the Lord Jesus **took the cup after supper**. In connection with **the cup**, He said that it was **the new covenant in** His **blood**. This refers to the covenant that God promised to the nation of Israel in Jeremiah 31:31–34. It is an unconditional promise by which He agreed to be merciful to their unrighteousness and to remember their sins and iniquities no more. The terms of the new covenant are also given in Hebrews 8:10–12. The covenant is in force at the present time, but unbelief keeps the nation of Israel from enjoying it. All who do trust the Lord Jesus receive the benefits that were promised. When the people of Israel turn to the Lord, they will enjoy the blessings of the new covenant; that will be during Christ's thousand-year reign on earth. The **new covenant** was ratified by the **blood** of Christ, and that is why He speaks of **the cup** as being **the new covenant in** His **blood**. The foundation of the new covenant was laid through the cross.

11:26 Verse 26 touches on the question as to how frequently the Lord's Supper should be observed. **For as often as you eat . . . and drink. . . .** No legalistic rule is laid down; neither is any fixed date given. It seems clear from Acts 20:7 that the practice of the disciples was to meet on the first day of the week to remember the Lord. That this ordinance was not intended simply for the early days of the church is abundantly proved by the expression **till He comes**. Godet beautifully points out that the Lord's Supper is "the link between His two comings, the monument of the one, the pledge of the other."[42]

In all this instruction concerning the Lord's Supper it is notable that there is not a word about a minister or priest officiating. It is a simple memorial service left for all the people of God. Christians gather together simply as believer-priests to thus proclaim the Lord's death **till He comes.**

11:27 Having discussed the origin and purpose of the Lord's Supper, the apostle now turns to the consequences of participating in it wrongly. Whoever **eats this bread or drinks this cup of the Lord in an unworthy manner will be guilty of the body and blood of the Lord**. We are all unworthy to partake of this solemn Supper. In that sense, we are unworthy of any of the Lord's mercy or kindness to us. But that is not the subject here. The apostle is not speaking of our own personal unworthiness. Cleansed by the blood of Christ, we can approach God in all the worthiness of His own beloved Son. But Paul is speaking here of the disgraceful conduct which characterized the Corinthians as they gathered together for the Lord's Supper. They were **guilty** of careless, irreverent behavior. To act thus is to **be guilty of the body and blood of the Lord.**

11:28 As we come to the Lord's Supper, we should do so in a judged condition. Sin should be confessed and forsaken; restitution should be made; apologies should be offered to those we have offended. In general we should make sure that we are in a proper state of soul.

11:29 To eat and to drink **in an** inconsistent **manner** is to eat and drink **judgment to** oneself, **not discerning the Lord's body**. We should realize that the Lord's body was given in order that our sins might be put away. If we go on living in sin, while at the same time partaking of the Lord's Supper, we are living a lie. F. G. Patterson writes, "If we eat the Lord's Supper with unjudged sin upon us, we do not discern the Lord's body which was broken to put it away."

11:30 Failure to exercise self-judgment resulted in God's disciplinary judgment upon some in the church at Corinth. **Many** were **weak and sick**, and not a few slept. In other words, physical illness had come upon some, and some were taken home to heaven. Because they did not judge sin in their lives, the Lord was required to take disciplinary action against them.

11:31 On the other hand, **if we** exercise this self-judgment, it will not be necessary to so chasten us.

11:32 God is dealing with us as with His own children. He loves us too dearly to allow us to go on in sin. Thus we soon feel the shepherd's crook on our necks pulling us back to Himself. As someone has said, "It is possible for the saints to be fit for heaven (in Christ) but not fitted to remain on the earth in testimony."

11:33 When the believers **come together** for the love feast, or agapē, they should **wait for one another**, and not selfishly proceed without regard for the other saints. "Waiting for one another" is in contrast to verse 21, "each one takes his own supper ahead of others."

11:34 But if anyone is hungry, let him eat at home. In other words, the love feast, linked as it was with the Lord's Supper, was not to be mistaken for a common meal. To disregard its sacred character would be to **come together for judgment.**

And the rest I will set in order when I come. Undoubtedly there were other minor matters which had been mentioned to the apostle in the letter from the Corinthians. Here he assures them that he will deal with these matters personally when he visits them.

E. Concerning the Gifts of the Spirit and Their Use in the Church (Chaps. 12–14)

Chapters 12–14 deal with the gifts of the Spirit. There had been abuses in the assembly in Corinth, especially in connection with the gift of tongues, and Paul writes in order to correct those abuses.

There were believers in Corinth who had received the gift of tongues, which means that they were given the power to speak foreign languages without ever having studied those languages.[43] But instead of using this gift to magnify God and edify other believers, they were using it to show off. They stood up in the meetings and spoke in languages which no one else understood, hoping that others would be impressed by their linguistic proficiency. They exalted the sign-gifts above the others, and claimed superior spirituality for those who spoke in tongues. This led to pride on the one hand, and to feelings of envy, inferiority, and worthlessness on the other. It was therefore necessary for the apostle to correct these erroneous attitudes and to establish controls in the exercise of the gifts, especially tongues and prophecy.

12:1 He does **not want** the saints at Corinth **to be ignorant** in the matter of **spiritual** manifestations or **gifts**. The literal reading here is **"Now concerning** 'spirituals,' **brethren, I do not want you to be ignorant."** Most versions supply the word *gifts* to complete the sense. However, the next verse suggests that Paul might have been thinking not only of manifestations of the Holy Spirit but of evil spirits as well.

12:2 Before conversion the Corinthians had been idolaters, enslaved by evil spirits. They lived in fear of the spirits and were **led** about by these diabolical influences. They witnessed supernatural manifestations of the spirit world and heard spirit-inspired utterances. Under the influence of evil spirits, they sometimes surrendered self-control, and said and did things beyond their own conscious powers.

12:3 Now that they are saved, the believers must know how to judge all spirit-manifestations, that is, how to discern between the voice of evil spirits and the authentic voice of the Holy Spirit. The crucial test is the testimony that is given concerning the Lord Jesus. If a man says, **"Jesus is accursed,"** you can be sure that he is demon-inspired, because evil spirits characteristically blaspheme and curse the name of Jesus. **The Spirit of God** would never lead anyone to speak of the Savior in this way; His ministry is to exalt the Lord Jesus. He leads people to **say that Jesus is Lord**, not just with their lips, but with the warm, full confession of their hearts and lives.

Notice that the three Persons of the Trinity are mentioned in verse 3 and also in verses 4–6.

12:4 Paul next shows that while there is a variety **of gifts** of the Holy Spirit in the church, there is a basic, threefold unity, involving the three Persons of the Godhead.

First of all, **there are diversities of gifts, but the same Spirit**. The Corinthians were acting as if there was only one gift — tongues. Paul says, "No, your unity is not found in the possession of one *common* gift, but rather in possession of the Holy Spirit who is the Source of *all* the gifts."

12:5 Next the apostle points out that **there are differences of ministries**

or services in the church. We don't all have the same work. But what we have in common is that whatever we do is done for **the same Lord** and with a view to serving others (not self).

12:6 Then again, though **there are diversities of activities** as far as spiritual gifts are concerned, **it is the same God who** empowers each believer. If one gift seems more successful or spectacular or powerful than another, it is not because of any superiority in the person possessing it. It is God who supplies the power.

12:7 The **Spirit** manifests Himself in the life of **each** believer by imparting some gift. There is no believer who does not have a function to perform. And the gifts are given **for the profit of** the entire body. They are not given for self-display or even for self-gratification but in order to help others. This is a pivotal point in the entire discussion.

That leads quite naturally to a list of some of the gifts of the Spirit.

12:8 **The word of wisdom** is the supernatural power to speak with divine insight, whether in solving difficult problems, defending the faith, resolving conflicts, giving practical advice, or pleading one's case before hostile authorities. Stephen so demonstrated the word of wisdom that his adversaries "were not able to resist the wisdom and the Spirit by which he spoke" (Acts 6:10).

The word of knowledge is the power to communicate information that has been divinely revealed. This is illustrated in Paul's use of such expressions as "Behold, I tell you a mystery" (1 Cor. 15:51) and "For this we say to you by the word of the Lord" (1 Thess. 4:15). In that primary sense of conveying new truth, the word of knowledge has ceased, because the Christian faith has been once for all delivered to the saints (Jude 3). The body of Christian doctrine is complete. In a secondary sense, however, **the word of knowledge** may still be with us. There is still a mysterious communication of divine knowledge to those who live in close fellowship with the Lord (see Psalm 25:14). The sharing of that knowledge with others is **the word of knowledge**.

12:9 The gift of **faith** is the divine ability to remove mountains of difficulty

in pursuing the will of God (13:2) and to do great exploits for God in response to some command or promise of God as found in His word or as communicated privately. George Müller is a classic example of a man with the gift of faith. Without ever making his needs known to anyone but God, he cared for 10,000 orphans over a period of sixty years.

The **gifts of healings** have to do with the miraculous power to heal diseases.

12:10 **Working of miracles** could include casting out demons, changing matter from one form to another, raising the dead, and exercising power over the elements. Philip worked miracles in Samaria, and thereby gained a hearing for the gospel (Acts 8:6, 7).

The gift of **prophecy**, in its primary sense, signified that a person received direct revelations from God and transmitted them to others. Sometimes the prophets predicted future events (Acts 11:27, 28; 21:11); more often they simply expressed the mind of God. Like the apostles, they were concerned with the foundation of the church (Eph. 2:20). They themselves were not the foundation, but they laid the foundation in what they taught concerning the Lord Jesus. Once the foundation was laid, the need for the prophets ceased. Their ministry is preserved for us in the pages of the NT. Since the Bible is complete, we reject any so-called prophet who claims to have additional truth from God.[44]

In a weaker sense, we use the word "prophet" to describe any preacher who declares the word of God authoritatively, incisively, and effectively. Prophecy can also include the ascription of praise to God (Luke 1:67, 68) and the encouragement and strengthening of His people (Acts 15:32).

Discerning of spirits describes the power to detect whether a prophet or other person is speaking by the Holy Spirit or by Satan. A person with this gift has special ability to discern if a man is an imposter and an opportunist, for instance. Thus Peter was able to expose Simon as one who was poisoned by bitterness and in the bond of iniquity (Acts 8:20–23).

The gift of **tongues**, as has been mentioned, is the ability to speak a foreign language without ever having learned it.

Tongues were given for a sign, especially to Israel.

The interpretation of tongues is the miraculous power to understand a language which the person has never known before and to convey the message in the local language.

It is perhaps significant that this list of gifts begins with those that are connected primarily with the intellect and closes with those dealing primarily with the emotions. The Corinthians had reversed this in their thinking. They exalted the gift of tongues above the other gifts. They somehow thought that the more a man had of the Holy Spirit, the more he was carried off by a power beyond himself. They confused power with spirituality.

12:11 All the gifts mentioned in verses 8–10 are produced and controlled by **the same Spirit**. Here again we see that He does not give the same gift to everyone. He distributes **to each one individually as He wills**. This is another important point — the Spirit sovereignly apportions the gifts. If we really grasp this, it will eliminate pride on the one hand, because we don't have anything that we didn't receive. And it will eliminate discontent on the other hand, because Infinite Wisdom and Love decided what gift we should have, and His choice is perfect. It is wrong for everyone to desire the same gift. If everyone played the same instrument, you could never have a symphony orchestra. And if a body consisted only of tongue, it would be a monstrosity.

12:12 **The** human **body** is an illustration of unity and diversity. **The body is one**, yet **has many members**. Although all the believers are different and perform different functions, yet they all combine to make one functioning unit — the **body**.

So also is Christ is more precisely translated: "So also is *the* Christ." "The Christ" here refers not only to the glorified Lord Jesus Christ in heaven, but to the Head in heaven and to His members here on earth. All believers are members of the Body of Christ. Just as the human body is a vehicle by which a person expresses himself to others, so the Body of Christ is the vehicle on earth by which He chooses to make Himself known to the world. It is an evidence of wonderful grace that the Lord would ever allow the expression "the Christ" to be used to include those of us who are members of His body.

12:13 Paul goes on to explain how we became members of the Body of Christ. **By** (or in) **one Spirit we were all baptized into one body**. The more literal translation here is *"in*[45] one Spirit." This may mean that the Spirit is the element in which we were baptized, just as water is the element in which we are immersed in believer's baptism. Or it may mean that the Spirit is the Agent who does the baptizing, thus **by one Spirit**. This is the more probable and understandable meaning.

The baptism of the Holy Spirit took place on the Day of Pentecost. The church was born at that time. We partake of the benefits of that baptism when we are born again. We become members of the **Body** of Christ.

Several important points should be noted here: First, the baptism of the Holy Spirit is that divine operation which places believers in the Body of Christ. It is not the same as water baptism. This is clear from Matthew 3:11; John 1:33; Acts 1:5. It is not a work of grace subsequent to salvation whereby believers become more spiritual. **All** the Corinthians had been **baptized** in the Spirit, yet Paul rebukes them for being carnal — not spiritual (3:1). It is *not* true that speaking in tongues is the invariable sign of being baptized by the Spirit. **All** the Corinthians had been **baptized**, but not all spoke in tongues (12:30). There *are* crisis experiences of the Holy Spirit when a believer surrenders to the Spirit's control and is then empowered from on high. But such an experience is *not* the same as the baptism of the Spirit, and should not be confused with it.

The verse goes on to say that believers **have all been made to drink into one Spirit**. This means that they partake of the **Spirit** of God in the sense that they receive Him as an indwelling Person and receive the benefits of His ministry in their lives.

12:14 Without a variety of members you could not have a human **body**. There must be **many** members, each one different from the others, working in

obedience to the head and in cooperation with the others.

12:15   When we see that diversity is
essential to a normal, healthy body, it
will save us from two dangers — from
belittling ourselves (vv. 15–20) and from
belittling others (vv. 21–25). It would be
absurd for **the foot** to feel unimportant
because it can't do the work of **a hand**.
After all, the foot can stand, walk, run,
climb, dance — and kick, as well as a
host of other things.

12:16   **The ear** shouldn't try to become a dropout because it is **not an eye**.
We take our ears for granted till deafness
overtakes us. Then we realize what a tremendously useful function they perform.

12:17   **If the whole body were an
eye**, you would have a deaf oddity fit
only for a circus sideshow. Or if the
body had only ears, it wouldn't have a
nose to detect when the gas was escaping and soon wouldn't even be able to
hear because it would be unconscious or
dead.

The point that Paul is driving at is
that if the body were all tongue, it would
be a freak, and a monstrosity. And yet
the Corinthians were so overemphasiz-
ing the gift of tongues that they were,
in effect, creating a local fellowship that
would be *all tongue*. It could talk, but that
was all it could do!

12:18   **God** has not been guilty of
such folly. In His matchless wisdom, He
has arranged the different **members
. . . in the body just as He pleased**. We
should give Him credit for knowing
what He is doing! We should be profoundly grateful for whatever gift He
has given us and joyfully use it for His
glory and for building up others. To be
envious of someone else's gift is sin. It
is rebellion against God's perfect plan for
our lives.

12:19   It is impossible to think of a
body with only **one member**. So the Corinthians should remember that if they
all had the gift of tongues, then they
would not have a functioning **body**.
Other gifts, though less spectacular and
less sensational, are nonetheless necessary.

12:20   As God has ordained, there
are **many members, yet one body**. These
facts are obvious to us in connection

with the human body, and they should
be equally obvious to us in connection
with our service in the church.

12:21   Just as it is folly for one person to envy another's gift, so it is equally
foolish for anyone to depreciate another's gift or feel that he doesn't need the
others. **The eye cannot say to the hand,
"I have no need of you"; nor again the
head to the feet, "I have no need of
you."** The eye can see things to be done,
but it can't do them. It depends on the
hand for that. Again, the head might
know that it is necessary to go to a certain place, but it depends on the feet to
take it there.

12:22   Some **members of the body
. . . seem to be weaker** than others. The
kidneys, for instance, don't seem to be
as strong as the arms. But the kidneys
are indispensable whereas the arms are
not. We can live without arms and legs,
or even without a tongue, but we cannot
live without heart, lungs, liver, or brain.
Yet these vital organs never put themselves on public display. They just carry
on their functions unostentatiously.

12:23   Some **members** of the body
are attractive while others are not so elegant. We compensate by putting clothes
over those that are not so beautiful.
Thus there is a certain mutual care
among the members, minimizing the differences.

12:24   Those **parts** of the body that
are **presentable** don't need extra attention. **But God** has combined all the differing members of **the body** into an or-
ganic structure. Some members are
comely, some homely. Some do well in
public, some not so well. Yet God has
given us the instinct to appreciate all the
members, to realize that they are all in-
terdependent, and to counterbalance the
deficiencies of those that are not so
handsome.

12:25   The mutual care of the members prevents division or **schism in the
body**. One gives to another what is
needed, and receives in return the help
which only that other member can give.
This is the way it must be in the church.
Overemphasis on any one gift of the
Spirit will result in conflict and schism.

12:26   What affects **one member** affects **all**. This is a well-known fact in the
human body. Fever, for instance, is not

confined to one part of the body, but affects the whole system. So it is with other types of sickness and pain. An eye doctor often can detect brain tumor, kidney disease, or liver infection by looking into the eye. The reason is that, although all these members are distinct and separate, yet they all form part of the one body, and they are so vitally linked together that what affects one member affects all. Therefore, instead of being discontent with our lot, or, on the other hand, instead of feeling a sense of independence from others, we should have a real sense of solidarity in the Body of Christ. Anything that hurts another Christian should cause us the keenest sorrow. Likewise, if we see another Christian **honored**, we should not feel jealous, but we should **rejoice with** him.

12:27 Paul reminds the Corinthians that they **are the body of Christ**. This cannot mean *the* Body of Christ in its totality. Neither can it mean *a* Body of Christ, since there is only one Body. It can only mean that they collectively formed a microcosm or miniature of the Body of Christ. **Individually** each one is a member of that great cooperative society. As such he should fulfill his function without any feeling of pride, independence, envy, or worthlessness.

12:28 The apostle now gives us another list of gifts. None of these lists is to be considered as complete. **And God has appointed these in the church: first apostles.** The word **first** indicates that not all are apostles. The twelve were men who had been commissioned by the Lord as His messengers. They were with Him during His earthly ministry (Acts 1:21, 22) and, with the exception of Judas, saw Him after His resurrection (Acts 1:2, 3, 22). But others besides the twelve were apostles. The most notable was Paul. There were also Barnabas (Acts 14:4, 14); James, the Lord's brother (Gal. 1:19); Silas and Timothy (1 Thess. 1:1; 2:6). Together with the NT prophets, the apostles laid the doctrinal foundation of the church in what they taught about the Lord Jesus Christ (Eph. 2:20). In the strict meaning of the word, we no longer have apostles. In a wider sense, we still have messengers and church-planters sent forth by the Lord. By calling them *missionaries* instead of apostles, we avoid

creating the impression that they have the extraordinary authority and power of the early apostles.

Next are the **prophets**. We have already mentioned that prophets were spokesmen of God, men who uttered the very word of God in the day before it was given in complete written form. **Teachers** are those who take the word of God and explain it to the people in an understandable way. **Miracles** might refer to raising the dead, casting out demons, etc. **Healings** have to do with the instantaneous cure of bodily diseases, as mentioned previously. **Helps** are commonly associated with the work of deacons, those entrusted with the material affairs of the church. The gift of **administrations**, on the other hand, is usually applied to elders or bishops. These are the men who have the godly, spiritual care of the local church. Last is the gift of **tongues**. We believe that there is a significance in the order. Paul mentions apostles first and tongues last. The Corinthians were putting tongues *first* and disparaging the apostle!

12:29, 30 When the apostle asks if every believer has the same gift — whether apostle, prophet, teacher, miracles, healings, helps, governments, tongues, interpretations of tongues — the grammar in the original shows that he expects and requires a "No" answer.[46] Therefore any suggestion, expressed or implied, that *everyone* should have the gift of tongues, is contrary to the word of God and is foreign to the whole concept of the body with its many different members, each with its own function.

If, as stated here, not everyone has the gift of tongues, then it is wrong to teach that tongues are the sign of the baptism of the Spirit. For, in that case, not everyone could expect that baptism. But the truth is that *every* believer has already been baptized by the Spirit (v. 13).

12:31 When Paul says: **"But earnestly desire the best gifts,"** he is speaking to the Corinthians as a local church, not as individuals. We know this because the verb is plural in the original. He is saying that as an assembly they should desire to have in their midst a good selection of gifts that edify. The best gifts are those that are most useful rather than those that are spectacular. All gifts are given by the Holy Spirit and none should be despised. Yet the fact is that some are of greater benefit to the body than others. These are the ones that every local fellowship should ask the Lord to raise up in the assembly.

And yet I show you a more excellent way. With these words Paul introduces the Love Chapter (1 Cor. 13). What he is saying is that the mere possession of gifts is not as important as the exercise of these gifts in love. Love thinks of others, not of self. It is wonderful to see a man who is unusually gifted by the Holy Spirit, but it is still more wonderful when that man uses that gift to build up others in the faith rather than to attract attention to himself.

People tend to divorce chapter 13 from its context. They think it is a parenthesis, designed to relieve the tension over tongues in chapters 12 and 14. But that is not the case. It is a vital and continuing part of Paul's argument.

The abuse of tongues had apparently caused strife in the assembly. Using their gifts for self-display, self-edification, and self-gratification, the "charismatics" were not acting in love. They received satisfaction out of speaking publicly in a language they had never learned, but it was a real hardship on others to have to sit and listen to something they did not understand. Paul insists that all gifts must be exercised in a spirit of love. The aim of love is to help others and not to please self.

And perhaps the "non-charismatics" had overreacted in acts of unlove. They might even have gone so far as to say that all tongues are of the devil. Their Greek tongues might have been worse than the "charismatic" tongues! Their lovelessness might have been worse than the abuse of tongues itself.

So Paul wisely reminds them all that love is needed on both sides. If they would act in love toward one another, the problem would be largely solved. It is not a problem that calls for excommunication or division; it calls for love.

13:1 Even if a person could **speak** in all languages, human and angelic, but didn't use this ability for the good of others, it would be no more profitable or pleasant than the **clanging**, jangling sound of metals crashing against each other. Where the spoken word is not understood, there is no profit. It is just a nerve-racking din contributing nothing to the common good. For tongues to be beneficial, they must be interpreted. Even then, what is said must be edifying. **The tongues of angels** may be figurative for exalted speech, but it does not mean an unknown language, because whenever angels spoke to men in the Bible, it was in the common speech, easily understood.

13:2 Likewise one might receive marvelous revelations from God. He might **understand** the great **mysteries** of God, tremendous truths hitherto unrevealed but now made known to him. He might receive a great inflow of divine **knowledge**, supernaturally imparted. He might be given that heroic **faith** which is able to **remove mountains**. Yet if these wonderful gifts are used only for his own benefit and not for the edifying of other members of the Body of Christ, they are of no value, and the holder is **nothing**, that is, he is of no help to others.

13:3 If the apostle gave all his **goods to feed the poor**, or even gave his **body to be burned**, these valiant acts would not profit him unless they were done in a spirit of **love**. If he were merely trying to attract attention to himself and seek a name for himself, then his display of virtue would be valueless.

13:4 Someone has said: "This did not start out to be a treatise on love, but like most literary gems of the NT, it was introduced in connection with some local situation." Hodge has pointed out that the Corinthians were impatient, discontented, envious, inflated, selfish, indecorous, unmindful of the feelings and interests of others, suspicious, resentful, and censorious.

And so the apostle now contrasts the characteristics of true love. First of all, **love suffers long and is kind**. Long-suffering is patient endurance under provocation. Kindness is active goodness, going forth in the interests of others. **Love does not envy** others; rather it is pleased that others should be honored and exalted. **Love does not parade itself, is not puffed up**. It realizes that whatever it has is the gift of God, and that there is nothing in man of which to be proud. Even gifts of the Holy Spirit are sovereignly bestowed by God and should not make a person proud or haughty, no matter how spectacular the gift might be.

13:5 Love **does not behave rudely**. If a person is truly acting in love, he will be courteous and considerate. Love **does not** selfishly **seek its own**, but is interested in what will assist others. Love **is not provoked**, but is willing to endure slights and insults. Love **thinks no evil**, that is, it does not attribute bad motives to others. It does not suspect their actions. It is guileless.

13:6 Love **does not rejoice in iniquity, but rejoices in the truth.** There is a certain mean streak in human nature which takes pleasure in what is unrighteous, especially if an unrighteous act seems to benefit one's self. This is not the spirit of love. Love **rejoices** with every triumph of **the truth**.

13:7 The expression **bears all things** may mean that love patiently endures **all things**, or that it hides or conceals the faults of others. The word **bears** may also be translated "covers." Love does not needlessly publicize the failures of others, though it must be firm in giving godly discipline when necessary.

Love **believes all things**, that is, it tries to put the best possible construction on actions and events. Love **hopes all things** in the sense that it earnestly desires that all things work out for the best. Love **endures all things** in the way of persecution or ill treatment.

13:8 Having described the qualities that characterize those who exercise their gift in love, the apostle now takes up the permanence of love, as contrasted with the temporary character of gifts. **Love never fails.** Throughout eternity, love will go on in the sense that we will still love the Lord and love one another. These gifts, on the other hand, are of temporary duration.

There are two principal interpretations of verses 8–13. One traditional view is that the gifts of prophecy, tongues, and knowledge will cease when believers enter the eternal state. The other view is that these gifts have already ceased, and that this occurred when the Canon of Scripture was completed. In order to present both views, we will paraphrase verses 8 through 12 under the labels ETERNAL STATE and COMPLETED CANON.

ETERNAL STATE

Love will never cease. In contrast, the prophecies which exist at the present time will be ended when God's people are home in heaven. While there is the gift of knowledge just now, this will be stopped when we reach the final consummation in glory. (When Paul says knowledge. . . will vanish away, he cannot mean that there will be no knowledge in heaven. He must be referring to the gift of knowledge whereby divine truth was supernaturally imparted.)

13:9 In this life our knowledge is partial at best, and so are our prophecies. There are many things we do not understand in the Bible, and many mysteries in the providence of God.

COMPLETED CANON

Love will never cease. While there are prophecies (at the time of Paul), the need for such direct revelations would end when the last book of the NT was completed. Tongues were still in use in Paul's day, but they would cease in and of themselves when the sixty-six books of the Bible were finished, because they would no longer be necessary to confirm the preaching of the apostles and prophets (Heb. 2:3, 4). Knowledge of divine truth was being given by God to the apostles and prophets, but this would also stop when the complete body of Christian doctrine was once for all delivered.

We, i.e., the apostles, know in part (in the sense that we are still receiving inspired knowledge by direct revelation from God), and we prophesy in part (because we can only express the partial revelations we are receiving).

13:10 But when that which is perfect has come, i.e., when we reach the perfect state in the eternal world, then the gifts of partial knowledge and partial prophecy will be done away.

13:11 This life may be compared to childhood, when our speech, understanding, and thoughts are very limited and immature. The heavenly state is comparable to full adulthood. Then our childish condition will be a thing of the past.

13:12 As long as we are on earth, we see things dimly and indistinctly, as if we were looking in a blurry mirror. Heaven, by contrast will be like seeing things face to face, i.e., without anything between to obscure the vision. Now our knowledge is partial, but then we shall know just as we also are known — which means more fully. We will never have perfect knowledge, even in heaven. Only God is omniscient. But our knowledge will be vastly greater than it is now.

But when that which is perfect has come, i.e., when the Canon is completed by the last book's being added to the NT, then periodic or piecemeal revelations of divine truth will be stopped, and the telling forth of this truth will be done away. There will be no more need for partial revelations since the complete word of God will be here.

The sign gifts were connected with the childhood of the church. The gifts were not childish; they were necessary gifts of the Holy Spirit. But once the full revelation of God was available in the Bible, the miracle gifts were no longer needed and were put aside. The word child[47] here means a baby without the full power of speech.

Now (during the apostolic age) we see in a mirror, dimly. No single one of us (apostles) has received God's full revelation. It is being given to us in portions, like parts of a puzzle. When the Canon of Scripture is completed, the obscurity will be removed and we will see the picture in its entirety. Our knowledge (as apostles and prophets) is partial at present. But when the last book has been added to the NT, we will know more fully and intimately than ever before.

13:13 Faith, hope, and **love** are what Kelly calls "the main moral principles characteristic of Christianity." These graces of the Spirit are superior to the gifts of the Spirit, and they are more lasting, too. In short, the *fruit* of the Spirit is more important than the *gifts* of the Spirit.

And **love** is **the greatest** of the graces because it is most useful to others. It is not self-centered but others-centered.

Now before leaving this chapter, there are a few observations to be made. As mentioned above, a widely accepted interpretation of verses 8–12 is that they contrast conditions in this life with those in the eternal state.

But many devout Christians hold to the COMPLETED CANON view, believing that the purpose of the sign gifts was to confirm the preaching of the apostles before the word of God was given in

final written form, and that the need for these miracle gifts passed when the NT was completed. While this second view merits serious consideration, it can hardly be proved decisively. Even if we believe that the sign gifts largely passed away at the end of the apostolic era, we cannot say with finality that God could not, if He wished, use these gifts today. Whichever view we hold, the abiding lesson is that while the gifts of the Spirit are partial and temporary, the fruit of the Spirit is eternal and is more excellent. If we practice love, it will save us from the misuse of gifts and from the strife and divisions that have arisen as a result of their abuse.

14:1 The connection with the previous chapter is apparent. Christians should **pursue love**, and this will mean that they will always be trying to serve others. They should also earnestly **desire**

spiritual gifts for their assembly. While it is true that gifts are distributed by the Spirit as He wishes, it is also true that we can ask for gifts that will be of greatest value in the local fellowship. That is why Paul suggests that the gift of prophecy is eminently desirable. He goes on to explain why prophecy, for instance, is of greater benefit than tongues.

14:2 He who speaks in a tongue without interpretation is not speaking for the benefit of the congregation. God understands what he is saying but the people don't because it is a foreign language to them. He might be setting forth marvelous truths, hitherto unknown, but it does no good because it is all unintelligible.

14:3 The man who prophesies, on the other hand, builds people up, encourages them, and comforts them. The reason for this is that he is speaking in the language of the people; that is what makes the difference. When Paul says that the prophet builds up, stirs up, and binds up, he is not giving a definition. He is simply saying that these results follow when the message is given in a language the people know.

14:4 Verse 4 is commonly used to justify the private use of tongues for self-edification. But the fact that the word "church" is found nine times in this chapter (vv. 4, 5, 12, 19, 23, 28, 33, 34, 35) offers rather convincing evidence that Paul is not dealing with a believer's devotional life in the privacy of his room, but with the use of tongues in the local assembly. The context shows that, far from advocating the use of tongues for self-edification, the apostle is condemning any use of the gift in the church that does not result in helping *others*. Love thinks of others and not of self. If the gift of tongues is used in love, it will benefit others and not only oneself.

He who prophesies edifies the church. He is not parading his gift for personal advantage, but speaking constructively in a language the congregation can understand.

14:5 Paul does not despise the gift of tongues; he realizes that it is a gift of the Holy Spirit. He could not and would not despise anything that comes from the Spirit. When he says "I wish you all spoke with tongues," he is renouncing any selfish desire to limit the gift to himself and a favored few. His desire is similar to one expressed by Moses: "O, that all the Lord's people were prophets, and that the Lord would put His Spirit upon them" (Num. 11:29b). But in saying this, Paul knew that it was not God's will that all believers should have any one gift (see 12:29, 30).

He would *rather* that the Corinthians prophesied, because in so doing they would be building up one another, whereas when they spoke in tongues without interpretation, their listeners would not understand and therefore would not be benefited. Paul preferred edification to display. "What astonishes is far less important for the spiritual mind than what edifies," as Kelly expresses it.[48]

The expression unless indeed he interprets could mean "unless the one speaking in tongues interprets" or "unless someone interprets."

14:6 Even if Paul himself came to Corinth speaking with tongues, it would not profit them unless they could understand what he said. They would have to be able to recognize what he was saying as revelation and knowledge, or prophesying and teaching. Commentators agree that revelation and knowledge have to do with inward reception, whereas prophesying and teaching have to do with the giving out of the same. Paul's point in this verse is that in order to profit the church, a message must be understood. He goes on to prove this in the following verses.

14:7 First of all, he uses the illustration of musical instruments. Unless a flute or harp makes a distinction in the notes, no one will know what is being piped or played. The very idea of enjoyable music includes the thought of distinction in notes, a definite rhythm, and a certain amount of clarity.

14:8 The same is true of a trumpet. The call to arms must be clear and distinct, otherwise no one will prepare for battle. If the trumpeter merely stands up and blows one long blast in a monotone, no one will stir.

14:9 So it is with the human tongue. Unless the speech we utter is intelligible, no one will know what is being said. It would be as profitless as **speaking into the air**. (In verse 9, "tongue" means the organ of speech, not a foreign language.) There is a practical application in all of this, namely, that ministry or teaching should be clear and simple. If it is "deep" and over the heads of the people, then it will not profit them. It might result in bringing a certain measure of gratification to the speaker, but it will not help the people of God.

14:10 Paul passes to another illustration of the truth he has been setting forth. He speaks of the **many** different **kinds of languages in the world**. Here the subject is broader than human languages; it includes the communications of other creatures. Perhaps Paul is thinking of the various birdcalls and the squeals and grunts used by animals. We know, for instance, that there are certain mating, migratory, and feeding calls used by birds. Also there are certain sounds used by animals to warn of danger. Paul is simply stating here that all of these voices have a definite meaning. **None of them is without significance.** Each one is used to convey some definite message.

14:11 It is true also with human speech. Unless a person speaks with articulate sounds, no one can understand him. He might as well be repeating meaningless gibberish. Few experiences can be more trying than the attempt to communicate with one who does not understand your language.

14:12 In view of this, the Corinthians should mingle their zeal **for spiritual gifts** with the desire to edify **the church**. "Make the edification of the church your aim in this desire to excel," Moffatt translates it. Notice that Paul never discourages them in their zeal for spiritual gifts, but seeks to guide and instruct them so that in the use of these gifts they will reach the highest goal.

14:13 If a man **speaks in a tongue**, he should **pray that he may interpret**. Or the meaning might be to pray that *someone* may interpret.[49] It is possible that a man who has the gift of tongues might also have the gift of interpretation, but

that would be the exception rather than the rule. The analogy of the human body suggests different functions for different members.

14:14 If a man, for instance, prays **in a tongue** at a meeting of the church, his **spirit prays** in the sense that his feelings find utterance, though not in the commonly used language. But his **understanding is unfruitful** in the sense that it doesn't benefit anyone else. The congregation doesn't know what he is saying. As we will explain in the notes on 14:19, we take the phrase **my understanding** to mean "other people's understanding of me."

14:15 **What is the conclusion then?** It is simply this: Paul **will** not only **pray with the spirit, but** he **will also pray** in such a manner as to be understood. This is what is meant by the expression: **"I will also pray with the understanding."** It does not mean that he will pray with his *own* understanding, but rather that he will pray so as to help others to understand. Likewise he **will sing with the spirit**, and **also sing** so as to be understood.

14:16 That this is the correct meaning of the passage is made abundantly clear by verse 16. If Paul gave thanks with his own spirit, but not in such a way as to be understood by others, how could one who did not understand the language he was using **say "Amen"** at the close?

He who occupies the place of the uninformed means a person who is sitting in the audience and does not know the language that is being used by the speaker. This verse incidentally authorizes the intelligent use of the **"Amen"** in public gatherings of the church.

14:17 Speaking in a foreign language, one might indeed really be giving **thanks** to God, but others are **not edified** if they do not know what is being said.

14:18 The apostle apparently had the ability to speak **more** foreign languages than **all** of them. We know that Paul had learned some languages, but here the reference is undoubtedly to his gift of tongues.

14:19 In spite of this superior language ability, Paul says that he **would rather speak five words with** his **under-**

standing, that is, so as to be understood, **than ten thousand words in a** foreign **tongue**. He was not at all interested in using this gift for self-display. His chief aim was to help the people of God. Therefore he determined that when he spoke he would do so in such a way that others would understand him.

The expression **my understanding** is what is known as an "objective genitive."[50] It does not mean what I myself understand, but what others understand when I speak.

Hodge demonstrates that the context here has to do, not with Paul's own understanding of what he spoke in tongues, but of other people's understanding him:

> That Paul should give thanks to God that he was more abundantly endowed with the gift of tongues, if that gift consisted in the ability to speak in languages which he himself did not understand, and the use of which, on that assumption, could according to his principle benefit neither himself nor others, is not to be believed. Equally clear is it from this verse that to speak with tongues was not to speak in a state of mental unconsciousness. The common doctrine as to the nature of the gift is the only one consistent with this passage. Paul says that although he could speak in foreign languages more than the Corinthians, he would rather speak five words *with his understanding*, i.e., so as to be intelligible, than ten thousand words in an unknown tongue. *In the church*, that is, in the assembly, that I might teach others also (katēcheō) to instruct orally, Gal. 6:6. This shows what is meant by speaking *with the understanding*. It is speaking in such a way as to convey instruction.[51]

14:20 Paul next exhorts the Corinthians against immaturity in their thinking. Children prefer amusement to usefulness, flashy things to stable ones. Paul is saying, "Don't take a childish delight in these spectacular gifts which you use for self-display. There is one sense in which you should be childlike, and that is in the matter of **malice** or evil. But in other matters, you should think with the maturity of men."

14:21 Next the apostle quotes from Isaiah to show that tongues are a sign to *unbelievers* rather than to believers. God said that because the children of Israel had rejected His message and had mocked it, He would speak to them through a foreign language (Isa. 28:11). The fulfillment of this took place when the Assyrian invaders came into the land of Israel, and the Israelites heard the Assyrian language being spoken in their midst. This was a sign to them of their rejection of God's word.

14:22 The argument here is that since God intended **tongues** as **a sign** to **unbelievers**, the Corinthians should not insist on using them so freely in gatherings of believers. It would be better if they prophesied, since prophesying was a sign for believers and **not for unbelievers**.

14:23 **If the whole church comes together in one place, and all** the Christians **speak with tongues** without interpretation, what would strangers coming in think about it all? It would not be a testimony to them; rather they would think that the saints were mental cases.

There is an *apparent* contradiction between verse 22 and verses 23–25. In verse 22, we are told that tongues are a sign to unbelievers whereas prophecy is for believers. But in verses 23–25, Paul says that tongues used in the church might only confuse and stumble unbelievers whereas prophecy might help them.

The explanation of the seeming contradiction is this: The unbelievers in verse 22 are those who have rejected the word of God and closed their hearts to the truth. Tongues are a sign of God's judgment on them, as they were on Israel in the Isaiah passage (v. 21). The unbelievers in verses 23–25 are those who are willing to be taught. They are open to hear the word of God, as is evidenced by their presence in a Christian assembly. If they hear Christians speaking in foreign languages without interpretation, they will be hindered, not helped.

14:24 If strangers enter a meeting where the Christians are prophesying rather than speaking in tongues, the visitors hear and understand what is being said and they are **convinced by all** and **convicted by all**. What the apostle is emphasizing here is that no real conviction of sin is produced unless the listeners understand what is being said. When tongues are being used with no interpretation, then obviously visitors are not helped at all. Those who prophesy would, of course, do it in the language in current use in that area, and as a result listeners would be impressed by what they heard.

14:25 **The secrets of** a man's **heart are revealed** by prophecy. He feels that the speaker is addressing him directly. The Spirit of God works conviction in his soul. **And so, falling down on his face, he will worship God and report that God is truly among** these people.

And so Paul's point in verses 22–25 is that tongues without interpretation produce no conviction among unbelievers, whereas prophecy does.

14:26 Because of the abuses that had entered the church in connection with the gift of tongues, it was necessary for the Spirit of God to set forth certain regulations to control the use of this gift. In verses 26–28, we have such controls.

What happened when the early church came **together**? It appears from verse 26 that the meetings were very informal and free. There was liberty for the Spirit of God to use the various gifts which He had given to the church. One man, for instance, would read **a psalm**, and then another would set forth some **teaching**. Another would speak in **a** foreign **tongue**. Another would present **a revelation** which he had received directly from the Lord. Another would interpret the tongue that had already been given. Paul gives tacit approval to this "open meeting" where there was liberty for the Spirit of God to speak through different brothers. But having stated this, he sets forth the first control in the exercise of these gifts. Everything must **be done** with a view to **edification**. Just because a thing is sensational or spectacular does not mean that it has any place in the church. In order to be acceptable, ministry must have the effect of building up the people of God. That is what is meant by **edification** – spiritual growth.

14:27 The second control is that in any one meeting no more than **three** may speak in tongues. **If anyone speaks in a tongue, let there be two or at the most three.** There was to be no such thing as a meeting where a multitude of people would arise to show their proficiency in foreign languages.

Next we learn that the two or three who were permitted to speak in tongues in any one meeting must do so **in turn**. That means that they must not speak at the same time, but one after the other. This would avoid the bedlam and disorder of several speaking at once.

The fourth rule is that there must be an **interpreter. Let one interpret.** If a man got up to speak in a foreign language, he must first determine that there was someone present to interpret what he was about to say.

14:28 **If there** was **no interpreter** present, then he must **keep silent in church**. He could sit there and **speak** inaudibly **to himself and to God** in this foreign language, but he was not permitted to do so publicly.

14:29 Rules for governing the prophetic gift are set forth in verses 29–33a. First of all, **two or three prophets** were to speak and **the others** were to **judge**. No more than **three** were to take part in any one meeting, and the Christians who listened were to determine whether this was truly a divine utterance or whether the man might be a false prophet.

14:30 As we have mentioned previously, a prophet received direct communications from the Lord and revealed them to the church. But it is possible that after giving this revelation, he might go on to preach to the people. So the apostle lays down the rule that if a prophet is speaking and **anything is revealed to another** prophet sitting in the audience, then **the first** is required to stop speaking to make way for the one who has received the latest revelation. The reason, as suggested, is that the longer the first man talks, the more apt he is to speak by his own power rather than by inspiration. In continued speech there is always the danger of shifting from God's words to one's own words. Revelation is superior to anything else.

14:31 The prophets should be given the opportunity to speak **one by one**. No one prophet should take all the time. In that way, the greatest benefit would result to the church — **all** would be able to **learn** and **all** would **be** exhorted or **encouraged**.

14:32 A very important principle is set forth in verse 32. Reading between the lines, we suspect that the Corinthians had the false idea that the more a man was possessed by the Spirit of God, the less self-control he had. They felt that he was carried away in a state of ecstasy and they contended, according to Godet, that the more spirit, the less intelligence or self-consciousness there would be. To them, a man under the control of the Spirit was in a state of passivity, and could not control his speech, the length of time he spoke, or his actions in general. Such an idea is thoroughly refuted by the passage of Scripture before us. **The spirits of the prophets are subject to the prophets.** That means that he is not carried away without his consent, or against his will. He cannot evade the instructions of this chapter on the pretense that he just couldn't help it. He himself can determine when or how long he should speak.

14:33 **For God is not the author of confusion but of peace.** In other words, if a meeting is the scene of pandemonium and disorder, then you can be *sure* that the Spirit of God is not in control!

14:34 As is well-known, the verse divisions and even the punctuation of the NT were added centuries after the original manuscripts were written. The last clause of verse 33 makes much greater sense modifying the church practice in verse 34 than a universal truth about the omnipresent God (some Greek Testaments and English translations use this punctuation). For instance, the ASV reads: "As in all the churches of the saints, let the women keep silent in the churches: for it is not permitted unto them to speak; but let them be in subjection, as also saith the law." The instructions which Paul is giving to the Corinthian saints do not apply to them alone. These are the same instructions that have been addressed to **all the churches of the saints**. The uniform testimony of the NT is that while women have many valuable ministries, it is not given to them to have a public ministry to the whole church. They are entrusted with the unspeakably important work of the home and of raising children. But they are not allowed to speak publicly in the assembly. Theirs is to be a place of submission to the man.

We believe that the expression **as the law also says** has reference to the woman's being submissive to the man. This is clearly taught in the law, which here probably means the Pentateuch primarily. Genesis 3:16, for instance, says "your desire shall be for your husband. And he shall rule over you."

It is often contended that what Paul is forbidding in this verse is for the women to chatter or gossip while the service is going on. However, such an interpretation is untenable. The word here translated speak (*laleō*) did not mean to chatter in Koinē Greek. The same word is used of God in verse 21 of this chapter, and in Hebrews 1:1. It means to speak authoritatively.

14:35 Indeed, women are not permitted to ask questions publicly in the church. **If they want to learn something**, they should **ask their own husbands at home**. Some women might try to evade the previous prohibition against speaking by asking questions. It is possible to teach by the simple act of questioning others. So this verse closes any such loophole or objection.

If it is asked how this applies to an unmarried woman or a widow, the answer is that the Scriptures do not try to take up each individual case, but merely set forth general principles. If a woman does not have a husband, she could ask her father, her brother, or one of the elders of the church. Actually, this may be translated, "Let them ask their men-folks[52] at home." The basic rule to be remembered is that **it is shameful for women to speak in church**.

14:36 Apparently the Apostle Paul realized that his teaching here would cause considerable contention. How right he was! To meet any arguments, he uses irony in verse 36 by asking: **Or did the word of God come originally from you? Or was it you only that it reached?** In other words, if the Corinthians professed to know more about these matters than the apostle, he would ask them if they, as a church, produced **the word of God**, or if they were the **only** ones who had received it. By their attitude they seemed to set themselves up as an official authority on these matters. But the facts are that no church originated the word of God, and no church has exclusive rights to it.

14:37 In connection with all the foregoing instructions, the apostle here emphasizes that they are not his own ideas or interpretations, but that they **are the commandments of the Lord**, and any man who is **a prophet** of the Lord or who is truly **spiritual** will **acknowledge** that that is the case. This verse is a sufficient answer to those who insist that some of Paul's teachings, especially those concerning women, reflected his own prejudices. These matters are not Paul's private view; they are **the commandments of the Lord**.

14:38 Of course, some would not be willing to accept them as such, and so the apostle adds that **if anyone is ignorant, let him be ignorant**. If a person refuses to acknowledge the inspiration of these writings and to bow to them obediently, then there is no alternative but for him to continue in his ignorance.

14:39 To sum up the preceding instructions on the exercise of gifts, Paul now tells the **brethren** to **desire earnestly to prophesy**, but **not** to **forbid** men **to speak with tongues**. This verse shows the relative importance of these two gifts — one they were to **desire earnestly**, while the other they were **not** to ban. Prophecy was more valuable than tongues because sinners were convicted through it and saints edified. Tongues without interpretation served no other purpose than to speak to God and to one's self, and to display one's own proficiency with a foreign language, a proficiency that had been given to them by God.

14:40 Paul's final word of admonition is that **all things** must **be done decently and in order**. It is significant that this control should be placed in this chapter. Down through the years, those who have professed to have the ability to speak in tongues have not been noted for the orderliness of their meetings. Rather, many of their meetings have been scenes of uncontrolled emotion and general confusion.

To summarize, then, the Apostle Paul sets forth the following controls for the use of tongues in the local church:

1. We must not forbid the use of tongues (v. 39).
2. If a man speaks in a tongue, there must be an interpreter (vv. 27c, 28).
3. Not more than three may speak in tongues in any one meeting (v. 27a).
4. They must speak one at a time (v. 27b).
5. What they say must be edifying (v. 26b).
6. The women must be silent (v. 34).
7. Everything must **be done decently and in order** (v. 40).

These are the abiding controls which apply to the church in our day.

IV. PAUL'S ANSWER TO DENIERS OF THE RESURRECTION (Chap. 15)

This is the great resurrection chapter. Some teachers had entered the church at Corinth, denying the possibility of bodily resurrection. They did not deny the fact of life after death, but probably suggested that we would simply be spirit beings and not have literal bodies. The apostle here gives his classic answer to these denials.

A. Certainty of the Resurrection (15:1–34)

15:1, 2 Paul reminds them of the good news which he had **preached** to them, which they had **received**, and **in which** they now stood. This was not a new doctrine for the Corinthians, but it was necessary that they should be reminded of it at this critical time. It was this **gospel** by which the Corinthians had been **saved**. Then Paul adds the words **if you hold fast that word which I preached to you — unless you believed in vain**. It was by the gospel of the resurrection that they had been saved — unless, of course, there was no such thing as resurrection, in which case they could not have been saved at all. The **if** in this passage does not express any doubt as to their salvation, nor does it teach that they were saved by holding fast. Rather, Paul is simply stating that if there is no such thing as resurrection, then they weren't saved at all. In other words, those who denied bodily resurrection were launching a frontal attack on the whole truth of the gospel. To Paul, the resurrection was fundamental. Without it there was no Christianity. Thus this verse is a challenge to the Corinthians to hold fast the gospel which they had received in the face of the attacks which were currently being made against it.

15:3 Paul had **delivered to** the Corinthians the message **which** he had **also received** by divine revelation. The first cardinal doctrine of that message was **that Christ died for our sins according to the Scriptures**. This emphasizes the substitutionary character of the death of Christ. He did not die for His own sins, or as a martyr; He **died for our sins**. He **died** to pay the penalty that **our sins** deserved. This was all **according to the Scriptures. The Scriptures** here refer to the OT Scriptures, since the NT was not yet in written form. Did the OT Scriptures actually predict that Christ would die for the sins of the people? The answer is an emphatic "Yes!" Isaiah 53, verses 5 and 6, are sufficient proof of this.

15:4† The burial of Christ was prophesied in Isaiah 53:9, and His resurrection in Psalm 16:9, 10. It is important to notice how Paul emphasizes the testimony of **the Scriptures**. This should always be the test in all matters relating to our faith: "What do the Scriptures say?"

15:5 In verses 5–7, we have a list of those who were eyewitnesses of the resurrection. First of all, the Lord appeared to **Cephas** (Peter). This is very touching indeed. The same faithless disciple who had denied his Lord three times is graciously privileged to have a private appearance of that same Lord in resurrection. Truly, how great is the grace of the Lord Jesus Christ! **Then** the Lord also appeared to **the twelve** disciples. Actually the twelve were not all together at this time, but the expression **the twelve** was used to denote the body of disciples, even though not complete at any one particular moment. It should be stated that not all the appearances which are recorded in the Gospels are mentioned in this list. The Spirit of God selects those resurrection appearances of Christ which are most pertinent for His use.

15:6 The Lord's appearance to **over five hundred brethren** is commonly believed to have taken place in Galilee. At the time Paul wrote, most of these brethren were still living, although some had

gone home to be with the Lord. In other words, should anyone wish to contest the truthfulness of what Paul was saying, the witnesses were still alive and could be questioned.

15:7 There is no way of knowing which **James** is referred to here, although most commentators assume him to be the Lord's half-brother. Verse 7 also tells us that the Lord appeared to **all the apostles**.

15:8 Paul next speaks of his own personal acquaintance with the risen Christ. This took place on the road to Damascus, when he saw a great light from heaven and met the glorified Christ face to face. **One born out of due time** means an abortion or an untimely birth. Vine explains it as meaning that in point of time, Paul speaks of himself as inferior to the rest of the apostles, just as an immature birth comes short of a mature one. He uses it as a term of self-reproach in view of his past life as a persecutor of the church.

15:9 As the apostle thinks of the privilege he had of meeting the Savior face to face, he is filled with a spirit of unworthiness. He thinks of how he **persecuted the church of God** and how, in spite of that, the Lord called him to be an apostle. Therefore he bows himself in the dust as **the least of the apostles**, and **not worthy to be called an apostle**.

15:10 He hastens to acknowledge that whatever he now is, he is **by the grace of God**. And he did not accept this grace as a matter of fact. Rather it put him under the deepest obligation, and he labored tirelessly to serve the Christ who saved him. Yet in a very real sense it was not Paul himself, **but the grace of God which was** working **with** him.

15:11 Now Paul joins himself with the other apostles and states that no matter which of them it was who preached, they were all united in their testimony as to the gospel, and particularly as to the resurrection of Christ.

15:12 In verses 12–19, Paul lists the consequences of the denial of bodily resurrection. First of all, it would mean that Christ Himself has not risen. Paul's logic here is unanswerable. Some were saying that there is no such thing as bodily resurrection. All right, Paul says, if that is the case, then Christ has not risen. Are you Corinthians willing to admit this? Of course they were not. In order to prove the possibility of any fact, all you have to do is to demonstrate that it has already taken place once. To prove the fact of bodily resurrection, Paul is willing to base his case upon the simple fact that **Christ** has already **been raised from the dead.**

15:13 But if there is no resurrection of the dead, then obviously **Christ is not risen**. Such a conclusion would involve the Corinthians in hopeless gloom and despair.

15:14 If Christ is not risen, then the **preaching** of the apostles was **empty**, or having no substance. Why was it **empty**? First of all, because the Lord Jesus had promised that He would rise from the dead on the third day. If He did *not* rise at that time, then He was either an imposter or mistaken. In either case, He would not be worthy of trust. Secondly, apart from the resurrection of Christ, there could be no salvation. If the Lord Jesus did not rise from the dead, then there would be no way of knowing that His death had been of any greater value than any other person's. But in raising Him from the dead, God testified to the fact that He was completely satisfied with the redemptive work of Christ.

Obviously, if the apostolic message was false, then **faith** would be **empty** too. There would be no value in trusting a message that was false or empty.

15:15 It would not simply be a matter that the apostles were preaching a false message; actually it would mean that they had been testifying against **God**. They **testified of God that He raised up Christ** from the dead. If God didn't do this, then the apostles had been bringing **false** witness against Him.

15:16 If resurrection is an utter impossibility, then there can be no exception to it. On the other hand, if resurrection had taken place once, for instance in the case of Christ, then it can no longer be thought of as an impossibility.

15:17 If Christ has not been raised, the **faith** of believers **is futile** and devoid of power. And there is no forgiveness of **sins**. Thus to reject the resurrection is to reject the value of the work of Christ.

15:18 As for those who had died believing **in Christ**, their case would be absolutely hopeless. If Christ did not rise, then their faith was just a worthless thing. The expression **fallen asleep** refers to the bodies of believers. Sleep is never used of the soul in the NT. The soul of the believer departs to be with Christ at the time of death, while the body is spoken of as sleeping in the grave.

We should also say a word concerning the word **perished**. This word *never* means annihilation or cessation of being. As Vine has pointed out, it is not loss of *being*, but rather loss of *well-being*. It speaks of ruin as far as the purpose for which a person or thing was created.

15:19 If Christ is not risen, then living believers are in as wretched a condition as those who have died. They, too, have been deceived. They **are of all men the most pitiable**. Paul is here doubtless thinking of the sorrows, sufferings, trials, and persecutions to which Christians are exposed. To undergo such afflictions for a false cause would be pathetic indeed.

15:20 The tension is relieved as Paul triumphantly announces the fact of the resurrection of Christ and of the blessed consequences that follow. **But now Christ is risen from the dead, ... the firstfruits of those who have fallen asleep**. There is a difference in the Scripture between the resurrection *of* the dead and the resurrection *from* the dead. The previous verses have been dealing with the resurrection of the dead. In other words, Paul has been arguing in a general way that the dead do indeed rise. But Christ rose *from* the dead. This means that when He rose, not all the dead rose. In this sense it was a limited resurrection. Every resurrection is a resurrection of the dead, but only that of Christ and of believers is a resurrection *from among* dead people.

15:21 It was **by man** that **death** first **came** into the world. That **man** was Adam. Through his sin, death came upon all men. God sent His Son into the world as a **Man** in order to undo the work of the first man and to raise believers to a state of blessedness such as they could never have known in Adam. Thus it was by the **Man** Christ Jesus that there **came the resurrection of the dead**.

15:22 Adam and **Christ** are presented as federal heads. This means that they acted for other people. And all who are related to them are affected by their actions. **All who are descended from Adam die. So in Christ all shall be made alive**. This verse has sometimes been taken to teach universal salvation. It is argued that the same ones who die in Adam will be made alive in Christ, and that all will eventually be saved. But that is not what the verse says. The key expressions are **in Adam** and **in Christ**. **All who are in Adam die**. **All who are in Christ shall be made alive**, that is, only believers in the Lord Jesus Christ will be raised from the dead to dwell eternally with Him. The **all** who **shall be made alive** is defined in verse 23 as those who are Christ's at His Coming. It does not include Christ's enemies, for they shall be put under His feet (v. 25), which, as someone has said, is a strange name for heaven.

15:23 Next we have the groups or classes involved in the first resurrection. First is the resurrection of **Christ** Himself. He is spoken of here as **the firstfruits**. Firstfruits were a handful of ripened grain from the harvest field before the actual harvest started. They were a pledge, a guarantee, a foretaste of what was to follow. The expression does not necessarily mean that Christ was the first one to rise. We have instances of resurrection in the OT, and the cases of Lazarus, the widow's son, and Jairus' daughter in the NT. But Christ's resurrection was different from all of these in that, whereas they rose to die again, Christ rose to die no more. He rose to live in the power of an endless life. He rose with a glorified body.

The second class in the first resurrection is described as **those who are Christ's at His coming**. This includes those who will be raised at the time of the Rapture, and also those believers who will die during the Tribulation and will be raised at the end of that time of trouble, when Christ comes back to reign. Just as there are stages in the coming of Christ, so there will be stages in the resurrection of His saints. The first resurrection does not include all who have ever died, but only those who have died with faith in Christ.

Some teach that only those Christians who have been faithful to Christ, or who have been overcomers will be raised at this time, but the Scriptures are very clear in refuting this. All **who are Christ's** will be raised at His coming.

15:24 The expression **then comes the end** refers, we believe, to **the end** *of the resurrection*. At the close of Christ's Millennial Reign, when He shall have put down all His enemies, there will be the resurrection of the wicked dead. This is the last resurrection ever to take place. All who have ever died in unbelief will stand before the Judgment of the Great White Throne to hear their doom.

After the Millennium and the destruction of Satan (Rev. 20:7–10), the Lord Jesus will deliver **the kingdom to God the Father**. By that time He will have abolished **all rule and all authority and power**. Up to this time the Lord Jesus Christ has been reigning *as the Son of Man*, serving as God's Mediator. At the end of the thousand-year reign, God's purposes on earth will have been perfectly accomplished. All opposition will have been put down and all enemies destroyed. The reign of Christ *as Son of Man* will then give way to the eternal kingdom in heaven. His reign *as Son of God* in heaven will continue forever.

15:25 Verse 25 emphasizes what has just been said, namely, that Christ's reign will continue until every trace of rebellion and enmity has been put down.

15:26 Even during Christ's Millennial Reign, people will continue to die, especially those who openly rebel against the Lord. But at the Judgment of the Great White Throne, **death** and Hades will be cast into the Lake of Fire.

15:27 God has decreed that **all things** shall be **put** under the **feet** of the Lord Jesus. Of course, in putting **all things under Him**, God necessarily excepted Himself. Verse 27 is rather hard to follow because it is not clear to whom each pronoun is referring. We might paraphrase it as follows: "For God has put all things under Christ's feet. But when God says, all things are put under Christ, it is obvious that God is excluded, who put all things under Christ."

15:28 Even after **all things** have been put in subjection to the Son, He

Himself will continue to be **subject** to **God** forever.

> God has made Christ ruler, administrator of all His plans and counsels. All authority and power is put in His hands. There is a time coming when He will render His account of the administration committed to Him. After He has brought everything into subjection, He will hand the kingdom back to the Father. Creation will be brought back to God in a perfect condition. Having accomplished the work of redemption and restoration for which He became Man, He will retain the subordinate place that He took in Incarnation. If He should cease to be man after having brought to pass all that God purposed and designated, the very link that brings God and man together would be gone. (Selected)

15:29 Verse 29 is perhaps one of the most difficult and obscure verses in all the Bible. Many explanations have been offered as to its meaning. For instance, it is contended by some that living believers may be baptized for those who have died without having undergone this rite. Such a meaning is quite foreign to the Scriptures. It is based on a single verse and must be rejected, not having the collective support of other Scripture. Others believe that baptism for the dead means that in baptism we reckon ourselves to have died. This is a possible meaning, but it does not fit in too well with the context.

The interpretation which seems to suit the context best is this: At the time Paul wrote, there was fierce persecution against those who took a public stand for Christ. This persecution was especially vicious at the time of their baptism. It often happened that those who publicly proclaimed their faith in Christ in the waters of baptism were martyred shortly thereafter. But did this stop others from being saved and from taking their place in baptism? Not at all. It seemed as though there were always new replacements coming along to fill up the ranks of those who had been martyred. As they stepped into the waters of baptism, in a very real sense **they** were being **baptized for**, or *in the place of* (Gk. *huper*) the dead. Hence **the dead** here refers to those who died as a result of their bold witness for Christ. Now the apostle's argument here is that it would be foolish to be thus baptized to fill up the ranks of those who had died if there is no such thing as resurrection from the dead. It would be like sending replacement troops to fill up the ranks of an army that is fighting a lost cause. It would be like fighting on in a hopeless situation. **If the dead do not rise at all, why then are they baptized for the dead?**

15:30 And why do we stand in jeopardy every hour? The Apostle Paul was constantly exposed to danger. Because of his fearlessness in preaching Christ, he made enemies wherever he went. Secret plots were hatched against him in an effort to take his life. He could have avoided all this by abandoning his profession of Christ. In fact, it would have been wise for him to abandon it if there was no such thing as resurrection from the dead.

15:31 I affirm, by the boasting in you which I have in Christ Jesus our Lord, I die daily might be paraphrased: "As surely as I rejoice over you as my children in Christ Jesus, every day of my life I am exposed to death."

15:32 The apostle now recalls the fierce persecution which he encountered **at Ephesus**. We do not believe that he was actually thrown into the arena with wild beasts, but rather that he is speaking here of wicked men as wild **beasts**. Actually, as a Roman citizen, Paul could not have been forced to fight with wild animals. We do not know to what incident he refers. However, the argument is clear that the apostle would have been foolish to engage in such dangerous warfare as he had if he were not assured of resurrection from the dead. Indeed it would have been much wiser for him to adopt the philosophy: **"If the dead do not rise, 'Let us eat and drink, for tomorrow we die!'"**

We sometimes hear Christians say that if this life were all, then they would still rather be Christians. But Paul disagrees with such an idea. If there were no resurrection, we would be better off to make the most of *this* life. We would live for food, clothing, and pleasure. This would be the only heaven we could look forward to. But since there *is* a resurrection, we dare not spend our lives for these things of passing interest. We must live for "then" and not for "now."

15:33 The Corinthians should **not be deceived** on this score. **Evil company corrupts good habits.** Paul is referring to the false teachers who had come into the church at Corinth, denying the resurrection. The Christians should realize that it is impossible to associate with **evil** people or evil teachings without being corrupted by them. Evil doctrine inevitably has an effect on one's life. False teachings do not lead to holiness.

15:34 The Corinthians should **awake to righteousness** and **not sin**. They should not be deluded by these evil teachings. **Some do not have the knowledge of God. I speak this to your shame.** This verse is commonly interpreted to mean that there are still men and women who have never heard the gospel story, and that Christians should be ashamed of their failure to evangelize the world. However, while this may be true, we believe that the primary meaning of the passage is that there were men in the fellowship at Corinth who did **not have the knowledge of God**. They were not true believers, but wolves in sheep's clothing, false teachers who had crept in unawares. It was to the **shame** of the Corinthians that these men were allowed to take their place with the Christians and to teach these wicked doctrines. The carelessness which let ungodly people enter the assembly resulted in lowering the congregation's whole moral tone, thus preparing an opening for the intrusion of all kinds of error.

B. Consideration of Objections to the Resurrection (15:35–57)

15:35 In verses 35–49, the apostle goes into greater detail concerning the actual mode of the resurrection. He anticipates two questions which would inevitably arise in the minds of those who questioned the fact of bodily resurrection. The first is: **"How are the dead raised up?"** The second is: **"And with what body do they come?"**

15:36 The first question is answered in verse 36. A common illustration from nature is used to illustrate the possibility of resurrection. A seed must fall into the ground and die before the plant can come forth. It is wonderful indeed to think of the mystery of life that is hidden in every tiny seed. We may dissect the seed and study it under the microscope, but the secret of the life principle remains an unfathomable mystery. All we know is that the seed falls into the ground and from that unlikely beginning there springs forth life from the dead.

15:37 The second question is taken up next. Paul explains that when you **sow** a seed, **you do not sow the** plant **that shall** eventually result, **but** you sow a bare **grain — perhaps wheat or some other grain**. What do we conclude from this? Is the plant the same as the seed? No, the plant is not the same as the seed; however, there is a very vital connection between the two. Without the seed there would have been no plant. Also, the plant derives its features from the seed. So it is in resurrection.

The resurrection body has identity of kind and continuity of substance with that which is sown, but it is purified from corruption, dishonor, and weakness, and made incorrupt, glorious, powerful, and spiritual. It is the same body, but it is sown in one form and raised in another. (Selected)

15:38 **God** produces **a body** according to the seed that was sown, and **each seed** has its own type of plant as a result. All the factors which determine the size, color, leaf, and flower of the plant are somehow contained in the seed that is sown.

15:39 To illustrate the fact that the glory of the resurrection body will be different from the glory of our present bodies, the Apostle Paul points out that **all flesh is not the same** kind. For instance, there is human **flesh, flesh of animals**, flesh **of fish**, and flesh **of birds**. These are distinctly different, and yet they are all flesh. There is similarity without exact duplication.

15:40 And just as there is a difference between the splendor of heavenly **bodies** (the stars, etc.) and bodies which are associated with this earth, so there is a difference between the body of the believer now and the one which he will have after death.

15:41 Even among the celestial bodies themselves, there is a difference of **glory**. For instance, **the sun** is brighter than **the moon, and one star differs from another in** brightness.

Most commentators agree that Paul is still emphasizing that the glory of the resurrection body will be different from the glory of the body which we have on earth at the present time. They do not think that verse 41, for instance, indicates that in heaven there will be differences of glory among believers themselves. However, we tend to agree with Holsten that "the way in which Paul emphasizes the diversities of the heavenly bodies implies the supposition of an analogous difference of glory between the risen." It is clear from other passages of Scripture that we shall not all be identical in heaven. Although all will resemble the Lord Jesus morally, that is, in freedom from sin, it does not follow that we shall all *look* like the Lord Jesus physically. He will be distinctly recognizable as such throughout all eternity. Likewise, we believe that each individual Christian will be a distinct personality recognizable as such. But there will be differences of reward granted at the Judgment Seat of Christ according to one's faithfulness in service. While all will be supremely happy in heaven, some will have greater *capacity* for enjoying heaven. Just as there will be differences of suffering in hell, according to the sins that a man has committed, so there will be differences of enjoyment in heaven, according to what we have done as believers.

15:42 Verses 42–49 show the contrast between what the believer's body is now and what it will be in its eternal state. **The body is sown in corruption, it is raised in incorruption.** At the present time, our bodies are subject to disease and death. When they are placed in the grave, they decompose and return to dust. But it will not be so with the resurrection body. It will no longer be subject to sickness or decay.

15:43 The present body **is sown in dishonor.** There is nothing very majestic or glorious about a dead body. However, this same body will be **raised in glory**. It will be free from wrinkles, scars, the marks of age, overweight, and the traces of sin.

It is sown in weakness, it is raised in power. With the coming of old age, **weakness** increases until death itself strips a man of all strength whatever. In eternity, the body will not be subject to these sad limitations, but will be possessed of powers that it does not have at the present time. For instance, the Lord Jesus Christ in resurrection was able to enter a room where the doors were locked.

15:44 **It is sown a natural body, it is raised a spiritual body.** Here we must be very careful to emphasize that spiritual does *not* mean nonmaterial. Some people have the idea that in resurrection we will be disembodied spirits. That is not at all the meaning of this passage, nor is it true. We know that the resurrection body of the Lord Jesus was composed of flesh and bones because He said, "A spirit does not have flesh and bones as you see I have" (Luke 24:39). The difference between **a natural body** and **a spiritual body** is that the former is suited to life here on earth whereas the latter will be suited to life in heaven. The former is usually soul-controlled whereas the latter is spirit-controlled. **A spiritual body** is one that will be truly the servant of the spirit.

God created man spirit, soul, and body. He always mentions the spirit first, because His intention was that the spirit should be in the place of preeminence or dominance. With the entrance of sin, something very strange happened. God's order seems to have been upset, and the result is that man always says "body, soul, and spirit." He has given the body the place which the spirit should have had. In resurrection it will not be so; the spirit will be in the place of control which God originally intended.

15:45 **And so it is written, "The first man Adam became a living being." The last Adam became a life-giving spirit.** Here again the first man Adam is contrasted with the Lord Jesus Christ. God breathed into Adam's nostrils the breath of life and he became a living being (Gen. 2:7). All who are descended from him bear his characteristics. **The last Adam**, the Savior, **became a life-giving spirit** (John 5:21, 26). The difference is that in the first case, Adam *was given* physical life, whereas in the second case Christ *gives* eternal life to others. Erdman explains:

As the descendants of Adam, we are made like him, living souls inhabiting mortal bodies, and bearing the image of an earthly parent. But as the followers of Christ, we are yet to be clothed with immortal bodies and to bear the image of our heavenly Lord.[53]

15:46 The apostle now sets forth a fundamental law in God's universe, namely, **the spiritual is not first, but the natural, and afterward the spiritual**. This can be understood in several ways. Adam, **the natural** man, came first on the stage of human history; then Jesus, **the spiritual** Man. Second, we are born into the world as **natural** beings; then when we are born again, we become **spiritual** beings. Finally, we first receive **natural** bodies, then in resurrection we will receive **spiritual** bodies.

15:47 The first man was of the earth, made of dust. This means that his origin was **of the earth** and that his characteristics were earthly. He was **made of the dust** of the ground in the first place, and in his life he seemed in a very real sense to be earth-bound. **The second Man is the Lord**[54] **from heaven.**

15:48 Of the two men mentioned in verse 45, Jesus was the second. He existed from all eternity, but as Man, he came after Adam. He came from heaven, and everything He did and said was **heavenly** and spiritual rather than earthly and soulish.

As it is with these two federal heads, so it is with their followers. Those who are born of Adam inherit his characteristics. Also those who are born of Christ are a **heavenly** people.

15:49 As we have borne the characteristics of Adam as to our natural birth, **we shall**[55] **also bear the image of** Christ in our resurrection bodies.

15:50 Now the apostle turns to the subject of the transformation that will take place in the bodies of believers, both living and dead, at the time of the Lord's Return. He prefaces his remarks with the statement **that flesh and blood cannot inherit the kingdom of God**. By this he means that the present body which we have is not suited to **the kingdom of God** in its eternal aspect, that is, our heavenly home. It is also true that **corruption** cannot **inherit incorruption**.

In other words, our present bodies which are subject to disease, decay, and decomposition, would not be suited for life in a state where there is no corruption. This raises the problem, then, of how the bodies of living believers can be suited for life in heaven.

15:51 The answer is in the form of **a mystery**. As previously stated, **a mystery** is a truth previously unknown, but now revealed by God to the apostles and made known through them to us.

We shall not all sleep, that is, not all believers will experience death. Some will be alive when the Lord returns. But whether we have died or are still alive, **we shall all be changed**. The truth of resurrection itself is not a mystery, since it appears in the OT, but the fact that not all will die and also the change of living saints at the Lord's Return is something that had never been known before.

15:52 The change will take place instantly, **in the twinkling of an eye, at the last trumpet. The last trumpet** here does not mean the end of the world, or even the last trumpet mentioned in Revelation. Rather, it refers to the **trumpet** of God which will sound when Christ comes into the air for His saints (1 Thess. 4:16). When the **trumpet** sounds, **the dead will be raised incorruptible, and we shall be changed**. What a tremendous moment that will be, when the earth and the sea will yield up the dust of all those who have died trusting in Christ down through the centuries! It is almost impossible for the human mind to take in the magnitude of such an event; yet the humble believer can accept it by faith.

15:53 We believe that verse 53 refers to the two classes of believers at the time of Christ's Return. **This corruptible** refers to those whose bodies have returned to the dust. They will **put on incorruption. This mortal**, on the other hand, refers to those who are still alive in body but are subject to death. Such bodies will **put on immortality.**

15:54 When the dead in Christ are raised and the living changed with them, **then shall be brought to pass the saying that is written, "Death is swallowed up in victory"** (Isa. 25:8). How magnificent!

C. H. Mackintosh exclaims:

> What are death, the grave, and decomposition in the presence of such power as this? Talk of being dead four days as a difficulty! Millions that have been mouldering in the dust for thousands of years shall spring up in a moment into life, immortality and eternal glory, at the voice of that blessed One.[56]

15:55 This verse may well be a taunt song which believers sing as they rise to meet the Lord in the air. It is as if they mock **Death** because for them it has lost its **sting**. They also mock **Hades** because for them *it* has lost the battle to keep them as its own. **Death** holds no terror for them because they know their sins have been forgiven and they stand before God in all the acceptability of His beloved Son.

15:56 **Death** would have no **sting** for anyone if it were not for **sin**. It is the consciousness of sins unconfessed and unforgiven that makes men afraid to die. If we know our sins are forgiven, we can face death with confidence. If, on the other hand, sin is on the conscience, death is terrible — the beginning of eternal punishment.

The strength of sin is the law, that is, **the law** condemns the sinner. It pronounces the doom of all who have failed to obey God's holy precepts. It has been well said that if there were no sin, there would be no death. And if there were no law, there would be no condemnation.

> The throne of death rests on two bases: sin, which calls for condemnation, and the law which pronounces it. Consequently, it is on these two powers that the work of the Deliverer bore.[57]

15:57 Through faith in Him, we have **victory** over death and the grave. Death is robbed of its sting. It is a known fact that when certain insects sting a person, they leave their stinger imbedded in the person's flesh, and being thus robbed of their "sting," they die. In a very real sense death stung itself to death at the cross of **our Lord Jesus Christ**, and now the King of Terrors is robbed of his terror as far as the believer is concerned.

C. Concluding Appeal in Light of the Resurrection (15:58)

In view, then, of the certainty of the resurrection and the fact that faith in Christ is not in vain, the Apostle Paul exhorts his **beloved brethren** to **be steadfast, immovable, always abounding in the work of the Lord, knowing that** their **labor is not in vain in the Lord**. The truth of resurrection changes everything. It provides hope and steadfastness, and enables us to go on in the face of overwhelming and difficult circumstances.

V. PAUL'S FINAL COUNSEL (Chap. 16)

A. Concerning the Collection (16:1–4)

16:1 The first verse of chapter 16 concerns a **collection** which was to be taken up by the church in Corinth and sent to needy **saints** in Jerusalem. The exact cause of their poverty is not known. Some have suggested that it was a result of famine (Acts 11:28–30). Possibly another reason is that those Jews who professed faith in Christ were ostracized and boycotted by their unbelieving relatives, friends, and fellow countrymen. They doubtlessly lost their jobs and in countless ways were subjected to economic pressures designed to force them to give up their profession of faith in Christ. Paul had already **given orders to the churches of Galatia** in connection with this very matter, and he now instructs the Corinthians to respond in the same manner that the Galatian saints had been exhorted to do.

16:2 Although the instructions given in verse 2 were for a specific collection, yet the principles involved are of abiding value. First of all, the laying by of funds was to be done **on the first day of the week**. Here we have a very strong indication that the early Christians no longer regarded the Sabbath or seventh day as an obligatory observance. The Lord had risen on the first day of the week, the Day of Pentecost was on the first day of the week, and the disciples gathered together on the first day of the week to break bread (Acts 20:7). Now they are to **lay something aside** for the saints **on the first day of the week**.

The second important principle is that the instructions concerning the collections were for **each one**. Rich and poor, slave and free, all were to have a part in the sacrifice of giving of their possessions.

Further, this was to be done systematically. **On the first day of the week** they were to **lay something aside, storing up**. It was not to be haphazard, or reserved for special occasions. The gift was to be set aside from other money and devoted to special use as occasion demanded. Their giving was also to be proportionate. This is indicated by the expression **as he may prosper**.

That there be no collections when I come. The Apostle Paul did not want this to be a matter of last-minute arrangement. He realized the serious possibility of giving without due preparation of heart or pocketbook.

16:3 Verses 3 and 4 give us very valuable insight into the care that should be taken with funds that are gathered in a Christian assembly. It is noticeable, first, that the funds were not to be entrusted to any one person. Even Paul himself was not to be the sole recipient. Secondly, we notice that the arrangements as to who would carry the money were not made arbitrarily by the Apostle Paul. Rather, this decision was left to the local assembly. When they selected the messengers, Paul would **send** them **to Jerusalem**.

16:4 If it was decided that it would be well for the apostle to **go** to Jerusalem **also**, then the local brethren would accompany him there. Notice that he says "they will go with me" rather than "I will go with them." Perhaps this is an allusion to Paul's authority as an apostle. Some commentators suggest that the factor that would determine whether or not Paul went would be the size of the gift, but we hardly believe that the great apostle would be guided by such a principle.

B. Concerning His Personal Plans (16:5–9)

16:5 Paul discusses his personal plans in verses 5–9. From Ephesus, where he wrote this letter, he planned to **pass through Macedonia**. Then he hoped to move south to Corinth.

16:6–8 Possibly Paul would **spend the winter with** the saints in Corinth and then they would speed him on his way, **wherever** he would **go** from there. For the present, then, he would not see them en route to Macedonia, but he did look forward to staying with them later for a while, **if the Lord** would so permit. Before leaving for Macedonia, Paul expected to **tarry in Ephesus until Pentecost**. It is from verse 8 that we learn that the Epistle was written from Ephesus.

16:9 Paul realized that there was a golden opportunity for serving Christ at that time at Ephesus. At the same time he realized that **there** were **many adversaries**. What an unchanging picture this verse gives us of Christian service: On the one hand, there are the fields white already to harvest; on the other, there is a sleepless foe who seeks to obstruct, divide, and oppose in every conceivable way!

C. Closing Exhortations and Greetings (16:10–24)

16:10 The apostle adds a word concerning **Timothy**. If this devoted young servant of the Lord came to Corinth, they should receive him **without fear**. Perhaps this means that Timothy was naturally of a timid disposition, and that they should not do anything to intensify this tendency. Perhaps, on the other hand, it means that he should be able to come to them **without** any **fear** of not being accepted as a servant of the Lord. That the latter is probably the proper meaning is indicated by Paul's words: **"For he does the work of the Lord, as I also do."**

16:11 Because of Timothy's faithful service for Christ, **no one** should **despise him**. Instead, an earnest effort should be made to **send him on his journey in peace, that he** might return to Paul in due time. The apostle was looking forward to a reunion with Timothy and **with the brethren**.

16:12 Now **concerning . . . brother Apollos,** Paul had **strongly urged him to** visit Corinth **with the brethren**. Apollos did not feel that this was God's will for him **at the time**, but he indicated that he would go to Corinth **when he** had the opportunity. Verse 12 is valuable to us in showing the loving spirit that prevailed among the servants of the Lord. Someone has called it a beautiful picture of "unjealous love and respect." It also shows the liberty that prevailed for each servant of the Lord to be guided by the Lord without dictation from any other source. Even the Apostle Paul himself was not authorized to tell Apollos what to do. In this connection Ironside commented: "I would not like to tear this chapter out of my Bible. It helps me to understand God's way of guiding His servants in their ministry for Him."[58]

16:13, 14 Now Paul delivers some pithy exhortations to the saints. They are to **watch** constantly, to **stand fast in the faith**, to **be brave** and to **be strong**. Perhaps Paul is thinking again of the danger of false teachers. The saints are to be on guard all the time. They are not to give up an inch of vital territory. They are to behave with true courage. Finally, they are to **be strong** in the Lord. In **all that** they **do**, they are to manifest **love**. This will mean lives of devotion to God and to others. It will mean a giving of themselves.

16:15 Next follows an exhortation concerning **the household of Stephanas**. These dear Christians were **the firstfruits of Achaia**, that is, the earliest converts in **Achaia**. Apparently from the time of their conversion, they had addicted **themselves to the ministry** (service) **of the saints**. They set themselves to serve the people of God. **The household of Stephanas** was mentioned previously in 1:16. There Paul states that he baptized that household. Many have insisted that **the household of Stephanas** included infants, and have sought thereby to justify the baptism of babies. However, it seems rather clear from this verse that there were no infants in this household, since it is distinctly stated that they **devoted themselves to the ministry of the saints.**

16:16 The apostle exhorts the Christians to **submit to such, and to everyone who** helps in the work **and labors**. We learn from the general teaching of the NT that those who set themselves apart for the service of Christ should be shown the loving respect of all the people of God. If this were done more generally, it would prevent a great deal of division and jealousy.

16:17 **The coming of Stephanas, Fortunatus, and Achaicus** had brought joy to Paul's heart. They **supplied what was lacking on the part** of the Corinthians. This may mean that they showed kindness to the apostle which the Corinthians had neglected to do. Or more probably it means that what the Corinthians were *unable* to do because of their distance from Paul, these men had accomplished.

16:18 They brought news from Corinth to Paul, and conversely they brought back news from the apostle to their home assembly. Again Paul commends them to the loving respect of the local church.

16:19 **The churches of Asia** refers to the congregations in the *province* of Asia (*Asia Minor* today), of which Ephesus was the capital. **Aquila and Priscilla** were apparently living in Ephesus at this time. At one time they had lived in Corinth, and thus were known to the saints there. **Aquila** was a tentmaker by trade, and had worked with Paul in this occupation. The expression **the church that is in their house** gives us a view of the simplicity of assembly life at that time. Christians would gather together in their homes for worship, prayer, and fellowship. Then they would go out to preach the gospel at their work, in the market place, in the local prison, and wherever their lot was cast.

16:20 **All the brethren** in the assembly join in sending their loving greetings to their fellow believers in Corinth. The apostle enjoins his readers to **greet one another with a holy kiss**. At that time, the **kiss** was a common mode of greeting, even among men. **A holy kiss** means a greeting without sham or impurity. In our sex-obsessed society, where perversion is so prevalent, the widespread use of the kiss as a mode of greeting might present serious temptations and lead to gross moral failures. For that reason, the handshake has largely taken the place of the kiss among Christians in English-speaking cultures. Ordinarily we should not allow cultural considerations to excuse us from strict adherence to the words of Scripture. But in a case like this, where literal obedience might lead to sin or even the appearance of evil because of local cultural conditions, we are probably justified in substituting the handshake for the kiss.

16:21 Paul's usual habit was to dictate his letters to one of his co-workers. However, at the end he would take pen in hand, add a few words in his own writing, and then give his characteristic **salutation**. That is what he does at this point.

16:22 Accursed translates the Greek word *anathema*. Those who do **not love the Lord Jesus** are condemned already, but their doom will be manifest at the coming of the Lord Jesus Christ. A Christian is one who loves the Savior. He loves the Lord Jesus more than anyone or anything in the world. Failure to love God's Son is a crime against God Himself. Ryle comments:

> St. Paul allows no way of escape to the man who does not love Christ. He leaves no loophole or excuse. A man may lack clear head-knowledge and yet be saved. He may fail in courage, and be overcome by the fear of man, like Peter. He may fall tremendously, like David, and yet rise again. But if a person does not love Christ he is not in the way of life. The curse is yet upon him. He is on the broad road that leadeth to destruction.[59]

O Lord, come! translates *maranatha*, an Aramaic expression used by the early Christians. If spaced "maran atha" it means "Our Lord has come," and if spaced "marana tha" it means Our **Lord, come!**

16:23 Grace was Paul's favorite theme. He loved to open and end his Letters on this exalted note. It is one of the true marks of his authorship.

16:24 Throughout the entire Epistle we have l tened to the heartbeat of this devoted apostle of Christ. We have listened to him as he sought to edify, comfort, exhort, and admonish his children in the faith. There was no doubt of his **love** for them. When they read these closing words, perhaps they would feel ashamed that they had allowed false teachers to come in, questioned Paul's apostleship, and turned away from their original love for him.

ENDNOTES

[1](1:18) Albert Barnes, *Notes on the New Testament, 1 Corinthians,* p.14.

[2](1:19) S. Lewis Johnson, "First Corinthians," *The Wycliffe Bible Commentary,* p. 1232.

[3](1:27) Erich Sauer, *The Dawn of World Redemption,* p. 91.

[4](1:30) Robert Traill, *The Works of Robert Traill, Vol. 2,* Edinburgh: Banner of Truth Trust, reprinted 1975, p. 234.

[5](1:30) Arthur T. Pierson, *The Ministry of Keswick, First Series,* p. 104.

[6](2:14) Vance Havner, further documentation unavailable.

[7](3:9) Charles R. Erdman, *The First Epistle of Paul to the Corinthians,* p. 40.

[8](3:15) E. W. Rogers, *Concerning the Future,* p. 77.

[9](3:18) Frédéric L. Godet, *Commentary on First Corinthians,* p. 195.

[10](4:8) H. P. Barker, *Coming Twice,* p. 80.

[11](5:2) Erdman, *First Corinthians,* p. 55.

[12](6:9) Some differentiate between "entering" the kingdom and "inheriting" the kingdom. They teach that a believer could conceivably not conquer a major sin in his life and yet be saved. He would "enter" the kingdom but have little or no inheritance (reward) in it. However, this passage deals with the unrighteous, i.e., the unregenerate.

[13](6:13) Erdman, *First Corinthians,* p. 63.

[14](6:17) A. T. Pierson, *Knowing the Scriptures,* p. 147.

[15](6:20) Edward Herbert Bates. *Spiritual Thoughts from the Scriptures of Truth,* p. 137.

[16](6:20) The NU text omits the reference to the spirit here.

[17](7:5) Larry Christenson, *The Christian Family,* p. 24.

[18](7:14) W. E. Vine, *First Corinthians,* p. 97.

[19](7:15) J. M. Davies, further documentation unavailable.

[20](7:17) W. E. Vine, *The Divine Plan of Missions,* p. 63.

[21](7:19) William Kelly, *Notes on the First Epistle to the Corinthians,* p. 123.

[22](7:29) Harry A. Ironside, *First Epistle to the Corinthians,* p. 223.

[23](7:29) Vine, *First Corinthians,* p. 104.

[24](7:33) *Ibid.,* p. 105.

²⁵(7:36) However, the standard Greek word for *virginity* is the abstract noun *parthenia*, and if Paul meant this, one wonders why he used the simple word for "virgin," as in Matthew 1:23.

²⁶(7:38) The "himself" has been supplied; it is not in the Greek.

²⁷(8:12) Barnes, *1 Corinthians*, p. 147.

²⁸(9:17) Charles C. Ryrie, *The Ryrie Study Bible, New King James Version*, p. 1771.

²⁹(9:20) The NU text adds the explanatory words here, "though not being myself under the law."

³⁰(9:20) William Arnot, *The Church in the House*, pp. 467, 468.

³¹(9:21) Charles C. Ryrie, *The Grace of God*, p. 83.

³²(9:22) NU omits "as," but it seems important to Paul's argument — he didn't *actually* become weak.

³³(9:27) Much of the problem stems from the KJV translation "castaway." The word *a-dokimos* simply means "not-approved." As an athletic term, it translates very well by our English "disqualified."

³⁴(10:5) Godet, *First Corinthians*, pp. 59, 60.

³⁵(10:22) Kelly, *First Corinthians*, p. 166.

³⁶(10:28) NU omits the repetition.

³⁷(11:5) It is clear from verses 4 and 5 that in situations involving prayer and prophesying, a woman should be *covered* whenever it is proper for a man to be *uncovered*. Women who have difficulty knowing what to do and when to do it should observe the man's example and do the opposite.

³⁸(11:7) Vine, *Expository Dictionary, under Glory, ,* p. 154.

³⁹(11:18) F. B. Hole, "The Administration of the Mystery" (booklet), p. 5.

⁴⁰(11:19) The Greek word is *haireseis*, but here it does not have the *later* meaning "heresies." See note on Titus 3:10.

⁴¹(11:19) Greek usually uses *opheilo* for *moral* necessity. Here Paul uses the regular word for *logical* necessity, *dei*.

⁴²(11:26) Godet, *First Corinthians*, p. 163.

⁴³(12:Intro) *Glossa* ("tongue") is the ordinary Greek word for "language." Similarly, formal English still occasionally says, e.g., "the French tongue."

⁴⁴(12:10) Much of what some people call "prophecy" today is either merely a re-wording of Bible texts or actual error that does not come true. Both are often in a poor imitation of King James English, as though God could not communicate in today's language!

⁴⁵(12:13) The Greek word *en* can be translated *in, with* or *by* with equal accuracy (context permitting), but we consider "in" the most "literal" because it is related to Greek *en*.

⁴⁶(12:29, 30) These questions start with *me* in Greek, suggesting a paraphrase such as, "Surely, all don't speak in tongues?" — and so forth.

⁴⁷(13:11) The word is *nepios* (cf. Heb. 5:13).

⁴⁸(14:5) Kelly, *First Corinthians*, p. 229.

⁴⁹(14:13) However, there is no indication in the original that the subject of "may interpret" is different from that of "speaks."

⁵⁰(14:19) The literal rendering is "understanding of me." The "of me" is in the genitive and is the *object* of the action suggested by the noun. The same *form* can be a *subjective* genitive. The context determines which is best.

⁵¹(14:19) Charles Hodge, *First Corinthians*, p. 292.

⁵²(14:35) The same Greek word *andres* can mean "husbands," "males" or "men-(folks)."

⁵³(15:45) Erdman, *First Corinthians*, p. 148.

⁵⁴(15:47) NU text omits "the Lord."

⁵⁵(15:49) The majority of Greek mss. have an exhortation here: "Let us bear . . . ."

⁵⁶(15:54) C. H. Mackintosh, *The Mackintosh Treasury: Miscellaneous Writings by C. H. Mackintosh*, p. 125.

⁵⁷(15:56) Godet, *First Corinthians*, p. 446.

⁵⁸(16:12) Ironside, *First Corinthians*, p. 542.

⁵⁹(16:22) J. C. Ryle, *Holiness*, p. 235.

BIBLIOGRAPHY

Barnes, Albert. *Notes on the New Testament.* (Vol. V, 1 Corinthians). London: Blackie & Son, n.d.

Bates, Edward Herbert. *Spiritual Thoughts from the Scriptures of Truth.* London: Pickering & Inglis, n.d.

Davies, J. M. *The Epistles to the Corinthians*. Bombay: Gospel Literature Service, 1975.

Erdman, Charles R. *The First Epistle of Paul to the Corinthians*. Philadelphia: Westminster Press, 1928.

Godet, F. L. *The First Epistle to the Corinthians*. Grand Rapids: Zondervan Publishing House, 1971.

Grant, F. W. "1 Corinthians," *The Numerical Bible*. Vol. 6, Acts to 2 Corinthians. New York: Loizeaux Bros., 1901.

Hodge, Charles. *An Exposition on the First Epistle to the Corinthians*. New York: George H. Doran Company, 1857.

Ironside, H. A. *Addresses on the First Epistle to the Corinthians*. New York: Loizeaux Brothers, 1955.

Johnson, S. Lewis. "First Corinthians," in *The Wycliffe Bible Commentary*. Chicago: Moody Press, 1962.

Kelly, William. *Notes on the First Epistle to the Corinthians*. London: G. Morrish, 1878.

Luck, G. Coleman. *First Corinthians*. Chicago: Moody Press, 1958.

Morgan, G. Campbell. *The Corinthian Letters of Paul: An Exposition of I and II Corinthians*. New York: Fleming H. Revell Company, 1946.

Morris, Leon. *The First Epistle of Paul to the Corinthians*. Grand Rapids: Wm. B. Eerdmans Publishing Company, 1966.

Robertson, Archibald and Alfred Plummer. *A Critical and Exegetical Commentary on the First Epistle of St. Paul to the Corinthians*. Edinburgh: T. & T. Clark, 1911.

Vine, W. E. *First Corinthians*. London: Oliphants Ltd., 1951.

THE SECOND EPISTLE TO THE CORINTHIANS

Introduction

"The transparency of the revelation of Paul [in 2 Corinthians] is to me unequaled in all sacred literature." — Sadler

I. Unique Place in the Canon

If 1 Corinthians is very widely studied and preached from, 2 Corinthians is widely neglected by preachers. Yet this is a very *important* Epistle. No doubt its difficult-to-translate and ironic style have helped to cause this neglect. The large number of italicized words in the KJV and NKJV shows how much must be supplied to make this emotional Letter acceptable English.

The Epistle is *difficult*. The meaning of many verses is obscure, to say the least. There are several explanations for this: (1) Paul uses a great deal of satire, but it is sometimes difficult to be sure just *when* he is doing so. (2) To fully understand some sections, we would have to have further information as to Paul's exact travels, the travels of his companions, and the letters he wrote. (3) The Epistle is intensely personal, and the words are often the language of the heart. These are not always the easiest to understand.

But the difficulties should not discourage us. Fortunately, they do not affect the basic truths of the Epistle, but only the details.

Finally, 2 Corinthians is a *much-loved* and *much-quoted* Epistle. After studying it, you will better understand why.

II. Authorship[†]

That Paul wrote 2 Corinthians is denied by virtually no one, though some

[†]See p. i.

have theories of "interpolations" here and there. However, the unity of the Letter (with typical Pauline digressions!) is apparent.

The *external evidence* for 2 Corinthians is strong, but a bit later than for 1 Corinthians. Surprisingly, Clement of Rome does not quote from it, but Polycarp, Irenaeus, Clement of Alexandria, Tertullian, and Cyprian all do. Marcion lists it as the third of the ten Pauline Epistles he accepts. It is also listed in the Muratorian Canon. From A.D. 175 on, the evidence for 2 Corinthians is abundant.

The *internal evidence* for Pauline authorship is overwhelming. Except for Philemon, it is Paul's most personal and least doctrinal Letter. The minute personal references, idiosyncrasies of the apostle, and the obviously close ties with 1 Corinthians, Galatians, Romans, and Acts all support the traditional view that Paul wrote the Letter. The same writer and same congregation as in the universally recognized First Epistle are clearly in evidence.

III. Date

Second Corinthians was probably written less than a year after 1 Corinthians, from Macedonia (some subscriptions to early translations spec.fy Philippi). A date of A.D. 57 is commonly received, but many choose 55 or 56, and Harnack opted for 53.

IV. Background and Theme[†]

One reason we love 2 Corinthians so greatly is because it *is* so personal. We seem to get closer to the heart of Paul here than in any of his other writings. We feel something of the tremendous enthusiasm he had for the work of the Lord. We catch a sense of the dignity of life's greatest calling. We read with silent amazement the catalog of sufferings which he endured. We experience the hot flush of indignation with which he answered his unscrupulous critics. In short, Paul seems to let us into every secret of his soul.

Paul's first visit to Corinth is recorded in Acts 18. It took place on his Second Missionary Journey, just after he had delivered his memorable Mars Hill address in Athens.

In Corinth, Paul worked as a tentmaker with Aquila and Priscilla, and preached the gospel in the synagogue. Silas and Timothy came from Macedonia to join him in this evangelistic work, which lasted at least eighteen months (Acts 18:11).

When most Jews rejected his preaching, Paul turned to the Gentiles. As souls were saved — both Jews and Gentiles — the Jewish leaders brought the apostle before the proconsul, Gallio. But the latter threw the case out of court as one over which he did not have jurisdiction.

After the trial, Paul stayed in Corinth many days, and then left for Cenchrea, Ephesus, and the long trip back to Caesarea and Antioch.

On his Third Missionary Journey, he

†*See p. ii.*

returned to Ephesus and stayed there for two years. During this stay, a delegation from Corinth visited him, asking Paul's advice on many matters. It was in answer to these queries that 1 Corinthians was written.

The apostle later became very anxious to find out how the Corinthians had reacted to his Letter, especially to the section concerning the discipline of a sinning member. So he left Ephesus for Troas where he hoped to meet Titus. However, failing to do so, he crossed over into Macedonia. It was here that Titus came with news, both good and bad. The saints had disciplined the sinning saint — and this discipline had resulted in his spiritual recovery. That was *the good news*. But the Christians had never sent the money to the needy saints at Jerusalem, as they had intended to do. That was not so good. Finally, Titus reported that the false teachers were active at Corinth, undermining the apostle's work and questioning his authority as a servant of Christ. This was *the bad news*!

These then are the circumstances that called forth the Second Epistle to the Corinthians, written from Macedonia.

In the First Epistle, Paul is seen primarily as a teacher, but in the Second he occupies the role of a pastor. If you listen carefully, you will hear the heartbeat of one who really loved the people of God and gave himself for their welfare.

So let us now embark on this grand adventure, and as we study these "thoughts that breathe and words that burn," let us do so with a prayer for the illumination of God's Holy Spirit.

OUTLINE

Commentary

I. PAUL'S EXPOSITION OF THE MINISTRY (Chaps. 1–7)

A. Salutation (1:1, 2)

1:1 **Paul** introduces himself at the outset of his letter as **an apostle of Jesus Christ by the will of God**. It is important that he should strike this note at the very beginning, because there were those in Corinth who raised the question as to whether Paul had ever really been commissioned by the Lord. His answer is that he did not choose the ministry by his own will, neither was he ordained by men, but he had been sent into the work by Christ Jesus through **the will of God**. His call to the apostleship took place on the road to Damascus. It was an unforgettable experience in his life, and it was the consciousness of this divine call that sustained the apostle during many bitter hours. Oftentimes when, in the service

of Christ, he was pressed beyond measure, he might well have given up and gone home if he had not had the assurance of a divine call.

The fact that **Timothy** is mentioned in verse 1 does not mean that he helped to compose the Letter. It only signifies that he was with Paul at the time the Epistle was written. Beyond this fact, there is a great deal of uncertainty about Timothy's movements during this period.

The letter is addressed **to the church of God which is at Corinth, with all the saints who are in all Achaia**. The expression **church of God** means that it was an assembly of believers belonging to **God**. It was not a heathen assembly, or some nonreligious gathering of people, but a company of born-again Christians, called out from the world to belong to the Lord. Doubtless as Paul wrote these words, he remembered how he had first gone to Corinth and preached the gospel there. Men and women steeped in idolatry and sensuality had trusted Jesus Christ as Lord, and had been saved by His marvelous grace. In spite of all the difficulties that had later come into the assembly at Corinth, the heart of the apostle doubtless rejoiced to think of the mighty change which had come into the lives of these dear people. The letter is addressed not only to Corinth but to **all the saints who are in Achaia**. **Achaia** represented the southern part of Greece; whereas Macedonia, of which we shall also be reading in this Epistle, was the northern section of that same country.

1:2 **Grace . . . and peace** form the lovely salutation that we have come to associate with the beloved Apostle Paul. When he wishes to describe his greatest desires for the people of God, he does not wish for them material things such as silver and gold. He knows only too well that these can quickly vanish. But rather he wishes for them spiritual blessings, such as **grace** and **peace**, which include every good thing that can come to a poor sinner on this side of heaven. Denney says, "Grace is the first and last word of the gospel; and peace — perfect spiritual soundness — is the finished work of Christ in the soul."[1] These blessings flow **from God our Father and the Lord Jesus Christ. God our Father** is the source, and **the Lord Jesus Christ** is the channel. Paul does not hesitate to place **the Lord Jesus Christ** side by side with **God** the **Father**, because, as a member of the Trinity, **Christ** is equal with the **Father**.

B. The Ministry of Comfort in Suffering (1:3–11)

1:3 From verse 3 through verse 11, the apostle bursts forth into thanksgiving for the **comfort** that has come to him in the midst of his distress and affliction. Undoubtedly, the **comfort** was the good news which Titus had brought to him in Macedonia. The apostle then goes on to show that whether he is afflicted or comforted, all turns out for the eventual good of the believers to whom he ministers. The thanksgiving is addressed to **the God and Father of our Lord Jesus Christ**. This is the full title of **God** in the

NT. No longer is He addressed as the God of Abraham, the God of Isaac, or the God of Jacob. Now He is **the God and Father of the Lord Jesus Christ**. This name, incidentally, implies the great truth that the Lord Jesus is both God and Man. God is the *God* of our Lord Jesus Christ; this refers to His relation to **Jesus**, the Son of Man. But God is also the *Father* **of our Lord Jesus Christ**; this refers to His relationship to Christ, the Son of God. In addition, God is described as **the Father of mercies and the God of all comfort**. It is from Him that all **mercies** and comforts flow.

1:4 In all Paul's afflictions, he was conscious of God's comforting presence. Here he gives one of the many reasons why God comforted him. It was so that he in turn might **be able to comfort** others **with the** very same **comfort with which** he was **comforted by God**. To us, the word "comfort" usually means consolation in time of sorrow. But as it is used in the NT, it has a wider meaning. It refers to the encouragement and exhortation that come to us from one who is beside us in time of need. There is a practical lesson in this verse for us all. We should remember when we are comforted that we should seek to pass on this comfort to others. We should not avoid the sick room or the house of death, but rather fly to the side of any who are in need of our encouragement. We are not comforted to be *comfortable* but to be *comforters*.

1:5 The reason Paul can comfort others is that the comforts **of Christ** are equal to the sufferings that are endured for Him. **The sufferings of Christ** here cannot mean the Savior's atoning sufferings. These were unique, and no man can share them. But Christians can and do suffer because of their association with the Lord Jesus. They suffer reproach, rejection, hostility, hatred, denial, betrayal, etc. These are spoken of as **the sufferings of Christ** because He endured them when He was on earth, and because He still endures them when the members of His Body experience them. In all our afflictions, He is afflicted (see Isa. 63:9). But Paul's point here is that there is a rich compensation for all these sufferings, namely, there is a corresponding share in the **consolation** of

Christ and this **consolation** is abundantly sufficient.

1:6 The apostle could see good emerging both from his afflictions and his comfort. Both were sanctified by the cross. **If he was afflicted, it** resulted in **consolation and salvation** for the saints — not the salvation of their souls, but the strength that would see them through their trials. They would be encouraged and challenged by Paul's endurance, and would reason that if God could give him grace **to suffer**, He could give them grace too. When Samuel Rutherford found himself in "the cellar of adversity," as he often did, he began to look around for some of the Lord's "best wines." Perhaps he learned to do this from the example of Paul, who always seemed to be able to trace the rainbow through his tears.

The comfort which the apostle received would fill the Corinthians with **consolation** and inspire them to patient endurance as they passed through the same kind of persecution as he did. Only those who have gone through deep testings know how to speak a fitting word to others who are called upon to go through the same. A mother who has lost an only child can better comfort another mother who has just been crushed by that heartache. Or, best of all, a Father who has lost an only Son can best console those who have lost loved ones.

1:7 The apostle now expresses his confidence that just as the Corinthians had known what it was to suffer on behalf of Christ, so they would experience the comforting help of Christ. **Sufferings** never come alone for the Christian. They are always followed by the **consolation** of Christ. We, too, can be confident of this, as Paul was.

The Living Bible paraphrases verses 3–7 as follows:

What a wonderful God we have — He is the Father of our Lord Jesus Christ, the source of every mercy, and the one who so wonderfully comforts and strengthens us in our hardships and trials. And why does He do this? So that when others are troubled, needing our sympathy and encouragement, we can pass on to them the same help and comfort God has given us. . . . In our trouble God has comforted us — and this, too, to help you: to show

you from our personal experience how God will tenderly comfort you when you undergo these same sufferings. He will give you the strength to endure.

1:8 Having spoken in general terms of affliction and comfort, Paul now mentions more specifically a severe testing through which he had recently gone. He does not want the Corinthian **brethren to be ignorant** of the **trouble which** befell him **in Asia**. (**Asia** here does not mean the continent, but rather a province in the western section of what is now Asia Minor.) Just what was the **trouble** to which the apostle refers here? Perhaps it refers to the dangerous riot which took place in Ephesus (Acts 19:23–41). Some suggest that it was a deadly sickness, and still others think that it might refer to disheartening news from Corinth. Fortunately, the value and enjoyment of such a passage does not depend on knowing the exact details.

The trouble was, however, so serious that Paul was weighed down greatly, so **beyond** the ordinary natural powers of endurance that he **despaired even of life** itself.

Phillip's paraphrase of this verse is helpful: "At that time we were completely overwhelmed; the burden was more than we could bear; in fact we told ourselves that this was the end."

1:9 The apostle's outlook was so grim that he had the feelings of a man sentenced to **death**. If someone had asked him, "Is it going to be life or death?" he would have had to answer, "Death." God allowed His servant to be brought to this place of extremity in order **that** he would **not trust in** himself **but in** the **God who raises the dead**. The **God who raises the dead** is here used doubtlessly as a synonym for the omnipotent God. One who can raise the dead is the only hope of a man who is doomed to die, as the apostle considered himself to be.

1:10 In the King James tradition (and the majority of manuscripts) Paul is speaking of deliverance in its three tenses: past (**delivered**), present (**does deliver**), and future (**will . . . deliver**).[2] If the riot in Ephesus is in view, then Paul refers to the way in which it stopped suddenly and he escaped (Acts 20:1).

The apostle knows that the same God who **delivered** him in the past is able to **deliver** him day by day, and **will** continue to **deliver** him until that final, grand moment when he will be completely released from the tribulations and persecutions of this world.

1:11 Here Paul generously assumes that the Corinthian Christians had been praying for him while he was going through this time of deep testing. Actually, many of the believers had become critical of the great apostle, and there could have been a serious question whether they were remembering him before the throne of grace at all. However, he is willing to give them the benefit of the doubt. The expression **the gift granted to us through many** refers to **the gift** of Paul's deliverance which was brought about through the prayers of **many persons**. He sees his escape as a direct result of the intercession of the saints. He says that because many had prayed, **many persons** can now give **thanks** because their prayers were answered.

C. Explanation of Paul's Change of Plans (1:12–2:17)

1:12 The reason Paul feels he can depend on the prayers of the believers is that he has always been straightforward in his dealings with them. He can boast of his integrity toward them, and his conscience bears witness to the fact that his conduct was characterized by **simplicity and godly sincerity**, that is, the transparent genuineness that comes from God. He did not stoop to the methods of **fleshly** men, **but** acted openly before all with the undeserved strength (**grace**) which **God** supplied. This should have been apparent in a special way to the Corinthians.

1:13 The integrity which characterized his past dealings with the Corinthians is true also of this letter. He is **writing** exactly what he means. There is no need for them to read between the lines. The meaning is on the surface, simple and obvious. It is exactly **what** they **read or understand**, and he hopes that they will continue to acknowledge it **even to the end**, that is, as long as they live.

1:14 The assembly in Corinth had acknowledged Paul **in part**, that is, some

of the believers had acknowledged him but not all. The loyal ones understood these two facts — that they would be proud of him and that he would be proud of them **in the day of the Lord Jesus. The day of the Lord Jesus** looks forward particularly to the Judgment Seat of Christ when the service of the redeemed will be evaluated and rewarded. When Paul looked forward to that tribunal, he invariably saw the faces of those who had been saved through his ministry. They would be his joy and crown of rejoicing, and they, in turn, would rejoice that he had been God's instrument to lead them to Christ.

1:15 The expression **in this confidence** means with the **confidence** that they rejoiced in him as a true apostle of Jesus Christ, and as one whose sincerity was above question. He wanted **to come to** them with the assurance of their trust, esteem, and affection. He **intended to come** first to them **before** he went into Macedonia, and then again on the return from Macedonia. They would thus have had a **second benefit** in the sense of two visits rather than one.

1:16 The "second benefit" is further explained by verse 16. As mentioned, the plan was that when Paul left Ephesus he would cross over into Achaia, where Corinth was located, and then travel north into **Macedonia**. After having preached there, he would retrace his steps south to Corinth. He hoped that the Corinthian believers would then help him **on** his **way to Judea** —probably by their hospitality and prayers, but not by their money, since he later states his determination not to accept funds from them (11:7–10).

1:17 Paul's original plan never came to pass. He journeyed from Ephesus to Troas, and when he did not find Titus, he went directly to Macedonia, omitting Corinth from his itinerary. So here he asks, **"Therefore when I was planning this, did I do it lightly?"** This is probably exactly what his detractors were saying. "Fickle, changeable Paul! He says one thing and does another! Could such a man be a true apostle?" The apostle challenges the Corinthians as to whether he is undependable. When he plans, does he **plan according to** fleshly motives with the result that it is **Yes** one minute and **No** the next? Is he guided simply by considerations of comfort and expediency? Phillips catches the spirit of this verse in his paraphrase: "Because we had to change this plan, does it mean that we are fickle? Do you think I plan with my tongue in my cheek, saying 'Yes' and meaning 'No'?"

1:18 Paul seems to pass from his **word** concerning his travel plans to his preaching. Perhaps his critics were saying that if he was undependable in his ordinary conversation, then his preaching could not be trusted.

1:19 Paul argues that his actions were not untrustworthy because the Savior he preached was the divine, unchangeable One in whom there was no vacillation or changeableness. When he first visited Corinth with **Silvanus and Timothy** (Acts 18:5), they had preached the trustworthy **Son of God**. "The message was not unstable because it concerned **the Son of God** who was not vacillating." The argument is that no one who preaches the Lord Jesus in the Spirit could possibly act the way his critics had accused him. Denney says, "Paul's argument here could have been used by a hypocrite, but no critic could ever have invented it." How could he preach a faithful God and himself be unfaithful to his own word?

1:20 **All the promises of God**, no matter how many they are, find their fulfillment *in Christ*. All who find **in Him** the fulfillment of God's promises add their **Amen**:

> We open our Bibles at a promise, we look up to God, and God says, "You can have all that through Christ." Trusting Christ, we say, "Amen" to God. God speaks through Christ, and we believe in Christ; Christ reaches down and faith stretches up, and every promise of God is fulfilled in Jesus Christ. In and through Him we appropriate and take them to ourselves and say, "Yes, Lord; I trust You." This is the believing yes.[3]

All of this is **to the glory of God through us**. Denney writes: "He is glorified when it dawns on human souls that He has spoken good concerning them beyond their utmost imaginings, and when that good is seen to be indubitably safe and sure in His Son."

The two words **through us**, remind

the Corinthians that it was **through** the preaching of men like Silvanus, Timothy, and Paul that they had ever come to claim the promises of God in Christ. If the apostle was a fraud, as his enemies charged, then could it be that God had used a cheat and a liar to effect such marvelous results? The answer, of course, is no.

1:21 Paul next shows that the Corinthians and he were all bound in the same bundle of life. **God** had established them in the faith, confirming them **in Christ** by the ministry of the word of God. He had also **anointed** them with **the Spirit**, qualifying, empowering, and teaching them.

1:22 He **also** had **sealed** them and **given** them **the Spirit in** their **hearts as a guarantee**. Here we have two more ministries of the Holy Spirit. The seal is the mark of ownership and security. **The Spirit** indwelling the believer is the mark that the believer now belongs to God and that he is eternally secure. The seal, of course, is invisible. People do not know that we are Christians by some badge we wear, but only by the evidences of a Spirit-filled life. God has also **given** them **the Spirit in** their **hearts as a guarantee** or downpayment in pledge that the entire inheritance will follow. When God saves a man, He gives him the indwelling Holy **Spirit**. Just as surely as a man receives **the Spirit**, so surely will he enter into the full inheritance of God. The same kind of blessings which the Holy Spirit makes real in our lives today will be ours in full measure in a day yet future.

1:23 From verse 23 through verse 4 of chapter 2, Paul returns to the charge of vacillation that had been made against him and gives a straightforward explanation of why he did not visit Corinth as planned. Since no man could discern the real inward motives of Paul's action, he calls **God** to **witness** to this fact. If the apostle had visited **Corinth** at the time planned, he would have had to deal very firmly with the situation there. He would have had to deliver a personal rebuke to the saints because of their carelessness in tolerating sin in the assembly. It was **to spare** them pain and sadness that Paul delayed his trip **to Corinth**.

1:24 But having said that, the Apostle Paul would not want anyone to think that he was acting as a dictator over the Corinthians. And so he adds here, **"Not that we have dominion over your faith, but are fellow workers for your joy; for by faith you stand."** It was not that the apostle wanted to lord it **over** their Christian **faith**. He did not want them to think of him as a tyrant. Rather, he and his co-workers were merely helpers of their **joy**, that is, he only wanted to do what would assist them in their Christian pathway and thus add to their enjoyment.

The latter part of verse 24 may also be rendered "for *in* faith you stand *fast*." That is, there was no need for them to be corrected as to their faith, for in that sphere they stood firm enough. The matters he sought to correct were not matters of doctrine as much as of practical behavior in the church.

2:1 This verse continues the thought from the last two verses of chapter 1. Paul further explains that the reason he did not go to Corinth as planned was that he did not want to cause them the **sorrow** that would inevitably follow a rebuke from him. The words **I determined . . . I would not come again to you in sorrow** seems to imply that he had made a sorrowful or painful visit subsequent to the first visit recorded in Acts 18:1–17. Such an interim visit may also be implied in 2 Corinthians 12:14; 13:1.

2:2 If the apostle came to Corinth with a personal rebuke to the Christians, he would of course sadden them. In that case, he too would be saddened because they were the very people to whom he was looking for joy. As Ryrie puts it, "If I hurt you, who will be left to make me glad but sad people? That wouldn't be any comfort."

2:3 Rather than cause this mutual **sorrow** through a personal visit, the Apostle Paul decided to write a letter. His hope was that the Letter would accomplish the desired result, that the Corinthians would exercise discipline in connection with the offending brother, and that Paul's next visit would not be clouded by strained relations between this people he so dearly loved and himself.

Does the letter referred to in the first part of verse 3 refer to the First Epistle of Paul to the Corinthians, or to some other letter which no longer exists today? Many believe that it could not be 1 Corinthians because of the description in verse 4, that it was written out of much affliction and anguish of heart, and with many tears. Other scholars feel that the description here fits the First Epistle very well. It is possible that Paul wrote a stern letter to Corinth that is no longer available. Presumably he wrote it after the sorrowful visit (2 Cor. 2:1) and appointed Titus to deliver it. Such a letter may be referred to in 2:4, 9; 7:8, 12.

Whichever view is correct, the thought in verse 3 is that Paul **wrote** them as he did so that when he visited them, he would not **have sorrow over** the sadness of those who should give him **joy**. He had confidence that the same things that brought **joy** to him would bring **joy** to them also. In the context, this means that the godly handling of the discipline problem would result in mutual rejoicing.

2:4 In this verse we have keen insight into the heart of a great pastor. Paul was deeply pained by the fact that sin had been tolerated in the assembly at Corinth. It caused him **much affliction and anguish of heart**, and hot **tears** of sorrow flowed down his cheeks. It is obvious that the apostle was more affected by sin in Corinth than the Corinthians themselves were. They should not interpret this letter as an attempt to hurt their feelings, but rather as a proof of his **love** for them. He hoped that, by his writing, they would have sufficient time to remedy the situation, so that his subsequent visit to them would be a joyful one. "Faithful are the wounds of a friend." We should not resent it if we are counseled or warned in a godly manner. Rather, we should realize that any person who would do this really has an interest in us. Righteous rebuke should be taken as from the Lord, and we should be grateful for it.

2:5 From verse 5 through verse 11, the apostle refers more directly to the incident that had caused the difficulty. Notice the extreme grace and Christian consideration which he shows. Not once does he name the offense or the offender. The expression **"if anyone has

caused grief" may refer to the incestuous man of 1 Corinthians 5:1, or to someone else who had caused trouble in the assembly. We will assume that it refers to the former. Paul did not regard it as a personal offence against himself. It had caused **grief** to **all** the believers **to some extent**.

2:6 The believers at Corinth had agreed on disciplinary action for the offender. Apparently they had excommunicated him from the church. As a result of this action, he had become truly repentant and had been restored to the Lord. Now Paul tells the Corinthians that the man's **punishment** has been **sufficient**. They should not needlessly prolong it. In the latter part of the verse, we find the expression **which was inflicted by** "the many" (lit.). Some believe that "the many" means **the majority**. Others insist that it means *all* the members *except* the one disciplined. The latter deny that a **majority** decision is sufficient in church matters. They say that where the Spirit of God is allowed to lead, there should be unanimous action.

2:7, 8 Now that the man has become thoroughly repentant, the Corinthians should **forgive and** seek to strengthen **him** by receiving him back into their fellowship. If they do not do this, there is the danger that he might be **swallowed up with too much sorrow**, that is, he might despair of the reality of his forgiveness and go on in constant gloom and discouragement.

The Corinthians could **reaffirm** their **love to him** by opening wide their arms and receiving him back with joy and tenderness.

2:9 In writing the First Epistle to the Corinthians, Paul had **put** the saints **to the test**. Here was an opportunity for them to show whether they were **obedient** to the word of the Lord, as ministered to them by the Apostle Paul. He had suggested at that time that they should put the man out of the fellowship of the church. That is exactly what they did, thus proving themselves to be truly **obedient**. Now Paul would have them go one step further, that is, to receive the man back.

2:10 Phillips paraphrases verse 10, "If you will forgive a certain person, rest assured that I forgive him too. Insofar as I had anything personally to forgive, I do forgive him, as before Christ." Paul wants the saints to know that he is thoroughly in fellowship with them as they forgive the repentant offender. If he had had **anything** to forgive, he does **forgive** it for the sake of the Corinthians, and as **in the presence of Christ**.

The emphasis in this letter on church discipline is an index of its importance. Yet it is a subject that is all but neglected in many evangelical churches today. It is another instance where we can profess to believe in the inspiration of the Scriptures, yet refuse to obey them when it suits our purposes.

2:11 Just as there is danger for an assembly if it does not take disciplinary action when called for, so there is a danger of not exercising forgiveness when true repentance has taken place. **Satan** is always ready to step into a situation such as this with his cunning devices. In the first case, he will wreck the testimony of an assembly through tolerated sin, and in the second, he will overwhelm the repentant person with overmuch sorrow, if the assembly does not restore him. If Satan can't destroy by immorality, he will try by the unmeasured sorrow following repentance.

Commenting on the expression **"we are not ignorant of his devices"**, J. Sidlow Baxter says:

> Satan uses all manner of stratagems to turn souls from the truth: a sieve to "sift" them (Luke 22:31), "devices" to trick (as in our text), "weeds" to "choke" (Matt. 13:22), "wiles" to intrigue (Eph. 6:11), the roaring of a lion to terrify (1 Pet. 5:8), the disguise of an angel to deceive (2 Cor. 11:14) and "snares" to entangle them (2 Tim. 2:26).[4]

2:12 Paul now resumes the subject of his change in plans where he left off in verse 4. He had not gone to Corinth as he previously announced he would. The previous verses explained that his failure to visit Corinth was to avoid doing so in a harsh spirit of rebuke. In verses 12 through 17, Paul tells exactly what did happen to him at this important point in his ministry. As mentioned before, Paul left Ephesus and journeyed **to Troas** in hopes of meeting Titus there and receiving news from Corinth. When he got to Troas, some wonderful **door** of opportunity **opened** out before him **by the Lord** for preaching **Christ's gospel.**

2:13 In spite of this golden opportunity, Paul's **spirit** was troubled. **Titus** was not there to meet him. The burden of the Corinthian church lay heavily on the apostle's heart. Should he stay in Troas and preach the gospel of Christ? Or should he press on into Macedonia? His decision was made; he would cross over into **Macedonia**. One wonders what the reaction of the Corinthians was when they read these words. Did they realize, perhaps with a trifle of shame, that it was *their* behavior which caused such restlessness in the life of the apostle, and which resulted in his having to refuse a wonderful gospel opportunity in order to learn of their spiritual welfare?

2:14 Paul was not defeated. No matter where he went in the service of Christ there was victory. And so he bursts out in thanksgiving: **But thanks be to God who always leads us in triumph in Christ**. A.T. Robertson says:

> Without a word of explanation, Paul leaps out of the Slough of Despond and sprints like a bird to the heights of joy. He soars aloft like an eagle, with proud scorn of the valley beneath him.[5]

Paul here borrows a figure from the triumphal processions of Roman conquerors. Returning home after glorious victories, they would lead their captives along the streets of the capital. Incense bearers would march along both sides, and the **fragrance** of the incense would permeate the scene. So Paul pictures the Lord marching as a conqueror from Troas to Macedonia, and leading the apostle in His train. Wherever the Lord goes, through His servants, there is victory. **The fragrance of** the **knowledge** of Christ is diffused through the apostle in every place. F. B. Meyer writes:

> Wherever they went men knew Jesus better; the loveliness of the Master's character became more apparent. Men became aware of a subtle fragrance, poured upon the air, which attracted them to the Man of Nazareth.[6]

Thus Paul does not feel that he has suffered a defeat in his warfare with Satan, but the Lord has won a victory and Paul shares it.

2:15 In the triumphal processions to which Paul refers, the fragrance of the incense meant glorious victory to the conquerors, but it spoke of doom for the captives. Thus the apostle notes that the preaching of the gospel has a twofold effect. It signifies one thing **among those who are being saved**, and something altogether different **among those who are perishing**. To those who accept it, it is a pledge of a glorious future; to others it is an omen of doom. But **God** is glorified in either case, for to Him it is **the fragrance** of grace in the one case and of justice in the other. F. B. Meyer states it well:

> When, therefore, we are told that we may be to God a sweet savour of Christ, it must be meant that we may so live as to recall to the mind of God what Jesus was in His mortal career. It is as though, as God watches us from day to day, He should see Jesus in us, and be reminded (speaking after the manner of men) of that blessed life which was offered as an offering and a sacrifice to God for a sweet smelling savour.[7]

2:16 To the saved, Christians **are the aroma of life leading to life**, but to the perishing, **the aroma of death leading to death**. We are what Phillips calls "the refreshing fragrance of life itself," bringing life to those who believe, but the "deathly smell of doom" to those who refuse to believe. This twofold effect is beautifully illustrated in an incident in the OT. When the ark of God was captured by the Philistines, it caused death and destruction as long as it was among them (1 Sam. 5). But when it was brought back to the house of Obed-Edom, it brought blessing and prosperity for him and for his household (2 Sam. 6:11). As Paul contemplates the tremendous responsibility of preaching the message that has such far-reaching consequences, he cries out, **"And who is sufficient for these things?"**

2:17 The connection between verse 17 and verse 16 is better seen if we supply the words "We are." "Who is sufficient for these things? We are, because we **are not . . . peddling the word of God"**, etc. (But this still must be understood in conjunction with 3:5 where Paul says that his sufficiency is from God.) The **so many**[8] refers to the Judaizing teachers who sought to turn the Corinthians away from the apostle. What were these men like? Paul says they peddled, huckstered, or made merchandise of **the word of God**. They had mercenary motives. They tried to turn the ministry into a profitable profession. This same word for **peddling** was also used of those who adulterated wine, often by adding to it. And so these false teachers sought to adulterate the word of God by adding their own doctrines to it. They sought, for instance, to mix law and grace.

Paul was not one of those who adulterated or merchandised the word of God. Rather, he could describe his ministry by four significant expressions. The *first* is **as of sincerity**. This means "as of transparency." His ministry was an honest one. There was no trickery or subterfuge in connection with it. Everything was out in the open. Robertson humorously explains the meaning of this expression: "Paul's berries were as good at the bottom as at the top."[9]

Secondly, he describes his service **as from God**. In other words, everything he spoke was **from God**. God was the source of his message, and it was **from God** he derived the strength to carry on. *Then* he adds **in the sight of God**. This means that the apostle served the Lord, conscious of the fact that **God** was always looking down upon him. He had a real sense of responsibility to God and realized that nothing could be hidden from the eye of God. *Then finally* he adds, **we speak . . . in Christ**. This means that he spoke in the name of **Christ**, with the authority of **Christ**, and as a spokesman for **Christ**.

D. Paul's Credentials for the Ministry (3:1–5)

3:1 In the latter part of 2:17, the apostle had used four distinct expressions to describe his ministry. He realized that this might sound to some, especially his critics, as if he were commending himself. And so he begins this chapter with the question, **Do we begin again to commend ourselves?** The **again** does not imply that he had commended himself previously. Rather, it simply means that he had been *accused* of doing so, and now he anticipates the repetition of such a charge against him.

Or do we need, as some others, epistles of commendation to you or letters of commendation from you? The **some others** to whom Paul is here referring are the false teachers of 2:17. They came to Corinth with **epistles of commendation**, perhaps from Jerusalem. And possibly when they left Corinth, they carried with them **letters of commendation from** the assembly there. Letters of commendation *were* used in the early church by Christians traveling from one place to the other. The apostle does not at all seek to discourage such a practice in this verse. Instead he is stating rather subtly that the *only* thing these false teachers had to commend them was the letter they carried! Otherwise they had no credentials to offer.

3:2 The Judaizers who had come to Corinth raised questions as to Paul's apostolic authority. They denied that he was a true servant of Christ. Perhaps they raised such doubts in the Corinthians' minds in order that the latter might demand a letter of recommendation from the Apostle Paul the next time he visited them. He has already asked them if he needs such a letter. Had he not come to Corinth when they were heathen idolaters? Had he not led them to Christ? Had not the Lord set His seal upon the ministry of the apostle by giving him precious souls in Corinth? That is the answer. The Corinthians themselves were Paul's **epistle, written in** his heart but **known and read by all men**. In his case there was no need of a letter written with pen and ink. They were the fruit of his ministry, and they were enshrined in his affections. Not only that, but they were **known and read by all men** in the sense that their conversion was a well-known fact in the whole area. People realized that a change had come over these people, that they had turned to God from idols, and that they were now living separated lives. They were the evidence of Paul's divine ministry.

3:3 At first glance, verse 3 seems to contradict verse 2. Paul had said that the Corinthians were his epistle; here he says that they are **an epistle of Christ**. In verse 2, he says that the epistle is written in his heart; in the latter part of verse 3, it seems clear that Christ has written the epistle on the hearts of the

Corinthians themselves. How can these differences be reconciled? The answer is that in verse 2 Paul is stating that the Corinthians were his letter of recommendation. Verse 3 gives the explanation. Perhaps we might get the connection by joining the two verses as follows: "You are our epistle . . . because **you are clearly** declared to be **an epistle of Christ.**" In other words, the Corinthians were Paul's letter of recommendation because it was clear to all that the Lord had done a work of grace in their lives. They were obviously Christians. Since Paul had been the human instrument in bringing them to the Lord, they were his credentials. This is the thought in the expression **ministered by us.** The Lord Jesus is the One who had done the work in their lives, but He did it through the ministry of Paul.

Whereas the letters of recommendation used by Paul's enemies were written **with ink,** Paul's epistle was written **by the Spirit of the living God** and was therefore divine. **Ink,** of course, is subject to fading, erasure, and destruction, but when **the Spirit of . . . God** writes in human hearts, it is forever. Then Paul adds that the epistle of Christ has been written **not on tablets of stone but on tablets** that are hearts **of flesh.** People visiting Corinth did not see Christ's epistle engraved on some great monument in the middle of the market place, but rather the letter was written in the hearts and lives of the Christians there.

As Paul contrasted **tablets of stone** and **tablets** that are hearts **of flesh,** there is little doubt that he also had in mind the difference between the law and the gospel. The law had, of course, been inscribed on tablets of stone on Mount Sinai, but under the gospel, God secures obedience through the message of grace and love that is written in human hearts. Paul will take up this subject in greater detail shortly, so he merely alludes to it here.

3:4 As we have listened to Paul speak with such confidence about his apostleship and the ministry the Lord had committed to him, we might well ask, "How can you dare to speak with such assurance in the matter, Paul?" The answer is given here in verse 4. Defense of his apostleship might seem like self-commendation, but here he denies that. He says that his confidence is **toward God,** i.e., confidence that can withstand God's scrutiny. He does not have any confidence in himself or in his own ability, but **through Christ,** and in the work which Christ had done in the lives of the Corinthians, he finds proof of the reality of his ministry. The remarkable change in the lives of the Corinthians commended the apostle.

3:5 Here, again, Paul disclaims any adequacy in or of himself that would enable him to reckon himself to be an apostle of Jesus Christ. The power for his ministry did **not** come **from** within, **but** from above. The apostle was not anxious to take credit for himself. He realized that if **God** had not made him sufficient for the ministry, then nothing would have been accomplished.

E. The Old and New Covenants Contrasted (3:6–18)

3:6 Having discussed *his own* credentials, and his qualification for the ministry, Paul now launches into an extended account of the ministry itself. In the verses to follow, he contrasts the Old Covenant (the law) and **the new covenant** (the gospel). There is a good reason why he should do so at this point. Those who were criticizing him so severely in Corinth were the Judaizers. These were the men who sought to mix law and grace. They taught Christians that they must observe certain portions of the Law of Moses in order to be fully accepted by God. And so the apostle is here going to demonstrate the superiority of the New Covenant to the Old. He prefaces his remarks by saying that God has made him competent as a servant of **the new covenant.** A covenant, of course, is a promise, an agreement, or a testament. The Old Covenant was the legal system delivered by God to Moses. Under it, blessing was conditioned upon obedience. It was a covenant of works. It was an agreement between God and man, that if man did his part, God would do His also. But because it depended on man, it could not produce righteousness. **The new covenant** is the gospel. Under it, God covenants to bless man freely by His grace through the redemption that is in Christ Jesus. Everything under the

New Covenant depends on God and not on man. Therefore, the New Covenant is able to accomplish what the Old could never do.

Paul gives several striking contrasts between the law and the gospel. He begins here in verse 6 with the first by saying, **Not of the letter, but of the Spirit; for the letter kills, but the Spirit**, or **spirit** (NKJV mg.) **gives life**. This is widely interpreted to mean that if you just take the outward, literal words of Scripture and try to be obedient to the letter without desiring to be obedient to the full spirit of the passage, then it harms you rather than helps you. The Pharisees were an illustration of this. They were scrupulous in their tithing to the very minutest extent, but they did not show mercy and love to others (Matt. 23:23). While this is a valid *application* of this passage, it is not the *interpretation*. In verse 6 the *letter* refers to the Law of Moses, and the *spirit* refers to the gospel of the grace of God. When Paul says that **the letter kills**, he is speaking of the ministry of the law. The law condemns all who fail to keep its holy precepts. "By the law is the knowledge of sin" (Rom. 3:20). "Cursed is everyone who does not continue in all things which are written in the book of the law, to do them" (Gal. 3:10). God never intended the law to be the means of giving life. Rather it was designed to bring the knowledge of sin and to convict of sin. The New Covenant is here called *spirit*. It represents the spiritual fulfillment of the types and shadows of the Old Covenant. What the law demanded but could never produce is now effected by the gospel.

J. M. Davies summarizes:

This ministry of the "letter" that killeth is illustrated in the 3000 killed at Sinai, at the inauguration of the Old Covenant; and the ministry of the Spirit, the life-giving ministry, is illustrated in the 3000 saved on the day of Pentecost.[10]

3:7 Verses 7 and 8 continue the contrast between the two covenants. Here the apostle is particularly contrasting the **glory** which attended the giving of the law with the glory which is connected with the gospel. The words **glory** and **glorious** are found in chapters 3 and 4

seventeen times. The Old Covenant is called **the ministry of death, written and engraved on stones**. This can only refer to the Ten Commandments. They threatened death to all who did not keep them (Ex. 19:13). Paul does *not* say that there was no glory connected with the giving of the law. That certainly was not the case. When God gave the Ten Commandments to Moses on Mount Sinai, there were great manifestations of the divine presence and power (Ex. 19). In fact, as Moses stood there communing with God, his own face began to shine, a reflection of the splendor of God. Thus **the children of Israel could not look steadily at the face of Moses because of the glory of his countenance**. It was too dazzling for them to view constantly. But then Paul adds the significant words **which glory was passing away**. This means that the bright shining which appeared on the face of Moses was not permanent. It was a temporary, passing glory. The spiritual meaning of this is that the **glory** of the Old Covenant was temporary. The law had a very definite function. It was given to reveal sin. It was a display of the holy requirements of God, and in that sense was glorious. But it was given until the time of Christ, who is the fulfillment of the law for righteousness to those who believe (Rom. 10:4). It was a *shadow*; He is the *substance*. It was a picture of better things to come, and those things find their reality in the Savior of the world.

3:8 Now if the law did have this glorious character, how much **more glorious** is the **ministry of the Spirit**? The expression **"the ministry of the Spirit"** refers to the gospel. The Spirit of God works through the preaching of the gospel, and in turn the Spirit of God is ministered to those who receive the good news of salvation. The **will** in **"how will the ministry of the Spirit"** does not express future time but the inevitable consequence. If one fact or condition exists, then another **will** certainly follow.

3:9 Here the Old Covenant is called **the ministry of condemnation**. That was its result. It brought **condemnation** to all men, because no one could perfectly keep the law. Yet there was a certain **glory** connected with it. It had a real purpose and a real usefulness for that time. But **the ministry of righteousness exceeds much more in glory**. Hodge says, "The ministration of righteousness is that ministration which reveals a righteousness by which men are justified, and thus freed from the condemnation pronounced upon them by the law."[11] The glories of the gospel are not the kind that appeal to physical sight but those deep and lasting excellencies that appeal to the spirit. The glories of Calvary far eclipse the glories of Sinai.

3:10 Although in one sense the law **was made glorious**, yet when you compare it with the *New* Covenant it really **had no glory** at all. The verse expresses to us a strong comparison and says that when the two covenants are placed side by side, one completely outshines the other, that is, the New Covenant surpasses the Old. A. T. Robertson states, "The greater glory dims the less. In one point at least, the old seems to have no glory at all, because of the superabundant glory of the new covenant."[12] Denney comments: "When the Sun shines in His strength, there is no other glory in the sky."[13]

3:11 **For if what is passing away was glorious** (literally, with glory), **what remains is much more glorious** (literally, glorious in glory). We should notice the two prepositions, *with* and *in*. The thought is that glory accompanied the giving of the law, but it is the very element of the New Covenant. Glory was in attendance when the Old Covenant was delivered, but the gospel of God's grace is **glorious** *in itself*.

This verse also contrasts the transient, temporary character of the law and the permanent character of the gospel. **What is passing away** can only refer to the Ten Commandments — "the ministry of death, written and engraved on stones" (v. 7). Thus this verse refutes the claims of Seventh Day Adventists, who say that the ceremonial law has been done away but not the Ten Commandments.

3:12 The **hope** which Paul refers to here is the sharp conviction that the glory of the gospel will never fade or become dim. Because of this strong assurance, he speaks the word with **great boldness**. He had nothing to hide. There is no reason to use a veil. In many reli-

gions of the world today, there are supposed mysteries. New converts must be initiated into these deep secrets. They pass from one order to the next. But with the gospel it is not so. Everything is clear and open. The gospel speaks plainly and with full assurance on such subjects as salvation, the Trinity, heaven, and hell.

3:13 **Unlike Moses, who put a veil over his face so that the children of Israel could not look steadily at the end of what was passing away**. The background to verse 13 is found in Exodus 34:29–35. There we learn that when Moses came down from Mount Sinai, after having been in the presence of the Lord, he did not know that his face was shining. The children of Israel were afraid to come near him because of the glory of his face. But he beckoned them to come near, and they did so. Then he gave them as commandments all that the Lord had told him. In Exodus 34:33 we read: "When Moses had finished speaking with them, he put a veil on his face." In 2 Corinthians 3:13, the apostle explains why Moses did this. He did it **so that the children of Israel could not look steadily at the end of what was passing away**. The glory on his face was a fading glory. In other words, the law which God had given to him had a transient glory. It was fading even then, and Moses did not want them to see **the end** of it. It was not that Moses wanted to hide the glory itself, but rather the *passing* of the glory. F. W. Grant has beautifully stated, "The glory on the face of Moses must give way to the glory in Another Face."[14] That has taken place with the coming of the Lord Jesus Christ. The result is that the minister of the New Covenant does not have to hide his face. The glory of the gospel will never grow dim or fade away.

3:14 **But their minds were blinded**. The children of Israel did not realize the true significance of what Moses was doing. And down through the centuries it has been so with the Jewish people. Even at the time of Paul's writing they still clung to the law as a means of salvation and would not accept the Lord Jesus Christ.

For until this day the same veil remains unlifted in the reading of the Old

Testament. In other words, at the time the apostle wrote, when the Jews read **the Old Testament**, they did not discover the secret which Moses hid from their forefathers beneath the **veil**. They did not realize that the glory of the law was a passing glory, and that the law had found its fulfillment in the Lord Jesus Christ.

The veil is taken away in Christ. The word *veil* here is in italics (supplied by translators), and some suggest that it is *not* the veil but *the Old Covenant* which is done away in Christ. An even more likely meaning is that *the difficulty in understanding* **the Old Testament** vanishes when a person comes to Christ. Hodge puts it well:

> The Old Testament Scriptures are intelligible only when understood as predicting and prefiguring Christ. The knowledge of Christ . . . removes the veil from the Old Testament.[15]

3:15 Here the figure changes slightly. In the OT illustration, the veil was over the *face* of Moses, but now **a veil lies on** the *hearts* of the Jewish people. They are still trying to obtain righteousness on the principle of *doing*, never realizing that the work has already been *done* by the Savior on the cross of Calvary. They are seeking to gain salvation by their own merit, not realizing that the law utterly condemns them and that they should flee to the arms of the Lord for mercy and grace.

3:16 The **one** in verse 16 may refer to the heart of an *individual* Jew, or it may refer to Israel *nationally*. When either **turns to the Lord** and accepts Jesus as Messiah, then **the veil is taken away**, the obscurity is gone. Then the truth dawns that all the types and shadows of the law find their fulfillment in God's beloved Son, the Messiah of Israel. If the *nation* of Israel is in view, then the verse points forward to a day yet future when a believing remnant will turn **to the Lord**, as prophesied in Romans 11:25, 26, 32.

3:17 Paul has been emphasizing that Christ is the key to the OT. Here he re-emphasizes that truth by saying, **Now the Lord is the Spirit**. Most versions, including NKJV, capitalize **Spirit**, interpreting it as the Holy Spirit. But the context suggests that the Lord is the spirit of the OT just as "the testimony of Jesus is the spirit of prophecy" (Rev. 19:10). All the types and shadows of the OT find their fulfillment in Christ. **Where the Spirit**[16] **of the Lord is, there is liberty** means that wherever Jesus Christ is recognized as Lord or Jehovah, **there is liberty**, that is, freedom from the bondage of the law, freedom from obscurity in reading the Scriptures, and freedom to gaze upon His face without a veil between.

3:18 In the Old Covenant, Moses alone was allowed to see the glory of the Lord. Under the New Covenant, **we all** have the privilege **of beholding . . . the glory of the Lord**. Moses' face had to be veiled after he had finished speaking with the people, but we can have an **unveiled face**. We can keep our face **unveiled** by confessing and forsaking sin, by being completely honest with God and ourselves. As a veteran missionary to India once said, we must "drop the veils of sin, of make-believe, all play-acting, all putting up of unreal fronts, all attempts at compromises, all halfway measures, all Yes and No."

The next step is **beholding as in a mirror the glory of the Lord. The mirror** is the word of God. As we go to the Bible, we see the Lord Jesus revealed in all His splendor. We do not yet see Him face to face, but only as mirrored in the word.

And note that it is **the glory of the Lord** that we behold. Here Paul is not thinking so much of the moral beauty of Jesus as a Man here on earth, but rather of His present glory, exalted at the right hand of God. The glory of Christ, as Denney points out, is that:

> He shares the Father's throne, that He is the Head of the Church, possessor and bestower of all the fulness of divine grace, the coming Judge of the world, conqueror of every hostile power, intercessor for His own, and, in short, bearer of all the majesty which belongs to His kingly office.[17]

As we are occupied with the glory of the risen, ascended, exalted Lord Jesus Christ, **we are being transformed into the same image**. Here, in a word, is the secret of Christian holiness — occupation with Christ. Not by occupation with self; that brings only defeat. Not by occupation with others; that brings disappointment. But by occupation with **the glory of the Lord**, we become more and more like Him.

This marvelous, transforming process takes place **from glory to glory**, that is, from one degree of **glory** to another. It is not a matter of instant change. There is *no experience* in the Christian life that will reproduce His image in a moment. It is a process, not a crisis. It is not like the fading glory of the law, but an ever-increasing glory.

The power for this wonderful process is the Holy Spirit of God — **just as by the Spirit of the Lord**. As we behold the Lord of glory, study Him, contemplate Him, gaze on Him adoringly, **the Spirit of the Lord** works in our life the marvelous miracle of increasing conformity to Christ.

Darby points out how Stephen was changed by beholding:

> We see it in Stephen when he is stoned, and he looks up and sees the glory of God and Jesus. Christ had said, "Father, forgive them; for they know not what they do"; and the view of Jesus in the glory of God draws from Stephen the prayer, "Lord, lay not this sin to their charge." And again on the cross, Christ says, "Father, into Thy hands I commend my spirit"; and Stephen says, "Lord Jesus, receive my spirit." He is changed into Christ's image.[18]

Consider then the transcendent glory of the New Covenant. Whereas only *one* man had the glory on his face in the Old Covenant, today it is the blood-bought privilege of *every* child of God. Also, instead of merely reflecting the glory of God in our faces, **we all** in the New Covenant **are** actually **being transformed** (lit., *metamorphosed*) **into the same image from glory to glory, just as by the Spirit of the Lord**. Whereas Moses' face reflected glory, our faces radiate glory from inside.

Thus Paul brings to a close his rather mystical and deeply spiritual exposition of the New Covenant and of how it compares with the Old.

F. Obligation to Preach a Clear Gospel (4:1–6)

4:1 In the first six verses of chapter 4, Paul emphasizes the solemn responsibility of every servant of Christ to make the message of the gospel plain. There can be no veil. Nothing must be hidden or mysterious. All must be clear, honest, and sincere.

Paul has been speaking of the marvelous way in which God had qualified him to be an able servant of the New Covenant. He now takes up the thread of thought from that point. Realization of the tremendous dignity of the Christian **ministry** prevents such a man as Paul from losing **heart**. Of course, there is much to discourage and depress in Christian service, but the Lord gives mercy and grace to help in every time of need. Thus, no matter what the discouragements may be, the encouragements are always greater.

Paul did **not lose heart**. He did not act cowardly, but rather courageously, in the face of seemingly insurmountable barriers.

4:2 Phillips gives a colorful paraphrase of verse 2:

> We use no hocus-pocus, no clever tricks, no dishonest manipulation of the Word of God. We speak the plain truth and so commend ourselves to every man's conscience in the sight of God.

Here doubtless the apostle is thinking once again of the false teachers who had come into the Corinthian church. Their methods were the same as are always used by forces of evil, namely, shameful enticements to sin, crafty juggling of the truth, use of tricky arguments, and adulteration of the word of God. With regard to the latter expression, **nor handling the word of God deceitfully**, Paul doubtless alludes to the favorite pastime of these men — of seeking to mix law and grace.

The apostle's method was very different. It is expressed in the words, **but by manifestation of the truth commending ourselves to every man's conscience in the sight of God. Manifestation of the truth** may take two forms. We manifest **the truth** when we tell it out in a plain, understandable manner. But we also manifest it when we live it in our lives before others so that they can see it by our example. Paul used both of these methods. He preached the gospel, and he obeyed the gospel in his own life. In doing so, he sought to commend himself to every man's conscience in the sight of God.

4:3 The apostle has been speaking of the tremendous care he used in seeking to make the truth of God clear to men, both by precept and by practice. If the **gospel is veiled** or hidden to some, it certainly is not God's fault, and Paul does not want it to be his fault either. And yet even as he writes the words, he is aware that there are those who simply cannot seem to take it in. Who are they? It is **those who are perishing**. Why are they thus blinded? The answer is given in the following verse.

4:4 Satan is the culprit. He is here called **the god of this age**. He has succeeded in putting a veil over the minds of the unbelieving ones. He would keep them in perpetual darkness, **lest the light of the gospel of the glory of Christ ... should shine on them** that they might be saved.

In our physical universe, the sun is always shining. We do not always see it, but the reason for that is that something has come between the sun and us. So it is with the gospel. **The light of the gospel** is always shining. God is always seeking to shine into the hearts of men. But Satan puts various barriers between unbelievers and God. It may be the cloud of pride, or of rebellion, or of self-righteousness, or any one of a hundred other things. But all of these serve effectively to hinder **the light of the gospel** from shining in. Satan simply does not want men to be saved.

The gospel has to do with **Christ in glory**. It is not the Carpenter of Nazareth who is presented to the believer's view. It is not simply Christ outstretched on the cross of shame. But it is the Lord Jesus Christ who has died, been buried, who has risen again, and who is even now at the right hand of God in heaven. He is the object of the believer's faith — the glorified Son of God in heaven.

4:5 In this one verse we have both the poorest theme for a preacher, and the best theme. The poorest theme is **ourselves**, while the best theme is *Christ Jesus the Lord.*

Apparently the Judaizers had a great habit of preaching about themselves. Paul separates himself from such a company. He would not waste the people's time by preaching on such an unworthy subject. His theme was **Christ Jesus the Lord**. He sought to bring men and women to the place where they were willing to bow the knee to Jesus Christ and to pay their homage to Him as Lord of their lives.

The apostle introduced his team as **your bondservants for Jesus' sake**. In so doing, he effectively hid himself and his co-workers in the background. They were only slaves, ready to help in any way that would bring men to the Lord Jesus.

4:6 Paul here compares the conversion of a sinner to the entrance of light at the dawn of creation.

Originally **God commanded light to shine out of darkness**. He said, " 'Let there be light,' and there was light" (Gen. 1:3).

Now Paul is saying here that **the same God** who originally **commanded light to shine out of darkness has shone in our hearts**. This is very beautiful. In the first creation God *commanded* the light to shine. But in the new creation, **God** Himself shines into **our hearts**. How much more personal this is!

The events in the early part of Genesis 1 are a picture of what takes place in the new creation. God originally created man as an innocent being. But sin came in, and with it came gross darkness.

As the gospel is preached, the Spirit of God moves on the heart of a person, just as He moved on the face of the deep after the original creation.

Then God shines into the heart of this person, showing him that he is a guilty sinner and needs a Savior. "The material creation in Genesis began with light and so also does the spiritual creation. God 'shines in our hearts' by the Holy Ghost, and then spiritual life begins" (Selected).

The verse goes on to explain to us why **God has shone in our hearts**. In the KJV and NKJV it reads, **to give the light of the knowledge of the glory of God in the face of Jesus Christ**. It sounds from this that His purpose is just *to give us* **the light of the knowledge of the glory of God**. But J. N. Darby suggests a significant change in this verse in his New Translation: *"For the shining forth* of the knowledge of the glory of God in the face of Jesus Christ."* In other words,

God does not shine in our hearts simply **to give** us this **knowledge**, but rather that through us the knowledge might *shine to others.* "We are not the terminals of our blessings or exercises, but the channels." (Selected)

A Scriptural illustration of this is found in the life of Paul himself. On the road to Damascus, God shone in his heart. He realized that the One whom he had hated and who he thought was buried in a Judean tomb was the Lord of glory. From that day he went out to spread **the light of the knowledge of the glory of God** as it is found **in the face of Jesus Christ.**

G. An Earthen Vessel with a Heavenly Destiny (4:7–18)

4:7 Having spoken of the obligation to make the message plain, the Apostle Paul now thinks of the human instrument to which the wonderful gospel treasure had been committed. The **treasure** is the glorious message of the gospel. The **earthen vessel,** on the other hand, is the frail human body. The contrast between the two is tremendous. The gospel is like a precious diamond that scintillates brilliantly every way in which it is turned. To think that such a precious diamond has been entrusted to such a frail, fragile earthenware vessel!

> Earthen vessels, marred, unsightly,
> Bearing Wealth no thought can know;
> Heav'nly Treasure, gleaming brightly —
> Christ revealed in saints below!
>
> Vessels, broken, frail, yet bearing
> Through the hungry ages on,
> Riches giv'n with hand unsparing,
> God's great Gift, His precious Son!
>
> O to be but emptier, lowlier,
> Mean, unnoticed and unknown,
> And to God a vessel holier,
> Filled with Christ, and Christ alone!
>
> Naught of earth to cloud the Glory!
> Naught of self the light to dim!
> Telling forth Christ's wondrous story,
> Broken, empty — filled with Him!
> — *Tr. Frances Bevan*

Why has God ordained that **this treasure** should be **in earthen vessels?** The answer is so **that the excellence of the power may be of God and not of us.** God does not want men to be occupied with the human instrument, but rather with His own power and greatness. And so He deliberately commits the gospel message to weak, often uncomely human beings. All the praise and glory must go to the Creator and not to the creature.

> It is a secret joy to find
> The task assigned beyond our powers;
> For thus, if ought of good be wrought,
> Clearly the praise is His, not ours.
> — *Houghton*

Jowett says:

> There is something wrong when the vessel robs the treasure of its glory, when the casket attracts more attention than the jewel which it bears. There is a very perverse emphasis when the picture takes second place to the frame, and when the ware which is used at the feast becomes a substitute for the meal. There is something deadly in Christian service when "the excellency of the power" is of us and not of God. Such excellency is of a very fleeting kind, and it will speedily wither as the green herb and pass into oblivion.[19]

As Paul penned verse 7, it is almost certain he was thinking of an incident in Judges 7. There it is recorded that Gideon equipped his army with trumpets, empty pitchers, and lamps within the pitchers. At the appointed signal, his men were to blow their trumpets and break the pitchers. When the pitchers were broken, the lamps shone out in brilliance. This terrified the enemy. They thought there was a vast host after them, instead of just three hundred men. The lesson is that, just as in Gideon's case the light only shone forth when the pitchers were broken, so it is in connection with the gospel. Only when human instruments are broken and yielded to the Lord can the gospel shine forth through us in all its magnificence.

4:8 The apostle now goes on to explain that because the treasure has been committed to earthen vessels, there is seeming defeat on the one hand, yet perpetual victory on the other. There is weakness to all outward appearance, but in reality incomparable strength. When he says, **We are hard pressed on every side, yet not crushed,** he means that he is constantly **pressed** by adversaries and difficulties, yet not completely hindered from uttering the message freely.

Perplexed, but not in despair. From the human standpoint, Paul often did not know there could possibly be a solution to his difficulties, and yet the Lord never allowed him to reach the place of **despair**. He was never brought into a narrow place from which there was no escape.

4:9 Persecuted, but not forsaken. At times, he could feel the hot breath of the enemy on the back of his neck, yet the Lord never abandoned him to his foes. **Struck down, but not destroyed** means that Paul was many times seriously "wounded in action," yet the Lord raised him up again to go with the glorious news of the gospel.

The *New Bible Commentary* paraphrases verses 8 and 9: "Hemmed in, but not hamstrung; not knowing what to do, but never bereft of all hope; hunted by men, but never abandoned by God; often felled, but never finished."

We may wonder why the Lord allowed His servant to go through such testings and trials. We would think that he could have served the Lord more efficiently if He had allowed his pathway to be free from troubles. But this Scripture teaches the very opposite. God, in His marvelous wisdom, sees fit to allow His servants to be touched by sickness, sorrow, affliction, persecution, difficulties, and distresses. All are designed to break the earthen pitchers so that the light of the gospel might shine out more clearly.

4:10 The life of the servant of God is one of constant **dying**. Just as **the Lord Jesus** Himself, in His lifetime, was constantly exposed to violence and persecution, so those who follow in His steps will meet the same treatment. But it does not mean defeat. This is the way of victory. Blessing comes to others as we thus die daily.

It is only in this way that the life of Jesus can be apparent in our bodies. **The life of Jesus** does not here mean primarily His life as a Man on earth, but His present **life** as the exalted Son of God in heaven. How can the world see the life of Christ when He is not personally or physically present in the world today? The answer is that as we Christians suffer in the service of the Lord, His life is **manifested in our body**.

4:11 This thought of **life** from **death** is continued in verse 11. It is one of the deepest principles of our existence. The

meat we eat and by which we live comes through the death of animals. It is so in the spiritual realm. "The blood of the martyrs is the seed of the church." The more the church is persecuted and afflicted and hunted and pursued, the more Christianity spreads.

And yet it is difficult for us to accept this truth. When violence comes to a servant of the Lord, we normally think of it as a tragedy. Actually, this is God's normal way of dealing. It is not the exception. Constant exposure **to death for Jesus' sake** is the divine manner in which **the life of Jesus** is **manifested in our mortal** bodies.

4:12 Here the apostle sums up all that he has said by reminding the Corinthians that it was through his constant suffering that **life** came to them. In order for Paul ever to go to Corinth with the gospel, he had to suffer untold hardships. But it was worth it all, because they had trusted in the Lord Jesus and now had eternal life. Paul's physical suffering and loss meant spiritual gain to others. Robertson says, "His dying was working out for the good of those who were benefited by his ministry."[20]

Oftentimes we have the tendency to cry out to the Lord in sickness, asking Him to deliver us from it, so that we might serve Him better. Perhaps we should sometimes thank God for such afflictions in our lives, and glory in our infirmities that the power of Christ might rest upon us.

4:13 The apostle has been speaking of the constant frailty and weakness of the human vessel to which the gospel is entrusted. What then is his attitude toward all this? Is he defeated and discouraged and dismayed? The answer is no. Faith enables him to go on preaching the gospel, because he knows that beyond the sufferings of this life lie unspeakable glories.

In Psalm 116:10 the psalmist says, **"I believed and therefore I spoke."** He trusted in the Lord, and therefore what he said was the result of that deep-seated faith. Paul is here saying that the same is true in his case. He had the same spirit of faith which the Psalmist had when he uttered those words. Paul says, **"We also believe and therefore speak."**

The afflictions and persecutions of Paul's life did not seal his lips. Wherever there is true faith, there must be the expression of it. It cannot be silent.

If on Jesus Christ you trust,
　Speak for Him you surely must;
Though it humble to the dust,
　If you love Him, say so.

If on Jesus you believe
　And the Saviour you receive
Lest you should the Spirit grieve,
　Don't delay, but say so.

4:14 If it seems strange to us that Paul was not shaken by the constant danger of death, we find the answer in verse 14. This is the secret of his fearlessness in uttering the Christian message. He knew that this life was not all. He knew that for the believer there was the certainty of resurrection. The same God **who raised up the Lord Jesus** would **also raise up** the Apostle Paul **with Jesus and** would **present** him **with** the Corinthians.

4:15 With the certain and sure hope of resurrection before him, the apostle was willing to undergo terrible hardships. He knew that all such sufferings had a twofold result. They abounded in blessing for the Corinthians, and thus caused **thanksgiving to abound to the glory of God**. These two motives actuated Paul in all he said and did. He was concerned with **the glory of God** and the blessing of his fellow men.

Paul realized that the more he suffered, the more the **grace** of God was made available to others. The more people who were saved, the more **thanksgiving** ascended to **God**. And the more **thanksgiving** ascended to **God**, the more **God** was glorified.

The *Living Bible* seems to capture the spirit of the verse in this paraphrase:

These sufferings of ours are for your benefit. And the more of you who are won to Christ, the more there are to thank him for his great kindness, and the more the Lord is glorified.

4:16 Paul had been explaining his willingness to undergo all kinds of suffering and danger because he had before him the certain hope of resurrection. **Therefore** he did **not lose heart**. Although on the one hand, the process of physical decay was going on constantly,

yet on the other hand there was a spiritual renewal which enabled him to go on in spite of every adverse circumstance.

The fact that the **outward man is perishing** needs little explanation or comment. It is all too evident in our bodies! But Paul is here rejoicing in the fact that God sends daily supplies of power for Christian service. Thus it is true, as Michelangelo said, "The more the marble wastes, the more the statue grows."

Ironside comments:

We are told that our material bodies are completely changed every seven years. . . Yet we have a consciousness of being the same persons. Our personality is unchanged from year to year, and so with regard to the greater change as yet to come. The same life is in the butterfly that was in the grub.[21]

4:17 After reading the terrible afflictions which the Apostle Paul endured, it may seem hard for us to understand how he could speak of them as **light affliction**. In one sense, they were not at all light. They were bitter and cruel.

But the explanation lies in the *comparison* which Paul makes. The afflictions viewed by themselves might be ever so heavy, but when compared with the **eternal weight of glory**[22] that lies ahead, then they are **light**. Also the **light affliction is but for a moment**, whereas the glory is **eternal.** The lessons we learn through afflictions in this world will yield richest fruit for us in the world to come.

Moorehead observes: "A little joy enters into us while we are in the world; we shall enter into joy when there. A few drops here; a whole ocean there."[23]

There is a pyramid in this verse which, as F. E. Marsh has pointed out, does not tire the weary climber but brings unspeakable rest and comfort to his soul.

Glory
Weight of glory
Eternal weight of glory
Exceeding and eternal weight of glory
More exceeding and eternal weight of glory
Far more exceeding and eternal
weight of glory[24]

4:18 In this verse **look** does not merely describe human vision; rather it conveys the idea of regarding a thing as important. As far as **the things which are seen** are concerned, they are not the goal of one's existence. Here they refer primarily to the hardships, trials, and sufferings which Paul endured. These were incidental to his ministry; the great object of his ministry was what is **not seen**. This might include the glory of Christ, the blessing of one's fellow men, and the reward that awaits the faithful servant of Christ at the Judgment Seat.

Jowett comments:

> To be able to see the first is sight; to be able to see the second is insight. The first mode of vision is natural, the second mode is spiritual. The primary organ in the first discernment is intellect; the primary organ in the second discernment is faith. . . . All through the Scriptures this contrast between sight and insight is being continually presented to us, and everywhere we are taught to measure the meagerness and stinginess of the one, and set it over the fulness and expansiveness of the other.[25]

H. Living in the Light of Christ's Judgment Seat (5:1–10)

The verses to follow are closely linked with what has gone before. Paul has been speaking of his present sufferings and distresses, and the future glory which lay before him. This brings him face to face with the subject of death. In this section we have one of the greatest unfoldings of death in all the word of God, and the Christian's relationship to it.

5:1 In verse 1, the apostle speaks of our present mortal body as **our earthly house, this tent**. A **tent** is not a permanent dwelling, but a portable one for pilgrims and travelers.

Death is spoken of as the dissolving of **this tent**. The **tent** is taken down at the time of death. The body goes into the grave, whereas the spirit and soul of the believer go to be with the Lord.

Paul opens the chapter with the assurance that if his **earthly house** should be **destroyed** (as a result of the sufferings mentioned in the preceding chapter) he knows he has **a building from God, a house not made with hands, eternal in the heavens**. Notice the distinction between **tent** and **building**. The temporary **tent** is taken down, but a new, permanent **house** awaits the be-

liever in the land beyond the skies. This is **a building from God**, in the sense that God is the One who gives it to us.

Furthermore, it is **a house not made with hands**. Why should Paul say this? Our present bodies are not made with hands; so why should he emphasize that our future, glorified bodies will not be made with hands? The answer is that the expression **not made with hands** means "not of this creation." This is made clear in Hebrews 9:11, where we read, "But Christ came as High Priest of the good things to come, with the greater and more perfect tabernacle *not made with hands, that is, not of this creation*." What Paul is saying in 2 Corinthians 5:1 is that whereas our present bodies are suited to life on this earth, our future, glorified bodies will not be of this creation. They will be especially designed for life in heaven.

The believer's future body is also described as **eternal in the heavens**. It is a body that will no longer be subject to disease, decay, and death, but one that will endure forever in our heavenly home.

It might sound from this verse as if a believer receives this building from God the moment he dies, but that is not the case. He does not get his glorified body until Christ comes back for His church (1 Thess. 4:13–18). What happens to the believer is this. At the time of death, his spirit and soul go to be with Christ where he is consciously enjoying the glories of heaven. His body is placed in the grave. At the time of the Lord's return, the dust will be raised from the grave, God will fashion it into a new, glorified body, and it will then be reunited with the spirit and the soul. Between death and Christ's coming for His saints, the believer might be said to be in a disembodied condition. However, this does not mean that he is not fully conscious of all the joy and bliss of heaven. He is!

Before leaving verse 1 we should mention that there are three principal interpretations of the **house not made with hands, eternal in the heavens**:

1. Heaven itself.
2. An intermediate body between death and resurrection.
3. The glorified body.

The house can scarcely be heaven itself, because it is said to be **eternal** *in* the heavens and *"from* heaven" (5:2). As far as an intermediate body is concerned, the Scriptures never mention such a body. Moreover, the house not made with hands is described as *eternal* in the heavens, which would not be true of an intermediate body. The third view — that the house is the resurrection body of glory — seems to be the correct one.

5:2 **In this** present mortal body, we are often forced to **groan** because of the way it limits us and impedes us in our spiritual lives. What we greatly desire is to **be clothed with our habitation which is from heaven**.

In this verse, the apostle seems to change his figure from a tent to clothing. A suggested explanation of this is that Paul was a tentmaker and realized that similar material used for tents was also used for clothing. At any rate, the meaning is clear that he longed to receive his glorified body.

5:3 What does **naked** mean in this verse? Does it mean that the person is unsaved and therefore without any covering of righteousness before God? Does it mean that the person, though saved, will be without reward at the Judgment Seat of Christ? Or does it mean that the saved person does not have a body between the time of death and resurrection, and is naked in the sense that he is a disembodied spirit?

This writer understands it to mean disembodied or unclothed. Paul is saying that his earnest desire is not for death, and for the disembodied state that goes with it, but rather for the coming of the Lord Jesus Christ when all those who have died will receive their glorified bodies.

5:4 That our interpretation of verse 3 is valid seems to be borne out by verse 4. The apostle says that **we who are in this** present earthly **tent groan, being burdened, not because we want to be unclothed, but further clothed, that mortality may be swallowed up by life**. In other words, he did not look forward to the state *between* death and the Rapture as the ideal hope of the believer, but to what will take place *at* the Rapture when believers will receive a body that will no longer be subject to death.

5:5 It is **God . . . who has prepared us for this very** purpose, namely, the redemption of the body. This will be the climax of His glorious purposes for us. At the present time we are redeemed as to our spirit and soul, but then redemption will include the body as well. Just think of it — God made us with this goal in view — the glorified state — a house not made with hands, eternal in the heavens!

And how can we be sure that we will have a glorified body? The answer is that **God . . . has given us the Spirit as a guarantee**. As explained previously, the fact that every believer possesses the indwelling **Spirit** of God is a pledge that *all* God's promises to the believer will be fulfilled. He is a token of what is to come. **The Spirit** of God is Himself **a guarantee** that what God has already given to us in part will one day be ours in full.

5:6 It was the deep assurance of these precious realities that enabled Paul to be always of good courage. He knew that as long as he was **at home in the body**, he was **absent from the Lord**. This was certainly not the ideal state for Paul, but he was willing that it should be so if he could serve Christ down here and be a help to the people of God.

5:7 The fact that **we walk by faith, not by sight** is abundant proof that we are absent from the Lord. We have never gazed upon the Lord with our physical eyes. Only through faith have we ever seen Him. As long as we are at home in the body, we have a life that is less close and intimate than the life of actual sight.

5:8 Verse 8 resumes the thought of verse 6 and completes it. Paul is of good courage in view of the blessed hope that lies before him, and he can say that he is **well pleased rather to be absent from the body and to be present with the Lord**. He has what Bernard calls a case of "heavenly homesickness."

This verse might seem to contradict what the apostle has just been saying. In the preceding verses he has been longing for the glorified body. But here he says that he is willing **rather to be absent from the body and to be present with the Lord**, that is, willing rather to be in the disembodied state that exists between death and the Rapture.

But there is no contradiction. There are three possibilities for the Christian, and it is simply a matter of which is most to be preferred. There is the present life on earth in this mortal body. There is the state between death and the coming of Christ, a disembodied state, but one in which the spirit and soul are consciously enjoying Christ's presence. Finally, there is the consummation of our salvation when we receive our glorified bodies at the coming again of the Lord Jesus. Paul is simply teaching in this passage that the first state is good, the second is better, and the third is best of all.

5:9 The believer should **make it his aim to be well pleasing to** the Lord. While his salvation is not dependent on works, his reward in a coming day will be directly proportionate to his faithfulness to the Lord. A believer should always remember that *faith* is linked with *salvation*, and *works* are linked with *reward*. He is saved by grace through faith, not of works; but once he is saved, he should be ambitious to perform good works, and for so doing he will receive rewards.

Notice that Paul wanted to **be well pleasing to Him, whether present or absent**. This means that his service on earth was designed to bring pleasure to the heart of his Lord, whether Paul was still here on earth or whether he was standing before the Judgment Seat of Christ.

5:10 One motive for being well pleasing to Christ is that **we must all appear before** His **judgment seat**. Actually it is not just a matter of *appearing* there, but of being *made manifest*. The NEB correctly says, "We must all have our lives laid open before the tribunal of Christ." It is one thing to appear in a doctor's office and quite another thing to be X-rayed by him there. **The judgment seat of Christ** will reveal our lives of service for Christ exactly as they have been. Not only the *amount* of our service, but also its *quality*, and even the very *motives* that prompted it will be brought into review.

Although sins after conversion will have an effect on our service, a believer's sins, as such, will not be brought into review for judgment at this solemn time.

That judgment took place over 1900 years ago, when the Lord Jesus bore our sins in His body on the tree. He fully paid the debt that our sins deserved, and God will never bring those sins into judgment again (John 5:24). **The judgment seat of Christ** has to do with our service for the Lord. It will not be a matter of whether we are saved or not; that is already an assured fact. But it is a matter of reward and loss at that time.

I. Paul's Good Conscience in the Ministry (5:11–6:2)

5:11 This verse is commonly taken to mean that since Paul was aware of God's terrible judgment on sin and the horrors of hell, he went everywhere seeking to persuade men to accept the gospel. While true, we believe this is not the primary meaning in this particular passage.

Paul is not here speaking so much of the terror of the Lord for the unsaved as of the *reverential awe* in which he sought to serve **the Lord** and to please Him. As far as God is concerned, the apostle knows that his life is an open book. But he would like the Corinthians also to be persuaded of his integrity and faithfulness in the ministry of the gospel. And so he says, in effect:

Since we know the fear **of the Lord, we** try to **persuade men** as to our integrity and sincerity as ministers of Christ. But whether we succeed in persuading men or not, **we are** well-known to **God.** And we hope that this will be the case in the **consciences** of you Corinthians as well!

This explanation seems to fit best with the context.

5:12 Immediately Paul realizes that what he has just said might be misinterpreted as self-praise. He does not want anyone to think that he is indulging in *that*! And so he adds, **we do not commend ourselves again to you**. This does not mean that he ever *had* commended himself to them, but he had been *accused* of doing so time and again, and he here seeks to disabuse their minds of any such idea.

Why then has he been giving such a prolonged defense of his ministry? Paul's answer is **"We . . . give you opportunity to boast on our behalf, that** you may have an answer for those who boast in appearance and not in heart." He was not interested in commending himself. Rather he realized that he was being sharply criticized by the false teachers in the presence of the Corinthian saints. He wanted the believers to know how to answer these attacks on him, and so he was giving them this information that they might be able to defend him when he was condemned in their presence.

He describes his critics as those who boast in appearance and not in heart (compare 1 Sam. 16:7). In other words, they were interested in outward show, but not in inward reality, integrity, and honesty. Physical appearance or eloquence or seeming zeal meant everything to them. "To the externalists, superficial appearances were everything and sincerity of heart counted for nothing" (Selected).

5:13 It would seem from this verse that the apostle had even been accused of insanity, of fanaticism, of various forms of mental disturbances. He does not deny that he lived in what Denney has called a state of "spiritual tension." He simply says that if he is beside himself, it is for God. Anything that might seem like insanity to his critics was really his deep-hearted devotion for the Lord. He was consumed with a passion for the things of God. If, on the other hand, he was of sound mind, it was for the sake of the Corinthians. What the verse says, in short, is that all of Paul's behavior could be explained in one of two ways: either it was zeal for God, or it was for the welfare of his fellow believers. In both cases, his motives were entirely unselfish. Could his critics say that of themselves?

5:14 No one who studies the life of the apostle can fail to wonder what made him serve so tirelessly and unselfishly. Here, in one of the greatest sections of all his letters, he gives the answer — the love of Christ.

Does the love of Christ here refer to His love for us or to our love for Him? There can be no question that it is His love for us. The only reason that we love at all is because He first loved us. It is His love that compels us, moves us along, as a person is moved along in a

crowd of Christmas shoppers. As Paul contemplated the marvelous love which Christ had shown to him, he could not help but be moved along in service for his wonderful Lord.

In dying for all, Jesus acted as our Representative. When He died we all died — in Him. Just as Adam's sin became the sin of his posterity, so Christ's death became the death of those who believe on Him (Rom. 5:12–21; 1 Cor. 15:21, 22).

5:15 The apostle's argument is irresistible. Christ died for all. Why did He die for all? So that those who live through faith in Him should live no longer for themselves, but for Him. The Savior did not die for us so that we might go on living our own petty, selfish lives the way we want to live them. Rather He died for us so that we might henceforth turn over our lives to Him in willing, glad devotion. Denney explains:

> In dying our death, Christ has done for us something so immense in love, that we ought to be His, and only His for ever. To make us His is the very object of His death.[26]

5:16 Perhaps Paul is here referring back to verse 12, where he described his critics as those who boast in appearance, and not in heart. Now he takes up that subject again by teaching that when we come to Christ, there is a new creation. From now on we do not judge men in a carnal, earthly way, according to appearances, human credentials, or national origin. We see them as precious souls for whom Christ died. He added that even though he had known Christ according to the flesh, that is, as merely another man, yet he did not know Him in that way any more. In other words, it was one thing to know Jesus as a next-door neighbor in the village of Nazareth, or even as an earthly messiah, and quite another thing to know the glorified Christ who is at the right hand of God at this present time. We know the Lord Jesus more intimately and more truly today as He is revealed to us through the word by the Spirit, than those knew Him who judged Him simply according to human appearances when He was on earth.

David Smith comments:

Though the Apostle had once shared that Jewish ideal of a secular Messiah, he had now attained to a loftier conception. Christ was for him the risen and glorified Savior, truly not known according to the flesh, but according to the spirit; not by historic tradition, but by immediate and vital fellowship.[27]

5:17 If anyone is in Christ, that is, saved, **he is a new creation**. Before conversion, one might have judged others according to human standards. But now all that is changed. **Old** methods of judging **have passed away; behold, all things have become new**.

This verse is a favorite with those who have recently been born again, and is often quoted in personal testimonies. Sometimes in being thus quoted, it gives quite a false impression. Listeners are apt to think that when a man is saved, old habits, evil thoughts, and lustful looks are forever done away, and everything becomes literally new in a person's life. We know that this is not true. The verse does not describe a believer's practice but rather his position. Notice it says that if anyone is **in Christ**. The words **in Christ** are the key to the passage. **In Christ, old things have passed away** and **all things have become new**. Unfortunately, "in me" not all this is true as yet! But as I progress in the Christian life, I desire that my practice may increasingly correspond to my position. One day, when the Lord Jesus returns, the two will be in perfect agreement.

5:18 All things are of God. He is the Source and Author of them **all**. There is no ground for human boasting. It is this same **God who has reconciled us to Himself through Jesus Christ, and has given us the ministry of reconciliation**.

This splendid statement of the scriptural doctrine of reconciliation is found in *A New and Concise Bible Dictionary*:

By the death of the Lord Jesus on the cross, God annulled in grace the distance which sin had brought in between Himself and man, in order that all things might, through Christ, be presented agreeably to himself. Believers are already reconciled, through Christ's death, to be presented holy, unblamable, and unreprovable (a new creation). God was in Christ, when Christ was on earth, reconciling the world unto Himself, not imput-

ing unto them their trespasses; but now that the love of God has been fully revealed in the cross, the testimony has gone out world-wide, beseeching men to be reconciled to God. The end is that God may have His pleasure in man.[28]

5:19 The ministry of reconciliation is here explained as the message **that God was in Christ reconciling the world to Himself**. There are two possible understandings of this statement, both of which are scripturally correct. First of all, we may think of it as saying **that God was in Christ**, in the sense that the Lord Jesus Christ is Deity. This is certainly true. But then we could also understand it as meaning **that God was, in Christ, reconciling the world to Himself**. In other words, He was **reconciling the world**, but He was doing it **in** the person of the Lord Jesus **Christ**.

Whichever interpretation we accept, the truth remains clear that God was actively removing the cause of the estrangement that had come between Himself and man by dealing with sin. God does not need to be reconciled, but man *does* need to be reconciled to Him.

Not imputing their trespasses to them. At first reading, it might seem that this verse teaches universal salvation, that all men are saved through the work of Christ. But such a teaching would be completely in disagreement with the rest of the word of God. God has provided a way by which men's trespasses might not be imputed to them, but while that way is available to all, it is effective only in those who are in Christ. The trespasses of unsaved men are definitely reckoned to them, but the moment these men trust the Lord Jesus as Savior, they are reckoned righteous in Him, and their sins are blotted out.

In addition to His reconciling work, God **has** also **committed to** His servants **the word of reconciliation**. In other words, He has entrusted them with the marvelous privilege of going forth and preaching this glorious message to all men everywhere. Not to angels did He give such a sacred charge, but to poor, feeble man.

5:20 In the previous verse the apostle said he has been given the message of reconciliation. He has been sent forth to preach this message to mankind. We would like to suggest that from 5:20 through 6:2 we have a *summary* of the word of reconciliation. In other words, Paul lets us listen to the message which he preached to the unsaved as he went from country to country and continent to continent. It is important to see this. Paul is not here telling the Corinthians to be reconciled to God. They are already believers in the Lord Jesus. But he is telling the Corinthians that this is the message which he preaches to the unsaved wherever he goes.

An ambassador is a minister of state, representing his own ruler in a foreign land. Paul always speaks of the Christian ministry as an exalted and dignified calling. Here he likens himself to an envoy sent by **Christ** to the world in which we live. He was a spokesman for God, and **God** was **pleading through** him. This seems rather strange language to apply to an ambassador. Usually we do not think of an ambassador as **pleading**, but that is the glory of the gospel, that, in it, God is actually on bended knee and with tear-dimmed eye begging men and women to **be reconciled to** Himself. If any enmity exists, it exists on man's part. God has removed any barriers to complete fellowship between Himself and man. The Lord has done all he can possibly do. Now man must lay down his arms of rebellion, must cease his stubborn revolt, and must **be reconciled to God**.

5:21 This verse gives us the doctrinal foundation for our reconciliation. How has God made reconciliation possible? How can He receive guilty sinners who come to Him in repentance and faith? The answer is that the Lord Jesus has effectively dealt with the whole problem of our sins, so now we can be reconciled to God.

In other words, God **made** Christ **to be sin for us** — Christ **who knew no sin — that we might become the righteousness of God in Him**.

We must beware of any idea that on the cross of Calvary the Lord Jesus Christ actually became *sinful* in Himself. Such an idea is false. Our sins were placed *on* Him, but they were not *in* Him. What happened is that God made Him to be a sin-offering on our behalf. Trusting in Him, we are reckoned righteous by God. The claims of the law have

been fully satisfied by our Substitute.

What a blessed truth it is that the One **who knew no sin** was **made sin for us, that we** who knew no righteousness **might become the righteousness of God in Him**. No mortal tongue will ever be able to thank God sufficiently for such boundless grace.

6:1 Some understand that in this verse Paul is addressing the Corinthians and encouraging them to make full use of **the grace** that had been shown to them.

We rather think that Paul is still giving an account of the message which he preached to the unsaved. He has already told unbelievers of the marvelous grace which has been offered to them by God. Now he further begs them **not to receive** such **grace in vain**. They should not allow the seed of the gospel to fall in barren soil. Rather they should respond to such a marvelous message by receiving the Savior of whom it tells.

6:2 Paul now quotes from Isaiah 49:8. If we go back and study that chapter, we find that God is in controversy with His people because of their rejection of the Messiah. In verse 7 you see the Lord Jesus rejected by the nation, and we know that His rejection led to His death. But then in verse 8 we have the words of Jehovah, assuring the Lord Jesus that His prayer has been heard and that God would help and preserve Him.

In the day of salvation I have helped you. This refers to the resurrection of the Lord Jesus Christ. The **acceptable time** and **the day of salvation** would be ushered in by Christ's resurrection from among the dead.

In his preaching of the gospel, Paul seizes upon this marvelous truth and announces to his unsaved listeners, **Behold, now is the accepted time; behold, now is the day of salvation**. In other words, the era of which Isaiah had prophesied as **the day of salvation** has already come, so Paul urges men to trust the Savior while it is still **the day of salvation**.

J. Paul's Behavior in the Ministry (6:3–10)

6:3 Here Paul switches from the message which he preached to his own behavior in the Christian **ministry**. He realized that there are always people who are looking for an excuse not to listen to the message of salvation, and if they can find that excuse in the inconsistent life of the preacher, so much the better. So he reminds the Corinthians that he gave **no offense in anything, that** the **ministry** might **not be blamed**. As we pointed out previously, the ministry here does not refer to some dignified, ecclesiastical office, but rather to the service of Christ. The idea of human ordination is not involved. The **ministry** belongs to all who are Christ's.

6:4 In verses 4 through 10 the apostle describes the way he sought to carry out his ministry — a manner that was above reproach. Conscious that he was a servant of the Most High, he always sought to behave in a manner worthy of such a calling. On this section Denney finely comments:

> The fountains of the great deep are broken up with him as he thinks of what is at issue; he is in all straits, as he begins, and can speak only in disconnected words, one at a time; but before he stops, he has won his liberty, and pours out his soul without restraint.[29]

Verses 4 and 5 describe the physical sufferings which Paul endured and which attested him as a sincere, faithful servant of the Lord. The next two verses have to do with the Christian graces which he exhibited. Then in verses 8 through 10 he lists the contrasting experiences which are so typical of the Christian ministry.

In much patience doubtless describes Paul's longsuffering toward individuals, local churches, and all the afflictions which were calculated to move him from his pathway of steadfastness.

Tribulations might refer to actual persecutions which he endured for the name of Christ.

Needs convey the idea of the privations he suffered, probably of food, clothing, and lodging.

Distresses might well include the unfavorable circumstances in which he often found himself.

6:5 Paul suffered many **stripes** as stated in Acts 16:23. His **imprisonments** are later referred to in 2 Corinthians 11:23, and doubtless the **tumults** refer to the riots and uproars which often fol-

lowed his preaching of the gospel. (The message that Gentiles could be saved in the same way as Jews caused some of the most violent outbursts.) Paul's **labors** might include his tent-making but also doubtless other forms of manual labor, to say nothing of his travels. **Sleeplessness** describes his constant need for being on the alert against the wiles of the devil and the efforts of his enemies to harm him. **Fastings** might include voluntary abstinence from food, but here it more probably means hunger that was forced by poverty.

6:6 Paul's ministry was conducted **by purity**, that is, in chastity and holiness. He could never be justly accused of immorality.

It was also conducted **by knowledge**, and this perhaps refers to the fact that it was not a ministry of ignorance but of divinely imparted **knowledge**. This is wonderfully shown by the breadth of divine truth revealed in Paul's Epistles.

The Corinthians should not need any proof of his **longsuffering**! The patient way in which he had put up with their sins and failings should have been proof enough! Paul's **kindness** was shown in his unselfish giving of himself for others, in his loving attitude toward the people of God, and in his sympathetic demeanor.

The expression **by the Holy Spirit** doubtless means that all Paul did was done in the Spirit's power and in subjection to Him.

By sincere love suggests that the **love** which was so obvious in the life of the Apostle Paul toward others was not pretended or hypocritical, but genuine. It characterized all his actions.

6:7 By the word of truth may indicate that all of Paul's ministry was carried out in obedience to **the word of truth**, or it may mean that it was an honest ministry, consistent with the type of message which he preached, namely, **the word of truth**.

By the power of God doubtless signifies that the apostle did not carry on his work in his own power, but in simple dependence on the strength which **God** provides. Some have also suggested that this may be a reference to the miracles which the apostle was empowered to perform because he was an apostle.

The armor of righteousness is described in Ephesians 6:14–18. It pictures an upright, consistent character. Someone has said, "When a man is clothed in practical righteousness, he is impregnable." If our conscience is void of offense toward God and man, the devil has little to shoot at.

There is some doubt as to the exact meaning of the expression **on the right hand and on the left**. One of the more probable explanations is that in ancient warfare the sword was held in the right hand and the shield in the left. The sword spoke of offensive combat and the shield of defensive. In that case, Paul would here be saying that a good Christian character is the best offense and defense.

6:8 Here and in verses 9 and 10 Paul describes some of the sharp contrasts that are found in service for the Lord Jesus. The true disciple experiences the mountain tops and the valleys, as well as all the territory that lies between. It is a life of **honor and dishonor**, of victory and seeming defeat, of commendation and criticism. The true servant of God is the object of **evil report and good report**. Some speak well of his zeal and courage, whereas others have only condemnation for him. He is treated as a deceiver or impostor, **and yet** he is **true** for all that. He is no impostor, but a genuine servant of the Most High God.

6:9 In one sense Paul was **unknown**, unappreciated, and misunderstood as far as the world was concerned, and yet he was **well known** to God and to his fellow believers.[30]

His life was one of daily **dying, and** yet **behold** he lived! Threatened, hunted, pursued, persecuted, and imprisoned, he won his freedom only to preach the gospel with greater zeal. This is further emphasized in the expression **as chastened, and yet not killed. Chastened** here has to do with the punishment which he endured at the hands of men. Many times, perhaps, they thought they had brought his tumultuous life to a close — only to hear of his exploits for Christ in other cities!

6:10 There was sorrow in connection with the ministry, and **yet** Paul was **always rejoicing**. Needless to say, he sorrowed over rejection of the gospel message, over the failures of God's people, and over his own shortcomings. Yet, when he thought of the Lord, and of the promises of God, there was always great cause to look up and rejoice.

Paul was a **poor** man as far as this world's goods are concerned. We do not read of his having property and wealth. Yet think of the lives that have been enriched through his ministry! Though he possessed **nothing**, yet in a sense he had **all things** that really counted.

"In these climacteric sentences," writes A. T. Robertson, "Paul lets his imagination loose and it plays like lightning on the clouds."[31]

K. Paul's Appeal for Openness and Affection (6:11–13)

6:11 And now the apostle bursts into an impassioned appeal for the **Corinthians** to open their hearts to him. He had **spoken openly** and frankly to them of his love. Since the mouth speaks out of the abundance of the heart, Paul's opened mouth spoke of a heart that was wide with affection for these people. That this is the general meaning of the verse is indicated by the following words: **our heart is wide open**, that is, ready to receive them in love.

As Tozer expressed it: "Paul was a little man with a vast interior life; his great heart was often wounded by the narrowness of his disciples. The sight of their shrunken souls hurt him much."[32]

6:12 Any restriction in **affections** between the Corinthians and Paul is not in himself but in them. They might have limited love toward him, so that they were not sure whether they should receive him or not, but he was not at all limited in his love toward them. The lack of love was on their side, not Paul's.

6:13 If they want to recompense his love to them (he is speaking to those who were his **children** in the faith), they should allow their affections toward him to **be** more **open**. Paul felt toward them as a father. They should love him as their father in the faith. Only God could bring this about, but they should allow Him to do it in their lives.

The Moffatt translation catches the idea of verses 11 through 13 nicely:

O Corinthians, I am keeping nothing back from you; my heart is wide open for you.

"Restraint?" — that lies with you, not me. A fair exchange now, as the children say! Open your hearts wide to me.

L. Paul's Appeal for Scriptural Separation (6:14–7:1)

6:14 The connection between verses 13 and 14 is this: Paul has told the saints to be open in their affections toward him. Now he explains that one way to do this is to separate from all forms of sin and unrighteousness. Doubtless he is thinking, in part, of false teachers who had invaded the assembly at Corinth.

Mention of the unequal yoke suggests Deuteronomy 22:10: "You shall not plow with an ox and a donkey together." The ox was a clean animal and the donkey unclean, and their step and pull are unequal. By way of contrast, when believers are yoked with the Lord Jesus, they find that His yoke is easy and His burden is light (Matt. 11:29, 30).

This section of 2 Corinthians is one of the key passages in all the word of God on the subject of separation. It is clear instruction that the believer should separate himself from **unbelievers**, iniquity, darkness, Belial, idols.

It certainly refers to the marriage relationship. A Christian should not marry an unsaved person. However, in cases where a believer is *already* married to an unbeliever, this passage does not justify separation or divorce. God's will in such a case is that the marriage relationship should be maintained with a view to the eventual salvation of the unsaved member (1 Cor. 7:12–16).

In addition to this, it refers to business. A Christian should not go into partnership with one who does not know the Lord. It applies clearly to secret orders or fraternities: How could one who is faithful to Christ consistently go on in an association where the name of the Lord Jesus is unwelcome? Its application to social life would be as follows: A Christian should maintain contact with the unsaved in an effort to win them to Christ, but he should never engage in their sinful pleasures or in any of their activities in such a way as to lead them to think he is no different than they. Then this section would also apply to religious matters: A faithful follower

of Christ would not want to hold membership in a church where unbelievers were knowingly admitted as members.

Verses 14 through 16 cover all the important relationships of life:

Righteousness and *lawlessness* describe the whole sphere of moral behavior.

Light and *darkness* have to do with intelligence as to the things of God.

Christ and *Belial* have to do with the realm of authority, in other words, the person or thing whom one acknowledges as master in his life.

Believer and *unbeliever* have to do with the realm of faith.

The temple of God and *idols* take in the whole subject of a person's worship.

Righteousness and **lawlessness** can have no fellowship together: they are moral opposites. Neither can **light** have **communion with darkness**. When **light** enters a room, the **darkness** is dispelled. Both cannot exist together at the same time.

6:15 The name **Belial** means "worthlessness" or "wickedness." Here it is a name for the evil one. Can there ever be peace between **Christ** and Satan? Obviously not! Neither can there be fellowship between **a believer** and **an unbeliever**. To attempt it is treason against the Lord.

6:16 **Idols** have nothing to do with **the temple of God**. That being the case, how can believers traffic with idols, since they are **the temple of the living God**. Idols here, of course, mean not only carved images but any objects which come between the soul and Christ. They could be money or pleasure or fame or material things.

The apostle finds abundant proof that we are **the temple of the living God** in such passages as Exodus 29:45, Leviticus 26:12 and Ezekiel 37:27. Denney says:

> [Paul] expects Christians to be as much in earnest as Jews to keep the sanctity of God's house inviolate; and now, he says, that house are we: it is ourselves we have to keep unspotted from the world.[33]

6:17 That being so, Paul issues a challenging call to **come out**. He quotes from Isaiah 52:11. These are God's plain instructions to His people concerning separation from evil. Christians are not to stay in the midst of it, as part of it, in order to remedy it. God's program is **come out**. The **unclean** thing in this verse is primarily the heathen world, no doubt, but it also applies to any form of evil, whether commercial, social, or religious.

The verse should *not* be used to teach separation from other believers. Christians are exhorted to endeavor "to keep the unity of the Spirit in the bond of peace."

6:18 It is often very hard for Christians to sever ties that have existed for years in order to be obedient to the word of God. It would seem that God anticipates such a difficulty in verse 18. He has already said in verse 17, "I will receive you," and now He adds, **"I will be a Father to you, and you shall be My sons and daughters, says the LORD Almighty."** The recompense for standing with Christ outside the camp of evil is to know fellowship with the **Father** in a new and more intimate way. It does not mean that we become sons and daughters by obedience to His word, but that we are *manifestly* His **sons and daughters** when we behave in this way, and we will experience the joys and delights of sonship in a way we never have before.

"The blessedness of true separation is nothing less than the glorious companionship of the great God Himself" (Selected).

The problem abounds on every hand today among evangelical Christians in liberal and neo-orthodox churches. They are continually asking, "What shall I do?" God's answer is found here. They should leave a fellowship where the Lord Jesus is not honored and exalted as God's well-beloved Son and the Savior of the world. They can do more for God outside such a fellowship than they will ever accomplish inside it.

7:1 This verse is closely linked with what has gone before. It does not begin a new paragraph but closes the paragraph that began with 6:14.

The **promises** referred to in this verse are those quoted in verses 17 and 18 of the previous chapter. "I will receive you . . . will be a Father to you . . . you shall be My sons and daughters." In view of these marvelous **promises** of God, we should **cleanse ourselves from all filthiness of the flesh and spirit**. Defilement of **the flesh** includes all forms

of physical impurity, whereas filthiness of the **spirit** covers one's inward life, motives, and thoughts.

But God not only gives the negative side, there is also the positive. **Perfecting holiness in the fear of God**. We are not only to put aside that which is defiling, but we are to become increasingly conformed to the Lord Jesus Christ in our daily lives. This verse does not suggest that it is ever possible to become perfectly holy while still here on earth. Practical sanctification is a process that goes on through our lifetime. We grow in likeness to the Lord Jesus Christ until the day when we see Him face to face, and then we shall be like Him throughout all eternity. It is as we have a reverential fear or awe of God that we have a desire in our hearts to become holy. May we all learn to say with the godly McCheyne, "Lord, make me as holy as it is possible for a man to be on this side of heaven."

M. Paul's Joy at the Good News from Corinth (7:2–16)

7:2 **Open your hearts to us.** There was no reason why the Corinthians should not do this, Paul goes on to say, because he had **wronged no one**, he had **corrupted no one**, he had **cheated no one**. Whatever his critics might be saying against him, the Apostle Paul had not injured anyone, he had not taken advantage of anyone financially.

7:3 Nothing Paul has said or is saying is intended **to condemn** the Corinthians in any way. He had repeatedly assured them that his deep affection for them would continue in life and in death.

7:4 Because he felt so intimately attached to the saints at Corinth, the apostle felt at liberty to use **great boldness of speech** when addressing them directly. But if his frankness to them was great, so also was his **boasting** about them in the presence of others. Thus they should not misinterpret his bluntness as indicating any lack of love; rather they should realize that he was truly proud of them and that he spoke highly of them wherever he went. Probably the particular aspect of their Christian life which evoked sincere commendation from Paul was their willing attitude in connection with the collection for the poor saints in Jerusalem. The apostle will come to that subject directly, but here he only makes a passing allusion to it.

I am filled with comfort. I am exceedingly joyful in all our tribulation. These expressions are explained in the verses to follow. Why was Paul so **joyful** in spite of **all** his **tribulation**? The answer is that Titus brought him a good report concerning the Corinthians, and this proved to be a source of tremendous cheer and encouragement to him.

7:5 We have previously mentioned how Paul left Ephesus and journeyed to Troas in search of Titus. Not finding him there, he crossed over **to Macedonia**. Now he explains that even his arrival in Macedonia did not give him the **rest** he sought. He was still disquieted, still **troubled**, still persecuted. On the **outside**, the enemy was hammering away mercilessly, while on the **inside** there were **fears** and anxieties — connected, no doubt, with the fact that he had not yet made contact with Titus.

7:6 Then **God** stepped in and **comforted** Paul **by the coming of Titus**. At this time the apostle experienced the truth of Proverbs 27:17, "As iron sharpens iron, so a man sharpens the countenance of his friend." Picture the joyful meeting between these two devoted servants of Christ, Paul's questions tumbling out one on top of the other, and Titus trying to answer them as quickly as possible! (See also Prov. 25:25.)

7:7 But it was **not only** the joyful reunion with his friend that made Paul so glad; rather it was the report of how **comforted** Titus had been with the response of the Corinthians to Paul's letter.

It was good news to hear that the Corinthians longed to see the Apostle Paul. This was in spite of the determined efforts on the part of the false teachers to alienate the affections of the saints from Paul. Not only were they anxious to see him, but they evidenced real **mourning**. This **mourning** may have been over the careless attitude they had taken by tolerating sin in the assembly, or it may have been over the distress and anxiety they had caused the apostle. In addition to this **mourning**, Titus reported their genuine regard for Paul and their **earnest desire** to please him.

Thus the apostle's rejoicing was **not**

just in the **coming** of Titus, but in these evidences of the fact that the Corinthians had been obedient to Paul's instructions and that they still felt kindly toward him.

7:8 **For even if I made you sorry with my letter, I do not regret it; though I did regret it. For I perceive the same epistle made you sorry, though only for a while.**

The **letter** Paul refers to may be what we know as 1 Corinthians, or it may be a second letter, now lost to us, which dealt with the saints rather severely.

With regard to Paul's **regret** over having written the **letter**, this point should be made clear. Assuming he refers to 1 Corinthians, it does not at all affect the subject of inspiration. The things which the apostle wrote were the very commandments of the Lord; yet Paul himself was still a man, prone to the discouragements and anxieties of other men. Williams comments:

> The distinction between the writer and inspiration appears in verse 8. He knew that his first letter was inspired. Its words were "the commandments of the Lord," but as a feeble, anxious, and affectionate man, he trembled lest the effect of the communications should estrange the Corinthians from him, and should cause them pain. This is an interesting instance of the difference between the individuality of the Prophet and the message of the Holy Spirit given to him.[34]

To summarize, Paul is saying this: When the Corinthians first read his letter, it came as a rebuke to them, and they were pained. After sending the letter, the apostle anticipated their reaction to it, and this made him sorry. Not that he was conscious of having done any wrong; that is not the thought here at all. Rather he was sorry that in carrying out his work for the Lord, it was necessary that others should at times be cast into unhappiness temporarily in order that God's purposes might be worked out in their lives.

In the latter part of verse 8, Paul emphasizes that though the letter had **made** them **sorry**, yet it was **only for a while**. The first effect of the letter was to cause pain. But the sorrow did not last.

The whole process which the apostle is describing here may be likened to the work of a surgeon. In order for him to remove a dangerously infected part from the human body, it is necessary for him to cut deep into the flesh. He does not rejoice in thus causing pain to the patient, though he knows it must be done if the patient is to regain his health. Especially if the patient is a close friend, the surgeon is keenly aware of the suffering that will be necessary. But he realizes that this suffering is only temporary, and he is willing that it should be so in order that the final outcome might be favorable.

7:9 Paul did **not rejoice** in having inflicted pain on the Corinthians **but that** their temporary **sorrow** led them **to** the place of **repentance**. In other words, their sorrow led them to a change of mind resulting in a change of life. **Repentance**, says Hodge, "is not merely a change of purpose, but includes a change of heart which leads to a turning from sin with grief and hatred thereof unto God."[35]

The sorrow of the Corinthians was according to the will of God; it was the kind of sorrow that God likes to see. Because their sorrow and repentance were of a genuine, **godly** nature, they suffered no permanent ill effects from the rebuke delivered to them by the Apostle Paul.

7:10 This verse contrasts **godly sorrow** and **the sorrow of the world. Godly sorrow** means grief which comes into a man's life after he has committed a sin and which leads to his repentance. He realizes that God is speaking to him, and so he takes sides with God against himself and against his sin.

When Paul says that **godly sorrow produces repentance leading to salvation**, he is not necessarily thinking of the salvation of the soul (although that could be true also). After all, the Corinthians were already saved. But here **salvation** is used to describe *deliverance* from any type of sin, bondage, or affliction in a person's life.

There is a question whether the expression **not to be regretted** refers to repentance or salvation. Since it is equally true that no one ever regrets **repentance** *or* **salvation**, we can leave the question open.

The sorrow of the world is not true repentance but mere remorse. It **produces** bitterness, hardness, despair, and eventually **death**. It is illustrated in the life of Judas. He was not sorry for the results which his sin brought to the Lord Jesus, but only remorseful because of the terrible harvest which he himself reaped from it.

7:11 The apostle points to the experience of the Corinthians as an example of what he said in the first part of verse 10. The **very thing** which he had spoken concerning godly sorrow was manifest in their own lives. We would say today, "As evidence of this very fact **that you sorrowed in a godly manner.**" Then he goes on to state various results of their godly sorrow.

First of all, it produced **diligence**, or earnest care, in them. If this passage refers to the case of discipline described in the First Epistle, then this expression means that although at first they had been indifferent, they subsequently became very concerned about the whole matter.

Secondly he says, **what clearing of yourselves**. This does not mean that they tried to *justify* or excuse themselves, but rather that by taking resolute action, they tried to clear themselves of any further guilt or blame in the matter. Their change in attitude led to this change in action.

What indignation may refer to their attitude toward the sinner because of the reproach he brought on the name of Christ. But more probably it refers to their attitude toward themselves for ever having allowed such a thing to go on for so long without taking action on it.

What fear doubtless means they acted in the **fear** of the Lord, but it may also include the thought that they feared a visit from the apostle, if he had to come with a rod.

What vehement desire literally means "what longing." Most commentators agree that this refers to a genuine longing which had been awakened in their souls for a visit from Paul. However, it could also mean a strong **desire** to see the wrong righted and the evil corrected.

What zeal has been variously explained as meaning **zeal** for the glory of God, for the restoration of the sinner, for their own cleansing from defilement in the matter, or for taking sides with the apostle.

What vindication means "what punishment or what avenging." The thought simply is that they took corrective action against the offender in the assembly. They were determined that sin must be punished.

Paul then adds: **In all things you proved yourselves to be clear in the matter.** Of course, we are not to understand by this that they were never to blame, but simply that they had done everything they could to take the proper action and to act as they should have acted in the first place.

7:12 There are four major problems in this verse. First, which letter does Paul refer to in this expression, **I wrote to you**? Second, who is the man **who had done the wrong**? Third, who is the man **who suffered wrong**? Finally, should the last part of the verse be translated **our care for you**, or "your care for us"?

The letter could be the one we know as 1 Corinthians, or it could be a subsequent letter which was not preserved for us. The wrongdoer could be the incestuous man of 1 Corinthians 5, or it could be some rebel in the church. If Paul is speaking of the incestuous man, then the injured person was the man's own father. On the other hand, if the wrongdoer was a rebel, then the injured person was Paul himself or some unidentified victim.

In the KJV and NKJV, the latter part of the verse reads: **but that our care for you in the sight of God might appear to you**. But most modern versions are similar to the NASB: "that your earnestness on our behalf might be made known to you in the sight of God."

7:13 Because his letter had had the desired effect, Paul was **comforted**. The Corinthians had repented and taken sides with him. In addition, he was encouraged by the enthusiasm **Titus** showed concerning the saints; he had **been refreshed by** his contact with them.

7:14 Apparently before the apostle sent Titus to Corinth, he had spoken to him glowingly about the believers there. Now he is saying his **boasting** did not prove to be untrue. All that he had said about the Corinthians was verified by the experience of **Titus** in their midst. Just as everything the apostle had ever said to the Corinthians was true, **so** his

boasting to Titus had been **found true** also.

7:15 Obviously Titus did not know what kind of a reception he would get when he reached southern Greece. Perhaps he had anticipated the worst. But when he did arrive, the Corinthians gave him a cordial welcome, and not only so, they endeared themselves to him all the more by being obedient to the instructions which he carried from the Apostle Paul.

When the apostle says that they received Titus **with fear and trembling**, he does not mean abject terror or cowardly fear, but rather a sense of reverence before the Lord in the matter and a scrupulous desire to please.

7:16 When Paul says he had **confidence in** the saints **in everything**, we must not make his words say more than he intended. They certainly do not mean that he considered the Corinthians to be beyond the possibility of sin or failure. But rather they mean that the **confidence** which he had placed in them, and of which he had boasted to Titus, had not been in vain. They had proved themselves *worthy* of his trust. It doubtless includes the idea also that since they had taken a proper attitude in reference to the matter discussed in the First Epistle, he feels justified in having full **confidence in** them.

This verse completes the first section of 2 Corinthians, a section which, as we have seen, has been devoted to a description of the apostle's ministry and a determined effort on Paul's part to strengthen the bonds which existed between the Corinthians and himself. The next two chapters handle "the grace of giving."

II. PAUL'S EXHORTATION TO COMPLETE THE COLLECTION FOR THE JERUSALEM SAINTS (Chaps. 8, 9)

A. Good Examples of Generous Giving (8:1–9)

8:1 Paul wanted the believers to know the very unusual way in which **the grace of God** had manifested itself among the Christians in **the churches of Macedonia** (northern Greece). Philippi and Thessalonica were two of the cities where churches had been planted.

The particular way in which these Macedonians showed that they had received **the grace of God** was by their *generosity*.

8:2 These Christians had been going through **a great trial of affliction**. Ordinarily, people thus tested would seek to save their money to provide for their future. And especially so if they were not very prosperous, as was the case with the Macedonians. They did not have very much money at all. Yet their Christian **joy** was so overflowing that when the need of the saints in Jerusalem was presented to them, they reversed all ordinary behavior and gave in a most liberal manner. They were able to combine **affliction, joy, poverty,** and **liberality**.

8:3 There were other unique features about their generosity. Their giving not only equaled **their ability**; it went **beyond their ability**. Also **they were freely willing**, that is, they gave spontaneously, without having to be pressured, coaxed, or cajoled.

8:4 So urgent were they in the matter that they begged Paul for the privilege of sharing in the relief of the Jerusalem saints. Perhaps the apostle hesitated to accept their kindness, knowing how poor they were themselves at the time. But they would not take "no" for an answer. They wanted to be allowed to give.

8:5 Probably Paul had **only** expected or **hoped** that they would act as most other mortals do: they give grudgingly at first, then increase the amount of the gift as greater pressure is brought to bear upon them. But not so the Macedonians! These beloved Christians **first gave** the greatest gift — **themselves**. Then afterwards it was an easy thing for them to give their money. When Paul says **they gave themselves to the Lord, and then to us by the will of God**, he simply means that first there was the complete committal of their lives to Christ, then they willingly gave themselves to Paul in the sense that they wanted to help in the collection for Jerusalem. They said to Paul, in effect, "We have given ourselves to the Lord, and now we give ourselves to you as His administrator. You tell us what to do, since

you are an apostle of Christ, our Lord."

"Contributions to the work of the Lord," says G. Campbell Morgan, "are only valuable as they are the gifts of those who are themselves yielded to God."

8:6 The apostle was so elated over the example of the Macedonians that he now wanted the Corinthians to imitate them. And so he says that he **urged Titus** to **complete** the work which he had begun at Corinth. In other words, when Titus had first visited the Corinthians, he had brought up this whole matter of the collection with them. Now when he goes back, he is instructed to see that good intentions are translated into *action*.

8:7 Since the Corinthians were so outstanding in many ways (and they were), Paul now wants them to excel in the matter of giving. He gives them credit for abounding **in faith, in speech, in knowledge, in all diligence** (earnestness), **and in** their **love for** him. In the First Epistle, Paul had commended them for their knowledge and speech. Here he adds several other virtues, doubtless as a result of Titus' visit.

The expression **in faith** may describe strong faith in God, the *gift* of faith, or *faithfulness* in their dealings with their fellow men.

In speech doubtless refers to their proficiency in the use of tongues, a subject which occupied considerable place in the First Epistle.

In knowledge may refer to the charismatic gift or to the breadth of their grasp of divine truths.

In all diligence describes their zeal and earnestness in the things of God.

Finally, their **love for** Paul is mentioned as being praiseworthy. Now Paul would like to add another expression to the list, namely, "in all generosity." Denney warns of:

> . . . the man who abounds in spiritual interests, who is fervent, prayerful, affectionate, able to speak in the Church, but unable to part with his money.[36]

8:8 Paul is not commanding this in a harsh, legalistic manner. Rather, he would like to put the **sincerity of** their **love** to the test, and especially so in the light of the eagerness or earnestness of the Macedonian Christians in this matter. When Paul states that he did **not** say this **by commandment**, he does not mean that it is not inspired. He simply means that the giving should come from a willing heart, because "God loves a cheerful giver."

8:9 It is at this point that the Apostle Paul introduces one of the greatest verses in this grand letter. Against a background of the petty circumstances of life in Macedonia and in Corinth he paints a lovely portrait of the most generous Person who ever lived.

The word **grace** is used in a variety of ways in the NT, but here the meaning is unmistakably that of generosity. How generous was the Lord Jesus? He was so generous that He gave *all He had* for our sakes **that** we **through His poverty might become** eternally **rich**.

Moorehead comments:

> He was rich in possessions, power, homage, fellowship, happiness. He became poor in station, circumstances, in His relations with men. We are urged to give a little money, clothing, food. He gave Himself.[37]

This verse teaches the pre-existence of the Lord Jesus. When was He **rich**? Certainly not when He came into the world as the Babe of Bethlehem! And certainly not during His thirty-three years of wandering "as a homeless stranger in the world His hands had made." He was rich in a bygone eternity, dwelling with the Father in the courts of heaven. But **He became poor**. This refers not only to Bethlehem but to Nazareth, Gethsemane, Gabbatha, and Golgotha. And it was all for our sakes, **that** we **through His poverty might become rich**.

If this is true, and it certainly is, then it should be our greatest joy to give all that we are and have to Him. No argument could be more forceful than this in the midst of Paul's discussion of Christian giving.

B. Good Advice to Complete the Collection (8:10, 11)

8:10 Now the apostle returns to the Corinthians. They had thought of making a collection for the poor saints before the Macedonians had decided to do it.

The Corinthians had actually begun to do it before the Macedonians started their fund. To be consistent, they should finish what they began **a year ago**. It would be to their advantage, because it would prove their sincerity and consistency.

8:11 Whatever their reason for delay, Paul tells them that they should disregard it and **complete** the thing which they had shown **a readiness** to do. They should do it according to the ability which they then had and not according to what they might like to do in the future if their wealth increased.

C. Three Good Principles for Generous Giving (8:12–15)

8:12 It seems the Corinthians had delayed in making a collection for the needy saints at Jerusalem hoping that they would be able to send more at a later date. They are here reminded, however, that it is not a question of how much they send at all. If there is a real desire in their heart to have fellowship in this good matter, then God accepts their gift, however small it may be. It's the heart attitude that counts.

8:13 Paul's purpose is not to put the Corinthians under financial strain. His thought is **not that** the Jerusalem church **should be eased** and the Corinthian church **burdened** or impoverished.

8:14 This verse describes God's program for the relief of want in the church of the Lord Jesus Christ. The Lord's purpose is that whenever a need exists in one area among Christians, then there should be a flow of funds from other areas to that needy spot. This constant flow and interflow of funds would result in an **equality** among the churches world-wide.

Thus, at the time Paul was writing, there would be a flow of funds from Corinth, Macedonia, and other places to Jerusalem. But perhaps in the future the saints at Jerusalem might be well cared for, whereas there might be definite **lack** in Corinth. In such an instance the flow of funds would be reversed. That is what Paul means by this verse. Now the need was in Jerusalem, but sometime in the future it might be in Corinth, and in that case others would help them.

8:15 This principle of equality is

emphasized by a quotation from Exodus 16:18. When the children of Israel went out to gather the manna, some were able to gather more than others. But it didn't matter. When the manna was distributed, each man received the same amount — one omer, or about five pints. So **"He who gathered much had nothing left over, and he who gathered little had no lack."** If anyone tried to *hoard* manna, it bred worms!

The equalization didn't happen by miracle or magic. It happened because those who had too much *shared* with those who didn't have enough. Hodge observes:

> The lesson . . . taught in Exodus and by Paul is that, among the people of God, the superabundance of one should be employed in relieving the necessities of others; and that any attempt to countervail this law will result in shame and loss. Property is like manna; it will not bear hoarding.[38]

Along the same lines is this selection from an unknown source:

> God intends each man to have a share of the good things of life. Some gather more, however, and some less. Those who have more should share with those who have less. God permits the unequal distribution of property, not so that the rich shall selfishly enjoy it, but share it with the poor.

D. Three Good Brethren to Prepare the Collection (8:16–24)

8:16 In these next two verses **Titus** is commended for the excellent attitude he has taken in the matter. First, **God** is thanked for putting **the same earnest care for** the Corinthians **into the heart of Titus**. Paul had found a kindred spirit in his fellow worker. The **same** burden which the apostle had for the Corinthians, he found to be shared by **Titus.**

8:17 Paul had exhorted Titus to go to Corinth with this Letter, but the exhortation was not necessary. He wanted to go **of his own accord**.

The clause **he went to you** probably means "he is going to you." It illustrates the epistolary aorist tense, which views the action not at the time when Paul wrote the Letter but when the Corinthians read it. Titus was unquestionably the one who carried this Letter to Corinth.

He didn't leave for Corinth until Paul finished the Letter.

8:18 Verses 18 through 22 describe two other Christian brethren who would accompany Titus on his mission. The first one is described in verses 18 through 21, and the second in verse 22. Both are unnamed.

This section of Scripture is valuable in showing the precautions which the Apostle Paul took in handling funds lest there be any basis for accusing him of mishandling the money.

The first **brother** referred to was one who was worthy of **praise** because of his work **in the gospel**. There is a great difference of opinion as to who is meant. Some say Luke, others Silas, some Trophimus. But perhaps by trying to guess we miss the whole spirit of the passage. Is it not intentional that he is unnamed? True discipleship often involves obscurity. This was so with the little maid who was used so greatly in the life of Naaman, the leper. It was also true with the little boy who put his lunch at the disposal of the Lord Jesus.

8:19 This unnamed brother **was also chosen by the churches** to make the journey necessitated by **this gift**. In other words, he was appointed to be one of the messengers to carry this freely-given contribution. The apostle looked upon himself and the others as servants or administrators of this gracious work. They did it for **the glory of the Lord Himself**. And they wanted it to demonstrate their willingness and eagerness to serve the poor saints in Jerusalem.

8:20 The apostle was too wise a man to handle this money alone, or to commit it to any one other man. He insisted on its being handled by a group of two or three or more. That is what he means here in verse 20. To avoid any possibility of misrepresentation or scandal, he ensured that the handling of **this lavish gift** might be done in such a way that no evil speaking could result.

8:21 **Providing honorable things** means making sure that things are done honestly. Paul was anxious that his actions should not only be honest **in the sight of the Lord**, but that they should also be above reproach **in the sight of men**. Morgan notes: "It is the business of the Christian community to do its business in such a way that men of the world will have no cause to suspect anything contrary to righteousness in its affairs."[39]

This verse, incidentally, is nearly the same as Proverbs 3:3, 4 in the Septuagint.

8:22 Here we have another unknown **brother** whom Paul had appointed to help in this important matter. He had **often proved diligent** in many matters, and now he showed special diligence with regard to this particular errand, **because of the great confidence** he had **in** the Corinthians.

At this point the NKJV says, **because of the great confidence which** we have in you. The words **we have** are supplied (italics), and many prefer that he has be understood instead. Then Paul would be commending him not only for his past faithfulness, but because of his keen interest on this particular occasion by reason of his **confidence** in the Corinthians.

8:23 Therefore, Paul says that **if anyone inquires about** these three men, the Corinthians could tell them that **Titus** is Paul's **partner and fellow worker** for the Corinthians, and that these other two **brethren** are **messengers of the churches** and **the glory of Christ**. The expression **the glory of Christ** is certainly an exalted description of these men. It is because they are deputies **of the churches** that they are so called. They make the work of the Lord shine before the eyes of men. They are a credit to the Lord and reflect His glory.

8:24 In view of all this, the Corinthians should give them a good reception and should justify Paul's **boasting** about them by entrusting to them the generous gift for the saints at Jerusalem. This would be **proof** to the surrounding **churches** of their Christian **love**. Phillips translates the verse, "So do let them, and all the Churches, see how genuine is your love, and justify all the nice things we have said about you!"

E. Appeal to the Corinthians to Justify Paul's Boasting of Them (9:1–5)

9:1 It was quite unnecessary for Paul **to write to** the Corinthians **concerning** the subject of sending financial help

to needy **saints** — yet he proceeded to do so anyway. Perhaps there is a trace of irony in this verse. Actually, in some respects it was not necessary for him to write to them. They had shown a willingness from the outset to participate in the collection for Jerusalem. As far as willingness was concerned, they were to be commended. But they simply had not carried out their original intentions. That is why he feels it necessary to enlarge on the **superfluous.**

9:2 There was no question about their **willingness**. From the time the subject was first broached they had shown **zeal** and earnestness. In fact, Paul had boasted about them to the Christians in Macedonia. He told them **that Achaia was ready a year ago. Achaia**, the southern part of Greece, is here used to refer to Corinth, since Corinth was located there. When **the Macedonians** heard that the Christians in Corinth had been ready for a year, many of them (the Macedonians) were **stirred up**; they caught the contagion of Christian giving and decided to give themselves to it wholeheartedly.

9:3 When Paul says here that he has **sent the brethren**, he really means he is sending them. The past tense views it from the perspective of the readers rather than the writer. **The brethren** are the three mentioned in the previous chapter: Titus and two unnamed Christians. They were being sent so that Paul's boasting concerning the Corinthians would not be in vain with regard to the collection. The mission of the three brethren would be to ensure that the collection was prepared by the time that Paul got there.

9:4 When the apostle would make the trip from Macedonia south to Corinth, it was not unlikely that one of the Macedonian believers would accompany him on the trip. How embarrassing it would be to the Apostle Paul **if**, after boasting of the Corinthians, he should bring one of those **Macedonians** and **find** that the Corinthians had actually done nothing about the gift for Jerusalem! In such an event Paul's confidence in the Corinthians would have been put to shame, **not to mention** that the Corinthians themselves would then have real cause to be ashamed for their neglect.

Phillips' translation of this verse is colorful:

> For, between ourselves, it would never do if some of the Macedonians were to accompany me on my visit to you and find you unprepared for this act of generosity! We (not to speak of you) should be horribly ashamed, just because we had been so proud and confident of you.

9:5 This then is why Paul **thought it necessary to exhort** these three **brethren to go to** Corinth before he himself went. They would **prepare** their **generous gift beforehand, which** they **had previously promised** for the Jerusalem saints.

That it may be ready as a matter of generosity and not as a grudging obligation. There was no thought that these funds should be wrung out of the saints as by extortion but that it should be a manifestation of their **generosity**, given through their own free will.

F. The Good Rewards of Generous Giving (9:6–15)

9:6 In verses 6 through 15 the Apostle Paul lists some of the wonderful rewards and benefits of Christian giving. First, he sets forth the law of the harvest. It is a well-known fact in agriculture that a generous sowing of seed is necessary if there is to be a generous harvest. Perhaps the farmer is ready to put the seed in the ground. Shall he sow liberally or shall he take some of the grain and use it as food during the months ahead? The thought here is that if **he sows** it liberally, he **will also reap** out of all proportion to what he **sows**.

We should remember this with regard to agriculture — the farmer does not reap the exact amount of grain he sows, but much more proportionately. So it is in Christian giving: it is not a question of receiving back exactly what one has given but receiving back far out of proportion to the amount of the gift. Of course, the return is not so much in money as in spiritual blessings.

9:7 Each one is to **give as he purposes in his heart**. It will be necessary for him to consider what is necessary for his own immediate needs. He will have to think of just obligations which he will incur in the course of normal life. But then above that, he should think of the needs of his fellow Christians, and of the claims of Christ upon him. Taking all these considerations into view, he should give **not grudgingly or of necessity**. It is possible to give and yet not be happy about it. It is also possible to give under the pressure of emotional appeals or public embarrassment. None of these things will do. **God loves a cheerful giver.** It has often been pointed out that our word *hilarious* comes from the word translated **cheerful** (*hilaron*).

Does God really need our money? No, the cattle on a thousand hills belong to Him, and if He needed anything, He would not tell us (Psalm 50:10–12). But our heart's attitude is what is important to Him. He loves to see a Christian who is so filled with the joy of the Lord that he wants to share what he has with others.

God loves a cheerful giver because, as Jowett says:

> Cheerful giving is born of love, and therefore it is a lover loving a lover and rejoicing in the communion. Giving is the language of loving; indeed, it has no other speech. "God so *loved* that He *gave!*" Love finds its very life in giving itself away. Its only pride in possession is the joy of surrender. If love has all things, it yet possesses nothing. [40]

9:8 Here we have a promise that, if a person really wants to be generous, God will see that he is given the opportunity. **Grace** is here used as a synonym for resources. **God is able** to supply us with resources so that we will not only have a **sufficiency** ourselves, but so that we will be able to share what we have with others and thus **have an abundance for every good work**.

Notice the *alls* of this verse. **All grace, always** (that is, *at all times*), **all sufficiency, all things, every good work**.

9:9 Now the apostle quotes from Psalm 112:9. The expression **He has dispersed abroad** refers to the act of sowing seed. The verse describes a man who has been generous in his sowing of the seed, or more particularly in his deeds of kindness. The specific kindness in which he engaged was giving **to the poor**. Is he the loser by such action? No! **His righteousness endures forever.** This means that if we disperse kindness as a sower scatters his seed, we will be laying up for ourselves treasures in heaven. The results of our kindness will endure **forever**.

9:10 The illustration of **the sower** continues. The same God **who supplies seed to the sower and bread for food** is careful to make sure that those who show kindness to others will reap certain rewards. Some of those rewards are now listed. First, He will **multiply the seed you have sown.** That is, He will give greater opportunity and more abundant results from showing kindness to His people. Furthermore, He will **increase the fruits of your righteousness.** The Corinthians were righteous in giving to the saints at Jerusalem. As a result of that giving they would receive fruit by way of eternal reward. As God increased their ability to give, and they increased in generosity, the rewards would **increase** accordingly.

9:11 It is certainly clear from this section that a person never impoverishes himself by giving to the Lord. Rather, every act of kindness has a reflex action, and the reward is all out of proportion to the gift given. Thus Paul says here that the Christians, by their giving, would be **enriched in everything for** further displays of great **liberality.** As the apostles looked on and saw the Corinthians growing in the grace of giving, they (the apostles) would give thanks **to God.**

9:12 When the gift from the Corinthians was put to work in Jerusalem, it would not only supply **the needs of the saints** there but would also result in many people giving thanks **to God.** We have noticed, time and again, the emphasis Paul puts on **thanksgivings.** Anything which resulted in the Lord being thanked assumed great importance in Paul's eyes.

9:13 There are still other benefits that would result from the Corinthians' gift. It would be a definite **proof** to the Judean Christians that there really had been a work of **Christ** in the lives of these Gentile converts. At one time the Jewish Christians had real doubts about such converts as the Corinthians. Perhaps they did not consider them to be full-fledged Christians. But this kindness would be to them a great **proof** of the reality of the faith of the Corinthians, and **they** would **glorify God for** what **the gospel of Christ** had done in Achaia, as well as for the **liberal** contribution which had been made to them.

9:14 And that is not all! Two more benefits follow. Because of the gift from Corinth to Jerusalem, the Jewish Christians would henceforth be careful to pray for the saints in Corinth, and there would be strong ties of affection. The saints in Jerusalem would **long for** the Corinthians because of **the exceeding grace of God** which the latter had shown.

9:15 At this point Paul simply bursts out into an exclamation! This verse has been a puzzle to many Bible scholars. They cannot see that it is closely connected with what has gone before. And they wonder what is meant by **His indescribable gift.**

But it seems to us that as the Apostle Paul reaches the end of his section on Christian giving, he is forced to think of the greatest Giver of all — **God** Himself. He thinks, too, of the greatest **gift** of all — the Lord Jesus Christ. And so he would leave his Corinthian brethren on this high note. They are children of God and followers of Christ. Then let them follow such worthy examples!

III. PAUL'S VINDICATION OF HIS APOSTLESHIP (Chaps. 10–13)

The last four chapters of this Epistle deal primarily with Paul's defense of his apostleship. The words of the Apostle Peter seem especially appropriate in describing this particular portion of Paul's writings: "In which are some things hard to understand." Paul is obviously answering charges made against him by his critics, but we are forced to form our own conclusions as to what the charges were by studying the text of Paul's answers. Throughout this section the apostle uses a great deal of irony. The difficulty is in knowing just *when* he is doing so!

However, it is a most rewarding portion of God's precious word, and we would certainly be much poorer without it.

A. Paul's Reply to His Accusers (10:1–12)

10:1 In verses 1–6 we have the apostle's answer to those who accused him of acting in accordance with the methods of worldly men.

First, he introduces himself simply as **I, Paul, myself**. Second, he pleads with the saints instead of acting in a dictatorial manner. Third, he bases his appeal on **the meekness and gentleness of Christ**. He is, of course, thinking of the pathway of the Lord Jesus when He was on earth as a Man. This, incidentally, is one of Paul's few references to the Savior's life on earth. Ordinarily, the apostle refers to Christ as the ascended, glorified One at the right hand of God.

In further description of himself, Paul says, **I who in presence am lowly among you, but being absent am bold toward you**. This obviously is spoken in irony. What his critics said was that Paul was cowardly when he was present with the people, but when he was **absent** he was **bold** as a lion. His boldness, they said, was evident in the overbearing attitude which he took in his letters.

10:2 This verse is connected with the *first part* of verse 1. There Paul started to say that he pleaded with the Corinthians, but he did not tell what was the content of his entreaty. Here he explains: **"I beg you that when I am present I may not be bold with that confidence by which I intend to be bold against some, who think of us as if we walked according to the flesh."** He did not want **to be bold** toward them as he intended **to be bold** toward those who accused him of acting in a carnal manner.

10:3 Here the thought is that **although** the apostles were living in bodies of **flesh**, they did not wage the Christian warfare **according to** fleshly methods or motives.

10:4 **The weapons of** the Christian **warfare are not carnal**. The Christian, for instance, does not use swords, guns, or the strategy of modern warfare in spreading the Christian gospel from shore to shore. But those are not the only carnal weapons of which the apostle is speaking. The Christian does not use wealth, glory, power, fluency, or cleverness to accomplish his aims.

Rather, he uses methods that are **mighty in God for pulling down strongholds**. Faith in the living God, prayer, and obedience to the word of God are the effective weapons of every true soldier of Jesus Christ. It is by these that **strongholds** are razed.

10:5 This verse tells us what is meant by "strongholds" in verse 4.

Paul saw himself as a soldier warring against the proud reasonings of man, **arguments** which oppose the truth. The true character of these **arguments** is described in the expression **against the knowledge of God**. It could be applied today to the reasonings of scientists, evolutionists, philosophers, and religionists who have no room for God in their scheme of things. The apostle was in no mood to sign a truce with these. Rather he felt committed to bring **every thought into captivity to the obedience of Christ**. All men's teachings and speculations must be judged in the light of the teachings of the Lord Jesus Christ. Paul would not condemn human reasoning as such, but would warn that we must not allow our intellects to be exercised in defiance of the Lord and in disobedience to Him.

10:6 As a soldier of Christ, the apostle was also **ready to punish all disobedience, when** the Corinthians had shown their **obedience** first of all. He was not going to act against the false teachers at Corinth until he was, first, sure of the **obedience** of the believers in all things.

10:7 The first sentence may be a question: **"Do you look at things according to the outward appearance?"** (NKJV). It may be a statement of fact: "You are looking only on the surface of things" (NIV). Or it may be an imperative: "Look at what is before your eyes" (RSV), that is, "Face the facts."

If we take it as a statement, it means that the Corinthians were prone to judge a man by whether or not he had a commanding presence, impressive eloquence, or great powers of logic. They were swayed by external appearance rather than by inward reality.

If anyone is convinced in himself

that he is Christ's, let him again consider this in himself, that just as he is Christ's, even so we are Christ's. Here Paul may be referring to those who said, "I am of Christ" (1 Cor. 1:12), probably meaning to the exclusion of others. He answers that no one has an exclusive claim on Christ. He belongs to the Lord Jesus as truly as they.

Whoever the exclusive Christians were, Paul does not deny they belonged to Christ. Therefore, in this passage he can hardly be referring to the false apostles and deceitful workers who transformed themselves into apostles of Christ (11:14). It seems that in this Letter Paul is dealing with different adversaries, some saved and some unsaved.

10:8 As an apostle of the Lord Jesus Christ, Paul had been given **authority** in connection with the churches he established. The aim of this authority was to build up the saints in their most holy faith. The false teachers, on the other hand, were exercising an authority among the Corinthians which they had never received from the Lord. Not only so, but they were exercising this authority in a manner to tear down the saints rather than build them up. So Paul says that even if he boasted more abundantly in the **authority, which the Lord gave** him, he would not be put to shame for it. His claims would eventually prove to be true.

10:9 He has said this in order that he might not **seem to terrify** the Christians **by** his **letters**. In other words, if the apostle should boast of his God-given authority, he does not want the Christians to think he is trying to scare them. That would be playing into the hands of his critics. Rather the Corinthians should remember that his authority was given to him for building them up, and that is how he used it.

10:10 Here we are permitted to listen to the very charge which was made against the Apostle Paul. His opponents charged him with writing threatening **letters**, but they said **his bodily presence is weak, and his speech contemptible**.

10:11 All who made such charges should **consider** that **when** Paul was going to be **present** with them, he would be the same as they said he was in his **letters**. This does not mean that Paul ad-

mitted to being overbearing in his letters. That was what they *said* about him. But he is saying that he would deal severely with them when he met them face to face. There would be no cowardliness about him.

10:12 It is obvious that the false teachers were in the habit of comparing themselves with others. They would hold up Paul before the gaze of the Corinthians in such a way as to make him a laughingstock. They considered themselves to be the inner circle. They were the elite ones. According to them, no one could stand by them and be seen in a favorable light. So Paul says in obvious satire, **"For we dare not class ourselves or compare ourselves with those who commend themselves. But they, measuring themselves by themselves, and comparing themselves among themselves, are not wise."** Bold as they accused Paul to be in his Letter, he here says he is not bold enough to number himself **with those who commend themselves**, or with those whose only standard of measurement is their own life.

It should be obvious that if a person's only standard is himself, then he is always right! There is no room for improvement. Those who do this **are not wise**. As has been well said, "It is the bane of all cliques and coteries to ignore all excellence out of their own party."

B. Paul's Principle: To Break New Ground for Christ (10:13–16)

10:13 In verses 13–16 Paul states his intention of boasting only in **the sphere** of ministry **which God** had given to him. He made it a practice not to intrude into someone else's work when he wanted to boast. This is an obvious reference to the Judaizers. It was *their* practice to work their way into churches already established by the Apostle Paul or some other Christian, and there build upon another man's foundation. When they boasted, they were actually boasting in something that was the work of another.

Paul says he **will not boast** concerning matters which lie outside **the sphere** of his own service for Christ. Rather, he will make his boast in the places and persons where God had honored his ministry. That would include Corinth, since he had gone there with the gospel and a church had been formed as a result.

Arthur S. Way aptly translates:

> But I — I do not vaunt of prerogatives beyond my legitimate province. I confine myself within the limits of the sphere of operations allotted to me by God — and that province certainly included my mission to you.

Actually, Paul had been commissioned by the Lord to take the gospel to the Gentiles. This commission would, of course, include Corinth. The apostles in Jerusalem had agreed to this, but now false teachers were coming from Jerusalem and invading the provinces which God had given to the Apostle Paul.

10:14 The apostle is not indulging in excessive boasting. God had appointed a sphere of service to him. That sphere included Corinth. He had come to Corinth, preached the gospel, and planted a church. If he had not come as far as Corinth, he could be accused of boasting beyond his proper limit.

He had undergone trial, testing, affliction, and difficulties in order that he might reach the Corinthians. Now others were invading the sphere which he had pioneered, and they were probably boasting loudly about their achievements.

The NIV translates this difficult verse: "We are not going too far in our boasting, as would be the case if we had not come to you, for we did get as far as you with the gospel of Christ."

10:15 The apostle is determined that he will **not** boast of matters which were not directly the result of his own service for Christ. That is the very thing of which the Judaizers were guilty: they boasted in other men's labors. They tried to steal Paul's sheep, assassinated his character, contradicted his teaching, and assumed a false authority.

Paul's hope was that when the Corinthians' **faith increased**, and he could move on, their **faith** would express itself in practical help that would enable him to go into still further regions as God's apostle. As he thus extended his ministry, he would follow his rule consistently.

The troubles at Corinth were so occupying his time that he was hindered from fulfilling his mission to the regions beyond.

10:16 The rule was **to preach the gospel in the regions beyond** the Corinthians (probably meaning Western Greece, Italy, and Spain) **and not to boast in another man's sphere of accomplishment**. The Apostle Paul did not intend to trespass on others' fields of labor or to glory in what other men had done before he got to a certain place.

C. Paul's Supreme Goal: The Commendation of the Lord (10:17, 18)

10:17 If anyone **glories**, he should **glory in the LORD**. Doubtless this means he should **glory** only in what **the LORD** has been pleased to do through him. This seems to be the general direction of the apostle's argument.

10:18 After all, self-commendation is not what wins God's approval. The question that Paul's critics should face is this: Has the Lord commended you by so blessing your ministry that souls have been saved, that saints have been established in the faith, and that churches have been planted? Can you demonstrate the approval of the Lord by pointing to those who have been converted through your preaching? This is what counts. Paul was willing and able to show such proof of the Lord's commendation of his ministry.

In this chapter and the next, Paul indulges in what he calls folly. He is going to engage in the foolish business of speaking well of himself. It is not that he wants to do this at all. It was positively distasteful to him. But he asks the Corinthians to bear with him as he thus makes a fool of himself.

Apparently the false teachers had engaged in a great deal of boasting. They doubtless gave glowing accounts of their service and of their spectacular successes. Paul had never done this. He had preached Christ and not himself.

The Corinthians seemed to prefer the boasting type of ministry, and so Paul asks them to let him engage in it for a while.

D. Paul's Assertion of His Apostleship (11:1–15)

11:1 Oh, that you would bear with me in a little folly — and indeed you do bear with me. Paul wishes they would put up with him as he indulges in boasting. But then he senses that they are already doing it, so the request is unnecessary.

11:2 Three reasons are then given why he should make this request of them. The first reason is that he was **jealous for** the Corinthians **with godly jealousy**. He had **betrothed** them **to one husband, that** he might **present** them **as a chaste virgin to Christ**. Paul felt a personal responsibility for the spiritual welfare of the Corinthian saints. His desire was that in a coming day, i.e., at the Rapture, he could present them to the Lord Jesus, uncorrupted by the false teachings that were then prevalent. It was because he was thus jealous over them that he was willing to indulge in what seemed to be folly.

11:3 The second reason for Paul's playing the fool was his **fear** that the saints might be deceived and their **minds** might **be corrupted from the simplicity** and purity of devotion to **Christ**. Here **simplicity** means singleheartedness. He wanted them to be devoted to the Lord Jesus alone, and not to allow their hearts' affections to be drawn away by anyone else. Then, too, he wanted them to be unspotted in their devotedness to the Lord.

The apostle remembers how **the serpent deceived Eve by his craftiness**. He did it with an appeal to her mind or intellect. That is exactly what the false teachers were doing in Corinth. Paul would have the heart of the Corinthian virgin to be undivided and unspotted.

Note that Paul treats the account of Eve and the serpent as fact, not myth.

11:4 The third reason why the apostle was willing to indulge in a little folly was that the Corinthians had shown a readiness to listen to false teachers.

When anyone came to Corinth actually preaching **another Jesus**, and professing to dispense **a different spirit** than the Holy Spirit, and proclaiming **a different gospel**, the Corinthians put up with such a one quite willingly. They showed a lovely toleration of these views. Paul is saying sarcastically, "If you do that with others, why don't you do it with me?"

The final words, **"you may well put up with it!"** must be understood as

irony. The apostle is not endorsing their acceptance of heresy, but chiding them for their gullibility and lack of discernment.

11:5 The reason they should be willing to put up with Paul is that he is **not at all inferior to the most eminent apostles**. The expression, **most eminent**, is used in sarcasm. The literal (and modern-sounding!) rendering is "the super-apostles."

The Reformers quoted this verse to refute the papal notion that Peter was the chief apostle and that the popes inherited this primacy.

11:6 Though Paul might have been **untrained in speech**, he certainly was **not** deficient **in knowledge**. This should have been obvious to the Corinthians, because it was from the apostle that they had received their **knowledge** of the Christian faith. Whatever Paul's deficiencies might have been as far as eloquence was concerned, he apparently had made himself intelligible to the saints at Corinth. They themselves would have to bear witness to this.

11:7 If his unpolished speech was not the reason the Corinthians had taken such a negative attitude toward him, perhaps it was because he had committed an offense **in humbling** himself **that** they **might be exalted**. The rest of the verse explains what he means here. When the apostle was with the Corinthians he did not receive any financial assistance from them. Perhaps they felt he had committed a sin in taking such a humble place that they might have a high one.

11:8 The expression, **"I robbed other churches,"** is a figure of speech known as hyperbole. It is an exaggerated statement designed to produce a real effect on the mind. Paul does not mean he literally robbed other churches, of course, but it simply means that while he was serving the Lord at Corinth he received financial assistance from **other churches** so that he might serve the Corinthians without any remuneration at all from them.

11:9 There were times during his stay at Corinth when the Apostle Paul was actually **in need**. Did he make known that **need** to the Corinthians and insist on help from them? He certainly did not. Some **brethren who came from**

Macedonia supplied what he **lacked** in material things.

In every way possible the apostle **kept** himself **from being burdensome to** the Corinthians, and he intended to continue so doing. With regard to the Corinthians, he would not insist on his right as an apostle to be cared for by them.

11:10 Paul is determined that **no one** will rob him of his ground of **boasting in the regions of Achaia**, where Corinth is located. He is doubtless referring here to his critics who used his abstinence as an argument against him. They said he realized he was not a true apostle, and that is why he did not insist on being supported by the Christians (1 Cor. 9). In spite of the charges of his critics, he will continue to boast that he served the Corinthians without taking any money from them.

11:11 **Why** will he boast like this? **Because** he does **not love** the Corinthians? **God knows** this is not so! His heart was full of the deepest affection for them. It seemed that no matter what the apostle did, he was criticized. If he had taken money from the Corinthians, his opponents would have said he was just preaching for what he got out of it. By not taking money from them he subjected himself to the charge that he did not really **love** them. But **God knows** the truth of the matter, and Paul is content to leave it with Him.

11:12 It seems clear that the Judaizers expected, demanded, and received money from the Corinthians. Like most cultists, they would not have served unless it paid them financially. Paul was determined to **continue** his policy of not receiving money from the believers in Corinth. If the false teachers wanted to engage in a boasting match with him, let them follow his policy. But he knew they would never be able to boast of serving without monetary reward. Thus he cut out this ground of boasting from under them.

11:13 Paul's real estimate of these men, pent up so far in the Letter, at last bursts forth. He can contain himself no longer! He must call them what they are. **Such are false apostles** in the sense that they never were commissioned by the Lord Jesus Christ. They either assumed the office themselves or had it conferred on them by other men. They are **deceitful workers**, and this describes the methods by which they went about from church to church seeking to gain adherents to their false teachings. **Transforming themselves into apostles of Christ**, they pretended to represent Him. Paul has no desire to be on the same level as **such** men.

The things which the apostle says of these Judaizing teachers are true of false teachers in the present day. "Evil, we all know, could never tempt us if we saw it simply as it is; disguise is essential to its power; it appeals to man through ideas and hopes which he cannot but regard as good" (Selected).

11:14 The apostle has just said that his critics in Corinth posed falsely as apostles of Christ. But he is not surprised at this when he thinks of the tactics of their master: **And no wonder! For Satan himself transforms himself into an angel of light.**

Satan is commonly pictured today as a horned, evil-looking red creature with a tail. But such, of course, is far removed from the manner in which he presents himself to men.

Others think of Satan in connection with a poor drunkard, wallowing in the gutter on Skid Row. But this, too, is a false impression of what Satan is really like.

This verse tells us that he masquerades as **an angel of light**. Perhaps by way of illustration we might say he poses as a minister of the gospel, wearing religious clothing, and standing in the pulpit of a fashionable church. He uses religious words such as *God, Jesus*, and *the Bible*. But he deludes his hearers, teaching that salvation is by good works or by human merit. He does not preach redemption through the blood of Christ.

11:15 J. N. Darby once stated that Satan is never more satanic than when he carries a Bible. This is the thought in verse 15. If Satan himself poses falsely, it is not surprising if his agents do the same. How do they pose? As false teachers? As atheists? As infidels? The answer is no. They pose as **ministers of righteousness**. They profess to be **ministers** of religion. They profess to lead people in the way of truth and **righteousness**, but they are agents of the evil one.

Their **end will be according to their works**. They destroy — they **will** be destroyed. Their deeds lead men to their doom; they themselves will be led to final perdition.

E. Paul's Sufferings for Christ Support His Apostleship (11:16–33)

11:16 In saying all this, Paul hopes that **no one** will **think** of him as a boasting **fool**. But if they insist on doing so, yet let them **receive** him **as a fool** so that he **also** might **boast a little**.

Notice the **also** in the latter part of this verse: **that I also may boast a little**. This word has real significance. The false teachers were doing plenty of boasting. Paul says, in effect, "Even **if** you have to look on me as **a fool**, which I am not, even then **receive me** so that I may do a little boasting like these other men do."

11:17 This verse has two possible interpretations. Some suggest that what Paul is saying here, though it was truly inspired, was **not** given to him by commandment of **the Lord**.

The other interpretation is that what Paul is doing here, that is, boasting, is **not according to the Lord** in the sense that it did not follow the Lord's example. The Lord Jesus never boasted.

Phillips apparently adopts the first view by translating: "I am not now speaking as the Lord commands me but as a fool who must be 'in on' this business of boasting."

But we prefer the second view —that **boasting** was **not according to the Lord**, and that Paul was acting in seeming foolishness by thus engaging in self-glory. Ryrie comments: "He had to indulge in it [boasting], he says, against his natural instincts, so that he could call some significant facts to their attention."[41]

11:18 The Corinthians had recently heard a great deal from men who were engaging in self-glory according to corrupt human nature. If the Corinthians thought that the false teachers had sufficient cause for glorying, let them consider his boasts and see if they were not well-grounded.

11:19 Paul again resorts to satire. What he was asking them to do with himself, they were doing with others daily. They considered themselves too **wise** to be taken in by foolishness. But that was exactly what was happening, as he goes on to explain.

11:20 They were willing to **put up with** the type of man described.

Who was the man described? It is obvious from what follows that he was the Judaizing teacher, the false apostle who was preying on the Corinthians. First, he brought them **into bondage**. This speaks undoubtedly of the slavery of the law (Acts 15:10). He taught that faith in Christ was not sufficient for salvation, but that people must also obey the Law of Moses.

Second, he devoured the saints, in the sense that he made heavy financial demands on them. He did not serve them for the sake of love, but was interested in the monetary return.

The expression, **one takes from you**, is a metaphor for fishing or hunting. The false teacher tried to make these people his prey, leading them about as he desired.

It was characteristic of these men that they exalted themselves by pride and boastfulness. By criticizing others, they always tried to make themselves appear greater in the sight of men.

Finally, they struck the believers **on the face**, a great indignity. We need not hesitate to understand this literally, because arrogant churchmen down through the years have actually struck their parishioners as a way of asserting their authority.

The apostle marvels that the Corinthians were willing to **put up with** such abusive treatment from these false teachers, and yet they were not willing to bear with him in his loving warnings and admonitions to them.

Darby states: "It is wonderful what people will suffer from what is false — very much more than they will endure from what is true."[42]

11:21 In this verse some have suggested that Paul is saying: "I speak thus, by way of disparaging myself, as though when I was with you in person, I had been weak and afraid to assert my authority in the way which these men do."

Another suggestion is that the meaning is: "In saying this, I disparage myself, because if that is strength, then I have been weak." Phillips' translation agrees with this latter view: "I am almost ashamed to say that I never did brave strong things like that to you."

Paul says that if the way the false teachers acted is real strength, then he has to say to his shame that he never showed that kind of strength, but rather weakness. Yet he quickly adds that in whatever aspect these other men had reason to be bold, he certainly had the same right to be bold as they. Moffatt states it well with these words: "but let them vaunt as they please, I am equal to them (mind, this is the role of a fool!)." With that introduction the Apostle Paul launches into one of the most magnificent sections in this Epistle, showing his right to the claim as a true servant of the Lord Jesus Christ.

You will remember that the question had been raised in the church at Corinth as to whether Paul was a true apostle. What credentials could he show that he had received a divine call? How could he prove to anyone's satisfaction that he was equal to the twelve apostles, for instance?

He is ready with his answer, but perhaps it is not exactly what we would expect. He does not bring forth a diploma to show he had graduated from some seminary. Neither does he bring an official letter, signed by the brethren in Jerusalem, stating that they had ordained him to the work. He does not present his personal accomplishments or skills. Rather, he brings before us a moving record of sufferings he had endured in the work of the gospel. Do not miss the drama and the pathos of this portion of 2 Corinthians. Picture the intrepid Paul as he hastens ceaselessly over land and sea on his missionary journeys, constrained by the love of Christ, and willing to endure untold hardships if only men might not perish for want of the gospel of Christ. Rarely can we read these verses without being deeply moved and greatly shamed.

11:22 The false teachers made much of their Jewish ancestry. They claimed to be full-blooded **Hebrews**, descended from Israel, and of **the seed of Abraham**. They still labored under the delusion that this family tree gave them favor in the sight of God. They did not realize that God's ancient people, Israel, had now been set aside by God because of their rejection of the Messiah. They did not realize that as far as God was concerned, there was now no difference between Jew and Gentile: all were sinners, and all needed to be saved through faith in Christ alone.

It is useless for them to boast in this regard. Their lineage did not give them any superiority over Paul, since he, too, was a Hebrew, an Israelite, and of **the seed of Abraham**. But these were not the things which proved him to be an apostle of Christ. And so he hurries on to the main portion of his argument: in one respect they could not excel him — in hardships and sufferings.

11:23 They were **ministers of Christ** by profession; he was a servant "in devotion, labor and suffering." The Apostle Paul could never forget he was a follower of the *suffering* Savior. He realized that the servant is not above his master, and that an apostle could not expect better treatment in the world than his Master had received. Paul reckoned that the more faithfully he served Christ and reproduced the Savior, the more abundantly he would suffer at the hands of men. To him, suffering was the mark or badge of Christ's servants. Though he felt like **a fool** in thus boasting, necessity demanded that he speak the truth, and the truth was that these false teachers were not noted for their suffering. They chose the easy path. They avoided reproach, persecution, and dishonor. For this reason Paul felt they were in a poor position to attack him as a servant of Christ.

Let us now look at the catalog of hardships which Paul enumerates as supporting his claim to be a true apostle.

In labors more abundant. He thinks of the scope of his missionary journeys, how he had traveled widely throughout the Mediterranean area to make Christ known.

In stripes above measure. Here we have a description of the beatings which he received at the hands of the enemies of Christ, both heathen and Jewish.

In prisons more frequently. The only one of these imprisonments recorded in the Scripture, up to this time in Paul's career, is that of Acts 16:23, where he and Silas were thrown into the jail at Philippi. Now we learn that this was only one of many imprisonments, that Paul was no stranger to the dungeon.

In deaths often. Undoubtedly, as the apostle wrote this, he thought of his close escape from death at Lystra (Acts 14:19). But he could also look back on other similar times when life was all but gone as a result of his persecutions.

11:24 The Law of Moses forbade the Jews to inflict more than forty stripes at one time (Deut. 25:3). In order to make sure that they did not break this law, it was common for the Jews to inflict only thirty-nine stripes. These would be inflicted, of course, only in what they considered to be cases of deep guilt. The Apostle Paul here informs us that his own people according to the flesh had given him the full measure of punishment on **five** different occasions.

11:25 Three times I was beaten with rods. The only case mentioned in the NT is that which occurred at Philippi (Acts 16:22). But there were two other times when Paul suffered this painful and humiliating treatment.

Once I was stoned. This is no doubt the occasion at Lystra, to which we have already referred (Acts 14:19). This stoning was so severe that Paul's body was dragged out of the city, supposedly dead.

Three times I was shipwrecked. Not all Paul's trials were directly from the hands of men. At times he was tossed about by the convulsions of nature. None of the shipwrecks mentioned here is recorded for us. (The shipwreck in Acts 27 on the way to Rome occurred later in Paul's history.)

A night and a day I have been in the deep. Again, no experience recorded in Acts seems to answer to this. There is a question whether the deep here refers to a dungeon, or the sea. If it means the sea, was Paul on a raft or in an open boat? If not, he could only have survived such an experience in the water by direct, miraculous intervention by the Lord.

11:26 In journeys often. If you turn to the maps at the back of most Bibles, you will usually find one labeled "The Missionary Journeys of St. Paul." As you follow the lines showing the general routes he traveled, and realize how primitive transportation facilities were in those days, you will realize a little more the depth of meaning of this expression!

Then Paul goes on to list eight different types of dangers which he encountered. There were **perils of waters**, referring to swollen rivers and streams. There were **perils of robbers**, since many of the routes which he traveled were infested with outlaws. He faced **perils from his own countrymen**, the Jews, as well as from **the Gentiles** to whom he sought to bring the gospel. There were **perils in the city**, such as Lystra, Philippi, Corinth, and Ephesus. Also he faced **perils in the wilderness**, probably referring to the thinly populated areas in Asia Minor and Europe. He met **perils in the sea** — from storms, hidden rocks, and perhaps pirates. Finally, there were **perils among false brethren**, no doubt referring to those Jewish legalists who posed as Christian teachers.

11:27 Weariness refers to Paul's incessant work, while **toil** carries with it the thought of the exhaustion and suffering connected with work.

In sleeplessness often. On many of his trips it would doubtless be necessary for him to sleep out in the open. But with dangers besetting him on every hand, it would be necessary for him to pass many a sleepless night, watching for the approach of danger.

In hunger and thirst, in fastings often. The great apostle was often forced to go hungry and thirsty as he went about serving the Lord. **Fastings** here may mean those of a voluntary nature, but more probably they were forced on him through food shortages.

In cold and nakedness. Sudden changes in weather, combined with the fact that he was often poorly shod and inadequately clothed, added these extreme forms of discomfort to his life. Hodge comments:

The greatest of the apostles here appears before us, his back lacerated by frequent scourgings, his body worn by hunger, thirst, and exposure; cold and naked, persecuted by Jews and Gentiles, driven from place to place without any certain dwelling. This passage, more than any other, makes even the most laborious of the modern ministers of Christ hide their face in shame. What have they ever done or suffered to compare with what this apostle did? It is a consolation to know that Paul is now as pre-eminent in glory, as he was here in suffering.[43]

11:28 Besides the other things, that is, those that were out of course or exceptional, Paul **daily** carried the steady burden of **all the** Christian **churches** on his heart. How significant it is that this climaxes all the other trials! Paul was a true pastor. He loved and cared for the Lord's people. He was not a hireling shepherd, but a true undershepherd of the Lord Jesus. That is exactly what he is seeking to prove in this portion of Scripture, and from the standpoint of every reasonable person, he certainly has won his point. His burden for the churches reminds us of the saying, "Church making is heartbreaking. Church mending is never ending."

11:29 This verse is closely linked with the previous verse. In verse 28 the apostle was saying he carried about daily the care of all the churches. Here he explains what he means. If he hears of some Christian who **is weak**, he feels that weakness himself. He endures the sufferings of others sympathetically. If he learns that some brother in Christ has been offended, he burns **with indignation**. What affects the people of God affects him. He sorrows in their tragedies and rejoices in their triumphs. And all this exhausts the nervous energy of a servant of Christ. How well Paul knew it!

11:30 Not his successes, not his gifts or abilities, but his weaknesses, his reproaches, the indignities he endured — these form the subject of his boasting. These are not the things that men usually boast about, or that make them famous.

11:31 In thinking of his sufferings and indignities, Paul's mind instinctively goes back to the most humiliating moment in his entire career. If he is going to glory in the things that concern his weakness, then he cannot fail to mention the experience he had at Damascus. For any man to boast of such a humiliating experience is so contrary to human nature that Paul here calls on **God** to attest the truthfulness of what he says.

11:32 Fuller details of this episode are given in Acts 9:19–25. After his conversion near **Damascus**, Paul began to preach the gospel in the synagogues there. At first his preaching aroused curious interest, but after a while the Jews plotted to kill him. They set a watch at the gates day and night, **desiring to arrest** him.

11:33 One night the disciples took the apostle, placed him **in a basket**, and lowered him **through a window in the wall** of the city to the ground outside. He was then able to escape.

But why does Paul mention this incident? J. B. Watson suggests:

> He takes hold of what men made an occasion of shame and ridicule and sets it in the light of being another proof that the paramount interest in his life was to serve the Lord Christ, for whose sake he was prepared to sacrifice his personal pride and appear as a coward in the eyes of men.[44]

F. Paul's Revelations Support His Apostleship (12:1–10)

12:1 The apostle wishes he didn't have **to boast** at all. It is not becoming or **profitable**, but under the circumstances it is necessary. So he will pass on from the lowest, most humiliating event in his ministry to the highest, most exalted. He will tell about a personal audience with the **Lord** Himself.

12:2 Paul knew **a man** who had this experience **fourteen years ago**. Although Paul does not identify him, there is no question but that he himself is the person referred to. In speaking of such an exalted experience, he will not mention himself personally, but will simply speak in a general way. The **man** referred to was **in Christ**, that is, a Christian.

12:3 Paul does not know **whether** he was **in the body or out of the body** at the time. Some have conjectured that this might have happened during one of Paul's persecutions, such as the one at Lystra. They say that he might have actually died and gone to heaven. But the text certainly does not demand such an interpretation. In fact, if Paul did not know whether he was **in the body or out of the body**, that is, alive or dead, at the time, it would be strange if any modern commentators could throw additional light on the subject!

The important thing is that this man **was caught up to the third heaven**. Scripture implies the existence of three heavens. The first is the atmosphere above us, that is, the blue sky. The second is the stellar heaven. The third is the highest heaven where the throne of God is.

It is clear from what follows that Paul was actually in the same place of bliss as that to which the Lord Jesus took the repentant thief after his death, that is, to God's dwelling place.

12:4 Paul **heard** the language of **Paradise** and understood what was spoken, but he was not allowed to repeat any of it when he came back to the earth. The **words** were **inexpressible** in the sense that they were too sacred to be uttered and therefore not for publication. G. Campbell Morgan writes:

There are some who seem eager to talk of visions and revelations which they have had. The question is as to whether such eagerness is not proof that the visions and revelations are not "of the Lord." When they are granted (and they certainly are granted to the servants of God under certain circumstances), they produce a reverent reticence. They are too solemn, too overwhelming, to be lightly described or discussed, but the effect of them will be apparent in all life and service.[45]

12:5 When boasting of weakness, the apostle didn't mind mentioning himself. But when boasting of visions and revelations of the Lord, he would not apply them directly to himself, but would rather speak of the experience impersonally as having occurred to some man he knew. He was not denying that he was the one who had the experience, but was simply refusing to involve himself directly and personally.

12:6 There are many other great experiences of which the apostle could **boast**. If he should **desire** to engage in this boasting, he would **not be a fool** in doing so. Anything he would say would be **the truth**. But he is not going to do it, because he does not want **anyone** to **think** more highly of him than they actually find him **to be or** than they hear **from** him.

12:7 This whole section is a most accurate description of the life of a servant of Christ. It has its moments of deep humiliation, such as the event at Damascus. Then it has its mountain top experiences, such as Paul's exhilarating revelation. But normally after a servant of the Lord has enjoyed one of these experiences, the Lord allows him to suffer some **thorn in the flesh**. That is what we have here.

We learn many priceless lessons from this verse. First, it is proof that even divine revelations of the Lord do not correct **the flesh** in us. Even after the apostle had listened to the language of Paradise, he still had the old nature, and was in danger of falling into the snare of pride. As R. J. Reid has said:

"A man in Christ" is safe in the presence of God as he listens to the untranslatable things spoken in paradise, but he needs "a thorn in the flesh" upon his return to earth, for the flesh in him would boast of his paradise experience.[46]

What was Paul's **thorn in the flesh**? All we can say for sure is that it was some bodily trial which God allowed to come into his life. No doubt the Lord purposely failed to specify exactly what the **thorn** was so that tried and tested saints down through the years might feel a closer kinship with the apostle as *they* suffer. Perhaps it was some form of eye disease,[47] perhaps an earache, perhaps malaria, perhaps migraine headaches, perhaps something connected with Paul's speech. Moorehead states: "The precise nature of it has been concealed perhaps that all afflicted ones may be encouraged and helped by Paul's unnamed yet painful experience."[48] Our trials may be very different from Paul's, but they should produce the same exercise and fruits.

The apostle describes the **thorn in the flesh** as **a messenger of Satan to buffet** him. In one sense it represented an effort on Satan's part to hinder Paul in the work of the Lord. But God is greater than Satan, and He used the **thorn** to further the work of the Lord by keeping Paul humble. Successful service for Christ depends on a weak servant. The weaker he is, the more the power of Christ accompanies his preaching.

12:8 **Three times** Paul **pleaded with the Lord** that the thorn in the flesh **might depart from** him.

12:9 Paul's prayer was answered,

but not in the way he had hoped. In effect, God said to Paul, "I will not remove the thorn, but I will do something better: I will give you grace to bear it. And just remember, Paul, that although I have not given you what you asked for, yet I am giving you what you need most deeply. You want my power and strength to accompany your preaching, don't you? Well, the best way to have that happen is for you to be kept in a place of weakness."

This was God's repeated answer to Paul's thrice repeated prayer. And it continues to be God's answer to his suffering people throughout the world. Better than the removal of trials and sufferings is the companionship of the Son of God in them, and the assurance of His strength and enabling grace.

Notice that God says, **My grace IS sufficient for you**. We don't have to ask Him to make His grace sufficient. It already **IS**!

The apostle is completely satisfied with the Lord's answer, so he says, **"Therefore most gladly I will rather boast in my infirmities, that the power of Christ may rest upon me."**

When the Lord explained the wisdom of His actions, Paul said in effect that that was the only way he would want it to be. So instead of complaining and grumbling about the thorn, he would **rather boast in** his **infirmities**. He would get down on his knees and thank the Lord for them. He would gladly endure them if only the power of Christ might rest upon him. J. Oswald Sanders puts it well:

> The world's philosophy is, "What can't be cured must be endured." But Paul radiantly testifies, "What can't be cured can be enjoyed. I enjoy weakness, sufferings, privations, and difficulties." So wonderful did he prove God's grace to be, that he even welcomed fresh occasions of drawing upon its fullness. "I gladly glory . . . I even enjoy — my thorn."[49]

Emma Piechynska, the wife of a Polish nobleman, led a long life of frustration and disappointment. Yet her biographer paid a remarkable tribute to her triumphant faith: "She made magnificent bouquets out of the refusals of God!"

12:10 Naturally speaking, it is quite impossible for us to **take pleasure** in the type of experiences listed here. But the key to the understanding of the verse is found in the expression, **for Christ's sake**. We should be willing to endure in His cause, and in the furtherance of His gospel, things which we would not ordinarily endure for ourselves or for the sake of some loved one.

It is when we are conscious of our own weakness and nothingness that we most depend on the power of God. And it is when we are thus cast on Him in complete dependence that His power is manifested to us, and we are truly **strong**.

William Wilberforce, who led the fight to abolish slavery in the British Empire, was physically weak and frail, but he had deep faith in God. Boswell said of him, "I saw what seemed to me a shrimp become a whale."

In this verse Paul is obeying the word of the Lord in Matthew 5:11, 12. He is rejoicing when men reviled and persecuted him.

G. Paul's Signs Support His Apostleship (12:11–13)

12:11 At this point Paul seems to be weary of his seeming boastfulness. He feels he has **become a fool in boasting** as he has done. He should not have done it, but the Corinthians really **compelled** him. They should have been the ones to commend him when his critics leveled their cruel attacks against him. Though he was **nothing** in himself, yet he was certainly not behind **the most eminent apostles** in whom they gloried.

12:12 He reminds them that when he went to Corinth and preached the gospel, God attested the preaching with **the signs of an apostle**. These signs were miracle powers given to the apostles by God so that their hearers might know that they were indeed sent by the Lord.

The words **signs and wonders and mighty deeds** do not describe three different types of miracles, but rather miracles viewed in three different aspects. **Signs** were miracles that conveyed a definite meaning to human intelligence. **Wonders**, on the other hand, were so remarkable that they stirred up human emotions. **Mighty deeds** were performances that were obviously of superhuman power.

It is nice to notice that Paul says that **the signs of an apostle** *were accomplished* among them. He uses the passive voice. He does not claim credit for them himself, but says God did them through him.

12:13 As far as the display of miracles was concerned, the Corinthians were not a bit **inferior to other churches**. They witnessed as many of these, at the hands of the Apostle Paul, as the **other churches** which he visited. In what sense then were they **inferior to** any of **the other churches**? The only difference Paul can see is that he had not been **burdensome** to the Corinthians. That is, he had not insisted on financial assistance from them. If this made them **inferior**, then Paul asks them to **forgive** him **this wrong**. This was the only "sign" of an apostle he did not insist on!

H. Paul's Pending Visit to Corinth (12:14–13:1)

12:14 Now for the third time I am ready to come to you. This can be understood to mean the apostle had been *ready* to visit Corinth three times, but that he had only *been there* once. He did not go the second time, because he did not want to deal harshly with the believers. Now he is **ready** to go **the third time**, and this will be his second visit.

Or it may mean he was about to make his **third** visit. The first is recorded in Acts 18:1. The second was the sorrowful visit (2 Cor. 2:1; 13:1). This will be **the third**.

When he does come, Paul is determined that **he will not be burdensome to** them. He means, of course, he will not accept any financial return from them. He will be independent of them as far as his support is concerned. The reason for this is that he was not after their material wealth but after themselves. Paul was more interested in people than he was in things.

He wants to play the part of a parent, as far as the Corinthians are concerned. **Children ought not to lay up for the parents, but the parents for the children.** This is simply a statement of life as we know it. In the normal course of events,

it is **the parents** who work hard and diligently to see that the **children** have food and clothing. The **children** ordinarily do not take this care for **the parents**. So Paul is saying he would like to be permitted to act as a parent to them.

One should be careful not to read too much into this sentence. It does *not* mean that parents ought to lay up wealth for the future of their children. This has nothing to do with future needs, but only with present necessities. Paul was thinking only of the supply of his immediate needs as he was serving the Lord in Corinth. He was determined that he would not depend on the saints there. There was no thought in his mind that they ought to be laying up a nest egg for his old age or that he should be doing that for them.

12:15 Here we have a beautiful glimpse into the unquenchable love of the Apostle Paul for the people of God in Corinth. He was willing **gladly** to give himself in tireless service and sacrifice for their souls, that is, for their spiritual welfare. He loved them more abundantly than the false teachers who were in their midst did, yet he was **loved less** by them. But that did not make any difference. Even if he had no hope of return of love from them, he would keep on loving them. In this he was truly following the Lord.

12:16 The apostle takes up the very words which his critics were using against him. They were saying, in effect, "Well, granted that Paul himself did not take money from you directly. However, he used trickery to get it. He sent delegates to you, and they took money back to him."

12:17 If I did not sponge off you directly, **did I** send others who did? The apostle asks the Corinthians directly if these charges against him were true.

12:18 He answers his own question. The expression, **I urged Titus**, probably means **I urged Titus** *to visit you*. But Paul did not send him alone. He **sent** another **brother** along **with him** lest there might be a breath of suspicion about Paul's motives. What happened when Titus reached Corinth? Did he insist on his rights? Did he ask the Corinthians to support him? Did he try to make a gain of them? No, it appears from this passage that Titus worked for his living by engaging in some secular occupation. That is suggested by the questions, **"Did we not walk in the same spirit? Did we not walk in the same steps?"** In other words, both Titus and Paul followed the same policy of working so that they would not have to be supported by the Corinthians.

12:19 The Corinthians would think, from all that Paul had said, that his aim was simply to **excuse** himself **to** them as if they were his judges. On the contrary, what he really was doing was writing these things to them as in the presence of **God**, in order that they might be built up. He wanted to strengthen them in the Christian life and warn them against the perils that were facing them. He was more interested in helping them than in defending his own reputation.

The supplied words (italics) in the expression, *we do* all things, might perhaps better read *we write* all these things (cf. 2 Cor. 13:10).

12:20 Paul desired that when he visited Corinth, he might find the Christians going along happily one with another, having renounced the false teachers, and having acknowledged the authority of the apostles.

Also when he visited them, he wanted to come with joy and not with heaviness. He would be greatly grieved if he should find **contentions, jealousies, outbursts of wrath, selfish ambitions**, and other forms of carnal conflict.

12:21 After all, these Corinthians were Paul's joy and crown of rejoicing. They were his glorying. He certainly did not want to come to them and have to be ashamed of them. Neither did he want to have to **mourn** over **many who** had **sinned** and had **not repented of** their **uncleanness, fornication, and lewdness**.

To whom does Paul refer as the **many** who had **practiced** these sins? It is only reasonable to assume they were in the church in Corinth; otherwise he would not be discussing them in this way in a Letter to the church. But it cannot be assumed that they were true believers. It specifically says they **practiced** these sins, and Paul elsewhere makes it clear

that anyone whose life is characterized by such behavior cannot inherit the kingdom of God (1 Cor. 6:9, 10). The apostle would **mourn** over them because they had not repented and would therefore have to be excommunicated.

Darby points out that this chapter opens with the third heaven and closes with vile sins on earth. Between the two, he notes that there is the remedy — the power of Christ resting on the Apostle Paul.[50]

13:1 Paul was about to visit Corinth. When he did, the cases of sin among the believers would be investigated. Such investigations would proceed according to the divine principle laid down in Deuteronomy 19:15: **"By the mouth of two or three witnesses every word shall be established."** Paul did not mean he would be conducting the trial. This would be done by the local church, and he would act as a counselor in the matter.

I. Paul's Apostleship Supported by the Corinthians Themselves (13:2–6)

13:2 On his second visit, otherwise unrecorded, Paul had warned them he would deal severely with the offenders. **Now** although **absent**, he foretells them all that when he comes **again** he **will not spare those who have** been sinning.

13:3 The Corinthians had been deceived by the false teachers into doubting that Paul was a true apostle. In fact, they actually challenged him to give them some **proof** that he was an authentic spokesman for God. What were his credentials that **Christ** was really **speaking** through him? The apostle begins his reply by quoting their impertinent request: **"since you seek a proof of Christ speaking in me . . ."**

Then in a parenthesis, he reminds them that Christ had revealed Himself to them through him in a **mighty** way. There had been nothing **weak** about the tremendous revolution in their lives when they believed the gospel message.

13:4 Mention of the words "weak" and "mighty" reminded Paul of the paradox of strength out of weakness which was seen in the Savior's life and is seen in the lives of His servants. Our Lord **was crucified in weakness, yet He lives**

by the power of God. So His followers are feeble in themselves, yet the Lord demonstrates His **power** through them. When Paul says, **we shall live with Him by the power of God toward you**, he is not speaking of the resurrection. Rather he means that when he visits them, he will demonstrate the mighty **power of God** in dealing with those who were sinning. They said he was weak and contemptible; he will show them he can be strong in exercising discipline!

13:5 This verse connects with the first part of verse 3 as follows: "Since you seek a proof of Christ speaking in me . . . **examine yourselves as to whether you are in the faith.**" They themselves were the proof of his apostleship. It was through him that they were led to the Savior. If they wanted to see his credentials, they should look at themselves.

Verse 5 is often misused to teach that we should look *within ourselves* for assurance of salvation, but this could lead to discouragement and doubt. Assurance of salvation comes first and foremost through the word of God. The moment we trust Christ we can know on the authority of the Bible that we have been born again. As time goes on, we do find other evidences of the new life — a new love for holiness, a new hatred of sin, love of the brethren, practical righteousness, obedience, and separation from the world.

But Paul is not telling the Corinthians to engage in self-examination as a proof of their salvation. Rather he is asking them to find in their salvation a proof of his apostleship.

There were only two possibilities: either **Jesus Christ** was **in** them, or they were **disqualified**, spurious. The word translated **disqualified** was used to describe metals which, when tested, were found to be false. So the Corinthians were either true believers, or they were **disqualified** by failure to pass the test.

13:6 If they concluded that they were genuinely saved, then it must follow that the Apostle Paul was genuine and **not disqualified**. The wonderful transformation that took place in the lives of the Corinthians could scarcely have come through a false teacher.

J. Paul's Desire to Do the Corinthians Good (13:7–10)

13:7 Paul now continues the subject of the discipline of sinning members of the church at Corinth. He states he is praying **to God that** the Corinthians would **do no evil** by countenancing sin in their midst, but that they would work ceaselessly toward the discipline and restoration of the sinning members. He does not pray this in order that he himself might **appear approved**, or might be seen in a better light. He does not want them to do it simply because he could then point to their obedience as an evidence of his authority. That is not the thought at all. He wants them to do it because it is *right* and *honest*. And he would rather have them do that, even **though** it meant that he might **seem disqualified**.

Here again we have an evidence of the unselfishness of Paul. In his prayer life his thoughts were constantly on what was for the good of others and not for his own recognition. If Paul went to Corinth with a rod, asserted his authority, and succeeded in gaining obedience to his instructions concerning discipline, then he could use this as an argument against the false teachers. He could say this was evidence of his lawful authority. But he would rather that the Corinthians take the necessary action themselves, in his absence, even if that might put him in an unfavorable light as far as the legalists were concerned.

13:8 The **we** of this verse probably refers to the apostles. Paul is saying that all they do must be done with a view to the furtherance of **the truth** of God, and not with any selfish motives in view. Even in the matter of discipline, no thought of personal vindictiveness must enter. All must be carried out with a view to the glory of God and the good of one's fellow Christians.

13:9 Here again the apostle expresses his utter unselfishness as far as the Corinthians were concerned. If his weakness, humiliation, and reproach resulted in their being strengthened in the things of God, then he was **glad**. While he thus rejoiced, he also prayed **that** they might **be made complete**. With regard to the subject of dealing with sinful offenders in their midst, Paul prayed that they might become **complete** and entire. That the whole will of God might be worked out in their lives was his fervent desire. As Hodge puts it, "Paul prayed that they might be perfectly restored from the state of confusion, contention and evil into which they had fallen."[51]

13:10 It was with their perfecting in view that he wrote this Letter to them. He would rather write while **absent** from them that these results might be secured, than that **being present** he **should** have to **use sharpness**, as authorized by **the Lord**. But even if he were **present** and dealt severely with them, it would still be **for** their **edification and not for** their **destruction**.

K. Paul's Gracious Trinitarian Farewell (13:11–14)

13:11 The apostle now draws this rather stormy Epistle to an abrupt close. After bidding them **farewell** (the Greek greeting literally means "rejoice"), he delivers four exhortations. First, they should **become complete**. The verb is the same as the one used of mending nets in Matthew 4:21, and can also mean "mend your ways." The Corinthians were to stop quarreling and sinning, and live in harmony with each other.

Be of good comfort may also be understood as "be encouraged" or "be exhorted." They had been given strong admonitions by the Apostle Paul. Here he tells them to receive these admonitions in a good spirit and to act on them.

Be of one mind. The only way, of course, in which Christians can **be of one mind** is to have *the mind of Christ*. It is to think as He thinks, to bring all their thoughts and reasonings in subjection to Himself.

Live in peace. It is evident from 12:20 that there had been disputes and wranglings among them. This is always the case when legalism is allowed to enter. So Paul here told them first to discipline the offenders and to get along with their fellow Christians in peace.

If they do this, **the God of love and peace will be with them**. Of course, in one sense the Lord is *always* with His

people. But this means He will manifest Himself to them in a special nearness and dearness if they are obedient in these regards.

13:12 The **holy kiss** was a characteristic greeting among Christians in the days of the apostles. It is designated as **a** *holy* kiss, meaning it was not just a symbol of artificial affection, but that it was sincere and pure. It is still practiced by Christians in many countries today. However, in some countries, kissing among men could be misinterpreted as a sign of homosexuality. Practicing such a tradition would not be obligatory if it brought serious reproach on the Christian testimony. In such cases a holy handshake would be preferable. Hodge says:

> It is not a command of perpetual obligation, as the spirit of the command is that Christians should express their mutual love in the way sanctioned by the age and community in which they live.[52]

13:13 The greetings from **all the saints** would remind the Corinthians of the breadth of the fellowship into which they had been brought, and would also tell them that other churches were looking on to see their progress and obedience to the Lord.

13:14 Here we have one of the lovely benedictions of the NT, and the only one that embraces all three members of the Trinity.

Lenski concludes:

> With the picture of the great apostle spreading his hands over the Corinthians with this profound New Testament benediction his voice sinks into silence. But the benediction remains upon our hearts.[53]

ENDNOTES

[1] (1:2) James Denney, *The Second Epistle to the Corinthians*, p. 11.

[2] (1:10) The critical (NU) text has one past and two future tenses.

[3] (1:20) H. W. Cragg, *The Keswick Week*, p. 126.

[4] (2:11) J. Sidlow Baxter, *Awake My Heart*, taken from the Nov. 10 reading, "Intoxication with Error."

[5] (2:14) A. T. Robertson, *The Glory of the Ministry*, p. 32.

6(2:14) Frederick Brotherton Meyer, *Paul*, p. 77.

7(2:15) *Ibid.*, p. 78.

8(2:17) The majority text is worded very strongly: "as the rest"; no doubt this is hyperbole, as so often is the case in 2 Corinthians.

9(2:17) Robertson, *Ministry*, p. 47.

10(3:6) J. M. Davies, *The Epistles to the Corinthians*, pp. 168, 169.

11(3:9) Charles Hodge, *A Commentary on the Second Epistle to the Corinthians*, p. 61.

12(3:10) Robertson, *Ministry*, p. 70.

13(3:10) Denney, *Second Corinthians*, p. 123.

14(3:13) F. W. Grant, "2 Corinthians," *The Numerical Bible*, VI:547.

15(3:14) Hodge, *Second Corinthians*, p. 71.

16(3:17) The NKJV translators took this as a reference to the Holy Spirit, and so capitalized it. The original was in *all* capitals (uncials), hence either is possible.

17(3:18) Denney, *Second Corinthians*, pp. 139, 140.

18(3:18) J. N. Darby, *Notes on I and II Corinthians*, pp. 189, 190.

19(4:7) J. H. Jowett, *Life in the Heights*, p. 65.

20(4:12) Robertson, *Ministry*, p. 157.

21(4:16) H. A. Ironside, further documentation unavailable.

22(4:17) In Hebrew the word for "glory" is derived from the root "to be heavy," which probably suggested Paul's wording.

23(4:17) William C. Moorehead, *Outline Studies in the New Testament: Acts to Ephesians*, p. 191.

24(4:17) F. E. Marsh, *Fully Furnished*, p. 103.

25(4:18) Jowett, *Life in the Heights*, pp. 68, 69.

26(5:15) Denney, *Second Corinthians*, p. 199.

27(5:16) David Smith, further documentation unavailable.

28(5:18) *A New and Concise Bible Dictionary*, p. 652.

29(6:4) Denney, *Second Corinthians*, p. 230.

30(6:9) "As unknown and yet well known" is fittingly inscribed on the tombstone of John Nelson Darby (1800-1882), who had a worldwide ministry not unlike that of Paul.

31(6:10) Robertson, *Ministry*, p. 238.

32(6:11) A. W. Tozer, *The Root of the Righteous*, 1955.

33(6:16) Denney, *Second Corinthians*, p. 246.

34(7:8) George Williams, *Student's Commentary on the Holy Scriptures*, p. 904.

35(7:9) Hodge, *Second Corinthians*, p. 182.

36(8:7) Denney, *Second Corinthians*, p. 267.

37(8:9) Moorehead, *Acts to Ephesians*, pp. 179, 180.

38(8:15) Hodge, *Second Corinthians*, p. 206.

39(8:21) G. Campbell Morgan, *Searchlights from the Word*, p. 345.

40(9:7) Jowett, *Life in the Heights*, p. 78.

41(11:17) Charles C. Ryrie, *The Ryrie Study Bible, New King James Version*, p. 1797.

42(11:20) J. N. Darby, *Notes on I and II Corinthians*, p. 236.

43(11:27) Hodge, *Second Corinthians*, p. 275.

44(11:33) J. B. Watson, further documentation unavailable.

45(12:4) Morgan, *Searchlights*, p. 346.

46(12:7) R. J. Reid, *How Job Learned His Lesson*, p. 69.

47(12:7) See Galatians 4:15 and 6:11.

48(12:7) Moorehead, *Acts to Ephesians*, p. 197.

49(12:9) J. Oswald Sanders, *A Spiritual Clinic*, pp. 32, 33.

50(12:21) Darby, *I and II Corinthians*, p. 253.

51(13:9) Hodge, *Second Corinthians*, p. 309.

52(13:12) *Ibid.*, p. 312.

53(13:14) R. C. H. Lenski, *The Interpretation of St. Paul's First and Second Epistles to the Corinthians*, p. 1341.

BIBLIOGRAPHY

Darby, J. N. *Notes on I and II Corinthians*. London: G. Morrish, n.d.

Davies, J. M. *The Epistles to the Corinthians*. Bombay: Gospel Literature Service, 1975.

Denney, James. *The Second Epistle to the Corinthians*. London: Hodder & Stoughton, 1894.

Erdman, C. R. *Second Epistle of Paul to the*

Corinthians. London: Philadelphia: Westminster Press, 1929.

Grant, F. W. "2 Corinthians," *The Numerical Bible*. Vol. 6, Acts – 2 Corinthians. New York: Loizeaux Brothers, 1901.

Hodge, Charles. *The Second Epistle to the Corinthians*. London: The Banner of Truth Trust, 1959.

Hughes, Philip E. *Commentary on the Second Epistle to the Corinthians*. Grand Rapids: Wm. B. Eerdmans Publishing Co., 1962.

Kelly, William. *Notes on the Second Epistle*

to the Corinthians. London: G. Morrish, 1882.

Lenski, R. C. H. *The Interpretation of St. Paul's First and Second Epistles to the Corinthians*. Columbus: Wartburg Press, 1937.

Luck, G. Coleman. *Second Corinthians*. Chicago: Moody Press, 1959.

Robertson, A. T. *The Glory of the Ministry*. New York: Fleming H. Revell Co., 1911.

Wilson, Geoffrey B. *2 Corinthians: A Digest of Reformed Comment*. London: The Banner of Truth Trust, 1973.

THE EPISTLE TO THE GALATIANS

Introduction

*"The 'Magna Charta' of spiritual freedom for the whole world
and for all time."* — Charles R. Erdman

I. Unique Place in the Canon

A large percentage of English-speaking peoples, as well as many French people, are of Celtic origin — that is, Scottish, Irish, Welsh, or Breton. These ethnic groups especially will be fascinated to know that one of Paul's earliest letters was written to their ancestors ("Galatia," "Celt," and "Gaul" are all related words).

About 278 B.C. a large number of these European Gauls migrated to what is today Turkey. Their boundaries became fixed and their state was named "Galatia." Many people think they can see "Celtic" traits in such things as the changeableness of the Galatians (in Acts 13 and Galatians 3:1, e.g.).

Be that as it may, the Epistle to the Galatians fulfills a crucial role in early Christianity. Though often seen as a "first draft" of Romans (since it covers the gospel of grace, Abraham, the law, etc., in a similar manner), Galatians is a stern, impassioned effort to save Christianity from becoming just a messianic sect of legalistic Judaism. How the Galatians themselves reacted we do not know, but the gospel of grace, apart from the works of the law, *did* triumph, and Christianity went on to become a global faith.

During the Reformation, Galatians became so important to Luther that he referred to the book as "my Kaethe" (his affectionate name for his wife). His *Commentary on Galatians* influenced not merely scholars, but the common folk, and is still in print and studied.

II. Authorship[†]

The genuineness of Galatians as a Pauline Epistle has never seriously been in question. It is quoted as Paul's by Polycarp, Ignatius, Justin Martyr, Origen, Irenaeus, Tertullian, and Clement of Alexandria. It is listed in the Muratorian Canon as Paul's and, probably due to its strong anti-Judaizing language, receives first place in Marcion's *Apostolicon*. The *external evidence* is thus very strong.

The *internal evidence* for Paul's authorship starts with the personal references in 1:1 and 5:2, and the remark near the end (6:11) that he wrote it in "large letters." This is widely taken to refer to a possible eye disease of the apostle. Supporting evidence includes the fact that the Galatians once would have been willing to pluck their *eyes* out for Paul. Many historical notes dovetail with Acts. The dispute over circumcision and whether Paul was a real apostle were flaming issues in the 50's and 60's but dead issues soon afterward.

III. Date

The date of the Epistle depends on the precise meaning of the expressions "the churches of Galatia" and "Galatians." If it refers to the southern part of Asia Minor, an earlier date, even before the Jerusalem Council, is likely. If the northern part is meant, a later date is called for.

Geographically the term "Galatia" was used for the north and *politically* it was used for the south — the Roman province of Galatia.

The North Galatian theory was standard until the 1800's and is largely held by German scholars still. There is no evidence that Paul ever ministered to the

†See p. i.

"Galatians" of that area, but this certainly does not rule it out.

Especially since Sir William Ramsay made it popular, the South Galatian theory has been widely held in Great Britain and North America. Since Luke gives much space in Acts to Paul's missionary work in this area (Antioch in Pisidia, Iconium, Lystra, and Derbe), it would seem likely that the apostle would have written to his converts there. Since Paul evangelized southern Galatia on his First Missionary Journey and revisited it on his Second, an early date is possible for Galatians. If the letter was penned *before* the Jerusalem Council of Acts 15 (A.D. 49), this would explain why the question of circumcision was still a very live issue. Theodor Zahn, a leading conservative German scholar, dates Galatians during Paul's Second Missionary Journey, from Corinth. This would make it his very earliest Epistle.

If the northern theory is correct, Galatians was probably written in the 50's, perhaps as early as 53, but probably later.

If, as we believe, the southern theory is correct, and especially if Galatians was written before Paul attended the Jerusalem Council, which decided the issue of circumcision for Gentile Christians, the book can be dated A.D. 48.

IV. Background and Theme[†]

During his early missionary journeys, the Apostle Paul visited Asia Minor, preaching the glorious message that salvation is by faith in Christ alone. Many

†See p. ii.

of his hearers were saved, and churches were formed, several of them in Galatia. The inhabitants of Galatia were known to be restless, warlike, and changeable.

After Paul had left this area, false teachers entered the churches and introduced wrong doctrine. They taught that salvation was by faith in Christ *plus* keeping the law. Their message was a mixture of Christianity and Judaism, of grace and law, of Christ and Moses. They also tried to turn the Galatians away from Paul by saying he was not a genuine apostle of the Lord and, therefore, his message was not reliable. They sought to destroy confidence in the message by undermining confidence in the messenger. Many of the Galatian Christians were affected by their evil suggestions.

What sorrow and disappointment must have filled Paul's heart when such news from Galatia reached him! Had his labors among these people been in vain? Could the Christians still be rescued from these Judaistic, legalistic teachings? Paul was stirred to swift and decisive action. He took up his pen and wrote this indignant letter to his beloved children in the faith. In it, he sets forth the true character of salvation as being given by grace from beginning to end, not earned by law-keeping either in whole or in part. Good works are not a condition of salvation, but a fruit of it. The Christian has died to the law; he leads a life of holiness, not by his own efforts, but by the power of the indwelling Holy Spirit of God.

OUTLINE

III. PRACTICAL: PAUL DEFENDS CHRISTIAN FREEDOM IN
THE SPIRIT (5:2–6:18)

    A. The Peril of Legalism (5:2–15)
    B. Power for Holiness (5:16–25)
    C. Practical Exhortations (5:26–6:10)
    D. Conclusion (6:11–18)

Commentary

I. PERSONAL: PAUL DEFENDS HIS AUTHORITY (Chaps. 1, 2)

A. Paul's Purpose in Writing (1:1–10)

1:1 At the outset, **Paul** insists that his call as **an apostle** was divine. It did **not** originate with **men, nor** was it communicated from God **through** some **man.** It came directly **through Jesus Christ and God the Father who raised Him from the dead**. A man who is thus called by God alone and is responsible to God alone has freedom to preach God's message without fear of man. So the apostle was independent of the twelve apostles and of everybody else, both as to his message and his ministry.

In this verse, the deity of Christ is both stated and implied. It is stated in the expression **nor through man, but through Jesus Christ**. It is implied by the way in which Paul links together **Jesus Christ and God the Father**, putting them on equality with one another. Then **God the Father** is mentioned as the One **who raised** Jesus **from the dead**. Paul had good reason to remind the Galatians of this. The resurrection was proof of God's complete satisfaction with the work of Christ for our salvation. Apparently, the Galatians were not wholly satisfied with the Savior's work, because they were trying to improve on it by adding their own efforts at law-keeping.

Paul was called by the *risen* Christ, in contrast to the twelve apostles, who were called by the Lord Jesus during His earthly ministry. Ever afterward, the resurrection formed an important part of his message.

1:2 The apostle associates himself with **all the brethren who** were **with** him. These **brethren** joined in appealing to the Galatians to hold on to the truth of the gospel. This Letter **to the churches of Galatia** shows a deliberate lack of warmth. Ordinarily Paul addressed believers as "the church of God," "saints," or "the faithful in Christ Jesus." He often expressed thanks for the Christians, or praise for their virtues. Frequently he mentioned individuals by name. But there is none of that here. The seriousness of the error in the Galatian churches caused him to be stern and cool toward them.

1:3 **Grace and peace** are two of the great words of the gospel. **Grace** is God's undeserved kindness toward ungodly sinners. Instead of asking man to *do*, it tells what God has *done*, and invites men to receive salvation as a free gift. Scofield says, "Instead of looking for good men whom it may approve, grace is looking for condemned, guilty, speechless, and helpless men whom it may save, sanctify, and glorify."

Peace is the result of grace. When a sinner receives the Savior, he has **peace** with God. He rests in the knowledge that the penalty for his sins has been paid, that all his sins have been forgiven, and that he will never be condemned. But grace not only *saves*; it *keeps* as well. And we need not only the blessing of *peace with God* but *the peace of God* also. These are the blessings which Paul wishes for the Galatians as he opens his Letter. Surely the Galatians realized that these blessings could never come by the law. The law brought a curse on all who broke its precepts. It never brought peace to a single soul.

1:4 Paul next reminds his readers of the tremendous cost of their salvation. Note the words: our Lord Jesus Christ, **who gave Himself for our sins**. If He **gave Himself** to settle the sin question, then it is both unnecessary and impossible for us to add to such a work, or to help atone for our sins by law-keeping.

Christ is the sole and sufficient Savior. Christ died to **deliver us from this present evil age**. This includes not only the moral and political corruption of this age, but also the religious world which mixes rituals and ceremonies with faith in Christ. It was especially timely, therefore, for the Galatians to be reminded that they were going back into the very system from which Christ had died to rescue them! Christ's redemption was **according to the will of our God and Father**. This places the credit where it belongs — not in man's puny efforts, but rather in the sovereign will of God. It emphasizes that Christ is God's way of salvation and that there is no other.

Verse 4 should be a reminder that God is not interested in improving the world, or making men comfortable in it, but in delivering men from it. Our priorities should coincide with His.

1:5 According to the gospel of grace, all the **glory** for man's salvation goes to God the Father and to the Lord Jesus Christ. Man cannot share this glory as a co-savior by keeping the law.

Each phrase in these five verses is meaningful, much truth being expressed in a few words. Paul has stated in embryo the two main subjects which will occupy the rest of the Epistle — *his own authority as an apostle* and *his gospel of the grace of God*. He is now ready to speak directly to the Galatians concerning the problem at hand.

1:6, 7 Paul confronts the Galatians at once on their readiness to accept error. He is amazed that they should so suddenly surrender the truth of the gospel, and he solemnly labels their action as deserting God for a false gospel. God had **called** them into **the grace of Christ**; now they were putting themselves under the curse of the law. They had accepted the true gospel; now they were abandoning it for **a different gospel** which was not good news at all. It was just a perverted message, a mixture of grace and law.

1:8, 9 Paul twice pronounces the solemn curse of God on anyone who preaches **any other gospel**. God has only one message for doomed sinners: He offers salvation by grace through faith, entirely apart from law-keeping. Those who proclaim any other way of salvation must necessarily be doomed. How very serious it is to preach a message that results in the eternal destruction of souls! Paul was not tolerant of such false teachers and neither should we be. John Stott warns:

> We are not to be dazzled, as many people are, by the person, gifts or office of teachers in the church. They may come to us with great dignity, authority and scholarship. They may be bishops or archbishops, university professors or even the pope himself. But if they bring a gospel other than the gospel preached by the apostles and recorded in the New Testament, they are to be rejected. We judge them by the gospel; we do not judge the gospel by them. As Dr. Alan Cole expresses it, "The outward person of the messenger does not validate his message; rather, the nature of the message validates the messenger."[1]

Notice that the apostle says **an angel from heaven**, not "an angel from God." **An angel from heaven** could conceivably bring a false message, but an angel from God could not. Language could not express more clearly the uniqueness of the gospel. It is the *only* way of salvation. Self-effort or human merit have no part. The gospel alone offers salvation without money or price. Whereas the law has a curse for those who fail to *keep* it, the gospel has a curse for those who seek to *change* it.

1:10 Paul is probably reminded at this point that his enemies accused him of changing the message to suit his audience, so he asks, in effect, "In insisting that there is only one gospel, am I trying to please **men, or God**?" Obviously he is not trying to **please men**, because they hate the suggestion that there is only one way to heaven. If Paul changed his message to suit **men**, he **would not be a bondservant of Christ**; in fact, he would be inviting the wrath of God to fall upon himself.

B. Paul's Defense of His Message and Ministry (1:11–2:10)

1:11, 12 The apostle now presents six arguments in defense of his message and ministry. First, the gospel was received by divine revelation and independently of man. It was **not according to man** in the sense that man did not originate it. A moment's reflection will confirm this. Paul's gospel makes everything of God and nothing of man. This is not the kind of salvation that men would devise! Paul **neither received it from** some other person, **nor was** he **taught it** through books. **It came** to him by direct **revelation** from **Jesus Christ** Himself.

1:13, 14 Secondly, Paul's failure to include Jewish law in his gospel could not be laid to any ignorance of **Judaism** on his part. By birth and training, he was steeped in the law. By personal choice, he became a notorious persecutor of **the church**. In passionate zeal **for the traditions of** his **fathers**, he surpassed many other Jews of his own age. Therefore, his gospel of salvation by faith apart from the law could certainly not be attributed to any ignorance of the law. Why then did he omit it from his preaching? Why did his gospel run counter to his background, his natural inclinations, and his whole religious development? Simply because it was not the result of his own thinking, but was given to him directly by God.

1:15–17 Thirdly, the first few years of his ministry were carried on independently of the other **apostles**. Paul now demonstrates his independence of other men in connection with his gospel. After his conversion, he **did not immediately confer with** human leaders, **nor did** he **go up to Jerusalem** where the other **apostles** were. Instead, he **went to Arabia**, then **returned again to Damascus**. His determination to avoid Jerusalem was not out of disrespect for his fellow-apostles; it was rather because he had been commissioned by the risen Lord Himself and given a unique ministry to the Gentiles (2:8). Hence his gospel and his service needed no human authorization. He was independent of man altogether.

Several expressions in these verses deserve careful consideration. Note the expression in verse 15: **God . . . separated me from my mother's womb**. Paul realized that even before his birth, he had been set apart by God for a special work. He adds that God **called me through His grace**, referring to his conversion on the road to Damascus. If he had received what he deserved at that

moment, he would have been cast into hell. But Christ, in wonderful grace, saved him and sent him out to preach the faith he had sought to destroy. In verse 16 he shows that God intended **to reveal His Son in** him. This gives us a wonderful view of God's purpose in calling us — to reveal His Son in *us*, so that we may represent the Lord Jesus to the world. He reveals Christ to our hearts (v. 16) in order that He may display Christ through us (vv. 16–23) in order that God may be glorified in this display (v. 24). Paul's special assignment was to preach Christ among the Gentiles.

In verse 17 he says, **"I went to Arabia."** Every servant of the Lord needs a time of seclusion and meditation. Moses had his forty years on the backside of the desert. David was alone with God while he tended sheep on the hillsides of Judea.

1:18–20 Fourthly, when Paul finally visited Jerusalem, he met only **Peter** and **James**. Apart from that, he was relatively unknown to the churches in Judea (1:21–24). To demonstrate further his independence of the other apostles, Paul recounts that he did not visit Jerusalem until at least **three years** after his conversion. He went up to make the acquaintance of **Peter**[2] — a personal, not an official visit (Acts 9:26–29). While there, he also met **James, the Lord's brother**. His stay with Peter lasted only **fifteen days** — scarcely long enough for a training course! Moreover, the text indicates he was on perfect equality with these servants of the Lord.

1:21–24 After that, he spent much of his time in **the regions of Syria and Cilicia** — so much so that **the churches of Judea** did not know him personally. All they knew was that this one who had treated the Christians so cruelly was now a Christian himself and was preaching Christ to others. Because of this **they glorified God** for what He had done in the life of Paul. (Do others glorify God because of the change in our lives?)

2:1 Fifthly, during Paul's later visit to Jerusalem, the apostles there agreed that his gospel was divine (2:1–10). Because the church began at Jerusalem, and the apostles more or less made that city their headquarters, certain Christians felt that the church there was "the mother church." Thus Paul had to contend with the charge that he was somewhat inferior because he was not one of the Jerusalem apostles. He replies with a detailed account of his later trip **to Jerusalem**. Whether this was **fourteen years** after his conversion, or after his first trip, we do not know. We do know that he received a revelation from Christ to go, together **with Barnabas**, his coworker, and **Titus**, a Gentile converted through Paul's ministry. The Judaizers had insisted that Titus be circumcised for full salvation. The Apostle Paul was adamantly opposed because he realized that the truth of the gospel was at stake. (Later when Paul himself circumcised Timothy, no important principle was involved — Acts 16:3.)

E. F. Kevan says:

> Paul saw that circumcision for justification was not the innocent little rite that the unthinking man might assume it to be. To undergo circumcision was to seek to be justified by a legalistic method of law-keeping, and thus to deny the very foundations of grace.[3]

2:2 When Paul reached Jerusalem he **communicated to them that gospel which** he preached **among the Gentiles, but privately to those who were of reputation, lest by any means** he **might run, or had run, in vain**. Why did Paul speak **privately** to the spiritual leaders rather than to the entire assembly? Did he want them to approve his gospel, in case he had been preaching something false? Obviously not! This is contrary to all that the apostle has been saying. He has insisted that his message was divinely revealed to him. He had no doubts that the doctrine he preached was the truth. The real explanation must be sought elsewhere. It was a matter of common courtesy to speak to the leaders first. It was also desirable that the leaders should be thoroughly convinced as to the genuineness of Paul's gospel. If they had any questions or difficulties, Paul wanted to answer them at the outset. Then he could go before the church with the full support of the other apostles. In dealing with a large number of people, there is always the danger that emotional appeals will sway the group. Therefore, Paul desired to present his

gospel **privately** at first, in an atmosphere free from possible mass hysteria. Had Paul acted otherwise, a serious dispute might have arisen, dividing the church into a Jewish wing and a Gentile one. Then the purpose of Paul's trip to Jerusalem would have been defeated. This is what he means by **lest by any means I might run, or had run, in vain.**

2:3 The whole question of legalism was brought to a head in the case of **Titus**. Would the Jerusalem church receive this Gentile convert into fellowship, or would it insist that he first **be circumcised**?[4] After considerable discussion and debate, the apostles decided that circumcision was not necessary for salvation. Paul had won a resounding victory.[5]

2:4 The underlying reason why Paul was led to go to Jerusalem is made clear by linking the beginning of verse 2 with the beginning of verse 4: "I went up by revelation . . . **and this occurred because of false brethren secretly brought in."** This refers to what had previously taken place in Antioch (Acts 15:1, 2). Some Jewish teachers from Jerusalem, posing as Christians, had somehow been **secretly** brought into the church at Antioch and were teaching that circumcision was essential for salvation.

2:5 Paul and Barnabas opposed them vigorously. To settle the matter, Paul, Barnabas, and others went to Jerusalem to obtain an opinion from the apostles and elders there.

2:6 Those who were esteemed as leaders in Jerusalem **added nothing** to him, either to his message or to himself as an apostle. This was remarkable. In the previous chapter, he had emphasized that his contact with the other apostles had been minimal. Now when he finally did confer with them, they agreed that he had been preaching the same gospel as they. What an important point this is! These Jewish leaders agreed that his gospel was not defective in any way. Though Paul had been independent of them, and had not been taught by them, yet the gospel they preached was exactly the same as his own. (Paul does not intend to belittle the other apostles, he simply states that **whatever they were**, namely, companions of the

Lord Jesus when He was on earth, did not give them any superior authority in his estimation. God does not accept man's person as far as such external distinctions are concerned.)

2:7, 8 The apostles in Jerusalem recognized that Paul had, by undeserved favor, been commissioned to take the gospel to **the uncircumcised** (the Gentiles) just as **Peter** had been sent to the Jews. Both men preached the same gospel, but primarily to different nationalities.

2:9, 10 Even **James, Cephas** (Peter), and **John**, apparently **pillars** of the church, **perceived** that God was working through Paul, and **gave** him **and Barnabas the right hand of fellowship** in taking the gospel **to the Gentiles**. This was not an official ordination, but an expression of their loving interest in Paul's work. The only suggestion they made was that Paul and Barnabas should **remember the poor, the very thing which** Paul states he **was eager to do.**

C. Paul Rebukes Peter (2:11–21)

2:11 As Paul's sixth and final answer to the attacks on his apostleship, he tells how it was necessary for him to rebuke the Apostle **Peter**[6] — considered by many Jewish Christians as the chief of the apostles. (This passage effectively refutes the notion that Peter was the infallible leader of the church.)

2:12 When Peter first came to Antioch, **he would eat with the Gentiles** in the full enjoyment of his Christian liberty. By Jewish tradition, he could not have done this. Some time later, a group **came** down **from James** in Jerusalem to Antioch for a visit. They claimed to represent James, but he later denied this (Acts 15:24). They were probably Jewish Christians who were still clinging to certain legal observances. When they arrived, Peter stopped having fellowship with the Gentiles, **fearing** that the news of his behavior would get back to the legalist faction in Jerusalem. In doing this, he was denying one of the great truths of the gospel — that all believers are one in Christ Jesus, and that national differences do not affect fellowship. Findlay says: "By refusing to eat with uncircumcised men, he affirmed implicitly that, though believers in Christ, they were still to him 'common and unclean,' that the Mosaic rites imparted a higher sanctity than the righteousness of faith."

2:13 Others followed Peter's example, including **Barnabas**, Paul's valued co-laborer. Recognizing the seriousness of this action, Paul boldly accused Peter of **hypocrisy**. Paul's rebuke is given in verses 14–21.[7]

2:14 As a Christian, Peter knew that God no longer recognized national differences; he had lived as a Gentile, eating their foods, etc. By his recent refusal to eat with Gentiles, Peter was implying that observances of Jewish laws and customs was necessary for holiness, and that the Gentile believers would have to **live as Jews**.

2:15 Paul seems to be using irony here. Did not Peter's conduct betray a lingering conviction concerning the superiority of the **Jews**, and the despised position of the **Gentiles**? Peter should have known better, because God had taught him before the conversion of the Gentile Cornelius to call no man common or unclean (Acts 10 and 11:1–18).

2:16 Jews who had been saved knew that there was no salvation in **the law**. The law condemned to death those who failed to obey it perfectly. This brought the curse on all, because all have broken its sacred precepts. The Savior is here presented as the only true object of faith. Paul reminds Peter that "**even we** *Jews*" came to the conclusion that salvation is **by faith in Christ and not by** law-keeping. What was the sense now of Peter's putting Gentiles under the law? The law told people what to do but gave them no power to do it. It was given to reveal sin, not to be a savior.

2:17 Paul and Peter and others had sought justification in **Christ** and in Christ alone. Peter's actions at Antioch, however, seemed to indicate that he was not completely justified, but had to go back under the law to complete his salvation. If this is so, then Christ is not a perfect and sufficient Savior. If we go to Him to have our sins forgiven, but then have to go elsewhere in addition, is not Christ **a minister of sin** in failing to fulfill His promises? If, while we are professedly depending on Christ for justification, we then go back to the law (which can only condemn us as sinners), do we act as Christians? Can we hope for Christ's approval on such a course of action that in effect makes Him **a minister of sin**? Paul's answer is an indignant **Certainly not!**

2:18 Peter had abandoned the whole legal system for faith in Christ. He had repudiated any difference between Jew and Gentile when it came to finding favor with God. Now, by refusing to eat with Gentiles, he is building up **again** what he once **destroyed**. In so doing, he proves himself to be **a transgressor**. Either he was wrong in leaving the law for Christ, or he is wrong now in leaving Christ for the law!

2:19 The penalty for breaking the law is death. As a sinner, I had broken the law. Therefore, it condemned me to die. But Christ paid the penalty of the broken law for me by dying in my place. Thus when Christ died, I died. He died to the law in the sense that He met all its righteous demands; therefore, in Christ, I too have **died to the law.**

The Christian has **died to the law**; he has nothing more to do with it. Does this mean that the believer is at liberty to break the Ten Commandments all he wants? No, he lives a holy life, not through fear of the law, but out of love to the One who died for him. Christians who desire to be under the law as a pattern of behavior do not realize that this places them under its curse. Moreover, they cannot touch the law in one point without being responsible to keep it completely. The only way we can **live to God** is by being dead to the law. The law could never produce a holy life; God never intended that it should. His way of holiness is explained in verse 20.

2:20 The believer is identified **with Christ** in His death. Not only was *He* crucified on Calvary, *I* was **crucified** there as well — in Him. This means the end of me as a sinner in God's sight. It means the end of me as a person seeking to merit or earn salvation by my own efforts. It means the end of me as a child of Adam, as a man under the condemnation of the law, as my old, unregenerate self. The old, evil "I" has been crucified; it has no more claims on my daily life. This *is* true as to my standing before God; it *should* be true as to my behavior.

The believer does not cease to live as a personality or as an individual. But the one who is seen by God as having died is not the same one who lives. **It is no longer I who live, but Christ** who **lives in me**. The Savior did not die for me in order that I might go on living my life as I choose. He died for me so that from now on He might be able to live His life in me. **The life which I now live in** this human body, **I live by faith in the Son of God**. Faith means reliance or dependence. The Christian lives by continual dependence on Christ, by yielding to Him, by allowing Christ to live His life in him.

Thus the believer's rule of life is Christ and not the law. It is not a matter of striving, but of trusting. He lives a holy life, not out of fear of punishment, but out of love to **the Son of God, who loved** him **and gave Himself for** him.

Have you ever turned your life over to the Lord Jesus with the prayer that His life might be manifest in your body?

2:21 The grace of God is seen in His unconditional gift of salvation. When man tries to earn it, he is making it void. It is no longer by grace if man deserves it or earns it. Paul's final thrust at Peter is effective. If Peter could obtain favor with God by Jewish observances, **then Christ died** for nothing; He literally threw His life away. Christ died because man could obtain **righteousness** in no other way — not even by law-keeping.

Clow says:

> The deepest heresy of all, which corrupts churches, leavens creeds with folly, and swells our human hearts with pride, is salvation by works. "I believe," writes John Ruskin, "that the root of every schism and heresy from which the Christian Church has suffered, has been the effort to earn salvation rather than to receive it; and that one reason why preaching is so ineffective is that it calls on men oftener to work for God than to behold God working for them."[8]

II. DOCTRINAL: PAUL DEFENDS JUSTIFICATION BY FAITH (3:1–5:1)

A. The Great Truth of the Gospel (3:1–9)

3:1 Their actions exhibited a lack of

understanding and reason. To turn to law from grace is to be **bewitched**. It is to be lulled as by a magic spell and unwarily to accept falsehood for truth. When Paul asks: **"Who has bewitched you?"**, the *who* is singular (Gk., *tis*),[9] not plural, perhaps suggesting that the devil was the author of this false teaching. Paul himself had preached **Jesus Christ** to the Galatians **as crucified**, emphasizing that the cross was to separate them forever from the curse and bondage of the law. How could they return to the law and thus disregard the cross? Had not the truth laid hold of them practically?

3:2 One question should be sufficient to settle the whole matter. Let them go back to the time of their conversion — the time when the Holy Spirit came to dwell in their bodies. How **did** they **receive the Spirit**? By doing, or by believing? Obviously it was by believing. No one ever received the Spirit by keeping **the law.**

3:3 If they could not *obtain* salvation by works, could they expect to grow in holiness or Christian maturity by the law? If the power of **the Spirit** was necessary to save them, could they complete the process by fleshly efforts?

3:4 When the Galatians first trusted in Christ, they exposed themselves to bitter persecution, perhaps partly at the hands of Jewish zealots who hated the gospel of grace. Was all that suffering **in vain**? In going back to the law were they not saying that the persecutors were right after all? **If indeed it was in vain**. Paul expresses continued hope that they will return to the gospel for which they once **suffered**.

3:5 There is a question whether **He** (or *he*)[10] in verse 5 refers to God, to Paul, or to someone else who was ministering to the Galatians at the time he was writing the Letter. Ultimately, it must apply to God, since only **He** can supply **the** Holy **Spirit**. However, in a secondary sense, it could apply to a Christian worker as the instrument through whom God performs His will. This would give a very exalted view of the Christian ministry. Someone has said: "Real Christian work of any sort is conveying the Holy Spirit to others; it is actually the dispensing of the Spirit."

If the apostle is speaking of himself, he is probably thinking of the miracles which accompanied his preaching and their reception of Christ (Heb. 2:4). However, the tense of the verb indicates not something that happened in the past, but something going on at the time of writing. Paul is probably referring to the miraculous gifts bestowed by the Holy Spirit on believers after their conversion, as described in 1 Corinthians 12:8–11.

Does He do it by the works of the law, or by the hearing of faith? The answer is: **By the hearing of faith**. The indwelling of the Holy Spirit and His subsequent work in the believer are never earned nor merited, but are always given by grace and received by **faith**. Thus the Galatians should have realized from their own experiences that blessing comes by faith and not by law-keeping.

For his second proof, Paul now turns to the very Scriptures which the false teachers were using to show the necessity of circumcision! What did the OT really say?

3:6 Paul had demonstrated that God's dealings with the Galatians were entirely on the basis of faith. Now he shows that men were saved in the same way even in OT times. The question in verse 5 was: "Does He do it by the works of the law, or by the hearing of faith?" The answer was: "By the hearing of faith." With that answer in mind, verse 6 opens, **just as Abraham. . . .** He was justified in the same way — by the hearing of faith.

Perhaps the Jewish teachers were using Abraham as their hero and example, basing their argument for the necessity of circumcision on his experience (Gen. 17:24, 26). If so, Paul will fight them on their own ground. How then was Abraham saved? **Abraham believed God.** It was not by any meritorious act at all. He simply **believed God**. There is no merit attached to that; in fact, a man is a fool not to believe God. Believing God is the only thing man can do in connection with salvation, which leaves him no ground for boasting. It is not a "good work," involving human effort. It gives no place to the flesh. What is more right than for a creature to trust his Creator or a child his Father?

Justification is an act of God by which He declares righteous all who believe on

Him. God can properly deal with sinners in this way because Christ died as a substitute for sinners on Calvary's cross, paying the debt of their sins. Justification does not mean that God makes the believer righteous and sinless in himself. He reckons him to be righteous on the basis of the work of the Savior. God gives the trusting sinner a righteous standing which makes him fit for heaven, then expects him to live righteously in gratitude for what He has done for him. The important thing to note here is that justification has nothing to do with law-keeping. It is entirely on the principle of faith.

3:7 Doubtless the Jewish teachers were maintaining that in order to be real sons of Abraham, the Galatians had to be circumcised. Paul refutes this. The real **sons of Abraham** are not those who are born Jews, or those who become Jewish converts, but those who are saved by faith. In Romans 4:10, 11, Paul shows that Abraham was reckoned righteous *before* he was circumcised. In other words, he was justified while he was still on *Gentile* ground.

3:8 The OT is depicted as a prophet, looking down the centuries and **foreseeing that God would justify the Gentiles** as well as Jews on the principle of **faith**. The blessing of **the Gentiles by faith** was not only foreseen by the OT, but was actually announced to Abraham in Genesis 12:3 — "In you all the families of the earth shall be blessed."

When we first read this quotation from Genesis, we find it difficult to see how Paul found such a meaning in it. Yet the Holy Spirit, who wrote that verse in the OT, knew that it contained the gospel of salvation by faith to all nations. Since Paul was writing by inspiration of the same Holy Spirit, he was enabled to explain to us the underlying meaning: **In you** — that is, along with Abraham, in the same way as Abraham. **All the nations** — the Gentiles as well as the Jews. **Shall be blessed** — be saved. How was Abraham saved? **By faith.** How will the nations be saved? In the same way as Abraham — by faith. Moreover, they will be saved as Gentiles, not by becoming Jews.

3:9 All **those who** exercise **faith** in

God **are** justified **with believing Abraham**, according to the testimony of the Jewish Scriptures.

B. Law Versus Promise (3:10–18)

3:10 Paul shows from the Sacred Writings that, far from conferring a blessing, the law can only **curse**. This verse does not say "As many as have broken the law," but: **As many as are of the works of the law**, that is, all who seek to obtain favor with God on the basis of obeying the law. They **are under the curse**, that is, condemned to death. **For it is written** (in Deut. 27:26) **"Cursed is everyone who does not continue. . . ."** It is not enough to keep the law for a day, or a month, or a year. One must **continue** to keep it. Obedience must be complete. It is not enough to keep just the Ten Commandments. All six hundred and some laws in the five books of Moses must be obeyed!

3:11 The false teachers are once again refuted from the OT. Paul quotes the prophet Habakkuk to show that God has always justified men **by faith** and not by law. The quotation in the original Greek word order reads: "The just (or righteous) by faith shall live." In other words, those who have been reckoned righteous by faith, not by works, shall have eternal life. The justified-by-faith-ones **shall live.**

3:12 The law does not ask men to believe. It does not even ask men to *try* to keep the commandments. It calls for strict, complete, and perfect obedience, as was so clearly taught in Leviticus. It is a contrary principle to faith. The law says: "Do and live." Faith says: "Believe and live." Paul's argument then is this: The just person shall live by faith. A person under **law** does **not** live by **faith.** Therefore, he is not *just* before God. When Paul says: **"The man who does them shall live by them,"** he is stating a theoretical axiom or ideal but one that is impossible to attain.

3:13 To redeem is to buy back, or to deliver by paying the price. **The curse of the law** is death — the penalty for breaking its commandments. Christ has delivered those under law from paying the penalty of death demanded by the law. (Paul is undoubtedly speaking primarily of believing Jews when he uses the pronoun **us**, although the Jews were representatives of the entire human race.)

Cynddylan Jones says:

> The Galatians imagined that Christ only half purchased them, and that they had to purchase the rest by their submission to circumcision and other Jewish rites and ceremonies. Hence their readiness to be led away by false teachers and to mix up Christianity and Judaism. Paul says here: (according to the Welsh translation) "Christ hath *wholly* purchased us from the curse of the law."[11]

Christ redeemed men by dying in their place, enduring the dreadful wrath of God against sins. The **curse** of God fell on Him as man's Substitute. He did not become sinful in Himself, but man's sins were placed upon Him.

Christ did not redeem men **from the curse of the law** by keeping the Ten Commandments perfectly during His lifetime. Scripture does not teach that His perfect obedience to the law is reckoned to us. Rather He delivered men from the law by bearing its dreadful curse in death. Apart from His death there could be no salvation. The law taught that when condemned criminals were hanged on a tree, it was a sign of their being under the curse of God (Deut. 21:23). Here the Holy Spirit sees in that passage a prophecy of the manner in which the Savior would die to bear the curse for His creatures. He was hung between heaven and earth as though unworthy of either. In His death by crucifixion, He is said to have been hanged **on a tree** (Acts 5:30; 1 Pet. 2:24).

3:14 God had promised to bless Abraham and to bless all the world through him. **The blessing of Abraham** is really salvation by grace through faith. The penalty of death required by God must first be paid. So the Lord Jesus was made a curse in order that God might reach out to both Jews and Gentiles in grace. Now in Christ (a descendant of Abraham), the nations are blessed.

God's promise to Abraham in Genesis 12:3 does not mention the Holy Spirit. But Paul tells us here, by inspiration of God, that the gift of the Holy **Spirit** was included in God's uncondi-

tional covenant of salvation with Abraham. It was there in embryo. The Holy Spirit could not come as long as the law was in the way. Christ had to die and be glorified before the Spirit could be given (John 16:7).

The apostle has demonstrated that salvation is by faith, not law, by (1) the experience of the Galatians, and (2) the witness of the OT Scriptures. He now turns to an illustration from everyday life.

Paul's argument in this section may be summarized as follows: In Genesis 12:3, God promised to bless all families of the earth in Abram. This promise of salvation included Gentiles as well as Jews. In Genesis 22:18, God also promised: "In your seed all the nations of the earth shall be blessed." He said *seed* (singular), not "seeds" (plural). God was referring to One Person, the Lord Jesus Christ, who was a direct descendant of Abraham (Luke 3:34). In other words, God promised to bless all nations, Gentile as well as Jewish, through Christ. The promise was unconditional; it required neither good works nor legal obedience. It was a simple promise meant to be received in simple faith.

Now the law, given to Israel 430 years later, could not add conditions to the promise nor alter it in any way. In human affairs this would be unrighteous; in divine matters it would be unthinkable. The conclusion therefore is that God's promise of blessing to the Gentiles is through Christ, by faith and not by law-keeping.

3:15 In human affairs, when a **covenant** or will is signed and sealed, no one would think of changing the document or adding to it. If human testaments cannot be broken, how much less can God's!

3:16 No doubt the Judaizers had argued that although the promises were originally made to Abraham and to his seed (the people of Israel) by faith, yet these same people of Israel were subsequently put under the law. Therefore, the Galatians, though originally saved by faith, must now observe the Ten Commandments. Paul answers: **The promises** were made **to Abraham and his Seed** (singular). "Seed" may sometimes denote a multitude, yet here it denotes one Person, namely Christ. (We ourselves would probably never see this in reading the OT, but the Spirit of God enlightens us.)

3:17 God's promise to Abraham was unconditional; it did not depend on works at all. God simply agreed to give Abraham a Seed (Christ). Though he had no child, Abraham believed God, thus believing also in the Christ to come, and he was justified. The coming of the **law — four hundred and thirty years later** could not affect **the promise** of salvation in any way. It could neither revoke the promise nor add conditions to it.

Perhaps the Judaizers were suggesting that the law, coming 430 years after the promise, had the effect of annulling it. "Not at all!" Paul says, in effect: "The promise was like a will, and had been ratified by a death (the covenant sacrifice, Gen. 15:7–11; see also Heb. 9:15–22). It could not be revoked."

The 430 years are reckoned from the time that God confirmed the Abrahamic Covenant to Jacob, just as Jacob was preparing to enter Egypt (Gen. 46:1–4), and they extend to the giving of the law about three months after the exodus.

3:18 **The inheritance** must be either by faith or by works. It cannot be by both. Scripture makes it clear that it was given **to Abraham by** unconditional **promise**. So it is with salvation. It is offered as an unconditional gift. Any thought of working for it is excluded.

C. The Purpose of the Law (3:19–29)

3:19 **What purpose then does the law serve?** If, as Paul contended, the law did not annul or add conditions to the promise God made to Abraham, **what** *was* the **purpose** of the law? The law was intended to reveal sin in its true character as transgression. Sin existed before the law, but man did not recognize it as transgression until the law came. Transgression is the violation of a known law.

The law was given to a nation of sinners. They could never obtain righteousness by keeping it because they did not have the power to obey it. The law was meant to show men what hopeless sinners they were, so they would cry out to God to save them by His grace. God's covenant with Abraham was an uncon-

ditional promise of blessing; the law resulted only in cursing. The law demonstrated the unworthiness of man to receive free and unconditional blessing. If man is to be blessed, it must be by the grace of God.

The Seed is Christ. Therefore, the law was given as a temporary measure until the coming of Christ. The promised Abrahamic blessing was to come through Him. A contract between two parties involves **a mediator**, a go-between. The law involved two contracting parties — God and Israel. Moses served as go-between (Deut. 5:5). The angels were God's messengers in delivering the law to Moses (Deut. 33:2; Ps. 68:17; Acts 7:53; Heb. 2:2). The participation of Moses and the angels spoke of distance between God and His people, of a people unfit for His presence.

3:20 If there was only one contracting party, and he made an unconditional promise, requiring nothing from the other party, there would be no need of **a mediator**. The fact that the law required a mediator implied that man must keep his part of the agreement. This was the weakness of the law; it called for obedience from those who did not have the power to give it. When **God** made His promise to Abraham, He was the sole contracting Party. This was the strength of the promise: everything depended on God and nothing on man. No mediator was involved, because none was needed.[12]

3:21 Did **the law** set aside **the promises** or take their place? **Certainly not!** If it were possible to give **a law** by which sinners could achieve the perfection required by God, then certainly salvation would have been by law-keeping. God would not have sent the Son of His love to die for sinners if He could have achieved the same result in some less costly way. But the law had plenty of both *time* and *people* to demonstrate that it could not save sinners. In this sense it was "weak through the flesh" (Rom. 8:3). All the law could do was show men their hopelessness and impress on them that salvation could only be by the free grace of God.

3:22 The OT showed that all men are sinners, including those under the law. It was necessary that man should be thus thoroughly convinced of sin, in order **that the promise** of salvation **by faith in Jesus Christ might be given to those who believe**. The key words in verse 22 are **faith, given**, and **believe**. There is no mention of "doing" or "law-keeping."

3:23 **Faith** here is the Christian faith. It refers to the era ushered in by the death, burial, resurrection, and ascension of the Lord Jesus, and the preaching of the gospel at Pentecost. Before that time, the Jews **were kept under guard** as if in a prison or in custody. They were fenced in by the law's requirements, and since they could not fulfill these, they were restricted to the way of **faith** for salvation. The people under law were thus confined until the glorious news of deliverance from the bondage of the law was announced in the gospel.

3:24 **The law** is pictured as a guardian and guide of children, or as a **tutor**.[13] This emphasizes the thought of teaching; the law taught lessons concerning the holiness of God, the sinfulness of man, and the need for atonement. Here the word is used to describe one who exercises discipline and general supervision over minors, or the immature.

The words **to bring us** are not in the original, but were supplied by the translators of the King James tradition. If we leave them out, the verse teaches that the law was a Jewish guardian up **to Christ**, that is, until the coming of Christ, or with the coming of Christ in view. There is a sense in which the law preserved the people of Israel as a distinct nation by regulations concerning marriage, property, foods, etc. When "the faith" came, it was first announced to this nation that had been so miraculously kept in ward through the centuries. Justification **by faith** was promised on the basis of the finished work of Christ, the Redeemer.

3:25 The law is the **tutor**, but once the Christian **faith** has been received, believing Jews **are no longer under** the law. How much less Gentiles, such as the Galatians, who were *never* under the tutor! Verse 24 teaches that man is *not justified by law*; verse 25 teaches that the *law is not the rule of life* for one who is justified.

3:26 Notice the change in pronouns from "we" to **you**. In speaking of the Jews as "we", Paul showed that they were kept under law until the coming of Christ. The law maintained them as a separate people to whom justification by faith might be preached. When they were justified, they ceased to be under law, and their distinctive character as Jews ceased. The pronoun **"you"** from here to the end of the chapter includes both saved Jews and saved Gentiles. Such people **are all sons of God through faith in Christ Jesus**.

3:27 Union with **Christ**, which takes place at the time of conversion, is confessed in water baptism. This baptism does not make a person a member of Christ or an inheritor of the kingdom of God. It is a public identification with Christ, which Paul speaks of as a "putting on" of **Christ**. Just as a soldier proclaims himself a member of the army by "putting on" his uniform, so a believer identifies himself as one who belongs to Christ by being **baptized** in water. By this act he publicly expresses submission to Christ's leadership and authority. He portrays visibly that he is a son of God.

It is certain that the apostle is *not* suggesting that water baptism unites a person to Christ. That would be a blatant repudiation of his basic thesis that salvation is by faith alone.

Nor is Paul likely referring here to Spirit baptism, which places a believer in the body of Christ (1 Cor. 12:13). The baptism of the Holy Spirit is invisible. There is nothing about it that corresponds to a public "putting on" of Christ.

This is a baptism that is *unto* Christ (JND). Just as the Israelites were baptized *unto* Moses, identifying themselves with him as their leader, so believers today are baptized *unto* Christ, signifying their recognition of Him as rightful Lord.

By baptism the believer signifies also the burial of the flesh and its efforts to obtain righteousness. He signifies the end of the old way of life and the beginning of the new one. In water baptism the Galatians confessed that they had died with Christ and had been buried with Him. Just as Christ died to the law, so they were dead to the law, and should not therefore desire to be under it as a rule of life. Just as Christ has, by His death, broken down the distinction between Jew and Gentile, so they have died to such national differences. They **have put on Christ** in the sense that they now live a completely new life — the life of Christ.

3:28 The law made distinctions between these classes. For instance, the distinction between Jew and Gentile is insisted on in Deuteronomy 7:6; 14:1, 2. In his morning prayer, a Jewish man thanked God that He had not made him a Gentile, a slave, or a woman. **In Christ Jesus** these differences disappear, that is, as far as acceptance with God is concerned. A Jew is not preferred over a Gentile, a free man is not more favored than a slave, nor is a man more privileged than a woman. All are on the same level because they are **in Christ Jesus**.

This verse must not be pressed into meaning something it does not say. As far as everyday life is concerned (not to mention public ministry in the church), God *does* recognize the distinction between male and female. The NT contains instructions addressed to each; it also speaks separately to slaves and masters. But in obtaining blessing from God, these things do not matter. The great thing is to be **in Christ Jesus**. (This refers to our heavenly position, not to our earthly condition.) Before God the believing Jew is not a bit superior to the converted pagan! Govett says: "All the distinctions which the law made are swallowed up in the common grave which God has provided." Therefore, how foolish it is for Christians to seek further holiness by setting up differences which Christ has abolished.

3:29 The Galatians were deluded into thinking that they could become Abraham's seed by keeping the law. Paul shows otherwise. Christ is the seed of Abraham; the inheritance promised to Abraham was fulfilled in Christ. When sinners believe on Him, they become one with Him. Thus they become **Abraham's seed** and, in Christ, they inherit all of God's blessings.

D. Children and Sons (4:1–16)

4:1, 2 The picture is of a wealthy father who intends to turn over control of his wealth to the son when he reaches maturity. However, **as long as he is** still **a child**, the heir's status is like that of **a slave**. He is continually told to do this and not to do that. He has **stewards** who manage his property and **guardians** in charge of his person. Thus, although the inheritance is surely his, he does not enter into it until he has grown up.

4:3 This was the condition of the Jews under law. They **were children**, being ordered around by the law just like slaves. They **were in bondage** under the **elements of the world**, meaning the elementary principles of the Jewish religion. The ceremonies and rituals of Judaism were designed for those who did not know God the Father as He is revealed in Christ. An illustration might be found in a child learning the rudiments of spelling by using blocks, or learning to identify objects by means of pictures. The law was full of shadows and pictures, appealing to the spiritual senses by means of the physical and external. Circumcision is an example of this. Judaism was physical, external, and temporal; Christianity is spiritual, internal, and permanent. These externals were a form of **bondage** to the **children.**

4:4[†] The fullness of the time refers to the time appointed by the Heavenly Father when the heirs would become of age (see v. 2).

In this verse we have, in a few words, a marvelous statement as to the deity and humanity of the Savior. He is the eternal Son of God; yet He **was born of a woman**. If Jesus had been only a man, it would be gratuitous to say that He **was born of a woman**. How else could a mere man be born? The expression, in our Lord's case, witnesses to His unique Person and the unique mode of His birth.

Born into the world as an Israelite, He was therefore **born under the law**. As Son of God, the Lord Jesus would never have been under the law; He was the One who gave it. But, in condescending grace, He put Himself **under the law** that He had made, in order that He might magnify it in His life, and bear its curse in His death.

4:5 The law demanded a price from those who failed to keep it — the price of death. Before God could bring men

[†]See p. xviii.

into the wonderful position of sonship, this price had to be paid. So the Lord Jesus, coming into the world as a member of the human race and of the Jewish nation, paid the price which the law demanded. Because He is God, His death was infinite in value, that is, it was sufficient to pay for any number of sinners. Because He was Man, He could die as a substitute for man. Govett says: "Christ, by nature Son of God, became Son of man, that we, by nature sons of man, might become sons of God. Wonderful exchange!"

As long as men were slaves, they could not be **sons**. Christ delivered them from the bondage of the law in order that they might be adopted **as sons**. Notice here the distinction between becoming a *child* of God and a *son* of God (compare Rom. 8:14, 16). The believer is born into the family of God as a *child* (see John 1:12). The emphasis here is on the fact of divine birth, not on the privileges and responsibilities of sonship. The believer is adopted into the family as a *son*. Every Christian is a son immediately and is brought into the inheritance of which he is an heir. Thus the instructions to Christians in the NT assume no infancy among the saints. All are treated as mature sons.

Adoption in Roman culture differed from that in modern life. We think of adoption as taking someone else's child to be one's own. But in the NT, **adoption** means putting believers into the position of mature sons with all the privileges and responsibilities of that position.

4:6 In order that those who **are sons** of God might realize the dignity of this position, **God sent** the Holy **Spirit** at Pentecost to indwell them. The Spirit creates an awareness of sonship, causing the saint to address God as **Father.** "**Abba, Father**" is a familiar form of address, combining the Aramaic and Greek words for "father." No slave could address the head of a family in this fashion; it was reserved for members of the family, and expresses love and confidence. Note the Trinity in this verse — **Spirit, Son** and **Father** — in that order.

4:7 The believer is **no longer a slave**; he is not under the law. Now he is **a son** of God. Since Christ, as God's

Son, is the heir of all God's riches, the Christian is **an heir of God through Christ**.[14] All that God has is his by faith.

In rabbinical schools in Israel today a student is not allowed to read the Song of Solomon or Ezekiel 1 until he is forty years old. The Song of Solomon is considered too sexually explicit for a younger mind, and Ezekiel 1 contains a description of the glory of the ineffable God. The Talmud tells that when a certain person under forty began to read Ezekiel 1, fire came out from the page and consumed him. What this shows is that a person under law is not considered a *man* until he is forty. (The well-known *bar mitzvah* at age thirteen only makes a Jewish boy a "son of the covenant" — the meaning of the term — and thus responsible to keep the law.) Up to the age of forty the Orthodox man is considered a minor.

Not so with believers under grace. The moment they are saved the whole inheritance is theirs. They are treated as adult, mature sons and daughters, and the whole Bible is theirs to read, enjoy, and obey.

In light of these truths Harrison's exhortation is very appropriate:

> Child of His love, all things are yours — He tells you this in 1 Corinthians 3:22, 23 to arouse you to a realization of riches beyond your utmost powers of imagination to comprehend. Consider the universe. Whose is it, but His and yours? Then live royally.[15]

4:8 The Galatians had once been under bondage to idols. Before their conversion, they had been heathens who worshiped idols of wood and stone — false **gods**. Now they were turning to another type of bondage — bondage to the law.

4:9 **How** could they excuse their conduct? They had come to know **God**, or, if they didn't know Him in a deep experiential way, at least they were **known by** Him, that is, they were saved. Yet they were turning from His power and riches (of which they were heirs) **to weak and** poor things, the things connected with the law, such as circumcision, holy days, and rules of diet. They were again putting themselves **in bondage** to things that could neither save nor enrich but could only impoverish them.

Paul labels the law and all its ceremonies as **weak and beggarly**. God's laws were beautiful in their time and place, but they are positive hindrances when substituted for the Lord Jesus. It is idolatry to turn from Christ to law.

4:10, 11 The Galatians were observing the Jewish calendar with its Sabbaths, its festivals, **and seasons**. Paul expresses fear for those who profess to be Christians, yet seek to find favor with God by legal observances. Even unregenerate people can observe **days and months and years.** It gives some people intense satisfaction to feel there is something they can do in their own strength to win God's smile. But this implies that man has some strength, and hence, to that extent, he does not need the Savior.

If Paul could write in this manner to the Galatians, what would he write to professing Christians today who are seeking to attain holiness by legal observances? Would he not condemn the traditions brought into Christianity from Judaism — a humanly ordained priesthood, distinctive vestments for the priest, Sabbath-keeping, holy places, candles, holy water, and so forth?

4:12 Apparently the Galatians had forgotten their gratitude to Paul when he first preached the gospel to them. But he addresses them as **"Brethren"** in spite of their failures and his fears for them. Paul had been a Jew under law. Now, in Christ, he was free from the law. So he says, **"Become like me** —delivered from the law and no longer living under it." The Gentile Galatians had never been under law, and were not under it now. Thus the apostle says: **"I became like you**. I, who was a Jew, now enjoy the freedom from law which you Gentiles always had."

You have not injured me at all. It is not exactly clear what Paul had in mind here. Perhaps he is saying that he had no feeling of personal injury as a result of their treatment of him. That they should have turned away from him to the false teachers was not so much a blow at him personally as a blow at the truth of God and thus an injury to their own selves.

4:13 The **gospel** was **first . . . preached** to them in **physical infirmity.**[16]

God often uses weak, despised, poor instruments to accomplish His work in order that the glory will be His and not man's.

4:14 Paul's illness was a **trial** to himself and to those who listened to him. However, the Galatians did not reject him because of his physical appearance or because of his speech. Instead, they **received** him **as an angel of God**, that is, a messenger sent by God, and **even as Christ Jesus** Himself. Since he represented the Lord, they received him as they would receive the Lord (Matt. 10:40). They accepted Paul's message as the very word of God. This should be a lesson to all Christians concerning their treatment of the Lord's messengers. When we receive them cordially, we receive Him in the same way (Luke 10:16).

4:15 When they first heard the gospel, they acknowledged what a rich **blessing** it was to their souls. So great was their appreciation that they would have given their **own eyes** to Paul, if it were possible. (This might be an indication that Paul's "thorn in the flesh" was an eye disease.) But where is this sense of gratitude now? Unfortunately, it has vanished like the morning dew.

4:16 What accounted for their changed attitude toward Paul? He was still preaching the same message, earnestly contending for **the truth** of the gospel. If this made him their **enemy**, then their position was dangerous indeed.

E. Bondage or Freedom (4:17–5:1)

4:17 The motives of the false teachers differed from Paul's: they wanted a following, whereas he was interested in the spiritual welfare of the Galatians (4:17–20). The false teachers were zealous in their efforts to win the affections of the Galatians, but their motives were not sincere. **They want to exclude you**. The Judaizers wanted to cut the Galatians off from the Apostle Paul and from other teachers. They wanted a following, and sought to form a sect in order to get it. Stott warns: "When Christianity is turned into a bondage to rules and regulations, its victims are inevitably in subjection, tied to the apron strings of their teachers, as in the Middle Ages."[17]

4:18 Paul says, in effect, "I do not

mind others fussing over you, even when I am absent from you, as long as they are doing so with pure motives and for a **good** cause."

4:19 By calling the Galatians his **little children**, Paul would remind them that it was he who had pointed them to Christ. He is undergoing birth-pangs again for them, not this time seeking their salvation, but rather that **Christ** might be **formed in** them. Christlikeness is God's full objective for His people (Eph. 4:13; Col. 1:28).

4:20 This verse might mean that Paul was puzzled as to the true status of the Galatians. Their defection from the truth had left him with **doubts**. He would like to be able **to change** his **tone** and speak with certainty and conviction about them. Or perhaps he was perplexed as to their reaction to his Letter. He would rather be speaking with them in person. Then he could better express himself by changing the **tone** of his voice. If they were receptive to his rebukes, he could be tender. If, however, they were haughty and rebellious, he could be stern. As it was, he was perplexed about them; he could not tell what their reaction to his message would be.

Since the Jewish teachers made so much of Abraham and insisted that believers must follow his example by being circumcised, Paul turns to Abraham's domestic history to show that legalism is slavery and cannot be mixed with grace.

God had promised that Abraham would have a son, even though he and Sarah were too old, naturally speaking, to have children. Abraham believed God and thus was justified (Gen. 15:1–6). Sometime afterward, Sarah became discouraged, waiting for the promised son, and suggested that Abraham should have a child by her slave-girl, Hagar. Abraham followed her advice, and Ishmael was born. This was not the heir promised by God, but the son of Abraham's impatience, carnality, and lack of trust (Gen. 16).

Then, when Abraham was one hundred years old, the child of promise, Isaac, was born. Obviously this birth was miraculous; it was made possible only by the mighty power of God (Gen. 21:1–5). At the customary feast in obser-

vance of the weaning of Isaac, Sarah saw Ishmael mocking her son. She thereupon ordered Abraham to expel Ishmael and his mother from the home, saying, "The son of this bondwoman shall not be heir with my son, namely, with Isaac" (Gen. 21:8–11). This is the background for the argument which the apostle now takes up.

4:21 Law in this verse is used in two different senses. The first refers to law as a means of attaining holiness, and the second to the OT books of the law (Genesis through Deuteronomy), particularly Genesis. Paul is saying, **"Tell me, you who desire to** obtain favor with God by law-keeping, **do you not** listen to the message of the book of **the law?"**

4:22, 23 The **two sons** were Ishmael and Isaac. The **bondwoman** was Hagar, and the **freewoman** was Sarah. Ishmael was born as a result of Abraham's scheming intervention. Isaac, on the other hand, was given to Abraham by **promise** of God.

4:24 The story is **symbolic**; it has a deeper meaning than at first appears. The real significance of the events is not expressly stated, but is implied. Thus, the true story of Isaac and Ishmael represents deep spiritual truth, which Paul now proceeds to explain.

The two women represent **two covenants: Hagar** the covenant of law, and Sarah the covenant of grace. The law was given at **Mount Sinai**. Strangely enough, the word "Hagar" in the Arabic language means "Rock," and the Arabs called Mt. Sinai "the Rock."

4:25 The covenant given at **Sinai** produced slavery; thus **Hagar**, a slave-girl, was a fitting type of the law. **Hagar** represents **Jerusalem**, the capital of the Jewish nation, and the center for the unsaved Israelites who were still seeking to obtain righteousness by keeping the law. These, together **with their children**, their followers, are **in bondage**. For Paul to link unbelieving Israelites with Hagar rather than with Sarah, with Ishmael rather than with Isaac, was a stinging characterization.

4:26 The capital city of those who are justified by faith is the heavenly **Jerusalem**. It **is the mother of** all believers, both Jew and Gentile.

4:27 This quotation from Isaiah 54:1

is a prediction that the children of the heavenly city will be more numerous than those of earthly Jerusalem. Sarah was the woman who for so long was **barren**. Hagar was the woman **who has a husband**. In what way are we to understand the eventual triumph of Sarah, or the heavenly Jerusalem? The answer is that the **children** of promise include all those, Gentiles as well as Jews, who come to God by faith — **many more** than the children of Hagar who abide under the law.

4:28 True believers are born not of the will of man nor of the will of the flesh, but of God. It is not natural descent that counts, but divine miraculous birth by faith in the Lord Jesus.

4:29 Ishmael mocked Isaac, and it has always been true that those born of the flesh have **persecuted** those **born** of **the Spirit**. Consider the sufferings of our Lord and of the Apostle Paul at the hands of unsaved men. It may seem to us a trivial offense that Ishmael should mock Isaac, but Scripture records it, and Paul sees in it a principle that still abides — the enmity between **the flesh** and **the Spirit.**

4:30 Let the Galatians then appeal to **Scripture**, and they will hear this verdict. Law and grace cannot be mixed; it is impossible to inherit God's blessings on the basis of human merit or fleshly effort.

4:31 Those who have trusted Christ have no connection with the law as a means of obtaining divine favor. They are children of the freewoman, and they follow the social condition of their mother.

5:1 The last verse of chapter 4 describes the believer's position — he is free. This first verse of chapter 5 refers to his practice — he should live as a **free** man. Here we have a very good illustration of the difference between law and grace. The law would say: "If you earn your freedom, you will become free." But grace says: "You have been made free at the tremendous cost of the death of Christ. In gratitude to Him, you should **stand fast therefore in the liberty with which Christ has made** you **free.**" Law commands but does not enable. Grace provides what law demands, then enables man to live a life consistent with his position by the power of the Holy Spirit and rewards him for doing it.

As C. H. Mackintosh says, "The law demands strength from one who has none, and curses him if he cannot display it. The gospel gives strength to one who has none, and blesses him in the exhibition of it."[18]

> "Run, John, and live," the law commands,
> But gives me neither legs nor hands;
> Far better news the Gospel brings,
> It bids me fly and gives me wings.

III. PRACTICAL: PAUL DEFENDS CHRISTIAN FREEDOM IN THE SPIRIT (5:2–6:18)

A. The Peril of Legalism (5:2–15)

5:2 Legalism makes Christ of no value. The Judaizers insisted on the necessity of Gentile believers being **circumcised** for salvation. Paul, speaking with the authority of an apostle, insists that to depend on circumcision is to make **Christ** of no benefit. Says Jack Hunter:

> In the Galatian situation, circumcision to Paul was not a surgical operation, nor merely a religious observance. It represented a system of salvation by good works. It declared a gospel of human effort apart from divine grace. It was law supplanting grace; Moses supplanting Christ; for to add to Christ was to take from Christ. Christ supplemented was Christ supplanted; Christ is the only Savior — solitary and exclusive. Circumcision would mean excision from Christ.[19]

5:3 Legalism requires men **to keep the whole law**. People under law cannot accept the easy commandments and reject the others. If a person attempts to please God by being circumcised, then he is under obligation **to keep the whole law**. Thus a man is entirely under law, or not under law at all. Obviously, if he is entirely under law, Christ is valueless to him. The Lord Jesus is not only a *complete* Savior, but also an *exclusive* one. Paul is not referring in this verse to any who might have been circumcised in the past, but only to those who might undergo this rite as a necessity for complete justification, to those who assert the obligations of law-keeping for their acceptance with God.

5:4 Legalism means the abandonment of **Christ** as one's only hope of righteousness. This verse has given rise to considerable discussion. Many different interpretations have been offered, but these may be grouped broadly in three classes, as follows:

1. Many hold that Paul here teaches that it is possible for a person to be truly saved, then to fall into sin, and therefore to fall from grace and be forever lost. This has come to be known as "the falling away doctrine."

We believe such an interpretation to be unsound for two compelling reasons: First, the verse does not describe saved persons who fall into sin. In fact, there is no mention of falling into sin. Rather, the verse is speaking of those who are living moral, respectable, upright lives and hope to be saved thereby. Thus the passage acts as a boomerang on those who use it to support the falling away doctrine. They teach that a Christian must keep the law, live a perfect life and otherwise refrain from sinning in order to remain saved. However, this Scripture insists that all who seek to be justified by works of law or self-effort **have fallen from grace.**

Secondly, this interpretation contradicts the over-all, consistent testimony of the NT to the effect that every true believer in the Lord Jesus Christ is eternally saved, that no sheep of Christ will ever perish, and that salvation depends entirely on the finished work of the Savior, and not on man's feeble efforts (John 3:16, 36; 5:24; 6:47; 10:28).

2. A second interpretation of the verse is that it refers to those who were originally saved by faith in the Lord Jesus, but who subsequently put themselves under the law to retain their salvation or to achieve holiness. In other words, they were saved by grace, but now seek to be kept by law. In this case, to fall from grace is, as Philip Mauro put it, "to turn from God's way of perfecting His saints by the work of the Spirit in them, and to seek that end through the observance of external rites and ceremonies, which men of the flesh can observe as well as saints of God."

This view is unscriptural, first because the verse does not describe Christians who seek holiness or sanctification, but rather unsaved persons

who seek *justification* by law-keeping. Note the wording — **you who attempt to be justified by law**. And second, this explanation of the verse implies the possibility of saved people being subsequently severed from Christ, and this is inconsistent with right views of the grace of God.

3. The third interpretation is that Paul is speaking of people who might profess to be Christians but who are not truly saved. They are seeking to be justified by keeping the law. The apostle is telling them that they cannot have two saviors; they must choose either Christ or the law. If they choose the law, then they are severed from Christ as their only possible hope of righteousness; they **have fallen from grace**. Hogg and Vine express it clearly:

Christ must be everything or nothing to a man; no limited trust or divided allegiance is acceptable to Him. The man who is justified by the grace of the Lord Jesus Christ is a Christian; the man who seeks to be justified by the works of the law is not.[20]

5:5 The apostle shows that the hope of the true believer is far different from that of the legalist. The Christian waits **for the hope of righteousness**. He hopes for the time when the Lord will come, when he will receive a glorified body, and when he will sin no more. Notice that it does not say that the Christian hopes for righteousness; he already has a right standing before God through the Lord Jesus Christ (2 Cor. 5:21). But he waits for the moment when he will be completely righteous in himself. He does not hope to achieve this by anything that he can do, but rather **through the Spirit** and **by faith**. The Holy Spirit is going to do it all, and the believer simply looks to God in faith to bring it to pass. The legalist, on the other hand, hopes to earn righteousness by his own works, law-keeping, or religious observances. It is a vain hope, because righteousness cannot be achieved in this way.

Notice that Paul uses the pronoun **we** in this verse, referring to true Christians, whereas in verse 4 he uses the pronoun "you" when speaking to those who seek justification by works of law.

5:6 Legalism **avails** nothing. As far

as a person who is **in Christ Jesus** (that is, a Christian) is concerned, **circumcision** does not make him any better, and **uncircumcision** does not make him any worse. What God looks for in the believer is **faith working through love. Faith** is complete dependence on God. **Faith** is not idle; it manifests itself in unselfish service to God and man. The motive of all such service is **love**. Thus **faith** works **through love**; it is prompted by **love**, not by law. This is a truth found many times in the Scriptures — that God is not interested in rituals, but in the reality of a godly life.

5:7 Legalism is disobedience to **the truth**. The Galatians had made a good start in the Christian life, but someone had **hindered** them. It was the Judaizers, the legalists, the false apostles. By accepting their erroneous teachings, the saints were disobeying **the truth** of God.

5:8 Legalism is not a divine teaching. **Persuasion** here means belief or doctrine. **Him who calls you** refers to God. Thus the belief that circumcision and law-keeping should be added to faith in Christ does not come from God but from the devil.

5:9 Legalism leads to more and more evil. **Leaven** in the Scripture is a common symbol of evil. Here it refers to the evil doctrine of the Judaizers. The natural tendency of **leaven**, or yeast, to affect all the meal with which it comes in contact is used here to show that **a little** error must inevitably lead to more. Evil is never static. It must defend its lies by adding more lies. Legalism is like garlic; there is no such thing as a little of it. If a few people in a church hold false doctrine, they will get more and more followers, unless sternly dealt with.

5:10 Legalism brings judgment on its teachers. Paul was confident that the Galatians would reject the false teachings. His **confidence** was **in the Lord**, which may mean that the Lord had given assurance to Paul on this matter. Or, knowing the Lord as he did, he was sure that the Great Shepherd would restore His wandering sheep, perhaps even through the Letter which Paul was then writing to them.

As for the false teachers themselves, they would be punished by God. It is a serious thing to teach error and thereby

to wreck a church (1 Cor. 3:17). It is much worse, for instance, to teach that drunkenness is permissible than to be a drunkard yourself, for the false teacher makes scores of others like himself.

5:11 Legalism does away with **the offense of the cross**. Paul now answers the absurd charge that even he at times preached the necessity of circumcision. He is still suffering **persecution** at the hands of the Jews. This **persecution** would stop instantly if he preached **circumcision**, because that would mean he had abandoned preaching **the cross**. The cross is an **offense** to man. It offends him or stumbles him because it tells him that there is nothing he can do to earn salvation. It gives no place to the flesh and its efforts. It spells an end to human works. If Paul were to introduce works by preaching circumcision, then he would be setting aside the whole meaning of the cross.

5:12 The apostle's wish that the troublemakers **would . . . cut themselves off** may be understood literally; he wishes that they were castrated. They were zealous in using the knife to circumcise others; now let the knife be used to make them eunuchs. It is probably preferable to take the words figuratively; in other words, Paul wishes that the false teachers were cut off from the Galatians altogether.

The gospel of grace has always been accused of permitting men to live as they like. People say: "If salvation is by faith alone, then there is no control over a person's conduct afterwards." But the apostle is quick to point out that Christian liberty does not mean license to sin. The believer's standard is the life of the Lord Jesus, and love for Christ impels him to hate sin and love holiness.

Perhaps it was especially necessary for Paul to warn his readers against license here. When men have been under the restraints of law for some time and are then granted their freedom, there is always the danger of going from the extreme of bondage to that of carelessness. The proper balance is that liberty which lies between law and license. The Christian is free from the law, but not lawless.

5:13 Christian **liberty** does not permit sin; it rather encourages loving service. **Love** is seen as the motive of all

Christian behavior, whereas under law, the motive is fear of punishment. Findlay says: "Love's slaves are the true freemen."

The Christian's freedom is *in Christ Jesus* (2:4), and this excludes any possible thought that it might ever mean freedom to sin. We must never turn our freedom into a base of operations **for the flesh**. Just as an invading army will seek to gain a beachhead and use it as a base of operations for further conquest, so the flesh will utilize a little license to expand its territory.

A proper outlet for our freedom is this: "Make it a habit to be slaves one to another."

A. T. Pierson says:

> True freedom is found only in obedience to proper restraint. A river finds liberty to flow, only between banks: without these it would only spread out into a slimy, stagnant pool. Planets, uncontrolled by law, would only bring wreck to themselves and to the universe. The same law which fences us in, fences others out; the restraints which regulate our liberty also insure and protect it. It is not control, but the right kind of control, and a cheerful obedience which make the free man.[21]

5:14 At first, it seems strange that Paul should introduce the **law** here after emphasizing all through the Epistle that believers are not under it. He is not urging his readers to go back to the law; he is showing that what the law demanded but could not produce is the very thing that results from the exercise of Christian liberty.

5:15 Legalism invariably leads to quarreling, and apparently it had done so in Galatia. How strange! Here were people who wanted to be under the law. The law requires them to love their neighbors. Yet the very reverse has happened. They have been backbiting and devouring one another. This behavior springs from the flesh, to which the law gives a place, and on which it acts.

B. Power for Holiness (5:16–25)

5:16 The believer should **walk in the Spirit**, not in the flesh. To **walk in** (or by) **the Spirit** is to allow Him to have His way. It is to remain in communion with Him. It is to make decisions in the light of His holiness. It is to be occupied with Christ, because the Spirit's ministry is to engage the believer with the Lord Jesus. When we thus **walk in the Spirit, the flesh**, or self-life, is treated as dead. We cannot be occupied at the same time with Christ and with sin.

Scofield says:

> The problem of the Christian life is based on the fact that so long as the Christian lives in this world he is, so to speak, two trees — the old tree of the flesh, and the new tree of the divine nature implanted by the new birth; and the problem itself is, how to keep barren the old tree and to make fruitful the new tree. The problem is solved by walking in the Spirit.[22]

This verse and those that follow show that **the flesh** is still present with the Christian; the idea of the eradication of the sinful nature is thus refuted.

5:17 **The Spirit** and **the flesh** are in constant conflict. God could have removed the fleshly nature from believers at the time of their conversion, but He did not choose to do so. Why? He wanted to keep them continually reminded of their own weakness; to keep them continually dependent on Christ, their Priest and Advocate; and to cause them to praise unceasingly the One who saved such worms. Instead of removing the old nature, God gave us His own Holy Spirit to indwell us. God's Spirit and our flesh are perpetually at war, and will continue to be at war until we are taken home to heaven. The believer's part in the conflict is to yield to the Spirit.

5:18 Those who are Spirit-led **are not under the law**. This verse might be understood in two ways: **Led by the Spirit** is a description of all Christians. Therefore, no Christians are **under the law**; they are not depending on self-effort. It is the **Spirit** who is resisting the motions of evil within them, not they themselves. Also, to be **led by the Spirit** means to be lifted above the flesh and to be occupied with the Lord. When one is so occupied, he is not thinking of the law or the flesh. The Spirit of God does not lead people to look to the law as a means of justification. Rather, He points them to the risen Christ as the only ground of acceptance before God.

5:19–21 We have mentioned before that the law appeals to the energy of the flesh. What kind of **works** does fallen human nature produce? There is no difficulty in identifying **the works of the flesh**. They are **evident** to all. **Adultery**[23] is unfaithfulness in the marriage relationship. **Fornication** is unlawful sexual intercourse. **Uncleanness** is moral evil, sensuality. **Lewdness** is shameless conduct involving absence of restraint. **Idolatry** is not only the worship of idols, but also the immorality that accompanies demon worship. **Sorcery** is witchcraft, the Greek word being related to drugs (*pharmakeia*). Because drugs were used in sorcery, the word came to mean intercourse with evil spirits, or the use of magic spells. It may also include superstitions, "bad luck," etc. **Hatred** means strong feelings of malice directed toward individuals. **Contentions** are discord, variance, quarrels. **Jealousies** are distrust, suspicions. **Wrath** is **outbursts** of hot anger or passions. **Selfish ambitions** are self-centered strivings to be "number one," even at others' expense. **Dissensions** are separations caused by disagreements. **Heresies** are sects formed by men with self-willed opinions. **Envy** is displeasure at the success or prosperity of others. **Murders**[24] are unlawful killing of others. **Drunkenness** refers to intoxication caused by strong drink. **Revelries** are riotous gatherings for entertainment, accompanied by drunkenness.

Paul warns his readers, as he had told them before, **that those who practice such things will not inherit the kingdom of God**. The passage does not teach that a drunkard cannot be saved, but it does say that those whose lives are *characterized* by the above catalog of fleshly works are not saved.[25]

Why should Paul write in this manner to churches of Christians? The reason is that not all who profess to be saved are true children of God. Thus throughout the NT the Holy Spirit often follows the presentation of wonderful spiritual truths with the most solemn warnings to all who profess the name of Christ.

5:22, 23 It is significant that the apostle distinguishes between the *works* of the flesh, and the **fruit of the Spirit**. Works are produced by human energy. **Fruit** is grown as a branch abides in the vine (John 15:5). They differ as a factory and a garden differ. Note that **fruit** is singular, not plural. The Holy Spirit produces one kind of **fruit**, that is, Christlikeness. All the virtues now listed describe the life of the child of God. Dr. C. I. Scofield has pointed out that every one of them is foreign to the soil of the human heart.

Love is what God is, and what we ought to be. It is beautifully described in 1 Corinthians 13, and told out in all its fullness at the cross of Calvary. **Joy** is contentment and satisfaction with God and with His dealings. Christ displayed it in John 4:34. **Peace** could include the peace of God as well as harmonious relations among Christians. For peace in the life of the Redeemer, see Luke 8:22–25. **Longsuffering** is patience in afflictions, annoyances, and persecutions. Its supreme example is found in Luke 23:34. **Kindness** is gentleness, perhaps best explained in the attitude of the Lord toward little children (Mark 10:14). **Goodness** is kindness shown to others. To see goodness in action, we have but to read Luke 10:30–35. **Faithfulness** may mean trust in God, confidence in our fellow Christians, fidelity, or reliability. This latter is probably the meaning here. **Gentleness** is taking the lowly place as Jesus did when He washed His disciples' feet (John 13:1–17). **Self-control** means literally holding oneself in, especially regarding sex. Our lives should be disciplined. Lust, passions, appetites, and temper should be ruled. We should practice moderation. As Samuel Chadwick points out:

> In newspaper English the passage reads something like this: the fruit of the Spirit is an affectionate, lovable disposition; a radiant spirit and a cheerful temper; a tranquil mind and a quiet manner; a forbearing patience in provoking circumstances and with trying people; a sympathetic insight and tactful helpfulness; generous judgment and a big-souled charity; loyalty and reliableness under all circumstances; humility that forgets self in the joy of others; in all things self-mastered and self-controlled, which is the final mark of perfection. How striking this is in relation to 1 Cor. 13![26]

Paul closes this list with the cryptic comment: **"Against such there is no law."** Of course not! These virtues are pleasing to God, beneficial to others, and good for ourselves. But how is this fruit produced? Is it by man's effort? Not at all. It is produced as Christians live in communion with the Lord. As they gaze upon the Savior in loving devotion, and obey Him in daily life, the Holy Spirit works a wonderful miracle. He transforms them into the likeness of Christ. They become like Him by beholding Him (2 Cor. 3:18). Just as the branch derives all its life and nourishment from the vine, so the believer in Christ derives his strength from the True Vine, and is thus able to live a fruitful life for God.

5:24 Those who are Christ's have crucified the flesh. The verb tense[27] here indicates something that happened decisively in the past. It actually occurred at the time of our conversion. When we repented, there was a sense in which we nailed the old, evil, corrupt nature to the cross with all its affections and lusts. We determined that we would no longer live to cater to our fallen nature, that it would no longer dominate it. Of course, this decision has to be renewed continually in our lives. We must constantly keep the flesh in the place of death.

5:25 If here carries the thought of "since." Since we have eternal life by the work of **the** Holy **Spirit** in us, let us live out the new life by the power of **the** same **Spirit**. The law never could give life, and was never intended to be the Christian's rule of life.

C. Practical Exhortations (5:26—6:10)

5:26 In this verse there are three attitudes to be avoided:

1. Conceit — **Let us not become conceited**, literally holding of false or empty opinion (of ourselves). God does not want Christians to be boastful or conceited braggarts; it does not fit in with being a sinner saved by grace. Men living under law often become proud of their miserable achievements, and taunt those who do not come up to their standards, and legalistic Christians will often run down other Christians who don't have the same lists of borderline things that they condemn.

2. Provocation — **Provoking one another**. It is a denial of the Spirit-filled life to provoke or challenge other people to measure up to one's own private viewpoints. One never knows the problems and temptations of another person's heart, never having walked in his shoes.

3. Envy — **Envying one another**. Envy is specifically the sin of wanting something that belongs to someone else to which one has no right or claim. Envy begrudges another person's superior success, talents, possessions, or good looks. Persons of few talents or weak character are apt to envy those who seem to be more successful lawkeepers. All such attributes are foreign to grace. A true believer should esteem others better than himself. Lawkeepers desire false glory. True greatness is to serve unnoticed, to labor unseen.

6:1 Here is a lovely statement on how a sinning believer is to be treated by other Christians. It is in sharp contrast to the law, of course, which called down judgment on offenders. To be **overtaken in any trespass** describes a man who has committed an act of sin rather than one who is habitually sinful. Such a person is to be dealt with by **spiritual** Christians. A carnal Christian might, by a hard, cold attitude, do more harm than good. Then, too, the offender will not be likely to receive the admonition of one who is himself out of touch with the Lord.

This verse raises an interesting question. If a man is truly spiritual, would he admit it? Are not spiritual people most conscious of their shortcomings? Who then would do the work of restoration, if doing so marked him as a spiritual man? Would it not betray a lack of modesty? The answer is this: A truly spiritual man will never boast of his condition, but he will have the tender heart of a shepherd, making him want to restore the transgressor. He will not act in a spirit of pride or superiority, but **in a spirit of gentleness**, remembering that he **also** might **be tempted.**

6:2 Burdens refers to failures, temptations, testings, and trials. Instead of standing off at a distance and criticizing, we should fly to the side of a brother in trouble or distress and help him in every possible way.

The law of Christ includes all the commandments of the Lord Jesus for His people found in the NT. It may be summarized by the commandment, "that you love one another" (John 13:34; 15:12). We fulfill this when we **bear one another's burdens**. **The law of Christ** is far different from that of Moses. Moses' Law promised life for obedience, but gave no power to obey, and could only encourage obedience by the fear of punishment. **The law of Christ**, on the other hand, is loving instruction for those who already have life. Believers are enabled to keep its precepts by the power of the Holy Spirit, and their motivation is love to Christ.

6:3 We are all made out of the same dust. When we see a brother sin, we should remember that it might have been ourselves. For a Christian to have a superiority complex is a form of self-deception. Certainly we should never think that bearing others' burdens is beneath our dignity.

6:4 This seems to be a warning against the habit of comparing ourselves with others, and finding cause for satisfaction. The apostle points out that we will be examined individually and not in comparison with others at the Judgment Seat of Christ. Therefore, we should take heed to ourselves, so that we might be able to rejoice in *our* **work** rather than in *others'* failures.

6:5 In verse 2, Paul teaches that we should share one another's sorrows, sufferings, and problems in this present life. In verse 5, the thought is that every one of us will have to **bear his own load** of responsibility at the Judgment Seat of Christ.

6:6 Believers are responsible to support their Christian teachers. To **share in all good things** means **to share** with them the material **things** of life, and also to sustain them with prayer and godly interest.

6:7 Although others may not notice our neglect of God's servants, He sees it, and gives a harvest accordingly. We **reap** what we sow, and we reap in greater quantities than we sow. When the farmer **sows** wheat, he reaps wheat, sometimes thirtyfold, sixtyfold, or a hundredfold. Scofield remarks that "the Spirit is not speaking here to sinners about their sins, but to saints about their meanness."

Of course, it is true in a wider sense that "those who plow iniquity and sow trouble reap the same" (Job 4:8) and that those who "sow the wind . . . reap the whirlwind" (Hos. 8:7). J. A. Froude, the historian, said, "One lesson, and only one, history may be said to repeat with distinctness, that the world is built somehow on moral foundations, that in the long run, it is well with the good, and in the long run it is ill with the wicked."[28]

6:8 Although it is true in a general sense that we reap whatever we sow, it should be noticed that this reminder follows an exhortation on Christian giving. Viewed in that light, we see that sowing **to the flesh** means spending one's money on oneself, one's own pleasures and comforts. Sowing **to the Spirit** is using one's money for the furtherance of God's interests.

Those who do the former reap a harvest of disappointment and loss right here on earth because they learn as they grow older that the flesh they lived to please is decaying and dying. Then in the age to come they lose eternal rewards. Those who sow **to the Spirit will of the Spirit reap everlasting life**. There are two ways in which eternal life (same word translated **everlasting**) is used in the Bible: (1) It is the present possession of every believer (John 3:36). (2) It is that which the believer receives at the end of his life here on earth (Rom. 6:22). Those **who sow to the Spirit** enjoy eternal life here and now in a way which other Christians do not. Then, too, they will reap the rewards which accompany faithfulness when they reach their heavenly home.

6:9 Lest any should become discouraged, Paul reminds his readers that the rewards are certain, even if not immediate. You do not harvest a field of wheat the day after you sow the seed. So in the spiritual realm, the rewards surely follow faithful sowing **in due season**.

6:10 **The household of faith** includes all who are saved, without regard to denominations or divisions. Our kindness is not to be limited to believers, but is to be shown to them in a special way. It is not *negative* — how little harm, but *positive* — how much **good** we can do that is to be our objective. John Wesley said it so succinctly: "Do all the good you can, in all the ways you can, to all the people you can, as long as ever you can."

D. Conclusion (6:11–18)

6:11 See with what large letters I have written to you with my own hand! Instead of dictating it to an assistant, as he usually did, Paul had written the letter himself. The **large letters** with which he wrote might have indicated his deep feeling in seeking to combat the legalists and how serious he considered the Judaizing error to be, or that Paul's eyesight was poor, as many have suggested from this and other passages. We feel that the latter view is correct.

6:12 The Judaizers wanted to make a **good showing in the flesh** by building up a large group of followers. They could do this by insisting on circumcision. People are often quite willing to observe rites and ceremonies as long as they are not required to change their habits. It is common today to build up a large church membership by lowering the standards. Paul sees through the insincerity of these false teachers and accuses them of seeking to avoid **persecution for the cross of Christ**. The cross signifies the condemnation of the flesh and its efforts to please God. The cross spells death for the fleshly nature and its noblest efforts. The cross means separation from evil. Therefore, men hate the glorious message of the cross, and persecute those who preach it.

6:13 The legalists were not really interested in keeping **the law**. What they wanted was an easy way to obtain converts, so that they could **boast** of a long list of followers. Boice says: "It was an attempt to win others to that which was itself bankrupt; for not even those who were circumcised were able to keep the law."

6:14 Paul's ground for boasting is not in the flesh of men, but **in the cross of our Lord Jesus Christ**. On that **cross** the world died to Paul and Paul to the world. When a man is saved, the world says goodbye to him, and he says goodbye **to the world**. He is spoiled as far as **the world** is concerned because he is no longer interested in its fleeting pleasures;

the world has lost its attraction for him, because he has found One who completely satisfies. Findlay says: "He can never believe in it, never take pride in it, nor do homage to it any more. It is stripped of its glory and robbed of its power to charm or govern him." Thus **the cross** is a great barrier or dividing line between the world and the child of God.

6:15 Although at first sight it might not seem so, this verse is one of the most important statements of Christian truth in the entire Epistle.

Circumcision was an external observance, a ritual. The Jewish teachers made everything depend on the observance of this ceremony. **Circumcision** was the foundation of Judaism. Paul sweeps it aside with a flourish — "circumcision is nothing." Neither ritual nor Judaism nor legalism counts. Then Paul adds — **nor uncircumcision**. There are those who pride themselves on their absence of ritual. Their whole church service is a revolt against ceremony. This is of no value either.

What really counts with God is **a new creation**. He wants to see the transformed life. Findlay writes: "The true Christianity is that which turns bad men into good, which transforms the slaves of sin into sons of God." All men are in one of two creations. As born into the world, they are sinful, helpless, and condemned. All their efforts to save themselves, or to assist God in their salvation by good character or good works, are futile, and leave them unchanged. The **new creation** is headed by the risen Christ, and includes all who have been redeemed from sin and given new life in Him. Because the **new creation** is all of Christ from start to finish, it excludes any thought of gaining God's favor through character or works. A life of holiness is produced, not by the observance of ritual, but by yielding to Christ and permitting Him to live His life in the believer. The **new creation** is not an improvement of or addition to the old, but something entirely different.

6:16 Of what **rule** is Paul speaking here? It is the **rule** of the new creation. He pronounces the double blessing of **peace and mercy** on all those who judge teaching by the question — "Is it of the new creation?" — and who reject all that is not.

And upon the Israel of God. Many have taken this to mean the church. However, **the Israel of God** refers to those Jews by natural birth who accept the Lord Jesus as Messiah. There was neither peace nor mercy for those who walked under the law, but both are the portion of those in the new creation.

6:17 Paul, once the slave of the law, had been delivered from that bondage by the Lord Jesus. Now he belonged to the Lord as a willing slave. Just as slaves were branded with the mark of their master, so Paul had the ownership **marks of the Lord Jesus** on his **body**. What were they? They were the scars which he received at the hands of his persecutors. Now he says: "Don't let anyone try to reclaim me. Don't talk to me about the brand-mark of circumcision, indicating bondage to the law. I wear the brand of my new Master, Jesus Christ."

6:18 The apostle is now about to lay down his pen. But he must close with an added word. What will it be? **GRACE** — the word which so characterizes his gospel. **Grace**, not law. It was the theme on which he began (1:3); it is the theme with which he closes. **The grace of our Lord Jesus Christ be with your spirit. Amen.**

LEGALISM

On completing a study of Galatians, one might conclude that Paul defeated the teachers of legalism so effectively that the issue would never trouble the church again. History and experience prove otherwise! Legalism has become so important a part of Christendom that most people believe that it actually belongs.

Yes, the legalists are still with us. What else shall we call those professed ministers of Christ who teach, for instance, that confirmation, baptism, or church membership are necessary for salvation; that the law is the believer's rule of life; that we are saved by faith but kept by works? What is it but Judaism brought over into Christianity when we are asked to accept a humanly ordained priesthood with its distinctive clothing, buildings patterned after the temple with their carved altars and elaborate rituals, and a church calendar with its Lenten season, its feasts, and its fasts?

And what is it but the Galatian heresy when believers are warned that they must keep the Sabbath if they are to be saved at last? Modern preachers of legalism are making tremendous inroads among those who profess faith in Christ, and for this reason every believer should be warned of their teaching and instructed how to answer them.

The prophets of the Sabbath usually begin by preaching the gospel of salvation by faith in Christ. They use beloved evangelical hymns to lure the unwary, and appear to place much emphasis on the Scriptures. But before long, they put their followers under the Law of Moses, especially the commandment concerning the Sabbath. (The Sabbath is the seventh day of the week, or Saturday.)

How do they dare to do this in the light of Paul's clear teaching that the Christian is dead to the law? How do they get around the plain statements of Galatians? The answer is that they make a sharp distinction between the moral law and the ceremonial law. The moral law is the Ten Commandments. The ceremonial law covers the other regulations given by God, such as rules concerning unclean foods, leprosy, offerings to God, and so forth.

The moral law, they say, has never been revoked. It is an expression of God's eternal truth. To commit idolatry, murder, or adultery will always be contrary to God's law. The ceremonial law, however, has been done away in Christ. Therefore, they conclude, when Paul teaches that the Christian is dead to the law, he is speaking about the ceremonial law and not the Ten Commandments.

Since the moral law is still in effect, Christians are bound to keep it, they insist. This means that they must keep the Sabbath, that they must do no work on that day. They assert that one of the popes of the Roman Catholic Church ordered the change from Sabbath-observance to observance of Sunday, in utter violation of Scriptures.

This reasoning sounds very logical and appealing. However, its great condemning feature is that it is entirely contrary to God's word! Note the following points:

1. In 2 Corinthians 3:7–11, the Ten Commandments are definitely stated to be "done away" for the believer in Christ. In verse 7, the law is described as "the ministry of death, written and engraved on stones." This could only mean the moral law, not the ceremonial law. Only the Ten Commandments were engraved in stones by the finger of God (Ex. 31:18). In verse 11, we read that the ministry of death, though glorious, is *done away*. Nothing could be more decisive than this. The Sabbath has no claim on the Christian.

2. No Gentile was ever commanded to keep the Sabbath. The law was given to the Jewish nation only (Ex. 31:13). Although God Himself rested on the seventh day, He did not command anyone else to do so until He gave the law to the children of Israel.

3. Christians did not switch from the Sabbath to the first day of the week because of the decree of any pope. We set aside the Lord's Day in a special way for worship and for service because the Lord Jesus rose from the dead on that day, a proof that the work of redemption was completed (John 20:1). Also, on that day the early disciples met to break bread, showing forth the Lord's death (Acts 20:7), and it was the day appointed by God for the Christians to set apart their offerings as the Lord had prospered them (1 Cor. 16:1, 2). Furthermore, the Holy Spirit was sent down from heaven on the first day of the week.

Christians do not "observe" the Lord's Day as a means of achieving holiness, or from fear of punishment; they set it apart because of loving devotion to the One who gave Himself for them.

4. Paul does not distinguish between the moral law and the ceremonial law. Rather, he insists that the law is a complete unit, and that a curse rests on those who seek to attain righteousness by it, yet fail to keep it all.

5. Nine of the Ten Commandments are repeated in the NT as moral instruction for the children of God. They deal with things that are inherently right or wrong. The one command-

ment which is omitted is the law of the Sabbath. The keeping of a day is not inherently right or wrong. There is no instruction to Christians to keep the Sabbath. Rather the Scripture distinctly states that the Christian *cannot be condemned* for failing to keep it! (Col. 2:16).

6. The penalty for breaking the Sabbath in the OT was death (Ex. 35:2). But those who insist on believers keeping the Sabbath today do not carry out the penalty on offenders. They thus dishonor the law and destroy its authority by failing to insist that its demands be met. They are saying, in effect, "This is God's law and you must keep it, but nothing will happen if you break it."

7. Christ, and not the law, is the believer's rule of life. We should walk as He walked. This is an even higher standard than was set by the law (Matt. 5:17–48). We are empowered to live holy lives by the Holy Spirit. We want to live holy lives because of our love for Christ. The righteousness demanded by the law is fulfilled by those who do not walk according to the flesh but according to the Spirit (Rom. 8:4).

Thus, the teaching that believers must keep the Sabbath is directly contrary to Scripture (Col. 2:16), and is simply a "different gospel" upon which God's word pronounces a curse (Gal. 1:7, 9).

May each one be given wisdom from God to discern the evil doctrine of legalism in whatever form it may appear! May we never seek justification or sanctification through ceremonies or human effort, but depend completely and only on the Lord Jesus Christ for every need. May we always remember that legalism is an insult to God because it substitutes the shadow for the Reality — ceremonialism for Christ. ‡

ENDNOTES

[1](1:8, 9) John Stott, *Only One Way: The Message of Galatians*, pp. 27, 28.

[2](1:18–20) The critical text reads *Cephas* (Aramaic form of *Peter*).

[3](2:1) E. F. Kevan, *The Keswick Week 1955*, p. 29.

[4](2:3) Circumcision is a minor surgical operation performed on the male. When

God ordained it for Abraham and his descendants, He intended it as a sign of His covenant with them, namely, that He would be their God and they would be His people (Gen. 17:1–11). It was not only a physical mark, but also a spiritual symbol. Abraham was circumcised as a sign that he had trusted in God (Rom. 4:11). The Jews soon forgot the *spiritual* meaning of circumcision, and carried it out simply as a ceremony. Thus the rite became valueless as far as God was concerned.

In the NT, circumcision is no longer commanded since God is now dealing in grace with Gentiles and Jews alike. In the early days of the church, a group of Jewish believers insisted that circumcision was necessary for salvation. Hence this party was known as "the circumcision" (Gal. 2:12).

⁵(2:3) A fairly full account of this meeting at Jerusalem is given in Acts 15. It should be studied carefully.

⁶(2:11) See note 2.

⁷(2:13) The punctuation, including quotation marks, is editorial. Some interpreters end the quotation here and view vv. 15–21 as Paul's *later explanation* of what he said to Peter.

⁸(2:21) W. M. Clow, *The Cross in the Christian Experience*, p. 114.

⁹(3:1) While Greek has separate singular and plural forms for *who*, an answer in the plural could not be ruled out here.

¹⁰(3:5) The most ancient manuscripts were all in "capitals." (Lower case letters evolved later.) Hence, while capitalization is editorial, the capital **H** for *He* is well taken in context.

¹¹(3:13) J. Cynddylan Jones, *Studies in the Gospel According to St. John*, p. 113.

¹²(3:20) Though there seems to be a contradiction between the argument here and the fact that Christ is later spoken of as the Mediator of the New Covenant (Heb. 9:15), the word *mediator* is used in two different senses in these two places. Moses served as a mediator simply by receiving the law from God and delivering it to the people of Israel. He was the go-between, or the people's representative. Christ is Mediator of the New Covenant in a far higher sense. Before God could righteously dispense the blessings of this covenant, the Lord Jesus

had to die. Just as death alone puts a person's last will and testament into force, so the New Covenant had to be sealed with His blood. He had to give Himself a ransom for all (1 Tim. 2:6). Christ not only insures the blessings of the covenant for His people, but also maintains His covenant people in a world that is antagonistic toward them. This He does as High Priest and Advocate, and this is also a part of His mediatorial work.

¹³(3:24) The Greek word *paidagōgos* (whence the English *pedagogy*) literally means a "child-leader." Such a person, usually a slave, was to see that the child got to and from school. Sometimes he taught as well.

¹⁴(4:7) The critical text reads simply *an heir through God*.

¹⁵(4:7) Norman B. Harrison, *His Side Versus Our Side*, p. 71.

¹⁶(4:13) Several theories have been advanced as to Paul's "infirmity." Some eye disease, among several that are common in the Middle East, is a likely candidate. Malaria, migraine, epilepsy, and other problems have also been suggested.

¹⁷(4:17) Stott, *Galatians*, p. 116.

¹⁸(5:1) C. H. Mackintosh, *Genesis to Deuteronomy*, pp. 232, 233.

¹⁹(5:2) Jack Hunter, *What the Bible Teaches, Galatians – Philemon*, p. 78.

²⁰(5:4) C. F. Hogg and W. E. Vine, *Epistle of Paul the Apostle to the Galatians*, p. 241.

²¹(5:13) Arthur T. Pierson, further documentation unavailable.

²²(5:16) C. I. Scofield, *In Many Pulpits with Dr. C. I. Scofield*, p. 234.

²³(5:19–21) The critical text (NU) omits *adultery*. The word *fornication* (*porneia*) is often translated *sexual immorality*, which would include adultery. However, it is unlikely Paul would fail to specifically mention this rampant sin of marital infidelity in a catalogue of the flesh's vices.

²⁴(5:19–21) The critical text omits *murders* (*phonoi*). Since this word looks so much like the previous word (*phthonoi*, "envy"), it would be easy to delete it in copying.

²⁵(5:19–21) See note on 1 Corinthians 6:9.

²⁶(5:22, 23) Samuel Chadwick, quoted by James A. Stewart, *Pastures of Tender Grass*, p. 253.

[27](5:24) English usage demands that the aorist *estaurōsan* be translated as a present perfect, but the aorist indicative stresses the deed, *not* lasting results.

[28](6:7) J. A. Froude, further documentation unavailable.

BIBLIOGRAPHY

Cole, Alan. *The Epistle of Paul to the Galatians*. Grand Rapids: Wm. B. Eerdmans Publishing Company, 1965.

Eadie, John. *Commentary on the Epistle of Paul to the Galatians*. Edinburgh: T. and T. Clark, 1884.

Harrison, Norman B. *His Side Versus Our Side*. Minneapolis: The Harrison Service, 1940.

Hogg, C. F., and W. E. Vine. *Epistle to the Galatians*. Glasgow: Pickering and Inglis, 1922.

Ironside, Harry A. *Expository Messages on the Epistle to the Galatians*. New York: Loizeaux Brothers, 1941.

Kelly, William. *Lectures on the Epistle of Paul the Apostle to the Galatians*. London: G. Morrish, n.d.

Lightfoot, J. B. *The Epistle of St. Paul to the Galatians*. Grand Rapids: Zondervan Publishing House, 1962.

Mackintosh, C. H. *Genesis to Deuteronomy*. Neptune, N.J.: Loizeaux Bros.

Stott, John. R. *Only One Way: The Message of Galatians*. Downers Grove, IL: InterVarsity Press, 1968.

THE EPISTLE TO THE EPHESIANS†

Introduction

"The crown of St. Paul's writings."   – J. Armitage Robinson
"Paul's third heaven epistle."   – A. T. Pierson

I. Unique Place in the Canon

In some ways Ephesians is a typical Pauline Epistle: the salutation, the thanksgiving, the development of doctrine followed by the application of that doctrine as our duty, and the closing greetings. Yet Ephesians, while a genuine letter, is almost like a sermon or even a Christian service with prayers and a doxology. In this letter, as Moorehead writes, "We pass into the stillness and hush of the sanctuary. . . .Here prevails the atmosphere of repose, of meditation, of worship and peace."[1]

In spite of the fact that so many commentators agree with Robinson's evaluation quoted above, some modern scholars, abandoning eighteen or nineteen centuries of Christian teaching, claim Paul could not have written Ephesians. But is this a valid viewpoint in light of the facts?

II. Authorship††

As far as the *external evidence* that Ephesians is an authentic Pauline Epistle, the case is solid and strong. No other Pauline Epistle has such an early and continuous stream of witnesses, starting with Clement of Rome, Ignatius, Polycarp, and Hermas, and going on with Clement of Alexandria, Irenaeus, and Hippolytus. Marcion included it in his "canon," though calling it "Laodiceans." The Muratorian Canon also lists Ephesians as by Paul.

Internal evidence includes the fact that the author twice *says* he is Paul (1:1 and 3:1), and the contents of the letter are so similar (in *some* respects) to Colossians that they must have been written close to one another in time. The structure of Ephesians, as was mentioned, is typically Pauline. Granted, Paul does introduce some new thoughts in this book, but if a writer cannot do so without being accused of being a forger, the opportunities for biblical writers helping to mature the saints will prove difficult indeed!

The German liberal Schleiermacher was probably the first to reject Pauline authorship. Many moderns have followed suit, such as Moffatt and Goodspeed. Vocabulary, style, "advanced" doctrine, and other subjective arguments are mustered to deny this book to the apostle. However, every one of these theories can be answered satisfactorily. In light of the overwhelming external evidence and the large number of scholarly commentators who see Ephesians as not merely in the spirit of Paul, but, as Coleridge expressed it, his very "divinest writing," the letter should be accepted as genuine.

III. Date

Along with Colossians, Philippians, and Philemon, Ephesians is one of the so-called "Prison Epistles." *Which* imprisonment is involved (3:1; 4:1) has been debated. While some believe it was Paul's two-year stay in Caesarea, or even an unproven Ephesian imprisonment, the weight of evidence seems to come down on the first Roman imprisonment (soon after A.D. 60). Like Colossians (4:7–9), this letter was carried to the province of Asia by Tychicus (6:21, 22). This explains the similarity of doctrinal content, the same ideas being fresh in the apostle's mind as he wrote these letters.

†See p. xxvii.
††See p. i.
1903

IV. Background and Theme[†]

The main subject of Ephesians is what Paul calls "the mystery." By that he does not mean something that cannot be explained, but rather a wonderful truth never revealed before but now made known.

This sublime truth, which forms the theme of the book, is the announcement that believing Jews and believing Gentiles are now one in Christ Jesus. They are fellow members of the church, the Body of Christ. At the present time they are seated in Christ in heavenly places. In the future they will share His glory as Head over all things.

The mystery is found in each of Ephesians' six chapters.

In chapter 1 it is called the mystery of God's will, and looks forward to the time when all things in heaven and on earth will be headed up in Christ (vv. 9, 10). Believing Jews (v. 11, "we") and believing Gentiles (v. 13, "you") will have their share in the glory of that day. They will reign with Him over the whole universe as His Body and His fullness (vv. 22, 23).

Chapter 2 describes the process by which Jews and Gentiles are saved by the grace of God; how they are reconciled to God and to one another; how, in union with Christ, they become one new man; and how they form a holy temple in which God dwells by His Spirit.

Chapter 3 gives the most complete explanation of the mystery. There it is spoken of as the mystery of "the Christ" (v. 4, JND), meaning Christ, the Head, and all believers, His Body. In this Body,

[†]See p. ii.

believing Gentiles are fellow heirs, fellow members, and fellow partakers of God's promise (v. 6).

Chapter 4 emphasizes the unity of the Body and God's plan for its growth to maturity (vv. 1–16).

In chapter 5, the mystery is called Christ and the church (v. 32). The relationship between Christ and the church is the pattern for the relationship between a believing husband and wife.

Finally, in chapter 6, Paul speaks of the mystery of the gospel, for which he was an ambassador in chains (vv. 19, 20).

Try to imagine the impact of this news on the Gentile believers to whom it was sent. Not only were they saved by grace through faith, the same as the Jews, but for the first time they occupied a place of equal privilege with them. They were in no way inferior as far as their standing before God was concerned. And they were destined to be enthroned with Christ as His Body and His Bride, sharing the glory of His universal reign.

Another important theme of Ephesians is *love* (Greek, *agapē*, the love expressed through the will). Paul starts and ends his Epistle with this concept (1:4; 6:24), and uses the verb and noun more in Ephesians than anywhere else in his Letters. This may show the Holy Spirit's foreknowledge, because while thirty years in the future the large and active congregation would still be obeying the command to fight false doctrine, our Lord tells them in His Letter to Ephesus that He held it against them that they had left their first *love* (Rev. 2:4).

OUTLINE

II. THE BELIEVER'S PRACTICE IN THE LORD (Chaps. 4–6)

  A. Appeal for Unity in the Christian Fellowship (4:1–6)

  B. Program for Proper Functioning of the Members of the Body (4:7–16)

  C. Appeal for a New Morality (4:17–5:21)

  D. Appeal for Personal Piety in the Christian Household (5:22–6:9)

  E. Exhortations Concerning the Christian Warfare (6:10–20)

  F. Paul's Personal Greetings (6:21–24)

Commentary

I. THE BELIEVER'S POSITION IN CHRIST (Chaps. 1–3)

A. Salutation (1:1, 2)

1:1 The name **Paul** means "small." Although physically he may have fitted this description, spiritually his influence was enormous. He introduces himself as **an apostle of Jesus Christ**. This means he was commissioned by the ascended Lord to perform a special mission. That mission was to preach *the gospel* to the Gentiles and to teach the great truth concerning *the church* (3:8, 9). Since Ephesians deals with the church, and since this truth was first revealed to the apostles and prophets (3:5), it is fitting that Paul should introduce himself as **an apostle**. It was not a mark of pride to do so; rather it was an explanation of how he could speak with authority on the subject. The source of his authority is expressed in the words, **by the will of God**. Paul did not choose his work as an occupation. And no men appointed him to it. It was a divine call from beginning to end (Gal. 1:1).

The letter is addressed **to the saints who are in Ephesus, and faithful in Christ Jesus. Saints** are people who have been separated to God from the world. It is a name which is applied in the NT to all born-again believers. Basically the word refers to a believer's position **in Christ** rather than to what he is in himself. **In Christ** all believers are **saints**, even though in themselves they are not always saintly. For instance, Paul addressed the Corinthians as saints (1 Cor. 1:2), even though it is clear from what follows that they were not all living holy lives. Yet God's will is that our practice should correspond to our position: **saints** should be saintly.

And faithful in Christ Jesus. The word, **faithful**, means "believing ones" and is thus a description of all true Christians. Of course, believers should also be **faithful** in the sense that they are reliable and trustworthy. But the primary thought here is that they had acknowledged **Christ Jesus** to be their only Lord and Savior.

Two of the oldest manuscripts omit the words, **in Ephesus**, although they stand in most manuscripts. Many scholars think this was a circular letter, written to be read by local gatherings of Christians in several places, of which the church at Ephesus was the most prominent. Fortunately the question affects neither the authenticity of the letter nor its value for us.

1:2 Next comes the apostle's greeting to the saints. Every word is loaded with spiritual significance — unlike many of the empty greetings we use today.

Grace means divine assistance for daily living. Paul's readers had already been saved by the grace of God, His undeserved favor to the lost. But now they needed strength **from God** to face the problems, trials, and sorrows of life. That is what the apostle wishes for them here.

Peace means a spirit at rest in all the changing circumstances of life. The saints had already experienced peace *with* God when they were converted. But day by day they needed the **peace** *of* God, that is, the calm, settled repose that is independent of circumstances and that results from taking everything to God in prayer (Phil. 4:6, 7).

It is worth noticing that **grace** comes first, then **peace**. This is always the order. Only after **grace** has dealt with the sin question can **peace** be known. And only through the undeserved strength which God gives from day to day can the believer experience **peace**, perfect **peace**, in all the changing moods of life.

Grace (*charis*) was a characteristically Greek word. The Jews use the word **peace** (Hebrew: *shālōm*) as a greeting. Put them together and we have, in miniature, the gospel for the whole world. When we unite them we also have the truth of the NT church which Paul expounds so fully in Ephesians — Jew and Gentile formed into one Body in Christ.

Grace . . . and peace come **from God our Father and the Lord Jesus Christ**. Paul did not hesitate to put the **Lord Jesus** on the same level as **God** the Father: he honored the Son just as he honored the **Father**. So should we (John 5:23).

Let us not overlook the marvelous conjunction of the words **God our Father**. The word, **God**, taken by itself might convey the impression of One who is infinitely high and unapproachable. The name, **Father**, on the other hand, speaks of One who is intimately near and accessible. Join the two by the pronoun, **our**, and we have the staggering truth that the high and lofty **God**, who inhabits eternity, is the loving **Father** of everyone who has been born again through faith in the **Lord Jesus.**

The full title of our Savior is **Lord Jesus Christ**. As **Lord** He is our absolute Master, with full rights to all we are and have. As **Jesus** He is our Savior from sin. As **Christ** He is our divinely anointed Prophet, Priest, and King. How much His name unfolds to every listening ear!

B. Paul's Praise to God for the Blessings of Grace (1:3–14)

1:3 Following his brief salutation, the apostle lifts his voice in a magnificent hymn of praise, soaring into some of the sublimest heights of NT worship. Here we have the overflow of a heart that adores God for the blessings of grace. In these verses (3–14) Paul traces God's activity in salvation from eternity past through time and on into eternity future. And this necessarily involves a discussion of the mystery of God's will — believing Jews and Gentiles as co-sharers of the glorious inheritance.

He begins by calling on all who know

God to bless Him, that is, to bring joy to His heart by praise and worshiping love. The **blessed** One is **the God and Father of our Lord Jesus Christ**. At certain times Jesus addressed God as God (Matt. 27:46). At other times He spoke of Him as Father (John 10:30). The **blessed** One is also the Blesser. We bless Him by praising Him. He blesses us and makes us glad by showering us with the riches of His grace.

He **has blessed us with every spiritual blessing in the heavenly places in Christ**. Here is a pyramid of grace:

blessing
spiritual blessing
every spiritual blessing
every spiritual blessing in the
heavenly places
every spiritual blessing in the heavenly
places in Christ

Notice first how unstinted are His heart and hand — **every spiritual blessing**. Notice, too, that these are *spiritual* blessings. The simplest way to explain this is to contrast them with the blessings of Israel under the law. In the OT, a faithful, obedient Jew was rewarded with long life, a large family, abundant crops, and protection from his enemies (Deut. 28:2–8). The blessings of Christianity, in contrast, are **spiritual**, that is, they deal with treasures that are nonmaterial, invisible, and imperishable. It is true that the OT saints also enjoyed some spiritual blessings, but as we shall see, the Christian today enjoys blessings that were unknown in previous times.

Our blessings are *in the heavenly places*, literally "*in the heavenlies*." Instead of being material blessings in earthly places, they are **spiritual** blessings *in the heavenly places*. The expression, **in the heavenly places**, is used five times in Ephesians:

1:3 The sphere of our **spiritual** blessing
1:20 The scene of Christ's present enthronement
2:6 The scene of our present enthronement in Christ
3:10 The locale from which angels witness God's wisdom exhibited in the church
6:12 The region which is the source of our present conflict with evil spirits

When we put these passages together,

we have a truly scriptural definition of **the heavenly places**. As Unger put it, they are "the realm of the believer's position and experience as a result of his being united to Christ by the baptism of the Spirit." All **spiritual** blessings are *in Christ*. It was He who procured them for us through His finished work at Calvary. Now they are available through Him. Everything that God has for the believer is in the Lord Jesus. In order to receive the blessings, we must be united to Christ by faith. The moment a man is *in Christ*, he becomes the possessor of them all. Chafer writes, "To be in Christ, which is the portion of all who are saved, is to partake of all that Christ has done, all that He is, and all that He ever will be."[2]

In Christ is one of the key expressions of Ephesians. There are two closely related lines of truth in the NT — the truth of the believer's position and the truth of his practice.

First, the believer's position. Everyone in the world is either "in Adam" or "in Christ." Those who are "in Adam" are in their sins and therefore condemned before God. There is nothing they can do in themselves to please God or gain His favor. They have no claim on God, and if they were to receive what they deserve, they would perish eternally.

When a person is converted, God no longer looks upon him as a condemned child of Adam. Rather He sees him as being **in Christ**, and He accepts him on that basis. It is important to see this. The believing sinner is not accepted because of what he is in himself, but because he is **in Christ**. When he is **in Christ**, he stands before God clothed in all the acceptability of Christ Himself. And he will enjoy God's favor and acceptance as long as Christ does, namely, forever.

The believer's position, then, is what he is **in Christ**. But there is another side to the picture — the believer's practice. This is what he is in himself. His position is perfect, but his practice is imperfect. Now God's will is that his practice should increasingly correspond to his position. It never will do so perfectly until he is in heaven. But the process of sanctification, growth, and increasing Christlikeness should be going on con-

tinually while he is here on earth.

When we understand the difference between the believer's standing and his state, it enables us to reconcile such seemingly opposite verses as the following:

Believers are perfect (Heb. 10:14)	Believers should be perfect (Matt. 5:48)
Believers are dead to sin (Rom. 6:2)	Believers should reckon themselves dead to sin (Rom. 6:11)
Believers are a holy nation (1 Pet. 2:9)	Believers should be holy (1 Pet. 1:15)

The first column deals with position, the second with practice.

Paul's Letter to the Ephesians itself is divided into two halves that parallel this truth: (Chaps. 1–3): Our position — what we are in Christ; (Chaps. 4–6): Our practice — what we should be in ourselves. The first half has to do with doctrine, the second half with duty. In the first three chapters our position is often described by such phrases as "in Christ," "in Christ Jesus," "in Him," "in whom." In the last three chapters the phrase, "in the Lord," is often used to express the believer's responsibility to Christ as Lord. Someone has well said that the first part of the letter pictures the believer in the heavenlies in Christ, whereas the last part views him in the kitchen.

Now we are ready to consider some of the **spiritual** blessings **in the heavenly places** which are ours **in Christ**.

1:4 The first is what is commonly known as election. **Just as He chose us in Him before the foundation of the world, that we should be holy and without blame before Him in love.**

Notice first the positive fact of election in the words, **He chose us**. Then there is the positional aspect of the truth, **in Him**: it is in the Person and work of the Lord Jesus that all God's purposes for His people are brought to pass. The time of God's election is indicated by the expression, **before the foundation of the world**. And the purpose is **that we should be holy and without blame before Him in love**. This purpose will not be completely realized until we are with Him in heaven (1 John 3:2), but the process should be going on continually in our lives down here.

Prayer: "Lord, make me holy now,
    since this is Your eventual
    purpose for me. Amen."

DIVINE ELECTION

The doctrine of election raises serious problems in the human mind, so we must consider more fully what the Bible does (and does not) teach on this subject.

First, it teaches that God does choose men to salvation (2 Thess. 2:13). It addresses believers as those who are "elect according to the foreknowledge of God" (1 Pet. 1:2). It teaches that people can know whether they are elect by their response to the gospel: those who hear and believe it are elect (1 Thess. 1:4–7).

On the other hand, the Bible never teaches that God chooses men to be lost. The fact that He chooses some to be saved does not imply that He arbitrarily condemns all the rest. He never condemns men who deserve to be saved (there are none), but He does save some who ought to be condemned. When Paul describes the elect, he speaks of them as "vessels of mercy which He had prepared beforehand for glory" (Rom. 9:23); but when he turns to the lost, he simply says, "vessels of wrath prepared for destruction" (Rom. 9:22). God prepares vessels of mercy to glory, but He does not prepare men for destruction: they do this for themselves by their own unbelief.

The doctrine of election lets God be God. He is sovereign, that is, He can do as He pleases, though He never pleases to do anything unjust. If left alone, all men would be lost. Does God have the right to show mercy to some?

But there is another side to the story. The same Bible that teaches sovereign election also teaches human responsibility. No one can use the doctrine of election as an excuse for not being saved. God makes a bona fide offer of salvation to all people everywhere (John 3:16; 3:36; 5:24; Rom. 10:9, 13). Anyone can be saved by repenting of his sins and believing on the Lord Jesus Christ. Therefore, if a person is lost, it is because he chooses to be lost, not because God desires it.

The fact is that the same Bible teaches election and free salvation to all who will receive it. Both doctrines are found in a single verse: "All that the Father gives Me will come to Me, and the one who comes to Me I will by no means cast out" (John 6:37). The first half of the verse speaks of God's sovereign choice; the last half extends the offer of mercy to all.

This poses a difficulty for the human mind. How can God choose some and yet offer salvation freely to all men? Frankly, this is a mystery. But the mystery is on our side, not on God's. The best policy for us is to believe both doctrines because the Bible teaches both. The truth is not found somewhere between election and man's free will, but in both extremes. W. G. Blaikie summarizes:

> Divine sovereignty, human responsibility and the free and universal offer of mercy are all found in Scripture, and though we are unable to harmonize them by our logic, they all ought to have a place in our minds.[3] ‡

1:5 The second spiritual blessing from the treasury of God's grace is predestination, or foreordination. Though somewhat related to election, it is not the same. Election pictures God's choice of people to salvation. But predestination is an advance on this: it means that God determined ahead of time that all who would be saved would also be adopted into His family **as sons**. He could have saved us without making us His sons, but He chose to do both.

Many translations link the last two words of verse 4 with verse 5 as follows: **in love having predestined us**.

This reminds us of the unique affection that prompted God to deal with us so graciously.

We have the fact of our glorious **adoption** in the phrase, **having predestined us to adoption as sons**. In the NT, **adoption** means placing a believer in the family of God as a mature, adult son with all the privileges and responsibilities of sonship (Gal. 4:4–7). The Spirit of adoption plants within the believer the instinct to address God as Father (Rom. 8:15).

Our **adoption as sons** is **by Jesus**

Christ. God could never have brought us into this position of nearness and dearness **to Himself** as long as we were in our sins. So the Lord Jesus came to earth, and by His death, burial, and resurrection He settled the sin question to God's satisfaction. It is the infinite value of His sacrifice on Calvary that provides a righteous basis on which God can adopt us **as sons**.

And it is all **according to the good pleasure of His will**. This is the sovereign motivation behind our predestination. It answers the question, "Why did He do it?" Simply because it was His **good pleasure**. He could not be satisfied until He had surrounded Himself with sons, conformed to the image of His only begotten Son, with Him and like Him forever.

1:6 To the praise of the glory of His grace, by which He has made us accepted in the Beloved. As Paul has contemplated the grace of God first in electing us and then in predestining us to be His sons, he punctuates his meditation with this refrain that is at once an exclamation, an explanation, and an exhortation. It is an *exclamation* — a holy gasp at the transcendent glories of such grace. It is an *explanation* that the object and the result of all God's gracious dealings with us is His own **glory**. Eternal adoration is due to Him for such matchless favor. Notice the terms of His **grace** — **He** (freely) **made us accepted**. The recipients of His **grace** — **us**. The channel of His **grace** — **in the Beloved**. Finally, it is an *exhortation*. Paul is saying, "Let us **praise** Him for His glorious **grace**". Before we go any farther, let us do it!

> Great God of wonders! All Thy ways
> Display Thine attributes divine;
> But the bright glories of Thy grace
> Above Thine other wonders shine:
> Who is a pard'ning God like Thee?
> Or who has grace so rich and free?
> *— Samuel Davies*

1:7 As we trace the sublime sweep of God's eternal plan for His people, we come next to the fact of **redemption**. This describes that aspect of the work of Christ by which we are freed from the bondage and guilt of sin and introduced into a life of liberty. The Lord Jesus is the Redeemer (**In Him we have redemp-tion**). We are the redeemed. **His blood** is the ransom price; nothing less would do.

One of the results of redemption is **the forgiveness of sins**. **Forgiveness** is not the same as **redemption**; it is one of its fruits. Christ had to make full satisfaction for our sins before they could be forgiven. This was done at the cross. And now —

> Stern justice can demand no more
> And mercy can dispense her store.

The measure of our **forgiveness** is given in the words, **according to the riches of His grace**. If we can measure **the riches of** God's **grace**, then we can measure how fully He has forgiven us. His **grace** is infinite! So is His **forgiveness**!

1:8 It was in grace that He chose us, predestined us, and redeemed us. But that is not all. God has superabounded that same grace **toward us in all wisdom and prudence**. This means He has graciously shared His plans and purposes with us. His desire is that we should have intelligence and insight into His plans for the church and for the universe. And so He has taken us into His confidence, as it were, and has revealed to us the great goal toward which all history is moving.

1:9 Paul now explains the particular way in which God has abounded toward us in all wisdom and prudence, namely, by making **known to us the mystery of His will**. This is the dominant theme of the Epistle — the glorious truth concerning Christ and the church. It is a **mystery**, not in the sense that it is mysterious, but that it is a sacred secret previously unknown but now revealed to the saints. This glorious plan originated in the sovereign will of God, quite apart from any outside influences: it was **according to His good pleasure**. And the grand subject of the plan is the Lord Jesus Christ; this is indicated by the clause, **which He purposed in Himself.**

1:10 Now Paul begins a more detailed explanation of the secret of God's plan, and in this chapter he is thinking particularly of the future aspect of the mystery. Chapters 2 and 3 will add further light on the present aspect of the mystery.

The time which Paul has in view is indicated by the expression, **the dispensation** (administration, Gk., *oikonomia*) **of the fullness of the times**. We understand this to refer to the Millennium, when Christ will return to the earth to reign as King of kings and Lord of lords. God has a special economy or plan of administration for the final era of human history on this earth.

The plan is "to head up all things in the Christ" (JND). During the Millennial Reign, **all things in heaven** and **on earth** will be summed up **in Christ**. The Savior who is now rejected and disowned will then be the preeminent One, the Lord of all, the object of universal worship. This is God's goal — to set up **Christ** as Head over **all things**, heavenly and earthly, in the kingdom.

The extent of the dominion of Christ is found in the words, "the things in the heavens and the things upon the earth" (JND). Bellett writes:

This is a secret never made known before. In the prophet Isaiah, we get a beautiful picture of the millennial earth; but do we ever get the millennial heavens with Christ at their head? Was it ever said by Isaiah that all things in heaven and earth should be headed up in the glorified Man?[4]

Verse 10 is sometimes used to support the false doctrine of universal salvation. It is twisted to suggest that eventually everything and everyone will be restored and reconciled in Christ. But that is quite foreign to the passage. Paul is speaking about universal *dominion*, not universal salvation!

1:11 One vital feature of the mystery is that believing Jews and believing Gentiles have their share in this grand program of God. The apostle speaks of the mystery in relation to Jewish believers in verses 11 and 12; in relation to Gentile believers in verse 13; then he combines them both in verse 14.

As for the Christians of Jewish ancestry, Paul writes, **In Him also we have obtained an inheritance**. Their right to a share is not based on their former national privileges, but solely on their union with Christ. The **inheritance** here looks forward to the time when they and all true believers will be manifested to an amazed world as the Body of Christ, the Bride of the Lamb.

From all eternity these Jewish Christians were marked out for this place of privilege by the sovereign will of God, **being predestined according to the purpose of Him who works all things according to the counsel of His will.**

1:12 The purpose of this predestination was **that** they **should be to the praise of His glory**. In other words, they are trophies of the grace of God, exhibiting what He can do with such unlikely raw materials, and thus bringing **glory** to Him.

The apostle speaks of himself and other believing Jews as **we who first trusted in Christ**. He is thinking of the godly remnant of Jews who responded to the gospel in the early days of Christianity. The good news was first preached to the Jews. Most of the nation of Israel flatly rejected it. But the godly remnant believed on the Lord Jesus. Paul was one of that number.

It will be different when the Savior returns to the earth the second time. Then the nation will look on Him whom they pierced and will mourn for Him as for an only Son (Zech. 12:10). "And so all Israel will be saved, as it is written: 'The Deliverer will come out of Zion, and He will turn away ungodliness from Jacob' " (Rom. 11:26).

Paul and his Christian contemporaries of Jewish background trusted in the Messiah before the rest of the nation. That is why he uses the description, "we . . . who have trusted beforehand in Christ" (FWG).

Those who "fore-hoped" in Messiah will reign with Him over the earth. The rest of the nation will be the earthly subjects of His kingdom.

1:13 Now Paul switches from believers who had been born Jews to those who had been born Gentiles; he indicates this by changing from "we" to **you**. Those who have been saved from paganism have a share in the mystery of God's will, as well as converted Jews. And so the apostle here traces the steps by which the Ephesians and other Gentiles had been brought into union with Christ.

They **heard** the gospel.

They **believed** in Christ.

They **were sealed with the Holy Spirit of promise.**

First they **heard the word of truth, the gospel of** their **salvation.** Basically, this refers to the good news of **salvation** through faith in the Lord Jesus. But in a wider sense it includes all the teachings of Christ and the apostles.

Having heard this message, they made a commitment of themselves to Christ by a decisive act of faith. The Lord Jesus is the true object of faith. **Salvation** is found in Him alone.

As soon as they **believed,** they **were sealed with the Holy Spirit of promise.** This means that every true believer receives the **Spirit** of God as a sign that he belongs to God and that he will be kept safe by God until the time he receives his glorified body. Just as in legal matters a seal indicates ownership and security, so it does in divine affairs. The indwelling Spirit brands us as God's property (1 Cor. 6:19, 20), and guarantees our preservation until the day of redemption (Eph. 4:30).

Our seal is called **the Holy Spirit of promise.** First, He is the *Holy* Spirit; this is what He is in Himself. Then, He is the Spirit of *promise.* He was promised by the Father (Joel 2:28; Acts 1:4), and by the Lord Jesus (John 16:7). In addition, He is the guarantee that all God's promises to the believer will be fulfilled.

Verse 13 rounds out the first of many mentions of the Trinity in this Letter:

God the Father (v. 3)

God the Son (v. 7)

God the Spirit (v. 13)

1:14 Again Paul changes his pronouns. He merges the "we" of verses 11 and 12 with the "you" of verse 13 to form the **our** of verse 14. By this deft literary device, he drops a hint of what he will more fully explain in chapters 2 and 3 — the union of believing Jews and believing Gentiles to form a new organism, the church.

The Holy Spirit is **the guarantee of our inheritance.** This is a downpayment, pledging that the full amount will be paid. It is the same in kind as the full payment, but not the same in amount.

As soon as we are saved, the Holy Spirit begins to reveal to us some of the riches that are ours in Christ. He gives us foretastes of the coming glory. But how can we be sure that we will get the full inheritance some day? The Holy Spirit Himself is the earnest or **guarantee.**

As the seal, He guarantees that we ourselves will be kept safely for the inheritance. As the earnest, He guarantees the **inheritance** will be kept securely for us.

The Spirit is the **guarantee until the redemption of the purchased possession.** The **guarantee** looks forward to the full **redemption,** just as the firstfruits look forward to the complete harvest. The Spirit's role as earnest will cease when **the purchased possession** is redeemed. But what does Paul mean by **the purchased possession?**

1. He may mean **our inheritance.** All that God possesses is ours through the Lord Jesus: we are heirs of God and joint heirs with Jesus Christ (Rom. 8:17; 1 Cor. 3:21–23). The universe itself has been defiled through the entrance of sin, and needs to be reconciled and purified (Col. 1:20; Heb. 9:23). When Christ returns to the earth to reign, this groaning creation will be delivered from the bondage of corruption into the glorious liberty of the children of God (Rom. 8:19–22).

2. The expression, **the purchased possession,** may mean the believer's body. Our spirits and souls were redeemed when we first believed, but the redemption of our bodies is still future. The fact that we suffer, grow old, and die proves that our bodies have not yet been redeemed. When Christ returns for us (1 Thess. 4:13–18), our bodies will be fashioned anew so they can be conformed to the body of His glory (Phil. 3:21). Then they will be fully and forever redeemed (Rom. 8:23).

3. Finally, **the purchased possession** may refer to the church (1 Pet. 2:9: "His own special people"). In this case, its redemption also looks forward to the Rapture, when Christ will present the church to Himself a glorious church without spot or wrinkle or any such thing (Eph. 5:27). Some believe that in this view, God's own **possession** may also include the OT saints.

Whichever view we hold, the ultimate result is the same — **to the praise of His glory**. God's marvelous plan for His people will then have reached a glorious consummation, and He will be the object of continual praise. Three times in this chapter Paul has reminded us that the intended goal and inevitable result of all God's actions is that He should be magnified and glorified.

To the praise of the glory of His grace (v. 6)

That we should be to the praise of His glory (v. 12)

To the praise of His glory (v. 14)

C. Paul's Thanksgiving and Prayers for the Saints (1:15–23)

1:15 In the preceding passage, extending from verse 3 through verse 14 (a single sentence in Greek!), the apostle has traced the thrilling sweep of God's program from eternity past to eternity future. He has ranged over some of the most awe-inspiring thoughts that can occupy our minds, thoughts so exalted that Paul now shares with his readers his deep prayer burden for their spiritual enlightenment in such concepts. His great desire for them is that they might appreciate their glorious privileges in Christ and the tremendous power which was required to give Christ to the church as Head over all creation.

The introductory **Therefore** looks back to all that God has done and will yet do for those who are members of the body of Christ, as described in verses 3–14.

After I heard of your faith in the Lord Jesus and your love for all the saints. It was when he received this information that Paul was assured his readers were possessors of the spiritual blessings just described, and was driven to prayer for them. Their **faith in the Lord Jesus** brought the miracle of salvation to their lives. Their **love for all the saints** demonstrated the transforming reality of their conversion.

Those Bible scholars who do not think this Letter was written exclusively to the Ephesians point to this verse as evidence. Paul speaks here of having heard of the faith of his readers — as if he had never met them. But he had spent at least three years in Ephesus

(Acts 20:31). They therefore conclude the Letter was sent to several local congregations, of which Ephesus was only one.

Fortunately the question does not affect the lessons we can learn from the verse. For instance, we see that the **Lord** is presented as the true object of faith: **your faith in the Lord Jesus**. We are not told to believe in a creed, in the church, or in Christians. Saving faith is in the risen, exalted Christ at God's right hand.

Another lesson for us is the expression, **your love for** *all* **the saints**. Our love should not be limited to those of our own area of fellowship, but should flow out to all who have been cleansed by the blood of Christ, to all the household of faith.

A third lesson is found in the combination of **faith** and **love**. Some people say they have faith, but it is hard to find any love in their lives. Others profess great love but are quite indifferent to the necessity of faith in Christ. True Christianity combines sound doctrine and sound living.

1:16 The faith and love of the believers impelled Paul to praise the Lord for them and to pray for them unceasingly. Scroggie puts it nicely:

> Thanksgiving is for the foundation already laid, but intercession is for the superstructure going up. Thanksgiving is for past attainments, but intercession is for future advancements. Thanksgiving is for the actual in their experience, but intercession is for the possible in God's purpose for them.

1:17 What a privilege it is to have this glimpse into the prayer life of a man of God. In fact, there are two such glimpses in this Letter — here and in 3:14–21. Here the prayer is for spiritual illumination; there it is for spiritual strength. Here the prayer is addressed to **God**; there to the Father. But in every case Paul's prayers were unceasing, specific, and appropriate to the current needs of the people. Here the prayer is addressed to **the God of our Lord Jesus Christ, the Father of glory**. The expression, **the Father of glory**, may mean that God is either:

1. the Source or Originator of all glory,
2. the One to whom all glory belongs, or

3. the Father of the Lord Jesus, who is the manifestation of God's glory.

The prayer continues that He **may give to you the spirit of wisdom and revelation in the knowledge of Him**. The Holy Spirit is the Spirit **of wisdom** (Isa. 11:2), and of **revelation** (1 Cor. 2:10). But since every believer is indwelt by Him, Paul cannot be praying that his readers might receive the Person of the Holy Spirit but rather that they might receive a special measure of illumination from Him.

Revelation deals with the imparting of knowledge; **wisdom** has to do with the proper use of it in our lives. The apostle is not thinking of knowledge in general but of the specific **knowledge** (Gk., *epignōsis*) **of Him**. He wants the believers to have a deep, spiritual, and experimental **knowledge** of God — a **knowledge** that cannot be gained by intellectual ability, but only by the gracious ministry of the Spirit.

Dale explains:

These Ephesian Christians had already Divine illumination, or they would not have been Christians at all; but Paul prayed that the Divine Spirit who dwelt in them would make their vision clearer, keener, stronger, that the Divine power and love and greatness might be revealed to them far more fully. And perhaps in these days in which men are making such rapid discoveries in inferior provinces of thought, discoveries so fascinating and so exciting as to rival in interest, even for Christian men, the manifestation of God in Christ, there is exceptional need for the church to pray that God would grant it a *"spirit of wisdom and revelation"*; if He were to answer that prayer we should no longer be dazzled by the knowledge which relates to "things seen and temporal," it would be outshone by the transcendent glory of "things unseen and eternal."[5]

1:18 We have seen that the source of spiritual illumination is God; the channel is the Holy Spirit; and the supreme subject is the full knowledge of God. Now we come to the organs of enlightenment: **the eyes of your hearts** (NKJV margin[6]) **being enlightened**.

This figurative expression teaches us that proper understanding of divine realities is not dependent on our having keen intellects but rather tender **hearts**.

It is a matter of the affections as well as of the mind. God's revelations are given to those who love Him. This opens up wonderful possibilities for every believer, because though we may not all have high I.Q.'s, we can all have loving **hearts.**

Next Paul specifies the three particular areas of divine knowledge which he desires for the saints:

1. **the hope of His calling**
2. **the riches of the glory of His inheritance in the saints**
3. **The exceeding greatness of His power toward us who believe**

The hope of His calling points forward to the future; it means that eventual destiny which He had in mind for us when He called us. It includes the fact that we shall be with Christ and like Him forever. We shall be manifested to the universe as sons of God and reign with Him as His spotless Bride. We hope for this, not in the sense that there is any doubt about it, but rather because it is that aspect of our salvation which is still future and to which we look forward.

The riches of the glory of His inheritance in the saints is the second tremendous vastness for believers to explore. Notice the way in which Paul stacks words upon words in order to produce the effect of immensity and grandeur:

His inheritance
His inheritance in the saints
The glory of His inheritance in the saints
The riches of the glory of His inheritance
in the saints

There are two possible ways of understanding this, and both are so meaningful that we present both. According to the first, **the saints** are **His inheritance**, and He looks on them as a treasure of incomparable worth. In Titus 2:14 and 1 Peter 2:9, believers are described as "His own special people." It is certainly an exhibition of unspeakable grace that vile, unworthy sinners, saved through Christ, could ever occupy such a place in the heart of God that He would speak of them as **His inheritance**.

The other view is that the **inheritance** means all that *we* will inherit. In brief, it means the whole universe put under the reign of Christ, and we, His Bride, reigning with Him over it. If we really appreciate the wealth of the glory of all He has in store for us, it will spoil us for the attractions and pleasures of this world.

1:19 Paul's third petition for the saints is that they might have a deep appreciation of the **power** which God engages to bring all this to pass: **the exceeding greatness of His power toward us who believe**.

F. B. Meyer says, "It is *power*. It is *His* power. It is *great* power; nothing less would suffice. It is *exceeding* great power, beyond the furthest cast of thought."[7]

This is the power which God used in our redemption, which He uses in our preservation, and which He will yet use in our glorification. Lewis Sperry Chafer writes:

> Paul wants to impress the believer with the greatness of the power which is engaged to accomplish for him everything that God has purposed according to His work of election, predestination and sovereign adoption.[8]

1:20 To further emphasize the magnitude of this power, the apostle next describes the greatest exhibition of divine **power** the world has ever known, namely, the power that **raised** Christ out **from** among **the dead** and enthroned Him at God's **right hand**. Perhaps we would think that the creation of the universe was the greatest display of God's might. Or God's miraculous deliverance of His people through the Red Sea. But no! The NT teaches that Christ's resurrection and ascension required the greatest outflow of divine energy.

Why was this? It seems that all the hosts of hell were massed to frustrate God's purposes by keeping Christ in the tomb, or by preventing His ascension once He was raised. But God triumphed over every form of opposition. Christ's resurrection and glorification were a shattering defeat for Satan and his hosts, and a glorious spectacle of victorious power.

No one is sufficient to describe such power. So Paul borrows several words from the vocabulary of dynamics in his description of the power which is employed on our behalf: **"according to** that *working* of the *strength* of **His** *might* which He *energized* in Christ when He

raised Him from the dead." The words seem to bend under the weight of the idea. It is hardly necessary for us to distinguish between the different words; it is enough to marvel at the immensity of the power and to worship our God for His omnipotence!

Meyer exclaims:

> A marvelous lift was there! From the grave of mortality to the throne of the eternal God, who only has immortality. From the darkness of the tomb to the insufferable light. From this small world to the center and metropolis of the universe. Open the compasses of your faith to measure this measureless abyss. Then marvel at the power which bore your Lord across it.[9]

As far as the Scriptures are concerned, the resurrection of Christ was the first such event in human history (1 Cor. 15:23). Others had been raised from the dead, but they died again. The Lord Jesus was the first to rise in the power of an endless life. Following Christ's resurrection and ascension, God **seated Him at His right hand in the heavenly places**. The **right hand** of God signifies the place of privilege (Heb. 1:13), power (Matt. 26:64), distinction (Heb. 1:3), delight (Ps. 16:11), and dominion (1 Pet. 3:22).

The location is further described as **in the heavenly places**. This indicates that the phrase includes the dwelling place of God. That is where the Lord Jesus is today in a literal body of flesh and bones, a glorified body no longer capable of dying. Where He is, we soon shall be.

1:21 The glorification of our Savior is further described as **far above all principality and power and might and dominion, and every name that is named, not only in this age but also in that which is to come**. The Lord Jesus is superior to every ruler or authority, human or angelic, now and forever.

In the heavenlies there are different ranks of angelic beings, some evil and some good. They have different degrees of power. Some, for instance, might correspond to our human offices of president, governor, mayor, or ward alderman. No matter how great their rule, authority, **power**, and **dominion** might be, Christ is **far above** them.

And this is true **not only in** the **age**

in which we live **but also in** the coming **age**, that is, the literal Thousand-Year Reign of Christ on earth. He will then be King over all kings and Lord over all lords. He will be exalted above all created beings; no exception can be named.

1:22 In addition, God has **put all** created **things under His feet**. This signifies universal dominion, not only over men and angels, but over all the rest of His creation, animate and inanimate. The writer of Hebrews reminds us that at the present time we do not see all things put under Him (Heb. 2:8). That is true. Though universal dominion belongs to Christ, He does not exercise it as yet. Men, for instance, still rebel against Him and deny Him or resist Him. But God has decreed that His Son will yet wield the scepter of universal dominion, and it is as certain as if it were a present reality.

What follows is almost incredible. This One whose nail-scarred hand will exercise sovereign authority over all the universe — God has given this glorious One **to the church**! Here Paul makes a startling revelation concerning the mystery of God's will; step by step he has been leading up to this climactic announcement. With graphic skill he has been describing the resurrection, glorification, and dominion of Christ. While our hearts are still awestruck at the contemplation of this all-glorious Lord, the apostle says, "It is in His capacity as **head over all things** that Christ has been given **to the church**."

If we read this verse carelessly, we might understand it to say that Christ is the Head of **the church**. While that is true enough, the verse says a lot more. It says that **the church** is closely associated with Him who has been given universal sway.

In verse 21 we learned that Christ is far above every *creature* in heaven and on earth, in this age and in the coming age. In the first part of verse 22 we learned that **all things** as well as all created beings are in subjection **under His feet**. Now we learn that the unique calling of **the church** is to be associated with Him in His boundless dominion. **The church** will share His rule. All the rest of creation will be under His rule.

1:23 In this final verse of chapter 1,

we learn how close is the relationship between Christ and the church. Two figures are given: (1) The church **is His body**; (2) It is **the fullness of Him who fills all in all**.

No relationship could be closer than that of the head and the **body**. They are one in vital union and indwelt by one Spirit. The church is a company of people called out from the world between Pentecost and the Rapture, saved by marvelous grace, and given the unique privilege of being the **body** of Christ. No other group of believers in any age ever has had or will have this distinction.

The second description of the church is **the fullness of Him who fills all in all**. This simply means that the church is the complement of Christ, who is everywhere at one and the same time. A complement is that which fills up or completes. It implies two things which when brought together constitute a whole. Just as a body is the complement of the head, so the church is the complement of Christ.

But lest anyone should think this implies any imperfection or incompleteness in Christ, Paul quickly adds, **the fullness of Him who fills all in all**. Far from His needing anything to fill up any lack of completeness, the Lord Jesus is Himself the One **who fills all in all**, who permeates the universe and supplies it with all that it needs.

Admittedly, this is too much for us to understand. We can only admire the infinite mind and plan of God while admitting our own inability to comprehend it.

D. God's Power Manifest in the Salvation of Gentiles and Jews (2:1–10)

2:1 The chapter break should not obscure the vital connection between the latter part of chapter 1 and the verses that follow. There we watched the mighty power of God as it raised Christ from the grave and crowned Him with glory and honor. Now we see how that same power has worked in our own lives, raising us from spiritual death and seating us in Christ in the heavenlies.

This passage resembles the first chapter of Genesis. In each we have: (1) a scene of desolation, chaos, and ruin (Gen. 1:2a; Eph. 2:1–3); (2) the introduction of divine power (Gen. 1:2b; Eph. 2:4); (3) the creation of new life (Gen. 1:3–31; Eph. 2:5–22).

When Ephesians 2 opens, we are spiritual corpses in death valley. When it closes, we are not only seated in Christ in the heavenlies; we form a habitation of God through the Spirit. In between we have the mighty miracle that brought about this remarkable transformation.

The first ten verses describe God's power in the salvation of Gentiles and Jews. No Cinderella ever advanced from such rags to such riches!

In verses 1 and 2 Paul reminds his Gentile readers that before their conversion they **were dead**, depraved, diabolical, and disobedient. They **were** spiritually **dead** as a result of their **trespasses and sins**. This means they were lifeless toward God. They had no vital contact with Him. They lived as if He did not exist. The cause of death was **trespasses and sins**. **Sins** are any form of wrongdoing, whether consciously committed or not, and thoughts, words, or deeds which fall short of God's perfection. **Trespasses** are sins which are committed in open violation of a known law. In a wider sense they may also include any form of false steps or blunders.

2:2 The Ephesians had been depraved as well as dead. They **walked according to the course of this world**. They conformed to the spirit of this age. They indulged in the sins of the times. The world has a mold into which it pours its devotees. It is a mold of deceit, immorality, ungodliness, selfishness, violence, and rebellion. In a word, it is a mold of depravity. That is what the Ephesians had been like.

Not only so, their behavior was diabolical. They followed the example of the devil, **the prince of the power of the air**. They were led around by the chief ruler of evil spirits, whose realm is the atmosphere. They were willingly obedient to the god of this age. This explains why the unconverted often stoop to vile forms of behavior lower than that of animals.

Finally, they were disobedient, walking according to **the spirit who now works in the sons of disobedience**. All unsaved people are **sons of disobedience** in the sense that they are character-

ized by **disobedience** to God. They are energized by Satan and are therefore disposed to defy, dishonor, and disobey the Lord.

2:3 Paul's switch of the personal pronoun from *you* to *we* indicates he is now speaking primarily of Jewish believers (although what he says is also true of everyone before conversion). Three words describe their status: carnal, corrupt, and condemned.

Among whom also we all once conducted ourselves in the lusts of our flesh. It was among the sons of disobedience that Paul and his fellow Christians also walked prior to their new birth. Their life was *carnal*, concerned only with the gratification of fleshly desires and appetites. Paul himself had lived an outwardly moral life on the whole, but now he realized how self-centered it was. And what he was in himself was a lot worse than anything he had ever done.

The unconverted Jews were also *corrupt*, **fulfilling the desires of the flesh and of the mind**. This indicates an abandonment to every natural desire. **Desires of the flesh and of the mind** may range all the way from legitimate appetites to various forms of immorality and perversion; here the emphasis is probably on the grosser sins. And notice, Paul refers to sins of thought as well as to sinful acts.

F. B. Meyer warns:

> It is as ruinous to indulge the desires of the *mind* as those of the *flesh*. By the marvelous gift of imagination we may indulge unholy fancies, and throw the reins on the neck of the steeds of passion — always stopping short of the act. No human eye follows the soul when it goes forth to dance with satyrs or to thread the labyrinthine maze of the islands of desire. It goes and returns unsuspected by the nearest. Its credit for snow-white purity is not forfeited. It is still permitted to watch among the virgins for the Bridegroom's advent. But if this practice is unjudged and unconfessed, it marks the offender a son of disobedience and a child of wrath.[10]

This is Paul's final description of the unsaved Jews: they were **by nature children of wrath, just as the others**. This means they had a natural predisposition to anger, malice, bitterness, and hot temper. They shared this with the rest of mankind. Of course, it is also true that they are under the **wrath** of God. They are appointed to death and judgment. Notice that man's three enemies are mentioned in verses 2 and 3: the world (v. 2), the devil (v. 2), and the flesh (v. 3).

2:4 The words, **But God**, form one of the most significant, eloquent, and inspiring transitions in all literature. They indicate that a stupendous change has taken place. It is a change from the doom and despair of the valley of death to the unspeakable delights of the kingdom of the Son of God's love.

The Author of the change is **God** Himself. No one else *could* have done it, and no one else *would* have done it.

One characteristic of this blessed One is that He **is rich in mercy**. He shows **mercy** to us by not treating us the way we deserve to be treated (Ps. 103:10). "Though it has been expended by Him for six millennia, and myriads and myriads have been partakers of it, it is still an unexhausted mine of wealth," as Eadie remarks.[11]

The reason for His intervention is given in the words, **because of His great love with which He loved us**. His love is great because He is its source. Just as the greatness of a giver casts an aura of greatness on his gift, so the surpassing excellence of God adds superlative luster to His love. It is greater to be loved by the mighty Sovereign of the universe, for instance, than by a fellow human being. God's love is great because of the price He paid. Love sent the Lord Jesus, God's only begotten Son, to die for us in agony at Calvary. God's love is great because of the unsearchable riches it showers on its objects.

2:5 And God's love is great because of the extreme unworthiness and unloveliness of the persons loved. **We were dead in trespasses**. We were enemies of God. We were destitute and degraded. He loved us in spite of it all.

As a result of God's love for us, and as a result of the redeeming work of Christ, we have been: (1) **made alive together with Christ**; (2) raised up with Him; (3) seated in Him.

These expressions describe our spiritual position as a result of our union

with Him. He acted as our Representative — not only *for* us, but *as* us. Therefore when He died, we died. When He was buried, we were buried.

When *He* was **made alive**, raised, and seated in the heavenlies, so were *we*. All the benefits of His sacrificial work are enjoyed by us because of our link with Him. To be **made alive together with** Him means that converted Jews and converted Gentiles are now associated with Him in newness of life. The same power that gave Him resurrection life has given it to us also.

The marvel of this causes Paul to interrupt his train of thought and exclaim, **By grace you have been saved**. He is overwhelmed by the fathomless favor which God has shown to those who deserved the very opposite. That is **grace**!

We have already mentioned that mercy means we do not get the punishment we deserve. **Grace** means we *do* get the salvation we do *not* deserve. We get it as a gift, not as something we earn. And it comes from One who was not compelled to give it. A. T. Pierson says:

> It is a voluntary exercise of love for which He is under no obligation. What constituted the glory of grace is that it is an utterly unfettered, unconstrained exercise of the love of God toward poor sinners.[12]

2:6 Not only have we been made alive with Christ; we have also been **raised up** with Him. Just as death and judgment are behind Him, they are behind us also. We stand on the resurrection side of the tomb. This is our glorious position as a result of our union with Him. And because it is true of us positionally, we should live as those who are alive from the dead.

Another aspect of our position is that we are seated in Him **in the heavenly places in Christ**. By our union with Him we are seen as already delivered from this present evil world and seated **in Christ** in glory. This is how God sees us. If we appropriate it by faith, it will change the character of our lives. We will no longer be earthbound, occupied with the trivial and the transient. We will seek those things which are above, where Christ is seated at the right hand of God (Col. 3:1).

The key to verses 5 and 6 is the

phrase, **in Christ Jesus**. It is in Him that we have been made alive, raised, and seated. He is our Representative; therefore His triumphs and His position are ours. George Williams exclaims, "Amazing thought! That a Mary Magdalene and a crucified thief should be the companions in glory of the Son of God."

2:7 This miracle of transforming grace will be the subject of eternal revelation. Throughout the endless ages God will be unveiling to the heavenly throng what it cost Him to send His Son to this jungle of sin, and what it cost the Lord Jesus to bear our sins at the cross. It is a subject that will never be exhausted. Again Paul builds words upon words to suggest something of its immensity:

> His kindness toward us
> His grace in His kindness toward us
> The riches of His grace in His kindness toward us
> The exceeding riches of His grace in His kindness toward us

Now it follows that if God will be disclosing this throughout eternity, then we will be learning forever and ever. Heaven will be our school. God will be the Teacher. **His grace** will be the subject. We will be the students. And the school term will be eternity.

This should deliver us from the idea that we will know everything when we get to heaven. Only God knows everything, and we will never be equal with Him.[13]

It also raises the interesting question: How much will we know when we get to heaven? And it suggests the possibility that we can prepare for the heavenly university by majoring in the Bible right now.

2:8 The next three verses present as clear a statement of the simple plan of salvation as we can find in the Bible.

It all originates with the **grace** of God: He takes the initiative in providing it. Salvation is given to those who are utterly unworthy of it, on the basis of the Person and work of the Lord Jesus Christ.

It is given as a present possession. Those who are saved can know it. Writing to the Ephesians, Paul said, **You have been saved**. He knew it, and they knew it.

The way we receive the gift of eternal life is **through faith**. **Faith** means that man takes his place as a lost, guilty sinner, and receives the Lord Jesus as his only hope of salvation. True saving faith is the commitment of a person to a Person.

Any idea that man can earn or deserve salvation is forever exploded by the words, **and that not of yourselves**. Dead people can *do* nothing, and sinners *deserve* nothing but punishment.

It is the gift of God. A gift, of course, is a free and unconditional present. That is the only basis on which God offers salvation. **The gift of God** is *salvation* **by grace** and **through faith**. It is offered to all people everywhere.

2:9 It is **not of works**, that is, it is not something a person can earn through supposedly meritorious deeds. It cannot be earned, for instance, by:

1. Confirmation
2. Baptism
3. Church membership
4. Church attendance
5. Holy Communion
6. Trying to keep the Ten Commandments
7. Living by the Sermon on the Mount
8. Giving to charity
9. Being a good neighbor
10. Living a moral, respectable life

People are not saved by **works**. And they are *not* saved by faith *plus* **works**. They are **saved through faith** *alone*. The minute you add works of any kind or in any amount as a means of gaining eternal life, salvation is no longer by grace (Rom. 11:6). One reason that **works** are positively excluded is to prevent human boasting. If anyone could be saved by his **works**, then he would have reason to **boast** before God. This is impossible (Rom. 3:27).

If anyone could be saved by his own good works, then the death of Christ was unnecessary (Gal. 2:21). But we know that the reason He died was because there was no other way by which guilty sinners could be saved.

If anyone could be saved by his own good works, then he would be his own savior, and could worship himself. But this would be idolatry, and God forbids it (Ex. 20:3).

Even if someone could be saved through faith in Christ plus his own good works, you would have the impossible situation of two saviors — Jesus and the sinner. Christ would then have to share the glory of saviorhood with another, and this He will not do (Isa. 42:8).

Finally, if anyone could contribute to his salvation by works, then God would owe it to him. This, too, is impossible. God cannot be indebted to anyone (Rom. 11:35).

In contrast to works, faith excludes boasting (Rom. 3:27), because it is non-meritorious. A man has no reason to be proud that he has trusted the Lord. Faith in Him is the most sane, rational, sensible thing a person can do. To trust one's Creator and Redeemer is only logical and reasonable. If we cannot trust Him, whom can we trust?

2:10 The result of salvation is that **we are His workmanship** — the handiwork of God, not of ourselves. A born-again believer is a masterpiece of God. When we think of the raw materials He has to work with, His achievement is all the more remarkable. Indeed, this masterpiece is nothing less than a new creation through union with Christ, for "if anyone is in Christ, he is a new creation; old things have passed away; behold, all things have become new" (2 Cor. 5:17).

And the object of this new creation is found in the phrase, **for good works**. While it is true that we are not saved *by* **good works**, it is equally true that we are saved **for** good works. **Good works** are not the *root* but the *fruit*. We do not work *in order to be saved*, but *because we are saved*.

This is the aspect of the truth that is emphasized in James 2:14–26. When James says that "faith without works is dead," he does not mean we are saved by faith plus works, but by the kind of faith that results in a life of **good works**. **Works** prove the reality of our faith. Paul heartily agrees: **we are His workmanship, created in Christ Jesus for good works**.

God's order then is this:
Faith –> Salvation –> Good Works –> Reward
Faith leads to salvation. Salvation results in **good works**. Good works will be rewarded by Him.

But the question arises: What kind of **good works** am I expected to do? Paul answers, **Good works, which God prepared beforehand that we should walk in them**. In other words, God has a blue-print for every life. Before our conversion He mapped out a spiritual career for us. Our responsibility is to find His will for us and then obey it. We do not have to work out a plan for our lives, but only accept the plan which He has drawn up for us. This delivers us from fret and frenzy, and insures that our lives will be of maximum glory to Him, of most blessing to others, and of greatest reward to ourselves.

In order to find out the **good works** He has planned for our individual lives, we should: (1) confess and forsake sin as soon as we are conscious of it in our lives; (2) be continually and unconditionally yielded to Him; (3) study the word of God to discern His will, and then do whatever He tells us to do; (4) spend time in prayer each day; (5) seize opportunities of service as they arise; (6) cultivate the fellowship and counsel of other Christians. God prepares us **for good works**. He prepares **good works** for us to perform. Then He rewards us when we perform them. Such is His grace!

E. The Union of Believing Jews and Gentiles in Christ (2:11–22)

In the first half of chapter 2 Paul traced the salvation of individual Gentiles and Jews. Now he advances to the abolition of their former national differences, to their union in Christ, and to their formation into the church, a holy temple in the Lord.

2:11 In verses 11 and 12 the apostle reminds his readers that prior to their conversion they were **Gentiles** by birth and therefore outcasts as far as the Jews were concerned. First, they were despised. This is indicated by the fact that the Jews called them **Uncircumcision**. This meant the Gentiles did not have the surgical sign in their flesh that marked the Israelites as God's covenant people. The name "uncircumcised" was an ethnic slur, similar to the names that people use today for despised nationalities. We can feel something of its sting when we hear David say concerning the Gentile Goliath, "Who is this uncircumcised Philistine, that he should defy the armies of the living God?" (1 Sam. 17:26).

The Jews, by contrast, spoke of themselves as **the Circumcision**. This was a name of which they were proud. It identified them as God's chosen earthly people, set apart from all the other nations of the earth. Paul seems to take exception to some of their boasting by saying their circumcision was only **made in the flesh by hands**. It was merely physical. Though they had the outward sign of God's covenant people, they did not have the inward reality of true faith in the Lord. "For he is not a Jew who is one outwardly, nor is circumcision that which is outward in the flesh; but he is a Jew who is one inwardly; and circumcision is that of the heart, in the Spirit, not in the letter; whose praise is not from men but from God" (Rom. 2:28, 29).

But whether or not the Jews were circumcised in heart, the point in verse 11 is that in their own eyes they were *the* people and the Gentiles were despised. This enmity between Jews and Gentiles was the greatest racial and religious difference the world has ever known. The Jew enjoyed a position of great privilege before God (Rom. 9:4, 5). The Gentile was a foreigner. If he wanted to worship the true God in the appointed way, he actually had to become a Jewish convert (cf. Rahab and Ruth). The Jewish temple in Jerusalem was the only place on earth where God had placed His name and where men could approach Him. Gentiles were forbidden to enter the inner temple courts on pain of death.

In His interview with a Gentile woman from the region of Tyre and Sidon, the Lord Jesus tested her faith by picturing the Jews as children in the house and the Gentiles as little dogs under the table. She acknowledged she was only a little dog, but asked for some crumbs the children might drop. Needless to say, her faith was rewarded (Mark 7:24–30). Here in Ephesians 2:11 the apostle is reminding his readers that they were formerly Gentiles and therefore despised.

2:12 The Gentiles were also **without Christ**: they had no Messiah. It was to the nation of Israel that He was promised. Although it was predicted that blessing would flow to the nations through the ministry of the Messiah (Isa. 11:10; 60:3), yet He was to be born a Jew and to minister primarily "to the lost sheep of the house of Israel" (Matt. 15:24). In addition to being without the

Messiah, the Gentiles were **aliens from the commonwealth of Israel**. An alien is one who does not "belong." He is a stranger and foreigner, without the rights and privileges of citizenship. As far as the community of **Israel** was concerned, the Gentiles were on the outside, looking in. And they were **strangers from the covenants of promise**. God had made **covenants** with the nation of **Israel** through such men as Abraham, Isaac, Jacob, Moses, David, and Solomon. These **covenants** promised blessings to the Jews. For all practical purposes, the Gentiles were outside the pale. They were without **hope**, both nationally and individually. Nationally, they had no assurance that their land, their government, or their people would survive. And individually their outlook was bleak: they had **no hope** beyond the grave. Someone has said that their future was a night without a star. Finally, they were **without God in the world**. This does not mean they were atheists. They had their own gods of wood and stone, and worshiped them. But they did not know the one and only true God. They were God–less in a godless, hostile world.

2:13 The words, **But now**, signal another abrupt transition (cf. 2:4). The Ephesian Gentiles had been rescued from that place of distance and alienation, and had been elevated to a position of nearness to God. This was brought about at the time of their conversion. When they trusted the Savior, God placed them **in Christ Jesus** and accepted them in the beloved One. From then on they were as **near** to God as Christ is, because they were **in Christ Jesus**. The cost of effecting this marvelous change was **the blood of Christ**. Before these Gentile sinners could enjoy the privilege of nearness to God, they had to be cleansed from their sins. Only **the blood of Christ** shed at Calvary could do this. When they received the Lord Jesus by a definite act of faith, all the cleansing value of His precious blood was credited to their account.

Jesus not only **brought** them **near**; He also created a new society in which the ancient enmity between Jew and Gentile was forever abolished. Up to NT times, all the world was divided into two classes — Jew and Gentile. Our Savior has introduced a third — the church of God (1 Cor. 10:32). In the verses that follow, we see how believing Jews and believing Gentiles are now made one in Christ, and are introduced into this new society, where there is neither Jew nor Gentile.

2:14 For He Himself is our peace. Notice it does not say, "He made peace." That, of course, is true too, as we will see in the next verse. Here the fact is that **He Himself** *is* our peace. But how can a person *be* peace?

This is how: When a Jew believes on the Lord Jesus, he loses his national identity; from then on he is "in Christ." Likewise, when a Gentile receives the Savior, he is no longer a Gentile; henceforth he is "in Christ." In other words, believing Jew and believing Gentile, once divided by enmity, are now **both one** in Christ. Their union with Christ necessarily unites them with one another. Therefore a Man **is** the **peace**, just as Micah predicted (Mic. 5:5).

The scope of His work as **our peace** is detailed in verses 14–18.

First is the work of union which we have just described. He **has made both one** — that is, both believing Jews and Gentiles. They are no longer Jews or Gentiles, but Christians. Strictly speaking, it is not accurate even to speak of them as Jewish Christians or Gentile Christians. All fleshly distinctions, such as nationality, were nailed to the cross.

The second phase of Christ's work might be called demolition: **He . . . has broken down the middle wall of separation**. Not a literal wall, of course, but the invisible barrier set up by the Mosaic Law of commandments contained in ordinances which separated the people of Israel from the nations. This has often been illustrated by the wall which restricted non-Jews to the Court of the Gentiles in the temple area. On the wall were No Trespassing signs which read: "Let no one of any other nation come within the fence and barrier around the Holy Place. Whoever is caught doing so will himself be responsible for the fact that his death will ensue."

2:15 A third aspect of Christ's work

was abolition of **the enmity** that smoldered between Jew and Gentile and also between man and God. Paul identifies the law as the innocent cause of the enmity, that is, **the law of commandments contained in ordinances**. The Law of Moses was a single legislative code; yet it was made up of separate, formal commandments; these in turn consisted of dogmas or decrees covering many, if not most, areas of life. The law itself was holy, just, and good (Rom. 7:12), but man's sinful nature used the law as an occasion for hatred. Because the law actually did set up Israel as God's chosen earthly people, many Jews became arrogant and treated the Gentiles with contempt. The Gentiles struck back with deep hostility, which we have come to know all too well as anti-Semitism. But how did Christ remove the law as the cause of **enmity**? First, He died to pay the penalty of the law that had been broken. He thus completely satisfied the righteous claims of God. Now the law has nothing more to say to those who are "in Christ"; the penalty has been paid for them in full. Believers are not under law but under grace. However, this does not mean they can live as they please; it means they are now enlawed to Christ, and should live as *He* pleases.

As a result of abolishing the hostility stirred up by the law, the Lord has been able to usher in a new creation. He has made in Himself **from the two**, that is, from believing Jew and believing Gentile, **one new man** — the church. Through union with Him, the former combatants are united with one another in this **new** fellowship. The church is **new** in the sense that it is a kind of organism that never existed before. It is important to see this. The NT church is not a continuation of the Israel of the OT. It is something entirely distinct from anything that has preceded it or that will ever follow it. This should be apparent from the following:

1. It is **new** that a Gentile should have equal rights and privileges with a Jew.
2. It is **new** that both Jews and Gentiles should lose their national identities by becoming Christians.
3. It is **new** that Jews and Gentiles

should be fellow members of the Body of Christ.

4. It is **new** that a Jew should have the hope of reigning with Christ instead of being a subject in His kingdom.

5. It is **new** that a Jew should no longer be under the law.

The church is clearly a **new** creation, with a distinct calling and a distinct destiny, occupying a unique place in the purposes of God. But the scope of Christ's work does not stop there. He has also made **peace** between Jew and Gentile. He did this by removing the cause of hostility, by imparting a new nature, and by creating a new union. The cross is God's answer to racial discrimination, segregation, anti-Semitism, bigotry, and every form of strife between men.

2:16 In addition to reconciling Jew and Gentile to one another, Christ has reconciled **them both to God**. Though Israel and the nations were normally bitterly opposed to each other, there was one sense in which they were united — in their hostility to God. The cause of this hostility was sin. By His death on the cross, the Lord Jesus removed **the enmity** by removing the cause. Those who receive Him are reckoned righteous, forgiven, redeemed, pardoned, and delivered from the power of sin. The enmity is gone; now they have peace with **God**. The Lord Jesus unites believing Jew and Gentile **in one body**, the church, and presents this Body to **God** with all trace of antagonism gone.

God never needed to be reconciled to us; He never hated us. But we needed to be reconciled to Him. The work of our Lord on the cross provided a righteous basis on which we could be brought into His presence as friends, not as foes.

2:17 In verse 14 Christ *is* our peace. In verse 15 He *made* peace. Now we find that **He came and** *preached* **peace**. When and how did He come? First, He came personally in resurrection. Second, He came representatively by the Holy Spirit. He **preached peace** in resurrection; in fact, **peace** was one of the first words He spoke after rising from the dead (Luke 24:36; John 20:19, 21, 26). Then He sent out the apostles in the power of the Holy Spirit and **preached peace** through them

(Acts 10:36). The good news of **peace** was presented to **you who were afar off** (Gentiles) **and to those who were near** (Jews), a gracious fulfillment of God's promise in Isaiah 57:19.

2:18 The practical proof that a state of peace now exists between members of the one Body and God is that they **have access** at any time into the presence of God. This is in sharp contrast to the OT economy, in which only the high priest could go into the Holy of Holies, the place of God's presence. And he could enter there on only one day of the year. Eadie points up the contrast:

> But now the most distant Gentile who is in Christ really and continuously enjoys that august spiritual privilege, which the one man of the one tribe of the one nation on the one day of the year, only typically and periodically possessed.[14]

Through prayer any believer can enter the throne room of heaven, kneel before the Sovereign of the universe, and address Him as **Father**.

The normal order to be followed in prayer is given here. First, it is **through Him** (the Lord Jesus). He is the one Mediator between God and man. His death, burial, and resurrection removed every legal obstacle to our admission to God's presence. Now as Mediator He lives on high to maintain us in a condition of fellowship with the Father. We approach God in His name; we have no worthiness of our own, so we plead His worthiness. The participants in prayer are **we both** — believing Jews and believing Gentiles. The privilege is that we **have access.** Our Helper in prayer is the Holy Spirit — **by one Spirit**. "The Spirit helps in our weaknesses. For we do not know what we should pray for as we ought, but the Spirit Himself makes intercession for us with groanings which cannot be uttered" (Rom. 8:26).

The One we approach is **the Father**. No OT saint ever knew God as Father. Before the resurrection of Christ, men stood before God as creatures before the Creator. It was after He rose that He said, "Go to my brethren and say to them, 'I am ascending to My Father and your Father, and to My God and your God' " (John 20:17). As a result of His redemptive work, believers were then able for the first time to address God as **Father**. In verse 18 all three Persons of the Trinity are directly involved in the prayers of the humblest believer: he prays to God the **Father**, approaching Him **through** the Lord Jesus Christ, in the power of the Holy **Spirit**.

2:19 In the last four verses of this chapter, the Apostle Paul lists some of the overwhelming new privileges of believing Gentiles. They **are no longer strangers and foreigners**. Never again will they be aliens, dogs, uncircumcision, outsiders. Now they are **fellow citizens with** all **the saints** of the NT period. Believers of Jewish ancestry have no advantage over them. All Christians are first-class citizens of heaven (Phil. 3:20, 21). They are also **members of the household of God**. Not only have they been "super-naturalized" into the divine kingdom; they have been adopted into the divine family.

2:20 Finally, they have been made members of the church, or as Paul pictures it here, they have become stones in the construction of a holy temple. With great detail the apostle describes this temple — its **foundation**, its **chief cornerstone**, its cohesive agent, its unity and symmetry, its growth, and its other unique features.

This temple is *built on the foundation of the apostles and prophets*. This refers to **the apostles and prophets** of the NT era; it could not possibly refer to OT prophets, because they knew nothing about the church. It does not mean that **the apostles and prophets** *were* the foundation of the church. Christ is **the foundation** (1 Cor. 3:11). But they laid the foundation in what they taught about the Person and work of the Lord Jesus. The church is founded on Christ as He was revealed by the confession and teaching of **the apostles and prophets**. When Peter confessed Him as the Christ, the Son of the living God, Jesus announced that His church would be built on that rock, namely, on the solid truth that He is the anointed of God and God's unique Son (Matt. 16:18). In Revelation 21:14 the apostles are associated with the twelve foundations of the holy Jerusalem. They are not the foundation but are linked with it, because they first taught the great truth concerning Christ and the church. The **foundation** of a building needs to be laid only once. **The apostles and prophets** did this work once for all. **The foundation** they laid is preserved for us in the writings of the NT, though they themselves are with us no longer. In a secondary sense, there are men in all ages whose ministry is apostolic or prophetic. Missionaries and church planters are apostles in a lower sense, and those who preach the word for edification are prophets. But they are not apostles and prophets in the primary sense.

Jesus Christ is not only **the foundation** of the temple; He is its **chief cornerstone** as well. No one picture or type can adequately portray Him in His manifold glories or in His varied ministries. There are at least three possible explanations of **the chief cornerstone**, all of which point to the Lord Jesus Christ as the unique, preeminent, and indispensable Head of the church.

1. We generally think of **the cornerstone** as one that lies at a lower front corner of a building. Since the rest of the structure seems to be supported by it, it has come to signify something of fundamental importance. In that sense it is a true type of the Lord. Also, since it joins two walls together, there may be a suggestion of the union of believing Jews and Gentiles in the church through Him.

2. Some Bible scholars believe that the word translated **the chief cornerstone** refers to the keystone of an arch. This stone occupies the highest place in the arch and provides support for the other stones. So Christ is the preeminent One in the church. He is also the indispensable One: remove Him and the rest will collapse.

3. A third possible understanding of the term is that it is the capstone of a pyramid. This stone occupies the highest place in the structure. It is the only stone of that size and shape. And its angles and lines determine the shape of the whole pyramid. So Christ is the Head of the church. He is unique as to His Person and ministry. And He is the One who gives the church its

unique features. First, its **foundation**:

2:21 The words, **in whom**, refer to Christ: He is the source of the church's life and growth. Blaikie says:

> In him we are added to it; in him we grow in it; in him the whole temple grows towards the final consummation, when the *topstone* shall be brought out with shouts of 'Grace, grace unto it.'[15]

The unity and symmetry of the **temple** are indicated by the expression, **the whole building, being fitted together**. It is a unity made up of many individual members. Each member has a specific place in the **building** for which he or she is exactly suited. Stones excavated from the valley of death by the grace of God are found to fit together perfectly. The unique feature of this building is that it **grows**. However, this feature is not the same as the growth of a building through the addition of bricks and cement. Think of it rather as the growth of a living organism, such as the human body. After all, the church is not an inanimate building. Neither is it an organization. It is a living entity with Christ as its Head and all believers forming the Body. It was born on the day of Pentecost, has been growing ever since, and will continue to grow until the Rapture.

This growing building of living materials is described as **a holy temple in the Lord**. The word Paul used for **temple** referred not to the outer courts but to the inner shrine (Gk., *naos*), not the suburbs but the sanctuary. He was thinking of the main building of the temple complex, which housed the Most Holy Place. There God dwelt and there He manifested Himself in a bright, shining cloud of glory.

There are several lessons for us here: (1) God indwells the church. Saved Jews and Gentiles form a living sanctuary in which He dwells and where He reveals His glory. (2) This **temple** is **holy**. It is set apart from the world and dedicated to Him for sacred purposes. (3) As **a holy temple**, the church is a center from which praise, worship, and adoration ascend to God through the Lord Jesus Christ.

Paul further describes this **holy temple** as being **in the Lord**. In other words, the Lord Jesus is its source of holiness. Its members are **holy** positionally through union with Him, and they should be **holy** practically out of love for Him.

2:22 In this wonderful temple, believing Gentiles have an equal place with believing Jews. It should thrill us to read this, as it must have thrilled the Ephesians and others when they heard it for the first time. The tremendous dignity of the believers' position is that they form **a dwelling place of God in the Spirit**. This is the purpose of the temple — to provide a place where **God** can live in fellowship with His people. The church is that place. Compare this with the position of the Gentiles in the OT. At that time they could not get near God's dwelling. Now they themselves *form* a good part of it!

And notice the ministry of each of the Persons of the Godhead in connection with the church: (1) **In whom**, that is, in Christ. It is through union with Him that we are built into the temple. (2) **A dwelling place of God**. This temple is the home of God the Father on earth. (3) **In the Spirit**. It is in the Person of the Holy **Spirit** that **God** indwells the church (1 Cor. 3:16).

And so the chapter that began with a description of Gentiles who were dead, depraved, diabolical, and disobedient, closes with those same Gentiles cleansed from all guilt and defilement, and forming **a dwelling place of God in the Spirit!**

F. A Parenthesis on the Mystery (3:1–13)

3:1 Paul begins a statement in verse 1 that is interrupted in verse 2 and not resumed till verse 14. The intervening verses form a parenthesis, the theme of which is the mystery — Christ and the church.

What makes this of special interest is that this present Church Age is itself a parenthesis in God's dealings. This can be explained as follows: During most of the period of history recorded in the OT, God was dealing primarily with the Jewish people. In fact, from Genesis 12 through Malachi 4 the narrative centers almost exclusively on Abraham and his descendants. When the Lord Jesus came to earth, He was rejected by Israel. As a result, God set aside that nation temporarily as His chosen, earthly people. We are now living in the Church Age, when Jews and Gentiles are on the same level before God. After the church has been completed and is taken home to heaven, God will resume His program with Israel nationally. The hands on the prophetic clock will begin to move once more. So the present age is sort of a parenthesis between God's past and future dealings with Israel. It is a new administration in the divine program — unique and separate from anything before or after it.

In verses 2–13 Paul gives a fairly detailed explanation of this parenthesis. Is it an undesigned coincidence that in doing so he uses a literary parenthesis to explain a dispensational parenthesis?

The apostle opens the section, **For this reason I, Paul, the prisoner of Christ Jesus for you Gentiles**. The phrase, **For this reason**, looks back to what he had just been saying about the place of privilege into which believing Gentiles are brought as a result of their union with Christ.

It is generally believed that this Letter was written during Paul's first Roman imprisonment. But he does not speak of himself as a prisoner of Rome. That might have indicated a sense of defeat, a feeling of self-pity, or a craving for sympathy. Paul calls himself **the prisoner of Christ Jesus**; this speaks of acceptance and dignity and triumph. Ruth Paxson puts it well:

> There is no smell of prison in Ephesians, for Paul is not bound in spirit. He is there as the prisoner of Rome, but this he will not admit, and claims to be the prisoner of Jesus Christ. What is the secret of such victorious other-worldliness? Paul's spirit is with Christ in the heavenlies, though his body languishes in prison.[16]

His imprisonment was definitely on behalf of **the Gentiles**. Throughout his ministry he ran into bitter opposition for teaching that believing Gentiles now enjoyed equal rights and privileges with believing Jews in the Christian church. What finally triggered his arrest and trial before Caesar was a false charge that he had taken Trophimus, an Ephesian, into the temple area that was out of bounds

for Gentiles (Acts 21:29). But behind the charge was the already fierce hostility of the religious leaders.

3:2 Now Paul breaks his train of thought and launches into a discourse on the mystery, in what we have already referred to as a literary parenthesis dealing with a dispensational parenthesis.

The **if** in verse 2 (**if indeed you have heard . . .**) might create the impression that the apostle's readers did not know of his special mission to the Gentiles. In fact, this verse is sometimes used to prove that Paul did not know the persons to whom he wrote and that therefore the Letter could not have been written to the beloved Ephesians. But "if" often carries the meaning of "since." Thus Phillips paraphrases it, "For you must have heard. . . ." They had surely known that this special ministry had been committed to him. He describes that ministry as a **dispensation of the grace of God**. Here **dispensation** refers to a stewardship. A steward is one who is appointed to administer the affairs of someone else. Paul was God's steward, charged with setting forth the great truth regarding the NT church. It was a stewardship of God's **grace** in at least three senses:

1. As to the one chosen. It was undeserved favor to Paul that selected him for such a high privilege.
2. As to the contents of the message. It was the message of God's free and unmerited kindness.
3. As to its recipients. The Gentiles were quite unworthy people to be so favored.

Yet this stewardship of **grace** was given to Paul in order that he in turn might impart it to the Gentiles.

3:3 He had not learned **the mystery** from anyone else, nor had he discovered it through his own intelligence. It was **made known to** him by direct **revelation** from God. We are not told where this happened, or how; all we know is that in some miraculous way God showed Paul His plan for a church composed of converted Jews and converted Gentiles. We have already mentioned that a **mystery** is a sacred secret hitherto unknown, humanly unknowable, and now divinely revealed. The apostle had alluded to **the mystery** briefly in 1:9–14, 22, 23; 2:11–22.

3:4 What he had already written on the subject was sufficient to demonstrate to his readers that he had a God-given insight into **the mystery of** the **Christ**. Blaikie paraphrases this passage as follows:

> With reference to which, *i.e.*, to what I wrote afore: to make that more intelligible I write on the subject more fully now, so that you shall see that your instructor is thoroughly informed in this matter of the mystery. . . .[17]

Darby's translation, "the mystery of *the* Christ," suggests that it is the mystical Christ that is in view here, that is, the Head *and* the Body. (For another instance of the name **Christ** including both the Lord Jesus and His people, see 1 Cor. 12:12.)

3:5 Verses 5 and 6 give us the most complete definition we have of the mystery. Paul explains what a mystery is, then he explains what the mystery of the Christ is.

First, it is a truth **which in other ages was not made known to the sons of men**. This means it is futile to look for it in the OT. There may be types and pictures of it there, but the truth itself was unknown at that time.

Second, it is a truth which **has now been revealed by the** Holy **Spirit** to God's **holy apostles and prophets**. God was the Revealer; the **apostles and prophets** were the ones set apart to receive the revelation; **the** Holy **Spirit** was the channel through whom the revelation came to them.

Unless we see that the **apostles and prophets** were those of the NT, not the OT period, this verse is contradictory. The first part says this truth was not revealed in other ages; therefore it was unknown to the OT prophets. How then could it be made known in Paul's day by men who had been dead for centuries? The obvious meaning is that the great truth of Christ and the church was made known to men of the Church Age like Paul who were specially commissioned by the risen Lord to serve as His spokesmen or mouthpieces. (Paul does not claim to be the *only* one to whom this sacred secret was disclosed; he was one among many, though he was the foremost in transmitting the truth to Gentiles of his day, and to succeeding generations through his Epistles.)

It is only fair to mention that many Christians take quite a different view from that given above. They say the church actually did exist in the OT; that Israel was then the church; but that the truth of the church has now been more fully revealed. They say, "The mystery was not known in other ages *as* it is now revealed. It was known *but not to the same extent as now*. We have a *fuller revelation*, but we are still the Israel of God, that is, a continuation of God's people." To support their argument, they point to Acts 7:38 in the 1611 KJV, where the nation of Israel is called "the church (NKJV, NASB,: *congregation*) in the wilderness." It is true that God's chosen people are spoken of as the congregation in the wilderness, but this does not mean they have any connection with the *Christian* church. After all, the Greek word *ekklēsia* is a general term which can mean any assembly, congregation, or called-out group. It is not only applied to Israel in Acts 7:38; the same word, translated *assembly*, is used in Acts 19:32, 41 of a heathen mob. We have to determine from the context *which* "church" or assembly is meant.

But what about the argument that verse 5 means the church existed in the OT though it was not as fully revealed then as now? This is answered in Colossians 1:26, which states flatly that the mystery was "hidden from ages and from generations, but now has been revealed to His saints." It is not a question of the degree of revelation but of the fact of it.

3:6 Now we come to the central truth of the mystery, namely, that in the church of the Lord Jesus Christ, believing **Gentiles** are **fellow heirs**, fellow members, and fellow **partakers of His promise in Christ through the gospel**. In other words, converted **Gentiles** now enjoy equal title and privileges with converted Jews.

First, they are **fellow heirs**. As far as the inheritance is concerned, they share equally with saved Jews. They are heirs of God, joint heirs with Jesus Christ, and **fellow heirs** with all the redeemed.

Then they are fellow members **of the same body**. They are at no distance or disadvantage now, but share a position of equality with saved Jews in the church.

Finally, they are fellow **partakers** of the **promise in Christ through the gospel**. The **promise** here may mean the Holy Spirit (Acts 15:8; Gal. 3:14), or it may take in all that is promised in **the gospel** to those who are **in Christ** Jesus. **Gentiles** are copartners with Jews in all of this.

None of this was true in the OT dispensation, nor will it be true in the coming kingdom of Christ.

In the OT, Israel held a distinct place of privilege before God. A Jew would have laughed at any suggestion that a Gentile held an equal share with him in the promises of God. It simply was not true. The prophets of Israel did predict the call of the Gentiles (Isa. 49:6; 56:6, 7), but they nowhere hinted that Gentiles would be fellow members of a body in which Jews did not have any priority.

In the coming kingdom of our Lord, Israel will be the head of the nations (Isa. 60:12); Gentiles will be blessed, but it will be through Israel (Isa. 60:3; 61:6; Zech. 8:23).

The calling of Israel was primarily, though not exclusively, to temporal blessings in earthly places (Deut. 28; Amos 9:13–15). The calling of the church is primarily to spiritual blessings in heavenly places (Eph. 1:3). Israel was called to be God's chosen earthly people. The church is called to be the heavenly Bride of Christ (Rev. 21:2, 9). Israel will be blessed under the rule of Christ in the Millennium (Hos. 3:5); the church will reign with Him over the entire universe, sharing His glory (Eph. 1:22, 23).

Therefore it should be clear that the church is not the same as Israel or the kingdom. It is a new society, a unique fellowship, and the most privileged body of believers we read about in the Bible. The church came into being after Christ ascended and the Holy Spirit was given (Acts 2). It was formed by the baptism of the Holy Spirit (1 Cor. 12:13). And it will be completed at the Rapture, when all who belong to Christ will be taken home to heaven (1 Thess. 4:13–18; 1 Cor. 15:23, 51–58).

3:7 Having emphasized the equal partnership of Gentiles and Jews in the church, Paul now moves on to discuss his own ministry in connection with it (vv. 7–9).

First, he **became a minister** of the gospel. Wuest writes, "The word 'minister' is misleading, since it is the technical word used today to designate the pastor of a church." It never means that in the NT. The basic meaning of the word is *servant*; Paul simply meant he served the Lord in connection with the mystery.

The ministry was in the nature of an undeserved gift: **according to the gift of the grace of God given to me**. And it was not only a display of **grace**; it also demonstrated God's **power** in effectually reaching the proud, self-righteous Pharisee, saving his soul, commissioning him as an apostle, empowering him to receive revelations, and strengthening him for the work. So Paul says **the gift** was given to him **by the effective working of His power.**

3:8 The apostle speaks of himself as **less than the least of all the saints**. This might seem like mock humility to some. Actually it is the true self-estimate of one who is filled by the Holy Spirit. Anyone who sees Christ in His glory realizes his own sinfulness and uselessness. In Paul's case there was the added memory that he had persecuted the Lord Jesus (Acts 9:4) by persecuting the church of God (Gal. 1:13; Phil. 3:6). In spite of this, the Lord had commissioned him in a special way to take the gospel to **the Gentiles** (Acts 9:15; 13:47; 22:21; Gal. 2:2, 8). Paul was the apostle to **the Gentiles** as Peter was to the Jews. His ministry was twofold: it concerned the gospel, and it concerned the church. First, he told men how to be saved, then he led them on into the truth of the NT church. For him evangelism was not an end in itself but a step toward establishing and strengthening indigenous NT churches.

The first function of his ministry was to **preach among the Gentiles the unsearchable riches of Christ**. Blaikie expresses it well:

Two attractive words, *riches* and *unsearchable*, conveying the idea of the things that are most precious being infinitely abundant. Usually precious things are rare; their very rarity increases their price; but here that which is most precious is also boundless — riches of compassion and love, of merit, of sanctifying, comforting and transforming power, all without limit, and capable of satisfying every want, craving, and yearning of the heart, now and evermore.[18]

When a person trusts the Lord Jesus, he immediately becomes a spiritual billionaire; in Christ he possesses inexhaustible treasures.

3:9 The second part of Paul's ministry was **to make all see what is** "the administration of the mystery" (JND), in other words, to enlighten them as to how **the mystery** is being worked out in practice. God's plan for this present age is to call out of the Gentiles a people for His name (Acts 15:14), a Bride for His Son. All that is involved in this plan is the administration (*stewardship*, NKJV margin[19]) **of the mystery**. **All** here must mean **all** *believers*. Unsaved people could not be expected to understand the deep truths of **the mystery** (1 Cor. 2:14). Paul therefore is referring to **all** in the sense of saved people of **all** *kinds* — Jews and Gentiles, slave and free.

This **mystery** had **from the beginning of the ages been hidden in God**. The plan was itself in the mind of God eternally, but here the thought is that He kept it a secret throughout **the ages** of human history. Once again we notice the care the Holy Spirit takes to impress us with the fact that the assembly, or church universal is something new, unique, unprecedented. It was not known before to anyone but God. The secret was **hidden in God who created all things**. He **created** the material universe, He **created the ages**, and He **created** the church — but in His wisdom He decided to withhold any knowledge of this new creation until the First Advent of Christ.

3:10 One of God's present purposes in connection with the mystery is to reveal His **manifold wisdom** to the angelic hosts of heaven. Paul again uses the metaphor of a school. God is the Teacher. The universe is the classroom. Angelic dignitaries are the students. The lesson is on "The multi-faceted **wisdom of God**." **The church** is the object lesson. From heaven the angels are compelled to admire His unsearchable judgments and marvel at His ways past

finding out. They see how God has triumphed over sin to His own glory. They see how He has sent heaven's Best for earth's worst. They see how He has redeemed His enemies at enormous cost, conquered them by love, and prepared them as a Bride for His Son. They see how He has blessed them with all spiritual blessings in the heavenlies. And they see that through the work of the Lord Jesus on the cross, more glory has come to God and more blessing has come to believing Jews and Gentiles than if sin had never been allowed to enter. God has been vindicated; Christ has been exalted; Satan has been defeated; and the church has been enthroned in Christ to share His glory.

3:11 The mystery itself, its concealment, its eventual disclosure, and the manner in which it exhibits the wisdom of God are all **according to the eternal purpose which He accomplished in Christ Jesus our Lord**. Before the world was made, God knew Satan would fall and man would follow him in sin. And He had already prepared a counterstrategy, a master plan. This plan has been worked out in the incarnation, death, resurrection, ascension, and glorification of Christ. The whole program centered in Christ and has been realized through Him. Now God can save ungodly Jews and Gentiles, make them members of the Body of Christ, conform them to the image of His Son, and honor them in a unique way as the Bride of the Lamb throughout eternity.

3:12 As a result of Christ's work and our union with Him, we now have the unspeakable privilege of entering into God's presence at any time, in full confidence of being heard, and without any fear of being scolded (Jas 1:5). Our **boldness** is the respectful attitude and absence of fear we have as children addressing their Father. Our **access** is our liberty to speak to God in prayer. Our **confidence** is the assurance of a welcome, a hearing, and a wise and loving answer. And it is all **through faith in Him**, that is, our **faith in** the Lord Jesus Christ.

3:13 In view of the dignity of his ministry and the wonderful results that flowed from it, Paul encouraged the saints not to be disheartened when they thought of his sufferings. He was glad to endure **tribulations** in carrying out his mission to the Gentiles. Rather than being discouraged by his troubles, he says, in effect, they should be proud he was counted worthy to suffer for the Lord Jesus. They should rejoice to think of the benefit of his **tribulations** to them and to other Gentiles. They should see his current imprisonment as **glory**, not disgrace.

G. Paul's Prayer for the Saints (3:14–19)

3:14 Now the apostle picks up the thought he had begun in verse 1 and had interrupted with a parenthetical section on the mystery. Therefore, the words, **For this reason**, refer back to chapter 2 with its description of what the Gentiles had been by nature and what they had become through union with Christ. Their astonishing rise from poverty and death to riches and glory drives Paul to pray they will always live in the practical enjoyment of their exalted position.

His posture in prayer is indicated: **I bow my knees**. This does not mean kneeling must always be the posture of the body, though it should always be the posture of the soul. We may pray as we walk, sit, or recline, but our spirits should be bowed in humility and reverence.

The prayer is addressed **to the Father**. In a general sense, God is the Father of all mankind, meaning He is their Creator (Acts 17:28, 29). In a more restricted sense, He is the Father of all believers, meaning He has begotten them into His spiritual family (Gal. 4:6). In a unique sense He is **the Father of our Lord Jesus Christ**, meaning They are equal (John 5:18).

3:15 The particular role of the Father which Paul has in view is as the One **from whom the whole family in heaven and earth is named**. This may mean:

1. All the redeemed in heaven and on earth look to Him as Head of the family.
2. All created beings, angelic and human, owe their existence to Him not only as individuals but as families as well. Families in heaven include the various grades of angelic creatures. Families on earth are the different races springing from Noah and now divided into various nations.

3. All fatherhood in the universe derives its name from Him. The Fatherhood of God is the original and the ideal; it is the prototype of every other paternal relationship. Phillips translates the verse, "from whom all fatherhood, earthly or heavenly, derives its name."

3:16 We cannot help but be struck by the vastness of Paul's request: **That He would grant you,** *according to the riches of His glory*. He is going to ask that the saints might **be** spiritually **strengthened**. But to what extent? Jamieson, Fausset, and Brown answer: "in abundance, consonant to the riches of His glory; not 'according to' the narrowness of our hearts."[20] Preachers often point out that there is a difference between the expressions "out of the riches" and **according to the riches**. A wealthy person might give a trifling amount; it would be *out of* his riches, but *not in proportion* to them! Paul asks that God will give strength **according to** the riches of His perfections. Since the Lord is infinitely rich in glory, let the saints get ready for a deluge! Why should we ask so little of so great a King? When someone asked a tremendous favor of Napoleon it was immediately granted because, said Napoleon, "He honored me by the magnitude of his request."

> Thou art coming to a King,
> Large petitions with thee bring;
> For His grace and power are such,
> None can ever ask too much.
> – *John Newton*

Now we come to Paul's specific prayer requests. Instead of a series of disconnected petitions, we should think of them as a progression in which each petition lays the groundwork for the next. Picture them as a pyramid: the first request is the bottom layer of stones. As the prayer advances, Paul builds toward a glorious climax.

The first request is that they would **be strengthened with might through His**

Spirit in the inner man. The blessing sought is *spiritual* power. Not the power to perform spectacular miracles, but the spiritual vigor needed to be mature, stable, intelligent Christians. The One who imparts this power is the Holy **Spirit**. Of course, He can give us strength only as we feed on the word of God, as we breathe the pure air of prayer, and as we get exercise in daily service for the Lord.

This power is experienced **in the inner man**, that is, the spiritual part of our nature. It is **the inner man** that delights in the law of God (Rom. 7:22). It is **the inner man** that is renewed day by day, even though the outward man is perishing (2 Cor. 4:16). Though it is of God, our **inner man** needs strength, growth, and development.

3:17 The second step is **that Christ may dwell in your hearts through faith**. This is the result of the Spirit's invigoration: we are strengthened in order **that Christ may dwell in** our **hearts**. Actually, the Lord Jesus takes up His personal residence in a believer at the time of conversion (John 14:23; Rev. 3:20). But that is not the subject of this prayer. Here it is not a question of His being *in* the believer, but rather of His feeling *at home* there! He is a permanent Resident in every saved person, but this is a request that He might have full access to every room and closet; that He might not be grieved by sinful words, thoughts, motives, and deeds; that He might enjoy unbroken fellowship with the believer. The Christian heart thus becomes the home of Christ, the place where He loves to be — like the home of Mary, Martha, and Lazarus in Bethany. The heart, of course, means the center of the spiritual life; it controls every aspect of behavior. In effect, the apostle prays that the lordship of Christ might extend to the books we read, the work we do, the food we eat, the money we spend, the words we speak — in short, the minutest details of our lives.

The more we are strengthened by the Holy Spirit, the more we will be like the Lord Jesus Himself. And the more we are like Him, the more He will "settle down and feel completely at home in our hearts" (KSW).

We enter into the enjoyment of His indwelling **through faith**. This involves constant dependence on Him, constant surrender to Him, and constant recognition of His "at home-ness." It is **through faith** that we "practice His presence," as Brother Lawrence quaintly put it.

Up to this point Paul's prayer has involved each member of the Trinity. The Father is asked (v. 14) to strengthen the believers through His Spirit (v. 16) **that Christ** might be completely at home in their **hearts** (v. 17). One of the great privileges of prayer is that we can engage the eternal Godhead to work in behalf of others and ourselves.

The result of Christ's unrestricted access is that the Christian becomes **rooted and grounded in love**. Here Paul borrows words from the worlds of botany and building. The root of a plant provides nourishment and support. The groundwork of a building is the foundation on which it rests. As Scroggie says, "Love is the soil in which our life must have its roots; and it is the rock upon which our faith must ever rest."[21] To be **rooted and grounded in love** is to be established **in love** as a way of life. The life of **love** is a life of kindness, selflessness, brokenness, and meekness. It is the life of Christ finding expression in the believer (see 1 Cor. 13:4–7).

3:18 The preceding requests have outlined a program of spiritual growth and development which prepares the child of God to be fully able to grasp **with all the saints what is the width and length and depth and height**.

Before we consider the dimensions themselves, let us notice the expression, **with all the saints**. The subject is so great that no one believer can possibly grasp more than a small fraction of it. So there is need to study, discuss, and share with others. The Holy Spirit can use the combined meditations of a group of exercised believers to throw a flood of additional light on the Scriptures.

The dimensions are generally taken to refer to the love of Christ, although the text does not say this. In fact, the love of Christ is mentioned separately in the following clause. If the love of Christ is intended, then the connection might be shown as follows:

Width   — The world (John 3:16)
Length — Forever (1 Cor. 13:8)
Depth   — Even the death of the cross (Phil. 2:8)
Height — Heaven (1 John 3:1–2)

F. B. Meyer expresses it well:

There will always be as much horizon before us as behind us. And when we have been gazing on the face of Jesus for millenniums, its beauty will be as fresh and fascinating and fathomless as when we first saw it from the gate of Paradise.[22]

But these dimensions may also refer to the mystery which holds such an important place in Ephesians. In fact, it is easy to find these dimensions in the text itself:

1. The **width** is described in 2:11–18. It refers to the wideness of God's grace in saving Jews and Gentiles, and then incorporating them into the church. The mystery embraces both these segments of humanity.

2. The **length** extends from eternity to eternity. As to the past, believers were chosen in Christ before the foundation of the world (1:4). As to the future, eternity will be a perpetual unfolding of the exceeding riches of His grace in His kindness toward us through Christ Jesus (2:7).

3. The **depth** is vividly portrayed in 2:1–3. We were sunk in a pit of unspeakable sin and degradation. Christ came to this jungle of filth and corruption in order to die in our behalf.

4. The **height** is seen in 2:6, where we have not only been raised up with Christ, but enthroned in Him in the heavenlies to share His glory.

These are the dimensions, then, of immensity and, indeed, infinity. As we think of them, "all we can do," Scroggie says, "is to mark the order in this tumult of holy words."

3:19 The apostle's next request is that the saints might **know** by experience **the** knowledge-surpassing **love of Christ**. They could never explore it fully, because it is an ocean without shores, but they could learn more and more about it from day to day. And so he prays for a deep, experimental knowledge and enjoyment of the wonderful **love** of our wonderful Lord.

The climax in this magnificent prayer is reached when Paul prays **that you may be filled with** (lit. *unto,* Gk. *eis*) **all the fullness of God**. **All the fullness** of the Godhead dwells in the Lord Jesus (Col. 2:9). The more He dwells in our hearts by faith, the more we are **filled** unto **all**

the fullness of God. We could never be filled *with* all the fullness of God. But it is a goal toward which we move.

And yet having explained this, we must say there are depths of meaning here we have not reached. As we handle the Scriptures, we are aware that we are dealing with truths that are greater than our ability to understand or explain. We can use illustrations to throw light on this verse, for example, the thimble dipped in the ocean is filled with water, but how little of the ocean is in the thimble! Yet when we have said all this, the mystery remains, and we can only stand in awe at God's word and marvel at its infinity.

H. Paul's Doxology (3:20, 21)

3:20 The prayer closes with a soul-inspiring doxology. The preceding requests have been vast, bold, and seemingly impossible. But God **is able to do** more in this connection than **we** can **ask or think**. The extent of His ability is seen in the manner in which Paul pyramids words to describe superabundant blessings:

Able
Able to do
Able to do what **we ask**
Able to do what **we think**
Able to do what **we ask or think**
Able to do all that we ask or think
Able to do above all that we ask or think
Able to do abundantly above all that we ask or think
Able to do exceedingly abundantly above all that we ask or think

The means by which God answers prayer is given in the expression, **according to the power that works in us**. This refers to the Holy Spirit, Who is constantly at work in our lives, seeking to produce the fruit of a Christlike character, rebuking us because of sin, guiding us in prayer, inspiring us in worship, directing us in service. The more we are yielded to Him, the greater will be His effectiveness in conforming us to Christ.

3:21 To Him be glory in the church by Christ Jesus to all generations, forever and ever. Amen. God is the worthy object of eternal praise. His wisdom and power are displayed in the angelic hosts; in sun, moon, and stars; in animals, birds, and fish; in fire, hail, snow, and mist; in wind; in mountains, hills, trees;

in kings and people, old men and young; in Israel and the nations. All these are intended to praise the name of the Lord (Ps. 148).

But there is another group from which endless **glory** will be given to God, that is, **the church** — Christ the Head and believers, the Body. This redeemed community will be an eternal witness to His matchless, marvelous grace. Williams writes:

> The eternal glory of God as God and Father will be made visible throughout all ages in the Church and in Christ Jesus. Amazing statement! Christ and the Church as One Body will be the vehicle of that eternal demonstration.[23]

Even now the church should be giving glory to His name "in the services of praise, in the pure lives of its members, in its world-wide proclamation of the Gospel, and in its ministries to human distress and need" (Erdman).

The duration of this praise is **to all generations, forever and ever**. As we hear Paul call for eternal praise to God in the church and in Christ Jesus, the response of our hearts is a hearty **Amen!**

II. THE BELIEVER'S PRACTICE IN THE LORD (Chaps. 4–6)

A. Appeal for Unity in the Christian Fellowship (4:1–6)

4:1 There is a major break at this point in Ephesians. The previous chapters have dealt with the Christian's calling. In the last three chapters, he is urged to **walk worthy of** his **calling**. The position into which grace has lifted us was the dominant theme up to now. From here on it will be the practical outworking of that position. Our exalted standing in Christ calls for corresponding godly conduct. So it is true that Ephesians moves from the heavenlies in chapters 1–3, to the local church, to the home, and to general society in chapters 4–6. As Stott has pointed out, these closing chapters teach that "we must cultivate unity in the church, purity in our personal lives, harmony in our homes and stability in our combat with the powers of evil."

For the second time Paul refers to

himself as a **prisoner** — this time as a **prisoner of the Lord**. Theodoret comments: "What the world counted ignominy, he counts the highest honor, and he glories in his bonds for Christ, more than a king in his diadem."

As one who was imprisoned as a result of faithfulness and obedience to the Lord, Paul exhorts his readers **to walk worthy of** their **calling**. He does not command or direct. With tenderness and gentleness he appeals to them in the language of grace.

The word, **walk**, is found seven times in this Letter (2:2, 10; 4:1, 17; 5:2, 8, 15); it describes a person's entire lifestyle. A **worthy** walk is one that is consistent with a Christian's dignified position as a member of the Body of Christ.

4:2 In every sphere of life, it is important to show a Christlike spirit. This consists of:

Lowliness — a genuine humility that comes from association with the Lord Jesus. **Lowliness** makes us conscious of our own nothingness and enables us to esteem others better than ourselves. It is the opposite of conceit and arrogance.

Gentleness — the attitude that submits to God's dealings without rebellion, and to man's unkindness without retaliation. It is best seen in the life of Him who said, "I am gentle and lowly in heart." Wright comments:

> What an astonishingly wonderful statement! The One who made the worlds, who flung the stars into space and calls them by name, who preserves the innumerable constellations in their courses, who weighs the mountains in scales and the hills in a balance, who takes up the isles as a very little thing, who holds the waters of the ocean in the hollow of His hand, before whom the inhabitants of the earth are as grasshoppers, when He comes into human life finds Himself as essentially meek and lowly in heart. It is not that He erected a perfect human ideal and accommodated Himself to it; He *was* that.[24]

Longsuffering — an even disposition and a spirit of patience under prolonged provocation. This has been illustrated as follows: Imagine a puppy and a big dog together. As the puppy barks at the big dog, worrying and attacking him, the big dog, who could snap up the puppy with one bite, patiently puts up with the puppy's impertinence.

Bearing with one another in love — that is, making allowance for the faults and failures of others, or differing personalities, abilities, and temperaments. And it is not a question of maintaining a façade of courtesy while inwardly seething with resentment. It means positive love to those who irritate, disturb, or embarrass.

4:3 **Endeavoring to keep the unity of the spirit in the bond of peace.** In forming the church, God had eliminated the greatest division that had ever existed among human beings — the rift between Jews and Gentiles. In Christ Jesus these distinctions were abolished. But how would it work out in their life together? Would there still be lingering antagonisms? Would there be a tendency to form a "Jewish Church of Christ" and a "Church of the Nations"? To guard against any divisions or smoldering animosities, Paul now pleads for unity among Christians.

They should give diligence **to keep the unity of the Spirit**. The Holy **Spirit** has made all true believers one in Christ; the Body is indwelt by one **Spirit**. This is a basic **unity** that nothing can destroy. But by quarreling and bickering, believers can act as if it were not so. **To keep the unity of the Spirit** means to live at peace with one another. **Peace** is the ligament which binds the members of the Body together in spite of their wide natural differences. A common reaction when differences arise is to divide and start another party. The spiritual reaction is this: "In essentials, unity. In doubtful questions, liberty. In all things, charity." There is enough of the flesh in every one of us to wreck any local church or any other work of God. Therefore, we must submerge our own petty, personal whims and attitudes, and work together in **peace** for the glory of God and for common blessing.

4:4 Instead of magnifying differences, we should think of the seven positive realities which form the basis of true Christian unity.

One body. In spite of differences in race, color, nationality, culture, language, and temperament, there is only **one body**, made up of all true believers from Pentecost to the Rapture. Denominations, sects, and parties hinder the outworking of this truth. All such manmade divisions will be swept away when the Savior returns. Therefore, our watchword at the present time should be, "Let names and sects and parties fall, and Jesus Christ be all in all."

One Spirit. The same Holy **Spirit** who indwells each believer individually (1 Cor. 6:19) also indwells the Body of Christ (1 Cor. 3:16).

One hope. Every member of the church is called to one destiny — to be with Christ, to be like Him, and to share His glory endlessly. The **one hope** includes all that awaits the saints at the Return of the Lord Jesus and thereafter.

4:5 **One Lord**. "For even if there are so-called gods, whether in heaven or on earth (as there are many gods and many lords), yet for us there is one God, . . . and one Lord Jesus Christ, through whom are all things, and through whom we live" (1 Cor. 8:5, 6; see also 1 Cor. 1:2).

One faith. This is the Christian **faith**, the body of doctrine "once for all delivered to the saints" (Jude 3), and preserved for us in the NT.

One baptism. There is a twofold sense in which this is true. First, there is **one baptism** by the Spirit, by which those who trust Christ are placed in the body (1 Cor. 12:13). Then there is **one baptism** by which converts confess their identification with Christ in death, burial, and resurrection. Though there are different modes of baptism today, the NT recognizes one believers' baptism, in the name of the Father and of the Son and of the Holy Spirit. By being baptized, disciples express allegiance to Christ, the burial of their old self, and a determination to walk in newness of life.

4:6 **One God**. Every child of God recognizes **one God and Father of all** the redeemed, who is:

Above all — He is the supreme Sovereign of the universe.

Through all — He acts through all, using everything to accomplish His purposes.

In you all — He dwells in all believers, and is present in all places at one and the same time.

B. Program for Proper Functioning of the Members of the Body (4:7–16)

4:7 The doctrine of the unity of the Body of Christ has a twin truth, namely, the diversity of its members. Each member has a particular role assigned. No two members are alike, and no two have exactly the same function. The part to be played by each one is assigned **according to the measure of Christ's gift**, that is, He does it as He sees fit. If **Christ's gift** here means the Holy Spirit (John 14:16, 17; Acts 2:38, 39), then the thought is that the Holy Spirit is the One who assigns some gift to every saint, and who also gives the ability to exercise that gift. As each member fulfills his appointed work, the Body of Christ grows both spiritually and numerically.

4:8† In order to assist each child of God to find and fulfill his function, the Lord has given some special **gifts** of ministry, or service to the church. These should not be confused with the gifts mentioned in the previous verse. Every believer has some gift (v. 7), but not everyone is one of the **gifts** named in verse 11: these are special **gifts** designed for the growth of the body.

First, we find that the Giver of those special **gifts** is the risen, ascended, glorified Lord Jesus Christ. Paul quotes Psalm 68:18 as a prophecy that the Messiah would ascend to heaven, would conquer His foes and lead them **captive**, and, as a reward for His victory, would receive **gifts** for **men**.

4:9 But this raises a problem! How could the Messiah ascend to heaven? Had He not lived in heaven with God the Father from all eternity? Obviously, if He was to ascend to heaven, He must first come down from heaven. The prophecy of His Ascension in Psalm 68:18 implies a prior descent. So we might paraphrase verse 9 as follows: **"Now** when it says in Psalm 68 'He ascended' — what does it mean but that He also first descended into the lower parts of the earth."** We know that this is exactly what happened. The Lord Jesus **descended** to Bethlehem's manger, to the death of the cross, and to the grave. **The lower parts of the earth** have sometimes been taken to refer to hades

†See p. xxiii.

or hell. But that would not fit in with the argument here: His Ascension necessitated a previous descent to earth but not to hell. In addition, the Scriptures indicate that Christ's spirit went to heaven, not hell, when He died (Luke 23:43, 46).

The New English Bible translates this verse: "Now the word 'ascended' implies that he also descended to the lowest level, down to the very earth."

4:10 The prophecy of Psalm 68:18 and the descent implied in the prophecy were exactly fulfilled by the Incarnation, death, and burial of the Lord Jesus. The One **who descended** from heaven **is also the One who** conquered sin, Satan, demons, and death, and **who ascended far above** the atmosphere and stellar **heavens, that He might fill all things**.

He does **fill all things** in the sense that He is the source of all blessing, the sum of all virtues, and the supreme Sovereign over all. "There is not a place between the depth of the cross and the height of the glory which He has not occupied," writes F. W. Grant.[25]

The central thought in verses 8–10 is that the Giver of the gifts is the ascended Christ. There were no such gifts before He went back to heaven. This lends further support to the contention that the church did not exist in the OT; for if it did, it was a church without gifts.

4:11 The names of the gifts are now given. To our surprise we find they are men, not natural endowments or talents. **He Himself gave some to be apostles, some prophets, some evangelists, and some pastors and teachers**.

Apostles were men who were directly commissioned by the Lord to preach the word and to plant churches. They were men who had seen Christ in resurrection (Acts 1:22). They had power to perform miracles (2 Cor. 12:12) as a means of confirming the message they preached (Heb. 2:4). Together with NT prophets, their ministry was primarily concerned with the foundation of the church (Eph. 2:20). The apostles referred to in this passage mean only those who were apostles *after* the Ascension of Christ.

Prophets were spokesmen or mouthpieces of God. They received direct revelations from the Lord and passed them on to the church. What they spoke by the Holy Spirit was the word of God.

In the primary sense we no longer have apostles and prophets. Their ministry ended when the foundation of the church was laid, and when the NT canon was completed. We have already emphasized that Paul is speaking here of NT **prophets**; they were given by Christ after His Ascension. To think of them as OT prophets introduces difficulties and absurdities into the passage.

Evangelists are those who preach the good news of salvation. They are divinely equipped to win the lost to Christ. They have special ability to diagnose a sinner's condition, probe the conscience, answer objections, encourage decisions for Christ, and help the convert find assurance through the word. Evangelists should go out from a local church, preach to the world, then lead their converts to a local church where they will be fed and encouraged.

Pastors are men who serve as undershepherds of the sheep of Christ. They guide and feed the flock. Theirs is a ministry of wise counsel, correction, encouragement, and consolation.

The work of **pastors** is closely related to that of elders in a local church, the principal difference being that a pastor is a gift whereas the elder is an office. The NT pictures a number of pastors in a local church (Acts 20:17, 28; 1 Pet. 5:1, 2) rather than one pastor or presiding elder.

Teachers are men who are divinely empowered to explain what the Bible says, interpret what it means, and apply it to the hearts and consciences of the saints. Whereas an evangelist may preach the gospel from a passage out of context, the teacher seeks to show how the passage fits into the context.

Because **pastors and teachers** are linked in this verse, some conclude only one gift is intended, that it should read "pastor-teachers." But this is not necessarily so. A man may be a teacher without having the heart of a shepherd. And a pastor may be able to use the word without having the distinctive gift of teaching. If **pastors and teachers** are the same persons here in verse 11, then, by

the same rule of grammar,[26] so are apostles and prophets in 2:20.

One final word. We should be careful to distinguish between divine gifts and natural talents. No unsaved person, however talented, could be an evangelist, pastor, or teacher in the NT sense. Neither could a Christian, for that matter, unless he has received that particular gift. The gifts of the Spirit are supernatural. They enable a man to do what would be humanly impossible for him.

4:12 We come now to the function or purpose of the gifts. It is **for the equipping of the saints for the work of the ministry, for the edifying of the body of Christ**. The process is this:

1. The gifts equip **the saints**.
2. **The saints** then serve.
3. The **body** is then built up.

The ministry is not a specialized occupation limited to men with professional training. The word simply means *service*. It includes every form of spiritual service. And what this verse teaches is that every believer should be "in the ministry."

The gifts are given to perfect or equip all Christians to serve the Lord, and thus to build up **the body of Christ**. Vance Havner explains in his inimitable way:

> Every Christian is commissioned, for every Christian is a missionary. It has been said that the Gospel is not merely something to come to church to hear but something to go from the church to tell — and we are all appointed to tell it. It has also been said, 'Christianity began as a company of lay witnesses; it has become a professional pulpitism, financed by lay spectators!' Nowadays we hire a church staff to do 'full-time Christian work,' and we sit in church on Sunday to watch them do it. Every Christian is meant to be in full-time Christian service . . . There is indeed a special ministry of pastors, teachers and evangelists — but for what? . . . For the perfecting of the saints for their ministry.[27]

These divinely given men should not serve in such a way as to make people perpetually dependent on them. Instead, they should work toward the day when the saints will be able to carry on by themselves. We might illustrate this as follows:

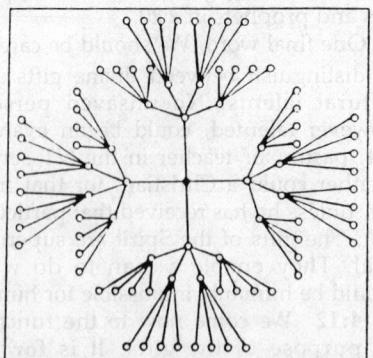

The circle in the center depicts, let us say, the gift of a teacher. He ministers to those in the circle around him so that they are equipped, that is, built up in the faith. Then they go forth and minister to others according to the gifts God has given them. In this way the church grows and expands. It is the divine method of producing growth in **the body of Christ**, both in size and spirituality.

Limitation of Christian service to a select class of men hinders the development of God's people, stifles the cause of world evangelism, and stunts the growth of the church. The distinction between clergy and laity is unscriptural and perhaps the greatest single hindrance to the spread of the gospel.

4:13 Verse 13 answers the question, "How long will this growth process continue?" The answer is **till we all come to** a state of **unity**, maturity, and conformity.

Unity. When the Lord takes His church home to heaven, we will all arrive at **the unity of the faith**. "Now we see in a mirror dimly" with regard to many matters. We have differences of opinion on a host of subjects. Then we will all be fully agreed. And we will reach **the unity of . . . the knowledge of the Son of God**. Here we have individual views of the Lord, of what He is like, of the implications of His teachings. Then we will see Him as He is, and know as we are known.

Maturity. At the Rapture we will also reach full growth or maturity. Both as individuals and as the Body of Christ, we will achieve perfection of spiritual development.

Conformity. And we will be conformed to Him. Everyone will be morally like **Christ**. And the universal church will be a full-grown Body, perfectly suited to its glorious Head. "The fulness of Christ is the Church itself, the fulness of Him that filleth all in all" (FWG). **The measure of the stature** of the church means its complete development, the fulfillment of God's plan for its growth.

4:14 When the gifts operate in their God-appointed manner, and the saints are active in service for the Lord, three dangers are avoided — immaturity, instability, and gullibility.

Immaturity. Believers who never become involved in aggressive service for Christ never emerge from being spiritual **children**. They are undeveloped through lack of exercise. It was to such that the writer to the Hebrews said, "For though by this time you ought to be teachers, you need someone to teach you again. . . ." (Heb. 5:12).

Instability. Another danger is spiritual fickleness. Immature Christians are susceptible to the grotesque novelties and fads of professional quacks. They become religious gypsies, moving **to and fro** from one appealing fantasy to another.

Gullibility. Most serious of all is the danger of deception. Those who are babes are unskillful in the word of righteousness, their senses are not exercised to discern between good and evil (Heb. 5:13, 14). They inevitably meet some false cultist who impresses them by his zeal and apparent sincerity. Because he uses religious words, they think he must be a true Christian. If they had studied the Bible for themselves, they would be able to see through his deceitful juggling of words. But now they are **carried about** by his **wind of doctrine** and led by unprincipled **cunning** into a form of systematized error.

4:15 The last two verses in the paragraph describe the proper process of growth in the Body of Christ. First, there is the necessity of doctrinal adherence: **but, speaking the truth**. . . . There can be no compromise as to the fundamentals of the faith. Second, there must be a right spirit: **but, speaking the truth in love**. If it is spoken in any other way, the result is a one-sided testimony. Blaikie admonishes:

> Truth is the element in which we are to live, move, and have our being. . . . But truth must be inseparably married to love; good tidings spoken harshly are not good tidings. The charm of the message is destroyed by the discordant spirit of the messenger.[28]

Then as the gifts equip the saints, and as the saints engage in active service, they **grow up in all things into** Christ. Christ is the aim and object of their growth, and the sphere of growth is **in all things**. In every area of their lives they become more like **Him**. As the Head has His way in the church, His Body will give an ever more accurate representation of Him to the world!

4:16 The Lord Jesus is not only the goal of growth, He is the source of growth as well. **From** Him **the whole body** is involved in the **growth** process. The marvelous integration of the members of the Body is described by the phrase, **joined and knit together**. This means that every member is exactly designed for his own place and function, and perfectly **joined** to every other member so as to make a complete, living organism. The importance, yes, the indispensability of every member is next indicated: **joined and knit together by what every joint supplies**. The human body consists primarily of bones, organs, and flesh. The bones are bound together by joints and ligaments, and the organs also are attached by ligaments. Each joint and ligament fulfills a role in the growth and usefulness of the body. So it is in **the body** of Christ. No member is superficial; even the most humble believer is necessary.

As each believer fulfills his proper role, **the body** grows as a harmonious, well-articulated unit. In a very real sense, **the body causes growth of the body**, paradoxical as it sounds. This simply means that **growth** is stimulated by **the body** itself as the members feed on the Bible, pray, worship, and witness for Christ. As Chafer said, "The Church, like the human body, is self-developing." In addition to growth in size, there is a building up **of itself in love**.

This speaks of the mutual concern of the members for one another. As Christians abide in Christ and fulfill their proper function in the church, they grow closer to one another **in love** and unity.

C. Appeal for a New Morality (4:17–5:21)

4:17 Here begins the apostle's eloquent appeal for a new morality, an appeal which extends to 5:21. Testifying **in the Lord**, that is, by authority of **the Lord** and by divine inspiration, he urges the Christians to put off every trace of their past life, as if it were a muddy coat, and to put on the virtues and excellencies of the Lord Jesus Christ. **You should no longer walk as the rest of the Gentiles walk**. They were no longer **Gentiles**; they were Christians. There should be a corresponding change in their lives. Paul saw the Christless world of the nations sunk in ignorance and degradation. Seven terrible things characterized them. They were:

Aimless. They walked **in the futility of their mind**. Their life was empty, purposeless, and fruitless. There was great activity but no progress. They chased bubbles and shadows, and neglected the great realities of life.

4:18 *Blind.* "They live blindfold in a world of illusion" (JBP). **Their understanding** was **darkened**. First, they had a native incapacity to understand spiritual truths, and then, because of their rejection of the knowledge of the true God, they suffered blindness as a judgment from the Lord.

Ungodly. They were **alienated from the life of God**, or at a great distance from Him. This was brought about by their willful, deep-seated ignorance and by the hardness of their hearts. They had rejected the light of God in creation and in conscience, and had turned to idolatry. Thereafter they had plunged farther and farther from God.

4:19 *Shameless.* They were **past feeling**. W. C. Wright explains:

> Moule translates it: "having got over the pain." How expressive! When conscience is at first denied, there is a twinge of pain; there is a protest that can be heard. But if the voice is silenced, presently the voice becomes less clear and clamant; the pro-

test is smothered; the twinge is less acute, until at last it is possible to "get over the pain."[29]

Sordid. They consciously gave **themselves over to lewdness**, that is, to vile forms of behavior. The cardinal sin of the Gentiles was and still is sexual immorality. They descended to unparalleled depths of depravity; the walls of Pompeii tell the story of shame and lost decency. The same sins characterize the Gentile world today.

Indecent. In their sexual sin, they worked **all uncleanness**. There is a suggestion here that they gave themselves up to every kind of **uncleanness** as if they were carrying on a trade or business in **lewdness**.

Insatiable. **With greediness**. They were never satisfied. They never had enough. Their sin created an enormous appetite for more of the same thing.

4:20 How different all this was from the **Christ** whom the Ephesians had come to know and love! He was the personification of purity and chastity. He knew no sin, He did no sin, there was no sin in Him.

4:21 The **if** in **if indeed you have heard Him and have been taught by Him** is not meant to cast doubt on the conversion of the Ephesians. It simply emphasizes that all those who had **heard** Christ and had **been taught by Him** had come to know Him as the essence of holiness and godliness. To have heard Christ means to have **heard Him** with the hearing of faith — to have accepted Him as Lord and Savior. The expression, **taught by Him**, refers to the instruction the Ephesians received as they walked in fellowship with Him subsequent to their conversion. Blaikie remarks: "All truth acquires a different hue and a different character when there is a personal relation to Jesus. Truth apart from the Person of Christ has little power."[30] **As the truth is in Jesus**. He not only teaches the truth; He is truth incarnate (John 14:6). The name **Jesus** takes us back to His life on earth, since that is His name in Incarnation. In that spotless life which He lived as a Man in this world, we see the very antithesis of the walk of the Gentiles which Paul has just described.

4:22 In the school of Christ we learn that at the time of conversion we put away our **old man which grows corrupt** through **deceitful lusts**. **The old man** means all that a person was before his conversion, all that he was as a child of Adam. It is corrupted as a result of giving in to **deceitful**, evil cravings which are pleasant and promising in anticipation but hideous and disappointing in retrospect. As far as his position in Christ is concerned, the believer's **old man** was crucified and buried with Christ. In practice, the believer should reckon it to be dead. Here Paul is emphasizing the positional side of the truth — we have **put off the old man** once for all.

4:23 A second lesson the Ephesians learned at the feet of Jesus was that they were being **renewed in the spirit of** their **mind**. This points to a complete aboutface in their thinking, a change from mental impurity to holiness. The Spirit of God influences the thought processes to reason from God's standpoint, not from that of unsaved men.

4:24 The third lesson is that they had **put on the new man** once for all. **The new man** is what a believer is in Christ. It is the new creation, in which old things have passed away and all things have become new (2 Cor. 5:17). This **new** kind of **man** is **according to God**, that is, **created** in His likeness. And it manifests itself **in true righteousness and holiness**. **Righteousness** means right conduct toward others. **Holiness** is "piety towards God, which puts Him in His place," as F. W. Grant defines it.[31]

4:25 Paul now moves from the believers' standing to their state. Because they have put off the old man and have put on the new man through their union with Christ, they should demonstrate this startling reversal in their everyday lives.

They can do this, first, by **putting away lying** and putting on truthfulness. **Lying** here includes every form of dishonesty, whether it is shading of the truth, exaggeration, cheating, failure to keep promises, betrayal of confidence, flattery, or fudging on income taxes. The Christian's word should be absolutely trustworthy. His yes should mean yes, and his no, no. The life of a Christian becomes a libel rather than a Bible when he stoops to any form of tampering with truthfulness.

Truth is a debt we owe to all men. However, when Paul uses the word, **neighbor**, here, he is thinking particularly of our fellow believers. This is clear from the motive given: **for we are members of one another** (cf. Rom. 12:5; 1 Cor. 12:12–27). It is as unthinkable for one Christian to lie to another as it would be for a nerve in the body to deliberately send a false message to the brain, or for the eye to deceive the rest of the body when danger is approaching.

4:26 A second area for practical renewal in our lives is in connection with sinful **wrath** and righteous anger. There are times when a believer may be righteously **angry**, for instance, when the character of God is impugned. In such cases anger is commanded: **Be angry**. Anger against evil can be righteous. But there are other times when anger is sinful. When it is an emotion of malice, jealousy, resentment, vindictiveness, or hatred because of personal wrongs, it is forbidden. Aristotle said, "Anybody can become angry — that is easy; but to be angry with the right person, to the right degree, at the right time, for the right purpose, and in the right way — that is *not* easy."

If a believer gives way to unrighteous **wrath**, he should confess and forsake it quickly. Confession should be made both to God and to the victim of his anger. There should be no nursing of grudges, no harboring of resentments, no carrying over of irritations. **Do not let the sun go down on your wrath**. Anything that mars fellowship with God or with our brethren should immediately be made right.

4:27 Unconfessed sins of temper provide **the devil** with a foothold or a base of operations. He is capable of finding plenty of these without our deliberately helping him. Therefore, we must not excuse malice, wrath, envy, hatred, or passion in our lives. These sins discredit the Christian testimony, stumble the unsaved, offend believers, and harm ourselves spiritually and physically.

4:28 Now Paul turns his attention to the contrasting behavior patterns of stealing and sharing. The old man steals;

the new man shares. Put off the old; put on the new! The fact that Paul would ever address such instruction as **"Let him who stole steal no longer"** to believers disproves any notion that Christians are sinlessly perfect. They still have the old, evil, selfish nature that must be reckoned dead in daily experience. Stealing may take many forms — all the way from grand larceny to nonpayment of debts, to witnessing for Christ on the employer's time, to plagiarism, to the use of false measurements, and to falsifying expense accounts. Of course, this prohibition against stealing is not new. The Law of Moses forbade theft (Ex. 20:15). It is what follows that makes the passage distinctively Christian. Not only should we refrain from stealing, we should actually **labor** in an honorable occupation in order to be able to share with others who are less fortunate. Grace, not law, is the power of holiness. Only the positive power of grace can turn a thief into a philanthropist.

This is radical and revolutionary. The natural approach is for men to work for the supply of their own needs and desires. When their income rises, their standard of living rises. Everything in their lives revolves around self. This verse suggests a nobler, more exalted view of secular employment. It is a means of supplying a modest standard of living for one's family, but also of alleviating human **need**, spiritual and temporal, at home and abroad. And how vast that **need** is!

4:29 The apostle now turns to the subject of speech, and contrasts that which is worthless with that which edifies. **Corrupt** speech generally means conversation that is filthy and suggestive; this would include off-color jokes, profanity, and dirty stories. But here it probably has the wider sense of any form of conversation that is frivolous, empty, idle, and worthless. Paul deals with obscene and vile language in 5:4; here he is telling us to abandon profitless speech and substitute constructive conversation. The Christian's speech should be:

Edifying. It should result in, building up the hearers.

Appropriate. It should be suitable to the occasion.

Gracious. It should **impart grace to the hearers**.

4:30 And do not grieve the Holy Spirit of God, by whom you were sealed for the day of redemption. If this is taken in connection with the preceding verse, it means that worthless talk grieves the Spirit. It may also be linked to verses 25–28 to indicate that lying, unrighteous anger, and stealing also hurt Him. Or in a still wider sense, it may be saying that we should abstain from anything and everything that grieves Him.

Three powerful reasons are suggested:

1. He is the *Holy* Spirit. Anything that is not holy is distasteful to Him.

2. He is the Holy Spirit of **God**, a member of the blessed Trinity.

3. We **were sealed** by Him **for the day of redemption**. As mentioned previously, a seal speaks of ownership and security. He is the seal that guarantees our preservation until Christ returns for us and our salvation is complete. Interestingly enough, Paul here uses the eternal security of the believer as one of the strongest reasons why we should *not* sin.

The fact that He can be grieved shows that the Holy Spirit is a Person, not a mere influence. It also means He loves us, because only a person who loves can be grieved. The favorite ministry of God's Spirit is to glorify Christ and to change the believer into His likeness (2 Cor. 3:18). When a Christian sins, He has to turn from this ministry to one of restoration. It grieves Him to see the believer's spiritual progress interrupted by sin. He must then lead the Christian to the place of repentance and confession of sin.

4:31 All sins of temper and tongue should be put away. The apostle lists several of them. Though it is not possible to distinguish each one precisely, the overall meaning is clear:

Bitterness — Smoldering resentment, unwillingness to forgive, harsh feeling.

Wrath — Bursts of rage, violent passion, temper tantrums.

Anger — Grouchiness, animosity, hostility.

Clamor — Loud outcries of anger,

bawling, angry bickering, shouting down of opponents.

Evil speaking — Insulting language, slander, abusive speech.

Malice — Wishing evil on others, spite, meanness.

4:32 The foregoing sins of temper should be terminated, but the vacuum must be filled by the cultivation of Christlike qualities. The former are natural vices; the following are supernatural virtues:

Kindness — An unselfish concern for the welfare of others, and a desire to be helpful even at great personal sacrifice.

Tenderheartedness — A sympathetic, affectionate, and compassionate interest in others, and a willingness to bear their burden.

Forgiveness — A readiness to pardon offenses, to overlook personal wrongs against oneself, and to harbor no desire for retaliation.

The greatest example of One who forgives is God Himself. The basis of His forgiveness is the work of Christ at Calvary. And we are the unworthy objects. God could not forgive sin without proper satisfaction being made. In His love He provided the satisfaction which His righteousness demanded. **In Christ**, that is, in His Person and work, God found a righteous basis on which He could forgive us.

Since He forgave us when we were in debt "millions of dollars," we ought to forgive others when they owe us "a few dollars" (Matt. 18:23–28. JBP). Lenski counsels:

> The moment a man wrongs me I must forgive him. Then *my* soul is free. If I hold the wrong against him I sin against God and against him and jeopardize my forgiveness with God. Whether the man repents, makes amends, asks my pardon or not, makes no difference. I have instantly forgiven him. He must face God with the wrong he has done; but that is his affair and God's and not mine save that I should help him according to Matt. 18:15, etc. But whether this succeeds or not and before this even begins, I must forgive him.[32]

5:1 God's example of forgiveness in 4:32 forms the basis of Paul's exhortation here. The connection is this: God in Christ has forgiven you. Now **be imita-**

tors of God in forgiving one another. A special motive is appended in the words, **as dear children**. In natural life, children bear the family likeness and should seek to uphold the family name. In spiritual life, we should manifest our Father to the world and seek to walk worthy of our dignity as His beloved **children.**

5:2 Another way in which we should resemble the Lord is by walking **in love**. The rest of the verse explains that to **walk in love** means to give ourselves for others. This is what Christ, our perfect Example, did. Amazing fact! He loved us. The proof of His love is that He gave Himself for us in death at Calvary.

His gift is described as **an offering and a sacrifice to God. An offering** is anything given to God; **a sacrifice** here includes the additional element of death. He was the true burnt **offering**, the One who was completely devoted to do the will of God, even to the death of the cross. His **sacrifice** of unspeakable devotion is eulogized as being **for a sweet-smelling aroma**. F. B. Meyer comments, "In love so measureless, so reckless of cost, for those who were naturally so unworthy of it, there was a spectacle which filled heaven with fragrance and God's heart with joy."[33]

The Lord Jesus pleased His Father by giving Himself for others. The moral is that we too can bring joy to God by giving ourselves for others.

> Others, Lord, yes, others!
> Let this my motto be;
> Help me to live for others
> That I may live like Thee.
> – *Charles D. Meigs*

5:3 In verses 3 and 4 the apostle reverts to the topic of sexual sins and decisively calls for saintly separation from them. First, he mentions various forms of sexual immorality:

Fornication. Whenever it is mentioned in the same verse as adultery, **fornication** means illicit intercourse among *unmarried* persons. However, when, as here, the word is not distinguished from adultery, it probably refers to *any* form of sexual immorality, and the NKJV usually so translates it. (Our word "pornography," literally, "whore-writing," is related to the word translated **fornication**.)

Uncleanness. This too may mean immoral acts, but perhaps it can also include impure pictures, obscene books, and other suggestive materials that go along with lives of indecency and that feed the fires of passion.

Covetousness. While we generally think of this as meaning the lust for money, here it refers to sensual desire — the insatiable greed to satisfy one's sexual appetite outside the bounds of marriage. (See Ex. 20:17: "You shall not covet . . . your neighbor's wife. . . .")

These things should **not even be named among** Christians. It goes without saying that they should never have to be named as *having been committed* by believers. They should not even be *discussed* in any way that might lessen their sinful and shameful character. There is always the greatest danger in speaking lightly of them, making excuses for them, or even discussing them familiarly and continually. Paul accents his exhortation with the phrase, **as is fitting for saints**. Believers have been separated from the corruption that is in the world; now they should live in practical separation from dark passion, both in deed and word.

5:4 Their speech should also be free from every trace of:

Filthiness. This refers to dirty stories, suggestive jokes with a sexual coloring, and all forms of obscenity and indecency.

Foolish talking. This means empty conversation that is worthy of a moron. Here it may include gutter language.

Coarse jesting. This means jokes or talk with unsavory, hidden meanings. To talk about something, to joke about it, to make it a frequent subject of conversation is to introduce it into your mind, and to bring you closer to actually doing it.

It is always dangerous to joke about sin. Instead of using his tongue for such unworthy and unbecoming talk, the Christian should deliberately cultivate the practice of expressing **thanks** to God for all the blessings and mercies of life. This is pleasing to the Lord, a good example to others, and beneficial to one's own soul.

5:5 There is no room for doubt as to God's attitude toward immoral persons: they have no **inheritance in the kingdom of Christ and God**. This verdict is in sharp contrast to the world's current attitude that sex offenders are sick and need psychiatric treatment. Men say immorality is a sickness; God calls it sin. Men condone it; God condemns it. Men say the answer is psychoanalysis; God says the answer is regeneration.

Three offenders are specified, the same three found in verse 3 — the **fornicator**, the **unclean person**, and the **covetous man**. Here the thought is added that a **covetous** person **is an idolater**. One reason he **is an idolater** is that he has a false impression of what God is like: his concept of God is a Being who approves sensual greed, otherwise, he would not dare be covetous. Another reason why covetousness is idolatry is that it puts the person's own will above the will of God. A third reason is that it results in the worship of the creature rather than the Creator (Rom. 1:25).

When Paul says that such persons have no **inheritance in the kingdom**, he means precisely that. People whose lives are characterized by these sins are lost, are in their sins, and are on the way to hell. They are not in the invisible **kingdom** at the present time; they will not be in **the kingdom** when Christ returns to reign; and they will be forever shut out from the everlasting **kingdom** in heaven. The apostle is not saying these are people who, though they are in **the kingdom**, will suffer loss at the Judgment Seat of Christ. The subject is salvation, not rewards. They may profess to be Christians, but they prove by their lives that they were never saved. They *can* be saved, of course, by repentance and faith in the Lord Jesus. But if they are genuinely converted, they will no longer practice these sins.

Notice that the deity of Christ is implied in the expression, **the kingdom of Christ and God**. **Christ** is put on an equal level with **God** the Father as Ruler in **the kingdom**.

5:6 Many people of the world adopt an increasingly lenient and tolerant attitude toward sexual immorality. They say the gratification of bodily appetites is needful and beneficial, and that their repression produces warped, inhibited personalities. They say morals are entirely a matter of the culture in which we

live, and that since "pre-marital," "extra-marital," and "gay" sex (which God's word condemns as fornication, adultery, and perversion) are accepted in our culture, they ought to be legalized. Surprisingly enough, some of the leading spokesmen in favor of making sexual sins acceptable are men who hold high positions in the professing church. Thus, the laymen who always thought immorality was immoral are now being assured by prominent clergymen that such an attitude is passé.

Christians should not be hoodwinked by such double talk. **Because of these things the wrath of God comes upon the sons of disobedience**. The Lord's attitude toward such sins as fornication and adultery was seen in Numbers 25:1–9: twenty-four thousand Israelites were slain because they sinned with the women of Moab. The Lord's attitude toward homosexuality was displayed when Sodom and Gomorrah were destroyed by brimstone and fire from heaven (Gen. 19:24, 28).

But God's **wrath** is displayed not only in such supernatural acts of punishment. Those who practice sexual sins experience His judgment in other ways. There are physical effects, such as venereal disease and AIDS. There are mental, nervous, and emotional disorders arising from a sense of guilt. There are changes in the personality — the effeminate often becomes even more so (Rom. 1:27). And of course there will be the final, eternal judgment of God on fornicators and adulterers (Heb. 13:4). No mercy will be shown to **sons of disobedience** — to those who are descended from disobedient Adam and who willfully follow him in disobeying God (Rev. 21:8).

5:7 Believers are solemnly warned to have no part in such ungodly behavior. To do so is to dishonor the name of Christ, to wreck other lives, to ruin one's own testimony, and to invite a torrent of retribution.

5:8 To enforce his urgent imperative in verse 7, the apostle now gives a pithy discourse on **darkness** and **light** (vv. 8–14). The Ephesians **were once darkness, but now** they **are light in the Lord**. Paul does not say they were *in* the darkness, but that they themselves *were* the personification of **darkness**. Now, through union with the Lord, they have become **light**. He is light; they are in Him; so **now** they **are light in the Lord**. Their state should henceforth correspond with their standing. They should **walk as children of light**.

5:9 This parenthesis explains the type of **fruit** produced by those who walk in the light.

The fruit of the Spirit[34] consists of **all forms of goodness, righteousness, and truth**. **Goodness** here is an inclusive term for all moral excellence. **Righteousness** means integrity in all dealings with God and men. **Truth** is honesty, equity, and reality. Put them all together and you have the light of a Christ-filled life shining out in a scene of dismal darkness.

5:10 Those who walk in the light not only produce the type of fruit listed in the preceding verse, but also find **out what is acceptable to the Lord**. They put every thought, word, and action to the test. What does **the Lord** think about this? How does it appear in His presence? Every area of life comes under the searchlight — conversation, standard of living, clothes, books, business, pleasures, entertainments, furniture, friendships, vacations, cars, and sports.

5:11 Believers should **have no fellowship with the unfruitful works of darkness**, either by participation or by any attitude that might indicate tolerance or leniency. These **works of darkness** are **unfruitful** as far as God and men are concerned. It was this feature of utter barrenness that once prompted Paul to ask the Roman Christians, "What fruit did you have then in the things of which you are now ashamed?" (Rom. 6:21). Then too they are **works of darkness**: they belong to the world of dim lights, drawn drapes, locked doors, secret rooms. They reflect man's natural preference for **darkness** and his abhorrence of light when his deeds are evil (John 3:19). The believer is called not only to abstain from **the unfruitful works of darkness**, but positively he is called to **expose them**. He does this in two ways: first, by a life of holiness, and second, by words of correction spoken under the direction of the Holy Spirit.

5:12 Now the apostle explains why the Christian must have no complicity with moral corruption and must rebuke it. The vile sins which people commit in secret are so debased that **it is shameful even to** mention them, let alone commit them. The unnatural forms of sin which man has invented are so bad that even to describe them would defile the minds of those who listened. So the Christian is taught to refrain from even talking about them.

5:13 **Light makes manifest** whatever is in the darkness. So a holy Christian life reveals by contrast the sinfulness of unregenerate lives. And appropriate words of rebuke reveal sin in its true character also. Blaikie illustrates:

> As, for instance, when our Lord reproved the hypocrisy of the Pharisees — their practices had not seemed to the disciples very evil before, but when Christ threw on them the pure light of truth, they were made manifest in their true character — they appeared and they still appear, odious.[35]

The latter part of verse 13 may better read: **for whatever** *is made* **manifest is light**.[36] This simply means that when Christians exercise their ministry as light, others are brought to the light. Wicked men are transformed into children of light through the reproving ministry of **light**.

It is not a rule without exceptions, of course. Not everyone who is exposed to the light becomes a Christian. But it is a general principle in the spiritual realm that light has a way of reproducing itself. We find an illustration of the principle in 1 Peter 3:1, where believing wives are taught to win their unbelieving husbands to Christ by the example of their lives: "Wives, likewise, be submissive to your own husbands, that even if some do not obey the word, they, without a word, may be won by the conduct of their wives." Thus the light of Christian wives triumphs over the darkness of heathen husbands, and the latter become light.

5:14 The life of the believer should always be preaching a sermon, should always be exposing the surrounding darkness, should always be extending this invitation to unbelievers:

**"Awake, you who sleep,
Arise from the dead,
And Christ will give you light."**

This is the voice of light speaking to those who are sleeping in darkness and lying in spiritual death. The light calls them to life and illumination. If they answer the invitation, **Christ will** shine on them and **give** them **light.**

5:15 In the next seven verses, Paul contrasts foolish footsteps and careful conduct by a series of negative and positive exhortations. The first is a general plea to his readers to **walk not as fools but as wise.** As mentioned previously, **walk,** is one of the key words of the Epistle: it is mentioned seven times to describe "the whole round of the activities of the individual life." To **walk circumspectly** is to live in the light of our position as God's children. To **walk as fools** means to descend from this high plane to the conduct of worldly men.

5:16 The walk of wisdom calls us to redeem **the time** or buy up the opportunities. Every day brings its opened doors, its vast potential. **Redeeming the time** means living lives noted for holiness, deeds of mercy, and words of help. What lends special urgency to this matter is the **evil** character of **the days** in which we live. They remind us God will not always strive with man, the day of grace will soon close, the opportunities for worship, witness, and service on earth will soon be forever ended.

5:17 So we should **not be unwise, but understand what the will of the Lord is.** This is crucial. Because of the abounding evil and the shortness of the time, we might be tempted to spend our days in frantic and feverish activity of our own choosing. But this would amount to nothing but wasted energy. The important thing is to find out God's **will** for us each day and do it. This is the only way to be efficient and effective. It is all too possible to carry on Christian work according to our own ideas and in our own strength, and be completely out of **the will of the Lord.** The path of wisdom is to discern God's **will** for our individual lives, then to obey it to the hilt.

5:18 And do not be drunk with wine, in which is dissipation. In our North American culture, such a command seems almost shocking and unnecessary, since total abstinence is the rule among so many Christians. But we must remember that the Bible was written for believers in all cultures, and in many

countries wine is still a fairly common beverage on the table. The Scriptures do not condemn the use of wine, but they do condemn its abuse. The use of wine as a medicine is recommended (Prov. 31:6; 1 Tim. 5:23). The Lord Jesus made wine for use as a beverage at the wedding in Cana of Galilee (John 2:1–11).

But the use of wine becomes abuse under the following circumstances and is then forbidden:

1. When it leads to excess (Prov. 23:29–35).
2. When it becomes habit-forming (1 Cor. 6:12b).
3. When it offends the weak conscience of another believer (Rom. 14:13; 1 Cor. 8:9).
4. When it hurts a Christian's testimony in the community and is therefore not to the glory of God (1 Cor. 10:31).
5. When there is any doubt in the Christian's mind about it (Rom. 14:23).

Paul's recommended alternative to being **drunk with wine** is being **filled with the Spirit.** This connection too may startle us at first, but when we compare and contrast the two states, we see why the apostle links them in this way.

First, there are certain similarities:

1. In both conditions, the person is under a power outside himself. In one case it is the power of intoxicating liquor (sometimes called "spirits"); in the other case it is the power of **the Spirit.**
2. In both conditions, the person is fervent. On the Day of Pentecost, the fervency produced by **the Spirit** was mistaken for that produced by new wine (Acts 2:13).
3. In both conditions, the person's walk is affected — his physical walk in the case of drunkenness and his moral behavior in the other instance.

But there are two ways in which the two conditions present sharp contrasts:

1. In the case of drunkenness, there is **dissipation** and debauchery. The Spirit's filling never produces these.
2. In the case of drunkenness, there is loss of self-control. But the fruit of **the Spirit** is self-control (Gal. 5:23).

A believer who is filled **with the Spirit** is never transported outside himself where he can no longer control his actions; the spirit of a prophet is always subject to the prophet (1 Cor. 14:32).

Sometimes in the Bible, the filling **with the Spirit** seems to be presented as a sovereign gift of God. For instance, John the Baptist was **filled with the** Holy **Spirit** from his mother's womb (Luke 1:15). In such a case, the person receives it without any prior conditions to be met. It is not something for which he works or prays; the Lord gives it as He pleases. Here in Ephesians 5:18 the believer is *commanded* to **be filled with the Spirit**. It involves action on his part. He must meet certain conditions. It is not automatic but the result of obedience.

For this reason the Spirit's filling should be distinguished from certain other of His ministries. It is *not* the same as any of the following functions:

1. *The baptism* by the Holy Spirit. This is the work of the Spirit which incorporates the believer in the body of Christ (1 Cor. 12:13).
2. *The indwelling.* By this ministry the Comforter takes up His residence in the body of the Christian and empowers him for holiness, worship, and service (John 14:16).
3. *The anointing.* **The Spirit** Himself is the anointing who teaches the child of God the things of the Lord (1 John 2:27).
4. *The earnest* and *the seal.* We have already seen that the Holy Spirit as the earnest guarantees the inheritance for the saint, and as the seal He guarantees the saint for the inheritance (Eph. 1:13, 14).

These are some of the ministries of the Spirit which are realized in a person the moment he is saved. Everyone who is in Christ automatically has the baptism, the indwelling, the anointing, the earnest, and the seal.

But the filling is different. It is not a once-for-all crisis experience in the life of a disciple; rather it is a continuous process. The literal translation of the command is "Be being filled with the Spirit." It may begin as a crisis experience, but it must continue thereafter as a moment-by-moment process. Today's filling will not do for tomorrow. And certainly it is a state greatly to be desired. In fact, it is the ideal condition of the believer on earth. It means that the Holy Spirit is having His way relatively ungrieved in the life of the Christian, and that the believer is therefore fulfilling his role in the plan of God for that time.

How then can a believer **be filled with the Spirit**? The Apostle Paul does not tell us here in Ephesians; he merely commands us to **be filled**. But from other parts of the word, we know that in order to **be filled with the Spirit** we must:

1. Confess and put away all known sin in our lives (1 John 1:5–9). It is obvious that such a holy Person cannot work freely in a life where sin is condoned.
2. Yield ourselves completely to His control (Rom. 12:1, 2). This involves the surrender of our will, our intellect, our body, our time, our talents, and our treasures. Every area of life must be thrown open to His dominion.
3. Let the word of Christ dwell in us richly (Col. 3:16). This involves reading the word, studying it, and obeying it. When the word of Christ dwells in us richly, the same results follow (Col. 3:16) as follow the filling of **the Spirit** (Eph. 5:19).
4. Finally, we must be emptied of self (Gal. 2:20). To be filled with a new ingredient a cup must first be emptied of the old. To **be filled with** *Him*, we must first be emptied of *us*.

An unknown author writes:

Just as you have left the whole burden of your sin, and have rested on the finished work of Christ, so leave the whole burden of your life and service, and rest upon the present inworking of the Holy Spirit. Give yourself up, morning by morning, to be led by the Holy Spirit and go forth praising and at rest, leaving Him to manage you and your day. Cultivate the habit all through the day, of joyfully depending upon and obeying Him, expecting Him to guide, to enlighten, to reprove, to teach, to use, and to do in and with you what He wills. Count upon His working as a fact, altogether apart from sight or feeling. Only let us believe in and obey the

Holy Spirit as the Ruler of our lives, and cease from the burden of trying to manage ourselves; then shall the fruit of the Spirit appear in us as He wills to the glory of God.

Does a person know it when he is **filled with the Spirit**? Actually, the closer we are to the Lord, the more we are conscious of our own complete unworthiness and sinfulness (Isa. 6:1–5). In His presence, we find nothing in ourselves to be proud of (Luke 5:8). We are not aware of any spiritual superiority over others, any sense of "having arrived." The believer who is **filled with the Spirit** is occupied with Christ and not with self.

At the same time, he may have a realization that God is working in and through his life. He sees things happen in a supernatural way. Circumstances click miraculously. Lives are touched for God. Events move according to a divine timetable. Even forces of nature are on his side; they seem chained to the chariot wheels of the Lord. He sees all this; he realizes that God is working for and through him; and yet he feels strangely detached from it all as far as taking any credit is concerned. In his inmost being, he realizes it is all of the Lord.

5:19 Now the apostle gives four results of being filled with the Spirit. First, Spirit-filled Christians speak **to one another in psalms and hymns and spiritual songs**. The divine infilling opens the mouth to talk about the things of the Lord, and enlarges the heart to share these things with others. While some see all three categories as parts of the Book of Psalms, we understand only **psalms** to mean the inspired writings of David, Asaph, and others. **Hymns** are noninspired songs which ascribe worship and praise directly to God. **Spiritual songs** are any other lyrical compositions dealing with spiritual themes, even though not addressed directly to God.

A second evidence of the filling is inward joy and praise to God: **singing and making melody in your heart to the Lord**. The Spirit-filled life is a fountain, bubbling over with joy (Acts 13:52). Zacharias is an illustration: when he was filled with the Holy Spirit, he sang with all his heart to the Lord (Luke 1:67–79).

5:20 A third result is thanksgiving:

giving thanks always for all things to God the Father in the name of our Lord Jesus Christ. Where the Spirit reigns, there is gratitude **to God**, a deep sense of appreciation, and a spontaneous expression of it. It is not occasional, but continual. Not only for the pleasant things, but for all things. Anyone can be thankful for sunshine; it takes the power of the Spirit to be thankful for the storms of life.

The shortest, surest way to all happiness is this:

Make it a rule to thank and praise God for everything that happens to you. For it is certain that whatever seeming calamity comes to you, if you thank and praise God for it, you turn it into a blessing. If you could work miracles, you could not do more for yourself than by this thankful spirit: for it needs not a word spoken and turns all that it touches into happiness. (Selected)

5:21 The fourth test of being Spirit-filled is **submitting to one another in the fear of God**. Erdman admonishes:

It is a phrase too often neglected. . . . It names a test of spirituality which Christians too seldom apply. . . . Many persons feel that shouts of hallelujah and exulting songs and the utterance of praise in more or less "unknown tongues" are all proofs of being "filled with the Spirit." These all may be spurious and deceitful and without meaning. Submission to our fellow Christians, modesty of demeanor, humility, unwillingness to dispute, forbearance, gentleness — these are the unmistakable proofs of the Spirit's power. . . .Such mutual submission to their fellow Christians should be rendered "in the fear of Christ," that is, in reverence to him who is recognized as the Lord and Master of all.[37]

These then are results of the Spirit's filling — speaking, singing, thanking, and submitting. But there are at least four others:

1. Boldness in rebuking sin (Acts 13:9–12), and in testifying for the Lord (Acts 4:8–12, 31; 13:52–14:3).
2. Power for service (Acts 1:8; 6:3, 8; 11:24).
3. Generosity, not selfishness (Acts 4:31, 32).
4. Exaltation of Christ (Acts 9:17, 20) and of God (Acts 2:4, 11; 10:44, 46).

We should earnestly desire to be

filled with the Spirit, but only for the glory of God, not for our own glory.

D. Appeal for Personal Piety in the Christian Household (5:22–6:9)

5:22 Though a new section begins here, there is a close link with the preceding verse. There Paul had listed subjection to one another as one of the results of the divine infilling. In the section from 5:22 to 6:9, he cites three specific areas in the Christian household where submission is the will of God:

Wives should **submit to** their *own husbands.*

Children should submit to their *parents.*

Bondservants should submit to their *masters.*

The fact that all believers are one in Christ Jesus does not mean that earthly relationships are abolished. We must still respect the various forms of authority and government which God has instituted. Every well-ordered society rests on two supporting pillars — authority and submission. There must be some who exercise authority and some who submit to that rule. This principle is so basic that it is found even in the Godhead: "But I want you to know that . . . the head of Christ is God" (1 Cor. 11:3). God ordained human government. No matter how wicked a government may be, yet from God's standpoint it is better than no government, and we should obey it as far as we can without disobeying or denying the Lord. The absence of government is anarchy, and no society can survive under anarchy.

The same is true in the home. There must be a head, and there must be obedience to that head. God ordained that the place of headship be given to the man. He indicated this by creating man first, then creating woman for the man. Thus, both in the order and purpose of creation, He put man in the place of authority and woman in the place of submission.

Submission never implies inferiority. The Lord Jesus is submissive to God the Father, but in no way is He inferior to Him. Neither is the woman inferior to the man. In many ways she may be superior — in devotedness, in sympa-

thy, in diligence, and in heroic endurance. But **wives** are commanded to **submit to** their **own husbands, as to the Lord**. In submitting to the authority of her husband, a wife is submitting to the Lord's authority. This in itself should remove any attitude of reluctance or rebellion.

History abounds with illustrations of the chaos resulting from disobedience to God's pattern. By usurping the place of leadership, and acting for her husband, Eve introduced sin into the human race, with all its catastrophic results. In more recent times many of the false cults were started by women who usurped a place of authority which God never intended them to have. Women who leave their God-appointed sphere can wreck a local church, break up a marriage, and destroy a home.

On the other hand, there is nothing more attractive than a woman fulfilling the role which God has assigned to her. A full-length portrait of such a woman is given in Proverbs 31 — an enduring memorial to the wife and mother who pleases the Lord.

5:23 The reason for the wife's submission is that her **husband is** her **head**. He occupies the same relation to her that Christ occupies to the church. **Christ is head of the church; and He is the Savior of the body**. (The word Savior here can have the meaning of Preserver, as it has in 1 Tim. 4:10, JND). So **the husband is head of the wife**, and he is her preserver as well. As **head** he loves, leads, and guides; as preserver he provides, protects, and cares for her.

We all know there is great revulsion against this teaching in our day. People accuse Paul of being a bigoted bachelor, a male chauvinist, a woman-hater. Or they say his views reflect the social customs of his day but are no longer applicable today. Such statements are, of course, a frontal attack on the inspiration of the Scriptures. These are not merely Paul's words; they are the words of God. To refuse them is to refuse Him and invite difficulty and disaster.

5:24 Nothing could more exalt the role of the wife than comparing it to the role of **the church** as the Bride of **Christ**. The church's submission is the pattern to be followed by the wife. She is to be

subject in everything — that is, everything that is in accordance with the will
of God. No wife would be expected to
obey her husband if he required her to
compromise her loyalty to the Lord
Jesus. But in all the normal relationships
of life, she is to obey her husband, even
if he is an unbeliever.

5:25 If the foregoing instructions to
wives stood alone, if there were no correspondingly high instructions to **husbands**, then the presentation would be
one-sided, if not unfair. But notice the
beautiful balance of truth in the Scriptures, and the corresponding standard
they require of the **husbands**. **Husbands**
are not told to keep their wives in subjection; they are told to **love** their **wives
just as Christ also loved the church**. It
has been well said that no wife would
mind being submissive to a husband
who loves her as much as **Christ** loves
the church. Someone wrote of a man
who feared he was displeasing God by
loving his wife too much. A Christian
worker asked him if he loved her more
than Christ loved the church. He said
no. "Only when you go beyond that,"
said the worker, "are you loving your
wife too much." Christ's love for **the
church** is presented here in three majestic movements extending from the past
to the present to the future. In the past,
He demonstrated His love for **the
church** by giving **Himself for her**. This
refers to His sacrificial death on the
cross. There He paid the greatest price
in order to purchase a Bride for Himself.
Just as Eve was brought forth from the
side of Adam, so, in a sense, **the church**
was created from the wounded side of
the Savior.

5:26 At the present time His love
for the church is shown in His work of
sanctification: **that He might sanctify
and cleanse her with the washing of
water by the word**. To **sanctify** means to
set apart. Positionally the church is already sanctified; practically she is being
set apart day by day. She is going through a process of moral and
spiritual preparation, similar to the one-
year course of beauty culture which
Esther took before being presented to
King Ahasuerus (Est. 2:12–16). The process of sanctification is carried on by the

washing of water by the word. In simple
terms this means that the lives of believers are cleansed as they hear the words
of Christ and obey them. Thus Jesus said
to the disciples, "You are already clean
because of the word which I have spoken to you" (John 15:3). And He linked
sanctification with the word in His high
priestly prayer: "Sanctify them by Your
truth. Your word is truth" (John 17:17).
Just as the blood of Christ cleanses once
for all from the guilt and penalty of sin,
so the word of God cleanses continually
from the defilement and pollution of sin.
This passage teaches that the church is
being bathed at the present time, not
with literal water, but with the cleansing
agent of the word of God.

5:27 In the past, Christ's love was
manifested in our *redemption*. In the present, it is seen in our *sanctification*. In the
future, it will be displayed in our *glorification*. He Himself will **present her to
Himself a glorious church, not having
spot or wrinkle or any such thing, but
. . . holy and without blemish**. She will
then reach the acme of beauty and spiritual perfection.

A. T. Pierson rightly can exclaim:

Think of it — when the omniscient eye
looks upon us at the last, He will not find
anything that to His immaculate holiness
can be so much as a pimple or a mole on
a human face. How incredible![38]

F. W. Grant concurs:

No sign of old age about it, no defect;
nothing will suit Him then but the bloom
and eternity of an eternal youth, the
freshness of affections which will never
tire, which can know no decay. The
Church will be holy and blameless then.
After all that we have known of her history, it would be strange to read that, if
we did not know how gloriously God
maintains His triumph over sin and evil.[39]

5:28 After soaring off on this magnificent rhapsody dealing with Christ's
love for the church, Paul now returns to
remind husbands that this is the pattern
they are to imitate: **So husbands ought
to love their own wives as their own
bodies**. In imitation of Christ's love, they
should **love their own wives** as being indeed **their own bodies**.

In the Greek, the word "own" occurs

six times in verses 22–33. This emphatic use of the word "own" reminds us that monogamy is God's will for His people. Although He permitted polygamy in the OT, He never approved it.

It is also interesting to notice the varied ways in which Paul describes the close relationship of the husband and the wife. He says that in loving his wife, a man is loving his own body (v. 28a); **himself** (vv. 28b, 33); and "his own flesh" (v. 29). Since marriage involves a true union of persons, and two become one flesh, a man **who loves his wife** is, in a very real sense, loving **himself.**

5:29 Man is born with the instinct to care for his own body. He feeds, clothes, and bathes it; he protects it from discomforts, pain, and harm. Its continued survival depends on this care. This solicitous interest is a pale shadow of the care **the Lord** has for **the church.**

5:30 For we are members of His body. The grace of God is amazing! It not only saves us from sin and hell, but incorporates us into Christ as **members of His** mystical **Body.** What volumes this speaks concerning His love for us: He cherishes us as His own Body. What care: He nourishes, sanctifies, and trains us. What security: He will not be in heaven without His **members.** We are united to Him in a common life. Whatever affects the members affects the Head also.

5:31 The apostle now quotes Genesis 2:24 as presenting God's original concept in instituting the marriage relationship. First, the man's relationship to his parents is superseded by a higher loyalty, that is, his loyalty to his wife. In order to realize the high ideal of the marital relationship, he leaves his parents **and** is **joined to his wife.** The second feature is that husband and wife **become one flesh**: there is a real union of two persons. If these two basic facts were kept in mind, they would eliminate in-law troubles on the one hand, and marital strife on the other.

5:32 This is a great mystery, but I speak concerning Christ and the church. Paul now climaxes his discussion of the marriage relationship by announcing this wonderful truth, hitherto unknown, namely, that as a wife is to

her husband, so **the church** is to **Christ.**

When Paul says the **mystery** is **great,** he does not mean it is very mysterious. Rather he means that the implications of the truth are tremendous. The **mystery** is the wonderful purpose which was hidden in God in previous ages, but which has now been revealed. That purpose is to call out of the nations a people to become the Body and Bride of His glorious Son. The marriage relationship thus finds its perfect antitype in the relation between **Christ and the church.**

> One spirit with the Lord:
> Jesus, the glorified,
> Esteems the church for which He bled,
> His body and His bride.
> – *Mary Bowley Peters*

5:33 This final verse is a sentence summary of what the apostle has been saying to husbands and wives. To the husbands the concluding admonition is this: **let each one of you**, without exception, **love his wife as** being **himself.** Not merely as you might love yourself, but in recognition of the fact that she is one with you. To the wives the word is: **see that** you continually **respect** and obey your **husband.** Now stop and think for a moment! What would happen if these divine instructions were widely followed by Christian people today? The answer is obvious. There would be no strife, no separation, no divorce. Our homes would be more like foretastes of heaven than they often are.

6:1 In chapter 5 we learned that one of the results of being filled with the Spirit is being submissive to one another. We saw that a Spirit-filled wife, for instance, is submissive to her husband. Now we learn that Spirit-filled **children** willingly submit to the authority of their parents. The fundamental duty of all children is to **obey** their **parents in the Lord.** Whether the children are Christians or whether the parents are Christians does not make any difference. The parent-child relationship was ordained for all mankind, not just for believers. The command to **obey . . . in the Lord** means, first, that children should **obey** with the attitude that in doing so they are obeying **the Lord**: their obedience should be as if to Him. Second, it means they should **obey** in all matters which are in accordance with the will of God. If their parents ordered them to sin, they should not be expected to comply. In such a case they should courteously refuse and suffer the consequences meekly and without retaliation. However, in all other cases they must be obedient.

Four reasons are given why they should obey. First, it **is right**. It is a basic principle built into the very structure of family life that those who are immature, impulsive, and inexperienced should submit to the authority of parents, who are older and wiser.

6:2 The second reason is that it is scriptural. Here Paul quotes Exodus 20:12: **Honor your father and mother** (see also Deut. 5:16). This command to **honor** parents is the **first** of the Ten Commandments with a specific **promise** of blessing attached to it. It calls for children to respect, love, and obey their parents.

6:3 The third reason is that it is for the best interests of the children: **that it may be well with you**. Think of what would happen to a child who received no instruction and no correction from his parents! He would be personally miserable and socially intolerable.

The fourth reason is that obedience promotes a full life: **and you may live long on the earth**. In the OT, a Jewish child who obeyed his parents did enjoy a long life. In this Gospel Age, it is not a rule without exceptions. Filial obedience is not always connected with longevity. A dutiful son may die at an early age. But it is true in a general way that the life of discipline and obedience is conducive to health and longevity, whereas a life of rebellion and recklessness often ends prematurely.

6:4 The instructions to children are now balanced with advice **to fathers**. They should **not provoke** their **children** to anger with unreasonable demands, with undue harshness, with constant nagging. Rather children should be nurtured **in the training and admonition of the Lord**. **Training** means discipline and correction, and may be verbal or corporal. **Admonition** means warning, rebuke, reproof. Child-training should be "in the **Lord**," that is, carried out in accordance

with His will as revealed in the Bible by one who acts as His representative.

Susannah Wesley, the mother of seventeen children, including John and Charles, once wrote:

> The parent who studies to subdue self-will in his child, works together with God in the renewing and saving of a soul. The parent who indulges it, does the Devil's work, makes religion impractical, salvation unattainable, and does all that in him lies to damn his child, soul and body forever.[40]

6:5 The third and final sphere of submission in the Christian household is that of servants to **masters**. The word Paul uses is **bondservants** or slaves, but the principles apply to servants or employees of all types.

The first duty of employees is to **those who are** their **masters according to the flesh**. The expression, **masters according to the flesh**, reminds us that the employer has jurisdiction as far as physical or mental work is concerned, but he cannot dictate in spiritual matters or command the conscience.

Second, servants should be respectful. **Fear and trembling** do not mean cowering servility and abject terror; they mean a dutiful respect and a **fear** of offending the Lord and the employer.

Third, service should be conscientious, or **in sincerity of heart**. We should endeavor to deliver sixty minutes of work for every hour of pay.

Next, our work should be **as to Christ**. These words show that there should be no real distinction between the secular and the sacred. All that we do should be for Him — with a view to pleasing and honoring Him and to attracting others to Him. The most menial and commonplace tasks in life are ennobled and dignified when they are done for the glory of God. Even washing dishes! That is why some Christian housewives have this motto over their kitchen sink: "Divine service held here three times daily."

6:6 We should always be diligent, not only when the boss is looking, but conscious that our Master is always looking. It is a natural tendency to slack off when the employer is away, but it is a form of dishonesty. The Christian's standards of performance should not vary according to the geographical location of the foreman. A customer once urged a Christian sales clerk to give him more than he was paying for, assuring him that his employer was not looking. The sales clerk replied, "My Master is always looking!" As servants of Christ, we should be **doing the will of God from the heart**, that is, with a sincere desire to please Him. Erdman says:

> Labor is immeasurably dignified by such considerations as these. The task of the humblest slave may be ennobled by being rendered in such a way as to please Christ, with such good will, with such hearty readiness and zeal, as to merit the approval of the Lord.[41]

6:7 Then, too, we should serve **with good will**. Not with an outward display of compliance while we are inwardly seething with resentment, but cheerfully and willingly. Even if a master is overbearing, abusive, and unreasonable, our work can still be done **as to the Lord and not to men**. It is this type of supernatural behavior that speaks the loudest in the kind of world in which we live.

6:8 A great incentive to do all as if to Christ is the assurance that He will reward every such good work. **Whether** a person **is a slave or free** makes no difference. The Lord notes all the jobs, pleasant or disagreeable, that are done for Him, and He will reward each worker.

Before leaving this section on slaves, some comments should be made:

1. The NT does not condemn slavery as such. In fact, it likens the true believer to a slave (bondservant) of Christ (v. 6). But the abuses of slavery have disappeared wherever the gospel has gone — mainly by moral reformation.

2. The NT has more to say to slaves than it has to kings. This may be a reflection of the fact that not many wise, mighty, or noble are called (1 Cor. 1:26). Probably most Christians are found in the lower economic and social brackets. The emphasis on slaves also shows that the most menial servants are not excluded from the choicest blessings of Christianity.

3. The effectiveness of these instructions to slaves is seen in the fact that in the early days of Christianity, Christian slaves frequently brought higher prices at the auction than heathen bondservants. It should be true today that Christian employees are worth more to their employers than those who have never been touched by the grace of God.

6:9 **Masters** should be guided by the **same** general principles as servants. They should be fair, kind, and honest. They should be particularly careful to refrain from abusive and **threatening** language. If they exercise discipline in this area, they will never have to resort to physical abuse of their servants. And they should always remember that they have a **Master also**, the same **Master** who **is in heaven** that the slave has. Earthly distinctions are leveled in the presence of the Lord. Both master and servant will one day give an account to Him.

E. Exhortations Concerning the Christian Warfare (6:10–20)

6:10 Paul is coming to the close of his Epistle. Addressing all the family of God, he makes a stirring appeal to them as soldiers of Christ. Every true child of God soon learns that the Christian life is a warfare. The hosts of Satan are committed to hinder and obstruct the work of Christ and to knock the individual soldier out of combat. The more effective a believer is for the Lord, the more he will experience the savage attacks of the enemy: the devil does not waste his ammunition on nominal Christians. In our own strength we are no match for the devil. So the first preparatory command is that we should be continually strengthened **in the Lord and in the** boundless resources **of His might**. God's best soldiers are those who are conscious of their own weakness and ineffectiveness, and who rely solely on Him. "God has chosen the weak things of the world to put to shame the things which are mighty" (1 Cor. 1:27b). Our weakness commends itself to **the power of His might**.

6:11 The second command is concerned with the need for divine **armor**. The believer must **put on the whole armor of God that** he **may be able to**

stand against the stratagems **of the devil**. It is necessary to be completely armed; one or two pieces will not do. Nothing less than the whole panoply which God provides will keep us invulnerable. **The devil** has various stratagems — discouragement, frustration, confusion, moral failure, and doctrinal error. He knows our weakest point and aims for it. If he cannot disable us by one method, he will try for another.

6:12 This warfare is not a matter of contending against godless philosophers, crafty priests, Christ-denying cultists, or infidel rulers. The battle is against demonic forces, against battalions of fallen angels, against evil spirits who wield tremendous power. Though we cannot see them, we are constantly surrounded by wicked spirit-beings. While it is true that they cannot indwell a true believer, they can oppress and harass him. The Christian should not be morbidly occupied with the subject of demonism; neither should he live in fear of demons. In the armor of God, he has all he needs to hold his ground against their onslaughts. The apostle speaks of these fallen angels as **principalities** and **powers**, as **rulers of the darkness of this age**, and as **spiritual hosts of wickedness in the heavenly places**. We do not have sufficient knowledge to distinguish between these; perhaps they refer to spirit-rulers with differing degrees of authority, such as presidents, governors, mayors, and aldermen, on the human scale.

6:13 As Paul wrote, he was probably guarded by a Roman soldier in full armor. Always quick to see spiritual lessons in the natural realm, he makes the application: we are flanked by formidable foes; we must **take up the whole armor of God, that** we **may be able to withstand** when the conflict reaches its fiercest intensity, and still be found standing when the smoke of battle has cleared away. **The evil day** probably refers to any time when the enemy comes against us like a flood. Satanic opposition seems to occur in waves, advancing and receding. Even after our Lord's temptation in the wilderness, the devil left Him for a season (Luke 4:13).

6:14 The first piece of armor mentioned is the belt of **truth**. Certainly we must be faithful in holding the **truth** of God's word, but it is also necessary for the **truth** to hold us. We must apply it to our daily lives. As we test everything by the **truth**, we find strength and protection in the combat.

The second piece is **the breastplate of righteousness**. Every believer is clothed with the righteousness of God (2 Cor. 5:21), but he must also manifest integrity and uprightness in his personal life. Someone has said, "When a man is clothed in practical righteousness, he is impregnable. Words are no defense against accusation, but a good life is." If our conscience is void of offense toward God and man, the devil has nothing to shoot at. David put on **the breastplate of righteousness** in Psalm 7:3–5. The Lord Jesus wore it at all times (Isa. 59:17).

6:15 The soldier must have his **feet shod with the preparation of the gospel of peace**. This suggests a readiness to go out with the good news **of peace**, and therefore an invasion into enemy territory. When we relax in our tents, we are in deadly peril. Our safety is to be found in following the beautiful feet of the Savior on the mountains, bearing glad tidings and publishing peace (Isa. 52:7; Rom. 10:15).

> Take my feet and let them be
> Swift and beautiful for Thee
> – *Frances Ridley Havergal*

6:16 In addition, the soldier must take **the shield of faith** so that when **the fiery darts of the wicked one** come zooming at him, they will hit the shield and fall harmlessly to the ground. **Faith** here is firm confidence in the Lord and in His word. When temptations burn, when circumstances are adverse, when doubts assail, when shipwreck threatens, **faith** looks up and says, "I believe God."

6:17 **The helmet** God provides is **salvation** (Isa. 59:17). No matter how hot the battle, the Christian is not daunted, since he knows that ultimate victory is sure. Assurance of eventual deliverance preserves him from retreat or surrender. "If God is for us, who can be against us?" (Rom. 8:31).

Finally, the soldier takes **the sword of the Spirit, which is the word of God**. The classic illustration of this is our Lord's use of this **sword** in His encounter with Satan. Three times He quoted the word of God — not just random verses but the appropriate verses which the Holy Spirit gave Him for that occasion (Luke 4:1–13). **The word**[42] **of God** here does not mean the whole Bible, but the particular portion of the Bible which best suits the occasion.

David Watson says:

> God gives us all the protection that we need. We must see that there is a "ring of truth" about our walk with the Lord, that our lives are right ("righteous") with God and with one another, that we seek to make peace wherever we go, that we lift up that shield of faith together to quench the flaming darts of the evil one, that we protect our minds from fears and anxieties that easily assail, and that we use God's word to good effect in the power of the Spirit. Remember it was by the repeated sword thrusts of God's word that Jesus overcame his adversary in the wilderness.[43]

6:18 **Prayer** is not mentioned as a part of the armor; but we would not be overrating its importance if we say that it is the atmosphere in which the soldier must live and breathe. It is the spirit in which he must don the armor and face the foe. **Prayer** should be continual, not sporadic; a habit, not an isolated act. Then too the soldier should use all kinds of **prayer**: public and private; deliberate and spontaneous; supplication and intercession; confession and humiliation; praise and thanksgiving.

And **prayer** should be **in the Spirit**, that is, inspired and led by Him. Formal prayers recited merely by rote (without giving thought to their meaning) — of what value are they in combat against the hosts of hell? There must be vigilance in **prayer: watchful to this end**. We must watch against drowsiness, mind-wandering, and preoccupation with other things. **Prayer** requires spiritual keenness, alertness, and concentration. And there must be **perseverance** in prayer. We must keep on asking, seeking, knocking (Luke 11:9). **Supplication** should be made **for all the saints**. They

are engaged in the conflict too, and need to be supported in **prayer** by their fellow soldiers.

6:19 Regarding Paul's personal request, **and for me**, Blaikie remarks:

> Mark the *unpriestly* idea! So far from Paul having a store of grace for all the Ephesians, he needed their prayers that, out of the one living store, the needful grace might be given to him.[44]

Paul was writing from prison. Yet he did not ask prayer for his early release. Rather he asked for **utterance** in opening his **mouth boldly** to declare **the mystery of the gospel**. This is Paul's final mention of **the mystery** in Ephesians. Here it is presented as the reason for his bonds. Yet he has no regrets. Quite the contrary! He wants to broadcast it more and more.

6:20 Ambassadors are generally granted diplomatic immunity from arrest and imprisonment. But men will tolerate almost anything better than they will tolerate the gospel. No other subject stirs such emotion, arouses such hostility and suspicion, and provokes such persecution. So Christ's representative was **an ambassador in chains**. Eadie states it well:

> A legate from the mightiest Sovereignty, charged with an embassy of unparalleled nobleness and urgency, and bearing with him credentials of unmistakable authenticity, is detained in captivity.[45]

The particular part of Paul's message that stirred the hostility of narrow religionists was the announcement that believing Jews and believing Gentiles are now formed into one new society, sharing equal privileges, and acknowledging Christ as Head.

F. Paul's Personal Greetings (6:21–24)

6:21, 22 Paul was sending **Tychicus** from Rome to Ephesus to let the saints know how he was getting along. He commends **Tychicus** as **a beloved brother and faithful minister** (servant) **in the Lord**. There are only five references to this man in the NT. He was one of the party that traveled with Paul from Greece to Asia (Acts 20:4). He was the apostle's messenger to the Christians at Colosse (Col. 4:7); to Ephesus (cf. 6:21

with 2 Tim. 4:12) and possibly to Titus in Crete (Titus 3:12). His twofold mission at this time was to inform the saints concerning Paul's welfare in prison, and also to encourage their **hearts**, allaying any unnecessary fears.

6:23 In the closing verses, we have Paul's characteristic greetings — *peace* and *grace*. In combining these two, he wishes for his readers the sum of all blessings. Also in combining the characteristic Jewish and Gentile words, he may be making a final veiled reference to the mystery of the gospel — Jew and Gentile now made one in Christ. In verse 23 he desires that his readers may have **peace** and **love with faith**. **Peace** would garrison their hearts in every circumstance of life. **Love** would enable them to worship God and work with one another. **Faith** would empower them for exploits in the Christian warfare. All these blessings come **from God the Father and the Lord Jesus Christ**, a fact that would be impossible if They were not equal.

6:24 Finally the beloved apostle wishes **grace** for **all those who love our Lord Jesus Christ** with an incorruptible, sincere love. True Christian love has the quality of permanence: its flame may flicker and grow low at times, but it is never extinguished.

The Roman prison has long since given up its noble inmate. The great apostle has entered into his reward and seen the face of his Beloved. But the Letter is still with us — as fresh and alive as the day it came from his heart and pen. In the twentieth century it still speaks to us words of instruction, inspiration, conviction, and exhortation.

In concluding our commentary on Ephesians we find ourselves in hearty agreement with the words of H. W. Webb-Peploe:

There is perhaps no writing in the Book of God so majestic and so wonderful: and therefore, how impossible it is for any man, as a messenger even from God Himself, to do justice to it in the space allotted to us! I hope we may draw nigh to it, simply seeking for teachings upon holiness, teachings by which we may be sent forth to live a nobler and higher life than hitherto, and by which we may be enabled to glorify God.[46]

ENDNOTES

[1](Intro) William G. Moorehead, *Outline Studies in Acts and the Epistles*, p. 214.

[2](1:3) Lewis Sperry Chafer, *The Ephesian Letter*, p. 74.

[3](Excursus) W. G. Blaikie, "Ephesians," *Pulpit Commentary*, XLVI:3.

[4](1:10) John G. Bellett, *Brief Notes on the Epistle to the Ephesians*, pp. 6, 7.

[5](1:17) R. W. Dale, *The Epistle to the Ephesians; Its Doctrines and Ethics*, p. 133.

[6](1:18) Both the oldest and the vast majority of existing mss. read *hearts* (lit. *kardias*, the singular), not *understanding* (*dianoias*). The marginal reading is thus undoubtedly correct.

[7](1:19) F. B. Meyer, *Key Words of the Inner Life*, p. 92.

[8](1:19) Chafer, *Ephesian Letter*, p.57.

[9](1:20) Meyer, *Key Words*, p. 93.

[10](2:3) *Ibid*, p. 140.

[11](2:4) John Eadie, *Commentary on the Epistle to the Ephesians*, p. 141.

[12](2:5) A. T. Pierson, "The Work of Christ for the Believer," *The Ministry of Keswick, First Series*, pp. 118, 119.

[13](2:7) First Corinthians 13:12 and 1 John 3:2 are sometimes used to prove that we will be omniscient in heaven. However, the first reference deals only with recognition of one another in heaven and the second with moral and physical likeness to Christ.

[14](2:18) Eadie, *Ephesians*, p. 187.

[15](2:21) Blaikie, "Ephesians," XLVI:68.

[16](3:1) Ruth Paxson, *The Wealth, Walk and Warfare of the Christian*, p. 57.

[17](3:4) Blaikie, "Ephesians," XLVI:104.

[18](3:8) *Ibid*, XLVI:105, 106.

[19](3:9) The Greek word for *stewardship* or *dispensation*, especially in the large (uncial) letters of the earliest mss., could easily be mistaken for the similar-looking word for *fellowship* (cf. OIKONOMIA and KOINŌNIA). The margin is correct; the traditional reading has very weak support.

[20](3:16) Jamieson, Fausset, and Brown, *Commentary Practical and Explanatory on the Whole Bible*, VI:408.

[21](3:17) W. Graham Scroggie, "Paul's Prison Prayers," the Ministry of Keswick, Second Series, p. 49.

[22](3:18) Meyer, *Key Words*, pp. 53, 54.

²³(3:21) George Williams, *The Student's Commentary on the Holy Scriptures*, p. 925.

²⁴(4:2) Walter C. Wright, *Ephesians*, p. 85.

²⁵(4:10) F. W. Grant, "Ephesians," *The Numerical Bible, Acts to 2 Corinthians*, VI:341.

²⁶(4:11) "Granville Sharp's rule" states that (in Greek) two nouns of office, title, or quality joined by *kai* (*and*), with only the first having the definite article, refer to the same person. A good example of this construction is "our God and Savior Jesus Christ" in 2 Peter 1:1, where the liberal RSV translators felt constrained by grammar to be stronger for the deity of Christ than even the King James. (The grammatical rule was not clearly defined till the late 1700's.) In the plural, as here, the rule does not always apply, though the construction at least closely associates the two nouns (cf. "Scribes and Pharisees," etc.).

²⁷(4:12) Vance Havner, *Why Not Just Be Christians*, p. 63.

²⁸(4:15) Blaikie, "Ephesians," XLVI: 150.

²⁹(4:19) Wright, *Ephesians*, p. 100.

³⁰(4:21) Blaikie, "Ephesians," XLVI: 151.

³¹(4:24) Grant, "Ephesians," p. 344.

³²(4:32) R. C. H. Lenski, *The Interpretation of St. Paul's Epistles to the Galatians, to the Ephesians, and to the Philippians*, p. 588.

³³(5:2) Meyer, *The Heavenlies*, p. 25.

³⁴(5:9) The NU text reads *light* (*phōtos*) for *Spirit* (*Pneumatos*).

³⁵(5:13) Blaikie, "Ephesians," XLVI: 209.

³⁶(5:13) Bishop Ellicott and Dean Alford preferred this translation.

³⁷(5:21) Charles R. Erdman, *Ephesians*, p. 106.

³⁸(5:27) Pierson, "The Work of Christ," p. 138.

³⁹(5:27) Grant, "Ephesians," VI:350.

⁴⁰(6:4) Quoted by William W. Orr in *Bible Hints on Rearing Children*, p. 19.

⁴¹(6:6) Erdman, *Ephesians*, p. 119.

⁴²(6:17) Paul does not use the widely known word *logos* here, but *rhēma* (related to our word *rhetoric*), an expressed word or saying, here a specific "word" from God for a specific need. Sometimes *logos* and *rhēma* are virtually synonymous.

⁴³(6:17) David Watson, *Discipleship*, p. 183.

⁴⁴(6:19) Blaikie, "Ephesians," XLVI: 260.

⁴⁵(6:20) Eadie, *Ephesians*, p. 480.

⁴⁶(6:24) H. W. Webb-Peploe, "Grace and Peace in Four Pauline Epistles," *The Ministry of Keswick, First Series*, p. 69.

BIBLIOGRAPHY

Bellett, John G. *Brief Notes on the Epistle to the Ephesians*. London: G. Morrish, n.d.

Blaikie, W. G. "Ephesians," *Pulpit Commentary, Vol. XLVI*. New York: Funk & Wagnalls, n.d.

Chafer, Lewis Sperry. *The Ephesian Letter*. Findlay, Ohio: Dunham Publishing Company, 1935.

Dale, R. W. *The Epistle to the Ephesians: Its Doctrine and Ethics*. London: Hodder and Stoughton, 1893.

Eadie, John. *Commentary on the Epistle to the Ephesians*. Grand Rapids: Zondervan Publishing House, 1957.

Erdman, Charles R. *The Epistle of Paul to the Ephesians*. Philadelphia: Westminster Press, 1931.

Flint, V. Paul. *Epistle to the Ephesians: To the Praise of His Glory*. Oak Park, IL: Emmaus Bible School, n.d.

Meyer, Frederick Brotherton. *Key Words of the Inner Life: Studies in the Epistle to the Ephesians*. Fleming H. Revell Company, 1893.

———. *The Heavenlies*. Westchester, IL: Good News Publishers, n.d.

Paxson, Ruth. *The Wealth, Walk and Warfare of the Christian*. New York: Fleming H. Revell Co., 1939.

Wright, Walter C. *Ephesians*. Chicago: Moody Press, 1954.

THE EPISTLE TO THE PHILIPPIANS

Introduction

"A little volume of graciousness, bound within the covers of grace."
— J. H. Jowett

I. Unique Place in the Canon

A denomination's "First Church" in any town or city has special prestige in the eyes of its adherents. Imagine, then, the importance of the first known church — before there were any denominations — not merely in a single town, but in all of Europe! Such was the congregation at Philippi, in ancient Macedonia (northern Greece). How Christians in the West should rejoice (and even non-Christians, if they knew of the blessed by-products of Christianity they enjoy) that Paul heeded "the Macedonian call" and turned west, not east, in his evangelization of the Roman Empire! Perhaps the continent of Asia would today be sending Christian missionaries to Europe and North America instead of vice versa, had not the gospel taken hold in Europe.

The Philippian assembly was generous, sending support to Paul time and again. And that, humanly speaking, is the reason for this "thank you letter."

But Philippians is much, much more. It is truly the Epistle of joy — forms of "joy" and "rejoice" occurring over twelve times in its four chapters. Paul knew how to rejoice in good times or hard times (4:11). Also, there is little controversy or negative admonition in this "upbeat" Letter.

The key reason Christians *can* rejoice is that the Son of God was willing to come to earth as a Man — and a Bondservant at that! Not stopping at healing and teaching, He went all the way to death — even death on a cross. Philippians 2:5–11 expresses this great truth in a beautiful paragraph that many believe

is an early Christian hymn, either quoted by Paul or original with him. Even this passage is included to teach unity through humility. Doctrine is never divorced from duty in the NT, as it often is among modern church people — with sad results.

This, then, is Philippians, one of the most cheerful and attractive books in the whole word of God.

II. Authorship[†]

Since most scholars regard the Pauline authorship of Philippians as indisputable, we cite the evidence largely for completeness. Some scholars think they see traces of *two* letters combined in Philippians, or at least that the Bondservant passage (2:5–11) is interpolated. No manuscript evidence exists for these theories.

The *external evidence* is strong. Those who quote the Letter early — often specifically mentioning it as by Paul — include Ignatius, Clement of Rome, Polycarp, Irenaeus, Clement of Alexandria, and Tertullian. Both Marcion's "canon" and the Muratorian Canon ascribe the book to Paul.

Besides the obvious reference to Paul in 1:1, the entire style and wording ring with Pauline tones. The arguments against Pauline authorship tend to be petty, such as maintaining that the reference to "bishops and deacons" in 1:1 demands a date later than Paul's lifetime. This would be true if we read back *later* ideas of bishops into the first century. But Paul uses *bishops* (*episkopoi*, the Greek work for overseers or superintendents) both in the Pastoral Epistles and Acts 20:28 as synonymous with *elders*. Also,

†*See p. i.*

it should be noted that the single congregation addressed had a *plurality* of bishops.

H. A. A. Kennedy beautifully sums up the *internal evidence*:

> Perhaps no Pauline epistle bears more conclusively the stamp of authenticity. There is an artlessness, a delicacy of feeling, a frank outpouring of the heart which could not be simulated.[1]

III. Date

Like Ephesians, Colossians, and Philemon, Philippians was written from prison, hence the category "Prison (or Captivity) Epistles." But while the other three were almost assuredly written and sent at nearly the same time (about A.D. 60), Philippians is clearly written a little later. Marcion specifically says that Paul wrote Philippians from Rome, and this fits well with 1:13 and 4:22, which verses suggest Rome as the place of origin. Paul spent two years under arrest in Rome; hints found in the Letter suggest that Philippians was written near the end of that time. For example, 1:12–18 would imply a certain length of time for preaching in the Eternal City since Paul arrived. That Paul's case was about to be decided (and probably in a positive way — by release) seems indicated in 1:12, 13, 19, 23–26.

These facts, plus allowing time for letters, visits, and gifts of money that are alluded to in the Epistle, give us a date of late A.D. 61.

IV. Background and Theme[†]

It was a momentous day in the history of Christian missions when the Apostle Paul came as far as Troas on his Second Missionary Journey. Troas was located on the northwest coast of Asia Minor, across the Aegean Sea from Greece. One night, in a vision, a man of Macedonia appeared to the apostle, saying, "Come over to Macedonia, and help us" (Acts 16:9). Immediately Paul arranged to sail for Macedonia with Timothy, and also with Luke and Silas. They first set foot on *European* soil at Neapolis, then journeyed inland to Philippi. The latter city was at that time a Roman colony, governed by Roman officials, and granting the rights and privileges of Roman citizenship to its inhabitants.

On the Sabbath, the gospel preachers went down by the riverside where a group of women were in the habit of gathering for prayer (Acts 16:13). One of these was Lydia, a seller of purple from the city of Thyatira. When she accepted the gospel message, she became the first known convert to Christianity on the continent of Europe.

But Paul's stay in Philippi did not prove entirely peaceful. A young woman possessed with a spirit of divination (foretelling future events) met the servants of the Lord and for some time followed them, crying out, "These men are the servants of the Most High God, who proclaim to us the way of salvation" (Acts 16:17). Not willing to accept the testimony of one possessed by an evil spirit, the apostle commanded the demon to come out of her. When her masters, who had profited from this girl's predictions, saw what had happened, they were furious with Paul. They dragged him and Silas into the market place to face the representatives of Rome. These magistrates, in turn, commanded that they should be beaten and thrown into prison.

What happened in that Philippian jail is now well-known. At midnight, Paul and Silas were praying and singing praises to God. Suddenly there was a great earthquake, opening all the doors of the prison and causing the prisoners' chains to be loosed. The jailer, thinking that the prisoners had escaped, was about to kill himself when Paul reassured him that his inmates had not fled. Then the jailer cried out, "Sirs, what must I do to be saved?" The memorable answer came back, "Believe on the Lord Jesus Christ and you will be saved" (Acts 16:31). God's grace had won another trophy at Philippi. In the morning, the local authorities urged Paul and his companions to leave town as quickly as possible. This Paul refused to do. He reminded them that they had beaten him, a Roman citizen, and had imprisoned him without a fair trial. After continued appeals from the magistrates to leave the city, Paul and his companions first went to visit in the home of Lydia and then took their leave (Acts 16:40).

[†]*See p. ii.*

About ten years later, Paul wrote to the Philippians. He was in prison again. The Philippians had heard that Paul was in prison, so they sent a gift of money to him. Epaphroditus had been commissioned to carry this gift to Paul. After delivering it, he decided to stay there a while and help the apostle in his troubles. Epaphroditus himself became ill in carrying out these duties; in fact, he nearly died. But God had mercy on him and raised him back to health once again. He is now ready to go back to Philippi, to his home assembly, and so the apostle is sending back this Letter of acknowledgment with him.

Philippians is one of the most personal and affectionate of Paul's Epistles. It reveals clearly that this congregation held a very special place of esteem in his affection. As we read it, we detect the very tender bond that existed between the great apostle and this church which he had founded.

OUTLINE

I. PAUL'S GREETING, PRAISE, AND PRAYER (1:1–11)

II. PAUL'S IMPRISONMENT, PROSPECTS, AND PLEA FOR PERSEVERANCE (1:12–30)

III. EXHORTATION TO UNITY BASED ON CHRIST'S EXAMPLE OF HUMILITY AND SACRIFICE (2:1–16)

IV. THE CHRISTLIKE EXAMPLE OF PAUL, TIMOTHY, AND EPAPHRODITUS (2:17–30)

V. WARNING AGAINST FALSE TEACHERS (3:1–3)

VI. PAUL'S HERITAGE AND PERSONAL ACHIEVEMENTS RENOUNCED FOR CHRIST (3:4–14)

VII. EXHORTATION TO A HEAVENLY WALK, AS EXEMPLIFIED BY THE APOSTLE (3:15–21)

VIII. APPEAL FOR HARMONY, MUTUAL ASSISTANCE, JOY, FORBEARANCE, PRAYERFULNESS, AND A DISCIPLINED THOUGHT LIFE (4:1–9)

IX. PAUL'S THANKS FOR FINANCIAL GIFTS FROM THE SAINTS (4:10–20)

X. CLOSING GREETINGS (4:21–23)

Commentary

I. PAUL'S GREETING, PRAISE, AND PRAYER (1:1–11)

1:1 Paul and Timothy are linked together at the opening of this Epistle. This does not mean that Timothy helped to write the Letter. He had been with Paul when he first visited Philippi, so he was known to the saints there. Now **Timothy** is with **Paul** as the apostle opens this Letter.

Paul was now an older man (Phmn. 9), while Timothy was still quite young. Thus youth and age were yoked together in the service of the Best of masters. Jowett puts it nicely: "It is the union of springtime and autumn; of enthusiasm and experience; of impulse and wisdom; of tender hope and quiet and rich assurance."[2]

Both are described as **bondservants of Jesus Christ**. Both loved their Master. The ties of Calvary bound them to the service of their Savior forever.

The Letter is addressed **to all the saints in Christ Jesus who are in Philippi, with the bishops and deacons**. The word *all* recurs in this Epistle quite frequently. Paul's affectionate interest went out to **all** the Lord's people.

The saints in Christ Jesus who are in Philippi describes the dual position of the believers. As to their spiritual status, they were set apart by God **in Christ**

Jesus. As to their geographical location, they were at **Philippi**. Two places at the same time!

Then the apostle mentions **the bishops and deacons**. **The bishops** were the elders or overseers in the assembly — those who took a pastoral interest in the flock of God and who led the flock by their godly example. The **deacons**, on the other hand, were the servants of the church who were probably chiefly concerned with its material affairs, such as finances, etc.

There were only these three groups in the church — **saints, bishops, and deacons**. If there had been a clergyman in charge, Paul would have mentioned him also. Instead he speaks only of **bishops** (plural) and **deacons** (also plural).

Here we have a remarkable picture of the simplicity of church life in the early days. **The saints** are mentioned first, then their *spiritual guides*, and last their *temporal servants*. That is all!

1:2 In Paul's characteristic greeting, he wishes the saints **grace . . . and peace**. The former is not so much the grace which comes to a sinner at the time of his conversion as the **grace** which he must constantly obtain at the throne of grace to help in every time of need (Heb. 4:16). Likewise, the **peace** which Paul craves for them is not so much peace with God, which is theirs already, as the **peace** of God which comes through prayer and thanksgiving (4:6, 7).

Both blessings come **from God our Father and the Lord Jesus Christ**. The apostle honors the Son even as he honors the Father (John 5:23). There is no mistaking that to Paul, Jesus Christ is God.

1:3 Now Paul bursts into a song of thanksgiving. But that is nothing new for the apostle. The walls of the Philippian jail had echoed the songs of Paul and Silas on their first visit there. As he writes these words, he is probably a prisoner in Rome — but he is still singing "songs in the night." The indomitable Paul! **Every remembrance** of the Philippians awakened thanksgiving in his heart. Not only were they his children in the faith, but in many ways they had proved to be a model church.

1:4 **In every prayer**, he made sup-

plication for the Philippians **with joy**. To him it was a sheer delight to pray for them — not dull drudgery. From this and many similar passages in Paul's writing, we learn that he was a man of prayer. It is not necessary to search further for the reason he was so wonderfully used of God. When we remember the extent of his travels and the host of Christians he knew, we marvel that he maintained such a personal, intimate interest in them all.

1:5 The specific reason for his thanksgiving was their **fellowship** in furthering **the gospel from the first day until now**. **Fellowship** might include financial assistance, but it extends also to prayer support and a wholehearted devotion to the spread of the good news. When Paul mentions **the first day**, one cannot help wondering if the jailor was still alive when this Letter was publicly read to the assembly at Philippi. If so, this mention of Paul's introduction to the Philippian believers would certainly have struck a responsive chord in his heart.

1:6 As the apostle thinks of the good start the believers have made in the Christian life, he is **confident** that God will finish the **good work** He **has begun**.

> The work which His goodness began,
> The arm of His strength will complete;
> His promise is Yea and Amen,
> And never was forfeited yet.
> *– Augustus M. Toplady*

Good work may refer to their salvation, or it may mean their active financial participation in the furtherance of the gospel. **The day of Jesus Christ** refers to the time of His coming again to take His people home to heaven and probably also includes the Judgment Seat of Christ, when service for Him will be reviewed and rewarded.

1:7 Paul feels justified in being thankful for the Philippians. In his **heart** he treasures a lasting memory of how loyally they stood with him, whether he was on trial, in prison, or traveling about **in the defense and confirmation of the gospel**. **The defense of the gospel** refers to the ministry of answering the critics, while the **confirmation of the gospel** relates rather to establishing the message more firmly in the hearts of those who are already believers. W. E. Vine says:

"The gospel both overthrows its foes and strengthens its friends."[3] **Grace** here means the undeserved strength from God to carry on the work of the Lord in the face of severe opposition.

1:8 The memory of their faithful cooperation makes the apostle **long** to be with them again. He calls **God** to **witness how greatly** he yearns **for them with the affection of Jesus Christ**. Paul's expression of love is all the more remarkable when we remember that he had been born a Jew and was writing to people of Gentile descent. The grace of God had broken down the ancient hatred, and now they were all one in Christ.

1:9 Thanksgiving now gives way to prayer. Will Paul ask wealth, comfort, or freedom from trouble for them? No, he asks that their **love** might constantly increase **in knowledge and all discernment**. The primary aim of the Christian life is to **love** God and to **love** one's fellow man. But love is not just a matter of the emotions. In effective service for the Lord, we must use our intelligence and exercise **discernment**. Otherwise, our efforts are apt to be futile. So Paul is here praying not only that the Philippians will continue in the display of Christian love, but also that their **love** will be exercised in full **knowledge and all discernment.**

1:10 Love that is thus enlightened will enable them to discern the things that are more **excellent**. In all realms of life, some things are good and others are better. The good is often the enemy of the best. For effective service, these distinctions must be made.

Love that is enlightened will also enable them to avoid what is questionable or downright wrong. Paul would have them **sincere**,[4] that is, utterly transparent, and blameless in view of **the day of Christ**. To be **without offense** does not mean to be sinless. We all commit sins, but the blameless person is the one who confesses and forsakes the sin, asking forgiveness from those who were wronged and making restitution whenever possible.

The day of Christ, as in verse 6, refers to the Rapture and the subsequent judgment of the believer's works.

1:11 The final petition of the apostle's prayer is that the Christians might be **filled with the fruits of righteousness**, that is, with **the fruits** which **righteousness** produces, or with all the Christian virtues that make up a righteous life. The source of these virtues is **Jesus Christ**, and their object is **the glory and praise of God**. This petition of Paul is exactly parallel to the words in Isaiah 61:3, "that they may be called trees of righteousness (**being filled with the fruits of righteousness**), the planting of the Lord (**which are by Jesus Christ**), that He may be glorified (**to the glory and praise of God.**)"

"The word 'fruit,' " Lehman Strauss writes, ". . . is associated closely with our relation to Christ and His expectation of us. The branches on a vine are intended to bear fruit."[5]

II. PAUL'S IMPRISONMENT, PROSPECTS, AND PLEA FOR PERSEVERANCE (1:12–30)

1:12 The prayer is ended. Paul next rehearses his blessings, that is, the benefits that have resulted from his imprisonment. Jowett calls this section "The Fortune of Misfortune."

The apostle would have the **brethren know that the things which happened** to him, that is, his trial and imprisonment, have resulted in **the furtherance of the gospel** rather than its hindrance, as might have been expected. This is another wonderful illustration of how God overrules the wicked plans of demons and men and brings triumph out of seeming tragedy and beauty from ashes. "Man has his wickedness, but God has His way."

1:13 First of all, Paul's **chains** have become **evident** as being **in Christ**. By this he means that it has become widely known that he was imprisoned as a result of his testimony for Christ and not as a criminal or evildoer.

The real reason for his **chains** became well-known throughout the **palace guard** and in all other places. **Palace guard** may mean either: (1) The whole praetorian **guard**, that is, the Roman soldiers who guarded the **palace** where the emperor dwelt, or (2) The whole praetorium itself. The praetorium was the **palace** and here would include all of its occupants. In any event, Paul is saying that his imprisonment has served as a testimony to the representatives of the Roman imperial power where he was.

T. W. Drury writes:

The very chain which Roman discipline riveted on the prisoner's arm secured to his side a hearer who would tell the story of patient suffering for Christ, among those who, the next day, might be in attendance on Nero himself.[6]

1:14 A second favorable outcome of his imprisonment was that other Christians were thereby encouraged to be more fearless in testifying for the Lord Jesus. Persecution often has the effect of transforming quiet and bashful believers into courageous witnesses.

1:15 The motive in some hearts was jealousy and rivalry. They preached **Christ** out of **envy** and contentiousness.

Others had sincere and pure motives; they preached Christ **from good will**, in an honest effort to help the apostle.

1:16 The jealous preachers thought that by doing this they might make Paul's imprisonment more bitter. Their message was good, but their temper was bad. It is sad to think that Christian service can be carried on in the energy of the flesh, motivated by greed, strife, pride, and envy. This teaches the necessity for watching our motives when we serve the Lord. We must not do it for self-display, for the advancement of a religious sect, or for the defeat of other Christians.

Here is a good example of the necessity for our love to be exercised in knowledge and discernment.

1:17 Others were preaching the gospel **out of** pure and sincere **love, knowing that** Paul was determined to defend **the gospel**. There was nothing selfish, sectarian, or cruel in their service. They knew very well that Paul had been committed to prison because of his bold stand for **the gospel**. So they determined to carry on the work while he was thus confined.

1:18 Paul refuses to be downcast by the wrong motives of some. **Christ is** being **preached** by both groups, and that is for him a great cause for rejoicing.

It is remarkable that under such difficult circumstances, Paul does not feel sorry for himself or seek the sympathy of others. Rather he is filled with the joy of the Lord and encourages his readers to rejoice also.

1:19 The outlook is encouraging. The apostle knows that the whole course of events will lead to his **deliverance. Deliverance** (KJV, "salvation") here does not mean the salvation of Paul's soul, but rather his liberation from prison. The means which God will use in effecting his release will be the **prayer** of the Philippians and the ministry or help of the **Spirit of Jesus Christ**. Marvel here at the importance which Paul puts on the prayers of a feeble band of believers. He sees them as sufficiently powerful to thwart the purposes and the mighty power of Rome. It is true; Christians can influence the destiny of nations and change the course of history through prayer.

The supply of the Spirit of Jesus Christ means the power of the Holy **Spirit** stretched forth in his behalf — the strength which the Spirit would supply to him. In general, it refers to "the boundless resources which the Spirit supplies to enable believers to stand fast, regardless of what the circumstances may be."

1:20 As he thought of the prayers of the Christians and the assistance of the Holy Spirit, he expressed his eager desire and **hope** that he might never **be ashamed**, but rather that he might always have a fearless and outspoken witness for Christ.

And no matter what the outcome of judicial processes might be — whether he was to be freed or put to **death** — his ambition was that **Christ** should **be magnified in** his **body**. To magnify does not mean to make Christ greater. He is already great, and nothing we can do will make Him greater. But to magnify means to cause Christ to be esteemed or praised by others. Guy King shows how Christ can **be magnified** by our bodies in **life:**

. . . magnified by lips that bear happy testimony to Him; magnified by hands employed in His happy service; magnified by feet only too happy to go on His errands; magnified by knees happily bent in prayer for His kingdom; magnified by shoulders happy to bear one another's burdens.[7]

Christ can also **be magnified** in our bodies **by death** — bodies worn out in His service; bodies pierced by savage spears; bodies torn by stones or burned at the stake.

1:21 Here, in a nutshell, is Paul's philosophy of life. He did not live for money, fame, or pleasure. The object of his life was to love, worship, and serve the Lord Jesus. He wanted his life to be like the life of **Christ**. He wanted the Savior to live out His life through him.

And to die is gain. To die is to be with Christ and to be like Him forever. It is to serve Him with unsinning heart and with feet that will never stray. We do not ordinarily think of death as one of our gains. Sad to say, the outlook today seems to be that "to live is earthly gain, and to die would be the end of gain." But, says Jowett: "To the Apostle Paul, death was not a darksome passageway, where all our treasures rot away in a swift corruption; it was a place of gracious transition, 'a covered way that leadeth into light.' "[8]

1:22 If it is God's will for Paul to **live on** a while longer **in the flesh**, then that will mean fruitful **labor** for him. He will be able to give further help to the Lord's people. But it was a difficult decision for him — whether to go to the Savior whom he loved, or to remain on earth in the Lord's service, to which he was also very attached. He did not know which to **choose.**

1:23 To be **hard pressed between the two** means to be required to make a difficult decision between **two** possibilities — that of going home to heaven or that of remaining on earth as an apostle of Christ Jesus.

He ardently longed **to depart and be with Christ, which is far better**. If he only considered his own interests, this is doubtless the choice he would make.

Notice that Paul did not believe in any theory of soul-sleep. He believed that the Christian goes to **be with Christ** at the time of death and that he is in the conscious enjoyment of the presence of the Lord. How ridiculous it would be for him to say, as some do today: "To live is Christ; to sleep is gain." Or, "To depart and to sleep is far better." "Sleep" is used in the NT of the believer's *body* at the time of death (1 Thess. 4:14),

never of his soul. Soul-sleep is a myth.

Notice, too, that death is not to be confused with the coming of the Savior. At the time of death, we go to **be with Him**. At the time of the Rapture, He comes to us.

1:24 **For** the sake of the Philippians, it was **more needful** for Paul to live on earth a while longer. One cannot help but be impressed with the unselfishness of this great-hearted man. He does not think of his own comfort or ease, but rather of what will best advance the cause of Christ and the welfare of His people.

1:25 **Being confident of this** — that he was still needed on earth to instruct, comfort, and encourage the saints — Paul knew that he would not be put to death at this time. How did he know? We believe that he lived so close to the Lord that the Holy Spirit was able to communicate this knowledge to him. "The secret of the Lord is with those who fear Him." (Ps. 25:14). Those who dwell deep in God, in quiet meditation, hear secrets that are drowned out by the noise, rush, and bustle of life today. You have to be near to hear. Paul was near.

By remaining in the flesh, Paul would be able to promote their spiritual **progress and** increase the **joy** that was theirs through trusting in the Lord.

1:26 Through his being spared for longer life and service on earth, the Philippians would have added cause for **rejoicing** in the Lord when he would visit them once again. Can you not imagine how they would throw their arms around him and kiss him, and praise the Lord with great joy when he would arrive at Philippi? Perhaps they would say, "Well, Paul, we prayed for you, but honestly, we never expected to see you here again. But how we praise the Lord that He has given you back to us once more!"

1:27 Now Paul adds a word of caution: **"Only let your conduct be worthy of the gospel of Christ."** Christians should be Christlike. Citizens of heaven should behave accordingly. We should be in practice what we are in position.

In addition to this plea for consistency, the apostle makes an appeal for constancy. Specifically, he desires **that whether** he comes to them personally, or, being **absent**, hears reports about them, he may know that they are standing **fast** with a common **spirit**, and unitedly laboring earnestly **for the faith of the gospel**, that is, the Christian faith. Christians face a common foe; they should not fight each other but should unite against the enemy.

1:28 Neither were they to be **terrified by** the enemies of the gospel. Fearlessness in the face of persecution has a twofold meaning. First, it is an omen of destruction to those who fight against God. Secondly, it is a sign **of salvation** to those who brave the wrath of the foe. **Salvation** is probably used here in its future tense, referring to the eventual deliverance of the saint from trial and the redemption of his body as well as his spirit and soul.

1:29 The Philippians should remember that it is a privilege **to suffer** for **Christ** as well as **to believe in Him.**

Dr. Griffith John wrote that once when he was surrounded by a hostile heathen crowd and was beaten, he put his hand to his face and when he withdrew it, saw that it was bathed in blood. "He was possessed by an extraordinary sense of exaltation, and he rejoiced that he had been counted worthy to suffer for His Name." Is it not remarkable that even suffering is exalted by Christianity to such a lofty plane? Truly, even "an apparent trifle burns with the fire immortal when it is in communion with the Infinite." The cross dignifies and ennobles.

1:30 The connection of this verse with the previous one is better understood if we supply the words "Since you are engaged in":

The privilege of suffering for Christ has been granted to you, since you are engaged in **the same** kind of **conflict which you saw in me** when I was in Philippi **and now hear** that I am still waging.

III. EXHORTATION TO UNITY BASED ON CHRIST'S EXAMPLE OF HUMILITY AND SACRIFICE (2:1–16)

Although the church at Philippi was exemplary in many respects, and Paul had occasion to commend the saints warmly, yet there was an undercurrent of strife. There was a difference of opinion between two women, Euodia and Syntyche (4:2). It is helpful to keep this in mind because in chapter 2 the apostle is dealing directly with the cause and cure of contentions among the people of God.

2:1 The **if** in this verse is not the "if" of doubt but of argument. The verse lists four great considerations which should draw believers together in harmony and cooperation. The apostle is saying, in effect: "*Since* there is so much encouragement **in Christ,** *since* His **love** has such a tremendous persuasiveness, *since* **the** Holy **Spirit** brings us all together in such a wonderful **fellowship,** and *since* there is so much tender **affection and mercy** in Christianity, we should all be able to get along in happy harmony with one another."

F. B. Meyer describes these four motives as:

1. The persuasiveness of Christ.
2. The tender care that love gives.
3. The sharing of the Spirit.
4. Humaneness and pity.[9]

It is clear that the apostle is making an appeal for unity based on common devotion to Christ and common possession of the Holy Spirit. With all that there is **in Christ,** the members of His Body should have unity of purpose, affection, accord, sympathy.

2:2 If these foregoing arguments carry any weight with the Philippians, then Paul begs them, on the basis of such arguments, that they should **fulfill** his **joy.** Up to this time, the Philippians had indeed given Paul much joy. He does not deny that for a moment, but now he asks that they should fill the cup of his joy to overflowing. They could do this **by being like-minded, having the same love,** and **being of one accord** and **of one mind.**

Does this mean that all Christians are expected to think and act alike? The word of God nowhere gives such a suggestion. While we are definitely expected to agree on the great fundamentals of the Christian faith, it is obvious that on many minor matters there will be a great deal of difference of opinion. *Uniformity* and *unity* are not the same thing. It is possible to have the latter without the former. Although we might not agree on minor matters, yet we can submerge our own opinions, where no real principle is involved, for the good of others.

To be **like-minded** really means to have the mind of Christ, to see things as He would see them, and to respond as He would respond. To have **the same love** means to show **the same love** to others that the Lord has shown to us, a love that did not count the cost. To be **of one accord** means to work together in harmony toward a common goal. Finally, to be **of one mind** means to act so unitedly as to show that Christ's mind is directing our activities.

2:3 **Nothing** whatever should **be done through selfish ambition or conceit**, since these are two of the greatest enemies of unity among the people of God. **Selfish ambition** is the desire to be number one, no matter what the cost. **Conceit** speaks of pride or self-display. Wherever you find people who are interested in gathering a clique around themselves or in promoting their own interests, there you will find the seeds of contention and strife. The remedy is found in the latter part of the verse. **In lowliness of mind let each esteem others better than himself.** This does not mean that we must consider criminals as having better moral characters than our own, but rather that we should live for others unselfishly, putting their interests above our own. It is easy to read an exhortation like this in the word of God, but quite another thing to appreciate what it really means, and then put it into actual practice. To **esteem others better than** ourselves is utterly foreign to the human mind, and we cannot do it in our own strength. It is only as we are indwelt and empowered by the Holy Spirit that it can ever be practiced.

2:4 The cure of troubles among the people of God is to be more concerned with the **interests of others** than with the things of our **own** lives. In a very real way the word **others** forms the key of this chapter. It is as we give our lives in devoted service for others that we rise above the selfish strife of men.

> Others, Lord, yes, others,
> Let this my motto be;
> Help me to live for others,
> That I might live like Thee.
> – *Charles D. Meigs*

2:5 **Let this mind be in you which was also in Christ Jesus.** Paul is now going to hold up before the eyes of the Philippians the example of the Lord Jesus Christ. What kind of attitude did He exhibit? What characterized His behavior toward others? Guy King has well described the mind of the Lord Jesus as: (1) The selfless mind; (2) The sacrificial mind; (3) The serving mind. The Lord Jesus consistently thought of others.[10]

> He had no tears for His own griefs,
> But sweat-drops of blood for mine.
> – *Charles H. Gabriel*

2:6 When we read that Christ Jesus was **in the form of God**, we learn that He existed from all eternity as **God**. It does not mean that He merely resembled God, but that He actually *is* God in the truest sense of the word.

Yet He **did not consider it robbery to be equal with God.** Here it is of utmost importance to distinguish between personal and positional equality with God. As to His Person, Christ always *was*, *is*, and *will be* equal with God. It would be impossible for Him to give that up. But positional equality is different. From all eternity Christ was positionally equal with His Father, enjoying the glories of heaven. But He **did not consider** this position something that He had to hold on to at all costs. When a world of lost mankind needed to be redeemed, He was willing to relinquish His positional equality **with God** — the comforts and joys of heaven. He **did not consider** them something that He had to grasp forever and under all circumstances.

Thus He was willing to come into this world to endure the contradiction of sinners against Himself. God the Father was never spit on or beaten or crucified. In this sense, the Father was greater than the Son — not greater as to His Person, but rather as to His position and the manner in which He lived. Jesus expressed this thought in John 14:28: "If you loved Me, you would rejoice because I said, 'I am going to the Father,' for My Father is greater than I." In other words, the disciples should have rejoiced to learn that He was going home to heaven. While on earth, He had been cruelly treated and rejected. He had been in lower circumstances than His Father. In that sense, His Father was greater. But when He went back to heaven, He would be equal with the Father in *His circumstances* as well as in *His Person*.

Gifford explains:

Thus it is not the nature or essence . . .but the *mode of existence* that is described in this second clause ["did not consider it robbery to be equal with God"]; and one mode of existence may be changed for another, though the essential nature is immutable. Let us take St. Paul's own illustration, 2 Cor. viii.9, "Though He was rich, yet for your sakes He became poor, that you through His poverty might become rich." Here in each case there is a change of the *mode of existence*, but not of the nature. When a poor man becomes rich, his *mode of existence* is changed, but not his nature as man. It is so with the Son of God; from the rich and glorious *mode of existence* which was the fit and adequate manifestation of His divine nature, He for our sakes descended, in respect of His human life, to the infinitely lower and poorer *mode of existence* which He assumed together with the nature of man.[11]

2:7 But made Himself of no reputation. The literal translation is: "But He emptied Himself." The question immediately arises, "Of what did the Lord Jesus empty Himself?"

In answering this question, one must use the greatest care. Human attempts to define this emptying have often ended by stripping Christ of His attributes of Deity. Some say, for instance, that when the Lord Jesus was on earth, He no longer had all-knowledge or all-power. He was no longer in all places at one and the same time. They say He voluntarily laid aside these attributes of Deity when He came into the world as a Man. Some even say He was subject to the limitations of all men, that He became liable to error, and accepted the common opinions and myths of His day!

This we utterly deny. The Lord Jesus did not lay aside any of the attributes of God when He came into the world.

He was still omniscient (all-knowing).

He was still omnipresent (present in all places at one and the same time).

He was still omnipotent (all-powerful).

What He did was to empty Himself of His

positional equality with God and to veil the glory of Deity in a body of human flesh. The glory was all there, though hidden, but it did shine forth on occasions, such as on the Mount of Transfiguration. There was no moment in His life on earth when He did not possess all the attributes of God.

Aside He threw His most divine array,
And hid His Godhead in a veil of clay,
And in that garb did wondrous love
    display,
Restoring what He never took away.

As mentioned before, one must use great care in explaining the words "He emptied Himself." The safest method is to let the succeeding expressions provide the explanation. He emptied Himself by **taking the form of a bondservant, and coming in the likeness of men**. In other words, He emptied Himself by taking upon Himself something He never had before — *humanity*. He did not lay aside His deity, only His place in heaven, and that only temporarily.

If He had been a mere man, this would not have been an act of emptying. We do not empty ourselves by being born into the world. But for God to become Man — that is the emptying of Himself. In fact, only God could do it.

Taking the form of a bondservant. The Incarnation and life of the Savior may be summarized by those lovely words of John 13:4: "Jesus . . . laid aside His garments, took a towel and girded Himself." The towel or apron is the badge of service. It was used by slaves. And it was used by the blessed Lord Jesus because He came "not to be served, but to serve, and to give His life a ransom for many" (Matt. 20:28). But let us pause to remind ourselves of the train of thought in this passage. There were contentions among the saints at Philippi. Paul exhorts them to have the mind of Christ. The argument, in brief, is that if Christians are willing to take the lowly place, to serve others, and to give their lives in sacrifice, there will be no quarrels. *People who are willing to die for others do not generally quarrel with them.*

Christ always existed, but came into the world **in the likeness of men**, meaning "as a real Man." The humanity of the Lord is as real as His deity. He is true God and true Man. But what a mystery this is! No created mind will ever be able to understand it.

2:8 Each section of this passage describes the increasing depth of the humiliation of God's beloved Son. He was not only willing to leave the glory of heaven! He emptied Himself! He took the form of a bondservant! He became Man! But now we read that **He humbled Himself**! There was no depth to which He would not stoop to save our guilty souls. Blessed be His glorious name forever!

He humbled Himself by becoming **obedient to the point of death**. This is marvelous in our eyes! He obeyed even though it cost Him His life. **Obedient to the point of death** means He obeyed to the end. Truly He was the Merchant who went and sold all that He had to buy the pearl of great price (Matt. 13:46). **Even the death of the cross. Death** by crucifixion was the most shameful form of execution. It might be compared to the gallows, the electric chair, or the gas chamber — reserved only for murderers. And that was the form of **death** reserved for heaven's Best when He came into this world. He was not allowed to die a natural death in bed. His was not to be an accidental death. He must die **the** shameful **death of the cross.**

2:9 Now there is an abrupt change. The previous verses describe what the Lord Jesus did. He took the path of self-renunciation. He did not seek a name for Himself. He humbled Himself.

But now we turn to a consideration of what *God* has done. If the Savior humbled Himself, **God also has highly exalted Him**. If He did not seek a name for Himself, **God has given Him the name which is above every name**. If He bent His knees in service to others, God has decreed that **every knee** shall **bow** to Him.

And what is the lesson in this for the Philippians — and for us? The lesson is that the way up is down. We should not exalt ourselves but be the servants of others, that God may exalt us in due time.

God exalted Christ by raising Him from the dead and opening the heavens to receive Him back to His own right hand. Not only that — **God has given Him the name which is above every name.**

Scholars are divided as to what this **name** is. Some say it is the name *Jesus*, which contains the name of *Jehovah*. In Isaiah 45:22, 23, it is decreed that every knee will bow to the name of Jehovah (God).

Others feel that **the name which is above every name** is simply a figurative way of saying the highest place in the universe, a position of supremacy and dominion. Both explanations are acceptable.

2:10 God was so completely satisfied with the redemptive work of Christ that He determined that **every knee should bow** to Him — of beings **in heaven, on earth**, and **under the earth**. This does not mean that all these beings will be saved. Those who do not *willingly* bow the knee to Him now will one day be *compelled* to do so. Those who will not be reconciled in the day of His grace will be subjugated in the day of His judgment.

2:11 In matchless grace, the Lord journeyed from glory to Bethlehem, to Gethsemane, and to Calvary. God, in return, will honor Him with universal homage and the universal acknowledgment of His lordship. Those who have denied His claims will one day admit that they have played the fool, that they have greatly erred, and that Jesus of Nazareth is indeed the Lord of glory.

Before leaving this magnificent passage on the Person and work of the Lord Jesus, we should repeat that it was introduced in connection with a minor problem in the church at Philippi. Paul did not set out to write a treatise on the Lord. Rather, he was merely seeking to correct selfishness and party spirit in the saints. The cure of their condition is the mind of Christ. Paul brings the Lord into every situation. "Even in dealing with matters most delicate, distressing and distasteful," Erdman writes, "he is able to state truth in such striking beauty as to make it appear like a precious jewel embedded in a clod of earth."[12]

2:12 Having set forth the example of Christ in such brilliant luster, the apostle is now ready to press home the exhortation based on it.

The Philippians had **always obeyed** Paul when he was present with them. **Now much more in** his **absence**, they should **work out** their **own salvation with fear and trembling.**

Again we come to a passage of Scripture concerning which there has been much confusion. At the outset, we should be very clear that Paul is not teaching that salvation can be earned by works. Throughout his writings, he repeatedly emphasizes that salvation is not by works but by faith in the Lord Jesus Christ. What then does the verse mean?

1. It may mean that we are to **work out** the salvation which God has placed within us. God has given us eternal life as a free gift. We are to live it out by lives of practical holiness.

2. **Salvation** here may mean the solution of their problem at Philippi. They had been plagued with squabbles and strife. The apostle has given them the remedy. Now they are to apply the remedy by having the mind of Christ. Thus they would **work out** their **own salvation**, or the solution of their difficulty.

The salvation spoken of here is not that of the soul, but deliverance from the snares which would hinder the Christian from doing the will of God. In a similar vein, Vine describes it as the present entire experience of deliverance from evil.

Salvation has many different meanings in the NT. We have already noticed that in 1:19 it means deliverance from prison. In 1:28 it refers to the eventual salvation of our bodies from the very presence of sin. The meaning in any particular case must be determined in part, at least, by the context. We believe that in this passage **salvation** means the solution of the problem that was vexing the Philippians, that is, their contentions.

2:13 Now Paul reminds them that it is possible for them to work out their salvation because **it is God who works in** them **both to will and to do for His good pleasure**. This means that **it is God** who puts within us the wish or desire to do His will in the first place. Then He also **works in** us the power to carry out the desire.

Here again we have the wonderful merging of the divine and human. In one sense, we are called on to work out

our salvation. In another sense, it is only God who can enable us to do it. We must do our part, and God will do His. (However, this does not apply to the forgiveness of sins, or to the new birth. Redemption is wholly the work of God. We simply believe and enter in.)

2:14 As we do His good pleasure, we should do it without grumbling or questioning: "Not somehow but triumphantly." **Complaining and disputing** usually lead to graver offenses.

2:15 By refraining from complaints and disputes, we **may** be **blameless and harmless** (sincere and guileless). To be **blameless** means that no charge can be sustained against a person (see Dan. 6:4). A **blameless** person may sin, but he apologizes, confesses, and makes it right whenever possible. To be **harmless** here means to be sincere or without deceit.

Children of God should be **without fault in the midst of a crooked and perverse generation**. By lives without blemish, God's children will stand out all the more clearly against the dark background of this world.

This leads Paul to think of them **as lights** in a dark night. The darker the night, the brighter the light appears. Christians are **lights** or light-bearers. They cannot create any light, but they can reflect the glory of the Lord so that others may see Jesus in them.

2:16 Holding fast (KJV "forth") **the word of life**. As lights we shine, but that does not excuse us from witnessing with our voices. There should be the twofold testimony of life and lips.

If the Philippians fulfill these functions, the apostle knows he will have some ground for glorying **in the day of Christ**. He feels a responsibility not only to see souls saved but also to present every man perfect in Christ (Col. 1:28).

The day of Christ refers to the time of His return and of the judgment of the believer's service (1:6, 10). If the Philippians are faithful in their labor for the Lord, it will be evident in that day that Paul's service had **not** been **in vain**.

IV. THE CHRISTLIKE EXAMPLE OF PAUL, TIMOTHY, AND EPAPHRODITUS (2:17–30)

In the preceding section, Paul has set

forth the Lord Jesus as the prime example of the lowly mind. But some might be tempted to say, "Oh, but He is God and we are only mortals." So Paul now gives three examples of men who exhibited the mind of Christ — himself, Timothy, and Epaphroditus. If Christ is the sun, then these three are moons, reflecting the glory of the sun. They are lights in a dark world.

2:17 The apostle uses a very beautiful illustration to describe the service of the Philippians and of himself. He borrows the picture from the common practice among both Jews and pagans of pouring out **a drink offering** or libation over a **sacrifice** as it was being offered.

He speaks of the Philippians as the offerers. Their **faith** is the **sacrifice**. Paul himself is the **drink offering**. He would be happy to be **poured out** in martyrdom **on the sacrifice and service of** their **faith**.

Williams comments:

> The apostle compares the self-sacrifice and energy of the Philippians with his own, magnifying theirs and minimizing his. They were both laying down their lives for the sake of the gospel, but their action he regards as the great sacrifice, and his as only the drink offering poured out upon it. Under this beauteous figure of speech, he speaks of his possible approaching death as a martyr.[13]

If this should be his lot, he would be **glad and rejoice** that it should be so.

2:18 **For the same reason**, the Philippians should **be glad and rejoice with** Paul. They should not look on his possible martyrdom as a tragedy but congratulate him on such a glorious homegoing.

2:19 Up to this point, Paul has cited two examples of self-sacrificing love — the Lord Jesus and himself. Both were willing to pour out their lives to death. Two more examples of selflessness remain — **Timothy** and **Epaphroditus**.

The apostle hopes **to send Timothy** to Philippi in the near future so that he **may be encouraged** by news concerning them.

2:20 Among Paul's companions, Timothy was unique in his unselfish care for the spiritual condition of the Philippians. There was **no one** else whom Paul could send to them with the same confidence. This is a high commendation in-

deed for one as young as Timothy!

2:21 The others had become engulfed in the ocean of **their own** private interests. They had become so engrossed with the cares of this life that they had no time for **the things which are of Christ Jesus**. Does this have a message for us today in our little world of homes, refrigerators, television sets, and other *things*? (see Luke 8:14.)

2:22 Timothy was the apostle's child in the faith, and he played the part with true faithfulness. They knew **his proven character**, his real worth, **that as a son** serves with **his father**, so Timothy **served with** Paul **in** the work of preaching **the gospel**.

2:23, 24 Because Timothy had thus proved himself, Paul hoped **to send him** to the Philippians as soon as he learned the outcome of his appeal to Caesar. This is doubtless the apostle's meaning in the expression **as soon as I see how it goes with me**. He hopes that his appeal will be successful, and that he will be set free so that he might visit the Philippians once more.

2:25 Next we see the mind of Christ in **Epaphroditus**. Whether this is the same man as the Epaphras of Colossians 4:12, we cannot be sure. At any rate, he lived in Philippi and was a messenger for the assembly there.

Paul speaks of him as: (1) **my brother**; (2) my **fellow worker**; (3) my **fellow soldier**. The first title speaks of affection, the second of hard work, and the third of conflict. He was a man who could work with others, and this is certainly a great essential in Christian life and service. It is one thing for a believer to work independently, having everything his own way. It is far more difficult to work with others, to play "second fiddle," to allow for individual differences, to submerge one's own desires and opinions for the good of the group. Let us be **fellow workers** and **fellow soldiers**!

In addition, Paul speaks of him as **your messenger and the one who ministered to my need**. This gives us another valuable clue into his personality. He was willing to do common or menial work. Many today are only interested in work that is public and pleasant. How thankful we should be for those who carry on the routine work quietly and inconspicuously! By doing the hard work, Epaphroditus humbled himself. But God exalted him by recording his faithful service in Philippians 2 for all future generations to read.

2:26 The saints had sent Epaphroditus to help Paul—a journey of at least 700 miles. The faithful messenger took **sick** as a result; indeed, he came very close to death. This caused him grave concern — not the fact that he was so sick, but the fear that the saints might hear about it. If they did, they would reproach themselves for sending him on this journey and for thus endangering his life. Surely in Epaphroditus we see "a heart at leisure from itself."

Many Christians have the unfortunate habit of dwelling at great length on their illnesses or operations. Too often this is but a manifestation of the hyphenated sins of the self-life: self-pity, self-occupation, self-display.

2:27 Epaphroditus had been **sick** near to **death, but God had mercy on him**. This section is valuable to us for the light it throws on the subject of divine healing:

1. First of all, sickness is not always the result of sin. Here is a man who was sick because of the faithful discharge of his duties (see v. 30), ". . .for **the work of Christ he came close to death.**"

2. Secondly, we learn that it is not always God's will to heal instantly and miraculously. It appears that Epaphroditus' illness was prolonged and his recovery gradual (see also 2 Tim. 4:20; 3 Jn. 2).

3. Thirdly, we learn that healing is a mercy from God and not something we can demand from Him as being our right.

Paul adds that **God had mercy** not only on Epaphroditus **but on** himself **also, lest** he **should have sorrow upon sorrow**. The apostle already had considerable grief in connection with his imprisonment. If Epaphroditus had died, he would have had additional sorrow.

2:28 Now that Epaphroditus had recovered so well, Paul has **sent him** back home **the more eagerly**. The Philippians would **rejoice** to have their beloved brother back again, and this would lessen Paul's sorrow also.

2:29 Not only should they **receive** Epaphroditus joyfully, but they should also **esteem** this dear man of God. It is a great dignity and privilege to be engaged **in** the service of **the Lord**. The saints should recognize this, even when it concerns one with whom they are very familiar.

2:30 As mentioned previously, Epaphroditus' illness was directly connected with his tireless service for **Christ**. This is of great value in the eyes of the Lord. It is better to *burn out* for Christ than to *rust out*. It is better to die in the service of Jesus than to be counted a mere statistic among those who die from illness or accident.

Does **"to supply what was lacking in your service toward me"** suggest that the Philippians had neglected Paul and that Epaphroditus had done what they should have done? This seems unlikely, since it was the saints at Philippi who had sent Epaphroditus to Paul in the first place.

We suggest that their lack of **service** refers to their *inability* to visit Paul in person and help him directly because of their distance from Rome. Instead of rebuking them, the apostle is merely stating that Epaphroditus did, as their representative, what they were unable to do in person.

V. WARNING AGAINST FALSE TEACHERS (3:1–3)

3:1 Finally, my brethren does not mean that Paul is about to close his Epistle. The literal meaning is "As for the rest . . . ." The same word is used again in 4:8.

He exhorts them to **rejoice in the Lord**. The Christian can always find real joy in **the Lord**, no matter what his circumstances may be. "The source of all his singing is high in heaven above." Nothing can really affect his joy unless it first robs him of his Savior, and this clearly is impossible. Natural happiness is affected by pain, sorrow, sickness, poverty, and tragedy. But Christian joy rides high over all the billows of life. Proof of this is found in the fact that Paul gives this exhortation from prison. Surely we can take the advice from such a man as he!

He does not find it irksome to repeat himself to the Philippians because he knows it is for their safety. But how does he repeat himself? Does this refer to the preceding expression where he urges them to **rejoice in the Lord**? Or does it mean the verses to follow where he warns them against the Judaizers? We believe that the latter is in view. Three times in verse 2 he uses the word **beware**. To use this repetition is **not tedious** for him, but for them it is a true safeguard.

3:2 They are to **beware of dogs, ... of evil workers**, and **of the mutilation**. All three expressions probably refer to the same group of men — false teachers who sought to put Christians under the laws of Judaism and taught that righteousness could be obtained by lawkeeping and ritual.

First of all, they were **dogs**. In the Bible, **dogs** are unclean animals. The term was used by Jews to describe Gentiles! In eastern countries, dogs were homeless creatures, running wild in the streets and scrounging food as best they could. Here Paul turns the tables and applies the term to those Jewish false teachers who were seeking to corrupt the church. They were really the ones who were living on the outside, trying to exist on rituals and ceremonies. They were "picking up the crumbs when they might sit down to a feast."

Secondly, they were **evil workers**. Professing to be true believers, they gained admission into Christian fellowships in order to spread their false teachings. The results of their work could only be evil.

Then Paul also calls them **the mutilation**. This is a sarcastic term to describe their attitude toward circumcision. Doubtless they insisted that a person must be circumcised in order to be saved. But all they meant by this was the physical, literal act of circumcision. They were not at all concerned with its spiritual meaning. Circumcision speaks of death to the flesh. It means that the claims of the fleshly nature should not be allowed. While they insisted on the literal act of circumcision, they gave full rein to the flesh. There was no heart acknowledgment that the flesh had been put to death at the cross. Paul was saying that they were mere mutilators of the flesh, who did not distinguish between the ceremony and its underlying meaning.

3:3 In contrast with these, Paul states that **we** (true believers) **are the circumcision** — not those who happen to be born of Jewish parents or who have been literally circumcised, but those who realize that the flesh profits nothing, that man can do nothing in his own strength to win God's smile of approval. Then Paul gives three characteristics of those who are the true circumcision:

1. They **worship God in** (or by) **the Spirit**. That is, theirs is a true spiritual worship, not one of mere ceremonies. In true worship, a person enters into the presence of God by faith, and pours out his love, praise, adoration and homage. Soulish worship, on the other hand, is occupied with beautiful buildings and ecclesiastical furniture, with elaborate ceremonies, with brocaded priestly garments, and with whatever appeals to the emotions.

2. Members of the true circumcision **rejoice** (or glory) **in Christ Jesus**. He alone is the ground of their boasting. They do not pride themselves in personal attainments, in cultural background, or in faithfulness to sacraments.

3. They **have no confidence in the flesh**. They do not think they can be saved through fleshly efforts in the first place or be kept by their own strength thereafter. They do not expect any good from their Adamic nature and are therefore not disappointed when they find none!

VI. PAUL'S HERITAGE AND PERSONAL ACHIEVEMENTS RENOUNCED FOR CHRIST (3:4–14)

3:4 As Paul thought of how these men boasted in their fleshly advantages and attainments, a smile doubtless formed on his lips. If they could brag, how much **more so** could he! In the next two verses, he shows how that to a preeminent degree he possessed those natural assets in which man normally glories. "He seemed to have belonged to almost every kind of aristocracy which excites the dreams and kindles the aspirations of men."

Concerning these two verses, Arnot has said: "The whole stock-in-trade of the self-righteous Pharisee is inventoried here. He delights to display the filthy rags and make a show of them openly."

You will notice that Paul speaks of: pride of ancestry (v. 5a); pride of orthodoxy (v. 5b); pride of activity (v. 6a); pride of morality (v. 6b).

3:5 Here, then, is the list of Paul's natural and fleshly advantages:

circumcised the eighth day — he was a Jew by birth, not an Ishmaelite or a convert to Judaism.

of the stock of Israel — a member of God's chosen earthly people.

of the tribe of Benjamin — a tribe that was considered an aristocratic leader (Judg. 5:14), and the one that gave Israel its first king.

a Hebrew of the Hebrews — he belonged to that segment of the nation that had held onto its original language, customs, and usages.

concerning the law, a Pharisee — the Pharisees had remained orthodox, whereas the Sadducees had abandoned the doctrine of the resurrection.

3:6 concerning zeal, persecuting the church — Paul sincerely thought that he had been doing God's service when he had attempted to wipe out the "sect" of Christians. He saw in it a threat to his own religion and therefore felt he must exterminate it.

concerning the righteousness which is in the law, blameless — this cannot mean that Paul had perfectly kept the law. He confesses in Romans 7:9, 10 that such was not the case. He speaks of himself as being **blameless**, not sinless. We can only conclude that when Paul had violated any part of the law, he was careful to bring the sacrifice required. In other words, he had been a stickler in seeking to observe the rules of Judaism to the letter.

Thus, as to birth, pedigree, orthodoxy, zeal, and personal righteousness, Saul of Tarsus was an outstanding man.

3:7 But now the apostle makes the great renunciation. Here he gives us his own "Profit and Loss Statement." On one side he lists the above-mentioned items, the things that had been **gain to** him. On the other side he writes the single word **Christ**. They all amount to nothing when compared with the treasure which he had found in Christ. He **counted** them **loss for Christ**. Guy King says, "All financial gain, all material gain, all physical gain, all intellectual gain, all moral gain, all religious gain — all these are no gains at all compared with the Great Gain."[14]

As long as he trusted in these things, he could never have been saved. Once he was saved, they no longer meant anything to him because he had seen the glory of the Lord, and all other glories seemed like nothing in comparison.

3:8 In coming to Christ for salvation, Paul had renounced **all things** and counted them worthless when compared to **the excellence of the knowledge of Christ Jesus**, his **Lord. The excellence of the knowledge** is a Hebrew way of saying "the excellent knowledge" or "the surpassing worth of knowing."

Ancestry, nationality, culture, prestige, education, religion, personal attainments — all these the apostle abandoned as grounds for boasting. Indeed, he counted **them as** dung or **rubbish** in order that he might **gain Christ.**

Although the present tense is used in this verse and in the one following, Paul is looking back primarily to the time of his conversion. In order to **gain Christ**, he had had to turn his back on the things he had always been taught to prize most highly. If he were to have Christ as his gain, he had to say "goodbye" to his mother's religion, his father's heritage, and his own personal attainments.

And so he did! He completely severed his ties with Judaism as a hope of salvation. In doing so, he was disinherited by his relatives, disowned by his former friends, and persecuted by his fellow countrymen. He literally **suffered the loss of all things** when he became a Christian.

Because the present tense is used in verse 8, it sounds as if Paul was still seeking to **gain Christ**. Actually, he had won Christ when he first acknowledged Him as Lord and Savior. But the present tense indicates that this is still his attitude — he still counts all else **as rubbish** when compared to the value of knowing the Lord Jesus. The great desire of his heart is: "That Christ may be my gain." Not gold, or silver, or religious reputation, but Christ.

3:9 And be found in Him. Here again it sounds as if Paul was still trying to be found in Christ. The fact is that he is looking back to the tremendous decision which faced him before he was saved. Was he willing to abandon his own efforts to earn salvation, and simply trust in Christ? He had made his choice. He had abandoned all else in order to be found in Christ. The moment he believed on the Lord Jesus, he stood in a new position before God. No longer was he seen as a child of sinful Adam, but now he was seen *in Christ*, enjoying all the favor which the Lord Jesus enjoys before God the Father.

Likewise he had renounced the filthy rags of his own self-righteousness, which he had sought to win by keeping the law, and had chosen the **righteousness** of God which is bestowed on everyone who receives the Savior. **Righteousness** is here spoken of as a garment or covering. Man needs righteousness in order to stand before God in favor. But man cannot produce it. And so, in grace, God gives *His own* **righteousness** to those who receive His Son as Lord and Savior. "He (God) made Him (Christ) who knew no sin *to be* sin for us, that we might become the righteousness of God in Him" (2 Cor. 5:21).

Again we would like to emphasize that verses 8 and 9 do not suggest that Paul had not yet received the righteousness of God. On the contrary, this became his possession when he was regenerated on the road to Damascus. But the present tense simply indicates that the results of that important event continued up to the present and that Paul still considered Christ to be worth far more than anything he had given up.

3:10 As we read this verse, we come to the supreme emotion of the apostle's life. F. B. Meyer calls it "The Soul's Quest for the Personal Christ."

The most frequent treatment of this passage is to "spiritualize" it. By this is meant that **sufferings, death,** and **resurrection** are not to be taken literally. Rather, they are used to describe certain spiritual experiences, such as mental suffering, dying to self, and living the resurrected life, etc. However, we would like to suggest that the passage should be taken literally. Paul is saying he wants to live as Christ lived. Did Jesus suffer? Paul wants to suffer too. Did Jesus die? Then Paul wants to die by martyrdom in his service for Christ. Did Jesus rise from among the dead? Then Paul wishes to do the same. He realized that the servant is not above his Master. Thus, he desired to follow Christ in **His sufferings, death,** and **resurrection**. He does not say that all must adopt this view, but for him there could be no other pathway.

That I may know Him. To **know Him** means to gain practical day-by-day acquaintance with Him in such an intimate way that the apostle himself would become more Christlike. He wants the life of Christ to be reproduced in himself.

And the power of His resurrection. The **power** that raised the Lord from the dead is set forth in Scripture as the greatest display of might which the universe has ever seen (Eph. 1:19, 20). It would seem as if all the hosts of evil were determined to keep His body in the tomb. God's mighty power defeated this infernal army by raising the Lord Jesus from the dead on the third day. This same **power** is placed at the disposal of all believers (Eph. 1:19), to be appropriated by faith. Paul is stating his ambition to experience this power in his life and testimony.

And the fellowship of His sufferings. It takes divine strength to suffer for Christ. That is why **the power of His resurrection** is put before **the fellowship of His sufferings**.

In the life of the Lord, suffering preceded glory. So then it must be in the life of Paul. He must share Christ's **sufferings**. He realized that there would be nothing of an atoning value in his own sufferings as there was in Christ's, but he knew, too, that it would be inconsistent for him to live in luxury and ease in a world where his Lord was rejected, scourged, and crucified. Jowett comments: "He was not contented to share the triumph of Olivet; he wanted to feel something of the pang and chill and loneliness of Gethsemane."[15]

Being conformed to His death. As

mentioned before, this is usually explained as meaning that Paul wanted to live the crucified life, to die practically to sin, self, and the world. But we feel that such an interpretation robs the passage of its shocking force. It does mean that, but also much more. Paul was a passionately devoted follower of the One who died on the cross of Calvary. Not only that, he was present when the first martyr of the Christian church died; in fact, he was an accomplice in murdering him! We believe Paul was actually anxious to pour out his life in the same way. Perhaps he would have felt embarrassed to meet Stephen in heaven if he had come by any more comfortable route than martyrdom. Jowett agrees:

Many Christians are satisfied with expenditure in which there is no "shedding of blood." They give away what they can easily spare. Their gifts are detached things, and the surrender of them necessitates no bleeding. They engage in sacrifice as long as it does not involve life; when the really vital is demanded, they are not to be found. They are prominent at all triumphant entries, and they willingly spend a little money on colorful decorations — on banners and palm branches; but when "Hurrahs" and "Hosannas" change into ominous murmurs and threats, and Calvary comes into sight, they steal away into safe seclusion.

But here is an Apostle who joyfully anticipates this supreme and critical demand. He is almost impatient at his own dribblings of blood-energy in the service of the kingdom! He is eager if need be to pour it out![16]

In a similar vein Hudson Taylor wrote:

There is a needs-be for us to give *ourselves* for the life of the world. . . .Fruit-bearing involves cross-bearing. "Except a corn of wheat fall into the ground and die, it abideth alone." We know how the Lord Jesus became fruitful — not by bearing His cross only, but by dying on it. Do we know much of fellowship with Him in this? There are not two Christs — an easy-going Christ for easy-going Christians, and a suffering, toiling Christ for exceptional believers. There is only one Christ. Are we willing to abide in Him and so to bear fruit?[17]

Finally, C. A. Coates says:

The knowledge of Christ in glory was the supreme desire of Paul's heart, and this desire could never exist without producing an intense longing to reach Him in the place where He is. Hence the heart that longs after Him instinctively turns to the path by which He reached that place in glory, and earnestly desires to reach Him in that place by the very path which He trod. The heart asks, "How did *He* reach that glory? Was it through resurrection? And did not sufferings and death necessarily precede resurrection?" Then the heart says, "Nothing would please me so well as to reach Him in resurrection glory by the very path which took *Him* there." It is the martyr spirit. Paul wanted to tread as a martyr the pathway of suffering and death, that he might reach resurrection and glory by the same path as the blessed One who had won his heart.[18]

3:11 Here again we are faced with a problem of interpretation. Are we to take this verse literally, or are we to spiritualize it? Various explanations have been offered, the principal of which are as follows:

1. Paul was not sure that he would be raised from the dead, so he was straining every muscle to insure his participation in the resurrection. Such a view is impossible! Paul always taught that resurrection was by grace and not by human works. In addition, he expressed the definite confidence that he would participate in the resurrection (2 Cor. 5:1–8).

2. Paul was not speaking of a physical resurrection at all, but was referring to his desire to live the resurrection life while still here on earth. Perhaps the majority of commentators hold this view.

3. Paul was talking about physical resurrection, but he was not expressing any doubt about his participation in it. Rather he was saying that he was not concerned about the sufferings that might lie before him en route to the resurrection. He was willing to undergo severe trials and persecutions, if that was what lay between the present time and the resurrection. The expression **"if, by any means"** does not necessarily express doubt (see Acts 27:12; Rom. 1:10; 11:14), but strong desire or expectation that does not count the cost.

We agree with the third interpretation. The apostle wanted to be conformed to Christ. Since Christ had suffered, died, and been raised from among the dead, Paul wanted nothing better than this for himself. We fear that our own desire for comfort, luxury, and ease often causes us to remove the sharp, cutting edges of some of these Bible verses. Would it not be safer to take them at their face value — literally — unless that sense is impossible in the light of the rest of the Bible?

Before leaving this verse, we should notice that Paul is speaking of **the resurrection from** *among* **the dead**. This is not a resurrection of all the dead. Rather, it describes a **resurrection** in which some will be raised, but others will remain in the grave. We know from 1 Thessalonians 4:13–18 and 1 Corinthians 15:51–57 that believers will be raised at the coming of Christ (some at the Rapture and some at the end of the Tribulation), but the rest of the dead will not be raised until after Christ's Thousand-Year Reign on earth; cf. Rev. 20:5.

3:12 The apostle did not consider that he was **already perfected. Perfected** refers not to the resurrection in the previous verse, but to the whole subject of conformity to Christ. He had no idea that it was possible to achieve a state of sinlessness or to arrive at a condition in life where no further progress could be achieved. He realized that "satisfaction is the grave of progress."

Thus he pressed on in order that the purpose for which the Lord Jesus had saved him might be fulfilled in him. The apostle had been apprehended by **Christ Jesus** on the road to Damascus. What was the purpose of this momentous meeting? It was that Paul might from then on be a pattern-saint, that God might show through him what Christ can do in a human life. He was not yet perfectly conformed to Christ. The process was still going on, and Paul was deeply exercised that this work of God's grace might continue and deepen.

3:13 This man who had learned to be content with whatever material things he had (4:11) never could be content with his spiritual attainments. He did **not count** himself to have "arrived," as we would say today. What then did he do?

But one thing I do. He was a man of single purpose. He had one aim and ambition. In this he resembled David, who said, "One thing have I desired of the Lord."

Forgetting those things which are behind would mean not only his sins and failures but also his natural privileges, attainments, and successes which he had described earlier in this chapter, and even his spiritual triumphs.

And reaching forward to those things which are ahead: namely, the privileges and responsibilities of the Christian life, whether worship, service, or the personal development of Christian character.

3:14 Looking at himself as a runner in a race, Paul describes himself as exerting every effort **toward the goal for the prize of the upward call of God in Christ Jesus**.

The goal is the finish line at the end of the race track. **The prize** is the award presented to the winner. Here **the goal** would be the finish of life's race, and perhaps more particularly the Judgment Seat of Christ. **The prize** would be the crown of righteousness which Paul elsewhere describes as the prize for those who have run well (2 Tim. 4:8).

The upward call of God in Christ Jesus includes all the purposes that God had in mind in saving us. It includes salvation, conformity to Christ, joint-heirship with Him, a home in heaven, and numberless other spiritual blessings.

VII. EXHORTATION TO A HEAVENLY WALK, AS EXEMPLIFIED BY THE APOSTLE (3:15–21)

3:15 As many as are mature should share Paul's willingness to suffer and die for Christ and to bend every effort in the quest for likeness to the Lord Jesus. This is the mature view of the Christian faith. Some would call it extreme, radical, or fanatical. But the apostle states that those who are full-grown will see that this is the only sane, logical, reasonable response to the One who shed His life-blood for them on Calvary.

If in anything you think otherwise, God will reveal even this to you. Paul realizes that not all will agree with him in adopting such a dangerous philosophy. But he expresses the confidence that if a person is really willing to know the truth of the matter, **God will reveal** it to him. The reason we have such an easy-going, complacent Christianity today is because we do not want to know the truth; we are not willing to obey the demands of ideal Christianity. **God** is willing to show the truth to those who are willing to follow it.

3:16 Then the apostle adds that, in the meantime, we should live up to whatever light the Lord has given us. It would not do to mark time until we came to a fuller knowledge of what is required of us as Christians. While we wait for the Lord to reveal the full implications of the cross to us, we should obey whatever **degree** of truth we have received.

3:17 Now Paul turns to exhortation, first by encouraging the Philippians to be followers, or imitators of himself. It is a tribute to his exemplary life that he could ever write such words. We often hear the expression in jest, "Do as I say, not as I do." Not so the apostle! He could hold up his own life as a model of wholehearted devotion to Christ and to His cause.

Lehman Strauss comments:

Paul considered himself the recipient of God's mercy that he might be a "pattern"; thus his whole life, subsequent to his conversion, was dedicated to presenting to others an outline sketch of what a Christian should be. God saved Paul in order that he might show by the example of his conversion that what Jesus Christ did for him He can and will do for others. Was not this the special object our Lord had in view in extending His mercy to you and me? I believe He has saved us to be a pattern to all future believers. Are we serving as examples of those who have been saved by His grace? May it be so![19]

And note those who so walk, as you have us for a pattern. This refers to any others who were living the same kind of life as Paul. It does not mean to mark them out disapprovingly, as in the next verse, but to observe them with a view to following in their steps.

3:18 Just as verse 17 describes those whom believers *should* follow, this passage tells of those we *should not* follow. The apostle does not identify these men specifically. Whether they were the Judaizing false teachers mentioned in verse 2, or professed Christian teachers who turned liberty into license, and used grace as a pretext for sin, he does not say.

Paul had warned the saints about these men previously, and he does so again with **weeping**. But why the tears in the midst of such a stern denunciation? Because of the harm these men did among the churches of God. Because of the lives they ruined. Because of the reproach they brought on the name of Christ. Because they were obscuring the true meaning of the cross. Yes, but also because true love weeps even when denouncing **the enemies of the cross of Christ**, just as the Lord Jesus wept over the murderous city of Jerusalem.

3:19 These men were destined to eternal perdition. This does not mean annihilation, but the judgment of God in the lake of fire forever.

Their **god** was **their belly**. All their activities, even their professed religious service, were directed toward the purchase of food (and perhaps drink) for the gratification of their bodily appetite. F. B. Meyer described these men with keen insight: "There is no chapel in their life. It is all kitchen."

Their **glory** was **in their shame**. They boasted in the very things they should have been ashamed of — their nakedness and their immoral behavior.

They were occupied with **earthly things**. For them, the important things in life were food, clothing, honor, comfort, and pleasure. Eternal issues and heavenly things did not disturb their groveling in the muck of this world. They carried on as if they were going to live on earth forever.

3:20 The apostle now contrasts the heavenly-minded attitude of the true believer.

At the time the Epistle was written, Philippi was a colony of Rome (Acts 16:12). The Philippians were citizens of Rome, enjoying its protection and privileges. But they were also citizens of their local government. Against this backdrop, the apostle reminds the believers that their **citizenship is in heaven**. Moffatt translates it: "But we are a colony of heaven."

This does not mean that Christians are not *also* citizens of earthly countries

Other Scriptures clearly teach that we are to be subject to governments because they are ordained by God (Rom. 13:1–7). Indeed, believers should be obedient to the government in all matters not expressly forbidden by the Lord. The Philippians owed allegiance to the local magistrates, and also to the Emperor in Rome. So believers have responsibilities to earthly governments, but their first loyalty is to the Lord in heaven.

Not only are we citizens of heaven, but **we also eagerly wait for the Savior** from heaven! **Eagerly wait for** is strong language (in the original) to express the earnest expectation of something believed to be imminent. It means literally to thrust forward the head and neck as in anxious expectation of hearing or seeing something.

3:21 When the Lord Jesus comes from heaven, He will change these bodies of ours. There is nothing vile or evil about the human body in itself. The evil lies in the wrong uses to which it is put.

But it is a **lowly body**, a body of humiliation. It is subject to wrinkles, scars, age, suffering, sickness, and death. It limits and cramps us!

The Lord will **transform** it into a body of glory. The full extent of the meaning of this we do not know. It will no longer be subject to decay or death, to the limitations of time or of natural barriers. It will be a real body, yet perfectly suited to conditions in heaven. It will be like the resurrection **body** of the Lord Jesus.

This does not mean that we will all have the same physical appearance! Jesus was distinctly recognizable after His resurrection, and doubtless each individual will have his or her own individual physical identity in eternity.

Also, this passage does not teach that we shall be like the Lord Jesus as far as the attributes of God are concerned. We shall never have all-knowledge or all-power; neither shall we be in all places at one and same time.

But we shall be morally like the Lord Jesus. We shall be forever free from sin. This passage does not give us enough to satisfy our curiosity, but it is enough to inspire comfort and stimulate hope.

According to the working by which He is able even to subdue all things to Himself. The transformation of our bodies will be accomplished by the same divine power which the Lord will later use **to subdue all things to Himself.** He is "able to save" (Heb. 7:25). He is "able to aid" (Heb. 2:18). He is "able to keep" (Jude 24). Now in this verse we learn that He is **able to subdue.** "This is . . . our God forever and ever: He will be our guide even to death" (Ps. 48:14).

VIII. APPEAL FOR HARMONY, MUTUAL ASSISTANCE, JOY, FORBEARANCE, PRAYERFULNESS, AND A DISCIPLINED THOUGHT LIFE (4:1–9)

4:1 On the basis of the wonderful hope which the apostle had set before the minds of the believers in the previous verse, he now exhorts them to **stand fast in the Lord.** This verse is filled with endearing names for the believers. First of all, Paul calls them his **brethren.** But not only his brethren — his **beloved brethren.** Then he adds the thought that he longs for them, that is, he longs to be with them again. Further, he speaks of them as his **joy and crown.** Doubtless he means that they are his **joy** at the present time and will be his **crown** at the Judgment Seat of Christ. Finally, he closes the verse with the expression **beloved.** The apostle really loved people, and doubtless this is one of the secrets of his effectiveness in the work of the Lord.

4:2 Euodia and **Syntyche** were women in the church at Philippi who were having difficulty getting along together. We are not given details as to the cause of their disagreement (and perhaps it is just as well!).

The apostle uses the word **implore** twice to show that the exhortation is addressed just as much to one as to the other. Paul urges them **to be of the same mind in the Lord.** It is impossible for us to be united in all things in daily life, but, as far as the things of **the Lord** are concerned, it is possible for us to submerge our petty, personal differences in order that the Lord may be magnified and His work advanced.

4:3 There is considerable speculation as to the identity of the **true companion** (or yoke-fellow[20]) whom Paul addresses in this verse. Timothy and Luke have both been suggested, but Epaphroditus is probably the person spoken of. He is exhorted to **help these women who** had **labored** with Paul **in the gospel**. We take it that these women were Euodia and Syntyche, and that the Apostle Paul is giving what experience has proven to be sound advice. Often when two people have been quarreling, the quarrel can best be settled by taking it to an independent third party — someone with mature, spiritual judgment. It is not that he acts arbitrarily in the case and hands down a decision, but rather that by appealing to the word of God, he is able to show the contending persons the scriptural solution to their problem.

Care should be taken in interpreting the expression "[they] **labored with me in the gospel**." By no stretch of the imagination can this be taken to mean that they preached the gospel with the Apostle Paul. There are many ways in which women can labor in the gospel — by hospitality to the servants of Christ, by home visitation, by teaching younger women and children — without assuming a ministry of public teaching or preaching.

Another co-laborer named **Clement** is mentioned. Nothing further is known of him with certainty. Then Paul mentions **the rest of** his **fellow workers, whose names are in the Book of Life**. This is a lovely way of expressing the eternal and unspeakable blessedness that attaches to faith in Christ and service for Him.

4:4 Turning now to the entire church, Paul repeats the favorite exhortation. The secret of his exhortation is found in the words **in the Lord**. No matter how dark the circumstances of life may be, it is always possible for the Christian to **rejoice in the Lord**.

Jowett shares his experience regarding Christian joy:

Christian joy is a mood independent of our immediate circumstances. If it were dependent on our surroundings, then, indeed, it would be as uncertain as an unprotected candle burning on a gusty night. One moment the candle burns clear and steady, the next moment the blaze leaps to the very edge of the wick,

and affords little or no light. But Christian joy has no relationship to the transient setting of the life, and therefore it is not the victim of the passing day. At one time my conditions arrange themselves like a sunny day in June; a little later they rearrange themselves like a gloomy day in November. One day I am at the wedding; the next day I stand by an open grave. One day, in my ministry, I win ten converts for the Lord; and then, for a long stretch of days, I never win one. Yes, the days are as changeable as the weather, and yet the Christian joy can be persistent. Where lies the secret of its glorious persistency?

Here is the secret. "Lo! I am with you *all the days.*" In all the changing days, "He changeth not, neither is weary." He is no fairweather Companion, leaving me when the year grows dark and cold. He does not choose my days of prosperous festival, though not to be found in my days of impoverishment and defeat. He does not show Himself only when I wear a garland, and hide Himself when I wear a crown of thorns. He is with me "all the days" — the prosperous days and the days of adversity; days when the funeral bell is tolling, and days when the wedding bell is ringing. "All the days." The day of life — the day of death — the day of judgment.[21]

4:5 Now Paul urges them to **let their gentleness be known to all men**. This has also been translated yieldedness, sweet reasonableness, and willingness to give up one's own way. The difficulty does not lie in *understanding* what is meant, but in *obeying* the precept **"to all men."**

The Lord is at hand may mean that the Lord is now present, or that the Lord's coming is near. Both are true, though we favor the latter view.

4:6 Is it really possible for a Christian to **be anxious for nothing**? It is possible as long as we have the resource of believing prayer. The rest of the verse goes on to explain how our lives can be free from sinful fretting. Everything should be taken to the Lord in **prayer. Everything** means *everything*. There is nothing too great or small for His loving care!

Prayer is both an act and an atmosphere. We come to the Lord at specific times and bring specific requests before Him. But it is also possible to live in an *atmosphere* of prayer. It is possible that the mood of our life should be a prayerful mood. Perhaps the word *prayer* in this verse signifies the overall attitude of our life, whereas **supplication** signifies the specific **requests** which we bring to the Lord.

But then we should notice that our **requests** should **be made known to God with thanksgiving**. Someone has summarized the verse as saying that we should be "anxious in nothing, prayerful in everything, thankful for anything."

4:7 If these attitudes characterize our lives, **the peace of God, which surpasses all understanding, will guard** our **hearts and minds through Christ Jesus. The peace of God** is a sense of holy repose and complacency which floods the soul of the believer when he is leaning hard upon God.

> Stayed upon Jehovah,
> Hearts are fully blessed;
> Finding, as He promised,
> Perfect peace and rest.
>
> – *Frances Ridley Havergal*

This **peace surpasses all understanding**. People of the world cannot understand it at all, and even Christians possessing it find a wonderful element of mystery about it. They are surprised at their own lack of anxiety in the face of tragedy or adverse circumstances.

This **peace** garrisons the heart and the thought life. What a needed tonic it is, then, in this day of neuroses, nervous breakdowns, tranquilizers, and mental distress.

4:8 Now the apostle gives a closing bit of advice concerning the thought life. The Bible everywhere teaches that we can control what we think. It is useless to adopt a defeatist attitude, saying that we simply cannot help it when our minds are filled with unwelcome thoughts. The fact of the matter is that we *can* help it. The secret lies in positive thinking. It is what is now a well-known principle — the expulsive power of a new affection. A person cannot entertain evil thoughts and thoughts about the Lord Jesus at the same time. If, then, an evil thought should come to him, he should immediately get rid of it by meditating on the Person and work of Christ.

The more enlightened psychologists and psychiatrists of the day have come to agree with the Apostle Paul on this matter. They stress the dangers of negative thinking.

You do not have to look very closely to find the Lord Jesus Christ in verse 8. Everything that is **true, noble, just, pure, lovely, of good report**, virtuous, and **praiseworthy** is found in Him. Let us look at these virtues one by one: **True** means not false or unreliable, but genuine and real. **Noble** means honorable or morally attractive. **Just** means righteous, both toward God and man. **Pure** would refer to the high moral character of a person's life. **Lovely** has the idea of that which is admirable or agreeable to behold or consider. **Of good report** has also been translated "of good repute" or "fair sounding." **Virtue**, of course, speaks of moral excellence; and **praiseworthy**, something that deserves to be commended.

In verse 7, Paul had assured the saints that God would garrison their hearts and thoughts in Christ Jesus. But he is not neglectful to remind them that they, too, have a responsibility in the matter. God does not garrison the thought-life of a man who does not *want* it to be kept pure.

4:9 Again the Apostle Paul sets himself forth as a pattern saint. He urges the believers to practice **the things which** they **learned** from him and which they **saw in** his life.

The fact that this comes so closely after verse 8 is significant. Right living results from right thinking. If a person's thought-life is pure, then his life will be pure. On the other hand, if a person's mind is a fountain of corruption, then you can be sure that the stream that issues from it will be filthy also. And we should always remember that if a person thinks an evil thought long enough, he will eventually do it.

Those who are faithful in following the example of the apostle are promised that **the God of peace will be with** them. In verse 7, the peace of God is the portion of those who are prayerful; here the **God of peace** is the Companion of those who are holy. The thought here is that God will make Himself very near and dear in present experience to all whose lives are embodiments of the truth.

IX. PAUL'S THANKS FOR FINANCIAL GIFTS FROM THE SAINTS (4:10–20)

4:10 In verses 10–19, Paul speaks of the relationship which existed between the church at Philippi and himself in connection with financial assistance. No one could ever tell how meaningful these verses have been for saints of God who have been called upon to go through times of financial pressure and reverses!

Paul rejoices that **now at last**, after a period of time had elapsed, the Philippians had sent him practical assistance in the work of the Lord. He does not blame them for the period of time in which no help was received; he gives them credit that they wanted to send gifts to him but that they **lacked opportunity** to do so. Moffatt translates: "For what you lacked was never the care but the chance of showing it."

4:11 In handling the whole subject of finances, it is lovely to see the delicacy and courtesy which Paul employs. He does not want them to think that he is complaining about any shortage of funds. Rather, he would have them know that he is quite independent of such mundane circumstances. He had **learned ... to be content**, no matter what his financial condition might be. Contentment is really greater than riches, for "if contentment does not produce riches, it achieves the same object by banishing the desire for them."

"It is a blessed secret when the believer learns how to carry a high head with an empty stomach, an upright look with an empty pocket, a happy heart with an unpaid salary, joy in God when men are faithless" (Selected).

4:12 Paul knew **how to be abased**, that is, by not having the bare necessities of life; and he also knew **how to abound**, that is, by having more given to him at a particular time than his immediate needs required. **Everywhere and in all things** he had **learned both to be full and to be hungry, both to abound and to suffer need**. How had the apostle

learned such a lesson? Simply in this way: he was confident that he was in the will of God. He knew that wherever he was, or in whatever circumstances he found himself, he was there by divine appointment. If he was **hungry**, it was because God wanted him to be hungry. If he was **full**, it was because his Lord had so planned it. Busily and faithfully engaged in the service of his King, he could say, "Even so, Father, for so it seemed good in Your sight."

4:13 Then the apostle adds the words which have been a puzzle to many: **"I can do all things through Christ who strengthens me."** Could he possibly mean this literally? Did the apostle really believe that there was nothing he could not do? The answer is this: When the Apostle Paul said that he could **do all things**, he meant **all things** which were God's will for him to do. He had learned that the Lord's commands are the Lord's enablements. He knew that God would never call on him to accomplish some task without giving the necessary grace. **All things** probably applies not so much to great feats of daring as to great privations and hungerings.

4:14 In spite of what he had said, he wants the Philippians to know that they **have done well** in having **shared in** his **distress**. This probably meant the money they sent to supply his needs during his imprisonment.

4:15 In the past, the **Philippians** had excelled in the grace of **giving**. During the early days of Paul's ministry, **when** he **departed from Macedonia, no church shared with** him financially except the Philippians.

It is remarkable how these seemingly unimportant details are recorded forever in God's precious word. This teaches us that what is given to the Lord's servants is given to the Lord. He is interested in every cent. He records all that is done as to Him, and He rewards with good measure, pressed down, shaken together, and running over.

4:16 Even when he was **in Thessalonica,** they **sent aid once and again for** his needs. It is apparent that the Philippians were living so close to the Lord that He was able to direct them in their giving. The Holy Spirit placed a burden on their hearts for the Apostle Paul. They responded by sending money to him **once and again**, that is, twice. When we remember that Paul was in Thessalonica only a short time, it makes their care for him there all the more remarkable.

4:17 The utter unselfishness of Paul is indicated in this verse. He was more elated by their gain than by their **gift**. Greater than his desire for financial help was his longing that **fruit** should abound **to the account** of the believers. This is exactly what happens when money is given to the Lord. It is all recorded in the account books and will be repaid a hundredfold in a coming day.

All that we have belongs to the Lord, and when we give to Him, we are only giving Him what is His own. Christians who argue as to whether or not they should tithe their money have missed the point. A tithe or tenth part was commanded to Israelites under the law as the minimum gift. In this age of grace, the question should not be, "How much shall I give the Lord?" but rather, "How much dare I keep for myself?" It should be the Christian's desire to live economically and sacrificially in order to give an ever-increasing portion of his income to the work of the Lord that men might not perish for want of hearing the gospel of Christ.

4:18 When Paul says **I have all** he means **I have all** *I need*, **and abound**. It seems strange in this day of twentieth-century commercialism to hear a servant of the Lord who is not begging for money, but who, on the contrary, admits having sufficient. The unrestrained begging campaigns of the present day are an abomination in the sight of God and a reproach to the name of Christ. They are completely unnecessary. Hudson Taylor once said, "God's work carried on in God's way will never lack God's resources." The trouble today is that we have failed to distinguish between working for God and the work of God. It is possible to engage in so-called Christian service which might not be the will of God at all. Where there is an abundance of money, there is always the greatest danger of embarking on ventures which might not have the divine

sanction. To quote Hudson Taylor once again: "What we greatly need to fear is not insufficient funds, but too much unconsecrated funds."

The love-gift which **Epaphroditus** brought from the Philippians to Paul is described as a **sweet-smelling aroma, an acceptable sacrifice, well pleasing to God**. The only other time these words are used, they refer to Christ Himself (Eph. 5:2). Paul dignifies the sacrificial giving of the Philippians by describing what it meant to God. It ascended as a fragrant **sacrifice** to Him. It was both **acceptable** and **well pleasing.**

Jowett exclaims:

> How vast, then, is the range of an apparently local kindness! We thought we were ministering to a pauper, and in reality we were conversing with the King. We imagined that the fragrance would be shut up in a petty neighborhood, and lo, the sweet aroma steals through the universe. We thought we were dealing only with Paul, and we find that we were ministering to Paul's Savior and Lord.[22]

4:19 Now Paul adds what is perhaps the best-known and best-loved verse in this entire chapter. We should notice that this promise follows the description of their faithful stewardship. In other words, because they had given of their material resources to God, even to the point where their own livelihood was endangered, **God** would **supply** their every **need**. How easy it is to take this verse out of context and use it as a soft pillow for Christians who are squandering their money on themselves with seldom a thought for the work of God! "That's all right. God will supply all your need."

While it is true in a general sense that **God** does **supply** the needs of His people, this is a specific promise that those who are faithful and devoted in their giving to Christ will never suffer lack.

It has often been remarked that God supplies the needs of His people — not *out of* His riches, **but according to His riches in glory by Christ Jesus**. If a millionaire gave a dime to a child, he would be giving *out of* his riches. But if he gave a hundred thousand dollars to some worthy cause, he would be giving *according to* his riches. God's supply is **accord-**

ing to His riches in glory by Christ Jesus, and nothing could be richer than that!

Williams calls verse 19 a note drawn upon the bank of faith:

My God — the name of the Banker.

Shall supply — the promise to pay.

All your need — the value of the note.

According to His riches — the capital of the bank.

In glory — the address of the bank.

By Christ Jesus — the signature at the foot, without which the note is worthless.[23]

4:20 Thinking of God's abundant provision causes the apostle to break out into praise. This is suitable language for every child of God who daily experiences God's gracious care, not only in the supply of material things, but also in providing guidance, help against temptation, and the quickening of a languishing devotional life.

X. CLOSING GREETINGS (4:21–23)

4:21 Thinking of the believers as they are gathered together and listening to the Letter which he was writing to them, Paul greets **every saint in Christ Jesus** and sends greetings from **the brethren who are with** him.

4:22 We are compelled to love this verse for its reference to **Caesar's household**. Our imaginations are strongly tempted to run riot. Who are the members of Nero's household referred to here? Were they some of the soldiers who had been assigned to watch the Apostle Paul, and who had been saved through his ministry? Were they slaves or freedmen who worked in the palace? Or might the expression include some officials of the Roman government? We cannot know with certainty, but here we have a lovely illustration of the truth that Christians, like spiders, find their way into king's palaces (Prov. 30:28)! The gospel knows no boundaries. It can penetrate the most forbidding walls. It can plant itself in the very midst of those who are seeking to exterminate it. Truly, the gates of Hades shall not prevail against the church of Jesus Christ!

4:23 Now Paul closes with his characteristic greeting. **Grace** sparkled on the first page of this Letter, and now is found again at the close. Out of the abundance of a man's heart his mouth speaks. Paul's heart was filled to overflowing with the greatest theme of all the ages — **the grace of** God through **Christ** — and it is not at all surprising that this precious truth should flood over into every channel of his life.

Paul Rees concludes for us:

> The greatest of humans has written his warmest of letters. The love-task is finished. The day is done. The chain is still there upon the apostolic wrist. The soldier is still on guard. Never mind! Paul's spirit is free! His mind is clear! His heart is glowing!

And next morning Epaphroditus strides away to Philippi![24]

ENDNOTES

[1](Intro) H. A. A. Kennedy, "Philippians," *The Expositor's Greek Testament*, III:407.

[2](1:1) J. H. Jowett, *The High Calling*, p. 2.

[3](1:7) W. E. Vine, *The Epistles to the Philippians and Colossians*, p. 23.

[4](1:10) By derivation the word translated "sincere" (eilikrinēs) means "unmixed," or possibly "sun-proof." If the latter, it has the same idea as English "sincere" (lit. "without wax"). An honest sculptor would keep chipping away to remove a flaw in a white marble statue. An "insincere" one would fill the gouge up with wax. But, in the sun, a statue with a wax filling would soon expose the sculptor's cover-up.

[5](1:11) Lehman Strauss, *Devotional Studies in Philippians*, p. 63.

[6](1:13) T. W. Drury, *The Prison Ministry of St. Paul*, p. 22.

[7](1:20) Guy King, *Joy Way*, p. 33.

[8](1:21) Jowett, *Calling*, p. 34.

[9](2:1) F. B. Meyer, *Devotional Commentary on Philippians*, pp. 77-79.

[10](2:5) King, *Joy Way*, p. 51.

[11](2:6) E. H. Gifford, *The Incarnation*, pp. 44, 45.

[12](2:11) Charles R. Erdman, further documentation unavailable.

[13](2:17)George Williams, *The Student's Commentary on the Holy Scriptures*, p. 931.

[14](3:7) King, *Joy Way*, p. 81.

[15](3:10) Jowett, *Calling*, p. 217.

[16](3:10) *Ibid.*, pp. 81, 82.

[17](3:10) Hudson Taylor, quoted by Mrs. Howard Taylor in *Behind the Ranges*, p. 170.

[18](3:10) C. A. Coates, *The Paths of Life and Other Addresses*, p. 127.

[19](3:17) Strauss, *Philippians*, p. 202.

[20](4:3) "Yoke-fellow" (Gk. *su(n)zugos*) may be a proper name (Synzygus). Though it has not yet been found elsewhere, it is the sort of name a slave especially might receive.

[21](4:4) Jowett, *Day by Day*, pp. 169-171.

[22](4:18) *Ibid*, p. 225.

[23](4:19) Williams, *Student's Commentary*, p. 934.

[24](4:23) Paul Rees, *The Adequate Man*, p. 127.

Bibliography

Erdman, C. R. *The Epistle of Paul to the Philippians*. Philadelphia: Westminster Press, 1928.

Gifford, E. H. *The Incarnation: A Study of Philippians*. London: Hodder & Stoughton, 1897.

Jowett, J. H. *The High Calling*. London: Andrew Melrose, 1909.

Kelly, William. *Lectures on Philippians and Colossians*. London: G. Morrish, n.d.

Kennedy, H. A. A. "Philippians," *The Expositor's Greek Testament, Vol. III*. Grand Rapids: Wm. B. Eerdmans Publishing Co., 1961.

King, Guy H. *Joy Way*. London: Marshall, Morgan & Scott, Ltd., 1954.

Meyer, F. B. *Devotional Commentary on Philippians*. Grand Rapids: Kregel Publications, 1979.

Rees, Paul. *The Adequate Man*. Westwood, N.J.: Fleming H. Revell Co., 1959.

Strauss, Lehman. *Devotional Studies in Philippians*. Neptune, N.J.: Loizeaux Bros. Publishers, 1959.

Vine, W. E. *The Epistles to the Philippians and Colossians*. London: Oliphants, 1955.

THE EPISTLE TO THE COLOSSIANS

Introduction

"To go into [Colossians] itself, to rethink its inspired thought that is clothed in inspired language, to let the light and the power of this thought fill the soul and mold the life, this is enrichment for time and for eternity."
— R. C. H. Lenski

I. Unique Place in the Canon

Most of Paul's Letters were written to congregations in large or important cities: Rome, Corinth, Ephesus, Philippi. Colosse was a town that had seen better days. Even the assembly there did not become well-known in early church history. In short, were it not for this inspired Epistle to the Christians there, Colosse would today be a name known only to students of ancient history.

Although the place was insignificant, the Letter that the apostle sent there is very important. Along with John 1 and Hebrews 1, Colossians 1 presents the most marvelous exposition of the absolute deity of our Lord Jesus Christ. Since this doctrine is fundamental to all Christian truth, its value cannot be overstressed.

The Letter also has rich instruction on relationships, cultic religion, and the Christian life.

II. Authorship†

There is no proof that anyone questioned the Pauline authorship of Colossians until the nineteenth century, so complete is the positive evidence. The *external evidence* is especially strong. Those who quote the Letter, often naming Paul as the author, include Ignatius, Justin Martyr, Theophilus of Antioch, Irenaeus, Clement of Alexandria, Tertullian, and Origen. Both the Canons of Marcion and Muratori accept Colossians as authentic.

The *internal evidence* includes the simple fact that thrice the writer *says* he is Paul (1:1, 23; 4:18) and the contents

agree with those statements. The exposition of doctrine followed by duty is typical of the apostle. Perhaps the most persuasive proof of authenticity is the strong link with Philemon, which everyone accepts as Pauline. Five of the same men mentioned in that little Letter also show up in Colossians. Even such a critic as Renan was impressed with the Philemon parallels, and *he had doubts about Colossians*.

The arguments *against* Pauline authorship center on vocabulary, the doctrine of Christ, and apparent references to Gnosticism. Regarding the first point, new vocabulary in Colossians replaces some of Paul's favorite words. Salmon, a conservative British scholar of the past century, rather wittily counters the argument: "I cannot subscribe to the doctrine that a man writing a new composition must not, on pain of losing his identity, employ any word that he has not used in a former one."[1] Regarding the Christology of Colossians, it dovetails with that of Philippians and John, and only those who desire to transform the deity of Christ into a second century development from paganism should have any trouble with this doctrine.

As to Gnosticism, the liberal Scottish scholar Moffatt thought that the early stage of Gnosticism presented in Colossians could well have existed in the first century.[2]

Thus the Pauline authorship of Colossians rests on a firm foundation.

III. Date

As one of the "Prison Epistles," Colossians could conceivably come from

†*See p. i.*

Paul's two-year incarceration in Caesarea (Acts 23:23; 24:27). However, since the evangelist Philip was his host there, it seems unlikely that the apostle would neglect to mention him, Paul being such a courteous and gracious Christian. A possible Ephesian imprisonment has also been suggested, though this is much less likely. The favored time for this Letter and Philemon is in the middle of Paul's first Roman imprisonment, about A.D. 60 (Acts 28:30, 31).

Fortunately, as is usually true, an understanding of this book does not depend on a full knowledge of the circumstances under which it was written.

IV. Background and Theme†

Colosse was a city in the province of Phrygia, in the area now known as Asia Minor. It was located ten miles east of Laodicea and thirteen miles southeast of Hierapolis (see 4:13). It was also located about one hundred miles east of Ephesus, at the mouth of a pass in the Cadmian mountain range (a narrow glen twelve miles long) on the military route from the Euphrates to the West. Colosse was on the Lycus (Wolf) River, which flows westward into the Maeander River shortly after it passes Laodicea. There the water from the hot springs from Hierapolis joins the cold waters from Colosse, producing a "lukewarm" condition at Laodicea. Hierapolis was both a health center and a religious center, while Laodicea was the metropolis of the valley. Colosse had been larger previous to NT times. The name is thought possibly to relate to the word "colossus," from the fantastic shapes of its limestone formations.

We do not know exactly how the gospel first reached Colosse. At the time Paul wrote this Letter, he had never met the believers there (2:1). It is generally believed that Epaphras was the one who first brought the good news of salvation to this city (1:7). Many believe that he was converted through Paul when the apostle spent the three years at Ephesus. Phrygia is a part of Proconsular Asia, and Paul was in Phrygia (Acts 16:6; 18:23), but not Colosse (2:1).

We do know from the Letter that a false teaching which in its full-blown form became known as Gnosticism was beginning to threaten the church at Colosse. The Gnostics prided themselves on their knowledge (Gk., *gnōsis*). They claimed to have information superior to that of the apostles and tried to create the impression that a person could not be truly happy unless he had been initiated into the deepest secrets of their cult.

Some of the Gnostics denied the true humanity of Christ. They taught that "the Christ" was a divine *influence* that came out from God and rested on the Man, Jesus, at His baptism. They further taught that the Christ left Jesus just before His crucifixion. The result, according to them, was that Jesus died, but the Christ did not.

Certain branches of Gnosticism taught that between God and matter there are various levels or grades of spirit beings. They adopted this view in an effort to explain the origin of evil. A. T. Robertson explains:

> The Gnostic speculation concerned itself primarily with the origin of the universe and the existence of evil. They assumed that God is good and yet there is evil in existence. Their theory was that evil is inherent in matter. And yet the good God could not create evil matter. So they postulated a series of emanations, aeons, spirits, angels that came in between God and matter. The idea was that one aeon came from God, another aeon from this aeon, and so on till there was one far enough away from God for God not to be contaminated by the creation of evil matter and yet close enough to have power to do the work.[3]

Some Gnostics, believing that the body was inherently sinful, practiced asceticism, a system of self-denial or even self-torture, in an effort to attain a higher spiritual state. Others went to the opposite extreme, living in carnal indulgence, saying that the body didn't matter or have any affect on a person's spiritual life!

It seems that traces of two other errors were found in Colosse. These were antinomianism and Judaism. Antinomianism is the teaching that under grace a person does not need to practice self-control but may give full vent to his bodily appetites and passions. Old Testament Judaism had degenerated into a

†See p. ii.

system of ceremonial observances by which a man hoped to achieve righteousness before God.

The errors which existed in Colosse are still with us today. Gnosticism has reappeared in Christian Science, Theosophy, Mormonism, Jehovah's Witnesses, Unity, and other systems. Antinomianism is characteristic of all who say that because we are under grace, we can live as we please. Judaism was originally a God-given revelation, whose forms and ceremonies were intended to teach spiritual truths in a typical way, as the Epistle to the Hebrews and other parts of the NT show. This lapsed into a system in which the forms themselves were considered to be meritorious, and so the spiritual meaning was often largely ignored. It has its counterpart today in the many religious systems which teach that a person can gain merit and favor with God by his own works, ignoring or denying his sinful state and need of salvation from God alone.

In Colossians, the Apostle Paul mas-

terfully counteracts all these errors by displaying the glories of the Person and work of our Lord Jesus Christ.

This Epistle bears a striking resemblance to Paul's Letter to the Ephesians. However, it is a resemblance without repetition. Ephesians views believers as seated with Christ in heavenly places. Colossians, on the other hand, sees believers on earth, with Christ their glorified Head in heaven. The emphasis in *Ephesians* is that the *believer* is *in Christ. Colossians* speaks of *Christ in the believer,* the hope of glory. In Ephesians, the thrust is on the church as the "Body" of Christ, "the fullness of Him who fills all in all" (Eph. 1:23). Hence the unity of the Body of Christ is stressed. In Colossians, the headship of Christ is set forth extensively in chapter 1, with the necessity of our "holding fast to the Head" (2:18, 19), being submissive to Him. Fifty-four of the 155 verses in Ephesians are similar to verses found in Colossians.

OUTLINE

Commentary

I. THE DOCTRINE OF THE PRE-EMINENCE OF CHRIST (Chaps. 1, 2)

A. Salutation (1:1, 2)

1:1 In the days when the NT was written, it was customary to begin a let-

ter with the name of the writer. Thus **Paul** introduces himself as **an apostle of Jesus Christ by the will of God. An apostle** was one who had been especially sent forth by the Lord Jesus as a messenger. In order to confirm the message that they preached, apostles were given the power to perform miracles (2 Cor. 12:12). In addition, we read that when the apostles laid their hands on believers in certain cases, the Holy Spirit was given (Acts 8:15–20; 19:6). There are no apostles in the world today in the strict sense of the word, and it is folly for men to claim to be successors of the original twelve. Ephesians 2:20 is taken by many to indicate that the work of those with the distinctive gift of apostles and prophets had to do chiefly with the founding of the church, in contrast with the work of evangelists, pastors, and teachers (Eph. 4:11), which continue throughout this dispensation.

Paul traces his apostleship to **the will of God** (see also Acts 9:15; Gal. 1:1). It was not an occupation which he had chosen for himself or for which he had been trained by men. Neither was the office given to him by human ordination. It was not "from men" (as the source), neither "through men" (as the instrument). Rather, his entire ministry was carried out under the solemn realization that God Himself had chosen him to be an apostle.

With Paul at the time this Letter was written was **Timothy our brother**. It is good to notice here a complete lack of officialism in Paul's attitude toward Timothy. Both were members of a common brotherhood and there was no thought of a hierarchy of church dignitaries with pompous titles and distinguishing clothing.

1:2 The Letter is addressed to **the saints and faithful brethren in Christ who are in Colosse**. Here are two of the lovely names that are given in the NT to all Christians. **Saints** means that they are separated to God from the world and that as a result they should lead holy lives. **Faithful brethren** indicates that they are children of a common Father through faith in the Lord Jesus; they are believing brothers and sisters. Christians are also called disciples and believers in other sections of the NT.

In Christ speaks of their *spiritual* position. When they were saved, God placed them in Christ, "accepted in the beloved." Henceforth, they had His life and nature. Henceforth, they would no longer be seen by God as children of Adam or as unregenerate men, but He

would now see them in all the acceptability of His own Son. The expression **in Christ** conveys more of intimacy, acceptance, and security than any human mind can understand. The *geographical* location of these believers is indicated by the expression **who are in Colosse**. It is doubtful that we would ever have heard of this town had it not been that the gospel was preached there and souls were saved.

Paul now greets the saints with the lovely salutation: **Grace to you and peace from God our Father and the Lord Jesus Christ.** No two words could better embrace the blessings of Christianity than **grace and peace**. **Grace** was a common Greek expression, while **peace** was the common Jewish greeting; and the words were used at meeting or parting. Paul united them, and elevated their meaning and use. **Grace** pictures God stooping down to sinful, lost humanity in loving and tender compassion. **Peace** summarizes all that results in the life of a person when he accepts God's grace as a free gift. R. J. Little said: "Grace can mean many things, and is like a blank check. Peace is definitely part of the Christian's heritage, and we should not allow Satan to rob us of it." The order of the words is significant: **grace** first, then **peace**. If God had not first acted in love and mercy toward us, we would still be in our sins. But because He took the initiative and sent His Son to die for us, we now can have peace with God, peace with man, and the peace of God in our souls. Even having said all this, one despairs of ever adequately defining such tremendous words as these.

B. Paul's Thanksgiving and Prayer for the Believers (1:3–14)

1:3 Having greeted these saints in terms which have become the watchword of Christianity, the apostle does something else which is very characteristic of him — he falls to his knees in **thanks** and prayer. It seems that the apostle always began his prayer with praise to the Lord, and this is a good example for us to follow. His prayer is addressed **to the God and Father of our Lord Jesus Christ**. Prayer is the unspeakable privilege of having audience with the Sovereign of the universe. But it may be asked: "How could a mere man dare to stand in the awful presence of the infinitely high God?" The answer is found in our text. The glorious and majestic God of the universe is **the Father of our Lord Jesus Christ**. The One who is infinitely high has become intimately nigh. Because as believers in Christ we share His life, God is our Father also (John 20:17). We can draw near through Christ. **Praying always for you.** Taken by itself, this expression does not seem remarkable, but it takes on new meaning when we remember that this describes Paul's interest in people he had never met. We often find it difficult to remember our own relatives and friends before the throne of grace, but think of the prayer list the Apostle Paul must have kept! He prayed not only for those he knew but also for Christians in faraway places whose names had been mentioned to him by others. Truly Paul's untiring prayer life helps us to understand him better.

1:4 He had heard of the Colossians' **faith in Christ Jesus and of** their **love to all the saints**. He first mentions their **faith in Christ Jesus.** That is where we must always begin. There are many religious people in the world today who are constantly talking about their love for others. But if you question them, you find that they do not have any **faith in** the Lord **Jesus**. Such love is hollow and meaningless. On the other hand, there are those who profess to have **faith in Christ**, yet you look in vain for any evidence of **love** in their lives. Paul would likewise question the sincerity of their faith. There must be true **faith** in the Savior, and this faith must be evidenced by a life of **love** to God and to one's fellow man.

Paul speaks of **faith** as being **in Christ Jesus**. It is very important to notice this. The Lord Jesus Christ is always set forth in Scripture as the Object of faith. A person might have unbounded faith in a bank, but that faith is only valid as long as the bank is reliable. The faith itself will not insure the safety of one's money if the bank is poorly managed. So it is in the spiritual life. Faith in itself is not sufficient. That faith must be centered in the Lord Jesus Christ.

Since He can never fail, no one who trusts Him will ever be disappointed.

The fact that Paul had heard of their **faith** and of their **love** shows that they certainly were not secret believers. In fact, the NT gives little encouragement to anyone who seeks to go on as a secret disciple. The teaching of the Word of God is that if a person has truly received the Savior, then it is inevitable that he will make public confession of Christ.

The love of the Colossians went out to **all the saints**. There was nothing local or sectarian about their love. They did not love only those of their own fellowship, but wherever they found true believers, their love flowed out freely and warmly. This should be a lesson to us that our love should not be narrow or limited to our own local fellowship, or to missionaries from our own country. We should recognize the sheep of Christ wherever they are found, and manifest our affection to them wherever possible.

1:5 It is not entirely clear how this verse connects with what has gone before. Is it connected with verse 3: We give thanks...**because of the hope which is laid up for you in heaven**? Or is it connected with the latter part of verse 4: Your love for all the saints, **because of the hope which is laid up for you in heaven**? Either interpretation is possible. The apostle could be giving thanks, not only for their faith and their love, but also for the future inheritance which would one day be theirs. On the other hand, it is also true that faith in Christ Jesus and love to all the saints are exercised in view of that which lies before us. In any case, we can all see that Paul is here listing the three cardinal virtues of the Christian life: faith, love, and **hope**. These are also mentioned in 1 Corinthians 13:13 and 1 Thessalonians 1:3; 5:8. Lightfoot says: "Faith rests on the past; love works in the present; hope looks to the future."[4]

In this verse, **hope** does not mean the attitude of waiting or looking forward to something, but rather it refers to that for which a person hopes. Here it means the fulfillment of our salvation when we shall be taken to heaven and will enter into our eternal inheritance. The Colossians had heard about this **hope** previously, perhaps when Epaphras preached the gospel to them. What they had heard is described as the **word of the truth of the gospel**. The **gospel** is here described as a message of *true* good news. Perhaps Paul was thinking of the *false* teachings of the Gnostics when he wrote this. Someone has defined "truth" as that which God says about a thing (John 17:17). **The gospel** is true because it is God's word.

1:6 The truth of the gospel had **come to** the Colossians even **as it** had **in all the** then-known **world**. This must not be taken in an absolute sense. It could not mean that *every man and woman* in the world had heard the gospel. It may mean, in part, that some from *every nation* had heard the good news of salvation (Acts 2). It may also mean that the gospel was for all men, and was being spread abroad without purposeful limitation. Paul is also describing the inevitable results which it produced. In Colosse and **in all** the other parts of **the world** where the gospel was preached, it bore **fruit** and was **growing** (NKJV margin⁵). This is stated to show the supernatural character of the gospel. In nature, a plant does not usually bear fruit and increase at the same time. Many times, it has to be pruned in order to bear fruit, for if it is allowed to grow wild, the result is that all the life of the plant goes into leaves and branches rather than into fruit. But the gospel does both at the same time. It bears **fruit** in the salvation of souls and in the upbuilding of the saints, and it also spreads from city to city and from nation to nation.

This is precisely the effect that the gospel had in the lives of the Colossians **since the day** they **heard and knew the grace of God in truth**. There was numerical growth in the church at Colosse and, in addition, there was spiritual growth in the lives of the believers there.

It appears that great strides had been made in the first century, and that the gospel did reach Europe, Asia, and Africa, going farther than many persons have supposed. Still, there is no ground for thinking that it covered the entire earth. **The grace of God** is used here as a lovely description of the gospel message. What could more beautifully summarize the glad tidings than the wonderful truth of God's grace bestowed on

guilty men who deserve God's wrath!

1:7 The apostle clearly states that it was **from Epaphras** that the believers had heard the gospel message and had come to know it experientially in their lives. Paul commends Epaphras as a **dear fellow servant** and **a faithful minister of Christ on** their **behalf**. There was nothing of bitterness or jealousy about the Apostle Paul. It did not bother him to see another preacher receiving commendation. In fact, he was the first to express his appreciation for other servants of the Lord.

1:8 It was from Epaphras that Paul himself had heard of the Colossians' **love in the Spirit**. This was not a merely human affection, but it was that genuine **love** for the Lord and for His people which is created by the indwelling **Spirit** of God. This is the only reference to the Holy Spirit in this Epistle.

1:9 Having concluded this thanksgiving, Paul now begins to make specific intercession for the saints. We have already mentioned how broad were the apostle's prayer interests. We should further point out that his requests were always specifically suited to the need of the people of God in any particular location. He did not pray in generalities. Here he seems to make four separate requests for the Colossians: (1) spiritual insight; (2) a worthy walk; (3) abundant power; (4) a thankful spirit.

There was nothing mean or stingy about his requests. This is especially obvious in verses 9, 10, and 11 by his use of the words *all, fully,* and *every*. (1) **All wisdom and spiritual understanding** (v. 9). (2) "fully pleasing" (v. 10). (3) "Every good work" (v. 10). (4) "All might" (v. 11). (5) "All patience and longsuffering" (v. 11).

For this reason connects with the preceding verses. It means *because of Epaphras' report* (vv. 4, 5, 8). From the first time he had **heard** about these dear saints at Colosse and their faith, love, and hope, the apostle had made it his practice to pray for them. First, he prayed that they might **be filled with the knowledge of** God's **will in all wisdom and spiritual understanding**. He did not ask that they should be satisfied with the boasted knowledge of the Gnostics. He would have them enter into the full

knowledge of God's **will** for their lives as revealed in His word. This knowledge is not of a worldly or carnal nature; it is characterized by spiritual **wisdom and spiritual understanding** — **wisdom** to apply the knowledge in the best way, and **understanding** to see what agrees and what conflicts with God's will.

1:10 There is a very important connection between verse 10 and verse 9. Why did the Apostle Paul want the Colossians to be filled with the knowledge of God's will? Was it so they might become mighty preachers or sensational teachers? Was it so they might attract large followings to themselves, as the Gnostics sought to do? No, the true purpose of spiritual wisdom and understanding is to enable Christians to **walk worthy of the Lord, fully pleasing Him**. Here we have a very important lesson on the subject of guidance. God does not reveal His will to us in order to satisfy our curiosity. Neither is it intended to cater to our ambition or pride. Rather the Lord shows us His will for our lives in order that we might please Him in all that we do.

Being fruitful in every good work. Here is a helpful reminder that although a person is not saved *by* good works, he most certainly is saved *for* good works. Sometimes in emphasizing the utter worthlessness of good works in the salvation of souls, we may create the impression that Christians do not believe in good works. Nothing could be further from the truth! We learn in Ephesians 2:10 that "we are His workmanship, created in Christ Jesus for good works." Again, Paul wrote to Titus: "This is a faithful saying, and these things I want you to affirm constantly, that those who have believed in God should be careful to maintain good works" (Tit. 3:8).

Not only did Paul want them to bear fruit **in every good work**, but also to increase **in the knowledge of God**. How is this done? First of all, it is done through the diligent study of God's word. Then it is also found in obeying His teachings and serving Him faithfully. (The latter seems to be the prominent thought here.) As we do these things, we enter into a deeper **knowledge of** the Lord. "Then shall we know,

if we follow on to know the Lord (Hos. 6:3, KJV).

Notice the repetition of words dealing with knowledge in chapter 1 and realize that there is a definite advance in thought with each use. In verse 6, they *"knew* the grace of God." In verse 9, they had "the *knowledge* of His will." In verse 10, they were *"increasing* in the *knowledge* of God." Perhaps we could say that the first refers to salvation, the second to study of the Scriptures, and the third to service and Christian living. Sound doctrine should lead to right conduct, which expresses itself in obedient service.

1:11 The apostle's third request is that the saints might be **strengthened with all might, according to His glorious power**. (Note the progression: *filled*, v. 9; *fruitful*, v. 10; *fortified*, v. 11.) The Christian life cannot be lived by mere human energy. It requires supernatural strength. Therefore Paul desires that the believers might know the power of the risen Son of God, and he furthermore desires that they should know this **according to His glorious power**. The request is not that this power might be *out of* His glorious power, but **according to** it. **His glorious power** is limitless and that is just the scope of the prayer. Peake writes: "The equipment with power is proportional not simply to the recipient's need, but to the Divine supply."[6]

Why did Paul want the Christians to have this power? Was it so they might go out and perform spectacular miracles? Was it so they might raise the dead, heal the sick, cast out demons? Once again the answer is "No." This power is needed so that the child of God may have **all patience and longsuffering with joy**. This deserves careful attention! In parts of Christendom today, great emphasis is placed upon so-called miracles, such as speaking in tongues, healing the sick, and similar sensational acts. But there is a greater miracle than all of these in the age in which we live: A child of God suffering patiently and thanking God in the midst of the trial!

In 1 Corinthians 13:4, longsuffering is connected with kindness; here with **joy**. We suffer because we cannot escape sharing the groaning of creation. To maintain **joy** within and kindness to others requires God's power, and is Christian victory. The difference between **patience** and **longsuffering** has been defined as the difference between enduring without complaint and enduring without retaliation. God's grace has achieved one of its greatest objects in the life of the believer who can suffer patiently and praise God in the midst of the fiery trial.

1:12 **Giving thanks** in this verse refers to the Colossians, not Paul (it is plural in the original). Paul is praying that they might not only be strengthened with all might but that they also might have a thankful spirit, that they might never fail to express their gratitude **to the Father**, who **qualified** them **to be partakers of the inheritance of the saints in the light**. As sons of Adam, we were not fit to enjoy the glories of heaven. In fact, if unsaved people could somehow be taken to heaven, they would not enjoy it, but would rather be in the deepest misery. Appreciation of heaven requires a fitness for it. Even as believers in the Lord Jesus, we do not have any fitness for heaven in ourselves. The only title to glory which we have is found in the Person of the Lord Jesus Christ:

> I stand upon His merit,
> I know no other stand,
> Not e'en where glory dwelleth,
> In Immanuel's land.
> – *Anne Ross Cousin*

When God saves someone, He instantly bestows on that person fitness for heaven. That fitness is Christ. Nothing can improve on that. Not even a long life of obedience and service here on earth makes a person more fit for heaven than he was the day he was saved. Our title to glory is found in His blood. While the inheritance is **in the light** and "reserved in heaven," we believers on earth have the Holy Spirit as the "guarantee of our inheritance." Therefore we can rejoice in what lies ahead for us, while enjoying even now the "firstfruits of the Spirit."

1:13 In making us "qualified . . . to be partakers of the inheritance of the saints in the light," God **has delivered us from the power of darkness and conveyed us into the kingdom of the Son of His love** (cf. 1 Jn. 2:11). This can be illustrated by the experience of the children of Israel, as recorded in Exodus. They had been living in Egypt, groaning under the lashes of the taskmasters there. By a marvelous act of divine intervention, God delivered them out of that fearful bondage and led them through the wilderness to the promised land. Similarly, as sinners we were in bondage to Satan, but through Christ we have been **delivered from** his clutches and now we are subjects of Christ's **kingdom**. Satan's kingdom is one of **darkness** — an absence of light, warmth, and joy; while the **kingdom** of Christ is one of **love**, which implies the presence of all three.

The kingdom of Christ is seen in Scripture in several different aspects. When He came to the earth the first time, He offered a literal kingdom to the nation of Israel. The Jews wanted deliverance from the Roman oppressor, but they did not want to repent of their sins. Christ could only reign over a people who were in proper spiritual relationship to Him. When that was made clear to them, they rejected their King and crucified Him. Since then, the Lord Jesus has gone back to heaven and we now have the kingdom in mystery form (Matt. 13). This means that the kingdom does not appear in visible form. The King is absent. But all who accept the Lord Jesus Christ during this present age acknowledge Him as their rightful Ruler, and thus they are subjects of His kingdom. In a coming day, the Lord Jesus will come back to earth, set up His kingdom with Jerusalem as capital, and reign for one thousand years. At the end of that time, Christ will put down all enemies under His feet and then deliver up the kingdom to God the Father. That will inaugurate the eternal kingdom, which will continue throughout eternity.

1:14 Having mentioned the kingdom of the Son of God's love, Paul now launches into one of the grandest passages in all the word of God on the Person and work of the Lord Jesus. It is hard for us to know whether he has finished his prayer, or whether it continues through these verses we are about to study. But it is not of great importance, because even if the following verses are not pure prayer, they certainly are pure worship.

Sturz has pointed out that "in this amazing passage which exalts Jesus Christ more than any other, His name does not appear even once in any form." While this is remarkable in one sense, yet it is not to be wondered at. For who else but our blessed Savior could ever fulfill the description which is given to us here? The passage reminds us of Mary's question to the gardener: "Sir, if You have carried Him away, tell me where You have laid Him, and I will take Him away" (John 20:15). She did not name Him. There *was* only one Person to her mind.

Christ is first presented as the One **in whom we have redemption . . . ,[7] the forgiveness of sins.** Redemption describes the act whereby we were bought from the slave market of sin. The Lord Jesus, as it were, put a price tag on us. How highly did He value us? He said, in effect, "I value them so highly that I am willing to shed My blood to purchase them." Since we have been purchased at such a tremendous cost, it should be clear to us that we no longer belong to ourselves; we have been bought with a price. Therefore we should not live our lives the way we choose. Borden of Yale pointed out that if we take our lives and do what we want with them, we are taking something that does not belong to us, and therefore we are thieves!

Not only has He redeemed us; He has given us **the forgiveness of sins**. This means that God has cancelled the debt which our sins incurred. The Lord Jesus Christ paid the penalty on the cross; it never needs to be paid again. The account is settled and closed, and God has not only forgiven, but He has removed our sins as far as the east is from the west (Ps. 103:12).

C. The Glories of Christ the Church's Head (1:15–23)

1:15 In the next four verses, we have the Lord Jesus described: (1) in His relationship to God (v. 15); (2) in His relationship to creation (vv. 16, 17); and (3) in His relationship to the church (v. 18).

The Lord is here described as **the image of the invisible God. Image** carries with it at least two ideas. First, it

conveys the thought that the Lord Jesus has enabled us to see what God is like. God is Spirit and is therefore invisible. But in the Person of Christ, God made Himself visible to mortal eyes. In that sense the Lord Jesus is **the image of the invisible God**. Whoever has seen Him has seen the Father (see John 14:9). But the word **image** also conveys the idea of "representative." God had originally placed Adam on the earth to represent His interests, but Adam failed. Therefore, God sent His only begotten Son into the world as His Representative to care for His interests and to reveal His heart of love to man. In that sense, He is the image of God. The same word **image** is used in 3:10, where believers are said to be the image of Christ.

Christ is also **the firstborn over all creation**, or "of every created being." What does this mean? Some false teachers suggest that the Lord Jesus is Himself a created being, that He was the first Person whom God ever made. Some of them are even willing to go so far as to admit that He is the greatest creature ever to come from the hand of God. But nothing could be more directly contrary to the teaching of the word of God.

The expression "firstborn" has at least three different meanings in Scripture. In Luke 2:7, it is used in *a literal sense*, where Mary brought forth her firstborn Son. There it means that the Lord Jesus was the first Child to whom she gave birth. In Exodus 4:22, on the other hand, it is used in *a figurative sense*. "Israel is My son, even My firstborn." In that verse there is no thought of an actual birth having taken place, but the Lord is using this word to describe the distinctive place which the nation of Israel had in His plans and purposes. Finally, in Psalm 89:27, the word "firstborn" is used to designate *a place of superiority*, of supremacy, of uniqueness. There God says that He will make David His firstborn, higher than the kings of the earth. David was actually the last-born son of Jesse according to the flesh. But God determined to give him a place of unique supremacy, primacy, and sovereignty.

Is not that exactly the thought of Colossians 1:15 — **the firstborn over all creation**? The Lord Jesus Christ is God's unique Son. In one sense all believers are sons of God, but the Lord Jesus is God's Son in a way that is not true of any other. He existed before all creation and occupies a position of supremacy over it. His is the rank of eminence and dominion. The expression **firstborn over all creation** has nothing to do with birth here. It simply means that He is God's Son by an eternal relationship. It is a title of priority of *position*, and not simply one of time.

1:16 False teachers use verse 15 (especially in the KJV) to teach that the Lord Jesus was a created being. Error can usually be refuted from the very passage of Scripture which the cultists use. That is the case here. Verse 16 states conclusively that the Lord Jesus is not a creature, but the very Creator. In this verse we learn that **all things** — the whole universe of things — **were created** not only **by Him** but **through Him and for Him**. Each of these prepositions conveys a different thought. First of all, we read that **by Him all things were created**. Here the thought is that the power to create was in His Being. He was the Architect. Later in the verse we learn that **all things were created through Him**. This speaks of Him as the Agent in creation. He was the Person of the Godhead through whom the creative act was performed. Also, all things were created **for Him**. He is the One for whom all things were created, the goal of creation.

Paul goes to great lengths to emphasize that **all things were created through** Christ, whether things **in heaven**, or things **on earth**. This leaves no loopholes for anyone to suggest that although He created some things, He Himself was created originally.

The apostle then goes on to state that the Lord's creation included things **visible and** things **invisible**. The word **visible** needs no explanation, but doubtless the Apostle Paul realized that when he said **invisible** he would arouse our curiosity. Therefore, he proceeds to give a break-down of what he means by things **invisible**. They include **thrones, dominions, principalities**, and **powers**. We believe that these terms refer to angelic beings, although we cannot distinguish between the different ranks of these intelligent beings.

The Gnostics taught that there were

various ranks and classes of spirit beings between God and matter, and that Christ belonged to one of these classes. In our day the Spiritists claim that Jesus Christ is an advanced spirit of the sixth sphere. Jehovah's Witnesses teach that before our Lord came into the world, He was a created angel and none other than the archangel Michael! Here Paul vigorously refutes such absurd notions by stating in the clearest possible terms that the Lord Jesus Christ is the Creator of angels — in fact, of all beings, whether **visible** or **invisible**.

1:17   He is before all things, and in Him all things consist. Paul says, "He **is** before all things," not "He *was* before all things." The present tense is often used in the Bible to describe the timelessness of Deity. The Lord Jesus said, for instance: "Before Abraham was, I AM" (John 8:58).

Not only did the Lord Jesus exist before there was any creation, but also **in Him all things consist**. This means that He is the Sustainer of the universe and the Source of its perpetual motion. He controls the stars and the sun and the moon. Even while He was here on earth He was the One who was controlling the laws by which our universe functions in an orderly manner.

1:18 The dominion of the Lord Jesus not only covers the natural universe, but it also extends to the spiritual realm. **He is the head of the body, the church**. All believers in the Lord Jesus during this dispensation are formed into what is known as **the body** of Christ, or **the church**. Just as a human body is a vehicle by which the person expresses himself, so the Body of Christ is that vehicle which He has on earth by which He chooses to express Himself to the world. And **He is the head of** that **body**. The head speaks of guidance, dictation, control. He occupies the place of **preeminence** in the church.

He is **the beginning**. We understand this to mean **the beginning** of the new creation (see Rev. 3:14), the source of spiritual life. This is further explained by the use of the expression **the firstborn from the dead**. Here again we must be careful to emphasize that this does not mean that the Lord Jesus was the first to rise from the dead. There were cases of resurrection in the OT as well as in the NT. But the Lord Jesus was the first to rise from the dead *to die no more*, He was the first to rise with a glorified body, and He rose as the Head of a new creation. His resurrection is unique, and is the pledge that all who trust in Him will also rise. It proclaims Him as supreme in the spiritual creation.

Alfred Mace put it well:

> Christ cannot be second anywhere. He is "firstborn of every creature," because He has created everything (Col. 1:15, 16). He is also firstborn from the dead in connection with a redeemed and heavenly family. Thus creation and redemption hand the honors of supremacy to Him because of Who He is and of what He has done; "that in all things He might have the preeminence." He is first everywhere.[8]

The Lord Jesus has thus a double preeminence — first in creation, and then in the church. God has decreed that in *all things* **HE may have the preeminence.** What an answer this is to those who, in Paul's day (and our own), would seek to rob Christ of His deity, and to make of Him only a created being, however exalted!

As we read **that in all things He may have the preeminence**, it is only proper that we should ask ourselves, "Does He have the preeminence in my life?"

1:19 Darby translates verse 19 as follows: "For in Him all the fullness of the Godhead was pleased to dwell." The King James tradition could make it sound as if at some point in time the Father (notice italics for words not in the Greek) was pleased to make all fullness dwell in the Son. The real meaning is that **the fullness** of the Godhead always dwelt in Christ.

Gnostic heretics taught that Christ was a kind of "halfway house" to God, a necessary link in the chain. But there were other, better links on ahead. "Go on from Him," they urged, "and you will reach the fullness." "No," Paul answers, "Christ is Himself the complete fullness!"

All fullness *dwells* in Christ. The word for **dwell** here means to dwell permanently,[9] and not simply to visit temporarily.

1:20 Verse 19 is connected with verse 20 as follows: "For it pleased *the Father* **by Him** (Christ) **to reconcile all things to Himself . . . having made**

peace through the blood of His cross." In other words, it was not only the Godhead's good pleasure that all fullness should dwell in Christ (v. 19), but also that Christ should **reconcile all things to Himself**.

There are two reconciliations mentioned in this chapter: (1) The reconciliation of **things** (v. 20), and (2) the reconciliation of persons (v. 21). The first is still future, whereas the second is past for all who have believed in Christ.

RECONCILIATION

To reconcile means to restore to a right relationship or standard, or to make peace where formerly there was enmity. The Bible never speaks of God as needing to be reconciled to man, but always of man being reconciled to God. The carnal mind is enmity toward God (Rom. 8:7), and because of this, man needs to be reconciled.

When sin entered the world, man became estranged from God. He adopted an attitude of hostility toward God. Therefore, he needed to be reconciled.

But sin affected all of creation, not just the human family.

1. Certain of the angels had sinned sometime in the past. (However, there is no indication in God's word that these angels will ever be reconciled. They are "reserved in everlasting chains under darkness for the judgment of the great day," Jude 6.) In Job 4:18, Eliphaz states that God charged His angels with folly.

2. The animal creation was affected by the entrance of sin: "For the earnest expectation of the creation eagerly waits for the revealing of the sons of God. For the creation was subjected to futility. . . . For we know that the whole creation groans and labors with birth pangs together until now" (Rom. 8:19–22). The fact that animals suffer sickness, pain, and death is evidence that they are not exempt from the curse of sin.

3. The ground was cursed by God after Adam sinned (Gen. 3:17). This is evidenced by weeds, thorns, and thistles.

4. In the book of Job, Bildad tells us that even the stars are not pure in God's sight (Job 25:5), so apparently sin has affected the stellar world.

5. Hebrews 9:23 says that things in heaven itself needed to be purified. We do not know all that is meant by this, but perhaps it suggests that heavenly things have been defiled through the presence of Satan, who has access to God as the accuser of the brethren (Job 1:6, 7; Rev. 12:10). Some think this passage refers to the dwelling place of God; others to the stellar heavens. The latter suggests that it is in the stellar spaces that Satan has access to God. In any case, all agree that the throne of God is certainly not defiled by sin.

One of the purposes of the death of Christ was to make possible the reconciliation of persons and things to God. In order to do this, He had to remove the cause of enmity and alienation. This He effectively did by settling the sin question to God's entire satisfaction.

The scope of reconciliation is indicated in Colossians 1, as follows. (1) All who believe on the Lord Jesus Christ are already reconciled to God (v. 21). Although Christ's reconciling work is sufficient for all mankind, it is only effective for those who avail themselves of it. (2) Eventually all things will be reconciled, whether things on earth or things in heaven (v. 20). This refers to the animal creation, and to inanimate things that have been defiled by sin. However, it does not refer to Satan, to other fallen angels, or to unbelieving men. Their eternal doom is clearly pronounced in the Scriptures.

Reconciliation is not said to extend to "things under the earth." There is a difference between reconciliation and subjugation. The latter is described in Philippians 2:10: "That at the name of Jesus every knee should bow, of those in heaven, and of those on earth, and of those under the earth." Or, as Darby translates it, "of heavenly and earthly and infernal beings." All created beings, even fallen angels, will eventually be compelled to bow to the Lord Jesus, but this does not mean that they will be reconciled. We emphasize this because Colossians 1:20 has been used to teach the false doctrine of universal salvation — namely, that Satan himself, fallen angels, and unbelieving men will all be reconciled to God eventually. Our passage limits the extent of reconciliation

by the phrase things on earth or things in heaven. "Things under the earth," or infernal things, are not included. ‡

1:21 Paul reminds the Colossians that reconciliation in their case was already an accomplished fact. Before their conversion, the Colossians had been Gentile sinners, **alienated** from God and **enemies** of His in their minds because of their **wicked works** (Eph. 4:17, 18). They desperately needed to be reconciled, and the Lord Jesus Christ, in His matchless grace, had taken the initiative.

1:22 He reconciled them **in the body of His flesh through death**. It was not by His life but by His **death**. The expression **the body of His flesh** simply means that the Lord Jesus effected reconciliation by dying on the cross in a real human **body** (not as a spirit being, which the Gnostics claimed Him to be). Compare Hebrews 2:14–16, where Christ's Incarnation is declared a necessity in order to effect redemption. The Gnostic concept denied this.

The wonderful result of this reconciliation is expressed in the words **to present you holy, and blameless, and above reproach in His sight**. What marvelous grace, that ungodly sinners can be delivered from their past evil life and conveyed into such a realm of blessing!

Well might C. R. Erdman say: "In Christ is found a God who is near, who cares, who hears, who pities and who saves."[10]

The full efficacy of Christ's reconciliation with regard to His people will be seen in a coming day when we are presented to God the Father without sin, stain, or any charge against us, and when, as worshipers, we shall gladly acknowledge Christ as the Worthy One (Rev. 5).

1:23 Now the Apostle Paul adds one of those **if**[11] passages which have proved very disconcerting to many children of God. On the surface, the verse seems to teach that our continued salvation depends on our continuing **in the faith**. If this is so, how can this verse be reconciled with other portions of the word of God, such as John 10:28, 29, which declare that no sheep of Christ can ever perish?

In seeking to answer this question,

we would like to state at the outset that the eternal security of the believer is a blessed truth which is set forth clearly in the pages of the NT. However, the Scriptures also teach, as in this verse, that true faith always has the quality of permanence, and that one who has really been born of God will go on faithfully to the end. Continuance is a proof of reality. Of course there is always the danger of backsliding, but a Christian falls only to rise again (Prov. 24:16). He does not forsake the faith.

The Spirit of God has seen fit to put many of these so-called "if" passages in the word of God in order to challenge all who profess the name of Christ as to the reality of their profession. We would not want to say anything that might dull the sharp edge of these passages. As someone has said: "These 'ifs' in Scripture look on professing Christians here in the world and they come as healthy tests to the soul."

Pridham comments on these challenging verses as follows:

> The reader will find, on a careful study of the Word, that it is the habit of the Spirit to accompany the fullest and most absolute statements of grace by warnings which imply a ruinous failure on the part of some who nominally stand in faith. . . . Warnings which grate harshly on the ears of insincere profession are drunk willingly as medicine by the godly soul. . . . The aim of all such teaching as we have here is to encourage faith, and condemn, by anticipation, reckless and self-confident professors.[12]

Doubtless with the Gnostics primarily in mind, the apostle is urging the Colossians **not** to be **moved away from the hope** that accompanies **the gospel**, or which the **gospel** inspires. They should **continue in the faith** which they learned from Epaphras, **grounded and steadfast.**

Again Paul speaks of the gospel as having been **preached to every creature** (or "all creation") **under heaven**. The gospel goes out to all creation, but it has not as yet reached literally every creature. Paul is arguing the worldwide proclamation of the gospel as a testimonial to its genuineness. He sees in this the evidence that it is adaptable to the needs of mankind everywhere. The verse does not mean that every person in the world at that time had heard the gospel. It was not a fact accomplished, but a process going on. Also, the gospel had reached to all the Bible world, that is, the Mediterranean world.

Paul speaks of himself as **a minister**, a Latin word that simply means "a servant." It has nothing of officialdom about it. It does not denote a lofty office so much as humble service.

D. The Ministry Committed to Paul (1:24–29)

1:24 The last six verses of chapter 1 describe Paul's ministry. First of all, it was carried out in an atmosphere of suffering. Writing from prison, Paul can say that he **now** rejoices **in** his **sufferings for** the saints, that is, on their account. As a servant of the Lord Jesus Christ, he was called upon to endure untold hardships, persecutions, and **afflictions**. These to him were a privilege — the privilege of filling up that which was left behind of **the afflictions of Christ**. What does the apostle mean by this? First of all, this cannot refer to the *atoning* sufferings of the Lord Jesus Christ on the cross. Those were finished once and for all, and no man could ever share in them. But there is a sense in which the Lord Jesus still suffers. When Saul of Tarsus was struck to the ground on the road to Damascus, he heard a voice from heaven saying, "Saul, Saul, why do you persecute Me?" Saul had not been consciously persecuting the Lord — he had only been persecuting the Christians. He learned, however, that in persecuting believers, he was persecuting their Savior. The Head in heaven feels the sufferings of His Body on earth.

Thus, the Apostle Paul looks on all the suffering that Christians are required to go through for the sake of the Lord Jesus as being part of the sufferings of Christ which still remain. They include suffering for righteousness' sake, suffering for His sake (bearing His reproach), and for the gospel's sake.

But **the afflictions of Christ** refer not only to sufferings *for* Christ. They also describe *the same kind of* sufferings that the Savior endured when He was here, though far less in degree.

The afflictions endured by the apostle

in his **flesh** were **for the sake of** Christ's **body**, namely, **the church**. The sufferings of unsaved people are, in a sense, purposeless. There is no high dignity attached to them. They are only a foretaste of the pangs of hell to be endured forever. But not so the sufferings of Christians. When they suffer for Christ, Christ in a very real way suffers with them.

1:25 **Of which I became a minister.** Paul had already used this expression at the close of verse 23. Now he repeats it. However, there is a difference in these two usages. The apostle had a twofold ministry: first, he was commissioned to preach the gospel (v. 23); and secondly, he was sent forth to teach the marvelous mystery of the church (v. 25). There is a real lesson in this for every true servant of Christ. We are not expected simply to lead men to Christ by the gospel and then abandon them to get along as best they can. Rather, we are expected to direct our evangelistic efforts to the formation of local NT churches where the converts can be built up in their most holy faith, including the truth of the church. The Lord wants His babes to be directed to feeding stations where they will be nourished and where they can grow.

Thus in Colossians 1 we have seen (1) Christ's twofold preeminence, (2) Christ's twofold reconciliation, and (3) Paul's twofold ministry. Here in verse 25, when Paul says, **"of which I became a minister,"** he is referring to his ministry with regard to the church and not the gospel. This is clear from the expression which follows: **According to the stewardship** (or "dispensation") **from God given to me for you**. A steward is one who cares for the interests or property of another. Paul was a steward in the sense that the great truth of the church was entrusted to him in a very special way. While the mystery of the Body of Christ was not revealed to him alone, yet he was chosen as the one who would carry this precious truth to the Gentiles. It includes the unique position of the church in its relation to Christ and the dispensations, with its constitution, its distinctive hope and destiny, and the many other truths concerning its life and order which God gave to Paul and the other apostles.

When he says, **which was given to me for you**, he is thinking of the Colossians as Gentile believers. The Apostle Peter had been sent to preach to the Jewish people, while Paul had been entrusted with a similar mission to the Gentiles.

One of the most difficult expressions in this chapter is **to fulfill the word of God**. Exactly what does Paul mean by this? First of all, we know that he does not mean that he completed the word of God by adding the last book to it. As far as we know, the book of Revelation, written by John, was the last book to be added to the NT in point of time. In what sense, then, did Paul **fulfill** or complete **the word of God**?

First of all, **to fulfill** may mean to declare fully, to make known. Thus, Paul had declared the whole counsel of God. We would suggest secondly that he fulfilled the word of God doctrinally. The great truth of the mystery forms the capstone of the NT revelation. In a very real way, it completes the circle of subjects that are covered in the NT. While other books were written later than Paul's, yet they do not contain any great mysteries of the faith that are not found in the writings of the Apostle Paul. In a very real sense the revelations concerning the mystery of the church filled up the word of God. Nothing that was added later was new truth in the same sense.

1:26 That Paul's fulfilling of the word of God had to do with **the mystery** is borne out in this verse, namely, **the mystery which has been hidden from ages and from generations, but now has been revealed to His saints**. In the NT, a mystery is a truth not previously revealed, but now made known to the sons of men through the apostles and prophets of the NT. It is a truth that man could never have arrived at by his own intelligence but which God has graciously deigned to make known.

This verse is one of the many in the NT which teach that the truth of the church was not known in the OT period. It had **been hidden from ages and from generations** (Eph. 3:2–13; Rom. 16:25–27). Thus it is wrong to speak of the church as having begun with Adam or Abraham. The church began on the Day of Pentecost, and the truth of the church was revealed by the apostles. The church in the NT is not the same as Israel in the Old. It is something that never previously existed.

Israel began with God calling Abraham out from Ur of the Chaldees, giving up the rest of the nations to their sins and idolatry. He made a nation out of Abraham's seed, distinct from all others and separate from them. The church is the reverse of this, and is a union of believers from all races and nationalities into one Body, morally and spiritually separated from all others. That the church is not the continuation of Israel can be seen from a number of things, one being the figure of the "olive tree" which Paul uses in Romans 11 to show that the nation of Israel retains its identity, though the individual Jew who believes in Christ becomes part of the church (Col. 3:10, 11).

1:27 The truth of **this mystery** may be summarized as follows: (1) The church is the Body of Christ. All true believers are members of the Body, and are destined to share Christ's glory forever. (2) The Lord Jesus is the Head of the Body, providing its life, nourishment, and direction. (3) Jews have no preference as to admission to the church; neither are Gentiles at any disadvantage. Both Jew and Gentile become members of the Body through faith and form one new man (Eph. 2:15; 3:6). That Gentiles could be saved was not a hidden truth in the OT; but that converted Gentiles would be fellow members of the Body of Christ, to be His companions in glory, and to reign with Him, was a truth never previously known.

The particular aspect of the mystery which Paul is emphasizing in verse 27 is that the Lord Jesus is willing to dwell within the Gentile heart. **Christ in you, the hope of glory.** This was spoken to the Colossians, who were Gentiles. F. B. Meyer exclaims: "That He should dwell in the heart of a child of Abraham was deemed a marvelous act of condescension, but that He should find a home in the heart of a Gentile was incredible." And yet that is exactly what was involved in the mystery — "that the Gentiles should be fellow heirs, of the same body, and partakers of His promise in Christ through the gospel" (Eph. 3:6). To

emphasize the importance of this truth, the apostle does not merely say "this mystery" or "the glory of this mystery," but **the riches of the glory of this mystery**. He piles words upon words in order to impress his readers with the fact that this is a glorious truth that deserves their closest attention.

Which is Christ in you, the hope of glory. The indwelling **Christ** is the believers' **hope of glory**. We have no other title to heaven than the Savior Himself. The fact that He indwells us makes heaven as sure as if we were already there.

1:28 The expression **Him we preach** is significant. The **Him**, of course, refers back to the Lord Jesus Christ (v. 27). Paul is saying that he preached a Person. He did not spend his time on politics or philosophy, but concentrated on the Lord Jesus Himself, because he realized that Christianity is Christ. **Warning every man and teaching every man in all wisdom, that we may present every man perfect in Christ Jesus**. Here we have further insight into the ministry of the beloved apostle. It was a man-to-man ministry. He warned the unsaved of the awful wrath to come, and he taught the saints the great truths of the Christian faith.

Then we see the emphasis which he placed on follow-up work. He felt a real sense of responsibility toward those whom he had pointed to the Savior. He was not satisfied to see souls saved and then to pass on. He wanted to **present every man perfect in Christ Jesus**. Paul pictures himself as a priest offering up sacrifices to God. The sacrifices here are men and women. In what condition does he offer them to the Lord? Are they weak or mere babes in Christ? No, he wants them to be mature, full-grown, adult Christians. He wants them to be well-grounded in the truth. Do we share a similar burden for those whom we have led to Christ?

1:29 It was toward this goal that the apostle labored, as well as all the other apostles. And yet he realized that he was not doing this in his own strength, but **according to His working which** worked **in him mightily**. In other words, he realized that it was only as he was empowered by the Lord that he was able to serve Him at all. He was conscious of the fact that the Lord was **working in** him **mightily** as he went from place to place planting churches and feeding the saints of God.

Verses 28 and 29 are especially helpful in Phillips' translation:

> So, naturally, we proclaim Christ. We warn everyone we meet, and we teach everyone we can, all that we know about Him, so that, if possible, we may bring every man up to his full maturity in Christ. This is what I am working at all the time, with all the strength that God gives me.

E. Christ's Sufficiency Against the Perils of Philosophy, Legalism, Mysticism, and Asceticism (2:1–23)

2:1 This verse is closely linked with the last two verses of chapter 1. There the Apostle Paul had been describing his strivings, by teaching and preaching, to present every believer mature in Christ. Here his strivings are of a different nature. Now they are spoken of as **great conflict** in prayer. And here this **great conflict** is in behalf of those he had never met. From the first day he had heard of the Colossians, he had prayed for them as well as for **those in** the neighboring city of **Laodicea**, and for other Christians whom he had not as yet met (see Rev. 3:14–19 for the later sad state of the church there).

Verse 1 is a comfort to those who are never privileged to engage in public ministry. It teaches that we need not be limited by what we can do in the presence of people. We can serve the Lord in the privacy of our rooms on our knees. If we do serve publicly, our effectiveness depends largely on our private devotions before God.

2:2 The exact content of Paul's prayer is given in this verse. The first part of the prayer is **that their hearts may be encouraged**. The Colossians were in danger of the teachings of the Gnostics. Therefore, **encouraged** here means confirmed or strengthened.

The second part of the prayer is that they might be **knit together in love**. If the saints went on in happy, loving fellowship with one another, they would present a solid flank against the onslaughts of the foe. Also, if their hearts were warm in love to Christ, He would reveal to them the deeper truths of the Christian faith. It is a well-known principle of Scripture that the Lord reveals His secrets to those who are close to Him. John, for instance, was the apostle who leaned on Jesus' chest, and it was no coincidence that he was also the one to whom the great revelation of Jesus Christ was given.

Next Paul prayed that they might enter into **all** the **riches of the full assurance of understanding**. The more they entered into an **understanding** of the Christian faith, the more fully convinced they would be of its truthfulness. The more firmly grounded the Christians were in the faith, the less would be the danger of their being led away by the false teachings of the day.

The expression **full assurance** is used three times in the NT. (1) Full assurance of *faith* — we rest on God's word, His testimony to us (Heb. 10:22). (2) Full assurance of *understanding* — we know and are assured (Col. 2:2). (3) Full assurance of *hope* — we press on with confidence as to the outcome (Heb. 6:11).

The climax of Paul's prayer is found in the words **to the knowledge of the mystery of God, both of the Father and of Christ**.

What does Paul mean when he says that they may know **the mystery of God . . . and of Christ**? He is still referring to the truth of the church — Christ, the Head of the Body, and all believers members of the Body. But the particular aspect of the mystery which he has in mind is the headship of Christ. He is anxious that the saints should acknowledge this truth. He knows that if they realize the greatness of their Head, they will not be drawn away by Gnosticism or the other evil cults that threatened them.

Paul wants the saints to use Christ, to utilize His resources, to draw upon Him in every emergency. He wants them to see that Christ, who, as Alfred Mace puts it:

> . . . is *in* His people, is possessed of every attribute of deity, and of infinite, unutter-

able, measureless resources, so that they did not need to go outside of Him for anything. "To them God willed to make known what are THE RICHES of the glory of THIS MYSTERY among the Gentiles: WHICH IS CHRIST IN YOU, the hope of glory" (Col. 1:27). The truth of this, known in power, is the sure and certain antidote for Laodicean pride, rationalistic theology, traditional religion, demon-possessed spiritualistic mediums, and every other form of opposition or counterfeit. [13]

2:3 In Christ **are hidden all the treasures of wisdom and knowledge**. The Gnostics, of course, boasted of an understanding far surpassing anything found within the pages of divine revelation. Their wisdom was something in addition to what was found in Christ or Christianity. But here Paul is saying that **all the treasures of wisdom and knowledge** are hidden in Christ, the Head. Therefore, there is no need for believers to go beyond what is written in the Scriptures. **The treasures** in Christ are hidden from unbelief; and even the believer needs to know Christ intimately to enter into them.

Christ is *in* the believer as Head, center and resource. By the vastness of His unsearchable riches, by the pre-eminent wealth of His infinite greatness, by all that He is essentially as God, by all He has accomplished in creation and in redemption, by His personal, moral and official glories, He crowds out the whole army of professors, authors, mediums, critics, and all others arrayed against Him. (Selected)

There is more in this verse than meets the eye. All **knowledge** is found in Christ. He is the incarnation of truth. He said: "I am the way, the truth, and the life." Nothing that is true will ever conflict with His words or His works. The difference between **knowledge** and **wisdom** has often been explained as follows: **Knowledge** is the understanding of truth, whereas **wisdom** is the ability to apply what truth has been learned.

2:4 Because all wisdom and knowledge are in Christ, Christians should not be deluded with the **persuasive words** of false cultists. If a man does not have the truth, then he must seek to attract a following through the clever presentation of his message. That is exactly what her-

etics always do. They argue from probabilities and build a system of teaching on deductions. On the other hand, if a man is preaching the truth of God, then he does not need to depend on such things as eloquence or clever arguments. The truth is its own best argument and, like a lion, will defend itself.

2:5 This verse shows how intimately aware the Apostle Paul was of the problems and perils facing the Colossians. He pictures himself as a military officer looking over the assembled troops as they stand ready for inspection. The two words **order** and **steadfastness** are military terms. The first describes the orderly array of a company of soldiers, whereas the second pictures the solid flank which is presented by them. Paul rejoices as he sees (**in spirit** though not in body) how the Colossians were standing true to the word of God.

2:6 Now he encourages them to go on in the same way in which they had originally begun, that is, by faith. **As you therefore have received Christ Jesus the Lord, so walk in Him.** The emphasis here seems to be on the word **Lord**. In other words, they had acknowledged that in Him there was complete sufficiency. He was enough, not only for salvation, but for the whole of their Christian life. Now Paul urges the saints to go on acknowledging the lordship of Christ. They should not stray from Him by accepting the teachings of men, however convincing they may sound. The word **walk** is one that is often used of the Christian life. It speaks of action and progress. You cannot walk and remain in the same place. So it is in the Christian life; we are either going forward or backward.

2:7 Paul first uses an expression from agriculture, then one from architecture. The expression **rooted** refers to what took place at the time of our conversion. It is as if the Lord Jesus Christ is the soil and we find our roots in Him, drawing all our nourishment from Him. This emphasizes, too, the importance of having our roots deep, so that when opposing winds blow, we will not be moved (Matt. 13:5, 20, 21).

Then Paul switches to the figure of a building. **Built up in Him.** Here the

Lord Jesus is suggested as the foundation, and we are being **built** on **Him**, the Rock of Ages (Luke 6:47–49). We were **rooted** once for all, but we are being **built up**.

And established in the faith. The word **established** might also be translated "confirmed," and the thought is that this is a process that goes on continuously through the Christian life. The Colossians had been taught the fundamentals of Christianity by Epaphras. As they continued on in the Christian pathway, these precious truths would be continually confirmed in their hearts and lives. Conversely, 2 Peter 1:9 indicates that failure to progress in spiritual life results in doubt and loss of the joy and blessing of the gospel.

Paul concludes this description with the words **abounding in it with thanksgiving**. He does not want Christians to be coldly doctrinal, but he wants their hearts to be captivated by the marvelous truths of the gospel so that they in turn will overflow in praise and thankfulness to the Lord. **Thanksgiving** for the blessings of Christianity is a wonderful antidote against the poison of false doctrine.

Arthur Way translates verse 7 as follows: "Be like trees fast-rooted, like buildings steadily rising, feeling His presence about you, and even (for to this your education has led up) unshaken in your faith, and overflowing with thanksgiving."

2:8 Now Paul is ready to deal directly with the specific errors that had threatened the believers in the Lycus Valley, where Colosse was situated. **Beware lest anyone cheat you through philosophy and empty deceit.** False teachings seek to rob men of what is worthwhile, but offer nothing substantial in its place. **Philosophy** means literally "the love of wisdom." It is not evil in itself, but becomes evil when men seek wisdom apart from the Lord Jesus Christ. Here the word is used to describe man's attempt to find out by his own intellect and research those things which can only be known by divine revelation (1 Cor. 2:14). It is evil because it exalts human reason above God and worships the creature more than the Creator. It is characteristic of the liberals of our day,

with their boasted intellectualism and rationalism. **Empty deceit** refers to the false and valueless teachings of those who profess to offer secret truths to an inner circle of people. There is really nothing to it. But it gathers a following by catering to man's curiosity. Also it appeals to their vanity by making them members of the "select few."

The **philosophy and empty deceit** which Paul attacks are **according to the tradition of men, according to the basic principles of the world, and not according to Christ. The tradition of men** here means religious teachings which have been invented by men but which have no true foundation in the Scriptures. (A tradition is a fixation of a custom which began as a convenience, or which suited some particular circumstance.) **The basic principles of the world** refer to Jewish rituals, ceremonies, and ordinances by which men hoped to obtain God's favor.

The Law of Moses had served its purpose as a type of things to come. It had been a "primary school" to prepare the heart for the coming Christ. To return to it now would be to play into the hands of the false teachers who conspired to use a discarded system to displace the Son of God. (Daily Notes of the Scripture Union)

Paul would have the Colossians test all teaching by whether or not it agreed with the doctrines of **Christ**. Phillips' translation of this verse is helpful: "Be careful that nobody spoils your faith through intellectualism or high sounding nonsense. Such stuff is at best founded on men's ideas of the nature of the world, and disregards Christ!"

2:9 It is marvelous to see how the Apostle Paul constantly brings his readers back to the Person of Christ. Here he gives one of the most sublime and unmistakable verses in the Bible on the deity of the Lord Jesus Christ. **For in Him dwells all the fullness of the Godhead bodily.** Note the intended accumulation of evidence as to the fact that Christ is God. First of all, you have His deity: "For in Him dwells . . . **the Godhead bodily.**" Secondly, you have what someone has called the amplitude of deity: "For in Him dwells *the fullness of* **the Godhead bodily.**" Finally, you have what has been called the absolute completeness of deity: "For in Him dwells *all* **the fullness of the Godhead bodily."** (This is an effective answer to the various forms of Gnosticism that deny the deity of the Lord Jesus — Christian Science, Jehovah's Witnesses, Unity, Theosophy, Christadelphianism, etc.)

Vincent says: "The verse contains two distinct assertions: (1) That the fulness of the Godhead eternally dwells in Christ . . . ; (2) The fulness of the Godhead dwells in Him . . . as one having a human body."[14] Many of the cults mentioned above would admit that some form of divinity dwelt in Jesus. This verse is identifying **all the fullness of the Godhead** with Him, in His manhood. The argument is clear — if there is such a sufficiency in the Person of the Lord Jesus Christ, why be satisfied with teachings which slight or ignore Him?

2:10 The apostle is still trying to impress on his readers the all-sufficiency of the Lord Jesus Christ, and of the perfect standing which they have **in Him**. It is a marvelous expression of the grace of God that the truth of verse 10 should follow that of verse 9. In Christ dwells all the fullness of the Godhead bodily, and the believer is **complete in Him**. This does not mean, of course, that the believer is indwelt by all the fullness of the Godhead. The only One of whom that was ever true, or ever shall be true, is the Lord Jesus Christ. But what this verse teaches is that the believer has in Christ all that is needed for life and godliness. Spurgeon gives a good definition of our completeness. He says we are (1) Complete without the aid of Jewish ceremony. (2) Complete without the help of philosophy. (3) Complete without the inventions of superstition. (4) Complete without human merit.

This One in whom we are complete **is the head of all principality and power**. The Gnostics were greatly taken up with the subject of angels. Mention of this is made later on in this chapter. But Christ is head over all the angelic beings, and it would be ridiculous to be occupied with angels when we can have the Creator of angels as the object of our affections and enjoy communion with Him.

2:11 Circumcision was the typical rite of Judaism. It is a minor surgical operation in which the knife was applied to the flesh of the male child. Spiritually it signified death to the flesh, or a putting aside of the evil, corrupt, unregenerate nature of man. Unfortunately, the Jewish people became occupied with the literal ceremony but neglected its spiritual meaning. In trying to achieve favor with God through ceremonies and good works, they were saying in effect that there was something in human flesh which could please God. Nothing could be further from the truth.

In the verse before us physical circumcision is not in view, but rather that spiritual **circumcision** which is true of everyone who has put his faith and trust in the Lord Jesus. This is clear from the expression **the circumcision made without hands**. What the verse is teaching is this: Every believer is circumcised **by the circumcision of Christ. The circumcision of Christ** refers to His death on the cross of Calvary. The thought is that when the Lord Jesus died, the believer died also. He died to sin (Rom. 6:11), to the law, to self (Gal. 2:20), and to the world (Gal. 6:14). (This circumcision was "màde without hands" in the sense that human hands can have no part in it by way of merit. Man cannot deserve or earn it. It is God's work.) Thus he has put off **the body of the sins of the flesh**. In other words, when a person is saved, he becomes associated with Christ in His death, and renounces any hope of earning or deserving salvation through fleshly efforts. Samuel Ridout writes: "Our Lord's death has not only put away the fruit, but condemned and set aside the very root which bore it."

2:12 Paul now turns from the subject of circumcision to that of **baptism**. Just as circumcision speaks of death to the flesh, even so **baptism** speaks of the burial of the old man. Thus we read: **Buried with Him in baptism, in which you also were raised with Him through faith in the working of God, who raised Him from the dead.** The teaching here is that we have not only died with Christ, but we have been **buried with Him**. This was typified at our baptism. It took place at the time of our conversion, but we expressed it in public confession when we went into the waters of baptism. Baptism is burial, the burial of all that we were as children of Adam. In baptism we acknowledge that nothing in ourselves could ever please God, and so we are putting the flesh out of God's sight forever. But it does not end with burial. Not only have we been crucified with Christ and buried with Him, but we have also risen with Him to walk in newness of life. All of this takes place at the time of conversion. It is **through faith in the working of God, who raised** Christ **from the dead**.

2:13 The Apostle Paul now makes the application of all this to the Colossians. Before their conversion, they had been **dead in** their **trespasses**. This means that because of their sins, they were spiritually dead toward God. It does not mean that their spirits were dead, but simply that there was no motion in their spirits toward God and there was nothing they could do to win God's favor. Not only were they **dead in** sins, but also Paul speaks of **the uncircumcision of** their **flesh. Uncircumcision** is often used in the NT to describe the Gentile peoples. The Colossians had been Gentiles. They had not been members of God's earthly people, the Jews. Therefore, they had been in a position of distance from God, and had given full rein to the flesh with its lusts. But when they heard the gospel and believed on the Lord Jesus Christ, they had been **made alive together with** Christ, and **all** their **trespasses** had been **forgiven**. In other words, what had really happened to the Colossians was that their whole lifestyle had been changed. Their history as sinners had come to an end, and now they were new creatures in Christ Jesus. They were living on the resurrection side. Therefore they should say "goodbye" to all that characterized them as men in the flesh.

2:14 Paul now goes on to describe something else that was included in the work of Christ. **Having wiped out the handwriting of requirements that was against us, which was contrary to us. And He has taken it out of the way, having nailed it to the cross. The handwriting of requirements that was against us** describes the law. In a sense, the Ten

Commandments were against us, condemning us because we did not keep them perfectly. But the Apostle Paul is thinking not only about the Ten Commandments, but also about the ceremonial law that was given to Israel. In the ceremonial law, there were all kinds of commandments with regard to holy days, foods, and other religious rituals. These were all a part of the prescribed religion of the Jews. They pointed forward to the coming of the Lord Jesus. They were shadows of His Person and His work. In His death on the cross, He took all this out **of the way**, nailing it **to the cross** and canceling it as a bill is canceled when the debt is paid. As Meyer put it: "By the death of Christ on the cross, the law which condemned men lost its penal authority, inasmuch as Christ by His death endured for man the curse of the law and became the end of the law."[15] Kelly summarizes neatly: "The law is not dead, but we have died to it."

Paul's language here very likely refers to an ancient practice of nailing the written evidence of a canceled debt in a public place as a notice to all that the creditor had no more claim on the debtor.

2:15 By His death on the cross and His subsequent resurrection and ascension, the Lord Jesus also conquered evil **powers**, making **a public spectacle of them**, and **triumphing over them**. We believe that this is the same triumph that is described in Ephesians 4, where the Lord Jesus is said to have led captivity captive. His death, burial, resurrection, and ascension were a glorious triumph over all the hosts of hell and of Satan. As He passed up through the atmosphere on His way back to heaven, He passed through the very domain of the one who is the prince of the power of the air.

Perhaps this verse carries special comfort for those who have been converted from demonism but who might still be obsessed with a fear of evil spirits. There is nothing to fear if we are in Christ, because He has **disarmed principalities and powers**.

2:16 Once again the Apostle Paul is ready to make the application of what he has just been stating. We might summarize the foregoing as follows: The Colossians had died to all efforts to please God by the flesh. They had not only died, but they had been buried with Christ and had risen with Christ to a new kind of life. Therefore they should be done forever with the Judaizers and Gnostics, who were trying to draw them back to the very things to which the Colossians had died. **So let no one judge you in food or in drink, or regarding a festival or a new moon or sabbaths.** All human religions place men under bondage to ordinances, rules, regulations, and a religious calendar. This calendar usually includes annual observances (holy days), monthly festivals (new moons), or weekly holidays (sabbaths). The expression **"Therefore let no one judge you"** means that a Christian cannot be justly condemned by others if, for instance, he eats pork, or if he fails to observe religious festivals or holy days. Some false cults, such as Spiritism, insist on their members abstaining from meats. For centuries Roman Catholics were not supposed to eat meat on Friday. Many churches require abstinence from certain foods during Lent. Others, like the Mormons, say that a person cannot be a member in good standing if he drinks tea or coffee. Still others, notably the Seventh Day Adventists, insist that a person must keep the Sabbath in order to please God. The Christian is not under such ordinances. For a fuller treatment of the law, the Sabbath, and legalism, see the excurses at Matthew 5:18, 12:8, and Galatians 6:18.

2:17 The Jewish religious observances were **a shadow of things to come, but the substance** (or body) **is** Christ's. They were instituted in the OT as a pre-picture. For instance, the Sabbath was given as a type of the rest which would be the portion of all who believed on the Lord Jesus Christ. Now that the Lord Jesus has come, why should men continue to be occupied with the shadows? It is the same as being occupied with a picture when the very person pictured is present.

2:18 It is rather difficult to know the exact meaning of this verse, because we are not fully acquainted with all that the Gnostics taught. Perhaps it means that these people pretended to be so humble

that they would not dare to approach God directly. Perhaps the Gnostics taught that they must approach God through angels, and so in their supposed **humility** they worshiped **angels** rather than the Lord. We have something similar to this in the world today. There are Roman Catholics who say that they would not think of praying directly to God or to the Lord Jesus, and so their motto is "To Jesus through Mary." This seems to be a **false humility** on their part and a worshiping of a created being. Christians should not allow anyone to rob them of their reward by such unscriptural practices. The word is clear that there is "one Mediator between God and men, the Man Christ Jesus" (1 Tim. 2:5).

The Apostle Paul goes on with the obscure expression: **intruding into those things which he has not**[16] **seen.** The Gnostics professed to have deep, secret mysteries, and in order to learn what these mysteries were, a person had to be initiated. Perhaps the secrets included many so-called visions. Supposed visions are an important element in such present-day heresies as Mormonism, Spiritism, Catholicism, and Swedenborgianism. Those who were members of the inner circle were naturally proud of their secret knowledge. Paul therefore adds: **Vainly puffed up by his fleshly mind.** They took a superior attitude toward others and created the impression that one could be happy only through entering into these deep secrets. We might pause here to say that much of this is characteristic of the secret fraternal organizations of our day. The Christian who is walking in fellowship with his Lord will have neither time nor sympathy for such organizations.

The important point to notice in this verse is that the various religious practices of these men were performed according to their own will. They had no scriptural authority. They did not act in subjection to Christ. They became **vainly puffed up by** the **mind** of their flesh because they were doing exactly what they themselves wanted to do, in independence of the Lord; yet their conduct appeared to be humble and religious.

2:19 And not holding fast to the Head. The Lord Jesus is here spoken of as the **Head** of the Body. "To hold to the Head" means to live with the consciousness that Christ is **Head**, drawing the supply of all our needs from His exhaustless resources, and doing all for His glory. It means looking to the Lord in glory for sustenance and direction, and keeping in touch with Him. This is further explained in the expression that follows: **from whom all the body, nourished and knit together by joints and ligaments, grows with the increase that is from God**. The various parts of the human body are connected by **joints and ligaments**. The body in turn is joined to the head. The body looks to the head for guidance and direction. That is just the thought that the Apostle Paul is emphasizing here. The members of Christ's Body on earth should find all their satisfaction and sufficiency in Him, and not be lured away by the convincing arguments of these false teachers.

Holding fast to the Head emphasizes the necessity for a moment-by-moment dependence on the Lord. Yesterday's help will not do for today. We can't grind grain with the water that has passed over the dam. It should also be added here that where Christians do hold to the Head, the result will be spontaneous action which will coordinate with other members of the Body.

2:20 The **basic principles of the world**, as used in this verse, refer to rituals and ordinances. For instance, the rituals of the OT were rudiments of the world in the sense that they taught the elementary **principles** of religion, the ABC's (Gal. 4:9–11). Perhaps Paul is also thinking of the rituals and ordinances connected with Gnosticism and other religions. In particular, the apostle is dealing with asceticism, springing from a Judaism which had already *lost* its standing with God, or from Gnosticism or any other cult which *never* had any standing with God. Since the Colossians had **died with Christ**, Paul asks them why there was still a desire to **subject** themselves **to** such **regulations**; to do so would be to forget that they had severed their ties with the world. Perhaps the question will arise in some minds: "If a Christian is dead to ordinances, why does he still retain baptism and the Lord's Supper?" The most obvious answer is that these

two ordinances of the Christian Church are taught in the NT. However, they are not "means of grace," making us more fit for heaven or helping us to gain merit before God. Rather, they are simple acts of obedience to the Lord, indicating respectively, identification with Christ and remembrance of Him in His death. They are not so much laws to be kept as privileges to be enjoyed.

2:21 This verse is better understood if we supply the words "such as" at the beginning. In other words, Paul is saying in verse 20, "Why, as though living in the world, do you submit yourselves to regulations — such as (v. 21) **Do not touch, do not taste, do not handle?**" Strangely enough, some have taught that Paul was here *commanding* the Colossians not to touch, taste, or handle! This, of course, is the very opposite of the meaning of the passage.

It should be mentioned here that some authorities, such as William Kelly, believe that the order of the clauses in this verse should be: "Handle not; Neither taste; Nor even touch." This order would describe an increasing severity in the practice of asceticism.

2:22 The meaning is still further explained in verse 22. These are prohibitions which are manmade, as is indicated by the expression **according to the commandments and doctrines of men**. Is this the essence of true religion, to be occupied with meats and drinks, rather than with the living Christ Himself?

Weymouth translates verses 20–22 as follows:

> If you have died with Christ and have escaped from the world's rudimentary notions, why, as though your life still belonged to the world, do you submit to such precepts as "Do not handle this"; "Do not taste that"; "Do not touch that other thing" — referring to things which are all intended to be used up and to perish — in obedience to mere human injunctions and teachings?

2:23 **These** practices of man's religion all create a seeming **appearance of wisdom in self-imposed religion, false humility**, and severity to **the body. Self-imposed religion** means that these people adopt a form of worship according to their own ideas of what is right, rather than according to God's word. They seem to be religious but it is not true Christianity. **False humility** has already been explained — they pretend to be too humble to approach God directly, and so they use angelic mediators. **Neglect of the body** refers to the practice of asceticism. It is the belief that through self-denial or self-torture, man can achieve a higher state of holiness. This is found in Hinduism and other mystical religions of the East.

What is the value of all these practices? Perhaps it is best expressed in the closing part of this verse: **of no value against the indulgence of the flesh**. All of these put on a fine appearance outwardly, but they do not succeed in checking **the indulgence of the flesh**. (Even the well-intentioned temperance pledges fail to achieve their goal.) Every false system utterly fails to make men better. While creating the impression that there is something the flesh can do to merit God's favor, they are unable to restrain the passions and lusts of the flesh. The Christian attitude is that we have died to the flesh with all its passions and lusts, and from now on we live to the glory of God. We do this, not out of fear of punishment, but rather out of love to the One who gave Himself for us. A. T. Robertson put it well: "It is love that makes us really free to do right. Love makes the choice easy. Love makes the face of duty beautiful. Love makes it sweet to keep up with Christ. Love makes the service of goodness freedom."

II. THE BELIEVER'S DUTY TO THE PREEMINENT CHRIST (Chaps. 3, 4)

A. The Believer's New Life: Putting Off the Old Man and Putting on the New (3:1–17)

3:1 **If then you were raised with Christ, seek those things which are above, where Christ is, sitting at the right hand of God.** The **If** of this verse does not express any doubt in the mind of the Apostle Paul. It is what has been called the "If" of argument, and may be translated *since*: "Since then you were raised together with Christ. . . ."

As mentioned in chapter 2, the be-

liever is seen as having died with Christ, having been buried with Him, and having risen with Him from among the dead. The spiritual meaning of all this is that we have said goodbye to the former way of life, and have entered upon a completely new type of life, that is, the life of the risen Lord Jesus Christ. Because we have been **raised with Christ**, we should **seek those things which are above**. We are still on earth, but we should be cultivating heavenly ways.

3:2 The Christian should not be earth-bound in his outlook. He should view things not as they appear to the natural eye but in reference to their importance to God and to eternity. Vincent suggests that "seek" in verse 1 marks the practical striving and that **set your mind** in verse 2 describes the inward impulse and disposition. The expression **set your mind** is the same as that in Philippians 3:19: "who set their mind on earthly things." A. T. Robertson writes: "The baptized life means that the Christian is seeking heaven and is thinking heaven. His feet are upon the earth, but his head is with the stars. He is living like a citizen of heaven here on earth."[17]

During World War II, a young Christian enthusiastically reported to a mature servant of Christ, "I understand our bombers were over the enemy's cities again last night." To this, the older believer replied, "I did not know that the church of God had bombers." He obviously was looking at things from the divine standpoint, rather than taking pleasure in the destruction of women and children.

F. B. Hole explains our position clearly:

> The counterpart to our identification with Christ in His death is our identification with Him in His resurrection. The effect of the first is to disconnect us from man's world, man's religion, man's wisdom. The effect of the other is to put us into touch with God's world and with all that is there. The first four verses of chapter III unfold the blessedness into which we are introduced.[18]

3:3 When Paul says that the believer has **died**, he is referring to position, and not to practice. Because of our identification with Christ in His death, God wants us to consider ourselves as having **died** with Him. Our own hearts are always ready to dispute this fact, because we feel so very much alive to sin and temptation. But the wonderful thing is that as we by faith reckon ourselves to have died with Christ, it becomes a moral reality in our lives. If we live as those who have died, then our lives will become increasingly conformed to the life of the Lord Jesus Christ. Of course, we will never reach perfection in this life, but it is a process that should be going on in every believer.

Not only have we **died**, but also our **life is hidden with Christ in God**. The things that concern and interest the worldly man are found on this planet on which we live. However, the things that are of greatest concern to the believer are all bound up in the Person of the Lord Jesus Christ. His destiny and ours are inseparable. Paul's thought is that since our **life is hidden with Christ in God**, we should not be occupying ourselves with the petty things of this world, and especially the religious world about us.

But there is another thought connected with the expression **your life is hidden with Christ in God**. The world does not see our spiritual life. Men do not understand us. They think it is strange that we do not live like they do. They do not comprehend our thoughts, our motives, or our ways. Just as it is said of the Holy Spirit that the world "neither sees Him, nor knows Him," so it is with our spiritual life; it **is hidden with Christ in God**. First John 3:1 tells us: "Therefore the world does not know us, because it did not know Him." The real separation from the world lies in the fact that the world does not understand, but rather misunderstands the believer.

3:4 To climax his description of the believer's portion in Christ, the apostle now looks on to Christ's coming again. **When Christ who is our life appears, then you also will appear with Him in glory.** At the present time we are raised with Him and enjoying a life that is not seen or understood by men. But the day is coming when the Lord Jesus will return for His saints. Then we **will appear with Him in glory**. Men will understand us then and realize why we behaved as we did.

3:5 In verse 3, we were told that we died. Here we are told to **put to death** our **members which are on the earth**. In these two verses we have a very clear illustration of the difference between a believer's standing and state. His standing is that he has died. His state should be that of reckoning himself dead to sin by putting **to death** his **members which are on the earth**. Our standing is what we are in Christ. Our state is what we are in ourselves. Our standing is the free gift of God through faith in the Lord Jesus Christ. Our state represents our response to God's grace.

Here we should also notice the difference between law and grace. God does not say, "If you live a life of freedom from sin, then I will give you a position of death with Christ." That would be law. Our position would depend on our own efforts, and needless to say, no one would ever attain that position. Instead of that, God says: "I freely give to all who believe on the Lord Jesus a position of favor in My sight. Now go out and live a life that is consistent with such a high calling." That is grace!

When the apostle says that we should **put to death** our **members which are on the earth**, he does *not* mean that we should literally destroy any of the members of our physical body! The expression is figurative, and is explained in the phrases that follows. The word **members** is used to signify the various forms of lust and hatred that are enumerated.

Fornication is generally used to describe unlawful sexual intercourse or immorality, especially between single people (Matt. 15:19; Mark 7:21). Sometimes it is broader, and is translated sexual immorality. **Uncleanness** refers to impurity of thought, word, or action. It speaks of moral filth rather than physical dirtiness here. **Passion** denotes strong and unbridled lust. **Evil desire** speaks of intense and often violent craving. **Covetousness** in general means greediness or the desire to have more, but here it may refer especially to an unholy desire to satisfy sexual appetite which **is idolatry**.

The list begins with acts and moves on to motives. The various forms of sexual sin are described, then they are traced to their lair, namely, the covetous heart of man. The word of God is clear in teaching that there is nothing inherently wrong in sex. God made man with the power for reproduction. But the sin comes when those things which God has so graciously bestowed upon His creatures are used for vile, illicit purposes. Sexual sin was the cardinal offense of the pagan world in Paul's day, and doubtless it still holds first place. Where believers are not yielded to the Holy Spirit, sexual sins often come into their lives and prove their downfall.

3:6 Men think that they can commit these outrageous sins and escape punishment. The heavens seem to be silent, and man increases in his boldness. But God is not mocked. **The wrath of God** comes down **upon the sons of disobedience** for these things. These sins have their consequences in this life; people reap in their own bodies the results of sexual immorality. In addition they will reap a terrible harvest of judgment in a day yet future.

3:7 Paul reminds the Colossians that they once indulged in these sins before their conversion. But the grace of God had come in and delivered them from impurity. That was a chapter in their life which was now covered by the blood of Christ. They now had a new life which empowered them to live for God. See Galatians 5:25: "If we live in the Spirit, let us also walk in the Spirit."

3:8 Since they had been redeemed at such a tremendous cost, they should now **put off** all these things like a dirty garment. Not only does the apostle refer to the various forms of unholy lust listed in verse 5, but also to the types of wicked hatred which he is about to enumerate.

Anger is, of course, a strong spirit of dislike or animosity, a vengeful spirit, a settled feeling of hatred. **Wrath** describes an intense form of anger, probably involving violent outbursts. **Malice** is wicked conduct toward another with the idea of harming his person or reputation. It is an unreasonable dislike that takes pleasure in seeing others suffer. **Blasphemy** here means reviling, that is, strong, intemperate language used against another person. It means scolding in a harsh, insolent manner. **Filthy**

language means shameful speaking, and describes that which is lewd, indecent, or corrupt. It is disgraceful, impure language. In this catalog of sin the apostle goes from motives to acts. Bitterness starts in the human heart and then manifests itself in the various ways which have been described.

3:9 In verse 9 the apostle is saying in effect, "Let your state be consistent with your standing." **You have put off the old man**; now put him off practically by refraining from lies. Lying is one of the things that belongs to **the old man**, and it has no place in the life of the child of God. Every day in our lives we are tempted to distort the truth. It may be by withholding information on an income tax form, or by cheating on an examination, or even by exaggerating the details of a story. Lying becomes doubly serious when we injure another by a false statement, or by creating a false impression.

3:10 Not only have we put off the old man, but we **have put on the new man, who is renewed in knowledge according to the image of Him who created him**. Just as the old man refers to all that we were as sons of Adam, with an unregenerate nature, so **the new man** refers to our new position as children of God. There has been a new creation, and we are new creatures. God's purpose is that this new man should always be growing more and more like the Lord Jesus Christ. We should never be satisfied with our present attainments, but should always press on to the goal of increasing conformity to the Savior. He is our example and the rule of our lives. In a coming day, when we stand before the Judgment Seat of Christ, we will be judged not by how much better our lives were than others but rather by how our life measured up to the life of the Lord Jesus Himself.

The image of God is not seen in the shape of our bodies, but in the beauty of the renewed mind and heart. Holiness, love, humility, meekness, kindness, and forgiveness — these make up the divine character. (Daily Notes of the Scripture Union)

3:11 In the new creation of which

the apostle has been speaking, **there is neither Greek nor Jew, circumcised nor uncircumcised, barbarian, Scythian, slave nor free, but Christ is all and in all**. Differences of nationality, religion, culture, and social level are not the things that count. As far as standing before God is concerned, all believers are on the same level, and in local church fellowship this same attitude should be adopted.

This does not mean that there are no distinctions in the church. Some have the gift of evangelist, some of pastor, and some of teacher. Some men are elders in the church and some are deacons. Thus, the verse does not disparage proper distinctions.

Neither should the verse be taken to teach that the distinctions listed have been abolished in the world. Such is not the case. There is still the **Greek** and the **Jew, Greek** here standing for the Gentile peoples in general. There are **the circumcised** and **the uncircumcised**. These two expressions are generally used in the NT to describe Jew and Gentile respectively. However, here they might refer more particularly to the ritual itself as practiced by the Jewish people, and as disregarded by the Gentiles.

There is still the **barbarian** (uncultured person) and the **Scythian**. These two expressions are not here set in contrast to one another. The **Scythians** were barbarians, but were generally considered to be the more extreme form; they were the wildest and most savage of the barbarians. The final contrast is between **slave** and **free**. **Free** refers to those who never had been in bondage, but were born free. For the Christian these worldly distinctions are no longer of importance. It is Christ who really counts. He is everything to the believer and in everything. He represents the center and circumference of the Christian's life.

Bishop Ryle states this truth boldly:

The three words — Christ is all — are the essence and substance of Christianity. If our hearts can really go along with them, it is well with our souls. . . . Many give Christ a certain place in their religion but not the place which God intended Him to fill. Christ alone is not "all in all" to their souls. No! It is either Christ and the church — or Christ and the sacraments — or Christ and His ordained ministers — or Christ and their own repentance — or Christ and their own goodness — or Christ and their own prayers — or Christ and their own sincerity and charity, on which they practically rest their souls.[19]

3:12 In verse 10, Paul said that we have put on the new man. Now he gives some practical ways in which this can be done in our everyday lives. First of all, he addresses the Colossians as **the elect of God**. This refers to the fact that they had been chosen by God in Christ before the foundation of the world. God's electing grace is one of the mysteries of divine revelation. We believe the Scripture clearly teaches that God, in His sovereignty, has chosen men to belong to Christ. We do not believe that God has ever chosen anyone to be damned. Such a teaching is directly contrary to Scripture. Just as we believe in God's electing grace, we also believe in man's responsibility. God does not save men against their will. The same Bible that says "elect according to the foreknowledge of God" also says "whoever calls on the name of the Lord shall be saved."

Next Paul addresses the Colossians as **holy and beloved. Holy** means sanctified, or set apart (same word as "saints") to God from the world. We are positionally holy, and we should be practically holy in our lives as well. Because we are the objects of God's love, it gives us a desire to please Him in every way.

Now Paul describes the Christian graces which we are to **put on** as a garment. **Tender mercies** speaks of a heart of compassion. **Kindness** speaks of the unselfish spirit of doing for others. It is an attitude of affection or goodwill. **Humility** means lowliness, the willingness to be humbled and to esteem others better than oneself. **Meekness** does not speak of weakness, but rather the strength to deny oneself and to walk in grace toward all men. Vine says:

The common assumption is that when a man is meek, it is because he cannot help himself; but the Lord was "meek" because He had the infinite resources of God at His command. Described negatively, meekness is the opposite to self-assertiveness and self-interest; it is equanimity of spirit that is neither elated nor cast down, simply because it is not occupied with self at all.[20]

If **humility** is the "absence of pride," then **meekness** is "the absence of passion." **Longsuffering** speaks of patience under provocation and of the long endurance of offense. It combines joy and a kind attitude toward others, along with perseverance in suffering.

3:13   Bearing with one another describes the patience we should have with the failings and odd ways of our brethren. In living with others, it is inevitable that we will find out their failures. It often takes the grace of God for us to put up with the idiosyncrasies of others, as it must for them to put up with ours. But we must bear with one another. **Forgiving one another, if anyone has a complaint against another.** There are few disputes among the people of God which could not be solved quickly if these injunctions were heeded. Forgiveness should be exercised toward others when they have offended. We often hear the complaint: "But he was the one who offended me. . . ." That is exactly the type of situation in which we are called upon to forgive. If the other person had not offended us, there would have been no need for forgiveness. If we had been the one who had committed the offense, then we should have gone and asked for pardon. Forbearance suggests our not taking offense; forgiveness — not holding it. There could scarcely be any greater incentive to forgiveness than is found in this verse: **Even as Christ forgave you, so you also must do.** How did **Christ** forgive us? He forgave us without a cause. So should we. He forgave us freely. So should we. He forgave and He forgot. So should we. Both as to manner and extent, we should follow our blessed Lord in this wonderful attitude.

3:14   Love is here spoken of as the outer garment, or the belt, which binds all the other virtues together in order to make up **perfection**. It holds together in symmetry all parts of the Christian character. It is possible that a person might manifest some of the virtues above without really having love in his heart. And so Paul is emphasizing here that what

we do must be done in a genuine spirit of **love** for our brethren. Our actions should not be grudging but should be born out of wholehearted affection. The Gnostics thought of knowledge as **the bond of perfection**, but Paul corrects this view by insisting that **love** is **the bond of perfection.**

3:15   The peace of God should act as an umpire **in** our **hearts**. If in anything we are in doubt, we should ask ourselves the questions: "Does it make for peace?" or "Would I have peace in my heart if I went ahead and did it?"

This verse is especially helpful when seeking guidance from the Lord. If the Lord really wants you to embark upon a certain course of action, He will most assuredly give you **peace** about it. If you do not have that peace, then you should not proceed. As has been said: "Darkness about going is light about staying."

Christ called us to enjoy His peace, both as individuals and also in the church. Do not overlook the importance of the latter part of this verse: **To which also you were called in one body.** One way in which we could enjoy peace would be to live in isolation from all other Christians. But this is not God's purpose. He has set the solitary in families. God's intention is that we should gather together in local churches. Although living with other Christians may try our patience at times, yet God in this way can develop virtues in the Christian's life which He could not produce in any other manner. So we should not shirk our responsibilities in the local church, nor give them up when we are annoyed or provoked. Rather we should seek to live compatibly with our fellow believers and help them in all we do and say.

And be thankful. This refrain is repeated over and over again in Paul's writings. There must have been a good reason: The Spirit of God must consider a **thankful** spirit very important. And we believe that it is! — important not only for a person's spiritual life, but for his physical welfare as well. Doctors have found out what the Scriptures have taught through the years — that a cheerful, **thankful** attitude of mind is beneficial for the body, and that worry, depression, and a complaining spirit are definitely harmful to one's health. Usually we think of thankfulness as something that is determined by our immediate circumstances, but Paul here shows that it is a grace to be cultivated. We are responsible to be **thankful**. Of all peoples of the world, we have the most for which to give thanks (compare Deut. 33:29). The fault is not in any lack of subject matter, but only in our selfish hearts.

3:16 There is disagreement as to how verse 16 should be punctuated. There was no punctuation in the original language of the NT, and the meaning of such a verse as this is largely determined by the punctuation marks that are used. We suggest the following: **Let the word of Christ dwell in you richly in all wisdom, teaching and admonishing one another; in psalms, hymns, and spiritual songs, singing with grace in your hearts to the Lord.**

There are thus three sections to the verse. First, we are to **let the word of Christ dwell in** us **richly. The word of Christ** refers to the teachings of Christ as found in the Bible. As we saturate our hearts and minds with His holy word, and seek to walk in obedience to it, then **the word of Christ** is really at home in our hearts.

The second thought is that **in all wisdom** we should be **teaching and admonishing one another**. Every Christian has a responsibility to his brothers and sisters in Christ concerning this matter. **Teaching** has to do with doctrine, whereas **admonishing** has to do with duty. We owe it to our brethren to share our knowledge of the Scripture with them, and to seek to help by practical and godly counsel. When **teaching and admonishing** are given **in wisdom**, they are more likely to find acceptance than when we speak with force but unwisely or without love.

The third thing is that with **psalms and hymns and spiritual songs** we should sing **with grace in** our **hearts to the Lord. Psalms** describe those inspired utterances which are found in the book by that name, which were sung as part of Israel's worship. **Hymns**, on the other hand, are generally understood as songs of worship and praise addressed to God

the Father or to the Lord Jesus Christ. For example:

Jesus! the very thought of Thee
With sweetness fills my breast;
But sweeter far Thy face to see,
And in Thy presence rest.
– *Attributed to Bernard of Clairvaux*

These **hymns** are not inspired in the same sense as the **psalms. Spiritual songs** refer to religious poetry describing Christian experience. An illustration of this might be found in the words:

O what peace we often forfeit,
O what needless pain we bear,
All because we do not carry
Everything to God in prayer.
– *Joseph Scriven*

Using these various types of songs we should sing **with grace** or thanksgiving, **in** our **hearts to the Lord**. At this point it might be well to say that the Christian should use discernment in the type of music he uses. Much of the so-called "Christian" music of today is light and frothy. A great deal of this music is utterly contrary to Scripture, and still more is so similar to the world's "pop" and rock that it is a discredit to the name of Christ.

Verse 16 is very similar to Ephesians 5:18, 19, where we read: "And do not be drunk with wine, in which is dissipation; but be filled with the Spirit, speaking to one another in psalms, hymns, and spiritual songs, singing and making melody in your heart to the Lord." In Colossians 3:16, the main difference is that instead of saying "be filled with the Spirit," Paul says: **"Let the word of Christ dwell in you richly."** In other words, being filled with the Spirit and being filled with God's word are both requisites for living joyful, useful, fruitful lives. We shall not be filled with the Spirit unless we are saturated with God's word; and the study of God's word will not be effective unless we yield up our inmost being to the control of the Holy Spirit. Can we not therefore conclude that to be filled with the Spirit means to be filled with God's word? It is not some mysterious, emotional crisis that comes in the life, but rather day by day feeding on the Scriptures, meditating on them, obeying them, and living by them.

3:17 Verse 17 is an all-inclusive rule

by which to judge our conduct as Christians. Young people today especially have a difficult time deciding whether certain things are right or wrong. This verse, committed to memory, can prove to be the key for unlocking many of these problems. The great test should be: Can I do this **in the name of the Lord Jesus** Christ? Would this be to His glory? Could I expect His blessing to rest on it? Would I want to be doing it when He comes back again? Notice that this test should apply to the words we speak and to the deeds we do. Obedience to this command ennobles all of life. It is a precious secret when the Christian learns to do all as to the Lord and for His glory. Once again the apostle adds the word, **"Giving thanks to God the Father through Him."** Thanks! *Thanks!* **Thanks**! It is a perpetual duty for those saved by grace and destined for the courts of heaven.

B. Appropriate Behavior for Members of the Christian Household (3:18—4:1)

Paul now gives a series of exhortations to members of the Christian household. The series continues through 4:1. He has advice for wives and husbands, for children and parents, and for servants and masters. At first, it may seem like an abrupt change to turn from the subjects which have occupied Paul to such mundane matters as home life. But actually this is most significant.

THE CHRISTIAN HOME

God considers the home to be a very important force in the Christian life. The well-known statement, "The hand that rocks the cradle rules the world," has truth in it beyond what appears on the surface. The family unit was designed by God for the preservation of much that is worthwhile in life. As less and less attention is devoted to the home, even so our civilization deteriorates rapidly. Paul's first Letter to Timothy teaches in a special way that God has ordained home life as the means of developing spiritual qualities, so that one's fitness for leadership in the church grows out of his proved character in the home.

In the verses to follow we have some of the fundamental principles to guide in the establishment of a Christian home. In studying this section, we should be aware of the following "musts."

1. There must be a family altar — a time each day when the family gathers for the reading of the Holy Scriptures and for prayer.

2. The father must have his place of authority in the home, and he must exercise it in wisdom and love.

3. The wife and mother should realize that her first responsibility to God and to the family is in the home. In general, it is not wise for the wife to have an outside job. There are, of course, exceptional cases.

4. The husband and wife should present a godly example to their children. They should be united on all matters, including the disciplining of the children, when necessary.

5. The family unit should be maintained. It is all too possible to become so engrossed in business, social life, and even in Christian service that the children suffer from lack of affection, companionship, instruction, and discipline. Many parents have had to confess mournfully over a wayward son or daughter: "And while your servant was busy here and there, he was gone" (1 Kgs. 20:40).

6. With regard to the disciplining of children, three cardinal rules have been suggested. Never punish in anger. Never punish unjustly. Never punish without explaining the reason.

7. It is good for children to learn to bear the yoke in their youth (Lam. 3:27), to learn the discipline of work and of accepting responsibility, and the value of money.

8. Above all, Christian parents should avoid being ambitious for their children in a carnal, worldly way, but should constantly hold before them the service of our Lord as the most profitable way in which to spend their lives. For some, it might mean full-time service on a mission field; for others, it might mean service for the Lord in a secular occupation. But in either case, work for the Lord should be the primary consideration. Whether at home, at work, or wherever we may be, we should be conscious of the fact that we

represent our Savior, and so every word and act should be worthy of Him, and should, in fact, be governed by Him. ‡

3:18 The first injunction of the apostle is addressed to **wives**. They are enjoined to **submit to their own husbands, as is fitting in the Lord**. According to the divine plan, the husband is head of the house. The woman has been given the place of submission to her husband. She is not to dominate or to lead, but to follow his leadership, wherever she can do so without compromising her loyalty to Christ. There are, of course, instances in which the woman cannot obey her husband and still be faithful to Christ. In such an instance, her first loyalty is to the Lord Jesus. Where a Christian woman has a backward husband, this verse indicates that she should help him to fulfill his proper place in the home, rather than for her to usurp it because she may be more clever.

3:19 The balance which is presented to us in the word of God is beautiful. The apostle does not stop with this advice to wives; he now goes on to show that **husbands**, too, have a responsibility. They are to **love** their **wives, and not to be bitter toward them**. If these simple precepts were followed, many of the problems of married life would disappear, and homes would be happier in the Lord. Actually no wife would be likely to object to submitting to a husband who truly loves her. It has been noted that the husband is not told to make his wife obey him. If she does not, he should take it to the Lord. The submission should be her voluntary act "as is fitting in the Lord."

3:20 Children are admonished: **obey your parents in all things, for this is well pleasing to the Lord**. In all ages, families have been held together by two simple principles — authority and obedience. Here we have the latter. Notice that this obedience is to be **in all things**. This means not only in the things that are agreeable, but those which are not so naturally pleasing.

Christian children who have unsaved parents are often placed in a difficult position. They want to be true to the Lord, and yet at the same time they are faced with demands made upon them by their parents. In general, we feel that if they honor their parents, God will in turn honor them. As long as they are living in the home of their parents, they have a very definite obligation to perform. Of course, they should not do anything that would be contrary to the teachings of Christ, but ordinarily they would not be called upon to do such. Often they will be called upon to do things that might seem very distasteful to them, but as long as it is not distinctly wrong or sinful, they can determine to do it as to the Lord. In this way they can be a good testimony to their parents and seek to win them to the Lord.

3:21 Fathers should **not provoke** their **children, lest they become discouraged**. It is interesting that this advice is addressed to **fathers** and not to mothers. Does it not reveal that the danger of a father committing this fault is greater than that of a mother? Kelly suggests that mothers are probably more prone to spoil the children.

3:22 From verse 22 to the end of the chapter, the Spirit of God addresses **bondservants** or slaves. It is interesting to note the amount of space devoted in the NT to slaves. This is not without significance. It shows that no matter how low a person's social status may be, he still can attain the very highest in the Christian life through faithfulness to the word of God. Perhaps it also reflects the foreknowledge of God that most Christian people would occupy places of service rather than positions of authority. For instance, there is very little instruction in the NT that refers to rulers of nations, but there is considerable advice for those who devote their lives in the service of others. Slaves in the days of Paul usually received very little consideration, and doubtless it struck the early Christians as unusual that so much attention was given to them in these Letters. But it shows how the grace of God reaches down to men, no matter how menial their position might be. C. H. Mackintosh notes: "The slave is not shut out from the service of God. By simply doing his duty in the sight of God, he can adorn the doctrine and bring glory to God."

Bondservants are told to **obey in all things** those who are their **masters according to the flesh**. There is a gentle reminder here that these masters are only **masters according to the flesh**. They have another Master who is above all and who sees all that is done to the lowliest of His children. Slaves are not to serve **with eyeservice, as menpleasers, but in sincerity of heart, fearing God**. (For a good example of this in the OT, see Genesis 24:33.) Especially when a person is oppressed, it is a temptation to slack off in work when the master is not looking. But the Christian servant will realize that his Master is always looking, and so even though his earthly circumstances may be very bitter, he will work as to the Lord. **In sincerity of heart** means that he will have a pure motive — only to please the Lord Jesus.

It is interesting that there is no express prohibition against slavery in the NT. The gospel does not overthrow social institutions by revolution. However, wherever the gospel has gone, slavery has been uprooted and eliminated. This does not mean that these instructions are therefore without meaning for us. All that is said here may very well be applied to employees and employers.

3:23 **Whatever** is done should be done **heartily** (literally "from the soul") **as to the Lord and not to men**. In every form of Christian service as well as in every sphere of life, there are many tasks which people find obnoxious. Needless to say, we try to avoid such work. But this verse teaches us the very important lesson that the humblest service can be glorified and dignified by doing it for the Lord. In this sense, there is no difference between secular and sacred work. All is sacred. Rewards in heaven will not be for prominence or apparent successes; they will not be for talents or opportunities; but rather for faithfulness. Thus obscure persons will fare very well in that day if they have carried out their duties faithfully as to the Lord. Two mottoes which are often hung over the kitchen sink are: "Not somehow, but triumphantly," and "Divine service held here three times daily."

3:24 **The Lord** is keeping the records at the present time, and everything done as to Him will command His attention. "The kindness of God will repay the kindness of men." Those who have little of earthly inheritance **will receive the reward of the inheritance** in heaven. Let us remember this the next time we are called upon to do something that we do not like to do, whether in the church, in the home, or at work; it is a testimony for Christ to do it uncomplainingly, and to do the best possible job.

3:25 Paul does not specify just whom he has in mind in verse 25. Perhaps we would most naturally think of an unjust master, one who oppresses his servants. Maybe a Christian servant has become weary of obeying his unjust demands. "Never mind," Paul is saying, "the Lord knows all about it, and He will take care of the wrongs, too."

But although this might include masters, it is addressed primarily to servants. Slipshod service, cheating, loafing, or other forms of insincerity will not go unnoticed. **There is no partiality** with God. He is the Master of all, and the distinctions that prevail among men mean nothing to Him. If slaves rob their masters (as Onesimus apparently did), they will have to give an account to the Lord.

4:1 This verse logically goes with the closing verse of chapter 3. **Masters** should **give** their **bondservants what is just and fair**. They should not withhold from them a proper wage, but should pay them well for the work they have done. This is addressed directly to Christian employers. God hates the oppression of the poor, and the gifts of a man who has grown rich through unfair labor practices are unacceptable to the Lord. God says in effect: "You keep your money; I don't like the way you made it" (see Jas. 5:1–4). Masters should not be high-minded but should fear. They **also have a Master in heaven**, One who is just and righteous in all His ways.

Before closing this section it is interesting to note how the Apostle Paul repeatedly brings these matters of everyday life under the searchlight of the lordship of Christ as follows: (1) Wives — as is fitting in the Lord (v. 18). (2) Children — well-pleasing to the Lord (v. 20). (3) Servants — fearing the Lord (v. 22). (4) Servants — as to the Lord (v. 23).

C. The Believer's Prayer Life and Witness by Life and Speech (4:2–6)

4:2 Paul never tires of exhorting the

people of God to be diligent in their **prayer** life. Doubtless one of the regrets we all will have when we get to heaven will be that we did not spend more time in prayer, especially when we will realize the extent to which our prayers were answered. There is a great deal of mystery in connection with the whole subject of prayer, many questions which cannot be answered. But the best attitude for the Christian is not to seek to analyze, dissect, or understand prayer's deeper mysteries. The best approach is to keep praying in simple faith, leaving aside one's intellectual doubts.

Not only are we to **continue earnestly in prayer**, but we are also to be **vigilant in it**. This immediately reminds us of the Lord Jesus' request to the disciples in the Garden of Gethsemane: "Watch and pray, lest you enter into temptation." They were not vigilant, and so fell sound asleep. Not only are we to watch against sleep, but also against wandering thoughts, listlessness, and unreality. And we are to watch to see that we are not robbed of time for prayer (Eph. 6:18). Then again, our prayers are to be **with thanksgiving**. Not only are we to be thankful for past answers to prayer, but in faith we can also thank the Lord for prayers He has not answered. Guy King summarizes nicely: "His love wants the best for us; His wisdom knows the best for us; and His power gets the best for us."[21]

4:3 Paul asks that the Colossians remember to pray **also for** him, and for the servants of the Lord who are with him in Rome. It is beautiful to notice that he does not ask that he might be released from prison, but rather **that God would open a door** to him for preaching **the word**. The apostle wanted God to open doors for him. What an important lesson there is for us in this! It is all too possible for us to go around opening doors for ourselves in Christian service. But this is a peril to be avoided. If the Lord opens the doors for us, then we can confidently enter them, knowing that He is leading. On the other hand, if we open the doors for ourselves, then we cannot be sure that we are in the center of the Lord's will, and we might soon be stooping to carnal means to carry on the so-called

work of the Lord. Paul's specific request is that **a door for the word** might be opened to him **to speak the mystery of Christ, for which** he was **in chains**. The **mystery of Christ** in this verse is the truth of the church, and particularly that aspect of it which might be defined by the expression "Christ for the Gentiles." That was the special aspect of the gospel message which had been committed to Paul to preach. It was because he dared to suggest that Gentiles could be saved in the same way as Jews that the Jewish leaders finally succeeded in having him sent to Rome as a prisoner.

There are some who teach that the great mystery of the church was revealed to Paul while he was in prison. They therefore put great emphasis on the "Prison Epistles" while seeming to underestimate the importance of the Gospels and other books of the NT. But it is clear from this verse that the preaching of the mystery was the *cause* of his imprisonment and therefore must have been revealed to him some time before his arrest.

4:4 He is anxious to **make it manifest**, that is, to preach it in such a clear manner that it will be readily understood by the people. This should be the desire of every Christian who seeks to make Christ known. There is no virtue in being "deep." We should aim to reach the masses of humanity and, in order to do so, the message must be presented simply and clearly.

4:5 Christians should **walk in wisdom toward those who are outside**. In their everyday behavior, they should realize that they are being carefully watched by unbelievers. The world is more interested in our walk than in our talk. In the language of Edgar Guest: "I'd rather see a sermon, than hear one, any day." This does not mean that the Christian should not also confess Christ with his lips, but the point is that his walk should correspond with his talk. It should never be said of him, "High talk, low walk."

Redeeming the time means "buying up opportunities." Every day of our lives we face opportunities for witnessing to the saving power of the Lord Jesus Christ. As these opportunities come along, we should be ready to snap them up. The word "buying" implies that there is often a cost involved. But whatever the cost may be, we should be ready to share our precious Savior with those who do not know Him.

4:6 Our **speech** should **always be with grace, seasoned with salt, that we may know how** we **ought to answer each one**. If our conversation is to be always **with grace**, it must be courteous, humble, and Christlike. It should be free from gossip, frivolity, uncleanness, and bitterness. The expression **seasoned with salt** may have a number of meanings. Some commentators think that although our language should be gracious, it should be equally honest and without hypocrisy. Other think of **salt** as that which heightens flavor, and so Paul is saying that our conversation should never be dull, flat, or insipid, but should always be worthwhile and profitable. Lightfoot says that heathen writers used "salt" as a figure of speech for "wit." Paul changes wit to wisdom. Perhaps the best way to explain the expression is to study the language of the Lord Jesus. To the woman taken in the act of adultery, He said: "Neither do I condemn you: go, and sin no more." Here we have the grace and the salt. First of all, the grace, "neither do I condemn you"; then the salt, "go, and sin no more." Then again the Lord Jesus said to the woman at Jacob's well: "Give Me a drink. . . . Go, call your husband." The first speaks of grace, whereas the second reminds us more of salt.

That you may know how you ought to answer each one. Perhaps the Apostle Paul is here thinking particularly of the Gnostics who came to the Colossians with their plausible doctrines. They should be ready to **answer** these false teachers with words of wisdom and faithfulness.

D. Glimpses of Some of Paul's Associates (4:7–14)

4:7 Tychicus was apparently the one who was chosen by the Apostle Paul to carry this Letter from Rome to Colosse. Maclaren pictures how amazed Tychicus would have been if told that "these bits of parchment would outlast all the ostentatious pomp of the city, and that his name, because written in them, would be known to the end of time all over the world."

Paul here assures the saints that when Tychicus arrives he will **tell** them **all the news** of the apostle's affairs. Again it is nice to read the combination of titles which Paul bestows on this brother. He calls him **a beloved brother, faithful minister, and fellow servant in the Lord**. How much more to be coveted are titles such as these than high-sounding ecclesiastical names that are given to church officials in our day!

4:8 Tychicus' trip to Colosse would serve two purposes. First of all, he would give the saints a firsthand account of Paul and his companions in Rome, and also he would **comfort** the **hearts** of the Colossians. Here again, **comfort** probably has more the idea of "strengthen" or "encourage" (see 2:2) than that of consoling. His ministry to them would have the general effect of helping them to stand against the false teaching that was then prevalent.

4:9 The mention of the name **Onesimus** brings before us the lovely story unfolded in Paul's Letter to Philemon. Onesimus was the runaway slave who sought to escape from punishment by fleeing to Rome. Somehow he had come in contact with Paul, who, in turn, had pointed him to Christ. Now Onesimus is going to travel back to his former master, Philemon, in Colosse. He will carry Paul's Letter to Philemon, while Tychicus carries the Letter to the church at Colosse. Picture the excitement among the believers in Colosse when these two brethren arrived with the Letters from Paul! Doubtless they sat up late in the evening, asking questions about conditions in Rome and hearing of Paul's courage in the service of his Savior.

4:10 Not much is known about **Aristarchus** except that he had previously been arrested in connection with his service for the Lord, as recorded in Acts 19:29. Now he is Paul's **fellow prisoner** in Rome.

Mark is here identified as **the cousin of Barnabas**. This young man had started out with Paul and Barnabas in missionary labors. Because of his failure,

Paul decided that he should be left at home, but Barnabas insisted on taking him with him. This caused a rift between the two older workers. However, it is good to learn that Mark's failure was not final, and he is now restored to the confidence of the beloved Paul.

If Mark should visit Colosse, the saints there are told to **welcome him**. The expression **about whom you received instructions** does not necessarily mean that the Colossians had previously received instructions concerning Mark. It may refer to the instructions which Paul is now giving to them: **If he comes to you, welcome him**. The tense of the verb **received** may simply mean that by the time the Colossians read this Letter, they would have received instructions. The mention of Mark, the writer of the Second Gospel, reminds us that we are *all* writing a gospel day by day:

> We each write a gospel, a chapter a day,
> By deeds, looks and likes, the things
>   that we say,
> Our actions betray us — words faithful
>   and true —
> Say, "What is the gospel according
>   to you?"

4:11 Another co-worker of Paul is spoken of as **Jesus, who is called Justus. Jesus** was a common name then, as it still is in certain countries. It was the Greek equivalent of the Hebrew name "Joshua." No doubt this man was **called Justus** because his Christian friends would feel the incongruity of anyone having the same name as the Son of God.

The three foregoing men were all converted Jews. Indeed they were the **only** three former Jews who were **fellow workers** with Paul **for the kingdom of God**, men who had **proved to be a comfort to** him.

4:12 As Paul is bringing his Letter to a close, **Epaphras** reminds him to be sure to send his own personal greetings to the dear saints in Colosse. Epaphras, a native of Colosse, was constantly remembering the believers **in** his **prayers**, asking the Lord that they might **stand perfect and complete in all the will of God**.

4:13 Paul bears **witness** to the fact **that** Epaphras travailed in prayer not only for those in Colosse, but also for the Christians **in Laodicea and those in Hierapolis**. This man had a personal interest in the people of God with whom he was acquainted. Doubtless he had a very long prayer list, and it would not be at all surprising if he remembered each one in prayer every day. "He prays hard for you all the time, that you may stand fast, ripe in conviction, and wholly devoted to doing God's will" (NEB).

4:14 Now Paul sends greetings from **Luke, the beloved physician, and Demas**. Here we have a study in contrasts. **Luke** had traveled with Paul considerably and had probably ministered to him both physically and spiritually during his times of sickness, persecution, and imprisonment.

Demas, on the other hand, had gone on with the apostle for a while, but it was necessary at last for the apostle to say of him: "Demas has forsaken me, having loved this present world, and has departed for Thessalonica" (2 Tim. 4:10).

E. Greetings and Instructions (4:15–18)

4:15 Greetings are now sent to **the brethren who are in Laodicea**, to **Nymphas, and the church that** was **in his house**. We read again of the church in Laodicea in Revelation 3:14–22. The church there became lukewarm about the things of God. It became utterly materialistic and self-satisfied. Thinking that all was well, the people did not realize their own nakedness. Manuscripts differ as to whether Nymphas (a man) or Nympha (a woman) is addressed. But it is sufficient to notice that there was a church in that home in Colosse. In those days the Christians did not have elaborate edifices such as are used today. However, most of us will readily agree that the power of God in a local church is far more important than an elaborate building or fine furnishings. Power is not dependent upon the latter; luxurious church buildings often serve as a hindrance to power.

4:16 **When this epistle** had been **read** in Colosse, it was to be sent to **the church of the Laodiceans** to be read there also. Undoubtedly this was done, but from what we learn in Revelation 3, it seems that the Laodiceans did not heed the message of this Letter, at least in a lasting way.

Paul also directs that **the epistle from Laodicea** should be read in Colosse. There is no way of knowing what Letter is referred to. Some believe that Paul's so-called Letter to the Ephesians was the one in view. Some ancient manuscripts omit the words "in Ephesus" in Ephesians 1:1. This has led commentators to believe that the Letter to the Ephesians might have been a circular Letter which was supposed to be read in several different churches — for instance, Ephesus, Laodicea, then Colosse. This view is also strengthened by the fact that so few personal references are made in *Ephesians* compared to the number made in Colossians.[22]

4:17 **Archippus** is told to **take heed to the ministry which** he had **received in the Lord**, and to **fulfill it**. Here again, we do not have definite information as to what **ministry** is referred to. Many have believed that **Archippus** was a son of Philemon, and that he was active in the church at Colosse. The verse will become much more meaningful to us if we assume that our name is Archippus, and if we hear the Spirit of God saying to us: **"Take heed to the ministry which you have received in the Lord, that you may fulfill it."** Each one of us has been given some service by the Lord, and we will some day be required to give an account of what we have done with it.

4:18 At this point, the apostle took the pen in his **own hand** and signed his closing **salutation** with his Gentile name **Paul**. Doubtless as he did so the **chains** on his hands proved an inconvenience in writing, but it reminded him to say to the Colossians: **Remember my chains**. "The sound of pen and chains together is the final sign that the preacher's chains cannot bind the Word of God."[23] Then he closed the Epistle with the words **Grace be with you. Amen.** A. T. Robertson writes: "There is no richer word than the word 'grace,' for it carries in it all of God's love as seen in the gift of His Son for us."[24] **Amen.**

ENDNOTES

[1](Intro) George Salmon, *A Historical Introduction to the Study of the Books of the New Testament*, p. 384.

[2](Intro) *New Bible Commentary*, p. 1043.

[3](Intro) A. T. Robertson, *Paul and the Intellectuals*, p. 16.

[4](1:5) J. B. Lightfoot, *Saint Paul's Epistles to the Colossians and to Philemon*, p. 134.

[5](1:6) Both NU and M texts add "and growing."

[6](1:11) A. S. Peake, "Colossians," *The Expositor's Greek Testament*, III:499.

[7](1:14) The words "through His blood" definitely occur in the parallel passage in Ephesians 1:7, but here they are neither in the oldest (NU) nor in the majority (M) of Greek mss.

[8](1:18) Alfred Mace, further documentation unavailable.

[9](1:19) The strengthened form of *oikeō* used here (*katoikeō*) suggests settling down and being at home.

[10](1:22) Charles R. Erdman, *Epistle of Paul to the Colossians and Philemon*, p. 46.

[11](1:23) The Greek language has two words for "if" (*ei* and *ean*) and several grammatical constructions to note the type of condition the writer or speaker envisions. Here the *ei* with the indicative *epimenete* is a first class condition (Paul takes it for granted that they *will* continue).

[12](1:23) Pridham, further documentation unavailable.

[13](2:2) Alfred Mace, further documentation unavailable.

[14](2:9) Marvin Vincent, *Word Studies in the New Testament*, II:906.

[15](2:14) H. A. W. Meyer, *Critical and Exegetical Handbook to the Epistles to the Philippians and Colossians*, p. 308.

[16](2:18) The word *not* is omitted in the NU text, but the resultant meaning would be much the same. Whether they actually saw anything or not, it was all carnal emptiness.

[17](3:2) Robertson, *Intellectuals*, p. 149.

[18](3:2) F. B. Hole, *Paul's Epistles, Volume Two*, p. 105.

[19](3:11) J. C. Ryle, *Holiness*, pp. 436, 455.

[20](3:12) W. E. Vine, *Expository Dictionary of New Testament Words*, p. 56.

[21](4:2) Guy King, *Crossing the Border*, p. 111.

[22](4:16) On the other hand, since Paul spent three years at Ephesus, he would have known *so many* people there that it would have been precarious to choose

a handful for fear of offending the rest.

²³(4:18) *New Bible Commentary*, p. 1051.

²⁴(4:18) Robertson, *Intellectuals*, p. 211.

BIBLIOGRAPHY

(Colossians and Philemon)

Carson, Herbert M. *The Epistles of Paul to the Colossians and to Philemon*. Grand Rapids: Wm. B. Eerdmans Publishing Co., 1960.

English, E. Schuyler. *Studies in the Epistle to the Colossians*. New York: Our Hope Press, 1944.

Erdman, Charles R. *Epistles of Paul to the Colossians and Philemon*. Philadelphia: Westminster Press, 1933.

King, Guy. *Crossing the Border*. London: Marshall, Morgan and Scott, Ltd., 1957.

Lightfoot, J. B. *Saint Paul's Epistle to the Colossians and to Philemon*. Grand Rapids: Zondervan Publishing House, reprint of 1879 edition by MacMillan.

Maclaren, Alexander. "Colossians and Philemon," *The Expositor's Bible*. London: Hodder and Stoughton, 1888.

Meyer, H. A. W. *Critical and Exegetical Handbook to the Epistles to the Philippians and Colossians*. New York: Funk and Wagnalls, 1884.

Nicholson, W. R. *Popular Studies in Colossians: Oneness with Christ*. Grand Rapids: Kregel Publications, 1903.

Peake, Arthur S. "Colossians," *The Expositor's Greek Testament*. Vol. 3. Grand Rapids: Wm. B. Eerdmans Publishing Co., 1961.

Robertson, A. T. *Paul and the Intellectuals*. Nashville: Sunday School Board of the Southern Baptist Convention, 1928.

Rutherfurd, John. *St. Paul's Epistles to Colossae and Laodicea*. Edinburgh: T. & T. Clark, 1908.

Sturz, Richard. *Studies in Colossians*. Chicago: Moody Press, 1955.

Thomas, W. H. Griffith. *Studies in Colossians and Philemon*. Grand Rapids: Baker Book House, 1973.

Vine, W. E. *The Epistle to the Philippians and Colossians*. London: Oliphants, 1955.

THE FIRST EPISTLE TO
THE THESSALONIANS

Introduction

"This letter, more than any other of Paul's, is characterised by simplicity,
gentleness, and affection . . . here there is no controversy."

— W. Graham Scroggie

I. Unique Place in the Canon

The first book by any famous author is usually highly prized as indicating earliest emphasis and gift of communication. First Thessalonians may well be Paul's first inspired Letter. The amazing amount of Christian teaching that the apostle was able to fit into his short stay at Thessalonica is clearly indicated by the many doctrines he discusses as already known by the Thessalonians.

Today the Rapture and Second Advent of our Lord are widely believed and looked for by evangelical Christians. This was not always so. The revival of interest in this doctrine, especially through the writings of the early Brethren in Great Britain (1825-1850) was largely based on 1 Thessalonians. Without this short Letter we would be terribly deprived in our understanding of the various aspects of Christ's return.

II. Authorship†

That 1 Thessalonians is an authentic Pauline Letter is denied by virtually no Bible scholars. The support for this is sufficient, as J. E. Frame says, "unless one is prepared to assert that Paul never lived or that no letter from him has survived."[1]

External evidence that Paul is the author is found in Polycarp, Ignatius, and Justin, as well as the Marcionite Canon and the Muratorian Canon (early lists of Christian Scriptures — one heretical and one orthodox).

Internal evidence is the use of Pauline vocabulary and style, and the outlook of a tender-hearted, spiritual father. The historical allusions coincide with Acts. Both in 1:1 and 2:18 the writer calls himself Paul.

III. Date

First Thessalonians was written from Corinth during Paul's eighteen-month stay there, not long after Timothy came to Paul (1 Thess. 3:6; 2:17). Since Gallio (Acts 18) is believed to have arrived as proconsul in the early summer of A.D. 51, Paul must have gone there in early 50 and written 1 Thessalonians soon after. Nearly all scholars date the book in the early 50's, and it is probably safe to date the Letter more precisely in A.D. 50 or 51, only twenty years after our Lord's Ascension.

IV. Background and Themes††

It was during Paul's Second Missionary Journey that the light of the gospel first broke in on the darkness of Thessalonica (Acts 17:1–10).

After Paul and Silas had been released from jail in Philippi, they traveled to Thessalonica via Amphipolis and Apollonia. Thessalonica at that time was a strategic city, both commercially and politically. True to form, Paul went to the Jewish synagogue and showed from the OT that the Messiah had to suffer and rise from the dead. He then went on to declare that Jesus of Nazareth was the promised Messiah. That lasted for three Saturdays. Some of the Jews were convinced, and took their place with Paul and Silas as Christian believers. Also,

†*See p. i.*   **2021**   ††*See p. ii.*

many of the Greek proselytes and quite a few of the leading women of the city were converted. Then the backlash started. Those Jews who did *not* believe rounded up some of the hoodlums from the marketplace, incited a riot, and besieged the house of Jason, where Paul and Silas had been staying. When they didn't find the preachers in the house, they dragged Jason and some of the other believers before the city rulers (politarchs), accusing them of having turned the world upside down. It was an unintended compliment! Then they charged the Christians with plotting to overthrow Caesar by promoting another King named Jesus. The politarchs were troubled. They required Jason and his colleagues to post bail, probably adding strict orders for his guests to get out of town. Then Jason and the others were released.

The Christian brethren in Thessalonica decided that it would be wise for the preachers to leave town, so they sent them by night to Berea.

The remarkable thing is that when Paul and Silas departed, they left behind a congregation of believers who were instructed in the doctrines of the faith and who were unmoved by the persecution they endured. It would be easy to conclude from Acts 17:2 that Paul and his companions were in Thessalonica for only three Sabbaths. However, that may have been only the duration of their teaching ministry *in the synagogue*. Paul and his team may have spent as long as three months *in the city*. The apostle's Letters to them show that the Thessalonians had a broad acquaintance with Christian doctrine, and they could scarcely have received this in three or four weeks.

From Berea, Paul went to Athens (Acts 17:15). There he heard that the believers in Thessalonica were being persecuted. He tried to visit them, but Satan hindered (1 Thess. 2:17, 18), so he sent Timothy to them (3:1, 2). Timothy brought back a report that was, on the whole, encouraging (3:6–8), and this prompted the apostle to write this Letter. In it, he defends his ministry against slanderous attacks; he calls for separation from the prevailing immorality of that culture; he corrects misapprehensions about those who had died in Christ; he rebukes those who had quit working in view of Christ's coming; and he urges the saints to respect their spiritual leaders.

One of the most important themes of 1 Thessalonians is the return of the Lord Jesus. It is mentioned at least once in each of the five chapters. G. R. Harding Wood put these references together and came up with the following excellent synopsis:

The Christian who is expecting the return of the Lord Jesus has no room for: (1) Idols in his heart (1:9, 10); (2) Slackness in his service (2:9, 19); (3) Divisions in his fellowship (3:12, 13); (4) Depression in his mind (4:13–18); or (5) Sin in his life (5:23).[2]

OUTLINE

C. The Life that Speaks to Outsiders (4:11, 12)
D. The Hope that Comforts Believers (4:13–18)
E. The Day of the Lord (5:1–11)
F. Varied Exhortations to the Saints (5:12–22)

IV. FINAL GREETINGS TO THE THESSALONIANS (5:23–28)

Commentary

I. SALUTATION (1:1)

The Letter opens with the names of three men who had been accused of turning the world upside down. The charge was intended as a slander; it was actually a tribute.

Paul was the author of the Epistle. **Silvanus and Timothy** were traveling with him at the time, so he included their names. **Silvanus** is probably the same as the Silas who sang a duet with Paul in the prison at Philippi (Acts 16:25). **Timothy** is the young brother from Lystra who had joined Paul just before the trip to Thessalonica (Acts 16:1).

The letter was written **to the church of the Thessalonians in God the Father and the Lord Jesus Christ**. The word we translate as *church* was used at that time to describe any kind of an assembly, so Paul wants to make it clear that this is not a heathen assembly but one that is related to **God** as **Father and** to **Jesus Christ** as **Lord**.

The greeting **grace . . . and peace** embraces the best blessings that anyone could enjoy this side of heaven. **Grace** is God's undeserved favor in every aspect of our lives. **Peace** is the unruffled quietness which defies the crashing, crushing circumstances of life. **Grace** is the cause and **peace**, the effect. Paul repeats the dual divine names as the co-equal source of the blessings, this time putting the possessive personal pronoun **our** in front of **Father**.[3]

II. PAUL'S PERSONAL RELATIONS WITH THE THESSALONIANS (1:2–3:13)

A. Paul's Commendation of the Thessalonians (1:2–10)

1:2, 3 Whenever Paul prayed he mentioned the Thessalonians. (Are we as faithful in remembering our Christian brothers and sisters?) And it was always with **thanks** that he prayed for them, **remembering** their **work of faith**, their **labor of love**, and their **patience of hope**.

Their **work of faith** probably refers primarily to their conversion to God. This description of **faith** as a **work** reminds us of the time some people asked Jesus, "What shall we do, that we may work the works of God?" Jesus answered them, "This is the work of God, that you believe in Him whom He sent" (John 6:28, 29). In this sense, faith is an act or deed. But it is not toil by which a man earns merit or in which he can boast. In fact, it is the only work that man can perform without robbing Christ of His glory as Savior and without denying his own status as a helpless sinner. Faith is a non-meritorious work by which the creature acknowledges his Creator and the sinner acknowledges his Savior. The expression **work of faith** also includes the *life* of faith which follows conversion.

In addition to their **work of faith**, Paul remembered their **labor of love**. This speaks of their service for God motivated by **love** to the Lord Jesus. Christianity is not a life to be endured for duty's sake, but a Person to be served for love's sake. To be His slave is perfect freedom, and "love for Him makes drudgery divine." Compared to love, the profit motive is a cheap, tawdry inducement. Love for Christ draws forth service that the dollar could never inspire. The Thessalonians were living testimonies to this fact.

Finally, Paul was thankful for their **patience of hope**. This speaks of their steadfast waiting for Jesus. They had been undergoing persecution as a result of their valiant stand for Christ. But no cracks had appeared in what Phillips calls their "sheer dogged endurance."

The place of remembrance is indicated by the phrase **in the sight of our God and Father**. As Paul entered the presence of God in prayer, he rehearsed the spiritual birth and growth of the saints and breathed out his thanksgiving for their faith, love, and hope.

1:4 The apostle was assured that these saints had been chosen **by God** before the foundation of the world. But how did he know? Did he have some supernatural insight? No, he knew they were among the elect by the way they had received the gospel.

The doctrine of **election**⁴ teaches that God chose certain people in Christ before the foundation of the world (Eph. 1:4). It does *not* teach that He chose some to be damned. If men are finally lost, it is because of their own sin and unbelief.

The same Bible that teaches election also teaches human responsibility or man's free choice. God makes a *bona fide* offer of salvation to all people everywhere. Whoever comes to Christ will find a warm welcome.

These two doctrines, election and freedom of choice, create an irreconcilable conflict in the human mind. But the Bible teaches both and so we should believe both even if we can't harmonize them.

We do not know who the elect are, and so we should carry the gospel to all the world. Sinners should not use the doctrine of election as an excuse for not believing. If they will repent and believe on the Lord Jesus Christ, God will save them.

1:5 By **our gospel** Paul does not imply a different message from that of the other apostles. The contents were the same; the difference was in the messengers. The Thessalonians had not treated the message as a mere religious lecture; they had, of course, received it in word, but not **in word only**.

It was **in power, and in the Holy Spirit, and in much assurance** that it came to them: (1) **In power**. The message worked in their lives with supernatural energy, producing conviction of sin, repentance, and conversion. (2) **In the Holy Spirit**. This power was produced by the Holy Spirit. (3) **In much assurance**. Paul preached with great confidence in the message. The Thessalonians accepted it with **much assurance** as the word of God. The result in their lives was full assurance of faith.

Paul now reminds them of his own conduct while he was with them. He not only preached the gospel, but lived a consistent life. The best sermon is a holy life.

1:6 Thus Paul could say, **"You became followers of us and of the Lord."** One would have expected him to say "of the Lord and of us," mentioning the Lord first. But here he is giving the order of their experience. Their first introduction to the Lord Jesus was in the life of the apostle.

It is sobering to think that people are supposed to be able to see Christ in us. We should be able to say with Paul, "Imitate me, just as I also imitate Christ" (1 Cor. 11:1).

Notice that they received the word with **affliction** and **joy**. This is how they had imitated the Lord and the apostles. Externally there was **affliction**; internally there was **joy**. It is an unusual combination! For the man of the world, it is impossible to experience joy and affliction simultaneously; to him, sorrow is the opposite of joy. The Christian has a **joy of the Holy Spirit** that is independent of circumstances; to him, the opposite of joy is sin.

The **affliction** they endured was the persecution which followed their conversion.

1:7 The Thessalonians became model Christians. First of all, their example of joy in the midst of persecution was an example to believers **in Macedonia and Achaia**, that is, to all the Christians in Greece.

1:8 But their testimony didn't stop there. They became reproducing Christians. Like ripples in a pool, **the word of the Lord** spread out in ever-widening circles: first **in Macedonia and Achaia**, then **in every place**. Soon the news of their **faith toward God** became so widespread that Paul didn't have to speak about it; the people already knew.

We are not intended to be termini of our blessings, but channels through which they can flow to others. God shines in our hearts so that the light might shine out to others (2 Cor. 4:6, JND translation). If we have really drunk the water of salvation, then rivers of living water will flow forth to those around us (John 7:37, 38).

1:9 It was a matter of common conversation that when the apostle and his colleagues went to Thessalonica, they had received a royal welcome. Also it had become a matter of common knowledge that a startling transformation had taken place in the lives of many people. They had **turned to God from** their pagan **idols** and had yielded their will to God as bondslaves.

Notice that they **turned to God from idols**, not from idols to God. It wasn't that they had become fed up with their idols and then decided to give God a chance. No, they **turned to God** and found Him so satisfying that they dropped their idols.

> It's that look that melted Peter,
> It's that face that Stephen saw,
> It's that heart that wept with Mary,
> Can alone from idols draw.
> — *Ora Rowan*

Let us never lose the sense of thrill and awe that is implicit in this account. Two men go into a heathen city with the word of the Lord. They preach the gospel in the power of the Spirit. The miracle of regeneration takes place: men and women become so enraptured with the Savior that they abandon their idols. Next you have a local assembly of believers praising God, living lives of holiness, bravely enduring persecution, and winning others to Christ. Truly the Lord's service is the prince of callings!

1:10 Not only were the Thessalonians serving the living and true God (in contrast to idols which are lifeless and false), but they were waiting for the Lord Jesus. Notice the details of their expectation:

1. The Person — **His Son**
2. The Place — **from heaven**
3. The Pledge — **whom He raised from the dead**
4. The Precious Name — **even Jesus**
5. The Prospect — **who delivers us from the wrath to come**

Thus we have in verses 9 and 10 the three aspects of the Thessalonians' experience:

Turning (compare work of faith, v. 3)
Serving (compare labor of love, v. 3)
Waiting (compare patience of hope, v. 3)

G. R. Harding Wood[5] analyzes them as follows:

Following — looking to God
Serving — looking on the fields
Waiting — looking for Jesus

The Thessalonians were waiting for God's **Son from heaven**. This implies the possibility of His coming during their lifetime, in fact, *at any moment* during their lifetime. The imminent return of the Lord Jesus is the Christian's hope. It is found in many passages of the NT, of which the following are a few:

Luke 12:36 — "And you yourselves be like men who wait for their master."

Romans 8:23 — ". . . waiting for the adoption, the redemption of our body."

1 Corinthians 11:26 — "For as often as you eat this bread and drink this cup, you proclaim the Lord's death till He comes."

2 Corinthians 5:2 — "For in this we groan, earnestly desiring to be clothed with our habitation which is from heaven."

Galatians 5:5 — "For we through the Spirit eagerly wait for the hope of righteousness by faith."

Philippians 3:20 — "We also eagerly wait for the Savior, the Lord Jesus Christ."

Philippians 4:5 — "The Lord is at hand."

Titus 2:13 — "Looking for the blessed hope and glorious appearing of our great God and Savior Jesus Christ."

Hebrews 9:28 — "To those who eagerly wait for Him He will appear a second time, apart from sin, for salvation."

James 5:7–9 — "Therefore, be patient, brethren, until the coming of the Lord . . . for the coming of the Lord is at hand . . . the Judge is standing at the door."

1 Peter 4:7 — "But the end of all things is at hand."

1 John 3:3 — "And everyone who has this hope in Him purifies himself, just as He is pure."

Jude 21 — ". . . looking for the mercy of our Lord Jesus Christ unto eternal life."

Revelation 3:11 — "I am coming quickly!" 22:7 — "Behold, I am coming quickly!" 22:12 — "And behold, I am coming quickly . . . " 22:20 — " 'Surely . . . quickly.' Amen. Even so, come, Lord Jesus!"

The Christian knows that he may be required to pass through death, but he also knows that the Lord may come at any moment and that, in that event, he will enter heaven without dying.

No prophecy of the Scripture needs to be fulfilled before the coming of Christ for His people. It is *the next great event* in God's program.

We cannot be looking for the Lord's return at any moment if some event or period of time has to intervene. The pretribulation Rapture position is the only one that permits the believer to look for Christ's coming today. Other views force abandonment of the imminency of His return.

The One we look for is Jesus, our Deliverer **from the wrath to come**. This description of the coming Savior may be understood in two ways:

1. He delivers us from the eternal punishment of our sins. On the cross He endured the **wrath** of God against our sins. Through faith in Him, we have the value of His work reckoned to our account. Henceforth there is no condemnation for us because we are in Christ Jesus (Rom. 8:1).

2. But He also delivers us from the coming period of judgment when the **wrath** of God will be poured out on the world that has rejected His Son. This period is known as the Tribulation and the time of Jacob's Trouble (Dan. 9:27; Matt. 24:4–28; 1 Thess. 5:1–11; 2 Thess. 2:1–12; Rev. 6:1–19:10).

B. Review of Paul's Ministry, Message, and Conduct at Thessalonica (2:1–12)

2:1 In the latter part of 1:5, Paul briefly alluded to his personal character and conduct while he was at Thessalonica. Now he launches into a more thorough review of his ministry, message, and lifestyle.

The point is that the primary ministry of a Christian is the ministry of *character*. What we are is far more important than anything we ever say. Our uncon-

scious influence speaks more loudly than our conscious influence. James Denney said:

A Christian's character is the whole capital he has for carrying on his business. In most other callings, a man may go on, no matter what his character is, provided his balance at the bank is on the right side; but a Christian who has lost his character has lost everything.[6]

The missionary martyr Jim Elliot wrote in his journal:

In spiritual work, if nowhere else, the character of the worker decides the quality of his work. Shelley and Byron may be moral free-lancers and still write good poetry. Wagner may be lecherous and still produce fine music, but it cannot be so in any work for God. Paul could refer to his own character and manner of living for proof of what he was saying to the Thessalonians. Nine times over in this first epistle he says, "You know," referring to the Thessalonians' firsthand observation of Paul's private as well as public life. Paul went to Thessalonica and lived a life that more than illustrated what he preached; it went beyond illustration to convincing proof. No wonder so much work in the Kingdom is shoddy; look at the moral character of the worker.[7]

Perhaps in these verses the apostle is defending himself against the false accusation of his critics. At any rate, he first reminds the Thessalonians that his ministry was successful. They themselves were living evidence that his work had been fruitful. They knew that his visit **was not in vain**. They themselves had been converted and a congregation had been established.

2:2 Then, too, his ministry was courageous. The bitter opposition and outrageous treatment **at Philippi**, including his imprisonment there with Silas, did not daunt, discourage, or intimidate him. He pressed on to Thessalonica. There, with the courage which only God can give, he preached **the gospel** in the face of **much conflict**. A less robust person could have thought of numerous theological reasons why God was calling him to more congenial audiences. But not Paul! He preached the message fearlessly despite great opposition, a direct result of the Spirit's filling.

2:3 The apostle's **exhortation** to believe the gospel was true in its source, pure in its motive, and dependable in its method. As to its source, it did not spring from false doctrine but from the truth of God. As to its motive, the apostle looked on the Thessalonians unselfishly, with their good in view, and not with any ulterior, impure desire. As to its method, there was no clever plot to deceive them. Apparently his jealous enemies were accusing him of heresy, lustful desire, and craftiness.

2:4 To Paul the ministry was a sacred stewardship. He was the steward, **approved by God**, and **the gospel** was the precious treasure that had been **entrusted** to him by God. His responsibility was to please God by the faithful proclamation of the message, no matter what man's reaction might be. It was clear to him that he couldn't please both God and man, so he chose to please **God, who tests our hearts** and then rewards accordingly.

A steward is obligated to please the one who pays him. Preachers may sometimes be tempted to hold back the full truth for fear of repercussion from those who contribute to their support. But God is the Master, and He knows when the message is watered down or suppressed.

2:5 In verses 5–12 Paul gives an account of his behavior at Thessalonica; in doing so, he has left a splendid pattern for all servants of Christ.

First of all, he never stooped to flattery or insincerity in order to achieve results. His words were honest and transparent, and his motives were free from hypocrisy.

Second, he never used the work of the Lord as **a cloak** under which he could hide a selfish desire to get rich. His service was not a false front **for covetousness**.

To disprove any charge of flattery, he appeals to the saints. But to disprove any thought of **covetousness**, he appeals to **God**, who is the only One who can read the heart.

2:6 Here we have another impressive insight into the character of this great man of God. **As apostles of Christ**, he and his colleagues were entitled to financial support (here called **glory**) from the Thessalonians. But they were deter-

mined that they would not be burdensome to them, so they worked day and night to provide for their own needs. It was a different story in Corinth. There Paul worked so as not to give his critics any ground for accusing him of preaching for money. In Thessalonica he worked because the saints were poor and persecuted, and he did not want to be an added burden to them.

2:7 Instead of lording it over God's heritage, he was **gentle among** them **as a nursing mother** caring for **her own children**. Paul realized that new converts need **nursing**, and he carried on this ministry with all the solicitude of a devoted **mother**.

2:8 So deep was his affectionate concern for them, he was anxious to share with them rather than to receive from them. His was not a cold, perfunctory dispensing of **the gospel of God** but a pouring out of his very soul. He loved them, and love is heedless of cost. Like his Master, he did not come to be served, but to serve and to give his life (Mark 10:45).

2:9 A further evidence of Paul's unselfishness is here: we see him working as a tentmaker in order to earn a living so that he could minister to the people without being **a burden to any of** them. While it is true that the gospel preacher is entitled to financial support from other Christians, it is commendable to see him foregoing this right, if necessary, from time to time. A true minister of Christ will continue to preach the gospel whether he receives money for it or has to work to finance himself. Notice the expressions **labor and toil** and **night and day**. The gospel didn't cost the Thessalonians a penny, but it cost Paul plenty.

2:10 The believers could testify to Paul's exemplary behavior toward them; and **God also** was a Witness that he was devout (or holy), just (or righteous), and blameless. Holy, that is, separated to God from sin. Righteous in character and in conduct. Blameless toward God and man. If the best sermon is a holy life, Paul was a great preacher. Not like another preacher whose eloquence was greater than his conduct: when he was in the pulpit, the people wished he would never leave it, but when he was out of it, they wished he would never enter it again!

2:11 In verse 7, he had compared himself to a nursing mother; now he changes the figure to that of a devoted **father**. If the former suggests tenderness and affection, the latter suggests wisdom and counsel. **As a father**, he **exhorted** them to live a holy life, he encouraged them to go on for the Lord in spite of persecutions, and he testified concerning the blessedness of obedience to the will and word of God.

2:12 The goal of Paul's ministry was that the saints might **walk worthy of God who calls** them **into His own kingdom and glory**.

In ourselves we are unworthy of God or of a place in heaven; the only worthiness we have is found in the Lord Jesus Christ. But as sons of God, we are expected to **walk worthy** of the high calling. We can do this by submitting ourselves to the control of the Holy Spirit and by confessing and forsaking sin in our lives continually.

All who are saved are subjects of God's **own kingdom**. At the present time that **kingdom** is invisible, and the King is absent. But the moral and ethical teachings of the kingdom apply to us today. When the Lord Jesus returns to reign, the **kingdom** will then be set up in visible form, and we will share the **glory** of the King in that day.

C. Review of the Thessalonians' Response to the Gospel (2:13–16)

2:13 Now the apostle picks up another theme which he had touched on in 1:5a — the Thessalonians' response to the preaching of the gospel. When they received the message, i.e., *heard* it, they did not receive, i.e., *accept* it as the word of men but as the word of God. The NKJV brings this out clearly:

> For this reason we also thank God without ceasing, because when you received the word of God which you heard from us, you welcomed it not as the word of men, but as it is in truth, the word of God, which also effectively works in you who believe.

Paul is deeply thankful for their re-

ception and acceptance of the message. This is another example of his selflessness. Most of us want others to believe what we say simply because *we* say it. But man's word forms a shaky foundation for faith. Only God can be fully trusted, and it is only when His word is trusted that results are produced in hearts and lives. This is what happened to the Thessalonians — the word was working **effectively** in their lives because they believed. Walter Scott wrote:

> His Word — the Bible — is inspired, or God-breathed, in all its books and parts as originally written. It is our only authority in all things, for all circumstances, and all times. There is needed a generation who shall tremble at the Word of God. It is life's chart; our guidance, our light, our moral safeguard. Thank God for the Sacred Volume.[8]

2:14 What results had the Bible produced in the lives of these believers? Not only had they been saved; they were enabled to stand firm in the face of severe persecution. This was good evidence of the reality of their conversion. By their steadfast endurance, they **became imitators of the** Christian **churches in Judea**. The only difference was that the Thessalonians **suffered** at the hands of their Gentile **countrymen**, whereas the believers in Judea were persecuted by **the Judeans**.

2:15 At this mention of the Judeans, Paul launches into an indictment of them as arch-opponents of the gospel. And who should know better than he? At one time he had been a ringleader of those Jews who attempted to liquidate the Christian faith. Then after his conversion he himself felt the sharp edge of the sword of their persecution.

The crowning sin of the Jews was killing **the Lord Jesus**. While the actual crucifixion was carried out by the Romans, it was the Jews who stirred them up to do it. This came as a climax to centuries of persecution of God's **prophets** sent to the nation of Israel (Matt. 21:33–39).

In the Christian era, they had already **persecuted** Paul and other apostles, mistakenly thinking that they were pleasing **God**. Their actions were displeasing to Him and they made themselves **contrary to all men**.

2:16 Not content to reject the gospel themselves, they were determined to prevent Paul and his associates from preaching the message **to the Gentiles**. Nothing infuriated them more than to hear that Gentiles could **be saved** in the same way as Jews.

In their opposition to the will of God, they were carrying on where their fathers had left off: **always to fill up the measure of their sins**. It was as if they were determined to keep the cup of their guilt full at all times.

But their doom is pronounced, for **wrath has come upon them to the uttermost**. Paul does not specify what he means by this **wrath**. Perhaps it is a general statement of impending judgment as a result of a full measure of guilt. We do know that within twenty years (A.D. 70) Jerusalem was destroyed and the surviving Jews were scattered throughout the earth.

From passages such as this, some have suggested that Paul was anti-semitic and that the NT is an anti-semitic book. The truth is that Paul had a deep love for his countrymen, the Jews, and was even willing to be cut off from Christ if it could have meant their salvation (Rom. 9:1–3). Though his ministry was primarily to the Gentiles, he never lost his burden for the evangelization of the Jews; at times this burden almost seems to have taken precedence over his primary mission.

What the apostle says here about the Judean leaders is historical fact and not personal invective. And we must remember that God moved him to write what he did. Anti-semitism is unchristian and cannot be justified under any circumstances. But it is not anti-semitic to say that the Jewish people are charged by God with the death of His Son (Acts 2:23), just as the Gentiles also are held responsible for their part (1 Cor. 2:8).

D. Explanation of Paul's Failure to Return to Thessalonica (2:17–20)

2:17 In the next four verses, the apostle explains his failure to return to Thessalonica. Perhaps his carping critics accused him of cowardice in not going back because of the opposition he had encountered there.

Paul first makes it clear that the separation was only physical. The expression **having been taken away from you** means that they were orphaned by the departure of their spiritual father. However, his affectionate interest in them had never waned. Notice the words that express the intensity of his love: **endeavored more eagerly . . . with great desire**.

2:18 Twice he had tried to go back to Thessalonica, but twice **Satan** had **hindered**. The exact nature of Satan's opposition is not always known.

Neither do we know how Paul could be sure it was the devil who **hindered** him and not the Lord. In Acts 16:6 we read that Paul and his party were forbidden by the Holy Spirit to preach the word in Asia. In the next verse, they tried to go to Bithynia but the Spirit would not permit them to go. How can we know when it is the Spirit and when it is the devil who is hindering? Perhaps one way is this: when we know that we are in the will of God, any hindrances that arise are not the Spirit's work but the devil's. Also, Satan can be expected to hinder whenever God is blessing. But God always overrules Satan's opposition. In this particular case, Paul's inability to go to Thessalonica resulted in the writing of this Letter. The Letter, in turn, has resulted in glory to God and blessing to us.

2:19 Why was the apostle so interested in going back to the Thessalonian believers? Because they were his children in the Lord. He had pointed them to Christ and felt responsible for their spiritual growth. He knew that he would have to give an account of them in a coming day. They were his **hope** of reward at the Judgment Seat of Christ. He wanted to be able to rejoice in them. They would be his **crown of rejoicing** before the **Lord Jesus Christ at His coming**.

It seems obvious from this verse that Paul expected to recognize the Thessalonians in heaven. And it follows that we too will know our loved ones in heaven.

In verse 19 Paul speaks of his children in the faith as being his **crown**. Elsewhere in the NT we read of other crowns: the crown of righteousness (2 Tim. 4:8); the crown of life (Jas. 1:12;

Rev. 2:10); the crown of glory (1 Pet. 5:4) — all of them incorruptible (1 Cor. 9:25).

2:20 The saints were his **glory and joy**. He had invested in human personality and his reward was spiritual sons and daughters who would worship the Lamb of God for all eternity.

THE COMING OF THE LORD

In verse 19, we have the first use of the word **coming** in 1 Thessalonians with regard to the Lord's return. Because this is the major theme of this Epistle, we are going to pause here and give an explanation of what we believe to be the scriptural teaching on the subject.

There are three principal Greek words used in the NT with reference to Christ's return:

parousia (pa-roo-SEE-ah): coming and subsequent presence

apokalupsis (apo-KAL-yoop-sis): unveiling, revelation

epiphaneia (epi-FAHN-ee-ah): manifestation

The word most commonly used is *parousia*. It means a *presence* or a *coming alongside*. Vine says it denotes both an arrival and a consequent presence. When we think of the Lord's coming, we should think of it not only as a momentary event but as a period of time.

Even in English, the word *coming* is used in this way. For instance, "Christ's coming to Galilee brought healing to multitudes." Here we do not mean the day He arrived in Galilee but the whole period of time He spent in that area. So when we think of Christ's coming, we should think of a period of time rather than an isolated event.

Now if we take all the occurrences of *parousia* in the NT, we find that they describe a period of time with (1) a beginning, (2) a course, (3) a manifestation, and (4) a climax.

1. The *beginning* of the *parousia* is the Rapture. It is described in the following passages (the word which translates *parousia* is italicized in each case):

For as in Adam all die, even so in Christ all shall be made alive. But each one in his own order: Christ the firstfruits, afterward those who are

Christ's at His *coming* (1 Cor. 15:22, 23).

But I do not want you to be ignorant, brethren, concerning those who have fallen asleep, lest you sorrow as others who have no hope. For if we believe that Jesus died and rose again, even so God will bring with Him those who sleep in Jesus. For this we say to you by the word of the Lord, that we who are alive and remain until the *coming* of the Lord will by no means precede those who are asleep. For the Lord Himself will descend from heaven with a shout, with the voice of an archangel, and with the trumpet of God. And the dead in Christ will rise first. Then we who are alive and remain shall be caught up together with them in the clouds to meet the Lord in the air. And thus we shall always be with the Lord. Therefore comfort one another with these words (1 Thess. 4:13–18).

Now, brethren, concerning the *coming* of our Lord Jesus Christ and our gathering together to him . . . (2 Thess. 2:1).

Therefore be patient, brethren, until the *coming* of the Lord. See how the farmer waits for the precious fruit of the earth, waiting patiently for it until it receives the early and latter rain. You also be patient. Establish your hearts, for the *coming* of the Lord is at hand (James 5:7, 8).

And now, little children, abide in Him, that when He appears, we may have confidence and not be ashamed before Him at His *coming* (1 John 2:28).

2. The *course* of the *parousia* includes the Judgment Seat of Christ when rewards will be given to believers for faithful service:

For what is our hope, or joy, or crown of rejoicing? Is it not even you in the presence of our Lord Jesus Christ at His *coming*? (1 Thess. 2:19).

Now may the God of peace Himself sanctify you completely; and may your whole spirit, soul, and body be preserved blameless at the *coming* of our Lord Jesus Christ (1 Thess. 5:23).

Another event which should probably be included in the *course* of the *parousia* is the Marriage Supper of the Lamb. From its location in the book of

Revelation, we know that it will take place prior to Christ's glorious reign. We include it here even though the word *coming* is not used in connection with it.

And I heard, as it were, the voice of a great multitude, as the sound of many waters and as the sound of mighty thunderings, saying, "Alleluia! For the Lord God Omnipotent reigns! Let us be glad and rejoice and give Him glory, for the marriage of the Lamb has come, and His wife has made herself ready." And to her it was granted to be arrayed in fine linen, clean and bright, for the fine linen is the righteous acts of the saints. Then he said to me, "Write: 'Blessed are those who are called to the marriage supper of the Lamb!' " (Rev. 19:6–9).

3. The *manifestation* of Christ's coming is His return to earth in power and great glory to reign as King of kings and Lord of lords. The Rapture will not be seen by the world; it takes place in a split second. But every eye will see Christ when He comes to reign. Therefore it is called the *manifestation* of His *parousia*. This is the third phase of His coming.

Now as He sat on the Mount of Olives, the disciples came to Him privately, saying, "Tell us, when will these things be? And what will be the sign of Your *coming*, and of the end of the age?" (Matt. 24:3).

For as the lightning comes from the east and flashes to the west, so also will the *coming* of the Son of Man be (Matt. 24:27).

But as the days of Noah were, so also will the *coming* of the Son of Man be (Matt. 24:37).

And [they] did not know until the flood came and took them all away, so also will the *coming* of the Son of Man be (Matt. 24:39).

So that He may establish your hearts blameless in holiness before our God and Father at the *coming* of our Lord Jesus Christ with all His saints (1 Thess. 3:13).

And then the lawless one will be revealed, whom the Lord will consume with the breath of His mouth and destroy with the brightness of His *coming* (2 Thess. 2:8).

For we did not follow cunningly devised fables when we made known to you the power and *coming* of our Lord Jesus Christ, but were eyewitnesses of His majesty (2 Pet. 1:16). [Here Peter is speaking about the manifestation of Christ's *parousia* as it was pre-pictured on the Mount of Transfiguration.]

4. Finally we have the *climax* of the *parousia*. It is referred to in the following verse:

Where is the promise of His *coming*? For since the fathers fell asleep, all things continue as they were from the beginning of creation (2 Pet. 3:4).

In this latter chapter we read of scoffers who will arise in the last days, denying the probability of Christ's return. What aspect of the *parousia* do they mean?

Are they referring to the Rapture? No. They probably know nothing about the Rapture. Are they referring to Christ's coming to reign? No. It is apparent that they are not. The entire context indicates that they are ridiculing the final punishment of all evildoers by the Lord. They mean a last, climactic judgment of God on the earth, or what they call "the end of the world." Their argument is that they have nothing to worry about. God hasn't intervened in history and He won't intervene in the future. So they feel free to continue in their evil words and deeds.

Peter answers their scoffing by pointing forward to the time, *after the thousand-year reign of Christ*, when the heavens and the earth as we now know them will be utterly destroyed. This climax of Christ's *parousia* is after the Millennium and at the inauguration of the eternal state.

In addition to *parousia*, the other two words used in the original language of the NT to describe the coming of the Lord are *apokalupsis* and *epiphaneia*.

Apokalupsis means an *unveiling* or a *Revelation*. Bible students are divided whether it *always* refers to the third phase of Christ's coming — His coming to the earth in power and glory — or whether it might also refer to the Rapture when He will be revealed to the church.

In the following verses it could refer either to the Rapture or to the coming back to the earth to reign over it:

So that you come short in no gift, eagerly waiting for the *revelation* of our Lord Jesus Christ (1 Cor. 1:7).

That the genuineness of your faith, being much more precious than gold that perishes, though it is tested by fire, may be found to praise, honor, and glory at the *revelation* of Jesus Christ (1 Pet. 1:7).

Therefore gird up the loins of your mind, be sober, and rest your hope fully upon the grace that is to be brought to you at the *revelation* of Jesus Christ (1 Pet. 1:13).

But rejoice to the extent that you partake of Christ's sufferings, that when His glory is *revealed*, you may also be glad with exceeding joy (1 Pet. 4:13).

In another passage this word seems to refer quite clearly to Christ's coming to reign:

And to give you who are troubled rest with us when the Lord Jesus is *revealed* from heaven with His mighty angels (2 Thess. 1:7).

Epiphaneia means a *manifestation* or an *appearing*. Again, some think it refers both to Christ's appearing for His saints and to His appearing with His saints; others say it refers only to the latter. The word is found in the following passages:

And then the lawless one will be revealed, whom the Lord will consume with the breath of His mouth and destroy with the *brightness* (lit., *manifestation*) of His coming (2 Thess. 2:8).

That you keep this commandment without spot, blameless until our Lord Jesus Christ's *appearing* (1 Tim. 6:14).

I charge you therefore before God and the Lord Jesus Christ, who will judge the living and the dead at His *appearing* and His kingdom (2 Tim. 4:1).

Finally, there is laid up for me the crown of righteousness, which the Lord, the Righteous Judge, will give to me on that Day, and not to me only but also to all who have loved His *appearing* (2 Tim. 4:8).

Looking for the blessed hope and glorious *appearing* of our great God and Savior Jesus Christ (Tit. 2:13).

The first and third verses clearly describe the appearing of Christ to the world. The others could conceivably refer to the Rapture also. The one thing that is clear is that both the Rapture and Christ's coming to reign are held before the believer as events for which he waits with eagerness. At the time of the Rapture, he will see the Savior and will receive his glorified body. When Christ returns to earth, the believer will appear with Him in glory (Col. 3:4). It is at this time also that the believer's rewards will be manifested. These rewards are given out previously at the Judgment Seat of Christ, but they are seen by all when Christ comes to reign. What are the rewards? In Luke 19:17–19 there is a hint that they have to do with local rule in the Millennium. One person is made ruler over ten cities, another over five.

By studying the various references to the Lord's coming, we have seen that it refers to a period of time rather than to a single event, and that this period of time has various phases or stages. There is a beginning, a course, a manifestation, and a climax. It begins with the Rapture, includes the Judgment Seat of Christ, will be visibly displayed when Christ returns to earth, and will end when the heavens and earth as we now know them are destroyed by fire. ‡

E. The Mission of Timothy to Thessalonica (3:1–10)

The words *your faith* occur five times in chapter 3 (vv. 2, 5, 6, 7, 10) and are a key to understanding the passage. The Thessalonians were passing through severe persecution, and Paul was anxious to know how their faith was standing up to the test. Thus the chapter is a lesson on the importance of follow-up work. It is not enough to lead sinners to the Savior. They must be helped to grow in grace and in the knowledge of the Lord.

3:1 In chapter 3 we continue to hear the heartbeat of Paul as he expresses his undying interest in the saints at Thessalonica. While he was **in Athens** he developed an intolerable craving to know how his converts were getting on. Satan had hindered his personal return. Finally he could not stand inaction any longer; he decided to send Timothy to the Thessalonians, while he remained **in Athens alone**. (The *we* is editorial.) There is a certain sadness to think of him there **alone**. The sights of a great city held no attraction for him; he was burdened with the care of the churches.

3:2 Notice the "degrees" after Timothy's name: **our brother and minister of God, and our fellow laborer in the gospel of Christ**. The word **minister**[9] here and elsewhere in the NT simply means *servant*. The idea of a separate class known as clergymen originated in later years.

What a privilege it was for Timothy to serve his apprenticeship under the beloved brother Paul! Now that he has proved himself, he is sent on a mission to Thessalonica alone.

The purpose of the trip was **to establish** the saints **and encourage** them **concerning** their **faith**. They had been persecuted because of their confession of Christ. This was a critical time for the young converts; Satan was probably dropping subtle suggestions that maybe they were wrong after all in becoming Christians!

It would be interesting to hear Timothy as he taught them to expect opposition, to bear it bravely, and to rejoice in it. They needed encouragement not to buckle under the pressure of opposition.

3:3 In the heat of persecution, it would be easy for the Thessalonians to think it strange that they should suffer so severely, and to wonder if God was displeased with them. Timothy reminded them that it wasn't strange at all: this is normal for Christians, so they shouldn't **be shaken** or lose heart.

3:4 Paul reminds them that even when he was in Thessalonica, he used to tell them that Christians were appointed to afflictions. His prediction came true in their own lives. How well they knew it!

Trials form a necessary discipline in our lives:

1. They prove the reality of our faith, and weed out those who are mere professors (1 Pet. 1:7).

2. They enable us to comfort and encourage others who are going through trials (2 Cor. 1:4).

3. They develop certain graces, such as endurance, in our character (Rom. 5:3).

4. They make us more zealous in spreading the gospel (Acts 4:29; 5:27–29; 8:3, 4).

5. They help to remove the dross from our lives (Job 23:10).

3:5 The apostle repeats the substance of verses 1 and 2: **when** further delay proved unendurable for him, he **sent** Timothy to find out how the Christians there were weathering the storm. His great anxiety was that the devil might have tricked them into giving up their aggressive Christian testimony in exchange for relaxation of the persecution. It is the ever-present temptation to swap loyalty to Christ for personal comfort, to by-pass the cross in pursuit of a crown. Who of us does not have to pray, "Forgive me, Lord, for so often finding ways to avoid the pain and sacrifice of discipleship. Strengthen me today to walk with You no matter what the cost."

If Satan had induced the saints to recant, then Paul felt his labor there would have been for nothing.

3:6 **Timothy** came back to Corinth **from** the Thessalonians with **good news**. First of all, he reassured Paul concerning their **faith and love**. They were not only standing true to the teachings of the Christian **faith**, but they were also manifesting the distinctive virtue of **love**. This is ever the test of reality — not just an orthodox acceptance of the Christian creed, but "faith working through love" (Gal. 5:6). Not just your "faith in the Lord Jesus" but also "your love for all the saints" (Eph. 1:15).

Was it significant that Timothy mentioned their **faith and love**, but omitted any reference to their hope? Had the devil shaken their confidence in the return of Christ? Possibly. As William Lincoln said, "The devil hates that doctrine because he knows the power of it in our lives." If their hope was defective, Paul certainly seeks to repair it in this Epistle of hope.

Timothy also reported that the Thessalonians had kind memories of the apostle and his friends, and that they were as anxious for a reunion as Paul, Silas, and Timothy were.

3:7 This news was like cold water to Paul's thirsty soul (Prov. 25:25). In all his distress and affliction, he was greatly encouraged **by** their **faith**.

3:8 He exclaims, **"For now we live, if you stand fast in the Lord."** The suspense of not knowing had been a living death to him. Now life quickly returned when he heard that all was well. What a commentary this is on the unselfish devotion of this great man of God!

3:9 Words failed to express adequately **to God** the **thanks** which filled Paul's heart. His cup of **joy** was overflowing every time he remembered them **before** his **God**.

3:10 Paul's prayer life was habitual, not spasmodic: **night and day**. It was intensely fervent: **praying exceedingly**. It was specific: **that we may see your face**. And it was altruistic: **that we may . . . perfect what is lacking in your faith**.

F. Paul's Specific Prayer (3:11–13)

3:11 The chapter closes with Paul's prayer for a return trip to them, and for the development of even greater love in them. The request is addressed to **our God and Father Himself, and our Lord Jesus Christ**. Then this plural subject is followed by a singular verb. This usage indicates the deity of Christ and the unity of the Godhead.

3:12 The Thessalonians had actually been commendable in manifesting true Christian love, but there is always room for development. And so he prays for a deeper measure: **may the Lord make you increase and abound in love**. Their **love** should embrace their fellow believers and all men, including their enemies. Its model or pattern should be the love of the apostles: **just as we do to you**.

3:13 The result of love in this life is blamelessness in the next. If we love one another and all mankind, we will stand **blameless in holiness before our God** when **Christ** comes **with all His saints**, for love is the fulfilling of the law (Rom. 13:8; Jas. 2:8).

Someone has paraphrased the prayer as follows: "The Lord enable you more and more to spend your lives in the interests of others, in order that He may so establish you in Christian character now, that you might be vindicated from every charge that might possibly be brought against you . . . ."

In chapter 2 we saw that the coming

of Christ has several stages or phases: a beginning, a course, a manifestation, and a climax. It is the third phase that is referred to in verse 13: **the coming of our Lord Jesus Christ with all His saints**. The Judgment Seat of Christ will have already taken place in heaven. The awards will already have been made. But these awards will be manifested to all when the Savior returns to earth as King of kings and Lord of lords.

Saints here probably means those believers who have been caught up to heaven at the time of the Rapture (1 Thess. 4:14). Some think that it means angels, but Vincent says it refers to *the holy and glorified people of God*. He points out that angels have nothing to do with anything in this Epistle, but that glorified believers are closely connected with the subject that was troubling the Thessalonians. He adds, "This does not exclude the attendance of angels on the Lord's coming, but when Paul speaks of such attendance, he says *with the angels of his power*, as in 2 Thessalonians 1:7."[10]

III. PRACTICAL EXHORTATIONS (4:1–5:22)

A. The Sanctification that Fulfills God's Will (4:1–8)

4:1 The word **finally** doesn't mean that Paul is about to close the Letter. It often indicates a change of subject, such as a shift to practical exhortations.

Three prominent words at the close of chapter 3 were *holiness, love,* and *coming*. These are three of the principal subjects of chapter 4: (1) Holiness (vv. 1–8), (2) Love (vv. 9, 10), and (3) Coming (vv. 13–18). The other main theme is industriousness (vv. 11, 12).

Chapter 4 opens with a plea to walk in holiness and thus to please God, and closes with the taking up of the saints. Paul was probably thinking of Enoch when he wrote this. Notice the similarity: (1) Enoch walked with God (Gen. 5:24a); (2) Enoch pleased God (Heb. 11:5b); and (3) Enoch was taken up (Gen. 5:24b; Heb. 11:5a). The apostle commends the believers for their practical holiness, but urges them to advance to new levels of accomplishment. Holiness is a process, not an achievement.

4:2 While he was with them, Paul repeatedly charged them, with the authority of **the Lord Jesus**, that they should please God by lives of practical holiness.

4:3 **The will of God** for His people **is** their **sanctification**. To sanctify means to set apart for divine use. In one sense, all believers have been set apart from the world to the service of the Lord; this is known as positional sanctification, and it is perfect and complete (1 Cor. 1:2; Heb. 10:10). However, in another sense, believers should sanctify themselves, that is, they should separate themselves from all forms of sin; this is known as practical or progressive sanctification. It is a process that will continue until the believer's death or the Lord's return. It is this latter use of the word that is found in verse 3. (See the discussion of sanctification under 5:23 below.)

The specific sin against which Paul warns is unlawful sexual activity, and in this section is probably the same as adultery. It is one of the principal sins of the heathen world. The admonition, **that you should abstain from sexual immorality**, is needed today as much as in the first century of the church.

4:4 The Christian program is for every one **to possess his own vessel in sanctification and honor**. The word **vessel** in this verse may mean a wife or it may mean the man's own body. It is used of a wife in 1 Peter 3:7 and of the body in 2 Corinthians 4:7.

The RSV understands it to mean a wife: "that each one of you know how to take a wife for himself in holiness and honor."

The NEB adopts the view that the body is meant: "every one of you must learn to gain mastery over his body, to hallow and honor it."

If we allow the context to decide, then **vessel** means the man's wife. The teaching is that each man should treat his wife honorably and decently, never stooping to any form of marital unfaithfulness. This reinforces monogamy as God's will for mankind (see also 1 Cor. 7:2).

4:5 The Christian view of marriage is in sharp contrast to that of the ungodly. As one commentator said, "When Jesus laid His hands on the woman in Luke 13:13, she was made straight. When pagan man touches a woman, she is made crooked."

The Gentiles think of sex as a means of gratifying the **passion of lust**. To them chastity is a weakness, and marriage a means of making sin legal. By their filthy conversation and their obscene writings on public walls, they glory in their shame.

4:6 Sexual immorality is a sin against God's Holy Spirit (1 Cor. 6:19); it is a sin against one's own body (1 Cor. 6:18); but it is also a sin against other persons. So Paul adds: **that no one should take advantage of and defraud his brother in this matter**. In other words, a Christian man must not go beyond the bounds of marriage and **defraud** a **brother** by stealing the affections of the brother's wife. Though these offenses are not generally punished in criminal courts today, **the Lord is the avenger of all such**. Sexual sins bring on a terrible harvest of physical and mental disorders in this life, but these are nothing compared to their eternal consequences, if they are unconfessed and unforgiven. Paul had **forewarned** the Thessalonians of this.

One of Britain's most gifted writers of the nineteenth century fell into sexual sin and ended in prison and disgrace. He wrote:

> The gods have given me almost everything. But I let myself be lured into long spells of senseless and sensual ease. . . . Tired of being on the heights, I deliberately went to the depths in search for new sensation. . . . *I grew careless of the lives of others*. I took pleasure where it pleased me and passed on. I forgot that every little action of the common day makes or unmakes character, and that therefore what one has done in the secret chamber, one has some day to cry aloud from the housetop. I ceased to be lord over myself. I was no longer the captain of my soul, and did not know it. I allowed pleasure to dominate me. I ended in horrible disgrace.[11]

He grew careless of the lives of others, or, as Paul would say, he transgressed and wronged **his brother in this matter**.

4:7 **God did not call us** on the basis of moral **uncleanness**, but in connection with lives of **holiness** and purity. He has called us from a cesspool of degradation, and has begun in us a lifelong process designed to make us more and more like Himself.

4:8 Anyone who **rejects this** instruction isn't simply despising the teaching of a **man**, such as Paul; he is defying, disregarding, flouting, and rejecting **God** Himself — **who has also given**[12] **us His** *Holy* **Spirit**. The word *Holy* is emphatic here. How can one who is indwelt by the **Holy Spirit** indulge in sexual sin?

Notice that all members of the Trinity are mentioned in this paragraph. The Father (v. 3), the Son (v. 2), and the **Holy Spirit** (v. 8). Wonderful thought! All three Persons in the Godhead are interested and involved in the sanctification of the believer.

The subject changes now from lust (vv. 1–8) to love (vv. 9–12), and the exhortation changes from abstain to abound.

B. The Love that Thinks of Others (4:9, 10)

4:9 Not only is the believer to have a controlled body; he should also have a heart of love for his brothers in the Lord. **Love** is the key word of Christianity as sin is of heathenism.

There was **no need** to **write** to the Thessalonians about this virtue. They were **taught by God to love** their brothers, both by divine instinct (1 John 2:20, 27) and by the instruction of Christian teachers. The believers at Thessalonica distinguished themselves by loving all the Christians in all of Macedonia. By commending them for it, Paul memorialized them forever.

4:10 As has been mentioned, brotherly kindness is not an achievement; it is something that must be practiced continually, and so Paul exhorts the believers to **increase more and more** in this grace.

Why is love of **the brethren** so important? Because where there is love, there is unity; and where there is unity, there is the Lord's blessing (Ps. 133:1, 3).

C. The Life that Speaks to Outsiders (4:11, 12)

4:11 Paul encouraged the saints to **aspire** to do three things. In today's par-

lance the three commands in this verse would be:

1. Don't seek after the limelight. Be content to be "little and unknown, loved and prized by Christ alone."

2. **Mind your own business** instead of butting into other people's affairs.

3. Be self-supporting. Don't be a parasite or a "moocher", sponging off others.

4:12 The fact that we are Christians and are looking for Christ's coming does not relieve us of the practical responsibilities of life. We should remember that the world is watching us. Men judge our Savior by us. We should **walk properly toward** unbelievers and be independent of them financially.

D. The Hope that Comforts Believers (4:13–18)

4:13 Old Testament believers had an imperfect and incomplete knowledge of what happened to a person at the time of death. To them *sheol* was an all-purpose word used to describe the disembodied state, both of believers and unbelievers.

They believed that everyone would die eventually, that apparently there would be one general resurrection at the end of the world, and then a final judgment. Martha reflected these sketchy views when she said, "I know that he (Lazarus) will rise again in the resurrection at the last day" (John 11:24).

The Lord Jesus brought "life and immortality to light by the gospel" (2 Tim. 1:10). Today we know that the believer departs to be with Christ at the time of death (2 Cor. 5:8; Phil. 1:21, 23). The unbeliever is said to be in Hades (Luke 16:22, 23). We know that not all believers will die, but that all will be changed (1 Cor. 15:51). We know that there will be more than one resurrection. At the Rapture, only believers will be raised (1 Cor. 15:23; 1 Thess. 4:16); the wicked dead will be raised at the end of the thousand-year reign of Christ (Rev. 20:5).

When Paul first went to Thessalonica, he taught the Christians about Christ's coming to reign and the events that would follow. But in the meantime, problems had arisen regarding those saints who had died. Would their bodies remain in the graves until the last day?

Would they be excluded from participation in Christ's coming and in His glorious kingdom? To answer their questions and to allay their fears, Paul now describes the order of events at the time of Christ's coming for his people.

The formula, **I do not want you to be ignorant, brethren**, is used to alert readers to an important announcement. Here the announcement concerns **those who have fallen asleep**, that is, those believers who have *died*. Sleep is used to describe the *bodies* of departed Christians, never their spirits or souls. Sleep is an appropriate simile of death, because in death a person seems to be sleeping. Even our word *cemetery* comes from a Greek word meaning "sleeping place" (*koimētērion*). And sleep is a familiar simile, because every night we act out this symbol of death, and every morning is like a resurrection.

The Bible does not teach that the soul sleeps at the time of death. The rich man and Lazarus were both conscious in death (Luke 16:19–31). When the believer dies, he is "present with the Lord" (2 Cor. 5:8). To die is to "be with Christ," a position which Paul speaks of as "gain" and as being "far better" (Phil. 1:21, 23). This would scarcely be true if the soul were sleeping!

Neither does the Bible teach annihilation. There is no cessation of being in death. The believer enjoys eternal life (Mark 10:30). The unbeliever suffers eternal punishment (Mark 9:48; Rev. 14:11).

With regard to those saints who have died, the apostle says that there is no need for hopeless sorrow. He does not rule out sorrow; Jesus wept at the grave of Lazarus, though He knew He would raise him in a few minutes (John 11:35–44). But he rules out the despairing grief of those who have no hope of heaven, of reunion, of anything but judgment.

The expression **others who have no hope** invariably reminds me of a funeral I attended where the stricken relatives clustered around the casket of an unsaved relative and wailed inconsolably, "Oh, Marie, my God, my God, Marie!" It was an unforgettable scene of unrelieved hopelessness.

4:14 The basis of the believer's hope is the resurrection of Christ. Just as surely as **we believe that Jesus died and rose again**, so we believe that those who have fallen asleep in Jesus will be raised and will participate in His coming. "For as in Adam all die, even so in Christ all shall be made alive" (1 Cor. 15:22). His resurrection is the pledge and proof of ours.

Notice the expression **sleep in Jesus** or "those who through Jesus sleep." Knowing that it is merely the Lover of our souls giving sleep to the bodies of His beloved ones robs death of its terror.

Our positive assurance concerning those who have died in Christ is that **God will bring** them **with Him**. This may be understood in two ways:

1. It may mean that at the time of the Rapture, God will raise the bodies of believers and bring them back to heaven with the Lord Jesus.

2. Or it may mean that when Christ comes back to the earth to reign, God will bring back with Christ those who have died in faith. In other words, the apostle is saying, "Don't worry that those who have died will miss out in the glory of the coming kingdom. God will bring them back with Jesus when the latter returns in power and great glory." (This is the generally preferred meaning.)

But how can this be? Their bodies are now lying in the grave. How can they come back with Jesus? The answer is given in verses 15–17. Before Christ comes to set up His kingdom, He will return to take His own people home to be with Him in heaven. Then at a later date, He will come back with them.

4:15 How did Paul know this? His answer is, **this we say to you by the word of the Lord**. He received this as *a direct revelation* from **the Lord**. We are not told how he received it — whether by a vision, by an audible voice, or by the inward impression of the Holy Spirit. But it is definitely a truth unknown to men up to that time.

Then he goes on to explain that when Christ returns, the living saints will not have any precedence or advantage over sleeping saints.

In this verse Paul speaks of himself as one who would be **alive** at Christ's **coming** (see also 1 Cor. 15:51, 52). However, in 2 Corinthians 4:14 and 5:1, he speaks of the possibility of his being among those who will be raised. The obvious conclusion is that we should look for the Lord to come at any moment, yet realize that we may be called to reach heaven by way of death.

4:16 The exact order of events at Christ's coming for His saints is now given. **The Lord Himself will descend from heaven**. He will not send an angel, but will come **Himself**!

It will be **with a shout, with the voice of an archangel, and with the trumpet of God**. Several explanations have been offered as to the significance of these commanding sounds, but frankly it is almost impossible to speak with finality about them:

1. Some feel that the **shout** is the voice of the Lord Jesus Himself which raises the dead (John 5:25; 11:43, 44) and changes the living. Others, like Hogg and Vine, say that the shout is the archangel's voice.

2. **The voice of** Michael, the **archangel**, is commonly understood as an assembling command for the OT saints, since he is so closely associated with Israel (Dan. 12:1; Jude 9; Rev. 12:4–7). Others think its purpose is to revive Israel nationally. And still others suggest **the voice of an archangel** summons the angels as a military escort to accompany the Lord and His saints through enemy territory back to heaven (cf. Luke 16:22).

3. **The trumpet of God** is the same as the last trumpet of 1 Corinthians 15:52, which has to do with the resurrection of believers at the time of the Rapture. It calls the saints to eternal blessing. It is not to be confused with the seventh trumpet of Revelation 11:15–18, which signals the final outpouring of judgment on the world during the Tribulation. The last **trumpet** *here* is the last for the church. The seventh trumpet of Revelation is the last for the unbelieving world (though it is never specifically called the "last trumpet").

The bodies of **the dead in Christ will rise first**. Whether this includes the OT saints is debatable. Those who think it does point out that the archangel's voice is heard at this time, and that he is

closely linked with the destinies of Israel (Dan. 12:1). Those who think that the OT saints will not be raised at the Rapture remind us that the phrase **in Christ** (**the dead in Christ**) is never applied to believers who lived before the Church Age; these believers will probably be raised at the end of the Tribulation (Dan. 12:2). In any case it is clear that this is definitely *not* a general resurrection. Not all the dead are raised at this time, but only **the dead in Christ**.

4:17 Then the living **shall be caught up together with them in the clouds to meet the Lord in the air**. The word *Rapture*, which we use to describe this first phase of the Lord's return, is derived from the verb used here in the Latin Bible meaning *caught up*.[13] A "rapture" is a snatching away or a catching up. It is used of Philip in Acts 8:39, of Paul in 2 Corinthians 12:2, 4, and of the male Child in Revelation 12:5.

The air is Satan's sphere (Eph. 2:2), so this is a triumphal gathering in open defiance of the devil right in his own stronghold.

Think of all that is included in these verses! The earth and the sea yielding up the dust of all the dead in Christ. Then the transforming miracle by which this dust is formed into glorified bodies, free forever from sickness, pain, and death. Then the space-flight to heaven. And all of this taking place in the twinkling of an eye (1 Cor. 15:52).

Men of the world have difficulty believing the account of the creation of man in Genesis 1 and 2. If they have difficulty with creation, what will they do with the Rapture — when God will recreate millions of people from the dust that has been buried, scattered, strewn, or swept up on the beaches of the world?

Men of the world are enthusiastic about space travel. But can their greatest exploits compare with the wonder of traveling to heaven in a split second without taking our own atmosphere with us, as the space men have to do when they go on short hops to outer space?

In connection with Christ's coming there is a sound to hear, a sight to see, a miracle to feel, a meeting to enjoy, and a comfort to experience.

It is also good to notice the recurrence of the word **Lord** in these verses: the *word* of the Lord (v. 15), the *coming* of the Lord (v. 15), the Lord *Himself* (v. 16), to **meet the Lord** (v. 17), to **always be with the Lord** (v. 17).

Forever **with the Lord**! Who can tell all the joy and blessedness that is included in these words?

4:18 Therefore comfort one another with these words. Thoughts of the Lord's coming do not produce terror for the believer. It is a hope that thrills and cheers and comforts.

INDICATIONS OF THE LAST TIMES

There are many indications that the Rapture may be near. We consider the following as straws in the wind:

1. The formation of the State of Israel in 1948 (Luke 21:29). The fig tree (Israel) is shooting forth, that is, putting forth its leaves (Luke 21:29–31). For the first time in centuries, the Jews have a national existence in their own homeland. This means that the kingdom of God is near.

2. The rise of many other nations (Luke 21:29). Jesus predicted that not only the fig tree would shoot forth but all the trees as well. We have recently witnessed the demise of colonial governments and the proliferation of new nations. It is an era of new nationalism.

3. The return of Israel to the land in unbelief (Ezek. 36:24, 25). Ezekiel prophesied that it would only be after their return that they would be cleansed from their sins. Israel today is largely an agnostic nation; only a small (but very vocal) segment of the people are orthodox Jews.

4. The ecumenical movement (Rev. 17, 18). We understand Babylon the Great to be a vast religious, political, and commercial system made up of apostate religious bodies that profess to be Christian, perhaps a merger of apostate Catholicism and apostate Protestantism. Christendom is becoming increasingly apostate (1 Tim. 4:1; 2 Thess. 2:3) and is moving toward a world super-church.

5. The worldwide increase in Spiritism (1 Tim. 4:1–3). It is sweeping over vast areas of the earth at this moment.

6. The drastic decline of moral standards (2 Tim. 3:1–5). The daily newspapers offer plenty of evidence of this.

7. Violence and civil disobedience (2 Thess. 2:7, 8). A spirit of lawlessness is abounding in the home, in national life, and even in the church.

8. People with a form of godliness but denying its power (2 Tim. 3:5).

9. The rise of the anti-Christian spirit (1 Jn. 2:18), manifested in the multiplication of false cults which profess to be Christian but deny every fundamental doctrine of the faith. They deceive by imitation (2 Tim. 3:8).

10. The tendency for nations to confederate along lines that approximate the line-up of the latter day. The European Common Market, based on what is known as the Treaty of Rome, may lead to the revival of the Roman Empire — the ten toes of iron and clay (Dan. 2:32–35).

11. Denial of the impending intervention of God in the affairs of the world by way of judgment (2 Pet. 3:3, 4).

To these could be added indications such as earthquakes in many countries, the threat of worldwide famine, and the increasing hostility among nations (Matt. 24:6, 7). The failure of governments to maintain law and order and to suppress terrorism creates the climate for a world dictator. The building of nuclear arsenals gives added meaning to such questions as, "Who is able to make war with him?" i.e., the beast (Rev. 13:4). Worldwide television facilities may be the means for fulfilling Scriptures describing events that will be seen simultaneously all over the planet (Rev. 1:7).

Most of these events are foreseen as occurring before Christ returns to the earth to reign. The Bible does not say they will take place before the Rapture but before His appearing in glory. If that is so, and if we see these trends developing already, then the obvious conclusion is that the Rapture must be near at hand. ‡

E. The Day of the Lord (5:1–11)

5:1 Bible teachers often apologize

for chapter breaks, explaining that the subject should continue without interruption. But here the chapter break is appropriate. Paul begins a new subject. He leaves his discussion of the Rapture and turns to the Day of the Lord. The words translated **but concerning** (Gk., *peri de*) indicate a new line of thought, as so often in 1 Corinthians.

For true believers the Rapture is a comforting hope, but what will it mean for those who are outside of Christ? It will mean the beginning of a period referred to here as **the times and the seasons**. This period is primarily Jewish in character. During this time God will resume His dealings with the nation of Israel, and the endtime events to which the OT prophets pointed will occur. When the apostles asked Jesus when He would set up His kingdom, He answered that it was not for them to know the times and the seasons (Acts 1:7). It seems that **the times and the seasons** cover the period prior to the setting up of the kingdom as well as the kingdom period itself.

Paul felt **no need** to **write to** the Thessalonians about **the times and the seasons**. For one thing, the saints would not be affected by them; they would be taken to heaven before these epochs began.

Also, **the times and the seasons** and the Day of the Lord are subjects that are found in the OT. The Rapture is a mystery (1 Cor. 15:51), never revealed until the time of the apostles.

5:2 The saints already knew about **the day of the Lord**. They knew that the exact time was unknown, and that it would come when least expected. What does Paul mean by **the day of the Lord**? It is certainly not a day of twenty-four hours, but a period of time with certain characteristics.

In the OT this term was used to describe any time of judgment, desolation, and darkness (Isa. 2:12; 13:9–16; Joel 2:1, 2). It was a time when God marched forth against the enemies of Israel and punished them decisively (Zeph. 3:8–12; Joel 3:14–16; Obad. 15–17; Zech. 12:8, 9). But it was also any occasion on which God punished His own people for their idolatry and backsliding (Joel 1:15–20; Amos 5:18; Zeph. 1:7–18). Basically it spoke of judgment on sin, of victory for the cause of the Lord (Joel 2:31, 32), and

untold blessing for His faithful people.

In the future, **the day of the Lord** will cover approximately the same period as the times and the seasons. It will begin after the Rapture and will include:

1. The Tribulation, i.e., the time of Jacob's trouble (Dan. 9:27; Jer. 30:7; Matt. 24:4–28; 2 Thess 2:2; Rev. 6:1–19:16).
2. The coming of Christ with His saints (Mal. 4:1–3; 2 Thess 1:7–9).
3. The thousand-year reign of Christ on the earth (Joel 3:18 [cf. v. 14]; Zech 14:8, 9 [cf. v. 1]).
4. The final destruction of the heavens and earth by fire (2 Pet. 3:7, 10).

The day of the Lord is the time when Jehovah will publicly intervene in human affairs. It is characterized by judgment on the enemies of Israel and on the apostate portion of the nation of Israel, by deliverance of His people, by establishment of Christ's kingdom of peace and prosperity, and glory for Himself.

The apostle reminds his readers **that the day of the Lord** will come **as a thief in the night**. It will be completely unexpected, taking men off guard. The world will be wholly unprepared.

5:3 This Day will also come deceptively, suddenly, destructively, inevitably, and inescapably.

There will be an air of confidence and security in the world. Then God's judgment will suddenly begin to descend with vast destructive force. **Destruction** does not mean loss of being, or annihilation; it means loss of well-being, or ruin as far as the purpose of one's existence is concerned. It will be as inevitable and unavoidable as **labor pains upon a pregnant woman**. From this judgment there will be no escape for unbelievers.

5:4 It is important to notice the change in pronouns from "they" and "them" in the previous verses to **you** and we in the following verses.

The Day of the Lord will be a time of wrath for the unsaved world. But what will it mean to us? The answer is that we are not in danger because we **are not in darkness**.

This Day will come as a thief in the night (v. 2). The only way it will **overtake** anyone is **as a thief**, and the only persons it will **overtake** will be those who are in the night, that is, the unconverted. It will not **overtake** believers at all, because they **are not in darkness**.

At first reading, this verse might seem to say that the Day of the Lord *will* overtake believers but *not as a thief*. But this is not so. It *will not overtake them at all* because when the thief comes to this world's night, the saints will be dwelling in eternal light.

5:5 All Christians are **sons of light and sons of the day**. They **are not of the night nor of darkness**. It is this fact that will exempt them from the judgment that God will pour out on the world that has rejected His Son. The judgments of the Day of the Lord are aimed only at those who are in moral darkness and spiritual night, at those who are alienated from God.

When it says here that Christians are **sons of the day**, it does not mean the Day of the Lord. To be **sons of the day** means to be people who belong to the realm of moral uprightness. The Day of the Lord is a time of judgment on those who belong to the realm of moral darkness.

5:6 The next three verses call believers to a life that is consistent with their exalted position. This means watchfulness and sobriety. We are to **watch** against temptation, laziness, lethargy, and distraction. Positively, we should **watch** for the Savior's return.

Sobriety here means not only being **sober** in conversation and in general demeanor but being temperate as far as food and drink are concerned.

5:7 In the natural realm, **sleep** is associated with **night**. So in the spiritual realm, careless indifference characterizes those who are sons of darkness, that is, the unconverted.

Men prefer to carry on their drunken revelry **at night**; they love darkness rather than light because their deeds are evil (John 3:19). The very name "night club" links the ideas of drinking and carousing with the darkness of night.

5:8 Those **who are of the day** should walk in the light as He is in the light (1 Jn. 1:7). This means judging and forsaking sin, and avoiding excesses of all kinds. It also means putting on the Christian armor and keeping it on. The armor consists of **the breastplate of faith and love** and the **helmet** of **the hope of salvation**. In other words, the armor is **faith**, **love**, and **hope** — the three cardinal elements of Christian character. It is not necessary to press the details of **the breastplate** and **helmet**. The apostle is simply saying that sons of light should wear the protective covering of a consistent, godly life. What preserves us from the corruption that is in the world through lust? **Faith**, or dependence on God. **Love** for the Lord and for one another. The **hope** of Christ's return.

Important Contrasts in Chapter Five

Unbelievers ("they")	Believers ("you")
sleeping	not sleeping
drunk	not drunk
in darkness	not in darkness
of the night and darkness	sons of light and sons of the day
overtaken unexpectedly by the Day of the Lord as a thief in the night	not overtaken unexpectedly by the Day of the Lord as a thief in the night.
sudden and inescapable destruction, as labor pains of a pregnant woman	not appointed to wrath but to obtain salvation

5:9 The Rapture has two aspects, **salvation** and **wrath**. For the believer it means the consummation of his **salvation** in heaven. For the unbeliever, it means the ushering in of a time of **wrath** on earth.

Since we are of the day, **God did not appoint us to** the **wrath** which He will pour out during the Tribulation Period, but rather to **salvation** in its fullest sense — freedom forever from the very presence of sin.

Some understand **wrath** here to refer to the punishment which unbelievers will suffer in hell. Of course it is true that God has not appointed us to that, but it is gratuitous to introduce that thought here. Paul is not talking about hell, but about future events on earth. The context deals with the Day of the Lord — the greatest period of **wrath** in the history of man on earth (Matt. 24:21). We do not have an appointment with the executioner but with the Savior.

Some say that the Tribulation is the time of Satan's wrath (Rev. 12:12), not the wrath of God. They say that the church will experience the wrath of Satan, but will be delivered from the wrath of God at the Second Coming of Christ. However, the following verses speak of the wrath of God and of the Lamb, and their setting is during the Tribulation Period: Revelation 6:16, 17; 14:9, 10, 19; 15:1, 7; 16:1, 19.

5:10 This verse emphasizes the tremendous price our Lord Jesus Christ paid to deliver us from wrath and insure our salvation. He **died for us, that whether we wake or sleep, we should live together with Him**.

There are two ways of understanding the expression **whether we wake or sleep**. Some scholars understand it to mean "living or dead" at the time of the Rapture. They point out that there will be two classes of believers at that time — those who have died in Christ, and those who are still living. So the thought would be that whether we are among the living or the dead at the time of Christ's return, **we** shall **live together with Him**. Christians who die lose nothing. The Lord explained this to Martha: "I am the resurrection and the life: he who believes in Me, though he may die [i.e., a Christian who dies before the Rapture], he shall live [he will be raised from among the dead]. And whoever lives and believes in Me [a believer who is alive at the time of the Rapture] shall never die . . ." (John 11:25, 26).

The other view held by scholars is that **wake or sleep** means "watchful or worldly." In other words, Paul is saying that whether we are spiritually alert or carnally indifferent to spiritual things, we will be caught up to meet the Lord. Our eternal salvation does not depend on our spiritual keenness during the closing moments of our time on earth. If truly converted, **we will live together with Him** when He comes again, whether we are on the tiptoes of expectancy or in the prone position of slumber. Our spiritual condition will determine our rewards, but our salvation depends on faith in Christ alone.

Those who hold this second view point out that the word for **wake** is the same word translated "watch" in verse 6. And the word for **sleep** is used in verses 6 and 7 to mean "insensitivity to divine things, involving conformity to the world" (Vine). But it is *not* the same

word used in 4:13, 14, 15 to mean death.[14]

5:11 In view of so great salvation, in love for so great a Savior, and in the light of His soon return, we should exhort one another by teaching, encouragement, and example, and we should build each other up with the word of God and with loving care. Because we will live together with Him then, we should live together with one another cooperatively now.

F. Varied Exhortations to the Saints (5:12-22)

5:12 Perhaps the elders of the church in Thessalonica had rebuked those who had quit working and were "mooching off" others. And no doubt the drones didn't take the rebuke too well! That may account for this exhortation to the leaders and to those led.

When Paul urges the saints **to recognize those who labor among** them, he means to respect and obey their spiritual guides. This is clear from the words **"and are over you in the Lord and admonish you."** Elders are undershepherds of God's sheep. Their responsibility is to teach, rule, and warn.

This verse is one of many in the NT that shows that there was no one-man rule in the apostolic churches. There was a group of elders in each congregation, pastoring the local flock. As Denney explains:

At Thessalonica there was not a single president, a minister in our sense, possessing to a certain extent an exclusive responsibility; the presidence was in the hands of a plurality of men.[15]

However, the absence of *one-man* rule does not justify *every-man* rule. The assembly should not be a *democracy*, but an *aristocracy*, the rule of the *best* qualified.

5:13 Elders serve as representatives of the Lord. Their work is the work of God. For that reason, they should be held in high regard and love.[16] The exhortation **"be at peace among yourselves"** is no incidental insertion. The number one problem among Christians everywhere is the problem of getting along with each other. Every believer has enough of the flesh in him to divide and wreck any local church. Only as empowered by the Spirit can we develop the love, brokenness, forbearance, kindness, tender-heartedness, and forgiveness that are indispensable for **peace**. A particular threat to **peace** which Paul may be warning against is the formation of cliques around human leaders.

5:14 This verse seems to be addressed to the spiritual leaders of the congregation; it tells them how to deal with problem brothers:

1. **Warn those who are unruly** — those who won't keep in step but insist on disturbing the peace of the church by their irresponsible behavior. Here the **unruly** are those who refuse to work. They are the same as those described in 2 Thessalonians 3:6–12, walking disorderly, not working, but being busybodies.

2. **Comfort the fainthearted** — those who need constant exhortation to rise above their difficulties and go on steadfastly for the Lord.

Concerning the KJV rendering, *Comfort the feeble-minded*, Ockenga remarks: "If the word meant feeble-minded we would still comfort them. They seem to gather when the gospel is preached." And isn't this a tribute to the gospel and to the Christian church? At least there is one sphere where they find sympathy, love, and consideration.

3. **Uphold the weak** — that is, help those who are spiritually, morally, or physically weak. Spiritual and moral support of those who are **weak** in the faith is probably the main idea, though we should not rule out financial help as well.

4. **Be patient with all** — show the grace of longsuffering when others tend to irritate and provoke.

5:15 Speaking now to Christians in general, Paul forbids any thought of retaliation. The natural reaction is to strike back, to return tit for tat. But the Christian should be so in fellowship with the Lord Jesus that he will react in a supernatural way. In other words, he will instinctively show kindness and love to other believers and to the unsaved as well.

5:16 Joy can be the constant experience of the Christian, even in the most adverse circumstances, because Christ is the source and subject of his joy, and Christ is in control of the circumstances. Incidentally, **"Rejoice always"** is the shortest verse in the Greek NT, even if "Jesus wept" is the shortest in the English.

5:17 Prayer should be the constant attitude of the Christian — not that he abandons his regular duties and gives himself wholly to prayer. He prays at certain regular times; he also prays extemporaneously as need arises; and he enjoys continual communion with the Lord by prayer.

5:18 Giving **thanks** to God should be the Christian's native emotion. If Romans 8:28 is true, then we should be able to praise the Lord at all times, in all circumstances, and for **everything**, just as long as in doing so we do not excuse sin.

These three good habits have been called the standing orders of the church. They represent **the will of God in Christ Jesus for** us. The words **in Christ Jesus** remind us that He taught us these things during His earthly ministry and He was the living embodiment of what He taught. By teaching and example, He revealed to us God's will concerning joy, prayer, and thanksgiving.

5:19 The next four verses seem to deal with behavior in the assembly.

To **quench the Spirit** means to stifle His work in our midst, to limit and hinder Him. Sin quenches the Spirit. Traditions quench Him. Man-made rules and regulations in public worship quench Him. Disunity quenches Him. Someone has said, "Cold looks, contemptuous words, silence, studied disregard, go a long way to quench Him. So does unsympathetic criticism." Ryrie says that the Spirit is quenched whenever His ministry is stifled in an individual or in the church.

5:20 If we link this verse with the previous one, then the thought is that we quench the Spirit when we **despise** prophesyings. For instance, a young brother may make some inelegant statement in public ministry. By criticizing him in such a way as to make him ashamed of his testimony for Christ we quench the Spirit.

In its primary NT sense, to prophesy meant to speak the word of God. The inspired utterances of the prophets are preserved for us in the Bible. In a secondary sense, to prophesy means to declare the mind of God as it has been revealed in the Bible.

5:21 We must evaluate what we hear and **hold fast what is good**, genuine, and true. The standard by which we **test** all preaching and teaching is the word of God. There will be abuses from time to time wherever the Spirit has liberty to speak through different brethren. But quenching the Spirit is not the way to remedy these abuses.

As Dr. Denney wrote:

An open meeting, a liberty of prophesying, a gathering in which any one could speak as the Spirit gave him utterance is one of the crying needs of the modern Church.[17]

5:22 Abstain from every form of evil may mean false tongues, prophecies, or teachings, or it may mean **evil** in general.

A. T. Pierson points out that there are seven distinct frames of mind for the Christian in verses 16-22:

1. The praiseful frame (16). Finding all God's dealings to be infinitely grand.

2. The prayerful frame (17). Prayer should never be unsuitable or unseemly.

3. The thankful frame (18). Even in circumstances not pleasant to the flesh.

4. The spiritual frame (19). He should have full liberty in and through us.

5. The teachable frame (20). *Any* channel which God chooses to use.

6. The judicial frame (21). Compare 1 John 4:1. Test all by the word of God.

7. The hallowed frame (22). If evil takes shape in your mind, avoid that evil.[18]

IV. FINAL GREETINGS TO THE THESSALONIANS (5:23-28)

5:23 Now Paul prays for the sanctification of the Christians. The source is **the God of peace**. The scope is found in the word **completely**, meaning "every part of your being."

This verse has been pressed into service by some to prove the "Holiness" doctrine of entire sanctification — that a believer can become *sinlessly perfect* in this life. However, that is not what Paul means when he prays, **the God of peace Himself sanctify you completely**. He is not praying for the eradication of the sin nature but rather that sanctification would extend to every part of their being — **spirit, soul, and body**.

SANCTIFICATION

There are four phases of sanctification in the NT — pre-conversion, positional, practical or progressive, and perfect.

1. Even before a person is saved, he is set apart in a position of external privilege. Thus we read in 1 Corinthians 7:14 that an unbelieving husband is sanctified by his believing wife. This is *pre-conversion sanctification.*

2. Whenever a person is born again, he is *positionally sanctified* by virtue of his union with Christ. This means that he is set apart to God from the world. It is referred to in such passages as Acts 26:18; 1 Corinthians 1:2; 6:11; 2 Thessalonians 2:13; Hebrews 10:10, 14.

3. But then there is *progressive sanctification*. This is a present setting apart of the believer to God from the world, sin, and self. It is the process by which he becomes more Christlike. This is the sanctification which Paul prays for the Thessalonians here. It is also found in 1 Thessalonians 4:3, 4; 2 Timothy 2:21. It is brought about by the Holy Spirit when we are obedient to the word of God (John 17:17; 2 Cor. 3:18). Such practical sanctification is a process that should continue as long as the believer is on earth. He will never achieve perfection or sinlessness on earth, but he should ever be pressing toward that goal.

4. *Perfect sanctification* refers to the believer's final condition in heaven. When he goes to be with the Lord, he will be morally like the Lord, completely and finally set apart from sin (1 Jn. 3:1-3). ‡

The apostle also prays for the preservation of the Thessalonians. This preservation should include the complete person — **spirit, soul, and body**. Notice the order. Man always says body, soul, and spirit. God always says **spirit, soul, and body**. In the original creation, the spirit was of first importance, the body last. Sin reversed the order; man lives for the body and neglects the spirit. When we pray for one another, we should follow the biblical order, putting spiritual welfare before physical needs.

From this verse and others, it is clear that we are tripartite beings. Our **spirit** is that part which enables us to have communion with God. Our **soul** has to do with our emotions, desires, affections, and propensities (John 12:27). Our **body** is the house in which our person dwells (2 Cor. 5:1).

All of our parts need to **be preserved** entire, that is, complete and sound. One commentator has suggested the needs for preservation as follows:

1. The spirit from (a) everything that would defile it (2 Cor. 7:1); (b) everything that would hinder the testimony of the Holy Spirit to the saints' relationship with God (Rom. 8:16); or (c) everything that would prevent the worship which He seeks (John 4:23; Phil 3:3).

2. The soul from (a) evil thoughts (Matt. 15:18, 19; Eph. 2:3); (b) fleshly appetites that war against it (1 Pet. 2:11); and (c) contention and strife (Heb. 12:15).

3. The body from (a) defilement (1 Thess. 4:3-8); and (b) evil uses (Rom. 6:19).

Some deny that the unsaved have a spirit. Perhaps they base this on the fact that they are spiritually dead (Eph. 2:1). However, the fact that the unsaved are spiritually dead does not mean that they have *no* spirit. It means that they are dead as far as fellowship with God is concerned. Their spirits may be very much alive, for example, as far as contact with the world of the *occult* is concerned, but they are dead *Godward*.

Lenski warns:

Many are satisfied with a partial Christianity, some parts of their life are still worldly. The apostolic admonitions constantly prod into all the corners of our nature so that none may escape purification.[19]

The prayer goes on to desire that God's sanctification and preservation will so extend to every part of their personalities that the believers will be **blameless at the coming of our Lord Jesus Christ**. This seems to point to the Judgment Seat of Christ, which follows the Rapture. At that time, the Christian's life, service, and testimony will be reviewed, and he will be rewarded or suffer loss.

5:24 As we learned in 4:3, our sanctification is the will of God. He has called us to eventually stand blameless before Him. Having begun this work in us, He will finish it (Phil. 1:6). **He who calls** us **is faithful** to His promise.

5:25 As Paul closes, he asks for the prayers of the saints. He never outgrew the need for prayer and neither do we. It is a sin to fail to **pray for** fellow believers.

5:26 Next he asks that **all the brethren** be greeted **with a holy kiss**. At that time, this was the accepted mode of greeting. In some countries it is still customary for men to kiss men, and women to kiss women. In still other cultures men kiss the women and vice versa. But more often than not this has led to abuses and has had to be abandoned.

The kiss was not instituted by the Lord as a prescribed form of greeting or taught by the apostles as obligatory. The Bible wisely allows for other modes of greeting in cultures where kissing might lead to sexual laxness. The Spirit of God seeks to guard against such irregularities by insisting that the **kiss** must be **holy**.

5:27 The apostle solemnly charges **that this epistle be read to all the holy[20] brethren**. Two points should be noted here:

1. Paul invests the Letter with the authority of the word of God. The OT was read publicly in the synagogues. Now **this epistle** will **be read** aloud in the churches.

2. The Bible is for all Christians, not for some inside circle or privileged class. All its truths are for all the saints.

Denney wisely insists:

There is no attainment in wisdom or in goodness which is barred against any man by the gospel; and there is no surer mark of faithlessness and treachery in a church than this, that it keeps its members in a perpetual pupilage or minority, discouraging the free use of Holy Scripture, and taking care that all it contains is not read to all the brethren.[21]

Notice that in verses 25-27 we have three keys to a successful Christian life: (1) prayer (v. 25); (2) love for fellow believers, which speaks of fellowship (v. 26); and (3) reading and study of the word (v. 27).

5:28 Finally we have Paul's characteristic close. He opened his First Epistle to the Thessalonians with grace, and now he closes it with the same theme. To the apostle Christianity is **grace** from beginning to end. **Amen**.

ENDNOTES

[1](Intro) James Everett Frame, *A Critical and Exegetical Commentary on the Epistles of St. Paul to the Thessalonians*, (ICC), p. 37.

[2](Intro) George Robert Harding Wood, *St. Paul's First Letter*, pp. 13, 14.

[3](1:1) The critical text omits "from God our Father and the Lord Jesus Christ," but it is found in the vast majority of mss. It would be easy to omit it in copying since it is nearly identical to the phrase used immediately preceding.

[4](1:4) See Ephesians 1 for an "Excursus on Divine Election."

[5](1:10) Wood, *First Letter*, p. 17.

[6](2:1) James Denney, *The Second Epistle to the Corinthians*, p. 100.

[7](2:1) Elliot, Elisabeth, ed., *The Journals of Jim Elliot*, p. 218.

[8](2:13) Walter Scott, further documentation unavailable.

[9](3:2) *Minister* is simply a Latin word for *servant*.

[10](3:13) Marvin Vincent, *Word Studies in the New Testament*, IV:34.

[11](4:6) Oscar Wilde, who left his lovely wife to engage in homosexuality.

[12](4:8) The critical (NU) text reads "who also gives."

[13](4:17) The Latin past participle *raptus*, from the verb *rapere*. Jerome's exact wording in the Vulgate is "rapiemur cum illis" (we shall be raptured with them).

[14](5:10) The words in the original are as follows: *wake* in 5:10 and *watch* in 5:6 are *grēgoreō* (the origin of the masculine name "Gregory," or "watchful"). *Sleep* in 5:6, 7 stands for *katheudō*, which can refer to literal sleep or "spiritual laziness

and indifference" (Arndt and Gingrich). In 4:13–15, *sleep* translates *koimaō*.

[15](5:12) James Denney, *The Epistles to Thessalonians*, p. 205.

[16](5:13) For a detailed exposition of elders, see comments on 1 Timothy 3:1-7 and Titus 1:5-9.

[17](5:21) Denney, *Thessalonians*, p. 244.

[18](5:22) Arthur T. Pierson, further documentation unavailable.

[19](5:23) R. C. H. Lenski, *The Interpretation of St. Paul's Epistles to the Colossians, to the Thessalonians, to Timothy, to Titus, and Philemon*, p. 364.

[20](5:27) The critical text omits "holy."

[21](5:27) Denney, *Thessalonians*, pp. 263, 264.

BIBLIOGRAPHY
(1 and 2 Thessalonians)

Buckland, A. R. *St. Paul's First Epistle to the Thessalonians*. Philadelphia: The Union Press, 1908.

_____. *St. Paul's Second Epistle to the Thessalonians*. Philadelphia: The Union Press, 1909.

Denney, James. *The Epistles to the Thessalonians*. New York: George H. Doran Company, n.d.

Eadie, John. *A Commentary on the Greek Text of the Epistles of Paul to the Thessalonians*. London: MacMillan, 1877.

Frame, James E. *A Critical and Exegetical Commentary on the Epistles of Paul to the Thessalonians, ICC*. New York: Chas. Scribner's Sons, 1912.

Hogg, C. F. and W. E. Vine, *The Epistles of Paul the Apostle to the Thessalonians*. London: C. A. Hammond, 1953.

Kelly, William. *The Epistles of Paul the Apostle to the Thessalonians*. London: C. A. Hammond, 1953.

_____. *Elements of Prophecy*. London: G. Morrish, 1976.

Morris, Leon. *The Epistles of Paul to the Thessalonians, TBC*. Grand Rapids: Wm. B. Eerdmans Publishing Company, 1957.

_____. *The First and Second Epistles to the Thessalonians, NIC*. Grand Rapids: Wm. B. Eerdmans Publishing Company, 1959.

Wood, George Robert Harding. *St. Paul's First Letter*. London: Henry E. Walter Ltd., 1952.

THE SECOND EPISTLE TO THE THESSALONIANS

Introduction

"As in the first Epistle, the apostle does not immediately grapple with the error, but prepares the hearts of the saints gradually and on all sides so as to clench the truth and exclude the error once it is exposed. This is the way of divine grace and wisdom; the heart is set right, and not the mere point of error or evil dealt with."
— William Kelly

I. Unique Place in the Canon

The important truths found in this little Letter are both doctrinal and practical. Paul further explains and corrects the Thessalonians' understanding of the Second Coming and the revelation about the man of sin. He also gives sound advice as to those who would use the Second Coming as an excuse not to work — don't let them eat, either!

II. Authorship[†]

If anything, the *external evidence* for 2 Thessalonians is even stronger than for 1 Thessalonians. Not only is it attested early by Polycarp, Ignatius, and Justin (as well as being found in the Marcionite Prologue and the Muratorian Canon), but Irenaeus quotes 2 Thessalonians by name.

Since it is so short, the Epistle does not have as much *internal evidence* as 1 Thessalonians, but it does complement and agree so well with that Epistle that few scholars hesitate to accept its Pauline authorship.

III. Date

Second Thessalonians was written in response to further problems and also the misunderstanding of parts of 1 Thessalonians. A few months or even weeks are all that are needed to pass between the writing of the two Letters. Paul, Sil-

vanus, and Timothy were still together (1:1), and Corinth is the only city where we read of their being together (Acts 18:1, 5). Hence the date is the early 50's, probably A.D. 50 or 51.

IV. Background and Themes[†]

There were three principal reasons for another Letter, even so soon after the first. The saints were being persecuted and needed to be encouraged (chap. 1). They were being misled as to the Day of the Lord and needed to be enlightened (chap. 2). Some were living in idleness in view of the Lord's Return and needed to be corrected (chap. 3).

With regard to the Day of the Lord, the believers were fearful that they were already in it. Their fears were strengthened by false rumors to the effect that Paul himself was teaching that the Day was now present. So the apostle sets the record straight.

It should be apparent that the Day of the Lord is not the same as the coming of the Lord, that is, the Rapture. The saints were not fearful that the Lord had come; they were fearful that they were in the Tribulation, the first phase of the Day of the Lord.

Paul had never taught that any events *had to occur before the Rapture.* But now he teaches that *before the Day of the Lord* begins, there will be a great apostasy, the restrainer will be removed, and the man of sin will be revealed.

†See p. i.
†See p. ii.

For the proper understanding of this Letter, nothing is more important than to see the distinction between the Rapture, the Day of the Lord, and Christ's Coming to reign. The Day of the Lord is defined in the notes on 1 Thessalonians 5:2. The distinction between the Rapture and the Revelation is made in an Excursus at 2 Thessalonians 1:7.

OUTLINE

I. SALUTATION (1:1, 2)

II. PAUL AND THE THESSALONIANS (1:3–12)
    A. Paul's Debt of Thanks (1:3–5)
    B. The Righteous Judgment of God (1:6–10)
    C. Paul's Prayer for the Saints (1:11, 12)

III. CONCERNING THE DAY OF THE LORD (2:1–12)
    A. An Appeal for Stability (2:1, 2)
    B. The Man of Sin (2:3–12)

IV. THANKSGIVING AND PRAYER (2:13–17)
    A. Paul's Thanks that the Saints Would Escape Judgment (2:13, 14)
    B. Paul's Prayer that the Saints Would Be Comforted and Established (2:15–17)

V. PRACTICAL EXHORTATIONS (3:1–15)
    A. For Mutual Prayer (3:1–5)
    B. For Dealing with the Insubordinate (3:6–15)

VI. BLESSING AND GREETING (3:16–18)

Commentary

I. SALUTATION (1:1, 2)

1:1 **Silvanus and Timothy** were with **Paul** when he wrote this Letter from Corinth. The Letter is addressed **to the church of the Thessalonians**; this reveals its human composition and geographical location. **In God our Father** distinguishes the assembly from a heathen gathering. **And in the Lord Jesus Christ** marks it out as a Christian congregation.[1]

1:2 The apostle does not wish fame, fortune, or pleasure for the saints, but **grace and peace**. **Grace** provides enablement for everything within the will of God, and **peace** gives serenity in every kind of circumstance. What more could a person desire for himself or for others?

Grace and peace are **from God our Father and the Lord Jesus Christ**. **Grace** precedes **peace**; we must know God's **grace** before we can experience His **peace**. Paul's mention **of God our Father and the Lord Jesus Christ** as co-sources of these blessings implies the equality of the Father and the Son.

II. PAUL AND THE THESSALONIANS (1:3–12)

A. Paul's Debt of Thanks (1:3–5)

1:3 The Letter begins with thanksgiving for the saints. To read this is to listen to the heartbeat of a true servant of Christ as he rejoices over his beloved spiritual children. To him thanksgiving was a continual duty to **God**, and it was an appropriate duty as well in view of the **faith** and **love** of the Christians. Their **faith** was making astonishing strides, and each one without exception was showing more and more **love** to the others. This was an answer to the apostle's prayer (1 Thess. 3:10, 12).

Notice the order: first **faith**, then

love. "Faith puts us in contact with the eternal spring of love in God Himself," writes C. H. Mackintosh, "and the necessary consequence is that our hearts are drawn out in love to all who belong to Him."

1:4 Their spiritual progress caused Paul and his associates to **boast** about them to other **churches of God**. They had remained steadfast and full of faith in spite of the **persecutions** they were enduring. **Patience** here means steadfastness or perseverance.

1:5 The fact that they were standing up so bravely under the persecutions and afflictions was an indication of the **righteous** dealings **of God**. He was supporting them, strengthening them, encouraging them. If they had not received His divine power, they would never have been able to demonstrate such patience and faith in suffering for Christ.

Their heroic endurance proved them **worthy of the kingdom of God**. It did not suggest that any personal merit entitled them to enter the kingdom; it is only through the merits of Christ that anyone will be there. But those who suffer on behalf of the kingdom here show that they are among those who will reign with Him in that coming day (Rom. 8:17; 2 Tim. 2:12).

E. W. Rogers, in commenting on the phrase **you may be counted worthy of the kingdom of God**, states:

This has to do with human responsibility. On the side of divine sovereignty we have been made meet to be partakers of the inheritance of the saints in light, and this meetness is solely due to our association with Christ in His death and resurrection. We are graced in the Beloved, altogether independent of anything in ourselves, either before or since we were saved. But God allows His people to go through persecutions and tribulations in order to develop in them the moral excellencies which make them "worthy citizens" of that kingdom.

Some of the apostles rejoiced that they were counted worthy to suffer for Jesus' name. Paul's prayer for the Thessalonians that God would count them worthy of their calling most certainly had nothing to do with adding anything to the work of Christ. The Cross makes the believer worthy of his position in the kingdom, but patience and faith in tribulation manifest such an one as morally worthy of it. Among members of any earthly society there are those who are discreditable as well as others. Paul prayed that it should not be so among these saints.[2]

B. The Righteous Judgment of God (1:6–10)

1:6 The **righteous** action of **God** is seen in two ways — punishment for the persecutors and then rest for the persecuted.

Williams says:

God's action in allowing His people to be persecuted, and in permitting the existence of their persecutors, had a double purpose — first, to test the fitness of His people for government (v. 5); and second, to manifest the fitness of their persecutors for judgment.[3]

1:7 Just as God will mete out punishment to the enemies of His people, so He will award **rest** to those who suffer for His sake.

We should not conclude from verse 7 that suffering saints will not obtain relief from trial until Christ comes back from heaven in flaming fire. When a believer dies, he obtains rest. Living believers will enjoy relaxation from all tensions at the time of the Rapture. What this verse is saying is that when the Lord pours out judgment on His adversaries, the saints will be seen by the world to be enjoying **rest**.

The time of God's righteous retribution is **when the Lord Jesus is revealed from heaven with His mighty angels**. Retribution for the ungodly and **rest** for believers are included in His coming. Which phase of Christ's coming is referred to here? It is clearly the third phase — the *manifestation* of His coming, when He returns with His saints to the earth.

THE RAPTURE AND REVELATION

But someone may ask, "How do you know that the Rapture and the Revelation are separate events?" The answer is that they are differentiated in the Scriptures in the following ways:

The Rapture

1. Christ comes to the air (1 Thess. 4:17).

2. He comes *for* His saints (1 Thess. 4:16, 17).

3. The Rapture is a mystery, i.e., a truth unknown in OT times (1 Cor. 15:51).

4. Christ's coming *for* His saints is never said to be preceded by celestial portents.

5. The Rapture is identified with the Day of Christ (1 Cor. 1:8; 2 Cor. 1:14; Phil. 1:6, 10).

6. The Rapture is presented as a time of blessing (1 Thess. 4:18).

7. The Rapture takes place in a moment, in the twinkling of an eye (1 Cor. 15:52). This strongly implies that it will not be witnessed by the world.

8. The Rapture seems to involve the church primarily (John 14:1–4; 1 Cor. 15:51–58; 1 Thess. 4:13–18).

9. Christ comes as the Bright and Morning Star (Rev. 22:16).

10. The Rapture is not mentioned in the Synoptic Gospels, but is alluded to several times in John's Gospel.

11. Those taken are taken for blessing (1 Thess. 4:13–18). Those left are left for judgment (1 Thess. 5:1–3).

12. No dating system is given for events preceding the Rapture.

13. The title "Son of Man" is never used in any of the passages dealing with the Rapture.

The Revelation

1. He comes to the *earth* (Zech. 14:4).

2. He comes *with* His saints (1 Thess. 3:13; Jude 14).

3. The Revelation is not a mystery; it is the subject of many OT prophecies (Ps. 72; Isa. 11; Zech. 14).

4. His coming *with* His saints will be heralded by signs in the heavens (Matt. 24:29, 30).

5. The Revelation is identified with the Day of the Lord (2 Thess. 2:1–12, NU Text).

6. The main emphasis of the Revelation is on judgment (2 Thess. 2:8–12).

7. The Revelation will be visible worldwide (Matt. 24:27; Rev. 1:7).

8. The Revelation involves Israel primarily, then also the Gentile nations (Matt. 24:1– 25:46).

9. He comes as the Sun of Righteousness with healing in His wings (Mal. 4:2).

10. The Revelation is characteristic in the Synoptics but hardly mentioned in John's Gospel.

11. Those taken are taken for judgment. Those left are left for blessing (Matt. 24:37–41).

12. An elaborate dating system is given for the Revelation, such as 1260 days, 42 months, 3½ years (see Dan. 7:25; 12:7, 11, 12; Rev. 11:2; 12:14; 13:5).

13. The revelation is spoken of as the coming of the Son of Man (Matt. 16:28; 24:27, 30, 39; 26:64; Mark 13:26; Luke 21:27).

Granted then that these are two separate events, yet how do we know that they do not occur at approximately the same time? How do we know that they are separated by an interval? Three lines of proof can be mentioned:

1. The first is based on Daniel's prophecy of seventy weeks (Dan. 9:25–27). We are now living in the par-

enthetical Church Age, between the sixty-ninth and seventieth weeks. The seventieth week is the Tribulation Period of seven years. The church is taken home to heaven before the Tribulation Period (Rom. 5:9; 1 Thess. 1:10; 1 Thess. 5:9; Rev. 3:10). The coming of Christ to reign takes place after the seventieth week (Dan. 9:24; Matt. 24).

2. The second line of proof for an interval of time between the Rapture and the Manifestation is based on the structure of the book of Revelation. In the first three chapters, the church is seen on earth. Chapters 4 through 19:10 describe the Tribulation Period when God's wrath will be poured out on the world that has rejected His Son. The church is never mentioned as being on earth during this period. The church is apparently taken to heaven at the close of chapter 3. In Revelation 19:11, Christ returns to earth to subdue His foes and to set up His kingdom — at the close of the Tribulation Period.

3. There is a third consideration which necessitates a time interval between Christ's coming *for* the saints and His coming *with* the saints. At the time of the Rapture, *all* believers are taken out of the world and are given their glorified bodies. Yet when Christ returns to reign, there will be believers on earth who will not as yet have glorified bodies and who will marry and raise children during the Millennium (Isa. 11:6, 8). Where do these believers come from? There must be a period of time between the Rapture and the Revelation during which they are converted. ‡

Now to return to verse 7, we have the arrival of **the Lord Jesus** in power and great glory. He is attended by **angels** through whom His power is exerted.

1:8 The **flaming fire** may be a reference to the Shekinah, the glory cloud which symbolizes God's presence (Ex. 16:10). Or it may be a picture of the fiery judgment which is about to be unleashed (Ps. 50:3; Isa. 66:15). Probably it is the latter.

When God takes **vengeance**, it is not vindictiveness, but righteous recompense. There is no thought of "getting even" but rather of meting out the punishment which His holy, righteous character demands. He has no pleasure in the death of the wicked (Ezek. 18:32).

Paul describes two classes marked out for retribution:

1. **Those who do not know God** — those who have rejected the knowledge of the true God as revealed in creation and in conscience (Rom. 1, 2).

They may never have heard the gospel.

2. **Those who do not obey the gospel of our Lord Jesus Christ** — those who have heard the gospel and have rejected it. The gospel is not simply a statement of facts to be believed, but a Person to be obeyed. Belief in the NT sense involves obedience.

1:9 **These shall be punished**. A god who doesn't punish sin is no god at all. The idea that a God of love must not punish sin overlooks the fact that God is also holy and must do what is morally right.

The nature of the punishment is here defined as **everlasting destruction**. The word translated "everlasting" or "eternal" (*aiōnios*) is used seventy times in the NT. Three times it may mean "ages of limited duration" (Rom. 16:25; 2 Tim. 1:9; Tit. 1:2). The other times it means eternal or endless. It is used in Romans 16:26 to describe the unending existence of God.

Destruction never means annihilation. It means loss of well-being, or ruin as far as the purpose of existence is concerned. The wineskins which the Lord Jesus described in Luke 5:37 were "destroyed" (same root word as used here). They did not cease to exist, but they were ruined as far as further usefulness was concerned.

This passage is often used by post-tribulationists to confirm their position. They understand it to say that believers will not obtain rest and their persecutors will not be punished until Christ comes back to reign, and this is admittedly at the end of the Tribulation. Therefore, they conclude that the hope of believers is the post-tribulation Rapture.

What they fail to see is that the Thessalonians to whom this was written have all died and are already enjoying rest with the Lord in heaven. Likewise, their persecutors have all died and are already suffering in Hades.

Why then does Paul seem to say that these conditions will not take place until Christ returns to earth in power and great glory? The reason is that this will be the time that these conditions will be *openly manifested to the world*. Then the world will see that the Thessalonians were right and their persecutors were wrong. The saints will be seen enjoying rest when they return with Christ in glory. The **destruction** of the Lord's enemies at the end of the Tribulation will be a public demonstration of the doom of all who have afflicted God's people in all ages.

It will help us to remember that Christ's coming to reign is a time of *manifestation*. What has been true all along will be unveiled for all the world to see. This is not true of the Rapture.

The punishment of the wicked also includes banishment **from the presence of the Lord and from the glory of His power**. To perish without Him is to be without Him forever.

1:10 His coming will be a time of glory for the Lord and of amazement for the spectators.

He will **be glorified in His saints**, that is, He will be honored because of what He has done in and through them. Their salvation, sanctification, and glorification will be tributes to His matchless grace and power.

He will **be admired among all those who believe**.[4] Amazed onlookers will gasp as they see what He has been able to do with such unpromising human beings!

And this will include the Thessalonian believers too, because they had received and believed the **testimony** of the apostles. They would share in the glory and triumph of **that Day**, namely, the Day of the Revelation of Jesus Christ.

By way of review, we might paraphrase verses 5–10 as follows: "Your patience in the midst of tribulation is very significant. In all this God is working out His righteous purposes. Your steadfast endurance of persecution shows that you are among the company of those who will share the glories of Christ's coming reign. On the one hand, God will measure out judgment to those who now trouble you. On the other hand, He will give rest to you who are now troubled, along with us also — Paul, Silvanus, and Timothy. He will judge your enemies when He comes from heaven with the angelic executors of His power in flaming fire, punishing those who are wilfully ignorant of God and those who are wilfully disobedient to the gospel. These will suffer everlasting destruction, even

banishment from the Lord's face and from the display of His power, when He returns to be glorified in all believers — including you, because you did believe the gospel message we preached to you."

C. Paul's Prayer for the Saints (1:11, 12)

1:11 In the preceding verses the apostle has been describing the glorious calling of the saints. They have been called to suffer persecution, which in turn fits them for rule in the kingdom. Now he prays that their lives in the meantime will be counted **worthy of** such a high **calling**, and that God's mighty **power** will enable them to obey every impulse to do good, and to accomplish every task undertaken in **faith**.

1:12 The result would be twofold. First, **the name of our Lord Jesus Christ** would **be glorified in** them. This means that they would give an accurate representation of Him to the world, and thus bring glory to Him. Then they, too, would be glorified **in Him**. Their association with Him, their Head, would bring honor to them as members of His Body.

Chapter 1 closes with the reminder that this prayer can be answered only **according to the grace of our God and the Lord Jesus Christ**. Thus he concludes a marvelous explanation of the meaning and outcome of suffering in the believer's life. Imagine how encouraged the Thessalonians were when they read this reassuring message!

III. CONCERNING THE DAY OF THE LORD (2:1–12)

A. An Appeal for Stability (2:1, 2)

2:1 Paul now undertakes to correct a misunderstanding that had arisen in the minds of the saints **concerning the coming of our Lord Jesus Christ** and the Day of the Lord. The saints were suffering such severe persecution that it was easy for them to think that they were already in the first part of the Day of the Lord, i.e., the Tribulation Period. And rumors were floating around that the *apostle himself* believed and taught that the Day of the Lord had arrived! So he must set the record straight.

A crucial question arises in verse 1 concerning the small word which Paul uses: **concerning** (Gk. *huper*). The problem is whether he is beseeching the saints "about" **the coming of our** Lord or "by" **the coming of our Lord**. If the first is the meaning, then the passage seems to teach that the Rapture and the Day of the Lord are one and the same event, since the following verses clearly deal with the Day of the Lord. If the second is the meaning, then Paul is appealing to them *on the basis of* the prior Rapture, that they should not think they were in the Day of the Lord. The question is debatable. We agree with William Kelly when he adopts the second view:

> The comfort of the Lord's coming is employed as a motive and means for counteracting the uneasiness created by the false presentation that the day (of the Lord) was there.[5]

We understand Paul to be saying, "I appeal to you on the basis of the Rapture that you should not fear that you are in the Day of the Lord. The Rapture must take place first. You will be taken home to heaven at that time and will thus escape the horrors of the Day of the Lord."

The expression **the coming of our Lord Jesus Christ and our gathering together to Him** seems to refer unmistakably to the Rapture. That is the time when we will be gathered to meet Him in the air.

2:2 It should be clear that the Rapture is not the same as the Day of the Lord. The Thessalonians were not worried that the Lord had come; they knew that He had not. But they *were* worried that the Day of the Lord had begun. The intense persecution they were enduring made them think they were in the Tribulation, the first phase of the Day of the Lord.

Rumors had been circulating that Paul himself had said that the Day of the Lord had arrived. Like most rumors, they were very garbled. One version intimated that Paul had received the information **by spirit**, that is, by a special revelation. According to another report, the news had come **by word**, that is, the apostle had publicly taught that the Tribulation had begun. **By letter as if from**

us is generally understood to refer to a forged letter, purportedly from Paul, that the Day of the Lord had started. The expression **as if from us** probably goes with **spirit**, **word**, and **letter**. None of these sources was to be trusted.

According to the KJV and NKJV (following the majority of manuscripts), the saints were afraid that **the day of Christ had come. The day of Christ** and similar expressions usually point forward to the Rapture and the Judgment Seat of Christ (1 Cor. 1:8; 5:5; 2 Cor. 1:14; Phil 1:6, 10; 2:15, 16).

But the Thessalonians were not in fear that the Day of Christ was at hand. That would have meant release from their sufferings. Most pre-tribulationists prefer the reading in the RV: "the day of the Lord is now present."[6] Paul's readers were afraid that the Day of God's *wrath* had begun.

B. The Man of Sin (2:3-12)

2:3 Now the apostle explains why they could not be in **that Day**. Certain events must take place first. After the Rapture, these events will begin to happen.

First of all there will be **the falling away**, or the apostasy.[7] What does this mean? We can only surmise that it refers to a wholesale abandonment of Christianity, a positive rejection of the Christian faith.

Then a great world figure will arise. As to his character, he is **the man of sin** or lawlessness,[8] that is, the very embodiment of sin and rebellion. As to his destiny, he is **the son of perdition**; he is doomed to eternal judgment.

The Scriptures contain many descriptions of important personages who will arise during the Tribulation, and it is difficult to know when different names apply to the same person. Some commentators believe that the man of sin will be a Jewish Antichrist. Others teach that he will be the Gentile head of the revived Roman Empire. Here are the names of some of the great rulers of the end times:

... the man of sin and son of perdition (2 Thess. 2:3)

... the Antichrist (1 Jn. 2:18)

... the little horn (Dan. 7:8, 24b–26)

... the king of fierce features (Dan. 8:23–25)

... the prince who is to come (Dan. 9:26)

... the willful king (Dan. 11:36)

... the worthless shepherd (Zech. 11:17)

... the beast out of the sea (Rev. 13:1–10)

... the beast out of the earth (Rev. 13:11–17)

... the scarlet beast with seven heads and ten horns (Rev. 17:4, 8–14)

... the king of the North (Dan. 11:6)

... the king of the South (Dan. 11:40)

... the false prophet (Rev. 19:20; 20:10)

... Gog, of the land of Magog (Ezek. 38:2–39:11) [not to be confused with the Gog of Rev. 20:8 who arises *after* the Millennium]

... the one who comes in his own name (John 5:43)

The man of sin has been given an intriguing variety of identifications down through the years. He has been equated with the Roman Catholic Church, the Pope, the Roman Empire, the final form of apostate Christendom, Judas reincarnated, Nero reincarnated, the Jewish State, Mohammed, Luther, Napoleon, Mussolini, and the embodiment of Satan.

2:4 He will violently oppose every form of divine worship and will enthrone himself **in the temple of God** in Jerusalem. This description clearly identifies him as Antichrist, the one who is *opposed to* Christ and who sets himself up *in the place of* Christ.[9]

Daniel 9:27 and Matthew 24:15 show that this blasphemous action of the Antichrist takes place in the middle of the Tribulation Period. Those who refuse to worship him will be persecuted and many will be martyred.

2:5 Paul used to tell the Thessalonians **these things** when he **was still with** them. However, with contradictory teaching being given to them which seemed to accurately describe the fierce persecutions they were then enduring, they had forgotten what the apostle had said. We all forget too easily and need to be constantly reminded of the great truths of the faith.

2:6 They knew **what** was **restraining** the full and open manifestation of

the man of sin, and what would continue to restrain him until the appointed time.

This brings us to the third great unanswered question in this chapter. The first is, "What is the apostasy?" The second is, "Who is the man of sin?" The third is, "What or who is the restrainer?"

In the first part of verse 6, the restrainer is described in an impersonal way ... **what is restraining**. But then in verse 7 it is a person — He who now restrains.[10] E. W. Rogers puts it clearly:

It is Something and Someone who wittingly, purposefully, and designedly holds it in check *with the view* to ensuring that the Man of Lawlessness is revealed in his own proper time.[11]

Seven of the more common views as to the identity of the restrainer are: (1) the Roman Empire, (2) the Jewish State, (3) Satan, (4) the principle of law and order as found in human government, (5) God, (6) the Holy Spirit, and (7) the true church as indwelt by the Spirit.

The Holy Spirit indwelling the church and the individual believer seems to fit the description of the restrainer more completely and accurately than any of the others. Just as the restrainer is spoken of as Something and Someone in this chapter, so the Spirit is spoken of in John 14:26, 15:26, 16:8, 13, 14 as both neuter (the Holy Spirit) and masculine (He).[12] As early as Genesis 6:3, the Holy Spirit is spoken of in connection with the restraint of evil. Then later He is seen in this same role in Isaiah 59:19b, John 16:7–11, and 1 John 4:4.

It is by the indwelling Spirit that believers are the salt of the earth (Matt. 5:13) and the light of the world (Matt. 5:14). Salt is a preservative, but it also hinders the spread of corruption. Light dispels darkness, the sphere in which men love to perform their evil deeds (John 3:19). When the Holy Spirit leaves the world as the permanent Indweller of the church (1 Cor. 3:16) and of individual believers (1 Cor. 6:19), the restraint of lawlessness will be gone.

2:7 Even when Paul wrote, **the mystery of lawlessness** was **already at work**. By this we understand that a tremendous spirit of disobedience to God was already stirring beneath the surface.

It was at work in **mystery** form — not that it was mysterious but rather that it was not yet fully manifested. It was still in germ form.

What has hindered the full display of this spirit? We believe that the presence of the Holy Spirit indwelling the church and indwelling every believer has been the restraining power. He will continue to exercise this function **until He is taken out of the way**, that is, at the Rapture.

But here an objection is raised. How can the Holy Spirit be removed from the world? As one of the Persons of the Godhead, isn't He omnipresent, that is, everywhere at all times? How then can He leave the world?

Of course, the Holy Spirit is omnipresent. He is always in all places at one and the same time. And yet there was a distinct sense in which He *came* to the earth on the Day of Pentecost. Jesus had repeatedly promised that He and the Father would send the Spirit (John 14:16, 26; 15:26; 16:7). How then did the Spirit come? He came as the permanent Indweller of the church and of every believer. Until Pentecost the Spirit had been *with* believers, but since Pentecost He has dwelt *in* them (John 14:17). Until Pentecost the Spirit was known to depart from believers — hence David's prayer, "Do not take your Holy Spirit from me" (Ps. 51:11b). After Pentecost the Spirit remains forever in believers of the Church Age (John 14:16).

The Holy Spirit will, we believe, *leave* the world in the same sense in which He *came* at Pentecost — that is, as the abiding Indweller of the church and of each believer. He will still be in the world, convicting people of sin and leading them to saving faith in Christ. His removal at the Rapture does not mean that no one will be saved during the Tribulation. Of course they will. But these people will not be members of the church, but rather the subjects of Christ's glorious kingdom.

2:8 After the church has been Raptured to heaven, **the lawless one will be revealed** to the world. In this verse, the apostle skips over the career of the Antichrist and describes his ultimate doom. It almost sounds as if he will be destroyed as soon as he is revealed. But

that of course is not so. He is allowed to conduct the reign of terror described in verses 9–12 before he is brought down at Christ's coming to reign.

If we are right in believing that the man of sin is revealed after the Rapture and that he continues until Christ's Revelation, then his mad career lasts approximately seven years — the length of the Tribulation Period.

The **Lord** Jesus **will consume** him **with the breath of His mouth** (cf. Isa. 11:4; Rev. 19:15), and will bring him to nothing by the manifestation **of His coming**. A word from Christ and the bright shining (Gk., *epiphaneia*) of His appearing (*parousia*) are all that are necessary to end the regime of this raging impostor.

The manifestation of Christ's coming, as has already been explained, is when He returns to the earth to take the throne and reign for one thousand years.

2:9 **The coming of the lawless one is** in accordance with **the working of Satan**. His career resembles that **of Satan** because he is energized by Satan. He will display all kinds of miracles and **signs and lying wonders**.

Here it is important to note that not all miracles are of God. The devil and his agents can perform miracles. The man of lawlessness will also perform them (Rev. 13:13–15).

A miracle indicates *supernatural* power but not necessarily *divine* power. The miracles of our Lord proved Him to be the promised Messiah, not simply because they were supernatural, but because they fulfilled prophecy and were of such a moral nature that Satan could not have done them without harming his own cause.

2:10 The Antichrist will unscrupulously use every form of wickedness to deceive the perishing people — those who heard the gospel during the Age of Grace but who had no **love** for **the truth**. If they had believed, they would have been **saved**. But now they are deceived by the miracles of the Antichrist.

2:11 God actually will **send them** a working of error that **they should believe the lie**. **The lie**, of course, is the Antichrist's claim to be God. These people refused to receive the Lord Jesus as God manifest in the flesh. When He was on earth, He warned men, "I have come in My Father's name, and you do not receive Me: if another comes in his own name, him you will receive" (John 5:43). So now they receive the man of sin who comes in his own name and demands worship as God. "Light rejected is light denied." If a person sets up an idol in his heart, God will answer him according to his idol (Ezek. 14:4).

The Antichrist will probably be Jewish (Ezek. 28:9, 10; Dan. 11:37, 38). Jews would not be deceived by one posing as the Messiah unless he claimed to be descended from the tribe of Judah and the family of David.

2:12 From this passage it seems that those who hear the gospel in this Age of Grace but who do not trust Christ will not have another opportunity to be saved after the Rapture. If men do not believe the Lord Jesus now, they will believe the Antichrist then. It says here that they **all** will be judged because of their unbelief and their love of evil. This is reminiscent of Luke 14:24, "For I say to you that none of those men who were invited shall taste my supper."

We know that many people will be saved during the Tribulation Period. One hundred and forty-four thousand Jews, for instance, will be saved and will be God's messengers in preaching the gospel of the kingdom throughout the world. Through their ministry many others will be saved. But it seems that those who will be saved are those who never heard the gospel clearly presented during this present age and who never deliberately refused the Savior.

IV. THANKSGIVING AND PRAYER (2:13–17)

A. Paul's Thanks that the Saints Would Escape Judgment (2:13, 14)

2:13 In the first twelve verses, Paul described the doom of the Antichrist and his followers. Now he turns to the Thessalonian Christians and thinks of their calling and destiny by way of contrast. As he does so, he expresses thanks to God for these **brethren beloved by the Lord**, and proceeds to give a summary of their salvation — past, present, and future.

God . . . chose you. The Bible clearly teaches that **God** chooses men to salvation, but it never teaches that He chooses some to be damned. Men are lost through their own deliberate choice. Apart from God's intervention, all would be lost. Does God have the right to choose some to be saved? Basically His desire is for all to be saved (1 Tim. 2:4; 2 Pet. 3:9). However, the Bible does not teach "Universalism," the theory that all will eventually be saved.

From the beginning. This has two possible readings. First, it may mean that God's choice was made before the foundation of the world (Eph. 1:4). Second, the expression may also be read "as first fruits," indicating that the Thessalonians, saved so early in the Christian dispensation, were chosen by God to be among the first of a great harvest of redeemed souls.

For salvation. This should be contrasted with the preceding verses. Unbelievers are doomed by their unbelief to eternal destruction, whereas believers are chosen **for salvation**.

Through sanctification by the Spirit. Here we have the Holy Spirit's preconversion work. He sets individuals apart to God from the world, convicts them of sin, and points them to Christ. Someone has well said, "If it had not been for Christ, there would have been no *feast*; if it had not been for the Holy Spirit, there would have been no *guests*!"

And belief in the truth. First you have God's part in salvation; now you have man's. Both are necessary. Some people can see only God's election, and they imply that man can do nothing about it. Others overemphasize man's part, and neglect God's sovereign choice. The truth lies in both extremes. Election and human responsibility are *both* Bible doctrines, and it is best to believe and teach both, even if we can't understand how both can be true.

2:14 To which He called you by our gospel. God *chose* us to salvation in eternity. **He called** us to it in time. The call refers to the moment when a person believes the truth. **Our gospel** does not mean that there are other genuine gospels. There is only one gospel, but there are many different preachers of it, and many different audiences. Paul is referring to the **gospel** of God which was preached by him.

For the obtaining of the glory of our Lord Jesus Christ. Here the apostle peers into the future and sees the ultimate outcome of salvation — to be with Christ and be like Him forever. J. N. Darby captures the thought in his beautiful hymn:

And is it so — I shall be like Thy Son?
Is this the grace which He for me has won?
Father of glory, thought beyond all thought!
In glory, to His own blest likeness brought!

Thus in verses 13 and 14 we have "a system of theology in miniature," a marvelous summary of the scope of God's purposes with His believing people. He has shown us that salvation "originates in a divine choice, is wrought out by divine power, is made effective through a divine message, and will be perfected in divine glory."

B. Paul's Prayer that the Saints Would Be Comforted and Established (2:15–17)

2:15 In view of their superlative calling, the saints are exhorted to **stand fast and hold the traditions which** they **were taught**, either by the apostles' words or by their Letters. The important thing to notice here is that the only **traditions** which are reliable and authoritative are the inspired utterances of the apostles. Jesus condemned the scribes and Pharisees for nullifying the commandments of God by *their* traditions (Matt. 15:6). And Paul warned the Colossians against *the traditions of men* (Col. 2:8). **The traditions** we should hold are the great truths which have been handed over to us in the sacred Scriptures.

This verse is sometimes used to justify the traditions of churches or of religious leaders. But any traditions which are contrary to the word of God are worthless and dangerous. If mere human traditions are accepted as equal with the Bible, who is to decide which traditions are right and which are wrong?

2:16 Having told out his message to the saints, the apostle now prays it in. He commonly follows his teaching with prayer (1 Thess. 5:23, 24; 2 Thess. 3:16). The prayer is addressed to **our Lord Jesus Christ Himself, and our God and Father**. We are accustomed to Paul's mentioning both divine Persons in the same breath, but it is unusual for him to mention the Son first. He is, of course, emphasizing their essential unity and complete equality. In the Greek, the plural subject (**Christ** and **God**) is followed by four singular verb forms (loved, gave, comfort, establish). What is this but a further indication of the unity of nature of the Son and Father in the Godhead?

God's past provision is introduced as an encouragement to trust Him for future courage and strength. He **loved us and** gave us **everlasting consolation and good hope by grace**. Doubtless this looks back to the greatest exhibition of God's love — the gift of His Son for us. Because we know that He settled the sin question at Calvary, we have eternal comfort now and the **hope** of a glorious future — and it is all through His marvelous **grace**.

2:17 The prayer itself is that God will **comfort** their **hearts and establish** them **in every good word and work**. Not just encouragement in the midst of distress, but strength to move forward in the battle. The word "retreat" wasn't in the apostle's vocabulary, and it shouldn't be in ours either.

Don't miss the expression **every good word and work**. Truth on our lips is not enough; it must be worked out in our life. So in our lives there should be the order of teaching and doing, doctrine and duty, preaching and practice.

V. PRACTICAL EXHORTATIONS (3:1–15)

A. For Mutual Prayer (3:1–5)

3:1 Paul felt the need for the prayers of the saints. This chapter opens with his request for prayer in three areas: (1) for the dissemination of the message; (2) for the triumph of the message; (3) for the preservation of the messengers.

He desires **that the word of the Lord**

may run swiftly — a graphic picture of the gospel sprinting from place to place in spite of obstacles (see Ps. 147:15).

He also desires that the word will produce the same marvelous spiritual and moral revolutions elsewhere that it did in Thessalonica.

3:2 The third request is that the apostle and his co-workers might **be delivered from unreasonable and wicked men**. He seems to be referring to some specific opposition, probably from Jews in Corinth (Acts 18:1–18). The choice of the word **unreasonable** was appropriate; there is nothing more irrational than people's opposition to the gospel and its messengers. It is something that baffles explanation. They may talk reasonably about politics, science, or a host of other subjects, but when it comes to the gospel, they lose all sense of reason.

3:3 Don't miss the beauty of the contrast between verse 2: "not all have faith" and verse 3: **But the Lord is faithful**. This teaches us to look away from faithless men to our never-failing God. He is **faithful** to confirm us to the end (1 Cor. 1:9). He is **faithful** to deliver us out of temptation (1 Cor. 10:13). He is **faithful** and just to forgive us our sins, and to cleanse us from all unrighteousness (1 John 1:9). And here He is **faithful** to **establish** and to **guard** us **from the evil one**, i.e., Satan.

3:4 Not all have faith . . . the Lord is faithful . . . **we have confidence** [faith] **in the Lord concerning you**. As Denney has remarked, "In the Lord you may depend on those who in themselves are weak, unstable, willful, foolish." Now Paul reminds the saints of their responsibility to **do the things** he commands them. Here again we have the wonderful and curious mingling of the divine and the human: God will keep you; now you keep the commandments. It is the same thought in 1 Peter 1:5: "Kept by the power of God" [His part], "through faith" [our part]. We also see it in Philippians 2:12, 13: "Work out your own salvation [our part], . . . for it is God who works in you [His part]."

3:5 In times of persecution it is easy to develop bitter thoughts toward others and to give up because of the duration and intensity of the suffering. It is for this reason that the apostle prays that the Thessalonians will love as **God** loves,

and will be steadfast as **Christ** is steadfast.

The KJV's "the patient waiting for Christ" is translated **the patience of Christ** in the NKJV. In the 1611 version it would mean steadfastness while *waiting* for Christ's Return. In the NKJV, it means showing the same **patience** or endurance which Christ showed as a Man on earth and which He still shows as Man in heaven.[13]

The Lord in this verse may refer to the Holy Spirit, and thus all three members of the Trinity would be mentioned, as they are in 2:13, 14.

B. For Dealing with the Insubordinate (3:6–15)

3:6 It seems clear that some of the saints at Thessalonica had stopped working for a living because they were so intently waiting for the Lord's return. Paul does not encourage this as a spiritual attitude, but proceeds to give definite instructions as to how to deal with such brethren.

His instructions are in the form of a command to **withdraw from every brother who walks disorderly**, that is one who does not keep in step with the others, but who refuses to work, and who sponges off others (see vv. 10, 11). Believers should show their disapproval of such a **brother** by refusing to mingle with him socially. The offense is not serious enough to warrant excommunication from the church, however.

The tradition which the Thessalonians **received from** Paul was one of tireless industry, hard work, and self-support.

3:7 He did not abandon his tentmaking just because he knew the Lord Jesus was coming again. He was indeed expecting Christ to come at any moment, but he was serving and working with the realization that the Lord might not come during his lifetime.

3:8 No one could accuse him of planting himself in someone's home and eating the food which someone else's toil had earned. He earned his own living while he was preaching the gospel. This meant long days and weary nights, but Paul was determined that he would **not be a burden to any of** them.

3:9 As a preacher of the gospel, the apostle had a right to be supported by those who were converted through his ministry (1 Cor. 9:6–14; 1 Tim. 5:18). But he preferred to forego his right in order that he might be **an example** of noble independence and unwearied diligence.

3:10 The Thessalonians had already been commanded not to support shirkers. If an able-bodied Christian refused to work, **neither** should **he eat**. Does this conflict with the fact that believers should always be kind? Not at all! It is not a kindness to encourage laziness. Spurgeon says, "The truest love to those who err is not to fraternize with them in their error but to be faithful to Jesus in all things."

3:11 Now the apostle uses a delightful play on words[14] to bring out the inconsistency of the pseudo-spirituality of these disorderly brothers. His words have been paraphrased variously as follows:

1. "Some who don't attend to business but are busybodies."
2. "Some that are not busy people but are busybodies."
3. "Some that are not busy in their own business but are over-busy in other people's business."
4. "Minding everybody's business but their own."

3:12 All **such** are commanded and exhorted **through our Lord Jesus Christ** to **work** without fanfare and earn **their own** living. This is a good testimony and glorifies God.

3:13 Those who have been working faithfully are encouraged to press on. It is the end of the race that counts, not the beginning; so they should **not grow weary in doing** the right thing.

3:14 But what about a man who refuses to **obey** the apostle's instructions? The other Christians should discipline him by refusing to have social fellowship with him. The purpose of this discipline is to shame him for his behavior and constrain him to mend his ways.

3:15 However, this discipline is not as strong as excommunication. Here the offender is still looked on **as a brother**. In excommunication, he is counted as "a heathen and a tax-collector" (Matt. 18:17).

The discipline of a believer always has in view his restoration to the Lord and to the people of God. It should not be carried out in a spirit of bitterness or enmity, but rather in Christian courtesy and firmness. He should **not** be treated **as an enemy, but** rather **as a brother**.

It seems strange to us today that Christians in Thessalonica were so ardently looking for the Lord's return that they abandoned their daily duties. That does not seem to be a peril to the church today! We have gone to the opposite extreme. We are so taken up with business and money-making that we have lost the freshness and thrill of the hope of His imminent coming.

VI. BLESSING AND GREETING (3:16–18)

3:16 This verse has been called "a peaceful close to a stormy Epistle." In it Paul prays that the suffering saints at Thessalonica may know the **peace** of **the Lord of peace** at all times and **in every way**.

The Christian is not dependent on anything in this world for his serenity. It is based entirely on the Person and work of the Lord Jesus. The world cannot give it or take it away. But we must appropriate it in all the circumstances of life. "Peace is not cessation from persecution, but is the calm of heart that comes from faith in God and that is independent of circumstances."

3:17, 18 At this point **Paul** apparently took the pen from the hand of his amanuensis (secretary) and wrote the closing **salutation**. He speaks of his greeting as being the **sign in every epistle** he writes. Some have understood this to mean that Paul's own handwriting at the end of each Letter proved it to be genuinely his. Others believe that the **sign** is the characteristic Pauline benediction: **the grace of our Lord Jesus Christ be with you all** (Rom. 16:24; 1 Cor. 16:23; 2 Cor. 13:14; Gal. 6:18; Eph. 6:24; Phil. 4:23; Col. 4:18; 1 Thess. 5:28; 1 Tim. 6:21; 2 Tim. 4:22; Tit. 3:15; Phmn. 25; and, if Paul wrote Hebrews, Heb. 13:25). From these references, we see that all his Epistles end on a **grace** note.

THE RAPTURE OF THE CHURCH

The truth of the Lord's return appears in each chapter of 1 Thessalonians and in the first two chapters of the Second Epistle. It is the unifying theme, the golden thread throughout the pattern.

But we must always remember that prophecy is not designed to intrigue our intellect or challenge our curiosity. Its purpose is to exert a transforming influence on our lives.

For believers the hope of the imminent return of Christ has practical implications of vast significance.

1. It should have a purifying influence on our lives (1 Thess. 5:23; 1 Jn. 3:3).

2. It should burden us to pray and work for the salvation of the lost (Gen. 19:14; Ezek. 33:6; Jude 21–23).

3. It should encourage us to persevere in spite of persecution and trial (Rom. 8:18; 2 Cor. 4:17; 1 Thess. 4:13–18).

4. It should make us reduce our holdings of material possessions; their value declines as His coming approaches (see Lev. 25:8–10, 14–16).

5. It should constrain us to apologize to anyone we have wronged and to make restitution where necessary (Matt. 5:24; Jas. 5:16).

6. It should inspire us to diligent service knowing that the night is coming when no one can work (Jn. 9:4; 1 Thess. 1:9,10a).

7. It should keep us in the attitude of expectancy (Luke 12:36) and abiding in Him so we will not be ashamed before Him as His coming (1 Jn. 2:28).

8. It should make us bold to confess Christ (Mark 8:38; Luke 9:26).

9. It should prove to be a comforting hope (John 14:1–3, 28; 1 Thess. 4:18; 2 Thess. 1:7; 2 Tim. 2:12).

10. It should be an encouragement to moderation, gentleness, and sweet reasonableness (Phil. 4:5).

11. It should be a motive for unity and love (1 Thess. 3:12, 13).

12. It should encourage an otherworldly attitude (Col. 3:1–4).

13. It should be a reminder of coming review and reward (Rom. 14:10–12; 1 Cor. 3:11–15; 2 Cor. 5:10).

14. It should be used as a powerful appeal in preaching the gospel (Acts 3:19–21; Rev. 3:3).

For those who are not believers, the truth of Christ's return should lead them to repent of their sins and make a full commitment of their lives to him as Lord and Savior. Only those who are in Christ will go to be with Him at the Rapture. The rest will be left behind for judgment.

What if it were today?

Because of the importance of Christ's coming in Thessalonians and in the Christian life, we add the following summaries:

Arguments for the Pretribulation Rapture

1. The first argument is based on imminency. There are many Scriptures that indicate that Christians should be looking for the Lord to come at any time. We should be watching and waiting, not knowing the time of His coming. If the church has to go through the Tribulation, then we cannot be looking for Him to come at any moment. In fact, He could not come for at least seven years, since we are not in the Tribulation now, and when it comes, it will last for seven years. The pretribulation view is the only one you can hold and still believe that Christ may come at any moment.

Here are some of the verses that indicate that we should be constantly looking for the Lord to come since we do not know the time of that event.

"Not only that, but we also who have the firstfruits of the Spirit, even we ourselves groan within ourselves, *eagerly waiting* for the adoption, the redemption of our body" (Rom. 8:23).

"For as often as you eat this bread and drink this cup, you *proclaim the Lord's death till He comes*" (1 Cor. 11:26 — Written to the Corinthians, this implied that the Lord might come in their lifetime.)

"For in this we groan, *earnestly desiring* to be clothed with our habitation which is from heaven" (2 Cor. 5:2 — Believers will be clothed with their glorified bodies at the Rapture.)

"For we through the Spirit *eagerly wait* for the hope of righteousness" (Gal. 5:5 — The hope of righteousness is the coming of the Lord and the glorified body which we will receive at that time.)

"For our citizenship is in heaven, from which we also *eagerly wait* for the Savior, the Lord Jesus Christ, who will transform our lowly body that it may be conformed to His glorious body, according to the working by which He is able even to subdue all things to Himself" (Phil. 3:20, 21).

"Let your gentleness be known to all men. *The Lord is at hand*" (Phil. 4:5).

"For they themselves declare concerning us what manner of entry we had to you, and how you turned to God from idols to serve the living and true God, and to *wait* for His Son from heaven, whom He raised from the dead, even Jesus who delivers us from the wrath to come" (1 Thess. 1:9, 10).

"*Looking* for the blessed hope and glorious appearing of our great God and Savior Jesus Christ" (Tit. 2:13).

"So Christ was offered once to bear the sins of many. To those who eagerly *wait* for Him He will appear a second time, apart from sin, for salvation" (Heb. 9:28).

"For yet *a little while*, and He who is coming will come and will not tarry" (Heb. 10:37).

"*Therefore be patient, brethren, until the coming of the Lord*. See how the farmer waits for the precious fruit of the earth, waiting patiently for it until it receives the early and latter rain. *You also be patient. Establish your hearts, for the coming of the Lord is at hand*. Do not grumble against one another, brethren, lest you be condemned. *Behold, the Judge is standing at the door!*" (Jas. 5:7–9).

"*But the end of all things is at hand*; therefore be serious and watchful in your prayers" (1 Pet. 4:7).

"And *everyone who has this hope in Him* purifies himself, just as He is pure" (1 Jn. 3:3).

"Keep yourselves in the love of God, *looking for the mercy of our Lord Jesus Christ unto eternal life*" (Jude 21. Here the mercy of our Lord Jesus Christ is His return to take His blood-bought people home to heaven).

"Behold, *I am coming quickly!* Hold fast what you have, that no one may take your crown" (Rev. 3:11).

"Behold *I am coming quickly!* Blessed is he who keeps the words of the prophecy of this book" (Rev. 22:7).

"And behold, *I am coming quickly*, and My reward is with Me, to give to every one according to his work" (Rev. 22:12).

"He who testifies to these things says, '*Surely I am coming quickly*.' Amen. Even so, come, Lord Jesus!" (Rev. 22:20).

There are other texts which, while they might not refer directly to the Rapture, yet add to the general impression that the coming of Christ is imminent. Throughout its history, the believing church has held that the time of Christ's coming is unknown and that therefore it could occur at any moment.

"*Watch therefore, for you do not know what hour your Lord is coming*. But know this, that if the master of the house had known what hour the thief would come, he would have watched and not allowed his house to be broken into. Therefore you also be ready, for the Son of Man is coming at an hour you do not expect" (Matt. 24:42–44).

"*But of that day and hour no one knows*, not even the angels in heaven, nor the Son, but only the Father. Take heed, *watch and pray; for you do not know when the time is*. It is like a man going to a far country, who left his house and gave authority to his servants, and to each his work, and commanded the doorkeeper to watch. *Watch therefore, for you do not know when the master of the house is coming* — in the evening, at midnight, at the crowing of the rooster, or in the morning — lest, coming suddenly, he find you sleeping. *And what I say to you, I say to all: Watch!*" (Mark 13:32–37).

"And you yourselves be like men who *wait* for their master, when he will return from the wedding, that when he comes and knocks they may open to him immediately" (Luke 12:36).

"So that you come short in no gift, *eagerly waiting* for the revelation of our Lord Jesus Christ" (1 Cor. 1:7).

"Christ Jesus, who is *about to judge living and dead*" (2 Tim. 4:1, JND).

"Little children, *it is the last hour*; and as you have heard that the Antichrist is coming, even now many antichrists have come, by which we know that *it is the last hour*" (1 Jn. 2:18).

"Therefore if you will not watch, I will come upon you as a thief, and you will not know what hour I will come upon you" (Rev. 3:3b).

"Behold, I am coming as a thief. *Blessed is he who watches*, and keeps his garments, lest he walk naked and they see his shame" (Rev. 16:15).

2. The second argument is based on the promise that the church will be delivered from the wrath to come. In Romans 5:9, Paul says that "we shall be saved from *wrath* through Him." First Thessalonians 1:10 describes the Lord Jesus as our Deliverer from the *wrath* to come. And in 1 Thessalonians 5:9 we learn that God has not appointed us to *wrath*, but to obtain salvation by our Lord Jesus Christ. The word "wrath" may refer to the wrath of the Tribulation Period, or it may refer to God's eternal judgment on unbelievers. In the Thessalonian Epistles, the context favors the wrath of the Tribulation (see 1 Thess. 5:2, 3; 2 Thess. 1:6–10; 2:10–21).

3. In Revelation 3:10, Christ promises to keep His people from (Greek *ek*, meaning "out of") the hour of trial, which shall come on all the world, to try them that dwell upon the earth.

4. The structure of the book of Revelation bears out the teaching of the pretribulation Rapture. In chapters 2 and 3 the church is seen on earth, but after chapter 3 it is never mentioned again as being on earth. In chapters 4 and 5 the saints are seen in heaven, wearing victor's crowns. Then follows the Tribulation on earth in chapters 6–19. The church saints are already in heaven.

5. The Tribulation Period will not begin until the man of sin has been revealed (2 Thess. 2:3). But the man of sin will not be revealed until first the restrainer is removed (2 Thess. 2:7, 8). The Holy Spirit certainly answers to the name of restrainer; He hinders or restrains the full development of evil as long as the church is in the world. He will be removed as the Indweller of the church at the time of the Rapture.

In one sense the Holy Spirit always was in the world and always will be. But there was a special sense in which He came at Pentecost, i.e., as the permanent Indweller of believers and of the church. It is in that sense that He will be removed at the Rapture. This does not mean that the Spirit of God will not carry on a ministry during the Tribulation. He will still convict and convert sinners. But He will not permanently indwell them and He will not incorporate them into the church. His ministry will be somewhat comparable to what it was in the OT period.

6. In 1 Thessalonians 4:18 the Rapture is spoken of as a comforting prospect. The Day of the Lord does not come as a comforter but as a thief in the night (1 Thess. 5:2). It is a time of sudden destruction (v. 3) and wrath (v. 9) from which there will be no escape (v. 3). In contrast, the Rapture is an ever-brightening hope, not an ever-frightening hope.

7. There must be an interval of time between Christ's coming for His saints and His coming with His saints. When Christ comes for His saints, *all* believers will be taken out of the world and will receive their *glorified bodies* (1 Cor. 15:51). Yet when Christ comes back to reign, there will be saved people who are still in their *natural bodies*, as is seen by the fact that they will be raising children (Isa. 65:20–25; Zech. 8:5). If the Rapture and the Revelation take place at the same time (the post-tribulation view), then where do these latter people come from?

There is a second reason why there must be an interval of time between the Rapture and the reign. The Judgment Seat of Christ must take place in heaven following the Rapture, when the Lord will judge the faithfulness of His saints and reward them accordingly (2 Cor. 5:10). The rewards given at this time will determine the extent of rule given to individual saints during the Millennium (Luke 19:17,19). If the Rapture and the coming to reign occurred simultaneously, there would be no time for the Judgment Seat of Christ to take place.

8. The only way the Day of the Lord will overtake anyone is as a thief in the night (1 Thess. 5:2). Yet Paul distinctly states that it will not overtake believers as a thief in the night (1 Thess. 5:4). Therefore it will not overtake believers at

all. Why not? Two reasons are given: (1) Believers are not children of the night but of the day (1 Thess. 5:4, 5). (2) God has not appointed believers to wrath (1 Thess. 5:9).

9. At the time of the Rapture, believers go to the Father's house (John 14:3), not straight back to the earth, as posttribulationists affirm.

10. The Tribulation is distinctly Jewish in character. It is called the time of *Jacob's* trouble (Jer. 30:7). Note the Jewish references in Matthew 24: Judea (v. 16), the Sabbath (v. 20), the holy place (v. 15). These terms have nothing to do with the church.

11. Several of the OT types point to a pretribulation Rapture. We do not *build* doctrine on types, but these types do fit the pretribulation view.

Enoch, a type of the church, was translated before the waters of God's judgment fell, whereas Noah and his family, types of the believing Jewish remnant, were preserved through the flood.

Lot was delivered from Sodom before the fires of judgment fell.

Abraham's offering of Isaac prefigures God offering His Son on Calvary. The first time Isaac is mentioned after that incident is when he went out to meet his bride and to take her back to his home. So Christ's first appearance after His Ascension will be when He comes to take His bride home to heaven.

Elijah was translated to heaven before judgment was meted out to the wicked Jezebel.

12. The first sixty-nine weeks of Daniel's prophecy (9:24–27) extend from the decree of Artaxerxes in 445 B.C. to the crucifixion of Christ. They have nothing to do with the church. Why then should the church be found in the seventieth week, which is the Tribulation Period? (Actually the Church Age occurs in an unmentioned parenthetical period between the sixty–ninth and seventieth weeks.)

**Arguments against the
Pretribulation Rapture and in favor
of a Post-tribulation Rapture.**

1. The promise in Revelation 3:10 is not that saints will be saved out of the Tribulation but that they will be kept through it (compare John 17:15).

Answer: The words translated "keep you from" in this verse literally mean "keep out of." The preposition in Greek (*ek*) means "out of." So the thought is not that the church will be preserved *in* or *through* the Tribulation, but that it will be kept *out of* it altogether.

The same words are used in John 17:15 where Jesus prays, "I do not pray that you shall take them out of the world, but that you should keep them from the evil one." Plummer comments, "Just as Christ is that *in* which his disciples live and move, so the evil one is that *out* of [*ek*] which He prays that they might be kept." The prayer has been answered; believers have been kept *out of* Satan's dominion, and translated into the kingdom of God's dear Son.

2. The Greek of Romans 5:3 says, ". . . *the* Tribulation works patience."

Answer: Paul is not saying that the only time that tribulation works patience is during *the* Tribulation Period. His argument clearly is that the tribulation that believers undergo in this life develops patience. Also, in Greek, as in French and Spanish, abstract nouns often have the article, hence the translation "tribulation" is correct.

3. Christians have always been promised Tribulation (John 16:33). There is no reason why we shouldn't go through it.

Answer: No one denies that "we must through many tribulations enter the kingdom of God" (Acts. 14:22). But there is a vast difference between the tribulation that is the portion of every believer and the Tribulation Period that awaits a Christ-rejecting world.

4. Second Thessalonians 1:7 shows that the saints will not obtain rest until the Lord Jesus returns to earth at the end of the Tribulation.

Answer: The Thessalonians to whom this was written have already received their rest in heaven. But the doom of their persecutors and the vindication of the saints will be *manifested* to the world when the Lord Jesus returns in power and great glory.

5. According to Acts 3:21, the heavens will hold the Lord Jesus until the times of restoration of all things, that is, the Millennium.

Answer: These words were spoken to *the men of Israel* (v. 4). *As far as the nation of Israel is concerned*, the statement is true. It agrees with the Savior's words to Jerusalem in Matthew 23:39, "You shall see Me no more till you say, 'Blessed is He who comes in the name of the Lord!' " That will take place at the end of the Tribulation Period. But the church will have been Raptured to heaven seven years earlier.

6. Psalm 110:1 says that Christ will sit at the right hand of God until all His enemies are destroyed. This will be at the end of the Tribulation.

Answer: In Revelation 20:8,9, we read of some who will be enemies of Christ at the end of the Millennium — that is 1000 years after the close of the Tribulation. The right hand of God may describe a position of honor and power as well as a geographical location.

7. In Titus 2:13, the blessed hope is the same as the glorious appearing. Therefore the Rapture takes place at the same time as the Revelation. Therefore, we do not look for a pretribulation Rapture but for Christ's coming to reign.

Answer: This argument is based on a rule of Greek syntax called Granville Sharp's rule which says: When two nouns connected by "and" (Gk. *kai*) are in the same case, and a definite article precedes the first noun but not the second, the second noun refers to the same person or thing the first noun does and is a further description of it. To give an example, Titus 2:13 says, "the glory of our great God and Savior Jesus Christ." The words "God" and "Savior" are connected by "and"; they are in the same case (objects of preposition "of"); the definite article (part of Greek for "our") precedes "God" but not "Savior." Therefore, according to Granville Sharp's rule, the word "Savior" refers to the same person as "God" and is a further description of Him. This proves, of course, that our Savior, Jesus Christ, is God.

Now in the same verse, it says in the Greek, "looking for the blessed hope and glorious appearing." Thus it is claimed that, according to Granville Sharp's rule, the blessed hope is the same as the glorious appearing, and since the glorious appearing is *generally* understood to be Christ's coming to reign, the believer's hope is not a pretribulation Rapture but Christ's coming in glory to the earth.

There are two answers to this. First of all, like all good rules, Granville Sharp's rule has exceptions. One is in Luke 14:23 where the Greek reads, "Go out into the highways and hedges." If the rule holds, then we must believe that highways are the same as hedges! A second exception is in Ephesians 2:20: "the foundation of the apostles and prophets." But no careful student would say that apostles and prophets are the same.

But even supposing that the blessed hope *is* the same as the glorious appearing, what is to prevent us from looking on the Rapture as Christ's glorious appearing to the church whereas the Revelation is His glorious appearing to the world? The words *apokalupsis* (revelation) and *epiphaneia* (shining forth or appearing) could refer to the Rapture as well as to Christ's coming to reign.

8. Other Scriptures which show that the believer's hope is Christ's coming to reign are 1 Corinthians 1:7; 1 Timothy 6:14; 2 Timothy 4:8; 1 Peter 1:7, 13; 4:13.

Answer: The words "revelation" and "appearing" used in these passages apply both to Christ's coming for His saints and to His coming with His saints. First, He reveals Himself and appears to the church, then later to the world.

But even if all the verses quoted did refer to Christ's coming to reign, it should be clear that the believer's hope embraces all the blessings of the prophetic future. We look forward to the Rapture, Christ's coming to reign, the Millennium, and the eternal state.

9. The traditional hope of the church has not been the pretribulation Rapture. This only began in the last 160 years or so through the teaching of J. N. Darby.

Answer: The NT church was waiting for God's Son from heaven. The saints did not know when He would come so they watched for Him at any time.

Arguments directed at what any person did or did not teach are called *ad hominem* (to the person) and are regarded as irrelevant to an issue. The question is "What does Scripture teach?", not "What did so-and-so teach?"

10. The last trumpet of 1 Corinthians 15:52 and the trumpet of God (1 Thess.

4:16) are connected with the Rapture and are the same as the seventh trumpet of Revelation 11:15. Since the seventh trumpet sounds at the end of the Tribulation when "the kingdoms of this world have become the kingdom of our Lord, and of His Christ," the return must be post-tribulational.

Answer: These trumpets are not all the same. The "last trumpet" is the same as the "trumpet of God." It announces the Rapture and signals the resurrection of believers and their translation to the Father's house. It is the "last trumpet" for the church. The seventh trumpet in Revelation 11:15 is the last in a series of judgments during the Tribulation. It is the last trumpet for unbelieving Israel and unbelieving Gentiles. The "last trumpet" of 1 Corinthians 15:52, also called the "trumpet of God" (1 Thess. 4:16), takes place before the Tribulation. The seventh trumpet takes place at the end of the Tribulation.

11. The first resurrection of Revelation 20:4, 5 takes place at the end of the Tribulation, and not seven years earlier, as the pretribulationists state.

Answer: The first resurrection is not an isolated event but a series. It began with the resurrection of Christ (1 Cor. 15:23). The next stage will be the resurrection of believers at the Rapture. The third stage will be the resurrection of Tribulation saints at the time of Christ's return to the earth (Rev. 20:4,5). In other words, the first resurrection includes the resurrection of Christ and of all true believers, no matter when they are raised. All unbelievers will be raised at the end of the Millennium to stand before the Great White Throne (Rev. 20:11–15).

12. In Matthew 13:24–30, the wheat and tares grow together until the end of the age, that is, until the end of the Tribulation.

Answer: True, but this parable is speaking of the kingdom of heaven and not of the church. There will be true and false people in the kingdom until the end of the Tribulation.

13. The Rapture couldn't be secret because there will be a shout, the voice of the archangel, and the trumpet of God (1 Thess. 4:16).

Answer: The teaching that the Rapture will be secret is based on the fact that it will take place in the twinkling of an eye (1 Cor. 15:52). It will be all over before the world has a chance to see anything or to know what has happened.

14. George Müller, Samuel Tregelles, Oswald Smith, and other noted men have held the post-tribulation view.

Answer: The argument proves nothing. There have been great men on both sides of the question.

15. Most references in the NT to Christ's coming refer to His coming to reign.

Answer: This does not deny the truth of the Rapture. Just because there are more references to heaven than to hell in the NT does not mean that there is no hell.

16. The church will not endure the wrath of God in the Tribulation, but it will endure the wrath of the Antichrist or the wrath of Satan.

Answer: Six times in the book of Revelation the wrath of the Tribulation Period is identified as the *wrath of God:*

"Then a third angel followed them, saying with a loud voice, 'If anyone worships the beast and his image, and receives his mark on his forehead or on his hand, he himself shall also drink of the wine of *the wrath of God*, which is poured out full strength into the cup of His indignation. He shall be tormented with fire and brimstone in the presence of the holy angels and in the presence of the Lamb' " (14:9, 10).

"So the angel thrust his sickle into the earth and gathered the vine of the earth, and threw it into the great winepress of *the wrath of God*" (14:19).

"Then I saw another sign in heaven, great and marvelous: seven angels having the seven last plagues, for in them *the wrath of God* is complete (15:1).

"Then one of the four living creatures gave to the seven angels seven golden bowls full of *the wrath of God* who lives forever and ever" (15:7).

"Then I heard a loud voice from the temple saying to the seven angels, 'Go and pour out the bowls of *the wrath of God* on the earth' " (16:1).

"Now the great city was divided into three parts, and the cities of the nations fell. And great Babylon was remembered before *God*, to give her the cup of the wine of the fierceness of *His wrath*" (16:19).

17. When Jesus says, "I am coming quickly" (Rev. 22:7,12, 20), it does not mean at any moment. Rather it means that His coming will be sudden.

Answer: It is a debated point. Even if it does mean "sudden," there are still verses like Hebrews 10:37, "For yet a little while, and He who is coming will come and will not tarry."

18. The restrainer in 2 Thessalonians 2:6–8 is not the Holy Spirit but the Roman government or the power of God.

Answer: This has been discussed in the notes on that passage.

19. Christ's coming couldn't have been imminent in the apostolic days because Peter and Paul both knew that they would die (John 21:18, 19; 2 Pet. 1:14, 15; 2 Tim. 4:6).

Answer: Paul sometimes spoke of himself as being alive when the Lord returns (1 Thess. 4:15) and sometimes as being among those believers who would die and be raised (Phil. 3:10, 11). That is the proper attitude for all of us. We expect the Lord to come in our lifetime, but we realize that we may die before the Rapture.

Peter believed that the end of all things was at hand (1 Pet. 4:7), and he condemned those scoffers who denied the Lord's coming by saying that "all things continue as they were from the beginning of creation" (2 Pet. 3:4).

20. The Lord's coming cannot be at any moment because the gospel must go out to all the world before He comes (Matt. 24:14).

Answer: This refers to *the gospel of the kingdom* (v. 14) which will go out to all the world during the Tribulation Period. The terms of this gospel are, "Believe on the Lord Jesus Christ and you will be saved, and when Christ comes, you will enter the Millennium with Him." It is the same way of salvation that we preach, but ours looks forward to the Rapture. In other words, we say, "Believe on the Lord Jesus Christ and you will be saved, and when Jesus comes, you will go to the Father's house with Him."

21. Passages like Matthew 28:19, 20

and Acts 1:8 speak of the gospel going out to "all the nations" and to "the end of the earth." This being so, it was not possible for the Lord to come during the lifetime of the apostles.

Answer: In Colossians 1:6, 23, Paul states that "all the world" and "every creature under heaven" had heard the gospel. In Romans 10:18, the gospel is said to have gone to the ends of the world. Of course, we understand that these passages refer to the known world at that time, the countries adjacent to the Mediterranean.

22. Paul's long term missionary plans, as given in Acts 18:21; 23:11; Romans 15:22–25, 30, 31, show that he did not expect the Lord to come in the immediate future.

Answer: Paul's plans were made, subject to the will of God (Acts 18:21; Rom. 1:10; 1 Cor. 4:19). He worked as if the Lord would not come back in his lifetime, but waited and watched as if He would return at any time.

23. Paul spoke of perilous times in the last days (1 Tim. 4:1–3; 2 Tim. 3:1–5). This presupposed a time lapse during which the Lord would not come.

Answer: Paul also said the mystery of iniquity was already working (2 Thess. 2:7), and John said it was "the last hour" in his day (1 Jn. 2:18). These men did not see any problem here that made the hope of Christ's imminent return impossible.

24. Parables such as Matthew 25: 14–30 and Luke 19:11–27 presuppose that a long period of time would elapse before the Lord returned. Therefore the early believers could not have been looking for the Lord to come at any moment.

Answer: Apparently the early believers did not base their doctrine on parables because they *were* looking for the Rapture! (1 Thess. 1:10). But quite apart from that, the "long time" of Matthew 25:19 is too indefinite to rule out imminency. The parable in Luke teaches that the *kingdom* would not appear immediately (Luke 19:11), but this does not preclude an any-moment Rapture of the *church*.

ENDNOTES

[1](1:1) There is still (or again) a NT as-

sembly of Christians in Thessalonica (today called Saloniki).

2(1:5) E. W. Rogers, *Concerning the Future*, p. 80.

3(1:6) George Williams, *The Student's Commentary on the Holy Scriptures*, p. 948.

4(1:10) Both the oldest (NU) and the majority (M) of mss. have "who have believed" here, undoubtedly the correct reading.

5(2:1) William Kelly, *Elements of Prophecy*, p. 253.

6(2:2) "Lord" (*Kurios*) is the critical (NU) reading. The traditional reading *Christos* (TR) of the KJ and NKJV is not (as sometimes) weakly supported; here it is the *majority* reading. Some scholars understand the "Day of Christ" as a reference to the final period of persecution, which can only begin when the man of sin has been revealed. Some of the Thessalonians wrongly thought that this period had already begun. By connecting this period with a post-Rapture event, Paul effectively refutes this notion.

7(2:3) Some theologians, such as J. Dwight Pentecost, translate *apostasia* as "departure," and refer it to the Rapture itself. If this is valid it is an air-tight verse for the pretribulational Rapture.

8(2:3) "Sin" is the TR and majority reading; "lawlessness" is the critical reading.

9(2:4) The Greek preposition (here a prefix) *anti* has both the meaning "against" and "in place of." Both meanings fit the Antichrist.

10(2:6) The Greek has a *neuter* article and participle in v. 6 and a *masculine* article and participle in v. 7.

11(2:6) Rogers, *Future*, p. 65.

12(2:6) The Holy Spirit is spoken of in the neuter for strictly grammatical reasons (the word *pneuma* is neuter). The masculine is used to stress His personality.

13(3:5) Both are valid translations of the genitive noun *Christou* (lit. "of Christ"). The KJV translates as an *objective* genitive (the "of-word" receiving the action suggested by the noun it modifies). The NKJV *subjective* genitive has Christ as the One showing the patience.

14(3:11) The Greek words are "not at all *ergazomenous* (working), but *periergazomenous* (working around or meddling around)." (Note the root *"erg"* — work.)

BIBLIOGRAPHY

See Bibliography at the end of *1 Thessalonians*.

THE PASTORAL EPISTLES

Introduction

"The Pastoral Epistles have played an important part in the history of the Christian Church and have amply justified their inclusion in the New Testament Canon. Their appeal lies in their blend of sound practical advice and theological statement, which has proved invaluable to Christians both personally and collectively."
— Donald Guthrie

I. The Meaning of the Term "Pastoral Epistles"

Since the 1700's, 1 and 2 Timothy and Titus have been called "the Pastoral Epistles." The description may be misleading or helpful, depending on how one understands it.

If the designation suggests that the Letters contain practical suggestions on how to care for the sheep of the Lord, then it has served its purpose well.

However, if it suggests that Timothy and Titus were settled clergymen (modern pastors) of the churches in Ephesus and Crete, respectively, then you have been misled.

Older editions of the King James Bible contain uninspired subscripts at the end of the Epistles which have lent credence to this historical error. For instance, at the end of 2 Timothy is this non-inspired addition:

> The second epistle unto Timotheus, ordained the first bishop of the church of the Ephesians, was written from Rome, when Paul was brought before Nero the second time.

And at the end of Titus is this explanation:

> It was written to Titus, ordained the first bishop of the church of the Cretians, from Nicopolis of Macedonia.

Albert Barnes, himself a clergyman, can scarcely be charged with prejudice when he comments:

> There is no evidence that Titus was the first bishop of the church there, or that

he was the first one there to whom might be properly applied the term bishop in the Scriptural sense. Indeed, there is positive evidence that he was not the first, for Paul was there with him, and Titus was "left" there to complete what he had begun.
>
> There is no evidence that Titus was "bishop" there at all in the prelatical sense of the term, or even that he was a settled pastor.
>
> These subscriptions are so utterly destitute of authority, and are so full of mistakes, that it is high time they were omitted in the editions of the Bible. They are no part of the inspired writings but are of the nature of "notes and comments," and are constantly doing something, perhaps much, to perpetuate error. The opinion that Timothy and Titus were "prelatical bishops," the one of Ephesus and the other of Crete, depends far more on these worthless subscriptions than on anything in the epistles themselves. Indeed, there is no evidence of it in the epistles, and, if these subscriptions were removed, no man from the New Testament would ever suppose that they sustained that office at all.[1]

Fortunately the subscriptions finally have been removed from modern versions of the NT, but the error they promulgated dies hard.

Timothy and Titus were sent to churches on temporary missions by the Apostle Paul to instruct the believers and to warn them against false teachers.

Since virtually all Bible scholars agree that these three Letters are from the *same period* and by the *same hand*, we will handle their authorship and authenticity as a unit.

II. Authorship of These Epistles[†]

Until 1804, when Schmidt denied that Paul wrote these Epistles, the entire church and even non-believers accepted them as genuine Letters of the great apostle.

Since that time it has grown ever more common to label these books as "forgeries," though "pious" ones (as if fraud could go with true piety!). Most liberals and some otherwise conservative people have trouble accepting the books as genuinely Pauline or at least *totally* so. Since there is much important teaching on how to guide a church and other important doctrines — *including warnings against heretics and unbelief in the latter days* — we feel it is necessary to give more detail on these Epistles' authenticity than any others except 2 Peter.

III. External Evidence

The external evidence for the Pastorals is very strong. In fact, if this were the only criterion for acceptance or rejection, they would win without question.

Irenaeus is the first known author to quote these Epistles directly. Tertullian and Clement of Alexandria ascribed them to Paul, as did the Muratorian Canon. Earlier fathers who seem to have known the Letters include Polycarp and Clement of Rome.

Marcion did not include these three Books in his "canon," according to Tertullian. This is probably not really a vote against their authenticity as much as against their *contents*. Marcion was the sort of cult leader to chafe under Paul's harsh attacks against incipient Gnosticism (see Introduction to Colossians) included in the Pastoral Epistles. Passages which this anti-Semitic heretic would especially dislike include 1 Timothy 1:8; 4:3; 6:20 and 2 Timothy 3:16, 17.

IV. Internal Evidence

Nearly all the attacks against Paul's having written the Pastoral Epistles are based on supposed evidence to the contrary *within* the Letters themselves.

Three main lines of evidence are alleged: historical, ecclesiastical, and linguistic. We will briefly examine and explain each of these three problems.

The historical problem. Several events and people in these books cannot be fitted into Acts or our knowledge of Paul's ministry from the other Epistles. Paul's leaving Trophimus sick at Miletus and his cloak and parchments at Troas do not fit in with his known travels.

This is an easy argument to refute. Yes, it is true they don't fit in with Acts; they don't *need* to. Philippians 1:25 suggests Paul was expecting to be released, and Christian tradition says that he was, and ministered for some years before he was re-imprisoned and beheaded. The events, friends, and enemies mentioned in the Pastorals are thus from this period of missionary work *between* the two imprisonments.

The ecclesiastical problem. It is said that the church organization is too late for Paul — second century, in fact. While it is true that bishops, elders, and deacons are discussed in the Pastorals, there is no evidence they were the "monarchical" type of bishops of the second and following centuries. In fact, Philippians 1:1, an earlier Epistle, mentions a plurality of bishops (overseers) in one church, not one bishop over a church, or the even later system of one bishop over several churches. Also, the words *elders* and *bishops* are used interchangeably in Timothy and Titus, whereas, starting in the second century, with persistent encouragement from Ignatius, one "bishop" was singled out to be over the other men as "presbyters."

The very basic teaching on church leaders thus clearly suggests the *apostolic* age, not the second century.

The linguistic argument. The strongest attack is based on the difference in style and vocabulary between these three Letters and the other ten we accept as by Paul. Some of Paul's favorite words and expressions are not found here, and many words not used in his other Letters are (36% new words). Statistical methodology is made to "prove" Paul "couldn't" have written these Letters. (The same method has challenged poems by Shakespeare with similar negative results.)

It is well to acknowledge that there are *actual problems* here. For once the theories are not almost completely based on prejudice against unpalatable scriptural doctrine. (However, the latter-day apostates who are attacked in the Pastorals do sound surprisingly like some of the very scholars who insist Paul is not the author of them.)

First of all, it is important to remember that these are the Letters of an old man facing death, one who has had much broadening travel and acquired many new friends since getting out of prison (2 Timothy is written from his second imprisonment). Everyone increases his vocabulary as he ages, reads, travels, and mixes with new people.

Second, we must realize the subject matter of these Letters — church officers, ethics, and apostasy — automatically calls for new words.

These Epistles are also far too short for a fair use of the statistical method. Perhaps most significantly, 80% of the NT vocabulary occurring only in the Pastorals is found in the Greek OT (LXX), as Guthrie states in his *Introduction*. Since Paul was ministering in Greek, it is obvious he knew the OT Scriptures in that language as well as in the Hebrew original. In short, these words which Paul is alleged to have used were at least part of his "recognition vocabulary." The church fathers who used Greek as their everyday language saw no problem in Pauline authorship of the Pastorals. (The fact that some *did* so for Hebrews shows they were sensitive to a writer's style.)

Putting all the answers to the arguments together, and especially when joined with the ancient and universal acceptance by orthodox believers of these Letters as from Paul's own hand, we also can accept them as such with a good conscience. In fact, the highly *ethical* content of these Epistles rules out a forger, "pious" or otherwise. These are the inspired words of God (2 Tim. 3:16, 17) communicated through the Apostle Paul.

V. Background and Themes of the Pastoral Epistles

Frankly, we do not have too much background for the period of Paul's life covered by these Epistles. The best we can do is to piece together the biographical statements which are found in the Letters themselves, and these are very sketchy.

There are several words and themes which recur frequently in these Letters. These give us an insight into the subjects which occupied Paul's mind increasingly as his ministry was drawing to a close.

Faith is one of the characteristic words. As the peril of apostasy increased, Paul sought to emphasize the great body of Christian doctrine which had been delivered to the saints. He described various attitudes which men had taken or would take toward faith.

1. Some suffered shipwreck concerning the faith (1 Tim. 1:19).
2. Some would depart from the faith (1 Tim. 4:1).
3. Some would deny the faith (1 Tim. 5:8).
4. Some would cast off their first faith (1 Tim. 5:12).
5. Some would stray from the faith (1 Tim. 6:10).
6. Some missed the mark concerning the faith (1 Tim. 6:21).

Clearly related is the expression *sound doctrine.* "Sound" here means more than correct or orthodox. It means healthy or health-giving. It is the word from which "hygiene" comes. Here, of course, it is spiritual hygiene. Note the following:

Sound doctrine (1 Tim. 1:10; 2 Tim. 4:3; Tit. 1:9; 2:1).

Wholesome words (1 Tim. 6:3).

Sound words (2 Tim. 1:13).

Sound in the faith (Tit. 1:13; 2:2).

Sound speech (Tit. 2:8).

The word *conscience* is mentioned six times, as follows:

1 Timothy 1:5, 19; 3:9; 4:2

2 Timothy 1:3

Titus 1:15

Godliness is emphasized as the practical proof of the soundness of one's doctrine — 1 Timothy 2:2, 10; 3:16; 4:7, 8; 5:4; 6:3, 5, 6, 11; 2 Timothy 3:5 (outward form of godliness only); 3:12; Titus 1:1; 2:12.

Being *sober* or *sober-minded* are qualities which the apostle felt were worthy of cultivation by his young assistants — 1 Timothy 2:9, 15; 5:6, 8; 2 Timothy 3:2, 11; Titus 1:8; 2:2, 4, 6, 12.

We should notice, too, the many *good* things which the apostle mentions:

Good conscience (1 Tim. 1:5, 19).

The law is good (1 Tim. 1:8).

A good warfare (1 Tim. 1:18).

Prayer is good (1 Tim. 2:3).

Good works (1 Tim. 2:10; 3:1; 5:10, 25; 6:18; 2 Tim. 2:21; 3:17; Tit. 1:16; 2:7, 14; 3:1, 8, 14).

Good behavior (1 Tim. 3:2).

Good testimony (1 Tim. 3:7).

A good standing (1 Tim. 3:13).

Every creature is good (1 Tim. 4:4).

A good minister (1 Tim. 4:6).

Good doctrine (1 Tim. 4:6).

Piety is good (1 Tim. 5:4).

The good fight of faith (1 Tim. 6:12; 2 Tim. 4:7).

Good confession (1 Tim. 6:13).

Good foundation (1 Tim. 6:19).

Good thing (2 Tim. 1:14; Tit. 2:3; 3:8).

A good soldier (2 Tim. 2:3).

Good people (2 Tim. 3:3; Tit. 1:8; 2:5).

Good fidelity (Tit. 2:10).

A final interesting word study concerns the medical terms which are found in these Letters. Some think that this is a reflection of the fact that Dr. Luke was a close companion of Paul at this time.

We have already mentioned that the word "sound" means health-giving and is used to describe doctrine, words, speech, and faith.

In 1 Timothy 4:2, Paul speaks of a seared conscience. "Seared" means cauterized as with a hot instrument.

The expression "obsessed with disputes" means sick about them, and refers to mental illness (1 Tim. 6:4).

"Cancer" in 2 Timothy 2:17 is translated "gangrene" in the Revised Version (the Greek word is the origin of this latter).

"Itching ears" (2 Tim. 4:3) is a final expression used by Paul in his diagnosis of these latter-day clinical cases.

With this background, let us now turn to the First Epistle to Timothy for a verse-by-verse study of its contents.

THE FIRST EPISTLE TO TIMOTHY

Introduction

"This Epistle would give Timothy some documentary proof of his authorization to act as the apostle's representative. Accordingly much of the Epistle is directly occupied with the personal life and activities of Timothy himself."
— D. Edmond Hiebert

I. Unique Place in the Canon

Those who would rob the church of the Pastoral Epistles as authentic Letters of the great Apostle Paul do severe damage to the faith. We suspect that the main problem for them does not really lie so much in the so-called "un-Pauline vocabulary," as it does in the *very* Pauline way these words are often put together! They condemn in advance the very things some of these people are doing and teaching.

The truth, beauty, and spiritual force of 1 Timothy comes through to anyone meditating on the text as such without preconceived notions. In fact, many who deny the Pauline authorship sense this so strongly that they feel forced to suggest that fragments of *genuine* Pauline Letters were woven into the alleged forger's excellent work! For example, the French skeptic of the past century, Ernest Renan, writes: "Some passages of these letters are so beautiful that we cannot help asking if the forger had not in his hands some authentic notes of Paul, which he has incorporated into his apocryphal composition."[1]

How much simpler to accept the nearly universal teaching of the church from earliest times that these are — *in their entirety* — "authentic notes of Paul"!

Very important revelation on church order, women's ministry, and church officers is found in 1 Timothy. How the man of God should live is clearly outlined by a model *par excellence*, Paul himself.

II. Authorship

See the Introduction to the Pastoral Epistles for a discussion of 1 Timothy's authorship.

III. Date

Nearly all conservatives agree that 1 Timothy is the first of the Pastorals to be written, with Titus soon after and 2 Timothy right before Paul's death. If Paul was released from house arrest in A.D. 61, allowing for his travels, a date between 64 and 66 is indicated. The Epistle was probably written from Greece.

IV. Background and Themes[†]

The theme of 1 Timothy is set forth quite clearly in 3:14, 15:

> These things I write to you, though I hope to come to you shortly; but if I am delayed, I write so that you may know how you ought to conduct yourself in the house of God, which is the church of the living God, the pillar and ground of the truth.

Paul states here quite simply that there is a standard of behavior for the church of God and that he is writing to Timothy to enable him to know it.

It is not enough to say to a child who is misbehaving, "Behave yourself!" if the child does not know what is expected in the way of good behavior. He must be told first what good behavior *is*. 1 Timothy does this for the child of God in relation to the church of God.

A summary glance at the various chapters supports the theme as outlined above. Chapter 2 shows us what that be-havior is in relation to public prayer and to women's role in public. Chapter 3 sets forth requirements for those who will be taking places of responsibility and leadership in the assembly. Chapter 5 stresses the congregation's responsibility toward widows.

OUTLINE

I. SALUTATION (1:1, 2)

II. PAUL'S CHARGE TO TIMOTHY (1:3–20)
   A. Charge to Silence False Teachers (1:3–11)
   B. Thanksgiving for the True Grace of God (1:12–17)
   C. Restatement of the Charge to Timothy (1:18–20)

III. INSTRUCTIONS CONCERNING CHURCH LIFE (2:1–3:16)
   A. Regarding Prayer (2:1–7)
   B. Regarding Men and Women (2:8–15)
   C. Regarding Elders and Deacons (3:1–13)
   D. Regarding Conduct in the Church (3:14–16)

IV. APOSTASY IN THE CHURCH (4:1–16)
   A. Warning Against the Impending Apostasy (4:1–5)
   B. Positive Instructions in View of the Impending Apostasy (4:6–16)

V. SPECIFIC INSTRUCTIONS CONCERNING VARIOUS CLASSES OF BELIEVERS (5:1–6:2)
   A. Different Age Groups (5:1, 2)
   B. Widows (5:3–16)
   C. Elders (5:17–25)
   D. Bondservants and Masters (6:1, 2)

VI. FALSE TEACHERS AND THE LOVE OF MONEY (6:3–10)

VII. CLOSING CHARGES TO TIMOTHY (6:11–21)

Commentary

I. SALUTATION (1:1, 2)

1:1 **Paul** first of all introduces himself as **an apostle of Jesus Christ. An apostle** is a "sent one," so Paul is simply stating that he had been divinely appointed to missionary work. Paul's authorship was **by the commandment of God our Savior and the Lord Jesus Christ, our hope**. This emphasizes that Paul had not chosen the ministry by himself as a means of livelihood; neither had he been ordained to this work by men. He had a definite call from God to preach, teach, and suffer. In this verse, **God** the Father is called **our Savior**. Usually in the NT, the Lord Jesus is spoken of as the Savior. But there is no contradiction. God is the **Savior** of men in the sense that He desires their salvation, He has sent His Son to accomplish the work of redemption, and He gives eternal life to all who accept the Lord Jesus by faith. Christ is the Savior in the sense that He actually went to the cross and finished the work that was necessary in order that God might righteously save ungodly sinners.

The Lord Jesus Christ is spoken of here as **our hope**. This reminds one of Colossians 1:27: "Christ in you, the hope of glory." Our only hope of getting to heaven is found in the Person and work of the Lord Jesus. In fact, all the bright prospects which are held out before us in the Bible are ours only because of our connection with Christ Jesus.

Note further Ephesians 2:14, where Christ is our peace, and Colossians 3:4, where He is our life. Christ is our peace, dealing with the problem of our sins in the past; Christ is our life, dealing with the problem of power for the present; and Christ is our hope, dealing with the problem of deliverance in the future.

1:2 The Letter is addressed **to Timothy**, who is described as **a true son in the faith (in the** realm **of faith)**. This may indicate that Timothy was saved through the apostle, perhaps during Paul's first visit to Lystra (Acts 14:6–20). But the general impression in Acts is that Timothy was already a disciple when Paul first met him (Acts 16:1, 2). In that case the expression **true son in the faith** means that Timothy exhibited the same spiritual and moral qualities as Paul; he was a **true** descendant of the apostle because he manifested the same character.

Stock says: "Happy is the young Christian worker who has such a leader, and happy is the Christian leader who 'hath his quiver full' of such 'true' children."

The usual salutation in NT Letters is "grace and peace." In 1 and 2 Timothy, Titus, and 2 John, this is enlarged to **grace, mercy and peace**. All of these latter Epistles were written to individuals rather than to churches, and this explains the addition of **mercy**.

Grace means all the divine resources needed for Christian life and service. **Mercy** speaks of God's compassionate care and protection for one who is needy and prone to fail. **Peace** means the inner tranquility that comes from leaning on the Lord. These three blessings come from **God our Father and Jesus Christ our Lord**. The deity of Christ is implied in this verse in that Paul speaks of Him as equal with the Father. The expression **Jesus Christ our Lord** stresses the Lordship of Christ. Whereas the word "Savior" occurs twenty-four times in the NT,

the word "Lord" occurs 522 times. We should be able to make a personal application of these important statistics.

II. PAUL'S CHARGE TO TIMOTHY (1:3–20)

A. Charge to Silence False Teachers (1:3–11)

1:3 It seems probable that after Paul's first imprisonment at Rome, he visited Ephesus with Timothy. When Paul moved on to Macedonia, he instructed Timothy to stay in Ephesus for a while to teach the word of God and to warn the believers against false teachers. From Macedonia, Paul apparently traveled south to Corinth, and it was perhaps from that city that he wrote this first Letter to Timothy. In verse 3, the apostle is saying in effect: "Just **as I** previously instructed you to stay **in Ephesus when I went into Macedonia**, so I am repeating those instructions now." It is not to be understood from this that Timothy was appointed pastor of the church at Ephesus. There is no such thought in the passage. Rather, he was there on a temporary mission, charging certain men in the assembly not to **teach** doctrines contrary to the Christian faith or supposed additions to it. The principal false doctrines in question were legalism and Gnosticism. Just in case Timothy was tempted to run away from these problems, Paul is telling him to stay on the job.

1:4 Timothy was also exhorted to charge these men not to pay attention **to fables and endless genealogies**. It is impossible for us to know definitely what these **fables** and **genealogies** were. Some connect them with legends that had arisen among some Jewish teachers. Others think they refer to the myths and generations of the Gnostics. It is interesting to notice that the false cults of today are characterized by these same things. Many fanciful stories have arisen with regard to the founders of false religions, and genealogies occupy an important place in Mormonism.

Such worthless subjects serve only to provoke questionings and doubts in people's minds. They do not produce **godly edification which is in faith**. The whole plan of redemption is designed by God, not to stir up doubts and **disputes**, but rather to induce **faith** in the hearts of men. These men in the Ephesian assembly should not be devoting their attention to such valueless themes as **fables and genealogies**, but rather should devote themselves to the great truths of the Christian faith, which will prove a blessing to men and will inspire **faith** rather than doubt.

1:5 Perhaps the most important thing to understand in this verse is that **commandment** does not refer to the Law of Moses or the Ten Commandments, but to the charge of verses 3 and 4. This is brought out clearly in the NKJV: **Now the purpose of the commandment is love.... ** Paul is saying that the goal or aim of the charge which he has just given Timothy is to produce not just orthodoxy but **love from a pure heart, from a good conscience, and from sincere faith**. These things always follow when the gospel of the grace of God is preached.

Love doubtless includes love to God, to one's fellow believers, and to the world in general. It must spring out of **a pure heart**. If one's inner life is unclean, then true Christian love can scarcely flow from it. This love must also be the by-product of **a good conscience**, that is, a **conscience** void of offense toward God and man. Finally, this love must be the outcome of **sincere** (literally, "unhypocritical") **faith**, that is, faith that does not wear a mask.

False teachings could never produce these things which Paul lists, and certainly they are never the outcome of fables and endless genealogies! It is the teaching of the grace of God that produces **a pure heart, a good conscience, a sincere faith**, and that therefore results in **love**.

Verse 5 gives us the test of all true teaching, namely, does it produce these results?

1:6 There were some who had **strayed** from these things, that is, from a pure heart, a good conscience, and sincere faith. The expression **turned aside** may mean either they aimed improperly or missed the mark. The former is no doubt the meaning here. It was not a question of these men having tried to

reach these things; they did not even aim for them. As a result, they **turned aside to idle talk**. Their preaching was aimless; it led nowhere; it failed to make men holy.

Paul frequently uses the word **some** in this Epistle. At the time he wrote 1 Timothy, these false teachers represented a minority in the church. When we come to 2 Timothy, we shall see that the word "some" is no longer prominent. The balance of power had changed. Departure had become much more general. The minority apparently had become the majority.

1:7 The false teachers referred to in the previous verses were Judaizers, who sought to mix Judaism and Christianity, law and grace. They maintained that faith in Christ was not sufficient for salvation. They insisted that a man must be circumcised or in other ways must keep the Law of Moses. They taught that the law was the believer's rule of life.

This false teaching has been present in every century of church history, and it is the plague which has been most successful in corrupting Christendom today. In its modern form, it states that although faith in Christ is necessary for salvation, a person must also be baptized, or join the church, or keep the law, or do penance, or tithe, or perform some other type of "good works." Those who teach this present-day legalism fail to realize that salvation is by faith in Christ without the deeds of the law. They do not realize that good works are the *result* of salvation and not the cause. A man does not become a Christian by doing these good works, but rather he does these good works because he is a Christian. They do not see that Christ, and not the law, is the believer's rule of life. They fail to understand that a man cannot be under the law without being under the curse. The law condemns to death all who fail to keep its sacred precepts. Since no man is able to obey the law perfectly, then all are condemned to death. But Christ has redeemed believers from the curse of the law because He was made a curse for us.

The apostle says of these self-styled **teachers of the law** that they did not understand **what they** were saying **nor the things** about which they were making confident affirmations. They could not speak intelligently about the law because they did not understand the purpose for which the law was given or the relationship of the believer to the law.

1:8 Paul makes it abundantly clear that there is nothing the matter with the law. "Therefore the law is holy, and the commandment holy and just and good" (Rom. 7:12). But the law must be used **lawfully**. It was never given as a means of salvation (Acts 13:39; Rom. 3:20; Gal. 2:16, 21; 3:11). The lawful use of **the law** is to so employ it in preaching and teaching as to produce conviction of sin. It should not be presented as a means of salvation or as a rule of life.

Guy King has pointed out that the three lessons which the law teaches are: "We ought. We haven't. We can't." When the law has done its work in the life of a sinner, then that person is ready to cry out to God, "Lord, save me by Your grace!"[2] Those who teach that the law is essential for salvation or sanctification are not consistent. They say that if a Christian breaks the law, then he need not be put to death. This is not establishing the authority of the law. Law without penalty is nothing but good advice.

1:9 The law is not made for a righteous person. If a man is righteous, he does not need a law. That is true of the Christian. When he is saved by the grace of God, he does not need to be placed under the Ten Commandments in order for him to live a holy life. It is not fear of punishment that makes a Christian live in a godly manner, but rather love for the Savior who died at Calvary.

The apostle goes on to describe the type of people for whom the law was given. Many Bible commentators have pointed out that there is a close connection between this description and the Ten Commandments themselves. The Ten Commandments are divided into two sections: the first four have to do with man's duty toward God (godliness), whereas the remaining six have to do with his duty toward his neighbor (righteousness). The following words seem to correspond to the first section of the Ten Commandments: **For the lawless and insubordinate, for the ungodly and for sinners, for the unholy and profane. . . .** The expression **for manslayers** is linked with the sixth commandment: **You shall not murder.** Here **manslayers** refers to murderers, and not just to a person who kills another accidentally.

1:10 The words **for fornicators, for sodomites** describe immoral heterosexuals and homosexuals. Here they are linked to the seventh commandment: "You shall not commit adultery." The phrase **for kidnappers** is obviously related to the eighth commandment: "You shall not steal." **For liars, for perjurers** (or false swearers) connects with the ninth commandment: "You shall not bear false witness against your neighbor."

The final words **and if there is any other thing that is contrary to sound doctrine** are not directly related to the tenth commandment, but rather seem to sweep back over all the commandments and summarize them.

1:11 It is difficult to decide how this verse is connected with what has gone before. It may mean that the sound doctrine mentioned in verse 10 **is according to the . . . gospel.** Or it may mean that all that Paul has been saying about the law in verses 8–10 is in perfect agreement with **the gospel** which he preached. Or again, it may mean that all that Paul has been saying about false teachers in verses 3–10 is in accord with **the gospel** message. While it is true that the gospel is **glorious**, the emphasis here may be on the fact that the gospel tells of *the glory* (the literal translation of **glorious**) of **God** in a wonderful way. It tells how the same God who is holy, righteous, and just is at the same time a God of grace, mercy, and love. His love provided what His holiness demanded; now those who receive the Lord Jesus are given eternal life.

This is the **gospel . . . which was committed** to the apostle's **trust.** It centers around the glorified Lord Jesus Christ and tells men that He is not only Savior but Lord as well.

B. Thanksgiving for the True Grace of God (1:12–17)

1:12 In the preceding passage, Paul has been describing the false teachers who were seeking to impose the law on the believers in Ephesus. He is now reminded of his own conversion. It was not through law-keeping but by the grace of God. The apostle had not been a righteous man but the chief of sinners. Verses 12–17 seem to illustrate the lawful use of the law from Paul's own experience. The law was not to him a way of salvation, but rather a means of conviction of sin.

First of all he bursts out into thanksgiving to **Christ Jesus** for His enabling grace. The emphasis is not on what Saul of Tarsus did for the Lord but what the Lord did for him. The apostle could never get over the wonder that the Lord Jesus not only saved him but **counted** him **faithful**, appointing him to His service. The law could never have shown such grace. Rather, its inflexible terms would have condemned the sinner Saul to death.

1:13 That Paul had broken the Ten Commandments before his conversion is abundantly evident from this verse. He speaks of himself as **formerly a blasphemer, a persecutor, and an insolent man**. As **a blasphemer**, he spoke evil concerning the Christians and their Leader, Jesus. As **a persecutor**, he sought to put Christians to death because he felt that this new sect posed a threat to Judaism. In carrying out his evil plan, he took delight in committing **insolent**, violent, and outrageous acts against the believers. Although it is not as obvious from the English words, there is an ascending scale of wickedness in the three words **blasphemer, persecutor, and insolent**. The first sin is a matter of words only. The second describes suffering inflicted on others for their religious beliefs. The third includes the idea of cruelty and abuse.

But Paul **obtained mercy**. He did not receive the punishment he deserved **because** he **did** these things **ignorantly in unbelief**. In persecuting Christians, he thought he was doing God's service. Since his parents' religion taught the worship of the true God, he could only conclude that the Christian faith was opposed to the Jehovah of the OT. With all the zeal and energy he possessed, he sought to defend the honor of God by killing the Christians.

Many insist that zeal and earnestness and sincerity are the important things

with God. But Paul's example shows that zeal is not enough. In fact, if a man is wrong, his zeal only makes the wrong more intense. The more zeal he has, the more damage he does!

1:14 Not only did Paul escape the punishment he deserved (mercy), but he also received **abundant** kindness which he did not deserve (**grace**). Where his sin had abounded, God's grace abounded much more (Rom. 5:20).

The fact that the **grace** of the Lord was not bestowed on Paul in vain is indicated by the words **"with faith and love which are in Christ Jesus."** The grace which came to Paul was accompanied by **faith and love which are in Christ Jesus**. It could, of course, mean that just as grace came from the Lord, so faith and love found their origin in Him. But the meaning seems to be clearer if we understand that God's grace was not refused by Paul, but that he responded by trusting the Lord Jesus and by loving this Blessed One whom he formerly had hated.

1:15 This is the first of five "faithful sayings" in the Pastoral Epistles. **This is a faithful saying** because it is the word of God, who can neither lie nor be mistaken. Men can afford to believe this statement with implicit trust. Indeed, to disbelieve it is unreasonable and unwise. It is **worthy of all acceptance** because it applies to all, tells what God has done for all, and extends the gift of salvation to all.

Christ Jesus emphasizes the deity of our Lord. The One who came from heaven to earth was first of all *God* (**Christ**) and then *Man* (**Jesus**). The preexistence of the Savior is suggested in the words He **came into the world**. Bethlehem was not the beginning of His existence. He had dwelt with God the Father from all eternity, but He came into the world as a Man on a specific errand. The calendar testifies to the fact that He came; we speak of this as A.D. 19—, the year of our Lord 19—. Why did He come? **To save sinners**. It was not to save good people (there were none!). Neither was it to save those who kept the law perfectly (none had done this either).

Here we come to the very heart of the difference between true Christianity and all other teachings. False religions tell man that there is something he can do or be in order to win favor with God. The gospel tells man that he is a sinner, that he is lost, that he cannot save himself, and that the only way he can get to heaven is through the substitutionary work of the Lord Jesus on the cross. The type of law teaching which Paul described earlier in this chapter gives a place to the flesh. It tells man exactly what he wants to hear, namely, that he can somehow contribute to his own salvation. But the gospel insists that all the glory for the work of salvation must go to Christ alone, that man does nothing but the sinning, and that the Lord Jesus does all the saving.

The Spirit of God brought Paul to the place where he realized he was the **chief** of sinners, or as some translate it: "a foremost one among sinners." If he was not the chief of sinners, then certainly he was in the front rank. Notice that the title "chief of sinners" is not given to a man steeped in idolatry or immorality, but rather to a deeply religious man, one who had been brought up in an orthodox Jewish home! His sin was doctrinal; he did not accept the word of God concerning the Person and work of the Lord Jesus Christ. Rejection of the Son of God is the greatest of sins.

Also, it should be noted that he says **of whom I am chief** — not "was" but **am**. The godliest saints are often the most conscious of their own sinfulness.

In 1 Corinthians 15:9 (written about A.D. 57), Paul called himself "the least of the apostles." Then in Ephesians 3:8 (written about A.D. 60), he called himself "less than the least of all saints." Now in 1 Timothy 1:15, written some years later, he calls himself the **chief** of **sinners**. Here we have an outline of Paul's progress in Christian humility.

Darby's translation of the expression **of whom I am chief** is "of whom I am (the) first." The thought is not so much that he was the worst sinner who ever lived but that he was first in relation to the nation of Israel. In other words, his conversion was a unique foreshadowing of the future conversion of the nation of Israel. He was "one born out of due time" (1 Cor. 15:8) in the sense that he was born again prior to the rebirth of his

people Israel. Just as he was saved by a direct revelation from heaven and apart from human instrumentality, so perhaps in this same way the Jewish remnant will be saved during the coming Tribulation Period. This interpretation seems to be borne out by the words "first" and "pattern" in verse 16.

1:16 This explains why Paul obtained mercy. It was so that he might be an exhibit of the **longsuffering** of **Jesus Christ**. Just as he had been the chief of sinners, so now he would be the chief display of the untiring grace of the Lord. He would be "Exhibit A," a living example, as William Kelly said, of "divine love rising above the most active hostility, of divine longsuffering exhausting the most varied and persistent antagonism."[3]

Paul's case would be **a pattern**. In the printing trade, pattern means a first proof. It signifies a specimen or a sample. Paul's conversion would be a **pattern** of what God would do with the nation of Israel when the Deliverer comes out of Zion (Rom. 11:26).

In a more general sense the verse means that none need despair, no matter how wicked they might be. They can console themselves that since the Lord has already saved the chief of sinners, they too can find grace and mercy by coming to Him as penitents. By believing on Him, they too can find **everlasting life.**

1:17 As Paul thinks of God's marvelous dealings with him in grace, he bursts out into this lovely doxology. It is difficult to know whether it is addressed to God the Father or to the Lord Jesus. The words **the King eternal** seem to refer to the Lord Jesus because He is called the "Kings of kings, and Lord of lords" (Rev. 19:16). However, the word **invisible** seems to refer to the Father, since the Lord Jesus was obviously visible to mortal eyes. The fact that we are not able to distinguish which Person of the Godhead is intended might serve as an indication of Their absolute equality.

The King eternal is spoken of, first of all, as **immortal**. This means incorruptible or imperishable. God in His essence is also **invisible**. Men have seen appearances of God in the OT, and the Lord Jesus fully revealed God to us in visible form, but the fact remains that God Himself is invisible to human eyes. Next He is spoken of as **God who alone is wise**. In the final analysis, all wisdom comes from God (Jas. 1:5).

C. Restatement of the Charge to Timothy (1:18–20)

1:18 The **charge** mentioned here is no doubt the charge Paul had given Timothy in verses 3 and 5 to rebuke false teachers. To encourage his **son Timothy** to carry out this important commission, the apostle reminds him of the circumstances which led to his call to Christian service.

According to the prophecies previously made concerning you seems to mean that before Paul met Timothy, a prophet had arisen in church and announced that Timothy would be used by the Lord in His service. A prophet was a spokesman for God who received revelations of God's will with regard to some particular course of action, and communicated these revelations to the church. Young Timothy was singled out by prophetic utterances and his future role as a servant of Jesus Christ was thus made known. If he should ever be tempted to lose heart or become discouraged in the work of the Lord, he should remember these **prophecies** and thus be inspired and stimulated to **wage the good warfare.**

1:19 In this warfare, he should hold **faith and a good conscience**. It is not enough just to be doctrinally accurate as to the Christian faith. One might be ever so orthodox, and yet not have **a good conscience**.

Hamilton Smith writes:

> Those who are gifted, and much before the public eye, have to beware, lest amid constant engagements, constant preaching, and public work before men, they neglect the secret life of godliness before God. Does not Scripture warn us that it is possible to preach with all the eloquence of men and angels, and yet be nothing? That which bears fruit for God, and will have its bright reward in the day to come, is the life of godliness from which all true service must flow.[4]

Some of those living in Paul's day had thrust a good conscience from them

and thus had **suffered shipwreck** as far as **the faith** was concerned. They have been likened to a foolish sailor who throws his compass overboard.

Those who had made **shipwreck** of the faith were true believers, but they simply had not maintained tender consciences. Their Christian life had started out like a gallant ship putting out to sea, but instead of returning to port with banners waving and a full cargo, they had foundered on the rocks and brought shame on themselves and their testimony.

1:20 We do not know whether **Hymenaeus and Alexander** are the ones mentioned in 2 Timothy 2:17 and 4:14. Neither do we know the nature of their blasphemy. All we are told is that they abandoned a good conscience and that they blasphemed. In the NT, **blaspheme**[5] does not always mean to speak evil of God. It might also be used to describe abusive or evil speaking against one's fellow men. It might be used to describe the lives of these men as well as the words of their lips. By making shipwreck of the faith, they had undoubtedly caused others to speak evil of the way of truth, and thus their lives were living blasphemies.

Theirs is the tragedy of once bright, effective Christians being sidetracked into error through the stifling of their consciences.

The apostle says that he **delivered** these men **to Satan**. Some scholars see in these words a simple reference to the act of excommunication. They understand them to mean that Paul had put these two men out of the local church and that this action was designed to bring them to repentance and to a restoration of fellowship with the Lord and with His people. The difficulty with this view is that excommunication was a function of the local church and not of an apostle. In 1 Corinthians 5 Paul did not excommunicate the incestuous man but counseled the Corinthians to do so.

The other major interpretation of this passage is that delivering **to Satan** was a power given to the apostles which is no longer in evidence today because there are no apostles. According to this view, the apostles had authority to turn a sinning person over **to Satan** for the infliction of physical suffering or, even in extreme cases, of death, as in the case of Ananias and Sapphira (Acts 5:1–11). The discipline here was obviously for corrective purposes — **that they may learn not to blaspheme**. It was not a question of damnation but of chastisement.

III. INSTRUCTIONS CONCERNING CHURCH LIFE (2:1–3:16)

A. Regarding Prayer (2:1–7)

Paul has concluded his first charge to Timothy concerning the false teachers, and now he moves on to the subject of prayer. It is generally agreed that this passage has to do with public prayer, although there is nothing in it that would not be equally applicable to one's private devotional life.

2:1 Prayer **for all men** is both a privilege and an obligation. It is a sheer privilege for us to have audience with God in behalf of our fellow men. And it is an obligation, too, for we are debtors to all with reference to the good news of salvation.

The apostle lists four aspects of prayer — **supplications, prayers, intercessions, and giving of thanks**. It is rather difficult to distinguish between the first three. In modern usage, **supplication** has the thought of strong and earnest pleading, but here the thought is more that of specific requests for specific needs. The word here translated **prayers** is a very general term, covering all kinds of reverent approaches to God. **Intercessions** describe those forms of petition in which we address God as our Superior in behalf of others. **Giving of thanks** describes prayer in which we rehearse the grace and kindness of our Lord, and pour out our hearts in gratitude to Him.

We might summarize the verse, then, by saying that in praying **for all men**, we should be humble, worshipful, trustful, and thankful.

2:2 Special mention is made here of **kings and all who are in authority**. These must occupy a special place in our prayers. Elsewhere, Paul has reminded

us that the authorities that exist are ordained of God (Rom. 13:1) and that they are ministers of God to us for good (Rom. 13:4).

This verse takes on special color when we remember that it was written in the days of Nero. The terrible persecutions which were inflicted on the Christians by this wicked ruler did not affect the fact that Christians should pray for their governmental heads. The NT teaches that a Christian is to be loyal to the government under which he lives, except when that government orders him to disobey God. In such a case his first responsibility is to God. A Christian should not engage in revolution or in violence against the government. He may simply refuse to obey any order that is contrary to the word of God and then quietly and submissively take the punishment.

The reason the apostle gives for praying for rulers is **that we may lead a quiet and peaceable life in all godliness and reverence**. It is for our own good that the government should be stable and that the country be preserved from revolution, civil war, turmoil, and anarchy.

2:3 That we should pray for all men, including kings and those in authority, **is good and acceptable in the sight of God**. It is **good** in itself and **acceptable in the sight of God our Savior**. The title which Paul gives to God here is significant. God's desire is for the salvation of all men. Therefore, to pray for all men is to promote the will of God in this regard.

2:4 This explains further what we have already pointed out in verse 3. **God desires all men to be saved** (Ezek. 33:11; John 3:16; 2 Pet. 3:9). Therefore, we should pray for **all men** everywhere.

This verse sets forth clearly the divine and the human aspects of salvation. The first half of the verse indicates that man must **be saved**. The verb here is passive; man cannot save himself but must **be saved** by God. This is the divine side of salvation.

In order to be saved, man must **come to the knowledge of the truth**. God does not save men against their will. He does not populate heaven with rebellious subjects. Man must come to Him who said:

"I am the Way, the Truth, and the Life." This is the human side.

From this, it should be clear that this verse does not teach universal salvation. Although God **desires** that **all men** should **be saved**, yet not all men will be saved. It was not initially God's will that the children of Israel should wander for thirty-eight years in the wilderness; yet they did it just the same. He permitted it, but it was not the pathway of blessing which He had planned for them.

2:5 The connection of this verse with what precedes is not entirely clear. However, the thought seems to be this: **God** is **one**; therefore, He is the God of all men, and prayer should be addressed to Him in behalf of all men. As the one God, He desires the salvation of all men. If He were one of many gods, He might be concerned only about His own worshipers.

Secondly, One is **Mediator between God and men**. This being so, no man can come to God in any other way. A **mediator** is a go-between, a middleman who can stand between two and communicate with both. Through Christ, Himself Man, God is enabled to approach men with forgiveness of sins. Consequently any poor sinner can approach Him, and will by no means be rejected.

Paul identifies the Mediator as **the Man, Christ Jesus**. This does not deny the deity of the Lord Jesus. In order to be the **Mediator between God and men**, He must be both God and Man. The Lord Jesus is God from all eternity, but He became Man in Bethlehem's manger. He represents the whole race of humanity. The fact that He is both God and Man is indicated in the name **Christ Jesus**. **Christ** describes Him as God's anointed One, the Messiah. **Jesus** is the name given to Him in Incarnation.

The verse effectively answers the teaching so common today that the blessed Virgin Mary or angels or saints are mediators between God and man. There is only **one Mediator**, and His name is **Christ Jesus.**

Verse 5 summarizes the messages of the OT and NT. **One God** was the message of the OT entrusted to Israel; **one Mediator** — the message of the NT entrusted to the church. As Israel failed in her responsibility by worshiping idols, so the professing church has failed in her responsibility by introducing other mediators — Mary, saints, clergy, etc.

2:6 The emphasis is on the fact that God desires the salvation of all men. Here this is further shown by the fact that Christ Jesus **gave Himself a ransom for all**. A **ransom** is a price paid to release or set another free. Notice that the **ransom** is **for all**. This means that the work of the Lord Jesus on Calvary's cross was sufficient to save **all** sinners. It does not mean that all will be saved, since man's will is also involved.

This verse is one of many which teach that the death of Christ was substitutionary. He died in behalf of **all**. Whether all will accept it is another question, but the fact remains that the redemptive work of Christ was sufficient in value **for all**.

To be testified in due time means that the testimony concerning Christ's substitutionary work was to be borne in its own time. The same God who desires the salvation of all men and provided the way of salvation for all men, has decreed that the gospel message should go out in this age in which we live. All of this is designed to demonstrate the overwhelming longing on the part of God to bless mankind.

2:7 As a final demonstration of God's desire for the salvation of all men, Paul states that he **was appointed a preacher and an apostle to the Gentiles**. Then, as now, Gentiles constituted the greater portion of the population of the world. It was not to one small segment of mankind, such as the Jews, that the apostle was sent, but rather to the Gentile nations.

He speaks of himself as **a preacher and an apostle** and **a teacher. A preacher** is literally a herald, a proclaimer of the gospel. The duties of **an apostle** may be somewhat broader — he not only preaches the gospel but plants churches, guides local churches in matters of order and discipline, and speaks with authority as one sent by the Lord Jesus Christ. **A teacher** expounds the word of God in such a manner that it will be understood by the people.

To give added emphasis to what he

is saying, Paul confirms his claim to be **a teacher of the Gentiles** by the words **"I am speaking the truth in Christ, and not lying."** The words **"in faith and truth"** may describe the faithful and honest way in which the apostle carried out his teaching ministry, but more probably they describe the contents of his teaching. In other words, he taught the Gentiles in matters pertaining to **faith** and **truth**.

B. Regarding Men and Women (2:8–15)

2:8 The subject of public prayer is now resumed, and this time our attention is directed to those who should lead the people of God in prayer. The introductory words **I desire** express Paul's active and inspired desire in this matter.

In the original language of the NT, there are two words which may be translated **men**. One word means mankind in general, whereas the other means **men** in contrast to women. It is the second word that is used here. The apostle's instruction is that public prayer should be led by **the men** rather than by the women. And it means all the men, not just the elders.

The expression **everywhere** may be taken to mean that any individual Christian may pray at any time, no matter where he may be. But since the subject here seems to be public prayer, it would be better to understand this verse as saying that wherever a mixed group of Christians is gathered together for prayer, it is **the men** and not the women who should lead in this exercise.

Three qualifications are added, applying to those who are to pray publicly. First of all, they should lift up **holy hands**. The emphasis here is not so much on the physical posture of the one praying as on his inward life. His hands should be **holy hands**. The **hands** here are figurative of the man's entire manner of life. Secondly, he should be **without wrath**. This points out the inconsistency of one who is given to displays of temper, rising in the local church to speak to God in behalf of those assembled. Finally, he should be without **doubting**. This may mean that he has faith in the ability and willingness of God to hear and answer prayer. We can summarize

these qualifications by saying that a man should exhibit holiness and purity *selfward*, love and peace *manward*, and unquestioning faith *Godward*.

2:9 Having discussed the personal requisites of the men who lead in public prayer, the apostle now turns to the things which should characterize **the women** who are in the congregation at such a time. First of all, he states that they should **adorn themselves in modest apparel, with propriety and moderation**. John Chrysostom gives a definition of **modest apparel** which can scarcely be improved upon:

> And what then is *modest apparel*? Such as covers them completely and decently, and not with superfluous ornaments; for the one is decent and the other is not. What? Do you approach God to pray with broidered hair and ornaments of gold? Are you come to a ball? a marriage-feast? a carnival? There such costly things might have been seasonable: here not one of them is wanted. You have come to pray, to ask pardon for your sins, to plead for your offences, beseeching the Lord. . . . Away with such hypocrisy![6]

Propriety means avoiding anything that would cause shame. It carries the thought of being modest and discreet. **Moderation** means that a woman will be moderate in her dress. On the one hand, she will not seek to attract attention to herself by expensive, conspicuous fashions. These might tend to provoke admiration or even jealousy from those who should be worshiping God. On the other hand, she should avoid attracting attention to herself by wearing clothes that are drab or old-fashioned. The Scriptures seem to teach a moderate, middle-of-the-road policy in regard to clothing.

Some of the excesses to be avoided are **braided hair, gold, pearls, or costly clothing. Braided hair** would not necessarily exclude simple braids, which might be very modest, but rather an elaborate adorning of the head with showy hairdos. The use of jewelry or expensive clothing as a means of self-exhibition is decidedly inappropriate at the time of prayer.

2:10 The positive side of women's adorning is brought before us in this verse. The adorning which is fitting **for**

women professing godliness is found in the performance of **good works**. Such "clothing" does not distract others from communion with God, but rather provokes such fellowship. Neither does it cause envy or jealousy in a wrong sense, but only encourages others to follow the example. **Good works** are a prominent theme in the Pastoral Epistles, forming a very necessary balance to sound doctrine.

2:11 As far as her part in public meetings of the church, **a woman** is to **learn in silence with all submission**. This is consistent with the rest of Scripture on this subject (1 Cor. 11:3–15; 14:34, 35).

2:12 When Paul says: **I do not permit a woman to teach**, he is speaking as inspired of God. This does not represent Paul's own personal prejudice, as some say. It is God who decrees that women should not have a public teaching ministry in the church. The only exceptions to this are that they are permitted to teach children (2 Tim. 3:15) and young women (Tit. 2:4). Neither is a woman **to have authority over a man**. That means that she must not have dominion over a man, **but** is **to be in silence** or quietness. Perhaps we should add that the latter part of this verse is by no means limited to the local assembly. It is a fundamental principle in God's dealings with mankind that man has been given the headship and that woman is in the place of subjection. This does not mean that she is inferior; that is certainly not true. But it does mean that it is contrary to God's will that the woman should have authority or dominion over the man.

2:13 To prove his point, Paul first of all goes to the creation of **Adam** and **Eve**. **Adam was formed first, then Eve.** The very order of the creation was significant. By creating man **first**, God intended him to be the head, the one who would exercise direction, the one who would have authority. The fact that woman was created second means that she should be in submission to her husband. By basing his argument on the order of creation, Paul rules out any thought that this is a matter of local culture.

2:14 The second proof refers to the entrance of sin into the human race. Instead of approaching **Adam** directly, the serpent went to Eve with his temptations and lies. According to God's intention, Eve should not have acted independently. She should have gone to Adam and put the matter before him. Instead of that, she allowed herself to be **deceived** by Satan and **fell into transgression**.

In this connection, it is noteworthy that false teachers today usually visit homes when the wife is most apt to be there alone, that is, when the husband will most probably be away at work.

Adam was not deceived. It appears that he sinned with his eyes open. There are those who suggest that when he saw that his wife had already fallen into sin, he wanted to maintain his unity with her, and so he himself plunged into sin. But the Scriptures do not state this. They merely state that **the woman** was **deceived**, but that **Adam was not.**

2:15 This is one of the most difficult verses in the Pastoral Epistles, and many explanations have been offered. Some think that it is a simple promise from God that a Christian mother **will be saved** from death in the physical act of **childbearing**. However, this is not always true, because some godly, devoted Christians have died in the act of bringing life into the world. Others think that **childbearing** (literally, "*the* childbearing") refers to the birth of the Messiah, and that women are saved through the One who was born of a woman. However, this scarcely seems to satisfy the sense of the passage, since men are saved in the same way. No one could reasonably suggest that the verse means that a woman receives eternal salvation by virtue of becoming a mother of children; this would be salvation by works, and works of a most unusual nature!

We would suggest the following as the most reasonable interpretation of the passage. First of all, salvation in this context does not refer to the salvation of her *soul*, but rather to the salvation of her *position* in the church. From what Paul has just said in this chapter, the impression might arise in the minds of some that the woman has no place in God's purposes and counsels; she is reduced to a nonentity. But Paul would dispute this claim.

Although it is true that no public ministry in the church is assigned to her, she does have an important ministry. God has decreed that woman's place is in the home, and more specifically in the ministry of raising children for the honor and glory of the Lord Jesus Christ. Think of the mothers of the leaders in the Christian church today! These women never mounted a public platform to preach the gospel, but in raising their children for God, they have been truly **saved** as far as position and fruitfulness for God are concerned.

Lilley writes:

> She shall be saved from the results of sin and be enabled to maintain a position of influence in the Church by accepting her natural destination as a wife and mother, provided this surrender is further ratified by bringing forth the fruit of sanctified Christian character.[7]

It may be asked at this point: "What about those women who never marry?" The answer is that in this passage God is dealing with women in general. The majority of Christian women do marry and bear children. As far as the exceptions are concerned, there are many other useful ministries committed to them and yet which do not involve public teaching or having authority over men.

Note the qualifying clause at the end of verse 15: **She will be saved in childbearing, if they continue in faith, love, and holiness, with self-control**. It is not exactly an unconditional promise. The thought is that if the husband and wife maintain a consistent Christian testimony, honor Christ in the home, and raise their children in the fear and admonition of the Lord, then the woman's position **will be saved**. But if the parents live careless, worldly lives, and neglect the training of their children, then these children may be lost to Christ and the church. In such a case, the woman does not achieve the true dignity which God has ordained for her.

Let no one think that because woman's ministry is private and in the home that it is any less important than that which is more public. It has been truly said: "The hand that rocks the cradle rules the world." In a coming day, at the Judgment Seat of Christ, it is faithfulness that will count, and this is something which can be exhibited in the home as well as in the pulpit.

C. Regarding Elders and Deacons (3:1–13)

3:1 The second **faithful saying** in 1 Timothy has to do with the work of bishops in the local church. **A bishop** is a Christian man of mature experience and understanding who assists in exercising godly care over the spiritual life of a local fellowship. He does not rule by lording it over God's heritage, but rather he leads by his spiritual example.

Today, "bishop" signifies a church official who exercises authority over many local congregations. But invariably in the NT there were several bishops in one church (Acts 14:23; 20:17; Phil. 1:1; Jas. 5:14).

A bishop is the same as an overseer. The same word translated **bishop** in this verse is translated "overseer" in Acts 20:28. A bishop, or overseer, is the same as an elder. The same men who are called elders in Acts 20:17 are called overseers in Acts 20:28 (cf. also Tit. 1:5 and 1:7). Elders are the same as presbyters, for although the latter word is not found in the NT, the English word "elder" translates the Greek word *presbuteros*. Thus, the words "bishop," "overseer," "elder," and "presbyter" all refer to the same person.

Actually, the word translated "elder" (*presbuteros*) is sometimes used to describe an older man, and not necessarily one who is a leader in the church (1 Tim. 5:1, Gk.), but at most other times "elder" describes a man recognized in a local church as one who exercises pastoral care among the people of God.

The NT envisages bishops or elders in every local church (Phil. 1:1). However, it would not be accurate to say that a church could not exist without bishops. From Titus 1:5, it seems clear that there were young churches in Crete in which elders had not as yet been recognized.

Only the Holy Spirit of God can make a man an elder. This is clear in Acts 20:28. The Holy Spirit lays a burden on a man's heart to take up this important work and also equips him for it. It is impossible to make a man a bishop by voting him into office or by ordaining him. The responsibility of the local assembly is to recognize those men in its midst who have been made elders by God the Holy Spirit (1 Thess. 5:12, 13). It is true that we find the appointment of elders in the book of Titus, but there it was simply a matter of Titus' singling out those men who had the qualifications of elders. At that time, the Christians did not have the NT in printed form, as we have it today. Therefore, they did not know what the exact qualifications for elders were. So Paul sent Titus to them with this information and instructed Titus to set apart those men who had been raised up by the Spirit of God for the work.

The recognition of elders by a local assembly might be quite informal. It often happens that Christians instinctively know who their elders are because they have acquainted themselves with the qualifications of elders in 1 Timothy 3 and Titus 1. On the other hand, the recognition of elders may be a more formal procedure. A local church might gather together for the express purpose of publicly recognizing the elders. In this case, the procedure usually is to read the pertinent Scripture passages, to have them expounded, and then to have the local Christians designate whom they consider to be the elders in that assembly. The names are then announced to the entire congregation. If a church does not have qualified elders, then its only resource is to pray that the Lord will raise up such men in days to come.

The Scripture does not specify any *number* of elders for a local church, though there *is always a plurality*. It is simply a matter of how many men respond to the leading of the Holy Spirit in this matter.

If a man desires the position of a bishop, he desires a good work. There is the tendency to think this is a dignified, ecclesiastical office, entailing little or no responsibility, whereas overseership is actually humble service among the people of God; it is **work.**

3:2 The qualifications of a bishop are given in verses 2–7. They stress four main prerequisites: personal character, the witness of the home, teaching apti-

tude, and a measure of experience. These are God's standards for any who would exercise spiritual leadership in the local church. Some argue today that no one can measure up to these standards. However, this is not true. Such an argument robs the Sacred Scriptures of their authority and permits men to take the place of a bishop who have never been qualified by the Holy Spirit.

A bishop, then, must be blameless. This means that no charge of serious wrong can be sustained against him. It does not mean that he is sinless, but rather that if he does commit some fault, he makes it right with both God and man. He must be irreproachable, not only having an untarnished reputation, but deserving it.

Secondly, he must be **the husband of one wife**. This requirement has been understood in several ways. Some suggest that it means that a bishop must be married. The argument is that a single man would not have the proper breadth of experience to deal with family problems as they arise. If this expression means that a bishop must be married, then it must also be argued in verse 4 than an elder must have children as well, following the same line of reasoning.

Others think that **the husband of one wife** means that if a bishop's first wife died, then he does not marry again. This is a very strict interpretation that might cast reflection on the holiness of the marriage relationship.[8]

A third interpretation is that the words mean that a bishop must not be divorced. This view has considerable merit, although it scarcely seems to be a complete explanation.

Another view is that a bishop must not have been guilty of any unfaithfulness or irregularity in his marriage. His moral life must be above question. This is certainly true, whatever else the passage might mean.

A final explanation is that this means that a bishop may not be a polygamist. This may seem a strange explanation to us, but it has considerable merit. On mission fields today, it often happens that a polygamist gets saved. Perhaps at the time of his conversion, he had four wives. He subsequently asks for baptism and reception into the local church.

What is the missionary to do? Someone answers that the man should put away three of his wives. However, this action causes grave difficulty. For one thing, he would ask which ones he should put away. He loves them all and is providing a home for them all. Also, if he should put away three wives, they would have no means of livelihood, and some of them might be plunged into prostitution in order to eke out an existence. God's solution of a problem like this would never be to remedy one sin by many worse sins. Christian missionaries in many places solve the problem by allowing the man to be baptized and to be received into the local church, but he can never be an elder in the church as long as he is a polygamist.

Temperate refers not only to matters of food and drink, but also to the avoidance of extremes in spiritual matters.

Sober-minded means that this man is not giddy or frivolous. He is serious, earnest, discerning, and discreet. He realizes that as "dead flies putrefy the perfumer's ointment, and cause it to give off a foul odor; so does a little folly to the one respected for wisdom and honor" (Eccl. 10:1).

A bishop must be **of good behavior**, that is, he must be well-ordered in his habits.

Hospitable signifies that he is a lover of strangers. His home is open to saved and unsaved alike, and he seeks to be a blessing to all who come beneath his roof.

An elder must be **able to teach**. As he visits those with spiritual problems, he must be able to turn to the Scriptures and explain the will of God in such matters. He must be able to feed the flock of God (1 Pet. 5:2) and to use the Scriptures in refuting those who bring false doctrines (Acts 20:29–31). It does not necessarily mean that a bishop must have the gift of teaching, but rather that in his house-to-house ministry, as well as in the assembly, he can set forth the doctrines of the faith and rightly divide the Word of Truth, and is ready and keen to do it.

3:3 The expression **given to wine** means addicted to alcoholic drinks. The bishop must not be a man who overindulges in **wine** and thus causes quarrels, that is, abusive brawlings.

Not violent means that this man does not use physical violence on another. For instance, if he is a master, he never hits his servant.

The words **not greedy for money** are not found in some ancient manuscripts, but are in the majority.[9] The love of money will bear evil fruit in the church as well as in the world.

An elder must be **gentle**. In his work in the church, he will need forbearance, patience, and a spirit of yieldedness.

He must **not** be **quarrelsome**, contentious, and arguing about every little thing. He does not insist on his own rights but is even-tempered and congenial.

A bishop must **not** be **covetous**, that is, a lover of money. Here the emphasis is on the word "lover." He is concerned with the spiritual life of the people of God and refuses to be distracted by a strong desire for material things.

3:4 In order to be recognized as an overseer, a man must rule **his own house well, having his children in submission** to him. This qualification would apply as long as a man's children are living in his home. After they have gone off and started to raise their own families, there would no longer be the same opportunity for demonstrating this subjection. If a man **rules his own house well**, he will avoid the extremes of undue harshness and of unrighteous leniency.

3:5 The argument here is clear. Unless **a man** shows fitness **to rule his own** home, **how will he** ever expect to **take care of the church of God**? In his own home, the number of persons is comparatively small. They are all related to him, and most of the members are very much younger than he. In the church, on the other hand, the numbers are apt to be much greater, and with this increase in numbers there goes a corresponding diversity of temperaments. It is obvious that if a man is unfit to rule in the smaller sphere, he would be clearly disqualified for the larger.

Verse 5 is important because it defines the work of an elder. It is to **take care of the church of God**. Notice it does not say "to rule" the church of God. An elder is not a despot, or even a benevolent ruler, but rather one who guides the people of God as a shepherd guides the sheep.

The only other time the expression "take care of" is used in the NT is in the story of the Good Samaritan (Luke 10:34). The same tender, compassionate care shown by the Good Samaritan to the victim of the robbers should be shown by the elder who cares for the church of God.

3:6 Not a novice. A recent convert to Christianity, or a person who is young in the faith, is not qualified to be a bishop. The work requires men of experience and understanding in the faith. The danger is that a novice might become **puffed up with pride** and then **fall into the same condemnation as the devil. Condemnation** of **the devil** does not mean the judgment which Satan brings on a man, but rather the judgment which fell on Satan himself because of his pride. He sought a high position for which he was not qualified, and as a result, he was brought low.

3:7 A bishop is a man who **must have a good** reputation in the community. **Those who are outside** refers to unsaved neighbors. Without this **good testimony**, he becomes subject to the accusations of men **and the snare of the devil**. The accusations may come from believers and unbelievers alike. **The snare of the devil** is the trap which Satan lays for those whose lives are not consistent with their profession. Once he has caught men in this trap, he holds them up to ridicule, scorn, and contempt.

3:8 The apostle now moves on from bishops to **deacons**. In the NT, a deacon is simply one who serves. It is generally understood that a deacon is one who cares for the temporal affairs of the local church, whereas bishops care for its spiritual life. This understanding of the duties of deacons is largely based on Acts 6:1–5, where men were appointed to care for the daily distribution of funds to widows in the church. Actually, the noun "deacon" is not used in this passage, but the verb form is used in verse 2: "It is not desirable that we should leave the word of God and serve (literally 'deacon') tables."

The qualifications for **deacons** are

very similar to those of bishops, although not quite as strict. One notable difference is that it is not required that a deacon should be apt to teach.

Deacons must be reverent, dignified, and worthy of respect. They must **not** be **double-tongued**, that is, they must not give conflicting reports to different persons or at different times. They must be consistent.

They must **not** be **given to** excess **wine**. The NT does not forbid the use of wine for medicinal purposes, or as a beverage in those countries where the water supply is polluted. But even though the moderate use of wine is permitted, the Christian must also consider his testimony in regard to this matter. Whereas in some countries it might be perfectly all right for a Christian to drink wine without having any adverse effect on his testimony, in other countries it might cause an unbeliever to stumble, should he see a Christian indulging in wine. Thus, although the use of wine might be lawful, it might not be expedient.

Deacons must **not** be **greedy for money**. As has been mentioned, one of the functions of a deacon might be to handle the funds of the local church. This exposes him to special temptation if he has a lust for money. He might be tempted to help himself. Judas was not the last treasurer to betray his Lord for mere money!

3:9 Deacons must hold **the mystery of the faith with a pure conscience**. This means that they must be sound in doctrine and in life. They must not only know the truth; they must live it. **The mystery of the faith** is a description of the Christian **faith**. Many of the doctrines of Christianity were kept secret throughout the OT period but were then revealed by the apostles and prophets of the NT. That is why the word **mystery** is used here.

3:10 Deacons should **first be tested**, as in the case of elders. This means that they should be observed for some time and perhaps even given some minor responsibilities in the local church. As they prove themselves to be trustworthy and faithful, then they can be advanced to greater responsibilities. **Then let them serve as deacons**, or simply, "let them minister." As with bishops, the emphasis is not so much on an ecclesiastical office as it is on service for the Lord and His people.

Whenever a man has been **found blameless** in his personal life and in his public life, he may be allowed to serve as a deacon. **Blameless** here refers particularly to the qualifications that have just been mentioned.

At this point it may be well to mention a few of the men who might be considered as deacons in a local church. The treasurer certainly would be one, and also the correspondent or secretary, the Sunday School superintendent, and the ushers.

3:11 This verse apparently refers to the **wives** of deacons, or to the wives of bishops and deacons. The **wives** of those who are given responsibilities in the church should certainly be women of Christian testimony and integrity, such as will help their husbands in their important work.

However, the same word used for "wives" may also be translated "women." This translation would permit the additional interpretation of women deacons. There were such women in the early church, e.g. Rom. 16:1, where Phoebe is spoken of as a servant (same word as "deacon") of the church at Cenchrea.[10] A clue as to the type of service which these women performed in the church is given in Romans 16:2, where Paul says of Phoebe that "she has been a helper of many and of myself also."

Whichever interpretation one accepts, these women **must be reverent**, dignified, and sober. They must **not** be **slanderers**, spending their time gossiping about others, passing on false and malicious reports designed to injure the reputation of others. They must be **temperate**, exhibiting self-control and restraint.

Finally, they must be **faithful in all things**. This might not only mean true to the Christian faith, but also dependable, loyal, and worthy of confidence. They should be able to keep personal confidences and family secrets.

3:12 The apostle now reverts to the subject of **deacons**. He first specifies that they must be **husbands of one wife**. The

various interpretations of this expression have been given in connection with verse 2 of this chapter. It is sufficient here to say that, like the bishops, the deacons must be above reproach in their married life.

They, too, must rule **their children and their own houses well**. The NT looks on failure to do this as a defect of Christian character. This does not mean that men must be autocratic and imperious, but it does mean that **their children** should be obedient and a testimony to the truth.

3:13 The clause **those who have served well as deacons obtain for themselves a good standing** is well illustrated in the cases of Philip and Stephen. In Acts 6:5, these two men are named among the seven deacons who were appointed. The work to which they were appointed was to handle the distribution of money to the widows in the church. As they were faithful in these duties, it seems that the Spirit of God advanced them to greater spheres of service; for, as the book of Acts continues, we find Philip serving as an evangelist and Stephen as a teacher. Having **served well as deacons**, they were promoted and given **a good standing** in the eyes of the local church. A person who faithfully discharges an assignment, even if it is a small matter, will soon come to be respected and esteemed for reliability and devotion.

In addition, Philip and Stephen were granted **great boldness in the faith which is in Christ Jesus**. This doubtless means that they were given great liberty in witnessing for Christ, in teaching, and in prayer. This was certainly true of Stephen in his remarkable address before he was martyred.

D. Regarding Conduct in the Church (3:14–16)

3:14 The apostle had written the preceding with the hope of seeing Timothy soon. **These things**, however, might refer not only to what precedes but also to what follows.

3:15 Paul recognized the possibility of being **delayed**, or even of his not getting to Ephesus at all. Actually, we do not know whether he ever was able to rejoin Timothy in Ephesus. And so if he tarried long, he wanted Timothy **to know how** believers **ought to conduct** themselves **in the house of God**.

In the preceding verses, Paul has been describing how bishops, deacons, and their wives ought to behave. Now he explains how Christians in general should behave in **the house of God**.

The house of God is here defined as **the church of the living God, the pillar and ground of the truth**. In the OT, God dwelt in the tabernacle and temple, but in the NT, He dwells in **the church**. It is spoken of as **the church of the living God**, and this contrasts it to a temple in which there are lifeless idols.

The church is spoken of as **the pillar and ground of the truth**. A pillar was not only used to support a structure, but oftentimes a pillar was set up in a public marketplace and notices were posted on it. It was thus a proclaimer. The church is the unit on earth which God has chosen to proclaim and display His **truth**. It is also the **ground of the truth**. Here **ground** carries the thought of foundation or supporting structure. This pictures the church as that which is entrusted with the defense and support of the truth of God.

3:16 This is a difficult verse. One difficulty is in discerning just how it fits in with what has preceded. One suggestion is that here we have an epitome of the truth, of which the church is the pillar and ground (v. 15). Another is that this verse gives the example and power of godliness which Paul insists is an integral part of proper behavior in the house of God. J. N. Darby said:

> This is often quoted and interpreted as if it spoke of the mystery of the Godhead, or the mystery of Christ's Person. But it is the mystery of godliness, or the secret by which all real godliness is produced — the divine spring of all that can be called piety in man. . . . Godliness springs from the knowledge of the incarnation, death, resurrection and ascension of the Lord Jesus Christ. . . . This is how God is known; and from abiding in this flows godliness.[11]

When Paul says that **the mystery of godliness** is **great**, he does not mean that it is very mysterious but that the previously unknown truth concerning the Person and work of the Lord Jesus is very marvelous and wonderful.

God[12] **was manifested in the flesh** refers to the Lord Jesus, and particulary to His Incarnation. True **godliness** was manifest in the flesh for the first time when the Savior was born as a Babe in Bethlehem's manger.

Does **justified in the Spirit** mean "justified in His own human spirit"? Or does it mean "justified by the Holy Spirit"? We understand it to mean the latter. He was vindicated by the Holy **Spirit** of God at His baptism (Matt. 3:15–17), transfiguration (Matt. 17:5), resurrection (Rom. 1:3, 4), and ascension (John 16:10).

The Lord Jesus was **seen by angels** at His birth, temptation, His agony in the Garden of Gethsemane, resurrection, and ascension.

From the day of Pentecost onward, He has been **preached among the Gentiles**. The proclamation has reached not only the Jewish people but the farthest corners of the earth.

Believed on in the world describes the fact that some from almost every tribe and nation have trusted the Lord Jesus. It does not say "believed on *by* the world." Although the proclamation has been worldwide, yet its reception has been only partial.

Received up in glory is generally agreed to refer to His Ascension to heaven after the work of redemption had been completed, and to His present position there. Vincent points out that it reads "*received up in* (not *into*) glory." It means "with attendant circumstances of pomp or majesty, as we say of a victorious general."

Some make this list of events chronological. For instance, they say that **manifested in the flesh** refers to the incarnation; **justified in the Spirit** refers to Christ's death, burial, and resurrection; **seen by angels** describes His ascension into heaven; **preached among the Gentiles** and **believed on in the world** are the events that followed His ascension; and, finally, **received up in glory** refers to a coming day when all His redeemed are gathered, raised from the dead, and received up with Him to glory. Then, and only then, will **the mystery of godliness** be complete, according to this view.

However, we see no reason that the order *must* be chronological. Some believe we have in this verse a fragment of an early Christian hymn. If so, it is rather similar to our gospel song "One Day":

Living, He loved me; dying, He saved me;
Buried, He carried my sins far away;
Rising, He justified freely forever:
One day He's coming — oh, glorious day!
                              – Charles H. Marsh

IV. APOSTASY IN THE CHURCH (4:1–16)

A. Warning Against the Impending Apostasy (4:1–5)

4:1 There are two ways in which **the Spirit** might be thought of as speaking **expressly**. First of all, what Paul is about to say was certainly given to him by divine revelation. But it might also mean that throughout the Scriptures, and particularly in the NT, it is **expressly** taught that the **latter times** will be characterized by departure from the faith.

Latter times means "in later times," periods of time subsequent to that time when the apostle was writing.

Some will depart from the faith. The word **some** is characteristic of 1 Timothy. What was a minority in this Epistle seems to have become the majority in 2 Timothy. The fact that these people **depart** or fall away **from the faith** does not mean that they were ever saved, but simply that they had professed to be Christians. They knew about the Lord Jesus Christ and had been told that He was the only Savior. They professed for a time to follow Him, but then they apostatized from the faith.

One can scarcely read this section without thinking of the rise of cults in our own day. The way these false systems have spread is accurately described here. A great part of their membership is made up of persons who were formerly in so-called Christian churches. Perhaps at one time these churches had been sound in the faith, but then they drifted toward the social gospel. The cultist teachers came along offering a more positive message, and these professing Christians were ensnared.

They give willing **heed** or assent to **deceiving spirits and doctrines of demons. Deceiving spirits** is used here in a figurative sense to describe the false teachers, indwelt by evil spirits, who deceive the unwary. **Doctrines of demons** does not mean teachings *about* demons, but rather **doctrines** which are inspired *by* **demons** or have their source in the demon world.

4:2 The word **hypocrisy** suggests "wearing a mask." How typical this is of the false cultists! They try to hide their true identity. They do not want people to know the system with which they are identified. They masquerade by using Bible terms and singing Christian hymns. Not only are they hypocrites, but they are liars as well. Their teaching is not according to the truth of God's word; they know this, and purposely deceive the people.

Their conscience is **seared with a hot iron.** Perhaps early in their lives their conscience had been tender, but they suppressed it so often and sinned against the light so much that now their conscience has become insensitive and hardened. They no longer have any scruples about contradicting the word of God and teaching things they know are untrue.

4:3 Two of the doctrines of demons are now stated. The first is the teaching that it is wrong **to marry.** This is directly contrary to the word of God. God Himself instituted marriage, and He did this before sin ever entered the world. There is nothing unholy about marriage, and when false teachers forbid marriage, they are attacking what God ordained.

An illustration of this teaching is the law **forbidding** certain priests and nuns **to marry.** However, even more directly, this verse refers to the teaching of spiritists called spiritual affinity by which, according to A. J. Pollock, "the marriage tie is derided, and in its practical working, men and women are seduced from their lawful partners to form unholy and unlawful links with their so-called spiritual affinities." We might also mention the attitude of Christian Science toward marriage. Its founder, Mrs. Eddy, thrice married, wrote:

Until it is learned that God is the Father of all, marriage will continue. . . . Matrimony, which was once a fixed fact among us, must lose its present adherence.[13]

The second teaching of demons is **to**

abstain from certain foods. Such teaching is found among spiritists, who claim that the eating of animal flesh hinders one in contacting the spirits. Also, among Theosophists and Hindus, there is a horror of sacrificing any kind of life because they believe that the soul of a man may come back and live in an animal or other creature.

The pronoun which may refer to marriage and to foods. Both were created by God to be shared by us with thanksgiving. He did not intend them only for the unregenerate but for those who believe and know the truth.

4:4 Every creature (or creation) of God is good. Both foods and marriage are creations of God, and are not to be refused if . . . received with thanksgiving. He instituted marriage for the propagation of human life (see Gen. 1:28), and food for the sustaining of life (Gen. 9:3).

4:5 The word of God sets apart both food and marriage for man's use. Food is thus sanctified in Genesis 9:3; Mark 7:19; Acts 10:14, 15; and 1 Corinthians 10:25, 26. Marriage is set apart in 1 Corinthians 7 and Hebrews 13:4.

They are also sanctified through prayer. Before partaking of a meal, we should bow our heads and give thanks for the food (see Matt. 14:19; Acts 27:35). By this act we are asking the Lord to sanctify the food to strengthen our bodies so that we might serve Him more acceptably. Before entering into marriage we should pray that God will bless the union for His glory, for the blessing of others, and for the good of the bride and groom.

It is a good testimony for Christians to give thanks for meals when in the presence of unsaved people. The blessing should not be showy or long, but neither should we try to conceal the fact that we are thanking God for our food.

B. Positive Instructions in View of the Impending Apostasy (4:6–16)

4:6 By instructing the brethren about these things mentioned in verses 1–5, Timothy will be a good minister of Jesus Christ. As mentioned previously, the word minister means "servant." He will be a servant, nourished in the

words of faith and of the good doctrine which he has carefully followed up to this time.

4:7 In this section, Paul is thinking of Christian service as a form of athletic contest. In verse 6, he spoke of the suitable diet for one who is serving Christ — he should be nourished in the words of the faith and of the good doctrine. In verse 7, he speaks of exercise that has godliness as its aim.

The apostle advises Timothy to reject profane and old wives' fables. He is not to combat them or spend a lot of time on them. Rather, he is to disdain them, to treat them with contempt. Old wives' fables make us think of Christian Science, which was founded by a woman, seems to appeal especially to elderly women, and teaches fables instead of truth.

Instead of wasting time on myths and fables, he should exercise himself to godliness. Such exercise involves reading and studying the Bible, prayer, meditation, and witnessing to others. Stock says, "There is no such thing as drifting into godliness; the 'stream of tendency' is against us." There must be exercise and effort.

4:8 Here two kinds of exercise are contrasted. Bodily exercise has certain values for the body, but these values are limited and of short duration. Godliness, on the other hand, is good for man's spirit, soul, and body, and is not only for time but for eternity as well. As far as this life is concerned, godliness yields the greatest joy, and as far as the life which is to come is concerned, it holds promise of bright reward and of capacity to enjoy the glories of that scene.

4:9 It is generally agreed that this verse refers back to the saying about godliness. The fact that godliness is of widespread and eternal value is a faithful saying and worthy of all acceptance. This is the third faithful saying in this Epistle.

4:10 For to this end we both labor and suffer reproach.[14] The end mentioned is the life of godliness. Paul states that this is the great goal toward which he exerts his finest efforts. This would not seem a worthy aim in life to unbelievers. But the Christian sees beyond the passing things of this world and sets his hope on **the living God**. This hope can never be disappointed for the very reason that He is **the living God, who is the Savior of all men, especially of those who believe. God** is **the Savior of all men** in the sense that He preserves them in the daily providences of life. But He **is** also **the Savior of all men** in the sense pointed out previously — that He has made adequate provision for the salvation **of all men**. He is the Savior of **those who believe** in a special way because they have availed themselves of His provision. We might say that He is the potential Savior of all men and the actual Savior of those who believe.

4:11 **These things** probably refers to what Paul has been saying in verses 6–10. Timothy is to **command and teach** such precepts, continually bringing them before the people of God.

4:12 At the time of this Letter, Timothy was probably between thirty and thirty-five years of age. In contrast with some of the elders in the assembly at Ephesus, he would be a comparatively young man. That is why Paul says here, **"Let no one despise your youth."** This does not mean that Timothy is to put himself on a pedestal and consider himself immune from criticism. Rather, it means he is to give nobody occasion to condemn him. By being **an example to the believers**, he is to avoid the possibility of justified criticism.

In word refers to Timothy's conversation. His speech should always be that which should characterize a child of God. He should not only avoid such speech as is distinctly forbidden, but also such as would not be edifying for his hearers.

In conduct refers to one's entire demeanor. Nothing about his deportment should cause reproach on the name of Christ.

In love suggests that **love** should be the motive for conduct, as well as the spirit in which it is carried out and the goal toward which it strives.

In spirit is lacking in most modern versions and commentaries that follow the critical text. However, the words do occur in the traditional and majority texts. Guy King decries the fact that *enthusiasm*, his insightful understanding of the phrase, is a:

> . . . quality strangely lacking from the make-up of many Christians. Plenty of enthusiasm for a football match, or for an election campaign, but so little of it for the service of GOD. How the magnificent enthusiasm of the Christian Scientists, the Jehovah's Witnesses, the Communists should put us to shame. Oh, for the flaming zeal again that once the church knew. This fine spirit will greatly help Timothy as he seeks to consolidate the position and to advance the line.[15]

In faith probably means "in faithfulness," and carries the idea of dependability and steadfastness.

Purity should characterize not only his acts but his motives as well.

4:13 This verse probably refers primarily to the local church, rather than to Timothy's personal life. He should **give attention** to the public **reading** of the Scriptures, **to exhortation**, and **to doctrine** or teaching. There is a definite order here. First of all, Paul emphasizes the public **reading** of the word of God. This was especially necessary at that time, since the distribution of the Scriptures was very limited. Few people had a copy of the word. After reading the Scriptures, Timothy was to exhort the believers on the basis of what had been read, and then he was to teach the great truths of the word of God. This verse reminds us of Nehemiah 8, and especially verse 8: "So they read distinctly from the book, in the Law of God; and they gave the sense, and helped them to understand the reading."

However, we should not leave out the thought of private devotions from this verse. Before Timothy could exhort and teach the word of God to others, he should first make it real in his own life.

4:14 We are not told exactly what **gift** had been given to Timothy — whether evangelist, pastor, or teacher. The general tenor of these Epistles would lead us to think that he was a pastor-teacher. However, we do know that **the gift . . . was given** to him **by prophecy with the laying on of the hands of the eldership**. First of all, it **was given** along with or **by prophecy**.

This simply means that a prophet in a local church at one time stood up and announced that the Spirit of God had imparted some **gift** to Timothy. The prophet did not confer the gift, but announced it. This was accompanied by **the laying on of the hands of the eldership**. Again we would emphasize that the presbyters, or elders, did not have the power to bestow the gift on Timothy. Rather, by laying their hands on him, they signified public recognition of what the Holy Spirit had already done.

The process is seen in Acts 13. In verse 2, the Holy Spirit singled out Barnabas and Saul for a specific work. Perhaps it was through a prophet that this word was transmitted. Then the local brethren fasted and prayed and laid their hands on Barnabas and Saul and sent them away (v. 3).

This same policy is followed by many local Christian communities today. When it becomes evident to the elders that a man has been given some gift of the Holy Spirit, they commend that man to the work of the Lord, indicating their confidence in him and their recognition of the Spirit's work in his life. Their commendation does not bestow a gift on him but merely recognizes that this has already been done by the Spirit of God.

There is a difference between what happened when the elders laid their hands on Timothy, as mentioned here, and when Paul laid his hands on Timothy, as described in 2 Timothy 1:6. In the former case, the action was in no way official, nor was it responsible for Timothy's gift. It only expressed fellowship with him in his work. In the latter case, Paul was actually the apostolic channel through whom the gift was imparted.

4:15 The words **meditate on these things** can be translated "cultivate" or "take pains with these things." This may well be the meaning here, since the next words are **give yourself entirely to them**. Paul is encouraging Timothy to give himself undividedly and undistractedly to the work of the Lord. He should be all-out in his efforts. In this way, his **progress** will **be evident to all**. Paul does not want Timothy to hit a plateau in his Christian service and then settle down into a comfortable rut. Rather, he wants

him to be always advancing in the things of the Lord.

4:16 Notice the order here. Timothy is first to **take heed to** himself **and** then **to the doctrine**. This emphasizes the importance of the personal life in any servant of Christ. If his life is wrong, he might be ever so orthodox in his doctrine, but it is of no avail. A. W. Pink has well said: "Service becomes a snare and an evil if it be allowed to crowd out worship and the cultivation of one's own spiritual life."

By continuing in the things Paul has been writing about, that is, reading, exhortation, and instruction, Timothy would **save both** himself **and those who** heard him. The word **save** here has nothing to do with the salvation of the soul. The chapter opened with a description of the false teachers who were causing havoc among the people of God. Paul is telling Timothy that by faithful adherence to a godly life and to the word of God, he **will save** himself from these false teachings and he will also rescue his hearers from them as well.

V. SPECIFIC INSTRUCTIONS CONCERNING VARIOUS CLASSES OF BELIEVERS (5:1–6:2)

A. Different Age Groups (5:1, 2)

5:1 This verse introduces a section on Timothy's behavior toward members of the Christian family among whom he would be working. Being younger and perhaps more aggressive, Timothy might be tempted to become impatient and resentful with some of the **older** men; hence, the admonition that he is **not** to **rebuke an older man** sharply, **but exhort him as a father**. It would be improper for him, as a younger man, to assault such a person with verbal blows.

There might also be the danger of this young servant of Christ manifesting an overbearing attitude toward **the younger men**. And so Paul tells him that he is to treat the younger men **as brothers**; he is to be just like one of them and not adopt a domineering attitude toward them.

5:2 Older women are to be regarded **as mothers** and treated with the dignity, love, and respect that is their due.

Purity should characterize all his dealings with **younger women**. Not only should he avoid what is positively sinful, but he should also steer clear of acts of indiscretion or any behavior which might have the appearance of evil.

B. Widows (5:3–16)

5:3 From verses 3–16, Paul takes up the subject of **widows** in the local church and the treatment which should be given to them.

First of all, the church should **honor** those **who are really widows. Honor** here not only carries the idea of respect but also includes the thought of financial help. A real widow is one who has no other means of support but is wholly cast upon the Lord for her maintenance. She has no living relatives who will care for her.

5:4, 5 A second class of **widows** is described in this verse. These are the ones who have **children or grandchildren**. In such cases, the **children** should learn to show practical godliness at home by repaying their mother (or grandmother) for all that she has done for them. The verse teaches clearly that **piety** begins **at home**. It is a poor testimony to the Christian faith to speak loudly about one's religion and then to neglect those who are linked to us by ties of nature!

It is **acceptable**[16] in the sight of **God** for Christians to take care of loved ones who are otherwise without support. In Ephesians 6:2, the Apostle Paul clearly teaches: "Honor your father and mother, which is the first commandment with promise." As mentioned previously, a real **widow** is one who is without financial resources and who must constantly look to **God** for the supply of her daily bread.

5:6, 7 In contrast to the godly widow of verse 5 is the one who gives herself to **pleasure**. There is some disagreement as to whether this woman is a true believer or a mere professor. We believe that she is a genuine Christian — but backslidden. She is **dead** as far as communion with God or usefulness for Him are concerned. Timothy is to warn such widows against living in **pleasure**

and is also to teach Christians to care for those who are related to them and are destitute.

5:8 The seriousness of failing to **provide for** one's **own** relatives, **and especially for those of** one's own immediate **household**, is emphasized here. It constitutes a denial of **the faith**. The Christian faith consistently maintains that those who are true believers should care for one another. When a Christian fails to do this, he denies by his actions the very truths which Christianity teaches. Such a person **is worse than an unbeliever** for the simple reason that many unbelievers show loving care for their own relatives. Also, a Christian can thus bring reproach on the name of the Lord in a way that an unbeliever cannot do.

5:9 It appears from this verse that a definite roll or list of names was kept in each local church, indicating those widows who were cared for by the church. Paul here specifies that no **widow** should be thus enrolled **under sixty years** of age.

The expression **the wife of one man** raises the same problem as the similar expression in connection with bishops and deacons. Similar interpretations of the expression have been given. It doubtless means that her married life must have been above reproach, without suspicion of moral wrong.

5:10 In order to be enrolled, a widow must also have a reputation for having performed such **good works** as should characterize a spiritual believer.

The words **if she has brought up children** doubtless means that she must have brought them up in such a manner as to reflect creditably on herself and her Christian home. There would be no virtue in simply rearing children, but only in bringing them up well.

Another mark of a godly widow is that she has shown hospitality to **strangers**. Over and over again in the NT, the grace of hospitality is mentioned and commended.

Washing the feet of visitors was the duty of a slave. So here the thought doubtless is that the widow has performed very menial services for her fellow Christians. But it might also mean to have **washed the saints' feet** in a spiritual way, with the washing of water by the word. This would not mean public ministry, but simply visiting in homes and using the word of God in such a way as to cleanse believers from defilement contracted in their daily walk.

Relief of **the afflicted** refers to acts of mercy performed for those who are sick, sorrowing, or otherwise in distress.

In short, in order to be enrolled on the list of a local assembly, this widow must have **diligently followed every good work**.

5:11 This is a difficult verse, but the meaning seems to be as follows: In general, it would be a mistake to make **younger widows** a charge of the local church. Being young, they would probably **desire to marry** again. This would not be wrong in itself, but the desire might become so strong at times that one of these young widows might even marry an unbeliever. The apostle speaks of this as to **grow wanton against Christ**. When it comes to a choice between marrying a pagan or remaining unmarried out of love to Christ and obedience to His word, the young widow is apt to **marry**. This would, of course, bring reproach on the local church which supported her.

5:12 Condemnation ("damnation," KJV) here does not mean eternal perdition, but simply that she has this judgment or **condemnation** for having **cast off** her **first faith**. At one time she professed the greatest loyalty and devotion to the Lord Jesus Christ, but now when the opportunity comes along to marry one who does not love Christ, she forgets her initial vows or pledges to Christ and goes off with the unbeliever, unfaithful to the Heavenly Bridegroom.

Paul is not criticizing young widows for marrying. As a matter of fact he urges them to marry (v. 14). What he finds fault with is their spiritual decline, their throwing divine principles to the wind in order to get a man.

5:13 For the local church to assume full financial responsibility for the younger widows might encourage them **to be idle**, with its associated evils. Instead of attending to their own responsibilities, they might become **gossips and busybodies**, occupying themselves with subjects that are none of their concern.

No action taken by a local church should ever encourage such behavior because, as mentioned before, it reflects unfavorably on the Christian testimony.

5:14 Paul **therefore** states that as a general principle, it is preferable that **younger widows marry, bear children**, and maintain a Christian home that is above reproach. Of course, Paul realized that it would not always be possible for every young widow to remarry. The initiative must ordinarily be taken by the man. But he is simply laying down a general principle to be followed whenever possible.

The adversary, or Satan, is always on the lookout for charges to hurl against the Christian testimony, and Paul seeks to guard against the possibility of there being any such legitimate causes **to speak reproachfully**.

5:15 What the apostle has been saying about young widows is not mere conjecture or speculation. It had **already** happened. **Some** had **turned aside after Satan**, in the sense that they had listened to the voice of **Satan** and had chosen an unbelieving partner in disobedience to the word of the Lord.

5:16 The subject now reverts to the obligation of relatives to care for their own. **If any believing man**[17] **or woman has** a widow in the family who needs support, then the believer should assume this responsibility so that **the church** will be free to care for those who are actually destitute and without near relatives.

This entire passage, verses 3–16, tells what the church *must* do under certain circumstances, not what it *may* do if it feels there are extenuating circumstances and if it is able to do so. The length of the paragraph shows that it is an important subject in the mind of the Holy Spirit, and yet it is one which is greatly neglected in most church circles today.

C. Elders (5:17–25)

5:17 The rest of this chapter deals with elders. First of all, Paul lays down the rule that **elders who rule well** should **be counted worthy of double honor**. Rule might better be translated "take the lead" (Darby). It is not a question of control, but of example. Such elders are **worthy of double honor. Honor** might mean respect, but it also includes the idea of financial reimbursement (Matt. 15:6). **Double honor** includes both ideas. First of all, he is **worthy of** respect from God's people because of his work, but also, if his time is devoted to this work fully, he is also **worthy of** financial help. **Those who labor in the word and doctrine** are probably the ones who spend so much time in preaching and teaching that they are not able to carry on regular employment.

5:18 Two Scriptures are introduced here to prove the statement that the elder is worthy of recompense. The first is Deuteronomy 25:4, and the second is taken from Luke 10:7. This verse is especially interesting in connection with the inspiration of the Scriptures. Paul takes one verse from the OT and one from the NT, places them side by side on the same level, and refers to them both as **the Scripture**. It is obvious from this that Paul considered the NT writings as of equal authority with the OT.

These Scriptures teach that **an ox** which is used in the harvesting process should not be deprived of a share of **the grain**. Also, a **laborer** is entitled to a portion of the fruit of his labor. So it is with elders. In spite of the fact that their work might not be physical, yet they are worthy of the support of God's people.

5:19 Since elders occupy a position of responsibility in the church, they become a special target of Satan's attack. For this reason the Spirit of God takes steps to guard them against false accusations. The principle is laid down that no disciplinary action should be taken **against an elder** unless the charge can be corroborated by the testimony of **two or three witnesses**. Actually, this same principle applies to disciplining any church member, but it is emphasized here because there was a special danger of elders being unjustly accused.

5:20 In the case of an elder who had been found guilty of **sinning** in such a way as to harm the testimony of the church, such a man should be publicly rebuked. This action impresses all believers with the seriousness of sin in connection with Christian service and serves as a strong deterrent in the lives of others.

Some commentators believe that verse 20 does not apply especially to elders, but to all Christians. Certainly the principle is applicable to all Christians, but the setting of the verse seems to link it directly with elders.

5:21 In dealing with matters of discipline in the local church, there are two dangers to be avoided. The first is **prejudice**, and the other is **partiality**. It is easy to be unfavorably prejudiced against a man and thus to prejudice the case. Also, it is all too easy to show **partiality** toward a man because of his wealth, position in the community, or his personality. Thus Paul solemnly charges Timothy in the sight of **God and the Lord Jesus Christ and** also in the sight of **the elect angels**, that he should obey these instructions without judging a matter before all the facts are known or without showing favor toward a man simply because he is a friend or well-known. Each case must be judged as in the sight of **God and the Lord Jesus**, and also in the sight of the **angels**. The angels are observers of the world in which we live, and they should see perfect righteousness in matters of discipline in the church. **The elect angels** are those who have not been involved in sin or rebellion against God, but kept their first estate.

5:22 When prominent men identify themselves with a local church, there is sometimes the tendency to advance them quickly to positions of responsibility. Here Timothy is warned against haste in recognizing newcomers. Neither should he identify himself with men whose characters are unknown to him, lest in so doing he **share in** their **sins**. Not only is he to **keep** himself morally clean but also **pure** in the sense of free from association with the sins of others.

5:23 It is not clear how this verse connects with the preceding. Perhaps the apostle wisely anticipated that Timothy's involvement in congregational problems and difficulties would have an adverse effect on his stomach. If so, Timothy would not be the first or the last to suffer from this affliction! More probably Timothy was the frequent victim of contaminated water that is still common in many parts of the world. The apostle's advice, **"No longer drink only water,"** means that Timothy should not use water to the exclusion of **a little wine**.

Paul advises the use of **a little wine for** his **stomach's sake** and his **frequent infirmities**. This verse is dealing only with the medicinal use of wine, and should never be stretched to condone its excessive use.

There is no doubt that it is real **wine** that is referred to here and not just grape juice. It is doubtful that grape juice even existed at this time, since grape juice is made by pasteurization, a process not yet known. The fact that it was real wine is implied in the expression **a little wine**. If it were not real wine, then there would be no sense in stipulating that only **a little** should be used.

This verse also sheds light on the subject of divine healing. Although Paul, as an apostle, doubtless had the power to heal all kinds of diseases, yet he did not always use it. Here he justifies the use of medicines in a case of stomach ailment.

5:24 In this verse the apostle seems to go back to the discussion in verse 22, where he had been warning Timothy against undue haste in laying hands on other men. Verses 24 and 25 explain this further.

Some men's sins are clearly evident and are so obvious that they may be compared to a trumpeter, blaring on in front of the man, announcing him to be a sinner, all the way **to** his **judgment**. But that is not the case with all. **Some men** who are sinners are not exposed until some time **later**.

In the first class, we might think of the drunkard who is known as such by the whole community. On the other hand, there is the husband who is carrying on a secret love affair with another woman. The community might not know about this at the time, but oftentimes the whole scandal is revealed at a **later** date.

5:25 It is somewhat similar in the case of good people. Some obviously seem to be good at once. Others are more retiring and modest, and it is only with the passing of time that their actual goodness becomes known. Even if we cannot see good, there may be some which will come to light later. The lesson to draw from all this is that we should not judge a person on first acquaintance,

but rather allow time for true character to show itself.

D. Bondservants and Masters (6:1, 2)

6:1 The conduct of slaves is now brought before us. They are spoken of as **bondservants** who **are under the yoke**, that is, **the yoke** of slavery. The apostle, first of all, speaks to slaves who have unsaved **masters**. Should slaves in such a case act insolently toward their masters? Should they rebel or run away? Should they do as little work as possible? On the contrary, they should **count their own masters worthy of all honor**. This means that they should give them due respect, work obediently and faithfully, and in general seek to be a help rather than a hindrance. The great motive for such diligent service is that the testimony for Christ is involved. If a Christian slave were to act rudely or rebelliously, then the master would blaspheme **the name of God** and the Christian faith. He would conclude that believers were a worthless lot.

The history of the early church reveals that Christian slaves generally commanded a higher price on the slave market than unbelievers. If a master knew that a certain slave on the auction block was a Christian, he would generally be willing to pay more for that slave, since he knew that the slave would serve him faithfully and well. This is high tribute to the Christian faith.

This verse reminds us that no matter how low a person's position may be on the social scale, yet he has every opportunity for witnessing for Christ and bringing glory to His name.

It has often been pointed out that the institution of slavery is not openly condemned in the NT. However, as the teachings of Christianity have spread, the abuses of slavery have been abolished.

Every true believer should realize that he is a bondslave of Jesus Christ. He has been bought with a price; he no longer belongs to himself. Jesus Christ owns him — spirit, soul, and body, and deserves the very best he has.

6:2 This verse deals with slaves **who have believing masters**. Doubtless there would be a very great temptation for such slaves to **despise** their masters. It is not at all unlikely that when the local church met together on Lord's Day evening for the breaking of bread (Acts 20:7), there would be Christian masters and Christian slaves seated around the table — all **brethren** in Christ Jesus. But the slaves were not, on this account, to think that the social distinctions of life were thereby abolished. Just because a master was a Christian did not mean that the slave did not owe him honor and service. The fact that the master was both a believer and a **beloved** brother should influence the slave to serve him faithfully.

Christian masters are here spoken of not only as faithful (**believers**) **and beloved**, but also as **those who are benefited**. This is generally taken to mean that they, too, are sharers in the blessing of salvation. However, the words might also be understood to mean that since both slaves and masters are interested in doing good, they should serve together, each trying to help the other.

The words **teach and exhort these things** doubtless refer to the preceding instructions to Christian slaves. The present-day application would be, of course, to the employer-employee relationship.

VI. FALSE TEACHERS AND THE LOVE OF MONEY (6:3–10)

6:3 Paul now turns his attention to those who might be disposed to teach new and strange doctrines in the church. These men do **not consent to wholesome words**. **Wholesome** here means health-giving words. Such were the **words** which were spoken by **our Lord Jesus Christ** when He was here on earth and which are found in the Gospels. Such also is the entire body of teaching found in the NT. This is **doctrine which accords with godliness** in the sense that it encourages and promotes godly behavior.

6:4 Such men are **proud**. They profess to have superior knowledge, but actually they know **nothing**. As Paul mentioned previously, they do not know what they are talking about.

They dote about **disputes and arguments over words**. The word **obsessed** literally means to be sick. These men are not spiritually healthy, and instead of teaching healthful words, as in the previous verse, they teach words that produce sick saints. They raise various questions that are not spiritually edifying and strive **over words**.

Since the things they talk about are not matters of Bible doctrine, there is no way of settling them decisively. As a result, their teaching stirs up **envy, strife, reviling**, and **evil suspicions**. Lenski says:

> In their questions and word battles, one envies the other because of the proficiency which he develops; there is strife as they vie with and contradict each other; blasphemies result, namely, denunciations couched in sacred words.[18]

6:5 These **wranglings** come from **men of corrupt**, that is, diseased, **minds**. Lenski comments trenchantly:

> The diseased state of the mind consists in a corruption and a disintegration — the mental faculties no longer function normally in the moral and the spiritual field. They do not react normally to the truth. All reality and its presentation in verity ought to produce the reaction of acceptance, especially the saving divine gospel realities should have this effect; all lies, falsities, perversions ought to produce rejection, most of all those in the moral and the spiritual field. . . . When it meets "the truth," the corrupted mind sees and seeks only objections; when it meets what differs from this truth, it sees and seeks reasons for accepting this difference.[19]

Also, these men are **destitute of the truth**. At one time, they had acquaintance with the truth, but because of their rejection of the light, they have been deprived of what **truth** they once had.

These men **suppose that godliness is a means of gain**. Apparently, they choose to be religious teachers as a profession in which they are well paid for a minimum of work. "They make the holiest of vocations a money-gaining craft."

This not only reminds us of the hireling shepherds who pose as Christian ministers but have no real love for the truth, but it also makes us think of the commercialism which has become so common in Christendom — the sale of indulgences, games of lottery, bazaars and sales, etc. **From such withdraw yourself.**[20] We are commanded to steer clear of such ungodly professors.

6:6 Just as the previous verse gave a false definition of gain, so this verse gives the true meaning of the word. The combination of **godliness with contentment is great gain.** Godliness without contentment would give a one-sided testimony. Contentment without godliness would not be distinctively Christian at all. But to have real **godliness** and at the same time to be satisfied with one's personal circumstances is more than money can buy.

6:7 This chapter bears a close resemblance to the teachings of the Lord Jesus in the Sermon on the Mount. Verse 7 reminds us of His instruction that we should trust our heavenly Father for the supply of our needs.

There are three times in life when we have empty hands — at birth, at the time we come to Jesus, and at death. This verse reminds us of the first and the last. **We brought nothing into the world, and it is certain that we can carry nothing out.**

Before Alexander the Great died, he said: "When I am dead, carry me forth on my bier, with my hands not wrapped in cloth, but laid outside, so that all may see that they are *empty.*" Bates comments on this:

> Yes, those hands which once wielded the proudest scepter in the world; which once held the most victorious sword; which once were filled with silver and gold; which once had power to save or to sign away life, were now EMPTY.[21]

6:8 Contentment consists of satisfaction with the basic necessities of life. Our heavenly Father knows that we need **food** and covering and has promised to supply these. Most of an unbeliever's life revolves around **food and clothing.** The Christian should seek first the kingdom of God and His righteousness, and God will see that he does not lack the essentials of life.

The word translated **clothing** here means covering and can include a place to live as well as clothes to wear. We should be **content** with **food, clothing,** and a place to live.

6:9 Verses 9–16 deal directly with those who have an insatiable **desire to be rich.** Their sin lies not in being wealthy, but in coveting to be so. **Those who desire to be rich** are people who are not content with food, clothes, and lodging, but are determined to have more.

Desiring **to be rich** leads a man **into temptation.** In order to achieve his goal, he is enticed to use dishonest and often violent methods. Such methods include gambling, speculation, fraud, perjury, theft, and even murder. Such a man also falls into **a snare** or a trap. The desire becomes so strong that he cannot deliver himself from it. Perhaps he promises himself that when he reaches a certain figure in the bank account he will stop. But he cannot. When he reaches that goal, he has the desire for more. The desire for money also brings with it cares and fears, which entangle the soul. People who determine to become wealthy fall **into many foolish . . . lusts.** There is the desire to "keep up with the Joneses." In order to maintain a social level in the community, they are often driven to sacrifice some of the really worthwhile values in life.

They also fall into **harmful lusts.** Greed for wealth causes men to endanger their health and jeopardize their souls. Indeed, that is the end toward which they are drifting. They become so occupied with material things that they become drowned **in destruction and perdition.** In their ceaseless quest for gold, they neglect their never-dying souls. Barnes warns:

> The destruction is complete. There is a total ruin of happiness, of virtue, of reputation, and of the soul. The ruling desire to be rich leads on a train of follies which ruins everything here, and hereafter. How many of the human family have thus been destroyed![22]

6:10 **The love of money is a root of all kinds of evil.** Not all evil in the universe springs from the **love of money.** But it is certainly one of the great sources of many varieties of **evil.** For instance, it leads to envy, strife, theft, dishonesty, intemperance, forgetfulness of God, selfishness, embezzlement, etc.

It is not money in itself which is spoken of, but **the love of money.** Money might be used in the service of the Lord in a variety of ways where only good would result. But here it is the inordinate desire for **money** that leads to sin and shame.

One particular evil of the love of money is now mentioned, that is, a wandering **from the** Christian **faith**. In their mad striving after gold, men neglect spiritual things, and it becomes difficult to tell whether they were ever really saved at all.

Not only did they lose their grip on spiritual values, but they **pierced themselves through with many sorrows**. Think of the **sorrows** connected with the greed for riches! There is the tragedy of a wasted life. There is the sorrow of losing one's children to the world. There is the grief of seeing one's wealth vanish overnight. There is the fear of meeting God, either unsaved or at least empty-handed.

Bishop J. C. Ryle summarizes:

> Money, in truth, is one of the most *unsatisfying* of possessions. It takes away some cares, no doubt; but it brings with it quite as many cares as it takes away. There is trouble in the getting of it. There is anxiety in the keeping of it. There are temptations in the use of it. There is guilt in the abuse of it. There is sorrow in the losing of it. There is perplexity in the disposing of it. Two-thirds of all the strifes, quarrels, and lawsuits in the world arise from one simple cause — *money!*[23]

The richest man in the world at one time owned oil wells, refineries, tankers, and pipelines; also hotels, a life insurance company, a finance company, and aircraft companies. But he surrounded his 700-acre estate with bodyguards, vicious dogs, steel bars, searchlights, bells, and sirens. In addition to being afraid of planes, ships, and crackpots, he feared disease, old age, helplessness, and death. He was lonely and gloomy and admitted that money could not buy happiness.[24]

VII. CLOSING CHARGES TO TIMOTHY (6:11–21)

6:11 Timothy here is addressed as a **man of God**. This title was often given to prophets in the OT and described a man who was godlike in his behavior.

It may indicate that Timothy had the gift of prophecy. The opposite of **man of God** is "man of sin," as found in 2 Thessalonians 2. The man of sin will be the very embodiment of sin. Everything about him will make men think of sin. Timothy is to be a **man of God**, a man who will make men think of God and glorify God.

In his service for Christ, Timothy should **flee** from conceit (v. 4), impurity (v. 5), a discontented spirit (vv. 6–8), foolish and harmful lusts (v. 9), and the love of money (v. 10). He should cultivate Christian character — the only thing he can take with him into heaven. Here the elements of Christian character are given as **righteousness, godliness, faith, love, patience, gentleness.**

Righteousness speaks of justice and integrity in our dealings with our fellow men. **Godliness** is Godlikeness. **Faith** might also mean faithfulness, or dependability. **Love** speaks of our affection for both God and our fellow men. **Patience** has been defined as steadfastness or endurance under trial, whereas **gentleness** is a kindly and humble disposition.

6:12 Not only is Timothy to *flee* and to *follow*, but he is also to **fight**. Here the word **fight** does not mean to combat, but rather to contend. The word is not taken from the battlefield but from the athletic contest. **The good fight** spoken of here is the Christian **faith** and the race connected with it. Timothy is to run well in that race. He is to **lay hold on eternal life**. This does not mean that he is to strive for salvation. That is already his possession. But here the thought is to live out in daily practice the **eternal life** which was already his.

Timothy had been called to this **eternal life** at the time of his conversion. Also, he had **confessed the good confession in the presence of many witnesses**. Perhaps this refers to his baptism, although it might also include his whole subsequent testimony for the Lord Jesus Christ.

6:13 The apostle now delivers a solemn charge to Timothy, and he does so in the presence of the two greatest Witnesses. First of all, the charge is given **in the sight of God who gives life to all things**. Perhaps in writing to Timothy,

Paul was conscious that one day he might have to lay down his life for his confession of the Lord Jesus. If that is the case, then it is good for this young warrior to remember that God is the One **who gives life to all things**. Even if men succeed in killing Timothy, yet his faith is in the One who raises the dead.

Secondly, the charge is given in the sight of **Christ Jesus**. He is the great example of **the good confession. Before Pontius Pilate**, He **witnessed the good confession**. Though this may refer to all the Savior's words and actions before the Roman governor, it perhaps points particularly to His statement in John 18:37: "For this cause I was born, and for this cause I have come into the world, that I should bear witness to the truth. Everyone who is of the truth hears My voice." This unfaltering confession was held before Timothy as an example to be followed in bearing witness to the truth.

6:14 Timothy is charged to **keep this commandment**. Some think this refers to the command to fight the good fight mentioned above. Others suggest it might refer to the entire charge which Paul has given to Timothy in this Epistle. Others think of the **commandment** as the message of the gospel, or the revelation of God as given in the word of God. We believe it is the charge to maintain the truth of the Christian faith.

The expressions **without spot, blameless** apply to Timothy rather than to the command. In keeping the **commandment**, Timothy is to maintain a testimony that is **without spot** and that will be unrebukable.

In the NT, **our Lord Jesus Christ's appearing** is constantly held before the believer. Faithfulness to Christ in this world will be rewarded at the Judgment of Christ. These rewards, in turn, will be manifested when the Lord Jesus comes back to the earth to set up His kingdom. It is then that the results of faithfulness or unfaithfulness will be clearly revealed.

6:15 Bible scholars are not agreed as to whether the pronouns in this verse and the next refer to God the Father or to the Lord Jesus Christ. Taken by itself, verse 15 seems to refer to the Lord Jesus, because He is definitely called **King of kings and Lord of lords** in Revelation 17:14. On the other hand, verse 16 seems to refer particularly to God the Father.

In any case, the meaning of verse 15 seems to be this: When the Lord Jesus Christ comes back to reign upon the earth, men will realize **who is the blessed and only Potentate**. The appearance will manifest who is the true **King**. At the time Paul wrote to Timothy, the Lord Jesus was the rejected One, and He still is. But a day is coming when it will be clearly shown that He is **the King** over all those who reign and He is **the Lord** over all those who rule as **lords**.

Blessed means not only worthy to be praised, but One who has in Himself the fullness of all blessing.

6:16 At the appearing of the Lord Jesus, men will also realize that it is God **alone** who **has immortality** or deathlessness. This means that He is the only One who has it *inherently*. Angels have had immortality conferred upon them, and at the resurrection, believers will receive bodies that are immortal (1 Cor. 15:53, 54), but God has **immortality** in Himself.

God is next spoken of as **dwelling in unapproachable light**. This speaks of the bright, shining glory which surrounds the throne of God. Man in his natural condition would be vaporized by this splendor. Only those who are accepted in the Beloved One and complete in Christ can ever approach God without being destroyed.

In His essential being, **no man has seen** God **or can see** Him. In the OT, men saw appearances of God, known as theophanies. In the NT, God has perfectly revealed Himself in the Person of His beloved Son, the Lord Jesus Christ.

However, it is still true that God is invisible to mortal eyes.

To this One, **honor and everlasting power** are due, and Paul closes his charge to Timothy with this ascription of homage to God.

6:17 Paul spoke earlier at length about those who desired to be rich. Here he deals with **those who are** already **rich**. Timothy should **command** them **not to be haughty**. This is a temptation to the wealthy. They are apt to look down on those who do not have a great deal of money as being uncouth, uncultured, and not very clever. This, of course, is not necessarily true. Great riches are not a sign of God's blessing in the NT, as they were in the OT. Whereas wealth was a token of divine favor under the law, the great blessing of the new dispensation is affliction.

The rich should not **trust in**, literally, "the uncertainty of **riches**." Money has a way of sprouting wings and flying away. Whereas great resources give the appearance of providing security, the fact is that the only sure thing in this world is the word of God.

Therefore, the rich are exhorted to trust **in the living God, who gives us richly all things to enjoy**. One of the great snares of riches is that it is difficult to have them without trusting in them. Yet this is really a form of idolatry. It is a denial of the truth that God is the One **who gives us richly all things to enjoy**. This latter statement does not condone luxurious living, but simply states that God is the Source of true enjoyment, and material things cannot produce this.

6:18 The Christian is reminded that the money he possesses is not his own. It is given to him as to a steward. He is responsible to use it for the glory of God and for the well-being of his fellow men. He should use it in the performance of **good works** and be **willing to share** it with the needy.

John Wesley's rule of life was, "Do all the good you can, by all the means you can, in all the ways you can, in all the places you can, at all the times you can, to all the people you can, as long as ever you can."

Willing to share expresses the idea that he should be ready to use it wherever the Lord may indicate.

6:19 This verse emphasizes the truth that it is possible for us to use our material things in such a way in this life that they will reap **eternal** dividends. By using our funds in the work of the Lord at the present time, we are **storing up . . . a good foundation for the time to come**. In this way, we **lay hold on** the **life** which is life indeed.

6:20 Now we come to Paul's final exhortation to **Timothy**. He is encouraged to **guard what was committed to** him. This probably refers to the true

doctrines of the Christian faith. It is not here a question of Timothy's soul or of his salvation, but rather of the truth of the gospel of the grace of God. Like money deposited in a bank, the truth entrusted to Timothy was to be preserved "entire and whole and unharmed."

He is to avoid **the profane and idle babble and contradictions of what is falsely called knowledge. Idle babble** or chatter is empty talk about matters which are not profitable.

Paul realized that Timothy would encounter a great deal of teaching which posed as true knowledge but which was actually opposed to the Christian revelation. Bishop Moule writes:

> The Gnostics of Paul's day claimed to lead their disciples "past the common herd of mere *believers* to a superior and gifted circle who should *know* the mysteries of being, and who by such *knowing* should live emancipated from the slavery of matter, ranging at liberty in the world of spirit."[25]

From all such Timothy should turn away.

This would refer, in our day, first of all to false cults, such as "Christian Science." This system claims to be Christian in character and also claims to have true **knowledge**, but it is **falsely** so-**called**. It is neither *Christian* nor *science*!

This verse may also be applied to many forms of natural science,[26] as taught in our schools today. Actually, no true finding of science will ever contradict the Bible, because the secrets of science were placed in the universe by the same One who wrote the Bible, God Himself. But many so-called facts of science are in reality nothing but unproved theories. Any such hypotheses which contradict the Bible should be rejected.

6:21 Paul realized that some professed Christians had been taken up with these false teachings and had **strayed concerning the faith**. These closing verses bring before us the great dangers of so-called intellectualism, rationalism, modernism, liberalism, and every other "ism" which disregards or waters down Christ.

Grace be with you. This benediction is Paul's "trademark," because only

God's **grace** can keep His people on the "strait and narrow" way. ▸**Amen**

ENDNOTES

Introduction to Pastoral Epistles

[1] Albert Barnes, *Notes on the New Testament: Thessalonians, Timothy, Titus, Philemon*, p. 289.

1 Timothy

[1] (Intro to 1 Timothy) Quoted from *L'Eglise chrétienne*, p. 95, by George Salmon in *A Historical Introduction to the Study of the Books of the New Testament*, p. 413.

[2] (1:8) Guy King, *A Leader Led*, p. 25.

[3] (1:16) William Kelly, *An Exposition of the Two Epistles to Timothy*, p. 22.

[4] (1:19) Hamilton Smith, further documentation unavailable.

[5] (1:20) The Greek word *blasphēmeō* (*defame, blaspheme*) is used for both God and man. Our English derivative is used almost exclusively for God and sacred things.

[6] (2:9) John Chrysostom, quoted by Alfred Plummer in *The Pastoral Epistles*, p. 101.

[7] (2:15) J. P. Lilley, *"The Pastoral Epistles,"* p. 94.

[8] (3:2) Christians who hold this view stress the elder's loyalty to the one woman implied in the Greek construction: "a one-woman-kind-of-man."

[9] (3:3) Since deacons must not be money-lovers (3:8), it seems unlikely that Paul would have omitted this quality for the even more responsible elders.

[10] (3:11) Probably it had not yet become a church *office* for women at this early date. See note in *Ryrie Study Bible, NKJV*, p. 1850.

[11] (3:16) J. N. Darby, "Notes of a Lecture on Titus 2:11–14," *The Collected Writings of J. N. Darby*, VII:333.

[12] (3:16) The sacred names of God, Christ, the Spirit, etc., were abbreviated in ancient mss. The Greek abbreviation for *God* looks exactly like the word for "who" plus a short horizontal stroke that differentiates a *theta* from an *omicron* and another stroke above the word to show it is an abbreviation. The mss. read variously "God" (TR and majority text),

"who" (NU) and "which." We accept the traditional reading of the majority of mss., followed by the KJV and NKJV.

[13] (4:3) Mary Baker Eddy, *Science and Health with Key to the Scriptures*, pp. 64, 65.

[14] (4:10) The critical (NU) text reads "we labor and strive."

[15] (4:12) King, *Leader*, p. 79.

[16] (5:4) Both the oldest and the majority of mss. lack "good and" before "acceptable." The shorter reading is no doubt original.

[17] (5:16) The omission of the believing *man* from this verse in the NU text is probably accidental. It seems highly unlikely that Paul would write only of those widows being cared for by believing *women*.

[18] (6:4) R. C. H. Lenski, *The Interpretation of St. Paul's Epistles to the Thessalonians, to Timothy, to Titus and to Philemon*, p. 700.

[19] (6:5) *Ibid*, pp. 701, 702.

[20] (6:5) The NU text omits this sentence.

[21] (6:7) Edward Herbert Bates, *Spiritual Thoughts from the Scriptures of Truth*, p.160.

[22] (6:9) Albert Barnes, *Notes on the New Testament: Thessalonians, Timothy, Titus, Philemon*, p. 199.

[23] (6:10) J. C. Ryle, *Practical Religion*, p. 215.

[24] (6:10) From news reports about the late Howard Hughes.

[25] (6:20) H. C. G. Moule, *Studies in II Timothy*, p. 91.

[26] (6:20) The Latin word *scientia* simply means "knowledge." The English derivative "science" (1611 text) now has a much narrower meaning, hence NKJV's change.

BIBLIOGRAPHY

(Pastoral Epistles)

Bates, Edward Herbert. *Spiritual Thoughts from the Scriptures of Truth*. London: Pickering & Inglis, n.d.

Bernard, J. H. *The Pastoral Epistles*. Cambridge: University Press, 1899.

Erdman, Charles R. *The Pastoral Epistles of Paul*. Philadelphia: Westminster Press, 1923.

Fairbairn, Patrick. *Commentary on the Pastoral Epistles*. Edinburgh: T. & T. Clark, 1874.

Guthrie, Donald. *The Pastoral Epistles*, (TBC). Grand Rapids: Wm. B. Eerdmans Publishing Co., 1957.

Hiebert, D. Edmond. *First Timothy*. Chicago: Moody Press, 1957.

_____. *Second Timothy*. Chicago: Moody Press, 1958.

_____. *Titus and Philemon*. Chicago: Moody Press, 1957.

Ironside, H. A. *Addresses, Lectures, Expositions on Timothy, Titus, and Philemon*. New York: Loizeaux Bros., 1947.

Kelly, William. *An Exposition of the Epistle of Paul to Titus*. London: Weston, 1901.

_____. *An Exposition of the Two Epistles to Timothy*, 3d Ed. Oak Park, IL: Bible Truth Publishers, n.d.

Kent, Homer A. *The Pastoral Epistles*. Chicago: Moody Press, 1958.

King, Guy H. *A Leader Led: A Devotional Study of I Timothy*. Fort Washington, Pa.: Christian Literature Crusade, 1944.

_____. *To My Son: An Expositional Study of II Timothy*. Fort Washington, Pa.: Christian Literature Crusade, 1944.

Lilley, J. P. *"The Pastoral Epistles."* Handbooks for Bible Classes. Edinburgh: T. & T. Clark, 1901.

Lock, Walter. *A Critical and Exegetical Commentary on the Pastoral Epistles* (*ICC*). Edinburgh: T. & T. Clark, 1924.

Moule, H. C. G. *Studies in II Timothy*. Grand Rapids: Kregel Publications, 1977.

Plummer, Alfred. *The Pastoral Epistles*. New York: George H. Doran Company, n.d.

Smith, Hamilton. *The Second Epistle to Timothy*. Wooler, Northumberland, England: Central Bible Hammond Trust Ltd., n.d.

Stock, Eugene. *Plain Talks on the Pastoral Epistles*. London: R. Scott, 1914.

Van Oosterzee, J. J. *"The Pastoral Letters."* *Lange's Commentary on the Holy Scriptures*. Vol. 23. Grand Rapids: Zondervan Publishing House, n.d.

Vine, W. E. *Exposition of the Epistles to Timothy*. London: Pickering & Inglis, 1925.

Wuest, Kenneth S. *The Pastoral Epistles in the Greek New Testament*. Grand Rapids: Wm. B. Eerdmans Publishing Co., 1953.

THE SECOND EPISTLE TO TIMOTHY

Introduction

"The Second Epistle to Timothy . . . is the expression of his [Paul's] heart, who outside Palestine, had, under God, founded and built the assembly of God on earth, and it was written in sight of its failure, and its departure from the principles on which he had established it."
— J. N. Darby

I. Unique Place in the Canon

The last words of famous people are generally cherished by those who loved the individuals. While 2 Timothy does not constitute literally Paul's last words, it is his last known writing to the Christians, originally sent to his beloved young lieutenant, Timothy.

Sitting in his dank dungeon in Rome, with only a hole in the ceiling for light, and awaiting execution by beheading, the spiritual, intelligent, and tender-hearted apostle, now aged and worn out from his long and arduous race for God, pens a final appeal to hold firmly to the truth and life that Timothy has been taught.

Like a number of "Second" Epistles, 2 Timothy deals with false teachers and the apostates of the last days. One cannot help but think that much of the frontal attack on the authenticity of 2 Timothy (and even more so of 2 Peter) is because the skeptical religious leaders who write these negative theories are themselves convicted of using religion as a cloak, the very crime about which Paul forewarns us (3:1-9).

No matter what some may say, 2 Timothy is much needed, and only too authentic!

II. Authorship

See the Introduction to the Pastoral Epistles for a discussion of 2 Timothy's authorship.

III. Date

Second Timothy was written from prison (traditionally the Mamertime Prison in Rome, still displayed to tourists). As a Roman citizen Paul could not be thrown to the lions or crucified, but "merited" execution with a sword by decapitation. Since he was killed under Nero, who died June 8, 68, the date for 2 Timothy is likely restricted to sometime between the autumn of 67 and the spring of 68.

IV. Theme[†]

The theme of 2 Timothy is well expressed in 2:15: "Be diligent to present yourself approved to God, a worker who does not need to be ashamed, rightly dividing the word of truth." In contrast to 1 Timothy, where collective, congregational conduct is emphasized, here individual responsibility and behavior are prominent. This theme may be stated as "Individual Responsibility in a Time of Collective Failure."

There is much collective failure in the professing church in this Letter. There has been great departure from the faith and from the truth. How does this affect the individual believer? Is he excused from seeking to hold to the truth and live a godly life? The answer of 2 Timothy is a decided *No!* "Be diligent to present yourself approved. . . ."

The situation of young Daniel in the court of Babylon (Dan. 1) illustrates this.

[†]*See p. ii.*

Because of the prolonged wickedness of the Israelites, he and a number of others had been taken captive to Babylon by Nebuchadnezzar. They were deprived of all the outward forms of the Jewish religion — sacrifices, priestly ministry, temple worship, etc. Indeed, these were soon to be entirely suspended when a few years later Jerusalem was destroyed and the entire nation was taken into captivity. Did Daniel, therefore, say to himself, "I might as well forget the Law and the Prophets and accommodate myself to the practices, standards, and morals here at Babylon"? History records the bright, glowing answer in his remarkable life of faith in circumstances seemingly so adverse.

Thus, too, the message of 2 Timothy speaks to the individual child of God who finds the collective church testimony of this day a far cry from the NT simplicity and holiness in which it began. He or she is still held responsible to "live godly in Christ Jesus" (2 Tim. 3:12).

OUTLINE

I. INTRODUCTORY GREETINGS TO TIMOTHY (1:1–5)

II. EXHORTATIONS TO TIMOTHY (1:6–2:13)
  A. To Fidelity (1:6–18)
  B. To Endurance (2:1–13)

III. FIDELITY VERSUS APOSTASY (2:14–4:8)
  A. Fidelity to True Christianity (2:14–26)
  B. The Coming Apostasy (3:1–13)
  C. The Man of God's Resource in View of the Apostasy (3:14–4:8)

IV. PERSONAL REQUESTS AND REMARKS (4:9–22)

Commentary

I. INTRODUCTORY GREETINGS TO TIMOTHY (1:1–5)

1:1 **Paul** introduces himself at the outset of the Letter as **an apostle of Jesus Christ**. He had been commissioned to special service by the glorified Lord. This appointment was not by men or through men, but directly through **the will of God**. Also, Paul speaks of his apostleship as being **according to the promise of life which is in Christ Jesus**. God has made **a promise** that all who believe **in Christ Jesus** will receive eternal **life**. Paul's call to be an **apostle** was in harmony with this **promise**. In fact, if there had been no such promise, there would have been no need of an apostle like Paul.

As Vine puts it: "It was according to the divine purpose that life, which was in Christ Jesus in the eternal past, should be given to us. It was consistent with this purpose that Paul should become an apostle."[1]

V. Paul Flint expounds the five references to life in this Epistle as 1:1, the *promise* of life; 1:10, the *presentation* of life; 2:11, the *participation* of life; 3:12, the *pattern* of life; and 4:1, the *purpose* of life.

1:2 **Timothy** is addressed as **a beloved son**. It cannot be definitely proved that Timothy was actually converted through the ministry of Paul. Their first recorded meeting is found in Acts 16:1 where Timothy is described as already being a disciple before Paul came to Lystra. At any rate, the apostle looked on him as **a beloved son** in the Christian faith.

As in 1 Timothy, Paul's greeting consists of **grace, mercy, and peace**. It was pointed out in the commentary on 1 Timothy that when writing to churches, Paul characteristically wishes for them grace and peace. When writing to Timothy, he adds the word **mercy**. Guy King has suggested that grace is needed for every service, mercy for every failure, and peace for every circumstance. Someone else has said, "Grace to the worthless, mercy to the helpless, and peace to the restless." Hiebert defines **mercy** as "the self-moved, spontaneous loving-kindness of God which causes Him to deal in compassion and tender affection with the miserable and distressed."[2]

These blessings flow **from God the Father and Christ Jesus our Lord**. Here is another instance where Paul honors *the Son* just as he honors the **Father**.

1:3 In his characteristic style, Paul next breaks into thanksgiving. As we read this, we should remember that he was writing from a Roman dungeon. He had been imprisoned for preaching the gospel and was now treated as a common criminal. The Christian faith was being actively suppressed by the Roman government, and many believers had already been put to death. In spite of all these adverse circumstances, Paul can begin his Letter to Timothy with the words, **"I thank God!"**

The apostle was now serving God **with a pure conscience, as** his Jewish **forefathers** had done. Although his forebears were not Christians, they were believers in the living God. They worshiped Him and sought to serve Him. They held "the hope and resurrection of the dead," as Paul pointed out in Acts 23:6. That is why he could further say, in Acts 26:6, 7a: "And now I stand and am judged for the hope of the promise made by God to our fathers. To this promise [of resurrection] our twelve tribes, earnestly serving God night and day, hope to attain."

Thus Paul could speak of his service for the Lord as being according to the example of his ancestors. The word he uses for **serve**[3] refers to loyalty and allegiance. He acknowledged the true God.

Next Paul speaks of his unceasing remembrance of Timothy **in** his **prayers, night and day**. Whenever the great apostle spoke to the Lord in prayer, he would be reminded of his beloved, young co-worker and would bring his name before the Throne of Grace. Paul knew that his own time of service was rapidly drawing

to a close. He knew that Timothy would be left alone, humanly speaking, to carry on his witness for Christ. He knew of the difficulties that would face him, and so he prayed continually for this young warrior of the faith.

1:4 How it must have touched Timothy's heart to read these words! The Apostle Paul had what Moule called a "home-sick yearning" **to see** him. This was certainly a mark of special love and esteem, and it speaks eloquently of the graciousness, tenderness, and humility of Paul.

Perhaps it was the last time they parted that Timothy broke down. His **tears** had made a deep impression on his elder co-worker. Hiebert suggests it was when Paul had been "torn from him" by the police or Roman soldiers.[4] Paul could not forget, and now he longs to be with Timothy again so **that** he might **be filled with joy**. He does not rebuke Timothy for those **tears**, as though they were unmanly, or as though there was no place for emotions in Christianity. J. H. Jowett used to say: "Tearless hearts can never be heralds of the passion. When our sympathy loses its pang, we can no longer be the servants of the passion."

1:5 In some way or other, Paul had been reminded of Timothy's **genuine faith**. His **faith** was sincere, true, and did not wear a mask.[5]

But Timothy was not the first in his family to be saved. Apparently, his Jewish **grandmother Lois** had heard the good news of salvation and accepted the Lord Jesus as Messiah. And her daughter **Eunice**, also a Jewess (Acts 16:1), had become a Christian. In this way, Timothy had come to learn the great truths of the Christian faith, and he represented the third generation in that family to trust the Savior. Nothing is said in the Scriptures as to whether Timothy's father was ever converted.

Although salvation cannot be inherited from believing parents, it certainly is true that there is a household principle in the Scriptures. It appears that God loves to save entire families. It is not His will that there should be a missing member.

Notice that **faith** is said to have **dwelt** in **Lois** and **Eunice**. It was not there as an occasional visitor, but as an abiding presence with them. Paul was **persuaded** that that was the case with Timothy **also**. It was a genuine faith that Timothy would maintain in spite of all the trials which he might have to face in connection with it.

II. EXHORTATIONS TO TIMOTHY (1:6–2:13)

A. To Fidelity (1:6–18)

1:6 Because of his godly family background and his own faith, Timothy is urged **to stir up the gift of God which is in** him. We are not told what **the gift of God** is. Some take it to mean the Holy Spirit. Others understand it to mean a special ability conferred by the Lord for some form of Christian service, for instance, the gift of an evangelist, pastor, or teacher. It seems clear that Timothy had been called into Christian service and had been given some special enablement. Here he is encouraged to kindle **the gift** into a living flame. He should not become discouraged by the general failure around him. Neither should he become professional in his service for the Lord and lapse into a comfortable routine. Rather, he should be concerned to use his gift more and more as the days grow darker and darker.

This **gift** was in Timothy **through the laying on of** the apostle's **hands**. This is not to be confused with the ordination service which is practiced in clerical circles today. This means exactly what it says — that **the gift** was actually given to Timothy at the moment Paul laid his **hands** upon him. The apostle was the channel by which the gift was conferred.

The question will immediately arise, "Does this take place today?" The answer is that it does not. The power to confer a gift by the laying on of hands was given to Paul as an apostle of Jesus Christ. Since we do not have apostles in that same sense today, we no longer have the power to perform apostolic miracles.

This verse should be studied in connection with 1 Timothy 1:18 and 4:14. Putting these three verses together, we find that the following is the order of events, as expressed by Vine. By prophetic utterance, Paul was guided to Timothy as one raised up for special service. By the formal act on the apostle's part, the Lord bestowed a gift on Timothy. The elders recognized what the Lord had done by laying on their hands. The latter action was not an act of ordination, conferring a gift or ecclesiastical position.[6]

Or, as Stock summarizes, "The gift came 'through' Paul's hands, but 'with' the presbyters' hands."

1:7 Facing martyrdom himself, Paul takes time out to remind Timothy that **God has not given us a spirit of fear** or cowardice. There is no time for fearfulness or timidity.

But God has given us a spirit **of power**. Unlimited strength is at our disposal. Through the enabling of the Holy Spirit, the believer can serve valiantly, endure patiently, suffer triumphantly, and, if need be, die gloriously.

God has also given us a spirit **of love**. It is our **love** for God that casts out fear and makes us willing to give ourselves for Christ, whatever the cost may be. It is our **love** for our fellow men that makes us willing to endure all kinds of persecutions and repay them with kindness.

Finally, God has given us a spirit **of a sound mind**, or discipline. The words **a sound mind** do not completely convey the thought. They might suggest that a Christian should be sane at all times, free from nervous breakdowns or other mental ailments. This verse has often been misused to teach that a Christian who is living close to the Lord could never be afflicted with any kind of mental ills. That is not a scriptural teaching. Many mental ills can be traced to *inherited* weaknesses. Many others may be the result of some *physical* condition not connected in any way with the person's spiritual life.

What this verse is teaching is that God has given us a spirit of self-control or self-mastery. We are to use discretion and not to act rashly, hastily, or foolishly. No matter how adverse our circumstances, we should maintain balanced judgment and act soberly.

1:8 Timothy is told that he should

not be ashamed. In verse 12, Paul states that he is not ashamed. Finally, in verse 16, we read that Onesiphorus was not ashamed.

It was a day when preaching the gospel was a crime. Those who sought to witness publicly for their Lord and Savior were persecuted. But this should not daunt Timothy. He should **not be ashamed** of the gospel, even though it involves suffering. Neither should he **be ashamed** of the Apostle Paul in prison. Already some of the Christians had turned their backs on him. Doubtless they feared that to identify themselves with him would invite persecution and possibly death.

Timothy was exhorted to take his **share** of **the sufferings** that accompany **the gospel** and to bear it **according to the power of God**. He should not try to avoid any disgrace that might be connected with it, but rather join with Paul in enduring such disgrace.

1:9 The apostle has been encouraging Timothy to be zealous (vv. 6, 7) and courageous (v. 8). Now Paul explains why this is the only reasonable attitude to take; it is found in God's wonderful dealings with us in grace. First of all, He **saved us**. This means that He delivered us from the penalty of sin. He constantly delivers us from the power of sin, and in a day yet future, He will deliver us from the very presence of sin. Also, He has freed us from the world and from Satan.

Again, God has **called us with a holy calling**. Not only has He delivered us from evil, but He has bestowed upon us all spiritual blessings in the heavenlies in Christ Jesus. The Christian's holy calling is described in some detail in Ephesians 1-3, especially in chapter 1. There we learn that we are chosen, predestined, adopted as sons, accepted in the Beloved, redeemed through His blood, forgiven, sealed with the Holy Spirit, and given the earnest of our inheritance. (In addition to this holy calling, we have a high calling, Phil. 3:14, and a heavenly calling, Heb. 3:1.)

This salvation and calling are **not according to our works**. In other words, they were given to us by God's grace. This means that we did not deserve them, but rather deserved the very op-

posite. We could not earn them; neither did we seek them. But God freely bestowed them upon us without condition or price.

This is further explained by the words **according to His own purpose and grace**. Why should God have so loved ungodly sinners that He was willing to send His only Son to die for them? Why should He go to such a cost to save them from hell and to bring them to heaven so that they could spend eternity with Him? The only possible answer is: **according to His own purpose and grace**. The reason for His action did not lie in us. Rather, it lay in His own great heart of love. He loved us because He loved us!

His favor **was given to us in Christ Jesus before time began**. This means that in the past eternity, God determined upon this wonderful plan of salvation. He determined to save guilty sinners through the substitutionary work of His dear Son. He decided to offer eternal life to as many as would accept Jesus Christ as Lord and Savior. The method by which we could be saved was planned not only before we were born, but even **before time began**.

1:10 The same gospel that was designed in eternity was **revealed** in time. It was **revealed by the appearing of our Savior Jesus Christ**. During the days of His flesh, He publicly proclaimed the good news of salvation. He taught men that He must die, be buried, and rise from the dead in order that God might righteously save ungodly sinners.

He **abolished death**. But how can this be, when we know that death is still very common in the world? The thought is that He annulled death, or put it out of commission. Before Christ's resurrection, death ruled as a cruel tyrant over men. It was a dreaded foe. The fear of death held men in bondage. But the resurrection of the Lord Jesus is a pledge that all who trust in Him will rise from the dead to die no more. It is in this sense that He has annulled death. He has robbed it of its sting. Death is now the messenger of God which brings the soul of the believer to heaven. It is our servant rather than our master.

Not only has the Lord Jesus annulled **death**, He has **brought life and immor-**

tality to **light through the gospel**. In the OT period, most men had a very vague and misty idea of life after death. They spoke of departed loved ones as in Sheol, which simply means the invisible state of departed spirits. Although they had a heavenly hope set before them, yet for the most part they did not understand it clearly.

Since the coming of Christ, we have much greater light on this subject. For instance, we know that when a believer dies, his spirit departs to be with Christ, which is far better. He is absent from the body and at home with the Lord. He enters into eternal life in all its fullness.

Christ has not only **brought life** to **light**, but also **immortality**. **Immortality** refers to the resurrection of the body. When we read in 1 Corinthians 15:53 that "this corruptible must put on incorruption," we know that even though the body is placed in the grave and returns to dust, yet at the coming of Christ that same body will be raised from the grave and fashioned into a body of glory, similar to that of the Lord Jesus Himself. The OT saints did not have this knowledge. It was **brought** to us through **the appearing of our Savior, Jesus Christ**.

1:11 It was to proclaim this glorious gospel that Paul **was appointed a preacher, an apostle, and a teacher of the Gentiles**. A **preacher** is a herald whose function is to publicly proclaim a message. **An apostle** is one who has been divinely sent, divinely equipped, and divinely empowered. A **teacher** is one whose function is to indoctrinate others; he explains the truth in an understandable manner so that others may respond by faith and obedience. **Of the Gentiles**[7] stresses his special ministry to the non-Jewish nations.

1:12 It was because of his faithful performance of duty that Paul was suffering imprisonment and loneliness. He had not hesitated to declare the truth of God. No fears for personal safety had sealed his lips. Now that he had been arrested and jailed, he still had no regrets. He was **not ashamed**, and neither should Timothy be ashamed. Although Paul could not be confident as to his personal safety, he was completely confident as to the One **whom** he had **believed**. Though Rome might succeed in

putting the apostle to death, men could not touch his Lord. Paul knew that the One whom he had trusted was **able**. Able to do what? **Able to keep what I have committed to Him until that Day**. Commentators are divided as to what Paul is referring to here. Some think that it is his soul's salvation. Others understand this to refer to the gospel. In other words, although the Apostle Paul himself might be put to death, yet the gospel could not be hindered. The more men sought to oppose it, the more it would prosper.

Perhaps it is best to take the expression in its broadest sense. Paul was persuaded that his entire case was in the best of hands. Even as he faced death, he had no misgivings. Jesus Christ was his Almighty Lord, and with Him there could be no defeat or failure. There was nothing to worry about. Paul's salvation was sure, and so was the ultimate success of his service for Christ here on earth.

That Day is a favorite expression of Paul. It refers to the coming of the Lord Jesus Christ, and particularly to the Judgment Seat of Christ when service for Him will be brought into review and when the kindness of God will reward the faithfulness of men.

1:13 This verse may be understood in two ways. First of all, Timothy is encouraged to **hold fast the pattern of sound words**. It is not just that he is to be loyal to the truth of God's word, but that he is to cling to the very expressions by which this truth is conveyed. Perhaps an illustration of this might help. In our day, it is sometimes suggested that we should abandon such old-fashioned expressions as "being born again" or "the blood of Jesus." People want to use more sophisticated language. But there is a subtle danger here. In abandoning the scriptural mode of expression, they often abandon the very truths which are communicated by these expressions. Therefore, Timothy should **hold fast the** very **pattern of** healthful **words**.

But the verse might also suggest that Paul's words were to serve as a model or pattern to Timothy. Everything that Timothy subsequently taught should harmonize with the outline that had been given to him. In carrying out his ministry, Timothy should do so **in faith and love which are in Christ Jesus. Faith** means not only trust, but dependence as well. **Love** includes not only **love** to God, but also **love** to our fellow believers and to the perishing world around us.

1:14 **That good thing** refers to the gospel. The message of redeeming love had been **committed** or entrusted to Timothy. He is not told to add to it or to improve on it in any way. His responsibility is to guard it through **the Holy Spirit who dwells in us**. As Paul wrote this Letter, he was conscious of the widespread departure from the faith which was menacing the church. Attacks would be made on the Christian faith from many different quarters. Timothy was admonished to stand true to the word of God. He would not have to do this in his own strength. The indwelling **Holy Spirit** would supply all that he needed for this task.

1:15 As the apostle thinks of the dark clouds gathering over the church, he is reminded of how the Christians **in Asia** had **turned away from** him. Since at the time this Letter was written Timothy was probably located in Ephesus, he knew exactly what the apostle was writing about.

It is likely that the Christians in Asia severed their connections with Paul when they learned that he had been arrested and imprisoned. They forsook him at the very time he needed them most. Probably their reason was that they feared for their own safety. The Roman government was on the lookout for all who sought to propagate the Christian faith. The Apostle Paul was one of the best-known representatives of Christianity. Any who dared to contact him publicly would be marked out at once as being sympathetic to the cause.

It is neither stated nor implied that these Christians forsook the Lord or the church. Nevertheless, it was an act of cowardice and unfaithfulness to desert Paul in this crisis hour.

Perhaps **Phygellus and Hermogenes** were leaders in the movement to dissociate themselves from Paul. At any rate, they brought upon themselves an immortality of shame and contempt for refusing to bear the reproach of Christ in fellowship with His servant. Guy King's comment is that "they couldn't help their ugly names, but they could have helped their ugly character."

1:16 There are two schools of thought with regard to **Onesiphorus**. Some think that he too had forsaken Paul, and that is why the apostle prays that **the Lord** will **grant mercy to** him. Others feel that he is mentioned as a happy exception to those who have just been described. We believe that the latter view is correct.

Paul asks that **the Lord** will **grant mercy to the household of Onesiphorus. Mercy** is the reward for those who have been merciful, according to Matthew 5:7. We are not told exactly how Onesiphorus **refreshed** Paul. Perhaps he brought food and clothing to the damp, dark Roman dungeon. At any rate, he **was not ashamed** to go to Paul in prison. No considerations of personal safety could prevent his helping a friend in time of need.

Jowett expressed it exquisitely:

It is a beautiful lineament in the character of Onesiphorus which is given in the Apostle's phrase, "He was not ashamed of my chain." . . . A man's chain often lessens the circle of his friends. The chain of poverty keeps many people away, and so does the chain of unpopularity. When a man is in high repute he has many friends. When he begins to wear a chain, the friends are apt to fall away. But the ministers of the morning breeze love to come in the shades of night. They delight to minister in the region of despondency, and where the bonds lie heaviest upon the soul. "He was not ashamed of my chain." The chain was really an allurement. It gave speed to the feet of Onesiphorus and urgency to his ministry.[8]

This verse has sometimes been misused to support prayers for the dead. The argument is that Onesiphorus had already died when Paul wrote this and that Paul was asking God to show mercy to him. There is not the vaguest hint that Onesiphorus was dead. Proponents of this view are idle babblers clutching at a straw to shore up an unbiblical practice.

1:17 When Onesiphorus **arrived in Rome**, he had at least three choices. First, he could have avoided any contact with the Christians. Secondly, he could have met with the believers secretly. Finally, he could boldly expose himself to danger by visiting Paul in prison. This would bring him into direct contact with the Roman authorities. To his everlasting credit, he chose the last policy. **He sought** Paul **out very zealously and found** him.

1:18 The apostle prays that this faithful friend might **find mercy from the Lord in that** coming **Day. Mercy** is here used in the sense of reward. **That Day**, as previously mentioned, refers to the time when rewards will be given, namely, the Judgment Seat of Christ.

In closing this section, the Apostle Paul reminds Timothy how Onesiphorus had served Paul **at Ephesus** in many different ways.

B. To Endurance (2:1–13)

2:1 To **be strong in the grace that is in Christ Jesus** means to be courageous with the strength which His **grace** provides, to go on faithfully for the Lord with the undeserved ability that comes through union with Him.

2:2 Not only is Timothy to be strengthened himself, but he is to provide for the spiritual strengthening of **others**. He is responsible to transmit to others the inspired teachings which he had received from the apostle. Paul was soon to pass off the scene. He had faithfully taught Timothy in the presence of **many witnesses**. Timothy's own day of service would be short at best, and he, too, should so order his ministry that others would be prepared to carry on as teachers.

This verse does *not* support the notion of apostolic succession. Neither does it refer to the present day practice of ordination of ministers. Rather, it is simply the Lord's instruction to the church to ensure a succession of competent teachers.

It has often been pointed out that there are four generations of believers in this verse, as follows:

1. The Apostle Paul.
2. Timothy and many witnesses.
3. Faithful men.
4. Others.

This Scripture emphasizes the importance of every-member evangelism. If each believer truly did his part the world

could be evangelized within a generation. However, this is merely hypothetical in the light of the perversity of man's will, the rival "evangelism" of world religions and the cults, and many other obstacles. Positively, however, one thing is certain: Christians could do a great deal better than the record so far!

Notice that Timothy is to **commit** the truth **to faithful men**, that is, men who are believers and who are themselves dependable. These men should be able **to teach others also**. This presupposes some competency as far as teaching ministry is concerned.

2:3 It has often been pointed out that Paul uses a wealth of similes in this chapter to describe Timothy: (1) Son (v. 1); (2) Soldier (vv. 3, 4); (3) Athlete (v. 5); (4) Farmer (v. 6); (5) Worker (v. 15); (6) Vessel (v. 21); (7) Servant (v. 24).

As a good soldier of Jesus Christ, Timothy should **endure**[9] suffering and **hardship**. (For a list of the many hardships Paul himself endured, see 2 Cor. 11:23–29.)

2:4 The soldier described in this verse is one who is on active duty. Not only so, but he is in the thick of the combat. No soldier in such grim circumstances **entangles himself with the affairs of this life**.

Does this mean that those who are in the Lord's service should never engage in secular occupations as well? Certainly not! Paul himself worked as a tentmaker while he was preaching the gospel and planting churches. He testified that his own hands ministered to his necessities.

The emphasis is on the word **entangles**. The soldier must not allow ordinary affairs of life to become the main object of existence. For instance, he must not make acquiring food and clothing the main aim of life. Rather, the service of Christ must always occupy the prominent place, while the things of this life are kept in the background. Kelly says: "To entangle oneself in the businesses of life means really to give up separation from the world by taking one's part in outward affairs as a bona fide partner in it."[10]

A soldier on duty keeps himself in readiness for orders from headquarters. His desire is to **please** the one **who enlisted him**. The believer, of course, has been enlisted by the Lord, and our love for Him should cause us to maintain a light hold on the things of this world.

2:5 The figure now changes to an athlete who **competes** in the games. In order to receive the reward, he must obey **the rules** of the game. So it is in Christian service. How many fall out before they reach the finish line, disqualified because they did not maintain an unquestioning obedience to the word of God!

What are some of the rules in connection with Christian service? (1) The Christian must practice self-discipline (1 Cor. 9:27). (2) He must not fight with carnal weapons, but with spiritual ones (2 Cor. 10:4). (3) He must keep himself pure. (4) He must not strive, but be patient.

Someone has said: "A spare-time Christian is a contradiction in terms; a man's whole life should be one strenuous endeavor to live out his Christianity in every moment and in every sphere of his life."

2:6 The hard-working farmer must be first to partake of the crops. According to all principles of righteousness, the one who labors to bring forth **the crops** has a prior right to participate in them.

While Darby agrees that the above is a possible rendering, he suggests that the sense of the passage is that the farmer must work in order to enjoy a share of the harvest. Therefore, he translates, "The husbandman must labour before partaking of the fruits." This preserves the thought of necessity: The soldier must endure; the athlete must keep the rules; the farmer must work hard.

2:7 But there is more in these three illustrations of Christian service than appears on the surface. Timothy is exhorted to consider them and to meditate on them. As he does so, Paul prays[11] that **the Lord** will **give** him **understanding in all things**. He will realize that the Christian ministry resembles warfare, athletics, and farming. Each of these occupations has its own responsibilities, and each brings its own reward.

2:8 At this point, the apostle reaches the high-water mark in his series of encouragements to young Timothy. He comes to the example of the Lord Jesus, and he can go no higher. His is an example of suffering followed by glory. **Remember that Jesus Christ, of the seed of David, was raised from the dead according to my gospel.** The thought is not that Timothy is to remember certain things *about* the Lord Jesus, but rather that he is to remember the Person Himself, alive **from the dead**.

In one sense, this verse is a brief summary of the gospel which Paul preached. The crucial point in that gospel is the resurrection of the Savior. Hiebert writes: "Not the vision of a crucified Jesus but the vision of a risen Lord is held up before Timothy."[12]

The expression **of the seed of David** is a simple statement that Jesus is the Christ, the descendant **of David**, in whom the Messianic promises of God are fulfilled.

Constant remembrance of the Savior's Person and work is essential for all who want to serve Him. Especially for those facing suffering and possible death, there is great encouragement in remembering that even the Lord Jesus Himself reached the glory of heaven by way of the cross and the grave.

2:9 It was for proclaiming the gospel outlined in verse 8 that Paul was now chained in a Roman prison. He was looked upon **as an evildoer**, as a common criminal. There was much to discourage. Not only was the Roman government determined to put him to death, but some of his own Christian friends had turned away from him.

And yet in spite of these bitter circumstances, Paul's happy spirit soars high above the dungeon walls. He forgets his own dismal outlook when he remembers that **the word of God is not chained**. As Lenski said so well, "The apostle's living voice may be smothered in his own blood, but what his Lord speaks through him still resounds in the wide world." Not all the armies in the world can hinder the word of God from going forth. They might just as well try to stop the rain or the snow from falling (Isa. 55:10, 11). Harvey says:

With irresistible, divine energy it is advancing in its career of triumph, even while its defenders suffer imprisonment and martyrdom. Men die, but Christ and His gospel live and triumph through the ages.[13]

2:10 Because of the irresistible nature of the gospel, Paul was willing to **endure all things for the sake of the elect. The elect** here refers to all those chosen by God for eternal salvation. While the Bible does teach that God chooses people to be saved, it nowhere says that He selects some to be damned. Those who are saved are saved by the sovereign grace of God. Those who are lost are lost by their own deliberate choice.

No one should quarrel with God over the doctrine of election. This doctrine simply allows God to be God, the Sovereign of the universe, who deals in grace, justice, righteousness, and love. He never does anything unfair or unkind, but He often shows favor that is completely unmerited.

The apostle realized that through his suffering for the sake of the gospel, souls were saved and that these very souls would one day participate in **eternal glory** with **Christ Jesus**. The vision of guilty sinners, saved by the grace of God and glorified together with Christ Jesus, was sufficient to inspire Paul to bear all things. In this, we are reminded of the words attributed to the godly Rutherford:[14]

> Oh, if one soul from Anwoth
> Meet me at God's right hand,
> My heaven shall be two heavens
> In Immanuel's land.

2:11 Verses 11-13 are thought by some to be from an early Christian hymn. Whether that is so or not, they certainly present some inflexible principles concerning man's relationship to the Lord Jesus Christ. Hiebert writes: "The central truth of these pithy statements is that faith in Christ identifies the believer with Him in everything while unbelief just as surely separates men from Him."[15] This is the fourth **faithful saying** in Paul's Letters to Timothy.

The first principle is that **if we died with** Christ, **we shall also live with Him**. This is true of every believer. In a spiritual sense, **we died with Him** the moment we trusted Him as our Savior. We were buried with Him, and we rose again with Him from among the dead. Christ died as our Representative and Substitute. We should have died for our

sins, but Christ died in our place. God reckons us to have **died with Him**, and this means that **we shall also live with Him** in heaven.

Perhaps this verse also has an application to those who die as Christian martyrs. Those who thus follow Him in death will likewise follow Him in resurrection.

2:12 In a sense, it is also true of all Christians that they **endure** and that they **shall also reign with** Christ. True faith always has the quality of permanence, and in this sense all believers do **endure**.

However, it should also be pointed out that not all will reign with Christ to the same extent. When He comes back to reign over the earth, His saints will return with Him and share in that rule. But the extent of one's rule will be determined by his faithfulness during this present life.

Those who **deny** Christ will be denied by Him. Here the thought is not of a temporary denial of the Savior under duress, as in the case of Peter, but a permanent, habitual denial of Him. These words describe an unbeliever — one who has never embraced the Lord Jesus by faith. All such will be denied by the Lord in a coming day, no matter how pious their profession might have been.

2:13 This verse also describes unbelievers. Dinsdale Young explains: "God cannot be inconsistent with Himself. It would be inconsistent with His character to treat the faithful and the unfaithful alike. He is evermore true to righteousness, whatever we are."[16]

The words should not be interpreted to teach that God's faithfulness will be demonstrated in upholding those who are unbelieving. Such is not the case. If men are unbelieving, **He** must be **faithful** to His own character and must treat them accordingly. As Van Oosterzee says, "He is just as faithful in His threatenings as in His promises."[17]

III. FIDELITY VERSUS APOSTASY (2:14–4:8)

A. Fidelity to True Christianity (2:14–26)

2:14 Timothy is to **remind them of**

these things, that is, the things of verses 11-13. But to whom does Paul refer with the word them? He probably refers in a general sense to all of Timothy's hearers and in a special sense to those who were introducing strange doctrines. This is evident from the remaining part of the verse, where those who obviously occupied the place of teachers or preachers are warned not to strive about words. Apparently there were those in Ephesus who made great issues over the technical meaning of certain words. Instead of building up the saints in the truth of God's word, they were only undermining the faith of some who heard them.

Dinsdale Young warns:

> It is so easy to become a theological crank — so readily are we engrossed with questions that are of no supreme moment. Life is too brief and too busy for the wasting of brain and heart on what is not formative of character.
> When a world awaits evangelization, it ill becomes us to be forever either sauntering or hurrying along doctrinal byways. Keep to the highways. Be true to the greater verities. Emphasize essentials, not incidentals. Do not emulate the victims of panic in the days of Shamgar and of Jael, who left the highways unoccupied and walked through byways.[18]

2:15 Timothy should be diligent to present himself approved to God. His efforts should be concentrated on becoming a worker who does not need to be ashamed. This he could do by rightly dividing the word of truth. This latter expression means to handle the Scriptures correctly, to "hew the line," or as Alford put it, "to manage rightly to treat truth fully without falsifying."[19]

2:16 Profane and idle babblings are teachings that are irreverent, evil, and useless. It is not profitable for the people of God and should be shunned. Timothy is not instructed to combat these teachings but rather to treat them with disdain, not even dignifying them with his attention.

One serious thing about these babblers is that they are never static. They always increase in ungodliness. It is so with all forms of error. Those who teach error must be continually adding to it. This explains the new dogmas and pronouncements that are constantly being issued by false religious systems. Needless to say, the more these doctrinal errors are expanded, the more ungodliness results.

2:17 The way in which evil teachings spread is compared to cancer. Most of us know only too well how this dread disease spreads rapidly in the human body, destroying tissue wherever it goes.

The word *cancer* can also be rendered "gangrene."[20] Gangrene refers to the mortification of part of the body when it is cut off from its normal supply of blood and nutrition.

Elsewhere in the NT, evil doctrine is likened to leaven, which, if allowed to spread, will eventually affect the whole lump of meal.

Two men are named whose teachings were corrupting the local church. They were Hymenaeus and Philetus. Because they failed to handle the word of truth correctly, they take their place with others in God's hall of shame.

2:18 Their false teaching is here exposed. They told the people that the resurrection was already past. Perhaps they meant that when a person was saved and was raised to newness of life with Christ, that was the only resurrection he could expect. In other words, they spiritualized the resurrection and scoffed at the idea of a literal raising of the body from the grave. Paul recognized this as a serious threat to the truth of Christianity.

Hamilton Smith says:

> If the resurrection is past already, it is evident that the saints have reached their final condition while yet on earth, with the result that the church ceases to look for the coming of the Lord, loses the truth of its heavenly destiny, and gives up its stranger and pilgrim character. Having lost its heavenly character, the church settles down on the earth, taking a place as part of the system for the reformation and government of the world.[21]

By overthrowing the faith of some, these men earned for themselves an undesirable entry in God's eternal book.

2:19 As Paul thinks of Hymenaeus and Philetus and their false teaching, he realizes afresh that dark days are coming upon the church. Unbelievers have been accepted into the local church. Spiritual life is at such a low ebb that it is often hard to tell true Christians from mere professors. Christendom is a mixed multitude, and the resulting confusion is devastating.

In the midst of such a condition, Paul finds comfort in the assurance that **the solid foundation of God stands**. This means that whatever has been established by **God** Himself will endure in spite of all the declension in the professing church.

Various explanations have been given as to what is meant by **the solid foundation of God**. Some suggest that it is the true church. Others say it refers to the promise of God, to the Christian faith, or to the doctrine of election. But is it not clear that the **foundation of God** refers to *anything that the Lord does*? If He sends out His word, nothing can hinder it. Hamilton Smith says: "No failure of man can set aside the foundation that God has laid, or prevent God from completing what He has commenced. . . . Those who are the Lord's, though hidden in the mass, cannot be ultimately lost."[22]

The **foundation of God** has a twofold **seal**. There is a divine side to it and a human side as well. From the divine side, **the Lord knows those who are His**. He **knows** them, not only in the sense of recognition, but of approval and appreciation. Lenski says He knows them "with appropriating and effective love."[23] The human side of the **seal** is that **everyone who names the name of Christ**[24] should **depart from iniquity**. In other words, those professing to be Christians can prove the reality of their profession by lives of holiness and godliness. The true Christian should have no dealings with unrighteousness.

A seal is a mark of ownership and also an emblem of guarantee and security. Thus the **seal** on God's **foundation** signifies His ownership of those who are true believers and the guarantee that all who have been converted will prove the reality of their new life by departing from unrighteousness.

2:20 In this illustration, we understand that the **great house** refers to Christendom in general. In a broad sense, Christendom includes believers and professors — those who are truly born again and those who are mere nominal Christians.

Vessels of gold and silver would therefore refer to genuine believers.

Vessels **of wood and clay** refer not to unbelievers in general, but to those in particular who were evil workers and who taught false doctrines, such as Hymenaeus and Philetus (v. 17).

Certain things should be noticed about these vessels. First of all, there is an important distinction between the materials of which the vessels are made. Secondly, there is a difference in the uses to which they are put. Finally, there is the distinction as to their ultimate destiny. The vessels of wood and clay are discarded after a while, but those of gold and silver are retained as valuable.

The expression **some for honor and some for dishonor** has been variously interpreted. Some suggest that **dishonor** simply means less honor. In that case, all the vessels would stand for true believers, but some are used for the highest purposes and some for the lowest. Others feel that the vessels **for honor** would refer to men like Paul and Timothy, whereas those **for dishonor** would refer to such men as Hymenaeus and Philetus.

2:21 The interpretation of this passage largely depends on one's understanding of the meaning of *the latter* in **"Therefore, if anyone cleanses himself from the latter."**

Does **latter** refer to the vessels of wood and clay? Does it refer to the false teachings that have been mentioned previously in this chapter? Or does it refer in a general way to evil men?

The most natural meaning seems to be to connect **latter** with vessels for dishonor. Timothy is instructed to separate himself from evil men and especially from evil teachers such as those Paul had just mentioned — Hymenaeus and Philetus.

Timothy is *not* instructed to leave the church. Neither is he told to leave Christendom as such. It would be impossible for him to do this without giving up his Christian profession, since Christendom includes all who profess to be believers. Rather, it is a question of separating from evildoers and avoiding contamination from wicked doctrine.

If a man keeps himself free from evil associations, **he will be a vessel for honor**. God can use only clean vessels in holy service. "Be clean, you who bear the vessels of the Lord" (Isa. 52:11). Such a man will also be **sanctified** in the sense that he will be set apart from evil to the service of God. He will be **useful for the Master** — a quality greatly to be desired by all who love the Lord. Finally, he will be **prepared for every good work**. He will be ready at all times to be used in whatever way his Master may dictate.

2:22 Not only is Timothy to separate himself from iniquitous men, but he is to separate himself from the **lusts** of the flesh. **Youthful lusts** may refer not only to physical appetites but also to the lust for money, fame, and pleasure. They may also include self-will, impatience, pride, and levity. As we have mentioned, Timothy was probably about thirty-five years of age at this time. Therefore, **youthful lusts** do not necessarily mean such lusts as would be particularly characteristic of a teenager but would include all the unholy desires that would present themselves to a young servant of the Lord and seek to divert him from the path of purity and righteousness.

Not only is Timothy to **flee**; he is also to follow. There is the negative and the positive.

He should **pursue righteousness**. This simply means that his dealings with his fellow men, saved and unsaved, should always be characterized by honesty, justice, and fairness.

Faith may mean faithfulness or absolute integrity. On the other hand, it may include a continual dependence on the Lord. Hiebert defines it as "sincere and dynamic confidence in God."[25]

Love cannot be limited here to love to God alone, but must also include love for one's brethren and for the world of lost sinners. Love always considers others; it is essentially unselfish.

Peace carries the idea of harmony and compatibility.

These virtues are to be followed **with those who call on the Lord out of a pure heart**. Just as in verse 21 Timothy was warned to separate himself from wicked men, so here he is taught to associate himself with Christians who are walking in purity before the Lord. He is not to follow the virtues of the Christian life in isolation, but rather he must take his place as a member in the Body and seek to work with his fellow members for the good of the Body.

2:23 In the course of his Christian ministry, Timothy would often be faced with trifling and stupid questions. Such questions would spring from an ignorant, uneducated mind and would have no real benefit connected with them. Such **disputes** should be refused because **they** only stir up **strife**. Needless to say, these are not questions connected with the great fundamentals of the Christian faith, but rather silly problems that would only succeed in wasting time and causing confusion and arguments.

2:24 The servant of the Lord here is literally the Lord's *bondservant*. It is fitting that this title should be used in a verse where gentleness and patience are encouraged.

Although the Lord's servant must contend for the truth, yet he must not be contentious or argumentative. Rather, he must **be gentle to all** and approach men with the purpose of instructing them rather than of winning an argument. He must be **patient** with those who are slow to understand and even with those who do not seem disposed to accept the truth of God's word.

2:25 The Lord's bondservant must exercise meekness and **humility** in dealing with **opposition**. A person wrongs his own soul by refusing to bow to the word of God. Such people need to be corrected lest they ignorantly go on with the mistaken notion that their view is in accordance with the Scriptures.

If God perhaps will grant them repentance, so that they may know the truth. At first, this might seem to suggest that there is some question as to God's willingness to grant repentance to these people. That, however, is not the case. The fact of the matter is that God is waiting to forgive them if only they will come to Him in confession and repentance. God does not withhold repentance from anyone, but men are so often unwilling to admit that they are wrong.

2:26 The servant of the Lord should so deal with erring men that **they may come to their senses and escape the snare of the devil**. They have **been taken captive by him to do his will**, and, as it were, bewitched or intoxicated by him.

B. The Coming Apostasy (3:1–13)

3:1 The apostle now gives Timothy a description of conditions that will exist in the world prior to the Lord's coming. It has often been pointed out that the list of sins that follows is very similar to the description of the ungodly heathen in Romans 1. The remarkable thing is that the very conditions that exist among the heathen in their savagery and uncivilized state will characterize professing believers **in the last days**. How solemn this is!

The last days referred to here are the days between the apostolic period and the appearing of Christ to set up His kingdom.

3:2 One cannot study these verses without being struck by the repetition of the word **lovers**. In verse 2, for instance, we find **lovers** of self and **lovers of money**. In verse 3, the expression "despisers of good" means literally "no-lovers-of good." In verse 4, we read of "lovers of pleasure rather than lovers of God."

In verses 2–5, nineteen characteristics of mankind during the last days are given. We shall simply list them and give synonyms that explain their meaning:

Lovers of themselves — self-centered, conceited, egotistical.

Lovers of money — greedy for money, avaricious.

Boasters — braggarts, full of great swelling words.

Proud — arrogant, haughty, overbearing.

Blasphemers — evil speakers, profane, abusive, foulmouthed, contemptuous, insulting.

Disobedient to parents — rebellious, undutiful, uncontrolled.

Unthankful — ungrateful, lacking in appreciation.

Unholy — impious, profane, irreverent, holding nothing sacred.

3:3 Unloving — hard-hearted, unnaturally callous, unfeeling.

Unforgiving — implacable, refusing to make peace, refusing efforts toward reconciliation.

Slanderers — spreading false and malicious reports.

Without self-control — men of uncontrolled passions, dissolute, debauched.

Brutal — savage, unprincipled.

Despisers of good — haters of whatever or whoever is good; utterly opposed to goodness in any form.

3:4 Traitors — treacherous, betrayers.

Headstrong — reckless, self-willed, rash.

Haughty — making empty pretensions, conceited.

Lovers of pleasure rather than lovers of God — those who love sensual pleasures but not God.

3:5 Outwardly these people seem religious. They make a profession of Christianity, but their actions speak louder than their words. By their ungodly behavior, they show that they are living a lie. There is no evidence of the power of God in their lives. While there might have been reformation, there never was regeneration. Weymouth translates: "They will keep up a make-believe of piety and yet exclude its power." Likewise Moffatt: "Though they keep up a form of religion, they will have nothing to do with it as a force." Phillips puts it: "They will maintain a façade of 'religion' but their conduct will deny its validity." They want to be religious and to have their sins at the same time (cf. Rev. 3:14–22). Hiebert warns: "It is the fearful portrayal of an apostate Christendom, a new paganism masquerading under the name of Christianity."[26]

From all **such people** Timothy is exhorted to **turn away**. These are the vessels described in the previous chapter from which he is to purge himself.

3:6 Among the corrupt men of the last days, Paul now singles out a particular group, namely, leaders and teachers of false cults. This detailed description of their character and methods finds its fulfillment in the cults of our present day.

First of all, we read that they **creep**

or worm their way **into households**. It is not by accident that this description reminds us of the movement of a serpent. If they revealed their true identity, they would not succeed in getting into many of these homes, but they use various subtle devices, such as speaking about God, the Bible, and Jesus (even if they do not believe what Scripture teaches about these).

Next it says that they **make captives of gullible women**. This is characteristic. They plan their visit when the husband is apt to be at work or elsewhere. History repeats itself. Satan approached Eve in the Garden of Eden and deceived her. She usurped authority over her husband, making the decision that should have been left to him. Satan's methods have not changed. He still approaches the womenfolk with his false teachings and leads them captive. These **women** are **gullible** in the sense that they are weak and unstable. They do not lack brains as much as they lack strength of character.

They are described as **loaded down with sins, led away by various lusts**. This suggests, first of all, that they are burdened under a sense of sin and feel a need in their lives. It is at this crucial time that the false cultists arrive. How sad it is that those who know the truth of God's word are not more zealous in reaching these anxious souls. Secondly, we read that they are **led away by various lusts**. Weymouth understands this to mean "led by ever-changing caprice." Moffatt calls them "wayward creatures of impulse." The thought seems to be that, conscious of their load of sin and seeking relief from it, they are willing to expose themselves to every passing wind of doctrine and to every religious novelty.

3:7 The expression **always learning** does not mean that they are continually learning more about the Lord Jesus and the word of God. Rather, it means that they are constantly delving into one cult after another, but **never able to come to the knowledge of the truth**. The Lord Jesus is Himself the Truth. These women seem to come ever so close to Him at times, but they are taken captive by the enemy of their souls and never attain the rest that is found only in the Savior.

It should be noted at this point that members of the various cults invariably say, "I am learning _____," mentioning the system by name. They can never speak with finality as to an accomplished redemption through faith in Jesus Christ.

This verse also makes us think of the vast present-day increase in knowledge in every realm of human endeavor, the tremendous emphasis on education so prevalent in modern life, and yet the abysmal failure of it all to bring men to the knowledge of the truth.

3:8 Three pairs of men are mentioned in this Epistle:

Phygellus and Hermogenes (1:15) — *ashamed* of the truth.

Hymenaeus and Philetus (2:17, 18) — *erred* concerning the truth.

Jannes and Jambres (3:8) — *resisted* the truth.

In this eighth verse, Paul returns to the leaders and teachers of false cults. He compares them to **Jannes and Jambres** who **resisted Moses**. Who were these men? Actually, their names are not mentioned in the OT, but it is generally understood that they were two of the chief Egyptian magicians who were called in by Pharaoh to imitate the miracles performed by Moses.

The question arises as to how Paul knew their names. This should present no difficulty, for if they were not passed down by Jewish tradition, it is not at all unreasonable that the names could have been given to him by divine revelation.

The important thing is that they **resisted Moses** by imitating his works, by counterfeit miracles. That is precisely the case with the false cultists. They withstand the work of God by imitating it. They have their own Bible, their own way of salvation — in short, they have a substitute for everything in Christianity. They withstand the truth of God by presenting a cheap perversion, and sometimes by resorting to magical arts.

These **men** are **of corrupt mind**. Arthur Way translates it: "their minds are rotten to the core." Their minds are distorted, debased, and depraved.

When tested concerning **the** Christian **faith**, they are found to be **disapproved** and spurious. The greatest single test that can be applied to them is to ask the simple question, "Is Jesus Christ God?" Many of them seek to hide their false doctrine by admitting that Jesus is the Son of God, but they mean that He is a son of God in the same sense that others are children of God. But when faced with the question, "Is Jesus Christ God?" they show their true colors. They not only deny the deity of Jesus Christ but usually become angry when so challenged. This is true of Christian Scientists, Spiritualists, Christadelphians, Jehovah's Witnesses, and "The Way."

3:9 Paul assures Timothy that these false teachers **will progress no further**. The difficulty here is that in every age they seem to be prospering on every hand, and nothing seems to hinder their advance in the world!

The probable meaning is that every system of error is eventually exposed. False systems come and go, one after the other. Although they might seem to prosper mightily, and even for a long time, yet the time comes when their falsity becomes evident to all. They can lead men up to a certain point, even offering a certain measure of reformation. But they fail in that they have no regeneration. They cannot offer a man freedom from the penalty and power of sin. They cannot give life.

Jannes and Jambres could imitate Moses to a certain extent by their acts of magic. However, when it came to producing life from death, they were utterly powerless. This is the very issue on which the false cults meet their defeat.

3:10 In marked contrast to these false teachers was the life and ministry of Paul. Timothy was well aware of the nine prominent features which characterized this servant of the Lord. He had followed Paul closely and could testify to the fact that here was a man who was faithful to Christ and His word.

The apostle's **doctrine** or teaching was true to the word of God and loyal to the Person of the Lord Jesus Christ. His **manner of life**, or conduct, was consistent with the message he preached. His **purpose** in life was to be separate from moral and doctrinal evil. **Faith** here may mean Paul's trust in the Lord, or his own personal fidelity. Timothy knew him as one who was utterly dependent

on the Lord, and at the same time, one who was honest and trustworthy. The apostle's **longsuffering** was seen in his attitude toward his persecutors and critics, and toward physical afflictions. As to **love**, he was selflessly devoted to the Lord and to his fellow men. The less he was loved by others, the more determined he was to love. **Perseverance** literally means "bearing up under," that is, fortitude or endurance.

3:11 Some of the **persecutions** and **afflictions**, or sufferings, of Paul are described in 2 Corinthians 11:23–28. However, he is thinking particularly of those with which Timothy would have been personally acquainted. Since Timothy's home was **Lystra**, he would know about the **persecutions** which came to Paul there and in the neighboring cities of **Antioch** and **Iconium**. The inspired record of these sufferings is given in the book of Acts — Antioch, Acts 13:45, 50; Iconium, Acts 14:3–6; Lystra, Acts 14:19, 20.

Paul exults in the fact that **the Lord** had **delivered** him **out of . . . all** of these crises. The Lord had not delivered *from* trouble, but He had delivered him **out of** the troubles. This is a reminder to us that we are not promised freedom from difficulties, but we are promised that the Lord will be with us and will see us through.

3:12 **Persecution** is an integral part of a devout Christian life. It is well that every young Timothy should be reminded of this. Otherwise, when he is called upon to go through deep waters, he might be tempted to think that he has failed the Lord or that the Lord is displeased with him for some reason. The fact is that **persecution** is inevitable for **all who desire to live** in a **godly** manner.

The reason for this **persecution** is simple. A **godly** life exposes the wickedness of others. People do not like to be thus exposed. Instead of repenting of their ungodliness and turning to Christ, they seek to destroy the one who has shown them up for what they really are. It is totally irrational behavior, of course, but that is characteristic of fallen man.

3:13 Paul had no illusions that the world would gradually become better and better, until finally all men would be converted. Rather, he knew by divine revelation that the very opposite would be the case. **Evil men and impostors will grow worse and worse**. They would become more subtle in their methods and more bold in their attacks. Not only would they deceive others, but they themselves would be ensnared by the very false teaching with which they sought to trap their hearers. After having peddled their lies for so long, they would actually come to believe them personally.

C. The Man of God's Resource in View of the Apostasy (3:14–4:8)

3:14 Time and time again, Timothy is reminded to **continue** steadfastly in the teachings of the word of God. This would be his great resource in a day when false doctrines would abound on every hand. If he knew and obeyed the Scriptures, he would not be led away by these subtle errors.

Timothy had not only **learned** the great truths of the faith, but he had become personally **assured** of them as well. Doubtless he would be told that such teachings were old-fashioned and not sufficiently cultural or intellectual. But he should not abandon truth for theories or human speculations.

The apostle further counsels him to remember **from whom** he had **learned** these truths. There is some difference of opinion as to whether the word **whom** refers to Paul himself, Timothy's mother and grandmother, or the apostles in general. In any case, the thought is that the Sacred Scriptures had been taught to him by those whose lives witnessed to the reality of their faith. They were godly people who lived with a single eye to the glory of God.

3:15 This is a most suggestive verse. The thought is that **from childhood** Timothy had known the sacred writings or letters. There is even the thought here that when his mother taught him his ABC's, she did so by using portions of the OT **Scriptures**. From infancy, he had been under the influence of the inspired writings, and under no circumstances should he forget that blessed Book which had molded his life for God and for good.

The Holy Scriptures are spoken of as being continually **able to make** men **wise**

for salvation. This means, first of all, that men learn the way of **salvation** through the Bible. It might also carry the thought that assurance of salvation comes through the word of God.

Salvation is **through faith which is in Christ Jesus**. We should mark this well. It is not through good works, baptism, church membership, confirmation, obeying the Ten Commandments, keeping the Golden Rule, or in any other way that involves human effort or merit. **Salvation** is **through faith** in the Son of God.

3:16 When Paul speaks of **all Scripture**, he is definitely referring to the complete OT, but also to those portions of the NT that were then in existence. In 1 Timothy 5:18, he quotes the Gospel of Luke (10:7) as Scripture. And Peter speaks of Paul's Epistles as Scriptures (2 Pet. 3:16). Today we are justified in applying the verse to the entire Bible.

This is one of the most important verses in the Bible on the subject of inspiration. It teaches that the Scriptures are God-breathed.[27] In a miraculous way, He communicated His word to men and led them to write it down for permanent preservation. What they wrote was the very word of God, inspired and infallible. While it is true that the individual literary style of the writer was not destroyed, it is also true that the very words he used were words given to him by the Holy Spirit. Thus we read in 1 Corinthians 2:13: "These things we also speak, not in words which man's wisdom teaches but which the Holy Spirit teaches; comparing spiritual things with spiritual." If this verse says anything at all, it says that the inspired writers used WORDS which the Holy Spirit taught. This is what is meant by *verbal* inspiration.

The writers of the Bible did not give their own private interpretation of things, but wrote the message which was given to them by God. "Knowing this first, that no prophecy of Scripture is of any private interpretation, for prophecy never came by the will of man, but holy men of God spoke as they were moved by the Holy Spirit" (2 Pet. 1:20, 21).

It is false to say that God simply gave the thoughts to the individual writers and allowed them to express these thoughts in their own words. The truth insisted on in the Scriptures is that the very words originally given by **God** to men were God-breathed.

Because the Bible is the word of God, it **is profitable**. Every portion of it **is profitable**. Although man might wonder about some of the genealogies or obscure passages, yet the Spirit-taught mind will realize that there is spiritual nourishment in every word that has proceeded from the mouth of God.

The Bible **is profitable for doctrine**, or teaching. It sets forth the mind of God with regard to such themes as the Trinity, angels, man, sin, salvation, sanctification, the church, and future events.

Again, it is profitable **for reproof**. As we read the Bible, it speaks to us pointedly concerning those things in our lives which are displeasing to God. Also, it is profitable for refuting error and for answering the tempter.

Again, the word is profitable **for correction**. It not only points out what is wrong but sets forth the way in which it can be made right. For instance, the Scriptures not only say, "Let him who stole steal no longer," but add, "Rather let him labor, working with his hands what is good, that he may have something to give to him who has need." The first part of the verse might be considered as **reproof**, whereas the second part is **correction**.

Finally, the Bible is profitable **for instruction in righteousness**. The grace of God teaches us to live godly lives, but the word of God traces out in detail the things which go to make up a godly life.

3:17 Through the word, **the man of God may be complete** or mature. He is **thoroughly equipped** with all that he needs to bring forth **every good work** which makes up the goal of his salvation (Eph. 2:8–10). This is in sharp contrast to the modern ideas of being equipped by means of academic degrees.

Lenski writes:

> The Scripture is thus absolutely incomparable; no other book, library, or anything else in the world is able to make a lost sinner wise for salvation; no other scripture, since it lacks inspiration of God, whatever profit it may otherwise afford, is profitable for these ends: teaching us

the true saving facts — refuting the lies and the delusions that deny these facts — restoring the sinner or fallen Christian to an upright position — educating, training, disciplining one in genuine righteousness. [28]

4:1 Paul now begins his final solemn charge to Timothy. He does so in the sight of **God and the Lord Jesus Christ**. All service should be carried out with the realization that it is watched by God's all-seeing eye.

In this verse, the Lord Jesus is spoken of as the One **who will judge the living and the dead at His appearing and His kingdom**. The English word **at** might suggest that when the Savior returns to earth to set up His kingdom, there will be a general resurrection and a general judgment. But in the original the Greek word *kata*[29] literally means "according to" or "in accordance with."

The Lord Jesus *is* the One **who will judge the living and the dead**, but no *time* is specified. Christ's **appearing and His kingdom** are presented by Paul as motives for faithful service.

We know from other Scriptures that the Second Coming of Christ is *not* the time when He will judge the living and the dead. *The wicked dead* will not be judged until the end of the Thousand-year Reign of Christ, according to Revelation 20:5.

The believer's service will be rewarded at the Judgment Seat of Christ, but these rewards will be manifested **at Christ's appearing and His kingdom**. It appears that rewards have to do with rule or administration during the Millennium. For instance, those who have been faithful will rule over ten cities (Luke 19:17).

4:2 In view of God's present observation of His servants and of His future reward, Timothy should herald **the word**. He should do so with a sense of urgency, availing himself of every opportunity. The message is **in season** at all times, even when some might think it to be **out of season**. As a servant of Christ, Timothy will be called upon to **convince**, that is, to prove or refute. He will have to **rebuke** what is false. He will be required to **exhort** or encourage sinners to believe and saints to go on for the Lord. In all of this, he must be unfailing in patient **longsuffering and** in the faithful **teaching** of sound doctrine.

4:3 In verses 3–6, the apostle gives two strong reasons for the charge he has just given. The first is that there will be a general turning away from wholesome **doctrine**. The second is that Paul's time of departure is at hand.

The apostle foresees a time when people will show a positive distaste for health-giving teaching. They will willfully turn away from those who teach the truth of God's word. Their **ears** will itch for doctrines that are pleasing and comfortable. To satisfy their lust for novel and gratifying doctrine, **they will** accumulate a group of **teachers** who will tell them what they want to hear.

4:4 The lust for inoffensive preaching will cause people to **turn their ears away from the truth** to myths. It is a poor exchange — to sacrifice truth for **fables** — but this is the wretched reward of those who refuse sound doctrine.

4:5 To **be watchful in all things** really means to be sober **in all things**. Timothy should be serious in his work, temperate, and well-balanced. He should not shun **afflictions** but should suffer willingly whatever hardships might come to him in his service for Christ.

There is some difference of opinion as to the expression **do the work of an evangelist.** Some think that Timothy actually *was* **an evangelist** and that here Paul was simply telling him to carry out this ministry. Others think that Timothy did not have the *gift* of evangelism, being perhaps a pastor or teacher, but that this should not prevent him from preaching the gospel as occasion arose. It seems likely that Timothy actually was **an evangelist** and that Paul's words are simply an encouragement for him to be all that evangelists should be.

In every respect, he should **fulfill** his **ministry**, devoting his finest talents to all the demands of his service.

4:6 The second reason for Paul's solemn charge to Timothy was his own approaching death. He was now about to be **poured out as a drink offering**. He likens the shedding of his blood in martyrdom to the pouring out of **a drink offering** over a sacrifice (see Ex. 29:40; Num. 15:1–10). Paul had previously likened his death to a drink offering in

Philippians 2:17. Hiebert says: "His whole life has been presented to God as a living sacrifice; now his death, comparable to the pouring out of the wine as the last act of the sacrificial ceremony, will complete the sacrifice."[30]

The time of my departure is at hand. The Greek word *analusis* (literally "up-loosing," whence English "analysis"), which Paul uses here to describe his **departure**, is a most expressive one, giving at least four different word pictures: (1) It was a seaman's word, used of the "un-loosing" of a ship from its anchorage. (2) It was a plowman's word, denoting the "unyoking" of a weary team of animals after a hard day. (3) It was a traveler's expression, suggesting the "striking" of a tent, preparatory to setting out on a march. (4) It was a philosopher's term, signifying the "solution" (analysis) of a problem. Here again we see the richness of the imagery used by the great apostle.

4:7 At first glance, it might seem as if Paul were boasting in this verse. However, such is not the case. The thought is not so much that he had fought *a* good fight, but rather that he had **fought** and was still fighting *the* **good fight**, namely, the fight of faith. He had spent his energies in the good contest. **Fight** here does not necessarily mean combat, but might just as well indicate an athletic contest.

Even as he wrote, he realized that **the** strenuous **race** was nearly over. He had been running on the course and was in sight of the goal.

Then, too, Paul had **kept the faith**. This means not only that Paul himself had continued to believe in and obey the great doctrines of **the** Christian **faith**, but also that, as a steward, he had guarded the doctrine which had been committed to him and had passed it on to others in its original purity.

4:8 The apostle here expresses confidence that the **righteousness** which he had manifested in his service would be rewarded by the righteous Lord at the Judgment Seat of Christ.

The Lord is here spoken of as **the righteous Judge**, but the thought is not that of a criminal court judge but of one at an athletic contest. Unlike earthly judges, He will have full and complete knowledge, He will not show respect of persons, He will evaluate motives as well as deeds, and His judgments will be accurate and impartial.

The crown of righteousness is the garland (here, not a diadem) which will be given to those believers who have exhibited **righteousness** in their service. Indeed, it will be given **to all** those **who have loved** Christ's **appearing**. If a man really longs with affection for the coming of Christ and lives in the light of that event, then his life will be righteous, and he will be rewarded accordingly. Here is a fresh reminder that the Second Coming of Christ, when truly believed and loved, exercises a sanctifying influence on one's life.

IV. PERSONAL REQUESTS AND REMARKS (4:9–22)

4:9 Paul, the aged, longs to have the companionship of his younger brother in the Lord. He therefore urges him to do his best **to come** to Rome in the near future. The apostle was feeling keenly the loneliness of his imprisonment in Rome.

4:10 One of the bitterest experiences in Christian service is to be forsaken by those who were formerly one's fellow laborers. **Demas** had been a friend of Paul's, a fellow believer, and a fellow worker. But now Paul was in prison, Christians were being persecuted, and the political climate was distinctly unhealthful for Christians. Instead of loving the Lord's appearing, **Demas** fell in love with **this present world**, and so left Paul and **departed for Thessalonica**. This does not necessarily mean that Demas gave up his Christian profession and became an apostate. Neither does it mean that he was not a true believer. Possibly his fears for his personal safety caused him to become a backslider.

The apostle then adds that **Crescens** had gone to **Galatia**, and **Titus** to **Dalmatia**. There is no suggestion of blame in these words; perhaps they had gone to these places on Christian service. This is the only mention of **Crescens** (whose name means "growing") in the Bible. We know nothing more about him. This should be an encouragement to all believers. No matter how humble their po-

sition in life may be, even an errand run for the Lord will not go unnoticed or unrewarded.

4:11 The beloved Doctor **Luke** was the only one who maintained contact with Paul in Rome. How much it must have meant to the apostle to have the spiritual encouragement and professional skill of this great man of God!

And how thankful we can be for the latter part of verse 11! It holds encouragement to all of us who have failed the Lord in our service that He will yet give us another opportunity to go forth for Him. **Mark** went with Paul and Barnabas on their First Missionary Journey, but then left them at Perga to return home. When it came time to go out on the Second Missionary Journey, Paul did not want to bring Mark along because of the young man's previous retreat. When Barnabas insisted that Mark should accompany them, the matter was resolved by Paul's leaving for Syria and Cilicia with Silas, while Barnabas and Mark went to Cyprus. Later on, Paul and Mark were reconciled, and here the apostle specifically asks for **Mark** as one who **is useful to** him **for ministry**.

4:12 Those who believe that Timothy was in Ephesus when Paul wrote this Letter to him suggest that the apostle sent **Tychicus to Ephesus** as a replacement during Timothy's approaching absence. They suggest that Paul's meaning here is: "But **Tychicus** I am commissioning to go **to Ephesus**."

4:13 **The cloak** mentioned here may be either an outer garment or a bag used for carrying books. It is generally understood to refer to the former here.

There is no agreement as to the difference between **the books** and **the parchments**.[31] Were they portions of Scripture? Were they some of Paul's Letters? Were they papers which he would be using at his trial? Were they blank pieces of papyrus or parchment which he wanted to use for writing? It is impossible to decide definitely. But the strong suggestion is that even in his imprisonment, the apostle wanted to keep busy with his writing and his reading.

An interesting true story is told in connection with this apparently unimportant Bible verse. F. W. Newman, Cardinal Newman's younger brother, once asked J. N. Darby how we could possibly be any the poorer if this verse were not in the Bible. Was it not of temporary value only? Would anything be lost if Paul had never written it? Darby promptly replied: "I would certainly have lost something; for this is the verse that saved me from selling my library. Every word, depend upon it, is from the Spirit, and is for eternal service."[32]

4:14 **Alexander the coppersmith** may have been the same one referred to by Paul in 1 Timothy 1:20 as having made shipwreck of the faith. In any event, he had done great **harm** to the apostle. We can only speculate as to the nature of his evil. Linking this verse with the verses that follow, it seems probable that **Alexander** testified against the apostle and brought false charges against him. Conybeare and Howson translate: "Alexander the coppersmith charged me with much evil." The apostle is confident that **the Lord** will **repay him according to his works**.

4:15 This verse anticipates Timothy's arrival in Rome. He **also must beware of** Alexander, lest he, too, suffer at the hands of this evil man. It is not unlikely that Alexander **greatly resisted** Paul's **words** by opposing his testimony at the public hearing.

4:16 Paul is probably still thinking of the events of the past few days. His **first defense** means the first opportunity which he was given to defend himself at this, his last trial.[33] It does seem sad indeed that **no one stood** up to speak a word in behalf of this valiant apostle whose writings have enriched the subsequent centuries. No one would undertake his defense, but there is no bitterness in his heart for all that. Like the Savior before him, he prays that it might **not be charged against them**.

4:17 He may have been forsaken by men, **but the Lord stood with** him. Not only so, but he was divinely strengthened to preach the gospel at his trial. The message went forth without hindrance, and a Gentile law court heard the message of salvation. Stock marvels:

All the Gentiles — what a throng of distinguished Romans may be included in

that simple phrase! — heard that day the message of God to mankind; all heard the Crucified and Exalted Jesus set forth as the One Savior. It is an overwhelming thought; the imagination fails to realize so tremendous a scene; it must have been one of the great moments of history; and what may not Eternity reveal to us of its results?[34]

The word **strengthened** in this verse is not a common one; it is found only eight times in the NT. It is used in Acts 9:22 at the beginning of Paul's public ministry: he "increased . . . in strength." Here it is used again, but now at the end of his public ministry — a touching reminder of the sustaining strength of the Lord throughout His servant's life.

The expression **"I was delivered out of the mouth of the lion"** is a way of saying that Paul was granted a temporary delay. The trial was continued. The danger was temporarily averted. Attempts have been made to identify the lion as Nero, the devil, and literal wild animals. But perhaps it is simpler to understand the word as meaning danger in general.

4:18 When the apostle said **the Lord** would **deliver** him **from every evil work**, he did not imply that he would be indefinitely delivered from execution. He knew that the time of his death was drawing near (v. 6). What then did he mean? Doubtless he meant that the Lord would save him from doing anything that would be a blot on the closing days of his testimony. The Lord would deliver him from recanting, from denying His name, from cowardice, or from any form of moral breakdown.

Not only so, but Paul was sure that the Lord would **preserve** him **for His heavenly kingdom**. The **heavenly kingdom** refers not to Christ's Millennial Reign on earth, but to heaven itself, where the rule of the Lord is acknowledged perfectly.

Here the apostle bursts into an ascription of **glory** to God **forever and ever**. **Forever and ever** is literally "to the ages of the ages" and the words represent the strongest expression of eternality possible in the Greek language. Technically, there are no "ages" in eternity, but since the human mind has no conception of timelessness, it is compelled to use expressions of time.

4:19 Now Paul sends greetings to a married couple who had served with him often in the gospel. **Prisca** (or Priscilla) **and Aquila** first met Paul in Corinth, and then traveled with him to Ephesus. They lived for a time in Rome (Rom. 16:3), and, like Paul, were tentmakers.

Onesiphorus was previously mentioned in 1:16 as one who had often refreshed the apostle and had not been ashamed of his imprisonment.

4:20 Perhaps **Erastus** is the same one who was treasurer of the city of **Corinth** (Rom. 16:23).

Trophimus is mentioned previously in Acts 20:4 and 21:29. Converted in Ephesus, he had accompanied Paul to Jerusalem. The Jews there thought that Paul had taken him into the temple. Here we read that Paul had **left** him **in Miletus sick**. This statement is important in showing that, although the apostle had the miraculous power of healing, he did not always use it. The miracle of healing was never employed as a matter of personal convenience, but rather as a testimony to unbelieving Jews as to the truth of the gospel.

4:21 Timothy should do his **utmost to come before winter** weather made travel difficult or impossible. His imprisoned friend in Rome needed his presence and was waiting for him. The repeated exhortations to Timothy **to come** are very touching (see 1:3, 4; 4:9).

Next we have greetings to Timothy from **Eubulus, Pudens, Linus, Claudia, and all the brethren**. These names might seem of little consequence, but they are a touching reminder, as Rodgers says, that "one of the special joys and privileges of Christian service is the way in which friendships are created and enriched."

4:22 And now Paul brings his last Epistle to a close. Speaking to Timothy in particular, he says, **"The Lord Jesus Christ[35] be with your spirit."** Then, addressing all those who were with Timothy at the time he received the Letter, the apostle adds: **"Grace be with your spirit. Amen."**

Here he lays down his pen. The Letter is finished. His ministry is ended.

But the fragrance of his life and testimony abides with us still, and we shall meet him again and talk with him about the grand themes of the gospel and the church.

ENDNOTES

[1](1:1) W. E. Vine, *Exposition of the Epistles to Timothy*, pp. 60, 61.

[2](1:2) D. Edmond Hiebert, *Second Timothy*, p. 26.

[3](1:3) The Greek word is *latreuō*, related to *latreia*, "worship" (cf. English "mariolatry," the adoration of Mary).

[4](1:4) Hiebert, *Second Timothy*, p. 31.

[5](1:5) The Greek for "genuine" is literally "unhypocritical." By derivation a hypocrite is a play-actor who answers from under (*hupo*) his mask.

[6](1:6) Vine, *Exposition*, under the verses listed.

[7](1:11) The critical (NU) text omits "of the Gentiles."

[8](1:16) J. H. Jowett, *Things that Matter Most*, p. 161.

[9](2:3) NU text reads "share."

[10](2:4) William Kelly, *An Exposition of the Two Epistles to Timothy*, p. 213.

[11](2:7) The critical (NU) text reads "the Lord will give you" (future indicative, not a prayer).

[12](2:8) Hiebert, *Second Timothy*, p. 59.

[13](2:9) Quoted by D. Edmond Hiebert in *Second Timothy*, p. 60.

[14](2:10) The beloved hymn "Immanuel's Land" was written by Anne Ross Cousin, but, it is said, using phraseology from Samuel Rutherford's writings.

[15](2:11) Hiebert, *Second Timothy*, p. 62.

[16](2:13) Dinsdale T. Young, *Unfamiliar Texts*, p. 253.

[17](2:13) J. J. Van Oosterzee, "The Pastoral Letters," *Lange's Commentary on the Holy Scriptures*, XI:95.

[18](2:14) Dinsdale T. Young, *The Enthusiasm of God*, p. 154.

[19](2:15) Henry Alford, *The Greek Testament*, III:384.

[20](2:17) The Greek word here is *gangraina*, but that does not necessarily mean that our English derivative is the best *translation*.

[21](2:18) Hamilton Smith, *The Second Epistle to Timothy*, p. 26.

[22](2:19) Smith, *ibid*.

[23](2:19) R. C. H. Lenski, *The Interpre-

tation of St. Paul's Epistles to the Colossians, to the Thessalonians, to Timothy, to Titus and to Philemon, p. 804.

²⁴(2:19) Both the NU and M texts read "Lord" for "Christ," which makes it close to Num. 16:5.

²⁵(2:22) Hiebert, *Second Timothy,* p. 76.

²⁶(3:5) Hiebert, *ibid.,* p. 86.

²⁷(3:16) The Greek word is *theopneustos.*

²⁸(3:17) Lenski, *Epistles, p. 841.*

²⁹*(4:1) The critical text reads kai ("and") for kata.*

³⁰(4:6) Hiebert, *Second Timothy,* pp. 109, 110.

³¹(4:13) Greek, *membranas.* These ex-pensive mss. were probably Bible books or perhaps commentaries.

³²(4:13) Quoted by H. A. Ironside, *Timothy, Titus and Philemon,* p. 255.

³³(4:16) Conceivably the trial at the end of Paul's *first* imprisonment is meant.

³⁴(4:17) Eugene Stock, *Plain Talks on the Pastoral Epistles,* pagination unavailable.

³⁵(4:22) NU text omits *Jesus Christ.*

BIBLIOGRAPHY

See Bibliography at the end of 1 Timothy.

THE EPISTLE TO TITUS

Introduction

"This is a short epistle, but it contains such a quintessence of Christian doctrine, and is composed in such a masterly manner, that it contains all that is needful for Christian knowledge and life." — Martin Luther

I. Unique Place in the Canon

Three short chapters written over nineteen centuries ago to a little-known missionary on an obscure island by an aging senior missionary — what possible relevance could these have for Christians in the "enlightened" twentieth century? Granted, if they were *only* the words of Paul (and most liberals will not even grant *that!*) they could have merely an interest for church history buffs or those majoring in early Christian thought.

But these are also "words which the Holy Spirit teaches," and as such have a contribution to make that *no other book* can fill. The handling of the subject of elders strengthens and supports the very similar teaching found in 1 Timothy. The repetition is not redundant, but like so many other parallels in the Bible, especially in the OT, merely emphasizes how much God desires His people to grasp certain principles.

Probably the most prized passage in Titus is 2:11–14, which is written with a lovely balanced style that enhances the doctrine of grace.

II. Authorship

See the Introduction to the Pastoral Epistles for a discussion of the authorship of the Epistle to Titus.

III. Date

Because of the similarity of themes and wording, Titus is believed by conservative scholars to have been written about the same time or soon after 1 Timothy. At any rate it came *between* 1 and 2 Timothy in time, not after 2 Timothy. While an exact date is impossible to give, sometime between A.D. 64 and 66 is likely. The place of origin is probably Macedonia.

IV. Theme†

Besides the general themes that Titus shares in common with the other two Pastoral Epistles (see Introduction to the Pastoral Epistles), Titus gives a fine concise summary of how a believer should adorn the doctrine of *grace* with *godliness* and *good works*. Many today who seem pleased with the doctrine of grace apparently have little interest in displaying it in good works, or even godliness. Such an attitude is wrong and suggests a misapprehension of true grace.

Paul sums up the theme perfectly: "This is a faithful saying, and these things I want you to affirm constantly, that those who have believed in God should be careful to maintain good works" (3:8a).

†See p. ii.

OUTLINE

Commentary

I. SALUTATION (1:1–4)

1:1 **Paul** was both **a bondservant of God and an apostle of Jesus Christ**. The first pictures him as a slave of the Supreme Master, the second as an envoy of the Sovereign Lord. The first speaks of submission, the second of authority. He became a **bondservant** by personal commitment, an **apostle** by divine appointment.

The goals of his ministry were to further **the faith of God's elect and the acknowledgement of the truth**. Furthering their **faith** may mean either bringing them *to faith* or conversion in the first place, or leading them on *in the faith* after salvation. Since the phrase, the **acknowledgement of the truth** seems to cover the second meaning, we understand the apostle to mean that his two basic aims were: (1) *evangelism* —furthering **the faith of God's elect**; (2) *education* — furthering their knowledge **of the truth**. It is an echo of Matthew 28:20 — preaching the gospel to all nations and teaching them to observe all things Christ commanded. In specifying without apology that it is **the faith of God's elect** he is called to promote, the apostle confronts us with the doctrine of election. Few doctrines of Scripture have suffered more misunderstanding, provoked more debate, and strained more intellects. Briefly, it teaches that God chose certain ones in Christ before the foundation of the world with the ultimate intention that they should be holy and blameless before Him (Eph. 1:4).[1]

Having spoken of his apostleship as being involved with **the faith of God's elect** and their **acknowledgement of the truth**, Paul now adds that this **truth ac-** **cords with godliness**. This means that the Christian faith is consistent with true holiness and is adapted to lead men to practical **godliness**. Soundness in faith demands purity in life. Nothing could be more incongruous than the preacher of whom it was said, "When he was in the pulpit, the people wished he would never leave it. When he was out of the pulpit, they wished he would never enter it!"

1:2 Paul's commission in connection with the gospel has a third great emphasis. It was not only concerned with: (1) *evangelism* — furthering the faith of God's elect, past tense; and (2) *education* — furthering their knowledge of the truth, present tense; but also (3) *expectation* — **in hope of eternal life**, future tense.

The NT speaks of **eternal life** as both a present possession and a future hope. The word **hope** does not imply uncertainty. The moment we trust Christ as Savior we have eternal life as a present possession (John 5:24) and become heirs to all the benefits of His redemptive work, but we will not experience the practical enjoyment of all of them until we reach our eternal home. We **hope** in the sense that we are looking forward to **eternal life** in its final form when we will receive our glorified bodies and be forever free from sin, sickness, sorrow, suffering, and death (Phil. 3:20, 21; Tit. 3:7).

The **hope** is sure because it was **promised** by God. Nothing is as sure as the word of **God, who cannot lie**, who cannot be deceived, and who would not deceive. There is no risk in believing what He says. In fact nothing is more reasonable than for the creature to believe his Creator.

God promised eternal life **before time**

began. This may be understood in two ways. First, God determined in past eternity to give eternal life to all who would believe on the Lord Jesus, and what He determined was the same as a promise. Or it may mean that all the blessings of salvation were contained in germ form in the promise of the Messiah found in Genesis 3:15. This was before the ages of time or dispensations began to unfold.

1:3 **In due time** God made known this glorious program of eternal life which He had decided on in past ages. He had not fully revealed it in OT times. Believers then had a very hazy idea of life after death. But the vagueness disappeared with the coming of the Savior. He "brought life and immortality to light through the gospel" (2 Tim. 1:10). And the good news was broadcast by Paul and the other apostles in fulfillment of **the commandment of God our Savior**, that is, in obedience to the Great Commission.

1:4 The Letter is addressed **to Titus**, Paul's **true son in** a **common faith**. But who is this Titus?

We have to piece together his biography from sparse references to him in three of Paul's Letters. A Greek by birth (Gal. 2:3), he was born again by faith in the Lord Jesus, possibly through Paul's ministry (Tit. 1:4). A battle was then raging over what was the true gospel. On one side were Paul and all those who taught salvation by grace through faith plus nothing. On the other side were the Judaizers who insisted that circumcision (and thus lawkeeping) was requisite for first-class citizenship in God's kingdom. Titus became a test case in the controversy. Paul and Barnabas took him to Jerusalem (Gal. 2:1) for a conference with the apostles and elders. The decision of the council was that a Gentile like Titus did not have to submit to Jewish laws and ceremonies in order to be saved (Acts 15:11). Gentiles did not have to become Jews. Jews did not have to become Gentiles. Rather, Jews and Gentiles became a new creation when they believed in Jesus.

Thereafter Titus became one of Paul's most valuable assistants, serving as a "trouble-shooter" in Corinth and Crete. The apostle first sent him from Ephesus to Corinth, presumably to cor-

rect doctrinal and ethical disorders in the assembly there. When Titus later rejoined Paul in Macedonia, Paul was overjoyed to hear that the Corinthians had responded positively to his apostolic admonitions (2 Cor. 2:12, 13; 7:5–7, 13–16). From Macedonia, Paul sent Titus to Corinth again, this time to expedite a collection for poor saints in Jerusalem (2 Cor. 8:6, 16, 17; 12:18). Paul described him as "my partner and fellow worker concerning you" (2 Cor. 8:23). We do not definitely know when Paul was with Titus in Crete, but it is generally believed to have been after the apostle's first imprisonment in Rome.

The last mention of Titus is in 2 Timothy 4:10. He was with Paul during part of his second imprisonment, but then Paul reports him as having left for Dalmatia, the Yugoslavia of today. Paul may have sent him there, though the general tone of the verse is that of a lonely and deserted man.

The apostle speaks of Titus as his **true son in** a **common faith**. This may mean that Paul was instrumental in Titus' conversion, but not necessarily. Paul also addressed Timothy as his true son in the faith (1 Tim. 1:2), yet it is possible that Timothy was already a disciple when Paul first met him (Acts 16:1). So the expression may mean that these younger men exhibited spiritual qualities similar to Paul's, and that in Christian service there was a filial bond.

For his young lieutenant Paul wishes **grace, mercy, and peace**. In this context, **grace** means the divine strength needed for life and service. **Mercy** is compassion on man's deep need. **Peace** means freedom from anxiety, panic, and distraction despite adverse circumstances. These come jointly **from God the Father and the Lord Jesus Christ our Savior**. In thus linking the Father and the Son as the sources of **grace, mercy, and peace**, the Spirit of God implies their complete equality.

II. ELDERS IN THE CONGREGATION (1:5–9)

1:5 When Paul left Crete, there were certain **things** that still needed to be **set in order**, there were false teachers to be silenced, and there was the pressing need for recognized spiritual guides in the assemblies. He left Titus to handle these matters.

We do not know how the Christian faith first came to Crete. Perhaps the best guess is that Cretans who were in Jerusalem on the Day of Pentecost (Acts 2:11) returned with the good news, and that local churches were subsequently established.

Neither can we be sure as to when Paul was in Crete with Titus. We know that he touched in at Crete on his voyage to Rome as a prisoner (Acts 27:12), but the circumstances would hardly have permitted active ministry in the churches. Since Acts makes no other reference to Paul's being in Crete, it is generally supposed that the visit took place after his first Roman imprisonment. Resorting to a little biblical detective work, we can reconstruct the following itinerary from various references in Paul's writings.

First Paul sailed from Italy to Crete on his way to Asia (Western Turkey today). Leaving Titus in Crete (Tit. 1:5), he traveled to Ephesus, the capital of Asia. At Ephesus he deputized Timothy to correct doctrinal errors that were creeping in there (1 Tim. 1:3, 4). Then he sailed across the Aegean Sea to Macedonia to fulfill his prior intention while in prison to visit Philippi as soon as he was free (Phil. 1:26). Finally, he traveled southwest across Greece to Nicopolis, where he planned to stay for the winter and where he expected Titus to join him (Tit. 3:12).

According to Homer, there were between ninety and one hundred cities in Crete as early as his time, and churches had apparently been formed in several of them. In each there was a need for responsible **elders** to be appointed.

ELDERS

Elders in the NT sense are mature Christian men of sterling character who provide spiritual leadership in a local assembly. The name elder, which refers to the spiritual maturity of the man, is translated from the Greek word *presbuteros*, (which turned into the English "presbyter"). The Greek word *episkopos*, translated "bishop," "overseer" or "guardian," is also used in reference

to elders, describing their function as undershepherds of God's flock.

The names "elders" and "bishops" are generally understood to refer to the same persons for the following reasons. In Acts 20:17, Paul called for the elders (*presbuteroi*) from Ephesus; in verse 28 he addressed them as guardians (*episkopoi*). In 1 Peter 5:1, 2, Peter similarly uses the terms interchangeably. The qualifications for bishops (*episkopoi*) in 1 Timothy 3 and those for elders (*presbuteroi*) in Titus 1 are substantially the same.

In modern usage, "bishop" has come to mean a prelate who supervises a diocese or a group of churches in a district. But the word never means this in the NT. The scriptural pattern is to have *several* bishops in *one* church rather than *one* bishop over *several* churches.

Nor should an elder be confused with the modern pastor, who is primarily responsible for preaching, teaching, and administering the sacraments in a local church. It is generally acknowledged that there was no such person in the early church. The primitive assemblies were composed of saints, bishops, and deacons (Phil. 1:1) — that is all. The clerical system did not rise until the second century.

A pastor in the NT sense is one of the special-service gifts which the risen, ascended Christ bestowed to build up the saints for the work of ministering (Eph. 4:11, 12). In many respects the work of pastors and elders is similar; both are called to tend and feed the flock of God. But the two are never equated. Conceivably, a pastor may have a traveling ministry, while an elder is usually associated with one local assembly.

The functions of elders are given in considerable detail:

1. They shepherd and care for the church of the Lord (Acts 20:28; 1 Tim. 3:5; 1 Pet. 5:2).

2. They are alert to protect the church from attacks, both from without and within (Acts 20:29–31).

3. They lead and rule, but by guiding, not driving (1 Thess. 5:12; 1 Tim. 5:17; Heb. 13:7, 17; 1 Pet. 5:3).

4. They preach the word, teach sound doctrine, and refute those who contradict it (1 Tim. 5:17; Tit. 1:9–11).

5. They moderate and arbitrate in doctrinal and ethical matters (Acts 15:5, 6; 16:4).

6. By their life they are an example to the flock (Heb. 13:7; 1 Pet. 5:3).

7. They seek to restore the believers who have been overtaken in any trespass (Gal. 6:1).

8. They keep watch over the souls of Christians in the local assembly as those who will have to give account (Heb. 13:17).

9. They exercise a ministry of prayer, especially with regard to the sick (Jas. 5:14, 15).

10. They are involved in the care of poor saints (Acts 11:30).

11. They share in the commendation of gifted men to the work to which God has called them (1 Tim. 4:14).

It is clear that in the early church, elders were appointed by the apostles and their representatives (Acts 14:23; Tit. 1:5). This does not mean, however, that the apostles and their delegates had the power to *make* a man an elder. In order to become a bishop, there must be both divine enablement and human willingness. Only the Holy Spirit can make a man a bishop or guardian (Acts 20:28), but the man must aspire to the work (1 Tim. 3:1). There must be this mingling of the divine and the human.

When local churches were first established in the apostolic days, there were no elders in them; all the believers were novices. But as time passed, the Lord prepared certain ones for this important ministry. Since the NT was not yet available in written form, Christians in general did not know the qualifications and duties of elders. Only the apostles and their assistants knew. On the basis of this knowledge, they singled out the men who met the divine standards and publicly named them as such.

Today we have the complete NT. We know what an elder is and what he is supposed to do. When we see qualified men who are actively serving as overseers, we recognize them (1 Thess. 5:12) and obey them (Heb. 13:17). It is not a question of *our* electing them but of recognizing those whom *God* has raised up for this work.

The qualifications of elders are found in 1 Timothy 3:1–7 and here in Titus.

Sometimes we hear the remark that if these are the requirements, then there are no bishops today. This idea downgrades the authority of the Scriptures by implying that they don't mean what they say. There is nothing unreasonable or unattainable in the standards given. We betray our own low spiritual state when we treat the Bible as excessively idealistic. ‡

1:6 Elders are men who are **blameless**, that is, of unquestioned integrity. No charge of false doctrine or irregular behavior can be proved against them. It does not mean that they are sinless, but that if they do minor wrongs, they are prompt to make them right by confession to God, by apology to the person(s) wronged, and by restitution, if applicable.

The second qualification, that they be **the husband of one wife**, has been understood in at least seven different ways: (1) a man must be married; (2) he must not be divorced; (3) he must not be remarried after divorce; (4) he must not be remarried after the death of his first wife; (5) he must not be a polygamist; (6) he must not have concubines or lesser wives; (7) in general, he must be a faithful husband and an example of strict morality.

If the phrase **husband of one wife** means that a man must be married, then by the same reasoning he must have children, because this same verse states that his **children** must be believers. Certainly it is preferable for an elder to have a family; he can deal more intelligently with family problems in the congregation. But it is doubtful that this verse prohibits any unmarried man from being an elder.

It probably does not mean that he must not be divorced under any circumstances, because the Savior taught that divorce is permissible in at least one instance (Matt. 5:32; 19:9).[2]

Neither can it be taken as an absolute prohibition of remarriage after divorce in all cases. For example, a believer who is entirely innocent might be divorced by an unbelieving wife who then remarries. In such a case, the Christian was not responsible. Since the first marriage was broken by the divorce and remarriage of his unbelieving partner, he is free to remarry.

The interpretation that eligibility for the work of an elder is forfeited if a man remarries after the death of his first wife is ruled out by the principle stated in 1 Corinthians 7:39: "A wife is bound by law as long as her husband lives; but if her husband dies, she is at liberty to be married to whom she wishes, only in the Lord."

Certainly the expression **the husband of one wife** means that an elder must not be a polygamist nor have a concubine or mistress. In summary, it means that his married life must be an example of purity to the flock.

In addition he must have **faithful children not accused of dissipation or insubordination**. More than most of us care to admit, the Bible holds parents responsible for the way their children turn out (Prov. 22:6). When a family is well-governed and well-trained in the word of God, the **children** generally follow the godly example of their parents. Although a father cannot determine the salvation of his children, he can prepare the way of the Lord by positive instruction in the word, by loving discipline, and by avoiding hypocrisy and inconsistency in his own life.

If children are spendthrifts and rebels against parental authority, the Scriptures lay the responsibility at the father's door. His indulgence and permissiveness have been to blame. If he cannot rule his own family well, it is unlikely that he would be a suitable elder, since the same principles apply in each case (1 Tim. 3:5).

There is a question whether this requirement concerning **faithful children** applies only as long as children are under parental authority in the home, or whether it includes those who are away from home. We favor the first view, remembering, however, that home training is one of the principal determinants of ultimate character.

1:7 A **bishop** is **a steward of God**. It is not *his* congregation that he helps to oversee. He is deputized to handle God's affairs in God's assembly. For the second time it is specified that he must be **blameless** — surely this is repetition for emphasis. Let there be no doubt — he must be a man who is above reproach

both doctrinally and morally. He must **not** be **self-willed**. If a man is headstrong, obstinately right with no possibility that those who differ might be, if he is unyielding and impatient of contradiction, then he is unsuited to be a spiritual leader. An elder is a moderator, not a dogmatic autocrat.

He must **not** be **quick-tempered**. If he has a volatile temperament, he has learned to bridle it. If he has a hot temper, he never lets it show.

He must **not** be **given to wine**. In our culture, this might seem so elementary as to scarcely need mentioning. But we must remember that the Bible was written for all cultures. In countries where wine is used by Christians as a common beverage, there is the danger of overindulgence and disorderly conduct. That lack of self-control is in view here.

The Bible distinguishes between the use of wine and its abuse. Its use in moderation as a beverage was allowed when Jesus turned the water into wine at the wedding in Cana (John 2:1–11). Its use for medicinal purposes is prescribed by Paul for Timothy (1 Tim. 5:23; see also Prov. 31:6). The abuse of wine and strong drink is condemned in Proverbs 20:1; 23:29–35. While total abstinence is not demanded in the word, there is one situation in which refraining is called for, namely, when drinking wine would offend a weaker brother or cause him to stumble (Rom. 14:21). This is the overriding consideration which causes great numbers of Christians in North American to abstain from alcohol entirely.

With the elder, the question is not the total prohibition of wine, but rather the excessive use of wine, which leads to brawling.

Neither should he be **violent**. He must not resort to the use of physical force by striking others. We have heard of officious clerics who gave an occasional blow to refractory members of their parish. This type of overbearing intimidation is forbidden for a bishop.

He must not be **greedy for money**, insatiably determined to get rich, but careless as to the means employed. It is true, as Samuel Johnson said, that "the lust of gold, unfeeling and remorseless, is the last corruption of degenerate man." A true elder can say with Paul:

"I have coveted no one's silver or gold or apparel" (Acts 20:33).

1:8 On the positive side, a bishop must be **hospitable**. His home should always be open to strangers, to those with personal problems, to the disheartened and the oppressed. It should be a place of happy Christian fellowship, where every guest is received as if he were the Lord Himself.

Next he must be **a lover of what is good** — good people and good things. His speech, his activities, and his associations should reveal that he is separated from all that is shady, questionable, or wrong.

He must be **sober-minded**. This means that he is prudent, discreet, and master of himself. The same word is used in Titus 2:2, 5, 6, 12, where it has the thought of being sensible, self-controlled, and sober.

In his dealings with others, the elder must be **just**. In relation to God he must be **holy**. In respect to himself he must be **self-controlled**. This is what Paul referred to in Galatians 5:22, 23: "The fruit of the Spirit is . . . self-control." It means that a person has every passion and appetite under control to obey Christ. While the power for this can only come from the Holy Spirit, there must be discipline and cooperation on the part of the believer.

1:9 The bishop must be sound in the faith. He must hold tenaciously to the spiritually healthful doctrines taught by the Lord Jesus and the apostles which have been preserved for us in the NT. Only then will he be able to give the saints a balanced diet of **sound doctrine**, and silence those who speak against the truth.

These are the qualifications of spiritual guides in the local assembly. It should be noticed that nothing is said about their physical prowess, educational attainments, social status, or business acumen. A hunchbacked street sweeper, homespun and unlettered, might be a qualified elder because of his spiritual stature. It is not true, as is sometimes suggested, that the same qualities that make a man successful in business also fit him for leadership in the church.

One other point should be men-tioned. The picture that emerges of a godly elder is not that of a man who arranges for speakers, disburses funds, contracts for building repairs, and that's all! The true elder is deeply and vitally involved in the spiritual life of the church by his instruction, exhortation, encouragement, rebuke, and correction.

III. ERROR IN THE CONGREGATION (1:10–16)

1:10 In the early church there was "the liberty of the Spirit," that is, freedom for the men to participate in the meetings as led by the Holy Spirit. Paul describes such an "open" meeting in 1 Corinthians 14:26: "How is it then, brethren? Whenever you come together, each of you has a psalm, has a teaching, has a tongue, has a revelation, has an interpretation. Let all things be done for edification." It is an ideal situation when the Spirit of God is thus free to speak through various members of the congregation. But human nature being what it is, wherever such liberty exists, you almost invariably find men rushing in to abuse it with false doctrine, unedifying nit-picking, or seemingly endless rambling, devoid of the Spirit.

This had happened in the Cretan congregations. Paul realized that there must be strong spiritual leadership to control the abuses and to preserve the liberty of the Spirit. He also realized that great care was needed in appointing elders who were fully qualified. So here he rehearses the conditions which called for prompt action in appointing elders in the churches.

Many insubordinate men had risen up to defy the authority of the apostles and deny their teachings. They were **both idle talkers and deceivers**. Their talk produced no spiritual benefits. Rather, it robbed people of the truth and led them into error.

The principal troublemakers were **those of the circumcision** party, that is, Jewish teachers who professed to be Christians and yet insisted that Christians must be circumcised and observe the ceremonial law. This was a practical denial of the all-sufficiency of the work of Christ.

1:11 Men like this must be muzzled. They must learn that the assembly is not a democracy, and that freedom of speech has limits. They had been overturning **whole households**. Does this suggest that they had been peddling their pernicious doctrines behind the scenes in private homes? It is a favorite method of the cults (2 Tim. 3:6). Their motives were suspect as well. They were out for money, using the ministry as a front for a lucrative business. Their message appealed to the legalistic streak in man, encouraging him to believe that he can gain God's favor by going through religious motions even though his life may be corrupt and defiled. They taught for **dishonest gain** what they had no right to teach.

1:12 Here Paul reminds Titus of the kind of people he is dealing with. The unusually blunt and caustic description was true of the false teachers in particular and of the **Cretans** in general. He quotes Epimenides, one of their own poetic spokesmen who lived around 600 B.C., as calling them inveterate **liars, evil beasts, lazy gluttons**. It seems that every people has national characteristics, but few could beat the Cretans in depravity. They were habitual and compulsive **liars**. They were like fierce animals, living to indulge gross and wild passions. Allergic to work and addicted to gluttony, they lived lives that were all kitchen and no chapel!

1:13 The apostle confirms the accuracy of the character sketch. Titus had unpromising raw materials to work with — enough to discourage any missionary! But Paul did not write the people off or counsel Titus to abandon them. Through the gospel there is hope for the worst of men. So Paul advises his assistant to **rebuke them sharply, that they may be sound** or healthy **in the** Christian **faith**. Some day these men might be not only exemplary believers, but also godly elders in the local churches. This passage overflows with encouragement for Christian workers in difficult fields of the world (and what field is not difficult?). Beyond the grossness, denseness, and unresponsiveness of the people, there is always the vision of their becoming gracious, pure, and fruitful saints.

1:14 In severely rebuking the false teachers, Titus was charged to warn them against **Jewish fables and commandments of men who turn from the truth**. The Judaizers lived in a world of religious fantasies and of rules centering around clean and unclean foods, the observance of days, and the avoidance of ceremonial defilement. It was of this which Paul wrote in Colossians 2:23: "These things indeed have an appearance of wisdom in self-imposed religion, false humility, and neglect of the body, but are of no value against the indulgence of the flesh."

1:15 What the apostle says next has given rise to such misinterpretation that it requires a detailed explanation. He writes: **"To the pure all things are pure, but to those who are defiled and unbelieving nothing is pure; but even their mind and conscience are defiled."**

If we take the words **to the pure all things are pure** out of context as a statement of *absolute* truth in *all* areas of life, we are in trouble! All things are *not* pure, even to those whose minds are pure. Yet people have actually used this verse to justify vile magazines, suggestive movies, and even immorality itself. This is what Peter speaks of as twisting the Scriptures "to their own destruction" (2 Pet. 3:16).

Let it be clearly understood that this verse has absolutely nothing to do with things that are sinful in themselves and condemned in the Bible. This proverbial saying must be understood in the light of the context. Paul has *not* been speaking about matters of clear-cut morality, of things that are inherently right or wrong. Rather, he has been discussing matters of moral indifference, things that were ceremonially defiling for a Jew living under the law but that are perfectly legitimate for a Christian living under grace. The obvious example is the eating of pork. It was forbidden to God's people in the OT, but the Lord Jesus changed all that when He said that nothing entering into a man can defile him (Mark 7:15). In saying this He pronounced all foods clean (Mark 7:19). Paul echoed this truth when he said: "But food does not commend us to God; for neither if we eat are we the better, nor if we do not eat are we the worse" (1 Cor. 8:8). When he says: **"To the pure all things are pure,"** he means that to the born again believer all foods are clean, **but to those who are defiled and unbelieving nothing is pure**. It is not what a person eats that defiles him but what comes out of his heart (Mark 7:20–23). If a man's inner life is impure, if he does not have faith in the Lord Jesus, then nothing is pure to him. The observance of dietary rules won't do a thing for him. More than anything else he needs to be converted, to receive salvation as a free gift rather than trying to earn it through rituals and legalism. The very minds and consciences of defiled people are corrupted. Their mental processes and their moral powers are defiled. It is not a question of external ceremonial defilement, but of inward corruption and depravity.

1:16 Obviously speaking of the false teachers, that is, the Judaizers, Paul says that **they profess to know God, but** by their **works they deny Him**. They pose as Christian believers, but their practice does not match their profession. To amplify his stinging castigation, the apostle denounces them as being **abominable, disobedient, and disqualified**. Their personal behavior was abhorrent. In God's eyes, theirs was a record of crass disobedience. As for good works toward God or man, they were worthless. Was it within the bounds of Christian love for Paul to speak about others in such strong language? The answer is an emphatic *yes*! Love never glosses over sin. These men were perverting the gospel, dishonoring the Person and work of the Lord Jesus, and deluding the souls of men. To be indulgent with such deceivers is sin.

IV. EXERCISE IN THE CONGREGATION (2:1–15)

2:1 The lives of the false teachers were a *libel* rather than a *Bible*. By their conduct they denied the great truths of the faith. Who can measure the damage to the Christian testimony by those who professed great sanctity but lived a lie? The task assigned to Titus (and to all true servants of the Lord) was to teach what **is proper for sound doctrine**. He was to close the awful chasm between the lips of God's people and their lives. Actually this is the keynote of the Epistle — the practical outliving of healthy doctrine in good works. The following verses give practical examples of what these good works should be.

2:2 First we come to **the older men** — not elders in the official sense, but men of physical age and maturity. They should be **sober**. Primarily this means moderate in the use of wine, but extends to mean careful in all areas of conduct. They should be **reverent** and dignified, yes, but please — not gloomy! Others have enough troubles of their own. The older men should be **temperate**, that is, balanced and discreet. They should be **sound in faith**. Age makes some people callous, bitter, and cynical. Those who are healthy in faith are thankful, optimistic, and good company. They should be sound **in love**. Love is not self-centered; it thinks of others and manifests itself in giving. And they should be vigorous **in patience**. Age has its infirmities and disabilities, often hard to take. Those who are sound in endurance bear up under their trials graciously and with fortitude.

2:3 **Older women** should also be **reverent in behavior**. Deliver us from giddy women whose thoughts are centered on frivolous matters! They should **not** be **slanderers**. The word Paul uses here is the Greek word for devil (*diabolos*). It is an apt word because malicious gossip is diabolical in its source and character. They should not be slaves to drink. In fact, they should not become enslaved by any food, beverage, or medicine. Although not assigned a *public* teaching ministry in the church, older women are commissioned to teach in the home. Who can measure the potential of such a ministry!

2:4 Specifically, an older woman should **admonish the young women**. Years of Bible study and practical experience enable her to pass on valuable counsel to those starting out in life. Otherwise each new generation is doomed to learn the hard way, repeating the mistakes of the past. While the responsibility for teaching is put on the **older**

women here, any wise young person will cultivate the friendship of godly older Christians and solicit their advice and correction.

A young woman should be taught to **love** her husband. But this means more than just kissing him when he leaves for work. It includes the myriad ways in which she can show that she really respects him — by acknowledging his headship in the home, by making no major decisions apart from him, by keeping an orderly home, by paying attention to personal appearance, by living within their means, by confessing promptly, by forgiving graciously, by keeping the lines of communication always open, by refraining from criticizing or contradicting her husband in front of others, and by being supportive when things go wrong.

They should be taught to **love their children** — by reading and praying with them, by being at home when they return from school or play, by disciplining firmly and fairly, and by molding them for the Lord's service rather than for the world — and hell.

2:5 Young women should be taught **to be discreet**. This means having a fine sense of what is appropriate for them as Christians and avoiding extremes. They should be **chaste**, faithful to their husbands and avoiding impurity in thought, word, or action. They should be good **homemakers**. They should realize that this is divine service which can be done for the glory of God. Older women should try to inculcate the high honor of serving the Lord in the home as a wife and mother rather than working in industry or business and neglecting the home and family. Young women should be taught how to be **good** — how to live for others, to be hospitable, to be gracious and generous, and not to be self-centered and possessive. They should be **obedient to their own husbands**, acknowledging them as head of the house. If a wife is more gifted and capable than her husband, rather than dominating him, she should encourage and aid him to be more active in home leadership and in serving the local church. If tempted to nag, she should resist the temptation and praise him instead. All of this is to keep **the word of God**

from being **blasphemed** or discredited. Throughout this Letter, Paul is conscious of the reproach brought upon the Lord's cause by the inconsistent lives of His people.

2:6 Paul did *not* urge Titus to teach the young women. For discretion's sake this ministry is left to the older women. But Titus is told to **exhort the young men**, and the particular admonition is that they should **be sober-minded** and control themselves. An appropriate word — since youth is the time of brimming zeal, restless energy, and burning drives. In every area of life, they need to learn continence and balance.

2:7 Paul has a special bit of advice for Titus too. As one charged with a public ministry in the churches, Titus has to exercise care to present a consistent **pattern of good works**. There should be a close parallel between his **doctrine** and his deportment. His teaching should be characterized by **integrity, reverence,** and **incorruptibility. Integrity** means that the teaching should correspond with the faith once-for-all delivered to the saints. By **reverence** Paul insists that the teaching should be dignified and sensible. **Incorruptibility**, a virtue unfortunately deleted here in most modern Bible versions,[3] has to do with the sincere teacher who cannot be corrupted from the way of truth.

2:8 Sound speech that cannot be condemned is free from anything to which exception might be taken. It should be free from side-issues, doctrinal novelties, fads, crudities, and the like. This type of ministry is irresistible. Those who oppose sound teaching are put to shame because they cannot find a chink in the believer's armor. There is no argument as effective as a holy life!

2:9 Special instructions are now given for slaves. We should remember that the Bible acknowledges the existence of institutions of which it does not necessarily approve. For instance, the OT records the polygamous lives of many of the patriarchs, yet polygamy was never God's will for His people. God has never approved of the injustices and cruelties of slavery; He will hold the masters responsible in a coming day. At the same time the NT does not advocate the overthrow of slavery by forcible revolution. Rather, it condemns and removes the abuses of slavery by the power of the gospel. History shows that the evils of slavery have disappeared wherever the word of God has been widely preached and taught.

But in the meantime, where slavery still exists, a slave is not excluded from the very best in Christianity. He can be a witness to the transforming power of Christ, and he can adorn the doctrine of God our Savior. More space in the NT is devoted to slaves than to rulers of nations! This may be a clue to their relative importance in the kingdom of God. Christian **bondservants** should be **obedient**, except when it would mean disobeying the Lord. In that case they would have to refuse and patiently suffer the consequences as Christians. They should give satisfaction in every respect, that is, be productive both as to quantity and quality. All such service can be done as to Christ and will be fully rewarded by Him. They should **not** talk **back** or be impudent. Many slaves had the privilege of leading their masters to the Lord Jesus in the early days of Christianity, largely because the difference between pagan slaves and themselves was so glaring.

2:10 One of the most obvious differences was that Christians did not succumb to the besetting sin of other slaves, namely, **pilfering**. The Christian ethic bound them to strict honesty. Is it any wonder that Christian slaves commanded higher prices at public auctions? In general they were taught to show complete and true **fidelity**. They were to be totally trustworthy and thus **adorn the doctrine of God our Savior** in every aspect of their lives and service. What was true of Christian bondservants then should be true of all Christian employees today.

2:11 The next four verses form a beautiful vignette of our salvation. But in admiring this literary gem, we must not divorce it from its setting. Paul has been urging consistent behavior on all members of the family of God. Now he shows that one of the great purposes of our salvation is to produce lives of unadulterated holiness.

For the grace of God ... has appeared. Here **the grace of God** is virtually synonymous with the Son of God.

God's grace **appeared** when the Lord Jesus visited our planet and especially when He gave Himself for our sins. He appeared for the salvation of **all men**. His substitutionary work is sufficient for the redemption of **all**. A bona fide offer of pardon and forgiveness is made **to all**. But only those who truly receive Him as Lord and Savior are saved. There is no suggestion here or elsewhere in the Bible that everyone will be saved at last. Universal salvation is a lie of the devil.

2:12 The same grace that saves us also trains us in the school of holiness. There are "No-No's" in that school which we must learn to renounce. The first is **ungodliness**, which means irreligion. The second is **worldly lusts** — not just sexual sins, but also the lust for wealth, power, pleasure, fame, or anything else that is essentially worldly.

On the positive side, grace teaches us to **live soberly, righteously** toward others, and **godly** in the pure light of His presence. These are the virtues that should characterize us in this world, where everything about us is going to be dissolved. It is the place of our pilgrimage and not our final home.

2:13 While living as aliens in the world, we are inspired by a magnificent **hope** — the **appearing** of the glory **of our great God and Savior Jesus Christ**. By this are we to understand the Rapture, when Christ appears in glory to the church and conveys it to heaven (1 Thess. 4:13–18)? Or does it refer to Christ's coming to reign, when He appears in glory to the world, puts down His foes, and sets up His kingdom (Rev. 19:11–16)? Basically we believe Paul is speaking of the first — Christ's coming for His bride, the church. But whether it is His coming as Bridegroom or as King, the believer should be prepared and looking for His **glorious** arrival.

2:14 As we await His Return we never forget the purpose of His First Coming and of His self-sacrifice. He **gave Himself** not only to save us from the guilt and penalty of sin but to **redeem us from every lawless deed**. It would have been a half-way salvation if the penalty of sin had been canceled but its dominion in our lives was left unconquered.

He also gave Himself to **purify for**

Himself His own special people. The 1611 King James quaintly[4] says "a peculiar people." Too often we *are* a peculiar people, but not in the way He intended! He didn't die to make us an odd or strange people, but a **people** who belong to Him in a **special** way — not to the world or to ourselves. And **He gave Himself for us that** we might be **zealous for good works**. We should have enthusiasm to perform acts of kindness in His name and for His glory. When we think of the zeal of men for sports, politics, and business, we should be provoked to jealousy and inspired to good deeds.

2:15 **These** are **things** that Titus was commissioned to teach — everything discussed in the foregoing verses, and particularly the purposes of the Savior's passion. He was to **exhort** or encourage the saints to lives of practical godliness and to **rebuke** any who contradicted the apostolic teachings either by word or by life. And he didn't have to be apologetic in carrying on a forceful ministry; let him do it **with all authority** and boldness of the Holy Spirit. **Let no one despise you.** Titus need have no qualms about his youth, his Gentile background, or any natural disability. He was speaking the word of God, and this made all the difference.

V. EXHORTATION IN THE CONGREGATION (3:1–11)

3:1 Titus was also to **remind** believers in the Cretan assemblies of their responsibilities toward their government. The Christian approach is that all governments are ordained of God (Rom. 13:1). A regime might be very unchristian or even anti-christian, but *any* government is better than no government at all. The absence of government is anarchy, and people cannot survive for long under anarchy. Even if a ruler does not know God personally, he is still "the anointed of the Lord" in his official position, and should be respected as such. Christians should be obedient **to rulers and authorities**. But if a government leaves its God-ordained sphere and commands a believer to disobey God, then the believer should refuse on the principle of Acts 5:29: "We ought to obey God

rather than men." If he is punished he should bear the punishment meekly as to the Lord. He should never join in rebellion against the government or seek its overthrow by violence.

THE CHRISTIAN AND THIS WORLD

Believers should obey the laws, including traffic laws, and pay their taxes and other levies. In general they should be law-abiding, respectful, obedient subjects. However, there are three areas in which Christians differ considerably as to their proper responsibility. These are the matters of voting, of seeking elected office, and of going to war with the armed forces. With regard to the first two, the following helpful guidelines are laid down in the Bible:

1. Christians are in the world but are not of it (John 17:14, 16).

2. The whole world system is in the hands of the wicked one, and has been condemned by God (1 Jn. 5:19b; 2:17; John 12:31).

3. The Christian's mission is not to improve the world, but to see men saved out of it.

4. While the believer is almost unavoidably a citizen of some earthly country, his primary citizenship is from heaven — so much so that he is to look upon himself as a pilgrim and an alien down here (Phil. 3:20; 1 Pet. 2:11).

5. No soldier on active duty should entangle himself with the affairs of this life, lest he displease the one who has enlisted him (2 Tim. 2:4).

6. The Lord Jesus said: "My kingdom is not of this world" (John 18:36). As His ambassadors, we should represent this truth to the world.

7. Politics tend to become corrupt by their very nature. Christians should separate themselves from iniquity (2 Cor. 6:17, 18).

8. In voting, a Christian would normally vote for a man thought to be upright and honest. But sometimes it is God's will to exalt the lowest of men (Dan. 4:17). How could we know and obey the will of God in such cases?

The other question is whether a believer should go to war when ordered by his country. There are strong arguments on both sides, but it seems to me that the balance of evidence is against participating. The principles listed above bear on the problem, but there are additional ones. (1) Our Lord said, "If My kingdom were of this world, My servants would fight" (John 18:36). (2) He also said, "All who take the sword will perish by the sword" (Matt. 26:52). (3) The whole idea of taking human life is opposed to the teaching of Him who said, "Love your enemies" (Matt. 5:44).

Those who are opposed to bearing arms can be grateful if they live in a country where they are allowed to register as conscientious objectors or noncombatants.

On the other hand, many Christian men *have* served in combat with honor. They have noted that the NT presents centurions (e.g. Cornelius and Julius) in a very favorable light. Also, figures of speech from military life are used to illustrate the *Christian* warfare (e.g. Eph. 6:10–17). If soldiering were inherently *wrong* it is hard to see how Paul could call on us to be "good soldiers of Jesus Christ." Whichever view a person holds, he should not judge or condemn those who disagree. There is room for differing opinions. ‡

An additional obligation of the Christian disciple is that he **be ready for every good work**. Not all jobs are honorable — much modern advertising is built on lies, and some businesses sell products that are harmful to man's spiritual, mental, and physical health. In all good conscience, these occupations should be avoided.

3:2 A Christian should **speak evil of no one**. Elsewhere the Bible specifically forbids speaking evil of a ruler (Ex. 22:28; Acts 23:5) — a command that all Christians should remember in the heat of a political campaign or in times of oppression and persecution. But here the injunction is broadened to protect everyone from ridicule, slander, insult, or verbal abuse. What oceans of grief and trouble could be avoided if Christians would obey this simple precept **to speak evil of no one**!

We should be **peaceable** and avoid quarreling. It takes two to generate a dispute. When someone tried to pick a quarrel with Dr. Ironside over a matter of minor importance which he had preached on, he would reply, "Well, dear brother, when we get to heaven, one of us is going to be wrong, and perhaps it will be me." That spirit put an end to all argument.

We should be **gentle**. It is hard to think about this quality without thinking of the Lord Jesus. He was mild-mannered and kind, peaceful and conciliatory. And we should show **all humility**, or courtesy, **to all men**. It seems so proper that courtesy should be taught as one of the Christian virtues. Essentially it means humbly thinking of others, putting others first, and saying and doing the gracious thing. Courtesy serves others before self, jumps at opportunities to assist, and expresses prompt appreciation for kindnesses received. It is never crude, vulgar, or rude.

3:3 Once again, in the midst of a strongly ethical section the apostle introduces a doctrinal classic on our salvation, with emphasis on the goal of salvation being a life of good works. The flow of thought is: (1) Our condition before salvation, verse 3; (2) the nature of our salvation, verses 4–7; (3) the practical result of salvation, verse 8. God's picture of us before our conversion is not flattering. Professing to know all the answers, **we were** actually **foolish**, unable to comprehend spiritual truths, and unwise in our choices and conduct. We were **disobedient** to God and perhaps to parents and other authorities as well. We were **deceived** by the devil and our own perverted judgment, always missing the right way and ending up on dead-end streets. We were **serving various** unclean habits, enslaved by an evil thought-life and besetting sins of all kinds. Life was a constant round of bitter **malice and envy** toward others. Unlovable and selfish, we were miserable and made others miserable. **Hateful and hating one another**: What a sad commentary on life among quarreling neighbors, warring fellow employees, cut-throat business competitors, and feuding families!

3:4 The dismal picture of man's depravity is interrupted by one of the great *buts* of Scripture. How thankful we can be for these nick-of-time conjunctions that signal God's marvelous intervention to save man from destroying himself! Someone has called them God's road-blocks on man's way to hell.

But when the kindness and love of God our Savior toward man appeared . . . This occurred when the Lord Jesus appeared to the world over nineteen hundred years ago. In another sense, God's goodness and lovingkindness **appeared** to us when we were saved. It was a manifestation of these attributes that He would send His beloved Son to die for a world of rebellious sinners. The word used for **love . . . toward men** is the Greek word from which *philanthropy* comes; it combines the thoughts of love, graciousness, and compassion. The title **God our Savior** refers to **God** the Father — **our Savior** in the sense that He sent His Son into the world as our Sacrifice for sin. The Lord Jesus is also called **God our Savior** (2:13) because He paid the necessary penalty in order that we might be pardoned and forgiven.

3:5 **He saved us** from the guilt and penalty of all our sins — past, present, and future. They were all future when the Savior died, and His death covered them all. But one of the simplest, clearest truths of the gospel is the most difficult for man to receive. It is that salvation is **not** based on good **works**; one doesn't become a Christian by living a Christian life. It is not good people who go to heaven. The consistent testimony of the Bible is that man cannot earn or merit salvation (Eph. 2:9; Rom. 3:20; 4:4, 5; 9:16; 11:6; Gal. 2:16; 3:11). Man cannot save himself by good works; all his righteous deeds are like polluted rags in God's sight (Isa. 64:6). He cannot become a Christian by living a Christian life for the simple reason that he has no power in himself to live a Christian life. It is not good people who go to heaven; it is sinners who have been saved by God's grace!

Good works do not earn salvation; they are the *result* of salvation. Wherever there is true salvation there will also be good works. So we read that God did not save us because of **works of righteousness which we have done, but according to His mercy**. Salvation is a work of **mercy** — not justice. Justice demands that the deserved punishment be administered; **mercy** provides a righteous way by which the punishment is averted.

God saved us by **the washing of regeneration**. Conversion is really a new creation (2 Cor. 5:17), and here that new creation is presented under the figure of a bath. It is the same figure used by the Lord Jesus when He taught the disciples that there is only one bath of regeneration but many necessary cleansings from defilement (John 13:10). That bath of regeneration has nothing to do with baptism. It is not a bodily cleansing by water, but a moral cleansing by the word of God (John 15:3). Baptism is not even a symbol of this bath; it rather depicts burial with Christ into death (Rom. 6:4).

Our new birth is also spoken of as a **renewing of the Holy Spirit**. The Spirit of God brings about a marvelous transformation — not putting new clothes on the old man, but putting a new man in the clothes! The Holy Spirit is the *Agent* in regeneration and the word of God is the *instrument*.

3:6 God **poured out** the Holy Spirit **on us abundantly**. Every believer is indwelt by the Spirit from the moment he is born again. The Spirit is sufficient to bring about the glorious renewal referred to. The Spirit is given **through Jesus Christ our Savior**. Just as the abundance of Pharaoh's court was mediated to Jacob's sons through Joseph, so the blessings of God, including the inexpressible blessing of His Spirit, are mediated to us through the Lord Jesus. Jesus is our "Joseph."

All three Persons of the Blessed Trinity are mentioned in connection with our salvation: God the Father, (v. 4); the Holy Spirit, (v. 5); and God the Son (v. 6).

3:7 The immediate result of our regeneration is **that having been justified by His grace we should become heirs according to the hope of eternal life**. Through the redemption that is in Christ Jesus, God reckons us righteous by an act of amazing grace. And we **become heirs** of all that God has prepared for those who love Him. Everything that is included in being with Christ and like Him for all eternity is our hope.

3:8 When Paul says **"This is a faithful saying"** are we to understand the preceding section, or the rest of the verse? The thrust of his argument seems to be that, having been saved from so much by such a great salvation, we should live in a manner worthy of our high calling.

Titus was to insist on these things (discussed in vv. 1–7) in his ministry in Crete so that believers would **be careful to maintain good works**. Although the expression **good works** may mean honorable occupations, the wider meaning — **good works** in general — is probably the right one. Teaching which calls for behavior that is consistent with one's Christian profession is excellent and **profitable**. All teaching should have a personal and practical application.

3:9 Of course, there are always traps to be avoided in the Christian ministry. In Paul's day there were stupid **disputes** over clean and unclean foods, Sabbath regulations, and observance of holy days. Arguments arose over **genealogies**, both angelic and human. There was bickering over intricate regulations that had been superimposed on the law. Paul was disgusted with them as being **unprofitable and useless**.

Servants of the Lord in our day may take Paul's advice to heart by avoiding the following tangents:

Pre-occupation with methods rather than with spiritual realities. For example, the ancient debates over whether to use fermented wine or grape juice, leavened or unleavened bread, a common cup or individual cups — as if these were important questions in the Bible!

Quibbling over words.

Majoring on one truth, or even one aspect of a truth, to the exclusion of all else.

Allegorizing the Scriptures until they become absurd.

Theological nit-picking that edifies no one.

Wandering from the word into political by-paths and into Christian crusades against this and that.

What a tragedy to spend precious time on these things while a world is perishing!

3:10 The **man** who majors on these minors is a **divisive** heretic.[5] He usually has one note on his violin and plays it to death. Soon he gathers around himself a coterie of people with a negative outlook, and the rest he drives away. He will divide an assembly rather than abandon his doctrinal hobbyhorse. No church should put up with such nonsense. If after one or two warnings, he refuses to desist, he should be expelled from the fellowship of the local church and the Christians should refrain from having social contact with him. Hopefully, this ostracism will bring him to repentance and to a more balanced handling of the word of God.

3:11 Lest anyone think that **such a person** is not a serious threat to the church, the apostle castigates him as **warped and sinning, being self-condemned**. His behavior is a perversion rather than a version of Christianity. He is **sinning** by forming a sect or party. He is **self-condemned** because he stubbornly clings to his wickedness after being warned by responsible Christians.

VI. CONCLUSION (3:12–15)

3:12 The Epistle closes with a few short directives to Titus. Paul planned to **send** either **Artemas, or Tychicus** to relieve Titus in Crete. We have met **Tychicus** before (Acts 20:4; Eph. 6:21; Col. 4:7), but **Artemas** we have not. It seems from 2 Timothy 4:12 that **Tychicus** was sent to Ephesus rather than to Crete, so **Artemas** was probably the replacement in Crete. As soon as he arrived, Titus was to go to **Nicopolis**, where Paul had determined to **spend the winter**. There were at least seven cities called Nicopolis in those days, but most commentators believe Titus chose the one in Epirus, in western Greece.

3:13 Titus was going to have visitors — **Zenas the lawyer and Apollos**. Perhaps they were the ones who brought the Letter from Paul to Titus. There were two kinds of lawyers in those days — scribes, who expounded the religious law, and advocates, who handled matters of civil law. We are left to decide which fraternity **Zenas** belonged to. I cast my vote for the former, suspecting he may have been called in to help Titus quell the interminable squabbles over the

Law of Moses (v. 9). If he was a civil lawyer, he was an honest one! The only other **Apollos** of whom we read in the NT is the one mentioned in Acts 18:24–28 and 1 Corinthians. Perhaps this is the same man. When Paul told Titus to **send** these two **on their journey with haste**, he included in his exhortation hospitality during their stay in Crete and everything necessary for their onward travel.

3:14 Titus was to teach the other Christians (**our people**) to show hospitality, to care for the sick and afflicted, and to be generous toward those who were in need. Instead of working merely to meet their own needs and wants, they should have the distinctly Christian vision of earning money in order to share with the less privileged (see Eph. 4:28b). This would save them from the misery of selfishness and the tragedy of a wasted, unfruitful life.

3:15 The closing greetings should not be thought of as trite and unimportant. In countries where Christians are few in number, despised, and persecuted, these kind words convey vast quantities of love, friendship, and encouragement. **All who** were **with** the apostle sent greetings to Titus, and Titus was asked to convey kind regards to all who loved Paul and his team **in the faith**. Finally, Paul closes the Letter on the theme that dominated his life — the **grace** of the Lord.

Grace be with you all. Amen.

ENDNOTES

[1](1:1) See Ephesians 1 and Romans 9 for fuller treatment of election.

[2](1:6) Many believe that while divorce is sometimes valid, a church *officer* should not be a divorced person.

[3](2:7) As so often (see NKJV footnotes), omissions are favored by the critical text, which is based largely on the oldest extant manuscripts, coming chiefly from Egypt. The KJV and NKJV favor the traditional text, (TR), which is usually, but by no means always, supported by the majority of manuscripts as well (majority text).

[4](2:14) It sounds quaint today because the meaning of "peculiar" has changed. The KJV is a very accurate translation; most so-called "errors" are (as here) due to nearly four centuries of changes in English.

[5](3:10) The word *heretic* (KJV) is from a Greek word meaning factious or *divisive* (NKJV). A person who splits churches usually teaches false or "heretical" doctrine, but this is a later development of the word *hairetikos* itself.

BIBLIOGRAPHY

See Bibliography at the end of 1 Timothy.

THE EPISTLE TO PHILEMON

Introduction

"A true little masterpiece in the art of letter-writing." — Ernest Renan

"We are all [the Lord's] Onesimi." — Martin Luther

I. Unique Place in the Canon

Some might suggest that we would be well able to do without this little Letter from Paul. They would be totally wrong. In the first place, it is universally recognized as an authentic personal Letter straight from the apostle's heart. As such it is a gem to start with. It has often been compared with a secular letter on the same subject — a runaway slave — by the Roman author Pliny the Younger to a friend. Except in the realm of elegant rhetoric, Paul's Letter comes out on top.

This little missive shows the courtesy, tact — with a dash of humor — and the loving heart of Paul. While it does not teach doctrine outright, it is a perfect illustration of the doctrine of "imputation" because of Paul's command to "charge that to my account." Just as Onesimus' failings were charged to Paul's "account" and Paul's ability to pay applied to Onesimus' helpless estate, so the Christian has his sins "imputed," or charged, to our Lord's account and our Lord's saving merits put on his own ledger. No wonder the great reformer, Martin Luther, wrote:

Here we see how St. Paul lays himself out for poor Onesimus, and with all his means pleads his cause with his master: and so sets himself as if he were Onesimus, and had himself done wrong to Philemon. Even as Christ did for us with God the Father, thus also St. Paul does for Onesimus with Philemon. . . . We are all His Onesimi, to my thinking.[1]

II. Authorship[†]

Everyone but the most negative critics accepts the Pauline authorship of Philemon. In fact, Renan was so sure of this authenticity that it made him question his own rejection of the authenticity of the closely related Colossian Epistle.

Since Philemon is so brief and so personal it is not surprising that there are not many early quotations from the Letter.

External Evidence

Philemon is quoted or alluded to in the writings of Ignatius, Tertullian, and Origen. Eusebius says it was one of the books accepted by all Christians (*homologoumena*). Marcion included it in his "canon" and it is also recognized by the Muratorian Canon.

Internal Evidence

Even in this short Letter Paul mentions himself by name three times (vv. 1, 9, 19). Verses 2, 23, 24 have close ties with Colossians 4:10-17, and so the two Epistles help support one another's authenticity. Thus the internal evidence agrees with the external.

III. Date

The Letter was sent at the same time as the Epistle to the Colossians (about A.D. 60), or about thirty years after the Ascension of our Lord.

IV. Background and Theme[††]

We have to piece together the story

[†]*See p. i.*
[††]*See p. ii.*

behind this Letter from the contents of the Epistle itself and from Paul's Letter to the Colossians. It appears that Philemon was a resident of Colosse (cf. Col. 4:17 with Phmn. v. 2) who had been converted through the Apostle Paul (v. 19). One of his slaves, Onesimus, had run away from him (vv. 15, 16) and there is a hint that Onesimus might have helped himself to some of his master's possessions as well (v. 18).

The fugitive reached Rome during the time that Paul was imprisoned there (v. 9). We can't be sure whether the apostle was actually behind bars at the time or whether it was within the period when he was allowed the freedom of his own rented house (Acts 28:30). By a curious chain of circumstances, Onesimus met Paul in the busy metropolis and was led to Christ through his ministry (v.

10). In the days that followed, a mutual bond of love developed (v. 12) and Onesimus proved to be a valued helper to the apostle (v. 13). But they both agreed that the proper thing would be for Onesimus to return to Philemon and make right the wrongs of the past. So Paul wrote this Letter to Philemon, interceding for Onesimus and presenting strong reasons why he should be graciously restored to his master's favor (v. 17). It was at this time that Paul also wrote the Letter to the Colossians. He assigned Tychicus to act as postman and sent Onesimus back to Colosse with him (Col. 4:7-9).

This is the most personal of all Paul's Letters. The Epistles to Timothy and Titus were also written to individuals but they deal with matters of assembly practice more than with personal affairs.

OUTLINE

Commentary

I. SALUTATION (Vv. 1–3)

V. 1 **Paul** introduces himself as **a prisoner** rather than as an apostle. He could have used his authority, but he prefers to appeal from what might seem a low place of disadvantage. Yet the apostle gilds this low place with the glory of heaven. He is **a prisoner of Christ Jesus**. Not for a minute will he grovel as a prisoner of Rome! He sees beyond the emperor to the King of kings. **Timothy** was with him as he wrote, and so he links this faithful disciple with him, though the Letter is obviously Paul's.

The main addressee is **Philemon**. His name means "affectionate," and apparently he was true to his name because Paul describes him as **our beloved friend and fellow laborer**.

V. 2 Since **Apphia** is a feminine name, most scholars assume that she

was Philemon's wife. The fact that the Letter is addressed in part to her reminds us that Christianity exalts womanhood.[2] Later we shall see how it also exalts slaves. Sanctified imagination has almost invariably identified **Archippus** as the son of Philemon. We can't be sure, but we do know that he was actively engaged in the Christian warfare. Paul honors him as a **fellow soldier**. We can picture him as a dedicated disciple of the Lord Jesus, on fire with a holy passion. In Colossians, Paul singled him out for special attention: "And say to Archippus, 'Take heed to the ministry which you have received in the Lord, that you may fulfill it' " (Col. 4:17).

If Philemon, Apphia, and Archippus give us a picture of a NT Christian family, the expression **the church in your house** calls up the image of a NT **church**. It seems clear from this that Philemon's **house** was the meeting place for an assembly of believers. It was there they gathered for worship, prayer, and Bible study. From there they went forth to witness for Christ in a world that would never welcome their message but would never forget it either. As they met together in Philemon's home, the Christians were all one in Christ Jesus. Rich and poor, male and female, master and slave — all were there as full-fledged members of the family of God. As soon as they returned to the work-a-day world, their social distinctions would reappear. But at the Lord's Supper, for instance, they were all on the common level of the holy priests. Philemon would have no precedence over Onesimus.

V. 3 Paul's characteristic greeting seems to embody the best he could desire for those he loved. **Grace** includes all the undeserved favor which God showers on His people. **Peace** here is the spiritual serenity and poise which stabilize the lives of those who are taught by His grace. Both blessings come **from God our Father and the Lord Jesus Christ**. This is full of significance. It means that the Lord Jesus is equal with **God** the **Father** in bestowing **grace** and **peace**. It would be blasphemy to give such honor to Christ if He were not truly and fully God.

II. PAUL'S THANKSGIVING AND PRAYER FOR PHILEMON (Vv. 4–7)

V. 4 Whenever Paul prayed for Philemon, he thanked **God** for this noble brother. We have every reason to believe that he was a choice trophy of the grace of God — the kind of man you would like to have as a friend and brother. Some commentators suggest that Paul is using diplomacy in these opening verses, that his purpose is to "soften" Philemon's heart to receive Onesimus back again. This ascribes an unworthy motive to the apostle and casts a shadow over the inspired text. Paul would not have said it if he had not sincerely meant it.

V. 5 There were two qualities in Philemon's character that gave great joy to Paul — his **love** and the **faith which** he had **toward the Lord Jesus and to-**ward all the saints**. His faith in Christ showed he had the root of divine life and his love **toward all the saints** showed that he had the fruit as well. His faith was productive.

In Ephesians 1:15, 16 and Colossians 1:3, 4 Paul expressed similar thanks for the saints to whom those Letters were addressed. However, in those places he put faith before love. Here he puts love before faith. Why the difference? Maclaren answers: "The order here is the order of analysis, digging down from manifestation to cause. The order in the parallel passages is the order of production ascending from root to flower."

There is another interesting feature of Paul's arrangement here. He divides the expression "Love toward all the saints" by inserting **faith . . . toward the Lord Jesus** after love. We might put it as follows: "love (and faith . . . toward the Lord Jesus) toward all the saints." The object of **faith** is **the Lord Jesus**. The object of **love** is the **saints**. But Paul wraps the faith clause with the love clause, as if to forewarn Philemon that he is about to have a special opportunity to manifest the reality of his faith by showing love to the slave Onesimus. Thus there is special emphasis in the word *all* — **all the saints**.

V. 6 The previous two verses expressed Paul's thanks for Philemon. This one discloses the nature of the apostle's prayer for him. The **sharing of your faith** means the practical kindness which Philemon showed to others. We can share our faith not only by preaching Christ but also by feeding the hungry, clothing the destitute, comforting the bereaved, relieving the distressed — yes, even by forgiving a runaway slave. Paul prayed then that Philemon's life of benevolence would lead many to acknowledge that all his good deeds came from **Christ Jesus**. There is tremendous power and influence in a life where the love of God is manifest. It is one thing to read about love in a book, but how compelling it is to see the Word become flesh in a human life!

V. 7 News of Philemon's overflowing generosity and self-sacrificial love traveled from Colosse to Rome, bringing **great joy**[3] **(or thanksgiving**, NKJV margin) and comfort to Christ's prisoner. It had been a great privilege for Paul to lead Philemon to the Lord, but now how rewarding it was to hear that his child in the faith was going on well for the Lord. How assuring it was to know that **the hearts of the saints** were being greatly **refreshed by** this beloved **brother**, and especially by his **love**. No one lives to himself, and no one dies to himself. Our actions affect others. We cannot measure the range of our influence. We have limitless potential for good or for evil.

III. PAUL'S PLEA FOR ONESIMUS (Vv. 8–20)

V. 8 Now Paul comes to the main purpose of the Letter. He is about to intercede for Onesimus. But how will he approach the subject? As an apostle, he could justifiably say to Philemon, "Now, my brother, it is your duty as a believer to forgive and restore this runaway, and that's exactly what I'm telling you to do." Paul could have ordered him to do it, and Philemon would no doubt have obeyed. But that would have been a hollow victory in this case.

V. 9 If the apostle did not win Philemon's heart, then Onesimus might have returned to an icy reception. Only obedience that was motivated by love would make the slave's status in the home tolerable. Perhaps as he wrote this, Paul thought of the Savior's words: "If you love Me, keep My commandments" (John 14:15). And so **for love's sake**, he preferred to **appeal** rather than to order. Would Philemon's love reach across the sea where an **aged** ambassador[4] of Christ was a prisoner for the Lord Jesus? Would he be moved by two considerations — Paul, **the aged, and now also a prisoner**? We do not know exactly how old the apostle was at this time. Estimates range from fifty-three to sixty-three. That might not seem old today, but he was probably prematurely old because of the way he had burnt himself out in the service of Christ. And now he was **a prisoner** for **Jesus Christ**. In mentioning this, he wasn't looking for sympathy, but he did hope that Philemon would weigh these factors in making his decision.

V. 10 In the original of this verse

the name *Onesimus* comes last. **"I appeal to you**, concerning a son of mine, **whom I have begotten while in my chains —** Onesimus."** By the time Philemon reached the name of his derelict slave, he was completely disarmed. Imagine his surprise when he learned that the "scoundrel" had been converted and, even more surprising, had been led to Christ through Paul, the prisoner!

One of the hidden delights of the Christian life is to see God working in marvelous, miraculous ways, revealing Himself in converging circumstances that cannot be explained by coincidence or chance. First Paul had led Philemon to the Lord. Then the apostle had later been arrested and taken to Rome for trial. Philemon's slave had run away and made his way to Rome. Somehow or other he had met Paul and had been converted. Master and slave were both born again through the same preacher but in widely separated places and under quite different circumstances. Was it a coincidence?

V. 11 The name Onesimus means **profitable**. But when he ran away, Philemon was probably tempted to call him a worthless rascal. Paul says, *in effect*, "Yes, he was useless as far as you were concerned, but now he is useful **to you and to me."** The slave who was returning to Philemon was a better slave than the one who had run away. It has been said that in NT times Christian slaves commanded a higher price on the market than others. It should be true today that Christian employees are more valuable as workers than unbelievers.

V. 12 The attitude of the NT toward slavery comes into focus in this Epistle. We notice that Paul does not condemn slavery or prohibit it. In fact, he sends Onesimus back to his master. But the abuses connected with slavery are condemned and prohibited throughout the NT. Maclaren writes:

> The New Testament . . . meddles directly with no political or social arrangements, but lays down principles which will profoundly affect these, and leaves them to soak into the general mind.[5]

Forcible revolution is not the Bible way to correct social evils. The cause of man's inhumanity lies in his own fallen nature. The gospel attacks the *root cause*, and offers a new creation in Christ Jesus.

It is conceivable that a slave who has a kind master might be better off than if he were independent. This is true, for instance, of believers, who are bondservants of the Lord Jesus. Those who are His slaves enjoy the truest form of freedom. In **sending** Onesimus **back** to Philemon, Paul was not doing an injustice to the slave. Both master and slave were believers. Philemon would be obligated to treat him with Christian kindness. Onesimus would be expected to serve with Christian faithfulness. The deep affection which the apostle had for Onesimus is expressed in the words **sending . . . my own heart**. Paul felt as if he were losing a part of himself.

We should notice that the important principle of restitution is set forth. Now that Onesimus was saved, was it necessary for him to return to his former master? The answer is definitely "Yes." Salvation removes the penalty and power of sin, but it does *not* cancel debts. The new Christian is expected to settle all unpaid accounts and to make right all wrongs, insofar as it is humanly possible. Onesimus was obligated to return to his master's service, and to repay any money which he might have stolen.

V. 13 The apostle's personal preference would have been **to keep** Onesimus **with** *him* in Rome. There were many things that the converted slave could have done for Paul while he was imprisoned for the gospel's sake. And this would have been an opportunity for Philemon to **minister** to the apostle — by providing an assistant. But it would have the drawback of being done without Philemon's knowledge or permission.

V. 14 Paul would not force a kindness from the slave's owner by keeping Onesimus with him in Rome. He would do **nothing** in connection with Onesimus **without** Philemon's **consent**. The kindness would be robbed of its beauty if it were done **by compulsion** and not by a free and loving willingness.

V. 15 It is a mark of spiritual maturity to be able to look beyond the adverse circumstances of the moment and see God working all things together for good to those who love Him (Rom. 8:28).

When Onesimus ran away, perhaps Philemon was filled with bitterness and a sense of financial loss. Would he ever see the slave again? Now Paul traces the rainbow through the dark clouds. Onesimus was lost to the family in Colosse for a while **that** they **might** have **him** back **forever**. This should be the comfort of Christians who lose believing relatives and friends in death. The separations are for a little while; the reunion will be eternal.

V. 16 Philemon was not only getting Onesimus back — he was receiving him under better conditions than he had ever known him before. It would no longer be the customary master-slave relationship. Onesimus was now **more than a slave**; he was **a beloved brother** in the Lord. Henceforth the fear motive would be replaced by the love motive. Paul had already enjoyed his fellowship as **a beloved brother**. But now he would no longer have him there in Rome. The apostle's loss would be Philemon's gain. He would now know Onesimus as a brother **both in the flesh and in the Lord**. The former slave would justify Paul's confidence both **in the flesh**, that is, by his devoted service in a physical way, and **in the Lord**, that is, by his fellowship as a believer.

V. 17 The apostle's request is startling both in its boldness and in its tenderness. He asks Philemon to **receive** Onesimus **as** he **would** receive the apostle himself. He says: **"If then you count me as a partner, receive him as you would me."** The words are reminiscent of the Savior's statements: "He who receives you receives Me, and he who receives Me receives Him who sent Me" (Matt. 10:40), and, "Inasmuch as you did it to one of the least of these My brethren, you did it to Me" (Matt. 25:40). They also remind us that God has accepted us in the Person of His Son, that we are as near and dear to God as Christ is.

If Philemon considered Paul **as a partner**, as one with whom he was in fellowship, then the apostle asks him to receive Onesimus on the same basis. This doesn't require that Onesimus be treated as a perpetual guest in the family with no obligation to work. He would still be a servant in the home, but one who belonged to Christ and was therefore a brother in the faith.

V. 18 The apostle doesn't say that Onesimus had stolen anything from Philemon, but this verse suggests such a possibility. Certainly theft was one of the cardinal sins of slaves. Paul is willing to accept responsibility for any loss that Philemon might have sustained. He recognizes that restitution should be made. The conversion of Onesimus did not cancel his debts to man. So Paul tells Philemon to **put that on** his **account**.

We cannot read this without being reminded of the enormous debt which we had contracted as sinners, and of how it was all charged to the account of the Lord Jesus at Calvary. He paid the debt in full when He died as our Substitute. We are also reminded here of Christ's ministry as our Advocate. When Satan, the accuser of the brethren, brings charges against us for wrongs we have done, our blessed Lord says in effect, "Charge that to My account." The doctrine of reconciliation is illustrated in this book. Onesimus had been estranged from Philemon because of wrongdoing. Through the ministry of Paul (we have every reason to believe) the distance and "enmity" were removed. The slave was reconciled to his master. So we were estranged from God because of our sin. But through the death and resurrection of Christ, the cause of enmity has been removed and believers are reconciled to God.

V. 19 Ordinarily Paul dictated his Letter to someone else, writing only the closing lines with his **own hand**. We can't be sure whether he wrote this entire Letter by hand, but at this point at least he took the pen and, in his familiar scrawl, committed himself to pay any debts incurred by Onesimus. He would do this in spite of the fact that Philemon owed him a considerable debt. Paul had led him to the Lord. He owed his spiritual life to the apostle, as far as the human instrument was concerned. But Paul would not press him for payment of the debt.

V. 20 Addressing Philemon as **brother**, the aged Paul asks only for some benefit in the Lord, some refreshment in Christ. He is pleading that Onesimus be received graciously, that

he be forgiven and restored to his place of service in the household — not now as a slave but as a brother in the family of God.

IV. CLOSING REMARKS (Vv. 21–25)

V. 21 The apostle had every **confidence** that Philemon would do **even more** than was requested. He himself had been freely forgiven by Christ. He would not do less, surely, for Onesimus. We have then a vivid illustration of Ephesians 4:32: "And be kind to one another, tenderhearted, forgiving one another, just as God in Christ also forgave you."

V. 22 But how would Paul know how Philemon had treated Onesimus? He hoped to visit Colosse and be a guest in Philemon's home. He expected to be released by the civil authorities in answer to the **prayers** of the Christians. And so he asks Philemon to **prepare a guest room for** him. Perhaps that would have been one of the first tasks assigned to Onesimus: "Get the guest room ready for our brother Paul." We do not know whether Paul ever reached Colosse. All we can do is assume that the **guest room** was ready for him, and that all the members of the household were eager to see him, their hearts having been knitted together in love.

V. 23 **Epaphras** may have been the one who planted the assembly in Colosse (Col. 1:7, 8; 4:12, 13). Now a **fellow prisoner** with Paul in Rome, he joins in sending greetings to Philemon.

V. 24 With Paul at this time were **Mark, Aristarchus, Demas,** and **Luke**. These names are also mentioned in Colossians 4:10, 14. Jesus, called Justus, is mentioned in Colossians 4, though omitted here for some reason. **Mark** was the writer of the Second Gospel. He had proved to be a faithful servant of the Lord after his early failure (2 Tim. 4:11, cf. Acts 13:13; 15:36–39). **Aristarchus**, a believer from Thessalonica, accompanied Paul on several journeys including the trip to Rome. In Colossians 4:10, Paul called him "my fellow prisoner." **Demas** later forsook Paul, having loved this present world (2 Tim. 4:10). **Luke**, the beloved physician, proved to be a faithful companion and helper to the end (2 Tim. 4:11).

V. 25 The Letter closes with Paul's characteristic benediction. He wishes the **grace of our Lord Jesus Christ** to **be with** Philemon's **spirit**. Life can hold no greater blessing than the unmerited favor of the Savior as one's moment-by-moment experience. To walk in the constant realization and enjoyment of His Person and work is all that heart can desire.

Paul laid down his pen and handed the Letter to Tychicus for delivery to Philemon. Little did he realize the extent to which the message of this Epistle would influence Christian behavior for centuries to follow. The Letter is a classic of love and courtesy, as applicable today as it was when it was written. **Amen**.

Colossians and to Philemon, pp. 317, 318 (translation updated by the present editor).

[2](V. 2) If one compares the status of Christian women with pagan and Muslim women, she (or he) will have to agree that the true "Liberator of women" is the Lord Jesus Christ.

[3](V. 7) The majority of mss. read *thanksgiving* (*charin*) for *joy* (*charan*).

[4](V. 9) The Greek words for "aged" (*presbutēs*) and *ambassador* (*presbeutēs*) are so similar that Bentley conjectured that Paul wrote "ambassador." The traditional mss. are totally against this conjecture, however nicely it may fit the context.

[5](V. 12) Alexander Maclaren, "Colossians and Philemon," *The Expositor's Bible*, p. 461.

ENDNOTES

[1](Intro) Martin Luther, quoted by J. B. Lightfoot, *Saint Paul's Epistles to the*

BIBLIOGRAPHY

See Bibliography at the end of Colossians.

THE EPISTLE TO THE HEBREWS

Introduction

"There is no portion of Scripture whose authorship is more disputed, nor any of which the inspiration is more indisputable."

— Conybeare and Howson

I. Unique Place in the Canon

The Epistle to the Hebrews is unique in the NT on many counts. While it does not start as a letter, it does so end, and is clearly addressed either to or from Italy (13:24), to a specific group, probably Hebrew Christians. It has been suggested that it was originally addressed to a small house church and therefore had no link with a large and famous congregation to keep alive the tradition of its origin and destination. The style is the most literary in the NT. It is poetic, and full of quotations from the Septuagint. It has a large vocabulary and uses the Greek language very precisely in verb tense and other details.

Though very *Jewish* in one sense (it has been compared to Leviticus), the warnings against drifting from the reality of Christ's death to mere religious ritual are always needed in *Christendom*. Hence the book's great importance.

II. Authorship[†]

Hebrews is anonymous, even though some earlier editions of the KJV printed Paul's name as part of the heading of the book. The early Eastern Church (Dionysius and Clement, both of Alexandria) suggested Paul as author. After much doubting, this view came to prevail from Athanasius onward, so that the West finally agreed. Few today, however, would maintain Pauline authorship. Origen agreed that the *contents* were Pauline, and there are some Pauline touches in it, but the style in the original is very different from Paul's. (This does not *rule*

out Pauline authorship, because a literary genius can alter his style.)

Several possible authors have been suggested through the years: Luke, whose style is similar, and who was familiar with Paul's preaching, Barnabas, Silas, Philip, even Aquila and Priscilla.

Luther suggested Apollos, a man who fits the style and content of the book: mighty in the OT Scriptures, and very eloquent (Alexandria, his home town, was noted for rhetoric). An argument against Apollos is that no Alexandrian tradition preserves such a theory, an unlikely situation if a native Alexandrian wrote it.

For some reason the Lord has seen fit to keep the author unknown. One suggestion is that Paul *did* write it but purposely veiled his authorship due to Jewish prejudice against him. While this is possible, the ancient words of Origen have never been bettered: "But who wrote the Epistle God alone knows for certain."

III. Date

In spite of the anonymous human *authorship*, it is possible to *date* the Epistle rather closely.

External evidence demands a first-century writing, since Clement of Rome used the book (c. A.D. 95). While Polycarp and Justin Martyr quote the Letter, they do not name the author. Dionysius of Alexandria quotes Hebrews as by Paul, and Clement of Alexandria says Paul wrote it in Hebrew and Luke translated it. (The book does not, however, read like a translation.) Irenaeus and

[†]*See p. i.*

Hippolytus did not think Paul wrote Hebrews, and Tertullian thought Barnabas did.

Internally it seems that the writer is a second generation Christian (2:3; 13:7), so it would not be *very* early like James or 1 Thessalonians (cf. 10:32). Since there is no mention of the Jewish Wars (starting in A.D. 66), and the temple sacrifices were still apparently going on (8:4; 9:6; 12:27; 13:10), a date perhaps before 66 and *certainly* before the destruction of Jerusalem (70) is called for. Persecutions are mentioned (12:4) but the believers had "not yet resisted to bloodshed." If Italy is the destination of the Letter, Nero's bloody persecution there (A.D. 64) would move the Letter back to mid-64 at the latest. A date of 63-65 is very likely.

IV. Background and Themes[†]

In a general way, Hebrews deals with the tremendous struggle involved in leaving one religious system for another. There is the violent wrenching of old ties, the stresses and tensions of alienation, and the formidable pressures exerted on the renegade to return.

But in this Epistle the problem was not just a question of leaving an old system for a new one of equal value. Rather it was a matter of leaving Judaism for Christ, and as the writer shows, this involved leaving shadows for the substance, ritual for reality, the prior for the ultimate, the temporary for the permanent — in short, the good for the best.

The problem also involved leaving the popular for the unpopular, the majority for the minority, and the oppressors for the oppressed. And this precipitated many serious problems.

The Letter was written to people of Jewish background. These Hebrews had heard the gospel preached by the apostles and others during the early days of the church, and had seen the mighty miracles of the Holy Spirit which confirmed the message. They had responded to the good news in one of three ways:

Some believed on the Lord Jesus Christ and were genuinely converted.

Some professed to become Christians, were baptized, and took their place in the local assemblies. However, they had never been born again by the Holy Spirit of God.

Others flatly rejected the message of salvation.

Our Epistle deals with the first two classes — truly saved Hebrews and those who had nothing but an outward veneer of Christianity.

Now when a Jew left the faith of his forefathers, he was looked on as a turncoat and an apostate (*meshummed*), and was often punished with one or more of the following:

.   Disinheritance by his family.
.   Excommunication from the congregation of Israel.
.   Loss of employment.
.   Dispossession.
.   Mental harassment and physical torture.
.   Public mockery.
.   Imprisonment.
.   Martyrdom.

Of course, there was always the escape route. If he would renounce Christ and return to Judaism, he would be spared from further persecution. As we read between the lines of this Letter, we can detect some of the strong arguments used to persuade him to return to Judaism:

.   The rich heritage of the prophets.
.   The prominent ministry of angels in the history of God's ancient people.
.   Association with the illustrious lawgiver Moses.
.   National ties with the brilliant military commander Joshua.
.   The glory of the Aaronic priesthood.
.   The sacred sanctuary where God chose to dwell among His people.
.   The covenant of the law given by God through Moses.
.   The divinely appointed furniture in the sanctuary, and the magnificent veil.
.   The services in the sanctuary, and especially the ritual on the great Day of Atonement (Yom Kippur, the most important day in the Jewish calendar).

We can almost hear the first-century Jews presenting all these glories of their ancient, ritualistic religion, then asking with a sneer, "And what do you Christians have? We have all this. What do you have? Nothing but a simple upper room, a table, and some bread and wine on the table! Do you mean to say that you have left all this for *that*?"

The Epistle to the Hebrews is really an answer to the question, "*What do you have?*" In a word the answer is *Christ*. In Him *we have*:

. One who is greater than the prophets.
. One who is greater than the angels.
. One who is greater than Moses.
. One who is greater than Joshua.
. One whose priesthood is superior to that of Aaron.
. One who serves in a better sanctuary.
. One who has introduced a better covenant.
. One who is the antitype of the typical furniture and veil.
. One whose once-for-all offering of Himself for sin is superior to the repeated sacrifices of bulls and goats.

Just as the stars fade from view in the greater glory of the sun, so the types and shadows of Judaism pale into insignificance before the greater glory of the Person and work of the Lord Jesus.

Yet there was still the problem of persecution. Those who professed to be followers of the Lord Jesus faced bitter, fanatical opposition. For true believers this could lead to the peril of discouragement and despair. They therefore needed to be encouraged to have faith in the promises of God. They needed endurance in view of the coming reward.

For those who were only nominal Christians, there was the danger of apostasy. After professing to receive Christ, they might utterly renounce Him and return to ritualistic religion. This was tantamount to trampling on the Son of God, profaning His blood, and insulting the Holy Spirit. For this willful sin there was no repentance or forgiveness. Against this sin there are repeated warnings in the Letter to the Hebrews. In 2:1 it is described as *drifting away* from the message of Christ. In 3:7–19 it is the sin of *rebellion* or of hardening the heart. In 6:6 it is *falling away* or committing apostasy. In 10:25 it is the *forsaking the assembling . . . together*. In 10:26 it is the *willfulness* or deliberate sin. In 12:16 it is spoken of as *selling one's birthright* for a single meal. Finally in 12:25 it is called a *refusal to hear* the One who is speaking from Heaven. But all these warnings are directed against different aspects of the same sin — the sin of *apostasy*.

The message of Hebrews is as timely today as it was in the first century of the church. We need to be constantly reminded of the eternal privileges and blessings that are ours in Christ. We need encouragement to endure in spite of opposition and difficulties, and all professing believers need to be warned against reverting to ceremonial religion after having tasted and seen that the Lord is good.

OUTLINE

I. CHRIST SUPERIOR IN HIS PERSON (1:1–4:13)
   A. Christ Superior to the Prophets (1:1–3)
   B. Christ Superior to the Angels (1:4–2:18)
   C. Christ Superior to Moses and Joshua (3:1–4:13)

II. CHRIST SUPERIOR IN HIS PRIESTHOOD (4:14–10:18)
   A. Christ's High Priesthood Superior to Aaron's (4:14–7:28)
   B. Christ's Ministry Superior to Aaron's (Chap. 8)
   C. Christ's Offering Superior to Old Testament Sacrifices (9:1–10:18)

III. WARNING AND EXHORTATIONS (10:19–13:17)
   A. Warning Not to Despise Christ (10:19–39)
   B. Exhortation to Faith by Old Testament Examples (Chap. 11)

Commentary

I. CHRIST SUPERIOR IN HIS PERSON (1:1–4:13)

A. Christ Superior to the Prophets (1:1–3)

1:1 No other NT Epistle comes to the point as quickly as this one. Without benefit of salutation or introduction, the writer plunges into his subject. It seems as if he were constrained by a holy impatience to set forth the superlative glories of the Lord Jesus Christ.

First, he contrasts God's revelation **by the prophets** with His revelation in His Son. **The prophets** were divinely inspired spokesmen for God. They were honored servants of Jehovah. The spiritual wealth of their ministry is preserved in the OT.

Yet their ministry was partial and fragmentary. To each one was committed a certain measure of revelation, but in every case it was incomplete.

Not only was the truth doled out to them in installments; they used **various** methods in communicating it to the people. It was presented as law, history, poetry, and prophecy. Sometimes it was oral, sometimes written. Sometimes it was by visions, dreams, symbols, or pantomime. But whatever the method used, the point is that God's former revelations to the Jewish people were preliminary, progressive, and **various** in the manner of presentation.

1:2 The periodic, partial, and differential prophecies of the OT have now been overshadowed by God's preeminent and final revelation in the person of **His Son**. The prophets were only channels through whom the divine word was communicated. The Lord Jesus Christ is Himself the final revelation of God to men. As John said, "No one has seen God at any time. The only begotten Son, who is in the bosom of the Father, He has declared Him" (John 1:18). The Lord Jesus said concerning Himself, "He

who has seen Me has seen the Father" (John 14:9). Christ speaks not only *for* God but *as* God.

To emphasize the infinite superiority of God's Son to the prophets, the writer first presents Him as **heir of all things**. This means that the universe belongs to Him by divine appointment and He will soon reign over it.

It was **through** Him that God **made the worlds**. Jesus Christ was the active Agent in creation. He brought into being the stellar heavens, the atmospheric heavens, the earth, the human race, and the divine plan of the ages. Every created thing, both spiritual and physical, was made by Him.

1:3 He is the outshining **of** God's **glory**, that is, all the perfections that are found in God the Father are found in Him also. He is the effulgence or radiance **of His glory**. All the moral and spiritual glories of God are seen in Him.

Further, the Lord Jesus is the exact **image** of God's essential being. This cannot, of course, refer to physical likeness because God is, in essence, a Spirit. It means that in every conceivable way Christ exactly represents the Father. No closer resemblance could be possible. The Son, being God, reveals to man by His words and ways exactly what God is like.

And He upholds the universe **by the word of His power**. Originally He spoke to bring the worlds into being (Heb. 11:3). Still He speaks and His powerful **word** sustains life, holds matter together, and maintains the universe in proper order. It is by Him that all things hold together (Col. 1:17). Here is a simple explanation of a profound scientific problem. Scientists grapple to discover what holds molecules together. We learn here that Jesus Christ is the great Sustainer, and He does it **by** His powerful **word**.

But the next glory of our Savior is the most amazing of all — **when He had by**

Himself purged our sins. The Creator and the Sustainer became the Sin-bearer. In order to create the universe, He only had to speak. In order to maintain and guide the universe, He only has to speak because no moral problem is involved. But in order to put away our sin once for all, He had to die on the cross of Calvary. It is staggering to think that the sovereign Lord would stoop to become the sacrificial Lamb. "Love so amazing, so divine, demands my soul, my life, my all," as Isaac Watts' hymn says.

Finally we have His exaltation as the enthroned Lord: He **sat down at the right hand of the Majesty on high**. He **sat down** — the posture of rest. This is not the rest following toil, but the rest of satisfaction in a finished work. This posture indicates that the work of redemption has been completed.

The right hand of the Majesty on high is the position of honor and privilege (Heb. 1:13). Because of His glorious triumph, God has highly exalted Him. The right hand is also the position of power (Matt. 26:64) and delight (Ps. 16:11). The nail-scarred hand of the Savior holds the scepter of universal dominion (1 Pet. 3:22).

In following the pathway of our Lord from creation to Calvary and then to glory, it seems we have quite lost sight of the prophets. Illustrious though they were, they have receded into the shadows. They bore witness to the coming Messiah (Acts 10:43). Now that He has come, they gladly retire from view.

B. Christ Superior to the Angels (1:4–2:18)

1:4 The next step in the argument of the Epistle demonstrates that Christ is superior to **the angels**. This was necessary because the Jewish people had a very high regard for the ministry of angels. After all, the law had been given through angels (Acts 7:53; Gal. 3:19), and angelic beings had appeared frequently throughout the history of God's ancient people. Perhaps it was argued that in leaving Judaism for Christ, a person would be cutting himself off from this important feature of his national and religious heritage. The truth is that, in gaining Christ, he gained One who is superior to angels in a twofold sense —

first as Son of God (1:4–14) and then as Son of Man (2:5–18).

Christ has **become so much better than the angels, as He has by inheritance obtained a more excellent name than they**. This speaks first of an acquired superiority, then of an inherent superiority.

The acquired superiority results from His resurrection, ascension, and exaltation as Lord and Christ. In incarnation He was made for a little while lower than the angels for the suffering of death (2:9). But God has exalted Him and enthroned Him in highest glory.

His inherent superiority has to do with His eternal relationship as Son of God. The **more excellent name** is the name of Son.

1:5 Two verses are now quoted from the OT identifying the Messiah as God's Son. First, in Psalm 2:7, God addresses Him as Son: **"You are My Son, today I have begotten You."** In one sense Christ is the eternally begotten Son. In another sense, He was begotten in incarnation. In a third sense, He was begotten in resurrection — the first-born from the dead (Col. 1:18). Paul used this verse in the synagogue at Antioch of Pisidia and applied it to Christ's First Advent (Acts 13:33).

But the main point is that God never addressed an angel as His **Son**. Angels collectively are spoken of as sons of God (Job 1:6; Ps. 89:6 [ASV margin]), but in that case it means nothing more than creatures. When the Lord Jesus is described as the Son of God, it signifies equality with God.

The second verse is from 2 Samuel 7:14: **"I will be to Him a Father, and He shall be to Me a Son."** Although the words might seem to have reference to Solomon, the Holy Spirit here identifies them as referring to David's greater Son. Here again the argument is that God never spoke of an angel in this way.

1:6 A third way in which Christ is greater than the angels is that He is to be the object of their worship, whereas they are His messengers and servants. To prove his point, the author quotes Deuteronomy 32:43 (LXX and DSS) and Psalm 97:7 (see NKJV margin).

The verse in Deuteronomy looks forward to the time **when He again brings** the firstborn into the world. In other words, it refers to the Second Advent of Christ. At that time He will be publicly worshiped by the angels. This can only mean that He is God. It is idolatry to worship any but the true God. Yet God here commands that the Lord Jesus Christ should be worshiped by the angels.

Firstborn may mean first in point of time (Luke 2:7) or first in rank or honor (Ps. 89:27). It has the latter meaning here and in Romans 8:29 and Colossians 1:15, 18.

1:7　By way of contrast with His preeminent Son, God makes His angels spirits [or winds] and His ministers a flame of fire. He is the Creator and Director of angels. They obey His will with the speed of wind and with the fervency of fire.

1:8†　Now follows a galaxy of glories in which the Son is seen to be incomparable. First He is addressed by God as God. In Psalm 45:6 God the Father hails the Messiah with the words, "Your throne, O God, is forever and ever." Here again the deity of Christ is unmistakable, and the argument comes from the traditional Hebrew text. (There is at least one quotation from the OT in every chapter of Hebrews.)

He is also the eternal Sovereign; His throne lasts forever and ever. His kingdom shall indeed "stretch from shore to shore, till moons shall wax and wane no more."

He is the righteous King. The psalmist speaks of Him as wielding a scepter of righteousness, which is a poetic way of saying that this King rules in absolute honesty and integrity.

1:9　His personal uprightness is evident from the fact that He has consistently loved righteousness and hated lawlessness. This doubtless refers primarily to His thirty-three years of life on earth, during which the eye of God could find no flaw in His character and no failure in His conduct. He proved His fitness to reign.

Because of this personal excellence, God has anointed Him with the oil of gladness more than His companions. This means that He has given Christ the place of supremacy above all other beings. The oil here may typify the Holy

Spirit; Christ was endued with the Spirit above all others (John 3:34). His companions include all those with whom He associated Himself, but the expression does not mean that they were His equals. Possibly it includes the angels, but more probably it refers to His Jewish brethren.

1:10　The Lord Jesus Christ is the Creator of heaven and earth. This is demonstrated from Psalm 102:25–27. In that psalm, the Messiah prays, "O my God . . . do not take me away" (v. 24). This prayer at Gethsemane and Calvary is answered by God the Father, "Of old You laid the foundation of the earth, and the heavens are the work of Your hands."

It should be noticed that God here in verse 10 addresses His Son as LORD, that is Jehovah. The conclusion is inescapable: the Jesus of the NT is the Jehovah of the Old.

1:11, 12　In verses 11 and 12 the creation's transience is contrasted with the Creator's perpetuity. His works will perish but He Himself will remain. Though the sun, moon, stars, mountains, oceans, and rivers appear to be enduring, the truth is that they have built-in obsolescence. The psalmist likens them to a garment: first, it becomes worn out; then it is folded up as unusable; then it is changed for something better.

Look out upon a range of snow-capped mountains, upon a glorious sunset, upon a star-studded sky. Then hear the majestic cadence of these words: Like a cloak You will fold them up, and they will be changed. But You are the same, and Your years will not fail.

1:13　A further quotation (Ps. 110:1) proves the Son's superiority. In that psalm God invites the Messiah, "Sit at My right hand, till I make Your enemies Your footstool." The question is asked, "To what angel did God ever say anything like that?" The answer is, of course, to none.

To be seated at the right hand of God signifies a position of highest honor and limitless power. To have all one's enemies as a footstool signifies universal subjugation and universal dominion.

1:14　The mission of the angels is not to rule but to serve. They are spirit

†See p. xviii.

beings whom God has created **to minister for those who will inherit salvation**. This may be understood in two ways: first, angels **minister** to those who are not yet converted; or, second, they serve those who are saved from the penalty and power of sin but not yet saved from the presence of sin, that is, those believers who are still on earth.

This means there are "guardian angels." Why should we be surprised at such a truth? It is certain there are evil spirits who wage unceasing conflict against God's elect (Eph. 6:12). Is it to be wondered at that there are holy angels who watch over those who are called to **salvation**?

But we must go back to the main point of the passage — not the existence of guardian angels, but the fact that angels are inferior to the Son of God just as servants are inferior to the Universal Sovereign.

2:1 The writer has just completed his argument that Christ is supremely better than the angels because He is the Son of God. Before showing that He is also superior as Son of Man, he pauses to inject the first of several solemn warnings that are found in the Epistle. This is a warning against drifting **away** from the message of the gospel.

Because of the greatness of the Giver and because of the greatness of His gift, those who hear the gospel must **give more** serious attention to it. There is always the danger of drifting **away** from the Person and slipping back into a religion of pictures. This means drifting into apostasy — the sin for which there is no repentance.

2:2 We have already mentioned that the Jews attached special importance to the ministry of angels in their history. Perhaps the leading instance of this was in the giving of the law when myriads of angelic beings were present (Deut. 33:2; Ps. 68:17). It is true that the law was **spoken through angels**. It is true that it was valid. It is true that **every** infraction was punished accordingly. These things are freely admitted.

2:3 But now the argument moves from the lesser to the greater. If those who broke the law were punished, what will be the fate of those who **neglect** the gospel? The law tells men what they must do; the gospel tells men what God has done. By the law is the knowledge of sin; by the gospel is the knowledge of **salvation**.

To **neglect so great a salvation** is more serious than to transgress the law. The law was given by God through angels, to Moses and then to the people. But the gospel was spoken directly by the Lord Jesus Himself. Not only so, it **was confirmed** to the early Christians by the apostles and by others **who heard** the Savior.

2:4 **God** Himself authenticated the message by **signs and wonders, with various miracles, and gifts of the Holy Spirit**. **Signs** were those miracles of the Lord and of the apostles which signified spiritual truths. For example, the feeding of the five thousand (John 6:1–14) formed the basis of the discourse on the Bread of Life which followed (John 6:25–59). **Wonders** were miracles which were intended to arouse amazement in the spectators; the raising of Lazarus illustrates this (John 11:1–44). **Miracles** were any displays of supernatural power which contravened the laws of nature. **Gifts of the Holy Spirit** were special enablements given to men to speak and act in a manner that was completely beyond their natural abilities.

The purpose of all these miracles was to attest to the truth of the gospel, especially to the Jewish people, who traditionally asked for some sign before they would believe. There is some evidence that the need of confirmatory miracles ceased when the NT became available in written form. But it is impossible to prove conclusively that the Holy Spirit *never* duplicates these miracles in other ages.

The words **according to His own will** indicate that these miraculous powers are given out by the Holy Spirit as He chooses. They are sovereign gifts of God. They cannot be demanded by men, or claimed in answer to prayer, because God has never promised them to all.

2:5 In the first chapter we saw that Christ is superior to the angels as the Son of God. Now it will be shown that He is also Superior as the Son of Man. It will help us in following the flow of thought if we remember that, to the Jewish mind, the thought of Christ's incarnation was incredible and the fact of His humiliation was shameful. To the Jews, Jesus was only a man, and therefore He belonged to a lower order than the angels. The following verses show that *even as Man*, Jesus was better than the angels.

First, it is pointed out that God did not decree that **the** habitable **world** of the future should be under the control of **angels. The world to come** here means the golden age of peace and prosperity which the prophets so frequently mentioned. We speak of it as the Millennium.

2:6 Psalm 8:4–6 is quoted to show that the eventual dominion over the earth has been given to man, not to angels. In a sense, man is insignificant, and yet God is **mindful of him**. In a sense, man is unimportant, yet God does **take care of him**.

2:7 In the scale of creation, man has been given a **lower** place **than the angels**. He is more limited as to knowledge, mobility, and power. And he is subject to death. Yet in the purposes of God, man is destined to be **crowned with glory and honor**. The limitations of his body and mind will be largely removed, and he will be exalted on the earth.

2:8 Everything will be put **under** man's authority in that coming day — the angelic hosts, the world of animals, birds, and fishes, the planetary system — in fact, every part of the created universe will be put **under** his control.

This was God's original intention for man. He told him, for instance, to "fill the earth and subdue it; have dominion over the fish of the sea, over the birds of the air, and over every living thing that moves on the earth" (Gen. 1:28).

Why then don't we see **all** things **in subjection under him**? The answer is that man lost his dominion because of his sin. It was Adam's sin that brought the curse on creation. Docile creatures became ferocious. The ground began to bring forth thorns and thistles. Man's control over nature was challenged and limited.

2:9 However, when the Son of Man returns to reign over the earth, man's dominion will be restored. Jesus, as Man, will restore what Adam lost, and more besides. So while we do not see

everything under man's control at the present time, **we** do **see Jesus**, and in Him we find the key to man's eventual rule over the earth.

For a little while, He was made **lower than the angels**, specifically, for the thirty-three years of His earthly ministry. His descent from heaven to Bethlehem, to Gethsemane, to Gabbatha, to Golgotha, and to the tomb, mark the stages in His humiliation. But now He is **crowned with glory and honor**. His exaltation is a result of His suffering and death; the cross led to the crown.

God's gracious purpose in it all was that Christ **might taste death for everyone**. The Savior died as our Representative and as our Substitute; that is, He died as man and He died for man. He bore in His body on the cross all God's judgment against sin so that those who believe on Him will never have to bear it.

2:10 It was entirely in keeping with the righteous character of God that man's dominion should be restored through the humiliation of the Savior. Sin had disturbed God's order. Before order could be brought out of chaos, sin must be dealt with righteously. It was consistent with the holy character of God that Christ should suffer, bleed, and die to put away sin.

The wise Planner is described as the One **for whom are all things and by whom are all things**. First He is the objective or goal of all creation; all things were made for His glory and pleasure. But He is also the Source or Originator of all creation; nothing was made apart from Him.

His great purpose was **bringing many sons to glory**. When we consider our own worthlessness, it staggers us to think that He would have even bothered with us, but it is because He is the God of all grace that He has called us to His eternal glory.

What is the cost of our glorification? The **captain** of our **salvation** had to be made **perfect through sufferings**. As far as His moral character is concerned, the Lord Jesus was always sinlessly perfect. He could never be made perfect in this respect. But He had to be made **perfect** *as our Savior*. In order to purchase eternal redemption for us, He had to suffer all the punishment that our sins deserved. We could not be saved by His spotless life; His substitutionary death was an absolute necessity.

God found a way of saving us that was worthy of Himself. He sent His only begotten Son to die in our place.

2:11 The next three verses emphasize the perfection of Jesus' humanity. If He is going to regain the dominion which Adam lost, then it must be demonstrated that He is true Man.

First, the fact is stated: **For both He who sanctifies and those who are being sanctified are all of one**, that is, they are all possessors of humanity. Or, ". . .have all one origin" (RSV), meaning that in their humanity, they all have one God and Father.

Christ is the One **who sanctifies**, that is, He sets apart or separates men to God from the world. Blessed are all those whom He thus sets apart!

A sanctified person or thing is one set apart from ordinary uses to be for God's own possession, use, and enjoyment. The opposite of sanctification is profanation.

There are four types of sanctification in the Bible: *pre-conversion sanctification, positional sanctification, practical sanctification,* and *perfect sanctification.* These types of sanctification are detailed in the Excursus at 1 Thessalonians 5:23, which should be read carefully.

The reader should be on the lookout for the various passages in Hebrews where sanctification is mentioned, and should seek to determine which type of sanctification is in view.

It is because He became a true Man that **He is not ashamed** to speak of His followers as **brethren**. Is it possible that the Eternal Sovereign of the universe should become man and identify Himself so closely with His creatures that He would call them brothers?

2:12 The answer is found in Psalm 22:22 where we hear Him say, **"I will declare Your name to My brethren."** The same verse also pictures Him as identified with His people in common worship, **"in the midst of the assembly I will sing praise to You."** In His dying agony, He looked forward to the day when He would lead the ransomed throng in **praise** to God the Father.

2:13 Two more verses are quoted from the Jewish Scriptures to prove Christ's humanity. In Isaiah 8:17 (LXX), He speaks of putting His **trust** in God. Implicit confidence in Jehovah is one of the greatest marks of true humanity. Then in Isaiah 8:18, the Lord is quoted as saying, "Here am I and the children whom the LORD has given me!" The thought is that they are members of a common family, acknowledging a common Father.

2:14 Those who consider the humiliation of the Son of Man to be shameful are now asked to consider four important blessings that flow from His passion.

The first is the destruction of Satan. How did this happen? There was a special sense in which God gave His children to Christ to sanctify, save, and emancipate. Since these children had human natures, the Lord Jesus assumed a body of flesh and blood. He set aside the outward display of His deity and veiled His Godhead in a "robe of clay."

But He did not stop at Bethlehem. "All the way to Calvary He went for me because He loved me so."

Through His **death**, He destroyed the one **who had the power of death, that is, the devil**. Destruction here means the loss of well-being rather than loss of being. It means to nullify or to bring to nothing. Satan is still actively opposing the purposes of God in the world, but he received a death wound at the cross. His time is short and his doom is sure. He is a defeated foe.

In what sense does the devil have **the power of death**? Probably the chief sense in which he has this power is in *demanding* death. It was through Satan that sin first entered the world. God's holiness decreed the death of all who sinned. So in his role as adversary, the devil can demand that the penalty be paid.

In heathen lands his power is also seen in the ability of his agents, the witch doctors, to pronounce a curse on a person and for that person to die without any natural cause.

There is no suggestion in Scripture that the devil can inflict death on a believer without the permission of God (Job 2:6), and therefore he cannot set the time of a believer's death. Through wicked men, he is sometimes permitted to kill the believer. But Jesus warned His disciples not to fear those who could destroy the body, but rather to fear God who can destroy both soul and body in hell (Matt. 10:28).

In the OT, Enoch and Elijah went to heaven without dying. No doubt this was because, as believers, they were reckoned to have died in the still-future death of Christ.

When Christ comes at the Rapture, all living believers will go to heaven without dying. But they too escape death because God's holiness was satisfied for them in the death of Christ. The risen Christ now has "the keys of Hades and of Death" (Rev. 1:18), that is, He has complete authority over them.

2:15 The second blessing traced to Christ's humiliation is emancipation from **fear**. Before the cross, the **fear of death** held men in lifelong servitude. Though there are occasional flashes of light in the OT concerning life after death, the general impression is one of uncertainty, horror, and gloom. What was hazy then is clear now because Christ brought life and immortality to light by the gospel (2 Tim. 1:10).

2:16 The third tremendous blessing is expiation of sin. In coming into the world, the Lord did **not give aid to angels, but He does give aid to the seed of Abraham**. "Give aid to" is a translation of *epilambanō*, "to take hold" (hence the KJV's "he took not on [him the nature of] angels; but he took on [him] the seed of Abraham"). While the verb might not have the idea of violent grasping which it carries elsewhere, the ideas of help and deliverance are suggested by its use here.

The seed of Abraham may mean Abraham's *physical* descendants, the Jews, or it may mean his *spiritual* seed — the believers of every age. The important point is that they are human, not angelic beings.

2:17 This being so, it was necessary that **He** should **be made like His brethren** in every respect. He assumed true and perfect humanity. He became subject to human desires, thoughts, feelings, emotions, and affections — with this important exception: He was without sin. His humanity was the ideal;

ours has been invaded by a foreign element, sin.

His perfect humanity fits Him to **be a merciful and faithful High Priest in things pertaining to God**. He can be **merciful** to man and **faithful** to God. His chief function as **High Priest** is to **make propitiation** [satisfaction] **for the sins of the people**. To accomplish this He did what no other High Priest ever did or could do — He offered *Himself* as a sinless sacrifice. He willingly died in our place.

2:18 The fourth blessing is help for the **tempted**. Because **He Himself has suffered** and has been **tempted, He is able to aid those who are** going through temptation. He can help others going through it because He has been there Himself.

Here again we must add a word of qualification. The Lord Jesus was **tempted** from without, but never from within. The temptation in the wilderness shows Him **being tempted** from without. Satan appeared to Him and sought to appeal to Him by external stimuli. But the Savior could never be tempted to sin by lusts and passions within, for there was no sin in Him and nothing to respond to sin. He **suffered, being tempted**. Whereas it pains us to resist temptation, it pained Him to be tempted.

C. Christ Superior to Moses and Joshua (3:1–4:13)

3:1 Moses was one of Israel's greatest national heroes. Therefore the third main step in the writer's strategy is to demonstrate Christ's infinite superiority to Moses.

The message is addressed to **holy brethren, partakers of the heavenly calling**. All true believers are **holy** as to their position, and they should be holy as to their practice. In Christ they are holy; in themselves they ought to be holy.

Their **heavenly calling** is in contrast to the earthly call of Israel. Old Testament saints were called to material blessings in the land of promise (though they did have a heavenly hope as well). In the Church Age, believers are called to spiritual blessings in the heavenlies now and to a heavenly inheritance in the future.

Consider Jesus. He is eminently worthy of our consideration as **the Apostle and High Priest of our confession**. In confessing Him as **Apostle**, we mean that He represents God to us. In confessing Him as **High Priest**, we mean that He represents us before God.

3:2 There is one aspect in which He was admittedly similar to Moses. He **was faithful to** God, just **as Moses also was faithful in** God's house. The **house** here does not mean only the tabernacle but also the entire sphere in which Moses represented God's interests. It is the **house** of Israel, God's ancient earthly people.

3:3 But there the similarity ends. In every other respect there is undisputed superiority. First the Lord Jesus is **worthy of more glory than Moses** because the builder of a **house has more honor than the house** itself. The Lord Jesus was the Builder of God's house; Moses was only a part of the house.

3:4 Second, Jesus is greater because He is God. **Every house** must have a builder. The One **who built all things is God**. From John 1:3, Colossians 1:16, and Hebrews 1:2, 10, we learn the Lord Jesus was the active Agent in creation. The conclusion is unavoidable — Jesus Christ is God.

3:5 The third point is that Christ is greater as a Son. **Moses** was a **faithful . . . servant** in all God's **house** (Num. 12:7), pointing men forward to the coming Messiah. He testified **of those things which would be spoken afterward**, that is, the good news of salvation in Christ. That is why Jesus said on one occasion, "If you believed Moses, you would believe Me; for he wrote about Me" (John 5:46). In His discourse with the disciples on the road to Emmaus, Jesus began at Moses and all the prophets, and "expounded to them in all the Scriptures the things concerning Himself" (Luke 24:27).

3:6 But Christ was faithful over God's house **as a Son**, not as a servant, and in His case, sonship means equality with God. God's house is **His own house**.

Here the writer explains what is meant by God's **house** today. It is composed of all true believers in the Lord Jesus: **whose house we are if we hold fast the confidence and the rejoicing of the hope firm to the end.**[1] At first this might seem to imply that our salvation is dependent on our holding fast. In that case, salvation would be by our endurance rather than by Christ's finished work on the cross. The true meaning is that we prove we are God's house if we hold fast. Endurance is a proof of reality. Those who lose confidence in Christ and in His promises and return to rituals and ceremonies show that they were never born again. It is against such apostasy that the following warning is directed.

3:7 At this point the writer interjects the second warning of the Epistle — a warning against hardening the heart. It had happened to Israel in the wilderness and it could happen again. So **the Holy Spirit** is still speaking through Psalm 95:7–11, as He did when He first inspired it, **"Today, if you will hear His voice."**

3:8 Whenever God speaks, we should be swift to hear. To doubt His word is to call Him a liar and to incur His wrath.

Yet that was Israel's history **in the wilderness**. It was a dreary record of complaint, lust, idolatry, unbelief, and rebellion. At Rephidim, for instance, they complained because of lack of water and doubted God's presence in their midst (Ex. 17:1–17). At the wilderness of Paran when the unbelieving spies returned with an evil report of discouragement and doubt (Num. 13:25–29), the people decided that they should go back to Egypt, the land of their slavery (Num. 14:4).

3:9 God was so highly incensed that He decreed that the people should wander in the wilderness for forty years (Num. 14:33–34). Of all those soldiers who came out of Egypt who were twenty years old or older, only two would ever enter the land of Canaan — Caleb and Joshua (Num. 14:28–30).

It is significant that just as Israel spent **forty years** in the wilderness, so the Spirit of God dealt with the nation of Israel for approximately forty years after the death of Christ. The nation hardened its heart against the message of Christ. In A.D. 70, Jerusalem was destroyed and the people were scattered among the Gentile nations.

3:10 God's keen displeasure with

Israel in the wilderness brought forth this stern denunciation. He accused them of a perpetual proneness to wander away from Him, and of a willful ignorance of His **ways**.

3:11 In His **wrath**, He **swore** that **they** would **not enter** His **rest**, that is, the land of Canaan.

3:12 Verses 12–15 give the application which the Holy Spirit draws for us from Israel's experience. As elsewhere in Hebrews, the readers are addressed as **brethren**. This does not mean that they were all true Christians. So all who profess to be believers should be constantly on guard against a pernicious **heart of unbelief** that might cause them to fall away **from the living God**. It is a constant menace.

3:13 One antidote is mutual exhortation. Especially in days of difficulty and distress, God's people should be **daily** urging others not to forsake Christ for religions that cannot deal with sin effectively.

Notice that this exhortation is not limited to a ministerial class but is the duty of all brethren. It should continue as long as it is called **"Today,"** that is, as long as God's offer of salvation by grace through faith continues. **"Today"** is the accepted time; it is the day of salvation.

To fall away is to **be hardened through the deceitfulness of sin**. Sin often looks beautiful in anticipation. Here it offers escape from the reproach of Christ, lower standards of holiness, rituals that appeal to the aesthetic senses, and the promise of earthly gain. But it is hideous in retrospect. It leaves a man with no forgiveness of sins, no hope beyond the grave, and no possibility of repentance.

3:14 Again we are reminded that **we have become** companions **of Christ if we hold** fast our first **confidence steadfast to the end**. Verses like this are often misused to teach that a person can be saved and then lost again. However, such an interpretation is impossible because the overwhelming testimony of the Bible is that salvation is freely bestowed by God's grace, purchased by Christ's blood, received by man's faith, and evidenced by his good works. True faith always has the quality of perma-

nence. We don't hold fast in order to retain our salvation, but as proof that we have been genuinely saved. Faith is the root of salvation; endurance is the fruit. Who are Christ's companions? The answer is, "Those who by their steadfastness in the faith prove that they really belong to Him."

3:15 Now the writer concludes the personal application of Israel's sad experience by repeating the words of Psalm 95:7, 8: **"Today, if you will hear His voice, do not harden your hearts as in the rebellion."** This poignant appeal, once directed to Israel, is now directed to any who might be tempted to forsake the good news and return to the law.

3:16 The chapter closes with a historical interpretation of Israel's apostasy. In a series of three questions and answers, the writer traces Israel's rebellion, provocation, and retribution. Then he states the conclusion.

Rebellion. The rebels are identified as **all who came out of Egypt, led by Moses**. Caleb and Joshua were the lone exceptions.

3:17 *Provocation*. It was these same rebels who provoked Jehovah for **forty years**. There were about 600,000 of them, and by the time the forty years were ended, the desert was dotted with 600,000 graves.

3:18 *Retribution*. These were the same ones who were excluded from the land of Canaan because of their disobedience.

The simple recital of these questions and answers should have a profound influence on any who might be tempted to leave the despised minority of true Christians for the vast majority of people who have an outward form of religion but deny the power of godliness. Is the majority always right? In this chapter of Israel's history, only two were right and over half a million were wrong!

A. T. Pierson emphasizes the seriousness of Israel's sin as follows:

Their unbelief was a fourfold provocation:

1. It was an assault on God's truth, and made Him a liar.

2. It was an assault upon His power, for it counted Him as weak and unable to bring them in.

3. It was an attack upon His immuta-

bility; for, although they did not say so, their course implied that He was a changeable God, and could not do the wonders He had once wrought.

4. It was also an attack upon His fatherly faithfulness, as though He would encourage an expectation He had no intention of fulfilling.[2]

Caleb and Joshua, on the contrary, honored God by accounting His word absolutely true, His power infinite, His disposition unchangingly gracious, and His faithfulness such that He would never awaken any hope which He would not bring to fruition.

3:19 *Conclusion.* It was **unbelief** that kept the rebellious children out of the promised land, and it is **unbelief** that keeps man out of God's inheritance in every dispensation. The moral is clear: beware of an evil heart of **unbelief**.

The following verses form one of the most difficult passages in the entire Letter. There is little agreement among the commentators as to the exact flow of the argument, although the over-all teaching of the section is fairly clear.

The theme of 4:1–13 is God's rest and the need of diligence in reaching it. It will be helpful for us at the outset if we notice that several kinds of rest are mentioned in the Bible:

1. God rested after the sixth day of creation (Gen. 2:2). This rest did not indicate weariness as a result of toil, but rather satisfaction with the work He had completed. It was the rest of complacency (Gen. 1:31). God's rest was interrupted by the entrance of sin into the world. Since that time He has been working ceaselessly. As Jesus said, "My Father has been working until now, and I have been working" (John 5:17).

2. Canaan was intended to be a land of rest for the children of Israel. Most of them never entered the land, and those who did, failed to find the rest that God intended for them. Canaan is used here as a type or picture of God's final, eternal rest. Many of those who failed to reach Canaan (Korah, Dathan, and Abiram, for example) picture present-day apostates who fail to reach God's rest because of their unbelief.

3. Believers today enjoy rest of conscience, knowing that the penalty for their sins has been paid through the finished work of the Lord Jesus. This is the rest which the Savior promised, "Come to Me . . . and I will give you rest" (Matt. 11:28).

4. The believer also enjoys a rest in serving the Lord. Whereas the preceding is a rest of salvation, this is a rest of service. "Take My yoke upon you and learn from Me . . . and you will find rest for your souls" (Matt. 11:29).

5. Finally there is the eternal rest which awaits the believer in the Father's house in heaven. This future rest, also called a Sabbath rest (Heb. 4:9), is the final rest of which the others are either types or foretastes. This rest is the principal subject (Heb. 4:1–13).

4:1 No one should think that the promise of **rest** is no longer valid. It has never had a complete and final fulfillment in the past; **therefore** the offer is still in effect.

But all who profess to be believers should make sure that they do not **come short of** the goal. If their profession is empty, there is always the danger of turning away from Christ and embracing some religious system that is powerless to save.

4:2 We have had good news **preached to us** — the good news of eternal life through faith in Christ. The Israelites also had good news preached to them — the good news of rest in the land of Canaan. But they did not benefit from the gospel of rest.

There are two possible explanations for their failure, depending on which manuscript reading of verse 2 we adopt. According to the NKJV, the reason for their failure was that the message was **not mixed with faith in those who heard it**. In other words, they did not believe it or act upon it.

The other reading (NKJV margin) is that "they were not united by faith with those who heeded it." The meaning here is that the majority of the Israelites were not united by faith with Caleb and Joshua, the two spies who believed the promise of God.

In either case, the prominent idea is that unbelief excluded them from the rest which God had prepared for them in the land of promise.

4:3 The continuity of thought becomes difficult in this verse. There seem to be three disjointed and unrelated clauses, yet we can see that there is a common thread in each clause — the theme of God's rest.

First we learn that **we who have believed** are the ones who **enter** God's **rest**. Faith is the key that opens the door. As has been pointed out already, believers today enjoy rest of conscience because they know that they will never be brought into judgment for their sins (John 5:24). But it is also true that those who believe are the only ones who will ever enter God's final rest in glory. It is probably this future rest that is primarily intended here.

The next clause reinforces the idea by stating it negatively: **as He has said: "So I swore in My wrath, 'They shall not enter My rest' "** (quoted from Ps. 95:11). Just as faith admits, so unbelief excludes. We who trust Christ are sure of God's rest; the unbelieving Israelites could not be sure of it because they did not believe God's word.

The third clause presents the most difficulty: it says, **although the works were finished from the foundation of the world**. Perhaps the simplest explanation is found by linking this with the preceding clause. There God had used the future tense in speaking of His rest: **They shall not enter My rest**. The future tense implies that God's rest is still a live option, even though some forfeited it through disobedience, and this rest is still available in spite of the fact that God's **works were finished from the foundation of the world**.

4:4 This verse is intended to prove from Scripture that **God rested** after the work of creation was completed. The author's vagueness in identifying the passage quoted does not indicate any ignorance on his part. It is merely a literary device in quoting a verse from a book that was not at that time divided into chapters and verses. The verse is adapted from Genesis 2:2: "And God rested on the seventh day from all His works."

Here the *past* tense is used and it might seem to indicate to some that God's rest belongs only to history and not to prophecy, that it has no relevance

for us today. But that is not the case.

4:5 To reinforce the idea that the reference to God's rest after creation does not mean that it is a closed issue, the writer again quotes with slight change from Psalm 95:11, where the *future* tense is used, **"They shall not enter My rest."** He is saying, in effect, "In your thinking, do not confine God's rest to what happened back in Genesis 2; remember that God later spoke about His rest as something that was still available."

4:6 Up to this point in the argument we have seen that, from the creation, God has been offering rest to mankind. The admission gate has been open.

The Israelites in the wilderness failed to **enter because of** their **disobedience**. But that did not mean that the promise was no longer in effect!

4:7 The next step is to show that even **in** the case of **David**, about 500 years after the Israelites were shut out from Canaan, God was still using the word **"Today"** as a day of opportunity. The writer had already quoted Psalm 95:7, 8 in Hebrews 3:7, 8, 15. He now quotes it again to prove that God's promise of rest did not cease with the Israelites in the wilderness. In David's time, He was still pleading with men to trust Him and **not** to **harden** their **hearts**.

4:8 Some Israelites did, of course, enter Canaan with **Joshua**. But even these did not enjoy the final **rest** which God has prepared for those who love Him. There was conflict in Canaan, and sin, sickness, sorrow, suffering, and death. If they had exhausted God's promise of rest, then He would not have offered it again in the time of David.

4:9 The preceding verses have been leading up to this conclusion: **There remains therefore a rest for the people of God**. Here the writer uses a different Greek word for **rest** (*sabbatismos*), which is related to the word *Sabbath*. It refers to the eternal rest which will be enjoyed by all who have been redeemed by the precious blood of Christ. It is a "Sabbath" keeping that will never end.

4:10 Whoever enters God's **rest** enjoys a cessation from labor, just **as God did** on the seventh day.

Before we were saved, we may have

tried to work for our salvation. When we realized that Christ had finished the work at Calvary, we abandoned our own worthless efforts and trusted the risen Redeemer.

After salvation, we expend ourselves in loving toil for the One who loved us and gave Himself for us. Our good works are the fruit of the indwelling Holy Spirit. We are often weary in His service, though not weary of it.

In God's eternal rest, we shall cease from our labors down here. This does not mean that we will be inactive in heaven. We shall still worship and serve Him, but there will be no fatigue, distress, persecution, or affliction.

4:11 The previous verses demonstrate that God's rest is still available. This verse says that diligence is necessary in order **to enter that rest**. We must **be diligent** to make sure that our only hope is Christ the Lord. We must diligently resist any temptation merely to profess faith in Him and then to renounce Him in the heat of suffering and persecution.

The Israelites were careless. They treated God's promises lightly. They hankered for Egypt, the land of their bondage. They were not diligent in appropriating God's promises by faith. As a result, they never reached Canaan. We should be warned by their example.

4:12 The next two verses contain a solemn warning that unbelief never goes undetected. It is detected first by **the word of God**. (The term used here for *word* is *logos*, the familiar word used by John in the prologue to his Gospel. However, this verse refers, not to the Living Word, Jesus, but to the written word, the Bible.) This **word of God** is:

living — constantly and actively alive.

powerful — energizing.

cutting — **sharper than any two-edged sword**.

dividing — **piercing** the **soul and spirit**, the two invisible, nonmaterial parts of man. Piercing the **joints and marrow**, the **joints** permitting the outward movements and the **marrow** being the hidden but vital life of the bones.

discerning — discriminating and judging with regard to **the thoughts**

and intents of the heart. It is the word that judges us, not we who judge the word.

4:13 Second, unbelief is detected by the living Lord. Here the pronoun shifts from the impersonal to the personal: **And there is no creature hidden from His sight**. Nothing escapes His notice. He is absolutely omniscient. He is constantly aware of all that is going on in the universe. Of course, the important point in the context is that He knows where there is real faith and where there is only an intellectual assent to facts.

II. CHRIST SUPERIOR IN HIS PRIESTHOOD (4:14–10:18)

A. Christ's High Priesthood Superior to Aaron's (4:14–7:28)

4:14 These verses take up again the strong current of the writer's thought which he had introduced in 3:1 — Christ as the **great High Priest** of His people. They present Him as the great resource of His needy people, able to keep them from falling. Also they change the emphasis "from the word as scrutinizer to the Lord as Sympathizer." When the word has thoroughly exposed us (vv. 12, 13), we can go to Him for mercy and grace.

Notice the excellencies of our wonderful Lord:

1. He is **a great High Priest**. There were many high priests under the Mosaic economy, but none was ever called great.

2. He **has passed through** the atmospheric heaven and the stellar heaven to the third heaven, the dwelling place of God. This speaks, of course, of His ascension and glorification at the Father's right hand.

3. He is human. **Jesus** was the name given to Him at His birth and it is the name that is particularly linked with His humanity.

4. He is divine. **The Son of God**, when used of Christ, speaks of His absolute equality with God the Father. His humanity qualified Him from our viewpoint; His deity, from God's viewpoint. No wonder He is called **a great High Priest**.

4:15 Then too we must consider His

experience. No one can truly **sympathize** with someone else unless he has been through a similar experience himself. As Man our Lord has shared our experiences and can therefore understand the testings which we endure. (He cannot sympathize with our wrongdoing because He never experienced it.)

> In every pang that rends the heart,
> The Man of Sorrows has a part.

He was **tempted** in every respect **as we are, yet without sin**. The Scriptures guard the sinless perfection of the Lord Jesus with jealous care, and we should too. He knew no sin (2 Cor. 5:21), He committed no sin (1 Pet. 2:22), and there is no sin in Him (1 Jn. 3:5).

It was impossible for Him to sin, either as God or as Man. As the perfect Man, He could do nothing of His own accord; He was absolutely obedient to the Father (John 5:19), and certainly the Father would never lead Him to sin.

To argue that His temptation was not meaningful if He could not sin is fallacious. One purpose of the temptation was to demonstrate conclusively that He could *not* sin.[3]

If you put gold to the test, the test is not less valid because the gold is pure. If there were impurity, the test would show it up. Similarly it is wrong to argue that if He could not sin, He was not perfectly human. *Sin is not an essential element in humanity*; rather it is a foreign intruder. Our humanity has been marred by sin; His is perfect humanity.

If Jesus could have sinned as a Man on earth, what is to prevent His sinning as a Man in heaven? He did not leave His humanity behind when He ascended to the Father's right hand. He was impeccable on earth and He is impeccable in heaven.

4:16 Now the gracious invitation is extended: draw near with confidence **to the throne of grace**. Our confidence is based on the knowledge that He died to save us and that He lives to keep us. We are assured of a hearty welcome because He has told us to **come**.

The people in OT days could not draw near to Him. Only the high priest could approach Him, and then only on one day of the year. We can go into His presence at any time of the day or night and **obtain mercy and find grace to help in time of need**. His **mercy** covers the things we should not have done, and His **grace** empowers us to do what we should do but do not have the power to do.

Morgan writes helpfully:

> I am never tired of pointing out that the Greek phrase translated "in time of need" is a colloquialism of which "in the nick of time" is the exact equivalent. "That we may receive mercy and find grace to help *in the nick of time*" — grace just when and where I need it. You are attacked by temptation. At the moment of assault, you look to Him, and the grace is there to help in the nick of time. There is no postponement of your petition until the evening hour of prayer. But there in the city street with the flaming temptation in front of you, turn to Christ with a cry for help, and the grace will be there in the nick of time.[4]

Up to this point, Jesus has been shown to be superior to the prophets, the angels, and Moses. We now turn to the important theme of priesthood to see that Christ's high priesthood is of a superior order to Aaron's.

When God gave the law to Moses on Mount Sinai, He instituted a human priesthood by which the people might draw near to Him. He decreed that the priests must be descended from the tribe of Levi and from the family of Aaron. This order is known as the Levitical or Aaronic priesthood.

Another divinely ordained priesthood is mentioned in the OT, that of the patriarch Melchizedek. This man lived in the days of Abraham, long before the law was given, and served both as a king and a priest. In the passage before us the author will show that the Lord Jesus Christ is a priest after the order of Melchizedek, and that this order is superior to the Aaronic priesthood.

In the first four verses we have a description of the Aaronic priest. Then in verses 5–10 Christ's fitness as a priest is detailed, mostly by way of contrast.

5:1 The first qualification of the Aaronic **priest** was that he had to be chosen **from among men**. In other words, he had to be a man himself.

He was appointed to act **for men** in relation **to God**. He belonged to a special caste of men who served as intermediaries between men and God. One of his principal functions was **to offer both gifts and sacrifices for sins**. **Gifts** refer to any offerings that were presented to God. **Sacrifices** refer to those special offerings in which blood was shed as atonement for sins.

5:2 He had to **have compassion on** human frailty and to deal gently with the ignorant and wayward. His own frail flesh equipped him to understand the problems his people were facing.

The reference in this verse to the **ignorant** and wayward is a reminder that the sacrifices in the OT were for sins not done willfully. No provision was made in the law for deliberate sin.

5:3 But while his being human was an advantage in that it identified the priest with the people, his sinful humanity was a disadvantage. He had **to offer sacrifices** for **himself** as well as for the **sins of the people.**

5:4 The office of priest was not something that men chose as a vocation. They had to be **called** to the work **by God, just as Aaron was**. God's call was limited to Aaron and his descendants. No one outside that family could serve in the tabernacle or the temple.

5:5[†] The writer now turns to **Christ** and demonstrates His fitness as a priest because of His divine appointment, His manifest humanity, and His acquired qualifications.

As to His appointment, its source was God Himself. It was a sovereign call, having nothing to do with human genealogy. It involved a better relationship than any earthly priest ever had. Our **Priest** is the unique **Son** of God, eternally **begotten**, begotten in incarnation, and begotten in resurrection.

5:6 Then Christ's priesthood is of a better order because in Psalm 110:4 God declared Him to be **a priest forever according to the order of Melchizedek**. This superiority will be explained more fully in chapter 7. The prominent thought here is that, unlike the Aaronic priesthood, this one is **forever**.

5:7 Christ is not only the sinless Son of God; He is also true Man. The

writer refers to the variety of human experiences through which He passed **in the days of His flesh** to prove this. Notice the words used to describe His life and especially His experience in the Garden of Gethsemane: **prayers and supplications, with vehement cries and tears**. They all speak of His career as a dependent Man, living in obedience to God, and sharing all man's emotions that are not connected with sin.

Christ's prayer was not that He might be saved from dying; after all, to die for sinners was His very purpose in coming to the world (John 12:27). His prayer was that He might be delivered *out of* death (JND), that His soul might not be left in Hades. This prayer was answered when God raised Him from the dead. He **was heard because of His godly fear**.

5:8 Now once again we come face to face with that profound mystery of the incarnation — how God could become Man in order to die for men.

Though He was a Son, or better, Son though He was — He was not *a* Son, that is, one of many, but He was the only begotten Son of God. In spite of this tremendous fact, **He learned obedience by the things which He suffered**. His entrance into this world as a Man involved Him in experiences which He would never have known had He remained in heaven. Each morning His ear was open to receive instructions from His Father for that day (Isa. 50:4). **He learned obedience** experimentally as the Son who was always subject to His Father's will.

5:9 And having been perfected. This *cannot* refer to His personal character because the Lord Jesus was absolutely perfect. His words, His works, and His ways were absolutely flawless. In what sense then was He **perfected**? The answer is in His office as our Savior. He could never have become our perfect Savior if He had remained in heaven. But through His incarnation, death, burial, resurrection, and ascension, He completed the work that was necessary to save us from our sins, and now He has the acquired glory of being the perfect Savior of the world.

Having returned to heaven, **He became the author of eternal salvation to** all who obey Him. He is the Source of salvation for all, but only those who obey Him are saved.

Here salvation is conditional on obeying Him. In many other passages salvation is conditional on faith. How do we reconcile this seeming contradiction? First of all, it is the obedience of faith (Rom. 1:5; 16:25–27): "the obedience which God requires is faith in His word." But it is also true that saving faith is the kind that results in obedience. It is impossible to believe, in the true NT sense, without obeying.

5:10 Having gloriously accomplished the fundamental work of priesthood, the Lord Jesus was addressed by God as High Priest "according to the order of Melchizedek."

It should be mentioned here that though Christ's priesthood is of the Melchizedekan order, yet His priestly functions are similar to those carried on by the Aaronic priests. In fact, the ministry of the Jewish priests was a foreshadow or picture of the work that Christ would accomplish.

5:11 At this point the author must digress. He would like to continue with the subject of Christ's Melchizedekan priesthood but he cannot. He is under divine constraint to rebuke his readers for their immaturity and at the same time to warn them seriously against the danger of falling away.

It is sadly true that our apprehension of divine truth is limited by our own spiritual condition. **Dull** ears cannot receive deep truths! How often it is true of us, as of the disciples, that the Lord has many things to say to us but we cannot bear them (John 16:12).

5:12 The writer reminds the Hebrews that they had been receiving instruction long enough now so that they should be teaching others. But the tragedy was that they still needed someone to teach them the ABCs of the word of God.

You ought to be teachers. God's order is that every believer should mature to the point where he can teach others. Each one teach one! While it is true that certain ones have a special gift of teaching, it is also true that every believer should engage in some teaching

ministry. It was never God's intention that this work should be limited to a few.

You have come to need milk and not solid food. In the physical realm, a child who never advances from milk to solids is impaired. There is a form of stunted growth in the spiritual realm as well (1 Cor. 3:2).

5:13 Professing believers who stay on a milk diet are unskilled in the word of righteousness. They are hearers of the word but not doers. They lose what they do not use, and remain in a state of perpetual infancy.

They do not have a keen sense of discernment in spiritual matters and are "tossed to and fro and carried about with every wind of doctrine, by the trickery of men, in the cunning craftiness of deceitful plotting" (Eph. 4:14).

5:14 Solid spiritual food is for the full-grown, for those who by reason of use have their senses exercised to discern both good and evil. By obeying the light they receive from God's word, these people are able to form spiritual judgments and save themselves from moral and doctrinal dangers.

In this context the particular sense in which the readers are urged to distinguish between good and evil is in relation to Christianity and Judaism. Not that Judaism was evil in itself; the Levitical system was introduced by God Himself. But it was intended to point forward to Christ. He is the fulfillment of the ceremonial types and shadows. Now that Christ has come, it is sinful to return to the pictures of Him. Anything that rivals Christ in the affections and loyalties of men is evil. Spiritually mature believers are able to discern between the inferiority of the Aaronic priesthood and the superiority of Christ's.

6:1 The warning which began in 5:11 continues throughout this chapter. It is one of the most controversial passages in the entire NT. Since so many godly Christians are disagreed on its interpretation, we must not speak with dogmatism. We present the explanation which seems most consistent with the context and with the rest of the NT.

First of all, the readers are exhorted to leave the elementary principles of

Christ, literally, "the word of the beginning of Christ" (FWG), or "the beginning word of Christ" (KSW). We understand this to mean the basic doctrines of religion that were taught in the OT and were designed to prepare Israel for the coming of the Messiah. These doctrines are listed in the latter part of verse 1 and in verse 2. As we shall seek to show, they are not the fundamental doctrines of Christianity but rather teachings of an elementary nature which formed the foundation for later building. They fell short of Christ risen and glorified. The exhortation is to leave these basics, not in the sense of abandoning them as worthless, but rather of advancing from them to maturity. The implication is that the period of Judaism was a time of spiritual infancy. Christianity represents full growth.

Once a foundation has been laid, the next step is to build upon it. A doctrinal **foundation** was laid in the OT; it included the six fundamental teachings which are now listed. These represent a starting point. The great NT truths concerning Christ, His Person, and His work, represent the ministry of maturity.

The first OT doctrine is **repentance from dead works**. This was preached constantly by the prophets as well as by the forerunner of the Messiah. They all called on the people to turn from **works** that were **dead** in the sense that they were devoid of faith.

Dead works here may also refer to works which formerly were right, but which now are **dead** since Christ has come. For example, all the services connected with temple worship are outmoded by the finished work of Christ.

Second, the writer mentions **faith toward God**. This again is an OT emphasis. In the NT, Christ is almost invariably presented as the object of faith. Not that this displaces faith in God; but a faith in God which leaves out Christ is now inadequate.

6:2 Instruction about **baptisms** refers not to Christian baptism,[5] but to the ceremonial washings which figured so prominently in the religious lives of the priests and people of Israel (see also 9:10).

The ritual of **laying on of hands** is described in Leviticus 1:4; 3:2; 16:21. The offerer or the priest laid his hands on the head of an animal as an act of identification. In figure, the animal bore away the sins of the people who were associated with it. This ceremony typified vicarious atonement. We do not believe that there is any reference here to the laying on of hands as practiced by the apostles and others in the early church (Acts 8:17; 13:3; 19:6).

Resurrection of the dead is taught in Job 19:25–27, Psalm 17:15, and it is implied in Isaiah 53:10–12. What was seen only indistinctly in the OT is brightly revealed in the New (2 Tim. 1:10).

The final foundational truth of the OT was **eternal judgment** (Ps. 9:17; Isa. 66:24).

These first principles represented Judaism, and were preparatory to the coming of Christ. Christians should not continue to be content with these but should press on to the fuller revelation they now have in Christ. The readers are urged to pass "from shadow to substance, from type to antitype, from husk to kernel, from the dead forms of the religion of their ancestors to the living realities of Christ."

6:3 The author expresses his desire to help them **do this**,[6] **if God permits**. However, the limiting factor will be on their side and not on God's. God will enable them to advance to full spiritual manhood, but they must respond to the word positively by exercising true faith and endurance.

6:4 We come now to the heart of the warning against apostasy. It applies to a class of people whom **it is impossible** to restore again to repentance. Apparently these people had once repented (though no mention is made of their faith in Christ). Now it is clearly stated that a renewed repentance is impossible.

Who are these people? The answer is given in verses 4 and 5. In examining the great privileges which they enjoyed, it should be noticed that all these things could be true of the unsaved. It is never clearly stated that they had been born again. Neither is any mention made of such essentials as saving faith, redemption by His blood, or eternal life.

They had **once** been **enlightened**.

They had heard the gospel of the grace of God. They were not in darkness concerning the way of salvation. Judas Iscariot had been enlightened but he rejected the light.

They **tasted the heavenly gift**. The Lord Jesus is the heavenly Gift. They had tasted of Him but had never received Him by a definite act of faith. It is possible to taste without eating or drinking. When men offered wine mixed with gall to Jesus on the cross, He tasted it but He would not drink it (Matt. 27:34). It is not enough to taste Christ; unless we eat the flesh of the Son of Man and drink His blood, that is, unless we truly receive Him as Lord and Savior, we have no life in us (John 6:53).

They had **become partakers of the Holy Spirit**. Before we jump to the conclusion that this necessarily implies conversion, we should remember that the Holy Spirit carries on a preconversion ministry in men's lives. He sanctifies unbelievers (1 Cor. 7:14), putting them in a position of external privilege. He convicts unbelievers of sin, of righteousness, and of judgment (John 16:8). He leads men to repentance and points them to Christ as their only hope. Men may thus partake of the Holy Spirit's benefits without being indwelt by Him.

6:5 They had **tasted the good word of God**. As they heard the gospel preached, they were strangely moved and drawn to it. They were like the seed that fell on rocky ground; they heard the word and immediately received it with joy, but they had no root in themselves. They endured for a while, but when tribulation or persecution arose on account of the word, they promptly fell away (Matt. 13:20, 21).

They had tasted **the powers of the age to come**. **Powers** here means "miracles." **The age to come** is the Millennial Age, the coming era of peace and prosperity when Christ will reign over the earth for one thousand years. The miracles which accompanied the preaching of the gospel in the early days of the church (Heb. 2:4) were a foretaste of signs and wonders which will be performed in Christ's kingdom. These people had witnessed these miracles in the first century, in fact, they might have

participated in them. Take, for instance, the miracles of the loaves and fishes. After Jesus had fed the five thousand, the people followed Him to the other side of the sea. The Savior realized that, though they had tasted a miracle, they did not really believe in Him. He said to them, "Most assuredly, I say to you, you seek Me, not because you saw the signs, but because you ate of the loaves and were filled" (John 6:26).

6:6 If they fall away,[7] after enjoying the privileges just enumerated, it is impossible **to renew them again to repentance**. They have committed the sin of apostasy. They have reached the place where the lights go out on the way to hell.

The enormous guilt of apostates is indicated in the words **since they crucify again for themselves the Son of God, and put Him to an open shame** (v. 6b). This signifies a deliberate, malicious spurning of Christ, not just a careless disregard of Him. It indicates a positive betrayal of Him, a joining of forces against Him, and a ridiculing of His Person and work.

APOSTASY

Apostates are people who hear the gospel, make a profession of being Christians, become identified with a Christian church, and then abandon their profession of faith, decisively repudiate Christ, desert the Christian fellowship, and take their place with enemies of the Lord Jesus Christ. Apostasy is a sin which can be committed only by unbelievers, not by those who are deceived but by those who knowingly, willfully, and maliciously turn against the Lord.

It should not be confused with the sin of the average unbeliever who hears the gospel but does nothing about it. For instance, a man may fail to respond to Christ after repeated invitations from the Holy Spirit. But he is not an apostate. He can still be saved if he will commit himself to the Savior. Of course, if he dies in unbelief, he is lost forever, but he is not hopeless as long as he is capable of exercising faith in the Lord.

Apostasy should not be confused with backsliding. A true believer may wander very far away from Christ.

Through sin his fellowship with God is shattered. He may even reach the point where he is no longer recognized as a Christian. But he can be restored to full fellowship as soon as he confesses and forsakes his sin (1 Jn. 1:9).

Apostasy is not the same as the unpardonable sin mentioned in the Gospels. That was the sin of attributing the miracles of the Lord Jesus to the prince of the demons. His miracles were actually performed in the power of the Holy Spirit. To attribute them to the devil was tantamount to blaspheming the Holy Spirit. It implied that the Holy Spirit was the devil. Jesus said that such a sin could never be forgiven, either in that age or in the age to come (Mark 3:22–30). Apostasy is similar to blasphemy against the Holy Spirit in that it is an eternal sin, but there the resemblance ends.

I believe that apostasy is the same as the sin leading to death, mentioned in 1 John 5:16b. John was writing about people who had professed to be believers and had participated in the activities of local churches. They then had imbibed the false teaching of the Gnostics and had spitefully left the Christian fellowship. Their deliberate departure indicated that they had never been truly born again (1 Jn. 2:19). By openly denying that Jesus is the Christ (1 Jn. 2:22), they had committed the sin leading to death, and it was useless to pray for their recovery (1 Jn. 5:16b).

Some earnest Christians are troubled when they read Hebrews 6 and similar passages. Satan uses these verses especially to unsettle believers who are having physical, mental, or emotional difficulties. They fear that they have fallen away from Christ and that there is no hope for restoration. They worry that they have drifted beyond redemption's point. The fact that they are even concerned about it is conclusive evidence that they are *not* apostates! An apostate would not have any such fears; he would brazenly repudiate Christ.

If the sin of apostasy does not apply to believers, to whom then does it apply in our day? It applies, for instance, to a young man who makes a profession of faith in Christ and seems to go on brightly for a while, but then something

happens in his life. Perhaps he experiences bitter persecution. Perhaps he falls into gross immorality. Or perhaps he goes off to college and is shaken by the anti-Christian arguments of atheistic teachers. With full knowledge of the truth, he deliberately turns away from it. He completely renounces Christ and viciously tramples on every sacred fundamental doctrine of the Christian faith. The Bible says it is impossible to restore such a one to repentance, and experience corroborates the Bible. We have known many who have apostatized from Christ, but we have never known one who has returned to Him.

As we approach the end of this age, we can expect a rising tide of apostasy (2 Thess. 2:3; 1 Tim. 4:1). Therefore the warning against falling away becomes more relevant with every day that passes. ‡

6:7 Now the writer turns to the world of nature to find a counterpart to the true believer (v. 7) and to the apostate (v. 8). In both cases the person is likened to the land. The privileges listed in verses 4 and 5 are compared to the invigorating **rain**. The crop of vegetation speaks of the ultimate response of the person to the privileges received. This in turn determines whether the land is blessed or cursed.

The true believer is like the land **which drinks in the rain**, brings forth useful vegetation, and is blessed by **God**.

6:8 The apostate is like land that also is well watered but it **bears** nothing but **thorns and briers**, the fruit of sin. It receives but never produces useful plants. Such land is worthless. It is condemned already. Its destiny **is to be burned**.

6:9 There are two strong indications in verses 9 and 10 that the apostates described in the preceding verses are unbelievers. First, there is the abrupt change in pronouns. In discussing apostates, the writer refers to them as "they." Now in addressing true believers, he uses the pronouns **you** and **your**.

The second indication is even clearer. Speaking to believers, he says, **"But, beloved, we are confident of better things** concerning you, yes, things that accompany salvation." The inference is that the things he had described in verses 4–6 and 8 do *not* accompany salvation.

6:10 Two of the things that accompany salvation were manifest in the lives of the saints — their **work and** their **labor of love**. Their faith manifested itself in a life of good works, and they had the hallmark of true Christianity — active **love** for the household of faith. They continued to serve the Lord's people for His sake.

6:11 The next two verses seem to be written to a different class of people; namely, to those of whom the writer was not sure. These were the ones who seemed to be in danger of drifting back into Judaism.

First, he desires **that** they will **show the same** earnestness as the true believers have shown in realizing **the full assurance of hope until the end**. He wants them to go on steadfastly for Christ until the final hope of the Christian is realized in heaven. This is a proof of reality.

6:12 They should **not become sluggish**, allowing their feet to drag and their spirits to lag. They should press on, imitating all true believers **who through faith and patience inherit the promises**.

6:13 The closing section of chapter 6 is linked with the exhortation in verse 12 to press on with confidence and patience. The example of **Abraham** is given as a stimulus and the certainty of the believer's hope is affirmed.

In one sense, the Christian may seem to be at a disadvantage. He has given up all for Christ, and has nothing material to show for it. Everything is in the future. How then can he be sure that His hope is not in vain?

The answer is found in God's **promise to Abraham**, a promise that included in germ form all that He would later bestow in the Person of Christ. When God made that promise, **He swore by Himself** since **He could swear by no one greater**.

6:14 The promise is found in Genesis 22:16, 17: "By Myself I have sworn, says the LORD . . . blessing I will bless you, and multiplying I will multiply your descendants. . . ." God pledged Himself to carry out this promise, and therefore its fulfillment was assured.

6:15 Abraham believed in God; he

patiently endured; and he received the fulfillment. Actually Abraham was not taking a chance in believing God. No risk was involved. The word of God is the surest thing in the universe. Any **promise** of God is as certain of fulfillment as if it had already taken place.

6:16 In human affairs, **men swear by** someone **greater** than themselves. In courts of law, for example, they promise to tell the truth and then add, "so help me, God." They appeal to God for confirmation that what they are going to say is true.

When men take **an oath** to confirm a promise, that normally ends all **dispute**. It is understood that the promise will be kept.

6:17 **God** wanted His believing people to be absolutely assured that what He promised would come to pass. Actually His bare promise would have been enough, but He wanted **to show** it to a greater extent than even by a promise. So He added **an oath** to the promise.

The heirs of promise are all those who by faith are children of faithful Abraham. The **promise** referred to is the promise of eternal salvation to all who believe on Him. When God made a promise of a seed to Abraham, the promise found its full and ultimate fulfillment in Christ, and all the blessings that flow from union with Christ were therefore *included* in the promise.

6:18 The believer now has **two** unchangeable **things** on which to rely — His word and His oath. It is impossible to imagine anything more secure or certain.[8] God promises to save all who believe on Christ; then He confirms it with an oath. The conclusion is inevitable: the believer is eternally secure.

In the remainder of chapter 6 the writer employs four figures to drive home the utter reliability of the Christian hope: (1) a city of refuge, (2) an anchor, (3) a forerunner, and (4) a High Priest.

First, those who are true believers are pictured as fleeing from this doomed world to the heavenly city of **refuge**. To encourage them in their flight, God has given them an unfailing **hope** based upon His word and His oath.

6:19 In the storms and trials of life this **hope** serves **as an anchor of the soul**. The knowledge that our glorification is as certain as if it had already happened keeps us from drifting on the wild waves of doubt and despair.

The **anchor** is not cast in the shifting sands of this world but takes hold in the heavenly sanctuary. Since our **hope** is the anchor, the meaning is that our hope is secured in God's very **Presence behind the veil**. Just as sure as the anchor is there, we shall be there also.

6:20 Jesus has gone into the inner shrine also as our **forerunner**. His presence there insures the ultimate entrance of all who belong to Him. It is no exaggeration to say that the simplest believer on earth is as certain of heaven as the saints who are already there.

D. Anderson-Berry writes:

> The word translated "forerunner" is found nowhere else in the New Testament. This expresses an idea never contemplated in the Levitical economy, for the high priest entered the holiest only as a representative. He entered where none could follow. But our Forerunner is a pledge that where He is, we also shall be. As Forerunner He (1) announced our future arrival there; (2) took possession of heaven's glories on our behalf; and (3) has gone to be able to bid His people welcome when they come, and to present them before the Majesty of heaven.[9]

The fourth figure is that of **High Priest**. Our Lord has **become High Priest forever according to the order of Melchizedek**. His eternal priesthood guarantees our eternal preservation. Just as surely as we have been reconciled to God by His death, so surely are we saved by His life as our Priest at God's right hand (Rom. 5:10).

This mention of **Jesus** as **High Priest** in **the order of Melchizedek** reminds us that this subject was interrupted at 5:10 when the author digressed on the extended warning against cast apostasy. Now he is ready to resume his theme that Christ's high priesthood is superior to Aaron's. He has skillfully returned to the main flow of argument.

7:1 Melchizedek was an enigmatic figure who appeared briefly on the stage of human history (Gen. 14:18–20), then disappeared. Centuries later his name was mentioned by David (Ps. 110:4). Then, after a lapse of additional centuries, it reappears in the book of Hebrews. One thing is apparent: God arranged the details of his life so that he would be an excellent type of our Lord Jesus Christ.

In these first three verses of chapter 7 we have some historical facts concerning him. We are reminded that he combined the offices of **king** and **priest** in his person. He was **king of Salem** (later called Jerusalem), and **priest of the Most High God**. He was the political and spiritual leader of his people. That is, of course, God's ideal — that there should be no separation between the secular and the sacred. When sinful man is reigning it is necessary to separate church and state. Only when Christ reigns in righteousness will it be possible to unite the two (Isa. 32:1,17).

Melchizedek encountered **Abraham** when the latter was **returning from** a military victory **and blessed him**. The significance of this act is reserved for verse 7. If we had only the OT Scriptures, we would never realize the deep significance of these seemingly irrelevant details.

7:2 Abraham gave a tenth part of the spoils of war to this mysterious king-priest. Again we must wait till verses 4, 6, 8–10 to learn the hidden meaning of Abraham's tithe.

In the Scriptures, a man's name stands for what he is. We learn about Melchizedek's name and his title: his name means **"king of righteousness"** and his title (**king of Salem**) means **"king of peace."**

It is not without meaning that **righteousness** is mentioned first, then **peace**. There cannot be peace unless first there is righteousness.

We see this clearly in the work of Christ. At the cross, "Mercy and truth . . . met together; righteousness and peace . . . kissed" (Ps. 85:10). Because the Savior met all the righteous demands of God against our sins, we can have peace with God.

7:3 The puzzle concerning Melchizedek deepens when we read that he had neither **father** nor **mother**, neither **genealogy**, birth, nor death. If we divorce these statements from their context, we would have to conclude that he was a visitor from heaven or from another planet, or that he was a special creation of God.

But the key to understanding lies in taking these statements in their context. The subject is priesthood. The writer is distinguishing between the Melchize-dekan priesthood and the Aaronic. In order to qualify for the Aaronic priesthood a man had to be born of the tribe of Levi and of the family of Aaron. Genealogy was all-important. Also, his qualification began at birth and ended at death.

Melchizedek's priesthood was quite different. He did not inherit the priesthood by being born into a priestly family. God simply picked him out and designated him as a priest. *As far as his priesthood was concerned*, there is no record of his **father** or **mother** or **genealogy**. In his case, this was of no importance, *and as far as the record is concerned*, no mention is made of his birth or death; therefore his priesthood continues.

We should not conclude that Melchizedek had no parents, that he was never born, and that he never died. That is not the point. The thought is that *as far as his priesthood was concerned*, there is no record of these vital statistics because his ministry as priest was not dependent on them.

He was not the Son of God, as some have mistakenly thought, but was **made like the Son of God** in this respect, that his priesthood continued without interruption.

Now the author is going to demonstrate that Melchizedek's priesthood is superior to Aaron's. There are three arguments in the proof: the argument concerning the tithes and blessing; the argument concerning a change that has taken place, replacing the Aaronic priesthood; and the argument concerning the perpetuity of the Melchizedekan priesthood.

7:4 In verses 4–10 we have the first argument. It opens with an unusual interjection, asking the readers to **consider** the greatness of Melchizedek. **Even the patriarch Abraham gave** him **a tenth of the spoils** of battle. Since Abraham was one of the greatest stars in the Hebrew firmament, it follows that Melchizedek must have been a star of even *greater* magnitude.

7:5 As far as the Levitical priests were concerned, they were authorized by **the law** to collect **tithes** from their fellow Hebrews. Both the priests and the people traced their descent from **Abra-**

ham, the father of the faithful.

7:6 **But** when Melchizedek **received tithes from Abraham**, it was an unusual and unconventional transaction. Abraham, called to be the father of the nation from which Messiah would come, was paying deference to one who was not connected with the chosen people. Melchizedek's priesthood leaped over racial barriers.

Another significant fact is that Melchizedek **blessed** Abraham. He said, "Blessed be Abram of God Most High, Possessor of heaven and earth" (Gen. 14:19, 20).

7:7 When one man blesses another man, it is understood that the superior blesses the inferior. This does not signify any personal or moral inferiority, of course, but simply an inferiority of position.

As we read these arguments based on the OT, we should try to picture the reactions of the Hebrew readers. They had always revered Abraham as one of their greatest national heroes, and rightly so. But now they learn that Abraham acknowledged a "non-Jewish" priest as his superior. Just think! This was in their Bible all the time and they had never noticed it.

7:8 In the Aaronic priesthood **tithes** were received by men who were subject to death. There was a constant succession of priests, each one serving his own generation, then passing on. In Melchizedek's case there is no mention of his having died. Therefore he can represent a priesthood which is unique in that it is perpetual.

7:9 In receiving tithes from **Abraham**, Melchizedek virtually received them from **Levi**. Since Levi was the head of the priestly tribe, it amounts to saying that the Aaronic priesthood **paid tithes** to Melchizedek and thus acknowledged the superiority of the latter.

7:10 By what chain of reckoning can it be said that Levi paid tithes to Melchizedek? Well, first of all, Abraham was actually the one who paid the tithes. He was the great-grandfather of Levi. Though Levi had not yet been born, he was **in the loins of** Abraham, that is, he was destined to be descended from the patriarch. Abraham really acted as a representative for all his posterity when he gave a tenth to Melchizedek. Therefore Levi, and the priesthood that sprang from him, took second place to Melchizedek and to his priesthood.

7:11 In verses 11–20 we find the second argument that shows Melchizedek's priesthood to be superior to Aaron's. The argument is that there has been a change in the priesthood. The priesthood of Christ has set aside the Levitical priesthood. This would not have been necessary if the latter had achieved its purpose fully and finally.

The fact is that **perfection** was not attainable **through the Levitical** system. Sins were never put away and the worshipers never obtained rest of conscience. The priesthood that was set up under the Law of Moses was not the ultimate one.

Another kind of priesthood is now in effect. The perfect Priest has now come, and His priesthood is **not** reckoned **according to the order of Aaron** but rather after **the order of Melchizedek**.

7:12 The fact that the **priesthood** has been **changed** forces the conclusion that the entire legal structure on which the priesthood was based has been changed also. This is a very radical announcement! Like a tolling bell, it rings out the old order of things and rings in the new. We are no longer under the law.

7:13 That there has been a change in the law is evident from the fact that the Lord Jesus **belongs to** a **tribe** which was barred from performing priestly function by the Levitical law.

7:14 It was **from** the tribe **of Judah** that **our Lord** was descended. The Mosaic legislation never authorized anyone from that tribe to be a priest. Yet Jesus is a Priest. How can that be? Because the law has been changed.

7:15 The author has additional evidence that there has been a vast change in the law of the priesthood. **Another** kind of **priest** has arisen **in the likeness of Melchizedek**, and His qualification for the office is quite different from that of Aaron's sons.

7:16 The Levitical priests became eligible by meeting the legal requirements concerning bodily descent. They had to

be born of the tribe of Levi and of the family of Aaron.

But what qualifies the Lord to be a Priest like Melchizedek is His **endless life**. It is not a question of pedigree but of personal, inherent power. He lives forever.

7:17 This is confirmed by the words of Psalm 110:4, where David points forward to the Messiah's priesthood: **"You are a priest forever according to the order of Melchizedek."** Here the emphasis is on the word **forever**. His ministry will never cease because His life will never end.

7:18 The law which set up the Aaronic priesthood has been annulled **because of its weakness and unprofitableness**. It has been canceled by the advent of Christ.

In what sense was the law weak and unprofitable? Was it not given by God Himself? Could God give anything that was impotent and useless? The answer is that God never intended this to be the ultimate law of priesthood. It was preparatory to the coming of God's *ideal* priesthood. It was a partial and temporary picture of that which would be perfect and final.

7:19 It was also weak and useless in the sense that it **made nothing perfect**. The people were never able to go into the presence of God in the Most Holy Place. This enforced distance between God and man was a constant reminder that the sin question was not settled once for all.

But now **a better hope** has been introduced **through which we draw near to God**. That **better hope** is the Lord Jesus Himself; those who have Him as their only hope have perfect access **to God** at any time.

7:20 Not only has there been a change in the order of priesthood and in the law of priesthood, but also, as we shall now see, there has been a change in the method of induction. The reasoning here revolves around the use of God's **oath** in connection with Christ's priesthood. The oath signifies the introduction of that which is unchangeable and everlasting. Rainsbury says, "Nothing less than the oath of Almighty God guarantees the efficacy and the eternity of the priesthood of our blessed Lord Jesus."[10]

7:21 The Aaronic priests were appointed **without an oath**. Therefore the implication is that their priesthood was intended to be provisional and not enduring.

But God addressed Christ **with an oath** in designating Him as a priest. The form of the oath is found in Psalm 110:4: **"The Lord has sworn and will not relent, 'You are a priest forever according to the order of Melchizedek.' "** Henderson says:

> God places behind Christ's commission the eternal verities of His throne, and the immutable attributes of His nature. If they can change, the new priesthood can change. Otherwise it cannot.[11]

7:22 It follows from this that **Jesus** is the **surety of a better covenant**. The Aaronic priesthood was a part of the Old Covenant. The priesthood of Christ is connected with the New **covenant**. Covenant and priesthood stand or fall together.

The *New* Covenant is an unconditional agreement of grace which God will make with the house of Israel and with the house of Judah when the Lord Jesus sets up His kingdom on earth (Jer. 31:33, 34). Believers today enjoy some of the blessings of the New Covenant but its complete fulfillment will not be realized until Israel is restored and redeemed nationally.

Jesus is the **surety of** the New **covenant** in the sense that He Himself is the Guarantee. By His death, burial, and resurrection, He provided a righteous basis on which God can fulfill the terms of the covenant. His endless priesthood is also vitally linked with the unfailing fulfillment of the terms of the covenant.

7:23 We now come to the third and final argument concerning the superiority of the Melchizedekan priesthood.

The priests of Israel were **many**. It is said that there were eighty-four high **priests** in the history of the nation, and of course, there were innumerable lesser priests. The office periodically changed hands because of the **death** of the incumbents. The ministry suffered from these inevitable interruptions.

7:24 In the case of Christ's priesthood, there is no such failure because He lives **forever**. His **priesthood** is never passed on to anyone else, and there is no interruption to its effectiveness. It is **unchangeable** and intransmissible.

7:25 Because He **lives** forever **He is also able to save to the uttermost those who come to God** by Him. We generally understand this to refer to His work in saving sinners from the penalty of sin, but actually the writer is speaking of Christ's work in saving saints from the power of sin. It is not so much His role as Savior as that of High Priest. There is no danger that any believers will be lost. Their eternal security rests on His perpetual **intercession for them. He is also able to save** them for all time because His present ministry for them at God's right hand can never be interrupted by death.

7:26 Christ's priesthood is superior to Aaron's because of His personal excellence. He is **holy** in His standing before God. He is **harmless** or guileless in His dealings with men. He is **undefiled** in His personal character. He is **separate from sinners** in His life at God's right hand. He **has become higher than the heavens** in His present and eternal splendor. It is **fitting for us** to have such a High Priest.

7:27 Unlike the Levitical priests, our High Priest **does not need** to offer sacrifices **daily; this He did once for all.** He does **not need** to offer **for His own sins** because He is absolutely sinless. A third amazing way in which He differs from the former priests is that **He offered up Himself** for the sins of the people. The Priest gave Himself as the sacrifice. Wonderful, matchless grace of Jesus!

7:28 **The law** sets up **priests** who are personally imperfect; they are characterized by **weakness** and failure; they are only ritually holy.

God's **oath**, given after the law, **appoints the Son** as a Priest **who has been perfected forever**. This oath was referred to in verse 21 of this chapter and quoted from Psalm 110:4.

There are momentous implications in the material we have just covered. Human priesthood has been superseded by a divine and eternal priesthood. How foolish, then, for men to set up priestly systems patterned after the OT and to intrude upon the functions of our great High Priest!

B. Christ's Ministry Superior to Aaron's (Chap. 8)

8:1 In the verses that follow, Christ's ministry is shown to be superior to Aaron's because He officiates in a better sanctuary (vv. 1–5) and in connection with a better covenant (vv. 7–13).

Now the writer has come to the **main point** of his argument. He is not summarizing what has been said but stating the main thesis to which he has been leading in the Epistle.

We have such a High Priest. There is a triumphant note in the words **we have**. They are an answer to those Jewish people who taunted the early Christians with the words, "We have the tabernacle; we have the priesthood; we have the offerings; we have the ceremonies; we have the temple; we have the beautiful priestly garments." The believers' confident answer is, "Yes, you have the shadows but we have the fulfillment. You have the ceremonies but we have Christ. You have the pictures but we have the Person. And our High Priest **is seated at the right hand of the throne of the Majesty in the heavens**. No other high priest ever sat down in recognition of a finished work, and none ever held such a place of honor and power."

8:2 He serves the people in **the sanctuary** of heaven. This is **the true** tent, of which the earthly tabernacle was a mere copy or representation. **The true tabernacle** was **erected** by **the Lord and not man**, as was the earthly tent.

8:3 Since one of the principal functions of a **high priest** is **to offer both gifts and sacrifices**, it follows that our High Priest must do this also.

Gifts is a general term covering all types of offerings presented to God. **Sacrifices** were gifts in which an animal was slain. What does Christ offer? The question is not answered directly until chapter 9.

8:4 This verse skips over the question of what Christ offers, and simply reminds us that **on earth He would not be** eligible to offer gifts in the tabernacle or temple. Our Lord was descended from Judah and not from the tribe of Levi or the family of Aaron. For this reason He was not qualified to serve in the earthly sanctuary. When we read in the Gospels that Jesus went into the temple (see Luke 19:45), we must understand that He went only into the area surrounding it, and not into the Holy Place or the Holy of Holies.

This of course raises the question whether Christ performed any high priestly functions when he was on earth, or was it only after He ascended that He began His priestly work? The point of verse 4 is that *He was not qualified on earth as a Levitical priest, and could not serve in the temple in Jerusalem.* But this does not mean that He could not perform the functions of *a Melchizedekan priest.* After all, His prayer in John 17 is a high priestly prayer, and His offering of Himself as the one perfect sacrifice at Calvary was certainly a priestly act (see 2:17).

8:5 The tabernacle on earth was a replica **of the heavenly** sanctuary. Its layout depicted the manner in which God's covenant people could approach Him in worship. First there was the door of the outer court, then the altar of burnt offering, then the laver. After that the priests entered the Holy Place and the high priest entered the Most Holy Place where God manifested himself.

The tabernacle was never intended to be the ultimate sanctuary. It was only a **copy and shadow**. When God called **Moses** up to Mount Sinai and told him to build the tabernacle, He gave him a definite blueprint to follow. This **pattern** was a type of a higher, **heavenly**, spiritual reality.

Why does the writer emphasize this so forcefully? Simply to impress on the minds of any who might be tempted to go back to Judaism that they were leaving the substance for the shadows when they should be going on from shadow to substance.

Verse 5 clearly teaches that the OT institutions were types of heavenly realities; therefore it justifies the teaching of typology when it is done in consonance with Scripture and without becoming fanciful.

8:6 This verse forms a transition between the subject of the superior sanctuary and the discussion of the **better covenant**.

First, there is a comparison. Christ's ministry is as superior to the ministry of the Aaronic priests as the **covenant** He mediates is superior to the old one.

Second, a reason is given: the **covenant** is **better** because it is enacted **on better promises**.

Christ's **ministry** is infinitely better. He offered Himself, not an animal. He presented the value of His own blood, not the blood of bulls and goats. He put away sins, not merely covered them. He gave believers a perfect conscience, not an annual reminder of sins. He opened the way for us to enter into the presence of God, not to stand outside at a distance.

He is also Mediator of a better covenant. As **Mediator** He stands between God and man to bridge the gap of estrangement. Griffith Thomas compares the covenants succinctly:

> The covenant is "better" because it is absolute not conditional, spiritual not carnal, universal not local, eternal not temporal, individual not national, internal not external.[12]

It is a **better covenant** because it is founded **on better promises**. The covenant of law promised blessing for obedience but threatened death for disobedience. It required righteousness but did not give the ability to produce it.

The New Covenant is an unconditional covenant of grace. It imputes righteousness where there is none. It teaches men to live righteously, empowers them to do so, and rewards them when they do.

8:7 That **first covenant** was not perfect, that is, it was not successful in achieving an ideal relationship between man and God. It was never intended to be the final covenant, but was preparatory to the coming of Christ. The fact that a **second** covenant is mentioned later shows that the **first** was not the ideal.

8:8 Actually the trouble was not with the first covenant itself: "the law is holy, and the commandment holy and just and good" (Rom. 7:12). The trouble

was with the people to whom it was given; the law had poor raw materials to work with. This is stated here: **Because finding fault with them, He says . . . .** He did not find fault with the covenant but with His covenant people. The first covenant was based on man's promise to obey (Ex. 19:8; 24:7), and therefore it was not destined to last very long. The New Covenant is a recital, from beginning to end, of what God agrees to do; this is its strength.

The writer now quotes Jeremiah 31:31–34 to show that in the Jewish Scriptures God had promised a New Covenant. The whole argument revolves around the word **new**. If the old was sufficient and satisfactory, why introduce a new one?

Yet God specifically promised to **make a new covenant with the house of Israel and with the house of Judah.** As mentioned previously, the **new covenant** has to do primarily with the nation of **Israel** and not with the church. It will find its complete fulfillment when Christ comes back to reign over the repentant and redeemed nation. In the meantime some of the blessings of the covenant are enjoyed by all believers. Thus when the Savior passed the cup of wine to His disciples, He said, "This is the new covenant in My blood. This do, as often as you drink it, in remembrance of Me" (1 Cor. 11:25).

Henderson quotes the following:

> And so we distinguish between the primary interpretation to Israel, and the secondary, spiritual application to the Church today. We now enjoy in the power of the Holy Spirit the blessings of the new covenant, and yet there will be still further and future manifestations for Israel according to God's promise.[13]

8:9 God specifically promised that the New Covenant would not be like **the covenant that** He **made with** them **when** He **took them by the hand** out **of Egypt.** How would it be different? He does not say, but perhaps the answer is implied in the remainder of the verse, **because they did not continue in My covenant, and I disregarded them, says the LORD.** The covenant of the law failed because it was conditional; it called for obedience from a people who did not produce it.

By making the New Covenant an *unconditional* covenant of grace, God avoids any possibility of failure since fulfillment depends on Himself alone and He cannot fail.

The quotation from Jeremiah contains a radical change. The words in the Hebrew text of Jeremiah 31:32 are "though I was a husband to them." Some early translations of Jeremiah read, "so I disregarded (or turned away from) them." The Holy Spirit, who inspired the words of Jeremiah and superintended the preservation of the Bible, directed the writer to the Hebrews to select this alternate reading.

8:10 Notice the repetition of the words **I will**. The Old Covenant tells what man must do; the New Covenant tells what God will do. **After** the **days** of Israel's disobedience are past, He **will put** His **laws in their mind** so that they will know them, and **on their hearts** so that they will love them. They will want to obey, not through fear of punishment but through love for Him. The laws will no longer be written in stone but on the fleshly tables of the heart.

I will be their God, and they shall be My people. This speaks of nearness. The OT told man to stand at a distance; grace tells him to come near. It also speaks of an unbroken relationship and unconditional security. Nothing will ever interrupt this blood-bought tie.

8:11 The New Covenant also includes universal knowledge of the Lord. During Christ's Glorious Reign, it will not be necessary for a man to **teach his neighbor** or **his brother** to **know the LORD**. Everyone will have an inward consciousness of Him, **from the least . . . to the greatest**: "The earth shall be full of the knowledge of the LORD as the waters cover the sea" (Isa. 11:9).

8:12 Best of all, the New Covenant promises mercy for an unrighteous people and eternal forgetfulness of **their sins**. The law was inflexible and unbending: "Every transgression and disobedience received a just reward" (Heb. 2:2).

Furthermore, the law could not deal effectively with sins. It provided for the atonement of sins but not for their removal. (The Hebrew word for atonement comes from the verb meaning *cover*.) The sacrifices prescribed in the law made a

man ceremonially clean, that is, they qualified him to engage in the religious life of the nation. But this ritual cleansing was external; it did not touch a man's inward life. It did not provide moral cleansing or give him a clear conscience.

8:13 The fact that God introduces a **New Covenant** means that the **first** is **obsolete**. Since this is so, there should be no thought of going back to the law. Yet that is exactly what some of the professing believers were tempted to do. The author warns them that the legal covenant is outmoded; a better covenant has been introduced. They should get in step with God.

C. Christ's Offering Superior to Old Testament Sacrifices (9:1–10:18)

9:1 In 8:3 the writer made passing mention of the fact that every high priest must have something to offer. He is now ready to discuss the offering of our great High Priest and to contrast it with the OT offerings. To introduce the subject he gives a rapid review of the layout of the tabernacle and of the regulations for worship.

9:2 The **tabernacle** was a tentlike structure in which God dwelt among the Israelites from the time of their encampment at Mount Sinai to the building of the temple. The area around the tabernacle was called the outer court. It was enclosed by a fence consisting of a series of bronze posts with linen cloth stretched between them. As the Israelite entered the tabernacle court through the gate at the east, he came to the altar of burnt offering, where the sacrificial animals were slain and burned; then to the laver, a large bronze stand containing water, in which the priests washed their hands and feet.

The tabernacle itself measured about 45 feet long, 15 feet wide, and 15 feet high. It was divided into two compartments. The first, the Holy Place, was 30 feet long and the second, the Most Holy Place, was 15 feet long.

The tent consisted of a wooden framework covered by goats' hair curtains and weatherproof drapes of animal skins. These coverings formed the top, back, and sides of the tent. The front of the tabernacle was an embroidered veil.

The Holy Place contained three articles of furniture:

1. The **table** of **showbread**, on which were twelve cakes of bread, representing the twelve tribes of Israel. These cakes were called "bread of the Presence" because they were set before the face or presence of God.
2. The golden **lampstand**, with seven arms reaching upward and holding oil-burning lamps.
3. The golden altar of incense, on which the holy incense was burned morning and evening.

9:3 **Behind the second veil** was **the Holiest of All** or the Holy of Holies. Here God manifested Himself in a bright shining cloud. It was the one spot on earth where He could be approached with the blood of atonement.

9:4 This second compartment of the original tabernacle contained **the ark of the covenant**, a large wooden chest **overlaid on all sides with gold**. Inside the chest were **the golden pot** holding **manna, Aaron's rod that budded, and the** two **tablets of the** law. (When the temple was erected later, there was nothing in the ark but the tablets of the law — see 1 Kgs. 8:9).

Verse 4 says that **the golden censer** was also in the Most Holy Place. The Greek word translated **censer**[14] can mean either the incense altar (mentioned in Ex. 30:6 as being in the Holy Place) or the **censer** with which the high priest carried the incense. The best explanation is the latter. The writer regarded the **censer** as belonging to the Most Holy Place because the high priest carried it in from the incense altar into the Holiest Place on the Day of Atonement.

9:5 The gold lid of the ark of the covenant was known as **the mercy seat**. On top of it were two golden figures known as **cherubim**. They faced each other, with wings overspread, and with heads bowed over the cover of the ark.

The writer stops with this brief description. It is not his purpose to go into great **detail**, but merely to outline the contents of the tabernacle and the way of approach to God which it depicted.

9:6 Since the writer is going to contrast Christ's offering with the offerings of Judaism, he must first of all describe those which were required by the law. There were many he could choose from, but he selects the most important in the whole legal system, the sacrifice which was offered on the great Day of Atonement (Lev. 16). If he can prove Christ's work to be superior to that of the high priest on the outstanding day of Israel's religious calendar, then he has won his point.

The priests had access to the outer tent, that is, the Holy Place. They went there continually in the performance of their ritual duties. The common people were not permitted in this room; they had to stay outside.

9:7 **Only one man** in the world could go into the Most Holy Place — **the high priest** of Israel. And that one man, out of one race, out of one tribe, out of one family, could enter on only one day of the year — the Day of Atonement. When he did enter, he was required to carry a basin of **blood, which he offered for himself and for the people's sins committed in ignorance**.

9:8 There were deep spiritual truths connected with this. **The Holy Spirit** was teaching that sin had created distance between man and God, that man must approach God through a mediator, and that the mediator could approach God only through the blood of a sacrificial victim. It was an object lesson to teach **that the way into** God's presence **was not yet** opened for worshipers.

Imperfect access continued **while the first tabernacle was still standing**. Darby's translation may be preferable here: "While as yet the first tabernacle has [its] standing." The tabernacle was displaced by the temple during the reign of Solomon, but it still had a standing until the death, burial, and resurrection of Christ. The principles it proclaimed concerning approach to God were still valid until the veil of the temple was ripped in two from the top to the bottom.

9:9 The tabernacle system **was symbolic for the present time**. A picture of something better to come, it was an imperfect representation of Christ's perfect work.

The **gifts and sacrifices** could never **make** the worshipers **perfect in regard to the conscience**. If complete remission of sins had been procured, then the offerer's **conscience** would have been free from the guilt of sin. But this never happened.

9:10 As a matter of fact, the Levitical offerings dealt **only with** ritual defilements. They were concerned with such externals as clean and unclean **foods and drinks**, and with ceremonial **washings** that would rid the people of ritual impurity, but they did not deal with moral uncleanness.

The offerings were concerned with a people who were in covenant relationship with God. They were designed to maintain the people in a position of ritual purity so that they could worship. They had nothing to do with salvation or with cleansing from sin. The people were saved by faith in the Lord, on the basis of the work of Christ still future.

Finally, the sacrifices were temporary. They were imposed **until the time of reformation**. They pointed forward to the coming of Christ and to His perfect offering. The Christian era is **the time of reformation** referred to here.

9:11 **Christ** has appeared **as High Priest of the good things to come,**[15] that is, of the tremendous blessings that He bestows on those who receive Him.

His sanctuary is a **greater and more perfect** tent. It is **not made with hands** in the sense that it is not constructed of this world's building materials. It is the sanctuary of heaven, the dwelling place of God.

> No temple made with hands,
>   His place of service is;
> In heaven itself He serves,
>   A heavenly priesthood His:
> In Him the shadows of the law
> Are all fulfilled, and now withdraw.
> — *Thomas Kelly*

9:12 Our Lord **entered the Most Holy Place once for all**. At the time of His Ascension, He went into God's presence, **having** finished the work of **redemption** at Calvary. We should never cease to rejoice over those words, **once for all**. The work is completed. Praise the Lord!

He offered **His own blood**, not the blood of bulls and goats. Animal blood had no power to put away sins; it was effective only in cases of technical offenses against religious ritual. But the blood of Christ is of infinite value; its power is sufficient to cleanse all the sins of all the people who have ever lived, all the people who are now living, and all the people who will ever live. Of course, its power is applicable only to those who come to Him by faith. But its cleansing potential is unlimited.

By His sacrifice He **obtained eternal redemption**. The former priests obtained annual atonement. There is a vast difference between the two.

9:13 To illustrate the difference between the sacrifice of Christ and the ceremonies of the law, the writer now turns to the ritual of the red **heifer**. Under the law, if an Israelite touched a dead body, he became ceremonially unclean for seven days. The remedy was to mix **the ashes of a heifer** with pure spring water and to sprinkle the defiled person on the third and seventh days. He then became clean.

Mantle says:

> The ashes were regarded as a concentration of the essential properties of the sin-offering, and could be resorted to at all times with comparatively little trouble and no loss of time. One red heifer availed for centuries. Only six are said to have been required during the whole of Jewish history; for the smallest quantity of the ashes availed to impart the cleansing virtue to the pure spring water (Numbers 19:17).[16]

9:14 If the ashes of a heifer had such power to cleanse from one of the most serious forms of outward defilement, **how much more** powerful is **the blood of Christ** to **cleanse** from inward sins of the deepest dye!

His offering was **through the eternal Spirit**. There is some difference of opinion as to the meaning of this expression. Some interpret it to mean, "through an eternal spirit," meaning the willing spirit in which He made His sacrifice in contrast to the involuntary character of animal offerings. Others understand it to mean, "through His eternal spirit." We rather believe that the *Holy Spirit* is in view; He made His sacrifice in the power of the Holy **Spirit**.

It was an offering made **to God**. He

was the spotless, sinless Lamb of God whose moral perfection qualified Him to be our Sin-bearer. The animal sacrifices had to be physically spotless; He was without blemish morally.

His **blood** cleanses the **conscience from dead works to serve the living God**. It is not merely a physical purging or a ceremonial cleansing but a moral renewal that purifies the conscience. It cleanses from those dead works which unbelievers produce in an effort to earn their own cleansing. It frees men from these lifeless works **to serve the living God**.

9:15 The previous verses stressed the superiority of the blood of the New Covenant to the blood of the Old. This leads to the conclusion of verse 15 — that Christ **is the Mediator of the New Covenant**. Wuest explains:

> The word "mediator" is the translation of *mesites* which refers to one who intervenes between two, to make or restore peace and friendship, to form a compact, or to ratify a covenant. Here the Messiah acts as a go-between or mediator between a holy God and sinful man. By His death on the cross, He removes the obstacle (sin) which caused an estrangement between man and God. When the sinner accepts the merits of Messiah's sacrifice, the guilt and penalty of his sin is his no more, the power of sin in his life is broken, he becomes the recipient of the divine nature, and the estrangement between himself and God, both legal and personal, disappears.[17]

Now those who are called may receive the promised **eternal inheritance**. Through Christ's work saints of the OT as well as of the New enjoy **eternal** salvation and **eternal** redemption.

The fact that qualifies believers of the pre-Christian era for the inheritance is that a **death** has occurred, that is, the death of Christ. His death redeems them from **transgressions under the** law.

There is a sense in which God saved OT people "on credit." They were justified by faith, just as we are. But Christ had not died as yet. Then how could God save them? The answer is that He saved them on the basis of what He knew Christ would accomplish. They knew little or nothing of what Christ would do at Calvary. But God knew, and He reckoned the value of that work

to their account when they believed whatever revelation He gave them of Himself.

In a sense a great debt of transgression had accumulated under the Old Covenant. By His death, Christ redeemed believers of the former dispensation from these **transgressions**.

The manner in which God saved them through the still-future work of Christ is known as the pretermission of sins. It is discussed in Romans 3:25, 26.

9:16 The author's mention of inheritance in verse 15 reminds him that before a last will and **testament** can be probated, evidence must be submitted that the **testator** has died. Usually a death certificate is sufficient evidence.

9:17 The testator may have drawn up his will many years previously and kept it secure in his safe, but it does not take effect until he dies. As long as he is alive, his property cannot be distributed to those named in the will.

9:18 Now the subject switches from a person's last will to the Old **Covenant** given by God through Moses. (The English words "covenant" and "testament" both translate the same Greek word, *diathēkē*.) Here too a death had to take place. It was ratified by the shedding of **blood**.

In ancient times every covenant was made valid by the sacrificial death of an animal. The blood was a pledge that the terms of the covenant would be fulfilled.

9:19 After **Moses** had recited the laws to Israel, **he took the blood of calves and goats, with water, scarlet wool, and hyssop, and sprinkled both the book** of the law **itself and all the people**. In this way Moses arranged the ceremony for the solemn sealing of the covenant.

In Exodus 24:1–11, we read that Moses **sprinkled** the altar and **the people**; no mention is made of sprinkling **the book**, or of the **water, scarlet wool**, and **hyssop**. It is best to view both accounts as complementary.

God, represented by the altar, and **the people** were the contracting parties. **The book** was the covenant. The sprinkled **blood** bound both parties to keep the terms of the covenant. The people promised to obey, and the LORD promised to bless them if they did.

9:20 As Moses sprinkled the blood he said, **"This is the blood of the covenant which God has commanded you."** This action pledged the life of the people if they failed to keep the law.

9:21 In a similar manner Moses **sprinkled with blood both the tabernacle and all the vessels** used in worship. This ritual is not found in the OT. No mention is made of blood in the consecration of the tabernacle in Exodus 40. However, the symbolism is clear. Everything that has any contact with sinful man becomes defiled and needs to be cleansed.

9:22 **Almost** everything under **the law** was **purified with blood**. But there were exceptions. For instance, when a man was to be numbered in a census among the children of Israel, he could bring a half-shekel of silver as "atonement money" instead of a blood offering (Ex. 30:11–16). The coin was a token symbolizing atonement for the man's soul in order for him to be reckoned as one of God's people. Another exception is found in Leviticus 5:11, where certain forms of ritual uncleanness could be dealt with by an offering of fine flour.

These exceptions dealt with *atonement* for, or *covering* of, sin, although generally speaking a blood offering was required even for atonement. But as far as **remission** of sin is concerned, there is no exception: **blood** must be shed.

9:23 The rest of chapter 9 compares and contrasts the two covenants.

First of all, the earthly tabernacle had to **be purified with** the blood of bulls and goats. As has been pointed out this was a ceremonial purification. It was a symbolic sanctification of a symbolic sanctuary.

The **heavenly** sanctuary was the reality of which the earthly tent was a copy. It has to be cleansed **with better sacrifices than these**, that is, with the **sacrifices of** Christ. The use of the plural to describe the single offering of Christ is a figure of speech known as the plural of majesty.

It may seem surprising that the heavenly places needed to **be purified**. Perhaps a clue is found in Job 15:15, "the heavens are not pure in His sight." Doubtless this is because Satan committed the first act of sin in heaven (Isa.

14:12–14), and because he still has access to the presence of God as the accuser of the brethren (Rev. 12:10).

9:24 **Christ** did **not** enter the manmade sanctuary, which was a pattern or figure **of the true** one, **but into heaven itself**. There He appears **in the presence of God for us**.

It is difficult to understand why anyone would want to leave the reality and go back to the copy, why anyone would leave the great High Priest serving in the heavenly sanctuary to return to the priests of Israel serving in a symbolic tent.

9:25 The Lord Jesus did not make repeated offerings, **as the** Aaronic **high priest** had to do. The latter went into **the Most Holy Place** on one day of the year — that is, the Day of Atonement, and he did not offer his own blood but the **blood** of sacrificial animals.

9:26 If Christ had made repeated offerings, that would have meant repeated suffering, since His offering was His own life. It is unthinkable that He should have suffered the agonies of Calvary periodically **since the foundation of the world**! And unnecessary too!

Under the New Covenant, there is:

1. Positive finality — **He has appeared once** for all. The work never needs to be repeated.
2. A propitious time — He appeared **at the end of the ages**, that is, after the Old Covenant had conclusively demonstrated man's failure and powerlessness.
3. A perfect work — He appeared, **to put away sin**. The emphasis is on the words **put away**. It was no longer a matter of annual atonement. Now it was eternal forgiveness.
4. A personal sacrifice — He put away sin **by the sacrifice of Himself**. In His own body He bore the punishment which our sins deserved.

> Bearing shame and scoffing rude,
> In my place condemned He stood;
> Sealed my pardon with His blood;
> Hallelujah! What a Saviour!
>   — *Philip P. Bliss*

9:27 Verses 27 and 28 seem to present another contrast between the Old Covenant and the New. The law condemned sinners **to die once, but after this the judgment**. The law was given to a people who were already sinners and who could not keep it perfectly. Therefore it became a means of condemnation to all who were under it.

9:28 The New Covenant introduces the infinite sacrifice of **Christ**; He **was offered once to bear the sins of many**. It presents the blessed hope of His imminent Return; **to those who eagerly wait for Him He will appear a second time**. But when He returns, it will not be to deal with the problem of **sin**: He finished that work at the cross. He will come to take His people home to heaven. This will be the culmination of their **salvation**; they will receive their glorified bodies and be forever beyond the reach of sin.

The expression, **those who eagerly wait for Him**, is a description of all true believers. All the Lord's people look for Him to return, though they may not agree on the exact order of events connected with His Coming.

The Bible does not teach that only a certain group of especially spiritual Christians will be taken to heaven at the time of the Rapture. It describes the participants as "the dead in Christ" and "we who are alive and remain" (1 Thess. 4:16, 17); this means all true believers, dead or living. In 1 Corinthians 15:23 the participants are identified as "those who are Christ's."

It has often been pointed out that we have three appearances of Christ in verses 24–28. They may be summarized as follows:

Verse 26: He *has* appeared. This refers to His First Advent when He came to earth to save us from the penalty of sin (the *past* tense of salvation).

Verse 24: He *now* appears. This is a reference to His present ministry in the presence of God to save us from the power of sin (the *present* tense of salvation).

Verse 28: He *will* appear. This speaks of His imminent Return when He will save us from the presence of sin (the *future* tense of salvation).

10:1 **The law** was only **a shadow of the good things** that were **to come**. It pointed forward to the Person and work of Christ but it was a poor substitute for reality. To prefer the law to Christ is like preferring a picture to the person represented. It is an *insult* to His majesty!

The weakness of the legal system is seen in the fact that its sacrifices had to be constantly repeated. This repetition proved their total inability to meet the claims of a holy God. Notice the expressions used to capture this idea of repetitiveness: **the same sacrifices**; **offer continually**; **year by year**.

The **sacrifices** were utterly unable to perfect the worshipers, that is, they never gave the people a **perfect** conscience as far as sin was concerned. The Israelites never enjoyed the consciousness of being cleared forever from the guilt of sin. They never had complete rest of conscience.

10:2 If the offerings had completely and finally absolved them from sin, **then would they not have ceased** making the annual trek to the tabernacle or temple? The regular recurrence of the sacrifices branded them as ineffectual. Whoever has to take medicine every hour to stay alive can hardly be said to be cured.

10:3 Instead of pacifying the conscience, the Levitical system stabbed it awake each year. Behind the beautiful ritual of the Day of Atonement lurked the annual reminder that sins were only being covered, not removed.

10:4 **The blood of bulls and goats** simply did **not** have the power to **take away sins**. As mentioned previously, these sacrifices dealt with ritual errors. They gave a certain ceremonial cleansing but they were utter failures as far as providing satisfaction for man's corrupt nature or for his evil deeds.

10:5 In contrast to the weakness of the Levitical offerings, we come now to the strength of the superlative sacrifice of Christ. By way of introduction, we are permitted to hear the Savior's soliloquy at the time of His incarnation. Quoting from Psalm 40, He noted God's dissatisfaction with the sacrifices and offerings of the Old Covenant. God had instituted these sacrifices, yet they were never His ultimate intention. They were never designed to put away sins but rather to point forward to the Lamb of God who would bear away the sin of the world. Could God be pleased with rivers of animal blood or with heaps of animal carcasses?

Another reason for God's dissatisfaction is that the people thought they were pleasing Him by going through ceremonies while their inward lives were sinful and corrupt. Many of them went through the dreary round of sacrifices with no repentance or contrition. They thought that God could be appeased with their animal sacrifices whereas He was looking for the sacrifice of a broken heart. They did not realize that God is not a ritualist!

Dissatisfied with the former sacrifices, God **prepared** a human **body** for His Son which was an integral part of His human life and nature. This, of course, refers to the unfathomable wonder of the Incarnation when the eternal Word became flesh so that, as Man, He might die for men.

It is interesting that the clause **a body You have prepared for Me**, adapted from Psalm 40:6, is capable of two other meanings. In that Psalm it reads, "My ears You have opened," and in the margin it says, "ears You have dug for Me." The open ear, of course, signifies that the Messiah was always ready to receive His instructions from God and to obey them instantly. The dug ear may be an allusion to the Hebrew slave (Ex. 21:1–6), whose ear was bored with an awl to the door as a sign that he willingly indentured himself to his master forever. In His Incarnation, the Savior said, in effect, "I love My Master . . . I will not go out free."

10:6 Continuing the quotation from Psalm 40, the Messiah repeated that God took **no pleasure in burnt offerings and sacrifices for sin**. The animals were unwilling victims whose blood was powerless to cleanse. Also they never represented God's ultimate desire. They were types and shadows looking forward to the sacrifice of Christ. As an end in themselves, they were valueless.

10:7 What did bring pleasure to God was the Messiah's willingness to do the **will** of **God**, no matter what the cost might be. He proved His willing obedience by offering Himself on the altar of sacrifice. As our Lord uttered those words, He was reminded that from the beginning to the end of the OT, it is witnessed of Him that He took wholehearted delight in accomplishing God's **will**.

10:8 In verses 8–10 the writer gives the spiritual significance of the soliloquy.

He sees it as signaling the demise of the old sacrificial system and the inauguration of the one perfect, complete, and final offering of Jesus Christ.

He repeats the quotation from Psalm 40 in condensed form to emphasize God's lack of **pleasure in** the sacrifices that were **offered according to the law**.

10:9 Then the writer sees significance in the fact that immediately after declaring God's displeasure with the old, the Messiah stepped forward, as it were, to do the thing that *would* please the heart of His Father.

The conclusion: **He takes away the first that He may establish the second**, that is, He abolishes the old system of offerings that were required by law, and introduces His own great sacrifice for sin. The legal covenant retires to the wings of the stage as the New Covenant moves to the center.

10:10 **By that will** of God, to which Jesus was utterly obedient, **we have been sanctified through the offering of the body of Jesus Christ once for all**. George Landis comments:

This is a positional sanctification, as is the case all through Hebrews with the exception of 12:14, and is true of all believers (1 Cor. 6:11) and not merely of a few "advanced Christians." It is accomplished by the will of God and the sacrifice of Christ. We are set apart **by** God, **to** God, and **for** God. It is not to be confused with the progressive work of God's Spirit in the believer through the Word (John 17:17–19; 1 Thess. 5:23).[18]

10:11 The ministry of **every** Aaronic **priest** is now contrasted sharply with that of Christ. The former stood **daily** in the performance of their duties. There was no chair in the tabernacle or temple. There could be no rest because their work was never completed. They **repeatedly** offered **the same sacrifices**. It was an unending routine which left sins untouched and the conscience unrelieved.

These **sacrifices** could **never take away sins**. "Aaron," writes A. B. Bruce, "though an important personage within the Levitical system, was after all but a sacerdotal drudge, ever performing ceremonies which had no real value."[19]

10:12 Our blessed Lord offered a single **sacrifice for sins**. None other would ever be needed!

No blood, no altar now,
The sacrifice is o'er!
No flame, no smoke ascends on high,
The lamb is slain no more.
But richer blood has flowed
From nobler veins
To purge the soul from guilt
And cleanse the reddest stains.
                                    — *Horatius Bonar*

Having finished the work of redemption, He "sat down in perpetuity at [the] right hand of God" (JND). This verse may correctly be punctuated to read either He "*offered one sacrifice for sins forever*," or that He "*forever sat down*." Both are true, but we tend to believe that the latter is the correct interpretation. He is seated uninterruptedly because sin's tremendous claim has been settled forever. He is seated **at the right hand of God**, the place of honor, power, and affection.

Someone may object that He cannot be seated *forever* since He will one day rise in judgment. There is no contradiction here, however. As far as making an offering for sin is concerned, He has sat down in perpetuity. As far as judgment is concerned, He is not seated forever.

10:13 He waits **till His enemies are made His footstool**, till the day when every knee will bow to Him, and every tongue acknowledge Him as Lord to the glory of God the Father (Phil. 2:10, 11). This will be the day of His public vindication on earth.

10:14 The surpassing value of His **offering** is seen in that by it **He has perfected forever** (or in perpetuity) **those who are being sanctified**. **Those who are being sanctified** here means all who have been set apart to God from the world, that is, all true believers. They have been **perfected** in a twofold sense. First, they have a perfect standing before God; they stand before the Father in all the acceptability of His beloved Son. Second, they have a perfect conscience as far as the guilt and penalty of sin are concerned; they know that the price has been paid in full and that God will not demand payment a second time.

10:15 **The Holy Spirit also witnesses to** the fact that under the New Covenant, sins would be effectively dealt with once and for all. He **witnesses to** it through the OT Scriptures.

10:16 In Jeremiah 31:31, **the LORD** promised to make a New **covenant** with His chosen earthly people.

10:17 **Then** in the very same passage, **He adds, "Their sins and their lawless deeds I will remember no more."** It is arresting that Jeremiah 31:34 contained this promise of full and final forgiveness of sins; yet some of those who lived in the day when the promise began to be fulfilled were disposed to return to the never-ending sacrifices of Judaism!

10:18 The promise of forgiveness under the New Covenant means that **there is no longer an offering for sin**. With these words, *no longer an offering for sin*, the author closes what we might call the doctrinal portion of the Epistle. He wants to have these words ringing in our hearts and minds as he now presses upon us our practical obligations.

III. WARNING AND EXHORTATIONS (10:19–13:17)

A. Warning Not to Despise Christ (10:19–39)

10:19 In OT times the people were kept at a distance; now in Christ we are brought near through **the blood** of His cross. Therefore we are encouraged to draw near.

This exhortation assumes that all believers are now priests because we are told to have **boldness to enter the Holiest by the blood of Jesus**. The common people during the Jewish economy were barred from the Holy Place and the Most Holy Place; only the priests could enter the first room, and only the high priest could enter the second. Now that is all changed. God has no special place where only a special caste of men may approach Him. Instead, all believers may come into His presence by faith at any time and from any place on earth.

Through the veil God bids me enter
By the new and living way;
Not in trembling hope I venture —
Boldly I His call obey;
There, with Christ my God, I meet
God upon the mercy-seat!

All the worth I have before Him
Is the value of the blood:

I present, when I adore Him
Christ, the First-fruits, unto God.
Him with joy doth God behold;
Thus is my acceptance told!
— *Author unknown*

10:20 Our approach is by **a new and living way**. **New** here may have the meaning of "newly slain" or "newly made". **Living** seems to be a reference to Jesus in resurrection, therefore, to a **living** Savior. This way was opened **through the veil, that is, His flesh**. This clearly teaches that **the veil** between the two compartments of the tabernacle was a type of the body of our Lord. In order for us to have access into God's presence, the veil had to be rent, that is, His body had to be broken in death. This reminds us that we cannot draw near by Christ's sinless life, but only by His vicarious death. Only through the mortal wounds of the Lamb can we go in. Every time we enter God's presence in prayer or worship, let us remember that the privilege was bought for us at tremendous cost.

10:21 We not only have great confidence when we enter the presence of God; we also have a great **High Priest over the house of God**. Even though we are priests (1 Pet. 2:9; Rev. 1:6), yet we still need a Priest ourselves. Christ is our great **High Priest**, and His present ministry for us assures our continued welcome before God.

10:22 **Let us draw near**. This is the believer's blood-bought privilege. How wonderful beyond all words that we are invited to have audience, not with this world's celebrities, but with the Sovereign of the universe! The extent to which we value the invitation is shown by the manner in which we respond to it.

There is a fourfold description of how we should be spiritually groomed in entering the throne room.

1. **With a true heart**. The people of Israel drew near to God with their mouth, and honored Him with their lips, but their heart was often far from Him (Matt. 15:8). Our approach should be with utter sincerity.

2. **In full assurance of faith**. We draw near with utter confidence in the promises of God and with the firm conviction that we shall have a gra-

cious reception into His presence.

3. **Having our hearts sprinkled from an evil conscience**. This can be brought about only by the new birth. When we trust Christ, we appropriate the value of His blood. *Figuratively* speaking, we sprinkle our hearts with it, just as the Israelites sprinkled their doors with the blood of the Passover lamb. This delivers us from an evil conscience. Our testimony is:

> Conscience now no more condemns us,
> For His own most precious blood
> Once for all has washed and cleansed us,
> Cleansed us in the eyes of God.
> — *Frances Bevan*

4. **And our bodies washed with pure water**. Again this is *symbolic* language. **Our bodies** represent our lives. The **pure water** might refer either to the word (Eph 5:25, 26), to the Holy Spirit (John 7:37–39), or to the Holy Spirit using the word in cleansing our lives from daily defilement. We are cleansed once for all from the guilt of sin by the death of Christ, but cleansed repeatedly from the defilement of sin by the Spirit through the word (see John 13:10).

Thus we might summarize the four requisites for entering God's presence as sincerity, assurance, salvation, and sanctification.

10:23 The second exhortation is to **hold fast the confession of our hope**. Nothing must be allowed to turn us from the staunch **confession** that our only **hope** is in Christ.

For those who were tempted to give up the future, unseen blessings of Christianity for the present, visible things of Judaism, there is the reminder that **He who promised is faithful**. His promises can never fail; no one who trusts in Him will ever be disappointed. The Savior will come, as He has **promised**, and His people will be with Him and like Him forever.

10:24 We should also be discovering ways of encouraging fellow believers to manifest **love** and to engage in **good works**. In the NT sense, **love** is not an emotion but an act of the will. We are *commanded* to **love**, therefore it is something we can and must *do*. **Love** is the root; **good works** are the fruit. By our example and by our teaching, we should **stir up** other believers to this kind of life.

> Loving hearts are gardens,
> Loving thoughts are roots,
> Loving words are flowers,
> And good works their fruits.
> — *Adapted*

10:25 Then we should continue to meet **together** and **not** desert the local fellowship, as **some** do. This may be considered as a general exhortation for all believers to be faithful in their church attendance. Without question we find strength, comfort, nourishment, and joy in collective worship and service.

It may also be looked on as a special encouragement for Christians going through times of persecution. There is always the temptation to isolate oneself in order to avoid arrest, reproach, and suffering, and thus to be a secret disciple.

But basically the verse is a warning against apostasy. To forsake the local assembly here means to turn one's back on Christianity and revert to Judaism. Some were doing this when this Letter was written. There was need to exhort one another, especially in view of the nearness of Christ's Return. When He comes, the persecuted, ostracized, despised believers will be seen to be on the winning side. Until then, there is need for steadfastness.

10:26 Now the writer introduces his fourth grim warning. As in the previous cases, it is a warning against apostasy, here described as a deliberate **sin**.

As has been indicated, there is considerable disagreement among Christians as to the real nature of this **sin**. The problem, in brief, is whether it refers to:

1. True Christians who subsequently turn away from Christ and are lost.

2. True Christians who backslide but who are still saved.

3. Those who profess to be Christians for a while, identify themselves with a local church, but then deliberately turn away from Christ. They were never truly born again, and now they never can be.

No matter which view we hold, there are admitted difficulties. We believe that the third view is the correct one because

it is most consistent with the over-all teaching of Hebrews and of the entire NT.

Here in verse 26 apostasy is defined as sinning deliberately **after** receiving **the knowledge of the truth**. Like Judas, the person has heard the gospel. He knows the way of salvation; he has even pretended to receive it; but then he deliberately repudiates it.

For such a person, **there no longer remains a sacrifice for sins**. He has decisively and conclusively rejected the once-for-all sacrifice of Christ. Therefore God has no other way of salvation to offer to him.

There is a sense in which all sin is willful, but the author here speaks of apostasy as a willful sin of extraordinary seriousness.

The fact that the author uses **we** in this passage does not necessarily mean that he includes himself. In verse 39 he definitely *excludes* himself and his fellow believers from those who draw back into perdition.

10:27 Nothing remains but a **certain fearful expectation of judgment**; there is no hope of escape. It is impossible to renew the apostate to repentance (6:4). He has knowingly and willfully cut himself off from God's grace in Christ. His fate is a **fiery indignation which will devour the adversaries**. It is pointless to haggle over whether this means literal fire. The language is obviously designed to denote punishment that is dreadfully severe.

Note that God classes apostates as **adversaries**. This indicates positive opposition to Christ, not a mild neutrality.

10:28 The doom of the lawbreaker in the OT is now introduced to form a backdrop against which to contrast the greater doom of the apostate. A man who broke **Moses' law** by becoming an idolater died **without mercy** when his guilt was proven by **the testimony of two or three witnesses** (Deut. 17:2–6).

10:29 The apostate will be counted worthy of **much worse punishment** because his privilege has been much greater. The enormity of his sin is seen in the three charges that are leveled against him:

1. He **has trampled the Son of God underfoot**. After professing to be a fol-

lower of Jesus, he now brazenly asserts that he wants nothing more to do with Him. He denies any need for Christ as Savior and positively rejects Him as Lord.

In Japan there is a crucifix which was used by the government in days of persecution. It was placed on the ground, and everybody had to tread on the face of the Crucified. The non-Christians did not hesitate to tread on His face; the real Christians refused and were killed. The story goes that the face of Jesus was worn down and marred by people trampling on it.

2. He has **counted the blood of the covenant by which he was sanctified a common thing**. He counts as useless and unholy the **blood** of Christ which ratified the New Covenant. He had been set apart by this **blood** in a place of external privilege. Through his association with Christian people, he had been sanctified, just as an unbelieving husband is sanctified by his believing wife (1 Cor. 7:14). But that does not mean that he was saved.

3. He has **insulted the Spirit of grace**. The Spirit of God had illuminated him concerning the good news, convicted him of sin, and pointed him to Christ as the only Refuge of the soul. But he had **insulted** the gracious **Spirit** by utterly despising Him and the salvation He offered.

10:30 Willful repudiation of God's beloved Son is a sin of immense magnitude. God will sit in judgment on all who are guilty of it. He has said, **"Vengeance is Mine, I will repay"** (see Deut. 32:35). **Vengeance** in this sense means full justice. When used of God it has no thought of vindictiveness or of "getting even." It is simply the meting out of what a person actually deserves. Knowing the character of God, we can be sure that He will do as He has said by repaying the apostate in just measure.

And again, "The LORD will judge His people." God will avenge and vindicate those who truly belong to Him, but here in verse 30, the obvious reference is to judgment of evil people.

If it causes difficulty to think of apostates being spoken of as **His people**, we should remember that they are His by creation and also for a while by profession. He is their Creator though not their Redeemer, and they once professed to be His people, even though they never knew Him personally.

10:31 The abiding lesson for all is this: do not be among those who **fall into** God's **hands** for judgment because **it is a fearful thing**.

Nothing in this passage of Scripture was ever intended to disturb and unsettle the minds of those who truly belong to Christ. The passage was purposely written in its sharp, searching, challenging style so that all who profess the name of Christ might be warned about the terrible consequences of turning away from Him.

10:32 In the remaining verses of chapter 10, the writer gives three strong reasons why the early Jewish Christians should continue steadfastly in their allegiance to Christ.

1. Their **former** experiences should stimulate them.

2. The nearness of the reward should strengthen them.

3. The fear of God's displeasure should deter them from going back.

First of all, then, their past experiences should stimulate them. After they professed faith in Christ, they became the targets of bitter persecution: their families disowned them, their friends forsook them, and their foes hounded them. But instead of producing cowardice and fear, these **sufferings** strengthened them in their faith. Doubtless they felt something of the exhilaration of being counted worthy to suffer dishonor for His name (Acts 5:41).

10:33 Sometimes their suffering was individual; they were taken out alone and publicly exposed to abuse and affliction. At other times, they suffered with other Christians.

10:34 They were not afraid to visit those who were prisoners for Christ, even though there was always the danger of guilt by association.

When their **goods** were confiscated by the authorities, they **accepted** it **joyfully**. They chose to be true to Jesus rather than to keep their material possessions. They knew that they had "an inheritance incorruptible and undefiled and that does not fade away" (1 Pet.

1:4). It was truly a miracle of divine grace that enabled them to value earthly wealth so lightly.

10:35 The second great consideration is this: the nearness of the **reward** should strengthen them. Having endured so much in the past, they should not capitulate now. The author says in effect, "Don't miss the harvest of your tears" (F. B. Meyer). They were now nearer to the fulfillment of God's promise than ever before. This was no time to turn back.

"Don't throw away your trust now — it carries with it a rich reward in the world to come" (JBP).

10:36 What they needed was **endurance**, the determination to remain under the persecutions rather than escape them by denying Christ. Then after having **done the will of God**, they would **receive** the promised reward.

10:37 The coming reward synchronizes with the Return of the Lord Jesus; hence the quotation from Habakkuk 2:3, **"For yet a little while, and He who is coming will come and will not tarry."** In Habakkuk the verse reads, "For the vision is yet for an appointed time; but at the end it will speak, and it will not lie. Though it tarries, wait for it; because it will surely come, it will not tarry."

Concerning this change Vincent says:

In the Hebrew, the subject of the sentence is the vision of the extermination of the Chaldees. . . . As rendered in the Septuagint either Jehovah or Messiah must be the subject. The passage was referred to Messiah by the later Jewish theologians and is so taken by our writer.[20]

A. J. Pollock comments:

The Old Testament passage and the altered quotation in the New Testament are alike verbally inspired and equally Scripture. The IT in Habakkuk refers to the vision — and deals with the coming of Christ to reign. IT becomes HE in Hebrews and refers to the Rapture.

Then he continues in a more general vein:

When an inspired writer quotes from the Old Testament he uses just as much of the passage quoted as suits the purpose of the Divine Mind, though never contradicting it; altering it often in order to convey, not the exact meaning of the Old Testament passage, but the fuller meaning intended to be conveyed by the Holy Spirit in the New Testament. . . . Now no one but God could so treat Scripture. The fact that it is done, and done largely, is another claim to inspiration. God is the Author of the Bible, and He can quote His OWN words, altering and adding to them to suit His purpose. But if any of us quote Scripture, we must do it with careful exactitude. We have no right to alter a jot or tittle. But the Author of the Book can do this. It matters little what pen He uses, whether it be Moses or Isaiah, Peter or Paul, or Matthew or John, it is all His writing.[21]

10:38 A final incentive to steadfast endurance is the fear of God's displeasure. Continuing the quotation from Habakkuk, the author shows that the life that pleases God is the life of **faith**: **Now the just**[22] **shall live by faith**. This is the life that values God's promises, that sees the unseen, and that perseveres to the end.

On the other hand the life that displeases God is that of the man who renounces the Messiah and returns to the obsolete sacrifices of the temple: **But if anyone draws back, My soul has no pleasure in him**.

10:39 The writer quickly dissociates himself and his fellow believers from **those who draw back to perdition**. This separates apostates from genuine Christians. Apostates **draw back** and are lost. True believers **believe** and thus preserve their souls from the doom of the renegade.

With this mention of faith ("believe" and "faith" are the same root word in Greek), the groundwork is laid for a fuller discussion of the life that pleases God. The illustrious eleventh chapter follows quite naturally at this point.

B. Exhortation to Faith by Old Testament Examples (Chap. 11)

11:1 This chapter deals with the vision and endurance of **faith**. It introduces us to men and women of the OT who had 20/20 spiritual vision and who endured tremendous shame and suffering rather than renounce their faith.

Verse 1 is not really a formal definition of faith; rather it is a description of what **faith** *does* for us. It makes **things hoped for** as real as if we already had them, and it provides unshakable **evi-**

dence that the unseen, spiritual blessings of Christianity are absolutely certain and real. In other words, it brings the future within the present and makes the invisible seen.

Faith is confidence in the trustworthiness of God. It is the conviction that what God says is true and that what He promises will come to pass.

Faith must have some revelation from God, some promise of God as its foundation. It is not a leap in the dark. It demands the surest evidence in the universe, and finds it in the word of God. It is not limited to possibilities but invades the realm of the impossible. Someone has said, "Faith begins where possibilities end. If it's possible, then there's no glory for God in it."

> Faith, mighty faith the promise sees,
> And looks to God alone;
> Laughs at impossibilities
> And cries, "It shall be done."
> – *Author unknown.*

There are difficulties and problems in the life of faith. God tests our faith in the crucible to see if it is genuine (1 Pet. 1:7). But, as George Müller said, "Difficulties are food for faith to feed on."

11:2 Because they walked by faith and not by sight, the OT worthies received divine approval. The rest of this chapter is an illustration of how God has borne witness to them.

11:3 **Faith** provides us with the only factual account of creation. God is the only One who was there; He tells us how it happened. We believe His word and thus we know. McCue states: "The conception of God pre-existent to matter and by His fiat calling it into being is beyond the domain of reason or demonstration. It is simply accepted by an act of faith."

By faith we understand. The world says, "Seeing is believing." God says, "Believing is seeing." Jesus said to Martha, "Did I not say to you that if you would believe you would see . . . " (John 11:40). The Apostle John wrote, "These things I have written to you who believe . . . that you may know" (1 Jn. 5:13). In spiritual matters faith precedes understanding.

The worlds were framed by the word of God. God spoke and matter came into being. This agrees perfectly with man's discovery that matter is essentially energy. When God spoke, there was a flow of energy in the form of sound waves. These were transformed into matter, and the world sprang into being.

The things which are seen were not made out of things which are visible. Energy is invisible; so are atoms, and molecules, and gases to the naked eye, yet in combination they become visible.

The fact of creation as set forth here in Hebrews 11:3 is unimpeachable. It has never been improved on and never will.

11:4 Adam and Eve are bypassed in the honor roll of faith. When Eve had to decide whether God or Satan was telling the truth, she decided that Satan was. However, this does not deny that they were subsequently saved by faith, as pictured by the coats of skin.

Abel must have had some revelation that sinful man can approach God only on the ground of shed blood. Perhaps he learned this from his parents who were restored to fellowship with God only after He had clothed them with the skins of animals (Gen. 3:21). At any rate, he exhibited **faith** by approaching God with the blood of a **sacrifice**. Cain's sacrifice was one of vegetables or fruit and was therefore bloodless. Abel illustrates the truth of salvation by grace through faith. Cain pictures man's futile attempt to save himself by good works.

George Cutting points out that "it was not the personal excellence of Abel that God looked at in counting him righteous, but the excellence of the sacrifice that he brought and his faith in it." And so it is with us: we are not justified because of our character or good works, but solely because of the excellence of the sacrifice of Christ and our acceptance of Him.

Abel was killed by Cain because law hates grace. Self-righteous man hates the truth that he cannot save himself and that he must cast himself on the love and mercy of God.

But Abel's testimony is perpetuated: **Through** his faith he **still speaks**. There is a sense in which faith enables a man's vocal chords to go on functioning long after his body is lying in the grave.

11:5 Sometime during his life **Enoch** must have received a promise from God that he would go to heaven without dying. Up to that time everyone had died — sooner or later. There was no record of anyone ever having been **taken away** without dying. But God promised and Enoch believed. It was the most sane, rational thing that Enoch could do; what is more reasonable than that the creature should believe his Creator?

And so it happened! Enoch walked with the invisible God for three hundred years (Gen. 5:21–24) and then he walked into eternity. **Before he was taken he had this testimony, that he pleased God**. The life of faith always pleases **God**; He loves to be trusted.

11:6 Without faith it is impossible to please Him. No amount of good works can compensate for lack of **faith**. After all is said and done, when a man refuses to believe God, he is calling Him a liar. "He who does not believe God has made Him a liar" (1 Jn. 5:10), and how can God be pleased by people who call Him a liar?

Faith is the only thing that gives God His proper place, and puts man in his place too. "It glorifies God exceedingly," writes C. H. Mackintosh, "because it proves that we have more confidence in His eyesight than in our own."

Faith not only believes that God exists, but it also trusts Him to reward **those who diligently seek Him**. There is nothing about God that makes it impossible for men to believe. The difficulty is with the human will.

11:7 The **faith** of **Noah** was based on God's warning that He was going to destroy the world with a flood (Gen. 6:17). There had never been a flood in human experience, in fact, there is some reason to believe that there had never been rainfall up to that time (Gen. 2:5, 6). Noah believed God and built **an ark**, even though he was probably very far from navigable waters. Doubtless he was the butt of many a joke. But Noah's faith was rewarded: **his household** was saved, **the world** was **condemned** by his life and testimony, and he **became heir of the righteousness which is** received on the basis of **faith**.

Perhaps many of the early Jewish Christians to whom this Letter was written often wondered why, if they were

right, they were such a small minority. Noah steps out from the pages of the OT to remind them that in his day only eight people were right and all the rest of the world perished!

11:8 Abraham was probably an idolater, living in Ur of the Chaldees, when God appeared to him and told him to move. With the obedience of **faith**, he left home and country, **not knowing** his ultimate destination. Doubtless his friends ridiculed him for such folly but his attitude was:

> I go on not knowing —
> I would not if I might,
> I'd rather walk in the dark with God
> Than walk alone in the light;
> I'd rather walk by faith with Him
> Than to walk alone by sight.
> — *Helen Annis Casterline*

The walk of faith often gives the impression to others of being imprudent and reckless, but the man who knows God, is content to be led blindfolded, **not knowing** the route ahead.

11:9 God had promised **the land** of Canaan to Abraham. In a very real sense it belonged to him. Yet the only parcel of ground he ever bought in it was a tomb for his dead. He was content to live **in tents**, the symbol of pilgrimage, instead of in a fixed abode. For the time being, he treated Canaan **as if it were a foreign country**.

The companions of his pilgrimage were his son and grandson. His godly example left its mark on them also; even though they were **heirs with him of the same promise** that the land would be theirs.

11:10 Why did Abraham hold such a light grip on real estate? Because **he waited for** *the* **city which has foundations, whose builder and maker is God**. He did not have his heart set on present, material things, but on the eternal. In the original there is a definite article before both **city** and **foundations** — **the city** and *the* **foundations**. In the reckoning of faith there is only one **city** worthy of the name and only one with sure **foundations**.

God is the architect of this heavenly city and He is its **builder** as well. It is the model city, without slums, polluted air, polluted water, or any of the other problems that plague our metropolitan centers.

11:11 **By faith Sarah** was miraculously empowered **to conceive** when she was about ninety years old. The record clearly states that **she was past** the time of life when she could bear a child. But she knew that God had promised her a baby, and she knew He could not go back on His word. She had shatterproof faith that He would do what He **had promised**.

11:12 Abraham was about ninety-nine when Isaac was born. Humanly speaking it was just about impossible for him to become a father, yet God had promised a numerous posterity and so it must be.

Through Isaac, Abraham became the father of an **innumerable** earthly family, the Hebrew nation. Through Christ, he became father of an **innumerable** spiritual family, that is, true believers of every subsequent age. The **sand by the seashore** probably pictures the *earthly* progeny, while the **stars of the sky** illustrate the *heavenly* people.

11:13 The patriarchs **all died in faith**. They did not live to see the fulfillment of **the** divine **promises**. For instance, Abraham never saw his numerous progeny. The Hebrew nation never occupied all the land that had been promised to it. The OT saints never saw the fulfillment of the promise of the Messiah. But their telescopic vision brought **the promises** near, so near that they are pictured as waving at them in joyful anticipation.

They realized that this world was not their final home. They were content to be **strangers and pilgrims**, refusing the urge to nestle to make themselves comfortable. Their desire was to pass through the world without taking any of its character upon themselves. Their hearts were set on pilgrimage (Ps. 84:5, Knox).

11:14 Their lives indicated **plainly that they** were seeking **a homeland**. Faith implanted a homing instinct in them which was never satisfied by the delights of Canaan. There was always a yen for a better land which they could call home.

11:15 In saying that they were seeking a homeland, the writer wants to make it clear that he is *not* referring to the land of their birth. If Abraham had desired to go back to Mesopotamia, he could have done so, but that was no longer home to him.

11:16 The true explanation is that they were seeking **a heavenly** homeland. This is rather remarkable when we remember that most of the promises to the people of Israel had to do with material blessings on this earth. But they had a heavenly hope as well, and this hope enabled them to treat this world as a foreign country.

This spirit of pilgrimage is especially pleasing to God. Darby writes, "He is not ashamed to be called the God of those whose heart and portion are in heaven." **He has prepared a city for them**, and there they find rest and satisfaction and perfect peace.

11:17 We now come to the greatest test of Abraham's **faith**. God told him to offer up his only son, **Isaac**, upon the altar. With unhesitating obedience, Abraham set forth to offer to God the dearest treasure of his heart. Was he oblivious of the tremendous dilemma? God had promised him numberless progeny. Isaac was **his only begotten son**. Abraham was now 117 and Sarah was 108!

11:18 The promise of a great host of descendants was to be fulfilled **in Isaac**. The dilemma was this: if Abraham killed Isaac, how could the promise ever be fulfilled? Isaac was now about seventeen and unmarried.

11:19 Abraham knew what God had promised; that was all that mattered. He concluded that if God required him to slay his son, **God** would **raise him up, even from the dead** in order to fulfill the promise.

Up to this time there had been no recorded case of resurrection from the dead. Human experience had no statistics to offer. In a real sense, Abraham invented the idea of resurrection. His faith in the promise of God drove him to the conclusion that God would have to raise Isaac.

In a figurative sense, he did receive Isaac back **from the dead**. He had committed himself to the fact that Isaac must be slain. God credited him with the act. But, as Grant put it so poignantly, the

Lord "spared Abraham's heart a pang He would not spare His own." He provided a ram to take Isaac's place, and the only begotten son was returned to his father's heart and home.

Before leaving this outstanding example of faith, there are two points that should be mentioned. First, God never really intended for Abraham to slay his son. Human sacrifices were never God's will for His people. He tested Abraham's faith and found it to be genuine; then He rescinded His order.

Second, Abraham's faith in the promise of a numerous progeny was tested over a period of one hundred years. The patriarch was seventy-five when the promise of a son was first given. He waited twenty-five years before Isaac was born. Isaac was seventeen when Abraham took him up on Mount Moriah to offer him to God. Isaac was forty when he married and was married twenty years before the twins were born. Abraham died when he was 175. At that time his descendants consisted of one son (seventy-five years old) and two grandchildren (fifteen years old). Yet during his lifetime, "He did not waver at the promise of God through unbelief, but was strengthened in faith, giving glory to God, and being fully convinced that what He had promised He was also able to perform" (Rom. 4:20, 21).

11:20 It is hard for our western minds to understand what was so unusual in the faith of **Isaac**, **Jacob**, and Joseph, as recorded in the next three verses. **Isaac**, for instance, achieved a place in faith's hall of fame because he invoked future blessings on **Jacob and Esau**. What was remarkable about that?

Before the children were born, the Lord announced to Rebekah that the boys would become the source of two nations and that the older (Esau) would serve the younger (Jacob). Esau was Isaac's favorite and, as the elder son, would normally have received the best portion from his father. But Rebekah and Jacob deceived Isaac, whose sight was now poor, into giving the best blessing to *Jacob*. When the plot was exposed, Isaac trembled violently. But he remembered God's word that the older would serve the younger, and in spite of his predilection for Esau, he realized that

God's overruling of his natural weakness must stand.

11:21 There were many inglorious chapters in the life of **Jacob**, but he is honored as a hero of faith nevertheless. His character improved with age and he died in a burst of glory. When he **blessed** Ephraim and Manasseh, **the sons of Joseph**, he crossed his hands so that the older son's blessing fell on Ephraim, the younger. In spite of Joseph's protests, Jacob insisted that the blessings must stand because this was the order which the Lord had specified. Though his physical sight was dim, his spiritual sight was keen. The closing scene of Jacob's life finds him worshiping while **leaning on the top of his staff**. C. H. Mackintosh summarizes in his usual lovely style:

The close of Jacob's career stands in most pleasing contrast with all the previous scenes of his eventful history. It reminds one of a serene evening after a tempestuous day: the sun, which during the day had been hidden from view by clouds, mists, and fogs, sets in majesty and brightness, gilding with his beams the western sky, and holding out the cheering prospect of a bright tomorrow. Thus it is with our aged patriarch. The supplanting, the bargain-making, the cunning, the management, the shifting, the shuffling, the unbelieving selfish fears, — all those dark clouds of nature and of earth seem to have passed away, and he comes forth, in all the calm elevation of faith, to bestow blessings, and impart dignities, in that holy skillfulness which communion with God can alone impart.[23]

11:22 Joseph's **faith** was also strong **when he was dying**. He believed God's promise that He would deliver **the people of Israel** out of Egypt. Faith enabled him to picture the exodus already. It was so sure to him that he instructed his sons to carry **his bones** with them for burial in Canaan. "Thus," writes William Lincoln, "while surrounded by Egypt's pomp and splendor, his heart was not there at all, but with his people in their future glory and blessing."[24]

11:23 It is really the **faith** of **his parents** and not of **Moses** himself that is in view here. As they looked on their baby, **they saw he was a beautiful child** — but it was more than *physical* beauty. They saw that he was a child of destiny, one whom God had marked out for a special work. Their faith that God's purposes would be worked out gave them courage to defy **the king's command** and to hide the child for **three months**.

11:24 **By faith Moses** himself was able to make several noble renunciations. Though reared in the luxury of Egypt's palace and assured of all the things that men strive for, he learned that "it is not the possession of things but the forsaking of them that brings rest" (J. Gregory Mantle).

First of all, he refused Egypt's fame. He was the adopted **son of Pharaoh's daughter** and therefore assured of a place in the social elite, perhaps even as Pharaoh's successor. But he had been born of better blood — a member of God's chosen earthly people. From this nobility he could not *step down* to Egypt's royalty. In his adult years he made his choice; he would not hide his true nationality to win a few short years of earthly fame. The result? Instead of occupying a line or two of hieroglyphics on some obscure tomb, he is memorialized in God's eternal Book. Instead of being found in a museum as an Egyptian mummy, he is famous as a man of God.

11:25 Second, he repudiated the **pleasures** of Egypt. Humble association **with the** suffering **people of God** meant more to him than the transient gratification of his appetites. The privileges of sharing ill-treatment with his own people was greater pleasure to him than dissipation in Pharaoh's court.

11:26 Third, he turned his back on **the treasures in Egypt**. Faith enabled him to see that the fabulous treasure houses of Egypt were worthless in the light of eternity. So he chose to suffer the same kind of **reproach** as the Messiah would later suffer. Loyalty to God and love for His people were valued by him more that the combined wealth of Pharaoh. He knew that these were the things that would count one minute after he died.

11:27 Then, he also renounced Egypt's *monarch*. Emboldened **by faith**, he made his exit from the land of bondage, careless of **the wrath of the king**. It was a clear break from the politics of this world. He feared Pharaoh so little because he feared God so much. He kept his eyes on "the blessed and only Potentate, the King of kings and Lord of lords, who alone has immortality, dwelling in unapproachable light, whom no man has seen or can see, to whom be honor and everlasting power. Amen" (1 Tim. 6:15, 16).

11:28 Finally, he rejected Egypt's *religion*. By instituting **the Passover** and by **sprinkling** the **blood**, he emphatically separated himself from Egyptian idolatry forever. He flung down the gauntlet in defiance of the religious establishment. For him, salvation was through the blood of the lamb, not through the waters of the Nile. As a result, the firstborn of Israel were spared while the **firstborn** of Egypt were slain by the destroyer.

11:29 At first **the Red Sea** seemed to spell disaster to the Hebrew refugees. With the enemy in hot pursuit, they seemed to be trapped. But in obedience to God's word, they moved forward and the waters parted: "The LORD caused the sea to go back by a strong east wind all that night, and made the sea into dry land, and the waters were divided" (Ex. 14:21). When **the Egyptians** tried to follow, their chariot wheels became clogged, the waters returned to their usual place, and Pharaoh's armies **were drowned**. Thus the Red Sea became a causeway of deliverance to Israel but a dead end of doom to the Egyptians.

11:30 The walled city of **Jericho** was the first military objective in the conquest of Canaan. Reason would claim that such an impregnable fortress could be taken only by superior forces. But faith's methods are different. God uses strategies that appear foolish to men in order to accomplish His purposes. He told the people to encircle the city **for seven days**. On the seventh day they were to march around it seven times. The priests were to give a loud blast on their trumpets, the people were to shout, and **the walls** would fall. Military experts would write off the method as ludicrous. But it worked! The weapons of the spiritual warfare are not worldly but have divine power to destroy strongholds (2 Cor. 10:4).

11:31 We do not know when **the harlot Rahab** became a worshiper of Jehovah, but it is clear that she did. She abandoned the false religion of Canaan to become a Jewish proselyte. Her faith received a rigorous test when the spies came to her home. Would she be loyal to her country and her fellow countrymen, or would she be true to the Lord? She decided to stand on the Lord's side, even if it meant betraying her country. By giving friendly welcome to **the spies**, she and her family were spared, while her disobedient neighbors perished.

11:32 At this point the writer asks a rhetorical question: **And what more shall I say?** He has given an imposing list of men and women who demonstrated faith and endurance in OT times. How many more must he give in order to make his point?

He has not run out of examples, but only out of time. It would take too long to go into details so he will satisfy himself to name a few and catalog some triumphs and testings of faith.

There was **Gideon** whose army was reduced from 32,000 to 300. First the timid were sent home, then those who thought too much of their own comfort. With a hard core of true disciples, Gideon routed the Midianites.

Then there was **Barak**. When called to lead Israel to battle against the Canaanites, he agreed only on the condition that Deborah would go with him. In spite of this cowardly facet in his character, God saw real trust and lists him among the men of faith.

Samson was another man of obvious weakness. Yet, in spite of that, God detected the faith that enabled him to kill a young lion with his hands, to destroy thirty Philistines in Ashkelon, to slay one thousand Philistines with the jawbone of a donkey, to carry away the gates of Gaza, and finally to pull down the temple of Dagon and slay more Philistines in his death than he had in his life.

Though an illegitimate child, **Jephthah** rose to be the deliverer of his people from the Ammonites. He illustrates the truth that faith enables a man to rise above his birth and environment and make history for God.

The faith of **David** shines out in his contest with Goliath, in his noble behavior toward Saul, in his capture of Zion, and in countless other episodes. In his psalms, we find his faith crystallized in penitence, praise, and prophecy.

Samuel was the last of Israel's judges and her first prophet. He was God's man for the nation at a time when the priesthood was marked by spiritual bankruptcy. He was one of the greatest leaders in Israel's history.

Add to this list **the prophets**, a noble band of God's spokesmen, men who were embodied consciences, who would rather die than lie, who would rather go to heaven with a good conscience than stay on earth with a bad one.

11:33 The writer now turns from naming people of faith to citing their exploits.

They **subdued kingdoms**. Here our minds turn to Joshua, to the judges (who were really military leaders), to David, and to others.

They **worked righteousness**. Kings like Solomon, Asa, Jehoshaphat, Joash, Hezekiah, and Josiah are remembered for reigns which, though not perfect, were characterized by **righteousness**.

They **obtained promises**. This may mean that God made covenants with them, as in the case of Abraham, Moses, David, and Solomon; or it may mean that they received the fulfillment of promises, thus demonstrating the truth of God's word.

They **stopped the mouths of lions**. Daniel is an outstanding example here (Dan. 6:22), but we should also remember Samson (Judg. 14:5, 6) and David (1 Sam. 17:34, 35).

11:34 They **quenched the violence of fire**. The fiery furnace succeeded only in burning the fetters of the three young Hebrews and setting them free (Dan. 3:25). Thus it proved to be a blessing in disguise.

They **escaped the edge of the sword**. David escaped Saul's malicious attacks (1 Sam. 19:9,10), Elijah escaped the murderous hatred of Jezebel (1 Kgs. 19:1–3), and Elisha escaped from the king of Syria (2 Kgs. 6:15–19).

They won strength **out of weakness**. Many symbols of **weakness** are found in the annals of faith. Ehud, for instance, was left-handed; yet he slew the king of Moab (Judg. 3:12–22). Jael, a member of "the weaker sex," killed Sisera with a tent peg (Judg. 4:21). Gideon used fragile earthen pitchers in the defeat of the

Midianites (Judg. 7:20). Samson used the jawbone of a donkey to slay one thousand Philistines (Judg. 15:15). They all illustrate the truth that God has chosen the weak things of the world to shame the strong (1 Cor. 1:27).

They **became valiant in battle**. Faith endowed men with strength beyond what was natural and enabled them to overcome in the face of insurmountable odds.

They put **to flight the armies of the aliens**. Though often under-equipped and greatly outnumbered, the armies of Israel walked off with the victory to the confusion of the foe and the amazement of everyone else.

11:35 Women received their dead by resurrection. The widow of Zarephath (1 Kgs. 17:22) and the woman of Shunem (2 Kgs. 4:34) are cases in point.

But faith has another face. In addition to those who performed dazzling feats, there were those who endured intense suffering. God values the latter as much as the former.

Because of their faith in the Lord, some were subjected to cruel torture. If they would have renounced Jehovah, they would have been released; but to them it was better to die and be raised again to heavenly glory than to continue this life as traitors to God. In the time of the Maccabees, a mother and her seven sons were put to death, one after the other, and in sight of each other, by Antiochus Epiphanes. They refused to accept release **that they might obtain a better resurrection**, that is, better than a mere continuation of life on earth. Morrison comments:

> So this is also a result of faith, *not* that it brings deliverance to a man, but that sometimes, when deliverance is offered, it gives him a fine courage to refuse it. There are seasons when faith shows itself in taking. There are seasons when it is witnessed in refusing. There is a deliverance that faith embraces. There is a deliverance that faith rejects. They were tortured, not accepting deliverance — that was the sign and seal that they were faithful. There are hours when the strongest proof of faith is the swift rejection of the larger room.[25]

11:36 Others were mocked and flogged, and were bound in prison. For faithfulness to God, Jeremiah endured all these forms of punishment (Jer. 20:1–6; 37:15). Joseph too was imprisoned because he would rather suffer than sin (Gen. 39:20).

11:37 They were stoned. Jesus reminded the scribes and Pharisees that their ancestors had murdered Zechariah in this way between the sanctuary and the altar (Matt. 23:35).

They were sawn in two. Tradition says that Manasseh used this method of executing Isaiah.

They **were tempted**.[26] This clause probably describes the tremendous pressures that were brought to bear on believers to compromise, to recant, to commit acts of sin, or in any way to deny their Lord.

They **were slain with the sword**. Uriah the prophet paid this price for his faithful proclamation of God's message to King Jehoiakim (Jer. 26:23); but the expression here refers to mass slaughter such as occurred in the times of the Maccabees.

They wandered about in sheepskins and goatskins, being destitute, afflicted, tormented. Moorehead comments:

> They might have rustled in silks and velvets and luxuriated in the palaces of princes had they denied God and believed the world's lie. Instead, they wandered about in sheepskins and goatskins, themselves accounted no better than goats or sheep, nay, they like these reckoned fit only for the slaughter.[27]

They suffered poverty, privation, and persecution.

11:38 The world treated them as if they were not worthy to live. But the Spirit of God burst forth here with the interjection that actually it was the other way around — **the world was not worthy** *of them*.

They wandered in deserts and mountains and **in dens and caves of the earth**. Dispossessed of homes, separated from families, pursued like animals, expelled from society, they endured heat and cold, distress and hardship, but they would not deny their Lord.

11:39 God has borne witness to the faith of these OT heroes, yet they died before receiving the fulfillment of **the promise**. They did not live to see the

Advent of the long awaited Messiah or to enjoy the blessings that would flow from His ministry.

11:40 **God** had reserved **something better for us**. He had arranged **that they should not be made perfect apart from us**. They never did enjoy a perfect conscience as far as sin was concerned; and they will not enjoy the full perfection of the glorified body in heaven until we are all caught up to meet the Lord in the air (1 Thess 4:13–18). The spirits of OT saints are already perfect in the presence of the Lord (Heb. 12:23), but their bodies will not be raised from among the dead until the Lord returns for His people. Then they will enjoy the perfection of resurrection glory.

To put it another way, the OT believers were not as privileged as we are. Yet think of their thrilling triumphs and tremendous trials! Think of their exploits and their endurance! They lived on the other side of the cross; we live in the full glory of the cross. Yet how do our lives compare with theirs? This is the cogent challenge of Hebrews 11.

C. Exhortation to Hope in Christ (Chap. 12)

12:1 We must bear in mind that Hebrews was written to people who were being persecuted. Because they had forsaken Judaism for Christ, they were facing bitter opposition. There was a danger that they might interpret their suffering as a sign of God's displeasure. They might become discouraged and give up. Worst of all, they might be tempted to return to the temple and its ceremonies.

They should not think that their sufferings were unique. Many of the witnesses described in chapter 11 suffered severely as a result of their loyalty to the Lord, yet they endured. If they maintained unflinching perseverance with their lesser privileges, how much more should we to whom the better things of Christianity have come.

They surround us as a **great cloud of witnesses**. This does *not* mean that they are spectators of what goes on on earth. Rather they witness to us by their lives of faith and endurance and set a high standard for us to duplicate.

This verse invariably raises the question, "Can saints in heaven see our lives on earth or know what is transpiring?" The only thing we can be sure they know is when a sinner is saved: "I say to you that likewise there will be more joy in heaven over one sinner who repents than over ninety-nine just persons who need no repentance" (Luke 15:7).

The Christian life is a race that requires discipline and endurance. We must strip ourselves of everything that would impede us. Weights are things that may be harmless in themselves and yet hinder progress; they could include material possessions, family ties, the love of comfort, lack of mobility, etc. In the Olympic races, there is no rule against carrying a supply of food and beverage, but the runner would never win the race that way.

We must also **lay aside . . . the sin which so easily ensnares us**. This may mean sin in any form, but especially the sin of unbelief. We must have complete trust in the promises of God and complete confidence that the life of faith is sure to win.

We must guard against the notion that **the race** is an easy sprint, that everything in the Christian life is rosy. We must be prepared to press on with perseverance through trials and temptations.

12:2 Throughout the race, we should look away from every other object and keep our eyes riveted on **Jesus**, the foremost Runner. A. B. Bruce comments:

> One stands out conspicuous above all the rest . . . the Man who first perfectly realised the idea of living by faith . . . , who undauntedly endured the bitter suffering of the cross, and despised the ignominy of it, sustained by a faith that so vividly realised coming joy and glory as to obliterate the consciousness of present pain and shame.[28]

He is the **author**, or pioneer, **of our faith** in the sense that He has provided us with the only perfect example of what the life of faith is like.

He is also the **finisher of our faith**. He not only began the race but finished it triumphantly. For Him the race course stretched from heaven to Bethlehem, then on to Gethsemane and Calvary, then out of the tomb and back to heaven. At no time did He falter or turn back. He kept His eyes fixed on the coming glory when all the redeemed would be gathered with Him eternally. This enabled Him to think nothing of **shame** and to endure suffering and death. Today He is seated **at the right hand of the throne of God.**

12:3 The picture now changes from a race to a fight against sin. Our undaunted Captain is the Lord Jesus; no one ever **endured such hostility from sinners** as He. Whenever we have a tendency to grow **weary and discouraged,** we should think of what He went through. Our trials will seem trifling by comparison.

12:4 We are engaged in a ceaseless **striving against sin**. Yet we **have not resisted** to the point of **bloodshed**, that is, to the point of death. *He did!*

12:5 The Christian view of suffering is now presented. Why do persecution, testings, trials, sickness, pain, sorrow, and trouble come into the life of the believer? Are they a sign of God's anger or displeasure? Do they happen by chance? How should we react to them?

These verses teach that these things are part of God's educative process for His children. Although they do not come from God, He permits them, then overrules them for His glory, for our good, and for the blessing of others.

Nothing happens by chance to the Christian. Tragedies are blessings in disguise, and disappointments are His appointments. God harnesses the adverse circumstances of life to conform us to the image of Christ.

So the early Hebrew believers were exhorted to remember Proverbs 3:11, 12, where God addresses them as **sons**. There He warns them against despising His discipline or losing courage under His rebuke. If they rebel or give up, they lose the benefit of His dealings with them and fail to learn His lessons.

12:6 When we read the word *chastening*, or *chastisement*, we tend to think of a whipping. But here the word means child training or education. It includes instruction, discipline, correction, and warning. All are designed to cultivate

Christian virtues and drive out evil. In this passage, the chastening was not punishment for wrongdoing, but training through persecution.

The passage in Proverbs distinctly states that God's discipline is a proof of His love, and no **son** of His escapes chastisement.

12:7 By remaining submissive to the **chastening** of **God**, we permit His discipline to mold us into His image. If we try to short-circuit His dealings with us, He may have to teach us over a longer period of time, using more instructive, and consequently, more difficult methods. There are grades in the school of God, and promotion comes only when we have learned our lessons.

So when testings come to us, we should realize that God is treating us as **sons**. In any normal father-son relationship, the father trains his **son** because he loves him and wants the best for him. God loves us too much to let us develop naturally.

12:8 In the spiritual realm, those who do not experience God's discipline are **illegitimate** children, not true **sons**. After all, a gardener does not prune thistles, but he does prune grapevines. As in the natural, so in the spiritual.

12:9 Most of us have experienced discipline from our **human fathers**. We did not interpret this as a sign that they hated us. We realized that they were interested in our welfare, **and we paid them respect**.

How **much more** should we respect the training of **the Father of spirits and live!** God is **the Father** (or source) of all beings that are spirit or that have a spirit. Man is a spirit dwelling in a human body. By being subject to God we enjoy life in its truest sense.

12:10 The discipline of earthly parents is not perfect. It lasts only for a time, that is, during childhood and youth. If it has not succeeded then, it can do no more. And it is **as seemed best to them**, according to what they think is right. Sometimes it may not be right.

But God's discipline is always perfect. His love is infinite and His wisdom is infallible. His chastenings are never the result of whim, but always for our profit. His objective **is that we may be**

partakers of His holiness. And godliness can never be produced outside God's school. Jowett explains:

> The purpose of God's chastening is not punitive but creative. He chastens "that we may share His holiness." The phrase "that we may share" has direction in it, and the direction points toward a purified and beautified life. The fire which is kindled is not a bonfire, blazing heedlessly and unguardedly, and consuming precious things; it is a refiner's fire, and the Refiner sits by it, and He is firmly and patiently and gently bringing holiness out of carelessness and stability out of weakness. God is always creating even when He is using the darker means of grace. He is producing the fruits and flowers of the Spirit. His love is always in quest of lovely things.[29]

12:11 At the time, all discipline seems painful. But **it yields the peaceable fruit of righteousness to those who have been trained by it**. That is why we often come across such testimonies, like this by Leslie Weatherhead:

> Like all men I love and prefer the sunny uplands of experience, where health, happiness, and success abound, but I have learned far more about God and life and myself in the darkness of fear and failure than I have ever learned in the sunshine. There are such things as the treasures of darkness. The darkness, thank God, passes. But what one learns in the darkness one possesses for ever. "The trying things," says Bishop Fenelon, "which you fancy come between God and you, will prove means of unity with Him, if you bear them humbly. Those things that overwhelm us and upset our pride, do more good than all that which excites and inspirits us."[30]

Or consider the following testimony by C. H. Spurgeon:

> I am afraid that all the grace I have got out of my comfortable and easy times and happy hours might almost lie on a penny. But the good that I have received from my sorrows and pains and griefs is altogether incalculable. What do I not owe to the hammer and the anvil, the fire and the file? Affliction is the best bit of furniture in my house.[31]

12:12 Believers should not cave in under the adverse circumstances of life; their lapse of faith might have an unfavorable influence on others. Drooping **hands** should be reinvigorated to serve the living Christ. **Feeble knees** should be strengthened for persevering prayer.

12:13 Faltering **feet** should be guided in **straight paths** of Christian discipleship. Williams writes:

> All who follow the Lord fully smooth the path of faith for feeble brethren; but those who do not follow fully, roughen the path for others' feet and create spiritual cripples.[32]

G. H. Lang gives a fine illustration:

> A weary traveler, tired of the road and the buffeting of the tempest, stands dispirited and limp. With shoulders bowed, hands hanging slack, knees bent and shaking, he is ready to give up and sink to the ground. Such can God's pilgrim become, as pictured by our writer.
>
> But one comes to him confident of mien, with kindly smile and firm voice, and says, "Cheer up, stand erect, brace your limbs, take heart of grace. You have already come far; throw not away your former toils. A noble home is at the end of the journey. See, yonder is the direct road to it; keep straight on; seek from the great Physician healing for your lameness. . . . Your Forerunner went this same hard road to the palace of God; others before you have won through; others are on the way; you are not alone; only press on! and you too shall reach the goal and win the prize."
>
> Happy is he who knows how to sustain with words him that is weary (Isaiah 50:4). Happy is he who accepts exhortation (Hebrews 13:22). And thrice happy is he whose faith is simple and strong so that he finds no occasion of stumbling in the Lord when His discipline is severe.[33]

12:14 Christians should strive for peaceable relations **with all people** and at all times. But this exhortation is especially needful when persecution is prevalent, when some are defecting from the faith, and when nerves are frayed. At such times it is all too easy to vent one's frustration and fears on those who are nearest and dearest.

We should also strive for the **holiness without which no one will see the Lord**. What is the **holiness** referred to here? To answer the question we should remind ourselves that *holiness* is used of believers in at least three different ways in the NT.

First of all, the believer becomes *positionally* holy at the time of his conversion; he is set apart to God from the world (1 Cor. 1:2; 6:11). By virtue of his union with Christ, he is sanctified forever. This is what Martin Luther meant when he said, "My holiness is in heaven." Christ is our holiness, that is, as far as our standing before God is concerned.

Then there is a *practical* sanctification (1 Thess. 4:3; 5:23). This is what we should be day by day. We should separate ourselves from every form of evil. This holiness should be progressive, that is, we should be growing more and more like the Lord Jesus all the time.

Finally, there is *complete* or *perfect* sanctification. This takes place when a believer goes to heaven. Then he is forever free from sin. His old nature is removed, and his state perfectly corresponds to his standing.

Now which holiness are we to **pursue**? Obviously it is practical sanctification that is in view. We do not strive after positional sanctification; it is ours automatically when we are born again. And we do not strive after the perfect sanctification that will be ours when we see His face. But practical or progressive sanctification is something that involves our obedience and cooperation; we must cultivate this holiness continually. The fact that we must follow it is proof that we do not fully attain it in this life. (See notes under 2:11 for a more detailed description of the various aspects of sanctification.)

Wuest writes:

> The exhortation is to the born-again Jews who had left the Temple, to live such consistent saintly lives, and to cling so tenaciously to their new-found faith, that the unsaved Jews who had also left the Temple and had outwardly embraced the New Testament truth, would be encouraged to go on to faith in Messiah as High Priest, instead of returning to the abrogated sacrifices of the Levitical system. These truly born-again Jews are warned that a limping Christian life would cause these unsaved Jews to be turned out of the way.[34]

But a difficulty remains! Is it true that we cannot see the Lord without practical sanctification? Yes, there is a sense in which this is true; but let us understand that this does not mean that we earn the right to see God by living holy lives. Jesus Christ is our only title to heaven.

What this verse means is that there must be practical **holiness** as a proof of new life within. If a person is not growing more holy, he is not saved. When the Holy Spirit indwells a person, He manifests His presence by a separated life. It is a matter of cause and effect; if Christ has been received, the rivers of living water will flow.

12:15 The next two verses seem to present four distinct sins to avoid. But there is a strong suggestion in the context that this is another warning against the single sin of apostasy and that these four sins are all related to it.

First of all, apostasy is a failure to obtain **the grace of God**. The person looks like a Christian, talks like a Christian, professes to be a Christian, but he has never been born again. He has come so near the Savior but has never received Him; so near and yet so far.

Apostasy is a **root of bitterness**. The person turns sour against the Lord and repudiates the Christian faith. His defection is contagious. Others are **defiled** by his complaints, doubts, and denials.

12:16 Apostasy is closely linked with immorality. A professing Christian may fall into gross moral sin. Instead of acknowledging his guilt, he blames the Lord and falls away. Apostasy and sexual sin are connected in 2 Peter 2:10, 14, 18 and Jude 8, 16, 18.

Finally, apostasy is a form of irreligion, illustrated by **Esau**. He had no real appreciation for the birthright; he willingly bartered it for the momentary gratification of his appetite.

12:17 Later Esau was remorseful at the loss of the older son's double portion, but it was too late. His father could not reverse the blessing.

So it is with an apostate. He has no real regard for spiritual values. He willingly renounces Christ in order to escape reproach, suffering, or martyrdom. He cannot be renewed to repentance. There may be remorse but no godly repentance.

12:18 Those who are tempted to return to the law should remember the terrifying circumstances that attended the giving of the law and should draw spiritual lessons from them. The scene was Mount Sinai, a literal, tangible **mountain** that was all on **fire**. It was enveloped in a pall or veil that made everything seem indistinct, obscure, and nebulous. A violent storm raged around it.

12:19 In addition to these natural disorders, there were terrible supernatural phenomena. **A trumpet** blasted away, and a **voice** thundered out so ominously that the people pled for it to stop.

12:20 They were completely unnerved by the divine edict that **"If so much as a beast touches the mountain, it shall be stoned** to death."[35] They knew that if it meant death to a dumb, uncomprehending animal, how much more surely would it mean death to those who understood the warning.

12:21 The entire scene was **so terrifying** and forbidding that **Moses** himself was **trembling**. All this speaks eloquently of the nature and ministry of the law. It is a revelation of God's righteous requirements and of His wrath against sin. The purpose of the law was not to provide the knowledge of salvation but to produce the knowledge of sin. It speaks of distance between God and man because of sin. It is a ministry of condemnation, darkness, and gloom.

12:22 Believers have not come to the forbidding terrors of Sinai but to the welcome of grace:

The burning mount and the mystic veil,
With our terrors and guilt are gone;
Our conscience has peace that can
    never fail,
'Tis the Lamb on high on the throne.
    — James G. Deck

Now every blood-brought child of God can say:

The terrors of law and of God,
With me can have nothing to do;
My Saviour's obedience and blood
Hide all my transgressions from view.
    — A. M. Toplady

"We *have* already arrived in principle where in full reality we shall be forever. The future is already the present. In today we possess tomorrow. On earth we own Heaven" (Selected).

We do not come to a tangible mountain on earth. Our privilege is to enter the sanctuary in heaven. By faith, we approach God in confession, praise, and prayer. We are not limited to one day of the year, but may enter the holiest at any

time with the knowledge that we are always welcome. God no longer says, "Stay at a distance"; He says, "Come near with confidence."

Law has its Mount Sinai but faith has its **Mount Zion**. This heavenly mountain symbolizes the combined blessings of grace — all that is ours through the redeeming work of Christ Jesus.

Law has its earthly Jerusalem but faith has its **heavenly** capital above. **The city of the living God** is in heaven, the city which has the foundations, whose Architect and Builder is God.

As we enter the presence of God, we are surrounded by an august gathering. First of all, there are myriads **of angels** who though untainted by sin cannot join with us in song because they do not know "the joy that our salvation brings."

12:23 Then we are with the **general assembly of the firstborn** ones **who are registered in heaven**. These are members of the **church**, the Body and Bride of Christ, who have died since Pentecost and are now consciously enjoying the Lord's presence. They await the Day when their bodies will be raised from the grave in glorified form and reunited with their spirits.

By faith we see **God the Judge of all**. No longer does darkness and gloom hide Him; to faith's vision His glory is transcendent.

The OT saints are there, **the spirits of just men made perfect**. Justified by faith, they stand in spotless purity because the value of Christ's work has been imputed to their account. They too await the time when the grave will yield up its ancient charges and they will receive glorified bodies.

12:24 **Jesus** is there, **the Mediator of the new covenant**. There is a difference between Moses as mediator of the Old Covenant and Jesus as **Mediator of the new**. Moses served as a mediator simply by receiving the law from God and delivering it to the people of Israel. He was the go-between, or the people's representative, offering the sacrifices by which the covenant was ratified.

Christ is **Mediator of the new covenant** in a far higher sense. Before God could righteously make this covenant, the Lord Jesus had to die. He had to seal the covenant with His own blood and give Himself a ransom for many (1 Tim. 2:6).

He secured the blessings of the New Covenant for His people by His death. He insures these blessings for them by His endless life. And He preserves His people to enjoy the blessings in a hostile world by His present ministry at God's right hand. All this is included in His mediatorial work.

Bearing the scars of Calvary, the Lord Jesus is exalted at God's right hand, a Prince and a Savior.

> We love to look up and behold Him there,
> The Lamb for His chosen slain;
> And soon shall His saints all His glories share,
> With their Head and their Lord shall reign.
>
> — James G. Deck

Finally, there is **the blood of sprinkling that speaks better things than** the blood of Abel. When Christ ascended, He presented to God all the value of **the blood** He shed at the cross. There is no suggestion that He literally carried His blood into heaven, but the merits of His blood have been made known in the sanctuary. Again, J. G. Deck puts truth into poetry:

> His precious blood is sprinkled there,
> Before and on the throne;
> And His own wounds in Heaven declare
> The work that saves is done.

His precious **blood** is contrasted with the blood **of Abel.** Whether we understand the latter as meaning the blood of Abel's sacrifice or Abel's own blood which was shed by Cain, it is still true that Christ's blood speaks more graciously. The blood of Abel's sacrifice said, "Covered temporarily"; Christ's blood says, "Forgiven forever." Abel's own blood cried, "Vengeance"; Christ's blood cries, "Mercy, pardon, and peace."

12:25 The closing verses of chapter 12 contrast God's revelation at Sinai with His revelation in and through Christ. The incomparable privileges and glories of the Christian faith are not to be treated lightly. God is speaking, inviting, wooing. To **refuse Him** is to perish.

Those who disobeyed the voice of God as it was heard in the law were punished accordingly. When privilege is greater, responsibility is also greater. In Christ, God has given His best and final revelation. Those who reject His voice as it now **speaks from heaven** in the gospel are more responsible than those who broke the law. **Escape** is impossible.

12:26 At Sinai God's voice caused an earthquake. But when He speaks in the future His voice will also produce a "heavenquake." This was, in substance, predicted by the prophet Haggai (2:6): "Once more (it is a little while) I will shake heaven and earth, the sea and dry land."

This shaking will take place during the period from the Rapture to the end of Christ's kingdom. Prior to Christ's coming to reign there will be violent convulsions of nature both on earth and in the heavens. Planets will be moved out of orbit causing raging tides and roaring seas. Then at the close of Christ's Millennial Reign, the earth, the stellar heavens, and the atmospheric heavens will be destroyed by fervent heat (2 Pet. 3:10–12).

12:27 When God said, **"Yet once more,"** He anticipated a complete and final **removal of** the heavens and the earth. This event will explode the myth that what we can see and touch and handle is real and that unseen things are unreal. When God ends the sifting and shaking process, only that which is real will **remain.**

12:28 Those who were occupied with the tangible, visible ritualism of Judaism were clinging to things that could be shaken. True believers have **a kingdom which cannot be shaken.** This should inspire the most fervent worship and adoration. We should unceasingly praise Him **with reverence and godly fear.**

12:29 **God is a consuming fire** to all who refuse to listen to Him. But even to His own, His holiness and righteousness are so great that they should produce profoundest homage and respect.

D. Exhortation to Various Christian Graces (13:1–17)

13:1 The practical section of Hebrews continues with six exhortations concerning graces that should be developed. First is **love** of the brethren. There should be a sense of family relationship toward all true Christians and a recognition of this kinship by loving words and acts (1 Jn. 3:18).

13:2 The readers are urged to show hospitality to **strangers**. This might refer primarily to believers who were fleeing from persecution and were hard-pressed to find food and lodging; to entertain them was to expose the host and hostess to danger. The verse may also be understood as a general encouragement to show hospitality to any believers who need it.

There is always the thrilling possibility that in doing this we may **unwittingly** entertain **angels!** This of course looks back to Abraham's experience with three men who were actually angelic beings (Gen. 18:1–15).³⁶ Even if we never have real angels in our homes, we may have men and women whose very presence is a benediction and whose godly influence on our family may have results that reach on into eternity.

13:3 The third exhortation concerns care for imprisoned believers. This almost certainly means those who were jailed because of their testimony for Christ. They would need food, warm clothing, reading matter, and encouragement. The temptation would be for other believers to shield themselves from association with **prisoners** and thus from the danger of guilt by association. They should **remember** that in visiting **prisoners**, they were visiting Christ.

Compassion should also be shown for the **mistreated**; again this doubtless means persecuted Christians. The readers should resist any tendency to shield themselves from the danger that such compassion might involve. For ourselves, we can broaden the application of the verse to include sympathy for all suffering saints. We should remember that we **are in the body also** and therefore subject to similar afflictions.

13:4 Marriage should be held in honor by all. We should remember that it was instituted by God before sin entered the world and that it is His holy will for mankind. To treat it as unclean, as ascetics do, or even to make jests and puns about it, as Christians sometimes

do, are alike forbidden in the Scripture.

Those who are married should be faithful to their vows and thus keep the marriage **bed undefiled**. In spite of modern man's smug laxness in this area, the fact remains that any sexual relations outside the bounds of marriage are sin. Adultery is not sickness; it is sin. And it is a sin which **God will** inevitably **judge**. No form of immorality will escape. He judges it in this life — through bodily ailments, broken families, mental and nervous afflictions, personality deformities. Unless it is pardoned through the blood of Christ, He will judge it in eternal fire.

Reformation Bishop Latimer reminded the immoral King Henry VIII of this in a way that was as convicting as it was courageous. He presented the king with a finely wrapped Bible. On the wrapping was inscribed the words, "Fornicators and adulterers God will judge."

13:5 The sixth virtue to cultivate is contentment. Remember that the adherents of Judaism were continually saying, "We have the tabernacle. We have the priesthood. We have the offerings. We have the beautiful ritual. What do you have?" Here the writer quietly says to the Christians: **Let your conduct be without covetousness; be content with such things as you have.** I should say so! What the Christian has is so infinitely greater than the best of Judaism — why shouldn't he **be content**? He has Christ; that is enough.

The love of silver can be a tremendous hindrance to the believer. Just as a small silver coin held before the eye comes between it and the sun, so **covetousness** breaks fellowship with God and hinders spiritual progress.

The greatest riches a person can have lie in possessing Him who promises, **"I will never leave you nor forsake you."** In Greek, strong negation is expressed by using two or more negatives. (This is the opposite of English structure in which a double negative makes a positive assertion.) In this verse the construction is very emphatic: it combines *five* negatives to indicate the impossibility of Christ deserting his own!

13:6 The words of Psalm 118:6 are the confident confession of the one who has Christ: **"The LORD is my helper; I will not fear. What can man do to me?"** The fact is that in Christ we have perfect security, perfect protection, perfect peace.

13:7 The readers are instructed to **remember** their leaders, the Christian teachers **who** spoke **the word of God to** them. What was **the outcome of their conduct**? They had not turned back to the Levitical system but had maintained their confession steadfast to the end. Perhaps some of them were martyred for Christ's sake. Theirs is the **faith** to imitate, the faith that clings to Christ and to Christian doctrine, and that brings God into every move in life. We are not all called to the same forms of service, but we are all called to a life of faith.

13:8 The connection of this verse with the preceding one is not clear. Perhaps the simplest way to understand it is as a summary of the teaching, the goal, and the faith of these leaders. The gist of their teaching was this: **Jesus Christ is the same yesterday, today, and forever.** The goal of their lives was **Jesus Christ — the same yesterday, today, and forever.** The foundation of their faith was that **Jesus** is the **Christ** (Messiah), **the same yesterday, today, and forever**.

13:9 Next follows a warning against the false teachings of legalism. The Judaizers insisted that holiness was connected with externals, such as ceremonial worship and clean foods, for example. The truth is that holiness is produced **by grace**, not by law. Legislation concerning clean and unclean foods was designed to produce *ritual* cleanness. But this is not the same thing as *inward* holiness. A man might be ceremonially clean and yet be filled with hatred and hypocrisy. Only God's grace can inspire and empower believers to live holy lives. Love for the Savior who died on account of our sins motivates us to "live soberly, righteously, and godly in the present age" (Tit. 2:12). After all, endless rules concerning foods and drinks have not profited their adherents.

13:10 Let us not miss the triumph of the words, **"We have an altar."** They are the Christian's confident answer to the repeated taunts of the Judaizers. Our **altar** is Christ, and therefore it includes

all the blessings that are found in Him. Those who are connected with the Levitical system **have no right to** partake of the better things of Christianity. They must first repent of their sins and believe in Jesus Christ as only Lord and Savior.

13:11 Under the sacrificial system, certain **animals** were slain and their blood was **brought into the** Most Holy Place **by the high priest** as a sacrifice **for sin. The bodies of those animals** were carried to a place away from the tabernacle environs and burned. **Outside the camp** means outside the outer fence that enclosed the tabernacle court.

13:12 The animals burned outside the camp were a type; the Lord **Jesus** was the antitype. **He** was crucified **outside the** city walls of Jerusalem. It was outside the camp of organized Judaism that He sanctified **the people with His own blood**.

13:13 The application for the early readers of the Epistle was this: they should make a clean break with Judaism. Once for all they should turn their backs on the temple sacrifices and appropriate the finished work of Christ as their sufficient sacrifice.

The application for us is similar: **the camp** today is the entire religious system that teaches salvation by works, by character, by ritual, or by ordinances. It is the modern church system with its humanly ordained priesthood, its material aids to worship, and its ceremonial trappings. It is corrupt Christendom, a church without Christ. The Lord Jesus is outside and we should **go forth to Him, . . . bearing His reproach**.

13:14 Jerusalem was dear to the hearts of those who served at the temple. It was the geographic center of their "camp." The Christian has **no** such **city** on earth; his heart is set on the heavenly city, the new Jerusalem, where the Lamb is all the glory.

13:15 In the NT all believers are priests. They are holy priests, going into the sanctuary of God to worship (1 Pet. 2:5), and they are royal priests going out into the world to witness (1 Pet. 2:9). There are at least three sacrifices which a believer-priest offers. First, there is the sacrifice of his person (Rom. 12:1). Then, here in verse 15 is the second: **the sacri-**

fice of praise. It is offered to God through the Lord Jesus. All our praise and prayer passes through Him before it reaches God the Father; our great High Priest removes all impurities and imperfections and adds His own virtue to it.

> To all our prayers and praises
> Christ adds His sweet perfume;
> And love the censer raises
> These odors to consume.
> — Mary B. Peters

The sacrifice of praise is the fruit of those lips that acknowledge His name. The only worship that God receives is that which flows from redeemed lips.

13:16 The third sacrifice is the offering of our possessions. We are to use our material resources in doing good, and in sharing with those who are in need. With such sacrificial living God is well pleased. It is the opposite of accumulating for self.

> The race of God's anointed priests
> Shall never pass away;
> Before His glorious Face they stand
> And serve Him night and day.
> Though reason raves, and unbelief
> Flows on a mighty flood,
> There are, and shall be, till the end,
> The hidden priests of God.
> His chosen souls, their earthly dross
> Consumed in sacred fire,
> To God's own heart their hearts ascend
> In flame of deep desire;
> The incense of their worship fills
> His Temple's holiest place;
> Their song with wonder fills the Heavens,
> The glad new song of grace.
> – Gerhard Tersteegen

13:17 In verses 7 and 8, the readers were instructed to remember their past leaders. Now they are taught to obey their present leaders. This probably refers primarily to the elders in the local church. These men act as representatives of God in the assembly. Authority has been given to them, and believers should be submissive to this authority. As undershepherds, the elders watch out for the souls of the flock. They will have to give account to God in a coming day. They will do it either joyfully or sadly, depending on the spiritual progress of their charges. If they have to do it sadly, that will mean loss of reward for the saints concerned. So it is to everyone's benefit to respect the lines of authority which God has laid down.

IV. CLOSING BENEDICTION (13:18–25)

13:18 As the writer comes to the close of his Letter, he adds a personal appeal for prayer. The rest of the verse suggests that he may have been under attack from critics. We can guess who the critics were — those who were coercing people to return to the worship of the Old Covenant. He protests that, in spite of any charges that were being brought against him, his conscience was clear and his desire was pure.

13:19 An added reason for prayer was that he might be restored to them the sooner. Perhaps this refers to release from prison. We can do no more than speculate on this point.

13:20 Then he adds one of the most beautiful benedictions of the Bible — one that takes its place with Numbers 6:24–26; 2 Corinthians 13:14; and Jude 24, 25. It is addressed to the God of peace. As has been mentioned, OT saints never had perfect peace of conscience. But under the New Covenant, we have peace with God (Rom. 5:1) and the peace of God (Phil. 4:7). The verse goes on to explain that this peace is the fruit of Christ's work. God raised our Lord Jesus from the dead as a sign that His work on the cross settled the sin question once for all.

Christ, as the good Shepherd, gave His life for the sheep (John 10:11). As the great Shepherd, He rose from the dead, having accomplished redemption (Heb. 13:20). As the Chief Shepherd, He is coming again to reward His servants (1 Pet. 5:4). We see Him as the good Shepherd in Psalm 22, as the great Shepherd in Psalm 23, and as the Chief Shepherd in Psalm 24.

He was brought back from the dead in accordance with the everlasting covenant. Wuest comments on this phrase:

The New Testament is called the eternal one, in contrast to the First Testament which was of a transitory nature. It was within the sphere of the eternal covenant that Messiah, having died for sinful man, was raised up from among those who are dead. He could not be a high priest after the order of Melchizedek if He was not raised from the dead. Sinful man needs a living Priest to give life to the believing sinner, not a dead priest merely to pay for his sins. Thus, it was provided within the New Testament that the priest who offered Himself for sacrifice would be raised from the dead.[37]

13:21 The prayer begun in verse 20 is that the saints might be equipped with **every good work to do** God's **will**. There is a curious mingling here of the divine and the human. God equips us with everything **good**. God works in us **what is well pleasing in His sight**. He does it **through Jesus Christ**. Then we do His will. In other words, He places the desire in us; He gives us the power to do it; then we do it; and He rewards us.

The prayer ends with the acknowledgment that Jesus Christ is worthy of **glory forever and ever**.

> Worthy of homage and of praise,
> Worthy by all to be adored;
> Exhaustless theme of heavenly lays
> Thou, Thou art worthy, Jesus Lord.
> – Miss F. T. Wigram

13:22 The writer now urges his readers to heed the **exhortation** of his Letter, that is, to abandon ritualistic religion and cleave to Christ with true purpose of heart.

He speaks of his Epistle as a brief one, and it is, considering how much more he could have said about the Levitical system and how it finds its fulfillment in Christ.

13:23 The mention **that our brother Timothy had been set free** here confirms many in their view that Paul wrote the Letter. There is the added touch that the writer plans to travel with Timothy, another possible sign pointing to Paul. But we cannot be sure, so it is best to leave the question open.

13:24 Greetings are sent to all the Christian leaders **and all the saints**. We should not overlook the many touches of Christian courtesy in the Epistles, and we should imitate them in our day.

Some believers **from Italy** were with the writer, and they too wanted to send their greetings. This suggests that the Letter was written to or from there.

13:25 It is especially fitting that this epistle of the New Covenant should end on a grace note: **Grace be with you all.** The New Covenant is an unconditional covenant of free grace, telling out God's

unbounded favor for unworthy sinners through the sacrificial work of the Lord Jesus Christ. **Amen.**

THE MESSAGE OF HEBREWS FOR TODAY

Does the Epistle to the Hebrews have a message for us in the twentieth century?

Although Judaism is not the dominant religion today that it was in the early days of the church, yet the legalistic spirit has permeated Christendom. In his well-known booklet, *Rightly Dividing the Word of Truth*, Dr. C. I. Scofield writes:

> It may be safely said that the *Judaizing of the Church* has done more to hinder her progress, pervert her mission, and destroy her spiritually, than all other causes combined. Instead of pursuing her appointed path of separation from the world and following the Lord in her heavenly calling, she has used Jewish Scriptures to justify herself in lowering her purpose to the civilization of the world, the acquisition of wealth, the use of an imposing ritual, the erection of magnificent churches . . . and the division of an equal brotherhood into "clergy" and "laity."[38]

The Letter calls on us to separate ourselves from all religious systems in which Christ is not honored as the only Lord and Savior and in which His work is not recognized as the once-for-all offering for sin.

Hebrews teaches us that the types and shadows of the OT system found their fulfillment in our Lord. He is our great High Priest. He is our Sacrifice. He is our Altar. He serves in the heavenly sanctuary and His priesthood will never end.

It teaches that all believers are priests, and that they have instant access into the presence of God by faith at any time. They offer the sacrifices of their person, their praise, and their possessions.

David Baron writes:

> To adopt the model of the Levitical priesthood in the Christian Church, which ritualism endeavors to do, is nothing else but an attempt, with unholy hands, to sew together again the veil which the blessed, reconciled God had Himself rent in twain;

and like saying, "stand aside, come not nigh to God" to those who are "made nigh by the blood of Christ."[39]

The book of Hebrews teaches us that we have a *better* covenant, a *better* Mediator, a *better* hope, *better* promises, a *better* homeland, a *better* priesthood, and *better* possessions — *better* than the best that Judaism could offer. It assures us that we have eternal redemption, eternal salvation, an eternal covenant, and an eternal inheritance.

It warns solemnly against the sin of apostasy. If a person professes to be a Christian, associates with a Christian church, then turns away from Christ and joins those who are enemies of the Lord, it is impossible for such a one to be renewed to repentance.

The Epistle to the Hebrews encourages true Christians to walk by faith and not by sight because this is the life that pleases Christ. It also encourages us to bear up steadfastly under sufferings, trials, and persecutions in order that we might receive the promised reward.

Hebrews teaches that because of their many privileges, Christians have a very special responsibility. The superiorities of Christ make them the most highly favored people in the world. If such privileges are neglected, they will suffer loss accordingly at the Judgment Seat of Christ. More is expected of them than of those who lived under the law; and more will be required in a coming day.

"Therefore let us go forth to Him, outside the camp, bearing His reproach" (13:13). ‡

ENDNOTES

[1](3:6) The NU text omits "firm to the end."

[2](3:18) Arthur T. Pierson, further documentation unavailable.

[3](4:15) Theologians summarize the doctrine as to whether or not Christ could sin in two Latin phrases: "non posse peccare" — *not possible to sin* and "posse non peccare" — *possible not to sin*. The true teaching is *non posse peccare*: He could not sin.

[4](4:16) G. Campbell Morgan, "Choice Gleanings Calendar."

[5](6:2) The words are not the same in the original: The usual word for "bap-

tism" is *baptisma*; here the word is *baptismoi*, "ritual washings."

[6](6:3) The majority text reads, "And let us do this. . . ."

[7](6:6) The NKJV margin is a better translation (since the form and context are the same as the previous clauses): "and have fallen away."

[8](6:18) The majority of mss. read "we have strong consolation" (indicative), rather than "might have strong consolation" (subjunctive). The former is even more certain.

[9](6:20) D. Anderson-Berry, *Pictures in the Acts*, p. 36ff.

[10](7:20) A. W. Rainsbury, "Able to Save to the Uttermost," *The Keswick Week, 1958*, p. 78.

[11](7:21) George Henderson, *Studies in the Epistle to the Hebrews*, p. 86.

[12](8:6) W. H. Griffith Thomas, *Hebrews: A Devotional Commentary*, p. 103.

[13](8:8) Henderson, *Hebrews*, p. 92.

[14](9:4) The word *thumiatērion* is a thing or place for burning incense.

[15](9:11) The NU text reads "that have come."

[16](9:13) J. Gregory Mantle, *Better Things*, p. 109.

[17](9:15) Kenneth S. Wuest, *Hebrews in the Greek New Testament*, p. 162, 163.

[18](10:10) George M. Landis, *Epistle to the Hebrews: On to Maturity*, p. 116.

[19](10:11) Alexander Balmain Bruce, *The Epistle to the Hebrews: The First Apology for Christianity*, p. 34.

[20](10:37) Marvin Vincent, *Word Studies in the New Testament*, II:1150.

[21](10:37) A. J. Pollock, *Modernism Versus the Bible*, p. 19.

[22](10:38) The NU text reads, "my just one."

[23](11:21) C. H. Mackintosh, *Genesis to Deuteronomy: Notes on the Pentateuch*, p. 133.

[24](11:22) William Lincoln, *Lectures on the Epistle to the Hebrews*, p. 106.

[25](11:35) G. H. Morrison, "Morrison on Luke," *The Glasgow Pulpit Series*, I:42.

[26](11:37) The critical (NU) text omits "were tempted."

[27](11:37) William G. Moorehead, *Outline Studies in the New Testament. Philippians to Hebrews*, p. 248.

[28](12:2) A. B. Bruce, *Hebrews*, pp. 415, 416.

[29](12:10) J. H. Jowett, *Life in the Heights*, pp. 247, 248.

[30](12:11) Leslie Weatherhead, *Prescription for Anxiety*, p. 32.

[31](12:11) C. H. Spurgeon, "Choice Gleanings Calendar."

[32](12:13) George Williams, *The Student's Commentary on the Holy Scriptures*, p. 989.

[33](12:13) G. H. Lang, *The Epistle to the Hebrews*, pp. 240, 241.

[34](12:14) Wuest, *Hebrews*, p. 222.

[35](12:20) The words "or shot with an arrow" are lacking in most mss., including the oldest. They are most likely a later addition.

[36](13:2) It is believed that one of these three was the Angel of the LORD, the pre-incarnate Christ.

[37](13:20) Wuest, *Hebrews*, p. 242.

[38](Excursus) C. I. Scofield, *Rightly Dividing the Word of Truth*, p. 17.

[39](Excursus) David Baron, *The New Order of Priesthood*, pp. 39, 40.

BIBLIOGRAPHY

Bruce, Alexander Balmain. *The Epistle to the Hebrews: The First Apology for Christianity*. Edinburgh: T. & T. Clark, 1908.

Govett, Robert. *Christ Superior to Angels, Moses and Aaron*. London: J. Nisbet, 1884.

Henderson, G. D. *Studies in the Epistle to the Hebrews*. Barkingside, England: G. F. Vallance, n.d.

Hewitt, Thomas. *The Epistle to the Hebrews, TBC*. Grand Rapids: Eerdmans, 1960.

Ironside, H. A. *Hebrews and Titus*. Neptune, N.J.: Loizeaux Brothers, 1932.

Kelly, William. *Introductory Lectures to the Epistle to the Hebrews and the Epistle to Philemon*. Oak Park IL: Bible Truth Publishers, n.d.

Landis, G. M. *Epistle to the Hebrews: On to Maturity*. Oak Park: Emmaus Bible School, 1964.

Lang, G. H. *The Epistle to the Hebrews*. London: Paternoster Press, 1951.

Lincoln, William. *Lectures on the Epistle to the Hebrews*. Boston: Believers' Book-Room, n.d.

Mantle, J. Gregory. *"Better Things": A Series of Bible Readings on the Epistle to the Hebrews*. New York: Christian Alliance Publishing Co., 1921.

Meyer, F. B. *The Way into the Holiest*. Grand Rapids: Zondervan Publishing House, 1950.

Moffatt, James. *A Critical and Exegetical Commentary on the Epistle to the Hebrews, ICC*. Edinburgh: T. & T. Clark, 1924.

Moule, H. C. G. *Studies in Hebrews*. Grand Rapids: Kregel Publications, 1977.

Newell, W. R. *Hebrews Verse by Verse*. Chicago: Moody Press, 1947.

Pfeiffer, Charles F. *The Epistle to the Hebrews*. Chicago: Moody Press, 1962.

Rainsbury, A. W. "Able to Save to the Uttermost," *The Keswick Week*. London: Marshall, Morgan and Scott Ltd., 1958.

Thomas, W. H. Griffith. *Hebrews: A Devotional Commentary*. Grand Rapids: Wm. B. Eerdmans Publishing Co., 1961.

Vine, W. E. *The Epistle to the Hebrews*. London: Oliphants Ltd., 1952.

Westcott, B. F. *The Epistle to the Hebrews*. London: MacMillan, 1889.

Wuest, K. S. *Hebrews in the Greek New Testament*. Grand Rapids: Eerdmans Publishing Co., 1947.

THE EPISTLE OF JAMES

Introduction

"[James is] a preacher who speaks like a prophet . . . in language which for forcibleness is without parallel in early Christian literature, excepting the discourses of Jesus."
— Theodor Zahn

I. Unique Place in the Canon

Martin Luther's low estimation of James' Epistle as a "right strawy Epistle" was dead wrong! Luther's misunderstanding of James' teaching on good works amid the Reformer's fierce battle with those who taught salvation by faith plus works caused him to err here. He is not the only one to misjudge this earliest of Christian Letters. Some have called the book "a string of pearls," suggesting there is no cohesion to the Letter, but just several well-developed paragraphs strung together!

Actually, this little book is a masterpiece of didactic writing. It has a strong Jewish flavor, even referring to the Christian assembly (2:2, Gk.) as a "synagogue" — merely the Greek word for congregation — yet soon to be used exclusively for *Jewish* congregations, as today.

James used nature to illustrate spiritual truth thirty times in five short chapters. Here one is reminded of the teaching of our Lord.

This is a very practical Epistle. It deals with some unpopular subjects, such as controlling one's tongue, the danger of kowtowing to the rich, and the need to show that our faith is real by our lives.

II. Authorship[†]

Many Bible names were changed in their journey from Hebrew through Greek, Latin, and French into English. None is more different from its source than "James," which translates Greek

"Iakobos", taken from Hebrew Yaakov ("Jacob"). The name *Jacob* ("James") was very popular among the Jews, and there are four men so named in the NT. Each one has been suggested as the writer of this Epistle, but with varying degrees of likelihood and scholarly support.

1. James *the Apostle*, son of Zebedee and brother of John (Matt. 4:21). If the Apostle James were the author, there would not have been the reluctance to accept this Letter for so long (see below). Also, James was martyred in A.D. 44, which is probably before the book was written.

2. James *the son of Alphaeus* (Matt. 10:3). He is almost *unknown* except that he is in the lists of apostles. The fact that the author could refer to himself as "James" with no distinguishing titles shows he was *well-known* at that time.

3. James *the father of Judas* (not Iscariot, Luke 6:16). This man was even more obscure and can safely be ruled out.

4. James *the half brother of our Lord* (Matt. 13:55; Gal. 1:19). This is almost surely the author of our Epistle. He is well-known, yet modest, since he doesn't mention his physical relationship to Christ (see also Introduction to Jude). This is the man who presided at the Jerusalem Council and stayed at that city until his death. He was notable as a very *Jewish* Christian, extremely strict in lifestyle. In short, he is remembered by history (Josephus) and church tradition as just such a Christian who would have written just such an Epistle.

†See p. i.

External Evidence

James has one of the weakest *external* testimonies, being only *alluded* to, not quoted, by the earliest church fathers. It is also not in the Muratorian Canon. This is probably because it was from Jerusalem, addressed to Eastern Jews and *seemed* to many people to contradict Paul on justification by faith.

However, James is quoted by Cyril of Jerusalem, Gregory of Nazianzus, Athanasius, and Jerome. Eusebius tells us that James was among books spoken against (*antilegomena*) by some Christians, but he himself quoted it as Holy Scripture.

Internal Evidence

The *internal evidence* for James is quite strong. It harmonizes with what we know of James' style from Acts and Galatians, and also with the history of the Dispersion known from other sources. There is no reason to forge such a book; it contains no major doctrinal additions (as a heretical second century forgery invariably does). Josephus tells us that James had a very good reputation for devotion to the law among Jews, but was martyred for witnessing for his Messiah when this was forbidden. This Jewish historian says that James was stoned by order of the high priest Ananias. Eusebius tells us James was thrown from the pinnacle of the temple and finally clubbed to death. Hegesippus combines both these traditions.

The argument that the Greek style of the Epistle of James is "too good" for a Palestinian Jew shows an unbecoming ignorance of the amazing intellectual talents of the chosen people.

III. Date

Josephus says James was killed in 62, so the Letter must predate that. Since the Epistle says nothing of the decisions on the law made at the Jerusalem Council (A.D. 48 or 49) over which meeting James presided (Acts 15), a date between A.D. 45 and 48 is widely accepted.

IV. Background and Themes[†]

While this may be the first book of the NT to be written, and thus has a strongly Jewish flavor, its teachings must not be relegated to another age. They are applicable to us today, and very much needed.

To achieve his goal, James draws heavily on the teachings of the Lord Jesus in the Sermon on the Mount. This will be readily seen by the following comparisons:

Subject	James	Parallel in Matthew
Adversity	1:2,12; 5:10	5:10–12
Prayer	1:5; 4:3; 5:13–18	6:6–13; 7:7–12
The Single Eye	1:8; 4:8	6:22,23
Wealth	1:10,11; 2:6,7	6:19–21, 24–34
Wrath	1:19,20; 4:1	5:22
The Law	1:25; 2:1, 12,13	5:17–44
Mere Profession	1:26,27	6:1–18
The Royal Law	2:8	7:12
Mercy	2:13	5:7
Faith and Works	2:14–26	7:15–27
Root and Fruit	3:11,12	7:16–20
True Wisdom	3:13	7:24
The Peacemaker	3:17,18	5:9
Judging Others	4:11,12	7:1–5
Rusted Treasures	5:2	6:19
Oaths	5:12	5:33–37

There are frequent references to the law in this Letter. It is called "the perfect law" (1:25), "the royal law" (2:8), and "the law of liberty" (2:12). James does not teach that his readers are under law for salvation or as a rule of life. Rather, portions of the law are cited as instruction in righteousness for those who are under grace.

There are many resemblances to the book of Proverbs in James. Like Proverbs, his style is rugged, vivid, graphic, and difficult to outline. The word *wisdom* recurs frequently.

Another key word in James is *breth-*

†*See p. ii.*

ren. It occurs fifteen times, and reminds us that James is writing to believers, even if at times he seems to address the unconverted also.

In some ways, the Letter of James is the most authoritarian in the NT. That is, James issues instructions more profusely than any of the other writers. In the short space of 108 verses, there are fifty-four commands (imperative forms).

OUTLINE

Commentary

I. SALUTATION (1:1)

The writer introduces himself as **James, a bondservant of God and of the Lord Jesus Christ**. If the author was the Lord's half-brother, as we believe, then a wonderful change had come into his life. At one time, he had not believed in the Lord Jesus (John 7:5). He may have shared the view that Jesus was out of His mind (Mark 3:21). But our Lord patiently sowed the seed of the word. Though unappreciated, He taught the great principles of the kingdom of God. Then the seed took root in the life of James. A mighty transformation resulted. The skeptic became a servant. And he wasn't ashamed to say so!

By calling himself **a bondservant of God and of the Lord Jesus Christ**, James correctly puts **God** and **the Lord Jesus** on the same level as equals. He honors the Son just as he honors the Father (John 5:23). James knew that "no man can serve two masters" (Matt. 6:24). Yet he spoke of himself as a servant of God and of the Lord Jesus. There is no contradiction here because God the Father and God the Son are co-equal.

The Letter is addressed **to the twelve tribes which are scattered abroad**, literally which are in the Dispersion (Gk., *Diaspora*). These people were Jews by birth, belonging to the **twelve tribes** of Israel. Because of Israel's sin, the people had been driven from their native land and were now dispersed in the countries surrounding the Mediterranean. The *original* dispersion took place when the ten tribes were carried into captivity by the Assyrians, 721 B.C. Some of these returned to the land in the days of Ezra and Nehemiah, but only a remnant. On the Day of Pentecost, devout Jews were visiting Jerusalem from every nation of the then-known world (Acts 2:4). These could properly be called Jews of the Dispersion. But a later dispersion of *Christian* Jews took place. In Acts 8:1, we read that the early Christians (mostly of Jewish ancestry) were scattered abroad throughout Judea and Samaria by the persecutions of Saul. This dispersion is referred to again where we read that believers were driven to Phoenicia, Cyprus, and Antioch. Therefore, the people to whom James wrote could have been Jews who had been dispersed in any one of these crisis times.

Since all true believers are strangers and pilgrims in this world (Phil. 3:20; 1 Pet. 2:11), we can apply this Letter to ourselves, even if it wasn't written directly to us.

A more difficult question is whether James is addressing non-Christian Jews, Jews who had been converted to Christ, or both believing and unbelieving Jews. Primarily the author seems to be writing to true, born again believers (1:18). Yet there are times when he seems to be addressing professing Christians or even the unconverted. This is one of the proofs of the very early date of the Letter: the rift between Hebrew Christians and unbelieving Jews was not yet an accomplished fact.

II. TRIALS AND TEMPTATIONS (1:2–17)

1:2 In this section James deals with the subject of temptation. He uses the word in two different senses. In verses 2–12, the temptations are what we might call *holy* **trials** or problems which are sent from God, and which test the reality of our faith and produce likeness to Christ. In verses 13–17, on the other hand, the subject is *unholy temptations*, which come from within, and which lead to sin. The Christian life is filled with problems. They come uninvited and unexpected. Sometimes they come singly and sometimes in droves. They are inevitable. James does not say *"if* **you fall into various trials"** but **when**. We can never get away from them. The question is, "What are we going to do about them?"

There are several possible attitudes we can take toward these testings and **trials** of life. We can rebel against them (Heb. 12:5) by adopting a spirit of defiance, boasting that we will battle through to victory by our own power. On the other hand, we can lose heart or give up under pressure (Heb. 12:5). This is nothing but fatalism. It leads to questioning even the Lord's care for us. Again, we can grumble and complain about our troubles. This is what Paul warns us against in 1 Corinthians 10:10. Another option — we can indulge in

self-pity, thinking of no one but ourselves, and trying to get sympathy from others. Or better, we can be exercised by the difficulties and perplexities of life (Heb. 12:11). We can say, in effect, "God has allowed this trial to come to me. He has some good purpose in it for me. I don't know what that purpose is, but I'll try to find out. I want His purposes to be worked out in my life." This is what James advocates: **"My brethren, count it all joy when you fall into various trials."** Don't rebel! Don't faint! Rejoice! These problems are not enemies, bent on destroying you. They are friends which have come to aid you to develop Christian character.

God is trying to produce Christlikeness in each of His children. This process necessarily involves suffering, frustration, and perplexity. The fruit of the Spirit cannot be produced when all is sunshine; there must be rain and dark clouds. Trials never seem pleasant; they seem very difficult and disagreeable. But afterwards they yield the peaceable fruit of righteousness to those who are trained by them (Heb. 12:11). How often we hear a Christian say, after passing through some great crisis, "It wasn't easy to take, but I wouldn't give up the experience for anything."

1:3 James speaks of **the testing of your faith**. He pictures faith as a precious metal which is being tried by the Assayer (God) to see if it is genuine. The metal is subjected to the fires of persecution, sickness, suffering, or sorrow. Without problems, we would never develop endurance. Even men of the world realize that problems strengthen character. Charles Kettering, noted industrialist, once said, "Problems are the price of progress. Don't bring me anything but problems. Good news weakens me."

1:4 **"But let patience have its perfect work,"** says James. Sometimes when problems come we become desperate and use frantic means to cut short the trial. Without consulting the Lord as to His purposes in the matter, we rush to the doctor, for instance, and gulp down large doses of medicine in order to shorten the trial. By doing this, we actually may be thwarting God's program in our lives. And it is just possible that we may have to undergo a longer trial in the future before His particular purpose is realized in us. We should not short-circuit the development of endurance in our lives. By cooperating with God we will become mature, well-rounded Christians, **lacking** in none of the graces of the Spirit.

We should never become despondent or discouraged when passing through trials. No problem is too great for our Father. Some problems in life are never removed. We must learn to accept them and to prove His grace sufficient. Paul asked the Lord three times to remove a physical infirmity. The Lord did not remove it, but gave Paul the grace to bear it (2 Cor. 12:8–10).

When we face problems in life that God obviously isn't going to remove, we should be submissive to His will. The gifted blind hymn-writer wrote these lines as a girl of eight:

> O what a happy soul am I
> Although I cannot see;
> I am resolved that in this world
> Contented I will be.
> How many blessings I enjoy
> That other people don't.
> To weep and sigh because I'm blind
> I cannot and I won't.
> — *Fanny Crosby*

Peace comes through submission to the will of God.

Some problems in life are removed when we have learned our lessons from them. As soon as the Refiner sees His reflection in the molten metal, He turns off the heat. Most of us lack wisdom to view the pressures of life from God's standpoint. We adopt a short-range view, occupying ourselves with the immediate discomfort. We forget that God's unhurried purpose is to enlarge us through pressure (Ps. 4:1, JND).

1:5 We don't have to face the problems of life in our own wisdom. **If**, in the time of trial, we lack spiritual insight, we should go to God and tell Him all about our perplexity and ignorance. All who are thus exercised to find God's purposes in the trials will be **liberally** rewarded. And they need not worry that God will scold them either; He is pleased when we are teachable and tractable. We all lack **wisdom**. The Bible does not give *specific* answers to the innumerable problems that arise in life. It does not solve

problems in so many words, but God's word does give us general principles. We must apply these principles to problems as they arise day by day. That is why we need wisdom. Spiritual wisdom is the practical application of our Lord's teachings to everyday situations.

1:6–8 We must approach God **in faith, with no doubting**. We must believe He loves and cares, and that nothing is impossible with Him. If we doubt His goodness and His power, we will have no stability in time of trouble. One minute we might be resting calmly on His promises, but the next we will feel that God has forgotten to be kind. We will be like the surge **of the sea**, rising to great heights, then falling back into valleys — troubled **and tossed**. God is not honored by the kind of faith that alternates between optimism and pessimism. He does not give divine insight to such vacillating, unstable men (vv. 7, 8). In verses 5–8, the source of wisdom is God; it is obtained by prayer; it is available to everybody; it is given liberally and without reproach; the crucial condition is that we **ask in faith, with no doubting**.

1:9 At first glance, verses 9–11 seem to introduce a completely new subject, or at least a parenthesis. James, however, is continuing with the subject of holy trials by giving specific illustrations. Whether a man is poor or rich, he can derive lasting spiritual benefits from the calamities and crises of life. For instance, when a **lowly brother** finds himself dissatisfied and discouraged, he can always rejoice that he is an heir of God, and a joint heir with Jesus Christ. He can find consolation in the truth that all things are his, and he is Christ's and Christ is God's. **The lowly brother** probably has no control over his humble circumstances. There is no reason to believe he is lazy or careless. But God has seen fit to place him in a low income bracket and that is where he has been ever since. Perhaps if he had been rich, he never would have accepted Christ. Now that he is in Christ, he is blessed with all spiritual blessings in the heavenlies. What should he do? Should he rebel against his station in life? Should he become bitter and jealous? No, he should accept from God the circumstances over which he has no control and rejoice in his spiritual blessings.

Too many Christians go through life rebelling against their sex, their age, their height, and even against life itself. Girls with a flair for baseball wish they were boys. Young people wish they were older, and old people want to be younger. Short people envy those who are tall, and tall ones wish they weren't so conspicuous. Some people even say, "I wish I were dead!" All this is absurd! The Christian attitude is to accept from God things which we cannot change. They are God's destiny for us, and we should make the most of them for His glory and for the blessing of others. We should say with the Apostle Paul: "By the grace of God I am what I am" (1 Cor. 15:10). As we forget our disabilities and lose ourselves in service for others, we will come to realize that spiritual people love us for what we are, not for our appearance, for instance.

1:10, 11 Next James turns to **the rich**. But strangely enough he does not say, "Let the rich man rejoice in his riches." Rather he says that the rich can rejoice that he is made low. He agrees with Jeremiah 9:23, 24:

Let not the wise man glory in his wisdom, let not the mighty man glory in his might, nor let the rich man glory in his riches; but let him who glories glory in this, that he understands and knows Me, that I am the LORD, exercising lovingkindness, judgment, and righteousness in the earth. For in these things I delight, says the LORD.

The rich man may actually find real cause for rejoicing should he be stripped of his material possessions. Perhaps business reverses would bring him to the Lord. Or if he is already a Christian, then he could take joyfully the spoiling of his goods knowing he has in heaven a better and more enduring possession (Heb. 10:34). Earthly riches are destined to pass away, like the **flower of the field** (Isa. 40:6, 7). If a man has nothing but material wealth, then all his plans will end at the grave. James dwells on the transiency of **grass** as an illustration of the fleeting life of a rich man and the limited value of his riches. He **will fade away in** the midst of **his pursuits**. The point is, of course, that neither sun nor

scorching wind can affect *spiritual* values. Any trial that weans us away from the love of passing things and sets our affections on things above is a blessing in disguise. Thus the same grace that exalts the lowly humbles the rich. Both are cause for rejoicing.

1:12 In concluding his discussion of holy trials, James pronounces a blessing on the person who stands up under afflictions. When such a man has stood the test or **has been approved, he will receive the crown of life. The crown** here is not the king's diadem but the victor's wreath, to be awarded at the Judgment Seat of Christ. There is no suggestion, of course, that eternal life is the reward for enduring testings, but those who have endured with fortitude will be honored for that kind of life, and will enjoy a deeper appreciation of eternal life in heaven. Everyone's cup will be full in heaven but people will have different sized cups — different capacities for enjoying heaven. This is probably what is in view in the expression **crown of life**; it refers to a fuller enjoyment of the glories of heaven.

Now let us make this section on holy trials practical in our own lives. How do we react when various forms of testing come into our lives? Do we complain bitterly against the misfortunes of life, or do we rejoice and thank the Lord for them? Do we advertise our trials or do we bear them quietly? Do we live in the future, waiting for our circumstances to improve, or do we live in the present, seeking to see the hand of God in all that comes to us? Do we indulge in self-pity and seek sympathy or do we submerge self in a life of service for others?

1:13 The subject now shifts to *unholy* temptations (vv. 13–17). Just as holy trials are designed to bring out the best in us, so unholy temptations are designed to bring out the worst in us. One thing must be clearly understood. When we are **tempted** to sin, the temptation does *not* come from **God**. God does test or try men, as far as their faith is concerned, but He never tempts a man to commit any form of evil. **He Himself** has no dealings with **evil**, and He does not entice to sin.

1:14 Man is always ready to shift responsibility for his sins. If he cannot blame God, he will adopt an approach of modern psychology by saying that sin is a sickness. In this way he hopes to escape judgment. But sin is not a sickness; it is a moral failure for which man must give account. Some even try to blame inanimate things for sin. But material "things" are not sinful in themselves. Sin does not originate there. James tracks the lion to its den when he says: **"Each one is tempted when he is drawn away by his own desires and enticed."** Sin comes from within us, from our old, evil, fallen, unregenerate nature. Jesus said, "Out of the heart proceed evil thoughts, murders, adulteries, fornications, thefts, false witness, blasphemies" (Matt. 15:19).

The word James uses for **desires** in verse 14 could refer to any form of desire, good or evil. The word itself is morally neutral. But with few exceptions it is used in the NT to describe evil desires, and that is certainly the case here. Lust is likened to an evil woman here parading her allurements and enticing her victims. Every one of us is tempted. We have vile lusts and impure appetites constantly urging us on in sin. Are we helpless victims then, when we are **drawn away by** our **own desires and enticed**? No, we may expel all thoughts of sin from our mind and concentrate on subjects that are pure and holy (Phil. 4:8). Also in the moment of fierce temptation, we may call on the Lord, remembering that "The name of the Lord is a strong tower: the righteous run to it, and are safe" (Prov. 18:10).

1:15 If that is so, why then do we sin? Here is the answer: **Then, when desire has conceived, it gives birth to sin**. Instead of expelling the vile thought, we may encourage, nourish, and enjoy it. This act of acquiescence is likened to sexual intercourse. Lust conceives and a hideous baby named SIN is born. Which is another way of saying that if we think about a forbidden act long enough, we will eventually do it. The whole process of lust conceiving and bringing forth sin is vividly illustrated in the incident of David and Bathsheba (2 Sam. 11:1–27).

And sin, when it is full-grown, brings forth death, says James. Sin is not a barren, sterile thing; it produces a brood of its own. The statement that **sin** produces **death** may be understood in several ways. First of all, the sin of Adam brought physical death on himself and on all his posterity (Gen. 2:17). But sin also leads to eternal, spiritual death — the final separation of the person from God and from blessing (Rom. 6:23a). There is a sense also in which sin results in death for a believer. For instance, in 1 Timothy 5:6 we read that a believing widow who lives in pleasure is dead while she lives. This means that she is wasting her life and utterly failing to fulfill the purpose for which God saved her. To be out of fellowship with God is for a Christian a form of living death.

1:16, 17 It is not unusual for people who fall into sin to blame God instead of themselves. They say, in effect, to their Creator, "Why have you made me this way?" But this is a form of self-deception. Only good gifts come from God. In fact, He is the source of **every good and every perfect gift**.

James describes God as **the Father of lights**. In the Bible the word *Father* sometimes has the meaning of Creator or Source (see Job 38:28). Therefore God is the Creator or Source **of lights**. But what is meant by **lights**? Certainly it includes the heavenly bodies — the sun, moon, and stars (Gen. 1:14–18; Ps. 136:7). But God is also the Source of all spiritual light as well. So we should think of Him as the Source of every form of light in the universe. **With whom there is no variation or shadow of turning**. God is unlike the heavenly bodies He has created. They are undergoing constant changes. He never does. Perhaps James is thinking not only of the declining brilliance of the sun and stars, but also of their changing relation to the earth as our planet rotates. Variableness characterizes the sun, moon, and stars. The expression **shadow of turning** may mean **shadow** caused by **turning**. This could have reference to the shadows cast on earth by the rotation of the earth around the sun. Or it could refer to eclipses. A solar eclipse, for instance, is produced when the moon's shadow falls on the earth. With God it is quite different; there is no variableness in Him, or **shadow** caused by **turning**. And His gifts are as **perfect** as Himself. Therefore it is unthinkable that He would ever entice man to sin. Temptation comes from man's own evil nature.

Let us test our faith on the subject of unholy temptations. Do we encourage evil thoughts to linger in our minds, or do we expel them quickly? When we sin, do we say that we couldn't help it? Do we blame God when we are tempted to sin?

III. THE WORD OF GOD (1:18–27)

James has been speaking of God as the Father of lights. Now he reminds us that He is our Father also, and that He has given us a unique role in His vast creation. We can fulfill that role by obedience to the word of truth (vv. 19–27).

1:18 This passage outlines the part played in the new birth by the word of God as it is applied to us by the Holy Spirit. We are told that **"Of His own will He brought us forth by the word of truth, that we might be a kind of firstfruits of His creatures." Of His own will** — this tells us what prompted Him to save us. He was not forced to do it by any merit in us. He did it **of His own** free **will**. His love to us was unmerited, unbought and unsought. It was entirely voluntary on His part. This should cause us to worship! **He brought us forth** — this describes the fact of the new birth. By this spiritual birth we become His children — a relationship that can never be changed since a birth can never be undone. **By the word of truth** — the Bible is the instrument of the new birth. In every genuine case of conversion, the Scriptures are involved, whether orally or in printed form. Apart from the Bible, we would not know the way of salvation. Indeed, we would not even know that salvation was available!

That we might be a kind of firstfruits of his creatures — there are three prominent thoughts in connection with the word **firstfruits**. First, the **firstfruits** of a harvest was the first sheaf of ripened grain. The Christians to whom James was writing were among the first believers in the Christian Dispensation. Of course, all believers are **a kind of firstfruits** of His creatures, but the pri-

mary reference is to the Jewish Christians to whom James wrote. Second, **the firstfruits** were offered to God in gratitude for His bounty and in recognition that all comes from Him and belongs to Him. Thus, all believers should present themselves to God as living sacrifices (Rom. 12:1, 2). Third, the **firstfruits** were a pledge of the full harvest to come. James likened his readers to the first sheaves of grain in Christ's harvest. They would be followed by others down through the centuries, but they were set forth as pattern saints to exhibit the fruits of the new creation. Eventually the Lord will populate the whole earth with others like them (Rom. 8:19–23). The full harvest will come when the Lord Jesus returns to reign over the earth. In the meantime, they were to yield the same kind of obedience to Christ which all the world will yield during the Millennium. And though the passage refers primarily to first-century Christians, yet it has an application for each one of us who honors the name of Christ.

1:19a The rest of this chapter gives practical instructions as to how we can be firstfruits of His creatures. It sets forth the practical righteousness which should characterize those who have been born again by the Word of Truth. We know that we were begotten by the word in order to manifest the truth of God. **So then**,[2] let us now discharge our responsibility.

We should **be swift to hear**. This is an unusual command, with almost a trace of humor in it. It's like saying, "Hurry up and hear!" It means that we should be ready **to hear** the word of God, as well as all godly counsel and admonition. We should be teachable by the Holy Spirit. We should be **slow to speak**. It is surprising how much James has to say about our speech! He cautions us to be guarded in our conversation. Even nature itself teaches us this. Epictetus noticed so long ago: "Nature has given to man one tongue, but two ears, that we may hear from others twice as much as we speak." Solomon would have agreed heartily with James. He once said, "He who guards his mouth preserves his life, but he who opens wide his lips shall have destruction" (Prov.

13:3). He also said, "In the multitude of words sin is not lacking, but he who restrains his lips is wise" (Prov. 10:19). Compulsive talkers eventually transgress.

1:19b, 20 We should be **slow to wrath**. A man who is quick-tempered **does not produce the** kind of **righteousness** which **God** expects from His children. Those who lose their temper give people a wrong impression about Christianity. It is still true that "he who is slow to anger is better than the mighty; and he who rules his spirit than he who takes a city" (Prov. 16:32).

1:21 Another way to manifest ourselves as firstfruits of His creatures is to **lay aside all filthiness and overflow of wickedness**. These vices are likened to soiled garments which are to be set aside once for all. **Filthiness** includes every form of impurity, whether spiritual, mental, or physical. The expression **"overflow of wickedness"** may refer to those forms of evil which are a holdover from our unconverted days. It may refer to sins which **overflow** from our lives and touch the lives of others. Or it may refer to abounding evil, in which case James is not so much describing an excess of evil, but the intensely wicked character which evil has. The over-all meaning is clear. In order to receive the truth of the word of God, we must be morally clean.

Another requirement for the reception of divine truth is **meekness**. It is all too possible to read the Bible without letting it speak to us. We can study it in an academic way without being affected by it. Our pride and hardness and sin make us unreceptive and unresponsive. Only those with submissive, humble spirits can expect to derive the maximum benefit from the Scriptures. "The humble He guides in justice, and the humble He teaches His way" (Ps. 25:9). "But on this one I will look: on him who is poor and of a contrite spirit, and who trembles at My word" (Isa. 66:2).

James speaks of the Scriptures as **the implanted word, which is able to save your souls**. The thought is that the word becomes a sacred deposit in the Christian's life when he is born again. The margin of the RV reads "the inborn word." This word is able to **save your souls**. The Bible is the instrument God uses in the new birth. He uses it in saving the soul not only from the penalty of sin, but from its power as well. He uses it in saving us not only from damnation in eternity, but from damage in *this life*.[3] It is doubtless this present, continuing aspect of salvation James is speaking of in verse 21.

1:22 It is not enough to receive the implanted word; we must obey it. There is no virtue in possessing the Bible or even in reading it as literature. There must be a deep desire to hear God speaking to us and an unquestioning willingness to do whatever He says. We must translate the Bible into action. The word must become flesh in our lives. There should never be a time when we go to the Scriptures without allowing them to change our lives for the better. To profess great love for God's word or even to pose as a Bible student is a form of self-deception unless our increasing knowledge of the word is producing increasing likeness to the Lord Jesus. To go on gaining an intellectual knowledge of the Bible without obeying it can be a trap instead of a blessing. If we continually learn what we ought to do, but do not do it, we become depressed, frustrated, and callous. "Impression without expression leads to depression." Also we become more responsible to God. The ideal combination is to read the word and obey it implicitly.

1:23, 24 Anyone who hears **the word** but does not change his behavior **is like a man** who takes a fleeting glance in the mirror each morning, then completely **forgets what** he saw. He derives no benefit from the mirror or from looking into it. Of course, there are some things about our appearance that cannot be changed. But at least we should be humbled by the sight! And when the mirror says "Wash" or "Shave" or "Comb" or "Brush," we should at least do as we are told. Otherwise the mirror is of no practical benefit to us.

It is easy to read the Bible casually or because of a sense of duty without being affected by what we read. We see what we ought to be but we quickly forget and live as if we were already perfect. This type of self-satisfaction prevents spiritual progress.

1:25 In contrast is the man **who looks into the** word of God and who habitually reduces it to practice. His contemplative, meditative gazing has practical results in his life. To him the Bible is **the perfect law of liberty**. Its precepts are not burdensome. They tell him to do exactly what his new nature loves to do. As he obeys, he finds true freedom from human traditions and carnal reasonings. The truth makes him free. This is the man who benefits from the Bible. He does not forget what he has read. Rather he seeks to live it out in daily practice. His simple childlike obedience brings incalculable blessing to his soul. **This one will be blessed in what he does**.

1:26, 27 **Useless religion** and **pure and undefiled religion** are contrasted. **Religion** here means the external patterns of behavior connected with religious belief. It refers to the outward forms rather than the inward spirit. It means the outer expression of belief in worship and service rather than the doctrines believed.

Anyone who **thinks he is religious**, but cannot control **his tongue, . . . this one's religion is useless**. He might observe all kinds of religious ceremonies which make him appear very pious. But he is deceiving himself. God is not satisfied with rituals; He is interested in a life of practical godliness.

An unbridled **tongue** is only one example of futile **religion**. Any behavior inconsistent with the Christian faith is worthless. The story is told of a grocer who apparently was a pious fraud. He lived in an apartment above his store. Every morning he would call down to his assistant, "John!"

"Yes, sir."

"Have you watered down the milk?"

"Yes, sir."

"Have you colored the butter?"

"Yes, sir."

"Have you put chicory in the coffee?"

"Yes, sir."

"Very well. Come up for morning devotions!"

James says that such **religion is useless**.

What God is looking for is the practical type of godliness which takes a compassionate interest in others and keeps one's own life clean. As examples of **pure and undefiled religion**, James praises the man who visits needy **orphans and widows**, and who keeps himself **unspotted from the world**.

In other words, the practical outworking of the new birth is found in "acts of grace and a walk of separation." Guy King describes these virtues as practical love and practical holiness.

We should put *our own faith* on trial with the following questions: Do I read the Bible with a humble desire to have God rebuke me, teach me, and change me? Am I anxious to have my tongue bridled? Do I justify my temper or do I want victory over it? How do I react when someone starts to tell an off-color joke? Does my faith manifest itself in deeds of kindness to those who cannot repay me?

IV. CONDEMNATION OF PARTIALITY (2:1–13)

The first half of chapter 2 denounces the practice of showing respect of persons. Favoritism is utterly foreign to the example of the Lord or to the teachings of the NT. There is no place in Christianity for snobbishness or discrimination.

2:1 First of all, the practice is distinctly forbidden. Note first that the admonition is addressed to believers; we are assured of this by the salutation **"My brethren." The faith of our Lord Jesus Christ** refers to the Christian faith. It is not a question of His trust or dependence, but rather of the body of truth which He gave to us. Putting all these thoughts together, we find that James is saying, **"My brethren**, in your practice of the Christian **faith**, do not show **partiality."** Snobbery and caste distinctions are utterly inconsistent with true Christianity. Servility to human greatness has no place in the presence of the Lord of Glory. Contempt for others because of birth, race, sex, or poverty is a practical denial of the faith. This commandment does not contradict other portions of the NT where believers are taught to pay proper respect to rulers, masters, elders, and parents. There are certain divinely ordained relationships which must be recognized (Rom. 13:7). In this passage it is a matter of showing obsequious deference to people because of their expensive clothing or other artificial distinctions.

2:2–4 This is confirmed by the vivid illustration which James gives in verses 2–4. Guy King has cleverly entitled this section "The Shortsighted Usher." The scene is the local **assembly**¹ of Christians. A distinguished looking gentleman, with fashionable clothing and expensive **gold rings** has just arrived. The usher bows and scrapes, then escorts the notable visitor to a prominent, conspicuous seat in the front. As soon as the usher gets back to the door, he finds that another visitor has arrived. This time it is **a poor man** in humble attire. (The expression **filthy clothes** does not necessarily mean that the man's clothes needed cleaning. He is dressed poorly, in keeping with his humble circumstances in life.) This time the usher adroitly seeks to save the congregation from embarrassment by offering the visitor standing room at the rear, or a place on the floor, in front of his own seat. It seems incredible that anyone would ever act in this way. We would like to think that the illustration is overdrawn, but when we look into our own heart, we find that we often do make these artificial class distinctions among ourselves, and thus **become judges with evil thoughts**.

Probably the most glaring example of it in the church today is the discrimination shown against people of other races and colors. Black believers have been ostracized in many instances or at least made to feel unwelcome. Converted Jews have not always been accepted cordially. Oriental Christians have tasted discrimination in varying degrees. It is admitted that there are enormous social problems in the whole area of racial relations. But the Christian must be true to divine principles. His obligation is to give practical expression to the truth that all believers are one in Christ Jesus.

2:5, 6a Partiality is utterly incongruous with the Christian faith. James demonstrates this in verses 5–13. He gives four strong reasons why it is ridiculous for a believer to favor the rich and look down on the poor.

First of all, it means that we dishonor a man whom **God** honors. **God** has **chosen the poor** people **of this world to be**

rich in faith and heirs of the kingdom which He promised to those who love Him. The poor are God's elect, God's elite, heirs of God, and lovers of God. Repeatedly we find in Scripture that it is the poor people, not the rich, who rally to the banner of Christ. Our Lord Himself said, "The poor have the gospel preached to them" (Matt. 11:5). It was the common people who heard Him gladly, not the wealthy or aristocratic (Mark 12:37). Not many noble are called, but the foolish, the weak, the base, the despised, and the insignificant (1 Cor. 1:26–29). Rich people are ordinarily poor in faith, because they trust their riches instead of the Lord. On the other hand, poor people have been **chosen** by God **to be rich in faith**. A survey of the citizens of His kingdom would reveal that most of them have been poor. In the kingdom, they will occupy positions of wealth and glory. How foolish, then, and how perilous it is to treat with contempt those who will one day be exalted in the kingdom of our Lord and Savior.

2:6b A second reason why it is foolish to show deference to **the rich** is that, as a class, they are the ones who have characteristically oppressed the people of God. The argument is involved, and even a little confusing at this point. The rich man referred to earlier in the chapter was undoubtedly a believer. That does not mean that the rich men mentioned in verse 6 are believers also. What James is saying is simply this: "Why show favoritism to people just because they are rich? If you do, you are honoring those who have been the first to bully you **and** to **drag you into the courts**." Calvin captured the argument tersely when he said, "Why honor your executioners?"

2:7 A third reason why it is foolish to be partial toward the rich is that they habitually use evil or harsh speech involving the name of Christ. This is the **noble name by which** believers **are called** — Christians, or followers of Christ. While railing against the Lord is not a sin on which the rich have a monopoly, yet it is true that those who persecute poor believers often accompany this persecution with the vilest language against the Savior. So why should believers show special favoritism toward anyone simply because he is rich? The traits which accompany riches are not ordinarily honoring to the Lord Jesus. The expression **that noble name by which you are called** might also be translated "that noble name which has been called upon you." Some see this as a reference to Christian baptism. Believers are baptized in the name of the Lord Jesus. This is the very **name** which the rich habitually **blaspheme**.

2:8 James' fourth argument is that showing deference to the rich violates **the law** that **"You shall love your neighbor as yourself."** It is called **the royal law** because it belongs to the King and because it is the king of all laws. Perhaps the usher excused his action toward the rich man by saying that he was just trying to love his neighbor as himself. But that wouldn't excuse his action toward the poor man. If we really loved our neighbors as ourselves, we would treat them all the way we would want to be treated. Certainly *we* would not want to be despised simply because we were poor. Then we should not show contempt to others for this reason.

Of all the teachings of the Bible this is certainly one of the most revolutionary — **You shall love your neighbor as yourself**. Think what it means! It means that we should care for others as we care for ourselves. We should be willing to share our material possessions with those who are not as privileged as we are. And above all, we should do all in our power to see that they have the opportunity to know our blessed Savior. Too often our decisions are based on how our actions affect ourselves. We are self-centered. We cater to the rich because of the hope of reward, either socially or materially. We neglect the poor because there is little prospect of their benefiting us in this way. **The royal law** forbids such selfish exploitation of others. It teaches us to **love** our **neighbor as** ourselves. And if we ask, "Who is my neighbor?" we learn from the story of the Good Samaritan (Luke 10:29–37) that our neighbor is any person who has a need which we can help to meet.

2:9 To **show partiality** is a violation of the royal law. It is both **sin** and transgression. **Sin** is any lack of conformity to the will of God, a failure to meet His

standards. Transgression is the breaking of a known law. Certain acts are sinful because they are basically and inherently wrong, but they become transgressions when there is a specific law which forbids them. **Partiality** is sinful because it is essentially wrong in itself. But it is also transgression because there is a law against it.

2:10 To break **one** part of the law is to be **guilty of all**. The law is like a chain of ten links. Break one link and the chain is broken. God does not allow us to keep the laws we like, and break others.

2:11 The same God who forbade **adultery also** forbade **murder**. A man may not be guilty of **adultery**, yet he may commit **murder**. Is he **a transgressor of the law**? Certainly he is! The spirit of the law is that we should love our neighbor as ourselves. **Adultery** is certainly a violation of this, but so is **murder**. And so is snobbishness and discrimination. If we commit any of these sins, we have failed to do what the law commands.

THE TEN COMMANDMENTS

Now we must pause in our discussion to consider a basic problem which arises at this point in James' argument. The problem is this: "Are Christians under the law or are they not?" It certainly seems that James has been enforcing the Ten Commandments on Christian believers. He specifically refers to the sixth and seventh commandments which forbid murder and adultery. Also he summarizes the last five commandments in the words: "You shall love your neighbor as yourself." Yet to put believers under the law, as a rule of life, contradicts other portions of the NT, such as Romans 6:14 — "You are not under law, but under grace"; Romans 7:6 — "We have been delivered from the law"; Romans 7:4 — "You also have become dead to the law through the body of Christ" (see also Gal. 2:19; 3:13, 24, 25; 1 Tim. 1:8, 9; Heb. 7:19.) The fact that Christians are not under the Ten Commandments is distinctly stated in 2 Corinthians 3:7–11.

Why then does James press the matter of the law on believers in this Age of Grace? First of all, Christians are *not* under the law as a rule of life. Christ, not the law, is the believer's pattern. Where there is law, there must also be penalty. The penalty for breaking the law is death. Christ died to pay the penalty of the broken law. Those who are in Christ are therefore delivered from the law and its penalty. But certain principles of the law *are* of abiding value. These precepts apply to all people of all ages. Idolatry, adultery, murder, and theft are basically and inherently wrong. They are just as wrong for believers as for unbelievers. Furthermore, nine of the Ten Commandments are repeated in the Epistles. The only one that is not repeated is the one concerning the Sabbath. Nowhere are Christians ever told to keep the Sabbath or seventh day of the week, for that commandment is ceremonial rather than moral. It was not basically wrong in itself for a Jew to work on the seventh day. It was wrong only because God set that day apart.

Finally, it should be mentioned that the nine commandments which are repeated in the Epistles are not given as *law* but as instruction in righteousness for the people of God. In other words, God does not say to Christians, "If you steal, you are condemned to death." Or "If you commit an immoral act, you will lose your salvation." Rather He says: "I have saved you by My grace. Now I want you to live a holy life out of love to Me. If you want to know what I expect of you, you will find it throughout the NT. There you will find nine of the Ten Commandments repeated. But you will also find the teachings of the Lord Jesus which actually call for *a higher standard of conduct than the law required.*" So James is not really putting believers under the law and its condemnation. He is not saying, "If you show respect of persons, you are breaking the law, and are thus condemned to death." ‡

2:12 What James is saying is, "As believers, you are no longer under the law of bondage, but you are under **the law of liberty — liberty** to do what is right. The Law of Moses required you to love your neighbor but did not give you the power, and condemned you if you failed. Under grace, you are given the power to love your neighbor and are re-

warded when you do it. You don't do it in order to be saved but because you are saved. You do it, not through fear of punishment, but through love for Him who died for you and rose again. When you stand before the Judgment Seat of Christ, you will be rewarded or suffer loss according to this standard. It will not be a question of salvation but of reward." The expression **"So speak and so do"** refers to words and deeds. Both profession and life should agree. In speech and act, believers should avoid partiality. Such violations of the law of liberty will be judged at the Judgment Seat of Christ.

2:13 Verse 13 must be understood in the light of the context. James is speaking to believers. There is no question of eternal punishment here; that penalty was paid once for all at Calvary's cross. Here it is a question of God's dealing with us in this world as children. If we do not show **mercy** to others, we are not walking in fellowship with God and can expect to suffer the consequences of a backslidden condition.

Mercy triumphs over judgment may mean that God would rather show **mercy** to us than discipline us (Mic. 7:18); judgment is His "strange work." It may mean we can rejoice in the face of judgment if we have shown mercy to others, but if we have not shown mercy to those whom we might justly condemn, we will not be shown mercy. Or it may mean that **mercy triumphs over judgment** in the sense that it is always greater than judgment. The general idea seems to be that if we show mercy to others, the judgment which might otherwise fall on us will be replaced by mercy.

Let us test ourselves then on this important subject of partiality. Do we show more kindness to those of our own race than those of other races? Are we more kindly disposed to the young than to the old? Are we more outgoing to good-looking people than to those who are plain or homely? Are we more anxious to befriend prominent people than those who are comparatively unknown? Do we avoid people with physical infirmities and seek the companionship of the strong and healthy? Do we favor the rich over the poor? Do we give the "cold shoulder" to "foreigners," those who speak our language with a foreign accent?

As we answer these questions, let us remember that the way we treat the least lovable believer is the way we treat the Savior (Matt. 25:40).

V. FAITH AND WORKS (2:14–26)

These verses are perhaps the most controversial in James' Letter. Even such a great worthy of the church as Luther thought he saw an irreconcilable conflict between James' teaching on justification by works and Paul's insistence on justification by faith. These verses are commonly misused to support the heresy that we are saved by faith plus works, called "synergism." In other words, we must trust the Lord Jesus as our Savior, but that is not enough. We must also add to His redemptive work our own deeds of charity and devotion.

The section might actually be entitled "Justification by Works," because there is a sense in which we *are* justified by works. In fact, in order to grasp the full truth of justification, we should clearly understand that there are six aspects of justification. We are justified by *grace* (Rom. 3:24). This simply means that we do not deserve to be justified; in fact, we deserve the very opposite. We are justified by *faith* (Rom. 5:1). Faith is the human response to God's grace. By faith, we accept the free gift. Faith is that which appropriates what God has done for us. We are justified by *blood* (Rom. 5:9). Here blood is the price which had to be paid in order to procure our justification. The debt of sin was met by the precious blood of Christ, and now God can justify ungodly sinners because a righteous satisfaction has been made. We are justified by *God* (Rom. 8:33). The truth here is that God is the Person who justifies. We are justified by *power* (Rom. 4:25). Our justification is linked to the power that raised Christ from the dead. His resurrection proves that God is satisfied. And we are justified by *works* (Jas. 2:24). Works are the outward proof of the reality of our faith. They give outward expression to what would otherwise be invisible. From this we see that the person is justified by grace, by faith, by

blood, by God, by power, and by works. Yet there is no contradiction at all. These statements simply present different aspects of the same truth. Grace is the principle upon which God justifies; faith is the means by which man receives it; blood is the price which the Savior had to pay; God is the active Agent in justification; power is the proof; and works are the result.

2:14 James insists that a faith that does not result in good works cannot save. There are two keys which greatly help in the understanding of this verse. First of all, James does *not* say "What does it profit . . . though a man has faith . . . ." Rather he says, **What does it profit . . . if someone says he has faith**. In other words, it is not a question of a man who truly *has* faith, and yet is not saved. James is describing the man who has nothing but a profession of faith. He *says* he has faith, but there is nothing about his life that indicates it. The second helpful key is brought out in the NASB. There, the verse closes with the question "Can *that*[5] faith save him?" In other words, can *that kind of faith* save? If it be asked what kind of faith James is referring to, the answer is found in the first part of the verse. He is speaking about a *say-so faith* that is not backed up by good works. Such a faith is worthless. It is all words, and nothing else.

2:15, 16 The futility of words without deeds is now illustrated. We are introduced to two people. One has neither adequate **daily food** nor clothing. The other has both, but is not willing to share them. Professing great generosity, the latter says to his poor brother, "Go and put on some clothing, and eat a good meal." But he doesn't raise a little finger to make this possible. What good are such words? They are positively worthless! They neither satisfy the appetite nor provide warmth **for the body**.

2:17 Thus also faith by itself if it does not have works, is dead. A **faith** without **works** is not real faith at all. It is only a matter of words. James is *not* saying that we are saved by faith *plus* works. To hold such a view would be to dishonor the finished work of the Lord Jesus Christ. If we were saved by faith plus works, then there would be two saviors — Jesus and ourselves. But the NT is very clear that Christ is the one and only Savior. What James is emphasizing is that we are not saved by a faith of words only but by that kind of faith which results in a life of good works. In other words, works are not the root of salvation but the fruit; they are not the cause but the effect. Calvin put it tersely: "We are saved by faith alone, but not by a faith that is alone."

2:18 True faith and good works are inseparable. James shows this by giving us a snatch from a debate between two men. The first man, who is genuinely saved, is the speaker. The second professes to have faith, but he does not demonstrate that faith by good works. The first is heard delivering an unanswerable challenge to the other. We might paraphrase the conversation: "Yes," the first man may correctly and justifiably **say, "you** say you **have faith**, but you do not have works to demonstrate it. I claim that faith must be backed up by a life of works. Prove to me that you have **faith without** a life of good **works**. You cannot do it. Faith is invisible. The only way others can know you have faith is by a life that demonstrates it. **I will show you my faith by my works."** The key to this verse lies in the word *show*: To **show** faith apart from works is impossible.

2:19, 20 The debate continues. The first man is still the speaker. A man's professed faith may be nothing more than mental assent to a well-known fact. Such intellectual agreement involves no committal of the person, and does not produce a transformed life. It is not enough to believe in the existence of **God**. True, this is essential, but it is not sufficient. **Even the demons believe** in the existence of God and they shudder at the thought of their eventual punishment by Him. **The demons believe** the fact, but they do not surrender to the Person. This is not saving faith. When a person truly believes on the Lord, it involves a commitment of spirit, soul, and body. This commitment in turn results in a changed life. **Faith** apart from **works** is head belief, and therefore **dead**[6] belief.

2:21 Two examples of the faith which works are now given from the OT. They involve **Abraham** — a Jew, and Rahab — a Gentile. **Abraham** was **justified by works** in offering up **Isaac his son on the altar**. In order to see this truth in its proper perspective, turn to Genesis 15:6. We read that Abraham believed in the LORD, and He counted it to him for righteousness. Here Abraham was justified by believing; in other words, he was justified by faith. It is not till we come to Genesis 22 that we find Abraham offering up his son. It is then that he was **justified by works**. As soon as Abraham believed in the LORD, he was justified in the sight of God. But then, seven chapters later, God put Abraham's faith to the test. Abraham demonstrated that it was genuine faith by his willingness to offer up Isaac. His obedience showed that his faith was not merely a head belief, but a heart commitment.

It has sometimes been objected that there was no one else present when Abraham offered up Isaac, and there was therefore no one to whom he could prove the reality of his faith. But the young men who had accompanied Abraham were not far away, waiting for Abraham and Isaac to return from the mount. Moreover, Isaac was there. Also, Abraham's willingness to slay his son in obedience to God's command has been preserved in the Bible record, thus demonstrating to all generations the reality of his faith.

2:22, 23 It is clear then that Abraham's faith inspired his works, **and by** his **works** his **faith was made perfect**. True faith and works are inseparable. The first produces the second, and the second evidences the first. In the offering of Isaac we see a practical demonstration of the faith of Abraham. It was the practical fulfillment of **the Scripture** which said that **Abraham** was justified by believing. His good works identified him as **the friend of God**.

2:24 We conclude from this, **then, that a man is justified by works, and not by faith only**. Again, this does *not* mean that he was justified by faith *plus* works. He was justified **by faith** Godward, and **by works** manward. God justified him the moment he believed. Man says, "Show me the reality of your faith." The only way to do this is by good works.

2:25 The second OT illustration **is Rahab the harlot**. She certainly was *not* saved by good character (she was a prostitute!). But she was **justified by works** because **she received the messengers** (or spies) **and sent them out another way**. Rahab was a Canaanite, living in the city of Jericho. She heard reports that a victorious army was advancing toward the city, and that no opposition had been successful against this army. She concluded that the God of the Hebrews was the true God, and decided to identify herself with this God, whatever the cost might be. When the spies entered the city, she befriended them. In doing so, she proved the genuineness of her faith in the true and living God. She was not saved by harboring the spies, but this act of hospitality proved that she was a genuine believer.

Some people misuse this passage to teach that salvation is partly by good works. But what *they* mean by good works is giving to charity, paying your debts, telling the truth, and going to church. Were these the good works of Abraham and Rahab? Certainly not! In Abraham's case, it was willingness to kill his son! In Rahab's case, it was treason! If you remove faith from these works, they would be evil rather than good. "Strip them of faith and they were not only immoral and unfeeling, but they would have been sinful." Mackintosh well says, "This section refers to lifeworks, not law-works. If you abstract faith from Abraham's and Rahab's works, they were bad works. Look at them as the fruit of faith and they were life-works."

So this is a not a passage that can be used to teach salvation by good works. It puts the user in the untenable position of teaching salvation by murder and treason!

2:26 James ends the passage with the statement, **"For as the body without the spirit is dead, so faith without works is dead also."** Here the matter is summarized very beautifully. James compares **faith** to the human **body**. He likens **works** to **the spirit. The body without the spirit is** lifeless, useless, valueless. **So faith without works is dead**, ineffective, worthless. Obviously it is a spurious faith, not genuine saving faith.

To summarize, then, James tests our faith by our answers to the following questions. Am I willing like Abraham to offer the dearest thing in my life to God? Am I willing like Rahab to turn traitor to the world in order to be loyal to Christ?

VI. THE TONGUE: ITS USE AND ABUSE (3:1–12)

The first twelve verses of chapter 3 deal with the tongue (also mentioned in 1:19, 26; 2:12; 4:11; 5:12). Just as an old-fashioned doctor examined a patient's tongue to assist in diagnosis, so James tests a person's spiritual health by his or her conversation. Self-diagnosis begins with sins of speech. James would agree with the modern wit who said, "Watch your tongue. It's in a wet place where it's easy to slip!"

3:1 The subject is introduced by a warning against the hasty desire to be a teacher of the word of God. Although the tongue is not specifically mentioned, the underlying thought is that one who uses his tongue in teaching the Scriptures assumes added responsibility before God and man. The words **"Let not many of you become teachers"** may be paraphrased: "Do not become unduly ambitious to be a teacher." This should not be interpreted as a prohibition against the use of his gift by one who has actually been called of God to teach. It is a simple warning that this ministry should not be undertaken lightly. Those who teach the Word of Truth will receive heavier **judgment** if they fail to practice what they teach.

It is a great responsibility to teach the Bible. The teacher must be prepared to obey what he sees in the word. He can never hope to lead others beyond what he himself has practiced. The extent of his influence on others will be determined by how much he himself has progressed. The teacher begets others in his own image; he makes them like himself. If he dilutes or explains away the clear meaning of any Scripture, he hinders the growth of his students. If he condones sin in any form, he fosters lives of unholiness. No other book makes such claims on its readers as the NT. It calls for total commitment to Jesus Christ. It insists that He must be Lord of every phase of the believer's life. It is a serious matter to teach from such a book!

3:2 James now moves from the specific ministry of teaching to the general area of conversation. We are **all** prone to **stumble in many** areas but if anyone can control his tongue, so that he does not commit the various sins of speech, that person is truly well-rounded and well-disciplined. If one can exercise control in speech, he should not have difficulty in practicing self-control in other areas of life as well. Of course, the Lord Jesus Christ is the only One who ever did this completely, but there is a sense in which each of us can become **perfect**, that is, mature, complete, thoroughly disciplined.

3:3 Five figures of speech, or pictures of the tongue are given. First of all, it is compared to a bridle. Bridles are the harnesses which go over the horses' heads and hold the **bits in the horses' mouths**. Connected to the bit are the reins. Though the bit itself is a very small piece of steel, yet if a person can control that bit, he can control the behavior of the horse. So the tongue can direct the life — either for good or for evil.

3:4 The second picture is that of a **rudder**. Compared with the ship itself, a **rudder** is **very small**. It weighs only a fraction of the weight of the ship. For example, the Queen Elizabeth weighed 83,673 gross tons. The rudder of that ship weighed only 140 tons — less than two-tenths of one percent of the total. Yet when the rudder is **turned**, it controls the direction of the ship itself. It seems incredible that a man can control so huge a vessel with such a relatively small device; yet this is exactly what happens. Thus we should not misjudge the power of the tongue by its size. Though it is a very small member of the body, and relatively hidden, yet it can boast of great accomplishments, both good and evil.

3:5, 6 A third simile of the tongue is a **fire**. A lighted match, carelessly thrown, may start a brush fire. This in turn may ignite **a forest** and leave a charred mass of ruins. What possibilities, then, a small match holds of destruction and devastation! One of the great catastrophes of history was the Chicago fire of 1871. Tradition has it that it started when Mrs. O'Leary's cow kicked over her lantern. Whether or not that was true, the fire burned for three days over three and one half square miles of the city. It killed 250 people, made 100,000 homeless, and destroyed property valued at $175,000,000. The tongue is like a small lighted match or a turned-over lantern. Its potentials for wickedness are almost infinite. James speaks of it as **a world of iniquity . . . among our members**. The word *world* here is used to express vastness. We sometimes use it in this sense; for example, a world full of trouble. We mean a tremendous amount of trouble. The tongue, though so small, has vast possibilities of iniquity in it.

The manner in which the flame of evil-speaking spreads is illustrated by the conversation between two women in Brooklyn. One said, "Tillie told me that you told her that secret I told you not to tell her." The other replied, "She's a mean thing. I told Tillie not to tell you I told her." The first speaker responded, "Well, I told Tillie I wouldn't tell you she told me — so don't tell her I did."

The tongue can defile **the whole body**. A person can corrupt his whole personality by using his tongue to slander, abuse, lie, blaspheme, and swear.

Chappel writes:

> The faultfinder injures himself. . . . The mud slinger cannot engage in his favorite pastime without getting some of the mud that he slings both upon his hands and upon his heart. How often we have come away from such an experience with a sense of defilement! Yet that was not our intention at all. We were vainly hoping that by slinging mud upon others we might enhance someone's estimate of our own cleanliness. We were foolish enough to believe that we could build ourselves up by tearing another down. We were blind enough to imagine that by putting a stick of dynamite under the house of our neighbor we could strengthen the foundations of our own. But this is never the case. In our efforts to injure others we may succeed, but we always inflict the deeper injury upon ourselves.[7]

The tongue **sets on fire the course** (or the wheel) **of nature**. This is the "wheel" set in motion at birth. It describes the whole round of human activity. An evil tongue pollutes not only a man's personal life, but it contaminates all his activities as well. It affects "the whole of wickedness in the whole of man for the whole of life." A wicked tongue **is set on fire by hell**. All evil speech has its source there. It is hellish in its very character. The word used for **hell** here is Gehenna; apart from this instance, it is used only by the Lord Jesus in the NT.

3:7 The fourth figure to which the tongue is likened is a wild, untamable creature. All kinds of beasts, birds, serpents and marine life can be tamed. It is not uncommon to see tame elephants, lions, tigers, birds of prey, serpents, porpoises, and even fish. Pliny lists among creatures that were tamed by men in his day: elephants, lions and tigers, among beasts; the eagle, among birds; asps and other serpents; crocodiles and various fishes, among the inhabitants of the water. To argue that not every kind of creature has actually been tamed is to miss the point of James' argument; there is no reason to believe there is any kind of creature that could not be tamed by man, given sufficient time and persistence.

Robert G. Lee expresses it eloquently:

What has man done with huge elephants? He has invaded their jungle homes, trapped them, trained them — scores of them — in carrying lumber, in pushing heavily laden wagons, in all kinds of labor. What has man done with many green-eyed Bengal tigers? He has caught them, taught them, and made them his playmates. What has man done with fierce, furious, strong African lions? He has captured numbers of them and has trained them to jump through hoops of fire, to ride horseback, to sit on high pedestals, to leave untouched — when hungry — beef placed between their paws, to lie down, to stand up, to run, to roar in obedience to man's spoken word, in obedience to the crack of man's whip. Why, once I saw (years ago at a circus) a lion open wide his cavernous and ravenous mouth and hold it open while a man, his trainer, thrust his head far down into the lion's mouth and held it there a full minute.

What has man done with the huge boa constrictor? With the great python? Go to the circus and see little women, frail as flowers, coil these hideous monsters about their bodies with impunity. Go to the animal show, consider how man has made the spotted leopard and the bloodthirsty jaguar harmless and dumb before

him. Go to the show and see the trained fleas, see the hungry jackal lie down with the meek lamb, see the dove and the eagle nest together, see the wolf and the rabbit romp in play.[8]

3:8 But man's success with wild animals does not extend to the area of his own **tongue**. If we are honest, we will have to admit that this is true in our own lives. Because of the fall, we have lost dominion over this small piece of flesh. Human nature does not have the ability or strength to govern this little member. Only God can bring it under control.

James next characterizes the tongue as **an unruly evil**. Linking this expression with the words **full of deadly poison** we suspect that James has in mind a restless serpent, with exceedingly poisonous venom. A drop or two would be fatal. So the tongue can poison minds and assassinate characters. We all know how easy it is to gossip about others. How often we have engaged in mudslinging in order to get even for supposed wrongs. And often for no reason at all we have belittled others, criticized them, downgraded them. Who can measure the harm done, the tears that have flowed, the broken hearts, the ruined reputations? And who can measure the misery it has brought to our own lives and to our families? The inward bitterness that has been aroused, the shame of having to apologize, the bad effects on our health. Parents who have openly indulged in criticism of fellow-believers have had to watch their children adopt the same critical spirit and wander off from Christian fellowship. The price we have to pay for the undisciplined use of our tongue is enormous.

What is the remedy? Pray daily that the Lord will keep us from gossip, censoriousness, and unkind speech. Don't talk unfavorably about anyone; love covers a multitude of sins (1 Pet. 4:8). If we have something against another person, let us go to him directly, discuss it in love, and pray together (Matt. 18:15; Luke 17:3). Let us try to see Christ in our brethren instead of magnifying minor failures. If we start to say something unkind or unprofitable, let us stop in the middle of the sentence and explain that to continue wouldn't be edifying. Some things are better left unsaid.

3:9, 10 It is inconsistent to use the tongue for both good and evil purposes. It is completely unnatural; there is nothing like it in nature. One minute a man blesses **God** with his tongue, the next he curses those who are **made in the** image **of God.** How incongruous that a common source should ever produce such opposite results! Such a state of affairs should not exist. The tongue that blesses God should help men instead of wounding them. All that we say should be subject to the threefold test: Is it true? Is it kind? Is it necessary? Constantly we should ask the Lord to set a watch before our lips (Ps. 141:3), and pray that the words of our mouths and the meditations of our hearts might be acceptable in the sight of Him who is our strength and Redeemer (Ps. 19:14). We should remember that our members in Romans 12:1 include our tongue.

3:11 No **spring** gives **fresh water and bitter** at the same time. The tongue should not do so either. Its outflow should be uniformly good.

3:12 Just as water from a fountain speaks of refreshment, so fruit from **a fig tree** speaks of nourishment. A **fig tree** cannot produce **olives**, neither can **a grapevine** bear **figs**. In nature, a tree produces only one kind of fruit. How is it, then, that the tongue can produce two kinds of fruit — good and evil?

This passage should not be confused with a similar one in Matthew 7:16–20. There we are warned against expecting good fruit from bad trees. Evil men can only produce wicked works. Here we are warned against using the tongue to produce two opposite kinds of fruit.

No spring can yield **salt water and fresh** water at the same time. It must be one or the other. These lessons from nature are intended to remind us that our speech should be consistently good.

Thus James puts us on trial as far as our speech is concerned. Before leaving this section, let us ask ourselves the following questions. Do I teach others things that I have not obeyed myself? Do I criticize others behind their back? Is my speech consistently clean, edifying, kind? Do I use "minced oaths" such as gosh, golly, gee, jeepers, good heavens,

heck? After a solemn meeting, do I engage in levity or talk about football scores? Do I pun on the Scriptures? In retelling a story, do I exaggerate in order to make people more impressed? Do I habitually tell the truth, even if it means loss of face, friends, or finances?

VII. WISDOM: THE TRUE AND THE FALSE (3:13–18)

James now discusses the difference between true wisdom and false. When he speaks about wisdom, he is not thinking of how much *knowledge* a man has, but how he *lives* his life from day to day. It is not the possession of knowledge but the proper application of it that counts. We have here a portrait of the truly wise man. Basically, this man is the Lord Jesus Christ; He is wisdom incarnate (Matt. 11:19; 1 Cor. 1:30). But also the wise person is one who manifests the life of Christ, one in whom the fruit of the Spirit is evident (Gal. 5:22, 23).

We have also a portrait of the worldly-wise man. He acts according to the principles of this world. He embodies all the traits that men glorify. His behavior gives no evidence of divine life within.

3:13 If a man is **wise and understanding**, he will demonstrate it by his **good conduct** coupled with the humble spirit that comes from **wisdom**. The Lord Jesus, the embodiment of true wisdom, was not proud and arrogant; He was meek and lowly in heart (Matt. 11:29). Therefore, all who are truly wise will have the hallmark of genuine humility.

3:14 The worldly-wise man is characterized by **bitter envy and** selfish ambition in his heart. His one passion in life is to advance his own interests. He is jealous of any competitors and ruthless in dealing with them. He is proud of his wisdom that has brought success. But James says that this isn't wisdom at all. Such boasting is empty. It is a practical denial of **the truth** that the man who is truly wise is truly humble.

3:15 Even in Christian service, it is possible to be bitterly jealous of other workers, and to seek a prominent place for oneself. There is always a danger that worldly-wise men will be given places of leadership in the church. We must constantly guard against allowing worldly principles to guide us in spiritual affairs. James calls this false wisdom **earthly, sensual,** and **demonic.** There is an intended downward progression in these three adjectives. **Earthly** means that this wisdom is not from heaven, but from this earth. **Sensual** means that it is not the fruit of the Holy Spirit, but of man's lower nature. **Demonic** means that it stoops to actions that resemble the behavior of demons rather than of men.

3:16 Whenever you find **envy and self-seeking,** you will also find **confusion,** disharmony, **and every** other kind of **evil.** How true! Think of the unrest and agitation in the world today — all because men reject true Wisdom and act according to their own supposed cleverness!

3:17 **The wisdom that** comes from God **is first pure.** In thought, word, and deed, it is clean. In spirit and body, in doctrine and practice, in faith and in morals, it is undefiled. It is also **peaceable.** This simply means that a wise man loves peace, and will do all he can to maintain peace without sacrificing purity. This is illustrated by Luther's story of the two goats that met on a narrow bridge over deep water. They could not go back and they did not dare to fight. "After a short parley, one of them lay down and let the other go over him, and thus no harm was done. The moral," Luther would say, "is easy: be content if your person is trod upon for peace's sake; your person, I say, not your conscience." True wisdom is **gentle.** It is forbearing, not overbearing; courteous, not crude. A wise man is a gentleman, respectful of the feelings of others. Says A. B. Simpson, "The rude, sarcastic manner, the sharp retort, the unkind cut — all these have nothing whatever in common with the gentle teaching of the Comforter."

The next characteristic is **willing to yield.** It means conciliatory, approachable, open to reason, ready to give in when truth requires it. It is the opposite of obstinate and adamant. Wisdom from above is **full of mercy and good fruits.** It is **full of mercy** to those who are in the wrong, and anxious to help them

find the right way. It is compassionate and kind. There is no vindictiveness in it; indeed, it rewards discourtesy with benevolence. It is **without partiality,** that is, it does not produce favoritism. It is impartial in its treatment of others. Finally, true wisdom is **without hypocrisy.** It is sincere and genuine. It does not pretend to be other than it actually is.

Now let us put all these thoughts together to form the portraits of two men — the truly wise man and the man with false wisdom. The man who is truly wise is genuinely humble. He estimates others to be better than himself. He does not put on airs, but does put others at ease right away. His behavior is not like that of the world around him; it is otherworldly. He does not live for the body but for the spirit. In words and deeds, he makes you think of the Lord Jesus. His life is pure. Morally and spiritually he is clean. Then too he is peaceable. He will endure insult and false accusation but will not fight back or even seek to justify himself. He is gentle, mild-mannered, and tenderhearted. And he is easy to reason with, willing to try to see the other person's viewpoint. He is not vindictive but always ready to forgive those who have wronged him. Not only so but he habitually shows kindness to others, especially to those who don't deserve it. And he is the same to all; he doesn't play favorites. The rich receive the same treatment as the poor; the great are not preferred above the common people. Finally, he is not a hypocrite. He doesn't say one thing and mean another. You will never hear him flatter. He speaks the truth and never wears a mask.

The worldly-wise man is not so. His heart is filled with envy and strife. In his determination to enrich himself, he becomes intolerant of every rival or competitor. There is nothing noble about his behavior; it rises no higher than this earth. He lives to gratify his natural appetites — just as the animals do. And his methods are cruel, treacherous, and devilish. Beneath his well-pressed suit is a life of impurity. His thought life is polluted, his morals debased, his speech unclean. He is quarrelsome with all who disagree with him or who cross him in any way. At home, at work, in social life, he is constantly contentious. And he is harsh and overbearing, rude and crude. People cannot approach him easily; he keeps them at arm's length. To reason with him quietly is all but impossible. His mind is already made up, and his opinions are not subject to change. He is unforgiving and vindictive. When he catches someone in a fault or error, he shows no mercy. Rather he unleashes a torrent of abuse, discourtesy, and meanness. He values people according to the benefit they might be to him. When he can no longer "use" them, that is, when there is no further hope of profit from knowing them, he loses interest in them. Finally, he is two-faced and insincere. You can never be sure of him — either of his words or actions.

3:18 James closes the chapter with the words, **"Now the fruit of righteousness is sown in peace by those who make peace."** This verse is a connecting link between what we have been discussing and what is to follow. We have just learned that true wisdom is peace-loving. In the next chapter we find conflict among God's people. Here we are reminded that life is like the farming process. We have the farmer (the wise man who is a peacemaker); the climate (**peace**); and the harvest (**righteousness**). The farmer wants to raise a harvest of righteousness. Can this be done in an atmosphere of quarrels and bickering? No, the sowing must take place under peaceful conditions. It must be done by those who are of a peaceful disposition. A harvest of uprightness will be produced in their own lives and in the lives of those to whom they minister.

Once again James has put our faith on trial, this time with regard to the type of wisdom we manifest in our everyday life. We must ask ourselves — "Do I respect the proud men of the world more than the humble believer in the Lord Jesus?" "Do I serve the Lord without caring who gets the credit?" "Or do I sometimes use questionable means in order to get good results?" "Am I guilty of flattery in order to influence people?" "Do I harbor jealousy and resentment in my heart?" "Do I resort to sarcasm and unkind remarks?" "Am I pure in thought, in speech, in morals?"

VIII. COVETOUSNESS: ITS CAUSE AND CURE (Chap. 4)

James has pointed out that the wise man is a peace-loving man. Now he is reminded of the tragic strife that often exists among God's people. What is the cause of it all? Why are there so many unhappy homes and so many churches torn by division? Why are there such bitter feuds among Christian workers in the homeland, and such conflicts among missionaries abroad? The reason is that we are ceaselessly striving to satisfy our lust for pleasures and possessions, and to outdo others.

4:1, 2a The sad fact is that there *are* **wars and fights** among Christians. To suggest that this paragraph does not apply to believers is unrealistic, and it robs the passage of all its value for us. What causes all this fighting? It arises from the strong **desires** within us which are constantly struggling to be satisfied. There is the lust to accumulate material possessions. There is the drive for prestige. There is the craving **for pleasure**, for the gratification of bodily appetites. These powerful forces are at work within us. We are never satisfied. We always want more. And yet it seems we are constantly frustrated in our desire to get what we want. The unfulfilled longing becomes so powerful that we trample on those who seem to obstruct our progress. James says, **"You murder."** He uses the word largely in a figurative sense. We don't literally kill, but the anger, jealousy, and cruelty which we generate are murder in embryo.

4:2b, 3 We **covet and cannot obtain**. We want to have more things and better things than others. And in the attempt, we find ourselves quarreling and devouring one another.

John and Jane have just been married. John has a fair job with a moderate salary. Jane wants a house as good as the other young couples at church. John wants a late model car. Jane wants fine furnishings and appliances. Some of these things have to be purchased on the installment plan. John's salary is hardly sufficient to bear the strain. Then a baby is born into the family; this means added expenses and a badly unbalanced budget. As Jane's demands mount, John becomes cross and irritable. Jane retaliates with backbiting and tears. Soon the walls of the house are vibrating with the crossfire. Materialism is destroying the home.

On the other hand, it may be that Jane is jealous. She feels that Bob and Sue Smith have a more prominent place in the assembly than she and John. Soon she makes snide remarks to Sue. As the battle between them increases in tempo, John and Bob become involved in the fighting. Then the other Christians take sides, and the congregation is divided — because of one person's lust for prominence.

Here then is the source of the bickering and strife among believers. It comes from the desire for more, and from jealousy of others. "Keeping up with the Joneses" is the polite name for it; more accurately we should call it greed, covetousness, and envy. The desire becomes so strong that people will do almost anything to gratify their lusts. They are slow to learn that true pleasure is not found in this way, but in contentment with food and clothing (1 Tim. 6:8).

Prayer is the right approach to this problem. "Don't argue. Don't fight. Pray." James says, **"You do not have because you do not ask."** Instead of taking these things to the Lord in prayer, we try to get what we want by our own efforts. If we want something which we do not have, we should ask God for it. If we do ask, and the prayer is unanswered, what then? It simply means that our motives were not pure. We did not want these possessions for the glory of God or for the good of our fellow men. We wanted them for our own selfish enjoyment. We wanted them to satisfy our natural appetites. God does not promise to answer such prayers.

What a profound lesson in psychology we have in these first three verses! If men were content with what God has given them, what staggering conflict and unrest would be avoided! If we loved our neighbors as ourselves, and were more interested in sharing than in acquiring, what peace would result! If we would follow the Savior's command to forsake all instead of to accumulate, to lay up treasures in heaven rather than on earth, what contentions would cease!

4:4 James condemns the inordinate love of material things as spiritual adultery.[9] God wants us to love Him first and foremost. When we love the passing things of this world, we are being untrue to Him.

Covetousness is a form of idolatry. It means that we strongly desire what God does not want us to have. That means that we have set up idols in our hearts. We value material things above the will of God. Therefore, covetousness is idolatry, and idolatry is spiritual unfaithfulness to the Lord.

Worldliness **is** also **enmity with God. The world** does not mean the planet on which we live, or the world of nature about us. It is the system which man has built up for himself in an effort to satisfy the lust of the eyes, the lust of the flesh, and the pride of life. In this system there is no room for God or His Son. It may be the world of art, culture, education, science, or even religion. But it is a sphere in which the name of Christ is unwelcome or even forbidden, except, of course, as an empty formality. It is, in short, the world of mankind outside the sphere of the true church. **To be a friend** of this system is to be **an enemy of God**. It was this world that crucified the Lord of life and glory. In fact, it was the *religious* world that played the key role in putting Him to death. How unthinkable it is that believers should ever want to walk arm-in-arm with the world that murdered their Savior!

4:5 Verse 5 is one of the most difficult in the Epistle: **Do you think that the Scripture says in vain, "The Spirit who dwells in us yearns jealously"?**

The first difficulty is that James seems to be quoting from the OT; yet these words are not found anywhere in the OT, or even in the Apocryphal books. There are two possible explanations. First of all, while the exact words are not found in the OT, James may have been quoting them as being the general teaching of the Scripture. The second solution of the problem is given by the RV. There the verse is broken into two questions: "Or think ye that the Scripture speaketh in vain? Doth the spirit which he made to dwell in us long unto envying?" Here the thought is that in condemning the competitive, worldly spirit, the Bible is not wasting words.

The second major difficulty in verse 5 is the meaning of the second part of the verse. The problem is whether the spirit is the *Holy* Spirit (as in the NKJV[10]) or the spirit of passionate *jealousy*. If the former is meant, then the thought is that the Holy Spirit whom God caused to dwell in us does not originate the lust and jealousy which cause strife; rather He **yearns** over us with jealousy for our entire devotion to Christ. If the latter is intended, then the meaning is that the spirit that dwells in us, that is, the spirit of lust and envy, is the cause of all our unfaithfulness to God.

4:6 **But He gives more grace.** In the first five verses we saw how wicked the old nature of the believer can be. Now we learn that we are not left to deal with the lusts of the flesh in our own strength. Thank God, **He gives more grace** or strength whenever it is needed (Heb. 4:16). He has promised, ". . . as your days, so shall your strength be" (Deut. 33:25).

He giveth more grace when the burdens
  grow greater,
He sendeth more strength when the
  labors increase,
To added affliction He addeth His mercy,
To multiplied trials His multiplied peace.
  – *Annie Johnson Flint*

To prove that God gives grace as it is needed, James quoted Proverbs 3:34, but here there is the added thought that it is **to the humble**, not the proud, that this **grace** is promised. **God resists the proud**, but He cannot resist the broken spirit.

4:7 In verses 7–10, we find six steps to be followed where there is true repentance. James has been crying out against the sins of the saints. His words have pierced our hearts like arrows of conviction. They have fallen like thunderbolts from the throne of God. We realize that God has been speaking to us. Our hearts have been bowed beneath the influence of His word. But the question now is, "What shall we do?"

The first thing to do is to **submit to God**. This means that we must be subject to Him, ready to listen to Him and obey Him. We must be tender and contrite, not proud and stiff-necked. Then we must **resist the devil**. We do this by closing our ears and hearts to his suggestions and temptations. We do it also by using the Scriptures as the Sword of the Spirit to repel him. If we resist him, **he will flee from** us.

4:8 Next we should **draw near to God**. We do this by prayer. We must come before Him in desperate, believing prayer, telling Him all that is on our heart. As we thus approach Him, we find that He will **draw near to** us. We thought He would be far from us because of our carnality and worldliness, but when we **draw near to** Him, He forgives us and restores us. The fourth step is: **Cleanse your hands, you sinners; and purify your hearts, you double-minded. Hands** speak of our actions and **hearts** represent our motives and desires. We **cleanse** our **hands** and **purify** our **hearts** through confession and forsaking sins, both outward and inward. As **sinners** we need to confess evil acts; as **double-minded** people we need to confess our mixed motives.

4:9 Confession should be accompanied by deep sorrow for sin. **Lament and mourn and weep! Let your laughter be turned to mourning and your joy to gloom**. When God visits us in conviction of sin, it is not time for levity. Rather it is a time when we should prostrate ourselves before Him and **mourn** over our sinfulness, powerlessness, coldness, and barrenness. We should humble ourselves and weep over our materialism, secularism, and formalism. Both inwardly and outwardly, we should manifest the fruit of godly repentance.

4:10 Finally, we should **humble** ourselves **in the sight of the Lord**. If we honestly take our place in the dust at His feet, **He will lift** us **up** in due time.

This then is the way we should respond when the Lord exposes us to ourselves. Too often it is not the case, however. Sometimes, for example, we are in a meeting when God speaks loudly to our hearts. We are stirred for the moment, and filled with good resolves. But when the meeting closes, the people engage in animated and lighthearted conversation. The whole atmosphere of the service is dispersed, the power is dissipated, and the Spirit of God is quenched.

4:11, 12 The next sin James deals with is censoriousness, or speaking **evil** against **a brother.** Someone has suggested that there are three questions we should answer before indulging in criticism of others — What good does it do your brother? What good does it do yourself? What glory for God is in it?

The royal **law** of love says that we should love our neighbor as ourselves. To **speak evil** against a brother, therefore, or to judge his motives, is the same as speaking against this **law** and condemning it as worthless. To break a law deliberately is to treat it with disrespect and contempt. It is the same as saying that the law is not good, and not worthy of obedience. "He who refuses obedience virtually says it ought not to be law." Now this puts the one **who speaks evil of a brother** in the strange position of being **a judge** rather than one who is to be judged. He sets himself up as being superior to the law rather than subject to it. But only God is superior to the law; He is the One who gave it and the One who judges by it. **Who** then has the audacity to usurp the *place* of *God* and **judge another?**[11]

4:13 The next sin which James denounces is self-confident, boastful planning in independence of God (vv. 13–16). He pictures a businessman who has a complete plan laid out for the future. Notice the details. He thought about the time (**today or tomorrow**); the personnel (**we**); the place (**such and such a city**); the duration (**spend a year there**); the activity (**buy and sell**); and the anticipated result (**make a profit**). What is missing in this picture? He never once takes God into his business. In life, it is necessary to make some plans for the future, but to do so in self-will is sinful. To say "we will" or "I will" is the essence of sin. Note for instance, the "I wills" of Lucifer in Isaiah 14:13, 14: "For you have said in your heart: 'I will ascend into heaven, I will exalt my throne above the stars of God; I will also sit on the mount of the congregation on the farthest sides of the north; I will ascend above the heights of the clouds, I will be like the Most High.'"

4:14 It is wrong to plan as if **tomorrow** were certain. "Do not say . . . tomorrow" (Prov. 3:28). We do not know what tomorrow holds. Our lives are as frail and unpredictable as a "puff of smoke" (JBP).

4:15 God should be consulted in all our plans, and they should be made in His will. We should live and speak in the realization that our destinies are in His control. We should say, **"If the Lord wills, we shall live and do this or that."** Thus, in the book of Acts, we find the Apostle Paul saying, "I will return again to you, God willing" (18:21), and in 1 Corinthians 4:19 he wrote, "I will come to you shortly, if the Lord wills." Sometimes Christians employ the letters "D.V." to express this sense of dependence on God. These letters are the initials of two Latin words, *Deo volente*, meaning *God willing*.

4:16 **But now you boast in your arrogance**, writes James. The Christians were priding themselves in their boastful plans for the future. They were arrogant in their confidence that nothing would interfere with their time schedule. They acted as if they were the masters of their own fate. **All such boasting is evil** because it leaves God out.

4:17 **Therefore to him who knows to do good and does not do it, to him it is sin**. In this context, **to do good** is to take God into every aspect of our lives, to live in moment by moment dependence on Him. If we know we should do this, yet fail to do it, we are clearly sinning. Of course, the principle is of broader application. In any area of life, the opportunity **to do good** makes us responsible to do it. If we know what is right, we are under obligation to live up to that light. Failure **to do** so **is sin** against God, against our neighbors, and against ourselves.

In chapter 4, James has put us on trial with regard to covetousness and conflict, with regard to evil-speaking, and with regard to planning without consulting the Lord. Let us therefore ask ourselves the following questions — Am I continually anxious to get more or am I content with what I have? Am I envious of those who have more than I? Do I pray before purchasing? When God speaks to me, do I submit or resist? Do I speak against my brothers? Do I make plans without consulting the Lord?

IX. THE RICH AND THEIR COMING REMORSE (5:1–6)

In one of the most searching and piercing sections of his Letter, James now launches into a denunciation of the sins of the rich. The words fall like hammer-blows, blunt and unsparing. In fact, the denunciation is so strong that these verses are seldom preached on.

James is here seen in the role of a prophet of social justice. He cries out against the failure of the rich to use their money for the alleviation of human need. He condemns those who have become rich by exploiting their workers. He rebukes their use of wealth for self-indulgence and luxurious living. Finally, he pictures the rich as arrogant oppressors of the righteous.

5:1 First he summons the **rich** to **weep and howl** because of the **miseries** which they were about to experience. Soon they would meet God. Then they would be filled with shame and remorse. They would see that they had been unfaithful stewards. They would wail over the opportunities they had missed. They would mourn over their covetousness and selfishness. They would be convicted about their unfair employment practices. They would see the sin of seeking security in material things rather than in the Lord. And they would shed hot tears over the way they had indulged themselves to the full. James mentions four cardinal sins of the rich. The first is the sin of hoarding wealth.

5:2 "Your richest goods are ruined," says James, "your hoard of clothes is moth-eaten; your gold and silver are tarnished. Yes, their very tarnish will be the evidence of your wicked hoarding and you will shrink from them as if they were red-hot" (JBP).

The Bible never says that it is a sin to be rich. A person, for instance, may inherit a fortune overnight and certainly he has not committed any sin in thus becoming rich. But the Bible does teach that it is wrong to hoard riches. The Lord Jesus expressly forbade the hoarding of wealth. He said, "Do not lay up for yourselves treasures on earth, where moth and rust destroy and where thieves break in and steal; but lay up for yourselves treasures in heaven, where neither moth nor rust destroys and where thieves do not break in and steal. For where your treasure is, there your heart will be also" (Matt. 6:19–21).

James speaks of wealth in four forms: **riches, garments,** gold, and silver. In Bible times, wealth was generally in the form of grain, oil, and other produce: clothing, gold, and silver. Perhaps when James says **"Your riches are corrupted,"** he means that the grain had become wormy and the oil had become rancid. The point is that these things had been hoarded to the point where they were spoiled. They could have been used at one time to feed the hungry; now they were worthless. **"Your garments are moth-eaten,"** he says. This doesn't happen to clothing that is in regular use. But when the closet is so crowded with garments that they are used very infrequently, they are subject to moth damage. To James it is morally wrong to hoard clothes like this when so many people in the world are in desperate need.

5:3 Your gold and silver are corroded, and their corrosion will be a witness against you, and will eat your flesh like fire, he continues. **Gold and silver** do not rust, but they do tarnish and become discolored, and under unfavorable storage conditions, they could conceivably corrode. Instead of putting their money to work, feeding the hungry, clothing the destitute, providing medicines for the sick, and spreading the gospel, the rich were saving their money for a "rainy day." It benefited no one, and eventually rotted away.

Corrosion, speaking of disuse and decay, will be a condemning testimony against the rich. If this was true of the rich people of James' day, how much more true is it of believers in our day? What will be our condemnation if we have had the means of spreading the gospel and have failed to use it? If we have hoarded material things when they might have been used in the salvation of souls? The expression **their corrosion . . . will eat your flesh like fire** means that their failure to use their riches for the good of others would cause them the keenest suffering and remorse. When their eyes would at last be opened to see the cruelty of their selfishness and greed (costly jewelry, elegant clothing, luxurious homes, high-priced cars), it would be a scalding, scorching experience.

5:4 The second sin James attacks is acquiring wealth by failure to pay proper wages. **The laborers who mowed** the **fields** were deprived of their rightful pay. Though the workers might protest, they were quite helpless to get redress. They had no one on earth to plead their cause successfully. However, their **cries** were heard by the **Lord of Sabaoth** (Hebrew for "hosts"). He who commands the armies of heaven is strong on behalf of earth's downtrodden masses. The Lord God Omnipotent will help and avenge them. Thus, the Bible condemns not only the hoarding of wealth but the acquisition of wealth by dishonest means. In addition to the sin of paying inadequate wages, James could also have mentioned falsifying income tax returns, cheating on weights and measures, bribing local inspectors or other officials, false advertising, and falsifying expense accounts.

5:5 Next James denounces the luxurious living of the rich. Expensive jewelry, elegant clothes, epicurean foods, and palatial homes — how could they squander their wealth on self when multitudes were in desperate need? Or to bring it down to our own day, how can we justify the affluence and extravagance of the church and of Christian people? We live in a world where thousands die daily of starvation. Over half the world's population has never heard of the Lord Jesus Christ. In such a world, how can we justify our sports cars, limousines, speed boats? How can we spend the Lord's money in expensive hotels, in high-class restaurants, in any form of self-indulgence? The clear teaching of the Scriptures, the appalling need of the world, the example of the Savior, and the simple instinct of compassion tell us that it is wrong to live in comfort, luxury, and ease as long as there is a single soul who has not heard the gospel.

Those who live **in pleasure and** are unrestrained in **luxury** are likened to those who nourish their **hearts as in a day of slaughter** — like animals, fattening themselves just before their execu-

tion, or like soldiers who spend their time looting when others are perishing around them.

5:6 The final charge against the rich is that they **condemned** and **murdered the just**, and **he** did **not resist** them. Some think that this **just**, righteous one is the Lord Jesus. However, His death was brought about by the religious rather than by the rich. It is probably best to think of **the just** as representing innocent people in general. James is thinking of the rough, highhanded way in which rich people have characteristically behaved toward their subordinates. They **have condemned** them by false accusation, by harsh language, and by threats. They have killed them, not directly perhaps, but by overworking and underpaying them. The innocent offered no resistance. To protest might result in further brutality, or dismissal from their job.

X. EXHORTATION TO PATIENCE (5:7–12)

5:7 James now turns to believers who were being oppressed, and encourages them to **be patient**. The motive for patience is **the coming of the Lord**. This may refer either to the Rapture or to Christ's coming to reign. Both are used in the NT as incentives to patient endurance.

The farmer illustrates the need of patience. He does not reap on the same day that he plants. Rather there is a long period of waiting. First there must come the **early** rain, causing the seed to germinate. Then at the end of the season is the **latter rain**, needed to bring the crop to successful fruition. Some see in this reference to **early and latter rain** a promise that the blessings of Pentecost at the beginning of the Church Age will be repeated before the Lord's Return, but the overall tenor of NT Scripture seems to discourage such an expectation. However, there is nothing to forbid our looking for a faithful remnant of believers on fire for God and bent on world evangelization. What better way to welcome the returning Savior?

5:8 The wrongs of earth will be made right when the Lord returns. Therefore His people should **be patient**, like the farmer. Their **hearts** should be established with the certainty of His **coming**.

5:9 During times of persecution and distress, it is not uncommon for the victims to turn against one another. It is a curious twist of human nature that in times of pressure we build up wrath against those we love most. Hence the warning: **Do not grumble against one another, brethren, lest you be condemned.**[12] This verse has a voice for servants of the Lord working together under trying circumstances. We should not let resentment build up. After all, **the Judge is** already **at the door**! He knows what we think. Soon we will stand before the Judgment Seat of Christ to give an account. We should not judge lest we be judged.

5:10 The OT **prophets** are brought forth **as an example of suffering and patience**. Note that **suffering** precedes **patience**. "Tribulation produces perseverance" (Rom. 5:3). As explained previously, patience in the NT means fortitude or steadfastness. Because of their faithfulness in declaring the word of the Lord, the prophets were persecuted unmercifully. Yet "they endured as seeing Him who is invisible" (Heb. 11:27, 32–40).

5:11 We look back upon prophets such as Isaiah, Jeremiah, and Daniel with a great deal of respect. We honor them for their lives of zeal and devotion. In this sense we call them **blessed**. We agree that they were right and the world was wrong. Well, we should remember that they went through great trials and sufferings, and that they endured with patience. If we want to be blessed, it is only reasonable to conclude that we will be called upon to do the same.

Job is a fine example of **perseverance** or fortitude. Few if any men in the history of the world have ever suffered so much loss in so short a time as **Job**. Yet he never cursed God, or turned from Him. In the end, his endurance was rewarded. God revealed Himself, as He always does, to be **compassionate and merciful**.

If we did not know what James calls **the end intended by the Lord** (the final issue or result which **the Lord** brings to pass), we might be tempted to envy the wicked. Asaph was jealous when he saw the prosperity of the wicked (Ps.

73:3–17). The more he thought about it, the more perturbed he became. Then he went into the sanctuary of God and understood their latter end. This dispelled all his envy. David had the same experience. In Psalm 17:15 he describes the portion of the believer in the life to come. In view of this, it pays the believer to be steadfast. In Job's case, **the end intended by the Lord** was that God gave him twice as much as he had before (Job 42:10–15).

5:12 Impatience in times of trial is also manifested in swearing. Here it is not a question of profanity, or cursing, primarily. Neither is it a matter of taking an oath in a court of law. The practice forbidden is the thoughtless use of the Lord's Name or some other name to attest the truthfulness of one's speech. The Christian should **not** have to **swear** by anyone or anything, either in **heaven** or on **earth**. Those who know him should be able to depend on the fact that his **"Yes"** means **"Yes"** and his **"No"** means **"No."**

This passage could also be applied to forbid such needless expressions as "For heaven's sake," "As God is my Judge," "By Jove" and such minced oaths as "gee" (contraction for Jesus), "gosh" and "golly" (slang for God).

Lest you fall into judgment (or **hypocrisy**, NKJV margin[13]), says James, perhaps thinking of the third commandment: "You shall not take the name of the LORD your God in vain, for the LORD will not hold him guiltless who takes His name in vain" (Ex. 20:7).

XI. PRAYER AND THE HEALING OF THE SICK (5:13–20)

The theme of the closing verses of the Epistle is prayer. The word occurs seven times, either as a noun or verb.

5:13 In every circumstance of life, we should go to the Lord in prayer. When in trouble, we should approach Him with earnest entreaties. In times of rejoicing, we should lift our hearts to Him in praise. He wants to be brought into all the changing moods of our lives.

We should see God as the first great Cause of all that comes to us in life. We should not look into what Rutherford called the "confused rolling of the wheels of second causes." It is defeat to allow ourselves to be victims of circumstances, or to wait for our circumstances to change. We should see no hand but His.

This is one of the most disputed portions of the Epistle, and perhaps of the entire NT. It brings us face to face with the place of healing in the life of the believer today.

Before looking at the verses in detail, it should be helpful to review what the Bible teaches about sickness and healing.

DIVINE HEALING

1. Christians agree that all sickness is, in a general way, the result of sin in the world. If sin had never entered, there would be no sickness.

2. Sometimes sickness is a *direct* result of sin in a person's life. In 1 Corinthians 11:30, we read of certain Corinthians who were sick because they participated in the Lord's Supper without judging sin in their lives, that is, without confessing and forsaking it.

3. Not all sickness is a direct result of sin in a person's life. Job was sick in spite of the fact that he was a most righteous man (Job 1:8). The man born blind was not suffering for sins he had committed (John 9:2, 3). Epaphroditus was sick because of his tireless activity in the work of the Lord (Phil. 2:30). Gaius was spiritually healthy but apparently physically unwell (3 Jn. v. 2).

4. Sometimes sickness is a result of satanic activity. It was Satan who caused Job's body to be covered with boils (Job 2:7). It was Satan who crippled the woman in Luke 13:10–17 so that she was bent double, unable to straighten herself up: "This woman . . . whom Satan has bound — think of it — for eighteen years" (13:16). Paul had a physical infirmity caused by Satan. He called it "a thorn in the flesh . . . a messenger of Satan to buffet me" (2 Cor. 12:7).

5. God can and does heal. In a very real sense, *all* healing is divine. One of the names of God in the OT is *Jehovah-Ropheka* — "the LORD who heals you" (Ex. 15:26). We should acknowledge God in every case of healing.

It is clear from the Bible that God uses different means in healing. Sometimes He heals through natural bodily processes. He has placed within the human body tremendous powers of recuperation. Doctors know that most complaints are better by morning. Sometimes He heals through medicines. Paul advised Timothy, for instance, to "use a little wine for your stomach's sake and your frequent infirmities" (1 Tim. 5:23). Sometimes He heals through "deliverance from underlying fears, resentments, self-preoccupation, and guilts, all of which produce illness." Sometimes He heals through physicians and surgeons. Jesus explicitly taught that sick people need a physician (Matt. 9:12). Paul spoke of Luke as "the beloved physician" (Col. 4:14), which certainly recognizes the need of doctors among Christians. God uses doctors in the ministry of healing. As Paré, the famous French surgeon said, "The surgeon dresses the wound; God heals it."

6. But God also heals miraculously. The Gospels contain many illustrations of this. It would be incorrect to say that God generally heals in this way, but neither should we say that He never does. There is nothing in the Bible to discourage us from believing that God can heal miraculously today.

7. Yet we must also be clear that it is not always God's will to heal. Paul left Trophimus sick at Miletus (2 Tim. 4:20). The Lord did not heal Paul of his thorn in the flesh (2 Cor. 12:7–10). If it were always God's will to heal, some would never grow old or die!

8. God has not promised to heal in every case; therefore, healing is not something we can demand from Him. In Philippians 2:27, healing is spoken of as a mercy, not something which we have a right to expect.

9. While it is true in a general sense that healing is in the "Atonement," yet not all the blessings that are in the Atonement have been given to us yet. For instance, the redemption of the body was included in Christ's work for us, but we will not receive it until Christ comes for His saints (Rom. 8:23). At that time also we will be completely and finally healed of all diseases.

10. It is not true that failure to be healed indicates a lack of faith. If it were, this would mean that some would live on indefinitely; but no one does. Paul, Trophimus, and Gaius were not healed,

and yet their faith was virile and active. ‡

5:14, 15 Returning to James 5, we see how it fits in with what the rest of the Bible teaches about healing:

> Is anyone among you sick? Let him call for the elders of the church, and let them pray over him, anointing him with oil in the name of the Lord. And the prayer of faith will save the sick, and the Lord will raise him up. And if he has committed sins, he will be forgiven.

If these were the only verses in the Bible on healing, we would assume that a Christian could be assured of healing from every illness that comes in life, if he met the conditions listed. However, we have already seen from other Scriptures that it is not always God's will to heal. Therefore we are forced to the conclusion that James is not talking about *every* kind of illness, but only about a certain form of sickness, that is, a sickness which is the result of certain specific circumstances. The key to understanding the passage is found in the words **"And if he has committed sins, he will be forgiven."** Healing in this section is connected with the forgiveness of sins.

Here is a man who has committed some sin, probably involving the testimony of the local church. Shortly afterward he is stricken with illness. He realizes that this sickness is a direct result of his sin. God is chastening him in order to bring him back into fellowship. He repents of his sin and confesses it to God. But since the sin has also involved the public testimony of the assembly, he calls **the elders** and makes a full confession to them as well. They **pray over him, anointing him with oil in the name of the Lord**. This **prayer of faith** saves **the sick** man, **and the Lord will raise him up**. It is a definite promise of the Lord that where sickness is a direct result of sin, and where that sin is confessed and forsaken in the manner described, the Lord will heal.

Someone will say, "How do you know that the man has committed sins and that he is brought to the place of repentance and confession?" The answer is that the closing part of verse 15 speaks about his **sins** being **forgiven**. And we know that sins are forgiven only as a result of confession (1 Jn. 1:9).

Someone else will object, "It doesn't say he *has* committed sins. It says **if he has committed sins.**" This is true, but the whole context has to do with confession of sins and the restoration of a backslider. Notice the following: "Confess your trespasses to one another, and pray for one another, that you may be healed." The drought mentioned in verses 17, 18 was a judgment of God on Israel because of sin. It was lifted after they returned to the Lord, acknowledging Him as the true God (1 Kgs. 18:39). Verses 19, 20 clearly deal with the recovery of a backslider, as we shall see.

The entire context of James 5:13–20 implies that the healing promised by God is for a person whose sickness is a result of sin, and who confesses the sin to **the elders**. The responsibility of **the elders** is to **pray over him, anointing him with oil**. Some interpret **the oil** here as signifying the use of *medicinal means*, since oil was a form of medicine in the days when James was writing (Luke 10:34). Another view is that the *ritual use of oil* is meant. This view is strengthened by the words **in the name of the Lord.** In other words, the anointing was to be done by His authority and in obedience to His word. Oil was sometimes used by the apostles when effecting miraculous cures (Mark 6:13). The healing power was not in the oil, but the oil symbolized the Holy Spirit in His healing ministry (1 Cor. 12:9).

Some will object that the ritual use of oil is inconsistent with the Age of Grace, with its de-emphasis on ceremonies and rites. However, we do use the bread and wine as symbols of Christ's body and blood, and we use water in baptism. Also women use head coverings in the assembly as symbols of their submission to man. Why then should we object to the ritual use of oil?

In response to the **prayer of faith**, God will heal the person. It is a **prayer of faith** because it is based on the promise of God's word. It is not at all a question as to how much faith the elders have, or how much faith the sick man has. The elders can pray with complete assurance because God has promised to raise up the man when the conditions described have been fully met.

To summarize, then, we believe that verses 14, 15 apply to a case where a person is sick as a direct result of some sin. When he realizes this and repents, he should **call for the elders of the** assembly and make a full confession to them. They should then **pray over him, anointing him with oil in the name of the Lord**. They can pray for his recovery in faith, since God here promises to heal the man.

5:16a Confess your trespasses[14] **to one another, and pray for one another, that you may be healed**. A casual reading of this statement might give the impression that we are to tell other people all about our secret sins. But that is not at all the thought! Primarily James means that when we sin against someone else, we should be prompt to confess this sin to the person we have wronged.

Also we should **pray for one another**. Instead of holding grudges and allowing resentments to build up, we should maintain ourselves in fellowship with others through confession and prayer.

Physical healing is linked with spiritual restoration. Notice how James links together confession, prayer, and healing. It is a clear intimation of the vital connection between the physical and the spiritual. Man is a tripartite being — spirit, soul, and body (1 Thess. 5:23). What affects one part of him affects all. In the OT, the priest was also the physician. It was he who diagnosed leprosy, and it was he who pronounced it cured, for instance. By thus combining the offices of priest and doctor in one person, the Lord indicated the close tie between the spirit and the body.

The field of psychosomatic medicine recognizes this link and searches for personal problems that might be causing physical troubles. But modern medicine does not have the remedy for sin. Deliverance from the guilt, defilement, power, and penalty of sin can come only on the basis of the blood of Christ, and through confession Godward and manward. More often than we are willing to admit, illnesses are caused by sin — such sins as gluttony, worry, anger, an unforgiving spirit, intemperance, jealousy, self-

ishness, and pride. Sin in the life brings sickness and sometimes death (1 Cor. 11:30). We should confess and forsake sin as soon as we are aware it has come into our lives. *All* sins should be confessed to God. In addition, sins against other people should be confessed to them as well. It is vital for our spiritual health and good for our physical health.

> **5:16b–18** Tremendous power is made available through a good man's earnest prayer. Do you remember Elijah? He was a man like us, but he prayed earnestly that it should not rain. In fact, not a drop fell on the land for three and a half years. Then he prayed again; the heavens gave the rain, and the earth sprouted with vegetation as usual (JBP).

This incident is recorded in 1 Kings 17:1–19:10. Ahab was king of Israel at the time. Through his wife Jezebel, he became a worshiper of Baal, and led the people into this vile form of idolatry. "Ahab did more to provoke the LORD God of Israel to anger than all the kings of Israel who were before him" (16:33). It was a direct result of sin that drought came upon Israel for three and a half years.

Then Elijah had the famous contest with the priests of Baal on Mt. Carmel. When the fire of the Lord fell and consumed the burnt offering, the altar, and the water, the people were convinced, and they turned back to the Lord. Elijah **prayed again** and the drought ended. The example of **Elijah** is given as an encouragement to us to pray for those who have sinned and wandered away from fellowship with God. **The effective fervent prayer of a righteous man avails much** or, as someone has paraphrased it: "The prayer of a man whose heart is right with God works wonders." Lest we be tempted to think of him as belonging to a higher creation than ourselves, James reminds us that **Elijah was a man** with the same kind of frail flesh. He was a mere man, subject to the same weaknesses and infirmities as other men.

5:19, 20 In the preceding verses we have seen the elders of the assembly being used in the restoration of a sinning saint. And we have seen Elijah being used in the restoration (partial and temporary) of a backsliding nation. Now we are exhorted to give ourselves to this far-reaching ministry.

Verse 19 describes a Christian brother who has wandered away **from the truth**, either in doctrine or in practice. Another brother makes this a matter of fervent, believing prayer, and thus lovingly **turns him back** to fellowship with God and with his brothers and sisters in Christ. How immense is the significance of this ministry! First of all, **he will save** his erring brother from dying prematurely under the chastening hand of God. Secondly, he will **cover a multitude of sins**. They are forgiven and forgotten by God. Also they are forgiven by fellow believers and veiled from the gaze of the outside world. We need this ministry today. In our zeal to evangelize the lost, perhaps we do not give sufficient attention to those sheep of Christ who have wandered from the fold.

Once again James has been prodding our consciences with regard to various areas of the Christian life. He has been asking us, for example: Do you lay up treasures on earth? Are your business methods strictly honest? Your income tax return, for instance? Do you live luxuriously, or do you live sacrificially so that others may come to know the Savior? When you sin against another person, are you willing to go to him and apologize? When you become ill, whom do you contact first — the doctor or the Lord? When you see a brother fall into sin, do you criticize him or try to restore him?

And so we come to the end of this practical, brief Epistle. In it we have seen faith on trial. We have seen faith tested by the problems of life, by unholy temptations, by obedience to the word of God. The man who says he has faith has been challenged to exhibit it by avoiding partiality or snobbishness and to prove it by a life of good works. The reality of faith is seen in a person's speech; the believer learns to yield his tongue to the lordship of Christ. True faith is accompanied by true wisdom; the life of envy and strife is exchanged for that of practical godliness.

Faith avoids the feuds, struggles, and jealousies that spring from covetousness and worldly ambition. It avoids a harsh, critical spirit. It avoids the self-confidence which leaves God out of life's plans. Faith stands trial by the way it earns and spends its money. In spite of oppression, it manifests fortitude and endurance in view of the Lord's Return. Its speech is uniformly honest, needing no oaths to attest it. Faith goes to God in all the changing moods of life. In sickness, it first looks for spiritual causes. By confession to God and to those who have been wronged, it removes these possible causes. Finally, faith goes out in love and compassion to those who have backslidden.

Your faith and mine are on trial each day. What is the Judge's verdict?

ENDNOTES

[1](1:14) The Greek word *epithumia* is just a strengthened form of "desire." The English word *lust* (cf. 1611 KJV) originally meant simply "strong desire" too, but has taken on definite sexual connotations.

[2](1:19) The words "So then" (Gk. *hōste*) are replaced by "Know" (*iste*) in some mss., and most modern versions that prefer the Alexandrian (NU) readings. However, the traditional reading best fits the context — a major break summing up what we should do in light of vv. 1–18.

[3](1:21) The same Greek word (*psuchē*) means both "life" and "soul" and it is not always certain which rendering is better. Also "save" (in Greek and English) does not necessarily refer to eternal salvation. It can refer to healing, deliverance, rescue, and other things. Thus, the expression "save your soul" could mean *in some contexts* "make a success of your *life*" (for Christ).

[4](2:2–4) The Greek word here is *sunagōgē* (congregation). Since this word later came to be used only for *Jewish* congregations ("synagogues"), this is an indication of the very early date of James. "Congregation" (Tyndale), "church" (KJV), and "assembly" (JND), are usually translations of the word *ekklēsia*, a (called-out) assembly. This was originally a political term (cf. General *Assembly* of the United Nations).

[5](2:14) However, in all fairness, it should be pointed out that the Greek does *not* have the word for "that" here,

but simply the definite article ("the"). While the article may sometimes have a demonstrative force, it could just be the ordinary article used with an abstract noun. Since this is admittedly interpretive, the NKJV, which had "that faith" in its 1st edition, reverted to the KJV reading in later editions.

6(2:20) The NU text reads "useless" for "dead."

7(3:5, 6) Clovis G. Chappel, *Sermons from the Psalms*, p.132.

8(3:7) Robert G. Lee, *Lord I Believe*, pp. 166-168.

9(4:4) Most mss. read "Adulterers and adulteresses," perhaps suggesting literal immorality in the congregations addressed. The Alexandrian mss. (NU) have only the feminine form "adulteresses," which would almost demand a non-literal meaning. The KJV and NKJV allow either meaning, physical and/or spiritual adultery.

10(4:5) The most ancient mss. had not yet developed separate forms for capital and small letters. Ideally, there would be an "S" that was somewhere between upper case and lower case for the many places in the NT where a passage is not clearly Spirit or spirit. Since there is no such form, translators and editors must decide according to context. Here and elsewhere good Bible scholars are divided.

11(4:11, 12) NU text reads *a neighbor*.

12(5:9) Both NU and M texts read "judged," but the context does suggest a negative verdict, so "condemned" is still valid.

13(5:12) The majority text has a most interesting variant reading here. The KJV (and NU) reading "into (lit. "under") judgment" is *hupo krisin*. The majority of mss., however, read *eis* ("into") *hupokrisin* ("hypocrisy"). If the little preposition "eis" were to drop out by mistake in copying, it would be natural to take the prefix on *hupokrisin* as a separate preposition and come up with "under judgment." While both expressions fit the immediate context, the whole Epistle of James, coming to a close here, could be said to be a warning against falling into religious *hypocrisy*.

14(5:16a) The NU text reads "Therefore confess your sins."

BIBLIOGRAPHY

Adamson, James. *The Epistle of James* (NIC). Grand Rapids: Wm. B. Eerdmans Publishing Company, 1976.

Brown, Charles. *The General Epistle of James: A Devotional Commentary*. Philadelphia: The Union Press, 1907.

Gaebelein, Frank. *The Practical Epistle of James*. Great Neck, N. Y.: Doniger & Raughley, Inc., 1955.

Johnstone, Robert. *Lectures Exegetical and Practical on the Epistle of James*. Minneapolis: Klock & Klock Christian Publishers (Reprint of 1871 ed.).

Kelly, William. *The Epistle of James*. London: F. E. Race, 1913.

King, Guy H. *A Belief that Behaves*. London: Marshall, Morgan & Scott, Ltd., 1954.

Zodhiates, Spiros. *The Behavior of Belief*. Grand Rapids: Wm. B. Eerdmans Publishing Co., 1959.

THE FIRST EPISTLE OF PETER

Introduction

"Did we not know who wrote this letter we should be forced to say: 'This is a rocklike man who writes thus, whose soul rests on a rock foundation, and who with his mighty testimony undertakes to fortify the souls of others against the pressure of the storms of suffering advancing upon them and to establish them upon the true rock basis.'"
— Wiesinger

I. Unique Place in the Canon

Christians in Muslim and Marxist countries are so used to repression, hostility, and even downright persecution that they almost come to expect it. For them 1 Peter is a tremendous practical help in accepting suffering as allowed by the Lord and as beneficial in producing certain desirable qualities, such as perseverance.

Christians in the West, especially English-speaking believers with their great biblical heritage, have not yet adjusted to public opposition to the faith. Until recently the state at least smiled on the family unit as basic to society and even encouraged attendance at "the church of your choice." No longer. The government, especially local government, seems to use its judges, educational institutions, and especially the media, to misrepresent, ridicule, and even defame Bible-believing Christians. Radio, television, films, newspapers, magazines, and official communiqués promote immorality, liquor, cheating, and even blasphemy. Christianity is now "counter-culture," and the sooner believers learn the lessons the Apostle Peter teaches in his First Letter, the more prepared they will be for the last years of the twentieth and first years of the twenty-first centuries — if our Lord tarries.

II. Authorship[†]

External Evidence

The *external evidence* that Peter wrote this Epistle is early and well-nigh universal. Eusebius counts 1 Peter as among the books accepted by all believers (*homologoumena*). Polycarp and Clement of Alexandria accept the book. The fact that it is not in Marcion's "canon" should cause no wonder, as he only accepted *Paul's* Letters. The Muratorian Canon does not list 1 Peter, but this may be due to the fragmentary nature of that document.

It is quite possible that 2 Peter 3:1 is the earliest attestation to 1 Peter. Even those who believe Peter did not write 2 Peter (see Introduction to 2 Peter) still see the Letter as early enough to be a valid witness to 1 Peter, if indeed 2 Peter 3:1 is meant to refer back to this earlier Letter.

Internal Evidence

The *internal evidence* that causes some to doubt Petrine authorship is the very good Greek that is used. Could a Galilean fisherman write so well? Many say "No." However, as our own culture will amply illustrate, men with a flair for words and public speech often become outstanding users of the standard language without formal college or seminary training. Peter had thirty years' experience preaching, not to mention the Holy Spirit's inspiration and the probable help from Silvanus in composing the Letter. When Acts 4:13 says that Peter and John were unlearned it merely means they lacked formal rabbinical training.

References to Peter's life and ministry

are ample in 1 Peter, as the following selection of details will demonstrate:

The writer implies in 1:8 that he had seen Jesus in a way his readers had not. He says, "whom having not seen *you* love," *not* ". . . *we* have not seen Him." We shall see in other passages that the writer had companied with the Lord.

The first ten verses of chapter 2 present Christ as the Cornerstone, and thus take us back to the incident at Caesarea Philippi (Matt. 16:13-20). When Peter confessed Jesus as the Christ, the Son of the living God, the Lord Jesus announced that His church would be built on that foundation, that is, on the truth that Christ is the Son of the living God. He is the Cornerstone and Foundation of the church.

The reference to living stones in 2:5 recalls the incident in John 1:42 where Simon's name was changed to Cephas (Aramaic) or Peter (Greek), which both mean *stone*. Through faith in Christ, Peter became a living stone. It is not surprising that he has so much to say about stones in chapter 2. In 2:7, the writer quotes Psalm 118:22: *"The stone which the builders rejected has become the chief cornerstone."* This is the same passage which Peter quoted when he was arraigned before the rulers, elders, and scribes in Jerusalem (Acts 4:11).

As we hear the apostle advising his readers to submit to governmental authorities (2:13-17), we think back to that time when Peter himself did not submit, but cut off the ear of the high priest's slave (John 18:10). So his advice, in addition to being inspired, has the ring of practical experience behind it!

Chapter 2:21-24 seems to indicate direct knowledge of the trial and death of the Lord Jesus. Peter could never forget the meek endurance and silent suffering of the Savior. In 2:24 we have a reference to the mode of the Savior's death — by crucifixion. The description seems to echo Peter's words in Acts 5:30 and 10:39.

When Peter spoke of his readers returning to the Shepherd and Overseer of their souls (2:25), he might well have been thinking of his own restoration (John 21:15-19), following his denial of the Lord.

The reminder that "love will cover a multitude of sins" (4:8) might refer back to Peter's questions, "Lord, how often shall my brother sin against me, and I forgive him? Up to seven times?" Jesus said to him, "I do not say to you, up to seven times, but up to seventy times seven" (Matt. 18:21, 22). In other words, indefinitely.

In 4:16 we are told that if anyone suffers as a Christian he should not be ashamed, but in that name should glorify God. Compare this with Acts 5:40-42 where Peter and the other apostles, after having been flogged, left the council, "rejoicing that they were counted worthy to suffer shame for His name."

The writer of the Epistle identifies himself as a witness of the sufferings of Christ (5:1). The expression, "a partaker of the glory that will be revealed," may be an allusion to the transfiguration. Peter was present, of course, on both occasions.

The gentle, pastoral counsel to "shepherd the flock of God which is among you" (5:2) reminds us of the Savior's words to Peter, "Feed My lambs. . . . Tend My sheep. . . . Feed My sheep" (John 21:15-17).

The language of 5:5, "be clothed with humility" is strongly reminiscent of the incident in John 13 where Jesus clothed Himself with the apron of a slave and washed His disciples' feet. In fact, the whole section on pride and humility (5:5, 6) is all the more meaningful when we remember Peter's proud assertion that he would never deny the Lord (Mark 14:29-31) and his subsequent threefold denial of the Savior (Mark 14:67-72).

A final reference that may relate to Peter's experience is found in 5:8: "Your adversary the devil walks about like a roaring lion, seeking whom he may devour." When Peter wrote this, was he thinking of the time when Jesus said to him, "Simon, Simon! Indeed, Satan has asked for you, that he may sift *you* as wheat . . . " (Luke 22:31)?

III. Date

Peter's teaching that government is generally helpful to those who wish to do right (1 Pet. 2:13-17) is thought by many to be too conciliatory to have been written *after* the start of Nero's fierce persecution of the Christians (A.D. 64). At any rate, the Letter cannot be very far removed from this period in time, probably 64 or 65.

IV. Background and Themes†

As has been noted, Peter is especially dealing with suffering in the Christian life. So far his readers seem to have undergone slander and ridicule for Christ (4:14, 15). Prison, confiscation of property, and violent death for many still apparently lay in the future. Suffering is not the only theme of this great Letter, however. The blessings inherited by accepting the gospel, the proper relationships of believers with the world, the state, the family, and the church, and instruction on elders and discipline are all included.

From "Babylon" — either the literal city on the Euphrates with its Jewish community, or spiritual Babylon on the Tiber (Rome) — the apostle sends this Letter to the eastern provinces of what is now Turkey.

OUTLINE

Commentary

I. THE BELIEVER'S PRIVILEGES AND DUTIES (1:1–2:10)

A. Salutation (1:1, 2)

1:1 The beloved fisherman introduces himself as **Peter, an apostle of Jesus Christ**. He had been commissioned by the Lord Jesus as one of the original twelve, called to be the herald of a glorious, transforming message. By responding to the divine tap on the shoulder, he had become a fisher of men.

All believers are called to represent Christ's interests here on earth. We are all supposed to be missionaries, whether at home or abroad. This is the central purpose of our life as Jesus' followers; all else is subordinate.

The Letter is addressed **to the pilgrims** or foreigners scattered throughout **Pontus, Galatia, Cappadocia, Asia, and Bithynia**. Who were these exiles?

Peter's use of the words **"of the Dispersion"** predisposes us to think that they were Jewish believers because James uses that same word concerning believers from the twelve tribes of Israel (Jas. 1:1). Also the word in John 7:35 describes Jews who were scattered among the Gentiles.

But it is quite probable that Peter is writing to the Gentile believers who had been dispersed by persecution among the surrounding nations. In doing so, he takes many of the names that were formerly given to God's earthly people and applies them to God's new society, the church. He calls them elect (1:2), a chosen generation, a royal priesthood, a holy nation, a people of God's possession (2:9). He also gives three other indications that he is writing to Gentile believers. He speaks of the empty way of life which had been handed down to them from their forefathers (1:14, 18). He describes them as those who in time past were not a people (2:10). Finally, in 4:3 he says that they had lived in previous times like Gentiles. So there is strong evidence that the Diaspora or Dispersion to which Peter writes is the Christian church, composed largely of those who were Gentiles before their conversion. If it be objected that Peter was preeminently the apostle to the Jews, that did not preclude his ministering to Gentiles. Certainly Paul, the apostle to the Gentiles, spent time ministering to the Jews.

1:2 The recipients of the Letter are further designated by a fourfold progression of their salvation which involved all three Persons of the Trinity.

First of all, they were **elect according to the foreknowledge of God the Father**. This means that in a past eternity, God chose them to belong to Himself. The doctrine of divine election is not always popular, but it does have this virtue — it allows God to be God. Attempts to make it palatable to man only succeed in detracting from the sovereignty of God. Any difficulty in reconciling God's election and human responsibility lies in man's mind, not in God's. The Bible teaches both doctrines, and we should believe both. The truth lies in both extremes, not somewhere between them.

God's choice is said to be **according to** His **foreknowledge**. Some understand this to mean that God elected those

whom He foreknew would trust the Savior. Others say that God knew very well that, left to himself, no sinner would trust the Savior, and so in His foreknowledge He marked out certain ones to be trophies of His grace. While there is unutterable mystery in God's choice, we can be sure that there is nothing unjust about it.

The second step in salvation is **sanctification of the Spirit**. This aspect of **sanctification** takes place before conversion.[1] It is a ministry of the Holy **Spirit** by which He sets people apart to belong to God (see also 2 Thess. 2:13). It logically follows election by God the Father. In *eternity* God foreknew and chose men. In *time* the Holy Spirit operates to make that election real in the lives of the individuals concerned.

The third step in the soul's salvation is the sinner's response to the work of the Holy Spirit. It is described as **obedience** to **Jesus Christ**. This means obeying the gospel by repenting of one's sins and receiving Christ as Savior. The concept of the gospel as something to be obeyed is a common one in the NT (see Rom. 2:8; 2 Thess. 1:8).

Finally, there is the **sprinkling** with His **blood**. We must not take this with absolute literalness and insist that when a person is saved, he is actually sprinkled with the blood of Jesus. This is figurative language. What it does say is that as soon as a person obeys the gospel, he receives all the benefits which flow from the shedding of Christ's blood on Calvary. The Savior's blood was shed once for all over 1900 years ago; it will never be shed again. But we receive forgiveness, redemption, and the other innumerable blessings that flow from that crimson tide as soon as we believe on Him.

Having traced the four steps in his readers' spiritual birth, Peter now wishes that **grace** and **peace** might be **multiplied** to them. They have already experienced the grace of God in salvation and the resulting peace with God. But day by day they will need **grace** or strength for the Christian life, and **peace** in the midst of a turbulent society. That is what the apostle wishes for them here in fullest abundance. James Denney said that "grace is the first and last word of the Gospel; and peace — perfect spiritual soundness — is the finished work of grace."

B. His Position as a Believer (1:3–12)

1:3 In verses 3–12, Peter sets forth the unique glories of our salvation. He begins by calling for praise to be given to the Author of salvation — **the God and Father of our Lord Jesus Christ**. This title presents God in a twofold relationship to the Lord Jesus. The name **God . . . of our Lord Jesus Christ** emphasizes the humanity of the Savior. The name **Father** underlines the deity of God's Son. The full name of the Son is given:

Lord — the One with the exclusive right to rule in hearts and lives.

Jesus — the One who saves His people from their sins.

Christ — God's Anointed One who has been exalted to heaven's highest place.

It is by God's **abundant mercy** that we have been born anew **to a living hope through the resurrection of Jesus Christ from the dead**. God is the source of this salvation. His great mercy is its cause. The new birth is the nature of it. A living hope is its present reward. **The resurrection of Jesus Christ** is the righteous basis of our salvation, as well as the foundation of our **living hope**.

As sinners, we had no hope beyond the grave. There was nothing ahead for us but the certainty of judgment and fiery indignation. As members of the first creation we were under the sentence of death. But in the redemptive work of Christ, God found a righteous basis upon which He can save ungodly sinners and still be just. Christ has paid the penalty of our sins. Full satisfaction has been made. The claims of justice have been met, and now mercy can flow out to those who obey the gospel. In the resurrection of Christ, God indicated His complete satisfaction with the sacrificial work of His Son. The resurrection is the Father's "Amen" to our Lord's cry, "It is finished!" Also, that resurrection is a pledge that all who die in Christ will be raised from among the dead. This is our **living hope** — the expectation of being

taken home to heaven to be with Christ and to be like Him forever. F. B. Meyer calls the **living hope** "the link between our present and future."

1:4 Verses 4, 5 describe this future aspect of salvation. When we are born again we have the certain hope of **an inheritance . . . in heaven**. The **inheritance** includes all that the believer will enjoy in heaven for eternity, and all that will be his through Christ (Ps. 16:5). The inheritance is **incorruptible and undefiled and** unfading: (1) **Incorruptible** means that it can never corrode, crack, or decay. It is death-proof. (2) **Undefiled** means that the inheritance itself is in perfect condition. No tarnish or stain can dim its purity. It is sin-proof. (3) **That does not fade away** means that it can never suffer variations in value, glory, or beauty. It is time-proof.

Earthly inheritances are uncertain at best. Sometimes the value of an estate drops sharply because of market declines. Sometimes wills are successfully contested by parties not mentioned in them. Sometimes people are deprived of an inheritance because of legal technicalities. But this divine inheritance is not subject to any of the changes of time, and there are no loopholes in the believer's title to it. It is kept in the safety-vault of heaven for the child of God.

1:5 Not only is the inheritance guarded for Christians, but they **are kept** or guarded for **it**. In this life an heir may die before an inheritance is divided. But the same grace that preserves the heavenly inheritance preserves us as heirs to enjoy it. God's election of His people can never be frustrated. Those who were chosen in eternity past are saved in time now and kept for eternity to come. The believer in Christ is eternally secure.

But there is a human as well as a divine side to eternal security. We **are kept by the power of God** — that is the divine side, but it is **through faith** — that is the human side. This does not mean that a person is saved only as long as he exercises faith. Where there is true **faith**, there will be continuance. Saving faith *always* has the quality of permanence.

The child of God is guarded by **the power of God for salvation ready to be**

revealed in the last time. This refers to salvation in its future tense. It has often been pointed out that there are three tenses of salvation: (1) A Christian *was saved* from the penalty of sin the moment he first trusted the Savior (Eph. 2:8). (2) He *is saved* daily from the power of sin as he allows the Savior to live His life through him (Rom. 5:10). (3) He *will be saved* from the presence of sin at the time of the Rapture (Heb. 9:28). His body will be changed and glorified, and be forever free from sin, sickness, and death. This future tense of salvation also includes the time when the saints will return to earth with Christ and will be clearly shown to be children of God (1 Jn. 3:2).

1:6 Because of this hope of the redemption of the body and of a glorious inheritance, believers can **greatly rejoice** even in the midst of **trials**. The Christians to whom Peter was writing were suffering persecution because of their testimony for Christ. Peter reminds them of one of the delightful paradoxes of Christianity — joy in the midst of sorrow. On the one hand, they can **rejoice** in the prospect of a kept inheritance for a kept people. On the other hand, they can find joy in the knowledge that the **various trials** are only for a little while, whereas the glory will be forever (see 2 Cor. 4:17). Commenting on the presence of joy in the midst of grief caused by numerous trials, J. H. Jowett wrote: "I never expected to find a fountain in so unpromising a waste."

1:7 There is further comfort for suffering saints in knowing that their sufferings are neither purposeless nor fruitless. The sufferings of the ungodly are only a foretaste of the pangs of hell which they will endure eternally. This is not true for the Christian. One of the many beneficial purposes of afflictions in this life for the child of God is to test the **genuineness of** his **faith**. Peter contrasts our faith with **gold**. Of all the substances known to man, gold is one of the most imperishable. It can be subjected to intense heat and might seem to be indestructible. But the truth is that gold **perishes** through use, pressure, and fire.

True **faith** is indestructible. The believer may undergo severe tests and trials, but instead of destroying his faith, they become food for faith to feed on.

Job probably sustained heavier losses in one day than any other man in the history of the world, yet he was able to say, "Though He slay me, yet will I trust Him" (Job 13:15). The three men in the Babylonian furnace were literally **tested by fire**. The fire proved their faith to be real. Also it burned away the ropes that held them, setting them free (Dan. 3:12–30). And during their flaming ordeal, they had the companionship of One "like the Son of God." **The genuineness of faith** can be proved only **by fire**. When prevailing conditions are favorable, it might be easy to be a Christian. But when public confession of Christ brings persecution and suffering, then the casual followers drift away and are lost in the crowd. A religion which costs nothing is worth nothing. Faith which refuses to pay the price is spurious. It is the kind of say-so faith that James condemns.

Genuine **faith** will result in **praise, honor, and glory** when **Jesus Christ** is revealed. This simply means that God will reward every instance of faith that stood the test. He will **praise** those who are joyful though surrounded by trouble. He will award **honor and glory** to tried and suffering believers who were able to accept their tribulations as a vote of confidence from Him.

This will be apparent when Jesus Christ comes back to earth to reign as King of kings and Lord of lords, and all those whom the world rejected will be shown clearly to be sons of God. A comparison of Scripture indicates that rewards will be announced at the Judgment Seat of Christ, in heaven, after the Rapture. But the public display of these rewards apparently takes place at the Second Advent of Christ.

1:8 Peter now discusses the present enjoyment of our salvation — Christ taken by faith. Though we have never **seen** Him with our eyes, we **love** Him.[2] **Though** we **do not see Him** at this time, **yet** we believe in Him. That is how we enter into the blessedness which He mentioned to Thomas, "Blessed are they who have not seen and yet have believed" (John 20:29).

William Lincoln writes:

> People talk a lot about love, but the true test of love to God and Christ is, that in

the trial it says — "I would not lose the favor and smile of God, so will rather suffer than grieve Him." Love will be content with a crust and the smile of God, rather than a better position and the popularity of the world without it. Such tests must come to all the true children of God; they winnow the chaff from the wheat. The gold comes out from the fire tried, and purified from its dross.[3]

Believing on Him we **rejoice with joy inexpressible and full of glory**. To be united to Him through faith is to have uninterrupted and eternal contact with the fountain of all pure **joy**. The Christian's joy is not dependent on earthly circumstances but on the risen, exalted Christ at God's right hand. It is no more possible to rob a saint of his joy than it is to unseat Christ from His place of glory. The two stand together.

1:9 Next, Peter deals with the present outcome of faith — **the salvation of** the soul. The salvation of the body is still future; it will take place when Christ comes for His saints. But as soon as we trust Christ by faith, we receive **the salvation of** our **souls**. The word here refers to the non-material part of man, his person apart from his body. It is the soul which is separated from the body at the time of death. In this passage it includes the spirit, by which we have God-consciousness. The soul is saved at the time of the new birth.

1:10 **This salvation** was the theme of many OT **prophets**. God's ancient spokesmen prophesied the undeserved favor which we would receive. But they did not fully understand what they were writing (see Dan. 12:8).

1:11 They apparently did not understand: (1) The identity of the Person who would appear as Messiah. (2) The **time** of His appearance. They were inspired by the Spirit of God to foretell **the sufferings of** the Messiah **and the glories that would follow**. But they did not understand that these two events would be separated by at least 1900 years. As has often been pictured, they saw the two mountain peaks — (a) Calvary, where Jesus suffered, and (b) Olivet, where He will return in glory. But they did not see the valley which lay between, that is, the present Age of Grace, in which we find ourselves able to see

both events, one past, one still future, with a clearer perspective than they.

1:12 **To them** the Spirit of God mysteriously **revealed** that they were serving generations yet unborn. While the prophets' words had meaning for their own generation, they were aware that their full meaning was not exhausted by events in their day.

This, of course, raises questions. Were not the OT prophets familiar with the truth of justification by faith? What was it that they did not understand about our salvation? In what sense did they serve **us** rather than **themselves**?

William Lincoln says:

The fullness of God's grace could not appear till Christ came. God could and did save sinners and take them to heaven, as He did Enoch before, but union with Christ and all that such union implies, could not be experienced until Christ died and rose again. O how God delights to heap honor upon His Son![4]

The things that were veiled to the prophets were now made clear. The Holy Spirit came down from heaven at Pentecost. He empowered the apostles to preach the good news that Jesus of Nazareth was the predicted Messiah, that He had died for the sins of men, had been buried, and had been raised the third day. They announced that salvation was offered as a free gift through faith in Christ. They declared that God's purpose during this age is to gather out of the nations a people for His name, and that the Lord Jesus would return to earth one day to take the scepter of universal government.

The immense privilege of believers in this age is seen not only in that they understand clearly what was veiled from the prophets, but also in the fact that **angels desire to look into** these truths of salvation. **Angels** have a prominent place in the NT as well as in the Old. They are mentioned in connection with the birth of Christ, His temptation, His agony in Gethsemane, and His resurrection. But as far as we know, there is no redemption for angels that have fallen. Christ did not come to intervene on behalf of angels, but on behalf of Abraham's descendants (Heb. 2:16). The church is an object lesson to angels, setting forth the manifold wisdom of God (Eph. 3:10). But it is not for them to know the joy that our salvation brings.

C. His Conduct in the Light of His Position (1:13–2:3)

1:13 Beginning here, there is a change in emphasis. Peter has been dealing with the glories of our salvation. At this point, he launches into a series of exhortations based on the foregoing. Jowett says: "The present appeal is based on the introductory evangel. . . . Spiritual impulse is created by the momentum of superlative facts. The dynamic of duty is born in the heart of the Gospel."[5]

First, Peter urges the saints to have a "girded" **mind**. The girding up of the **mind** is an interesting figure of speech. In eastern lands, people wore long, flowing robes. When they wanted to walk fast or with a minimum of hindrance, they would tie the robe up around their waist with a belt (see Ex. 12:11). In this way they girded up their loins. But what does Peter mean by **gird up the loins of your mind**? As they went out into a hostile world, believers were to avoid panic and distraction. In times of persecution, there is always the tendency to become rattled and confused. A girded mind is one that is strong, composed, cool, and ready for action. It is unimpeded by the distraction of human fear or persecution.

This state of mental solidarity is further encouraged by the words **be sober**. This means self-control in contrast to hysteria. The **sober** spirit is poised and stable.

Next, the saints are urged to have the optimistic, forward-looking mind: **rest your hope fully upon the grace that is to be brought to you at the revelation of Jesus Christ**. The assurance of Christ's Return is held out as a compelling motive for endurance through the storms and tribulations of life. **The revelation of Jesus Christ** is generally taken to refer to His coming back to earth when He will be revealed in glory. However, it could also refer to the Rapture when Christ will come for His saints.

1:14 In verses 14–16, the subject is the **obedient** mind. **Obedient children** should not indulge in the sins which characterized them in their former life. Now that they are Christians, they should pattern their life after the One whose name they bear. If they conform to the ungodly world, they are denying their heavenly character. The things they did in the days of their **ignorance** should be put away now that they have been illuminated by the Holy Spirit. **The former lusts** means the sins they indulged in while they were still ignorant of God.

1:15 Instead of imitating the ungodly world with its fads and fashions, our lives should reproduce the **holy** character of the One who called us. To be godly means to be Godlike. God is holy in all His ways. If we are to be like Him, we must be **holy** in all that we do and say. In this life we will never be *as* holy as He is, but we should **be holy** *because* He is.

1:16 Peter reaches back into the OT for proof that God expects His people to be like Himself. In Leviticus 11:44, the Lord said: **"Be holy, for I am holy."** Christians are empowered to live holy lives by the indwelling Holy Spirit. Old Testament saints did not have this help and blessing. But since we are more privileged, we are also more responsible. The verse Peter quotes from Leviticus acquires a new depth of meaning in the NT. It is the difference between the formal and the vital. Holiness was God's ideal in the OT. It has assumed a concrete, everyday quality with the coming of the Spirit of truth.

1:17 Not only are we exhorted to holiness but also to a reverent mind. This means a respectful **fear**, a deep appreciation of who God is. It especially means a realization that the One whom we address as **Father** is the same One who **judges** His children impartially **according to** their deeds. As we realize the extent of His knowledge and the accuracy of His judgment, we should live with a wholesome fear of displeasing Him. **The Father . . . judges** His own in this life; He has committed the judgment of sinners to the Lord Jesus (John 5:22).

Lincoln writes: "He is looking on, taking notice of all, whether there is integrity of purpose, intelligence of mind, and desire of heart to please Him."[6]

We are to pass **the time of** our **stay** on earth **in fear**. Christians are not at home in this world. We are living in a foreign country, exiled from heaven. We should not settle down as if this were our permanent dwelling. Neither should we imitate the behavior of the earth-dwellers. We should always remember our heavenly destiny and behave ourselves as citizens of heaven.

1:18 Before their conversion, believers were not different from the rest of the world. Their talk and walk were as empty and trivial as that of men around them. Their unconverted days are described as **your aimless conduct received by tradition from your fathers**. But they had been ransomed from that futile existence by a tremendous transaction. They had been rescued from the slavery of world-conformity by the payment of an infinite ransom. Was it by **silver or gold** that these kidnap victims had been freed (see Ex. 30:15)?

1:19 No, it was **with the precious blood of Christ** — like the blood of a perfect, unblemished **lamb**. Christ is **a lamb without blemish** or **spot**, that is, He is absolutely perfect, inwardly and outwardly. If a believer is ever tempted to return to worldly pleasures and amusements, to adopt worldly modes and patterns, to become like the world in its false ways, he should remember that Christ shed His **blood** to deliver him from that kind of life. To go back to the world is to re-cross the great gulf that was bridged for us at staggering cost. But even more — it is positive disloyalty to the Savior.

"Reason back from the greatness of the sacrifice to the greatness of the sin. Then determine to be done forever with that which cost God's Son His life."

1:20 Christ's work for us was no afterthought on God's part. The Redeemer was destined to die for us **before the** creation **of the world. But** at the end of the **times**, that is, at the end of the dispensation of law, He appeared from heaven to rescue us from our former way of life. Lincoln comments: "In these last times — the world's moral history was closed at the cross of Christ. It has shown itself fully and got to its end before God."[7]

Peter adds these considerations to impress us even more deeply with the importance of making a clean break with the world system from which Christ died to deliver us. We are in the world but not of it. We must not isolate ourselves from unregenerate men, but rather carry the gospel to them. Yet in our dealings and relationships with them, we must never share in or condone their sins. We are to show by our lives that we are children of God. The moment we become like the world, our testimony is weakened. There is no incentive for worldlings to be converted if they cannot see a difference — a change for the better in our lives.

1:21 Loyalty to the Lord Jesus is further demanded by the fact that it is **through Him** we have come to **believe in God**. He is the One who has revealed the Father's heart to us. As W. T. P. Wolston says: "it is not by creation nor providence nor law that man knows God, but by Christ."[8] The Father indicated His complete satisfaction with Christ's redeeming work by raising Him out **from** among **the dead** ones and honoring **Him** with the place of highest **glory** in heaven. The result of all this is **that** our **faith and hope are in God**. It is in Him, not in the present evil world system, that we live and move and have our being.

1:22 Now the Apostle Peter urges his readers to have the loving mind (1:22–2:3). First, he describes the new birth and points out that one of the changes that it brings is **love** for our **brethren** (1:22a). Next, he presses home the obligation to love (1:22b). Again he reverts to the new birth, and especially to the seed from which this new life has grown — the word of God (1:23–25). And once again he emphasizes the obligations that rest on those who have received the word (2:1–3).

In 1:22a, Peter first describes the new birth: **Since you have purified your souls. . . .** We understand, of course, that it is God who purifies our souls when we are saved; in the strict sense, we do not have the power for personal purity. But in this figure of speech those of us who have experienced purification are said to have attained it when we believed.

The means employed in this purification is **obeying the truth**. This is the second time Peter describes saving faith as an act of obedience (see 1:2). In Romans, Paul twice uses the phrase "the obedience of faith." In our thinking we should not try to separate belief and obedience. True faith is obeying faith. This can only be done **through the Spirit**.[9]

One of the goals of the new birth is **sincere love of the brethren**. In a very real sense, we are saved in order to love all our fellow Christians. By this **love**, we know that we have passed out of death into life (1 Jn. 3:14), and by it, the world knows that we are disciples of the Lord Jesus (John 13:35).

So the exhortation follows quite naturally — **love one another fervently with a pure heart**. This is one of the many instances in the NT where a declarative statement becomes the basis for an imperative. The declaration is this: **Since you have purified your souls . . . in sincere love of the brethren. . . .** Then the command: **love one another fervently with a pure heart**. The positional forms the basis for the practical. Our love should be warm, wholehearted, with all our strength, earnest, unceasing, and **pure**.

The exhortation to **love one another** is especially timely for a people undergoing persecution because it is well known that "under conditions of hardship, trivial disagreements take on gigantic proportions."

1:23 Again Peter takes his readers back to their new birth, and this time to the seed of that birth **the word of God**. The exhortations in 2:1–3 will be based on this.

The new birth is **not** brought about by **corruptible seed**, that is, it is not produced in the same way as a physical birth. Human life is brought into being by means of seed that must obey physical laws of decay and death. The physical life that is produced has the same quality as the seed from which it sprang; it too is of a temporary character.

The new birth is brought about **through the word of God**. As men hear or read the Bible they are convicted of their sins, convinced that Christ is the sole and sufficient Savior, and converted to God. No one is ever saved apart from the instrumentality in some way of the incorruptible word of God.

Samuel Ridout notes in *The Numerical Bible:*

> . . . the three "incorruptible" things we have in this first chapter — an incorruptible inheritance (v. 4), an incorruptible redemption (vv. 18, 19), and an incorruptible word by which we are born (v. 23). Thus we have a nature which is taintless, fitted for the enjoyment of a taintless inheritance and on the basis of a redemption which never can lose its value. How the stamp of eternal perfection is upon all, and what a fitting companion to these is that "incorruptible" ornament of a meek and quiet spirit (chap. iii. 4).[10]

The word **lives and abides forever**.[11] Though heaven and earth pass away, it will never pass away. It is settled forever in heaven. And the life it produces is eternal also. Those who are born anew through the word take on the everlasting character of the word.

In the human birth, the seed which produces a child contains, in germ form, all the characteristics of the child. What the child will eventually be is determined by the seed. For our present purposes, it is enough to see that as the seed is perishable, so is the human life which results from it.

1:24 The transitory character of human nature is emphasized by a quotation of Isaiah 40:6, 7. Human life is as impermanent **as grass**. Physical beauty is as short-lived as the flowers of the field. **The grass withers**, and the flowers droop and die.

1:25 In contrast, **the word of the LORD endures forever** (Isa. 40:8). Therefore, the new life of the believer is equally incorruptible. This incorruptible word is the message of good news which **was preached** to Peter's readers and which caused them to be born again. It was the source of their eternal life.

2:1 Because they are partakers of the divine life, Christians should put away once for all the following unloving acts:

Malice — the harboring of evil thoughts against another person. **Malice** nourishes antagonism, builds up grudges, and secretly hopes that revenge, harm, or tragedy will overtake another. George Washington Carver was refused admission at a university because he was black. Years later, when someone asked him the name of the university, he replied, "Never mind. That doesn't matter now." He harbored no malice.

Deceit — any form of dishonesty and trickery (and what a variety of forms it takes!). **Deceit** falsifies income tax returns, cheats on exams, lies about age, bribes officials, and pulls shady deals in business.

Hypocrisy — insincerity, pretense, sham. The hypocrite is a play-actor, pretending to be someone he is not. He pretends to be happily married when his home is actually a battlefield. He pretends to be spiritual on Sundays but he is as carnal as a goat on weekdays. He pretends interest in others but his motives are selfish.

Envy — bare-faced jealousy. Vine defines it as the feeling of displeasure produced by observing or hearing of the advantage or prosperity of others. It was **envy** that caused the chief priests to deliver Jesus up to Pilate for death (Matt. 27:18). **Envy** is still a killer. Women can look daggers at others because of their better homes and gardens, smarter clothes, or superior cooking. A man can praise another fellow's new car or speedboat but what he is thinking is, "I'll show him. I'll get something better."

Evil speaking — backbiting, malicious gossip, recrimination. Slander is the attempt to make oneself look cleaner by slinging mud at someone else. It may take very subtle forms such as: "Yes, she is a lovely person but she has this one failing. . . ." and then the knife is deftly thrust into her back. Or it may even have a religious pose: "I mention this only for your prayer fellowship, but did you know that he. . . ." and then the character is assassinated.

All of these sins are violations of the fundamental commandment to love our neighbor as ourselves. No wonder Peter tells us to decisively rid ourselves of them.

2:2 A second obligation flowing from our new birth is to have an insatiable craving for the **pure** spiritual **milk of the word**. The sins mentioned in the previous verse stunt spiritual growth; the good word of God nourishes it.

The phrase **as newborn babes** does not necessarily mean that Peter's readers were new believers; they may have been saved for several years. But young or old in the faith, they should thirst for the word just as infants cry for **milk**. We get some idea of the thirst of the healthy baby by the impatient, aggressive, determined way he sucks and swallows.

By the **pure milk of the word**, a believer grows up spiritually.[12] The ultimate goal toward which all spiritual growth in this life is moving is conformity to the image of our Lord Jesus Christ.

2:3 If indeed you have tasted that the Lord is gracious. What a tremendous impetus for thirsting for the pure spiritual milk! The **if** does not express any doubt; we *have* tasted and seen that the Lord is good (Ps. 34:8). His sacrifice for us was an act of unspeakable goodness and kindness (Tit. 3:4). What we have already tasted of His kindness should whet our appetites to feed more and more on Him. The sweet taste of nearness to Him should make us dread the thought of ever wandering away from Him.

D. His Privileges in the New House and Priesthood (2:4–10)

2:4 Now Peter moves from exhortation to a consideration of believers' privileges in the new house (the church) and in the new priesthood.

In the new order, Christ is central, and so we come **to Him**. Because Peter is thinking in terms of a building and of building materials, we are not surprised to find the Lord presented figuratively as **a stone**. First, He is that **living stone** — not an inanimate or dead stone but One who lives in the power of an endless life (Heb. 7:16).

Incredible as it may seem, He is **rejected by men**. In their stupid, selfish, amateurish blueprints for life, insignificant, shortsighted men can find no place for their Creator and Redeemer. Just as there was no room for Him in the inn, so there is no place for Him in the plan of their lives!

But it is not man's opinion that counts. In God's sight the Lord Jesus is **chosen . . . and precious**. He is **chosen** as not only the suitable stone but the indispensable One. And His value to **God** is inestimable; He is **precious** beyond computation.

If we are going to be used in God's building program we must come to Christ. Our only suitability to be building materials is derived from our identification with Him. We are only important as we contribute to His **glory**.

2:5 The **spiritual house** is built up of all believers in Christ, and is therefore the same as the church. The church has this in common with the temple of the OT that it is the dwelling place of God on earth (1 Kgs. 6:11–13; Eph. 2:22). But it is contrasted with the temple, a physical, tangible building made of beautiful but lifeless, perishable materials. The church is a structure built of **living stones**.

Now the figure changes swiftly from **a spiritual house** to the **holy priesthood** that functions in connection with the house. Believers are not only **living** building blocks in the house; they are **holy** priests as well. Under the Mosaic Law, the priesthood was limited to the tribe of Levi and the family of Aaron. And even those who were priests were forbidden to approach the Presence of God. Only the high priest could do that on one day of the year (Yom Kippur, the Day of Atonement) following the precisely ordained procedure outlined for the event by the Lord.

In the new dispensation, all believers are priests with instant access to the Throne Room of the universe, day or night. Their function is **to offer up spiritual sacrifices** (in contrast to the animal, bird, and meal offerings of the Mosaic Law). The spiritual sacrifices of the NT priest are:

1. The presentation of the body as a living sacrifice, holy and acceptable to God. This is an act of spiritual worship (Rom. 12:1).
2. The sacrifice of praise. "That is, the fruit of our lips, giving thanks to His name" (Heb. 13:15).
3. The sacrifice of good works. "Do not forget to do good. . . ." This

sacrifice is pleasing to God (Heb. 13:16).
4. The sacrifice of possessions, or pocketbook. "Do not forget . . . to share." This sacrifice also is pleasing to the Lord (Heb. 13:16).
5. The sacrifice of service. Paul speaks of his ministry to the Gentiles as a priestly offering (Rom. 15:16).

These sacrifices are **acceptable to God through Jesus Christ**. It is only **through Jesus Christ**, our Mediator, that we can approach God in the first place, and it is only He who can make our offerings acceptable to God. All that we do — our worship and our service — is imperfect, flawed by sin. But before it reaches the Father, it passes through the Lord Jesus. He removes all the sin, and when it reaches God the Father it is perfectly acceptable.

The high priest in the OT wore a gold plate on his turban with the words HOLINESS TO THE LORD (Ex. 28:36) inscribed on it. It was for any sin that might be involved in the offerings of the people (Ex. 28:38). So our High Priest wears a miter for us, for any human failure that may be involved in our sacrifices.

The priesthood of all believers is a truth that should be understood, believed, and joyfully practiced by every Christian. At the same time, it must not be abused. Though all believers are priests, not every priest has the right to preach or teach in the assembly. There are certain controls which must be observed.

1. Women are forbidden to teach or to have authority over men; they are to keep silent (1 Tim. 2:12).
2. Men who speak should do so as the oracles of God (1 Pet. 4:11). That means they should have a distinct assurance that they are speaking the words which God would have them speak on that particular occasion.
3. All believers have some gift, just as every member of the human body has some function (Rom. 12:6; 1 Cor. 12:7). But not all gifts involve public speaking. Not all have the special service gifts of evangelist, pastor, or teacher (Eph. 4:11).
4. A young man should rekindle the

gift of God that is within him (2 Tim. 1:6). If that gift involves preaching, teaching, or some other form of public speaking, he should be given opportunity to exercise it in the assembly.

5. The priesthood of believers is seen in operation in 1 Corinthians 14:26: "How is it then brethren? Whenever you come together, each of you has a psalm, has a teaching, has a tongue, has a revelation, has an interpretation. Let all things be done for edification."

In that same chapter are many controls limiting the public exercise of gifts in a congregation to insure order and edification. The universal priesthood of Christians must not be used to justify abuses in the local church.

2:6 Still thinking of the building, Peter reverts to Christ the stone, and in particular, to Christ as the **chief cornerstone**. By quoting from Isaiah 28:16, he shows that Christ's role as **cornerstone** was foretold in Scripture. He points out that God has determined that Christ will have this unique position, that He is an **elect** and **precious** stone, and that He is completely dependable. No one who trusts in Him will ever be disappointed.

The word translated **cornerstone**[13] in this passage may be understood in at least three ways, and each applies with equal validity and force to the Lord Jesus.

1. **A cornerstone** in modern architecture is placed at the base of one corner, where it binds two walls together and symbolizes the foundation on which the entire building rests. Christ is the **cornerstone**, the only genuine foundation (1 Cor. 3:10, 11), the One who has united believing Jews and Gentiles (like two walls in one building) into one new man (Eph. 2:13, 14).

2. Some scholars think that this stone is the *keystone* in an arch. It is the stone which completes the arch and holds the rest of the building together. Our Lord certainly meets this description. He is the topmost stone in the arch, and without Him there would be no strength or cohesion to the building.

3. A third view is that the stone is the *capstone* in a pyramid, occupying the highest place in the structure. It is

the only stone of that shape in the structure. Its shape determines the shape of the entire pyramid. It is the last stone to be put in place. So Christ is the Capstone of the church, the truly unique Stone. The church gets its character from Him. When He returns, the building will be completed.

He is a stone **elect** and **precious**. He is **elect** in the sense that God has selected Him to occupy the place of chief honor; He is **precious** because there is not another like Him.

He **who believes on Him will by no means be put to shame**. The original passage in Isaiah from which this is quoted is rendered "he who believes will not act hastily." Put these two together and you have the wonderful promise that those who have Christ as their **cornerstone** are saved from frustrating humiliation and from frantic haste.

2:7 In the preceding verses the Lord Jesus has been presented as the *living* stone, a *rejected* stone, a *precious* stone and the *cornerstone*. Now, without using the word, Peter seems to picture Him as the touchstone. A touchstone reveals whether certain minerals rubbed against it are genuine or spurious. It shows, for instance, whether a nugget is gold or fool's gold.

When people come in contact with the Savior, they are shown for what they really are. In their attitude toward Him they reveal themselves. To true believers, **He is precious**; unbelievers reject Him. The believer can get some small indication of *how* **precious** He is by trying to imagine what life would be like without Him. Not all earthly pleasures are "worth comparing for a moment with a Christ-filled life." He is "Chief among ten thousand" and "altogether lovely" (Song 5:10, 16).

But what about **those who are disobedient** or disbelieve?[14] The writer of Psalm 118 predicted that this precious stone would be rejected by the builders, but would later become the head of the corner.

There is a persistent legend in connection with the building of Solomon's temple that perfectly illustrates this prophecy. The stones for the temple were prepared in advance in a nearby quarry. As they were needed, they were raised up to the building site. One day the workers in the quarry sent up a stone of unique shape and proportions. The masons saw no place for it in the building so they carelessly pushed it over the hill where, in time, it became overgrown with moss and surrounded with weeds. As the temple neared completion, the masons called for a stone of certain dimensions. The men in the quarry replied, "We sent that stone up to you long ago." After careful search, the discarded stone was found and was set in its proper place in the temple.

The application is obvious. The Lord Jesus presented Himself to the nation of Israel at His First Advent. The people, and especially the rulers, had no room for Him in their scheme of things. They rejected Him and delivered Him to be crucified.

But God raised Him from the dead and seated Him at His own right hand in heaven. When the Rejected One returns to earth the second time, He will come as King of kings and Lord of lords. He will then be publicly manifested as **the chief cornerstone**.

2:8 Now the figure changes from Christ the touchstone and the head of the corner to Christ the **stone of stumbling**. Isaiah predicted that for those who did not believe, He would be a stone that will make men stumble and **a rock** that will make them fall (Isa. 8:14, 15).

This was literally fulfilled in the history of the nation of Israel. When their Messiah came, the Jews were offended by His origins and His simple way of life. They wanted a political demagogue and a military strongman. In spite of the most convincing proofs, they refused to accept Him as the promised Messiah.

But this does not apply only to Israel. For any who will not believe on Jesus, He becomes **a stumbling stone and a rock** that trips them. Men either bow before Him in repentance and faith to salvation or stumble over Him into hell. "What might have been their salvation is made the cause of their deeper condemnation." There can be no neutrality; He must be either Savior or Judge.

They stumble, being disobedient to the word. Why do **they stumble**? Not because of honest intellectual difficulties. Not because there is anything about the Lord Jesus that makes it impossible to believe in Him. **They stumble** because they willfully disobey **the word**. The trouble is in the human will. The reason men are not saved is because they do not want to be saved (John 5:40).

The latter part of verse 8, **to which they also were appointed**, seems to say that they were destined to disobey **the word**. Is this what it means? No, this verse teaches that all those who willfully disobey **the word** are destined to **stumble**. The words **to which they also were appointed** refer back to the entire preceding clause, **they stumble, being disobedient to the word**. God has decreed that all who refuse to bow to the Lord Jesus will **stumble**. If a man insists on going on in unbelief, then he is appointed to stumble. "Unwillingness to obey makes stumbling a foregone conclusion" (JBP).

2:9 Peter now turns again to the privileges of believers. They are **a chosen generation, a royal priesthood, a holy nation**, God's **special people**. God had promised these very privileges to the nation of Israel if they would obey Him:

> Now therefore, if you will indeed obey My voice and keep My covenant, then you shall be a special treasure to Me above all people, for all the earth is Mine. And you shall be to Me a kingdom of priests and a holy nation (Ex. 19:5, 6a).

Because of unbelief Israel failed to realize the promise of God, and the nation forfeited its place as God's own people. During the present age, the church occupies the favored place that Israel lost through disobedience.

Believers today are **a chosen generation, chosen** by God before the foundation of the world to belong to Christ (Eph. 1:4). But instead of being an earthly race with common ancestry and distinct physical characteristics, Christians are a heavenly people with a divine parentage and spiritual resemblances.

Believers are also **a royal priesthood**. This is the second **priesthood** mentioned in this chapter. In verse 5, believers are described as holy priests, offering up spiritual sacrifices. Now they are said to be **royal** priests, proclaiming the excellencies of God. As *holy* priests, they enter the sanctuary of heaven by faith to worship. As **royal** priests, they go out into the world to witness. This difference in priesthood is illustrated by the imprisonment of Paul and Silas at Philippi. As holy priests they sang praises to God at midnight; as **royal** priests they preached the gospel to their jailer (Acts 16:25, 31).

Believers are **a holy nation**. It was God's intention that Israel should be a nation distinguished by holiness. But the Israelites stooped to the sinful practices of their Gentile neighbors. So Israel has been set aside temporarily and the church is now God's **holy nation**.

Finally, Christians are a **people** for God's own possession. They belong to Him in a unique way and are of **special** value to Him.

The last part of verse 9 describes the responsibility of those who are God's new race, **priesthood, nation** and **people**. We should **proclaim** the excellencies **of Him who called** us **out of darkness into His marvelous light**. Once we were groping in the darkness of sin and shame. By a stupendous deliverance we have been transferred into the kingdom of His dear Son. The light is as clear and brilliant as the darkness was oppressive. How we should shout **the praises** of the One who did all this for us!

2:10 Peter closes this section by referring to the book of Hosea. Using the prophet's own tragic family life as an object lesson, God had pronounced judgment on the nation of Israel. Because of their unfaithfulness to Him, He said He would no longer have pity on them and that they would no more be His people (Hos. 1:6, 9). But the casting aside of Israel was not final, for the Lord also promised that in a future day, Israel would be restored:

". . . I will have mercy on her who had not obtained mercy; then I will say to those who were not My people, 'You are My people!' And they shall say, 'You are my God!' " (Hos. 2:23).

Some of the people to whom Peter was writing had once been part of the nation of Israel. Now they were members of the church. Through faith in Christ, they had become the people of God, while unbelieving Jews were still cast aside.

So Peter sees in the condition of the converted Jews of his day a partial fulfillment of Hosea 2:23. In Christ, they had become God's new people; in Christ, they had **obtained mercy**. This handful of saved Jews enjoyed the blessings promised to Israel through Hosea long before Israel nationally would enjoy them.

No one should conclude from this passage in Peter that because the church is now God's people, He is through with Israel as a nation. Neither should one assume that the church is now the Israel of God, or that the promises made to Israel now apply to the church. Israel and the church are separate and distinct entities, and an understanding of this distinction is one of the most important keys to interpreting the prophetic word.

Israel was God's chosen earthly people from the time of the call of Abraham to the coming of the Messiah. The nation's rebellion and faithlessness reached its awesome climax when Christ was nailed to the cross. Because of this crowning sin, God temporarily set aside Israel as His chosen people. They are His ancient earthly people today but not His chosen people.

During the present age, God has a new people — the church. This Church Age forms a parenthesis in God's dealings with Israel. When the parenthesis is closed, that is, when the church is caught away to heaven, God will resume His dealings with Israel. Then a believing portion of the nation will become God's people again.

The final fulfillment of Hosea's prophecy is still future. It will take place at the Second Advent. The nation that rejected its Messiah will "look on Me whom they pierced. Yes, they will mourn for Him as one mourns for his only son, and grieve for Him as one grieves for a firstborn" (Zech. 12:10). Then repentant, believing Israel will receive mercy and will become God's people once more.

The point Peter is making in verse 10 is that believing Jews today enjoy an advance fulfillment of Hosea's prophecy, while unbelieving Jews are still alienated from God. The complete and final fulfillment will take place when "the Deliverer will come out of Zion" and "turn away ungodliness from Jacob" (Rom. 11:26).

II. THE BELIEVER'S RELATIONSHIPS (2:11–4:6)

A. As a Pilgrim in Relation to the World (2:11, 12)

2:11 Most of the rest of 1 Peter concerns the conduct that should characterize the Christian in the various relationships of life. Peter reminds believers that they are **sojourners and pilgrims** in the world and that this fact should leave its stamp on all their behavior. They are **sojourners** in the sense that they are living in a foreign country where they do not have the rights of citizens. They are **pilgrims** in the sense that they are obliged to live for a while in a place which is not their permanent home.

The hymns of yesterday remind us of our pilgrimage. For instance:

Called from above, and heavenly men
 by birth
(Who once were but the citizens of earth),
As pilgrims here, we seek a heav'nly
 home,
Our portion in the ages yet to come.

We are but strangers here, we do not
 crave
A home on earth, which gave Thee but
 a grave:
Thy cross has severed ties which bound
 us here,
Thyself our treasure in a brighter sphere.
 – James G. Deck

But these sentiments have largely dropped from our hymnology. When the church has settled down in the world, it seems a bit hypocritical to be singing beyond our experience.

When we read the exhortation to **abstain from fleshly lusts which war against the soul**, we think immediately of sexual sins. But the application is wider than that; it refers to any strong desire that is inconsistent with the will of God. It would include over-indulgence in food or drink, catering to the body with excessive sleep, the determination to amass material possessions, or the hankering for worldly pleasures. All these things wage incessant warfare against our spiritual well-being. They hinder communion with God. They deter spiritual growth.

2:12 Not only must we exercise discipline in the area of fleshly indulgence, but we must also maintain our **conduct honorable**[15] **among the Gentiles**, that is, the pagan world. In our day we must not pattern our lives after the world. We should be marching to the beat of a different drummer.

Almost inevitably we will be criticized. At the time Peter wrote this Letter, writes Erdman:

> . . . the Christians were being slandered as irreligious because of not worshiping the heathen gods, as morons and ascetics because of refraining from popular vices, as disloyal to the government because of claiming allegiance to a heavenly King.[16]

Such criticism cannot be avoided. But under no circumstances should believers give the world a *valid* reason for such reproach. All slanders should be refuted by an unbroken record of good deeds. Then the accusers will be compelled to **glorify God in the day of visitation**.

A **day of visitation** is any time the Lord draws near, either in grace or in judgment. The expression is used in Luke 19:41–44. Jesus wept over Jerusalem because it did not know the time of its visitation, that is, Jerusalem did not realize that the Messiah had come in love and mercy. Here it may mean: (1) The day when God's grace will visit the critics and they are saved, or (2) the day of judgment when the unsaved will stand before God.

Saul of Tarsus illustrates the first interpretation. He had shared in accusing Stephen, but Stephen's good deeds triumphed over all opposition. When God visited Saul in mercy on the road to Damascus, the repentant Pharisee glorified God and went forth, like Stephen, to influence others by the radiance of a Christ-filled life. Jowett says:

> The beautiful life is to raise men's thoughts in homage to the glorious God. When they behold the Divine realized in the human, they too are to be wooed into heavenly fellowship. They are to be wooed, not by the eloquence of our speech, but by the radiance of our behavior. By the imposing grace of noble living we are to "put to silence the ignorance of

foolish men," and that silence will be for them the first stage in a life of aspiring consecration.[17]

In the second interpretation, the thought is that unsaved people will be compelled to **glorify God in the day of** judgment. They will have no excuse, for they not only heard the gospel, they saw it in the lives of their Christian relatives, friends, and neighbors. God will then be vindicated through the blameless conduct of His children.

B. As a Citizen in Relation to Government (2:13–17)

2:13 The next five verses deal with the Christian's relation toward government. The key word here is **submit**. In fact, the injunction to submit is found four times in the Epistle.

Citizens are to **submit** to the government (2:13).

Slaves are to *submit* to their masters (2:18).

Wives are to *submit* to their husbands (3:1).

Younger believers are to *submit* to the elders (5:5).

Lyall says:

The ultimate Christian answer to persecution, detractors and critics is that of a blameless life, conduct beyond reproach and good citizenship. In particular . . . submission is a supremely Christlike virtue.[18]

Human governments are instituted by God (Rom. 13:1). Rulers are God's servants (Rom. 13:4). Even if the rulers are not believers, they are still God's men officially. Even if they are dictators and tyrants, their rule is better than no rule at all. The complete absence of rule is anarchy, and no society can continue under anarchy. So any government is better than no government at all. Order is better than chaos. Believers should **submit to every** human institution **for the Lord's sake**. In doing so, they are fulfilling His will and doing the thing that pleases Him. These instructions apply to the emperor or to whoever is the supreme ruler. Even if Nero happens to be occupying the imperial palace, the general exhortation is to be subject to him.

2:14 The injunction of obedience applies to subordinate officials such as **governors**. They are authorized by God to punish offenders and to **praise** those who keep the law. Actually, government officials have little time or inclination to do the latter, but that does not alter the responsibility of the Christian to obey! The historian Arnold Toynbee observed that "as long as original sin remains an element in human nature, Caesar will always have plenty to do."

Of course, there are exceptions. There is a time when obedience is not required. If a human government orders a believer to act contrary to the revealed will of God, then the believer must disobey the government. In that case he has a higher responsibility; he should obey God rather than men (Acts 5:29). If punishment is meted out for his disobedience, he should endure it courageously. Under no circumstances should he rebel or seek to overthrow the government.

Technically, those who smuggle Bibles into closed countries are breaking the law. But they are obeying a law that has precedence over any human law — the command to go into all the world with the gospel. So they cannot be condemned on scriptural grounds.

Suppose the government orders a Christian into the armed forces. Is he obligated to obey and to bear arms? If he feels that this is in direct violation of God's word, he should first exhaust any options that are open to him in the status of a non-combatant or a conscientious objector. If these fail, then he would have to refuse induction and bear the consequences.

Many Christians do not have conscientious scruples about serving in the military forces. It is a matter in which each one should be fully convinced in his own mind, and allow liberty for others to disagree.

The questions as to whether a Christian should vote or engage in politics are of a different order. The government does not demand these things, so it is not a question of obedience or disobedience. Each one must act in the light of the principles of conduct and citizenship found in the Bible. Here too we must allow liberty for differing viewpoints and not insist that others see eye to eye with us.

2:15 God's **will** is that His people should live so honorably and unblamably that the unconverted will have no legitimate basis for accusation. By lives of exemplary conduct, Christians can and should expose the **ignorance** of the charges made against Christianity by **foolish men**.

Christians and the Christian faith are ceaselessly bombarded by **the ignorance of foolish men**. It may be in the university classroom; it may be in the science laboratory; it may be in the pulpit. Peter says that one of the best answers to such blasting is a holy life.

2:16 Act **as free** men. We are not in bondage or slavery to civil authorities. We need not live in servility or terror. After all, we are the Lord's free men. But that does not mean we are free to sin. **Liberty** does not mean license. Freedom does not include lawlessness. So we must never use our freedom as a pretext for evil. Sinful disobedience should never be justified by some pseudo-spiritual excuse. The cause of Christ is never advanced by evil masquerading in religious clothes.

If we live as **bondservants of God**, our relationship with governmental authorities will fall into proper place. We are to act in the light of His presence, obey Him in all things, do all for His glory. The best citizen is a believer who lives as a slave of the Lord. Unfortunately, most governments don't realize how much they owe to Christians who believe and obey the Bible.

Ponder the expression **bondservants of God**. "Heaven takes our most dreaded terms," F. B. Meyer writes, "and makes them sparkle in its own light, till what seemed the synonym of terror becomes the target of our noblest aims."[19]

2:17 No relationship of life can be left outside the sphere of Christian responsibility. So Peter here runs the gamut with four crisp commands.

Honor all people. We cannot always **honor** their words or their behavior, but we can remember that every single life is of more value than all the world. We can recognize that every person was made in the image and likeness of God. We must never forget that the Lord Jesus bled and died for even the most unworthy.

Love the brotherhood. We are to **love** all men, but we are especially obligated to love the members of our spiritual family. This is a love like God's love for us. It is utterly undeserved, it goes out to the loveless, it looks for no reward, and it is stronger than death.

Fear God. We **fear** Him when we reverence Him as the supreme Lord. Glorifying Him then becomes our number one priority. We **fear** doing anything that would displease Him and we **fear** misrepresenting Him before men.

Honor the king. Peter returns to the subject of human rulers for a final reminder. We are to respect our rulers as officials appointed by God for the maintenance of an ordered society. This means we must pay "taxes to whom taxes are due, customs to whom customs, fear to whom fear" (Rom. 13:7). Generally speaking, the Christian can live under any form of government. The only time he should disobey is when he is ordered to compromise his loyalty or obedience to the Lord Jesus Christ.

C. As a Servant in Relation to His Master (2:18–25)

2:18 It is significant that the NT gives more instructions to **servants** than to kings. Many of the early believers were **servants**, and the Scripture shows that most Christians came from the middle or lower strata of society (Matt. 11:5; Mark 12:37; 1 Cor. 1:26–29).

This passage is addressed to domestic **servants**, but the principles apply to employees of any kind. The basic appeal is to submit to the master with all respect. It is a built-in fact of life that in any society or organization, there must be authority on the one hand, and obedience to that authority on the other. It is for any servant's own good to submit to his master, otherwise he would not have employment. But it is much more important for a *Christian* to submit. More than his paycheck is involved; his testimony depends on it.

Obedience should not vary according to the temperament of the employer. Anyone can submit to an employer who is **good and gentle**. Believers are called to go beyond that and be respectful and obedient to the **harsh**, overbearing boss. This stands out as distinctly Christian behavior.

2:19 When we suffer unjustly, we win God's approval. He is pleased when He finds us so conscious of our relation to Him that we endure undeserved pain without vindicating self or fighting back. When we meekly take unjust treatment, we display Christ; this supernatural life gains God's "Well done."

2:20 There is no virtue in patient suffering for our own misdeeds. Certainly there is no glory for God in it. Such suffering will never mark us out as Christians, or make others want to become Christians. But suffering **patiently** for well-doing is the thing that counts. It is so unnatural, so other-worldly that it shocks people into conviction of sin and, hopefully, into salvation.

2:21 The thought of believers' suffering for righteousness' sake leads inevitably to this sublime passage on our great **example**, the Lord Jesus. No one was ever treated as unjustly as He, or bore it as patiently.

We have been called to act as He acted, suffering for the wrongs of others. The word used here for **example** carries the idea of a copybook that contains flawless penmanship. The pupil seeks to reproduce the original as closely as possible. When he copies the model carefully, his writing is quite good. But the further he moves away from it, the more the copy worsens. Our safety is in staying close to the Original.

2:22 Our Lord did not suffer for His own sins because He had none. "He knew no sin" (2 Cor. 5:21); He **committed no sin** (this verse); "in Him there is no sin" (1 Jn. 3:5).

His speech was never tainted by **deceit**. He never lied or even shaded the truth. Think about that! A Person once lived on this planet who was absolutely honest, absolutely free from trickery or **deceit**.

2:23 He was patient under provocation. **When He was reviled**, He **did not** pay back in kind. When blamed He did not answer back. When accused He did not defend Himself. He was wondrously free from the lust of self-vindication.

An unknown author has written:

It is a mark of deepest and truest humility to see ourselves condemned without cause, and to be silent under it. To be silent under insult and wrong is a very noble imitation of our Lord. When we remember in how many ways He suffered, who in no way deserved it, where are our senses when we feel called to defend and excuse ourselves?

When He suffered, He did not threaten. "No ungentle, threatening word escaped His silent tongue." Perhaps His assailants mistook His silence for weakness. If they had tried it they would have found it was not weakness but supernatural strength!

What was His hidden resource in bearing up under such unprovoked abuse? He trusted God **who judges righteously**. And we are called to do the same:

Beloved, do not avenge yourselves, but rather give place to wrath; for it is written, "Vengeance is Mine, I will repay," says the Lord. Therefore, "if your enemy hungers, feed him; if he thirsts, give him a drink, for in so doing you will heap coals of fire on his head." Do not be overcome by evil, but overcome evil with good (Rom. 12:19–21).

2:24 The Savior's sufferings were not only exemplary, but expiatory as well. We cannot imitate His sufferings in this respect, and Peter does not suggest that we should. Rather the argument seems to be as follows: The Savior's agony was not brought on by His own sins, for He had none. It was for **our sins** He was nailed to the cross. Because He has suffered for **our sins** once for all, we should never allow ourselves to get into the position where we have to suffer for them too. The fact that He died *for* them should cause us to die *to* them. And yet, it is not simply a matter of negative goodness; we should not only die to sin but **live to righteousness**.

By whose stripes you were healed. The word **stripes** is actually singular in the original, perhaps suggesting that His body was one massive welt. What should be our attitude toward sin when our healing cost the Savior so much? Theodoret comments: "A new and strange method of healing. The doctor suffered the cost, and the sick received the healing."

2:25 Before conversion, we **were like sheep going astray** — lost, torn, bruised, bleeding. Peter's mention of straying **sheep** is the last of six references to Isaiah 53 in this passage:

v. 21 *Christ . . . suffered for us* (cf. Isa. 53:4, 5).

v. 22 *He committed no sin, nor was deceit found in His mouth* (cf. Isa. 53:9).

v. 23 *When He was reviled, He did not revile in return* (cf. Isa. 53:7).

v. 24 *Who Himself bore our sins in His own body on the tree* (cf. Isa. 53:4, 11).

v. 24 *By whose stripes you were healed* (cf. Isa. 53:5).

v. 25 *For you were like sheep going astray* (cf. Isa. 53:6).

When we are saved, we return to the Shepherd — the good Shepherd who laid down His life for the sheep (John 10:11); the great Shepherd who "tends with sweet, unwearied care the flock for which He bled," and the Chief Shepherd who will soon appear to lead His sheep into the green pastures above — from which they will never stray.

Conversion is returning **to the** Guardian[20] **of our souls**. We were His by creation, but became lost through sin. Now we return to His keeping care, and are safe and secure forever.

D. As a Wife in Relation to Her Husband (3:1–6)

3:1 Peter has stressed the obligation of Christians to submit to human government and to earthly masters. He now takes up the submission of **wives** to their **husbands**.

Every wife is to **be submissive to** her husband, whether he is a believer or not. God has given to the man the place of headship, and it is His will that the woman should acknowledge the authority of the man. The relationship between husband and wife is a picture of that between Christ and the church. The woman should obey her husband just as the church should obey Christ.

This is considered passé in our society. Women are rising to places of authority over man, and our society is becoming increasingly matriarchal. In many churches, women seem to be more active and gifted than the men. But God's word stands. The headship of man is the divine order. No matter how reasonable the arguments may sound, nothing but trouble and chaos can ultimately result when woman usurps authority over the man.

Even when a woman's husband is an unbeliever, she should still respect him as her head. This will be a testimony to him of her faith in Christ. Her **conduct** as an obedient, loving, devoted wife may be used to win him to the Savior.

And she may win him **without a word**. This means that the wife need not be preaching to her husband constantly. Possibly great harm has been done by wives who nagged their husbands concerning the gospel, cramming it down their throats. The emphasis here is on the wife's winning her husband by living Christ daily before him.

But suppose a husband interferes with his wife in her Christian life. What should she do then? If he requires her to disobey a plain command of Scripture, then she must disobey her husband and be true to the Lord. If, however, the matter involves a Christian privilege rather than a clear duty, she should be subject to her husband and forego the privilege.

When Peter speaks about a Christian wife having a pagan husband, he does not thereby condone a believer's marrying an unbeliever. This is never God's will. The apostle is dealing primarily with cases where the wife was saved after marriage. Her obligation is to **be submissive** even to an unbelieving husband.

3:2 The unsaved husband may be impressed by the reverent and **chaste conduct** of his wife. The Spirit of God may use this to convict him of his own sinfulness, and he may come to faith in Christ.

George Müller told of a wealthy German whose wife was a devout believer. This man was a heavy drinker, spending late nights in the tavern. She would send the servants to bed, stay up till he returned, receive him kindly, and never scold him or complain. At times she would even have to undress him and put him to bed.

One night in the tavern he said to his cronies, "I bet if we go to my house, my wife will be sitting up, waiting for me.

She'll come to the door, give us a royal welcome, and even make supper for us, if I ask her."

They were skeptical at first, but decided to go along and see. Sure enough, she came to the door, received them courteously, and willingly agreed to make supper for them without the slightest trace of resentment. After serving them, she went off to her room. As soon as she had left, one of the men began to condemn the husband. "What kind of a man are you to treat such a good woman so miserably?" The accuser got up without finishing his supper and left the house. Another did the same and another till they had all departed without eating the meal.

Within a half hour, the husband became deeply convicted of his wickedness, and especially of his heartless treatment of his wife. He went to his wife's room, asked her to pray for him, repented of his sins, and surrendered to Christ. From that time on, he became a devoted disciple of the Lord Jesus. Won without a word!

George Müller advised:

> Don't be discouraged if you have to suffer from unconverted relatives. Perhaps very shortly the Lord may give you the desire of your heart, and answer your prayer for them. But in the meantime, seek to commend the truth, not by reproaching them on account of their behavior toward *you*, but by manifesting toward *them* the meekness, gentleness and kindness of the Lord Jesus Christ.[21]

3:3 The subject here seems to change to women's apparel, but actually the apostle is dealing primarily with the best ways for a wife to please and serve her husband. It is not her outward appearance that will influence him as much as her inner life of holiness and submission.

Various types of outward **adornment** are to be avoided:

1. **Arranging the hair**. Some think that this excludes even modest braids. It is more likely that Peter is speaking against the excess of mountainous coiffures with terraces of braids, which were popular in ancient Rome.
2. **Wearing gold**. Some interpret this as an absolute prohibition against any gold jewelry. Others see it as forbidding showy and extravagant displays.
3. **Putting on fine apparel**. Obviously, it is not the wearing of clothing that is forbidden, but the wearing of ostentatious dress. Read Isaiah 3:16–25 to see what God thinks about all forms of extravagant adornment.

CHRISTIAN DRESS

In the matter of clothing and jewelry, there are guidelines that apply to all believers, men as well as women. A first principle is expense. How much do we spend on clothes? Is it all necessary? Could the money be spent in better ways?

First Timothy 2:9 forbids expensive clothes: "not with . . . costly clothing." It is not a matter of whether or not we can afford them. It is sin for a Christian to spend money on expensive clothes, because God's word forbids it. Compassion forbids it too. The desperate plight of our neighbors in other lands, their enormous spiritual and physical needs, point up the callousness of spending money unnecessarily on clothing.

This applies not only to the quality of the clothes we buy but to the quantity as well. The closets of some Christians look like branch clothing stores. Often as they travel on vacation, a rod stretched over the back seat of the car holds an array of dresses, shirts, and suits that rivals the samples of a traveling clothing salesman.

Why do we do it? Is it not a matter of pride? We love to be complimented on our good taste, our fine appearance. The expense involved in buying clothes is only one principle that should guide us in its choice.

Another is modesty. Paul says "with propriety and moderation." One meaning of the word *propriety* is "decent." One of the functions of clothing is to hide man's nakedness. At least, that's the way it was in the beginning. But now clothing seems to be designed to reveal increasingly large areas of the anatomy. Man is thus glorying in his shame. It is not surprising to find ungodly men doing this, but it is rather shocking when Christians imitate them.

But modest can also mean attractive. This suggests that the Christian should dress neatly. There is no virtue in shabbiness, in untidiness. Oswald Chambers said that slovenliness is an insult to the Holy Spirit. The believer's clothes should be clean, pressed, in good repair, and well-fitting.

In general, the Christian must avoid fashions that attract attention to himself. That is not his function in life. He is not on earth as an ornament, but as a fruit-bearing branch of the Vine. We can attract attention to ourselves in many ways. Wearing clothes that are old-fashioned will do it. The Christian should also avoid wearing clothes that are uncommonly plain, or loud, or odd.

Finally, the Christian — and this may be a special problem for the young believer — should avoid clothes that are suggestive or provocative. We have already referred to fashions that are "revealing." But clothes can cover the whole body and still arouse unholy lust in others. Modern fashions are not designed to encourage spirituality. On the contrary, they reflect the obsession with sex in our age. The believer should never wear clothes that incite passions or make it hard for others to live a Christian life.

The great problem, of course, is the enormous social pressure to conform. This always has been true and always will be. Christians need plenty of spine to resist the extremes in fashion, to swim against the tide of public opinion, and to dress in a manner that befits the gospel.

If we make Christ the Lord of our wardrobe, all will be well. ‡

3:4 The clothing which makes a believer genuinely attractive is the beauty of **the hidden person**. Fashionable coiffures, costly jewelry, and fine clothing are perishable. In presenting this vivid contrast, Peter challenges us to make a choice. F. B. Meyer notes: "Plenty are there whose outward body is richly decked, but whose inner being is clothed in rags; whilst others, whose garments are worn and threadbare, are all glorious within."[22]

Men think jewels are precious; **God** considers **precious** the jewel of **a gentle and quiet spirit**.

3:5 Godly women of the OT **adorned themselves** by cultivating the moral and spiritual beauty of the inner life. One aspect of this beauty was a dutiful submission **to their own husbands**. These **holy women trusted in God**. They lived God-centered lives. Desiring to please Him in all things, they recognized His order in the home and were **submissive to their own husbands**.

3:6 **Sarah** is cited as an example. She **obeyed Abraham, calling him lord**. This takes us back to Genesis 18:12 where we read that Sarah said this "within herself." She did not go around and make a loud profession of submission to Abraham by publicly calling him *lord*. Rather, in her inward life, she recognized him as her head, and this recognition was displayed by her actions.

Those women who follow Sarah's example are her children. Jewish women are descendants of Sarah by natural birth. But to be her **daughters** in the best sense, they must imitate her personal character. Children should carry the family likeness.

They should **do good** and let nothing terrify them. This means that a Christian wife should fill her God-appointed role as an obedient helpmate, and not be terrified even if she must suffer the unreasonable conduct of an unbelieving husband, except, of course, when it becomes violent or life-threatening.

E. As a Husband in Relation to His Wife (3:7)

Now the apostle turns to **husbands** and shows the corresponding duties they must fulfill. They should live considerately with their wives, showing love, courtesy, and **understanding**. They should bestow the tender regard on their wives that is appropriate for members of the **weaker** sex.

In this day of the women's liberation movement, the Bible might seem out of step with the times in speaking of women as the **weaker vessels**. But it is a simple fact of life that the *average* woman is **weaker** than the man physically. Also, generally speaking, she does not have the same power to control her emotions and is more frequently guided by emotional reactions than by rational, logical thought. The handling of deep theological problems is not characteristically her forte. And, in general, she is more dependent than the man.

But the fact that a woman is **weaker** in some ways does not mean that she is inferior to man; the Bible never suggests this. Neither does it mean that she might not actually be stronger, or more competent in some areas. As a matter of fact, women are generally more devoted to Christ than men. And they usually are better able to bear prolonged pain and adversity.

A man's attitude toward his wife should recognize the fact that she is a fellow heir **of the grace of life**. This refers to a marriage in which both are believers. Though weaker than the man in some ways, the woman enjoys equal standing before God and shares equally the gift of everlasting life. Also she is more than her husband's equal in bringing new physical life into the world.

When there is discord, prayers are hindered. Bigg says: "The sighs of the injured wife come between the husband's prayers and God's hearing."[23] Also it is very difficult for a couple to pray together when something is disrupting their fellowship. For the peace and welfare of the home it is important for the husband and wife to observe a few basic rules:

1. Maintain absolute honesty in order to have a basis of mutual confidence.

2. Keep lines of communication open. There must be a constant readiness to talk things out. When steam is allowed to build up in the boiler, an explosion is inevitable. Talking things out includes the willingness for each to say, "I am sorry" and to forgive — perhaps indefinitely.

3. Overlook minor faults and idiosyncrasies. Love covers a multitude of sins. Don't demand perfection in others when you are unable to produce it in yourself.

4. Strive for unity in finances. Avoid overspending, installment buying, and the lust to keep up with the Joneses.

5. Remember that love is a commandment, not an uncontrollable emotion. Love means all that is included in

1 Corinthians 13. Love is courteous, for instance; it will keep you from criticizing or contradicting your partner in front of others. Love will keep you from quarreling in front of your children, which could undermine their security. In these and a hundred other ways, love creates a happy atmosphere in the home and rules out strife and separations.

F. As a Brother in Relation to the Fellowship (3:8)

That this verse deals primarily with the Christian and his relation to the fellowship seems evident from the exhortations to unity and brotherly love. The other three exhortations could have a wider application.

The word **Finally** does not mean that Peter is about to close his Epistle. He has been speaking to various classes of individuals such as servants, wives, and husbands. Now, as a finale, he has a word for **all of you**.

Let all of you be of one mind. It is not expected that Christians will see eye-to-eye on everything. That would be uniformity, not unity. The best formula is contained in the well-known expression: In fundamentals, unity; in non-essentials, liberty; in everything, love. We are to have **compassion for one another**. Literally, this means "to suffer with," and the admonition is especially appropriate when given to those undergoing persecution. The advice is for all times because no age is exempt from suffering.

Love as brothers. An unknown author writes:

> Providence does not ask us whom we would like to be our brethren — that is settled for us; but we are bidden to love them, irrespective of our natural predilections and tastes. You say, "That is impossible!" But remember that true love does not necessarily originate in the emotions, but in the will; it consists not in feeling but in doing; not in sentiment, but in action; not in soft words, but in noble and unselfish deeds.

Tenderhearted means having a heart sensitive to the needs and feelings of others. It refuses to turn cold, callous, or cynical in spite of abuse.

Courteous[24] — It seems so proper

that courtesy should be taught as one of
the Christian virtues. Essentially it
means humbly thinking of others, putting others first, and saying and doing
the gracious thing. Courtesy serves others before self, jumps at opportunities to
assist, and expresses prompt appreciation for kindnesses received. It is never
coarse, vulgar, or rude.

G. As a Sufferer in Relation to Perse-
cutors (3:9–4:6)

3:9 This whole Epistle is written
against a backdrop of persecution and
suffering. From this verse to 4:6 the subject is the Christian and his relation to
persecutors. Repeatedly, believers are
urged to suffer for righteousness' sake
without retaliating. We are not to repay
evil for evil or reviling for reviling. Instead we are to bless those who mistreat
us, and to repay insult with kindness.
As Christians, we are not called to harm
others but to do them good, not to curse
but to bless. Then God rewards this type
of behavior with **a blessing**.

3:10 In verses 10–12, Peter quotes
Psalm 34:12–16a to confirm that God's
blessing rests on the one who refrains
from evil deeds and evil speech, and
practices righteousness.

The force of the first verse is this: The
one who wishes to enjoy **life** to the hilt
and experience **good days** should **refrain**
from speaking **evil** or **deceit**. He should
not repay insult and lies in kind.

To **love life** is condemned in John
12:25, but there it means to live for self
and disregard the true purpose of life.
Here it means to live in the way God intended.

3:11 Not only evil speech, but **evil**
deeds are forbidden. To retaliate only
intensifies the conflict. It is stooping to
use the world's weapons. The believer
should repay **evil** with **good**, and promote **peace** by meekly enduring abuse.
Fire cannot be fought with fire.

The only way to overcome evil is to let
it run its course, so that it does not find
the resistance it is looking for. Resistance
merely creates further evil and adds fuel
to the flames. But when evil meets no opposition and encounters no obstacle but
only patient endurance, its sting is
drawn, and at last it meets an opponent

which is more than its match. Of course,
this can only happen when the last ounce
of resistance is abandoned, and the renunciation of revenge is complete. Then
evil cannot find its mark, it can breed no
further evil, and is left barren (Selected).

3:12 The LORD looks with approval
on those who act righteously. He is attentive **to their prayers**. Of course, the
Lord hears the prayers of all His people.
But He undertakes in a special sense the
cause of those who suffer for Christ's
sake without returning evil for evil.

**The face of the LORD is against those
who do evil.** This primarily refers to the
persecutors of His people. But it may
also include the believer who fights back
against his foes with physical violence
and intemperate language. **Evil** is evil,
and God opposes it wherever He finds
it — whether in the saved or in the lost.

In quoting Psalm 34:16, Peter left out
the closing words: " . . . to cut off the remembrance of them from the earth."
This omission was not an oversight. We
are living in the dispensation of the
grace of God; it is the acceptable year of
the Lord. The day of vengeance of our
God has not come as yet. When the Lord
Jesus returns as King of kings and Lord
of lords, He will punish evildoers and
cut off the remembrance of them from
the earth.

3:13 Peter resumes his argument
with a question: **"And who is he who
will harm you if you become followers
of what is good?"** The answer implied
is "No one." And yet the history of the
martyrs seems to prove that enemies of
the gospel do harm faithful disciples.

There are at least two possible explanations of this paradox:

1. Generally speaking, those who
follow a path of righteousness are not
harmed. A policy of nonresistance disarms the opposition. There may be exceptions, but as a rule, the one who
is eager for the right is protected from
harm by his very goodness.

2. The worst that the foe can do to
a Christian does not give eternal harm.
The enemy can injure his body but he
cannot damage his soul.

During World War II a Christian boy
of twelve refused to join a certain movement in Europe. "Don't you know that

we have power to kill you?" they said. "Don't you know," he replied quietly, "that I have power to die for Christ!" He had the conviction that no one was able to harm him.

3:14 But suppose a Christian **should suffer** persecution because of his loyalty to the Savior. What then? Three results follow:

1. God overrules the suffering for His own glory.
2. He uses the suffering to bring blessing to others.
3. He blesses the one who suffers for His name.

Don't be afraid of men, or terrified by **their threats**. How well the martyrs lived out this policy! When Polycarp was promised release if he would blaspheme Christ, he said, "Eighty six years I have served Christ and He has never done me wrong. How can I blaspheme my King and my Savior?" When the proconsul threatened to expose him to the wild beasts, he replied, "It is well for me to be speedily released from this life of misery." Finally the ruler threatened to burn him alive. Polycarp said, "I fear not the fire that burns for a moment: You do not know that which burns forever and ever."

3:15 In the last part of verse 14 and in this verse, Peter quotes from Isaiah 8:12b, 13, which says: "Nor be afraid of their threats, nor be troubled. The LORD of hosts, Him you shall hallow; Let Him be your fear, and let Him be your dread." Someone has said, "We fear God so little because we fear man so much."

The Isaiah passage speaks of *The LORD of hosts* as the One to be reverenced. Quoting it, Peter by inspiration of the Holy Spirit says, **sanctify the Lord God**[25] **in your hearts**.

To reverence the Lord means to make Him the Sovereign of our lives. All we do and say should be in His will, for His pleasure, and for His glory. The lordship of Christ should dominate every area of our lives — our possessions, our occupation, our library, our marriage, our spare time — nothing can be excluded.

Always be ready to give a defense to everyone who asks you a reason for the hope that is in you, with meekness and fear. This applies primarily to times when Christians are being persecuted because of their faith. The consciousness of the presence of the Lord Christ should impart a holy boldness and inspire the believer to witness a good confession.

The verse is also applicable to everyday life. People often ask us questions which quite naturally open the door to speak to them about the Lord. We should **be ready** to tell them what great things the Lord has done for us. This witnessing should be done in either case with gentleness and reverence. There should be no trace of harshness, bitterness or flippancy when we speak of our Savior and Lord.

3:16 The believer must have **a good conscience**. If he knows he is innocent of any crime, he can go through persecution with the boldness of a lion. If he has a bad conscience, he will be plagued with feelings of guilt and will not be able to stand against the foe. Even if a believer's life is blameless, the enemies of the gospel will still find fault with him and bring false charges against him. But when the case comes to trial, and the charges are found to be empty, the accusers will **be ashamed**.

3:17 If a Christian must **suffer**, which might sometimes be God's will for him, it should be **for doing good**. But he should not bring suffering on himself for his own misdeeds; there is no virtue in that.

3:18 The rest of chapter 3 presents **Christ** as the classic example of One who **suffered** for righteousness' sake, and reminds us that for Him, suffering was the pathway to glory.

Notice the six features of His sufferings: (1) They were expiatory, that is, they freed believing sinners from the punishment of their **sins**. (2) They were eternally effectual. He died once for all and settled the **sin** question. The work of redemption was completed. (3) They were substitutionary. **The just** died **for the unjust**. "The Lord has laid on Him the iniquity of us all" (Isa. 53:6b). (4) They were reconciling. Through His death we have been brought **to God**. The sin which caused alienation has been removed. (5) They were violent. His **death** was by execution. (6) Finally, they were climaxed by resurrection. He was raised from the dead on the third day. The expression **made alive by the Spirit** means that His resurrection was through the power of the Holy Spirit.

3:19 Verses 19, 20 constitute one of the most puzzling and intriguing texts in the NT. It has been made the pretext for such unbiblical doctrines as purgatory on the one hand and universal salvation on the other. However, among evangelical Christians, there are two commonly accepted interpretations.

According to the first, Christ went to Hades in spirit between His death and resurrection, and proclaimed the triumph of His mighty work on the cross. There is disagreement among proponents of this view as to whether **the spirits in prison** were believers, unbelievers, or both. But there is fairly general agreement that the Lord Jesus did not preach the gospel to them. That would involve the doctrine of a second chance which is nowhere taught in the Bible. Those who hold this view often link this passage with Ephesians 4:9 where the Lord is described as descending "into the lower parts of the earth." They cite this as added proof that He went to Hades in the disembodied state and heralded His victory at Calvary. They also cite the words of the Apostles' Creed — "descended into hell."

The second interpretation is that Peter is describing what happened in the days of Noah. It was the *spirit* of Christ who preached *through* Noah to the unbelieving generation before the flood. They were not disembodied spirits *at that time*, but living men and women who rejected the warnings of Noah and were destroyed by the flood. So *now* they are **spirits in** the **prison** of Hades.

This second view best fits the context and has the least difficulties connected with it. Let us examine the passage phrase by phrase.

By whom also He went and preached to the spirits in prison. The relative pronoun **whom** obviously refers back to *Spirit* at the end of verse 18. We understand this to mean the Holy Spirit. In 1:11 of this Letter the "Spirit of Christ," that is, the Holy Spirit, is described as speaking through the prophets of the OT. And in Genesis 6:3, God speaks of His Spirit, that is, the Holy Spirit, as nearing the limit of endurance with the antediluvians.

He went and preached. As already mentioned, it was Christ who preached, but He preached through Noah. In 2 Peter 2:5, Noah is described as a "preacher of righteousness." It is the same root word used here of Christ's preaching.

To the spirits *now* **in prison**. These were the people to whom Noah preached — living men and women who heard the warning of an impending flood and the promise of salvation in the ark. They rejected the message and were drowned in the deluge. They are now disembodied **spirits in prison**, awaiting the final judgment.

So the verse may be amplified as follows: **"by whom** (the Holy Spirit) **He** (Christ) **went and preached** (through Noah) **to the spirits** *now* **in prison** (Hades)."

But what right do we have to assume that **the spirits in prison** were the living men in Noah's day? The answer is found in the following verse.

3:20 Here the spirits in prison are unmistakably identified. Who were they? Those **who formerly were disobedient**. When **were** they **disobedient**? When **once the Divine longsuffering waited in the days of Noah, while the ark was being prepared**. What was the final outcome? Only **a few, that is, eight souls, were saved through water**.

It is well to pause here and remind ourselves of the general flow of thought in this Letter which was written against a general background of persecution. The Christians to whom Peter wrote were suffering because of their life and testimony. Perhaps they wondered why, if the Christian faith was right, they should be suffering rather than reigning. If Christianity was the true faith, why were there so few Christians?

To answer the first question, Peter points to the Lord Jesus. Christ suffered for righteousness' sake, even to the extent of being put to death. But God raised Him from the dead and glorified Him in heaven (see v. 22). The pathway to glory led through the valley of suffering.

Next Peter refers to **Noah**. For 120 years this faithful preacher warned that God was going to destroy the world with water. His thanks was scorn and rejection. But God vindicated him by saving him and his family through the flood.

Then there is the problem, "If we are right, why are there so few of us?" Peter answers: "There was a time when *only eight people in the world* were right and all the rest were wrong!" Characteristically in the world's history the majority has not been right. True believers are usually a small remnant, so one's faith should not falter because of the small number of the saved. There were only **eight** believers in Noah's day; there are millions today.

At the end of verse 20, we read that **a few, that is, eight souls, were saved through water**. It is not that they were saved *by* water; they were saved **through the water**. Water was not the savior, but the judgment **through** which God brought them safely.

To properly understand this statement and the verse that follows, we must see the typical meaning of the ark and of the flood. The ark is a picture of the Lord Jesus Christ. The flood of water depicts the judgment of God. The ark was the only way of salvation. When the flood came, only those who were inside were saved; all those on the outside perished. So Christ is the only way of salvation; those who are in Christ are as saved as God Himself can make them. Those on the outside could not be more lost.

The water was not the *means* of salvation, for all who were in the water drowned. The ark was the place of refuge. The ark went through the water of judgment; it took the full brunt of the storm. Not a drop of water reached those inside the ark. So Christ bore the fury of God's judgment against our sins. For those who are in Him there is no judgment (John 5:24).

The ark had water beneath it, and water coming down on top of it, and water all around it. But it bore the believing occupants **through the water** to safety in a renewed creation. So those who trust the Savior are brought safely through a scene of death and desolation to resurrection ground and a new life.

3:21 There is also an antitype which now saves us — baptism. Once again we are in difficult and controversial territory! This verse has been a battleground between those who teach baptismal regeneration and those who deny that baptism has any power to save.

BAPTISM

First let us see what it *may* mean, and then what it *cannot* mean.

Actually, there *is a baptism which saves us* — not our baptism in water, but a baptism which took place at Calvary almost 2000 years ago. Christ's death was a baptism. He was baptized in the waters of judgment. This is what He meant when He said, "I have a baptism to be baptized with, and how distressed I am till it is accomplished!" (Luke 12:50). The psalmist described this baptism in the words, "Deep calls unto deep at the noise of Your waterfalls; all Your waves and billows have gone over me" (Ps. 42:7). In His death, Christ was baptized in the waves and billows of God's wrath, and it is this baptism that is the basis for our salvation.

But we must accept His death for ourselves. Just as Noah and his family had to enter the ark to be saved, so we must commit ourselves to the Lord as our only Savior. When we do this, we become identified with Him in His death, burial, and resurrection. In a very real sense, we then have been crucified with Him (Gal. 2:20), we have been buried with Him (Rom. 6:4), and we have been brought from death to life with Him (Rom. 6:4).

All this is pictured in the believer's baptism. The ceremony is an outward sign of what has taken place spiritually; we have been baptized into Christ's death. As we go under the water, we acknowledge that we have been buried with Him. As we come up out of the water, we show that we have risen with Him and want to walk in newness of life.

An antitype which now saves us — baptism refers to Christ's baptism unto death on the cross and our identification with Him in it, which water baptism represents.

The verse *cannot* mean that we are saved by ritual baptism in water for the following reasons:

1. That would make water the savior, instead of the Lord Jesus. But He said, "I am the way" (John 14:6).

2. It would imply that Christ died in vain. If people can be saved by water, then why did the Lord Jesus have to die?

3. It simply doesn't work. Many who have been baptized have proved by their subsequent lives that they were never truly born again.

Neither can this verse mean that we are saved by *faith plus baptism*.

1. This would mean that the Savior's work on the cross was not sufficient. When He cried, "It is finished," it wasn't really so, according to this view, because baptism must be added to that work for salvation.

2. If baptism is necessary for salvation, it is strange that the Lord did not personally baptize anyone. John 4:1, 2 states that Jesus did not do the actual baptizing of His followers; this was done by His disciples.

3. The Apostle Paul thanked God that he baptized very few of the Corinthians (1 Cor. 1:14–16). This would be strange thanksgiving for an evangelist if baptism were essential for salvation! The fact that Paul did baptize some shows that he taught believer's baptism, but the fact that he baptized only a few shows that he did not consider it a requirement for salvation.

4. The penitent thief on the cross was not baptized, yet he was assured of being in Paradise with Christ (Luke 23:43).

5. The Gentiles who were saved in Caesarea received the Holy Spirit when they believed (Acts 10:44), showing that they then belonged to Christ (Rom. 8:9b). After receiving the Holy Spirit, that is, after being saved, they were baptized (vv. 47, 48). Therefore, baptism was not necessary for their salvation. They were saved first, then baptized in water.

6. In the NT, baptism is always connected with death and not with spiritual birth.

7. There are about 150 passages in the NT which teach that salvation is by faith alone. These cannot be contradicted by two or three verses that *seem* to teach that baptism is necessary for salvation. ‡

Therefore, when we read in verse 21, **Baptism . . . which now saves us**, it does not mean our baptism in literal water, but Christ's baptism unto death and our identification with Him in it.

Not the removal of the filth of the flesh. The ceremonial worship of the OT, with which Peter's Jewish-Christian readers were familiar, provided a sort of external cleansing. But it was not able to give the priests or the people a clear conscience with regard to sin. The **baptism** of which Peter is speaking is not a question of physical or even of ritual cleansing from defilement. Water does have the effect of removing dirt from the body, but it cannot provide a good conscience toward God. Only personal association with Christ in His death, burial, and resurrection can do that.

But the answer of a good conscience toward God. The question inevitably arises, "How can I have a righteous standing before God? How can I have a clear **conscience** before Him?" The answer is found in the baptism of which Peter has been speaking — Christ's baptism unto death at Calvary and one's personal acceptance of that work. By Christ's death the sin question was settled once for all.

Through the resurrection of Jesus Christ. How do I know that God is satisfied? I know because He raised **Christ** from the dead. A clear conscience is inseparably linked with **the resurrection of Jesus Christ**; they stand or fall together. The resurrection tells me that God is fully satisfied with the redemptive work of His Son. If Christ had not risen, we could never be sure that our sins had been put away. He would have died like any other man. But the risen Christ is our absolute assurance that the claims of God against our sins have been fully met.

As the hymn writer, James G. Deck, put it, "Our conscience has peace that can never fail: 'tis the Lamb on high, on the throne."

So it **now saves us** — **baptism ... the answer of a good conscience toward God, through the resurrection of Jesus Christ**. My only claim for a good conscience is based on the death, burial, and resurrection of the Lord Jesus. The order is as follows:

1. Christ was baptized unto death for me at Calvary.
2. When I trust Him as Lord and Savior, I am spiritually united with Him in His death, burial, and resurrection.
3. Through the knowledge that He has risen, my request for a clear conscience is answered.
4. In water baptism, I give visible expression to the spiritual deliverance I have experienced.

3:22 Who has gone into heaven and is at the right hand of God, angels and authorities and powers having been made subject to Him. The Lord Jesus Christ not only arose from among the dead, but He ascended to **heaven** from where He had originally come. He is there today, not as an invisible, intangible spirit-being, but as a living Man in a glorified body of flesh and bones. In that body He bears eternally the wounds He received at Calvary — eloquent and everlasting tokens of His love for us.

Our Lord is **at the right hand of God**, the place of:

Power: Since the right hand is generally stronger than the left, it has come to be associated with power (Matt. 26:64).

Honor: Christ is *"exalted to the right hand of God"* (Acts 2:33; 5:31).

Rest: In virtue of His finished work Christ *"sat down at the right hand of the Majesty on high"* (Heb. 1:3; see also 8:1; 10:12). This *rest* is the *rest* of satisfaction and complacency, not the rest that conquers weariness.

Intercession: Paul speaks of Christ being at the right hand of God where He *intercedes* for us (Rom. 8:34).

Preeminence: "At His right hand in the heavenly *places*, (He is) *far above all* principality and power and might and dominion, and every name that is named, not only in this age but also in that which is to come . . ." (Eph. 1:20, 21).

Dominion: In Hebrews 1:13, God the Father says to the Son, "Sit at My right hand, *till I make Your enemies Your footstool.*" Dominion is emphasized in 1 Peter 3:22: **" . . . at the right hand of God, with angels and authorities and powers having been made subject to Him."**

Angels and authorities and powers are doubtless intended to cover all ranks of heavenly beings. They are all servants of the risen, glorified Christ.

This then was our Lord's experience in suffering for well-doing. Men rejected Him, both in His pre-incarnate testimony through Noah and in His First Advent as the Son of Man. He was baptized in death's dark waters at Calvary. But God raised Him from the dead and glorified Him at His own right hand in heaven. In the eternal purposes of God, suffering had to precede glory.

This was the lesson both for Peter's original readers and also for us. We should not be upset if we experience opposition and even persecution for doing good, for we do not deserve better treatment than our Savior had when He was on earth. We should comfort ourselves with the promise that if we suffer with Him, we shall be glorified with Him (Rom. 8:17). Furthermore, the sufferings now are not worthy to be compared with the glory that awaits us (Rom. 8:18). The afflictions are light and momentary; the glory is eternal and weighty beyond all comparison (2 Cor. 4:17).

4:1 There is a close connection between this section and the preceding (cf. 3:18). We have been considering **Christ** as an example of One who **suffered** unjustly. He **suffered** at the hands of wicked men for the cause of righteousness. Since this was so, His followers should **arm** themselves **with the same mind**. They should expect to suffer for His name. They should be prepared to endure persecution because they are Christians.

Whoever **has suffered in the flesh**, that is, in the body, **has ceased from sin**. The believer is faced with two possibilities — sin or suffering. On the one hand, he can choose to live like the unsaved people around him, sharing their sinful pleasures, and thus avoid persecution. Or he can live in purity and godliness, bearing the reproach of Christ, and suffer at the hands of the wicked.

James Guthrie, a martyr, said just before he was hanged, "Dear friends, pledge this cup of suffering as I have done, before you sin, for sin and suffering have been presented to me, and I have chosen the suffering part."

When a believer deliberately chooses to suffer persecution as a Christian rather than to continue in a life of sin, he has **ceased from sin**. This does not mean that he no longer commits acts of sin, but that the power of sin in his life has been broken. When a man suffers because he refuses to sin, he is no longer controlled by the will of the flesh.

4:2 During the remainder of a believer's earthly life, he is not controlled by human passions **but by the will of God**. He prefers to suffer as a Christian rather than to sin like the unbelievers. He would rather die than deny his Lord. **The rest of his time in the flesh** means the remainder of one's life here on earth. The believer chooses to live these years for the glory of God rather than for the gratification of sensual appetites.

4:3 Peter is writing to some who, before their conversion, had lived in all the moral corruption of the Gentile world. There had been **enough of** that kind of life! As Christians, they were new creatures, and the old sins should be abandoned. The remaining years of life belonged to God and should be given to Him.

The sins listed still characterize the Gentile non-Christian world today — the sins of sex, liquor, and false religion.

Lewdness — unrestrained indulgence, primarily in sexual immorality.

Lusts — gratification of unlawful appetites of any kind, but probably referring especially to sexual sins.

Drunkenness — giving oneself over to the control of intoxicating beverages with the resulting weakening of willpower to resist temptation. There is a close link between drunkenness and immorality.

Revelries — riotous parties and late-night merrymaking.

Drinking parties — drinking bouts which lead to debauchery and brawls.

Abominable idolatries — the worship of idols, with all the immorality that is associated with such worship.

People become like what they worship. When they abandon the true God, their moral standards are automatically lowered. These lowered standards permit them to engage in all sorts of sinful pleasures for which they have an appetite. This is why idolatrous religions breed sin and degradation.

4:4 This verse describes the common experience of those who are saved from lives of outward corruption. Their former cronies think they have gone mad and accuse them of being religious fanatics. They think it a form of insanity that the Christians will no longer participate in dances, worldly parties, and sex orgies. The clean, moral life of a believer condemns the sinner; no wonder he hates the change!

4:5 Though the ungodly blaspheme Christians in this life, **they will give an account** for every word and deed at the Judgment of the Great White Throne. The Lord **is ready to judge the living and the dead**. Clearly it is unbelievers whom Peter has in mind here. The judgment of the living unbelievers will take place before the Millennium begins; the wicked dead will be judged at the close of Christ's reign on earth. Their condemnation will be proof of the righteousness of the children of God.

4:6 **It is for this reason** — the vindication of the children of God — **that the gospel was preached also to those who are dead**. Here again we come to a difficult passage. Does this mean that the gospel was preached to people after they had died or while they were still alive? And who were these people?

We understand this verse to refer to people to whom the gospel was preached while they were still alive on the earth and who believed on the Lord. Because of their valiant stand for the truth, they suffered at the hands of wicked men, and in some cases were martyred. These believers, though **judged**, or condemned, **according to men in the flesh**, were vindicated by God. They are now enjoying eternal life with Him.

They were not dead when the gospel

was preached to them. But they are dead now, as far as their bodies are concerned. Though men thought them mad, **God** honored them, and their spirits are now in heaven.

Preaching the gospel brings two results to those who believe — the blame of men and the approval of God. Barnes explains:

> The design in publishing the Gospel to them was, that though they might be judged by men in the usual manner, and put to death, yet that in respect to their higher and nobler nature, *the spirit*, they might live unto God.[26]

III. THE BELIEVER'S SERVICE AND SUFFERING (4:7–5:14)

A. Urgent Imperatives for the Last Days (4:7–11)

4:7 A series of admonitions is now introduced by the statement **"The end of all things is at hand."** This has been taken to mean either (1) the destruction of Jerusalem, (2) the Rapture, (3) the return of Christ to reign, or (4) the destruction of the heavens and the earth at the end of the Millennium. We think it probably refers to the last of these.

The first admonition is to **be serious and watchful in your prayers**. This was written in a time of persecution and means that the believer's prayer life should be free from the distractions of panic and emotional instability brought on by stress: his fellowship with God should be undisturbed by discordant circumstances.

4:8 He must pay attention to his fellowship with other believers (vv. 8, 9), and **have fervent love** for all members of the household of faith. Such a love will not publicize the faults and failings of other believers, but will protect them from public view. Someone has said, "Hatred makes the worst of everything. Love is entitled to bury things out of sight."

The statement **"love will cover a multitude of sins"** (Prov. 10:12) should not be taken as a doctrinal explanation of how sins are put away. The guilt and penalty of sins can only be removed by the blood of Christ. Neither should the statement be used to condone sin or to relieve an assembly from its responsibility to discipline an offender. It means that true love is able to overlook minor faults and failures in other believers.

4:9 One means of demonstrating love to the brethren is by practicing hospitality ungrudgingly. This counsel is especially needed during times of persecution when food supplies might be running low and when those who harbor Christians are subject to arrest and imprisonment, if not death itself.

Hospitality is a tremendous privilege. In practicing it, some have entertained angels unwittingly (Heb. 13:2). Any kindness shown to a child of God is reckoned as shown to the Lord Himself (Matt. 25:40). No matter how slight the kindness, it will be rewarded handsomely; even a cup of cold water given in the Lord's name will be rewarded (Matt. 10:42). Those who receive a prophet because he is a prophet shall receive a prophet's reward (Matt. 10:41) which, in Jewish reckoning, was superlative. Many Christians testify to the blessing that has come to their homes and their children through hospitality shown to servants of the Lord.

Jesus taught that we should entertain those who cannot repay us (Luke 14:12). This does not mean that we should *never* entertain relatives, friends, or neighbors who might entertain us in return. But our purpose should be to show kindness in the name of the Lord Jesus with no thought of being repaid. Certainly it is questionable whether believers should keep up a continuing round of banquets and parties with their own clique, while great sections of the world are still unevangelized.

4:10 **Each** believer **has received a gift** from the Lord, some special function to perform as a member of the Body of Christ (1 Cor. 12:4–11, 29–31; Rom. 12:6–8). These gifts are a stewardship from God. They are not to be used for selfish gain but for His glory and for the good of others. We are not meant to be the *terminals* of God's gifts to us; His grace reaches us but should not end with us. We are intended to be *channels* through whom the blessing can flow to others.

We are to be **good stewards of the manifold grace of God**. The **grace of God** here refers to the undeserved favor which He offers to man. **Manifold** literally means *multi-colored* or variegated. Phillips translates it "magnificently varied."

4:11 Even if a man is gifted to preach or teach, he must be sure that the words he speaks are the very words **God** would have him say on that particular occasion. This is what is meant by **the oracles of God**. It is not enough for a man simply to preach from the Bible. He should also have the assurance that he is presenting the particular message intended by God for that audience at that time.

Anyone who performs any kind of service should do it with the humble recognition that it is **God** who empowers him. Then the glory will go to **God** — to whom it belongs.

A man should not become proud no matter how highly gifted he is in Christian service. The gift did not originate by his own effort, but was given to him from above. In fact, he has nothing which he did not receive. All service should be performed so that **God** gets the credit.

As Peter points out, this honor is presented to the Father **through Jesus Christ** as Mediator, and also because of what God has done for us through Him. To this blessed Savior belongs praise and power **forever and ever. Amen.**

B. Exhortations and Explanations Concerning Suffering (4:12–19)

4:12 The rest of chapter 4 contains exhortations and explanations concerning suffering incurred for the name of Christ. The word "suffering" and its derivatives are used twenty-one times in this Epistle.

The natural attitude for a Christian is to look on persecution as **strange** and abnormal. We are surprised when we have to suffer. But Peter tells us that we should consider it as normal Christian experience. We have no right to expect better treatment from the world than our Savior received. All who desire to live a godly life in Christ Jesus will be persecuted (2 Tim. 3:12). It is especially true

that those who take a forthright stand for Christ become the object of savage attack. Satan doesn't waste his ammunition on nominal Christians. He turns his big guns on those who are storming the gates of Hades.

4:13 The privilege of sharing **Christ's sufferings** should cause us great rejoicing. We cannot of course share His atoning sufferings; He is the only Sin-Bearer. But we can share the same kind of **sufferings** He endured as a Man. We can share His rejection and reproach. We can receive the wounds and scars in our bodies which unbelievers would still like to inflict on Him.

If the child of God can **rejoice** today in the midst of suffering, how much more will he rejoice and **be glad** when Christ's **glory is revealed. When** the Savior comes back to earth as the Lion of the tribe of Judah, He will be **revealed** as the Almighty Son of God. Those who suffer now for His sake will be honored then with Him.

4:14 The early Christians rejoiced that they were counted worthy to suffer shame **for the name of Christ** (Acts 5:41). So should every Christian who has the privilege of being reviled for Christ's sake. Such suffering is a true indication that **the Spirit of glory and of God rests upon** us. This is the Holy **Spirit** who **rests upon** persecuted Christians as the glory cloud rested on the tabernacle in the OT, indicating the presence of God.

We know that **the Spirit** indwells every true child of God, but He **rests** in a special way **upon** those who are completely committed to the cause of Christ. They know the presence and power of the Spirit of God as others do not. The same Lord Jesus who **is blasphemed** by the persecutors **is glorified** by His suffering saints.[27]

4:15 A Christian should never bring suffering upon himself for wrongdoing. He should never be guilty of murder, stealing, evil in general, or meddling **in other people's matters**. There is no glory for God in this — only shame for the testimony of Christ.

4:16 But there is no disgrace **if anyone suffers as a Christian**. F. B. Meyer says this is true whether it means "the loss of business, reputation, and home;

desertion by parents, children, and friends; misrepresentation, hatred and even death."[28] Under the name of **Christian** it is possible **to glorify God** in all these trials. G. Campbell Morgan admonishes as follows:

> This is more than glorying in the name. It is so living worthily of all it means as to glorify God. If a man is known as a Christian and does not live as one, he dishonors God. To bear the name is to take a responsibility, a great and glorious one, but none the less a very solemn one.[29]

4:17 Peter contrasts the suffering of God's people in this life with the sufferings of the wicked in eternity. **The time has come for judgment to begin at the house of God**. **The time** referred to is the dispensation of the church, which began at Pentecost and will continue to the Rapture. **The house of God** refers to the church. During this age, the church is undergoing **judgment** by the unbelieving world. Believers are experiencing their sufferings now, just as Jesus did when He was on earth.

If that is so, what will be the fate **of those who do not obey the gospel of God**? If Christians suffer now for doing good, what will the unsaved suffer in eternity for all their ungodly deeds?

4:18 The same argument is contained in this verse, quoted from Proverbs 11:31: **"If the righteous will be recompensed on the earth, how much more the ungodly and the sinner."**

The righteous person **is scarcely saved** or **saved** with difficulty. From the divine standpoint his salvation was purchased at enormous cost. From the human standpoint, men are told, "Strive to enter through the narrow gate" (Luke 13:24). Believers are taught that "We must through many tribulations enter the kingdom of God" (Acts 14:22). With all the dangers and temptations that beset a Christian, it is only a miracle of divine grace that preserves him for the heavenly kingdom.

That being so, what will be the doom of those who have died in their sins, unrepentant and unsaved? A vivid illustration of this truth is found in the following anecdote from the writings of F. B. Meyer:

It was the earnest wish of a holy man that his death might be so triumphant that his unconverted sons might be convinced and attracted by the evident power of the Gospel to sustain and cheer in the dark passage of the valley. Instead of this, to his deep regret, his spirit lay under a cloud; he was oppressed with fear and misgiving; and the enemy was permitted to torment him to the uttermost. But these very facts were the ones which most profoundly impressed his children. "For," said the eldest, "we all know what a good man our father was; and yet see how deep his spiritual sufferings were. What then may *we* not expect, who have given no thought to the concerns of our souls?[30]

4:19 Peter insists that sufferings must be **according to the will of God**. Religious zealots may *invite* suffering by acting impulsively without divine guidance. Those with a martyr complex tempt God in a way that leads to dishonor. But the true pathway of suffering for Christians leads to eternal glory. In view of that, they should continue to do right, no matter what the cost may be, and entrust **their souls** to the **faithful Creator**.

It seems somewhat strange that Peter should introduce the Lord as **Creator** here rather than as Savior, High Priest, or Shepherd. Christ is our Creator in a twofold sense — we are His as part of the original creation and of the new creation (Eph. 4:24; Col. 3:10). In either case, we are the objects of His love and care. It is only reasonable that we should entrust ourselves to the One who made our souls and who saved them.

C. Exhortations and Salutations (5:1–14)

5:1 This final chapter of 1 Peter contains exhortations and greetings. First there is a word for **the elders**. By way of authority for delivering such a charge, Peter introduces himself as a **fellow elder and a witness of the sufferings of Christ, and also a partaker of the** impending **glory**. **Fellow elder** — what a far cry from claiming to be "supreme pontiff" of the church! **A witness** — Peter saw the Shepherd die for the sheep, and the memory of such love constrains him to care for them as a faithful undershepherd. **A partaker** —

soon the glory will dawn, Christ will appear, and we shall appear with Him in glory (Col. 3:4). Till then the Savior's commission remains, "Feed My lambs! . . . Tend My sheep!" (John 21:15–17).

5:2 Elders are mature men of Christian character who are qualified by the Holy Spirit to provide spiritual leadership in the assembly. The NT presupposes a plurality of elders — not one elder over a church or over a group of churches, but two or more elders in one assembly (Phil. 1:1). For the qualifications of elders see 1 Timothy 3:1–7 and Titus 1:6–9. In the early church before the NT was available in written form, elders were appointed by the apostles and their representatives, but only after sufficient time had elapsed in a new church for it to be evident who had the qualifications. Today, Christians should recognize and obey those who have the qualifications and who do the work of elders.

Shepherd the flock of God which is among you. The flock belongs to **God** but elders have been given the responsibility to serve as undershepherds. **Not by compulsion but willingly**.[31] Overseeing the flock is not a work into which men are coerced by election or appointment. The Holy Spirit provides the burden and ability, and the elders must respond with a willing heart. So we read in 1 Timothy 3:1, "If a man desires the position of a bishop, he desires a good work." Coupled with divine enablement must be human willingness.

Not for dishonest gain but eagerly. Financial reward must not be the motive for being an elder. This does not mean that an elder may not be supported by the local church; the existence of such "full-time elders" is indicated in 1 Timothy 5:17, 18. But it means that a mercenary spirit is incompatible with true Christian ministry.

5:3 The third phase of Peter's exhortation is this: **nor as being lords over those entrusted to you, but being examples to the flock**. Elders should be **examples**, not dictators. They should be walking out in front of the flock, not driving them from behind. They should not treat the flock as if it belonged to them. This strikes at the very heart of authoritarianism!

Many of the abuses in Christendom would be eliminated by simply obeying the three instructions in verses 2, 3. The first would abolish all *reluctance*. The second would spell the end of *commercialism*. The third would be the death of *officialism* in the church.

5:4 An elder's work involves a tremendous expenditure of physical and emotional energy. He must sympathize, counsel, reprove, rebuke, teach, discipline, and warn. At times it may seem a thankless task. But a special reward is promised to the faithful elder. **When the Chief Shepherd appears**, he **will receive** an unfading **crown of glory**. Frankly, we don't know too much about the promised crowns of Scripture — the crown of rejoicing (1 Thess. 2:19), the crown of righteousness (2 Tim. 4:8), the crown of life (Jas. 1:12; Rev. 2:10); and the crown of glory. We do not know whether they will be literal crowns that we can cast at the Savior's feet; whether they simply indicate the extent of responsibility that will be given to us during the reign of Christ (Luke 19:17–19); or whether they are facets of Christian character which we will bear throughout eternity. But we do know that they will be ample recompense for any tears, trials, and sufferings we have experienced down here.

5:5 Those who are **younger**, whether in years or in the faith, should be submissive **to the elders**. Why? Because these overseers have wisdom that comes from years of experience in the things of God. They have a deep, experiential knowledge of the word of God. And they are the ones to whom God has given responsibility for the care of His sheep.

All believers should **be clothed with humility**; it is a great virtue. Moffatt says, "Put on the apron of humility." Very appropriate — since the apron is the badge of a servant. A missionary to India once said, "If I were to pick out two phrases necessary for spiritual growth, I would pick out these: 'I don't know' and 'I am sorry.' And both phrases are the evidences of deep humility." Imagine a congregation where all the member have this humble spirit; where they esteem others better than themselves; where they outdo each other in performing the menial tasks. Such a church need not be imaginary; it could and should be an actuality.

If there were no other reason for being humble, this would be enough: **God resists the proud, but gives grace to the humble**. (Peter is quoting from the Greek version of Prov. 3:34.) Think of it — the mighty God opposed to our pride and determined to break it, contrasted with the mighty God powerless to resist a broken and contrite heart!

5:6 This humility is to be shown not only in relation to others but to **God** as well. In Peter's day the saints were passing through the fires of affliction. These trials, though not sent by God, were permitted by Him. The best policy, Peter says, is to take them humbly from the Lord's hand. He will sustain His people and **exalt** them **in due time**.

5:7 Believers are privileged to cast **all** their anxieties on the Lord with the strong confidence that **He cares**. Once again Peter is quoting from the Greek version of the OT (Ps. 55:22).

J. Sidlow Baxter points out that there are two kinds of care here:

> There is *anxious* care, in the words: "Casting all your care upon Him"; and there is *affectionate* care, in the words: "He careth for you." Over against all our own *anxious* care is our Savior's never-failing *affectionate* care.[32]

Worry is unnecessary; there is no need for us to bear the burdens when He is willing and able to bear them for us. Worry is futile; it hasn't solved a problem yet. Worry is sin. A preacher once said: "Worry is sin because it denies the wisdom of God; it says that He doesn't know what He's doing. It denies the love of God; it says He does not care. And it denies the power of God; it says that He isn't able to deliver me from whatever is causing me to worry." Something to think about!

5:8 Although we should not worry, we must **be sober** and **vigilant, because** we have a powerful **adversary, the devil**. To **be sober** means to be serious-minded, to take a realistic approach to life, to be intelligent concerning the stratagems of Satan. Pentecost well says:

> An individual who takes no cognizance of the nature or character of the world, one who is unmindful of the purposes and attacks of our adversary, the Devil, can afford to live in a lighthearted or flippant way. But for one who sees life as Jesus Christ sees it, there must be an entirely

new attitude, an entirely new outlook characterized by sobriety.[33]

There must also be constant vigilance, a preparedness to meet every attack of the wicked one. Here the **adversary** is described as **a roaring lion, seeking** someone to **devour**. **The devil** has different poses. Sometimes he comes like a snake, seeking to lure people into moral corruption. Sometimes he disguises himself as an angel of light, attempting to deceive people in the spiritual realm. Here, as **a roaring lion**, he is bent on terrorizing God's people through persecution.

5:9 We are not to surrender to his fury. Rather we must **resist him** through prayer and God's word. We do not have strength in ourselves to oppose him, but as we are firm **in** our **faith**, in our dependence on the Lord, we can **resist him**.

One of Satan's devices is to discourage us with the thought that our sufferings are unique. As we pass through the fire of affliction, it is easy to faint under the mistaken idea that no one else has as much trouble as we do. Peter reminds us that **the same sufferings are experienced** by our Christian **brotherhood** throughout **the world**.

5:10 True victory in persecution is to see God behind the scenes working out His wonderful purposes. No matter what our trials, we should remember first of all that He is **the God of all grace**. This lovely title of our God reminds us that His dealings with us are not based on what we deserve, but on His thoughts of love to us. No matter how fierce our testing, we can always be thankful we are not in hell where we ought to be.

A second strong consolation is that He has **called us to His eternal glory**. This enables us to look beyond the sufferings of this life to the time when we shall be with the Savior and be like Him forever. Just think of it! We have been picked up from the scrap heap and **called to His eternal glory**!

A third comfort is that suffering is just for **a while**. When contrasted with the **eternal glory**, life's afflictions are less than momentary.

The final encouragement is that God uses suffering to educate us and mold our Christian character. He is training us for reigning. Four aspects of this training process are listed.

Perfect — Trials make the believer fit; they supply needed elements in his character to make him spiritually mature.

Establish — Suffering makes Christians more stable, able to maintain a good confession, and to bear up under pressure. This is the same word the Lord Jesus used with Peter: "...strengthen [or establish] your brethren" (Luke 22:32).

Strengthen — Persecution is intended by Satan to weaken and wear out believers, but it has the opposite effect. It strengthens them to endure.

Settle — This verb is related to the word "foundation" in the original. God wants every believer to be firmly planted in a secure place in His Son and in His word.

Lacey says:

The inevitable suffering of the Christian life always yields the same blessed result in the character of believers; it will refine the faith, adjust the character, establish, strengthen and settle the people of God.[34]

5:11 In view of the marvelous way in which God overrules persecution and suffering for His **glory** and our good, it is little wonder that Peter bursts into this doxology: **"To Him be the glory and the dominion forever and ever. Amen."** Only to such a One is **glory** due; only in the hands of such a One is **dominion** safe!

5:12 **Silvanus** (probably the same man called Silas, the shorter form of the name), was the **faithful brother** to whom Peter dictated this Letter, and probably the messenger who delivered it. Peter's object in this Letter was to assure the believers of the Dispersion that the Christian faith which they held was the true faith — or, as he calls it, **the true grace of God**. Perhaps in the heat of persecution, they might be tempted to wonder if they had been right to embrace Christianity. Peter declares that they were right. They had found *God's truth* and should stand fast in it.

5:13 **She who is in Babylon, elect together with you, greets you; and so does Mark my son.**

It is impossible to state with certainty who or what is meant by **"She who is in Babylon, elect together with you."** Some of the main interpretations are: (1) The "brotherhood" (2:17; 5:9). In the Greek this abstract noun happens to be feminine. (2) Peter's wife. (3) Some locally prominent lady. It is also impossible to know which **Babylon** is meant. It could be: (1) The famous city on the Euphrates, where there were many Jews; (2) The military station by the same name on the Nile (unlikely); (3) Rome. In Revelation, the city of Babylon is generally understood as referring to Rome (17:1–9; 18:10, 21).

A third question arises over the mention of **Mark**. Is this Peter's own **son** in the flesh, or is he referring to John **Mark**, the writer of the Gospel? The latter is more probable. If that is so, then we are left to decide whether Mark was Peter's son because the latter had led him to Christ or whether the word **son** merely designates the close spiritual relationship between an elder and a younger Christian. The word Peter uses for **son**[35] is not the same word which Paul uses to describe his spiritual relationship with Timothy and Titus, and fits the ancient tradition that Mark's very vivid Gospel is based on Peter's eyewitness accounts.

5:14 The elder closes with a charge and a benediction. The charge is, **"Greet one another with a kiss of love."** The obligation of brotherly **love** is a standing order for the church, though the manner of expressing it may vary in cultures and times.

The benediction is: **"Peace to you all who are in Christ Jesus."** It is a tranquil word to use with storm-tossed saints, who are enduring affliction for the name of Christ. Jesus whispers **peace** to His blood-bought flock as they suffer for Him in the midst of a turbulent society.

Peace, perfect peace, death shadowing
   us and ours?
Jesus has vanquished death and all
   its powers.

— *Edward H. Bickersteth*

ENDNOTES

[1](1:2) There are other forms of sanctification which take place later. When a person is born again, he becomes

positionally sanctified because he is "in Christ" (Heb. 10:10, 14). Throughout his Christian life he should experience *practical* sanctification, that is, the process of becoming more like Christ (1 Pet. 1:15). In heaven he will achieve *perfect* sanctification, for he will never again sin (Col. 1:22). See Excursus on Sanctification after Hebrews 2:11.

²(1:8) The majority of Greek mss. read "known" (*eidotes*) rather than "seen" (*idontes*). The resultant meaning is about the same; i.e., they had not been personally acquainted with Jesus on earth.

³(1:8) William Lincoln, *Lectures on the First and Second Epistles of Peter*, p. 21.

⁴(1:12) *Ibid.*, p. 23.

⁵(1:13) J. H. Jowett, *The Redeemed Family of God*, p. 34.

⁶(1:17) Lincoln, *Lectures*, p. 30.

⁷(1:20) *Ibid.*, p. 33.

⁸(1:21) W. T. P. Wolston, *Simon Peter: His Life and Letters*, p. 270.

⁹(1:22) The critical (NU) text omits "through the Spirit."

¹⁰(1:23) Footnote in F. W. Grant, "1 Peter," *The Numerical Bible*, Hebrews to Revelation, p. 149.

¹¹(1:23) The NU text omits "forever."

¹²(2:2) The Alexandrian Text (NU in NKJV footnotes) reads "grow up to salvation." However, this reading could cast doubt on assurance of salvation.

¹³(2:6) Biblical Greek *lithon* (stone) *akro-* (top or tip) *gōniaion* (of corner), hence *cornerstone* or *capstone*.

¹⁴(2:7) The NU text reads "disbelieve" for "are disobedient," but since *believing* the gospel is also called *obeying* the Gospel, the meaning is about the same.

¹⁵(2:12) A literal rendering is *noble* or *lovely* (Gk. *kalos*, cf. English *calligraphy*, beautiful writing).

¹⁶(2:12) Charles R. Erdman, *The General Epistles*, p. 66.

¹⁷(2:12) Jowett, *Redeemed Family*, pp. 88, 89.

¹⁸(2:13) Leslie T. Lyall, *Red Sky at Night*, p. 81.

¹⁹(2:16) F. B. Meyer, *Tried by Fire*, p. 91.

²⁰(2:25) The Greek word is *episkopos*, "overseer" or "bishop."

²¹(3:2) George Müller, in a periodical called *The Word*, edited by Richard Burson, date unknown, pp. 33–35.

²²(3:4) Meyer, *Tried*, p. 117.

²³(3:7) Charles Bigg, *A Critical and Exegetical Commentary on the Epistles of St. Peter and St. Jude* (ICC), p. 155.

²⁴(3:8) Instead of "courteous" (*philophrones*), the NU text reads "humble" (*tapeinophrones*). Both are fine virtues that fit the context; which is chosen as original depends on one's view of NT textual criticism. We follow the KJ tradition here.

²⁵(3:15) The NU text reads "Christ as Lord" for "the Lord God." This would suggest that the Christ of the NT is the Jehovah Sabaoth of the OT.

²⁶(4:6) Albert Barnes, *Notes on the New Testament: James, Peter, John and Jude*, p. 191.

²⁷(4:14) The NU text lacks the last sentence of verse 14. Since "rests upon you" and "glorified" both end with the same letters in Greek (*-etai*) it would be easy to omit it by accident. This is technically called omission by "homoeoteleuton" (similar ending).

²⁸(4:16) F. B. Meyer, *Tried by Fire*, p. 27.

²⁹(4:16) G. Campbell Morgan, *Searchlights from the Word*, p. 366.

³⁰(4:18) Meyer, *Tried*, pp. 180-181.

³¹(5:2) The NU text reads "according to God" for "willingly." The traditional reading of KJ and NKJV (found in TR and majority text) fits the context much better as a *contrast to compulsion*.

³²(5:7) J. Sidlow Baxter, *Awake, My Heart*, p. 294. The beautiful play on words of the KJ tradition is not in the original Greek, where the two "cares" are unrelated words. It comes from the first printed *English* NT (1526), the work of the outstanding translator and martyr of the Inquisition, William Tyndale (1484-1536). His text reads "cast all youre care to hym: for he careth for you."

³³(5:8) J. Dwight Pentecost, *Your Adversary the Devil*, p. 94.

³⁴(5:10) Harry Lacey, *God and the Nations*, p. 92.

³⁵(5:13) The ordinary Greek word *huios*; Paul uses *teknon*, literally "born one" (Scots *bairn*) or child.

BIBLIOGRAPHY

(1 and 2 Peter)

Barbieri, Louis A. *First and Second*

Peter. Chicago: Moody Press, 1975.

Bigg, Charles. *A Critical and Exegetical Commentary on the Epistles of St. Peter and St. Jude* (ICC). Edinburgh: T. & T. Clark, 1901.

Grant, F. W. "I and II Peter," *The Numerical Bible,* vol. 7. New York: Loizeaux Bros., 1903.

Ironside, H. A. *Notes on James and Peter.* New York: Loizeaux Brothers, 1947.

Jowett, J. H. *The Redeemed Family of God.* London: Hodder & Stoughton, n.d.

Lenski, R. C. H. *The Interpretation of the Epistles of St. Peter, St. John & St. Jude.* Columbus: Wartburg Press, 1945.

Lincoln, William. *Lectures on the First and Second Epistles of Peter.* Kilmarnock: John Ritchie Publ., n.d.

Meyer, F. B. *Tried by Fire.* Fort Washington, PA: Christian Literature Crusade, 1983.

Stibbs, Alan M. *The First Epistle General of Peter.* Grand Rapids: Wm. B. Eerdmans Publishing Co., 1959.

Thomas, W. H. Griffith. *The Apostle Peter: His Life and Writings.* Grand Rapids: Kregel Publications, 1984.

Westwood, Tom. *The Epistles of Peter.* Glendale, California: The Bible Treasury Hour, Inc., 1953.

Wolston, W. T. P. *Simon Peter: His Life and Letters.* London: James Nisbet & Co., 1913.

THE SECOND EPISTLE OF PETER

Introduction

"[Second Peter] breathes Christ and awaits His consummation."
— E. G. Homrighausen

I. Unique Place in the Canon

The above introductory quotation is especially significant because its author, like so many today, denies that Peter wrote the Epistle. He also admits that "what we have is Petrine in character and spirit."[1] Ironically, these two statements sum up the unique contribution of 2 Peter very succinctly.

Amid the encroaching darkness of apostasy this short Letter is looking forward to our Lord's Coming. It is personally reminiscent of Peter's life and personality, yet does indeed breathe Christ to those who will let the little Letter speak for itself.

II. Authorship[†]

A leading conservative American NT scholar recently said, "Second Peter, like Daniel and Isaiah in the OT, is where we separate the men from the boys as to strict orthodoxy in biblical criticism." Modern commentators often do not even seek to disprove the Petrine authorship of 2 Peter; they assume it is a proven fact that Peter did *not* write the Epistle. There are more serious problems in accepting this book as authentic than any other NT book, but they are definitely not as strong as they are presented.

External Evidence

The usual citations of Polycarp, Ignatius, and Irenaeus cannot be mustered for 2 Peter. However, if, as the early church taught, Jude is after 2 Peter, we have a *first century* attestation of 2 Peter in the Epistle of Jude (see Introduction to Jude). The German scholar Zahn thinks we need no other. Next to Jude,

Origen is the first one to quote 2 Peter, and he is followed by Methodius of Olympus (a martyr under Emperor Diocletian) and Fumilian of Caesarea. Eusebius admits that the *majority* of Christians accepted 2 Peter, whereas he himself had doubts.

The Muratorian Canon lacks 2 Peter — but it also lacks 1 Peter, and furthermore it is a fragmentary document. While Jerome was aware of doubts as to 2 Peter's authenticity, he, along with the other leading church fathers, Athanasius and Augustine, accepted it as genuine. The whole church followed suit till Reformation times.

Why is 2 Peter much more weakly attested *externally* than other books? First of all, it is short, apparently not widely copied, and does not contain much unique material. This latter point is an argument in its favor: books by heretics always *added* doctrine contradicting or at least strangely supplementing apostolic doctrine. This suggests perhaps the main reason for the caution regarding 2 Peter in the early centuries: there were several "pseudepigrapha" (false writings) using Peter's name to promote Gnostic heresies, such as "The Apocalypse of Peter."

Finally it is important to know that while 2 Peter was one of several books questioned by some (antilegomena), it was *never rejected as spurious by any church*.

Internal Evidence

Those who reject Petrine authorship emphasize the difference in style between 1 Peter and 2 Peter. Jerome explained this as due to Peter's using a different amanuensis. However, the difference is not really as great between

1 Peter and 2 Peter as it is between the two Epistles together against the rest of the NT. Both Epistles use a wide, colorful vocabulary that has many coincidences with Peter's sermons in Acts and events in his life.

The references to events in Peter's past occurring in the book are used both *for* and *against* traditional authorship. Some who reject Petrine authorship say there should be *more allusions*; others say there are *too many* not to have been planned by a forger! But what would be the reason for forging such a book? While those rejecting authenticity have been most creative in attempting *theories*, no satisfactory ones have yet been produced.

But as we study the Epistle, we find several internal evidences that Peter was indeed the author:

In 1:3, the writer speaks of believers as having been called by the Lord's own glory and virtue. This takes us back to Luke 5:8 where the glory of the Lord so overpowered Peter that he cried, "Depart from me, for I am a sinful man, O Lord!"

When the writer gives a prescription whereby his readers may never stumble (1:5–10), we think immediately of Peter's fall, and of the sorrow it brought him.

Chapter 1 verse 14 is especially significant. The writer had been told of his death by the Lord Jesus. This fits perfectly with John 21:18, 19 where Jesus revealed to Peter that he would be killed in his old age.

In verses 13–15 of chapter 1, the words "tent" (tabernacle) and "decease" (exodus) are both words used by Luke in the account of the transfiguration (Luke 9:31–33).

One of the most convincing proofs that Peter wrote this Epistle is the reference in 1:16–18 to the transfiguration. The writer was present on the holy mountain. This means that he was either Peter, James, or John (Matt. 17:1). This second Letter claims to have been written by Peter (1:1), not by James or John.

In 2:14, 18 we find the words "enticing" and "allure." They come from the word *deleagō* — to catch with a lure. They are from the vocabulary of a fisherman, and are thus especially appropriate from Peter.

In 3:1 the author refers to a previous Letter, which is probably 1 Peter. He also speaks in 3:15 of Paul in very personal terms, which an apostle could certainly do.

A final word that harks back to Peter's experience is found in 3:17. The word "steadfastness" comes from the same root as the word "strengthen" which Jesus used in Luke 22:32. "When you have returned to Me, strengthen your brethren." It is also found as "establish" in 1 Peter 5:10 and 2 Peter 1:12.

Finally, as in the Pastoral Epistles, we suspect that Peter's trenchant condemnation of apostates has drawn out much of the modern hostility to 2 Peter as a genuine product of the apostle's life and pen.

As we study the Epistle, we may find other internal evidences that link it with the Apostle Peter. But the important thing is to turn to the Letter and see what the Lord is saying to us through it.

III. Date

The date of 2 Peter obviously hinges on its authenticity. Those who believe it is a forgery choose some date in the second century. Since we conclude that the church was correct in recognizing 2 Peter as canonical, both from a historical and a spiritual perspective, we would assign a date shortly before Peter's death (A.D. 67 or 68), that is, 66 or 67.

IV. Background and Themes[†]

Two main strands that militate against one another show up clearly in the fabric of the apostle's Letter: *the prophetic word* (1:19–21) and *libertinism* (chap. 2). Already on the horizon Peter sees false teachers who will bring in "destructive heresies" that allow loose and licentious lifestyles. These are people who ridicule the idea of coming judgment (3:1–7). What is seen as future in Peter's day is seen as having crept in by Jude's Epistle (v. 4). When Christendom lost its love for Christ's Coming and settled down in the world (under Constantine and following), the morals of the church went plummeting. The same is true today. The nineteenth century awakening of interest in prophetic truth

is waning today in many circles — and the loose living in some churches shows that Peter was inspired to write much needed truth for the entire Christian era.

OUTLINE

I. SALUTATION (1:1, 2)

II. CALL TO DEVELOP STRONG CHRISTIAN CHARACTER (1:3–21)

III. THE RISE OF FALSE TEACHERS PREDICTED (Chap. 2)

IV. THE RISE OF SCOFFERS PREDICTED (Chap. 3)

Commentary

I. SALUTATION (1:1, 2)

1:1 **Simon Peter** introduces himself as **a bondservant and apostle of Jesus Christ**. At once we are struck by his simplicity and humility. He was a bondslave by choice; an **apostle** by divine appointment. He uses no pompous titles or symbols of status. He has only a grateful acknowledgment of his obligation to serve the risen Savior.

All we are told about those to whom the Letter was written is that they had **obtained** the same **precious faith** as Peter and his colleagues. This may indicate that he was writing to Gentile believers, the point being that they had received the same kind of **faith** as believing Jews, a faith that was in no way deficient. All who are saved by the grace of God enjoy equal acceptance before Him, whether they are Jews or Gentiles, male or female, slave or free.

Faith means the sum total of all they had received when they embraced the Christian faith. He goes on to explain that this **faith** is **by the righteousness of our God and Savior Jesus Christ**. He means that it was a righteous thing for **God** to give this **faith** of equal standing to those who believe on the Lord **Jesus**. Christ's death, burial, and resurrection provide a just basis upon which God can show grace to sinners through faith. The debt of sin has been fully paid and now God can justify the ungodly sinner who believes on His Son.

The title **our God and Savior Jesus Christ** is one of many in the NT which

indicate the absolute deity of the Lord Jesus. If He is not God, then these words have no meaning.

1:2 The apostle's lofty prayer for his readers is that **grace and peace** might **be multiplied to** them **in the knowledge of God and of Jesus our Lord**. He wants them to have this **knowledge** by the sustaining, empowering **grace** of God in their everyday lives. He wants their hearts to be guarded by the **peace** of God that passes all understanding. But this is not to be given in small doses! He desires these blessings to **be multiplied** in volume, not added in small segments.

How can these blessings **be multiplied**? It is **in the knowledge of God and of Jesus our Lord**. The better we know **God**, the more we experience **grace and peace**. We do better by dwelling in the secret place of the Most High than by making occasional visits there. Those who live in the sanctuary rather than in the suburbs find the secret of God's **grace and peace**.

II. CALL TO DEVELOP STRONG CHRISTIAN CHARACTER (1:3–21)

1:3 This passage should be of immense interest to every Christian because it tells how we can keep from falling in this life and how we can be assured of a triumphal entry into the next.

First we are assured that God has made full provision for us to have a life of holiness. This provision is said to be an evidence of His **power**: **His divine** power has given to us all things that pertain to life and godliness. Just as His power saves us in the first place, so His power energizes us to live holy lives from then on. The order is — first **life**, then **godliness**. The gospel is the power of God to save from the penalty of sin and from its power, from damnation and from defilement.

The **all things that pertain to life and godliness** include the high priestly work of Christ, the ministry of the Holy Spirit, the activity of angelic agencies on our behalf, the new life we receive at conversion, and the instruction of the word of God.

The **power** to live a holy life comes **through the knowledge of Him who called us**. Just as **His divine power** is the source of holiness, so **the knowledge of Him** is the channel. To know Him is eternal life (John 17:3) and progress in knowing Him is progress in holiness. The better we get to know Him, the more we become like Him.

Our calling is one of Peter's favorite themes. He reminds us that: (1) We have been called out of darkness into His marvelous light (1 Pet. 2:9). (2) We have been called to follow Christ in a pathway of suffering (1 Pet. 2:21). (3) We have been called to return blessing for reviling (1 Pet. 3:9). (4) We have been called to his eternal glory (1 Pet. 5:10). (5) We have been called **by glory and virtue** (2 Pet. 1:3). This last reference means that He **called us** by revealing to us the wonders of His Person. Saul of Tarsus was called on the road to Damascus when he saw the glory of God. A later disciple testified, "I looked into His face and was forever spoiled for anything that was unlike Him." He was **called by** His **glory and** excellence.

1:4 Included among the "all things" which God's power has **given** to promote a life of holiness are His **exceedingly great and precious promises** in the word. It is estimated that there are at least 30,000 promises in the Bible. John Bunyan once said, "The pathway of life is strewn so thickly with the promises of God that it is impossible to take one step without treading upon one of them."

The **promises** of God are the last of seven **precious** things mentioned by Peter in his Letters. Our faith is more precious than gold (1 Pet. 1:7). The blood of Christ is precious (1 Pet. 1:19). Christ, the Living Stone, is precious in God's sight (1 Pet. 2:4). He is precious also as the Cornerstone (1 Pet. 2:6). To all who believe, He is precious (1 Pet. 2:7). The imperishable jewel of a gentle and quiet spirit is very precious in God's sight (1 Pet. 3:4). And finally, the **promises** of God are **precious** (2 Pet. 1:4).

Think of some of the promises that relate to the life of holiness. (1) Freedom from sin's dominion (Rom. 6:14). (2) Grace that is sufficient (2 Cor. 12:9). (3) Power to obey His commands (Phil. 4:13). (4) Victory over the devil (Jas. 4:7). (5) Escape when tempted (1 Cor. 10:13). (6) Forgiveness when we confess our sins (1 Jn. 1:9) — and forgetfulness too (Jer. 31:34). (7) Response when we call (Ps. 50:15).

No wonder Peter says the **promises** of God are **precious** and very **great**! These promises enable the believer to escape **the corruption that is in the world through lust**. God has promised all that we need to resist temptation. When passionate cravings come, we can claim the promises. They enable us to escape from the world's corruption — its sexual sin, its drunkenness, its filth, its misery, its treachery, and its strife.

The positive side is that by these same promises we **may be partakers of the divine nature**. This takes place primarily at the time of conversion. Then as we live in the practical enjoyment of what God has promised, we become more and more conformed to His image. For instance, He has promised that the more we think about Him, the more we will become like Him (2 Cor. 3:18). We make this promise a reality by reading the word, studying Christ as He is revealed in it, and following Him. As we do this, the Holy Spirit changes us into His likeness from one degree of glory to another.

1:5 Verses 3 and 4 show that God has given us all that is necessary for the divine life. Because He has, we must be diligent in cultivating it. God does not make us holy against our will or without our involvement. There must be desire, determination, and discipline on our part.

In the development of Christian character, Peter assumes **faith**. After all, he is writing to Christians — to those who have already exercised saving **faith** in the Lord Jesus. So he does not tell them to furnish faith; he assumes that they already have it.

What *is* necessary is that **faith** be supplemented by seven elements of holiness, not adding these one after another, but manifesting all the graces all the time.

Tom Olson's father used to read the passage to his sons as follows:

Add to your faith the virtue or courage of David; and to the courage of David the knowledge of Solomon; and to the knowledge of Solomon the patience of Job; and to the patience of Job the godliness of Daniel; and to the godliness of Daniel the brotherly kindness of Jonathan; and to the brotherly kindness of Jonathan the love of John.[2]

Lenski suggests:

The list of seven is arranged with reference to the pseudo-prophets (2:1) and to the way in which they live according to their pretended faith. For praise they supply disgrace; for knowledge, blindness; for self-control, libertinistic license; for perseverance in good, perseverance in evil; for godliness, ungodliness; for fraternal friendliness, dislike for God's children; for genuine love, its terrible absence.[3]

The first characteristic is **virtue**. This may mean piety, goodness of life, or moral excellence, though these seem to be covered later by the word "godliness." It may also be that **virtue** here means spiritual courage before a hostile world, the strength to stand for what is right.

We think of the courage of the martyrs. Archbishop Cranmer was ordered to sign a recantation or be burned at the stake. At first he refused, but then under enormous pressure, his right hand signed the recantation. Later he realized his mistake and notified his executioners to start the fire. At his own request, his hands were untied. Then he held his right hand in the fire and said, "This is the hand that wrote it, and therefore it shall suffer punishment first. This hand hath offended! Perish this unworthy right hand!"[4]

Courage is to be supplemented with **knowledge**, especially the knowledge of spiritual truth. This emphasizes the importance of studying the word of God and obeying its sacred precepts.

More about Jesus in His Word,
Holding communion with my Lord.
Hearing His voice in every line,
Making each faithful saying mine.
    — Eliza E. Hewitt

Through an experiential knowledge of the Bible we develop what Erdman calls "practical skills in the details of Christianity."

1:6 God calls every Christian to a life of discipline. Someone has defined this as the controlling power of the will under the operation of the Spirit of God. There must be discipline in prayer, discipline in Bible study, discipline in the use of time, discipline in curbing bodily appetites, discipline in sacrificial living.

Paul exercised such **self-control**. "Therefore I run thus: not with uncertainty. Thus I fight: not as one who beats the air. But I discipline my body and bring it into subjection, lest, when I have preached to others, I myself should become disqualified" (1 Cor. 9:26, 27).

Audubon, the great naturalist, was willing to undergo prolonged discomfort to learn more of the world of birds. Let Robert G. Lee tell it:

He counted his physical comforts as nothing compared with success in his work. He would crouch motionless for hours in the dark and fog, feeling himself well-rewarded, if, after weeks of waiting he secured one additional fact about a single bird. He would have to stand almost to his neck in the nearly stagnant water, scarcely breathing, while countless poisonous moccasin snakes swam past his face, and great alligators passed and repassed his silent watch.

"It was not pleasant," he said, as his face glowed with enthusiasm, "but what of that? I have the picture of the bird." He would do that for the picture of the bird.[5]

Because of the example of others, the urgent needs of a perishing world, the personal peril of wrecking our testimony, we should discipline ourselves so that Christ will have the best of our lives.

Self-control should be supplemented with **perseverance**, that is, patient endurance of persecution and adversity. We need to be constantly reminded that the Christian life is a challenge to endure. It is not enough to start off in a blaze of glory; we must persevere in spite of difficulties. The idea that Christianity is an unending round of mountaintop experiences is unrealistic. There is the daily routine, the menial task, the disappointing circumstance, the bitter grief, the shattered plan. **Perseverance** is the art of bearing up and pressing on in the face of all that seems to be against us.

The next virtue is **godliness**. Our lives should be like God, with all that means in the way of practical holiness. There should be such a supernatural quality in our conduct that others will know we are children of the heavenly Father; the family likeness should be unmistakable. Paul reminds us, ". . . godliness is profitable for all things, having promise of the life that now is and of that which is to come" (1 Tim. 4:8).

1:7 **Brotherly kindness** identifies us to the world as Christ's disciples: "By this all will know that you are My disciples, if you have love for one another" (John 13:35).

Love of the brethren leads to **love** for all mankind. This is not primarily a matter of the emotions but of the will. It is not a sentimental exhilaration to experience but a commandment to obey. In the NT sense, love is supernatural. An unbeliever cannot love as the Bible commands because he does not have divine life. It takes divine life to love one's enemies and to pray for one's executioners. Love manifests itself in giving. For instance, "God so loved the world, that He gave . . ." (John 3:16). "Christ also loved the church and gave . . ." (Eph. 5:25). We can show our love by giving our time, our talents, our treasures, and our lives for others.

T. E. McCully was the father of Ed McCully, one of five young missionaries slain by Auca Indians in Ecuador. One night as we were on our knees together, he prayed, "Lord, let me live long enough to see those fellows saved who killed our boys, that I may throw my arms around them and tell them I love them because they love my Christ." That

is Christian love — when you can pray like that for the guilty murderers of your son.

These seven graces make a full-orbed Christian character.

1:8 There is either advance or decline in the pathway of discipleship — no standing still. There is strength and security in moving forward; danger and failure in retreat.

Failure to persevere in the development of Christian character leads to barrenness, unfruitfulness, blindness, shortsightedness, and forgetfulness.

Barrenness. Only the life lived in fellowship with God can be truly effective. The guidance of the Holy Spirit eliminates **barren** activity and insures maximum efficiency. Otherwise, we are shadow-boxing, or sewing without thread.

Unfruitfulness. It is possible to have considerable **knowledge of** the **Lord Jesus Christ** and yet to be **unfruitful** in that knowledge. Failure to practice what we know leads inevitably to barrenness. Inflow without outgo killed the Dead Sea, and it kills productivity in the spiritual realm as well.

1:9 *Shortsightedness.* There are various degrees of impaired vision which are spoken of as blindness. Shortsightedness here specifies the form of blindness in which man lives for the present rather than the future. He is so occupied with material things that he neglects the spiritual.

Blindness. Whoever lacks the seven characteristics listed in verses 5–7 is blind. He is not aware of what is central in life. He lacks discernment of true spiritual values. He lives in a dark world of shadows.

Forgetfulness. Finally, the man who lacks the seven virtues **has forgotten that he was cleansed from his old sins**. The truth of his redemption has lost its grip on him. He is going back in the direction from which he was once rescued. He is toying with sins that caused the death of God's Son.

1:10 And so Peter exhorts his readers to confirm their **call and election**. These are two facets of God's plan of salvation. **Election** refers to His sovereign, *eternal* choice of individuals to belong to

Himself. **Call** refers to His action *in time* by which the choice is made evident. Our **election** took place before the world was made; our **call** takes place when we are converted. Chronologically, there is first **election**, then **call**. But in human experience we first become aware of His **call**, then we realize we were chosen in Christ from all eternity.

We cannot make our **call and election** more **sure** than they already are; God's eternal purposes can never be thwarted. But we can confirm them by growing in likeness to the Lord. By manifesting the fruit of the Spirit, we can provide unmistakable evidence that we truly belong to Him. A holy life proves the reality of our salvation.

Living a holy life will keep us from stumbling. It is not a question of falling into eternal perdition; the work of Christ delivers us from that. Rather, it refers to falling into sin, disgrace, or disuse. If we fail to progress in divine things, we are in danger of wrecking our lives. But if we walk in the Spirit, we will be spared from being disqualified for His service. God guards the Christian who moves forward for Him. The peril lies in spiritual idleness and blindness.

1:11 Not only is there safety in constant spiritual progress, there is also the promise of a richly-provided **entrance** into **the everlasting kingdom of our Lord and Savior Jesus Christ**. Peter refers here not to the *fact* of our entry but to the *manner* of it. The only basis of admission to the heavenly **kingdom** is faith in the Lord Jesus Christ. But some will have a more abundant **entrance** than others. There will be degrees of reward. And the rewards are here said to depend on the degree of one's conformity to the Savior.

1:12 As he considered the present and eternal implications of this subject, Peter determined to keep on reminding the believers of the importance of the development of Christian character. Even if they already knew it, they needed to be constantly reminded. And so do we. Even though we **are established in the present truth**, there is always the danger of a preoccupied moment or a forgetful hour. So the truth must be constantly repeated.

1:13 Not only was it Peter's intention, but it was his duty **to stir** the saints **up** through frequent reminders **as long as** he lived. He felt the fitness of keeping them from spiritual drowsiness as he approached the close of his life.

1:14 The **Lord** had already revealed to Peter the *fact* that he would die and the *manner* in which he would die (John 21:18, 19). Many years had elapsed since then. The aging apostle knew that in the normal course of events, his death was near. This knowledge gave added impetus to his determination to care for the spiritual welfare of God's people during whatever time remained.

He speaks of his death as laying aside his earthly dwelling or putting off his body or **tent**. Just as a tent is a temporary dwelling for travelers, so the body is the structure in which we dwell during our pilgrimage on earth. In death the tent is taken down. At the Rapture, the body will be raised and changed. In its eternal, glorified form the body is spoken of as a building and a house (2 Cor. 5:1).

The fact that Peter knew he would die does not negate the truth of the imminent Return of Christ for His saints, as is sometimes argued. The true church has always expected that Christ may come at any moment. Only by a special revelation did Peter know that he would not be alive when the Lord returned.

1:15 Not only did the apostle determine personally to remind the saints of the importance of spiritual progress, he also arranged to leave **a reminder** behind in permanent written form. Through his writings, the believers would be able to remind themselves at any time. As a result, Peter's Letters have shed light on the path of men and women now for over nineteen centuries, and will continue doing so till the Coming of our Savior. Also, reliable ancient tradition says that the Gospel of Mark is essentially the eyewitness reminiscences of his spiritual leader, the Apostle Peter.

The importance of written ministry is clear here. It is the written word that lasts. Through the written word, a man's ministry goes on while his body is lying in the grave.

The word Peter uses for **decease** here

is the word from which we get *exodus*. It is the same word used to describe the death of Christ in Luke 9:31. Death is not the cessation of being but the departure from one place to another.

These verses have special value to us as they show what is important to a man of God who is living in the shadow of death. **These things** occurs four times — verses 8, 9, 12 and 15. The great, basic truths of the Christian faith have enormous value when seen from the borders of the eternal world.

1:16 The closing verses of chapter 1 deal with the certainty of Christ's coming in glory. Peter deals first with the certainty of the apostolic witness, then with the certainty of the prophetic word. It is as if Peter joins the NT and the OT, and tells his readers to cling to this united testimony.

He emphasizes that the apostles' testimony was based on fact, not on myth. They **did not follow** cleverly **devised fables** or myths **when** they **made known to the readers the power and coming of our Lord Jesus Christ**.

The specific event to which he refers is the Transfiguration of Christ on the mount. It was witnessed by three of the apostles — Peter, James, and John. **The power and coming** is a literary way[6] of saying "the coming in power," or "powerful coming." The Transfiguration was a preview of Christ's **coming** in **power** to reign over all the earth. This is made clear in Matthew's account of the event. In Matthew 16:28 Jesus said, "Assuredly, I say to you, there are some standing here who shall not taste death till they see the Son of Man coming in His kingdom." The very next verses (17:1–8) describe the Transfiguration. On the mount, Peter, James, and John saw the Lord Jesus in the same glory He will have when He reigns for one thousand years. Before they died, those three apostles saw the Son of Man in the glory of His coming kingdom. Thus the Lord's words in Matthew 16:28 were fulfilled in 17:1–8.

Now Peter is emphatic that the apostolic account of the Transfiguration was not based on **fables** (in Greek, myths). This is the word that some modern theologians are using in their attack on the Bible. They are suggesting that we should "demythologize" the Scriptures.

Bultmann spoke of the "mythological element" in the NT. John A. T. Robinson called on Christians to recognize that much of the Bible contains myths:

> In the last century a painful but decisive step forward was taken in the recognition that the Bible does contain "myth," and that this is an important form of religious truth. It was gradually acknowledged, by all except extreme fundamentalists, that the Genesis stories of the Creation and Fall were representations of the deepest truths about man and the universe in the form of myth rather than history, and were none-the-less valid for that. Indeed, it was essential to the defense of Christian truth to recognize and assert that these stories were not history, and not therefore in competition with the alternative accounts of anthropology or cosmology. Those who did not make this distinction were, we can now see, playing straight into the hands of Thomas Huxley and his friends.[7]

To refute the charge of myths, Peter gives three proofs of the Transfiguration: the testimony of *sight*; the testimony of *hearing*; and the testimony of *physical presence*.

As to *sight*, the apostles **were eyewitnesses of** the Lord's **majesty**. John testified, "We beheld His glory, the glory as of the only begotten of the Father" (John 1:14).

1:17 Then there was the testimony of *hearing*. The apostles heard the **voice** of **God** saying, **"This is My beloved Son, in whom I am well pleased."** This audible expression of honor for the Lord Jesus **came to Him from the Excellent Glory**, that is, from the bright, shining glory cloud, called the Shekinah, which symbolized the presence of God.

1:18 Speaking of James, John, and himself, Peter emphasizes that they distinctly **heard** the **voice** of God **when** they **were with** the Lord **on the holy mountain**. Here is the testimony of three witnesses, which according to Matthew 18:16 is authoritative and competent.

Finally, Peter adds the testimony of *physical appearance*: **we were with Him on the holy mountain**. It was a real-life situation; there could be no question about that.

We do not know the **mountain** on which the Transfiguration took place. If it were identifiable, it would probably be littered with shrines by now.[8] It is called the holy mountain not because it was intrinsically sacred but because it was set apart as the site for a sacred event.

1:19 And so we have the prophetic word confirmed. The OT prophets had predicted Christ's coming in power and great glory. The events on the mount of Transfiguration **confirmed** those prophecies. What the apostles saw did not set aside the OT prophecies or make them any more certain, but simply added confirmation to the predictions. The apostles were given an advance glimpse of the glory of Christ's future kingdom.

F. W. Grant's translation of the rest of verse 19 is helpful. ". . . to which ye do well in taking heed (as to a lamp that shineth in an obscure place, until the day dawn and the morning star ariseth) in your hearts." Notice Grant's use of the parenthesis. According to his translation, we should link **heed** with **in your hearts**. In other words, we should pay attention in our hearts. In the NKJV and many other versions, **the day dawns and the morning star rises in your hearts**, and this presents practical difficulties of interpretation.

The prophetic word is the shining **light**. The dismal or **dark place** is the world. The dawning of **day** signals the end of this present Church Age (Rom. 13:12). The rising of **the morning star** pictures Christ's coming for His saints. Thus the sense of the passage is that we should always keep **the prophetic word** before us, treasuring it **in our hearts**, for it will serve as a **light** in this dark world until the age is ended and Christ appears in the clouds to take His waiting people home to heaven.

1:20 In the final two verses of the chapter, Peter emphasizes that the prophetic Scriptures originated with God and not with man; they were divinely inspired.

No prophecy of Scripture is of any private interpretation (or **origin**, margin). This statement has given rise to a great variety of interpretations. Some are absurd, such as the view that interpretation of the Bible is the right of the church alone and that individuals should not study it!

Other explanations may be true statements, although not the meaning of this passage. For instance, it is true that no verse should be interpreted by itself, but in the light of the context and of all the rest of Scripture.

But Peter here is dealing with the *origin* of the prophetic word, and not with the way men interpret it after it has been given. The point is that when the prophets sat down to write, they did not give their own **private interpretation** of events or their own conclusions. In other words **interpretation**[9] does not refer to the explaining of the word by those of us who have the Bible in written form; rather it refers to the *way* in which the Word came into being in the first place. D. T. Young writes:

> So the text, rightly understood . . . asserts that Scripture is not human in its ultimate origin. It is God's interpretation, not man's. We often hear of certain statements of Scripture as representing David's opinion, or Paul's opinion, or Peter's opinion. Yet, strictly speaking, we have no man's opinion in those Holy Writings. It is all God's interpretation of things. No prophecy of the Scripture represents an individual's interpretation: men spake as they were moved by the Holy Ghost.[10]

The translation in the NKJV margin, **origin**, is thus quite accurate, and, we believe, superior in context.

1:21 This verse confirms the explanation just given in verse 20. **For prophecy never came by the will of man**. As someone has said, "What they wrote was not a concoction of their own ideas, and it was not the result of human imagination, insight, or speculation."

The fact is that **holy men of God spoke**[11] **as they were moved by the Holy Spirit**. In some way which we cannot fully understand, God directed these **men** as to the very words to write, and yet He did not destroy the individuality or style of the writers. This is one of the key verses in the Bible on divine inspiration. In a day when many are denying the authority of the Scriptures, it is important that we stand firmly for the *verbal, plenary* inspiration of the *inerrant* word.

By *verbal* inspiration we mean that the *words* as originally penned by the forty or more human writers were God-breathed (see 1 Cor. 2:13). God did not give a general outline or some basic ideas, then let the writers phrase them as they wished. The very words they wrote were given **by the Holy Spirit**.

By *plenary* inspiration we mean that *all* the Bible is equally God-given from Genesis through Revelation. It is the word of God (see 2 Tim. 3:16). By *inerrant* we mean that the resultant word of God is totally *without error* in the original, not only in doctrine, but in history, science, chronology, and all other areas.

III. THE RISE OF FALSE TEACHERS PREDICTED (Chap. 2)

2:1 At the close of chapter 1 Peter referred to the prophets of the OT as men who spoke, not by their own will, but as moved by the Holy Spirit. Now he mentions that in addition to the true prophets in the OT period, **there were also false prophets**. And just as there will be bona fide teachers in the Christian era, **there will be false teachers** as well.

These **false teachers** take their place inside the church. They pose as ministers of the gospel. This is what makes the peril so great. If they came right out and said they were atheists or agnostics, people would be on guard. But they are masters of deception. They carry the Bible and use orthodox expressions — though using them to mean something entirely different. The president of a liberal theological seminary acknowledged the strategy as follows:

> Churches often change convictions without formally renouncing views to which they were previously committed, and their theologians usually find ways of preserving continuity with the past through re-interpretations.

W. A. Criswell describes the false teacher as follows:

> . . . a suave, affable, personable, scholarly man who claims to be the friend of Christ. He preaches in the pulpit, he writes learned books, he publishes articles in the religious magazines. He attacks Christianity from within. He makes the church and the school a lodging place for every unclean and hateful bird. He leavens the meal with the doctrine of the Sadducees.[12]

Where are these false teachers found? To mention perhaps the most obvious places, they are found in:

Liberal and Neo-Orthodox Protestantism

Liberal Roman Catholicism
Unitarianism and Universalism
Russellism (Jehovah's Witnesses)
Mormonism
Christian Science
Unity School of Christianity
Christadelphianism
Armstrongism (The "Radio Church of God")

While professing to be ministers of righteousness, they **secretly bring in** soul-destroying **heresies** alongside true Bible doctrine. It is a deliberately deceptive mixture of the false and the true. Primarily, they peddle a system of denials. Here are some of the denials which can be found among certain of the groups listed above:

They deny the verbal, plenary inspiration of the Bible, the Trinity, the deity of Christ, His virgin birth, and His death as a Substitute for sinners. They are especially vehement in their denial of the value of His shed blood. They deny His bodily resurrection, eternal punishment, salvation by grace through faith in the Lord Jesus Christ, the reality of miracles in the Bible.

Other false teachings common today are:

The Kenosis theory — the heresy that Christ emptied Himself of the attributes of deity. This means that He could sin, make mistakes, etc.

The "God is dead" fantasy, evolution, universal salvation, purgatory, prayers for the dead, etc.

The ultimate sin of false teachers is that they even deny the Master **who bought them**. While they may say nice things about Jesus, refer to His "divinity," His lofty ethics, His superb example, they fail to confess Him as God and as unique Savior.

Nels Ferré wrote, "Jesus never was or became God. . . . To call Jesus God is to substitute an idol for Incarnation."[13]

Methodist Bishop Gerald Kennedy agreed:

> I am frank to confess that the statement (that Christ is God) does not please me and it seems far from satisfactory. I would much prefer to have it say that God was in Christ, for I believe that the testimony of the New Testament taken as a whole is against the doctrine of the deity of

Jesus, although I think it bears overwhelming witness to the divinity of Jesus.[14]

In this and in many other ways, **false teachers** deny **the Lord who bought them**. Here we should pause to remind ourselves that while these false teachers to whom Peter refers had been *bought* by the Lord, they had never been *redeemed*. The NT distinguishes between purchase and redemption. All are purchased but not all are redeemed. Redemption applies only to those who receive Jesus Christ as Lord and Savior, availing themselves of the value of His shed blood (1 Pet. 1:18, 19).

In Matthew 13:44 the Lord Jesus is pictured as a man who sold all He had to buy a field. In verse 38 of that same chapter, the field is distinctly said to be the world. So by His death on the cross, the Lord *bought* the world and all who are in it. But He did not *redeem* the whole world. While His work was *sufficient* for the redemption of all mankind, it is only *effective* for those who repent, believe, and accept Him.

The fact that these false teachers were never truly born again is indicated by their destiny. They **bring on themselves swift destruction**. Their doom is eternal punishment in the lake of fire.

2:2 Peter predicts that they will attract a large following. They do this by scuttling the biblical standards of morality and encouraging the indulgence of the flesh. Here are two examples:

Anglican Bishop John A. T. Robinson wrote:

> . . . nothing can of itself always be labeled as "wrong." One cannot, for instance, start from the position "sex relations before marriage" or "divorce" are wrong or sinful in themselves. They may be in 99 cases or even 100 cases out of 100, but they are not intrinsically so, for the only intrinsic evil is lack of love.[15]

In the book *Called to Responsible Freedom*, published by the National Council of Churches, young people are counseled:

> In the personal, individual sense, then, what justifies and sanctifies sexuality is not the external marital status of the people before the law but rather what they feel toward each other in their hearts.

Measured in such a way, holding hands can be very wrong indeed while intimate sex-play can be right and good.[16]

As a result of this type of behavior, taught and practiced by false teachers, **the way of truth** is maligned. Unbelievers develop a deep contempt for Christianity.

2:3 These false teachers are greedy, both in the sexual and financial realms. They have chosen the ministry as a lucrative profession. Their great aim is to build up a large following and thus to increase their income.

They **exploit** people with **false words**. Darby said, "The devil is never more satanic than when he carries a Bible." So these men, with Bible in hand, pose as ministers of righteousness, give out well-known evangelical hymns, and use scriptural expressions. But all this is camouflage for heretical teachings and corrupt morals.

An awful condemnation awaits these religious fifth-columnists. **Their judgment has not been idle**; it has been arming itself for the slaughter. **Their destruction** has **not** been nodding its head in sleep; it has been wide awake, ready to pounce like a panther.

2:4 In verses 4–10, we have three OT examples of God's judgment on apostasy — the angels, the antediluvians, and the cities of Sodom and Gomorrah.

We assume that **the angels who sinned** are those also mentioned in Jude 6. There we learn that: (1) They did not keep their position. (2) They left their proper dwelling. Though we cannot be certain, there is strong reason to believe that these are the same as "the sons of God" mentioned in Genesis 6:2: "The sons of God saw the daughters of men, that they were beautiful; and they took wives for themselves of all whom they chose." Angels are called sons of God in Job 1:6; 2:1. The inference in Genesis 6 is that these sons of God left the angelic position assigned to them, exchanged their dwelling in heaven for one on earth, and intermarried with human wives. The children born to them were *nephilim*, which means "fallen ones" (Gen. 6:4). It seems clear from Genesis 6:3 that God was extremely displeased with these abnormal sexual unions.

Against this view it is generally argued that angels are sexless and therefore cannot marry. But the Bible does not say this. All it says is that *in heaven* they do not marry (Mark 12:25). Angels often appeared in human form in the OT. For example, the two angels whom Lot entertained in Sodom (Gen. 19:1) are described as men in verses 5, 10, 12. They had feet (v. 2) and hands (v. 10); they could eat (v. 3); they had physical strength (vv. 10, 16). It is obvious from the perverted desires of the men of Sodom that these angels had bodies that were capable of sexual abuse (v. 5).

God was outraged by this gross apostasy of **the angels** from His established order. Their doom was to be thrown **down to hell**, committed to pits of utter gloom until the final **judgment**.

2:5 The second illustration of God's direct intervention in punishing sin relates to the people who perished in **the flood**. Their wickedness had been great. Every imagination of the thoughts of their heart was only evil continually (Gen. 6:5). In God's sight the earth was corrupt and filled with violence (Gen. 6:11–13). The Lord was sorry that He had made men on the earth (Gen. 6:6). He was so grieved that He determined to blot them out (Gen. 6:7). He **did not spare the ancient world**, but brought **the flood** upon it to destroy its ungodly inhabitants.

Only **Noah** and his family found favor in the eyes of the Lord. They sought and found refuge in the ark, and rode safely above the storm of God's wrath and indignation.

Noah is described as **a preacher of righteousness**. Doubtless as he built the ark, his hammer blows were interspersed with warnings to the mocking spectators to turn from sin or face God's righteous punishment for their wickedness.

2:6 The third example of God's unsparing judgment concerns the destruction of **Sodom and Gomorrah**. These two cities, somewhere near what is now the southern area of the Dead Sea, were cesspools of sexual perversion. The people accepted homosexuality as a normal way of life. This sin is described in Romans 1:26, 27:

Even their women exchanged the natural use for what is against nature. Likewise also the men, leaving the natural use of the woman, burned in their lust for one another, men with men committing what is shameful, and receiving in themselves the penalty of their error which was due.

God did not look upon this unrestrained degeneracy as sickness but as sin. In order to show to all succeeding generations His extreme hatred of homosexuality, He rained fire and brimstone on Sodom and Gomorrah (Gen. 19:24), reducing them to ashes. The destruction was so complete that there is considerable doubt today as to the exact location of the cities. They serve as an example to any who would legalize this sin or condone it as a disease.

It is significant that liberal clergymen today are becoming increasingly outspoken in favor of sexual perversion. One official of the United Church of Christ, writing in *Social Action*, recommended that the church cease to discriminate against homosexuals in admission to seminaries, in ordination, and in employment on church staffs. Ninety Episcopal priests recently decided that homosexual acts between consenting adults are morally neutral. False religious teachers are in the forefront of movements to legalize this sin.

It is no accident that this Epistle, dealing with *apostasy*, should have so much to say about *immorality*; the two often go together. Apostasy often has its roots in moral failure. For instance, a man may fall into serious sexual sin. Instead of acknowledging his guilt and finding cleansing through the blood of Christ, he decides to cast off the knowledge of God, which condemns his actions, and live in practical atheism. A. J. Pollock tells of meeting a young man who had once professed to be a Christian but who was now full of doubts and denials. Mr. Pollock asked him, "My friend, what sin have you been indulging lately?" The young man hung his head, brought the conversation to a quick halt, and went away shamefacedly.[17]

2:7 The same God who visits destruction on the ungodly rescues the **righteous**. Peter illustrates this by the experience of **Lot**. If we had only the OT account of Lot, we might not think him a true believer at all. In the Genesis account, he almost appears as a status-seeking opportunist, willing to put up with sin and corruption in order to make a place and name for himself in the world. But Peter, writing by inspiration, tells us that he was a **righteous** man **who was oppressed by the filthy conduct of the wicked**. God saw that Lot had genuine faith, and that he loved righteousness and hated sin.

2:8 To emphasize that Lot really was a **righteous man** in spite of appearances to the contrary, Peter repeats that his soul was **tormented** daily by the things he heard and saw in Sodom. The vile immorality of the people caused him deep suffering.

2:9 The conclusion is that **the Lord knows how to deliver the godly** and to punish the ungodly. He can rescue His people from trial, and at the same time **reserve the unjust under punishment for the day of judgment**.

The wicked are reserved for hell (v. 9) and hell for the wicked (v. 17). By way of contrast, an inheritance is reserved for believers, and they are kept for the inheritance (1 Pet. 1:4, 5).

2:10 God's ability to keep wicked men under restraints until their final trial is **especially** true of the class of people described in this chapter — false teachers whose lives are contaminated by sexual **uncleanness**, who advocate rebellion against governmental **authority**, and who boldly hurl insults at high officials.

It is no secret that false religious leaders, posing as ministers of Christ, are often characterized by low moral standards. They not only indulge in illicit sexual activities themselves, but they openly advocate libertinism. The Episcopal Chaplain of a girls' school in Baltimore, Maryland, wrote:

We all ought to relax and stop feeling guilty about our sexual activities, thoughts and desires. And I mean this, whether those thoughts are heterosexual, homosexual or autosexual. . . . Sex is fun . . . and this means that there are no laws attached which you ought to do or not to do. There are no rules of the game, so to speak.[18]

It is also significant that liberal religious leaders are commonly in the fore-

front of movements that advocate the violent overthrow of the government. Modernistic ministers have been frequently affiliated with subversive political causes. A director of church and community affairs for the Presbytery of Philadelphia said, "I don't think we preclude this (the use of bombs and grenades by the church) in the future, if all non-violent means prove ineffectual."

These men are bold and willful. Their brazen repudiation of all duly constituted authority seems to have no limits. No language is too extreme for them to use in reviling their rulers. The fact that human governments are ordained by God (Rom. 13:1) and that it is forbidden to speak evil of them (Acts 23:5) does not influence such men in the least. They seem to delight in shocking people by their belligerent denunciation of **dignitaries** (Greek: "glories" or "glorious ones"). This is a general term that could include all those, whether angels or men, who have been vested with governmental authority by God. Here it probably means *human* rulers.

2:11 The audacity of these professed ministers of religion is without parallel in the angelic realm. Although **angels . . . are greater** than men **in power and might**, they do not pronounce **a reviling accusation against** the glorious ones **before the Lord**. Here the reference to the glorious ones seems to apply to *angels* who are in positions of authority.

It is generally thought that this obscure allusion to angels is the same as that in Jude 9: "Yet Michael the archangel, in contending with the devil when he disputed about the body of Moses, dared not bring against him a railing accusation, but said, 'The Lord rebuke you.' " We are not sure as to why there was a controversy over the body of Moses. The important point for us is this: Michael recognized that Satan has a position of authority in the world of demons, and although Satan had no jurisdiction over Michael, yet the latter would not revile him. Think, then, of the boldness of men who dare to do what holy angels shrink from doing! And think too of the corresponding judgment that will repay such defiance!

2:12 **These** apostate religious leaders resemble irrational animals. Instead of using the powers of reasoning which distinguish them from animals, they live as if the gratification of their bodily appetites is the very essence of existence. Just as many animals seem to have no higher destiny than to be killed and butchered, so the false teachers lunge forward to destruction, heedless of what is their true calling — to glorify God and to enjoy Him forever.

They **speak evil of the things they do not understand**. Their ignorance is never more glaring than when they criticize the Bible. Because they are devoid of divine life, they are utterly unable to understand the words, ways, and works of God (1 Cor. 2:14). Yet they pose as experts in the spiritual realm. A humble believer can see more on his knees than they can see on their tiptoes.

They will be destroyed in the same destruction as the animals. Since they choose to live like animals, they will die like them. Their death will not mean extinction, but they will die ingloriously and without hope.

2:13 In death they will suffer for their **unrighteousness**. As Phillips paraphrases it, "Their wickedness has earned them an evil end and they will be paid in full."

These people are so shameless and abandoned that they carry on their sinful activities in full daylight. Most men wait for the cover of darkness to **carouse** (John 3:19); hence the dim lights of the bar and the brothel (1 Thess. 5:7). The false teachers have cast off the restraints that usually hide sin in the shadows.

When they eat with Christian people, they are blots **and blemishes**, that is, unsightly, impure intruders, who luxuriate in their excessive eating and drinking. In his description of these same people, Jude says: "These are spots in your love feasts, while they feast with you without fear, serving only themselves" (Jude 12). When the false teachers attended the love feasts held in connection with the Lord's Supper in the early days of the church, they were utterly intemperate and totally unmindful of the spiritual significance of the feast. Instead of thinking of others, which love always does, they selfishly looked after themselves.

2:14 Even more scandalous is the fact that their **eyes** are **full of adultery and that cannot cease from sin**. This describes men who preach supposedly religious sermons, administer the ordinances, counsel the members of their congregation; yet their **eyes** are constantly looking for women with whom they might have an adulterous affair. Their thirst for lechery, disguised perhaps under the ministerial "cloth," seems to be limitless.

They entice **unstable souls**. Perhaps they misuse passages of Scripture to condone sin. Or they explain that matters of right and wrong are largely determined by our culture. Or they suavely reassure their dupes that nothing is wrong if it is done in love. It is easy for unsteady souls to reason that if a thing is all right for a religious leader, it certainly must be all right for a member of the laity.

They have hearts **trained in covetous practices**. They are not rank amateurs, but are schooled in the art of seduction. While the word **covetous** may cover any kind of excessive craving, the context here seems to point primarily to sexual greed.

As Peter thinks of this enormous travesty of Christianity, of the sin that these apostates cause to be associated with the name of Christ, he exclaims, **accursed children**! It is not that he is cursing them; he is simply foreseeing that they will experience the curse of God in all its fury.

2:15 In several ways, these false teachers resemble the prophet **Balaam the son of Beor**. They falsely pose as spokesmen for God (Num. 22:38). They induce others to sin (Rev. 2:14). But the chief likeness is that they use the ministry as a means of financial enrichment. **Balaam** was a Midianite prophet hired by the king of Moab to curse Israel. His motive for doing this was money.

2:16 On one of his attempts to curse Israel, Balaam and his donkey met the angel of the Lord (that is, the Lord Jesus in one of His pre-incarnate appearances). The donkey repeatedly refused to go on. When Balaam whipped it, the **donkey** rebuked him in human language (Num. 22:15–34). This was an astonishing phenomenon — **a dumb donkey speaking with** a human **voice** (and showing better sense than its master!). But the miracle did not shock Balaam out of his **madness.**

Lenski says:

> Balaam is a fearful example of a man who was "a prophet," whom God told what not to do, whom God hindered in his wrongdoing by even letting a dumb ass speak to him, but who in spite of everything secretly clung to his love for what he thought he could get out of unrighteousness, and so perished.[19]

God does not rebuke false teachers by dumb animals today. But there is every reason to believe that in other ways He often rebukes their madness and folly and encourages them to turn to the right way, which is Christ. God often uses the simple testimony of a humble believer to confound these men who pride themselves on their superior knowledge and on their ecclesiastical position. It may be by quoting a verse of Scripture or asking an incisive question, that a Spirit-filled "layman" leaves the modern-day Balaam to writhe in his humiliation and anger.

2:17 Peter likens the false teachers to waterless springs. Needy people go to them for refreshment and for relief from spiritual thirst but are disappointed. They **are wells without water**. They are also **clouds carried by a tempest**. The **clouds** hold promise of rain for land that has suffered from prolonged drought. But then a windstorm comes and drives the clouds away. Hopes are dashed; parched tongues are unsatisfied.

The nether gloom **of darkness** is **reserved for** these religious charlatans. Pretending to be ministers of the gospel, they actually have no good news to offer. People go to them for bread and get a stone. The penalty for such deception is an eternity[20] in **the blackness of darkness**.

2:18 They speak great swelling words of emptiness, or as Knox translates it, they use "fine phrases that have no meaning." This is an accurate description of the words of many liberal preachers and false cultists. They are accomplished orators, holding audiences spellbound by their grandiose rhetoric. Their erudite vocabulary attracts undiscerning people. What their sermons lack in content, they make up for in a dogmatic, forceful presentation. But when they have finished they have said nothing. As an example of this sort of sterile sermon, here is a quotation from a well-known theologian of our day:

> It is not a relationship of either parity or disparity, but of similarity. This is what we think and this is what we express as the true knowledge of God, although in faith we still know and remember that everything that we know as "similarity" is not identical with the similarity meant here. Yet we also know and remember, and again in faith, that the similarity meant here is pleased to reflect itself in what we know as similarity and call by this name, so that in our thinking and speaking similarity becomes similar to the similarity posited in the true revelation of God (to which it is, in itself, not similar) and we do not think and speak falsely but rightly when we describe the relationship as one of similarity.

The strategy of these false teachers is to **allure** people by promising unrestrained indulgence in every form of lust and passion. They teach that since our bodily appetites are God-given, they should not be restrained. To do so, they say, would cause severe personality disturbances. And so they advocate sexual experimentation before marriage and relaxed morals after marriage.

Their victims are **the ones who have actually escaped**[21] **from those who live in error.** These unsaved people once indulged freely in sinful pleasures, but they've had a change of heart. They decide to reform, to turn over a new leaf, and to start attending church. Instead of going to a Bible-believing church, they wander into a service where one of these false shepherds is holding forth. Instead of hearing the gospel of salvation through faith in Christ, they hear sin condoned and permissiveness encouraged. It all comes as rather a surprise; they had always thought that sin was wrong and that the church was against it. Now they learn that sin is given religious approval!

2:19 The apostate ministers talk a lot about freedom, but they mean freedom from divine authority and freedom to sin. Actually, this is not **liberty** but the worst form of **bondage. They themselves are slaves of corruption.** Bound by the chains of evil lusts and habits, they are powerless to break free.

2:20 Verses 20-22 refer, not to the false teachers themselves, but to their victims. They are people who had reformed but who had not been born again. **Through** a partial **knowledge of . . . Christ** and of Christian principles, they had turned from a life of sin and begun a moral house-cleaning.

Then they come under the influence of false teachers who mock puritanical virtue and crusade for liberation from moral inhibitions. They become involved again in the very sins from which they had been temporarily delivered. As a matter of fact, they sink lower than before, because now that religious restraints are gone, there is nothing to hold them back. So it is true that their **latter** state is **worse than** the first.

2:21 The greater a person's privilege, the greater his responsibility. The more a person knows of Christian standards, the more obligated he is to live up to them. **It would** be **better** never **to have known** God's holy requirements, **than having known** them to turn back to the filth of the world.

2:22 These people illustrate **the true proverb** concerning **a dog** that **returns to his own** disgusting **vomit** (see Prov. 26:11) and a washed **sow** that goes back **to her wallowing in the mire.** It is significant that Peter uses the **dog** and **sow** as illustrations. Under the Law of Moses, both of these were unclean animals. There is no suggestion in the proverb that they had experienced any change in their natures. They were unclean before they were delivered from the **vomit** and the mud, and they were *still* unclean when they returned to them.

So it is with the people of whom Peter wrote. They had undergone a moral reformation but they had never received a new nature. In the language of Matthew 12:43–45, their house was empty, swept, and put in order, but they had never invited the Savior to dwell in it. The unclean spirit which was cast out went and found seven other spirits more evil than himself to occupy the empty house. And the last state of that house

was worse than its initial condition.

This passage should not be used to teach that true believers may fall from grace and be lost. These people never were true believers. They never received a new nature. They demonstrated by their last state that their nature was still unclean and evil. The lesson is, of course, that reformation alone is not only insufficient, but is positively dangerous, because it can lull a person into a false security. Man can receive a new nature only by being born again. He is born again through repentance toward God and faith in our Lord Jesus Christ.

IV. THE RISE OF SCOFFERS PREDICTED (Chap. 3)

3:1 From the subject of false teachers in chapter 2, Peter turns to the certain rise of scoffers in the last days. In this Letter as in the previous one, he first encourages his readers to cling to the Bible.

3:2 They should remember the predictions of **the holy prophets** — found in the OT; and they should remember the teaching **of the Lord** as conveyed through **the apostles** — this is preserved in the NT. The Bible is the only true safeguard in days of declension.

3:3 The united testimony of the prophets and apostles was that **scoffers** would **come in the last days**, following **their own lusts.** Christians should remember this. They should not be bowled over by the arrogant and blasphemous denials of these men. Rather they should see in them a definite indication that the end of the age is nearing.

These mockers follow **their own** passions. Having rejected the knowledge of God, they fearlessly indulge their appetites. They advocate permissiveness with total disregard of any impending judgment.

3:4 Their primary scoff has to do with the coming of Christ. Their attitude is, **"Where is the promise of His coming?"** meaning, "Where is the *fulfillment* of the promise?" But what do they mean by **His coming**?

Do they mean Christ's coming for His saints, which we speak of as the Rapture (1 Thess. 4:13–18)? It is doubtful that these scoffers know anything about this first phase of the Lord's return.

Do they mean Christ's coming with His saints to set up His universal kingdom (1 Thess. 3:13)? It is possible that this could be included in their thinking.

But it seems clear from the rest of the passage that they are thinking of the *final judgment* of God on the earth, or what is commonly called the end of the world. They are thinking of the fiery destruction of the heavens and earth at the end of the Millennium.

What they really say is this: "You Christians have been threatening us with warnings about a terrible judgment upon the world. You tell us that God is going to intervene in history, punish the wicked, and destroy the earth. It's all a pack of nonsense. We have nothing to fear. We can live as we please. There is no evidence that God ever has intervened in history; why should we believe that He ever will?"

Their conclusion is based on the careless hypothesis that **"since the fathers fell asleep, all things continue as they were from the beginning of creation."** They say that nature invariably follows uniform laws, that there are no supernatural interventions, that there is a natural explanation for everything.

They believe in the law of uniformitarianism. This law states that existing processes in nature have always acted in the same manner and with essentially the same intensity as at present, and that these processes are sufficient to account for all the changes that have taken place.

There is a vital link between the law of uniformitarianism and the usual theories of evolution. The theory of the progressive development of living organisms from pre-existing types depends on the supposition that conditions have been fairly uniform. If this earth has been racked by cataclysms and catastrophes, then some of the presuppositions of Darwinian evolution are affected.

3:5 The scoffers deliberately ignore one fact — the flood. God *did* intervene at one time in the affairs of men, and the specific purpose of His intervention was to punish wickedness. If it happened once, it can happen again.

It is a withering indictment of these men that they are **willfully** ignorant. They pride themselves on being knowledgeable. They profess to be objective in their reasoning. They boast that they ad-

here to the principles of scientific investigation. But the fact is that they deliberately ignore a well-attested fact of history — the deluge. They should take a course in geology!

For this they willfully forget: that by the word of God the heavens were of old, and the earth standing out of the water and in the water, . . . perished. **The heavens** and **the earth** were formed **by the word of God**; He spoke and they came into being (Heb. 11:3). The **earth** was formed, Peter says, **out of the water and in the water**. We confess that there are depths in this statement that we cannot fully understand. We do know from Genesis 1:2 that the face of the earth was once covered with water. Then in verse 6 we read that God made a firmament or expanse to separate the water on the earth from the mist or cloud-cover over the earth. We assume from this that the earth had been covered by a thick mist of water in which life could not have been sustained. The firmament provided the clear atmosphere in which we can breathe. In Genesis 1:9, the continents were separated from the oceans; this may be what is referred to by the expression **"the earth standing out of water"** (see also Ps. 24:2).

Whatever the scientific implications of Peter's statement, we do know that the earth is a watery, cloud-covered world; three quarters of the surface is ocean, and much of it is veiled by mists. As far as we know, the earth is the only watery planet, and therefore the only one that can sustain human life.

3:6 From its inception, the earth was stored with the means of its own destruction. It had water in its subterranean depths, water in the seas, and water in the clouds above. Finally God released the waters from below and above (Gen. 7:11), the land was inundated, and all life outside the ark was destroyed.

The critics willfully disregard this fact of history. It is interesting that the flood has emerged in recent years as the object of bitter attack. But the record of it is written in stone, in the traditions of ancient peoples and modern, and best of all, in God's Holy word.

3:7 When God created the earth, He seeded it with sufficient water to destroy it. In the same manner, He seeded

the heavens and the earth with enough **fire** to destroy them.

In this nuclear age, we understand that matter is stored-up energy. The splitting of an atomic nucleus results in the fiery release of enormous quantities of energy. So all the matter in the world represents tremendous explosive potential. At present it is held together by the Lord (Col. 1:17, "in Him all things consist"). If His restraining hand were removed, the elements would melt. In the meantime **the heavens and the earth** are being **reserved for fire until the day of judgment and perdition of ungodly men**.

3:8 Why then the long delay in God's judgment? Well, first we should remember that God is timeless. He does not live in a sphere of time as we do. After all, time is determined by the relation of the sun to the earth, and God is not limited by this relationship.

With the Lord one day is as a thousand years, and a thousand years as one day. He can expand a day into a millennium, or compress a millennium into a day. He can either spread or concentrate His activities.

3:9 God has promised to end the history of ungodly men with judgment. If there seems to be delay, it is **not** because God is unfaithful to **His promise**. It is because He is patient. He does **not** want **any** to **perish**. His desire is **that all should come to repentance**. He purposely extends the time of grace so that men might have every opportunity to be saved.

In Isaiah 61:2 we read of the *year* of the Lord's favor and the *day* of His vengeance. This suggests that He delights to show mercy and that judgment is His strange work (Isa. 28:21). It may also indicate that He can extend His longsuffering 1000 years and condense His judgments into one day.

He waited 120 years before He sent the flood. Now He has waited several thousand years before destroying the world with fire.

3:10 But the day of the Lord will come. The day of the Lord refers to any period when God acts in judgment. It was used in the OT to describe any time when God punished evildoers and tri-

umphed over His foes (Isa. 2:12; 13:6, 9; Ezek. 13:5; 30:3; Joel 1:15; 2:1, 11, 31; 3:14; Amos 5:18, 20; Obad. 15; Zeph. 1:7, 14; Zech. 14:1; Mal. 4:5). In the NT it is a period of time with various stages:

1. It refers to the Tribulation, a seven-year period when God will judge unbelieving Israel (1 Thess. 5:2; 2 Thess. 2:2, NU Text).
2. It includes His return to earth when He will inflict vengeance on those who do not know God and who do not obey the gospel of the Lord Jesus (2 Thess. 1:7–10).
3. It is used of the Millennium when Christ will rule the earth with a rod of iron (Acts 2:20).
4. It refers to the final destruction of the heavens and the earth with fire. That is the meaning here in chapter 3.

It **will come as a thief** — that is, unexpectedly and destructively. **The heavens will pass away**. This certainly means the atmospheric heavens, and may mean the stellar heavens, but it cannot mean the third heaven — the dwelling place of God. As they pass away with a deafening explosion, **the elements will** be dissolved **with fervent heat. The elements** here refer to the constituent parts of matter. All matter will be destroyed in what resembles a universal nuclear holocaust.

Both the earth and the works that are in it will be burned up.[22] Not only the works of the natural creation, but all civilization will be consumed. The great capitals of the world, the imposing buildings, the phenomenal scientific productions are all marked for utter destruction.

3:11 Now Peter turns from the scoffers to the saints and presses home the obligations that devolve on them. **Therefore, since all these things will be dissolved, what manner of persons ought you to be in holy conduct and godliness.** Everything material has the stamp of oblivion upon it. The things of which men boast, the things for which they live are passing things at best. To live for material things is to live for the temporary. Common sense tells us to turn from the tinsel and toys of this world and live in holiness and **godliness**. It is a simple matter of living for eternity rather than time, of emphasizing the spiritual rather than the material, of choosing the permanent over the passing.

3:12 Believers should also be expectant. They should wait for and earnestly desire **the coming of the day of God**. Some use the words **"hastening the coming of the day of God"** to teach that we can hurry up the coming of the Lord by lives of devoted, unflagging service. But there are two difficulties in this teaching. First of all, the Day of God is *not* the coming of the Lord. Secondly, even if it were, there is real reason to question whether the time of Christ's coming can be altered by the zeal of His people.

The day of God refers to the eternal state. It follows the final phase of the Day of the Lord when the heavens and earth will be destroyed. **The day of God** is the Day of His complete and final triumph. For this reason it is a **day** we should wait for and earnestly desire.

In speaking of **the day of God**, Peter does not say "in which," but **because of which the heavens will be dissolved, being on fire, and the elements will melt with fervent heat. The day of God** is not the time in which the final destruction takes place. Instead, this ultimate judgment must occur before the Day of God can be ushered in.

3:13 In verse 12, believers were urged to wait for the Day of God. Here they are described as waiting **for the new heavens and a new earth in which righteousness dwells**. This supports the view that the Day of God refers to the eternal state when there will be **new heavens and a new earth**.

In Isaiah 65:17; 66:22, the **new heavens and new earth** are used to describe the Millennium as well as the eternal state. We know those passages include the Millennium because sin will be present (65:20) and children will be born (65:23). Peter applies the words exclusively to the eternal state; the existing heavens and earth will have already passed away.

Peter speaks of **righteousness** *dwelling* **in the new heavens** and **new earth**. At the present time grace reigns through righteousness (Rom. 5:21). In the Millen-

nium righteousness will *reign* (Isa. 32:1); in eternity, righteousness will *dwell*. In the earthly kingdom, Christ will rule with a rod of iron and righteousness will be enforced by Him. In that sense righteousness will reign. But in eternity, there will be no need for an iron rod. **Righteousness** will be at home. No sin will enter to mar the peace or beauty of that scene.

3:14 The truth concerning the new heavens and the new earth should deepen our desire to live holy "as to the Lord." It is not only a truth that we should hold but one that should hold us. Knowing that we shall soon stand before God should create within us a desire to be **without spot and blameless**, that is, to be morally clean. It should make us zealous to be found in a state of **peace**, not strife.

3:15 And consider that the longsuffering of our Lord is salvation. His delay in judgment is to give men full opportunity to be saved. As we consider the multiplying wickedness of men, we often wonder how the Lord can put up with it any longer. His forbearance is astonishing. But there is a reason for it. He does not desire the death of the wicked. He longs to see people turn from their wicked ways and be saved.

As also our beloved brother Paul, according to the wisdom given to him, has written to you. Several interesting points emerge in this allusion to **Paul**:

1. First, Peter speaks of **Paul** as **our beloved brother**, and this in spite of the fact that Paul had publicly rebuked Peter in Antioch for acting insincerely (Gal. 2:11–21). Obviously Peter had accepted the rebuke humbly. We should all be able to accept correction without harboring animosities.

2. Peter acknowledged that Paul was **given** divine **wisdom** in writing his Epistles. This is surely an intimation that Peter considered Paul's writings to be divinely inspired.

3. Peter's readers had apparently read one or more of Paul's Epistles. This may mean that the Epistles were addressed directly to them or that they were circulated in that area.

Which of Paul's Letters says **that the longsuffering of our Lord is salvation**?

Romans 2:4 reads: "Or do you despise the riches of His goodness, forbearance, and longsuffering, not knowing that the goodness of God leads you to repentance?"

3:16 In all his epistles Paul spoke of the great truths with which Peter has been dealing in his two Letters; truths such as the new birth, the deity of Christ, His life of sinless suffering, His substitutionary death, His resurrection, His ascension, His coming again, the Day of the Lord and the eternal state.

Some Bible truths are **hard to understand**, such as the Trinity, God's election and man's free will, the mystery of suffering, etc. It should not disturb us if we find matters in the Bible which are above our understanding. The word of God is infinite and inexhaustible. In studying it we must always be willing to give God credit for knowing things which we can never fully fathom.

Peter is not criticizing Paul's writings when he speaks of **things hard to understand**. It is not Paul's style of writing which is difficult to understand but the subjects which he treats. Barnes writes: "Peter refers not to the difficulties of understanding what Paul *meant*, but to the difficulty of comprehending the great *truths* which he taught."[23]

Instead of accepting them simply by faith, **untaught and unstable people twist** some of these difficult truths **to their own destruction**. Some false cults, for instance, twist the law into a way of salvation rather than a revealer of sin. Others make baptism the door to heaven. They do this not only with Paul's writings but with other Scriptures as well.

Notice that Peter here puts Paul's writings on the same level **as the rest of the Scriptures**, that is, the OT and whatever portions of the NT were then available. He acknowledges that the Pauline Epistles were part of the inspired sacred Scriptures.

3:17 Believers must be constantly on guard against the peril of **error**. The knowledge that there will always be false teachers who corrupt and imitate the truth should keep us alert. It is easy for the unsuspecting to be swept off their feet by the **error of the wicked** and to lose their spiritual balance.

3:18 Once again Peter teaches that continued progress in divine things is a great protection against the peril of false teachers. There must be a twofold growth — **in grace and** in **knowledge.** Grace is the practical demonstration of the fruit of the Spirit. Growth in **grace** is not increased head knowledge or tireless activity; it is increasing likeness to the Lord Jesus. **Knowledge** means acquaintance with the Lord through the word. Growth in **knowledge** means increasing study of and subjection to His words, works, and ways.

But Peter cannot close his Epistle with an exhortation to the saints. The climax must be **glory** to the Savior. And so we find the lovely doxology: **To Him be the glory, both now and forever. Amen.** This, after all, is the ultimate reason for our existence — to glorify Him — and therefore no concluding note to this Epistle could be more fitting.

ENDNOTES

[1](Intro) E. G. Homrighausen, "The Second Epistle of Peter," *Exposition, IB*, XII, 1957, p. 166.

[2](1:5) From the spoken ministry of Tom Olson, a personal friend of the author.

[3](1:5) R. C. H. Lenski, *The Interpretation of the Epistles of St. Peter, St. John and St. Jude*, p. 266.

[4](1:5) This famous story is widely recounted. See, for example, S. M. Houghton, *Sketches from Church History*, pp. 114-116.

[5](1:6) Robert G. Lee, *Seven Swords and Other Messages*, p. 46.

[6](1:16) When we use two words to give one meaning, such as "good and mad" to mean *very* mad, it is called a *hendiadys* (from the Greek for "one through two"). The Bible uses this figure of speech frequently, as here, so it is good to be able to recognize it.

[7](1:16) John A. T. Robinson, *Honest to God*, p. 32, 33.

[8](1:18) Roman Catholic tradition makes Mt. Tabor the site of the Transfiguration, and it does indeed have shrines on it. Historically this tradition is impossible, as Tabor is not a high mountain and the Gospels say it was "exceedingly high." Also, there was probably a

Roman garrison on Tabor in the time of our Lord, a poor backdrop for a private revelation! Mt. Hermon, a high snow-capped range north of Galilee is a very likely site.

[9](1:20) The Greek word *epilusis* can be translated "origin" (NKJV margin) as well as "interpretation."

[10](1:20) Dinsdale T. Young, *The Unveiled Evangel*, pp. 13, 14.

[11](1:21) The critical text (NU) reads "but men spoke from God."

[12](2:1) Wallie Amos Criswell, *The Evangel*, Largo, FL, November 1949, p. 1.

[13](2:1) Nels Ferré, *The Sun and the Umbrella*, pp. 35, 112.

[14](2:1) Gerald Kennedy, *God's Good News*, p. 125.

[15](2:2) Robinson, *Honest*, p. 118.

[16](2:2) NCC, *Called to Responsible Freedom*, p. 11.

[17](2:6) A. J. Pollock, *Why I Believe the Bible is the Word of God*, p. 23.

[18](2:10) *Pageant Magazine*, October, 1965.

[19](2:16) Lenski, *Interpretation*, pp. 326, 327.

[20](2:17) The word "forever" is omitted by NU here but not in the close parallel in Jude 13.

[21](2:18) The NU text here reads "are barely escaping."

[22](3:10) Instead of "burned up" (*katakaēsetai*) the NU text reads "found" (*heurethēsetai*), perhaps meaning "laid bare."

[23](3:16) Albert Barnes, *Notes on the New Testament*, X:268.

BIBLIOGRAPHY

See Bibliography at the end of 1 Peter.

THE FIRST EPISTLE OF JOHN

Introduction

"It is not Christ walking on the sea, but His ordinary walk, that we are called on here to imitate."
— Martin Luther

I. Unique Place in the Canon

John's First Epistle is like a family photograph album. It describes those who are members of the family of God. Just as children resemble their parents, so God's children have His likeness too. This Letter describes the similarities. When a person becomes a child of God, he receives the life of God — eternal life. All who have this life show it in very definite ways. For instance, they acknowledge Jesus Christ as their Lord and Savior, they love God, they love the children of God, they obey His commandments, and they do not go on sinning. These, then, are some of the hallmarks of eternal life. John wrote this Epistle so that all who have these family traits may *know* that they have eternal life (1 Jn. 5:13).

First John is unusual in many ways. Although it is a real Letter that was actually sent, neither the author nor the addressees are named. Doubtless they knew each other well. Another remarkable thing about this lovely book is that extremely deep spiritual truths are expressed in such short, simple sentences, with a vocabulary to match. Who says that deep truth must be put into complex sentences? We fear that what some people foolishly praise as "deep" preaching or writing is merely muddy or *unclear*.

First John merits long meditation and sincere study. The apparently repetitious style actually repeats with slight *differences* — and it is these shades of meaning that must be noted.

II. Authorship†

The *external evidence* for the author-

ship of 1 John is early and strong. Specifically quoting the Epistle as by John, the author of the Fourth Gospel, are: Irenaeus, Clement of Alexandria, Tertullian, Origen, and his pupil, Dionysius.

Like the author of Hebrews, the writer of 1 John does not mention his name. Unlike Hebrews, however, 1 John has convincing *internal evidences* of its authorship.

The first four verses show that the writer knew Christ well and spent time with Him. This narrows down the possibilities of authorship considerably and coincides with the tradition that it is the Apostle John.

Strengthening this is the apostolic tone of the Letter: the author writes with authority, with the tenderness of an older spiritual leader ("my little children"), and even with a dogmatic note.

The thought, vocabulary ("abide," "light," "new," "commandment," "word," etc.), and expressions ("eternal life," "lay down one's life," "pass from death into life," "Savior of the world," "take away sins," "works of the devil," and others), coincide with the Fourth Gospel and the two other Epistles by John.

Likewise the Hebrew style of parallelism and simple sentence structure characterize both the Gospel and this Epistle. In short, if we accept the Fourth Gospel as by John the Apostle we should have no trouble crediting the Epistle to him as well.

III. Date

Some believe that John wrote his three canonical Letters in the 60's from

Jerusalem before the Romans destroyed it. More commonly, a date late in the first century is accepted (A.D. 80-95). The fatherly tone of the Epistles goes well with the ancient tradition of the aged Apostle John being carried into the congregation and saying, "Little children, love one another."

IV. Background and Theme[†]

At the time John was writing, a false sect had arisen which became known as Gnosticism (Gk. *gnōsis* = knowledge). These Gnostics professed to be Christians but claimed to have *additional knowledge*, superior to what the apostles taught. They claimed that a person could not be completely fulfilled until he had been initiated into their deeper "truths." Some taught that matter was evil, and that therefore the Man Jesus could not be God. They made a distinction between Jesus and the Christ. "The Christ" was a divine emanation which came upon Jesus at His baptism and left before His death, perhaps in the Garden of Gethsemane. According to them, Jesus *did* die, but the Christ did *not* die. They insisted, as Michael Green put it, that "the heavenly Christ was too holy and spiritual to be soiled by permanent contact with human flesh." In short, they denied the Incarnation, that Jesus is the Christ, and that Jesus Christ is both God and Man. John realized that these people were not true Christians, and so he warned his readers against them by showing that the Gnostics did not have the marks of true children of God.

According to John, a person either is a child of God or he is not; there is no in-between ground. That is why this Epistle is filled with such extreme opposites as light and darkness, love and hatred, truth and lie, death and life, God and the devil. At the same time, it should be noted that the apostle likes to describe people by their habitual behavior. In discerning between Christians and non-Christians, for instance, he does not base his conclusion on a single act of sin, but rather on what characterizes the person. Even a broken clock tells the correct time twice in every twenty-four hours! But a good clock tells the correct time regularly. So the general, day-by-day behavior of a Christian is holy and righteous, and by this he is known as a child of God. John uses the word "know" a great many times. The Gnostics professed to *know* the truth, but John here sets forth the true facts of the Christian Faith, which can be *known* with certainty. He describes God as light (1:5); love (4:8, 16); truth (5:6); and life (5:20). This does not mean that God is not a Person, but rather that God is the source of these four blessings. John also speaks of God as righteous (2:29; 3:7); pure (3:3); and sinless (3:5).

While John does use simple *words*, the *thoughts* he expresses are often deep, and sometimes difficult to understand. As we study this book, therefore, we should pray that the Lord will help us to grasp the meaning of His word and to obey the truth as He reveals it to us.

†See p. ii.

OUTLINE

Commentary

I. PROLOGUE: THE CHRISTIAN FELLOWSHIP (1:1–4)

1:1 The doctrinal foundation of all true fellowship is the Person of the Lord Jesus Christ. There can be no true fellowship with those who hold false views concerning Him. The first two verses teach His eternity and the reality of His Incarnation. The same One who existed from all eternity with God the Father came down into this world as a real Man. The reality of His Incarnation is indicated by the fact that the apostles **heard** Him, saw Him **with** their **eyes**, gazed upon Him with deep meditation, and actually **handled** Him. The **Word of life** was not a mere passing illusion, but was a real Person in a body of flesh.

1:2 Verse two confirms that the One who **was with the Father**, and whom John calls **that eternal life**, became flesh and dwelt among us and was **seen** by the apostles.

The following lines by an unknown author show the practical implications of these first two verses for our lives:

> I am glad that my knowledge of eternal life is not built on the speculations of philosophers or even theologians but on the unimpeachable testimony of those who heard, saw, gazed at, and handled Him in whom it was incarnate. It is not merely a lovely dream, but solid fact, carefully observed and an accurately recorded fact.

1:3 The apostles did not keep this wonderful news as a secret, and neither should we. They realized that the basis of all fellowship is found here and so they declared it freely and fully. All who receive the testimony of the apostles have **fellowship with the Father, with His Son Jesus Christ**, and also with the apostles and all other believers. How wonderful that guilty sinners should ever be brought into **fellowship with** God **the Father and with His Son Jesus Christ**! And yet, that is the very truth which we have here.

His Son Jesus Christ. Jesus and Christ are one and the same Person, and that Person is the **Son** of God. **Jesus** is the name given to Him at birth, and therefore speaks of His perfect humanity. **Christ** is the name that speaks of Him as God's Anointed One, the Messiah. Therefore, in the name **Jesus Christ**, we have a witness to His humanity and to His deity. Jesus is "very God of very God" (Nicene Creed) and yet truly human.

1:4 But why does John thus **write** concerning the subject of fellowship? The reason is that our **joy may be full**. John realized that the world is not capable of providing true and lasting **joy** for the human heart. This **joy** can only come through proper relationship with the Lord. When a person is in fellowship with God and with the Lord Jesus, he has a deep-seated **joy** that cannot be disturbed by earthly circumstances. As the poet said, "The source of all his singing is high in heaven above."

II. MEANS OF MAINTAINING FELLOWSHIP (1:5–2:2)

1:5 Fellowship describes a situation where two or more persons share things in common. It is a communion or a partnership. John now undertakes to instruct his readers as to the requirements for fellowship with God. In doing so, he appeals to the teachings of the Lord Jesus when He was here on earth. Although the Lord is not quoted as having used these exact words, the sum and substance of His teaching was **that God is light and in Him is no darkness at all**. By this He meant **that God is** absolutely holy, absolutely righteous, and absolutely pure. God cannot look with favor on any form of sin. Nothing is hidden with Him, but "all things are naked and open to the eyes of Him to whom we must give account" (Heb. 4:13).

1:6 Now it follows that in order for a person to be in **fellowship with** God, there can be no hiding of sin. Light and darkness cannot exist in a person's life at the same time, any more than they can exist together in the room of a home. If a man is walking **in darkness**, he is not in fellowship with God. A man who says he has **fellowship with Him** and habitually walks **in darkness** was never saved at all.

1:7 On the other hand, **if** one walks **in the light**, then he can **have fellowship with** the Lord Jesus and with his fellow Christians. As far as John is concerned in this passage, a man is either in the light or in darkness. If he is in the light, he is a member of God's family. If he is in darkness, he does not have anything in common with God because there is no darkness in God at all. Those who walk in the light, that is, those who are Christians, **have fellowship with one another, and the blood of Jesus Christ** continually **cleanses** them **from all sin**. All God's forgiveness is based on the blood of His Son that was shed at Calvary. That **blood** provided God with a righteous basis on which He can forgive sins, and, as we sing, "the blood will never lose its power." It has lasting efficacy to cleanse us. Of course, believers must confess before they can receive forgiveness, but John deals with that in verse 9.

1:8 Then again, fellowship with God requires that we acknowledge **the truth** concerning ourselves. For instance, to deny that we have a sinful nature means self-deception and untruthfulness. Notice that John makes a distinction between **sin** (v. 8) and *sins* (v. 9). **Sin** refers to our corrupt, evil nature. *Sins* refers to evils that we have done. Actually what we are is a lot worse than anything we have ever done. But, praise the Lord, Christ died for our **sin** and our *sins*.

Conversion does not mean the eradication of the sin nature. Rather it means the implanting of the new, divine nature, with power to live victoriously over indwelling sin.

1:9 In order for us to walk day by day in fellowship with God and with our fellow believers, we must **confess our sins**: sins of commission, sins of omission, sins of thought, sins of act, secret sins, and public sins. We must drag them out into the open before God, call them by their names, take sides with God against them, and forsake them. Yes, true confession involves forsaking of sins: "He who covers his sins will not prosper: but whoever confesses and forsakes them will have mercy" (Prov. 28:13).

When we do that, we can claim the promise that God **is faithful and just to forgive**. He is **faithful** in the sense that He has promised to forgive and will abide by His promise. He is **just to forgive** because He has found a righteous basis for forgiveness in the substitutionary work of the Lord Jesus on the cross. And not only does He guarantee to forgive, but also **to cleanse us from all unrighteousness**.

The forgiveness John speaks about here is parental, not judicial. Judicial forgiveness means forgiveness from the penalty of sins, which the sinner receives when he believes on the Lord Jesus Christ. It is called judicial because it is granted by God acting as Judge. But what about sins which a person commits after conversion? As far as the penalty is concerned, the price has already been paid by the Lord Jesus on the cross of Calvary. But as far as fellowship in the family of God is concerned, the sinning saint needs parental forgiveness, that is, the forgiveness of His Father. He obtains it by confessing his sin. We need judicial forgiveness only once; that takes care of the penalty of all our sins — past, present, and future. But we need parental forgiveness throughout our Christian life.

When **we confess our sins**, we must believe, on the authority of the word of God, that He forgives us. And if He forgives us, we must be willing to forgive ourselves.

1:10 Finally, in order to be in fellowship with God, we must not deny that we have committed acts of sin. God has stated over and over in His word that all have sinned. To deny this is to **make** God **a liar**. It is a flat contradiction of His word, and a complete denial of the reason the Lord Jesus came to suffer, bleed, and die.

Thus we see that fellowship with God does not require lives of sinlessness, but rather requires that all our sins should be brought out into His presence, confessed, and forsaken. It means that we must be absolutely honest about our condition, and that there should be no hypocrisy or hiding of what we really are.

2:1 John gives us God's perfect standard for His people, and His gracious provision in the event of failure. The **little children** refers to all the members of the family of God. God's perfect standard is then set forth in the words **these things I write to you, that you may not sin**. Because God is perfect, His standard for His people is absolute perfection. He would not be God if He said: "These things I write to you so that you sin just as little as you can." God cannot condone sin in the least degree, and so He sets perfection before us as the goal. The Lord Jesus did this with the woman who was caught in the act of adultery; He said, "Neither do I condemn you, go and sin no more."

At the same time, the Lord knows our frame. He remembers that we are dust, and so He has graciously made provision for us in the event of failure. This is expressed in the words, **"if anyone sins, we have an Advocate with the Father, Jesus Christ the righteous." An advocate** is one who comes to the side of another person in time of need in order to help. This is exactly what the Lord Jesus does for us when we sin. He immediately comes to us in order to restore us to fellowship with Himself. Notice that it does not say, "If any man confesses his sins. . . ." As our Advocate, the Lord seeks to bring us to the place where we do confess and forsake our sin.

There is something very wonderful in this verse which we should not overlook. It says, **"And if anyone sins, we have an Advocate with the Father."** It does not say *with God*, but rather *with the Father*. He is still our **Father** even if we sin. This reminds us of the blessed truth that though sin in a believer's life breaks fellowship, it does not break relationship. When a person is born again, he becomes a child of God. God is henceforth his **Father**, and nothing can ever affect that relationship. A birth is something that cannot be undone. A son may disgrace his father, but he is still a son by the fact of birth.

Notice that our **Advocate** is **Jesus Christ the righteous**. It is good to have a **righteous** Defender. When Satan brings some accusation against a believer, the Lord Jesus can point to His finished work on Calvary and say, "Charge that to My account."

2:2 And the Lord Jesus is not only our Advocate, but He is also **the propitiation for our sins**. This means that by dying for us, He freed us from the guilt of our sins and restored us to God by providing the needed satisfaction and by removing every barrier to fellowship. God can show mercy to us because Christ has satisfied the claims of justice. It is not often that an advocate (or lawyer) pays for his client's sins; yet that is what our Lord has done, and most remarkable of all, He paid for them by the sacrifice of Himself.

John adds that He is the satisfying sacrifice **not for** our sins **only, but also for the whole world**. This does not mean that the whole world is saved. Rather it means that the work of the Lord Jesus is *sufficient* in value to save all the **world**, but it is only *efficient* to save those who actually put their trust in Him. It is because His work is sufficient for all men that the gospel can be offered to all the world. But if all men were automatically saved, there would be no need of preaching the gospel to them.

It is interesting that the superscription on the cross was written in Hebrew — the language of God's chosen people — and in Greek and Latin, the principal languages of the then-known world. It was thus proclaimed to all the world that Jesus Christ is a sufficient Savior for all men everywhere.

III. MARKS OF THOSE IN THE CHRISTIAN FELLOWSHIP: OBEDIENCE AND LOVE (2:3–11)

2:3 John is about to give the true marks of those who are in the Christian fellowship. The first is obedience. We can have assurance concerning our relationship with God if our life is characterized by a loving desire to do His will. These verses are doubtless aimed at the Gnostics who professed to have a superior knowledge of God, but who showed little interest in keeping the **commandments** of the Lord. John shows that such knowledge is hollow and worthless.

John describes the believer's obedience in a threefold way — keeping **His commandments** (v. 3); keeping *His word* (v. 5); walking *as He walked* (v. 6). There is a definite progress in thought. To **keep His commandments** is to obey the teachings of the Lord Jesus as found in the NT. To keep *His word* means not only obedience to what is written, but a desire to do what we know would please Him. To walk *as He walked* is the full expression of God's standard for His people; it means to live as Jesus lived.

2:4 John does not imply that the Christian life consists in faultless obedience to the will of God, but rather that the Christian habitually desires to **keep His commandments** and to do those things that are pleasing in His sight. John is looking at the over-all tenor of a person's life. If someone says he knows God but **does not keep His commandments**, then it is clear that he is not telling **the truth**.

2:5 On the other hand, when we keep **His word**, then **the love of God is perfected in** us. **The love of God** does not refer to our love for God, but rather

to His love for us. The thought is that God's **love** toward us has been brought to its goal when we keep **His word**. It accomplishes its aim and reaches its end in producing obedience to Him.

2:6 Therefore, whoever **says he abides in Him** should **walk just as** the Lord Jesus **walked**. His life, as set forth in the Gospels, is our pattern and guide. It is not a life which we can live in our own strength or energy, but is only possible in the power of the Holy Spirit. Our responsibility is to turn our lives over to Him unreservedly, and allow Him to live His life in and through us.

2:7 Another important mark of true believers is love for the brethren. John says that this is not a **new commandment** which he is writing, **but an old commandment which** they had **had from the beginning**. In other words, the Lord Jesus had taught His disciples to love one another **from the** very **beginning** of His earthly ministry.

The Gnostics were always parading their teachings as being new. But the apostle urges his readers to test everything by the teaching of the Lord Jesus when He was here on earth. There is always the danger of drifting away from that which was in **the beginning**.[1] John says, "Get back to the beginning, and you will know what is true."

2:8 Yet this commandment is not only an old commandment, but there is a sense in which it is also **new**. When the Lord Jesus was here, He not only taught His disciples to love one another, but He gave them a living example of what He meant. His life was characterized by love for others. The commandment was thus **true in Him** when He was here on earth. But now there is a sense in which the Old Commandment is new. In this dispensation, it is not only **true in** the Lord Jesus, but in believers also. These Christians had formerly been heathens, living in hatred and passion. Now they illustrated and embodied the great law of love in their lives.

Thus **the darkness is passing away** whenever men receive the light of the gospel. The darkness has not all vanished because many have not come to Christ, but Christ, **the true light, is already shining**, and whenever sinners turn to Him they are saved, and henceforth love their fellow believers.

2:9–11 In verses 9–11 we have the contrast between love that is false and that which is true. If one professes to be a Christian and yet **hates** those who are truly Christians, it is a sure sign that such a one **is in darkness until now**. This latter expression shows that it is not a case of backsliding that is in view. The man continues to be what he always was, namely, unsaved. On the other hand, the one **who** characteristically **loves his brother abides in the light, and there is no cause for stumbling in him**. This may mean that the man himself is not in danger of stumbling, or that he will not cause others to stumble. Either interpretation is true. If the Christian is really living in touch with the Lord, the light illuminates his own pathway, and no one else is offended because of any discrepancy between his profession and his practice. The Gnostics had a deep hatred for those who were true to God's word. This proved that they were **in darkness** and walked **in darkness, and** that they did **not know where** they were **going, because the darkness** had **blinded** their **eyes**.

As if to illustrate the brotherly love about which he has been speaking, the apostle now stops to address loving greetings to those who are members of the family of God.

IV. STAGES OF GROWTH IN THE FELLOWSHIP (2:12–14)

2:12 First he embraces the whole family with the expression **little children**.[2] Here there is no thought of age or spiritual development. John is speaking to all who belong to the Lord, and this is proved by the rest of the verse, **because your sins are forgiven you for His name's sake**. This is true of all Christians. It is a wonderful thing to know, as a present possession, the complete remission of our sins. Notice, too, that our **sins are forgiven for His name's sake**. It is for Christ's sake that God forgives us our sins.

2:13 **Fathers** are described as those who **have known** the One **who is from the beginning**, mature believers who have known the sweet companionship of

the Son of God and are satisfied with Him. **Young men** in the spiritual family are characterized by vigor and by combat. This is the period of conflict and of wrestling with the foe. **Young men . . . overcome the wicked one** because they have learned the secret of victory, namely, "Not I, but Christ living in me." The **little children** are the babes in the faith. They do not know very much, perhaps, but they do know **the Father**.

2:14 When John repeats his address to the **fathers**, it is the same as at the first. This is because they have achieved maturity in spiritual experience. Again the **young men** are addressed as those who **are strong** in the Lord and in the power of His might. They **have overcome the wicked one** because **the word of God abides in** them. The Lord Jesus was able to defeat Satan in the wilderness by quoting the Scriptures. This emphasizes the importance of constantly feeding on the Bible and having it ready to repel the attacks of Satan.

V. TWO DANGERS TO THE FELLOWSHIP: THE WORLD AND FALSE TEACHERS (2:15–28)

In verses 15–17, we have a strong warning against the world and all its false ways. Perhaps this is addressed primarily to the young men, for whom the world often holds a special attraction, but it is a warning that applies to all the Lord's people. The world here is not the planet on which we live, or the natural creation about us. Rather it is the system which man has built up in an effort to make himself happy without Christ. It may include the world of culture, the world of opera, art, education — in short, any sphere in which the Lord Jesus is not loved and welcomed. Someone has defined it as "human society insofar as it is organized on wrong principles, and characterized by base desires, false values, and egoism."

2:15, 16 We are plainly warned **not** to **love the world or the things** that are **in the world**, for the simple reason that love for the world is not compatible with **love** for the **Father. All that** the **world** has to offer may be described as **the lust of the flesh, the lust of the eyes, and the pride of life. The lust of the flesh** refers to such sensual bodily appetites as proceed from within our evil nature. **The lust of the eyes** applies to such evil desires as may arise from what we see. **The pride of life** is an unholy ambition for self-display and self-glory. These three elements of worldliness are illustrated in the sin of Eve. The tree was good for food; that is **the lust of the flesh**. The tree was pleasant to the eyes; that is **the lust of the eyes**. It was a tree to be desired to make one wise; this describes **the pride of life**.

As the *devil* is opposed to *Christ*, and the *flesh* is hostile to *the Spirit*, so the *world* is antagonistic to the *Father*. Appetite, avarice, and ambition are **not of the Father, but of the world**. That is, they do not proceed from **the Father**, but find their source in **the world**. Worldliness is the love for passing things. The human heart can never find satisfaction with things.

2:17 **The world is passing away, and the lust of it.** When a bank is breaking, smart people do not deposit in it. When the foundation is tottering, intelligent builders do not proceed. Concentrating on this world is like rearranging the deck chairs on the Titanic. So wise people do not live for a **world** that **is passing away. But he who does the will of God abides forever.** It is **the will of God** that delivers us from the temptation of **passing** things. This, incidentally, was the life verse of D. L. Moody, the great evangelist, and is inscribed on his tombstone: "He who does the will of God abides forever."

2:18 Another test of those who are in the Christian fellowship is the test of doctrine. The subject is introduced by a warning addressed to those who are babes in Christ against false teachers. Those who are young in the faith are especially susceptible to the lies of **the Antichrist**. John's readers had been taught that an **Antichrist** would arise prior to the coming of Christ and pretend to be Christ. Just as coming events cast their shadow before them, so prior to the rise of **the Antichrist, many antichrists** appear. These are false teachers who offer a false christ and a false gospel. It is remarkable that the day in which we live is characterized by the existence of many Christ-denying cults, and these all bear

testimony to the fact that the coming of the Savior is near.

2:19 These false teachers were professing Christians who once associated with the apostles. However, in heart they were not really one with true believers, and they showed this by going **out from** the fellowship. **If they had been of us, they would have continued with us.** Here we learn that true faith always has the quality of permanence. If a man has really been born again, he will go on for the Lord. It does not mean that we are saved by enduring to the end, but rather that those who endure to the end are really saved. The false teachers **went out that they might be made manifest, that none of them were of us.**

2:20 But this raises the question: "How can a young believer know what is truth and what is falsehood?" The answer is that we **have an anointing from the Holy One, and . . . know all things**, and this **anointing** refers to the Holy Spirit and **is from the Holy One**, the Lord Jesus Christ. When a person is saved, he receives the indwelling Holy Spirit, and He enables the believer to discern between truth and error. When John tells his young readers **"you know all things,"**[3] he does not mean this in an absolute sense. It is not that they have perfect knowledge, but rather that they have the capacity to recognize what is true and what is not. Thus the youngest, simplest believer has the capacity of discernment in divine things that an unsaved philosopher would not have. The Christian can see more on his knees than the worldling can see on his tiptoes. In the physical realm, when a baby is born, he is at once endowed with all the faculties of the human race. He has eyes, hands, feet, and brains. He never gets these later. Although they grow and develop, the whole person is there at the first. So it is when a person is born again. He has at that moment all the faculties that he will ever have, although there will be endless possibilities for developing them.

2:21 John did **not** write **because** his readers were ignorant of **the truth, but** rather to confirm them in the truth that they knew, and to remind them **that no lie is of the truth**. The Gnostics were teaching doctrines that were contrary to the word of God, and therefore they were lies. Their principal lie, the very basis of all their teaching, was their denial that Jesus is the Christ. As pointed out in the introduction, they taught that Jesus was a mere man and that the Christ came upon Him at His baptism. This is the great lie of some of the cults today. The Bible everywhere insists that the Jesus of the NT is the LORD (Jehovah) of the OT. It is not correct to say that the Christ came upon Jesus, but rather that Jesus is the Christ.

2:22 John is careful to point out that to deny the deity of the Lord **Jesus** is to deny **the Father** also. Some people like to believe that they worship God, but they do not want to have anything to do with the Lord Jesus Christ. The apostle says, **"He is antichrist who denies the Father and the Son."**

2:23 In John 8:19, 42, Jesus said that those who failed to recognize His deity and to love Him neither knew the Father nor had Him as their Father. Similarly, John says, **"Whoever denies the Son does not have the Father either; he who acknowledges the Son has the Father also."** Here we have the wonderful truth of the unity between **the Father** and **the Son**. You cannot have **the Father** unless you have **the Son**. This is a message which should be heeded by all Unitarians, Christian Scientists, Muslims, Modernists, Jehovah's Witnesses, and Jews.

2:24 The safeguard for young believers against the false teachers is to **let that abide in you which you heard from the beginning**. This refers to the teachings of the Lord Jesus and of all His apostles. Our great safety is to stay close to the word of God. We should test everything by "What do the Scriptures say?" If a teaching does not agree with the Bible, then we should reject it also. As Dr. Ironside used to say, "If it's new, it's not true, and if it's true, it's not new."

2:25 When we abide in the Christian doctrine, we give proof of the reality of our faith. And **the promise** of that faith is **eternal life**. When we accept the Lord Jesus, we receive His own life, namely, **eternal life**, and this life enables us to test all new and questionable doctrines.

2:26, 27 John wrote thus to the young believers concerning the false teachers by way of warning. He does not have any fear as to the eventual outcome when he remembers that his readers had **received . . . the anointing from** the Lord Jesus. As mentioned previously, **the anointing** is the Holy Spirit, and here we learn that the Holy Spirit **abides in you**. This is a positive statement that once the Holy Spirit is received, He will never be taken away. Because we have received the Holy Spirit, we **do not need any one** to **teach** us. This does not mean that we do not need Christian teachers in the church. God has made specific provision for such teachers in Ephesians 4:11. It means that the Christian does not need any teaching apart from what is found in the Word of God as to the truth of God. The Gnostics professed to have additional truth, but John is saying here that there is no need for additional truth. With the Word of God in our hands and the Spirit of God in our hearts, we have all that we need for instruction in the truth of God.

2:28 John addresses all the dear **children** of the family of God, and exhorts them to **abide in Him** so **that when He appears, we may have confidence and not be ashamed before Him at His coming.** The **we** here refers to the apostles, and the teaching is that if the Christians to whom John wrote did not go on faithfully for the Lord, the apostles who led them to Christ would **be ashamed** at Christ's **coming.** This verse emphasizes the importance of follow-up work in all evangelistic endeavors. It also suggests the possibility of shame when Christ comes.

VI. MARKS OF THOSE IN THE CHRISTIAN FELLOWSHIP (CONT.): RIGHTEOUSNESS, LOVE, AND THE CONFIDENCE IT BRINGS (2:29–3:24)

2:29 The fourth family trait is **righteousness**. We know in the physical realm that like begets like. So it is in the spiritual. **Everyone who practices righteousness is born of** God. Because God **is righteous**, it follows that all He does is righteous, and therefore everyone **born**

of Him is righteous. This is John's inescapable logic.

3:1 The thought of being born of God arrests John with wonder, and he calls on his readers to take a look at the wonderful **love** that brought us into the family of **God**. Love could have saved us without making us **children of God**. But the **manner of** God's **love** is shown in that he brought us into His family as **children. "Behold, what manner of love the Father has bestowed on us, that we should be called children of God!"**[4]

Now as we walk about from day to day, **the world does not** recognize **us** as children of God. The people of the world do not understand us nor the way we behave. Indeed, the world did not understand the Lord Jesus when He was here on earth. "He was in the world, and the world was made through Him, and the world did not know Him. He came to His own, and His own did not receive Him." Since we have the same characteristics as the Lord Jesus, we cannot expect the world to understand us, either.

3:2 However, understood or not, **now we are children of God**, and this is the guarantee of future glory. It **has not yet been revealed what we shall be, but we** do **know that when** Christ **is revealed, we shall be like Him, for we shall see Him as He is**. This does *not* mean that we will be *physically* like Jesus in heaven. The Lord Jesus will have His own definite appearance, and will bear the scars of Calvary throughout eternity. Each of us, we believe, will have his own distinct features and will be recognizable as such. The Bible does not teach that everyone will look alike in heaven. However, we will be morally like the Lord Jesus Christ. We will be free from the possibility of defilement, sin, sickness, sorrow, and death.

And how will this marvelous transformation be accomplished? The answer is that one look at Christ will bring it to pass. **For we shall see Him as He is.** Here in life, the process of becoming like Christ is going on, as we behold Him by faith in the word of God. But then the process will be absolutely complete when we **see Him as He is**: for to **see Him** is to **be like Him**.

3:3 **Everyone who has this hope** of seeing Christ and of being like Him, **purifies himself, just as He is pure**. It has long been recognized by Christians that the hope of the imminent return of Christ has a sanctifying influence in the life of the believer. He does not want to be doing anything that he would not want to be doing when Christ returns. Notice that it says **"purifies himself, just as He** (Christ) **is pure."** It does *not* say "just as He (Christ) purifies Himself." The Lord Jesus never had to purify Himself; He is pure. With us, it is a gradual process; with Him, it is a fact.

3:4 The opposite of purifying oneself is found in verse four: **"Whoever commits sin also commits lawlessness, and sin is lawlessness."** The word **commits** is literally *does* (Gk., *poieō*). It is a matter of continual behavior, expressed by the present, continuous tense. It is possible to have sin even if there is no law. Sin was in the world between the time of Adam and Moses, but this was before God's law had been given. Thus it is not entirely accurate to say "that sin is a transgression of the law" (1611 KJV), but rather that **sin is lawlessness**. It is insubordination to God, wanting one's own way, and refusing to acknowledge the Lord as rightful Sovereign. In essence it is placing one's own will above the will of God. It is opposition to a Living Person who has the right to be obeyed.

3:5 A Christian cannot go on practicing sin, because that would be a complete denial of the purpose for which the Lord Jesus came into the world. **He was manifested to take away our sins.** To go on in sin, therefore, is to live in utter disregard of the reason for His Incarnation.

Again, a Christian cannot go on in sin because that would be a denial of the One whose name he bears. **In Him there is no sin.** This is one of the three key passages in the NT dealing with the sinless humanity of the Lord Jesus Christ. Peter tells us that "He *did* no sin." Paul tells us that "He *knew* no sin." Now John, the disciple who knew the Lord in an especially intimate way, adds his testimony, "In Him *is* no sin."

3:6 **Whoever abides in Him does not sin. Whoever sins has neither seen**

Him, nor known Him. This verse contrasts the true believer with one who has never been born again. It can definitely be said of the true believer that he does not go on sinning. John is not here speaking about isolated acts of sin, but rather continued, habitual, characteristic behavior. This verse does not imply that when a Christian commits an act of sin, he loses his salvation. Rather it says that when a person sins habitually, it is conclusive that he was never regenerated.

The question naturally arises, "When does sin become habitual? How often does a person have to commit it for it to become characteristic behavior?" John does not answer this. Rather he puts each believer on guard, and leaves the burden of proof on the Christian himself.

3:7 Now while the Gnostics made great pretensions as to their knowledge, they were very careless about their personal lives. Therefore, John adds, **"Little children, let no one deceive you. He who practices righteousness is righteous, just as He is righteous."** There should be no confusion on this point — a man cannot have spiritual life and go on living in sin. On the other hand, a man can only practice righteousness through having the nature of Him who **is righteous**.

3:8 Some children are so like their parents that you couldn't lose them in a crowd. This is true of God's children and of the devil's children. **He who sins is of the devil, for the devil has sinned from the beginning.** Here again the thought is, "He who practices sin is of the devil." The devil has been sinning (continuous, characteristic behavior) from the beginning, that is, from the first time that he did sin. All his children follow him in this broad way. It should be added here that men become children of God through the new birth, but there is no birth in connection with the children of the devil. A man becomes a child of the devil simply by imitating his behavior, but no one is begotten as a child of the devil.

In contrast, the coming of the Lord Jesus was in order to **destroy** (or annul) **the works of the devil**. The Lord could have destroyed the devil with a single word, but instead of that, He came down to this world to suffer, bleed, and die

that He might annul **the works of the devil**. If it cost the Savior so much to put away sin, what should be the attitude of those who have trusted Him as Savior?

3:9 Verse nine repeats the impossibility of one who **has been born of God** going on in sin. Some Bible students think that this verse refers to the believer's new nature, and that while the old nature can and does sin, the new nature cannot sin. However, we believe that here again the apostle is contrasting the regenerate man with the unregenerate, and is speaking of constant or habitual behavior. The believer does not have the sin habit. He does not defiantly continue in sin.

The reason is that **His seed remains in him**. There is considerable disagreement among Bible students as to the meaning of this latter expression also. Some think that this **seed** refers to the new nature, others to the Holy Spirit, and still others to the word of God. All of these are true, and therefore are possible explanations. We take it that the **seed** refers to the new life which is imparted to the believer at the time of conversion. Here, then, is a statement that the divine life **remains in** the believer. He is eternally secure. Rather than being an excuse for the Christian to go out and sin, his eternal security is a guarantee he will not go on sinning. **He cannot sin** habitually **because he has been born of God.** This divine relationship precludes the possibility of continuance in sin as a lifestyle.

3:10a Here then is the fourth distinction of **the children of God and the children of the devil**. Those who do **not practice righteousness** are **not of God**. There is no in-between ground. There are none who are half-and-half. God's children are known by their righteous lives.

3:10b, 11 In this section we have a continuation of the second test of those who are in the family of God — the test of **love**. This is continued from 2:7–17. From the beginning of the Christian dispensation, it has been taught that **love** to one's brothers is a divine obligation. **Love** here is not used in the sense of friendliness or mere human affection, but it is *divine* **love**. It is loving others as Christ loved us. Actually, this cannot be done in one's own personal strength, but only as empowered by the Holy Spirit.

3:12 John goes back to the first recorded instance of a man who did not love his brother. **Cain** showed that he **was of the wicked one** by murdering **his brother**, Abel. The underlying reason for this is given in the words **"his works were evil and his brother's righteous."**

3:13 It is a basic principle in human life that wickedness hates righteousness, and this explains why **the world hates** the believer. The righteous life of the Christian throws the wickedness of the unbeliever into sharp relief. The latter hates this exposure and instead of changing his wicked behavior, he seeks to destroy what shows it up so clearly. It would be just as unreasonable for a person to destroy a ruler or straightedge for showing how crooked is the line that he has drawn.

3:14 **We know that we have passed from death to life, because we love the brethren.** It is a remarkable fact that when a person is saved, he has an entirely different attitude toward Christians. This is one of the ways he receives assurance of salvation. A person who does not love a true child of God may profess to be a Christian, but the Scripture says he **abides in death**. He always was dead spiritually, and that is what he still is.

3:15 In the eyes of the world, hatred is not a very wicked thing, but God calls it murder. A moment's reflection will show that it is murder in embryo. The motive is there, although the act might not be committed. Thus, **whoever hates his brother is a murderer**. When John says **that no murderer has eternal life abiding in him**, he does not mean that a murderer cannot be saved. He simply means that a man who characteristically hates his fellows is a potential murderer and is not saved.

3:16 Our Lord Jesus gave us the ultimate example of **love** when **He laid down His life for us**. Christ is here contrasted with Cain. He gives us love in its highest expression. In one sense, love is invisible, but we can see the manifestation of love. In the cross of Calvary we see the love that is love indeed. John draws the lesson from this that **we also ought to lay down our lives for the brethren**. This means that our lives should be a continual giving-out on behalf of other believers, and that we should be ready to die for them also if necessary. Most of us will never be required to die on behalf of others, but every one of us can manifest brotherly love by sharing our material things with those in need. That is what is emphasized in verse 17.

3:17 If verse 16 suggests the most we can do for our brethren, verse 17 suggests the least. John distinctly says that a man is not a Christian who **sees his brother in need** and yet withholds from him what is necessary to satisfy that need. This does not justify indiscriminate giving to everyone, because it is possible to harm a man by giving him money with which to buy what would not be good for him. However, the verse does raise very disturbing questions concerning the accumulation of wealth by Christians.

3:18 We should **not love in word or in tongue, but** rather **in deed and in truth**. In other words, it should not be a matter of affectionate terms only, neither should it be an expression of what is not true. But it should be manifested in actual deeds of kindness and should be genuine instead of false.

3:19 **By** the exercise of **this** real and active love to our brethren, we shall know **that we are of the truth**, and this will **assure our hearts** as we come **before Him** in prayer.

3:20 **For if our heart condemns us, God is greater than our heart, and knows all things.** The subject here is the attitude with which we come before God in prayer. This verse may be understood in two ways.

First of all, **if our heart condemns us, God is greater than our heart** in the sense that He is **greater** *in compassion*. While we may have intense feelings of unworthiness, yet God knows that basically we love Him and we love His people. He knows that we are His in spite of all our failures and sins.

The other view is that **if our heart condemns us, God is greater than our heart** in the matter of *judgment*. Whereas we only know our sins in a very limited way, God **knows** them fully and absolutely. He knows all that there is to blame in us, whereas we only know it in part. We lean to this latter viewpoint, although both are true and therefore possible.

3:21 Here is the attitude of one who has a clear conscience before God. It is not that this person has been living sinlessly, but rather that he has been quick to confess and forsake his sins. By doing this, he has **confidence** before **God** and boldness in prayer. Thus, **if our heart does not condemn us, we have confidence toward God**.

3:22 And whatever we ask we receive from Him, because we keep His commandments and do those things that are pleasing in His sight. To **keep His commandments** is to abide in Him. It is to live in close, vital intimacy with the Savior. When we are thus in fellowship with Him, we make His will our own will. By the Holy Spirit, He fills us with the knowledge of His will. In such a condition, we would not ask for anything outside the will of God. When we ask according to His will, **we receive from Him** the things **we ask for**.

3:23 God's **commandment** is **that we should believe on the name of His Son Jesus Christ, and love one another, as He gave us commandment.** This seems to summarize all the commandments of the NT. It speaks of our duty to God and to our fellow Christians. Our first duty is to trust in the Lord Jesus Christ. Then because true faith is expressed in right conduct, we should **love one another**. This is an evidence of saving faith.

Notice in this and other verses that John uses the personal pronouns **He** and **Him** to refer to both God the Father, and the Lord Jesus Christ without stopping to explain which one is intended. He dares to do this because the Son is as truly God as the Father, and it is no presumption to speak of Them in the same breath.

3:24a The first part of verse 24 ends the section on love as a test of the children of God: **Now he who keeps His commandments abides in Him, and He in him.** To obey Him is to abide in Him, and those who abide in Him are assured of His abiding presence also.

3:24b And by this we know that He abides in us, by the Spirit whom He has given us. The subject of confidence is introduced by the statement that assurance of God's abiding in us comes **by the** Holy **Spirit**. All believers have the Holy Spirit. He is the one who guides them into all truth and enables them to discern error.

VII. THE NEED TO DISCERN BETWEEN TRUTH AND ERROR (4:1–6)

4:1 Having mentioned the Holy Spirit, John is reminded that there are other **spirits** abroad in the world today, and that the children of God need to be warned against them. Thus he cautions the believer not to trust **every spirit**. The word **spirit** here probably refers primarily to teachers but not exclusively so. Just because a man speaks about the Bible, God, and Jesus does not mean that he is a true child of God. We are to **test the spirits, whether they are of God; because many false prophets have gone out into the world**. These are people who profess to accept Christianity, but teach another gospel altogether.

4:2 John gives the actual tests by which these men are to be proven. The great test of a teacher is, "What do you think of Christ?" **Every spirit that confesses that Jesus Christ has come in the flesh is of God.** It is not so much the confession of the historical fact, namely that Jesus was born into the world in a human body, but rather it is the confession of a living Person, **Jesus Christ come in the flesh**. It is the confession that acknowledges **Jesus** *as* the **Christ** Incarnate. And confessing Him means bowing to Him as Lord of one's life. Now if you ever hear a person presenting the Lord Jesus as the true Christ of God, you will know that he is speaking by the Spirit of God. The Spirit of God calls on men to acknowledge Jesus Christ as Lord and to commit their lives to Him. The Holy Spirit always glorifies Jesus.

4:3 And every spirit that does not confess that Jesus Christ has come in the flesh is not of God.[5] This is how you can detect the false teachers. They do **not confess** the **Jesus** who was described in the previous verse. **This is the spirit of the Antichrist, which** has been prophesied **and** which **is now already in the world**. There are many today who are willing to say acceptable things about Jesus, but they will not confess Him as God Incarnate. They will say that Christ is "divine," but not that He is *God*.

4:4 Humble believers are able to **overcome** these false teachers **because** they have the Holy Spirit within them, and this enables them to detect error and to refuse to listen to it.

4:5 The false teachers **are of the world** and **therefore**, the source of all that they **speak** is **the world. The world** is the spring of all that they teach, and therefore **the world hears them**. This reminds us that the approval of the world is not a test as to the truthfulness of one's teachings. If a man simply wants to be popular, all he needs to do is to speak as the world speaks, but if he is to be faithful to God, then he must face the disapproval of the world.

4:6 In verse 6, John speaks as representing the apostles. He says, **"We are of God. He who knows God hears us."** This means that all who are really born of God will accept the teaching of the apostles found in the NT. On the other hand, those who are not of God refuse the testimony of the NT, or they seek to add to or adulterate it.

VIII. MARKS OF THOSE IN THE CHRISTIAN FELLOWSHIP (CONT.) (4:7–5:20)

A. Love (4:7–21)

4:7, 8 Here John resumes the subject of love for one's brother. He emphasizes that **love** is a duty, consistent with the character of **God**. As has been mentioned previously, John is not thinking of love that is common to all men, but of that love to the children of God which has been implanted in those who have been born again. **Love is of God** as to its origin, **and everyone who loves is born of God and knows God. He who does not love does not know God; for God is love.** It does not say that God loves. That is true, but John is emphasizing that **God is love**. Love is His nature. There is no love in the true sense but that which finds its source in Him. The words **"God is love"** are well worth all the languages in earth or heaven. G. S. Barrett calls them:

. . . the greatest words ever spoken in human speech, the greatest words in the whole Bible. . . . It is impossible to suggest even in briefest outline all that these words contain, for no human and no created intellect has ever, or will ever, fathom their unfathomable meaning; but we may reverently say that this one sentence concerning God contains the key to all God's works and way . . . the mystery of creation, . . . redemption . . . and the Being of God Himself.[6]

4:9, 10 In the verses that follow, we have a description of the manifestation of God's love in three tenses. In the past, it was manifested to us as sinners in the gift of **His only begotten Son** (4:9–11). In the present, it is manifested to us as saints in His dwelling in us (4:12–16). In the future, it will be manifested to us in giving us boldness in the day of judgment.

First of all, then, we have God's love to us as sinners. **God has sent His only begotten Son into the world that we might live through Him** and **to be the propitiation**[7] **for our sins.** We were dead needing life, and we were guilty needing **propitiation**. The expression, **"His only begotten Son"** carries with it the idea of a unique relationship in which no other son could share. This makes the love of God all the more remarkable, that He would send **His** unique **Son** into the world that we might live through Him.

God's love was **not** shown to us because **we** first **loved** Him. We did not; in fact, we were His enemies and hated Him. In other words, He did not love us because we loved Him, but He loved us in spite of our bitter antagonism. And how did He show His love? By sending His **Son** as **the propitiation for our sins. Propitiation** means satisfaction, or a settling of the sin question.

Some liberals like to think of the love of God apart from the redemptive work of Christ. John here links the two as not being in the least contradictory. Denney comments:

Note the resounding paradox of this verse, that God is at once loving and wrathful, and His love provides the propitiation which averts His wrath from us. So far from finding any kind of contrast between love and propitiation, the apostle can convey no idea of love to anyone except by pointing to the propitiation.[8]

4:11 John now enforces the lesson of such love on us: **"If God so loved us, we also ought to love one another."** The **if** here does not express doubt, but rather is used in the sense of "since." Since God so showered His love on those who are now His people, **we also ought to love** those who are members with us of His blessed family.

4:12, 13 God's love is manifested to us at the present time in dwelling in us. The apostle says, **"No one has seen God at any time. If we love one another, God abides in us, and His love has been perfected in us."** In John 1:18 we read: "No one has seen God at any time. The only begotten Son, who is in the bosom of the Father, He has declared Him." In John's Gospel we see that the invisible God is made known to the world through the Lord Jesus Christ. Here we have the expression **"no one has seen God at any time"** repeated in John's Epistle. But now God is manifested to the world, not through Christ, for He has gone back to heaven and is now at the right hand of God. Instead God is now manifested to the world through believers. How stupendous that now *we* must be God's answer to man's need to see Him! And when we love one another, **His love** is **perfected in us**. This means that God's love to us has achieved its goal. We are never intended to be terminals of God's blessings, but channels only. God's love is given to us, not that we might hoard it for ourselves, but that it might be poured out through us to others. When we do love one another in this way, that is proof that we are **in Him, and He in us**, and that we are partakers of **His Spirit**. We should pause to marvel at His dwelling in us and our dwelling in Him.

4:14 John now adds the testimony of the apostolic company: **"We have seen and testify that the Father has sent the Son as Savior of the world."** This is a grand statement of divine love in action. **"The Father has sent the Son"** describes the boundless scope of Christ's work. W. E. Vine wrote that "the scope of His mission was as boundless as humanity, and only man's impenitence and unbelief put a limit to its actual effect."[9]

4:15 The blessing of being indwelt by **God** Himself is the privilege of all who confess **that Jesus is the Son of God**. Here again it is not the confession of merely intellectual assent, but a confession that involves the commitment of one's person to the Lord Jesus Christ. No closer relationship is possible than for a person to abide **in God** and to have **God** abiding **in him**. It is hard for us to visualize such a relationship, but we might compare it, in the natural realm, to a poker in the fire, a sponge in the water, or a balloon in the air. In each case, the object is in an element and the element is in the object.

4:16 **And we have known and believed the love that God has for us. God is love, and he who abides in love abides in God, and God in him. God is love**, and that love must find an object. The special object of God's love is the company of those who have been born into the family. If I am to be in fellowship with God, then I must love those He loves.

4:17 **Love has been perfected among us in this.** It is not our love that is made perfect, but God's love is made perfect with us. John is now taking us on to that future time when we will stand before the Lord. Will it be with **boldness** and confidence or will it be with cringing terror? The answer is that it will be with **boldness**, or confidence, because perfect love has settled the sin question once and for all. The reason for our confidence in that coming day is given in the words **"because as He is, so are we in this world."** The Lord Jesus is now in heaven, with judgment completely behind Him. He came into the world once and suffered the punishment which our sins deserved. But He has finished the work of redemption and now will never have to take up the sin question again. **As He is, so are we in this world.** That is, our sins were judged at the cross of Calvary, and we can confidently sing:

> Death and judgment are behind me,
> Grace and glory lie before;
> All the billows rolled o'er Jesus,
> There they spent their utmost power.
> — *Mrs. J. A. Trench*

Just as judgment is passed for Him, so we are beyond the reach of condemnation.

4:18 Because we have come to know God's **love**, we have **no fear** of perishing. **There is no fear in love; but**

perfect love casts out fear. It is His **perfect love** that **casts out** our **fear**. I am assured of the Lord's love first of all, because He sent His Son to die for me. Secondly, I know He loves me because He indwells me at the present moment. Thirdly, I can look to the future with confidence and without fear. Truly, **fear involves torment**, and **he who fears is not made perfect in love.** God's love has not been allowed to operate in the lives of those who are afraid of Him. They have never come to Him in repentance and received the forgiveness of sins.

4:19 We love Him[10] **because He first loved us.** The only reason **we love** at all is **because He first loved us.** The Ten Commandments require that a man should love his God and neighbor, but the law could not produce this love. How then could God obtain this love which His righteousness required? He solved the problem by sending His Son to die for us. Such wonderful love draws out our hearts to Him in return. We say, "You have bled and died for me; from now on I will live for You."

4:20 John emphasizes the futility of professing to **love God** while at the same time hating one's **brother**. As spokes get nearer to the center of the wheel, so they get nearer to one another. Thus, as we get closer to the Lord, the more we will love our fellow believers. Actually, we do not love the Lord a bit more than we love the humblest of His followers. John argues the impossibility of loving God **whom** we have **not seen** if we do not love our brothers whom we have **seen**.

4:21 John closes the section by repeating the **commandment** which **we have from Him, that he who loves God must love his brother also.**

B. Sound Doctrine (5:1a)

John now concludes the tests of life. Here he resumes the test of doctrine, or we might also call it the test of faith. In the first three verses, we are given the results of faith. These are, first, the divine birth, then love for God, then love for one's fellow believers, and finally obedience to God's commandments. First of all, then, we have the divine birth: **Whoever believes that Jesus is the Christ is born of God.** Belief here is not a mere intellectual assent to the fact, but

rather a committal of one's life to Jesus as the Christ.

C. Love and the Obedience It Produces (5:1b–3)

5:1b If we have been truly **born of God**, then we will love **Him**. And not only so, we will love His children as well. It is good to notice here that we are to love all believers, and not just those of a certain earthly communion or fellowship.

5:2, 3 The fourth result of faith is obedience to God's **commandments. By this we know that we love the children of God, when we love God and keep His commandments.** Those who are truly saved will be characterized by a desire to do the will of God. Our **love** for **God** is expressed in willing obedience to His commands. The Lord Jesus said, "If you love Me, keep My commandments."

When John says that **His commandments are not burdensome**, he does not mean that they are not difficult, but rather that they are the very things which born again people love to do. When you tell a mother to take good care of her baby, you are only telling her what she loves to do. The **commandments** of the Lord are the things which are best for us, and the things in which our new nature takes a wholehearted delight.

D. Faith that Overcomes the World (5:4, 5)

5:4 Next we learn the secret of victory over **the world**. The world system is a monstrous scheme of temptation, always trying to drag us away from God and from what is eternal, and seeking to occupy us with what is temporary and sensual. People of the world are completely taken up with the things of time and sense. They have become the victims of passing things.

Only the man who **is born of God** really **overcomes the world**, because by **faith** he is able to rise above the perishing things of this world and to see things in their true, eternal perspective. Thus the one who really **overcomes the world** is not the great scientist or philosopher or psychologist, but the simple believer who realizes that the things which are seen are temporary and that the things which are not seen are eternal. A sight of the glory of God in the face of Jesus dims the glory of this world.

5:5 As we have seen, the subject of this section is faith as a test of eternal life. John has just mentioned that **he who overcomes** is **he who believes that Jesus is the Son of God**. He now goes on to expound the truth concerning the work of the Lord Jesus Christ.

E. Sound Doctrine (5:6–12)

5:6 He says, **"This is He who came by water and blood."** A great deal of discussion has arisen over the meaning of these words. Some feel that the **water and blood** refer to that which flowed from the Savior's side (John 19:34). Others feel that the **water** refers to the Spirit of God and that the **blood** refers to the blood shed on Calvary. Still others believe it is a reference to natural birth, where **water and blood** are present. We would like to suggest a fourth interpretation that takes particular account of the Gnostic heresy which the apostle is seeking to combat in this Epistle.

As mentioned earlier, the Gnostics believed that Christ came upon Jesus at His baptism and left Him before His passion, namely in the Garden of Gethsemane. In other words, they would say, "The Christ did not die on the cross, but Jesus the man died." This, of course, robs His work of any atoning value for the sins of others. We suggest that John is using **water** as an emblem of Jesus' baptism and **blood** as a symbol of His atoning death. These were the two terminals of His public ministry. John is saying that Jesus was just as much the Christ when He died on the cross as when He was baptized in the Jordan. **This is He who came by water and by blood — not only by water** (which the Gnostics would concede), **but by water and by blood**. It seems that the human heart is perpetually trying to rid itself of the doctrine of the atonement. Men would like to have the Lord Jesus as a perfect Man, the ideal Example, who has given us a marvelous code of morals. But John here insists that the Lord Jesus is not only Perfect Man, but Perfect God also, and that the same One who was baptized in the Jordan River gave His life as a sacrifice for sinners. Men say to Christ, "Come down from the cross and we will believe on You." If they can just eliminate the cross from their thinking, they will be happy. But John says, "No. You cannot have the Lord Jesus Christ apart from His perfect redemptive work at Calvary."

It is the Spirit who bears witness, because the Spirit is truth. This means that the Holy **Spirit** of God always testifies to the truth concerning the Lord Jesus which John has been unfolding. He bears witness that Christ came not with water only, but with **water and** with **blood**, because this is the truth of God.

5:7, 8 It always disturbs some devout Christians to learn that parts of verses 7, 8, as found in the KJV and NKJV, are actually found in only a handful of Greek manuscripts of the NT.[11] But this does not at all affect the truth of the inspiration of the Scriptures. Some people think it is important to retain the words because they mention the three Persons of the Trinity. However, the truth of the Trinity does not depend on this passage alone, but is found in many other portions of the Scriptures.

Having stated in the previous verses the Person and work of Christ, John now goes on to state the trustworthiness of our belief in Him. He says that **there are three that bear witness** (the words "in earth" should not be included), **the Spirit, the water, and the blood; and these three agree as one**. Although the word of God should be sufficient for us, as a basis of faith, He condescends to give us a threefold witness concerning the truth. First of all, **the Spirit** of God bears witness to the truth that Jesus Christ is God and that He is the only Savior of the world. The witness of the Spirit is found in the written word of God.

Then there is the witness of **the water**. We believe that this refers to what happened at the baptism of the Lord Jesus. At that event, God opened the heavens and publicly proclaimed, "This is My beloved Son, in whom I am well pleased." Thus God the Father added His own witness to God the Spirit concerning the Person of Christ.

Finally, there is the witness of **the blood**. On the cross, the Lord Jesus bore witness concerning Himself that He was the Son of God. No one took His life from Him; He laid it down by Himself.

If He were a mere man, He could not have done this. The **blood** of the Lord Jesus Christ witnesses that the sin question has been settled once and for all to the satisfaction of God. All **these three** witnesses **agree as one**. That is, they are united in the testimony concerning the perfection of the Person and work of Christ.

5:9 Now John comes in with a telling argument: **"If we receive the witness of men, the witness of God is greater."** In everyday life, we constantly accept the word of our fellow men. If we did not, business would be at a standstill and social life would be impossible. We accept the testimony of men who may be mistaken and who may be deceivers. Now if we do this in everyday life, how much more should we trust the word of God, who cannot fail and cannot lie. It is most unreasonable not to believe God. His witness is absolutely credible.

5:10 When a man does accept His testimony concerning His **Son**, God seals the truth by giving the man **the witness of the Spirit in himself**. On the other hand, if a man disbelieves God, he makes **Him a liar; because he has not believed the testimony that God has given of His Son**. People think they can accept or reject God's testimony concerning Christ, but John would have them know that to reject it is to accuse God of dishonesty.

5:11 John now summarizes the Christian message: **"This is the testimony: that God has given us eternal life, and this life is in His Son."** What tremendous truths these are, namely, that God has given **eternal life** to men, and that the source of this **life is in His Son**.

5:12 From this, the conclusion is inevitable. **He who has the Son has life; and he who does not have the Son of God does not have life**. The teaching is unmistakable. Eternal life is not found in education or philosophy or science or good works or religion or the church. To have **life**, one must **have the Son of God**. On the other hand, **he who does not have the Son of God does not have life**, that is, true life: *Eternal* **life** is inseparable from Jesus Christ.

F. Assurance Through the Word (5:13)

We have now come to the concluding portion of the Epistle. First of all, John states in the clearest terms why he has written the preceding passages. The purpose is that those **who believe in the name of the Son of God may know that** they **have eternal life**. If you have the marks of those who are children of God, then you can **know** that you have been born into the family of God. This verse also teaches another precious truth, namely, that assurance of salvation comes through the word of God. John wrote these things so that people **may know that** they **have eternal life**. In other words, the Scriptures were written that those who believe on the Lord Jesus may have *assurance* that they are saved. There is no need of hoping or guessing or feeling or groping in the dark. It is not presumption for one to say that he is saved. John states in the clearest possible manner that those **who** truly **believe in** the Lord Jesus **may know that they have eternal life**.

G. Confidence in Prayer (5:14–17)

5:14, 15 When we know that we have eternal life, needless to say, we can go before the Lord with **confidence**. John describes this **confidence** in verses 14, 15. We know **that if we ask anything according to** God's **will, He hears** those prayers and will answer them. Indeed we should fear to pray for anything that is *not* in accordance with His will. Perhaps someone will say, "But how can I know the will of God?" In a general way, the answer is that God's will is revealed to us in the Sacred Scriptures, and so we should study the word in order that we might know better what God's will is and how we can pray more intelligently.

5:16 John gives an instance in which the believer can have confidence in prayer, but he also cites an example in which confidence is not possible. **If anyone sees his brother sinning a sin which does not lead to death, he will ask, and He will give him life for those who commit sin not leading to death**. This apparently is a case where a Christian sees a fellow believer engaging in some sinful activity. It is not a sin of a nature as to bring death on the person committing it. In such an instance, the believer can ask for the recovery of the erring person, and God **will give** the petitioner **life** for those who do not sin unto death.

On the other hand, **there is sin leading to death**, and the apostle says, **I do not say that he should pray about that**.

THE SIN
LEADING TO DEATH

It is impossible to say with finality just what **sin leading to death** is, and so perhaps the safest course to follow is to list various accepted interpretations and then tell which one we feel is most correct.

1. Some feel that the **sin leading to death** refers to sin persisted in by a believer and unconfessed by him. In 1 Corinthians 11:30, we read that some had died because they partook of the Lord's Supper without judging themselves.

2. Others feel that the sin of murder is referred to. If a Christian should, in a moment of passion, murder another person, then we should not feel at liberty to pray for his release from the death penalty, because God has already stated that it is His will that "whoever sheds man's blood, by man his blood shall be shed."

3. Still others feel that the sin referred to here is blasphemy against the Holy Spirit. The Lord Jesus said that those who attributed His miracles which were done in the power of the Holy Spirit to Beelzebub, the prince of demons, had committed the unpardonable sin, and that there was no forgiveness for this sin either in that age or in the age to come.

4. Others believe that it is some special form of sin such as that committed by Moses or Aaron, Ananias and Sapphira, and which God visits with summary judgment.

5. A final explanation is that the sin of apostasy is in view, and we believe that this is the explanation which fits in best with the context. An apostate is one who has heard the great truths of the Christian Faith, has become intellectually convinced that Jesus is the Christ, has even made a profession of Christianity, although he has never been truly saved. After having tasted the good things of Christianity, he completely renounces them and repudiates the Lord Jesus Christ. In He-

brews 6 we learn that this is sin leading to death. Those committing this sin have no way of escape, since "they crucify again for themselves the Son of God, and put Him to an open shame." In this entire Epistle, John has been speaking with the Gnostics in view. These false teachers had once been in the Christian fellowship. They had professed to be believers. They had known the facts of the faith, but then they had turned their backs on the Lord Jesus and accepted a teaching which completely denied His deity and the sufficiency of His atoning work. A Christian cannot have liberty in praying for the restoration of such because God has already indicated in His word that they have sinned unto death. ‡

5:17 **All unrighteousness is sin, and there is sin not leading to death.** There are distinct differences in the degrees of **sin**, and there are sins which are **not** of such a serious nature as to result in **death**.

H. Knowledge of Spiritual Realities (5:18–20)

5:18 Beginning with verse 18, John brings his Epistle to a majestic close by reiterating the great certainties of the Christian Faith. **We know that whoever is born of God does not sin.** Of this we can be sure, that one who has the divine nature does not go on practicing sin. The reason follows: **He who has been born of God keeps himself,**[12] **and the wicked one does not touch him.** As in 3:9, this refers to the true believer who perseveres or keeps himself through his divine nature. It is only such a person who remains unscathed by the wicked one.

5:19 The Christian answer to those who profess to have superior knowledge is this: **We know that we are of God, and the whole world lies under the sway of the wicked one.** With John, there is no mincing of words. He sees only two spheres — in Him or **under the sway of the wicked one**. All people are either saved or lost, and their position depends on their relationship to Jesus Christ. Hear this, you Gnostics!

5:20 The third great truth is that of the Incarnation. **We know that the Son of God has come.** This is the theme with which John opened his Epistle and with which he is now about to close it. The coming of the Lord Jesus revealed to us **Him who is true**, that is, **the true God**. God the Father can only be known through the Lord Jesus Christ. "The only begotten Son, who is in the bosom of the Father, He has declared Him." Then John adds: **and we are in Him who is true**, **in His Son Jesus Christ**. Again the emphasis is that it is only as we are in Jesus Christ that we can be in God. "No one comes to the Father except through Me." **This is the true God and eternal life.** In other words, John is teaching what the Gnostics denied, namely, that Jesus Christ is God, and that eternal life is found only in Him.

IX. CLOSING APPEAL (5:21)

Lastly, we have John's final exhortation: **"Little children, keep yourselves from idols."** The apostle is saying in effect, "Beware of any teachings which are opposed to these realities." He wants believers to guard themselves from any ideas concerning God, other than those which have been handed down to us by the apostles. Jesus Christ is God. Any other thought is idolatry. Here John is not speaking primarily of idols carved out of wood. An idol is a substitute or false god taking the place of the true. Here an idol is not so much a material thing as a false teaching.

Archbishop Alexander spoke of this appeal as "an eloquent shudder." We can think of no language that could improve on such a description, and so we close this commentary with John's *eloquent shudder*:

> **"Little children, keep yourselves from idols. Amen."**

ENDNOTES

[1](2:7) The critical (NU) text omits the second "from the beginning."

[2](2:12) The word *teknia* is from a word meaning *to bear* (children). The diminutive makes it "little born-ones," an exact counterpart to the tender Scots word "bairnies."

[3](2:20) The traditional (and majority) texts read "you know all things" (*panta*). The critical (NU) reads "you all (*pantes*)

know." It is easy to see why the difficult reading would be changed to the easy-to-understand "you all know."

[4](3:1) The NU text adds "And we are."

[5](4:3) The NU text omits the second "that" and "Christ has come in the flesh."

[6](4:7, 8) G. S. Barrett, *The First Epistle General of St. John*, pp. 170-173.

[7](4:9, 10) *Propitiation* means satisfaction made for sin through a sacrifice. In the original, the word is related to the Greek word for "mercy seat." Under Britain's C. H. Dodd, a successful crusade was mounted against the word (and doctrine) so that, following the lead of the liberal RSV, most modern Bibles have changed the word. Since it is a standard "sound word" for a theological truth, we should maintain it (as in KJV and NKJV).

[8](4:9, 10) James R. Denney, *The Death of Christ*, 2d. ed., p. 276. The first part of the quotation is apparently from an earlier edition.

[9](4:14) W. E. Vine, *The Epistles of John*, p. 85.

[10](4:19) NU text omits *Him*.

[11](5:7, 8) Erasmus added these words to later editions of his Greek NT under pressure from the pope (they occur in the official Roman Catholic *Latin* Bible, the Vulgate). Only *four very late Greek* mss. have these words, so it is unsafe to use them. Those cultists who go door to door denying the Blessed Trinity are quick to point out these facts, so it is wise to be aware of the problem.

[12](5:18) If the NU text "him" is read instead of "himself," then "He who has been born of God" will refer to Christ.

BIBLIOGRAPHY

Barrett, G. S. *The First Epistle General of St. John*. London: The Religious Tract Society, 1910.

Candlish, Robert S. *The First Epistle of John*. Grand Rapids: Zondervan Publishing House, n.d.

Findlay, George. *Fellowship in the Life Eternal*. London: Hodder & Stoughton, n.d.

Ironside, H. A. *Addresses on the Epistles*

of John. New York: Loizeaux Bros., n.d.

Kelly, William. *An Exposition of the Epistles of John the Apostle*. London: T. Weston, 1905.

Law, Robert. *The Tests of Life*. Edinburgh: T & T Clark, 1909.

Marshall, I. Howard. *The Epistles of John* (NIC). Grand Rapids: Wm. B. Eerdmans Publishing Company, 1978.

Mitchell, John G. *Fellowship: Three Letters from John*. Portland, Ore.: Multnomah Press, 1974.

Stott, John R. W. *The Epistles of John* (TBC). Grand Rapids: Wm. B. Eerdmans Publishing Company, 1964.

Vine, W. E. *The Epistles of John: Light, Love, Life*. Grand Rapids: Zondervan Publishing House, 1970.

Westcott, Brooke Foss. *The Epistles of St. John*. Cambridge: The MacMillan Company, 1892.

THE SECOND EPISTLE OF JOHN

Introduction

"[Second John] gives us a new aspect of the Apostle: it shews him to us as the shepherd of individual souls. . . . Whether it be addressed to a local Church, or . . . to a Christian lady, . . . it is for the sake of particular persons about whom he is greatly interested that he sends the letter."

— A. Plummer

I. Unique Place in the Canon

Along with 3 John this short note is all we have of the priceless *personal* correspondence of one of the most beloved early saints, the Apostle John.

Sometimes Christians are concerned about how "open" or "closed" they should be to others, especially to those who profess to be believers. Second and Third John answer this very practical question. Second John shows the importance of keeping our house (or house church) closed to heretics; 3 John encourages an "open door policy" to traveling preachers and missionaries.

II. Authorship[†]

The *external evidence* for 2 John is weaker than for 1 John, no doubt due to its size and private nature. Irenaeus quotes it, but, like several others, thought it was part of 1 John (chapter and verse divisions came centuries later). Origen doubted the Epistle, but Clement and Dionysius, both of Alexandria, quote it as John's. Cyprian specifically quotes verse 10 as by the Apostle John.

The *internal evidence* consists of the fact that the style and vocabulary match that of the Gospel and 1 and 3 John. Even though 2 and 3 John have different beginnings from 1 John, they are so similar that few would deny that they all came from the same hand and apparently from about the same time.

There is no compelling reason to doubt the traditional ascription of 2 John

to the apostle (see Introduction to 1 John for more details).

III. Date

As in the case of 1 John, two general periods are possible. Either an early date (60's) before the destruction of Jerusalem, or a late date (85-90) is indicated. If the former, it would probably be from Jerusalem; if the latter, it would be from Ephesus, where the aged apostle ended his days.

IV. Background and Theme[††]

The background of this Epistle is the widespread ministry of itinerant preachers in the early church, still practiced somewhat in certain circles. These evangelists and ministers of the word would receive hospitality, food, and sometimes money at the Christian homes and congregations they visited. Unfortunately, false teachers and religious charlatans were quick to step in and use this custom as a means for easy gain and to spread their heresies, such as Gnosticism (see Introduction to 1 John).

If it was important in the first century to warn of heretics and "religious profiteers," what would the Apostle John say if he could see today's patchwork quilt of sects, cults, and false religions?

The central theme of 2 John is that we should give no cooperation whatever to a person who is spreading error regarding the Person of our Lord (vv. 10, 11).

[†]*See p. i.*
[††]*See p. ii.*

2329

OUTLINE

I.   THE APOSTLE'S SALUTATION: GRACE, MERCY, AND PEACE (Vv. 1–3)

II. THE APOSTLE'S JOY: OBEDIENT CHILDREN (V. 4)

III. THE APOSTLE'S CHARGE: TO WALK IN LOVE (Vv. 5, 6)

IV. THE APOSTLE'S CONCERN: ANTICHRIST DECEIVERS (Vv. 7–11)

V.   THE APOSTLE'S HOPE: A PERSONAL VISIT (Vv. 12, 13)

Commentary

I. THE APOSTLE'S SALUTATION: GRACE, MERCY, AND PEACE (Vv. 1–3)

V. 1 In 2 John, the apostle introduces himself as **the elder**. This may refer to age or official position in the church. As to age, John was the last of the apostles who had companied with the Lord Jesus. As to official position, he surely was a bishop or overseer. Thus, we need not choose our explanation; both are correct.

The expression **"To the elect lady"** is not so easy to explain. Three views are commonly held. (1) Some believe that **the elect lady** is the church, elsewhere referred to as the Bride of Christ, or a particular local church. (2) Others think that the Letter was addressed to "the elect Kyria" — her name being Kyria. This name could be the Greek equivalent to the Aramaic name Martha (both mean "lady").[1] (3) Others feel that John is writing to an unnamed Christian **lady**, who with all other believers is among the **elect** of God — chosen in Christ before the foundation of the world.

We prefer the last view, and feel it is especially significant that this warning against anti-christian teachers should be found in a Letter addressed to a woman. Sin first entered the world through Eve's being deceived by Satan. "The woman being deceived, fell into transgression" (1 Tim. 2:14). Paul speaks of false teachers who make a special appeal to women; they get into the house and capture "gullible women loaded down with sins, led away by various lusts," who will listen to anyone and yet are "never able to come to the knowledge of the truth" (2 Tim. 3:6, 7). Even today the false cults visit homes during the daytime, when the man of the house is usually at work. Children need to be warned against false teachers also.

John states that he loves this **elect lady and her children . . . in truth.** Those who are saved find themselves in a wonderful fellowship, loving others whom they never would have loved, were it not for their common love for the truth of God. It is God's truth that binds hearts together — the hearts of **all those who have known the truth.**

V. 2 **Because of the truth** has two possible explanations. It may refer to the motive for loving all the saints, or it may give John's reason for writing this Letter. Both are valid meanings. **The truth which abides in us and will be with us forever.** Here **the truth** may refer to: (1) the Lord Jesus Christ. He said, "I am . . . the truth" (John 14:6); (2) the Holy Spirit. "The Spirit is truth" (1 Jn. 5:6; see John 14:16, 17); or (3) the Bible. "Your word is truth" (John 17:17). Should we not pause to marvel at our being sustained by these Three, and their being with us forever!

V. 3 John's greeting is **"grace, mercy, and peace will be with you."**[2] **Grace** is undeserved favor to those who deserve the opposite. **Mercy** is pity shown to those who are guilty and wretched. **Peace** is the harmonious relationship that *results from* God's **grace** and **mercy**. All three of these blessings are **from God the Father and from the Lord Jesus Christ**. The **Father** is the Source and the **Son** is the Channel. In addition, they are **in truth and love**, and never at the expense of either of these virtues.

II. THE APOSTLE'S JOY: OBEDI-ENT CHILDREN (V. 4)

Now John expresses his joy at hearing that some of the **children** of the elect lady were **walking in truth**. The **truth** is not just something to be believed with the mind, but something to be lived out in everyday behavior. Just as the Lord Jesus was the living embodiment of truth, so He expects our lives to be testimonies to the **truth**.

III. THE APOSTLE'S CHARGE: TO WALK IN LOVE (Vv. 5, 6)

V. 5 In verses 5 through 9, the apostle seems to give a short summary of his First Epistle. There he listed the tests of life. Now in these verses, he repeats at least three of them — the test of **love** (v. 5), the test of *obedience* (v. 6), and the test of *doctrine* (vv. 7–9).

V. 6 First, he reminds his readers of the commandment to **love** their fellow believers. **Love** here is essentially the unselfish giving of oneself for the benefit of others. It is not "What can I get out of that person?" but "What can I do for that person?" Then, **love** is shown to be a walking **according to His commandments**. We cannot truly love, in the divine sense, unless we are walking in obedience to the Lord and to the truth of God.

IV. THE APOSTLE'S CONCERN: ANTICHRIST DECEIVERS (Vv. 7–11)

V. 7 This brings us to the test of doctrine. The great question is: "Did God really become Man in the Person of Jesus Christ?" The answer is a resounding "Yes!" The Gnostics[3] believed that the divine Christ came upon Jesus of Nazareth for a period of time. But John insists that **Jesus Christ** was, is, and always will be God.

V. 8 Therefore, he warns his readers, **"Look to yourselves, that we do not lose those things we worked for, but that we may receive a full reward."** *In other words*, stand firm in the truth concerning the Lord Jesus Christ so that our labor

among you will not have been in vain, and so that **we** (the apostles and their followers) **will receive a full reward.**

V. 9 When John says, **"Whoever transgresses[4] and does not abide in the doctrine of Christ,"** he is speaking of false teachers. To transgress is to go beyond the allowed bounds. That is what the cults do; they claim to have new light and teach doctrines that God has not revealed in His word. They do not stay within the bounds of the Christian revelation, or abide **in the doctrine of Christ**, probably meaning the teachings which **Christ** Himself brought. It could also mean all that the Bible teaches *about* **Christ**. The apostle emphasizes in verse 9 that a cultist may claim to know God, but if he does not believe in the absolute deity and humanity of the Lord Jesus, he **does not have God** at all. God can only be known through His Son. "No one comes to the Father except through Me" (John 14:6).

Vv. 10, 11 This is the heart of the Epistle. It gives us valued advice on how to deal with false teachers who come to our doors. John does not refer to casual visitors but to anti-Christian propagandists. Should we invite them in? Give them a cup of coffee? Help them financially? Buy their literature? The answer is that we should **not receive** them or **greet** them. These people are enemies of Christ. To show them hospitality is to take sides with those who are against our Savior. It is possible that sometime we might let such a person into our house without knowing that he denies the Lord. These verses would not apply in such a case. But when we do know a man to be a false teacher, it would be disloyal to Christ to befriend him. These verses do not apply to visitors generally. We often have unbelievers as guests in an effort to win them to Christ. But here it is a question of religious teachers who deny the deity and humanity of Jesus Christ. C. F. Hogg explains:

Nothing should be done to give the impression that the offense against Christ is a matter of no great moment, or to put the delinquent in the way of influencing others.[5]

V. THE APOSTLE'S HOPE: A PERSONAL VISIT (Vv. 12, 13)

V. 12 John would have liked to say more to the elect lady. But he stops writing at this point in the hope of an early personal visit when he can speak **face to face**. How much more satisfactory it is to talk in personal encounter than to write **with paper and ink**! And how much more wonderful it will be to see the Savior face to face than to see Him by the eyes of faith, as at present! Truly then **our joy** will **be full**!

V. 13 So John closes: **"The children of your elect sister greet you."** We do not know who they were, but we shall meet them some day and enjoy fellowship with them and with the beloved Apostle John who penned this Letter, and best of all with the Savior Himself. **Amen.**

ENDNOTES

[1](V. 1) Less likely, the Greek word for elect (Eklektē, "Electa") could be taken as a proper name and the word "lady" as a title: "Lady Electa."

[2](V. 3) The critical (NU) and majority (M) texts read "us." The Greek words for *you/we*, for *you/us*, and *your/our* are only one letter different from each other, hence the copying problems in the mss. (See, e.g., V. 8, where the NU text reads *you*, not *we*.)

[3](V. 7) See Introduction to Colossians for a discussion of Gnosticism.

[4](V. 9) The NU text reads "goes ahead" or "*progresses*" (*proagōn*) instead of the "*transgresses*" (*parabainōn*) of the TR and majority text.

[5](Vv. 10, 11) C. F. Hogg, *What Saith the Scripture?*, p. 143.

BIBLIOGRAPHY

See Bibliography at the end of 1 John.

THE THIRD EPISTLE OF JOHN

Introduction

"Altogether this last glimpse of Christian life in the apostolic age is one on which the student may well linger. The state of things which is disclosed does not come near an ideal, but it witnesses to the freedom and vigour of a growing faith."

— B. F. Westcott

I. Unique Place in the Canon

Even 3 John, the shortest book in the NT (just one line shorter than 2 John in the original), illustrates the divine truth that "all Scripture . . . is profitable." Like 2 John, its key words are *love* and *truth*. But unlike 2 John, which shows the *firmness* of love in refusing to entertain those who do not teach the truth, 3 John shows the *tenderness* of love in helping those who have gone forward with the truth.

II. Authorship†

The *external evidence* for 3 John is similar to that of 2 John. These Letters are so short and so personal it is easy to see why they lack the greater spread of evidence that 1 John has.

Origen and Eusebius classed 3 John among the *antilegomena*, or disputed books. Clement and Dionysius, both of Alexandria, accepted 3 John, as did Cyril of Jerusalem. The evidence of the Muratorian Canon is unclear in this area.

The *internal evidence* couples this Letter very closely with 2 John, and also clearly with 1 John. Together the three support one another's authenticity.

There is no compelling reason to doubt the traditional view that John the Apostle wrote 3 John along with the other two Letters ascribed to him.

†*See p. i.*
††*See p. ii.*

III. Date

As in the case of 1 and 2 John, two general dates have been proposed. If John was writing from Jerusalem before the destruction of that city, a date in the 60's is likely. More commonly, scholars see the Letter as from a later period when John lived and served in Ephesus. Thus a date of 85-90 has been widely accepted.

IV. Background and Theme††

The historical backdrop of this little Letter gives us a vivid glimpse into church life in the latter half of the first century. With just a few concise strokes of the pen the apostle sketches in three characters: Gaius the hospitable and spiritual, Demetrius the commendable, and Diotrephes the self-seeking and unloving. Diotrephes may illustrate the strong self-willed personality that can show up in *any* church structure. On the other hand, he may show the trend toward one elder gaining precedence and rule over a formerly equal eldership. This latter trend evolved into the "monarchical episcopate" (rule of one dominant overseer, or bishop) of the second century and following.

OUTLINE

Commentary

I. SALUTATION (Vv. 1–4)

V. 1 As in his Second Epistle, John speaks of himself as **the elder**. He addresses the Letter to the **beloved Gaius, whom** he loves **in truth**. Although we do not know if this is the Gaius mentioned in Romans 16:23 or the one in Acts 20:4, it is surprising how much we do learn about him in these few verses. First of all, we gather that he was a much **beloved** believer, a man whose whole life commended him to his fellow Christians.

V. 2 But apparently he was not too well in body, since John wishes that his physical **health** might correspond to his spiritual vigor. When John says **I pray that you may prosper in all things** it is doubtful that he is thinking of wealth or material prosperity. Rather he is speaking of physical well-being, as suggested by the next phrase — **and be in health**.

Would we want *our* physical condition to correspond to our spiritual? Is it not sadly true that we take better care of our bodies than of our souls? That is why F. B. Meyer wryly remarked:

> It would not be desirable to express the wish of verse 2 to all our friends, because if their bodies were to correspond to the condition of their souls, they would suddenly fall into ill-health.[1]

Verse 2 flatly contradicts what is taught by many so-called "faith-healers." They contend that all sickness is a result of sin in the life, and that if a person isn't healed, it's because of a lack of faith. This certainly wasn't true in Gaius' case. His spiritual condition was good, but his physical condition was not so

good. This shows that one's spiritual state cannot be argued from the bodily one.

V. 3 The apostle **rejoiced greatly when** certain **brethren came and testified of the truth that** was in Gaius, and how he walked **in the truth**. It is good to have the truth in us but it is better to manifest the **truth** in our lives. We should not only hold the truth, but allow the truth to hold us. Men would rather see a sermon than hear one. Nothing counts more for God in an age of fact than a holy life.

V. 4 So important was this to John that he could say, **"I have no greater joy than to hear that my children walk in truth."** Perhaps most of us think of soul-winning as the greatest joy of the Christian life, and it is wonderful indeed to see men and women translated from the kingdom of darkness into the kingdom of the Son of His love. But who can measure the heartache to see those who professed to be saved, returning to their former life; like a sow returning to her wallowing in the mire and a dog to its vomit. On the other hand, what a thrill it is to see one's spiritual children going on for the Lord, from grace to grace. Again this emphasizes the importance of follow-up work in all our evangelistic endeavors.

II. THE GODLY GAIUS (Vv. 5–8)

V. 5 Gaius took a special delight in throwing open his home to those who had gone out preaching the gospel. He extended his gracious hospitality not only to those whom he knew, but to strangers as well.[2] John says that he was faithful in this ministry. It appears from the NT that hospitality is very important in God's sight. If we entertain the Lord's people, it is the same as if we entertain the Lord Himself (Matt. 25:40). On the other hand, failure to entertain His servants is looked upon as failure to entertain Him (Matt. 25:45). Through entertaining strangers, "some have unwittingly entertained angels" (Heb. 13:2). Many can testify that through the practice of hospitality, meals have been turned into sacraments (Luke 24:29–35), children have been converted, and families have been drawn closer to the Lord.

V. 6 Rewards are involved. Gaius' kindness was known to all **the church**. But more than that, his name is forever enshrined in God's Holy Word as one who had an open home and an open heart. And even more, Gaius will yet be rewarded at the Judgment Seat of Christ, for "he who receives a prophet in the name of a prophet shall receive a prophet's reward" (Matt. 10:41). He will share in the reward of all those preachers he entertained. This is a good point to remember for those who cannot preach: You can receive a preacher's reward by showing hospitality to preachers in the name of the Lord. God will pay back all good deeds! His kindness will crown the kindness of men.

Now John reminds Gaius that he **will do well** to **send them forward on their journey in a manner worthy of God**. To **send them forward on their journey** means not just a friendly farewell, but adequate supplies. This surely sets a high standard for us as we share our material things with those who preach and teach.

V. 7 A special reason is given why Gaius should be helpful to these itinerant evangelists: **Because they went forth for His name's sake taking nothing from the Gentiles.** These men looked to the Lord alone for the supply of their needs. They would not accept support from the unconverted. To do so would imply that their Master was too poor to provide for them. It might also give the unsaved a false ground of self-righteousness on which to rest. What a rebuke this is to the money-raising methods of Christendom today! And how it should remind us of the special obligation we have toward those servants of the Lord who go out in faith in the living God and who make their needs known to no one but the Lord.

V. 8 **We therefore ought to receive such, that we may become fellow workers for the truth**. To **receive**[3] them means to do everything possible to help them, for when we do, we help **the truth** in its onward march.

III. THE DICTATORIAL DIOTREPHES (Vv. 9–11)

V. 9 Apparently John had written along this line **to the church**, but his Letter was intercepted by a man named **Diotrephes**, who had an exaggerated view of his own importance. He was a virtual dictator in the assembly. His sin was pride of place, an inflated ego, and a violent jealousy for what he regarded as his own rights — which he doubtless defended as the autonomy of the local church. Diotrephes had forgotten that Christ is the Head of the church — if he ever knew it! He had forgotten that the Holy Spirit is the Vicar or Representative of Christ in the church. No mere man has the right to take charge, to make decisions, to receive, or to refuse. Such conduct is popery, and God hates it. Doubtless Diotrephes excused his behavior on the ground that he was contending for the truth. But that was, of course, a lie! He was doing untold harm to the truth by refusing the apostle on the pretext of being faithful to God. And not only John, but other brethren as well.

V. 10 Not only did he refuse these true believers, but he excommunicated those who *did* receive them. He was a power-mad creature, **prating against** God's true servants **with malicious words**. John will remember him on his next visit to that assembly! Such self-styled popes cannot stand being openly denounced from the word of God. Their continuance in power depends upon secret meetings and upon a reign of fear and intimidation.

V. 11 Gaius is exhorted to turn away from such **evil** behavior and to follow **what is good**. Good works are an evidence of relationship with **God**. That being so, the apostle seems to cast grave doubts on the spiritual state of Diotrephes.

IV. DEVOUT DEMETRIUS (V. 12)

Perhaps **Demetrius** was the bearer of this Letter. At any rate, he had **a good testimony from all, and from the truth itself**. F. B. Hole says:

> Note, it is not that he bore witness to the truth, but that the truth bore witness to him. Demetrius was not the standard by which truth was tested. The truth was the standard by which he was tested; and having been so tested, he stood approved.[4]

V. THE APOSTLE'S PLAN AND BENEDICTION (Vv. 13, 14)

John closes in much the same way as he closed his Second Epistle — delaying discussion until **face to face** reunion. We are indebted to him for these Letters, giving us an insight into life in the early days of Christianity, and setting forth timeless instruction for the people of God. Soon we shall speak face to face in heaven, and then we shall understand more fully the occasional obscurities of divine revelation.

ENDNOTES

[1](V. 2) F. B. Meyer, *Through the Bible Day by Day*, VII:164, 165.

[2](V. 5) The critical (NU) text reads *"especially* (Gk. *touto*, lit. "this") strangers."

[3](V. 8) The NU text reads "support" (*hupolambanein*) rather than the "receive" (*apolambanein*) of the TR and majority text.

[4](V. 12) F. B. Hole, further documentation unavailable.

BIBLIOGRAPHY

See Bibliography at the end of 1 John.

THE EPISTLE OF JUDE

Introduction

"An Epistle of few lines but full of the mighty words of heavenly grace."
— Origen

I. Unique Place in the Canon

Just as Luke begins Christian history with the Acts of the Apostles, Jude is chosen to write the next to the last book of the NT, which has been appropriately called "the Acts of the Apostates." Jude would have preferred to write about the common Christian Faith shared with his readers, but false teachings were becoming so prevalent that he was constrained to pen a plea to "contend earnestly for the faith which was once for all delivered to the saints."

Jude does not mince words! He pulls out all the stops, as it were, to unmask these notorious heretics, drawing illustrations from nature, the OT, and Jewish tradition (Enoch) to stir up the faithful.

In spite of its harsh language, the Epistle is a masterpiece of construction, studded with triads (e.g., the three evils in v. 11). The descriptions of the apostates are vivid and unforgettable.

The church is forever in debt to Jude for the beautiful benediction with which he ends his Letter. His Epistle may be short, but it is greatly needed in these days of ever-increasing apostasy.

II. Authorship[†]

External Evidence

In spite of its shortness, its use of non-canonical materials, and the fact that it is not by an apostle (v. 17), Jude is better attested as to *external evidence* than is 2 Peter.

Hermas, Polycarp, and probably Athenagoras use material borrowed from this Epistle. Tertullian specifically refers

to Jude's use of Enoch. Eusebius puts Jude among the disputed books (*antilegomena*). The Muratorian Canon lists Jude as genuine.

Internal Evidence

Jude (same name as Judas and Judah, Hebrew *Yehudah*) was a very popular Jewish name. Of the seven Judes or Judases in the NT, three have been suggested as the "Jude, . . . brother of James" who wrote this Epistle:

1. The Apostle Judas (not Iscariot, who had committed suicide). Since verse 17 apparently differentiates the writer from the apostles, and since it would strengthen his position if he could claim apostleship, he is an unlikely candidate.

2. Judas, a leader sent to Antioch with Paul, Barnabas, and Silas (Acts 15:22). This is a possibility, but no evidence links this man with the Letter.

3. Judas (Jude), a younger half-brother of our Lord and a brother of James (see Introduction to James). He is the strongest candidate, sharing with the Lord Jesus and with James in his use of nature illustrations and a trenchant, colorful style. We accept this view.

Like his brother James, Jude was too modest to exploit his natural relationship to the Savior. After all, it is spiritual relationship to the Lord Jesus that counts. Did Christ not say, "Whoever does the will of My Father in heaven is My brother and sister and mother" (Matt. 12:50)? On another occasion He taught that it was more blessed to hear the word of God and do it than to be a close blood-relative of His (Luke

†See p. i.

11:27, 28). Like James, Jude took the place of "a bondservant." Since both brothers disbelieved in their divine Half-brother until after the resurrection, this was a suitable spirit to show. Jude was married and took his wife around on his itinerant preaching tours (1 Cor. 9:5). Jude's grandsons were brought before Emperor Domitian in the 90's on the charge of being Christians. Seeing their hands hardened from years of farming, the emperor released them as harmless Jews.

III. Date

Whether Peter used Jude, or Jude adapted 2 Peter (or both used a common source) is debated. The similarities between the two are too great to be coincidental. Since Peter writes in his Second Epistle (2:1 and 3:3) that there *"will* be" false teachers and scoffers, and Jude says such men *"have* crept in" (v. 4), it is probable that Jude is the later writer. A date between 67 and 80 is likely. Since Jude makes no mention of the destruction of Jerusalem (A.D. 70), this could suggest it was yet to happen, making a date of 67–70 likely. It could also mean that it had happened some time ago (if Jude was written in A.D. 80, or even 85 — assuming Jude lived that long). Another possibility is that the event was still too traumatic for a sensitive Hebrew Christian to use as an illustration.

IV. Background and Theme[†]

Jude is concerned with apostasy. Even in his day, the church was already being infiltrated by religious Quislings, men who posed as servants of God but who were actually enemies of the cross of Christ. Jude's purpose is to expose these traitors and to describe their ultimate doom.

An apostate is a person who professes to be a true believer but who, as a matter of fact, has never been regenerated. He may be baptized and participate fully in the privileges of a local Christian fellowship. But after a while, he willfully abandons the Christian faith and maliciously renounces the Savior. He denies the deity of Christ, His re-

demptive work at Calvary, His bodily resurrection, or other fundamental doctrines.

It is not at all a question of backsliding; the apostate was never converted at all. He has no qualms about his deliberate spurning of God's only way of salvation. He is hardened in his unbelief and stubbornly opposed to the Christ of God.

Apostasy is not simply a question of *denying* the Savior. Peter did that. Peter was a true believer who buckled under the pressures of a crisis. But he really loved the Lord and demonstrated the reality of his faith by his subsequent repentance and restoration.

Judas Iscariot was an apostate. He professed to be a disciple; he traveled with the Lord Jesus for about three years. He even served as treasurer of the team, but finally he revealed his true self by betraying the Lord for thirty pieces of silver.

Apostasy is a sin leading to death, one that lies beyond the responsibility of believers' prayers (1 Jn. 5:16b). It is impossible to renew an apostate to repentance, since he crucifies to himself the Son of God, and puts Him to open shame (Heb. 6:6). For those who thus sin willfully after receiving the knowledge of the truth, "there no longer remains a sacrifice for sins, but a certain fearful expectation of judgment, and fiery indignation which will devour the adversaries" (Heb. 10:26, 27).

The seeds of apostasy were already sown in the early church. Paul warned the Ephesian elders that after his departure savage wolves would come in, not sparing the flock, and that from among themselves, men would rise up, speaking perverse things, to draw away disciples after themselves (Acts 20:29, 30). In his First Epistle, John spoke of those antichrists who had been in the Christian fellowship but who manifested their unreality by leaving it, that is, by abandoning their faith (1 Jn. 2:18, 19).

In 2 Thessalonians 2:2–4 we learn that there will be a great apostasy prior to the Day of the Lord. As we understand it, the order will be this:

First, the Lord will come into the air to take the church to the Father's house (John 14:1–3; 1 Thess. 4:13–18).

Then there will be a wholesale defection of those nominal Christians who are left behind.

Then the man of sin will make his public début on the world stage.

Then the Day of the Lord will begin — the seven-year Tribulation Period.

The man of sin will be the archapostate — not only opposing Christ but demanding that he himself be worshiped as God.

Peter gives a detailed portrait of the apostate false teachers who will arise in the last days (2 Pet. 2). In some respects his description closely parallels that which is given by Jude. The resemblance may be seen by comparing the following:

Jude	2 Peter
V. 4	2:1–3
V. 7	2:6
V. 8	2:10
V. 9	2:11
V. 10	2:12
V. 16	2:18

But actually the *differences* between the two passages are more significant than the *similarities*. Jude makes no mention of Noah, the flood, or Lot. Peter omits any mention of the Israelites who were saved out of Egypt, of Michael, Cain, Korah, or of Enoch's prophecy. He does not give as much information about the angels that sinned as Jude does. He speaks of the false teachers as denying the Master who bought them, whereas Jude elaborates by saying that they "turn the grace of our God into lewdness and deny the only Lord God and our Lord Jesus Christ" (Jude 4).

So instead of thinking of the two chapters as carbon copies, we should realize that the Holy Spirit has selected materials to suit His purpose in each case, and that the two chapters do not overlap as much as they might seem at first. Those who have studied the four Gospels and have compared Ephesians and Colossians realize that the Spirit of God never needlessly repeats Himself. There are spiritual meanings behind the similarities and differences, if only we have eyes to see them.

OUTLINE

    I. SALUTATION (Vv. 1, 2)

    II. THE APOSTATES UNMASKED (Vv. 3–16)

    III. THE BELIEVER'S ROLE IN THE MIDST OF APOSTASY (Vv. 17–23)

    IV. THE BEAUTIFUL BENEDICTION (Vv. 24, 25)

Commentary

I. SALUTATION (Vv. 1, 2)

V. 1 God used a righteous **Jude** to unmask the apostates, of whom another Jude, Judas Iscariot, was a prime example. All that we know *for certain* about the good **Jude** is that he was **a bondservant of Jesus Christ, and brother of James**.

In addressing the Letter, Jude gives three designations that are true of all believers. They **are called, sanctified[1] by God the Father, and preserved in Jesus Christ**. God has **called** these out of the world by the gospel to belong to Himself. They are set apart **by God** to be God's special and pure people. And they are marvelously **preserved** from danger, damage, defilement, and damnation until at last they are ushered in to see the King in His beauty.

V. 2 Jude wishes for his readers **mercy, peace, and love**. The greeting is peculiarly suited to those who were facing the onslaught of those whose aim was to subvert the faith. **Mercy** means God's compassionate comfort and care for His beleaguered saints in times of conflict and stress. **Peace** is the serenity and confidence that come from reliance on God's word and from looking above circumstances to the One who overrules all circumstances for the accomplishment of His own purposes. **Love** is the undeserved embrace of God for His dear people — a super-affection that should then be shared with others.

He wishes that these three blessings **be multiplied**. Not measured out by mere addition, but by multiplication!

II. THE APOSTATES UN-MASKED (Vv. 3–16)

V. 3 Jude had originally intended **to write** about the glorious **salvation** that is the **common** possession of all believers. But God's Spirit so influenced this yielded scribe that he sensed a change of direction. A simple doctrinal essay would no longer do; it must be a fervent appeal that would strengthen the readers. They must be stirred up **to contend earnestly for the faith**. Attacks were being made on the sacred deposit of Christian truth, and efforts were already launched to whittle away the great fundamental doctrines. God's people must stand uncompromisingly for the inspiration, inerrancy, authority, and sufficiency of God's Holy Word.

Yet in contending for the faith, the believer must speak and act as a Christian. As Paul wrote: "A servant of the Lord must not quarrel but be gentle to all, able to teach, patient" (2 Tim. 2:24). He must **contend** without being contentious, and testify without ruining his testimony.

What we **contend earnestly for** is **the faith which was once for all delivered to the saints**. Notice that! Not "once upon a time" but **once for all**. The body of doctrine is complete. The canon is finished. Nothing more can be added. "If it's new it's not true, and if it's true it's not new." When some teacher claims to have a revelation which is above and beyond what is found in the Bible, we reject it out of hand. The faith has been delivered and we neither need nor heed anything else. This is our answer to the leaders of false cults with their books that claim equal authority with the Scriptures.

V. 4 The nature of the threat is unveiled in verse 4. The Christian fellowship was being invaded by subversive elements. **Certain men** had wormed **in unnoticed**. It was an underground movement of stealth and deceit.

These fifth-columnists **long ago were marked out for this condemnation**. This seems to say that God selected these particular individuals to be doomed. But that is not the meaning. The Bible never teaches that some are chosen to be damned. When men are saved, it is through the sovereign grace of God. But when they are finally lost, it is because of their own sin and disobedience.

This expression teaches that the **condemnation** of apostates has been determined long beforehand. If men choose to fall away from the Christian Faith, then their **condemnation** is the same as that of the unbelieving Israelites in the wilderness, the rebel angels, and the Sodomites. They are not foreordained to fall away, but once they do apostatize by their own choice, they face the punishment predetermined for all apostates.

Two prominent features of these **ungodly** persons are their depraved conduct and their corrupt doctrine. In their behavior, they **turn the grace of God into lewdness**. They twist Christian liberty into license, and pervert freedom to serve into freedom to sin. In their doctrine, they **deny the only Lord**[2] **God and our Lord Jesus Christ**. They **deny** His absolute right to rule, His deity, His vicarious death, His resurrection — in fact, they **deny** every essential doctrine of His Person and work. While professing an expansive liberality in the spiritual realm, they are dogmatically and viciously opposed to the gospel, to the value of the precious blood of Christ, and to His being the only way of salvation.

Who are these men? They are supposed ministers of the gospel. They hold positions of leadership in Christendom. Some are bishops or church council members or seminary professors. But they all have this in common — they are against the Christ of the Bible and have invented for themselves a liberal[3] or Neo-Orthodox[4] "Christ", stripped of glory, majesty, dominion, and authority.

V. 5 There is no question about God's attitude toward these apostates. He has revealed it in the OT on more than one occasion. Jude now wants to **remind** his readers of three such example — the unbelieving Israelites, the angels that sinned, and the people of Sodom and Gomorrah.

The first example is Israel in the wilderness: **The Lord, having saved the people out of the land of Egypt, afterward destroyed those who did not believe** (see Num. 13, 14; 1 Cor. 10:5–10). God had promised the land of Canaan to the people. In that promise was all the enablement they needed. But they accepted the evil report of the spies at Kadesh and rebelled against the Lord. As a result, all those men who were twenty or over when they left Egypt perished in the wilderness, with the exception of Caleb and Joshua (see Heb. 3:16–19).

V. 6 The second example of rebellion and apostasy is **the angels** who sinned. All we know about them for certain is that they **did not keep** the **domain** that was assigned to them, they abandoned **their own abode**, and they are now restrained **in everlasting chains under darkness for** their final **judgment**.

It seems from Scripture that there have been at least two apostasies of angels. One was when Lucifer fell and presumably involved a host of other angelic beings in his rebellion. These fallen angels are not bound at the present time. The devil and his demons are actively promoting war against the Lord and His people.

The other apostasy of angels is the one referred to by Jude and also by Peter (2 Pet. 2:4). There is considerable difference of opinion among Bible students as to what event is referred to here. What we suggest is a personal viewpoint, not a dogmatic assertion of fact.

We believe that Jude is referring to what is recorded in Genesis 6:1–7. The sons of God left their proper estate as angelic beings, came down to the earth in human form, and married the daughters of men. This marital union was contrary to God's order and an abomination to Him. There may be a suggestion in verse 4 that these unnatural marriages produced offspring of tremendous strength and wickedness. Whether or not this is true, it is clear that God was exceedingly displeased with the wickedness of man at this time and determined to destroy the earth with a flood.

There are three objections to this

view: (1) The passage in Genesis does not mention angels, but only "sons of God." (2) Angels are sexless. (3) Angels do not marry.

It is true that angels are not specifically mentioned but it is also true that the term "sons of God" does refer to angels in Semitic languages (see Job 1:6; 2:1).

There is no Bible statement that angels are sexless. Angels sometimes appeared on earth in human form, having human parts and appetites (Gen. 18:2, 22; compare 19:1, 3–5).

The Bible does not say that angels do not marry but only that *in heaven* they neither marry nor give in marriage (Matt. 22:30).

Whatever historical incident may lie behind verse 6, the important point is that these angels abandoned the sphere which God had marked out for them and are now **in . . . chains** and in **darkness** until the time when they will receive their final sentence to perdition.

V. 7 The third OT apostasy which Jude mentions is that of **Sodom and Gomorrah and the cities around them** (Gen. 18:16–19:29). The introductory word **as** shows that the sin of the Sodomites had features in common with that of the angels. It was gross immorality that was utterly against nature and abhorrent to God.

The specific sin of perversion is discussed by Paul in Romans: "Their women exchanged the natural use for what is against nature. Likewise also the men, leaving the natural use of the woman, burned in their lust for one another, men with men committing what is shameful, and receiving in themselves the penalty of their error which was due" (Rom. 1:26b, 27). The men of Sodom, Gomorrah, Admah, and Zeboiim were greatly addicted to homosexuality. The sin is described here as **having . . . gone after strange flesh**, meaning that it is completely contrary to the natural order which God has ordained.

Is it mere coincidence that many modern day apostates are in the vanguard of those who publicly defend homosexuality and campaign for it to be legalized as long as it is done between consenting adults?

To all such libertines the cities of

Sodom and Gomorrah are exhibited **as an example** in **suffering the** punishment **of eternal fire**. That last expression **eternal fire** cannot mean that the fire which destroyed the wicked cities is eternal, but rather that in the thoroughness and vastness of its consuming power, it pictures the eternal punishment which will fall on all rebels.

V. 8 Jude reverts to the subject of present-day apostates, and launches into a description of their sins, their indictment, their counterparts in nature, their doom, and their ungodly words and deeds (vv. 8–16).

First of all is the matter of their sins. By dreaming **they defile the flesh**. Their thought life is polluted. Living in a world of filthy fantasies, they eventually find fulfillment of their dreams in sexual immorality, just like the men of Sodom.

They **reject authority**. They are rebels against God and against governmental institutions. Depend on them to be proponents of lawlessness and anarchy. Their names are on the membership rolls of organizations that are dedicated to the overthrow of government.

They **speak evil of** angelic **dignitaries**. It means nothing to them that "there is no authority except from God, and the authorities that exist are appointed by God" (Rom. 13:1b). They scorn the divine command, "You shall not . . . curse a ruler of your people" (Ex. 22:28). They speak contemptuously and spitefully against authority, whether it be divine, angelic, or human.

V. 9 In this respect they take liberties which even **Michael the archangel** would reject. When Michael disputed **with the devil about the body of Moses**, he did **not** dare rail **against him but** simply **said, "The Lord rebuke you!"** Here Jude shares with us an incident which is found nowhere else in the Bible. The question naturally arises, "Where did he get this information?"

Some say that the information was passed down by tradition. This may or may not be so.

The most satisfying explanation is that the information was supernaturally revealed to Jude by the same Holy Spirit who moved him to write the Epistle.

We have no definite knowledge why the dispute arose between Michael and Satan **about the body of Moses**. We do know that Moses was buried by God in a valley of Moab. It is not unlikely that Satan wanted to know the spot so that he could have a shrine built there. Then Israel would turn to the idolatrous worship of Moses' bones. As the angelic representative of the people of Israel (Dan. 10:21), Michael would strive to preserve the people from this form of idolatry by keeping the burial site secret.

But the important point is this. Even if **Michael** is an **archangel**, the one whom God will use to cast Satan down from heaven (Rev. 12:7–9), still he did not presume to speak reproachfully to the one who rules in the realm of demons. He left all such rebuking to God.

V. 10 Headstrong and brazen, the apostates **speak** disrespectfully in areas of which they are ignorant. They do not realize that in any ordered society, there must be authority and there must be subjection to that authority. And so they surge forward and swagger around in arrogant rebellion.

The area in which they are most knowledgeable is that of natural instincts, the gratification of sensual appetites. With the mindlessness of unreasoning animals, they abandon themselves to sexual gratification, and in the process **they corrupt** and destroy **themselves**.

V. 11 A stinging indictment is pronounced upon them. **Woe to them!** Because of their stubborn and unrepentant heart, they store up wrath for themselves in the Day of wrath and revelation of the righteous judgment of God (Rom. 2:5).

Their career is described as a plummeting fall of ever increasing velocity. First **they have gone in the way of Cain**. They have **run greedily in the error of Balaam**. Finally they **perished in the rebellion of Korah**. Error and apostasy are never static. They lead people pell-mell to the precipice, then over it to destruction.

The way of Cain is basically the rejection of salvation through the blood of a sacrificial victim (Gen. 4). It is the attempt to appease God by human efforts. C. H. Mackintosh says, "God's remedy to *cleanse* is rejected, and man's effort to *improve* is put in its place. This is 'the way of Cain.' " But, of course, reliance on human effort leads to a hatred of grace and to the objects of grace. And that hatred eventually leads to persecution and even murder (1 Jn. 3:15).

The error of Balaam is the desire to become personally wealthy by making a business out of the service of God. Balaam professed to be a prophet of God, but he was covetous, and willing to prostitute his prophetic gift for money (Num. 22–24). Five times Balak paid him to curse Israel, and he was more than willing to do it, but he was forcibly restrained by God. Many of the things that he said were true and beautiful, but for all that, he was a hireling prophet. He couldn't curse the men of Israel, but he eventually succeeded in luring them into sin with the daughters of Moab (Num. 25:1–5).

Like Balaam, the false teachers of today are suave and convincing. They can speak out of both corners of their mouths at once. They suppress the truth in order to increase their income. The principal point is that they are greedy, seeking to make the house of God a house of merchandise.

Christendom today is leavened by the sin of simony. If the profit motive could somehow be removed, much of what passes as Christian work would come to a screeching halt. C. A. Coates warns:

> Man is so base that he makes gain for himself out of God's things. The ultimate point of man's baseness is that he will make gain out of God's things for himself. The Lord has a definite judgment on it all. We can see how Christendom is full of it, and we have to watch it in ourselves lest that element come in.[5]

The third reason for the **woe** pronounced by Jude is that these false teachers have **perished in the rebellion of Korah**. Along with Dathan and Abiram, Korah rebelled against the leadership of Moses and Aaron and desired to intrude into the priestly office (Num. 16). In this they were actually spurning the Lord. For their insubordination, they were swallowed alive in a great earthquake. God thus showed His extreme displeasure at **rebellion** against those whom He has set up as His representatives.

V. 12 Next Jude chooses five similes from the world of nature to picture the character and destiny of the apostates. Moffatt says that "sky, land and sea are ransacked for illustrations of the character of these men."

They **are spots in** the **love feasts**[6] which were held by the early Christians in connection with the Lord's Supper. They fear neither God nor man, and care for themselves rather than for the flock. They lure others to besmirch the faith.

They are clouds without water, appearing to hold promise of refreshment to the parched countryside, but then **carried along** (NKJV margin)[7] **by the winds**, and leaving disappointment and disillusionment.

They are **late autumn trees**, stripped of leaves and **fruit. Twice dead** may be an intensive form meaning thoroughly dead — or it may mean dead in the root as well as the branches. Also they are **pulled up by the roots**, as if torn out of the ground by a strong wind and leaving no stump as a possible future source of life and growth.

V. 13 They are **raging waves of the sea**, ungovernable, boisterous, and furious. For all their noise and motion, there is nothing to show but the foam of their **shame**. They glory in what they should be ashamed of and leave nothing of substance and value behind.

Finally, they are like **wandering stars, for whom is reserved the blackness of darkness forever. Wandering stars** are celestial bodies that do not move in regular orbit. They are worthless as navigational aids. How appropriate a description of the false teachers! It is impossible to get spiritual direction from these religious meteors, falling stars, and comets who blaze brightly for a moment, then fizzle out into darkness like firework rockets.

V. 14 The doom of the apostates was foretold by **Enoch in the seventh** generation **from Adam**. It is a prophecy that is found only in Jude's Epistle. Some think it is taken from the apocryphal Book of Enoch, but there is no proof that that spurious book existed in the time of Jude. Kelly said:

> It [Enoch] has every mark of having been written subsequent to the destruction of Jerusalem [and therefore after Jude's Epistle was written], by a Jew who still buoyed himself up with the hope that God would stand by the Jews.[8]

While we do not know how Jude learned of this ancient prophecy, a simple and plausible explanation is that the Holy Spirit revealed the words to him just as He guided in all the rest of the Epistle.

The prophecy begins: **"Behold, the Lord comes⁹ with ten thousands of His saints."** The prediction will have a preliminary and partial fulfillment when the Lord Jesus returns to earth after the Tribulation to destroy His foes and to reign as King. It will have its complete and final fulfillment at the end of the Millennium when the wicked dead are judged at the Great White Throne.

V. 15 Christ comes **to execute judgment on all**. The rest of the verse shows that the **all** here means all *the ungodly*. True believers will not be included. Through faith in Christ, they have been granted immunity from judgment, as promised in John 5:24: "Most assuredly, I say to you, he who hears My word and believes in Him who sent Me has everlasting life, and shall not come into judgment, but has passed from death into life." As the Son of Man to whom all judgment has been committed, the Lord Jesus will **convict all who are ungodly among them of all their ungodly deeds which they have committed in an ungodly way, and of all the harsh things which ungodly sinners have spoken against Him.** Four times in this one verse we find the word **ungodly** occurring. The people are **ungodly**, their deeds are **ungodly**, the manner in which they perform these deeds is **ungodly**, and they further manifest their ungodliness by their blasphemies against the Lord. He will convict them of the whole **ungodly** business, not just in the sense of making them feel a deep sense of guilt, but convicting them by pronouncing sentence as a result of their proven guilt.

V. 16 Their ungodly words and deeds are now described in more detail. They are **grumblers**, complaining against the providences of God instead of being thankful for His mercies. The fact that God hates such griping is abundantly proved by His punishment of Israel in the wilderness.

They are always finding fault with the Lord. Why does He permit wars and suffering? Why doesn't He put an end to all the social injustice? If He is all-powerful, why doesn't He do something about the mess the world is in? They also find fault with God's people for being narrow-minded in creed and puritanical in conduct.

They live lustfully, indulging the passions of the flesh and being the loudest in advocating permissiveness in the sexual realm.

Their arrogant speech proves a real attention-getter. By their shocking espousal of political, economic, and social extremism, they make the headlines. And their bold, shameless repudiation of basic Christian doctrines, such as their assertion that God is dead, give them a certain notoriety among liberal theologians.

Finally, they are masters in the art of flattery, thereby gaining a following for themselves and a comfortable income as well.

This portrait is true and accurate. It is confirmed almost every day by the news media of the world.

III. THE BELIEVER'S ROLE IN THE MIDST OF APOSTASY (Vv. 17–23)

V. 17 Jude now turns away from the apostates to the believers' role in the midst of these hireling shepherds. First he reminds them that they have been forewarned as to the oncoming peril. Then he encourages them to maintain themselves in a strong spiritual condition. Finally, he counsels them to use discernment in ministering to those who have been victimized by the apostates.

The **apostles** had predicted the rise of false teachers. This can be seen in the ministry of *Paul* (Acts 20:29, 30; 1 Tim. 4:1–5; 2 Tim. 3:1–9); *Peter* (2 Pet. 2:1–22; 3:1–4); and *John* (1 Jn. 2:18, 19).

Vv. 18, 19 The gist of their message was that **in the last time, mockers** would appear, following **their own ungodly lusts**.

To this testimony Jude now adds the explanation that these scoffers have three prominent characteristics. They are **sensual persons**, which means that they think and act as natural men. They **cause divisions**, drawing disciples after themselves and perhaps dividing people into various classes according to their progress in apostasy. They do not have **the Spirit**. They were never born from above and therefore have a total incapacity to understand the things of God.

V. 20 The believer's resource, of course, is to stay close to the Lord and live in unbroken fellowship with Him. But how is this done? Jude gives four steps.

The *first* is **building yourselves up on your most holy faith**, that is, the *Christian* faith. We build up ourselves on it by studying and obeying the Bible. Constant familiarity with the word guides us positively in the way of righteousness, and warns us against the perils along the way. "Men may decry doctrine," H. Pickering says, "but it is creed that produces character and not character that produces creed."

The *second* step is **praying in the Holy Spirit**. This means to pray as guided by the **Spirit**, in accordance with the will of God as revealed in the Bible or as privately revealed by the **Spirit** in a subjective way to the believer. It is in contrast to prayers which are recited mechanically or spun off without any real spiritual involvement.

V. 21 *Then again* believers are to **keep** themselves **in the love of God**. Here **the love of God** can be compared to the sunshine. The sun is always shining. But when something comes between us and the sun, we are no longer in the sunshine. That's the way it is with **the love of God**. It is always beaming down upon us. But if sin comes between us and the Lord, then we are no longer enjoying His love in practice. We can **keep** ourselves in His **love** first of all by lives of holiness and godliness. And if sin should come between, then we should confess and forsake that sin immediately. The secret is to let nothing come between us and God.

Nothing between my soul and the Savior,
Naught of this world's delusive dream;
Nothing preventing the least of His favor,
Keep the way clear, let nothing between.
— *Charles A. Tindley*

Finally, we should be eagerly **looking for the mercy of our Lord Jesus Christ unto eternal life. The mercy of our Lord** here refers to His imminent return to take His people home to heaven. In days of darkness and apostasy, we are to keep the light of the blessed hope burning in our hearts. It will prove a comforting and purifying hope (1 Thess. 4:18; 1 Jn. 3:3).

V. 22 A certain measure of spiritual discernment is necessary in dealing with victims of apostasy. The Scriptures make a distinction between the way we should handle those who are active propagandists of false cults and those who have been duped by them. In the case of the leaders and propagandists, the policy is given in 2 John 10, 11: "If anyone comes to you and does not bring this doctrine, do not receive him into your house nor greet him; for he who greets him shares in his evil deeds." But in speaking of those who have been deceived by false teachers, Jude counsels making a **distinction**[10] and gives two separate courses of action.

On some we should **have compassion**. That is, we should show a compassionate interest in them and try to guide them out of doubts and disputations into a firm conviction of divine truth.

V. 23 Then there are those who are on the verge of the precipice, ready to fall over into the flames of apostasy. These we are to **save** by strong, resolute warning and instruction, **hating even the garment defiled by the flesh**. In the OT the clothing of a leper was contaminated and had to be burned (Lev. 13:47–52). Today in dealing with people who have fallen into sexual sins, we must remember that material objects, such as clothing, for example, often excite the passions. As we see these things or feel them, there is a mental association with certain sins. So in dealing with people who have become defiled, we must be careful to avoid anything which might prove a temptation in our own lives. An unknown author expressed it like this:

The clothes that belong to a man have about them the association and infection of sin, the contagion of evil. Whatever is associated with a life of sin should be cast off and renounced, if we are to be safe from the infection and contagion of this soul-destroying disease.

J. B. Mayor warns, "While it is the duty of the Christian to pity and pray for the sinner, he must view with loathing all that bears traces of the sin."[11]

IV. THE BEAUTIFUL BENEDICTION (Vv. 24, 25)

V. 24 Jude closes with a beautiful benediction. It is the ascription of praise and worship **to Him who is able**. He is able to save (Heb. 7:25), able to establish (Rom. 16:25), able to aid (Heb. 2:18), able to subdue (Phil. 3:21) — and here He **is able to keep**. He is able to keep us in perfect peace (Isa. 26:3), He is able to keep that which we have committed to Him until that Day (2 Tim. 1:12), He is able to do exceedingly abundantly above all that we ask or think (Eph. 3:20), and **He is able to keep us**[12] **from stumbling**. This latter promise is especially timely for the days of apostasy to which Jude is referring.

But the promise doesn't stop there. He is able to make us stand **faultless in the presence of His glory with exceeding joy**. This is truly stupendous! When we think of what we were — dead through our trespasses and sins; when we think of what we are — poor, weak, failing servants; and then to think that one day we will stand absolutely **faultless** in the Throne Room of the universe, rejoicing **with exceeding joy** — what grace is this!

V. 25 He is not only our Keeper and Perfecter — He is **God our Savior**.[13] It is a marvel that **God** should be so interested in us that He would also become **our Savior**, in the sense that He devised the plan whereby we are saved and He provided His sinless Son as the sacrificial Lamb. **Who alone is wise** — ultimately all wisdom comes from God (cf. Jas. 1:5). Our wisdom is merely derived from the fount of wisdom, the only **wise** God.

If *worship* (Old English "worth-ship") means ascribing to God what He is *worthy of*, it will be **glory, and majesty, dominion, and power. Glory** — the superlative honor He deserves for all He is

and all He has done for us. **Majesty** — the dignity and splendor He deserves as the Supreme Monarch of the universe. **Dominion** — the unchallenged sway which is His by sovereign right. And **power** or authority — the might and prerogative to rule all that His hands have made.

He was worthy of such praise in the past, He is worthy at the present time, and He will be worthy of it throughout eternity. Apostates and false teachers may seek to rob Him of **glory**, detract from His **majesty**, grumble against His **dominion**, and challenge His **power**. But all true believers find their greatest fulfillment in glorifying and enjoying Him **both now and forever**.

Amen.

ENDNOTES

[1](V. 1) Instead of "sanctified" (*hēgiasmenois*) the critical (NU) text reads "beloved" (*ēgapēmenois*). The strong condemnation of immorality in this letter is probably better introduced by its opposite, "sanctified."

[2](V. 4) The word "God" is omitted by the NU text. The two "Lords" are different words in the original. In "Lord Jesus" the usual word *Kurios* is used. In "Lord God" a synonym, *Despotēs*, occurs. (Our derivative "despot" is not a good *translation* due to its bad connotation in *English*.) Both words mean "Lord," "Master," or "Owner."

[3](V. 4) "Liberal" means free, but in religion it refers to those who deny major doctrines of the faith, such as inspiration, the virgin birth, the deity of Christ, and the blood atonement. So-called liberals are often open to any doctrine or religion — as long as it is *not* the orthodox biblical teaching.

[4](V. 4) The Neo- ("New") Orthodox are not really orthodox. They accept some of the teachings of the Bible, but use orthodox terminology to mask unbiblical unbelief. For example, the Bible "becomes" the word of God to the Neo-Orthodox if it "speaks to him." To the orthodox believer, the Bible *is* the word of God.

[5](V. 11) C. A. Coates, *An Outline of Mark's Gospel and other Ministry*, p. 125.

⁶(V. 12) They called the feast an *agapē*, literally "love."

⁷(V. 12) The best reading is "carried away" or "along," as in the oldest (NU) and also the majority of mss. (majority text). The reading of the TR, KJV, and NKJV ("carried about") has weak support.

⁸(V. 14) William Kelly, "Lectures on the Epistle of Jude," *The Serious Christian,* I:123.

⁹(V. 14) "Comes" translates the aorist (*ēlthe*). This may translate a Semitic prophetic perfect, a future event seen as so certain that it is expressed in the past.

¹⁰(V. 22) The textual variants here are further complicated by the fact that the Greek verb *diakrinomai* can mean "doubting" or "making a distinction." See NKJV footnotes on vv. 22, 23.

¹¹(V. 23) J. B. Mayor, *The Epistle of St. Jude and the Second Epistle of St. Peter,* p. 51.

¹²(V. 24) The majority text reads "them" for "you," meaning those sinning in the previous verses that spiritual Christians strive to save.

¹³(V. 25) As a constant reading of the textual notes in the NKJV NT will show, the NU text (largely Alexandrian) is very prone to be shorter ("omit") than the traditional and majority texts. Hence, when it *adds* something it is especially interest-ing. In verse 25, *three* additions are made, so that it reads:

"To the *only* God our Savior,
Through Jesus Christ our Lord,
Be glory and majesty,
Dominion and power,
Before all time," etc.

It *does* omit the word "wise," however. Perhaps Jude's perennially popular benediction was recited in this longer form in the Egyptian churches.

BIBLIOGRAPHY

Bigg, Charles. *The Epistles of St. Peter and St. Jude.* Edinburgh: T. & T. Clark Ltd., 1901.

Coder, S. Maxwell. *Jude: The Acts of the Apostates.* Chicago: Moody Press, 1958.

Green, Michael. *The Second Epistle General of Peter and the General Epistle of Jude.* Grand Rapids: Wm. B. Eerdmans Publishing Company, 1968.

Ironside, H. A. *Epistles of John and Jude.* New York: Loizeaux Bros., Inc., 1931.

Kelly, William. "Lectures on the Epistle of Jude," *The Serious Christian.* Vol. I. Charlotte, N.C.: Books for Christians, 1970.

Mayor, J. B. *The Epistle of St. Jude and the Second Epistle of St. Peter.* Grand Rapids: Baker Book House, 1965.

THE REVELATION OF JESUS CHRIST

Introduction

"Praise must fill our hearts when we read the words of this Prophecy and remember the grace which has saved us from all which is coming upon this age. Another blessing is the assurance of ultimate victory and glory."
— Arno C. Gaebelein

I. Unique Place in the Canon

The uniqueness of the last book of the Bible is apparent in the very first word — "Revelation," or in the original, *Apokalupsis*. This word, meaning *unveiling*, is the origin of our word *apocalyptic*, a type of writing found in Daniel, Ezekiel, and Zechariah in the OT, but only here in the New. It refers to the prophetic visions of the future that use symbols, figures, and other literary devices.

Not only does Revelation look *forward* to the *future* consummation of all things and the eventual triumph of God and the Lamb, but it also ties up the loose ends of the first sixty-five books of the Bible. In fact, that is how the book can best be understood, by knowing the whole Bible! The characters, symbols, events, numbers, colors, and so forth, are *nearly* all previously encountered in the word of God. Some have appropriately called the book "the Grand Central Station" of the Bible because it is here that the "trains" come in. What trains? The trains of thought begun in Genesis and the following books, such as the concepts of the scarlet line of redemption, the nation of Israel, the Gentile nations, the church, Satan the adversary of God's people, the Antichrist, and many more.

The Apocalypse (since the fourth century often erroneously labeled "The Revelation of St. John the Divine," but really "The Revelation of Jesus Christ" (1:1)), is the necessary culmination of the Bible. It tells us how everything is going to come out. Even a casual reading should be a stern warning to unbelievers to re-

pent and an encouragement to God's people to persevere!

II. Authorship†

The book itself tells us the author is John (1:1, 4, 9; 22:8), writing at the command of his Lord, Jesus Christ. Ancient, strong, and widespread *external evidence* supports the view that the John meant is the Apostle John, the son of Zebedee, who labored for many years in Ephesus (in Asia Minor where all seven churches addressed in chapters 2 and 3 were located). He was exiled by Domitian to Patmos,†† where he wrote the visions he was granted by our Lord. Later he returned to Ephesus, where he died at a ripe old age. Justin Martyr, Irenaeus, Tertullian, Hippolytus, Clement of Alexandria, and Origen, all ascribe the book to John. More recently a book called the *Apocryphon of John* (about A.D. 150), was found in Egypt that specifically attributes Revelation to John the brother of James.

The first opposition to the apostolic authorship was by Dionysius of Alexandria, but he didn't *want* it to be by John since he opposed the doctrine of the Millennium (Rev. 20). His vague and vacillating references first to John Mark and then to "John the Presbyter" as possible authors cannot counterbalance such strong testimony, although many modern scholars of the more liberal persuasion also reject John the Apostle as author. There is no evidence in church history of such an individual as "John the Presbyter" (Elder) other than the author of 2nd and 3rd John. These two Letters are in the same style as 1 John and also fit in well with John's Gospel in simplicity and vocabulary.

While the external evidence cited above is so strong, the *internal evidence* is not as clear. The vocabulary, rather rough "Semitic" Greek style (even containing a few expressions grammarians would call "solecisms"), and also the word order, convince many that the same person who wrote the Apocalypse could not have written the Gospel.

However, these differences can be explained, and are not without counterbalancing similarities between the two books.

Some, for example, accept an early date in the 50's or 60's for the *Revelation* (under Claudius' or Nero's reign) with the idea that John wrote his *Gospel* much later in the 90's when he had improved his mastery of Greek. However, this is not a necessary solution. It is quite possible that John had an amanuensis for his Gospel, and was strictly alone in his exile on Patmos. (The doctrine of inspiration is not affected either way, since God uses the individual style of the writer, not a generalized style for all Bible books.)

The general themes of light and darkness are found in both the Gospel of John and Revelation. Such words as "Lamb," "overcome," "word," "true," "living waters," and others tend to tie the two works together. Also, both John 19:37 and Revelation 1:7 quote Zechariah 12:10, yet do *not* use the word for "pierced" found in the Septuagint, but another word translated "pierced."[1]

A further reason for the differences in vocabulary and style in the Gospel and Revelation is the very different type of literature they represent. In addition, the great multitude of Hebraic phraseology in Revelation comes from drawing so widely upon the whole OT.

In conclusion, the traditional view that the Apostle John, the son of Zebedee and brother of James, wrote the Revelation has a firm historical foundation, and the problems can be explained without rejecting that authorship.

III. Date

An early date for Revelation is preferred by some, either in the 50's or late 60's. As was noted, this is partly to explain the less developed style of Revelation. Also, some believe that "666" (13:18) was a prediction of Nero,[2] who some believed would come back from the dead. This would suggest an early date. The fact that this did not happen did not affect the acceptance of the book. (Perhaps this suggests that it was written much *later* than Nero's time.)

Church fathers specifically indicate the latter part of Domitian's reign (about 96) as the time John was on Patmos receiving the Revelation. Since this is an early, informed, and widespread view among orthodox Christians, there is every reason to accept it.

IV. Themes and Scope[†]

A simple key to the understanding of the book of Revelation is to realize that it is divided into three main parts. Chapter 1 describes a vision in which John saw Christ robed as a Judge and standing in the midst of the seven churches. Chapters 2 and 3 have to do with the Church Age in which we now live. The remaining nineteen chapters have to do with future events following the close of the Church Age. We may divide the book as follows:

1. *The things which John saw*, that is, the vision of Christ as Judge of the churches.

2. *The things which are*: an outline of the Church Period from the death of the apostles to the time when Christ will take His saints to heaven (chaps. 2 and 3).

3. *The things which will take place after this*: an outline of future events from the Rapture of the saints to the Eternal State (chaps. 4–22). An easy way to remember the contents of this third section of the book is as follows:

   a. Chapters 4 through 19 describe the Tribulation, a period of at least seven years during which God will judge the unbelieving nation of Israel and unbelieving Gentiles as well. These judgments are described under the figures of:

      (1) Seven seals.
      (2) Seven trumpets.
      (3) Seven bowls.

†See p. ii.

b. Chapters 20–22 deal with Christ's Second Coming, His kingdom on earth, the Judgment of the Great White Throne, and the Eternal State.

In the Tribulation Period, the seventh seal contains the seven trumpets. Also the seventh trumpet contains the seven bowl judgments. Thus the Tribulation Period might be diagrammed as follows:

SEALS
1 2 3 4 5 6 7

TRUMPETS
1 2 3 4 5 6 7

BOWLS
1 2 3 4 5 6 7

The Parentheses in the Book

The above diagram gives the main line of thought through the book of Revelation. However, as the narrative proceeds, there are frequent interruptions to introduce the reader to various great personalities and events of the Tribulation Period. Some writers call these parentheses or insets. Some of the principal parentheses are:

1. The 144,000 sealed Jewish saints (7:1–8).
2. Gentile believers of this period (7:9–17).
3. The mighty angel with the little scroll (chap. 10).
4. The two witnesses (11:3–12).
5. Israel and the dragon (chap. 12).
6. The two beasts (chap. 13).
7. The 144,000 with Christ on Mount Zion (14:1–5).
8. The angel with the everlasting gospel (14:6, 7).
9. Preliminary announcement of Babylon's fall (14:8).
10. Warning to worshipers of the beast (14:9–12).
11. The harvest and the vintage (14:14–20).
12. The destruction of Babylon (17:1–19:3).

The Symbols in the Book

Much of the language of Revelation is symbolic. Numbers, colors, minerals, jewels, beasts, stars, and lampstands are all used to represent persons, things, or truths.

Fortunately some of these symbols are clearly explained in the book itself. For instance, the seven stars are the angels of the seven churches (1:20); the great dragon is the Devil, or Satan (12:9). Clues to the meaning of other symbols are found in other parts of the Bible. The four living creatures (4:6) are almost identical with the four living creatures of Ezekiel 1:5–14. In Ezekiel 10:20 they are identified as cherubim. The leopard, bear, and lion (13:2) remind us of Daniel 7 where these wild animals refer to the world empires of Greece, Persia, and Babylon respectively. Other symbols do not seem to be clearly explained in the Scriptures, and we must be extremely careful in seeking to interpret them.

The Scope of the Book

In studying Revelation, as in all Bible study, we must constantly keep in mind the distinction between the church and Israel. The church is a heavenly people, blessed with spiritual blessings, and called to share Christ's glory as His Bride. Israel is God's ancient, earthly people to whom God promised the land of Israel and a literal earthly kingdom under the rule of the Messiah. The true church is mentioned in the first three chapters, but is not seen again until the Marriage Supper of the Lamb in chapter 19:6–10. The Tribulation Period (4:1–19:5) is primarily Jewish in character.

Before closing this Introduction, it is only fair to say that not all Christians interpret the book of Revelation in the manner outlined above. Some think that the book was entirely fulfilled in the early history of the church. Others teach that Revelation presents a continuous picture of the Church Age from John's day to the end.

For all children of God, the book teaches the folly of living for things that will shortly pass away. It spurs us to witness to the perishing, and encourages us to wait with patience for the Lord's Return. For the unbeliever, the book is a solemn warning of the terrible doom that awaits all who reject the Savior.

OUTLINE

Commentary

I. THE THINGS WHICH JOHN HAD SEEN (Chap. 1)

A. Title and Salutation (1:1–8)

1:1, 2 The first verse announces the subject of the book, namely, the **things which must shortly take place**. The book of Revelation is primarily an unfolding of the future. This **revelation** of future events was given by God to **Jesus Christ**. The Lord Jesus, in turn, committed it to **His angel**, and the angel made it known **to His servant John**. John's purpose in writing the Book was to share the information with the Lord's **servants**, that is, with all true believers. In doing this, John **bore witness to the** prophetic **word** which **God** had spoken to him **and to the testimony** to which **Jesus Christ** had borne witness. In short, John testified **to all things that he saw** in heavenly visions.

1:3 It was obviously God's intention that this Book should be read in church because He promised a special blessing to the one **who reads** it aloud and to all **those** in the assembly **who hear** it and take it to heart. **The time** for the fulfillment of the prophecies was **near**.

1:4 John addresses the book **to the seven churches** located **in** the Roman province of **Asia**. This province was situated in Asia Minor (modern Turkey).

First, John wishes for these churches **grace . . . and peace. Grace** means the undeserved favor of God and the strength that is needed in the Christian life day by day. **Peace** is the resulting calm that enables the believer to face persecution, sorrow, and even death itself. Grace and peace are said to come from the Trinity. They come **from Him who is and who was and who is to come.** This refers to God the Father and gives the true meaning of the name Jehovah. He is the ever-existing One and the One who is always the same. It comes **from the seven Spirits who are before His throne.** This refers to God the Holy Spirit in His fullness, seven being the number of perfection and completeness. It is not surprising that the number seven is found fifty-four times in this final book of the Bible.

1:5 It comes **from Jesus Christ, the faithful witness, the firstborn from the dead, and the ruler over the kings of the earth.** This clearly describes God the Son. He is the dependable **witness.** As **firstborn from the dead,** He is the first One to rise **from the dead** to die no more, and the One who holds the place of honor and pre-eminence among all who are raised from the dead to enjoy eternal life. He is also **the ruler over** all earthly **kings.** Following his initial greetings, John writes a tribute of praise to the Lord Jesus. First of all, he speaks of the Savior as the One **who loved us** (*loves us,* margin[3]) **and washed us from our sins in His own blood.** Note the tenses of the verbs: *loves,* a present, continuous action; **washed,** a past, completed work. Note too the order: He *loves us,* and indeed **loved us** long before He **washed us.** And note the price He paid: **His own blood.** Honest self-evaluation forces us to confess that the cost was too high. We did not deserve to be washed at such an exorbitant price.

1:6 His love did not stop at washing us, though it could have done so. He made us a kingdom (NKJV margin) **and priests to His God and Father.** As holy **priests,** we offer spiritual sacrifices to God: our persons, our possessions, our praise, and our service. As royal **priests,** we tell forth the excellencies of Him who called us out of darkness into His marvelous light. If we meditate on such love,

we can only conclude that He is worthy of all the **glory,** honor, worship, and praise that we can heap on Him. And He is worthy of **dominion** over our lives, the church, the world, and the entire universe. **Amen.**

1:7 This blessed One **is coming** back to earth in chariots of **clouds.** His Advent will be neither local nor invisible, because **every eye will see Him** (cf. Matt. 24:29, 30). The people who were guilty of His crucifixion will be aghast. In fact, **all the tribes of the earth will** be plunged into mourning **because** He comes to judge His enemies and set up His kingdom. Believers do not mourn His Coming; they say, **"Even so, Amen."**

1:8 There is a change of speaker. The Lord Jesus introduces Himself as **the Alpha and the Omega** (the first and last letters of the Greek alphabet), **the Beginning and the End.**[4] He spans time and eternity, and exhausts the vocabulary of excellence. He is the source and goal of creation, and it is He who began and will end the divine program in the world. He **is** and **was** and **is to come,** eternal in His being and **the Almighty** in power.

B. The Vision of Christ in Judicial Robes (1:9–20)

1:9 Back to **John,** who introduces himself as a **brother and companion** of all believers **in the tribulation and kingdom and patience of Jesus Christ.** He here links **tribulation,** perseverance (**patience**), and the **kingdom.** Paul similarly linked them in Acts 14:22 when he exhorted the saints to "continue in the faith, . . . saying, 'We must through many tribulations enter the kingdom of God.' "

John was in prison **on the island** of **Patmos** in the Aegean Sea because of his loyalty to **the word of God and** to **the testimony of Jesus Christ.** But his prison became an anteroom of heaven as he received visions of glory and judgment.

1:10 John **was in the Spirit,** that is, walking in unclouded fellowship with Him and thus in a position to receive divine communications. This reminds us that a person must be near to hear. "The secret of the Lord is with those who fear Him" (Ps. 25:14). It was **on the Lord's Day,** that is, the first day of the week.

That was the day of Christ's resurrection, of two subsequent appearances to His disciples, of the descent of the Spirit at Pentecost. The disciples gathered to break bread on the Lord's Day, and Paul instructed the Corinthians to take a collection on the first day. Some think that John refers to the time of judgment about which he will be writing, but the expression is quite different in the original.[5]

Suddenly John **heard behind** him a **voice** with the clarity, volume, and tone **of a trumpet**.

1:11, 12 It was Jesus, directing him to **write in a book** what he was about to **see** and to **send it to the seven churches**. Turning to see the Speaker, John **saw seven golden lampstands**, each one having a base, a single vertical stem, and an oil-burning lamp at the top.

1:13 The Person **in the midst of the seven lampstands** was **One like the Son of Man**. There was nothing between Him and the individual **lampstands**, no agency, hierarchy, or organization. Each church was autonomous. In describing the Lord, says McConkey:

> The Spirit ransacks the realm of nature for symbols that might convey some faint conception to our dull and finite minds of the glory, splendor, and majesty of this coming One, who is the Christ of Revelation.[6]

His outer **garment** was the long robe of a judge. The **band** around His **chest** symbolizes the righteousness and faithfulness with which He judges (see Isa. 11:5).

1:14 **His head and hair were white like wool**, picturing His eternity, as the Ancient of Days (Dan. 7:9), and also the wisdom and purity of His judgments. **Eyes like a flame of fire** speak of perfect knowledge, infallible insight, and inescapable scrutiny.

1:15 The Lord's **feet were like** polished **brass, as if refined in a furnace**. Since brass is a consistent type of judgment, this supports the view that it is the *judicial office* that is primarily in view. **His voice** sounded like the waves of the sea, or a mountain cataract, majestic and awesome.

1:16 **He** held **in His right hand seven stars**, indicating possession,

power, control, and honor. **Out of His mouth went a sharp two-edged sword**, the word of God (Heb. 4:12). Here it refers to the keen and accurate verdicts concerning His people, as seen in the letters to the seven churches. **His countenance was** radiant as the **sun** at high noon, the dazzling splendor and transcendant glory of His deity.

Combining all these thoughts, we see Christ in all His perfections as supremely qualified to judge the seven churches. Later in the book He will judge His foes, but "judgment (must) begin at the house of God" (1 Pet. 4:17). Note, however, that it is a different kind of judgment in each case. The churches are judged with the purpose of purification and reward, the world with the purpose of punishment.

1:17 The sight of the Judge prostrated John **at His feet as** if **dead**, but the Lord revived him by revealing Himself as **the First and the Last**, a title of Jehovah (Isa. 44:6; 48:12).

1:18 The Judge is the Living One who **was dead** but is now **alive forevermore**. He has **the keys of Hades and of Death**, having control over both and uniquely able to raise the dead. **Hades** here stands for the soul and **Death** for the body. When a person dies, the soul is in **Hades**, a name used to describe the disembodied state. The body goes to the grave. For the believer the disembodied state is the same as being present with the Lord. At the resurrection, the soul is reunited with the glorified body and raptured (caught up) to the Father's house.

1:19 John must **write the things which** he had **seen** (chap. 1); **the things which are** (chaps. 2, 3); **and the things which will take place after this** (chaps. 4–22). This forms the general outline of the book.

1:20 The Lord then explained to John the hidden meaning **of the seven stars** and **the seven golden lampstands**. The **stars** represented **the angels** or messengers **of the seven churches**, whereas the **lampstands** represented **the seven churches** themselves.

Various explanations of **the angels** have been offered. Some say that they were angelic beings who represented the churches, just as angels represent nations (Dan. 10:13, 20, 21). Others say that they were the bishops (or pastors) of the churches, an explanation that lacks scriptural support. Still others say that they were human messengers who picked up the letters from John in Patmos and delivered them to the individual churches. The same Greek word (*angelos*) means either angel or messenger, but in this book the first meaning is very prominent.

Although the letters are addressed to **angels**, the contents are clearly intended for all in the churches.

The **lampstands** were light-bearers and were a fitting emblem of local **churches**, which are supposed to shine for God amid the darkness of this world.

II. THE THINGS WHICH ARE: LETTERS FROM OUR LORD (Chaps. 2, 3)

In chapters 2 and 3, we have individual letters addressed to the seven churches of Asia. The letters may be applied in at least three ways. First of all, they describe conditions that actually existed in the *seven local churches* at the time John was writing. Secondly, they give a view of Christendom on earth *at any one time* in its history. The features found in these letters have existed in part, at least, in every century since Pentecost. In this respect, the letters bear marked resemblances to the seven parables of Matthew 13. Finally, the letters give a *consecutive preview* of the history of Christendom, each church representing a distinct period. The general trend of conditions is downward. Many believe that the first three letters are consecutive and that the last four are concurrent, reaching to the time of the Rapture.

According to the third view, the epochs in the history of the church are generally listed as follows:

Ephesus: The church of the first century was generally praiseworthy but it had already left its first love.

Smyrna: From the first to the fourth century, the church suffered persecution under the Roman emperors.

Pergamos: During the fourth and fifth centuries, Christianity was recognized as an official religion through Constantine's patronage.

Thyatira: From the sixth to the fifteenth century, the Roman Catholic Church largely held sway in Western Christendom until rocked by the Reformation. In the East, the Orthodox Church ruled.

Sardis: The sixteenth and seventeenth centuries were the Post-Reformation period. The light of the Reformation soon became dim.

Philadelphia: During the eighteenth and nineteenth centuries, there were mighty revivals and great missionary movements.

Laodicea: The church of the last days is pictured as lukewarm and apostate. It is the church of liberalism and ecumenism.

There is a similarity in the structure of the letters. For instance, each opens with a salutation to an individual church; each presents the Lord Jesus in a role that is peculiarly fitting for that particular church; each describes His knowledge of the church's works, introduced by the words "I know." Words of commendation are addressed to all churches except Laodicea; reproof to all except Smyrna and Philadelphia. To each a special exhortation is given to hear what the Spirit is saying and in each a special promise is included for the overcomer.

Each church has its own distinctive character. Phillips has assigned the following titles, expressing these dominant features: *Ephesus*, the loveless church; *Smyrna*, the persecuted church; *Pergamos*, the over-tolerant church; *Thyatira*, the compromising church; *Sardis*, the sleeping church; *Philadelphia*, the church with opportunity; and *Laodicea*, the complacent church. Walvoord describes their problems as: (1) losing their first love; (2) fear of suffering; (3) doctrinal defection; (4) moral departure; (5) spiritual deadness; (6) not holding fast; and (7) lukewarmness.[7]

A. To Ephesus (2:1–7)

2:1 The Lord introduces Himself to **the church of Ephesus** as the One **who holds the seven stars in His right hand, who walks in the midst of the seven golden lampstands**. Most of the descriptions of the Lord in these letters are similar to that which is found in chapter 1.

2:2 This church was outstanding for

its plentiful **works**, its arduous **labor**, and its patient endurance. It did not tolerate **evil** men in its midst. It had the ability to discern false apostles and to deal with them accordingly.

2:3, 4 For the sake of Christ's name, it had endured trial and adversity with **patience** and had **labored** tirelessly. But the tragedy of Ephesus was that it had **left** its **first love**. The fire of its affection had died down. The glowing enthusiasm of its early days had disappeared. The Christians could look back to better days when their bridal love for Christ flowed warm, full, and free. They were still sound in doctrine and active in service, but the true motive of all worship and service was missing.

2:5 They should **remember** the good days of their early faith, **repent** of their diminishing of **first** love, and repeat the devoted service which characterized the outset of their Christian life. Otherwise He would **remove** the **lampstand** at Ephesus, that is, the assembly would cease to exist. Its testimony would die out.

2:6 A further word of commendation concerns their hatred of **the deeds of the Nicolaitans**. We cannot be positive who these people were. Some think they were followers of a religious leader named Nicolas. Others point out that the name means "rule over the laity" and see in this a reference to the rise of the clerical system.

2:7 Those who have ears to hear God's word are encouraged to listen to **what the Spirit says to the churches**.

Then a promise is held out to the overcomer. In general, an overcomer in the NT is one who believes that Jesus Christ is the Son of God (1 Jn. 5:5), in other words, a true believer. His faith enables him to overcome the world with all its temptations and allurements. Perhaps in each of the letters the word has an additional thought, connected with the condition in that particular church. Thus an overcomer in Ephesus may be one who shows the genuineness of his faith by repenting when he has backslidden from his first love. All such **will ...eat from the tree of life, which is in the midst of the Paradise of God**. This does not imply that they are saved by overcoming, but that their overcoming

proves the reality of their conversion experience. The only way men are saved is by grace through faith in Christ. All who are saved will **eat from the tree of life**, that is, they will enter into eternal life in its fullness in heaven.

Ephesus is often taken to describe the condition of the church soon after the death of the apostles.

B. To Smyrna (2:8–11)

2:8 **Smyrna** means *myrrh* or *bitterness*. Here Christ presents Himself as **the First and the Last, who was dead and came to life**. This description would be particularly comforting to those who faced the threat of death daily.

2:9 With special tenderness, the Lord tells His suffering saints that He knows their **tribulation** thoroughly. To outward appearances, they might be **poverty**-stricken, but as far as spiritual things were concerned, they were **rich**. As Charles Stanley said, "There was peculiar honor in being near and like Himself, who had nowhere to lay His head. I have learned this: Jesus is specially the partner of His poor servants."

The saints at Smyrna were being bitterly attacked by the Jews. Historians tell of the eagerness with which these Jews sought to aid in the martyrdom of Polycarp, for instance. As **Jews**, they claimed to be God's chosen people, but by their blasphemous behavior they showed that they were **a synagogue of Satan**.

2:10 The Christians should **not fear any of those things** they would soon **suffer**. Some of them would be imprisoned and **tested** by **tribulation** for **ten days**. This time period may refer to **ten** *literal* **days**; to **ten** distinct persecutions under the Roman emperors who preceded Constantine; or to **ten** years of persecution under Diocletian.

The believers were encouraged to **be faithful until death**, that is, to be willing to die rather than renounce their faith in Christ. They would receive **the crown of life**, a special reward for martyrs.

2:11 Again the willing hearer is encouraged to listen to the Spirit's voice. The overcomer is promised exemption from **the second death**. Here an overcomer is one who proves the reality of his faith by choosing to go to heaven with a good conscience rather than stay on earth with a bad one. He will not be affected by **the second death**, the doom of all unbelievers (20:6, 14).

C. To Pergamos (2:12–17)

2:12 **Pergamos** (or Pergamum) means *high tower* or *thoroughly married*. This letter presents the Lord as the One **who has the sharp two-edged sword**. This is the word of God (Heb. 4:12) with which He will judge evildoers in the assembly (see v. 16).

2:13 Pergamos was the Asian headquarters for the cult of emperor-worship: hence it is called the place of **Satan's throne**. In spite of the surrounding paganism, the church had remained loyal to Christ, even though one of its members, **Antipas**, had been martyred for his confession of the Lord Jesus. He was the first known Asian to die for refusing to worship the emperor.

2:14, 15 **But** the Lord must reprove the church for permitting men with evil doctrine to continue in the Christian fellowship. There were **those who** held **the doctrine of Balaam** and **of the Nicolaitans. The doctrine of Balaam** sanctioned eating **things sacrificed to idols** and **sexual immorality**. It also refers to the practice of preaching for hire (Num. 22–25; 31).

The doctrine of the Nicolaitans is not defined. Many Bible scholars feel that these were libertines, teaching that those under grace were free to practice idolatry and sexual sins.

Dr. C. I. Scofield, however, links the doctrine with the rise of the clerical system:

It is the doctrine that God has instituted an order of "clergy" or priests, as distinguished from the "laity." The word is formed from two Greek words, *niko*, conqueror or overcomer, and *laos*, the people. The New Testament knows nothing of a "clergyman," still less of a priest, except as all sons of God in this dispensation are "a royal priesthood." In the apostolic church there were offices: elders (or bishops) and deacons; and gifts: apostles, prophets, evangelists, pastors and teachers (Eph. 4:11). These might or might not be elders or deacons. But late in the apostolic period there emerged a disposition to arrogate to elders alone authority to administer ordinances, and, generally, to

constitute themselves a class between God and the people; they were the Nicolaitans. You will observe that what were "deeds" in the Ephesus or late apostolic period, had become a "doctrine" two hundred years later in the Pergamos or Constantine period.[8]

2:16 True believers are called on to **repent**. If they did, they would presumably expel the evil teachers from their midst. Otherwise the Lord Himself would **fight against** these evil men.

2:17 Obedient saints should **hear what the Spirit says to the churches**. The overcomer would be given **hidden manna** and a **white stone**. The overcomer in Pergamos may be the child of God who refuses to tolerate evil teaching in the local church. But what are **the hidden manna** and the **white stone**?

Manna is a type of Christ Himself. It may speak of heavenly food in contrast to foods offered to idols (v. 14). **Hidden manna** may be "some sweet, secret communion with Himself, known in the glory as the One who suffered here." The **white stone** has been explained in many ways. It was a token of acquittal in a legal case. It was a symbol of victory in an athletic contest. It was an expression of welcome given by a host to his guest. It seems clear that it is a reward given by the Lord to the overcomer and expressing individual approval by Him. Alford says that the **new name** indicates acceptance by God and title to glory.

Historically this church probably represents the time soon after Constantine, when the church was "thoroughly married" to the state. Thousands became nominal Christians, and the church tolerated pagan practices in its midst.

D. To Thyatira (2:18–29)

2:18 The name **Thyatira** means *perpetual sacrifice* or *continual offering*. In this letter the Son of God is seen as having **eyes like a flame of fire** and **feet like fine brass**. The **eyes** speak of piercing vision, and the brass **feet** speak of threatened judgment.

2:19 This church was outstanding in several ways. It was not lacking in good **works**, **love**, **service**, **faith**, and patient endurance. In fact, its **works** were increasing in quantity rather than declining.

2:20 But impure doctrine had been tolerated in the assembly with the result that **immorality** and idolatry were being practiced. The church had permitted a self-styled **prophetess** named **Jezebel**[9] to lead God's servants into sin. Just as Jezebel in the OT had corrupted God's people with fornication and idolatry, so this woman taught that Christians could engage in these practices without sinning. Perhaps she encouraged the believers to join the trade guilds of Thyatira, even though this involved honoring the guild god or goddess and participating in festivals where food was **sacrificed to idols**. She doubtless justified this compromise with the world on the ground that it would allegedly advance the cause of the church.

2:21–23 Because she refused **to repent**, the Lord was going to give her a **sick bed** of tribulation in place of her bed of lust. **Those who** committed **adultery** with her would be thrown into a bed of **great tribulation** and death **unless they** forsook her and escaped from her **deeds**. Then **all the churches** would **know** that the Lord is watching and that He rewards according to man's deeds. There was probably a literal prophetess in Thyatira named Jezebel. But Bible students have also seen here a reference to the rise of a false church system with its adoration of images, sale of indulgences, and priestly absolution from such sins as fornication.

2:24, 25 There was a faithful remnant in Thyatira (**the rest . . . as many as do not have this doctrine**) which had not been initiated into the secret doctrines and rites of Jezebel, otherwise known as **the depths of Satan. No other burden** of responsibility was placed on them than to **hold fast** the truth until Christ's Coming.

2:26–28 The overcomer in Thyatira was the true believer who steadfastly maintained the **works** of genuine Christianity. His reward would be to reign with Christ during the Millennium. He would have authority **over the nations** and would **rule them with a rod of iron**. All sin and rebellion would be punished severely and promptly. The Lord promised to give to the overcomer **the morning star**. The Lord Jesus is the Bright and Morning Star (22:16). Just as the **morning star** appears in the heavens before the sun rises, so Christ will appear as the Morning Star to rapture His church to heaven before He appears as the Sun of Righteousness to reign over the earth (1 Thess. 4:13–18; Mal. 4:2). Thus the overcomer is promised a part in the Rapture. He does not earn this by his works, but his works demonstrate the reality of his faith. Because he is genuinely converted, he will be given **the morning star**.

2:29 In this and the following three letters, the formula **"He who has an ear, let him hear . . ."** follows the promise to the overcomer rather than preceding it. This may indicate that from this point on, only those who overcome are expected to have an ear to **hear what the Spirit says to the churches**.

E. To Sardis (3:1–6)

3:1 **Sardis** means *those escaping* or *renovation.* The Lord reveals Himself as the One **who has the seven Spirits of God and the seven stars**. It is in the power of the Holy Spirit that He controls the churches and their messengers. Sardis was a church of lifeless profession. It had a reputation as a Christian assembly, but for the most part, it simply went through a formal, dull routine. It did not overflow with spiritual life. It did not sparkle with the supernatural.

3:2, 3 The Lord called it to a new zeal and a new endeavor to **strengthen** what little there remained for Him, for even that was showing signs of dying. The people had often started projects for God but had never brought them to completion. Christ warned them to **hold fast** the sacred deposit of truth and to **repent** of their lifelessness. Unless they awoke, He would **come** unexpectedly and deal with them in judgment.

3:4 There was a remnant **even in Sardis** which had not lost its Christian testimony. These believers who had **not defiled their garments** with worldliness would **walk with** Christ **in white**.

3:5 They were the overcomers, whose righteous acts marked them as true believers. Their **white garments** speak of the righteousness of their lives. Because they were manifestly true Christians, their names would not be blotted out of **the Book of Life**.

Some think that the **Book of Life** contains the names of all who have been given *physical* life. According to this view, those who show by their lives that they have been truly born again will not be removed from the book whereas, by implication, all others will.

Others see the book as a register of those who have *spiritual* life. They are promised that their names will not be blotted out, that is, that they will never lose their salvation. According to this view, the fact that some names will not be blotted out does not require that others will.

Because of the consistent teaching of the Scriptures that salvation is by grace, not by works, and because of the clear statements that the true believer is eternally secure (John 3:16; 5:24; 10:27–29), verse 5 cannot imply the possibility of a child of God ever being lost.

Our Lord adds the promise that He **will confess** the names of the overcomers **before** His **Father** and the **angels** of heaven.

3:6 Again men are called to hear this solemn warning against having a religious profession without ever having been born again.

The assembly at Sardis is often taken as a picture of the Post-Reformation period when the church became formal, ritualistic, worldly, and political. The Protestant state churches of Europe and the American colonies were leaders in this drift.

F. To Philadelphia (3:7–13)

3:7 **Philadelphia** means *love for the brethren*. To this church the Lord appears as **He who is holy, He who is true, He who has the key of David, He who opens and no one shuts, who shuts and no one opens.**

In other words, He has administrative power and uncontestable control:

The open door which Jewish synagogue and pagan cults were powerless to shut is the God-given opportunity to preach Christ to all who will hear. The key of David is an Old Testament allusion to the absolute sovereignty of God in opening doors and shutting mouths. See Isaiah 22:22.[10]

3:8 The assembly at Philadelphia re-

ceived only words of praise from the Lord. The saints had been faithful. They had been zealous for good **works**. In their own human weakness, they had trusted in the Lord. As a result, they had been able to preserve the truth by living it out in their lives. They had **not denied** Christ's **name**. Therefore, He would **set before** them **an open door** of opportunity that **no one** would be able to **shut**.

3:9 Those self-styled **Jews** who had opposed them so bitterly would be humbled before these simple believers. Those who claimed to be God's chosen people, though actually a **synagogue of Satan**, would be forced to admit that the despised Christians were actually the chosen flock.

3:10 **Because** the Philadelphians had maintained God's truth by living it before men, the Lord would **keep** them **from the hour of trial** which is to come upon all **who dwell on the earth**. This is a promise of exemption from the Tribulation Period described in chapters 6–19. Note that they will be kept from the *hour* of trial, that is, from the whole time period. Also they will be kept *out of* that period (Gk., *ek*), not through it.

"Those who dwell on the earth" is a technical term, meaning those who make this earth their home, "men of the world who have their portion in this life" (Ps. 17:14b).

3:11 Christ's coming is held before the saints as a motive to steadfast endurance. They should not let anyone rob them of the victor's **crown** when it is so near at hand.

3:12 The overcomer will be made a **pillar in the** inner sanctuary of **God**. Whatever else this may mean, it certainly carries the thought of strength, honor, and permanent security. He shall never leave this place of safety and joy. The overcomer will have three names written **on him: the name of . . . God, the name of the New Jerusalem, which comes down out of heaven from . . .** **God**, and the **new name** of the Lord Jesus. He will thus be identified as belonging to all three.

3:13 **He who has an ear** should listen to this message from **the Spirit** to **the churches**.

The church of Philadelphia is often taken as a symbol of the great evangelical awakening in the eighteenth and early nineteenth centuries, the recovery of the truth concerning the church and Christ's coming, and the worldwide missionary outreach. While evangelical Christians enjoyed a real measure of recovery during this period, yet Satan made a determined effort to leaven the church with legalism, ritualism, and rationalism.

G. To Laodicea (3:14–22)

3:14 The name **Laodicea** means either *the people ruling* or *the judgment of the people*. The Lord Jesus speaks of Himself as **the Amen, the Faithful and True Witness, the Beginning of the creation of God**. As **the Amen**, He is the embodiment of faithfulness and truth, and the One who guarantees and fulfills the promises of God. He is also the originator **of the creation of God**, both material and spiritual. The expression, **"the Beginning of the creation of God"** does not mean that He was the first Person to be created; He was never created. Rather, it means that He began all **creation**. It does not say that He *had* a beginning, but that He *is* **the Beginning**. He is the *origin* **of the creation of God**. And He is pre-eminent over all creation.

3:15–17 The church at Laodicea was **neither cold nor hot**. It was sickeningly **lukewarm**. The Lord would have preferred it to have been extreme in its indifference or its zeal. But no — it was **lukewarm** enough to deceive people into thinking that it was a church of God, and so disgustingly **lukewarm** about divine things as to nauseate the Most High. Furthermore, the church was characterized by pride, ignorance, self-sufficiency, and complacency.

3:18 The people were counseled **to buy from** the Lord **gold refined in the fire**. This may mean divine righteousness, which is bought without money or price (Isa. 55:1) but received as a gift through faith in the Lord Jesus. Or it may mean genuine faith, which when tested **in the fire**, results in praise, honor, and glory at the revelation of Jesus Christ (1 Pet. 1:7).

Also the people were counseled to buy **white garments**, that is, practical righteousness in everyday life. And they should **anoint** their **eyes with eye salve**, that is, gain true spiritual vision through the enlightenment of the Holy Spirit. This counsel was especially appropriate, since Laodicea was known as a center for banking, textiles, and medicines — especially eye salve.

3:19 The Lord's **love** for the church is seen in the fact that He rebukes and chastens it. If He did not care, He would not bother. With lingering tenderness, He calls on this nominal church to **be zealous and repent**.

3:20 In the closing verses, we have what Scofield calls "the place and attitude of Christ at the end of the church age." He is outside the professing church, politely knocking and inviting individuals (no longer the mass of the people) to leave the apostate church in order to have fellowship with Him.

Trench comments:

> Every man is lord of the house of his own heart; it is his fortress; he must open the gates of it. He has the mournful prerogative and privilege of refusing to open. But if he refuses, he is blindly at strife with his own blessedness, a miserable conqueror.[11]

3:21 The overcomer is promised that he will share the glory of Christ's **throne** and reign with Him over the millennial earth. Those who follow Him in humility, rejection, and suffering will also follow Him in glory.

3:22 Then for the last time, the hearer is solemnly advised to listen to the voice of **the Spirit**.

Whatever interpretation we take of the book of Revelation, it is undeniable that the church of Laodicea presents a vivid picture of the age in which we live. Luxury-living abounds on every hand while souls are dying for want of the gospel. Christians are wearing crowns instead of bearing a cross. We become more emotionally stirred over sports, politics, or television than we do over Christ. There is little sense of spiritual need, little longing for true revival. We give the best of our lives to the business world, then turn over the remnants of a wasted career to the Savior. We cater to our bodies which in a few short years will return to dust. We accumulate instead of forsake, lay up treasures on earth instead of in heaven. The general attitude is, "Nothing too good for the people of God. If I don't pamper myself, who will? Let's get ahead in the world and give our spare evenings to the Lord." This is our condition on the eve of Christ's Return.

III. THE THINGS WHICH WILL TAKE PLACE AFTER THIS (Chaps. 4–22)

We now come to the third main division of Revelation. The first three chapters described the Church Age from the time of the apostles until the Rapture. Beginning with this chapter, the subject is "things which must take place after this."

There is a definite break between chapters 3 and 4. From this point on, the church is never mentioned as being on earth. What then has happened to it? We believe that it was taken to heaven by the Lord at the end of chapter 3.

Once the saints have been translated to heaven, the Lord will resume His dealings with the nation of Israel. Then will begin the Tribulation. This is a seven-year period in which the Lord deals with the Jewish people concerning their rejection of the Messiah. Those who turn to Christ during the Tribulation will be saved to enter the glorious kingdom on earth, whereas those who refuse Him will be destroyed.

Large numbers of Jews will return to the land of Israel in unbelief at the outset of the Tribulation (Ezek. 36:24, 25). The Roman world power will make a treaty with the Israelis, guaranteeing them freedom of worship (Dan. 9:27). In fact, the first three and one-half years of the Tribulation will be relatively mild. The Lord Jesus described these years in Matthew 24:4–14.

At the middle of the Tribulation, an idolatrous image will be set up in the temple at Jerusalem and men will be ordered to worship it or be killed (Matt. 24:15). This will signal the beginning of the Great Tribulation, the Time of Jacob's Trouble, a period of suffering such as the world has never known or ever will know (Matt. 24:21).

Chapter 4 introduces us to the beginning of the Tribulation. The first scene is in heaven, where John is given a vision of the glory of God. The Lord frequently gave a vision of His glory to His prophets before permitting them to foretell the future (Isa. 6; Ezek. 1). In chapter 1, John saw Christ's glory before he was permitted to record the future history of the church. Now he is given a vision of God before he learns the judgments which will be poured out on unbelieving Israel and the Gentiles.

A. The Vision of God's Throne (Chap. 4)

4:1 The **voice** that invites John to heaven is the voice of Christ (cf. vv. 10–20). Many Bible students believe that John's entrance into heaven is a picture of the church's being taken home to be with the Lord at this time (1 Thess. 4:13–18; 1 Cor. 15:51–53). The Lord Jesus promises to **show** John **things which must take place after this**. These words are similar to the last part of 1:19 and support the use of that verse as an outline of the book.

4:2, 3 The Holy **Spirit** takes possession of John in a special way, and he **immediately** sees the eternal God sitting upon His **throne** in majesty and splendor.

Some, following the majority of manuscripts, omit the words **"And He who sat there was,"** making the **jasper** and **sardius** descriptive of the **throne** rather than of the Lord. However, these precious stones may also describe the Lord Himself. In the high priest's breastplate, the jasper represented Reuben, Jacob's firstborn, and the sardius represented Benjamin, his lastborn. The name Reuben means "Behold, a son," and Benjamin means "son of my right hand." Walvoord sees the two stones as including all the other stones, depicting all of God's people, and the Person on the throne as God in relation to the people of Israel.[12]

The **rainbow**, apparently a ring of green light **like an emerald**, is a pledge that God will keep His covenants, in spite of the coming judgments.

4:4 We cannot say with certainty who **the twenty-four elders** are. They are variously understood as angelic be-ings, as the redeemed people of both the OT and NT, and as NT saints only. The fact that they are crowned and en-throned suggests that they are saints who have been judged and rewarded.

4:5 It is clear that **the throne** here is one of judgment, with its terrifying **lightnings, thunderings, and voices**. The **seven lamps of fire** represent the Holy Spirit in His fullness and majesty. There is only one Spirit of God, but the seven represents perfection and completeness.

4:6 **The sea of glass like crystal** tells us that the throne is located in a place that is undisturbed by the restless, wild tossings of this world, or by the op-position of the wicked, who are like a troubled sea.

At **the throne** were **four living crea-tures, full of eyes in front and in back**. This speaks of clarity, breadth, and depth of vision.

4:7, 8 **The four living creatures** are difficult to identify. All we can say for certain is that they are created beings be-cause they worship God. They seem to be a combination of the cherubim in Eze-kiel 10 and the seraphim in Isaiah 6. Verse 7 describes cherubim and verse 8 pictures seraphim. These angelic beings are guardians of the throne of God. The cherubim seem to be associated with burning judgment and the seraphim with burning purification.

The description in verse 7 parallels the way Christ is presented in the Gos-pels:

> **lion** — Matthew — King;
> **calf** or ox — Mark — Servant;
> **man** — Luke — Son of Man;
> **eagle** — John — Son of God.

The living creatures sing ceaselessly of the holiness and eternity of God. Most manuscripts actually have the word **holy** nine times here, a strong trinitarian touch.

4:9, 10 **Whenever the living crea-tures** worship the eternal One **on the throne, . . . the twenty-four elders** pros-trate themselves, **worship** the eternal God, **and cast their crowns before the throne**.

4:11 Their worship acknowledges the **Lord** as **worthy** of **glory and honor and power** because He **created all**

things, and by His **will they exist**.

The vision prepares us for what is to follow. God is seen as the Almighty Ruler of the universe sitting on the throne of His glory, surrounded by wor-shiping creatures, and about to send judgment on the earth.

B. The Lamb and the Seven-Sealed Scroll (Chap. 5)

5:1 God is seen holding **a scroll** which has **seven seals** binding it. The scroll contains a record of the judgments that must fall on the earth before the Lord Jesus can set up His kingdom.

5:2, 3 **A strong angel** sends forth an appeal for someone **worthy to open the scroll and** break the **seals**, one by one. **No one**, celestial, terrestrial, or subterra-nean, was found qualified to unroll it or to read it. No angel, man, or demon has the wisdom and knowledge to execute judgment.

5:4 John **wept** copiously when it seemed **that no one was found worthy**. Did that mean that the wrongs of earth would go unrighted, that the righteous would never be vindicated, that the wicked would go unpunished? Did it mean that the kingdom would not come because the necessary purging of the earth would be thwarted?

5:5 **One of the elders** comforted John with the glad news that **the Lion of the tribe of Judah, the Root** (Creator and Progenitor) **of David**, was qualified **to open the scroll**, break **the seals**, and thus release the judgments. Jesus is qual-ified to be the Judge by His infinite wis-dom, by divine decree (John 5:22, 27), by personal excellence, and by His work at Calvary.

In Revelation our Lord is presented both as Lamb and Lion. As the Lamb of God, He is the sacrificial One, bearing away the sins of the world. As the Lion, He is the Judge, punishing His enemies. At His First Coming, He was the Lamb. At His Second Coming, He will be the Lion.

5:6 When John **looked**, he saw **the throne** surrounded **by the four living creatures** and **the elders. In the** middle **stood a** little **Lamb** which looked as if **it had been** freshly **slain**. The Lamb had **seven horns** (omnipotence) **and seven**

eyes (omniscience). His possession of **the seven Spirits of God** reminds us that the Lord Jesus was endued with the full measure of the Holy Spirit (John 3:34b). **The seven Spirits of God sent out into all the earth** suggest omnipresence.

5:7, 8 As soon as the Lamb **took the** judgment roll **out of the right hand of** God the Father, **the living creatures** and **elders** prostrated themselves **before the Lamb. Each had a harp and golden bowls full of incense**, representing **the prayers of the saints**, probably the prayers of martyrs crying to God to avenge their blood (6:10). Though they handled the prayers, there is no suggestion that they presented them to God or had any part in answering them.

5:9, 10 In their **new song**, they acclaimed the Lamb as **worthy** to execute judgment because of His redemptive work on the cross. There is a question whether they include themselves among the redeemed (**"have redeemed us to God"**) or whether it should read, as in some versions, "and did purchase for God with Your blood men from every tribe and tongue and people and nation".[13]

Beyond redemption, the Lord has made believers **kings**[14] **and priests** to worship Him, to witness for Him, and to **reign** with Him over **the** millennial **earth**.

5:11 The chorus widened as **many angels** joined **the living creatures and the elders**, a choir numbering millions, perhaps billions, all participating in perfect harmony.

5:12 Their tribute is one that believers will sing throughout eternity. **"Worthy is the Lamb who was slain to receive:**

power — over my life, the church, the world, the universe;

riches — all my silver and my gold;

wisdom — the finest of my intellectual powers;

strength — my physical strength for His service;

honor — a single, pure desire to magnify Him in all my ways;

glory — my entire life devoted to glorifying Him;

blessing" — all my powers of praise for Him.

5:13 Now the music becomes a diapason, a full, deep burst of harmonious song. **Every creature . . . in heaven and on the earth** joins in heaping eternal **blessing and honor and glory and power** on God the Father and on **the Lamb**.

This verse parallels Philippians 2:10 and 11, which insists that every knee will bow at the name of Jesus and every tongue confess Him Lord. No single, specific time is mentioned, but it will obviously be after the saved are raised to everlasting life and then after the unsaved are raised to everlasting judgment. Believers will have already acknowledged Jesus as Lord; unbelievers will then be compelled to honor Him. Universal homage to the Father and the Son is an assured fact.

5:14 The finale! As **the four living** ones say **"Amen"**, the **elders** fall **down** and worship the enthroned Lord **who lives forever and ever**.

C. The Opening of the Six Seals (Chap. 6)

6:1, 2 **When the Lamb opened** the first seal, **one of the four living creatures** cried out **"Come and see."**[15] In response, a rider, possibly the Antichrist, carrying **a bow**, came forth on **a white horse . . . conquering** and bent on conquest. This may represent what is known today as cold war. The **bow** poses the threat of war, but there is no mention of an arrow. Perhaps there is even the suggestion of missile warfare since the bow is a weapon of distant combat. This rider does not actually *cause* warfare; it is not until the second seal that peace is taken from the earth.

6:3, 4 **The second living creature** summoned the second rider to come forth. This one carried **a great sword** and rode on **a horse** which was **fiery red**. A **sword** is used in hand to hand combat. Thus the second seal contemplates invading armies in fierce person to person warfare. The second rider takes **peace from the earth**.

6:5, 6 In obedience to **the third living creature**, a rider holding a set **of scales** came forth on **a black horse**. This represents famine, which often follows war. **A voice in the** middle **of the four living creatures** announced that **wheat**

and **barley** were being sold at prohibitive prices. The **scales** were used to weigh the rationed grain and were thus a symbol of famine. The expression **do not harm the oil and the wine** is difficult. Some say that these were the food of the poor. If they were staple items, then they must be protected in order to preserve life. It seems more likely, however, that the luxury items of the rich are contemplated here: historically, even in famine the rich can get some luxuries.

6:7, 8 The **fourth living creature** called forth **a pale horse** with **Death and Hades** as its riders. **Death** is associated with the body and **Hades** with the spirit and soul. By means of war, famine, pestilence, and wild **beasts, a fourth of the** earth's inhabitants are destroyed. We might think that plagues are no longer a threat because of modern antibiotics and wonder drugs. However, the great killer diseases are not conquered but merely dormant. They can spread throughout the world as fast as jet aircraft can carry them.

6:9 Now we are introduced to the first martyrs of the Tribulation Period (Matt. 24:9), Jewish believers who go out and preach the gospel of the kingdom and who are **slain for** their **testimony**. Their **souls** are **under the altar** in heaven.

6:10 **They** cry out to the sovereign **Lord**[16] to **avenge** their **blood**. As mentioned previously, **"those who dwell on the earth"** refers to unbelievers who look upon the earth as their home.

6:11 **White** robes are **given to** the martyrs, a symbol of their righteousness. They are told to wait until the final complement of tribulation martyrs is **completed**.

6:12, 13 The opening of **the sixth seal** brought tremendous convulsions of nature. **A great earthquake** shook land and sea, and the starry heavens were thrown into disorder. **The sun** darkened and **the moon** turned red **like blood. Stars . . . fell to the earth** like ripe figs when the **fig tree is shaken** violently.

6:14 **The sky receded** as if it were a sheet of parchment being **rolled up. Every mountain and island was** displaced by tremendous upheavals.

6:15 Not surprisingly, all classes of society were seized with panic. Recognizing that God was pouring out His wrath, they **hid themselves in the caves and** among the **rocks of the mountains**.

6:16, 17 They preferred to be crushed by tumbling **mountains and rocks** than to endure the judgment of God and **the wrath of the Lamb**. Too late they realized that no rebel **is able to stand** up against the Lamb's indignation.

D. The Saved in the Great Tribulation (Chap. 7)

Chapter 7 comes between the sixth and seventh seals and introduces us to two important companies of believers. The chapter answers the question at the end of chapter 6, "Who is able to stand?" Those described in this chapter will stand in the sense that they will be spared to enter the Millennium with Christ.

7:1–4 The vision of **four angels standing at the four corners of the earth** and **holding** back **the four winds** means that a great storm is about to burst on the world. However, the angels are told to delay this terrible destruction until **the servants of God** have been **sealed on their foreheads**. Twelve thousand persons from each of **the** twelve **tribes** of **Israel** are then **sealed.**

7:5–8 The 144,000 are clearly Jewish believers, not members of some 20th century Gentile cult. These Jewish saints are saved during the early part of the Tribulation. The seal on their foreheads brands them as belonging to God and guarantees that they will be preserved alive during the ensuing seven years.

Two tribes are absent from the list: Ephraim and Dan. Perhaps they are omitted because they were leaders in idolatry. Some think that the Antichrist will come from Dan (Gen. 49:17). The tribes of **Joseph** and **Levi** are included in the list, **Joseph** doubtless taking the place of his son, Ephraim.

7:9 The people described in this section are Gentiles from **all nations, tribes, peoples, and tongues**. They stand **before the throne and before the Lamb with white robes** (the righteous acts of the saints, 19:8) and holding **palm branches**, which are a symbol of victory.

7:10 These are Gentiles who will be

saved during the Great Tribulation by trusting the Lord Jesus. In their song they celebrate their **salvation** and attribute it to their **God and to the Lamb**.

7:11, 12   The angels . . . and the elders and the four living creatures join in worshiping **God**, although the subject of redemption is missing from their praise. As the hymnwriter said, "Angels never felt the joy that our salvation brings." But they do chant His praises and pronounce Him worthy of seven distinct forms of **honor**.

7:13, 14 When **one of the elders** asked John **who** were **these** people **in white** and **where did they come from**, John confessed ignorance but a desire to know. Then the elder explained that they had **come out of the great tribulation, and** had **washed their robes and made them white in the blood of the Lamb**. "When we stand face to face with an inexplicable mystery," writes F. B. Meyer, "how comforting it is to be able to say in perfect faith, 'Thou knowest.'"

7:15 The elder went on to explain their present location and service. Bible students are not agreed as to whether this Gentile multitude is seen in heaven or on the millennial earth. The blessings described are true of either place. If the Millennium is in view, then the throne of God and **His temple** refer to the temple which will be located in Jerusalem during the Kingdom Age (Ezek. 40–44).

Notice the blessings that are described:

Perfect nearness: **Therefore they are before the throne of God**.

Perfect service: **and serve Him day and night in His temple**.

Perfect fellowship: **He who sits on the throne will dwell among them.**

7:16 Perfect satisfaction: **They shall neither hunger nor thirst anymore;**

Perfect security: **the sun shall not strike them, nor any heat;**

7:17 Perfect guidance: **for the Lamb who is in the midst of the throne will shepherd them and lead them to fountains of the waters of life** (NKJV margin).

Perfect joy: **God will wipe away every tear from their eyes.**

E.   The Seventh Seal and the Start of the Seven Trumpets (Chaps. 8, 9)

8:1 After the parenthesis of chapter 7, in which we saw two companies of Tribulation saints, we now come to **the seventh** and final **seal**. This is introduced by a thirty-minute **silence in heaven**, an awesome hush which precedes ever-deepening judgments.

8:2 No specific judgment is mentioned when the seventh seal is broken. The narrative moves directly to seven trumpet judgments. From this we infer that the seventh seal *consists of* the **seven trumpets**.

8:3, 4 The **angel** in this verse is often understood to be the Lord Jesus. He is called the Angel of Jehovah in the OT (Gen. 16:13; 31:11, 13; Judg. 6:22; Hos. 12:3, 4). **The prayers of all the saints** ascend to the Father through Him (Eph. 2:18). He takes **much incense** to **offer it with the prayers**. The **incense** speaks of the fragrance of His Person and work. By the time **the prayers** reach God the Father, they are perfectly flawless and perfectly effectual.

In the context, **the prayers** are those of Tribulation **saints**, beseeching God to punish their enemies, although the order is true of all prayer.

8:5 In answer to their prayers, **the angel . . . threw** flaming coals **to the earth**, causing loud explosions, **thunderings, lightnings and an earthquake**. As H. B. Swete says, "The prayers of the saints return to the earth in wrath."[17] Thus the seven trumpet judgments are introduced with violent disturbances of nature.

8:6 We have now come to the middle of the Tribulation. These trumpet judgments take us on to the time when Christ descends to the earth, destroys His foes, and ushers in His kingdom. The first four judgments affect man's natural environment; the last three affect man himself. Many commentators note the resemblance between these plagues and the ones which fell on Egypt (Ex. 7–12).

8:7 When the **first angel sounded, a third** part **of the earth** (NKJV margin), **trees**, and **grass** were **burned up** by **hail and fire . . . mingled with blood**. It is

best to take this literally as a terrible calamity on the areas from which man gets
most of his food.

8:8, 9 **Something like a great** flaming **mountain . . . was thrown into the
sea,** turning **a third of the sea** into
blood, destroying **a third** of the marine
life, and wrecking **a third of the ships**.
This would not only decrease man's local
food supply still further but would reduce his means of obtaining food from
distant places.

8:10, 11 This third trumpet signaled
the fall of a blazing **star** called **Wormwood,** causing **a third** of man's **water**
supply to become **bitter** at its sources.
Apparently the **bitter** water was also
poisonous, since **many men died**. It is
difficult to identify **Wormwood**. When
the trumpet sounds, these verses will be
all too clear to earth-dwellers. In the
study of prophecy, it is good to remember that there are many things that will
not be clear until they actually take
place.

8:12 It appears that the **sun, . . .
moon,** and **stars** will be damaged in such
a way that they will give only two-thirds
of their usual light. This fourth trumpet
resembles the plague of darkness in
Egypt.

8:13 An eagle (NKJV margin)[18] flying in mid-heaven pronounces a threefold **woe to the inhabitants of the earth,**
that is, those whose outlook is utterly
worldly, who are at home on the earth,
who are not true believers. The three remaining judgments are also known as
three woes because of their dire effect on
men.

9:1, 2 The **star fallen from heaven**
may be a **fallen** angel or even Satan himself. He had the **key** to the shaft of **the
bottomless pit** (the *abyss* in Greek). This
is the dwelling place of demons. When
he opened the entrance to the abyss, billows of **smoke** poured forth, as if from
a huge **furnace,** veiling the landscape in
darkness.

9:3, 4 Swarms of **locusts** emerged
from **the smoke,** capable of inflicting excruciating pain like the sting of **scorpions**. But their **power** was restricted.
They were forbidden **to harm** vegetation. Their victims were those **who** did
not have the seal of God on their fore-

heads, that is, all who were unbelievers.

9:5, 6 Although their sting was not
fatal, it inflicted **torment** that lasted **for
five months**. It was so intense that **men**
wanted **to die,** but they could not.
These locusts probably represent demons which, when released from the
pit, took possession of unsaved men and
women. This demon-possession caused
the most intense physical suffering and
mental torture, as it did with Legion in
Mark 5:1-20.

9:7 The description **of the locusts** is
designed to create an impression of conquest and victory. **Like horses prepared
for battle,** they were a conquering host.
Wearing **gold**-like **crowns,** they were authorized to rule in men's lives. With
human-appearing **faces,** they were creatures of intelligence.

9:8–10 With **hair like women's,**
they were attractive and seductive. With
lion-like **teeth,** they were ferocious and
cruel. With armor-like iron **breastplates,**
they were difficult to attack and destroy.
With **wings** that made a great sound,
they were terrifying and demoralizing.
Tails like scorpions equipped them to
torture both physically and mentally. **Their power . . . to hurt men five
months** meant unrelieved suffering.

9:11 **They had** a **king . . . whose
name in Hebrew is Abaddon** (destruction), **but in Greek . . . Apollyon** (destroyer). This is generally understood to
refer to Satan.

9:12 The first of three woes **is past**.
The worst is yet to come. The judgments
increase in intensity.

9:13–15 The mention of **the golden
altar which is before God** links the following judgment to the prayers of God's
oppressed people. The sixth trumpeter
releases **four angels who are bound at
the great river Euphrates**. These **four
angels,** perhaps demons, had been held
in readiness for this exact moment to go
forth and **kill a third of mankind**.

9:16, 17 Following them were **two**[19]
hundred million riders on horses with
breastplates that were **fiery red, hya-
cinth blue, and sulfur yellow**. The
horses' **heads** were like lions', and their
mouths belched **fire, smoke,** and sulfur
(**brimstone**).

9:18, 19 These three: **fire, smoke,**

and brimstone, represent **three plagues** which kill **a third of mankind**. Not only do the horses kill with **their mouths**, but they also wound with **their** serpentine **tails**.

There are many unanswered questions in this passage. Are the four angels in verse 14 the same as those in 7:1? Are the riders real men, or do they represent demons, diseases, or other destructive forces? What are the three plagues that are pictured by **fire, smoke**, and sulfur?

It is worth noticing that death is inflicted by the horses, not the riders. One writer suggests that the mighty army of horsemen might symbolize "some irresistible delusion of the devil, coming from the East." Hamilton Smith says:

> "Their power is in their mouth" may indicate that this delusion will be presented with all the persuasive eloquence of speech. But behind the delusion is the power of Satan, symbolized by their tails being like serpents.[20]

9:20, 21 Although two-thirds **of mankind** survived **these plagues, they did not repent**, but continued to bow down to **demons** and handmade **idols**, lifeless and impotent. They did not turn from **murders, sorceries** (drug related[21]), **sexual immorality**, and **thefts**. Punishment and suffering cannot change a sinner's character; only the new birth can do that.

F. The Mighty Angel and the Little Scroll (Chap. 10, 11)

10:1 John now sees **another mighty angel coming down from heaven**. The description leads many to believe that He is the Lord Jesus. He had a **rainbow on his head**, the sign of God's covenant. **His face was like the sun**, an expression of unveiled glory. His **feet** were like **pillars of fire**, the **pillars** speaking of strength and the **fire** of judgment.

10:2 He held **a little book** or scroll, no doubt a record of impending judgments. With **his right foot on the sea and his left foot on the land**, He claimed His right to worldwide dominion.

10:3–6 When He called out **with a loud voice, . . . seven thunders** sounded. Apparently John could understand the message of these thunders, but when he

was about to write, the angel forbade him. The angel then **swore by** God, the Creator, **that there should be delay no longer**.

10:7 **The mystery of God would be** fulfilled during the time of the seventh trumpet. **The mystery of God** has to do with God's plan to punish all evildoers and to usher in the kingdom of His Son.

10:8, 9 John was commanded to **eat** the **little book**, that is, he was to read and meditate on the judgments recorded in it.

10:10 As predicted by the angel, the scroll was **sweet as honey in** his **mouth, but bitter** in his **stomach**. For the believer, it is sweet to read of God's determination to glorify His Son where He was once crucified. It is sweet to read of the triumph of God over Satan and all his hosts. It is sweet to read of the time when the wrongs of earth will all be made right. But there is bitterness also connected with the study of prophecy. There is the bitterness of self-judgment which the prophetic Scriptures produce. There is the bitterness of viewing the judgments which must soon fall on apostate Judaism and Christendom. And there is the bitterness of contemplating the eternal doom of all who reject the Savior.

10:11 John was told that he **must prophesy again about many peoples, nations, tongues, and kings**. The remaining chapters of Revelation fulfill this mandate.

G. The Two Witnesses (11:1–14)

11:1, 2 John was now commanded to **measure the temple** and **the altar**, and to number the worshipers. Measuring here seems to carry the idea of preservation. He was *not* to measure **the court** of **the Gentiles** because it would be trampled by the nations **for forty-two months** — the latter half of the Tribulation Period (see Luke 21:24). **The temple** mentioned here is the one that will be standing in Jerusalem during the Tribulation. The act of numbering the worshipers may signify that God will preserve a remnant of worshipers for Himself. **The altar** pictures the means by which they will approach Him, that is, the work of Christ at Calvary.

11:3 God will raise up **two witnesses** during the last half of the Tribulation. **Clothed in sackcloth**, a symbol of mourning, they will cry out against the sins of the people and announce God's coming indignation.

11:4 The two witnesses are compared to **two olive trees** and **two lampstands**. As **olive trees** they are filled with the Spirit (oil). As **lampstands** they bear testimony to the truth of God in a day of darkness. (For an OT parallel see Zech. 4:2–14.)

11:5 For three and one half years, the witnesses are miraculously preserved from harm. **Fire** proceeding **from their mouth** consumes their foes, and even the effort **to harm them** is punished by death.

11:6 They **have power** to bring drought on the earth, **to turn** the waters **to blood, and to strike the earth with all plagues**. It is not surprising that they have been commonly associated with Moses and Elijah. Their power **to turn** the waters **to blood** and **to strike the earth with all plagues** reminds us of what Moses did in Egypt (Ex. 7:14–20; 8:1–12:29). Their power over fire and weather reminds us of Elijah's ministry (1 Kgs. 17:1; 18:41–45; 2 Kgs. 1:9–12).

McConkey says:

> They will warn the people who crowd the temple of the Man of Sin whom they come to worship. They will admonish them of the shortness of his time of triumph; of the coming of Jesus to destroy him; of the perils which the tribulation will bring; of the need of counting not their lives dear unto themselves when the test of life and death shall come; of their need to fear not him who can kill the body only but to fear Him who can cast both body and soul into hell; of the splendor and nearness of the King and His kingdom after they have suffered awhile; of the sureness that if they suffer with Him they shall reign with Him; and of the eternal peace, righteousness and glory that shall be theirs who endure unto the end, even though it may mean martyrdom in the great hour of trial through which they are passing. Mighty indeed will be their testimony from the Book.[22]

11:7 **When they finish their testimony, the beast** from the **bottomless pit** will **kill them**. This beast seems to be the same as the one in 13:8 — the head of the revived Roman Empire.

11:8 The **dead bodies** of the witnesses **lie in the street** of Jerusalem for three and one half days. Jerusalem is here **called Sodom** because of its pride, indulgence, prosperous ease, and indifference to the needs of others (see Ezek. 16:49). And it is called **Egypt** because of its idolatry, persecution, and enslavement to sin and unrighteousness.

11:9 People **from** all **nations** view **their dead bodies** but do **not allow** them to be buried, a tremendous indignity in almost all cultures.

11:10 Great rejoicing breaks out because their unpopular prophecies have been silenced, and people exchange **gifts**, much as they do today at Christmas time. The only prophets people love are dead ones.

11:11, 12 **After the three-and-a-half days, . . . God** raises them from the dead, much to the consternation of the populace, and takes them **to heaven** as **their enemies** watch.

11:13, 14 At **the same** time, Jerusalem is shaken by **a great earthquake**, one **tenth of the city** falls, and **seven thousand people** are **killed**. The survivors give **glory** to **God**, not genuine worship, but a grudging admission of His power. **The second woe is past**.

This does not mean that everything from 9:13 to 11:13 comprises the second woe. On the contrary, chapter 10 and 11:1–13 are a parenthesis between **the second woe** (sixth trumpet) and **the third woe** (seventh trumpet).

H. The Seventh Trumpet (11:15–19)

11:15 The blowing of the seventh trumpet reveals that the Great Tribulation is over and the reign of Christ has begun. **The kingdoms**[23] **of this world have become the kingdoms of our Lord and of His Christ, and He shall reign forever and ever!**

11:16, 17 Falling **on their faces** before **God**, the **twenty-four elders** express **thanks** to Him because He has assumed His **great power** and inaugurated His reign.

11:18 The unbelieving **nations** are **angry** with Him, and try to prevent His coronation. But now the time has come for Him to be angry with them, to judge those who do not have spiritual life, to **destroy** the destroyers. And it is time for the Lord to **reward** His own, **prophets** and people, **small and great**.

11:19 God has not forgotten **His covenant** with His people, Israel. When **the temple of God** is **opened in heaven, the ark of His covenant** appears, a symbol that all He promised to Israel will come to pass. There are **lightnings, noises, thunderings, an earthquake, and great hail**.

I. The Key Figures in the Tribulation (Chaps. 12–15)

12:1 **A great sign appeared in heaven**, namely, **a woman clothed with the sun, with the moon under her feet, and on her head a garland of twelve stars**. The **woman** is Israel. The **sun, moon** and **stars** depict the glory and dominion which has been promised to her in the coming kingdom, just as they pictured Joseph's ultimate rule over his father, mother, and brothers (Gen. 37:9–11).

12:2 The woman is **in labor**, awaiting the **birth** of a baby. Much of the history of Israel is telescoped in these verses, with no indication that time gaps exist between events, or that the events are necessarily in chronological order.

12:3 A second **sign** in heaven is **a fiery red dragon with seven heads and ten horns** and a diadem on each head. The **dragon** is Satan, but since the description parallels that of the revived Roman Empire in 13:1, it may be Satan energizing that world power.

12:4, 5 With a swish of **his tail**, the dragon sweeps **a third of the stars of heaven . . . to the earth**, a possible reference to war in heaven which takes place in the middle of the Tribulation and which results in fallen angels being cast from heaven to earth (see vv. 8, 9).

The dragon is ready **to devour** the **Child as soon as** He is **born** — fulfilled in the attempt of Herod the Great, vassal of Rome, to destroy the newborn King of the Jews. The **male Child** is clearly Jesus, destined **to rule all the nations with a rod of iron**. The record here jumps from His birth to His Ascension.

12:6 The present Church Age is

passed over between verses 5 and 6. In the middle of the Tribulation, a portion of the nation of Israel flees to a secret place of refuge in **the wilderness** (some think it is Petra). These people remain in hiding for three and one half years.

12:7 **War** breaks out **in heaven** with **Michael and his angels** on one side and **the dragon and his angels** on the other. This is in the middle of the Tribulation. Michael, the archangel, is associated with the affairs of the nation of Israel (Dan. 12:1).

12:8, 9 The dragon is so thoroughly defeated that he loses any right of access to **heaven**. He and his minions are **cast** down **to the earth**. This is not his final fate, however (see 20:1–3, 10). Notice John's description of him: **the great dragon, that serpent of old, the Devil, Satan**, the one **who deceives the whole world**.

12:10 The eviction of the dragon is followed by **a loud** cry **in heaven** that God's triumph and the day of His people's conquest have come. This anticipates the Millennial Kingdom. In the meantime, it is a glorious event that **the accuser of our brethren . . . has been cast down**.

12:11 The announcement continues. Persecuted Jewish believers **overcame** the evil one **by the blood of the Lamb and by the word of their testimony**. Their victory was based on the death of Christ and **their testimony** to the value of that death. In faithfulness to Him, they sealed **their testimony** with their blood.

12:12, 13 The **heavens** can **rejoice** over the dragon's departure, but it is bad news for **the earth and the sea! The devil . . . knows** his **time** is **short** and he is determined to pour out his wrath as widely as possible. The dragon's spleen is vented especially against Israel, the nation from which the Messiah came.

12:14 The faithful Jewish remnant is **given two wings of a great eagle**, enabling it to escape quickly to its **wilderness** hideout. (Some have conjectured that these **wings** speak of a great Air Force.) There the remnant is cared for and protected from the serpent's attacks for three and one half years (**a time, times, and half a time**).

12:15, 16 In an effort to foil Israel's escape, **the serpent** causes a great **flood** to follow the people, but an earthquake swallows the water and the devil is outwitted.

12:17 Furious over this humiliation, he seeks to wreak vengeance on Jews who had remained in the land — Jews who show the reality of their faith by keeping **the commandments of God** and by bearing **testimony** to **Jesus**.

13:1 Chapter 13 introduces us to two great beasts: one **beast rising up out of the sea**, and one out of the earth or land, that is, the land of Israel. There is no doubt that these beasts symbolize men who will play prominent roles during the Tribulation Period. They combine the features of the four beasts of Daniel 7:3-7. The first beast is the head of the revived Roman Empire, which will exist in a ten-kingdom form. He rises **out of the sea**, a type of the Gentile nations. He has **ten horns**. Daniel predicted that the Roman Empire would be revived in a ten-kingdom form (Dan. 7:24). He has **seven heads**. In 17:9, 10 these are said to be seven kings, a possible reference to seven different types of rulers or seven different stages of the empire. He has **ten** diadems **on his horns**. These speak of the power to rule, which was given to him by the dragon, Satan. He has a **blasphemous name on his heads**, and he makes claims for himself as if he were God and not a mere man.

13:2 **The beast** is **like a leopard, his feet like** a bear's, and **his mouth like** a lion's. In Daniel 7, the **leopard** symbolizes Greece; the **bear** is a type of Medo-Persia; and the **lion** represents Babylon. The revived Roman Empire thus resembles its predecessors in that it is swift to conquer like **a leopard**, powerful as **a bear**, and greedy as **a lion**. In short, it combines all the evil features of the preceding world empires. The empire and its ruler receive supernatural strength from Satan.

13:3 The beast has a mortal **wound** in one of its heads. Scofield explains: "Fragments of the ancient Roman Empire have never ceased to exist as separate kingdoms. It was the imperial form of government which ceased; the one head wounded to death."[24] The **deadly**

wound is **healed**. In other words, the empire is revived with an emperor as head, namely, **the beast**.

13:4 **The beast** is **worshiped** by men. They are not only amazed at him; they actually worship him as God. They also worship **the dragon**.

13:5, 6 The beast makes proud boasts and utters unspeakable **blasphemies**. He is allowed **to make war** (NKJV margin) **for forty-two months**. He speaks with callous irreverence against God's **name, His tabernacle**, and the hosts of **heaven**.

13:7 He makes **war** with God's people and overcomes many of them. They die rather than submit to him. His rule extends over all the world — the last world empire before Christ's Reign.

13:8 Those who are not true believers readily **worship** the beast. Because they never trusted Christ, their names were never **written in the Book of Life of the Lamb**. And because their names are not found among those of the redeemed, they are given over to error. They would not believe the truth; now they believe a lie.

13:9 This should be a warning to everyone to accept the light of God's word when it is available. The consequence of rejecting light is to have light denied.

13:10 True believers are assured that their persecutors **shall go into captivity** and **be killed with the sword**. This enables the **saints** to wait in **patience** and **faith**.

13:11 The second **beast** is another prominent figure of the Tribulation Period. He works in close cooperation with the first beast, even organizing an international campaign for the worship of the first beast and of a huge idol representing the Roman emperor. The second beast comes **up out of the earth** or land. If the land of Israel is in view, then this leader is almost surely a Jew. He is the False Prophet (see 16:13; 19:20; 20:10). He has **two horns like a lamb**, giving the appearance of gentleness and harmlessness, but also suggesting that He impersonates the Lamb of God. He speaks **like a dragon**, indicating that he is directly inspired and empowered by Satan.

13:12–14 He exercises all the authority of the first beast, meaning that the Roman emperor gives him unlimited authority to act on his behalf. He has supernatural powers, even causing fire to fall from heaven. The purpose of his miracles, of course, is to deceive the people into worshiping a man as God.

13:15 He gives animation to the great image, the abomination of desolation, so that it can actually speak. The penalty for refusing to worship it is death.

13:16 The second beast insists that people indicate their allegiance to the Roman emperor by wearing the mark of the beast on their right hand or on their foreheads.

13:17 In addition to this mark, the beast has a name and a mystical number. Unless a person takes the mark, name, or number of the beast, he will not be able to buy or sell. It is an effort to force men by economic means to forsake Christ for idolatry. This will be a severe test, but true believers will prefer death to renouncing their Savior.

13:18 The number of the beast is 666. Six is the number of man. The fact that it is one less than seven may suggest that man has fallen short of the glory or perfection of God. The three sixes are a trinity of evil.

One of the biggest questions raised in connection with chapter 13 is whether the *first* or *second* beast is the Antichrist. Basically, the argument for the first being the Antichrist is that he insists on being worshiped as God. Those who hold that the second beast is the Antichrist point out that no Jew would ever accept a Gentile as Messiah, and that since the second beast is a Jew, he must therefore be the false messiah.

14:1 The Lamb is seen standing on Mount Zion with one hundred and forty-four thousand followers, all of whom were sealed on their foreheads. This looks forward to the time when the Lord Jesus will come back to the earth and stand in Jerusalem with this group of believers from each of the twelve tribes of Israel. The one hundred and forty-four thousand are the same ones mentioned in chapter 7. They are now about to enter the kingdom of Christ.

14:2, 3 John hears music coming from heaven like the voice of many waters, and like the sound of loud thunder, and like harpists playing their harps. Only the hundred and forty-four thousand could learn that song.

14:4, 5 They are described as virgins, those who have not defiled themselves with women. They had kept themselves free from the terrible idolatry and immorality of this period and followed the Lamb in unquestioning obedience and devotion. Pentecost says, "They are called 'the firstfruits unto God and to the Lamb', that is, they are the first of the harvest of the tribulation period that will come into the millennium to populate the millennial earth."[25] They did not accept the lie of the Antichrist — that a mere man was to be worshiped. They were blameless as far as their steadfast confession of Christ was concerned.

14:6, 7 The angel flying in midheaven with the everlasting gospel seems to correspond with Matthew 24:14: "And this gospel of the kingdom will be preached in all the world as a witness to all the nations, and then the end will come." The subject of the gospel is given in verse 7. Men are commanded to fear God rather than the beast; to give glory to Him rather than to the idolatrous image; and to worship Him rather than a mere man. Of course, there is only one gospel — the good news of salvation through faith in Christ. But there are different emphases in different dispensations. During the Great Tribulation, the gospel will seek to turn men away from worship of the beast and prepare them for Christ's kingdom on earth.

14:8 The second angel announces Babylon's fall. This anticipates chapters 17 and 18. Babylon represents apostate Judaism and apostate Christendom, which will be a vast commercial and religious conglomerate with headquarters in Rome. All nations will have become drunk with the wine of the wrath of her fornication.

14:9, 10 We can fix the time of the third angel's pronouncement as being at the middle of the Tribulation, which is the same as the beginning of the Great Tribulation. The angel warns that any who agree to beast-worship in any of its forms will suffer God's **wrath** now and eternally. **The wine of** His **wrath** will be **poured out** on the earth during the Great Tribulation. But that will be only a foretaste of the pangs of eternal hell, where unbelievers **shall be tormented with fire and brimstone**.

14:11 This verse reminds us that hell consists of eternal and conscious punishment. The Bible never teaches that the wicked dead will be annihilated. **The smoke of their torment ascends** perpetually, and there is **no** relief **day or night**.

14:12 This will be a time when the saints will be called to endure patiently the savagery of the beast, to obey **God** by refusing to worship a man or an idol, and to hold fast their confession of **faith in Jesus**. The eventual doom of the wicked (vv. 9–11) serves to encourage the faithful to endure.

14:13 Believers **who die** during this period will not miss the blessings of the Millennial Kingdom. Man says, "Blessed are the living." God says, **"Blessed are the dead who die in the Lord."** And, **"Their works follow them."** Everything done for Christ and in His name for others will be richly rewarded — every kindness, sacrificial gift, prayer, tear, word of testimony.

14:14 If we compare this passage with Matthew 13:39–43 and 25:31–46, we learn that the harvest of the earth takes place at the Second Advent of our Lord. Here He is said to do the reaping; in Matthew 13:39 the angels are the reapers. Both are true; Christ does it through the agency of angels.

Christ is here seen descending **on a white cloud, . . . having on His head a golden crown, and in His hand a sharp sickle**.

14:15 An **angel** from **the temple** tells Him to **thrust in** His **sickle** because **the harvest of the earth is ripe**. This should not be looked on as an order; angels have no right to command God. Rather it is an entreaty or a message relayed from God the Father.

14:16 There are two ways of understanding this first harvest. First of all, it may picture the gathering of tribulation *believers* to enter the Millennium. According to this view, it would correspond to

the good seeds of Matthew 13, that is, the sons of the kingdom. Or it may be a harvest of *judgment*. If this is the case, the subjects of the judgment may be Gentiles, since Israel seems to be in view in the next harvest (vv. 17–20).

14:17 Now the record turns to the last terrible judgments that will fall on the unbelieving portion of the nation of Israel, the vine of the earth (see Ps. 80:8; Isa. 5:1–7; Jer. 2:21; 6:9). An **angel** comes **out of the temple which is in heaven**, equipped with **a sharp sickle**.

14:18 **Another angel** gives the signal to begin reaping. This angel has **power over fire**, which may symbolize the judgment to follow.

14:19 The mature grapes are gathered and thrown **into the great winepress of the wrath of God**. The trampling of grapes in the process of making wine is used here as a picture of crushing judgment.

14:20 This vintage takes place **outside the city** of Jerusalem, perhaps in the Valley of Jehoshaphat. The carnage will be so great that **blood** will flow in a stream 180 miles long and as deep as **the horses' bridles**. This would reach from Jerusalem to the south of Edom.

15:1 **Another sign in heaven** involves **seven angels having the seven last plagues**, which, when loosed, mark the completion of **the wrath of God**. From this we know that we are now toward the end of the Tribulation.

15:2 John sees a great company of people in heaven, **standing on a sea of glass mingled with fire**. He recognizes them as those who refused to worship **the beast** or **his image**. Doubtless they were martyred as a result.

15:3, 4 But now they are in heaven, singing **the song of Moses . . . and the song of the Lamb**, composed almost entirely of quotations from the OT. They testify to the righteousness of God's **judgments** in anticipation of what He is about to do to their murderers on earth. They praise **God Almighty** for His **works** and **ways**. In the context, this means His acts of judgment, though it may be applied to all His works and ways, of course. **King of the saints** should read **King of the** *nations* (NKJV margin).[26]

The song of Moses celebrated God's

redemption of His people from slavery in Egypt. **The song of the Lamb** celebrates the final deliverance from Satan and all foes of spiritual life. Thus, as A. T. Pierson has so aptly pointed out, "They mark the two bounds of Redemption history, and between them lies the whole history of God's ransomed people."[27]

God's judgments on the earth have shown Him to be a God of holiness. They will cause **all nations** to **fear, glorify**, and **worship** Him.

15:5 **After these things** John sees **the temple of the tabernacle of the testimony in heaven . . . opened**. This is apparently the heavenly reality of which the earthly temple was a pattern or copy (Heb. 9:23). It refers especially to the Most Holy Place.

15:6 **Seven angels** emerge, **clothed in pure, bright linen, and having their chests girded with golden bands**. This means that they are equipped to execute righteous judgment by which God will be glorified. These **angels** are about to unleash **the seven** last **plagues**.

15:7 **One of the four living creatures** hands a bowl to each angel. These **bowls** contain the final judgments of the Great Tribulation which affect all of God's enemies, not just a portion of them.

15:8 The fact that **no one** can **enter the temple till** these **seven plagues** are **completed** may mean that no priestly intercession can now delay God's wrath.

J. The Seven Bowl Judgments (Chap. 16)

16:1, 2 **A loud voice from the temple** orders **the seven angels** to **go and pour out the bowls of the wrath of God on the earth**. These judgments are similar to the trumpet judgments in nature and sequence but they are greater in intensity. The first bowl causes **foul and loathsome** sores to break out on **those who worshiped** the beast and **his image**.

16:3 The second plague turns the waters of the **sea** to **blood**, like that **of a dead man**, and all marine life dies.

16:4 The third **bowl** causes all **water** sources to become **blood**.

16:5, 6 At this point, **the angel of the waters** defends the justice of God's judgments. Men are only receiving the just recompense of their own sinful deeds. They had **shed blood** in abundance; now they are rewarded with **blood to drink** instead of water. **It is their just due**.

16:7 **The altar** probably symbolizes the souls of martyred saints (6:9). They had waited long and patiently for their persecutors to be punished.

16:8, 9 The fourth plague causes men to suffer severe sunburn or solar radiation. This does **not**, however, cause them to **repent**. Instead they curse **God** for sending this scorching heat on them.

16:10, 11 **The fifth angel** pours **out his** plague of **darkness** on the **kingdom of the beast**. This adds to men's suffering because they are not able to travel for relief from the preceding afflictions. But it does not soften their hearts. They only become more settled in their hatred of God.

16:12 When the sixth bowl is poured out, the **water** of the **Euphrates** dries up, permitting the armies **from the east** to march toward the land of Israel.

16:13, 14 John sees **three** frog-like **spirits** issuing from **the mouth of the dragon, . . . the beast and . . . the false prophet**, Satan's counterfeit trinity. These are demonic **spirits, performing** miracles to deceive the world's rulers, and to lure them to a climactic **battle** on the **great day of God Almighty**.

16:15 At the mention of that battle, the Lord interjects a special blessing on the tribulation saints, those who are watching for His Return, and who have kept themselves pure from the idolatrous worship of that day. He will come to the unsaved **as a thief**, unexpectedly and causing loss.

16:16 The armies of the world will gather at a **place called in Hebrew Armageddon** (NKJV margin, Megiddo).[28] This is commonly associated with the Plain of Esdraelon, with Megiddo on the southern rim. It is reported that Napoleon called it the cockpit of the world, that is, the ideal battlefield.

16:17 That this is the final bowl judgment is indicated by the **seventh angel's** announcement, **"It is done!"** The wrath of God is finished as far as the Tribulation Period is concerned.

16:18 When the last bowl is poured out, there are violent convulsions of nature: explosions, **thunderings, lightnings,** and an **earthquake** of unprecedented proportions.

16:19 **The great city** of **Babylon, divided into three parts,** drinks **the cup** of God's fury. He has not forgotten her idolatry, cruelty, and religious confusion. At this same time **the cities of the nations** are laid flat.

16:20 **Every island** and **the mountains** disappear as the earth reels.

16:21 One-hundred pound hailstones bombard the earth, but **men** blaspheme **God** rather than repent.

K. The Fall of Babylon the Great (Chaps. 17, 18)

17:1, 2 **One of the seven angels** invites John to witness **the judgment of the great harlot.** This is a great religious and commercial system with headquarters in Rome. Many believe that chapter 17 describes religious Babylon and chapter 18 the commercial aspect. Religious Babylon certainly includes apostate Christendom, both Protestant and Catholic. It may well represent the ecumenical church. Notice the description. The **harlot sits on many waters,** controlling great areas of the Gentile world. **The kings of the earth** have **committed fornication** with her; she has seduced political leaders with her compromise and intrigue. **The inhabitants of the earth** have become **drunk with the wine of her fornication;** vast numbers have come under her evil influence and have been reduced to staggering wretchedness.

17:3 The apostate church is seen **sitting on a scarlet beast.** We have already noted in chapter 13 that this beast is the revived Roman Empire (and sometimes the head of that empire). The beast is **full of** blasphemous **names** and has **seven heads and ten horns.**

17:4 For a while the false church seems to dominate the empire. She sits in full celestial state, wearing the symbols of her vast wealth and displaying **a golden cup full of** her idolatry and immorality.

17:5 **A name** of **mystery** is **on her forehead: Babylon the great, the mother of harlots and of the abominations of**

the earth. This is the church that has shed the blood of Christian martyrs down through the centuries, and is still doing it. She is drunk with their blood.

17:6 Like many others, John **marveled** when he **saw the woman,** intoxicated **with the blood of the saints.** This refers to **the saints** of all eras of church history, but especially to **the martyrs of Jesus** during the Tribulation.

17:7, 8 **The angel** offers to explain to John **the mystery of the woman and of the beast. The beast** that John **saw was** (the Roman Empire existed in the past); it **is not** (it broke up and no longer exists as a world-empire today); it **will ascend out of the bottomless pit** (it will reappear in a particularly diabolical form); **and go to perdition** (it will be utterly and finally destroyed). The revival of the empire and the appearance of its charismatic leader will cause the world of unbelievers to **marvel.**

17:9 The angel says that this calls for a **mind** with **wisdom. The seven heads are seven mountains on which the woman sits.** A traditional interpretation is that the harlot has her headquarters in Rome, which is built on seven hills.

17:10 Some commentators explain these **seven kings** as seven forms of Roman government; others explain them as seven literal emperors. Others say that the kings represent great world powers: Egypt, Assyria, Babylon, Persia, Greece, Rome, and the future revived Roman Empire.

17:11 **The eighth** king has been variously identified as the head of the revived Roman Empire and the Antichrist. The exact meaning of this prophecy may never be perfectly clear until it is fulfilled.

17:12 **The ten horns** may symbolize the future **kings** who will serve under the Roman **beast.** They will rule **for one hour,** that is, a short time (see v. 10b).

17:13 The ten kings unanimously yield **their power and authority** to the Roman **beast.** In other words, ten countries (or governments) surrender their national sovereignty to him.

17:14 This ten-kingdom empire goes to war against the Lord Jesus when He returns to earth at the end of the

Tribulation. But they meet their Waterloo in this battle. Though He is **the Lamb, He is** also **Lord of lords and King of kings**. His followers **are called, chosen, and faithful**.

17:15 The angel goes on to explain that **the waters** in verse 1 are **peoples, multitudes, nations, and tongues. The harlot sits** on **the waters** in the sense that she dominates vast segments of the populace.

17:16 It appears that the revived Roman Empire allows itself to be controlled, or at least influenced by the harlot church for a while. Then, however, it throws off this intolerable yoke and destroys her. The hated **harlot** is stripped, consumed, and burned by the beast on which she sat.

17:17 God is behind the scenes in all of this. It is He who causes the kingdoms to unite under the Roman beast and then to turn against the harlot. It is all **to fulfill His** sovereign **purpose**.

17:18 That great city is Mystery Babylon, ruling **over the kings of the earth**. But as we have seen, the woman has her headquarters in Rome.

18:1 Chapter 18 consists primarily of a funeral song, celebrating the fall of Babylon. As mentioned, this refers to the harlot church which is not only a vast religious system but perhaps the greatest commercial establishment in the world. It apparently controls the world market.

When **another angel** with **great authority** comes **down from heaven** to break the news, it is as if the lights go on. **His glory** illuminates **the earth**.

18:2 Babylon the great has **fallen** and its ruins have become the haunt for **demons, every foul spirit**, and **unclean**, hateful **birds**.

18:3 The reason for her fall is the utter corruption she has practiced with the nations and their **merchants**. She has made **all the nations** drunk with her passionate **fornication**.

18:4 Another voice from heaven warns God's people to **come out of** the doomed system on the eve of its destruction. Intercourse with her would mean sharing **her plagues**.

18:5, 6 Her sins have piled up **to heaven, and God has remembered her iniquities**, and is lashing out against

them. She is to receive **double** payment for her wicked deeds, not from God's people, but from the angel who is the instrument of His vengeance.

18:7 Her torment and sorrow will be proportionate to her self-aggrandizement and luxurious lifestyle. She thinks of herself **as queen**, sitting on top of everything and safe from **sorrow**.

18:8 Her judgment **will come in one day** and will involve **death and mourning and famine**. It is the mighty **Lord God** who will punish her **with fire**.

18:9, 10 The kings of the earth will **lament** over the **burning** of their former mistress. Their mourning, however, is not unselfish. They sorrow over the loss of pleasure and luxury. **Standing at a distance**, they marvel at the extent of **her torment** and the suddenness of her end.

18:11–13 The merchants mourn principally because their hope of gain is gone. **No one buys their merchandise anymore**.

The list of products in which Babylon traded seems to compass world trade: precious metals, jewelry, fabrics, **wood, ivory, bronze, iron, marble**, spices, perfumes, **wine, oil**, grains, livestock, **chariots, and bodies and souls of men**. Both the apostate church and the business world are guilty of trafficking in the **souls of men**, the church by the sale of indulgences, etc., and the business world by exploitation.

18:14 The businessmen, addressing the fallen system, lament that its hoped-for profits have vanished, and its riches and splendor have disappeared suddenly and forever.

18:15, 16 Like the kings, **the merchants . . . stand** aghast, **weeping and wailing** that such profits were lost in an hour. They recount the former luxury of the city, how the people were finely **clothed** and **adorned with** jewels.

18:17, 18 Now all that opulence has suddenly come **to nothing**, and the threat of a great depression hangs low. Those engaged in maritime commerce stand **at a distance** and cry, "What could ever compare with **this great city?**"

18:19 They throw **dust on their heads**, weep and wail over the city that had enriched the world maritime industry and now is ruined **in one hour**.

18:20 But while all these godless tears are being shed on earth, there is great rejoicing in **heaven**. At last **God has avenged** His **saints** (NKJV margin), **apostles**, and **prophets**. He has judged Babylon for the way she treated His people.

18:21 **A mighty angel** throws **a stone like a great millstone . . . into the sea**, a graphic picture of the final doom of **Babylon**.

18:22 **The sound of** its former activities, whether music, manufacturing, or milling is silenced forever.

18:23 Every **light** is extinguished and never again will the joy of a wedding be present. Why? Because Babylon's leaders hoodwinked **all the nations** with their **sorcery**.

18:24 She was guilty of **the blood of** God's **saints**, of **all** believers **who were slain** for their faith. Now He is rewarding her in full measure.

L. The Coming of Christ and His Millennial Kingdom (19:1–20:9)

19:1 **After these things** John hears a **great multitude in heaven**, praising the Lord for His righteous punishment of the great harlot. The song extols Him as **the Lord our God** to whom belong **salvation, glory, honor, and power**.

19:2 It vindicates Him for His destruction of **the great harlot**. It was consistent with His attributes of truth and righteousness that He should punish the whore for **her fornication** and for her cold-blooded slaughter of **His servants**.

19:3 The perpetual **smoke** ascending from the funeral pyre evokes a second **"Alleluia!"**, or "Praise the Lord."

19:4 **The twenty–four elders and the four living creatures** concur with a loud **"Amen!"** and a heartfelt **"Alleluia!"**

19:5 **A voice . . . from the throne** calls on all God's **servants** to join in magnifying the Lord for destroying the monstrous Babylon.

19:6 Now another song breaks out in heaven, as "loud as many waters' noise, loud as thunders to the ear." A great **"Alleluia"** swells in celebration of the reign of the **Lord God Omnipotent**!

19:7, 8 The Tribulation is past. Bab-ylon has been judged. Now **the marriage of the Lamb has come**. The church, the **wife** of Christ, has prepared **herself** for the soul-thrilling occasion. She is **arrayed in fine linen, clean and bright**, which is explained as symbolizing **the righteous acts of the saints**.[29]

19:9 An angel instructs John to **write** a benediction for all **who are called to the marriage supper of the Lamb**. The church is the heavenly Bride; those who are invited guests are the rest of the redeemed. The angel reinforces the importance of the blessing by insisting that it represents **the true sayings of God**.

19:10 John falls before the angel's **feet** in an act of **worship**, but is forbidden. Only God is to be worshiped. The angel is a **fellow servant** of John and of all who hold **the testimony of Jesus**. Then the angel adds, **"For the testimony of Jesus is the spirit of prophecy."** This means that the true purpose **of prophecy** is to bear testimony to the Person and work **of Jesus**. "Prophecy," says C. C. Ryrie, "is designed to unfold the loveliness of Jesus."[30]

The angel wanted men to **worship** God the Son, concerning whom he was bearing witness.

19:11 Finally we reach the event to which the rest of the book has been looking forward, the glorious coming of Christ to earth in order to put down His enemies and set up His kingdom. This is not the Rapture of the church; there Christ comes to the air *for* His saints. Here He comes to the earth *with* His saints.

Notice the description of our Lord. He is sitting on **a white horse**; here obviously it is a war horse since He is coming to conquer His enemies. His name is **Faithful and True**. He is **faithful** to His promises and **true** to His own character. **In righteousness He judges and makes war**. He can only rule over a kingdom where the people are willing to live under a reign of **righteousness**. Therefore He must first remove all things that offend.

19:12 **His eyes** are **like a flame of fire**, suggesting the penetrating power of His judgment. He can detect all rebellion and unbelief. **On His head** are **many** diadems. Others may wear the crown of victory, but only the Lord Jesus is spoken of as wearing the diadem of royalty. **He** has a **name** inscribed which **no one** knows **except Himself**. There are mysteries connected with the Person of Christ that no created being will ever be able to comprehend.

19:13 He is **clothed in a robe dipped in blood**, not the blood He shed on Calvary's cross, but the **blood** of His enemies whom He tramples in the winepress of the wrath of God. He is called by the **name, "The Word of God."** A *word* is a means of expressing thought. In Christ, God has fully expressed Himself to man.

19:14 He is accompanied by **the armies** of **heaven**, which are **clothed in fine linen** and riding **on white horses**. These armies are no doubt made up of the saints, but it is noteworthy that they are not required to fight. The Lord Jesus defeats His foes unaided.

19:15 From **His mouth** issues **a sharp sword** with which He strikes **the nations**. He comes to **rule them with a rod of iron** and to tread **the winepress of the fierceness and wrath of Almighty God**.

19:16 On His robe and on His thigh is **written:**

KING OF KINGS
AND LORD OF LORDS

Our Jesus is the Supreme Ruler; all others must submit to His reign.

19:17, 18 The great supper of God (NKJV margin) is the destruction of God's remaining foes before the kingdom is set up. The vultures are summoned to attend! They will feed on the carcasses of those who are slain by the Lord — people from every class of society, **both small and great**.

19:19, 20 In a desperate attempt to prevent Christ from taking the reins of government (Ps. 2), **the beast** allies with the **armies** of the world **to make war against** the Lord **and against His army**. But it is a futile attempt. Both **the beast** and **the false prophet** are **captured** and hurled **alive into the lake of fire burning with brimstone**.

19:21 The rest of the rebels are **killed with the sword** of the Lord, their bodies providing ample carrion for the vultures. The sword is an allusion to the word of God (see Eph. 6:17; 2 Thess. 2:8; Heb. 4:12; Rev. 1:16; 2:12, 16).

This brings us to the end of the Great Tribulation.

20:1 Before the Millennium begins, Satan must be restrained. To accomplish this, **an angel** comes **down from heaven** with **the key to the** abyss **and a** huge **chain in his hand**.

In one sense, our Lord bound Satan when He came to earth (Matt. 12:29). So this is another stage in his binding.

20:2 The angel seized Satan **and bound him for a thousand years**. John lists four names of the tempter: **dragon, serpent, Devil** (accuser), **and Satan** (adversary).

20:3 During the Millennium, the archenemy is confined to **the bottomless pit**. The abyss is sealed **so that he** cannot go forth to **deceive the nations**. Toward the end of Christ's Reign, **he** will **be released for** his last brief rebellion (vv. 7–10).

20:4 John now sees people enthroned in heaven with authority to rule. These are saints of the Church Age who will reign **with Christ** as His Bride. John also sees a company of martyrs, who had refused to take the mark of **the beast**. These are clearly tribulation saints who died for their faith. Both companies will reign **with Christ** during the golden age of peace and prosperity.

20:5 The first part of verse 5 must be understood as a parenthesis. **The rest of the dead** refers to unbelievers of all ages who will be raised at the end of the Millennium to stand before the Judgment of the Great White Throne.

The statement **This is the first resurrection** refers back to verse 4. **The first resurrection** is not a single event. It describes the **resurrection** of the righteous at various times. It includes **the resurrection** of Christ (1 Cor. 15:23), **the resurrection** of those who are Christ's when He raptures the church (1 Thess. 4:13–18), **the resurrection** of the two witnesses whose bodies will lie in the streets (Rev. 11:11), and **the resurrection** of tribulation saints who are described here (see also Dan. 12:2a). In other words, **the first resurrection** includes **the resurrection** of Christ and of all true believers, though they are raised at different times. It occurs in several stages.

20:6 Those who participate **in the first resurrection** are **blessed** because they will not be included in **the second death**, when all unbelievers will be cast into the lake of fire (v. 14). True believers **shall be priests of God and of Christ and shall reign with Him a thousand years**.

20:7, 8 When the thousand years **have expired, Satan will be released from** confinement, **and will go out** to **the four corners of the earth** in order to **deceive the nations** that are hostile to Christ, here called **Gog and Magog**. This reference to **Gog and Magog** must not be confused with a similar reference in Ezekiel 38 and 39. There Magog is a great land north of Israel, and Gog is its ruler. Here the words refer to the nations of the world in general. In Ezekiel, the setting is premillennial; here it is postmillennial.

20:9 After recruiting an army of ungodly rebels, the devil marches against Jerusalem, **the beloved city**. But **fire** comes **down from God out of heaven** and consumes the troops.

M. The Judgment of Satan and All Unbelievers (20:10–15)

20:10 **The devil** himself is **cast into the lake of fire** to join **the beast and the false prophet**.

It may seem surprising that Satan would be able to assemble an army of unbelievers at the end of the Millennium. However, it should be remembered that all children born during Christ's Reign will be born in sin and will need to be saved. Not all will accept Him as rightful King, and these will scatter throughout the earth, trying to get as far away from Jerusalem as possible.

Note that **the beast and the false prophet** are still in hell after one thousand years. This disproves the doctrine of annihilation, as does the statement, **And they will be tormented day and night forever and ever**.

20:11 Next we are introduced to **the great white throne** judgment. It is **great** because of the issues involved and **white** because of the perfection and purity of the decisions handed down. The Lord Jesus is sitting as Judge (John 5:22, 27). The expression **from whose face the earth and the heaven fled away** indicates

that this judgment takes place in eternity, after the destruction of the present creation (2 Pet. 3:10).

20:12 **The dead, small and great**, stand **before God**. These are the unbelievers of all ages. Two sets of **books** are **opened. The Book of Life** contains the names of all who have been redeemed by the precious blood of Christ. The other books contain a detailed record of the **works** of the unsaved. No one who appears at this judgment is registered in **the Book of Life**. The fact that his name is missing *condemns* him, but the record of his evil **works** determines the *degree* of his punishment.

20:13 **The sea** will yield up the bodies of those who have been buried in it. The graves, here represented by **Death**, will deliver up the bodies of all the unsaved who have been interred. **Hades** will give up the souls of all who died in unbelief. The bodies and souls will be reunited to stand before the Judge.

Just as there will be degrees of reward in heaven, so there will be degrees of punishment in hell. This will be based on their **works**.

20:14 When we read that **Death and Hades** are **cast into the lake of fire**, it means the complete persons: spirit, soul, and body. The text explains **that this is the second death**, and the NKJV margin adds, *the lake of fire*.

There is a difference between Hades and hell. For the unconverted who have died, Hades is a disembodied state of conscious punishment. It is a sort of holding tank, an intermediate condition where they await the Judgment of the Great White Throne.

For believers who have died, Hades is a state of disembodied blessedness in heaven, awaiting the resurrection and glorification of the body. When Jesus died, He went to Paradise (Luke 23:43), which Paul equates with the third heaven (2 Cor. 12:2, 4), the dwelling place of God. In Acts 2:27 the Lord's disembodied state is called Hades. God did not leave His soul in Hades, but clothed it with a glorified body.

Hell is the final prison of the wicked dead. It is the same as the lake of fire, Gehenna, and the second death.

20:15 The deciding factor at this judgment is whether one's name is **written in the Book of Life**. Actually if a person's name had been inscribed there, he would have already been a part of the first resurrection. So this verse applies only to those who stand before the Great White Throne.

N. The New Heaven and the New Earth (21:1–22:5)

21:1 There is a question whether chapters 21 and 22 deal with the Eternal State alone or whether they alternate between the Millennium and the Eternal State. Since the Millennium and eternity are similar in many ways, it is not surprising if they seem to merge at times in the writings of the Apostle John.

Here the Eternal State is called **a new heaven and a new earth**. These are not to be confused with the new heaven and earth described in Isaiah 65:17–25. There the Millennium is in view, because sin and death are still present. These will be completely excluded from the Eternal State.

21:2 John sees **the holy city, New Jerusalem, coming down out of heaven, prepared as a bride adorned for her husband**. The fact that it is never said to land on the earth leads some to see it as hovering over the new earth. The fact that the names of the tribes of Israel are on the gates indicates that redeemed Israel will have access to the city, even if they are not part of the church itself. The distinction between the church (the Bride, the Lamb's Wife, v. 9), Israel (v. 12), and the Gentile nations (v. 24) is maintained throughout.

21:3 John hears an announcement **from heaven** that **the tabernacle of God is with men and** that **He will dwell with them**. As **His people** they will enjoy communion with Him closer than ever dreamed of. **God Himself will be with them and be their God** in a nearer and dearer relationship.

21:4, 5 The expression **"God will wipe away every tear from their eyes"** does not mean that there will be tears in heaven. It is a poetic way of saying that there will *not* be! Neither will there be **death, nor sorrow, nor crying**. For God's people, these will be forever ended.

The One who sits **on the throne** will **make all things new**. His **words are true and faithful**, and will surely come to pass.

21:6 The ushering in of the Eternal State marks the conclusion of God's purposes for the earth on which we live. As **Alpha** and **Omega** are the first and last letters of the Greek alphabet, so He is **the Beginning and the End**, the Creator and the Object of creation, the One who began and the One who finishes, the Eternal One. It is He who gives **the water of life** (salvation) **freely to** whoever **thirsts** for it.

21:7 It is He who blesses the overcomer with total inheritance and a new intimacy as between Father and **son**. As mentioned previously, an overcomer is one who believes that Jesus is the Son of God (1 Jn. 5:5). By faith he overcomes the world (1 Jn. 5:4).

21:8 But not all are overcomers. Some are **cowardly**, afraid to confess Christ; **unbelieving**, unwilling to trust the sinner's Savior; *sinners* (NKJV marginal reading found in most mss.), all those who remain in their sins, whether guilty of the gross iniquities listed here or not; **abominable**, given over to disgusting immorality; **murderers**, malicious and savage killers; **sexually immoral**, practicing fornication and other forms of sexual sins; **sorcerers**, those who traffic with evil spirits; **idolaters**, insulting God by worshiping images; **and all liars**, compulsive deceivers. These will be assigned to **the lake of fire** as their final destiny.

21:9 One of the seven angels involved in the bowl judgments offered to give John a further, more detailed view of the New Jerusalem, which he called **the bride, the Lamb's wife**. This may mean that the city is the residence of **the bride**.

21:10, 11 Carried away in the Spirit to a great and high mountain, John again saw **Jerusalem descending out of heaven**, radiant with **the glory of God** and sparkling like a costly gem.

21:12, 13 It was surrounded by a massive **wall** in which were **twelve gates**, graced by **twelve angels** and bearing **the names of the twelve tribes of . . . Israel. Three gates** faced each direction of the compass.

The number *twelve* is used twenty-one times in this book and seven times in this chapter. It is commonly understood to stand for *government* or administration.

21:14 The **twelve foundations** of the walls bore **the names of the twelve apostles of the Lamb**. This may have reference to the fact that they laid the foundation of the church in what they taught concerning Christ (Eph. 2:20).

21:15, 16 With a **gold** measuring rod, the angel determined that **the city** was approximately **twelve thousand furlongs** (1400-1500 miles) in **length, breadth, and height**. Whether shaped like a cube or a pyramid, it extended far beyond the bounds of restored Israel.

21:17 The **wall** was **one hundred and forty-four cubits** thick. The expression **"according to the measure of a man, that is, of an angel"** means that the angel of verses 9 and 15 used units of measure employed by man.

21:18 The description of the **wall** (**jasper**) **and the city** (**pure gold**), while hard for us to visualize, is designed to create an image of magnificence and brilliance. In that, it succeeds.

21:19, 20 The twelve **foundations** were adorned with twelve **precious stones**, similar to those on the breastplate of the high priest that represent the twelve tribes of Israel. It is not possible to identify all the jewels with precision or to determine their spiritual meaning.

21:21 The twelve gates are twelve pearls, a reminder that the church is the pearl of great price for which the Savior sold all that He had (Matt. 13:45, 46).

The street of the city was pure gold, like transparent glass, which speaks of unspotted glory.

21:22, 23 Certain things are missing from the city. **No temple** is necessary because **the Lord God Almighty and the Lamb** are there. There is no **sun** or **moon** because **the glory of God** illuminates it, and **the Lamb is** the lamp.

21:24 Gentile **nations** will enjoy its beauty, **and the kings of the earth** will come with their tribute to the Lord.

21:25 There are no closed **gates** because there is perfect security and freedom of access. There is **no night there**; it is a land of fadeless day.

21:26 As mentioned, the wealth **of the nations** will flow to the city, all their **glory** and **honor**.

21:27 Nothing unclean will ever enter there, **but only those who are written in the Lamb's Book of Life**.

22:1, 2 A pure river of water of life

flows **from the throne of God and of the Lamb** through **the middle of** the **street. On either side of the river** grows **the tree of life** with its **twelve** kinds of fruit, no longer forbidden. This suggests God's ceaseless provision for every season. **The leaves of the tree** are **for the healing of the nations** is a figurative way of saying that they will enjoy perpetual health.

22:3–5 A. T. Pierson summarizes as follows:

"And there shall be no more curse," perfect sinlessness;

"but the throne of God and of the Lamb shall be in it," perfect government;

"and His servants shall serve Him," perfect service;

"They shall see His face," perfect communion;

"and His name shall be on their foreheads," perfect resemblance;

"And there shall be no night there," perfect blessedness;

"And they shall reign forever and ever," perfect glory.[31]

O. Closing Warnings, Comforts, Invitations, and Benedictions (22:6–21)

22:6 The interpreting angel reminds John again of the trustworthiness of all that he has revealed. **The Lord God** had **sent His angel to show His servants** the panorama of events that **must shortly take place**.

22:7 The climax, the high point of it all will be the glorious Advent of the Savior. He assures us that He will come **quickly**. This may mean either *soon* or *suddenly*, but *soon* is preferred. A special blessing is given to each one **who keeps the words of** this **prophecy**. We can do this by living in the hope of His Coming.

22:8, 9 When **John saw and heard these things**, he **fell down** at the angel's **feet**, but he was forbidden to do so. The **angel** was only a created being; only God should be worshiped.

22:10 John was **not** to **seal** up **the prophecy** because **the time** of fulfillment was near. To **seal** here means to postpone disclosure.

22:11 When the time of fulfillment comes, **the unjust** will be fixed in their impenitence. The **filthy** will have no further chance to change when the Lord returns to earth. But the **righteous** will continue to live righteously, and the **holy** to live in holiness.

22:12, 13 Again the Lord announces His soon Coming, this time with the promise of **reward to every one according to his work**. Again He identifies Himself as **the Alpha and the Omega**. The same One who created all things will draw the curtain on the stage of time.

22:14 This verse may read, **"Blessed are those who do His commandments"** or **"Blessed are those who wash their robes"** (margin). *Neither* reading teaches salvation by works but rather works as the fruit and proof of salvation. Only true believers have access **to the tree of life** and to **the** eternal city.

22:15 Forever excluded from heaven will be **dogs, sorcerers**, the **sexually immoral, murderers, idolaters**, and liars. **Dogs** here may refer to male prostitutes (Deut. 23:18), unclean Gentiles (Matt. 15:26), or Judaizers (Phil. 3:2).

22:16 The Lord **sent** His **angel** with this message to **the churches**. He speaks of Himself as **the Root and the Offspring of David**. As to His deity, He is David's *Creator*; as to His humanity, He is David's *Descendant*. **The Bright and Morning Star** appears in the sky before the sun rises. Christ will first come to the church as **the Bright and Morning Star**, that is, at the Rapture. Later he will come to the earth as the Sun of Righteousness with healing in His wings (Mal. 4:2).

22:17 There are two ways of understanding this verse. First, it may be a gospel appeal throughout, with **the Spirit, the bride**, and the hearer urging the thirsty to **come** to Christ for salvation. Or the first three uses of the word **come** may be prayers for Christ to return, followed by two invitations to the unsaved to **come** to Him for **the water of life** (salvation) and thus be ready for His return.

22:18, 19 If men add to the things written in **this book** of Revelation, they will suffer **the plagues** described in it. Since the subjects in this book are woven throughout the Bible, the verse, in effect, condemns any tampering with God's word. A similar judgment is pronounced on **anyone** who **takes away from the words of this prophecy**. This does not apply to minor differences of interpreta-

tion, but to an outright attack on the inspiration and completeness of the Bible. The penalty is eternal doom. **God shall take away his part from the tree of life** (NKJV margin).[32] It means that he will never share in the blessings of those who have eternal **life**.

22:20 Revelation closes with a promise and a blessing. The promise is that the Lord Jesus is **coming quickly**. As mentioned previously, this could mean *soon* or *suddenly*. The hope of a *sudden* return would not excite the same anticipation or watchfulness as the hope of a *soon* return. Every redeemed person responds to the blessed hope, **"Amen. Even so, come, Lord Jesus!"**

Just as Genesis is the book of beginnings, so Revelation is the book of consummation. Subjects that were introduced in the first book are brought to fruition in the last. Note the following:

GENESIS	REVELATION
Creation of heavens and earth (Gen. 1:1).	Destruction of heavens and earth (Rev. 20:11b). Creation of new heavens and new earth (Rev. 21:1).
Start of Satan's reign on earth (Gen. 3:1–7).	Satan cast into the Lake of Fire (Rev. 20:10).
Entrance of sin (Gen. 3:1–7).	Sin banished (Rev. 21:27).
Pronouncing of the curse on creation (Gen. 3:17–19).	The curse removed (Rev. 22:3).
Right to tree of life forfeited (Gen. 3:24b).	Access to tree of life restored (Rev. 22:2, 19 marg.)
Eviction of man from the Garden of Eden (Gen. 3:24a).	Man welcomed back to [Paradise] (Rev. 22:1–7)
Entrance of death into the world (Gen. 2:17; 5:5).	Death forever removed (Rev. 21:4).
Marriage of the first Adam (Gen. 4:1).	Marriage of the last Adam (Rev. 19:7).
Sorrow comes to mankind (Gen. 3:16).	Sorrow eliminated (Rev. 21:4).

22:21 And now we come to the final blessing of this wonderful book of Revelation, and of the word of God. It is a peaceful close to a book filled with the thunders of divine judgment.

John wishes for **"The grace of our Lord Jesus Christ** to **be with** God's people." There are three interesting variant readings in the manuscripts here.

1. In the critical (NU) text John wishes Christ's grace to *all* — which hardly fits Revelation's theme of impending wrath on the majority.

2. The traditional (TR, KJV, NKJV) reading is better. Christ's grace is wished to "you all" — many of the hearers and readers of Revelation will be true believers.

3. The best reading in light of the sharp contrasts between saints and sinners in this book is found in the majority text and NKJV margin: **"The grace of our Lord Jesus Christ be with all the saints. Amen."**

ENDNOTES

[1](Intro) The verb used in the Gospel and Revelation is *ekkentēsan*; in the Septuagint of Zechariah the form is *katorchēsanto*.

[2](Intro) In Hebrew and Greek the letters of the alphabet have numerical value. For example, aleph and alpha are 1, beth and beta are 2, etc. Hence every name can be added up. The Greek name for Jesus (*Iesous*), interestingly enough, adds up to 888. (Eight is the number of new beginning and resurrection.) It is believed that the letters of the Beast's name will actually equal 666. By slightly adjusting the spelling, "Nero Caesar" can be made to add up to 666, using this system. Other names also add up to 666, however, and one should avoid wild speculation.

[3](1:5) The marginal reading here is the first of very many in the NKJV, of Revelation where both the oldest (NU) and majority (M) of readings agree against the reading of the TR, KJV, and NKJV. The reason for this is that Erasmus, who published the first Greek NT (1516), had only one copy of Revelation, and it was faulty. Hence, there are the many small variations in the footnotes or margin. Fortunately, the other books of the NT were represented by mss. that agreed largely with a yet-to-be discovered mass of mss. In this commentary, only crucial changes have been noted. The combination of NU and M will be the original reading, we believe. Where they differ from one another, the majority text is to be preferred.

[4](1:8) The NU and M texts omit "the Beginning and the End."

[5](1:10) "The Day of the Lord" is *hē hēmera tou Kuriou* in Greek; "the Lord's (lit. "lordly") Day" is *"hē Kuriakē hēmera"* (whence "kirk, church").

[6](1:13) James H. McConkey, *The Book of Revelation: A Series of Outline Studies in the Apocalypse*, p. 9.

[7](2:1) John F. Walvoord, *The Revelation of Jesus Christ*, pp. 50-100.

[8](2:14, 15) Ella E. Pohle, *Dr. C. I. Scofield's Question Box*, p. 89.

[9](2:20) The majority text reads, "your wife (or woman) Jezebel."

[10](3:7) *Daily Notes of the Scripture Union*.

[11](3:20) Richard Chevenix Trench, *Commentary on the Epistles to the Seven Churches in Asia*, p. 225.

[12](4:3) Walvoord, *Revelation*, p. 104.

[13](5:9, 10) Both the NU and M texts have "them" and "they," which would mean that the elders are not singing about themselves, but about *others*. This *might* suggest that they are angelic beings.

[14](5:9, 10) NU text reads "kingdom."

[15](6:1, 2) The NU and M texts omit "and see."

[16](6:10) The Greek word here is strong: *Despotēs* (but without the negative connotation of the English derivative).

[17](8:5) Henry Barclay Swete, *The Apocalypse of St. John*, p. 109.

[18](8:13) "Angel" and "eagle" look somewhat similar in Greek also (*angelos* and *aetos*), hence the copying error. "Eagle" is correct.

[19](9:16, 17) The majority of mss. read "one hundred million."

[20](9:18, 19) Hamilton Smith, *The Revelation: An Expository Outline*, p. 57.

[21](9:20, 21) The Greek word here is *pharmakon*, "medicine, potion, drug" (cf. English "pharmacy").

[22](11:6) McConkey, *The Book of Revelation*, pp. 68, 69.

[23](11:15) The NU and M texts read "kingdom . . . has become."

[24](13:3) *The Scofield Reference Bible*, p. 1342.

[25](14:4, 5) J. D. Pentecost, *Things to Come*, p. 300.

[26](15:3, 4) "Saints" is a very weakly supported reading. Both the NU and M texts support "nations."

²⁷(15:3, 4) Arthur T. Pierson, *Knowing the Scriptures*, p. 248.

²⁸(16:16) "Armageddon" comes from Hebrew "Har" (Mount) Megiddo. The majority text reads simply "Megiddo."

²⁹(19:8) The 1611 text reads "righteousness," often interpreted by preachers as that *righteousness of Christ* which is *imputed* to the saints. While this is a sound doctrine, the Greek word *dikaiō-mata* rules out that understanding. The word is plural (not the abstract singular which is *dikaiōsunē*). Furthermore, it has a "passive" ending, *here* denoting something *done* (in this case, "righteous deeds"). Salvation is not in view in this passage.

³⁰(19:10) Charles C. Ryrie, *The Ryrie Study Bible, New King James Version*, p. 1953.

³¹(22:3–5) Pierson, *The Ministry of Keswick, First Series*, p. 144.

³²(22:18, 19) The reading "book of life" has *no* Greek mss. support here! The last six verses were missing in Erasmus' Greek copy of Revelation so he translated these verses back from the Latin Vulgate. This is a most unfortunate reading. It mars the literary "full-circle," that is, God's program from the banishment of man from the tree of life in Genesis 3 to its restoration to His saints at the end of the very last chapter in the Bible.

BIBLIOGRAPHY

Criswell, Wallie Amos. *Exposition of Sermons on Revelation*. Grand Rapids: Zondervan Publishing House, 1962.

Dennett, Edward. "The Seven Churches," *The Serious Christian*, Vol. XI. Charlotte, N.C.: Books for Christians, n.d.

Gaebelein, Arno C. *The Revelation*. New York: Publication Office "Our Hope," 1915.

Grant, F. W. *The Revelation of Christ*. New York: Loizeaux Brothers, n.d.

Ironside, H. A. *Lectures on the Revelation*. New York: Loizeaux Brothers, 1919.

Kelly, William. *Lectures on the Book of Revelation*, New Edition. London: G. Morrish, n.d.

Lenski, R. C. H. *The Interpretation of St. John's Revelation*. Minneapolis: Augsburg Publishing House, 1943.

McConkey, James H. *The Book of Revelation: A Series of Outline Studies in the Apocalypse*. Pittsburgh: Silver Publishing Co., 1921.

Morgan, G. Campbell. *The Letters of Our Lord*. Westwood, N.J.: Fleming H. Revell Co., n.d.

Morris, Leon. *The Revelation of Jesus Christ* (TBC). Grand Rapids: Wm. B. Eerdmans Publishing Co., 1969.

Mounce, Robert H. *The Book of Revelation* (NIC). Grand Rapids: Wm. B. Eerdmans Publishing Co., 1977.

Ryrie, Charles Caldwell. *Revelation*. Chicago: Moody Press, 1968.

Scott, Walter. *Exposition of the Revelation of Jesus Christ*. London: Pickering & Inglis Ltd., n.d.

Smith, Hamilton. *The Revelation: An Expository Outline*. Addison, IL: Bible Truth Publishers, n.d.

Stanley, Charles. *The Revelation of Jesus Christ*. New York: Loizeaux Brothers Publishers, n.d.

Swete, Henry Barclay. *The Apocalypse of St. John*. Grand Rapids: Wm. B. Eerdmans Publishing Company, n.d.

Tenney, Merrill C. *Interpreting Revelation*. Grand Rapids: Wm. B. Eerdmans Publishing Company, 1957.

Trench, Richard Chevenix. *Commentary on the Epistles to the Seven Churches in Asia*. Minneapolis: Klock and Klock Christian Publishers, 1978.

Walvoord, John F. *The Revelation of Jesus Christ*. Chicago: Moody Press, 1966.

BOOKS

Alford, Henry. *The Greek Testament*. 4 vols. Revised by Everett F. Harrison. Chicago: Moody Press, 1958.

Anderson, Sir Robert. *Misunderstood Texts of the New Testament*. London: Nisbet & Co., Ltd., 1916.

Anderson-Berry, D. *Pictures in the Acts*. Glasgow: Pickering & Inglis, n.d.

Arndt, William F. and F. Wilbur Gingrich. *A Greek-English Lexicon of the New Testament and Other Early Christian Literature*. Chicago: The University of Chicago Press, 1979.

Barker, H. P. *Coming Twice*. New York: Loizeaux Brothers, n.d.

Barnes, Albert. *Notes on the New Testament*. 10 vols. Grand Rapids: Kregel Publications, 1975.

Baron, David. *The New Order of Priesthood*. Findlay, Ohio: Dunham Publishing Company, 1955.

Barnhouse, D. G. *The Measure of Your Faith*. Book 69. Further documentation unavailable.

_____. *Words Fitly Spoken*. Wheaton: Tyndale House Publishers, 1969.

Baxter, J. Sidlow. *Awake My Heart*. Grand Rapids: Zondervan Publishing House, 1960.

_____. *Explore the Book*. 3 vols. London: Marshall, Morgan & Scott, 1955.

Bellett, James Gifford. *The Evangelists*. New York: Loizeaux Brothers, n.d.

Bonar, Andrew R. *Last Days of the Martyrs*. Kilmarnock: John Ritchie, Ltd., n.d.

Brookes, J. H. *I Am Coming*. Glasgow: Pickering & Inglis, 1895.

Chafer, L. S. *Systematic Theology*. 8 vols. Dallas: Dallas Seminary Press, 1947.

Chappel, Clovis G. *Sermons from the Psalms*. Nashville: Cokesbury Press, 1931.

Christenson, Larry. *The Christian Family*. Minneapolis: Bethany Fellowship, 1970.

Clow, W. M. *The Cross in Christian Experience*. New York: Hodder & Stoughton, 1908.

Cragg, H. W. *The Keswick Week, 1955*. London: Marshall, Morgan & Scott, 1955.

Darby, J. N. *The Collected Writings of John Nelson Darby*. Edited by William Kelly. 34 vols. and Index. Oak Park, IL: Bible Truth Publishers, 1971.

_____. *Synopsis of the Books of the Bible*. 5 vols. New York: Loizeaux Brothers, 1942.

Davidson, F., ed. *The New Bible Commentary*. Chicago: The InterVarsity Christian Fellowship, 1953.

Denney, James R. *The Death of Christ*. 2nd ed. Philadelphia: The Westminster Press, 1903.

Dillow, Joseph. *Speaking in Tongues*. Grand Rapids: Zondervan Publishing House, 1976.

Drury, T. W. *The Prison Ministry of St. Paul*. London: The Religious Tract Society, 1911.

*Eddy, Mary Baker. *Science and Health with Key to the Scriptures*. Boston: Allison V. Stewart, 1909.

Elliot, Elisabeth, ed. *The Journals of Jim Elliot*. Old Tappan, NJ: Fleming H. Revell Company, 1978.

Erdman, Charles R. *The General Epistles*. Philadelphia: The Westminster Press, 1919.

The Expositor's Greek Testament. 5 vols. Grand Rapids: Wm. B. Eerdmans Publishing Company, 1951.

Falwell, Jerry, ed. *Liberty Bible Commentary*. 2 vols. Lynchburg, Virginia: The Old-Time Gospel Hour, 1982.

*Ferré, Nels. *The Sun and the Umbrella*. New York: Harper & Brothers, 1953.

Fernald, James C., ed. *Funk & Wagnalls Standard Handbook of Synonyms, Antonyms, and Prepositions*. New York: Harper & Row, 1947.

Ford, Leighton. *The Christian Persuader*. New York: Harper & Row, 1966.

Gaebelein, Arno C. *The Annotated Bible*. 9 vols. Neptune, New Jersey: Loizeaux Brothers, rev. ed., 1970.

Gaebelein, Frank E., ed. *The New Scofield Reference Bible*. New York: Oxford University Press, 1967.

Gibbon, Edward. *The Decline and Fall of the Roman Empire*. Vol. II. Chicago: Belford, Charles and Co., n.d.

Gibbs, A. P. *Preach and Teach the Word*. Oak Park, IL: Emmaus Bible School, 1971.

Gook, Arthur. *Can A Young Man Find the Path?* London: Pickering & Inglis, 1949.

Grant, F. W. *Genesis in the Light of the*

New Testament. New York: Loizeaux Brothers, n.d.

———. *The Numerical Bible*. 7 vols. New York: Loizeaux Brothers, 1932.

Gray, James M. *Christian Workers' Commentary on the Whole Bible*. Westwood, NJ: Fleming H. Revell, 1953.

Grubb, Norman P. *C. T. Studd, Cricketer and Pioneer*. London: Lutterworth Press, 1957.

Guthrie, Donald. *New Testament Introduction*. 3 vols. London: The Tyndale Press, 1962.

Harrison, Everett F. *Introduction to the New Testament*. Grand Rapids: Wm. B. Eerdmans Publishing Company, 1964.

Havner, Vance. *Why Not Just Be Christians?* NY: Fleming H. Revell, 1964.

Hession, Roy. *The Calvary Road*. Philadelphia: Christian Literature Crusade.

Hodges, Zane C. and Arthur L. Farstad, eds. *The Greek New Testament According to the Majority Text*. Nashville: Thomas Nelson Publishers, 2d ed., 1985.

Hogg, C. F. *What Saith the Scripture?* London: Pickering & Inglis, 1947.

Hole, F. B. *Paul's Epistles, Volume Two*. Wooler, Northumberland, England: Central Bible Hammond Trust Ltd., n.d.

Houghton, S. M. *Sketches from Church History*. Edinburgh: The Banner of Truth Trust, 1980.

Hunter, Jack. *What the Bible Teaches, Galatians – Philemon*. Kilmarnock, Scotland: John Ritchie, Scotland: 1983, p. 78.

Ironside, Harry A. *Notes on James & Peter*. New York: Loizeaux Brothers, 1947.

Jamieson, Fausset and Brown. *A Commentary, Critical, Experimental, and Practical on the Old and New Testaments*. 6 vols. London: Wm. Collins and Co., n.d.

Jones, E. Stanley. *Christ's Alternative to Communism*. Nashville: Abingdon Press, 1935.

———. *Conversion*. Nashville: Abingdon Press, 1959.

———. *Growing Spiritually*. Nashville: Abingdon Press, 1978.

Jowett, J. H. *Life in the Heights*. London: Hodder & Stoughton, 1924.

———. *Things that Matter Most*. London: Jas. Clarke & Co., 1913.

Jukes, Andrew. *The Law of the Offerings*. London: Lamp Press, 1954.

*Kennedy, Gerald. *God's Good News*. New York: Harper & Brothers, 1955.

The Keswick Convention 1934, London: Pickering & Ingalis, 1934.

The Keswick Week 1955, London: Marshall, Morgan & Scott, Ltd., 1955.

Lacey, Harry. *God and the Nations*. Kilmarnock, Scotland: John Ritchie, 1944.

Lang, G. H. *The Churches of God*. London: Paternoster Press, n.d.

———. *The Parabolic Teaching of the Scripture*. Grand Rapids: Wm. B. Eerdmans Publishing Company, 1956.

Lange, J. P. *A Commentary on the Holy Scriptures*. 25 vols. Grand Rapids: Zondervan Publishing House, n.d.

Lee, Robert G. *Lord, I Believe*. Nashville: Broadman Press, 1927.

Lee, Robert G. *Seven Swords and Other Messages*, Grand Rapids: Zondervan Publishing House, 1958.

Lenski, R. C. H. *The Interpretation of the Epistle to the Hebrews and of the Epistle of James*. Minneapolis: Augsburg Publishing House, 1938.

———. *The Interpretation of St. Paul's Epistles to the Colossians, to the Thessalonians, to Timothy, to Titus and to Philemon*. Columbus, Ohio: The Wartburg Press, 1937.

———. *The Interpretation of St. Paul's Epistles to the Galatians, to the Ephesians, and to the Philippians*. Columbus, Ohio: The Wartburg Press, 1946.

Lyall, L. T. *Red Sky at Night*. London: Hodder & Stoughton, 1969.

Macartney, Clarence Edward. *Macartney's Illustrations*. New York: Abingdon Press, 1946.

Mackay, W. M. *The Men Whom Jesus Made*. London: Hodder & Stoughton, 1924.

Mackintosh, C. H. *Genesis to Deuteronomy: Notes on the Pentateuch*. 6 vols. New York: Loizeaux Brothers, 1879.

———. *The Mackintosh Treasury*. Neptune, NJ: Loizeaux Brothers, 1976.

Marsh, F. E. *Fully Furnished*. London: Pickering & Inglis, n.d.

Matheson, George. *Rest By the River*. London: Hodder & Stoughton, 1906.

McClain, Alva J. *The Greatness of the Kingdom*. Chicago: Moody Press, 1968.

Metzger, Bruce M. *The New Testament: Its Background, Growth, and Content*. Nashville: Abingdon Press, 1965.

Meyer, Frederick Brotherton. *Paul.* London: Morgan & Scott, n.d.

_____. *Through the Bible Day by Day.* 7 vols. Philadelphia: American S. S. Union, 1918.

Miller, J. R. *Come Ye Apart.* New York: Thomas Crowell & Co., 1887.

The Ministry of Keswick, First Series, 1892-1919. Grand Rapids: Zondervan Publishing House, 1963.

The Ministry of Keswick, Second Series, 1921-1956. Grand Rapids: Zondervan Publishing House, 1964.

Moorehead, William G. *Outline Studies in Acts and the Epistles.* Chicago: Fleming H. Revell, 1902.

_____. *Outline Studies in the New Testament: Acts to Ephesians.* Pittsburgh: United Presbyterian Board of Publications, 1902.

_____. *Outline Studies in the New Testament: Philippians to Hebrews.* Pittsburgh: United Presbyterian Board of Publications, 1905.

Morris, Leon. *Understanding the New Testament: 1 Timothy, 2 Timothy, Titus, Philemon, Hebrews, James.* Philadelphia: A. J. Holman Company, 1978.

Morrison, G. H. "Morrison on Luke," *The Glasgow Pulpit Series, Vol. I.* Chattanooga, TN: AMG Publishers, 1978.

Morgan, G. Campbell. *Searchlights from the Word.* London: Oliphants, 1970.

Murray, Andrew. *The Holiest of All.* Westwood, NJ: Fleming H. Revell, 1960.

Myers, F. W. H. *St. Paul.* London: Samuel Bagster & Sons Ltd., n.d.

Nee, Watchman. *Do All to the Glory of God.* NY: Christian Fellowship Publishers, Inc., 1974.

New and Concise Bible Dictionary. London: G. Morrish, 1897-1900.

Orr, J., ed. *International Standard Bible Encyclopedia.* 5 vols. Grand Rapids: Wm. B. Eerdmans Publishing Co., 1939.

Orr, William W. *Bible Hints on Rearing Children.* Wheaton, IL: InterVarsity Press, 1955.

Pentecost, J. D. *Your Adversary the Devil.* Grand Rapids: Zondervan Publishing House, 1969.

Pfeiffer, Charles F. and Everett F. Harrison, eds. *The Wycliffe Bible Commentary.* Chicago: Moody Press, 1962.

Phillips, J. B. *The Young Church in Action.* New York: The Macmillan Company, 1956.

Pierson, A. T. *"Knowing the Scriptures."* New York: Gospel Publishing House, 1910.

_____. "The Work of Christ for the Believer," *The Ministry of Keswick, First Series.* Grand Rapids: Zondervan Publishing House, 1963.

Pink, Arthur W. *The Attributes of God.* Swengel, Pennsylvania: Bible Truth Depot, n.d.

Pollock, A. J. *The Apostle Paul and His Missionary Labors.* New York: Loizeaux Brothers, n.d.

_____. *Modernism Versus the Bible.* London: Central Bible Truth Depot, n.d.

_____. *Why I Believe the Bible is the Word of God.* London: Central Bible Truth Depot, n.d.

Pohle, Ella E. *C. I. Scofield's Question Box.* Chicago: The Bible Institute Colportage Association, 1917.

Reid, R. J. *How Job Learned His Lesson.* New York: Loizeaux Brothers, n.d.

Robertson, A. T. *Word Pictures in the New Testament.* 6 vols. New York: Harper & Bros., 1930.

*Robinson, John A. T. *Honest to God.* Philadelphia: The Westminster Press, 1963.

Rogers, E. W. *Concerning the Future.* Chicago: Moody Press, 1962.

_____. *Jesus the Christ.* London: Pickering & Inglis, 1962.

Ryle, John Charles. *Expository Thoughts on the Gospels.* 3 vols. New York: Fleming H. Revell, 1858.

_____. *Holiness.* Grand Rapids: Baker Book House, 1979.

_____. *Practical Religion.* London: Jas. Clarke & Co., Ltd., 1959.

Ryrie, Charles C. *The Grace of God.* Chicago: Moody Press, 1975.

_____, ed. *The Ryrie Study Bible, New King James Version.* Chicago: Moody Press, 1985.

Salmon, George. *A Historical Introduction to the Study of the Books of the New Testament.* London: John Murray, 1894.

Sanders, J. Oswald. *A Spiritual Clinic.* Chicago: Moody Press, 1958.

_____. *Spiritual Problems.* Chicago: Moody Press, 1971.

Sauer, Erich. *The Dawn of World Redemption.* Grand Rapids: Wm. B. Eerdmans Publishing Company, 1953.

Scorer, C. G. *The Bible and Sex Ethics Today.* London: The Tyndale Press, 1967.

Scott, Walter. *Bible Handbook to the New Testament*. Charlotte, North Carolina: Books for Christians, 1977.

Scroggie, W. Graham. *Know Your Bible: A Guide to the Gospels*. London: Pickering & Inglis, 1948.

———. "Paul's Prison Prayers," *The Ministry of Keswick, Second Series*. Grand Rapids: Zondervan Publishing House, 1964.

Spurgeon, Charles H. *The Treasury of the New Testament*. London: Marshall, Morgan & Scott, n.d.

Stalker, James. *Life of St. Paul*. Fleming H. Revell, 1912.

Stevens, G. B. *The Theology of the New Testament*. New York: Chas. Scribner's Sons, n.d.

Stewart, James A. *Evangelism*. Swengel, PA: Reiner Publications, n.d.

———. *Pastures of Tender Grass*. Further documentation unavailable.

Stewart, James S. *The Life and Teaching of Jesus Christ*. Nashville: Abingdon Press, 1958.

———. *A Man in Christ*. New York: Harper & Row, 1935.

———. *Pastures of Tender Grass*, Philadelphia: Revival Literature, 1962.

Stonehouse, Ned B. *Origins of the Synoptic Gospels — Some Basic Questions*. Grand Rapids: Wm. B. Eerdmans Publishing Company, 1963.

Strombeck, J. F. *First the Rapture*. Moline, IL: Strombeck Agency, Inc., 1950.

Strong, A. H. *Systematic Theology*. Philadelphia: The Judson Press, 1943.

Swindoll, Charles. *Growing Strong in the Seasons of Life*. Portland: Multnomah Press, 1983.

Taylor, Mrs. Howard. *Behind the Ranges*. London: Lutterworth Press, 1944.

Thiessen, Henry Clarence. *Introduction to the New Testament*. Grand Rapids: Wm. B. Eerdmans Publishing Company, 1943.

Tozer, A. W. *That Incredible Christian*. India: Alliance Publications, 1964.

———. *The Root of the Righteous*. Chicago: Moody Press, 1955.

Trench, Richard Chevenix. *Synonyms of the New Testament*. London: Kegan Paul, Trench, Trubner & Co., Ltd., 1901.

Unger, Merrill F. *Unger's Bible Dictionary*. Chicago: Moody Press, 1966.

———. *Unger's Bible Handbook*. Chicago: Moody Press, 1966.

———. *Zechariah*. Grand Rapids: Zondervan Publishing House , 1963.

Van Oosterzee, J. J. "The Pastoral Letters." *Lange's Commentary on the Holy Scriptures*. Vol. 23. Grand Rapids: Zondervan Publishing House, n.d.

Velikovsky, I. *Earth in Upheaval*. New York: Doubleday and Co., 1955.

Vincent, Marvin R. *Word Studies in the New Testament*. 4 vols. Grand Rapids: Wm. B. Eerdmans Publishing Company, 1957.

Vine, W. E. *The Divine Plan of Missions*. London: Pickering & Inglis, n.d.

———. *Expository Dictionary of New Testament Words*. Old Tappan, NJ: Fleming H. Revell, 1966.

Walvoord, John F. and Roy B. Zuck, eds. *The Bible Knowledge Commentary: New Testament Edition*. Wheaton, Illinois: Victor Books, 1983.

Warfield, B. B. *Christology and Criticism*. New York: Oxford University Press, 1929.

Watson, David. *Discipleship*. London: Hodder and Stoughton, 1981.

Weatherhead, Leslie D. *Prescription for Anxiety*. London: Hodder & Stoughton, 1956.

Webb-Peploe, H. W. "Grace and Peace in Four Pauline Epistles," *The Ministry of Keswick, First Series*. Grand Rapids: Zondervan Publishing House, 1963.

Williams, George. *The Student's Commentary on the Holy Scriptures*. Grand Rapids: Kregel Publications, 1953.

Wuest, Kenneth S. *Ephesians and Colossians in the Greek New Testament*. Grand Rapids: Wm. B. Eerdmans Publishing Co., 1957.

———. *In These Last Days*. Grand Rapids: Wm. B. Eerdmans Publishing Co., 1954.

———. *Wuest's Expanded Translation of the Greek New Testament*. 3 vols. Grand Rapids: Wm. B. Eerdmans Publishing Co., 1956-1959.

Young, Dinsdale T. *The Enthusiasm of God*. London: Hodder & Stoughton, 1906.

———. *Neglected People of the Bible*. London: Hodder & Stoughton, 1901.

———. *Unfamiliar Texts*. London: Hodder & Stoughton, 1899.

———. *The Unveiled Evangel*. London: Robert Scott, 1912.

Zahn, Theodor. *Introduction to the New Testament*. 3 vols. Minneapolis: Klock & Klock Christian Publishers, 1977.

ARTICLES AND PERIODICALS

Christian Truth Magazine. various dates.

Daily Notes of the Scripture Union. London: C.S.S.M., various dates.

*Homrighausen, E. G. "The Second Epistle of Peter," *Exposition*, IB, XII, 1957.

Our Daily Bread. Grand Rapids: Radio Bible Class, various dates.

The Sunday School Times. Homer L. Payne. "What Is a Missionary Church?" Feb. 22, 1964.

Toward the Mark. Weston-super-Mare, Vol. 5, No. 6 (1976).

PAMPHLETS

Cutting, George. "The Old Nature and the New Birth." New York: Loizeaux Brothers, n.d.

Green, Samuel. "Scripture Testimony to the Deity of Christ." Oak Park, Illinois: Bible Truth Publishers, 1959.

Hole, F. B. "The Administration of the Mystery." London: Central Bible Truth Depot, n.d.

*National Council of Churches. "Called to Responsible Freedom."

Scofield, C. I. "Rightly Dividing the Word of Truth."

N.B. Works marked with an asterisk (*) are quoted to illustrate false teaching.

SUPPLEMENTS

Name	Nationality	Home Town	Occupation	Relationships	Chapters Written	Verses Written	Books Written
Matthew	Jew	Capernaum	Tax Collector	Apostle of Jesus Christ	28	1,071	Gospel of Matthew
Mark	Jew/Roman	Jerusalem	Missionary	Disciple of Peter	16	678	Gospel of Mark
Luke	Greek	Antioch	Physician	Disciple of Paul	52	2,158	Gospel of Luke Acts
John	Jew	Bethsaida or Capernaum	Fisherman	Apostle of Jesus Christ	50	1,414	Gospel of John 1 John 2 John 3 John Revelation
Paul	Jew	Tarsus	Tentmaker	Apostle of Jesus Christ	87 (100)*	2,033 (2,336)*	Romans 1 Corinthians 2 Corinthians Galatians Ephesians Philippians Colossians Philemon 1 Thessalonians 2 Thessalonians 1 Timothy 2 Timothy Titus (Hebrews?)
James	Jew	Nazareth	Carpenter?	Brother of Jesus Christ	5	108	James
Peter	Jew	Bethsaida	Fisherman	Apostle of Jesus Christ	8	166	1 Peter 2 Peter
Jude	Jew	Nazareth	Carpenter?	Brother of Jesus Christ	1	25	Jude

*Indicates total if Hebrews is assigned to Paul.

From *Talk Thru the Bible*. Reprinted by permission of Walk Thru the Bible Ministries.

THE THEMES OF THE NEW TESTAMENT LETTERS

PAUL'S LETTERS TO CHURCHES

BOOK	KEY WORD	THEME
Romans	Righteousness of God	Portrays the gospel from condemnation to justification to sanctification to glorification (1–8). Presents God's program for Jews and Gentiles (9–11) and practical exhortations for believers (12–16).
1 Corinthians	Correction of Carnal Living	Corrects problems of factions, immorality, lawsuits, and abuse of the Lord's Supper (1–6). Replies to questions concerning marriage, meat offered to idols, public worship, and the Resurrection (7–16).
2 Corinthians	Paul Defends His Ministry	Defends Paul's apostolic character, call, and credentials. The majority had repented of their rebellion against Paul, but there was still an unrepentant minority.
Galatians	Freedom from the Law	Refutes the error of legalism that had ensnared the churches of Galatia. Demonstrates the superiority of grace over law, and magnifies the life of liberty over legalism and license.
Ephesians	Building the Body of Christ	Extols the believer's position in Christ (1–3), and exhorts the readers to maintain a spiritual walk that is based upon their spiritual wealth (4–6).
Philippians	To Live Is Christ	Paul speaks of the latest developments in his imprisonment and urges his readers to a life-style of unity, humility, and godliness.
Colossians	The Preeminence of Christ	Demonstrates the preeminence of Christ in creation, redemption, and the relationships of life. The Christian is complete in Christ and needs nothing else.
1 Thessalonians	Holiness in Light of Christ's Return	Paul commends the Thessalonians for their faith and reminds them of his motives and concerns on their behalf. He exhorts them to purity of life and teaches them about the coming of the Lord.
2 Thessalonians	Understanding the Day of the Lord	Paul corrects false conclusions about the day of the Lord, explains what must precede this awesome event, and exhorts his readers to remain diligent.

PAUL'S LETTERS TO PEOPLE

BOOK	KEY WORD	THEME
1 Timothy	Leadership Manual for Churches	Paul counsels Timothy on the problems of false teachers, public prayer, the role of women, and the requirements for elders and deacons.
2 Timothy	Endurance in Ministry	A combat manual designed to build up and encourage Timothy to boldness and steadfastness in view of the hardships of the spiritual warfare.
Titus	Conduct Manual for Churches	Lists the requirements for elders and instructs Titus in his duties relative to the various groups in the churches.
Philemon	Forgiveness from Slavery	Paul appeals to Philemon to forgive Onesimus and to regard him no longer as a slave but as a brother in Christ.

LETTERS FROM OTHERS

BOOK	KEY WORD	THEME
Hebrews	Superiority of Christ	Demonstrates the superiority of Christ's person, priesthood, and power over all that preceded Him to encourage the readers to mature and to become stable in their faith.
James	Faith that Works	A practical catalog of the characteristics of true faith written to exhort James' Hebrew-Christian readers to examine the reality of their own faith.
1 Peter	Suffering for Christ	Comfort and counsel to those who were being maligned for their faith in Christ. They are encouraged to develop an attitude of submission in view of their suffering.
2 Peter	Guard Against False Prophets	Copes with internal opposition in the form of false teachers who were enticing believers into their errors of belief and conduct. Appeals for growth in the true knowledge of Christ.
1 John	Fellowship with God	Explores the dimensions of fellowship between redeemed people and God. Believers must walk in His light, manifest His love, and abide in His life.
2 John	Avoid Fellowship with False Teachers	John commends his readers for remaining steadfast in apostolic truth and reminds them to walk in love and avoid false teachers.
3 John	Enjoy Fellowship with the Brethren	John thanks Gaius for his support of traveling teachers of the truth, in contrast to Diotrephes, who rejected them and told others to do the same.
Jude	Contend for the Faith	This expose of false teachers reveals their conduct and character and predicts their judgment. Jude encourages his readers to build themselves up in the truth and contend earnestly for the faith.
Revelation	Revelation of the Coming Christ	The glorified Christ gives seven messages to the church (1–3). Visions of unparalleled judgment upon rebellious mankind are followed by the Second Advent (4–19). The Apocalypse concludes with a description of the new heaven and new earth and the marvels of the new Jerusalem (20–22).

From *Visual Survey of the Bible*. Reprinted by permission of the author.

Date	Event	Location	Matthew	Mark	Luke	John	Related References
	Luke's Introduction				1:1–4		Acts 1:1
	Pre-fleshly state of Christ					1:1–18	Heb. 1:1–14
	Genealogy of Jesus Christ		1:1–17		3:23–38		Ruth 4:18–22 1 Chr. 1:1–4

BIRTH, INFANCY, AND ADOLESCENCE OF JESUS AND JOHN THE BAPTIST IN 17 EVENTS

Date	Event	Location	Matthew	Mark	Luke	John	Related References
7 B.C.	(1) Announcement of Birth of John	Jerusalem (Temple)			1:5–25		Num. 6:3
7 or 6 B.C.	(2) Announcement of Birth of Jesus to the Virgin	Nazareth			1:26–38		Is. 7:14
c. 5 B.C.	(3) Song of Elizabeth to Mary	Hill Country of Judea			1:39–45		
	(4) Mary's Song of Praise				1:46–56		Ps. 103:17
5 B.C.	(5) Birth, Infancy, and Purpose for Future of John the Baptist	Judea			1:57–80		Mal. 3:1
	(6) Announcement of Jesus' Birth to Joseph	Nazareth	1:18–25				Is. 9:6, 7
5–4 B.C.	(7) Birth of Jesus Christ	Bethlehem	1:24, 25		2:1–7		Is. 7:14
	(8) Proclamation by the Angels	Near Bethlehem			2:8–14		1 Tim. 3:16
	(9) The Visit of Homage by Shepherds	Bethlehem			2:15–20		
	(10) Jesus' Circumcision	Bethlehem			2:21		Lev. 12:3
4 B.C.	(11) First Temple Visit with Acknowledgments by Simeon and Anna	Jerusalem			2:22–38		Ex. 13:2 Lev. 12
	(12) Visit of the Wise Men	Jerusalem & Bethlehem	2:1–12				Num. 24:17
	(13) Flight into Egypt and Massacre of Innocents	Bethlehem, Jerusalem & Egypt	2:13–18				Jer. 31:15
	(14) From Egypt to Nazareth with Jesus		2:19–23		2:39		
Afterward A.D. 7–8	(15) Childhood of Jesus	Nazareth			2:40, 51		
	(16) Jesus, 12 Years Old, Visits the Temple	Jerusalem			2:41–50		Deut. 16:1–8
Afterward	(17) 18-Year Account of Jesus' Adolescence and Adulthood	Nazareth			2:51, 52		1 Sam. 2:26

TRUTHS ABOUT JOHN THE BAPTIST

Date	Event	Location	Matthew	Mark	Luke	John	Related References
c. A.D. 25–27	John's Ministry Begins	Judean Wilderness	3:1	1:1–4	3:1, 2	1:19–28	Mal. 3:1
	Man and Message		3:2–12	1:2–8	3:3–14		Is. 40:3
	His Picture of Jesus		3:11, 12	1:7, 8	3:15–18	1:26, 27	Acts 2:38
	His Courage		14:4–12		3:19, 20		

BEGINNING OF JESUS' MINISTRY IN 12 EVENTS

Date	Event	Location	Matthew	Mark	Luke	John	Related References
c. A.D. 27	(1) Jesus Baptized	Jordan River	3:13–17	1:9–11	3:21–23	1:29–34	Ps. 2:7
	(2) Jesus Tempted	Wilderness	4:1–11	1:12, 13	4:1–13		Ps. 91:11
	(3) Calls First Disciples	Beyond Jordan				1:35–51	
	(4) The First Miracle	Cana in Galilee				2:1–11	
	(5) First Stay in Capernaum	(Capernaum is "His" city)				2:12	
A.D. 27	(6) First Cleansing of the Temple	Jerusalem				2:13–22	Ps. 69:9
	(7) Received at Jerusalem	Judea				2:23–25	
	(8) Teaches Nicodemus about Second Birth	Judea				3:1–21	Num. 21:8, 9
	(9) Co-Ministry with John	Judea				3:22–30	

Date	Event	Location	Matthew	Mark	Luke	John	Related References
A.D. 27	(10) Leaves for Galilee	Judea	4:12	1:14	4:14	4:1–4	
	(11) Samaritan Woman at Jacob's Well	Samaria				4:5–42	Josh. 24:32
	(12) Returns to Galilee			1:15	4:15	4:43–45	

A.D. 27–29   THE GALILEAN MINISTRY OF JESUS IN 55 EVENTS

Date	Event	Location	Matthew	Mark	Luke	John	Related References
A.D. 27	(1) Healing of the Nobleman's Son	Cana				4:46–54	
	(2) Rejected at Nazareth	Nazareth			4:16–30		Is. 61:1, 2
	(3) Moved to Capernaum	Capernaum	4:13–17				Is. 9:1, 2
	(4) Four Become Fishers of Men	Sea of Galilee	4:18–22	1:16–20	5:1–11		Ps. 33:9
	(5) Demoniac Healed on the Sabbath Day	Capernaum		1:21–28	4:31–37		
	(6) Peter's Mother-in-Law Cured, Plus Others	Capernaum	8:14–17	1:29–34	4:38–41		Is. 53:4
c. A.D. 27	(7) First Preaching Tour of Galilee	Galilee	4:23–25	1:35–39	4:42–44		
	(8) Leper Healed and Response Recorded	Galilee	8:1–4	1:40–45	5:12–16		Lev. 13:49
	(9) Paralytic Healed	Capernaum	9:1–8	2:1–12	5:17–26		Rom. 3:23
	(10) Matthew's Call and Reception Held	Capernaum	9:9–13	2:13–17	5:27–32		Hos. 6:6
	(11) Disciples Defended via a Parable	Capernaum	9:14–17	2:18–22	5:33–39		
A.D. 28	(12) Goes to Jerusalem for Second Passover; Heals Lame Man	Jerusalem				5:1–47	Ex. 20:10
	(13) Plucked Grain Precipitates Sabbath Controversy	En Route to Galilee	12:1–8	2:23–28	6:1–5		Deut. 5:14
	(14) Withered Hand Healed Causes Another Sabbath Controversy	Galilee	12:9–14	3:1–6	6:6–11		
	(15) Multitudes Healed	Sea of Galilee	12:15–21	3:7–12	6:17–19		
	(16) Twelve Apostles Selected After a Night of Prayer	Near Capernaum		3:13–19	6:12–16		
	(17) Sermon on the Mt.	Near Capernaum	5:1—7:29		6:20–49		
	(18) Centurion's Servant Healed	Capernaum	8:5–13		7:1–10		Is. 49:12, 13
	(19) Raises Widow's Son from Dead	Nain			7:11–17		Job 19:25
	(20) Jesus Allays John's Doubts	Galilee	11:2–19		7:18–35		Mal. 3:1
	(21) Woes Upon the Privileged		11:20–30				Gen. 19:24
	(22) A Sinful Woman Anoints Jesus	Simon's House, Capernaum			7:36–50		
	(23) Another Tour of Galilee	Galilee			8:1–3		
	(24) Jesus Accused of Blasphemy	Capernaum	12:22–37	3:20–30	11:14–23		
	(25) Jesus' Answer to a Demand for a Sign	Capernaum	12:38–45		11:24–26, 29–36		
	(26) Mother, Brothers Seek Audience	Capernaum	12:46–50	3:31–35	8:19–21		
	(27) Famous Parables of Sower, Seed, Tares, Mustard Seed, Leaven, Treasure, Pearl, Dragnet, Lamp Told	By Sea of Galilee	13:1–52	4:1–34	8:4–18		Joel 3:13
	(28) Sea Made Serene	Sea of Galilee	8:23–27	4:35–41	8:22–25		
	(29) Gadarene Demoniac Healed	E. Shore of Galilee	8:28–34	5:1–20	8:26–39		
	(30) Jairus' Daughter Raised and Woman with Hemorrhage Healed		9:18–26	5:21–43	8:40–56		
	(31) Two Blind Men's Sight Restored		9:27–31				

Date	Event	Location	Matthew	Mark	Luke	John	Related References
A.D. 28	(32) Mute Demoniac Healed		9:32–34				
	(33) Nazareth's Second Rejection of Christ	Nazareth	13:53–58	6:1–6			
	(34) Twelve Sent Out		9:35—11:1	6:6–13	9:1–6		1 Cor. 9:14
	(35) Fearful Herod Beheads John	Galilee	14:1–12	6:14–29	9:7–9		
Spring A.D. 29	(36) Return of 12, Jesus Withdraws, 5000 Fed	Near Bethsaida	14:13–21	6:30–44	9:10–17	6:1–14	
	(37) Walks on the Water	Sea of Galilee	14:22–33	6:45–52		6:15–21	
	(38) Sick of Gennesaret Healed	Gennesaret	14:34–36	6:53–56			
	(39) Peak of Popularity Passes in Galilee	Capernaum				6:22–71 7:1	Is. 54:13
A.D. 29	(40) Traditions Attacked		15:1–20	7:1–23			Ex. 21:17
	(41) Aborted Retirement in Phoenicia: Syro-Phoenician Healed	Phoenicia	15:21–28	7:24–30			
	(42) Afflicted Healed	Decapolis	15:29–31	7:31–37			
	(43) 4000 Fed	Decapolis	15:32–39	8:1–9			
	(44) Pharisees Increase Attack	Magdala	16:1–4	8:10–13			
	(45) Disciples' Carelessness Condemned; Blind Man Healed		16:5–12	8:14–26			Jer. 5:21
	(46) Peter Confesses Jesus Is the Christ	Near Caesarea Philippi	16:13–20	8:27–30	9:18–21		
	(47) Jesus Foretells His Death	Caesarea Philippi	16:21–26	8:31–37	9:22–25		
	(48) Kingdom Promised		16:27, 28	9:1	9:26, 27		Prov. 24:12
	(49) The Transfiguration	Mountain Unnamed	17:1–13	9:2–13	9:28–36		Is. 42:1
	(50) Epileptic Healed	Mt. of Transfiguration	17:14–21	9:14–29	9:37–42		
	(51) Again Tells of Death, Resurrection	Galilee	17:22, 23	9:30–32	9:43–45		
	(52) Taxes Paid	Capernaum	17:24–27				Ex. 30:11–15
	(53) Disciples Contend About Greatness; Jesus Defines; also Patience, Loyalty, Forgiveness	Capernaum	18:1–35	9:33–50	9:46–62		
	(54) Jesus Rejects Brothers' Advice	Galilee				7:2–9	
c. Sept. A.D. 29	(55) Galilee Departure and Samaritan Rejection		19:1		9:51–56	7:10	

A.D. 29–30	LAST JUDEAN AND PEREAN MINISTRY OF JESUS IN 42 EVENTS						
Oct. A.D. 29	(1) Feast of Tabernacles	Jerusalem				7:2, 11–52	
	(2) Forgiveness of Adulteress	Jerusalem				7:53—8:11	Lev. 20:10
A.D. 29	(3) Christ—the Light of the World	Jerusalem				8:12–20	
	(4) Pharisees Can't Meet the Prophecy Thus Try to Destroy the Prophet	Jerusalem—Temple				8:12–59	Is. 6:9
	(5) Man Born Blind Healed; Following Consequences	Jerusalem				9:1–41	
	(6) Parable of the Good Shepherd	Jerusalem				10:1–21	
	(7) The Service of the Seventy	Probably Judea				10:1–24	
	(8) Lawyer Hears the Story of the Good Samaritan	Judea (?)				10:25–37	
	(9) The Hospitality of Martha and Mary	Bethany				10:38–42	
	(10) Another Lesson on Prayer	Judea (?)				11:1–13	

Date	Event	Location	Matthew	Mark	Luke	John	Related References
A.D. 29	(11) Accused of Connection with Beelzebub				11:14–36		
	(12) Judgment Against Lawyers and Pharisees				11:37–54		Mic. 6:8
	(13) Jesus Deals with Hypocrisy, Covetousness, Worry, and Alertness				12:1–59		Mic. 7:6
	(14) Repent or Perish				13:1–5		
	(15) Barren Fig Tree				13:6–9		
	(16) Crippled Woman Healed on Sabbath				13:10–17		Deut. 5:12–15
Winter	(17) Parables of Mustard Seed and Leaven	{ Probably Perea			13:18–21		
A.D. 29	(18) Feast of Dedication	Jerusalem				10:22–39	Ps. 82:6
	(19) Withdrawal Beyond Jordan					10:40–42	
	(20) Begins Teaching Return to Jerusalem with Special Words About Herod	Perea			13:22–35		Ps. 6:8
	(21) Meal with a Pharisee Ruler Occasions Healing Man with Dropsy; Parables of Ox, Best Places, and Great Supper				14:1–24		
	(22) Demands of Discipleship	Perea			14:25–35		
	(23) Parables of Lost Sheep, Coin, Son				15:1–32		1 Pet. 2:25
	(24) Parables of Unjust Steward, Rich Man and Lazarus				16:1–31		
	(25) Lessons on Service, Faith, Influence				17:1–10		
	(26) Resurrection of Lazarus	{ Perea to Bethany				11:1–44	
	(27) Reaction to It: Withdrawal of Jesus					11:45–54	
A.D. 30	(28) Begins Last Journey to Jerusalem via Samaria & Galilee	{ Samaria, Galilee			17:11		
	(29) Heals Ten Lepers				17:12–19		Lev. 13:45, 46
	(30) Lessons on the Coming Kingdom				17:20–37		Gen. 6—7
	(31) Parables: Persistent Widow, Pharisee and Tax Collector				18:1–14		
	(32) Doctrine on Divorce		19:1–12	10:1–12			Deut. 24:1–4 Gen. 2:23–25
	(33) Jesus Blesses Children: Objections	Perea	19:13–15	10:13–16	18:15–17		Ps. 131:2
	(34) Rich Young Ruler	Perea	19:16–30	10:17–31	18:18–30		Ex. 20:1–17
	(35) Laborers of the 11th Hour		20:1–16				
	(36) Foretells Death and Resurrection	{ Near Jordan	20:17–19	10:32–34	18:31–34		Ps. 22
	(37) Ambition of James and John		20:20–28	10:35–45			
	(38) Blind Bartimaeus Healed	Jericho		10:46–52	18:35–43		
	(39) Interview with Zacchaeus	Jericho			19:1–10		
	(40) Parable: the Minas	Jericho			19:11–27		
	(41) Returns to Home of Mary and Martha	Bethany				{ 11:55— 12:1	
	(42) Plot to Kill Lazarus	Bethany				12:9–11	

Spring A.D. 30	JESUS' FINAL WEEK OF WORK AT JERUSALEM IN 41 EVENTS						
Sunday	(1) Triumphal Entry	Bethany, Jerusalem, Bethany	21:1–9	11:1–11	19:28–44	12:12–19	Zech. 9:9

Date	Event	Location	Matthew	Mark	Luke	John	Related References
Monday	(2) Fig Tree Cursed and Temple Cleansed	Bethany to Jerusalem	21:10–19	11:12–18	19:45–48		Jer. 7:11
	(3) The Attraction of Sacrifice	Jerusalem				12:20–50	Is. 6:10
Tuesday	(4) Withered Fig Tree Testifies	Bethany to Jerusalem	21:20–22	11:19–26			
	(5) Sanhedrin Challenges Jesus. Answered by Parables: Two Sons, Wicked Vinedressers and Marriage Feast	Jerusalem	21:23—22:14	11:27—12:12	20:1–19		Is. 5:1, 2
	(6) Tribute to Caesar	Jerusalem	22:15–22	12:13–17	20:20–26		
	(7) Sadducees Question the Resurrection	Jerusalem	22:23–33	12:18–27	20:27–40		Ex. 3:6
	(8) Pharisees Question Commandments	Jerusalem	22:34–40	12:28–34			
	(9) Jesus and David	Jerusalem	22:41–46	12:35–37	20:41–44		Ps. 110:1
	(10) Jesus' Last Sermon	Jerusalem	23:1–39	12:38–40	20:45–47		
	(11) Widow's Mite	Jerusalem		12:41–44	21:1–4		Lev. 27:30
	(12) Jesus Tells of the Future	Mt. Olives	24:1–51	13:1–37	21:5–36		Dan. 12:1
	(13) Parables: Ten Virgins, Talents. The Day of Judgment	Mt. Olives	25:1–46				Zech. 14:5
	(14) Jesus Tells Date of Crucifixion		26:1–5	14:1, 2	22:1, 2		
	(15) Anointing by Mary at Simon's Feast	Bethany	26:6–13	14:3–9		12:2–8	
	(16) Judas Contracts the Betrayal		26:14–16	14:10, 11	22:3–6		Zech. 11:12
Thursday	(17) Preparation for the Passover	Jerusalem	26:17–19	14:12–16	22:7–13		Ex. 12:14–28
Thursday P.M.	(18) Passover Eaten, Jealousy Rebuked	Jerusalem	26:20	14:17	22:14–16, 24–30		
	(19) Feet Washed	Upper Room				13:1–20	
	(20) Judas Revealed, Defects	Upper Room	26:21–25	14:18–21	22:21–23	13:21–30	Ps. 41:9
	(21) Jesus Warns About Further Desertion; Cries of Loyalty	Upper Room	26:31–35	14:27–31	22:31–38	13:31–38	Zech. 13:7
	(22) Institution of the Lord's Supper	Upper Room	26:26–29	14:22–25	22:17–20		1 Cor. 11:23–34
	(23) Last Speech to the Apostles and Intercessory Prayer	Jerusalem				14:1—17:26	Ps. 35:19
Thursday- Friday	(24) The Grief of Gethsemane	Mt. Olives	26:30, 36–46	14:26, 32–42	22:39–46	18:1	Ps. 42:6
Friday	(25) Betrayal, Arrest, Desertion	Gethsemane	26:47–56	14:43–52	22:47–53	18:2–12	
	(26) First Examined by Annas	Jerusalem				18:12–14, 19–23	
	(27) Trial by Caiaphas and Council; Following Indignities	Jerusalem	26:57, 59–68	14:53, 55–65	22:54, 63–65	18:24	Lev. 24:16
	(28) Peter's Triple Denial	Jerusalem	26:58, 69–75	14:54, 66–72	22:54–62	18:15–18, 25–27	
	(29) Condemnation by the Council	Jerusalem	27:1	15:1	22:66–71		Ps. 110:1
	(30) Suicide of Judas	Jerusalem	27:3–10				Acts 1:18, 19
	(31) First Appearance Before Pilate	Jerusalem	27:2, 11–14	15:1–5	23:1–7	18:28–38	
	(32) Jesus Before Herod	Jerusalem			23:6–12		
	(33) Second Appearance Before Pilate	Jerusalem	27:15–26	15:6–15	23:13–25	18:39—19:16	Deut. 21:6–9
	(34) Mockery by Roman Soldiers	Jerusalem	27:27–30	15:16–19			
	(35) Led to Golgotha	Jerusalem	27:31–34	15:20–23	23:26–33	19:16, 17	Ps. 69:21
	(36) 6 Events of First 3 Hours on Cross	Calvary	27:35–44	15:24–32	23:33–43	19:18–27	Ps. 22:18
	(37) Last 3 Hours on Cross	Calvary	27:45–50	15:33–37	23:44–46	19:28–30	Ps. 22:1
	(38) Events Attending Jesus' Death		27:51–56	15:38–41	23:45, 47–49		
	(39) Burial of Jesus	Jerusalem	27:57–60	15:42–46	23:50–54	19:31–37	Ex. 12:46
Friday- Saturday	(40) Tomb Sealed	Jerusalem	27:61–66		23:55, 56		Ex. 20:8–11
	(41) Women Watch	Jerusalem		15:47			

Date	Event	Location	Matthew	Mark	Luke	John	Related References
A.D. 30	**THE RESURRECTION THROUGH THE ASCENSION IN 12 EVENTS**						
Dawn of First Day (Sunday, "Lord's Day")	(1) Women Visit the Tomb	Near Jerusalem	28:1–10	16:1–8	24:1–11		
	(2) Peter and John See the Empty Tomb				24:12	20:1–10	
	(3) Jesus' Appearance to Mary Magdalene	Jerusalem		16:9–11		20:11–18	
	(4) Jesus' Appearance to the Other Women	Jerusalem	28:9, 10				
	(5) Guards' Report of the Resurrection		28:11–15				
Sunday Afternoon	(6) Jesus' Appearance to Two Disciples on Way to Emmaus			16:12, 13	24:13–35		1 Cor. 15:5
Late Sunday	(7) Jesus' Appearance to Ten Disciples Without Thomas	Jerusalem		16:14	24:36–43	20:19–25	
One Week Later	(8) Appearance to Disciples with Thomas	Jerusalem				20:26–31	
During 40 Days until Ascension	(9) Jesus' Appearance to Seven Disciples by Sea of Galilee	Galilee				21:1–25	
	(10) Appearance to 500	Mt. in Galilee					1 Cor. 15:6
	(11) Great Commission		28:16–20	16:15–18	24:44–49		
	(12) The Ascension	Mt. Olivet		16:19, 20	24:50–53		Acts 1:4–11

The Jewish Calendar

The Jews used two kinds of calendars:
Civil Calendar—official calendar of kings, childbirth, and contracts.
Sacred Calendar—from which festivals were computed.

NAMES OF MONTHS	CORRESPONDS WITH	NO. OF DAYS	MONTH OF CIVIL YEAR	MONTH OF SACRED YEAR
TISHRI	Sept.–Oct.	30 days	1st	7th
HESHVAN	Oct.–Nov.	29 or 30	2nd	8th
CHISLEV	Nov.–Dec.	29 or 30	3rd	9th
TEBETH	Dec.–Jan.	29	4th	10th
SHEBAT	Jan.–Feb.	30	5th	11th
ADAR	Feb.–Mar.	29 or 30	6th	12th
NISAN	Mar.–Apr.	30	7th	1st
IYAR	Apr.–May	29	8th	2nd
SIVAN	May–June	30	9th	3rd
TAMMUZ	June–July	29	10th	4th
AB	July–Aug.	30	11th	5th
*ELUL	Aug.–Sept.	29	12th	6th

The Jewish day was from sunset to sunset, in 8 equal parts:

FIRST WATCH ..... SUNSET TO 9 P.M.
SECOND WATCH ... 9 P.M. TO MIDNIGHT
THIRD WATCH ..... MIDNIGHT TO 3 A.M.
FOURTH WATCH ... 3 A.M. TO SUNRISE

FIRST WATCH ..... SUNRISE TO 9 A.M.
SECOND WATCH ... 9 A.M. TO NOON
THIRD WATCH ..... NOON TO 3 P.M.
FOURTH WATCH ... 3 P.M. TO SUNSET

*Hebrew months were alternately 30 and 29 days long. Their year, shorter than ours, had 354 days. Therefore, about every 3 years (7 times in 19 years) an extra 29-day-month, VEADAR, was added between ADAR and NISAN.

THE LIFE OF CHRIST
AND
CHRIST'S PUBLIC MINISTRY

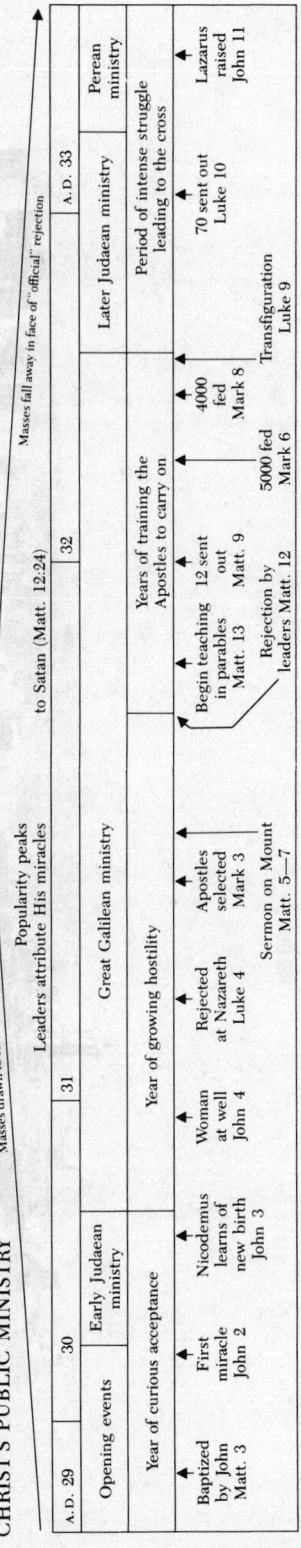

4 B.C.	A.D. 9 (Temple Discussion)	A.D. 29	A.D. 33
EARLY CHILDHOOD	YEARS AT NAZARETH (Luke 2:51, 52)	PUBLIC MINISTRY	

Birth — Luke 2:41–50

CHRIST'S PUBLIC MINISTRY

Masses drawn to His miracles and teachings

Popularity peaks — Leaders attribute His miracles to Satan (Matt. 12:24)

Masses fall away in face of "official" rejection

A.D. 29	30	31	32	A.D. 33

Opening events — Early Judaean ministry — Great Galilean ministry — Later Judaean ministry — Perean ministry

Year of curious acceptance — Year of growing hostility

Years of training the Apostles to carry on

Period of intense struggle leading to the cross

- Baptized by John — Matt. 3
- First miracle — John 2
- Nicodemus learns of new birth — John 3
- Woman at well — John 4
- Rejected at Nazareth — Luke 4
- Sermon on Mount — Matt. 5—7
- Apostles selected — Mark 3
- Begin teaching in parables — Matt. 13
- Rejection by leaders Matt. 12
- 12 sent out — Matt. 9
- 5000 fed — Mark 6
- 4000 fed — Mark 8
- Transfiguration — Luke 9
- 70 sent out — Luke 10
- Lazarus raised — John 11

From *Visual Survey of the Bible*. Reprinted by permission of the author.

The Old Testament prophet Micah had predicted that the Messiah would be born in this city (Micah 5:2), Bethlehem. It is a small city just 10 km. (6 mi.) south of Jerusalem.

Bethlehem, in the hill country of Judah—the home of David and the birthplace of Jesus (1 Sam. 16:1, 4; Luke 2:11).

Photo by Gustav Jeeninga

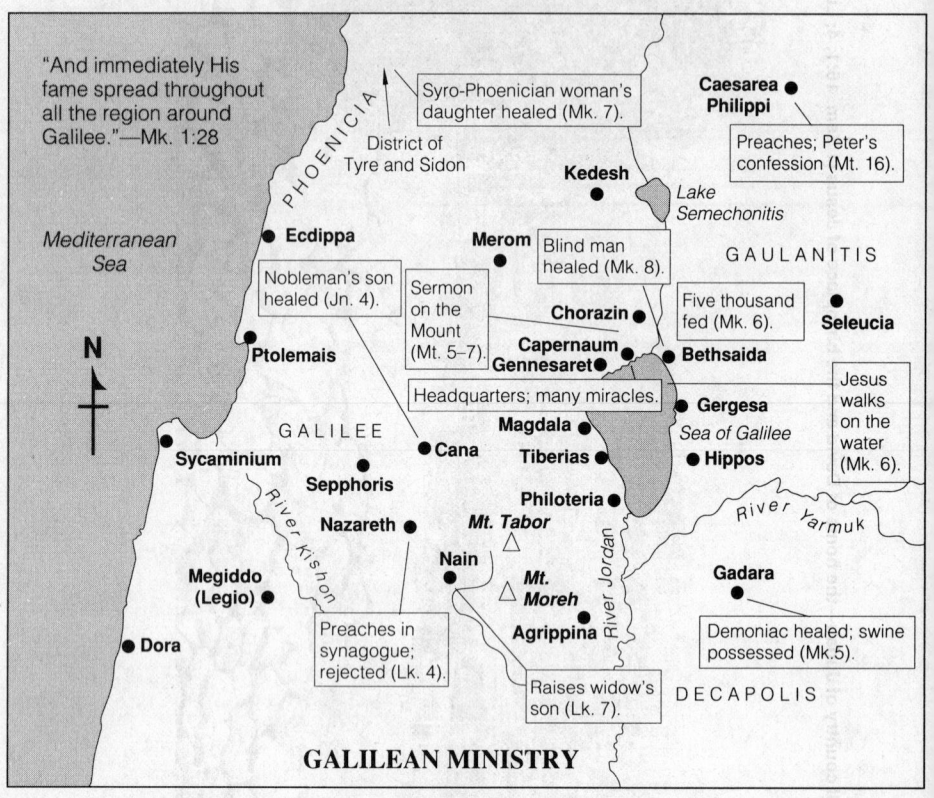

"And immediately His fame spread throughout all the region around Galilee."—Mk. 1:28

Mediterranean Sea

PHOENICIA

District of Tyre and Sidon

Syro-Phoenician woman's daughter healed (Mk. 7).

Caesarea Philippi

Preaches; Peter's confession (Mt. 16).

Kedesh

Lake Semechonitis

GAULANITIS

Ecdippa

Merom

Blind man healed (Mk. 8).

Five thousand fed (Mk. 6).

Seleucia

Nobleman's son healed (Jn. 4).

Sermon on the Mount (Mt. 5–7).

Chorazin

Ptolemais

Capernaum
Gennesaret

Bethsaida

Headquarters; many miracles.

Gergesa

Jesus walks on the water (Mk. 6).

N

GALILEE

Cana

Magdala

Sea of Galilee

Sycaminium

Sepphoris

Tiberias

Hippos

River Kishon

Nazareth

Philoteria

River Yarmuk

Mt. Tabor

Nain

Megiddo (Legio)

Mt. Moreh

River Jordan

Gadara

Preaches in synagogue; rejected (Lk. 4).

Agrippina

Demoniac healed; swine possessed (Mk.5).

Dora

Raises widow's son (Lk. 7).

DECAPOLIS

GALILEAN MINISTRY

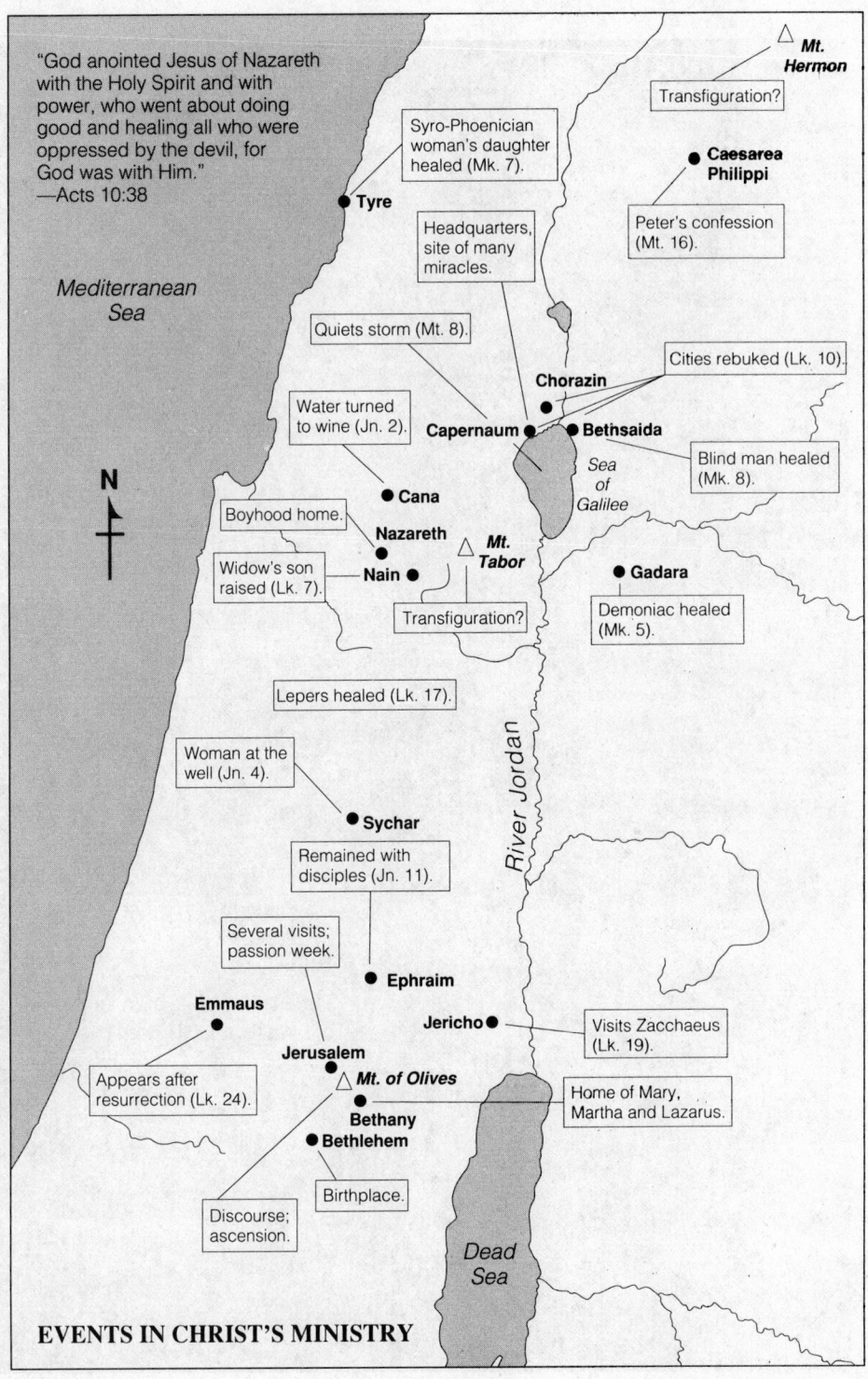

"God anointed Jesus of Nazareth with the Holy Spirit and with power, who went about doing good and healing all who were oppressed by the devil, for God was with Him."
—Acts 10:38

Mt. Hermon

Transfiguration?

Syro-Phoenician woman's daughter healed (Mk. 7).

Caesarea Philippi

Tyre

Peter's confession (Mt. 16).

Mediterranean Sea

Headquarters, site of many miracles.

Quiets storm (Mt. 8).

Cities rebuked (Lk. 10).

Chorazin

Water turned to wine (Jn. 2).

Capernaum **Bethsaida**

Sea of Galilee

Blind man healed (Mk. 8).

N

Cana

Boyhood home.

Nazareth

Mt. Tabor

Nain

Widow's son raised (Lk. 7).

Transfiguration?

Gadara

Demoniac healed (Mk. 5).

Lepers healed (Lk. 17).

Woman at the well (Jn. 4).

River Jordan

Sychar

Remained with disciples (Jn. 11).

Several visits; passion week.

Ephraim

Emmaus

Jericho

Visits Zacchaeus (Lk. 19).

Appears after resurrection (Lk. 24).

Jerusalem *Mt. of Olives*

Home of Mary, Martha and Lazarus.

Bethany
Bethlehem

Discourse; ascension.

Birthplace.

Dead Sea

EVENTS IN CHRIST'S MINISTRY

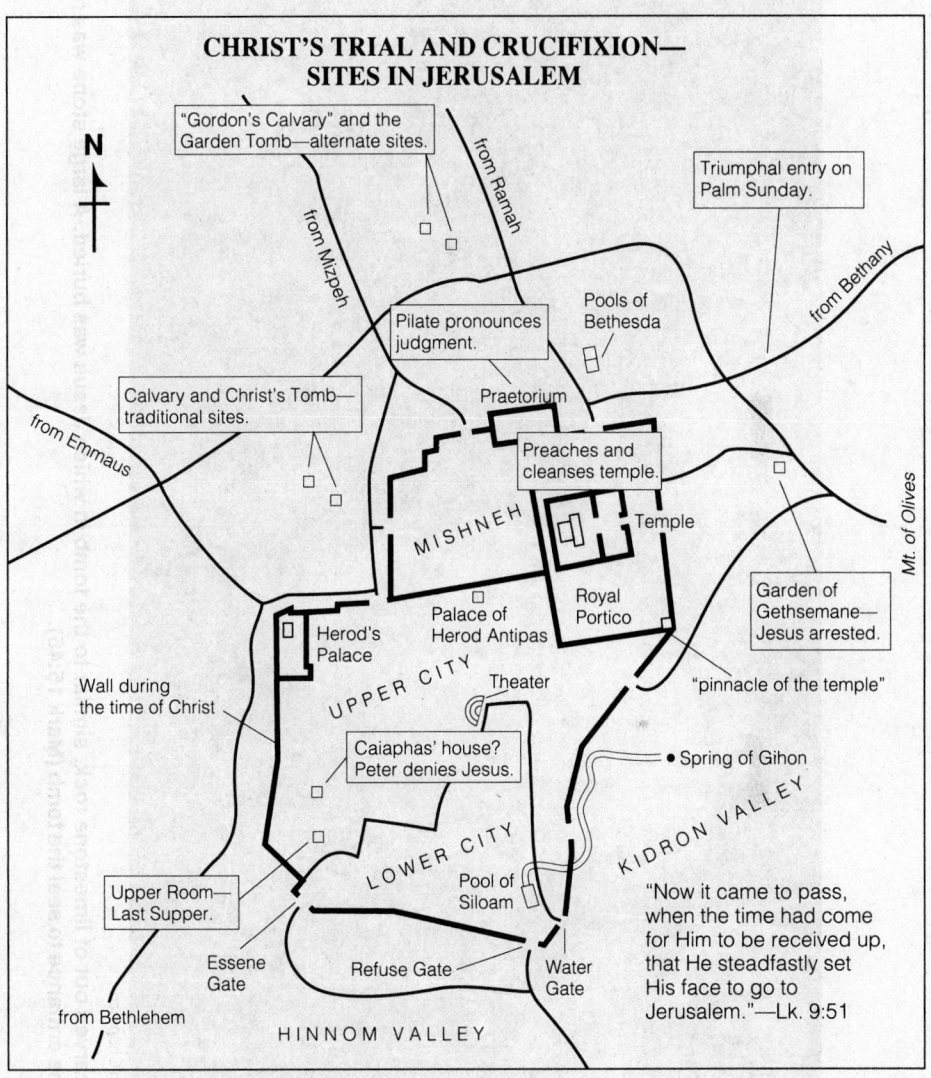

CHRIST'S TRIAL AND CRUCIFIXION—
SITES IN JERUSALEM

N

"Gordon's Calvary" and the
Garden Tomb—alternate sites.

from Ramah

Triumphal entry on
Palm Sunday.

from Mizpeh

from Bethany

Pools of
Bethesda

Pilate pronounces
judgment.

Calvary and Christ's Tomb—
traditional sites.

Praetorium

from Emmaus

Preaches and
cleanses temple.

MISHNEH

Temple

Mt. of Olives

Royal
Portico

Garden of
Gethsemane—
Jesus arrested.

Herod's
Palace

Palace of
Herod Antipas

Wall during
the time of Christ

UPPER CITY

Theater

"pinnacle of the temple"

Caiaphas' house?
Peter denies Jesus.

Spring of Gihon

LOWER CITY

KIDRON VALLEY

Upper Room—
Last Supper.

Pool of
Siloam

Essene
Gate

Refuse Gate

Water
Gate

"Now it came to pass,
when the time had come
for Him to be received up,
that He steadfastly set
His face to go to
Jerusalem."—Lk. 9:51

from Bethlehem

HINNOM VALLEY

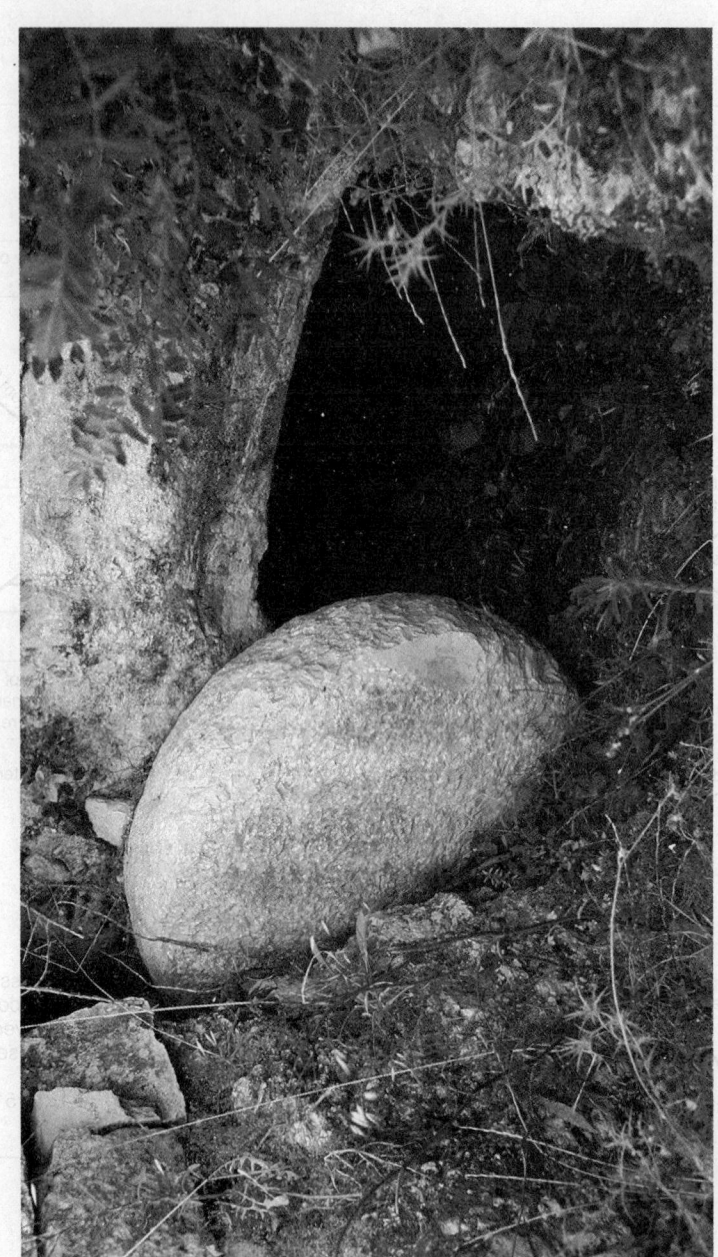

A tomb carved out of limestone rock, similar to the tomb in which Jesus was buried. A large stone was rolled across the entrance to seal the tomb (Mark 15:46).

FROM RESURRECTION TO ASCENSION—APPEARANCES

"But now Christ is risen from the dead, and has become the firstfruits of those who have fallen asleep."—1 Cor. 15:20

Mediterranean Sea

Ptolemais
Capernaum ● **Bethsaida**
Sea of Galilee

Jesus appears to His disciples as they fish (Jn. 21).

GALILEE

Tiberias

Nazareth

△ **Mt. Tabor**

River Yarmuk

● **Caesarea**

Jesus appears to the eleven disciples on a mountain in Galilee (Mt. 28).

SAMARIA

PEREA

River Jabbok

River Jordan

In Jerusalem, Jesus appears to: Mary Magdalene (Mk. 16); the other women (Mt. 28); the eleven disciples (Lk. 24); and Thomas (Jn. 20).

Resurrection.

Jesus appears to five hundred brethren and to James (1 Cor. 15), place unknown.

● **Joppa**

Emmaus ●

Jesus appears to two followers on the road to Emmaus (Lk. 24).

Jerusalem
● **Bethany**
△ **Mt. of Olives**

JUDEA

Ascension (Lk. 24).

Dead Sea

N

PROPHECIES OF THE MESSIAH FULFILLED IN JESUS CHRIST

Presented Here in Their Order of Fulfillment

PROPHETIC SCRIPTURE	SUBJECT	FULFILLED
Gen. 3:15, p. 7 "And I will put enmity between you and the woman, and between your seed and her Seed; He shall bruise your head, and you shall bruise His heel."	seed of a woman	**Gal. 4:4, p. 1189** "But when the fullness of the time had come, God sent forth His Son, born of a woman, born under the law,"
Gen. 12:3, p. 14 "I will bless those who bless you, and I will curse him who curses you; And in you all the families of the earth shall be blessed."	descendant of Abraham	**Matt. 1:1, p. 973** "The book of the genealogy of Jesus Christ, the Son of David, the Son of Abraham:"
Gen. 17:19, p. 18 "Then God said, 'No, Sarah your wife shall bear you a son, and you shall call his name Isaac; I will establish My covenant with him for an everlasting covenant, *and* with his descendants after him.'"	descendant of Isaac	**Luke 3:34, p. 1040** "*the son* of Jacob, *the son* of Isaac, *the son* of Abraham, *the son* of Terah, *the son* of Nahor,"
Num. 24:17, p. 157 "I see Him, but not now; I behold Him, but not near; a Star shall come out of Jacob; a Scepter shall rise out of Israel, and batter the brow of Moab, and destroy all the sons of tumult."	descendant of Jacob	**Matt. 1:2, p. 973** "Abraham begot Isaac, Isaac begot Jacob, and Jacob begot Judah and his brothers."
Gen. 49:10, p. 50 "The scepter shall not depart from Judah, nor a lawgiver from between his feet, until Shiloh comes; and to Him *shall be* the obedience of the people."	from the tribe of Judah	**Luke 3:33, p. 1040** "*the son* of Amminadab, *the son* of Ram, *the son* of Hezron, *the son* of Perez, *the son* of Judah."
Is. 9:7, p. 687 "Of the increase of *His* government and peace *there will be* no end, upon the throne of David and over His kingdom, to order it and establish it with judgment and justice from that time forward, even forever. The zeal of the LORD of hosts will perform this."	heir to the throne of David	**Luke 1:32, 33, p. 1037** "He will be great, and will be called the Son of the Highest; and the Lord God will give Him the throne of His father David. And He will reign over the house of Jacob forever, and of His kingdom there will be no end."
Ps. 45:6, 7, p. 565; 102:25–27, p. 596 "Your throne, O God, *is* forever and ever; a scepter of righteousness *is* the scepter of Your kingdom. You love righteousness and hate wickedness; therefore God, Your God, has anointed You with the oil of gladness more than Your companions." "Of old You laid the foundation of the earth, and the heavens *are* the work of Your hands. They will perish, but You will endure; yes, all of them will grow old like a garment; like a cloak You will change them, and they will be changed. But You *are* the same, and Your years will have no end."	anointed and eternal	**Heb. 1:8–12, p. 1248** "But to the Son He says: 'Your throne, O God, is forever and ever; a scepter of righteousness is the scepter of Your kingdom. You have loved righteousness and hated lawlessness; therefore God, Your God, has anointed You with the oil of gladness more than Your companions.' And: 'You, LORD, in the beginning laid the foundation of the earth, and the heavens are the work of Your hands; they will perish, but You remain; and they will all grow old like a garment; like a cloak You will fold them up, and they will be changed. But You are the same, and Your years will not fail.'"

PROPHETIC SCRIPTURE	SUBJECT	FULFILLED
c. 5:2 'But you, Bethlehem, Ephrathah, ugh you are little among the thousands Judah, *yet* out of you shall come forth to the One to be ruler in Israel, whose ngs forth *have been* from of old, from rlasting.''	born in Bethlehem	*Luke 2:4, 5, 7* "And Joseph also went up from Galilee, out of the city of Nazareth, into Judea, to the city of David, which is called Bethlehem, because he was of the house and lineage of David, to be registered with Mary, his betrothed wife, who was with child. . . . And she brought forth her first-born Son, and wrapped Him in swaddling cloths, and laid Him in a manger, because there was no room for them in the inn.''
n. 9:25 'Know therefore and understand, *that* m the going forth of the command to re- re and build Jerusalem until Messiah Prince, *there shall be* seven weeks and ty-two weeks; the street shall be built ain, and the wall, even in troublesome es.''	time for His birth	*Luke 2:1, 2* "And it came to pass in those days *that* a decree went out from Caesar Augustus that all the world should be registered. This census first took place while Quirinius was governing Syria.''
7:14 'Therefore the Lord Himself will give u a sign: Behold, the virgin shall con- ve and bear a Son, and shall call His me Immanuel.''	to be born of a virgin	*Luke 1:26, 27, 30, 31* "Now in the sixth month the angel Gabriel was sent by God to a city of Galilee named Nazareth, to a virgin betrothed to a man whose name was Joseph, of the house of David. The virgin's name *was* Mary. . . . Then the angel said to her, 'Do not be afraid, Mary, for you have found favor with God. And behold, you will conceive in your womb and bring forth a Son, and shall call His name Jesus.'''
: 31:15 "Thus says the Lord: 'A voice was heard Ramah, lamentation *and* bitter weeping, chel weeping for her children, refusing be comforted for her children, because ey *are* no more.'''	slaughter of children	*Matt. 2:16–18* "Then Herod, when he saw that he was deceived by the wise men, was exceedingly angry; and he sent forth and put to death all the male children who were in Bethlehem and in all its districts, from two years old and under, according to the time which he had determined from the wise men. Then was fulfilled what was spoken by Jeremiah the prophet, saying: 'A *voice was heard in Ramah, lamentation, weeping, and great mourning, Rachel weeping for her children, refusing to be comforted, because they were no more.*'''
os. 11:1 "When Israel *was* a child, I loved him, d out of Egypt I called My son.''	flight to Egypt	*Matt. 2:14, 15* "When he arose, he took the young Child and His mother by night and departed for Egypt, and was there until the death of Herod, that it might be fulfilled which was spoken by the Lord through the prophet, saying, '*Out of Egypt I called My Son.*'''
40:3–5 "The voice of one crying in the wilder- ess: 'Prepare the way of the Lord; make raight in the desert a highway for our od. Every valley shall be exalted, and ery mountain and hill shall be made low; e crooked places shall be made straight, d the rough places smooth; the glory of e Lord shall be revealed, and all flesh all see *it* together; for the mouth of the ɔRD has spoken.'''	the way prepared	*Luke 3:3–6* "And he went into all the region around the Jordan, preaching a baptism of repentance for the remission of sins, as it is written in the book of the words of Isaiah the prophet, saying: '*The voice of one crying in the wilderness: "Prepare the way of the Lord, make His paths straight. Every valley shall be filled and every mountain and hill brought low; and the crooked places shall be made straight and the rough ways made smooth; and all flesh shall see the salvation of God."*'''

PROPHETIC SCRIPTURE	SUBJECT	FULFILLED
Mal. 3:1, p. 964 "'Behold, I send My messenger, and he will prepare the way before Me. And the Lord, whom you seek, will suddenly come to His temple, even the messenger of the covenant, in whom you delight. Behold, He is coming,' says the LORD of hosts."	**preceded by a forerunner**	**Luke 7:24, 27, p. 1046** "When the messengers of John had parted, He began to speak to the multudes concerning John: 'What did you out into the wilderness to see? A re shaken by the wind? . . . This is *he* of wh it is written: *"Behold, I send My messen; before Your face, who will prepare Yo way before You."*'"
Mal. 4:5, 6, p. 965 "Behold I will send you Elijah the prophet before the coming of the great and dreadful day of the LORD. And he will turn the hearts of the fathers to the children, and the hearts of the children to their fathers, lest I come and strike the earth with a curse."	**preceded by Elijah**	**Matt. 11:13, 14, p. 984** "For all the prophets and the law prophesied until John. And if you are willing receive *it*, he is Elijah who is to come.
Ps. 2:7, p. 541 "I will declare the decree: the LORD has said to Me, "You *are* My Son, today I have begotten You."	**declared the Son of God**	**Matt. 3:17, p. 975** "And suddenly a voice *came* fre heaven, saying, 'This is My beloved Son, whom I am well pleased.'"
Is. 9:1, 2, p. 686 "Nevertheless the gloom *will* not *be* upon her who *is* distressed, as when at first He lightly esteemed the land of Zebulun and the land of Naphtali, and afterward more heavily oppressed *her, by* the way of the sea, beyond the Jordan, in Galilee of the Gentiles. The people who walked in darkness have seen a great light; those who dwelt in the land of the shadow of death, upon them a light has shined."	**Galilean ministry**	**Matt. 4:13–16, p. 976** "And leaving Nazareth, He came a dwelt in Capernaum, which is by the sea, the regions of Zebulun and Naphtali, tha might be fulfilled which was spoken by Isa the prophet, saying: *'The land of Zebu and the land of Naphtali, the way of the s beyond the Jordan, Galilee of the Genti The people who sat in darkness saw a gr light, and upon those who sat in the reg and shadow of death light has dawned.'*
Ps. 78:2–4, p. 582 "I will open my mouth in a parable; I will utter dark sayings of old, which we have heard and known, and our fathers have told us. We will not hide *them* from their children, telling to the generation to come the praises of the LORD, and His strength and His wonderful works that He has done."	**speaks in parables**	**Matt. 13:34, 35, p. 987** "All these things Jesus spoke to the m titude in parables; and without a paral He did not speak to them that it might fulfilled which was spoken by the proph saying: *'I will open My mouth in parables will utter things which have been kept cret from the foundation of the world.'*
Deut. 18:15, p. 191 "The LORD your God will raise up for you a Prophet like me from your midst, from your brethren. Him you shall hear."	**a prophet**	**Acts 3:20, 22, p. 1108** "And that He may send Jesus Christ, w was preached to you before. . . . For Mos truly said to the fathers, *'The LORD yo God will raise up for you a Prophet like from your brethren. Him you shall hear all things, whatever He says to you.'*
Is. 61:1, 2, p. 734 "The Spirit of the Lord GOD *is* upon Me, because the LORD has anointed Me to preach good tidings to the poor; He has sent Me to heal the brokenhearted, to proclaim liberty to the captives, and the opening of the prison to *those who are* bound; to proclaim the acceptable year of the LORD, and the day of vengeance of our God; to comfort all who mourn."	**to bind up the brokenhearted**	**Luke 4:18, 19, p. 1041** "*The Spirit of the LORD is upon Me, l cause He has anointed Me to preach t gospel to the poor. He has sent Me to he the brokenhearted, to preach deliveran to the captives and recovery of sight to l blind, to set at liberty those who are o pressed, to preach the acceptable year the LORD.'*
Is. 53:3, p. 727 "He is despised and rejected by men, a man of sorrows and acquainted with grief. And we hid; as it were, *our* faces from Him; He was despised, and we did not esteem Him."	**rejected by His own people, the Jews**	**John 1:11, p. 1075** "He came to His own, and His own d not receive Him." **Luke 23:18, p. 1068** "And they all cried out at once, sayir 'Away with this *Man,* and release to us B rabbas'"——

PROPHETIC SCRIPTURE	SUBJECT	FULFILLED
110:4, p. 602 "The LORD has sworn and will not re-⋅t, 'You *are* a priest forever according to ⋅ order of Melchizedek.'"	**priest after order of Melchizedek**	**Heb. 5:5, 6, p. 1250** "So also Christ did not glorify Himself to become High Priest, *but it* was He who said to Him: *'You are My Son, today I have begotten You.'* As *He* also *says* in another place: *'You are a priest forever according to the order of Melchizedek.'*";
ch. 9:9, p. 955 "Rejoice greatly, O daughter of Zion! ⋅out, O daughter of Jerusalem! Behold, ⋅ur King is coming to you; He *is* just and ⋅ving salvation, lowly and riding on a don-⋅y, a colt, the foal of a donkey."	**triumphal entry**	**Mark 11:7, 9, 11, p. 1023** "Then they brought the colt to Jesus and threw their garments on it, and He sat on it. . . . Then those who went before and those who followed cried out, saying: 'Hosanna! *Blessed is He who comes in the name of the* LORD!' . . . And Jesus went into Jerusalem and into the temple. So when He had looked around at all things, as the hour was already late, He went out to Bethany with the twelve."
8:2, p. 544 "Out of the mouth of babes and infants ⋅u have ordained strength, because of ⋅ur enemies, that You may silence the en-⋅y and the avenger."	**adored by infants**	**Matt. 21:15, 16, p. 995** "But when the chief priests and scribes saw the wonderful things that He did, and the children crying out in the temple and saying, 'Hosanna to the Son of David!' they were indignant and said to Him, 'Do You hear what these are saying?' And Jesus said to them, 'Yes. Have you never read, "*Out of the mouth of babes and nursing infants You have perfected praise*"?'"
53:1, p. 727 "Who has believed our report? And to ⋅om has the arm of the LORD been re-⋅aled?"	**not believed**	**John 12:37, 38, p. 1091** "But although He had done so many signs before them, they did not believe in Him, that the word of Isaiah the prophet might be fulfilled, which he spoke: '*Lord, who has believed our report? And to whom has the arm of the* LORD *been revealed?*'"
41:9, p. 563 "Even my own familiar friend in whom I ⋅sted, who ate my bread, has lifted up *his* ⋅el against me."	**betrayed by a close friend**	**Luke 22:47, 48, p. 1067** "And while He was still speaking, behold, a multitude; and he who was called Judas, one of the twelve, went before them and drew near to Jesus to kiss Him. But Jesus said to him, 'Judas, are you betraying the Son of Man with a kiss?'"
ch. 11:12, p. 957 "Then I said to them, 'If it is agreeable to ⋅u, give *me* my wages; and if not, refrain.' ⋅ they weighed out for my wages thirty ⋅ces of silver."	**betrayed for thirty pieces of silver**	**Matt. 26:14, 15, p. 1002** "Then one of the twelve, called Judas Iscariot, went to the chief priests and said, 'What are you willing to give me if I deliver Him to you?' And they counted out to him thirty pieces of silver."
35:11, p. 558 "Fierce witnesses rise up; they ask me ⋅ings that I do not know."	**accused by false witnesses**	**Mark 14:57, 58, p. 1029** "And some rose up and bore false witness against Him, saying, 'We heard Him say, "I will destroy this temple that *is* made with hands, and within three days I will build another made without hands."'"
53:7, p. 727 "He was oppressed and He was afflicted, ⋅t He opened not His mouth; He was led ⋅ a lamb to the slaughter, and as a sheep ⋅fore its shearers is silent, so He opened ⋅t His mouth."	**silent to accusations**	**Mark 15:4, 5, p. 1029** "Then Pilate asked Him again, saying, 'Do You answer nothing? See how many things they testify against You!' But Jesus still answered nothing, so that Pilate marveled."

PROPHETIC SCRIPTURE	SUBJECT	FULFILLED
Is. 50:6 "I gave My back to those who struck *Me*, and My cheeks to those who plucked out the beard; I did not hide My face from shame and spitting."	spat on and struck	**Matt. 26:67**, "Then they spat in His face and b Him; and others struck *Him* with the pal of their hands,"
Ps. 35:19. "Let them not rejoice over me who are wrongfully my enemies; nor let them wink with the eye who hate me without a cause."	hated without reason	**John 15:24, 25** "If I had not done among them the wo which no one else did, they would have sin; but now they have seen and also ha both Me and My Father. But *this happer* that the word might be fulfilled which written in their law, *'They hated Me wi out a cause.'*"
Is. 53:5 "But He *was* wounded for our transgressions, *He was* bruised for our iniquities; the chastisement for our peace *was* upon Him, and by His stripes we are healed."	vicarious sacrifice	**Rom. 5:6, 8** "For when we were still without streng in due time Christ died for the ungoc . . . But God demonstrates His own l toward us, in that while we were still s ners, Christ died for us."
Is. 53:12. "Therefore I will divide Him a portion with the great, and He shall divide the spoil with the strong, because He poured out His soul unto death, and He was numbered with the transgressors, and He bore the sin of many, and made intercession for the transgressors."	crucified with malefactors	**Mark 15:27, 28** "With Him they also crucified two re bers, one on His right and the other on I left. So the Scripture was fulfilled wh says, *'And He was numbered with the tra gressors.'*"
Zech. 12:10 "And I will pour on the house of David and on the inhabitants of Jerusalem the Spirit of grace and supplication; then they will look on Me whom they have pierced; they will mourn for Him as one mourns for *his* only *son*, and grieve for Him as one grieves for a firstborn."	pierced through hands and feet	**John 20:27** "Then He said to Thomas, 'Reach yc finger here, and look at My hands; a reach your hand *here*, and put *it* into I side. Do not be unbelieving, but beli ing.'"
Ps. 22:7, 8 "All those who see Me laugh Me to scorn; they shoot out the lip, they shake the head, *saying*, 'He trusted in the LORD, let Him rescue Him; let Him deliver Him, since He delights in Him!'"	sneered and mocked	**Luke 23:35** "And the people stood looking on. F even the rulers with them sneered, sayin 'He saved others; let Him save Himsel He is the Christ, the chosen of God.'"
Ps. 69:9 "Because zeal for Your house has eaten me up, and the reproaches of those who reproach You have fallen on me."	was reproached	**Rom. 15:3** "For even Christ did not please Himse but as it is written, *'The reproaches of tho who reproached You fell on Me.'*"
Ps. 109:4 "In return for my love they are my accusers, but I *give myself to* prayer."	prayer for His enemies	**Luke 23:34** "Then Jesus said, 'Father, forgive the for they do not know what they do.' A they divided His garments and cast lot
Ps. 22:17, 18. "I can count all My bones. They look *and* stare at Me. They divide My garments among them, and for My clothing they cast lots."	soldiers gambled for His clothing	**Matt. 27:35, 36** "Then they crucified Him, and divid His garments, casting lots, that it might fulfilled which was spoken by the proph *'They divided My garments among the and for My clothing they cast lots.'* Sitti down, they kept watch over Him there
Ps. 22:1 "My God, My God, why have You forsaken Me? *Why are You so* far from helping Me, *and from* the words of My groaning?"	forsaken by God	**Matt. 27:46** "And about the ninth hour Jesus cri out with a loud voice, saying, 'Eli, Eli, lar sabachthani?' that is, *'My God, My Go why have You forsaken Me?'*"

PROPHETIC SCRIPTURE	SUBJECT	FULFILLED
s. 34:20, p. 558 "He guards all his bones; not one of them broken."	**no bones broken**	*John 19:32, 33, 36, p. 1098* "Then the soldiers came and broke the legs of the first and of the other who was crucified with Him. But when they came to Jesus and saw that He was already dead, they did not break His legs. . . . For these things were done that the Scripture should be fulfilled, 'Not one of His bones shall be broken.'"
ech. 12:10, p. 957 "And I will pour on the house of David ad on the inhabitants of Jerusalem the pirit of grace and supplication; then they ill look on Me whom they have pierced; ey will mourn for Him as one mourns for s only *son*, and grieve for Him as one rieves for a firstborn."	**His side pierced**	*John 19:34, p. 1098* "But one of the soldiers pierced His side with a spear, and immediately blood and water came out."
. 53:9, p. 727 "And they made His grave with the icked—but with the rich at His death, ecause He had done no violence, nor *was ny* deceit in His mouth."	**buried with the rich**	*Matt. 27:57–60, p. 1005* "Now when evening had come, there came a rich man from Arimathea, named Joseph, who himself had also become a disciple of Jesus. This man went to Pilate and asked for the body of Jesus. Then Pilate commanded the body to be given to him. And when Joseph had taken the body, he wrapped it in a clean linen cloth, and laid it in his new tomb which he had hewn out of the rock; and he rolled a large stone against the door of the tomb, and departed."
s. 16:10, p. 547 "For You will not leave my soul in Sheol, or will You allow Your Holy One to see orruption." *s. 49:15, p. 567* "But God will redeem my soul from the ower of the grave, for He shall receive me. elah"	**to be resurrected**	*Mark 16:6, 7, p. 1031* "But he said to them, 'Do not be alarmed. You seek Jesus of Nazareth, who was crucified. He is risen! He is not here. See the place where they laid Him. But go *and* tell His disciples—and Peter—that He is going before you into Galilee; there you will see Him, as He said to you.'"
s. 68:18, p. 575 "You have ascended on high, You have *·d* captivity captive; You have received *·*ifts among men; even *among* the re- *·*ellious, that the LORD God might dwell *·*ere."	**His ascension to God's right hand**	*Mark 16:19, p. 1031* "So then after the Lord had spoken to them, He was received up into heaven, and sat down at the right hand of God." *1 Cor. 15:4, p. 1170* "And that He was buried, and that He rose again the third day according to the Scriptures." *Eph. 4:8, p. 1197* "Therefore He says: 'When He ascended on high, He led captivity captive, and gave gifts to men.'"

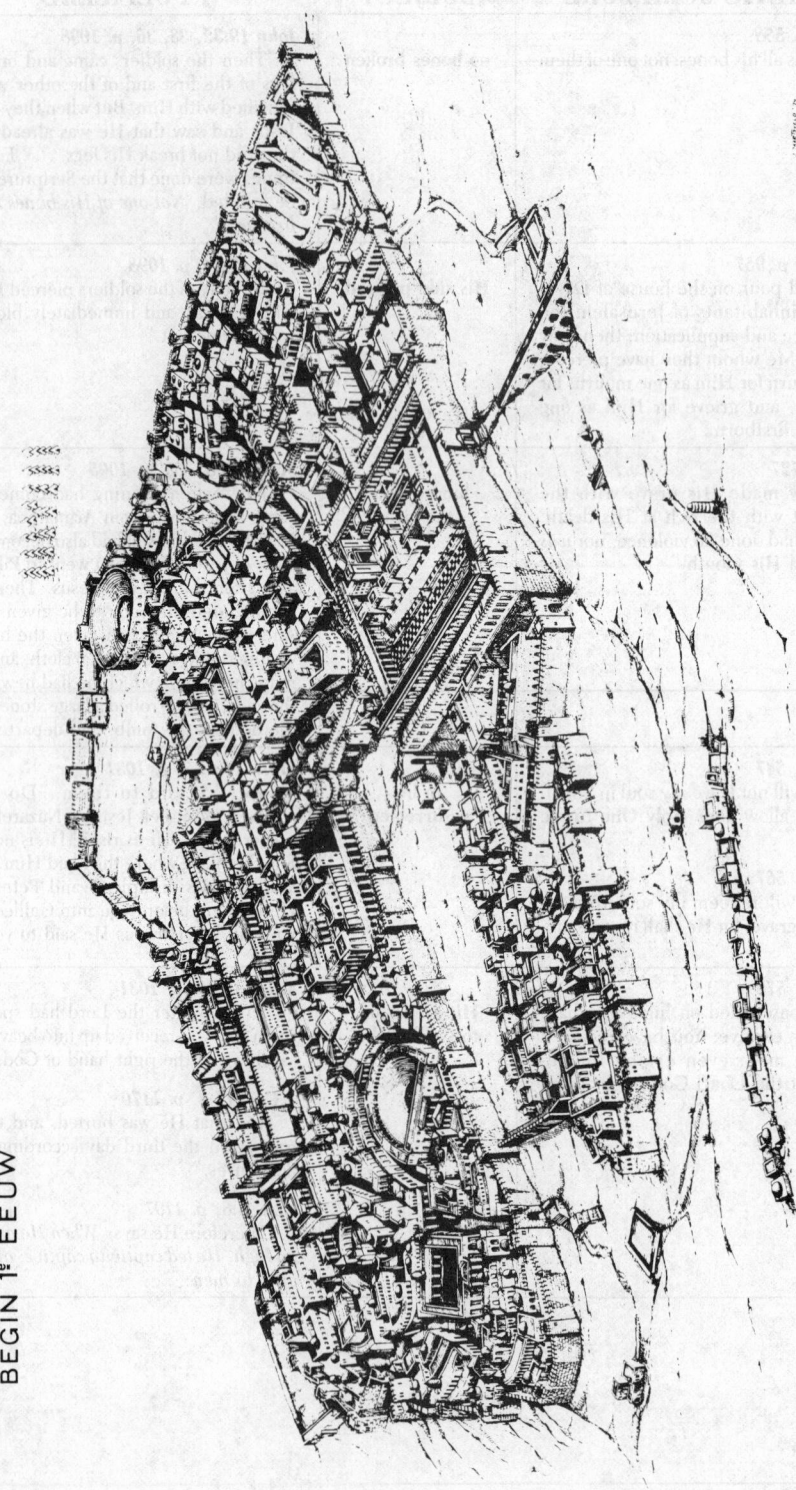

JERUZALEM
BEGIN 1ᵉ EEUW

An artist's sketch of what Jerusalem might have looked like in New Testament times. The beautiful Temple built by Herod appears within the square wall structure in the foreground.

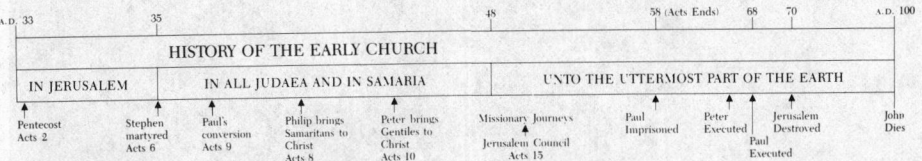

| A.D. 33 | | 35 | | | | | 48 | | 58 (Acts Ends) | 68 | 70 | A.D. 100 |

HISTORY OF THE EARLY CHURCH

| IN JERUSALEM | IN ALL JUDAEA AND IN SAMARIA | UNTO THE UTTERMOST PART OF THE EARTH |

Pentecost
Acts 2

Stephen
martyred
Acts 6

Paul's
conversion
Acts 9

Philip brings
Samaritans to
Christ
Acts 8

Peter brings
Gentiles to
Christ
Acts 10

Missionary Journeys

Jerusalem Council
Acts 15

Paul
Imprisoned

Peter
Executed

Jerusalem
Destroyed
Paul
Executed

John
Dies

THE BOOK OF ACTS IN OVERVIEW

"But ye shall receive power, after that the Holy Ghost is come upon you: and ye shall be witnesses unto me both in *Jerusalem*, and in all *Judaea*, and in *Samaria*, and unto the *uttermost part of the earth* " (Acts 1:8).

Chapters	Acts 1–7	Acts 8–12	Acts 13–28
Spread of the Church	The church in Jerusalem	The church in all Judaea and Samaria	The church to all the earth
The Gospel	Witnessing in the city	Witnessing in the provinces	Witnessing in the world
Theme	Power and progress of the church	Expansion of the church	Paul's three journeys and trials
People Addressed	Jews	Samaritans	Gentiles
Key Person	Peter	Philip	Paul
Time	2 years (A.D. 33–35)	13 years (A.D. 35–48)	14 years (A.D. 48–62)
Development	Triumph	Transition	Travels and trials

From *Visual Survey of the Bible.* Reprinted by permission of the author.

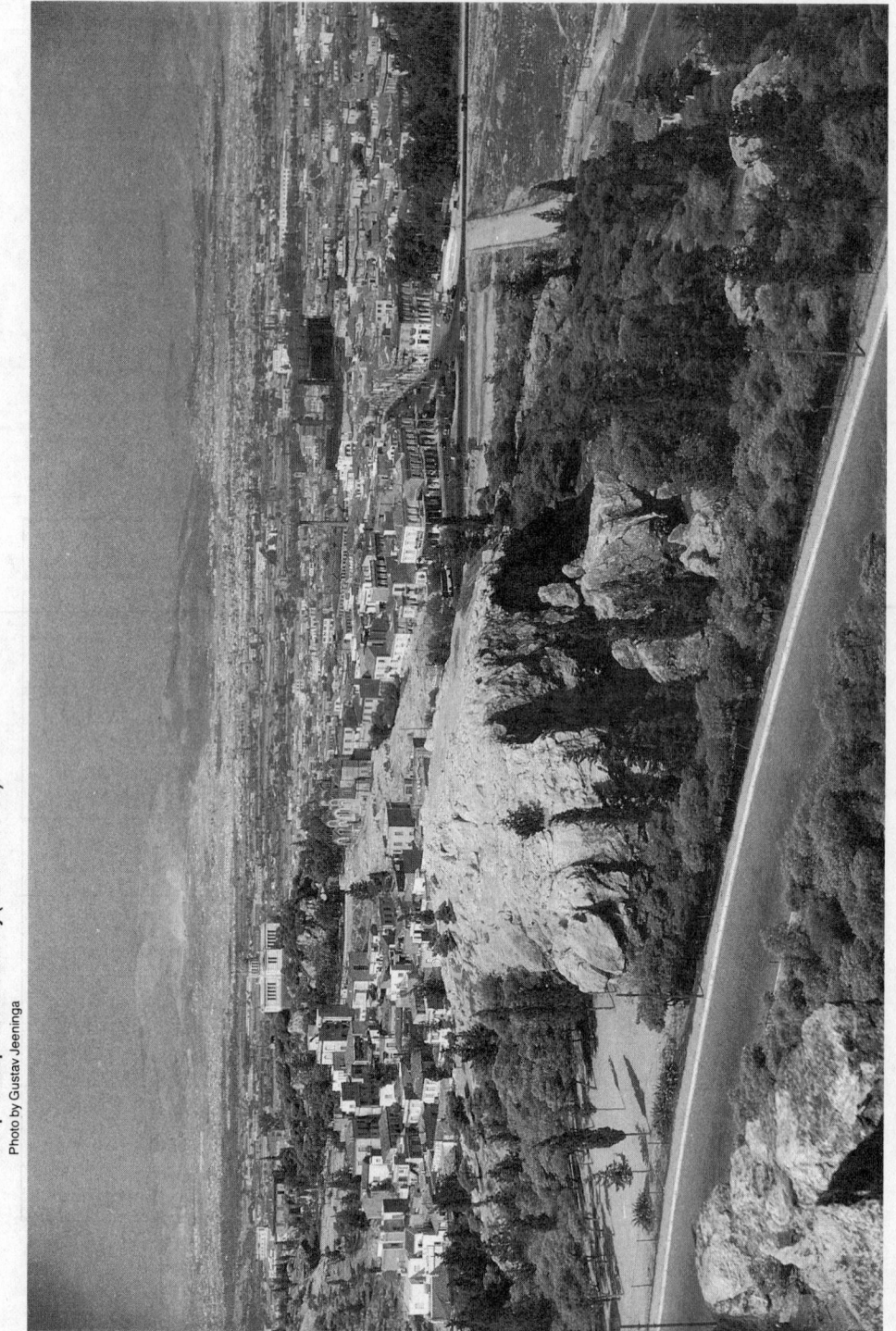

The Areopagus (Mars' Hill) is a little hill near the acropolis in Athens where Paul may have been brought before the philosophers of this city (Acts 17:16-34).

Photo by Gustav Jeeninga

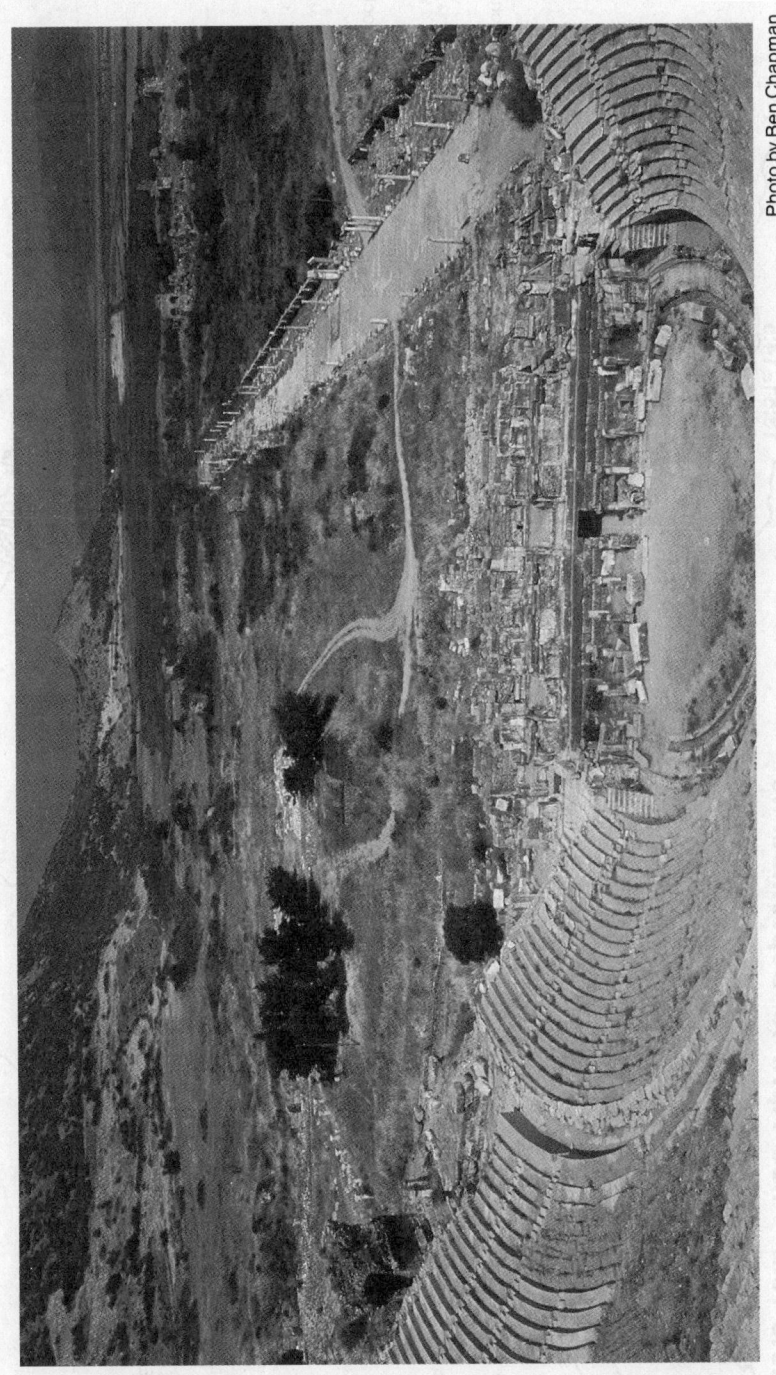

Photo by Ben Chapman

The great theater of the city of Ephesus, showing the marble boulevard leading to the nearby harbor, now silted in because of erosion.

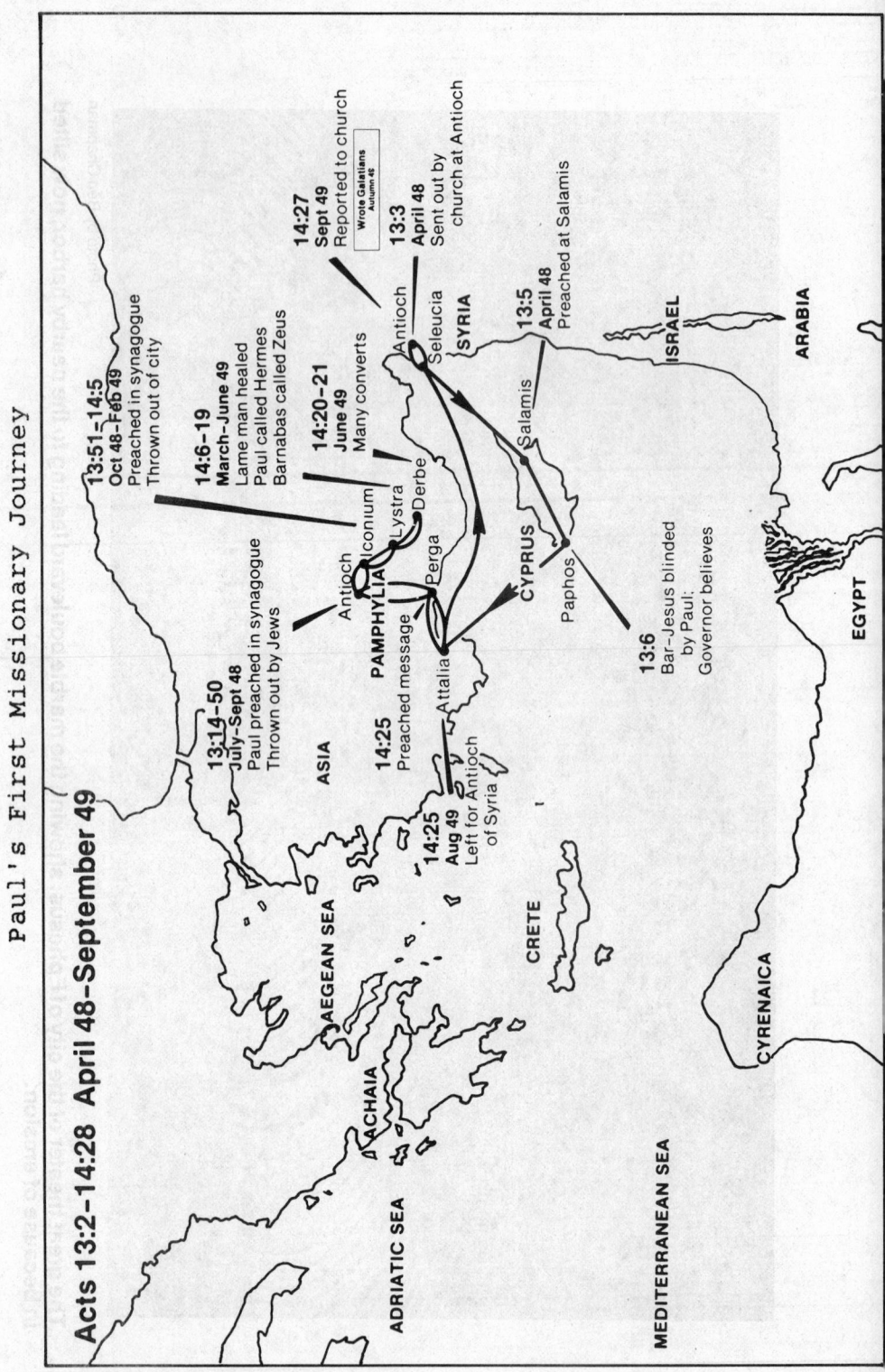

Paul's First Missionary Journey

Acts 13:2–14:28 April 48–September 49

13:51–14:5
Oct 48–Feb 49
Preached in synagogue
Thrown out of city

14:6–19
March–June 49
Lame man healed
Paul called Hermes
Barnabas called Zeus

14:20–21
June 49
Many converts

14:27
Sept 49
Reported to church

Wrote Galatians
Autumn 49

13:3
April 48
Sent out by
church at Antioch

13:5
April 48
Preached at Salamis

13:14–50
July–Sept 48
Paul preached in synagogue
Thrown out by Jews

14:25
Preached message

14:25
Aug 49
Left for Antioch
of Syria

13:6
Bar-Jesus blinded
by Paul; Governor believes

Antioch
Seleucia
SYRIA
Salamis
CYPRUS
Paphos
ISRAEL
ARABIA
EGYPT

Antioch
Iconium
Lystra
Derbe
Perga
PAMPHYLIA
Attalia

ASIA

AEGEAN SEA
ACHAIA
ADRIATIC SEA
CRETE
CYRENAICA
MEDITERRANEAN SEA

From *Talk Thru the Bible*. Reprinted by permission of Walk Thru the Bible Ministries.

Paul's Second Missionary Journey

Acts 15:36–18:22 April 50–September 52

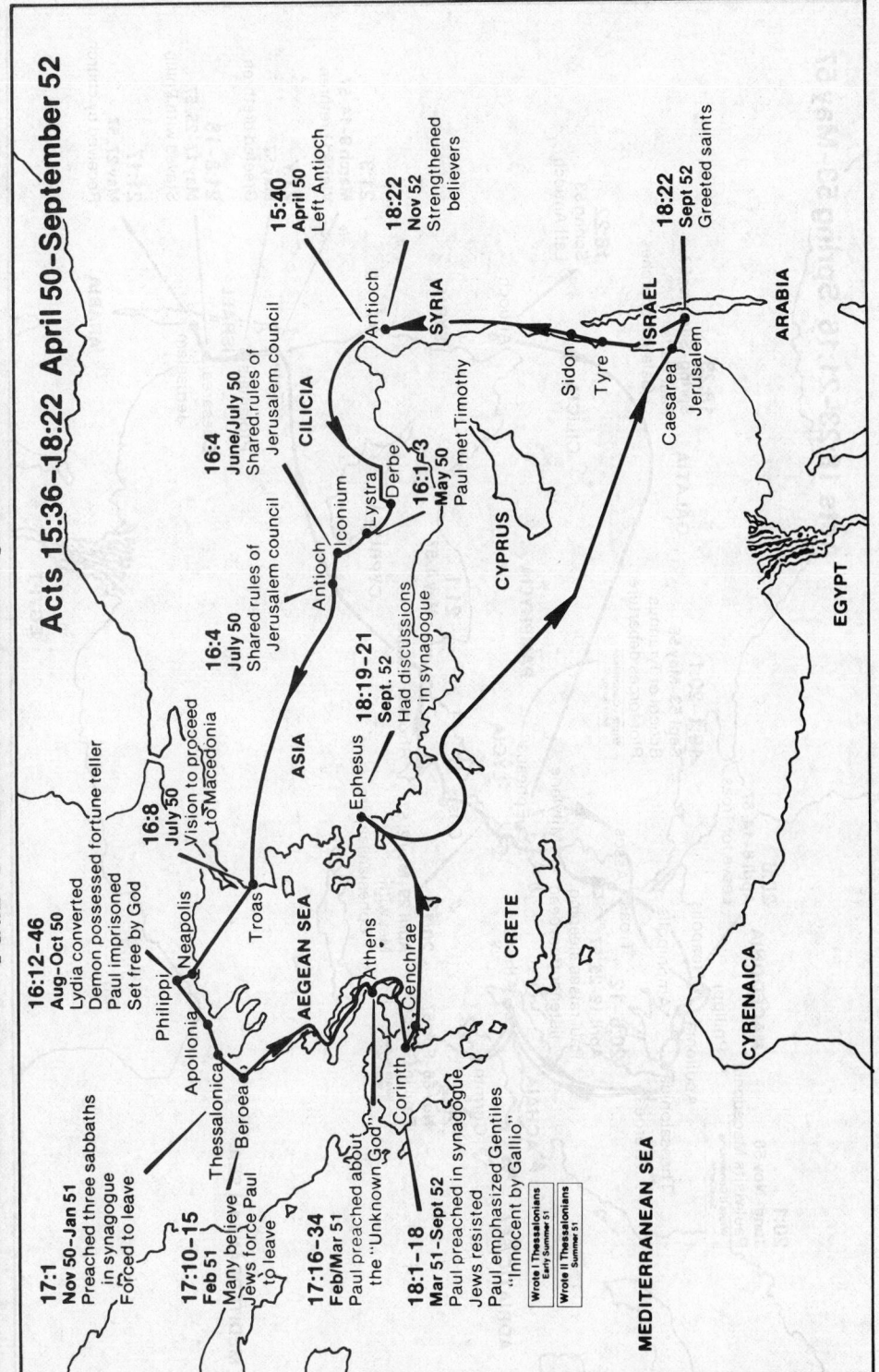

15:40
April 50
Left Antioch

18:22
Nov 52
Strengthened
believers

18:22
Sept 52
Greeted saints

16:4
June/July 50
Shared rules of
Jerusalem council

16:1-3
May 50
Paul met Timothy

16:4
July 50
Shared rules of
Jerusalem council

18:19–21
Sept. 52
Had discussions
in synagogue

16:8
July 50
Vision to proceed
to Macedonia

16:12-46
Aug–Oct 50
Lydia converted
Demon possessed fortune teller
Paul imprisoned
Set free by God

17:1
Nov 50–Jan 51
Preached three sabbaths
in synagogue
Forced to leave

17:10-15
Feb 51
Many believe
Jews force Paul
to leave

17:16-34
Feb/Mar 51
Paul preached about
the "Unknown God"

18:1-18
Mar 51–Sept 52
Paul preached in synagogue
Jews resisted
Paul emphasized Gentiles
"Innocent by Gallio"

Wrote I Thessalonians
Early Summer 51

Wrote II Thessalonians
Summer 51

SYRIA

CILICIA

ASIA

CYPRUS

CRETE

ISRAEL

ARABIA

EGYPT

CYRENAICA

AEGEAN SEA

MEDITERRANEAN SEA

Antioch

Derbe

Lystra

Iconium

Antioch

Ephesus

Troas

Neapolis

Philippi

Apollonia

Thessalonica

Beroea

Athens

Corinth

Cenchrae

Sidon

Tyre

Caesarea

Jerusalem

From *Talk Thru the Bible*. Reprinted by permission of Walk Thru the Bible Ministries.

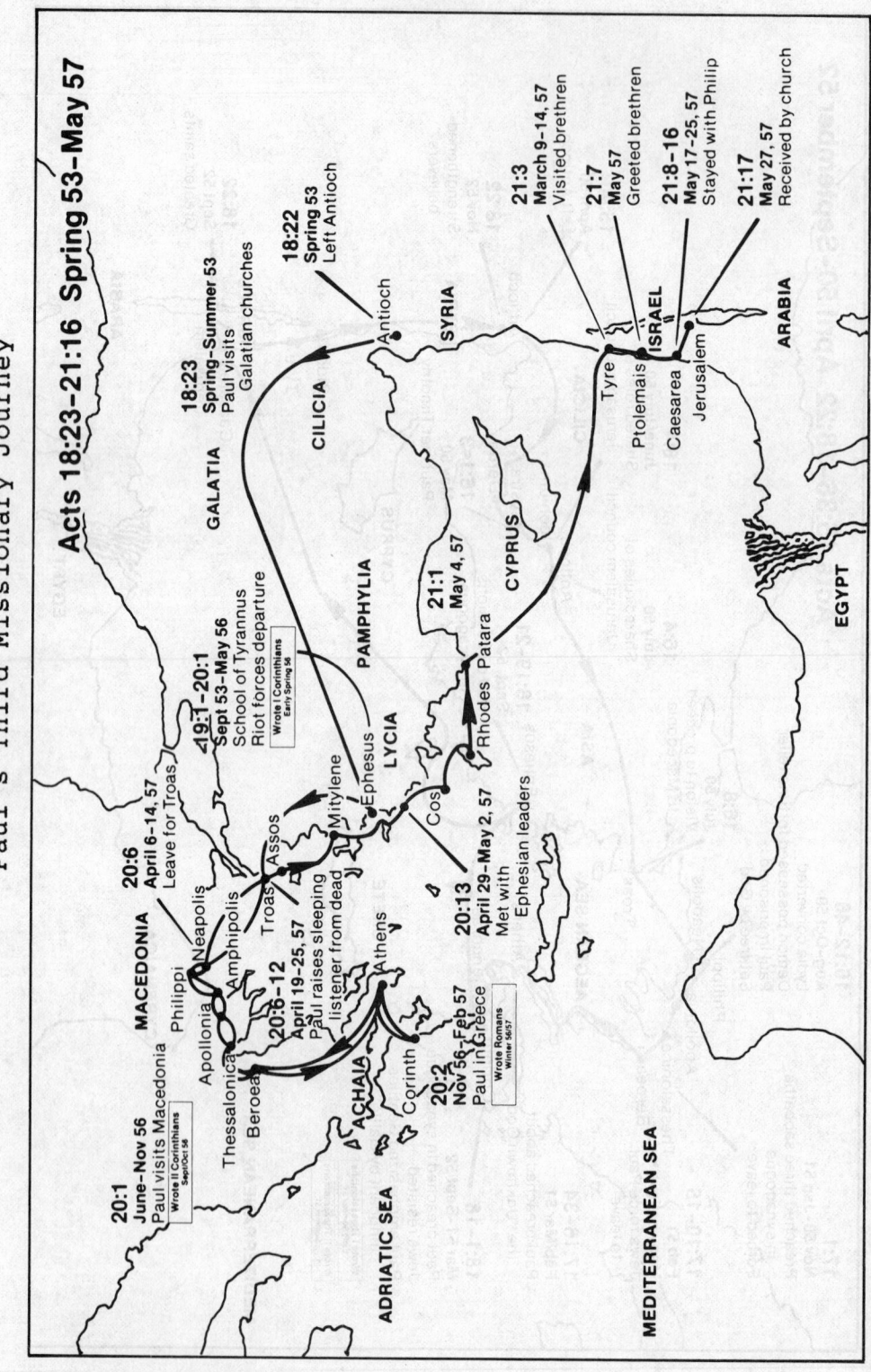

Paul's Third Missionary Journey

Acts 18:23–21:16 Spring 53–May 57

18:22 Spring 53 Left Antioch

18:23 Spring–Summer 53 Paul visits Galatian churches

21:3 March 9–14, 57 Visited brethren

21:7 May 57 Greeted brethren

21:8–16 May 17–25, 57 Stayed with Philip

21:17 May 27, 57 Received by church

ANTIOCH

SYRIA

CILICIA

GALATIA

ISRAEL

ARABIA

Tyre
Ptolemais
Caesarea
Jerusalem

21:1 May 4, 57

PAMPHYLIA

CYPRUS

LYCIA

19:1–20:1 Sept 53–May 56 School of Tyrannus Riot forces departure

Wrote I Corinthians Early Spring 56

Patara
Rhodes
Cos
Ephesus
Mitylene

EGYPT

20:6 April 6–14, 57 Leave for Troas

MACEDONIA
Neapolis
Philippi
Apollonia
Amphipolis
Thessalonica
Beroea

Assos
Troas

20:6–12 April 19–25, 57 Paul raises sleeping listener from dead

20:13 April 29–May 2, 57 Met with Ephesian leaders

20:1 June–Nov 56 Paul visits Macedonia

Wrote II Corinthians Sept/Oct 56

ACHAIA
Athens
Corinth

20:2 Nov 56–Feb 57 Paul in Greece

Wrote Romans Winter 56/57

ADRIATIC SEA

MEDITERRANEAN SEA

From *Talk Thru the Bible.* Reprinted by permission of Walk Thru the Bible Ministries.

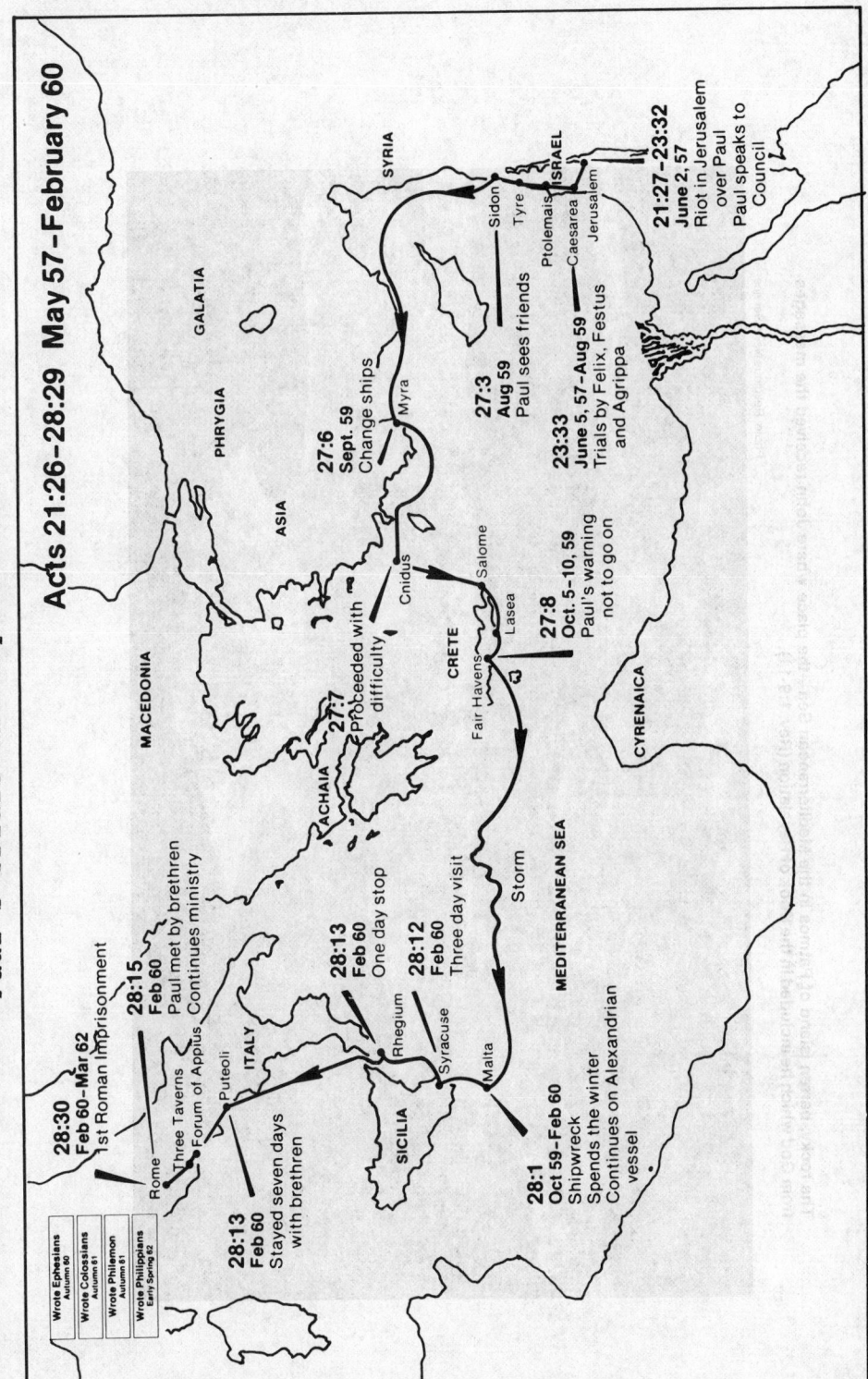

Paul's Trials and Imprisonments

Acts 21:26–28:29 May 57–February 60

21:27–23:32
June 2, 57
Riot in Jerusalem over Paul
Paul speaks to Council

23:33
June 5, 57–Aug 59
Trials by Felix, Festus and Agrippa

27:3
Aug 59
Paul sees friends

SYRIA

ISRAEL

Sidon
Tyre
Ptolemais
Caesarea
Jerusalem

27:6
Sept. 59
Change ships

Myra

GALATIA

PHRYGIA

ASIA

Cnidus

Salome

CRETE

Lasea

Fair Havens

27:8
Oct. 5–10, 59
Paul's warning not to go on

CYRENAICA

27:7
Proceeded with difficulty

MACEDONIA

ACHAIA

Storm

MEDITERRANEAN SEA

28:13
Feb 60
One day stop

28:12
Feb 60
Three day visit

Rhegium

Syracuse

SICILIA

Malta

28:1
Oct 59–Feb 60
Shipwreck
Spends the winter
Continues on Alexandrian vessel

28:15
Feb 60
Paul met by brethren
Continues ministry

28:30
Feb 60–Mar 62
1st Roman Imprisonment

Three Taverns
Forum of Appius
Puteoli

ITALY

Rome

28:13
Feb 60
Stayed seven days with brethren

| Wrote Ephesians Autumn 60 |
| Wrote Colossians Autumn 61 |
| Wrote Philemon Autumn 61 |
| Wrote Philippians Early Spring 62 |

From *Talk Thru the Bible*. Reprinted by permission of Walk Thru the Bible Ministries.

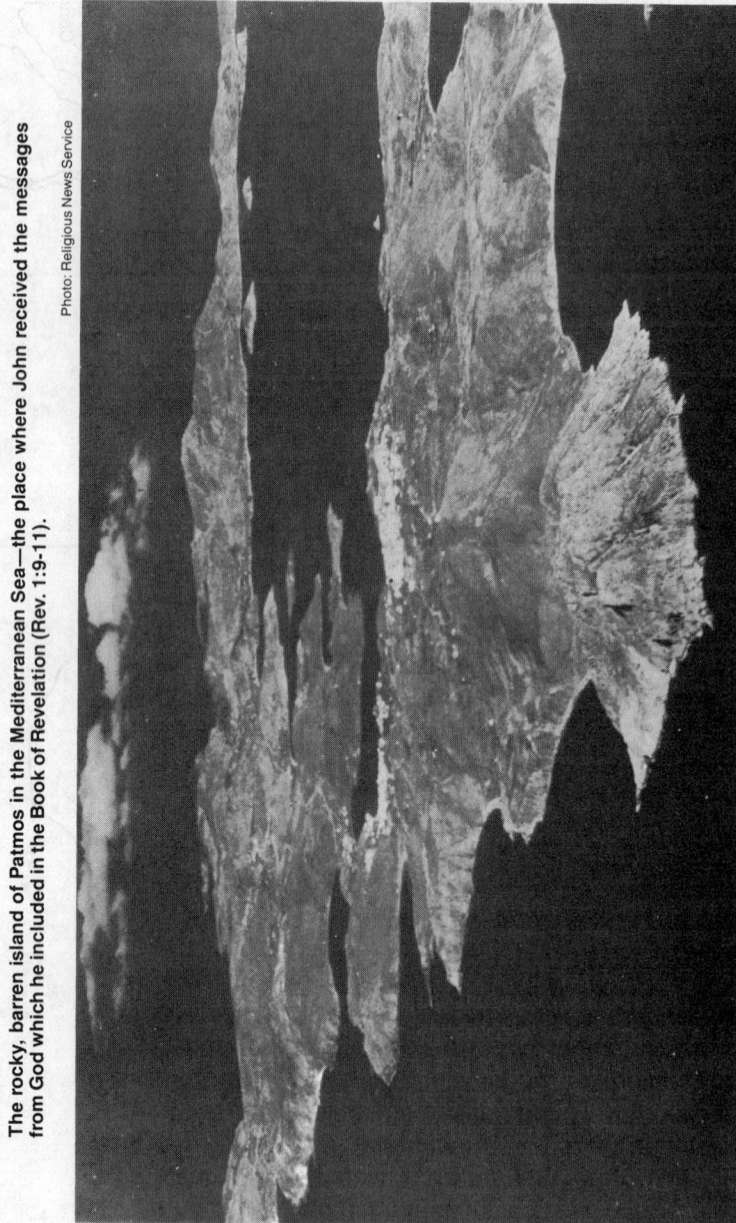

The rocky, barren island of Patmos in the Mediterranean Sea—the place where John received the messages from God which he included in the Book of Revelation (Rev. 1:9-11).

Photo: Religious News Service

People and Places of the Bible

This article identifies the most outstanding people and places whose proper names occur in the Bible, excluding the deuterocanonical books. The names are set out alphabetically as they are spelled in the New King James Version. People and places bearing the same name in Scripture are treated under separate entries with personal names listed first. Variant spellings are enclosed in brackets [ ], and the meaning of the name is then given in parentheses ( ). Under each entry, various individuals or places bearing this name are differentiated by boldface brackets, like this: [1]; [2]; and so on. Then follows a description of the entry with several Bible verses listed where the name occurs. (Not all verses are given. If the reader is considering a passage that is not cited in the section, he must choose the name that would most likely be identical with the person or place in his passage.)

No attempt has been made to designate each person as a Palite, Harodite, Gileadite, and so on. Many of these designations refer to the ancestor of an individual. In other cases, they refer to the person's city, district, or distinctive clan. It is often a guess as to which meaning is intended.

The meanings of the names are not infallibly accurate. They are simply interesting possibilities.

Many people and places in Scripture bear the same name. In dozens of cases, it cannot be determined whether an individual or place in one book is identical with the same use of the name in another book. In the ancient world, a person was often called by more than one name. Many of the place names are pre-Israelite, and their history is obscure and uncertain. Different names were used to refer to certain sites in different periods of history (e.g. Ararat and Armenia). These are grouped under the most familiar biblical name with the other names cross referenced to it. Modern place names are given under most of the biblical names.

In the transmission of Scripture, copyists occasionally made errors. Surely Enoch was not called Hanoc, nor Imna called Jimna, and so on. Yet which is original? Only in a few cases do we have any clues.

We find variant forms and contractions of names throughout the Bible. They probably presented little difficulty to an ancient reader. But this further complicates the identification problem for us. Often a Hebrew name refers to both a person and a place.

The Hebrew genealogies are abbreviated at many points. At times it is difficult to distinguish a man from his ancestor. Consider also the problem of trying to match an abbreviated list with a fuller list. Either the names in the abbreviated list are independent of the longer list or they are already included in it. In other words, we may find the same person included in two lists or two different people in two lists.

In a few cases, our English versions use the same word to transliterate several similar Hebrew names. In these instances, we have recorded a separate entry for each Hebrew name (e.g., Joash).

A

Aaron ("enlightened, rich, mountaineer"), the brother of Moses. He became the first high priest of Israel (Ex. 4:14, 30; 7:2, 19; 17:9-12; 29; Num. 12; 17).

Abdon ("service, servile"). [1] A judge of Israel for eight years (Judg. 12:13, 15). *See* Bedan. [2] A descendant of Benjamin who dwelt in Jerusalem (1 Chr. 8:23). [3] First-born son of Jehiel, mentioned in Chronicles (1 Chr. 8:30; 9:36). [4] One sent to Huldah to inquire of the meaning of the Law (2 Chr. 34:20). He is called Achbor in Second Kings 22:12. Possibly he is identical with [2].

Abdon ("servile"), a city belonging to the tribe of Asher, located at the present site of Khirbet Abdeh (Josh. 21:30; 1 Chr. 6:74). It was once called Hebron; *see* Hebron [2], the city.

Abed-Nego ("servant of Nebo; servant of Ishtar"), name given to Azariah, one of the three friends of Daniel who were carried captive to Babylon. He was thrown into a fiery furnace (Dan. 1:7; 2:49; 3:12-30).

Abel ("a breath, vapor; shepherd"), second son of Adam and Eve, slain by his brother Cain (Gen. 4:1-10; Heb. 11:4; 12:24).

Abel Keramim, a place east of the Jordan River, site of the battle in which Jephthah defeated the forces led by Ammon (Judg. 11:33).

Abez ("lofty"), a town in northern Palestine apportioned to the tribe of Issachar (Josh. 19:20).

Abi-Albon ("father of strength"), one of David's "valiant men" (2 Sam. 23:31). Also called Abiel (1 Chr. 11:32).

Abiasaph [Ebiasaph] ("my father has gathered"), a Levite whose descendants were gatekeepers of the tabernacle (Ex. 6:24; 1 Chr. 6:23; 9:19).

Abiathar ("father of super-excellence or preeminence"), the only priest to escape Saul's massacre at Nob, he was a high priest in David's time. He was deposed by Solomon (1 Sam. 22:20-23; 1 Kin. 2:27; 1 Chr. 15:11, 12). First Samuel 21 says that Ahimelech [1] was the high priest when David ate the show-bread, yet Mark 2:26 states this occurred in the days of Abiathar the high priest. Abiathar may have been assisting his father as high priest and thus could be so designated. Or, since Abiathar was more prominent in history than was his father Ahimelech, he is so mentioned here instead of Ahimelech. If this is so (and it seems to be), then Abiathar is called the "high priest" before he actually assumed that office.

Abigail ("father [i.e., cause] of delight"). [1] A wife of Nabal and afterward of David (1

Sam. 25:3, 14-44). [2] Mother of Amasa, whom Absalom made captain (2 Sam. 17:25; 1 Chr. 2:16, 17).

Abihu ("he is my father"), a son of Aaron, destroyed with his brother for offering strange fire to God (Ex. 6:23; Lev. 10:1).

Abijah [Abijam] ("Jehovah is my father"). [1] A son of Samuel and wicked judge of Israel (1 Sam. 8:2; 1 Chr. 6:28). [2] The wife of Hezron (1 Chr. 2:24). [3] Son of Rehoboam and successor to the throne of Judah, an ancestor of Christ (1 Chr. 3:10; 2 Chr. 11:20—14:1; Matt. 1:7). He was also known as Abijam (1 Kin. 15:1). [4] The seventh son of Becher the son of Benjamin (1 Chr. 7:8). [5] A descendant of Aaron appointed by David in connection with the priestly courses (1 Chr. 24:10; cf. Luke 1:5). [6] A son of Jeroboam I of Israel (1 Kin. 14:1-8). [7] A priest of Nehemiah's time who sealed the covenant (Neh. 10:7). Possibly the same as the priest mentioned in Nehemiah 12:1, 4, 17.

Abijam ("father of the sea [or west]"). *See* Abijah [3].

Abimelech ("father of the king"). [1] Many scholars believe the King(s) Abimelech(s) of Gerar in Genesis 20, 21, and 26 are not proper names but a royal title borne by the Philistine kings. The Psalm 34 title mentions Abimelech where Achish should occur. Since the story of Achish was well known, it seems improbable to regard this as a mistake, but rather a royal title of Achish, king of Gath. [2] A son of Gideon who tried to become king of Israel, and did reign for three years (Judg. 8:30—10:1). [3] *See* Ahimelech [2].

Abinadab ("father or source of liberality or willingness"). [1] A man of Judah in whose house the ark was placed (1 Sam. 7:1; 2 Sam. 6:3, 4; 1 Chr. 13:7). [2] A brother of David (1 Sam. 16:8; 17:13; 1 Chr. 2:13). [3] Son of Saul slain by the Philistines (1 Sam. 31:2; 1 Chr. 8:33; 9:39; 10:2). [4] Father of one of Solomon's officers (1 Kin. 4:11).

Abiram ("father of elevation"). [1] One who conspired against Moses and was destroyed (Num. 16:27; Ps. 106:17). [2] Firstborn son of Hiel who died when his father began to rebuild Jericho (1 Kin. 16:34; cf. Josh. 6:26).

Abishag ("my father was a wanderer"), a beautiful woman chosen to nurse the aged David (1 Kin. 1:3, 15; 2:17, 21, 22). This woman may also be the heroine of the Song of Solomon, where she is simply called "the Shulamite."

Abishai ("my father is Jesse; source of wealth"), a son of David's sister, Zeruiah. He was one of David's mighty men (1 Sam. 26:6-9; 2 Sam. 2:18; 10:10; 23:18).

Abner [Abiner] ("my father of light"), a shortened form of *Abiner;* the captain of the host under Saul and Ishbosheth (1 Sam. 14:50, 51; 26:5, 7; 2 Sam. 2; 3).

Abraham [Abram]. The founder of the Jewish nation and an ancestor of Christ. His name was changed from Abram ("the father is exalted") to Abraham ("father of multitudes") (Gen. 11—26; Matt. 1:1, 2).

Absalom ("father of peace"), a son of David who tried to usurp the throne from his father (2 Sam. 3:3; 13—19).

Achan [Achar] ("trouble"), one who stole part of the spoil of Jericho and brought "trouble" on his people. He was killed for this (Josh. 7:1-24). In First Chronicles 2:7, he is called *Achar*.

Achim ("woes"), ancestor of Christ (Matt. 1:14).

Achish ("serpent-charmer"). **[1]** A king of Gath to whom David fled for safety (1 Sam. 21; 27-29). **[2]** Another king of Gath who bore the same name but reigned during Solomon's time (1 Kin. 2:39, 40). However, many believe the kings to be identical.

Achor ("trouble"), a valley south of Jericho, in which Achan was stoned (Josh. 7:24); and which formed the northern boundary of Judah (Josh. 15:7).

Achzib [Chezib] ("false"). **[1]** A Canaanite city in the lowlands of Judah, captured by Joshua (Gen. 38:5; Josh. 15:44). **[2]** A seashore town on the northern side of Galilee near the Lebanon border (Josh. 19:29; Judg. 1:31).

Adam ("of the ground; firm"), the first man. His sin caused a curse to fall upon all the race (Gen. 2—3; 1 Cor. 15:22, 45). He is listed in the genealogy of Christ (Luke 3:38).

Adam ("red; of the earth"), a city on the east bank of the Jordan River that was given to the tribe of Reuben (Josh. 3:16).

Adino ("ornament"), a chief of David's mighty men (2 Sam. 23:8). Some identify him with Jashobeam **[1]**; others deny this.

Admah ("redness"), one of the Cities of the Plain that God destroyed with Sodom and Gomorrah (Gen. 19:25-29); its location may now be submerged by the southern end of the Dead Sea.

Adnah ("pleasure"). **[1]** A captain who joined David at Ziklag (1 Chr. 12:20). **[2]** A chief captain of Jehoshaphat (2 Chr. 17:14).

Adonijah ("Jehovah is my Lord"). **[1]** A son of David, executed by Solomon for trying to usurp the throne (2 Sam. 3:4; 1 Kin. 1:2). **[2]** One sent by Jehoshaphat to teach the law (2 Chr. 17:8). **[3]** One who sealed the new covenant with God after the Exile (Neh. 10:14-16).

Adoni-Zedek ("lord of justice or righteousness"), a king of Jerusalem defeated by Joshua (Josh. 10:1-27).

Adramyttium ("from Adramys, brother of Craesus"), a port city of Mysia in the northwestern part of the Roman province of Asia (Acts 27:2; cf. 16:7).

Adriatic ("from [the city] Adria of Italy"), originally a name referring to the sea east of Italy. In later times, the term included the Mediterranean between Greece and Sicily (Acts 27:27).

Adullam ("refuge"), a town of Judah near Succoth. David made the headquarters of his rebellion against Saul in a cave near this town (Josh. 12:7-15; 1 Sam. 22; 2 Sam. 23:13).

Aenon ("fountains"), a place noted for its abundant supply of water, where John baptized his converts. Most likely this site was at the head of the Valley of Shechem (John 3:23).

Agabus ("locust"), a prophet of Jerusalem who foretold suffering for Paul if he went to Jerusalem (Acts 11:28; 21:10).

Agrippa. *See* Herod.

Ahab ("father's brother [uncle]"). **[1]** The seventh king of Israel. He was wicked and idolatrous and married a woman of the same character—Jezebel (1 Kin. 16:28—22:40). **[2]** A false prophet killed by Nebuchadnezzar (Jer. 29:21, 22).

Ahasuerus. **[1]** The king of Persia whom Esther married. He is known as Xerxes to historians (Esth. 1:1; 2:16; 10:3). **[2]** The father of Darius the Mede (Dan. 9:1). **[3]** Another name for Cambyses, king of Persia (Ezra 4:6).

Ahaz ("he holds"). **[1]** The eleventh king of Judah and an ancestor of Christ (2 Kin. 15:38—16:20; Matt. 1:9). **[2]** A descendant of Benjamin (1 Chr. 8:35, 36; 9:41, 42).

Ahaziah [Azariah] ("Jehovah holds or sustains"). **[1]** The eighth king of Israel. He was weak and idolatrous (1 Kin. 22:51—2 Kin. 1:18). **[2]** The sixth king of Judah; he reigned only one year (2 Kin. 8:24-29; 9:16ff.). He was also known as Jehoahaz (2 Chr. 21:17; 25:23). His being called Azariah in Second Chronicles 22:6 is an error; over fifteen Hebrew manuscripts and all recent versions read Ahaziah. *See* Jehoahaz.

Ahihud ("brother of honor"). **[1]** A prince of Asher (Num. 34:27). **[2]** A member of the family of Ehud, descended from Benjamin (1 Chr. 8:7).

Ahijah ("Jehovah is brother; my brother is Jehovah"). **[1]** A prophet who prophesied the splitting away of the ten tribes (1 Kin. 11:29, 30; 14:2, 4, 5). **[2]** Father of Baasha who conspired against Nadab (1 Kin. 15:27, 33; 21:22). **[3]** A son of Jerahmeel (1 Chr. 2:25). **[4]** One of David's mighty men (1 Chr. 11:36). **[5]** One who sealed the new covenant with

God after the Exile (Neh. 10:26). **[6]** One set over the temple treasures (1 Chr. 26:20). *See also* Ahimelech.

Ahimaaz ("powerful brother"). **[1]** Father of Ahinoam, wife of Saul (1 Sam. 14:50). **[2]** One of Solomon's officers (1 Kin. 4:15). **[3]** Son of Zadok who remained loyal to David (2 Sam. 15:27, 36; 17:17, 20; 18:19–29).

Ahimelech ("brother of the king; my brother is king"). **[1]** A Hittite friend of David (1 Sam. 26:6). **[2]** A priest, son of Abiathar and grandson of **[3]** (2 Sam. 8:17; 1 Chr. 24:6). Some think the readings in these passages have been transposed (i.e., they speak of Ahimelech the son of Abiathar instead of Abiathar the son of Ahimelech). But this seems unlikely, especially in First Chronicles 24. He is called Abimelech in First Chronicles 18:16. The Septuagint has Ahimelech here also. **[3]** One of the priests of Nob slain for helping David (1 Sam. 21:1–8; 22:9–20). *See also* Abimelech; Ahijah.

Ahinoam ("pleasant brother"). **[1]** Wife of King Saul (1 Sam. 14:50). **[2]** A woman of Jezreel who married David (1 Sam. 25:43; 27:3; 1 Chr. 3:1).

Ahithophel ("brother of foolishness"), the real leader of Absalom's rebellion against David. When he saw that victory was impossible, he committed suicide (2 Sam. 15—17).

Ahitub ("a good brother; my brother is goodness"). **[1]** A son of Phinehas (1 Sam. 14:3; 22:9, 11, 12, 20). **[2]** Father of Zadok the high priest (2 Sam. 8:17; 15:27; 1 Chr. 6:7, 8). **[3]** A high priest of the same family who served during Nehemiah's time (1 Chr. 6:11; 9:11; Neh. 11:11).

Ai [Aiath; Aija] ("heap of ruins"). **[1]** One of the strongest Canaanite cities, located east of Bethel (Josh. 7:2; Neh. 11:31). In Isaiah 10:28 the Hebrew feminine form of the name (Aiath) occurs. **[2]** A city of the Ammonites, probably located near Heshbon (Jer. 49:3).

Aijalon [Ajalon] ("place of harts"). **[1]** A town located 22.5 km. (14 mi.) northwest of Jerusalem, designated as a Levitical city (Josh. 19:42; 21:24; 2 Chr. 28:18). **[2]** A site belonging to the tribe of Zebulun west of the Sea of Galilee, where the judge Elon was buried (Judg. 12:12). Its exact location is unknown.

Ain ("eye"). **[1]** A town of Judah near Rimmon, assigned to the Levites serving the tribe of Simeon (Josh. 15:32; 19:7; 21:16; 1 Chr. 4:32). **[2]** A site on the boundary line of the Promised Land, west of Riblah (Num. 34:11). Its exact location is unknown.

Akel Dama [Potter's Field] ("field of blood"), a field purchased by the priests of Jerusalem with the 30 pieces of silver that bought the betrayal of Jesus (Acts 1:19); also called Potter's Field (Matt. 27:7).

Alexander ("helper of man"). **[1]** A son of the Simon who bore Christ's cross (Mark 15:21). **[2]** A kinsman of Annas and a leading man in Jerusalem (Acts 4:6). **[3]** A Christian with Paul when the Ephesians had a riot (Acts 19:33). Perhaps the same as **[1]**. **[4]** A convert who apostatized (1 Tim. 1:20). **[5]** A person who did much harm to Paul (2 Tim. 4:14). Perhaps the same as **[4]**.

Alexandria ("city of Alexander the Great"), a city on the Mediterranean coast of Egypt, which served as Egypt's capital city for many years (Acts 27:6; 28:11–13).

Almon Diblathaim ("hiding place of two fig sacks"), a site between the Arnon River and Shittim where the Israelites camped during their wandering in the wilderness (Num. 33:46).

Alphaeus ("leader; chief"). **[1]** The father of Levi (Matthew) (Mark 2:14). **[2]** The father of the apostle James (Matt. 10:3; Mark 3:18; Acts 1:13). Some identify him with Clopas.

Alush ("crowd"), a site where the Israelites camped on their journey from Egypt to Mount Sinai (Num. 33:14).

Amana ("forth"), a range of mountains in Lebanon, probably south of the Amana [Abana] River (Song 4:8).

Amasa ("burden-bearer; people of Jesse"). **[1]** A nephew of David who became the commander of Absalom's army (2 Sam. 17:25; 19:13; 20:4–12). **[2]** One who opposed making slaves of captured Jews (2 Chr. 28:12).

Amaziah ("Jehovah has strength"). **[1]** Son and successor of Joash to the throne of Judah. He was murdered at Lachish (2 Kin. 12:21—14:20). **[2]** A man of the tribe of Simeon (1 Chr. 4:34). **[3]** A Levite descendant from Merari (1 Chr. 6:45). **[4]** An idolatrous priest of Bethel (Amos 7:10, 12, 14).

Amittai ("truthful"), father of the prophet Jonah (2 Kin. 14:25; Jon. 1:1).

Ammiel ("my people are strong; my kinsman is God"). **[1]** One of those who spied out the Promised Land (Num. 13:12). **[2]** Father of Machir, David's friend (2 Sam. 9:4, 5; 17:27). **[3]** A porter of the tabernacle in the time of David (1 Chr. 26:5).

Amminadab [Aminadab] ("my people are willing or noble"). **[1]** Aaron's father-in-law (Ex. 6:23). **[2]** A prince of Judah and ancestor of Christ (Num. 1:7; 2:3; Ruth 4:19, 20; Matt. 1:4). **[3]** A son of Kohath (1 Chr. 6:22). **[4]** One who helped to bring the ark of the covenant from the house of Obed-Edom (1 Chr. 15:10, 11).

Ammon. *See* Ben-Ammi.

Amnon ("upbringing; faithful"). **[1]** Eldest son of David, by Ahinoam, slain by Absalom

(2 Sam. 3:2; 13:1–39). [2] A son of Shimon of the family of Caleb (1 Chr. 4:20).

Amon ("workman" or "trustworthy"). [1] Governor of Samaria in Ahab's time (1 Kin. 22:26; 2 Chr. 18:25). [2] Son and successor of Manasseh to the throne of Judah; an ancestor of Christ (2 Kin. 21:19–25; Jer. 1:2; Zeph. 1:1; Matt. 1:10).

Amos ("burden-bearer; burdensome"). [1] A prophet during the reigns of Uzziah and Jeroboam (Amos 1:1; 7:10–12, 14). [2] An ancestor of Christ (Luke 3:25).

Amoz ("strong"), father of the prophet Isaiah (2 Kin. 19:2, 20; Is. 1:1; 2:1; 13:1).

Amram ("people exalted; red"). [1] A descendant of Levi and father or ancestor of Aaron, Moses, and Miriam (Ex. 6:18, 20; Num. 3:19; 26:58, 59). [2] One who had taken a foreign wife (Ezra 10:34).

Ananiah ("Jehovah has covered"), a town inhabited by the tribe of Benjamin after the Exile (Neh. 11:32).

Ananias ("Jehovah is gracious"). [1] A disciple struck dead for trying to deceive the apostles (Acts 5:1, 3, 5). [2] A disciple of Damascus who helped Paul after receiving a vision (Acts 9:10–17; 22:12). [3] A high priest in Jerusalem who opposed Paul (Acts 23:2; 24:1).

Anathoth ("answer"), a town of the tribe of Benjamin, located about 4 km. (2.5 mi.) northeast of Jerusalem (Josh. 21:18; Ezra 2:23); the birthplace of the prophet Jeremiah (Jer. 1:1; 11:21).

Andrew ("manly; conqueror"), the brother of Peter and one of the twelve apostles (Matt. 4:18; 10:2; John 1:40; 6:8).

Anna ("grace"), a prophetess of the tribe of Asher in Christ's time (Luke 2:36).

Annas ("grace of Jehovah"), high priest of the Jews who first tried Christ (Luke 3:2; John 18:13, 24; Acts 4:6).

Antioch ("speedy as a chariot"). [1] A Syrian city on the south side of the Orontes River, where the followers of Jesus were first called Christians (Acts 11:19–26). [2] A city of Phrygia near the border of Pisidia, visited by Paul and Barnabas on their missionary journey (Acts 13:14).

Antipas, a Christian martyr of Pergamos (Rev. 2:13).

Aphek [Aphik] ("strength"). [1] A city north of Sidon (Josh. 13:4). [2] A town assigned to the tribe of Asher but never captured from the Canaanites; located just southeast of Acco (Josh. 19:30; Judg. 1:31). [3] A town on the Plain of Sharon northeast of Joppa, whose king was killed by Joshua (Josh. 12:18). [4] A town between Shunem and Jezreel, whose soldiers fought in the war between Saul and the Philistines (1 Sam. 28:4; 29:1, 11; 31:1).

Apollonia ("city of Apollo"), a Macedonian town visited by Paul on his way to Thessalonica (Acts 17:1).

Apollos ("a destroyer"), a Jewish Christian, mighty in the Scriptures, who came to Ephesus and was instructed by Aquila and Priscilla (Acts 18:24; 19:1; 1 Cor. 1:12; 3:4–6; Titus 3:13).

Appii Forum ("marketplace of Appius"), a town in Italy about 64 km. (40 mi.) from Rome. Roman Christians met Paul here when he was brought to plead his case before Caesar (Acts 28:15).

Aquila ("eagle"), a pious Jewish Christian, husband of Priscilla and friend of Paul (Acts 18:2, 18, 26; Rom. 16:3; 1 Cor. 16:19).

Arabah ("steppe"), the depression of land holding the Sea of Galilee and the Dead Sea (Josh. 18:18). The "valley" of Joshua 11:2 probably refers to the Arabah.

Arabia ("desert"), a large peninsula bounded on the east by the Persian Gulf and the Gulf of Oman, on the west by the Red Sea, and on the south by the Indian Ocean. It was the home of many nomadic tribes, and was sometimes called the "East Country" (2 Chr. 21:16; Is. 13:20).

Ararat ("high land"), a mountainous, hilly land in western Asia (Jer. 51:27) later known as Armenia (Is. 37:38; 2 Kin. 19:37). Noah's ark rested on mountains in this area (Gen. 8:4).

Araunah ("Jehovah is firm"). *See* Ornan.

Archelaus ("people's chief"), the son of Herod the Great who succeeded his father as the ruler of Idumea, Judea, and Samaria (Matt. 2:22).

Archippus ("chief groom"), a "fellow-soldier" whom Paul addresses (Col. 4:17; Philem. 2).

Areopagus ("hill of Ares [Mars]"), a hill west of the acropolis in Athens, where Paul addressed several Greek philosophers; also known as Mars's Hill (Acts 17:19–34).

Aretas ("pleasing; virtuous"), Aretas IV, Philopatris. King of the Nabataeans whose deputy tried to seize Paul (2 Cor. 11:32).

Arimathea ("heights"), the home of a businessman named Joseph, who gained permission to bury the body of Jesus (Matt. 27:57; Luke 23:51).

Aristarchus ("the best ruler"), a faithful companion who accompanied Paul on his third missionary journey (Acts 19:29; 20:4; Col. 4:10).

Aristobulus ("best counselor"), a person in Rome whose household Paul saluted (Rom. 16:10).

Armageddon (Hebrew, *Har Megiddo*—"hill

of Megiddo"), the site of the final battle between Christ and Satan (Rev. 16:16).

Armenia. *See* Ararat.

Arnon ("rushing water"), a river that pours
into the Dead Sea (Num. 21:13; Josh. 13:16).

Artaxerxes ("fervent to spoil"). [1] A king
of Persia, Artaxerxes I Longimanus, at
whose court Ezra and Nehemiah were officials (Ezra 7:1, 7, 11, 12; Neh. 2:1; 5:14). [2]
Some suppose that Ezra 4:7 uses "Artaxerxes" to refer to the pseudo-Smerdis king of
Persia, but the reference is probably to [1].

Asa ("physician; healer"). [1] The third
king of Judah and an ancestor of Christ (1
Kin. 15:8—16:29; Matt. 1:7, 8). [2] Head of a
Levite family (1 Chr. 9:16).

Asahel ("God is doer; God has made"). [1]
A son of David's sister, Zeruiah. He was slain
by Abner (2 Sam. 2:18—32; 3:27, 30). [2] A Levite sent to teach the Law (2 Chr. 17:8). [3] A
Levite employed as an officer of the offerings
and tithes (2 Chr. 31:13). [4] Father of Jonathan, appointed to take a census of foreign
wives (Ezra 10:15).

Asaph ("collector; gatherer"). [1] One of
David's three chief musicians (1 Chr. 6:39;
15:17, 19). Author of Psalms 50, 73—83. [2]
Father of Joah the recorder to Hezekiah (2
Kin. 18:18, 37; 2 Chr. 29:13). [3] A Levite
whose descendants lived in Jerusalem (1 Chr.
9:15). [4] One whose descendants were por-
ters in David's time (1 Chr. 26:1). The text
should possibly read Abiasaph (q.v.). [5] A
keeper of the royal forests in Judah (Neh.
2:8).

Asenath ("dedicated to [the deity] Neit"),
the Egyptian wife of Joseph (Gen. 41:45, 50;
46:20).

Ashdod ("stronghold"), one of the five chief
Canaanite cities; the seat of the worship of
the fish god Dagon; located halfway between
present-day Jaffa and Gaza (Josh. 11:22; 1
Sam. 5:1). In the N.T. the city is called Azotus (Acts 8:40).

Asher ("happy"), a town on the southern
border of Manasseh (Josh. 17:7).

Ashkelon [Askelon] ("wandering"), one of
the five chief Canaanite cities, the seat of the
worship of the goddess Derceto; located
about 19 km. (12 mi.) north of the present-
day city of Gaza (Josh. 13:3; Jer. 47:5).

Ashpenaz, prince of Nebuchadnezzar's eunuchs who had charge of the captives from
Judah (Dan. 1:3).

Asia ("eastern"), the term used by the
Bible to refer to Asia Minor (1 Cor. 16:19;
Acts 2:9). It is sometimes used to refer to a
Roman province in Asia Minor (Acts 19:10;
Rev. 1:4).

Askelon. *See* Ashkelon.

Asshur [Assur] ("level plain"). [1] A son of

Shem (Gen. 10:22; 1 Chr. 1:17). Possibly the
people of Assyria are intended. [2] Genesis
10:11, if denoting a person, refers to a son of
Ham or to [1]. However, many scholars
translate: "From that land he [Nimrod] went
into Assyria [Asshur]."

Asshur [Assur] ("level plain"), a city in Assyria which was sometimes the capital, or
the nation itself may be referred to (Num.
24:22, 24).

Assur. *See* Asshur.

Assyria ("country of Assur"), a Semitic nation on the Tigris River, whose capital was
Nineveh (Gen. 2:14; 2 Kin. 15:10, 20).

Atad ("a thorn"), the campsite near Hebron
used by Joseph and his brothers as they prepared to take Jacob's body back to Canaan
(Gen. 50:11). The new name given the site
was a pun: the Canaanites saw the mourning
[Hebrew, *ēbhel*] of the Egyptians and called
the place *Abel* [Hebrew, *ābhel*]—"meadow";
Mizraim—"of the Egyptians."

Ataroth Addar [Ataroth Adar] ("crown of
Addar"), a village on the southern frontier of
Ephraim (Josh. 16:5; 18:13). The town is
probably to be identified with Ataroth (Josh.
16:2).

Athaliah ("whom Jehovah has afflicted; Jehovah is strong"). [1] The daughter of Jezebel, wife of King Jehoram, and afterwards
ruler of Israel for six years (2 Kin. 8:26; 11:1—
20; 2 Chr. 22:2—23:21). [2] A son of Jeroham
(1 Chr. 8:26). [3] Father of a returned exile
(Ezra 8:7).

Athens ("city of Athena"), the greatest
city of classical Greece, capital of the Greek
city-state of Attica, where Paul founded a
Christian church (Acts 17:15—18).

Attai ("seasonable; timely"). [1] One who
joined David at Ziklag (1 Chr. 12:11). [2] A
son of King Rehoboam (2 Chr. 11:20). [3] Descendant of Pharez (1 Chr. 2:35, 36).

Augustus (i.e., "consecrated" or "holy").
Acts 25:21, 25; 27:1 use the Greek rendering
of the title "reverend" in this fashion, since
Augustus had been dead many years.

Augustus Caesar, the imperial name of Oc-
tavian, a nephew of Julius Caesar who became emperor of Rome. During his reign,
Christ was born (Luke 2:1).

Azarel [Azareel] ("God is helper"). [1] One
who joined David at Ziklag (1 Chr. 12:6). [2]
One who ministered in the song service of
the temple (1 Chr. 25:18). [3] A prince of Dan
(1 Chr. 27:22). [4] One who took a foreign wife
(Ezra 10:41). [5] A priest of the family of Immer (Neh. 11:13). [6] One who played the
trumpet at the dedication of the new temple
(Neh. 12:36).

Azariah ("Jehovah has helped"). [1] *See*
Uzziah. [2] A ruler of Solomon's officers (1

Kin. 4:5). **[3]** A descendant of David's high priest (1 Kin. 4:2). **[4]** A descendant of Judah (1 Chr. 2:8). **[5]** A descendant of Jerahmeel (1 Chr. 2:38, 39). **[6]** A son of Ahimaaz (1 Chr. 6:9). **[7]** A high priest and grandson of **[6]** (1 Chr. 6:10, 11). **[8]** A son of Hilkiah the high priest under Josiah (1 Chr. 6:13, 14; 9:11; Ezra 7:1). **[9]** An ancestor of Samuel the prophet (1 Chr. 6:36). **[10]** A prophet who went to Asa (2 Chr. 15:1). **[11], [12]** Two sons of King Jehoshaphat (2 Chr. 21:2). **[13]** *See* Ahaziah **[2]**. **[14]** A captain who helped to place Joash on the throne (2 Chr. 23:1). **[15]** Another man who helped Joash (2 Chr. 23:1). **[16]** A high priest who opposed Uzziah (2 Chr. 26:17, 20). **[17]** A chief of Ephraim (2 Chr. 28:12). **[18]** A descendant of Kohath and father of Joel (2 Chr. 29:12). **[19]** One who helped cleanse the temple (2 Chr. 29:12). **[20]** A chief of the family of Zadok, priest in Hezekiah's time (2 Chr. 31:10, 13). **[21]** Ancestor of Zadok and Ezra (Ezra 7:3). **[22]** One who repaired the wall of Jerusalem (Neh. 3:23, 24). **[23]** One who came up to Jerusalem with Zerubbabel (Neh. 7:7). Perhaps this is another name of Seraiah (Ezra 2:2); if not, his name is omitted in this passage. **[24]** A priest who explained the Law (Neh. 8:7). **[25]** *See* Ezra **[1]**. **[26]** A prince of Judah (Neh. 12:33). **[27]** One who charged Jeremiah with false prophecy (Jer. 43:2). **[28]** A captive carried to Babylon with Daniel (Dan. 1:6, 7, 11, 19; 2:17). *See* Abed-Nego.

Azubah ("forsaken"). **[1]** The mother of King Jehoshaphat (1 Kin. 22:42; 2 Chr. 20:31). **[2]** Wife of Caleb, the son of Hezron (1 Chr. 2:18, 19).

B

Baal ("master; lord"). **[1]** A descendant of Reuben (1 Chr. 5:5). **[2]** The fourth of ten sons of Jehiel (1 Chr. 8:29, 30; 9:36).

Baal ("master"), a city of Simeon, identical with Baalath Beer (1 Chr. 4:33).

Baalath Beer ("mistress of a well"), a border town of the tribe of Simeon, sometimes called "Ramah of the South" (Josh. 19:8). It is identical with Baal (q.v.).

Baal Gad ("the lord of fortune; Gad is lord"), a town at the foot of Mount Hermon that marked the northern limit of Joshua's conquest (Josh. 11:17; 12:7).

Baal Hazor ("lord of Hazor [enclosure]"), the place near Ephraim where Absalom had Amnon killed (2 Sam. 13:23); the probable site is about 7 km. (4.5 mi.) northeast of Bethel.

Baal Hermon ("lord of Hermon"), the site of Canaanite rituals on the eastern slope of Mount Hermon, which marked the north-

west boundary of the half-tribe of Manasseh (Judg. 3:3; 1 Chr. 5:23).

Baalis ("lord of joy"), the king of the Ammonites after Jerusalem was taken (Jer. 40:14).

Baal Tamar ("lord of palms"), a place near Gibeah and Bethel in the territory of Benjamin, where the Israelites repelled the army of Gibeah (Judg. 20:33).

Baana [Baanah] ("son of grief; patient"). **[1]** One of Solomon's royal merchants (1 Kin. 4:12). **[2]** Another merchant of Solomon, responsible for Asher (1 Kin. 4:16). **[3]** Father of Zadok, the builder of the temple (Neh. 3:4). **[4]** Father of one of David's mighty men (2 Sam. 23:29; 1 Chr. 11:30). **[5]** A captain in Ishbosheth's army (2 Sam. 4:2, 5, 6, 9). **[6]** One who returned from the Exile with Zerubbabel (Ezra 2:2; Neh. 7:7; 10:27).

Baasha ("boldness"), the third king of Israel; war and wickedness characterized his reign (1 Kin. 15:16—16:13).

Babylon (meaning unknown). **[1]** The capital city of the Babylonian Empire, famous for its hanging gardens; a focal point of the Jewish captivity beginning in 586 B.C. (2 Kin. 17:24, 25; Is. 39:3, 6, 7). **[2]** Most scholars believe the references in First Peter 5:13 and Revelation 14:8; 18:2, 10–21 are to Rome. However, some believe Peter refers to **[1]**.

Balaam ("a pilgrim; lord [Baal] of the people"), a prophet that the king of Moab induced to curse Israel. Instead, God put words of blessing in his mouth (Num. 22—24; 31:8).

Balak ("void; empty"), the king of Moab that hired Balaam to curse Israel (Num. 22—24; Josh. 24:9).

Bani ("posterity"). **[1]** One of David's mighty men (2 Sam. 23:36). **[2]** A descendant of Merari (1 Chr. 6:46). **[3]** A descendant of Pharez (1 Chr. 9:4). **[4]** Father of a family that returned from the Babylonian Captivity (Ezra 2:10; 10:29). In Nehemiah 7:15, he is called Binnui. **[5]** One whose descendants had taken foreign wives during the Exile (Ezra 10:34). **[6]** A descendant of **[5]** who took a foreign wife during the Exile (Ezra 10:38). **[7]** A Levite who helped to repair the wall of Jerusalem (Neh. 3:17; 8:7). **[8]** A Levite who assisted in the devotions of the people (Neh. 9:4; 10:13). **[9]** One who sealed the new covenant with God after the Exile (Neh. 10:14). **[10]** A Levite whose son was an overseer of the Levites after the Exile. Perhaps the same as **[7]** or **[8]** (Neh. 11:22). **[11], [12], [13]** Three Levites who participated in the temple worship (Neh. 9:4, 5).

Bar, Aramaic for the Hebrew "ben," "son." "Bar" and "ben" are frequently prefixed to names to indicate direct relationship. Thus

Peter is called Bar-Jonah (son of Jonah) because his father was named Jonah (Matt. 16:17) and perhaps Nathanael was called Bartholomew (son of Tolmai) because his father was named Tolmai.

Barabbas ("father's son"), a murderer whom the people demanded that Pontius Pilate should release instead of Christ (Matt. 27:17, 20, 21, 26; Mark 15:7). *See* Bar.

Barak ("lightning"), the general of the judge Deborah; he helped to defeat Sisera (Judg. 4:6—5:15).

Barnabas ("son of consolation"), a Jewish Christian who traveled widely with Paul (Acts 4:36; 9:27; 11:22-30; Gal. 2:1). His original name was Joses, but he was named Barnabas by the apostles (Acts 4:36); obviously they considered him to be *their* consoler. *See* Bar.

Barsabas ("son of Saba"). *See* Bar; Joseph [11]; Juda [12].

Bartholomew ("son of Tolmai"), one of Jesus' twelve apostles (Matt. 10:3; Mark 3:18; Acts 1:13). He is probably the same as Nathanael (q.v.). *See* Bar.

Baruch ("blessed"). [1] Jeremiah's friend and scribe (Jer. 32:12, 13, 16; 36). [2] One who helped to rebuild the wall of Jerusalem (Neh. 3:20; 10:6). [3] A descendant of Perez who returned from the Exile (Neh. 11:5).

Basemath ("fragrant"). [1] A daughter of Solomon (1 Kin. 4:15). [2] A wife of Esau (Gen. 26:34). *See also* Esau. [3] Another wife of Esau, whom she married to appease his father (Gen. 36:3, 4, 10, 13).

Bathsheba ("the seventh daughter; daughter of the oath"), the beautiful wife of Uriah the Hittite, and afterward the wife of David (2 Sam. 11:3; 12:24; 1 Kin. 1:11—2:19). She was the mother of Solomon and an ancestor of Christ (Matt. 1:6). She is called Bathshua in First Chronicles 3:5.

Bathshua ("daughter of prosperity"). [1] Another name of Bathsheba (q.v.). [2] The wife of Judah. In Genesis 38:2 and First Chronicles 2:3, the KJV incorrectly renders her name as "daughter of Shua"; Bathshua is really a proper name.

Beautiful Gate, a portion of the east gate of Jerusalem where Peter and John healed a lame man (Acts 3:2).

Bedan ("son of judgment"). [1] A leader of Israel mentioned as a deliverer of the nation (1 Sam. 12:11). The Septuagint, Syriac, and Arabic read *Barak* instead; however, many think this is a reference to Abdon. [2] A descendant of Manasseh (1 Chr. 7:17).

Beeliada ("the lord knows"), a son of David (1 Chr. 14:7) also known as Eliada (2 Sam. 5:16; 1 Chr. 3:8).

Beer ("a well"). [1] A temporary encampment of the Israelites in the wilderness (Num. 21:16–18); possibly the same as Beer Elim (Is. 15:8). [2] A place where Jotham sought refuge from his brother Abimelech (Judg. 9:21); possibly the same as Beeroth.

Beer Lahai Roi ("well of the living one who sees me"), the well of Hagar, located between Kadesh and Bered on the road to Shur, about 80 km. (50 mi.) southwest of Beersheba (Gen. 16:14).

Beersheba ("well of oaths"), a city in southern Judah, site of Abraham's covenant with Abimelech; it is located about 45 km. (28 mi.) southwest of Hebron (Gen. 21:14, 22–31; Josh. 15:28).

Belshazzar (Hebrew form of the Babylonian name Bel-shar-usur—"[the god] Bel has protected the king [ship]"), the son of Nabonidus and co-regent in Babylon. He witnessed strange handwriting on the wall of his palace before his kingdom was overthrown by Persia (Dan. 5; 7:1; 8:1).

Belteshazzar (Hebrew form of the Babylonian name, Balat-usu-usur—"Protect his life!"), the name given to Daniel in Babylon (Dan. 1:7). *See* Daniel.

Benaiah ("Jehovah has built"). [1] The third leader of David's army, counselor to the kings, and loyal friend of both David and Solomon (2 Sam. 8:18; 20:23; 1 Kin. 1:8—2:46). [2] One of David's mighty men (2 Sam. 23:30; 1 Chr. 11:31). [3] Head of a family of the tribe of Simeon (1 Chr. 4:36). [4] One of David's priests (1 Chr. 15:18, 20, 24; 16:5, 6). [5] Father of one of David's counselors (1 Chr. 27:34).

Ben-Ammi ("son of my people"), the ancestor of the Ammonites (Gen. 19:38), born to Lot and his daughter.

Ben-Hadad ("son of [the god] Hadad"). [1] Ben-Hadad I, the king of Syria who made a league with Asa of Judah and invaded Israel (1 Kin. 15:18, 20; 2 Chr. 10:2, 4). [2] Ben-Hadad II, another king of Syria defeated by Ahab; he eventually laid siege to Samaria itself (1 Kin. 20; 2 Kin. 6:24; 8:7, 9). [3] The son of Hazael who reigned over Syria as the empire disintegrated (2 Kin. 13:3, 24, 25; Amos 1:4). [4] Possibly a general title of the Syrian kings (Jer. 49:27).

Benjamin ("son of the right hand"). [1] The youngest son of Jacob; his descendants became one of the twelve tribes of Israel (Gen. 35:18, 24; 42:4, 36; 43—45). [2] A descendant of Benjamin (1 Chr. 7:10). [3] A descendant of Harim (Ezra 10:32). [4] One who helped to repair the wall of Jerusalem (Neh. 3:23). [5] One who helped to dedicate the wall of Jerusalem (Neh. 12:34).

Ben-Oni ("son of my sorrow"), name given

to Rachel's child as she died bearing him; Jacob changed his name to Benjamin (q.v.).

Bernice ("victorious"), the immoral daughter of Herod Agrippa I. She and her brother Agrippa (with whom she was living in incest) sat in judgment on Paul (Acts 25:13, 23; 26:30).

Berothah [Berothai; Chun] ("of a well"), a town in northern Palestine between Hamath and Damascus, captured by David; also called Chun (2 Sam. 8:8; 1 Chr. 18:8; Ezek. 47:16).

Bethabara ("house at the ford"), a place on the eastern side of the Jordan River where John the Baptist baptized his converts (John 1:28). The majority of Greek manuscripts read Bethany here instead; however, this city was not identical with Bethany proper.

Bethany ("house of affliction; place of unripe figs"), a settlement on the hill leading to the Mount of Olives, about 2.6 km. (1.6 mi.) from Jerusalem (Mark 11:1; Luke 19:29).

Beth Aven ("house of idols"), a town of the tribe of Benjamin, located in the wilderness near Ai (Josh. 7:2; 18:12; 1 Sam. 13:5).

Bethel ("house of God"). A town located about 18 km. (11 mi.) north of Jerusalem; an important site throughout the history of Israel (cf. Gen. 13:3; 28:18, 19; Josh. 16:2; Judg. 21:19). It was formerly called Luz. The modern town of Bertin is located near the ruins.

Bethesda ("house of outpouring or overflowing water"), a pool near the Sheep Gate of Jerusalem reputed to have healing qualities (John 5:2, 3).

Beth Horon ("cave house"), twin towns located on the boundary between the territories of Ephraim and Benjamin. Upper Beth Horon was situated on a mountain pass between Jerusalem and the plain to the west. Lower Beth Horon was about 2 km. (1.5 mi.) farther northwest (Josh. 16:3; 18:13; 2 Chr. 8:5; 1 Kin. 9:17). The modern names for these towns are Beit 'Ur et Tahta (Lower) and Beit 'Ur el Foka (Upper).

Bethlehem ("house of bread"). [1] A town about 10 km. (6 mi.) south of Jerusalem; birthplace of Jesus Christ (Matt. 2:5) and Ephrath (Gen. 35:16, 19; Ruth 4:11; cf. Mic. 5:2). Only in later times was it known as Bethlehem. It was originally called Ephrathah (Ephrath) (Ruth 4:11; Gen. 35:16). [2] A city of the tribe of Zebulun located about 11 km. (7 mi.) northwest of Nazareth (Josh. 19:15).

Beth Nimrah ("house of the leopardess"), a fortified city built by the tribe of Gad east of the Jordan River (Num. 32:36); also called Nimrah (Num. 32:3).

Beth Peor ("house of Peor"), a site near

Pisgah where the Israelites placed their main camp while warring against Og (Deut. 3:29; 4:46).

Bethphage ("house of unripe figs"), a settlement near Bethany on the road from Jerusalem to Jericho, probably at the descent from the Mount of Olives (Matt. 21:1; Mark 11:1).

Bethsaida ("fish house"), a fishing town on the Sea of Galilee; birthplace of Philip, Andrew, and Simon (Matt. 11:21; Luke 9:10; Mark 6:45).

Beth Shean [Beth Shan] ("house of rest"), the southern border town of the region of Galilee; largest of the ten cities of the Decapolis (Josh. 17:11; 1 Chr. 7:29).

Beth Shemesh ("house of the sun"). [1] A town on the road from Ashkelon and Ashdod to Jerusalem; it is located about 38 km. (24 mi.) west of Jerusalem (Josh. 15:10). [2] A Canaanite city in the territory of Naphtali (Josh. 19:38; Judg. 1:33). [3] A city of the tribe of Issachar, probably on the Jordan River near the Sea of Galilee (Josh. 19:22). [4] Another name for the Egyptian city of Heliopolis (Jer. 43:13).

Bethuel [Bethul] ("dweller of God"), a town apportioned to the tribe of Simeon (Josh. 19:4; 1 Chr. 4:30). The town was also called Bethel (1 Sam. 30:27).

Beulah ("married"), Isaiah's name for the Promised Land after the Babylonian Captivity (Is. 62:4).

Bezalel ("God is protection"). [1] A chief worker and designer of the tabernacle (Ex. 31:2; 35:30; 36:1, 2). [2] One who had married a foreign wife (Ezra 10:30).

Bildad ("lord Adad; son of contention"), one of Job's three "friends" (Job 2:11; 8:1; 18:1; 25:1; 42:9).

Bilhah ("tender"), the handmaid of Rachel and mother of Dan and Naphtali (Gen. 29:29; 30:3–5, 7).

Boanerges, the surname bestowed upon James and John, the sons of Zebedee. It means "sons of thunder" (Mark 3:17).

Boaz ("fleetness; strength"), a Bethlehemite of Judah who became the husband of Ruth and an ancestor of Christ (Ruth 2–4; Matt. 1:5; Luke 3:32).

Bochim ("weepers"), a site near Gilgal where the Israelites repented of their sins (Judg. 2:1–5).

Buz ("contempt"). [1] The second son of Nahor, the brother of Abraham (Gen. 22:21). [2] A descendant of Gad (1 Chr. 5:14).

Buzi ("despised by Jehovah"), a descendant of Aaron and father of Ezekiel (Ezek. 1:3).

C

Caesar, the name of a branch of the aristocratic family of the Julii, which gained control of the Roman government; afterward it became a formal title of the Roman emperors. *See* Augustus Caesar; Tiberius Caesar; Claudius Caesar.

Caesarea ("city of Caesar"), a coastal city of Palestine that served as capital of the Roman province (Acts 8:40). Built by Herod the Great, it is located 37 km. (23 mi.) from the foot of Mount Carmel; also called Caesarea Maritima.

Caesarea Philippi ("Caesar's city of Philippi"), a town located at the foot of Mount Hermon; the northernmost extent of Jesus' ministry (Matt. 16:13–20).

Caiaphas ("depression"), the high priest who took a leading role in the trial of Jesus (Matt. 26:3, 57–68; John 11:49).

Cain ("acquired; spear"), the eldest son of Adam who killed his brother Abel (Gen. 4:1–25).

Calvary. *See* Golgotha.

Cana ("reeds"), a village of Galilee where Jesus performed the miracle of changing water into wine. It is located 16 km. (10 mi.) northeast of Nazareth (John 2:1, 11; 4:46).

Canaan ("low"), a son of Ham and grandson of Noah (Gen. 10:6–19; 1 Chr. 1:8, 13). Possibly a reference to the inhabitants of Canaan.

Canaan ("purple"), the native name of Palestine, the land given to Abraham and his descendants (Gen. 11:31; Ex. 6:4).

Capernaum ("village of Nahum"), a town on the northwest shore of the Sea of Galilee; an important center of Jesus' ministry (Matt. 4:13; Luke 4:31).

Carchemish ("city [fortress] of Chemosh"), a city west of the Euphrates River; the eastern capital of the Hittites (2 Chr. 35:20; Is. 10:9; Jer. 46:2).

Carmel ("orchard"). [1] A string of mountains that run about 24 km. (15 mi.) through central Palestine and jut into the Mediterranean Sea (Jer. 46:18). [2] A town in the mountains of Judah about 14 km. (9 mi.) south-southeast of Hebron (Josh. 15:55; 1 Sam. 25:5); modern Kermel.

Cephas. *See* Peter.

Chaldea ("demons"), the southern region of the Babylonian Empire (Jer. 50:10; Ezek. 11:24).

Cherith ("gorge"), a small stream east of the Jordan River, where birds fed the prophet Elijah (1 Kin. 17:3–5).

Chidon [Nachon] ("javelin"), the place where Uzzah was struck dead for touching the ark of the covenant (1 Chr. 13:9); in Second Samuel 6:6 the place is called Nachon. Its exact location is unknown.

Chileab ("restraint of father"), a son of David (2 Sam. 3:3); probably also called Daniel (1 Chr. 3:1).

Chinnereth [Chinneroth] ("harps"). [1] Another name for the Sea of Galilee (Num. 34:11; Josh. 12:3). [2] A city on the north shore of the Sea of Galilee (Deut. 3:17). [3] The region surrounding the city of Chinnereth (1 Kin. 15:20).

Chloe ("a tender sprout"), a Corinthian woman or an Ephesian woman who knew of the problems at Corinth (1 Cor. 1:11).

Chorazin ("secret"), a coastal city of the Sea of Galilee where Jesus Christ performed many miracles (Matt. 11:21; Luke 10:13).

Christ. *See* Jesus Christ.

Chun ("founding"). *See* Berothah.

Cilicia ("rolling"), a district of southeast Asia Minor. Paul was born in Tarsus, the principal city of this district (Acts 21:39).

Cities of Refuge, six Levitical cities set aside as sanctuaries for certain criminals: Bezer, Ramoth Gilead, Golan, Kedesh, Shechem, and Kirjath Arba (Deut. 4:41–43; Josh. 20:7–9).

Cities of the Plain, five cities located on the Plain of Jordan: Sodom, Gomorrah, Admah, Zeboim, and Zoar (Gen. 10:19; 13:10).

City of David. [1] Jebusite city of Zion captured by David's men. David made it his royal city and renamed it Jerusalem (2 Sam. 5:6–9; 1 Chr. 11:5, 7). [2] *See* Bethlehem.

City of Salt, a city in the wilderness of Judah near En Gedi (Josh. 15:62).

Claudia ("lame"), a Roman Christian who sent greetings to Timothy (2 Tim. 4:21).

Claudius Caesar ("lame ruler"), Roman emperor who banished the Jews from Rome (Acts 18:2).

Claudius Lysias ("lame dissolution"), a Roman officer, chief captain in Jerusalem (Acts 23:26).

Clement ("mild"), a co-worker with Paul at Philippi (Phil. 4:3).

Cleopas ("renowned father"), one of the disciples whom Jesus met on the way to Emmaus (Luke 24:18).

Colosse ("punishment"), a city in the district of Phrygia in Asia Minor (Col. 1:2).

Corinth ("ornament"), a Greek city located on the isthmus between the Peloponnesus and mainland Greece, about 64 km. (40 mi.) west of Athens (Acts 18:1; 1 Cor. 1:2).

Cornelius ("of a horn"), a Roman centurion who was converted to Christianity (Acts 10:1–31).

Corner Gate, a gate near the northwest corner of the wall of Jerusalem (2 Kin. 14:13).

Crete ("carnal"), a large island southeast of Greece (Titus 1:5).

Crispus ("curled"), a ruler of the Jewish synagogue at Corinth who was converted to Christ (Acts 18:7, 8; 1 Cor. 1:14).

Cyprus ("fairness"), an island in the northeastern Mediterranean Sea about 96 km. (60 mi.) east of Syria (Acts 13:4; 15:39).

Cyrus, founder of the Persian Empire; he returned the Jews to their land (Ezra 1:1-4, 7; 3:7; Is. 44:28; 45:1-4; Dan. 6:28).

D

Dalmanutha ("bucket"), a fishing village on the western coast of the Sea of Galilee (Mark 8:10).

Damascus ("sackful of blood"), an important Syrian trade center; Paul was converted on the road from Jerusalem to this city (Gen. 14:15; Acts 9:2).

Dan ("judge"), the fifth son of Jacob and ancestor of one of the twelve tribes of Israel (Gen. 30:6; 49:16, 17).

Dan ("judge"), a town of the tribe of Dan in the northwest portion of Palestine (Josh. 19:47; Judg. 20:1).

Daniel ("God is my judge"). [1] A prophet at the time of Nebuchadnezzar and Cyrus. His wisdom and faith earned him a position of esteem under Nebuchadnezzar and Darius (Dan. 1:1-6; 2; 6:1, 2). [2] One of the sons of David (1 Chr. 3:1). *See* Chileab. [3] A Levite of the line of Ithamar (Ezra 8:2; Neh. 10:6).

Darius ("he that informs himself"). [1] The sub-king of Cyrus who received the kingdom of Belshazzar (Dan. 5:30—6:28); also known as Darius the Mede. [2] The fourth king of Persia (Ezra 4:5; Hag. 1:1; Zech. 1:1); also called Hystaspis. [3] Darius II (Nothus) who ruled Persia and Babylon (Neh. 12:22).

Dathan ("fount"), a chief of the tribe of Reuben who tried to overthrow Moses and Aaron (Num. 16; 26:9; Deut. 11:6).

David ("beloved"), the great statesman, general, and king of Israel. He united the divided tribes of Israel and made many preparations for the temple, which his son Solomon would complete (1 Sam. 16—1 Kin. 2:11). He was an ancestor of Christ (Matt. 1:6).

Dead Sea. *See* Salt Sea.

Deborah ("bee"). [1] The nurse of Rebekah (Gen. 24:59; 35:8). [2] Prophetess and judge of Israel who helped to deliver her people from Jabin and Sisera (Judg. 4:4-14; 5).

Decapolis ("ten cities"), a league of ten cities forming a Roman district on the Plain of Esdraelon and the Upper Jordan Valley (Matt. 4:25).

Delaiah ("Jehovah has raised; Jehovah is deliverer"). [1] One of David's priests (1 Chr. 24:18). [2] A prince who urged Jehoiakim not to destroy the roll containing Jeremiah's prophecies (Jer. 36:12, 25).

Delilah ("longing; dainty one"), a woman whom the Philistines paid to find Samson's source of strength (Judg. 16).

Demetrius ("belonging to Demeter"). [1] A Christian praised by John (3 John 12). [2] A silversmith who led the opposition against Paul at Ephesus (Acts 19:24-41).

Derbe ("sting"), a city of southeastern Asia Minor, where Paul sought refuge after being stoned at Lystra (Acts 14:6-20).

Didymus. *See* Thomas.

Dinah ("justice"), the daughter of Jacob and Leah who was violated by Shechem; this resulted in a tribal war (Gen. 34).

Dionysius ("Bacchus"), a member of the supreme court at Athens converted by Paul (Acts 17:34).

Dorcas. *See* Tabitha.

Dothan ("two wells"), a city of the tribe of Manasseh west of the Jordan River and northeast of Samaria, near Mount Gilboa; here Joseph was sold into slavery (Gen. 37:17; 2 Kin. 6:13).

Drusilla ("watered by dew"), a Jewess, the daughter of Herod Agrippa I and wife of Felix; she and Felix heard a powerful message of Paul's (Acts 24:24, 25).

Dura ("fortress"), the Babylonian plain where King Nebuchadnezzar set up a golden idol (Dan. 3:1).

E

Ebenezer ("stone of help"). [1] The site of the defeat of Israel by the Philistines (1 Sam. 4:1-22). It was in the north of Sharon near Aphek. [2] Name of a stone Samuel erected to commemorate his victory over the Philistines (1 Sam. 7:12). The stone was possibly named after [1] to give the idea that Israel's defeat there had been reversed.

Eden ("pleasure"). [1] The garden that God created as the first residence of man (Gen. 2:15); its exact location is unknown. It may have been between the Tigris and Euphrates Rivers near the head of the Persian Gulf. [2] A region in Mesopotamia (2 Kin. 19:12; Is. 37:12).

Edom ("red"), name given to Esau, the elder son of Isaac, because of the red stew for which he sold his birthright (Gen. 25:30). *See* Esau; Obed-Edom.

Edom ("red"), a mountainous region south of Moab, which stretches from the Dead Sea to the Gulf of 'Aqabah. It was settled by the descendants of Esau, the Edomites (Gen. 32:3; Ex. 15:15).

Eglah ("calf"), one of David's wives (2 Sam. 3:5; 1 Chr. 3:3).

Eglon ("of a calf"), a town in the lowlands of Judah (Josh. 15:39); its exact location is unknown.

Egypt ("land of the soul of Ptah"), northeast corner of Africa where the Israelites were held in bondage until Moses led them to the Promised Land (Gen. 45:9; 47:6).

Ehud ("strong"). [1] A judge who delivered Israel from the oppression of Eglon of Moab (Judg. 3:15–30). [2] Great-grandson of Benjamin (1 Chr. 7:10; 8:6); perhaps the same as [1].

Elah ("oak"). [1] A chieftain of Edom (Gen. 36:41; 1 Chr. 1:52). [2] Father of a commissary officer under Solomon (1 Kin. 4:18). [3] The son and successor of Baasha, king of Israel. He was murdered by Zimri (1 Kin. 16:6–14). [4] The father of Hoshea, last king of Israel (2 Kin. 15:30; 17:1). [5] A son of Caleb, son of Jephunneh (1 Chr. 4:15). [6] A descendant of Benjamin (1 Chr. 9:8).

El Bethel ("God of Bethel"), name Jacob gave the scene of his vision at Luz (Bethel) (Gen. 35:7).

Eldad ("God is a friend"), one of two elders who received the prophetic powers of Moses (Num. 11:26, 27).

Eleazar ("God is helper"). [1] Third son of Aaron and successor to the high priest's office (Ex. 6:23; Num. 3:32; 20:28). [2] One sanctified to keep the ark of the covenant (1 Sam. 7:1). [3] One of David's mighty men (2 Sam. 23:9; 1 Chr. 11:12). [4] A descendant of Merari who had no sons (1 Chr. 23:21, 22; 24:28). [5] A priest who accompanied Ezra when he returned to Jerusalem (Ezra 8:33). [6] A priest who assisted at the dedication of the walls of Jerusalem (Neh. 12:42); possibly the same as [5]. [7] An ancestor of Jesus (Matt. 1:15).

Eliakim ("God is setting up"). [1] Successor of Shebna as master of Hezekiah's household (2 Kin. 18:18, 26; Is. 22:20). [2] Original name of King Jehoiakim (q.v.).

Eliezer ("God is help"). [1] Abraham's chief servant (Gen. 15:2). [2] The second son of Moses and Zipporah (Ex. 18:4; 1 Chr. 23:15, 17). [3] A descendant of Benjamin (1 Chr. 7:8). [4] A priest who assisted with bringing the ark of the covenant to Jerusalem (1 Chr. 15:24). [5] A prince of Reuben in the time of David (1 Chr. 27:16). [6] A prophet who rebuked Jehoshaphat (2 Chr. 20:37). [7] A leader who induced others to return to Jerusalem (Ezra 8:16).

Elihu ("God himself"). [1] One who joined David at Ziklag (1 Chr. 12:20). [2] A porter at the tabernacle at the time of David (1 Chr.

26:7). [3] The youngest "friend" of Job (Job 32:2, 4–6).

Elijah ("Jehovah is my God"). [1] A great prophet of God, he strenuously opposed idolatry. He was caught up in a chariot of fire to heaven (1 Kin. 17:1–2 Kin. 2:11; Matt. 17:3). [2] A chief of the tribe of Benjamin (1 Chr. 8:27). [3] One who married a foreign wife during the Exile (Ezra 10:26). [4] Another who took a foreign wife during the Exile (Ezra 10:21).

Elimelech ("my God is King"), the husband of Naomi and father-in-law of Ruth. He died in Moab (Ruth 1:2, 3; 2:1, 3; 4:3, 9).

Eliphaz ("God is dispenser"). [1] The leader of Job's three "friends" who confronted him (Job 2:11; 4:1; 15:1). [2] A son of Esau (Gen. 36:4, 10–12; 1 Chr. 1:35, 36).

Eliphelet [Elpelet] ("God is escape"). [1] The last of David's thirteen sons (2 Sam. 5:16; 1 Chr. 3:8; 14:7). [2] Another of David's sons (1 Chr. 3:6); called Elpelet in First Chronicles 14:5. [3] One of David's mighty men (2 Sam. 23:34).

Elisha [Elishah] ("God is Savior"). [1] The disciple and successor of Elijah; he held the prophetic office for 55 years (1 Kin. 19:16, 17, 19; 2 Kin. 2—6; Luke 4:27). [2] Eldest son of Javan and grandson of Noah (Gen. 10:4). Possibly the people of Cyprus or the inhabitants of Alasiya, a country near Cilicia. Others suggest it includes the Italians and Peloponnesians.

Elishama ("God is hearer"). [1] Grandfather of Joshua (Num. 1:10; 2:18; 1 Chr. 7:26). [2] A son of King David (2 Sam. 5:16; 1 Chr. 3:8). [3] Another son of David (1 Chr. 3:6); also called Elishua in Second Samuel 5:15 and First Chronicles 14:5. [4] A descendant of Judah (1 Chr. 2:41). [5] One of the "royal seed" and grandfather of Gedaliah (Jer. 41:1; 2 Kin. 25:25). [6] A scribe or secretary of Jehoiakim (Jer. 36:12, 20, 21). [7] A priest sent by Jehoshaphat to teach the Law (2 Chr. 17:8).

Elizabeth ("God is swearer; oath of God"), the wife of Zacharias and mother of John the Baptist (Luke 1:5–57).

Elkanah [Elkonah] ("God is possessing"). [1] Grandson of Korah (Ex. 6:24; 1 Chr. 6:23). [2] Father of the prophet Samuel and a descendant of [1] (1 Sam. 1:1–23; 2:11, 20). [3] A descendant of Levi (1 Chr. 6:25, 36). [4] A descendant of Levi (1 Chr. 6:26, 35); perhaps the same as [3]. [5] A Levite ancestor of Berechiah (1 Chr. 9:16). [6] One who joined David at Ziklag (1 Chr. 12:6). [7] A gatekeeper of the ark of the covenant (1 Chr. 15:23); perhaps the same as [6]. [8] An officer of King Ahaz (2 Chr. 28:7).

Elymas ("a sorcerer"), a false prophet who

opposed Saul and Barnabas at Paphos (Acts 13:8); he was also called Bar-Jesus (v. 6).

En Dor ("fountain of habitation"), a town of the tribe of Manasseh where Saul consulted a witch about his future (Josh. 17:11); probably modern Indur on the northeastern shoulder of the Little Hermon Mountain, 10 km. (6 mi.) southeast of Nazareth.

En Gedi ("fountain of the goat"), a town on the western shore of the Dead Sea assigned to the tribe of Judah; originally called Hazazon Tamar (2 Chr. 20:2; Josh. 15:62).

Enoch ("teacher"). [1] The eldest son of Cain (Gen. 4:17, 18). [2] A son of Jared and an ancestor of Christ (Gen. 5:18, 19, 21; 1 Chr. 1:3; Luke 3:37; Heb. 11:5).

Enoch ("initiated"), a city built by Cain (Gen. 4:17).

Enos [Enosh] ("mortal"), son of Seth and ancestor of Christ (Gen. 4:26; 5:6–11; 1 Chr. 1:1; Luke 3:38).

Enosh. *See* Enos.

Epaphras (shortened form of *Epaphroditus*—"lovely"), a Christian worker with Paul who served as missionary to Colosse (Col. 1:7; 4:12; Philem. 23).

Epaphroditus ("lovely"), a Philippian Christian who worked so strenuously that he lost his health (Phil. 2:25; 4:18).

Ephesus ("desirable"), a town on the western coast of Asia Minor between Miletus and Smyrna; an important trading center (Acts 19:1).

Ephod ("oracular"), father of a prince of the tribe of Manasseh (Num. 34:23).

Ephraim ("doubly fruitful"), the second son of Joseph by Asenath. Although Ephraim was the younger of the two sons of Joseph, he received the firstborn's blessing. He was an ancestor of one of the twelve tribes of Israel (Gen. 41:52; 46:20; 48; 50:23).

Ephrathah [Ephrath] ("fertility"), the second wife of Caleb (1 Chr. 2:19, 50; 4:4).

Ephron ("strong"), a Hittite from whom Abraham bought a field with a cave, which became Sarah's burial place (Gen. 23:8, 10, 13, 14; 49:30).

Erastus ("beloved"). [1] Christian sent with Timothy into Macedonia while Paul stayed in Asia (Acts 19:22). [2] An important person in Corinth sending greetings to Rome (Rom. 16:23). [3] One who remained at Corinth (2 Tim. 4:20). Perhaps some or all of the above are identical.

Esarhaddon ("Ashur has given a brother"), the son of Sennacherib and a powerful king of Assyria (2 Kin. 19:37; Ezra 4:2; Is. 37:38).

Esau ("hairy"), eldest son of Isaac and twin brother of Jacob. He is the progenitor of the tribe of Edom (Gen. 25:25). He sold his birthright to Jacob (Gen. 25:26–34; 27; 36).

Esther ("star; [the goddess] Ishtar"), the Persian name of Hadassah, who was chosen by Ahasuerus to be his queen. The book of Esther tells her story.

Ethan ("ancient"). [1] A wise man in the days of Solomon (1 Kin. 4:31; Ps. 89, title). [2] A descendant of Judah (1 Chr. 2:6, 8). He is possibly identical with [1]. [3] *See* Jeduthun. [4] A descendant of Levi (1 Chr. 6:42).

Ethbaal ("Baal's man; with Baal"), king of Sidon and father of Ahab's wife Jezebel (1 Kin. 16:31).

Ethiopia [Cush?] ("burnt face"), a nation located in the upper region of the Nile River (Ps. 68:31; Is. 18:1). It is not the same as modern Ethiopia.

Eubulus ("of good counsel"), one of the Roman Christians that remained loyal to Paul (2 Tim. 4:21).

Eunice ("conquering well"), the pious mother of Timothy (2 Tim. 1:5; cf. Acts 16:1).

Euphrates (meaning unknown), a major river of western Asia, which begins in Armenia and joins the Tigris River before flowing into the Persian Gulf. It formed the western boundary of Mesopotamia (Gen. 2:14; 15:18).

Eutychus ("fortunate"), a young man at Troas whom Paul restored to life (Acts 20:6–12).

Eve ("life; life-giving"), the first woman, Adam's wife (Gen. 3:20; 4:1; 2 Chr. 11:3).

Evil-Merodach (Babylonian, Arvil-Marduk—"the man of [the god] Marduk"), the king of Babylon who released Jehoiachin from imprisonment. He succeeded his father, Nebuchadnezzar (2 Kin. 25:27–30; Jer. 52:31).

Ezekiel ("God strengthens"), a prophet of a priestly family carried captive to Babylon. He prophesied to the exiles in Mesopotamia by the river Chebar, and is the author of the book bearing his name (Ezek. 1:3; 24:24).

Ezra ("help"). [1] Head of one of the courses of priests that returned from the Exile (Neh. 12:1). The full form of his name, *Azariah*, occurs in Nehemiah 10:2. [2] A descendant of Judah through Caleb (1 Chr. 4:17). [3] A prominent scribe and priest descended from Hilkiah the high priest (Ezra 7:1–12; 10:1; Neh. 8:1–13). *See* Azariah.

F

Felix ("happy"), Roman governor of Judea that presided over the trial of Paul at Caesarea (Acts 23:23–27; 24:22–27).

Festus ("swine-like"), successor of Felix to the governorship of Judea. He continued the trial of Paul begun under Felix (Acts 25; 26).

Fortunatus ("fortunate"), a Corinthian

Christian who cheered and comforted Paul at Ephesus (1 Cor. 16:17, 18).

G

Gad ("fortune"). [1] The seventh son of Jacob and an ancestor of one of the twelve tribes (Gen. 30:11; 49:19). [2] David's seer who frequently advised him (1 Sam. 22:5; 1 Chr. 21:9–19).

Gad ("lot; fortune"), the territory settled by the tribe of Gad, east of the Jordan River (1 Sam. 13:7; Josh. 13:24).

Gadara ("walls"), a town located east of the Jordan River, 11 km. (7 mi.) south of the Sea of Galilee (Mark 5:1; Luke 8:26). It was one of the Decapolis cities (q.v.). See also Gergesa.

Gaius ("lord"). [1] One to whom John's third epistle is addressed (3 John 1). [2] A native of Macedonia and a companion of Paul (Acts 19:29). [3] A man of Derbe who accompanied Paul as far as Asia (Acts 20:4). [4] The host to Paul when he wrote to the Romans (Rom. 16:23). [5] A convert whom Paul baptized at Corinth (1 Cor. 1:14); some think he is identical with [4].

Galilee ("circle"), one of the largest Roman districts of Palestine; the primary region of Jesus' ministry (Luke 3:1; 23:6).

Galilee, Sea of, a large lake in northern Palestine, fed by the Jordan River; several of Jesus' disciples worked as fishermen on this lake (John 6:1). The lake was also known as the Sea of Chinnereth, the Sea of Tiberias, and the Sea of Gennesaret. See also Chinnereth [1] and Gennesaret [2].

Gallio (meaning unknown), Roman proconsul of Achaia before whom Paul was tried in Corinth (Acts 18:12–17).

Gamaliel ("reward or recompense of God"). [1] A prince of the tribe of Manasseh (Num. 1:10; 2:20). [2] A great Jewish teacher of the Law. He persuaded his fellow Jews to let the apostles go free (Acts 5:33–40; 22:3).

Gath ("winepress"), one of the five chief Philistine cities; home of the giant Goliath (1 Sam. 17:4; 2 Kin. 12:17; 2 Chr. 26:6). Its exact location is not known.

Gaza ("strong"). [1] The southernmost of the five chief Philistine cities, located 72 km. (44.5 mi.) south of modern Jaffa and 4 km. (2.4 mi.) from the Mediterranean Sea. It was the scene of Samson's exploits (Josh. 11:22; Judg. 16:1–3; 2 Kin. 18:8; Jer. 25:20). [2] A town of the tribe of Ephraim located on a small plain near Shiloh (1 Chr. 7:28).

Gehazi ("valley of vision; diminisher"), the dishonest servant of Elisha (2 Kin. 4:12–37; 5:20–27; 8:4).

Gennesaret ("garden of the prince"). [1] The region on the northwest shore of the Sea of Galilee (Matt. 14:34). [2] Another name for the Sea of Galilee (Luke 5:1).

Gergesa ("pilgrims"), a town or district which would have been located on the eastern side of the Sea of Galilee. Its location is not certain, but some have suggested modern-day Kersa (Matt. 8:28).

Gershon [Gershom] ("exile"), an important priest, the eldest son of Levi (Gen. 46:11; Ex. 6:16; 1 Chr. 6:1). He is also called Gershom (1 Chr. 6:16, 17, 20; 15:7).

Gethsemane ("oil press"), a garden east of Jerusalem, beyond the Brook Kidron at the foot of Mount Olivet; the site of Christ's betrayal (Matt. 26:36–56).

Geuel ("salvation of God"), the spy sent out from Gad to bring back word about Canaan (Num. 13:15).

Gibeah ("hill"). [1] A Judean town about 16 km. (10 mi.) northwest of Hebron (Josh. 15:57). [2] A town midway between Jerusalem and Ramah; home and capital of King Saul (1 Sam. 10:26; 15:34). The town is called Gibeath in Joshua 18:28. [3] A town or hill in the territory of Ephraim (Josh. 24:33); probably near Timnah [1]. [4] A hill in Kirjath Jearim on which was located the house of Abinadab (2 Sam. 6:3, 4).

Gibeon ("hill height"), the chief city of the Hivites, assigned to the tribe of Benjamin; located 9 km. (5.5 mi.) north-northwest of Jerusalem (Josh. 11:19; 2 Sam. 20:1–9). Its modern name is El-Jib.

Gideon ("feller [i.e., great warrior]"), the great judge of Israel who delivered his people from Midian (Judg. 6—8); he was given the name Jerubbaal (q.v.).

Gihon ("stream; bursting forth"). [1] One of the four rivers of Eden [1] (Gen. 2:13). [2] An intermittent spring outside the walls of Jerusalem, south of the temple area (1 Kin. 1:38–45; 2 Chr. 32:30).

Gilgal ("rolling"). [1] The first campsite of the Israelites after they crossed the Jordan River into Canaan, probably near Jericho (Josh. 4:19–24). [2] A village 11 km. (7 mi.) northeast of Bethel, from which Elijah and Elisha began their journey (2 Kin. 2:1–4; 4:38); present-day Jiljilia.

Gog ("high; mountain") (. [1] A descendant of Reuben (1 Chr. 5:4). [2] A prince of Rosh, Meshech, and Tubal (Ezek. 38:2; 39:1, 11). In Revelation 20:8 Gog appears to have become a nation as is Magog, thus indicating the name is to be understood symbolically.

Golan ("passage"), a city of Bashan east of the Jordan River, assigned to the Levites as a city of refuge (Deut. 4:43; Josh. 21:27). It is probably the site of modern Sahem el-Jaulan, 27 km. (17 mi.) east of the Sea of Galilee.

Golgotha [Calvary] ("skull"), a hill just outside the walls of ancient Jerusalem; the site of Jesus' crucifixion (Matt. 27:33; John 19:17). Its exact location is unknown, but it was probably inside the walls of what is now called the "old city."

Goliath ("an exile or soothsayer"). **[1]** The Philistine giant who was slain by David (1 Sam. 17:4–54). **[2]** Another giant, possibly the son of **[1]** (2 Sam. 21:19).

Gomer. [1] Eldest son of Japheth (Gen. 10:2, 3; 1 Chr. 1:5, 6). Possibly a people inhabiting the north, probably including or identical with the Cimmerians of classical history. **[2]** The immoral wife of Hosea (Hos. 1:3; 3:1–4).

Gomorrah ("submersion"), one of the five Cities of the Plain destroyed along with Sodom (Gen. 18:20; 19:24, 28). Many scholars believe it was submerged by the southeastern tip of the Dead Sea.

Goshen ("drawing near"). **[1]** A cattle-raising district of the Nile delta assigned to the Israelites before they were placed in bondage (Gen. 46:28). **[2]** A town in the hill country of Judah (Josh. 15:51); probably modern Dahariyeh, about 21 km. (13 mi.) southwest of Hebron. **[3]** A region of Judah that probably derived its name from the town of Goshen (Josh. 10:41; 11:16).

Greece (meaning uncertain), a country of Southern Europe between Italy and Asia Minor; one of the most powerful nations of the ancient world (Dan. 8:21; Zech. 9:13; Acts 20:2).

H

Habakkuk ("love's embrace"), A prophet during the reigns of Jehoiakim and Josiah (Hab. 1:1; 3:1).

Hadassah ("myrtle"), the Hebrew name of Esther (q.v.).

Hagar ("wandering"), an Egyptian servant of Sarah; she became the mother of Ishmael by Abraham (Gen. 16:1–16; 21:14–17).

Haggai ("festive"), the first of the prophets who prophesied after the Babylonian Captivity (Ezra 5:1; Hag. 1:1, 3, 12).

Haggith ("festal"), the fifth wife of David and mother of Adonijah (2 Sam. 3:4; 1 Kin. 1:5, 11).

Ham, the youngest son of Noah. Because of his wickedness, his son Canaan was cursed (Gen. 5:32; 9:22–27).

Ham. [1] A name for Egypt used only in poetry (Ps. 78:51). **[2]** A place between Ashteroth Karnaim in Bashan and the Moabite country (Gen. 14:5). Possibly modern Ham about 5 mi. south of Irbid in the 'Ajlūn district.

Haman ("celebrated Human [Humban]"), the prime minister of Ahasuerus who plotted against the Jews (Esth. 3--9).

Hamath ("anger"). **[1]** A Hittite city on the Orontes River about 200 km. (125 mi.) north of Damascus; a supply base for Solomon's armies (2 Chr. 8:4). **[2]** The ideal northern boundary of Israel (Num. 13:21; 34:8).

Hamon Gog ("multitude of Gog"), the valley where Gog and his armies will be defeated in their final struggle against God's people (Ezek. 39:11–15).

Hanani ("gracious"). **[1]** A musician and head of one of the courses of the temple services (1 Chr. 25:4, 25). **[2]** The father of the prophet Jehu; cast into prison by Asa (1 Kin. 16:1, 7; 2 Chr. 16:7–10). **[3]** A priest who married a foreign wife (Ezra 10:20). **[4]** A brother of Nehemiah and a governor of Jerusalem under him (Neh. 1:2; 7:2). **[5]** A priest and musician who helped to purify the walls of Jerusalem (Neh. 12:36).

Hananiah ("Jehovah is gracious"). **[1]** A descendant of Benjamin (1 Chr. 8:24). **[2]** An officer of Uzziah (2 Chr. 26:11). **[3]** The father of a prince under Jehoiakim (Jer. 36:12). **[4]** The leader of the sixteenth division of David's musicians (1 Chr. 25:4, 23). **[5]** The grandfather of Irijah (Jer. 37:13). **[6]** A false prophet who opposed Jeremiah (Jer. 28). **[7]** One of Daniel's friends at Babylon (Dan. 1:7, 11, 19). *See also* Shadrach. **[8]** A son of Zerubbabel (1 Chr. 3:19, 21). **[9]** A Levite who married a foreign wife during the Exile (Ezra 10:28). **[10]** A druggist and priest who helped to rebuild the wall of Jerusalem (Neh. 3:8). **[11]** One who helped to rebuild the gate of Jerusalem (Neh. 3:30); perhaps the same as **[10]. [12]** A faithful Israelite placed in charge of Jerusalem (Neh. 7:2). **[13]** One who sealed the new covenant with God after the Exile (Neh. 10:23). **[14]** A priest present at the dedication of the walls of Jerusalem (Neh. 12:12, 41).

Hannah ("grace"), a prophetess, the mother of Samuel (1 Sam. 1).

Hanoch [Enoch] ("dedicated"). **[1]** A grandson of Abraham (Gen. 25:4). **[2]** The eldest son of Reuben, and founder of the Hanochite clan (Gen. 46:9; 1 Chr. 5:3). **[3]** Enoch, the son of Jared (1 Chr. 1:3).

Haran ("strong; enlightened"). **[1]** A brother of Abraham who died before his father (Gen. 11:26–31). **[2]** A descendant of Levi (1 Chr. 23:9). **[3]** A son of Caleb (1 Chr. 2:46).

Haran ("mountains"), a Mesopotamian city located 386 km. (240 mi.) northwest of Nineveh and 450 km. (280 mi.) north-northeast of Damascus (Gen. 11:31; 12:4, 5).

Hashabiah ("Jehovah is associated"). **[1]** A

descendant of Levi (1 Chr. 6:45). [2] Another descendant of Levi (1 Chr. 9:14). [3] A son of Jeduthun (1 Chr. 25:3). [4] A descendant of Kohath (1 Chr. 26:30). [5] A son of Kemuel who was a prince of the Levites (1 Chr. 27:17). [6] A chief of a Levite clan (2 Chr. 35:9). [7] A Levite who returned with Ezra from Babylon (Ezra 8:19). [8] A chief of the family of Kohath (Ezra 8:24). [9] One who repaired the wall of Jerusalem (Neh. 3:17). [10] One who sealed the covenant with Nehemiah (Neh. 10:11). [11] A Levite in charge of certain temple functions (Neh. 11:15). [12] An attendant of the temple (Neh. 11:22). [13] A priest in the days of Jeshua (Neh. 12:21). [14] A chief Levite (Neh. 12:24). [Note: It is quite possible that [9], [12], and [14] refer to the same person.]

Hattush ("contender"). [1] Descendant of the kings of Judah, perhaps of Shechaniah (1 Chr. 3:22). [2] A descendant of David who returned fro the Exile with Ezra (Ezra 8:2). [3] A priest who returned from the Exile with Zerubbabel (Neh. 12:2). [4] One who helped to rebuild the wall of Jerusalem (Neh. 3:10). [5] A priest who signed the covenant (Neh. 10:1, 4). [Note: Entries [1], [2], [3], and [5] may refer to the same person.]

Hazael ("God sees"), the murderer of Ben-Hadad II who usurped the throne of Syria (1 Kin. 19:15, 17; 2 Kin. 8:8–29).

Hazor ("enclosure"). [1] The capital of the Canaanite kingdom, later included in the territory of Naphtali in northern Palestine (Josh. 11:1, 10, 13); site of a major archaeological excavation. [2] A place in extreme southern Judah (Josh. 15:23); possibly modern el-Jebariyeh. [3] Another city in southern Judah (Josh. 15:25). Hezron was a district or region of the city or another name for the city itself (verse 25). [4] A village of the tribe of Benjamin, to which the Jewish exiles returned (Neh. 11:33); modern Khirbet Hazzur, 6 km. (4 mi.) north-northwest of Jerusalem. [5] A region of the Arabian Desert east of Palestine (Jer. 49:28, 30, 33).

Heber ("companion"). [1] A descendant of Asher (Gen. 46:17; 1 Chr. 7:31, 32). [2] The husband of Jael, who killed Sisera (Judg. 4:11, 17, 21; 5:24). [3] Head of a clan of Judah (1 Chr. 4:18). [4] A descendant of Benjamin (1 Chr. 8:17). [5] Used in Luke 3:35 to refer to Eber [1].

Hebron ("friendship"). [1] A city in the hills of Judah, 32 km. (20 mi.) south of Jerusalem (Gen. 13:18; Num. 13:22). [2] A town of the tribe of Asher, more frequently called Abdon (Josh. 21:30).

Hell ("conceal"), the place of woe for the departed. "Hades" is the New Testament name for "Sheol," which was conceived as a place where the souls of all dead resided (Ps. 16:10; Matt. 11:23; Acts 2:27). The KJV also has *hell* as its translation of *Gehenna*, a valley outside Jerusalem that Jesus used as a symbol of woe for lost souls. For believers, He said that Hades would be Paradise (Luke 23:43); for the godless, it would be "Gehenna" (cf. Luke 16:22, 23).

Heman ("faithful"). [1] A musician and seer appointed by David as a leader in the temple's vocal and instrumental music (1 Chr. 6:33; 15:17; 2 Chr. 5:12; 35:15). [2] A wise man with whom Solomon was compared (1 Kin. 4:31; 1 Chr. 2:6). He composed a meditative Psalm (Ps. 88, title).

Hermon ("devoted to destruction"), the highest mountain of the Anti-Lebanon range, marking the northeast boundary of Palestine (Deut. 3:8; Josh. 11:17; 1 Chr. 5:23).

Herod ("heroic"). [1] Herod the Great, the sly king of Judea when Christ was born. In order to maintain power, he murdered the children of Bethlehem, thinking that he would be killing the Messiah (Matt. 2:1–22; Luke 1:5). [2] Herod Antipas, son of the former, was tetrarch of Galilee and Perea. He was the murderer of John the Baptist (Matt. 14:1–10; Luke 13:31, 32; 23:7–12). [3] Herod Philip, son of Herod the Great, was tetrarch of Iturea and Trachonitis (Luke 3:1). [4] Herod Philip, another son of Herod the Great, is the Philip whose wife Herod Antipas lured away (Matt. 14:3). [5] Herod Agrippa I, tetrarch of Galilee and eventual ruler of his grandfather's (i.e., Herod the Great's) old realm. He bitterly persecuted Christians (Acts 12:1–23). [6] Herod Agrippa II, son of Agrippa I and king of various domains, witnessed the preaching of Paul (Acts 25:13–26; 26:1–32). *See also* Archelaus; Bernice; Drusilla.

Herodias ("heroic"), granddaughter of Herod the Great, wife of Antipas, and ultimate cause of John the Baptist's death (Matt. 14:3–9; Luke 3:19).

Hezekiah ("Jehovah is strength"). [1] One who returned from Babylon (Ezra 2:16; Neh. 7:21). He, or his representative, is called Hizkijah (a form of Hezekiah) in Nehemiah 10:17. [2] The twelfth king of Judah; an ancestor of Christ. He instituted religious reform and improved the overall safety and prosperity of the nation (2 Kin. 18–20; 2 Chr. 29–32; Matt. 1:9, 10). [3] A son of Neariah, a descendant of the royal family of Judah (1 Chr. 3:23).

Hiddekel ("sound"), an archaic name for the Tigris River (Gen. 2:14; Dan. 10:4). It is narrower than the Euphrates, but carries more water. It joins the Euphrates 100 miles from the Persian Gulf at Al Qurna.

Hiel ("God is living"), a man who rebuilt Jericho (1 Kin. 16:34) and sacrificed his sons, in fulfillment of Joshua's curse (Josh. 6:26).

Hilkiah ("Jehovah is protection" or "my portion"). **[1]** One who stood with Ezra at the reading of the Law (Neh. 8:4). **[2]** A Levite who kept the children of the temple officials (1 Chr. 6:45). **[3]** A gatekeeper of the tabernacle (1 Chr. 26:11). **[4]** Master of the household of King Hezekiah (2 Kin. 18:18, 26; Is. 22:20; 36:3). **[5]** A priest of Anathoth and father of Jeremiah (Jer. 1:1). **[6]** High priest and the discoverer of the Book of the Law in the days of Josiah (2 Kin. 22:4, 8; 23:4). **[7]** The father of Gemariah (Jer. 29:3). **[8]** A chief of priests who returned from captivity (Neh. 12:7) and his later descendants (Neh. 12:12, 21).

Hinnom, an unknown person who had a son(s) after whom a valley near Jerusalem was named. Human sacrifices took place there in Jeremiah's day, and garbage was later incinerated in this defiled place (Josh. 15:8; 18:16; Neh. 11:30; Jer. 7:31, 32).

Hinnom ("their riches"), a narrow valley southwest of Jerusalem (Josh. 15:8; 18:16; 2 Chr. 28:3).

Hiram [Huram] (abbreviated form of Ahiram, "My brother is the exalted"). **[1]** A king of Tyre who befriended David and Solomon (2 Sam. 5:11; 1 Kin. 5; 9:11; 10:11). **[2]** The skillful worker in brass whom Solomon secured from King Hiram (1 Kin. 7:13, 40, 45; 2 Chr. 4:11, 16). **[3]** A descendant of Benjamin (1 Chr. 8:5).

Hobab ("beloved"), the father-in-law or brother-in-law of Moses (Num. 10:29; Judg. 4:11). The phrase "father-in-law" in Judges 4:11 may possibly mean nothing more than "in-law," or perhaps Jethro was also named Hobab; but the identity is uncertain. *See also* Jethro.

Horeb ("desert"), a range of mountains on the Sinai Peninsula, of which Mount Sinai is the highest (Ex. 17:6); now called the Serbal range.

Hosea ("help; i.e., Jehovah is help"), a prophet of Israel; he denounced the idolatries of Israel and Samaria (Hos. 1:1, 2).

Hoshea [Hosea] ("Jehovah is help or salvation"). **[1]** A chief of the tribe of Ephraim in the days of David (1 Chr. 27:20). **[2]** The last king of Israel; he was imprisoned by Sargon of Assyria (2 Kin. 15:30; 17:1, 4, 6; 18:1). **[3]** One who sealed the covenant with Nehemiah (Neh. 10:23). **[3]** The original name of Joshua (q.v.).

Hur ("free; noble"). **[1]** One of the men who held up Moses' arms during the battle with Amalek (Ex. 17:10, 12; 24:14). **[2]** A son of Caleb (Ex. 31:2; 35:30; 38:22; 1 Chr. 2:19, 50; 4:1, 4). **[3]** A Midianite king slain by Israel

(Num. 31:8; Josh. 13:21). **[4]** An officer of Solomon on Mount Ephraim (1 Kin. 4:8). **[5]** The ruler of half of Jerusalem under Nehemiah (Neh. 3:9).

Huram. *See* Hiram.

Hushai ("quick"), a friend and counselor of David (2 Sam. 15:32, 37; 16:16–18; 17:5–15).

I

Ibzan ("famous; splendid"), a Bethlehemite who judged Israel for seven years (Judg. 12:8–10).

Iconium ("coming"), capital of the province of Lycaonia in Asia Minor (Acts 13:51; 14:1).

Iddo ("adorned"). **[1]** A prophet who wrote about the kings of Israel (2 Chr. 9:29; 2 Chr. 12:15). **[2]** A priest who returned to Jerusalem with Zerubbabel (Neh. 12:4); perhaps the same as **[1]**.

Igal ("Jehovah redeems") **[1]** One of the twelve spies sent to search out Canaan (Num. 13:7). **[2]** One of David's heroes (2 Sam. 23:36). **[3]** A descendant of the royal house of Judah (1 Chr. 3:22).

Illyricum ("joy"), a Roman province on the east coast of the Adriatic Sea, stretching from Italy on the north to Macedonia on the south (Rom. 15:19). It was later renamed Dalmatia.

Immer ("lamb"), a person or place in Babylonia (Ezra 2:59; Neh. 7:61); its exact location is unknown.

Imna [Jimna; Jimnah; Imnah] ("lugging") **[1]** A descendant of Asher (Gen. 46:17; 1 Chr. 7:35). **[2]** A son of Asher (Num. 26:44; 1 Chr. 7:30). **[3]** Father of Kore in Hezekiah's reign (2 Chr. 31:14).

Imnah. *See* Imna.

India (meaning unknown), a land on the eastern limit of the Persian Empire, surrounding the Indus River (Esth. 1:1; 8:9).

Ira ("watchful"). **[1]** A priest of David (2 Sam. 20:26). **[2]** One of David's thirty mighty men (1 Chr. 11:28; 2 Sam. 23:38) and a captain of the temple guard (1 Chr. 27:9). **[3]** Another of David's thirty (1 Chr. 11:40; 2 Sam. 23:26).

Isaac ("laughter"), the son of Abraham and Sarah, born to them in their old age. He was the father of Jacob and Esau and an ancestor of Christ (Gen. 21— 25; Matt. 1:2).

Isaiah ("salvation of Jehovah"), called the "prince of prophets"; his career lasted over sixty years. He foretold the coming of Christ (Is. 1:1; 7:14; 9:6; 52:12-53).

Iscariot. *See* Judah **[8]**.

Ishbosheth ("man of shame"), son and successor of King Saul. He reigned two years before being defeated by David (2 Sam. 2:8-15;

3:8, 14, 15; 4:5–12). He also was known as Esh-Baal (1 Chr. 8:33; 9:39).

Ishmael ("God hears"). **[1]** Son of Abraham and Hagar; his descendants are the Arabian nomads (Gen. 16:11–16; 17:18–26; 25:9–17; 28:9; 36:3). **[2]** The cunning son of Nethaniah and traitor of Israel (Jer. 40:8–41:18). **[3]** A descendant of Benjamin (1 Chr. 8:38). **[4]** Father of Zebadiah (2 Chr. 19:11). **[5]** A captain in the time of Jehoiada and Joash (2 Chr. 23:1). **[6]** A Levite who married a foreign wife during the Exile (Ezra 10:22).

Israel. *See* Jacob.

Israel ("who prevails with God"), the northern kingdom of the Hebrews in Palestine, inhabited by the ten tribes that followed Ishbosheth and Jeroboam. The cities of Jericho and Gezer marked its southern boundary (2 Chr. 35:18; cf. Gen. 32:32).

Issachar ("reward"). **[1]** Ninth son of Jacob and ancestor of one of the twelve tribes of Israel (Gen. 30:17, 18; 49:14, 15). **[2]** A tabernacle porter (1 Chr. 26:5).

Italy ("abounding with calves"), the peninsula jutting from the Alps into the Mediterranean Sea, bounded on the south by the straits of Messina (Acts 18:2; 27:1).

Ittai ("timely"), a Philistine friend and general of David (2 Sam. 15:11–22; 18:2, 4, 12).

J

Jabesh ("dry place"), father of Shallum, who killed Zechariah and reigned in his place (2 Kin. 15:10–14). *See also* Jabesh Gilead.

Jabesh Gilead ("dry"), a city of Gilead (Judg. 21:8; 1 Sam. 11:1). It may have been located at a site now called Wadi Yabis, about 32 km. (20 mi.) south of the Sea of Galilee.

Jabin ("intelligent; observed"). **[1]** A king of Hazor defeated by Joshua (Josh. 11:1). **[2]** Another king of Hazor who oppressed Israel and was defeated by Deborah (Judg. 4).

Jachin ("founding" or "he will establish"). **[1]** A son of Simeon (Gen. 46:10; Ex. 6:15; Num. 26:12). He is called Jarib in First Chronicles 4:24. **[2]** A priest in Jerusalem after the Babylonian Captivity (1 Chr. 9:10; Neh. 11:10). **[3]** Head of a family of Aaron (1 Chr. 24:17).

Jachin ("God establishes"), the right hand pillar of Solomon's porch on the temple of Jerusalem (1 Kin. 7:21).

Jacob ("supplanter; following after"). **[1]** Son of Isaac, twin of Esau, and an ancestor of Christ. He bought Esau's birthright and became the father of the Jewish nation (Gen. 25–50; Matt. 1:2). God changed his name from Jacob to Israel ("God strives"; Gen. 32:28; 35:10). **[2]** The father of Joseph, the husband of Mary (Matt. 1:15, 16).

Jaddua ("very knowing; known"). **[1]** One who sealed the covenant (Neh. 10:21). **[2]** The last high priest mentioned in the Old Testament (Neh. 12:11, 22).

Jael ("a wild goat"), wife of Heber who killed Sisera (Judg. 4:17–22; 5:6, 24).

Jahaziel ("God reveals"). **[1]** One who joined David at Ziklag (1 Chr. 12:4). **[2]** A priest who helped bring the ark of the covenant into Jerusalem (1 Chr. 16:6). **[3]** Son of Hebron (1 Chr. 23:19; 24:23). **[4]** A Levite who encouraged Jehoshaphat's army against the Moabites (2 Chr. 20:14). **[5]** A chief man whose son returned from Babylon (Ezra 8:5).

Jair ("Jehovah enlightens"). **[1]** A descendant of Judah through his father and of Manasseh through his mother (Num. 32:41; Deut. 3:14; 1 Kin. 4:13; 1 Chr. 2:22). **[2]** Judge of Israel for twenty-two years (Judg. 10:3–5). **[3]** The father of Mordecai, Esther's cousin (Esth. 2:5).

Jairus ("enlightened"), a ruler of a synagogue near Capernaum whose daughter Jesus raised from the dead (Luke 8:41).

James (Greek form of Jacob). **[1]** The son of Zebedee and brother of John called to be one of the Twelve. He was slain by Herod Agrippa I (Matt. 4:21; Mark 5:37; Luke 9:54; Acts 12:2). **[2]** The son of Alphaeus, another of the twelve apostles. He is probably the same as James "the less," the son of Mary. By "the less" is meant his age or height in relation to James the son of Zebedee (Matt. 10:3; Mark 15:40; Acts 1:13). **[3]** The brother of Jesus (Matt. 13:55). After Christ's resurrection, he became a believer (1 Cor. 15:7) and a leader of the church at Jerusalem (Acts 12:17; Gal. 1:19; 2:9). He wrote the epistle of James (James 1:1). **[4]** Unknown person mentioned as "the brother of Judas." Most view this as an incorrect translation and would render "Judas, the son of James" (Luke 6:16; Acts 1:13).

Japheth ("the extender; fair; enlarged"), second son of Noah, considered the father of the Indo-European races (Gen. 5:32; 6:10; 7:13; 9:18, 23, 27; 1 Chr. 1:4, 5).

Jason ("healing"). **[1]** Paul's host during his stay at Thessalonica (Acts 17:5–9). **[2]** A Jewish Christian kinsman of Paul who sent salutations to Rome (Rom. 16:21). Both are possibly identical.

Jebus ("manager"), another name for Jerusalem (Judg. 19:10, 11).

Jeconiah. *See* Jehoiachin.

Jedaiah ("Jehovah is knowing"). **[1]** A priest of Jerusalem (1 Chr. 9:10; 24:7; Ezra 2:36; Neh. 7:39). **[2]** A priest who returned with Zerubbabel (Neh. 11:10; 12:6, 19). **[3]** Another priest who came up with Zerubbabel (Neh. 12:7, 21). **[4]** One who brought gifts to the temple (Zech. 6:10, 14).

Jediael ("God knows"). [1] A son of Benjamin (1 Chr. 7:6, 10, 11). Possibly the same as Ashbel (1 Chr. 8:1). [2] One of David's mighty men (1 Chr. 11:45). [3] One who joined David at Ziklag (1 Chr. 12:20). [4] A descendant of Korah, son of Meshelemiah (1 Chr. 26:2).

Jedidiah ("beloved of Jehovah"), the name God gave Solomon through Nathan (2 Sam. 12:25).

Jeduthun ("a choir of praise"). [1] One of the three chief musicians of the service of song (1 Chr. 9:16; 25:1-6; Neh. 11:17). He was also named Ethan (1 Chr. 6:44; 15:17, 19). [2] The father of Obed-Edom (1 Chr. 16:38). Some believe him identical with [1].

Jehoahaz ("Jehovah upholds"). [1] Son and successor of Jehu on the throne of Israel. His reign was one of disaster (2 Kin. 10:35; 13:2-25). [2] The son of Josiah and ruler of Judah for three months before he was deposed by Pharaoh Necho (2 Kin. 23:30-34; 2 Chr. 36:1-4). He was also called Shallum before becoming king (1 Chr. 3:15; Jer. 22:11). [3] *See* Ahaziah [2].

Jehoash [Joash] ("Jehovah has given; Jehovah supports"). [1] The ninth king of Judah. Until the time of Jehoiada the priest's death Jehoash followed God; afterward, he brought idolatry and disaster to his country (2 Kin. 11:21—12:21). He is more frequently called by the shortened form of his name, Joash. [2] The twelfth king of Israel; he was successful in many military campaigns (2 Kin. 13:9—14:16). He is most frequently called Joash, an abbreviated form of his name.

Jehoiachin ("Jehovah establishes"), ruler of Judah when it was captured by Nebuchadnezzar. He was an ancestor of Christ (2 Kin. 24:8-16; 2 Chr. 36:9, 10; Matt. 1:11, 12). Jeconiah ("Jehovah is able") is an altered form of his name (1 Chr. 3:16, 17; Jer. 24:1) as is Coniah ("Jehovah is creating"; Jer. 22:24, 28; 37:1).

Jehoiada ("Jehovah knows"). [1] The father of one of David's officers (2 Sam. 8:18; 1 Kin. 1:8, 26). [2] The chief priest of the temple for many years of the monarchy. He hid Joash from Athaliah for 6 years (2 Kin. 11—12:9). [3] One who joined David at Ziklag (1 Chr. 12:27). [4] A counselor of David (1 Chr. 27:34). [5] One who helped to repair a gate of Jerusalem (Neh. 3:6). [6] A priest replaced by Zephaniah (Jer. 29:26).

Jehoiakim ("Jehovah sets up" or "Jehovah has established"), the name given to Eliakim by Pharaoh Necho when he made him king of Judah. The name probably means that Necho claimed Jehovah had authorized him to put Eliakim on the throne (2 Kin. 23:34—24:6). Not to be confused with Joiakim.

Jehonadab [Jonadab] ("Jehovah is liberal"). [1] Descendant of Rechab, who forbade his followers and descendants to drink wine and live in houses (Jer. 35:6-19; 2 Kin. 10:15, 23). [2] The sly son of David's brother, Shimeah (2 Sam. 13:3, 5, 32, 35).

Jehoram [Joram] ("Jehovah is high"), Joram is a shortened form of the name. [1] Son and successor of Jehoshaphat to the throne of Judah and an ancestor of Christ (2 Kin. 8:16-24; Matt. 1:8). [2] The ninth king of Israel, slain by Jehu (2 Kin. 1:17; 3:1-6; 9:24). [3] A priest commissioned to teach the people (2 Chr. 17:8).

Jehoshaphat [Joshaphat] ("Jehovah is judge"). [1] The recorder of David (2 Sam. 8:16; 20:24; 1 Kin. 4:3). [2] An officer of Solomon (1 Kin. 4:17). [3] Father of Jehu, who conspired against Joram (2 Kin. 9:2, 14). [4] A priest who helped to bring the ark of the covenant from Obed-Edom (1 Chr. 15:24). [5] Faithful king of Judah and an ancestor of Christ (1 Kin. 22:41-50; Matt. 1:8).

Jehoshaphat ("judged of God"), the valley where the Last Judgment will take place (Joel 3:2); tradition identifies it as the Kidron Valley (q.v.).

Jehu ("Jehovah is he"). [1] The prophet who brought tidings of disaster to Baasha of Israel (1 Kin. 16:1-12; 2 Chr. 19:2). [2] The tenth king of Israel (1 Kin. 19:16, 17; 2 Kin. 9; 10). His corrupt leadership weakened the nation. [3] A descendant of Hezron (1 Chr. 2:38). [4] A descendant of Simeon (1 Chr. 4:35). [5] One who joined David at Ziklag (1 Chr. 12:3).

Jeiel [Jehiel] ("God snatches away"). [1] A chief of the tribe of Reuben (1 Chr. 5:7). [2] An ancestor of Saul (1 Chr. 9:35). [3] One of David's mighty men (1 Chr. 11:44). [4] A singer and gatekeeper of the tabernacle (1 Chr. 15:18, 21; 16:5). [5] A descendant of Asaph (2 Chr. 20:14). [6] A scribe or recorder of Uzziah (2 Chr. 26:11). [7] A Levite in Hezekiah's time (2 Chr. 29:13). [8] A chief Levite in the days of Josiah (2 Chr. 35:9). [9] One who returned to Jerusalem with Ezra (Ezra 8:13). [10] One who married a foreign wife during the Exile (Ezra 10:43).

Jephthah ("an opposer"), a judge of Israel who delivered his people from Ammon (Judg. 11—12:7).

Jeremiah ("Jehovah is high"). [1] A dweller of Libnah whose daughter married King Josiah (2 Kin. 23:31; Jer. 52:1). [2] Head of a family of the tribe of Manasseh (1 Chr. 5:24). [3] One who joined David at Ziklag (1 Chr. 12:4). [4] A man of Gad who joined David at Ziklag (1 Chr. 12:10). [5] Another who joined

David at Ziklag (1 Chr. 12:13). **[6]** A priest who sealed the new covenant with God after the Exile (Neh. 10:2; 12:1, 12). **[7]** A descendant of Jonadab (Jer. 35:3). **[8]** A prophet whose activity covered the reigns of the last five kings of Judah. He denounced the policies and idolatries of his nation (Jer. 1; 20; 26; 36).

Jericho ("his sweet smell"), a fortified city of Canaan located about 8 km. (5 mi.) from the north end of the Dead Sea and 27 km. (17 mi.) west of the Jordan River (Num. 22:1; Deut. 32:49). Today it is the oldest continually inhabited city in the world.

Jeroboam ("enlarger; he pleads the people's cause"). **[1]** The first king of Israel after the division of the kingdom. He reigned for 22 years (1 Kin. 11:26–40; 12:1—14:20). **[2]** The thirteenth king of Israel; his Israel was strong but overtly idolatrous (2 Kin. 14:23–29).

Jeroham ("loved"). **[1]** A Levite, the grandfather of Samuel (1 Sam. 1:1; 1 Chr. 6:27). **[2]** A descendant of Benjamin (1 Chr. 9:8). **[3]** Head of a family of Benjamin (1 Chr. 8:27). **[4]** A priest whose son lived in Jerusalem after the Exile (1 Chr. 9:12; Neh. 11:12). **[5]** Father of two who joined David at Ziklag (1 Chr. 12:7). **[6]** Father of Azareel, prince of Dan (1 Chr. 27:22). **[7]** Father of one who helped Jehoiada to set Joash on the throne of Judah (2 Chr. 23:1).

Jerubbaal ("let Baal contend" or possibly "let Baal show himself great"), the name given to Gideon by his father (Judg. 6:32; 7:1; 8:29).

Jerubbesheth ("contender with the idol"), name given to Jerubbaal (Gideon) by those who wanted to avoid pronouncing Baal (2 Sam. 11:21).

Jerusalem ("possession of peace"), capital of the southern kingdom of Judah, located 48 km. (30 mi.) from the Mediterranean Sea and 29 km. (18 mi.) west of the Jordan River (Josh. 10:1; 2 Sam. 5:5).

Jeshurun ("blessed"), a symbolic name for Israel (Deut. 32:15; Is. 44:2).

Jesse ("Jehovah exists; wealthy"), father of David and an ancestor of Christ (Ruth 4:17, 22; 1 Sam. 17:17; Matt. 1:5, 6).

Jesus (Greek form of Joshua). **[1]** A Christian who, with Paul, sent greetings to the Colossians (Col. 4:11); he was also called Justus. **[2]** See Joshua.

Jesus Christ (*Jesus*—"Jehovah is salvation," *Christ*—"the anointed one"), the son of the Virgin Mary who came to earth to fulfill the prophecies of the King who would die for the sins of His people. The account of His ministry is found in the Gospels of Matthew, Mark, Luke, and John.

Jethro ("preeminence"), the father-in-law of Moses. He advised Moses to delegate the time-consuming administration of justice (Ex. 3:1; 4:18; 18:1–12). He is called Reuel in Exodus 2:18. In Numbers 10:29, the KJV calls him Raguel; but the Hebrew text reads Reuel.

Jezebel ("unexalted; unhusbanded"). **[1]** The wicked, idolatrous queen of Israel (1 Kin. 16:31; 18:4—21:25; 2 Kin. 9:7–37). **[2]** A false prophetess at Thyatira (Rev. 2:20). Possibly the name is symbolic and not the prophetess's real name.

Jezreel ("God sows"). **[1]** A descendant of Etam (1 Chr. 4:3). **[2]** The symbolic name of a son of Hosea (Hos. 1:4).

Jimna. *See* Imna.

Joab ("Jehovah is father"). **[1]** A son of Zeruiah, David's sister. He was captain of David's army (2 Sam. 2:13–32; 3:23–31; 18; 1 Kin. 2:22, 23). **[2]** A descendant of Judah (1 Chr. 2:54). Some scholars believe a city of Judah is referred to here. The name would include the four words that follow in the KJV and be written: Atroth beth joab. **[3]** One of the tribe of Judah (1 Chr. 4:14). **[4]** An ancestor of returned captives (Ezra 2:6; 8:9; Neh. 7:11).

Joanna [Joannas] ("God-given"). **[1]** An ancestor of Christ (Luke 3:27). **[2]** The wife of Chuza, Herod's steward, who ministered to Christ and the apostles (Luke 8:3; 24:10).

Joash (abbreviated form of Jehoash). **[1]** A man of Judah (1 Chr. 4:22). **[2]** Father of Gideon the judge (Judg. 6:11–32). **[3]** A son of Ahab (1 Kin. 22:26; 2 Chr. 18:25). **[4]** One who joined David at Ziklag (1 Chr. 12:3). **[5]** *See* Jehoash **[1]**. **[6]** *See* Jehoash **[2]**.

Joash ("Jehovah has aided"). **[1]** A son of Becher, a descendant of Benjamin (1 Chr. 7:8). **[2]** The keeper of David's stores of oil (1 Chr. 27:28).

Job ("hated; persecuted"). **[1]** A pious man of Uz. His endurance in fierce trial resulted in marvelous blessing (Job 1—3; 42; Ezek. 14:14, 20). **[2]** The third son of Issachar (Gen. 46:13); he is also called Jashub (Num. 26:24; 1 Chr. 7:1).

Jochebed ("Jehovah is honor or glory"), a descendant of Levi and mother of Moses (Ex. 6:20; Num. 26:59).

Joel ("Jehovah is God"). **[1]** The firstborn son of Samuel the prophet (1 Sam. 8:2; 1 Chr. 6:33; 15:17). **[2]** A descendant of Simeon (1 Chr. 4:35). **[3]** The father of Shemaiah, a descendant of Reuben (1 Chr. 5:4, 8). **[4]** A chief of the tribe of Gad (1 Chr. 5:12). **[5]** An ancestor of the prophet Samuel (1 Chr. 6:36). **[6]** A descendant of Tola (1 Chr. 7:3). **[7]** One of David's mighty men (1 Chr. 11:38). **[8]** A Levite in David's time (1 Chr. 15:7, 11; 23:8). **[9]**

A keeper of the treasures of the Lord's house (1 Chr. 6:22). **[10]** A prince of Manasseh west of the Jordan (1 Chr. 27:20). **[11]** A Levite who aided in cleansing the temple (2 Chr. 29:12). **[12]** One who married a foreign wife during the Exile (Ezra 10:43). **[13]** An overseer of the descendants of Benjamin in Jerusalem (Neh. 11:9). **[14]** A prophet in the days of Uzziah (Joel 1:1; Acts 2:16).

Johanan ("Jehovah is gracious"). **[1]** A captain who allied with Gedaliah after the fall of Jerusalem (2 Kin. 25:23; Jer. 40:8, 13). **[2]** Eldest son of Josiah, king of Judah (1 Chr. 3:15). **[3]** A son of Elioenai (1 Chr. 3:24). **[4]** Father of a priest in Solomon's time (1 Chr. 6:9, 10). **[5]**, **[6]** Two valiant men who joined David at Ziklag (1 Chr. 12:4, 12). **[7]** One who opposed making slaves of Judean captives in Ahaz's time (2 Chr. 28:12). **[8]** A returned exile (Ezra 8:12). **[9]** A priest who beckoned the exiles to Jerusalem (Ezra 10:6). **[10]** A son of Tobiah the Ammonite (Neh. 6:18). **[11]** A priest in the days of Joiakim (Neh. 12:22, 23).

John (a contraction of Jehohanan, "gift of God"). **[1]** The son of Zacharias and Elizabeth who came to prepare the way for the Messiah. He was called John the Baptist and was beheaded by Herod (Matt. 3; 11:7-18; 14:1-10; Luke 1:13-17). **[2]** A son of Zebedee and one of the twelve apostles. He is traditionally accorded the authorship of the Revelation, the Fourth Gospel, and the three epistles bearing his name (Matt. 4:21; 10:2; Acts 1:13; Gal. 2:9; Rev. 1:1). **[3]** A relative of the high priest Annas, who sat in judgment on Peter (Acts 4:6). **[4]** A missionary better known by his surname, Mark (q.v.). *See also* Johanan.

Joiakim ("Jehovah sets up"), the son of Jeshua who returned from the Babylonian Captivity (Neh. 12:10, 12, 26). Not to be confused with Jehoiakim.

Joiarib ("Jehovah knows"). **[1]** One whom Ezra sent to persuade ministers to return to the land of Israel (Ezra 8:16). **[2]** An ancestor of a family living in Jerusalem (Neh. 11:5). **[3]** A priest who returned from captivity (Neh. 11:10; 12:6, 19). He is called Jehoiarib in First Chronicles 9:10.

Joktan, a son of Eber of Shem's line (Gen. 10:25, 26; 1 Chr. 1:19, 20, 23). Perhaps the reference is to an Arabian tribe from whom many other Arabian groups sprang.

Jonadab. *See* Jehonadab.

Jonah [Jonas] ("a dove"). **[1]** The father of Simon Peter (John 1:42; 21:15-17). **[2]** A Hebrew prophet sent to preach to Nineveh in the days of Jeroboam II. He was the first Hebrew prophet sent to a heathen nation (2 Kin. 14:25; Jon. 1:1, 3, 5, 17; 2:10; Matt. 12:39-41).

Jonathan ("Jehovah is given"). **[1]** A priest of an idol shrine in the territory of Ephraim (Judg. 18:30). **[2]** A son of Abiathar the high priest (2 Sam. 15:27, 36; 17:17; 1 Kin. 1:42). **[3]** A son of Shimea, David's brother (2 Sam. 21:21; 1 Chr. 20:7). **[4]** One of David's mighty men (2 Sam. 23:32; 1 Chr. 11:34). **[5]** A grandson of Onam (1 Chr. 2:32, 33). **[6]** An uncle of David (1 Chr. 27:32). **[7]** Father of one who returned with Ezra (Ezra 8:6). **[8]** One involved with the foreign wife controversy (Ezra 10:15). **[9]** A descendant of Jeshua the high priest (Neh. 12:11). **[10]** A priest (Neh. 12:14). **[11]** A scribe in whose house Jeremiah was kept prisoner (Jer. 37:15, 20; 38:26). **[12]** One who joined Gedaliah after the fall of Jerusalem (Jer. 40:8). **[13]** A son of Saul and close friend of David (1 Sam. 14; 18:1-4; 31:2).

Joppa ("beauty"), a town on the coast of Palestine (2 Chr. 2:16; Acts 9:36).

Jordan (meaning uncertain), the major river of Palestine. It rises in a valley between Mount Lebanon and Hermon. It follows a twisting route to enter the north end of the Dead Sea (Gen. 13:10; Josh. 2:7).

Jose, an ancestor of Christ (Luke 3:29). Not to be confused with Joses.

Joseph ("increaser"). **[1]** The son of Jacob and Rachel. He was sold into slavery but became the prime minister of Egypt (Gen. 37; 39—50). **[2]** Father of one of the spies sent into Canaan (Num. 13:7). **[3]** A son of Asaph (1 Chr. 25:2, 9). **[4]** One who married a foreign wife during the Exile (Ezra 10:42). **[5]** A priest of the family of Shebaniah (Neh. 12:14). **[6]** The husband of Mary, mother of Jesus (Matt. 1:16-24; 2:13; Luke 1:27; 2:4). **[7]** A converted Jew of Arimathea in whose tomb Jesus was laid (Matt. 27:57, 59; Luke 15:43). **[8]** An ancestor of Christ (Luke 3:24). **[9]** Another ancestor of Christ (Luke 3:26). **[10]** Yet another ancestor of Christ (Luke 3:30). **[11]** A disciple considered to take the place of Judas Iscariot (Acts 1:23). He was also known as Barsabas and Justus.

Joses ("helped"). **[1]** One of the brothers of Christ (Matt. 13:55; Mark 6:3). **[2]** The son of Mary, the wife of Clopas (Matt. 27:56; Mark 15:40, 47). Not to be confused with Jose.

Joshaphat. *See* Jehoshaphat.

Joshua [Hoshea] ("Jehovah is salvation"). **[1]** The successor of Moses; the general who led the conquest of the Promised Land (Ex. 17:9-14; 24:13; Deut. 31:1-23; 34:9). Moses changed his name from Hoshea ("Jehovah is help"), to Joshua. **[2]** A native of Beth Shemeth in the days of Eli (1 Sam. 6:14, 18). **[3]** The governor of Jerusalem under Josiah (2 Kin. 23:8). **[4]** High priest at the rebuilding of the temple (Hag. 1:1, 12, 14; 2:2, 4; Zech. 3:1, 3, 6).

Josiah ("Jehovah supports"). **[1]** Godly king of Judah during whose reign the Book of the Law was found (1 Kin. 13:2; 2 Kin. 22:1–23:30). He was an ancestor of Christ (Matt. 1:10, 11). **[2]** A son of Zephaniah living in Jerusalem (Zech. 6:10).

Jotham ("Jehovah is perfect"). **[1]** The son of Gideon who managed to escape from Abimelech (Judg. 9:5, 7, 21, 57). **[2]** A son of Jahdai (1 Chr. 2:47). **[3]** The twelfth king of Judah and an ancestor of Christ (2 Kin. 15:5-38; Is. 1:1; 7:1; Matt. 1:9).

Judah [Judas; Jude] ("praise"). **[1]** A son of Jacob by Leah and an ancestor of Christ. He acquired the birthright Reuben lost. His descendants became one of the twelve tribes of Israel (Gen. 29:35; 37:26-28; 43:3-10; Matt. 1:2, 3; Luke 3:33). **[2]** An ancestor of one who helped to rebuild the temple (Ezra 3:9). **[3]** One who married a foreign wife during the Exile (Ezra 10:23). **[4]** Second in authority over Jerusalem after the Exile (Neh. 11:9). **[5]** One who came up to Jerusalem with Zerubbabel (Neh. 12:8). **[6]** A prince of Judah (Neh. 12:34). **[7]** A priest and musician (Neh. 12:36). **[8]** One of the twelve apostles. He betrayed his Lord and hanged himself (Matt. 10:4; 26:14, 25, 47; 27:3; Luke 6:16; 22:3, 47, 48). He was called Iscariot, apparently meaning "a man of Kerioth," a town 19 km. (12 mi.) from Hebron. **[9]** One of the brothers of Jesus (Matt. 13:55; Mark 6:3). He wrote the epistle bearing his name (Jude 1). **[10]** A Galilean who caused a rebellion against Rome (Acts 5:37). **[11]** One with whom Paul stayed at Damascus (Acts 9:11). **[12]** A prophet sent to Antioch with Silas (Acts 15:22, 27); he was surnamed Barsabas. **[13]** *See* Thaddaeus. **[14]**, **[15]** Two ancestors of Christ (Luke 3:26, 30).

Judah ("the praise of the Lord"), the territory of one of the original twelve tribes. Judah, along with Benjamin, formed the southern kingdom after Solomon's death. The uncertain border between Israel and Judah ran between Bethel in Israel and Ramah in Judah. Jerusalem was its capital (2 Chr. 13:18; 15:8).

Judea ("the praise of the Lord"), first mentioned as a Persian province (Ezra 5:8). Later it became a Roman province (Matt. 2:1). Its northern boundary was Joppa on the west to a point 16.1 km. (10 mi.) north of the Dead Sea on the east. Its southern boundary was about 7 miles southwest of Gaza, through Beersheba, to the southern end of the Dead Sea.

Justus ("just"). **[1]** A believer in Corinth with whom Paul lodged (Acts 18:7). **[2]** *See* Jesus **[2]**. **[3]** *See* Joseph **[11]**.

K

Kadesh. *See* Kadesh Barnea; also Meribah **[2]**.

Kadesh Barnea ("holy"), a wilderness on Palestine's southern frontier. It was on the border between the wilderness of Paran on the south and the wilderness of Zin on the north of the Sinai Peninsula (Num. 32:8; 34:4). It is also called simply Kadesh (Num. 13:26; 20:1). In Genesis 14:7 the region is called En Mishpat.

Kedesh ("holy"). **[1]** A city of the Canaanites near the northern border, defeated by Joshua (Josh. 12:22; 19:37). **[2]** Levitical city of refuge in Naphtali. It was sometimes called Kedesh Naphtali (Josh. 20:7; Judg. 4:6, 9). It is probably modern Kades, about 7.2 km. (4.5 mi.) northwest of Lake Huleh. **[3]** A Levitical city in Issachar (1 Chr. 6:72). **[4]** A city of Judah near Hazor and Ithan (Josh. 15:23).

Keilah ("fortress"), a town in the lowlands of Judah (1 Sam. 23:1, 13; Josh. 15:44). It is 8.5 mi. north of Hebron at Khirbet Kila.

Kemuel ("God stands" or "God's mound"). **[1]** A son of Nahor and a nephew of Abraham (Gen. 22:21). **[2]** A prince of Ephraim (Num. 34:24). **[3]** A Levite (1 Chr. 27:17).

Kenaz [Kenez] ("side" or "hunting"). **[1]** A duke of Edom (Gen. 36:42; 1 Chr. 1:53). **[2]** The fourth son of Eliphaz (Gen. 36:11, 15; 1 Chr. 1:36); perhaps the same as **[1]**. **[3]** Father of Othniel the judge (Josh. 15:17; Judg. 1:13). **[4]** A grandson of Caleb (1 Chr. 4:15).

Kidron ("obscure; making black or sad"), a valley in Jerusalem between the Mount of Ophel and the Mount of Olives (2 Sam. 15:23; John 18:1). Today it is called Wadi Sitti Maryan.

Kirjath Jearim ("city of woods"), originally one of the cities of the Gibeonites located at the northwestern boundary of Judah (Josh. 9:17; Judg. 18:12). It is identical with Baalah (Josh. 15:9); Kirjath Arim (Ezra 2:25), Kirjath Baal (Josh. 18:12), and Baale Judah (2 Sam. 6:2). It is thought to be modern Deir el-Azhar, about 13.4 km. (8.3 mi.) northwest of Jerusalem.

Kish [Cis] ("bow; power"). **[1]** A son of Gibeon (1 Chr. 8:30; 9:36). **[2]** A Levite in David's time (1 Chr. 23:21; 24:29). **[3]** A descendant of Levi who assisted in the cleansing of the temple under Hezekiah (2 Chr. 29:12). **[4]** Great-grandfather of Mordecai (Esth. 2:5). **[5]** The father of King Saul (1 Sam. 9:1, 3; 14:51; Acts 13:21).

Kishon [Kison] ("bending; crooked"), a river in central Palestine which rises in Mount Tabor and, flowing westward, drains the valley of Esdraelon [Jezreel] (Judg. 4:7,

13; 1 Kin. 18:40; Ps. 83:9). Next to the Jordan, it is the most important river in Palestine.

Korah ("baldness"). [1] A son of Esau by Aholibamah (Gen. 36:5, 14, 18; 1 Chr. 1:35). [2] A son of Eliphaz (Gen. 36:16). [3] A son of Hebron (1 Chr. 2:43). [4] Grandson of Kohath and ancestor of some sacred musicians (1 Chr. 6:22; Ps. 42; 45—46 titles). He was one of the leaders of the rebellion against Moses and Aaron; the earth swallowed them up (Num. 16:1-35).

Kore ("one who proclaims; quail"). [1] A Levite in charge of the freewill offerings in Hezekiah's time (2 Chr. 31:14). [2] A son of Asaph whose descendants were gatekeepers at the tabernacle (1 Chr. 9:19; 26:1, 19).

L

Laban ("white; glorious"), the brother of Rebekah and father of Rachel and Leah. Jacob served him for seven years in order to marry Rachel, but Laban tricked him by substituting Leah at the wedding festivals (Gen. 24—31).

Lamech ("strong youth; overthrower"). [1] Father of Noah and ancestor of Christ (Gen. 5:25-31; Luke 3:36). [2] Father of Jabal and Jubal; he is the first recorded polygamist (Gen. 4:18-26).

Laodicea ("just people"), a chief city of Phrygia in Asia Minor (Col. 2:1; 4:15; Rev. 1:11). It is located on the Lycos River, a tributary of the Meander.

Lazarus (abridged form of Eleazar, "God has helped"). [1] The brother of Mary and Martha whom Jesus raised from the dead (John 11:1—12:17). [2] A believing beggar who was carried to Abraham's bosom (Luke 16:19-31).

Leah ("weary"), Jacob's wife through the deception of her father, Laban (Gen. 29—31).

Lebbaeus. *See* Thaddaeus.

Lebanon ("white"), one of two ranges of mountains in northern Palestine (Deut. 1:7; Josh. 1:4). The second is called the Anti-Lebanons; Mount Hermon is its highest peak. Running for about 161 km. (100 mi.), the chain begins about 24.1 km. (15 mi.) southeast of Sidon and runs north to about 19.3 km. (12 mi.) north-northeast of Tripolis in Syria.

Lemuel ("Godward; dedicated"), an unknown king often supposed to be Solomon or Hezekiah, whose words are recorded in Proverbs 31:1-9.

Levi ("joined"). [1] The third son of Jacob who avenged Dinah's wrong (Gen. 34:25-31), and went to Egypt with his father (Gen. 29:34; Ex. 6:16). His descendants became the priests of Israel. [2] An ancestor of Christ (Luke 3:24). [3] An ancestor of Christ (Luke 3:29). [4] Another name of Matthew (q.v.).

Libya ("heart of the sea"), the Greek name for the continent of Africa, west of Egypt (Acts 2:10). The Hebrews called this region Phut [Put]. Even though the Hebrew text of Ezekiel 30:5 and 38:5 read Phut, the KJV rendered the word *Libya.*

Lois ("pleasing; better"), the pious grandmother of Timothy (2 Tim. 1:5).

Lot ("veiled"), Abraham's nephew who escaped from wicked Sodom (Gen. 13:1-14; Gen. 19).

Lucifer (Latin, "light-bearer"), an epithet for the king of Babylon (Is. 14:12). Lucifer translates a Hebrew word meaning "light-bearer." The title came to be applied to Satan.

Lucius ("morning born; of light"). [1] A prophet or teacher from Cyrene ministering at Antioch (Acts 13:1). [2] A Jewish Christian who saluted the community at Rome (Rom. 16:21). Perhaps the same as [1].

Luke ("light-giving"), evangelist, physician, and author of the Third Gospel and Acts (Col. 4:14; 2 Tim. 4:11; Philem. 24).

Lycaonia ("she-wolf"), an inland district of Asia Minor. Paul twice visited in the cities of Derbe and Lystra here (Acts 14:6-11). It was bordered on the north by Galatia and on the south by Cilicia.

Lydda ("a standing pool"), a town located on the plains of Sharon (Acts 9:32). It is identical with Lod (q.v.).

Lydia ("native of Lydia"), a woman convert of Thyatira (Acts 16:14, 15).

Lydia ("Lydus land"), a country and people in Northern Africa, west of Egypt (Ezek. 30:5).

Lysias. *See* Claudius Lysias.

Lystra ("that dissolves"), a city of Lycaonia in central Asia Minor. Paul was stoned here (Acts 14:6-21).

M

Maachah [Maacah] ("depression"). [1] The son of Nahor, Abraham's brother (Gen. 22:24). [2] One of David's wives and mother of Absalom (2 Sam. 3:3; 1 Chr. 3:2). [3] A king of Maachah (2 Sam. 10:6). Some translate "the king of Maacah." [4] Father of Achish, king of Gath (1 Kin. 2:39). He is called Maoch in First Samuel 27:2. [5] The mother of Asa, king of Judah (1 Kin. 15:10, 13; 2 Chr. 15:16). She is called Michaiah (2 Chr. 13:2). [6] Concubine of Caleb (1 Chr. 2:48). [7] Wife of Machir, son of Manasseh (1 Chr. 7:15, 16). [8] Wife of Jehiel (1 Chr. 8:29; 9:35). [9] Father of one of David's warriors (1 Chr. 11:43).

[10] Father of Shephatiah, ruler of Simeon (1 Chr. 27:16).

Macedonia (meaning unknown), a nation lying to the north of Greece proper (Acts 16:9; 18:5).

Magdala ("tower"), a village located on the western edge of the Sea of Galilee (Matt. 15:39). It is present-day el-Mejdel, 4.8 km. (3 mi.) north-northwest of Tiberias.

Mahalaleel [**Mahalalel**] ("God is splendor"). **[1]** Son of Cainan and an ancestor of Christ (Gen. 5:12, 13, 15; Luke 3:37). **[2]** One whose descendants lived at Jerusalem (Neh. 11:4).

Maher-Shalal-Hash-Baz ("the spoil hastens, the prey speeds"), symbolic name of Isaiah's son (Is. 8:1–4).

Mahlon ("mild; sickly"), the first husband of Ruth who died in Moab (Ruth 1:2–5).

Malachi ("messenger of Jehovah" or "my messenger"), the last of the prophets recorded in the Old Testament; he was contemporary with Nehemiah (Mal. 1:1).

Malchiah [**Malchijah; Melchiah**] ("Jehovah is king"). **[1]** A leader of singing under David's reign (1 Chr. 6:40). **[2]** An Aaronite whose descendants dwelt in Jerusalem after the Captivity (1 Chr. 9:12; Neh. 11:12). **[3]** Head of a priestly family (1 Chr. 24:9). **[4]**, **[5]**, **[6]** Three who married foreign wives during the Exile (Ezra 10:25, 31). **[7]**, **[8]**, **[9]** Three who helped to rebuild the wall of Jerusalem (Neh. 3:11, 14, 31). **[10]** A prince or Levite who stood beside Ezra as he read the Law (Neh. 8:4). **[11]** A priest who helped to purify the wall of Jerusalem (Neh. 10:3; 12:42). **[12]** Father of Pashhur (Jer. 21:1; 38:1).

Malchijah. *See* Malchiah.

Malchishua. *See* Melchishua.

Malluch ("counselor; ruling"). **[1]** A descendant of Levi (1 Chr. 6:44). **[2]**, **[3]** Two who took foreign wives during the Exile (Ezra 10:29, 32). **[4]** A priest who sealed the covenant (Neh. 10:4). **[5]** A leader who sealed the new covenant with God after the Exile (Neh. 10:27). **[6]** One of the priests who returned with Zerubbabel (Neh. 12:2); he is called Melichu in verse 14.

Malta ("affording honey"), an island located in the Mediterranean Sea (Acts 28:1). It is 96.5 km. (60 mi.) south of Sicily.

Mamre ("firmness; vigor"), an Amorite chief who allied with Abraham (Gen. 14:13, 24).

Manahath ("resting place; rest"), a city of Benjamin (1 Chr. 8:6).

Manasseh ("causing forgetfulness"). **[1]** The first son of Joseph (Gen. 41:51). His descendants became one of the twelve tribes of Israel and occupied both sides of the Jordan

(Josh. 16:4–9; 17). **[2]** The idolatrous successor of Hezekiah to the throne of Israel. He was an ancestor of Christ (2 Kin. 21:1–18; Matt. 1:10). **[3]** One whose descendants set up graven images at Laish (Judg. 18:30). Most scholars suggest that we should read Moses here instead. Perhaps a scribe felt an idolatrous descendant would cast reproach on the great lawgiver. A few manuscripts of the Septuagint, Old Latin, and the Vulgate read Moses here. **[4]**, **[5]** Two who had taken foreign wives (Ezra 10:30, 33).

Manoah ("rest"), the father of Samson the judge (Judg. 13:1–23).

Marah ("bitter"), the fountain of bitter water in the wilderness of Shur where the Israelites first halted after crossing the Red Sea (Ex. 15:23; Num. 33:8). The traditional site is 'Ain Hawarah, about 75.6 km. (47 mi.) from Suez.

Mark ("polite; shining"), a Christian convert and missionary companion of Paul (Acts 12:12, 25; 15:37, 39; Col. 4:10). Mark is his Latin name, John his Hebrew name. He wrote the Gospel bearing his name.

Martha ("lady"), sister of Mary and Lazarus in Bethany (Luke 10:38, 40, 41; John 11:1–39).

Mary (Greek form of Miriam, "strong"). **[1]** The mother of Jesus Christ; her song of faith (Luke 1:46–55) reveals her deep faith (Matt. 1:16–20; cf. John 2:1–11). **[2]** Mary the sister of Martha. She anointed the Lord with ointment and received His approval (Luke 10:39, 42; John 11:1–45). **[3]** A woman of Magdala in Galilee. She had been converted after having "seven devils" cast out of her (Matt. 27:56, 61; 28:1; Luke 8:2; John 19:25). **[4]** The mother of John Mark (Acts 12:12). **[5]** A Roman Christian to whom Paul sent greetings (Rom. 16:6). **[6]** Mary, the mother of Joses (Mark 15:47) and James (Luke 24:10), the "other Mary" (Matt. 28:1), and the Mary, wife of Clopas (John 19:25), are possibly to be identified as the same person (Mark 15:40).

Massah ("temptation"), the name of a spot in the vicinity of Horeb where the Israelites tempted God (Ex. 17:7; Deut. 6:16). *See also* Meribah **[1]**.

Mattaniah ("gift of Jehovah"). **[1]** The original name of King Zedekiah (2 Kin. 24:17). **[2]** A descendant of Asaph whose family dwelt at Jerusalem (1 Chr. 9:15; 2 Chr. 20:14; Neh. 11:17, 22; 13:13). **[3]** A son of Heman the singer (1 Chr. 25:4, 16). **[4]** One who helped to cleanse the temple (2 Chr. 29:13). **[5]**, **[6]**, **[7]**, **[8]** Four who married foreign wives during the Exile (Ezra 10:26, 27, 30, 37). **[9]** One of the gatekeepers (Neh. 12:25).

Matthat ("gift"). **[1]** Grandfather of Joseph

and ancestor of Jesus (Luke 3:24). **[2]** Another ancestor of Jesus (Luke 3:29).

Matthew ("gift of God"), one of the twelve apostles; he was a tax collector before his call. He was also known as Levi (Matt. 9:9; 10:3; Mark 2:14). He wrote the Gospel bearing his name.

Matthias ("God's gift"), a Christian chosen to become an apostle to fill the place of Judas (Acts 1:23, 26). He was surnamed Justus.

Mattithiah ("gift of Jehovah"). **[1]** A Levite in charge of "things that were baked in the pans" (1 Chr. 9:31). **[2]** A Levite singer and gatekeeper (1 Chr. 15:18, 21; 16:5). **[3]** A son of Jeduthun (1 Chr. 25:3, 21). **[4]** One who took a foreign wife during the Exile (Ezra 10:43). **[5]** One who stood with Ezra when he read the Law (Neh. 8:4).

Medad ("love"), one of the elders of the Hebrews on whom the Spirit fell (Num. 11:26, 27).

Media ("middle land"), a country of Asia located south of the Caspian Sea, west of Parthia, north of Elam, and east of the Yagros Mountains. During the 400s B.C. the Persians and Medes had a powerful empire here (Esth. 1:3, 14, 18; Dan. 8:20).

Melchishua [Malchishua], the third son of King Saul (1 Sam. 14:49; 31:2; 1 Chr. 8:33).

Melchizedek [Melchisedec] ("king of righteousness"), king and high priest of Salem. He was a prophetic symbol or "type" of Christ (Gen. 14:18–20; Ps. 110:4; Heb. 5–7).

Memphis ("abode of the good"), an ancient Egyptian city located on the western bank of the Nile in the central portion of the country (Hos. 9:6). It was also called Noph (Jer. 2:16).

Menahem ("comforter"), the idolatrous and cruel usurper of the throne of Israel who killed Shallum (2 Kin. 15:14–23).

Mephibosheth ("idol breaker"). **[1]** Son of Saul by his concubine Rizpah (2 Sam. 21:8). **[2]** A grandson of Saul. He was loyal to David, even though Ziba told David he was a traitor (2 Sam. 4:4; 9:6–13). He was also called Merib-Baal ("Baal contends") (1 Chr. 8:34; 9:40).

Merab ("increase"), daughter of Saul promised to David but given to Adriel (1 Sam. 14:49; 18:17, 19). Apparently she was a sister of Michal.

Meremoth ("strong; firm"). **[1]** A priest who weighed the gold and silver vessels of the temple (Ezra 8:33; Neh. 3:4, 21). **[2]** One who took a foreign wife during the Exile (Ezra 10:36). **[3]** One who sealed the new covenant with God after the Exile (Neh. 10:5; 12:3).

Meribah ("quarrel"). **[1]** The desert location where Moses smote the rock (Ex. 17:7). **[2]** Another name for Kadesh Barnea in the Wilderness of Zin, where the Hebrew people rebelled against Moses (Num. 20:13). In Deuteronomy 32:51 the place is called Meribah Kadesh.

Meribah Kadesh. *See* Meribah **[2]**.

Mesha ("freedom"). **[1]** A king of Moab who rebelled against Ahaziah (2 Kin. 3:4). **[2]** Eldest son of Caleb (1 Chr. 2:42). **[3]** A descendant of Benjamin (1 Chr. 8:9).

Meshach ("the shadow of the prince; who is this?"), the name given to Mishael after he went into Babylonian captivity. He was delivered from the fiery furnace (Dan. 1:7; 3:12–30).

Meshullam ("associate; friend"). **[1]** Grandfather of Shaphan, a scribe (2 Kin. 22:3). **[2]** A descendant of King Jehoiakim (1 Chr. 3:19). **[3]** Head of a family of Gad (1 Chr. 5:13). **[4]** A descendant of Ben-jamin (1 Chr. 8:17). **[5]** One whose son lived in Jerusalem (1 Chr. 9:7). **[6]** One who lived in Jerusalem (1 Chr. 9:8). **[7]** A descendant of Aaron and an ancestor of Ezra (1 Chr. 9:11; Neh. 11:11). He is also called Shallum (Ezra 7:2; 1 Chr. 6:12, 13). **[8]** A priest (1 Chr. 9:12). **[9]** An overseer of the temple work (2 Chr. 34:12). **[10]** A chief man who returned with Ezra to Jerusalem (Ezra 8:16). **[11]** One who assisted in taking account of those who had foreign wives after the Exile (Ezra 10:15). **[12]** One who took a foreign wife during the Exile (Ezra 10:29). **[13]**, **[14]** Two who rebuilt part of the wall of Jerusalem (Neh. 3:4, 6, 30; 6:18). **[15]** A prince or priest who stood with Ezra while he read the Law (Neh. 8:4). **[16]** A priest who sealed the new covenant with God after the Exile (Neh. 10:7). **[17]** One who sealed the new covenant with God after the Exile (Neh. 10:20). **[18]** One whose descendants lived in Jerusalem (Neh. 11:7). **[19]** A priest who assisted in the dedication of the wall of Jerusalem (Neh. 12:13, 33). **[20]** A descendant of Ginnethon (Neh. 12:16). **[21]** A Levite and gatekeeper after the Exile (Neh. 12:25).

Mesopotamia ("between two rivers"), a region located between the Tigris and Euphrates Rivers (Gen. 24:10; Deut. 23:4), excluding the mountain regions where the rivers take their rise and the low-lying plains of Babylon.

Methuselah, the longest living human recorded in the Bible, the grandfather of Noah and an ancestor of Christ (Gen. 5:21–27; Luke 3:37).

Micah [Micha, Michah—all probably contractions of Micaiah]. **[1]** Owner of a small private sanctuary (Judg. 17:1–5). **[2]** A descendant of Reuben (1 Chr. 5:5). **[3]** A son of Merib-Baal, Mephibosheth in Second Samuel 4:4 (1 Chr. 8:34). **[4]** A descendant of Kohath, son of Levi (1 Chr. 23:20; 24:24). **[5]**

The father of Abdon (2 Chr. 34:20). He is called Michaiah in Second Kings 22:12. [6] A prophet (Jer. 26:18; Mic. 1:1). [7] The son of Zichri (1 Chr. 9:15; Neh. 11:17). [8] One who signed the covenant (Neh. 10:11).

Michael ("who is like God?"). [1] One sent to spy out the land of Canaan (Num. 13:13). [2] A descendant of Gad (1 Chr. 5:13). [3] Another descendant of Gad (1 Chr. 5:14). [4] An ancestor of Asaph (1 Chr. 6:40). [5] A chief of the tribe of Issachar (1 Chr. 7:3). [6] One residing in Jerusalem (1 Chr. 8:16). [7] A warrior who joined David at Ziklag (1 Chr. 12:20). [8] Father of Omri, a prince of Issachar (1 Chr. 27:18). [9] A son of Jehoshaphat (2 Chr. 21:2). [10] An ancestor of one who returned from the Exile (Ezra 8:8).

Michaiah [Micaiah] ("who is like Jehovah?"). [1] Wife of Rehoboam (2 Chr. 13:2). She is also called Maachah (1 Kin. 15:2; 2 Chr. 11:20). See Maachah [5]. [2] See Micah [5]. [3] A prince of Judah (2 Chr. 17:7). [4] The son of Zaccur (Neh. 12:35). [5] One present at the dedication of the wall (Neh. 12:41). [6] A prophet who predicted Ahab's downfall (1 Kin. 22:8-28; 2 Chr. 18:7-27).

Michal ("who is like God?"), a daughter of Saul whom David married (1 Sam. 14:49). Michal "had no child unto the day of her death" (2 Sam. 6:23). Yet Second Samuel 21:8 states she had five sons. The KJV rendering, "whom she brought up for Adriel," is not a permissible translation—the Hebrew text states she bore them. A few Hebrew, Greek, and Syriac manuscripts read: "the five sons of Merab" instead of Michal, which seems a plausible solution to the problem. See First Samuel 18:19.

Midian ("contention"), a son of Abraham by Keturah and founder of the Midianites (Gen. 25:2, 4; 36:35; 1 Chr. 1:32).

Midian ("contention"), the land of the descendants of Midian beyond the Jordan. It included Edom, the Sinai Peninsula, and Arabian Petra (Ex. 2:15, 16; Judg. 6:1; Acts 7:29).

Miletus ("scarlet"), a coastal city of Ionia (Acts 20:15; 2 Tim. 4:20). It was 57.9 km. (36 mi.) south of Ephesus.

Miriam ("fat; thick; strong"). [1] The sister of Moses and Aaron. She rebelled against Moses with Aaron at Hazeroth (Ex. 2:4-10; Num. 12:1-15; 20:1). [2] A woman descendant of Judah (1 Chr. 4:17).

Mishael ("who is what God is?"). [1] One who carried away the dead Nadab and Abihu (Ex. 6:22; Lev. 10:4). [2] One who stood with Ezra at the reading of the Law (Neh. 8:4). [3] One of the companions of Daniel in Babylon (Dan. 1:6, 7, 11, 19). See Meshach.

Mithredath ("given by [the god] Mithra").

[1] The treasurer of Cyrus through whom he restored the temple vessels (Ezra 1:8). [2] One who wrote to the king of Persia protesting the restoration of Jerusalem (Ezra 4:7).

Mitylene ("purity"), the principal city of the Island of Lesbos off the western coast of Asia Minor (Acts 20:14).

Mizpah ("a watchtower"). [1] A mound of stones on Mount Gilead (Gen. 31:49). [2] A Hivite settlement in northern Palestine at the foot of Mount Hermon (Josh. 11:3). [3] A city in the lowlands of Judah (Josh. 15:38). It was just north of Eleutheropolis [Beit Jibrin]. [4] A town in Gilead east of the Jordan (Judg. 11:34). It is possibly identical with Ramath Mizpah. [5] A town of Benjamin just north of Jerusalem (Josh. 18:26; 1 Kin. 15:22). The exact site is uncertain. [6] A place in Moab (1 Sam. 22:3); perhaps modern Rujm el-Meshrefeh west-southwest of Madaba.

Mizraim. The second son of Ham (Gen. 10:6, 13; 1 Chr. 1:8, 11). Possibly the Egyptian people are intended.

Mnason ("remembering"), a Cyprian convert who accompanied Paul from Caesarea on Paul's last visit to Jerusalem (Acts 21:16).

Moab ("from my father"), the son of Lot by his daughter and an ancestor of the Moabites (Gen. 19:34-37).

Moab. A land that consisted of the plateau east of the Dead Sea between the wadis Arnon and Zered, though at certain periods extending to the north of the Arnon (Deut. 1:5; Num. 22—25).

Mordecai ("dedicated to Mars"). [1] A Jewish exile who became a vizier of Persia. He helped save the Jews from destruction (Esth. 2—10). [2] A leader who returned from the Babylonian Captivity (Ezra 2:2; Neh. 7:7).

Moreh ("stretching"). [1] The first stopping place of Abraham after he entered Canaan (Gen. 12:6). It was near Shechem. [2] A hill lying at the foot of the valley of Jezreel (Judg. 7:1). It is probably modern Jebel Dahy or Little Hermon about 12.9 km. (8 mi.) northwest of Mount Gilboa.

Moriah ("bitterness of the Lord"). [1] An elevation in Jerusalem on which Solomon built the temple (2 Chr. 3:1). Probably the same hilltop was used as the threshing floor of Araunah. The name Moriah was possibly ascribed by the Chronicler because of its traditional meaning (2 Sam. 24:18; 2 Chr. 3:1). [2] The hill on which Abraham was prepared to sacrifice Isaac (Gen. 22:2). The site is uncertain, but Samaritans identify Moriah with Moreh [1]. This seems unlikely.

Moses ("drawer-out; child; one-born"), the great prophet and lawgiver of Israel. He led his people from Egyptian bondage. The book of Exodus tells his story. He wrote the first five books of the Bible.

N

Naamah ("pleasant"). [1] Daughter of Lamech and Zillah (Gen. 4:22). [2] A wife of Solomon and mother of Rehoboam (1 Kin. 14:21; 2 Chr. 12:13).

Naaman ("pleasantness"). [1] A Syrian general who was healed of leprosy by bathing in the Jordan (2 Kin. 5; Luke 4:27). [2] Grandson of Benjamin (Gen. 26:38, 40). [3] A son of Benjamin and founder of a tribal family (Gen. 46:21).

Nabal ("foolish; wicked"), a wealthy Carmelite who refused David and his men food (1 Sam. 25).

Naboth ("a sprout"), the owner whom Jezebel had killed in order to obtain his vineyard (1 Kin. 21:1–18).

Nachon. *See* Chidon.

Nadab ("liberal"). [1] Firstborn son of Aaron, struck dead for offering "strange fire" to God (Ex. 6:23; Lev. 10:1–3). [2] A descendant of Jerahmeel (1 Chr. 2:28, 30). [3] A brother of Gibeon (1 Chr. 8:30). [4] Son of Jeroboam I; he ruled Israel for two years (1 Kin. 15:25–31).

Nahash ("oracle" or "serpent"). [1] The father of Abigail and Zeruiah (2 Sam. 17:25). [2] An Ammonite king that was defeated by Saul (1 Sam. 11:1, 2; 12:12). [3] Another king of Ammon (2 Sam. 10:2; 17:27; 1 Chr. 19:1, 2). Not to be confused with Ir-Nahash.

Nahor ("piercer"). [1] Grandfather of Abraham and ancestor of Christ (Gen. 11:22–25; Luke 3:34). [2] A brother of Abraham (Gen. 11:26, 27, 29; 22:20, 23; Josh. 24:2).

Nahum ("comforter"), one of the later prophets; he prophesied against Nineveh (Nah. 1:1). Not to be confused with Naum.

Nain ("beauty"), a village in Galilee where Christ resurrected a widow's son (Luke 7:11). It is located 3.2 km. (2 mi.) south of Mount Tabor and a little southwest of the Sea of Galilee.

Naioth ("habitation"), the place in Ramah where a community of prophets gathered around Samuel (1 Sam. 19:18–23; 20:1). Its location is not clearly identified. *See also* Ramah [2].

Naomi ("pleasantness; my joy"), mother-in-law to Ruth (Ruth 1:2–4:17).

Naphtali ("wrestling"), the sixth son of Jacob (Gen. 30:7, 8). His descendants became one of the twelve tribes.

Naphtali [Nephthalim] ("that struggles"), a territory assigned to the tribe of Naphtali, located in mountainous northern Palestine (Josh. 19:32–39; Matt. 4:13). It was bounded on the east by the Upper Jordan River and the Sea of Galilee and on the west by the territories of Zebulun and Asher.

Nathan ("gift"). [1] Prophet and royal advisor to David (2 Sam. 7:2-17; 12:1-25). [2] A son of King David and ancestor of Christ (2 Sam. 5:14; 1 Chr. 3:5; Luke 3:31). [3] Father of Igal (2 Sam. 23:36). [4] A descendant of Jerahmeel (1 Chr. 2:36). [5] A companion of Ezra (Ezra 8:16). [6] One of those who had married a foreign wife (Ezra 10:39). [7] Brother of Joel, one of David's valiant men (1 Chr. 11:38). [8] Father of Solomon's chief officer (1 Kin. 4:5). [9] A chief man of Israel (Zech. 12:12).

Nathanael ("God has given"), a Galilean called by Christ to be a disciple. He is probably to be identified with Bartholomew (John 1:45-49; 21:2; Acts 1:13). *See also* Bartholomew.

Nazareth ("sanctified"), the hometown of Jesus in lower Galilee, north of the Plain of Esdraelon [Jezreel] (Matt. 4:13; Mark 1:9). It is 8 km. (5 mi.) west-southwest of Tiberias, 32.2 km. (20 mi.) southwest of modern Tell Hum [Capernaum] and 141.6 km. (88 mi.) north of Jerusalem.

Nebo ("that prophesies"). [1] The mountain from which Moses saw the Promised Land (Deut. 32:49; 34:1). It is a peak in the Abarim Mountains east of the Jordan, opposite Jericho; probably modern Jebel en Neba 12.9 km. (8 mi.) east of the mouth of the Jordan. On a clear day, all of Palestine can be seen from this peak. [2] A city of Reuben that fell again to the Moabites (Num. 32:3, 38; 33:47). It is probably modern Khirbet el-Mekhayyet, south of Mount Nebo. [3] A city in Judah (Ezra 2:29; Neh. 7:33), probably modern Beth-Nube, near Lydda.

Nebuchadnezzar [Nebuchadrezzar](Babylonian, *Nabur-kudurri-utsur*— "may [the god] Nabu guard my boundary stones"), great king of the Babylonian Empire; he captured Jerusalem three times and carried Judah into captivity (2 Kin. 24:1, 10, 11; 25:1, 8, 22; Dan. 1—4).

Nehemiah ("Jehovah is consolation"). [1] Governor of Jerusalem; he helped rebuild the fallen city (Neh. 1:1; 8:9; 12:47). [2] A chief man who returned from the Exile (Ezra 2:2; Neh. 7:7). [3] One who repaired the wall of Jerusalem (Neh. 3:16).

Nepheg ("sprout; shoot"). [1] A brother of Korah (Ex. 6:21). [2] A son of David (2 Sam. 5:15; 1 Chr. 3:7; 14:6).

Ner ("light"). [1] An uncle (?) of Saul, father of Abner (1 Sam. 14:50). [2] Grandfather of Saul (1 Chr. 8:33; 9:39). These relationships are unclear. Abner may have been Saul's uncle. If so, Ner [1] and [2] are the same. He is also called Abiel (1 Sam. 9:1). It is also possible that Ner **[2]** (Abiel) had sons names Ner **[1]** and Kish, the father of Saul.

Nethanel ("God gives"). **[1]** Chief of Issachar whom Moses sent to spy out the land of Canaan (Num. 1:8; 2:5; 7:18, 23; 10:15). **[2]** Fourth son of Jesse (1 Chr. 2:14). **[3]** One of the trumpet blowers when the ark of the covenant was brought up (1 Chr. 15:24). **[4]** A Levite (1 Chr. 24:6). **[5]** A son of Obed-Edom and gatekeeper of the tabernacle (1 Chr. 26:4). **[6]** A prince commissioned by Jehoshaphat to teach the people (2 Chr. 17:7). **[7]** A Levite in the days of Josiah (2 Chr. 35:9). **[8]** A priest who married a foreign wife (Ezra 10:22). **[9]** A priest in the days of Joiakim (Neh. 12:21). **[10]** Levite musician at the purification ceremony (Neh. 12:36).

Nicanor ("conqueror"), one of the seven chosen in the ministry to the poor (Acts 6:5).

Nicodemus ("innocent blood"), a Pharisee and ruler of the Jews who assisted in Christ's burial (John 3:1–15; 7:50–52; 19:39–42).

Nicolas ("conqueror of the people"), one of the seven chosen to aid in the ministration to the poor (Acts 6:5).

Nile ("dark blue"), the greatest river of Egypt and the world's longest. It is simply referred to in Scripture as "the river" (Gen. 13:1; Ex. 2:3; 7:21). The Nile is about 6,669.3 km. (4,145 mi.) long.

Nimrah. *See* Beth Nimrah.

Nimrod ("valiant; strong"), a son of Cush (Gen. 10:8, 9; 1 Chr. 1:10). His kingdom included Babel, Erech, Accad, and Calneh, cities in Shinar, but also included Assyria.

Nineveh [Nineve] (meaning unknown), the capital of the Kingdom of Assyria (Nah. 1:1; cf. 3:1; Luke 11:32; Zeph. 2:13). It was located east of the Tigris River in the area north of the point the Tigris joins the Upper Zab. The ruins are now called Tell Kuyunjik and Tell Nebi Yunus.

Noah ("rest"), son of Lamech; the patriarch chosen to build the ark. Only his family survived the flood (Gen. 5:28–32; 6:8–22; 7—10). He was an ancestor of Christ (Luke 3:36).

Nod ("vagabond"), an unidentified land east of Eden to which Cain fled after the murder of Abel (Gen. 4:16). Some suppose it to be China, but this is speculation.

Noph. *See* Memphis.

Nun [Non] ("continuation; fish"). **[1]** A descendant of Ephraim (1 Chr. 7:27); possibly the same as **[2]**. **[2]** The father of Joshua (Ex. 33:11; 1 Kin. 16:34).

O

Obadiah ("servant of Jehovah"). **[1]** The governor or prime minister of Ahab who tried to protect the prophets against Jezebel

(1 Kin. 18:3–16). **[2]** A descendant of David (1 Chr. 3:21). **[3]** A chief of the tribe of Issachar (1 Chr. 7:3). **[4]** A descendant of King Saul (1 Chr. 8:38; 9:44). **[5]** A man of the tribe of Zebulun (1 Chr. 27:19). **[6]** A chief of the Gadites who joined David at Ziklag (1 Chr. 12:9). **[7]** One of the princes whom Jehoshaphat commissioned to teach the Law (2 Chr. 17:7–9). **[8]** A Levite overseer in work done on the temple (2 Chr. 34:12). **[9]** The chief of a family that returned to Jerusalem (Ezra 8:9). **[10]** One who sealed the covenant with Nehemiah (Neh. 10:5). **[11]** A gatekeeper for the sanctuary of the temple (Neh. 12:25). **[12]** The fourth of the "minor prophets." His message was directed against Edom (Obad. 1).

Obed ("servant"). **[1]** A son of Boaz and Ruth, father of Jesse, and ancestor of Christ (Ruth 4:17; Matt. 1:5; Luke 3:32). **[2]** A descendant of Judah (1 Chr. 2:37, 38). **[3]** One of David's warriors (1 Chr. 11:47). **[4]** A Levite gatekeeper in David's time (1 Chr. 26:7). **[5]** Father of Azariah, who helped make Joash king of Judah (2 Chr. 23:1).

Obed-Edom ("servant of [the god] Edom"). **[1]** A man who housed the ark for three months (2 Sam. 6:10–12; 1 Chr. 13:13, 14). **[2]** One of the chief Levitical singers and doorkeepers (1 Chr. 15:18, 21, 24; 16:5, 38; 26:4, 8, 15). **[3]** A temple treasurer or official, or perhaps the tribe that sprang from **[2]** (2 Chr. 25:24).

Oded ("aiding" or "restorer"). **[1]** Father of Azariah the prophet (2 Chr. 15:1). **[2]** A prophet of Samaria who persuaded the northern army to free their Judean slaves (2 Chr. 28:9– 5).

Olives, Mount of [Mount of Corruption; Olivet], a ridge east of Jerusalem and separated from Jerusalem by the Kidron Valley (2 Sam. 15:30; Mark 11:1; Acts 1:12). It is called the Mount of Corruption in Second Kings 23:13.

Omri ("Jehovah apportions; pupil"). **[1]** The sixth king of Israel and founder of the third dynasty. He founded Samaria and made it Israel's capital (1 Kin. 16:15–28). **[2]** A descendant of Benjamin, the son of Becher (1 Chr. 7:8). **[3]** A descendant of Perez living at Jerusalem (1 Chr. 9:4). **[4]** A prince of Issachar in the days of David (1 Chr. 27:18).

Onan ("vigorous"), the second son of Judah. He was slain by God for disobedience (Gen. 38:4–10; Num. 26:19).

Onesimus ("useful"), a slave on whose behalf Paul wrote an epistle to his master, Philemon (Col. 4:9; Philem. 10, 15).

Onesiphorus ("profit-bringer"), a loyal friend of Paul's who often refreshed him in prison (2 Tim. 1:16; 4:19).

Ophir ("fruitful region"), a region where Solomon mined gold (1 Kin. 9:28; 1 Chr. 29:4). The location is highly uncertain. Josephus thought it was India, but the African coast in modern Somaliland is more probable.

Ornan ("active"), a Jebusite from whom David bought a piece of land, on which Solomon's temple was erected (1 Chr. 21:15–25). He is called Araunah in Second Samuel 24:16.

Orpah ("fawn; youthful freshness"), daughter-in-law of Naomi (Ruth 1:4–14).

Othniel ("God is power"), Caleb's younger brother who liberated Israel from foreign rule (Judg. 1:13; 3:8–11; 1 Chr. 27:15).

Ozem ("strength"). [1] A brother of David (1 Chr. 2:15). [2] A son of Jerahmeel of Judah (1 Chr. 2:25).

P

Padan Aram [Padan] ("plain [tableland] of Aram"), the plain region of Mesopotamia from the Lebanon Mountains to beyond the Euphrates, and from the Taurus Mountains on the north to beyond Damascus on the south (Gen. 25:20; 28:2; 31:18). It is called simply Padan in Genesis 48:7.

Palestine [Palestina] ("which is covered"), an ill-defined region between the Jordan River and the Dead Sea on the east and the Mediterranean on the west (Ex. 15:14; Joel 3:4; Gen. 15:18). Its northern border is roughly the Lebanon Mountain range. It stretches in a southwesterly triangle to the Gulf of Aqaba on the Red Sea.

Paltiel ("God delivers"). [1] A prince of the tribe of Issachar (Num. 34:26). [2] The man who married David's wife (2 Sam. 3:15). He is called Phalti in First Samuel 25:44.

Pamphylia ("a nation made up of every tribe"), a southern coastal area in Asia Minor; its main city is Perga (Acts 13:13; 14:24; 27:5).

Paphos ("that which boils"), a town on the southwest extremity of Cyprus; it was visited by Paul and Barnabas (Acts 13:6–13). It is now called Baffa.

Paradise ("pleasure ground; park"), figurative name for the place where God dwells (2 Cor. 12:3) and the abode of the righteous (Luke 23:43; Rev. 2:7).

Paran ("beauty"), a wilderness seven days' march from Mount Sinai (Gen. 21:21; Num. 10:12; 1 Sam. 25:1). It is located east of the wilderness of Beersheba and Shurj, and it merges with the Wilderness of Sin with no clearly marked boundary. The area borders on Edom and Midian; it is sometimes called

Mount Paran (Hab. 3:3) and El Paran (Gen. 14:6).

Parmenas ("steadfast"), one of the seven deacons (Acts 6:5).

Pashhur ("splitter; cleaver"). [1] Head of a priestly family (Ezra 2:38; 10:22; Neh. 7:41). [2] A priest who sealed the covenant with God after the Exile (Neh. 10:1, 3). Possibly identical with [1]. [3] A priest, the "chief governor in the house of the Lord," who persecuted Jeremiah (Jer. 20:1–6). [4] Son of Melchiah, whose family returned to Jerusalem (1 Chr. 9:12; Neh. 11:12; Jer. 21:1; 38:1).

Patmos ("mortal"), a barren island to which John was banished (Rev. 1:9). It is in the Greek archipelagos and is now called Patino.

Paul (Latin, *Paulus*—"little"), the Roman name of Saul of Tarsus, a Pharisee who studied Jewish law under Gamaliel (Acts 21:39). He was converted and made an apostle to the Gentiles (Acts 26:12–20). Perhaps he used his Roman name in humility. The Book of Acts tells of his missionary journeys.

Pedaiah ("Jehovah delivers"). [1] Father of Joel (1 Chr. 27:20). [2] Grandfather of King Josiah (2 Kin. 23:36). [3] Son or grandson of Jeconiah (1 Chr. 3:18, 19). [4] One who helped to rebuild the wall of Jerusalem (Neh. 3:25). [5] One who stood with Ezra when he read the Law (Neh. 8:4; 13:13). [6] A descendant of Benjamin (Neh. 11:7).

Pelatiah ("Jehovah delivers"). [1] One who sealed the new covenant with God after the Exile (Neh. 10:22). [2] A descendant of David (1 Chr. 3:21). [3] A captain of Simeon (1 Chr. 4:42, 43). [4] A wicked prince seen in Ezekiel's vision (Ezek. 11:1, 13).

Peniel. *See* Penuel.

Penuel [Peniel] ("face of God"), an encampment of the Hebrews east of Jordan (Gen. 32:30, 31; Judg. 8:8, 17). It derived its name from the fact that Jacob had seen God face-to-face there.

Perga ("very earthy"), the capital of Pamphylia in Asia Minor during the Roman period (Acts 13:13).

Pergamos ("elevation"), a city of Mysia in northwest Asia Minor and the site of one of the seven churches of Asia (Rev. 2:12–17).

Persia ("cuts or divides"), a great empire including all of western Asia and parts of Europe and Africa (Ezek. 38:5; Ezra 1:8). Persia proper corresponded to what is now the province of Fars in Iran.

Peter ("stone; rock"), a fisherman called to be an apostle of Christ. He became one of the leaders of the early church (Matt. 4:18–20; 16:15–19; Acts 2). Christ changed this man's name from Simon to a name meaning "rock" (*Cephas* in Aramaic, *Peter* in Greek).

Pharaoh ("inhabitant of the palace"), royal title of Egyptian kings, equivalent to our word *king* (Gen. 12:15; 37:36; Ex. 2:15; 1 Kin. 3:1; Is. 19:11).

Philadelphia ("love of a brother"), a town of Lydia in Asia Minor. It was the site of one of the seven churches of Asia (Rev. 1:11; 3:7–13). It was 45.5 km. (28.3 mi.) southeast of Sardis.

Philemon ("friendship"), a convert at Colosse to whom Paul wrote an epistle on behalf of his runaway servant, Onesimus (Philem. 1, 5–7).

Philetus ("amiable"), a convert who was condemned by Paul because of his stand on the Resurrection (2 Tim. 2:17).

Philip ("lover of horses"). **[1]** One of the twelve apostles of Christ (Matt. 10:3; John 1:44–48; 6:5–9). **[2]** An evangelist mentioned several times in Acts (Acts 6:5; 8:5–13). **[3]** *See* Herod **[3]**, **[4]**.

Philippi ("pertaining to Philip"), a city of Macedonia founded by Philip the Great and named for him (Acts 16:12; 20:3–6). It lies inland about 16.1 km. (10 mi.) northwest of its seaport, Neapolis.

Philistia ("land of sojourners"), an area on the southwest coast of Palestine (Ps. 60:8; 87:4; 108:9). This land, which was the home of traditional enemies of Israel, was 80 km. (50 mi.) long and only 24 km. (15 mi.) wide.

Phinehas ("mouth of brass"). **[1]** Grandson of Aaron and high priest (Ex. 6:25; Num. 25:6–18; 1 Chr. 6:4; 9:20). **[2]** Younger son of Eli; he was a priest who abused his office (1 Sam. 1:3; 2:22–24, 34). **[3]** Father of Eleazar (Ezra 8:33).

Phoebe ("shining"), a servant of the church at Corinth or Cenchrea who helped Paul (Rom. 16:1).

Phoenicia ("land of palm trees"), a thin strip of territory between the Mediterranean Sea on the west and on the east the mountains of Lebanon (Acts 21:2; 11:19; 15:3). It included the hills running south from those mountains.

Phoenix ("land of palm trees"). **[1]** A harbor in southern Crete (Acts 27:12). **[2]** *See* Phoenicia.

Phrygia ("barren"), a large and important inland province of Asia Minor (Acts 2:10; 16:6).

Phut. *See* Libya.

Pilate. *See* Pontius Pilate.

Pisgah ("fortress"), the mountain ranges from which Moses viewed the Promised Land (Num. 21:20; Deut. 3:27). This part of the Abarim Range is near the northeast end of the Dead Sea.

Pisidia ("pitch"), an inland district of Asia

Minor with Antioch as its capital (Acts 13:14).

Pontius Pilate (Latin, *Pontius Pilatus*— "marine dart-carrier"), a Roman procurator of Judea. When Christ was brought before him for judgment, Pilate, fearing the Jews, turned Him over to the people even though he found Him not guilty (Matt. 27:2–24; John 18:28–40).

Pontus ("the sea"), a district in northeastern Asia Minor on the Pontus Euxinus (Acts 2:9; 1 Pet. 1:1).

Porcius Festus. *See* Festus.

Potiphar ("belonging to the sun-god"), Egyptian captain of the guard who became the master of Joseph (Gen. 37:36; 39:1).

Poti-Pherah ("given of the sun-god"), a priest of On; father-in-law of Joseph (Gen. 41:45, 50).

Potter's Field. *See* Akel Dama.

Praetorium. The Praetorium was originally the headquarters of a Roman camp, but in the provinces the name was used to designate the official residence. Jesus was brought to Pilate's Praetorium in Jerusalem (Mark 15:16).

Priscilla [Prisca] ("ancient one"), the wife of Aquila; a Jewish Christian deeply loyal to her faith (Acts 18:2, 18, 26; Rom. 16:3).

Prochorus ("choir leader"), one of the seven deacons (Acts 6:5).

Publius ("common; first"), governor of Malta who courteously received Paul and his company when they were shipwrecked (Acts 28:1–10).

Pul. *See* Tiglath-Pileser.

Put. *See* Libya.

R

Rabmag. This is not a proper name, but an official position of some sort. It is unclear whether it is a high religious or governmental position (Jer. 39:3, 13). Nergal-Sharezer of Babylonia bore this title.

Rabsaris, not a proper name, but an official position in the Babylonian and Assyrian governments. Its precise nature is unknown (Jer. 39:3, 13; 1 Kin. 18:17).

Rabshakeh, the title of an office in the Assyrian government. Its precise function is unknown, but suggestions include that of a field marshal or governor of the Assyrian provinces east of Haran (2 Kin. 18:17– 8; 19:4, 8).

Rachel ("ewe"), daughter of Laban, wife of Jacob, and mother of Joseph and Benjamin (Gen. 29—35).

Raguel. *See* Jethro.

Rahab ("broad"), the harlot of Jericho who helped the Hebrew spies and who became an ancestor of Christ (Josh. 2:1–21; 6:17–25; Matt. 1:5).

Ram [Aram] ("exalted"). [1] An ancestor of David and of Christ (Ruth 4:19; Matt. 1:3, 4; Luke 3:33). [2] Son of Jerahmeel of Judah (1 Chr. 2:27). [3] Head of the family of Elihu (Job 32:2).

Ramah ("elevated"). [1] A town in Benjamin near Gibeah, Geba, and Bethel (Josh. 18:25; Judg. 4:5; Is. 10:29; Matt. 2:18). It has been identified as modern Er-Ram 8 km. (5 mi.) north of Jerusalem. [2] The town where Samuel was born (1 Sam. 1:1). It is also called Ramathaim Zophim (1 Sam. 1:1). Its location is uncertain but has been identified with Ramah [1] and modern-day Rentis, about 14.5 km. (9 mi.) northeast of Lydda. It may be Arimathea. [3] A frontier town of Asher (Josh. 19:29). If not the same as Ramah [4] it may be Rameh, about 20.9 km. (13 mi.) south-southeast of Tyre. [4] A fortified city of Naphtali (Josh. 19:36). The site may be modern Rameh 27.4 km. (17 mi.) east-northeast of Acco. [5] *See* Ramoth Gilead.

Ramathaim Zophim. *See* Ramah [2].

Rameses ("child of the sun"), a fertile district of Egypt where the Israelites settled (Gen. 47:11; Ex. 12:37). It was possibly the Land of Goshen.

Ramoth Gilead [Ramoth] ("heights of Gilead"), the chief city of Gad. It was a city of refuge ascribed to the Levites (1 Kin. 4:13; 22:4). Sometimes it is called simply Ramoth (Deut. 4:43; Josh. 20:8). It has been identified with both Tell Ramith and Tell el-Hush.

Rapha ("fearful"). [1] The fifth son of Benjamin (1 Chr. 8:2). He is called Rephaiah in First Chronicles 9:43. [2] A descendant of King Saul (1 Chr. 8:37).

Rebecca. Greek form of Rebekah (q.v.).

Rebekah [Rebecca] ("flattering"), wife of Isaac and mother of Jacob and Esau (Gen. 22:23; 24—28).

Rechab ("companionship"). [1] A descendant of Benjamin who murdered Ishbosheth (2 Sam. 4:2, 5–9). [2] Founder of a tribe called Rechabites (2 Kin. 10:15; Jer. 35). [3] A descendant of Hemath (1 Chr. 2:55). [4] One who helped to build the wall of Jerusalem (Neh. 3:14).

Red Sea, a sea that divides Egypt and Arabia. It was across this body of water that the Israelites escaped from Egypt (Ex. 10:19). The Hebrews called it the Sea of Deliverance; others called it the Sea of Reeds.

Refuge, Cities of. *See* Cities of Refuge.

Refuse Gate. A gate in the southwest wall of Jerusalem (Neh. 2:13; 12:31).

Rehoboam ("freer of the people"), the son of Solomon; when he was king, ten tribes re-

volted from him and he set up the southern kingdom of Judah (1 Kin. 11:43; 12; 14). He was an ancestor of Christ (Matt. 1:7).

Rehoboth ("spaces"). [1] A well dug by Isaac in the Valley of Gerar (Gen. 26:22). It is probably modern Wadi Ruheibeh, 30.6 km. (19 mi.) southwest of Beersheba. [2] A suburb of Nineveh (Gen. 10:11). [3] A city somewhere in northern Edom (Gen. 36:37; 1 Chr. 1:48). Its location is unidentified.

Rephaim, Valley of ("valley of the giants"), the site in Judah where David defeated the Philistines (Is. 17:5; 2 Sam. 5:18). It lies between Jerusalem and Bethlehem, southwest of Jerusalem and the Valley of Hinnom. It is probably the present-day Valley el-Bukaa.

Reuben ("behold, a son"), eldest son of Jacob and Leah; he lost his birthright through sin against his father (Gen. 29:32; 35:22; 37:29). His descendants became one of the twelve tribes of Israel.

Reuel ("God is his friend"). [1] A son of Esau by Basemath (Gen. 36:4; 1 Chr. 1:35, 37). [2] Descendant of Benjamin (1 Chr. 9:8). [3] *See* Jethro.

Rezin ("dominion"). [1] The last king of Syria who, along with Pekah, fought Judah (2 Kin. 15:37; 16:5–10). [2] One whose descendants returned from the Babylonian Captivity (Ezra 2:48; Neh. 7:50).

Rhoda ("rose"), a maid in the house of Mary (Acts 12:12–15).

Riblah ("quarrel"). [1] A city on the Orontes where the sons of Zedekiah were slain (Jer. 39:5–7; 2 Kin. 23:33). It was 80 km. (50 mi.) south of Hamath. It may be modern Ribleh in the Plain of Coelesyria. [2] A border city of the Promised Land (Num. 34:11). It is perhaps modern Harmel northeast of the source of the Orontes.

Rimmon. [1] A town in southern Judah (Josh. 15:32; 1 Chr. 4:32; Zech. 14:10). It is identified with Khirbet Umm er-Ramāmīn, about 9 mi. from Beersheba. [2] A rock near Gibeah (Judg. 20:45–47; 21:13). It is possibly a limestone projection 3½ mi. east of Bethel. [3] A border town of Zebulun (1 Chr. 6:77). The town is called Dimnah in Joshua 21:35, a reading many scholars consider a corruption of Rimmon. The site is referred to in Joshua 19:13 as Remmonmethoar. Many translate verse 13: "[the border] goes out to Ittah-Kazin and goes to Kemmon and bends [methoar] to Neah."

Rome ("city of Romulus"), the capital of the great Roman Empire (Acts 23:11). It is located in Italy on the Tiber River.

Rufus ("red"). [1] A son of Simon of Cyrene (Mark 15:21). He was probably well-known to those to whom Mark wrote his Gospel. [2] A

Roman Christian (Rom. 16:13); some identify him with [1].

Ruth ("friendship; companion"), Moabite wife of Mahlon and Boaz; she was the great-grandmother of David and an ancestor of Christ (Ruth 1:4, 5, 14–16; 4:10; Matt. 1:5).

S

Salamis ("shaken"), a town located on the east end of Cyprus (Acts 13:5). It is 4.8 km. (3 mi.) northwest of modern Famagusta.

Salem ("perfect peace"), the city of Melchizedek (Gen. 14:18; Ps. 76:2). It is possibly modern Salim; however, many believe it to be Jerusalem.

Salim ("path"), the place where John baptized (John 3:23). It is near the waters of Aenon, which were probably north of Shechem, although the site is uncertain.

Salome ("clothing; strength"). [1] One of the women who saw the Crucifixion (Mark 15:40; 16:1). Matthew 27:56 mentions that the mother of the sons of Zebedee was present; she is probably to be identified with Salome. John 19:25 lists the sister of Jesus' mother among those near the cross; some scholars identify her with Salome, but others deny this. [2] The daughter of Herodias who danced before Herod (Matt. 14:6; Mark 6:22).

Salt, City of. *See* City of Salt.

Salt Sea [Dead Sea; East Sea], the body of water at the southern end of the Jordan Valley, which contains no marine life because of its heavy mineral contents (Gen. 14:3; Num. 34:12). Its modern name is the Dead Sea.

Samaria ("watch mountain"). [1] The capital of the northern kingdom of Israel (1 Kin. 20:1; 2 Chr. 18:2; Jer. 41:5). It was 67.6 km. (42 mi.) north of Jerusalem. [2] Another name for the kingdom of Israel (1 Kin. 13:32; 2 Kin. 17:24). [3] A district of Palestine in Christ's time (Luke 17:11–19). Galilee was on its north and Judea on the south.

Samson ("distinguished; strong"), judge of Israel for 20 years. His great strength and moral weakness have made him famous (Judg. 13:24; 14–16).

Samuel [Shemuel] ("asked of God; heard of God"), prophet and last judge of Israel. He anointed Saul and later David as king (1 Sam. 1:20; 3–13; 15–16; 19; 25:1; Heb. 11:32).

Sanballat ("strong"), a leading opponent of the Jews at the time they were rebuilding the walls of Jerusalem (Neh. 2:10; 4:1, 7; 6:1–14).

Sapphira ("beautiful; sapphire"), the dishonest wife of Ananias, who was struck dead by God (Acts 5:1–10).

Sarah [Sarai] ("princess"), the wife of Abraham and mother of Isaac (Gen. 17–18; 20–21; Heb. 11:11; 1 Pet. 3:6). Her name was changed from Sarai ("Jehovah is prince") to Sarah ("princess") because she would be the progenitor of a great nation (Gen. 17:15).

Sarai. *See* Sarah.

Sardis ("prince of joy"), the capital city of Lydia where a church was located (Rev. 1:11; 3:1, 4). It was on the east bank of the Pactolus River about 80.5 km. (50 mi.) east of Smyrna.

Sargon ("[the god] has established the king [ship]"), an important king of Assyria who finished the siege of Samaria and carried away Israel. He is called by name only once in Scripture (Is. 20:1).

Saul [Shaul] ("asked"). [1] The first king of Israel; God eventually gave him up. He tried several times to slay David, but was killed himself at Gilboa (1 Sam. 9–31). [2] The original name of Paul (q.v.). [3] The sixth king of Edom (Gen. 36:37, 38; 1 Chr. 1:48, 49).

Seir ("tempest"). [1] The valley and mountains of Arabah from the Dead Sea south to the Elanitic Gulf (Gen. 14:6; 32:3). Seir was the name of the mountain range in Edom and the name came to include the entire territory. [2] A ridge on Judah's border west of Kirjath Jearim (Josh. 15:10).

Sela ("a rock"). [1] The capital of Edom, located between the Dead Sea and the Gulf of 'Aqaba (2 Kin. 14:7; Is. 16:1). It is also called Petra. [2] A rock formation about 1,160 m. (3,800 ft.) above sea level, which dominates the city of Petra (cf. Judg. 1:36). It is now called Ummel-Bizarah.

Sennacherib (Babylonian, *Sin-ahi-eriba*— "[the god] Sin has substituted for my brother"), an Assyrian king who killed his brother to usurp the throne. He unsuccessfully invaded Judah. The amazing story of the destruction of his army is told in Second Kings 19 (2 Kin. 18:13; Is. 36:1; 37:17, 21, 37).

Seraiah ("Jehovah is prince; Jehovah has prevailed"). [1] A scribe of David (2 Sam. 8:17). In Second Samuel 20:25, he is called Sheva and Shavsha in First Chronicles 18:16. He is also called Shisha in First Kings 4:3. [2] Chief priest of Jerusalem (2 Kin. 25:18; 1 Chr. 6:14; Ezra 7:1). [3] One whom Gedaliah advised to submit to Chaldea (2 Kin. 25:23; Jer. 40:8). [4] The brother of Othniel (1 Chr. 4:13, 14). [5] A descendant of Simeon (1 Chr. 4:35). [6] A priest that returned to Jerusalem with Zerubbabel (Ezra 2:2). [7] A leader sent to capture Jeremiah (Jer. 36:26). [8] A prince of Judah who went to Babylon (Jer. 51:59, 61). [9] A son of Hilkiah dwelling in Jerusalem after the Exile (Neh. 11:11). [10] A chief of the priests who returned from Babylon (Neh. 12:1, 7).

Sergius Paulus. The Roman deputy of Cyprus who was converted because Elymas was struck blind (Acts 13:7).

Seth [Sheth] ("compensation; sprout"), son of Adam and Eve, and an ancestor of Christ (Gen. 4:25, 26; 1 Chr. 1:1; Luke 3:38).

Shabbethai ("sabbath-born"). [1] An assistant to Ezra (Ezra 10:15). [2] One who explained the Law to the people (Neh. 8:7). [3] A chief Levite in Jerusalem (Neh. 11:16). All three may be identical.

Shadrach ("servant of [the god] Sin"), the name given to Hananiah at Babylon. He was cast into a fiery furnace and rescued (Dan. 1:7; 3).

Shallum [Shallun] ("recompenser"). [1] The youngest son of Naphtali (1 Chr. 7:13). He is also called Shillem (Gen. 46:24; Num. 26:49). [2] A descendant of Simeon (1 Chr. 4:25). [3] A descendant of Judah (1 Chr. 2:40, 41). [4] One who usurped the throne of Israel and reigned for one month (2 Kin. 15:10-15). [5] Husband of Huldah the prophetess (2 Kin. 22:14; 2 Chr. 34:22). [6] *See* Jehoahaz [2]. [7] *See* Meshullam [7]. [8] A gatekeeper of the tabernacle (1 Chr. 9:17-19, 31; Ezra 2:42; Neh. 7:45). [9] Father of Jehizkiah (2 Chr. 28:12). [10], [11] Two who married foreign wives during the Exile (Ezra 10:24, 42). [12] One who helped to repair the wall of Jerusalem (Neh. 3:12). [13] One who helped to repair the gate of Jerusalem (Neh. 3:15). [14] An uncle of Jeremiah (Jer. 32:7). [15] Father of one who was a temple officer in the days of Jehoiakim (Jer. 35:4).

Shammah ("fame; renown"). [1] A grandson of Esau (Gen. 36:13, 17; 1 Chr. 1:37). [2] A son of Jesse (1 Sam. 16:9; 17:13). He is also called Shimeah or Shimea (2 Sam. 13:3; 21:21; 1 Chr. 20:7; 2:13). [3] One of David's mighty men or the father of one of David's mighty men (2 Sam. 23:11). [4] Another of David's mighty men (2 Sam. 23:33), called Shammoth in First Chronicles 11:27. [5] Yet another of David's mighty men (2 Sam. 23:25).

Shammua ("famous"). [1] One sent to spy out the land of Canaan (Num. 13:4). [2] One of David's sons (2 Sam. 5:14; 1 Chr. 14:4). In First Chronicles 3:5, he is called Shimea. [3] A Levite who led the temple worship after the Exile (Neh. 11:17). He is also called Shemaiah (1 Chr. 9:16). [4] The head of a priestly family in Nehemiah's day (Neh. 12:18).

Shaphan ("prudent; sly"). [1] A scribe of Josiah who read him the Law (2 Kin. 22:3; 2 Chr. 34:8-21). [2] Father of a chief officer under Josiah (2 Kin. 22:12; 2 Chr. 34:20). [3] Father of Elasah (Jer. 29:3). [4] Father of

Jaazaniah whom Ezekiel saw in a vision (Ezek. 8:11). Many scholars consider all of the above to be identical.

Shaphat ("judge"). [1] One sent to spy out the land of Canaan (Num. 13:5). [2] Father of Elisha the prophet (1 Kin. 19:16, 19; 2 Kin. 3:11; 6:31). [3] One of the family of David (1 Chr. 3:22). [4] A chief of Gad (1 Chr. 5:12). [5] One over David's herds in the valley (1 Chr. 27:29).

Sharon ("his song"). [1] A region that lies between the Mediterranean Sea from Joppa to Carmel and the central portion of Palestine (1 Chr. 27:29; Acts 9:35). [2] A district east of the Jordan occupied by the tribe of Gad (1 Chr. 5:16).

Shear-Jashub ("a remnant returns"), symbolic name given a son of Isaiah (Is. 7:3).

Sheba ("oath; covenant"). [1] A chief of Gad (1 Chr. 5:13). [2] One who rebelled against David and was beheaded for it (2 Sam. 20). [3] A grandson of Abraham (Gen. 25:3; 1 Chr. 1:32). [4] A descendant of Shem (Gen. 10:28; 1 Chr. 1:22). Some scholars identify [5] with [4]. They believe Sheba is a tribe or people and stress that close genealogical ties account for the occurrence of the name in both Ham's and Shem's genealogy. [5] A descendant of Ham (Gen. 10:7; 1 Chr. 1:9).

Sheba ("oath"). [1] A country in southwest Arabia (1 Kin. 10:1-13; 2 Chr. 9:1-12). Its capital was Ma'rib, which was about 60 miles east-northeast of San'a, the present capital of Yemen. [2] A town of Simeon mentioned after Beersheba (Josh. 19:2). Its location is uncertain.

Shechaniah [Shecaniah] ("Jehovah is a neighbor"). [1] Head of a family of the house of David (1 Chr. 3:21, 22). [2], [3] Two whose descendants returned from the Babylonian Captivity (Ezra 8:3, 5). [4] One who took a foreign wife during the Exile (Ezra 10:2). [5] Father of one who repaired the wall of Jerusalem (Neh. 3:29). [6] Father-in-law to one who opposed Nehemiah (Neh. 6:18). [7] A priest who returned from the Exile (Neh. 12:3). [8] A priest in the time of David (1 Chr. 24:11). [9] A priest in Hezekiah's day (2 Chr. 31:15).

Shechem ("shoulder"). [1] Son of Hamor who defiled Dinah; he and his family were soon destroyed for that act (Gen. 33:19; 34). [2] A descendant of Manasseh (Num. 26:31; Josh. 17:2). [3] Another descendant of Manasseh (1 Chr. 7:19).

Shechem ("portion"), an ancient city in central Palestine (Gen. 12:6; 33:18; Josh. 24:32; Acts 7:16), in the hill country of Ephraim. It is present-day Nablus, located about 66 km. (41 mi.) north of Jerusalem between Mount Ebal and Mount Gerizim.

Shelomith ("peacefulness"). [1] Mother of one stoned for blasphemy in the wilderness (Lev. 24:11). [2] Daughter of Zerubbabel (1 Chr. 3:19). [3] A descendant of Gershon (1 Chr. 23:9). [4] A descendant of Levi and Kohath (1 Chr. 23:18). [5] One over the treasures in the days of David (1 Chr. 26:25-28). [6] Child of Rehoboam (2 Chr. 11:20). [7] An ancestor of a family that returned from the Exile (Ezra 8:10). Not to be confused with Shelomoth.

Shem ("name; renown"), son of Noah and ancestor of Christ (Gen. 5:32; 6:10; 10:1; Luke 3:36).

Shemaiah ("Jehovah is fame" or "Jehovah hears"). [1] A prophet who warned Rehoboam against war (1 Kin. 12:22; 2 Chr. 11:2). [2] A descendant of David (1 Chr. 3:22). [3] Head of a family of Simeon (1 Chr. 4:37). [4] Son of Joel (1 Chr. 5:4). [5] A descendant of Merari (1 Chr. 9:14; Neh. 11:15). [6] One who helped to bring the ark of the covenant to the temple (1 Chr. 15:8, 11). [7] A Levite who recorded the allotment in David's day (1 Chr. 24:6). [8] A gatekeeper for the tabernacle (1 Chr. 26:4, 6, 7). [9] A Levite whom Jehoshaphat sent to teach the people (2 Chr. 17:8). [10] One who helped to cleanse the temple (2 Chr. 29:14). [11] A Levite in Hezekiah's day (2 Chr. 31:15). [12] A chief Levite in Josiah's day (2 Chr. 35:9). [13] One who returned with Ezra (Ezra 8:13). [14] A person sent to Iddo to enlist ministers (Ezra 8:16). [15], [16] Two who married foreign wives during the Exile (Ezra 10:21, 31). [17] One who helped to repair the wall of Jerusalem (Neh. 3:29). [18] One who tried to intimidate Nehemiah (Neh. 6:10). [19] One who sealed the new covenant with God after the Exile (Neh. 10:8). [20] One who helped to purify the wall of Jerusalem (Neh. 12:36). [21] One at the dedication of the wall of Jerusalem (Neh. 12:42). [22] Father of the prophet Urijah (Jer. 26:20). [23] One who wanted the priests to reprimand Jeremiah (Jer. 29:24, 31). [24] Father of a prince of the Jews (Jer. 36:12). [25] See Shammua [3]. [26] A prince of Judah who took part in the dedication of the wall (Neh. 12:34). [27] A Levite of the line of Asaph (Neh. 12:35). [28] A chief of the priests who returned with Zerubbabel (Neh. 12:6, 7).

Shemariah [Shamariah] ("whom Jehovah guards"). [1] One who joined David at Ziklag (1 Chr. 12:5). [2] A son of King Rehoboam (2 Chr. 11:19). [3], [4] Two who married foreign wives during the Exile (Ezra 10:32, 41).

Shemuel (variant form of Samuel—"asked of God"). [1] One appointed to divide the land of Canaan (Num. 34:20). [2] Head of a family of Issachar (1 Chr. 7:2). [3] See Samuel.

Shephatiah ("Jehovah is judge"). [1] A son of David by Abital (2 Sam. 3:4; 1 Chr. 3:3). [2] Father of Meshullam who dwelt in Jerusalem (1 Chr. 9:8). [3] A valiant man who joined David at Ziklag (1 Chr. 12:5). [4] A prince of Simeon (1 Chr. 27:16). [5] A son of Jehoshaphat (2 Chr. 21:2). [6] An ancestor of returned captives (Ezra 2:4; Neh. 7:9). [7] One of Solomon's servants whose descendants returned from the Babylonian Captivity (Ezra 2:57; Neh. 7:59). [8] An ancestor of returned captives (Ezra 8:8). He is possibly identical with [6]. [9] A descendant of Perez whose descendants dwelt in Jerusalem (Neh. 11:4). [10] A prince of Judah in Zedekiah's time (Jer. 38:1).

Sheshbazzar ("O Shamash [the god], protect the father"), the prince of Judah into whose hands Cyrus placed the temple vessels. Many believe he is the same as Zerubbabel, but others deny this. They claim Sheshbazzar was governor under Cyrus and Zerubbabel under Darius (Ezra 1:8, 11; 5:14-16).

Shihor [Sihor] ("blackness"), the east branch of the Nile River (1 Chr. 13:5; Jer. 2:18). Ideally, this was to be Israel's southern boundary.

Shiloh ("peace"), a town in Ephraim (Josh. 18:1-10; Judg. 21:19). It is halfway between Shechem and Bethel.

Shimea [Shimeah] ("[God] has heard [a prayer]"). [1] A descendant of Merari (1 Chr. 6:30). [2] Father of Berachiah (1 Chr. 6:39). [3] See Shammah [2]. [4] See Shammua [2]. [5] One of the family of King Saul whose descendants dwelt in Jerusalem (1 Chr. 8:32; 9:38). In the latter passage he is called Shimeam.

Shimei [Shimi] ("Jehovah is fame; Jehovah hear me"). [1] A son of Gershon and a grandson of Gershon (Ex. 6:17; Num. 3:18, 21; Zech. 12:13). [2] A descendant of Benjamin who cursed David when he was fleeing from Absalom (2 Sam. 16:5-13; 19:16-23). [3] A loyal officer of David (1 Kin. 1:8). [4] An officer of Solomon (1 Kin. 4:18). [5] Grandson of King Jeconiah (1 Chr. 3:19). [6] A man who had sixteen sons and six daughters (1 Chr. 4:26, 27). [7] A descendant of Reuben (1 Chr. 5:4). [8] A son of Libni (1 Chr. 6:29). [9] Father of a chief of Judah (1 Chr. 8:21). [10] A Levite (1 Chr. 23:9). [11] A Levite in the temple song service in the days of David (1 Chr. 25:17). [12] One in charge of many vineyards (1 Chr. 27:27). [13] One who helped to cleanse the temple (2 Chr. 29:14). [14] A Levite in charge of the temple offerings under Hezekiah (2 Chr. 31:12, 13). [15], [16], [17] Three men who took foreign wives during the Exile (Ezra 10:23, 33, 38). **[18]** Grandfather of Mordecai (Esth. 2:5).

Shimri ("Jehovah is watching"). **[1]** Head of a family of Simeon (1 Chr. 4:37). **[2]** Father of one of David's mighty men (1 Chr. 11:45). **[3]** Gatekeeper of the tabernacle in David's day (1 Chr. 26:10). **[4]** One who helped to cleanse the temple (2 Chr. 29:13).

Shinar ("watch of him that sleeps"), the plains later known as Babylonia or Chaldea, through which the Tigris and Euphrates Rivers flow (Gen. 10:10; Is. 11:11).

Shittim [Acacia Grove] ("thorns"). **[1]** The final Israelite encampment before crossing the Jordan. Here Moses bade farewell and the Law was completed (Num. 25:1; Josh. 2:1). It was in Moab, east of Jordan, opposite Jericho. **[2]** A dry and unfruitful valley (Joel 3:18). The name may not denote any particular valley, but it may refer to the Kidron Wadi which starts northwest of Jerusalem, moves toward the east and runs toward the Dead Sea. It may also be a portion of the Arabah around the Dead Sea.

Shur ("wall"), a desert in the northwest part of the Sinai Peninsula (Gen. 16:7; 25:18). It was outside the eastern border of Egypt and was probably a caravan route between Egypt and Beersheba.

Shushan [Susa] ("a lily"), the capital of Elam inhabited by the Babylonians; later a royal residence and capital of the Persian Empire (Neh. 1:1; Dan. 8:2). The city was also known as Susa. The site is modern Shush on the Ulai River.

Sidon ("hunting"), an ancient city of Canaan (Gen. 10:15, 19; Josh. 11:8; Luke 4:26).

Sihon ("great; bold"), an Amorite king that was defeated by Israel (Num. 21:21–31; Deut. 1:4; 2:24–32; Josh. 13:15–28).

Sihor. *See* Shihor.

Silas [Silvanus] ("forest; woody; third; asked"), an eminent member of the early church who traveled with Paul through Asia Minor and Greece and was imprisoned with him at Philippi (Acts 15:22, 32–34; 2 Cor. 1:19; 1 Thess. 1:1).

Siloam ("sent"). **[1]** A famous pool of Jerusalem at the south end of Hezekiah's tunnel (John 9:7). It is identical with Shiloah. **[2]** A tower on the Ophel ridge near Siloam (Luke 13:4).

Silvanus. *See* Silas.

Simeon [Simon] ("hearing"). **[1]** The second son of Jacob by Leah (Gen. 29:33; 34:25; 48:5; 49:5). His descendants became one of the twelve tribes of Israel. **[2]** A devout Jew who blessed the Christ child in the temple (Luke 2:25–34). **[3]** An ancestor of Jesus (Luke 3:30). **[4]** A disciple and prophet at An-

tioch (Acts 13:1); he was surnamed Niger ("black"). **[5]** Original name of Peter (q.v.). Simon is but another form of Simeon. Not to be confused with Shimeon.

Simon ("hearing"). **[1]** Original name of the apostle Peter (Matt. 4:18; 16:16, 17; Luke 4:38; Acts 10:18). **[2]** Another of the twelve apostles, called Simon the Canaanite, indicating his fierce loyalty either to Israel or to his faith (Matt. 10:4; Mark 3:18; Luke 6:15; Acts 1:13). **[3]** One of Christ's brothers (Matt. 13:55; Mark 6:3). **[4]** A leper of Bethany in whose house Christ was anointed (Matt. 26:6; Mark 14:3). **[5]** A Cyrenian who was forced to bear the cross of Christ (Matt. 27:32; Mark 15:21). **[6]** A Pharisee in whose house the feet of Christ were anointed (Luke 7:40, 43, 44). **[7]** The father of Judas Iscariot (John 6:71; 12:4; 13:2). **[8]** A sorcerer who tried to buy the gifts of the Holy Spirit (Acts 8:9, 13, 18, 24). **[9]** A tanner of Joppa with whom Peter lodged (Acts 9:43; 10:6, 17, 32).

Sin ("bush"). **[1]** A city on the eastern side of the Nile (Ezek. 30:15, 16). It is possibly Pelusium; but is also identified with Syene, which is present-day Aswan at the first cataract of the Nile. **[2]** A wilderness area located between the Gulf of Suez and Sinai (Ex. 16:1; Num. 33:11, 12).

Sinai ("a bush"). **[1]** An area in the center of the peninsula that lies between the horns of the Red Sea, the Gulf of Suez, and the Gulf of 'Aqaba (Ex. 16:1; Acts 7:30–38). **[2]** A mountain, called also Horeb, where the Israelites received the Ten Commandments (Ex. 19:18). The location of the site is uncertain, although it is generally agreed to be in central Sinai. The traditional site is Jebel Musa, but other possibilities are Mount Serbal and Ras es-Safsafeh.

Sion ("breastplate"). **[1]** Another name for Mount Hermon (Deut. 4:48). **[2]** *See* Zion.

Sirion ("breastplate"), the name given to Mount Hermon by the Sidonians (Deut. 3:9; Ps. 29:6).

Sisera ("mediation; array"). **[1]** Captain of the army of Jabin who was murdered by Jael (Judg. 4:1–22; 5:26, 28). **[2]** One whose descendants returned (Ezra 2:53; Neh. 7:55).

Smyrna ("myrrh"), a city on the western coast of Asia Minor (Rev. 2:8–11). It is 64.4 km. (40 mi.) north of Ephesus.

Sodom ("their secret"), one of the five Cities of the Plain (Gen. 10:19; Rom. 9:29), destroyed because of its wickedness. The exact location of the site is unknown, but it is in the Dead Sea area.

Solomon ("peace"), son of David by Bathsheba and king of a united, strong Israel for forty years. His wisdom and carnal sin stand out in his multi-faceted character (1 Kin.

1:11; 2:11). He was an ancestor of Christ (Matt. 1:6, 7).

Solomon's Pools. A repository of water built by Solomon near Bethlehem (Eccl. 2:6).

Solomon's Porch. A colonnade built by Solomon on the east side of the temple (John 10:23; Acts 3:11).

Sosthenes ("strong; powerful"). [1] Chief ruler of the synagogue at Corinth, beaten by the Greeks (Acts 18:17). [2] A believer who united with Paul in addressing the Corinthian church (1 Cor. 1:1). Some believe he was [1] after conversion.

Stephanas ("crown"), one of the first believers of Achaia (1 Cor. 1:16; 16:15-17).

Stephen ("crown"), one of the seven deacons. He became the first martyr of the church after Christ (Acts 6:5-9; 7:59; 8:2).

Succoth ("tents"). [1] A town where Jacob built himself a house (Gen. 33:17; Josh. 13:27). It was east of the Jordan between Peniel and Shechem. Its probable location is Deir 'Alla, about 1.6 km. (1 mi.) west of where the Jabbok bulges and turns south. [2] The first camping ground of the Israelites after leaving Egypt (Ex. 12:37; 13:20).

Supply Cities [Treasure House]. Designated cities at which the kings of the ancient world kept their treasures and tithes (Ex. 1:11; Ezra 5:17).

Susa. See Shushan.

Susanna ("lily"), one of the women who ministered to Christ and was His follower (Luke 8:3).

Sychar ("end"), a town of Samaria near Jacob's well (John 4:5).

Syria (a form of the word *Assyria*), the country lying north and east of Palestine (Judg. 10:6; 1 Kin. 10:29; Acts 15:23). It stretched far inland from the Mediterranean and was bounded by the Taurus Mountains to the north.

Syrtis Sands ("shallows"), two shoals off the coast of Africa between Carthage and Cyrene (Acts 27:17). The greater Syrtis is now called the Gulf of Sidra, the lesser Syrtis the Gulf of Gabes.

T

Tabel ("God is good"). [1] Father of a man the kings of Israel and Damascus planned to make king of Judah (Is. 7:6). [2] A Persian official who tried to hinder the rebuilding of the wall of Jerusalem (Ezra 4:7).

Taberah ("burning"), a place three days north of Mount Sinai where Israel was punished for murmuring against God (Num. 11:3; Deut. 9:22).

Tabitha ("gazelle"), the Christian woman of Joppa whom Peter raised from the dead

(Acts 9:36-42). Dorcas is the Greek form of the name.

Tabor ("purity"). [1] A mountain located in the northern part of the Valley of Jezreel (Judg. 4:6, 12, 14; Ps. 89:12). It is now called Jebel el-Tur and is 8.8 km. (5.5 mi.) southeast of Nazareth. [2] A town of Zebulun given to the Levites (1 Chr. 6:77). Its location is uncertain. It may be the Chisloth Tabor of Joshua 19:12 or Khirbet Dabural, which is on a hill between Tabor and Nazareth. [3] An oak (not a plain as in KJV) in Benjamin (1 Sam. 10:3).

Tahpenes. An Egyptian queen, wife of the pharaoh, who received the fleeing Hadad, an enemy of Solomon (1 Kin. 11:18-20).

Talmai ("bold; spirited"). [1] A man or clan defeated by Caleb (Num. 13:22; Josh. 15:14; Judg. 1:10). [2] King of Geshur and father-in-law of David (2 Sam. 3:3; 13:27).

Tamar ("palm"). [1] The wife of Er, mother of Perez, and an ancestor of Christ (Gen. 38:6, 11, 13; Ruth 4:12; Matt. 1:3). [2] The daughter of David violated by Amnon (2 Sam. 13:1-32). [3] A daughter of Absalom (2 Sam. 14:27).

Tarshish [Tarshishah] ("hard"). [1] A son of Javan and grandson of Noah (Gen. 10:4; 1 Chr. 1:7). Possibly a people who inhabited a region in Spain (Tartessus), near Gibraltar. [2] One of the seven princes of Persia (Esth. 1:14). [3] A descendant of Benjamin (1 Chr. 7:10).

Tarsus ("winged"), the most prominent city of Cilicia located on the river Cydnus in Asia Minor; it was the birthplace of Paul (Acts 9:11).

Tartan (meaning unknown), the title of a high Assyrian officer. There is evidence that the office was second only to the king. There are two Tartans mentioned in Scripture (2 Kin. 18:17; Is. 20:1).

Tattenai ("gift"), a Persian governor of Samaria in the days of Zerubbabel (Ezra 5:3; 6:6, 13).

Temple. The structure in which the Israelites worshiped and offered sacrifices to God. There were three temples: Solomon's, Zerubbabel's, and Herod's.

Terah ("turning; duration"), the father of Abraham and ancestor of Christ (Gen. 11:27-32; Luke 3:34).

Tertius ("third"), the scribe to whom the epistle to the Romans was dictated (Rom. 16:22). Some conjecture that he is Silas (q.v.).

Tertullus ("third"), an orator hired by the Jews to state skillfully their case against Paul before Felix (Acts 24:1-8).

Thaddaeus (a name derived from an Aramaic word for the female breast), one of the twelve apostles (Matt. 10:3; Mark 3:18). He is the same as Judas, the brother of James

(Luke 6:16; John 14:22; Acts 1:13). He was also named Lebbaeus ("heart").

Theophilus ("loved by God"), an unknown person, possibly a Roman official, to whom Luke addressed his Gospel and Acts (Luke 1:3; Acts 1:1).

Thessalonica ("victory at sea"), a city situated on the Macedonian coast at the head of the Thermaic Gulf (Acts 17:1, 11, 13; 27:2). It is known as Salonika today.

Thomas ("twin"), one of the twelve apostles of Jesus. When Christ rose from the dead, Thomas was most skeptical (Matt. 10:3; Mark 3:18; John 20:24-29). His Aramaic name is Didymus in Greek.

Three Inns. A station on the Appian Way near the modern city of Cisterna (Acts 28:15).

Thyatira ("sacrifice of labor"), a city between Pergamos and Sardis (Acts 16:14; Rev. 2:18-29). It was in Lydia in Asia Minor.

Tiberias ("good vision"), a city on the west coast of the Sea of Galilee (John 6:1; 21:1).

Tiberius ("son of [the river] Tiber"), third emperor of the Roman Empire (Luke 3:1).

Tibni ("intelligent"), one who rivaled Omri for the throne of Israel (1 Kin. 16:21, 22).

Tiglath-Pileser (Babylonian, *Tukulti-apil-Esharra*—"my trust is in the son of Asharra"), a king of Assyria who invaded Naphtali during the time of Pekah of Israel. He conquered northern Palestine and deported many from Naphtali (2 Kin. 15:29; 16:7, 10; 1 Chr. 5:6, 26). His native name was Pul (2 Kin. 15:19). Realizing he bore two names, we should translate First Chronicles 5:26, " ...God...stirred...Pul king of Assyria, that is, [not *and*] Tiglath-Pileser king of Assyria."

Timon ("honorable"), one of the seven deacons (Acts 6:1-6).

Timothy ("honored of God"), a young friend and convert of Paul; he traveled extensively with the apostle. He was from Lystra and was the son of Eunice, a Jewess, and a Greek father (Acts 16:1; 17:14, 15; 1 Tim. 1:2, 18; 6:20).

Titus ("pleasant"), a converted Grecian entrusted with a mission to Crete (2 Cor. 2:13; Gal. 2:1; Titus 1:4).

Tobiah [Tobijah] ("Jehovah is good"). [1] A Levite sent by Jehoshaphat to teach the Law (2 Chr. 17:8). [2] An ancestor of returning captives who had lost their genealogy (Ezra 2:60; Neh. 7:62). [3] An Ammonite servant of Sanballat who opposed Nehemiah (Neh. 2:10-20). [4] A leader who returned from the Babylonian Captivity (Zech. 6:10, 14).

Tobijah. *See* Tobiah.

Tophet [Topheth] ("a drum"), once a part of a king's garden in Hinnom; it became a place where people in Jerusalem sacrificed their children (Is. 30:33; Jer. 19:6, 11-14; 2 Kin. 23:10).

Troas ("penetrated"), an important city on the coast of Mysia (Acts 16:8; 2 Tim. 4:13). It was in northern Asia Minor and is also called Alexandria.

Trophimus ("a foster child"), a Christian convert and afterward a companion-in-travel with Paul (Acts 20:4; 21:29; 2 Tim. 4:20).

Tychicus ("fortunate"), a disciple and messenger of Paul (Acts 20:4; Eph. 6:21; 2 Tim. 4:12).

Tyrannus ("tyrant"), a Greek rhetorician or Jewish rabbi in whose school Paul taught at Ephesus (Acts 19:9).

Tyre ("rock"), a city on the central coast of Phoenicia noted for its commercial activity (Josh. 19:29; 2 Sam. 5:11; Jer. 25:22). It is located halfway between Acco and Sidon.

U

Ur. The city which Abram left to go to Haran (Gen. 11:28, 31). Ur is generally identified as ancient Ur (Uri), modern Tell el-Muqayyar located on the Euphrates in south Iraq.

Uriah [Urijah] ("Jehovah is my light"). [1] A Hittite soldier in David's army. He was killed in a fierce battle, for David, desiring to marry his wife, Bathsheba, had placed him on the front battle line (2 Sam. 11). [2] A priest under Ahaz who built a pagan altar on the king's command; then placed it in the temple (2 Kin. 16:10-16). [3] A prophet whose message of judgment so offended Jehoiakim that he murdered him (Jer. 26:20-23). [4] A priest, the father of Meremoth (Ezra 8:33; Neh. 3:4, 21). [5] A man who stood by Ezra when he read the Law (Neh. 8:4). Possibly the same as [4]. [6] A priest whom Isaiah took as a witness (Is. 8:2).

Urijah. *See* Uriah.

Uz [Huz] ("counsel; firmness"). [1] Eldest son of Aram (Gen. 10:23). Possibly the name refers to an Aramean tribe or people. [2] A son of Shem (1 Chr. 1:17). The Septuagint makes this Uz identical with [1] naming Aram as his father. It is also possible the Hebrew text was abbreviated here. [3] A son of Dishan, son of Seir (Gen. 36:28). [4] The son of Nahor by Milcah (Gen. 22:21).

Uz ("counsel; firmness"). [1] The country where Job lived (Job 1:1). The two most likely locations are Hauran, south of Damascus, and the area between Edom and north Arabia. [2] A kingdom not far from Edom (Jer. 25:20; Lam. 4:21). Perhaps identical with [1].

Uzza [Uzzah] ("strength"). [1] A man who

was struck dead by God when he touched the ark of the covenant (2 Sam. 6:2-7; 1 Chr. 13:6-10). [2] A descendant of Merari (1 Chr. 6:29). [3] A descendant of Ehud (1 Chr. 8:7). [4] An ancestor of a Nethinim family that returned from Babylon (Ezra 2:49; Neh. 7:51).

Uzziah ("Jehovah is strong" or "my strength is Jehovah"). [1] The eleventh king of Judah. When he attempted to offer incense unlawfully, God struck him with leprosy. He was also called Azariah (2 Kin. 15:1-8; 2 Chr. 26). He was an ancestor of Christ (Matt. 1:8, 9). [2] A Levite descended from Kohath and ancestor of Samuel (1 Chr. 6:24). [3] Father of Jehonathan (1 Chr. 27:25). [4] A priest who had married a foreign wife (Ezra 10:21). [5] A descendant of Judah (Neh. 11:4).

Uzziel ("God is my strength" or "God is strong"). [1] The ancestor of the Uzzielites; the son of Kohath (Ex. 6:18). [2] Captain of the sons of Simeon (1 Chr. 4:42). [3] A son of Bela and grandson to Benjamin (1 Chr. 7:7). [4] An assistant wall-builder (Neh. 3:8). [5] A Levite, son of Jeduthun, who helped to cleanse the temple (2 Chr. 29:14). [6] A musician set by David over the service of song in the temple (1 Chr. 25:4). Uzziel is the same as Azarel in verse 18.

V

Valley Gate. A gate in the southwest wall of Jerusalem leading to the Hinnom Valley (Neh. 2:13).

Vashti ("beautiful woman; best"), the queen of Persia who was divorced by King Ahasuerus because she refused to come to his great feast (Esth. 1:10-22).

W

Water Gate. A gate on the east side of Jerusalem, above the spring of Gihon (Neh. 8:1, 3).

Wilderness. The area in which the Israelites wandered for 40 years before entering Canaan (Deut. 1:1; Josh. 5:6). Several places are encompassed in the designation Wilderness; these are listed under their individual names (e.g., Paran, Zin. etc.).

Z

Zacchaeus ("pure"), a publican with whom Jesus lodged during His stay at Jericho (Luke 19:1-10).

Zacharias (Greek form of Zechariah—"memory of the Lord"). [1] The prophet whom the Jews stoned (Matt. 23:35; Luke 11:51). Some believe this prophet to be identical with Zechariah [11] or [16], though it is possible the reference is to an unknown prophet.

[2] A priest, father of John the Baptist (Luke 1).

Zadok ("righteous"). [1] A high priest in the time of David (2 Sam. 8:17; 15:24-36; 1 Kin. 1:8-45). [2] Father of Jerusha, wife of Uzziah and mother of Jotham, both kings of Israel (2 Kin. 15:33; 2 Chr. 27:1). [3] Son of Ahitub and father of Shallum or Meshullam (1 Chr. 6:12, 13; Ezra 7:2). [4] A young man of valor (1 Chr. 12:28). [5], [6] Two who repaired the wall of Jerusalem (Neh. 3:4, 29). [7] One who sealed the covenant with Nehemiah (Neh. 10:21). [8] A scribe under Nehemiah (Neh. 13:13). [9] An ancestor of Christ (Matt. 1:14).

Zalmunna ("withdrawn from protection"), a Midianite king slain by Gideon (Judg. 8:5-21).

Zaphnath-Paaneah ("savior of the world; revealer of secrets"), name given to Joseph by Pharaoh (Gen. 41:45).

Zarephath ("smelting place"), a town located near Zidon (Sidon) that was the residence of Elijah (1 Kin. 17:9).

Zealot, The. See Simon [2].

Zebedee ("the gift of Jehovah"), a fisherman of Galilee, husband of Salome, and father of the apostles James and John (Matt. 4:21; 27:56; Mark 1:19, 20).

Zebulun ("dwelling"), tenth son of Jacob and ancestor of one of the twelve tribes (Gen. 30:20; 49:13; 1 Chr. 2:1).

Zebulun ("dwelling"), the territory given to the tribe of Zebulun (Josh. 19:27, 34). It was north of Issachar, east of Asher, and southwest of Naphtali.

Zechariah ("Jehovah my righteousness"). [1] A chief of the tribe of Reuben (1 Chr. 5:7). [2] A Levite gatekeeper in the days of David (1 Chr. 9:21; 26:2, 14). [3] A Levite set over the service of song in the days of David (1 Chr. 15:18, 20; 16:5). [4] A priest in the days of David (1 Chr. 15:24). [5] A descendant of Levi through Kohath (1 Chr. 24:25). [6] A descendant of Levi through Merari (1 Chr. 26:11). [7] Father of Iddo (1 Chr. 27:21). [8] A prince of Jehoshaphat sent to teach the people (2 Chr. 17:7). [9] A Levite who encouraged Jehoshaphat against Moab (2 Chr. 20:14). [10] A son of Jehoshaphat (2 Chr. 21:2). [11] A son of Jehoiada who was stoned (2 Chr. 24:20). Also mentioned in Matthew 23:35 and Luke 11:51. [12] Prophet in the days of Uzziah (2 Chr. 26:5). [13] A Levite who helped to cleanse the temple (2 Chr. 29:13). [14] A descendant of Levi (2 Chr. 34:12). [15] A prince of Judah in the days of Josiah (2 Chr. 35:8). [16] A prophet in the days of Ezra. His book still exists (Ezra 5:1; 6:14; Zech. 1:1, 7; 7:1, 8). [17] A chief man of Israel (Ezra 8:3). [18] One who returned from the Exile

(Ezra 8:11). The chief man in Ezra 8:16 was probably [17] or [18]. [19] One who took a foreign wife during the Exile (Ezra 10:26). [20] A prince with Ezra (Neh. 8:4). [21] A descendant of Perez (Neh. 11:4). [22] One whose descendants dwelt in Jerusalem (Neh. 11:5). [23] A priest (Neh. 11:12). [24] A Levite trumpeter (Neh. 12:35, 36). [25] A priest who took part in the dedication ceremony (Neh. 12:41). [26] One whom Isaiah took as a witness (Is. 8:2). [27] Father of Abi or Abijah, mother of Hezekiah (2 Kin. 18:2). [28] Son and successor of Jeroboam II. He reigned only six months (2 Kin. 18:2).

Zedekiah ("Jehovah my righteousness; Jehovah is might"). [1] A false prophet who encouraged Ahab to attack the Syrians at Ramoth Gilead (1 Kin. 22:11, 24; 2 Chr. 18:10, 23). [2] A false prophet (Jer. 29:21–23). [3] A prince of Judah in the days of Jehoiakim (Jer. 36:12). [4] The last king of Judah; his rebellion spelled the doom of Judah (2 Kin. 24:18–25:7; 2 Chr. 36:11–21). He is probably referred to in First Chronicles 3:16 as a "son" or successor of Jeconiah. *See* Mattaniah [1].

Zephaniah ("Jehovah is darkness; Jehovah has treasured"). [1] A prophet in the days of Josiah (Zeph. 1:1). [2] A Levite or priest, ancestor of Samuel (1 Chr. 6:36). Possibly the same as Uriel [1]. [3] Son of Josiah the priest (Zech. 6:10, 14). [4] A priest who opposed Babylonian rule (2 Kin. 25:18; Jer. 21:1; 37:3).

Zered ("brook"), a brook and valley that marks the greatest limit of the Hebrews wandering in the wilderness (Num. 21:12; Deut. 2:13, 14). It was south of the Arnon, probably Wadi el-Hesa.

Zerubbabel ("seed of Babylon"). [1] The leader of a group who returned from Exile; he began the rebuilding of the temple (Ezra 3–5; Neh. 7:7; 12:1, 47). He was an ancestor of Christ (Matt. 1:12, 13). [2] An ancestor of Christ (Luke 3:27); perhaps the same as [1].

Zimri ("celebrated"). [1] A disobedient Israelite slain by Phinehas (Num. 25:14). [2] A captain who slew Elah (1 Kin. 16:9–20). [3] A son of Zerah of Judah (1 Chr. 2:6). [4] A descendant of Benjamin (1 Chr. 8:36; 9:42).

Zin ("swelling"), a wilderness on the southern border of Canaan, not to be confused with the wilderness of Sin. It was either a part of the Wilderness of Paran or bordered on the wilderness which contained Kadesh Barnea (Num. 20:1; 27:14; Josh. 15:1–3).

Zion [Sion] ("monument; fortress; set up"), one of the hills on which Jerusalem stood. It came to be applied to the temple and the whole of Jerusalem and its people as a community whose destiny depends on God (2 Sam. 5:7; Is. 8:18; Ps. 48:11; Joel 2:23). Zion also is a symbol of heaven (Rev. 14:1).

Ziphron ("rejoicing"), a place specified by Moses as the northern boundary of the Promised Land (Num. 34:9). It is probably Za'feranh southeast of Restan.

Zipporah ("little bird"), the wife of Moses and daughter of Reuel (Ex. 2:21; 4:25; 18:2).

NOTES

NOTES

NOTES